LAROUSSE

CONCISE
DICTIONARY

PORTUGUESE
ENGLISH

ENGLISH
PORTUGUESE

D0048823

LAROUSSE

CONTENTS
ÍNDICE

© Larousse, 2010
21, rue du Montparnasse, 75283 Paris Cedex 06, France

Published in the United States of America and Canada by:
Publicado nos Estados Unidos e Canadá por:

Éditions LAROUSSE
21, rue du Montparnasse, 75283 Paris Cedex 06, France
www.larousse.fr

ISBN 978 2 03 541039 9

Sales / Distribuição: Houghton Mifflin Harcourt, Boston
Library of Congress CIP Data has been applied for

31232009785017

LAROUSSE

DICIONÁRIO AVANÇADO

PORTUGUÊS INGLÊS

INGLÊS PORTUGUÊS

LAROUSSE

Project Management
Direção da obra

Luzia Araújo   Valerie Grundy

Editors
Redação

Alison Aiken	Maria Inês Alves
Laura Bocco	Shirley Brotherton-Pinniger
Salete Cechin	Karoll Ferreira
José A. Gálvez	Daniel Grassi
Mike Harland	Bill Martin
Viviane Possamai	Julia Rice
Christine Robinson	Sergio Tellaroli

Publishing Manager
Direção Geral

Janice McNeillie

Prepress
Diagramação

David Reid   Sharon McTeir

PREFACE

This CONCISE dictionary is a reliable and user-friendly tool for use in all language situations. It provides accurate and up-to-date information on written and spoken Portuguese and English as they are used today.

Its 90,000 words and phrases and 120,000 translations give you access to Portuguese texts of all types. The dictionary aims to be as comprehensive as possible in a book of this size, and includes many proper names and abbreviations, as well as a selection of the most common terms from computing, business and currents affairs.

Carefully construced entries and a clear page design help you to find the translation that you are looking for fast. Examples (from basic constructions and common phrases to idioms) have been included to help put a word in context and give a clear picture of how it is used.

The dictionary provides extra help for students of Portuguese with the inclusion of boxes on life and culture in Brazil that appear within the dictionary text itself, and a central section which gives fuller background details on political and cultural life in Brazil, as well as a useful communication guide.

A NOSSOS LEITORES

Este Dicionário AVANÇADO é a ferramenta de consulta ideal para toda uma gama de situações que vão da aprendizagem de uma língua estrangeira, em casa ou na escola, até as necessidades cotidianas no trabalho.

O Dicionário AVANÇADO Inglês-Português foi desenvolvido para responder com rapidez e eficiência às dificuldades com que nos defrontamos na leitura do inglês contemporâneo, bem como na redação de trabalhos escolares, cartas e relatórios.

Com suas mais de 90 mil palavras e expressões – e um número de traduções superior a 120 mil –, este dicionário permitirá ao leitor compreender com clareza toda uma variedade de textos, desde obras literárias e artigos jornalísticos até documentos comerciais, folhetos e manuais, possibilitando a realização de resumos e traduções com eficácia e apuro.

A atualidade das siglas e abreviações, bem como dos termos comerciais e de informática aqui incluídos, é outro fator a atestar a abrangência e contemporaneidade deste dicionário.

Valendo-se do tratamento claro e detalhado dado aqui ao vocabulário básico, dos muitos exemplos de construções gramaticais e de uso mais atualizado da língua, bem como dos indicadores de contexto a conduzir à tradução mais adequada, o usuário deste Dicionário AVANÇADO poderá expressar-se em inglês com precisão e segurança.

Especial atenção foi dedicada também à apresentação de cada entrada, tanto do ponto de vista de sua estrutura quanto da tipologia empregada, visando a facilitar a consulta e o entendimento.

Aliando precisão e praticidade, profundidade de conteúdo e facilidade de consulta, o Dicionário AVANÇADO é a obra ideal para todos aqueles que já superaram os níveis iniciais de aprendizagem da língua inglesa, demandando para o seu cotidiano – na escola, em casa ou no trabalho – um dicionário prático, mas abrangente.

ABREVIATURAS

ABBREVIATIONS

abreviatura	*abrev/abbr*	abbreviation
adjetivo	*adj*	adjective
advérbio	*adv*	adverb
antes de substantivo	*antes de subst*	before noun
artigo	*art*	article
auxiliar	*aux*	auxiliary
comparativo	*compar*	comparative
conjunção	*conj*	conjuction
contínuo	*cont*	continuous
definido	*def*	definite
demonstrativo	*dem/demos*	demonstrative
especialmente	*esp*	especially
interjeição	*excl*	exclamation
substantivo feminino	*f*	feminine noun
familiar	*fam*	informal
figurado	*fig*	figurative
formal	*fml*	formal
inseparável	*fus*	inseparable
geralmente	*ger/gen*	generally
humorístico	*hum*	humorous
indefinido	*indef*	indefinite
familiar	*inf*	informal
interjeição	*interj*	exclamation
invariável	*inv*	invariable
irônico	*irôn/iro*	ironic
literal	*lit*	literal
locução	*loc*	phrase
substantivo masculino	*m*	masculine noun
substantivo	*n*	noun
numeral	*num*	numeral
	o.s.	oneself
pejorativo	*pej*	pejorative
pessoal	*pess/pers*	personal
plural	*pl*	plural
possessivo	*poss*	possessive
particípio passado	*pp*	past participle
preposição	*prep*	preposition
pronome	*pron*	pronoun
passado	*pt*	past tense
marca registrada	®	registered trademark
relativo	*relat*	relative
substantivo	*s*	noun
	sb	someone, somebody
separável	*sep*	separable
singular	*sg*	singular
gíria	*sl*	slang
	sthg	something
sujeito	*suj/subj*	subject
superlativo	*superl*	superlative
substantivo incontável	*U*	uncountable noun

ABREVIATURAS

inglês britânico	*UK*
inglês americano	*US*
verbo	*v/vb*
verbo intransitivo	*vi*
verbo impessoal	*v impess/impers*
verbo pronominal	*vpr*
verbo transitivo	*vt*
vulgar	*vulg*
equivalente cultural	≃

ABBREVIATIONS

British English
American English
verb
intransitive verb
impersonal verb
pronominal verb
transitive verb
vulgar
cultural equivalent

CAMPOS SEMÂNTICOS

FIELD LABELS

administração	**ADMIN**	administration
aeronáutica	**AERON**	aeronautics
agricultura	**AGR**	agriculture
anatomia	**ANAT**	anatomy
arqueologia	**ARCHEOL**	archeology
arquitetura	**ARQUIT/ARCHIT**	architecture
astrologia	**ASTROL**	astrology
astronomia	**ASTRON**	astronomy
automóveis	**AUT(O)**	automobiles, cars
biologia	**BIOL**	biology
botânica	**BOT**	botany
química	**CHEM**	chemistry
ciências	**CIÊN/SCIENCE**	science
cinema	**CINE(MA)**	cinema
comércio	**COM(M)**	commerce
informática	**COMPUT**	information technology
construção	**CONSTR**	construction, building
costura	**COST**	sewing
culinária	**CULIN**	culinary, cooking
ecologia	**ECOLOG**	ecology
economia	**ECON**	economy
educação, escola	**EDUC**	education, school
eletricidade, eletrônica	**ELETR/ELEC**	electricity, electronics
esporte	**ESP**	sport
farmacologia	**FARM**	pharmacology
finanças	**FIN**	finance
física	**FÍS**	physics
fotografia	**FOTO**	photography
geografia	**GEOGR**	geography
geologia	**GEOL**	geology
geometria	**GEOM**	geometry
gramática	**GRAM(M)**	grammar
história	**HIST**	history
indústria	**IND**	industry
jornalismo	**JORN**	journalism
jurídico	**JUR**	juridical, legal
lingüística	**LING**	linguistics
literatura	**LITER**	literature
matemática	**MAT(H)**	mathematics
mecânica	**MEC**	mechanical engineering
medicina	**MED**	medicine
metalurgia	**METAL**	metallurgy
meteorologia	**METEOR**	meteorology
militar	**MIL**	military
mineralogia	**MIN**	mineralogy
mitologia	**MITOL/MYTH**	mythology
música	**MÚS/MUS**	music
náutica	**NAUT**	nautical
farmacologia	**PHARM**	pharmacology
fotografia	**PHOT**	photography
física	**PHYS**	physics
política	**POL(ÍT)**	politics
psicologia	**PSICOL/PSYCH**	psychology
química	**QUÍM**	chemistry
ferrovia	**RAIL**	railways
religião	**RELIG**	religion
escola	**SCH**	school
sociologia	**SOCIOL**	sociology

CAMPOS SEMÂNTICOS

bolsa de valores	**ST EX**	stock exchange
teatro	**TEATR/THEAT**	theatre
técnico, tecnologia	**TEC/TECH**	technical, technology
telecomunicações	**TELEC**	telecommunications
tipografia	**TIP/TYP**	printing, typography
televisão	**TV**	television
universidade	**UNIV**	university
veterinária	**VETER**	veterinary science
zoologia	**ZOOL**	zoology

FIELD LABELS

FONÉTICA

Vogais portuguesas
[a] pá cada
[ɛ] sé, seta, hera
[e] ler mês
[i] ir, sino, nave
[ɔ] nota, pó
[o] corvo, avô
[u] azul, tribo

Ditongos portugueses
[aj] faixa, mais
[ej] leite, rei
[ɛj] hotéis, pastéis
[ɔj] herói, bóia
[oj] coisa, noite
[uj] azuis, fui
[aw] nau, jaula
[ɛw] céu, véu
[ew] deus, seu
[iw] riu, viu

Vogais nasais
[ã] maçã, santo
[ẽ] lençol, sempre
[ĩ] fim, patim
[õ] onde, com, honra
[ũ] jejum, nunca

Ditongos nasais
[ãj] cãibra, mãe
[ãw] camarão, cão
[ẽj] bem, quem
[õj] cordões, leões

Semivogais portuguesas
[j] eleito, maio
[w] luar, quadro

Consoantes
[b] beijo, abrir
[d] dama, prenda

PHONETICS

English vowels
[ɪ] pit, big, rid
[e] pet, tend
[æ] pat, bag, mad
[ʌ] run, cut
[ɒ] pot, log
[ʊ] put, full
[ə] mother, suppose
[iː] bean, weed
[aː] barn, car
[ɔː] born, lawn
[uː] loop, loose
[ɜː] burn, learn, bird

English dipthongs
[eɪ] bay, late, great
[aɪ] buy, light, aisle
[ɔɪ] boy, foil
[əʊ] no, road, blow
[aʊ] now, shout, town
[ɪə] peer, fierce, idea
[eə] pair, bear, share
[ʊə] sure, tour

English semi-vowels
[j] you, spaniel
[w] wet, why, twin

English consonants
[p] pop, people
[b] bottle, bib

[dȝ]	dia, bonde	[t]	train, tip
[f]	faca, afinal	[d]	dog, did
[g]	grande, agora	[k]	come, kitchen
[ȝ]	gelo, cisne, anjo	[g]	gag, great
[l]	lata, feliz, cola	[tʃ]	chain, wretched
[ʎ]	malha, telha	[dȝ]	jet, fridge
[m]	mesa, cama	[f]	fib, physical
[n]	nada, banana	[v]	vine, live
[ɲ]	linha, sonho	[θ]	think, fifth
[ŋ]	anca, inglês	[ð]	this, with
[p]	pão, gripe	[s]	seal, peace
[s]	cima, desse, caça	[z]	zip, his
[ʃ]	noz, bis, caixa, chá	[ʃ]	sheep, machine
[t]	tema, lata, porta	[ȝ]	usual, measure
[tʃ]	tio, infantil	[h]	how, perhaps
[v]	vela, ave	[m]	metal, comb
[x]	rádio, terra	[n]	night, dinner
[z]	zelo, brisa	[ŋ]	sung, parking
		[l]	little, help
		[r]	right, carry

O símbolo fonético l(x)l em português indica que o 'r' final da palavra é apenas levemente pronunciado, exceto quando seguido de uma vogal: nesse caso, pronuncia-se lrl.

O símbolo ['] indica que a sílaba subseqüente é a tônica, sobre a qual recai o acento principal; [,] indica que a sílaba subseqüente é a subtônica, sobre a qual recai o acento secundário.

As regras de pronúncia aplicadas ao português refletem a língua falada no Rio de Janeiro.

The symbol l(x)l in Portuguese phonetics indicates that final 'r' is often barely sounded unless it is followed by a word beginning with a vowel, in which case it is pronounced lrl.

The symbol ['] indicates that the following syllable carries primary stress and [,] that the following syllable carries secondary stress.

Portuguese phonetics reflect the language as spoken in Rio de Janeiro.

COMO UTILIZAR ESTE DICIONÁRIO

Como encontrar a palavra ou expressão que procuramos?

A primeira coisa a fazer é perguntar:

Trata-se de uma palavra ou de uma abreviatura?
Seria um substantivo composto?
Uma expressão ou locução?
Trata-se de um verbo pronominal ou *phrasal verb*?

Palavras e abreviaturas

Em geral, encontraremos a palavra que procuramos no lugar que lhe corresponde na ordem alfabética. Se desejamos a tradução para o português de uma palavra inglesa, consultamos a parte inglês-português do dicionário; se desconhecemos o sentido de uma palavra do português, procuraremos por sua tradução na parte português-inglês. A palavra em **negrito**, que aparece no início de cada verbete do dicionário, chama-se "entrada".

Se duas palavras são escritas de forma idêntica, mas uma delas começa com **maiúscula**, a palavra em maiúscula aparecerá depois daquela que começa com letra minúscula.

> **ad** (*abbr of* **advertisement**) *n fam* **-1.** [in newspaper] anúncio *m.* **-2.** [onTV] propaganda *f.*
> **AD** (*abbr of* **Anno Domini**) d.C.

Palavras contendo **hífen**, **apóstrofe** ou **ponto** aparecem depois daquelas de mesma grafia, mas que não apresentam esses sinais gráficos.

> **its** [ɪts] *poss adj* o seu (a sua), dele (dela).
> **it's** [ɪts] = **it is**, **it has**.

Da mesma forma, uma palavra com **acento** figurará depois de outra de mesma grafia, mas sem acento.

> **do** [du] = **de + o**.
> **dó** ['dɔ] *m* **-1.** [piedade] pity; **ter ~ de alguém** to take pity on sb. **-2.** *MÚS* doh.

Em alguns casos, as entradas são seguidas de um pequeno **número sobrescrito**. Isso quer dizer que, imediatamente antes ou após, haverá outra entrada idêntica, também seguida de um número, mas com significado ou pronúncia diferente. São os chamados homógrafos. Atenção: certifique-se de não estar consultando a entrada errada! É necessário prestar muita atenção à categoria gramatical.

> **bow¹** [baʊ] ◇ *n* **-1.** [act of bowing] reverência *f-* **2.** [of ship] proa *f.* ◇ *vt* [lower] inclinar. ◇ *vi* **-1.** [make a bow] inclinar-se **-2.** [defer]: **to ~ to sthg** submeter-se a algo.
> ◆ **bow down** *vi* [give in]: **to ~ down (to sb)** render-se (a alguém).
> ◆ **bow out** *vi* afastar-se.
> **bow²** [baʊ] *n* **-1.** [gen & *MÚS*] arco *m.* **-2.** [knot] laço *m.*

Às vezes, vamos encontrar palavras precedidas de um losango negro (◆), chamadas "sub-entradas". Um exemplo disso são os verbos pronominais do português ou os *phrasal verbs* ingleses. Além disso, se buscamos uma palavra que possui duas formas, maiúscula e minúscula, com significados diferentes, nós encontraremos a forma em maiúscula como sub-entrada daquela em minúscula, precedida de um losango negro.

> **beneficiar** [16] [benefi'sja(x)] *vt* **-1.** [favorecer] to benefit. **-2.** [processar] to process. **-3.** [melhorar] to improve.
> ◆ **beneficiar-se** *vp* [favorecer-se] to profit.

> **ascension** [ə'senʃn] *n* [to throne] ascensão *f.*
> ◆ **Ascension** *n RELIG* Ascensão *f.*

Da mesma forma, se procuramos um substantivo cuja forma plural possui um significado distinto do singular (como **glass/glasses** em inglês; ou **bem/bens**, em português), encontraremos a palavra no plural como sub-entrada da forma singular, precedida do símbolo (➠).

glass [glɑ:s] ◇ n -**1.** *(U)* [material] vidro m -**2.** [for drinking] copo m -**3.** *(U)* [glassware] objetos mpl de cristal. ◇ *comp* de vidro.
➠ **glasses** npl [spectacles] óculos m inv; [binoculars] binóculos mpl.

Alguns substantivos aparecem como entradas já no plural, seja porque não existem no singular ou porque a forma singular é pouco freqüente. É o caso, por exemplo, de **scissors**, em inglês, ou **juros**, em português.

Substantivos compostos

O substantivo composto é uma expressão que, como tal, possui um significado próprio, mas que se compõe de mais de uma palavra (**virtual reality**, por exemplo, ou **café com leite**). Os substantivos compostos poderão ser encontrados na entrada correspondente a seu primeiro elemento. Assim sendo, **café com leite** aparecerá em **café**. Os demais compostos com o substantivo **café** como primeiro elemento - **café expresso**, **café pingado** - figuram em ordem alfabética.

No caso dos substantivos compostos do inglês, é característica deste dicionário listá-los como entradas, em ordem alfabética. Assim, **blood donor** aparecerá depois de **blood-curdling**, que, por sua vez, sucede a **blood count**.

café [ka'fɛ] m -**1.** [ger] coffee; ~ **(preto)** black coffee; ~ **com leite** white coffee *UK*, coffee with cream *US*; ~ **expresso** espresso; ~ **pingado** *coffee with a tiny drop of milk*; **ser** ~ **pequeno** *fam* [tarefa] to be small beer; [pessoa] to be small fry. -**2.** [desjejum]: ~ **(da manhã)** breakfast. -**3.** [estabelecimento] café.

blood count n contagem f de glóbulos sangüíneos.
blood-curdling adj de gelar o sangue.
blood donor n doador m, -ra f de sangue.

Se o composto, seja em inglês ou português, se tornou uma unidade autônoma - isto é, se seu significado conjunto já se destacou da soma de seus elementos -, ele é tratado à parte, sendo precedido de um losango negro.

Expressões e locuções

Expressões e locuções devem ser localizadas a partir do primeiro substantivo que as forma. Se a expressão não possui um substantivo, deve-se procurá-la pelo adjetivo ou, na ausência deste, pelo verbo. No interior de cada verbete, as expressões aparecem em **negrito**, com o símbolo ~ representando a entrada correspondente.

Algumas expressões de significado e valor gramatical próprio (as chamadas locuções), como **in spite of** (inglês) ou **atrás de** (português), figuram vinculadas a seu primeiro elemento importante, precedidas do símbolo (➠).

Isso possibilita destacar a diferença de sentido e função gramatical entre a locução em si e a entrada à qual ela está vinculada.

time [taɪm] ◇ n -**1.** *(U)* [general measurement, spell] tempo m; **to get the** ~ **to do sthg** ter tempo para fazer algo; **to take** ~ levar tempo; **to take** ~ **out to do sthg** tirar tempo para fazer algo; **it's high** ~ ... já é hora de ...; **to get** ~ **and a half** receber o pagamento combinado mais a metade; **to have no** ~ **for sb/sthg** não ter tempo a perder com alguém/algo; **to make good** ~ fazer uma boa média (de tempo); **to pass the** ~ passar o tempo; **to play for** ~ tentar ganhar tempo; **to take one's** ~ **(doing sthg)** dar-se seu tempo (para fazer algo)...

spite [spaɪt] ◇ n *(U)* rancor m; **to do sthg out of** *or* **from** ~ fazer algo por maldade. ◇ vt magoar.
➠ **in spite of** *prep* apesar de; **to do sthg in** ~ **of o.s.** [unintentionally] fazer algo a contragosto.

atrás [a'trajʃ] adv -**1.** [posição] behind; **lá** ~ back there. -**2.** [no tempo] ago. -**3.** [em classificação]: **estar/ficar** ~ **(de)** to be ranked behind; **não ficar** ~ *fam fig* not to be far behind.
➠ **atrás de** *loc prep* -**1.** [posição] behind. -**2.** [em seguimento a] after; **logo** ~ **de** right behind. -**3.** [em busca de - pessoa] after; [- objeto, explicação] looking for.

Verbos pronominais e *phrasal verbs*

A maioria dos verbos pronominais e *phrasal verbs* apresenta-se na entrada correspondente ao verbo em questão, precedida do símbolo (➧).

> **aclarar** [4] [akla'ra(x)] *vt* [questão, mistério] to clarify.
> ➧ **aclarar-se** *vp* to become clear.

Informações culturais

Para entender e falar melhor uma língua estrangeira, é necessário algum conhecimento acerca das especificidades culturais do(s) país(es) onde ela é falada. Contudo, uma entrada de dicionário não é o local apropriado para esse tipo de informação. Assim sendo, na parte inglês-português deste dicionário, o leitor de língua portuguesa encontrará **boxes** informativos dedicados a particularidades culturais dos países de língua inglesa.

> **GUY FAWKES NIGHT**
>
> Festividade britânica celebrada na noite de 5 de novembro, em comemoração ao complô católico encabeçado por Guy Fawkes, em 1605, que tinha por objetivo explodir as casas do Parlamento. Nessa noite, os britânicos acendem fogueiras, nas quais queimam uma efígie de Guy Fawkes, e soltam fogos de artifício, razão pela qual a noite é também conhecida como *Fireworks Night* ou *Bonfire Night*.

O box **Guy Fawkes' Night**, por exemplo, nos informa sobre uma peculiaridade histórico-cultural britânica para a qual não há equivalente no Brasil.

HOW TO USE THE DICTIONARY

How to find the word or expression you are looking for:

First ask yourself some basic questions:

Is it a single word, a hyphenated word or an abbreviation?
Is it a compound noun?
Is it a phrase?
Is it a reflexive verb?

Single words, hyphenated words and abbreviations

As a rule, you can find the word you are looking for in its alphabetical order. If you want to translate an English word into Portuguese, you should look on the English–Portuguese side of the dictionary, and if you want to know what a Portuguese term means, you should look on the Portuguese–English side. The word in **bold** at the start of each entry is called the 'headword'.

Entries beginning with a **capital** appear after those spelled the same way but with a small letter.

> **ad** (*abbr of* **advertisement**) *n fam* **-1.** [in newspaper] anúncio *m.* **- 2.** [on TV] propaganda *f.*
> **AD** (*abbr of* **Anno Domini**) d.C.

Words with a **hyphen**, a **full stop** or an **apostrophe** come after those spelled the same way but without any of these punctuation marks.

> **its** [ɪts] *poss adj* o seu (a sua), dele (dela).
> **it's** [ɪts] = **it is**, **it has**.

In some cases, the entry is followed by a number in **superscript**. This means that just before or just after there is another entry, also followed by a number, which is written the same way but which has a completely different meaning or pronunciation. You must take care not to choose the wrong entry.

> **bow¹** [baʊ] ◇ *n* **-1.** [act of bowing] reverência *f* **- 2.** [of ship] proa *f.* ◇ *vt* [lower] inclinar. ◇ *vi* **-1.** [make a bow] inclinar-se **- 2.** [defer]: **to ~ to sthg** submeter-se a algo.
> ◆ **bow down** *vi* [give in]: **to ~ down (to sb)** render-se(a alguém).
> ◆ **bow out** *vi* afastar-se.
> **bow²** [bəʊ] *n* **-1.** [gen & MUS] arco *m* **- 2.** [knot] laço *m.*

You will sometimes see words followed by a grey lozenge, called sub-entries. English phrasal verbs and Portuguese pronominal verbs fall into this category.

> **beneficiar** [16] [benefi'sja(x)] *vt* **-1.** [favorecer] to benefit. **- 2.** [processar] to process. **- 3.** [melhorar] to improve.
> ◆ **beneficiar-se** *vp* [favorecer-se] to profit.

If you are looking up a noun which has a form with an initial capital which has a different meaning from the form without a capital, you should look at the form without a capital.

> **ascension** [ə'senʃn] *n* [to throne] ascensão *f.*
> ◆ **Ascension** *n RELIG* Ascensão *f.*

If you are looking up a noun which, in the plural, has a different meaning from the noun in its singular form (like glass/glasses in English), you will find it under the singular form; the plural form will be there as a sub-entry, indicated by the symbol ➡.

> **glass** [glɑ:s] ◇ n -**1.** (U) [material] vidro m -**2.** [for drinking] copo m -**3.** (U) [glassware] objetos mpl de cristal. ◇ comp de vidro.
> ➡ **glasses** npl [spectacles] óculos m inv; [binoculars] binóculos mpl.

Some plural nouns appear as headwords in their own right when they are never or rarely used in the singular (e.g. **juros** in Portuguese, **scissors** in English).

Compound nouns

A compound is a word or expression which has a single meaning but is made up of more than one word, e.g. **point of order, kiss of life, virtual reality, International Monetary Fund.**

It is a feature of this dictionary that English compounds appear in the A–Z list in strict alphabetical order. The compound **blood donor** will therefore come after **blood-curdling** which itself follows **blood count.**

> **blood count** n contagem f de glóbulos sangüíneos.
> **blood-curdling** adj de gelar o sangue.
> **blood donor** n doador m, -ra f de sangue.

On the Portuguese-English side however you should look under the first element of the compound. So, for example, you will find **café com leite** at the entry **café.** If there is more than one compound within an entry they will appear in their alphabetical order within the entry, regardless of any preposition between the two parts of the compound. So at **café** you will find **café pingado** after **café expresso.**

Phrases

If looking for a phrase, you should look first under the noun that is used in the phrase. If there is no noun, then you should look under the adjective, and if there is no adjective, under the verb. Phrases appear in entries in bold, the symbol ~ standing for the headword.

> **time** [taɪm] ◇ n -**1.** (U) [general measurement, spell] tempo m; **to get the ~ to do sthg** ter tempo para fazer algo; **to take ~** levar tempo; **to take ~ out to do sthg** tirar tempo para fazer algo; **it's high ~ ...** já é hora de ...; **to get ~ and a half** receber o pagamento combinado mais a metade; **to have no ~ for sb/sthg** não ter tempo a perder com alguém/algo; **to make good ~** fazer uma boa média (de tempo); **to pass the ~** passar o tempo; **to play for ~** tentar ganhar tempo; **to take one's ~ (doing sthg)** dar-se seu tempo (para fazer algo)...

Some very fixed phrases like **in spite of** in English or **atrás de** in Portuguese are entered under the first important element and preceded by ➡.

> **spite** [spaɪt] ◇ n (U) rancor m; **to do sthg out of** OR **from ~** fazer algo por maldade. ◇ vt magoar.
> ➡ **in spite of** prep apesar de; **to do sthg in ~ of o.s.** [unintentionally] fazer algo a contragosto.

> **atrás** [a'trajʃ] adv -**1.** [posição] behind; **lá ~** back there. -**2.** [no tempo] ago. -**3.** [em classificação]: **estar/ficar ~ (de)** to be ranked behind; **não ficar ~** fam fig not to be far behind.
> ➡ **atrás de** loc prep -**1.** [posição] behind. -**2.** [em seguimento a] after; **logo ~ de** right behind. -**3.** [em busca de - pessoa] after; [- objeto, explicação] looking for.

Reflexive verbs

Portuguese reflexive verbs are entered under the main form, after the symbol ➤.

> **aclarar** [4] [akla'ra(x)] *vt* [questão, mistério] to clarify.
> ➤ **aclarar-se** *vp* to become clear.

Cultural information

An appreciation of the culture of a foreign country is key to being able to understand and speak its language well. Cultural information on Brazil is provided in this dictionary in boxes on the Portuguese–English side of the dictionary.

> **BOSSA NOVA**
>
> Musical movement born in Rio de Janeiro in the late 50s; the bossa nova revolutionized the samba, condensing its rhythmic wealth into a syncopated beat with polished jazz chords for piano and guitar. The bossa nova's delicate melody and subtle song were to have a great influence on western popular music through two of the art form's greatest exponents, Tom Jobim and João Gilberto.

TRADEMARKS

Words considered to be trademarks are marked with the symbol ®. However, neither the presence nor the absence of such designation should be regarded as affecting the legal status of any trademark.

MARCAS REGISTRADAS

O símbolo ® indica que a palavra em questão é uma marca registrada. Este símbolo, ou a sua eventual ausência, não afeta, no entanto, a situação legal da marca.

PORTUGUESE VERBS

Portuguese verbs have a number, which refers to the conjugation table given at the back of the dictionary. This number is not repeated for reflexive verbs when they are sub-entries.

VERBOS PORTUGUESES

Os verbos portugueses são seguidos de um número que remete à tabela de conjugação, ao final do dicionário. Esse número não se repete nos verbos pronominais tratados como sub-entrada.

LIST OF BRAZILIAN CULTURAL BOXES
LISTA DE BOXES CULTURAIS BRASILEIROS

AFOXÉS
AMAZÔNIA
BAHIA
BIODIVERSIDADE
BOSSA NOVA
BRASÍLIA
CACHAÇA
CAFÉ
CAIPIRINHA
CANDOMBLÉ
CAPOEIRA
CARNAVAL
CATARATAS DO IGUAÇU
CHORO
CORDEL
DITADURA MILITAR

ESPORTES
FAVELAS
FEIJOADA
FERNANDO DE NORONHA
FESTAS JUNINAS
FUTEBOL
GENOMA
GUARANÁ
ILHAS
JEITINHO BRASILEIRO
LÍNGUA PORTUGUESA
LITERATURA BRASILEIRA
MERCOSUL
MISTURA DE RAÇAS
MOEDA
MÚSICA

OURO PRETO
PANTANAL
PATRIMÔNIOS CULTURAIS
PAU-BRASIL
POROROCA
RIO DE JANEIRO
SAMBA
SANTOS-DUMONT
SÃO FRANCISCO
SECA
TELENOVELAS
TROPICALISMO
TUPI
VESTIBULAR

LISTA DE BOXES CULTURAIS INGLESES
LIST OF ENGLISH CULTURAL BOXES

A-LEVEL
APRIL FOOL'S DAY
BILL OF RIGHTS
BROADSHEET/BROADSIDE
BUILDING SOCIETY
CHURCH OF ENGLAND
THE CITY
CONGRESS
CONSTITUTION
DOWNING STREET
ELECTION
ENGLISH BREAKFAST
FLEET STREET
FOURTH OF JULY
FRATERNITY
-GATE

GREEN CARD
GUY FAWKES' NIGHT
HALLOWEEN
HOUSE OF COMMONS
HOUSE OF LORDS
HOUSE OF REPRESENTIVES
L
LABOR DAY
LICENSING HOURS
MEDICARE/MEDICAID
NATIVE AMERICAN
OXBRIDGE
PENTAGON
PILGRIM FATHERS
POPPY DAY
PRIMARIES

PUB
PUBLIC SCHOOL
SAINT PATRICK'S DAY
SAT
SENATE
SUPREME COURT
TABLOID
THANKSGIVING
WALL STREET
WESTMINSTER
WHITEHALL
WHITE HOUSE
WORLD SERIES
YANKEE

PORTUGUÊS - INGLÊS
PORTUGUESE-ENGLISH

a¹, A [a] *m* [letra] a, A.

a² [a] ⟨⟩ *artigo definido* ▷ **o.** ⟨⟩ *prep* **-1.** [introduz um complemento indireto] to; **mostrar algo a alguém** to show sthg to sb, to show sb sthg; **diga ao Zé para vir** tell Zé to come; **peça o chapéu ao Paulo** ask Paulo for the hat. **-2.** [relativo a direção] to; **fomos à praia** we went to the beach; **vamos ao cinema** we're going to the movies; **cheguei a Salvador ontem** I arrived in Salvador yesterday; **ele percorreu o país de norte a sul** he travelled the country from north to south. **-3.** [relativo a posição, lugar, distância]: **é à esquerda/direita** it's on the left/right; **fica na saída do teatro** it's on the way out of the theatre. **-4.** [introduz um complemento direto]: **amar a Deus** to love God; **ele criou o menino como a um filho** he raised the boy like his own son. **-5.** [relativo a quantidade, medida, preço]: **aos centos/às dezenas** by the hundred/dozen; **a quanto estão as pêras?** how much are the pears?; **a quilo/metro** by the kilo/metre. **-6.** [indica modo, maneira]: **feito à mão** handmade; **bater à máquina** to type; **ir a pé/cavalo** to go on foot/horseback; **viajar a trabalho/passeio** to go on a business/pleasure trip; **à moda da casa** house style; **sal a gosto** salt to taste; **pagar à vista/a prazo** to pay cash/on time; **a olho nu** with the naked eye. **-7.** [relativo a velocidade]: **dirigir a 60 km/h** to drive at 60 kph; **ela ia a 100km/h** she was doing 100 kph. **-8.** [indica frequência]: **três vezes ao dia** three times a day; **estou lá às terças e quintas** I'm there on Tuesdays and Thursdays. **-9.** [introduz complemento de tempo]: **as lojas abrem às nove horas** the shops open at nine (o'clock); **eles chegam daqui a 2 horas** they're arriving in two hours' time; **fica a dez minutos daqui** it's ten minutes from here; **à noite** at night. **-10.** [indica série]: **de ... a** a from ... to; **façam os exercícios de um a dez** do exercises one to ten. **-11.** [seguido de infinitivo para exprimir momento]: **ele começou a falar** he started speaking; **ele tropeçou ao subir no**

ônibus he tripped as he was getting on the bus. **-12.** [seguido de infinitivo indicando duas ações]: **ela saiu a cantar** she went out singing; **ele nunca aprendeu a assobiar** he never learned to whistle; **começou a chover** it started to rain. **-13.** [em locuções]: **a não ser que** unless; **à exceção de** except for; **a partir de** from; **a respeito de** regarding.

à [a] = **a + a.**

AA (*abrev de* Alcoólicos Anônimos) *m* AA.

AACC (*abrev de* Associação de Assistência à Criança com Câncer) *f Brazilian association for assistance to children with cancer.*

AACD (*abrev de* Associação de Assistência à Criança Defeituosa) *f Brazilian association for assistance to disabled children.*

aba ['aba] *f* **-1.** [de chapéu] brim. **-2.** [de casaca] tail.

abacate [aba'katʃi] *m* avocado.

abacateiro [abaka'tejru] *m* avocado tree.

abacaxi [abaka'ʃi] *m* **-1.** [fruta] pineapple. **-2.** *fam* [problema, dificuldade] difficulty; **ter ~s para resolver** to have some difficulties to sort out; **descascar um ~** to get out of a fix.

abade, dessa [a'badʒi, desa] *m, f* abbot (*f* abbess).

abadia [aba'dʒia] *f* abbey.

abafado, da [aba'fadu, da] *adj* **-1.** [ar, sala] stuffy. **-2.** [pessoa - sem ar] suffocated. **-3.** [som] muffled.

abafador [abafa'do(x)] *m* **-1.** [de bule de chá] cosy. **-2.** [de instrumento] mute.

abafamento [abafa'mẽntu] *m* **-1.** [sufoco] suffocation. **-2.** [de som] muffling.

abafar [4] [aba'fa(x)] ⟨⟩ *vt* **-1.** [sufocar] to suffocate. **-2.** [cobrir] to cover. **-3.** [apagar] to smother. **-4.** [amortecer] to muffle. **-5.** [ocultar] to cover up. ⟨⟩ *vi* **-1.** [sufocar] to suffocate. **-2.** *fam* [fazer sucesso] to steal the show.

abagunçado, da [abagũn'sadu, da] *adj* messed-up.

abagunçar [abagũn'sa(x)] *vt* to mess sthg up.

abaixado, da [abaj'ʃadu, da] ◇ *pp* ▷ **abaixar**. ◇ *adj* -**1.** [pessoa] stooped. -**2.** [persiana] lowered.
abaixar [4] [abaj'ʃa(x)] *vt* to lower; ~ **o volume** to turn down the volume.
➤ **abaixar-se** *vp* [curvar-se] to crouch down.
abaixo [a'bajʃu] ◇ *adv* -**1.** [posição] down; **mais** ~ lower down. -**2.** [direção] further down; **escada** ~ downstairs; **ladeira** ~ downhill; **rio** ~ downstream. -**3.** [em texto] below. ◇ *interj* down with; ~ **a opressão!** down with oppression!
➤ **abaixo de** *loc prep* -**1.** [em posição inferior] below. -**2.** [em número inferior etc] under.
abaixo-assinado [a͵bajʃuasi'nadu] *(pl* **abaixo-assinados)** *m* petition.
abajur [aba'ʒu(x)] *(pl* **-es**)͵ *m* -**1.** [pantalha] shade. -**2.** [lâmpada] table lamp.
abalado, da [aba'ladu, da] *adj* -**1.** [pessoa] shaken. -**2.** [saúde] impaired.
abalar [4] [aba'la(x)] *vt* -**1.** [prédio, fundações] to rock. -**2.** [pessoa] to shake. -**3.** [saúde] to impair.
➤ **abalar-se** *vp* [comover-se] to be moved.
abalizado, da [abali'zadu, da] *adj* -**1.** [profissional] skilled. -**2.** [opinião] expert.
abalo [a'balu] *m* -**1.** [tremor] tremor; ~ **sísmico** earth tremor. -**2.** [efeito ruim] setback. -**3.** *fig* [comoção] uproar.
abalroar [20] [abawro'a(x)] *vt* to collide with.
abanar [4] [aba'na(x)] *vt* -**1.** [com leque, jornal] to fan. -**2.** [com mão, lenço] to wave. -**3.** [rabo] to wag. -**4.** [cabeça] to shake.
➤ **abanar-se** *vp* [ventilar-se] to fan o.s.
abandonado, da [abãndo'nadu, da] *adj* -**1.** [desamparado] abandoned. -**2.** [descuidado] neglected.
abandonar [4] [abãndo'na(x)] *vt* -**1.** [desamparar] to abandon. -**2.** [negligenciar] to neglect. -**3.** [deixar - estudos, profissão] to give up; [- cônjuge] to leave. -**4.** [renegar] to reject.
➤ **abandonar-se** *vp* -**1.** [desleixar-se] to let o.s. go. -**2.** [entregar-se]: ~**-se a algo** to surrender o.s. to sthg.
abandono [abãn'donul] *m* -**1.** [ato] abandonment. -**2.** [estado] neglect. -**3.** [relaxamento] shabbiness. -**4.** [entrega] surrender.´
abarcar [12] [abax'ka(x)] *vt* -**1.** [abranger] to comprise. -**2.** [alcançar] to cover. -**3.** [monopolizar] to monopolize.
abarrotado, da [abaxo'tadu, da] *adj*: ~ **(de)** packed (with).
abarrotar [4] [abaxo'ta(x)] *vt*: ~ **algo (de)** to pack sthg (with).
abastado, da [abaʃ'tadu, da] *adj* well-off.
abastardar [4] [abaʃtax'da(x)] *vt* to bastardize.
abastecer [25] [abaʃte'se(x)] *vt*: ~ **algo (de)** to supply sthg (with).
➤ **abastecer-se** *vp*: ~**-se (de algo)** to stock up (with sthg).
abastecimento [abaʃtesi'mẽntul] *m* supply.
abate [a'batʃil] *m* slaughter.
abatedouro [abate'dorul] *m* [matadouro] slaughterhouse.
abater [5] [aba'te(x)] *vt* -**1.** [matar - animais] to

slaughter; [- pessoa] to kill. -**2.** [diminuir] to reduce. -**3.** [enfraquecer] to weaken. -**4.** [desanimar] to shatter.
abatido, da [aba'tʃidu, da] *adj* -**1.** [pálido] drawn. -**2.** [enfraquecido] weakened. -**3.** [desanimado] downcast.
abatimento [abatʃi'mẽntul] *m* -**1.** [palidez] paleness. -**2.** [fraqueza] weakness. -**3.** [desânimo] dejection. -**4.** [redução] reduction; **fazer um** ~ to give a discount.
abaulado, da [abaw'ladu, da] *adj* convex.
abdicação [abdʒika'sãwl] *(pl* **-ões)** *f* abdication.
abdicar [12] [abdʒi'ka(x)] ◇ *vt*: ~ **o trono (em favor de alguém)** to abdicate the throne (in favour of sb). ◇ *vi* to abdicate; ~ **de algo** *fig* to forgo sthg.
abdominal [abdomi'nawl] *(pl* **-ais)** *adj* abdominal.
➤ **abdominais** *mpl* sit-ups.
abecê [abe'sel] *m* -**1.** [alfabeto] ABC. -**2.** *fig* [rudimentos] fundamentals *(pl)*.
abecedário [abese'darjul] *m* alphabet.
abeirar [4] [abej'ra(x)] *vt* to bring near.
➤ **abeirar-se** *vp*: ~**-se de** to draw near to.
abelha [a'beʎa] *f* bee.
abelha-mestra [a͵eʎa'mɛʃtral] *(pl* **abelhas-mestras)** *f* queen bee.
abelhudo, da [abe'ʎudu, da] *adj* nosy.
abençoado, da [abẽn'swadu, da] *adj* -**1.** [bento] blessed. -**2.** [bem-sucedido] successful.
abençoar [20] [abẽn'swa(x)] *vt* to bless; **(que) Deus te abençoe!** God bless you!
aberração [abexa'sãwl] *(pl* **-ões)** *f* aberration.
aberrante [abe'xãntʃil] *adj* incongruous.
aberto, ta [a'bɛxtu, tal] ◇ *pp* ▷ **abrir**. ◇ *adj* -**1.** [ger] open. -**2.** [registro, torneira] turned on. -**3.** [sem cobertura - terraço] open-air; [- carro] convertible. -**4.** [céu] clear. -**5.** [embrulho, pacote etc] unwrapped. -**6.** [camisa etc] undone. -**7.** [sincero] frank. -**8.** [liberal] open-minded.
➤ **aberto** *m ESP* open.
abertura [abex'tural] *f* -**1.** [ger] opening; **cerimônia de** ~ opening ceremony. -**2.** [orifício] gap. -**3.** [início] start. -**4.** [de golfo, enseada] width. -**5.** [em roupa] neckline. -**6.** [em idéias] openness. -**7.** *FOT* aperture. -**8.** *MÚS* overture. -**9.** [*POL* - democrática] liberalization; [- de aeroporto, porto] deregulation.
abestalhado, da [abeʃta'ʎadu, da] *adj* moronic.
ABF *(abrev de* **Associação Brasileira de Franchising)** *f Brazilian franchising association.*
ABI *(abrev de* **Associação Brasileira de Imprensa)** *f Brazilian press association.*
abilolado, da [abilo'ladu, da] *adj fam* potty, loony.
abismado, da [abiʒ'madu, da] *adj* dismayed.
abismo [a'biʒmul] *m* -**1.** [precipício] abyss. -**2.** *fig* [grande diferença] chasm. -**3.** *fig* [situação difícil]: **estar à beira de um** ~ to be on the brink.
abissal [abi'sawl] *(pl* **-ais)** *adj* [região] deep.
abjeto, ta [ab'ʒɛtu, tal] *adj* abject.
ABL *(abrev de* **Academia Brasileira de Letras)** *f*

Brazilian academy of arts.

abnegação [abnega'sãw] *f* self-sacrifice.

abnegado, da [abne'gadu, da] *adj* self-sacrificing.

abnegar [14] [abne'ga(x)] *vi* [renunciar]: ~ **de algo** to renounce sthg.

➡ **abnegar-se** *vp* [sacrificar-se] to sacrifice o.s.

ABNT (*abrev de* **Associação Brasileira de Normas Técnicas**) *f Brazilian body overseeing technical standards*, ≃ BSI *UK*, ≃ ANSI *US*.

abóbada [a'bɔbada] *f* vault.

abóbora [a'bɔbora] *f* pumpkin.

abobrinha [abɔ'briɲa] *f* courgette *UK*, zucchini *US*.

abocanhar [4] [laboka'ɲa(x)] *vt*-**1.** [morder] to bite. -**2.** *fig* [apoderar-se de] to seize.

aboletar-se [abole'ta(x)si] *vp* to install o.s.

abolição [abolisãw] *f* abolition.

abolir [79] [abo'li(x)] *vt* to abolish.

abominação [abomina'sãw] (*pl* -ões) *f* abomination.

abominar [4] [abomi'na(x)] *vt* to loathe.

abominável [abomi'navew] (*pl* -eis) *adj* abominable.

abonado, da [abo'nadu, da] <> *adj* [rico] well-off. <> *m, f* [rico] well-off person; **os** ~**s** the well-off.

abonar [4] [abo'na(x)] *vt* -**1.** [gen] to back up. -**2.** [afiançar] to guarantee. -**3.** [aprovar] to approve. -**4.** [dar] to grant. -**5.** [adiantar] to advance. -**6.** [relevar] to excuse.

abono [a'bonu] *m* -**1.** [aprovação] approval. -**2.** [fiança] collateral. -**3.** [pagamento extra] bonus; ~ **de Natal** Christmas bonus. -**4.** [relevação] pardon.

abordagem [abox'daʒẽ] (*pl* -ns) *f* approach.

abordar [4] [abox'da(x)] *vt* -**1.** [ir a bordo de] to board. -**2.** [pessoa] to approach. -**3.** [assunto] to broach.

aborígine [abo'riʒeni] *adj* -**1.** [indígena] native. -**2.** [da Austrália] aboriginal.

➡ **aborígines** *mpl & fpl* -**1.** [população indígena] natives. -**2.** [da Austrália] Aborigines.

aborrecer [25] [aboxe'se(x)] *vt* -**1.** [amolar] to annoy. -**2.** [entediar] to bore.

➡ **aborrecer-se** *vp* -**1.** [amolar-se]: ~**-se com alguém** to get annoyed with sb. -**2.** [entediar-se]: ~**-se (com alguém/algo)** to get bored (with sb/sthg).

aborrecido, da [aboxe'sidu, da] *adj* -**1.** [amolado] annoyed. -**2.** [enfadonho] boring.

aborrecimento [aboxesi'mẽtu] *m* [amolação] annoyance.

abortar [4] [abox'ta(x)] <> *vi* [MED - espontaneamente] to have a miscarriage; [- intencionalmente] to have an abortion. <> *vt* [plano, greve, etc] to abort.

aborto [a'boxtu] *m* [MED - espontâneo] miscarriage; [- intencional] abortion.

abotoadura [abotwa'dura] *f* cuff-link.

abotoar [20] [abo'twa(x)] *vt* [roupa] to button.

abr. (*abrev de* **abril**) Apr.

abraçar [13] [abra'sa(x)] *vt* -**1.** [com os braços] to hug. -**2.** *fig* [seguir] to embrace.

➡ **abraçar-se** *vp* to hug each other.

abraço [a'brasu] *m* hug; **dar um** ~ **em alguém** to give sb a hug; **um** ~ [em cartas] best wishes.

abrandar [4] [abrãn'da(x)] <> *vt* -**1.** [dor] to ease. -**2.** [lei, palavreado] to moderate. <> *vi* -**1.** [ger] to soften. -**2.** [dor, ira, calor, vento] to die down.

abrangente [abrãn'ʒẽtʃi] *adj* all-embracing.

abranger [26] [abrãn'ʒe(x)] *vt* -**1.** [incluir] to include. -**2.** [entender] to grasp. -**3.** [conter em sua área] to comprise.

abrasar [4] [abra'za(x)] *vt* -**1.** [incendiar] to set alight. -**2.** [esquentar muito] to scorch.

abrasileirar [4] [abrazilej'ra(x)] *vt* to Brazilianize.

➡ **abrasileirar-se** *vp* [pessoa] to become Brazilianized.

abrasivo, va [abra'zivu, va] *adj* abrasive.

abreugrafia [abrewgra'fia] *f* X-ray.

abreviação [abrevja'sãw] (*pl* -ões) *f* -**1.** [de palavra] abbreviation. -**2.** [resumo] abridgement. -**3.** [diminuição] curtailment.

abreviar [16] [abre'vja(x)] *vt* -**1.** [pôr em abreviatura] to abbreviate. -**2.** [resumir] to abridge. -**3.** [tornar breve] to shorten.

abreviatura [abrevja'tura] *f* abbreviation.

abridor [abri'do(x)] (*pl* -es) *m*: ~ **de garrafa** bottle opener; ~ **de lata** can opener.

abrigar [14] [abri'ga(x)] *vt* -**1.** [albergar] to shelter. -**2.** [proteger]: ~ **alguém de algo** to protect sb from sthg.

➡ **abrigar-se** *vp* [albergar-se] to take shelter.

abrigo [a'brigu] *m* -**1.** [refúgio] shelter; ~ **anti-aéreo** bomb shelter. -**2.** [cobertura] cover. -**3.** [asilo] home.

abril [a'briw] *m* April; **primeiro de** ~ April Fool's Day; *veja também* **setembro**.

abrilhantar [4] [abriʎãn'ta(x)] *vt fig* enhance.

abrir [6] [a'bri(x)] <> *vt* -**1.** [ger] to open. -**2.** [pernas, braços] to stretch out. -**3.** [camisa etc] to undo. -**4.** [mapa] to open out. -**5.** [registro, torneira, água] to turn on. -**6.** [túnel] to bore. -**7.** [estrada] to make. -**8.** [exceção, precedente] to create. -**9.** [apetite] to whet. <> *vi* -**1.** [ger] to open. -**2.** [sinal de tráfego] to turn green. -**3.** [tempo] to clear up.

➡ **abrir-se** *vp* [confidenciar]: ~**-se com alguém** to confide in sb.

ab-rogação [abxoga'sãw] (*pl* -ões) *f* -**1.** [de lei] repeal. -**2.** [de uso, costume] discontinuation.

ab-rogar [14] [abxo'ga(x)] *vt* -**1.** [lei] to repeal. -**2.** [uso, costume] to discontinue.

abrolho [a'broʎu] *m* thorn.

abrupto, ta [a'bruptu, ta] *adj* -**1.** [súbito] sudden. -**2.** [áspero] abrupt.

abrutalhado, da [abruta'ʎadu, da] *adj* brusque.

ABS (*abrev de* **antilock braking system**) *m* ABS; **freios** ~ ABS brakes.

absenteísmo [absẽnte'iʒmu] *m* absenteeism.

absolutamente [abso,luta'mẽtʃi] *adv* -**1.** [completamente] absolutely. -**2.** [de modo nenhum] absolutely not.

absoluto, ta [abso'lutu, ta] *adj* absolute; **em ~** not at all.

absolver [5] [absow've(x)] *vt*: **~ alguém (de algo)** *JUR* to acquit sb (of sthg); *RELIG* to absolve sb (of sthg); [inocentar] to clear sb (of sthg).

absolvição [absowvi'sãw] *f* -**1.** *JUR* acquittal. -**2.** *RELIG* absolution.

absorção [absox'sãw] *f* -**1.** [de água, vapores, gases] absorption. -**2.** [de valores, cultura] absorption.

absorto, ta [ab'soxtu, ta] *adj* [concentrado] absorbed.

absorvente [absox'vẽntʃi] *adj* -**1.** [substância] absorbent. -**2.** [pessoa, leitura, trabalho] absorbing.

~ absorvente *m*: **~ higiênico** sanitary towel.

absorver [5] [absoxve(x)] *vt* to absorb; **~ energia** to use up energy; **~ tempo** to take up time.

~ absorver-se *vp* [concentrar-se]: **~-se em algo** to absorb o.s. in sthg.

abstêmio, mia [abʃ'temju, mja] <> *adj* abstemious. <> *m, f* teetotaller.

abstenção [abʃtẽn'sãw] (*pl* -**ões**) *f* -**1.** [de prazeres, de fumo] abstinence. -**2.** [do voto] abstention.

abster-se [1] [abʃ'texsil] *vp*: **~ (de algo/de fazer algo)** to abstain (from sthg/from doing sthg).

abstinência [abʃtʃi'nẽnsja] *f* abstinence.

abstração [abʃtra'sãw] *f* -**1.** [alheamento] abstraction. -**2.** [isolamento] isolation. -**3.** [concentração] concentration.

abstrair [68] [abʃtra'i(x)] *vt* -**1.** [afastar] to keep away from. -**2.** [isolar] to separate out.

~ abstrair-se *vp* -**1.** [alhear-se]: **~-se de** to distance o.s. from. -**2.** [concentrar-se]: **~-se em** to absorb o.s. in. -**3.** [abster-se]: **~-se de** to abstain from.

abstrato, ta [abʃ'tratu, ta] *adj* abstract.

absurdo, da [ab'suxdu, da] *adj* absurd.

~ absurdo *m* absurdity.

abulia [abu'abu'dabi] *f* apathy.

abundância [abũn'dãnsja] *f* -**1.** [grande quantidade] abundance; **em ~** in abundance. -**2.** [riqueza]: **ele vive com ~** he is a man of means.

abundante [abũn'dãntʃil] *adj*: **~ (em/de)** abundant (in/with).

abundar [4] [abũn'da(x)] *vi* to abound; **~ em** *ou* **de** to abound in *ou* with.

aburguesado, da [abuxge'zadu, da] *adj* bourgeois.

aburguesar [4] [abuxge'za(x)] *vt* to gentrify.

~ aburguesar-se *vp* -**1.** [pessoa] to become bourgeois. -**2.** [área] to become gentrified.

abusado, da [abu'zadu, da] *adj* forward.

abusar [4] [abu'za(x)] *vi* -**1.** [aproveitar-se, exceder-se] to go too far. -**2.** [praticar excessos]: **~ de algo** to abuse sthg. -**3.** [aproveitar-se]: **~ de alguém/algo** to take advantage of sb/sthg. -**4.** [sexualmente]: **~ de alguém** to abuse sb.

abusivo, va [abu'zivu, va] *adj* -**1.** [tratamento] abusive. -**2.** [preço] excessive.

abuso [a'buzul] *m*: **~ (de)** abuse (of); **~ de confiança** breach of trust; **~ sexual** sexual abuse.

abutre [a'butri] *m* vulture.

AC (*abrev de* **Estado do Acre**) *m* State of Acre.

a.C. (*abrev de* **antes de Cristo**) *adj* BC.

acabado, da [aka'badu, da] *adj* -**1.** [terminado] finished. -**2.** [móvel, roupa etc]: **bem/mal ~** well/badly finished. -**3.** [gasto] worn. -**4.** [abatido, exausto] exhausted. -**5.** [envelhecido] aged.

acabamento [akaba'mẽntul] *m* finish.

acabar [4] [aka'ba(x)] <> *vt* -**1.** [terminar] to finish. -**2.** [rematar] to finish off. <> *vi* -**1.** [terminar] to finish, to end; **~ bem/mal** to end well/badly; **~ de fazer algo** to finish doing sthg; [há pouco] to have just done sthg. -**2.** [terminar por]: **~ fazendo algo** to end up doing sthg. -**3.** [ter como consequência]: **~ em algo** to end up in sthg. -**4.** [ter como limite]: **~ em algo** to end in sthg. -**5.** [abolir]: **~ com algo** to put an end to sthg. -**6.** [destruir]: **~ com algo** to destroy sthg. -**7.** [tornar-se] to end up.

~ acabar-se *vp* -**1.** [terminar] to finish, to end. -**2.** [desgastar-se] to wear o.s. out.

acabrunhado, da [akabru'ɲadu, da] *adj* -**1.** [desanimado] disheartened. -**2.** [envergonhado] embarrassed.

acabrunhar [4] [akabru'ɲa(x)] *vt* -**1.** [desanimar] to dishearten. -**2.** [envergonhar] to embarrass.

acácia [a'kasja] *f* acacia.

academia [akade'mial] *f* -**1.** [escola] school. -**2.** [sociedade] academy; **Academia Brasileira de Letras** *Brazilian Academy of language and literature*. -**3.** *ESP* school; **~ de ginástica** gym.

acadêmico, ca [aka'demiku, ka] <> *adj* academic. <> *m, f* academic.

açafrão [asa'frãw] *m* saffron.

acalanto [aka'lãntul] *m* lullaby.

acalentar [4] [akalẽn'ta(x)] *vt* -**1.** [ninar] to lull. -**2.** *fig* [nutrir] to cherish. -**3.** [aconchegar] to cuddle.

acalmar [4] [akaw'ma(x)] <> *vt* [pessoa, ânimos] to calm. <> *vi* -**1.** [pessoa] to calm down. -**2.** [ventania] to abate. -**3.** [mar] to become calm.

~ acalmar-se *vp* [pessoa, ânimos] to calm down.

acalorado, da [akalo'radu, da] *adj* [discussão etc] heated.

acamado, da [aka'madu, da] *adj* bedridden.

açambarcar [12] [asãnbax'ka(x)] *vt* -**1.** [apropriar-se de] to appropriate. -**2.** [monopolizar] to corner.

acampamento [akãnpa'mẽntul] *m* -**1.** [atividade] camping; [lugar] campsite. -**2.** *MIL* encampment.

acampar [4] [akãn'pa(x)] <> *vt* to encamp. <> *vi* to camp.

acanhado, da [aka'ɲadu, da] *adj* shy.

acanhamento [akaɲa'mẽntul] *m* shyness.

acanhar-se [4] [aka'ɲaxsil] *vp*: **~ (de fazer algo)** to be shy (about doing sthg).

ação [a'sãwl] (*pl* -**ões**) *f* -**1.** [atuação] action. -**2.** [feito] act; **~ de graças** thanksgiving. -**3.** [capacidade de agir]: **sem ~** helpless. -**4.** [efeito] effect. -**5.** [enredo] plot; **filme de ~** action movie. -**6.** *JUR* legal action; **mover uma ~ contra alguém** to bring a legal action against sb; **~ judicial** lawsuit. -**7.** *FIN* share; **~ ordinária** ordinary share; **~ preferencial** preference share. -**8.** *MIL* action.

acarajé [akara'ʒɛl] *m bean fritter*.

acareação [akarja'sãw] (pl -ões) f confrontation.
acarear [15] [aka'rja(x)] vt to confront.
acariciar [16] [akari'sja(x)] vt to caress.
acarinhar [4] [akari'ɲa(x)] vt to caress.
acarretar [4] [akaxe'ta(x)] vt to cause.
acasalamento [akazala'mẽtul] m mating.
acasalar [4] [akaza'la(x)] vt to mate.
acaso [a'kazu] m chance; **essa descoberta foi um** ~ it was a chance discovery.
   ➡ **ao acaso** loc adv at random.
   ➡ **por acaso** loc adv by chance.
acastanhado, da [akaʃta'ɲadu, da] adj brown.
acatamento [akata'mẽtul] m - 1. [respeito]: ~ **(a)** respect (for). - 2. [cumprimento]: ~ **(a ou de)** deference (to).
acatar [4] [aka'ta(x)] vt - 1. [respeitar] to respect. - 2. [cumprir] to obey.
acautelar [4] [akawte'la(x)] vt to caution.
   ➡ **acautelar-se** vp: ~**-se (contra)** to guard (against).
acebolado, da [asebo'ladu, da] adj cooked with onions.
aceder [5] [ase'de(x)] vi: ~ **a algo** to accede to sthg; ~ **em fazer algo** to agree to do sthg.
aceitação [asejta'sãw] f - 1. [anuência] acceptance. - 2. [admissão, aprovação] approval. - 3. [receptividade] acceptability.
aceitar [4] [asej'ta(x)] vt - 1. [anuir a] to accept. - 2. [admitir, aprovar] to approve.
aceitável [asej'tavew] (pl -eis) adj acceptable.
aceito, ta [a'sejtu, ta] <> pp ⊳ **aceitar**. <> adj - 1. [pessoa, produto] well-received. - 2. [proposta, solução] accepted.
aceleração [aselera'sãw] f - 1. FÍS acceleration. - 2. [de processo etc] progress.
acelerado, da [asele'radu, da] adj quick.
acelerador [aselera'do(x)] (pl -es) m accelerator.
acelerar [4] [asele'ra(x)] <> vt - 1. AUTO to accelerate. - 2. [apressar] to hurry. <> vi AUTO to accelerate.
acelga [a'sewga] f chard.
acenar [4] [ase'na(x)] <> vt - 1. [sinalizar] to indicate. - 2. [fazer movimento com - cabeça] to nod; [- mãos] to wave. <> vi - 1. [sinalizar - com cabeça] to nod; [- com mãos,lenço] to wave. - 2. [prometer]: ~ **algo (a alguém)** to offer (sb) sthg.
acendedor [asẽde'do(x)] m [de bico de gás] lighter.
acender [5] [asẽ'de(x)] <> vt - 1. [cigarro, fósforo] to light. - 2. [lâmpada, luz] to switch on. - 3. fig [ânimo] to excite. <> vp [lâmpada, luz] to be turned on.
aceno [a'senu] m - 1. [gesto] gesture. - 2. [com a cabeça] nod. - 3. [com a mão] wave.
acento [a'sẽtu] m - 1. [gráfico] accent; ~ **agudo/circunflexo** acute/circumflex accent. - 2. [intensidade] stress.
acentuação [asẽtwa'sãw] f accentuation.
acentuado, da [asẽ'twadu, da] adj - 1. [palavra, vogal] accented. - 2. [sílaba] stressed. - 3. [proeminente] accentuated. - 4. [marcante] marked.

acentuar [4] [asẽ'twa(x)] vt - 1. [palavra, vogal] to stress. - 2. [enfatizar] to emphasize. - 3. [realçar] to accentuate.
acepção [asep'sãw] (pl -ões) f sense.
acerca [a'sexka] ➡ **acerca de** loc adv about, concerning.
acercar-se [12] [asex'kaxsi] vp: ~ **de** [ir] to go towards; [vir] to draw near to.
acerola [ase'rɔla] f fruit similar to Barbados Cherry, commonly drunk as a fruit juice, rich in vitamins and minerals.
acertado, da [asex'tadu, da] adj - 1. [relógio] correct. - 2. [medida, decisão] sensible. - 3. [combinado] arranged.
acertar [4] [asex'ta(x)] <> vt - 1. [relógio] to set. - 2. [combinar] to arrange. - 3. [contas] to settle. - 4. [igualar] to even up. - 5. [endireitar] to put right. - 6. [encontrar] to find. - 7. [fazer atingir]: ~ **algo em algo** to land sthg on sthg. - 8. [aplicar] to strike. <> vi - 1. [em adivinhação, jogo] to guess correctly. - 2. [atingir]: ~ **em algo/alguém** to hit sthg/sb.
acerto [a'sextu] m - 1. [em decisão, escolha] right decision. - 2. [acordo] agreement. - 3. [de contas] settling. - 4. [sensatez]: **com** ~ with sensitivity.
acervo [a'sexvu] m [patrimônio] collection.
aceso, sa [a'sezu, za] <> pp ⊳ **acender**. <> adj - 1. [cigarro, fósforo] lit. - 2. [lâmpada, luz] on. - 3. fig [pessoa] excited.
acessar [4] [ase'sa(x)] vt COMPUT to access.
acessível [ase'sivew] (pl -eis) adj - 1. [de acesso fácil] accessible. - 2. [que se pode obter] available. - 3. [tratável] approachable. - 4. [inteligível] comprehensible. - 5. [módico] affordable.
acesso [a'sɛsu] m - 1. [ger] access. - 2. [aproximação] approach; **de fácil** ~ accessible; **de difícil** ~ inaccessible. - 3. [trato]: **de fácil** ~ approachable. - 4. [ímpeto] fit. - 5. MED attack. - 6. COMPUT access; ~ **discado** dial-up access.
acessório, ria [ase'sɔrjul] adj accessory.
   ➡ **acessório** m accessory.
acetinado, da [aseti'nadu, da] adj satiny.
acetona [ase'tona] f [removedor de esmalte] nail polish remover.
achacar [12] [aʃa'ka(x)] vt - 1. [tachar]: ~ **alguém de algo** to accuse sb of sthg. - 2. fam [extorquir dinheiro de] to extort money from.
achado [a'ʃadul m - 1. [coisa encontrada] find. - 2. [descoberta] discovery. - 3. [pechincha] bargain. - 4. [coisa providencial] godsend. - 5. loc: **não se dar por** ~ to play dumb.
achaque [a'ʃakil m ailment.
achar [4] [a'ʃa(x)] <> vt - 1. [encontrar - procurando] to find; [- por acaso] to come across. - 2. [descobrir, encontrar] to find. - 3.: ~ **graça em algo** to find sthg amusing. - 4. [supor, opinar] to think; ~ **que ...** to think that ...; **acho que sim** I think so. <> vi [decidir]: ~ **de fazer algo** to decide to do sthg.
   ➡ **achar-se** vp - 1. [estar] to be. - 2. [considerar-se] to consider o.s.
achatar [4] [aʃa'ta(x)] vt - 1. [aplanar] to flatten. - 2. [rebaixar] to lower.

achegar-se [14] [aʃe'gaxsil *vp*: ~ **(a/de)** to get closer (to).

acidentado, da [asidẽn'tadu, da] <> *adj* **-1.** [terreno] rough. **-2.** [viagem, vida] turbulent. **-3.** [pessoa] injured. <> *m, f* [pessoa] injured person.

acidental [asidẽn'tawl] (*pl* **-ais**) *adj* **-1.** [fortuito] accidental. **-2.** [secundário] incidental.

acidentar-se [asidẽn'tarsil] *vp* **-1.** [sofrer acidente] to have an accident. **-2.** [vitimar-se] to be injured.

acidente [asi'dẽntʃil] *m* **-1.** [desastre] accident; ~ **de carro** car accident. **-2.** [eventualidade] circumstance; **por** ~ by chance. ~ **geográfico** geographic accident. ~ **de trabalho** accident at work, industrial accident. ~ **vascular cerebral** MED stroke.

acidez [asi'deʒl] *f* acidity.

ácido, da [ˈasidu, da] *adj* **-1.** QUÍM acid. **-2.** [bebida, fruta, sabor] acidic.
➡ **ácido** *m* **-1.** QUÍM acid; ~ **úrico** uric acid. **-2.** fam [droga] acid.

acima [a'sima] *adj* **-1.** [ger] above; **mais** ~ higher up. **-2.** [em direção à parte superior]: **morro** *ou* **ladeira** ~ uphill.
➡ **acima de** *loc prep* **-1.** [em posição superior] above. **-2.** [quantia, quantidade] more than.

acinte [a'sĩntʃil] *m* provocation.

acintosamente [asĩntoza'mẽntʃil] *adv* deliberately.

acintoso, osa [asĩn'tozu, ozal] *adj* provocative.

acinzentado, da [da, asĩnzẽ'tadul] *adj* greyish.

acionar [4] [asjo'na(x)l] *vt* **-1.** [mecanismo, medidas] to set in motion. **-2.** JUR to sue.

acionista [asjo'niʃtal] *mf* shareholder; ~ **majoritário/minoritário** majority/minority shareholder.

acirrado, da [asi'xadu, da] *adj* **-1.** [luta, discussão, ânimo] tough. **-2.** [ódio] bitter.

acirrar [4] [asi'xa(x)l] *vt* **-1.** [instigar]: ~ **alguém contra algo/alguém** to incite sb against sthg/sb. **-2.** [exacerbar] to stir up.

aclamação [aklama'sãwl] *f* **-1.** [ovação] ovation; **por** ~ by acclamation. **-2.** [proclamação] proclamation.

aclamar [4] [akla'ma(x)l] *vt* **-1.** [ovacionar] to applaud. **-2.** [proclamar] to proclaim.

aclarado, da [akla'radu, da] *adj* [questão, mistério] clarified.

aclarar [4] [akla'ra(x)l] *vt* [questão, mistério] to clarify.
➡ **aclarar-se** *vp* to become clear.

aclimatação [aklimata'sãwl] *f* acclimatization.

aclimatar [4] [aklima'ta(x)l] *vt*: ~ **algo/alguém a algo** to acclimatize sth/sb to sthg.
➡ **aclimatar-se** *vp*: ~**-se (a algo)** to acclimatize o.s. (to sthg).

aclive [a'klivil] *m* slope; **um caminho em** ~ an uphill slope.

ACM (*abrev de* **Associação Cristã de Moços**) *f* ≃ YMCA.

acne [ˈaknil] *f* acne.

aço [ˈasul] *m* steel; ~ **inoxidável** stainless steel.

acocorado, da [akoko'radu, da] *adj* squatting.

acocorar-se [4] [akoko'raxsil] *vp* to squat down.

ações [a'sõjʃl] *pl* ⊳ **ação**.

açoitar [4] [asoj'ta(x)l] *vt* **-1.** [com açoite] to whip. **-2.** [suj: vento, temporal] to lash.

açoite [a'sojtʃil] *m* whip.

acolá [ako'lal] *adv* over there.

acolchoado, da [akow'ʃwadu, da] *adj* [forrado] quilted.
➡ **acolchoado** *m* quilt.

acolchoar [20] [akow'ʃwa(x)l] *vt* [forrar] to quilt.

acolhedor, ra [akoʎe'do(x), ral] *adj* welcoming.

acolher [5] [ako'ʎe(x)l] *vt* **-1.** [ger] to welcome. **-2.** [hospedar] to put sb up. **-3.** [admitir] to receive.

acolhida [ako'ʎida] *f* **-1.** [hospedagem] hospitality. **-2.** [recepção] welcome.

acometer [5] [akome'te(x)l] *vt* **-1.** [atacar] to attack. **-2.** [suj: doença, desejo, sentimento] to strike.

acomodação [akomoda'sãwl] (*pl* **-ões**) *f* **-1.** [alojamento] accommodation. **-2.** [aposento, instalação] room. **-3.** [arranjo, arrumação] layout. **-4.** [adaptação] adaptation.

acomodado, da [akomo'dadu, da] *adj* **-1.** [alojado, instalado] settled. **-2.** [conformado] reconciled.

acomodar [4] [akomo'da(x)l] *vt* **-1.** [alojar, instalar] to accommodate. **-2.** [adaptar]: ~ **algo a** *ou* **com algo** to adapt sthg to sthg.
➡ **acomodar-se** *vp* **-1.** [alojar-se, instalar-se] to settle o.s. **-2.** [conformar-se] to reconcile o.s.

acompanhado, da [akõnpa'ɲadu, da] *adj* accompanied.

acompanhamento [akõnpaɲa'mẽntul] *m* **-1.** [de processo, doença] monitoring. **-2.** MÚS accompaniment. **-3.** CULIN side order, side dish.

acompanhante [akõnpa'ɲãntʃil] *mf* companion.

acompanhar [4] [akõnpa'ɲa(x)l] <> *vt* **-1.** [ger] to accompany. **-2.** [processo, doença] to monitor. **-3.** [suj: problema, preocupações] to stay with. **-4.** [mar-gear] to run parallel to. **-5.** [compreender] to keep up with. **-6.** [combinar]: ~ **algo com algo** to accompany sthg with sthg. **-7.** CULIN to go with. <> *vi* MÚS to accompany.

Aconcágua [akõn'kagwal] *n*: **o (Monte)** ~ (Mount) Aconcagua.

aconchegado, da [akõnʃe'gadu, da] *adj* snug, cosy.

aconchegante [akõnʃe'gãntʃil] *adj* cosy.

aconchegar [14] [akõnʃe'ga(x)l] *vt* **-1.** [nos braços] to cuddle. **-2.** [na cama, nas cobertas] to tuck up *ou* in.
➡ **aconchegar-se** *vp* **-1.** [nos braços] to snuggle. **-2.** [na cama, nas cobertas] to tuck o.s. up *ou* in.

aconchego [akõn'ʃegul] *m* warmth.

acondicionamento [akõndʒisjona'mẽntul] *m* packaging.

acondicionar [4] [akõndʒisjo'na(x)l] *vt* **-1.** [embrulhar] to wrap. **-2.** [embalar] to package.

aconselhar [4] [akõnse'ʎa(x)l] *vt* **-1.** [dar conselho a]: ~ **alguém (a fazer algo** *ou* **a que faça algo)** to advise sb (to do sthg). **-2.** [recomendar] to recommend.
➡ **aconselhar-se** *vp* to seek advice; ~**-se com**

alguém to seek the advice of sb.

aconselhável [akõnse'ʎavɛw] *(pl* -eis) *adj* advisable.

acontecer [25] [akõnte'se(x)] *vi* to happen.

acontecimento [akõntesi'mẽntu] *m* event.

acoplado, da [ako'pladu, da] *adj* [conectado - peças] connected; [- naves espaciais] docked.

acoplar [4] [ako'pla(x)] *vt* to couple.

acordado, da [akox'dadu, da] *adj* -1. [desperto] awake; **sonhar** ~ to daydream. -2. [combinado] agreed.

acordar [4] [akox'da(x)] ⟨⟩ *vt* -1. [despertar] to wake. -2. [combinar]: ~ **algo/fazer algo** to arrange sthg/to do sthg; ~ **que** to agree that. ⟨⟩ *vi* -1. [despertar] to wake. -2. [concordar]: ~ **em algo/fazer algo** to agree to sthg/to do sthg.

acorde [a'kɔxdʒi] *m* MÚS chord.

acordeão [akox'dʒjãw] *(pl* -ões) *m* accordion.

acordeonista [akoxdʒjo'niʃta] *mf* accordionist.

acordo [a'koxdu] *m* agreement; **chegar a um** ~ to arrive at an agreement; **de** ~ agreed; **de** ~ **com** [conforme] according to; **estar de** ~ **(com alguém/em fazer algo)** to be in agreement (with sb/to do sthg); **de comum** ~ by common accord.

Açores [a'soriʃ] *npl*: **os** ~ the Azores.

acorrentar [4] [akoxẽn'ta(x)] *vt* to chain.

acossado, da [ako'sadu, da] ⟨⟩ *adj* [perseguido] persecuted, hounded. ⟨⟩ *m, f* victim.

acossar [4] [ako'sa(x)] *vt* -1. [perseguir] to pursue. -2. [acuar] to corner.

acostamento [akoʃta'mẽntu] *m* hard shoulder.

acostumado, da [akoʃtu'madu, da] *adj* -1. [habitual] usual. -2. [habituado]: **estar** ~ **a** *ou* **com algo** to be used to sthg; **estar** ~ **a fazer algo** to be in the habit of doing sthg.

acostumar [4] [akoʃtu'ma(x)] ⟨⟩ *vt*: ~ **alguém/algo a algo** to accustom sb/sthg to sthg; ~ **alguém a fazer algo** to accustom sb to doing sthg. ⟨⟩ *vi*: ~ **com algo** to get used to sthg.

→ **acostumar-se** *vp* to accustom o.s.; ~-**se a algo/a fazer algo** to accustom o.s. to sthg/to doing sthg.

acotovelar [4] [akotove'la(x)] *vt* -1. [para chamar a atenção] to nudge. -2. [empurrar] to elbow.

→ **acotovelar-se** *vp* [empurrar-se] to elbow one's way.

açougue [a'sogi] *m* butcher's.

açougueiro, ra [aso'gejru, ra] *m* butcher.

acovardado, da [akovax'dadu, da] *adj* intimidated.

acovardar [4] [akovax'da(x)] *vt* [amedrontar] to intimidate.

→ **acovardar-se** *vp* -1. [amedrontar-se] to be intimidated. -2. [perder o ânimo] to become disheartened.

acre ['akri] *adj* -1. [ácido, amargo] acrid. -2. *fig* [áspero] harsh.

Acre ['akri] *n* Acre.

acreditar [4] [akredʒi'ta(x)] ⟨⟩ *vt* -1. [crer] to believe. -2. [abonar] to confirm. ⟨⟩ *vi* -1. [crer]: ~

em algo/alguém to believe in sthg/sb. -2. [confiar]: ~ **em algo/alguém** to have confidence in sthg/sb.

acrescentar [4] [akresẽn'ta(x)] *vt* to add.

acrescer [25] [akre'se(x)] ⟨⟩ *vt* [adicionar]: ~ **algo (a algo)** to add sthg (to sthg). ⟨⟩ *vi*: **acresce que** ... in addition to which ...

acréscimo [a'krɛsimu] *m* -1. [adição] addition. -2. [aumento] increase.

acrílico [a'kriliku] *m* acrylic.

acrimônia [akri'monja] *f* acrimony.

acrobacia [akroba'sia] *f* acrobatics *(pl)*.

acrobata [akro'bata] *mf* acrobat.

acuado, da [a'kuadu, da] *adj* [acossado] cornered.

acuar [4] [a'kwa(x)] ⟨⟩ *vt* to corner. ⟨⟩ *vi* to retreat.

açúcar [a'suka(x)] *m* sugar; ~ **mascavo** brown sugar.

açucarado, da [asuka'radu, da] *adj* sugary.

açucareiro [asuka'rejru] *m* sugar bowl.

açude [a'sudʒi] *m* dam.

acudir [61] [aku'dʒi(x)] ⟨⟩ *vt* to run to help. ⟨⟩ *vi* to rush to sb's aid.

acuidade [akwi'dadʒi] *f* sharpness.

acumulação [akumula'sãw] *(pl* -ões) *f* accumulation.

acumulado, da [akumu'ladu, da] *adj* -1. [juros] accrued. -2. [prêmio] rollover.

acumular [4] [akumu'la(x)] *vt* -1. [ajuntar] to accrue. -2. [amontoar] to accumulate. -3. [reunir] to collate. -4. [cargos] to combine.

acúmulo [a'kumulu] *m* accumulation.

acupuntura [akupũn'tural] *f* acupuncture.

acupunturista [akupũntu'riʃtal *mf* acupuncturist.

acusação [akuza'sãw] *(pl* -ões) *f* -1. [incriminação] accusation. -2. [promotoria]: **a** ~ the prosecution.

acusado, da [aku'zadu, da] *m, f* [réu] defendant.

acusar [4] [aku'za(x)] *vt* -1. [gen]: ~ **alguém (de algo)** to accuse sb (of sthg). -2. JUR : ~ **alguém de algo** to charge sb with sthg. -3. [recebimento] to acknowledge. -4. [mostrar] to reveal.

acústico, ca [a'kuʃtʃiku, ka] *adj* acoustic.

→ **acústica** *f* FÍS acoustics.

AD *(abrev de* **Anno Domini)** AD.

adaga [a'daga] *f* dagger.

adágio [a'daʒul *m* -1. MÚS adagio. -2. [provérbio] adage.

adaptação [adapta'sãw] *(pl* -ões) *f* adaptation.

adaptado, da [adap'tadu, da] *adj* adapted.

adaptador [adapta'do(x)] *(pl* -res) *m*: ~ **de rede** COMPUT network adaptor.

adaptar [4] [adap'ta(x)] *vt* -1. [fixar] to fit. -2. [peça teatral, música, linguagem] to adapt.

→ **adaptar-se** *vp* [ambientar-se] to adapt o.s.

adega [a'dɛgal *f* cellar.

ademais [adʒi'majʃ] *adv* [além disso] moreover.

adendo [a'dẽndul *m* addendum.

adentro [a'dẽntrul *adv*: **casa/noite** ~ into the house/night; **mar** ~ out to sea.

adepto, ta [a'dɛptu, tal *m, f*: ~ **(de)** follower (of).

adequadamente [adekwada'mēntʃi] *adv* adequately.

adequado, da [ade'kwadu, da] *adj* appropriate.

adequar [23] [ade'kwa(x)] *vt*: ~ **algo a algo** to adapt sthg to sthg.

adereço [ade'resu] *m* -1. [enfeite] decoration. -2. [jóia] adornment.

aderência [ade'rēnsja] *f* -1. [de cola] adherence. -2. [a partido, campanha etc] support.

aderente [ade'rēntʃi] ◇ *adj* [substância] adhesive. ◇ *mf* [adepto] adherent.

aderir [57] [ade'ri(x)] *vi* -1. [colar-se] to stick. -2. [a partido, campanha] to adhere. -3. [a moda, estilo de vida] to follow.

adesão [ade'zãw] (*pl* -ões) *f* [a partido, campanha] adhesion; **jantar de** ~ fund-raising dinner; **documento de** ~ petition.

adesivo, va [ade'zivu, va] *adj* adhesive.

◆ **adesivo** *m* Sellotape® *UK*, Scotch tape® *US*.

adestrador, ra [adeʃ'trado(x), ra] *m, f* [de animais] trainer.

adestramento [adeʃtra'mēntu] *m* training.

adestrar [4] [adeʃ'tra(x)] *vt* to train.

adeus [a'dewʃ] ◇ *m* farewell. ◇ *interj* goodbye!

adiamento [adʒja'mēntu] *m* [prorrogação] postponement.

adiantado, da [adʒjãn'tadu, da] *adj* -1. [trabalho] ahead of schedule. -2. [relógio] fast. -3. [pagamento] advance *(antes de subst)*. -4. [aluno, povo] advanced.

◆ **adiantado** *adv*: **pagar** ~ to pay in advance; **cheguei** ~ **ao encontro** I arrived early for the meeting.

adiantamento [adʒjãnta'mēntu] *m* -1. [progresso] progress. -2. [de quantia, salário] advance.

adiantar [4] [adʒjãn'ta(x)] ◇ *vt* -1. [trabalho] to get ahead with. -2. [relógio] to put forward. -3. [quantia, salário] to advance. -4. [dizer antecipadamente] to anticipate. ◇ *vi* -1. [relógio] to be fast. -2. [trazer benefício]: ~ **fazer algo** to be worth doing sthg.

◆ **adiantar-se** *vp* -1. [em trabalho, estudos] to get ahead. -2. [avançar]: ~**se para** to go towards. -3. [sobrepujar]: ~**se a alguém** to surpass sb.

adiante [a'dʒjãntʃi] *adv* -1. [na frente] ahead; **mais** ~ [no espaço] further on; [no tempo] later on; **logo** ~ just ahead. -2. [em explicação, narração]: **ir** ~ to go ahead. -3.: **levar algo** ~ [obra, plano] to go ahead with sthg.

adiar [16] [a'dʒja(x)] *vt* to postpone.

adição [adʒi'sãw] (*pl* -ões) *f* -1. [acréscimo] addition. -2. *MAT* sum.

adicionar [4] [adʒisjo'na(x)] *vt* -1. [acrescentar] to add. -2. *MAT* to add up.

adido, da [a'dʒidu, da] *m, f* [em embaixada] attaché.

adiposo, osa [adʒi'pozu, oza] *adj* adipose.

aditivo [adʒi'tʃivu] *m* additive.

adivinhação [adʒiviɲa'sãw] *f* -1. [previsão] prediction. -2. [conjetura] guess. -3. [decifração] solution.

adivinhar [4] [adʒivi'ɲa(x)] *vt* -1. [presente, futuro] to predict. -2. [resposta, causa, intenção] to guess. -3. [enigma, mistério] to solve.

adivinho, nha [adʒi'viɲu, ɲal *m,f* fortune-teller.

◆ **adivinha** *f* [adivinhação] riddle.

adjacências [adʒa'sēnsjaʃ] *fpl* neighbourhood.

adjacente [adʒa'sēntʃi] *adj* adjacent.

adjetivo [adʒɛ'tʃivu] *m* adjective.

adjudicação [adʒudʒika'sãw] (*pl* -ões) *f* *JUR* adjudication.

adjudicar [12] [adʒudʒi'ka(x)] *vt JUR* : ~ **algo a alguém** to adjudicate sthg for sb.

adjunto, ta [ad'ʒũntu, ta] ◇ *adj* [assistente] assistant. ◇ *m, f* -1. [assistente] assistant. -2. *GRAM* adjunct.

administração [adʒiminiʃtra'sãw] (*pl* -ões) *f* -1. [ger] administration; ~ **de empresas** [curso] business studies; ~ **pública** public administration. -2. [pessoal] management.

◆ **Administração** *f* [governo] Administration.

administrador, ra [adʒiminiʃtra'do(x), ra] (*mpl* -es, *fpl* -s) *m, f* administrator.

administrar [4] [adʒiminiʃ'tra(x)] *vt* -1. [gerir] to manage. -2. [dar] to administer.

administrativo, va [adʒiminiʃtra'tʃivu, va] *adj* administrative.

admiração [adʒimira'sãw] *f* -1. [respeito] admiration. -2. [surpresa] surprise.

admirado, da [adʒimi'radu, da] *adj* -1. [respeitado] admired. -2. [surpreso]: ~ **(de)** astonished (at).

admirador, ra [adʒimira'do(x), ra] *m, f* admirer.

admirar [4] [adʒimi'ra(x)] ◇ *vt* -1. [respeitar, contemplar] to admire. -2. [surpreender] to surprise. ◇ *vi* [surpreender] to be astounding; **não é de** ~ **(que ...)** it's no wonder (that ...).

◆ **admirar-se** *vp* -1. [mutuamente] to admire each other. -2. [surpreender-se]: ~**se (de algo)** to be surprised (at sthg); **não me admiro!** I'm not surprised!

admirável [adʒimi'ravɛw] (*pl* -eis) *adj* -1. [excelente] admirable. -2. [assombroso] amazing.

admissão [adʒimi'sãw] (*pl* -ões) *f* -1. [ger] admission. -2. [contratação] employment.

admissível [adʒimi'sivew] (*pl* -eis) *adj* acceptable.

admitir [6] [adʒimi'tʃi(x)] *vt* -1. [ger] to admit. -2. [aceitar] to tolerate. -3. [consentir em] to permit. -4. [contratar] to take on. -5. [comportar] to allow.

admoestação [adʒmweʃta'sãw] (*pl* -ões) *f* -1. [advertência] warning. -2. [reprimenda] reprimand.

admoestar [4] [adʒmweʃ'ta(x)] *vt* -1. [advertir]: ~ **alguém de** *ou* **sobre** to warn sb of *ou* about. -2. [repreender]: ~ **alguém (de)** to reprimand sb (for).

ADN (*abrev de* ácido desoxirribonucleico) *m* DNA.

adoçante [ado'sãntʃi] *m* sweetener.

adoção [ado'sãw] (*pl* -ões) [-õjʃ] *f* adoption.

adoçar [13] [ado'sa(x)] *vt* -1. [café, chá] to sweeten. -2. *fig* [velhice, vida] to ease.

adocicado, da [adosi'kadu, da] *adj* slightly sweet.

adoecer [25] [adwe'se(x)] ◇ *vi*: ~ **(de)** to fall ill (with). <> *vt* to make ill.

adoentado, da [adwẽn'tadu, da] *adj* ill.

adoidado, da [adoj'dadu, da] <> *adj* [amalucado] mad. <> *adv fam* [muito] madly.

adolescência [adole'sẽnsja] *f* adolescence.

adolescente [adole'sẽntʃi] <> *adj* adolescent. <> *mf* adolescent.

adoração [adora'sãw] *f* adoration.

adorar [4] [ado'ra(x)] *vt* -**1.** [divindade] to adore. -**2.** [gostar muito de] to love.

adorável [ado'ravɛw] (*pl* -**eis**) *adj* lovely.

adormecer [25] [adoxme'se(x)] <> *vi* -**1.** [dormir] to fall asleep. -**2.** [ficar dormente] to go numb. <> *vt* [causar sono a] to make sleepy.

adormecido, da [adoxme'sidu, da] *adj* -**1.** [que está dormindo] asleep. -**2.** [dormente] numb.

adornar [4] [adox'na(x)] *vt* to adorn.

adorno [a'doxnu] *m* adornment; **de** ~ decorative.

adotar [4] [ado'ta(x)] *vt* to adopt.

adotivo, va [ado'tʃivu, va] *adj* adoptive.

adquirir [6] [adʒiki'ri(x)] *vt* -**1.** [comprar] to buy. -**2.** [conseguir] to acquire.

adrede [a'dredʒi] *adv* on purpose.

adrenalina [adrena'lina] *f* adrenalin.

Adriático [a'drjatʃikul] *n:* **o (mar)** ~ the Adriatic (Sea).

adro ['adru] *m* churchyard.

adstringente [adʒiʃtrĩ'ʒẽntʃi] <> *adj* astringent. <> *m* astringent lotion.

aduana [a'dwana] *f* customs (*pl*).

aduaneiro, ra [adwa'nejru, ra] *adj* customs (*pl*).

adubar [4] [adu'ba(x)] *vt* to fertilize.

adubo [a'dubu] *m* [fertilizante] fertilizer; ~ **orgânico/químico** organic/chemical fertilizer.

adulação [adula'sãw] *f* flattery.

adulador, ra [adula'do(x), ra] <> *adj* flattering. <> *m, f* flatterer.

adular [4] [adu'la(x)] *vt* to flatter.

adulteração [aduwtera'sãw] (*pl* -**ões**) *f* -**1.** [de texto] falsification. -**2.** [de alimento, medicamento] adulteration.

adulterar [4] [aduwte'ra(x)] *vt* -**1.** [texto] to falsify. -**2.** [alimento, medicamento] to adulterate.

adultério [aduw'tɛrju] *m* adultery.

adúltero, ra [a'duwteru, ra] <> *adj* adulterous. <> *m, f* adulterer (*f* adulteress). •

adulto, ta [a'duwtu, ta] <> *adj* adult. <> *m, f* adult.

adunco [a'dũnku] *adj* [nariz] hooked.

adventício, cia [adʒvẽn'tʃisju, sja] <> *adj* -**1.** [forasteiro] alien. -**2.** [casual] chance. <> *m, f* [forasteiro] outsider.

advento [adʒ'vẽntul] *m* advent.

advérbio [adʒ'vɛxbjul] *m* adverb.

adversário, ria [adʒivex'sarju, rja] *m, f* adversary.

adversidade [adʒivexsi'dadʒi] *f* adversity.

adverso, sa [adʒi'vɛxsu, sa] *adj* -**1.** [difícil] adverse. -**2.** [desfavorável]: ~ **a algo** unfavourable to sthg. -**3.** [contrário]: ~ **a algo** opposed to sthg.

advertência [adʒivex'tẽnsja] *f* -**1.** [aviso] warning. -**2.** [repreensão] reprimand.

advertir [54] [adʒivex'tʃi(x)] *vt* -**1.** [prevenir, avisar] to warn. -**2.** [repreender] to reprimand.

advindo, da [ad'vĩndu, da] *adj:* ~ **de** resulting from.

advir [67] [adʒ'vi(x)] *vi* -**1.** [resultar]: ~ **de** to result from. -**2.** [suceder]: ~ **(a)** to happen to.

advocacia [adʒivoka'sia] *f* advocacy.

advogado, da [adʒivo'gadu, da] *m, f* lawyer; ~ **do diabo** devil's advocate.

advogar [14] [adʒivo'ga(x)] <> *vt* -**1.** JUR to advocate. -**2.** *fig* [defender] to defend. <> *vi* -**1.** [exercer a profissão de advogado] to practise law. -**2.** [interceder]: ~ **por algo/alguém** to represent sthg/sb.

aéreo, rea [a'ɛrju, rja] *adj* -**1.** AERON air (antes de subst). -**2.** [pessoa] absent-minded.

aerobarco [aɛro'baxkul] *m* hovercraft.

aeróbico, ca [ae'rɔbiku, ka] *adj* aerobic.
➤ **aeróbica** *f* aerobics (sg).

aeroclube [aɛro'klubi] *m* flying club.

aerodinâmico, ca [aɛrodʒi'nãmiku, ka] *adj* aerodynamic.
➤ **aerodinâmica** *f* aerodynamics (pl).

aeródromo [ae'rɔdromul] *m* airfield.

aeroespacial [aɛroʃpa'sjawl] (*pl* -**ais**) *adj* aerospace (antes de subst).

aerofoto [aɛro'fɔtul] *f* aerial photograph.

aerograma [aɛro'gramal] *m* aerogramme UK, aerogram US.

aeromoça [aɛro'mosa] *f* air stewardess, flight attendant.

aeromodelismo [a,ɛromode'liʒmul] *m* -**1.** [técnica] model aeroplane making. -**2.** ESP model aeroplane flying.

aeronauta [aɛro'nawtal] *m, f* airline pilot.

aeronáutica [aɛro'nawtʃikal] *f* -**1.** [ciência] aeronautics (sg). -**2.** MIL air force.

aeronave [aɛro'navil] *f* aircraft.

aeroporto [aɛro'poxtul] *m* airport.

aerossol [aɛro'sɔwl] (*pl* -**óis**) *m* aerosol.

afã [a'fã] *m* -**1.** [ânsia - por sucesso] longing; [- de agradar] eagerness; [- para fazer algo] urge. -**2.** [entusiasmo, vontade] enthusiasm.

afabilidade [afabili'dadʒi] *f* affability.

afagar [14] [afa'ga(x)] *vt* -**1.** [person] to caress. -**2.** [animal, hair] to stroke.

afago [a'fagul] *m* stroke, caress.

afamado, da [afa'madu, da] *adj* famous.

afanar [4] [afa'na(x)] *vt fam* [roubar] to nick, to steal.

afasia [afa'zia] *f* aphasia.

afastado, da [afaʃ'tadu, da] *adj* -**1.** [praia, terras] remote. -**2.** [casa] isolated. -**3.** [parente] distant. -**4.** [pernas] apart.

afastamento [afaʃta'mẽntul] *m* -**1.** [distanciamento] withdrawal. -**2.** [de cargo] removal.

afastar [4] [afaʃ'ta(x)] *vt* **1.** [tirar do caminho] to push out of the way. -**2.** [apartar] to put aside. -**3.** [pôr de lado] to part. -**4.** [distanciar] to keep away *(sep)*. **-5.** [de cargo] to remove. **-6.** [frustrar] to thwart.

➤ **afastar-se** *vp* **-1.** [distanciar-se - no espaço] to move aside *(sep)*; [- de amigos etc] to part. **-2.** [sair] to leave. **-3.** [de cargo] to take leave from.

afável [a'favɛw] *(pl -eis) adj* affable.

afazeres [afa'zeriʃ] *mpl* affairs; ~ **domésticos** housework *(sg)*.

Afeganistão [afeganiʃ'tãw] *n* Afghanistan.

afegão, gã [afegiãw, ga] <> *adj* Afghan. <> *m, f* Afghan.

afeição [afej'sãw] *f* affection; **sentir** ~ **por alguém/algo** to feel affection for sb/sthg.

afeiçoado, da [afej'swadu, da] *adj* attached.

afeiçoar-se [20] [afej'swaxsi] *vp*: ~ **a alguém/algo** to become attached to sb/sthg.

afeito, ta [a'fejtu, ta] *adj*: ~ **a** accustomed to.

aferidor [aferi'do(x)] *m* [instrumento] meter.

aferir [57] [afe'ri(x)] *vt* **-1.** [conferir] to check. **-2.** [avaliar] to estimate. **-3.** [cotejar]: ~ **algo/alguém por algo** to judge sthg/sb by sthg.

aferrado, da [afe'xadu, da] *adj* [apegado] attached.

aferrar-se [4] [afe'xaxsi] *vp* [apegar-se]: ~ **a algo** to cling to sthg.

aferrolhar [4] [afexo'ʎa(x)] *vt* **-1.** [com ferrolho] to bolt. **-2.** *fig* [aprisionar] to lock up *(sep)*.

aferventar [4] [afexvẽn'ta(x)] *vt* to boil.

afetação [afeta'sãw] *f* affectation.

afetado, da [afe'tadu, da] *adj* affected.

afetar [4] [afe'ta(x)] *vt* to affect.

afetividade [afetʃivi'dadʒi] *f* **-1.** affection. **-2.** *PSIC* affectivity.

afetivo, va [afe'tʃivu, va] *adj* **-1.** affectionate, kind. **-2.** *PSIC* affective.

afeto [a'fɛtu] *m* **-1.** affection. **-2.** *PSIC* affect.

afetuoso, osa [afe'tuozu, ɔza] *adj* affectionate.

afiado, da [a'fjadu, da] *adj* sharp.

afiançar [13] [afjãn'sa(x)] *vt* **-1.** [réu] to bail out. **-2.** [dívida, empréstimo] to guarantee.

afiar [16] [a'fja(x)] *vt* [faca, tesoura] to sharpen.

aficionado, da [afisjo'nadu, da] *m, f* enthusiast.

afigurar-se [4] [afigu'raxsi] *vp* to seem, to appear.

afilado, da [afi'ladu, da] *adj* fine.

afilhado, da [afi'ʎadu, da] *m, f* godchild.

afiliação [afilja'sãw] *f* affiliation.

afiliado, da [afi'ljadu, da] *m, f* affiliate.

afiliar [16] [afi'lja(x)] *vt* to affiliate.

➤ **afiliar-se** *vp*: ~**-se a algo** to join sthg.

afim [a'fĩ] *(pl -ns) adj* **-1.** [objetivos] similar. **-2.** [almas] kindred.

afinação [afina'sãw] *(pl -ões)* [sõjʃ] *f MÚS* tuning.

afinado, da [afi'nadu, da] *adj* **-1.** [instrumento] tuned. **-2.** [pessoa]: ~ **com** attuned to.

afinal [afi'naw] *adv* **-1.** [por fim] finally, in the end; ~ , **ele vem ou não vem?** so is he coming or not?; ~ **(de contas)** in the end. **-2.** [pensando bem] all things considered.

afinar [4] [afi'na(x)] <> *vt* **-1.** [voz, instrumento] to tune. **-2.** [idéias, sentimentos]: ~ **algo com algo** to

attune sthg to sthg. **-3.** [estilo, modos] to refine. <> *vi* **-1.** [emagrecer] to slim down. **-2.** [concordar]: ~ **com alguém em algo** to see eye to eye with sb over sthg. **-3.** [dar-se bem]: ~ **com alguém** to get on with sb.

afinco [a'fĩŋku] *m* perseverance; **com** ~ assiduously.

afinidade [afini'dadʒi] *f* **-1.** [semelhança] affinity. **-2.** [parentesco]: **são primas por** ~ they look on each other as cousins.

afins [a'fĩʃ] *pl* ▷ **afim**.

afirmação [afixma'sãw] *(pl -ões) f* **-1.** [declaração] assertion. **-2.** [auto-afirmação] self-assertion.

afirmar [4] [afix'ma(x)] *vt* **-1.** [declarar] to declare. **-2.** [confirmar] to assert.

➤ **afirmar-se** *vp* **-1.** [estabelecer-se] to establish o.s. **-2.** [sentir-se seguro] to assert o.s.

afirmativamente [afixmatʃiva'mẽntʃi] *adv*: **responder** ~ to reply in the affirmative.

afirmativo, va [afixma'tʃivu, va] *adj* affirmative.

➤ **afirmativa** *f* assertion.

afivelar [4] [afive'la(x)] *vt* to buckle.

afixar [4] [afik'sa(x)] *vt* [aviso, cartaz] to affix.

aflição [afli'sãw] *(pl -ões) f* **-1.** [sofrimento] distress *(U)*. **-2.** [ansiedade] anxiety. **-3.** [desconforto]: **dar** ~ **a alguém** to unsettle sb.

afligir [52] [afli'ʒi(x)] *vt* **-1.** [fazer sofrer] to distress. **-2.** [causar ansiedade a] to trouble. **-3.** [suj: mal] to torment.

➤ **afligir-se** *vp*: ~**-se (com)** to worry (about).

aflitivo, va [afli'tʃivu, va] *adj* distressing.

aflito, ta [a'flitu, ta] *adj* distressed; **estar** ~ **com algo/para fazer algo** to be desperate about sthg/to do sthg.

aflorar [4] [aflo'ra(x)] *vi* **-1.** [vir à tona] to come to the surface. **-2.** [surgir] to surface.

afluência [aflu'ẽnsja] *f* **-1.** [de líquido] flow. **-2.** [de pessoas] flood. **-3.** [riqueza] affluence.

afluente [aflu'ẽntʃi] <> *adj* [rico] affluent. <> *m* [curso de rio] tributary.

afluir [74] [a'flwi(x)] *vt*: ~ **a ou para/de** to flow into *ou* towards/from; [pessoas] to flock to *ou* towards/from.

afobação [afoba'sãw] *f* **-1.** [agitação, atrapalhação] turmoil. **-2.** [pressa] haste. **-3.** [ansiedade] anxiety.

afobado, da [afo'badu, da] *adj* **-1.** [ger] flustered. **-2.** [ansioso] upset.

afobamento [afoba'mẽntul *m* = afobação.

afobar [4] [afo'ba(x)] *vt* **-1.** [ger] to fluster. **-2.** [deixar ansioso] to perturb.

➤ **afobar-se** *vp* **-1.** [ficar agitado] to get flustered. **-2.** [apressar-se] to fret. **-3.** [ficar ansioso] to worry.

afofar [4] [afo'fa(x)] *vt* **-1.** [almofada] to fluff up. **-2.** [terra] to loosen.

afogado, da [afo'gadu, da] *adj* **-1.** [pessoa] drowned. **-2.** [motor] flooded. **-3.** [em dívidas] weighed down. **-4.** [em trabalho] swamped.

afogador [afoga'do(x)] *(pl -es) m AUTO* choke.

afogamento [afoga'mẽntul *m* drowning.

afogar [14] [afo'ga(x)] <> *vt* **-1.** [pessoa] to drown.

- **2.** [motor] to flood. - **3.** [pensamentos, sentimento] to quell. ⬦ *vi* - **1.** [pessoa] to drown. - **2.** [motor] to flood.

➤ **afogar-se** *vp* [pessoa] to drown o.s.

afoito, ta [a'fojtu, ta] *adj* in a hurry *(depois de subst/de verbo)*.

afonia [afo'nia] *f* aphonia.

afônico, ca [a'foniku, ka] *adj* silent.

afora [a'fɔra] ⬦ *adv*: **pelo mundo** ~ throughout the world; **mar** ~ across the sea; **pela vida** ~ throughout life; **sair** *ou* **ir por aí** ~ to go off; **porta** ~ out the door. ⬦ *prep* apart from.

aforismo [afo'riʒmu] *m* aphorism.

afortunado, da [afoxtu'nadu, da] *adj* fortunate.

Afoxés [a'foʃɛʃ] *mpl traditional groups who parade through the streets during Carnival.*

AFOXÉS

Religious procession related to *candomblé*; *afoxés* were made up of groups of black people, who took to the streets and sang to the sound of percussion instruments such as *atabaques* and *agogôs*. Nowadays, *afoxés* are carnival displays typical of Bahia. The most popular one is known as *Filhos de Gandhi* ('Sons of Gandhi').

---

afrescalhado, da [afreʃka'ʎadu, da] *adj fam* camp.

afresco [a'freʃku] *m* fresco.

África ['afrika] *n* Africa.

africano, na [afri'kãnu, na] ⬦ *adj* African. ⬦ *m, f* African.

afro-americano, na [afrwameri'kãnu, na] ⬦ *adj* Afro-American. ⬦ *m, f* Afro-American.

afro-brasileiro, ra [afrobrazi'lejru, ra] *adj* Afro-Brazilian.

afrodisíaco, ca [afrodʒi'ziaku, ka] *adj* aphrodisiac.

➤ **afrodisíaco** *m* aphrodisiac.

afronta [a'frõnta] *f* affront.

afrontado, da [afrõn'tadu, da] *adj* [ultrajado] outraged.

afrontar [4] [afrõn'ta(x)] *vt* - **1.** [ultrajar] to outrage. - **2.** [atacar] to confront.

afrouxar [4] [afro'ʃa(x)] ⬦ *vt* - **1.** [soltar] to loosen. - **2.** [relaxar] to relax. ⬦ *vi* - **1.** [soltar-se] to come undone. - **2.** [pessoa] to give up.

afta ['afta] *f* mouth ulcer.

afugentar [4] [afuʒẽn'ta(x)] *vt* to chase away.

afundar [4] [afũn'da(x)] ⬦ *vt* - **1.** [fazer ir ao fundo - pessoa] to force to the ground; [- âncora] to drop. - **2.** [aprofundar] to deepen. ⬦ *vi* to sink.

➤ **afundar-se** *vp* - **1.** *fam* [em exame] to fail. - **2.** [embrenhar-se - em afazeres] to become engulfed; [- no matagal] to go deep. - **3.** [imergir] to sink. - **4.** [perder-se] to lose o.s.

afunilar [4] [afuni'la(x)] *vt* - **1.** [dar forma de funil] to shape into a funnel. - **2.** [estreitar] to narrow.

➤ **afunilar-se** *vp* [estreitar-se - rio] to narrow; [- análise] to be narrowed down.

agá [a'ga] *m* aitch.

agachado, da [aga'ʃadu, da] *adj* squat.

agachar-se [7] [aga'ʃaxsi] *vp* - **1.** [acocorar-se] to squat. - **2.** *fig* [aviltar-se] to grovel.

agarrado, da [aga'xadu, da] *adj* - **1.** [preso com força]: ~ **a** *ou* **em algo** clinging to *ou* onto sthg. - **2.** [apegado]: ~ **a** *ou* **com alguém** clinging to *ou* onto sb.

agarramento [agaxa'mẽntu] *m* [entre namorados] clinch; **ser pego de** ~ **com alguém** to be caught in a clinch with sb.

agarrar [4] [aga'xa(x)] ⬦ *vt* - **1.** [segurar com força] to grasp. - **2.** [capturar] to catch. ⬦ *vi* - **1.** [segurar com força]: ~ **em** to hold on to. - **2.** [goleiro] to defend.

➤ **agarrar-se** *vp* - **1.** [segurar com força]: ~ **-se a** *ou* **em** to hold on to. - **2.** [abraçar-se fortemente] to cling to each other.

agasalhado, da [agaza'ʎadu, da] *adj* warmly wrapped.

agasalhar [4] [agaza'ʎa(x)] *vt* to wrap up warmly.

➤ **agasalhar-se** *vp* to wrap o.s. up warmly.

agasalho [aga'zaʎu] *m* - **1.** [casaco, manta] warm clothing. - **2.** [suéter] jumper.

ágeis ['aʒejʃ] *pl* ⊃ **ágil**.

agência [a'ʒẽnsja] *f* - **1.** [empresa] agency; ~ **de notícias** news agency; ~ **de viagens** travel agency. - **2.** [sucursal] branch; ~ **de correios** post-office branch.

agenciamento [a'ʒẽsjamẽntul] *m* - **1.** [negociação] negotiation. - **2.** [representação] representation. - **3.** [obtenção, busca] recruitment.

agenciar [16] [a'ʒẽsja(x)] *vt* - **1.** [ger] to manage. - **2.** [servir de agente a] to act as agent for.

agenda [a'ʒẽnda] *f* - **1.** [de compromissos] diary; ~ **eletrônica** electronic organizer. - **2.** [programação - de reunião] agenda; [- de semana] schedule.

agendar [4] [aʒẽnda(x)] *vt* to schedule.

agente [a'ʒẽntʃi] ⬦ *m, f* [pessoa] agent; ~ **secreto** secret agent; ~ **de viagens** travel agent. ⬦ *m* - **1.** [ger] agent. - **2.** *GRAM* subject.

agigantado, da [aʒigãn'tadu, da] *adj* gigantic.

agigantar [4] [aʒigãn'ta(x)] *vt* to magnify; **o vento agigantou as ondas** the wind swelled the waves.

ágil ['aʒiw] *(pl* **ágeis***) adj* agile.

agilidade [aʒili'dadʒi] *f* agility.

agilizar [4] [aʒili'za(x)] *vt* to activate.

ágio ['aʒju] *m* interest.

agiota [a'ʒjota] *m, f* [usurário] usurer.

agir [52] [a'ʒi(x)] *vi* to act; ~ **bem/mal** to act properly/wrongly.

agitação [aʒita'sãw] *(pl* **-ões***) f* - **1.** [movimento - de garrafa] shaking; [- de líquido] stirring; [- de braços] waving. - **2.** *PSIC* [excitação] agitation. - **3.** [inquietação] restlessness. - **4.** [rebuliço] agitation. - **5.** [política, social] unrest.

agitado, da [aʒi'tadu, da] *adj* - **1.** [excitado] agitated. - **2.** [inquieto] disturbed. - **3.** [tumultuado] unsettled. - **4.** [mar] rough.

agitador, ra [aʒita'do(x), ra] *m, f* agitator.

agitar [4] [aʒi'ta(x)] ⬦ *vt* - **1.** [movimentar - garrafa etc] to shake; [- líquido] to stir; [- braços] to wave.

-2. [excitar] to unnerve. **-3.** [inquietar] to worry. **-4.** [sublevar] to agitate. **-5.** *fam* [fazer, organizar] to organize. ⬥ *vi* [movimentar]: **'agite antes de usar'** 'shake before use'.

➠ **agitar-se** *vp* **-1.** [inquietar-se] to become agitated. **-2.** [movimentar-se - na cama] to be restless; [- na rua, no trabalho etc] to run around.

agito [a'ʒitu] *m fam* excitement.

aglomeração [aglomera'sãw] (*pl* -ões) *f* **-1.** [de coisas] stack. **-2.** [de pessoas] mass; **~ urbana** built-up area.

aglomerado [aglome'radu] *m* **-1.** [de coisas] pile. **-2.** [de pessoas] mass.

aglomerar [4] [aglome'ra(x)] *vt* to mass.
➠ **aglomerar-se** *vp* [pessoas] to swarm.

aglutinação [aglutʃina'sãw] *f* **-1.** [fusão] agglutination. **-2.** [combinação] almagamation.

aglutinar [4] [aglutʃi'na(x)] *vt* **-1.** [com cola] to glue. **-2.** [palavras, sufixo] to agglutinate.

ago. (*abrev de* **agosto**) Aug.

agonia [ago'nia] *f* **-1.** [ger] agony; **que ~!** *fig* what a pain! **-2.** [de moribundo] death throes (*pl*). **-3.** *fig* [declínio] decline.

agoniado, da [ago'njadu, da] *adj* **-1.** [aflito] distressed. **-2.** [irritado] irritated.

agoniar [16] [ago'nja(x)] *vt* **-1.** [afligir] to distress. **-2.** [irritar] to irritate.

agonizante [agoni'zãntʃi] *adj* dying.

agonizar [4] [agoni'za(x)] *vi* to be dying.

agora [a'gɔra] ⬥ *adv* **-1.** [neste momento] now; **e ~?** now what?; **~ mesmo** right now; [há pouco] just now; **até ~** until now; **de ~ em diante** from now on. **-2.** [atualmente] nowadays. **-3.** [doravante] from now on. ⬥ *conj* [mas] now.

agorafobia [,agorafo'bia] *f* agoraphobia.

agorinha [ago'riɲa] *adv* just now.

agosto [a'goʃtu] *m* August; *veja também* **setembro.**

agourar [4] [ago'ra(x)] ⬥ *vt* [pressagiar] to portend. ⬥ *vi* [fazer mau agouro] to bode ill.

agourento, ta [ago'rẽntu, ta] *adj* **-1.** [supersticioso] superstitious. **-2.** [que anuncia desgraças] ominous; **que mulher mais agourenta!** what a prophet of doom that woman is!

agouro [a'goru] *m* omen; **mau ~** bad omen.

agraciar [16] [agra'sja(x)] *vt* **-1.** [condecorar] to decorate. **-2.** [preso, exilado] to pardon.

agradabilíssimo, ma [agradabi'lisimu, ma] *adj* = *superl de* **agradável**.

agradar [4] [agra'da(x)] ⬥ *vt* [causar prazer a] to please. ⬥ *vi* **-1.** [satisfazer]: **~ (a) alguém** to please sb. **-2.** [aprazer]: **~ a** to delight. **-3.** [ser agradável] to please, to be pleasing.

agradável [agra'davɛw] (*pl* -eis) *adj* pleasant.

agradecer [25] [agrade'se(x)] ⬥ *vt*: **~ algo** to say thank you for sthg. ⬥ *vi* **-1.** [dizer obrigado] to say thank you; **~ a alguém por algo** to thank sb for sthg. **-2.** [ficar grato] to be grateful.

agradecido, da [agrade'sidu, da] *adj* grateful.

agradecimento [agradesi'mẽntu] *m* [gratidão] thanks (*pl*), thank you; **carta de ~** thank-you letter.

➠ **agradecimentos** *mpl* thanks.

agrado [a'gradu] *m*: **fazer um ~ a alguém** [presentear] to give sb a present; [acariciar] to be affectionate with sb.

agrário, ria [a'grarju, rja] *adj* agrarian.

agravamento [agrava'mẽntu] *m* worsening.

agravante [agra'vãntʃi] ⬥ *adj* aggravating. ⬥ *m* [o que piora a situação]: **o agravante é que ...** the annoying thing is that ...

agravar [4] [agra'va(x)] ⬥ *vt* [piorar] to worsen. ⬥ *vi JUR*: **~ de algo** to appeal against sthg.
➠ **agravar-se** *vp* [piorar] to worsen.

agravo [a'gravu] *m JUR* appeal.

agredir [58] [agre'dʒi(x)] *vt* **-1.** [atacar] to attack. **-2.** [insultar] to insult. **-3.** *fig* [afetar] to offend.

agregado, da [agre'gadu, da] ⬥ *adj* attached. ⬥ *m, f* [hóspede] guest.
➠ **agregado** *m CONSTR* aggregate.

agregar [4] [agre'ga(x)] *vt* to add; **~ algo a algo** to add sthg to sthg.
➠ **agregar-se** *vp* [associar-se]: **~-se a algo** to join sthg.

agressão [agre'sãw] (*pl* -ões) *f* aggression.

agressividade [agresivi'dadʒi] *f* aggressiveness.

agressivo, va [agre'sivu, va] *adj* aggressive.

agressor, ra [agre'so(x), ra] *m, f* aggressor.

agreste [a'grɛʃtʃi] ⬥ *adj* rural. ⬥ *m stony, unfertile area of north-eastern Brazil*.

agrião [agri'ãw] (*pl* -ões) *m* watercress.

agrícola [a'grikola] *adj* agricultural.

agricultor, ra [agrikuw'to(x), ra] *m, f* farmer.

agricultura [agrikuw'tural] *f* agriculture.

agridoce [agri'dosi] *adj* **-1.** [comida] sweet and sour. **-2.** [emoções] bitter-sweet.

agroindústria [agrwĩn'duʃtrja] *f* agro-industry.

agronomia [agrono'mia] *f* agronomy.

agrônomo, ma [a'gronomu, ma] *m, f* agronomist.

agropecuário, ria [agrope'kwarju, rja] *adj* mixed-farming (*antes de subst*).
➠ **agropecuária** *f* mixed farming.

agrotóxico [agro'tɔksikul] *m* pesticide.

agrupamento [agrupa'mẽntu] *m* collection.

agrupar [4] [agru'pa(x)] *vt* to collect.
➠ **agrupar-se** *vp* to be grouped together.

agrura [a'grura] *f* scourge.

água [a'gwa] *f* **-1.** water; **~ benta** holy water; **~ boricada** boric acid; **~ corrente** running water; **~ doce/salgada** fresh/salt water; **peixe de ~ doce** freshwater fish; **~ mineral/gasosa/sem gás** mineral/sparkling/still water; **~ oxigenada** hydrogen peroxide; **~ potável** drinking water; **~ de rosas** rose water; **~ sanitária** chemically purified water; **claro como ~** crystal-clear; **com ~ na boca** watering at the mouth; **ir nas ~s de alguém** to go with sb's wishes. **-2.** *fig* [plano]: **ir por ~ abaixo** to go down the drain.
➠ **águas** *fpl* **-1.** [chuvas] rainwater (*sg*). **-2.** [minerais, termais] waters, thermal springs.

aguaceiro [agwa'sejru] *m* downpour.

água-com-açúcar [ˌagwakwa'suka(x)] *adj (inv)* sentimental.

água-de-coco [ˌagwadʒi'kokul] *f* coconut milk.

água-de-colônia [ˌagwadʒiko'lonja] (*pl* águas-de-colônia) *f* eau-de-Cologne.

aguado, da [a'gwadu, da] *adj* watered-down.

água-furtada [ˌagwafux'tada] (*pl* águas-furtadas) *f* garret.

água-marinha [ˌagwama'riɲa] (*pl* águas-marinhas) *f* aquamarine.

aguar [22] [a'gwa(x)] *vt* -1. [diluir] to water down. -2. [regar] to water.

aguardar [4] [agwax'da(x)] <> *vt* to await. <> *vi* to wait; ~ por to wait for.

aguardente [agwax'dẽntʃi] *f* brandy; ~ de cana cachaça.

aguarrás [agwa'xaʃ] *f* turpentine.

água-viva [ˌagwa'viva] (*pl* águas-vivas) *f* jellyfish.

aguçado, da [agu'sadu, da] *adj* -1. [ger] sharp. -2. [apetite] keen; [interesse] lively.

aguçar [13] [agu'sa(x)] *vt* -1. [ger] to sharpen. -2. [estimular] to stimulate.

agudeza [agu'deza] *f* sharpness.

agudo, da [a'gudu, da] *adj* -1. [ger] acute. -2. [penetrante] sharp. -3. [nota, voz] shrill.

agüentar [4] [agwẽn'ta(x)] <> *vt* -1. [ger] to bear; ~ fazer algo to be able to bear to do sthg. -2. [tolerar] to put up with. <> *vi* -1. [resistir] to support; não ~ de algo to be unable to bear sthg. -2. *loc:* ~ a mão *fam* [esperar] to hold on; [resistir a situação difícil] to hang on.
    ◆ **agüentar-se** *vp* [permanecer] to remain.

aguerrido, da [age'xidu, da] *adj* -1. [afeito à guerra] warlike. -2. [combativo] bellicose.

águia ['agja] *f* -1. [ave] eagle. -2. *fig* [pessoa] talented person.

agulha [a'guʎa] *f* needle.

ah [a] *interj* ah!

ai [ˌaj] <> *interj* -1. [de dor] ouch! -2. [de cócegas] eek! -3. [suspiro] oh! -4. [lamento] oh dear! -5. [gemido] oh no! <> *m* [de dor] groan.
    ◆ **ai de** *loc adj* damn.

aí [a'i] <> *adv* -1. [ger] there; espera ~! wait there! -2. [em lugar indeterminado]: por ~ around. -3. [para lugar indeterminado]: sair por ~ (afora) to go off somewhere. -4. [junto, em anexo] herewith. -5. [nesse caso, então] then. -6. [aproximadamente]: por ~ around. -7. [em data, período]: ~ pelos anos 60 around the 60s. -8. [e assim por diante]: e por ~ afora and so on and so forth. -9. *fam* [saudando]: e ~! hi! <> *interj* -1. [animando] go on! -2. [maliciando]: ~ ... hein? well, now ...

aiatolá [ajato'la] *m* ayatollah.

aidético, ca [aj'dɛtʃiku, ka] <> *adj* suffering from AIDS. <> *m, f* AIDS sufferer, person with AIDS.

AIDS (*abrev de* Acquired Immunodeficiency Syndrome) *f* AIDS.

ainda [a'ĩnda] *adv* -1. [ger] still; ~ não not yet; ~

(assim) still. -2. [um dia] one day. -3. [ao menos]: se ~ ... if at least.
    ◆ **ainda agora** *loc adv* just now.
    ◆ **ainda bem** *loc adv* just as well.
    ◆ **ainda por cima** *loc adv* still; ele não ajuda, e ~ por cima reclama he's not helping, and on top of that he's complaining.
    ◆ **ainda que** *loc conj* even if.

aipim [aj'pĩ] (*pl* -ns) *m* cassava.

aipo ['ajpu] *m* celery.

airoso, osa [aj'rozu, ɔza] *adj* elegant.

ajardinado, da [aʒaxdʒi'nadu, da] *adj* with garden.

ajardinar [4] [aʒaxdʒi'na(x)] *vt* to turn into a garden.

ajeitar [4] [aʒej'ta(x)] *vt* -1. [endireitar] to straighten. -2. [arrumar] to tidy up. -3. [acomodar] to tuck up.
    ◆ **ajeitar-se** *vp* -1. [arrumar-se] to tidy o.s. up. -2. [a emprego] to adapt. -3. [acomodar-se] to settle down. -4. [adaptar-se]: ~-se com algo to get used to sthg.

ajoelhado, da [aʒwe'ʎadu, da] *adj* kneeling.

ajoelhar [4] [aʒwe'ʎa(x)] *vi* to kneel.
    ◆ **ajoelhar-se** *vp* to kneel down.

ajuda [a'ʒuda] *f* -1. [auxílio] help; dar ~ a alguém (em algo) to help sb (with sthg); sem ~ without help; vir em ~ de alguém to come to sb's aid. -2. *ECON & POL* aid; ~ de custo financial assistance.

ajudante [aʒu'dãntʃi] *mf* assistant.

ajudar [4] [aʒu'da(x)] <> *vt* -1. [auxiliar]: ~ alguém (em algo) to help sb (with sthg); ~ alguém a fazer algo to help sb do sthg. -2. [facilitar] to help. -3. [missa] to serve at. <> *vi* -1. [auxiliar] to help; ~ a alguém to help sb; ~ em algo to help with sthg. -2. [facilitar] to help.
    ◆ **ajudar-se** *vp* to help each other.

ajuizado, da [aʒwi'zadu, da] *adj* sensible.

ajuizar [4] [aʒwi'za(x)] *vt* -1. *JUR* [levar a juízo] to bring before a court. -2. [formar juízo sobre] to form an opinion on.

ajuntamento [aʒũnta'mẽntul] *m* -1. [de pessoas] gathering. -2. [de objetos] pile.

ajuntar [4] [aʒũn'ta(x)] *vt* -1. [reunir] to assemble. -2. [amontoar] to pile up. -3. [acrescentar] to add.

ajustar [4] [aʒuʃ'ta(x)] *vt* -1. [regular] to adjust. -2. [adaptar]: ~ algo a algo [idéias, procedimento] to adapt sthg to sthg; ~ algo em algo [peça] to fit sthg into sthg. -3. [apertar] to tighten. -4. [acertar] to agree; ~ contas to settle accounts.
    ◆ **ajustar-se** *vp* [adaptar-se] to adapt.

ajustável [aʒuʃ'tavew] (*pl* -eis) *adj* adjustable.

ajuste [a'ʒuʃtʃi] *m* -1. [acordo] agreement. -2. [de peça - encaixe] fitting; [- aperto] tightening. -3. [regulagem] adjustment. -4. [acerto]: ~ de contas settlement of accounts; *fig* settling of scores.

AL (*abrev de* Estado de Alagoas) *n* State of Alagoas.

ala ['ala] *f* -1. [ger] wing. -2. [de escola de samba] group; a ~ das baianas *the section of the carnival parade made up of women wearing typical Bahia costumes.*

Alá [a'la] *m* Allah.

alagadiço, ça [alaga'dʒisu, sa] adj subject to flooding (depois de verbo).

alagado, da [ala'gadu, da] adj flooded.

alagamento [alaga'mẽntu] m flooding.

alagar [14] [ala'ga(x)] vt to flood.

Alagoas [ala'goaʃ] n Alagoas.

ALALC (abrev de Associação Latino-Americana de Livre Comércio) f Latin-American free trade association.

alambique [alãn'biki] m still (for making alcohol).

alameda [ala'medal f avenue.

alaranjado, da [alarãn'ʒadu, da] adj orange-coloured.

alarde [a'laxdʒi] m -1. [ostentação] ostentation; **fazer ~ de algo** to show off sthg. -2. [bazófia] boastfulness; **fazer ~ de algo** to brag about sthg.

alardear [15] [alax'dʒja(x)] vt -1. [ostentar] to parade. -2. [gabar-se de] to brag about.

alargamento [alaxga'mẽntu] m [de estrada] widening.

alargar [14] [alax'ga(x)] vt -1. [estrada] to widen. -2. [roupa] to let out.

alarido [ala'ridu] m [gritaria, algazarra] uproar.

alarmante [alax'mãntʃi] adj alarming.

alarmar [4] [alax'ma(x)] vt to alarm.

➡ **alarmar-se** vp to become alarmed.

alarme [a'laxmi] m alarm; **campainha de ~** alarm bell; **dar o ~** to sound the alarm.

alarmista [alax'miʃta] adj alarmist.

Alasca [a'laʃka] n Alaska.

alastrar [4] [alaʃ'tra(x)] vt [propagar, espalhar] to spread.

➡ **alastrar-se** vp to spread.

alavanca [ala'vãŋka] f -1. [peça] lever; **~ de mudanças** AUTO gear lever. -2. fig [meio de ação] lever.

alavancagem [alavãŋ'kaʒẽ] f ECON leverage.

alavancar [alavaŋ'ka(x)] vt [promover] to launch; ECON to leverage.

albanês, esa [awbã'neʃ] <> adj Albanian. <> m, f Albanian.

➡ **albanês** m [língua] Albanian.

Albânia [aw'bãnja] n Albania.

albergue [aw'bɛxgi] m -1. [hospedaria] hostel; [para jovens] youth hostel. -2. [asilo] refuge.

albino, na [aw'binu, na] <> adj albino. <> m, f albino.

álbum ['awbũ] (pl -ns) m album.

albumina [awbu'mina] f albumin.

ALCA (abrev de Área de Livre Comércio das Américas) f FTAA.

alça ['awsa] f -1. [de mala, vestido] strap. -2. [em arma]: **~ de mira** sights (pl).

alcachofra [awka'ʃofra] f artichoke.

alcaçuz [awka'suʒ] m liquorice plant.

alçada [aw'sada] f -1. [competência] competence; **ser da ~ de alguém** to be sb's responsibility. -2. JUR jurisdiction.

álcali ['awkalil m alkali.

alcalino, na [awka'linu, na] adj alkaline.

alcançar [13] [awkãn'sa(x)] vt -1. [ger] to reach. -2. [pegar] to catch. -3. [entender] to grasp. -4. [conseguir] to attain.

alcançável [awkãn'savew] (pl -eis) adj attainable.

alcance [aw'kãnsi] m -1. [de arma, míssil] range. -2. [de pessoa]: **ao meu/ao teu ~** within my/your reach; **ao ~ da vista** within sight; **fora do ~ de** [objeto, pessoa] out of reach of; [entendimento] beyond the grasp of. -3. [importância]: **de pequeno/grande ~** of minor/major importance.

alçapão [awsa'pãw] (pl -ões) m -1. [portinhola] trapdoor. -2. [armadilha] trap.

alcaparra [awka'paxa] f caper.

alçar [13] [aw'sa(x)] vt -1. [levantar - carga, viga] to lift; [- braço] to raise. -2. [voz] to raise. -3. [vôo] to rise.

➡ **alçar-se** vp [a cargo] to rise.

alcatéia [awka'tɛja] f [de lobos] pack.

alcatra [aw'katra] f rump steak.

alcatrão [awka'trãw] m tar.

álcool ['awkow] (pl -óis) m alcohol.

alcoólatra [aw'kɔlatra] <> adj alcoholic. <> mf alcoholic.

alcoólico, ca [aw'kwɔliku, ka] adj alcoholic.

alcoolismo [awko'liʒmu] m alcoholism.

alcoolizado, da [awkoli'zadu, da] adj [pessoa] drunk.

Alcorão [awko'rãw] m Koran.

alcova [aw'kova] f dressing room.

alcoviteiro, ra [awkovi'tejru, ra] m, f gossip.

alcunha [aw'kuɲa] f nickname.

aldeão, deã [aw'dʒjãw, dja] (mpl -ões, -ãos, fpl -s) m, f villager.

aldeia [aw'deja] f village; **~ de pescadores** fishing village.

aldraba [aw'draba] f [de bater] door-knocker.

aleatório, ria [alea'tɔrju, rja] adj random.

alecrim [ale'krĩ] m rosemary.

alegação [alega'sãw] (pl -ões) f allegation.

alegado, da [ale'gadu, da] adj alleged.

➡ **alegado** m JUR allegation.

alegar [14] [ale'ga(x)] vt to allege; **~ que** to allege that; JUR to allege that.

alegoria [alego'ria] f allegory.

alegórico, ca [ale'gɔriku] adj allegorical; ▷ carro.

alegrar [4] [ale'gra(x)] vt to cheer up.

➡ **alegrar-se** vp to be happy; **alegre-se!** cheer up!

alegre [a'lɛgri] adj -1. [pessoa] cheerful. -2. [festa, bar, voz] lively. -3. [cor] bright. -4. [embriagado] merry.

alegria [ale'gria] f -1. [qualidade] cheerfulness. -2. [satisfação] contentment. -3. [júbilo] joy.

aléia [a'lɛja] f -1. [alameda] alley. -2. [passagem] alley.

aleijado, da [alej'ʒadu, da] <> adj crippled. <> m, f cripple.

aleijar [4] [alej'ʒa(x)] vt to cripple.

aleitamento [alejtamẽntu] m breastfeeding.

além [a'lẽj] <> m [o outro mundo]: **o ~** the beyond. <> adv -1. [em lugar afastado] over there. -2. [mais

adiante] further on; **mais** ~ further.
- **além de** *loc prep* **-1.** [mais adiante de] beyond.
- **2.** [do outro lado de, acima de] beyond. **-3.** [afora] apart from.
- **além disso** *loc conj* besides.
- **além do mais** *loc conj* furthermore.
Alemanha [ale'mãɲa] *n* Germany.
alemão, mã [ale'mãw, mã] <> *adj* German. <> *m, f* German.
- **alemão** *m* [língua] German.
alentado, da [álẽntadu, da] *adj* **-1.** [animoso] brave. **-2.** [volumoso] bulky. **-3.** [corpulento] stout.
alentar [4] [alẽnta(x)] *vt* to comfort.
alento [a'lẽntu] *m* **-1.** [ânimo] courage. **-2.** [fôlego] breath.
alergia [alex'ʒia] *f* **-1.** MED allergy; **ter** ~ **a algo** to be allergic to sthg. **-2.** *fig* [aversão] allergy; **ter** ~ **a algo/alguém** to be allergic to sthg/sb.
alérgico, ca [a'lɛxʒiku, ka] *adj* **-1.** MED : ~ **(a)** allergic (to). **-2.** *fig* [averso]: ~ **a algo** to.
alerta [a'lɛxta] <> *adj* alert. <> *adv* alert. <> *m* warning.
alertar [4] [alex'ta(x)] *vt* : ~ **alguém (de/sobre algo)** to alert sb (to sthg).
alfabético, ca [awfa'bɛtʃiku, ka] *adj* alphabetical.
alfabetização [awfabetʃiza'sãw] *f* **-1.** [ato] teaching to read and write. **-2.** [estado] literacy.
alfabetizado, da [awfabetʃi'zadu, da] *adj* literate.
alfabetizar [4] [awfabetʃi'za(x)] *vt* to teach to read and write.
alfabeto [awfa'bɛtu] *m* alphabet.
alface [aw'fasi] *f* lettuce.
alfafa [aw'fafa] *f* alfalfa.
alfaiataria [awfajata'ria] *f* tailor's shop.
alfaiate [awfa'jatʃi] *m* tailor.
alfândega [aw'fãndega] *f* **-1.** [administração] customs (pl). **-2.** [local] customs house.
alfandegário, ria [awfãnde'garju, rja] *adj* customs (antes de subst).
alfazema [awfa'zema] *f* lavender.
alfinetada [awfine'tada] *f* **-1.** [picada de alfinete] pin-prick. **-2.** [dor] sharp pain. **-3.** *fig* [dito] stinging remark; **dar uma** ~ **em alguém** to make a stinging remark to sb.
alfinetar [4] [awfine'ta(x)] *vt* **-1.** COST to pin. **-2.** *fig* [criticar] to criticize.
alfinete [awfi'netʃi] *m* **-1.** COST pin. **-2.** [prendedor]: ~ **de fralda** nappy pin; ~ **de segurança** safety pin. **-3.** [jóia] pin.
alfineteira [awfine'tejra] *f* **-1.** [caixa] pin box. **-2.** [almofadinha] pincushion.
alforje [aw'fɔxʒi] *m* saddlebag.
alga [ˈawga] *f* seaweed.
algarismo [awga'riʒmu] *m* number.
algazarra [awga'zaxa] *f* shouting; **fazer** ~ to make a racket.
álgebra [ˈawʒebra] *f* algebra.
algébrico, ca [aw'ʒɛbriku, ka] *adj* MAT algebraic.
algemar [4] [awʒe'ma(x)] *vt* to handcuff.

algemas [aw'ʒemaʃ] *fpl* handcuffs.
algo [ˈawgu] <> *pron* **-1.** (em frases afirmativas) something. **-2.** (em frases interrogativas) anything. <> *adv* somewhat.
algodão [awgo'dãw] *m* cotton; ~ **(hidrófilo)** cotton wool; **uma camisa de** ~ a cotton shirt.
algodão-doce [awgo doãw'dosi] (pl algodões-doces) *m* candyfloss.
algodoeiro [awgo'dwejru] *m* cotton plant.
algoritmo [awgo'xitʃimu] *m* algorithm.
algoz [aw'gɔʒ] *m* **-1.** [carrasco] executioner. **-2.** [pessoa cruel] cruel person.
alguém [aw'gẽj] <> *pron indef* **-1.** [alguma pessoa] someone; ~ **quebrou este vaso** someone broke this vase; **tem** ~ **lá embaixo** there's someone downstairs **-2.** [em frases interrogativas] anybody, anyone; ~ **me telefonou?** did anybody phone me?; ~ **quer mais café?** does anybody want more coffee?; **tem** ~ **aí?** is anybody there?; ~ **mais** anybody else. **-3.** [determinada pessoa] somebody; **ele sabia que haveria** ~ **à sua espera** he knew there would be somebody waiting for him; **você é** ~ **que admiro muito** you are somebody I admire greatly. **-4.** *fig* [pessoa importante] somebody; **se um dia eu me tornar** ~, **lembrarei dos velhos amigos** if one day I become somebody, I'll remember my old friends; **ele é** ~ **na empresa?** is he somebody in the company?; **ser** ~ **(na vida)** to be somebody in life. <> *m* [uma pessoa]: **esse** ~ that person; **um** ~ a person.
algum, ma [aw'gũ, ma] (mpl **-ns**, fpl **-s**) <> *adj* **-1.** [indeterminado] some; **ela morou** ~ **tempo em Londres** she lived for some time in London; **me dê** ~ **dinheiro** give me some money; ~ **dia vamos te visitar** some day we'll come and see you **-2.** [em interrogativas, negativas] any; ~ **problema?** any problems?; **de jeito** *ou* **modo** ~ in no way; **não há problema** ~ there's no problem, there aren't any problems; **em parte alguma do país** nowhere in the country; **coisa alguma** nothing; **não há melhora alguma** there is no improvement, there isn't any improvement. <> *pron* **-1.** [indicando pessoa] somebody; **alguns preferem cinema, outros, teatro** some people prefer the cinema, others the theatre **-2.** [indicando coisa] one; **abra a caixa de bombons e prove alguns** open the box of sweets and try some **-3.** [em interrogativas: pessoa] anybody **-4.** [em interrogativas: coisa] any; ~ **dia** one *ou* some day; **alguma coisa** something, anything; **alguma vez** sometime.
- **alguns** *pron pl* some.
- **alguma** *f* [evento, feito]: **deve ter lhe acontecido alguma** something must have happened to him; **esse menino aprontou alguma** that boy has been up to something.
alheamento [aʎea'mẽntu] *m* [indiferença] indifference.
alhear [15] [aʎeia(x)] *vt* **-1.** [desviar] to turn. **-2.** [bens] to separate.
- **alhear-se** *vp* [distanciar-se] to distance o.s.
alheio, alheia [a'ʎeju, a'ʎeja] *adj* **-1.** [de outra

pessoa]: **um problema** ~ somebody else's problem. -**2.** [irrelevante]: ~ **a** irrelevant to. -**3.** [afastado, abstraído]: ~ **(a)** unaware (of).

➤ **alheios** mpl [estranhos] outsiders.

alho ['aʎul m garlic; **confundir** ~**s com bugalhos** to confuse two different things.

alho-poró [aʎupo'rɔ] (pl **alhos-porós**) m leek.

alhures [a'ʎuriʃ] adv elsewhere.

ali [a'li] adv -**1.** [naquele lugar] there; ~ **dentro/fora** in/out there; **logo** ~ right there; **por** ~ around there. -**2.** [naquele momento] then.

aliado, da [a'ljadu, da] ◇ adj allied. ◇ m, f ally.

➤ **Aliados** mpl: os Aliados the Allies.

aliança [a'ljãnsa] f -**1.** [pacto] alliance. -**2.** [anel] wedding ring.

aliar [16] [a'lja(x)] vt [qualidades] to combine.

➤ **aliar-se** vp [nações] to become allied.

aliás [a'ljajʃ] adv -**1.** [a propósito] as a matter of fact. -**2.** [diga-se de passagem] incidentally. -**3.** [ou por outra] or rather.

álibi ['alibi] m alibi.

alicate [ali'katʃi] m pliers (pl); ~ **de unhas** nail clippers (pl).

alicerçado, da [alisex'sadu, da] adj based.

alicerce [ali'sɛxsi] m CONSTR foundation.

aliciamento [alisia'mẽntu] m [sedução] seduction.

aliciar [16] [ali'sja(x)] vt -**1.** [atrair, seduzir] to entice. -**2.** [convocar] to recruit. -**3.** [subornar] to bribe.

alienação [aljena'sãw] f -**1.** [falta de consciência, participação] lack of awareness. -**2.** PSIC : ~ **mental** mental illness. -**3.** [de bens] assignment.

alienado, da [alje'nadu, da] adj -**1.** [não participante] alienated. -**2.** [louco] insane. -**3.** [bens] assigned.

alienar [4] [alje'na(x)] vt -**1.** [tornar não participante] to alienate. -**2.** [afastar] to drive away. -**3.** [bens] to assign.

➤ **alienar-se** vp [afastar-se] to withdraw.

alienígena [alje'niʒena] mf alien.

alijar [4] [ali'ʒa(x)] vt -**1.** [carga] to jettison. -**2.** [isentar]: ~ **alguém de algo** to free sb of sthg.

➤ **alijar-se** vp [isentar-se]: ~-**se de algo** to be released from sthg.

alimentação [alimẽta'sãw] f -**1.** [ato] feeding. -**2.** [dieta] diet. -**3.** [de máquina, impressora] feeding. -**4.** ELETR supply.

alimentador [alimẽnta'do(x)] m: ~ **de papel** paper feed.

alimentar [4] [alimẽn'ta(x)] (pl -**es**) ◇ adj alimentary. ◇ vt -**1.** [ger] to feed. -**2.** [nutrir] to feed. -**3.** [esperança] to feed. ◇ vi [nutrir] to provide nourishment.

➤ **alimentar-se** vp to feed o.s.; ~-**se de algo** to live on sthg.

alimentício, cia [alimẽn'tʃisju, sja] adj -**1.** [qualidades] nutritious; **gêneros** ~**s** foodstuffs. -**2.** [pensão] maintenance.

alimento [ali'mẽntu] m -**1.** [comida] food. -**2.** [nutrição] nourishment.

alínea [a'linja] f indent.

alinhado, da [ali'nadu, da] adj -**1.** [posto em linha reta] in a row. -**2.** [elegante] elegant. -**3.** [correto] correct.

alinhamento [alina'mẽntu] m -**1.** [enfileiramento] row. -**2.** [de estrada] direction. -**3.** TIP justifying.

alinhar [4] [ali'na(x)] vt -**1.** [enfileirar] to line up. -**2.** [estrada] to straighten. -**3.** TIP to justify.

alinhavar [4] [alina'va(x)] vt COST to tack UK, to baste.

alinhavo [ali'navul m tacking UK, basting.

alíquota [a'likwota] f tax rate.

alisar [4] [ali'za(x)] vt -**1.** [tornar liso - cama, cabelo] to smooth; [- tábua] to plane. -**2.** [acariciar] to caress.

alistamento [aliʃta'mẽntu] m -**1.** [em partido] enrolment. -**2.** MIL enlistment.

alistar [4] [aliʃ'ta(x)] vt -**1.** [em partido] to enrol. -**2.** MIL to enlist.

➤ **alistar-se** vp -**1.** [em partido] to enrol. -**2.** MIL to enlist.

aliteração [alitera'sãw] f alliteration.

aliviado, da [ali'vjadu, da] adj -**1.** [pessoa - tranqüilizado] relieved; [- folgado] slackened. -**2.** [consciência] relieved. -**3.** [embarcação] lightened.

aliviar [16] [ali'vja(x)] ◇ vt -**1.** [gen] to relieve. -**2.** [folgar] to slacken. -**3.** [desafogar]: ~ **alguém de algo** to unburden sb of sthg. -**4.** [embarcação] to lighten. ◇ vi -**1.** [diminuir] to ease. -**2.** [confortar] to comfort.

➤ **aliviar-se** vp to be relieved; ~-**se de algo** to be relieved of sthg.

alívio [a'livju] m relief; **que** ~! what a relief!

alma ['awma] f -**1.** [essência humana] soul. -**2.** [espírito desencarnado] spirit; ~ **do outro mundo** ghost. -**3.** [pessoa]: **não ver viva** ~ not to see a living soul. -**4.** [caráter] heart; ~ **gêmea** soulmate. -**5.** [entusiasmo] heart and soul; **com** ~ with enthusiasm. -**6.** [bondade]: **pessoa sem** ~ heartless person. -**7.** fig [de negócio, empresa, partido] essence.

almaço [aw'masul adj [papel] foolscap.

almanaque [awma'nakil m almanac.

almejar [4] [awme'ʒa(x)] ◇ vt to long for; ~ **fazer algo** to long to do sthg. ◇ vi: ~ **por algo** to long for sthg.

almirantado [awmirãn'tadul m -**1.** [corporação] admiralty. -**2.** [posto] admiralship.

almirante [awmi'rãntʃil m admiral.

almoçar [13] [awmo'sa(x)] ◇ vt to have for lunch. ◇ vi to have lunch.

almoço [aw'mosul m lunch; **na hora do** ~ at lunchtime; ~ **americano** buffet lunch; ~ **de negócios** business lunch.

almofada [awmo'fadal f cushion.

almofadinha [awmofa'dʒiɲal f [para alfinetes] pincushion.

almôndega [aw'mõndegal f meatball.

almoxarifado [awmoʃari'fadul m warehouse.

almoxarife [awmoʃa'rifil mf warehouseperson.

alô [a'lol ◇ interj [ao telefone] hello! ◇ m hello.

alocação [aloka'sãwl (pl -**ões**) f allocation.

alocar [12] [alo'ka(x)] vt to allocate.

aloirado, da [aloj'radu, da] *adj* fair-haired.
alojamento [aloʒa'mẽntu] *m* **-1.** [ger] accommodation. **-2.** MIL billet.
alojar [4] [alo'ʒa(x)] *vt* **-1.** [hospedar] to accommodate. **-2.** MIL to billet. **-3.** [armazenar] to store.
  ➡ **alojar-se** *vp* **-1.** [hospedar-se] to stay. **-2.** [acampar] to camp.
alongamento [alõŋga'mẽntu] *m* **-1.** [ger] lengthening. **-2.** [de prazo] extension. **-3.** [ginástica] stretching.
alongar [14] [alõŋ'ga(x)] *vt* **-1.** [ger] to lengthen. **-2.** [perna, braço] to stretch. **-3.** [conversa] to prolong.
  ➡ **alongar-se** *vp* **-1.** [corpo] to stretch. **-2.** [conversa] to prolong. **-3.** [sobre assunto] to expand.
alopata [alo'pata] *mf* allopath.
alopatia [alopa'tʃia] *f* allopathy.
aloprado, da [alo'pradu, da] *adj fam* crazy.
alourado, da [alow'radu, da], **aloirado, da** [aloj'radu, da] *adj* fair-haired.
alpaca [aw'paka] *f* alpaca.
alpargata [aw'paxgata] *f* espadrille.
alpendre [aw'pẽndri] *m* [telheiro] porch.
alpercata [awpex'kata] = **alpargata**.
Alpes ['awpiʃ] *npl*: **os ~** the Alps.
alpinismo [awpi'niʒmu] *m* mountaineering.
alpinista [awpi'niʃta] *mf* mountaineer.
alpino, na [aw'pinu, na] *adj* Alpine.
alpiste [aw'piʃtʃi] *m* [planta] canary grass.
alqueire [aw'kejri] *m measure for land area =* *4.84 hectares in Rio de Janeiro, Minas Gerais e Goiás and 2.42 hectares in São Paulo.*
alquimia [awki'mia] *f* alchemy.
alquimista [awki'miʃta] *mf* alchemist.
alta ['awta] *f* ▷ **alto.**
alta-fidelidade [ˌawtafideli'dadʒi] *f* hi-fi.
altaneiro, ra [awta'nejru, ra] *adj* haughty.
altar [aw'ta(x)] (*pl* **-es**) *m* altar.
altar-mor [awˌta(x)'mɔ(x)] (*pl* **altares-mores**) *m* high altar.
alta-roda [ˌawta'xɔda] (*pl* **altas-rodas**) *f* high society.
alta-tensão [ˌawtatẽnsãw] (*pl* **altas-tensões**) *f* high voltage.
altear [15] [awte'a(x)] *vt* **-1.** [construção] to build. **-2.** [preço, voz] to raise. **-3.** [posição]: **~ sua posição numa firma** to move up within a company.
alteração [awtera'sãw] (*pl* **-ões**) *f* **-1.** [modificação - em gosto, clima, programação] change; [- de texto, roupa] alteration. **-2.** [perturbação] worry. **-3.** [tumulto] commotion.
alterado, da [awte'radu, da] *adj* **-1.** [modificado - gosto, clima, programação] changed; [- texto, roupa] altered. **-2.** [perturbado] worried.
alterar [4] [awte'ra(x)] *vt* **-1.** [modificar] to change. **-2.** [perturbar] to worry.
  ➡ **alterar-se** *vp* [perturbar-se] to be worried.
altercar [12] [awtex'ka(x)] *vi*: **~ (com)** to quarrel (with).
alternado, da [awtex'nadu, da] *adj* alternated.
alternância [awtex'nãnsja] *f* alternation.

alternar [4] [awtex'na(x)] ◇ *vt*: **~ algo (com)** to alternate sthg (with). ◇ *vi*: **~ com** to alternate with.
  ➡ **alternar-se** *vp* [revezar-se] to alternate; [pessoas] to take turns.
alternativo, va [awtexna'tʃivu, va] *adj* alternative.
  ➡ **alternativa** *f* alternative.
alteza [aw'teza] *f*: **Sua Alteza** Your Highness.
altissonante [awtʃiso'nãntʃi] *adj* **-1.** [voz] booming. **-2.** [orquestra] majestic.
altitude [awtʃi'tudʒi] *f* altitude.
altivez [awtʃi'veʒ] *f* **-1.** [arrogância] presumption. **-2.** [dignidade] dignity.
altivo, va [aw'tʃivu, va] *adj* **-1.** [arrogante] presumptuous. **-2.** [digno] dignified.
alto, ta ['awtu, ta] *adj* **-1.** [ger] high; [forte] loud; **ler em voz ~** to read aloud. **-2.** [em estatura] tall. **-3.** *(antes de subst)* [superior] high; **de ~ luxo** of great luxury. **-4.** *(antes de subst)* [importante - cargo] top; [- negócio] big. **-5.** [avançado]: **altas horas (da noite)** late; **altas horas da madrugada** early hours of the morning. **-6.** *(antes de subst)* [grave - risco] high; [- perigo] grave; **alta traição** high treason. **-7.** GEOGR upper. **-8.** HIST high; **alta Antigüidade** early antiquity. **-9.** [MÚS - tom, nota] high; [- voz, saxofone] alto. **-10.** *fam* [embriagado] high.
  ➡ **alto** ◇ *m* **-1.** [topo] top. **-2.** MÚS [saxofone] alto. **-3.** [mando, poder]: **do ~** from above. ◇ *adv* **-1.** [falar] aloud. **-2.** [voar] high. ◇ *interj*: **alto!** stop!
  ➡ **alta** *f* **-1.** MED to be discharged; **dar/receber ~** to discharge/to be discharged. **-2.** [de preços] rise. **-3.** [de cotação] rise; **estar em ~** [cotação] to be rising; *fam* [reputação] to be in favour; *fam* [moda] to be highly fashionable.
  ➡ **por alto** *loc adv* roughly.
alto-astral [ˌawtwaʃ'trawl] (*pl* **-ais**) *fam* ◇ *m* cool; **estar de ~** to be cool. ◇ *adj* cool.
alto-falante ['awtufa'lãntʃil] (*pl* **-s**) *m* loudspeaker.
alto-mar [ˌawtu'ma(x)] (*pl* **altos-mares**) *m* open sea.
alto-relevo [ˌawture'levu] (*pl* **altos-relevos**) *m* high relief; **em ~** in relief.
altruísmo [awtru'iʒmu] *m* altruism.
altruísta [awtru'iʃta] ◇ *adj* altruistic. ◇ *mf* [pessoa] altruist.
altruístico, ca [awtru'iʃtʃiku, ka] *adj* altruistic.
altura [aw'tura] *f* **-1.** [ger] height; **a dez mil metros de ~** at an altitude of ten thousand metres. **-2.** [de som, volume] level. **-3.** [momento] time; **nessa ~ do campeonato** *fam fig* at this stage. **-4.** [localização]: **na ~ de** close to; **a loja fica na avenida principal, mas em que ~?** the shop is on the main road, but how far up? **-5.** [nível]: **à ~ de** equal to.
  ➡ **alturas** *fpl* RELIG [céu]: **as ~s** the heavens; **pôr algo/alguém nas ~s** *fig* to praise sthg/sb highly.
aluado, da [alu'adu, da] *adj* crazy, lunatic.
alucinação [alusina'sãw] (*pl* **-ões**) *f* hallucination.
alucinado, da [alusi'nadu, da] ◇ *adj* **-1.** PSIC

hallucinated. **-2.** *fig* [apaixonado]: ~ **por** crazy about. **-3.** *fig* [desvairado] frantic. <> *m, f* PSIC lunatic.

alucinante [alusi'nãntʃi] *adj fam* **-1.** [enlouquecedor] maddening. **-2.** [ótimo, incrível] amazing.

alucinar [4] [alusi'na(x)] <> *vt* **-1.** [enlouquecer] to drive crazy. **-2.** [apaixonar] to drive wild. **-3.** PSIC to cause to hallucinate. <> *vi* PSIC to be hallucinogenic.

alucinógeno, na [alusi'nɔʒenu, na] *adj* hallucinogenic.

➡ **alucinógeno** *m* hallucinogen.

aludir [6] [alu'dʒi(x)] *vi:* ~ **a** to allude to.

alugar [14] [alu'ga(x)] *vt* **-1.** [tomar de aluguel - carro, traje] to hire; [- apartamento] to rent. **-2.** [dar em aluguel - carro, traje] to hire out; [- apartamento] to rent out. **-3.** *fam* [incomodar] to annoy.

aluguel [alu'gɛwl] (*pl* **-eis**) *m* **-1.** [ato - carro] rental; [- apartamento] renting. **-2.** [pagamento] rent.

alumínio [alu'minju] *m* aluminium *UK*, aluminum *US*.

alunissagem [aluni'saʒẽ] (*pl* **-ns**) *f* lunar landing.

alunissar [4] [aluni'sa(x)] *vi* to land on the moon.

aluno, na [a'lunu, na] *m, f* pupil; ~ **externo** day pupil; ~ **interno** boarder.

alusão [alu'zãw] (*pl* **-ões**) *f* allusion; **fazer uma** ~ **a** to allude to, to make a reference to.

alusivo, va [alu'zivu, va] *adj* allusive.

alvará [awva'ra] *m* permit.

alvejante [awve'ʒãntʃi] <> *adj* bleaching. <> *m* bleach.

alvejar [4] [awve'ʒa(x)] *vt* **-1.** [mirar em] to aim at. **-2.** [branquear] to bleach, to whiten.

alvenaria [awvena'ria] *f* masonry; **de** ~ stonework.

alvéolo [al'vɛwlu] *f* **-1.** [cavidade] cavity. **-2.** [ANAT - do pulmão]: ~ **pulmonar** alveolus; [- de dente] cavity.

alvo, va ['awvu, 'va] *adj* white.
➡ **alvo** *m* **-1.** [mira] target; **acertar no** ~ to hit the target. **-2.** *fig* [objeto]: **ser** ~ **de** to be the target of.

alvorada [awvo'rada] *f* dawn.

alvorecer [25] [awvore'se(x)] <> *m* [alvorada] daybreak. <> *vi* [amanhecer] to dawn.

alvoroçar [4] [awvoro'sa(x)] *vt* **-1.** [agitar] to stir up. **-2.** [entusiasmar] to excite.
➡ **alvoroçar-se** *vp* **-1.** [agitar-se] to be startled. **-2.** [entusiasmar-se] to get excited.

alvoroço [awvo'rosul] *m* [agitação] commotion; **fazer** ~ to cause a commotion.

alvura [aw'vura] *f* **-1.** [branqueza] whiteness. **-2.** [pureza] innocence.

AM <> *f* (*abrev de* **Amplitude Modulation**) AM. <> *m* (*abrev de* **Estado do Amazonas**) *State of Amazon.*

ama ['ama] *f* ⊳ **amo.**

amabilidade [amabili'dadʒi] *f* **-1.** [delicadeza, cortesia] courtesy. **-2.** [de gesto, palavra] kindness.

amabilíssimo, ma [amabi'lisimu, ma] *superl* ⊳ **amável.**

amaciante [ama'sjãntʃi] *m:* ~ **de roupas** fabric conditioner.

amaciar [16] [ama'sja(x)] <> *vt* **-1.** [tornar macio] to soften. **-2.** [bife] to tenderize. **-3.** [motor] to run in. <> *vi* [motor] to run in.

ama-de-leite [ˌãmadʒi'lejtʃi] (*pl* **amas-de-leite**) *f* wet nurse.

amado, da [a'madu, da] <> *adj* **-1.** [ger] favourite. **-2.** [person] beloved. <> *m, f* beloved, love.

amador, ra [ama'do(x)] (*mpl* **-es**, *fpl* **-s**) <> *adj* amateur. <> *m, f* amateur.

amadorismo [amado'riʒmu] *m* **-1.** [diletantismo] dilettantism. **-2.** *pej* [antiprofissionalismo] amateurism.

amadorístico, ca [amado'riʃtʃiku, ka] *adj* amateurish.

amadurecer [25] [amadure'se(x)] <> *vt* **-1.** [fruta] to ripen. **-2.** *fig* [pessoa] to mature. <> *vi* **-1.** [fruta] to ripen. **-2.** *fig* [pessoa] to mature. **-3.** *fig* [idéia, projeto] to come to fruition.

âmago ['ãmagul] *m* **-1.** [cerne - de madeira] heart; [- de questão] heart. **-2.** [essência] essence. **-3.** [alma, interior] heart.

amainar [4] [amaj'na(x)] *vi* **-1.** [tormenta, tempestade] to die down. **-2.** [ira] to subside. **-3.** [distúrbio, bombardeio] to ease off.

amaldiçoar [20] [amawdi'swa(x)] *vt* to curse.

amálgama [a'mawgama] *m* amalgam.

amalgamar [4] [amawga'ma(x)] *vt* to amalgamate.

amalucado, da [amalu'kadu, da] *adj* crazy.

amamentação [amamẽta'sãw] (*pl* **-ões**) *f* breastfeeding.

amamentar [4] [amamẽ'ta(x)] *vt* & *vi* to breastfeed.

amanhã [amã'ɲa] <> *adv* tomorrow; ~ **de manhã** tomorrow morning; ~ **à noite** tomorrow night; ~ **de tarde** tomorrow afternoon/evening; **depois de** ~ the day after tomorrow. <> *m* tomorrow.

amanhecer [25] [amãɲe'se(x)] <> *m* dawn; **ao** ~ at dawn. <> *vi* **-1.** [dia] to dawn. **-2.** [pessoa]: **hoje amanheci com dor de cabeça** today I woke up with a headache.

amansar [4] [amã'sa(x)] <> *vt* **-1.** [animal] to break in. **-2.** *fig* [pessoa etc] to calm down. <> *vi* **-1.** [animal] to become tame. **-2.** *fig* [pessoa etc] to relent.

amante [a'mãntʃi] *mf* lover.

amanteigado, da [amãntej'gadu, da] *adj* **-1.** [torrada, pão] buttered. **-2.** [biscoito] buttery.

Amapá [ama'pa] *n* Amapá.

amar [4] [a'ma(x)] <> *vt* **-1.** [sentir amor por] to love. **-2.** [fazer amor com] to make love to. <> *vi* [sentir amor] to be in love.
➡ **amar-se** *vp* **-1.** [mutuamente] to love each other. **-2.** [fazer amor] to make love.

amarelado, da [amare'ladu, da] *adj* yellowish.

amarelar [4] [amare'la(x)] *vt* [tornar amarelado]

to turn yellow. ◇ *vi fam* [acovardar-se] to pale.
amarelinha [amarɛ'liɲa] *f* hopscotch.
amarelo, la [ama'rɛlu, la] *adj* yellow.
➤ **amarelo** *m* yellow.
amarfanhar [4] [amaxfa'ɲa(x)] *vt* to crumple.
amargar [14] [amax'ga(x)] ◇ *vt* - **1.** [tornar amargo] to make bitter. - **2.** *fig* [fazer sofrer] to embitter. ◇ *vi* - **1.** [tornar-se amargo] to go bitter. - **2.** *loc*: **ser de** ~ to be the last straw.
amargo, ga [a'maxgu, ga] *adj* bitter.
amargor [amax'go(x)] *m* - **1.** [sabor amargo] bitter taste. - **2.** [sensação de desgosto] bitterness.
amargura [amax'gura] *f* - **1.** [ger] bitterness. - **2.** *fig* [sofrimento] bitterness.
amargurado, da [amaxgu'radu, da] *adj* - **1.** [pessoa] bitter. - **2.** [expressão, texto] acrimonious.
amargurar [4] [amaxgu'ra(x)] *vt* - **1.** [afligir] to make bitter. - **2.** [tornar sofrido] to sour.
amarra [a'maxa] *f* - **1.** [corrente, cabo - de âncora] moorings *(pl)*; [- de vela] sheet. - **2.** [grilhão] shackle.
amarrado, da [ama'xadu, da] *adj* - **1.** [atado] tied up. - **2.** *fig* [cara] glowering. - **3.** *fam fig* [comprometido] committed.
amarrar [4] [ama'xa(x)] *vt* - **1.** [atar] to tie. - **2.** *NÁUT* to moor. - **3.** *fig*: ~ **a cara** to glower.
➤ **amarrar-se** *vp fam* - **1.** [apaixonar-se]: ~**-se em alguém** to become attached to sb. - **2.** [gostar muito]: ~**-se em algo** to be keen on sthg.
amarronzado, da [amaxõn'zadu, da] *adj* brownish.
amarrotar [4] [amaxo'ta(x)] ◇ *vt* to crumple. ◇ *vi* to be crumpled.
ama-seca [ˌama'sɛka] *(pl* **amas-secas)** *f* nanny.
amasiar-se [7] [amazi'axsi] *vp dated* to live together; ~ **com alguém** to live with sb.
amassado, da [ama'sadu, da] *adj* [tecido, roupa, papel] crumpled; [carro] smashed up.
amassar [4] [ama'sa(x)] *vt* - **1.** [massa] to knead; [bolo, pão] to mix. - **2.** [roupa] to crease. - **3.** [papel] to crumple. - **4.** [carro] to smash up.
amável [a'mavew] *(pl* -**eis)** *adj* friendly.
amazona [ama'zona] *f* - **1.** [mulher que anda a cavalo] horsewoman. - **2.** [mulher guerreira] Amazon.
Amazonas [ama'zonaʃ] *n* - **1.** [rio]: **o** ~ the Amazon. - **2.** [estado] Amazonas.
Amazônia [ama'zonja] *n* Amazonia.

AMAZÔNIA

The area of *Amazônia* exceeds 7 million km², over half of which is in Brazilian territory. The Amazon basin has the most extensive river network and the greatest flow of freshwater in the world; it is also home to the world's largest tropical forest. Its enormous biodiversity includes over 60,000 species of trees, some of which can reach a height of 100m or more.

---

amazônico, ca [ama'zoniku, ka] *adj* Amazonian.
Amã [a'mã] *n* Amman.
âmbar ['ãnba(x)] *m* amber.

AmBev (*abrev de* **American Beverage Company**) *f* ≃ AmBev, *Brazilian drinks manufacturer*.
ambição [ãnbi'sãw] *(pl* -**ões)** *f* ambition.
ambicionar [4] [ãnbisjo'na(x)] *vt* to set one's sights on.
ambicioso, osa [ãnbi'sjozu, ɔza] ◇ *adj* ambitious. ◇ *m, f* go-getter.
ambidestro, tra [ãnbi'deʃtru, tra] *adj* ambidextrous.
ambiental [ãnbjẽn'taw] *(pl* -**ais)** *adj* environmental.
ambientalista [ãnbjẽnta'liʃta] ◇ *adj* environmental. ◇ *mf* environmentalist.
ambientar [4] [ãnbjẽn'tar] *vt* - **1.** [filme, enredo] to set. - **2.** [adaptar] to acclimatize.
➤ **ambientar-se** *vp* [adaptar-se] to mingle.
ambiente [ãn'bjẽntʃi] ◇ *adj* ambient. ◇ *m* - **1.** [gen & *COMPUT*] environment. - **2.** [em sala, boate] area. - **3.** *fig* [atmosfera] atmosphere.
ambigüidade [ãnbigwi'dadʒi] *f* ambiguity.
ambíguo, gua [ãn'bigwu, gwa] *adj* ambiguous.
âmbito ['ãnbitu] *m* [campo de ação] field.
ambivalência [ãnbiva'lẽnsja] *f* ambivalence.
ambivalente [ãnbiva'lẽntʃil] *adj* ambivalent.
ambos, bas ['ãnbuʃ, baʃ] ◇ *adj* both. ◇ *pron* both.
ambrosia [ãnbro'zia] *f a sweet dish of eggs and milk*.
ambulância [ãnbu'lãnsja] *f* ambulance.
ambulante [ãnbu'lãntʃil] ◇ *adj* - **1.** [vendedor, pipoqueiro - na calçada] street *(antes de subst)*; [- de porta em porta] door-to-door *(antes de subst)*. - **2.** [biblioteca, posto médico] mobile. - **3.** *fam fig*: **ele é uma enciclopédia** ~ he's a walking encyclopedia. ◇ *mf* [vendedor ambulante] street vendor.
ambulatório [ãnbula'tɔrju] *m* outpatient department.
ameaça [a'mjasa] *f* threat; ~ **de bomba** bomb scare; ~ **de enfarte** risk of heart attack; ~ **de morte** death threat.
ameaçador, ra [amjasa'do(x), ra] *adj* threatening, menacing.
ameaçar [13] [amja'sa(x)] *vt* to threaten; ~ **fazer algo** to threaten to do sthg; ~ **alguém de morte** to threaten sb with death.
amealhar [4] [amja'ʎa(x)] ◇ *vt* [juntar] to amass. ◇ *vi* [poupar] to save up.
ameba [a'mɛba] *f* amoeba *UK*, ameba *US*.
amedrontador, ra [amedrõnta'do(x), ra] *adj* frightening.
amedrontar [4] [amedrõn'ta(x)] *vt* to frighten.
➤ **amedrontar-se** *vp* to feel afraid.
ameia [a'meja] *f* battlement.
ameixa [a'mejʃa] *f* - **1.** [fresca] plum. - **2.** [seca] prune.
amém [a'mẽ] ◇ *interj* amen! ◇ *m fig*: **dizer** ~ **a** to give in to.
amêndoa [a'mẽndwa] *f* almond.
amendoado, da [amẽn'dwadu, da] *adj* [olhos] almond-shaped.
amendoeira [amẽn'dwejra] *f* almond tree.

amendoim [amẽn'dwĩ] (pl -ns) m peanut; ~ torrado roasted peanut.

amenidade [ameni'dadʒi] f -1. [suavidade] mildness. -2. [delicadeza] gentleness.

➤ **amenidades** fpl [futilidades] trivialities.

amenizar [4] [ameni'za(x)] vt -1. [abrandar] to reduce. -2. [tornar agradável] to make pleasant. -3. [briga, conflito] to settle. -4. [facilitar] to lighten.

ameno, na [a'menu, na] adj -1. [brando - sabor] mild; [- repreensão] quiet; [- pena] light. -2. [agradável] pleasant.

América [a'mɛrikal] n America; ~ **Central** Central American; ~ **do Norte** North America; ~ **do Sul** South America; ~ **Hispânica** Spanish America; ~ **Latina** Latin America.

americanizado, da [amerikãni'zadu, da] adj Americanized.

americanizar [amerikãni'za(x)] vt to Americanize.

americano, na [ameri'kãnu, na] <> adj American. <> m, f American.

ameríndio, dia [ame'rĩndʒu, dʒa] <> adj Amerindian. <> m, f Amerindian.

amesquinhar [4] [ameʃki'ɲa(x)] vt [tornar mesquinho] to demean.

➤ **amesquinhar-se** vp -1. [tornar-se avaro] to become mean. -2. [humilhar-se] to demean o.s.

ametista [ame'tʃiʃta] f amethyst.

amianto [a'mjãntu] m asbestos.

amicíssimo, ma [ami'sisimu, ma] superl ➤ amigo.

amido [a'midu] m starch.

amigar-se [14] [ami'gaxsi] vp [amancebar-se] to live together; ~ **com alguém** to live with sb.

amigável [ami'gavɛw] (pl -eis) adj friendly.

amígdala [a'migdala] f tonsil.

amigdalite [amigda'litʃi] f tonsillitis.

amigo, ga [a'migu, ga] <> adj friendly. <> m, f friend; ~ **do peito** bosom buddy; ~ **secreto** ou **oculto** [jogo] a game of present swapping in which you draw a person's name from a hat and then anonymously give them a present after a certain period of time; [pessoa] the person to whom the present is given in this game.

amigo-da-onça, amiga-da-onça [ˌamiguda'õsa, ˌamigada'õsal] m, f fam false friend.

amistoso, osa [amiʃ'tozu, ɔza] adj friendly.

➤ **amistoso** m ESP friendly.

amiúde [a'mjudʒi] adv often.

amizade [ami'zadʒi] f -1. [relação] friendship; fazer ~ (com alguém) to make friends (with sb); ~ **colorida** fam casual relationship. -2. [estima] friendliness; **ela o tratou com** ~ she treated him in a friendly manner.

amnésia [am'nɛzja] f amnesia.

amo, ma [ˈamo, ma] m, f master (f mistress).

➤ **ama** f [governanta] nanny.

amolação [amola'sãw] (pl -ões) f [incômodo, aborrecimento] hassle.

amolado, da [amo'ladu, da] adj -1. [afiado] sharp. -2. [aborrecido] annoyed.

amolador [amola'do(x)] m [de facas] knife sharpener.

amolar [4] [amo'la(x)] <> vt -1. [faca] to sharpen. -2. [incomodar, aborrecer] to annoy. <> vi [causar incômodo] to be annoying.

➤ **amolar-se** vp [aborrecer-se] to get annoyed.

amoldar [4] [amow'da(x)] vt [adaptar, ajustar]: ~ **algo (a)** to adapt sthg (to).

➤ **amoldar-se** vp [adaptar-se, ajustar-se]: ~-se (a) to adapt (to).

amolecer [25] [amole'se(x)] <> vt -1. [tornar mole] to soften. -2. fig [abrandar] to mollify. <> vi -1. [tornar-se mole] to soften. -2. fig [tornar-se brando] to relent.

amônia [a'monja] f ammonia.

amoníaco [amo'niaku] m ammonia.

amontoado [amõn'twadu] m pile.

amontoar [20] [amõn'twa(x)] vt to pile up.

➤ **amontoar-se** vp to pile up.

amor [a'mo(x)] (pl -es) m love; ~ **livre** free love; **fazer** ~ to make love; **pelo** ~ **de Deus!** for God's sake!; **ser um** ~ **(de pessoa)** to be a gem (of a person).

amora [a'mɔra] f mulberry.

amoral [amo'raw] (pl -ais) <> adj amoral. <> mf unscrupulous person.

amora-preta [aˌmɔra'pretal] (pl amoras-pretas) f mulberry.

amordaçar [13] [amoxda'sa(x)] vt to gag.

amoreco [amo'rɛku] m: **um** ~ a darling.

amorenado, da [amore'nadu, da] adj swarthy.

amorfo, fa [a'mɔxfu, fa] adj -1. [sem forma] amorphous. -2. fig [pessoa] dreary.

amornar [4] [amox'na(x)] <> vt to warm up. <> vi to cool down.

amoroso, osa [amo'rozu, ɔza] adj [pessoa] loving; **um caso** ~ a love affair.

amor-perfeito [aˌmoxpex'fejtu] (pl amores-perfeitos) m heartsease.

amor-próprio [aˌmox'prɔprju] (pl amores-próprios) m -1. [auto-estima] self-esteem. -2. [orgulho] conceitedness.

amortecedor [amoxtese'do(x)] (pl -es) m shock absorber.

amortização [amoxtiza'sãw] (pl -ões) f -1. [pagamento parcial] part payment. -2. FIN [de ações] amortization.

amortizar [4] [amoxti'za(x)] vt -1. [pagar parte de] to repay (in part). -2. FIN [ações] to amortize.

amostra [a'mɔʃtra] f sample; ~ **grátis** free sample.

amostragem [amoʃ'traʒẽ] (pl -ns) f -1. [coleta, seleção] sampling. -2. [amostra] selection. -3. [em estatística] cross sample.

amotinado, da [amotʃi'nadu, da] adj mutinous.

amotinar [4] [amotʃi'na(x)] vt to lead into mutiny.

➤ **amotinar-se** vp to mutiny.

amparar [4] [ãnpa'ra(x)] vt -1. [escorar, segurar] to hold. -2. [ajudar] to support.

➤ **amparar-se** vp [escorar-se, segurar-se]: ~-se

(contra/em) to lean (against/on).

amparo [ãn'paru] *m* -**1.** [apoio] hold. -**2.** [ajuda] support.

amperagem [ãnpe'raʒɛl] *f* [eletr] amperage.

ampère [ãn'pɛri] *m* amp, ampere.

ampliação [ãnplia'sãw] (*pl* -**ões**) *f* -**1.** [aumento - de forma, imagem] enlargement; [- de ângulo] widening. -**2.** [extensão] extension. -**3.** [desenvolvimento - de estudos] broadening; [- de negócio] expansion. -**4.** [FOT - processo] blow-up; [- exemplar] enlargement.

ampliar [16] [ãnpli'a(x)] *vt*-**1.** [aumentar- forma, imagem] to enlarge; [- ângulo] to widen. -**2.** [estender] to extend. -**3.** [desenvolver- estudos] to broaden; [- negócio] to expand.

amplificação [anplifika'sãw] (*pl* -**ões**) *f* -**1.** [aumento - de forma, imagem] enlargement; [- de ângulo] widening. -**2.** [de som] amplification.

amplificador [ãnplifika'do(x)] (*pl* -**es**) *m* [de som] amplifier.

amplificar [12] [ãnplifi'ka(x)] *vt*-**1.** [aumentar- forma, imagem] to enlarge; [- ângulo] to widen. -**2.** [som] to amplify.

amplitude [ãnpli'tudʒi] *f* -**1.** [espaço] spaciousness. -**2.** *fig* [abrangência] scope. -**3.** *TEC* amplitude.

amplo, pla ['ãnplu, 'pla] *adj* -**1.** [espaçoso] spacious. -**2.** [abrangente] broad. -**3.** [lato]: **no sentido mais ~ da palavra** in the broadest sense of the word. -**4.** *(antes de subst)* [ilimitado] ample.

ampola [ãn'pola] *f* ampoule *UK*, ampule *US*.

ampulheta [ãnpu'ʎeta] *f* hour-glass.

amputação [ãnputa'sãw] (*pl* -**ões**) *f* amputation.

amputar [4] [ãnpu'ta(x)] *vt* to amputate.

Amsterdã [amiʃtex'dã] *n* Amsterdam.

amuado, da [a'mwadu, da] *adj* [aborrecido] sulking.

amuar [4] [a'mwa(x)] *vt* [aborrecer] to annoy.

➤ **amuar-se** *vp* [aborrecer-se]: **~-se (com** *ou* **contra)** to get annoyed (with).

amulatado, da [amula'tadu, da] *adj* mulatto-looking.

amuleto [amu'letu] *m* amulet.

anã [a'nã] *f* ▷ **anão**.

anacrônico, ca [ana'kroniku, ka] *adj* anachronistic.

anacronismo [anakro'niʒmul] *m* anachronism.

anafilático, ca [anafi'latiku, ka] *adj* ▷ **choque**.

anagrama [ana'grãma] *m* anagram.

anágua [a'nagwal] *f* petticoat.

anais [a'najʃ] *mpl* annals.

anal [a'naw] (*pl* -**ais**) *adj* anal.

analfabetismo [anawfabe'tʃiʒmul] *m* illiteracy.

analfabeto, ta [anawfa'bɛtu, ta] <> *adj* illiterate. <> *m, f* illiterate.

analgésico, ca [anaw'ʒɛziku, ka] *adj* analgesic.
➤ **analgésico** *m* [remédio] painkiller, analgesic.

analisar [4] [anali'za(x)] *vt* -**1.** [examinar, avaliar] to analyse. -**2.** *PSIC* to put through analysis.

análise [a'nalizil] *f* [ger & *PSIC*] analysis; **~s clínicas** clinical tests.

analista [ana'liʃta] *mf* -**1.** [ger & *PSIC*] analyst; **~ de sistemas** systems analyst.

analítico, ca [ana'litʃiku, ka] *adj* analytical.

analogia [analo'ʒia] *f* analogy; **por ~** by analogy.

análogo, ga [a'nalogu, ga] *adj* analogous.

ananás [ana'naʃ] (*pl* -**ases**) *m* pineapple.

anão, ã [a'nãw, ã] (*mpl* -**ões**, *fpl* -**s**) *m, f* dwarf.

anarquia [anax'kia] *f* -**1.** [ausência de governo] anarchy. -**2.** *fig* [bagunça] shambles.

anárquico, ca [a'naxkiku, ka] *adj* -**1.** [sistema, sociedade] anarchic. -**2.** *fig* [caótico] chaotic.

anarquismo [anax'kizmul] *m* anarchism.

anarquista [anax'kiʃta] <> *adj* [partido, sociedade] anarchist. <> *mf* -**1.** [militante] anarchist. -**2.** *fig* [bagunceiro, agitador] agitator.

anarquizar [4] [anaxki'za(x)] *vt fig* -**1.** [tornar anárquico] to reduce to anarchy. -**2.** [incitar à desordem] to incite to riot. -**3.** [abagunçar] to make a mess of. -**4.** [desmoralizar, ridicularizar] to ridicule.

ANATEL (*abrev de* **Agência Nacional de Telecomunicações**) *f Brazilian state telecommunications regulator,* ≃ Oftel *UK,* ≃ ODTR *US*.

anátema [a'natemal] *m* [maldição, estigma] anathema.

anatomia [anato'mia] *f* anatomy.

anatômico, ca [ana'tomiku, ka] *adj* anatomical.

anca ['ãŋka] *f* -**1.** [de pessoa] hip. -**2.** [de animal] haunch.

ancestral [ãn'seʃtrawl] (*pl* -**ais**) <> *adj* ancestral, age-old. <> *mf* ancestor.
➤ **ancestrais** *mpl* ancestors.

anchova [ãn'ʃoval] *f* anchovy.

ancião, ciã [ã'sjãw, sjãl] (*mpl* -**ões**, *fpl* -**s**) <> *adj* aged. <> *m, f* venerable person.

ancinho [ãn'siɲul] *m* rake.

anciões [ã'sjõjʃl] *pl* ▷ **ancião**.

âncora ['ãŋkoral] *f ECON*: **~ cambial** exchange rate pegging.

ancoradouro [ãŋkora'dorul] *m* anchorage.

ancorar [4] [ãŋko'ra(x)] <> *vt* -**1.** -[fundear] to anchor. -**2.** *fig* [basear] to base. <> *vi* [fundear] to base.
➤ **ancorar-se** *vp fig* [basear-se] to be based.

andada [ãn'dadal] *f* walk; **dar uma ~** to take a walk.

andaime [ãn'dãjmil] *m* scaffolding.

andamento [ãnda'mẽntul] *m* -**1.** [prosseguimento] progress; **dar ~ a algo** to set in motion; **estar em ~** to be under way. -**2.** [direção] direction. -**3.** *MÚS* tempo.

andança [4] [ãn'dãnsaʃ] *f* [viagem] travel.

andar [4] [ãn'da(x)] (*pl* -**es**) <> *m* -**1.** [jeito de caminhar] walk. -**2.** [pavimento] storey *UK*, story *US*. <> *vi* -**1.** [caminhar] to walk. -**2.** [usar como transporte]: **~ de bicicleta/a cavalo** to ride a bicycle/horse; **~ de avião/carro/trem** to go by plane/car/train. -**3.** [movimentar-se] to go. -**4.** [errar] to wander. -**5.** [progredir, funcionar] to go. -**6.** [passar] to go, to pass. -**7.** [conviver]: **~ com alguém** to get along with sb. -**8.** [ter caso amoroso]: **~ com alguém** to be going out with sb. -**9.** [estar] to be; **~ em** *ou* **por** to be travelling in; ~ **fazendo algo** to be doing sthg. **-10. :** ~ **por** to be around. **-11.** [ir-se]: **ir andando** to be on one's way. **-12.** [apressar-se]: **anda (com isso)!** get a move on! <> *vt* [percorrer] to do; **andamos 50 quilômetros em um dia** we did 50 kms in one day.

andarilho, lha [ãnda'riʎu, ʎa] *m, f* walker.

Andes ['ãndiʃ] *npl*: **os** ~ the Andes.

andino, na [ãn'dinu, na] <> *adj* Andean. <> *m, f* Andean.

andorinha [ãndo'riɲa] *f* swallow.

Andorra [ãn'doxa] *n*: **(o principado de)** ~ (the principality of) Andorra.

andrógino, na [ãn'drɔʒinu, na] *adj* androgynous.

anedota [ane'dɔta] *f* joke.

anel [a'nɛwl (*pl* **-éis**) *m* **-1.** [ger] ring. **-2.** [de corrente] circuit. **-3.** [de cabelo] lock.

anelado, da [ane'ladu, da] *adj* curly.

anemia [ane'mia] *f* anaemia *UK*, anemia *US*.

anêmico, ca [a'nemiku, ka] *adj* anaemic *UK*, anemic *US*.

anestesia [aneʃte'zia] *f* **-1.** [efeito] anaesthesia *UK*, anesthesia *US*. **-2.** [anestésico] anaesthetic *UK*, anesthetic *US*; **tomar** ~ to have an anaesthetic; ~ **geral/local** general/local anaesthetic.

anestesiado, da [aneʃte'zjadu, da] *adj* [paciente] anaesthetized.

anestesiar [16] [aneʃte'zja(x)] *vt* **-1.** [entorpecer] to anaesthetize *UK*, anesthetize *US*. **-2.** [aplicar anestesia] to give an anaesthetic to *UK*, to give an anesthetic to *US*.

anestésico, ca [aneʃ'tɛziku, ka] *adj* anaesthetizing *UK*, anesthetizing *US*.

◆ **anestésico** *m* anaesthetic *UK*, anesthetic *US*.

anexação [aneksa'sãw] (*pl* **-ões**) *f* **-1.** [de cláusulas, documentos] attachment. **-2.** [de terras, país] annexation.

anexado, da [ane'ksadu, da] *adj* COMPUT attached.

anexar [4] [anek'sa(x)] *vt* COMPUT: ~ **um arquivo** to attach a file.

anexo [a'nɛksu] *m* COMPUT attachment.

ANFAVEA (*abrev de* **Associação Nacional dos Fabricantes de Veículos Automotores**) *f* Brazilian *association of automobile manufacturers.*

anfetamina [ãnfeta'mina] *f* amphetamine.

anfíbio, bia [ãn'fibju, bja] *adj* amphibious.

◆ **anfíbio** *m* amphibian.

anfiteatro [ãnfi'tʃjatru] *m* amphitheatre *UK*, amphitheater *US*.

anfitrião, triã [ãnfi'trjãw, trjã] (*mpl* **-ões**, *fpl* **-s**) *m, f* host (*f* hostess).

angariar [16] [ãnga'rja(x)] *vt* to attract.

angelical [ãnʒeli'kawl (*pl* **-ais**) *adj* angelic.

angina [ãn'ʒina] *f*: ~ **(do peito)** angina (pectoris).

anglicano, na [ãngli'kanu, na] <> *adj* Anglican. <> *m, f* Anglican.

anglicismo [ãngli'siʒmul *m* Anglicism.

anglófono, na [ãŋ'glɔfonu, na] <> *adj* English-speaking. <> *m, f* English speaker.

anglo-saxão, xã [ˌãŋglosak'sãw, sã] (*mpl* **-ões**, *fpl* **-ãs**) <> *adj* Anglo-Saxon. <> *m, f* Anglo-Saxon.

anglo-saxônico, ca [ˌãŋglosak'soniku, ka] (*mpl* **-s**, *fpl* **-s**) *adj* Anglo-Saxon.

Angola [ãŋ'gola] *n* Angola.

angolano, na [ãŋgo'lãnu, na] <> *adj* Angolan. <> *m, f* Angolan.

angorá [ãŋgo'ra] <> *adj* angora. <> *m* [tecido] angora. <> *mf* [gato] angora.

angra ['ãŋgra] *f* bay.

angu [ãŋ'gul *m* **-1.** [ger] ≃ porridge. **-2.** *fam fig* [confusão, problema]: **um** ~**-de-caroço** a tough nut to crack.

angular [ãŋgu'la(x)] *adj* angular.

ângulo ['ãŋgulul *m* **-1.** [ger] angle; ~ **agudo/obtuso/reto** acute/obtuse/right angle. **-2.** [canto] corner. **-3.** [de mira] angle (of vision).

anguloso, sa [ãŋgu'lozu, lɔza] *adj* angled.

angústia [ãŋ'guʃtʃja] *f* anguish.

angustiado, da [ãŋguʃ'tʃjadu, da] *adj* anguished.

angustiante [ãŋguʃ'tʃjãntʃil *adj* harrowing.

angustiar [16] [ãŋguʃ'tʃja(x)] *vt* to cause anguish to.

◆ **angustiar-se** *vp* to become distressed; ~ **-se com algo** to be distressed by sthg; ~**-se de** *ou* **por** to be distressed about.

anil [a'niwl *m* [cor] blue.

animação [anima'sãw] *f* **-1.** [entusiasmo] enthusiasm. **-2.** [alegria] jollity. **-3.** [movimento] hustle and bustle. **-4.** CINE animation.

animado, da [ani'madu, da] *adj* **-1.** [entusiasmado] spirited. **-2.** [alegre, movimentado] lively.

animador, ra [anima'do(x), ra] (*mpl* **-es**, *fpl* **-s**) <> *adj* encouraging. <> *m, f* animator.

animal [ani'mawl (*pl* **-ais**) <> *adj* **-1.** [ger] animal. **-2.** *fam pej* [pessoa] brutal. <> *mf fam pej* [pessoa - bruto] brute; [- ignorante] ass. <> *m* ZOOL animal; ~ **doméstico** [de estimação] domestic animal; [de criação] livestock.

animalesco, ca [anima'leʃku, ka] *adj* animal.

animar [4] [ani'ma(x)] *vt* **-1.** [ger] to liven up. **-2.** [encorajar]: ~ **alguém (a fazer algo)** to encourage sb (to do sthg). **-3.** [entusiasmar] to enthuse. **-4.** [fomentar, estimular] to stimulate. **-5.** [dar animação] to animate. **-6.** RELIG [dar vida a] to bring to life.

◆ **animar-se** *vp* **-1.** [tomar coragem]: ~**-se (a fazer algo)** to resolve (to do sthg). **-2.** [entusiasmar-se] to become enthusiastic. **-3.** [debate, conversa, festa] to liven up. **-4.** [alegrar-se] to cheer up. **-5.** RELIG [ganhar vida] to come to life.

ânimo ['ãnimu] <> *m* **-1.** [coragem] courage. **-2.** [entusiasmo] enthusiasm; **perder o** ~ to lose courage; **recobrar o** ~ to regain one's resolve. **-3.** [estímulo] life; **representar um novo** ~ **para** o give a new lease of life to. <> *interj*: ~**!** come on!

animosidade [animozi'dadʒi] *f* animosity.

aninhar [4] [aniˈɲa(x)] ◇ vt **-1.** [acolher, aconchegar] to cuddle. **-2.** [abrigar] to shelter. ◇ vi [fazer ninho] to nest.

➤ **aninhar-se** vp **-1.** [aconchegar-se] to nestle. **-2.** [fazer ninho] to nest.

aniquilação [anikilaˈsãw] f **-1.** [anulação] rescission. **-2.** [esgotamento] exhaustion. **-3.** [destruição] annihilation; ~ **moral** moral decay. **-4.** fig [ruína] ruin.

aniquilar [4] [anikiˈla(x)] vt **-1.** [anular] to rescind. **-2.** [esgotar] to exhaust. **-3.** [destruir] to annihilate. **-4.** fig [arruinar] to ruin.

➤ **aniquilar-se** vp **-1.** [esgotar-se] to be exhausted. **-2.** fig [moralmente] to destroy o.s.

anis [aˈniʃ] (pl -es) m aniseed; **licor de** ~ anisette.

anistia [aniʃˈtʃia] f amnesty.

anistiado, da [aniʃˈtʃiadu, da] ◇ adj amnestied. ◇ m, f person granted amnesty.

aniversariante [anivexsaˈrjãntʃi] ◇ adj: **a cidade** ~ the city that is celebrating its anniversary. ◇ mf [pessoa] birthday boy (f birthday girl).

aniversariar [16] [anivexsaˈrja(x)] vi **-1.** [pessoa] to celebrate one's birthday/anniversary. **-2.** [cidade] to celebrate its anniversary.

aniversário [anivexˈsarju] m **-1.** [de acontecimento] anniversary. **-2.** [de nascimento] birthday. **-3.** [festa] birthday party.

anjo [ˈãnʒu] m angel; ~ **da guarda** guardian angel.

Ankara [ãŋˈkara] n Ankara.

ano [ˈãnu] m [período] year; **no** ~ **de 1969, o homem foi à Lua** in 1969, man went to the moon; **os** ~**s 70** the 1970s; ~ **bissexto** leap year; ~ **civil** calendar year; ~ **corrente** current year; ~ **financeiro** financial year; ~ **fiscal** tax year; ~ **letivo** academic year; **este** ~ this year; **há** ~**s** ou **faz** ~**s que** it's years since; **faz** ~**s que não o vejo** it's years since I saw him, I haven't seen him for years; **(no)** ~ **passado** last year; **(no)** ~ **que vem** next year; **por** ~ a year, per year.

➤ **anos** mpl [idade]: **tenho vinte** ~ **(de idade)** I'm twenty (years old); **quantos** ~**s você tem?** how old are you?; **ela faz nove** ~**s em outubro** she'll be nine in October.

ano-bom [ˌãnuˈbõ] (pl anos-bons) m [festa] New Year.

anões [aˈnõjʃ] pl ▷ anão.

anoitecer [25] [anojteˈse(x)] ◇ m nightfall; **ao** ~ at nightfall. ◇ vi **-1.** [cair a noite]: **quando anoiteceu, acendemos as luzes** when it got dark we turned on the lights. **-2.** [estar em algum lugar ao anoitecer] to be somewhere when night falls; **anoitecemos na estrada** night fell while we were on the road.

ano-luz [ˌãnuˈluʃ] (pl anos-luz) m light year.

anomalia [anomaˈlia] f abnormality.

anômalo, la [aˈnomalu, la] adj abnormal.

anonimato [anoniˈmatu] m anonymity; **ficar no** ~ to remain in anonymity; **viver no** ~ to live in anonymity.

anônimo, ma [aˈnonimu, ma] adj anonymous.

ano-novo [ˌãnuˈnovu] (pl anos-novos) m **-1.** [período] new year. **-2.** [festa] New Year.

anoraque [anoˈrakil] m anorak.

anorexia [anorekˈsia] f anorexia.

anoréxico, ca [anoˈreksiku, ka] ◇ adj anorexic. ◇ m, f anorexic.

anormal [anoxˈmaw] (pl -ais) ◇ adj **-1.** [ger] abnormal. **-2.** [incomum] unusual. **-3.** [extraordinário] extraordinary. **-4.** [deficiente] retarded. ◇ m **-1.** [pessoa excepcional] abnormal person. **-2.** fam pej [idiota] cretin.

anormalidade [anoxmaliˈdadʒi] f **-1.** [anomalia] abnormality. **-2.** [situação] abnormal situation.

anotação [anotaˈsãw] (pl -ões) f note.

anotar [4] [anoˈta(x)] vt **-1.** [tomar nota de] to note down. **-2.** [apor observações a] to annotate.

anseio [ãnˈseju] m desire; **no** ~ **de fazer algo** in one's eagerness to do sthg.

ânsia [ˈãnsja] f **-1.** [desejo]: **ter** ~ **(por algo/de fazer algo)** to be longing for sthg/to do sthg; ~**s de vômito** nausea. **-2.** [ansiedade] anxiety.

ansiar [17] [ãnˈsja(x)] vi: ~ **por algo/por fazer algo** to long for sthg/to do sth.

ansiedade [ãnsjeˈdadʒi] f **-1.** [ger] anxiety; **com** ~ anxiously. **-2.** [desejo] longing.

ansioso, osa [ãnˈsjozu, ɔza] adj [angustiado, desejoso] anxious; **o presidente aguarda** ~ **o resultado das eleições** the president is anxiously awaiting the election results.

anta [ˈãnta] f **-1.** ZOOL tapir. **-2.** fam pej [idiota]: **ser uma** ~ to be an ass.

antagônico, ca [ãntaˈgoniku, ka] adj [contrário] antagonistic; **opiniões antagônicas** conflicting opinions.

antagonismo [ãntagoˈniʒmu] m **-1.** [oposição] antagonism; ~ **de idéias** conflict of ideas. **-2.** [rivalidade] competition.

antagonista [ãntagoˈniʃta] ◇ adj **-1.** [candidato, partido] opposing. **-2.** [opinião, idéia] conflicting. ◇ mf [rival] opponent.

antártico, ca [ãnˈtaxtʃiku, ka] adj Antarctic.

➤ **Antártico** n: **o (oceano)** ~ the Antarctic (Ocean).

Antártida [ãnˈtaxtʃida] n: **a** ~ Antarctica.

ante [ˈãntʃi] prep **-1.** [diante de] before; **jurar** ~ **a Bíblia** to swear on the Bible; **jurar** ~ **o juiz** to swear before the judge. **-2.** [em conseqüência de] as a result of.

ante- [ˈãntʃi-] prefixo ante-.

antebraço [ãntʃiˈbrasul] m forearm.

antecedência [ãnteseˈdẽnsja] f: **com** ~ in advance; **com uma semana de** ~ a week in advance.

antecedente [ãnteseˈdẽntʃi] ◇ adj [precedente] preceding. ◇ m **-1.** [precedente] predecessor. **-2.** GRAM, MAT antecedent.

➤ **antecedentes** mpl [pessoais] track record (sg); **ter bons** ~**s** to have a clean record; ~**s criminais** criminal record (sg).

anteceder [5] [ãnteseˈde(x)] ◇ vt [preceder, chegar antes de] to precede. ◇ vi [preceder] ~ **a** to precede.

➥ **anteceder-se** *vp* [antecipar-se]: ~ **(a)** to be ahead (of).

antecessor, ra [ãntese'so(x), ra] ◇ *adj* preceding. ◇ *m, f* predecessor.

antecipação [ãntesipa'sãw] (*pl* -ões) *f* - **1.** [adiantamento]: **a** ~ **de metas** the early achievement of goals; **a** ~ **do comunicado provocou uma crise** the bringing forward of the announcement caused a crisis. - **2.** [salarial] advance. - **3.** [antecedência]: **com** ~ in advance; **com uma semana/um mês de** ~ a week/month in advance.

antecipadamente [ãntesi,pada'mẽntʃi] *adv* in advance.

antecipado, da [ãntesi'padu, da] *adj* - **1.** [pagamento] advance (*antes de subst*). - **2.** [eleições] early.

antecipar [4] [ãntesi'pa(x)] *vt* - **1.** [fazer ocorrer mais cedo] to bring forward. - **2.** [adiantar-se a] to anticipate.

➥ **antecipar-se** *vp* [adiantar-se]: ~-**se a algo/alguém** to pre-empt sthg/sb; ~-**se a alguém em algo** to steal a march on sb in sthg.

antegozar [4] [ãntego'za(x)] *vt* to have a foretaste of.

antemão [ãnte'mãw] ➥ **de antemão** *loc adv* beforehand.

antena [ãn'tena] *f* - **1.** [ger] antenna; **de** ~**s ligadas** with one's antennae out. - **2.** *RÁDIO, TV* aerial; ~ **parabólica** satellite dish.

anteontem [ãntʃi'õntẽ] *adv* the day before yesterday.

anteparo [ãnte'paru] *m* [proteção] screen.

antepassado, da [,ãntepa'sadu, da] *m, f* ancestor.

antepenúltimo, ma [ãntepe'nuwtʃimu, ma] *adj* last but two, antepenultimate.

antepor [45] [ãnteẽpo(x)] *vt* - **1.** [contrapor]: ~ **algo a algo** to respond to sthg with sthg. - **2.** [preferir]: ~ **algo a algo** to prefer sthg to sthg.

➥ **antepor-se** *vp* [contrapor-se]: ~-**se a algo** to place o.s. in front of sthg.

anterior [ãnte'rjo(x)] (*pl* -es) *adj* - **1.** [prévio]: ~ **(a)** before. - **2.** [antigo]: ~ **(a)** previous (to). - **3.** [em posição] front; **membro** ~ forelimb; **músculo** ~ anterior muscle.

anteriormente [ãnterioxẽmẽntʃi] *adv* [previamente] previously; ~ **a algo** prior to sthg.

antes ['ãnʃiʃ] *adv* - **1.** [previamente] beforehand; **o quanto** ~ as soon as possible; **pouco** ~ a little before. - **2.** [antigamente] in the past; **como** ~ as ever; **de** *ou* **que** ~ as before. - **3.** [de preferência] rather. - **4.** [ao contrário] on the contrary.

➥ **antes de** *loc prep* before; ~ **de fazer algo** before doing sthg; ~ **da hora/do tempo** early; ~ **de tudo** above all.

➥ **antes que** *loc conj* before; **fui embora** ~ **que chovesse** I left before it rained.

ante-sala [,ãnte'sala] (*pl* -s) *f* antechamber.

antever [40] [ãnte've(x)] *vt* to foresee.

antevéspera [,ãnte'vɛʃpera] *f*: **(na)** ~ the day before yesterday.

antevisão [,ãnte'vizãw] *f* - **1.** [visão antecipada]: **ter**

uma ~ **de** to foresee. - **2.** [pressentimento] premonition.

anti- ['ãntʃi-] *prefixo* anti-, non-.

antiácido, da [ãn'tʃjasidu, da] *adj* antacid.
➥ **antiácido** *m* antacid.

antiaderente [ãntʃjade'rẽntʃi] (*pl* -s) ◇ *adj* non-stick. ◇ *m* non-stick surface.

antiaéreo, rea [ãntʃja'ɛrju, rja] *adj* anti-aircraft; **abrigo** ~ bomb shelter.

antialérgico, ca [ãntʃja'lɛxʒiku, ka] *adj* hypoallergenic.
➥ **antialérgico** *m* antihistamine.

antiamericano, na [ãntʃjameri'kãnu, na] *adj* anti-American.

antibiótico, ca [ãntʃi'bjɔtʃiku, ka] *adj* antibiotic.
➥ **antibiótico** *m* antibiotic.

anticaspa [ãntʃi'kaʃpa] *adj* anti-dandruff.

anticlímax [ãntʃi'klimãks] *m inv* anticlimax.

anticoagulante [ãntʃikwagu'lãntʃi] ◇ *adj* anticoagulant. ◇ *m* anticoagulant.

anticomunista [ãntʃikomu'niʃta] ◇ *adj* anti-communist. ◇ *mf* [pessoa] anti-communist.

anticoncepcional [ãntʃikõnsepsjo'naw] (*pl* -ais) ◇ *adj* contraceptive. ◇ *m* [pílula, dispositivo] contraceptive.

anticongelante [ãntʃikõnʒe'lãntʃi] ◇ *adj* antifreeze. ◇ *m* antifreeze.

anticorpo [ãntʃi'koxpu] *m* antibody.

anticorrosivo [ãntʃikoxo'zivul] *adj* - **1.** non-corrosive. - **2.** [proteção] anti-corrosive.

antidemocrático, ca [ãntʃidemo'kratʃiku, ka] *adj* anti-democratic.

antidepressivo, va [ãntʃidepre'sivu, va] *adj* antidepressant.
➥ **antidepressivo** *m* antidepressant.

antiderrapante [ãntʃidexa'pãntʃi] *adj* non-skid.

antídoto [ãn'tʃidotu] *m* antidote.

antiestético, ca [ãntʃjeʃ'tɛtʃiku, ka] *adj* tasteless.

antiético, ca [ãn'tʃjɛtʃiku, ka] *adj* unethical.

antigamente [ãntʃiga'mẽntʃi] *adv* in the past; **de** ~ old-fashioned.

antigo, ga [ãn'tʃigu, ga] *adj* - **1.** [ger] old. - **2.** [antiquado, remoto] old-fashioned. - **3.** (*antes de subst*) [anterior] former, previous. - **4.** (*antes de subst*) [veterano] longstanding; **ser** ~ **no clube** to be a longstanding member of the club; **ser** ~ **na empresa** to be a longstanding member of staff; **ser** ~ **no cargo** to be an old hand at the job. - **5.** *HIST* [da Antigüidade] ancient.
➥ **antigos** *mpl HIST* [homens] ancients.

antigüidade [ãntʃigwi'dadʒi] *f* - **1.** [idade] age. - **2.** [em cargo, função] seniority. - **3.** [peça, monumento] antique.
➥ **Antigüidade** *f* [época] antiquity.
➥ **antigüidades** *fpl* - **1.** [peças] antiques; **loja de** ~**s** antique shop. - **2.** [monumentos] ancient monuments.

anti-higiênico, ca [ãntʃji'ʒeniku, ka] (*mpl* -s, *fpl* -s) *adj* unhygienic.

anti-histamínico, ca [ãntʃji'iʃta'miniku, ka] *adj* antihistamine.
➤ **anti-histamínico** *m* antihistamine.
anti-horário [ãntʃjo'rarju] *adj*: **sentido/movimento** ~ anticlockwise direction/movement.
antiinflacionário, ria [ãntʃiflasjo'narju, rja] *adj* anti-inflationary.
antiinflamatório, ria [ãntʃiĩnflama'tɔriu, rja] <> *adj* anti-inflammatory. <> *m* anti-inflammatory.
antilhano, na [ãntʃi'ʎanu, na] <> *adj* West Indian. <> *m, f* West Indian.
Antilhas [ãn'tʃiʎas] *npl*: **as** ~ the West Indies.
antílope [ãn'tʃilopi] *m* antelope.
antinatural [ãntʃinatu'raw] (*pl* -ais) *adj* unnatural.
antinuclear [ãntʃinukle'a(x)] *adj* anti-nuclear.
antipático, ca [ãntʃi'patʃiku, ka] *adj* unpleasant.
antipatizar [4] [ãntʃipatʃi'za(x)] *vi*: ~ **com alguém** to dislike sb.
antipatriótico, ca [ãntʃipa'trjotʃiku, ka] *adj* unpatriotic.
antiperspirante [ãntʃipexʃpi'rantʃil] <> *adj* antiperspirant. <> *mf* antiperspirant.
antipoluente [ãntʃipo'lwẽntʃi] <> *adj* -1. [sistema, proteção] anti-pollution. -2. [material] non-polluting. <> *m* anti-pollution agent.
antiquado, da [ãntʃi'kwadu, da] *adj* antiquated.
antiquário, ria [ãntʃi'kwarju, rja] *m, f* [comerciante] antique dealer.
➤ **antiquário** *m* [loja] antique shop.
antiquíssimo, ma [ãntʃi'kisimu, ma] *superl* ▷ antigo.
anti-semita [ãntʃise'mita] (*pl* -s) <> *adj* anti-Semitic. <> *mf* [pessoa] anti-Semite.
anti-séptico, ca [antʃi'sɛptʃiku, ka] *adj* antiseptic.
➤ **anti-séptico, antisséptico** *m* [desinfetante] antiseptic.
anti-social [ãntʃiso'sjaw] (*pl* -ais) *adj* antisocial.
antisséptico [ˌãntʃi'sɛptʃiku] = **anti-séptico**.
antitabagismo [ãntʃitaba'ʒizmu] *m* anti-smoking.
antitabagista [ãntʃitaba'ʒista] <> *adj* anti-smoking. <> *mf* anti-smoker.
antitérmico, ca [ãntʃi'tɛxmiku, ka] *adj* antipyretic.
➤ **antitérmico** *m* [comprimido] antipyretic.
antiterrorismo [ãntʃitexo'riʒmu] *m* anti-terrorism.
antiterrorista [ãntʃitexo'riʃta] <> *adj* anti-terrorist. <> *mf* anti-terrorist.
antítese [ãn'tʃitezi] *f* antithesis.
antivírus [ãntʃi'viruʃ] *m inv* -1. BIOL antivirus. -2. COMPUT antivirus program.
antolhos [ã'tɔʎuʃ] *mpl* blinkers.
antologia [ãntolo'ʒia] *f* anthology.
antológico, ca [ãnto'lɔʒiku, ka] *adj* outstanding.
antônimo [ãn'tonimu] *m* antonym.
antro [ˈãntru] *m* -1. [caverna] cave. -2. [de animal] lair. -3. [de bandidos etc] den.

antropofagia [ãntropofa'ʒia] *f* cannibalism.
antropófago, ga [ãntro'pɔfagu, ga] <> *adj* cannibalistic. <> *m, f* cannibal.
antropologia [ãntropolo'ʒia] *f* anthropology.
antropólogo, ga [ãntro'pɔlogu, ga] *m, f* anthropologist.
anual [a'nwaw] (*pl* -ais) *adj* annual, yearly.
anuário [a'nwarju] *m* yearbook.
anuidade [anwi'dadʒi] *f* annuity.
anuir [74] [a'nwi(x)] *vi* to agree; ~ **a** *ou* **em algo** to agree to *ou* on sthg; ~ **a** *ou* **em fazer algo** to agree to do sthg.
anulação [anula'sãw] (*pl* -ões) *f* -1. [cancelamento, invalidação] cancellation. -2. [casamento] annulment. -3. [pena] revocation. -4. [gol] disallowance.
anular [4] [anu'la(x)] <> *vt* -1. [cancelar, invalidar] to cancel. -2. [casamento] to annul. -3. [pena] to revoke. -4. [gol] to disallow. -5. [sobrepujar] to cancel out. <> *adj* -1. [forma] circular. -2. [dedo] ring. <> *m* [dedo] ring finger.
anunciante [anũn'sjãntʃi] *m* COM advertiser.
anunciar [16] [anũn'sja(x)] *vt* -1. [ger] to announce. -2. COM [produto] to advertise.
anúncio [a'nũnsju] *m* -1. [comunicado] announcement. -2. [cartaz, aviso] notice. -3. [publicitário] advertisement; ~**s classificados** classifieds.
ânus [ˈãnuʃ] *m inv* anus.
anuviar [16] [anuvi'a(x)] *vt* to cloud.
➤ **anuviar-se** *vp* -1. [o céu] to become cloudy. -2. *fig* [rosto] to cloud.
anverso [ãn'vɛxsu] *m* obverse.
anzol [ãn'zɔw] (*pl* -óis) *m* hook.
ao [aw] = **a** + **o**.
aonde [a'õndʒi] *adv* where; ~ **quer que ...** wherever ...
aos [awʃ] = **a** + **os**.
AP (*abrev de* **Estado do Amapá**) *n State of Amapá*.
apadrinhar [4] [apadri'ɲa(x)] *vt* -1. [criança] to be godfather to. -2. [noivo] to be best man to. -3. *fig* [proteger] to take under one's wing. -4. *fig* [patrocinar] to sponsor.
APAE (*abrev de* **Associação de Pais e Amigos dos Excepcionais**) *f Brazilian association of parents and friends of the disabled*.
apagado, da [apa'gadu, da] *adj* -1. [fogo] extinguished. -2. [desligado] out *(depois de verbo)*. -3. [com borracha] rubbed out *UK*, erased *US*. -4. [desvanecido] faded. -5. *fig* [sem brilho] lacklustre. -6. *fig* [pessoa] dull.
apagador [apaga'do(x)] *m* board eraser.
apagão [apa'gãw] (*pl* -ões) *m* [blecaute] power cut.
apagar [14] [apa'ga(x)] <> *vt* -1. [fogo] to put out. -2. [vela] to blow out. -3. [luz, lanterna] to turn out. -4. [lustre] to dim. -5. [com borracha, apagador] to rub out. -6. [fazer desvanecer-se] to fade. -7. [abrandar] to dull. -8. COMPUT [eliminar] to delete. -9. *fam fig* [matar] to wipe out. <> *vi fam fig* [adormecer] to crash out.
➤ **apagar-se** *vp* -1. [extingüir-se] to die out. -2. [desligar-se] to go out. -3. [desvanecer-se] to fade. -4. [abrandar-se] to dull.

apaixonado, da [apaiʃoˈnadu, da] *adj* **-1.** [enamorado] in love; **estar** ~ **(por alguém)** to be in love (with sb). **-2.** [exaltado] impassioned. **-3.** [aficcionado]: **ser** ~ **(por algo)** to be passionate about sthg.

apaixonante [apaiʃoˈnãntʃi] *adj* exciting.

apaixonar-se [4] [apaiʃoˈnaxsi] *vp* **-1.** [enamorarse]: ~ **(por alguém)** to fall in love (with sb). **-2.** [aficcionar-se]: ~ **(por algo)** to become passionate (about sthg).

apalermado, da [apalexˈmadu, da] *adj* idiotic.

apalpar [4] [apawˈpa(x)] *vt* to feel.

➡ **apalpar-se** *vp* [examinar-se] to examine o.s.

apanhado [apãˈnadu] *m* **-1.** [resumo] summary. **-2.** [de flores] bunch.

apanhar [4] [apãˈna(x)] ◇ *vt* **-1.** [ger] to catch. **-2.** [pegar] to pick out. **-3.** [alcançar] to get. **-4.** [pegar do chão] to pick up. **-5.** [agarrar] to grab. **-6.** [colher] to pick. **-7.** [ir buscar] to fetch. **-8.** [tomar condução] to take. ◇ *vi* **-1.** [ser espancado] to be beaten; ~ **de alguém** to take a beating from sb; ~ **de algo** to be beaten with sthg. **-2.** *ESP* [perder] to lose. **-3.** *fig* [ter dificuldades] to go through a lot.

apara [aˈpara] *f* **-1.** [madeira] shaving. **-2.** [papel] shred.

aparador [aparaˈdo(x)] (*pl* **-es**) *m* [móvel] sideboard.

aparafusar [4] [aparafuˈza(x)] *vt* **-1.** [parafuso] to screw in. **-2.** [prender] to screw.

aparar [4] [apaˈra(x)] *vt* **-1.** [cabelo, barba, unhas] to trim. **-2.** [unhas] to clip. **-3.** [golpe] to fend off. **-4.** [tábua, folhas] to smooth out.

aparato [apaˈratu] *m* **-1.** [pompa] ceremony. **-2.** [conjunto - de ferramentas] collection; [- de armas] apparatus. **-3.** *fig* [de conceitos, análises] structure.

aparecer [25] [apareˈse(x)] *vt* **-1.** [ger] to appear. **-2.** [ser perceptível] to be apparent. **-3.** [comparecer] to turn up; *fam* [fazer visita] to drop in. **-4.** *fam pej* [exibir-se] to show off.

aparecimento [aparesiˈmẽntu] *m* appearance.

aparelhado, da [apareˈʎadu, da] *adj* **-1.** [preparado] prepared. **-2.** [madeira] planed.

aparelhagem [apareˈʎaʒẽ] (*pl* **-ns**) *f* **-1.** [equipamento] equipment; [de som] sound system. **-2.** [da madeira] planing. **-3.** *NÁUT* rigging.

aparelhar [4] [apareˈʎa(x)] *vt* **-1.** [preparar] to equip. **-2.** *NÁUT* to rig.

➡ **aparelhar-se** *vp* [preparar-se] to equip o.s.

aparelho [apaˈreʎu] *m* **-1.** [conjunto] set; ~ **de chá** tea set; ~ **de jantar** dinner service. **-2.** [equipamento] equipment; ~ **de som** sound system. **-3.** [máquina] machine; ~ **de barbear** shaving equipment; ~ **de rádio/TV** radio/television set; ~ **eletrodoméstico** domestic appliance. **-4.** *PESCA* tackle. **-5.** *POL* hideout. **-6.** *ANAT* system; ~ **digestivo** digestive system; ~ **fonador** voice box.

aparência [apaˈrẽnsja] *f* **-1.** [aspecto] appearance; **sob a** ~ **de** in the guise of; **na** ~ by all appearances. **-2.** [ilusão] show.

➡ **aparências** *fpl* [exterioridades] appearances; **as** ~**s enganam** *prov* one shouldn't judge by appearances; **manter as** ~**s** to keep up appearances; **salvar as** ~**s** to save appearances.

aparentado, da [apaˈrẽntadu, da] *adj* **-1.** [que tem parentesco] related; **ser** ~ **de alguém** to be related to sb; **bem** ~ well connected. **-2.** [que tem boa aparência]: **bem** ~ smart.

aparentar [4] [aparẽnˈta(x)] *vt* **-1.** [parecer] to seem. **-2.** [fingir] to pretend.

aparente [apaˈrẽntʃi] *adj* **-1.** [falso] feigned. **-2.** [visível] visible.

aparição [apariˈsãw] (*pl* **-ões**) *f* apparition.

apartamento [apaxtaˈmẽntu] *m* **-1.** [residência] apartment, flat *UK*. **-2.** [de hotel] hotel suite.

apartar [4] [apaxˈta(x)] *vt* **-1.** [separar] to split. **-2.** [briga] to break up.

➡ **apartar-se** *vp* [afastar-se] to split from.

aparte [aˈpaxtʃi] *m* [observação] aside; **fazer um** ~ to make an aside.

apartheid [apaxˈtajdʒi] *m* apartheid.

apartidário, ria [apaxtʃiˈdarju, rja] *adj* non-partisan.

aparvalhado, da [apaxvaˈʎadu, da] *adj* **-1.** [idiota] idiotic. **-2.** [sem reação]: **ficar** ~ to be stunned.

apatetado, da [apateˈtadu, da] *adj* [trapalhão] foolish.

apatia [apaˈtʃia] *f* indifference.

apático, ca [aˈpatʃiku, ka] *adj* indifferent.

apátrida [aˈpatrida] *mf* stateless person.

apavorado, da [apavoˈradu, da] *adj* terrified.

apavoramento [apavoraˈmẽntu] *m* panic, terror.

apavorante [apavoˈrãntʃi] *adj* terrifying.

apavorar [4] [apavoˈra(x)] ◇ *vt* to terrify. ◇ *vi* to be terrifying.

➡ **apavorar-se** *vp* to become terrified.

apaziguar [21] [apaziˈgwa(x)] *vt* to calm.

➡ **apaziguar-se** *vp* **-1.** to calm down. **-2.** [inimigos] to make peace.

apear [aˈpja(x)] *vi* to dismount.

apedrejar [4] [apedreˈʒa(x)] *vt* to stone.

apegado, da [apeˈgadu, da] *adj* [afeiçoado]: ~ **(a)** attached (to).

apegar-se [14] [apeˈgaxsi] *vp* [afeiçoar-se]: ~ **a algo/alguém** to become attached to sthg/sb.

apego [aˈpegu] *m* [afeição] attachment; **ter** ~ **por** to be attached to.

apelação [apelaˈsãw] (*pl* **-ões**) *f* **-1.** [apelo] appeal. **-2.** *JUR* appeal. **-3.** *fam* [vulgarização] solicitation.

apelante [apeˈlãntʃi] *mf* appellant.

apelar [4] [apeˈla(x)] *vi* **-1.** [recorrer]: ~ **a** to appeal to; ~ **(para a violência)** to turn nasty. **-2.** [invocar]: ~ **a** [compreensão, amizade] to call upon. **-3.** *JUR* : ~ **a** **(de)** to appeal (against). **-4.** [vulgarmente] to turn nasty.

apelidar [4] [apeliˈda(x)] *vt*: ~ **alguém de algo** to nickname sb sthg.

apelido [apeˈlidu] *m* [alcunha] nickname; **chato é** ~**! ele é insuportável!** *fam* boring's an understatement! he's odious!

apelo [aˈpelu] *m* appeal; ~ **a alguém/algo** appeal to sb/sthg.

apenas [a'penaʃl ◇ *adv* [só] only. ◇ *conj* [logo que] as soon as.

apêndice [a'pĕndʒisil *m* appendix.

apendicite [apĕndʒi'sitʃil *f* appendicitis.

Apeninos [ape'ninuʃl *npl*: **os** ~ the Apennines.

apequenar [4] [apeke'na(x)l *vt* - **1.** [tornar pequeno] to lessen. - **2.** *fig* [rebaixar, humilhar] to belittle.

   apequenar-se *vp fig* [rebaixar-se, humilhar-se] to belittle o.s.

aperceber-se [5] [apexse'bexsil *vp*: ~ **de** to realise.

aperfeiçoamento [apexfejswa'mĕntul *m* [aprimoramento] improvement.

aperfeiçoar [20] [apexfej'swa(x)l *vt* to improve.

   aperfeiçoar-se *vp* [aprimorar-se] to improve; ~-se em algo to improve in *ou* at sthg.

aperitivo, va [aperi'tʃivu, val *adj* appetizing.

   aperitivo *m* - **1.** [bebida] aperitif. - **2.** [petisco] appetizer.

aperreação [apexja'sãwl (*pl* -ões) *f* - **1.** [aborrecimento] vexation. - **2.** [situação difícil] hardship.

aperreado, da [ape'xjadu, dal *adj* - **1.** [aborrecido] vexed. - **2.** [em situação difícil] troubled.

aperrear [15] [ape'xja(x)l *vt* - **1.** [aborrecer] to annoy. - **2.** [afligir] to vex.

   aperrear-se *vp* - **1.** [aborrecer-se] to become vexed. - **2.** [afligir-se] to be anxious.

apertado, da [apex'tadu, dal ◇ *adj* - **1.** [ger] tight. - **2.** [passagem] narrow. - **3.** [poltrona, sala, teatro] cramped. - **4.** [difícil] hard. - **5.** [sem tempo] pressed. - **6.** [sem dinheiro] strapped for cash; **orçamento** ~ tight budget. - **7.** *fam* [para ir ao banheiro]: **estar** ~ to be desperate to go to the bathroom. - **8.** [coração]: **estar com o coração** ~ to be anguished. ◇ *adv* [com dificuldade] only just.

apertar [4] [apex'ta(x)l ◇ *vt* - **1.** [cingir]: ~ **algo (contra/entre)** to clasp sthg (against/between); ~ **alguém (contra/entre)** to clasp sb (against/between); ~ **a mão de alguém** [cumprimentar] to shake sb's hand. - **2.** [espremer] to squeeze. - **3.** [incomodar por ser justo] to constrict. - **4.** [tornar mais justo] to tighten. - **5.** [pressionar - botão] to do up; [- gatilho] to squeeze. - **6.** *fig* [intensificar] to tighten up on. - **7.** [passo, ritmo] to speed up. - **8.** [cortar] to cut. - **9.** [coração] to wring. - **10.** *fig* [pessoa] to put pressure on. ◇ *vi* - **1.** [roupa, sapato] to be tight. - **2.** [chuva, frio, fome] to intensify. - **3.** [prazo] to run out. - **4.** [estrada, rio] to narrow.

   apertar-se *vp* - **1.** [cortar gastos] to tighten one's belt. - **2.** [ficar sem dinheiro] to be pressed for cash. - **3.** [com a roupa] to squeeze o.s. into.

aperto [a'pextul *m* - **1.** [em cumprimento]: ~ **de mãos** handshake. - **2.** *fig* [apuro] problem; **passar um** ~ to have a rough time. - **3.** *fig* [financeiro] hardship.

apesar [ape'za(x)l *prep*: ~ **de** in spite of; ~ **de que** even though; ~ **disso** in spite of this.

apetecer [25] [apete'se(x)l *vi* to be appetizing; ~ **a alguém** to appeal to sb.

apetecível [apete'sivewl (*pl* -eis) *adj* - **1.** [prato,

receita] appetizing. - **2.** *fig* [idéia proposta] attractive.

apetite [ape'tʃitʃil *m* appetite; **abrir o** ~ to whet the appetite; **bom** ~! enjoy your meal!; **ter um** ~ **de sucesso/riqueza/poder** to have an appetite for success/wealth/power.

apetitoso, osa [apetʃi'tozu, ɔzal *adj* tasty.

apetrechar [4] [apetre'ʃa(x)l *vt*: ~ **alguém (com/para algo)** to equip sb (with/for sthg).

   apetrechar-se *vp*: ~-se (com/para algo) to equip o.s. (with/for sthg).

apetrechos [ape'treʃuʃl *mpl* - **1.** [de guerra] equipment *(U)*. - **2.** [de pesca] tackle *(U)*.

ápice ['apisil *m* - **1.** [cimo] top, summit. - **2.** *fig* [apogeu] peak.

apicultura [apikuw'tural *f* bee-keeping.

apiedar-se [4] [apje'daxsil *vp*: ~ **(de alguém/algo)** to feel sorry (for sb/sthg).

apimentado, da [apimĕn'tadu, dal *adj* - **1.** [com muita pimenta] peppery. - **2.** *fig* [sensual] spicy.

apimentar [4] [apimĕn'ta(x)l *vt* to pepper.

apinhado, da [api'ɲadu, dal *adj* crowded; ~ **de gente** crowded with people.

apinhar [4] [api'ɲa(x)l *vt* [lotar] to crowd.

   apinhar-se *vp* - **1.** [aglomerar-se] to crowd. - **2.** [lotar]: ~-se (de gente) to be crowded (with people).

apitar [4] [api'ta(x)l ◇ *vi* - **1.** [com apito] to whistle. - **2.** *fam fig* [ter autoridade] to know a lot; **ele apita muito em medicina** he knows a lot about medicine; **ele não apita nada em casa** he's not the one who wears the trousers. ◇ *vt* [ESP - arbitrar] to referee; [- falta, pênalti] to whistle.

apito [a'pitul *m* [instrumento, silvo] whistle.

aplacar [12] [apla'ka(x)l ◇ *vt* - **1.** [serenar] to subdue. - **2.** [abrandar] to assuage. ◇ *vi* - **1.** [serenarse] to die down. - **2.** [abrandar-se] to calm down.

   aplacar-se *vp* to calm down.

aplainar [4] [aplaj'na(x)l *vt* - **1.** [madeira] to plane. - **2.** [nivelar] to level out.

aplanar [4] [apla'na(x)l *vt* - **1.** [nivelar] to level out. - **2.** [alisar] to smooth. - **3.** *fig* [obstáculos] to smooth out.

aplaudir [6] [aplaw'di(x)l ◇ *vt* to applaud; ~ **alguém/algo de pé** to give sb/sthg a standing ovation. ◇ *vi* to clap, to applaud.

aplauso [a'plawzul *m* - **1.** [ger] applause; **o filme recebeu o** ~ **da crítica** the film received critical acclaim. - **2.** *fig* [aprovação] approval; **as medidas contra o crime contam com meu** ~ I applaud the measures against crime.

aplicação [aplika'sãwl (*pl* -ões) *f* - **1.** [ger] application. - **2.** [ornato] adornment.

aplicado, da [apli'kadu, dal *adj* - **1.** [esforçado] hard-working. - **2.** [prático] applied.

aplicar [12] [apli'ka(x)l ◇ *vt* - **1.** [ger] to apply. - **2.** [injeção] to give. - **3.** *FIN* to invest. ◇ *vi FIN* to invest.

   aplicar-se *vp* - **1.** [esforçar-se]: ~-se em/para algo to work hard at/for sthg. - **2.** [adequar-se]: ~-se a algo to apply to sthg.

aplicativo, va [aplika'tʃivu, val *adj COMPUT*: **programa** ~ application.

➥ **aplicativo** *m COMPUT* application.

aplicável [apli'kavew] (*pl* -eis) *adj* -1. [ger] applicable. -2. [apropriado] appropriate.

aplique [a'pliki] *m* -1. [de luz] wall light. -2. [peruca] hairpiece.

APM (*abrev de* Associação de Pais e Mestres) *f* ≃ PTA.

apocalipse [apoka'lipsi] *m* apocalypse.

apocalíptico, ca [apoka'liptʃiku, ka] *adj* -1. [do Apocalipse] apocalyptic. -2. [terrível] terrifying. -3. [difícil de entender] enigmatic.

apócrifo, fa [a'pɔkrifu, fa] *adj* apocryphal.

➥ **apócrifo** *m* [texto] apocrypha (*pl*).

apoderar-se [4] [apode'raxsi] *vp*: ~ **de algo** to take over sthg.

apodrecer [25] [apodre'se(x)] ◇ *vi* -1. [comida] to go off. -2. [dente] to rot. -3. *fam* [pessoa]: ~ **em** to rot in. ◇ *vt* [tornar podre] to rot.

apodrecimento [apodresi'mẽntu] *m* rot.

apogeu [apo'ʒew] *m* -1. [de império, carreira, romance] crowning point. -2. *ASTRON* apogee.

apoiar [16] [apo'ja(x)] *vt* -1. [ger] to support. -2. [firmar]: ~ **algo em** *ou* **sobre algo** to rest sthg on sthg. -3. [fundamentar]: ~ **algo em** *ou* **sobre algo** to base sthg on sthg.

➥ **apoiar-se** *vp* -1. [amparar-se mutuamente] to support one another. -2. [firmar-se] to lean. -3. [fundamentar-se] to be based on.

apoio [a'poju] *m* -1. [ger] support; ~ **moral** moral support. -2. [patrocínio] sponsorship; ~ **cultural** cultural sponsorship. -3. [alicerce] foundations (*pl*). -4. *fig* [fundamento] basis.

apólice [a'pɔlisi] *f* policy; ~ **de seguro** insurance policy.

apolítico, ca [apo'litʃiku, ka] *adj* apolitical.

apologia [apolo'ʒia] *f* defence.

apologista [apolo'ʒiʃta] *mf* apologist.

apontador [apõnta'do(x)] (*pl* -es) *m* -1. [de lápis] pencil sharpener. -2. [de jogo] marker.

apontamento [apõnta'mẽntu] *m* [anotação] notes (*pl*).

apontar [4] [apõn'ta(x)] ◇ *vt* -1. [ger] to point out. -2. [arma] to aim. -3. [citar] to name. -4. [notas] to make notes. -5. [jogo] to mark. -6. [lápis] to sharpen! ◇ *vi* -1. [com arma]: ~ **para** to aim at; apontar! aim! -2. [com o dedo]: ~ **para** to point at. -3. [aparecer] to appear.

apoplético, ca [apo'plɛtʃiku, ka] *adj* apoplectic.

apoquentar [4] [apokẽnta(x)] *vt* to annoy.

➥ **apoquentar-se** *vp* to get annoyed.

aporrinhação [apoxiɲa'sãw] (*pl* -ões) *f mfam* annoyance.

aporrinhar [4] [apoxi'ɲa(x)] *vt mfam* to annoy.

aportar [4] [apox'ta(x)] *vi* [desembarcar, ancorar]: ~ **em** to dock in.

aportuguesar [4] [apoxtuge'za(x)] *vt* to make Portuguese.

➥ **aportuguesar-se** *vp* to become Portuguese.

após [a'pɔjʃ] *prep* after.

aposentado, da [apozẽn'tadu, da] ◇ *adj* -1.

[pessoa] retired. -2. [sapato] discarded. -3. [carro, máquina] disused. ◇ *m, f* retired person.

aposentadoria [apozẽntado'ria] *f* -1. [condição] retirement. -2. [vencimentos] pension.

aposentar [4] [apozẽn'ta(x)] *vt* -1. [pessoa] to pension off. -2. [máquina] to discard.

➥ **aposentar-se** *vp* to retire.

aposento [apo'zẽntu] *m* bedroom.

apossar-se [4] [apo'saxsi] *vp*: ~ **de algo** to take possession of sthg.

aposta [a'pɔʃta] *f* bet.

apostar [4] [apoʃ'ta(x)] ◇ *vt* to bet; ~ **que** to bet that. ◇ *vi*: ~ **em** to bet on.

apostila [apoʃ'tʃila] *f* -1. [nota marginal] marginal note. -2. [matéria de aula] handout.

apóstolo [a'pɔʃtulu] *m* apostle.

apóstrofo [a'pɔʃtrofu] *m* apostrophe.

apoteose [apote'ɔzi] *f* apotheosis.

aprazer [32] [apra'ze(x)] *vi*: ~ **a alguém** to please sb.

aprazível [apra'zivew] (*pl* -eis) *adj* pleasant.

apreçar [13] [apre'sa(x)] *vt* [dar valor a] to value.

apreciação [apresja'sãw] (*pl* -ões) *f* -1. [análise] consideration. -2. [julgamento] assessment.

apreciador, ra [apresja'do(x), ra] *m, f* aficionado.

apreciar [16] [apre'sja(x)] *vt* -1. [ger] to appreciate. -2. [gostar de] to enjoy.

apreciativo, va [apresja'tʃivu, va] *adj* appreciative.

apreciável [apre'sjavew] (*pl* -eis) *adj* -1. [estimável] considerable. -2. [significativo] notable.

apreço [a'presu] *m* [estima, consideração] consideration.

apreender [5] [aprjẽn'de(x)] *vt* -1. [tomar] to seize; ~ **algo a alguém** to seize sthg from sb. -2. [compreender] to understand, to comprehend.

apreensão [aprjẽn'sãw] (*pl* -ões) *f* -1. [tomada] seizure. -2. [percepção] understanding, comprehension. -3. [preocupação] apprehension.

apreensivo, va [aprjẽn'sivu, va] *adj* apprehensive.

apregoar [20] [apre'gwa(x)] *vt* to proclaim.

aprender [5] [aprẽn'de(x)] ◇ *vt* to learn. ◇ *vi* to learn; ~ **a fazer algo** to learn to do sthg; ~ **de cor** to learn by heart.

aprendiz [aprẽn'dʒiʒ] (*pl* -es) *mf* learner.

aprendizado [aprendʒi'zadu] (*pl* -es) *m*, **aprendizagem** *f* [aprẽndʒi'zaʒẽl] learning.

apresentação [aprezẽnta'sãw] (*pl* -ões) *f* [ger] presentation.

apresentador, ra [aprezẽnta'do(x), ra] *m, f* -1. [de seminário, painel] speaker. -2. *RÁDIO,TV* presenter.

apresentar [4] [aprezẽn'ta(x)] *vt* -1. [ger] to present; ~ **uma comunicação** to give a talk. -2. [fazer] to make. -3. [moção, recurso] to introduce.

➥ **apresentar-se** *vp* -1. [dar-se a conhecer] to introduce o.s. -2. [comparecer] to present o.s. -3. [manifestar-se] to arise. -4. [candidatar-se] to put o.s. forward.

apresentável [aprezẽn'tavew] (*pl* -eis) *adj* presentable.

apressado, da [apre'sadu, da] *adj* hurried; **estar** ~ to be in a hurry.

apressar [4] [apre'sa(x)] *vt* to hurry.

→ **apressar-se** *vp* to hurry.

aprimorado, da [aprimo'radu, da] *adj* improved.

aprimoramento [aprimora'mẽntul] *m* improvement.

aprimorar [4] [aprimo'ra(x)] *vt* to improve.

→ **aprimorar-se** *vp*: ~-se **(em algo)** to try hard (at sthg).

aprisionamento [aprizjona'mẽntul] *m* -**1.** [de pessoa] imprisonment. -**2.** [de passarinho] captivity.

aprisionar [4] [aprizjo'na(x)] *vt* -**1.** [prender] to imprison. -**2.** [meter em prisão] to put in prison. -**3.** [capturar] to keep in captivity.

aprofundamento [aprofũnda'mẽntul] *m* in-depth examination.

aprofundar [4] [aprofũn'da(x)] *vt* -**1.** [ger] to deepen. -**2.** [investigação] to intensify. -**3.** [conhecimentos] to improve. -**4.** [divergências] to increase.

→ **aprofundar-se** *vp* -**1.** [no solo, no mar] to go down. -**2.** [em investigações, análise] to intensify. -**3.** [em área de conhecimento] to immerse o.s. -**4.** [em selva, mato] to penetrate deeper.

aprontar [4] [aprõnta(x)] ⟨⟩ *vt* -**1.** [preparar] to prepare. -**2.** [terminar] to complete. -**3.** *fam* [briga, confusão] to cause. ⟨⟩ *vi fam* [criar confusão] to play up.

→ **aprontar-se** *vp* -**1.** [vestir-se, arrumar-se] to get ready. -**2.** [preparar-se] to prepare o.s.

apropriação [aproprja'sãw] (*pl* -**ões**) *f* -**1.** [assenhoramento] takeover. -**2.** [tomada] seizure. -**3.** COM [adequação]: ~ **de custos** cost adjustment.

apropriado, da [apro'prjadu, da] *adj* -**1.** [adequado] appropriate. -**2.** [tomado] seized.

apropriar [16] [apro'prja(x)] *vt* [adequar] to adapt.

→ **apropriar-se** *vp*: ~-se **de algo** to take possession of sthg.

aprovação [aprova'sãw] (*pl* -**ões**) *f* -**1.** [ger] approval. -**2.** [em exame] pass.

aprovar [4] [apro'va(x)] *vt* -**1.** [apoiar] to approve. -**2.** [sancionar] to approve. -**3.** [em exame] to pass.

aproveitador, ra [aprovejta'do(x), ra] (*mpl* -**es**, *fpl* -**s**) ⟨⟩ *adj* opportunistic. ⟨⟩ *m, f* opportunist.

aproveitamento [aprovejta'mẽntul] *m* -**1.** [uso] good use. -**2.** [nos estudos] improvement; **ter um bom** ~ to do well.

aproveitar [4] [aprovej'ta(x)] ⟨⟩ *vt* -**1.** [tirar proveito de]: **aproveitei que chovia para descansar** I took advantage of the rainy weather to have a rest. -**2.** [não desperdiçar] to make the most of, to put to good use. -**3.** [usar] to use. ⟨⟩ *vi* [tirar proveito]: ~ **para fazer algo** to take opportunity to do sthg; **aproveite!** make the most of it!; **aproveite enquanto é tempo!** make the most of it while you can!, make hay while the sun shines!

→ **aproveitar-se** *vp*: ~-se **de algo/alguém** to take advantage of sthg/sb.

aproveitável [aprovej'tavewl] (*pl* -**eis**) *adj* reusable.

aprovisionamento [aprovizjona'mẽntul] *m* supply.

aprovisionar [4] [aprovizjo'na(x)] *vt* [abastecer] to supply.

aprox. (*abrev de* **aproximadamente**) *adv* approx.

aproximação [aprosima'sãw] (*pl* -**ões**) *f* -**1.** [chegada] approach. -**2.** [estimativa] approximation. -**3.** [de países] coming together. -**4.** [de pontos de vista] similarity.

aproximado, da [aprosi'madu, da] *adj* approximate.

aproximar [4] [aprosi'ma(x)] *vt* -**1.** [precipitar] to bring forward. -**2.** [cálculo] to approximate. -**3.** [pessoas, países] to bring together. -**4.** [levar para perto] to draw up. -**5.** [fazer parecer perto] to bring closer.

→ **aproximar-se** *vp* -**1.** [achegar-se] to approach. -**2.** [pessoas, países] to draw closer. -**3.** [assemelhar-se] to be similar.

aprumado, da [apru'madu, da] *adj* -**1.** [vertical] straight. -**2.** *fig* [altivo] upright. -**3.** [elegante] elegant.

aprumo [a'prumu] *m* -**1.** [posição vertical] straightness. -**2.** [altivez] rectitude. -**3.** [elegância] elegance.

aptidão [aptʃi'dãw] (*pl* -**ões**) *f* -**1.** [ger] aptitude. -**2.** [jeito]: **ter** ~ **para** to have an aptitude for.

apto, ta l'aptu, ta] *adj* suitable; ~ **para** fit for.

Apto. (*abrev de* **apartamento**) *m* Flat no. UK, Apt. US.

apunhalar [4] [apuɲa'la(x)] *vt* -**1.** [esfaquear] to stab. -**2.** *fig* [trair] to stab in the back.

apuração [apura'sãw] (*pl* -**ões**) *f* -**1.** [de votos] counting. -**2.** [de fatos, informações] examination. -**3.** [de conta] checking.

apurado, da [apu'radu, da] *adj* -**1.** [ger] refined. -**2.** [aguçado] sharp.

apurar [4] [apu'ra(x)] *vt* -**1.** [tornar puro] to purify. -**2.** [refinar] to refine. -**3.** [aprimorar] to perfect. -**4.** [aguçar] to sharpen. -**5.** [averiguar] to verify. -**6.** [votos] to count. -**7.** [conta] to check.

→ **apurar-se** *vp* -**1.** [tornar-se puro] to become pure. -**2.** [no trajar] to smarten o.s. up. -**3.** [aprimorar-se] to become perfect.

apuro [a'purul *m* -**1.** [esmero] care. -**2.** [dificuldade] fix; **estar em** ~**s** to be in a fix. -**3.** [aperto financeiro] hardship.

aquarela [akwa'rɛla] *f* water colour.

aquariano, na [akwa'rjãnu, na] *m, f* ASTROL Aquarian.

aquário [a'kwarjul *m* [para peixes] aquarium.

→ **Aquário** *m* ASTROL Aquarius.

aquático, ca [a'kwatʃiku, ka] *adj* aquatic; **pólo/ massagem** ~ water polo/massage; **ginástica** ~ aquarobics; **esportes** ~**s** aquatics.

aquecedor [akese'do(x)] (*pl* -**es**) *adj* heating.

→ **aquecedor** *m* heater.

aquecer [25] [aˈʀe'se(x)] ⟨⟩ *vt* -**1.** [ger] to warm up. -**2.** [esquentar] to heat. ⟨⟩ *vi* -**1.** [esquentar] to become hot. -**2.** [dar calor] to give warmth.

→ **aquecer-se** *vp* -**1.** [ger] to warm up. -**2.**

[esquentar-se] to warm o.s. **-3.** *fig* [debate] to become heated.

aquecimento [akesi'mẽntul *m* **-1.** [ger] heating; ~ **central** central heating. **-2.** [econômico] warming. **-3.** *ESP* [muscular] warm up; **ir para o** ~ to go for a warm-up.

àquela [a'kɛla] = **a + aquela**.

aquele, aquela [a'keli, a'kɛla] <> *adj* that, those *pl*.<> *pron* that one; ~ **ali** that one there; ~ **que** [relativo a pessoa] the one who, those who *pl*; [relativo a objeto] the one which; **peça àquele homem/àquela mulher** ask that man/woman.

àquele [a'keli] = **a + aquele**.

aquém [a'kẽj] *adv* **-1.** [deste lado] this side; ~ **de** on this side of. **-2.** [abaixo]: ~ **de** below.

aqui [a'ki] *adv* **-1.** [neste lugar] here; ~ **dentro/ fora** in/out here; ~ **e agora** here and now; ~ **mesmo** right here; **eis** ~ here is; **por** ~ round here; **estar por** ~ **(com algo/alguém)** to be up to here (with sthg/sb). **-2.** [neste momento] at that point; **até** ~ up to now. **-3.** [nisto] on this point.

aquiescência [akje'sẽnsja] *f* acquiescence.

aquiescer [25] [akje'se(x)] *vi*: ~ **a** to accede to; ~ **em** to agree to.

aquietar [4] [akje'ta(x)] *vt* to quieten.

~ **aquietar-se** *vp* to quieten down.

aquilatar [4] [akila'ta(x)] *vt* **-1.** [metais] to assay. **-2.** [estimar] to weigh up.

aquilino, na [aki'linu, na] *adj* [nariz] aquiline.

aquilo [a'kilu] *pron* that; **você chama aquilo de carro!** you call that a car!

àquilo [a'kilu] = **a + aquilo**.

aquinhoar [20] [akiɲo'a(x)] *vt* to endow.

aquisição [akizi'sãw] (*pl* **-ões**) *f* acquisition.

aquisitivo, va [akizi'tʃivu, va] *adj* [poder] acquisitive.

ar [a(x)] (*pl* **-ares**) *m* **-1.** [ger] air; **o avião está no** ~ the plane is in the sky; **ao** ~ **livre** in the open air; **tomar** ~ **(fresco)** to get some (fresh) air; ~ **condicionado** [atmosfera] air conditioning; **ir pelos ares** to be blown sky-high; **corrente de** ~ draught. **-2.** *RÁDIO, TV*: **no** ~ on the air; **ir ao** ~ to be broadcast, to go on the air; **sair do** ~ to come off the air. **-3.** *fig* [aspecto] appearance. **-4.** *loc*: **apanhar as coisas no** ~ to pick things up quickly; **dar o** ~ **de sua** *ou* **da graça** to show up; **estar no** ~ to be up in the air; **ficar no** ~ to be confused.

~ **ares** *mpl* **-1.** [clima] air; **mudar de ares** to get a change of air. **-2.** [pose] airs (*pl*).

árabe ['arabi] <> *adj* Arab. <> *m, f* Arab. <> *m* [língua] Arabic.

arabesco [ara'beʃku] *m* arabesque.

Arábia Saudita [a,rabjasaw'dʒita] *n* Saudi Arabia.

arábico, ca [a'rabiku, ka] *adj* **-1.** [da Arábia] Arabian. **-2.** [algarismo] Arabic. **-3.** [goma]: **goma arábica** gum arabic.

Aracajú [araka'ʒu] *n* Aracajú.

arado [a'radu] *m* plough.

aragem [a'raʒẽ] (*pl* **-ns** [a'raʒẽʃ]) *f* breeze.

Aral [a'raw] *n*: **o mar de** ~ the Aral Sea.

aramado, da [ara'madu, da] *adj* [estádio] fenced in.

~ **aramado** *m* **-1.** [cerca] wire fencing. **-2.** [porta-objetos] wire basket/rack.

arame [a'rãmi] *m* [cabo] wire; ~ **farpado** barbed wire.

aranha [a'rãɲa] *f* spider.

aranha-caranguejeira [a,rãɲakarãŋge'ʒejra] (*pl* **aranhas-caranguejeiras**) *f* bird-eating spider.

arapuca [ara'puka] *f* **-1.** [armadilha, cilada] trap; **cair numa** ~ to fall into a trap. **-2.** *fam fig* [estabelecimento] shady company.

araque [a'raki] *m*: **de** ~ *fam* rubbish.

arar [4] [a'ra(x)] *vt* to plough.

arara [a'rara] *f* macaw; **estar/ficar uma** ~ to be hopping mad.

araruta [ara'ruta] *f* arrowroot.

arbitragem [axbi'traʒẽ] (*pl* **-ns**) *f* **-1.** [julgamento] arbitration. **-2.** [*ESP* - ato] adjudication; [- decisão] decision; [- os juízes] referees (*pl*).

arbitrar [4] [axbi'tra(x)] *vt* **-1.** [questão, litígio] to arbitrate. **-2.** *ESP* [partida, campeonato] to referee. **-3.** [adjudicar]: ~ **algo a alguém** to award sb sthg.

arbitrariedade [axbitrarje'dadʒi] *f* arbitrariness.

arbitrário, ria [axbi'trarju, rja] *adj* arbitrary.

arbítrio [ax'bitrju] *m* **-1.** [resolução] judgment; **deixar algo ao** ~ **de alguém** to leave sthg to the discretion of sb. **-2.** [faculdade] free will.

árbitro ['axbitru] *m* **-1.** [de questão, litígio] mediator. **-2.** [juiz] judge. **-3.** [*ESP* - em futebol, box] referee; [- em tênis] umpire.

arborizado, da [axbori'zadu, da] *adj* **-1.** [bairro, terreno] wooded. **-2.** [rua] tree-lined.

arborizar [4] [axbori'za(x)] *vt* to plant with trees.

arbusto [ax'buʃtu] *m* bush.

arca ['axka] *f* **-1.** [caixa] chest. **-2.** [barca]: **Arca de Noé** Noah's Ark.

arcabouço [axka'bosu] *m* **-1.** [linhas gerais] outline. **-2.** *ARQUIT* [estrutura] framework.

arcada [ax'kada] *f* **-1.** [de arcos] arcade; ~ **dentária** dental arch. **-2.** [arco] arch.

arcaico, ca [ax'kajku, ka] *adj* **-1.** [antigo] archaic. **-2.** [antiquado] antiquated.

arcaizante [axkaj'zãntʃil *adj* archaic.

arcanjo [ax'kãnʒu] *m* archangel.

arcar [12] [ax'ka(x)] *vi*: ~ **com algo** to take responsibility for sthg.

arcebispo [axse'biʃpu] *m* archbishop.

arco ['axku] *m* **-1.** [ger] arch; **em** ~ arched. **-2.** [arma, instrumento musical] bow; ~**-e-flecha** *ESP* archery. **-3.** *GEOM , ELETR & MAT* arc. **-4.** [de barril] hoop.

arco-da-velha [,axkuda'veʎa] *m*: **coisas do** ~ fantastic things; **história do** ~ tall story.

arco-e-flecha [axkuiflɛʃa] (*pl* **arcos-e-flechas**) *m* **-1.** *ESP* archery. **-2.** [arma] bow and arrow.

arco-íris [ax'kwirif] (*pl* **arcos-íris**) *m inv* rainbow.

ar-condicionado [,a(x)kõndʒisjo'nadul (*pl* **ares-condicionados**) *m* [aparelho] air conditioning.

ardência [ax'dẽnsja] *f* burning.

ardente [ax'dẽntʃi] *adj* burning.

arder [5] [ax'de(x)] *vi* **-1.** [ger] to burn; ~ **em chamas** to be in flames; ~ **em febre** [pessoa] to have a burning fever. **-2.** [ferimento] to sting.

ardido, da [ax'dʒidu, da] *adj* **-1.** [costas, olhos] stinging. **-2.** [pimenta, comida] hot.

ardil [ax'dʒiw] (*pl* **-is**) *m* cunning.

ardiloso, losa [axdʒi'lozu, lɔza] *adj* [pessoa] cunning.

ardor [ax'do(x)] (*pl* **-es**) *m* [paixão] ardour.

ardoroso, rosa [axdo'rozu, rɔza] *adj* amorous.

ardósia [ax'dɔzja] *f* slate.

árduo, dua ['axdwu, dwa] *adj* **-1.** [escarpado] arduous. **-2.** [difícil] hard. **-3.** [sofrimento] painful.

área ['arja] *f* **-1.** [ger] area; ~ **interditada** forbidden territory; ~ **de serviço** service point. **-2.** [de conhecimento etc] field.

areal [a'rejw] (*pl* **-ais**) *m* sandy area.

arear [15] [a'rja(x)] *vt* [polir] to polish.

areia [a'reja] *f* sand; ~ **movediça** quicksand; **ser muita** ~ **para o caminhão de alguém** to be too hot for sb to handle.

arejado, da [are'ʒadu, da] *adj* **-1.** [ventilado] airy. **-2.** [fig] [pessoa, cabeça] open-minded.

arena [a'rena] *f* **-1.** [ger] arena. **-2.** [de circo] ring. **-3.** [de teatro] amphitheatre.

arenito [are'nitu] *m* sandstone.

arenoso, osa [are'nozu, ɔza] *adj* sandy.

arenque [a'rẽŋkil] *m* herring.

ares ['ariʃ] ⊳ **ar**.

aresta [a'rɛʃta] *f* [quina] edge.

arfar [4] [ax'fa(x)] *vi* **-1.** [ofegar] to pant. **-2.** NÁUT to pitch.

argamassa [axga'masa] *f* mortar.

Argel [ax'ʒɛw] *n* Algeria.

Argélia [ax'ʒɛlja] *n* Algeria.

argelino, na [axʒe'linu, na] ⋄ *adj* Algerian. ⋄ *m, f* Algerian.

Argentina [axʒẽn'tʃina] *n*: **(a)** ~ Argentina.

argentino, na [axʒẽn'tʃinu, na] ⋄ *adj* Argentinian. ⋄ *m, f* Argentinian.

argila [ax'ʒila] *f* clay.

argiloso, losa [axʒi'lozu, lɔza] *adj* [terreno] clay.

argola [ax'gɔla] *f* **-1.** [aro] ring. **-2.** [de porta] knocker.

argúcia [ax'gusja] *f* **-1.** [agudeza] shrewdness. **-2.** [sutileza] subtlety.

argüição [axgwi'sãw] (*pl* **-ões**) *f* oral exam.

argüir [75] [ax'gwi(x)] *vt* [alunos, candidatos] to examine.

argumentação [axgumẽnta'sãw] (*pl* **-ões**) *f* argument, reasoning.

argumentar [4] [axgumẽn'ta(x)] ⋄ *vt* [alegar] to argue. ⋄ *vi* [expor argumentos] to argue one's case.

argumento [axgu'mẽntul] *m* **-1.** [em teoria, debate] argument. **-2.** [de filme, TV, romance] theme, plot.

arguto, ta [ax'gutu, ta] *adj* **-1.** [agudo] shrewd. **-2.** [sutil] subtle.

ária ['arja] *f* MÚS aria.

ariano, na [a'rjãnu, na] ⋄ *adj* Aryan. ⋄ *m, f*

-1. [pessoa] Aryan. **-2.** ASTROL Arian.

aridez [ari'deʒ] *f* **-1.** [de clima, estação] dryness. **-2.** [de terra, região] aridity. **-3.** *fig* [de teoria, pensamento] barrenness.

árido, da ['aridu, da] *adj* **-1.** [clima, estação] dry. **-2.** [terra, região] arid. **-3.** *fig* [teoria, pensamento] barren.

arisco, ca [a'riʃku, ka] *adj* **-1.** [insociável] antisocial. **-2.** [animal] untameable.

aristocracia [ariʃtokra'sial] *f* aristocracy.

aristocrata [ariʃto'kratal] *mf* aristocrat.

aristocrático, ca [ariʃto'kratʃiku, ka] *adj* aristocratic.

aritmético, ca [aritʃ'mɛtʃiku, ka] *adj* arithmetic. ➠ **aritmética** *f* arithmetic.

arma ['axma] *f* **-1.** [ger] weapon; **depor as** ~ **s** to lay down arms; ~ **biológica/química** biological/chemical weapon; ~ **branca** knife (*or other weapon with a blade*); ~ **de fogo** firearm; ~ **nuclear** nuclear weapon. **-2.** MIL [do Exército] force. ➠ **armas** *fpl* **-1.** [forças armadas] forces. **-2.** [brasão] arms.

armação [axma'sãw] (*pl* **-ões**) *f* **-1.** [de barraca, estrutura, peças] framework. **-2.** [estrutura] frame. **-3.** [de óculos] frames (*pl*). **-4.** [de onda] point near a shoreline where the waves start to break. **-5.** [de tempestade] gathering. **-6.** *fam* [golpe] con. **-7.** *fam* [programa, aventura] move.

armada [ax'mada] ➠ **Armada** *f* navy.

armadilha [axma'diʎa] *f* trap; **cair numa** ~ to fall into a trap.

armador, ra [axma'do(x), ra] *m, f* **-1.** [NÁUT - dono] shipowner; [- firma] ship chandler's. **-2.** [operário] ship chandler.

armadura [axma'dura] *f* **-1.** [de cavaleiro] armour. **-2.** [de ouriço, besouro] shell. **-3.** ELETR armature. **-4.** CONSTR framework.

armamentista [axmamẽn'tʃiʃta] *adj* ⊳ **corrida**.

armamento [axma'mẽntul] *m* **-1.** [armas] armament. **-2.** NÁUT fitting out.

armar [4] [ax'ma(x)] ⋄ *vt* **-1.** [com arma] to arm. **-2.** [carregar] to load. **-3.** [gatilho] to cock. **-4.** [montar] to assemble. **-5.** [preparar] to set up. **-6.** [saia etc] to give body to. **-7.** *fam* [planejar - golpe] to plot; [- programa, aventura] to plan. **-8.** *fam* [provocar] to cause. **-9.** NÁUT to fit out. ⋄ *vi fam* [urdir trama] to scheme; ~ **contra** to plot against. ➠ **armar-se** *vp* **-1.** [com armas] to arm o.s. **-2.** *fig* [munir-se]: ~ **-se de** to arm o.s with.

armarinho [axma'riɲul] *m* haberdasher's *UK*, notions store *US*.

armário [ax'marjul] *m* **-1.** [de roupa] wardrobe; ~ **embutido** fitted wardrobe. **-2.** [de cozinha etc] cupboard.

armazém [axma'zẽl] (*pl* **-ns**) *m* **-1.** [depósito] warehouse. **-2.** [loja] store.

armazenagem [axmaze'naʒẽl] *f*, **armazenamento** [axmazena'mẽntul] storage.

armazenar [4] [axmaze'na(x)] *vt* to store.

Armênia [ax'menja] *n* Armenia.

armênio, nia [ax'menju, njal] ⋄ *adj* Armenian. ⋄ *m, f* Armenian.

➤ **armênio** m [língua] Armenian.

arminho [ax'miɲu] m ermine.

armistício [axmiʃ'tʃisju] m armistice.

aro ['aru] m -**1.** [ger] rim. -**2.** [argola] ring. -**3.** [de porta] frame.

aroma [a'roma] m -**1.** [de perfume] scent. -**2.** [de café, comida] aroma.

aromático, ca [aro'matʃiku, ka] adj -**1.** [essência, erva] aromatic. -**2.** [tempero, comida] spicy.

arpão [ax'pãw] (pl -ões) m harpoon.

arpejo [ax'peʒu] m arpeggio.

arpoar [20] [ax'pwa(x)] vt to harpoon.

arpões [ax'põjʃ] pl ⊳ **arpão.**

arqueado, da [ax'kjadu, da] adj -**1.** [pernas] bandy. -**2.** [sobrancelhas] arched.

arquear [16] [ax'kja(x)] vt to arch.

➤ **arquear-se** vp to bend.

arqueiro, ra [ax'kejru, ra] m, f -**1.** [atirador] archer. -**2.** [goleiro] goalkeeper.

arqueologia [axkjolo'ʒia] f archaeology.

arqueológico, ca [axkjo'lɔʒiku, ka] adj archaeological.

arqueólogo, ga [ax'kjɔlogu, ga] m, f archaeologist.

arquétipo [ax'kɛtʃipu] m archetype.

arquibancada [axkibãŋ'kada] f -**1.** [local] terrace; **ir de** ~ to sit on the terraces. -**2.** [público] terraces (pl).

arquimilionário, ria [axkimiljo'narju, rja] ◇ adj multimillionaire. ◇ m, f [pessoa] multimillionaire.

arquipélago [axki'pɛlagu] m archipelago.

arquitetar [4] [axkite'ta(x)] vt to design.

arquiteto, ta [axki'tɛtu, ta] m, f architect.

arquitetônico, ca [axkite'toniku, ka] adj architectural.

arquitetura [axkite'tura] f architecture.

arquivamento [axkiva'mẽntul m -**1.** [de documentos, fichas etc] filing. -**2.** [de projeto, processo] shelving.

arquivar [4] [axki'va(x)] vt -**1.** [ger] to file. -**2.** [projeto, processo] to shelve.

arquivista [axki'viʃta] mf archivist.

arquivo [ax'kivu] m -**1.** [ger] file; ~ **morto** dead file; **abrir/fechar um** ~ to open/close a file. -**2.** [local] archive. -**3.** [móvel] filing cabinet. -**4.** [de instituição] file.

arraia [a'xaja] f [peixe] ray.

arraial [axa'jaw] (pl -ais) m [povoado] village.

arraia-miúda [a,xajami'uda] f hoi polloi (pl).

arraigado, da [axaj'gadu, da] adj -**1.** [costume, idéia, mentalidade] deep-rooted. -**2.** fig [defensor, admirador] staunch.

arraigar [14] [axaj'ga(x)] vi [criar raízes] to put down roots.

➤ **arraigar-se** vp -**1.** [ger] to take root. -**2.** [pessoa] to settle down.

arrancada [axãŋ'kada] f -**1.** [puxão] tug. -**2.** [partida] start. -**3.** [em competição, disputa] spurt; **dar uma** ~ to jump ahead.

arrancar [12] [axãŋ'ka(x)] ◇ vt -**1.** [tirar]: ~ **algo**

de alguém to pull sthg off sb; ~ **algo (de algo)** [pétala, botão] to pull sthg (off sthg); [folha] to tear sthg (out of sthg); [raiz] to pull sthg up (out of sthg). -**2.** [conseguir]: ~ **algo de alguém** to draw sthg from sb. -**3.** [fazer sair]: ~ **alguém de algum lugar** to turf sb out of somewhere. ◇ vi -**1.** [dar partida] to start off. -**2.** [em competição] to put on a spurt.

➤ **arrancar-se** vt fam [fugir]: ~-**se (de)** to scarper (from).

arranco [a'xãŋko] m [puxão] tug.

arranha-céu [a,xãɲa'sɛw] (pl **arranha-céus**) m skyscraper.

arranhão [axã'ɲãw] (pl -ões) m scratch; **ele saiu sem muitos arranhões dessa situação** he came out of that situation relatively unscathed.

arranhar [4] [axa'ɲa(x)] ◇ vt -**1.** [ger] to scratch. -**2.** fig [tocar mal] to bash away at. -**3.** fig [idioma] to scratch by. ◇ vi [provocar arranhão] to scratch.

➤ **arranhar-se** vp to scratch o.s.

arranjador, ra [axãnʒa'dor, ra] m, f MÚS arranger.

arranjar [4] [axãn'ʒa(x)] vt -**1.** [ger] to arrange. -**2.** [resolver] to sort out. -**3.** [conseguir] to obtain. -**4.** [contrair] to catch. -**5.** [encontrar] to find.

➤ **arranjar-se** vp [virar-se] to get by.

arranjo [a'xãnʒu] m -**1.** [ger] arrangement. -**2.** [acordo] deal. -**3.** [mamata] scam.

arranque [a'xãŋki] m ⊳ **motor.**

arrasado, da [axa'zadu, da] adj -**1.** [devastado] razed, devastated. -**2.** [arruinado] ruined. -**3.** [deprimido] devastated. -**4.** [muito cansado] worn out.

arrasador, ra [axaza'do(x), ra] adj -**1.** [devastador] crippling. -**2.** [notícia, crítica] devastating. -**3.** [vitória] overwhelming.

arrasar [4] [axa'za(x)] vt -**1.** [devastar] to raze. -**2.** [arruinar] to destroy. -**3.** [com críticas] to demolish.

➤ **arrasar-se** vp -**1.** [ser devastado] to be devastated. -**2.** [destruir-se] to be destroyed. -**3.** [arruinar-se] to collapse in ruins. -**4.** [em exame, competição] to flop.

arrastado, da [axaʃ'tadu, da] adj -**1.** [demorado] sluggish. -**2.** [lento] slow.

arrastão [axaʃ'tãw] (pl -tões) m -**1.** [PESCA - rede] dragnet; [- ato] haul. -**2.** [puxão] tug. -**3.** fig [assalto] mobbing.

arrasta-pé [a,xaʃta'pɛ] (pl **arrasta-pés**) m fam shindig.

arrastar [4] [axaʃ'ta(x)] ◇ vt -**1.** [ger] to drag. -**2.** fig [impelir]: ~ **alguém a algo** to lead sb into sthg. ◇ vi [roçar] to drag.

➤ **arrastar-se** vp -**1.** [rastejar] to crawl. -**2.** [andar com dificuldade] to drag o.s. -**3.** [decorrer lentamente] to drag on.

arrasto [a'xaʃtu] m -**1.** [ato] dragging. -**2.** [rede] trawl. -**3.** fís [força] drag.

arrazoado, da [axa'zwadu, da] adj [discurso, argumento] reasoned.

➤ **arrazoado** m [defesa] defence.

arrazoar [20] [axa'zwa(x)] vi [argumentar] to argue.

arrear [15] [a'xja(x)] vt [montaria] to harness.

arrebanhar [4] [axeba'ɲa(x)] *vt* -**1**. [gado] to herd. -**2**. *fig* [reunir] to gather.

arrebatado, da [axeba'tadu, da] *adj* -**1**. [impetuoso] impetuous. -**2**. [exaltado] fiery.

arrebatador, ra [axebata'do(x), ra] *adj* fiery.

arrebatamento [axebata'mẽntu] *m* -**1**. [impetuosidade] impetuousness. -**2**. [exaltação] fervour.

arrebatar [4] [axeba'ta(x)] *vt* -**1**. [arrancar]: ~ algo de algo/alguém to grab sthg from sthg/sb. -**2**. [carregar] to drag off. -**3**. *fig* [aplausos] to draw. -**4**. *fig* [coração] to break.

⟶ **arrebatar-se** *vp* -**1**. [exaltar-se] to get carried away. -**2**. [maravilhar-se] to be entranced.

arrebentação [axebẽnta'sãw] *f* [local] *point close to a shoreline at which the waves break.*

arrebentado, da [axebẽn'tadu, da] *adj* -**1**. [em mau estado] broken. -**2**. [ferido] battered. -**3**. [muito cansado] worn out.

arrebentar [4] [axebẽn'ta(x)] <> *vt* -**1**. [quebrar, romper] to break. -**2**. [estragar] to wreck. -**3**. [ferir] to smash; ~ alguém [surrar] to give sb a bashing; ~ a cara de alguém to smash sb's face in. <> *vi* -**1**. [quebrar-se, romper-se] to snap. -**2**. [bomba] to explode. -**3**. *fig* [guerra, revolução] to break out. -**4**. *fam fig* [fazer sucesso]: ~ (em algo) to have a smashing win (at sthg).

⟶ **arrebentar-se** *vp* [ferir-se] to smash o.s.up.

arrebitado, da [axebi'tadu, da] *adj* -**1**. [para cima] turned up. -**2**. [bumbum, nariz] pert.

arrebitar [4] [axebi'ta(x)] *vt* to turn up.

arrecadação [axekada'sãw] (*pl* -ões) *f* -**1**. [coleta] collection. -**2**. [receita] revenue.

arrecadar [4] [axeka'da(x)] *vt* to collect.

arrecife [axe'sifi] *m* reef.

arredar [4] [axe'da(x)] *vt* [retirar] to remove; ~ (o) pé (de) [de lugar] to budge from; [de intenção, princípios] to budge (from).

⟶ **arredar-se** *vp* [retirar-se] to withdraw.

arredio, dia [axe'dʒiu, dʒia] *adj* [pessoa] withdrawn.

arredondado, da [axedõn'dadu, da] *adj* round.

arredondar [4] [axedõn'da(x)] *vt* -**1**. [formato] to round off. -**2**. [conta] to round up.

arredores [axe'dɔriʃ] *mpl* -**1**. [cercanias] neighbourhood. -**2**. [periferia] outskirts.

arrefecer [25] [axefe'se(x)] <> *vt* -**1**. [tornar frio] to cool. -**2**. [febre] to lower. -**3**. *fig* [desanimar] to cool. <> *vi* -**1**. [tornar-se frio] to cool down. -**2**. [ger] to subside.

ar-refrigerado [ˌa(x)xefriʒe'radu] (*pl* ares-refrigerados) *m* -**1**. [aparelho] air-conditioner. -**2**. [sistema] air-conditioning.

arregaçar [13] [axega'sa(x)] *vt* to roll up.

arregalado, da [axega'ladu, da] *adj* staring.

arregalar [4] [axega'la(x)] *vt* to open wide.

arreganhado, da [axega'ɲadu, da] *adj* gaping.

arreganhar [4] [axega'ɲa(x)] *vt* -**1**. [gola de blusa] to open. -**2**. [boca] to open in a grin.

arregimentar [4] [axeʒimẽn'ta(x)] *vt* to drum up.

arreio [a'xeju] *m* [cavalo] harness.

arrematar [4] [axema'ta(x)] *vt* -**1**. [ger] to finish off. -**2**. [dizer concluindo] to conclude. -**3**. [em leilão - comprar] to bid successfully for; [- vender] to auction off.

arremate [axe'matʃi] *m* -**1**. [ger] finishing off. -**2**. [conclusão] finish.

arremessar [4] [axeme'sa(x)] *vt* to throw.

⟶ **arremessar-se** *vp* to throw o.s.

arremesso [axe'mesu] *m* [lançamento] throw; ~ de peso *ESP* shot-put.

arremeter [5] [axeme'te(x)] *vi* to charge; ~ contra to attack.

arremetida [axeme'tʃida] *f* attack.

arrendamento [axẽnda'mẽntu] *m* leasing, hiring, rental.

arrendar [4] [axẽn'da(x)] *vt* -**1**. [dar] to let, to lease. -**2**. [tomar] to rent, to take a lease on.

arrepender-se [5] [axepẽn'dexsi] *vp* to repent; ~ de algo/de fazer algo to regret sthg/doing sthg.

arrependido, da [axepẽn'dʒidu, da] *adj* repentent, sorry.

arrependimento [axepẽndʒi'mẽntu] *m* -**1**. [remorso] regret. -**2**. [de crime] remorse. -**3**. *RELIG* repentance.

arrepiado, da [axe'pjadu, da] *adj* -**1**. [eriçado - cabelo] standing on end (*depois de subst/verbo*); [- pele] goose-pimpled. -**2**. *fig* [assustado] terrified.

arrepiar [16] [axe'pja(x)] *vt* -**1**. [eriçar - cabelo] to cause to stand on end; [- pele] to give goose pimples. -**2**. [fig] [assustar] to terrify; (ser) de ~ os cabelos to be enough to make your hair stand on end.

⟶ **arrepiar-se** *vp* [ficar eriçado - cabelo] to stand on end; [- pessoa] to shiver.

arrepio [axe'piw] *m* shiver; dar ~s (a alguém) *fig* to send shivers up sb's spine.

arresto [a'xɛʃtu] *m JUR* confiscation.

arrevesado, da [axeve'zadu, da] *adj* -**1**. [obscuro] obscure. -**2**. [confuso] complicated.

arriado, da [a'xjadu, da] *adj* -**1**. [muito cansado] dead beat. -**2**. [devido a doença] drained.

arriar [16] [a'xja(x)] <> *vt* -**1**. [abaixar - cortina, calça] to lower; [- pneu] to let down. -**2**. [cansar muito] to exhaust. -**3**. [pôr de cama] to lay up. <> *vi* -**1**. [pneu, bateria] to go flat. -**2**. [vergar] to sag. -**3**. [desanimar] to lose heart.

arrimo [a'ximu] *m* support; ~ de família family support.

arriscado, da [axiʃ'kadu, da] *adj* -**1**. [perigoso] hazardous, risky. -**2**. [audacioso] daring.

arriscar [12] [axiʃ'ka(x)] <> *vt* -**1**. [pôr em perigo] to put at risk. -**2**. [palpite] to risk. <> *vi* [tentar] to take the risk; quem não arrisca não petisca *prov* nothing ventured nothing gained.

⟶ **arriscar-se** *vp* [pôr-se em perigo] to take a risk; ~-se a fazer algo to risk doing sthg.

arritmia [axitʃ'mia] *f* arrhythmia.

arrivista [axi'viʃta] <> *adj* opportunistic. <> *mf* opportunist.

arroba [a'xobal] *f COMPUT* at.

arrochado, da [axo'ʃadu, da] *adj* -**1**. [apertado] tight. -**2**. [difícil] tricky.

arrochar [4] [axo'ʃa(x)] vt -**1.** [apertar] to squeeze. -**2.** fig [diminuir] to shrink. -**3.** fam fig [pressionar] to grill.

arrocho [a'xoʃu] m -**1.** [diminuição] lessening; ~ **salarial** wage squeeze. -**2.** [dificuldade financeira] hardship. -**3.** fam fig [pressão] grilling; **dar um ~ em alguém** to give sb a grilling.

arrogância [axo'gãnsja] f arrogance.

arrogante [axo'gãntʃil] adj arrogant.

arrogar-se [14] [axo'gaxsil] vp to claim.

arroio [a'xoju] m stream.

arrojado, da [axo'ʒadu, da] adj -**1.** [ger] bold. -**2.** [ousado] daring. -**3.** [temerário] rash.

arrojar [4] [axo'ʒa(x)] vt [atirar]: ~ **algo (em/contra algo)** to hurl sthg (at/against sthg).

arrolamento [axola'mẽntu] m -**1.** [levantamento] register. -**2.** [lista] list.

arrolar [4] [axo'la(x)] vt [listar] to list.

arrolhar [4] [axo'ʎa(x)] vt [garrafa] to cork.

arromba [a'xõnba] ◆ **de arromba** loc adj fam fantastic.

arrombamento [axõnba'mẽntu] m [abertura forçada]: **foi necessário o ~ da porta** it was necessary to break down the door.

arrombar [4] [axõn'ba(x)] vt -**1.** [ger] to break into. -**2.** [porta] to break down.

arrotar [4] [axo'ta(x)] ◇ vi [dar arroto] to belch. ◇ vt -**1.** [cheiro] to burp. -**2.** fam fig [alardear] to boast about.

arroto [a'xotu] m burp; **dar** ou **soltar um ~** to let out a burp.

arroubo [a'xobu] m [enlevo] moment of ecstasy; ~ **de algo** outpouring of sthg.

arroz [a'xoʒ] m rice; ~ **à grega** Greek risotto, rice with ham, smoked bacon, sweet peppers, onion and peas; ~ **doce** rice pudding.

arrozal [axo'zaw] (pl -ais) m paddy field.

arroz-doce [axoʒ'dosil] m CULIN rice pudding sprinkled with cinnamon and cloves.

arruaça [a'xwasa] f riot; **fazer ~** to run riot.

arruaceiro, ra [axwa'sejru, ra] ◇ adj rowdy. ◇ m, f rioter.

arruela [a'xwɛla] f washer.

arruinado, da [axwi'nadu, da] adj ruined.

arruinar [4] [axwi'na(x)] vt -**1.** [arrasar] to demolish. -**2.** [destruir] to destroy. -**3.** [causar falência] to ruin.
◆ **arruinar-se** vp [ruir] to be ruined.

arrulhar [4] [axu'ʎa(x)] vi -**1.** [pombo] to coo. -**2.** fig [namorados] to bill and coo.

arrulho [a'xuʎu] m -**1.** [de pombo] cooing. -**2.** [de namorados] wooing.

arrumação [axuma'sãw] f -**1.** [arranjo] arrangement. -**2.** [de quarto, armário] tidying; **fazer uma ~ em algo** to tidy sthg up. -**3.** [de malas, bagagem] packing.

arrumadeira [axuma'dejra] f [criada] maid.

arrumar [4] [axu'ma(x)] vt -**1.** [pôr em ordem] to arrange; ~ **a vida** fam fig to set one's life in order. -**2.** [quarto, armário] to tidy. -**3.** [malas, bagagem] to pack. -**4.** [vestir, aprontar] to straighten up. -**5.** [conseguir] to get.

◆ **arrumar-se** vp -**1.** [vestir-se, aprontar-se] to get ready. -**2.** [na vida] to set o.s. up. -**3.** [virar-se] to fend for o.s. -**4.** fam [na vida amorosa]: ~**-se (com alguém)** to hitch up (with sb).

arsenal [axse'naw] (pl -ais) m arsenal.

arsênico [ax'senikul] m arsenic.

arsênio [ax'senju] m arsenic.

arte [ˈaxtʃil] f -**1.** [ger] art; ~ **abstrata/figurativa** abstract/figurative art; ~ **dramática** theatre; ~ **moderna** modern art. -**2.** [arte-final] artwork. -**3.** [ofício] art. -**4.** [técnica] art; ~ **culinária** cuisine; ~ **marcial** martial art; ~**s e ofícios** arts and crafts. -**5.** [primor]: **com ~** skilfully. -**6.** [astúcia] cunning. -**7.** fam [travessura] mischief; **fazer ~** to get up to mischief.

◆ **artes** fpl -**1.** [visuais] arts; ~**s gráficas** graphic arts; ~**s plásticas** plastic arts. -**2.** [curso]: **(belas) ~s** fine arts. -**3.** [artifício]: **por ~s de** through the artful wiles of.

artefato [axte'fatul] m -**1.** [instrumento] artefact. -**2.** [produto] goods (pl); ~**s de madeira/couro** wooden/leather goods.

arteiro, ra [axẽtejru, ra] adj mischievous.

artéria [ax'terja] f artery.

arterial [axte'rjaw] (pl -ais) adj arterial.

arteriosclerose [axterjoʃkle'rɔzi] f arteriosclerosis.

artesã [axte'zãl] f ▷ **artesão**.

artesanal [axteza'naw] (pl -ais) adj craftwork.

artesanato [axteza'natu] m craftwork.

artesão, sã [axte'zãw, zãl] (mpl -ãos, fpl -s) m, f craftsmán (f craftswoman).

ártico, ca [ˈaxtʃikul] adj Arctic.
◆ **Ártico** n: **o Ártico** the Arctic; **o Oceano Glacial Ártico** the Arctic Ocean.

articulação [axtʃikula'sãw] (pl -ões) f -**1.** [ligação] connection. -**2.** ANAT joint. -**3.** POL link.

articulado, da [axtʃiku'ladu, da] adj -**1.** [membro, boneco] articulated. -**2.** [pessoa - ao falar] articulate; [- bem relacionado] well connected.

articular [4] [axtʃiku'la(x)] vt -**1.** [ligar] to link. -**2.** [pronunciar] to articulate. -**3.** [organizar] to put together.
◆ **articular-se** vp -**1.** [ligar-se] to be joined. -**2.** [organizar-se] to organize o.s.; ~**-se em** to be organised in.

articulista [axtʃiku'liʃta] mf JORN article writer.

artífice [ax'tʃifisil] mf -**1.** [artesão] craftsman (f craftswoman). -**2.** [criador, mentor] author.

artificial [axtʃifi'sjaw] (pl -ais) adj -**1.** [ger] artificial. -**2.** [dissimulado] false.

artificialidade [axtʃifisjali'dadʒil] f artificiality.

artifício [axtʃi'fisju] m -**1.** [processo] artifice. -**2.** [subterfúgio] trick. -**3.** [dissimulação] pretence.

artigo [ax'tʃigu] m article; ~ **de luxo** luxury item; ~**s esportivos** sports goods; ~**s de toucador** toiletries; ~ **de fundo** editorial.

artilharia [axtʃiʎa'rial] f artillery.

artilheiro, ra [axtʃi'ʎejru, ra] m, f -**1.** [atirador] gunner. -**2.** FUT striker.

artimanha [axtʃi'mãɲa] m -**1.** [estratagema]

stratagem. **-2.** [astúcia] cunning.
artista [ax'tʃiʃta] *mf* **-1.** [ger] artist. **-2.** [ator] actor (*f* actress). **-3.** [pessoa manhosa] crafty person.
artístico, ca [ax'tʃiʃtʃiku, ka] *adj* artistic.
artrite [ax'tritʃi] *f* arthritis.
artrose [ax'trɔzi] *f* arthrosis.
arvorar [4] [axvo'ra(x)] *vt* **-1.** [cruz, bandeira] to hoist. **-2.** [elevar]: ~ **alguém em algo** to hold sb up as sthg.
➼ **arvorar-se** *vp* [elevar-se]: ~**-se em algo** to claim to be sthg.
árvore ['axvori] *f* **-1.** [vegetal] tree; ~ **genealógica** family tree; ~ **de Natal** Christmas tree. **-2.** TEC shaft.
arvoredo [axvo'redu] *m* grove.
as [aʃ] ▷ **a**.
ás, ases ['ajʃ, 'azeʃ] ◇ *mf* [pessoa exímia]: ~ **de algo** ace at sthg. ◇ *m* [carta] ace.
às [ajʃ] = **a + as**.
asa ['aza] *f* **-1.** [de pássaro, avião, inseto] wing; **dar** ~**s à imaginação** to give free rein to one's imagination. **-2.** [de xícara] handle.
asa-delta [‚aza3'dɛwta] (*pl* **asas-delta**) *f* **-1.** [veículo] hang-glider. **-2.** [esporte] hang-gliding.
ascendência [asẽn'dẽnsja] *f* **-1.** [antepassados] descent. **-2.** [influência, domínio] influence; **ter** ~ **sobre** to hold sway over.
ascendente [asẽn'dẽntʃi] ◇ *adj* rising. ◇ *m, f* [antepassado] ancestor.
ascender [5] [asẽn'de(x)] *vi* to rise.
ascensão [asẽn'sãw] (*pl* **-ões**) *f* **-1.** [ger] rise. **-2.** [subida] climb.
ascensorista [asẽnso'riʃta] *mf* lift operator.
asceta [a'sɛta] *mf* ascetic.
ASCII (*abrev de* **American Standard Code for Information Interchange**) *m* ASCII.
asco ['aʃku] *m* disgust; **dar** ~ **a alguém** to make sb sick; **ser um** ~ to be a disgrace; **ter** ~ **de** to detest.
asfaltado, da [aʃfaw'tadu, da] *adj* asphalted.
asfaltar [4] [aʃfaw'ta(x)] *vt* to asphalt.
asfalto [aʃ'fawtu] *m* asphalt.
asfixia [aʃfik'sia] *f* asphyxia.
asfixiante [aʃfik'sjãntʃi] *adj* **-1.** [substância, ambiente] asphyxiating. **-2.** *fig* [calor] suffocating. **-3.** *fig* [regime, disciplina] oppressive.
asfixiar [16] [aʃfik'sja(x)] *vt* **-1.** [matar por asfixia] to asphyxiate. **-2.** [sufocar] to be suffocating. **-3.** *fig* [oprimir] to suppress.
➼ **asfixiar-se** *vp* **-1.** [morrer por asfixia] to be asphyxiated. **-2.** [sufocar-se] to gasp for breath.
Ásia ['azja] *n* Asia; ~ **Central** Central Asia.
asiático, ca [a'zjatʃiku, ka] ◇ *adj* Asian. ◇ *m, f* Asian.
asilo [a'zilu] *m* **-1.** [para orfãos, anciãos] home. **-2.** [refúgio] refuge. **-3.** POL asylum; ~ **político** political asylum.
asma ['aʒma] *f* asthma.
asmático, ca [aʒ'matʃiku, ka] ◇ *adj* asthmatic. ◇ *m, f* [pessoa] asthmatic.

asneira [aʒ'nejra] *f* **-1.** [ação] blunder; **dizer/fazer uma** ~ to say/do something stupid. **-2.** [condição] stupidity.
asno ['aʒnu] *m* **-1.** [animal] ass, donkey. **-2.** *fam fig* & *pej* [idiota] silly ass.
aspargo [aʃ'paxgu] *m* asparagus.
aspas ['aʃpaʃ] *fpl* quotation marks; **entre** ~ in inverted commas.
aspecto [aʃ'pɛktu] *m* **-1.** [aparência] look; **ter bom/mau** ~ [pessoa] to look right/dodgy; [coisa] to look good/bad. **-2.** [faceta] aspect; **em todos os** ~**s** in every way. **-3.** [ângulo] angle; **sob este** ~ from this angle. **-4.** [visão, detalhe] view.
aspereza [aʃpe'reza] *f* **-1.** [no tato] roughness. **-2.** *fig* [severidade, rispidez] harshness.
aspergir [64] [aʃpex'ʒi(x)] *vt* to sprinkle.
áspero, ra ['aʃperu, ra] *adj* **-1.** [ao tato] rough. **-2.** *fig* [severo, ríspido] harsh.
asperso, sa [aʃ'pexsu, sa] *pp* ▷ **aspergir**.
aspiração [aʃpira'sãw] (*pl* **-ões**) *f* **-1.** [de ar - por pessoa] inhalation; [- por máquina] suction. **-2.** LING aspiration. **-3.** [desejo]: **ter** ~ **a algo** to aspire to sthg.
aspirador [aʃpira'do(x)] (*pl* **-es**) *m*: ~ **(de pó)** vacuum cleaner; **passar o** ~ **(em)** to vacuum, to hoover.
aspirante [aʃpi'rãntʃi] *mf* **-1.** [candidato]: **ser** ~ **(a algo)** to be a candidate (for sthg). **-2.** MIL & NÁUT cadet.
aspirar [4] [aʃpi'ra(x)] ◇ *vt* **-1.** [sugar] to aspirate, to suck in. **-2.** [ar - pessoa] to inhale; [- máquina] to suction. **-3.** LING to aspirate. ◇ *vi* **-1.** [desejar]: ~ **a algo** to aspire to sthg. **-2.** [respirar] to breathe. **-3.** [soprar brisa] to blow.
aspirina® [aʃpi'rinal *f* aspirin®.
asqueroso, osa [aʃke'rozu, ɔza] *adj* disgusting.
assadeira [asa'dejra] *f* roasting dish.
assado, da [a'sadu, da] *adj* roast.
➼ **assado** *m* roast.
assadura [asa'dura] *f* **-1.** [em bebê] nappy rash. **-2.** [em adulto] rash.
assalariado, da [asala'rjadu, da] ◇ *adj* wage-earning. ◇ *m, f* wage earner.
assaltante [asaw'tãntʃi] *mf* **-1.** [na rua] mugger. **-2.** [de banco] robber. **-3.** [de casa] burglar.
assaltar [4] [asaw'ta(x)] *vt* **-1.** [atacar] to attack. **-2.** [roubar - na rua] to mug; [- banco] to rob; [- casa] to break into. **-3.** *fig* [acometer] to assail.
assalto [a'sawtu] *m* **-1.** [ataque] attack. **-2.** [na rua] mugging. **-3.** [a banco] robbery. **-4.** [a casa] burglary.
assanhado, da [asa'ɲadu, da] *adj* **-1.** [excitado, irrequieto] excited. **-2.** [criança] excitable. **-3.** [desavergonhado] brazen. **-4.** [namorador] passionate.
assanhar [4] [asa'ɲa(x)] *vt* **-1.** [excitar, agitar] to excite. **-2.** [sensualmente] to arouse.
➼ **assanhar-se** *vp* **-1.** [excitar-se, agitar-se] to become excited. **-2.** [sensualmente] to become aroused.
assar [4] [a'sa(x)] ◇ *vt* **-1.** [no forno] to roast. **-2.** [na grelha] to grill. ◇ *vi* to roast.

assassinar [4] [asasi'na(x)] *vt* -**1**. [matar] to murder. -**2**. *POL* to assassinate.

assassinato [asasi'natu], **assassínio** [asa'sinju] *m* -**1**. [de pessoa comum] murder. -**2**. *POL* assassination.

assassino, na [asa'sinu, na] <> *adj* deadly. <> *m, f* -**1**. [de pessoa comum] killer, murderer. -**2**. *POL* assassin.

assaz [a'saʒ] *adv* quite.

asseado, da [a'sjadu, da] *adj* clean, neat.

assediar [16] [ase'dʒja(x)] *vt* -**1**. [sitiar] to besiege. -**2**. [perseguir] to hound. -**3**. [importunar]: ~ **alguém (com)** to pester sb (with). -**4**. [sexualmente] to harass.

assédio [a'sɛdʒju] *m* -**1**. [cerco] siege. -**2**. [insistência] hounding; **ele se acostumou com o ~ dos repórteres** he became used to being hounded by reporters; ~ **sexual** sexual harassment.

assegurar [4] [asegu'ra(x)] *vt* -**1**. [garantir] to ensure; ~ **alguém de algo** to assure sb of sthg; ~ **algo a alguém** to assure sb sthg; ~ **alguém de que** to assure sb that. -**2**. [afirmar] to give an assurance.

  ➡ **assegurar-se** *vp*: ~**-se de fazer algo** to make sure of doing sthg.

asseio [a'seju] *m* cleanliness, neatness.

assembléia [asẽn'blɛja] *f* -**1**. [reunião] meeting; ~ **geral** annual general meeting. -**2**. [órgão] assembly; **Assembléia Legislativa** Legislative Assembly.

assemelhar [4] [aseme'ʎa(x)] *vt* [tornar semelhante] to liken.

  ➡ **assemelhar-se** *vp* [ser parecido] to look alike; ~**-se a algo/alguém** to look like sthg/sb.

assenhorear-se [15] [aseɲo'rjaxsil] *vp*: ~ **de** to take possession of.

assentado, da [asẽn'tadu, da] *adj* -**1**. [firme] secure. -**2**. [combinado] arranged. -**3**. [ajuizado] sound. -**4**. [em terras] landed.

assentamento [asẽnta'mẽntul] *m* -**1**. [registro] registration. -**2**. [nota] entry. -**3**. [em terras] settling.

assentar [4] [asẽn'ta(x)] <> *vt* -**1**. [firmar] to set. -**2**. [colocar] to place. -**3**. [tijolos] to lay. -**4**. [em terras] to settle. -**5**. *fig* [basear] to base. -**6**. [anotar, registrar] to note down. -**7**. [estabelecer] to establish. -**8**. [determinar] to agree. -**9**. [decidir] to resolve. <> *vi* -**1**. [ger] to settle. -**2**. *fig* [cair]: ~ **a** *ou* **em alguém** to suit sb.

  ➡ **assentar-se** *vp* -**1**. [firmar-se] to be founded. -**2**. *fig* [basear-se] to be based. -**3**. *fig* [ajuizar-se] to settle down.

assente [a'sẽntʃi] <> *pp* ⊳ **assentar**. <> *adj* [combinado, fixo] agreed.

assentir [56] [asẽn'tʃi(x)] *vi* -**1**. [concordar]: ~ **(em)** to agree (to). -**2**. [aceder]: ~ **(a)** to accede (to).

assento [a'sẽntu] *m* -**1**. [para sentar] seat. -**2**. *fig* [base]: **ter ~** to be based on.

assepsia [asep'sia] *f* *MED* asepsis.

asséptico, ca [a'sɛptʃiku, ka] *adj* aseptic.

assertiva [asex'tʃival] *f* assertion.

assessor, ra [ase'so(x), ra] *m, f* -**1**. [consultor] consultant. -**2**. [assistente] adviser; ~ **de comunicação** public relations, PR; ~ **de imprensa** press adviser. -**3**. *POL* aide.

assessoramento [asesora'mẽntul] *m* assistance.

assessorar [4] [aseso'ra(x)] *vt* -**1**. [prestar consultoria]: ~ **alguém (em algo)** to advise sb (on sthg). -**2**. [assistir] to assist.

assessoria [aseso'ria] *f* -**1**. [consultoria] consultancy. -**2**. [assistência] assistance. -**3**. [setor, órgão, conselho] advisors *(pl)*; ~ **de comunicação** public relations, PR; ~ **de imprensa** press advisors *(pl)*.

asseveração [asevera'sãw] *(pl* -**ões)** *f* -**1**. [afirmação] assertion. -**2**. [garantia] affirmation.

asseverar [4] [aseve'ra(x)] *vt* -**1**. [afirmar] to assert. -**2**. [garantir] to affirm.

assexuado, da [asek'swadu, da] *adj* asexual.

assiduidade [asidwi'dadʒi] *f* -**1**. [a aulas, trabalho] regular attendance. -**2**. [diligência] diligence; **com ~** diligently.

assíduo, dua [a'sidwu, dwa] *adj* -**1**. [a aulas, trabalho] regularly attending. -**2**. [diligente] diligent.

assim [a'sĩ] <> *adv* -**1**. [deste modo] just like that; ~ **sendo** that being the case; **como ~?** how do you mean? -**2**. [igualmente] the same; **algo ~** [algo parecido] something similar; **e ~ por diante** and so on; ~ **como** [tal como] just like; [também] as well as. -**3**. [deste tamanho]: **ser grande ~** to be this big. <> *conj* [então] so; ~ **mesmo, mesmo ~** even so.

  ➡ **assim que** *loc conj* as soon as.

assimétrico, ca [asi'mɛtriku, ka] *adj* -**1**. [ger] asymmetrical. -**2**. *ESP* asymmetric.

assimilação [asimila'sãw] *(pl* -**ões)** *f* -**1**. [ger] assimilation. -**2**. [de alimento] absorbtion.

assimilar [4] [asimi'la(x)] *vt* -**1**. [ger] to assimilate. -**2**. [apropriar-se de] to absorb. -**3**. [comparar]: ~ **algo (a algo)** to compare sthg (to sthg).

assinalado, da [asina'ladu, da] *adj* -**1**. [marcado] marked. -**2**. [eminente] distinguished. -**3**. [notável] outstanding.

assinalar [4] [asina'la(x)] *vt* -**1**. [marcar] to mark. -**2**. [distinguir] to indicate. -**3**. [especificar] to specify. -**4**. [observar] to point out. -**5**. [celebrizar] to distinguish.

assinante [asi'nãntʃi] *mf* subscriber.

assinar [4] [asi'na(x)] <> *vt* -**1**. [firmar] to sign. -**2**. [ser assinante de] to subscribe to. <> *vi* [firmar] to sign.

assinatura [asina'tura] *f* -**1**. [firma] signature. -**2**. [subscrição] subscription.

assistência [asif'tẽnsja] *f* -**1**. [ger] assistance, aid; ~ **jurídica** legal aid; ~ **médica** medical aid; ~ **técnica** technical assistance; ~ **social** social work. -**2**. [presença] attendance. -**3**. [espectadores] audience. -**4**. [ambulância] emergency assistance.

assistente [asif'tẽntʃi] <> *adj* [auxiliar] assistant. <> *mf* -**1**. [auxiliar] assistant; ~ **social** social worker. -**2**. [espectador - em jogo] spectator; [- em teatro, cinema] member of the audience.

assistir [6] [asiʃ'tʃi(x)] ◇ *vt* - **1.** [socorrer] to assist. - **2.** [auxiliar] to assist. - **3.** [fazer companhia a] to attend. ◇ *vi* - **1.** [estar presente]: ~ **a** [ver] to watch; [testemunhar] to witness; [comparecer a] to attend. - **2.** [caber]: ~ **a alguém** to pertain to sb.

assoalho [a'swaʎu] *m* floor.

assoar [20] [a'swa(x)] *vt* to blow (one's nose).

assoberbado, da [asobex'badu, da] *adj* [de trabalho] snowed under.

assoberbar [4] [asobex'ba(x)] *vt*: ~ **alguém (de trabalho)** to overload sb (with work).

assobiar [aso'bja(x)] *m* = **assoviar**.

assobio [aso'biw] *m* = **assovio**.

associação [asosja'sãw] (*pl* -ões) *f* - **1.** [ger] association; ~ **de moradores** residents' association. - **2.** [parceria, aliança] partnership.

associado, da [aso'sjadu, da] ◇ *adj* - **1.** [relacionado] associated. - **2.** [sócio] associate. - **3.** [médico, advogado etc] associate. ◇ *m, f* [sócio] associate, partner.

associar [16] [aso'sja(x)] *vt* relacionar; ~ **algo a algo** to associate sthg with sthg.

    associar-se *vp* - **1.** COM [formar associação] to form a partnership. - **2.** [entrar de sócio]: ~**-se a** to become a member of.

assolar [4] [aso'la(x)] *vt* to devastate.

assomar [4] [aso'ma(x)] *vi* - **1.** [aparecer]: ~ **(a)** to appear (at). - **2.** [subir]: ~ **a** to climb.

assombração [asõnbra'sãw] (*pl* -ões) *f* ghost.

assombrar [4] [asõn'bra(x)] *vt* - **1.** [assustar] to frighten. - **2.** [rondar] to haunt. - **3.** [impressionar] to amaze.

assombro [a'sõnbru] *m* - **1.** [admiração] astonishment. - **2.** [espanto, maravilha]: **ser um** ~ to be amazing.

assombroso, osa [asõn'brozu, rɔza] *adj* amazing.

assoprar [4] [aso'pra(x)] ◇ *vt* - **1.** [vela] to blow out. - **2.** [vidro] to blow. - **3.** *fam* [resposta, palpite] to whisper. ◇ *vi* [brisa, vento] to blow.

assoviar [16] [aso'vja(x)], **assobiar** [aso'bja(x)] *vi* & *vt* to whistle.

assovio [aso'viw], **assobio** [aso'bju] *m* whistling, whistle; **dar um** ~ to whistle.

assumido, da [asu'midu, da] *adj fam* - **1.** [declarado] acknowledged. - **2.** [homossexual]: **ser um gay** ~ to be openly gay.

assumir [6] [asu'mi(x)] ◇ *vt* - **1.** [chamar a si] to assume. - **2.** [reconhecer - filho] to recognize; [- erro] to admit. - **3.** [tomar posse de] to take up. - **4.** [adotar, adquirir] to take on. - **5.** [homossexualidade] to come out. ◇ *vi* [tomar posse] to take office.

Assunção [asũn'sãw] *n* [cidade] Asunción.

assuntar [4] [asũn'ta(x)] ◇ *vt* - **1.** [prestar atenção a] to notice. - **2.** [verificar] to find out about. ◇ *vi* [meditar]: ~ **(em)** to reflect (on).

assunto [a'sũntu] *m* [tema] subject; ~ **urgente** urgent business; **não ter** ~ *fig* to have nothing to talk about.

assustadiço, ça [asuʃta'dʒisu, sa] *adj* nervous.

assustador, ra [asuʃta'do(x), ra] (*mpl* -es, *fpl* -s)

adj - **1.** [amedrontador] terrifying. - **2.** [alarmante] alarming.

assustar [4] [asuʃ'ta(x)] ◇ *vt* - **1.** [amedrontar] to frighten. - **2.** [alarmar] to alarm. ◇ *vi* - **1.** [amedrontar] to be terrifying. - **2.** [alarmar] to be alarming.

    assustar-se *vp*: ~**-se (com)** [amedrontar-se] to be terrified (by); [alarmar-se] to be alarmed (by).

asteca [aʃ'tɛkal ◇ *adj* Aztec. ◇ *mf* Aztec.

asterisco [aʃte'riʃku] *m* asterisk.

astigmatismo [aʃtʃigma'tʃiʒmu] *m* astigmatism.

astral [aʃ'trawl (*pl* -ais) ◇ *adj* ASTRO astrological. ◇ *m* [humor, ambiente] mood.

astrologia [aʃtrolo'ʒial *f* astrology.

astrólogo, ga [aʃ'trɔlogu, ga] *m, f* astrologist.

astronauta [aʃtro'nawta] *mf* astronaut.

astronáutica [aʃtro'nawtʃika] *f* astronautics (*sg*).

astronave [aʃtro'navi] *f* spaceship.

astronomia [aʃtrono'mia] *f* astronomy.

astronômico, ca [aʃtro'nomiku, ka] *adj* astronomical.

astúcia [aʃ'tusja] *f* - **1.** [esperteza] shrewdness. - **2.** [ardil] ruse.

astuto, ta [aʃ'tutu, ta] *adj* - **1.** [esperto] shrewd. - **2.** [ardiloso] cunning.

at. (*abrev de* atenção a) attn.

ata [l'ata] *f* [de reunião] minutes (*pl*).

atacadista [ataka'dʒiʃta] ◇ *adj* COM [comércio, mercado, vendedor] wholesale. ◇ *mf* [vendedor] wholesaler.

atacado, da [ata'kadu, da] *adj fam* [pessoa]: **estar** *ou* **andar** ~ to be in a foul mood.

    atacado *m* COM: **no/por** ~ wholesale.

atacante [ata'kãntʃil ◇ *adj* attacking. ◇ *mf* attacker.

atacar [12] [ata'ka(x)] ◇ *vt* - **1.** [lançar ataque contra] to attack. - **2.** [acometer] to strike at. - **3.** *fig* [combater] to tackle. - **4.** *fig* [criticar] to hit out at. ◇ *vi* - **1.** [lançar ataque] to attack. - **2.** [vírus] to strike. - **3.** ESP [time, jogador] to go on the attack. ◇ *interj*: atacar! charge!

atado, da [a'tadu, da] *adj* - **1.** [desajeitado] clumsy. - **2.** [confuso, perplexo] bewildered.

atadura [ata'dura] *f* bandage.

atalho [a'taʎu] *m* COMPUT shortcut.

atapetar [4] [atape'ta(x)] *vt* to carpet.

ataque [a'taki] *m* - **1.** [ger] attack; ~ **aéreo** air strike; ~ **cardíaco** heart attack; ~ **epilético** epileptic fit; ~ **histérico** fit of hysteria; ~ **de nervos** attack of nerves; ~ **de riso** fit of laughter; **ter um** ~ **(de raiva)** *fam* to have a fit (of rage). - **2.** [FUT - de time] attack; [- campo, ação]: **no** ~ on the attack.

atar [4] [a'ta(x)] *vt* to tie; **não** ~ **nem desatar** [pessoa] to shilly-shally; [negócio, namoro] to be getting nowhere.

atarantado, da [atarãn'tadu, da] *adj* - **1.** [dia] hectic. - **2.** [pessoa] flustered.

atarantar [4] [atarãn'ta(x)] *vt* to fluster.

atarefado, da [atare'fadu, da] *adj* busy.

atarracado, da [ataxa'kadu, da] *adj* - **1.** [pessoa]

thickset. **-2.** [pescoço, perna] thick.

atarraxar [4] [ataxa'ʃa(x)] *vt* to screw.

ataúde [ata'udʒi] *m* coffin.

atávico, ca [a'taviku, ka] *adj* atavistic.

atazanar [4] [ataza'na(x)] *vt* to taunt.

até [a'tɛ] <> *prep* **-1.** [no espaço] as far as, up to; de ... ~ ... from ... to ... **-2.** [no tempo] until, till; ~ que enfim! at long last!; ir ~ o fim com algo to see sthg through; ~ agora so far, up until now. **-3.** [prazo - antes de] before; [- extensão] until. **-4.** [despedida]: **até!** see you!; ~ amanhã until tomorrow; ~ já see you soon; ~ logo bye for now; ~ a vista until next time. **-5.** [com quantidades] up to. <> *adv* [mesmo, inclusive] even.

◆ **até que** *loc conj* **-1.** [até quando] until. **-2.** [bem que]: ~ que admittedly.

atear [15] [ate'a(x)] *vt* **-1.** [fogo]: ~ fogo a algo to set fire to sthg. **-2.** *fig* [espalhar] to inflame.

atéia [a'tɛja] *f* ▷ **ateu.**

ateliê [ate'lje] *m* studio.

atemorizado, da [atemori'zadu, da] *adj* frightened.

atemorizador, ra [atemoriza'do(x), ra] *adj* alarming.

atemorizante [atemori'zãntʃi] *adj* frightening.

atemorizar [4] [atemori'za(x)] *vt* **-1.** [assustar] to frighten. **-2.** [intimidar] to alarm.

Atenas [a'tenaʃ] *n* Athens.

atenção [atēn'sãw] (*pl* -ões) <> *f* **-1.** [interesse] attention; chamar a ~ (de) [atrair] to catch the eye (of); chamar a ~ de alguém [advertir] to warn sb; prestar ~ (a) to pay attention (to). **-2.** [cuidado] care. **-3.** [cortesia] consideration *(U)*. <> *interj*: ~! [cuidado] beware!; [exigindo concentração] pay attention!; [em aeroporto, conferência] your attention please!

atencioso, osa [atēn'sjozu, ɔsa] *adj* **-1.** [que presta atenção] attentive. **-2.** [polido, cortês] considerate.

atendente [atēn'dēntʃi] *mf* auxiliary.

atender [5] [atēn'de(x)] <> *vt* **-1.** [satisfazer] to attend to. **-2.** [deferir] to grant. **-3.** [receber] to receive. **-4.** [responder] to answer. **-5.** [em loja] to serve. **-6.** [cuidar de - convidado, hóspede] to look after; [- paciente, ferido] to tend. <> *vi* **-1.** [satisfazer]: ~ a to attend to. **-2.** [responder]: ~ (a) to answer; ~ por [por nome, apelido] to answer to. **-3.** [loja, vendedor] to serve; ~ bem/mal to give good/bad service. **-4.** [dar atenção]: ~ a to heed.

atendimento [atēndʒi'mēntu] *m* **-1.** [serviço] service; ~ médico medical care; horário de ~ opening times. **-2.** [recepção]: tivemos pronto ~ no ministério we were dealt with swiftly at the ministry.

ateniense [ate'njēnsil] <> *adj* Athenian. <> *m, f* Athenian.

atentado [atēn'tadu] *m* **-1.** [ataque] attack; ~ a bomba/tiros bomb/gun attack; ~ terrorista terrorist attack. **-2.** [contra pessoa] attempt on one's life. **-3.** [contra edifício, monumento]: ~ (a/contra) attack (on/against). **-4.** [crime, ofensa]: ~

(a algo) attack (on sthg); ~ ao pudor indecent exposure.

atentar [4] [atēn'ta(x)] *vi* **-1.** [prestar atenção]: ~ para ou a to pay attention to. **-2.** [cometer atentado]: ~ contra (a vida de) alguém to make an attempt on sb's life; ~ contra algo [violar, ofender] to offend against sthg.

atento, ta [a'tēntu, ta] *adj* **-1.** [interessado, concentrado] attentive. **-2.** [cuidadoso] painstaking.

atenuação [atenwa'sãw] (*pl* -ões) *f* **-1.** [de pressão, pena] reduction. **-2.** [de combate] subduing. **-3.** [de dor] easing.

atenuante [ate'nwãntʃi] <> *adj* extenuating. <> *m* JUR extenuating circumstance.

atenuar [4] [ate'nwa(x)] *vt* **-1.** [pressão, pena] to reduce. **-2.** [combate] to die down. **-3.** [dor] to ease.

aterrador, ra [atexa'do(x), ra] *adj* terrifying.

aterragem [ate'xaʒēj] (*pl* -ns) *f* = aterrissagem.

aterrar [4] [ate'xar] *vt* [cobrir com terra] to level.

aterrissagem [atexi'saʒēj] (*pl* -ns) *f* landing.

aterrissar [atexi'sa(x)], **aterrizar** [atexi'za(x)] [4] *vi* to land.

aterro [a'texul] *m* [área aterrada] levelling.

aterrorizado, da [atexori'zadu, da] *adj* terrified.

aterrorizante [atexori'zãntʃi] *adj* terrifying.

aterrorizar [4] [atexori'za(x)] *vt* to terrorize.

ater-se [1] [a'texsi] *vp* **-1.** [limitar-se]: ~ a to keep to. **-2.** [fiar-se por] to rely on.

atestado, da [ateʃ'tadu, da] *adj* certified.

◆ **atestado** *m* **-1.** [certificado] certificate; ~ médico medical certificate; ~ de óbito death certificate; passar um ~ to issue a certificate. **-2.** *fig* [prova] confirmation. **-3.** JUR testimony.

atestar [4] [ateʃ'ta(x)] *vt* **-1.** [certificar] to certify. **-2.** [provar] to confirm. **-3.** [testemunhar] to vouch for.

ateu, atéia [a'tew, a'tɛja] <> *adj* atheist. <> *m, f* atheist.

atinado, da [atʃi'nadu, da] *adj* [sensato] sensible.

atinar [4] [atʃi'na(x)] <> *vt* **-1.** [descobrir, acertar] to work out. **-2.** [perceber] to realize. <> *vi* **-1.** [encontrar]: ~ com to come up with. **-2.** [ter consciência de]: ~ em to be aware of.

atingir [52] [atʃĩn'ʒi(x)] *vt* **-1.** [ger] to reach. **-2.** [acertar] to hit. **-3.** [objetivo] to achieve. **-4.** *fig* [ferir] to wound. **-5.** [afetar] to affect. **-6.** [compreender] to grasp.

atingível [atʃĩn'ʒivew] (*pl* -eis) *adj* achievable, attainable.

atípico, ca [a'tʃipiku, ka] *adj* untypical, atypical.

atirado, da [atʃi'radu, da] *adj fam* [pessoa] forward.

atirador, ra [atʃira'do(x), ra] *m, f* shot, shooter.

atirar [4] [atʃi'ra(x)] <> *vt* **-1.** [lançar]: ~ algo (em) to throw sthg (into); ~ algo (por) to throw sthg (through). **-2.** [fig] [olhares, beijos] to cast. <> *vi* [dar disparo]: ~ (em) to fire (at).

◆ **atirar-se** *vp* **-1.** [lançar-se]: ~-se (a/em) to throw o.s. (at); *fig* [dedicar-se] to throw o.s. into; ~-se contra to throw onself against. **-2.** *fam* [insinuar-se amorosamente] to come on to.

atitude [atʃi'tudʒil *f* **-1.** [modo de agir] response; **tomar uma** ~ [reagir, tomar uma providência] to take a stance. **-2.** [postura] attitude.

ativa [a'tʃival *f* ▷ **ativo**.

ativação [ativa'sãw] (*pl* **-ões**) *f* [aceleração, intensificação] acceleration.

ativar [4] [atʃi'va(x)] *vt* **-1.** [acionar] to turn on. **-2.** [bomba] to activate. **-3.** [estimular] to stimulate.

atividade [atʃivi'dadʒi] *f* **-1.** [ger] activity; ~ **extracurricular** extracurricular activity; **entrar em** ~ to be put into action; **em** ~ [aparelho] functioning; [pessoa] on the go. **-2.** [ocupação] pursuit. **-3.** [movimento intenso] bustle.

ativo, va [a'tivu, va] *adj* **-1.** [ger] active. **-2.** [que trabalha] working. **-3.** [ágil, movimentado] lively.

⟶ **ativo** *m* COM assets *(pl)*.

⟶ **ativa** *f* MIL: **estar na** ~ to be in active service; **da** ~ staff *(antes de subst)*.

atlântico, ca [at'lãntʃiku, ka] *adj* Atlantic.

⟶ **Atlântico** *n*: **o (oceano) Atlântico** the Atlantic Ocean.

atlas ['atlaʃ] *m inv* atlas.

Atlas ['atlaʃ] *n*: **o** ~ the Atlas Mountains.

atleta [a'tlɛta] *mf* athlete.

atlético, ca [a'tlɛtʃiku, ka] *adj* athletic.

atletismo [atle'tʃiʒmu] *m* athletics *(sg)*.

atmosfera [atmoʃ'fɛra] *f* **-1.** GEOGR atmosphere. **-2.** *fig* [ambiente] mood.

atmosférico, ca [atmoʃ'fɛriku, ka] *adj* atmospheric.

ato ['atu] *m* **-1.** [ger] act; ~ **sexual** sexual act; ~ **falho** Freudian slip; **em** ~ **contínuo** straight away; **no** ~ [imediatamente] on the spot. **-2.** [cerimônia] action; ~ **público** public ceremony. **-3.** POL [decreto]: ~ **(institucional)** act, law.

à-toa [a'toa] *adj* **-1.** [sem importância] insignificant. **-2.** [simples] simple.

atoalhado, da [atwa'ʎadu, da] *adj* towelling.

atolado, da [ato'ladu, da] *adj* **-1.** [carro, rua] muddy. **-2.** *fig* [pessoa]: ~ **(de coisas para fazer)** snowed under (with things to do).

atolar [4] [ato'la(x)] *vt* to get bogged down.

⟶ **atolar-se** *vp fig* [pessoa] to be snowed under.

atoleiro [ato'lejru] *m* **-1.** [de lama] quagmire. **-2.** *fig* [situação] morass.

atômico, ca [a'tomiku, ka] *adj* atomic.

atomizador [atomiza'do(x)] *m* atomizer, spray.

átomo ['atomu] *m* atom.

atonal, nais [a'tonaw, aiʃ] *adj* MÚS atonal.

atônito, ta [a'tonitu, ta] *adj* astonished.

ator, atriz [a'to(x), a'triʒ] (*mpl* **-res**, *fpl* **-zes**) *m, f* actor, actress.

atordoado, da [atox'dwadu, da] *adj* dazed.

atordoamento [atoxdwa'mẽntu] *m* bewilderment.

atordoante [atox'dwãntʃi] *adj* deafening.

atordoar [20] [atox'dwa(x)] *vt* to daze.

atormentado, da [atoxmẽn'tadu, da] *adj* tormented.

atormentar [4] [atoxmẽn'ta(x)] *vt* to torment.

atóxico, ca [a'toksiku, ka] *adj* non-toxic.

ATP (*abrev de* **Associação dos Tenistas Profissionais**) *f* ATP.

atração [atra'sãw] (*pl* **-ões**) *f* **-1.** FÍS attraction. **-2.** [de cinema, teatro] main attraction. **-3.** [propensão] pull. **-4.** [sexual] attraction.

atracar [12] [atra'ka(x)] *vt & vi* NÁUT to moor.

⟶ **atracar-se** *vp* **-1.** *fig* [em briga] to come to blows. **-2.** *fam fig* [amorosamente] to clinch.

atraente [atra'ẽntʃi] *adj* **-1.** [objeto, efeito] eye-catching. **-2.** [proposta, vantagem] appealing. **-3.** [pessoa] attractive.

atraiçoar [20] [atraj'swa(x)] *vt* to betray.

atrair [68] [atra'i(x)] *vt* **-1.** [fascinar] to attract. **-2.** [chamar a si] to bring. **-3.** [aliciar] to entice.

atrapalhação [atrapaʎa'sãw] (*pl* **-ões**) *f* [confusão] muddle.

atrapalhar [4] [atrapa'ʎa(x)] ⟷ *vt* **-1.** [confundir] to muddle. **-2.** [perturbar] to upset. **-3.** [dificultar] to confound. ⟷ *vi* [perturbar] to be disturbing.

⟶ **atrapalhar-se** *vp* [confundir-se] to get into a muddle.

atrás [a'trajʃ] *adv* **-1.** [posição] behind; **lá** ~ **back there. -2.** [no tempo] ago. **-3.** [em classificação]: **estar/ficar** ~ **(de)** to be ranked behind; **não ficar** ~ *fam fig* not to be far behind.

⟶ **atrás de** *loc prep* **-1.** [posição] behind. **-2.** [em seguimento a] after; **logo** ~ **de** right behind. **-3.** [em busca de - pessoa] after; [- objeto, explicação] looking for.

atrasado, da [atra'zadu, da] *adj* **-1.** [ger] slow. **-2.** [tardio] late. **-3.** [país, povo, costume] backward. **-4.** [pagamento, conta] overdue. **-5.** [número, edição] back.

⟶ **atrasados** *mpl* arrears.

atrasar [4] [atra'za(x)] ⟷ *vt* **-1.** [fazer demorar] to delay. **-2.** [retardar] to hold back. **-3.** [relógio] to put back. **-4.** [pagamento] to be late with. ⟷ *vi* **-1.** [demorar] to be delayed. **-2.** [publicação] to be late. **-3.** [relógio] to be slow. **-4.** [pagamento] to arrive late. **-5.** [em trabalho, encomenda] to fail to keep up.

⟶ **atrasar-se** *vp* [pessoa]: ~**-se (para)** to be late (for).

atraso [a'trazu] *m* **-1.** [demora] delay; **chegar com** ~ to arrive late; **um** ~ **de vida** a drag. **-2.** [de pagamento] late payment. **-3.** [de país, povo, costumes] backwardness.

atrativo, va [atra'tʃivu, va] *adj* attractive.

⟶ **atrativo** *m* attraction.

atravancar [12] [atravãŋ'ka(x)] *vt* **-1.** [bloquear] to block. **-2.** [lotar] to clutter.

através [atra'vɛʃ] *adv* [de lado a lado] through.

⟶ **através de** *loc adv* **-1.** [por entre] amongst. **-2.** [pelo centro de] through. **-3.** [no decorrer de] through. **-4.** [por meio de] by means of. **-5.** [por via de] through.

atravessado, da [atrave'sadu, da] *adj* **-1.** [de través] askew; ~ **sobre** (lying) across. **-2.** [cruzado] crossed. **-3.** [passado de lado a lado] (stuck) across. **-4.** *fig* [irritado] irritated; **estar com alguém** ~ **na garganta** to be fed up with sb.

atravessar [4] [atrave'sa(x)] *vt* **-1.** [ger] to cross.

- **2.** [pôr de través] to place across. - **3.** [transpassar] to pierce. - **4.** *fig* [passar por] to go through.

atrelar [4] [atre'la(x)] *vt* - **1.** [prender] to tie up, to tether. - **2.** [ligar] to attach; ~ **algo a algo** to attach sthg to sthg.

atrever-se [5] [atre'vexsi] *vp*: ~ **(a fazer algo)** to dare (to do sthg):

atrevido, da [atre'vidu, da] *adj* - **1.** [petulante] impertinent. - **2.** [ousado] bold.

atrevimento [atrevi'mēntu] *m* - **1.** [petulância] insolence. - **2.** [ousadia - condição] boldness; [- ato] effrontery.

atribuição [atribwi'sãw] (*pl* -ões) *f* - **1.** [ato] attribution. - **2.** [prerrogativa] prerogative.
  ➡ **atribuições** *fpl* [poderes] powers.

atribuir [74] [atri'bwi(x)] *vt* - **1.** [imputar]: ~ **algo a alguém/algo** to attribute sthg to sb/sthg. - **2.** [conceder]: ~ **algo a alguém** to award sb sthg.

atribulação [atribula'sãw] (*pl* -ões) *f* adversity.

atribulado, da [atribu'ladu, da] *adj* wretched.

atribular [4] [atribu'la(x)] *vt* to afflict.
  ➡ **atribular-se** *vp* to be distressed.

atributo [atri'butu] *m* attribute.

átrio ['atriu] *m* - **1.** [vestíbulo] hallway. - **2.** [pátio] courtyard.

atritar [atri'ta(x)] *vt* to rub.

atrito [a'tritu] *m* - **1.** [fricção] friction. - **2.** *fig* [conflito] conflict; **entrar em** ~ to have a misunderstanding.

atriz [a'triʒ] *f* ➣ **ator**.

atrocidade [atrosi'dadʒil] *f* atrocity.

atrofia [atro'fia] *f* atrophy.

atrofiado, da [atro'fjadu, da] *adj* atrophied.

atrofiar [16] [atro'fja(x)] ◇ *vt* to cripple. ◇ *vi* to atrophy.
  ➡ **atrofiar-se** *vp* to become atrophied.

atropeladamente [atropelada'mēntʃi] *adv* [atabalhoadamente] chaotically.

atropelamento [atropela'mēntu] *m* [de pedestre] running over.

atropelar [4] [atrope'la(x)] *vt* - **1.** [pedestre] to run over. - **2.** [esbarrar em, empurrar] to crash into. - **3.** *fig* [precipitar]: ~ **as coisas** to rush things.

atropelo [atro'pelu] *m* - **1.** [confusão] turmoil. - **2.** [dificuldade, aflição] headache, problem.

atroz [a'troʒ] *adj* - **1.** [cruel] atrocious. - **2.** [terrível] terrible.

atuação [atwa'sãw] (*pl* -ões) [-õjʃ] *f* - **1.** [ger] performance. - **2.** [participação] role.

atual [a'twaw] (*pl* -ais) *adj* - **1.** [corrente] present. - **2.** [moderno] current.

atualidade [atwali'dadʒil] *f* - **1.** [período atual] present time. - **2.** [modernidade] modernity.
  ➡ **atualidades** *fpl JORN* news (*sg*).

atualização [atwaliza'sãw] (*pl* -ões) *f* updating.

atualizado, da [atwali'zadu, da] *adj* up-to-date.

atualizar [4] [atwali'za(x)] *vt* to update.
  ➡ **atualizar-se** *vp* [pessoa] to bring o.s. up to date.

atualmente [atwaw'mēntʃil] *adv* - **1.** [no momento] currently. - **2.** [hoje em dia] nowadays.

atuante [a'twāntʃi] *adj* active.

atuar [4] [a'twa(x)] *vi* - **1.** [ger] to act. - **2.** [participar de]: ~ **em** to act on/in. - **3.** [contribuir para]: ~ **para** *ou* **por** to work for *ou* towards. - **4.** [influenciar]: ~ **sobre** to influence.

atum [a'tũ] (*pl* -ns) *m* tuna.

aturar [4] [atu'ra(x)] *vt* to endure, to put up with.

aturdido, da [atur'dʒidu, da] *adj* stunned.

aturdir [6] [atux'dʒi(x)] ◇ *vt* to stun. ◇ *vi* to deafen.

audácia [aw'dasja] *f* - **1.** [intrepidez] boldness. - **2.** [insolência] audacity; **que** ~! what a cheek!

audacioso, sa [awda'sjozu, ɔza] *adj* - **1.** [pessoa] intrepid. - **2.** [ato] gallant. - **3.** [decisão] bold.

audaz [aw'daʒ] (*pl* -es) *adj* [intrépido] audacious.

audição [awdʒi'sãw] (*pl* -ões) *f* - **1.** [ger] hearing. - **2.** [concerto] audition.

audiência [aw'dʒjēnsja] *f* - **1.** [ger] audience; **dar uma** ~ to grant an audience. - **2.** [mídia - RÁDIO] listeners (*pl*); [- TV] viewers (*pl*); **índices de** ~ ratings (*pl*). - **3.** *JUR* hearing.

áudio ['awdʒul] *m* audio.

audiovisual [ˌawdʒuvi'zwaw] (*pl* -ais) ◇ *adj* audiovisual. ◇ *m* projector.

auditar [4] [awdʒi'ta(x)] *vt FIN* to audit.

auditivo, va [awdʒi'tʃivu, va] *adj* auditory.

auditor, ra [awdʒi'to(x), ra] *m, f* - **1.** *FIN* auditor. - **2.** [juiz] judge, magistrate. - **3.** [ouvinte] listener.

auditoria [awdʒito'ria] *f* - **1.** [serviço] audit; **fazer a** ~ **de** to carry out an audit of. - **2.** [empresa] firm of accountants.

auditório [awdʒi'tɔrjul] *m* - **1.** [recinto] courtroom. - **2.** [platéia] auditorium.

audível [aw'dʒivewl] (*pl* -eis) *adj* audible.

auê [aw'e] *m fam* [confusão] uproar; **fazer um** ~ to create an uproar.

auferir [57] [awfe'ri(x)] *vt* to obtain.

auge ['awʒil] *m* height.

augurar [4] [awgu'ra(x)] *vt* - **1.** [prognosticar] to foretell. - **2.** [indicar] to augur. - **3.** [desejar] to wish.

augúrio [aw'gurjul] *m* - **1.** [prognóstico] prophecy. - **2.** [sinal] indication.

aula ['awla] *f* [escola] - **1.** lesson; **dar** ~ to teach. - **2.** [universidade] lecture; ~ **inaugural** introductory lecture.

aumentar [4] [awmēn'ta(x)] ◇ *vt* - **1.** [ger] to increase. - **2.** [adicionar]: ~ **algo (a)** to add sthg (to/onto). ◇ *vi* - **1.** [ger] to increase. - **2.** [crescer] to grow.

aumento [aw'mēntul] *m* - **1.** [ger] price increase. - **2.** [de salário] rise *UK*, raise *US*. - **3.** [crescimento] increase. - **4.** [ampliação] magnification.

aura ['awra] *f* - **1.** [halo] halo. - **2.** *fig* [ar] aura.

áureo, rea ['awrju, rja] *adj* golden.

auréola [aw'rewla] *f* halo.

aurora [aw'rɔra] *f* dawn.

auscultar [4] [awʃkuw'ta(x)] *vt* - **1.** *MED* to sound, to auscultate. - **2.** *fig* [sondar] to sound (out).

ausência [aw'zēnsja] *f* - **1.** [falta de presença] absence. - **2.** *fig* [inexistência] lack.

ausentar-se [7] [awzēn'taxsi] *vp* to absent o.s.

ausente [aw'zẽntʃi] ⬦ *adj* **-1.** [não-presente] absent. **-2.** [omisso] neglectful. ⬦ *mf* [não-presente] absent.

auspiciar [16] [awʃpi'sja(x)] *vt* [prenunciar] to augur.

auspício [awʃ'pisju] *m* **-1.** [prenúncio] sign. **-2.** [patrocínio]: **sob os ~s de** under the auspices of.

auspicioso, osa [awʃpi'ʃjozu, ɔza] *adj* auspicious.

austeridade [awʃteri'dadʒi] *f* **-1.** [severidade, seriedade] severity. **-2.** [em gastos] austerity.

austero, ra [awʃ'tɛru, ra] *adj* **-1.** [severo] strict. **-2.** [em gastos] austere.

austral [awʃ'traw] (*pl* **-ais**) *adj* southern.

Austrália [awʃ'tralja] *n* Australia.

australiano, na [awʃtra'ljãnu, na] ⬦ *adj* Australian. ⬦ *m, f* Australian.

Áustria ['awʃtrja] *n* Austria.

austríaco, ca [awʃ'triaku, ka] ⬦ *adj* Austrian. ⬦ *m, f* Austrian.

autarquia [awtax'kia] *f* autocracy.

autárquico, ca [aw'taxkiku, ka] *adj* autocratic.

autenticação [awtẽntʃi'kasãw] (*pl* **-ões**) *f* COMPUT verification.

autenticar [12] [awtẽntʃi'ka(x)] *vt* to authenticate.

autenticidade [awtẽntʃisi'dadʒi] *f* [genuinidade] authenticity.

autêntico, ca [aw'tẽntʃiku, ka] *adj* **-1.** [genuíno] authentic. **-2.** [original] original. **-3.** *(antes de subst)* *pej* [verdadeiro] real.

autismo [aw'tʃiʒmu] *m* autism.

autista [aw'tʃiʃta] ⬦ *adj* autistic. ⬦ *mf* autistic.

auto ['awtu] *m* **-1.** JUR (legal) brief. **-2.** TEATRO medieval allegorical play.
　➡ **autos** *mpl* JUR legal papers.

auto-adesivo, va [ˌawtwade'zivu, va] (*mpl* **-s**, *fpl* **-s**) ⬦ *adj* self-adhesive. ⬦ *m* sticker.

auto-afirmação [ˌawtwafixma'sãw] *f* self-assertion.

autobiografia [awtobjogra'fia] *f* autobiography.

autobiográfico, ca [awtubjo'grafiku, ka] *adj* autobiographical.

autoconfiança [awtukõn'fjãnsa] *f* self-confidence.

autoconhecimento [awtukoɲesi'mẽntu] *m* self-knowledge.

autocontrole [awtukõn'troli] *m* self-control.

autocrata [awto'krata] ⬦ *adj* autocratic. ⬦ *mf* autocrat.

autocrítica [awto'kritika] *f* self-criticism; **fazer uma ~** to admit to one's faults.

autóctone [aw'tɔktoni] ⬦ *adj* native. ⬦ *mf* [nativo] native.

autodefesa [awtude'feza] *f* self-defence.

autodenominar-se [7] [awtudenomi'naxsi] *vp* to call o.s.

autodestruição [awtudeʃtruj'sãw] *f* self-destruction.

autodeterminação [awtudetexmina'sãw] *f* self-determination.

autodidata [awtodʒi'data] ⬦ *adj* self-taught. ⬦ *mf* self-taught person.

autodisciplina [awtudʒisi'plina] *f* self-discipline.

autodomínio [ˌawtodo'minju] *m* self-control.

autódromo [aw'tɔdromu] *m* racetrack.

auto-escola [ˌawtwiʃ'kɔla] (*pl* **auto-escolas**) *f* driving school.

auto-estima [ˌawtwiʃ'tʃima] *f* self-esteem.

auto-estrada [ˌawtwiʃ'trada] (*pl* **auto-estradas**) *f* motorway *UK*, freeway *US*.

autografar [4] [awtogra'fa(x)] *vt* to sign.

autógrafo [aw'tɔgrafu] *m* autograph.

automação [awtoma'sãw] *f* = **automatização**.

automático, ca [awto'matʃiku, ka] *adj* automatic.

automatização [awtomatʃiza'sãw] (*pl* **-ões**) *f* automation.

automatizar [4] [awtomatʃi'za(x)] *vt* to automate.

autômato [aw'tomatu] *m* **-1.** [aparelho] robot. **-2.** *fig* [pessoa] automaton.

automedicar-se [7] [awtumedʒi'kaxsi] *vp* to self-medicate.

automobilismo [awtomobi'liʒmu] *m* motor racing.

automobilista [awtomobi'liʃta] *mf* ESP racing driver.

automóvel [awto'mɔvɛw] (*pl* **-eis**) *m* car.

autonomia [awtono'mia] *f* **-1.** [independência] autonomy. **-2.** [de veículo] range; **~ de vôo** flight range.

autônomo, ma [aw'tonomu, ma] ⬦ *adj* **-1.** [independente] autonomous. **-2.** [trabalhador] autonomist. ⬦ *m, f* [trabalhador] autonomist.

autopeça [awto'pɛsa] *f* spare part *(for car)*.

autópsia [aw'tɔpsja] *f* autopsy.

autor, ra [aw'to(x), ra] (*mpl* **-es**, *fpl* **-s**) *m, f* author.

autoral [awto'raw] (*pl* **-ais**) *adj* authorial.

auto-retrato [ˌawtoxe'tratu] (*pl* **auto-retratos**) *m* self-portrait.

autoria [awto'ria] *f* **-1.** LITER authorship; **ser de ~ de alguém** to be written by sb. **-2.** [de crime] perpetration.

autoridade [awtori'dadʒi] *f* **-1.** [ger] authority; **ter/não ter ~** to have/not to have authority. **-2.** [perito]: **ser uma ~ em algo** to be an authority on sthg.

autoritário, ria [awtori'tarju, ja] *adj* authoritarian.

autoritarismo [awtorita'riʒmu] *m* authoritarianism.

autorização [awtoriza'sãw] (*pl* **-ões**) *f* permission; **dar ~ a alguém (para algo/para fazer algo)** to give sb permission (for sthg/to do sthg).

autorizar [4] [awtori'za(x)] *vt* **-1.** [permitir] to authorize. **-2.** [capacitar] to enable.

auto-serviço [ˌawtusex'visu] (*pl* **auto-serviços**) *m* self-service.

auto-suficiente [ˌawtusufi'sjẽntʃi] (*pl* **-s**) *adj*

self-sufficient; **ser** ~ **em algo** to be self-sufficient in sthg.

auto-sugestão [‚awtusuʒeʃ'tãw] (pl -ões) f auto-suggestion.

autuar [4] [aw'twa(x)] vt to report; ~ **alguém em flagrante** to catch sb red-handed.

auxiliar [16] [awsi'lja(x)] (pl -es) <> adj -1. [ger] assistant. - **2.** [enfermeiro] auxiliary. <> mf assistant; ~ **administrativo** administrative assistant. <> vt to assist.

auxílio [aw'silju] m assistance; **prestar** ~ **a** to give assistance to.

auxílio-desemprego [aw‚siljudʒizĩn'pregu] (pl **auxílios-desemprego**) m unemployment benefit.

auxílio-doença [aw‚silju'dwẽnsa] (pl **auxílios-doença**) m sickness benefit.

auxílio-natalidade [aw‚siljunatali'dadʒil (pl **auxílios-natalidade**) m maternity grant.

av. (abrev de avenida) f Av.

avacalhado, da [avaka'ʎadu, da] adj -1. [camisa, cabelo] dishevelled. - **2.** [trabalho] slipshod.

avacalhar [ava'kaʎa(x)] vt -1. [pôr em ridículo] fam to make a travesty of. - **2.** [executar com desleixo] fam to make a mess of.

aval [a'vaw] (pl -ais) m -1. [ger] backing. - **2.** [garantia] warranty.

avalanche [ava'lãnʃil, **avalancha** f avalanche.

avaliação [avalja'sãw] (pl -ões) f -1. [de preço, prejuízos] estimate. - **2.** [de qualidade, vantagens] appraisal. - **3.** [opinião] opinion. - **4.** EDUC assessment.

avaliar [16] [ava'lja(x)] vt -1. [preço, prejuízo] to estimate. - **2.** [imóvel] to value. - **3.** [qualidade, vantagens, idéia] to evaluate. - **4.** EDUC to assess.

avalista [ava'liʃta] mf backer.

avançado, da [avãn'sadu, da] adj -1. [adiantado] jutting out. - **2.** [hora] late. - **3.** [nível] advanced. - **4.** [idéia, pessoa] progressive.

avançar [13] [avã'sa(x)] <> vi -1. [adiantar-se] to move forward. - **2.** [estender-se] to spread. - **3.** [atacar, investir] to advance. - **4.** [atirar-se]: ~ **em algo** to throw o.s. upon sthg. <> vt [adiantar] to advance.

avanço [a'vãsul m -1. [de tropa] advance. - **2.** [adiantamento] headway. - **3.** [melhora] step in the right direction. - **4.** [progresso] progress.

avantajado, da [avãnta'ʒadu, da] adj imposing.

avante [a'vãntʃi] <> adv -1. [adiante] ahead. - **2.** [para diante] onward. <> interj forward!

avarento, ta [ava'rẽntu, ta] <> adj miserly. <> m, f miser.

avareza [ava'reza] f avarice.

avaria [ava'ria] f -1. [de veículo, máquina] breakdown. - **2.** [de carga, casco] damage.

avariado, da [ava'rjadu, da] adj -1. [veículo, máquina] broken down. - **2.** [carga, casco] damaged.

avariar [16] [ava'rja(x)] <> vt to break down. <> vi -1. to spoil. - **2.** [casco] to be damaged.

avaro, ra [a'varu, ra] <> adj avaricious. <> m, f miser.

ave ['avil f bird; ~ **de rapina** bird of prey.

aveia [a'veja] f oat.

avelã [ave'lã] f hazelnut.

aveludado, da [avelu'dadu, da] adj velvety.

avenida [ave'nida] f avenue.

avental [avẽn'taw] (pl -ais) m -1. [proteção] apron. - **2.** [vestido] pinafore dress.

aventar [4] [avẽn'ta(x)] vt to air.

aventura [avẽn'tural f -1. [experiência] adventure. - **2.** [amorosa] love affair.

aventurar [4] [avẽntu'ra(x)] vt to risk.

➤ **aventurar-se** vp to venture (forth); ~-**se a fazer algo** to dare to do sthg.

aventureiro, ra [avẽntu'rejru, ra] <> adj adventurous. <> m, f adventurer (f adventuress).

averiguação [averigwa'sãw] (pl -ões) f -1. [investigação] investigation. - **2.** [verificação] check.

averiguar [21] [averi'gwa(x)] vt -1. [investigar] to investigate. - **2.** [verificar] to check.

avermelhado, da [avexme'ʎadu, da] adj reddish.

aversão [avex'sãw] (pl -ões) f aversion; **ter** ~ **a algo** to have an aversion to sthg.

avesso, ssa [a'vesul adj [lado] wrong.

➤ **avesso** m [lado] underside; **virar pelo** ~ [blusa etc] to turn inside out; fig [revirar] to turn upside down.

➤ **às avessas** loc adj [oposto]: **ser um santo às avessas** to be anything but a saint.

avestruz [aveʃ'truʃ] (pl -es) f ostrich.

aviação [avja'sãw] f -1. [sistema] aviation. - **2.** [força aérea] air force.

aviador, ra [avja'do(x), ra] m, f pilot, aviator.

aviamento [avja'mẽntul m -1. COST trimmings (pl). - **2.** [de receita médica] preparation.

avião [a'vjãw] (pl -ões) m -1. [veículo] aeroplane; ~ **a jato** jet plane; **ir de** ~ to fly. - **2.** fam [mulher] stunner. - **3.** gír [droga] drug pedlar.

aviar [16] [a'vja(x)] vt [receita médica] to make up.

avicultor, ra [avikuw'to(x), ra] m, f poultry breeder.

avicultura [avikuw'tural f poultry breeding.

avidez [avi'deʒ] f -1. [desejo] eagerness; **com** ~ eagerly. - **2.** [cobiça] greed.

ávido, da ['avidu, da] adj -1. [desejoso] eager. - **2.** [cobiçoso] greedy.

aviltamento [aviwta'mẽntul m [degradação] degradation.

aviltar [4] [aviw'ta(x)] vt [degradar] to weaken.

➤ **aviltar-se** vp [degradar-se] to degenerate.

avinagrado, da [avina'gradu, da] adj sour.

avisar [4] [avi'za(x)] <> vt -1. [informar] to warn; ~ **alguém de algo** to inform sb of sthg. - **2.** [advertir]: ~ **alguém de algo** to warn sb about/of sthg. <> vi -1. [informar] to give warning. - **2.** [advertir] to give fair warning; **estou avisando** ... I'm warning you ...

aviso [a'vizul m -1. [placa] notice. - **2.** [notificação] notification; ~ **de crédito** credit note. - **3.** [informação] sign. - **4.** [advertência] warning sign; ~ **prévio** [notificação, período] notice.

avistar [4] [aviʃ'ta(x)] vt to catch sight of.

➤ **avistar-se** vp [ter entrevista] to meet; ~-**se**

com alguém to have a meeting with sb.
avivar [4] [avi'va(x)] *vt* **-1.** [ger] to revive. **-2.** [memória] to rekindle.
avizinhar-se [4] [avizi'ɲaxsi] *vp* [aproximar-se] to draw near.
avo ['avu] *m* [fração] fractional part.
avô [a'vo], **avó** [a'vɔ] *m, f* grandfather (*f* grandmother).
    ➠ **avós** *pl* grandparents.
avoado, da [avo'adu, da] *adj* scatty.
avolumar [4] [avolu'ma(x)] *vt* [aumentar- em volume] to swell; [- em quantidade] to increase.
    ➠ **avolumar-se** *vp* **-1.** [em volume] to rise. **-2.** [em quantidade] to increase.
avós [a'vɔʃ] *pl* ▷ **avô**.
avulso, sa [a'vuwsu, sa] *adj* loose.
    ➠ **avulso** *m* flyer.
avultado, da [avuw'tadu, da] *adj* large.
avultar [4] [avuw'ta(x)] ⬦ *vt* [fazer crescer] to increase. ⬦ *vi* **-1.** [sobressair] to tower above. **-2.** [crescer] to grow.
axila [ak'sila] *f* armpit.
axioma [ak'sjoma] *m* axiom.
axiomático, ca [aksio'matʃiku, ka] *adj* axiomatic.
azaléia [aza'lɛja] *f* azalea.
azar [a'za(x)] (*pl* **-es**) *m* bad luck; ~! tough!; **que** ~! damn!; ~ **o seu!** your loss!; **dar** ~ to bring bad luck; **estar com** ~ to be down on one's luck.
azaração [azara'sãw] (*pl* **-ões**) *f fam* flirtation.
azarado, da [aza'radu, da] *adj* jinxed.
azarar [4] [aza'ra(x)] *fam* ⬦ *vt* to woo. ⬦ *vi* to pull.
azedar [4] [aze'da(x)] ⬦ *vt* **-1.** [comida, leite] to cause to go sour. **-2.** *fig* [pessoa] to irritate. ⬦ *vi* [leite, vinho] to go sour.
azedo, da [a'zedu, da] *adj* **-1.** [sabor] sour. **-2.** *fig* [pessoa] bitter.
azedume [aze'dumi] *m* **-1.** [em sabor] bitterness. **-2.** *fig* [em pessoa] bitterness.
azeite [a'zejtʃi] *m*: ~ **(de oliva)** (olive) oil.
azeitona [azej'tona] *f* olive.
Azerbaijão [azexbaj'ʒãw] *n* Azerbaijan.
azerbaijano, na [azexbaj'ʒãnu, na] ⬦ *adj* Azerbaijani. ⬦ *m, f* Azerbaijani.
azeviche [aze'viʃi] *m* [cor] jet black.
azia [a'zia] *f* heartburn.
aziago, ga [azi'agu, ga] *adj* ill-omened.
azucrinar [4] [azukri'na(x)] *vt* to annoy.
azul [a'zuw] (*pl* **azuis**) ⬦ *adj* blue; **está tudo** ~ *fig* everything is rosy. ⬦ *m* blue.
azulado, da [azu'ladu, da] *adj* bluish.
azul-claro, ra [a'zuwklaru, ra] ⬦ *adj* light blue. ⬦ *m* light blue.
azulejado, da [azule'ʒadu, da] *adj* tiled.
azulejar [4] [azule'ʒa(x)] *vt* to tile.
azulejo [azu'leʒu] *m* (ornamental) tile.
azul-escuro, ra [a'zuwiʃkuru, ra] ⬦ *adj* dark blue. ⬦ *m* dark blue.
azul-marinho [a,zuwma'riɲu] ⬦ *adj inv* ultramarine. ⬦ *m* ultramarine.

azul-turquesa [a,zuwtux'keza] ⬦ *adj inv* turquoise. ⬦ *m* turquoise.

b, B [be] *m* [letra] b, B.
BA (*abrev de* **Estado da Bahia**) *n* State of Bahia.
B2B (*abrev de* **business-to-business**) *m* B2B.
baba ['baba] *f* dribble.
babá [ba'ba] *f* nursemaid.
babaca [ba'baka] *mfam adj* stupid.
baba-de-moça [,babadʒi'mosa] (*pl* **babas-de-moça**) *m, f CULIN* egg and coconut pudding.
babado, da [ba'badu, da] *adj* [molhado de baba] dribbly.
    ➠ **babado** *m* **-1.** [em roupa etc] frill. **-2.** *fam* [caso] gossip.
babador [baba'do(x)] *m* bib.
babaquice [baba'kisi] *f fam* [estupidez] stupidity.
babar [4] [ba'ba(x)] ⬦ *vt* to dribble on. ⬦ *vi* **-1.** [deitar baba] to dribble. **-2.** *fam* [ficar impressionado] to drool.
    ➠ **babar-se** *vp* **-1.** [deitar baba em si] to dribble. **-2.** *fig* [gostar muito de]: ~-**se por** to drool over.
babosa [ba'bɔsa] *f* aloe.
baboseira [babo'zejra] *f* [tolice, bobagem] nonsense.
baby-sitter [,bejbi'site(x)] (*pl* **baby-sitters**) *mf* baby-sitter.
bacalhau [baka'ʎaw] *m* cod.
bacalhoada [bakaʎo'ada] *f* a dish made with salt cod boiled with potatoes, cabbage, whole onions and other vegetables, mixed with hard-boiled eggs and olives and seasoned with vinegar and olive oil.
bacana [ba'kãna] ⬦ *adj* cool. ⬦ *mf fam* [pessoa] toff.
bacanal [baka'naw] (*pl* **-ais**) *f* bacchanal.
BACEN (*abrev de* **Banco Central do Brasil**) *n* central bank of Brazil.
bacharel [baʃa'rɛw] (*pl* **-éis**) *mf*: ~ **em Artes/Direito/Economia** Arts/Law/Economics graduate.
bacharelado [baʃare'ladu] *m* **-1.** [grau] degree. **-2.** [curso] undergraduate course.
bacharelar-se [4] [baʃare'laxsi] *vp*: ~ **(em algo)** to obtain a degree (in sthg).
bacia [ba'sia] *f* **-1.** [ger] basin. **-2.** [sanitária] lavatory. **-3.** *ANAT* pelvis.
bacilo [ba'silu] *m* bacillus.

➤ **bacilos** *mpl* bacilli.

backbone [bak'bonl] (*pl* **backbones**) *m* backbone.

background [bɛk'grawndʒil] (*pl* **-s**) *m* background.

backup [bɛ'kapil] (*pl* **-s**) *m* backup.

baço, ça l'basu, 'sal ◇ *adj* **-1.** [pele] dull. **-2.** [metal] tarnished. ◇ *m ANAT* spleen.

bacon l'bejkõl *m* bacon.

bactéria [bak'tɛrjal *f* bacterium.

➤ **bactérias** *fpl* bacteria.

badalação [badala'sãw] (*pl* **-ões**) *f fam* [movimento, diversão] movement.

badalado, da [bada'ladu, dal *fam adj* **-1.** [movimentado, divertido] swinging. **-2.** [famoso, falado] much talked about.

➤ **badalada** *f* [de sino] peal.

badalar [4] [bada'la(x)] ◇ *vt* [tocar] to ring. ◇ *vi* **-1.** [tocar] to peal. **-2.** *fam* [sair, divertir-se] to go out and enjoy o.s.

badalo [ba'dalul *m* **-1.** [de sino] peal. **-2.** *fam* [diversão] fun.

badejo [ba'deʒul *m* serran.

baderna [ba'dɛxnal *f* **-1.** [bagunça] mess. **-2.** [tumulto] revelry.

badulaque [badu'lakil *m* trinket.

➤ **badulaques** *mpl* odds and ends.

bafafá [bafa'fal *m fam* [tumulto] hoo-ha.

bafo l'baful *m* breath; ~**-de-onça** *fam* bad breath.

bafômetro [ba'fometrul *m* breathalyzer.

baforada [bafo'radal *f* [fumaça] blast.

bagaço [ba'gasul *m* [de fruta] remains of fruit (*once juice has been extracted*); **estar/ficar um** ~ *fig* to be drained, to be exhausted.

bagageiro [baga'ʒejrul *m AUTO* luggage rack.

bagagem [ba'gaʒẽl (*pl* **-ns**) *f* **-1.** [equipagem] luggage. **-2.** *fig* [conhecimentos, experiência] experience.

bagatela [baga'tɛlal *f fig* [ninharia] next to nothing.

Bagdá [bag'dal *n* Baghdad.

bago l'bagul *m* **-1.** [fruto] berry. **-2.** [uva] grape. **-3.** [de chumbo] shot. **-4.** *vulg* [testículo] ball.

baguete [ba'gɛtʃil *f* baguette.

bagulho [ba'guʎul *m* **-1.** [objeto] trinket. **-2.** *fig* & *pej* [pessoa]: **ser um** ~ to be ugly.

bagunça [ba'gũnsal *f* mess.

bagunçado, da [bagũn'sadu, dal *adj* cluttered.

bagunçar [bagũn'sa(x)], *vt* **-1.** [fazer confusão em] to clutter. **-2.** *fig* [atrapalhar, tumultuar] to upset.

bagunceiro, ra [bagũn'sejru, ral *adj* [pessoa - desordeiro] disorderly; [- relaxado] untidy.

Bahamas [ba'amaʃ] *npl*: **as** ~ the Bahamas.

Bahia [ba'ial *n* Bahia.

baia l'bajal *f* stall.

baía [ba'ial *f* bay.

baiana [ba'jãnal *f*: **rodar a** ~ to make a fuss.

baiano, na [baj'ãnu, nal ◇ *adj* Bahian. ◇ *m, f* Bahian.

baião [baj'ãwl (*pl* **-ões**) *m* [ritmo, dança] baião, *popular music from north-eastern Brazil.*

baila l'bajlal *f*: **trazer à** ~ to raise (the issue); **vir à** ~ to come to light.

bailado [baj'ladul *m* dance.

bailar [4] [baj'la(x)] *vt* & *vi* to dance.

bailarino, na [bajla'rinu, nal *m, f* dancer.

baile l'bajlil *m* ball; ~ **de carnaval** carnival ball; ~ **à fantasia** fancy-dress party; ~ **funk** funk party; **dar um** ~ **em** *fig* [superar] to crush.

bainha [ba'iɲal *f* **-1.** [de arma] sheath. **-2.** *COST* hem.

baioneta [bajo'netal *f* bayonet; ~ **calada** bayoneted rifle.

bairrista [baj'xiʃtal ◇ *adj* **-1.** [que defende interesse do bairro] community-based. **-2.** [muito patriota] regionalistic. ◇ *mf* **-1.** [do local] local. **-2.** [patriota] regionalist.

bairro l'bajxul *m* neighbourhood.

baita l'bajtal *adj* (antes de subst) **-1.** [soco, sucesso] tremendous. **-2.** [gripe, resfriado] terrible. **-3.** [abraço] huge.

baixa l'bajʃal *adj* ⊳ **baixo**.

baixada [baj'ʃadal *f GEOGR* valley.

baixa-mar l bajʃa'ma(x)l (*pl* **baixa-mares**) *f* low tide.

baixar [4] [baj'ʃa(x)] *vt COMPUT* [fazer download]: ~ **um arquivo** to download a file.

baixaria [bajʃa'rial *f* **-1.** [ger] depravity. **-2.** [escândalo] disgrace.

baixela [baj'ʃɛlal *f* dinner service.

baixeza [baj'ʃezal *f* low-mindedness.

baixio [baj'ʃiul *m* sandbank.

baixista [baj'ʃiʃtal *mf* bass player.

baixo, xa l'bajʃu, ʃal *adj* **-1.** [ger] low. **-2.** [pessoa] short. **-3.** [cabeça, olhar] lowered. **-4.** [bairro, cidade] lower. **-5.** [metal] base. **-6.** (antes de subst) [rio] downriver. **-7.** (antes de subst) [época] late. **-8.** (antes de subst) [vil, grosseiro] base; ~ **nível** *fam* [baixaria] disgrace; **palavrão de** ~ **nível** swear word.

➤ **baixo** ◇ *m* **-1.** [MÚS - instrumento] bass; [- cantor] bass player. **-2.** *fam* [bairro] lower town. ◇ *adv* **-1.** [a pouca altura] low. **-2.** *fig* [em posição inferior]: **estar/ficar por** ~ to be/become disheartened. **-3.** [falar] softly.

➤ **baixa** *f* **-1.** [ger] drop; **em baixa** falling. **-2.** [de serviço] sick-leave; **dar** *ou* **ter baixa (de)** to go on *ou* take sick-leave (from). **-3.** *MIL* loss.

➤ **para baixo** *loc adv* downwards.

➤ **por baixo (de)** *loc adv* underneath.

baixo-astral [ˌbajʃwaʃ'traw] *m fam* glumness; estar/ficar de ~ to be/become glum.

baixote, ta [baj'ʃɔtʃi, ta] <> *adj* shortish. <> *m, f* shortish person.

bajulação [baʒula'sãw] (*pl* -ões) *f* adulation.

bajulador, ra [baʒula'do(x), ra] <> *adj* adulatory. <> *m, f* adulator.

bajular [4] [baʒu'la(x)] *vt* to adulate.

bala ['bala] *f* -**1**. [munição] bullet; ~ de festim blank cartridge. -**2**. [doce] boiled sweet. -**3**. *loc*: estar/ficar uma ~ *fam* to be/go ballistic.

balada [ba'lada] *f* ballad.

balaio [ba'laju] *m* basket.

balança [ba'lãnsa] *f* scales (*pl*); ~ comercial balance of trade.

➤ **Balança** *f* ASTRO Libra.

balançar [13] [balãn'sa(x)] <> *vt* -**1**. [fazer oscilar - bebê, navio] to rock; [- quadril] to wiggle; [- galho, carro, avião] to shake. -**2**. [compensar] to counterbalance. <> *vi* -**1**. [oscilar] to shake. -**2**. [em balanço, cadeira] to rock.

➤ **balançar-se** *vp* [sacudir-se] to sway.

balancear [15] [balãn'sja(x)] *vt* -**1**. AUTO to balance (*wheels*). -**2**. [compensar] to counterbalance.

balancete [balãn'setʃi] *m* COM balance.

balanço [ba'lãnsu] *m* -**1**. [de criança] swing. -**2**. [ação] swinging. -**3**. ECON : ~ de pagamentos balance of payments.

balangandã [balãngãn'dã] *m* amulet.

balão [ba'lãw] (*pl* -ões) *m* -**1**. [dirigível] airship. -**2**. [de brinquedo] balloon; soltar um ~ to release a balloon. -**3**. [sonda] probe; ~ meteorológico metereological balloon. -**4**. [tanque]: ~ de oxigênio oxygen cylinder. -**5**. [em estrada etc] *place for doing U-turns.* -**6**. [em história em quadrinhos] bubble.

balão-de-ensaio [baˌlãwdʒĩn'saju] (*pl* balões-de-ensaio) *m* -**1**. [instrumento] pilot balloon. -**2**. *fig* [boato]: soltar um ~ to spread a rumour.

balão-sonda [baˌlãw'sõnda] (*pl* balões-sondas) *m* pilot balloon.

balaustrada [balawʃ'trada] *f* balustrade.

balaústre [bala'uʃtri] *m* baluster.

balbuciar [16] [bawbu'sja(x)] <> *vt* to stammer. <> *vi* to babble.

balbúrdia [baw'buxdʒja] *f* hustle and bustle.

balcão [baw'kãw] (*pl* -ões) *m* -**1**. [sacada] balcony. -**2**. [de loja] counter. -**3**. DE TEATRO dress circle; ~ nobre balcony; ~ simples upper circle.

Balcãs ['bawkãʃ] *npl* os ~ the Balkans.

balcânico, ca [baw'kãniku, ka] <> *adj* Balkan. <> *m, f* Balkan.

balconista [bawko'niʃta] *mf* shop assistant.

balde ['bawdʒi] *m* bucket.

baldeação [bawdʒja'sãw] (*pl* -ões) *f* transfer; fazer ~ to change.

baldio, dia [baw'dʒiu, dʒia] *adj* gone to wasteland.

balé [ba'lɛ] *m* ballet.

baleeira [bale'ejra] *f* whaler.

baleia [ba'leja] *f* -**1**. ZOOL whale. -**2**. *fam fig & pej* [pessoa]: ser uma ~ to look like a beached whale.

baleiro, ra [ba'lejru, ra] <> *m, f* [vendedor] sweet seller. <> *m* [pote] sweet jar.

Bali ['bali] *n* Bali.

balido [ba'lidu] *m* bleating.

balística [ba'liʃtʃika] *f* ballistics (*sg*).

baliza [ba'liza] *f* -**1**. [estaca] goalpost. -**2**. [bóia] buoy. -**3**. [luminosa] beacon. -**4**. ESP goal.

balizamento [baliza'mẽntu] *m* beaconing, signposting.

balneário [baw'njarju] *m* baths (*pl*).

balões [ba'lõjʃ] *pl* ➤ **balão**.

balofo, fa [ba'lofu, fa] <> *adj* puffy. <> *m, f* puffed-up person.

balsa ['bawsa] *f* -**1**. [jangada] raft. -**2**. [barca] catamaran. -**3**. [salva-vidas] lifeboat.

bálsamo ['bawsamu] *m* balsam.

Báltico ['bawtʃiku] *n*: o (mar) ~ the Baltic (Sea).

baluarte [ba'lwaxtʃil] *m* stronghold.

balzaquiana [bawza'kjana] *f woman in her late twenties or early thirties.*

bamba ['bãnba] *fam* <> *adj* [perito] expert. <> *mf* [perito] expert.

bambear [15] [bãn'bja(x)] <> *vt* [afrouxar] to loosen. <> *vi* -**1**. [tornar-se frouxo] to work itself loose. -**2**. *fig* [hesitar] to falter.

bambo, ba ['bãnbu, ba] *adj* -**1**. [corda, laço, parafuso] loose. -**2**. [perna] faltering.

bambolê [bãnbo'le] *m* hula hoop.

bamboleante [bãnbo'ljãntʃi] *adj* -**1**. [que balança] swaying. -**2**. [sem firmeza - parafuso, cordo] loose; [- estaca] wobbly.

bambolear [15] [bãnbo'lja(x)] <> *vt* [balançar] to sway. <> *vi* to sway.

bambu [bãn'bu] *m* -**1**. [planta] bamboo. -**2**. [vara] bamboo-stick.

bambuzal [bãnbu'zaw] (*pl* -ais)) *m* bamboo thicket.

banal [ba'naw] (*pl* -ais) *adj* mundane.

banalidade [banali'dadʒi] *f* simplicity.

banalizar [4] [banali'za(x)] *vt* to make commonplace.

banana [ba'nãna] <> *f* [fruta] banana; dar uma ~ (para alguém) *vulg fig* to say 'up yours!' (to sb). <> *mf fam fig & pej* [bobo, idiota] fool.

bananada [bana'nada] *f* banana sweetmeat.

bananal [bana'naw] (*pl* -ais)) *m* banana plantation.

bananeira [bana'nejra] *f* banana tree; plantar ~ *fig* to do a handstand.

banca ['bãŋka] *f* -**1**. [de jogo] game of chance. -**2**. [estande]: ~ (de jornal) newspaper stand. -**3**. [comissão]: ~ (examinadora) (examination) board. -**4**. [escritório] desk. -**5**. [mesa de trabalho] worktop; botar ~ to boss about.

bancada [bãŋ'kada] *f* -**1**. [banco] bench. -**2**. [POL - de partido] bench; [- de estado] representatives (*pl*). -**3**. [mesa de trabalho] workbench.

bancar [12] [bãŋ'ka(x)] *vt* -**1**. [financiar] to back. -**2**. [comportar-se como] to play.

bancário, ria [bãŋ'karju, rjal ◇ *adj* bank. ◇ *m, f* [empregado] bank employee.

bancarrota [bãŋka'xotal *f* bankruptcy; **ir à ~ to** go bankrupt.

banco ['bãŋkul *m* -**1.** [ger] bank; **~ 24 horas** 24-hour bank; **~ de sangue** blood bank. -**2.** [assento] bench; **~ dos réus** prisoners'' dock. -**3.** COMPUT : **~ de dados** databank. -**4.** GEOL : **~ de areia** sandbank.

banda ['bãndal *f*: COMPUT **~ larga** broadband.

bandagem [bãda'ʒẽl (*pl* -ns) *f* bandage.

Band-aid® [bãn'dejdʒl *m* Band-Aid®.

bandalheira [bãnda'ʎejral *f* roguery.

bandear-se [15] [bãn'dʒjaxsil *vp*: **~ para** *ou* **a to** side with.

bandeira [bãn'dejra, ral *f* -**1.** [ger] flag; **~ branca** white flag; **~ a meio pau** flag at half-mast; **jurar a ~ to** swear to the flag; **~ dois** taxi night-rate. -**2.** [estandarte] standard. -**3.** [de porta] fanlight. -**4.** *loc*: **dar ~ de que** to let it be known that.

bandeirante [bãndej'rãntʃil ◇ *m* [explorador] expedition member. ◇ *f* [moça] Girl Guide.

bandeirinha [bãn'dejriɲal *m* ESP linesman.

bandeirola [bãndej'rɔlal *f* banderole.

bandeja [bãn'deʒal *f* tray; **dar de ~ to** proffer.

bandejão [bãnde'ʒãwl (*pl* -ões) *m* [UNIV - refeição] meal on a tray; [- refeitório] canteen.

bandido, da [bãn'dʒidu, dal ◇ *m, f* -**1.** [marginal] bandit. -**2.** [mau-caráter] rogue. ◇ *adj fam fig* [malvado, ruim] cruel.

banditismo [bãndʒi'tʃiʒmul *m* banditry.

bando ['bãndul *m* -**1.** [de pessoas, animais] flock; **em ~ in** flocks. -**2.** [quadrilha] gang. -**3.** [facção] group. -**4.** [monte] stack.

bandô [bãn'dol *m* pelmet.

bandoleiro, ra [bãndo'lejru, ral *m, f* bandit.

bandolim [bãndo'lĩl (*pl* -ns) *m* mandolin.

bandolinista [bãndoli'niʃtal *mf* mandolin player.

bangalô [bãŋga'lol *m* bungalow.

Bangkok [bãŋ'kɔkl *n* Bangkok.

bangue-bangue [bãŋgi'bãŋgil *m*: **(filme de) ~** Western (movie).

banguela [bãŋ'gɛlal *adj* toothless.

banha ['bãɲal *f* -**1.** [no homem] fat. -**2.** [de porco] lard.

banhar [4] [bã'ɲa(x)l *vt* -**1.** [dar banho em] to bathe. -**2.** [mergulhar]: **~ algo (em)** to dip sthg (into). -**3.** [molhar]: **~ algo (com/em)** to bathe sthg (with/in). -**4.** [rio, mar] to wash.

➡ **banhar-se** *vp* -**1.** [tomar banho] to bathe. -**2.** [molhar-se]: **~-se em algo** to become bathed in sthg.

banheira [bã'ɲejral *f* -**1.** [para banho] bathtub. -**2.** *fam fig* [carro] charabanc.

banheiro [bã'ɲejrul *m* toilet; **~ feminino/masculino** ladies'/men's toilet.

banhista [bã'ɲiʃtal *mf* bather.

banho ['bãɲul *m* -**1.** [ger] immersion; **tomar um ~ de algo** to immerse o.s. in sthg. -**2.** [de entusiasmo] wave. -**3.** [para asseio]: **~ (de chuveiro)** shower;

tomar ~ to have a shower; **tomar ~ (de banheira)** to take a bath; **~ de assento** hip bath; **~ de espuma** foam bath. -**4.** [na praia, em clube etc]: **tomar um ~ de mar/piscina** to swim in the sea/pool; **tomar um ~ de sol** to sunbathe. -**5.** *fam fig* [surra]: **dar um ~ em alguém** to wipe sb out. -**6.** *loc*: **dar um ~ de algo em alguém** [derramar] to drench sb in sthg; **vai tomar ~!** *fam* get away!

banho-maria [ˌbãɲuma'rial (*pl* banhos-marias, banhos-maria) *m* CULIN double boiler, bain-marie.

banimento [bani'mẽntul *m* banishment.

banir [79] [ba'ni(x)l *vt* to banish.

banjo ['bãnʒul *m* banjo.

banner ['banexl (*pl* banners) *m* COMPUT banner.

banqueiro, ra [bãŋ'kejru, ral *m, f* banker.

banqueta [bãŋ'ketal *f* banquette.

banquete [bãŋ'ketʃil *m* banquet.

banquetear [15] [bãŋke'tʃja(x)l *vt* [festejar] to give a banquet in honour of.

➡ **banquetear-se** *vp* [participar de banquete] to treat o.s. to a wonderful meal.

baque ['bakil *m* -**1.** [choque] shock; **levar um ~ to** be given a shock; **ele levou um baque com a notícia** the news gave him a shock. -**2.** [ruído] thud. -**3.** [queda] fall.

baquear [15] [ba'kja(x)l *vi* -**1.** [cair] to fall. -**2.** *fig* [abalar-se] to be shaken.

bar ['ba(x)l (*pl* -es) *m* bar.·

baralho [ba'raʎul *m* pack.

barão [ba'rãwl (*pl* -ões) *m, f* baron.

barata [ba'ratal *f* cockroach; **estar entregue às ~s** [pessoa] to let o.s. go; [projeto, construção] to fall into a state of neglect.

baratear [15] [bara'tʃja(x)l *vt* to mark down.

barateiro, ra [bara'tʃejru, ral *adj* cut-price.

baratinado, da [baratʃi'nadu, dal *adj* -**1.** [sobrecarregado, apressado] stressed. -**2.** [transtornado - pessoa] upset; [- idéia, atitude] disturbed.

baratinar [4] [baratʃi'na(x)l *vt* -**1.** [atrapalhar, assoberbar] to stress. -**2.** [transtornar] to upset.

barato, ta [ba'ratu, tal ◇ *adj* -**1.** [produto, serviço, preço] cheap. -**2.** [barateiro] cut-price. -**3.** *fam* [ordinário] common or garden. ◇ *adv* [cobrar etc] cheaply. ◇ *m* -**1.** *gír droga* high. -**2.** *fam* [legal]: **que ~!** how cool!; **ser um ~ to** be cool.

barba ['baxbal *f* -**1.** [de homem] beard; **fazer a ~ to** shave; **fazer algo nas ~s de alguém** *fig* to do sthg under sb's nose; **pôr as ~s de molho** *fig* to lie low. -**2.** [de animal] whiskers.

barbada [bax'badal *f* -**1.** *fam* [facilidade]: **ser uma ~ to** be a piece of cake. -**2.** *gír turfe* [palpite] dead cert.

barbado, da [bax'badu, dal *adj* bearded.

Barbados [bax'baduʃl *n* Barbados.

barbante [bax'bãntʃil *m* string.

barbaramente [baxbara'mẽntʃil *adv* -**1.** [cruelmente] brutally. -**2.** [demasiadamente] atrociously.

barbaridade [baxbari'dadʒil *f* -**1.** [crueldade] barbarity. -**2.** [expressando espanto]: **que ~!** great! -**3.** [tolice] absurdity.

barbárie [bax'barjel *f* barbarity.

barbarismo [baxba'riʒmuʃ] *m* barbarism.

bárbaro, ra ['baxbaru, ra] *adj* **-1.** [terrível] barbaric. **-2.** [ótimo] great.

barbatana [baxba'tãna] *f* fin.

barbeador [barbja'do(x)] (*pl* **-es**) *m* razor.

barbear [15] [bax'bja(x)] *vt* to shave.

➡ **barbear-se** *vp* to shave.

barbearia [baxbja'ria] *f* barbershop.

barbeiragem [baxbej'raʒẽ] *f fam* [no trânsito] bad driving; **fazer uma** ~ to drive badly.

barbeiro, ra [bax'bejru, ra] <> *adj fam* [motorista] careless. <> *m* **-1.** [quem corta cabelos, barba] barber. **-2.** [barbearia] barbershop. **-3.** [inseto] kissing bug.

barbicha [bax'biʃa] *fam* <> *f* [cavanhaque] goatee. <> *m* [pessoa de cavanhaque] man with a goatee.

barbitúrico [baxbi'turiku] *m* barbiturate.

barbudo, da [bax'budu, da] <> *adj* bearded. <> *m* bearded man.

barca ['baxka] *f* ship.

barcaça [bax'kasa] *f* barge.

barco ['baxku] *m* boat; ~ **a motor** motor boat; ~ **a remo** rowing boat; ~ **a vela** sailing boat; **deixar** o ~ **correr** *fig* to let matters run their course; **estar no mesmo** ~ *fig* to be in the same boat; **tocar** o ~ **para frente** *fig* to carry on with one's life.

barganha [bax'gãɲa] *f* bargain.

barganhar [4] [baxgã'ɲa(x)] *vt & vi* to bargain.

barítono, na [ba'ritonu, na] <> *adj* baritone. <> *m* baritone.

barlavento [baxla'vẽtu] *m NÁUT* windward; **a** ~ to windward.

barman ['baxmɛ] (*pl* **-s**) *m* barman.

barões [ba'rõjʃ] *pl* ➡ **barão**.

barômetro [ba'rometru] *m* barometer.

baronesa [baro'neza] *f* ➡ **barão**.

barqueiro, ra [bax'kejru, ra] *m, f* boatman.

barra ['baxa] *f* **-1.** [ger] bar; ~ **de chocolate** chocolate bar; ~ **s paralelas** parallel bars. **-2.** [de metal] ingot; ~ **de direção** tiller. **-3.** [de madeira] pole. **-4.** [de balé] barre. **-5.** [traço] score. **-6.** [acabamento] trimming. **-7.** [faixa] strip. **-8.** *GEOGR* sandbar. **-9.** *loc*: **agüentar a** ~ *fam* to stick it out; **forçar a** ~ to make things difficult; **ser uma** ~ *fam* [ser difícil] to be a pain.

barraca [ba'xaka] *f* **-1.** [ger] tent. **-2.** [em feira] stall. **-3.** [de madeira] hut.

barracão [baxa'kãw] (*pl* **-ões**) *m* **-1.** [telheiro] shed. **-2.** [habitação] big house.

barraco [ba'xaku] *m* shack.

barragem [ba'xaʒẽ] (*pl* **-ns**) *f* **-1.** [represa] dam. **-2.** [barreira] barrage.

barranco [ba'xãŋku] *m* **-1.** [ribanceira] ravine. **-2.** [escarpa] escarpment. **-3.** [precipício] precipice.

barra-pesada [ˌbaxape'zada] (*pl* **barras-pesadas**) *fam adj* **-1.** [violento] threatening. **-2.** [difícil] tough.

barrar [4] [ba'xa(x)] *vt* **-1.** [obstruir] to block. **-2.** [excluir] to bar.

barreira [ba'xejra] *f* **-1.** [escarpa] embankment. **-2.** *fig* [dificuldade] barrier. **-3.** [fronteira] roadblock. **-4.** *ESP* hurdle.

barrento, ta [ba'xẽtu, ta] *adj* clayey.

barrete [ba'xetʃi] *m* [gorro] (woolly) hat.

barrica [ba'xika] *f* barrel.

barricada [baxi'kada] *f* barricade.

barriga [ba'xiga] *f* **-1.** *ANAT* belly. **-2.** [saliência] bulge. **-3.** *loc*: **chorar de** ~ **cheia** to complain for no reason; **tirar a** ~ **da miséria** to get one's fill.

barrigudo, da [baxi'gudu, da] *adj* pot-bellied.

barril [ba'xiw] (*pl* **-is**) *m* cask.

barro ['baxu] *m* clay.

barroco, ca [ba'xoku, ka] *adj* baroque.

barrote [ba'xɔtʃi] *m* beam.

barulheira [baru'ʎejra] *f* din.

barulhento, ta [baru'ʎẽtu, ta] *adj* noisy.

barulho [ba'ruʎu] *m* **-1.** [ruído] noise. **-2.** *fig* [confusão] fuss.

basco, ca ['baʃku, ka] <> *adj* Basque. <> *m, f* Basque.

➡ **basco** *m* [língua] Basque.

basculante [baʃku'lãtʃi] *m* swivel window.

base ['bazi] *f* **-1.** [ger] base; ~ **monetária** monetary base. **-2.** [camada] base coat. **-3.** *fig* [fundamento] basis; **com** ~ **em** based on; **na** ~ **de** with the support of.

baseado, da [ba'zjadu, da] *adj* [fundamentado] based.

➡ **baseado** *m fam* [droga] spliff.

basear [15] [ba'zja(x)] *vt*: ~ **algo em algo** to base sthg on sthg.

➡ **basear-se** *vp*: ~**-se em algo** to base o.s. on sthg.

básico, ca ['baziku, ka] *adj* basic.

basílica [ba'zilika] *f* basilica.

basquete [baʃ'ketʃi], **basquetebol** [baʃketʃi'bɔw] *m* basketball.

basta ['baʃta] <> *m*: **dar um** ~ **em** to stop. <> *interj* that's enough!

bastante [baʃ'tãtʃi] <> *adj* **-1.** [suficiente] enough. **-2.** [numeroso] many. <> *adv* enough.

bastão [baʃ'tãw] (*pl* **-ões**) *m* stick.

bastar [4] [baʃ'ta(x)] *vi* [ser suficiente] to be enough.

➡ **bastar-se** *vp* [ser auto-suficiente]: ~**-se a si próprio** to be self-sufficient.

bastardo, da [baʃ'taxdu, da] *adj* bastard.

bastião [baʃtʃi'ãw] (*pl* **-ões**) *m* **-1.** [fortificação] bastion. **-2.** *fig* [sustentáculo] bastion.

bastidor [baʃtʃi'do(x)] *m* [moldura] frame.

➡ **bastidores** *mpl* **-1.** *TEATRO* wings. **-2.** [lado secreto] shadowy side.

bastões [baʃ'tõjʃ] *pl* ➡ **bastão**.

bata ['bata] *f* **-1.** [blusa] blouse. **-2.** [jaleco] white coat, overall.

batalha [ba'taʎa] *f* **-1.** [ger] battle. **-2.** *fig* [esforço] struggle.

batalhador, ra [bataʎa'do(x), ra] *adj* hardworking.

batalhão [bata'ʎãw] (pl -ões) m - **1.** MIL battallion. - **2.** [multidão] crowd.

batalhar [4] [bata'ʎa(x)] vi - **1.** [combater] to battle. - **2.** fig [lutar] to fight.

batata [ba'tata] f potato; ~ **frita** chips UK, fries US; ~ **da perna** calf (of the leg).

batata-doce [ba,tata'dosi] (pl **batatas-doces**) f sweet potato.

bate-boca [,batʃi'boka] (pl **bate-bocas**) m quarrel.

bate-bola [,batʃi'bɔla] (pl **bate-bolas**) m warm-up.

batedeira [bate'dejra] f - **1.** [para fazer bolos etc] whisk. - **2.** [para fazer manteiga] churn.

batedor [bate'do(x)] m - **1.** [polícia] escort. - **2.**: ~ **de carteiras** [ladrão] bag-snatcher.

batelada [bate'lada] f- **1.** [carregamento] boat-load. - **2.** fig [granda quantidade]: **uma** ~ **de** a large number of.

batente [ba'tẽntʃi] m - **1.** [ombreira] doorpost. - **2.** fam [trabalho] work; **pegar firme no** ~ to toil away.

bate-papo [,batʃi'papu] (pl **bate-papos**) m fam chat.

bater [5] [ba'te(x)] <> vt- **1.** [ger] to beat; ~ **o pé** to stamp one's foot. - **2.** [datilografar]: ~ **algo (à máquina)** to type sthg out. - **3.** [fechar com força] to slam. - **4.** [foto] to take. - **5.** [usar todo dia] to wear every day. - **6.** fam [furtar]: ~ **carteira** to pick-pocket. <> vi - **1.** [dar pancadas]: ~ **em alguém/ algo** to hit sb/sthg. - **2.** [colidir]: ~ **em algo** to collide with sthg. - **3.** [horas, sino] to strike. - **4.** [coração] to beat. - **5.** loc: **não** ~ **bem** fam [ser meio doido] to be off one's rocker.

➤ **bater-se** vp: ~-**se por** to fight for.

bateria [bate'ria] f - **1.** [de cozinha] set of kitchen utensils. - **2.** [MÚS - instrumentos de percussão] percussion; [- conjunto de pratos, caixa e bombo] drum kit. - **3.** ELETR battery.

baterista [bate'riʃta] mf [MÚS - percussionista] percussionist; [- que toca bateria] drummer.

batido, da [ba'tʃidu, da] <> adj - **1.** [ger] beaten. - **2.** [comum demais] worn out. <> adv [às pressas] in a hurry.

➤ **batida** f - **1.** [ger] beat. - **2.** [de relógio, sino] strike. - **3.** [à porta] knock. - **4.** AUTO collision. - **5.** [bebida] crush.

batina [ba'tʃina] f RELIG cassock.

batismal [batʃiʒ'maw] (pl -**ais**) adj baptismal.

batismo [ba'tʃiʒmu] m baptism.

batistério [batʃiʃ'tɛrju] m baptistery.

batizado, da [batʃi'zadu, da] <> adj baptized. <> m baptism.

batizar [4] [batʃi'za(x)] vt - **1.** [ger] to baptize. - **2.** [apelidar] to nickname.

batom [ba'tõ] (pl -**ns**) m lipstick.

batucada [batu'kada] f street gathering for samba music and expression.

batucar [12] [batu'ka(x)] vi - **1.** MÚS to dance and sing the batuque. - **2.** [martelar] to hammer.

batuque [ba'tuki] m Afro-Brazilian dance.

batuta [ba'tuta] <> f [de maestro] baton. <> adj

fam [exímio]: **ser** ~ **em algo** to be a maestro in sthg.

baú [ba'u] m trunk.

baunilha [baw'niʎa] f vanilla.

bazar [ba'za(x)] (pl -**es**) m - **1.** [ger] bazaar. - **2.** [loja] bazaar.

bazuca [ba'zuka] f bazooka.

BB (abrev de **Banco do Brasil**) m Brazilian state-owned bank.

BC (abrev de **Banco Central do Brasil**) m central bank of Brazil.

bê-á-bá [bea'ba] m - **1.** [abecedário] alphabet. - **2.** fig [noções básicas] ABC.

beatitude [beatʃi'tudʒi] f beatitude.

beato, ta [be'atu, ta] <> adj - **1.** [beatificado] blessed. - **2.** [fanático religioso] churchy. <> m - **1.** [quem foi beatificado] beatified person. - **2.** [devoto] worshipper.

bêbado, da [l'bebadu, da] <> adj drunk. <> m, f - **1.** [que bebe regularmente] drunkard. - **2.** [que bebeu demais] drunk.

bebê [be'be] m baby.

bebedeira [bebe'dejra] f - **1.** [estado do bêbado] drunkenness; **tomar uma** ~ to get drunk. - **2.** [ato de se embebedar] drinking bout.

bêbedo [l'bebedu] adj ➤ **bêbado**.

bebedouro [bebe'doru] m - **1.** [aparelho] drinking fountain. - **2.** [para animais] drinking trough.

beber [5] [be'be(x)] <> vt - **1.** [tomar líquido] to drink. - **2.** [absorver] to soak up. <> vi - **1.** [tomar bebida alcoólica] to have a drink. - **2.** [embriagar-se] to get drunk.

bebericar [12] [beberi'ka(x)] <> vt [beber degustando] to sip. <> vi [beber pouco] to sip.

beberrão, rrona [bebe'xãw, xona] <> adj [que bebe muito] heavy drinking. <> m [ébrio] heavy drinker.

bebida [be'bida] f - **1.** [líquido potável] drink. - **2.** [alcoólica] (alcoholic) drink.

bebível [be'bivew] (pl -**eis**) adj [tolerável] drinkable.

beca [l'bɛka] f - **1.** [toga] robe. - **2.** fig [magistratura] magistrature.

beça [l'bɛsa] f: **à** ~ [em grande quantidade] in large numbers; [ao extremo] **gostei à** ~ **da nova revista** I enjoyed the new magazine very much.

beco [l'beku] m alley; **estar num** ~ **sem saída** to be in a catch-22 situation.

bedelho [be'deʎu] m latch; **meter o** ~ **em** [intrometer-se] to stick one's oar in.

beduíno, na [be'dwinu, na] <> adj Bedouin. <> m, f Bedouin.

bege [l'bɛʒi] <> adj inv beige. <> m beige.

begônia [be'gonja] f begonia.

beiço [l'bejsu] m lip.

beiçudo, da [bej'sudu, da] adj pouting.

beija-flor [,bejʒa'flo(x)] (pl **beija-flores**) m hummingbird.

beijar [4] [bej'ʒa(x)] vt to kiss.

➤ **beijar-se** vp to kiss.

beijo [l'bejʒu] m kiss; **dar um** ~ **em alguém** to give sb a kiss.

beijoca [bej'ʒɔka] f *fam* smackeroo.

beira ['bejra] f edge; **à ~ de** [na borda] on the edge of; *fig* on the brink of.

beirada [bej'rada] f **-1.** [beira] side. **-2.** [bocado] slither.

beira-mar [ˌbejra'ma(x)] f: **à ~** by the sea.

beirar [4] [bej'ra(x)] vt **-1.** [caminhar à beira de] to walk alongside. **-2.** [estar à beira de] to be on the edge of. **-3.** [estar próximo de] to be close to.

Beirute [bej'rutʃi] n Beirut.

beisebol [bejze'bɔw] m baseball.

belas-artes [ˌbɛla'zaxtʃiʃ] fpl fine arts.

beldade [bew'dadʒi] f **-1.** [beleza] beauty. **-2.** [mulher bonita] beautiful woman.

beleléu [bele'lɛw] loc adv fam: **ir para o ~** [morrer] to die; [desaparecer] to disappear; [fracassar] to fail.

Belém [be'lẽj] n **-1.** [no Brasil] Belém. **-2.** [na Palestina] Bethlehem.

beleza [be'leza] f **-1.** [de lugar etc] beauty. **-2.** [mulher bela] beautiful woman; **ser uma ~** [pessoa, lugar] to be beautiful.

belga ['bɛwga] <> adj Belgian. <> m, f Belgian.

Bélgica ['bɛwʒika] n Belgium.

Belgrado [bew'gradu] n Belgrade.

beliche [be'liʃi] m bunk bed.

bélico, ca ['bɛliku, ka] adj war (antes de subst).

belicoso, cosa [beli'kozu, kɔza] adj **-1.** [aguerrido] quarrelsome. **-2.** [pronto para a guerra] bellicose. **-3.** [que incita à guerra] war-mongering.

beligerante [beliʒe'rãntʃi] adj belligerent.

beliscão [beliʃ'kãw] (pl **-ões**) m pinch; **dar um ~ alguém** to pinch sb.

beliscar [12] [beliʃ'ka(x)] <> vt **-1.** [pessoa] to pinch. **-2.** fig [comida] to pick at (food). <> vi fig [comer] to pick at one's food.

beliscões [beliʃ'kõjʃ] pl ⊳ **beliscão**.

Belize [be'lizi] n Belize.

belo, la ['bɛlu, la] <> adj **-1.** [perfeito] lovely. **-2.** [sublime] wonderful. **-3.** (antes de subst) [considerável] fine. **-4.** (antes de subst) [gratificante] excellent. **-5.** [indefinido]: **um ~ dia ...** one fine day ... <> m [estética] beauty.

Belo Horizonte [ˌbɛlori'zõntʃi] n Belo Horizonte.

bel-prazer [ˌbɛwpra'ze(x)] m: **ao seu ~** to one's heart's content.

beltrano [bew'trãnu] m so-and-so.

bem ['bẽj] <> adv **-1.** [ger] well. **-2.** [muito, bastante] very. **-3.** [exatamente] exactly; **~ ali** right there. **-4.** [de bom grado]: **~ que eu gostaria de ajudar, mas não posso** I'd very much like to help, but I can't. **-5.** [expressando opinião]: **estar ~** [de saúde] to be well; [de aspecto] to look good; [financeiramente] to be well-off; **cair ~** [comida] to go down well; **fazer ~ a alguém** [suj: exercício etc] to be good for sb; **ficar** ou **cair ~** [atitude] to be suitable; **ficar ~ em alguém** [roupa] to suit sb well. **-6.** [saudando]: **tudo ~?** fam how are you?; **tudo ~** [em resposta] fine. **-7.** [concordando]: **tá ~** all right. **-8.** [em conclusão, introdução] well now. **-9.** [em congratulação]: **muito ~!** well done! <> m **-1.** [ger] good. **-2.** [pessoa amada] loved one. **-3.** fam [forma de

tratamento]: **meu ~** my darling. **-4.** [patrimônio] assets (pl).

⇒ **bens** mpl **-1.** [patrimônio] assets. **-2.** [produtos]: **~ de consumo** consumer goods.

⇒ **bem como** loc adv as well as.

⇒ **nem bem** loc adv scarcely.

⇒ **se bem que** loc conj even though.

bem-acabado, da [bẽjaka'badu, da] (mpl **-s**, fpl **-s**) adj well-finished.

bem-agradecido, da [bẽjagrade'sidu, da] (mpl **-s**, fpl **-s**) adj grateful.

bem-apessoado, da [bẽjape'swadu, da] (mpl **-s**, fpl **-s**) adj presentable.

bem-arrumado, da [bẽjaxu'madu, da] (mpl **-s**, fpl **-s**) adj **-1.** [pessoa] well dressed. **-2.** [casa] well appointed.

bem-casado, da [bẽjka'zadu, da] (mpl **-s**, fpl **-s**) adj happily married.

bem-comportado, da [bẽjkõnpox'tadu, da] (mpl **-s** [-ʃ], fpl **-s** [-ʃ]) adj well behaved.

bem-conceituado, da [bẽjkõnsej'twadu, da] (mpl **-s** [-ʃ], fpl **-s** [-ʃ]) adj well respected.

bem-disposto, ta [bẽjdʒiʃ'poʃtu, ta] adj good-humoured.

bem-educado, da [bẽjedu'kadu, da] (mpl **-s**, fpl **-s**) adj well bred.

bem-estar [bẽjʃ'ta(x)] m well-being.

bem-feito, ta [bẽj'fejtu, ta] (mpl **-s**, fpl **-s**) adj **-1.** [bem-acabado] well made. **-2.** [de belas formas] elegant. **-3.** [quando algo ruim ocorre]: **~ serves you right!**

bem-humorado, da [bẽjumo'radu, da] (mpl **-s**, fpl **-s**) adj good-humoured.

bem-intencionado, da [bẽjĩntẽnsjo'nadu, da] (mpl **-s**, fpl **-s**) adj well meaning.

bem-me-quer [bẽjmi'kɛ(x)] m daisy.

bem-nascido, da [bẽjna'sidu, da] (mpl **-s**, fpl **-s**) adj well born.

bem-passado, da [bẽjpa'sadu, da] (mpl **-s**, fpl **-s**) adj [carne] well cooked.

bem-sucedido, da [bẽjsuse'dʒidu, da] (mpl **-s**, fpl **-s**) adj successful.

bem-te-vi [bẽjtʃi'vi] (pl **bem-te-vis**) m great kiskadee.

bem-vindo, da [bẽj'vĩndu, da] adj welcome.

bem-visto, ta [bẽj'viʃtu, ta] (mpl **-s**, fpl **-s**) adj respected.

benchmarking [bɛnʃmarkiŋ] m ECON benchmarking.

benção [bẽnsãw] (pl **-ções**) f blessing.

bendito, ta [bẽn'dʒitu, ta] adj [abençoado] blessed.

bendizer [29] [bẽndʒi'ze(x)] vt **-1.** [falar bem de] to praise. **-2.** [abençoar] to bless.

beneficência [benefi'sẽnsja] f **-1.** [bondade] kindness. **-2.** [caridade] charity.

beneficente [benefi'sẽntʃi] adj **-1.** [bondoso] kind. **-2.** [caridoso] charitable.

beneficiado, da [benefi'sjadu, da] <> adj [que se beneficiou] benefitting. <> m [beneficiário] beneficiary.

beneficiar [16] [benefi'sja(x)] *vt* **-1.** [favorecer] to benefit. **-2.** [processar] to process. **-3.** [melhorar] to improve.
➡ **beneficiar-se** *vp* [favorecer-se] to profit.
beneficiário, ria [benefi'sjarju, rja] ⟷ *adj* favoured. ⟷ *m* [herdeiro beneficiado] beneficiary.
benefício [bene'fisju] *m* benefit.
benéfico, ca [be'nɛfiku, ka] *adj* **-1.** [ger] beneficial. **-2.** [favorável] favourable.
benemérito, ta [bene'meritu, ta] ⟷ *adj* **-1.** [que merece o bem] deserving. **-2.** [digno de honras] praiseworthy. **-3.** [ilustre] renowned. ⟷ *m* worthy person.
beneplácito [bene'plasitu] *m* [aprovação] approval.
benevolência [benevo'lẽnsja] *f* **-1.** [boa-vontade] benevolence. **-2.** [complacência] friendliness. **-3.** [afeto] kindness.
benevolente [benevo'lẽntʃi] *adj* **-1.** [bondoso] kindly. **-2.** [complacente] friendly.
benévolo, la [benɛ'volu, la] *adj* **-1.** [benevolente] benevolent. **-2.** [tolerante] tolerant.
benfazejo, ja [bẽnfa'zeʒu, ʒal] *adj* [benéfico] beneficial.
benfeitor, ra [bẽnfej'to(x), ra] ⟷ *adj* [benévolo] benevolent. ⟷ *m* [aquele que faz benfeitoria] benefactor.
benfeitoria [bẽnfejto'ria] *f* **-1.** [obra de melhoria] improvement. **-2.** [benefício] benefit.
bengala [bẽŋ'gala] *f* walking stick.
benigno, na [be'nignu, na] *adj* **-1.** [benévolo] gentle. **-2.** [complacente] friendly. **-3.** *MED* benign.
benjamim [bẽnʒa'mĩ] *(pl* **-ns)** *m ELETR* adaptor.
benquisto, ta [bẽn'kiʃtu, ta] *adj* **-1.** [querido] loved. **-2.** [bem-aceito] welcomed.
bens ['bẽjʃ] *pl* ⊳ **bem.**
bento, ta ['bẽntu, ta] ⟷ *pp* ⊳ **benzer.** ⟷ *adj* holy.
benzedeira [bẽnze'dejra] *f* healer.
benzer [5] [bẽn'ze(x)] *vt* [abençoar] to bless.
➡ **benzer-se** *vp* [fazer o sinal-da-cruz] to make the sign of the cross.
benzina [bẽn'zina] *f* benzine.
berbere [bex'bɛri], **berber** [bex'bɛ(x)] ⟷ *adj* Berber. ⟷ *mf* Berber.
➡ **berbere** *m* [língua] Berber.
berçário [bex'sarju] *m* nursery.
berço ['bexsu] *rm* **-1.** cradle. **-2.** *loc*: nascer em ~ de ouro to be born with a silver spoon in one's mouth.
Berlim [bex'lĩ] *n* Berlin.
berimbau [berĩ'baw] *m MÚS* berimbau, *small Brazilian percussion instrument.*
berinjela [berĩ'ʒɛla] *f* aubergine *UK*, eggplant *US*.
berlinda [bex'lĩda] *f*: estar na ~ to be the butt of jokes.
berloque [bex'lɔki] *m* trinket.
bermuda [bex'muda] *f* Bermuda shorts *(pl).*
berrante [bex'ãntʃi] *adj* gaudy.
barrar [4] [ba'xa(x)] *vt* to bar.

berreiro [be'xejru] *m* **-1.** [gritaria] shouting. **-2.** [choradeira] wailing.
berro ['bɛxu] *m* bellow; estar aos ~s to be bellowing; falar aos ~s to talk too loud.
besouro [be'zoru] *m* beetle.
besta ['beʃta] *fam* ⟷ *adj* **-1.** [pedante] pedantic. **-2.** [idiota] idiotic; fazer alguém de ~ to make a fool of sb. **-3.** [surpreso]: ficar ~ to be dumbfounded. **-4.** [insignificante] insignificant. ⟷ *f* **-1.** [animal] beast. **-2.** *fam* [pessoa pedante] pedant. **-3.** *fam* [pessoa idiota] fool.
bestalhão, lhona [beʃta'ʎãw, ʎona] *(mpl* **-lhões,** *fpl* **-s)** ⟷ *adj* **-1.** [pateta] idiotic. **-2.** [ignorante] ignorant. ⟷ *m* **-1.** [paspalhão] simpleton. **-2.** [ignorante] ignoramus.
bestial [beʃ'tjaw] *(pl* **-ais)** *adj* **-1.** [brutal] bestial. **-2.** [repugnante] depraved.
bestialidade [beʃtʃjali'dadʒi] *f* bestiality.
bestificar [12] [beʃtʃifi'ka(x)] *vt* **-1.** [bestializar] to bestialize. **-2.** [assombrar] to dumbfound. **-3.** [imbecilizar] to stupefy.
best-seller [,bɛʃt'sɛle(x)] *(pl* **-s)** *m* best-seller.
besuntar [4] [bezũn'ta(x)] *vt* **-1.** [untar]: ~ de *ou* com to grease with. **-2.** [lambuzar]: ~ de *ou* com to smear.
beterraba [bete'xaba] *f* beetroot.
betoneira [beto'nejra] *f* cement mixer.
betume [be'tumi] *m* bitumen.
bexiga [be'ʃiga] *f ANAT* bladder.
bezerro, rra [be'zexu, xa] *m,f* calf; pensar na morte da bezerra to daydream.
bibelô [bibe'lo] *m* [objeto decorativo] knick-knack.
bíblia ['biblja] *f* bible.
➡ **Bíblia** *f* Bible.
bíblico, ca ['bibliku, ka] *adj* biblical.
bibliografia [bibljogra'fia] *f* bibliography.
biblioteca [bibljo'tɛka] *f* library.
bibliotecário, ria [bibljote'karju, rja] *m, f* librarian.
biblioteconomia [bibljotekono'mia] *f* librarianship.
biboca [bi'bɔka] *f* **-1.** [casebre] hut. **-2.** [venda] small shop.
bica ['bika] *f* water outlet; suar em ~s to be streaming with perspiration.
bicada [bi'kada] *f* peck.
bicama [bi'kãma] *f* sofa bed.
bicampeão, peã [bikãnpjãw, pja] *(mpl* **-peões,** *fpl* **-s)** ⟷ *adj* twice champion. ⟷ *m* twice champion.
bicar [12] [bi'ka(x)] *vt* **-1.** [dar bicadas] to peck. **-2.** [bebericar] to sip.
bicarbonato [bikaxbo'natu] *m* bicarbonate.
bicentenário, ria [bisẽnte'narju, rja] ⟷ *adj* bicentennial. ⟷ *m* bicentenary.
bíceps ['biseps] *m (inv)* biceps.
bicha ['biʃa] *f* **-1.** [lombriga] earthworm. **-2.** *fam pej* [efeminado] fairy.
bichado, da [bi'ʃadu, da] *adj* worm-eaten.
bicheiro [bi'ʃejru] *m* [em jogo do bicho] bookie *(collecting money for illegal lottery bets).*

bicho [ˈbiʃu] *m* **-1.** [animal] animal. **-2.** [inseto, piolho] insect. **-3.** *fam* [pessoa feia]: **ser um ~** to be enough to scare one's own mother. **-4.** *fam* [sujeito] mate. **-5.** [loc]: **ver que ~ dá** to see what will come of it; **virar ~** *fig* to turn nasty.

bicho-da-seda [ˌbiʃudaˈseda] (*pl* **bichos-da-seda**) *m* silkworm.

bicho-de-sete-cabeças (*pl* **bichos-de-sete-cabeças**) *fam m* **-1.** [coisa difícil]: **ser um ~** to be hideous; **fazer um ~ de algo** to make a mountain out of a molehill. **-2.** [coisa que amedronta]: **ser um ~** to be a hideous thing.

bicho-do-mato [ˌbiʃuduˈmatul] (*pl* **bichos-do-mato**) *m fig* [pessoa] loner.

bicho-papão [ˌbiʃopaˈpãw] (*pl* **bichos-papões**) *m* **-1.** [imagem] bogeyman. **-2.** *fig* [coisa ou pessoa que amedronta]: **o diretor é severo mas não é nenhum ~** the manager is strict but he won't eat you; **a idéia do fim do mundo é um ~** the idea of the end of the world is a terrifying prospect.

bicicleta [besiˈklɛta] *f* bicycle; **~ ergométrica** ergonometric bicycle; **andar de ~** to ride a bike.

bicicletário [bisikleˈtarju] *m* cycle rack.

bico [ˈbiku] *m* **-1.** [de ave] beak. **-2.** [ponta] tip. **-3.** *fam* [boca] mouth; **abrir o ~** to pipe up; **calar o ~** to pipe down. **-4.** [chupeta] teat. **-5.** *fam* [biscate] odd job. **-6.** ANAT : **~ do peito** nipple. **-7.** [de gás] burner.

bico-de-papagaio [ˌbikudʒipapaˈgaju] (*pl* **bicos-de-papagaio**) *m* **-1.** [doença] osteophyte on the spinal column. **-2.** [nariz adunco] hooked nose.

bicolor [bikoˈlo(x)] *adj* bicoloured.

bicudo, da [biˈkudu, da] <> *adj* **-1.** [que tem bico] beaked. **-2.** [pontiagudo] pointed. **-3.** *fam* [difícil] painful. <> *m* [peixe] boulengerella.

BID (*abrev de* **Banco Interamericano de Desenvolvimento**) *m* IDB.

bidê [biˈde] *m* bidet.

bidimensional [bidʒimẽsjoˈnaw] (*pl* **-ais**) *adj* two-dimensional.

Bielo-Rússia [bjɛloˈxusja] *n* Belarus.

bielo-russo, sa, bielorusso, sa [bjɛloˈxusu, sa] <> *adj* Belorussian. <> *m, f* Belorussian.

bienal [bjeˈnaw] (*pl* **-ais**) <> *adj* biennial. <> *f* biennial.

biênio [ˈbjenju] *m* two years.

bife [ˈbifi] *m* **-1.** CULIN steak; **~ a cavalo** steak with a fried egg; **~ a milanesa** steak milanese. **-2.** [pele humana]: **tirar um ~** to nick one's skin.

bifocal [bifoˈkaw] (*pl* **-ais**) *adj* bifocal.

bifurcado, da [bifuxˈkadu, da] *adj* forked.

bifurcar [12] [bifuxˈka(x)] *vi* to fork.

➤ **bifurcar-se** *vp* to fork.

bigamia [bigaˈmia] *f* bigamy.

bígamo, ma [ˈbigamu, ma] <> *adj* bigamous. <> *m, f* bigamist.

bigode [biˈgodʒi] *m* moustache.

bigodudo, da [bigoˈdudu, da] *adj* moustached.

bigorna [biˈgoxna] *f* anvil.

bijuteria [biʒuteˈria] *f* piece of jewellery.

bilateral [bilateˈraw] (*pl* **-ais**) *adj* bilateral.

bilhão [biˈʎãw] (*pl* **-ões**) *num* billion.

bilhar [biˈʎa(x)] (*pl* **-es**) *m* **-1.** [jogo] billiards *(sg)*. **-2.** [estabelecimento] billiard hall.

bilhete [biˈʎetʃi] *m* **-1.** [ger] ticket; **~ de ida** one-way ticket; **~ de ida e volta** return ticket. **-2.** [mensagem] note; **dar o ~ azul** to sack; **receber o ~ azul** to be given the sack.

bilheteiro, ra [biʎeˈtejru, ra] *m, f* ticket clerk.

bilheteria [biʎeteˈria] *f* ticket office.

bilhões [biˈʎõjʃ] *pl* ➪ **bilhão**.

biliar [biliˈa(x)] *adj* bilious; **vesícula ~** gall bladder.

bilíngüe [biˈlĩgwi] *adj* bilingual.

bilionário, ria [biljoˈnarju, rja] <> *adj* billionaire. <> *m, f* billionaire.

bílis [ˈbiliʃ] *f (inv)* bile.

bimensal [bimẽˈsaw] (*pl* **-ais**) *adj* fortnightly, twice-monthly.

bimestral [bimeʃˈtraw] (*pl* **-ais**) *adj* two-monthly.

bimestre [biˈmeʃtri] *m* two-month period.

bimotor [bimoˈto(x)] <> *adj* twin-engined. <> *m* twin-engined plane.

binário, ria [biˈnarju, rja] *adj* binary.

bingo [ˈbĩgu] *m* bingo.

binóculo [biˈnɔkulu] *m* binoculars *(pl)*.

binômio [biˈnomju] *m* MAT binomial.

biodegradável [bjwdegraˈdavew] (*pl* **-eis**) *adj* biodegradable.

biodiversidade [bjwdʒivexsiˈdadʒi] *f* biodiversity.

BIODIVERSIDADE

Over 20% of the world's existing plants can be found in Brazil; the country's animal biodiversity is equally rich: Brazilian fauna includes not only 10% of all amphibians and mammals in the world, but also 17% of the planet's existing birds.

---

bioengenharia [biowẽʒeɲaˈria] *f* bioengineering.

biofísica [bjoˈfizika] *f* biophysics *(sg)*.

biografia [bjograˈfia] *f* biography.

biográfico, ca [bjoˈgrafiku, ka] *adj* biographical.

biógrafo, fa [biˈjɔgrafu, fa] *m, f* biographer.

biologia [bjoloˈʒia] *f* biology.

biológico, ca [bjoˈlɔʒiku, ka] *adj* biological.

biólogo, ga [biˈjɔlogu, ga] *m, f* biologist.

biombo [ˈbjõbu] *m* screen.

biônico, ca [biˈjoniku, ka] *adj* **-1.** [relativo à biônica] bionic. **-2.** *irôn & POL* undemocratically appointed *politician.*

biópsia [bjɔpˈsia] *f* biopsy.

bioquímica [bjoˈkimika] *f* biochemistry.

biorritmo [bjoˈxitʃmu] *m* biorhythm.

BIOS (*abrev de* **Basic Input/Output System**) *m* BIOS.

biosfera [bjosˈfɛra] *f* biosphere.

bipartidário, ria [bipaxtʃiˈdarju, rja] *adj* bipartisan.

bipartidarismo [bipaxtʃida'riʒmu] *m* bipartisanship.

bípede ['bipedʒi] *adj* biped.

biqueira [bi'kejra] *f* **-1.** [ger] tip. **-2.** [calha] gutter.

biquíni [bi'kinil] *m* bikini.

BIRD (*abrev de* **Banco Internacional de Reconstrução e Desenvolvimento**) *m* IBRD.

birita [bi'rita] *f fam* (alcoholic) drink.

Birmânia [bix'mãnja] *n* Burma.

birmanês, esa [bixma'neʃ, ezal] <> *adj* Burmese. <> *m, f* Burmese.
    birmanês *m* [língua] Burmese.

birosca [bi'rɔʃka] *f* **-1.** [pequena mercearia] small shop. **-2.** [botequim] snack bar.

birra ['bixa] *f* **-1.** [teimosia] temper; **fazer** ~ to throw a tantrum. **-2.** [irritação, zanga]: **ficar de** ~ **com alguém** to be at loggerheads with sb.

birrento, ta [bi'xẽntu, ta] *adj* wilful.

biruta [bi'ruta] <> *adj* [pessoa] mad. <> *m* [pessoa] madman. <> *f* [dispositivo] windsock.

bis ['biʃ] <> *m* encore; **pedir um** ~ to demand an encore; **fazer** *ou* **dar um** ~ to give an encore. <> *interj* encore!

bisar [4] [bi'za(x)] *vt* **-1.** [pedir repetição de] to demand an encore. **-2.** [repetir] to give an encore.

bisavô, vó [biza'vo, vɔ] *m, f* great-grandfather (*f* great-grandmother).
    bisavós *mpl* great-grandparents.

bisbilhotar [4] [biʒbiʎo'ta(x)] <> *vt* [examinar] to pry. <> *vi fam* [fazer mexericos] to gossip.

bisbilhoteiro, ra [biʒbiʎo'tejru, ra] <> *adj* **-1.** [curioso] nosy. **-2.** [mexeriqueiro] gossipy. <> *m, f* **-1.** [pessoa curiosa] nosy parker. **-2.** [pessoa mexeriqueira] gossip.

bisbilhotice [biʒ'biʎo'tʃisil] *f* **-1.** [curiosidade] meddling. **-2.** [mexerico] gossip.

biscate [biʃ'katʃi] *m fam* odd job.

biscateiro, ra [biʃka'tejru, ra] *m, f* odd-job man.

biscoito [biʃ'kojtu] *m* biscuit; ~ **amanteigado** buttery biscuit.

bisnaga [biʒ'nagal] *f* **-1.** [pão] baguette. **-2.** [tubo] tube.

bisneto, ta [biʒ'nɛtu, ta] *m, f* great-grandchild.

bisonho, nha [bi'zɔɲu, ɲal] *adj* **-1.** [inexperiente] inexperienced. **-2.** [novato] novice.

bispado [biʃ'padul] *m* **-1.** [diocese] diocese. **-2.** [dignidade episcopal] episcopate.

bispo ['biʃpul] *m* bishop.

bissexto, ta [bi'sejʃtu, ta] *adj*: **ano** ~ leap year.
    bissexto *m* 29 February.

bissexual [bisek'swawl] (*pl* -ais) <> *adj* bisexual. <> *m* bisexual.

bisturi [biʃtu'ri] *m* scalpel.

bit ['bitʃi] *m* COMPUT bit.

bitmap ['bitimapil] *m* COMPUT bitmap.

bitola [bi'tɔlal] *f* gauge.

bizarro, a [bi'zaxu, xal] *adj* bizarre.

blablablá [blabla'bla] *m fam* chatter.

black-tie [blɛk'taj] *m* black tie, dinner jacket.

blasé [bla'ze] *adj* blasé.

blasfemar [4] [blaʃfe'ma(x)] <> *vt* RELIG to take in vain. <> *vi* **-1.** RELIG to swear. **-2.** [praguejar]: ~ **contra** to defame.

blasfêmia [blaʃ'femja] *f* **-1.** RELIG blasphemy. **-2.** [ultraje] defamation.

blasfemo, ma [blaʃ'femu, ma] *adj* [palavras] blasphemous.
    blasfemo *m* [pessoa] blasphemer.

blazer ['blejzɛ(x)] (*pl* -es) *m* blazer.

blecaute [ble'kawtʃil] *m* blackout.

blefar [4] [ble'fa(x)] <> *vi* **-1.** [em jogo] to bluff. **-2.** [tapear] to deceive. <> *vt* [tapear] to trick.

blefe ['blɛfi] *m* **-1.** [truque] trick. **-2.** [no jogo] bluff.

blindado, da [blĩ'dadu, da] *adj* armoured.

blindagem [blĩ'daʒẽl] *f* armour.

blitz ['blitiʃ] (*pl* blitze) *f* blitz.

bloco ['blɔku] *m* **-1.** [ger] block. **-2.** [papel] pad. **-3.** [grupo]: ~ **de Carnaval** group of carnival revellers.
    em bloco *loc adv* en bloc.

bloquear [15] [blo'kja(x)] *vt* **-1.** [cercar] to surround. **-2.** [impedir] to block off. **-3.** PSIC to block.

bloqueio [blo'kejul *m* **-1.** [cerco] blockade. **-2.** [obstrução] obstacle; MED, PSIC blockage. **-3.** ECON : ~ **econômico** economic blockade.

blue chip [bluw'ʃipil] (*pl* blue chips) *f* ECON blue chip.

blues ['bluwʃ] *m* (*inv*) MÚS blues.

blusa ['bluzal *f* blouse.

BM (*abrev de* **Banco Mundial**) *m* World Bank.

BM & F (*abrev de* **Bolsa de Mercadorias e Futuros**) *f Brazilian commodities and futures market.*

BNDES (*abrev de* **Banco Nacional de Desenvolvimento Econômico e Social**) *m Brazilian bank for financing economic and social development.*

BNH (*abrev de* **Banco Nacional da Habitação**) *m national bank for financing low-paid workers to buy their own homes.*

BO (*abrev de* **Boletim de Ocorrência**) *m Brazilian crime report.*

boa ['boal *f* ⊳ bom.

boa-fé [‚boa'fɛ] *f* **-1.** [ger] good faith; **agir de** ~ to act in good faith. **-2.** [ingenuidade] naivety.

boa-gente [‚boa'ʒẽntʃi] *adj* (*inv*) trustworthy.

boa-noite [‚boa'nojtʃi] (*pl* boas-noites) *f* good night.

boa-pinta [‚boa'pĩtal (*pl* boas-pintas) *fam* <> *adj* good-looking. <> *m* looker.

boa-praça [‚boa'prasal (*pl* boas-praças) *UK fam adj* kind-hearted.

boas-festas [‚boaʒ'fɛʃtaʃ] *fpl inv* [felicitações - no Natal] Happy Christmas; [- no Ano-Novo] Happy New Year.

boas-vindas [‚boaʒ'vĩdaʃ] *fpl inv* welcome.

boa-tarde [‚boa'taxdʒil (*pl* boas-tardes) *f* good afternoon.

boataria [bwata'rial *f* rumour.

boate ['bwatʃil *f* nightclub.

boateiro, ra [bwa'tejru, ra] <> *adj* gossipy. <> *m, f* rumour-monger.

boato ['bwatu] *m* rumour.

boa-vida [ˌboa'vida] (*pl* **boas-vidas**) *m* bon vivant.

Boa Vista [ˌboa'viʃta] *n* Boa Vista.

bobagem [bo'baʒẽ] (*pl* **-ns**) ⬦ *f* **-1**. [coisa supérflua] frippery. **-2**. [dito] rubbish. **-3**. [fato sem importância] trifle. ⬦ *adj* [desaconselhável]: **ser ~ fazer algo** to be foolish to do sthg.

bobalhão, lhona [boba'ʎaw, ʎona] (*mpl* **-lhões**, *fpl* **-s**) *m, f* fool.

bobeada [bo'bjada] *f fam* foolishness; **dar uma ~** to be a fool.

bobear [15] [bo'bja(x)] *vi* **-1**. [fazer besteira] to make a mistake. **-2**. [deixar-se enganar] to be tricked. **-3**. [descuidar-se] to be careless. **-4**. [perder uma chance] to blow it.

bobeira [bo'bejra] *f* mistake; **marcar ~** *fam* [ser enganado] to be a fool; [perder uma chance] to blow it.

bobina [bo'bina] *f* bobbin.

bobo, ba ['bobu, ba] ⬦ *adj* foolish. ⬦ *m, f* fool.

  ➧ **bobo** *m*: **~ da corte** court jester.

bobó [bo'bɔ] *m CULIN* : **~ (de camarão)** shrimp bobó.

boboca [bo'bɔka] ⬦ *mf* idiot. ⬦ *adj* idiotic.

boca ['boka] *f* **-1**. [ger] mouth; **~ do estômago** *MED* cardia; **~ da noite** nightfall; **cala a ~!** *fam* shut up! **-2**. [de calça] top. **-3**. *fam* [emprego] opening. **-4**. *fam* [pessoa para alimentar] mouth to feed. **-5**. *POL* : **~ de urna** ballot-box slit. **-6**. *loc*: **bater ~** to argue; **botar a ~ no trombone** *fam* [denunciar] to complain loudly; **falar da ~ para fora** not to mean what one is saying.

  ➧ **de boca** *loc adv* unwritten.

boca-a-boca [ˌboka'boka] ⬦ *m MED* mouth-to-mouth resuscitation. ⬦ *adj*: **respiração ~** kiss of life.

boca-de-fumo [ˌbokadʒi'fumu] (*pl* **bocas-de-fumo**) *f fam* drug-dealing patch.

boca-de-sino [ˌbokadʒi'sinu] *adj inv* flared, bell-bottomed.

bocadinho [boka'dʒiɲu] *m* **-1**. [pequena quantidade]: **um ~ (de)** a little bit (of). **-2**. [tempo curto]: **um ~** a little bit.

bocado [bo'kadu] *m* **-1**. [grande quantidade]: **um ~ de** quite a lot of. **-2**. [pedaço, porção]: **um ~ (de)** a bit (of). **-3**. [mordida] mouthful.

  ➧ **um bocado** *loc adv* [bastante] quite.

bocal [bo'kaw] (*pl* **-ais**) *m* **-1**. [ger] mouth. **-2**. *MÚS* mouthpiece.

boçal [bo'saw] (*pl* **-ais**) *adj* **-1**. [ignorante] stupid. **-2**. [grosseiro] rude.

boçalidade [bosali'dadʒi] *f* **-1**. [ignorância] stupidity. **-2**. [grosseria] rudeness.

boca-livre [ˌboka'livri] (*pl* **bocas-livres**) *f* **-1**. [em evento] free meal. **-2**. [em serviços públicos] gravy train, *a place where a blind eye is turned to the misappropriation of public funds.*

bocejar [4] [bose'ʒa(x)] *vi* to yawn.

bocejo [bo'seʒu] *m* yawn.

boceta [bu'seta] *f vulg* [vulva] cunt.

bochecha [bu'ʃeʃa] *f* cheek.

bochechar [4] [boʃe'ʃa(x)] ⬦ *vt* to rinse one's mouth with. ⬦ *vi* to rinse one's mouth.

bochecho [bo'ʃeʃu] *m* mouthwash.

bochechudo, da [boʃe'ʃudu, da] *adj* chubby-cheeked.

bocó [bo'kɔ] *adj* **-1**. [infantil] childish. **-2**. [tolo] silly.

bodas ['bodaʃ] *fpl* wedding anniversary *(sg)*; **~ de ouro** golden wedding *(sg)*; **~ de prata** silver wedding *(sg)*.

bode ['bɔdʒi] *m* **-1**. *ZOOL* billy goat; **~ expiatório** *fig* scapegoat. **-2**. *fam* [problema]: **dar ~** to be hell to pay.

bodega [bo'dɛga] *f* **-1**. *fam* [coisa sem valor] rubbish. **-2**. [taberna] tavern.

boêmia [bo'emja] *f* bohemian lifestyle.

Boêmia [bo'emja] *n* Bohemia.

boêmio, mia [bo'emju, mja] ⬦ *adj* **-1**. [vida etc] bohemian. **-2**. [da Boêmia] Bohemian. ⬦ *m, f* **-1**. [pessoa boêmia] bohemian. **-2**. [da Boêmia] Bohemian.

bofe ['bɔfi] *m fam* **-1**. [pulmão] lungs *(pl)*. **-2**. *fam* [pessoa feia] monster.

bofetada [bofe'tada] *f* slap in the face.

bofetão [bofe'tãw] (*pl* **-ões**) *m* hard slap on the face.

Bogotá [bogo'ta] *n* Bogotá.

boi ['boj] *m* ox.

bói ['bɛj] *m* office boy.

bóia ['bɔja] *f* **-1**. *NÁUT* buoy; **~ salva-vidas** lifebuoy. **-2**. *fam* [comida] grub.

boiada [bo'jada] *f* drove of oxen.

bóia-fria [ˌbɔja'fria] (*pl* **bóias-frias**) *m* agricultural dayworker.

boiar [4] [bo'ja(x)] *vi* **-1**. [flutuar] to float. **-2**. *fam* [não entender]: **estar/ficar boiando** to be thrown by.

boicotar [4] [bojko'ta(x)] *vt* to boycott.

boicote [boj'kɔtʃi] *m* boycott.

boiler ['bɔjle(x)] (*pl* **-s**) *m* boiler.

boina ['bojna] *f* cap.

bojo ['boʒu] *m* **-1**. [saliência] bulge. **-2**. [de navio] belly.

bojudo, da [bo'ʒudu, da] *adj* rounded.

bola ['bɔla] *f* **-1**. [objeto] ball; **ser bom de ~** to play football very well; **~ de futebol** football; **~ de gude** marble; **~ de neve** snowball; *fig* [situação] snowball. **-2**. *ESP* [jogada] shot. **-3**. *fam fig* [cabeça]: **não ser bom da ~** to be not right in the head. **-4**. *fam fig* [pessoa engraçada]: **ser uma ~** to be a good laugh. **-5**. *loc*: **dar ~ para alguém** [flertar] to flirt with sb; **dar ~ para algo** [dar importância a] to care about sthg; **não dar ~ (para)** [ignorar] to ignore; **não dar ~ para algo** [não dar importância a] to ignore sthg; **pisar na ~** *fig* to make a mistake; **trocar as ~s** to get mixed up.

bolacha [bo'laʃa] *f* **-1**. [biscoito] biscuit; **~ d'água** water biscuit. **-2**. *fam* [bofetada]: **dar uma ~ em alguém** to slap sb; **levar uma ~ de alguém** to be slapped by sb. **-3**. [em bares, restaurantes] coaster.

boláda [bo'lada] f **-1.** [pancada] hit *(with a ball)*. **-2.** [vez]: **de uma** ~ **só** in one go. **-3.** [de dinheiro] jackpot.

bolar [4] [bo'la(x)] <> vt to devise. <> vi to be successful.

boléia [bo'lɛja] f lorry driver's seat.

boletim [bole'tʃĩ] (*pl* **-ns**) *m* **-1.** [publicação] bulletin. **-2.** *EDUC* school report. **-3.** [nota] memo; ~ **médico** medical report.

boleto [bo'letu] *m* requisition.

bolha ['boʎa] <> f **-1.** [em líquido, material] bubble. **-2.** [na pele] blister. <> *mf fam* [pessoa] bore.

boliche [bo'liʃi] *m* **-1.** [jogo] pool. **-2.** [estabelecimento] pool room.

bolinagem [bolina'ʒẽ] (*pl* **-ns**) f *fam* touching up.

bolinar [4] [boli'na(x)] vt *fam* to touch up.

bolinho [bo'liɲu] *m* croquette; ~ **de bacalhau** salt cod croquette.

Bolívia [bo'livja] *n* Bolivia.

boliviano, na [boli'vjãnu, na] <> *adj* Bolivian. <> *m, f* Bolivian.

bolo ['bolu] *m* **-1.** *CULIN* cake. **-2.** [quantidade]: **um** ~ **de** a load of. **-3.** *fam* [confusão] commotion; **dar o maior** ~ to cause a commotion; **deu o maior** ~ **quando ...** there was a great to-do when ... **-4.** [em jogo etc] stake. **-5.** *loc*: **dar o** ~ **em alguém** to stand sb up.

bolor [bo'lo(x)] *m* mould.

bolorento, ta [bolo'rẽntu, ta] *adj* mouldy.

bolota [bo'lɔta] f **-1.** [fruto do carvalho] acorn. **-2.** [caroço] lump.

bolsa ['bowsa] f **-1.** [acessório] purse. **-2.** *EDUC*: ~ **(de estudos)** bursary. **-3.** *FIN*: ~ **(de valores)** stock market. **-4.** *MED*: ~ **d'água** amniotic sac.

bolsista [bow'siʃta] *EDUC* <> *adj* scholarship *(antes de subst)*. <> *mf* scholarship holder.

bolso ['bowsu] *m* pocket; **de** ~ pocket *(antes de subst)*.

bom, boa ['bõ, 'boa] (*mpl* **bons**, *fpl* **boas**) *adj* **-1.** [ger] good; **ser** ~ **em algo** to be good at sthg; **ficar** ~ to be well made/done. **-2.** [curado] well. **-3.** [seguro] safe. **-4.** [amplo, confortável] spacious. **-5.** [em saudação]: **tudo** ~? how are you? **-6.** [pedindo opinião, permissão]: **está** ~? all right?
➡ **bom** <> *interj*: **que** ~! how great! <> *m*: **o** ~ **é que ...** the good thing is that ...
➡ **bons** *mpl* [pessoas honradas]: **os bons** the great.
➡ **boa** *fam* <> *adj f* [boazuda] sexy. <> f *irôn* [situação difícil]: **meter-se numa boa** to put o.s. in a tight spot; **livrar-se de uma boa** to get out of a tight spot.
➡ **às boas** *loc adv*: **viver às boas com alguém** to get on well with sb; **voltar às boas (com alguém)** to make up (with sb).

bomba ['bõba] f **-1.** [explosivo] bomb; ~ **atômica** atomic bomb; ~ **de hidrogênio** hydrogen bomb. **-2.** [fogo de artifício] rocket. **-3.** [máquina, aparelho] pump; ~ **d'água** water pump; ~ **de ar** air pump; ~ **de gasolina** petrol pump; ~

de incêndio fire extinguisher. **-4.** *fig* [acontecimento] shock. **-5.** *fig* [coisa ruim]: **ser uma** ~ to be a flop. **-6.** *EDUC*: **levar** ~ **(em algo)** to fail at sthg. **-7.** [trabalho mal-acabado]: **estar/ficar uma** ~ to be/end up shoddy. **-8.** [doce] bombe.

bombachas [bõ'baʃaʃ] *fpl* gaucho pants.

bombardear [15] [bõbax'dʒja(x)] vt to bombard.

bombardeio [bõbax'deju] *m* bombardment.

bomba-relógio [ˌbõbaxe'lɔʒju] (*pl* **bombas-relógios**, **bombas-relógio**) f time bomb.

bombástico, ca [bõ'baʃtʃiku, ka] *adj* **-1.** [estrondoso] deafening. **-2.** *fig* [empolado] bombastic.

bombear [15] [bõ'bja(x)] vt & vi to pump.

bombeiro [bõ'bejru] *m* **-1.** [de incêndios] firefighter. **-2.** [encanador] plumber.

bombom [bõ'bõ] (*pl* **-ns**) *m* sweetie.

bombordo [bõ'bɔxdu] *m* *NÁUT* port.

bom-tom [bõ'tõ] *m* good manners; **ser de** ~ to be socially acceptable.

bonachão, ona [bona'ʃãw, ɔna] (*mpl* **-ões**, *fpl* **-s**) *adj* kind-hearted.

bonaerense [bonaj'rẽsi] <> *adj* Buenos Aires *(antes de subst)*. <> *mf* person from Buenos Aires.

bonança [bo'nãsa] f **-1.** *NÁUT* calm. **-2.** *fig* [tranqüilidade] calm.

bondade [bõ'dadʒi] f **-1.** [qualidade] kindness. **-2.** [benevolência] goodness; **ter a** ~ **de fazer algo** to be kind enough to do sthg.

bonde ['bõdʒi] *m* **-1.** [veículo] tram; **pegar o** ~ **andando** *fig* to come in (a conversation) half way. **-2.** *fam* [mulher feia] ugly woman.

bondoso, sa [bõ'dozu, ɔza] *adj* kind.

boné [bo'nɛ] *m* cap.

boneca [bo'nɛka] f **-1.** [ger] doll; ~ **de pano** rag doll. **-2.** *fam* [homosexual] queen.

boneco [bo'nɛku] *m* **-1.** [ger] stencil. **-2.** [brinquedo] doll. **-3.** *fig* [fantoche] puppet.

bonificação [bonifika'sãw] (*pl* **-ões**) f **-1.** [gratificação] bonus. **-2.** [desconto] discount.

boníssimo, ma [bo'nisimu, ma] *superl* ▷ **bom**.

bonitão, tona [boni'tãw, tona] (*mpl* **-ões**, *fpl* **-s**) *adj* handsome.

bonito, ta [bo'nitu, ta] *adj* **-1.** [ger] beautiful. **-2.** *iron* [lamentável] lovely.
➡ **bonito** *adv* [bem] well.

bonitona [boni'tona] f ▷ **bonitão**.

bons ['bõjʃ] *pl* ▷ **bom**.

bônus ['bonuʃ] *m* *(inv)* **-1.** [prêmio] prize. **-2.** [debênture] share.

boot ['butil] (*pl* **boots**) *m* *COMPUT* [inicialização] boot-up; **dar** ~ to reboot.

boquiaberto, ta [bokja'bɛxtu, ta] *adj* gaping.

boquinha [bo'kiɲa] f **-1.** [boca pequena] small mouth. **-2.** *fig* [refeição]: **fazer uma** ~ snack.

borboleta [boxbo'leta] f **-1.** *ZOOL* butterfly. **-2.** [roleta] turnstile.

borboletear [15] [boxbole'tʃja(x)] vi **-1.** [vaguear] to flutter. **-2.** *fig* [devanear] to daydream.

borbotão [boxbo'tãw] (*pl* -ões) *m*: aos borbotões in spurts.

borbulhante [boxbu'ʎãntʃi] *adj* fizzy.

borbulhar [4] [boxbu'ʎa(x)] *vi* to bubble.

borda ['bɔxda] *f* -**1.** edge. -**2.** [lençol] hem. -**3.** [jardim] border. -**4.** [rio] bank. -**5.** [piscina] side.

bordadeira [boxda'dejra] *f* embroiderer.

bordado, da [box'dadu, da] *adj* embroidered.

➡ **bordado** *m* embroidery.

bordão [box'dãw] (*pl* -ões) *m* -**1.** [cajado] crook. -**2.** *fig* [arrimo] prop. -**3.** [MÚS - corda] bass string; [- nota] lowest note. -**4.** [frase] slogan.

bordar [4] [box'da(x)] *vt & vi* to embroider.

Bordeaux [box'do] *n* Bordeaux.

bordejar [4] [boxde'ʒa(x)] *vi* NÁUT to tack.

bordel [box'dɛw] (*pl* -eis) *m* brothel.

bordo ['bɔxdu] *m* -**1.** [de navio] board; **a** ~ on board. -**2.** [ao bordejar] tack.

bordô [box'do] ◇ *adj* burgundy. ◇ *n* Bordeaux.

bordoada [box'dwada] *f* beating.

bordões [box'dõjʃ] *pl* ⊳ **bordão**.

boreste [bo'rɛstʃi] *m* NÁUT starboard; **a** ~ to starboard.

boricado, da [bori'kadu, da] *adj* boric.

borla ['bɔxla] *f* -**1.** [pendão] tassel. -**2.** [pompom] pompom.

borocoxô [boroko'ʃo] *adj* feeble.

borra ['bɔxa] *f* -**1.** [de café] grounds *(pl)*. -**2.** [de vinho] dregs *(pl)*.

borra-botas [ˌbɔxa'bɔtaʃ] *mf inv* good-for-nothing.

borracha [bo'xaʃa] *f* -**1.** [ger] rubber. -**2.** [para apagar] rubber, eraser. -**3.** [mangueira] hose-pipe.

borrachudo [boxa'ʃudu] *m* black fly.

borracheiro [boxa'ʃejru] *m* -**1.** [pessoa] tyre fitter. -**2.** [oficina] tyre-fitting workshop.

borrado, da [bo'xadu, da] *adj* -**1.** [manchado] stained. -**2.** *fam* [de fezes] foul.

borrão [bo'xãw] (*pl* -ões) *m* stain.

borrar [4] [bo'xa(x)] *vt* -**1.** [manchar] to stain. -**2.** [riscar] to cross out. -**3.** [pintar] to smear. -**4.** *fam* [de fezes] to foul.

➡ **borrar-se** *vp vulg* [de fezes] to shit o.s.; ~-se **(de medo)** *fig* to be shitting o.s.

borrasca [bo'xaʃka] *f* -**1.** [tempestade] thunderstorm. -**2.** [em alto mar] squall.

borrifar [4] [boxi'fa(x)] *vt* to spray.

borrifo [bo'xiflu] *m* spray.

borrões [bo'xõjʃ] *pl* ⊳ **borrão**.

Bósnia-Herzegovina [ˌbɔʒnjexzego'vina] *n* Bosnia-Herzegovina.

bósnio, nia ['bɔʒnju, nja], **bosniano, na** [boʒni'ãnu, na] ◇ *adj* Bosnian. ◇ *m, f* Bosnian.

bosque ['bɔʃki] *m* wood.

bossa ['bɔsa] *f* -**1.** [ger] bump. -**2.** *fam* [charme] appeal; **ter** ~ to be appealing. -**3.** *fam* [aptidão]: **ter** ~ **(para algo)** to have an aptitude for (sthg). -**4.** MÚS: ~ **nova** bossa nova.

BOSSA NOVA

Musical movement born in Rio de Janeiro in the late 50s; the bossa nova revolutionized the samba, condensing its rhythmic wealth into a syncopated beat with polished jazz chords for piano and guitar. The bossa nova's delicate melody and subtle song were to have a great influence on western popular music through two of the art form's greatest exponents, Tom Jobim and João Gilberto.

bosta ['bɔʃta] *f* -**1.** [de animal] dung. -**2.** [de ser humano] excrement.

bota ['bɔta] *f* boot; ~**s de borracha** wellington boots, rubber boots; **bater as** ~**s** [morrer] to kick the bucket; **onde Judas perdeu as** ~**s** God-forsaken place.

bota-fora [ˌbɔta'fɔra] (*pl* **bota-foras**) *m* [despedida] send-off.

botânico, ca [bo'taniku, ka] ◇ *adj* botanic. ◇ *m, f* botanist.

➡ **botânica** *f* botany.

botão [bo'tãw] (*pl* -ões) *m* -**1.** [ger] button; **falar/pensar com os seus botões** to think to o.s. -**2.** [de jogo] counter. -**3.** [de flor] bud.

botar [4] [bo'ta(x)] ◇ *vt* -**1.** [ger] to put; ~ **algo em dia** to bring sthg up to date; ~ **fora** to throw away. -**2.** [roupa, sapatos] to put on. -**3.** [defeito] to point out. ◇ *vi loc*: ~ **para quebrar** [empreender mudanças] to make sweeping changes; [fazer sucesso] to be a huge hit.

bote ['bɔtʃi] *m* -**1.** [barco] boat; ~ **inflável** inflatable boat; ~ **salva-vidas** lifeboat. -**2.** [golpe - com arma] thrust; [- salto] leap; [- de cobra] lunge; **dar o** ~ to lunge.

boteco [bo'tɛku] (*pl* -s), **botequim** [bote'kĩ] (*pl* -ns) *m* tavern.

boticário, ria [botʃi'karju, rja] *m, f* dispensing chemist.

botijão [botʃi'ʒãw] (*pl* -ões) *m* cylinder.

botina [bo'tʃina] *f* ankle-boot.

botões [bo'tõjʃ] *pl* ⊳ **botão**.

Bovespa (*abrev de* **Bolsa de Valores do Estado de São Paulo**) *f São Paulo stock exchange*.

bovino, na [bo'vinu, na] *adj* bovine.

boxe ['bɔksi] *m* -**1.** ESP boxing. -**2.** [em banheiro] shower cubicle.

boxeador [boksja'do(x)] *m* boxer.

boy ['bɔj] *m* = **bói**.

bps [bepe'esi] (*abrev de* **bit por segundo**) COMPUT bps.

BR *abrev de* **Brasil**.

braça ['brasa] *f* NÁUT fathom.

braçada [bra'sada] *f* -**1.** [de flores] armful. -**2.** [em natação] stroke.

braçadeira [brasa'dejra] *f* -**1.** [para o braço] armband. -**2.** [de cortina] tie-back. -**3.** [metálica] clasp. -**4.** ESP [correia] wristband.

braçal [bra'saw] (*pl* -ais) *adj* physical; **trabalho** ~ physical work.

bracelete [brase'letʃi] *m* bracelet.

braço ['brasu] *m* -**1.** [ger] arm; **cruzar os** ~**s** to fold one's arms; *fig* [ficar impassível] to do nothing; *fig* [fazer greve] to go on strike; **de ~s cruzados** with arms folded; *fig* [impassível] impassively; **dar o ~ a alguém** to give one's arm to sb; **de ~ dado** arm in arm; **no ~** [à força] by force; **~ direito** *fig* right arm. **-2.** [de toca-discos] arm. **-3.** [de balança] pointer. **-4.** [trabalhador] hand. **-5.** [ramo] limb. **-6.** *loc*: **meter o ~ em alguém** to beat sb up; **não dar o ~ a torcer** to stick to one's guns; **receber (alguém) de ~s abertos** to welcome (sb) with open arms.

bradar [4] [bra'da(x)] ◇ *vt* to proclaim. ◇ *vi* to shout.

Bradesco (*abrev de* **Banco Brasileiro de Descontos**) *m largest private Brazilian bank.*

brado ['bradu] *m* shout.

braguilha [bra'giʎa] *f* flies *UK (pl)*, fly *US*.

braile ['brajli] *m* Braille.

bramido [bra'midu] *m* **-1.** [ger] roar. **-2.** [grito] scream.

bramir [79] [bra'mi(x)] *vi* **-1.** [ger] to roar. **-2.** [gritar] to scream.

branco, ca ['brãŋku, ka] ◇ *adj* **-1.** [ger] white; **arma ~** weapon with a blade. **-2.** [versos] blank. ◇ *m, f* [pessoa] White.
 ◆ **branco** *m* **-1.** [cor] white; **~ do olho** white of the eye. **-2.** [espaço] blank space. **-3.** [esquecimento] blank; **me deu um ~** my mind went blank.
 ◆ **em branco** ◇ *loc adj* [espaço] blank. ◇ *loc adv* **-1.** [sem preencher] blank. **-2.** [sem dormir]: **deixar algo em ~** to leave sthg blank. **-2.** [sem dormir]: **passar a noite em ~** to have a sleepless night. **-3.** [sem comemorar]: **passar uma data em ~** not to celebrate an important date.

brancura [brãŋ'kura] *f* whiteness.

brandir [79] [brãn'dʒi(x)] *vt* to brandish.

brando, da ['brãndu, da] *adj* **-1.** [ger] mild. **-2.** [fraco - ação] weak; [- febre] mild. **-3.** [fogo, forno] warm.

brandura [brãn'dura] *f* mildness.

branquear [15] [brãŋ'kja(x)] *vt & vi* to whiten.

brasa ['braza] *f* **-1.** [de carvão] embers *(pl)*; **na ~** in the embers. **-2.** [incandescência] heat; **em ~** red-hot. **-3.** *loc*: **mandar ~** *fam* to get cracking; **puxar a ~ para a sua sardinha** *fam* to look after number one.

brasão [bra'zãw] *(pl -ões)* *m* coat of arms.

braseiro [bra'zejru] *m* brazier.

Brasil [bra'ziw] *n*: **(o) ~** Brazil.

brasileiro, ra [brazi'lejru, ra] ◇ *adj* Brazilian. ◇ *m, f* Brazilian.

Brasília [bra'zilja] *n* Brasilia.

brasões [bra'zõjʃ] *pl* ▷ **brasão**.

Bratislava [bratʃiʒ'lava] *n* Bratislava.

bravata [bra'vata] *f* bravado.

bravio, via [bra'viw, via] *adj* **-1.** [selvagem] wild. **-2.** [feroz] fierce.

bravo, va ['bravu, va] ◇ *adj* **-1.** [corajoso] brave. **-2.** [animal] wild. **-3.** [mar] rough. ◇ *m, f* [pessoa] intrepid person.
 ◆ **bravo** *interj* bravo!

bravura [bra'vura] *f* **-1.** [coragem] courage. **-2.** [de animal] wildness.

brecar [12] [bre'ka(x)] ◇ *vt* **-1.** [frear] to brake. **-2.** [conter] to curb. ◇ *vi* [frear] to brake.

brecha ['brɛʃa] *f* **-1.** [ger] gap. **-2.** [fenda, abertura] opening. **-3.** [prejuízo] hole. **-4.** *fam* [oportunidade] break.

brechó [bre'ʃɔ] *m* second-hand shop.

brega ['brɛga] *adj fam* [cafona] tacky.

brejo ['brɛʒu] *m* swamp; **ir para o ~** *fam* to go out the window.

brenha ['breɲa] *f* thicket.

breu ['brew] *m* **-1.** pitch; **escuro como ~** pitch black. **-2.** [escuridão] darkness.

breve ['brɛvi] ◇ *adj* **-1.** [ger] short. **-2.** [rápido] fleeting. **-3.** [conciso] brief; **ser ~** to be brief. **-4.** *MÚS* [nota] short. ◇ *adv* [dentro de pouco tempo] soon; **até ~** see you soon; **(dentro) em ~** soon. ◇ *m RELIG* [escapulário] scapular. ◇ *f MÚS* breve.

brevê [bre'vel] *m* diploma.

brevemente [ˌbrɛvi'mẽntʃi] *adv* **-1.** [dentro de pouco tempo] shortly. **-2.** [de modo conciso] concisely.

brevidade [brevi'dadʒi] *f* **-1.** [curteza] shortness. **-2.** [rapidez] brevity. **-3.** *CULIN* cassava-flour cake.

bricabraque [brika'braki] *m* **-1.** [conjunto] bric-a-brac. **-2.** [loja] junk shop.

bridge ['bridʒi] *m* bridge.

briga ['briga] *f* **-1.** [luta] brawl; **partir para a ~** to roll up one's sleeves; **~ de foice** long, drawn-out brawl; **~ de galo** cockfight. **-2.** [desavença] dispute. **-3.** [rixa] fight.

brigada [bri'gada] *f* brigade.

brigadeiro [briga'dejru] *m* **-1.** *MIL* brigadier. **-2.** *CULIN* confectionery made with condensed milk and chocolate, very common at birthday parties.

brigão, gona [bri'gãw, gɔna] *(mpl -ões, fpl -s)* ◇ *adj* brawling. ◇ *m, f* brawler.

brigar [4] [bri'ga(x)] *vi* **-1.** [ger] to fight; **~ por algo** to fight for sthg. **-2.** [desavir-se] to fall out.

brilhante [bri'ʎãntʃi] ◇ *adj* **-1.** [que reluz] sparkling. **-2.** *fig* [notável] brilliant. ◇ *m* [diamante] sparkler.

brilhar [4] [bri'ʎa(x)] *vi* **-1.** [reluzir] to shine. **-2.** *fig* [distinguir-se] to excel.

brilho ['briʎu] *m* **-1.** [luz] shine. **-2.** [de cor] brightness. **-3.** [de metal etc] gleam. **-4.** *fig* [distinção] excellence; **dar ~ a** to make sthg shine; **com ~** brilliantly. **-5.** *fig* [esplendor] splendour. **-6.** *gír* [cocaína] coke.

brim [brĩ] *m* coarse cloth.

brincadeira [brĩŋka'dejra] *f* **-1.** [divertimento] play. **-2.** [jogo] game. **-3.** [gracejo] joke; **de ~** as a joke;

~ **de mau gosto** joke in bad taste; **deixe de** ~! stop kidding!; **fora de** ~ seriously. - **4.** *fam* [coisa fácil] child's play; **não ser** ~ to be no joke.

brincalhão, ona [brĩŋka'ʎãw, ɔna] (*mpl* -**ões**, *fpl* -**s**) *adj* playful.

brincar [12] [brĩŋ'ka(x)] <> *vi* - **1.** [divertir-se] to play; ~ **de algo/de fazer algo** to play with/at doing sthg; ~ **de esconder** to play hide-and-seek. - **2.** [gracejar]: ~ **com alguém** to joke with sb; **está brincando?** are you kidding?; **estar (só) brincando** to be (only) joking. - **3.** [no Carnaval] to party. <> *vt* [Carnaval] to celebrate.

brinco ['brĩŋku] *m* - **1.** [adorno] earring. - **2.** *fig* [primor]: **estar/ficar um** ~ to be shiny.

brindar [4] [brĩn'da(x)] <> *vt* - **1.** [no ato de beber] to toast. - **2.** [presentear]: ~ **alguém (com algo)** to make sb a present (of sthg). - **3.** [conceder]: ~ **alguém com algo** to reward sb with sthg. <> *vi* [no ato de beber]: ~ **a algo** to drink a toast to sthg.

brinde ['brĩndʒi] *m* - **1.** [no ato de beber] toast; **erguer um** ~ **(a)** to raise one's glass (to). - **2.** [presente] free gift.

brinquedo [brĩŋ'kedu] *m* toy.

brio ['briw] *m* - **1.** [honra, dignidade] honour; **mexer com os** ~**s de alguém** to attack sb's honour. - **2.** [galhardia] dignity.

brioche [bri'ɔʃi] *m* brioche.

brioso, osa ['brjozu, ɔza] *adj* noble.

brisa ['briza] *f* breeze.

brita ['brita] *f* CONSTR gravel.

britadeira [brita'dejra] *f* pneumatic drill.

britânico, ca [bri'tãniku, ka] <> *adj* British. <> *m, f* British person, Briton.

broa ['broa] *f* cornflour bread; ~ **de milho** maize-flour bread.

broca ['brɔka] *f* drill.

brocado [bro'kadu] *m* brocade.

broche ['brɔʃi] *m* brooch.

brochura [bro'ʃura] *f* - **1.** [livro] binding; **em** ~ in paperback. - **2.** [folheto] brochure.

brócolis ['brɔkoliʃ] *mpl* broccoli *(sg).*

bronco, ca ['brõŋku, ka] *adj* - **1.** [rude] ill-mannered. - **2.** [burro] slow-witted.

➤ **bronca** *f fam* [repreensão] telling-off; **dar uma** ~ **em alguém** to give sb a telling-off; **levar uma** ~ **(de alguém)** to be given a telling-off (by sb).

bronquear [15] [brõŋ'kja(x)] *vi fam* to get furious; ~ **com alguém** to tell sb off.

brônquio ['brõŋkju] *m* bronchus.

bronquite [brõŋ'kitʃi] *f* bronchitis.

bronze ['brõzil] *m* bronze.

bronzeado, da [brõ'zeadu, da] *adj* tanned.

➤ **bronzeado** *m* tan; **pegar um** ~ to get a suntan.

bronzeador [brõzea'do(x)] (*pl* -**es**) *adj* suntan (*antes de subst*).

➤ **bronzeador** *m* suntan lotion.

bronzear [15] [brõ'zja(x)] *vt* to tan.

➤ **bronzear-se** *vp* to sunbathe.

brotar [4] [bro'ta(x)] *vi* - **1.** [germinar, desabrochar - planta] to sprout; [- muda] to begin; [- flor] to

blossom. - **2.** [manar] to flow; ~ **de** to spurt from. - **3.** *fig* [esperança, suspeita, paixão] to grow.

broto ['brotu] *m* - **1.** [de vegetal] sprout; ~ **de bambu** bamboo shoot; ~ **de feijão** bean sprout. - **2.** [de flor] shoot. - **3.** [jovem] sapling.

brotoeja [bro'tweʒa] *f* rash.

broxa [brɔ'ʃa] <> *f* [pincel] brush. <> *m vulg* [homem impotente] dickless guy. <> *adj vulg* [impotente] dickless.

bruços ['brusuʃ] *mpl*: **de** ~ lying face down.

bruma ['bruma] *f* mist.

brumoso, osa [bru'mozu, ɔza] *adj* misty.

brusco, ca ['bruʃku, ka] *adj* - **1.** [repentino] sudden. - **2.** [tosco, grosseiro] coarse.

brutal [bru'taw] (*pl* -**ais**) *adj* - **1.** [violento, bárbaro] brutal. - **2.** [tremendo, grande] tremendous.

brutalidade [brutali'dadʒi] *f* brutality.

brutamontes [bruta'mõntʃiʃ] *m inv* [homem corpulento] hulk.

bruto, ta ['brutu, ta] *adj* - **1.** [rude, grosseiro] brutish. - **2.** [tosco] coarse. - **3.** *(antes de subst)* [tremendo, grande] tremendous. - **4.** [violento] brutal. - **5.** [produto] raw; **em** ~ raw. - **6.** [sem decréscimo] gross.

bruxa ['bruʃa] *f* - **1.** [feiticeira] witch. - **2.** [mariposa] moth. - **3.** *fam pej* [mulher má] bad woman. - **4.** *fam pej* [mulher feia] hag.

bruxaria [bruʃa'ria] *f* witchcraft.

Bruxelas [bru'ʃɛlaʃ] *n* Brussels.

bruxo ['bruʃul] *m* sorcerer.

Bucareste [buka'rɛʃtʃi] *n* Bucharest.

bucha ['buʃa] *f* - **1.** [de parafuso] Rawlplug®. - **2.** [para buracos] lid. - **3.** [de arma] wad. - **4.** [de balão] wick.

➤ **na bucha** *loc adv fam* [sem demora] promptly.

bucho ['buʃu] *m* - **1.** [de boi] maw. - **2.** *fam* [pessoa feia]: **ser um** ~ to look gross.

buço ['busu] *m* down.

bucólico, ca [bu'kɔliku, ka] *adj* bucolic.

Budapeste [buda'peʃtʃi] *n* Budapest.

budismo [bu'dʒiʒmu] *m* Buddhism.

budista [bu'dʒiʃta] <> *adj* Buddhist. <> *mf* Buddhist.

bueiro [bu'ejru] *m* gutter.

Buenos Aires [bwenu'zajriʃ] *n* Buenos Aires.

búfalo ['bufalu] *m* buffalo.

bufante [bu'fãntʃi] *adj* bouffant.

bufar [4] [bu'fa(x)] *vi* - **1.** [ofegar] to pant. - **2.** [de raiva] to fume.

bufê, buffet [bu'fe] *m* buffet.

bug ['bugi] (*pl* bugs) *m* COMPUT bug.

bugiganga [buʒĩŋ'gãŋga] *f* piece of junk.

bujão [bu'ʒãw] (*pl* -**ões**) *m* cylinder; ~ **de gás** gas cylinder.

bula ['bula] *f* - **1.** MED information leaflet. - **2.** RELIG: ~ **(papal)** papal bull.

bulbo ['buwbu] *m* bulb.

buldôzer [buw'doze(x)] (*pl* -**es**) *m* bulldozer.

bule ['buli] *m* pot.

Bulgária [buw'garja] *n* Bulgaria.

búlgaro, ra ['buwgaru, ra] <> *adj* Bulgarian. <> *m, f* Bulgarian.

búlgaro *m* [língua] Bulgarian.

bulhufas [bu'ʎufaʃ] *pron fam* [coisa nenhuma]: **não entender/ouvir** ~ to understand/hear nothing.

buliçoso, osa [buli'sozu, ɔza] *adj* -**1.** [agitado] turbulent. -**2.** [vivo] lively.

bulimia [buli'mia] *f* bulimia.

bulir [61] [bu'li(x)] <> *vt* [mover] to ruffle. <> *vi* -**1.** [mover-se] to sway. -**2.** [tocar, mexer]: ~ **em** to fiddle with sthg. -**3.** [provocar]: ~ **com alguém** to taunt sb.

bumbum [bũn'bũ] (*pl* -**ns**) *m fam* bottom, bum.

bunda ['bũnda] (*pl* -**ns**) *f fam* bottom, bum.

bunda-mole [͵bũnda'mɔli] (*pl* **bundas-moles**) *mf fam* wimp.

buquê [bu'ke] *m* bouquet; ~ **de flores** bouquet of flowers.

buraco [bu'raku] *m* -**1.** [ger] hole; ~ **da fechadura** keyhole. -**2.** [de agulha] eye. -**3.** [jogo] rummy.

burburinho [buxbu'riɲu] *m* -**1.** [agitação] clamour. -**2.** [rumor] murmur.

burguês, guesa [bux'geʃ, geza] <> *adj* bourgeois. <> *m, f* [pessoa] bourgeois.

burguesia [buxge'zia] *f* bourgeoisie; **alta** ~ upper middle class.

burilar [4] [buri'la(x)] *vt* -**1.** [lavrar] to engrave. -**2.** *fig* [aprimorar] to perfect.

burla ['buxla] *f* -**1.** [fraude] double-dealing. -**2.** [zombaria] jeering.

burlar [4] [bux'la(x)] *vt* -**1.** [fraudar, lesar] to cheat. -**2.** [enganar] to deceive. -**3.** [lei] to defraud.

burlesco, ca [bux'leʃku, ka] *adj* burlesque.

burocracia [burokra'sia] *f* bureaucracy.

burocrata [buro'krata] *m f* bureaucrat.

burocrático, ca [buro'kratʃiku, ka] *adj* bureaucratic.

burocratizar [4] [burokratʃi'za(x)] *vt* to bureaucratize.

burrice [bu'xisi] *f* -**1.** [estupidez] stupidity. -**2.** [ato, dito] something stupid; **foi** ~ **minha ter aceitado a proposta** it was silly of me to accept that offer.

burro, a ['buxu, xa] <> *adj* stupid. <> *m, f* [pessoa imbecil] ass.

➡ **burro** *m* ZOOL donkey; ~ **de carga** beast of burden; *fig* workhorse; **dar com os** ~**s n'água** to lose out.

➡ **pra burro** *fam loc adv*: **ele pinta mal pra** ~ **he** paints terribly; **a mulher do hotel era feia pra** ~ the woman in the hotel was terribly ugly.

bursite [bux'sitʃi] *f* bursitis.

busca ['buʃka] *f* search; **em** ~ **de** in search of; **dar** ~ **a** to search for.

buscador [buʃka'do(x)] *m* COMPUT search engine.

busca-pé [buʃka'pɛ] (*pl* -**s**) *m* firecracker.

buscar [12] [buʃ'ka(x)] *vt* -**1.** [procurar] to search for. -**2.** [tratar de obter] to seek. -**3.** [pegar, trazer] to fetch; **ir** ~ to go and fetch; **mandar** ~ to send for. -**4.** [esforçar-se por]: ~ **fazer algo** to try to do sthg. -**5.** COMPUT to search.

bússola ['busola] *f* compass.

bustiê [buʃ'tʃje] *m* bustier.

busto ['buʃtu] *m* -**1.** [ger] bust; **ela tem 85 cm de** ~ her bust size is 85 cm. -**2.** [torso] torso.

butique [bu'tʃiki] *f* boutique.

buzina [bu'zina] *f* horn, hooter.

buzinada [buzi'nada] *f* honk; **dar uma** ~ to honk.

buzinar [4] [buzi'na(x)] <> *vt* -**1.** AUTO to honk. -**2.** *fig* [dizer com insistência] to harp on; ~ **algo nos ouvidos de alguém** to harp on about sthg to sb. <> *vi* AUTO to honk.

búzio ['buzju] *m* [concha] conch; **jogar** ~**s** [espirit] to cast shells (*in fortune telling*).

byte ['bajtʃi] *m* COMPUT byte.

C

c, C ['se] *m* [letra] c, C.

➡ **C** *abrev de* **celsius**.

cá ['ka] *adv* -**1.** [lugar] here; **vem** ~**!** come here!; **de** ~ **para lá** from here to there; **do lado de** ~ this side; **mais para** ~ closer. -**2.** [tempo]: **de uma semana para** ~ for the past week; **de uns tempos para** ~ recently; **de lá para** ~ since then. -**3.** [na intimidade]: ~ **comigo** to myself; ~ **entre nós** just between ourselves.

CA (*abrev de* **Centro Acadêmico**) *m* centre in a *Brazilian university where students meet to discuss problems concerning their course etc.*

caatinga [ka'tʃĩga] *f* caatinga.

cabal [ka'baw] (*pl* -**ais**) *adj* -**1.** [pleno, completo] utter. -**2.** [exato] complete. -**3.** [prova] ultimate.

cabala [ka'bala] *f* -**1.** [doutrina] cabbala. -**2.** *fig* [maquinação] cabal.

cabalístico, ca [kaba'liʃtʃiku, ka] *adj* cabalistic.

cabana [ka'bãna] *f* hut.

cabaré [kaba'rɛ] *m* cabaret.

cabeça [ka'besa] <> *f* -**1.** [ger] head; **de** ~ [calcular] in one's head; **de** ~ head first; **de** ~ **erguida** *fig* with one's head held high; **por** ~ per head; **só faz o que lhe dá na** ~ he only does what he has a mind to; **meter na** ~ to get into one's head; **não bater bem da** ~ to be off one's rocker; **não estar com** ~ **para fazer algo** not to be in the mood to do sthg; **passar pela** ~ to cross one's mind; **subir à** ~ [suj: sucesso, dinheiro] to go to one's head; **ter a** ~ **no lugar** [ser ajuizado] to be level-headed; ~ **fria** *fig* cool-headed; **com a** ~ **no ar** with one's head in the clouds; ~ **a** ~ neck and neck. -**2.** [inteligência] mind; **usar a** ~ to use one's head. -**3.** [pessoa inteligente] brains. -**4.** [topo, parte de cima]: **de** ~ **para baixo** upside down. -**5.**

cabeçada [kabe'sada] *f* - **1.** [pancada] headbutt; **dar uma ~ em alguém** to headbutt sb; **dar uma ~ em algo** to bang one's head on sthg; **dar uma ~** *fig* to take a knock. - **2.** *FUT* header.

[de lista] top. - **6.** *fam* [de glande] glans. - **7.** [loc]: **fazer a ~ de alguém** to influence sb's thinking; **levar na ~** *fam* to take a hard knock; **não esquentar a ~** *fam* not to get hot and bothered; **perder a ~** to lose one's head; **quebrar a ~** to rack one's brains. <> *mf* head.

cabeça-de-vento [ka͜besadʒi'vẽntu] (*pl* cabeças-de-vento) *mf* scatterbrain.

cabeça-dura [ka͜besa'dura] (*pl* cabeças-duras) <> *adj* [teimoso] headstrong. <> *mf* headstrong person.

cabeça-feita [ka͜besa'fejta] (*pl* cabeças-feitas) *adj fam* [pessoa responsável] level-headed.

cabeçalho [kabe'saʎu] *m* - **1.** [de livro] title. - **2.** [de página, capítulo] heading.

cabecear [15] [kabe'sja(x)] *FUT vt* [bola] to head.

cabeceira [kabe'sejra] *f* head; **livro de ~** bedside book.

cabeçudo, da [kabe'sudu, da] *adj* - **1.** [de cabeça grande] big-headed. - **2.** *fam* [teimoso] pig-headed.

cabedal [kabe'daw] (*pl* -ais) *m* wealth.

cabeleira [kabe'lejra] *f* - **1.** [natural] head of hair. - **2.** [peruca] wig.

cabeleireiro, ra [kabelej'rejru, ra] *m, f* [profissional] hairdresser.

  ➤ **cabeleireiro** *m* [salão] hairdressing salon.

cabelo [ka'belu] *m* [ger] hair; **~ liso/crespo/pixaim** straight/curly/woolly hair; **de arrepiar os ~s** *fig* hair-raising.

cabeludo, da [kabe'ludu, da] *adj* - **1.** hairy. - **2.** *fam fig* [complicado, obsceno] hairy.

  ➤ **cabeludo** *m fam* [homem] hairy man.

caber [34] [ka'be(x)] *vi* - **1.** [ger] to fit; **não ~ em si de** *fam fig* to be overwhelmed with; **~ (em)** to fit (in); **~ por** to fit through; **~ fazer algo** to have to do sthg. - **2.** [ser oportuno] to be time to. - **3.** [ser compatível]: **~ em algo** to be compatible with sthg. - **4.** [competir]: **~ a alguém fazer algo** to be the responsibility of sb to so sthg. - **5.** [partilha]: **~ a alguém** to be allocated to sb.

cabide [ka'bidʒi] *m* [de armário] clothes hanger; [de pé] coat hanger; [de parede] coat hook; **~ de empregos** *fig* [pessoa] Jack-of-all-trades (but master of none); *fig* [empresa estatal] jobs-for-the-boys organisation.

cabideiro [kabi'dejru] *m* - **1.** [de pé] coat hanger. - **2.** [de parede] coat hook.

cabimento [kabi'mẽntu] *m* [adequação] sense; **ter/não ter ~** to make/not to make sense.

cabine [ka'bini] *f* - **1.** [ger] cabin. - **2.** [telefônica] phone box *UK*, phone booth *US*. - **3.** [guarita] sentry box. - **4.** *FERRO* [compartimento] carriage, compartment trunck. - **5.** *AERON* [de comando] cockpit. - **6.** [vestuário] changing room.

cabisbaixo, xa [kabiʒ'bajʃu, ʃa] *adj* crestfallen.

cabível [ka'bivew] (*pl* -eis) *adj* fitting.

cabo [ˈkabu] *m* - **1.** [de panela, faca, vassoura] handle.

- **2.** [fim] end. - **3.** *CORDA* : **~ de aço** iron cable. - **4.** *ELETR* cable. - **5.** *GEOGR* cape. - **6.** *MIL* corporal. - **7.** *POL* : **~ eleitoral** electoral canvasser. - **8.** [fim]: **dar ~ de** [pessoa] to kill; [problema] to put an end to; [tarefa] to finish; **levar algo a ~** [tarefa, projeto] to see sthg through; **ao ~ de** by the end of; **de ~ a rabo** [de uma extremidade a outra] from one end to the other; [do início ao fim] from the beginning to the end.

caboclo, cla [ka'boklu, cla] <> *adj* - **1.** [pele] copper-coloured. - **2.** [pessoa] bumpkinish. <> *m, f* - **1.** [mestiço de banco com índio] caboclo. - **2.** [pessoa da roça] bumpkin.

cabotino, na [kabo'tʃinu, na] <> *adj* theatrical. <> *m, f* show-off.

Cabo Verde [͜kabu'vexdʒi] *n* Cape Verde.

cabra [ˈkabra] <> *f* [animal] goat. <> *m fam* - **1.** [homem] guy. - **2.** [capanga] gunman.

cabra-cega [͜kabra'sɛga] (*pl* cabras-cegas) *f* blind man's buff.

cabra-macho [͜kabra'maʃul (*pl* cabras-machos) *m* tough guy.

cabreiro, ra [ka'brejru, ra] *adj fam* [desconfiado] suspicious.

cabresto [ka'breʃtu] *m* [para cavalos] halter.

cabrito [ka'britul *m* kid.

caça [ˈkasa] <> *f* - **1.** [ato] hunt; **~ às bruxas** witch-hunt; **à ~ de** in pursuit of. - **2.** [animal - caçado por homem] game; [- caçado por outro animal] prey; game. - **3.** [passatempo] hunting. <> *m AERON* fighter.

caçada [ka'sada] *f* [jornada] hunting trip.

caçador, ra [kasa'do(x), ra] (*mpl* -es, *fpl* -s) *m, f* hunter.

caça-minas [͜kasa'minaʃ] *m inv* minesweeper.

caça-níqueis [͜kasa'nikejʃ] *m inv* - **1.** [máquina] slot-machine. - **2.** *fam* [empresa, loja] cowboy outfit.

cação [ka'sãw] (*pl* -ões) *m* dogfish.

caçapa [ka'sapa] *f* pocket (*on billiard table*).

caçar [13] [ka'sa(x)] <> *vt* - **1.** [animais] to hunt. - **2.** [a tiro] to shoot. - **3.** [buscar - documentos, prova, tesouro] to search for; [- recompensa] to seek. - **4.** [perseguir] to hunt down. - **5.** *fam* [marido] to hunt for. <> *vi* [andar à caça] to hunt.

cacareco [kaka'rɛku] *m* piece of junk.

  ➤ **cacarecos** *mpl* junk (*sg*).

cacarejar [4] [kakare'ʒa(x)] *vi* to cluck.

cacarejo [kaka'reʒul *m* clucking.

caçarola [kasa'rɔla] *f* casserole.

cacau [ka'kaw] *m* - **1.** [fruto] cacao. - **2.** [semente] cocoa bean. - **3.** [pó] cocoa.

cacetada [kase'tada] *f* whack; **dar uma ~ (em algo/alguém)** to whack (sthg/sb).

cacete [ka'setʃi] <> *adj* [tedioso] tedious. <> *m* - **1.** [porrete] truncheon. - **2.** *vulg* [pênis] rod.

  ➤ **pra cacete** *mfam* <> *loc pron*: **gente pra ~** shitloads of people. <> *loc adv*: **chato/bom/forte pra cacete** bloody boring/good/strong.

cachaça [ka'ʃasa] *f* sugar-cane brandy.

CACHAÇA

Cachaça is the most popular alcoholic drink in Brazil; it is a fermented drink, obtained from the distillation of sugar-cane sap, and it is very high in alcohol. Its popularity can be measured by the many names that Brazilians give this drink, such as *pinga*, *caninha*, *branquinha*, *mel*, among many others.

cachaceiro, ra [kaʃa'sejru, ra] <> *adj* drunken. <> *m, f* drunkard.

cache [ka'ʃe] *m COMPUT* cache.

cachê [ka'ʃe] *m* fee *(for performance)*.

cacheado, da [ka'ʃjadu, da] *adj* curly.

cachecol [kaʃe'kɔw] (*pl* **-óis**) *m* scarf.

cachimbo [ka'ʃĩbu] *m* pipe.

cacho ['kaʃu] *m* **-1.** [ger] bunch. **-2.** [de cabelos - anel] lock; [- mecha] strand.

cachoeira [ka'ʃwejra] *f* waterfall.

cachorra [ka'ʃoxa] *f* ⊳ **cachorro**.

cachorrada [kaʃo'xada] *f* **-1.** [matilha] pack of dogs. **-2.** *fam fig* [canalhice] scam; **fazer uma ~ com alguém** to scam sb.

cachorrinho, nha [kaʃo'xiɲu, ɲa] *m, f* [filhote] puppy.

➡ **cachorrinho** *m* [nado] doggy-paddle.

cachorro, rra [ka'ʃoxu, ra] *m, f* **-1.** [cão] dog; **soltar os ~s (em cima de alguém)** *fig* to lash out (at sb); **estar matando ~ a grito** to be scraping the barrel. **-2.** *fam pej* [patife] bastard.

➡ **cachorra** *f*: **estar com a ~** *fig* to be in a bad mood.

cachorro-quente [ka,ʃoxu'kẽtʃi] (*pl* **cachorros-quentes**) *m* hot dog.

cacife [ka'sifi] *m* stake; **ter ~ para** *fig* [ter dinheiro para] to be able to afford; [ter condições de] to have what it takes.

cacique [ka'siki] *m* **-1.** [indígena] cacique, tribal chief. **-2.** *fig* [chefão] boss.

caco ['kaku] *m* **-1.** [de vidro etc] shard. **-2.** *fam* [pessoa]: **estar um ~** [estar velho] to be a wreck; [estar desgastado] to be a wreck; [estar exausto] to be wiped out.

caçoar [20] [ka'swa(x)] *vi* to mock; **~ de algo/alguém** to make fun of sthg/sb.

cações [ka'sõjʃ] *pl* ⊳ **cação**.

cacoete [ka'kwetʃi] *m* tic.

cacto [ka'ktu] *m* cactus.

caçula [ka'sula] <> *adj* youngest. <> *mf* youngest child.

CAD (*abrev de* **Computer Aided Design**) *m* CAD.

cada ['kada] *adj (inv)* **-1.** [valor de unidade] each; **uma coisa de ~ vez** one thing at a time; **~ (um)** [em preço] each; **~ qual**, **~ um** each one. **-2.** [todo] every; **a ~** every; **aumentar a ~ dia** to increase from day to day; **em ~ dez pessoas, uma sofre de ...** one out of ten people suffers from ... **-3.** [valor progressivo]: **~ vez** more and more. **-4.** [valor intensivo] such; **me acontece ~ uma!** would you believe it!

cadafalso [kada'fawsu] *m* gallows *(pl)*.

cadarço [ka'daxsu] *m* shoelace.

cadastramento [kadaʃtra'mẽtu] *m* registration.

cadastrar [4] [kadaʃ'tra(x)] *vt* **-1.** [registrar] to register. **-2.** *COMPUT* [dados] to record.

➡ **cadastrar-se** *vp* [inscrever-se] to register o.s.

cadastro [ka'daʃtru] *m* **-1.** [registro] register. **-2.** [ato] registration. **-3.** [ficha de criminoso] criminal record. **-4.** [de banco, clientes] records *(pl)*. **-5.** [de imóveis] land registry. **-6.** *COMPUT* [de dados] data record.

cadáver [ka'davε(x)] (*pl* **-es**) *m* corpse.

cadavérico, ca [kada'vεriku, ka] *adj* **-1.** [exame] post-mortem *(antes de subst)*. **-2.** [pessoa, palidez, rosto] cadaverous.

cadê [ka'de] *adv fam* where is/are.

cadeado [ka'dʒjadu] *m* padlock.

cadeia [ka'deja] *f* **-1.** [ger] chain. **-2.** [prisão] prison. **-3.** [série, seqüência] series *(inv)*; **~ de montanhas** mountain range. **-4.** [de emissoras de TV] network.

cadeira [ka'dejra] *f* **-1.** [ger] chair; **~ de balanço** rocking chair; **~ de rodas** wheelchair; **~ cativa** [em estádio] reserved place; **falar de ~** to speak with authority. **-2.** [disciplina] subject. **-3.** [em teatro] seat.

➡ **cadeiras** *fpl ANAT* hips.

cadela [ka'dεla] *f* [cão] bitch ⊳ **cão**.

cadência [ka'dẽsja] *f* **-1.** [ritmo] rhythm. **-2.** [de estilo, fala] cadence.

cadenciado, da [kadẽ'sjadu, da] *adj* **-1.** [ritmado] rhythmic. **-2.** [pausado] measured.

cadente [ka'dẽtʃi] *adj* [estrela] falling.

caderneta [kadex'neta] *f* **-1.** [livrete] note pad. **-2.** [escolar] mark sheet. **-3.** *FIN:* **~ de poupança** savings account.

caderno [ka'dεxnu] *m* **-1.** [de notas] notebook. **-2.** [de jornal] section.

cadete [ka'detʃi] *m* cadet.

cadinho [ka'dʒiɲu] *m* **-1.** [recipiente] crucible. **-2.** *fig* [local] melting pot.

caducar [12] [kadu'ka(x)] *vi* **-1.** [prazo, documento, lei] to expire. **-2.** [pessoa] to become senile.

caduco, ca [ka'duku, ka] *adj* **-1.** [prazo, documento, lei] expired. **-2.** [pessoa] senile. **-3.** *BOT* deciduous.

caduquice [kadu'kisi] *f* [senilidade] senility.

cães ['kãjʃ] *pl* ⊳ **cão**.

cafajestada [kafaʒeʃ'tada] *f fam* con; **fazer uma ~ com alguém** to pull a fast one on sb.

cafajeste [kafa'ʒεʃtʃi] *fam* <> *adj* **-1.** [canalha] crooked. **-2.** [vulgar] vulgar. <> *mf* [pessoa canalha] con man.

café [ka'fε] *m* **-1.** [ger] coffee; **~ (preto)** black coffee; **~ com leite** white coffee *UK*, coffee with cream *US*; **~ expresso** espresso; **~ pingado** *coffee with a tiny drop of milk*; **ser ~ pequeno** *fam* [tarefa] to be small beer; [pessoa] to be small fry. **-2.** [desjejum]: **~ (da manhã)** breakfast. **-3.** [estabelecimento] café.

CAFÉ

The *cafézinho*, so greatly enjoyed by the Brazilians, played a decisive role in the country's history. Coffee was the main export at the end of the nineteenth century; it propelled Brazilian industrialisation, bringing about the opening of roads and railways throughout the central south of the country. Coffee was a determining factor in the development of São Paulo as the industrial and financial centre of Brazil.

café-com-leite [ˌkafɛkõnˈlejtʃi] *adj inv* [cor] coffee-coloured.

cafeeiro, ra [kafeˈejru, ra] <> *adj* [setor, indústria] coffee *(antes de subst).* <> *m* coffee bush.

cafeicultor, ra [kafejkuwˈto(x), ra] *m, f* coffee planter.

cafeína [kafeˈina] *f* caffeine.

cafetã [kafeˈtã] *f* kaftan.

cafetão, tina [kafeˈtãw, tʃina] *(mpl* -ões, *fpl* -s) *m, f* pimp.

cafeteira [kafeˈtejra] *f* coffee pot.

cafetina [kafeˈtʃina] *f* ▷ **cafetão**.

cafezal [kafeˈzaw] *(pl* -ais) *m* coffee plantation.

cafezinho [kafɛˈziɲu] *m fam* small black coffee.

cafona [kaˈfona] <> *adj* [pessoa, roupa, música] tacky. <> *mf* [pessoa] tacky person.

cafonice [kafoˈnisi] *f* tackiness.

cafundó-do-judas [kafũnˌdɔduˈʒudaʃ] *m*: **no** ~ out in the sticks.

cafuné [kafuˈnɛ] *m*: **fazer** ~ **em alguém**: **fazer em alguém** to scratch sb's head gently.

cagada [kaˈgada] *f vulg* crap.

cágado [ˈkagadu] *m* terrapin.

caganeira [kagaˈnejra] *f vulg* runs *(pl).*

cagão, gona [kaˈgãw, gona] *(mpl* -ões, *fpl* -s) *m, f fam* [medroso, tímido] wimp.

cagar [14] [kaˈga(x)] *vulg* <> *vi* -**1.** [defecar] to have a crap. -**2.** *fig* [menosprezar]: ~ **para alguém/algo** not to give a shit about sb/sthg. <> *vt fig* [impôr]: ~ **regras** to be full of shit.
    ➡ **cagar-se** *vp* [defecar nas calças] to shit o.s.; ~ **-se de medo** *fig* to be shit scared.

caiado, da [kaˈjadu, da] *adj* ≃ whitewashed.

caiaque [kaˈjakil] *m* kayak.

caiar [16] [kaˈja(x)] *vt* to whitewash.

caibro [ˈkajbru] *m* joist.

caído, da [kaˈidu, da] *adj* -**1.** [derrubado] fallen. -**2.** [pendente] droopy. -**3.** *fig* [abatido] depressed. -**4.** *fig* [apaixonado]: **estar** ~ **por alguém** to be in love with sb. -**5.** *fig* [desanimado] subdued. -**6.** *fig* [feio] saggy.
    ➡ **caída** *f* [queda] fall.

caimento [kajˈmẽntu] *m* [de roupa] hang.

caipira [kajˈpira] *fam* <> *adj* provincial. <> *mf* [pessoa - do interior] country bumpkin; [- sem traquejo social] boor.

caipirinha [kajpiˈriɲa] *f* caipirinha, *cocktail made with sugar-cane brandy and lime juice.*

CAIPIRINHA

One of the most typical alcoholic beverages of Brazil; *caipirinha* is prepared with slices or chunks of lemon, *cachaça*, ice and sugar. It is an essential accompaniment to Brazilian *feijoadas* and barbecues, and probably originates from the interior of the state of São Paulo, which would explain its name: *caipira* is the name given to those who were born there. Variations of *caipirinha* include *caipirosca* (made with vodka instead of *cachaça*) and *caipiríssima* (made with rum).

cair [68] [kaˈi(x)] *vi* -**1.** [ger] to fall; ~ **de joelhos** to fall to one's knees; ~ **de quatro** to fall on all fours; *fig* [surpreender-se] to fall over backward; **estar caindo de sono** *fig* to be dropping with tiredness; ~ **em** to fall into; ~ **nas garras de alguém** *fig* to fall into sb's clutches. -**2.** [desabar] to collapse. -**3.** [desprender-se - dente, cabelo, folha] to fall out; [- botão] to fall off. -**4.** [deixar-se enganar] to fall for. -**5.** [entregar-se a]: ~ **em** [na farra] to join in. -**6.** *EDUC* [em prova] to crop up. -**7.** *loc*: ~ **bem/mal** [penteado, roupa, cor] to suit/not to suit; [frase, atitude] to go down well/badly; [comida, bebida] to agree/not to agree with; **estar caindo aos pedaços** to be falling to pieces; ~ **em si** [reconhecer o erro] to accept one's mistake; [voltar à realidade] to come down to earth; **não ter onde** ~ **morto** to have nothing to one's name.

cais [ˈkajʃ] *m inv* quay.

Cairo [ˈkajru] *n* Cairo.

caixa [ˈkajʃa] <> *f* -**1.** [ger] box; ~ **acústica** loudspeaker; ~ **de fósforos** matchbox. -**2.** [para correspondência]: ~ **de correio** postbox *UK*, mailbox *US*; ~ **postal** *ou* **de coleta** postal box. -**3.** [mecanismo]: ~ **de chave** console; ~ **de luz** fuse-box; ~ **de marchas** *ou* **de mudanças** gearbox. -**4.** [máquina]: ~ **registradora** cash till. -**5.** [seção] till. -**6.** [banco] savings bank; ~ **dois** undeclared assets; ~ **econômica** national savings bank. -**7.** *ANAT*: ~ **craniana** cranium; ~ **torácica** thorax. -**8.** *TIP*: ~ **alta/baixa** upper/lower case. <> *m* -**1.** [máquina]: ~ **eletrônico** cashpoint. -**2.** [livro] ledger; ~ **dois** fraudulent books *(pl).* <> *mf* [funcionário] cashier.

caixa-d'água [ˈkajʃaˈdagwa] *(pl* caixas-d'água) *f* water tank.

caixa-de-fósforos [ˈkajʃadʒiˈfɔʃforuʃ] *f fam* [habitação, carro] matchbox.

caixa-forte [ˈkajʃaˈfɔxtʃi] *(pl* caixas-fortes) *f* safe.

caixão [kajˈʃãw] *(pl* -ões) *m* [ataúde] coffin.

caixa-preta [ˈkajʃaˈpreta] *(pl* caixas-pretas) *f AERON* black box.

caixeiro, ra [kajˈʃejru, ra] *m, f* -**1.** [balconista] sales assistant. -**2.** [entregador] delivery person.

caixeiro-viajante, caixeira-viajante [kajˌʃejruvjaˈʒãntʃi, kajˌʃejravjaˈʒãntʃil] *m, f* commercial traveller.

caixilho [kajˈʃiʎu] *m* [moldura] frame.

caixões [kajˈʃõjʃ] *pl* ▷ **caixão**.

caixote [kaj'ʃɔtʃi] *m* crate.

caju [ka'ʒu] *m* cashew.

cajueiro [ka'ʒwejru] *m* cashew tree.

cal ['kaw] *f* -**1.** [substância] lime, quicklime. -**2.** [extinta] slaked lime. -**3.** [para caiar] whitewash.

calabouço [kala'bosu] *m* dungeon.

calada [ka'lada] *f*: **na ~ da noite** in the dead of night.

calado, da [ka'ladu, da] *adj* quiet.

calafetagem [kalafe'taʒẽ] (*pl* -**ns**) *f* caulking.

calafetar [4] [kalafe'ta(x)] *vt* to stop up.

calafrio [kala'friw] *m* shiver; **ter ~s** to have the shivers.

calamar [kala'ma(x)] *m* squid.

calamidade [kalami'dadʒi] *f* calamity.

calamitoso, tosa [kalami'tozu, tɔza] *adj* calamitous.

calão [ka'lãw] *m*: **(baixo) ~** foul language.

calar [4] [ka'la(x)] <> *vt* -**1.** [ocultar] to keep quiet about. -**2.** [silenciar] to silence; **cala a boca!** shut up! -**3.** [conter] to ignore. -**4.** *euf* [armas, canhões] to silence. <> *vi* -**1.** [manter-se em silêncio] to keep quiet. -**2.** [repercutir]: **~ em** to reverberate through.

➡ **calar-se** *vp* [parar de falar] to go quiet, to stop talking.

calça ['kawsa] *f* trousers *UK* (*pl*), pants *US* (*pl*).

calçada [kaw'sada] *f* pavement *UK*, sidewalk *US*.

calçadão [kawsa'dãw] (*pl* -**ões**) *m* pavement.

calçadeira [kawsa'dejra] *f* shoehorn.

calçado, da [kaw'sadu, da] *adj* -**1.** [caminho, rua] paved. -**2.** [pessoa, pé] with shoes on (*depois de subst*).

➡ **calçado** *m* [sapato, tênis] footwear.

calçamento [kawsa'mẽntu] *m* paving.

calcanhar [kawka'ɲa(x)] (*pl* -**es**) *m* heel.

calcanhar-de-aquiles [kawka‚naxdʒia'kiliʃ] (*pl* calcanhares-de-aquiles) *m* Achilles' heel.

calção [kaw'sãw] (*pl* -**ões**) *m* shorts (*pl*); **~ de banho** swim shorts (*pl*).

calcar [12] [kaw'ka(x)] *vt* -**1.** [pisar] to tread on. -**2.** [comprimir]: **~ algo em** to press sthg into. -**3.** *fig* [basear]: **~ algo em** to base sthg on.

calçar [13] [kaw'sa(x)] *vt* -**1.** [sapatos, luvas] to put on; [tamanho] to take a size. -**2.** [pavimentar] to pave. -**3.** [pôr calço em] to wedge.

➡ **calçar-se** *vp* [pôr sapatos] to put one's shoes on.

calcário, ria [kaw'karju, rja] *adj* -**1.** [substância, pedra] chalky, calcareous. -**2.** [água] hard.

➡ **calcário** *m* [rocha] limestone.

calcificação [kawsifika'sãw] *f* calcification.

calcificar [12] [kawsifi'ka(x)] *vt* to calcify.

➡ **calcificar-se** *vp* to calcify.

calcinha [kaw'siɲa] *f* panties (*pl*).

cálcio ['kawsju] *m* calcium.

calço ['kawsu] *m* [cunha] wedge.

calções [kal'sõjʃ] *pl* ▷ **calção**.

calculadora [kawkula'dora] *f* calculator.

calcular [4] [kawku'la(x)] <> *vt* -**1.** [fazer a conta de] to calculate. -**2.** [avaliar, estimar] to estimate. -**3.**

[imaginar] to imagine. -**4.** [supor, prever]: **~ que** to guess that. <> *vi* [fazer contas] to calculate.

calculável [kawku'lavew] (*pl* -**eis**) *adj* calculable.

calculista [kawku'liʃta] <> *adj* calculating. <> *mf* opportunist.

cálculo ['kawkulu] *m* -**1.** [conta] calculation. -**2.** [estimativa] estimate. -**3.** *MAT* calculus. -**4.** *MED* stone; **~ renal** kidney stone.

calda ['kawda] *f* syrup.

caldeira [kaw'dejra] *f* *TEC* boiler.

caldeirão [kawdej'rãw] (*pl* -**ões**) *m* cauldron.

caldo ['kawdu] *m* -**1.** [sopa] broth; **~ verde** green vegetable and potato soup. -**2.** [sumo] juice; **~ de cana** sugar-cane juice. -**3.** [tempero]: **~ de carne/galinha** beef/chicken stock. -**4.** *fig* [mistura]: **~ de cultura** melting pot of cultures. -**5.** *fam* [mergulho]: **dar um ~ em alguém** to duck sb.

calefação [kalefa'sãw] *f* heating.

caleidoscópio [kalejdoʃ'kɔpju] *m* kaleidoscope.

calejado [kale'ʒadu] *adj* -**1.** [mão, pé] calloused. -**2.** *fig* [vivido] experienced. -**3.** *fig* [endurecido] hardened.

calejar [4] [kale'ʒa(x)] *vt* -**1.** [mãos, pés] to cause to become calloused. -**2.** *fig* [endurecer] to harden.

calendário [kalẽn'darju] *m* calendar.

calha [ka'ʎa] *f* -**1.** [sulco] channel. -**2.** [para a chuva] gutter.

calhamaço [kaʎa'masu] *m* tome.

calhambeque [kaʎãn'bɛki] *m* *fam* jalopy.

calhar [4] [ka'ʎa(x)] *vi* -**1.** [acontecer]: **~ que** to happen that. -**2.** [concidir] to happen that; **calhou de elas usarem vestidos iguais** they happened to be wearing the same dress. -**3.** [convir]: **vir a ~** to come at just the right time.

calhau [ka'ʎaw] *m* pebble.

calibrado, da [kali'bradu, da] *adj* -**1.** [pneu] balanced. -**2.** *fam* [meio embriagado] tipsy.

calibragem [kali'braʒẽj] (*pl* -**ns**) *f* calibration.

calibrar [4] [kali'bra(x)] *vt* -**1.** [pneu] to balance. -**2.** [instrumento] to calibrate.

calibre [ka'libri] *m* [de cano] calibre.

cálice ['kalisi] *m* -**1.** [taça] liqueur glass. -**2.** *RELIG* chalice.

cálido, da ['kalidu, da] *adj* warm.

caligrafia [kaligra'fia] *f* -**1.** [arte] calligraphy. -**2.** [letra] handwriting.

calista [ka'liʃta] *mf* chiropodist *UK*, podiatrist *US*.

calma ['kawma] *f* ▷ **calmo**.

calmante [kaw'mãntʃi] <> *adj* calming. <> *m* tranquillizer.

calmaria [kaw'maria] *f* lull.

calmo, ma ['kawmu, ma] *adj* [ger] calm.

➡ **calma** *f* -**1.** [quietude] tranquillity. -**2.** [serenidade] serenity; **calma!** just a moment!; **manter/perder a ~** to keep/lose one's composure.

calo ['kalu] *m* [endurecimento da pele] callus; [no pé] corn; **pisar nos ~s de alguém** *fig* to hit a raw nerve.

calombo [ka'lõnbu] *m* -**1.** [ger] lump. -**2.** [em estrada] bump.

calor [ka'lo(x)] *m* -**1.** [ger] heat; **estar com ~**,

sentir ~ to be/feel hot; **fazer** ~ to be hot. **-2.** [quentura] warmth.

calorão [kalo'rãw] *m* [tempo] heatwave.

calorento, ta [kalo'rẽntu, ta] *adj* **-1.** [pessoa] sensitive to heat. **-2.** [local] hot.

caloria [kalo'ria] *f* calorie.

caloroso, osa [kalo'rozu, ɔza] *adj* **-1.** [ger] warm. **-2.** [manifestação, protesto] fervent.

calota [ka'lɔta] *f AUTO* hubcap.

calote [ka'lɔtʃi] *m fam* [de dívida] bad debt; **dar o** ~ **em alguém** to welsh on sb.

caloteiro, ra [kalo'tejru, ra] <> *adj* unreliable. <> *m, f* bad payer.

calouro, ra [ka'loru, ra] *m, f* **-1.** *EDUC* fresher *UK*, freshman *US*. **-2.** [novato] novice.

calúnia [ka'lunja] *f* calumny.

caluniador, ra [kalunja'do(x), ra] <> *adj* slanderous. <> *m, f* slanderer.

caluniar [16] [kalu'nja(x)] *vt* to slander.

calunioso, niosa [kalu'njozu, njɔza] *adj* slanderous.

calvário [kaw'varju] *m* **-1.** [via crucis] way of the cross. **-2.** *fig* [sofrimento] bitter trial.

calvície [kaw'visi] *f* baldness.

calvo, va ['kawvu, va] *adj* bald.

cama ['kãma] *f* bed; ~ **de casal** double bed; ~ **de solteiro** single bed; **estar de** ~ [estar doente] to be bedridden.

camada [ka'mada] *f* **-1.** [ger] layer. **-2.** [de tinta] coat.

camafeu [kama'few] *m* cameo.

câmara ['kãmara] *f* **-1.** [ger] chamber; ~ **de gás** gas chamber; ~ **mortuária** burial chamber; ~ **alta/baixa** upper/lower house; ~ **de comércio** chamber of commerce; **Câmara dos Deputados** House of Representatives; ~ **municipal** town council. **-2.** *CINE & FOTO* camera; ~ **escura** darkroom. **-3.** *TV* television camera; **em** ~ **lenta** in slow motion. **-4.** [de pneu]: ~ **(de ar)** inner tube.

◆ **câmara** *mf* [cinegrafista] cameraman.

◆ **de câmara** *loc adj MÚS* chamber.

câmara-ardente [ˌkãmaraax'dẽntʃi] *(pl* **câmaras-ardentes)** *f*: **estar exposto em** ~ to lie in wake.

camarada [kama'rada] *adj* **-1.** [amigável] friendly. **-2.** [preço] good.

camaradagem [kamara'daʒẽ] *(pl* **-ns)** *f* **-1.** [convivência] companionship. **-2.** [procedimento] good turn; **por** ~ out of friendship.

câmara-de-ar [ˌkãmara'dʒja(x)] *(pl* **câmaras-de-ar)** *f* inner tube.

camarão [kama'rãw] *(pl* **-ões)** *m* **-1.** [comum] shrimp. **-2.** [graúdo] prawn.

camareiro, ra [kama'rejru, ra] *m, f* **-1.** [in hotel] chambermaid, room cleaner. **-2.** [on boat] cabin cleaner.

camarilha [kama'riʎa] *f* clique.

camarim [kama'rĩ] *(pl* **-ns)** *m* dressing room.

Camarões [kama'rõjʃ] *n* Cameroon.

camaronês, esa [kamaro'nejʃ, ɛza] <> *adj* Cameroonian. <> *m, f* Cameroonian.

camarote [kama'rɔtʃi] *m* **-1.** *NÁUT* cabin. **-2.** *TEATRO* box.

cambada [kãn'bada] *f* **-1.** [porção] load. **-2.** [súcia] bunch.

cambalacho [kãnba'laʃu] *m* scam.

cambaleante [kãnba'ljãntʃi] *adj* unsteady.

cambalear [15] [kãnba'lja(x)] *vi* to stagger.

cambalhota [kãnba'ʎɔta] *f* somersault; **dar uma** ~ to somersault.

cambial [kãn'bjaw] *(pl* **-ais)** *adj* exchange.

cambiar [4] [kãn'bja(x)] <> *vt* **-1.** [moeda] to exchange. **-2.** [transformar]: ~ **algo em** to change sthg into. <> *vi* [trocar]: ~ **de** to change.

câmbio ['kãnbju] *m* **-1.** [ger] exchange; ~ **livre** free trade; ~ **negro** black economy; ~ **oficial/paralelo** official/parallel exchange; [taxa] exchange rate. **-2.** *AUTO* [mudança] gear stick.

cambista [kãn'biʃta] *mf* **-1.** [de moeda] money changer. **-2.** [de ingressos] (ticket) tout.

Camboja [kãn'bɔʒa] *n* Cambodia.

cambojano, na [kãnbo'ʒãnu, na] <> *adj* Cambodian. <> *m, f* Cambodian.

camburão [kãnbu'rãw] *(pl* **-ões)** *m* police van.

camélia [ka'mɛlja] *f* camellia.

camelo [ka'melu] *m* **-1.** [animal] camel. **-2.** *fig* [pessoa burra] idiot.

camelô [kame'lo] *m* pedlar.

câmera ['kãmera] <> *f* camera. <> *mf* [operador] camera operator.

cameraman [ˌkãmera'mẽj] *(pl* **cameramen)** *mTV & CINE* camera operator.

caminhada [kami'nada] *f* **-1.** [passeio] walk. **-2.** [extensão] trek.

caminhão [kami'nãw] *(pl* **-ões)** *m* lorry *UK*, truck *US*.

caminhar [kami'na(x)] *vi* **-1.** [andar] to walk. **-2.** [progredir] *fig* to progress; ~ **para** to lead to.

caminho [ka'miɲu] *m* **-1.** [via, estrada] road. **-2.** [extensão, direção] way; **havia um obstáculo no meio do** ~ there was an obstruction in the way; **cortar** ~ to take a short cut; **ser meio** ~ **andado** *fig* to be half way there. **-3.** *fig* [meio] way. **-4.** *fig* [rumo] route.

caminhoneiro, ra [kamiɲo'nejru, ra] *m, f* lorry driver *UK*, truck driver *US*.

caminhonete [kamjo'nɛtʃi], **camioneta** [kamio'nɛta] *f* van.

camisa [ka'miza] *f* shirt; ~ **esporte** sports shirt; ~ **pólo** polo shirt; ~ **social** dress shirt; **mudar de** ~ *ESP & fig* to change sides.

camisa-de-força [kaˌmizadʒi'foxsa] *(pl* **camisas-de-força)** *f* straitjacket.

camisa-de-vênus [kaˌmizadʒi'venuʃ] = **camisinha**.

camisão [kami'sãw] *(pl* **-ões)** *m* smock.

camiseta [kami'zeta] *f* T-shirt.

camisinha [kami'ziɲa] *f* condom.

camisola [kami'zɔla] *f* nightdress.

camomila [kamo'mila] *f* camomile; **de** ~ camomile.

campainha [kãmpa'iɲa] *f* bell.

campal [kãn'pawl] (*pl* -**ais**) *adj* -**1.** [relativo ao campo] rural. - **2.** [ao ar livre]: **missa** ~ open-air mass.

campanário [kãnpa'narjul] *m* bell tower.

campanha [kãn'pãɲa] *f* -**1.** [ger] campaign; **fazer** ~ (**de/contra**) to campaign for/against. - **2.** [planície] plain.

campeão, ã [kãn'pjãw, ã] (*mpl* -**ões**, *fpl* -**s**) <> *adj* [time etc] champion. <> *m, f* champion.

campeonato [kãnpjo'natu] *m* championship.

campestre [kãn'pɛʃtri] *adj* rural.

campina [kãn'pina] *f* -**1.** [prado] meadow. - **2.** [planície] plain.

camping [kãn'pĩŋ] *m* -**1.** [atividade] camping. - **2.** [lugar] campsite.

campismo [kãn'piʒmu] *m* camping.

campista [kãn'piʃta] *mf* camper.

campo ['kãnpu] *m* -**1.** [ger] field. - **2.** [zona rural] countryside; **casa de** ~ country house. - **3.** [área] camp; ~ **de aviação** airfield; ~ **de concentração** concentration camp. - **4.** *ESP*: ~ **de futebol** football pitch; ~ **de golfe** golf course; ~ **de tênis** tennis court. - **5.** *fig* [âmbito] field; ~ **de ação** field of action. - **6.** *fig* [ocasião] scope. - **7.** *loc*: **embolar o meio de** ~ to mess it all up.

➤ **de campo** *loc adj* [pesquisa] field.

Campo Grande [ˌkãnpu'grãndʒil] *n* Campo Grande.

camponês, esa ['kãnpo'neʃ, eza] (*mpl* -**eses**, *fpl* -**s**) <> *adj* rural. <> *m, f* countryman (*f* countrywoman).

campus ['kãnpuʃ] *m inv* campus.

camuflado, da [kamu'fladu, da] *adj* camouflaged.

camuflagem [kamu'flaʒẽ] (*pl* ns) *f* camouflage.

camuflar [4] [kamu'fla(x)] *vt* -**1.** [dissimular] to camouflage. - **2.** *fig* [disfarçar] to disguise.

camundongo [kamũn'dõŋgu] *m* mouse.

camurça [ka'muxsa] *f* suede; **de** ~ suede.

cana ['kãna] *f* -**1.** [ger] cane. - **2.** *fam* [cachaça] gutrot, cachaça, *sugar-cane brandy.* - **3.** *fam* [cadeia] jail; **ir em** ~ to be locked up.

Canadá [kana'da] *n*: **(o)** ~ Canada.

cana-de-açúcar [ˌkãnadʒja'suka(x)] (*pl* **canas-de-açúcar**) *f* sugar cane.

canadense [kana'dẽnsi] <> *adj* Canadian. <> *mf* Canadian.

canal [ka'naw] (*pl* -**ais**) *m* -**1.** [ger] canal; **canais competentes** proper channels. - **2.** *GEOGR,TV* channel. - **3.** [conduto] pipe. - **4.** *fig* [meio, via] channel.

canalha [ka'naʎa] <> *adj* despicable. <> *mf* rotter.

canalização [kanaliza'sãw] (*pl* -**ões**) *f* -**1.** [ato] piping. - **2.** [tubulação] plumbing.

canalizar [4] [kanali'za(x)] *vt* -**1.** [rios] to channel. - **2.** [pôr canos de esgotos] to lay with pipes. - **3.** [abrir canais] to canalize. - **4.** *fig* [dirigir] to channel.

canapé [kana'pɛl] *m* couch.

canapê [kana'pel] *m* canapé.

Canárias [ka'narjaʃ] *npl*: **as (Ilhas)** ~ the Canary Islands, the Canaries.

canário [ka'narjul] *m* canary.

canastra [ka'naʃtra] *f* -**1.** [cesto] large basket. - **2.** [jogo] canasta.

canastrão, trona [kanaʃ'trãw, trona] (*mpl* -**ões**, *fpl* -**s**) *m, f TEATRO* ham actor.

canavial [kana'vjawl] (*pl* -**ais**) *m* cane field.

canavieiro, ra [kana'vjejru, ral] *adj* cane-growing.

Canberra [kãn'bɛxa] *n* Canberra.

canção [kãn'sãw] (*pl* -**ões**) *f* song.

cancela [kãn'sɛla] *f* gate.

cancelamento [kãnsela'mẽntu] *m* -**1.** [passagem] cancellation. - **2.** [processo] overruling.

cancelar [4] [kãnse'la(x)] *vt* -**1.** [anular] to cancel. - **2.** [riscar] to cross out. - **3.** [desistir de] to call off. - **4.** [suprimir - atividade, pagamento] to cancel; [- regalia] to revoke.

câncer ['kãse(x)] (*pl* -**es**) *m MED* cancer; ~ **de mama** breast cancer.

➤ **Câncer** *m ASTRO* Cancer; **ser** ~ to be a Cancer; **Trópico de** ~ Tropic of Cancer.

canceriano, na [kãnse'rjãnu, na] <> *adj ASTRO* Cancerian. <> *m, f* Cancerian.

cancerígeno, na [kãnse'riʒenu, na] *adj MED* carcinogenic.

cancerologista [kãnserolo'ʒiʃta] *mf* cancer specialist.

canceroso, rosa [kãnse'rozu, rɔza] <> *adj* cancerous. <> *m, f* cancer patient.

cancha ['kãnʃa] *f* -**1.** [raia] track. - **2.** *fig* [experiência] track record.

canções [kãn'sõjʃ] *pl* ⊳ **canção**.

candeeiro [kãn'djejru] *m* lamp.

candelabro [kãnde'labrul] *m* -**1.** [castiçal] candlestick. - **2.** [lustre] chandelier.

candente [kãn'dẽntʃi] *adj* -**1.** [ardente] red-hot. - **2.** *fig* [inflamado] inflamed.

candidatar-se [7] [kãndʒida'taxsi] *vp* -**1.** [à presidência da república] to stand for. - **2.** [à vaga] to apply for.

candidato, ta [kãndʒi'datu, ta] *m* -**1.** *POL* candidate. - **2.** [pretendente - a vaga] applicant; [- a exame] candidate.

candidatura [kãndʒida'tura] *f* -**1.** [ger] candidature. - **2.** [proposta] application.

cândido, da ['kãndʒidu, da] *adj* -**1.** [imaculado] candid. - **2.** *fig* [inocente] naive.

candomblé [kãndõn'blɛl] *m* -**1.** [religião] *Yoruba religious tradition in Bahia and its ceremony.* - **2.** [local] Candomblé shrine.

CANDOMBLÉ

Afro-Brazilian religion that worships West-African gods, known as *orixás*. The temples where *candomblé* ceremonies take place are called *terreiros* and the celebrations are held to the sound of percussion instruments, such as *atabaques*. One of the better known celebrations is the feast of Iemanjá, the queen of the oceans and seas, celebrated on 31st December in Rio de Janeiro and on 2nd February in Bahia, when devotees throw offerings into the sea.

candura [kãn'dura] *f* **-1.** [alvura] candour. **-2.** *fig* [inocência] naivety.

caneca [ka'nɛka] *f* mug.

caneco [ka'nɛku] *m* tankard.

canela [ka'nɛla] *f* **-1.** [especiaria] cinnamon. **-2.** ANAT shin.

canelada [kane'lada] *f* kick in the shins.

caneta [ka'neta] *f* pen; ~ **esferográfica** ballpoint pen; ~ **marca-texto** highlighter; ~ **pilot** felt-tip pen.

caneta-tinteiro [ka,netatʃĩn'tejru] (*pl* **canetas-tinteiros**) *f* fountain pen.

canga [ˈkãŋga] *f* [de praia] beach wrap.

cangaceiro [kãŋga'sejru] *m* bandit. '

cangote [kãn'gɔtʃi] *m* (back of the) neck.

canguru [kãŋgu'ru] *m* kangaroo.

cânhamo [ˈkãɲamu] *m* hemp.

canhão [ka'ɲãw] (*pl* **-ões**) *m* **-1.** MIL cannon. **-2.** *fam fig* [mulher feia] hag.

canhestro, tra [ka'ɲeʃtru, tra] *adj* **-1.** [desajeitado] clumsy. **-2.** [acanhado] awkward.

canhões [ka'ɲõjʃ] *pl* ▷ **canhão**.

canhoto, ta [ka'ɲotu, ta] ⬦ *adj* left-handed. ⬦ *m, f* left-handed person.
⬥ **canhoto** *m* [em talão] stub.

canibal [kani'baw] (*pl* **-ais**) ⬦ *adj* cannibalistic. ⬦ *m, f* cannibal.

canibalismo [kaniba'liʒmu] *m* cannibalism.

caniço [ka'nisu] *m* **-1.** PESCA rod. **-2.** *fam* [perna fina] pin.

canil [ka'niw] (*pl* **-is**) *m* kennel.

caninha [ka'niɲa] *f* sugar-cane alcohol.

canino, na [ka'ninu, na] *adj* **-1.** [ger] canine. **-2.** [fome] ravenous.
⬥ **canino** *m* [dente] canine.

canivete [kani'vetʃi] *m* penknife.

canja [ˈkãʒa] *f* **-1.** CULIN thin broth of rice and chicken. **-2.** *fig* [coisa fácil]: **ser** ~ to be a cinch. **-3.** MÚS: **dar uma** ~ to do a turn.

canjica [kãn'ʒika] *f a sweet dish of maize, coconut milk and cinnamon.*

cano [ˈkãnu] *m* **-1.** [tubo] pipe; ~ **de esgoto** sewer pipe. **-2.** [de arma] barrel. **-3.** [de bota] leg. **-4.** [trambique] swindle. **-5.** *loc*: **entrar pelo** ~ to come a cropper.

canoa [ka'noa] *f* canoe.

canoagem [ka'nwaʒẽ] *f* canoeing.

canoeiro, ra [ka'nwejru, ra] *m, f* canoeist.

canonização [kanoniza'sãw] (*pl* **-ões**) *f* canonization.

canonizar [4] [kanoni'za(x)] *vt* **-1.** [santificar] to canonize. **-2.** [consagrar] to endorse.

cansaço [kãn'sasu] *m* weariness.

cansado, da [kãn'sadu, da] *adj* **-1.** [fatigado] tired. **-2.** [enfastiado] weary.

cansar [4] [kãn'sa(x)] ⬦ *vt* **-1.** [fatigar] to tire. **-2.** [entediar] to bore. **-3.** [aborrecer] to annoy. ⬦ *vi* **-1.** [ficar cansado] to get tired; ~ **de algo/alguém** to get tired of sthg/sb; ~ **de fazer algo** to be tired of doing sthg. **-2.** [fazer ficar cansado] to be tiring. **-3.** [aborrecer] to be boring. **-4.** [desistir]: ~ **de**

fazer algo to weary of doing sthg.
⬥ **cansar-se** *vp* **-1.** [fatigar-se] to get tired. **-2.** [entediar-se]: ~**-se de algo** to get bored with sthg. **-3.** [aborrecer-se]: ~**-se de algo** to become weary of sthg.

cansativo, va [kãnsa'tʃivu, va] *adj* **-1.** [fatigante] tiring. **-2.** [enfadonho] boring.

canseira [kãn'sejra] *f* **-1.** [cansaço] weariness. **-2.** *fam* [esforço] hassle.

cantada [kãn'tada] *f* smooth talk.

cantado, da [kãn'tadu, da] *adj* sung.

cantar [4] [kãn'ta(x)] ⬦ *vt* **-1.** [ger] to sing. **-2.** [dizer em voz alta] to sing out. **-3.** *fam* [tentar seduzir] to sweet talk. ⬦ *vi* MÚS to sing.

cântaro [ˈkãntaru] *m* pitcher.

cantarolar [4] [kãntaro'la(x)] *vt & vi* to hum.

canteiro [kãn'tejru] *m* **-1.** [jardim]: ~ **de flores** flower bed. **-2.** [construção]: ~ **de obras** work site. **-3.** [operário] stone mason.

cantiga [kãn'tʃiga] *f* ballad.

cantil [kãn'tʃiw] (*pl* **-is**) *m* **-1.** [frasco] flask. **-2.** [ferramenta] plane.

cantina [kãn'tʃina] *f* canteen.

canto [ˈkãntu] *m* **-1.** [ger] corner. **-2.** [de triângulo] angle. **-3.** [lugar retirado] quiet corner. **-4.** [MÚS - som musical] song; ~ **gregoriano** Gregorian chant; [- arte] singing.

cantoneira [kãnto'nejra] *f* **-1.** [como reforço] angle iron. **-2.** [como enfeite] corner plate. **-3.** [para fotos] corner slot. **-4.** [prateleira] corner shelf.

cantor, ra [kãn'to(x), ra] (*mpl* **-es**, *fpl* **-s**) *m, f* singer.

cantoria [kãnto'ria] *f* singing.

canudo [ka'nudu] *m* **-1.** [tubo] tube. **-2.** [para beber] straw. **-3.** *fam* [diploma] certificate.

cão [ˈkãw] (*pl* **cães**) *mf* **-1.** ZOOL dog; ~ **de caça** hound; ~ **de guarda** guard dog. **-2.** *loc*: **quem não tem** ~ **caça com gato** there is more than one way to skin a cat.
⬥ **de cão** *loc adj* [dia, férias etc] dreadful.

caolho, lha [ka'oʎu, ʎa] ⬦ *adj* **-1.** [zarolho] one-eyed. **-2.** [estrábico] cross-eyed. ⬦ *m, f* **-1.** [pessoa zarolha] one-eyed person; **ele é um** ~ he only has one eye. **-2.** [pessoa estrábica] cross-eyed person.

caos [ˈkawʃ] *m inv* chaos.

caótico, ca [ka'ɔtʃiku, ka] *adj* chaotic.

capa [ˈkapa] *f* **-1.** [ger] cover; ~ **dura** hard cover; **de** ~ **dura** hardback. **-2.** [roupa] cape; ~ **(de chuva)** rain cape. **-3.** *fig* [aparência] cloak.

capacete [kapa'setʃi] *m* helmet.

capacho [ka'paʃu] *m* **-1.** [tapete] door mat. **-2.** *fig* [pessoa servil] toady.

capacidade [kapasi'dadʒi] *f* **-1.** [ger] capacity. **-2.** [habilidade] ability. **-3.** *fig* [sumidade] genius.

capacitar [4] [kapasi'ta(x)] *vt* **-1.** [habilitar]: ~ **alguém a fazer algo** to prepare sb to do sthg. **-2.** [convencer]: ~ **alguém de algo** to convince sb of sthg.
⬥ **capacitar-se** *vp* [convencer-se]: ~**-se de algo** to become convinced of sthg.

capado, da [ka'padu, da] ⬦ *adj* [castrado]

castrated. <> *m* gelded pig.
capar [4] [ka'pa(x)] *vt* to castrate.
capataz [kapa'taʒ] *m* foreman.
capaz [ka'paʃ] (*pl* -es) *adj* -1. [competente] competent. -2. [apropriado] capable. -3. [provável]: **é ~ de nevar** it might snow. -4.: **ser ~ de fazer algo** [dispor-se a, ter coragem de] to be capable of doing sthg.
capcioso, osa [kap'sjozu, ɔza] *adj* [pergunta] trick.
capela [ka'pɛla] *f* chapel.
capelão [kape'lãw] (*pl* -ães) *m* chaplain.
capenga [ka'pẽŋga] <> *adj* lame. <> *mf* cripple.
capengar [14] [kapẽŋ'ga(x)] *vi* to limp.
CAPES (*abrev de* **Coordenação de Aperfeiçoamento de Pessoal de Nível Superior**) *f Brazilian educational body that finances postgraduate studies.*
capeta [ka'peta] *m* -1. [diabo] devil. -2. *fam* [traquinas] troublemaker.
capilar [kapi'la(x)] *adj* -1. [do cabelo] hair (*antes de subst*). -2. [vaso] capillary.
capim [ka'pĩ] *m* grass.
capinar [4] [kapi'na(x)] *vt* [limpar] to weed.
capita ['kapita] ➝ **per capita** *loc adj* per capita.
capital [kapi'taw] (*pl* -ais) <> *adj* -1. [essencial] major. -2. [pena] capital. <> *m* ECON capital; **~ de giro** working capital; **~ de risco** venture capital. <> *f* [cidade] capital.
capitalismo [kapita'liʒmu] *m* capitalism.
capitalista [kapita'liʃta] <> *adj* capitalist. <> *mf* capitalist.
capitalização [kapitaliza'sãw] *f* ECON capitalization.
capitalizar [4] [kapitali'za(x)] *vt* -1. ECON to capitalize. -2. *fig* [tirar proveito de] to capitalize on.
capitanear [15] [kapita'nja(x)] *vt* -1. MIL to command. -2. [dirigir] to head.
capitania [kapitã'nia] ➝ **capitania do porto** *f* port authority.
capitão, ã [kapi'tãw, ã] (*mpl* -ães, *fpl* -s) *m, f* -1. [ger] captain. -2. [chefe] leader.
capitulação [kapitula'sãw] (*pl* -ões) *f* [rendição] surrender.
capitular [kapitu'la(x)] <> *vi* to capitulate. <> *adj* capitular. <> *f* [letra] capital.
capítulo [ka'pitulu] *m* chapter.
capô [ka'po] *m* AUTO bonnet *UK*, hood *US*.
capoeira [ka'pwejra] *f* [dança] capoeira, *acrobatic game in dance form that is very popular in north-eastern Brazil.*

capoeirista [kapwej'riʃta] *mf* person who does capoeira dancing.
capota [ka'pɔta] *f* AUTO hood.
capotar [4] [kapo'ta(x)] *vi* to overturn.
caprichar [4] [kapri'ʃa(x)] *vi*: **~ (em)** to take delight in.
capricho [ka'priʃul *m* -1. [esmero] care. -2. [vontade] whim. -3. [teimosia] obstinacy.
caprichoso, osa [kapri'ʃozu, ɔza] *adj* -1. [cuidadoso] meticulous. -2. [voluntarioso] capricious. -3. [teimoso] obstinate.
capricorniano, na [kaprikox'njãnu, na] <> *adj* Capricorn. <> *m, f* Capricorn.
Capricórnio [kapri'kɔxnju] *m* ASTRO Capricorn; **ser de ~** to be a Capricorn; **Trópico de ~** Tropic of Capricorn.
cápsula ['kapsula] *f* capsule.
captação [kapta'sãw] (*pl* -ões) *f* ECON: **~ de recursos** fund-raising.
captar [4] [kap'ta(x)] *vt* -1. [atrair] to win. -2. [sintonizar] to pick up. -3. [água] to collect. -4. [compreender] to catch.
captura [kap'tura] *f* capture.
capturar [kaptu'ra(x)] *vt* to capture.
capuz [ka'puʃ] (*pl* -es) *m* hood.
caquético, ca [ka'kɛtʃiku, ka] *adj* doddering.
caqui [ka'ki] *m inv* kaki fruit.
cáqui ['kaki] <> *adj inv* khaki. <> *m* drill.
cara ['kara] <> *f* -1. [rosto] face; **~ a ~** face to face; **ser a ~ de alguém** to be the image of sb. -2. [aspecto] look; **estar com uma ~ boa** [pessoa] to look well; [comida] to look good; **ficar com ~ de tacho** to be dumbfounded. -3. [de moeda] side. -4. *fam* [coragem] nerve. <> *m* -1. *fam* [sujeito] guy. -2. *loc*: **amarrar a ~** to sulk; **dar as ~s (em)** to show up for; **dar de ~ com alguém** to bump into sb; **encher a ~** *fam* to have a skinful; **estar com ~ de que** [parecer que] to look like; **estar na ~** to be staring one in the face; **meter a ~ em algo** *fig* to put one's back into sthg; **não ir com a ~ de alguém** not to be keen on sb.
carabina [kara'bina] *f* rifle.
Caracas [ka'rakaʃ] *n* Caracas.
caracol [kara'kɔw] (*pl* -óis) *m* -1. [molusco] snail. -2. [de cabelo] curl.
➝ **de caracol** *loc adj* [escada] spiral.
caractere [karak'tɛri] *m* character.
caracteres [karak'tɛriʃ] *pl* ▷ **caráter**.
➝ **caracteres** *mpl* -1. [características individuais] characteristics. -2. [legendas, créditos] credits.
característico, ca [karakte'riʃtʃiku, ka] *adj* characteristic.
➝ **característica** *f* characteristic.
caracterização [karakteriza'sãw] (*pl* -ões) *f* -1. [descrição] characterization. -2. [TEATRO - maquilagem] make-up; [- indumentária] wardrobe.
caracterizar [4] [karakteri'za(x)] *vt* -1. [descrever] characterize. -2. [TEATRO - maquilagem] to make up; [- indumentária] to dress.
➝ **caracterizar-se** *vp* [distinguir-se]: **~-se por** to be characterized by.

cara-de-pau [ˌkaradʒiˈpawl] fam ◇ adj shameless. ◇ mf shameless person.

caralho [karaˈʎul] vulg ◇ interj fuck!, fuck me! ◇ m [pênis] dick, cock.

caramanchão [karamãnˈʃãw] (pl -ões) m pergola.

caramba [kaˈrãnba] interj my goodness! UK, gee! US; está frio/quente pra ~ it's incredibly cold/hot.

carambola [karãmˈbɔla] f star fruit.

caramelado, da [karameˈladu, da] adj caramelized.

caramelo [karaˈmɛlu] m -1. [calda] caramel. -2. [bala] toffee.

cara-metade [ˌkarameˈtadʒi] (pl caras-metades) f better half.

caramujo [karaˈmuʒu] m shellfish.

caranguejo [karãŋˈgejʒu] m crab.

carão [kaˈrãw] (pl -ões) m ticking off; **passar um ~ em alguém** to tick sb off.

carapaça [karaˈpasa] f carapace.

carapuça [karaˈpusa] f -1. [gorro] cap. - 2. [indireta]: **enfiar a ~** to take it personally.

caraquenho, nha [karaˈkẽɲu, ɲa] ◇ adj Caracas (antes de subst). ◇ m, f person from Caracas.

caratê [karaˈte] m karate.

caráter [kaˈrate(x)] (pl -es) m [índole, natureza, cunho] character; **uma pessoa de ~ /sem ~** a person of good moral fibre/with no moral fibre.

➦ **a caráter** loc adv [vestir-se] in character.

caravana [karaˈvãna] f caravan.

carboidrato [kaxbwiˈdratu] m carbohydrate.

carbônico, ca [kaxˈbóniku, ka] adj carbonic.

carbonizar [4] [kaxboniˈza(x)] vt to carbonize.

carbono [kaxˈbonu] m QUÍM carbon; **de ~** carbon (antes de subst).

carburador [kaxburaˈdo(x)] (pl -es) m carburettor UK, carburator US.

carcaça [kaxˈkasa] f -1. [esqueleto] carcass. - 2. [armação] frame. - 3. [de navio] hull.

cárcere [ˈkaxseri] m jail.

carcereiro, ra [kaxseˈrejru, ra] m jailer.

carcomer [kaxkoˈme(x)] vt [roer] to eat into.

carcomido, da [kaxkoˈmidu, da] adj -1. [roído] worm-eaten. -2. [gasto] frayed. -3. fig [rosto] pockmarked.

cardápio [kaxˈdapju] m menu.

cardeal [kaxˈdʒjaw] (pl -ais) ◇ m RELIG cardinal. ◇ adj [ponto] cardinal.

cardíaco, ca [kaxˈdʒiaku, ka] ◇ adj cardiac, heart; **ataque ~** heart attack; **ser ~** to have heart trouble. ◇ m, f heart patient, person with heart problems.

cardigã [kaxdʒiˈgã] m cardigan.

cardinal [kaxdʒiˈnaw] (pl -ais) adj cardinal.

cardiologista [kaxdʒoloˈʒiʃta] mf cardiologist.

cardiovascular [ˌkaxdʒjovaʃkuˈla(x)] (pl -es) adj cardiovascular.

cardume [kaxˈdumi] m shoal.

careca [kaˈrɛka] ◇ adj bald; **estar ~ de saber algo** to know sthg full well. ◇ m bald man. ◇ f bald patch.

carecer [25] [kareˈse(x)] vt -1. [não ter]: ~ **de** to lack. - 2. [precisar]: ~ **de** to need.

careiro, ra [kaˈrejru, ra] adj pricey.

carência [kaˈrẽnsja] f -1. [falta]: ~ **de** lack of. -2. [falta de afeto]: ~ **afetiva** lack of care. -3. [em seguro, financiamento]: **período de** ~ moratorium.

carente [kaˈrẽntʃi] adj -1. [desprovido] lacking. -2. [pobre] needy.

carestia [kareʃˈtʃia] f -1. [custo alto] high cost. -2. [escassez] scarcity.

careta [kaˈreta] ◇ adj -1. fam [conservador - pessoa] fuddy-duddy; [- roupa, festa] dated. -2. fam [que não usa drogas] clean. ◇ f [com o rosto] grimace; **fazer ~** to pull faces.

caretice [kareˈtʃisi] f fam [convencionalismo]: **meu pai é a ~ em pessoa** my father is as old-fashioned as they come.

carga [ˈkaxga] f -1. [ato] loading. -2. [carregamento] cargo; ~ **aérea** air freight. -3. [fardo] load. -4. [de arma de fogo] charge. -5. [de caneta] cartridge. -6. ELETR: ~ **elétrica** electric charge. -7. fig [peso] burden. - 8. fig [responsabilidade] load; ~ **horária** working hours.

carga-d'água [ˌkaxgaˈdagwa] (pl cargas-d'água) f [chuva] downpour.

➦ **cargas-d'água** fpl [motivo]: **por que cargas-d'água ...?** why on earth ...?

cargo [ˈkaxgu] m -1. [função] post. -2. [responsabilidade] responsibility.

cargueiro, ra [kaxˈgejru, ra] adj cargo.

➦ **cargueiro** m cargo ship.

cariado, da [kaˈriadu, da] adj [dente] decayed.

cariar [16] [kaˈrja(x)] ◇ vt to rot. ◇ vi to decay.

Caribe [kaˈribi] n: **o (mar do)** ~ the Caribbean (Sea).

caribenho, nha [kariˈbẽɲu, ɲa] ◇ adj Caribbean. ◇ m, f Caribbean.

caricatura [karikaˈtura] f -1. [desenho] caricature. - 2. fig [reprodução mal-feita] distortion.

caricatural [karikatuˈraw] (pl -ais) adj grotesque.

caricaturista [karikatuˈriʃta] mf caricaturist.

carícia [kaˈrisja] f caress.

caridade [kariˈdadʒi] f -1. [benevolência] charity. -2. [esmola] alms (pl).

caridoso, osa [kariˈdozu, ɔza] adj charitable.

cárie [ˈkari] f caries.

carimbar [4] [karĩnˈba(x)] vt to stamp.

carimbo [kaˈrĩnbu] m stamp.

carinho [kaˈriɲu] m -1. [afago] caress. -2. [cuidado] care.

carinhosamente [kariɲozaˈmẽntʃi] adv -1. [afetuosamente] affectionately. -2. [cuidadosamente] carefully.

carinhoso, osa [kariˈɲozu, ɔza] adj affectionate.

carioca [kaˈrjɔka] ◇ adj carioca. ◇ mf carioca.

carisma [kaˈriʒma] m charisma.

carismático, ca [kariʒ'matʃiku, ka] *adj* charismatic.

caritativo, va [karita'tʃivu, va] *adj* charitable.

carnal [kax'naw] (*pl* **-ais**) *adj* **-1.** [da carne, do corpo] carnal. **-2.** [consanguíneo] blood- *(antes de subst)*.

carnaval [kaxna'vaw] (*pl* **-ais**) *m* **-1.** [festa popular] carnival. **-2.** *fig* [desordem] mess. **-3.** *fig* [estardalhaço] racket.

CARNAVAL

The greatest of all Brazilian festivals; *carnaval* officially lasts for four days, from Saturday until Shrove Tuesday. Although its most famous display is the parade of the Samba Schools of Rio de Janeiro, broadcast throughout the entire country, *carnaval* is celebrated in different ways in the various Brazilian states. In Salvador (BA), it is characterized by the parade of the *afoxés* and the *trios-elétricos*, drawing behind them vast numbers of revellers. Recife and Olinda (PE) celebrate *carnaval* with a parade of revellers partying to the sound of the *frevo*.

---

carnavalesco, ca [kaxnava'leʃku, ka] *adj* **-1.** [relativo ao carnaval] carnival. **-2.** [extravagante] over the top.
➡ **carnavalesco** *m* **-1.** [folião] reveller. **-2.** [organizador] carnival planner.

carne ['kaxni] *f* **-1.** [ger] flesh; **em ~ e osso** in the flesh; **em ~ viva** raw; **ser de ~ e osso** *fig* to be only human, after all. **-2.** *CULIN* meat; **~ assada** roast meat. **-3.** [parentesco] flesh and blood.

carnê [kax'ne] *m* [de pagamento] slate.

carne-de-sol [ˌkaxnidʒi'sɔw] (*pl* **carnes-de-sol**) *f* *CULIN lightly dried meat*.

carneiro [kax'nejru] *m* lamb.

carne-seca [ˌkaxni'seka] (*pl* **carnes-secas**) *f* *CULIN* dried meat.

carniça [kax'nisa] *f* carrion; **pular ~** to play leapfrog.

carnificina [kaxnifi'sina] *f* carnage.

carnívoro, ra [kax'nivoru, ra] *adj* carnivorous.
➡ **carnívoro** *m* carnivore.

carnoso, osa [kax'nozu, ɔza] *adj* **-1.** [semelhante à carne] meaty. **-2.** [fruto] fleshy. **-3.** [folha] pulpy.

carnudo, da [kax'nudu, da] *adj* **-1.** [lábios] full. **-2.** [fruta, perna] plump.

caro, ra ['karu, ra] *adj* **-1.** [ger] expensive. **-2.** [querido, custoso] dear.
➡ **caro** *adv* **-1.** [por alto preço] for a high price. **-2.** *fig* [com alto custo] dear.

carochinha [karo'ʃina] *f* ➪ **história**.

caroço [ka'rosu] *m* stone.

carola [ka'rɔla] <> *adj* pious. <> *mf* pious person.

carona [ka'rona] *f* lift; **dar/pegar ~** to give/hitch a lift; **ir/viajar de ~** to hitchhike.

Cárpatos ['kaxpatuʃ] *npl*: **os ~** the Carpathians.

carpete [kax'petʃi] *m* fitted carpet.

carpintaria [kaxpĩta'ria] *f* **-1.** [ofício] carpentry. **-2.** [oficina] carpenter's shop.

carpinteiro, ra [kaxpĩ'tejru] *m, f* carpenter.

carranca [ka'xãŋka] *f* **-1.** *fam* [cara fechada] sour face. **-2.** [em embarcação] figurehead.

carrancudo, da [kaxãŋ'kudu, da] *adj* surly.

carrapato [kaxa'patu] *m* **-1.** [inseto] tick. **-2.** *fam* [pessoa dependente] hanger-on.

carrapicho [kaxa'piʃu] *m* **-1.** [arbusto] burr. **-2.** [carapinha] Afro hairstyle.

carrasco [ka'xaʃku] *m* **-1.** [algoz] executioner. **-2.** *fig* [tirano] tyrant.

carreata [ka'xjata] *f* motorcade.

carregado, da [kaxe'gadu, da] *adj* **-1.** [caminhão etc]: **~ (de)** laden with. **-2.** [fisionomia] sullen. **-3.** [ambiente] dismal. **-4.** [estilo] dark. **-5.** [céu] threatening.

carregador [kaxega'do(x)] (*pl* **-es**) *m, f* **-1.** [de bagagem] porter. **-2.** [transportador] carrier.

carregamento [kaxega'mẽntu] *m* **-1.** [ato] loading. **-2.** [carga] load.

carregar [14] [kaxe'ga(x)] <> *vt* **-1.** [ger] to load. **-2.** [levar] to transport. **-3.** *fig* [sentimento etc] to carry. **-4.** [bateria] to charge. **-5.** [impregnar] to fill. <> *vi* **-1.** [pôr em demasia]: **~ em** to overdo. **-2.** [exagerar]: **~ em** to overstate.

carreira [ka'xejra] *f* **-1.** [correria] run. **-2.** [profissão] career. **-3.** [fileira]: **~ de algo** row of sthg. **-4.** *NÁUT* slipway. **-5.** [turfe] racecourse. **-6.** [trilha] track.

carreirista [kaxej'riʃta] *mf* careerist.

carreta [ka'xeta] *f* **-1.** [caminhão] truck. **-2.** [carroça] cart.

carretel [kaxe'tɛw] (*pl* **-éis**) *m* **-1.** [cilindro] reel. **-2.** [molinete] fishing reel.

carretilha [kaxe'tʃiʎa] *f* **-1.** [roldana] pulley. **-2.** [cortadeira] pastry cutter.

carrilhão [kaxi'ʎãw] (*pl* **-ões**) *m* **-1.** [sinos] carillon. **-2.** [relógio] chime.

carrinho [ka'xiɲu] *m* **-1.** [para transportar criança] pushchair *UK*, stroller *US*. **-2.** [para transportar comida etc] trolley; **~ de chá** tea trolley *UK*, tea cart *US*; **~ de feira** shopping trolley; **~ de mão** handcart.

carro ['kaxu] *m* **-1.** [veículo] car; **~ alegórico** float; **~ de bombeiro** fire engine; **~ de passeio** car; **~ de praça** taxi. **-2.** [vagão] waggon. **-3.** [de bois] cart. **-4.** [de máquina de escrever] carriage. **-5.** *loc*: **pôr o ~ adiante dos bois** to put the cart before the horse.

carro-bomba [ˌkaxu'bõnba] (*pl* **carros-bombas**, **carros-bomba**) *m* car bomb.

carroça [ka'xɔsa] *f* **-1.** [de tração animal] cart. **-2.** [calhambeque] trap.

carroceria [kaxose'ria] *f* car body.

carro-chefe [ˌkaxu'ʃefi] (*pl* **carros-chefes**) *m* leading float.

carrocinha [kaxo'siɲa] *f* dog wagon.

carro-forte [ˌkaxu'fɔxtʃi] (*pl* **carros-fortes**) *m* armoured car.

carrossel [kaxo'sɛw] (*pl* **-éis**) *m* roundabout *UK*, merry-go-round *US*.

carruagem [ka'xwaʒẽ] (*pl* **-ns**) *f* carriage.

carta ['kaxta] *f* **-1.** [missiva] letter; **~ registrada** registered letter. **-2.** [de baralho] playing card;

dar as ~s to deal the cards. -**3.** [mapa] map. -**4.** [constituição]: ~ **magna** charter.

  ➤ **carta branca** f: **dar/ter** ~ **branca** to give/ have carte blanche.

carta-bomba [ˌkaxta'bõnba] (pl **cartas-bombas**, **cartas-bomba**) f letter bomb.

cartada [kax'tada] f -**1.** [em jogo] card play. -**2.** fig [ato arriscado] risk; **jogar a última** ~ to play one's last card.

cartão [kax'tãw] (pl -**ões**) m card; ~ **de crédito** credit card; ~ **de telefone** phone card; ~ **de embarque** boarding card; ~ **de visita** business card.

cartão-postal [kaxˌtãwpoʃtaw] (pl **cartões-postais**) m postcard.

cartaz [kax'taʃ] (pl -**es**) m -**1.** [anúncio] poster. -**2.** [popularidade]: **ter** ~ to be popular. -**3.** CINE & TEATRO : **estar em** ~ to be showing.

carteado [kax'tʃjadu] m card game.

carteira [kax'tejra] f -**1.** [para dinheiro]: ~ **(de notas)** wallet. -**2.** [mesa] desk. -**3.** [documento]: ~ **de identidade** identity card; ~ **de estudante** student card; ~ **de investimentos** ECON investment portfolio; ~ **de sócio** membership card; ~ **de motorista** driving licence UK, driver's license US; ~ **profissional** ou **de trabalho** employment contract. -**4.** [de cigarros] pack. -**5.** [de títulos, ações] portfolio.

carteiro, ra [kax'tejru, ra] m, f postman (f postwoman).

cartel [kax'tɛw] (pl -**éis**) m COM cartel.

cartela [kax'tɛla] f [mostruário] card.

cartilagem [kaxtʃi'laʒẽ] (pl -**ns**) f ANAT cartilage.

cartões [kax'tõjʃ] mpl ❯ **cartão**.

cartografia [kaxtogra'fia] f cartography.

cartola [kax'tola] ❱❯ f [chapéu] top hat. ❱❯ m -**1.** fam [pessoa importante] snob. -**2.** pej & FUT club manager who abuses his position.

cartolina [kaxto'lina] f card.

cartomante [kaxto'mãntʃi] mf card reader.

cartório [kax'tɔrju] m -**1.** [arquivo] archive. -**2.** [de registro civil] registry office. -**3.** [de registro de imóveis] Land Registry.

cartucho [kax'tuʃu] m -**1.** [de arma] cartridge. -**2.** [invólucro] tube; **queimar o último** ~ fig to play one's last card.

cartum [kax'tũ] (pl -**ns**) m cartoon.

cartunista [kaxtu'niʃta] mf cartoonist.

caruncho [ka'rũnʃu] m woodworm.

carvalho [kax'vaʎu] m oak.

carvão [kax'vãw] (pl -**ões**) m -**1.** [combustível] coal; ~ **vegetal** charcoal. -**2.** [tição] cinder.

casa [ˈkaza] f -**1.** [ger] house; ~ **de campo** country house; ~ **popular** council house; ~ **geminada** semi-detached house. -**2.** [lar] home; **em** ~ at home; **ir para** ~ to go home; **você é da** ~ [convidado, hóspede] make yourself at home. -**3.** [estabelecimento] building; ~ **de câmbio** bureau de change; **Casa da Moeda** Mint; ~ **noturna** nightclub; ~ **de saúde** hospital. -**4.** [de botões] buttonhole. -**5.** MAT place. -**6.** [instalação]:

~ **de máquinas** engine housing.

casaca [ka'zaka] f cloak; **virar a** ~ to be a turncoat.

casacão [kaza'kãw] (pl -**ões**) m overcoat.

casaco [ka'zaku] m coat; ~ **de pele** fur coat.

casa-grande [ˌkaza'grãndʒi] (pl **casas-grandes**) f main house.

casal [ka'zaw] (pl -**ais**) m -**1.** [homem e mulher] couple. -**2.** [de filhos] pair.

casamenteiro, ra [kazamẽn'tejru, ra] adj matchmaking; **Santo Antônio, o santo** ~ St Anthony the matchmaker.

casamento [kaza'mẽntu] m -**1.** [ger] marriage. -**2.** [cerimônia] wedding; ~ **civil/religioso** civil/ religious wedding.

casar [4] [ka'za(x)] ❱❯ vt -**1.** [ger] to marry. -**2.** [emparelhar] to pair. ❱❯ vi [em matrimônio]: ~ **(com alguém)** to marry (sb); ~ **no civil/no religioso** to have a civil/religious wedding.

  ➤ **casar-se** vp -**1.** [em matrimônio] to marry. -**2.** [combinar-se] to go.

casarão [kaza'rãw] (pl -**ões**) m large house.

casca [ˈkaʃka] f -**1.** [de pão] crust. -**2.** [de ferida] scab. -**3.** [de ovo] shell. -**4.** [de fruta] peel. -**5.** fig [aparência] sullenness.

casca-grossa [ˌkaʃka'grɔsa] (pl **cascas-grossas**) mf uncouth person.

cascalho [kaʃ'kaʎu] m gravel.

cascão [kaʃ'kãw] (pl -**ões**) m -**1.** [crosta] hard crust. -**2.** [de sujeira] grime.

cascata [kaʃ'kata] f -**1.** [queda d'água] waterfall. -**2.** fam [mentira] fib. -**3.** fam [bazófia] bragging.

cascateiro, ra [kaʃka'tejru, ra] fam ❱❯ adj bullshit. ❱❯ m, f bullshitter.

cascavel [kaʃka'vɛw] (pl -**éis**) ❱❯ m ZOOL rattlesnake. ❱❯ f fig [mulher] cow.

casco [ˈkaʃku] m -**1.** [de navio] hull. -**2.** [de tartaruga] shell. -**3.** [garrafa] cask. -**4.** [crânio] scalp.

cascudo, da [kaʃ'kudu, da] adj [de casca dura] crusty.

  ➤ **cascudo** m -**1.** [inseto] horn-shelled insect. -**2.** [pancada] rap on the head; **dar um** ~ **em alguém** to rap sb on the head.

casebre [ka'zɛbri] m hovel.

caseiro, ra [ka'zejru, ra] ❱❯ adj -**1.** [produto] home-made. -**2.** [trabalho] home- (antes de subst). -**3.** [roupa] homespun. -**4.** [pessoa] family man. ❱❯ m, f [empregado] caretaker.

caserna [ka'zɛxna] f MIL barracks (pl).

casmurro, rra [kaʒ'muxu, xa] adj -**1.** [teimoso] stubborn. -**2.** [sorumbático] gloomy.

caso [ˈkazu] ❱❯ m -**1.** [fato] matter; **o** ~ **é que** ... the fact is that ... -**2.** [circunstância]: **em todo** ~ anyway; **neste** ~ in that case; **no** ~ **de** should there be; ~ **de emergência** emergency. -**3.** [história] story. -**4.** [amoroso] affair. -**5.** [problema]: **criar** ~ to cause a problem. -**6.** MED, GRAM case. -**7.** loc: **fazer pouco** ~ **de** to take little account of; **não vem ao** ~ it's not relevant; **ser um** ~ **perdido** to be a lost cause. ❱❯ conj if.

casório [ka'zɔrju] m fam splicing.

caspa ['kaʃpal f dandruff.

Cáspio ['kaʃpju] n: o (mar) ~ the Caspian (Sea).

casquinha [kaʃ'kiɲal f -1. [de sorvete] cone. -2. [de pele] scab.

cassado, da [ka'sadu, da] m, f person deprived of his/her civil rights.

cassar [4] [ka'sa(x)] vt -1. POL to annul. -2. [licença, direitos] to quash.

cassete [ka'sɛtʃil <> adj inv [fita, gravador] tape- (antes de subst). <> m [gravador] tape.

cassetete [kase'tɛtʃil m truncheon.

cassino [ka'sinul m casino.

casta ['kaʃtal f -1. [camada social] caste. -2. fig [raça] race.

castanha [kaʃ'tãɲal f ⊏> castanho.

castanha-do-pará [kaʃ,tãɲadupa'ral (pl casta- nhas-do-pará) m Brazil nut.

castanheiro [kaʃtã'ɲejrul m chestnut tree.

castanho, nha [kaʃ'tãɲu, ɲal adj [olhos etc] brown.

➤ **castanha** f [fruto] chestnut; ~ de caju cashew.

castanholas [kaʃtã'ɲɔlaʃl fpl castanets.

castelo [kaʃ'tɛlul m castle.

castiçal [kaʃtʃi'sawl (pl -ais) m candlestick.

castiço, ça [kaʃ'tʃisu, sal adj -1. [puro] top-breed. -2. [de boa casta] well-bred. -3. fig [vernáculo] vernacular.

castidade [kaʃtʃi'dadʒil f chastity.

castigar [14] [kaʃtʃi'ga(x)] vt -1. [punir] to punish. -2. fam [tocar] to bash out.

➤ **castigar-se** vp [penitenciar-se] to do penance.

castigo [kaʃ'tʃigul m -1. [punição] punishment; estar/ficar de ~ to be being punished. -2. fig [mortificação] torture; ser um ~ to be torture.

casto, ta ['kaʃtu, tal adj chaste.

castrado, da [kaʃ'tradu, dal adj castrated.

castrar [4] [kaʃ'tra(x)] vt -1. [capar] to castrate. -2. fig [impedir] to muzzle. -3. fig [personalidade] to castrate.

casual [ka'zwawl (pl -ais) adj chance (antes de subst).

casualidade [kazwali'dadʒil f chance; por ~ by chance.

casulo [ka'zulul m -1. [de insetos] cocoon. -2. [de sementes] boll.

cata ['katal f: à ~ de algo/alguém in search of sthg/sb.

cataclismo [kata'kliʒmul m -1. [dilúvio] flood. -2. GEOL cataclysm. -3. fig [desastre] cataclysm. -4. fig [convulsão social] revolt.

catacumbas [kata'kũbaʃl fpl catacombs.

catalão, lã [kata'lãw, lãl <> adj Catalan. <> m, f Catalan.

➤ **catalão** m [língua] Catalan.

catalisador, ra [kataliza'do(x), ral adj catalytic.

➤ **catalisador** m catalyst.

catalogar [14] [katalo'ga(x)] vt to catalogue.

catálogo [ka'talogul m catalogue; ~ (de telefo- nes) telephone directory.

Catalunha [kata'lũɲal n Catalonia.

catapora [kata'pɔral f chickenpox.

catar [4] [ka'ta(x)] vt -1. [procurar] to search for. -2. [pegar, recolher] to pick up. -3. [tirar, limpar de] to pick out; ~ piolhos to delouse. -4. [escolher] to pick over; ~ feijão/arroz to pick over beans/ rice.

catarata [kata'ratal f -1. [queda d'água] waterfall. -2. MED cataract.

CATARATAS DO IGUAÇU

Situated in the interior of the National Park of Iguaçu (PR), on the border between Brazil and Argentina, the Iguaçu falls pour out 13 million litres of water per second from an altitude that varies between 40 and 90 metres. Its 275 waterfalls are spread, on the Brazilian side, over a width of 800 metres. The almost 90m high *Garganta do Diabo* is its most famous fall.

catarro [ka'taxul m catarrh.

catarse [ka'taxsil f catharsis.

catástrofe [ka'taʃtrofil f catastrophe.

catastrófico, ca [kataʃ'trɔfiku, kal adj cata- strophic.

catatau [kata'tawl (pl -ais) m fam: um ~ de a pile of.

cata-vento [kata'vẽntul (pl cata-ventos) m weathervane.

catecismo [kate'siʒmul m catechism.

cátedra ['katedral f -1. UNIV chair. -2. RELIG throne.

catedral [kate'drawl (pl -ais) f cathedral.

catedrático, ca [kate'dratʃiku, kal <> m, f chair. <> adj chair.

categoria [katego'rial f -1. [grupo] category. -2. [qualidade] quality; de (alta) ~ high quality. -3. [social] standing. -4. [cargo] position.

categórico, ca [kate'gɔriku, kal adj categoric.

categorização [kategoriza'sãwl (pl -ões) f cate- gorization.

categorizar [4] [kategori'za(x)] vt to classify.

catequese [kate'kɛzil f religious instruction.

catequizar [4] [kateki'za(x)] vt -1. RELIG to teach doctrine to. -2. fig [doutrinar] to indoctrinate.

cateter [kate'tɛ(x)] m MED catheter.

cateterismo [katete'riʒmul m MED catheteriza- tion.

catinga [ka'tʃĩgal f [mau-cheiro] stench.

cativante [katʃi'vãntʃil adj entrancing.

cativar [4] [katʃi'va(x)] vt -1. [escravizar] to capture. -2. [seduzir] to captivate.

cativeiro [katʃi'vejrul m -1. [escravidão] slavery. -2. [prisão] captivity.

cativo, va [ka'tʃivu, val <> adj -1. [preso] captive. -2. [sujeito]: ~ a attracted by. -3. [cadeira] exclusive. <> m, f -1. [escravo] slave. -2. [prisionei- ro] prisoner.

catolicismo [katoli'siʒmul m Catholicism.

católico, ca [ka'tɔliku, kal adj -1. RELIG Catholic. -2. fig [correto, tradicional]: não ser muito ~ to be unconventional. -3. fig [bem, de bom humor]: ele não está muito ~ he's not in a good mood.

catorze [ka'toxzil num fourteen; veja também seis.

catucar [12] [katu'ka(x)] *vt* = cutucar.
caução [kaw'sãw] (*pl* -ões) *f* - **1.** [cautela] care. - **2.** [garantia] pledge. - **3.** *JUR* bail.
Cáucaso ['kawkazu] *n* Caucasus.
caucionar [4] [kawsjo'na(x)] *vt* - **1.** [garantir] to pledge. - **2.** *JUR* to stand bail for.
cauções [kaw'sõjʃ] *fpl* ▷ caução.
cauda ['kawda] *f* - **1.** [de animal] tail. - **2.** [de vestido] train.
caudaloso, osa [kawda'lozu, ɔza] *adj* torrential.
caudilho [kaw'dʒiʎu] *m* military commander.
caule ['kawli] *m* stem.
causa ['kawza] *f* - **1.** [ger] cause. - **2.** [motivo] reason; **por ~ de** because of.
causador, ra [kawza'do(x), ra] ◇ *adj* causal. ◇ *m, f* cause.
causar [4] [kaw'za(x)] *vt* to cause.
cáustico, ca ['kawʃtʃiku, ka] *adj* caustic.
cautela [kaw'tɛla] *f* - **1.** [precaução] precaution; **com ~** with care. - **2.** [título] share certificate. - **3.** [de penhor] pawn ticket.
cautelar [kawte'la(x)] *adj* precautionary.
cauteloso, osa [kawte'lozu, ɔza] *adj* cautious.
cauterizar [4] [kawteri'za(x)] *vt* to cauterize.
cava ['kava] *f* ▷ cavo.
cavaco [ka'vaku] *m*: **~s do ofício** part of the job.
cavala [ka'vala] *f* [peixe] mackerel.
cavalar [kava'la(x)] *adj* excessive.
cavalaria [kavala'ria] *f* - **1.** *MIL* cavalry. - **2.** [cavalos] herd of horses. - **3.** [ordem] chivalry.
cavalariça [kavala'risa] *f* [estrebaria] stable.
cavalariço [kavala'risu] *m* [estribeiro] groom *UK*, stableman *US*.
cavaleiro, ra [kava'lejru] *m, f* [quem monta] horseman (*f* horsewoman).
➤ **cavaleiro** *m* [medieval] knight.
cavalete [kava'letʃi] *m* - **1.** [de pintor] easel. - **2.** [de mesa] trestle. - **3.** [para instrumento] bridge.
cavalgar [14] [kavaw'ga(x)] *vt & vi* to ride.
cavalheiresco, ca [kavaʎej'reʃku, ka] *adj* noble.
cavalheiro [kava'ʎejru] ◇ *m* gentleman. ◇ *adj* [educado] well-bred.
cavalo [ka'valu] *m* - **1.** *ZOOL* horse; **a ~** on horseback. - **2.** [em xadrez] knight. - **3.** *fig* [pessoa agressiva] pig; **ele agiu como um ~** he behaved like a pig. - **4.** [cavalo-vapor] horsepower. - **5.** *loc*: **fazer um ~ de batalha** to make a fuss about nothing; **pode tirar o ~ da chuva que ela não vai aceitar sua proposta** you can forget that, as she's not going to accept your proposal.
cavalo-de-pau [kavaludʒi'paw] (*pl* cavalos-de-pau) *m* wheel spin.
cavalo-de-Tróia [ka'valudʒitrɔja] (*pl* cavalos-de-Tróia) *m* *COMPUT* Trojan horse.
cavalo-marinho [ka,valuma'riɲu] (*pl* cavalos-marinhos) *m* sea-horse.
cavanhaque [kava'ɲaki] *m* goatee.
cavaquinho [kava'kiɲu] *m* small guitar.
cavar [4] [ka'va(x)] ◇ *vt* - **1.** [ger] to dig. - **2.** [emprego] to search long and hard. ◇ *vi* [escavar] to dig.
cave ['kavi] *f* cellar.

caveira [ka'vejra] *f* - **1.** [crânio] skull. - **2.** *fig* [rosto macilento] cavernous face. - **3.** *loc*: **fazer a ~ de alguém** to run sb down.
caverna [ka'vɛxna] *f* cavern.
cavernoso, osa [kavɛx'nozu, ɔza] *adj* cavernous.
caviar [ka'vja(x)] *m* caviar.
cavidade [kavi'dadʒi] *f* cavity.
cavilha [ka'viʎa] *f* peg.
cavo, va ['kavu, va] *adj* [côncavo] hollow.
➤ **cava** *f* [de manga] armhole.
caxias [ka'ʃiaʃ] ◇ *adj (inv)* scrupulous. ◇ *mf (inv)* hard taskmaster.
caxumba [ka'ʃũnba] *f* mumps (*sg*).
CBF (*abrev de* Confederação Brasileira de Futebol) *f* Brazilian football federation.
c/c (*abrev de* conta corrente) *f* c/a.
CD [se'de] (*abrev de* Compact Disc) *m* CD.
CDB (*abrev de* Certificado de Depósito Bancário) *m* type of investment offered by Brazilian banks.
CDC (*abrev de* Código de Defesa do Consumidor) *m* Brazilian consumer protection legislation.
CD-i (*abrev de* Compact Disc-Interativo) *m* CD-I.
CD-ROM (*abrev de* Compact Disc-Read Only Memory) *m* CD-ROM.
CE ◇ *f* (*abrev de* Comunidade Européia) EC. ◇ *m* (*abrev de* Estado do Ceará) State of Ceará.
cear [15] ['sja(x)] ◇ *vt* to have for supper. ◇ *vi* to have supper.
Ceará [sja'ra] *n* Ceará.
CEASA (*abrev de* Companhia de Entrepostos e Armazéns S.A) *m* Brazilian company of fruit and vegetable wholesalers.
cebola [se'bola] *f* onion.
cebolinha [sebo'liɲa] *f* chive.
CEBRAP (*abrev de* Centro Brasileiro de Análise e Planejamento) *m* independent research centre for the study of Brazilian society.
cê-cedilha [,sese'dʒiʎa] (*pl* cês-cedilhas) *m* c-cedilla.
cê-dê-efe [sede'ɛfi] (*pl* cê-dê-efes) *mf fam* - **1.** [com o trabalho] workaholic. - **2.** [com os estudos] swot.
cedente [se'dẽntʃi] *mf* transferor.
ceder [5] [se'de(x)] ◇ *vt* - **1.** [dar] to hand over. - **2.** [emprestar] to loan. ◇ *vi* - **1.** [aquiescer]: **~ a algo** to give in to sthg. - **2.** [diminuir] to fall. - **3.** [afrouxarse] to loosen. - **4.** [curvar-se ao peso] to give way. - **5.** [sucumbir]: **~ a algo** to give way to sthg. - **6.** [transigir] to give in.
cedilha [se'diʎa] *f* cedilla.
cedo ['sedu] *adv* [de manhãzinha] early; **mais ~ ou mais tarde** sooner or later; **o mais ~ possível** as soon as possible; **quanto mais ~ melhor** the sooner the better.
cedro ['sɛdru] *m* cedar.
cédula ['sɛdula] *f* - **1.** [dinheiro] banknote. - **2.** [em votação]: **~ eleitoral** ballot paper.
CEF (*abrev de* Caixa Econômica Federal) *f* Brazilian state-owned bank financing loans for house purchase.
cefaléia [sefa'lɛja] *f* headache.

cegar [14] [se'ga(x)] *vt* **-1.** [ger] to blind. **-2.** [suj: paixão, raiva] to make blind. **-3.** [tesoura etc] to blunt.

cego, ga ['sɛgu, ga] <> *adj* **-1.** [ger] blind. **-2.** [tesoura] blunt. <> *m, f* blind person.

➡ **às cegas** *loc adv* **-1.** [sem ver] blindly. **-2.** [sem saber] in the dark.

cegonha [se'goɲa] *f* [ave] stork; **esperar a chegada da** ~ *fam* to be pregnant.

cegueira [se'gejra] *f* blindness.

ceia ['seja] *f* supper; **a última** ~ *RELIG* the Last Supper; ~ **de Natal** Christmas Eve midnight supper.

ceifa ['sejfa] *f* **-1.** [ato] harvest. **-2.** [época] harvest-time. **-3.** *fig* [destruição, mortandade] death-toll.

ceifar [4] [sej'fa(x)] <> *vt* **-1.** [trigo, espigas] to harvest. **-2.** *fig* [vidas] to take. <> *vi* [colher] to harvest.

Ceilão [sej'lãw] *n* Ceylon.

cela ['sɛla] *f* cell.

celebração [selebra'sãw] (*pl* **-ões**) *f* **-1.** [realização] celebration. **-2.** [comemoração] commemoration.

celebrado, da [sele'bradu, da] *adj* [afamado] celebrated.

celebrar [4] [sele'bra(x)] *vt* **-1.** [ger] to celebrate. **-2.** [exaltar] to glorify.

célebre ['sɛlebri] *adj* famous.

celebridade [selebri'dadʒi] *mf* celebrity.

celebrizar [4] [selebri'za(x)] *vt* [conferir fama a] to make famous.

➡ **celebrizar-se** *vp* to become famous.

celeiro [se'lejru] *m* **-1.** [para cereais] granary. **-2.** [depósito] store.

célere ['sɛleri] *adj* quick.

celeste [se'lɛʃtʃi] *adj* heavenly.

celestial [seleʃ'tʃjaw] (*pl* **-ais**) *adj* celestial.

celeuma [se'lewma] *f* hubbub.

celibatário, ria [seliba'tarju, rja] <> *adj* celibate. <> *m, f* unmarried person.

celibato [seli'batu] *m* celibacy.

celofane [selo'fãni] <> *adj* [papel] cellophane. <> *m* cellophane.

celsius [sew'siuʃ] *adj* Celsius.

celta ['sɛwta] <> *adj* Celtic. <> *mf* [pessoa] Celt. <> *m* [língua] Celtic.

célula ['sɛlula] *f* cell; ~ **fotoelétrica** photo-electric cell.

celular [selu'la(x)] <> *adj* cellular. <> *m* TELEC cellular phone.

celulite [selu'litʃi] *f* cellulite.

celulose [selu'lɔzi] *f* cellulose.

cem ['sɛ̃] *num* **-1.** [cardinal] one/a hundred; ~ **por cento** one/a hundred per cent; *veja também* **seis**. **-2.** [muitos]: ~ **vezes** hundreds of times.

➡ **cem por cento** <> *loc adj*: **ser** ~ **por cento** to be one hundred per cent. <> *loc adv* [totalmente] completely.

cemitério [semi'tɛrju] *m* cemetery.

cena ['sena] *f* **-1.** [de peça, filme, novela] scene; ~**s externas** outdoor scenes. **-2.** [palco] stage; **levar à** ~ to stage; **em** ~ on stage. **-3.** [acontecimento]

spectacle. **-4.** [escândalo]: **fazer uma** ~ to make a scene.

cenário [se'narju] *m* **-1.** [ger] scene. **-2.** [em teatro, cinema, TV] scenery. **-3.** [panorama] sight.

cenho ['seɲu] *m* frown.

cênico, ca ['seniku, ka] *adj* TEATRO stage (*antes de subst*); **artes cênicas** performing arts.

cenografia [senogra'fia] *f* scenography.

cenógrafo, fa [se'nɔgrafu, fa] *m, f* scenographer.

cenoura [se'noura] *f* carrot.

censo ['sẽsu] *m* census.

censor, ra [sẽso(x), ra] *m, f* censor.

censura [sẽ'sura] *f* **-1.** [crítica] criticism. **-2.** [repreensão] reprimand. **-3.** [condenação] condemnation. **-4.** [prática] censure. **-5.** [organismo] board of censors. **-6.** [proibição] censorship. **-7.** [corte] cut.

censurado, da [sẽsu'radu, da] *adj* [proibido] censored.

censurar [4] [sẽsu'ra(x)] *vt* **-1.** [criticar] to criticise. **-2.** [repreender] to reprove. **-3.** [condenar] to condemn. **-4.** [examinar] to censor. **-5.** [proibir] to ban. **-6.** [cortar] to cut.

censurável [sẽsu'ravew] (*pl* **-eis**) *adj* [decisão, comportamento] open to criticism.

centavo [sẽ'tavu] *m* cent; **estar sem um** ~ to be penniless.

centeio [sẽ'teju] *m* rye.

centelha [sẽ'teʎa] *f* spark.

centena [sẽ'tena] *f* hundred; **às** ~**s** in their hundreds; **uma** ~ **de vezes** a hundred times.

centenário, ria [sẽte'narju, rja] <> *adj*: **um homem** ~ a hundred-year-old man; **ele é** ~ he is a hundred years old. <> *m, f* [pessoa] centenarian.

➡ **centenário** *m* [comemoração] centenary.

centésimo, ma [sẽ'tɛzimu, ma] <> *num* hundredth. <> *m, f* [pessoa] hundredth.

➡ **centésimo** *m* hundredth.

centígrado, da [sẽ'tʃigradu] *adj* centigrade (*depois de subst*).

➡ **centígrado** *m* centigrade.

centilitro [sẽtʃi'litru] *m* centilitre.

centímetro [sẽ'tʃimetru] *m* centimetre.

cento ['sẽtu] *num*: ~ **e dez** one/a hundred and ten; **por** ~ per cent; *veja também* **seis**.

centopéia [sẽto'pɛja] *f* centipede.

central [sẽ'traw] (*pl* **-ais**) <> *adj* **-1.** [ger] central. **-2.** *fig* [problema, ponto, argumento] central. <> *f* **-1.** [agência, delegacia]: ~ **de polícia** police station; ~ **de atendimento** call centre; ~ **de correios** post office; ~ **telefônica** telephone exchange. **-2.** [usina]: ~ **elétrica** power station; ~ **nuclear** nuclear power station.

centralização [sẽtraliza'sãw] *f* centralization.

centralizar [4] [sẽtrali'za(x)] *vt* to centralize.

centrar [4] [sẽ'tra(x)] <> *vt* **-1.** [ger] to centre. **-2.** FUT [bola, passe]: ~ to kick into the centre. <> *vi* FUT to shoot.

centrífuga [sẽtri'fuga], **centrifugadora** [sẽtri'fuga'dora] *f* centrifuge.

centro ['sẽtru] *m* **-1.** [ger] centre; ~ **de gravidade** centre of gravity; ~ **da Terra** centre of the

Earth; ~ **de mesa** centrepiece; **ser o ~ das atenções** to be the centre of attention; ~ **comercial** shopping centre *UK*, shopping mall *US*; ~ **cultural** cultural centre; ~ **espírita** spiritualist centre; ~ **financeiro** financial centre; ~ **industrial** industrial centre; ~ **produtor** manufacturing centre; ~ **de atendimento** service centre; ~ **de processamento de dados** data processing centre. **-2.** [de cidade] (city) centre; **ir ao ~** to go downtown. **-3.** [metrópole] metropolis.

centroavante [ˌsẽntrwˈvãntʃi] *m* centre forward.

CEP (*abrev de* **Código de Endereçamento Postal**) *m* ≃ post code *UK*, ≃ zip code *US*.

CEPAL (*abrev de* **Comissão Econômica para a América Latina**) *f* ECLAC.

cepo [ˈsepu] *m* **-1.** [toro] log. **-2.** [para decapitação] block.

cera [ˈsera] *f* **-1.** [ger] wax. **-2.** [para polir] wax polish. **-3.** *fam fig* [manha] sham; **fazer ~** to sham.

cerâmica [seˈrãmika] *f* **-1.** [ger] ceramics. **-2.** [fábrica] pottery. **-3.** [argila cozida] ceramic.

ceramista [seraˈmiʃta] *mf* potter, ceramicist.

cerca [ˈsexka] *f* [de arame, madeira, ferro] fence; ~ **viva** hedge.

➡ **cerca de** *loc prep* around.

cercado, da [sexˈkadu, da] *adj* fenced.

➡ **cercado** *m* **-1.** [terreno] enclosure. **-2.** [para animais] pen. **-3.** [para crianças] playground.

cercanias [sexkaˈniaʃ] *fpl* **-1.** [arredores] outskirts. **-2.** [vizinhança] neighbourhood.

cercar [12] [sexˈka(x)] *vt* **-1.** [ger] to surround. **-2.** [pôr cerca em] to fence.

➡ **cercar-se** *vp* [rodear-se]: ~**-se de** to surround o.s. with.

cercear [15] [sexˈsja(x)] *vt* [liberdade, privilégios] to restrict.

cerco [ˈsexku] *m* [assédio] siege; **fechar o ~ a** to close in on, to clamp down on; **pôr ~ a** to lay siege to.

cerda [ˈsexda] *f* [de escova de dentes] bristle.

cereal [seˈrjal] (*pl* -ais) *m* cereal.

cerebral [sereˈbrawl] (*pl* -ais) *adj* **-1.** ANAT cerebral. **-2.** [intelectual] intellectual.

cérebro [ˈserebru] *m* **-1.** ANAT brain. **-2.** *fig* [líder, mentor]: **o ~** the brains (*sg*).

cereja [seˈreʒa] *f* cherry.

cerejeira [sereˈʒejra] *f* **-1.** [árvore] cherry tree. **-2.** [madeira] cherry wood.

cerimônia [seriˈmonja] *f* **-1.** [solenidade] ceremony; ~ **de posse** investiture. **-2.** [formalidade] formality; **fazer ~** to stand on ceremony; **sirva-se sem ~!** just help yourself!

cerimonial [serimoˈnjawl] (*pl* -ais) *m* [protocolo] ceremonial.

cerimonioso, osa [serimoˈnjozu, ɔza] *adj* ceremonious.

cerne [ˈsexni] *m* **-1.** [de madeira] heartwood. **-2.** *fig* [de questão] heart.

ceroulas [seˈrolaʃ] *fpl* long johns.

cerração [sexaˈsãw] *f* [neblina] fog.

cerrado, da [seˈxadu, da] *adj* **-1.** [fechado - porta, olhos] closed; [- punhos, dentes] clenched. **-2.** [intenso] [bombardeio] heavy. **-3.** [denso, espesso] thick.

➡ **cerrado** *m* [vegetação] *dense, low vegetation found in northern and central Brazil*.

cerrar [4] [seˈxa(x)] *vt* [fechar - porta, olhos] to close; [-punhos, centes] to clench.

➡ **cerrar-se** *vp* **-1.** [fechar-se] to close; ~**-se em** to shut oneself in. **-2.** [céu] to become dark.

certa [ˈsexta] *f* ➡ **certo.**

certame [sexˈtãmi] *m* [concurso, competição] contest.

certeiro, ra [sexˈtejru, ra] *adj* accurate.

certeza [sexˈteza] *f* certainty; **tem ~?** are you sure?; **ter ~ de algo** to be sure about sthg; **ter ~ de que** to be sure that; **com ~** definitely.

certidão [sextʃiˈdãw] (*pl* -ões) *f* certificate; ~ **de casamento** marriage certificate; ~ **de nascimento** birth certificate.

certificação [sextʃifikaˈsãw] (*pl* -ões) *f* certification.

certificado [sextʃifiˈkadu] *m* certificate.

certificar [12] [sextʃifiˈka(x)] *vt* **-1.** [assegurar]: ~ **alguém de algo/de que** to assure sb of sthg/that. **-2.** [atestar] to affirm.

➡ **certificar-se** *vp*: ~**-se de que/de algo** to make sure that/of sthg.

certo, ta [ˈsextu, ta] <> *adj* **-1.** [ger] right. **-2.** [correto, certeiro] correct. **-3.** [sensato, acertado] sensible. **-4.** [infalível, seguro] certain; **ser ~ que** to be certain that. **-5.** [com razão]: **estar ~** to be right. **-6.** [com certeza]: **estar ~ de que/de algo** to be sure that/of sthg. <> *pron* **-1.** (*antes de subst*) [um, algum] right; **certa vez** once. **-2.** *loc* : **dar ~** to work; **está ~** [está bem] all right.

➡ **certo** <> *m* **-1.** [correto] (what is) right; **ele não sabe distinguir entre o ~ e o errado** he doesn't know the difference between right and wrong. **-2.** [verdade] truth. <> *adv* **-1.** [certamente] certainly. **-2.** [corretamente] correctly.

➡ **certa f: na certa** definitely.

➡ **ao certo** *loc adv* for sure.

➡ **por certo** *loc adv* definitely.

cerveja [sexˈveʒa] *f* [bebida] beer.

cervejaria [sexveʒaˈria] *f* **-1.** [fábrica] brewery. **-2.** [estabelecimento] *beer bar, usually serving food if wanted*.

cervical [sexviˈkawl] (*pl* -ais) *adj* cervical.

cerzir [58] [sexˈzi(x)] <> *vt* to darn. <> *vi* to do invisible mending.

cesariana [sezaˈrjãna], **cesárea** [seˈzarja] *f* Caesarean.

cessação [sesaˈsãw] *f* ending.

cessão [seˈsãw] (*pl* -ões) *f* **-1.** [cedência] assignment. **-2.** [transferência] transfer.

cessar [4] [seˈsa(x)] <> *vi* to come to an end; ~ **com algo/de fazer algo** to stop sthg/doing sthg; **sem ~** non-stop. <> *vt* **-1.** [fogo] to cease. **-2.** [trabalho] to stop.

cessar-fogo [seˌsaxˈfogu] *m* (*inv*) ceasefire.

cessões [seˈsõjʃ] *pl* ➡ **cessão.**

cesta [ˈseʃta] *f* **-1.** [ger] basket; ~ **básica** *basic* monthly supplies that the average lower-middle-class family needs in order to survive. **-2.** [conteúdo] basketful. **- 3.** [ESP - aro] basket; [- ponto] stitch.

cesto ['sɛʃtu] m basket; ~ **de roupa suja** laundry basket.

CETESB (abrev de **Companhia Estadual de Tecnologia de Saneamento Básico e Defesa do Meio Ambiente**) f São Paulo environment agency.

ceticismo [setʃi'siʒmu] m scepticism.

cético, ca ['sɛtʃiku, ka] <> adj sceptical. <> m, f sceptic.

cetim [se'tʃĩ] m satin.

cetro ['sɛtru] m sceptre.

céu ['sɛw] m **- 1.** [firmamento] sky; **a ~ aberto** [ao ar livre] in the open; [mineração] open-cast; **cair do ~ fig** to be heaven-sent; **mover ~s e terra fig** to move heaven and earth. **- 2.** RELIG heaven. **- 3.** ANAT : ~ **da boca** roof of the mouth.

cevada [se'vada] f barley.

cevar [4] [se'va(x)] vt **- 1.** [alimentar] to feed. **- 2.** [fazer engordar] to fatten.

CFC (abrev de **clorofluorocarboneto**) m CFC.

chá ['ʃa] m **- 1.** [ger] tea; ~ **completo** afternoon tea; ~ **de camomila/menta** camomile/mint tea; ~ **preto** black tea. **- 2.** [reunião] tea party; ~ **beneficente** fund-raising tea; ~ **dançante** tea dance. **- 3.** loc: depois de aparecer vários dias seguidos, ele tomou um ~ de sumiço having turned up several days in a row he's gone missing; **tomar ~ de cadeira** to be a wallflower; **levei o maior ~ de cadeira no consultório ontem** I waited for ages at the doctor's yesterday.

chã ['ʃã] f plain.

chacal [ʃa'kaw] (pl **-ais**) m jackal.

chácara ['ʃakara] f **- 1.** [no campo] smallholding. **- 2.** [na cidade] large town house. **- 3.** [casa de campo] country house.

chacina [ʃa'sina] f slaughter.

chacinar [4] [ʃasi'na(x)] vt to slaughter.

chacoalhar [4] [ʃakwa'ʎa(x)] <> vt [agitar] to shake. <> vi [sacudir] to shake.

chacota [ʃa'kɔta] f **- 1.** [deboche] ridicule. **- 2.** [objeto de deboche] butt of ridicule.

chacrinha [ʃa'kriɲa] fam f **- 1.** [reunião] meeting. **- 2.** pej [bagunça] mess.

chá-de-panela [ˌʃadʒipa'nɛla] (pl **chás-de-panela**) m (bridal) shower US, party at which presents are given to a bride-to-be.

chafariz [ʃafa'riʃ] (pl **-es**) m fountain.

chafurdar [4] [ʃafux'da(x)] vi: ~ **em** [lama etc] to wallow in; fig [vícios etc] to become involved in.

chaga ['ʃaga] f **- 1.** [ferida] wound. **- 2.** fig [mal] scourge.

chalé [ʃa'lɛ] m cottage.

chaleira [ʃa'lejra] f kettle.

chama ['ʃama] f flame; **em ~s** in flames.

chamada [ʃa'mada] f **- 1.** [telefônica] call; **fazer uma ~ a cobrar** to make a reverse charge call UK, to call collect US. **- 2.** [verificação de presença] roll call. **- 3.** JORN headline. **- 4.** [repreensão]: **dar**

uma ~ **em alguém** to reprimand sb.

chamar [4] [ʃa'ma(x)] <> vt **- 1.** [ger] to call; **ela decidiu chamá-la de Júlia** she decided to call her 'Júlia'. **- 2.** [com gesto] to hail. **- 3.** [convocar] to summon; [para função]: ~ **alguém para algo** to call sb for sthg. **- 4.** [convidar] to invite; ~ **a atenção** [suj: pessoa, roupa] to attract attention; [para aspecto etc] to draw attention; ~ **a atenção de alguém** [repreender] to reprimand sb. **- 5.** [acordar] to wake. **- 6.** [qualificar]: ~ **algo/alguém de algo** to call sthg/sb sthg. <> vi **- 1.** [dar sinal para vir] to call over; **chamei, mas ela não quis vir** I called her over but she didn't want to come. **- 2.** [para acudir]: ~ **por alguém** to call out for sb; ~ **por socorro** to call for help. **- 3.** [telefone] to ring.

➡ **chamar-se** vp [ter por nome] to be called; **como você se chama?** what's your name?

chamariz [ʃama'riʒ] m **- 1.** [isca] bait. **- 2.** [seta, anúncio] advert. **- 3.** fig [engodo] illusion.

chamativo, va [ʃama'tʃivu, va] adj flashy.

chamego [ʃa'megu] m state of excitement; **estar/ficar de ~ com alguém** to caress sb.

chaminé [ʃami'nɛ] f chimney.

champanha [ʃãm'pãɲa], **champanhe** [ʃãm'paɲi] m ou f champagne.

chamuscar [12] [ʃamuʃ'ka(x)] vt **- 1.** [roupa] to scorch. **- 2.** [cabelo] to singe. **- 3.** [pessoa, braço] to burn.

➡ **chamuscar-se** vp to burn o.s.

chance ['ʃãsi] f chance; **dar uma ~ a ou para alguém/algo** to give sb/sthg a chance; **ele tem boas ~s de ganhar** he has a good chance of winning.

chancela [ʃãn'sɛla] f seal.

chancelaria [ʃãnsela'ria] f **- 1.** [repartição] chancery. **- 2.** [ministério do exterior] foreign ministry.

chanceler [ʃãnse'lɛ(x)] mf **- 1.** [ministro] minister. **- 2.** [chefe de governo] head of government.

chanchada [ʃãn'ʃada] f **- 1.** CINE blue movie. **- 2.** TEATRO pornographic play.

chantagear [15] [ʃãnta'ʒja(x)] vt to blackmail.

chantagem [ʃãn'taʒẽ] (pl **-ns**) f blackmail.

chantagista [ʃãnta'ʒiʃta] mf blackmailer.

chão ['ʃãw] m **- 1.** [piso] floor. **- 2.** [solo] ground.

chapa ['ʃapa] <> f **- 1.** [folha] sheet; ~ **de metal/ aço** metal/steel sheet. **- 2.** [para grelhar] hotplate; **bife na ~** steak on the griddle. **- 3.** AUTO [placa] number plate UK, license plate US; ~ **fria** false number plate UK, false license plate US. **- 4.** [de impressão] plate. **- 5.** FOT shot. **- 6.** [radiografia] X-ray. **- 7.** POL [eleitoral] roll. <> mf [camarada] mate.

chapelaria [ʃapela'ria] f **- 1.** [loja] hat shop. **- 2.** [fábrica] millinery factory.

chapeleiro, ra [ʃape'lejru, ra] m, f milliner.

chapéu [ʃa'pɛw] m hat; **de tirar o ~** fantastic.

chapéu-coco [ʃaˌpɛw'koku] (pl **chapéus-cocos**) m bowler hat.

chapinha [ʃa'piɲa] f [de garrafa] stopper.

charada [ʃa'rada] f [enigma] puzzle; **matar uma ~** to solve a problem.

charco ['ʃaxku] m puddle.

charge [ˈʃaxʒi] f cartoon.

chargista [ʃaxˈʒiʃta] mf cartoonist.

charlatão, tã [ʃaxlaˈtãw, tã] (mpl **-ães**, fpl **-s**) <> adj charlatan. <> m, f impostor.

charme [ˈʃaxmi] m charm; **fazer** ~ to play it cool.

charmoso, osa [ʃaxˈmozu, ɔza] adj charming.

charrete [ʃaˈxɛtʃi] f chariot.

charter [ˈʃaxte(x)] <> adj inv charter. <> m charter plane.

charuto [ʃaˈrutu] m cigar.

chassi [ʃaˈsil] m **-1.** [ger] chassis. **-2.** ARTE [de tela] stretcher.

chateação [ʃatʃjaˈsãw] (pl **-ões**) f **-1.** [aborrecimento] boredom. **-2.** [maçada] bore.

chatear [15] [ʃaˈtʃja(x)] <> vt **-1.** [aborrecer] to annoy. **-2.** [incomodar] to bother. **-3.** [enfadar] to irritate. **-4.** [implicar com] to tease. <> vi **-1.** [aborrecer] to be boring. **-2.** [incomodar] to be annoying.
◆ **chatear-se** vp [aborrecer-se] to become bored.

chatice [ʃaˈtʃisil] f boredom.

chato, ta [ˈʃatu, tal] <> adj **-1.** [superfície, forma] flat; **ele tem pés** ~**s** he's got flat feet. **-2.** [filme, música] boring. **-3.** [desagradável] unwelcome. **-4.** [embaraçoso] tricky. <> m, f bore; **um** ~ **de galochas** a drag.
◆ **chato** m [coisa desagradável]: **o** ~ **é que vamos passar o final de semana trabalhando** the annoying thing is we're going to spend the weekend working.
◆ **chata** f [embarcação] boat.

chatura [ʃaˈtural] f fam drag.

chauvinismo [ʃawviˈniʒmul] m chauvinism.

chauvinista [ʃoviˈniʃta] mf chauvinist.

chavão [ʃaˈvãw] (pl **-ões**) m hackneyed phrase.

chave [ˈʃavil] f **-1.** [de fechadura] key; ~ **mestra** master key. **-2.** [ferramenta] spanner; ~ **de fenda** ou **para fusos** screwdriver; ~ **de porcas** wrench; ~ **inglesa** adjustable spanner UK, monkey wrench US. **-3.** ELETR switch. **-4.** [golpe] blow; ~ **de braço** armlock. **-5.** [sinal gráfico] curly bracket. **-6.** fig [de problema] key.

-chave [ˈʃliavil] sufixo key- (prefixo).

chaveiro [ʃaˈvejrul] m **-1.** [utensílio] key-rack. **-2.** [profissional] locksmith.

chavões [ʃaˈvõjʃ] pl ▷ **chavão**.

checar [12] [ʃeˈka(x);] vt to check.

check-up [ʃeˈkapil] (pl **check-ups**) m check-up.

chefe [ˈʃɛfil] mf **-1.** [superior] head; ~ **de estado** head of state; ~ **de família** head of the family; ~ **de turma** shift supervisor. **-2.** fam [garçom] waiter. **-3.** fam [freguês] mate.

chefia [ʃeˈfial] f **-1.** [direção] management. **-2.** [repartição, sala] management office.

chefiar [16] [ʃeˈfja(x)] vt to lead.

chega [ˈʃegal] m fam [repreensão]: **dar um** ~ **(para lá) em alguém** to tear a strip off sb.

chegada [ʃeˈgadal] f **-1.** [vinda, regresso] arrival. **-2.** [aproximação] approach. **-3.** ESP finishing line.

chegado, da [ʃeˈgadu, dal] adj **-1.** [ger] close. **-2.** [propenso]: **ser** ~ **a** to be very fond of.

chegar [14] [ʃeˈga(x)] <> vi **-1.** [a um lugar]: ~ **em** to arrive at; ~ **em casa** to arrive home; ~ **de** to arrive from. **-2.** [aproximar-se] to approach; **chega aqui** fam come here; **chega para cá** move over here. **-3.** [afastar-se]: **chega para lá** [ir embora] go away; [deslocar-se] move over. **-4.** [verão, noite, hora] to arrive. **-5.** [bastar] to be enough; **chegar!** that's enough! **-6.** [alcançar] to reach; **não** ~ **aos pés de** [não ser comparável a] to come nowhere near. **-7.** [conseguir]: ~ **a (ser) algo** to succeed in becoming sthg; ~ **a fazer algo** to manage to do sthg. **-8.** [ir ao extremo]: ~ **a fazer algo** to reach the point of doing sthg. **-9.** fam [partir]: **vou chegando** I'm pushing off. <> vt **-1.** [aproximar]: ~ **algo para cá** to bring sthg over here. **-2.** [afastar]: ~ **algo para lá/parao lado** to move sthg over there/to one side.
◆ **chegar-se** vp [aproximar-se] to come closer.

cheio, cheia [ˈʃeju, ˈʃejal] adj **-1.** [ger] full; ~ **de** full of; ~ **de manchas** covered in stains; ~ **de dedos** fam fig [receoso] full of apprehension; [tímido] timid; ~ **de frescura** fam fig finicky; ~ **da nota** fam [rico] loaded; ~ **de si** [orgulhoso] proud; [arrogante] full of o.s. **-2.** [gordo] plump. **-3.** fam [farto]: **estar** ~ **(de alguém/algo)** to be fed up with sb/sthg.
◆ **cheia** f **-1.** [de rio] flood. **-2.** [época] flood season.
◆ **em cheio** loc adv: **acertar em** ~ to hit the mark.

cheirar [4] [ʃejˈra(x)] <> vt **-1.** [flor, perfume, comida] to smell. **-2.** [cocaína] to snort. <> vi **-1.** [flor, perfume, comida] to smell; ~ **a** [ter cheiro de] to smell of; fig [parecer] to smack (of); ~ **bem/mal** to smell nice/bad; **isto não me cheira bem** it makes me feel uncomfortable. **-2.** [cocaína]: **passou a noite cheirando** he spent the whole night snorting (coke).

cheiroso, osa [ʃejˈrosu, ɔzal adj scented; **estar** ~ to be scented.

cheiro-verde [ˌʃeju'vexdʒil (pl **cheiros-verdes**) m parsley and spring onion.

cheque [ˈʃɛkil m cheque; ~ **em branco** blank cheque; ~ **compensado** cleared cheque; ~ **cruzado** crossed cheque; ~ **especial** guaranteed cheque; ~ **nominal** nominative cheque; ~ **ao portador** bearer cheque; ~ **pré-datado** pre-dated cheque; ~ **voador** ou **sem fundos** bounced cheque.

chiado [ˈʃjadul m **-1.** [de roda, porta] squeak. **-2.** [de passarinho] chirp.

chiar [16] [ˈʃja(x)] vi **-1.** [emitir chio - pessoa, respiração] to wheeze; [- vento] whistle. **-2.** fam [reclamar] to kick up a stink.

chibata [ʃiˈbatal f [vara] stick.

chiclete [ʃiˈklɛtʃil m chewing gum; ~ **de bola** bubble gum.

chicória [ʃiˈkɔrjal f chicory.

chicote [ʃiˈkɔtʃil m whip.

chicotear [15] [ʃikoˈtʃja(x)] vt to whip.

chifrada [ʃiˈfradal f horn thrust.

chifrar [4] [ʃi'fra(x)] *vt* **-1.** [toureiro, tronco] to gore. **-2.** *fam fig* [marido, namorada] to two-time.

chifre ['ʃifri] *m* [de animal] horn; **pôr ~s em** *fam fig* [em marido, namorada] to two-time.

chifrudo, da [ʃi'frudu, da] *adj* **-1.** [animal] large-horned. **-2.** *fam fig* [marido, namorada] two-timed.

Chile ['ʃilil *n* Chile.

chileno, na [ʃi'lenu, na] <> *adj* Chilean. <> *m, f* Chilean.

chilique [ʃi'likil *m fam* faint; **ter um ~** to have a fit.

chilrear [15] [ʃiw'xja(x)] *vi* to chirp.

chilreio [ʃiw'xeju] *m* chirping.

chimarrão [ʃima'xãw] (*pl* **-ões**) *m herbal tea.*

chimpanzé [ʃĩpãn'zɛ] *m* chimpanzee.

China ['ʃinal *n*: **(a)** ~ China.

chinelo [ʃi'nɛlul *m* slipper; **botar no ~** *fam* [superar] to outdo.

chinês, esa [ʃi'neʃ, ezal (*pl* **-eses**, *fpl* **-s**) <> *adj* Chinese. <> *m, f* [da China] Chinese.

chinfrim [ʃĩn'frĩl (*pl* **-ns**) *adj* worthless.

chip ['ʃipil *m* COMPUT microchip.

Chipre ['ʃipril *n* Cyprus.

chique ['ʃikil *adj* chic.

chiqueiro [ʃi'kejrul *m* **-1.** [de porcos] pigsty. **-2.** *fam fig* [bagunça] pigsty.

chispa ['ʃiʃpal *f* [faísca] spark.

chispar [4] [ʃiʃ'pa(x)] *vi* [correr] to race.

chita ['ʃital *f* printed cotton.

choça ['ʃosal *f* hut.

chocalhar [4] [ʃoka'ʎa(x)l <> *vt* to rattle. <> *vi* [soar] to rattle.

chocalho [ʃo'kaʎul *m* **-1.** MÚS maraca. **-2.** [brinquedo] rattle. **-3.** [de gado, cavalo] bell.

chocante [ʃo'kãntʃil *adj* **-1.** [assustador, ofensivo] shocking. **-2.** *fam* [ótimo] wicked.

chocar [12] [ʃo'ka(x)l <> *vt* **-1.** [assustar, ofender] to shock. **-2.** ZOOL to hatch. <> *vi* **-1.** [causar espanto, ofensa] to shock. **-2.** ZOOL to brood.

➤ **chocar-se** *vp* **-1.** [colidir]: **~-se (contra)** to collide (with). **-2.** [assustar-se]: **~-se (com)** to be shocked (by). **-3.** [discordar]: **~-se em relação a** to clash over.

chocho, cha ['ʃoʃu, ʃal *adj* **-1.** [sem graça] dull. **-2.** [fruta, ovo] rotten.

choco, ca ['ʃoku, kal *adj* **-1.** [ave] sitting. **-2.** [ovo - fertilizado] fertilized; [- estragado] addled.

chocolate [ʃoko'latʃil *m* chocolate.

chofer [ʃo'fɛ(x)] (*pl* **-es**) *mf* driver.

chofre ['ʃofril ➤ **de chofre** *loc adv* [subitamente] suddenly.

chopada [ʃo'padal *f fam* beer-drinking session.

chope ['ʃopil *m* beer.

choque ['ʃɔkil *m* **-1.** [ger] shock; **estado de ~** state of shock; **dar um ~ (em alguém)** to give (sb) a shock; **levar** *ou* **tomar um ~** to get a shock. **-2.** [colisão] crash. **-3.** [conflito, confronto] clash.

choradeira [ʃora'dejral *f* **-1.** [choro] crying. **-2.** [lamúria] grumbling. **-3.** [pedido] complaining.

choramingar [ʃoramĩn'ga(x)l *vi* to whine.

choramingas [14] [ʃora'mĩngaʃl *mf* crybaby.

choramingo [ʃora'mĩngul *m* whine.

chorão, ona [ʃo'rãw, onal (*mpl* **-ões**, *fpl* **-onas**) <> *adj* moaning. <> *m, f* [pessoa] crybaby.

➤ **chorão** *m* BOT weeping willow.

chorar [4] [ʃo'ra(x)l <> *vi* **-1.** [verter lágrimas] to cry. **-2.** *fig* [barganhar] to haggle. <> *vt* **-1.** [lágrima] to cry; **~ a morte de alguém** to mourn the death of sb. **-2.** *fig* [barganhar] to haggle. **-3.** *loc*: **~ as mágoas** to pour out; **~ miséria** to moan about poverty.

chorinho [ʃo'riɲul *m* MÚS = choro.

choro ['ʃorul *m* **-1.** [pranto] crying. **-2.** MÚS *a type of traditional Brazilian music started at the end of the nineteenth century.*

CHORO

One of the more polished expressions of Brazilian music, the *choro,* or *chorinho,* is an instrumental musical genre characterized by virtuosity and improvisation. *Choro* originated in Rio de Janeiro towards the end of the nineteenth century and is derived from the polka and the maxixe, a precursor of the samba. It is generally performed to the accompaniment of percussion instruments, guitars, a *cavaquinho* (small four-stringed guitar), a mandolin and certain wind instruments such as the flute or the clarinet.

---

chorona [ʃo'ronal *f* ▷ **chorão.**

choroso, osa [ʃo'rozu, ɔzal *adj* tearful.

choupana [ʃo'pãnal *f* hut.

chouriço [ʃo'risul *m* chorizo.

chove-não-molha [ˌʃovináw'mɔʎal *m inv fam* shilly-shallying.

chover [47] [ʃo've(x)l *v impess* **-1.** METEOR to rain; **~ a cântaros** to pour down with rain; **nem que chova canivete** *fig* come what may. **-2.** *fig* [cair do alto] to shower. **-3.** *fig* [sobrevir em demasia] to pour in.

chuchu [ʃu'ʃul *m fruit-bearing climbing plant*; **está frio pra ~** *fam* it's bloody cold; **tinha comida pra ~** *fam* there was loads of food at the party.

chucrute [ʃu'krutʃil *m* choucroute, sauerkraut.

chulé [ʃu'lɛl *m* smell of feet.

chulear [15] [ʃu'lja(x)l *vt* to hem.

chulo, lo ['ʃulu, lal *adj* vulgar.

chumaço [ʃu'masul *m* **-1.** [enchimento] padding. **-2.** [de algodão, gaze] wadding.

chumbado, da [ʃũn'badu, dal *adj fam* worn out.

chumbar [4] [ʃũn'ba(x)l *vt* **-1.** [soldar] to solder. **-2.** [grade, portão] to secure. **-3.** [rede, anzol] to drop.

chumbo ['ʃũnbul *m* lead.

chupado, da [ʃu'padu, dal *adj fam* [magro] skinny.

➤ **chupada** *f* [chupadela] suck.

chupão [ʃu'pãwl (*pl* **-ões**) *fam m* **-1.** [beijo] slurpy kiss. **-2.** [marca] love bite.

chupar [4] [ʃu'pa(x)l *vt* to suck.

chupeta [ʃu'petal *f* **-1.** [de criança] dummy *UK*, comforter *US*. **-2.** *fam* AUTO: **fazer uma ~** to use jump-leads.

churrascaria [ʃuxaʃka'rial *f* *restaurant specializing in grilled and spit-roasted meat*; **~**

rodízio restaurant where diners may pick and choose from food offered.

churrasco [ʃuˈxaʃkul m **-1.** [carne] barbecued meat. **-2.** [refeição] barbecue.

churrasqueira [ʃuxaʃˈkejral f rotisserie.

churrasquinho [ʃuxaʃˈkiɲul m kebab.

chutar [4] [ʃuˈta(x)] ◇ vt **-1.** [objeto, pessoa] to kick. **-2.** fam [resposta] to take a stab at. **-3.** fam [funcionário, namorado]: ~ **alguém** to give sb the push. ◇ vi **-1.** [dar chute] to kick. **-2.** fam [em prova] to take a pot shot. **-3.** loc: ~ **alto** to tell tall stories.

chute [ˈʃutʃi] m **-1.** [pontapé] kick. **-2.** fam [mentira] bullshit. **-3.** fam [dispensa] push; **dar um** ~ **em alguém** to give sb the push.

chuteira [ʃuˈtejral f football boot; **pendurar as** ~**s** [aposentar-se] to hang up one's boots.

chuva [ˈʃuval f **-1.** METEOR rain; ~ **ácida** acid rain; ~ **fina** drizzle; ~ **de granizo** ou **pedra** hail; **tomar** ~ to get wet in the rain; **estar na** ~ fig to be drunk. **-2.** fig [de papel picado etc] shower.

chuvarada [ʃuvaˈradal f downpour.

chuveirada [ʃuvejˈradal f shower.

chuveiro [ʃuˈvejrul m shower.

chuviscar [12] [ʃuviʃˈka(x)] vi to drizzle.

chuvisco [ʃuˈviʃkul m **-1.** [chuva] drizzle. **-2.** CULIN confection made of egg-yolk and sugar.

chuvoso, osa [ʃuˈvozu, ɔzal adj rainy.

Cia (abrev de **Companhia**) f Co.

cianeto [sjaˈnetul m cyanide.

cibercafé [sibexˈkafel m cybercafé.

ciberespaço [sibereʃˈpasul m cyberspace.

cibernética [sibexˈnetʃikal f cybernetics (sg).

cibernético, ca [sibexˈnetʃiku, kal adj cybernetic.
    ◆ **cibernética** f cybernetics.

ciberpunk [sibexˈpũŋkil mf net hacker.

CIC (abrev de **Cartão de Identificação do Contribuinte**) m Brazilian tax-payer's identity card for individual contributions.

cicatriz [sikaˈtriʃl (pl -**es**) f scar.

cicatrização [sikatrizaˈsãwl f healing.

cicatrizar [4] [sikatriˈza(x)] ◇ vt **-1.** [fechar] to heal. **-2.** [cobrir de cicatrizes] to scar. ◇ vi [fechar-se] to heal.

cicerone [siseˈronil mf guide.

ciceronear [sˈronja(x)] vt to act as a guide for.

ciciar [16] [siˈsja(x)] vi to whisper.

cíclico, ca [ˈsikliku, kal adj cyclic.

ciclismo [siˈkliʒmul m cycling.

ciclista [siˈkliʃtal mf cyclist.

ciclo [ˈsiklul m cycle; ~ **básico** UNIV foundation course.

ciclone [siˈklonil m cyclone.

ciclotimia [siklotʃiˈmial f PSIC cyclothymia.

ciclotímico, ca [siklоˈtʃimiku, kal ◇ adj cyclothymic. ◇ m, f cyclothymic.

ciclovia [sikloˈvial f bicycle lane.

cidadã [sidaˈdãl f ▷ **cidadão**.

cidadania [sidadaˈnial f citizenship.

cidadão, dã [sidaˈdãw, dal (pl -**ãos**, fpl -**s**) m, f citizen.

cidade [siˈdadʒil f **-1.** [centro urbano] city; [pequena] small town; ~ **satélite** satellite town. **-2.** [bairro central] town. **-3.** fig [população] city.

Cidade do Cabo [si,dadʒiduˈkabul n Cape Town.

Cidade do México [si,dadʒiduˈmɛʃikul n Mexico City.

cidadela [sidaˈdɛlal f citadel.

cidra [ˈsidral f citron.

ciência [ˈsjẽnsjal f **-1.** [saber] science; ~**s econômicas** economics; ~**s humanas** humanities; ~**s ocultas** occultism (sg); ~**s sociais** social science (sg). **-2.** [da vida, do amor] art. **-3.** [conhecimento] knowledge; **dar** ~ **de algo (a alguém)** to tell sb sthg; **tome** ~ take this on board.

ciente [ˈsjẽntʃil adj learned; **estar** ~ **(de algo)** to be aware of sthg.

cientificismo [sjẽntʃifiˈsiʒmul m scientific spirit.

científico, ca [sjẽnˈtʃifiku, kal adj scientific.

cientista [sjẽnˈtʃiʃtal mf scientist.

cifra [ˈsifral f **-1.** [ger] cipher. **-2.** [soma, quantia] sum. **-3.** MÚS figure.

cifrão [siˈfrãwl (pl -**ões**) m dollar sign.

cifrar [siˈfra(x)] vt to write in code.

cigano, na [siˈgãnu, nal ◇ adj gipsy. ◇ m, f gipsy.

cigarra [siˈgaxal f **-1.** ZOOL cicada. **-2.** [campainha] buzzer.

cigarreira [sigaˈxejral f [estojo] cigarette case.

cigarrilha [sigaˈxiʎal f cheroot.

cigarro [siˈgaxul m cigarette.

cilada [siˈladal f **-1.** [ger] trap. **-2.** [emboscada] ambush.

cilindrada [silĩˈdradal f cubic capacity.

cilíndrico, ca [siˈlĩdriku, kal adj cylindrical.

cilindro [siˈlĩdrul m GEOM, AUTO cylinder.

cílio [ˈsiljul m eyelash.

cima [ˈsimal f: **lá em** ~ [no topo, no alto] up there; [em andar superior] upstairs; **andar de** ~ upstairs; **ainda por** ~ on top of that; **de** ~ from the top; **de** ~ **de** from the top of; **de** ~ **para baixo** from top to bottom; **em** ~ **de** on top of; **em** ~ **da mesa** on the table; **para** ~ upwards; **por** ~ **de** over; **dar em** ~ **de alguém** to chat sb up; **estar por** ~ to be quids in; **tudo em** ~? fam everything all right?

cimentado, da [simẽnˈtadu, dal adj **-1.** CONSTR cemented. **-2.** [consolidado] sealed.

cimentar [4] [simẽnˈta(x)] vt to cement.

cimento [siˈmẽntul m cement; ~ **armado** reinforced concrete.

cimo [ˈsimul m top.

cinco [ˈsĩŋkul num five; veja também **seis**.

cindir [6] [sĩnˈdʒi(x)] vt **-1.** [separar] to separate. **-2.** [cortar] to cut through.

cineasta [siˈnjaʃtal mf cinematographer.

cinéfilo, la [siˈnɛfilu, lal m, f film enthusiast.

cinegrafista [sinegraˈfiʃtal mf cameraman (f camerawoman).

cinema [siˈnemal m cinema; ~ **mudo** silent film.

cinematografia [sinematogra'fial f cinemato-graphy.

cinematográfico, ca [sinemato'grafiku, kal adj cinematographic.

Cingapura [sĩŋga'pural n Singapore.

cingir [52] [sĩn'ʒi(x)] vt - 1. [ger] to encircle. - 2. [pôr à cintura] to gird.

cínico, ca l'siniku, kal ⬦ adj shameless. ⬦ m, f immoral person.

cinismo [si'niʒmul m impudence.

cinqüenta [sĩŋ'kwẽntal num fifty; veja também seis.

cinqüentão, tona [sĩŋkwẽn'tãw, tɔnal (mpl -ões, fpl -s) ⬦ adj quinquagenarian. ⬦ m, f quin-quagenarian.

cinta l'sĩntal f - 1. [faixa] belt. - 2. [feminina] girdle.

cinta-liga [ˌsĩnta'ligal (pl cintas-ligas) f suspen-der belt.

cintilante [sĩntʃi'lãntʃil adj scintillating.

cintilar [4] [sĩntʃi'la(x)] vi to scintillate.

cinto l'sĩntul m belt; ~ **de segurança** safety belt.

cintura [sĩn'tural f waist.

cinturão [sĩntu'rãw] (pl -ões) m belt; ~ **verde** green belt.

cinza l'sĩzal ⬦ adj inv [cor] grey. ⬦ m [cor] grey. ⬦ f [de combustão] ash.

➡ **cinzas** fpl ashes.

cinzeiro [sĩn'zejrul m ashtray.

cinzel [sĩn'zɛwl (pl -éis) m chisel.

cinzelar [4] [sĩnze'la(x)] vt - 1. [lavrar] to chisel. - 2. [gravar] to engrave. - 3. fig [frase, verso] to polish.

cinzento, ta [sĩn'zẽntu, tal adj grey.

cio l'siwl m rut; **estar no** ~ to be in a rut.

cioso, ciosa l'sjozu, 'sjɔzal adj jealous.

CIPA (abrev de **Comissão Interna de Prevenção de Acidentes**) f Brazilian commission for preven-tion of accidents at work, ≃ HSE UK, ≃ OHSA US.

cipreste [si'prɛʃtʃil m cypress.

cipriota [sipri'ɔtal ⬦ adj Cypriot. ⬦ m, f Cypriot.

circense [six'sẽnsil adj circus (antes de subst).

circo l'sixkul m circus.

circuito [six'kujtul m circuit.

circulação [sixkula'sãwl f circulation.

circulante [sirku'lãntʃil adj - 1. [itinerante] itiner-ant. - 2. ECON: **capital** ~ ready capital.

circular [4] [sixku'la(x)l (pl -es) ⬦ adj [formato] circular. ⬦ m [ônibus] shuttle. ⬦ f [carta, ofício] circular. ⬦ vt -1. [rodear] to circle. - 2. [dar voltas por] to surround. ⬦ vi -1. [ger] to circulate. -2. [percorrer] to wander.

círculo l'sixkulul m - 1. GEOM circle; ~ **vicioso** vicious circle. - 2. fig [meio, grupo] circle.

circunavegação [sixkũnavega'sãwl f circumna-vigation.

circunavegar [14] [sixkũnave'ga(x)l vt to circum-navigate.

circuncidado [sixkũnsi'dadul adj circumcised.

circuncidar [4] [sixkũnsi'da(x)l vt to circumcise.

circuncisão [sixkũnsi'zãwl f circumcision.

circundante [sixkũn'dãntʃil adj surrounding.

circundar [4] [sixkũn'da(x)l vt to surround.

circunferência [sixkũnfe'rẽnsjal f circumfer-ence.

circunflexo [sixkũn'flɛksul GRAM ⬦ adj circum-flex. ⬦ m circumflex.

circunscrever [6] [sixkũnʃkre've(x)l vt -1. [ger] to contain. - 2. [inscrever] to circumscribe. - 3. [res-tringir] to restrict.

➡ **circunscrever-se** vp [restringir-se] to be re-stricted.

circunscrição [sixkũnʃkri'sãwl (pl -ões) f [reparti-ção] division; ~ **eleitoral** electoral constituency.

circunscrito, ta [sixkũnʃ'kritu, tal ⬦ pp ⊳ **circunscrever**. ⬦ adj circumscribed.

circunspe(c)ção [sixkũnʃpe(k)sãwl (pl -ões) f circumspection.

circunspecto, ta [sixkũnʃ'pɛktu, tal adj circum-spect.

circunstância [sixkũnʃ'tãnsjal f -1. [ger] circum-stance. - 2. JUR : ~**s atenuantes/agravantes** at-tenuating/aggravating circumstances. - 3. [caso] event.

circunstanciado, da [sixkũnʃtãn'sjadu, dal adj detailed.

circunstantes [sixkũnʃ'tãntʃiʃl mpl onlookers.

cirrose [si'xɔzil f cirrhosis.

cirurgia [sirux'ʒial f surgery; ~ **plástica** plastic surgery; ~ **estética** aesthetic surgery UK, esthetic surgery US; ~ **reconstrutora** ou **repara-dora** reconstructive surgery.

cirurgião, ã [sirux'ʒjãwʒjã, al (pl -ões, fpl -s) m, f surgeon.

cirurgião-dentista, cirurgiã-dentista [si-rux.ʒjãwdẽn'tʃiʃta, sirux.ʒjãdẽntʃiʃtal (mpl **cirurgi-ões-dentistas**, fpl **cirurgiãs-dentistas**) m, f dental surgeon.

cirúrgico, ca [si'ruxʒiku, kal adj surgical; **ataque** ou **bombardeio** ~ fig surgical strike.

cisão [si'zãwl (pl -ões) f -1. [divisão] split. - 2. [discor-dância] division.

cisco l'siʃkul m dust.

cisma l'siʒmal ⬦ m schism. ⬦ f [mania] crazy idea.

cismado, da [siʒ'madu, dal adj wary.

cismar [4] [siʒ'ma(x)] ⬦ vt [convencer-se de]: ~ **que** to be convinced that. ⬦ vi - 1. [decidir]: ~ **de** ou **em fazer algo** to determine upon doing sthg. - 2. [implicar]: ~ **com** to clash with. - 3. [insis-tir]: ~ **em** to insist on.

cisne l'siʒnil m swan.

cisões [si'zõjʃl pl ⊳ **cisão**.

cisterna [siʃ'tɛxnal f cistern.

cistite [siʃ'tʃitʃil f cystitis.

citação [sita'sãwl (pl -ões) f -1. [de trecho, autor] quotation. - 2. JUR citation.

citadino, na [sita'dʒinu, nal adj citizen.

citar [4] [si'ta(x)] vt -1. [trecho, autor] to quote. - 2. JUR to summons.

cítrico, ca l'sitriku, kal adj -1. [fruta] citrus. - 2. [ácido] citric.

ciúme ['sjumił] *m* jealousy; **ficar com** ~ *ou* ~**s to** become jealous; **ter** ~ *ou* ~**s de alguém** to be jealous of sb.

ciumeira [sju'mejrał] *f* jealousy.

ciumento, ta [sju'mẽntu, ta] *adj* jealous.

cívico, ca ['siviku, ka] *adj* civic.

civil [si'viwł] (*pl* **-is**) <> *adj* **-1.** [direito, tribunal] civil. **- 2.** [vida, traje] civilian. <> *mf* [pessoa] civilian. <> *m* [casamento civil]: **casar-se no** ~ to have a civil wedding.

civilidade [sivili'dadʒił] *f* courtesy.

civilização [siviliza'sãw] (*pl* **-ões**) *f* civilization.

civilizadamente [civilizada'mẽntʃił] *adv* **-1.** [com educação] politely. **- 2.** [com ordem] in a civilized manner.

civilizador, ra [siviliza'do(x), ra] *adj* civilizing.

civilizar [4] [sivili'za(x)] *vt* to civilize.

⏵ **civilizar-se** *vp* to become civilized.

civismo [si'viʒmu] *m* public spirit.

cl. (*abrev de* **centilitro**) *m* cl.

clã ['kłã] (*pl* **clãs**) *m* clan.

clamar [4] [kla'ma(x)] <> *vt* to clamour. <> *vi:* ~ **por/contra algo** to clamour for/to protest against sthg.

clamor [kla'mo(x)] (*pl* **-es**) *m* clamour *UK*, clamor *US*.

clamoroso, osa [klamo'rozu, ɔza] *adj* clamorous.

clandestino, na [kłãndeʃ'tʃinu, na] *adj* clandestine.

claque ['kłaki] *f* **-1.** *TEATRO* paid participating audience. **- 2.** [de fãs, seguidores] group of fans.

clara ['kłara] *f* ▷ **claro**.

clarabóia [kłara'bɔja] *f* skylight.

clarão [kla'rãw] (*pl* **-ões**) *m* **-1.** [de raio, flash] flash. **- 2.** [claridade] brightness.

clarear [15] [kla'rja(x)] <> *vt* **- 1.** [iluminar] to light up. **- 2.** [dia, céu] to brighten. <> *vi* **-1.** [amanhecer] to get light. **- 2.** [dia, céu] to brighten.

clareira [kla'rejra] *f* [em floresta] glade, clearing.

clareza [kla'reza] *f* clarity; **com** ~ clearly.

claridade [klari'dadʒi] *f* [luz] clarity.

clarim [kla'rĩ] (*pl* **-ns**) *m* bugle.

clarinete [klari'netʃi] *m* clarinet.

clarividência [klarivi'dẽnsja] *f* far-sightedness.

clarinetista [klarine'tʃiʃta] *mf* clarinettist *UK*, clarinetist *US*.

clarividente [klarivi'dẽntʃi] <> *adj* **-1.** [sagaz] wise. **- 2.** [prudente] cautious. **- 3.** [vidente] clairvoyant. <> *mf* [vidente] clairvoyant.

claro, ra ['kłaru, ra] *adj* **-1.** [ger] bright; **dia** ~ daylight. **- 2.** [límpido, nítido, explícito] clear; **deixar** ~ **que** to make explicit; **estar** ~ **(que/por que)** to be obvious (that/why); **ser** ~ **(que)** to be obvious (that); **ser** ~ **como água** to be crystal clear.

⏵ **claro** <> *adv* [evidentemente]: **claro!** of course!; ~ **que sim!/que não!** of course!/of course not! <> *m* **-1.** [em escrita] space. **- 2.** [em pintura] highlight.

⏵ **clara** *f:* ~ **(de ovo)** egg white.

⏵ **às claras** *loc adv* in broad daylight.

⏵ **em claro** *loc adv:* **passar a noite em** ~ to have a sleepless night.

clarões [kla'rõjʃ] ▷ **clarão**.

classe ['klasi] *f* **-1.** [ger] class; ~ **média** middle class; ~ **trabalhadora** *ou* **operária** working class; ~ **executiva** business class; ~ **turística** tourist class; **primeira** ~ first class. **- 2.** [categoria]: **de primeira** ~ first class; **ela tem** ~ she's got class; **com** ~ charmingly; **de** ~ classy.

clássico, ca ['klasiku, ka] *adj* **-1.** [ger] classic; **música** ~ classical music. **- 2.** [da Antigüidade] classical.

⏵ **clássico** *m* [obra-prima] classic.

classificação [klasifika'sãw] (*pl* **-ões**) *f* **-1.** [ger] classification. **- 2.** [qualificação] label. **- 3.** [para cinema e TV] rating.

classificado, da [klasifi'kadu, da] <> *adj* classified. <> *m, f* [em concurso, competição] classified entrant.

⏵ **classificado** *m* [anúncio] classified advertisement, classified ad.

⏵ **classificados** *mpl JORN* [seção] classifieds.

classificar [12] [klasifi'ka(x)] *vt* to classify.

⏵ **classificar-se** *vp* **-1.** [ser aprovado] to pass. **- 2.** [obter posição de]: ~**-se em primeiro lugar** to be first.

classificatório, ria [klasifika'tɔrju, rja] *adj* classifying.

classudo, da [kla'sudu, da] *adj fam* classy.

claudicante [klawdʒi'kãntʃi] *adj* [capengante] hobbling.

claudicar [12] [klawdʒi'ka(x)] *vi* **-1.** [mancar] to limp. **- 2.** *fig* [ir mal] to limp along.

claustro ['klawʃtru] *m* cloister.

claustrofobia [klawʃtrofo'bia] *f* claustrophobia.

claustrofóbico, ca [klawʃtro'fɔbiku, ka] *adj* claustrophobic.

cláusula ['klawzula] *f* clause.

clausura [klaw'zura] *f* **-1.** [recinto] enclosure. **- 2.** [vida] seclusion.

clave ['klavi] *f MÚS* clef.

clavícula [kla'vikula] *f* clavicle, collarbone.

clemência [kle'mẽnsja] *f* **-1.** [qualidade] leniency. **- 2.** [perdão] clemency.

clemente [kle'mẽntʃi] *adj* clement.

cleptomaníaco, ca [klɛptoma'niaku, ka] *m, f* kleptomaniac.

clérigo ['klɛrigu] *m* clergyman.

clero ['klɛru] *m* clergy.

clicar [12] [kli'ka(x)] *vi* to click.

cliché [kli'ʃe] *m* **-1.** *FOT* proof. **- 2.** [chavão] cliché. **- 3.** [tipográfico] type. **- 4.** *JORN* edition; **segundo** ~ second edition.

cliente [kli'ẽntʃi] *m COMPUT* client.

clientela [kliẽn'tɛla] *f* **-1.** clientele. **- 2.** [de médico] patients (*pl*).

clientelismo [kliẽnte'liʒmu] *m POL* political patronage.

clima ['klima] *m* **-1.** *METEOR* climate. **- 2.** *fam fig* [atmosfera] atmosphere.

climático, ca [kli'matʃiku, ka] adj climatic.

clímax ['klimaks] m inv - **1.** [ger] climax. - **2.** [auge] peak.

clinicar [12] [klini'ka(x)] vi to be in clinical practice.

clínico, ca ['kliniku, ka] <> adj clinical. <> m, f [médico] doctor; ~ **geral** general practitioner, GP.
➤ **clínica** f- **1.** [local] clinic. - **2.** [prática] medicine; **clínica geral** general practice.

clipe ['klipi] m - **1.** [videoclipe] clip. - **2.** [para papéis] paper clip.

clitóris [kli'tɔriʃ] m inv clitoris. ·

clonagem [klo'naʒẽ] (pl -ns) f BIOL cloning.

clonar [klo'na(x)] vt BIOL to clone.

clone ['klonil] m clone.

cloro ['klɔru] m chlorine.

clorofila [kloro'fila] f chlorophyll.

clorofórmio [kloro'fɔxmju] m chloroform.

close ['klozi] m close-up; **dar um ~ (em)** to take a close-up (of).

CLT (abrev de **Consolidação das Leis do Trabalho**) f Brazilian legislation regulating the rights and responsibilities of workers.

clube ['klubi] m club.

cm (abrev de **centímetro**) m cm.

CNH (abrev de **Carteira Nacional de Habilitação**) f driving licence UK, driver's license US.

coabitar [4] [koabi'ta(x)] vi: ~ **(com alguém)** to live (with sb).

coação [koa'sãw] f force.

coadjuvante [kwadʒu'vãntʃil] <> adj back-up; **ator ~** supporting actor; **criminoso ~** accomplice. <> mf - **1.** CINE, TEATRO, TV supporting role. - **2.** [cúmplice] accomplice.

coadjuvar [4] [kwadʒu'va(x)] vt - **1.** [ajudar] to collaborate in. - **2.** CINE, TEATRO, TV to support.

coador [kwa'do(x)] (pl -es) m - **1.** [crivo] sieve. - **2.** [de café] filter. - **3.** [para legumes] colander.

coadunar [4] [koadu'na(x)] vt - **1.** [idéias, propostas] to combine. - **2.** [pessoas] to unite.
➤ **coadunar-se** vp [combinar-se] to be combined; **~-se com** to tie in with.

coagir [52] [kwa'ʒi(x)] vt: ~ **alguém (a fazer algo)** to coerce sb (into doing sthg).

coagulação [kwagula'sãw] (pl -ões) f [do sangue] clotting.

coagular [4] [kwagu'la(x)] <> vt [solidificar] to clot. <> vi - **1.** [sangue] to clot. - **2.** [leite] to curdle.
➤ **coagular-se** vp - **1.** [sangue] to clot. - **2.** [leite] to curdle.

coágulo ['kwagulu] m [de sangue] clot.

coalhado, da [kwa'ʎadu, da] adj [leite] curdled.
➤ **coalhada** f clabber.

coalhar [4] [kwa'ʎa(x)] vt & vi to curdle.
➤ **coalhar-se** vp to curdle.

coalho [ko'aʎu] m clot.

coalizão [kwali'zãw] (pl -ões) f coalition.

coar [20] ['kwa(x)] vt - **1.** [líquido] to filter. - **2.** [café] to percolate.

co-autor, ra [ˌkoaw'to(x), ra] (mpl -res, fpl -ras) m, f co-author.

co-autoria [ˌkoawto'ria] (pl -s) f co-authorship.

coaxar [4] [kwa'ʃa(x)] <> m [de sapo] croak. <> vi [sapo] to croak.

cobaia [ko'baja] f guinea pig.

cobalto [ko'bawtu] m cobalt.

coberto, ta [ko'bɛxtu, ta] <> pp ▷ **cobrir.** <> adj covered.
➤ **coberta** f - **1.** [colcha, cobertor] bed cover. - **2.** [cobertura] covering. - **3.** [telhado] roofing.

cobertor [kobex'to(x)] (pl -es) m [de lã] blanket; fam ~ **de orelha** lover.

cobertura [kobex'tura] f - **1.** [ger] cover; **dar ~ a** to cover up. - **2.** [apartamento] penthouse. - **3.** [calda] topping. - **4.** JORN coverage.

cobiça [ko'bisa] f greed.

cobiçar [13] [kobi'sa(x)] vt to covet.

cobiçoso, osa [kobi'sozu, ɔza] adj - **1.** [pessoa] greedy. - **2.** [olhar, interesse] avid.

cobra ['kɔbra] <> adj fam [perito] ace. <> f - **1.** ZOOL snake. - **2.** pej [mau-caráter] snake. <> mf fam [perito] ace.

cobrador, ra [kobra'do(x), ra] (mpl -es, fpl -s) m, f - **1.** [recebedor, caixa] debt collector; ~ **de impostos** tax collector. - **2.** [de ônibus] conductor.

cobrança [ko'brãnsa] f - **1.** [de taxa, passagem, ingresso] fee. - **2.** fig [exigência] demands (pl). - **3.** ESP penalty; ~ **de pênalti** FUT penalty kick.

cobrar [4] [ko'bra(x)] vt - **1.** [taxa, passagem, ingresso] to collect. - **2.** [preço] to charge. - **3.** fig [promessa, favor] to exact. - **4.** ESP to take a penalty; ~ **um pênalti** FUT to take a penalty.

cobre ['kɔbri] m - **1.** [metal] copper. - **2.** [dinheiro, moeda] coin.

cobrir [59] [ko'bri(x)] vt - **1.** [ger] to cover. - **2.** [ocultar] to conceal. - **3.** [envolver] to wrap up. - **4.** [exceder] to exceed. - **5.** [encher]: ~ **algo/alguém de algo** to cover sthg/sb with sthg. - **6.** ZOOL [fêmea] to breed.
➤ **cobrir-se** vp - **1.** [ocultar-se, resguardar-se] to hide o.s. - **2.** [com cobertor] to cover o.s. - **3.** [encher-se]: ~-**se de** to cover o.s with.

coca ['kɔka] f coca.

cocada [ko'kada] f coconut ice UK, coconut candy US.

cocaína [koka'ina] f cocaine.

coçar [13] [ko'sa(x)] <> vt to scratch. <> vi to itch.
➤ **coçar-se** vp to scratch o.s; **não tenho tempo nem para me ~** I haven't got time to blink.

cócar [ko'ka(x)] m crest.

cóccix ['kɔksis] m inv coccyx.

cócegas ['kɔsigaʃ] fpl: **fazer ~ em alguém** to tickle sb; **sentir ~** to feel itchy.

coceguento, ta [kose'gẽntu, ta] adj ticklish.

coceira [ko'sejra] f [sensação] itch.

cocheira [ko'ʃejra] f stable; **informação de ~** fam inside information.

cocheiro [ko'ʃejru] m coachman.

cochichar [4] [koʃi'ʃa(x)] vi to whisper.

cochicho [ko'ʃiʃu] m whisper.

cochilar [4] [koʃi'la(x)] vi - **1.** [dormir um pouco] to take a nap. **-2.** [dormitar] to doze off.

cochilo [ko'ʃilu] *m* nap; **tirar um** ~ to take a nap.

coco ['koku] *m* **-1.** [fruta] coconut. **-2.** *fam fig* [cabeça] nut.

cocô [ko'ko] *m fam* poo; **fazer** ~ to have a poo.

cócoras ['kɔkoraʃ] ◆ **de cócoras** *loc adv* squatting.

cocoricar [12] [kokori'ka(x)] *vi* to crow.

cocuruto [koku'rutu] *m* **-1.** [de morro] top. **-2.** [no chão] mound. **-3.** [da cabeça] crown.

codificação [kodʒiʃika'sãw] (*pl* **-ões**) *f* COMPUT coding.

codificador [kodʒifika'do(x)] *m* COMPUT encoder.

codificar [12] [kodʒifi'ka(x)] *vt* **-1.** [ger] to encode. **-2.** [direito, leis] to codify.

código ['kɔdʒigu] *m* [ger] code; ~ **de barras** bar code; ~ **civil** civil code; ~ **de ética profissional** code of professional ethics.

código-fonte ['kɔdʒigu'fõntʃi] (*pl* **códigos-fonte**) *m* COMPUT source code.

codinome [kodʒi'nɔmi] *m* code name.

codorna [ko'dɔxna] *f* quail.

co-editar [4] [koedʒi'ta(x)] *vt* to co-edit.

co-editor, ra [koedʒi'to(x), ra] (*mpl* **-res**, *fpl* **-ras**) *m, f* co-editor.

coeficiente [koefi'sjẽntʃi] *m* **-1.** MAT coefficient. **-2.** *fig* [fator] factor.

coelho ['kweʎu] *m* rabbit; **matar dois** ~**s de uma cajadada só** to kill two birds with one stone.

coentro ['kwẽntru] *m* coriander.

coerção [koex'sãw] *f* coercion.

coercivo, va [koex'sivu, va], **coercitivo, va** [koexsi'tʃivu, va] *adj* coercive.

coerência [koe'rẽnsja] *f* coherence.

coerente [koe'rẽntʃi] *adj* coherent.

coesão [koe'zãw] *f* cohesion.

coeso, sa ['kwεzu, za] *adj* **-1.** [unido, ligado] united. **-2.** [coerente] coherent.

coexistência [koeziʃ'tẽnsja] *f* coexistence.

coexistir [6] [koeziʃ'tʃi(x)] *vi* to coexist.

COFINS (*abrev de* **Contribuição para o Financiamento da Seguridade Social**) *m Brazilian employer's social security contributions, based on profits.*

cofre ['kɔfri] *m* safe; **os** ~**s públicos** the public coffers.

cofre-forte [ˌkofri'fɔxtʃi] (*pl* **cofres-fortes**) *m* strongroom.

cogitar [4] [koʒi'ta(x)] ◇ *vt* **-1.** [considerar] to consider. **-2.** [planejar]: ~ **fazer algo** to consider doing sthg. ◇ *vi* [refletir] to deliberate; ~ **sobre algo** to think about sthg.

cognato [kog'natu] *m* cognate; **falso** ~ false cognate.

cognome [kog'nɔmi] *m* nickname.

cognominar [4] [kognomi'na(x)] *vt*: ~ **alguém** to give a cognomen to sb.

cogumelo [kogu'mεlu] *m* **-1.** [comestível] mushroom. **-2.** [venenoso] toadstool.

COI (*abrev de* **Comitê Olímpico Internacional**) *m* IOC.

coibição [kojbi'sãw] (*pl* **-ões**) *f* restraint.

coibir [77] [koj'bi(x)] *vt* to restrain; ~ **alguém de fazer algo** to restrain sb from doing sthg.

coice ['kojsi] *m* **-1.** [de animal] backward kick; **dar um** ~ **em** *fig* to give sb a kick in the teeth. **-2.** [de arma] butt.

coifa ['kojfa] *f* [para fogão] extractor hood.

coincidência [koĩnsi'dẽnsja] *f* coincidence; **que** ~**!** what a coincidence!; **ser uma** ~ to be a coincidence.

coincidente [koĩnsi'dẽntʃi] *adj* coincidental.

coincidentemente [koĩnsidẽntʃi'mẽntʃi] *adv* coincidentally.

coincidir [6] [koĩnsi'di(x)] *vi* **-1.** [eventos, datas] to coincide. **-2.** [concordar]: ~ **(em)** to agree (upon).

coisa ['kojza] *f* **-1.** [ger] thing. **-2.** [assunto] topic. **-3.** *loc:* ~ **do arco da velha** [feito] incredible thing; **deu uma** ~ **nele** *fam* sthg came over him; **ele não diz** ~ **com** ~ he talks absolute rubbish; **que** ~**!** goodness me!; **a festa foi uma** ~ [ser ótimo] the party was amazing; **ser uma** ~ [ser terrível] to be dreadful.

◆ **coisa de** *loc adv* roughly.

◆ **coisas** *fpl fam* [genitais] private parts.

coisíssima [koj'zisima] *f*: **ele não é corrupto** ~ **nenhuma** [de modo algum] no way is he corrupt; **ele não sabia** ~ **nenhuma** he knew absolutely nothing.

coitado, da [koj'tadu, da] ◇ *adj* [pessoa] wretched; **coitado!** poor thing!; **coitado do povo que ...** poor people who ... ◇ *m, f* poor wretch.

coito ['kojtu] *m* sex; ~ **anal** anal sex.

cola ['kɔla] *f* **-1.** [adesivo] glue. **-2.** *fam* EDUC [ato] cribbing. **-3.** *fam* EDUC [objeto] crib.

colaboração [kolabora'sãw] (*pl* **-ões**) *f* **-1.** [ajuda] cooperation. **-2.** [em jornal etc] freelance work.

colaborador, ra [kolabora'do(x), ra] *m, f* **-1.** [ajudante] collaborator. **-2.** [de jornal etc] freelance.

colaborar [4] [kolabo'ra(x)] *vi* **-1.** [ajudar] to cooperate; ~ **em algo/com alguém** to cooperate on sthg with sb. **-2.** [em jornal etc]: ~ **em algo** to freelance on sthg.

colação [kola'sãw] (*pl* **-ões**) *f* [concessão] bestowal; ~ **de grau** conferment of a degree.

colagem [ko'laʒẽ] (*pl* **-ns**) *f* **-1.** [ato] glueing. **-2.** ARTE collage.

colante [ko'lãntʃi] *adj* [roupa] clinging.

colapso [ko'lapsu] *f* collapse; **entrar em** ~ to collapse; ~ **cardíaco** heart failure; ~ **nervoso** nervous breakdown.

colar [4] [ko'la(x)] (*pl* **-es**) *vt* COMPUT to paste.

colarinho [kola'riɲu] *m* **-1.** [de camisa] collar. **-2.** *fam* [de cerveja] head; **com/sem** ~ with/without a head.

colarinho-branco [kolaˌriɲu'brãŋku] (*pl* **colarinhos-brancos**) *m* white-collar worker; **crime do** ~ white-collar crime.

colateral [kolate'raw] (*pl* **-ais**) *adj* collateral.

colcha ['kowʃa] *f* bedspread; ~ **de retalhos** *fig* mishmash.

colchão [kow'ʃãw] (*pl* **-ões**) *m* mattress.

colcheia [kow'ʃeja] f MÚS quaver UK, eighth note US.

colchete [kow'ʃetʃi] m -1. [de roupa] hook; ~ de gancho hook and eye; ~ de pressão press stud. -2. [sinal] bracket.

colchões [kow'ʃõjʃ] pl ⊳ colchão.

colchonete [kowʃo'nɛtʃi] m bolster.

coleção [kole'sãw] (pl -ões) f collection.

colecionador, ra [kolesjona'do(x), ra] (mpl -res, fpl -s) m, f collector.

colecionar [4] [kolesjo'na(x)] vt to collect.

colega [ko'lɛga] mf -1. [amigo] friend. -2. [de escola] schoolfriend. -3. [de trabalho] colleague.

colegial [kole'ʒjaw] (pl -ais) ⟨⟩ adj school (antes de subst). ⟨⟩ mf schoolboy (f schoolgirl).

colégio [ko'lɛʒju] m -1. [escola] school. -2. [de intelectuais] college. -3. [de clérigos] chapter. -4. [de eleitores]: ~ eleitoral electoral college.

coleguismo [kole'giʒmu] m esprit de corps.

coleira [ko'lejra] f dog collar.

cólera ['kɔlera] ⟨⟩ f [ira] anger. ⟨⟩ m MED cholera.

colérico, ca [ko'lɛriku, ka] ⟨⟩ adj [irado] angry. ⟨⟩ m, f MED cholera victim.

colesterol [koleʃte'rɔw] m cholesterol.

coleta [ko'lɛta] f collection; ~ de dados fact-gathering.

coletânea [kole'tãnja] f collectanea.

coletar [4] [kole'ta(x)] vt to collect.

colete [ko'letʃi] m waistcoat UK, vest US; ~ salva-vidas life jacket.

coletividade [koletʃivi'dadʒi] f community.

coletivo, va [kole'tʃivu, va] adj -1. [de muitos] collective. -2. [transporte, banheiro] public.
◆ **coletivo** m -1. [ônibus] public transport. -2. [futebol] trials. -3. [ling] collective noun.

coletor, ra [kole'to(x), ra] m, f [de impostos] collector.

colheita [ko'ʎejta] f -1. [ger] harvest. -2. [produto] crop.

colher [5] [ko'ʎɛ(x)] (pl -es [ko'ʎɛriʃ]) ⟨⟩ f -1. [talher] spoon; ~ de chá teaspoon; ~ de sobremesa dessertspoon; ~ de sopa tablespoon; dar uma ~ de chá a alguém fig to do sb a favour. -2. [ferramenta]: ~ de pedreiro trowel. ⟨⟩ vt -1. [fruta, verdura, safra] to pick. -2. [dados] to gather.

colherada [koʎe'rada] f spoonful.

colibri [koli'bri] m hummingbird.

cólica ['kɔlika] f colic; ~ menstrual period pains (pl).

colidir [6] [koli'dʒi(x)] vi [chocar-se] to collide; ~ com/contra to collide with/against.

coligação [koliga'sãw] (pl -ões) f coalition; ~ partidária ou eleitoral political coalition.

coligar [14] [koli'ga(x)] vt to bind together.
◆ **coligar-se** vp to unite; ~-se com to align o.s with.

coligir [52] [koli'ʒi(x)] vt to compile.

colina [ko'lina] f hill.

colírio [ko'lirju] m eyewash; ser um ~ para os olhos de alguém fam to be a sight for sore eyes.

colisão [koli'zãw] (pl -ões) f collision.

colite [ko'litʃi] f colitis.

collant [ko'lã] m tights (pl).

colméia [kow'mɛja] f beehive.

colo ['kɔlu] m -1. [ger] neck. -2. [regaço] lap; no ~ on one's lap.

colocação [koloka'sãw] (pl -ões) f -1. [ato] fitting. -2. [posição, emprego] position. -3. [em concurso, competição] place. -4. [observação] observation.

colocar [12] [kolo'ka(x)] vt -1. [ger] to place. -2. [dar emprego a] to employ. -3. [situar - no espaço] to site. -4. [instalar - ar-condicionado] to install; [- pneu] to fit; [- carpete] to lay; [- cortina] to hang. -5. [levantar] to raise.
◆ **colocar-se** vp -1. [pôr-se] to position o.s. -2. [em concurso, competição] to be placed. -3. [imaginar-se]: **coloque-se no meu lugar** put yourself in my place.

Colômbia [ko'lõnbja] n Colombia.

colombiano, na [kolõn'bjãnu, na] ⟨⟩ adj Colombian. ⟨⟩ m, f Colombian.

cólon ['kɔlõ] m ANAT colon.

colônia [ko'lonja] f -1. [ger] colony; **Brasil** ~ colonial Brazial. -2. [para crianças]: ~ de férias summer camp. -3. [perfume] cologne; **água de** ~ eau de cologne.

colonial [kolo'njaw] (pl -ais) adj colonial.

colonialismo [kolonja'liʒmu] m colonialism.

colonização [koloniza'sãw] f colonization.

colonizador, ra [koloniza'do(x), ra] ⟨⟩ adj [nação, esforço] colonizing. ⟨⟩ m, f [pessoa] settler.

colonizar [4] [koloni'za(x)] vt to colonize.

colono, na [ko'lonu, na] m, f -1. [povoador] colonist. -2. [cultivador] smallholder.

coloquial [kolo'kjaw] (pl -ais) adj colloquial.

coloquialismo [kolokja'liʒmu] m familiar tone.

colóquio [ko'lɔkju] m -1. [congresso] symposium. -2. ant [conversa] conversation.

coloração [kolora'sãw] (pl -ões) f colouration.

colorido, da [kolo'ridu, da] adj multi-coloured UK, multi-colored US.
◆ **colorido** m colour UK, color US.

colorir [79] [kolo'ri(x)] vt -1. [dar cor a] to colour UK, to color US. -2. fig [avivar] to brighten.

colossal [kolo'saw] (pl -ais) adj colossal.

colosso [ko'losu] m [ger] colossus.

coluna [ko'luna] f -1. [ger] column; ~ social society column. -2. [pilar] pillar. -3. ANAT: ~ vertebral spinal column.

colunável [kolu'navew] (pl -eis) ⟨⟩ adj [pessoa, festa] glamorous. ⟨⟩ mf [celebridade] celebrity.

colunista [kolu'niʃta] mf columnist; ~ social society columnist.

com [kõ] prep -1. with; **ela mora** ~ **um amigo** she lives with a friend; ~ **quem você vai?** who are you going with? -2. [relativo a modo] with; ~ **cuidado** with care; [relativo a instrumento] with; **ela escreve** ~ **a mão direita** she writes with her right hand; ~ **o tempo, a mulher conseguiu superar o trauma** with time, the woman managed to overcome the trauma -3. [indica causa] with, because of; **só ~ muito esforço é que ele conseguiu** only with a lot of effort did he manage to do it; **estar ~ dor de cabeça** to have a headache; **estar ~ fome** to be hungry; **estar ~ pressa** to be in a hurry. **- 4.** [apesar de] in spite of; **~ todo esse trabalho ele ainda encontra tempo para estudar** in spite of all that work, he still finds time to study; **você vai jogar bola ~ chuva?** are you going to play football in the rain?; **~ 86 anos, ele continua cheio de energia** at 86, he is still full of energy. **- 5.** *(em loc prep)* with; **~ relação a** in relation to; **~ vistas a** with an aim to; **de acordo ~** in accordance with; **em parceria ~** in partnership with.

coma [ˈkoma] *m MED* coma; **estado de ~** comatose state; **em ~** in a coma.

comadre [koˈmadri] *f* **- 1.** [madrinha] *a godmother in relation to her godchild's parents; a child's mother in relation to its godparents.* **- 2.** [amiga] friend. **- 3.** [urinol] bedpan.

comandante [komãnˈdãntʃi] *mf* **- 1.** *MIL, NÁUT* commander. **- 2.** [dirigente] leader.

comandar [4] [komãnˈda(x)] *vt* **- 1.** *MIL, NÁUT* to command. **- 2.** [dirigir] to head.

comando [koˈmãndu] *m* [ger] command.

comarca [koˈmaxka] *f* area of jurisdiction.

combalido, da [kõnbaˈlidu, da] *adj* enfeebled.

combate [kõnˈbatʃi] *m* **- 1.** [luta, oposição] fight. **- 2.** [bélico] skirmish; **fora de ~** *fig* flat on one's back.

combatente [kõnbaˈtẽntʃi] *mf* combatant.

combater [5] [kõnbaˈte(x)] *vt* [lutar contra, opor-se a] to struggle. *vi* [belicamente] to fight.

combinação [kõnbinaˈsãw] *(pl -ões) f* **- 1.** [ger] combination. **- 2.** *QUÍM* compound. **- 3.** [acordo, plano] agreement. **- 4.** [peça de roupa] slip.

combinar [4] [kõnbiˈna(x)] *vt* **- 1.** [associar, reunir] to combine. **- 2.** [encontro, jantar] to fix; **combinado!** agreed! **- 3.** [plano, fuga] to plan. *vi* **- 1.** [planejar]: **combinamos de ir ao cinema** we fixed up to go to the cinema. **- 2.** [cores, roupas] to match; **~ com algo** to go with sthg.

comboio [kõnˈboju] *m* **- 1.** [ger] convoy. **- 2.** *FERRO* train.

combustão [kõnbuʃˈtãw] *(pl -ões) f* combustion.

combustível [kõnbuʃˈtʃivɛw] *(pl -eis)* *adj* combustible. *m* fuel.

começar [13] [komeˈsa(x)] *vt* to start. *vi* to begin, to start; **~ a fazer algo** to start doing sthg, to start to do sthg; **~ por** to begin with; **para ~** [em primeiro lugar] first of all.

começo [koˈmesu] *m* beginning.

comédia [koˈmɛdʒja] *f* comedy.

comediante [komeˈdʒjãntʃi] *mf* comedian.

comedido, da [komeˈdʒidu, da] *adj* **- 1.** [moderado] moderate. **- 2.** [prudente] prudent.

comedimento [komedʒiˈmẽntu] *m* [moderação] moderation.

comedir-se [70] [komeˈdʒixsi] *vp* [conter-se] to restrain o.s.

comemoração [komemoraˈsãw] *(pl -ões) f* celebration.

comemorar [4] [komemoˈra(x)] *vt* to celebrate.

comemorativo, va [komemoraˈtʃivu, va] *adj* commemorative.

comensal [komẽnˈsãw] *(pl -ais) mf* dinner guest.

comentar [4] [komẽnˈta(x)] *vt* **- 1.** [fato, festa, incidente] to comment on. **- 2.** [observar]: **~ que** to remark that. **- 3.** *ESP* [partida] to commentate.

comentário [komẽnˈtarju] *m* commentary; **fazer um ~** to do a commentary; **sem ~s** no comment; **~ esportivo** sports commentary; **~ político** political commentary.

comentarista [komẽntaˈriʃta] *mf* commentator; **~ esportivo** sports commentator; **~ político** political commentator.

comer [5] [koˈme(x)] *(pl -es)* *vt* **- 1.** [alimentar-se de] to eat. **- 2.** *fig* [suprimir] to swallow. **- 3.** *fig* [corroer] to corrode. **- 4.** *fig* [consumir] to devour. **- 5.** [em damas, xadrez] to take. **- 6.** *vulg fig* [sexualmente] to fuck. *vi* [alimentar-se] to eat; **dar de ~ a alguém** to feed sb; **~ por quatro** [comer demais] to stuff o.s.

comer-se *vp:* **~-se de raiva/vontade** to be consumed with anger/desire.

comercial [komexˈsjaw] *(pl -ais)* *adj* commercial. *m* [anúncio] advertisement, commercial.

comercialização [komexsjalizaˈsãw] *(pl -ões) f* commercialization.

comercializar [4] [komexsjaliˈza(x)] *vt* to market.

comercializável [komexsjaliˈzavew] *(pl -eis) adj* marketable.

comerciante [komexˈsjãntʃi] *mf* businessman (*f* businesswoman).

comerciar [18] [komexˈsja(x)] *vi* to trade; **~ com** to trade with.

comerciário, ria [komexˈsjarju, rja] *m, f* trader.

comércio [koˈmɛxsju] *m* **- 1.** [compra e venda] trade. **- 2.** [tráfico] trafficking. **- 3.** [estabelecimento] premises. **- 4.** [mercado comercial] business. **- 5.** *fig* [troca de idéias, influências] exchange.

comes [ˈkomiʃ] *mpl fam:* **~ e bebes** food and drink.

comestíveis [komeʃˈtʃivejʃ] *mpl* comestibles.

comestível [komeʃˈtʃivɛw] *(pl -eis) adj* edible.

cometa [koˈmeta] *m* comet.

cometer [5] [komeˈte(x)] *vt* to commit.

cometimento [kometʃiˈmẽntu] *m* **- 1.** [de crime, pecado, infração] committing. **- 2.** [empreendimento] undertaking.

comichão [komiˈʃãw] *(pl -ões) f* itch; **ter ou sentir ~** to have/feel an itch.

comicidade [komisiˈdadʒi] *f* comedy.

comício [koˈmisju] *m* rally; **~ relâmpago** short public rally.

cômico, co [ˈkomiku, ka] *adj* comical. *m, f* [comediante] comedian.

comida [koˈmida] *f* **- 1.** [alimento] food. **- 2.** [refeição] meal; **~ caseira** home cooking.

comigo [koˈmigu] *pron:* **ela não fala ~** she won't speak to me; **o livro dele está ~** I've got his book; **matemática é** ~ **mesmo** maths is my thing; **ela acenou, mas pensei que não era** ~ she nodded, but I thought that she didn't agree with me; **isto não é justo, pensei** ~ that isn't fair, I thought to myself; **deixa** ~**!** leave it with me!

comilança [komi'lãnsa] *f* spread, blowout.

comilão, lona [komi'lãw, lona] (*mpl* **-ões**, *fpl* **-s**) ◇ *adj* gluttonous. ◇ *m, f* glutton.

cominho [ko'miɲul *m* cumin.

comiserar-se [4] [komize'raxsil *vp* to feel pity; ~ **(de)** to feel pity for.

comissão [komi'sãw] (*pl* **-ões**) *f* **-1.** [comitê] committee; **Comissão Parlamentar de Inquérito** Parliamentary Investigative Committee. **-2.** [gratificação] commission.

comissário, ria [komi'sarju, rja] *m, f* agent; ~ **de bordo** air steward (*f* air stewardess).

comissionar [4] [komisjo'na(x)] *vt* **-1.** [encarregar] to commission. **-2.** [confiar] to entrust.

comitê [komi'te] *m* committee; ~ **executivo** executive committee.

comitiva [komi'tʃiva] *f* retinue.

commodity [comɔ'dʒitʃi] (*pl* **commodities**) *f* ECON commodity.

como ['komul ◇ *adv* **-1.** [ger] as. **-2.** [de que modo] how; ~**?** [o que você disse?] I'm sorry?; ~ **assim?** how do you mean? **-3.** [comparativo]: **ser** ~ **algo/alguém** to be like sthg/sb. **-4.** [exclamativo]: **como!** what!; **e** ~**!** *fam* and how!; ~ **não!** [pois não] of course! ◇ *conj* **-1.** [porque] because. **-2.** [conforme] as.
➤ **como que** *loc adv*: ~ **que por um golpe de mágica, tudo desapareceu** as if by magic, everything disappeared.
➤ **como quer que** *loc conj* however.
➤ **como quiser** *loc adv* as; **fazer algo** ~ **quiser** to do as one wishes.
➤ **como se** *loc conj* as if.

comoção [komo'sãw] (*pl* **-ões**) *f* **-1.** [abalo] shock. **-2.** [revolta] unrest.

cômoda ['komoda] *f* chest of drawers.

comodidade [komodʒi'dadʒil *f* **-1.** [conforto] comfort. **-2.** [conveniência] convenience.

comodismo [komo'dʒiʒmul *m* indolence.

comodista [komo'dʒiʃta] ◇ *adj* passive. ◇ *mf* passive person.

cômodo, da ['komodu, da] *adj* **-1.** [confortável] comfortable. **-2.** [conveniente] appropriate.
➤ **cômodo** *m* [aposento] room.

comovente [komo'vẽntʃi], **comovedor, ra** [komove'do(x), ra] *adj* moving.

comover [5] [komo've(x)] ◇ *vt* to move. ◇ *vi* to be moving.
➤ **comover-se** *vp* to be moved.

comovido, da [komo'vidu, da] *adj* moved.

compactador [kõmpak'tado(x)] *m* COMPUT (file) compressor.

compactar [kõmpzk'ta(x)] *vt* COMPUT: ~ **arquivos** to compress files.

compacto, ta [kõm'paktu, ta] *adj* **-1.** [pequeno] compact. **-2.** [denso, comprimido] dense.

➤ **compacto** *m* [disco] compact disc, CD.

compadecer-se [25] [kõnpade'sexsil *vp*: ~ **de** to take pity on.

compadecido, da [kõnpade'sidu, da] *adj* compassionate.

compadecimento [kõnpadesi'mẽntul *m* [piedade] compassion.

compadre [kõn'padril *m* **-1.** [padrinho do filho] *a godfather in relation to his godchild's parents ou a child's father in relation to its godparents.* **-2.** *fam* [companheiro] companion; **meu** ~ my friend.

compaixão [kõnpaj'ʃãw] *f* **-1.** [piedade] compassion. **-2.** [misericórdia] mercy.

companheirismo [kõnpaɲej'riʒmul *m* companionship.

companheiro, ra [kõnpa'ɲejru, ra] *m, f* **-1.** [que acompanha] companion; ~ **de viagem** travelling companion. **-2.** [colega] colleague. **-3.** [marido, namorado] partner. **-4.** *fam* [amigo] mate.

companhia [kõnpa'ɲia] *f* [ger] company; **em** ~ **de** in the company of; **fazer** ~ **a alguém** to keep sb company.

comparação [kõnpara'sãw] (*pl* **-ões**) *f* comparison.

comparar [4] [kõnpa'ra(x)] *vt*: ~ **algo/alguém (com)** to compare sthg/sb (with).
➤ **comparar-se** *vp*: ~**-se com** to compare o.s. to; **isto não se compara com ...** this does not bear comparison with ...

comparável [kõnpa'ravew] (*pl* **-eis**) *adj* comparable.

comparecer [25] [kõnpare'se(x)] *vi*: ~ **(a)** to appear (at).

comparecimento [kõnparesi'mẽntul *m* presence; ~ **às urnas** turnout at the ballot-boxes.

comparsa [kõn'paxsal *mf* **-1.** [cúmplice] accomplice. **-2.** TEATRO extra.

compartilhar [4] [kõmpaxtʃi'ʎa(x)] ◇ *vt* [partilhar] to share. ◇ *vi* [participar]: ~ **de** to share in.

compartimentar [4] [kõnpaxtʃimẽn'ta(x)] *vt* to split (*into separate rooms, parts etc*).

compartimento [kõnpaxtʃi'mẽntul *m* **-1.** [divisão] compartment; ~ **de carga** cargo bay. **-2.** [aposento] room.

compartir [6] [kõnpax'tʃi(x)] *vt* & *vi* = **compartilhar**.

compassado, da [kõnpa'sadu, da] *adj* **-1.** [pausado] measured. **-2.** [cadenciado] rhythmic. **-3.** [comedido] moderate.

compassivo, va [kõnpa'sivu, va] *adj* compassionate.

compasso [kõn'pasul *m* **-1.** [instrumento] pair of compasses. **-2.** MÚS beat. **-3.** [ritmo] time; **dentro/fora do** ~ in/out of time.

compatibilidade [kõnpatʃibili'dadʒil *f* compatibility.

compatível [kõnpa'tʃivɛw] (*pl* **-eis**) *adj* compatible.

compatriota [kõnpatri'ɔtal *mf* compatriot.

compelir [57] [kõnpe'li(x)] *vt*: ~ **alguém a**

fazer algo to force sb to do sthg.
compêndio [kõn'pẽndʒiu] *m* **-1.** [livro] textbook.
-2. [síntese] summary.
compenetração [kõnpenetra'sãw] *f* **-1.** [concentração] concentration. **-2.** [convicção] conviction.
compenetrado, da [kõnpene'tradu, da] *adj* **-1.** [concentrado] concentrated. **-2.** [convicto] convinced.
compenetrar [4] [kõnpene'tra(x)] *vt* [convencer] to convince.
→ **compenetrar-se** *vp* **-1.** [convencer-se]: ~-**se de** to become convinced of. **-2.** [concentrar-se] to concentrate.
compensação [kõnpẽnsa'sãw] (*pl* -**ões**) *f* **-1.** [reparação] compensation; **em** ~ to make up for it. **-2.** [equilíbrio] balance. **-3.** [de cheque] clearance.
compensado [kõnpẽn'sadu] *m* [madeira] plywood.
compensador, ra [kõnpẽnsa'do(x), ra] *adj* compensatory.
compensar [4] [kõnpẽn'sa(x)] ⟨⟩ *vt* **-1.** [dar reparo a] to make up for. **-2.** [equilibrar] to compensate for. **-3.** [cheque] to clear. ⟨⟩ *vi* [valer a pena] to pay.
competência [kõnpe'tẽnsja] *f* **-1.** [habilidade] competence. **-2.** [responsabilidade] responsibility; **ser da** ~ **de alguém** to be the responsibility of sb.
competente [kõnpe'tẽntʃi] *adj* **-1.** [hábil] competent. **-2.** [responsável] responsible.
competição [kõnpetʃi'sãw] (*pl* -**ões**) *f* **-1.** [disputa, concorrência] competition. **-2.** *ESP* [prova] contest.
competidor, ra [kõnpetʃi'do(x), ra] *m, f ESP* competitor.
competir [57] [kõnpe'tʃi(x)] *vi* to compete; ~ **com** to compete with.
competitividade [kõnpetʃitʃivi'dadʒi] *f* competitiveness.
competitivo, va [kõnpetʃi'tʃivu, va] *adj* competitive.
compilação [kõnpila'sãw] *f* compilation.
compilar [4] [kõnpi'la(x)] *vt* to compile.
complacência [kõnpla'sẽnsja] *f* complacency.
complacente [kõnpla'sẽntʃi] *adj* complacent.
compleição [kõnplej'sãw] (*pl* -**ões**) *f* build.
complementar [4] [kõnplemẽn'ta(x)] (*pl* -**es**) ⟨⟩ *adj* additional. ⟨⟩ *vt* to complement.
complemento [kõnple'mẽntu] *m* **-1.** [acréscimo] addition; ~ **alimentar** food supplement; ~ **salarial** additional wages. **-2.** *GRAM* object.
completamente [kõm‚pleta'mẽntʃi] *adv* completely.
completar [4] [kõnple'ta(x)] *vt* **-1.** [terminar] to complete. **-2.** [idade] to reach. **-3.** [com gasolina *etc*] to fill up.
completo, ta [kõn'plɛtu, ta] *adj* **-1.** [trabalho] finished. **-2.** [idade]: **ele tem 16 anos** ~**s** he is 16 years old. **-3.** [tanque] full.
→ **por completo** *loc adv* [inteiramente] completely.
complexado, da [kõnplek'sadu, da] *adj* hung-up; **estar/ficar** ~ to have a complex.
complexidade [kõnpleksi'dadʒi] *f* complexity.

complexo, xa [kõm'plɛksu, sa] *adj* complex.
→ **complexo** *m* complex; ~ **de Édipo** Oedipus complex; ~ **de inferioridade** inferiority complex.
complicação [kõnplika'sãw] (*pl* -**ões**) *f* **-1.** [ger] complexity. **-2.** *MED* complication.
complicado, da [kõnpli'kadu, da] *adj* complicated; **ser** ~ to be complicated.
complicar [12] [kõnpli'ka(x)] *vt* [tornar complexo] to complicate.
→ **complicar-se** *vp* to worsen.
complô [kõn'plo] *m* conspiracy.
componente [kõnpo'nẽntʃi] *m* component.
compor [45] [kõn'po(x)] ⟨⟩ *vt* **-1.** [formar, integrar] to comprise. **-2.** [música, versos] to compose. **-3.** [discurso, livro] to write. **-4.** [enfeitar] to arrange. **-5.** *POL* [aliança, acordo] to constitute. **-6.** *TIP* to typeset. ⟨⟩ *vi* **-1.** [música] to compose. **-2.** *TIP* to typeset.
→ **compor-se** *vp* **-1.** [ser integrado por]: ~-**se de** to consist of. **-2.** [controlar-se] to compose o.s.
comporta [kõn'pɔxta] *f* floodgate.
comportamento [kõnpoxta'mẽntu] *m* **-1.** [de pessoa] behaviour; **bom/mau** ~ good/bad behaviour. **-2.** [reação] reaction.
comportar [4] [kõnpox'ta(x)] *vt* **-1.** [suportar] to hold. **-2.** [conter] to contain.
→ **comportar-se** *vp* **-1.** [pessoa] to behave; ~ **se bem/mal** to behave well/badly. **-2.** [reagir] to behave.
composição [kõnpozi'sãw] (*pl* -**ões**) *f* **-1.** [ger] composition. **-2.** [de trem, metrô] formation. **-3.** *TIP* typesetting.
compositor, ra [kõnpozi'to(x), ra] (*mpl* -**es**, *fpl* -**s**) *m, f* **-1.** *MÚS* composer. **-2.** *TIP* typesetter; ~ **tipográfico** typesetter.
composto, ta [kõn'poʃtu, ta] ⟨⟩ *pp* ▷ **compor.** ⟨⟩ *adj* composed.
→ **composto** *m QUÍM* compound.
compostura [kõnpoʃ'tura] *f* composure; **perder a** ~ to lose one's composure.
compota [kõn'pɔta] *f* stewed fruit, fruit compote.
compra [ˈkõnpra] *f* **-1.** [ato] purchase; **fazer** ~**s** to shop; **ir às** ~**s** to go shopping. **-2.** [coisa comprada] shopping.
comprador, ra [kõnpra'do(x), ra] *m, f* purchaser, buyer.
comprar [4] [kõn'pra(x)] *vt* **-1.** [adquirir] to buy. **-2.** *fig* [subornar] to bribe. **-3.** *loc*: ~ **briga** to pick a fight; ~ **a briga de alguém** to take up sb's cause.
comprazer-se [32] [kõnpra'zexsi] *vp*: ~ **com** *ou* **em fazer algo** to take pleasure in doing sthg.
compreender [5] [kõnprjẽn'de(x)] *vt* **-1.** [entender] to understand. **-2.** [abranger] to comprise.
compreensão [kõnprjẽ'sãw] *f* **-1.** [entendimento intelectual] comprehension. **-2.** [aceitação] understanding. **-3.** [percepção] realization.
compreensível [kõnprjẽ'sivew] (*pl* -**eis**) *adj* understandable.
compreensivo, va [kõnprjẽ'sivu, va] *adj* **-1.**

[pessoa, atitude] understanding. **-2.** [medida] comprehensive.

compressa [kõn'prɛsa] *f* compress.

compressão [kõnpre'sãw] (*pl* **-ões**) *f* compression.

compressor, ra [kõnpre'so(x), ra] *adj* ▷ **rolo**.

comprido, da [kõn'pridu, da] *adj* **-1.** [longo] long. **-2.** [alto] tall.

comprimento [kõnpri'mẽntu] *m* length; **três metros de** ~ three metres in length, three metres long.

comprimido, da [kõnpri'midu, da] *adj* compressed.

➤ **comprimido** *m* tablet.

comprimir [6] [kõnpri'mi(x)] *vt* **-1.** [reduzir sob pressão - ar, volume] to compress; [- barriga] to pull in. **-2.** [apertar] to squeeze.

comprometedor, ra [kõnprometɛ'do(x), ra] *adj* compromising.

comprometer [5] [kõnprome'te(x)] *vt* **-1.** [ger] to compromise. **-2.** [empenhar] to commit.

➤ **comprometer-se** *vp* **-1.** [assumir compromisso]: ~**-se (com)** to make a commitment (to). **-2.** [ser envolvido]: ~**-se (em)** to become involved (in).

comprometido, da [kõnprome'tʃidu, da] *adj* **-1.** [ocupado] busy. **-2.** [amorosamente] engaged.

compromisso [kõnpro'misu] *m* **-1.** [encontro *etc*] appointment. **-2.** [promessa] promise; **assumir um** ~ to undertake. **-3.** [obrigação] obligation; **sem** ~ under no obligation. **-4.** [acordo] agreement; **solução de** ~ compromise solution. **-5.** [namoro, noivado] engagement.

comprovação [kõnprova'sãw] (*pl* **-ões**) *f* **-1.** [prova] proof. **-2.** ADMIN [de gastos] evidence.

comprovante [kõnpro'vãntʃi] ◇ *adj* confirming. ◇ *m* receipt.

comprovar [4] [kõnpro'va(x)] *vt* to confirm.

compulsão [kõnpuw'sãw] (*pl* **-ões**) *f* compulsion; **ter** ~ **por** to have a compulsion for.

compulsivo, va [kõnpuw'sivu, va] *adj* compulsive.

compulsório, ria [kõnpuw'sɔrju, rja] *adj* compulsory.

compunção [kõnpũn'sãw] *f* compunction.

compungir [52] [kõnpũn'ʒi(x)] ◇ *vt* to move. ◇ *vi* to be moving.

computação [kõnputa'sãw] *f* **-1.** [ato] computation. **-2.** [ciência, curso] computing.

computador [kõnputa'do(x)] (*pl* **-es**) *m* computer.

computadorizar [4] [kõnputadori'za(x)] *vt* to computerize.

computadorizado, da [kõmputa'dori'zadu, da] *adj* computerized.

computar [4] [kõnpu'ta(x)] *vt* **-1.** [contar] to count. **-2.** [calcular] to compute, to calculate. **-3.** [incluir] to include.

cômputo ['kõnputul] *m* **-1.** [contagem] counting. **-2.** [cálculo] estimate.

comum [ko'mũ] (*pl* **-ns**) ◇ *adj* **-1.** [ordinário] ordinary. **-2.** [mútuo] mutual; **ter algo em** ~ to

have sthg in common. **-3.** [usual] common. ◇ *m* [usual] usual thing; **o** ~ **é ficarmos em casa aos domingos** we usually stay at home on Sundays; **fora do** ~ [extraordinário] out of the ordinary.

comuna [ko'muna] *mf fam* [comunista] Commie.

➤ **comuna** *f* ADMIN commune.

comungar [14] [komũn'ga(x)] *vi* **-1.** RELIG to receive Communion. **-2.** *fig* [partilhar]: ~ **de algo** to share sthg.

comunhão [komu'nãw] (*pl* **-ões**) *f* **-1.** [união] unity; ~ **de bens** [em matrimônio] joint ownership of property. **-2.** RELIG Communion.

comunicação [komunika'sãw] (*pl* **-ões**) *f* **-1.** [ato] communication. **-2.** [ciência] communications *(sg)*; ~ **de massa** mass media; ~ **social** the media. **-3.** [mensagem] message. **-4.** [em congresso, simpósio] speech. **-5.** [ligação] link.

comunicador, ra [komunika'do(x), ra] *m, f* communicator.

comunicar [12] [komuni'ka(x)] ◇ *vt* **-1.** [informar sobre]: ~ **algo a alguém** to inform sb of sthg. **-2.** [ligar] to link. ◇ *vi* [ligar-se]: ~ **com** to be connected to.

➤ **comunicar-se** *vp* **-1.** [dialogar, entender-se] to communicate. **-2.** [entrar em contato]: ~**-se com** to contact.

comunicativo, va [komunika'tʃivu, va] *adj* communicative.

comunidade [komuni'dadʒi] *f* community; **Comunidade Européia** European Community.

comunismo [komu'niʒmu] *m* communism.

comunista [komu'niʃta] ◇ *adj* communist. ◇ *mf* communist.

comunitário, ria [komuni'tarju, rja] *adj* community.

comutador [komuta'do(x)] *m* switch.

comutar [4] [komu'ta(x)] *vt* **-1.** JUR to commute. **-2.** [trocar] to exchange.

concatenação [kõnkatena'sãw] (*pl* **-ões**) *f* [encadeamento] (close) linkage.

concatenar [4] [kõnkate'na(x)] *vt* to link together.

côncavo, va ['kõnkavu, va] *adj* concave.

➤ **côncavo** *m* hollow.

conceber [5] [kõnse'be(x)] ◇ *vt* [gerar] to conceive. ◇ *vi* [engravidar] to conceive.

concebível [kõnse'bivew] (*pl* **-eis**) *adj* [imaginável] conceivable.

conceder [5] [kõnse'de(x)] *vt* **-1.** [dar, outorgar] to concede. **-2.** [permitir]: ~ **que alguém faça algo** to allow sb to do sthg. **-3.** [admitir]: ~ **que** to admit that.

conceito [kõn'sejtu] *m* **-1.** [idéia] concept. **-2.** [opinião] opinion. **-3.** [reputação] reputation. **-4.** EDUC [nota] grade.

conceituação [kõnsejtua'sãw] (*pl* **-ões**) *f* **-1.** [definição] conceptualization. **-2.** [avaliação] rating.

conceituado, da [kõsej'twadu, da] *adj* respected.

conceituar [4] [kõnsej'twa(x)] *vt* **-1.** [formular conceito de] to conceptualize. **-2.** [avaliar] to assess.

concentração [kõnsẽntra'sãw] (*pl* -ões) *f* -**1.** [ger] concentration. -**2.** *ESP* athletic briefing and training usually the day before an important event.

concentrado, da [kõsẽn'tradu, da] *adj* -**1.** [ger] concentrated. -**2.** [centralizado] centralized. -**3.** [aglomerado] gathered together.

➥ **concentrado** *m* [substância] concentrate.

concentrar [4] [kõsẽn'tra(x)] *vt* -**1.** [ger] to concentrate. -**2.** [centralizar] to centralize. -**3.** [aglomerar] to bring together, to mass.

➥ **concentrar-se** *vp* -**1.** [aglomerar-se] to mass. -**2.** [pessoa, atenção, esforço]: ~-se (em algo) to concentrate (on sthg).

concepção [kõnsep'sãw] (*pl* -ões) *f* -**1.** [geração] conception. -**2.** [conceito] concept. -**3.** [opinião] opinion.

concernente [kõnsex'nẽntʃi] *adj*: ~ a concerning.

concernir [54] [kõnsex'ni(x)] *vi*: ~ a to concern; no que me concerne, ... as far as I'm concerned, ...

concerto [kõn'sextu] *m MÚS* concert.

concessão [kõnse'sãw] (*pl* -ões) *f* -**1.** [ger] concession; fazer uma ~ a to make a concession to. -**2.** [entrega - de empréstimo, licença *etc*] granting; [- de prêmio] awarding. -**3.** [permissão] permission.

concessionário, ria [kõnsesjo'narju, rja] *m, f* concessionaire.

➥ **concessionária** *f* [empresa] agency.

concha ['kõnʃa] *f* -**1.** [de molusco] shell. -**2.** [para líquidos] ladle.

conchavo [kõn'ʃavu] *m* conspiracy; fazer um ~ to form a conspiracy.

conciliação [kõnsilja'sãw] (*pl* -ões) *f* reconciliation.

conciliador, ra [kõnsilja'do(x), ra] <> *adj* conciliatory. <> *m, f* [pessoa] conciliator.

conciliar [16] [kõnsi'lja(x)] *vt* to reconcile.

conciliatório, ria [kõnsilja'tɔrju, rja] *adj* conciliatory.

conciliável [kõnsi'ljavew] (*pl* -eis) *adj* reconcilable.

concílio [kõn'silju] *m RELIG* council.

concisão [kõnsi'sãw] *f* concision.

conciso, sa [kõn'sizu, za] *adj* concise.

conclamar [4] [kõnkla'ma(x)] *vt* -**1.** [bradar] to shout. -**2.** [aclamar] to acclaim. -**3.** [convocar]: ~ alguém a fazer algo to incite sb to do sthg; ~ alguém para algo to call on sb for sthg.

conclave [kõn'klavi] *m* conclave.

concludente [kõnklu'dẽntʃi] *adj* conclusive.

concluir [74] [kõŋklu'i(x)] *vt* -**1.** [terminar] to conclude. -**2.** [deduzir] to deduce.

conclusão [kõŋklu'zãw] (*pl* -ões) *f* [ger] conclusion; chegar a uma ~ [chegar a uma dedução] to reach a conclusion; [chegar a um acordo] to come to an agreement; ~: *fam* [resultado] upshot.

conclusivo, va [kõŋklu'zivu, va] *adj* conclusive.

concomitante [kõnkomi'tãntʃi] *adj* concomitant; ~ a simultaneous with.

concordância [kõŋkox'dãnsja] *f* agreement.

concordante [kõŋkox'dãntʃi] *adj* corroborating.

concordar [4] [kõŋkox'da(x)] <> *vt*: ~ que to agree that. <> *vi* to agree; ~ com algo/alguém to agree with sthg/sb; ~ em fazer algo to agree to do sthg; não concordo! I disagree!

concordata [kõŋkox'data] *f* -**1.** *FIN* composition; entrar em ~ to make a composition; pedir a ~ to seek a composition. -**2.** *RELIG* concordat.

concórdia [kõŋ'kɔxdʒja] *f* -**1.** [harmonia] concord. -**2.** [paz] peace.

concorrência [kõŋko'xẽnsja] *f* -**1.** [ger] competition. -**2.** *fig* [licitação] tender; abrir uma ~ to call to tender.

concorrente [kõŋko'xẽntʃi] *adj* -**1.** [competidor] competitor. -**2.** [candidato] candidate.

concorrer [5] [kõŋko'xe(x)] *vi* -**1.** [ger] to compete; ~ com alguém to compete with sb; ~ a algo [ger] to apply for sthg; *POL* to be running for sthg. -**2.** [contribuir]: ~ para algo to contribute to sthg.

concorrido, da [kõŋko'xidu, da] *adj* -**1.** [disputado] disputed. -**2.** *fam* [festa, bar *etc*] popular.

concretamente [kõnkreta'mẽntʃi] *adv* [em termos reais] really, actually.

concretização [kõnkretʃiza'sãw] (*pl* -ões) *f* realization.

concretizar [4] [kõŋkreti'za(x)] *vt* to realize.

➥ **concretizar-se** *vp* [sonho, projeto, anseio] to be realized.

concreto, ta [kõŋ'krɛtu, ta] *adj* [sólido] concrete.

➥ **concreto** *m* concrete; ~ armado reinforced concrete.

concretude [kõnkre'tudʒi] *f* concrete nature.

concunhado, da [kõnku'ɲadu, da] *m, f* the brother-in-law or sister-in-law of one's husband or wife.

concupiscência [kõnkupi'sẽnsja] *f* -**1.** [ambição] ambition. -**2.** [lascívia] lust.

concupiscente [kõŋkupis'sẽntʃi] *adj* materialistic.

concursado, da [kõŋkux'sadu, da] <> *adj* referring to a person who has been successful in a competitive examination giving access to a position, particularly in public office.

concurso [kõŋ'kuxsu] *m* -**1.** [exame] competitive examination; ~ público public competitive examination. -**2.** [sorteio] lottery.

concussão [kõŋku'sãw] (*pl* -ões) *f* -**1.** *MED* concussion. -**2.** *fig* [desfalque] embezzlement.

condado [kõn'dadu] *m* county.

condão [kõn'dãw] *m* ▷ varinha.

conde, dessa ['kõndʒi, dʒesa] *m, f* count (*f* countess).

condecoração [kõndekora'sãw] (*pl* -ões) *f* -**1.** [cerimônia] investiture. -**2.** [insígnia] decoration.

condecorar [4] [kõndeko'ra(x)] *vt* to decorate.

condenação [kõndena'sãw] (*pl* -ões) *f* -**1.** *JUR* conviction. -**2.** [reprovação] condemnation.

condenar [4] [kõnde'na(x)] *vt* -**1.** [ger] to condemn; ~ alguém a algo to sentence sb to sthg. -**2.** *JUR* [declarar culpado] to find guilty. -**3.** *fig* [interditar] to condemn. **- 4.** *fig* [desenganar] to disillusion; ~ **um paciente** to give up hope of saving a patient.

condenável [kŏnde'navewl] (*pl* **-eis**) *adj* [reprovável] reprehensible.

condensação [kŏndĕnsa'sãwl] (*pl* **-ões**) *f* condensation.

condensar [4] [kŏndĕn'sa(x)l *vt* to condense.
➡ **condensar-se** *vp* to condense.

condescendência [kŏndesĕn'dĕnsja] *f* condescension.

condescendente [kŏndesĕn'dĕntʃil *adj* condescending.

condescender [5] [kŏndesĕn'de(x)l *vi* to acquiesce; ~ **a** *ou* **em** to agree to.

condessa [kŏn'desal *f* ▷ **conde**.

condição [kŏndʒi'sãwl (*pl* **-ões**) *f* **- 1.** [ger] position; **de** ~ **humilde** of humble position; **de** ~ [rico] wealthy; **na** ~ **de** in the capacity of. **- 2.** [exigência] condition; **com a** ~ **de que** on condition that. **- 3.** [natureza] nature; ~ **humana** human condition.
➡ **condições** *fpl* **- 1.** [ger] conditions; **condições atmosféricas** atmospheric conditions; **condições próprias/impróprias de banho** [praia] suitable/unsuitable conditions for swimming; **condições de vida** living conditions; **condições de trabalho** working conditions. **- 2.** [estado] condition *(sg)*; **em boas condições (de uso)** in good (working) order; **sem condições** [em mau estado] in poor condition. **- 3.** [capacidade] requirement; **estar em condições de fazer algo** to be able do sthg; **ter condições de fazer algo** to be able to do sthg. **- 4.** [meios] means.

condicionado, da [kŏndʒisjo'nadu, dal *adj* conditioned; **estímulo/reflexo** ~ conditioned stimulation/reflex; **venda** ~ conditional sale.

condicionamento [kŏndʒisjona'mĕntul *m* conditioning; ~ **físico** physical condition.

condigno, na [kŏn'dʒignu, nal *adj* **- 1.** [adequado] adequate. **- 2.** [merecido] worthy.

condimentar [4] [kŏndʒimĕn'ta(x)l *vt* to season.

condimento [kŏndʒi'mĕntul *m* condiment.

condizente [kŏndʒi'zĕntʃil *adj*: ~ **com** appropriate for.

condizer [29] [kŏndʒi'ze(x)l *vi*: ~ **com** to match.

condoer-se [28] [kŏndo'exsil *vp*: ~ **de** to be sorry for.

condolência [kŏndo'lĕnsjal *f* sympathy.
➡ **condolências** *fpl* condolences.

condomínio [kŏndo'minjul *m* **- 1.** [conjunto de casas, apartamentos] condominium. **- 2.** [pagamento] service charge.

condômino, na [kŏn'dominu, nal *m, f* [co-proprietário] *person living in a condominium.*

condução [kŏndu'sãwl (*pl* **-ões**) *f* **- 1.** [ato] transportation. **- 2.** [transporte] transport. **- 3.** [ônibus] bus. **- 4.** *FÍSICA* conduction.

conducente [kŏndu'sĕntʃil *adj*: ~ **a** conducive to.

conduta [kŏn'dutal *f* conduct, behaviour; **má** ~ bad behaviour.

conduto [kŏn'dutul *m* **- 1.** [tubo] tube. **- 2.** [cano] pipe. **- 3.** [canal] channel.

condutor, ra [kŏndu'to(x), ral (*mpl* **-es**, *fpl* **-s**) ⬦ *adj* [de eletricidade] conductor. ⬦ *m, f* [de veículo] driver.
➡ **condutor** *m* *ELETR* conductor.

conduzir [72] [kŏndu'zi(x)l ⬦ *vt* **- 1.** [levar]: ~ **algo/alguém (a)** to transport sthg/sb (to). **- 2.** [empresa, equipe] to lead. **- 3.** *ELETR* to conduct. ⬦ *vi* [levar]: ~ **a** to lead to.
➡ **conduzir-se** *vp* [portar-se] to behave.

cone ['konil *m* cone.

conectar [4] [konek'ta(x)l *vt* to connect.
➡ **conectar-se** *vp* to connect; ~ **à internet** to connect to the Internet.

conectividade [konektʃivi'dadʒil *f* connectivity.

cônego ['konegul *m* canon.

conexão [konek'sãwl (*pl* **-ões**) *f* **- 1.** [ger & *COMPUT*] connection; ~ **discada** *ou* **dial-up** dial-up connection; ~ **a cabo** cable connection. **- 2.** [nexo] link. **- 3.** [relação] relationship.

conexo, xa [ko'nɛksu, sal *adj* connected.

confabulação [kŏnfabula'sãwl (*pl* **-ões**) *f* **- 1.** [conspiração] conspiracy. **- 2.** [conversa] chat.

confabular [4] [kŏnfabu'la(x)l *vi* **- 1.** [conspirar] to conspire. **- 2.** [conversar] to chat; ~ **com** to chat with.

confecção [kŏnfek'sãwl (*pl* **-ões**) *f* **- 1.** [ger] making. **- 2.** [fábrica de roupas] clothing factory.

confeccionar [4] [kŏnfeksjo'na(x)l *vt* [fabricar, fazer] to make.

confederação [kŏnfedera'sãwl (*pl* **-ões**) *f* confederation.

confeitar [4] [kŏnfej'ta(x)l *vt* [bolo] to sugar-coat.

confeitaria [kŏnfejta'rial *f* cake shop.

confeiteiro, ra [kŏnfej'tejru, ral *m, f* confectioner.

conferência [kŏnfe'rɛsjal *f* **- 1.** [verificação] check. **- 2.** [palestra] lecture; **fazer uma** ~ to give a lecture.

conferencista [kŏnferĕn'siʃtal *m f* [palestrante] speaker.

conferente [kŏnfe'rĕntʃil *mf* [em uma verificação] checker, controller.

conferir [57] [kŏnfe'ri(x)l ⬦ *vt* **- 1.** [verificar] to check. **- 2.** [cotejar, comparar] to compare. **- 3.** [dar]: ~ **algo a alguém/algo** to invest sb/sthg with sthg. **- 4.** [título, encargo] to confer. ⬦ *vi* **- 1.** [estar correto]: ~ **(com)** to agree (with). **- 2.** [garantir] to make sure.

confessar [4] [kŏnfe'sa(x)l ⬦ *vt* **- 1.** [fazer confissão de] to confess. **- 2.** *RELIG* [ouvir confissão de] to hear confession. ⬦ *vi* **- 1.** [fazer confissão] to make a confession. **- 2.** *RELIG* to confess.
➡ **confessar-se** *vp* **- 1.** *RELIG* to confess. **- 2.** [admitir ser] to confess to being; ~ **-se culpado** *JUR* to plead guilty.

confessionário [kŏnfesjo'narjul *m* confessional.

confesso, sa [kŏn'fesu, sal *adj* confessed.

confessor [kŏnfe'so(x)l *m* *RELIG* confessor.

confete [kõn'fɛtʃi] *m* confetti; **jogar ~** *fam* [bajular] to please sb.

confiabilidade [kõnfjabili'dadʒi] *f* [credibilidade] reliability.

confiado, da [kõn'fjadu, da] *adj* [atrevido] cheeky.

confiança [kõn'fjãnsa] *f* **-1.** [segurança] confidence. **-2.** [fé] trust; **digno de ~** worthy of trust; **ter ~ em alguém** to have confidence in sb; **de ~** trustworthy. **-3.** *fam* [intimidade] familiarity; **dar ~ a alguém** to allow sb to treat one in a familiar way.

confiante [kõn'fjãntʃi] *adj* **-1.** [seguro] confident. **-2.** [esperançoso]: **~ (em)** trusting (in).

confiar [16] [kõn'fja(x)] <> *vi:* **~ em** to trust in. <> *vt* **-1.** [entregar]: **~ algo a alguém** to entrust sthg to sb. **-2.** [contar]: **~ algo a alguém** to confide in sb about sthg.

confiável [kõn'fjavew] *(pl -eis) adj* reliable.

confidência [kõnfi'dẽnsja] *f* confidence; **em ~** in confidence.

confidencial [kõnfidẽn'sjaw] *(pl -ais) adj* confidential.

confidenciar [16] [kõnfidẽn'sja(x)] *vt :* **~ algo a alguém** to confide sthg to sb.

confidente [kõnfi'dẽntʃi] *m f* confidant *(f* confidante*)*.

configuração [kõnfigura'sãw] *(pl -ões) f* **-1.** [disposição - de objetos, peças] arrangement; [- de astros] configuration. **-2.** [forma] shape. **-3.** *COMPUT* configuration.

configurar [4] [kõnfigu'ra(x)] *vt* to represent.

confinamento [kõnfina'mẽntu] *m* confinement.

confinar [4] [kõnfi'na(x)] <> *vt* [isolar, enclausurar]: **~ alguém/algo em** to confine sb/sthg to/in. <> *vi* **~ confinar-se** *vp* [isolar-se, enclausurar-se] to isolate o.s.

confins [kõn'fĩʃ] *mpl* [limite extremo] ends; **nos ~ de Judas** *fam* in the back of beyond.

confirmação [kõnfixma'sãw] *(pl -ões) f* confirmation.

confirmar [4] [kõnfix'ma(x)] *vt* [comprovar] to confirm.

~ confirmar-se *vp* **-1.** [cumprir-se] to be confirmed. **-2.** [justificar-se] to be justified.

confiscar [12] [kõnfiʃ'ka(x)] *vt* to confiscate.

confisco [kõn'fiʃku] *m* confiscation.

confissão [kõnfi'sãw] *(pl -ões) f* [de falta, crime] confession.

conflagração [kõnflagra'sãw] *(pl -ões) f* **-1.** [guerra] war. **-2.** [revolução] revolution.

conflagrar [4] [kõnfla'gra(x)] *vt* [levar à guerra] to convulse.

conflitante [kõnfli'tãntʃi] *adj* conflicting.

conflito [kõn'flitu] *m* [ger] conflict; **~ de gerações** generation gap; **entrar em ~ (com)** to clash (with).

confluência [kõn'flwẽnsja] *f* **-1.** [de rios] confluence. **-2.** [de estradas, ruas] junction.

confluente [kõn'flwẽntʃi] *adj* **-1.** [rio] confluent. **-2.** [estrada, rua] merging.

confluir [kõn'flui(x)] *vi* to merge.

conformação [kõnfoxma'sãw] *(pl -ões) f* **-1.** [resignação] resignation. **-2.** [forma] shape.

conformado, da [kõnfox'madu, da] *adj* [resignado] resigned.

conformar [4] [kõnfox'ma(x)] *vt* [formar] to shape.

~ conformar-se *vp* **-1.** [resignar-se]: **~-se com** to resign o.s. to. **-2.** [acomodar-se]: **~-se a** *ou* **com** to conform to *ou* with.

conforme [kõn'fɔxmi] <> *prep* [de acordo com, segundo] in accordance with. <> *conj* **-1.** [ger] as. **-2.** [de acordo com] according to. **-3.** [dependendo de] depending on.

~ conformes *mpl:* **dentro dos ~s** *fam* in accordance with the requirements.

conformidade [kõnfoxmi'dadʒi] *f* [acordo] agreement; **em ~ com** in accordance with.

conformismo [kõnfox'miʒmu] *m* conformity.

conformista [kõnfox'miʃta] *mf* conformist.

confortante [kõnfox'tãntʃi] *adj* comforting.

confortar [4] [kõnfox'ta(x)] *vt* [consolar] to comfort.

confortável [kõnfox'tavɛw] *(pl -eis) adj* comfortable.

conforto [kõn'foxtu] *m* comfort.

confraria [kõnfra'ria] *f* fraternity.

confraternização [kõnfratexniza'sãw] *(pl -ões) f* fraternization.

confraternizar [4] [kõnfratexni'za(x)] <> *vt* **-1.** [reunir, ligar] to socialize. **-2.** [reconciliar] to reconcile. <> *vi* **-1.** [reunir-se, ligar-se] to unite. **-2.** [comemorar] to celebrate.

confrontação [kõnfrõnta'sãw] *(pl -ões) f* **-1.** [comparação] comparison. **-2.** [acareação] confrontation.

confrontar [4] [kõnfrõn'ta(x)] *vt* **-1.** [comparar] to compare. **-2.** [acarear] to confront.

~ confrontar-se *vp* [defrontar-se] to face each other.

confronto [kõn'frõntu] *m* **-1.** [comparação] comparison. **-2.** [choque] confrontation.

confundir [6] [kõnfũn'di(x)] *vt* **-1.** [ger] to confuse; **~ algo com** to confuse sthg with. **-2.** [misturar] to muddle. **-3.** [trocar] to mix up.

~ confundir-se *vp* to become confused; **~-se com** to become confused with.

confusão [kõnfu'zãw] *(pl -ões) f* **-1.** [mistura] muddle. **-2.** [troca] mixing up; **fazer ~** [confundir-se] to become confused. **-3.** [indistinção] confusion. **-4.** [caos] mess. **-5.** [problema] hassle; **dar ~** to cause a hassle. **-6.** [tumulto] melee.

confuso, sa [kõn'fuzu, za] *adj* **-1.** [obscuro] obscure. **-2.** [misturado] muddled. **-3.** [indistinto] hazy. **-4.** [atrapalhado] confused.

congelado, da [kõnʒe'ladu, da] *adj* frozen.

~ congelado *m* frozen food *(inv)*.

congelador [kõnʒela'do(x)] *(pl -es) m* freezer.

congelamento [kõnʒela'mẽntu] *m* **-1.** [de água, alimento *etc*] freezing. **-2.** *ECON* [de preços, salários] freeze.

congelar [4] [kõnʒe'la(x)] <> *vt* [água, rio, alimento] to freeze. <> *vi* **-1.** [ficar congelado] to freeze. **-2.**

[sentir frio] to be freezing.
➤ **congelar-se** *vp* [ficar congelado] to freeze.
congênere [kõn'ʒeneri] *adj* similar.
congênito, ta [kõnʒenitu, ta] *adj* congenital.
congestão [kõnʒeʃ'tãw] (*pl* -ões) *f* congestion; ~ nasal nasal congestion.
congestionado, da [kõnʒeʃtjo'nadu, da] *adj* -1. [trânsito] congested. -2. [nariz, artéria] blocked.
congestionamento [kõnʒeʃtjona'mẽntu] *m* -1. [engarrafamento] congestion; ~ de tráfego traffic congestion. -2. [de nariz, artéria] blockage.
congestionar [4] [kõnʒeʃt[jo'na(x)] *vt* -1. [trânsito]: ~ o trânsito to cause traffic congestion. -2. [nariz, artéria] to block.
➤ **congestionar-se** *vp* -1. [trânsito] to become congested. -2. [nariz, artéria] to become blocked.
conglomeração [kõŋglomera'sãw] (*pl* -ões) *f* conglomeration.
conglomerado [kõŋglome'radu] *m* conglomerate.
conglomerar [4] [kõŋglome'ra(x)] *vt* -1. [reunir] to conglomerate. -2. [empresas] to merge.
Congo ['kõŋgu] *n*: o ~ the Congo.
congolês, esa [kõŋgo'leʃ, eza] <> *adj* Congolese. <> *m, f* Congolese.
congratular [4] [kõŋgratu'la(x)] *vt*: ~ alguém (por algo) to congratulate sb (on sthg).
congregação [kõŋgrega'sãw] (*pl* -ões) *f* -1. RELIG congregation. -2. [reunião] coming together.
congregar [14] [kõŋgre'ga(x)] *vt* [reunir] to bring together.
➤ **congregar-se** *vp* [reunir-se] to congregate.
congressista [kõŋgre'siʃta] *m f* -1. [participante] delegate *(at a conference)*. -2. POL congressman (*f* congresswoman).
congresso [kõŋ'gresu] *m* -1. [conferência] conference. -2. POL: o Congresso Congress.
conhaque [ko'nakil] *m* cognac.
conhecedor, ra [konese'do(x), ra] (*mpl* -es, *fpl* -s) <> *adj* [ciente]: ~ (de) aware (of). <> *m, f* [especialista]: ~ (de) specialist (in).
conhecer [25] [kone'se(x)] *vt* -1. [ger] to know. -2. [entender de] to understand. -3. [pessoa pela primeira vez] to meet; ~ alguém de nome/de vista to know sb by name/sight. -4. [loja, casa *etc*] to see. -5. [país] to visit. -6. [reconhecer]: ~ algo/alguém (por) to recognize sthg/sb (by).
➤ **conhecer-se** *vp* -1. [a si próprio] to know o.s. -2. [pessoas] to know one another; [pela primeira vez] to meet.
conhecido, da [kone'sidu, da] <> *adj* -1. [famoso] well-known; ~ por known for. -2. [sabido] wise. -3. [notório] notorious. <> *m, f* [pessoa] acquaintance.
conhecimento [konesi'mẽntu] *m* -1. [saber] knowledge; ~ de causa due knowledge; **levar algo ao** ~ **de alguém** to bring sthg to the attention of sb; **não tomar** ~ **de** [não dar importância a] not to attach importance to; **ser de** ~ **geral que** to be general knowledge that; **ter** ~ **de** to be aware of; **tomar** ~ **de** to find out about. -2.

[conhecido] acquaintance. -3. COM: ~ aéreo air waybill.
➤ **conhecimentos** *mpl* -1. [noções] knowledge *(sg)*. -2. [relações, conhecidos] friends.
cônico, ca ['koniku, ka] *adj* conical.
conivência [koni'vẽnsja] *f* connivance.
conivente [koni'vẽnt[il] *adj* conniving; **ser** ~ **com** to connive in.
conjetura [kõnʒe'tural] *f* conjecture; **fazer** ~**s (sobre)** to make conjectures (about).
conjeturar [4] [kõnʒetu'ra(x)] *vt* to conjecture.
conjugação [kõnʒuga'sãw] (*pl* -ões) *f* -1. [união] union. -2. GRAM conjugation.
conjugado, da [kõnʒu'gadu, da] *adj* -1. [apartamento, sala] adjoining. -2. GRAM conjugated.
➤ **conjugado** *m* [apartamento] adjoining apartment.
conjugal [kõnʒu'gaw] (*pl* -ais) *adj* marital; **vida** ~ married life.
conjugar [14] [kõnʒu'ga(x)] *vt* -1. [unir] to combine. -2. GRAM to conjugate.
➤ **conjugar-se** *vp* [unir-se] to be connected.
cônjuge ['kõnʒuʒil] *m* spouse.
conjunção [kõnʒũn'sãw] (*pl* -ões) *f* -1. [união] combination. -2. GRAM conjunction.
conjuntivite [kõnʒũnt[i'vit[il] *f* conjunctivitis.
conjunto, ta [kõn'ʒũntu, ta] *adj* combined, joint.
➤ **conjunto** *m* -1. [grupo] combination. -2. [totalidade]: **o** ~ **de** the whole of; **em** ~ together. -3. MÚS group. -4. [residencial] complex; ~ **habitacional** housing complex. -5. [traje] suit. -6. MAT set.
conjuntura [kõnʒũn'tural] *f* conjuncture.
conluio [kõn'lujul] *m* collusion.
conosco [ko'noʃkul] *pron pess* with us.
conotação [konotaʃãw] (*pl* -ões) *f* connotation.
conotar [4] [kono'ta(x)] *vt* to connote.
conquanto [kõŋ'kwãntul] *conj* although.
conquista [kõŋ'kiʃta] *f* conquest.
conquistador, ra [kõŋkiʃta'do(x), ra] <> *adj* -1. [exército, país] conquering. -2. [sedutor] seductive. <> *m, f* -1. [de terras, país] conqueror. -2. [sedutor-homem] lady-killer; [- mulher] femme fatale.
conquistar [4] [kõŋkiʃ'ta(x)] *vt* -1. [subjugar] to conquer. -2. [alcançar] to achieve. -3. [ganhar] to win. -4. [seduzir] to seduce.
consagração [kõnsagra'sãw] (*pl* -ões) *f* -1. [aclamação] acclaim. -2. [exaltação] acclamation; **fazer a** ~ **de** to be an acclamation of. -3. [dedicação] dedication. -4. [aceitação] acceptance. -5. RELIG consecration.
consagrar [4] [kõnsa'gra(x)] *vt* -1. [levar à aclamação] to lead to the acclamation of. -2. [exaltar] to glorify. -3. [dedicar] to dedicate. -4. [tornar aceito] to become accepted. -5. RELIG to consecrate.
➤ **consagrar-se** *vi* -1. [atingir a aclamação] to achieve acclaim. -2. [dedicar-se]: ~**-se a algo** to dedicate oneself to sthg.
consangüíneo, nea [kõnsãn'gwinju, nja] <> *adj* related by blood. <> *m, f* [parente] blood relation.

consciência [kõn'sjẽnsja] *f* **-1.** [conhecimento] awareness; ~ **de classe** class-consciousness; ~ **política** political awareness; **ter/tomar** ~ **de** to be/become aware of. **-2.** [sentidos]: **perder a** ~ to lose consciousness. **-3.** [moral] conscience; **estar com a** ~ **limpa/pesada** to have a clear/guilty conscience. **-4.** [cuidado, responsabilidade] care.

consciencioso, osa [kõnsjẽn'sjozu, oza] *adj* conscientious.

consciente [kõnʃ'sjẽntʃi] <> *adj* conscious. <> *m* PSIC consciousness.

conscientemente [kõnsjẽntʃi'mẽntʃi] *adv* consciously.

conscientizar [4] [kõnsjẽntʃi'za(x)] *vt* [dar conhecimento a]: ~ **alguém (de algo)** to raise sb's awareness (of something).

➡ **conscientizar-se** *vp* [tomar consciência de]: ~ **-se (de algo)** to become aware (of sthg).

cônscio, cia [ˈkõnsju, sja] *adj* lucid.

consecução [kõnseku'sãw] *f* attainment.

consecutivo, va [kõnseku'tʃivu, va] *adj* consecutive.

conseguinte [kõnse'gĩntʃi] ➡ **por conseguinte** *loc conj* consequently.

conseguir [55] [kõnse'gi(x)] *vt* **-1.** [obter] to obtain. **-2.** [alcançar] to achieve; ~ **fazer algo** to manage to do sthg.

conselheiro, ra [kõnse'ʎejru, ra] *m, f* **-1.** [ger] adviser. **-2.** [membro de conselho] councillor.

conselho [kõ'seʎu] *m* **-1.** [advertência] advice; **dar um** ~ **a alguém** to give sb a piece of advice. **-2.** [órgão] council; ~ **administrativo** board of directors; ~ **de Estado** Council of State; ~ **de ministros** Cabinet; ~ **de guerra** council of war.

consenso [kõn'sẽnsu] *m* consensus.

consensual [kõnsẽn'swaw] (*pl* **-ais**) *adj* consensual.

consentimento [kõnsẽntʃi'mẽntu] *m* consent.

consentir [56] [kõnsẽn'tʃi(x)] <> *vt* **-1.** [permitir] to grant. **-2.** [aprovar] to approve. <> *vi* [concordar, anuir]: ~ **em algo** to consent to sthg; ~ **em fazer algo** to agree to do sthg.

consequência [kõnse'kwẽnsja] *f* [resultado] consequence; **em** ~ **de** because of, owing to; **por** ~ consequently.

consequente [kõnse'kwẽntʃi] *adj* **-1.** [resultante] consequent. **-2.** [coerente] coherent.

consertar [4] [kõnsex'ta(x)] *vt* **-1.** [reparar] to repair. **-2.** [remediar] to rectify.

conserto [kõn'sextu] *m* repair.

conserva [kõn'sɛrva] *f* preserve; **em** ~ preserved.

conservação [kõnsexva'sãw] *f* **-1.** [ger] conservation. **-2.** [preservação] preservation.

conservacionista [kõnsexvasjo'niʃta] <> *adj* conservationist. <> *mf* conservationist.

conservado, da [kõnsex'vadu, da] *adj* **-1.** [carro, casa] well kept. **-2.** [pessoa] well preserved.

conservador, ra [kõnsexva'do(x), ra] <> *adj* conservative. <> *m, f* conservative.

conservadorismo [kõnsexvado'riʒmu] *m* conservatism.

conservante [kõnser'vãntʃi] *m* preservative.

conservar [4] [kõnsex'va(x)] *vt* **-1.** [preservar] to preserve. **-2.** [sabor, qualidade etc] to conserve. **-3.** [manter] to maintain.

➡ **conservar-se** *vp* **-1.** [pessoa] to be well preserved. **-2.** [permanecer] to remain.

conservatório [kõnsexva'tɔrju] *m* conservatoire.

consideração [kõnsidera'sãw] (*pl* **-ões**) *f* **-1.** [ger] consideration; **levar em** ~ to take into consideration; **falta de** ~ **(com alguém)** lack of consideration (towards sb). **-2.** [pensamento] thought.

considerado, da [kõnside'radu, da] *adj* respected.

considerar [4] [kõnside'ra(x)] *vt* **-1.** [ger] to consider. **-2.** [respeitar, estimar]: ~ **muito alguém/algo** to have a high regard for sb/sthg.

➡ **considerar-se** *vp* [julgar-se] to consider o.s.

considerável [kõnside'ravɛw] (*pl* **-eis**) *adj* considerable.

consignação [kõnsigna'sãw] (*pl* **-ões**) *f* **-1.** [registro] report. **-2.** COM consignment; **venda por** ~ sale on consignment; **em** ~ on consignment. **-3.** [de verbas] allocation.

consignar [4] [kõnsig'na(x)] *vt* **-1.** [produtos] to consign. **-2.** [registrar] to record. **-3.** [verbas] to allocate.

consigo [kõn'sigu] *pron pess* with him/her/you/it.

consistência [kõnsiʃ'tẽnsja] *f* consistency; **ganhar** ~ to thicken.

consistente [kõnsiʃ'tẽntʃi] *adj* **-1.** [sólido] solid. **-2.** [espesso] thick. **-3.** [coerente, sólido] consistent.

consistir [6] [kõnsiʃ'tʃi(x)] *vi* [constituir-se]: ~ **em** to consist of; ~ **em fazer algo** to consist in doing sthg.

consoante [kõn'swãntʃi] <> *adj* LING consonant. <> *f* LING consonant. <> *prep* [de acordo com] according to.

consolação [kõnsola'sãw] (*pl* **-ões**) *f* comfort.

consolador, ra [kõnsola'do(x), ra] *adj* comforting.

consolar [4] [kõnso'la(x)] *vt* to comfort.

➡ **consolar-se** *vp*: ~**-se (com)** to console o.s. (with).

console [kõn'soli] *m* console.

consolidação [kõnsolida'sãw] (*pl* **-ões**) *f* [estabilização] consolidation.

consolidar [4] [kõnsoli'da(x)] <> *vt* **-1.** [estabilizar, ratificar] to consolidate. **-2.** [fratura] to calcify. <> *vi* [tornar-se sólido] to solidify.

consolo [kõn'solu] *m* **-1.** [consolação] comfort. **-2.** *vulg* [consolo-de-viúva] dildo.

consomê [kõnso'me] *m* consommé.

consonância [kõnso'nãnsja] *f* consonance; **em** ~ **com** in accordance with.

consórcio [kõn'sɔxsju] *m* **-1.** [união] partnership. **-2.** [de interesses, necessidades] uniting. **-3.** COM consortium.

consorte [kõn'sɔxtʃi] *m, f* consort.

conspícuo, cua [kõʃ'pikwu, kwa] *adj* **-1.** [evidente] conspicuous. **-2.** [ilustre] remarkable.

conspiração [kõʃpira'sãw] (*pl* -ões) *f* conspiracy.

conspirador, ra [kõʃpira'do(x), ra] *m, f* conspirator.

conspirar [4] [kõʃpi'ra(x)] ◇ *vi:* ~ **(contra)** to conspire (against). ◇ *vt* to plot.

conspiratório, ria [kõʃpira'tɔrju, rja] *adj* conspiratorial.

constância [kõʃ'tãnsja] *f* **-1.** [de ruído, incômodo] persistence. **-2.** [no amor] constancy. **-3.** [perseverança] perseverance. **-4.** [de idéias, opiniões] constancy.

constante [kõʃ'tãntʃi] *adj* **-1.** [ger] constant. **-2.** [pessoa, amor] faithful. **-3.** [que consta]: ~ **de** pertaining to.

constar [4] [kõʃ'ta(x)] *vi* **-1.** [informação]: ~ **(em** ou **de)** to appear (in). **-2.** [ser assegurado]: ~ **que** to be said that. **-3.** [ser do conhecimento de]: **não lhe constava que o preço tivesse subido** he was not aware that the price had risen. **-4.** [constituir-se]: ~ **de** to consist of.

constatação [kõʃtata'sãw] (*pl* -ões) *f* **-1.** [observação] observation. **-2.** [comprovação] confirmation.

constatar [4] [kõʃta'ta(x)] *vt* **-1.** [observar] to notice. **-2.** [comprovar] to prove.

constelação [kõʃtela'sãw] (*pl* -ões) *f* constellation.

consternação [kõʃtexna'sãw] (*pl* -ões) *f* [desalento, desolação] dismay.

consternado, da [kõʃter'nadu, da] *adj* dismayed.

consternar [4] [kõʃtex'na(x)] *vt* to discourage.

constipação [kõʃtʃipa'sãw] (*pl* -ões) *f* **-1.** [prisão de ventre] constipation. **-2.** [resfriado] cold.

constipado, da [kõʃtʃi'padu, da] *adj* **-1.** [resfriado]: **estar** ~ to have a cold. **-2.** [com prisão de ventre] constipated.

constitucional [kõʃtʃitusjo'naw] (*pl* -ais) *adj* constitutional.

constitucionalidade [kõʃtʃitusjonali'dadʒi] *f* constitutionality.

constituição [kõʃtʃitwi'sãw] (*pl* -ões) *f* **-1.** [formação] make-up. **-2.** [consistência] composition. **-3.** *POL* [carta] constitution.

constituinte [kõʃtʃi'twĩtʃi] ◇ *adj* **-1.** [componente] constituent. **-2.** *POL* representative. ◇ *mf* *POL* [deputado] deputy.

➠ **Constituinte** *f POL* [assembléia]: **a Constituinte** the Constituent Assembly.

constituir [74] [kõʃtʃi'twi(x)] *vt* **-1.** [compor, ser] to constitute. **-2.** [criar, estabelecer] to establish.

➠ **constituir-se** *vp* **-1.** [estabelecer-se como]: ~ **se em algo** to establish o.s. as sthg. **-2.** [ser]: ~ **se em algo** to be sthg, to constitute sthg.

constitutivo, va [kõʃtʃitu'tʃivu, va] *adj* **-1.** [formador] constituent. **-2.** [indispensável] essential. **-3.** [característico] characteristic.

constrangedor, ra [kõʃtrãʒe'do(x), ra] *adj* **-1.** [embaraçador] embarrassing. **-2.** [repressivo] repressive.

constranger [26] [kõʃtrãn'ʒe(x)] *vt* **-1.** [embaraçar] to embarrass. **-2.** [reprimir, refrear] to curb. **-3.** [coagir]: ~ **alguém a fazer algo** to force sb to do sthg.

➠ **constranger-se** *vp* [ficar embaraçado] to be embarrassed.

constrangimento [kõʃtrãnʒi'mẽntu] *m* **-1.** [embaraço] embarrassment. **-2.** [repressão] restriction.

construção [kõʃtru'sãw] (*pl* -ões) *f* **-1.** [edifício] building; **em** ~ under construction *(depois de verbo)*. **-2.** [intelectual, imaginária] feat.

construir [73] [kõʃtru'i(x)] *vt* to build.

construtivo, va [kõʃtru'tʃivu, va] *adj* constructive.

construtor, ra [kõʃtru'to(x), ra] (*mpl* -es, *fpl* -s) ◇ *adj* building *(antes de subst)*. ◇ *m, f* builder.

➠ **construtora** *f* [empresa] building company.

cônsul ['kõsuw] (*pl* -es) *m* consul.

consulado [kõsu'ladu] *m* consulate.

consulente [kõsu'lẽntʃi] *mf* advice seeker.

cônsules ['kõsuliʃ] *pl* ➢ **cônsul**.

consulesa [kõsu'leza] *f* **-1.** [diplomata] consul. **-2.** [esposa] consul's wife.

consulta [kõn'suwta] *f* **-1.** [sobre problema, dúvida] query; **fazer uma** ~ **a alguém** to consult sb. **-2.** *MED* consultation; **horário de** ~ surgery hours; **ter uma** ~ **(com)** to have an appointment (with).

consultar [4] [kõsuw'ta(x)] *vt* to consult; ~ **alguém sobre algo** to consult sb about sthg.

consultivo, va [kõsuw'tʃivu, va] *adj* consultative.

consultor, ra [kõsuw'to(x), ra] *m, f* consultant.

consultoria [kõsuwto'ria] *f* [serviço] consultancy; **empresa de** ~ consultancy.

consultório [kõsuw'tɔrju] *m* **-1.** *MED* consulting room. **-2.** *JORN:* ~ **sentimental** agony column.

consumação [kõsuma'sãw] (*pl* -ões) *f* **-1.** [realização] realization, carrying out. **-2.** [completude] completion. **-3.** [de casamento] consummation. **-4.** [em restaurante, bar]: ~ **mínima** minimum order.

consumado, da [kõsu'madu, da] *adj* **-1.** [realizado] realized, carried out. **-2.** [completado] completed. **-3.** [casamento] consummated.

consumar [4] [kõsu'ma(x)] *vt* **-1.** [realizar] to realize, to carry out. **-2.** [completar] to complete. **-3.** [casamento] to consummate.

➠ **consumar-se** *vp* **-1.** [realizar-se] to be realized, to be carried out. **-2.** [completar-se] to be completed. **-3.** [casamento] to be consummated. **-4.** [profecia] to come true.

consumidor, ra [kõsumi'do(x), ra] (*mpl* -es, *fpl* -s) ◇ *adj* consumer. ◇ *m, f* consumer.

consumir [6] [kõsu'mi(x)] ◇ *vt* **-1.** [ger] to consume. **-2.** [comprar] to purchase. **-3.** [corroer, devorar] to corrode. **-4.** *fig* [desgastar] to consume. ◇ *vi* [comprar] to consume.

➠ **consumir-se** *vp* **-1.** [combustível, fogo] to burn

itself out. **-2.** *fig* [pessoa] to wear o.s. out.

consumismo [kõnsu'miȝmu] *m* consumerism.

consumista [kõnsu'miʃta] *adj* consumerist.

consumo [kõ'sumu] *m* **-1.** [ger] consumption. **-2.** [compra] sale; **bens de** ~ consumer goods; **sociedade de** ~ consumer society. **-3.** [de drogas] use.

conta ['kõnta] *f* **-1.** [ger] account; **pôr na** ~ to charge to one's account; **abrir uma** ~ to open an account; ~ **conjunta** joint account; ~ **corrente** current account; ~ **negativa** overdrawn account; ~ **de poupança** savings account. **-2.** [cálculo] counting; **acertar** *ou* **ajustar contas com alguém** *fig* to settle a score with sb; **demais da** ~ *fig* in excess; **fazer** ~**s** to make calculations; **pedir as** ~**s** *fig* [demitir-se] to resign; **perder a** ~ **de algo** to lose count of sthg; **ser a** ~ **certa** to be the correct amount; **afinal de** ~**s** after all. **-3.** [em restaurante] bill; **a** ~**, por favor!** the bill, please!; **pedir a** ~ to ask for the bill. **-4.** [fatura] invoice; ~ **de gás/luz/telefone** gas/electricity/telephone bill. **-5.** [consideração]: **levar algo em** ~ to take sthg into account; **dar(-se)** ~ **de** to realize. **-6.** [justificação, razão]: **à** ~ **de** on account of; **por** ~ **de** because of. **-7.** [informação, satisfação] account; **dar** ~ **de** to give an account of; **prestar** ~**s de** to account for. **-8.** [responsabilidade, capacidade]: **dar** ~ **de** to manage; **deixar por** ~ **de alguém** to leave to sb; **não ser da** ~ **de alguém** to be nobody's business; **tomar** ~ **de alguém/algo** [cuidar, encarregar-se de] to look after sb/sthg; **tomar** ~ **de** [difundir-se por] to take over. **-9.** [de colar] bead. **-10.** *loc*: **dar** ~ **do recado** to do well; **fazer de** ~ **que** [imaginar] to pretend; [fingir] to pretend; **ficar por** ~ to get angry; **ter alguém em alta** ~ to hold sb in high esteem.

➡ **por conta própria** *loc adv* on one's own account; **trabalhar por** ~ **própria** to be self-employed.

contábil [kõn'tabiw] (*pl* **-eis**) *adj* accountancy (*antes de subst*).

contabilidade [kõntabili'daȝil] *f* **-1.** [ofício] accountancy; ~ **de custos** cost accounting. **-2.** [setor] accounts department.

contabilista [kõntabi'liʃta] *m f* accountant.

contabilizar [4] [kõntabili'za(x)] *vt* **-1.** [registrar] to keep accounts. **-2.** [calcular] to count.

contado, da [kõn'tadu, da] *adj* accounted for; **estar com o dinheiro** ~ to have every penny accounted for; **ele está com seus dias** ~**s** his days are numbered.

contador [kõnta'do(x)] (*pl* **-es**) *m, f* **-1.** COM accountant. **-2.** [narrador]: ~ **de histórias** storyteller.

➡ **contador** *m* TEC meter.

contadoria [kõntado'ria] *f* accounts department.

contagem [kõn'taȝẽ] (*pl* **-ns**) *f* **-1.** [ato] counting; ~ **regressiva** countdown. **-2.** [escore] score.

contagiante [kõnta'ȝjãntʃi] *adj* contagious.

contagiar [16] [kõnta'ȝja(x)] *vt* **-1.** [infectar] to infect. **-2.** *fig* [influenciar] to affect.

➡ **contagiar-se** *vp* **-1.** [infectar-se] to become infected. **-2.** *fig* [influenciar-se] to be affected.

contágio [kõn'taȝju] *m* contagion.

contagioso, osa [kõnta'ȝjozu, za] *adj* contagious.

conta-gotas [ˌkõnta'gotaʃ] *m inv* dropper.

contaminação [kõntamina'sãw] (*pl* **-ões**) *f* contamination.

contaminado, da [kõntami'nadu, da] *adj* **-1.** [infectado, poluído] contaminated. **-2.** [por doença] infected.

contaminar [4] [kõntami'na(x)] ◇ *vt* [contagiar] to contaminate. ◇ *vi fig* [corromper] to corrupt.

contanto [kõn'tãntu] ➡ **contanto que** *loc adv* provided that.

contar [4] [kõn'ta(x)] ◇ *vt* **-1.** [enumerar] to count. **-2.** [narrar] to tell. **-3.** [supor]: ~ **que** to expect. ◇ *vi* **-1.** [fazer contas] to count. **-2.** [importar] to matter. **-3.**: ~ **com** [ger] to count on; [dispor] to have. **-4.** [pretender]: ~ **(em) fazer algo** to intend to do sthg. **-5.** [incluir]: ~ **algo/alguém entre algo** to count sthg/sb as (being) sthg.

contatar [4] [kõnta'ta(x)] *vt* to contact.

contato [kõn'tatu] *m* contact.

contêiner [kõn'tejne(x)] *m* container.

contemplação [kõntẽnpla'sãw] *m* contemplation.

contemplar [4] [kõntẽn'pla(x)] *vt* **-1.** [olhar] to contemplate. **-2.** [premiar] to reward.

➡ **contemplar-se** *vp* [olhar-se] to look at o.s.

contemplativo, va [kõntẽnpla'tʃivu, va] *adj* contemplative.

contemporaneidade [kõntẽnporãnej'dadȝil] *f* contemporary nature.

contemporâneo, nea [kõntẽmpo'ranju, nja] ◇ *adj* contemporary. ◇ *m, f* contemporary.

contemporizar [4] [kõntẽnpori'za(x)] ◇ *vt* [acalmar] to calm. ◇ *vi* [transigir]: ~ **(com)** to compromise (with).

contenção [kõntẽn'sãw] *f* **-1.** [diminuição - de despesas] cutback; [- de gestos, palavras] restraint. **-2.** [interrupção de fluxo] containment.

contencioso, osa [kõntẽn'sjozu, ɔza] *adj* contentious.

contenda [kõn'tẽnda] *f* dispute.

contentamento [kõntẽnta'mẽntu] *m* **-1.** [alegria] happiness. **-2.** [satisfação] contentment.

contentar [4] [kõntẽn'ta(x)] *vt* **-1.** [satisfazer] to content. **-2.** [agradar] to please.

➡ **contentar-se** *vp* [satisfazer-se]: ~**-se com** to be satisfied with.

contente [kõn'tẽntʃi] *adj* happy.

contento [kõn'tẽntu] ➡ **a contento** *loc adv* satisfactorily.

conter [1] [kõn'te(x)] *vt* **-1.** [controlar] to control. **-2.** [ter] to contain.

➡ **conter-se** *vp* [controlar-se] to restrain o.s.

conterrâneo, nea [kõnte'xãnju, nja] ◇ *adj* fellow (*antes de subst*); **é um amigo** ~ he is a friend who comes from the same place as me. ◇ *m, f* compatriot.

contestação [kõnteʃta'sãw] (*pl* -ões) *f* -**1**. [negação] dispute. -**2**. [impugnação] challenge. -**3**. [oposição] opposition. -**4**. [réplica] reply.

contestar [4] [kõnteʃ'ta(x)] <> *vt* -**1**. [negar] to dispute. -**2**. [impugnar] to challenge. <> *vi* -**1**. [opor-se] to oppose. -**2**. [responder]: ~ **(a)** to reply (to).

contestatório, ria [kõnteʃta'tɔrju, rja] *adj* contentious; **movimento** ~ protest movement.

contestável [kõnteʃ'tavew] (*pl* -**eis**) *adj* questionable.

conteúdo [kõn'tjudu] *m* contents (*pl*).

contexto [kõn'teʃtu] *m* context.

contextualização [kõnteʃtwaliza'sãw] (*pl* -ões) *f* contextualization.

contextualizar [kõnteʃtwali'za(x)] *vt* to put into context.

contido [kõn'tʃidu] *adj* -**1**. [encerrado] contained. -**2**. [reprimido] repressed.

contigo [kõn'tʃigu] *pron pess* with you.

contíguo, gua [kõn'tʃigwu, gwa] *adj* adjacent; ~ **a** next to.

continência [kõntʃi'nẽnsja] *f* MIL salute; **fazer** *ou* **bater** ~ **(a alguém)** to salute (sb).

continental [kõntʃinẽn'taw] (*pl* -**ais**) *adj* continental.

continente [kõntʃi'nẽntʃi] *m* continent.

contingência [kõntʃĩn'ʒẽnsja] *f* contingency.

contingente [kõntʃĩn'ʒẽntʃi] <> *adj* contingent. <> *m* contingent.

continuação [kõntʃinwa'sãw] (*pl* -ões) *f* continuation.

continuar [4] [kõntʃi'nwa(x)] <> *vt* [prosseguir] to continue. <> *vi* -**1**. [perdurar] to continue. -**2**. [prolongar-se] to go on. -**3**. [prosseguir]: ~ **em algo** to continue with sthg; ~ **fazendo algo** *ou* **a fazer algo** to continue doing sthg/to do sthg. <> *v de ligação (antes de adjetivo)* [expressa qualidade, estado]: **a cidade continua bonita** the city is still beautiful.

continuidade [kõntʃinwi'dadʒi] *f* continuity.

contínuo, nua [kõn'tʃinwu, nwa] <> *adj* -**1**. [sem interrupção] continuous. -**2**. [constante] constant. <> *m* [pessoa] office junior.

contista [kõn'tʃiʃta] *mf* story writer.

conto ['kõntu] *m* story; ~ **de fadas** *ou* **da carochinha** fairy tale.

conto-do-vigário ['kõntuduvi'garju] (*pl* **contos-do-vigário**) *m* confidence trick; **cair no** ~ to be tricked; **passar o** ~ **em alguém** to try to con sb.

contorção [kõntox'sãw] (*pl* -ões) *f* contortion.

contorcer [25] [kõntox'se(x)] *vt* to warp.
➤ **contorcer-se** *vp* to writhe.

contornar [4] [kõntox'na(x)] *vt* -**1**. [rodear] to go around. -**2**. *fig* [resolver] to get around.

contornável [kõntox'navew] (*pl* -**eis**) *adj* surmountable.

contorno [kõn'toxnu] *m* outline.

contra ['kõntra] <> *prep* [ger] against. <> *adv* against. <> *m* -**1**. [dificuldade] hard knock. -**2**. [contestação] objection; **dar o** ~ to object; **pesar os prós e os** ~**s** to weigh up the pros and the cons; **ser do** ~ to object on principle.

contra-almirante [ˌkõntraawmi'rãntʃi] (*pl* **contra-almirantes**) *m* rear admiral.

contra-argumento [ˌkõntraaxgu'mẽntul] (*pl* **contra-angumentos**) *m* counter-argument.

contra-atacar [12] [ˌkõntraata'ka(x)] *vt* to counter-attack.

contra-ataque [ˌkõntra'taki] (*pl* **contra-ataques**) *m* counter-attack.

contrabaixista [ˌkõntra'bajʃiʃta] *mf* double-bass player.

contrabaixo [ˌkõntra'bajʃul] *m* -**1**. [instrumento] double bass. -**2**. [músico] bassist.

contrabalançar [13] [ˌkõntrabalãn'sa(x)] *vt* to counterbalance; ~ **algo com algo** to compensate sthg with sthg.

contrabandear [15] [ˌkõntrabãn'dʒja(x)] *vt* to smuggle.

contrabandista [ˌkõntrabãn'dʒiʃta] *mf* smuggler.

contrabando [ˌkõntra'bãndul] *m* -**1**. [ato] smuggling. -**2**. [mercadoria] contraband; **fazer** ~ to smuggle.

contração [kõntra'sãw] (*pl* -ões) *f* contraction.

contracapa [ˌkõntra'kapal] *f* inside cover.

contracenar [4] [ˌkõntrase'na(x)] *vi*: ~ **(com)** to perform (with).

contracepção [ˌkõntrasep'sãw] (*pl* -ões) *f* contraception.

contraceptivo, va [ˌkõntrasep'tʃivu, val] *m* contraceptive.

contracheque [ˌkõntra'ʃɛki] *m* payslip.

contradição [ˌkõntradʒi'sãw] (*pl* -ões) *f* contradiction; **entrar** *ou* **cair em** ~ to contradict o.s.

contraditório, ria [ˌkõntradʒi'tɔrju, rja] *adj* contradictory.

contradizer [29] [ˌkõntradʒi'ze(x)] *vt* to contradict.
➤ **contradizer-se** *vp* to contradict o.s.

contrafeito, ta [ˌkõntra'fejtu, tal] *adj* constrained.

contrafilé [ˌkõntrafi'lɛl] *m* rump steak.

contragosto [kõntra'goʃtul] ➤ **a contragosto** *loc adv* unwillingly.

contraído, da [kõntra'idu, da] *adj* -**1**. [tenso] tense. -**2**. [assumido] agreed. -**3**. [adquirido] contracted.

contra-indicação [ˌkõntraĩndʒika'sãw] (*pl* **contra-indicações**) *f* [de remédio] contraindication.

contra-indicado [ˌkõntraĩndʒi'kadul] (*pl* **contra-indicados**) *adj* -**1**. [remédio] contraindicated. -**2**. [medida, solução] inadvisable.

contra-indicar [12] [ˌkõntraĩndʒi'ka(x)] *vt* to contraindicate.

contrair [68] [kõntra'i(x)] *vt* -**1**. [ger] to contract. -**2**. [assumir]: ~ **matrimônio** to get married; ~ **dívidas** to run up debts; ~ **compromisso** to take on responsibilities. -**3**. [adquirir- doenças] to catch; [- hábitos] to acquire.
➤ **contrair-se** *vp* [encolher-se] to contract.

contralto [kõn'trawtu] *m* -**1.** [voz] contralto. -**2.** [tom de instrumento] alto. - **3.** [cantora] contralto.

contramão [‚kõntra'mãw] <> *adj* -**1.** [em sentido contrário] one-way. -**2.** [inconveniente] out of one's way. <> *f*: **na** ~ **on the wrong side of the road.**

contramestre [‚kõntra'mɛʃtri] *m* -**1.** [em fábrica etc] foreman. -**2.** [náut] first mate.

contra-ofensiva [‚kõntraofẽn'siva] (*pl* **contra-ofensivas**) *f* counteroffensive.

contra-oferta [‚kõntrao'fɛxta] (*pl* **contra-ofertas**) *f* counteroffer.

contraparente [‚kõntrapa'rẽntʃi] *m* -**1.** [distante] distant relative. -**2.** [afim] in-law.

contrapartida [‚kõntrapar'tʃida] *f* -**1.** [oposto] opposite. -**2.** [compensação]: **em** ~ in compensation.

contrapeso [‚kõntra'pezu] *m* counterbalance.

contrapor [45] [‚kõntra'po(x)] *vt* [confrontar] to confront; ~ **algo a algo** to set sthg against sthg.
    ➡ **contrapor-se** *vp* [opor-se]: ~-**se a algo** to be opposed to sthg.

contraproducente [‚kõntraprodu'sẽntʃi] *adj* counterproductive.

contra-regra [‚kõntra'xɛgra] (*pl* **contra-regras**) *mf* stage manager.

contra-revolução [‚kõntraxevolu'sãw] (*pl* **contra-revoluções**) *f* counter-revolution.

contrariado, da [kõntra'rjadu, da] *adj* annoyed.

contrariar [16] [kõntra'rja(x)] *vt* -**1.** [vontade, interesse] to thwart. -**2.** [declaração, informação] to contradict. -**3.** [desobedecer - ordem, instrução] to disobey; [- lei] to break. -**4.** [descontentar] to annoy.
    ➡ **contrariar-se** *vp* -**1.** [descontentar-se] to get annoyed. -**2.** [contradizer-se] to contradict o.s.

contrariedade [kõntrarje'dadʒi] *f* nuisance.

contrário, ria [kõn'trarju, rja] *adj* -**1.** [lado] opposite. -**2.** [ponto de vista, decisão] opposing; **ser** ~ **a algo** to be against sthg; **caso** ~ otherwise.
    ➡ **contrário** *m* opposite; **do** ~ otherwise; **pelo** *ou* **ao** ~ on the contrary; **ao** ~ [de outra maneira] the other way round; [roupa] back to front.

contra-senso [‚kõntra'sẽnsu] (*pl* **contra-sensos**) *m* nonsense (*inv*).

contrastante [kõntraʃ'tãntʃi] *adj* contrasting.

contrastar [4] [kõntraʃ'ta(x)] <> *vt*: ~ **algo com algo** to contrast sthg with sthg. <> *vi* to contrast; ~ **em algo** to contrast in sthg.

contraste [kõn'traʃtʃi] *m* contrast.

contratação [kõntrata'sãw] (*pl* **-ões**) *f* recruitment.

contratante [kõntra'tãntʃi] <> *adj* contracting. <> *mf* contractor.

contratar [4] [kõntra'ta(x)] *vt* to recruit.

contratempo [‚kõntra'tẽnpu] *m* -**1.** [imprevisto] setback. -**2.** [dificuldade] hurdle. -**3.** [aborrecimento] upset.

contrato [kõn'tratu] *m* -**1.** [documento] contract. -**2.** [acordo] agreement.

contratual [kõntra'twaw] (*pl* **-ais**) *adj* contractual.

contravenção [‚kõntravẽn'sãw] (*pl* **-ões**) *f* contravention.

contraventor, ra [‚kõntravẽn'to(x), ra] *m, f* offender.

contribuição [kõntribwi'sãw] (*pl* **-ões**) *f* -**1.** [ger] contribution. -**2.** [tributo - sindical] dues (*pl*); [- fiscal] tax.

contribuinte [kõntri'bwĩntʃi] *m f* -**1.** [colaborador] contributor. -**2.** [aquele que paga imposto] taxpayer.

contribuir [74] [kõntri'bwi(x)] *vi* -**1.** [ger] to contribute; ~ **com algo (para algo)** [fornecer, colaborar] to contribute sthg (for/to sthg). -**2.** [ter parte em um resultado]: ~ **para algo** to contribute to · sthg.

contrição [kõntri'sãw] *f* contrition.

contrito, ta [kõn'tritu, ta] *adj* contrite.

controlar [4] [kõntro'la(x)] *vt* to control.
    ➡ **controlar-se** *vp* [dominar-se] to control o.s.

controlável [kõntro'lavew] (*pl* **-eis**) *adj* controllable.

controle [kõn'troli] *m* control; ~ **remoto** remote control.

controvérsia [kõntro'vɛrsja] *f* controversy; **em** ~ controversial.

controverso, sa [kõntro'vɛrsu, sa] *adj* controversial.

contudo [kõn'tudu] *conj* however.

contumácia [kõntu'masja] *f* -**1.** obstinacy. -**2.** *JUR* contempt of court.

contumaz [kõntu'majʒ] *adj* obstinate.

contundente [kõntũn'dẽntʃi] *adj* -**1.**: **por instrumento** ~ with a blunt instrument. -**2.** *fig* [decisivo] decisive.

contundir [5] [kõntũn'dʒi(x)] *vt* to bruise.
    ➡ **contundir-se** *vp* to bruise o.s.

conturbação [kõntuxba'sãw] (*pl* **-ões**) *f* -**1.** [perturbação] commotion. -**2.** [motim] riot.

conturbar [4] [kõntux'ba(x)] *vt* -**1.** [perturbar] to disturb. -**2.** [amotinar] to stir up.
    ➡ **conturbar-se** *vp* -**1.** [perturbar-se] to become troubled. -**2.** [amotinar-se] to rebel.

contusão [kõntu'zãw] (*pl* **-ões**) *f* bruise.

conúbio [kõ'nubju] *m* [aliança] alliance.

convalescença [kõnvaleʃ'sẽnsa] *f* convalescence.

convalescente [kõnvale'sẽntʃi] <> *adj* convalescent. <> *mf* convalescent patient.

convalescer [25] [kõnvale'se(x)] *vi* to convalesce.

convenção [kõnvẽn'sãw] (*pl* **-ões**) *f* convention; ~ **social** social convention.

convencer [25] [kõnvẽn'se(x)] <> *vt* [persuadir]: ~ **alguém (de algo)** to convince sb (of sthg); ~ **alguém a fazer algo** to persuade sb to do sthg. <> *vi fig* [agradar] to impress.
    ➡ **convencer-se** *vp* [persuadir-se]: ~-**se de algo** to convince o.s. of sthg.

convencido, da [kõnvẽn'sidu, da] *adj* -**1.** [convicto] convinced. -**2.** *fig* [presunçoso] conceited.

convencimento [kõnvẽnsi'mẽntu] *m* -**1.** [convicção] conviction. -**2.** *fig* [presunção] conceit.

convencional [kõvẽnsjo'naw] (pl -ais) adj -1. [ger] conventional. -2. pej [comum] commonplace.

convencionar [4] [kõvẽnsjo'na(x)] vt to agree on.

conveniado, da [kõve'njadu, da] <> adj associated. <> m, f associate.

conveniência [kõve'njẽnsja] f convenience; **ser da ~ de alguém** to be suitable for sb.
➡ **conveniências** fpl [regras sociais] decorum; **loja de ~s** convenience store.

conveniente [kõve'njẽntʃi] adj -1. [ger] convenient. -2. [oportuno] opportune.

convênio [kõ'venju] m -1. [acordo] agreement. -2. [entre instituições] accord.

convento [kõ'vẽntu] m convent.

convergência [kõver'gẽnsja] f convergence.

convergente [kõvex'ʒẽntʃi] adj convergent.

convergir [64] [kõvex'ʒi(x)] vi -1. [mesma direção]: **~ para** to converge on. -2. [ter a mesma tendência]: **~ (para)** to aim (at). -3. [afluir]: **~ (de/para)** to converge (from/towards).

conversa [kõ'vɛxsa] f -1. [diálogo] chat; **~ fiada** ou **mole** chit-chat. -2. [mentira]: **~ (fiada)** nonsense (inv). -3. loc: **passar uma ~ em alguém** to soft-soap sb; **ir na ~ de alguém** to be taken in by sb.

conversação [kõvexsa'sãw] (pl -ões) f conversation.

conversador, deira [kõvexsa'do(x), dejra] adj chatty.

conversado [kõvex'sadu] adj [problema, assunto] discussed; **estamos ~s** there is nothing more to be said.

conversa-fiada [kõnˌvɛxsa'fjada] (pl conversas-fiadas) mf [pessoa] loudmouth.

conversão [kõvex'sãw] (pl -ões) f conversion.

conversar [4] [kõvex'sa(x)] vi to talk, to hold a conversation.

conversibilidade [kõvexsibili'dadʒi] f convertibility.

conversível [kõvex'sivew] (pl -eis) <> adj convertible. <> m AUTO convertible.

conversor [kõvex'so(x)] m -1. [dispositivo] transformer. -2. COMPUT converter.

converter [5] [kõvex'te(x)] vt -1. [transformar]: **~ algo/alguém em algo** to convert sthg/sb into sthg. -2. [trocar]: **~ algo em algo** to change sthg into sthg. -3. POL & RELIG: **~ alguém a** to convert sb to.
➡ **converter-se** vp POL & RELIG: **~-se (a)** to convert (to).

convertido, da [kõvex'tʃidu, da] <> adj converted. <> m, f POL & RELIG convert.

convés [kõ'vɛʃ] (pl -veses) m deck.

convexo, xa [kõ'veksu, sa] adj convex.

convicção [kõvik'sãw] (pl -ões) f conviction; **ter ~ de que** to be convinced that.

convicto, ta [kõ'viktu, ta] <> adj -1. [convencido] convinced. -2. [réu] convicted. <> m, f [presidiário] convict.

convidado, da [kõvi'dadu, da] m, f guest.

convidar [4] [kõvi'da(x)] <> vt -1. [ger] to invite. -2. fig [induzir]: **~ alguém a** to invite sb to. <> vi fig [induzir]: **~ a** to be conducive to.
➡ **convidar-se** vp -1. [invitar-se] to invite o.s. -2. [oferecer-se] to put o.s. forward.

convidativo, va [kõvida'tʃivu, va] adj inviting.

convincente [kõvĩ'sẽntʃi] adj convincing.

convir [67] [kõ'vi(x)] vi -1. [concordar]: **~ (com alguém) em algo** to agree (with sb) about sthg; **você há de ~ que** you have to agree that. -2. [ser conveniente, proveitoso]: **~ a alguém** to be convenient for sb. -3. [condizer]: **~ a alguém** to be appropriate for sb.

convite [kõ'vitʃi] m invitation.

conviva [kõ'viva] m f guest.

convivência [kõvi'vẽnsja] f -1. [convívio] closeness. -2. [familiaridade] familiarity.

conviver [5] [kõvi've(x)] vi -1. [coexistir] to coexist. -2. [lidar]: **~ com** to cope with.

convívio [kõ'vivju] m [convivência] closeness.

convocação [kõvoka'sãw] (pl -ões) f [chamamento] summons.

convocar [12] [kõvo'ka(x)] vt -1. [chamar] to summon. -2. [reunir] to convene. -3. MIL to call up.

convosco [kõ'voʃku] pron pess with you.

convulsão [kõvuw'sãw] (pl -ões) f -1. MED convulsion. -2. fig upheaval.

convulsionar [4] [kõvuwsjo'na(x)] vt -1. [pôr em convulsão] to convulse. -2. fig [povo, país] to agitate.

convulsivo, va [kõvuw'sivu, va] adj convulsive.

cookie ['koki] (pl cookies) m COMPUT cookie.

cooper ['kupe(x)] m jogging; **fazer ~** to go jogging.

cooperação [kwopera'sãw] (pl -ões) f cooperation.

cooperante [kwope'rãntʃi] adj cooperative.

cooperar [4] [kwope'ra(x)] vi: **~ (com)** to cooperate (with).

cooperativo, va [kwopera'tʃivu, va] adj cooperative.
➡ **cooperativa** f cooperative.

coordenação [kooxdena'sãw] f [ato] coordination.

coordenada [kooxde'nada] f -1. fam [orientação] instructions. -2. GEOM coordinate.

coordenar [koorde'na(x)] m to coordinate.

copa ['kɔpa] f -1. [cômodo] pantry. -2. [parte superior] crown. -3. ESP cup.
➡ **copas** fpl [naipe] hearts.

copeiro, ra [ko'pejro, ra] m, f domestic servant (who waits at table).

Copenhague [kõpe'nagil] n Copenhagen.

cópia ['kɔpja] f -1. [ger] copy. -2. [fotocópia] photocopy.

copiadora [kopja'dora] f -1. [loja] print shop. -2. [máquina] photocopier.

copiar [16] [ko'pja(x)] vt to copy.

copidescar [kopi'deʃka(x)] vt [revisar] to copy edit.

copidesque [kopi'dɛʃkil] <> *m* [redação final] copy-editing. <> *mf* [redator] copy editor.

co-piloto, ta [kopi'lotu, ta] (*mpl* **co-pilotos**, *fpl* **co-pilotas**) *m, f* copilot.

copioso, piosa [ko'pjozu, pjɔza] *adj* -**1.** [ger] copious. -**2.** [refeição] copious.

copista [ko'piʃta] *mf* [copiador] copyist.

copo ['kɔpu] *m* -**1.** [recipiente] glass. -**2.** [conteúdo] glassful. -**3.** *loc*: **ser um bom** ~ to be a heavy drinker.

COPOM (*abrev de* **Comitê de Política Monetária**) [ko'põ] *m* [econ] Monetary Policy Committee.

cópula *f* [coito] copulation.

copular [ko'pula(x)] *vi* to copulate.

copyright [kopi'xajtʃi], **copirraite** [kopi'xajtʃi] *m* copyright.

coque ['kɔki] *m* bun.

coqueiro [ko'kejru] *m* coconut palm.

coqueluche [koke'luʃi] *f* -**1.** [doença] whooping cough. -**2.** *fig* [moda]: **o bambolê foi** ~ **nos anos setenta** the hula hoop was all the rage in the seventies.

coquete [ko'kɛtʃi] *adj* coquettish.

coquetel [koke'tɛw] (*pl* -**éis**) *m* -**1.** [drinque] cocktail. -**2.** [festa] cocktail party.

coqueteleira [kokete'lejra] *f* cocktail shaker.

cor ['ko(x)] (*pl* -**es**) *f* -**1.** [tom] colour; ~ **de burro quando foge** *hum* undefinable color. -**2.** [de pele] complexion; **ficar sem** ~ to go pale. -**3.** *fig* [feição] tone.
 de cor *loc adv* by heart.

coração [kora'sãw] (*pl* -**ões**) *m* [ger] heart; **abrir o** ~ [confidenciar] to open one's heart; **ter um** ~ **de ouro** [ser bondoso] to have a good heart.

corado, da [ko'radu, da] *adj* -**1.** [na face] ruddy. -**2.** [avermelhado] reddish. -**3.** *fig* [envergonhado] shamefaced. -**4.** *CULIN* sautéed.

coragem [ko'raʒẽ] *f* courage.

corajoso, osa [kora'ʒozu, ɔza] *adj* courageous.

coral [ko'raw] (*pl* -**ais**) <> *m* -**1.** [ger] coral. -**2.** *MÚS* choir. <> *f* [cobra] coral snake. <> *adj* coral.

corante [ko'rãntʃi] <> *adj* colouring. <> *m* dye.

corar [4] [ko'ra(x)] <> *vt CULIN* to brown. <> *vi* [enrubescer] to blush.

corcova [kox'kɔva] *f* hump.

corcunda [kox'kũnda] <> *adj* hunchbacked. <> *mf* hunchback.

corda ['kɔrda] *f* -**1.** [ger] spring; **dar** ~ **em** to wind up. -**2.** [fio] rope; **pular** ~ skipping. -**3.** [varal] clothesline. -**4.** *loc*: **dar** ~ **para alguém** *fig* [alimentar a conversa] to get sb going; [flertar] to flirt with sb; **estar com a** ~ **toda** *fig* to be really wound up.
 cordas *fpl* -**1.** *ANAT*: ~ **s vocais** vocal cords. -**2.** *MÚS*: **quarteto de** ~ **s** string quartet.

cordão [kor'dãw] (*pl* -**ões**) *m* -**1.** [corda fina] twine. -**2.** [jóia] chain. -**3.** [cadarço] shoelace. -**4.** [bloco carnavalesco] carnival block. -**5.** *ANAT*: ~ **umbilical** umbilical cord.

cordato, ta [kox'datu, ta] *adj* sensible.

cordeiro [kor'dejru] *m* lamb.
 cordeiros *mpl fig* [seguidores] disciples.

cordel [kor'dɛw] (*pl* -**éis**) *m* -**1.** [barbante] string. -**2.** *LITER*: **(literatura de)** ~ popular Brazilian literature.

> **CORDEL**
>
> A popular form of literature, typical of the north-east of Brazil; the *cordel* ('string') consists of a small booklet, made up usually of a single sheet of paper folded over three times, to make eight pages. The *cordel* tells stories, in verse, of the people of the north-east. In order to sell these booklets in the street or at fairs, it is customary to hang them up with pieces of twine, hence the name *cordel*.

cor-de-rosa [kordʒi'xɔza] <> *adj* -**1.** [cor] pink. -**2.** *fig* [feliz] rose-tinted. <> *m* [cor] pink.

cordial [kor'dʒjaw] (*pl* -**ais**) *adj* -**1.** [gentil] cordial. -**2.** [afetuoso] warm.

cordialidade [koxdʒjali'dadʒi] *f* -**1.** [gentileza] cordiality. -**2.** [afeição] warmth.

cordilheira [kordʒi'ʎejra] *f* mountain range.

cordões *pl* ⊳ **cordão**.

coreano, na [ko'rjãnu, na] <> *adj* Korean. <> *m, f* Korean.

Coréia *n* Korea; ~ **do Norte** North Korea; ~ **do Sul** South Korea.

coreografia [korjogra'fia] *f* choreography.

coreógrafo, fa [ko'rjɔgrafu, fa] *m, f* choreographer.

coreto [ko'retu] *m* bandstand.

corisco [ko'riʃku] *m* -**1.** [ger] flash. -**2.** *fig* bright spark.

corista [ko'riʃta] *m, f* -**1.** [em coro] chorister. -**2.** [vedete] chorus girl.

coriza [ko'riza] *f* runny nose.

corja ['kɔxʒa] *f* gang.

córnea ['kɔxnja] *f* cornea.

cornear [15] [kox'nja(x)] *vt* -**1.** [com os chifres] to gore. -**2.** *fam* [trair] to two-time.

córner ['kɔxne(x)] *m* corner (kick).

corneta [kox'neta] *f* cornet.

corneteiro, ra [koxne'tejru, ra] *m, f* bugler.

cornija [kox'niʒa] *f* [em parede] cornice.

corno ['kɔxnu] *m* -**1.** [de animal] horn. -**2.** *vulg* [pessoa] cuckold.

cornudo, da [kox'nudu, da] <> *adj* [animal] horned.
 cornudo *m vulg* [pessoa] cuckold.

coro ['koru] *m* -**1.** [ger] chorus; **em** ~ in chorus. -**2.** [cantores] choir. -**3.** [balcão] organ loft.

coroa [ko'roa] <> *f* -**1.** [ger] crown. -**2.** [de flores] garland. -**3.** [calvície] bald spot. <> *mf* [pessoa] *fam* old fogey.

coroação [korwa'sãw] (*pl* -**ões**) *f* coronation.

coroar [20] [koro'a(x)] *vt* -**1.** [ger] to crown. -**2.** [premiar] to reward.

coroinha *m* altar server.

corolário [koro'larju] *m* corollary.

coronário, ria [koro'narju, rja] *adj* coronary.

coronel [koro'nɛw] (*pl* -**éis**) *m* -**1.** *MIL* colonel. -**2.** *POL* political baron.

coronha [ko'roɲa] f butt.

coronhada [koro'ɲada] f blow with a rifle butt.

corpete [kox'petʃi] m bodice.

corpo ['koxpu] m - 1. [ger] body; ~ de baile dance group; ~ de bombeiros fire department; ~ diplomático diplomatic corps; ~ docente faculty; [tronco] trunk; [carne] flesh; [formas] body. - 2. [cadáver] corpse, body. - 3. [consistência]: tomar ~ to thicken. - 4. JUR: ~ de delito material fact. - 5. MED: ~ estranho foreign body. - 6. loc: fazer ~ mole to skulk; tirar o ~ fora to duck out.

corporação [koxpora'saw] (pl -ões) f corporation.

corporal [koxpo'raw] (pl -ais) adj corporal.

corporativismo [koxporatʃi'viʒmu] m corporatism.

corporativista [koxporatʃi'viʃta] <> adj [relativo ao corporativismo] corporate. <> mf [partidário] corporatist.

corporativo, va [koxpo'ratʃivu, va] adj corporative.

corpulência [koxpu'lẽsja] f corpulence.

corpulento, ta [koxpu'lẽtu, ta] adj corpulent.

correção [koxe'saw] (pl -ões) f - 1. [ato] marking; ~ monetária inflationary adjustment. - 2. [qualidade] exactness.

corre-corre [kɔxi'kɔxi] m mad rush.

corredor, ra [koxe'do(x), ra] (mpl -es, fpl -s) m, f [atleta] runner.
- **corredor** m [passagem - em casa] corridor; [- em avião, etc] aisle.

córrego ['kɔxegu] m brook.

correia [ko'xeja] f - 1. [tira] strap. - 2. [em máquina] belt. - 3. [em carro] fan belt.

correio [ko'xeju] m - 1. [serviço] mail. - 2. [correspondência] post; agência dos ~s post office. - 3. fig [carteiro] postman UK, mailman US. - 4. COMPUT: ~ eletrônico email.

correlação [koxela'saw] (pl -ões) f correlation.

correlacionar [koxelasjo'na(x)] vt to correlate.
- **correlacionar-se** vp to correlate.

correligionário, ria [koxeliʒjo'narju, rja] <> adj partisan. <> m, f - 1. POL fellow party member. - 2. RELIG coreligionist.

corrente [ko'xẽtʃi] <> adj - 1. [atual] current. - 2. [comum] common. - 3. [fluente - língua] fluent; [- estilo] flowing. - 4. [água] running. <> f - 1. [ger] current; ~ marítima marine current; remar contra a ~ fig to swim against the tide. - 2. [corrente] chain. - 3. [vento]: ~ de ar draught.

correnteza [koxẽ'teza] f current.

correntista [koxẽ'tʃiʃta] mf account holder.

correr [5] [ko'xe(x)] <> vi - 1. [ger] to run. - 2. [passar] to fly past. - 3. [circular] to circulate. - 4. [espalhar-se] to spread. - 5. [despesas]: ~ por conta de alguém to go on sb's tab. <> vt - 1. [percorrer]: ~ a fazenda to go all over sthg. - 2. [passar de leve] to run. - 3. [olhar rapidamente]: corri os olhos pela revista I ran my eyes over the magazine. - 4. [estar exposto a]: ~ o risco de algo to run the risk of sthg.

correria [koxe'ria] f rushing about.

correspondência [koxeʃpõ'dẽsja] f correspondence.

correspondente [koxeʃpõ'dẽtʃi] <> adj corresponding. <> mf correspondent; ~ de guerra war correspondent.

corresponder [5] [koxeʃpõ'de(x)] vi - 1. [ger]: ~ a to correspond to. - 2. [retribuir]: ~ a to reciprocate.
- **corresponder-se** vp to correspond with.

corretagem [koxe'taʒẽ] f - 1. [atividade] brokerage. - 2. [remuneração] commission.

corretamente [ko,xɛta'mẽtʃi] adv correctly.

corretivo, va [koxe'tʃivu, va] adj [que corrige] corrective.
- **corretivo** m [castigo] punishment.

correto, ta [ko'xɛtu, ta] adj - 1. [ger] correct. - 2. [íntegro] honest.

corretor, ra [koxe'to(x), ra] (mpl -es, fpl -s) m, f [agente] broker; ~ de imóveis estate agent UK, realtor US; ~ de Bolsa stockbroker.
- **corretora** f [instituição] agency.

corrida [ko'xida] f - 1. [ato] running. - 2. ESP racing. - 3. [de táxi] fare.

corrido, da [ko'xidu, da] adj [rápido] rushed.

corrigir [52] [koxi'ʒi(x)] vt - 1. [retificar] to correct. - 2. [eliminar] to repair. - 3. [repreender] to tell off. - 4. [atenuar] to attenuate.
- **corrigir-se** vp [emendar-se] to correct o.s.

corrimão [koxi'maw] (pl -ãos, -ões) m handrail.

corrimento [koxi'mẽtu] m discharge.

corriqueiro, ra [koxi'kejru, ra] adj everyday.

corroborar [4] [koxobo'ra(x)] vt to corroborate.

corroer [28] [koxo'e(x)] vt - 1. [carcomer] to eat away. - 2. [danificar] to corrode. - 3. fig [depravar] to undermine.

corromper [5] [koxõ'pe(x)] vt - 1. [perverter] to pervert. - 2. [subornar] to corrupt. - 3. [adulterar] to tamper with.
- **corromper-se** vp [perverter-se] to become corrupt.

corrompido, da [koxõ'pidu, da] adj [pervertido] corrupted; arquivo ~ COMPUT corrupted file.

corrosão [koxo'saw] (pl -ões) f - 1. [de metais] corrosion. - 2. GEOL erosion.

corrosivo, va [koxo'zivu, va] adj corrosive.

corrupção [koxup'saw] (pl -ões) f - 1. [perversão] pervertion. - 2. [suborno] corruption.

corrupto, ta [ko'xuptu, ta] adj corrupt.

Córsega ['kɔxsega] n Corsica.

cortada [kox'tada] f ESP smash; dar uma ~ to smash the ball; dar uma ~ em alguém fig to cut sb short.

cortado, da [kox'tadu, da] adj - 1. [ger] cut. - 2. [relações] severed. - 3. fig [coração] broken.
- **cortado** m fig [apuro] struggle.

cortador [koxta'do(x)] m cutter.

cortante [kox'tãtʃi] adj - 1. [ger] cutting. - 2. [que corta] sharp.

cortar [4] [kox'ta(x)] <> vt - 1. [ger] to cut. - 2. [árvore] to cut down. - 3. [suprimir] to cut out. - 4. AUTO to stall. **-5.** [interromper] to interrupt. **-6.** [pôr fim a] to end. **-7.** [encurtar]: ~ **caminho** to take a short cut. <> *vi* **-1.** [ter bom gume] to cut. **-2.** *ESP* to smash the ball.

⬌ **cortar-se** *vp* [ferir-se] to cut o.s.

corte¹ ['kɔxtʃi] *m* **-1.** [ger] cut. **-2.** [gume] cutting edge; **ter bom** ~ to be sharp; **estar sem** ~ to be blunt. **-3.** [porção de tecido]: ~ **de algo** length of sthg. **-4.** *ELETR*: ~ **de luz** power cut.

corte² ['kɔxtʃi] *f* **-1.** [ger] court. **-2.** *fig* [de admiradores *etc*] entourage. **-3.** [cortejar]: **fazer a** ~ **a alguém** to court sb.

cortejar [4] [koxte'ʒa(x)] *vt* to court.

cortejo [kox'teʒu] *m* **-1.** [séquito] cortege. **-2.** [procissão] procession.

cortês [kox'teʃ] *adj* polite.

cortesão, sã [koxte'zãw, zã] (*mpl* -**ãos, -ões,** *fpl* -**s**) <> *adj* courtly. <> *m, f* courtier. <> *f* courtesan.

cortesia [koxte'zia] *f* **-1.** [delicadeza] courtesy. **-2.** [presente] complimentary gift. **-3.** [mesura] bow.

cortiça [kox'tʃisa] *f* cork.

cortiço [kox'tʃisu] *m* **-1.** [para abelhas] beehive. **-2.** [habitação] slum dwelling.

cortina [kox'tʃina] *f* **-1.** [peça] curtain. **-2.** *fig* [nuvem] screen.

cortisona [koxtʃi'zona] *f* cortisone.

coruja [ko'ruʒa] <> *f ZOOL* owl. <> *adj* [pai, mãe] doting.

corvo ['koxvu] *m* crow.

cós ['kɔʃ] *m inv* **-1.** [tira de pano] waistband. **-2.** [cintura] waist.

coser [5] [ko'ze(x)] <> *vt* to stitch. <> *vi* to sew.

cosmético, ca [koʒ'mɛtʃiku, ka] *adj* cosmetic.

⬌ **cosmético** *m* cosmetic.

cósmico, ca ['kɔʒmiku, ka] *adj* cosmic.

cosmo ['kɔʒmu] *m* cosmos.

cosmonauta [kɔʒmo'nawta] *mf* cosmonaut.

cosmopolita [kɔʒmopo'lita] <> *adj* cosmopolitan. <> *mf* [pessoa] cosmopolitan person.

costa ['kɔʃta] *f* [litoral] coast.

costado [koʃ'tadu] *m NÁUT* [forro] hull cladding.

Costa do Marfim [ˌkɔʃtadumax'fĩ] *n* Ivory Coast.

Costa Rica [ˌkɔʃta'xika] *n* Costa Rica.

costa-riquense [ˌkɔʃtaxi'kẽnsil], **costarriquenho, nha** [ˌkɔʃtaxi'kẽɲu, ɲa] <> *adj* Costa Rican. <> *m, f* Costa Rican.

costas ['kɔʃtaʃ] *fpl* **-1.** [ger] back. **-2.** [encosto] backrest. **-3.** *loc*: **carregar nas** ~ *fig* to shoulder the burden; **ter** ~ **quentes** *fig* to be under sb's wing.

costela [koʃ'tɛla] *f* rib.

costeleta [koʃte'leta] *f* **-1.** *CULIN* chop. **-2.** [suíças] sideburns.

costumar [4] [koʃtu'ma(x)] *vt* **-1.** [ter o hábito de]: ~ **fazer algo** to be in the habit of doing sthg; **costumo correr todas as manhãs** I usually go running every morning. **-2.** [habituar] to accustom.

costume [koʃ'tumi] *m* **-1.** [hábito] habit; **ter o** ~ **de**

fazer algo to be in the habit of doing sthg; **como de** ~ as usual. **-2.** [roupa] costume.

⬌ **costumes** *mpl* [de um povo] customs.

costumeiro, ra [koʃtu'mejru, ra] *adj* usual, customary.

costura [koʃ'tura] *f* **-1.** [ger] sewing; **alta** ~ haute couture. **-2.** [linha de junção] seam.

costurar [4] [koʃtu'ra(x)] <> *vt* **-1.** *COST* to stitch. **-2.** *fig* [texto] to tidy up. <> *vi* **-1.** *COST* to sew. **-2.** *fam AUTO* to weave in and out.

costureira [koʃtu'rejra] *f* seamstress.

costureiro [koʃtu'rejru] *m* [estilista] couturier.

cota ['kɔta] *f* **-1.** [quinhão] quota. **-2.** [prestação, parcela] instalment.

cotação [kota'sãw] (*pl* -**ões**) *f* **-1.** [ato] quoting. **-2.** [preço] quote. **-3.** *fig* [possibilidade de êxito] chance. **-4.** *fig* [conceito] reputation.

cotado, da [ko'tadu, da] *adj* **-1.** [com bom preço] well priced. **-2.** *fig* [favorito] favourite. **-3.** *fig* [conceituado] respected. **-4.** [avaliado] valued.

cotar [4] [ko'ta(x)] *vt* **-1.** [ger] to quote. **-2.** [avaliar]: ~ **algo/alguém em** to value sthg/sb at.

cotejar [4] [kote'ʒa(x)] *vt* to compare.

cotejo [ko'teʒu] *m* comparison.

cotidiano, na [kotʃi'dʒianu, na] *adj* everyday.

⬌ **cotidiano** *m* routine.

cotizar [4] [kotʃi'za(x)] *vt* **-1.** [distribuir por cotas] to allocate. **-2.** [cotar] to value, to assess.

⬌ **cotizar-se** *vp* to club together.

coto *m* **-1.** [mus] koto. **-2.** [zool] feather follicle.

cotonete [koto'nɛʃil] *m* cotton bud.

cotovelada [kotove'lada] *f* **-1.** [batida] hefty nudge. **-2.** [cutucada] nudge.

cotovelo [koto'velu] *m* **-1.** *ANAT* elbow; **falar pelos** ~**s** *fig* to talk non-stop. **-2.** [de estrada *etc*] bend.

couraça [ko'rasa] *f* **-1.** [armadura] breastplate. **-2.** [de animal] plating. **-3.** *NÁUT* armour plate.

couraçado, da [kora'sadu, da] *adj* [que tem couraça] armoured.

⬌ **couraçado** *m NÁUT* battleship.

couro ['koru] *m* **-1.** [de animal] hide; [curtido] leather; ~ **cru** rawhide; **de** ~ leather. **-2.** [humano]: ~ **cabeludo** scalp. **-3.** *loc*: **não dar no** ~ to underperform.

couve ['kovi] *f* spring greens.

couve-de-bruxelas [ˌkovidʒibru'ʃelaʃ] (*pl* **couves-de-bruxelas**) *f* Brussels sprout.

couve-flor [ˌkovi'flo(x)] (*pl* **couves-flores**) *f* cauliflower.

couvert [ko've(x)] *m* cover charge.

cova ['kɔval *f* **-1.** [sepultura] grave. **-2.** [caverna] cavern. **-3.** [buraco] hole.

covarde [ko'vaxdʒil] <> *adj* cowardly. <> *mf* coward.

covardia [kovax'dʒia] *f* cowardice.

coveiro [ko'vejru] *m* gravedigger.

covil [ko'viw] (*pl* -**is**) *m* **-1.** [ger] den. **-2.** *fig* [casebre] hovel.

covinha [ko'viɲa] *f* dimple.

coxa ['koʃa] *f ANAT* thigh; ~ **de galinha** *CULIN*

chicken drumstick; **fazer (algo) nas** ~**s** *vulg* to do it any old how.

coxear [15] [koˈʃja(x)] *vi* to limp.

coxia [koˈʃia] *f* aisle.

coxo, xa [ˈkoʃu, ʃa] *adj* -**1.** [ger] lame. -**2.** [móvel] wobbly (*on account of having one leg shorter than the others*).

cozer [5] [koˈze(x)] *vt* to cook.

cozido, da [koˈzidu, da] *adj* cooked.
 ➡ **cozido** *m* stew.

cozinha [koˈziɲa] *f* -**1.** [cômodo] kitchen. -**2.** [arte] cookery; ~ **brasileira** Brazilian cuisine; **aula/livro de** ~ cookery class/book.

cozinhar [4] [koziˈɲa(x)] <> *vt* -**1.** [cozer] to cook. -**2.** *fig* [adiar] to put off. <> *vi* to cook.

cozinheiro, ra [koziˈɲejru, ra] *m, f* cook.

CPD (*abrev de* **Centro de Processamento de Dados**) *m* data-processing department.

CPF (*abrev de* **Cadastro de Pessoa Física**) *m* Brazilian tax-payer's identity card for individual contributions, ≈ NI number *UK*, ≈ social security number *US*.

CPMF (*abrev de* **Contribuição Provisória sobre Movimentação Financeira**) *f* Brazilian tax on bank transactions.

crachá [kraˈʃa] *m* badge.

crack [1] [ˈkraki] *m* crack (cocaine).

crack [2] [ˈkraki] (*pl* **cracks**) *m* COMPUT hack.

cracker (*pl* **crackers**) *m* COMPUT hacker.

crânio [ˈkrãnju] *m* -**1.** ANAT skull. -**2.** *fam* [gênio]: **ser um** ~ to be a brainbox.

crápula [ˈkrapula] *mf* villain.

craque [ˈkraki] <> *mf* [pessoa exímia]: **ser um** ~ **em algo** to be an expert in sthg. <> *m* FUT football star *UK*, soccer star *US*.

crase [ˈkrazi] *f* LING crasis.

crasso, ssa [ˈkrasu, sa] *adj* -**1.** [grosseiro] crass. -**2.** [espesso] viscous.

cratera [kraˈtɛra] *f* crater.

cravar [4] [kraˈva(x)] *vt* -**1.** [fazer penetrar] to drive in. -**2.** [engastar] to set. -**3.** *fig* [fixar]: ~ **os olhos em alguém** to stare at sb.

cravejar [4] [kraveˈʒa(x)] *vt* -**1.** [com cravos] to nail. -**2.** [com pedras preciosas] to set.

cravo [ˈkravu] *m* -**1.** [flor] carnation. -**2.** [prego] nail. -**3.** MÚS harpsichord. -**4.** [especiaria] clove. -**5.** [na pele] blackhead.

crawl [ˈkrɔw] *m* ESP crawl.

creche [ˈkrɛʃi] *f* crèche.

credenciais [kredẽnsiˈajʃ] *fpl* [qualificações] credentials.

credenciamento [kredẽnsiaˈmẽntu] *m* accreditation.

credenciar [16] [kredẽnˈsja(x)] *vt* -**1.** [dar credenciais a] to accredit. -**2.** [habilitar] to qualify.
 ➡ **credenciar-se** *vp* JORN to be accredited.

crediário [kreˈdʒjarju] *m* hire purchase.

credibilidade [kredʒibiliˈdadʒi] *f* credibility.

creditar [4] [kredʒiˈta(x)] *vt* -**1.** [depositar] to deposit. -**2.** [inscrever como credor]: ~ **alguém em** to credit sb with. -**3.** [atribuir]: ~ **algo a algo/**

alguém to put sthg down to sb/sthg.

crédito [ˈkrɛdʒitu] *m* -**1.** [ger] credit; **digno de** ~ creditworthy. -**2.** FIN credit; **venda a** ~ sale on credit. -**3.** [boa reputação] credibility.

credo [ˈkrɛdu] *m* -**1.** [crença] belief. -**2.** [reza]: **o Credo** the Creed.

credor, ra [kreˈdo(x), ra] (*mpl* -**es**, *fpl* -**s**) <> *adj* -**1.** FIN credit (*antes de subst*). -**2.** [merecedor] deserving. <> *m, f* FIN creditor.

credulidade [kreduliˈdadʒi] *f* credulity.

crédulo, ula [ˈkredulu, la] <> *adj* gullible. <> *m, f* gullible person.

cremação [kremaˈsãw] (*pl* -**ões**) *f* cremation.

cremar [4] [kreˈma(x)] *vt* to cremate.

crematório [kremaˈtɔrju] *m* crematorium.

creme [ˈkremi] <> *adj inv* [cor] cream. <> *m* -**1.** [ger] cream; ~ **de leite** dairy cream; ~ **chantilly** whipped cream. -**2.** [cosmético] face cream. -**3.** [pasta]: ~ **dental** toothpaste. -**4.** [flavour]: **sorvete de** ~ vanilla ice cream.

cremoso, osa [kreˈmozu, ɔza] *adj* creamy.

crença [ˈkrẽnsa] *f* -**1.** RELIG belief. -**2.** [convicção] conviction.

crendice [krẽnˈdʒiʃi] *f* superstition.

crente [ˈkrẽntʃi] <> *adj* -**1.** [que tem fé] believing. -**2.** [protestante] Protestant. -**3.** [convencido]: **estar** ~ **que** to be sure that. <> *mf* -**1.** [quem tem fé] believer. -**2.** [protestante] Protestant.

crepitação [krepitaˈsãw] (*pl* -**ões**) *f* crackling.

crepitante [krepiˈtãntʃi] *adj* crackling.

crepitar [4] [krepiˈta(x)] *vi* to crackle.

crepom [kreˈpõ] <> *adj* [papel] crêpe. <> *m* [tecido] crêpe.

crepuscular [krepuʃkuˈla(x)] *adj* twilight.

crepúsculo [kreˈpuʃkulu] *m* -**1.** [ao amanhecer] dawn. -**2.** [ao anoitecer] dusk. -**3.** *fig* [declínio] twilight.

crer [37] [ˈkre(x)] <> *vt* [ger] to believe. <> *vi* [acreditar]: ~ **em** to believe in.

crescendo [kreˈsẽndu] *m* crescendo.

crescente [kreˈsẽntʃi] <> *adj* -**1.** [tamanho] growing. -**2.** [formato] crescent. <> *m* [fase da lua] crescent moon.

crescer [4] [kreˈse(x)] *vi* -**1.** [aumentar] to grow. -**2.** CULIN to rise.

crescido, da [kreˈsidu, da] *adj* grown-up.

crescimento [kresiˈmẽntu] *m* growth.

crespo, pa [ˈkreʃpu, pa] *adj* -**1.** [anelado] curly. -**2.** [áspero] rough.

Creta [ˈkreta] *n* Crete.

cretinice [kretʃiˈnisi] *f* stupidity.

cretino, na [kreˈtʃinu, na] <> *adj* cretinous. <> *m, f* cretin.

cria [ˈkria] *f* offspring (*inv*).

criação [krjaˈsãw] (*pl* -**ões**) *f* -**1.** [ger] creation. -**2.** [de animais] raising. -**3.** [de filhos] upbringing.
 ➡ **de criação** *loc adj* adopted.

criado-mudo [ˌkrjaduˈmudu] (*pl* **criados-mudos**) *m* bedside table.

criador, ra [kriaˈdo(x), ra] (*mpl* -**es**, *fpl* -**s**) <> *adj* creative. <> *m, f* -**1.** [autor] creator. -**2.** [de animais] breeder.

⬥ Criador m [Deus]: **o Criador** the Creator.
criança [kri'ãnsa] f - **1.** [infante] child. - **2.** [pessoa infantil] child.
criançada [krjãn'sada] f: **a ~** the kids (pl).
criancice [krjãn'sisi] f childishness.
criar [16] [kri'a(x)] vt - **1.** [produzir] to create. - **2.** [fundar] to found. - **3.** [educar] to bring up. - **4.** [animais] to raise. - **5.** [plantas] to cultivate.
⬥ criar-se vp [educar-se] to grow up.
criatividade [kriatʃivi'dadʒil f creativity.
criativo, va [kria'tʃivu, va] adj creative.
criatura [kria'tura] f creature.
crime ['krimi] m crime.
criminal [krimi'naw] (pl -ais) adj criminal.
criminalidade [kriminali'dadʒi] f criminality.
criminalista [krimina'liʃta] m f criminologist.
criminoso, osa [krimi'nozu, ɔza] ⬥ adj criminal. ⬥ m, f criminal.
crina ['krina] f mane.
crioulo, la ['krjolu, la] ⬥ adj - **1.** [comida, dialeto] Creole. - **2.** [negro] black. ⬥ m, f [pessoa negra] black person.
cripta ['kripta] f crypt.
criptografar [kriptogra'fa(x)] vt COMPUT to encrypt.
criptografia [kriptogra'fia] f COMPUT cryptography.
críquete ['krikétʃi] m cricket.
crisântemo [kri'zãntemul m chrysanthemum.
crise ['krizi] f - **1.** MED attack. - **2.** [escassez] shortage. - **3.** [fase difícil] crisis. - **4.** fig [acesso] fit; **ter uma ~** to have a fit.
crisma ['kriʒma] f confirmation.
crismar [kriʒ'ma(x)] vt REL to confirm.
crista ['kriʃta] f - **1.** [de galo] comb. - **2.** [cume] crest.
cristal [kriʃ'taw] (pl -ais) m crystal.
cristaleira [kriʃta'lejra] f display cabinet.
cristalino, na [kriʃta'linu, na] adj crystalline.
cristalização [kriʃtaliza'sãw] (pl -ões) f crystallization.
cristalizar [4] [kriʃtali'za(x)] ⬥ vt [tornar cristalino] to crystallize. ⬥ vi [tornar-se cristalino] to crystallize.
⬥ cristalizar-se vp [consolidar-se] to crystallize.
cristandade [kriʃtãn'dadʒi] f Christianity.
cristão, ã [kriʃ'tãw, ã] ⬥ adj Christian. ⬥ mf Christian.
cristianismo [kriʃtʃjã'niʒmu] m Christianity.
cristo ['kriʃtu] m fig [vítima] victim.
Cristo ['kriʃtu] m Christ.
critério [kri'tɛrju] m criterion.
criterioso, osa [krite'rjozu, ɔza] adj selective.
criticar [12] [kritʃi'ka(x)] vt - **1.** [censurar] to criticize. - **2.** [analisar] to review.
crítico, ca ['kritʃiku, ka] ⬥ adj critical. ⬥ m, f [pessoa] critic.
⬥ crítica f - **1.** [censura] criticism (inv); **ser alvo de ~s** to be criticized. - **2.** [análise] review. - **3.** [os críticos]: **a ~** critics (pl).
crivar [4] [kri'va(x)] vt - **1.** [com balas, facadas] to

riddle. - **2.** [fig] [com perguntas] to bombard.
crível ['krivew] (pl -eis) adj believable.
crivo ['krivu] m - **1.** [peneira] sieve. - **2.** fig [escrutínio] scrutiny.
Croácia [kro'asja] n Croatia.
croata [kro'ata] ⬥ adj Croat. ⬥ mf Croat.
crocante [kro'kãntʃi] adj crunchy.
crochê [kro'ʃe] m crochet.
crocodilo [kroko'dʒilu] m crocodile.
cromado, da [kro'madu, da] adj chromium-plated.
cromo ['kromu] m chrome.
cromossomo [kromo'somu] m [genética] chromosome.
cromoterapia [ˌkromotera'pia] f colour therapy.
crônica ['kronika] f - **1.** HIST & LITER chronicle. - **2.** JORN column.
crônico, ca ['kroniku, ka] adj - **1.** [ger] chronic. - **2.** [inveterado] inveterate.
cronista [kro'niʃta] m f - **1.** HIST & LITER chronicler. - **2.** JORN columnist.
cronograma [krono'grãma] m schedule.
cronologia [kronolo'ʒia] f chronology.
cronológico, ca [krono'lɔʒiku, ka] adj chronological.
cronometrar [4] [kronome'tra(x)] vt to time.
cronômetro [kro'nometru] m stopwatch.
croquete [kro'kɛtʃi] m croquette.
croqui [kro'ki] m sketch.
crosta ['kroʃta] f - **1.** [de pão, terra] crust. - **2.** [de ferida] scab.
cru, crua ['kru, 'krua] adj - **1.** [não cozido] raw. - **2.** [não refinado] crude. - **3.** fig [duro] harsh.
crucial [kru'sjaw] (pl -ais) adj - **1.** [ger] crucial. - **2.** [difícil] important.
crucificação [krusifika'sãw] (pl -ões) f RELIG: **a ~** the Crucifixion.
crucificar [12] [krusifi'ka(x)] vt to crucify.
crucifixo [krusi'fiksu] m crucifix.
cruel [kru'ɛw] (pl -éis) adj - **1.** [perverso] cruel. - **2.** [doloroso] cruel. - **3.** [violento] violent.
crueldade [kruew'dadʒi] f cruelty.
cruento, ta [kru'ẽntu, ta] adj bloody.
crustáceos [kruʃ'tasjuʃ] mpl crustacea (pl).
cruz ['kruʃ] (pl -es ['kruziʃ]) f cross.
⬥ Cruz Vermelha f Red Cross.
cruzada [kru'zada] f crusade.
cruzado, da ['kru'zadu, da] adj crossed.
⬥ cruzado m [moeda] cruzado (former Brazilian currency).
cruzador [kruza'do(x)] m NÁUT cruiser.
cruzamento [kruza'mẽntu] m - **1.** [de estradas] junction. - **2.** [de raças] crossbreeding.
cruzar [4] [kru'za(x)] ⬥ vt - **1.** [ger] to cross. - **2.** [animais] to crossbreed. ⬥ vi - **1.** [rua]: **~ com to** intersect. - **2.** [navio] to cruise. - **3.** fig [encontrar]: **~ com alguém** to bump into sb.
⬥ cruzar-se vp [encontrar-se] to bump into each other.
cruzeiro [kru'zejru] m - **1.** NÁUT cruise. - **2.** [moeda]

cruzeiro *(former Brazilian currency)*.

CTI *(abrev de* Centro deTerapia Intensiva) *m* ICU.

cu [ˈkul *m vulg* arse; **fazer ~-doce** to act cool; **~ -do-mundo** arsehole.

cuba [ˈkubal *f* vat.

Cuba [ˈkubal *n* Cuba.

cubano, na [ˈkubãnu, nal <> *adj* Cuban. <> *m*, *f* Cuban.

cúbico, ca [ˈkubiku, kal *adj* cubic.

cubículo [kuˈbikulul *m* cubicle.

cubismo [kuˈbiʒmul *m* cubism.

cubista [kuˈbiʃtal <> *adj* cubist. <> *mf* cubist.

cubo [ˈkubul *m* **-1.** [ger] cube. **-2.** GEOM hexahedron. **-3.** MAT cube. **-4.** AUTO: **~ de roda** wheel hub.

cuca [ˈkukal *fam f* **-1.** [cabeça] head. **-2.** [mente] intellect; **fundir a ~** [baratinar] to do one's head in; [confundir] to addle one's brain. **-3.** CULIN sponge cake.

cuca-fresca [ˌkukaˈfreʃkal *(pl* cucas-frescas) *mf fam* cool person.

cuco [ˈkukul *m* **-1.** [ave] cuckoo. **-2.** [relógio] cuckoo clock.

cucuia [kuˈkujal *f fam:* **ir para a ~** to go out the window.

cu-de-ferro [ˌkudʒiˈfɛxul *(pl* cus-de-ferro) *fam* <> *adj* anal-retentive. <> *mf* anal-retentive.

cueca [ˈkwɛkal *f* underpants *(pl)*.

cueiro [kuˈejrul *m* nappy *UK*, diaper *US*.

Cuiabá [kujaˈbal *n* Cuiabá.

cuíca [ˈkwikal *f* cuíca, *an instrument resembling a drum whose sound is produced by vibrating a cord on the inside*.

cuidado, da [kwiˈdadu, dal *adj* [tratado]: **bem/mal ~** well/badly cared for.

◆ cuidado *m* **-1.** [ger] care; **~!** careful! **-2.** [encargo]: **sob os ~s de** in the care of.

cuidadoso, osa [kwidaˈdozu, ɔzal *adj* careful.

cuidar [4] [kwiˈda(x)] *vi* [tratar]: **~ de alguém/algo** to take care of sb/sthg.

◆ cuidar-se *vp* **-1.** [tratar-se] to take care of o.s. **-2.** [prevenir-se] to be careful.

cujo, ja [ˈkuʒu, ʒal *pron rel* **-1.** [de quem] whose. **-2.** [de que] whose.

culatra [kuˈlatral *f* gun breech.

culinário, ria [kuliˈnarju, rjal *adj* culinary.

◆ culinária *f* cookery.

culminante [kuwmiˈnãntʃil *adj* culminating.

culminar [4] [kuwmiˈna(x)] *vi:* **~ com algo** to culminate with sthg.

culote [kuˈlɔtʃil *m* **-1.** [calça] jodphurs *(pl)*. **-2.** [nas coxas] big thighs *(pl)*.

culpa [ˈkuwpal *f* **-1.** [falta] fault; **pôr a ~ em** to blame; **ter ~ de** to be to blame for. **-2.** JUR guilt.

culpabilidade [kuwpabiliˈdadʒil *f* guilt.

culpado, da [kuwˈpadu, dal <> *adj* guilty. <> *m*, *f* criminal.

culpar [4] [kuwˈpa(x)] *vt:* **~ alguém (de)** [atribuir a culpa] to blame sb (for); [acusar] to accuse sb (of).

◆ culpar-se *vp* to take the blame o.s.

cultivar [4] [kuwtʃiˈva(x)] *vt* to cultivate.

◆ cultivar-se *vp* [instruir-se] to cultivate one's mind.

cultivável [kuwtʃiˈvavewl *(pl* -eis) *adj* arable.

cultivo [kuwˈtʃivul *m* cultivation.

culto, ta [ˈkuwtu, tal *adj* **-1.** [instruído] well educated. **-2.** [civilizado] civilized.

◆ culto *m* **-1.** RELIG ritual. **-2.** [veneração] worship.

cultura [kuwˈtural *f* **-1.** [conhecimento] culture. **-2.** [civilização] civilization. **-3.** [cultivo] culture. **-4.** [criação - de animais] breeding; [- de germes, bactérias] culture.

cultural [kuwtuˈrawl *(pl* -ais) *adj* cultural.

cumbuca [kũnˈbukal *f* gourd.

cume [ˈkumil *m* **-1.** [topo] summit. **-2.** *fig* [apogeu] apex.

cúmplice [ˈkũnplisil *mf* **-1.** [co-autor] accomplice. **-2.** *fig* [parceiro] partner.

cumplicidade [kũnplisiˈdadʒil *f* complicity.

cumpridor, ra [kũnpriˈdo(x), ral *adj* [responsável]: **é ~ da sua palavra** he keeps his word.

cumprimentar [4] [kũnprimẽnˈta(x)] *vt* **-1.** [saudar] to greet. **-2.** [elogiar] to compliment.

◆ cumprimentar-se *vp* [saudar-se] to greet one another.

cumprimento [kũnpriˈmẽntul *m* **-1.** [saudação] congratulation. **-2.** [elogio] compliment. **-3.** [realização] fulfilment.

cumprir [6] [kũnˈpri(x)] <> *vt* **-1.** [dever, obrigação] to fulfill. **-2.** [lei] to obey. **-3.** [promessa] to keep. **-4.** [caber] to be sb's responsibility. <> *vi* [convir] to be necessary, to be convenient.

◆ cumprir-se *vp* [concretizar-se] to come true.

cumulativo, va [kumulaˈtʃivu, val *adj* cumulative.

cúmulo [ˈkumulul *m* height.

cunha [ˈkuɲal *f* wedge.

cunhado, da [kuˈɲadu, dal *m, f* brother-in-law, sister-in-law.

cunhar [4] [kuˈɲa(x)] *vt* **-1.** [moedas] to mint. **-2.** [palavras] to create.

cunho [ˈkuɲul *m* **-1.** [marca] mark. **-2.** *fig* [selo] stamp. **-3.** *fig* [caráter] nature.

cunilíngua [kuniˈlĩŋwal *f* cunnilingus.

cupê [kuˈpel *m* coupé.

cupido [kuˈpidul *m* cupid.

cupim [kuˈpĩl *(pl* -ns) *m* termite.

cupincha [kuˈpĩʃal *m f* mate.

cupom [kuˈpõl *(pl* -ns) *m* coupon.

cúpula [ˈkupulal *f* **-1.** [abóbada] dome. **-2.** [chefia] leadership.

cura [ˈkural <> *f* **-1.** [ger] cure; **não ter ~** *fig* to be incurable. **-2.** [recuperação] recovery. <> *m* [pároco] curate.

curado, da [kuˈradu, dal *adj* **-1.** [pessoa, doença] cured. **-2.** [ferimento] healed. **-3.** [carne, queijo] cured.

curador, ra [kuraˈdo(x), ral *m, f* **-1.** JUR [de menores] guardian. **-2.** [de instituições] caretaker. **-3.** [de arte] curator.

curandeiro, ra [kurãnˈdejru, ral *m* healer.

curar [4] [ku'ra(x)] ◇ *vt* **-1.** [pessoa, doença] to cure; ~ **alguém de algo** to cure sb of sthg. **-2.** [ferimento] to heal. ◇ *vi* [sarar] to heal.
◆ **curar-se** *vp* **-1.** [sarar] to heal. **-2.** [emendar-se] to mend one's ways.

curativo [kura'tʃivu] *m* dressing.

curável [ku'ravew] (*pl* **-eis**) *adj* curable.

Curdistão [kuxdʒiʃ'tãw] *n* Kurdistan.

curdo, da ['kurdu, da] ◇ *adj* Kurdish. ◇ *m, f* [pessoa] Kurd.
◆ **curdo** *m* [língua] Kurdish.

curetagem [kure'taʒẽ] (*pl* **-ns**) *f* curettage.

curinga [ku'rĩga] *m* **-1.** [ger] joker.- **2.** *COMPUT:* (**caractere**) ~ wild card.

curiosidade [kurjozi'dadʒi] *f* curiosity.

curioso, osa [ku'rjozu, ɔza] ◇ *adj* **-1.** [ger] curious. **-2.** [bisbilhoteiro] nosy. **-3.** [interessante] interesting. ◇ *m, f* **-1.** [pessoa interessada] bystander. **-2.** [amador] amateur.
◆ **curioso** *m* [coisa singular]: **o** ~ **é ...** the strange thing is ...
◆ **curiosos** *mpl* [espectadores] onlookers.

Curitiba [kuri'tʃiba] *n* Curitiba.

curral [ku'xaw] (*pl* **-ais**) *m* corral.

currar [4] [ku'xa(x)] *vt fam* to rape.

currículo [ku'xikulu] *m* **-1.** [histórico] curriculum vitae *UK*, resume *US*. **-2.** [matérias] curriculum.

curriculum vitae [ku,xikulũn'vitaj] *m (inv)* curriculum vitae *UK*, resume *US*.

cursar [4] [kux'sa(x)] *vt* **-1.** [curso] to study. **-2.** [escola] to attend.

cursinho [kur'siɲu] *m* [pré-vestibular] *preparatory course for university entry*.

cursivo, va [kux'sivu, va] *adj* [letra] cursive.

curso ['kursu] *m* **-1.** [ger] flow. **-2.** [rumo] course. **-3.** [andamento]: **em** ~ current. **-4.** [*EDUC*- nível] key stage *UK*, grade *US*; [- estabelecimento] school; ~ **de férias** summer school; ~ **normal** teacher training course *(for primary school)*; ~ **de primeiro grau** primary school *UK*, grade school *US*; ~ **de segundo grau** secondary school *UK*, high school *US*; ~ **superior** degree course; ~ **supletivo** supplementary course.

cursor [kux'so(x)] (*pl* **-es**) *m COMPUT* cursor.

curta-metragem [,kuxtame'traʒẽ] (*pl* **curtas-metragens**) *m* short film.

curtição [kuxtʃi'sãw] *f* **-1.** [de couro] tanning. **-2.** *fam* [prazer] fun.

curtido, da [kux'tʃidu, da] *adj* **-1.** [couro] tanned. **-2.** *fig* [sofrido] fed up. **-3.** *fig* [endurecido] hardboiled.

curtir [6] [kux'tʃi(x)] *vt* **-1.** [couro] to tan. **-2.** [sofrer] to suffer. **-3.** *fam* [desfrutar de] to enjoy.
◆ **curtir-se** *vp fam*: **eles se curtem muito** they really hit it off.

curto, ta ['kuxtu, ta] ◇ *adj* **-1.** [com pouco comprimento] short. **-2.** [breve] brief. **-3.** [limitado] intellectually limited. ◇ *m ELETR* = **curto-circuito**.

curto-circuito [,kuxtusix'kujtu] (*pl* **curtos-circuitos**) *m ELETR* short circuit.

curva ['kuxva] *f* **-1.** [de rua *etc*] bend; ~ **fechada** sharp bend, hairpin bend. **-2.** [arqueamento] curve. **-3.** *GEOM* arc. **-4.** [em gráfico] curve.
◆ **curvas** *fpl* [de mulher] curves.

curvado, da [kux'vadu, da] *adj* curved, bent.

curvar [4] [kux'va(x)] ◇ *vt* **-1.** [arquear] to arch. **-2.** *fig* [dominar] to subdue. ◇ *vi* [envergar] to stoop.
◆ **curvar-se** *vp* **-1.** [envergar-se] to bend down. **-2.** [prostrar-se] to bow. **-3.** *fig* [submeter-se]: ~**-se a** to give in to.

curvatura [kuxva'tura] *f* curvature.

curvilíneo, nea [kuxvi'linju, nja] *adj* [forma, objeto, linha] curvilinear.

curvo, va ['kuxvu, va] *adj* **-1.** [arqueado] curved. **-2.** [sinuoso - estrada, caminho] bendy; [- rio] meandering.

cuscuz [kuʃ'kuʃ] *m* couscous.

cusparada [kuʃpa'rada] *f* gob of spittle.

cuspe ['kuʃpi] *m* spittle.

cuspida [kuʃ'pida] *f fam*: **dar** ~**s em** to spit on *ou* at.

cuspido, da [kuʃ'pidu, da] *adj* **-1.** [telefone] crackling. **-2.** [pessoa] affronted.

cuspir [61] [kuʃ'pi(x)] ◇ *vt* to spit. ◇ *vi* to spit; ~ **no prato em que comeu** *fig* to bite the hand that feeds you.

custa ['kuʃta] *f*: **à** ~ **de** at the expense of.
◆ **custas** *fpl JUR* costs.

custar [4] [kuʃ'ta(x)] ◇ *vt* **-1.** [preço] to cost; **custe o que** ~ whatever the cost; *fig* ~ **os olhos da cara** to cost an arm and a leg. **-2.** *fig* [acarretar] to cause; **não** ~ **nada fazer algo** not to cost anything to do sthg. ◇ *vi* **-1.** [produto, serviço]: ~ **barato/caro** to be cheap/expensive. **-2.** [ser difícil, penoso]: **não custava você ter ajudado ...** it wouldn't have hurt you to help me ...; ~ **caro** to cost a great deal. **-3.** [ter dificuldade]: ~ **a fazer algo** to find sthg hard to do. **-4.** [demorar] to be late; ~ **a fazer algo** to take a lot of doing.

custear [15] [kuʃ'tja(x)] *vt* to defray.

custeio [kuʃ'teju] *m* defrayal.

custo ['kuʃtu] *m* **-1.** [preço] cost; ~ **de vida** cost of living. **-2.** *fig* [dificuldade]: **ser um** ~ **fazer algo** to be difficult to do sthg; **a todo** ~ at all costs.

custódia [kuʃ'tɔdʒja] *f* custody.

CUT (*abrev de* **Central Única dos Trabalhadores**) *f central trade union body*, ≃ TUC *UK*.

cutelaria [kutela'ria] *f* cutlery.

cutelo [ku'tɛlu] *m* cutlass.

cutia [ku'tʃia] *f* agouti.

cutícula [ku'tʃikula] *f* cuticle.

cútis ['kutʃiʃ] *f inv* cutis.

cutucada [kutu'kada] *f* **-1.** [com o cotovelo] nudge. **-2.** [como o dedo] poke.

cutucar [12] [kutu'ka(x)], **catucar** [katu'ka(x)] *vt* **-1.** [com o cotovelo] to nudge. **-2.** [com o dedo] to poke.

C.V. (*abrev de* curriculum vitae) *m* CV.

CVM (*abrev de* **Comissão de Valores Mobiliários**) *f* *regulatory body overseeing the sale of shares*, ≃ FSA *UK*.

czar, ina [ˈkza(x), ina] *m, f* czar (*f* czarina).

d, D [de] *m* [letra] d, D.

da [da] = **de + a**.

DAC (**Departamento de Aviação Civil**) *m* civil *aviation department*, ≃ CAA.

dadaísmo [dadaˈiʒmu] *m* dadaism.

dadaísta [dadaˈiʃta] ◇ *adj* Dadaist. ◇ *mf* Dadaist.

dádiva [ˈdadiva] *f* **-1.** [donativo] donation. **-2.** [dom] gift.

dadivoso, osa [dadʒiˈvozu, ɔza] *adj* generous.

dado, da [ˈdadu, da] *adj* **-1.** [ger] given. **-2.** [presenteado] presented. **-3.** [afável] friendly. **-4.** [afeito]: **ser ~ a algo** to be fond of sthg.

➤ **dado** *m* **-1.** [em jogo] dice. **-2.** [informação] data.

➤ **dados** *mpl* COMPUT data.

➤ **dado que** *loc conj* given that.

daí [daˈi] = **de + aí**.

Dakar [daˈka(x)] *n* Dakar.

dali [daˈli] = **de + ali**.

dália [ˈdalja] *f* dahlia.

dálmata [ˈdawmata] *m* Dalmatian.

daltônico, ca [dawˈtoniku, ka] ◇ *adj* colour-blind. ◇ *m, f* colour-blind person.

dama [ˈdama] *f* **-1.** [mulher] lady; **~ de companhia** companion; **~ de honra** bridesmaid. **-2.** POL: **primeira-~** first lady. **-3.** [em uma área específica] grande dame. **-4.** [em xadrez, baralho] queen.

➤ **damas** *fpl* [jogo] checkers.

damasco [daˈmaʃku] *m* **-1.** [fruta] apricot. **-2.** [tecido] damask.

Damasco [daˈmaʃku] *n* Damascus.

danação [danaˈsãw] *f* **-1.** [maldição] damnation. **-2.** *fam* [travessura] mischief.

danado, da [daˈnadu, da] ◇ *adj* **-1.** [amaldiçoado] damned. **-2.** [zangado] annoyed. **-3.** [travesso] mischievous. **-4.** [incrível] unbelievable. **-5.** [hábil]: **ser ~ para algo** to be incredibly good at sthg. ◇ *m* **-1.** [pessoa amaldiçoada] cursed person. **-2.** *fam* [esperto] joker.

danar-se [4] [daˈnaxsi] *vp* [zangar-se] to become furious; **dane-se!** *fam* to hell with it!

dança [ˈdãsa] *f* dance; **~ folclórica** folkdance; **~ de salão** ballroom dance; **~ do ventre** belly dance.

dançante [dãnˈsãntʃi] *adj* dancing; **chá ~** tea dance.

dançar [13] [dãnˈsa(x)] ◇ *vi* **-1.** [bailar] to dance. **-2.** *fam* [sair-se mal] to flop. **-3.** *fam* [deixar de acontecer] to fall through. ◇ *vt* [bailar] to dance.

dançarino, na [dãnsaˈrinu, na] *m, f* ballet dancer.

danceteria [dãnseteˈria] *f* dancehall.

danificar [12] [danifiˈka(x)] *vt* to damage.

➤ **danificar-se** *vp* to get damaged.

daninho, nha [daˈniɲu, ɲa] *adj* harmful; **erva daninha** weed.

dano [ˈdanu] *m* damage.

danoso, osa [daˈnozu, ɔza] *adj* [nocivo]: **~ a** damaging to.

Danúbio [daˈnubju] *n*: **o ~** the Danube.

daquela [daˈkɛla] = **de + aquela** ▷ aquele.

daquele [daˈkeli] = **de + aquele** ▷ aquele.

daqui [daˈki] = **de + aqui** ▷ aqui.

daquilo [daˈkilu] = **de + aquilo** ▷ aquilo.

dardo [ˈdaxdu] *m* **-1.** [seta] dart. **-2.** ESP javelin.

dar [11] [ˈda(x)] ◇ *vt* **-1.** [entregar, presentear] to give; **~ algo a alguém** to give sb sthg, to give sthg to sb. **-2.** [produzir] to yield. **-3.** [causar, provocar] to give; **isto me dá sono/pena** this makes me sleepy/sad; **isto vai ~ muito que fazer** this is going to be a lot of work; **o amor só dá problemas** love is nothing but trouble. **-4.** [filme, programa]: **deu no noticiário hoje** it was on the news today. **-5.** [exprime ação] to give; **~ um berro** to cry out; **~ um pontapé em alguém** to kick sb; **~ um passeio** to go for a walk. **-6.** [festa, concerto] to have, to hold; **vão ~ uma festa** they're going to have *ou* throw a party. **-7.** [dizer] to say; **ele me deu boa-noite** he said good night to me. **-8.** [ensinar] to teach; **o que é que você está dando nas suas aulas?** what do you teach in your class?; **ela dá aula numa escola** she teaches at a school; **eu gostaria de ~ aulas de inglês** I would like to teach English. **-9.** [aprender, estudar] to do; **o que é que estão dando em Inglês?** what are you doing in English at the moment?; **estamos dando o verbo "to be"** we're doing the verb "to be". ◇ *vi* **-1.** [horas]: **já deram cinco horas** it's just gone five o'clock. **-2.** [condizer]: **~ com** to go with; **as cores não dão umas com as outras** the colours clash. **-3.** [proporcionar]: **~ de beber a alguém** to give sb sthg to drink; **~ de comer a alguém** to feed sb. **-4.** [em locuções]: **dá igual/no mesmo** it doesn't matter; **~ ares de** to look like; **~ à luz** to give birth; **~ de si** to give of o.s.

➤ **dar com** *v + prep* [encontrar, descobrir] to meet; **dei com ele no cinema** I met him at the movies.

➤ **dar em** *v + prep* [resultar]: **a discussão não vai ~ em nada** the discussion will come to nothing.

➤ **dar para** *v + prep* [servir para, ser útil para] to be good for; [suj: varanda, janela] to look onto; [suj: porta] to lead to; [ser suficiente para] to be enough for; [ser possível] to be possible; **dá para você fazer isso hoje?** could you do it today?; **dá para ir a pé?** is it within walking distance?; **não vai ~ para eu chegar na hora** I won't be able to get there on time.

◆ **dar por** *v + prep* [aperceber-se de] to notice.

◆ **dar-se** *vp*: **~-se bem/mal com alguém** to get on well/badly with sb; **o professor deu-se mal com a brincadeira** the teacher did not appreciate the joke; **~-se por vencido** to give up.

das [daʃ] = de + as.

DAT (*abrev de* **digital audio tape**) *f* DAT.

data ['data] *f* -**1.** [em carta *etc*] date; **~ de nascimento** date of birth. -**2.** [época] time; **de longa ~** of long standing.

● **data-base** [ˌdataˈbazi] (*pl* **datas-bases**) *f* baseline date.

datação [dataˈsãw] (*pl* -**ões**) *f* dating.

data-limite [ˌdataliˈmitʃi] (*pl* **datas-limites**) *f* deadline.

datar [4] [daˈta(x)] <> *vt* -**1.** [pôr data em] to date. -**2.** [considerar que existe]: **~ algo de** to date sthg at. <> *vi* [existir]: **~ de** to date from.

datilografar [4] [datʃilograˈfa(x)] *vt* to type.

datilografia [datʃilograˈfial] *f* typing.

datilógrafo, fa [datʃiˈlɔgrafu, fa] *m*, *f* typist.

dativo [daˈtʃivu] *m* GRAM dative.

DC (*abrev de* **Depois de Cristo**) AD.

DDT (*abrev de* **Dicloro-Difenil-Tricloretana**) *m* DDT.

de [dʒi] *prep* -**1.** [indica posse] of; **o lápis do Mário** Mário's pencil; **o carro daquele homem** that man's car; **a recepção do hotel** the hotel reception; **a casa é dela** it's her house, the house is hers; **as fases da lua** the phases of the moon. -**2.** [indica matéria] (made) of; **um bolo ~ chocolate** a chocolate cake; **um relógio ~ ouro** a gold watch. -**3.** [indica conteúdo] of; **um copo d'água** a glass of water. -**4.** [usado em descrições, determinações]: **uma camiseta ~ manga curta** a short-sleeved T-shirt; **uma nota ~ 50 reais** a 50-real note; **o senhor ~ preto** the man in black. -**5.** [indica assunto] about; **fale da viagem** tell me about the trip; **um livro ~ informática** a book about *ou* on computers; **um livro ~ geografia** a geography book. -**6.** [indica origem] from; **sou ~ Salvador** I'm from Salvador; **os habitantes do bairro** the locals; **um produto do Brasil** a Brazilian product. -**7.** [indica tempo]: **o jornal das nove** the nine o'clock news; **partimos às três da tarde** we left at three in the afternoon; **trabalho das nove às cinco** I work from nine to five. -**8.** [indica uso]: **a sala ~ espera** the waiting room; **uma máquina ~ calcular** a calculator; **a porta d'entrada** the front door. -**9.** [usado em denominações, nomes] of. -**10.** [indica causa, modo]: **chorar ~ alegria** to cry with joy; **está tudo ~ pernas para o ar** everything is upside down; **morrer ~ frio** to freeze to death; **ele viajou ~ carro** he travelled by car. -**11.** [indica autor] by; **um filme ~ Glauber Rocha** a film by Glauber Rocha; **o último livro ~ Ferreira Gullar** Ferreira Gullar's latest book. -**12.** [introduz um complemento]: **cheio ~ gente** full of people, crowded; **desconfiar ~ alguém** to distrust sb;

difícil ~ esquecer hard to forget; **gostar ~ algo/alguém** to like sthg/sb. -**13.** [em comparações]: **do que** than; **teu carro é mais rápido do que este** your car is faster than this one. -**14.** [em superlativos] of; **o melhor ~ todos** the best of all. -**15.** [dentre] of; **uma daquelas cadeiras** one of those chairs; **um dia destes** one of these days; **um desses hotéis serve** one of those hotels will do. -**16.** [indica série]: **~ dois em dois dias** every two days; **~ quinze em quinze minutos** every fifteen minutes; **~ três em três metros** every three metres.

deão [dʒiˈãw] (*pl* **deãos, deães**) *m* dean.

debaixo [deˈbajʃu] *adv* underneath.

◆ **debaixo de** *loc prep* under.

debalde [deˈbawdʒi] *adv* in vain.

debandada [debãnˈdada] *f* -**1.** [fuga] stampede. -**2.** [confusão]: **em ~** in disarray.

debandar [4] [debãnˈda(x)] <> *vt* [dispersar] to break up. <> *vi* [pôr-se em fuga] to scatter.

◆ **debandar-se** *vp* [dispersar-se] to break up.

debate [deˈbatʃi] *m* -**1.** [discussão] debate. -**2.** [disputa] discussion.

debatedor, ra [debateˈdo(x), ra] *m*, *f* debater.

debater [5] [debaˈte(x)] <> *vt* -**1.** [discutir] to debate. -**2.** [questionar] to dispute. <> *vi* [discutir] to discuss.

◆ **debater-se** *vp* [agitar-se] to struggle.

débeis ['dɛbejʃ] *pl* ▷ **débil**.

debelar [4] [debeˈla(x)] *vt* -**1.** [ger] to overcome. -**2.** [dominar] to defeat.

debênture [deˈbẽnturi] *f* COM debenture.

débil ['dɛbiw] (*pl* -**eis**) <> *adj* -**1.** [fraco] weak. -**2.** PSIC retarded. <> *mf* PSIC: **~ mental** mentally retarded person; *fam* [idiota] fool.

debilidade [debiliˈdadʒi] *f* -**1.** [fraqueza] weakness. -**2.** PSIC: **~ mental** mental retardation.

debilitação [debilitaˈsãw] *f* [enfraquecimento] debilitation.

debilitante [debiliˈtãntʃil] *adj* debilitating.

debilitar [4] [debiliˈta(x)] *vt* to debilitate.

◆ **debilitar-se** *vp* to weaken.

debilóide [debiˈlɔjdʒil] *fam* <> *adj* stupid. <> *mf* dunderhead.

debitar [4] [debiˈta(x)] *vt* to debit.

débito ['dɛbitu] *m* debit.

debochado, da [deboˈʃadu, da] *adj* scornful.

debochar [4] [deboˈʃa(x)] *vi*: **~ de algo/alguém** to scorn sb/sthg.

deboche [deˈbɔʃi] *m* scorn.

debruçar [13] [debruˈsa(x)] *vt* to lean.

◆ **debruçar-se** *vp* to lean over.

debulhar [4] [debuˈʎa(x)] *vt* -**1.** [grãos] to thresh. -**2.** [cascа] to shell.

◆ **debulhar-se** *vp*: **~-se em lágrimas** *fig* to dissolve into tears.

debutante [debuˈtãntʃil] *f* debutante.

debutar [4] [debuˈta(x)] *vi* to make one's debut.

década ['dɛkada] *f* decade.

decadência [dekaˈdẽnsja] *f* decadence.

decadente [deka'dẽntʃi] *adj* decadent.

decair [68] [deka'i(x)] *vi* **-1.** [deteriorar] to deteriorate. **-2.** [pender] to wither. **-3.** [diminuir] to diminish.

decalcar [12] [dekaw'ka(x)] *vt* to trace.

decalque [de'kawki] *m* tracing.

decano [de'kãnu] *m* **-1.** [membro mais antigo] oldest member. **-2.** [de universidade] dean.

decantar [4] [dekãn'ta(x)] *vt* **-1.** [líquido] to decant. **-2.** [exaltar] to sing the praises of.

decapitar [4] [dekapi'ta(x)] *vt* to decapitate.

decatleta [deka'tlɛta] *mf ESP* decathlete.

decatlo [de'katlu] *m* decathlon.

decência [de'sẽnsja] *f* decency.

decênio [de'senju] *m* decade.

decente [de'sẽntʃi] *adj* **-1.** [digno] decent. **-2.** [decoroso] demure. **-3.** [apropriado, asseado - roupa] decent; [- restaurante, casa] clean. **-4.** [bem-feito] well done.

decentemente [desẽntʃi'mẽntʃi] *adv* **-1.** [dignamente, com decoro] decently. **-2.** [adequadamente] satisfactorily.

decepar [4] [dese'pa(x)] *vt* to cut off.

decepção [desep'sãw] (*pl* **-ões**) *f* **-1.** [desapontamento] disappointment. **-2.** [desilusão] disillusion.

decepcionado, da [desepsjo'nadu, da] *adj* **-1.** [desapontado] disappointed. **-2.** [desiludido] disillusioned.

decepcionar [4] [desepsjo'na(x)] *vt* **-1.** [desapontar] to disappoint. **-2.** [desiludir] to disillusion.

➡ **decepcionar-se** *vp* [desapontar-se]: ~**-se com algo/alguém** to be disappointed with sthg/sb.

decerto [dʒi'sextu] *adv* surely.

decibel [desi'bɛw] (*pl* **-éis**) *m* decibel.

decididamente [desidʒida'mẽntʃi] *adv* **-1.** [com certeza] certainly. **-2.** [resolutamente] decidedly.

decidido, da [desi'dʒidu, da] *adj* **-1.** [resolvido] resolved. **-2.** [resoluto] resolute.

decidir [6] [desi'dʒi(x)] <> *vt* **-1.** [resolver] to resolve. **-2.** [deliberar] to decide; ~ **que** to decide that; ~ **fazer algo** to decide to do sthg. **-3.** [concluir] to decide. <> *vi* **-1.** [tomar decisão]: ~ **(sobre algo)** to make a decision (about sthg). **-2.** [optar]: ~ **entre** to decide between.

➡ **decidir-se** *vp* **-1.** [tomar decisão] to make a decision; ~**-se a fazer algo** to decide to do sthg. **-2.** [optar]: ~**-se por** to opt for.

decifrar [4] [desi'fra(x)] *vt* **-1.** [ler, interpretar] to decipher. **-2.** [entender] to unravel.

decifrável [desi'fravew] (*pl* **-eis**) *adj* decipherable.

décima ['dɛsima] ▷ **décimo**.

decimal [desi'maw] (*pl* **-ais** [dɛsi'majʃ]) <> *adj* decimal. <> *m* decimal.

décimo, ma ['dɛsimu, ma] *num* tenth.

➡ **décimo** *m* tenth part; *veja também* **sexto**.

decisão [desi'zãw] (*pl* **-ões**) *f* **-1.** [deliberação] decision; **tomar uma** ~ to make a decision. **-2.** [qualidade] decisiveness.

decisivo, va [desi'zivu, va] *adj* **-1.** [deliberativo, crítico] decisive. **-2.** [terminante] deciding.

declamação [deklama'sãw] *f* recitation, declamation.

declamar [4] [dekla'ma(x)] <> *vt* [recitar] to recite. <> *vi* **-1.** [recitar] to declaim. **-2.** *pej* [falar com afetação] to posture.

declaração [deklara'sãw] (*pl* **-ões**) *f* **-1.** [documento] written declaration. **-2.** [depoimento] testimony; ~ **de amor** declaration of love; **fazer uma** ~ to make a declaration. **-3.** [inventário] statement; ~ **de imposto de renda** income tax declaration.

declarado, da [dekla'radu, da] *adj* **-1.** [patenteado] declared. **-2.** [confessado] self-declared.

declarante [dekla'rãntʃi] *mf JUR* declarant.

declarar [4] [dekla'ra(x)] *vt* **-1.** [ger] to declare; ~ **que** to declare that. **-2.** [confessar] to confess.

➡ **declarar-se** *vp* **-1.** [manifestar-se]: ~**-se a favor de/contra** to declare o.s for/against. **-2.** [confessar-se] to confess o.s. to be. **-3.** [designar-se] to declare o.s.

declinação [deklina'sãw] (*pl* **-ões**) *f* **-1.** *GRAM* declension. **-2.** [diminuição] reduction. **-3.** [declive] slope.

declinar [4] [dekli'na(x)] <> *vt* **-1.** [ger] to decline. **-2.** [revelar] to disclose. <> *vi* **-1.** [astro] to set. **-2.** [mesa, terreno] to slope. **-3.** [dia, tarde] to draw to a close.

declínio [de'klinju] *m* decline.

declive [de'klivi] *m* [de terreno] slope.

decô [de'ko] *adj* decor.

decodificador [dekodʒifika'do(x)] *m COMPUT & TV* decoder.

decodificar [12] [dekodʒifi'ka(x)] *vt COMPUT & TV* to decode.

decolagem [deko'laʒẽ] (*pl* **-ns**) *f* take-off.

decolar [4] [deko'la(x)] *vi* to take off.

decompor [45] [dekõn'po(x)] *vt* **-1.** [separar elementos de] to break down. **-2.** [dividir em partes] to dissect. **-3.** [estragar] to rot. **-4.** [alterar] to change.

➡ **decompor-se** *vp* **-1.** [estragar-se] to rot. **-2.** [alterar-se] to change o.s.

decomposição [dekõnpozi'sãw] (*pl* **-ões**) *f* **-1.** [apodrecimento] rotting. **-2.** [divisão em partes] dissection. **-3.** [separação de elementos] breakdown. **-4.** [alteração] change. **-5.** [desorganização] break-up.

decomposto, ta [dekõn'poʃtu, ta] <> *pp* ▷ **decompor.** <> *adj* **-1.** [putrefato] rotten. **-2.** [dividido] dissected.

decoração [dekora'sãw] (*pl* **-ões**) *f* decoration.

decorador, ra [dekora'do(x), ra] *m, f* [profissional] decorator.

decorar [4] [deko'ra(x)] *vt* **-1.** [memorizar] to learn by heart. **-2.** [ornamentar] to decorate.

decorativo, va [dekora'tʃivu, va] *adj* decorative.

decoro [de'korul] *m* **-1.** [decência] decency; **com** ~ properly. **-2.** [dignidade] dignity.

decoroso, osa [deko'rozu, ɔza] *adj* decent.

decorrência [deko'xẽnsja] *f* consequence; **em** ~ **de** as a consequence of.

decorrente [deko'xẽntʃil *adj*: ~ de resulting from.

decorrer [5] [deko'xe(x)] <> *m* [decurso]: **no ~ de** in the course of, during. <> *vi* **-1.** [derivar]: ~ **de** to stem from. **-2.** [passar] to pass.

decorrido, da [deko'xidu, da] *adj* [terminado]: **decorrida a votação, ...** once the voting was over, ...

decotado, da [deko'tadu, da] *adj* low-cut.

decotar [4] [deko'ta(x)] *vt* to cut a low neckline in.

decote [de'kɔtʃi] *m* décolletage.

decrépito, ta [de'krɛpitu, ta] *adj* decrepit.

decrepitude [dekrepi'tudʒil *f* [caducidade] decrepitude.

decrescente [dekre'sẽntʃil *adj* falling.

decrescer [25] [dekre'se(x)] *vi* to decrease.

decréscimo [de'krɛsimul *m* decrease.

decretação [dekreta'sãwl (*pl* **-ões**) *f* decreeing.

decretar [4] [dekre'ta(x)] <> *vt* **-1.** [ordenar] to decree. **-2.** [determinar] to determine. <> *vi* [ordenar] to decree.

decreto [de'krɛtul *m* **-1.** [ordem] decree; [judicial] fiat. **-2.** *loc*: **nem por ~** not for all the tea in China.

decreto-lei [de,krɛtu'lejl (*pl* **decretos-lei**) *m* law by decree.

decúbito [de'kubitul *m*: **em ~ dorsal/lateral** lying on one's back/side.

decurso [de'kuxsul *m* course; **no ~ de** in the course of.

dedal [de'dawl (*pl* **-ais**) *m* thimble.

dedão [de'dãwl (*pl* **-ões**) *m* **-1.** [polegar] thumb. **-2.** [do pé] big toe.

dedetização [dedetʃiza'sãwl (*pl* **-ões**) *f* fumigation.

dedetizar [4] [dedetʃi'za(x)] *vt* to fumigate.

dedicação [dedʒika'sãwl (*pl* **-ões**) *f* **-1.** [devotamento] dedication. **-2.** [amor] devotion.

dedicado, da [dedʒi'kadu, da] *adj* dedicated.

dedicar [12] [dedʒi'ka(x)] *vt* [devotar]: ~ **algo a alguém** to devote sthg to sb; [oferecer] to dedicate.
➡ **dedicar-se** *vp* [devotar-se]: ~**-se a algo/alguém** to devote o.s to sthg/sb; ~**-se a fazer algo** to devote o.s to doing sthg.

dedicatória [dedʒika'tɔrjal *f* dedication.

dedilhar [4] [dedʒi'ʎa(x)] <> *vt* [cordas, música] to strum. <> *vi* [tamborilar] to drum one's fingers.

dedo [ˈdedul *m* **-1.** [da mão] finger; ~ **anular** ring finger; ~ **indicador** forefinger; ~ **mindinho** *ou* **mínimo** little finger; ~ **polegar** thumb. **-2.** [do pé] toe. **-3.** [quantidade]: **um ~ de algo** a finger of sthg. **-4.** *loc*: **cheio de ~s** finicky; **não levantar um ~** not to lift a finger.
➡ **a dedo** *loc adv* [escolher] with care.

dedo-duro [ˌdedu'durul (*pl* **dedos-duros**) *mf* **-1.** [POL, crime] squealer. **-2.** [criança] tell-tale.

dedões [de'dõjʃl *pl* ▷ **dedão**.

dedução [dedu'sãwl (*pl* **-ões**) *f* deduction.

dedurar [4] [dedu'ra(x)] *fam vt* **-1.** [crime] to squeal. **-2.** [criança] to tell tales.

dedutível [dedu'tʃivewl (*pl* **-eis**) *adj* deductible.

dedutivo, va [dedu'tʃivu, val *adj* deductive.

deduzir [72] [dedu'zi(x)] <> *vt* **-1.** [subtrair] to subtract. **-2.** [concluir] to deduce. <> *vi* [tirar dedução] to deduce.

defasado, da [defa'zadu, da] *adj* out of phase.

defasagem [defa'zaʒẽl (*pl* **-ns**) *f* [discrepância] gap.

defecar [12] [defe'ka(x)] *vi* to defecate.

defecção [defɛk'sãwl (*pl* **-ões**) *f* defection.

defectivo, va [defɛk'tʃivu, val *adj* defective.

defeito [de'fejtul *m* **-1.** [físico] defect. **-2.** [moral] flaw. **-3.** [falha] fault; **com ~** out of order; **pôr ~ em algo** [criticar] to find fault with sthg.

defeituoso, osa [defej'twozu, ɔzal *adj* **-1.** [com falha] faulty. **-2.** [físico] defective.

defender [5] [defẽn'de(x)] *vt* **-1.** [proteger]: ~ **algo/alguém (contra** *ou* **de)** to defend sthg/sb (against). **-2.** [sustentar] to stand up for.
➡ **defender-se** *vp* [proteger-se]: ~**-se (contra** *ou* **de)** to defend o.s (against).

defensável [defẽn'savewl (*pl* **-eis**) *adj* defensible.

defensivo, va [defẽn'sivu, val *adj* defensive.
➡ **defensiva** *f* **-1.** [meios de defesa] defences *UK*, defenses *US*. **-2.** [atitude]: **estar/ficar na ~** to be/stay on the defensive.

defensor, ra [defẽn'so(x), ral (*mpl* **-es**, *fpl* **-s**) *m, f* **-1.** [de causa *etc*] defender. **-2.** *JUR* defendant.

deferência [defe'rẽnsjal *f* **-1.** [respeito] deference. **-2.** [condescendência] acquiescence.

deferente [defe'rẽntʃil *adj* **-1.** [atencioso] deferential. **-2.** [condescendente] acquiescent.

deferir [57] [defe'ri(x)] <> *vt* **-1.** [atender] to grant. **-2.** [conceder]: ~ **algo a alguém** to award sthg to sb. <> *vi* **-1.** [atender]: ~ **a algo** to yield to sthg. **-2.** [acatar]: ~ **a algo** to respect sthg.

defesa [de'fezal *f* **-1.** [proteção] defence. **-2.** *JUR* defence lawyer. **-3.** *FUT* defence. **-4.** *UNIV*: ~ **de tese** viva.

defeso, sa [de'fezu, zal *adj* [proibido] forbidden.

deficiência [defi'sjẽnsjal *f* **-1.** [carência] deficiency. **-2.** *MED*: ~ **física/mental** physical/mental disability.

deficiente [defi'sjẽntʃil <> *adj* deficient. <> *mf* *MED*: ~ **(físico/mental)** physically/mentally disabled.

déficit [ˈdɛfisitʃl *m ECON*: ~ **público** public deficit.

deficitário, ria [defisi'tarju, rjal *adj* [orçamento, saldo] negative; [empresa] loss-making.

definhamento [defiɲa'mẽntul *m* [debilitação] debilitation, wasting away.

definhar [4] [defi'ɲa(x)] <> *vt* to drain. <> *vi* to waste away.

definição [defini'sãwl (*pl* **-ões**) *f* **-1.** [explicação] explanation. **-2.** [decisão] decision. **-3.** [de imagem] definition.

definido, da [defi'nidu, da] *adj* **-1.** [exato, claro] defined. **-2.** *GRAM* definite.

definir [6] [defi'ni(x)] *vt* **-1.** [fixar, explicar] to define. **-2.** [decidir] to determine.
➡ **definir-se** *vp* **-1.** [pronunciar-se]: ~**-se sobre/contra/a favor de** to come out for/against/in favour of. **-2.** [decidir-se] to make up one's mind.

-3. [descrever-se]: ~**-se como** to describe o.s. as.

definitivamente [defini͏ˌtʃiva'mẽntʃi] *adv* **-1.** [para sempre] definitively. **-2.** [decididamente] definitely.

definitivo, va [defini'tʃivu, va] *adj* **-1.** [final] definitive. **-2.** [permanente] permanent; **em caráter** ~ definitively.

deflagrar [4] [defla'gra(x)] <> *vt* **-1.** [causar a explosão] to ignite. **-2.** *fig* [provocar] to inflame. <> *vi* **-1.** [explodir] to explode. **-2.** *fig* [irromper] to erupt.

deflorar [4] [deflo'ra(x)] *vt* [mulher] to deflower.

deformação [defoxma'sãw] (*pl* -ões) *f* distortion.

deformar [4] [defox'ma(x)] *vt* **-1.** [tornar disforme] to deform. **-2.** [deturpar] to distort.

➡ **deformar-se** *vp* [tornar-se disforme] to become deformed.

deformidade [defoxmi'dadʒi] *f* deformity.

defraudar [4] [defraw'da(x)] *vt* to defraud.

defrontar [4] [defrõn'ta(x)] <> *vi* **-1.** [estar]: ~ **com** to face onto. **-2.** [deparar]: ~ **com** to come upon. <> *vt* **-1.** [encarar] to face. **-2.** [confrontar] to compare.

➡ **defrontar-se** *vp* [deparar-se]: ~**-se com** to come face to face with.

defronte [de'frõntʃi] <> *adv* [em frente] opposite. <> *prep*: ~ **a/de** in front of.

defumado, da [defu'madu, da] *adj* smoked.

defumador [defuma'do(x)] *m* **-1.** [recipiente] burner. **-2.** [substância] *substance used in burners for its smell.*

defumar [4] [defu'ma(x)] *vt* **-1.** [curar] to cure. **-2.** [perfumar] to perfume.

defunto, ta [de'fũntu, ta] <> *adj* [morto] dead. <> *m, f* [cadáver] corpse.

degelar [4] [deʒe'la(x)] <> *vt* [descongelar] to defrost. <> *vi* [derreter-se] to melt.

degelo [de'ʒelu] *m* thaw.

degeneração [deʒenera'sãw] *f* **-1.** [ger] degeneration. **-2.** [depravação] corruption.

degenerado, da [deʒene'radu, da] *adj* degenerate.

degenerar [4] [deʒene'ra(x)] *vi* **-1.** [ger] to degenerate. **-2.** [depravar-se] to become depraved.

➡ **degenerar-se** *vp* [depravar-se] to be led astray.

degenerativo, va [deʒenera'tʃivu, va] *adj* degenerative.

deglutição [deglutʃi'sãw] (*pl* -ões) *f* swallowing.

deglutir [6] [deglu'tʃi(x)] <> *vt* & *vi* to swallow.

degola [de'gɔla] *f* **-1.** [decapitação] decapitation. **-2.** [demissão] large-scale redundancy. **-3.** *ESP* sacking.

degolar [4] [dego'la(x)] *vt* to behead.

degradação [degrada'sãw] *f* degradation.

degradante [degra'dãntʃi] *adj* [aviltante] demeaning.

degradar [4] [degra'da(x)] *vt* **-1.** [privar] to strip. **-2.** [aviltar] to demean.

➡ **degradar-se** *vp* [aviltar-se] to demean o.s.

dégradé [degra'de] *adj* gradational.

degrau [de'graw] *m* **-1.** [de escada] step. **-2.** *fig* [meio] means.

degredar [degre'da(x)] *vt* to exile.

degredo [de'gredu] *m* **-1.** [pena] exile. **-2.** [lugar] place of exile.

degringolar [4] [degrĩngo'la(x)] *vi* **-1.** [cair] to fall down. **-2.** *fig* [deteriorar-se] to go off the rails. **-3.** *fig* [desordenar-se - esquema] to get in a mess; [- fila, jogo] to become disorderly. **-4.** [arruinar-se] to go bankrupt.

degustação [deguʃta'sãw] (*pl* -ões) *f* tasting.

degustar [4] [deguʃ'ta(x)] *vt* **-1.** [provar] to taste. **-2.** [saborear] to savour.

deificar [12] [dejfi'ka(x)] *vt* to deify.

deitada [dej'tada] *f fam*: **dar uma** ~ to have a lie-down.

deitado, da [dej'tadu, da] *adj* **-1.** [pessoa] lying down *(depois de verbo)*. **-2.** [objeto] set down *(depois de verbo)*.

deitar [4] [dej'ta(x)] <> *vt* **-1.** [pessoa] to lay down. **-2.** [objeto] to set down. <> *vi* [pessoa] to lie down; ~ **e rolar** *fig* to call the shots.

➡ **deitar-se** *vp* [pessoa] to go to bed.

deixa ['dejʃa] *f* **-1.** [dica] hint. **-2.** *TEATRO* cue. **-3.** [chance] opportunity.

deixar [4] [dej'ʃa(x)] <> *vt* **-1.** [ger] to leave. **-2.** [abandonar] to abandon. **-3.** [demitir-se de] to resign. **-4.** [consentir]: ~ **alguém fazer/que alguém faça algo** to allow sb to do sthg; ~ **passar algo** to overlook sthg. **-5.** [tornar possível]: **não** ~ **alguém fazer algo** not to allow sb to do sthg. **-6.** [esperar] to let. **-7.** [ignorar]: ~ **algo/alguém pra lá** to let sthg/sb be. **-8.** [não considerar, esquecer] to forget; **me deixa (em paz)!** leave me alone! <> *vi* **-1.** [parar]: ~ **de fazer algo** to stop doing sthg. **-2.** [não se preocupar]: **pode** ~ it's fine; **deixa pra lá!** forget it! **-3.** [expressando pedido]: **não deixe de ir no concerto!** make sure you go to the concert! **-4.** *loc*: ~ **(muito) a desejar** to leave much to be desired.

➡ **deixar-se** *vp* [permitir-se]: ~**-se fazer algo** to allow o.s. to do sthg.

dejeto [de'ʒɛtu] *m* dejection.

dela ['dɛla] = **de + ella.**

delação [dela'sãw] (*pl* -ões) *f* **-1.** [denúncia] accusation. **-2.** [acusação] charge.

delas ['dɛlaʃ] = **de + ellas.**

delatar [4] [dela'ta(x)] *vt* **-1.** [denunciar] to denounce. **-2.** [acusar] to accuse. **-3.** [informar] to inform.

➡ **delatar-se** *vp* [denunciar-se] to betray o.s.

delator, ra [dela'to(x), ra] *m, f* informer.

délavé [dela've] *adj* faded.

dele ['deli] = **de + ele.**

delegação [delega'sãw] (*pl* -ões) *f* delegation; ~ **de poderes** transfer of powers.

delegacia [delega'sia] *f* police station; ~ **de polícia** police station.

delegado, da [dele'gadu, da] *m, f* delegate; ~ **de polícia** chief of police.

delegar [14] [dele'ga(x)] *vt* **-1.** [dar]: ~ **algo a alguém** to delegate sthg to sb. **-2.** [enviar] to send sb as a delegate.

deleitar [4] [delej'ta(x)] *vt* to delight.

➡ **deleitar-se** *vp*: ~**-se com** to rejoice in.

deleite [de'lejtʃi] *m* delight.

deleitoso, osa [delej'tozu, ɔza] *adj* delightful.

deles ['deliʃ] = **de + eles**.

deletar [4] [dele'ta(x)] *vt* COMPUT to delete.

deletério, ria [dele'tɛrju, rja] *adj* harmful.

delgado, da [dew'gadu, da] *adj* **-1.** [fino] slim. **-2.** [esbelto] slender.

deliberação [delibera'sãw] (*pl* **-ões**) *f* **-1.** [discussão] discussion; **em** ~ under discussion. **-2.** [decisão] decision.

deliberadamente [deliberada'mẽntʃi] *adj* [propositalmente] deliberately.

deliberado, da [delibe'radu, da] *adj* **-1.** [decidido] wilful. **-2.** [propositado] deliberate.

deliberar [4] [delibe'ra(x)] ⬦ *vt* [decidir] to decide. ⬦ *vi* [refletir sobre]: ~ **sobre** to ponder upon.

deliberativo, va [delibera'tʃivu, va] *adj* deliberative.

delicadeza [delika'dezal *f* **-1.** [ger] delicacy. **-2.** [leveza] fineness. **-3.** [fragilidade] fragility. **-4.** [apuro]: ~ **de detalhes** attentiveness to detail. **-5.** [cortesia] politeness.

delicado, da [deli'kadu, da] *adj* **-1.** [ger] delicate. **-2.** [sensível] urbane. **-3.** [cortês] polite.

delícia [de'lisja] *f* **-1.** [deleite] delight. **-2.** [coisa saborosa]: **ser/estar uma** ~ to be delicious. **-3.** [pessoa encantadora]: **ser uma** ~ to be a delight.

deliciar [16] [deli'sja(x)] *vt* to delight.

➡ **deliciar-se** *vp*: ~**-se com algo** to be delighted with sthg.

delicioso, osa [deli'sjozu, ɔza] *adj* **-1.** [vinho, doce] delicious. **-2.** [passeio] delightful.

delimitação [delimita'sãw] (*pl* **-ões**) *f* demarcation.

delimitar [4] [delimi'ta(x)] *vt* **-1.** [demarcar] to mark the limits of. **-2.** [restringir] to outline.

delineador [delinja'do(x)] *m* eyeliner.

delinear [15] [deli'nja(x)] *vt* to outline.

delinqüência [delĩ'kwẽnsja] *f* delinquency.

delinqüente [delĩ'kwẽntʃil ⬦ *adj* delinquent. ⬦ *mf* delinquent.

delirante [deli'rãntʃi] *adj* **-1.** PSIC delirious. **-2.** [extravagante, aloucado] wild. **-3.** [maravilhoso] wonderful.

delirar [4] [deli'ra(x)] *vi* **-1.** PSIC to be delirious. **-2.** [sentir intensamente]: ~ **de algo** to be overcome with sthg.

delírio [de'lirju] *m* **-1.** PSIC delirium. **-2.** [excitação] excitement. **-3.** [êxtase] ecstasy.

delirium tremens [de'lirjũ 'trɛmẽns] *m* delirium tremens.

delito [de'litu] *m* **-1.** [falta] sin. **-2.** [crime] crime.

delonga [de'lõŋga] *f* delay; **sem mais** ~ without further delay.

delongar [14] [de'lõŋ'ga(x)] *vt* [retardar] to postpone.

➡ **delongar-se** *vp* **-1.** [demorar-se] to delay. **-2.** [prolongar-se] to prolong.

delta ['dɛwta] *m* delta.

demagogia [demago'ʒia] *f* demagogy.

demagógico, ca [dema'gɔʒiku, ka] *adj* demagogic.

demagogo, ga [dema'gogu, ga] *m, f* demagogue.

demais [de'majʃ] ⬦ *adv* **-1.** [em demasia, muitíssimo] too much. **-2.** *fam* [ótimo]: **estar/ser** ~ to be amazing. ⬦ *pron* [outros]: **os/as** ~ the others.

demanda [de'mãnda] *f* **-1.** ECON demand. **-2.** JUR lawsuit. **-3.** [disputa] dispute. **-4.** [pedido] request.

demandar [4] [demãn'da(x)] *vt* **-1.** JUR to sue. **-2.** [exigir] to demand. **-3.** [pedir] to request.

demão [de'mãw] (*pl* **-s**) *f* coat.

demarcação [demaxka'sãw] (*pl* **-ões**) *f* **-1.** [delimitação] demarcation. **-2.** [separação] boundary.

demarcado, da [demax'kadu, da] *adj* **-1.** [delimitado] demarcated. **-2.** [separado] set apart.

demarcar [12] [demax'ka(x)] *vt* **-1.** [delimitar] to demarcate. **-2.** [fixar] to define. **-3.** [separar] to distinguish between.

demarcatório, ria [demaxka'tɔrju, rja] *adj* boundary (*antes de subst*).

demasia [dema'zia] *f* excess; **em** ~ in excess.

demasiadamente [demazjada'mẽntʃil *adv* **-1.** [demais] excessively. **-2.** [muito] too.

demasiado, da [dema'zjadu, da] ⬦ *adj* excessive. ⬦ *adv* too much; **por** ~ too.

demência [de'mẽnsja] *f* **-1.** MED dementia. **-2.** [loucura] insanity.

demente [de'mẽntʃi] *adj* **-1.** MED demented. **-2.** [louco] insane.

demérito, ta [de'mɛritu, ta] *adj* unworthy.

➡ **demérito** *m* [desmérito] unworthiness.

demissão [demi'sãw] (*pl* **-ões**) *f* **-1.** [solicitado pelo empregador] dismissal. **-2.** [solicitado pelo empregado] resignation; **pedir** ~ to tender one's resignation.

demissionário, ria [demisjo'narju, rja] *adj* resigning.

demitir [6] [demi'tʃi(x)] *vt* to dismiss.

➡ **demitir-se** *vp* to resign.

democracia [demokra'sia] *f* democracy.

democrata [demo'krata] *mf* democrat.

democrático, ca [demo'kratʃiku, ka] *adj* **-1.** [relativo a democracia] democratic. **-2.** [indiferente às classes sociais] egalitarian.

democratização [demokratʃiza'sãw] *f* democratization.

democratizar [4] [demokratʃi'za(x)] *f* **-1.** [tornar democrático] to democratize. **-2.** [popularizar] to make accessible.

➡ **democratizar-se** *vp* [tornar-se democrático] to become democratic.

démodé [demo'del *adj* outmoded.

demografia [demogra'fia] *f* demography.

demográfico, ca [demo'grafiku, ka] *adj* demographic.

demolição [demoli'sãw] (*pl* -ões) *f* -1. demolition. -2. *fig* [ger] de reputação] destruction; [- de obstáculo] elimination.

demolidor, ra [demo'lido(x), ra] <> *adj* demolition (*antes de subst*). <> *m, f* demolition expert.

demolir [79] [demo'li(x)] *vt* -1. [destruir] to demolish. -2. *fig* [- reputação] to destroy; [- obstáculo] to overcome.

demoníaco, ca [demo'niaku, ka] *adj* demonic.

demônio [de'monju] *m* demon.

demonstração [demõnʃtra'sãw] (*pl* -ões) *f* -1. [ger] demonstration. -2. [apresentação] display.

demonstrar [4] [demõnʃ'tra(x)] *vt* -1. [ger] to demonstrate. -2. [afeto, antipatia *etc*] to show. -3. [habilidades, talentos] to display.

◆ demonstrar-se *vp* [revelar-se] to show o.s.

demonstrativo, va [demõnʃtra'tʃivu, va] *adj* demonstrative.

demonstrável [demõnʃ'travew] (*pl* -eis) *adj* demonstrable.

demora [de'mɔra] *f* [atraso] delay; **sem ~** without delay.

demorado, da [demo'radu, da] *adj* delayed.

demorar [4] [demo'ra(x)] <> *vt* [retardar] to delay. <> *vi* -1. [tardar] to be late; **~ a fazer algo** to take a long time to do sthg. -2. [permanecer] to stay.

◆ demorar-se *vp* -1. [tardar] to be late; **~-se a fazer algo** to take a long time to do sthg. -2. [permanecer] to remain.

demover [5] [demo've(x)] *vt* -1. [dissuadir]: **~ alguém de algo/fazer algo** to dissuade sb from sthg/doing sthg. -2. [remover] to move.

◆ demover-se *vp* [dissuadir-se]: **~-se de algo** to dissuade o.s. from sthg.

DENARC (*abrev de* Departamento de Investigações sobre Narcóticos) *m* Brazilian police narcotics department.

DENATRAN (*abrev de* Departamento Nacional de Trânsito) *m* Brazilian national department responsible for transport law.

dendê [dẽn'de] *m* -1. *BOT* palm. -2. [azeite] palm oil.

denegrir [58] [dene'gri(x)] *vt* [escurecer] to blacken.

dengo ['dẽngu] *m* -1. [faceirice] foppery. -2. [manha] affectation.

dengoso, osa [dẽn'gozu, ɔza] *adj* whining.

dengue ['dẽngi] *f* MED dengue.

denodado, da [deno'dadu, da] *adj* -1. [ousado] daring. -2. [impetuoso] impetuous.

denominação [denomina'sãw] (*pl* -ões) *f* -1. [nomeação] name. -2. [designação] designation. -3. REL denomination.

denominador, ra [denomina'do(x), ra] *adj* designatory.

◆ denominador *m* MAT denominator; **~ comum** common denominator.

denominar [4] [denomi'na(x)] *vt* -1. [nomear] to name. -2. [designar] to designate.

◆ denominar-se *vp* to be called.

denotar [4] [deno'ta(x)] *vt* -1. [indicar] to indicate. -2. [significar] to denote.

densidade [dẽnsi'dadʒi] *f* density; **de alta/dupla ~** high/double density.

denso, sa ['dẽnsu, sa] *adj* -1. [ger] dense. -2. [espesso] thick.

dentada [dẽn'tada] *f* bite.

dentado, da [dẽn'tadu, da] *adj* serrated.

dentadura [dẽnta'dura] *f* -1. [natural] set of teeth. -2. [postiça] denture.

dental [dẽn'taw] (*pl* -ais) *adj* dental; **pasta ~** toothpaste.

dentário, ria [dẽn'tarju, rja] *adj* dental.

dente ['dẽntʃi] *m* -1. [ger] tooth; **~ de leite** milk tooth; **~ de siso** wisdom tooth; **falar entre os ~s** to mutter. -2. [de elefante] tusk. -3. [alho] clove.

dente-de-leão [dẽntʃidʒi'lãw] (*pl* dentes-de-leão) *m* dandelion.

dentição [dẽntʃi'sãw] *f* -1. [processo] dentition. -2. [as dentes] teething; **primeira/segunda ~** milk/second teeth.

dentifrício, cia [dẽntʃi'frisju, sja] *adj* dental.

◆ dentifrício *m* toothpaste.

dentista [dẽn'tʃiʃta] *mf* dentist.

dentre ['dẽntri] *prep* among.

dentro ['dẽntru] <> *adv* in; **aí/lá ~** in there. <> *prep* -1.: **~ de** [no interior de] inside; [no tempo] within; **por ~** [na parte interna] inside. -2. *loc*: **estar por ~ (de algo)** *fam* to be in touch (with sthg); **não dei uma ~** *fam* I didn't get a single thing right.

dentuço, ça [dẽn'tusu, sa] <> *adj* buck-toothed. <> *m, f* [pessoa] buck-toothed person.

◆ dentuça *f* [arcada] buck-teeth.

denúncia [de'nũnsja] *f* -1. [acusação] accusation. -2. [à polícia] report. -3. [JUR - de pessoa, crime] condemnation; [- de contrato] termination; **~ vazia** unfettered right to forfeiture.

denunciar [16] [denũn'sja(x)] *vt* -1. [acusar] to denounce. -2. [divulgar] to expose. -3. [JUR - pessoa, crime] to condemn; [- contrato] to terminate. -4. [evidenciar] to reveal.

◆ denunciar-se *vp* -1. [delatar-se] to confess. -2. [trair-se] to betray o.s.

deparar [4] [depa'ra(x)] *vi*: **~ com** to come across.

departamental [depaxtamẽn'taw] (*pl* -ais) *adj* departmental.

departamento [departa'mẽntu] *m* department.

depauperado, da [depawpe'radu, da] *adj* -1. [empobrecido] impoverished. -2. [enfraquecido] exhausted.

depauperar [4] [depawpe'ra(x)] *vt* -1. [empobrecer] to impoverish. -2. [debilitar] to weaken.

◆ depauperar-se *vp* [debilitar-se] to become weak.

depenar [4] [depe'na(x)] *vt* -1. [ave] to pluck. -2. [pessoa] to lift. -3. [casa] to clean out.

dependência [depẽn'dẽnsja] *f* -1. [ger] dependency. -2. [cômodo] room.

dependente [depẽn'dẽntʃi] <> *adj* [subordinado]

dependent. <> *mf* dependant.

depender [5] [depẽn'de(x)] *vi* **-1.** [ger]: ~ **de** to depend upon. **- 2.** [financeiramente]: ~ **de** to be dependent upon. **- 3.** [de droga]: ~ **de** to be dependent on.

dependurar [4] [depẽndu'ra(x)] *vt* [pendurar]: ~ algo (em algo) to hang sthg (on sthg).

  ◆ **dependurar-se** *vp*: ~-se em algo to hang from sthg.

depilação [depila'sãw] (*pl* -ões) *f* depilation.

depilador, ra [depila'do(x), ra] *m, f beautician who does hair-removal.*

depilar [4] [depi'la(x)] *vt* to remove hair from.

  ◆ **depilar-se** *vp* **-1.** [com cera - na estética] to have a wax; [- em casa] to wax. **- 2.** [com lâmina] to shave.

depilatório, ria [depila'tɔrju, rja] *adj* hair-removing.

  ◆ **depilatório** *m* hair removal cream/wax.

deplorar [4] [deplo'ra(x)] *vt* to lament.

deplorável [deplo'ravew] (*pl* -eis) *adj* **-1.** [lamentá-
· vel] lamentable. **- 2.** [detestável] deplorable.

depoente [depo'ẽntʃi] *m* JUR witness.

depoimento [depoj'mẽntu] *m* **-1.** [ger] statement. **- 2.** [ato] testimony.

depois [de'pojʃ] <> *adv* **-1.** [posteriormente] after; logo ~ straight after. **- 2.** [além disso] besides. <> *prep*: ~ **de fazer algo** after doing sthg.

  ◆ **depois que** *loc conj* after.

depor [45] [de'po(x)] <> *vt* **-1.** [colocar] to put down. **- 2.** [destituir] to depose. **- 3.** JUR: ~ **que** to testify that. **- 4.** [expressar] to express. <> *vi* JUR: ~ (a favor/contra) to testify (for/against).

  ◆ **depor-se** *vp* [depositar-se] to settle.

deportação [depoxta'sãw] (*pl*-ões) *f* deportation.

deportar [4] [depox'ta(x)] *vt* to deport.

deposição [depozi'sãw] (*pl* -ões) *f* [destituição] deposition.

depositante [depozi'tãntʃi] *mf* depositor.

depositar [4] [depozi'ta(x)] *vt* to deposit.

  ◆ **depositar-se** *vp* [assentar] to settle.

depositário, ria [depozi'tarju, rja] *m, f* **-1.** [quem recebe em depósito] depositary. **- 2.** *fig* [confidente] confidant.

depósito [de'pɔzitul] *m* **-1.** [ger] deposit. **- 2.** [reservatório] depository.

depravação [deprava'sãw] (*pl* -ões) *f* **-1.** [perversão] perversion. **- 2.** [degeneração] degeneration.

depravado, da [depra'vadu, da] <> *adj* depraved. <> *m, f* depraved person.

depravar [4] [depra'va(x)] *vt* **-1.** [corromper] to corrupt. **- 2.** [estragar] to ruin.

  ◆ **depravar-se** *vp* [corromper-se] to become corrupted.

depreciação [depresja'sãw] (*pl* -ões) *f* [desvalorização] depreciation.

depreciar [16] [depre'sja(x)] *vt* **-1.** [desvalorizar] to devalue. **- 2.** [subestimar] to undervalue.

  ◆ **depreciar-se** *vp* **-1.** [desvalorizar-se] to fall in value. **- 2.** [subestimar-se] to underestimate o.s.

depredação [depreda'sãw] (*pl*-ões) *f* **-1.** [destruição] destruction. **- 2.** [pilhagem] robbery.

depredador, ra [depreda'do(x), ra] <> *adj* harmful, damaging. <> *m, f* damaging person.

depredar [4] [depre'da(x)] *vt* **-1.** [destruir] to destroy. **- 2.** [saquear] to loot.

depreender [5] [deprjẽn'de(x)] *vt* **-1.** [compreender] to conclude. **- 2.** [deduzir] to deduce.

depressa [de'prɛsal] *adv* quickly.

depressão [depre'sãw] (*pl* -ões) *f* **-1.** PSIC depression. **- 2.** [en terreno, superfície] dip. **- 3.** *fig* [abatimento] despondency.

depressivo, va [depre'sivu, va] *adj* depressive.

deprimente [depri'mẽntʃi] *adj* depressing.

deprimido, da [depri'midu, da] *adj* depressed.

deprimir [6] [depri'mi(x)] *vt* to depress.

  ◆ **deprimir-se** *vp* to become depressed.

depto (*abrev de* departamento) *m* dept.

depuração [depura'sãw] (*pl* -ões) *f* purification.

depurar [4] [depu'ra(x)] *vt* to purify.

  ◆ **depurar-se** *vp* to become purified.

deputado, da [depu'tadu, da] *m, f* **-1.** POL deputy. **- 2.** [delegado] representative.

deque ['dɛkil] *m* decking.

DER (*abrev de* Departamento de Estradas de Rodagem) *m Brazilian highways department.*

deriva [de'rival] *f* drift; à ~ drifting; ir à ~ to drift.

derivação [deriva'sãw] (*pl* -ões) *f* **-1.** GRAM derivation. **- 2.** *fig* [origem] origin.

derivado, da [deri'vadu, da] *adj* [proveniente]: ~ de derived from.

  ◆ **derivado** *m* derivative.

  ◆ **derivada** *f* MAT derivative.

derivar [4] [deri'va(x)] *vi* **-1.** [resultar]: ~ **de** to derive from. **- 2.** [ficar à deriva] to drift. **- 3.** GRAM: ~ de to stem from.

derivativo, va [deriva'tʃivu, va] *adj* derivative.

  ◆ **derivativo** *m* [distração] distraction.

dermatologia [dexmatolo'ʒial] *f* dermatology.

dermatológico, ca [dexmato'lɔgiku, ka] *adj* dermatological.

dermatologista [dexmatolo'ʒiʃtal] *mf* dermatologist.

derradeiro, ra [dexa'dejru, ra] *adj* final.

derramamento [dexama'mẽntul] *m* **-1.** [de água, leite] spillage. **- 2.** [de lágrimas] flow; ~ **de sangre** bloodshed.

derramar [4] [dexa'ma(x)] *vt* **-1.** [ger] to spill **- 2.** [espalhar] to strew

  ◆ **derramar-se** *vp* [verter] to spill.

derrame [de'xãmil *m* **-1.** [de líquido] spillage. **- 2.** [de lágrimas, sangue] flow. **- 3.** MED haemorrhage; ~ cerebral brain haemorrhage.

derrapagem [dexa'paʒẽl (*pl* -ns) *f* skid.

derrapar [4] [dexa'pa(x)] *vi* to skid.

derredor [dexe'do(x)] *adv fml*: em ~ (de) around.

derreter [5] [dexe'te(x)] <> *vt* to melt. <> *vi* [liquefazer-se] to melt.

  ◆ **derreter-se** *vp* **-1.** *fig* [comover-se]: ~ (com algo) to be moved (by sthg). **- 2.** *fig* [apaixonar-se]: ~-se todo (por alguém) to fall completely (for sb).

derretido, da [dexe'tʃidu, da] *adj* **-1.** [liquefeito] melted. **-2.** *fig* [comovido] moved. **-3.** *fig* [apaixonado] besotted.

derrocada [dexo'kada] *f* **-1.** [desmoronamento] destruction. **-2.** [ruína] ruin.

derrota [de'xɔta] *f* **-1.** [fracasso] defeat. **-2.** NÁUT course.

derrotado, da [dexo'tadu, da] *adj* defeated.

derrotar [4] [dexo'ta(x)] *vt* to defeat.

derrotista [dexo'tʃiʃta] <> *adj* defeatist. <> *mf* defeatist.

derrubar [4] [dexu'ba(x)] *vt* **-1.** [fazer cair] to knock down. **-2.** [vencer] to overcome. **-3.** [destituir] to overthrow. **-4.** [destruir] to defame. **-5.** [prostrar] to lay low. **-6.** *fam* [prejudicar] to knock.

desabafar [4] [dʒizaba'fa(x)] <> *vt*: ~ algo (com alguém) to share sthg (with sb). <> *vi*: ~ (com alguém) to open up (to sb).
➡ **desabafar-se** *vp*: ~-se (com alguém) to open up (to sb).

desabafo [dʒiza'baful] *m* outpouring.

desabalado, da [dʒizaba'ladu, da] *adj* **-1.** [excessivo] enormous. **-2.** [espavorido]: **sair/correr** ~ to go/run headlong.

desabamento [dʒizaba'mẽntul] *m* collapse.

desabar [4] [dʒiza'ba(x)] *vi* **-1.** [ruir] to tumble down. **-2.** [cair com força] to fall heavily.

desabitado, da [dʒizabi'tadu, da] *adj* unoccupied.

desabituar [4] [dʒizabi'twa(x)] *vt*: ~ alguém de algo/de fazer algo to wean sb off sthg/doing sthg.
➡ **desabituar-se** *vp*: ~-se de algo/de fazer algo to wean o.s. off sthg/doing sthg.

desabonar [4] [dʒizabo'na(x)] *vt* to discredit.

desabotoar [20] [dʒizabo'twa(x)] *vt* to unbutton.
➡ **desabotoar-se** *vp* to open up.

desabrigado, da [dʒizabri'gadu, da] <> *adj* **-1.** [sem casa] homeless. **-2.** [exposto] unsheltered. <> *m, f* [pessoa] homeless person; **os** ~**s** the homeless.

desabrigar [dʒiza'briga(x)] *vt* [tirar do abrigo] to leave without shelter.

desabrigo [dʒiza'brigul] *m* **-1.** [falta de abrigo] lack of shelter. **-2.** *fig* [abandono] lack of protection.

desabrochar [4] [dʒizabro'ʃa(x)] *vi* **-1.** [flor] to bloom. **-2.** *fig* [pessoa] to blossom.

desacatar [4] [dʒizaka'ta(x)] <> *vt* **-1.** [afrontar] to disrespect. **-2.** [desprezar] to disregard. <> *vi* *fam* [causar espanto] to stun.

desacato [dʒiza'katul] *m* **-1.** [afronta] disrespect. **-2.** [desprezo] disregard. **-3.** *fam* [pessoa]: **ser um** ~ to be a show-off.

desaceleração [dʒizaselera'sãw] *f* deceleration.

desacelerar [4] [dʒizasele'ra(x)] *vt* to slow down.

desacerto [dʒiza'sextul] *m* **-1.** [erro] mistake. **-2.** [tolice] blunder.

desacomodar [4] [dʒizakomo'da(x)] *vt* **-1.** [desorganizar] to disarrange. **-2.** [desalojar] to ask to leave.

desacompanhado, da [dʒizakõnpa'ɲadu, da] *adj* unaccompanied.

desaconselhar [4] [dʒizakõnse'ʎa(x)] *vt*: ~ algo (a alguém) to warn (sb) against sthg.

desaconselhável [dʒizakõnse'ʎavεw] (*pl* -eis) *adj* not recommended *(depois de verbo)*.

desacordado, da [dʒizakox'dadu, da] *adj* senseless.

desacordo [dʒiza'koxdul] *m* **-1.** [falta de acordo] disagreement. **-2.** [desarmonia] disharmony.

desacostumado, da [dʒizakoʃtu'madu, da] *adj*: ~ (a) unaccustomed (to).

desacostumar [4] [dʒizakoʃtu'ma(x)] *vt*: ~ alguém de algo to wean sb off sthg.
➡ **desacostumar-se** *vp* [desabituar-se]: ~-se de algo/de fazer algo to wean o.s. off sthg/doing sthg.

desacreditado, da [dʒizakredʒi'tadu, da] *adj* discredited.

desacreditar [4] [dʒizakredi'ta(x)] *vt* to discredit.
➡ **desacreditar-se** *vp* [perder o crédito] to become discredited.

desafeto [dʒiza'fεtul] *m* opponent.

desafiador, ra [dʒizafja'do(x), ral] <> *adj* challenging. <> *m, f* challenger.

desafiar [16] [dʒiza'fja(x)] *vt* **-1.** [propor luta] to challenge. **-2.** [afrontar] to defy.

desafinação [dʒizafina'sãw] (*pl* -ões) *f* disharmony.

desafinado, da [dʒizafi'nadu, da] *adj* out of tune.

desafinar [4] [dʒizafi'na(x)] <> *vt*: ~ un instrumento to put an instrument out of tune. <> *vi* to be out of tune.

desafio [dʒiza'fiwl] *m* **-1.** [provocação] challenge. **-2.** LITER & MÚS *literary/musical competition between two people.*

desafivelar [4] [dʒizafive'la(x)] *vt* to unclasp.

desafogado, da [dʒizafo'gadu, da] *adj* **-1.** [pessoa - de preocupações, de opressão] relieved; [- de trabalho] unencumbered. **-2.** [trânsito] clear.

desafogar [14] [dʒizafo'ga(x)] <> *vt* **-1.** [desoprimir - garganta] to clear; [- espírito] to free. **-2.** [desabafar] to relieve. **-3.** [aliviar]: ~ alguém (de algo) to relieve sb (of sthg). <> *vi* [desabafar-se]: ~ (com alguém) to open up (to sb).
➡ **desafogar-se** *vp* [desabafar-se] to unburden o.s.

desafogo [dʒiza'fogul] *m* **-1.** [alívio] relief; **dar** ~ **a algo** to relieve sthg. **-2.** [de trabalho] break.

desaforado, da [dʒizafo'radu, da] *adj* insulting.

desaforo [dʒiza'forul] *m* insult; **eu não levo** ~ **para casa** I'm not going to take it lying down.

desafortunado, da [dʒizafoxtu'nadu, da] *adj* unfortunate.

desagasalhado, da [dʒizagaza'ʎadu, da] *adj* unsheltered.

deságio [de'zaʒiul] *m* ECON discount.

desagradar [4] [dʒizagra'da(x)] <> *vt* to displease. <> *vi*: ~ a alguém to displease sb.
➡ **desagradar-se** *vp* to be displeased.

desagradável [dʒizagra'davewl] (*pl* -eis) *adj* unpleasant.

desagrado [dʒiza'gradul *m* displeasure.

desagravo [dʒiza'gravul *m* -**1.** [reparação de agravo] recompense; **de** ~ to make amends. -**2.** *JUR* reparation.

desagregação [dʒizagrega'sãw] (*pl* -**ões**) *f* -**1.** [dissolução] break-up. -**2.** [separação] division.

desagregar [14] [dʒizagre'ga(x)] *vt* -**1.** [dissolver] to dissolve. -**2.** [separar] to split.

➡ **desagregar-se** *vp* [dissociar-se] to split.

desaguar [22] [dʒiza'gwa(x)] ◇ *vi* [vazar-se]: ~ **em** to flow into. ◇ *vt* [drenar] to drain.

desajeitado, da [dʒiza'ʒej'tadu, da] *adj* clumsy.

desajuizado, da [dʒizaʒwi'zadu, -da] *adj* senseless.

desajustado, da [dʒizaʒuʃ'tadu, da] ◇ *adj* -**1.** *PSIC* maladjusted. -**2.** [desajuntado] in need of adjustment. ◇ *m, f PSIC* maladjusted person.

desajustamento [dʒizaʒuʃta'mẽntul *m PSIC* maladjustment.

desajustar [4] [dʒizaʒuʃ'ta(x)] *vt* -**1.** *PSIC* to disturb. -**2.** [desajuntar] to undo.

desajuste [dʒiza'ʒuʃtʃil *m* -**1.** *PSIC* maladjustment. -**2.** [de peças, máquina] loosening.

desalentado, da [dʒizalẽn'tadu, da] *adj* discouraged.

desalentar [4] [dʒizalẽn'ta(x)] ◇ *vt* to discourage. ◇ *vi* to lose heart.

➡ **desalentar-se** *vp* to become discouraged.

desalento [dʒiza'lẽntu] *m* discouragement.

desalinhado, da [dʒizali'ɲadu, da] *adj* dishevelled.

desalinhar [dʒiza'liɲa(x)] *vt* -**1.** [tirar do alinhamento] to break up. -**2.** [desarrumar] to mess up.

desalinho [dʒiza'liɲul *m* dishevelment.

desalmado, da [dʒizaw'madu, da] *adj* soulless.

desalojar [4] [dʒizalo'ʒa(x)] ◇ *vt*: ~ **alguém de** to remove sb from. ◇ *vi* to quit.

desamarrar [4] [dʒizama'xa(x)] ◇ *vt* [desfazer] to untie. ◇ *vi NÁUT* to lift anchor.

desamarrotar [4] [dʒizamaxo'ta(x)] *vt* to smooth.

desamassar [4] [dʒizama'sa(x)] *vt* to straighten out.

desambientado, da [dʒizãnbjẽn'tadu, da] *adj* disorientated.

desamor [dʒiza'mo(x)] *m* antipathy.

desamparado, da [dʒizãnpa'radu, da] *adj* -**1.** [pessoa - abandonado] abandoned; [- sem ajuda] unassisted. -**2.** [lugar] abandoned.

desamparar [4] [dʒizãnpa'ra(x)] *vt* [abandonar] to abandon.

desamparo [dʒizãn'parul *m* -**1.** [abandono] abandonment. -**2.** [falta de ajuda] helplessness.

desandar [4] [dʒizãn'da(x)] *vi* -**1.** *fam* [clara, maionese] to separate. -**2.** [começar]: ~ **a rir** to burst out laughing; ~ **a chorar** to burst into tears; ~ **a correr** to break into a run; ~ **a falar** to start speaking.

desanimação [dʒizanima'sãw] *f* dejection.

desanimado, da [dʒizani'madu, da] *adj* despondent.

desanimador, ra [dʒizanima'do(x), ral *adj* disheartening.

desanimar [4] [dʒizani'ma(x)] ◇ *vt* -**1.** [fazer perder o ânimo]: ~ **alguém** to dishearten sb. -**2.** [desencorajar]: ~ **alguém de fazer algo** to discourage sb from doing sthg. ◇ *vi* -**1.** [perder o ânimo] to become disheartened; ~ **de fazer algo** to become disheartened about doing sthg. -**2.** [ser desencorajador] to be discouraging.

desânimo [dʒi'zãnimul *m* despondency.

desanuviar [16] [dʒizanu'vja(x)] *vt* -**1.** [céu] to clear. -**2.** *fig* [pessoa, mente] to calm.

➡ **desanuviar-se** *vp* -**1.** [céu] to clear. -**2.** *fig* [pessoa, mente] to become calm.

desaparafusar [4] [dʒizaparafu'za(x)] *vt* to unscrew.

desaparecer [25] [dʒizapare'se(x)] *vi* to disappear.

desaparecido, da [dʒizapare'sidu, da] ◇ *adj* missing. ◇ *m, f* [pessoa] missing person.

desaparecimento [dʒizaparesi'mẽntul *m* -**1.** [sumiço] disappearance. -**2.** [falecimento] loss.

desapegado, da [dʒizape'gadu, da] *adj* detached.

desapegar [14] [dʒizape'ga(x)] *vt*: ~ **alguém de algo/alguém** to detach sb from sthg/sb.

➡ **desapegar-se** *vp*: ~-**se de algo/alguém** to detach o.s. from sthg/sb.

desapego [dʒiza'pegul *m* -**1.** [desamor] lack of love. -**2.** [indiferença] indifference.

desapertar [4] [dʒizapex'ta(x)] *vt* to loosen.

desapiedado, da [dʒizapje'dadu, da] *adj* ruthless.

desapontador, ra [dʒizapõnta'do(x), ral *adj* disappointing.

desapontamento [dʒizapõnta'mẽntul *m* disappointment.

desapontar [4] [dʒizapõn'ta(x)] *vt* to disappoint.

➡ **desapontar-se** *vp* to be disappointed.

desapossar [4] [dʒizapo'sa(x)] *vt*: ~ **alguém de algo** to deprive sb of sthg.

➡ **desapossar-se** *vp*: ~-**se de algo** to deprive o.s. of sthg.

desapreço [dʒiza'presul *m* discontent.

desaprender [5] [dʒizaprẽn'de(x)] ◇ *vt* to forget. ◇ *vi*: ~ **a fazer algo** to forget how to do sthg.

desapropriação [dʒizaproprja'sãw] (*pl* -**ões**) *f* dispossession.

desapropriar [16] [dʒizapro'prja(x)] *vt* -**1.** [desapossar]: ~ **alguém de algo** to deprive sb of sthg. -**2.** [expropriar]: ~ **algo (de alguém)** to expropriate sthg (from sb).

desaprovação [dʒizaprova'sãw] (*pl* -**ões**) *f* disapproval.

desaprovar [4] [dʒizapro'va(x)] *vt* -**1.** [reprovar] to disapprove. -**2.** [censurar] to censure.

desarmado, da [dʒizax'madu, da] *adj* -**1.** [ger] disarmed. -**2.** [sem arma] unarmed.

desarmamento [dʒizaxma'mẽntul *m* disarmament.

desarmar [4] [dʒizax'ma(x)] *vt* **-1.** [ger] to disarm. **-2.** [barraca, brinqueda] to take down. **-3.** [arma] to disable.

desarmar-se *vp* [criminoso] to hand over one's arms.

desarmonia [dʒizaxmo'nia] *f* **-1.** [falta de harmonia] disharmony. **-2.** *fig* [divergência] discord.

desarraigar [14] [dʒizaxaj'ga(x)] *vt* **-1.** [arrancar] to uproot. **-2.** [extinguir] to stamp out.

desarranjado, da [dʒizaxãn'ʒadu, da] *adj* **-1.** [desarrumado] untidy. **-2.** *MED:* **estar** ~ to be queasy.

desarranjar [4] [dʒizaxãn'ʒa(x)] *vt* [desarrumar] to make untidy.

desarranjo [dʒiza'xãnʒu] *m* disorder.

desarregaçar [dʒizaxega'sa(x)] *vt* [mangas] to roll down.

desarrumado, da [dʒizaxu'madu, da] *adj* untidy.

desarrumar [4] [dʒizaxu'ma(x)] *vt* **-1.** [ger] to make untidy. **-2.** [mala] to unpack.

desarticulado, da [dʒizaxtʃiku'ladu, da] *adj* **-1.** [deslocado] dislocated. **-2.** [desfeito] broken up.

desarticular [4] [dʒizaxtʃiku'la(x)] *vt* to dislocate.

desarvorado, da [dʒizaxvo'radu, da] *adj* disorientated.

desassociar [16] [dʒizaso'sja(x)] *vt:* ~ **algo/alguém (de)** to dissociate sthg/sb (from).

desassociar-se *vp:* ~**-se (de)** to dissociate o.s. (from).

desassossego [dʒizaso'segu] *m* uneasiness.

desastrado, da [dʒizaʃ'tradu, da] *adj* clumsy.

desastre [dʒi'zaʃtri] *m* **-1.** [acidente] accident. **-2.** *fig* [fracasso]: **ser um** ~ to be a disaster.

desastroso, osa [dʒizaʃ'trozu, ɔza] *adj* disastrous.

desatar [4] [dʒiza'ta(x)] <> *vt* **-1.** [desfazer] to undo. **-2.** [desprender] to loosen. <> *vi* [começar]: ~ **a fazer algo** to start to do sthg suddenly.

desatarraxar [4] [dʒizataxa'ʃa(x)] *vt* to undo.

desatenção [dʒizatẽn'sãw] *f* **-1.** [distração] lack of attention. **-2.** [descortesia] lack of courtesy.

desatento, ta [dʒiza'tẽntu, ta] *adj* inattentive.

desatinado, da [dʒizatʃi'nadu, da] <> *adj* mad. <> *m, f* mad person.

desatinar [4] [dʒizatʃi'na(x)] <> *vt* to drive mad. <> *vi* to go mad.

desatino [dʒiza'tʃinu] *m* idiocy.

desativar [4] [dʒizatʃi'va(x)] *vt* **-1.** [tornar inativo] to close down. **-2.** [desmontar] to deactivate.

desatolar [4] [dʒizato'la(x)] *vt* to pull out of the mud.

desatrelar [4] [dʒizatre'la(x)] *vt* **-1.** [cão] to unleash. **-2.** [cavalo] to unharness.

desatualizado, da [dʒizatwali'zadu, da] *adj* out-of-date.

desautorizar [4] [dʒizawtori'za(x)] *vt* **-1.** [não permitir] to disallow. **-2.** [fazer perder a autoridade] to discredit.

desavença [dʒiza'vẽnsa] *f* **-1.** [briga] enmity. **-2.** [dissensão] dissent.

desavergonhado, da [dʒizavexgo'ɲadu, da] *adj* unashamed.

desavisado, da [dʒizavi'zadu, da] *adj* not made aware.

desbancar [12] [dʒiʒbãŋ'ka(x)] *vt:* ~ **alguém (em algo)** to outdo sb (at sthg).

desbaratar [4] [dʒiʒbara'ta(x)] *vt* **-1.** [dissipar]: ~ **algo (em algo)** to squander sthg (on sthg). **-2.** [arruinar] to destroy. **-3.** [vencer] to defeat.

desbastar [4] [dʒiʒbaʃ'ta(x)] *vt* to thin (out).

desbocado, da [dʒiʒbo'kadu, da] *adj fig* lewd.

desbotado, da [dʒiʒbo'tadu, da] *adj* faded.

desbotar [4] [dʒiʒbo'ta(x)] *vt* to fade.

desbragadamente [dʒiʒbragada'mẽntʃi] *adv* shamelessly.

desbravador, ra [dʒiʒbrava'do(x), ra] *m, f* **-1.** [de terra, mata] explorer. **-2.** [de animais] tamer.

desbravar [4] [dʒiʒbra'va(x)] *vt* **-1.** [terras, matas] to explore. **-2.** [animais selvagens] to tame. **-3.** [cavalo] to break in.

desbundante [dʒiʒbũn'dãntʃi] *adj fam* amazing.

desbundar [4] [dʒiʒbũn'da(x)] *vi fam* [perder compostura] to freak out.

desbunde [dʒiʒ'bũndʒi] *m fam* sensation.

desburocratizar [4] [dʒiʒburokratʃi'za(x)] *vt* to get rid of bureacracy from.

descabelado, da [dʒiʃkabe'ladu, da] *adj* with untidy hair *(depois de subst)*.

descabelar [4] [dʒiʃkabe'la(x)] *vt fam* to ruffle the hair of.

descabelar-se *vp fam* to ruffle one's hair.

descabido, da [dʒiʃka'bidu, da] *adj* **-1.** [absurdo] ridiculous. **-2.** [impróprio] inappropriate.

descadeirado, da [dʒiʃkadej'radu, da] *adj* **-1.** [com dor nas cadeiras]: **estar** ~ to have painful hips. **-2.** [exausto] exhausted.

descalabro [dʒiʃka'labru] *m* disaster, ruin.

descalçar [13] [dʒiʃkaw'sa(x)] *vt* to take off.

descalçar-se *vp* to take off one's shoes/gloves.

descalço, ça [dʒiʃ'kawsu, sa] *adj* barefoot.

descambar [4] [dʒiʃkãn'ba(x)] *vi* **-1.** [para o lado]: ~ **para** to topple towards. **-2.** [degenerar]: ~ **em** to degenerate into.

descampado, da [dʒiʃkãn'padu, da] *adj* uninhabited.

descampado *m* open country.

descansado, da [dʒiʃkãn'sadu, da] *adj* **-1.** [tranqüilo] calm. **-2.** [lento] slow.

descansar [4] [dʒiʃkãn'sa(x)] <> *vt* **-1.** [ger] to rest. **-2.** *fig* [tranqüilizar] to calm. <> *vi* **-1.** [repousar] to rest. **-2.** *fig* [tranqüilizar-se] to calm down. **-3.** *ant & fig* [morrer] to be at rest.

descanso [dʒiʃ'kãnsu] *m* **-1.** [repouso] rest. **-2.** [folga] break. **-3.** [para travessa *etc*] trivet.

descaracterizar [4] [dʒiʃkara(k)teri'za(x)] *vt* to destroy the character of.

descarado, da [dʒiʃka'radu, da] <> *adj* shameless. <> *m, f* shameless person.

descaramento [dʒiʃkara'mẽntu] *m* shamelessness.

descarga [dʒiʃ'kaxga] *f* **-1.** [ato] unloading. **-2.** [vaso sanitário] flush; **dar a ~** to flush. **-3.** [de arma] fire. **-4.** *ELETR*: **~ elétrica** electrical discharge.

descarregar [14] [dʒiʃkaxe'ga(x)] <> *vt*-**1.** [carga] to unload. **-2.** [arma] to fire. **-3.** *ELETR* to discharge. **-4.** [desabafar] to give vent to. <> *vi* [bateria] to go flat.

descarrilamento [dʒiʃkaxila'mẽntu] *m* derailment.

descarrilar [4] [dʒiʃkaxi'la(x)] *vt & vi* to derail.

descartar [4] [dʒiʃkax'ta(x)] *vt* to discard.

descartar-se *vp*: **~-se de** [de carta, pessoa] to get rid of; [de compromisso] to free o.s. of.

descartável [dʒiʃkax'tavɛw] (*pl* -**eis**) *adj* disposable.

descascador [dʒiʃkaʃka'do(x)] *m* peeler.

descascar [12] [dʒiʃkaʃ'ka(x)] <> *vt* to peel. <> *vi* -**1.** [perder a casca] to lose its shell. **-2.** [perder a pele] to peel; **com tanto sol, estou descascando todo** with all this sun, I'm peeling all over.

descaso [dʒiʃ'kasu] *m* negligence.

descendência [desẽn'dẽnsja] *f* descendancy.

descendente [desẽn'dẽntʃi] <> *adj* descendent; **ser ~ de** to be a descendant of. <> *mf* [pessoa] descendant.

descender [5] [desẽn'de(x)] *vi* -**1.** [pessoa]: **~ de** to be descended from. **-2.** [palavra]: **~ de** to stem from.

descentralização [dʒisẽntraliza'sãw] *f* decentralization.

descentralizar [4] [dʒiʃsẽntrali'za(x)] *vt* to decentralize.

descer [25] [de'se(x)] <> *vt* -**1.** [escada] to go down. **-2.** [carga] to take down. <> *vi* -**1.** [ger] to go down. **-2.** [de ônibus] to get off.

descida [de'sida] *f* [declive] descent.

desclassificação [dʒiʃklasifika'sãw] (*pl* -**ões**) *f* disqualification.

desclassificar [12] [dʒiʃklasifi'ka(x)] *vt* -**1.** [eliminar] to disqualify. **-2.** [desmoralizar] to disgrace.

descoberto, ta [dʒiʃko'bɛxtu, ta] <> *pp* >
descobrir. <> *adj* -**1.** [ger] discovered. **-2.** [exposto] uncovered. **-3.** *BANCO* [conta] overdrawn.

descoberta *f* discovery.

a descoberto *loc adv* *FIN* [saque] overdrawn, in the red.

descobridor, ra [dʒiʃkobri'do(x), ra] *m, f* discoverer.

descobrimento [dʒiʃkobri'mẽntu] *m* [de continentes] discovery.

descobrir [59] [dʒiʃko'bri(x)] *vt* -**1.** [ger] to discover. **-2.** [tirar a proteção de] to uncover. **-3.** [estátua] to unveil.

descobrir-se *vp* [tirar a coberta] to appear.

descolado, da [dʒiʃko'ladu, da] *adj* *fam* trendy, cool.

descolar [4] [deʃko'lar] <> *vt* -**1.** [desgrudar]: **~ algo (de)** to detach sthg (from). **-2.** *fam* [conseguir]

to fix up. <> *vi* [afastar-se]: **~ de alguém** to move away from sb.

descolorir [79] [dʒiʃkolo'ri(x)] <> *vt* [tirar a cor] to discolour. <> *vi* [perder a cor] to fade.

descomedido, da [dʒiʃkome'dʒidu, da] *adj* immoderate.

descompassado, da [dʒiʃkõnpa'sadu, da] *adj* -**1.** [ritmo] out of time. **-2.** [desmedido] excessive. **-3.** [desordenado] untidy.

descompor [45] [dʒiʃkõn'po(x)] *vt* [desordenar] to muddle.

descomposto, osta [dʒiʃkõn'poʃtu, ɔʃta] <> *pp* > **descompor**. <> *adj* -**1.** [desalinhado] confused. **-2.** [desfeito] disordered. **-3.** [desfigurado] upset.

descompostura [dʒiʃkõnpoʃ'tura] *f* -**1.** [repreensão] reprimand; **passar uma ~ em alguém** to reprimand sb. **-2.** [insulto] affront.

descompressão [dʒiʃkõnpre'sãw] (*pl* -**ões**) *f* decompression.

descomprometido, da [dʒiʃkõnprome'tʃidu, da] *adj* no longer compromised (*depois de verbo*).

descomunal [dʒiʃkomu'naw] (*pl* -**ais**) *adj* -**1.** [gigantesco] huge. **-2.** [fora do comum] unusual.

desconcentrar [4] [dʒiʃkõnsẽn'tra(x)] *vt* to distract.

desconcentrar-se *vp* to lose concentration.

desconcentrado, da [dʒiʃkõnsex'tadu, da] *adj* lacking concentration.

desconcertado, da [dʒiʃkõnsex'tadu, da] *adj* -**1.** [confuso] confused. **-2.** [frustrado] upset.

desconcertante [dʒiʃkõnsex'tãntʃi] *adj* -**1.** [desorientador] confusing. **-2.** [frustrante] upsetting.

desconcertar [dʒiʃkõnsex'ta(x)] *vt* -**1.** [desorientar] to confuse. **-2.** [frustrar] to upset.

desconcertar-se *vp* -**1.** [desarranjar-se] to break down. **-2.** [perturbar-se] to become bewildered. **-3.** [frustrar-se] to be upset.

desconectar [4] [dʒiʃkonek'ta(x)] *vt* to disconnect.

desconectar-se *vp* [comput] to be disconnected.

desconexo, xa [dʒiʃko'nɛksu, ksa] *adj* -**1.** [incoerente] incoherent. **-2.** [desunido] disconnected.

desconfiado, da [dʒiʃkõn'fjadu, da] *adj* distrustful.

desconfiança [dʒiʃkõn'fjãnsa] *f* distrust.

desconfiar [16] [dʒiʃkõn'fja(x)] <> *vt* [conjeturar]: **~ que** to fear that. <> *vi* -**1.** [ficar suspeitoso] to suspect. **-2.** [não confiar em]: **~ de** to be distrustful of. **-3.** [suspeitar de]: **~ de** to be suspicious of.

desconfortável [dʒiʃkõnfor'tavɛw] (*pl* -**eis**) *adj* uncomfortable.

desconforto [dʒiʃkõn'foxtu] *m* discomfort.

descongelar [4] [dʒiʃkõnʒe'la(x)] *vt* to defrost.

descongestionante [dʒiʃkõnʒeʃtʃjo'nãntʃi] <> *adj* decongestant. <> *m* decongestant.

descongestionar [4] [dʒiʃkõnʒeʃtʃjo'na(x)] *vt* -**1.** to decongest. **-2.** *fig* [trânsito, rua] to clear.

desconhecer [25] [dʒiʃkoɲe'se(x)] *vt* -**1.** [ignorar]

not to know. **-2.** [estranhar] not to recognize. **-3.** [ser ingrato a] to be ungrateful for.

desconhecido, da [dʒiʃkoɲe'sidu, da] <> *adj* [incógnito] unknown. <> *m, f* [pessoa] unknown person.

desconhecimento [dʒiʃkoɲesi'mẽntul] *m* ignorance.

desconjuntado, da [dʒiʃkõnʒũn'tadu, da] *adj* dislocated.

desconjuntar [4] [dʒiʃkõnʒũn'ta(x)] *vt* to dislocate.

desconsideração [dʒiʃkõnsidera'sãw] (*pl*-ões) *f* **-1.** [desrespeito] disrespect. **-2.** [ofensa] insult.

desconsiderar [4] [dʒiʃkõnside'ra(x)] *vt* to overlook.

desconsolado, da [dʒiʃkõnso'ladu, da] *adj* disconsolate.

desconsolar [4] [dʒiʃkõnso'la(x)] <> *vt* to sadden. <> *vi* to become saddened.

➤ **desconsolar-se** *vp* to become dispirited.

descontar [4] [dʒiʃkõn'ta(x)] *vt* **-1.** [deduzir]: ~ algo (de) to deduct sthg (from). **-2.** [título de crédito - pagar] to pay off; [- receber] to receive. **-3.** *fam* [revidar]: ~ algo (em alguém) to pay sthg back (to sb). **-4.** *fig* [não fazer caso de] to take no notice of.

descontentamento [dʒiʃkõntẽnta'mẽntul] `m` **-1.** [desprazer] displeasure. **-2.** [insatisfação] dissatisfaction.

descontentar [4] [dʒiʃkõntẽn'ta(x)] *vt* to displease.

➤ **descontentar-se** *vp* to be displeased.

descontente [dʒiʃkõn'tẽntʃil] *adj* displeased.

descontínuo, nua [dʒiʃkõn'tʃinwu, nwa] *adj* discontinued.

desconto [dʒiʃ'kõntul] *m* discount; **com** ~ at a discount; **dar um** ~ *fig* to make allowances.

descontração [dʒiʃkõntra'sãw] *f* relaxation.

descontraído, da [dʒiʃkõntra'idu, da] *adj* relaxed.

descontrair [68] [dʒiʃkõntra'i(x)] *vt* to relax.

➤ **descontrair-se** *vp* to relax.

descontrolado, da [dʒiʃkõntro'ladu, da] *adj* uncontrolled.

descontrolar [4] [dʒiʃkõntro'la(x)] *vt* to lose control of.

➤ **descontrolar-se** *vp* **-1.** [pessoa] to lose control of o.s. **-2.** [situação] to get out of control.

descontrole [dʒiʃkõn'trolil] *m* lack of control.

desconversar [4] [dʒiʃkõnvex'sa(x)] *vi* to change the subject.

descorar [4] [dʒiko'ra(x)] <> *vt* [desbotar] to discolour. <> *vi* [empalidecer] to turn pale.

descortês, tesa [dʒiʃkox'teʃ, tezal *adj* discourteous.

descortesia [dʒiʃkoxte'zial] *f* discourtesy.

descortinar [4] [dʒiʃkoxtʃi'na(x)] *vt* **-1.** [avistar] to reveal. **-2.** [correndo a cortina] to unveil. **-3.** [revelar]: ~ algo a alguém to reveal sthg to sb.

descoser [5] [dʒiʃko'ze(x)], **descosturar** [dʒiʃkoʃtu'ra(x)] <> *vt* to unstitch. <> *vi* to come unstiched.

descrédito [dʒiʃ'krɛdʒitul] *m* discredit.

descrença [dʒiʃ'krẽnsal] *f* disbelief.

descrente [dʒiʃ'krẽntʃil] *adj* disbelieving.

descrer [37] [dʒiʃ'kre(x)] *vi* to disbelieve: ~ de algo/alguém not to believe in sthg/sb.

descrever [5] [dʒiʃkre've(x)] *vt* **-1.** [expor] to describe. **-2.** [traçar] to trace.

descrição [dʒiʃkri'sãw] (*pl*-ões) *f* description.

descritivo, va [dʒiʃkri'tʃivu, va] *adj* descriptive.

descuidado, da [dʒiʃkuj'dadu, da] *adj* **-1.** [desleixado] uncared-for. **-2.** [irrefletido] careless.

descuidar [4] [dʒiʃkuj'da(x)] *vi*: ~ de algo to neglect sthg.

➤ **descuidar-se** *vp*: ~-se de algo to become careless about sthg.

descuido [dʒiʃ'kujdul] *m* **-1.** [ger] carelessness. **-2.** [erro] error.

desculpa [dʒiʃ'kuwpal] *f* **-1.** [ger] excuse. **-2.** [perdão] forgiveness; **pedir** ~s a alguém por algo to ask sb forgiveness for sthg.

desculpar [4] [dʒiʃkuw'pa(x)] *vt* **-1.** [perdoar]: ~ alguém (por algo) to forgive sb (for sthg). **-2.** [justificar] to give as an excuse.

➤ **desculpar-se** [justificar-se]: ~-se (com alguém) por algo to apologize (to sb) for sthg.

desculpável [dʒiʃkuw'pavew] (*pl*-eis) *adj* forgiveable.

descumprir [6] [dʒiʃkũn'pri(x)] *vt* to disobey.

desde ['deʒdʒil] *prep* **-1.** [tempo] since; ~ então from then on; ~ já straight away. **-2.** [espaço] from.

➤ **desde que** *loc conj* **-1.** [tempo] since. **-2.** [visto que] as. **-3.** [contanto que] as long as.

desdém [deʒ'dẽl] *m* disdain.

desdenhar [4] [deʒde'ɲa(x)] *vt* **-1.** [desprezar] to despise. **-2.** [escarnecer] to scorn.

desdenhoso, osa [deʒde'ɲozu, ɔzal] *adj* disdainful.

desdentado, da [dʒiʒdẽn'tadu, da] *adj* toothless.

desdita [dʒiʒ'dʒital] *f* bad luck.

desdizer [29] [dʒiʒdʒi'ze(x)] *vt* **-1.** [negar] to deny. **-2.** [desmentir] to contradict.

➤ **desdizer-se** *vp* [negar o que havia dito] to retract.

desdobramento [dʒiʒdobra'mẽntul] *m* unfolding, development.

desdobrar [4] [dziʒdo'bra(x)] *vt* **-1.** [abrir] to unfold. **-2.** [dividir]: ~ algo em algo to divide sthg into sthg. **-3.** [aumentar] to develop.

➤ **desdobrar-se** *vp* **-1.** to unfold. **-2.** [empenhar-se]: ~-se (em algo) *fig* to make an effort (at sthg).

deseducar [12] [dʒizedu'ka(x)] *vt* **-1.** [educar mal] to educate poorly. **-2.** [estragar] to spoil.

desejar [4] [deze'ʒa(x)] *vt* **-1.** [querer] to wish; ~ que to hope that; ~ fazer algo to want to do sthg. **-2.** [ambicionar]: ~ algo to wish for sthg; ~ fazer algo to wish to do sthg. **-3.** [formulando votos]: ~ algo a alguém to wish sb sthg. **-4.** [sexualmente] to desire. <> *vi*: deixar a ~ to leave sthg to be desired.

desejável [dese'ʒavew] (*pl* **-eis**) *adj* desirable.

desejo [de'zeʒu] *m* **-1.** [ger] desire. **-2.** [ambição] wish. **-3.** [de grávida] craving.

desejoso, osa [dese'ʒosu, ɔsa] *adj*: ~ **de algo/de fazer algo** keen for sthg/to do sthg.

deselegância [dʒizele'gãnsja] *f* inelegance.

deselegante [dʒizele'gãntʃi] *adj* inelegant.

desembaçar [13] [dʒizĩba'sa(x)] *vt* to wipe the steam of.

desembainhar [4] [dʒizẽmbaj'ɲa(x)] *vt* to unsheathe; [sword] to draw.

desembalar [4] [dʒizĩba'la(x)] *vt* to unwrap.

desembaraçado, da [dʒizẽmbara'sadu, da] *adj* **-1.** [desinibido] uninhibited. **-2.** [livre] free. **-3.** [expedito] prompt. **-4.** [cabelo, novelo] loose.

desembaraçar [13] [dʒizĩbara'sa(x)] *vt* **-1.** [livrar] to free. **-2.** [desemaranhar] to loosen. **-3.** [liberar] to unencumber.

◆ **desembaraçar-se** *vp* **-1.** [desinibir-se] to open up. **-2.** [livrar-se]: ~**-se de algo/alguém** to free o.s. of sthg/sb.

desembaraço [dʒizĩba'rasu] *m* **-1.** [desinibição] ease. **-2.** [agilidade] agility.

desembarcar [12] [dʒizĩbax'ka(x)] <> *vt* **-1.** [carga] to unload. **-2.** [passageiros] to disembark. <> *vi* [descer de transporte] to disembark.

desembargador, ra [dʒizẽmbaxga'do(x), ra] *m, f* high court judge.

desembarque [dʒizĩ'baxki] *m* disembarcation.

desembestar [dʒizĩbeʃ'ta(x)] *vi* [disparar] to bolt.

desembocadura [dʒizĩboka'dura] *f* discharge.

desembocar [12] [dʒizĩbo'ka(x)] *vi* [rio, rua]: ~ **em** to discharge into.

desembolsar [4] [dʒizĩbow'sa(x)] *vt* [gastar] to spend.

desembolso [dʒizĩ'bowsu] *m* [gasto] expenditure.

desembrulhar [4] [dʒizĩbru'ʎa(x)] *vt* to unwrap.

desembuchar [4] [dʒizĩbu'ʃa(x)] *fam* <> *vt* [confessar] to get off one's chest. <> *vi* to open up.

desempacotar [4] [dʒizĩpako'ta(x)] *vt* to unpack.

desempatar [4] [dezĩpa'ta(x)] <> *vt ESP:* ~ **a partida** to score a deciding point or goal in a match. <> *vi* to decide; **a eleição só desempatou no final** the election was only decided at the finish.

desempate [dʒizĩ'patʃi] *m ESP* decision.

desempenhar [4] [dʒizĩpe'ɲa(x)] *vt* **-1.** [ger] to perform. **-2.** [cumprir] to carry out.

desempenho [dʒizĩ'peɲu] *m* performance.

desempregado, da [dʒizĩpre'gadu, da] <> *adj* unemployed. <> *m, f* unemployed person.

desempregar [14] [dʒizĩpre'ga(x)] *vt* to sack, to lay off.

◆ **desempregar-se** *vp* to lose one's job.

desemprego [dʒizĩ'pregu] *m* unemployment.

desencadear [15] [dʒizĩŋka'dʒja(x)] *vt* [provocar] to unleash.

◆ **desencadear-se** *vp* [irromper] to break out.

desencaixar [4] [dʒizĩŋkaj'ʃa(x)] *vt* to dislocate.

◆ **desencaixar-se** *vp* to become dislocated.

desencaixotar [4] [dʒizĩŋkajʃo'ta(x)] *vt* to take out of a box.

desencalhar [4] [dʒizĩŋka'ʎa(x)] <> *vt NÁUT* to set loose. <> *vi* **-1.** *NÁUT* to free itself. **-2.** *fam* [pessoa] to get hitched.

desencaminhar [4] [dʒizĩŋkami'ɲa(x)] *vt* to lead astray.

◆ **desencaminhar-se** *vp* to go astray.

desencantar [4] [dʒizĩŋkãn'ta(x)] *vt* **-1.** [desiludir] to disillusion. **-2.** [de feitiço *etc*] to free from a spell. **-3.** [encontrar] to unearth.

◆ **desencantar-se** *vp* [desiludir-se] to become disenchanted.

desencanto [dʒizĩŋ'kãntu] *m* [desilusão] disenchantment.

desencardir [6] [dʒizĩŋkax'di(x)] *vt* to clean.

desencargo [dʒizĩŋ'kaxgu] *m* [cumprimento] carrying out; **por** ~ **de consciência** to clear one's conscience.

desencarregar-se [14] [dʒizẽŋkaxe'gaxsi] *vp* [desobrigar-se]: ~ **de algo** to unburden o.s. of sthg.

desencavar [4] [dʒizĩŋka'va(x)] *vt* to dig up.

desencontrado, da [dʒizĩŋkõn'tradu, da] *adj* **-1.** [contrário] contrary. **-2.** [desalinhado] out of step.

desencontrar [4] [dʒizĩŋkõn'tra(x)] *vt* [fazer que não se encontrem] to send in different directions.

◆ **desencontrar-se** *vp* **-1.** [não se encontrar]: ~**-se (de)** to diverge (from). **-2.** [perder-se um do outro] to fail to meet one another.

desencontro [dʒizĩŋ'kõntru] *m* **-1.** [falta de encontro] failure to meet. **-2.** [divergência] difference.

desencorajar [4] [dʒizĩŋkora'ʒa(x)] *vt* to discourage.

desencostar [4] [dʒizĩŋkoʃ'ta(x)] *vt*: ~ **algo/alguém (de)** to move sthg/sb away (from).

◆ **desencostar-se** *vp*: ~**-se de algo** to stop leaning against sthg.

desenferrujar [4] [dʒizĩfexu'ʒa(x)] *vt* **-1.** [metal] to remove rust from. **-2.** *fig* [pernas] to stretch; [língua] to polish, brush up.

desenfreado, da [dʒizĩfre'adu, da] *adj* wild.

desenganado, da [dʒizĩŋga'nadu, da] *adj* [sem cura] incurable; [desiludido] disenchanted.

desenganar [4] [dʒizĩŋga'na(x)] *vt* **-1.** [doente] to give up hope for. **-2.** [desiludir] to disillusion.

◆ **desenganar-se** *vp* [desiludir-se]: ~**-se de algo/alguém** to have no illusions about sthg/sb.

desengano [dʒizĩ'gãnu] *m* [desilusão] disillusionment.

desengarrafar [4] [dʒizĩŋgaxa'fa(x)] *vt* **-1.** [líquido] to pour from a bottle. **-2.** *fig* [trânsito] to clear.

desengatar [4] [dʒizĩŋga'ta(x)] *vt* to uncouple.

desengonçado, da [dʒizẽŋgõ'sadu, da] *adj* **-1.** [desconjuntado] disjointed. **-2.** [desajeitado] clumsy.

desengrenado, da [dʒizĩŋgre'nadu, da] *adj AUTO* in neutral.

desengrenar [4] [dʒizĩŋgre'na(x)] *vt AUTO* to put into neutral.

desenhar [4] [deze'ɲa(x)] <> *vt* **-1.** [traçar] to outline. **-2.** *TEC* to design. **-3.** *ARTE* to draw. <> *vi* [traçar desenhos] to draw up.
  ◆ **desenhar-se** *vp* [figurar-se] to take shape.

desenhista [deze'ɲiʃta] *m, f* designer.

desenho [de'zeɲu] *m* **-1.** [expressão de formas] drawing. **-2.** *ARTE & TEC* design; ~ **industrial** technical drawing. **-3.** *CINE:* ~ **animado** (animated) cartoon.

desenlace [dʒizẽn'lasi] *m* unfolding, development.

desenredar [4] [dʒizẽnxe'da(x)] *vt* **-1.** [desembaraçar]: ~ **alguém de** to extricate sb from. **-2.** [resolver] to resolve. **-3.** [descobrir] to unravel.
  ◆ **desenredar-se** *vp* [desembaraçar-se]: ~**-se de** to extricate o.s. from.

desenrolar [4] [dʒizẽnxo'la(x)] <> *m* to progress. <> *vt* **-1.** [estender] to unroll. **-2.** [expor] to unfold.
  ◆ **desenrolar-se** *vp* **-1.** [desenroscar-se] to uncurl o.s. **-2.** [mostrar-se] to open out.

desentender-se [5] [dʒizẽntẽn'dexsil *vp:* ~ **(com)** to disagree (with).

desentendido, da [dʒizẽntẽn'dʒidu, da] *adj:* **fazer-se de** ~ to pretend not to understand.
  ◆ **desentendido** *m* person who does not understand.

desentendimento [dʒizĩntẽndʒi'mẽntu] *m* misunderstanding.

desenterrar [4] [dʒizẽnte'xa(x)] *vt* **-1.** [ger] to dig up. **-2.** [exumar] to exhume. **-3.** [descobrir] to unearth.

desentortar [4] [dʒizẽntox'ta(x)] *vt* to straighten.

desentrosado, da [dʒizẽntro'zadu, da] *adj* out of line.

desentupir [61] [dʒizẽntu'pi(x)] *vt* to unblock.

desenvolto, ta [dʒizẽn'vowtu, ta] *adj* wanton.

desenvoltura [dʒizĩnvow'tura] *f* lack of inhibition.

desenvolver [5] [dʒizĩnvow've(x)] *vt* **-1.** [ger] to develop. **-2.** [melhorar] to improve. **-3.** [teorizar sobre] to expand on. **-4.** [correr] to run.
  ◆ **desenvolver-se** *vp* **-1.** [crescer] to develop. **-2.** [progredir] to progress.

desenvolvido, da [dʒizẽvow'vidu, da] <> *pp* ⊳ **desenvolver.** <> *adj* **-1.** [concebido] conceived. **-2.** [adiantado] advanced. **-3.** [crescido] developed.

desenvolvimento [dʒizĩnvowvi'mẽntul *m* **-1.** [crescimento] development. **-2.** [concepção] conception.

desequilibrado, da [dʒizekili'bradu, da] <> *adj* **-1.** [sem equilíbrio] unbalanced. **-2.** *PSIC* unstable. <> *m, f PSIC* unstable person.

desequilibrar [4] [dʒizekili'bra(x)] *vt* **-1.** [fazer perder o equilíbrio] to unbalance.
  ◆ **desequilibrar-se** *vp* **-1.** *PSIC* to become

unstable. **-2.** *fig* [descontrolar] to get out of control.

desequilíbrio [dʒizeki'librju] *m* **-1.** [falta de equilíbrio] lack of balance. **-2.** *PSIC* instability.

deserção [dezex'sãw] (*pl* -ões) *f* desertion.

deserdar [4] [dezex'da(x)] *vt* to disinherit.

desertar [4] [dezex'ta(x)] <> *vt* [abandonar] to abandon. <> *vi* **-1.** *MIL* to desert. **-2.** [abandonar]: ~ **de algo** to abandon sthg. **-3.** [bandear]: ~ **para algo** to go over to sthg.

deserto, ta [de'zɛxtu, ta] *adj* deserted.
  ◆ **deserto** *m* desert.

desertor, ra [dezex'to(x), ra] *m, f* deserter.

desesperado, da [dʒizeʃpe'radu, da] *adj* **-1.** [sem esperança] desperate. **-2.** [irritado] irritated. **-3.** [intenso - briga, competição] fierce; [- amor] intense.

desesperador, ra [dʒizeʃpera'do(x), ra] *adj* **-1.** [sem esperança] hopeless. **-2.** [irritante] irritating.

desesperança [dʒiziʃpe'rãnsa] *f* despair.

desesperar [4] [dʒizeʃpe'ra(x)] <> *vt* **-1.** [arrasar] to dishearten. **-2.** [irritar] to drive mad. <> *vi* [perder a esperança] to give up hope.
  ◆ **desesperar-se** *vp* **-1.** [perder a esperança] to give up hope. **-2.** [afligir-se] to get upset.

desespero [dʒiziʃ'perul *m* **-1.** [desesperança] despair. **-2.** [aflição] despondency; **levar alguém ao** ~ to lead sb to despair.

desestabilizar [4] [dʒiziʃtabili'za(x)] *vt* to destabilize.
  ◆ **desestabilizar-se** *vp* to become destabilized.

desestimulante [dʒiziʃtʃimulãntʃil] *adj* discouraging.

desestimular [4] [dʒiziʃtʃimu'la(x)] *vt* to discourage.

desfaçatez [dʒiʃfasa'teʃ] *f* effrontery.

desfalcar [12] [dʒiʃfaw'ka(x)] *vt* **-1.** [reduzir] to reduce. **-2.** [privar] to deprive. **-3.** [defraudar] to defraud.

desfalecer [25] [dʒiʃfale'se(x)] *vi* **-1.** [desmaiar] to faint. **-2.** [esmorecer] to lose heart.

desfalque [dʒiʃ'fawkil *m* **-1.** [redução] reduction. **-2.** [privação] loss. **-3.** [fraude] fraud.

desfavorável [dʒiʃfavo'ravɛwl (*pl* -eis) *adj* **-1.** [desvantajoso] unfavourable. **-2.** [oposto] adverse.

desfazer [31] [dʒiʃfa'ze(x)] <> *vt* **-1.** [desmanchar] to undo. **-2.** [dispersar] to disperse. **-3.** [acabar com] to put an end to. **-4.** [anular] to annul. <> *vi* ~ **de** *ou* **em** [desdenhar] to despise.
  ◆ **desfazer-se** *vp* **-1.** [desmanchar-se] to come undone. **-2.** [dispersar-se] to disperse. **-3.** [acabarse] to end. **-4.** [desembaraçar-se]: ~**-se de algo** to get rid of sthg. **-5.** [despojar-se]: ~**-se de algo** to be stripped of sthg. **-6.** *fig* [desmanchar-se]: ~**-se em lágrimas** to burst into tears; ~**-se em sorrisos** to break into smiles; ~**-se em gentilezas** to be desperate to please.

desfechar [4] [dʒiʃfe'ʃa(x)] *vt* **-1.** [disparar] to fire. **-2.** [insultos] to loose off.

desfecho [dʒiʃ'feʃul *m* ending.

desfeita [dʒiʃ'fejtal *f* insult.

desfeito, ta [dʒʃ'fejtu, ta] <> *pp* ⊳ **desfazer.**

◇ *adj* -**1.** [desmanchado] undone. - **2.** [acabado] ended. - **3.** [desarrumada] untidy. - **4.** [anulado] annulled.

desferir [57] [dʒiʃfe'ri(x)] *vt* [aplicar] to direct.

desfiado, da [dʒiʃ'fjadu, da] *adj* -**1.** [meia, tecido] frayed. - **2.** *fig* [assunto, tema] well-worn.

desfiar [16] [dʒiʃ'fja(x)] ◇ *vt* -**1.** [tecido *etc*] to unravel. - **2.** [terço] to unthread. - **3.** [galinha] to cut up. ◇ *vi* [tecido *etc*] to unravel.

desfigurar [4] [dʒiʃfigu'ra(x)] *vt* -**1.** [transformar] to disfigure. - **2.** *fig* [adulterar] to adulterate.

◆ **desfigurar-se** *vp* [transformar-se] to alter.

desfiladeiro [dʒiʃfila'dejru] *m* ravine.

desfilar [4] [dʒiʃfi'la(x)] ◇ *vt* [exibir] to parade. ◇ *vi* [passar em desfile - soldado] to march past; [- manequim, escola de samba] to parade.

desfile [dʒiʃ'filil] *m* [passar em desfile - soldado] march past; [- manequim, escola de samba] parade.

desforra [dʒiʃ'fɔxa] *f* revenge.

desfraldar [4] [dʒiʃfraw'da(x)] *vt* to unfurl.

desfrutar [4] [dʒiʃfru'ta(x)] ◇ *vt* to enjoy. ◇ *vi*: ~ de algo to enjoy sthg.

desfrute [dʒiʃ'frutʃil] *m* [prazer] enjoyment.

desgarrado, da [dʒiʒga'xadu, da] *adj* [perdido] lost.

desgarrar-se [4] [dʒiʒga'xaxsil] *vp* [perder-se]: ~ de algo to lose sight of sthg; ~ (do caminho) to lose one's way.

desgastante [dʒiʒgaʃ'tãntʃil] *adj* -**1.** [estressante] stressful. - **2.** [cansativo] tiring. - **3.** [desprestigiante] damaging.

desgastar [4] [dʒiʒgaʃ'ta(x)] *vt* -**1.** [ger] to wear out. - **2.** [gastar] to wear away. - **3.** [desprestigiar] to damage.

desgaste [dʒiʒ'gaʃtʃil] *m* -**1.** [deterioração] deterioration. - **2.** [dano] harm.

desgostar [4] [dʒiʒgoʃ'ta(x)] ◇ *vt* [contrariar] to displease. ◇ *vi* [não gostar]: ~ de algo to dislike sthg.

◆ **desgostar-se** *vp* [deixar de gostar]: ~-se de algo/de fazer algo to no longer enjoy sthg/doing sthg.

desgosto [dʒiʒ'goʃtu] *m* -**1.** [desprazer] displeasure. - **2.** [pesar] regret.

desgostoso, osa [dʒiʒgoʃ'tozu, ɔza] *adj* -**1.** [triste] sad. - **2.** [contrariado] displeased.

desgovernado, da [dʒiʒgovex'nadu, da] *adj* -**1.** [país] misruled. - **2.** [veículo, animal] out of control.

desgraça [dʒiʒ'grasa] *f* -**1.** [infortúnio] misfortune. - **2.** [miséria] penury. - **3.** *fig* [pessoa inábil]: ser uma ~ to be a disgrace. - **4.** *loc:* cair em ~ [perder o prestígio] to fall from grace.

desgraçado, da [dʒiʒgra'sadu, da] ◇ *adj* -**1.** [desafortunado] unfortunate. - **2.** [miserável] wretched. - **3.** [vil] vile. - **4.** *m fam* [grande] hellish. ◇ *m, f* -**1.** [desafortunado] unfortunate. - **2.** [pessoa vil] beggar.

desgraçar [13] [dʒiʒgra'sa(x)] *vt* to disgrace.

desgravar [4] [dʒiʒgra'va(x)] *vt* to wipe.

desgrenhado, da [dʒiʒgre'ɲadu, da] *adj* -**1.** [despenteado] tousled. - **2.** [desarrumado] untidy.

desgrenhar [4] [dʒiʒgre'ɲa(x)] *vt* [despentear] to tousle.

desgrudar [4] [dʒiʒgru'da(x)] *vt* -**1.** [descolar]: ~ algo de algo to unstick sthg from sthg. - **2.** [afastar]: ~ alguém de alguém/algo *fig* to drag sb away from sb/sthg.

◆ **desgrudar-se** *vp* [afastar-se] to break away.

desguarnecer [25] [dʒiʒgwaxne'se(x)] *vt* -**1.** MIL to unman. - **2.** [despojar]: ~ algo/alguém de algo to take sthg/sb away from sthg.

desidratação [dezidrata'sãwl (*pl* -ões) *f* dehydration.

desidratante [dʒidra'tãntʃil *adj* dehydrating.

desidratar [4] [dʒidra'ta(x)] *vt* to dehydrate.

◆ **desidratar-se** *vp* to become dehydrated.

design [dʒi'zajnil (*pl* -s) *m* design.

designação [dezigna'sãwl (*pl* -ões) *f* -**1.** [nome] designation. - **2.** [escolha] appointment.

designar [4] [dezig'na(x)] *vt* -**1.** [denominar] to designate. - **2.** [simbolizar] to symbolize. - **3.** [determinar] to award. - **4.** [escolher]: ~ alguém para algo to appoint sb as sthg.

designer [dʒi'zajnɛ(x)] (*pl* -s) *mf* designer.

desígnio [de'zignjul *m* design.

desigual [dezi'gwawl (*pl* -ais) *adj* -**1.** [diferente] different. - **2.** [irregular] irregular. - **3.** [injusto] unfair.

desigualdade [dʒizigwaw'dadʒil *f* -**1.** [diferença] difference. - **2.** [injustiça] inequality.

desiludir [6] [dʒizilu'dʒi(x)] *vt*: ~ alguém (de algo /de fazer algo) to dissuade sb (from sthg/from doing sthg); ~ alguém (com algo) to disappoint sb) with sthg).

◆ **desiludir-se** *vp*: ~-se (com algo) to be disappointed (by sthg).

desilusão [dʒizilu'zãwl (*pl* -ões) *f* disappointment.

desimpedido, da [dʒizĩmpe'dʒidu, da] *adj* -**1.** [desatravancado] clear. - **2.** [livre de compromisso] unencumbered.

desimpedir [70] [dʒizĩmpe'dʒi(x)] *vt* to clear.

desinchar [4] [dʒizĩn'ʃa(x)] *vt* to reduce.

desincompatibilizar [4] [dʒizĩŋkõmpatʃibili'-za(x)] *vt* to get rid of incompatibility between.

◆ **desincompatibilizar-se** *vp* to cease to be incompatible.

desincumbir-se [6] [dʒizĩŋkũn'bixsil *vp*: ~ de algo to be released from sthg.

desinência *f* GRAM ending.

desinfetante [dʒizĩnfe'tãntʃil ◇ *adj* disinfectant. ◇ *m* disinfectant.

desinfetar [4] [dʒizĩnfe'ta(x)] *vt* MED to disinfect.

desinflamar [4] [dʒizĩnfla'ma(x)] ◇ *vt* to reduce inflammation in/on. ◇ *vi* to become less inflamed.

desinibido, da [dʒizini'bidu, da] *adj* uninhibited.

desinibir [6] [dʒizini'bi(x)] *vt* to make less inhibited.

◆ **desinibir-se** *vp* to lose one's inhibitions, to come out of o.s.

desintegração [dʒizĩntegra'sãw] *f* disintegration.

desintegrar [4] [dʒizĩnte'gra(x)] *vt* to cause to disintegrate.

➤ **desintegrar-se** *vp* to disintegrate.

desinteressado, da [dʒizĩntere'sadu, da] *adj* **-1.** [sem interesse] disinterested. **-2.** [despreendido] detached.

desinteressar [4] [dʒizĩntere'sa(x)] *vt* : ~ **alguém de algo** to destroy sb's interest in sthg.

➤ **desinteressar-se** *vp*: ~-**se de algo** to lose interest in sthg.

desinteresse [dʒizĩnte'resi] *m* **-1.** [falta de interesse] lack of interest. **-2.** [despreendimento] detachment.

desintoxicação [dʒizĩntoksika'sãw] (*pl* **-ões**) *f* detoxification.

desintoxicar [12] [dʒizĩntoksi'ka(x)] *vt* to detoxify.

desistência [deziʃ'tẽnsja] *f* withdrawal.

desistir [6] [deziʃ'tʃi(x)] *vi* to give up; ~ **de algo** /**de fazer algo** to give up sthg/doing sthg.

desjejum [dʒiʒe'ʒũ] (*pl* **-ns**) *m* breakfast.

deslanchar [4] [dʒiʒlãn'sa(x)] *vi* **-1.** [dar partida] to set off. **-2.** [progredir rápido] to take off.

deslavado, da [dʒiʒla'vadu, da] *adj* brazen.

desleal [dʒiʒ'ljaw] (*pl* **-ais**) *adj* disloyal.

deslealdade [dʒiʒleaw'dadʒi] *f* disloyalty.

desleixado, da [dʒiʒlej'ʃadu, da] *adj* messy.

desleixo [dʒiʒ'lejʃu] *m* mess.

desligado, da [dʒiʒli'gadu, da] *adj* **-1.** ELETR switched off. **-2.** [desconectado] disconnected. **-3.** [afastado]: ~ **de** detached from. **-4.** *fig* [despreendido] indifferent. **-5.** *fig* [distraído] absent-minded.

desligar [14] [dʒiʒli'ga(x)] <> *vt* ELETR to switch off; ~ **o carro** to switch off the engine. <> *vi fam* [despreocupar-se] to switch off.

➤ **desligar-se** *vp* **-1.** [afastar-se]: ~-**se de** to switch off from. **-2.** *fig* [despreender-se]: ~-**se de** to abandon. **-3.** *fig* [distrair-se] to switch off.

deslizamento [dʒiʒliza'mẽntu] *m* slip; ~ **de terra** landslide.

deslizante [dʒiʒli'zãntʃi] *adj* slippery.

deslizar [4] [dʒiʒli'za(x)] *vi* **-1.** [movimentar-se - cisnes, dançarino] to glide; [- terra, encosta] to slide. **-2.** [escorregar] to slip. **-3.** *fig* [falhar] to make a slip.

deslize [dʒiʒ'lizil] *m* **-1.** [escorregão] slip. **-2.** *fig* [falha] blunder. **-3.** *fig* [engano] slip.

deslocado, da [dʒiʒlo'kadu, da] *adj* **-1.** MED dislocated. **-2.** [transferido] transferred. **-3.** *fig* [desambientado] out of place.

deslocamento [dʒiʒloka'mẽntu] *m* **-1.** MED dislocation. **-2.** [movimentação] movement.

deslocar [12] [dʒiʒlo'ka(x)] *vt* **-1.** MED to dislocate. **-2.** [transferir] to transfer. **-3.** [mover] to move.

➤ **deslocar-se** *vp* [mover-se] to move around.

deslumbrado, da [dʒiʒlũn'bradu, da] *adj* dazzled.

deslumbramento [dʒiʒlũnbra'mẽntu] *m* dazzle.

deslumbrante [dʒiʒlũn'brãntʃi] *adj* dazzling.

deslumbrar [4] [dʒiʒlũn'bra(x)] <> *vt* to dazzle. <> *vi* to be dazzling.

➤ **deslumbrar-se** *vp* to be dazzled.

desmaiado, da [dʒiʒma'jadu, da] *adj* **-1.** MED unconscious. **-2.** [pálido] pale.

desmaiar [4] [dʒiʒmaj'a(x)] *vi* to faint.

desmaio [dʒiʒ'maju] *m* faint.

desmamar [4] [dʒiʒma'ma(x)] <> *vt* to wean. <> *vi* to be weaned.

desmancha-prazeres [dʒiʒˌmãnʃapra'zeriʃ] *mf inv* killjoy.

desmanchar [4] [dʒiʒmãn'ʃa(x)] *vt* **-1.** [desfazer] to undo. **-2.** [acabar com] to break off.

➤ **desmanchar-se** *vp* **-1.** [dissolver-se] to come undone. **-2.** *fig* [expandir-se]: ~-**se em algo** to be lavish with sthg.

desmantelar [4] [dʒiʒmãnte'la(x)] *vt* **-1.** [desmontar] to dismantle. **-2.** [desmoronar] to demolish.

➤ **desmantelar-se** *vp* **-1.** [desmontar-se] to fall apart. **-2.** [desmoronar-se] to collapse.

desmarcar [12] [dʒiʒmax'ka(x)] *vt* **-1.** [tirar as marcas de] to remove markings from. **-2.** [adiar] to postpone.

desmascaramento [dʒiʒmaʃkara'mẽntu] *m* unmasking.

desmascarar [4] [dʒiʒmaʃka'ra(x)] *vt* **-1.** [revelar] to reveal. **-2.** [desmoralizar] to demoralize.

desmatamento [dʒiʒmata'mẽntu] *m* deforestation.

desmatar [4] [dʒiʒma'ta(x)] *vt* to deforest.

desmazelado, da [dʒiʒmaze'ladu, da] *adj* slovenly.

desmazelar-se [7] [dʒiʒmaze'laxsi] *vp* to become slovenly.

desmazelo [dʒiʒma'zelu] *m* slovenliness.

desmedido, da [dʒiʒme'dʒidu, da] *adj* immense.

desmembramento [dʒiʒmẽnbra'mẽntu] *m* dismembering.

desmembrar [4] [dʒiʒmẽn'bra(x)] *vt* to divide up.

➤ **desmembrar-se** *vp* to divide.

desmemoriado, da [dʒiʒmemo'rjadu, da] *adj* forgetful.

desmentido [dʒiʒmẽn'tʃidul] *m* contradiction.

desmentir [56] [dʒiʒmẽn'tʃi(x)] *vt* **-1.** [negar] to deny. **-2.** [discrepar de] to disagree with. **-3.** [contradizer] to contradict.

➤ **desmentir-se** *vp* [contradizer-se] to contradict o.s.

desmerecer [25] [dʒiʒmere'se(x)] *vt* **-1.** [menosprezar] to despise. **-2.** [não merecer] not to deserve.

desmesurado, da [dʒiʒmezu'radu, da] *adj* excessive.

desmiolado, da [dʒiʒmjo'ladu, da] *adj* **-1.** [sem juízo] brainless. **-2.** [esquecido] forgetful.

desmistificação [dʒiʒmitʃifica'sãw] (*pl* **-ões**) *f* demystification.

desmistificar [12] [dʒiʒmiʃtʃifi'ka(x)] *vt* to demystify.

desmitificar [dʒiʒmitʃifi'ka(x)] *vt* to dispel the myth about.

desmontar [4] [dʒiӡmõn'ta(x)] <> *vt* **-1.** [separar as partes de] to dismantle. **-2.** *fig* [destruir] to destroy. <> *vi* [apear]: ~ **(de algo)** to dismount (from sthg).

desmontável [dʒiӡmõn'tavɛwl] (*pl* **-eis**) *adj* that can be taken apart, knockdown *US*.

desmoralização [dʒiӡmoraliza'sãw] *f* demoralization.

desmoralizante [dʒiӡmorali'zãntʃi], **desmoralizador, ra** [dʒiӡmoraliza'do(x), ra] *adj* demoralizing.

desmoralizar [4] [dʒiӡmorali'za(x)] *vt* to demoralize.

➡ **desmoralizar-se** *vp* to be demoralized.

desmoronamento [dʒiӡmorona'mẽntu] *m* landslide.

desmoronar [4] [dʒiӡmoro'na(x)] <> *vt* to knock down. <> *vi* to collapse.

desmotivado, da [dʒiӡmotʃi'vadu, da] *adj* demotivated.

desmunhecar [12] [dʒiӡmuɲe'ka(x)] *vi fam* to be camp.

desnatado, da [dʒiӡna'tadu, da] *adj* skimmed.

desnecessário, ria [dʒiӡnese'sarju, rja] *adj* unnecessary.

desnível [dʒiӡ'nivɛw] (*pl* **-eis**) *m* unevenness.

desnivelar [4] [dʒiӡnive'la(x)] *vt* to make uneven.

desnorteado, da [dʒiӡnox'tʃjadu, da] *adj* [perturbado] bewildered.

desnorteante [dʒiӡnox'tʃjãntʃi] *adj* bewildering.

desnortear [15] [dʒiӡnox'tʃja(x)] *vt* **-1.** [desorientar] to disorientate. **-2.** *fig* [perturbar] to confuse.

➡ **desnortear-se** *vp* **-1.** [perder-se] to get lost. **-2.** *fig* [perturbar-se] to become confused.

desnudar [4] [dʒiӡnu'da(x)] *vt* **-1.** [despir] to undress. **-2.** *fig* [revelar] to reveal.

➡ **desnudar-se** *vp* [despir-se] to undress.

desnutrição [dʒiӡnutri'sãw] *f* malnutrition.

desnutrido, da [dʒiӡnu'tridu, da] *adj* malnourished.

desobedecer [25] [dʒizobede'se(x)] *vi*: ~ **(a)** to disobey.

desobediência [dʒizobe'dʒjẽnsja] *f* disobedience.

desobediente [dʒizobe'dʒjẽntʃi] *adj* disobedient.

desobrigar [14] [dʒizobri'ga(x)] *vt*: ~ **alguém de algo/de fazer algo** to release sb from sthg/doing sthg.

desobstruir [74] [dʒizobʃtru'i(x)] *vt* to clear.

desocupação [dʒizokupa'sãw] *f* emptiness.

desocupado, da [dʒizoku'padu, da] <> *adj* **-1.** [ocioso] idle. **-2.** [disponível] available. **-3.** [vazio] empty. <> *m, f* **-1.** [desempregado] unemployed person. **-2.** [vagabundo] layabout.

desocupar [4] [dʒizoku'pa(x)] *vt* **-1.** [deixar livre] to leave free. **-2.** [esvaziar] to empty.

desodorante [dʒizodo'rãntʃi] *m* deodorant.

desodorizar [4] [dʒizodori'za(x)] *vt* to deodorize.

desolação [dezola'sãw] *f* **-1.** [tristeza] sadness.

-2. [devastação] devastation.

desolado, da [dezo'ladu, da] *adj* **-1.** [triste] sad. **-2.** [devastado] devasted.

desolador, ra [dezola'do(x), ra] *adj* [entristecedor] devastating.

desolar [4] [dezo'la(x)] *vt* to devastate.

desonestidade [dʒizoneʃtʃi'dadʒi] *f* dishonesty.

desonesto, ta [dʒizo'nɛʃtu, ta] <> *adj* **-1.** [indigno] contemptible. **-2.** [mentiroso] dishonest. <> *m, f* [pessoa indigna] despicable person.

desonra [dʒi'zõnxa] *f* dishonour.

desonrar [4] [dʒizõn'xa(x)] *vt* to dishonour.

➡ **desonrar-se** *vp* to disgrace o.s.

desonroso, osa [dʒizõn'xozu, ɔza] *adj* dishonourable.

desopilar [4] [dʒizopi'la(x)] *vt* **-1.** *MED* to clear an obstruction from. **-2.** [mente] to relieve.

desoprimir [6] [dʒizopri'mi(x)] *vt* to free from oppression.

desordeiro, ra [dʒizox'dejru, ra] <> *adj* rowdy. <> *m, f* rowdy person.

desordem [dʒi'zɔxdẽ] (*pl* **-ns**) *f* **-1.** [bagunça] mess. **-2.** [tumulto] commotion.

desordenar [4] [dʒizoxde'na(x)] *vt* to upset.

desorganização [dʒizoxganiza'sãw] *f* confusion.

desorganizar [4] [dʒizoxgani'za(x)] *vt* to throw into confusion.

➡ **desorganizar-se** *vp* to be disorganized.

desorientação [dʒizorjẽnta'sãw] *f* disorientation.

desorientar [4] [dʒizorjẽn'ta(x)] *vt* **-1.** [desnortear] to disorientate. **-2.** [perturbar] to bewilder. **-3.** *PSIC* to disturb.

➡ **desorientar-se** *vp* **-1.** [desnortear-se] to become disorientated. **-2.** [perturbar-se] to become disconcerted.

desossar [4] [dʒizo'sa(x)] *vt* to bone.

desovar [4] [dʒizo'va(x)] <> *vi* [pôr ovos] to lay eggs. <> *vt fig* [livrar-se de] to get rid of.

despachado, da [dʒiʃpa'ʃadu, da] *adj* **-1.** [enviado] dispatched. **-2.** [eficiente] efficient.

despachante [dʒiʃpa'ʃãntʃi] *mf* forwarding agent.

despachar [4] [dʒiʃpa'ʃa(x)] *vt* **-1.** [enviar] to send. **-2.** [resolver] to dispatch. **-3.** [atender] to attend to. **-4.** [mandar embora] to get rid of.

despacho [dʒiʃ'paʃu] *m* **-1.** [resolução] determination. **-2.** *ESPIRIT* religious offering.

despedaçar [13] [dʒiʃpeda'sa(x)] *vt* **-1.** [quebrar em pedaços] to smash. **-2.** *fig* [magoar]: ~ **o coração de alguém** to break sb's heart.

➡ **despedaçar-se** *vp* [quebrar-se em pedaços] to smash.

despedida [dʒiʃpe'dʒida] *f* [ato] farewell.

despedir [70] [dʒiʃpe'dʒi(x)] *vt* [demitir] to dismiss.

➡ **despedir-se** *vp* [dizer adeus]: ~**-se (de alguém)** to say goodbye (to sb).

despeitado, da [dʒiʃpej'tadu, da] *adj* **-1.** [invejoso] envious. **-2.** *fam* [que tem o peito magro] flat.

despeito [dʒiʃ'pejtu] *m* [inveja] spite.

➤ **a despeito de** *loc conj* [apesar de] despite.

despejar [4] [dʒiʃpeˈʒa(x)] *vt* - **1.** [inquilino] to evict. - **2.** [entornar] to pour.

despejo [dʒiʃˈpeʒul] *m* [de inquilino] eviction.

despencar [12] [dʒiʃpēŋˈka(x)] *vi* [cair]: ~ **de algo** to fall from sthg.

despender [5] [dʒiʃpēnˈde(x)] *vt* to spend.

despenhadeiro [dʒiʃpeɲaˈdejrul *m* precipice.

despensa [dʒiʃˈpēnsal *f* pantry.

despentear [15] [dʒiʃpēnˈtʒja(x)] *vt* to tousle.

➤ **despentear-se** *vp* *fig* to let one's hair down.

despercebido, da [dʒiʃpexseˈbidu, dal *adj* unnoticed.

desperdiçar [13] [dʒiʃpexdʒiˈsa(x)] *vt* to waste.

desperdício [dʒiʃpexˈdʒisjul *m* waste.

despersonalizar [4] [dʒiʃpexsonaliˈza(x)] *vt* to depersonalize.

despertador [dʒiʃpextaˈdo(x)] (*pl* -**es**) *m* alarm clock.

despertar [4] [dʒiʃpexˈta(x)] ⟨⟩ *m* awakening. ⟨⟩ *vt* - **1.** [acordar] to wake. - **2.** [provocar] to awaken. - **3.** *fig* [tirar]: ~ **alguém de algo** to rouse sb from sthg. ⟨⟩ *vi* - **1.** [ger] to wake up. - **2.** *fig* [sair]: ~ **de algo** to rouse o.s. from sthg.

desperto, ta [dʒiʃˈpextu, tal *adj* awake.

despesa [dʒiʃˈpezal *f* expense.

despido, da [dʒiʃˈpidu, dal *adj* - **1.** [nu] naked. - **2.** *fig* [desprovido]: ~ **de algo** lacking sthg.

despir [57] [dʒiʃˈpi(x)] *vt* [roupa, pessoa] to undress.

➤ **despir-se** *vp* - **1.** [tirar a roupa] to get undressed. - **2.** *fig* [despojar-se]: ~**-se de algo** to abandon sthg.

despistar [4] [dʒiʃpiʃˈta(x)] *vt* to mislead.

desplante [dʒiʃˈplãntʃi] *m* *fig* cheek.

despojado, da [dʒiʃpoˈʒadu, dal *adj* - **1.** [privado]: ~ **de algo** stripped of sthg. - **2.** [desprendido] generous. - **3.** [sem enfeite] unadorned.

despojamento [dʒiʃpoʒaˈmēntul *m* [privação, abandono] shedding.

despojar [4] [dʒiʃpoˈʒa(x)] *vt* - **1.** [roubar] to rob. - **2.** [espoliar] to clean out.

➤ **despojar-se** *vp* [privar-se]: ~**-se de algo** to renounce sthg.

despojos [dʒiʃˈpoʒoʃ] *mpl* remains; ~ **mortais** mortal remains.

despoluir [74] [dʒiʃpoˈlwi(x)] *vt* to clean up.

despontar [4] [dʒiʃpõnˈta(x)] *vi* to rise.

desportista [dʒiʃpoxˈtʃiʃtal ⟨⟩ *adj* sporty. ⟨⟩ *mf* sportsman (*f* sportswoman).

desporto [dʒiʃˈpoxtul *m* sport.

déspota [ˈdɛʃpotal ⟨⟩ *adj* despotic. ⟨⟩ *mf* despot.

despotismo [deʃpoˈtʃiʒmul *m* despotism.

despovoado, da [dʒiʃpoˈvwadu, dal *adj* uninhabited.

desprazer [dʒiʃpraˈze(x)] *m* displeasure.

despregado, da [dʒiʃpreˈgadu, dal *adj* loose.

despregar [14] [dʒiʃpreˈga(x)] ⟨⟩ *vt*: ~ **algo (de)** to unfasten sthg (from); **não despregou os olhos de mim** *fig* he didn't take his eyes off me. ⟨⟩ *vi* to come undone.

➤ **despregar-se** *vp* [soltar-se] to come loose.

desprender [5] [dʒiʃprēnˈde(x)] *vt* - **1.** [soltar]: ~ **alguém/algo (de algo)** to untie sthg (from sthg). - **2.** [escalar] to release.

➤ **desprender-se** *vp* - **1.** [soltar-se]: ~**-se (de algo)** to get free (from sthg). - **2.** [exalar]: ~**-se de algo** to extricate o.s. from sthg.

desprendido, da [dʒiʃprēnˈdʒidu, dal *adj* detached.

desprendimento [dʒiprēndʒiˈmēntul *m* [desapego] detachment.

despreocupado, da [dʒiʃpreokuˈpadu, dal *adj* carefree.

despreparado, da [dʒiʃprepaˈradu, dal *adj* unprepared.

despreparo [dʒiʃpreˈparul *m* lack of preparation.

desprestigiar [16] [dʒiʃpreʃtʃiˈʒja(x)] *vt* to discredit.

despretensioso, osa [dʒiʃpretēnˈsjozu, ɔzal *adj* unpretentious.

desprevenido, da [dʒiʃpreveˈnidu, dal *adj* [distraído] unaware; **ser pego** ~ to be taken by surprise.

desprezar [4] [dʒiʃpreˈza(x)] *vt* - **1.** [menosprezar] to despise. - **2.** [não dar importância] to scorn. - **3.** [não considerar] to disregard.

desprezível [dʒiʃpreˈzivewl (*pl* -**eis**) *adj* - **1.** [vil] despicable. - **2.** [ínfimo] least.

desprezo [dʒiʃˈprezul *m* - **1.** [desdém] disdain. - **2.** [repulsa] revulsion.

desproporção [dʒiʃpropoxˈsãwl (*pl* -**ões**) *f* inequality.

desproporcional [dʒiʃpropoxsjoˈnawl (*pl* -**ais**) *adj*: ~ **(a)** disproportionate (to).

despropositado, da [dʒiʃpropoziˈtadu, dal *adj* unreasonable.

despropósito [dʒiʃproˈpɔzitul *m* - **1.** [disparate] absurdity. - **2.** *fig* [excesso]: **un** ~ more than enough.

desproteger [26] [dʒiʃproteˈʒe(x)] *vt* to abandon.

desprotegido, da [dʒiʃproteˈgidu, dal *adj* [desamparado] vulnerable.

desprover [41] [dʒiʃproˈve(x)] *vt*: ~ **alguém (de algo)** to deprive sb (of sthg).

➤ **desprover-se** *vp*: ~**-se de algo** to strip o.s. of sthg.

desprovido, da [dʒiʃproˈvidu, dal *adj*: ~ **de algo** lacking sthg.

despudor [dʒiʃpuˈdo(x)] *m* shamelessness.

despudorado, da [dʒiʃpudoˈradu, dal *adj* shameless.

desqualificar [12] [dʒiʃkwalifiˈka(x)] *vt* - **1.** [tornar indigno] to render unfit. - **2.** [inabilitar] to disqualify; ~ **alguém (para)** to disqualify sb (from).

➤ **desqualificar-se** *vp* [inabilitar-se]: ~**-se (para)** to be eliminated (from).

desquitar-se [4] [dʒiʃkiˈtaxsil *vp* to get divorced.

desquite [dʒiʃˈkitʃil *m* divorce.

desratização [dʒiʒxatizaˈsãwl *f* extermination of rats and mice.

desratizar [4] [dʒiʒxati'za(x)] *vt* to exterminate rats and mice.

desregrado, da [dʒiʒxe'gradu, da] <> *adj* **-1.** [desordenado] disorderly. **-2.** [devasso] dissolute. <> *m, f* [devasso] debauched person.

desregulado, da [dʒiʃregu'ladu, da] *adj* [motor, aparelho] poorly adjusted.

desregular [4] [dʒiʒxegu'la(x)] *vt* irregular.

desrespeitar [4] [dʒiʒxeʃpej'ta(x)] *vt* **-1.** [desacatar] to disregard. **-2.** [desobedecera] to disobey.

desrespeito [dʒiʒxeʃ'pejtu] *m*: ~ **(a)** disrespect (for).

desrespeitoso, osa [dʒiʒxeʃpej'tozu, ɔza] *adj* disrespectful.

dessa ['dɛsa] = de + esse.

desse ['desi] = de + esse.

destacado, da [dʒiʃta'kadu, da] *adj* **-1.** [separado] detached. **-2.** [proeminente] eminent.

destacamento [dʒiʃtaka'mẽntu] *m* detachment.

destacar [12] [dʒiʃta'ka(x)] *vt* **-1.** [ger] to detach. **-2.** [fazer sobressair] to highlight.

➤ **destacar-se** *vp* [fazer-se notar] to be outstanding.

destacável [dʒiʃta'kavɛw] (*pl* **-eis**) *adj* detachable.

destampado, da [dʒiʃtãn'padu, da] *adj* uncovered.

destampar [4] [dʒiʃtãn'pa(x)] *vt* to remove the lid from.

destapar [4] [dʒiʃta'pa(x)] *vt* to uncover.

destaque [dʒiʃ'takil *m* **-1.** [realce] prominence. **-2.** [pessoa ou assunto relevante] highlight.

desta ['dɛʃta] = de + esta.

deste ['deʃtʃi] = de + este.

destemido, da [dʒiʃte'midu, da] *adj* fearless.

destempero [dʒiʃtẽn'perul *m* **-1.** [disparate] blunder. **-2.** *fam* [diarréia] diarrhoea. **-3.** *fam* [grande quantidade] mountain.

desterrar [4] [dʒiʃte'xa(x)] *vt* to exile.

desterro [dʒiʃ'texul *m* exile.

destilação [deʃtʃila'sãw] *f* distillation.

destilar [4] [deʃtʃi'la(x)] *vt* to distil.

destilaria [deʃtʃila'rial *f* distillery.

destinação [deʃtʃina'sãw] (*pl* **-oes**) *f* destination.

destinar [4] [deʃtʃi'na(x)] *vt* **-1.** [reservar] to put aside. **-2.** [aplicar] to allocate.

➤ **destinar-se** *vp* **-1.** [ser designado]: ~**-se a** to be intended for. **-2.** [dedicar-se] to dedicate oneslf.

destinatário, ria [deʃtʃina'tarju, rja] *m, f* addressee.

destino [deʃ'tʃinul *m* **-1.** [direção] destination. **-2.** [aplicação] purpose. **-3.** [futuro] destiny.

destituição [deʃtʃitwi'sãw] *f* destitution.

destituir [74] [deʃtʃi'twi(x)] *vt* **-1.** [privar]: ~ **alguém de algo** to deprive sb of sthg. **-2.** [demitir]: ~ **alguém (de algo)** to deprive sb (of sthg).

destoante [dʒiʃto'ãntʃil *adj* **-1.** [desafinado] discordant. **-2.** [divergente] divergent.

destoar [20] [dʒiʃto'a(x)] *vi* **-1.** [desafinar] to be out of tune. **-2.** [divergir]: ~ **de algo** to diverge from

sthg. **-3.** [não condizer]: ~ **de algo** to clash with sthg.

destorcer [25] [dʒiʃtox'se(x)] *vt* [endireitar] to straighten.

destorcido, da [dʒiʃtox'sidu, da] *adj* untwisted.

destrambelhado, da [dʒiʃtränbe'ʎadu, da] *adj* **-1.** [aloprado] foolish. **-2.** [desajeitado] awkward. **-3.** [sem propósito] hair-brained.

destrancar [12] [dʒiʃträŋ'ka(x)] *vt* to unlock.

destratar [4] [dʒiʃtra'ta(x)] *vt* to offend.

destravar [4] [dʒiʃtra'va(x)] *vt* **-1.** [porta] to unlock. **-2.** [língua] to loosen.

destreza [deʃ'trezal *f* skill.

destrinchar [4] [dʒiʃtrĩ'ʃa(x)] *vt* **-1.** [resolver] to unravel. **-2.** [detalhar] to detail.

destro, tra ['dɛʃtru, tral *adj* dexterous.

destroçar [13] [dʒiʃtro'sa(x)] *vt* **-1.** [ger] to destroy. **-2.** [despedaçar] to pull to pieces.

destroços [dʒiʃ'trosuʃl *mpl* wreckage *(sg)*.

destróier [dʒiʃ'trɔje(x)] *m* destroyer.

destronar [4] [dʒiʃtro'na(x)] *vt* to dethrone.

destroncar [12] [dʒiʃtrõŋ'ka(x)] *vt* **-1.** [deslocar] to dislocate. **-2.** [decepar] to cut off.

destruição [dʒiʃtruj'sãw] *f* destruction.

destruidor, ra [dʒiʃtruj'do(x), ra] <> *adj* destructive. <> *m, f* destroyer.

destruir [74] [dʒiʃtru'i(x)] <> *vt* **-1.** [ger] to destroy. **-2.** [aniquilar] to annihilate. <> *vi* [ter efeito negativo] to be destroying.

➤ **destruir-se** *vp* **-1.** [a si próprio] to destroy o.s. **-2.** [um ao outro] to destroy one another.

destrutivo, va [dʒiʃtru'tʃivu, val *adj* destructive.

desumano, na [dʒizu'mãnu, nal *adj* inhuman.

desunião [dʒiʒun'jãwl *f* **-1.** [separação] separation. **-2.** [discórdia] discord.

desunir [6] [dʒizu'ni(x)] *vt* [separar] to separate.

desusado, da [dʒizu'zadu, da] *adj* out of date.

desvairado, da [dʒiʒvaj'radu, da] <> *adj* **-1.** [louco] crazy. **-2.** [descontrolado] uncontrolled. <> *m, f* **-1.** [pessoa louca] crazy person. **-2.** [pessoa descontrolada] person who is quite out of control.

desvalido, da [dʒiʒva'lidu, da] *adj* **-1.** [desamparado] destitute. **-2.** [miserável] wretched.

desvalorização [dʒiʒvaloriza'sãw] (*pl* **-ões**) *f* devaluation.

desvalorizar [4] [dʒiʃvalori'za(x)] *vt & vi* to devalue.

➤ **desvalorizar-se** *vp* to undervalue o.s.

desvanecer [25] [dʒiʒvane'se(x)] *vt* [dissipar] to dispel.

➤ **desvanecer-se** *vp* **-1.** [dissipar-se] to disappear. **-2.** [desbotar-se] to fade.

desvanecido, da [dʒiʒvane'sidu, da] *adj* **-1.** [dissipado] dispelled. **-2.** [desbotado] faded.

desvantagem [dʒiʒvãn'taʒẽl (*pl* **-ns**) *f* disadvantage; **em** ~ at a disadvantage.

desvantajoso, osa [dʒiʒvãnta'ʒozu, ɔzal *adj* disadvantageous.

desvão [dʒiʒ'vãwl *m* loft.

desvario [dʒiʒva'riwl *m* madness.

desvelar [4] [dʒiʒve'la(x)] vt -**1.** [provocar vigília] to keep awake. -**2.** [descobrir] to uncover; ~ **uma estátua** to unveil a statue. -**3.** [aclarar] to clear up.

➤ **desvelar-se** vp to stay awake.

desvelo [dʒiʒ'velul m [zelo] zeal.

desvencilhar [4] [dʒiʒvẽnsi'ʎa(x)] vt [soltar]: ~ **algo/alguém (de algo)** to save sthg/sb (from sthg).

➤ **desvencilhar-se** vp -**1.** [soltar-se]: ~-**se (de algo)** to free o.s. (from sthg). -**2.** fig [livrar-se]: ~ **de alguém/algo** to get rid of sb/sthg.

desvendar [4] [dʒiʒvẽn'da(x)] vt -**1.** [tirar a venda de] to remove the blindfold from. -**2.** [revelar] to reveal.

desventura [dʒiʒvẽn'tura] f misfortune.

desviar [16] [dʒiʒ'vja(x)] vt -**1.** [mudar a direção de] to deviate. -**2.** fig [roubar] to misappropriate.

➤ **desviar-se** vp [mudar a direção] to deviate.

desvincular [4] [dʒiʒvĩŋku'la(x)] vt: ~ **algo de algo** to dissociate sthg from sthg.

➤ **desvincular-se** vp: ~-**se de algo/alguém** to break ties with sthg/sb.

desvio [dʒiʒ'viw] m -**1.** [mudança de direção] diversion. -**2.** [da coluna vertebral] curvature. -**3.** fig deviation. -**4.** [roubo] misappropriation.

desvirar [4] [dʒiʒvi'ra(x)] vt to turn back to the normal position.

desvirginar [4] [dʒiʒvixʒi'na(x)] vt to deflower.

desvirtuar [4] [dʒiʒvix'twa(x)] vt to misconstrue.

detalhadamente [detaʎada'mẽntʃil adv in detail.

detalhado, da [deta'ʎadu, da] adj detailed.

detalhar [4] [deta'ʎa(x)] vt to detail.

detalhe [de'taʎil m detail; **entrar em** ~**s** to go into detail.

detalhista [deta'ʎiʃta] adj meticulous.

detecção [detek'sãwl f detection.

detectar [4] [detek'ta(x)] vt to detect.

detector [detek'to(x)] (pl -**es**) m detector.

detenção [detẽn'sãwl (pl -**ões**) f detention.

détente [de'tãntʃil f POL détente.

detento, ta [de'tẽntu, ta] m, f prisoner.

detentor, ra [detẽn'to(x), ra] m, f holder.

deter [1] [de'te(x)] vt -**1.** [parar] to stop. -**2.** [prender] to detain. -**3.** [manter, reter] to keep. -**4.** [reprimir] to hold back. -**5.** [ter em seu poder] to retain.

➤ **deter-se** vp -**1.** [parar] to stop. -**2.** [ficar] to remain. -**3.** [reprimir-se] to hold back. -**4.** [ocupar-se]: ~-**se em algo** to dwell on sthg.

detergente [detex'ʒẽntʃil <> adj cleansing. <> m detergent.

deterioração [deterjora'sãwl f deterioration.

deteriorar [4] [deterjo'ra(x)] <> vt -**1.** [estragar] to spoil. -**2.** [piorar] to damage. <> vi [piorar] to worsen.

➤ **deteriorar-se** vp -**1.** [estragar] to become spoiled. -**2.** fig [piorar] to deteriorate.

determinação [detexmina'sãwl (pl -**ões**) f -**1.** [empenho] determination. -**2.** [ordem] order.

determinado, da [detexmi'nadu, da] adj -**1.** [resoluto] determined. -**2.** [estabelecido] fixed. -**3.**

(antes de subst) [certo] certain; **em ~ momento ...** at a certain moment.

determinante [detexmi'nãntʃil <> adj determining. <> m MAT determinant.

determinar [4] [detexmi'na(x)] vt -**1.** [ger] to determine. -**2.** [precisar] to state.

➤ **determinar-se** vp [decidir-se]: ~-**se a fazer algo** to decide to do sthg.

detestar [4] [deteʃ'ta(x)] vt to detest.

➤ **detestar-se** vp to detest o.s.

detestável [deteʃ'tavewl (pl -**eis**) adj detestable.

detetive [dete'tʃivil m f detective.

detidamente [detʃida'mẽntʃil adv minutely.

detido, da [de'tʃidu, da] adj -**1.** [retido] retained. -**2.** [preso] detained.

detonação [detona'sãwl (pl -**ões**) f detonation.

detonar [4] [deto'na(x)] <> vt [arma, bomba] to detonate. <> vi -**1.** [arma, bomba] to detonate. -**2.** [trovão] to thunder.

DETRAN (abrev de **Departamento Estadual de Trânsito**) m Brazilian state department responsible for licensing of drivers and vehicles, ≃ DVLA.

detrás [de'trajʃl adv behind.

➤ **detrás de** loc prep behind.

➤ **por detrás** loc adv from behind.

detrimento [detri'mẽntul m: **em ~ de** to the detriment of.

detrito [de'tritul m detritus.

deturpação [detuxpa'sãwl (pl -**ões**) f corruption.

deturpar [4] [detux'pa(x)] vt -**1.** [adulterar] to distort. -**2.** [corromper] to corrupt.

deus, sa [de'wʃ, sal (mpl -**ses**, fpl -**sas**) m, f god.

➤ **Deus** m God; **Deus e o mundo** [todo o mundo] the world and his wife; **graças a Deus!** thank God!; **meu Deus do céu!** my goodness!

deus-dará [,dewʃda'ral m -**1.**: **ficar ao ~** [à ventura] to be left unattended. -**2.**: **viver ao ~** [a esmo] to have no aims in one's life.

deus-nos-acuda [,dewʃnuʃa'kudal m commotion.

devagar [dʒiva'ga(x)] <> adv slowly. <> adj inv fam -**1.** [lento] slow. -**2.** [sem graça] boring; **ser ~ quase parando** to go at a snail's pace.

devagarinho [dʒivaga'riɲul adv nice and slowly.

devanear [15] [deva'nja(x)] vi to muse.

devaneio [deva'nejul m reverie.

devassa [de'vasal f official inquiry.

devassado, da [deva'sadu, da] adj open.

devassidão [devasi'dãwl f licentiousness.

devasso, ssa [de'vasu, sal <> adj debauched. <> m, f debauched person.

devastar [4] [devaʃ'ta(x)] vt -**1.** [assolar] to devastate. -**2.** [despovoar] to drive people out of.

deve [de'vil m COM debit.

devedor, ra [deve'do(x), ra] <> adj [firma, pessoa] in debt. <> m, f debtor.

dever [5] [de've(x)] (pl -**es**) <> m -**1.** [obrigação] duty; **cumprir seu ~** to do one's duty. -**2.** EDUC: ~ **(de casa)** homework; **fazer o ~ (de casa)** to do one's homework. <> vt -**1.** [dinheiro, favores]: ~

algo (a alguém) to owe sthg (to sb). **-2.** [expressando probabilidade]: **deve fazer sol amanhã** it ought to be sunny tomorrow; **deve ser meia-noite** it must be midnight; **ela deve chegar à noite** she should arrive in the evening; **deve ter acontecido alguma coisa** something must have happened. **-3.** [expressando sugestão]: **você deve sair cedo** you ought to go out early. **-4.** [expressando necessidade]: **devo praticar mais esportes** I should do more sport. **-5.** [expressando obrigação]: **você deve ser pontual sempre** you must always be on time. ⬦ *vi* [ter dívida]: **ele deve muito na praça** she owes a lot at the market; **ela deve a todos os amigos** she owes a lot to all her friends, she's in debt to all her friends.

➤ **dever-se a** *vp* [ser consequência de] to be due to.

deveras [de'vɛraʃ] *adv* really.

devidamente [de‚vida'mẽntʃi] *adv* duly.

devido, da [de'vidu, da] *adj* due; **no ~ tempo** in due course.

➤ **devido a** *loc adv* due to.

devoção [devo'sãw] *f* **-1.** RELIG devotion. **-2.** [dedicação] dedication.

devolução [devolu'sãw] (*pl* -ões) *f* return.

devoluto, ta [devo'lutu, ta] *adj* **-1.** [vago, vazio] vacant. **-2.** [jur] repossessed.

devolver [5] [devow've(x)] *vt* **-1.** [restituir] to return. **-2.** [replicar] to respond to. **-3.** [vomitar] to throw up.

devorar [4] [devo'ra(x)] *vt* **-1.** [ger] to consume. **-2.** [comida] to devour. **-3.** *fig* [livro] to read voraciously.

devotar [4] [devo'ta(x)] *vt* : **~ algo a algo/alguém** to devote sthg to sthg/sb.

➤ **devotar-se** *vp* : **~-se a algo/alguém** to devote o.s. to sthg/sb.

devoto, ta [de'votu, ta] ⬦ *adj* devout. ⬦ *m, f* devotee.

dez ['dɛʒ] *num* ten; *veja também* **seis**.

dez. (*abrev de* **dezembro**) Dec.

dezembro [de'zẽnbru] *m* December; *veja também* **setembro**.

dezena [de'zena] *f* **-1.** [ger] ten. **-2.** [em jogo]: **ganhei na ~** I got ten numbers right.

dezenove [deze'nɔvi] *num* nineteen; *veja também* **seis**.

dezesseis [deze'sejʃ] *num* sixteen; *veja também* **seis**.

dezessete [deze'sɛtʃi] *num* seventeen; *veja também* **seis**.

dezoito [de'zoitu] *num* eighteen; *veja também* **seis**.

DF (*abrev de* **Distrito Federal**) *m* Federal District.

dia ['dʒia] *m* **-1.** [gen] day; **bom ~!** good morning!; **de um ~ para outro** from one day to the next; **no ~ anterior/seguinte** the previous/next day; **mais ~, menos dia** sooner or later; **o ~ todo** all day long; **todo ~, todos os ~s** all day, every day; **todo santo ~** every single day. **~ cheio** busy day; **um ~ daqueles** one of those days. **-2.** [data] date; **no ~ dez** on the tenth; **~ de Reis** Twelfth

Night; **~ santo** feast day. **-3.** [luz do sol]: **de ~** in the daytime. **-4.** [atualidade]: **do ~** today's; **em ~** up-to-date; **hoje em ~** nowadays. **-5.** [horário de trabalho]: **~ de folga** day off; **~ útil** working day.

➤ **dias** *mpl* **-1.** [época]: **nos meus ~s** in my day. **-2.** [vida]: **ele está com seus ~s contados** his days are numbered.

dia-a-dia *m* daily routine.

diabetes [dʒia'bɛtʃiʃ] *m ou f* diabetes.

diabético, ca [dʒia'bɛtʃiku, ka] ⬦ *adj* diabetic. ⬦ *m, f* diabetic.

diabo ['dʒiabul] ⬦ *m* devil; **aconteceu o ~** it all happened; **comer o pão que o ~ amassou** to go through hell; **dizer** *ou* **falar o ~ de alguém** to bad-mouth sb; **estar com o ~ no corpo** to be restless; **fazer o ~** to run riot. ⬦ *adj fam*: **o ~ de carro parou** the damned car has stopped. ⬦ *interj* damn!

➤ **como o diabo** *loc adv fam*: **é feia como o ~!** she's as ugly as sin!

diabólico, ca [dʒia'bɔliku, ka] *adj* diabolical.

diabrura [dʒia'brura] *f* devilish trick.

diacho ['dʒiaʃu] *interj fam* what the devil!

diácono ['dʒiakonu] *m* deacon.

diadema [dʒia'dema] *m* diadem.

diáfano, na ['dʒiafãnu, na] *adj* diaphanous.

diafragma [dʒia'fragma] *m* diaphragm.

diagnosticar [12] [dʒiagnoʃtʃi'ka(x)] *vt* diagnose.

diagnóstico [dʒiag'nɔʃtʃiku] *m* diagnosis.

diagonal [dʒiago'naw] (*pl* -ais) ⬦ *adj* diagonal. ⬦ *f* diagonal.

diagrama [dʒia'grãma] *m* diagram.

diagramador, ra [dʒiagrama'do(x), ra] *m, f* typesetter.

diagramar [4] [dʒiagra'ma(x)] *vt* to work as a typesetter.

dialética [dʒia'lɛtʃika] *f* dialectic.

dialeto [dʒia'lɛtu] *m* dialect.

diálise ['dʒializi] *f* dialysis.

dialogar [14] [dʒialo'ga(x)] *vi* **-1.** [conversar]: **~ (com)** to talk (to). **-2.** [negociar]: **~ (com)** to negotiate (with).

diálogo ['dʒialogu] *m* dialogue.

dial-up *m COMPUT* dial-up.

diamante [dʒia'mãntʃi] *m* diamond.

diâmetro ['dʒiãmetru] *m* diameter.

diante ➤ **por diante** *loc adv* : **e assim ~** and so on.

➤ **diante de** *loc adv* in the face of; **~ de algo/alguém** in front of sthg/sb.

➤ **daqui por diante** *loc adv* from now on.

dianteira [dʒiãn'tejra] *f* lead; **na ~** ahead.

dianteiro, ra [dʒiãn'tejru, ra] *adj* front.

diapasão [dʒiapa'zãw] *m* tuning fork.

diapositivo [dʒiapozi'tʃivul] *m* slide.

diário, ria ['dʒiarju, rja] *adj* daily.

➤ **diário** *m* **-1.** [caderno] diary; **~ de bordo** logbook. **-2.** [para viagem] journal. **-3.** [jornal] daily paper. **-4.** *COM* ledger.

➤ **diária** *f* [de hotel] daily rate.

➤ **Diário Oficial** *m* official gazette.

diarista [dʒja'riʃta] *m f* diarist.

diarréia [dʒja'xeja] *f* diarrhoea.

dica ['dʒika] *f fam* hint.

dicção [dʒik'sãw] *f* diction.

dicionário [dʒisjo'narju] *m* dictionary.

dicionarista [dʒisjona'riʃta] *mf* lexicographer.

dicotomia [dʒikoto'mia] *f* dichotomy.

didata [dʒi'data] *mf* teacher.

didático, ca [dʒi'datʃiku, ka] *adj* -**1.** [pessoa] didactic. -**2.** [explicação] instructive.

➡ **didática** *f* didactics.

DIEESE (*abrev de* **Departamento Intersindical de Estatísticas e Estudos Sócio-Econômicos**) *m trade union body for the support of workers in São Paulo.*

diesel ['dʒizɛwl] *m* diesel; **motor (a)** ~ diesel engine.

dieta ['dʒjɛtal] *f* diet; **fazer** ~ to diet.

dietético, ca [dʒje'tɛtʃiku, ka] *adj* dietary; **chocolate** ~ diet chocolate; **bebida** ~ diet drink.

dietista [dʒje'tʃiʃta] *mf* dietician.

difamação [dʒifama'sãw] (*pl* -ões) *f* slander.

difamador, ra [dʒifama'do(x), ra] <> *adj* slanderous. <> *m, f* slanderer.

difamar [4] [dʒifa'ma(x)] *vt* to slander.

difamatório, ria [dʒifama'tɔrju, rja] *adj* defamatory.

diferença [dʒife'rẽnsal] *f* -**1.** [desigualdade] difference. -**2.** [distinção]: **fazer** ~ **entre** to distinguish between; **fazer** ~ to make a difference. -**3.** [prejuízo]: **fazer** ~ **para alguém** to matter to sb. -**4.** [discordância]: **ter** ~**(s) com alguém** to have one's differences with sb. -**5.** MAT remainder.

diferenciação [dʒiferẽnsja'sãw] *f*: **fazer** ~ **entre** to differentiate between.

diferencial [dʒiferẽn'sjaw] (*pl* -ais) <> *adj* differential. <> *m* AUTO differential. <> *f* MAT differential.

diferenciar [16] [dʒiferẽn'sja(x)] *vt*: ~ **algo/alguém (de)** to distinguish sthg/sb (from).

➡ **diferenciar-se** *vp* to differ.

diferente [dʒife'rẽntʃi] <> *adj* different; ~ **de** different from UK, different than US. <> *adv* differently.

diferir [57] [dʒife'ri(x)] *vi*: ~ **(em algo)** to differ (on sthg); ~ **de algo/alguém** to differ from sthg/sb.

difícil [dʒi'fisiw] (*pl* -eis) <> *adj* -**1.** [ger] difficult, hard. -**2.** [delicado] tricky. -**3.** [improvável]: **acho muito** ~ **ele vir hoje** I think it is very unlikely he will come today. <> *adv*: **falar /escrever** ~ to use fancy words. <> *m*: **o** ~ **é** the trouble is.

dificílimo, ma [dʒifi'silimu, ma] *superl* extremely difficult.

dificilmente [dʒifisiw'mẽntʃi] *adv*: ~ **voltarei a falar com ele** it will be hard for me ever to speak to him again.

dificuldade [dʒifikuw'dadʒi] *f* -**1.** [ger] problem; **pôr** ~ **em algo/em fazer algo** to object to sthg/to doing sthg; **ter** ~**s com algo** to have problems

with sthg; **ter** ~ **em fazer algo** to have difficulty in doing sthg. -**2.** [qualidade de difícil] difficulty. -**3.** [impedimento] snag. -**4.** [relutância]: **ter** ~ **em fazer algo** to be loath to do sthg. -**5.** [situação crítica] trouble; **em** ~**(s)** in trouble; **meter-se em** ~**s** to get into trouble; **passar** ~**(s)** to have a hard time.

dificultar [4] [dʒifikuw'ta(x)] *vt* to complicate.

difteria [dʒifte'rial] *f* diphtheria.

difundir [6] [dʒifũn'di(x)] *vt* to spread.

difusão [dʒifu'zãw] *f* transmission.

difuso, sa [dʒi'fuzu, za] *adj* diffuse.

digerir [57] [dʒiʒe'ri(x)] *vt* to digest.

digestão [dʒiʒeʃ'tãw] *f* digestion.

digestivo, va [dʒiʒeʃ'tʃivu, va] *adj* digestive.

digitação [dʒiʒita'sãw] (*pl* -ões) *f* COMPUT keying-in.

digitador, ra [dʒiʒita'do(x), ra] *m, f* keyboarder.

digital [dʒiʒi'taw] (*pl* -ais) *adj* -**1.** [ger] digital. -**2.** [dos dedos] finger.

digitalizado, da [dʒiʒitali'zadu, da] *adj* COMPUT digitized.

digitalizar [4] [dʒiʒitali'za(x)] *vt* COMPUT to digitize.

digitar [4] [dʒiʒi'ta(x)] *vt* COMPUT to key in.

dígito ['dʒiʒitul] *m* digit.

digladiar-se [16] [dʒigla'dʒjaxsil] *vp* -**1.** [com espada] to fight with a sword. -**2.** *fig* [lutar] to battle it out.

dignamente [dʒigna'mẽntʃil] *adv* with dignity.

dignar-se [7] [dʒig'naxsil] *vp*: ~**-se a fazer algo** to deign to do sthg.

dignidade [dʒigni'dadʒil] *f* -**1.** [cargo] office. -**2.** [decência, honra] dignity; **com** ~ with dignity.

dignificar [12] [dʒignifi'ka(x)] *vt* to dignify.

dignitário, ria [dʒigni'tarju, rjal] *m, f* dignitary.

digno, na ['dʒignu, nal] *adj* worthy; **ser** ~ **de algo /de fazer algo** to be worthy of sthg/doing sthg.

digressão [dʒigre'sãw] (*pl* -ões) *f* digression.

dilaceração [dʒilasera'sãw] *f* laceration.

dilacerante [dʒilase'rãntʃil] *adj* agonizing.

dilacerar [4] [dʒilase'ra(x)] *vt* [despedaçar] to tear to pieces.

➡ **dilacerar-se** *vp* [afligir-se] to be torn apart.

dilapidação [dʒilapida'sãw] *f* -**1.** [destruição] dilapidation. -**2.** [esbanjamento] squandering.

dilapidar [4] [dʒilapi'da(x)] *vt* -**1.** [derrubar] to reduce to rubble. -**2.** [esbanjar] to squander.

dilatação [dʒilata'sãw] *f* dilation.

dilatador, ra [dʒitala'do(x), ra] <> *adj* MED dilator. <> *m* MED dilator.

dilatar [4] [dʒila'ta(x)] *vt* -**1.** [ampliar] to dilate. -**2.** [adiar] to delay.

dilema [dʒi'lemal] *m* dilemma.

diletante [dʒile'tãntʃil] <> *adj* dilettantish. <> *mf* dilettante.

diletantismo [dʒiletãn'tʃiʒmul] *m* dilettantism.

diligência [dʒili'ʒẽnsjal] *f* -**1.** [cuidado] diligence. -**2.** [presteza] promptness. -**3.** [pesquisa] enquiry. -**4.** [veículo] stagecoach. -**5.** JUR formality.

diligenciar [16] [dʒiliʒẽn'sja(x)] *vt* to strive for.

diligente [dʒili'ʒẽntʃil] *adj* diligent.

diluente [dʒil'wẽntʃi] <> adj diluent. <> m diluent.

diluição [dʒilwi'sãw] f dilution.

diluir [74] [dʒi'lwi(x)] vt: ~ algo (em algo) to dilute sthg (in sthg).

dilúvio [dʒi'luviw] m flood.

dimensão [dʒimẽn'sãw] (pl -ões) f -1. [ger] dimension. -2. [tamanho] size.

dimensionar [4] [dʒimẽnsjo'na(x)] vt to dimension.

diminuição [dʒiminwi'sãw] f reduction.

diminuir [74] [dʒimi'nwi(x)] <> vt -1. [reduzir] to reduce. -2. [subtrair]: ~ algo de ou em algo to deduct sthg from sthg. <> vi [reduzir-se] to lessen; ~ de peso/largura to decrease in weight/width.

diminutivo [dʒiminu'tʃivul m GRAM diminutive.

diminuto, ta [dʒimi'nutu, ta] adj minute.

dinâmico, ca [dʒi'nâmiku, ka] adj dynamic.

  ◆ **dinâmica** f -1. MEC dynamics (pl). -2. fig [atividade] dynamic; ~ de grupo teamwork.

dinamismo [dʒina'miʒmu] m dynamism.

dinamitar [4] [dʒinami'ta(x)] vt to dynamite.

dinamite [dʒina'mitʃi] f dynamite.

dinamizar [4] [dʒinami'za(x)] vt to motivate.

Dinamarca [dʒina'marka] n Denmark.

dinamarquês, esa [dʒinamax'keʃ, eza] <> adj Danish. <> m, f Dane.

  ◆ **dinamarquês** m [língua] Danish.

dínamo ['dʒinamul m dynamo.

dinastia [dʒinaʃ'tʃia] f dynasty.

dinheirão [dʒiɲej'rãw] m fam: um ~ a mint.

dinheiro [dʒi'ɲejru] m money; ~ vivo hard cash.

dinossauro [dʒino'sawru] m dinosaur.

diocese [dʒjo'sɛzi] f diocese.

dióxido ['dʒjɔksidu] m QUÍM dioxide; ~ de carbono carbon dioxide.

diploma [dʒi'ploma] m diploma.

diplomacia [dʒiploma'sial f -1. [ciência] diplomacy. -2. [representantes] diplomatic corps. -3. fig [tato] tact; com ~ tactfully.

diplomado, da [dʒiploma'du, da] <> adj [formado] graduated. <> m, f graduate.

diplomar [4] [dʒiplo'ma(x)] vt to graduate.

  ◆ **diplomar-se** vp: ~-se (em algo) to get a diploma/degree (in sthg).

diplomata [dʒiplo'mata] mf -1. [representante] diplomat. -2. fig [negociador hábil] mediator.

diplomático, ca [dʒiplo'matʃiku, ka] adj diplomatic.

dique ['dʒikil m dyke.

direção [dʒire'sãw] (pl -ões) f -1. [rumo, sentido] direction; em ~ a towards, headed for. -2. [de empresa] management. -3. [de partido] leadership. -4. [de filme, peça de teatro] direction. -5. [de jornal] editors. -6. [diretores] board of directors. -7. AUTO steering.

direcionamento [dʒiresiona'mẽntul m COMPUT forwarding.

direcionar [4] vt to channel.

direita [dʒi'rejta] f ▷ direito.

direitinho [dʒirej'tʃiɲul adv just right.

direitista [dʒirej'tʃiʃta] mf right-winger.

direito, ta [dʒi'rejtu, ta] adj -1. [lado] right-hand. -2. [destro] right. -3. [digno] honest. -4. [arrumado] straight.

  ◆ **direito** <> m -1. JUR law; ~ civil civil law. -2. [prerrogativa] right. -3. [lado] right side. <> adv properly.

  ◆ **direita** f -1. [lado direito] right-hand side; à ~ on ou to the right. -2. POL right; ser de ~ to be right-wing.

  ◆ **direitos** mpl: ~ autorais copyright (sg); ~ humanos human rights.

diretamente [dʒirɛta'mẽntʃi] adv straight.

diretas [dʒi'rɛtaʃ] fpl POL direct elections.

direto, ta [dʒi'rɛtu, ta] adj -1. [ger] direct. -2. TV [transmissão] live.

  ◆ **direto** adv straight.

diretor, ra [dʒire'to(x), ra] (mpl -res, fpl -ras) m, f -1. [de escola] head. -2. [de empresa, teatro, cinema] director. -3. [de jornal] editor.

diretoria [dʒireto'ria] f -1. [de escola] headship. -2. [de empresa] directorship.

diretório [dʒire'tɔriw] m -1. [conselho] board; ~ acadêmico students' union. -2. COMPUT directory; ~ raiz root directory.

diretriz [dʒire'triʒ] f directive.

DIRF (abrev de Declaração de Imposto de Renda na Fonte) f Brazilian declaration of income tax at source.

dirigente [dʒiri'ʒẽntʃi] mf leader.

dirigir [52] [dʒiri'ʒi(x)] <> vt -1. [administrar - empresa, hotel] to manage; [- filme, peça de teatro] to direct. -2. AUTO to drive. -3. [bicicleta] to ride. -4. [atenção, esforços]: ~ esforços para algo to direct one's energy towards sthg. -5. [enviar] to address. <> vi AUTO to drive.

  ◆ **dirigir-se** vp -1. [encaminhar-se]: ~-se a to go to. -2. [falar com]: ~-se a alguém to speak to sb.

dirimir [6] [dʒiri'mi(x)] vt to settle.

discagem [dʒiʃ'kaʒẽl f dialling; ~ direta direct dialling.

discar [12] [dʒiʃ'ka(x)] vt to dial.

discente [dʒiʃ'sẽntʃi] adj student.

discernimento [dʒisexni'mẽntu] m discernment.

discernir [54] [dʒisex'ni(x)] vt -1. [perceber] to recognize. -2. [distinguir]: ~ entre algo e algo to distinguish between sthg and sthg.

discernível [dʒisex'nivew] (pl -eis) adj perceptible.

disciplina [dʒisi'plina] f discipline.

disciplinador, ra [dʒisiplina'do(x), ra] adj disciplinary.

disciplinar [4] [dʒisipli'na(x)] <> adj disciplinary. <> vt to discipline.

  ◆ **disciplinar-se** vp to discipline o.s.

discípulo, la [dʒi'sipulu, la] m, f disciple.

disc-jóquei [dʒisk'ʒɔkej] (pl disc-jóqueis) mf disc jockey.

disco ['dʒiʃkul m -1. [ger] disc; ~ voador flying

saucer. **-2.** *MÚS* record; ~ **laser** compact disc; **mudar o** ~ *fig* to stop banging on; **não mudar o** ~ to keep banging on. **-3.** [de telefone] dial. **-4.** *COMPUT* disk; ~ **flexível/rígido** floppy/hard disk; ~ **de sistema** system disk.

discordância [dʒiʃkox'dãnsja] *f* **-1.** [ger] disagreement. **-2.** [resultados, opinião, gosto] difference.

discordante [dʒiʃkox'dãntʃi] *adj* at variance.

discordar [4] [dʒiʃkox'da(x)] *vi*: ~ **(de algo/alguém)** to disagree (with sthg/sb).

discórdia [dʒiʃ'kordʒja] *f* discord.

discorrer [5] [dʒiʃko'xe(x)] *vi*: ~ **sobre algo** to talk about sthg (at length).

discoteca [dʒiʃko'tɛka] *f* **-1.** [boate] discotheque. **-2.** [coleção de discos] record collection.

discotecário, ria [dʒiʃkote'kariw, rja] *m, f* disc jockey.

discrepância [dʒiʃkre'pãnsja] *f* discrepancy.

discrepante [dʒiʃkre'pãntʃi] *adj* differing.

discrepar [4] [dʒiʃkre'pa(x)] *vi*: ~ **de algo/alguém** to differ from sthg/sb.

discretamente [dʒiʃkreta'mẽntʃi] *adv* discreetly.

discreto, ta [dʒiʃ'krɛtu, ta] *adj* **-1.** [roupa] modest. **-2.** [pessoa] discreet.

discrição [dʒiʃkri'sãw] *f* discretion.

discriminação [dʒiʃkrimina'sãw] *f* **-1.** [diferenciação] differentiation. **-2.** [segregação] discrimination.

discriminador, ra [dʒiʃkrimina'do(x), ra] *adj* biased.

discriminar [4] [dʒiʃkrimi'na(x)] *vt* **-1.** [listar] to itemize. **-2.** [segregar] to isolate.

discriminatório, ria [dʒiʃkrimina'tɔrju, rja] *adj* **-1.** [lista] itemized. **-2.** [medida] discriminatory.

discursar [4] [dʒiʃkux'sa(x)] *vi*: ~ **(sobre)** to make a speech (about).

discurso [dʒiʃ'kuxsu] *m* speech.

discussão [dʒiʃku'sãw] (*pl* -ões) *f* **-1.** [debate] discussion. **-2.** [briga] argument.

discutido, da [dʒiʃku'tʃidu, da] <> *pp* ▷ discutir. <> *adj* much-discussed.

discutir [6] [dʒiʃku'tʃi(x)] <> *vt* [debater]: ~ **algo (com alguém)** to discuss sthg (with sb). <> *vi* [brigar]: ~ **(com alguém)** to argue (with sb).

discutível [dʒiʃku'tʃivew] (*pl* -eis) *adj* arguable.

disenteria [dʒizẽnte'rja] *f* dysentery.

disfarçado, da [dʒiʃfax'sadu, da] *adj* disguised.
➡ **disfarçada** *f*: **dar uma** ~ **(em algo)** to mask (sthg).

disfarçar [13] [dʒiʃfax'sa(x)] *vt* [dissimular] to disguise.
➡ **disfarçar-se** *vp* [fantasiando-se]: ~-**se de algo** to disguise o.s. as sthg.

disfarce [dʒiʃ'faxsi] *m* disguise.

disfasia [dʒiʃfa'zja] *f MED* dysphasia.

disforme [dʒiʃ'fɔxmi] *adj* [horrendo] deformed.

disfunção [dʒiʃfũn'sãw] (*pl* -ões) *f* dysfunction.

dislexia [dʒiʃlek'sja] *f* dyslexia.

disléxico, ca [diʒ'lɛksiku, ka] *adj* dyslexic.

díspar ['dʒiʃpa(x)] *adj* disparate.

disparado, da [dʒiʃpa'radu, da] *adj* [lançado - tiro, flecha] fired; [- pedra] hurled.
➡ **disparado** *adv* **-1.** [a toda velocidade] at full speed. **-2.** [com grande superioridade] by far.
➡ **disparada** *f*: **em** ~ like a shot.

disparar [4] [dʒiʃpa'ra(x)] <> *vt* [desfechar, lançar - tiro, flecha] to fire; [- pedra] to hurl. <> *vi* **-1.** [descarregar-se] to fire. **-2.** [correr] to shoot off.

disparatado, da [dʒiʃpara'tadu, da] *adj* absurd.

disparate [dʒiʃpa'ratʃi] *m* nonsense.

disparidade [dʒiʃpari'dadʒi] *f* disparity.

disparo [dʒiʃ'parul] *m* shot.

dispêndio [dʒiʃ'pẽndʒul] *m* expense.

dispendioso, osa [dʒiʃpẽn'djozu, ɔza] *adj* costly.

dispensa [dʒiʃ'pẽnsa] *f* dispensation.

dispensar [4] [dʒiʃpẽn'sa(x)] *vt* **-1.** [prescindir] to do without. **-2.** [conceder]: ~ **algo a alguém** to grant sthg to sb. **-3.** [eximir]: ~ **alguém (de algo)** to excuse sb (from sthg).

dispensável [dʒiʃpẽn'savew] (*pl* -eis) *adj* expendable.

dispepsia [dʒiʃpep'sja] *f* dyspepsia.

dispersão [dʒiʃpex'sãw] *f* dispersal.

dispersar [4] [dʒiʃpex'sa(x)] *vt* to disperse.
➡ **dispersar-se** *vp* to disperse.

dispersivo, va [dʒiʃpex'sivu, va] *adj* **-1.** [pessoa] easily distracted. **-2.** [barulho] distracting.

display *m* display.

displicência [dʒiʃpli'sẽnsja] *f* carelessness.

displicente [dʒiʃpli'sẽntʃi] *adj* careless.

disponibilidade [dʒiʃponibili'dadʒi] *f* availability; **em** ~ openly available.

disponível [dʒiʃpo'nivɛw] (*pl* -eis) *adj* available.

dispor [45] [dʒiʃ'po(x)] <> *m*: **ao** ~ **de alguém** at sb's disposal. <> *vt* **-1.** [arrumar] to arrange. **-2.** [determinar] to decide. <> *vi* **-1.** [usar]: ~ **de** to have at one's disposal; **disponha!** go ahead! **-2.** [ter]: ~ **de** to have available.
➡ **dispor-se** *vp* **-1.** [decidir-se] to decide. **-2.** [propor-se] to be prepared.

disposição [dʒiʃpozi'sãw] *m* **-1.** [arrumação] arrangement. **-2.** [ânimo, vontade]: **minha** ~ **para trabalhar hoje é pouca** I don't feel much like working today. **-3.** [subordinação]: **à** ~ **de** available to.

dispositivo [dʒiʃpozi'tʃivul] *m* **-1.** [mecanismo] mechanism, device; ~ **intra-uterino** intrauterine device. **-2.** *JUR* provision. **-3.** *fig* [meio] measures (*pl*).

disposto, ta [dʒiʃ'poʃtu, ta] *adj* **-1.** [arrumado] arranged. **-2.** [animado] in a good mood; ~ **a algo/a fazer algo** willing for sthg/to do sthg.

disputa [dʒiʃ'putal] *f* **-1.** [briga] dispute. **-2.** [competição] contest.

disputar [4] [dʒiʃpu'ta(x)] <> *vt* **-1.** [concorrer a] to enter. **-2.** [competir por] to compete for. <> *vi* [rivalizar]: ~ **com algo/alguém** to rival sthg/sb.

disquete [dʒiʃ'kɛtʃi] *m COMPUT* floppy disk.

dissabor [dʒisa'bo(x)] *m* annoyance.

dissecar [12] [dʒise'ka(x)] vt **-1.** [corpo] to dissect.
-2. fig [analisar] to examine in detail.
disse-me-disse ['dʒisimi'dʒisil] m inv gossip.
disseminação [dʒisemina'sãw] f spread.
disseminar [4] [dʒisemi'na(x)] vt to spread.
➤ **disseminar-se** vp to spread.
dissensão [dʒisẽn'sãw] (pl **-ões**) f dissension.
dissentir [56] [dʒisẽn'tʃi(x)] vi **-1.** [discordar]: ~ **de**
algo/alguém to disagree with sthg/sb. **-2.** [discrepar]: ~ **de algo** to be at odds with sthg.
dissertação [dʒisexta'sõw] (pl **-ões**) f **-1.** [tratado]
dissertation. **-2.** [discurso] lecture.
dissertar [4] [dʒisex'ta(x)] vi: ~ **(sobre algo)** to
lecture (on sthg).
dissidência [dʒisi'dẽnsja] f **-1.** [divergência] difference of opinion. **-2.** [cisão] breakaway. **-3.** [dissidentes] dissidents (pl).
dissidente [dʒisi'dẽntʃi] <> adj dissident. <>
mf dissident.
dissídio [dʒi'sidʒu] m dispute; ~ **coletivo** collective dispute.
dissimilar [4] [dʒisimi'la(x)] vt to dissimilate.
dissimulação [dʒisimula'sãw] f **-1.** [fingimento]
pretence UK, pretense US. **-2.** [disfarce] disguise.
dissimular [4] [dʒisimu'la(x)] <> vt **-1.** [disfarçar]
to disguise. **-2.** [fingir] to feign. <> vi [disfarçar] to
dissimulate.
dissipação [dʒisipa'sãw] f dissipation.
dissipar [4] [dʒisi'pa(x)] vt **-1.** [dispersar] to
disperse. **-2.** [esbanjar] to squander.
➤ **dissipar-se** vp to vanish.
disso ['dʒisu] = de + isso.
dissociação [dʒisosia'sãw] (pl **-ões**) f dissociation.
dissociar [16] [dʒiso'sja(x)] vt: ~ **algo de algo** to
dissociate sthg from sthg.
dissolução [dʒisolu'sãw] f dissolution.
dissoluto, ta [dʒiso'lutu, ta] adj dissolute.
dissolver [5] [dʒisow've(x)] vt to dissolve.
➤ **dissolver-se** vp **-1.** [extinguir-se] to break up.
-2. [desmanchar-se] to dissolve.
dissonância [dʒiso'nãnsja] f **-1.** MÚS discord. **-2.**
[som desagradável] cacophony. **-3.** fig [desarmonia]
incongruity.
dissonante [dʒiso'nãntʃi] adj **-1.** MÚS discordant.
-2. [sons] jarring. **-3.** fig [desarmônico] incongruous.
dissuadir [6] [dʒiswa'di(x)] vt: ~ **alguém (de algo/de fazer algo)** to dissuade sb (from
sthg/doing sthg).
dissuasão [dʒiswa'zãw] f dissuasion.
dissuasivo, va [dʒiswa'zivu, va] adj dissuasive.
distância [dʒiʃ'tãnsja] f **-1.** [espaço] distance;
manter-se à ~ **de** to keep at a distance from.
-2. fig [intervalo] gap. **-3.** [diferença] difference.
distanciamento [dʒiʃtãnsja'mẽntu] m separation.
distanciar [16] [dʒiʃtãn'sja(x)] vt to separate.
➤ **distanciar-se** vp to move away.
distante [dʒiʃ'tãntʃi] adj **-1.** [longe] distant. **-2.** fig
[alheado] aloof.

distar [4] [dʒiʃ'ta(x)] vi: a cidade não dista muito,
estamos chegando lá the city isn't very far, we're
nearly there; fig os poetas distam muito dos escritores de prosa poets are very different from
prose writers; o Rio dista 420 km de São Paulo
Rio is 420 km from São Paulo.
distender [5] [dʒiʃtẽn'de(x)] vt [ger] to stretch;
[músculo] to pull.
distensão [dʒiʃtẽn'sãw] (pl **-ões**) f **-1.** MED
relaxation. **-2.** POL calm.
distinção [dʒiʃtĩn'sãw] (pl **-ões**) f [ger] distinction;
[honraria] honour.
distinguir [53] [dʒiʃtĩŋ'gi(x)] vt **-1.** [caracterizar] to
typify. **-2.** [discernir] to distinguish. **-3.** [separar] to
differentiate. **-4.** [perceber] to make out. **-5.**
[premiar] to decorate.
➤ **distinguir-se** vp [sobressair-se] to stand
out.
distintivo, va [dʒiʃtʃĩn'tʃivu, va] adj distinctive.
➤ **distintivo** m badge.
distinto, ta [dʒiʃ'tʃĩntu, ta] adj **-1.** [diferente]
different. **-2.** [perceptível] distinct. **-3.** [ilustre]
distinguished. **-4.** [elegante - pessoa] refined; [-
roupa] elegant; [- postura] distinguished.
disto ['dʒiʃtu] = de + isto.
distorção [dʒiʃtox'sãw] (pl **-ões**) f distortion.
distorcer [25] [dʒiʃtox'se(x)] vt to distort.
distração [dʒiʃtra'sãw] (pl **-ões**) f **-1.** [descuido]
carelessness. **-2.** [diversão] distraction.
distraído, da [dʒiʃtra'idu, da] adj **-1.** [desatento]
inattentive. **-2.** [alheio] absent-minded.
distrair [68] [dʒiʃtra'i(x)] vt **-1.** [divertir] to amuse.
-2. [entreter] to entertain. **-3.** [desviar a atenção]: ~
alguém (de) to distract sb (from).
➤ **distrair-se** vp **-1.** [divertir-se] to amuse o.s.
-2. [alhear-se] to lose concentration.
distribuição [dʒiʃtribwi'sãw] (pl **-ões**) f distribution.
distribuidor, ra [dʒiʃtribwi'do(x), ra] (mpl **-es**, fpl
-s) m, f [pessoa] distributor.
➤ **distribuidor** m AUTO distributor.
➤ **distribuidora** f FIN broker.
distribuir [74] [dʒiʃtri'bwi(x)] vt **-1.** [repartir] to
distribute. **-2.** [atribuir] to allocate. **-3.** [entregar]
to deliver. **-4.** [dispor] to arrange. **-5.** [levar] to
supply. **-6.** [dirigir] to bestow.
distrito [dʒiʃ'tritu] m **-1.** [divisão administrativa]
district; ~ **eleitoral** electoral constituency. **-2.**
[policial] administrative area of a town or city in
which there is at least one police station, police
district US.
➤ **Distrito Federal** m [no Brasil] Brasilia.
distúrbio [dʒiʃ'tuxbju] m **-1.** [agitação]
disturbance. **-2.** [sublevação] riot. **-3.** MED & PSIC
problem.
ditado [dʒi'tadu] m **-1.** [exercício escolar] dictation.
-2. [provérbio] saying.
ditador, ra [dʒita'do(x), ra] (mpl **-es**, fpl **-s**) m, f **-1.**
POL dictator. **-2.** fig [pessoa autoritária] despot.
ditadura [dʒita'dura] f dictatorship.

DITADURA MILITAR

In Brazil, in 1964, as happened in many South American countries throughout the 60s and 70s, a military coup deposed the country's president. The hardening of the military regime, especially from 1968 onwards, curtailed the civil liberties of the Brazilian people for two decades, stopping them from electing their rulers by direct vote until 1989. The growing protests of the civilian population, expressed through widespread popular demonstrations from the end of the 70s onwards, gradually restored the democratic freedoms of the country. The military government brought about some economic growth, but deepened foreign debt, increased the inequality of national income distribution and reinforced social inequality, evils which beset Brazil to this day.

ditame [dʒi'tãmi] *m* [preceito] rule.

ditar [4] [dʒi'ta(x)] *vt* -**1.** [texto] to dictate. -**2.** [impor] to impose.

ditatorial [dʒitato'rjaw] (*pl* -**ais**) *adj* [autoritário] dictatorial.

dito, ta ['dʒitu, ta] <> *pp* ⊳ **dizer.** <> *adj* aforementioned.
 ◆ **dito** *m* [provérbio] saying.

dito-cujo, dita-cuja [ˌdʒitu'kuʒu, ˌdʒita'kuʒa] (*mpl* **ditos-cujos,** *fpl* **ditas-cujas**) *m, f fam:* **o ~** the said person.

ditongo [dʒi'tõŋgu] *m* diphthong.

ditoso, osa [dʒi'tozu, ɔza] *adj* [venturoso] fortunate.

DIU (*abrev de* **Dispositivo Intra-Uterino**) *m* IUD.

diurético, ca [dʒju'rɛtʃiku, ka] *adj* diuretic.
 ◆ **diurético** *m* diuretic.

diurno, na ['dʒjuxnu, na] *adj* daytime.

divã [dʒi'vã] *m* couch.

divagação [dʒivaga'sãw] (*pl* -**ões**) *f* -**1.** [devaneio] daydream. -**2.** [digressão] digression.

divagar [14] [dʒiva'ga(x)] *vi* -**1.** [vaguear]: **~ por** to wander about. -**2.** [devanear] to daydream. -**3.** [desviar-se do assunto] to digress.

divergência [dʒivex'ʒẽnsja] *f* -**1.** [discordância] divergence. -**2.** [desacordo] disagreement.

divergente [dʒivex'ʒẽntʃi] *adj* divergent.

divergir [64] [dʒivex'ʒi(x)] *vi* -**1.** [afastar-se] to branch off. -**2.** [discordar]: **~ (de alguém)** to disagree (with sb).

diversão [dʒivex'sãw] (*pl* -**ões**) *f* -**1.** [entretenimento] entertainment, amusement. -**2.** [passatempo] pastime.

diversidade [dʒivexsi'dadʒi] *f* -**1.** [variedade] diversity. -**2.** [divergência] difference.

diversificação [dʒivexsifika'sãw] (*pl* -**ões**) *f* diversification.

diversificar [12] [dʒivexsifi'ka(x)] <> *vt* [tornar diverso] to diversify. <> *vi* [variar] to vary.

diverso, sa [dʒi'vɛxsu, sa] *adj* [diferente] different.
 ◆ **diversos** *adj pl* [vários] various.

divertido, da [dʒivex'tʃidu, da] *adj* entertaining, amusing.

divertimento [dʒivextʃi'mẽntu] *m* entertainment, amusement.

divertir [54] [dʒivex'tʃi(x)] *vt* to entertain, to amuse.
 ◆ **divertir-se** *vp* to have a good time.

dívida ['dʒivida] *f* debt; **~ pública** national debt; **~ externa** foreign debt.

dividendo [dʒividẽndu] *m* dividend.

dividido, da [dʒivi'dʒidu, da] *adj* [em sentimento] divided.

dividir [6] [dʒivi'dʒi(x)] <> *vt* -**1.** [ger] to divide. -**2.** [repartir] to share. -**3.** [separar] to split. -**4.** [demarcar] to mark out. <> *vi* MAT to divide.
 ◆ **dividir-se** *vp* -**1.** [separar-se] to split up. -**2.** [divergir] to be divided.

divindade [dʒivĩn'dadʒi] *f* divinity.

divisa [dʒi'viza] *f* -**1.** [fronteira] border. -**2.** [insígnia] emblem. -**3.** [slogan] slogan.
 ◆ **divisas** *fpl* FIN foreign exchange *(sg).*

divisão [dʒivi'zãw] (*pl* -**ões**) *f* -**1.** [partilha] sharing. -**2.** MAT division. -**3.** [discórdia] disagreement. -**4.** [compartimento] compartment.

divisar [4] [dʒivi'za(x)] *vt* -**1.** [avistar] to make out. -**2.** [marcar] to delimit.

divisível [dʒivi'zivew] (*pl* -**eis**) *adj* divisible.

divisor, ra [dʒivi'zo(x), ra] <> *adj* [separador] separating. <> *m* MAT divisor.

divisório, ria [dʒivi'zɔrju, rja] *adj* dividing.
 ◆ **divisória** *f* partition.

divorciado, da [dʒivox'sjadu, da] <> *adj* divorced. <> *m, f* divorcé (*f* divorcée).

divorciar [16] [dʒivox'sja(x)] *vt* -**1.** [cônjuge] to divorce. -**2.** [separar] to separate.
 ◆ **divorciar-se** *vp* -**1.** [cônjuges]: **~-se (de)** to get divorced (from). -**2.** *fig* [afastar-se] to cut o.s. off.

divórcio [dʒi'vɔxsju] *m* divorce.

divulgação [dʒivuwga'sãw] *f* -**1.** [de notícias] publication. -**2.** [de doutrina, conhecimento, cultura] spread. -**3.** [de segredo] disclosure. -**4.** [de produto] marketing.

divulgador, ra [dʒivuwga'do(x), ra] *m, f* discloser.

divulgar [14] [dʒivuw'ga(x)] *vt* -**1.** [notícias] to publicize. -**2.** [doutrina, conhecimento, cultura] to spread. -**3.** [segredo] to disclose. -**4.** [produto] to market.

dizer [29] [dʒi'ze(x)] <> *vt* -**1.** [ger] to tell. -**2.** [falar] to say; **~ que** to say that; **~ que sim/não** to say yes/no; **~ algo (a alguém)** to tell (sb) sthg; **~ uma prece** to say a prayer. -**3.** [aconselhar, pensar, opinar] to say. -**4.** [significar] to mean; **esse título não me diz nada** the title means nothing to me; **querer ~** to mean; **quer ~, ...** that is to say, ... -**5.** [atrair] to appeal. <> *vi* [falar]: **tive uma idéia! - diga!** I've had an idea! - tell me!; **dito e feito** no sooner said than done. <> *v impess* [afirmar]: **dizem que** it is said that; **a bem ~** [na verdade] in fact; **que dirá** [quanto mais] let alone; [muito menos] even less.
 ◆ **dizer-se** *vp* [afirmar de si mesmo] to claim to be.
 ◆ **dizeres** *mpl* [dito] sayings.
 ◆ **até dizer chega** *loc adv* beyond belief.

por assim dizer *loc adv* so to speak.

dizimar [4] [dʒizi'ma(x)] *vt* -**1.** [destruir em parte] to decimate. -**2.** *fig* [dissipar] to squander.

dízimo ['dizimu] *m RELIG* tithe.

DJ [di'ʒej] (*abrev de* **Disc jockey**) *m* DJ.

dl (*abrev de* **decilitro**) *m* dl.

DLL (*abrev de* **Dynamic Link Library**) *f* DLL.

dm (*abrev de* **decímetro**) *m* dm.

DNA (*abrev de* **ácido desoxirribonucleico**) *m* DNA.

do [du] = **de + o**.

dó ['dɔ] *m* -**1.** [piedade] pity; **ter ~ de alguém** to take pity on sb. -**2.** *MÚS* doh.

doação [dwa'sãw] (*pl* -**ões**) *f* donation.

doador, ra [dwa'do(x), ra] *m, f* donor.

doar [20] ['dwa(x)] *vt*: **~ algo (a alguém/algo)** to donate sthg (to sb/sthg).

dobra ['dɔbra] *f* -**1.** [parte voltada] fold. -**2.** [prega] pleat. -**3.** [vinco] crease.

dobradiça [dobra'disa] *f* hinge.

dobradinha [dobra'diɲa] *f* -**1.** *CULIN* tripe dish. -**2.** *fam* [dupla] pair.

dobrado, da [do'bradu, da] *adj* -**1.** [com dobras] folded. -**2.** [flexionado] bent. -**3.** [duplicado] doubled.

dobrar [4] [do'bra(x)] <> *vt* -**1.** [fazer dobras em] to fold. -**2.** [flexionar] to bend. -**3.** [duplicar] to double. -**4.** [circundar] to turn. -**5.** *fig* [fazer ceder] to win sb over. <> *vi* -**1.** [duplicar-se] to double. -**2.** [sino] to toll. -**3.** [envergar] to bend.

dobrar-se *vp* -**1.** [curvar-se] to stoop. -**2.** *fig* [ceder] to give in.

dobro ['dobru] *m* double.

DOC (*abrev de* **Documento de Operação de Crédito**) *m Brazilian certificate of credit transfer between accounts*.

doca ['dɔka] *f* dock.

doce ['dosi] <> *adj* -**1.** [no sabor] sweet. -**2.** [terno] gentle. -**3.** [água] fresh. <> *m* -**1.** *CULIN* dessert, pudding. -**2.** [loc]: **fazer ~** *fam* to play hard to get; **ser um ~ (de pessoa)** to be a sweetie.

doce-de-coco [,dosidʒi'kokul] (*pl* **doces-de-coco**) *m* [pessoa]: **ser um ~** to be a sweetie.

doceiro, ra [do'sejru, ra] *m, f* confectioner.

docemente [dosi'mẽntʃi] *adv* gently.

docência [do'sẽnsja] *f* teaching.

docente [do'sẽntʃi] <> *adj* teaching. <> *mf* teacher.

dócil ['dɔsiw] (*pl* -**eis**) *adj* docile.

docilidade [dosili'dadʒi] *f* docility.

documentação [dokumẽnta'sãw] *f* -**1.** [em arquivos] documentation. -**2.** [pessoal] papers.

documental [dokumẽn'taw] (*pl* -**ais**) *adj* documentary.

documentar [4] [dokumẽn'ta(x)] *vt* to document.

documentário [dokumẽn'tarju] *m* documentary.

documento [doku'mẽntu] *m* document.

doçura [do'sura] *f* -**1.** [gosto doce] sweetness. -**2.** [suavidade] gentleness.

doença ['dwẽnsa] *f* -**1.** *MED* illness. -**2.** *fig* [mania] obsession.

doente ['dwẽntʃi] <> *adj* -**1.** *MED* sick, ill. -**2.** *fam* [fanático] obsessed. <> *mf* [pessoa] patient.

doentio, tia [dwẽn'tʃiw, tʃia] *adj* -**1.** [débil] sickly. -**2.** [mórbido] unhealthy.

doer [48] ['dwe(x)] *vi* -**1.** [fisicamente] to hurt. -**2.** [causar pena, dó]: **~ (a alguém)** to distress (sb).

dogma ['dɔgma] *m* -**1.** *RELIG* doctrine. -**2.** [opinião] dogma.

dogmático, ca [dog'matʃiku, ka] *adj* dogmatic.

doidão, dona [doj'dãw, dɔna] (*mpl* -**ões**, *fpl* -**s**) *fam adj* -**1.** [maluco] crazy. -**2.** [sob efeito de droga]: **estar ~** to be high.

doideira [doj'dejra], **doidice** [doj'dʒizi] *f* -**1.** [ato de maluco] madness. -**2.** [imprudência] foolishness. -**3.** [exagero]: **ser uma ~** to be crazy.

doidivanas [dojdʒi'vãnaʃ] *mf inv fam* tearaway.

doido, da ['dojdu, da] <> *adj* -**1.** [maluco] mad. -**2.** [imprudente, insensato] foolish. -**3.** [excêntrico] crazy. -**4.** [exagerado] insane. -**5.** [apaixonado]: **ser ~ por** to be mad about. -**6.** [encantado] thrilled. <> *m, f* [pessoa] madman (*f* mad woman).

doído, da [do'idu, da] *adj* -**1.** [dolorido] sore. -**2.** [doloroso] painful. -**3.** [magoado] pained.

doidona [doj'dona] *adj f* ⊳ **doidão**.

dois, duas ['dojʃ, 'duaʃ] *num* two; *veja também* **seis**.

dois-pontos [,dojʃ'põntuʃ] *m inv* colon (*punctuation mark*).

dólar ['dɔla(x)] (*pl* -**es**) *m* dollar.

dolarização [dolariza'sãw] *f* dollarization.

dolarizar [dolari'za(x)] *vt* to base on the dollar.

doleiro, ra [do'lejru, ra] *m, f* dollar dealer.

dolo ['dɔlu] *m* fraud.

dolorido, da [dolo'ridu, da] *adj* sore.

doloroso, osa [dolo'rozu, ɔza] *adj* painful.

dolorosa *f fam* [conta] tab.

doloso, osa [do'lozu, ɔza] *adj* premeditated; **crime ~** premeditated crime.

dom ['dõ] (*pl* -**ns**) *m* -**1.** [dádiva] gift. -**2.** [aptidão] knack. -**3.** [virtude] talent.

dom. (*abrev de* **domingo**) *f* Sun.

domador, ra [doma'do(x), ra] (*mpl* -**es**, *fpl* -**s**) *m, f* tamer.

domar [4] [do'ma(x)] *vt* -**1.** [animal] to tame. -**2.** [subjugar] to subdue. -**3.** [reprimir] to repress.

doméstica [do'mɛʃtʃika] *f* ⊳ **doméstico**.

domesticado, da [domeʃtʃi'kadu, da] *adj* domesticated.

domesticar [12] [domeʃtʃi'ka(x)] *vt* to domesticate.

doméstico, ca [do'mɛʃtʃiku, ka] *adj* domestic.

doméstica *f* maid.

domiciliar [domisi'lja(x)] *adj* home; **prisão ~** house arrest.

domicílio [domi'silju] *m* residence; **entrega a ~** home delivery.

dominação [domina'sãw] *f* domination.

dominador, ra [domina'do(x), ra] <> *adj* domineering. <> *m, f* [pessoa] ruler.

dominante [domi'nãntʃi] *adj* dominant.

dominar [4] [domi'na(x)] <> *vt* -**1.** [controlar] to dominate. -**2.** [conhecer] to master. -**3.** [abranger] to overlook. <> *vi* -**1.** [ter influência]: ~ **em** to hold sway over. -**2.** [predominar]: ~ **em** to stand out in.
→ **dominar-se** *vp* [controlar-se] to control o.s.

domingo [do'mĩŋgu] *m* Sunday; ~ **de Páscoa** Easter Sunday; ~ **de Ramos** Palm Sunday; *veja também* **sexta-feira**.

domingueiro, ra [domĩŋ'gejru, ra] *adj* Sunday.

dominical [domini'kaw] (*pl* -**ais**) *adj* -**1.** RELIG dominical. -**2.** [relativo a domingo] Sunday (*antes de subst*).

dominicano, na [domini'kãnu, na] <> *adj* Dominican. <> *m, f* Dominican.

domínio [do'minju] *m* -**1.** [dominação]: ~ (**sobre**) control (over). -**2.** [posse] power. -**3.** [território] domain. -**4.** [controle] command. -**5.** [conhecimento] mastery. -**6.** COMPUT domain.

dom-juan (*pl* **dom-juans**) *m* Don Juan.

domo ['domu] *m* dome.

dona ['dona] *f* ⊳ **dono**.

donatário, ria [dona'tarju, rja] *m, f* recipient.

donde ['dõde] = **de** + **onde**.

dondoca [dõ'dɔka] *f fam* socialite.

dono, na ['donu, na] *m, f* [proprietário, senhor] owner; ~ **da bola** *fam* big boss; ~ **da verdade** know-all *UK*, know-it-all *US*; **ser** ~ **de seu nariz** to lead one's own life.
→ **dona** *f* -**1.** [título - de casada] Mrs, Ms; [- de solteira] Miss, Ms. -**2.** *fam* [mulher] madam.
→ **dona de casa** *f* housewife.

dons *pl* ⊳ **dom**.

donzela [dõ'zɛla] *f* virgin.

dopado, da [do'padu, da] *adj* -**1.** [pessoa] drugged. -**2.** [cavalo] doped.

dopar [4] [do'pa(x)] *vt* -**1.** [pessoa] to drug. -**2.** [cavalo] to dope.
→ **dopar-se** *vp* to take drugs.

doping *m* ESP doping.

dor ['do(x)] (*pl* -**es**) *f* -**1.** [física] pain. -**2.** [pesar] grief.

doravante [dora'vãntʃi] *adv* from now on.

dor-de-cotovelo [ˌdoxdʒikoto'velu] (*pl* **dores-de-cotovelo**) *f fam* jealousy.

dor-d'olhos ['do(x)dɔ'ʎuʃ] (*pl* **dores-d'olhos**) *f fam* eye infection.

dormência [dox'mẽsja] *f* numbness.

dormente [dor'mẽntʃi] *adj* numb.
→ **dormente** *m* [ferro] sleeper.

dormida [dox'mida] *f* [sono] sleep; **dar uma** ~ to have a sleep.

dormideira [doxmi'dejra] *f* -**1.** [sonolência] drowsiness. -**2.** BOT poppy.

dormido, da [dox'midu, da] *adj fam* [da véspera] yesterday's.

dorminhoco, ca [doxmi'ɲoku, ka] <> *adj* sleepy. <> *m, f* sleepyhead.

dormir [59] [dor'mi(x)] <> *vi* -**1.** [cair no sono] to sleep. -**2.** [ter relações sexuais]: ~ **com alguém** to sleep with sb. <> *vt* -**1.** [sesta, noite]: **dormi uma deliciosa noite** I had a wonderful night's sleep;

dormimos uma sesta ótima esta tarde we had a really good nap this afternoon. -**2.** *loc:* ~ **como uma pedra** to sleep like a log; *fig* ~ **no ponto** [bobear] to miss the boat.

dormitar [4] [doxmi'ta(x)] *vi* to doze.

dormitório [dormi'tɔrju] *m* -**1.** [coletivo] dormitory. -**2.** [quarto] bedroom.

dorsal [dox'saw] (*pl* -**ais**) *adj* dorsal; **coluna** ~ spine, spinal column.

dorso ['doxsu] *m* back.

dos [duʃ] = **de** + **os**.

DOS (*abrev de* Disc Operating System) *m* DOS.

dosagem [do'zaʒẽ] (*pl* -**ns**) *f* dosage.

dosar [4] [do'za(x)] *vt* -**1.** [regular - medicamento, drinque] to measure out; [- palavras] to measure. -**2.** [misturar] to mix.

dose ['dɔzi] *f* -**1.** [remédio] dose. -**2.** [bebida] measure; ~ **cavalar** massive dose; **ser** ~ **para leão** *fam* to be too much.

dossiê [do'sje] *m* dossier.

dotação [dota'sãw] (*pl* -**ões**) *f* allocation.

dotado, da [do'tadu, da] *adj* -**1.** [que tem dote] gifted. -**2.** [possuidor]: ~ **de** endowed with.

dotar [4] [do'ta(x)] *vt* -**1.** [em casamento]: ~ **alguém de algo** to give sthg to sb as a dowry. -**2.** [favorecer]: ~ **alguém/algo de algo** to endow sb/sthg with sthg. -**3.** [prover]: ~ **algo de algo** to provide sthg with sthg.

dote ['dɔtʃi] *m* -**1.** [bens] dowry. -**2.** *fig* [dom natural] gift.

DOU (*abrev de* Diário Oficial da União) *m official Brazilian government publication*, ≃ Weekly Information Bulletin *UK*, ≃ Federal Register *US*.

dourado, da [do'radu, da] *adj* golden; **peixinho** ~ goldfish.
→ **dourado** *m* -**1.** [cor] golden colour. -**2.** [peixe] gilthead.

dourar [4] [do'ra(x)] *vt* to gild; ~ **a pílula** to sugar the pill.

douto, ta ['dotu, ta] *adj*: ~ (**em**) learned (in).

doutor, ra [do'to(x), ra] (*mpl* -**es**, *fpl* -**s**) *m, f* -**1.** MED doctor. -**2.** UNIV: ~ (**em**) doctor (of). -**3.** [conhecedor]: ~ **em** expert on.

doutorado [doto'radu] *m* doctorate.

doutorando, da [doto'rãndu, da] *m* candidate for doctorate.

doutrina [do'trina] *f* doctrine.

doutrinar [4] [dotri'na(x)] <> *vt* -**1.** [ensinar] to teach. -**2.** [convencer] to indoctrinate. <> *vi* to give instruction.

download [do'lodi] (*pl* **downloads**) *m* COMPUT download; **fazer (um)** ~ to download.

doze ['dozi] *num* twelve; *veja também* **seis**.

DP (*abrev de* Distrito Policial) *m* police district.

Dr. (*abrev de* Doutor) *m* Dr.

Dra. (*abrev de* Doutora) *f* Dr.

draga ['draga] *f* dredger.

dragagem [dra'gaʒẽ] (*pl* -**ns**) *f* dredging.

dragão [dra'gãw] (*pl* -**ões**) *m* dragon.

drama ['drama] *m* -**1.** TEATRO play. -**2.** *fig* [catástrofe] tragedy. **-3.** *loc*: **fazer** ~ to make a scene; **ser um** ~ to be a nightmare.

dramalhão [drama'ʎãw] (*pl* **-ões**) *m pej* melodrama.

dramático, ca [dra'matʃiku, ka] *adj* dramatic.

dramatização [dramatʃiza'sãw] (*pl* **-ões**) *f TEATRO* dramatization.

dramatizar [4] [dramatʃi'za(x)] <> *vt* to dramatize. <> *vi fig* [ser dramático] to exaggerate.

dramaturgia [dramatux'ʒia] *f* play-writing.

dramaturgo, ga [drama'turgu, ga] *m, f* dramatist, playwright.

drapeado, da [dra'pjadu, da] *adj* draped.

◆ **drapeado** *m* [caimento] hang.

drástico, ca ['draʃtʃiku, ka] *adj* drastic.

drenagem [dre'naʒẽ] (*pl* **-ns**) *f* drainage.

drenar [4] [dre'na(x)] *vt* to drain.

dreno ['drenu] *m* **-1.** [tubo] drainpipe. **-2.** *MED* drain, drainage tube.

driblar [4] [dri'bla(x)] *vt* **-1.** *FUT* to dribble. **-2.** *fig* [enganar] to dodge.

drible ['dribli] *m FUT* dribble.

drinque ['drĩŋki] *m* drink.

drive ['drajvi] (*pl* **drives**) *m COMPUT* disk drive.

driver ['drive(x)] (*pl* **drivers**) *m COMPUT* driver; ~ **de vídeo** video driver; ~ **de impressora** printer driver.

droga ['drɔga] <> *f* **-1.** [medicamento, entorpecente] drug. **-2.** *fam fig* [coisa ruim]: **ser uma** ~ to be a disaster. <> *interj fam* damn!

drogado, da [dro'gadu, da] <> *adj* drugged. <> *m, f* [pessoa] drug addict.

drogar [4] [dro'ga(x)] *vt* to drug.

◆ **drogar-se** *vp* to take drugs.

drogaria [droga'ria] *f* chemist's (shop) *UK*, drugstore *US*.

dromedário [drome'darju] *m* dromedary.

dropes ['drɔpiʃ] *m inv* drop (*sweet*).

dualidade [ˌdwali'dadʒi] *f* duality.

duas ['duaʃ] *num* ⊳ **dois**.

duas-peças [ˌduaʃ'pɛsaʃ] *mpl* two-piece.

dubiedade [dubje'dadʒi] *f* [ambigüidade] dubiousness.

dúbio, bia ['dubju, bja] *adj* dubious.

dublado, da [du'bladu, da] *adj CINE* dubbed.

dublador, ra [dubla'do(x), ra] *m, f CINE* dubber.

dublagem [du'blaʒẽ] (*pl* **-ns**) *f CINE* dubbing.

dublar [4] [du'blax] *vt CINE* to dub.

dublê [du'ble] *mf* double.

Dublin *n* Dublin.

dublinense [dubli'nẽsi] <> *adj* Dublin (antes de subst). <> *mf* Dubliner.

ducado [du'kadu] *m* duchy.

ducentésimo, ma [dusẽn'tɛzimu, ma] *num* two-hundredth.

ducha ['duʃa] *f* **-1.** [jorro de água] shower; **tomar uma** ~ to take a shower. **-2.** [boxe] shower (cubicle).

duelar [dwe'la(x)] *vi* **-1.** [combater] to fight a duel. **-2.** *fig* [confrontar] to confront each other.

duelo ['dwɛlu] *m* duel.

duende ['dwẽndʒi] *m* goblin.

dueto ['dwetu] *m* duet.

dulcíssimo, ma [duw'sisimu, ma] *adj* very sweet.

dumping ['dãnpĩŋ] *m COM* dumping.

duo ['duw] *m* [dueto] duo.

duodeno [dwo'denu] *m* duodenum.

dupla ['dupla] *f* ⊳ **duplo**.

duplex *m* duplex.

duplicação [duplika'sãw] (*pl* **-ões**) *f* [de receita etc] doubling.

duplicar [12] [dupli'ka(x)] <> *vt* **-1.** [dobrar] to double. **-2.** [aumentar] to redouble. <> *vi* [dobrar] to double.

duplicata [dupli'kata] *f* **-1.** [título] trade note. **-2.** [cópia] duplicate.

duplicidade [duplisi'dadʒi] *f fig* [falsidade] duplicity.

duplo, pla ['duplu, pla] *adj* double; **dupla cidadania** dual nationality.

duque, duquesa ['duki, du'keza] *m, f* duke (f duchess).

durabilidade [durabili'dadʒi] *f* durability.

duração [dura'sãw] *f* duration.

duradouro, ra [dura'doru, ra] *adj* lasting.

duramente [dura'mẽntʃi] *adv* **-1.** [severamente] strongly. **-2.** [cruelmente] harshly.

durante [du'rãntʃi] *prep* during.

durão, rona [du'rãw, rona] (*mpl* **-ões**, *fpl* **-s**) *adj* strict.

durar [4] [du'ra(x)] *vi* to last.

durável [du'ravew] (*pl* **-eis**) *adj* lasting, durable.

durex® [du'rɛkiʃ] *m* [fita adesiva] Sellotape® *UK*, Scotch tape® *US*.

dureza [du'reza] *f* **-1.** [rijeza] hardness. **-2.** [rigor] harshness. **-3.** [crueldade] callousness. **-4.** *fam* [dificuldade]: **ser uma** ~ to be a hardship. **-5.** *fam* [falta de dinheiro]: **estar na maior** ~ to be hard up.

duro, ra ['duru, ra] *adj* **-1.** [ger] harsh. **-2.** [carne, material, água] hard. **-3.** [vida, trabalho, tarefa] tough. **-4.** *fam* [sem dinheiro]: **estar** ~ to be hard up. **-5.** *loc*: **dar** ~ **(para algo/ fazer algo)** to work flat out (for sthg/to do sthg).

durona [du'rona] *f* ⊳ **durão**.

dúvida ['duvida] *f* doubt; **sem** ~ without a doubt.

duvidar [4] [duvi'da(x)] <> *vt*: ~ **que** to doubt that. <> *vi*: ~ **de alguém/algo** to doubt sb/sthg.

duvidoso, osa [duvi'dozu, ɔza] *adj* **-1.** [incerto] doubtful. **-2.** [suspeito] dubious.

duzentos, tas [du'zẽntuʃ, taʃ] *num* two hundred; *veja também* **seis**.

dúzia ['duzja] *f* dozen; **meia** ~ half a dozen.

DVD (*abrev de* **Digital Video Disk**) *m* DVD.

E

e, E [ɛ] m [letra] e, E.
ébano ['ɛbanul] m ebony.
ébrio, ébria ['ɛbrju, 'ɛbrjal] <> adj drunk. <> m, f drunkard.
EBTU (abrev de **Empresa Brasileira de Transportes Urbanos**) f Brazilian company for urban transport planning.
ebulição libuli'sãwl f -1. [de líquido] boiling. -2. fig [agitação] excitement.
e-business [ɛbusi'nɛɛsil m ECON e-business.
eclampsia f eclampsia.
eclesiástico, ca lekle'zjastʃiku, kal adj ecclesiastical.
➜ **eclesiástico** m [membro do clero] clergyman.
eclético, ca le'klɛtʃiku, kal adj eclectic.
eclipsar [4] leklip'sa(x)l vt to eclipse.
eclipse le'klipsil m eclipse.
eclodir [6] leklo'dʒi(x)l vi -1. [surgir] to emerge. -2. [estourar] to break out.
eclosão leklo'zãwl (pl -ões) f -1. [aparecimento] emergence. -2. [desenvolvimento] development. -3. [de flor] blooming.
eclusa le'kluzal f lock (on waterway).
eco ['ɛkul m echo.
ecoar [20] le'kwa(x)l vt & vi to echo.
ecologia lekolo'ʒial f ecology.
ecológico, ca leko'lɔʒiku, kal adj ecological.
ecólogo, ga le'kɔlogu, gal m, f ecologist.
e-commerce [ɛko'mɛxsil m ECON e-commerce.
economia lekono'mial f -1. [ger] economy; ~ doméstica domestic economy; ~ dirigida managed economy; ~ de mercado market economy; ~ mista mixed economy; fazer ~ to economize. -2. [estudo] economics; ~ política political economy.
➜ **economias** fpl [poupança] savings.
econômico, ca leko'nomiku, kal adj -1. [ger] economical. -2. [relativo à economia] economic.
economista lekono'miʃtal mf economist.
economizar [4] lekonomi'za(x)l <> vt -1. [gastar, usar com moderação] to economize on. -2. [acumular] to save. <> vi [fazer economia] to economize.
ecossistema [ɛkosiʃ'temal m ecosystem.
ECT (abrev de **Empresa Brasileira de Correios e Telégrafos**) f Brazilian postal service, ~ The Post Office UK, ~ USPS US.
ecumênico, ca leku'meniku, kal adj ecumenical.
eczema lek'zemal m eczema.
ed. (abrev de **edifício**) m building.
edema le'demal m oedema UK, edema US.
éden ['ɛdɛ̃n] m Eden.
edição ledʒi'sãwl (pl -ões) f -1. [ger] edition; ~ atualizada revised edition; ~ pirata pirate copy. -2. [publicação] publication; -3. [seleção] editing.
edificação ledʒifika'sãwl (pl -ões) f -1. [ger] building. -2. fig [moral, religiosa] edification. -3. fig [instrução] instruction.
edificante ledʒifi'kãntʃil adj -1. [moralizante] edifying. -2. [instrutivo] instructive.
edificar [12] ledʒifi'ka(x)l <> vt -1. [construir] to build. -2. fig [moralmente] to edify. <> vi fig [moralmente] to inspire.
edifício ledʒi'fisjul m building.
Édipo ['ɛdʒipul m ▷ complexo.
edital ledʒi'tawl (pl -ais) m proclamation.
editar [4] ledʒi'ta(x)l vt -1. [ger] to produce. -2. [livro, revista] to publish. -3. [preparar texto] to edit.
edito le'dʒitul m edict.
editor, ra ledʒi'to(x), ral <> adj [casa] publishing. <> m, f -1. [ger] editor. -2. [dono de editora] publisher. -3. RÁDIO & TV producer; ~ de imagem ou de VT video editor. -4. COMPUT: ~ de texto text editor.
➜ **editora** f [estabelecimento] publisher.
editoração ledʒitora'sãwl f editing; ~ eletrônica electronic publishing.
editorar [4] ledʒito'ra(x)l vt [editar] to edit.
editoria ledʒito'rial f section.
editorial ledʒitor'jawl (pl -ais) <> adj editorial. <> m editorial.
editorialista ledʒitorja'liʃtal mf editorial writer.
edredom ledre'dõl (pl -ns) m eiderdown.
educação leduka'sãwl f -1. [ensino] education; ~ física/sexual physical/sex education. -2. [criação] upbringing. -3. [polidez] manners; falta de ~ bad manners.
educacional ledukasjo'nawl (pl -ais) adj educational.
educado, da ledu'kadu, dal adj [polido] well-mannered.
educador, ra leduka'do(x), ral m, f instructor.
educandário ledukãn'darjul m educational establishment.
educar [12] ledu'ka(x)l vt -1. [instruir] to educate. -2. [criar] to bring up. -3. [adestrar] to instruct.
➜ **educar-se** vp [instruir-se] to teach o.s.
educativo, va leduka'tʃivu, val adj educational.
EEUU (abrev de **Estados Unidos da América do Norte**) mpl USA.
efeito le'fejtul m effect; fazer ~ to have an effect; levar a ~ to put into effect; para todos os ~ s to all intents and purposes; sob o ~ de as a result of; ~ colateral side effect; ~ s especiais CINE special effects; ~ estufa greenhouse effect.

efemérides [efe'mεridʒiz] *fpl* **-1.** [notícia diária] daily news. **-2.** [registro] *section of a newspaper listing events that happened in the past on the day of issue.*

efêmero, ra [e'femeru, ra] *adj* [passageiro] ephemeral.

efervescência [efexve'sẽnsja] *f* **-1.** [de líquido] effervescence. **-2.** *fig* [agitação] excitement.

efervescente [eferve'sẽntʃi] *adj* **-1.** [líquido, comprimido] effervescent. **-2.** *fig* [agitado] excited.

efervescer [25] [efexve'se(x)] *vi* **-1.** [líquido] to effervesce. **-2.** *fig* [agitar-se] to become excited.

efetivamente [efεˌtʃiva'mẽntʃi] *adv* **-1.** [permanentemente] permanently. **-2.** [realmente] actually.

efetivar [4] [efetʃi'va(x)] *vt* **-1.** [realizar] to carry out. **-2.** [admitir] to employ.

efetividade [efetʃivi'dadʒi] *f* effectiveness.

efetivo, va [efe'tʃivu, va] *adj* **-1.** [positivo] effective. **-2.** [permanente] permanent. **-3.** [seguro] certain.

efetivo *m* **-1.** MIL military strength. **-2.** COM liquid assets.

efetuar [4] [efe'twa(x)] *vt* to carry out.

eficácia [efi'kasja] *f* **-1.** [de pessoa] efficiency. **-2.** [de medida, tratamento] effectiveness.

eficaz [efi'kaʃ] (*pl* **-es**) *adj* **-1.** [pessoa] efficient. **-2.** [medida, tratamento] effective.

eficiência [efi'sjẽnsja] *f* efficiency.

eficiente [efi'sjẽntʃi] *adj* efficient.

efígie [e'fiʒi] *f* effigy.

efusão [efu'zãw] (*pl* **-ões**) *f* **-1.** [de líquido, gás] spillage. **-2.** *fig* [demonstração] outburst.

efusivo, va [efu'zivu, va] *adj fig* [expansivo] effusive.

e.g. (*abrev de exempli gratia*) e.g.

Egeu [e'gewl] *n*: **o (mar)** ~ the Aegean (Sea).

égide ['εʒidʒi] *f fig* [proteção]: **sob a** ~ **de** under the aegis of.

egípcio, cia [e'ʒipsju, ja] <> *adj* Egyptian. <> *m*, *f* Egyptian.

Egito [e'ʒitul] *n* Egypt.

ego ['εgul] *m* ego.

egocêntrico, ca [ego'sẽntriku, ka] <> *adj* egocentric. <> *m*, *f* egocentric person.

egocentrismo [egosẽn'triʒmul] *m* egocentricity.

egoísmo [e'gwiʒmul] *m* egoism.

egoísta [e'gwiʃta] <> *adj* egotistic. <> *mf* [pessoa] egotist.

egrégio, gia [e'greʒju, ʒja] *adj* (*antes de subst*) [ilustre] distinguished.

egresso, ssa [e'grεsu, sa] *adj* graduate.

egresso *m* **-1.** [ex-detento] ex-prisoner. **-2.** [ex-frade] former monk.

égua ['εgwa] *f* mare.

ei [ej] *interj* hey!

ei-lo ['ejlul] = **eis** + **o**.

eira ['ejra] *f*: **sem** ~ **nem beira** without a penny to one's name.

eis ['ejʃ] *adv* here is/are.

eixo ['ejʃul] *m* **-1.** [de rodas] axle. **-2.** [de máquina] shaft. **-3.** MAT axis. **-4.** [trecho] area (*between two points*). **-5.** *loc*: **entrar nos** ~**s** to be on the right track; **sair dos** ~**s** to lose control.

ejaculação [eʒakula'sãw] (*pl* **-ões**) *f* ejaculation.

ejacular [4] [eʒaku'la(x)] *vt & vi* to ejaculate.

ejetar [4] [eʒe'ta(x)] *vt* to eject.

ela ['εla] ⊳ **ele**.

elã [e'lã] *m* enthusiasm.

elaboração [elabora'sãw] (*pl* **-ões**) *f* preparation.

elaborador, ra [elabora'do(x), ra] *m*, *f* maker.

elaborar [4] [elabo'ra(x)] *vt* to prepare.

elasticidade [elaʃtʃisi'dadʒi] *f* elasticity.

elástico, ca [e'laʃtʃiku, ka] *adj* **-1.** [tecido etc] elastic. **-2.** *fig* [flexível] adaptable.

elástico *m* **-1.** [para prender notas *etc*] rubber band. **-2.** [para roupa] elastic. **-3.** [para cabelo] elastic band.

ele, ela ['eli, 'εla] (*mpl* **eles**, *fpl* **elas**) *pron pess* (*de* + *ele* = *dele; de* + *ela* = *dela; em* + *ele* = *nele; em* + *ela* = *nela*) **-1.** [pessoa] he (*f* she); ~ **é médico** he is a doctor; **ela foi embora** she has gone away; **elas viajaram** they travelled; **eles têm uma filha** they have one daughter; **que só** ~ as only he can be/do; ~ **mesmo** *ou* **próprio** him himself. **-2.** [animal, coisa] it; **o cachorro?** ~ **uivou a noite inteira** the dog? it howled all night long; **ela dá flor em novembro** it flowers in November; **o relatório? aqui está** ~ the report? here it is; **eles já foram vendidos** they have already been sold; ~ **mesmo itself**. **-3.** (*depois de prep*) [pessoa] him, her, it; **este livro pertence a** ~ this book belongs to him; **jantei com** ~ I had dinner with them; **todos olharam para eles** ~ everybody looked at them; **sou mais velho que** ~ I am older than him; **decidimos ir sem ela** we decided to go without her; **deram um tiro nele** they shot him; **aquele é o carro dele** that's his car; **os jornais só falam dela** the newspapers talk about nothing but her. **-4.** *loc*: **agora é que são elas** there's the rub; **ser elas por elas** to be tit for tat.

elefante [ele'fãntʃi] *m* elephant; ~ **branco** *fig* white elephant.

elefantíase [elefãn'tʃjazi] *f* elephantiasis.

elefantino, na [elefãn'tʃinu, na] *adj* elephantine.

elegância [ele'gãnsja] *f* elegance; **com** ~ elegantly.

elegante [ele'gãntʃi] *adj* elegant.

eleger [26] [ele'ʒe(x)] *vt* **-1.** [por meio de votos] to elect. **-2.** [escolher] to select.

elegia [ele'ʒia] *f* elegy.

elegível [ele'ʒivewl] (*pl* **-eis**) *adj* eligible.

eleição [elej'sãw] (*pl* **-ões**) *f* **-1.** [por meio de votos] election. **-2.** [escolha] selection.

eleito, ta [e'lejtu, ta] <> *pp* ⊳ **eleger**. <> *adj* **-1.** [por votos] elected. **-2.** [escolhido] selected.

eleitor, ra [elej'to(x), ra] (*mpl* **-es**, *fpl* **-s**) *m*, *f* voter.

eleitorado [elejto'radul *m* electorate; **conhecer o seu** ~ *fam fig* to know who one is dealing with.

eleitoral [elejto'rawl] (*pl* **-ais**) *adj* electoral.

eleitoreiro, ra [elejto'rejru, ra] *adj pej* vote-catching.

elementar [elemẽn'ta(x)] (*pl* **-es**) *adj* **-1.** [rudimentar] elementary. **-2.** [fundamental] fundamental.

elemento [ele'mẽntu] *m* **-1.** [ger] element; **estar no seu** ~ to be in one's element. **-2.** [indivíduo] individual; **bom/mau** ~ good/bad lot.
➤ **elementos** *mpl* **-1.** [ger] elements. **-2.** [dados] facts.

elencar [elẽn'ka(x)] *vt* [listar] to list.

elenco [e'lẽnku] *m* **-1.** *TEATRO* cast list. **-2.** [rol] list.

elepê [eli'pe] *m* LP.

eletivo, va [ele'tʃivu, va] *adj* elective.

eletricidade [eletrisi'dadʒi] *f* electricity.

eletricista [eletri'siʃta] *mf* electrician.

elétrico, ca [e'lɛtriku, ka] *adj* **-1.** *ELETR* electric. **-2.** *fig* [agitado] excited.

eletrificar [4] [eletrifi'ka(x)] *vt* to electrify.

eletrizante [eletri'zãntʃi] *adj fig* electrifying.

eletrizar [4] [eletri'za(x)] *vt* **-1.** *ELETR* to electrify. **-2.** *fig* [arrebatar] to thrill.

Eletrobras (*abrev de* **Centrais Elétricas Brasileiras S/A**) *f* Brazilian electricity company.

eletrocardiograma [e,lɛtrokaxdʒo'grãma] *m* *MED* electrocardiogram.

eletrochoque [elɛtro'ʃɔki] *m* electroconvulsive therapy.

eletrocutar [4] [eletroku'ta(x)] *vt* to electrocute.

eletrodinâmica [elɛtrodʒi'nãmika] *f* *FÍS* electrodynamics *(sg)*.

eletrodo [ele'trodul] *m* electrode.

eletrodomésticos [eletrodo'mɛʃtʃikuʃ] *mpl* domestic appliances.

eletroeletrônico, ra [elɛktro'eletroniko, ka] <> *adj* electronics. <> *m, f* electronic device.

eletroencefalograma [e,lɛtrwẽnsɛfalo'grãma] *m* electroencephalogram.

eletromagnético, ca [elɛtromag'nɛtʃiku, ka] *adj* electromagnetic.

elétron *m* electron.

eletrônica [ele'tronika] *f* electronics *(sg)*.

eletrônico, ca [ele'troniku, ka] *adj* electronic.

elevação [eleva'sãw] (*pl* **-ões**) *f* **-1.** [ger] elevation. **-2.** [aumento] rise.

elevado, da [ele'vadu, da] *adj* **-1.** [alto] high. **-2.** [nobre] noble.
➤ **elevado** *m* [via] flyover.

elevador [eleva'do(x)] (*pl* **-es**) *m* lift *UK*, elevator *US*.

elevar [4] [ele'va(x)] *vt* **-1.** [erguer] to lift up. **-2.** [aumentar] to raise. **-3.** [exaltar] to acclaim.
➤ **elevar-se** *vp* to rise.

eliminação [elimina'sãw] (*pl* **-ões**) *f* elimination.

eliminar [4] [elimi'na(x)] *vt* **-1.** [ger] to eliminate. **-2.** [descartar] to exclude.

eliminatório, ria [elimina'tɔrju, rja] *adj* eliminatory.
➤ **eliminatória** *f* **-1.** *ESP* heat. **-2.** *EDUC* test.

elipse [e'lipsi] *f* ellipsis.

elite [e'litʃi] *f* elite.

elitismo [eli'tʃiʒmu] *m* elitism.

elitista [eli'tʃiʃta] *adj* elitist.

elitizar [4] [elitʃi'za(x)] *vt* to class among the elite.

elixir [eli'ʃi(x)] *m* elixir.

elo ['ɛlu] *m* link.

elocução [eloku'sãw] *f* elocution.

elogiar [16] [elo'ʒja(x)] *vt* to praise.

elogio [elo'ʒiu] *m* praise.

elogioso, osa [elo'ʒozu, ɔza] *adj* flattering.

El Salvador *n* El Salvador.

elucidação [elusida'sãw] (*pl* **-ões**) *f* clarification.

elucidar [4] [elusi'da(x)] *vt* to explain.

elucidativo, va [elusida'tʃiva, va] *adj* explanatory.

elucubração [elukubra'sãw] (*pl* **-ões**) *f* meditation.

elucubrar [4] [eluku'bra(x)] <> *vt* [intelectualmente] to dream up. <> *vi* [refletir, pensar] to muse.

em [ẽ] *prep* (*em + o = no*; *em + a = na*) **-1.** [lugar - dentro de] in; **no bolso/estojo/quarto** in the pocket/case/bedroom; **na bolsa/caixa/sala** in the purse/box/living room; [- num certo ponto de] at; ~ **casa** at home; **no trabalho** at work; **nas ruas** on the streets; **moramos na capital** we live in the capital; **depositei o dinheiro no banco** I deposited the money in the bank; [- sobre] on; **o bife mal cabia no prato** the steak hardly fitted on the plate; **havia um vaso de flores na mesa** there was a vase of flowers on the table; [- cidade, país] in; ~ **Londres/São Paulo** in London/São Paulo; ~ **Porto/Rio de Janeiro** in Oporto/Rio de Janeiro; ~ **Portugal** in Portugal; **no Brasil** in Brazil; **na França** in France; **nos Estados Unidos** in the United States. **-2.** [tempo] in; **inaugurado** ~ **1967** officially opened in 1967; **ele tirou férias** ~ **maio** he took his holidays in May; ~ **7 de setembro de 1622** on 7th September 1622; **comemoram a liberdade no 25 de abril** freedom is celebrated on 25th April; **no Natal** at Christmas; **na Semana Santa** during Holy Week; **ela fez tudo** ~ **uma semana** she did everything in one week; **o serviço ficará pronto** ~ **dois dias** the work will be ready in two days' time; **naquela época** at that time in those days; ~ **breve** soon. **-3.** [introduzindo o objeto indireto] in; **enfiar/esquecer/guardar algo** ~ to slip/forget/keep sthg in; **acreditar** ~ to believe in; **pensar** ~ to think of; **ele caiu num buraco** he fell in a hole; **ela caiu/no chão** she fell on the floor; **ela entrou na sala** she entered the room; **vou no jornaleiro e já volto** I am going to the newsagent's and I'll be right back. **-4.** [assunto] in; **doutorado** ~ **sociologia** graduated in sociology; **ele é perito** ~ **balística** he is an expert in ballistics. **-5.** [modo] in; **ele falou** ~ **voz baixa** he spoke in a low voice; **ela falou** ~ **português** she spoke in Portuguese; **ele dirige** ~ **alta velocidade** he drives fast; **ela pagou** ~ **libras/reais** she paid in pounds sterling/reals; **o preço aumentou** ~ **10%** the price has gone up by 10%; **ele gasta tudo o que ganha** ~ **livros** he spends all he earns on books; **bife na chapa** grilled steak. **-6.** [estado]: **a multidão** ~ **euforia** the rejoicing crowd; **ela ainda está** ~ **convalescença** she is still convalescing; **um carro usado** ~ **boas condições** a well-kept second-hand car; **países** ~ **guerra** countries at war. **-7.** [material]: **estátua** ~ **bronze**

bronze statue; **camisa** ~ **viscose** rayon shirt. **- 8.** (*em loc adv, loc prep*) on; **com base** ~ based on/in; **de tempos** ~ **tempos** from time to time; ~ **busca de** in search of; ~ **caso de** in case of; ~ **geral** in general; ~ **meio a** in the middle of; **na verdade** in truth; **no mínimo/máximo** at least/the most.

emagrecer [25] [emagre'se(x)] ⟨> *vt* [causar perda de peso] to cause to lose weight. ⟨> *vi* **-1.** [perder peso] to lose weight. **- 2.** [definhar] to slim down.

emagrecimento [emagresi'mēntul *m* slimming.

e-mail *m* e-mail.

emanar [4] [ema'na(x)] *vi* **-1.** [exalar-se]: ~ **de** to emanate from. **- 2.** [originar-se]: ~ **de** to stem from.

emancipação [emãnsipa'sãw] (*pl* **-ões**) *f* **-1.** [de mulheres, escravos] emancipation. **- 2.** [de menor] coming of age. **- 3.** [de país] liberation.

emancipado, da [emãnsi'padu, da] *adj* liberated.

emancipar [4] [emãnsi'pa(x)] *vt* **-1.** [ger] to emancipate. **- 2.** [país] to liberate.

➤ **emancipar-se** *vp* **-1.** [mulheres] to become emancipated. **- 2.** [menor] to come of age. **- 3.** [país] to become free.

emaranhado, da [emarã'ɲadu, da] *adj* [embaraçado] tangled.

➤ **emaranhado** *m* [confusão] confusion.

emaranhar [4] [emarã'ɲa(x)] *vt* **-1.** [enredar] to tangle. **- 2.** *fig* [complicar] to confuse.

➤ **emaranhar-se** *vp* [enredar-se] to become entangled.

embaçado, da [ēnba'sadu, da] *adj* **-1.** [vidro] misted up. **- 2.** [olhos] misty.

embaçar [13] [ēnba'sa(x)] *vt* **-1.** [vidro] to mist up. **- 2.** [olhos] to mist.

embaciado, da [ēnba'sjadu, da] *adj* **-1.** [metal] tarnished. **- 2.** [vidro] misted up. **- 3.** [olhos] misty.

embaciar [16] [ēnba'sja(x)] ⟨> *vt* **-1.** [vidro] to mist up. **- 2.** [olhos] to mist. ⟨> *vi* **-1.** [metal] to tarnish. **- 2.** [vidro, olhos] to cloud.

embainhar [4] [ēnbaj'ɲa(x)] *vt* **-1.** [espada] to sheathe. **- 2.** [roupa] to hem.

embaixada [ēnbaj'ʃada] *f* **-1.** [local] embassy. **- 2.** [cargo] ambassadorial duties. **- 3.** [funcionários] embassy staff.

embaixador, ra [ēnbajʃa'do(x), ra] (*mpl* **-es**, *fpl* **-s**) *m, f* ambassador.

embaixatriz [ēnbajʃa'triʃ] *f* [esposa do embaixador] ambassadress.

embaixo [ēn'bajʃu] *adv* **-1.**: ~ **de** underneath. **- 2.**: **aí** ~ down there. **- 3.**: **lá** ~ downstairs.

➤ **embaixo de** *loc prep* under.

embalado, da [ēnba'ladu, da] ⟨> *adj* **-1.** [empacotado] wrapped, packed. **- 2.** [acelerado] fast. **- 3.** [drogado] high. ⟨> *adv* [aceleradamente] more quickly.

embalagem [ēnba'laʒẽ] (*pl* **-ns**) *f* **-1.** [ato] wrapping, packing. **- 2.** [invólucro] package.

embalar [4] [ēnba'la(x)] *vt* **-1.** [acondicionar] to wrap. **- 2.** [berço] to rock. **- 3.** [balanço] to swing.

➤ **embalar-se** *vp* [balançar-se] to rock o.s.

embalo [ēn'balu] *m* **-1.** [balanço] rocking. **- 2.** [impulso] push. **- 3.** [euforia causada por droga] high. **- 4.** *fam* [festa]: **festa de** ~ swinging party.

embalsamado, da [ēnbawsa'madu, da] *adj* **-1.** [cadáver] embalmed. **- 2.** [perfumado] scented.

embalsamar [4] [ēnbaws'ma(x)] *vt* **-1.** [cadáver] to embalm. **- 2.** [perfumar] to perfume.

embananado, da [ēnbana'nadu, da] *fam adj* **-1.** [situação] snarled up. **- 2.** [pessoa] in a hole, in trouble.

embananar [4] [ēnbana'na(x)] *vt* [situação] to complicate.

➤ **embananar-se** *vp fam* [pessoa] to be in a hole, to be in trouble.

embaraçar [13] [ēnbara'sa(x)] *vt* **-1.** [obstruir] to block. **- 2.** [acanhar] to embarrass. **- 3.** [cabelos] to tangle. **- 4.** [dificultar] to complicate.

➤ **embaraçar-se** *vp* [embaralhar-se] to become embroiled.

embaraço [ēnba'rasul *m* **-1.** [obstáculo] obstacle. **- 2.** [acanhamento] embarrassment. **- 3.** [dificuldade] difficult situation.

embaraçoso, osa [ēnbara'sozu, ɔza] *adj* embarrassing.

embaralhar [4] [ēnbara'ɲa(x)] *vt* **-1.** [cartas] to shuffle. **- 2.** [confundir] to jumble.

➤ **embaralhar-se** *vp* [confundir-se] to become confused.

embarcação [ēnbaxka'sãw] (*pl* **-ões**) *f* vessel.

embarcadouro [ēnbaxka'dorul *m* quay.

embarcar [12] [ēnbax'ka(x)] ⟨> *vt* **-1.** [pessoa] to board. **- 2.** [carga] to load. ⟨> *vi* **-1.**: ~ **(em)** [subir a bordo] to board; [viajar] to travel. **- 2.** *fam* [cair na conversa]: ~ **em algo** to fall for sthg.

embargado, da [ēnbax'gadu, da] *adj* **-1.** [impedido] blocked. **- 2.** [contido] carefully controlled.

embargar [14] [ēnbax'ga(x)] *vt* **-1.** [JUR - apreender] to seize; [- impedir] to block. **- 2.** [conter] to control.

embargo [ēn'baxgu] *m* **-1.** *JUR* seizure. **- 2.** [obstáculo] impediment.

embarque [ēn'baxki] *m* **-1.** [de pessoa] boarding. **- 2.** [de carga] loading.

embasamento [ēnbaza'mēntul *m* **-1.** [base] foundation. **- 2.** *fig* [fundamento] basis.

embasar [4] [ēnba'za(x)] *vt* **-1.** [alicerçar] to lay the foundations of. **- 2.** [fundamentar] to base.

embasbacado, da [ēnbaʒba'kadu, da] *adj* astounded.

embasbacar [12] [ēnbaʒba'ka(x)] *vt* to astound.

➤ **embasbacar-se** *vp* to be astounded.

embate [ēn'batʃi] *m* **-1.** [colisão] crash. **- 2.** [choque] shock. **- 3.** [resistência] resistance.

embebedar [4] [ēnbebe'da(x)] *vt & vi* to intoxicate.

➤ **embebedar-se** *vp* to become intoxicated.

embeber [5] [ēnbe'be(x)] *vt* **-1.** [ensopar]: ~ **algo em algo** to soak sthg in sthg. **- 2.** [absorver] to soak up.

➤ **embeber-se** *vp* [absorver-se]: ~~**-se em** to be absorbed in.

embelezador, ra [ẽnbeleza'do(x), raᴵ *adj* beautifying.

embelezar [4] [ẽnbele'za(x)] *vt* [tornar belo] to beautify.

➡ **embelezar-se** *vp* [enfeitar-se] to make o.s. beautiful.

embevecer [25] [ẽnbeve'se(x)] *vt* to delight.

➡ **embevecer-se** *vp* to be delighted.

embevecido, da [ẽnbeve'sidu, daᴵ *adj* delighted.

embicar [12] [ẽnbi'ka(x)] ⬦ *vt* [tornar bicudo] to sharpen. ⬦ *vi* -1. [esbarrar] to meet. -2. [implicar]: ~ com algo/alguém to become entangled with sthg/sb. -3. [dirigir-se]: ~ para to head towards.

embirrar [4] [ẽnbi'xa(x)] *vi* -1. [teimar]: ~ em to insist upon. -2. [antipatizar]: ~ com to take a disliking to. -3. [ficar birrento] to be obstinate.

embocadura [ẽnboka'duraᴵ *f* -1. [de rio] mouth. -2. [de instrumento] mouthpiece.

embolar [4] [ẽnbo'la(x)] ⬦ *vt* [emaranhar] to entangle. ⬦ *vi* -1. [engalfinhar-se]: ~ com alguém to grapple with sb. -2. [encaroçar] to make lumpy.

➡ **embolar-se** *vp* [engalfinhar-se]: ~-se (com alguém) to become locked in battle (with sb).

embolia [ẽnbo'lial *f* embolism.

êmbolo ['ẽnbolul *m* -1. [bomba] piston. -2. [seringa] plunger. -3. *MED* embolism.

embolorado, da [ẽnbolo'radu, daᴵ *adj* [mofado - pão, fruta] mouldy; [- roupa, casa] musty.

embolorar [4] [ẽnbolo'ra(x)] *vi* to become mouldy.

embolsar [4] [ẽnbow'sa(x)] *vt* -1. [receber] to pocket. -2. [pagar] to pay.

embonecar [12] [ẽnbone'ka(x)] *vt* to doll up.

➡ **embonecar-se** *vp* to doll o.s. up.

embora [ẽn'bɔral ⬦ *conj* although. ⬦ *adv*: ir ~ to go; vá-se ~! go away!

emborcar [12] [ẽnbox'ka(x)] *vt* -1. [canoa] to overturn. -2. [vasilha] to turn upside down.

emboscada [ẽnboʃ'kadaᴵ *f* ambush.

embotado, da [ẽnbo'tadu, daᴵ *adj* -1. [enfraquecido] weakened. -2. [insensível] numb.

embotar [4] [ẽnbo'ta(x)] *vt* to blunt.

Embraer (*abrev de* Empresa Brasileira de Aeronáutica) *f* Brazilian aeronautical company.

embranquecer [25] [ẽnbrãŋke'se(x)] ⬦ *vt* to whiten. ⬦ *vi* to turn white.

Embratel (*abrev de* Empresa Brasileira de Telecomunicações S/A) *f* Brazilian telecommunications company.

embravecer [25] [ẽnbrave'se(x)] ⬦ *vt* to make wild. ⬦ *vi* to become furious.

➡ **embravecer-se** ⬦ *vp* to become furious.

embreagem [ẽnbre'aʒẽl (*pl* -ns) *f* clutch.

embrear [15] [ẽm'brja(x)] ⬦ *vt* to engage (the clutch). ⬦ *vi* to engage the clutch.

embrenhar-se [15] [ẽnbre'ɲaxsil *vp*: ~-se em/ por to conceal o.s. in.

embriagado, da [ẽnbrja'gadu, daᴵ ⬦ *adj* -1. [bêbado] drunk. -2. *fig* [enlevado] intoxicated. ⬦ *m, f* [pessoa bêbada] drunk.

embriagante [ẽnbrja'gãntʃil *adj* intoxicating.

embriagar [14] [ẽnbrja'ga(x)] ⬦ *vt* to intoxicate. ⬦ *vi* [embebedar] to intoxicate.

➡ **embriagar-se** *vp* [enlevar-se] to become intoxicated.

embriaguez [ẽnbrja'geʒl *f* -1. [ebriedade] drunkenness. -2. *fig* [enlevo] intoxication.

embrião [ẽn'brjãwl (*pl* -ões) *m* embryo.

embrionário, ria [ẽnbrjo'narju, jaᴵ *adj* [relativo a embrião] embryonic.

embromação [ẽnbroma'sãwl (*pl* -ões) *f* -1. [embuste] deception. -2. [protelação] delaying tactic.

embromador, ra [ẽnbroma'do(x), raᴵ *fam* ⬦ *adj* -1. [enrolador] dishonest. -2. [trapaceiro] fraudulent. ⬦ *m, f* -1. [pessoa enroladora] cheat. -2. [pessoa trapaceira] fraud.

embromar [4] [ẽnbro'ma(x)] ⬦ *vt* -1. [enrolar] to fool. -2. [enganar] to bamboozle. ⬦ *vi* -1. [protelar] to procrastinate. -2. [fazer rodeios] to beat about the bush.

embrulhada [ẽnbru'ʎadaᴵ *f fam* [confusão] muddle.

embrulhar [4] [ẽnbru'ʎa(x)] *vt* -1. [empacotar] to wrap. -2. *fig* [estômago] to upset. -3. [confundir] to screw up. -4. [enganar] to trick.

➡ **embrulhar-se** *vp* [enrolar-se] to get into a muddle.

embrulho [ẽn'bruʎul *m* -1. [pacote] package. -2. [confusão] confusion.

embrutecer [25] [ẽnbrute'se(x)] ⬦ *vt* to make brutal. ⬦ *vi* to brutalize.

➡ **embrutecer-se** *vp* to become brutalized.

emburrado, da [ẽnbu'xadu, daᴵ *adj* [aborrecido] sulky.

emburrar-se [4] [ẽnbu'xaxsil *vp* [aborrecer-se] to sulk.

embuste [ẽn'buʃtʃil *m* -1. [mentira] deception. -2. [armadilha] trick.

embusteiro, ra [ẽnbuʃ'tejru, raᴵ ⬦ *adj* deceitful. ⬦ *m, f* [pessoa] trickster.

embutido, da [ẽnbu'tʃidu, daᴵ *adj* [armário, estante] built-in.

embutir [6] [ẽnbu'tʃi(x)] *vt* -1. [armário] to build in. -2. [pedra, marfim] to inlay.

emenda [e'mẽndaᴵ *f* -1. [correção] correction. -2. *JUR* amendment. -3. *COST* repair. -4. [ligação] join.

emendar [4] [emẽn'da(x)] *vt* -1. [corrigir] to correct. -2. *JUR* to amend. -3. [reparar] to redress. -4. [ligar] to join.

➡ **emendar-se** *vp* [corrigir-se] to mend one's ways.

emergência [emex'ʒẽnsjaᴵ *f* -1. [ger] emergency. -2. [surgimento] emergence.

emergente [emex'ʒẽntʃil *adj* emerging.

emergir [78] [emex'ʒi(x)] *vi* to emerge.

emérito, ta [e'mɛritu, taᴵ *adj* emeritus.

emigração [emigra'sãwl (*pl* -ões) *f* -1. [de pessoas] emigration. -2. [de aves] migration.

emigrado, da [emi'gradu, daᴵ ⬦ *adj* emigrant. ⬦ *m, f* emigré.

emigrante [emi'grãntʃi] <> *adj* emigrant. <> *mf* emigré.
emigrar [4] [emi'gra(x)] *vi* **-1.** [pessoa] to emigrate. **-2.** [ave] to migrate.
eminência [emi'nẽsja] *f* **-1.** [ger] eminence. **-2.** [título, tratamento] Eminence. **-3.** [pessoa importante] important person; ~ **parda** eminence grise.
eminente [emi'nẽntʃi] *adj* **-1.** [ilustre] eminent. **-2.** [elevado] high.
emir [e'mi(x)] *m* emir.
emirado [emi'radu] *m* emirate.
Emirados Árabes Unidos *n*: **os** ~ the United Arab Emirates.
emissão [emi'sãw] (*pl* **-ões**) *f* **-1.** [ger] emission. **-2.** [de moeda, títulos, passagens aéreas] issue. **-3.** *RÁDIO & TV* transmission.
emissário, ria [emi'sarju, rja] *m, f* [mensageiro] emissary.
➤ **emissário** *m* [esgoto] outlet.
emissor, ra [emi'so(x), ra] (*mpl* **-es**, *fpl* **-s**) *adj FIN* issuing.
➤ **emissor** *m* [transmissor] transmitter.
➤ **emissora** *f* transmitter.
emitente [emi'tẽntʃi] <> *adj FIN* issuing. <> *mf FIN* issuer.
emitir [6] [emi'tʃi(x)] <> *vt* **-1.** [ger] to issue. **-2.** [sons, raios] to emit. **-3.** [opinião, idéias] to transmit. <> *vi FIN* to issue money.
emoção [emo'sãw] (*pl* **-ões**) *f* emotion.
emocional [emosjo'naw] (*pl* **-ais**) *adj* emotional.
emocionante [emosjo'nãntʃi] *adj* **-1.** [comovente] moving. **-2.** [empolgante] gripping.
emocionar [4] [emosjo'na(x)] <> *vt* **-1.** [comover] to move. **-2.** [excitar] to thrill. <> *vi* [provocar emoção] to thrill.
➤ **emocionar-se** *vp* [comover-se]: ~-**se com algo/alguém** to get emotional about sthg/sb.
emoldurar [4] [emowdu'ra(x)] *vt* to frame.
emoticom [ɛmo'tikõl] (*pl* **-ns**) *m COMPUT* emoticon.
emotividade [emotʃivi'dadʒi] *f* emotiveness.
emotivo, va [emo'tʃivu, va] *adj* emotional.
empacar [12] [ẽnpa'ka(x)] *vi* **-1.** [recusar-se a andar] to stand stock still. **-2.** [não progredir] to stand still. **-3.** [parar] to dry up; ~ **em algo** to get bogged down in sthg.
empacotar [4] [ẽnpako'ta(x)] <> *vt* [embalar] to wrap up. <> *vi fam* [morrer] to snuff it.
empada [ẽn'pada] *f CULIN* pie.
empadão [ẽnpa'dãw] (*pl* **-ões**) *m* pie.
empalhar [4] [ẽnpa'ʎa(x)] *vt* **-1.** [animal] to stuff. **-2.** [cadeira, garrafa] to cover in wickerwork.
empalidecer [25] [ẽnpalide'se(x)] <> *vt* [tornar pálido] to cause to turn pale. <> *vi* [perder a cor] to turn pale.
empanada [ẽnpa'nada] *f CULIN* large pie.
empanturrado, da [ẽnpãntu'xadu, da] *adj* stuffed full.
empanturrar [4] [ẽnpãntu'xa(x)] *vt*: ~ **alguém de algo** to stuff sb with sthg.
➤ **empanturrar-se** *vp*: ~-**se de algo** to stuff o.s with sthg.

empapar [4] [ẽnpa'pa(x)] <> *vt* [ensopar] to drench. <> *vi* [fazer papo] to soak through.
➤ **empapar-se** *vp* [ensopar-se] to get drenched.
empapuçado, da [ẽnpapu'sadu, da] *adj* [olhos] puffy; [roupa] puffed.
empapuçar [ẽnpapu'sa(x)] *vt* [inchar] to stuff.
emparedar [4] [ẽnpare'da(x)] *vt* [enclausurar] to shut away.
➤ **emparedar-se** *vp* [isolar-se] to shut o.s. away.
emparelhado, da [ẽnpare'ʎadu, da] *adj* [lado a lado] paired.
emparelhar [4] [ẽnpare'ʎa(x)] <> *vt* [por em pares] to pair up. <> *vi* **-1.** [equivaler]: ~ **(em algo)** to be equal (in sthg). **-2.** [equiparar-se]: ~ **com** to be equal to. **-3.** [correr parelhas]: ~ **(com alguém)** to draw alongside.
➤ **emparelhar-se** *vp* [empatar] to become equal.
empastar [4] [ẽnpaʃ'ta(x)] *vt* **-1.** [ger] to plaster. **-2.** [tornar pastoso] to make a paste of.
empatar [4] [ẽnpa'ta(x)] <> *vi* [em jogo]: ~ **com** to draw with. <> *vt* **-1.** [impedir] to hinder. **-2.** [ocupar] to take up. **-3.** [aplicar] to tie up.
empate [ẽn'patʃi] *m* [jogo, votação] tie; **dar** ~ to end in a draw.
empatia [ẽnpa'tʃia] *f* empathy.
empecilho [ẽnpe'siʎu] *m* obstacle.
empedernido, da [ẽnpedex'nidu, da] *adj* harsh.
empedrar [4] [ẽnpe'dra(x)] *vt* [cobrir com pedras] to pave.
empenado, da [ẽnpe'nadu, da] *adj* **-1.** [deformado] warped. **-2.** [fora de prumo] leaning.
empenar [4] [ẽnpe'na(x)] <> *vt* [entortar] to warp. <> *vi* [entortar-se] to warp.
empenhado, da [ẽnpe'nadu, da] *adj* **-1.** [disposto] determined. **-2.** [penhorado] pawned.
empenhar [4] [ẽnpe'na(x)] *vt* **-1.** [dar em penhor] to pawn. **-2.** [aplicar] to apply. **-3.** [comprometer] to pledge.
➤ **empenhar-se** *vp* [aplicar-se]: ~-**se (para fazer algo)** to commit o.s. (to do sthg); ~-**se em algo** to get into debt over sthg.
empenho [ẽn'penu] *m* **-1.** [diligência] commitment; **pôr todo o** ~ **em algo** to put all one's effort into sthg. **-2.** [compromisso] commitment. **-3.** [penhor] pledge.
emperiquitado, da [ẽnperiki'tadu, da] *adj* flashy.
emperiquitar-se [7] [ẽnperiki'taxsi] *vp* to get dolled up.
emperrado, da [ẽnpe'xadu, da] *adj* **-1.** [entravado] jammed. **-2.** [teimoso] stubborn.
emperrar [4] [ẽnpe'xa(x)] <> *vi* [tornar-se imóvel] to stick. <> *vt* **-1.** [entravar] to cause to stick. **-2.** [dificultar] to bog down.
empertigado, da [ẽnpextʃi'gadu, da] *adj* upright.
empertigar-se [14] [ẽnpextʃi'gaxsi] *vp* to stand up straight.
empestar [15] [ẽnpeʃ'ta(x)] *vt* **-1.** [contaminar] to infest. **-2.** [infectar com mau cheiro]: ~ **algo (com**

algo) to stink out sthg (with sthg).

empilhadeira [ẽnpiʎa'dejra] f fork-lift truck.

empilhar [4] [ẽnpi'ʎa(x)] vt [amontoar] to stack.

empinado, da [ẽnpi'nadu, da] adj straight.

empinar [4] [ẽnpi'na(x)] <> vt -1. [peito, corpo, nariz] to thrust out. -2. [pipa] to empty. <> vi [cavalo] to rear.

empipocado, da [ẽnpipo'kadu, da] adj spotty.

empipocar [12] [ẽnpipo'ka(x)] vi [corpo, superfície, massa] to come out in spots.

empírico, ca [ẽn'piriku, ka] adj empirical.

emplacar [12] [ẽnpla'ka(x)] vt -1. [veículo] to put a number plate on. -2. fam fig [idade] to make it to.

emplastrar [4] [ẽnplaʃ'tra(x)] vt to put in plaster.

emplastro [ẽn'plaʃtru] m [medicamento] plaster.

empobrecer [25] [ẽnpobre'se(x)] <> vt -1. [tornar pobre] to impoverish. -2. [o solo] to deplete. <> vi [tornar-se pobre] to become poor.

empobrecimento [ẽnpobresi'mẽntul] m -1. [ger] impoverishment. -2. [do solo] depletion.

empoeirado, da [ẽnpoej'radu, da] adj dusty.

empoeirar [4] [ẽnpoej'ra(x)] vt to cover in dust.

empolado, da [ẽnpo'ladu, da] adj -1. [pele] blistered. -2. fig [linguagem, estilo] pompous.

empolar [4] [ẽnpo'la(x)] <> vt [pele] to cause to swell. <> vi [pele] to blister.

◆ **empolar-se** vp -1. [pele] to become blistered. -2. [tornar-se soberbo] to become puffed up.

empolgação [ẽnpowga'sãw] f enthusiasm; **com ~** with enthusiasm.

empolgante [ẽnpow'gãntʃi] adj thrilling.

empolgar [14] [ẽnpow'ga(x)] vt to fill with enthusiasm.

◆ **empolgar-se** vp [entusiasmar-se] to become enthusiastic.

emporcalhar [4] [ẽnpoxka'ʎa(x)] vt to dirty.

◆ **emporcalhar-se** vp [pessoa] to get dirty.

empório [ẽn'pɔrjul m -1. [mercado] market. -2. [armazém] department store.

empossado, da [ẽmpo'sadu, da] adj newly appointed.

empossar [4] [ẽnpo'sa(x)] vt [dar posse a] to install in office.

empreendedor, ra [ẽnprjẽnde'do(x), ra] <> adj [ativo] enterprising. <> m, f [pessoa] entrepreneur.

empreender [5] [ẽnprjẽn'de(x)] vt to undertake.

empreendimento [ẽnprjẽndʒi'mẽntul] m undertaking.

empregado, da [ẽnpre'gadu, da] m, f [funcionário] employee.

◆ **empregada** f [em casa de família]: **empregada (doméstica)** maid.

empregador, ra [ẽnprega'do(x), ra] m, f employer.

empregar [14] [ẽnpre'ga(x)] vt -1. [ger] to use. -2. [dar emprego a] to employ. -3. [ocupar] to put to use.

◆ **empregar-se** vp [obter trabalho] to get a job.

empregatício, cia [ẽnprega'tʃisju, sjal adj employment.

emprego [ẽn'pregul m -1. [trabalho] job. -2. [local de trabalho] work. -3. [uso] use.

empreguismo [ẽnpre'giʒmul m nepotism.

empreitada [ẽnprej'tadal f -1. [trabalho, empresa] contract. -2. [tarefa] venture. -3. [empresa] undertaking.

empreiteira [ẽnprej'tejral f contracting company.

empreiteiro [ẽnprej'tejrul m contractor.

empresa [ẽn'prezal f -1. [firma] company; **~ estatal/privada** state-owned/privately-owned company. -2. [empreendimento] enterprise.

empresariado [ẽnpreza'rjadul m employers (pl).

empresarial [ẽnpreza'rjawl (pl -ais) adj company.

empresário, ria [ẽnpre'zarju, rja] m, f -1. [dono de empresa] employer. -2. [de artista, jogador] agent.

emprestado, da [ẽnpreʃ'tadu, da] adj loaned; **pedir algo ~** to borrow sthg.

emprestar [4] [ẽnpreʃ'ta(x)] vt to lend.

empréstimo [ẽn'prɛʃtʃimul m [de dinheiro] loan.

emproado, da [ẽnpro'adu, da] adj arrogant.

empulhação [ẽnpuʎa'sãwl (pl -ões) f [logro] hoax.

empurra-empurra [ẽnpu͵xẽn'puxal (pl empurras-empurras ou empurra-empurras) m pushing and shoving.

empurrão [ẽnpu'xãw] (pl -ões) m shove; **dar um ~** to give a shove; **levar um ~** to be shoved.

empurrar [4] [ẽnpu'xa(x)] vt -1. [impelir com força] to shove; **'empurre'** [aviso] 'push' -2. [impingir] to palm off.

emudecer [25] [emude'se(x)] <> vt [fazer calar] to silence. <> vi [calar-se] to go quiet.

emulação [emula'sãw] f -1. [competição] rivalry. -2. [estímulo] ambition.

emular [4] [emu'la(x)] <> vt -1. [rivalizar com] to compete with. -2. [imitar] to emulate. <> vi [competir]: **~ com** to compete with.

emulsão [emuw'zãwl (pl -ões) f QUÍM emulsion; **~ fotográfica** photographic emulsion.

enaltecer [25] [enawte'se(x)] vt to honour.

enamorado, da [enamo'radu, da] adj in love.

enamorar-se [4] [enamo'raxsil vp: **~-se de** ou **por alguém** to fall in love with sb.

encabeçar [4] [ẽŋkabe'sa(x)] vt -1. [vir à frente de] to head. -2. [chefiar] to lead.

encabulação [ẽŋkabula'sãw] f -1. [acanhamento] embarrassment. -2. [constrangimento] constraint.

encabulado, da [ẽŋkabu'ladu, da] adj -1. [acanhado] embarrassed. -2. [envergonhado] ashamed.

encabular [4] [ẽŋkabu'la(x)] <> vt [envergonhar] to embarrass. <> vi [acanhar-se] to be embarrassed.

◆ **encabular-se** vp -1. [acanhar-se] to be embarrassed. -2. [envergonhar-se] to be ashamed.

encaçapar [4] [ẽŋkasa'pa(x)] vt -1. [bola] to pocket. -2. fam [surrar] to spank.

encadeamento [ẽŋkadʒia'mẽntul m chain.

encadear [15] [ẽŋka'dʒja(x)] *vt* [concatenar] to link.
◆ **encadear-se** *vp* [concatenar-se] to become linked.

encadernação [ẽŋkadexna'sãw] (*pl* -ões) *f* bookbinding.

encadernado, da [ẽŋkadex'nadu, da] *adj* bound.

encadernar [4] [ẽŋkadex'na(x)] *vt* to bind.

encaixar [4] [ẽŋkaj'ʃa(x)] <> *vt* -1. [inserir]: ~ algo (em algo) to fit sthg (into sthg). -2. [encaixotar] to box. <> *vi* [entrar no encaixe] to fit.
◆ **encaixar-se** *vp* to fit.

encaixe [ẽŋ'kajʃi] *m* -1. [ato] entrance. -2. [cavidade] groove. -3. [junção] joint.

encaixotar [4] [ẽŋkajʃo'ta(x)] *vt* to box.

encalacrado, da [ẽŋkala'kradu, da] *adj* in trouble.

encalacrar [4] [ẽŋkala'kra(x)] *vt* to lead into difficulties.
◆ **encalacrar-se** *vp* to get into difficulties.

encalço [ẽŋ'kawsu] *m*: estar no ~ de algo/alguém to be in pursuit of sthg/sb.

encalhado, da [ẽŋka'ʎadu, da] *adj* -1. [embarcação] aground. -2. [mercadoria] unsaleable. -3. *fam* [pessoa solteira] on the shelf.

encalhar [4] [ẽŋka'ʎa(x)] *vi* -1. [embarcação] to run aground. -2. [mercadoria] to remain unsold. -3. [processo] to grind to a halt. -4. *fam* [pessoa solteira] to be left on the shelf.

encaminhar [4] [ẽŋkami'ɲa(x)] *vt* -1. [dirigir] to direct. -2. [orientar] to guide. -3. [dar andamento] to get going.
◆ **encaminhar-se** *vp* [dirigir-se]: ~-se para/a to set out for/to.

encampar [4] [ẽŋkãm'pa(x)] *vt* -1. *JUR* to rescind. -2. [empresa] to take into administration.

encanador, ra [ẽŋkana'dox, ra] (*mpl* -es, *fpl* -s) *m*, *f* plumber.

encanamento [ẽŋkana'mẽntu] *m* [sistema] plumbing.

encanar [4] [ẽŋka'na(x)] *vt* -1. [canalizar] to channel. -2. *fam* [prender] to lock up.

encantado, da [ẽŋkãn'tadu, da] (*mpl* -es, *fpl* -s) *adj* [ger] enchanted.

encantador, ra [ẽŋkãnta'do(x), ra] (*mpl* -es, *fpl* -s) *adj* -1. [fascinante] charming. -2. [deslumbrante] fantastic.

encantamento [ẽŋkãnta'mẽntu] *m* -1. [magia] enchantment. -2. [deslumbramento] fascination.

encantar [4] [ẽŋkãn'ta(x)] *vt* -1. [enfeitiçar] to bewitch. -2. [fascinar] to charm. -3. [deslumbrar] to fascinate.
◆ **encantar-se** *vp*: ~-se com algo to be enchanted by sthg.

encanto [ẽŋ'kãntu] *m* -1. [ger] charm. -2. *fam* [pessoa]: ser um ~ to be a charming person.

encapado, da [ẽŋka'padu, da] *adj* covered.

encapar [4] [ẽŋka'pa(x)] *vt* to cover.

encapetado, da [ẽŋkape'tadu, da] *adj* [criança] mischievous.

encapetar-se [ẽŋkape'ta(x)si] *vp* [endiabrar-se] to go into a tantrum.

encapotar [4] [ẽŋkapo'ta(x)] *vt* [cobrir] to wrap.
◆ **encapotar-se** *vp* [cobrir-se] to wrap o.s. up.

encaracolado, da [ẽŋkaraco'ladu, da] *adj* curly.

encaracolar [4] [ẽŋkarako'la(x)] <> *vt* [cabelo] to curl. <> *vi* [cabelo] to curl.

encarar [4] [ẽŋka'ra(x)] *vt* -1. [fitar] to stare at. -2. [enfrentar] to face up to. -3. [considerar] to consider.

encarcerar [4] [ẽŋkaxse'ra(x)] *vt* [prender] to incarcerate.

encardido, da [ẽŋkar'dʒidu, da] *adj* -1. [roupa] soiled. -2. [pele] grimy.

encardir [6] [ẽŋkax'dʒi(x)] <> *vt* -1. [roupa] to soil. -2. [pele] to make grimy. <> *vi* [ficar mal lavado] to be badly washed.

encarecer [25] [ẽŋkare'se(x)] <> *vt* -1. [tornar mais caro] to make more expensive. -2. [elogiar] to praise. <> *vi* [ficar mais caro] to go up in price.

encarecidamente [ẽŋkaresida'mẽntʃi] *adv* [insistentemente]: pedir ~ to ask insistently.

encarecimento [ẽŋkaresi'mẽntu] *m* increase in price; ~ da vida rise in the cost of living.

encargo [ẽŋ'kaxgu] *m* -1. [ger] duty. -2. [responsabilidade] responsibility.

encarnação [ẽŋkaxna'sãw] (*pl* -ões) *f* -1. [ger] incarnation. -2. [personificação]: ser a ~ de algo to be the embodiment of sthg. -3. *fam* [implicância] teasing.

encarnado, da [ẽŋkax'nadu, da] *adj* [vermelho] red.

encarnar [4] [ẽŋkax'na(x)] <> *vi* -1. [alma, espírito] to represent. -2. [implicar] *fam*: ~ em alguém to tease sb. <> *vt* -1. [personificar] to personify. -2. *TEATRO* to play.

encaroçar [13] [ẽŋkaro'sa(x)] *vi* -1. [pele] to come up in bumps. -2. [molho, massa] to be lumpy.

encarregado, da [ẽŋkaxe'gadu, da] <> *adj*: ~ de algo/fazer algo in charge of sthg/with doing sthg. <> *m*, *f* person in charge; ~ de negócios chargé d'affaires.

encarregar [14] [ẽŋkaxe'ga(x)] *vt*: ~ alguém de algo to put sb in charge of sthg.
◆ **encarregar-se** *vp*: ~-se de algo/fazer algo to take charge of sthg/doing sthg.

encartar [4] [ẽŋkax'ta(x)] *vt* to insert.

encarte [ẽŋ'kaxtʃi] *m* -1. [em publicação] insertion. -2. [de disco, CD] insert.

encasquetar [4] [ẽŋkaʃke'ta(x)] *vt*: ~ que to be convinced that; ~ uma idéia to be obsessed with an idea.

encefalograma [ẽnsɛfalo'grãma] *m* encephalogram.

encenação [ẽnsena'sãw] *f* -1. *TEATRO* staging. -2. [produção] production. -3. *fig* [fingimento] play-acting.

encenar [4] [ẽnse'na(x)] *vt* -1. *TEATRO* to stage. -2. [produzir] to produce. -3. *fig* [fingir] to play-act.

enceradeira [ẽnsera'dejra] *f* floor-polisher.

encerado, da [ẽnse'radu, da] *adj* waxed.
◆ **encerado** *m* [oleado] tarpaulin.

encerar [4] [ẽnse'ra(x)] *vt* to polish.

encerramento [ẽnsexa'mẽntuɭ] *m* closure.

encerrar [4] [ẽnse'xa(x)] *vt* **-1.** [acabar]: ~ algo **(com algo)** to close sthg (with sthg). **-2.** [confinar] to shut. **-3.** [conter] to contain.

➡ **encerrar-se** *vp* [enclausurar-se]: ~-se **(em)** to shut o.s. up (in).

encestar [4] [ẽnseʃ'ta(x)] *ESP* [basquete] *vt & vi* to score.

encetar [4] [ẽnse'ta(x)] *vt* [começar] to start.

encharcado, da [ẽnʃax'kadu, da] *adj* **-1.** [alagado] flooded. **-2.** [ensopado] soaking wet.

encharcar [12] [ẽnʃar'ka(x)] *vt* **-1.** [alagar] to flood. **-2.** [ensopar] to drench.

➡ **encharcar-se** *vp* [ensopar-se] to become soaked.

enchente [ẽn'ʃẽntʃi] *f* flood.

encher [5] [ẽn'ʃe(x)] <> *vt* **-1.** [ger] to fill; ~ o saco **(de alguém)** *m fam* to piss sb off. **-2.** [fartar]: ~ **algo (de)** to saturate sthg (with). **-3.** [balão, bola, pneu] to inflate. <> *vi* [tornar-se cheio] to become full.

➡ **encher-se** *vp* **-1.** [tornar-se cheio] to become full. **-2.** [fartar-se]: ~-se de to have too much of. **-3.** [aborrecer-se] to become fed up.

enchimento [ẽnʃi'mẽntuɭ] *m* **-1.** [ato] filling. **-2.** [coisa com que se enche] stuffing.

enchova [ẽn'ʃova] *f* anchovy.

encíclica [ẽn'siklika] *f RELIG* encyclical.

enciclopédia [ẽnsiklo'pɛdʒja] *f* **-1.** [obra] encyclopedia. **-2.** *fam* [pessoa sábia] walking encyclopedia.

enciclopédico, ca [ẽnsiklo'pɛdʒiku, ka] *adj* encyclopedic.

enciumar-se [4] [ẽnsju'maxsi] *vp* to be jealous.

enclausurar [4] [ẽnklawzu'ra(x)] *vt* to shut away.

➡ **enclausurar-se** *vp* to shut o.s. away.

encoberto, ta [ẽnko'bɛxtu, ta] <> *pp* ▷ **encobrir**. <> *adj* **-1.** [céu, tempo] overcast. **-2.** [escondido] hidden. **-3.** [disfarçado] concealed.

encobrir [59] [ẽnko'bri(x)] *vt* **-1.** [ger] to conceal. **-2.** [esconder] to hide.

➡ **encobrir-se** *vp* **-1.** [esconder-se] to hide. **-2.** [disfarçar-se] to disguise o.s. **-3.** [céu, sol] to become overcast.

encolerizar [4] [ẽnkoleri'za(x)] *vt* [pessoa] to enrage.

➡ **encolerizar-se** *vp* [pessoa] to get angry.

encolher [5] [ẽnko'ʎe(x)] <> *vt* **-1.** [contrair] to tuck in; ~ os ombros to shrug one's shoulders. **-2.** [diminuir o tamanho de] to shrink. <> *vi* [roupa] to shrink.

➡ **encolher-se** *vp* **-1.** [espremer-se] to squeeze up. **-2.** [de frio] to shrivel.

encomenda [ẽnko'mẽnda] *f* **-1.** [mercadoria] order; **fazer uma** ~ to order; **feito sob** ~ made to order. **-2.** [pacote] parcel.

encomendar [4] [ẽnkomẽn'da(x)] *vt* **-1.** [obra, compra]: ~ **algo a alguém** to order sthg from sb. **-2.** *RELIG* to commend.

encompridar [4] [ẽnkõnpri'da(x)] *vt* to lengthen.

encontrão [ẽnkõn'trãw] (*pl* -ões) *m* **-1.** [esbarrão]

bump; **dar um** ~ to shove. **-2.** [empurrão] shove.

encontrar [4] [ẽnkõn'tra(x)] <> *vt* **-1.** [pessoa - por acaso] to meet; [- em certa condição] to find. **-2.** [coisa perdida, procurada] to find. **-3.** [dificuldades] to come up against. **-4.** [solução, erro] to discover. <> *vi*: ~ **com alguém** [por acerto] to meet up with sb; [por acaso] to meet sb.

➡ **encontrar-se** *vp* **-1.**: ~-se **(com alguém)** [por acerto] to have a meeting (with sb); [por acaso] to meet (sb). **-2.** [estar] to be. **-3.** [colidir] to collide. **-4.** *PSIC* to find o.s.

encontro [ẽn'kõntru] *m* meeting; **ir ao** ~ **de** to go to meet; **de** ~ **a** [contra] against; **o carro foi de** ~ **ao muro** the car crashed into the wall; [em contradição a] in contrast with.

encorajamento [ẽnkoraʒa'mẽntuɭ] *m* encouragement.

encorajar [4] [ẽnkora'ʒa(x)] *vt* to encourage.

encorpado, da [ẽnkor'padu, da] *adj* **-1.** [forte] corpulent. **-2.** [espesso - tecido] thick; [- vinho] full-bodied.

encorpar [4] [ẽnkox'pa(x)] *vt* **-1.** [fazer crescer] to make grow. **-2.** [engrossar] to thicken.

encosta [ẽn'kɔʃta] *f* hillside.

encostar [4] [ẽnkoʃ'ta(x)] <> *vt* **-1.** [aproximar] to put against. **-2.** [quase fechar] to leave ajar. **-3.** [estacionar] to pull up. **-4.** [deitar] to rest. **-5.** *fig* [pôr de lado] to put aside. <> *vi* **-1.** [tocar]: ~ **em algo/alguém** to lean against sthg/sb. **-2.** [bater]: ~ **a mão em alguém** to hit sb with one's hand.

➡ **encostar-se** *vp* **-1.** [deitar-se] to recline. **-2.** [apoiar-se] to lean. **-3.** *fig* [aproveitar-se de]: ~-se **em alguém** to lean on sb. **-4.** *fig* [fugir de trabalho] to lie back.

encosto [ẽn'kɔʃtu] *m* [espaldar] back.

encouraçado, da [ẽnkora'sadu, da] *adj* ironclad.

➡ **encouraçado** *m NÁUT* battleship.

encravado, da [ẽnkra'vadu, da] *adj* **-1.** [unha] ingrown. **-2.** [pêlo] ingrowing.

encravar [4] [ẽnkra'va(x)] *vt*: ~ **algo (em algo)** to imbed sthg (in sthg).

encrenca [ẽ'ŋkrẽnka] *f* **-1.** [problema] tight spot. **-2.** [briga] fight; **meter-se numa** ~ to get caught up in a fight.

encrencar [12] [ẽnkrẽn'ka(x)] <> *vt* [meter em complicação] to embarrass. <> *vi* **-1.** [quebrar - carro] to break down; [- computador] to go down. **-2.** [complicar-se] to become complicated. **-3.** *fam* [implicar]: ~ **com alguém/algo** to take issue with sb/sthg.

encrenqueiro, ra [ẽnkrẽn'kejru, ra] *adj* troublemaking.

encrespado, da [ẽnkreʃ'padu, da] *adj* **-1.** [cabelo] tightly-curled. **-2.** [mar] choppy.

encrespar [4] [ẽnkreʃ'pa(x)] *vt* **-1.** [cabelo] to curl. **-2.** [mar] to ripple.

➡ **encrespar-se** *vp* **-1.** [mar] to become choppy, to get choppy. **-2.** *fig* [irritar-se] to become angry, to get angry.

encruar [4] [ẽnkru'a(x)] *vi* to harden.

encruzilhada [ẽŋkruziˈʎada] f crossroads (sg).
encucado, da [ẽŋkuˈkadu, da] adj perturbed.
encucar [12] [ẽŋkuˈka(x)] vi to become confused.
encurralado, da [ẽŋkuxaˈladu, da] adj [cercado] cornered.
encurralar [4] [ẽŋkuxaˈla(x)] vt to herd.
encurtar [4] [ẽŋkuxˈta(x)] vt to shorten.
end. (abrev de **endereço**) m add.
endêmico, ca [ẽnˈdemiku, ka] adj endemic.
endemoninhado, da [ẽndemoniˈɲadu, da] adj -**1**. [pessoa - possuído] possessed; [- levado] mischievous. -**2**. [expressão, olhar] diabolical.
endereçamento [ẽnderesaˈmẽntu] m -**1**. [ger] address. -**2**. COMPUT addressing.
endereçar [13] [ẽndereˈsa(x)] vt -**1**. [sobrescrever] to address. -**2**. [enviar] to send.
endereço [ẽndeˈresu] m address; ~ eletrônico e-mail address.
endeusar [4] [ẽndewˈza(x)] vt to deify.
endiabrado, da [ẽndʒjaˈbradu, da] adj mischievous.
endinheirado, da [ẽndʒiɲejˈradu, da] adj well-off.
endireitar [4] [ẽndʒirejˈta(x)] vt -**1**. [descurvar] to straighten. -**2**. [arrumar] to tidy.
  endireitar-se vp [corrigir-se] to go straight.
endividado, da [ẽndʒiviˈdadu, da] adj in debt.
endividamento [ẽndʒividaˈmẽntu] m state of being in debt.
endividar-se [4] [ẽndʒiviˈdaxsi] vp to fall into debt.
endócrino, na [ẽnˈdɔkrinu, na] adj endocrine.
endocrinologia [ẽnˌdokrinoloˈʒial f endocrinology.
endocrinologista [ẽnˌdokrinoloˈʒiʃtal mf endocrinologist.
endoidar [4] [ẽndojˈda(x)] vi to go mad; **meu relógio endoidou** my watch has gone haywire.
endoidecer [25] [ẽndojdeˈse(x)] ⟨⟩ vt to drive mad. ⟨⟩ vi to go mad.
endoscopia [ẽndoʃkoˈpial f endoscopy.
endossar [4] [ẽndoˈsa(x)] vt to endorse.
endosso [ẽnˈdosul m endorsement.
endurecer [25] [ẽndureˈse(x)] ⟨⟩ vt to harden. ⟨⟩ vi-**1**. [ficar duro] to go hard. -**2**. [ficar difícil] to be hard. -**3**. fig [tornar-se frio]: ~ **(com alguém)** to harden (towards sb).
endurecimento [ẽnduresiˈmẽntul m hardening.
enegrecer [25] [enegreˈse(x)] vt & vi to darken.
ENEM (abrev de **Exame Nacional do Ensino Médio**) m exam taken at the end of middle education in Brazil.
enema [eˈnemal m enema.
energético, ca [enexˈʒɛtʃiku, ka] adj energizing.
  energética f energy.
energia [enexˈʒial f energy; ~ **atômica/nuclear/solar** atomic/nuclear/solar energy.
enérgico, ca [eˈnɛxʒiku, ka] adj energetic.
energizante [enexʒiˈzãntʃil adj energizing.
energizar [4] [enexʒiˈza(x)] vt to energize.
enervante [enexˈvãntʃil adj annoying.

enervar [4] [enexˈva(x)] vt to annoy.
  enervar-se vp to get annoyed.
enevoado, da [eneˈvwadu, da] adj misty.
enfadar [4] [ẽnfaˈda(x)] vt to bore.
  enfadar-se vp to get bored.
enfado [ẽnˈfadul m boredom.
enfadonho, nha [ẽnfaˈdoɲu, ɲal adj boring.
enfaixar [4] [ẽnfajˈʃa(x)] vt to bandage.
enfartar [4] [ẽnfaxˈta(x)] vi to have a clot.
enfarte [ẽnˈfaxtʃil m MED clot.
ênfase [ˈẽnfazil f emphasis; **dar** ~ **a** to emphasize.
enfastiado, da [ẽnfaʃˈtʃjadu, da] adj bored.
enfastiar [16] [ẽnfaʃˈtʃja(x)] vt to bore.
  enfastiar-se vp to get bored.
enfático, ca [ẽnˈfatʃiku, ka] adj emphatic.
enfatizar [4] [ẽnfatʃiˈza(x)] vt to emphasize.
enfear [15] [ẽnfeˈa(x)] ⟨⟩ vt to make ugly. ⟨⟩ vi to become ugly.
enfeitar [4] [ẽnfejˈta(x)] vt to decorate.
  enfeitar-se vp to dress up.
enfeite [ẽnˈfejtʃil m decoration.
enfeitiçar [13] [ẽnfejtʃiˈsa(x)] vt -**1**. [lançar feitiço] to bewitch. -**2**. fig [fascinar] to charm.
enfermagem [ẽnfexˈmaʒẽl f nursing.
enfermaria [ẽnfexmaˈrial f sickroom.
enfermeiro, ra [ẽnfexˈmejru, ral m, f nurse.
enfermidade [ẽnfexmiˈdadʒil f illness.
enfermo, ma [ẽnˈfexmu, mal ⟨⟩ adj sick. ⟨⟩ m, f sick person.
enferrujado, da [ẽnfexuˈʒadu, da] adj [oxidado] rusty.
enferrujar [4] [ẽnfexuˈʒa(x)] ⟨⟩ vt to rust. ⟨⟩ vi to go rusty.
enfezado, da [ẽnfeˈzadu, da] adj annoyed.
enfezar [4] [ẽnfeˈza(x)] vt to annoy.
  enfezar-se vp to get annoyed.
enfiar [16] [ẽnˈfja(x)] vt -**1**. [introduzir]: ~ **algo (em algo)** to thread sthg (onto sthg). -**2**. [vestir] to slip on. -**3**. [pôr] to put.
  enfiar-se vp [meter-se]: ~-**se em algo** to slip into sthg.
enfileirar [4] [ẽnfilejˈra(x)] vt to put in line.
  enfileirar-se vp to get in line.
enfim [ẽnˈfil adv finally; **até que** ~ finally; ~ **sós!** alone at last!
enfisema [ẽnfiˈzemal f emphysema.
enfocar [12] [ẽnfoˈka(x)] vt to focus.
enfoque [ẽnˈfɔkil m focus.
enforcamento [ẽnfoxkaˈmẽntul m [de pessoa] hanging.
enforcar [ẽfoxˈka(x)] vt -**1**. [pessoa] to hang. -**2**. fam fig [dia de trabalho, aula] to skip.
  enforcar-se vp [pessoa] to hang o.s.
enfraquecer [25] [ẽnfrakeˈse(x)] ⟨⟩ vt to weaken. ⟨⟩ vi to grow weak.
  enfraquecer-se vp to weaken o.s.
enfraquecido, da [ẽnfrakeˈsidu, da] adj weakened.
enfraquecimento [ẽnfrakesiˈmẽntul m weakening.

enfrentamento [ênfrênta'mêntul] *m* clash, confrontation.

enfrentar [4] [ênfrên'ta(x)] *vt* to face.

enfronhado, da [ênfro'ɲadu, dal] *adj*: **bem ~ em algo** well-versed in sthg.

enfronhar [4] [ênfro'ɲa(x)] *vt*: **~ alguém em algo** to instruct sb in sthg.

➤ **enfronhar-se** *vp*: **~-se em algo** to become knowledgeable about sthg.

enfumaçado, da [ênfuma'sadu, dal] *adj* smoky.

enfumaçar [13] [ênfuma'sa(x)] *vt* to make smoky.

enfurecer [25] [ênfure'se(x)] *vt* to infuriate.

➤ **enfurecer-se** *vp* to get infuriated.

enfurecido, da [ênfure'sidu, dal] *adj* infuriated.

enfurnar-se [4] [ênfux'naxsil] *vp*: **~-se em** to hide o.s. in.

engaiolar [4] [êngajo'la(x)] *vt* to put in a cage.

engajado, da [êŋga'ʒadu, dal] *adj* engaged.

engajamento [êŋgaʒa'mêntul] *m* **-1.** [ger] engagement. **-2.** [de trabalhadores] taking on.

engajar [4] [êŋga'ʒa(x)] *vt* [trabalhadores] to take on.

➤ **engajar-se** *vp* **-1.** POL: **~-se (em)** to engage o.s. (in). **-2.** MIL: **~-se (em)** to become engaged (in). **-3.** [em campanha, luta]: **~-se em** to get involved (in). **-4.** [trabalhador]: **~-se (em)** to be engaged (in).

engalfinhar-se [4] [êŋgawfi'ɲaxsil] *vp* to get entangled.

engambelar [4] [êŋgãnbe'la(x)] *vt* to deceive.

enganação [êŋgana'sãw] *f* deception.

enganador, ra [êŋgana'do(x), ral] *adj* deceptive.

enganar [4] [êŋga'na(x)] *vt* **-1.** [iludir] to deceive. **-2.** [trair] to cheat.

➤ **enganar-se** *vp* **-1.** [iludir-se] to fool o.s. **-2.** [cometer um erro] to make a mistake.

enganchar [4] [êŋgãn'ʃa(x)] <> *vt*: **~ algo (em algo)** to hook sthg up (to sthg). <> *vi*: **~ (em algo)** to catch (in sthg).

engano [êŋ'gãnul] *m* [equívoco] error; [em telefonema]: **ser ~** to be a wrong number.

engarrafado, da [êŋgaxa'fadu, dal] *adj* **-1.** [bebida] bottled. **-2.** [rua, trânsito] blocked.

engarrafamento [êŋgaxafa'mêntul] *m* **-1.** [de bebida] bottling. **-2.** [no trânsito] traffic jam.

engarrafar [4] [êŋgaxa'fa(x)] *vt* **-1.** [bebida] to bottle. **-2.** [rua, trânsito] to block.

engasgar [14] [êŋgaʒ'ga(x)] <> *vt* [na garganta] to choke. <> *vi* to choke.

➤ **engasgar-se** *vp* [na garganta] to choke o.s.

engasgo [êŋ'gaʒgul] *m* [na garganta] choking.

engastar [4] [êŋgaʃ'ta(x)] *vt* to set.

engaste [êŋ'gaʃtʃil] *m* [stone] setting.

engatar [4] [êŋga'ta(x)] *vt* **-1.** [atrelar]: **~ algo (em algo)** to couple sthg (with sthg). **-2.** [engrenar] to get into gear. **-3.** [iniciar] to start.

engate [êŋ'gatʃil] *m* connection.

engatilhar [4] [êŋgatʃi'ʎa(x)] *vt* **-1.** [arma] to cock. **-2.** *fig* [resposta etc] to prepare.

engatinhar [4] [êŋgatʃi'ɲa(x)] *vi* **-1.** [bebê] to crawl. **-2.** *fig* [ser principiante]: **~ em algo** to feel one's way in sthg.

engavetamento [êŋgaveta'mêntul] *m* **-1.** [de carros] smash. **-2.** [de papéis] putting into a drawer. **-3.** [de projeto, processo] *fig* shelving.

engavetar [4] [êŋgave'ta(x)] <> *vt* **-1.** [papéis etc] to put into a drawer. **-2.** *fig* [processo, projeto] to shelve. <> *vi* [carros] to concertina.

➤ **engavetar-se** *vp* [carros] to concertina.

engendrar [4] [êŋʒên'dra(x)] *vt* to create.

engenharia [êŋʒeɲa'rial] *f* engineering; **~ genética** genetic engineering.

engenheiro, ra [êŋʒe'ɲejru, ral] *m, f* engineer.

engenho [êŋ'ʒeɲul] *m* **-1.** [habilidade] inventiveness. **-2.** [máquina] engine. **-3.** [moenda] mill. **-4.** [fazenda de cana de açúcar] sugar plant.

engenhoca [êŋʒe'ɲokal] *f pej* [aparelho] Heath-Robinson device.

engenhoso, osa [êŋʒe'ɲozu, ɔzal] *adj* ingenious.

engessado, da [êŋe'sadu, dal] *adj* plastered.

engessar [4] [êŋʒe'sa(x)] *vt* to put in plaster.

englobar [4] [êŋglo'ba(x)] *vt* to encompass.

engodo [êŋ'godul] *m* **-1.** [isca] bait. **-2.** [farsa] flattery.

engolir [59] [êŋgo'li(x)] *vt* **-1.** [ger] to swallow. **-2.** *fig* [sobrepujar]: **~ alguém** to eclipse sb.

engomado, da [êŋgo'madu, dal] *adj* starched.

engomar [4] [êŋgo'ma(x)] *vt* to starch.

engordar [4] [êŋgox'da(x)] <> *vt* to fatten. <> *vi* to put on weight; **açúcar engorda** sugar is fattening.

engordurado, da [êŋgoxdu'radu, dal] *adj* greasy.

engordurar [4] [êŋgoxdu'ra(x)] *vt* to grease.

engraçadinho, nha [êŋgrasa'dʒiɲu, ɲal] <> *adj* [pequeno, gracioso] cute. <> *m, f pej* clown.

engraçado, da [êŋgra'sadu, dal] *adj* amusing.

engraçar-se [13] [êŋgra'saxsil] *vp*: **~ para o lado de alguém** to take advantage of sb.

engradado [êŋgra'dadul] *m* crate.

engrandecer [25] [êŋgrãnde'se(x)] *vt* to elevate.

➤ **engrandecer-se** *vp* to elevate o.s.

engravidar [4] [êŋgravi'da(x)] <> *vt* to make pregnant. <> *vi* to become pregnant.

engraxar [4] [êŋgra'ʃa(x)] *vt* to polish.

engraxate [êŋgra'ʃatʃil] *mf* shoe shiner.

engrenagem [êŋgre'naʒêl] (*pl* **-ns**) *f* **-1.** AUTO gear. **-2.** *fig* [política, social] mechanism.

engrenar [4] [êŋgre'na(x)] *vt* **-1.** AUTO to put in gear. **-2.** [iniciar] to start.

engrossar [4] [êŋgro'sa(x)] <> *vt* **-1.** [aumentar] to enlarge. **-2.** [encorpar] to thicken. **-3.** [tornar grave] to deepen. <> *vi fig* [ser grosseiro]: **~ (com alguém)** to be rough (with sb).

enguia [êŋ'gial] *f* eel.

enguiçado, da [êŋgi'sadu, dal] *adj* **-1.** [com defeito] broken down. **-2.** [emperrado] bogged down.

enguiçar [13] [êŋgi'sa(x)] *vi* **-1.** [carro] to break down. **-2.** [relógio] to stop.

enguiço [êŋ'gisul] *m* breakdown.

engulho [êŋ'guʎul] *m* nausea.

enigma [e'nigmal] *m* enigma.

enigmático, ca [enigi'matʃiku, ka] *adj* enigmatic.
enjaular [19] [ẽʒaw'la(x)] *vt* to put in a cage.
enjeitado, da [ẽʒej'tadu, da] *adj* rejected.
enjeitar [4] [ẽʒej'ta(x)] *vt* **-1.** [rejeitar] to reject. **-2.** [abandonar] to abandon.
enjoado, da [ẽ'ʒwadu, da] *adj* **-1.** [nauseado] nauseous. **-2.** *fig* [cansado]: ~ de algo/de fazer algo fed up with sthg/with doing sthg. **-3.** *fig* [chato] boring.
enjoar [20] [ẽ'ʒwa(x)] <> *vt* **-1.** [nausear] to make nauseous. **-2.** *fig* [cansar] to bore. <> *vi* **-1.** [nausear-se] to feel sick. **-2.** *fig* [cansar-se]: ~ de algo /de fazer algo to become bored with sthg/with doing sthg.
enjoativo, va [ẽʒwa'tʃivu, va] *adj* nauseating.
enjôo [ẽ'ʒou] *m* **-1.** [náusea] sickness; ~ de gravidez morning sickness. **-2.** *fig* [aborrecimento]: ser um ~ to be a bore.
enlaçar [13] [ẽla'sa(x)] *vt* **-1.** [prender com laço] to tie up. **-2.** [envolver] to bog down.
enlace [ẽ'lasi] *m* **-1.** [união] union. **-2.** [casamento] marriage.
enlameado, da [ẽla'mjadu, da] *adj* **-1.** [com lama] muddy. **-2.** *fig* [vilipendiado] muddied.
enlamear [15] [ẽla'mja(x)] *vt* to muddy.
enlatado, da [ẽla'tadu, da] *adj* canned.
enlatado *m* **-1.** [comida em lata] canned food. **-2.** *pej* [série de TV] trash TV.
enlatar [15] [ẽla'ta(x)] *vt* to can.
enlevar [4] [ẽle'va(x)] *vt* to entrance.
enlevar-se *vp* **-1.** [extasiar-se] to become entranced. **-2.** [absorver-se]: ~-se em to become absorbed in.
enlevo [ẽ'levu] *m* enchantment.
enlouquecer [25] [ẽloke'se(x)] <> *vt* to drive mad. <> *vi* to go mad.
enlouquecido, da [ẽloke'sidu, da] *adj* crazed.
enlouquecimento [ẽlokesi'mẽtu] *m* (growing) insanity.
enluarado, da [ẽlwa'radu, da] *adj* moonlit.
enobrecer [25] [enobre'se(x)] *vt* to ennoble.
enobrecer-se *vp* to glorify o.s.
enojado, da [eno'ʒadu, da] *adj* disgusted.
enojar [4] [eno'ʒa(x)] *vt* to disgust.
enojar-se *vp* [sentir nojo]: enojava-se com o cheiro de frango the smell of chicken made him/her sick.
enorme [e'nɔxmi] *adj* enormous.
enormidade [enoxmi'dadʒi] *f* enormity; uma ~ de a vast quantity of.
enquadramento [ẽkwadra'mẽtu] *m* CINE & FOTO frame.
enquadrar [4] [ẽkwa'dra(x)] <> *vt* **-1.** [ajustar]: ~ algo em algo to frame sthg in sthg. **-2.** [autuar] to charge. <> *vi* [combinar]: ~ com to fit in with.
enquadrar-se *vp* [ajustar-se]: ~-se (em algo) to fit in (with sthg).
enquanto [ẽ'kwãntu] *conj* **-1.** [ger] while. **-2.** [considerado como]: isso é interessante ~ experiência it's interesting as an experience; ~ isso meanwhile.

por enquanto *loc adv* for the time being.
enquete [ẽ'ketʃil] *f* survey.
enraivecer [25] [ẽxajve'se(x)] *vt* to anger.
enraivecer-se *vp* to become angry.
enraizar [4] [ẽxaj'za(x)] *vt* to root.
enraizar-se *vp* to take root.
enrascada [ẽxaʃ'kada] *f* tight spot; meter-se numa ~ to get into a tight spot.
enrascado, da [ẽxaʃ'kadu, da] *adj* in a fix (depois de verbo).
enrascar-se [12] [ẽxaʃ'kaxsil] *vp* to get in a fix.
enredar [4] [ẽnre'da(x)] *vt* **-1.** [emaranhar] to twist. **-2.** *fig* [enganar] to deceive.
enredar-se *vp* **-1.** [pessoa] to become entangled. **-2.** [peixe] to fall into a net.
enredo [ẽ'xedu] *m* plot.
enrijecer [25] [ẽxiʒe'se(x)] *vt* to stiffen.
enrijecer-se *vp* to become stiff.
enriquecer [25] [ẽxike'se(x)] <> *vt* to enrich. <> *vi* to become rich.
enriquecer-se *vp*: ~-se com algo to become rich in sthg.
enriquecimento [ẽxikesi'mẽtu] *m* **-1.** [financeiro] increase in wealth. **-2.** [cultural] enrichment.
enrolado, da [ẽxo'ladu, da] *adj* **-1.** [embrulhado] ~ em algo rolled up in sthg. **-2.** [cabelo] coiled. **-3.** *fam* [confuso] screwed up.
enrolar [4] [ẽxo'la(x)] <> *vt* **-1.** [dar forma de rolo] to roll. **-2.** [embrulhar]: ~ algo/alguém em algo to wrap sthg/sb up in sthg. **-3.** *fam* [complicar] to screw up. **-4.** *fam* [enganar] to take in. <> *vi fam* [protelar] to put things off.
enrolar-se *vp* **-1.** [agasalhar-se]: ~-se em algo to wrap o.s. up in sthg. **-2.** *fam* [confundir-se] to screw things up.
enroscar [4] [ẽxoʃ'ka(x)] *vt*: ~ algo em to entwine sthg in.
enroscar-se *vp* **-1.** [encolher-se de frio] to curl up. **-2.** [embolar-se] to become entangled.
enrouquecer [25] [ẽxoke'se(x)] <> *vt* to make hoarse. <> *vi* to become hoarse.
enrubescer [25] [ẽxube'se(x)] <> *vt* to redden. <> *vi* to blush, go red.
enrugado, da [ẽxu'gadu, da] *adj* wrinkled.
enrugar [14] [ẽxu'ga(x)] *vt & vi* to wrinkle.
enrustido [ẽxuʃ'tʃidul] *m* [homossexual] closet gay.
ensaboar [20] [ẽsa'bwa(x)] *vt* to wash with soap.
ensaboar-se *vp* to soap o.s.
ensaiar [4] [ẽsa'ja(x)] *vt* to practise UK, to practice US.
ensaio [ẽ'saju] *m* **-1.** [experiência] trial. **-2.** TEATRO rehearsal. **-3.** LITER essay.
ensaísta [ẽsa'iʃta] *mf* essayist.
ensangüentado, da [ẽsãngwẽn'tadu, da] *adj* blood-stained.
ensangüentar [4] [ẽsãngwẽn'ta(x)] *vt* to stain with blood.
enseada [ẽn'sjada] *f* inlet.
ensebado, da [ẽnse'badu, da] *adj* greasy.

ensebar [4] [ẽnse'ba(x)] *vt* to grease.

ensejar [4] [ẽnse'ʒa(x)] *vt*: ~ **algo a alguém** to offer the opportunity of sthg to sb.

ensejo [ẽn'seʒul *m* opportunity.

ensimesmado, da [ẽnsimeʒ'madu, dal *adj* introverted.

ensinamento [ẽnsina'mẽntul *m* instruction.

ensinar [4] [ẽnsi'na(x)] *vt*: ~ **alguém a fazer algo** to teach sb how to do sthg; ~ **algo a alguém** to teach sthg to sb.

ensino [ẽn'sinul *m* **-1.** [transmissão de conhecimento] teaching. **-2.** [educação] education; ~ **fundamental/medio** primary/secondary education; ~ **superior** higher education; ~ **supletivo** *speeded-up education programme for adults who missed out on a full schooling.*

ensolarado, da [ẽnsola'radu, dal *adj* sunny.

ensombrecido, da [ẽnsõnbre'sidu, dal *adj* gloomy.

ensopado, da [ẽnso'padu, dal *adj* **-1.** *CULIN* stewed. **-2.** *fig* [encharcado] soaking.
➠ **ensopado** *m CULIN* stew.

ensopar [4] [ẽnso'pa(x)] *vt* to soak.

ensurdecedor, ra [ẽnsuxdese'dox, ral (*mpl* **-es**, *fpl* **-s**) *adj* deafening.

ensurdecer [25] [ẽnsuxde'se(x)] *vt* to deafen.

entabular [4] [ẽntabu'la(x)] *vt* to open.

entalado, da [ẽnta'ladu, dal *adj* stuck.

entalar [4] [ẽnta'la(x)] <> *vt* [apertar] to squeeze. <> *vi* [encravar] to stick.

entalhador, ra [ẽntaʎa'do(x), ral *m, f* wood-carver.

entalhar [4] [ẽnta'ʎa(x)] *vt* to carve.

entalhe [ẽn'taʎil *m* groove.

entanto [ẽn'tãntul ➠ **no entanto** *loc adv* however.

então [ẽn'tãwl *adv* then; **até** ~ up until then; **desde** ~ since then; **e** ~? well then?; **para** ~ so that; **pois** ~ then.

entardecer [25] [ẽntaxde'se(x)] <> *vi* to get late. <> *m* sunset.

ente [ˈẽntʃil *m* **-1.** [ser] being. **-2.** [corporação, órgão] entity.

enteado, da [ẽn'tʒjadu, dal *m, f* stepchild, stepson (*f* stepdaughter).

entediante [ẽnte'dʒjãntʃil *adj* boring.

entediar [16] [ẽnte'dʒa(x)] *vt* to bore.
➠ **entediar-se** *vp* to get bored.

entendedor, ra [ẽntẽnde'do(x), ral <> *adj* knowledgeable. <> *m, f* expert; **a bom** ~ **meia palavra basta** a word is sufficient to the wise.

entender [5] [ẽntẽn'de(x)] <> *vt* **-1.** [compreender] to understand; **dar a** ~ to give the impression. **-2.** [ouvir] to hear. **-3.** [interpretar] to perceive. **-4.** [deduzir]: ~ **que** to see (that). <> *vi* **-1.** [inferir] **o que você** ~ **por isso?** what do you deduce from it? **-2.** [conhecer]: ~ **de** to know about. <> *m*: **no** ~ **de alguém** in the opinion of sb.
➠ **entender-se** *vp* **-1.** [comunicar-se] to get along. **-2.** [chegar a um acordo]: ~**se (com alguém)** to see eye to eye (with sb). **-3.** [ter o uso da razão]:

desde que me entendo por gente, gosto de música for as long as I can remember, I've liked music.

entendido, da [ẽntẽn'dʒidu, dal <> *adj* **-1.** [perito] expert; ~ **em algo** expert in sthg. **-2.** *fam* [homossexual] gay. <> *m, f* **-1.** [perito] expert. **-2.** *fam* [homossexual] gay.
➠ **bem entendido** *loc adv* understood.

entendimento [ẽntẽndʒi'mẽntul *m* **-1.** [compreensão] understanding. **-2.** [juízo] perception. **-3.** [acordo] agreement.

enternecer [25] [ẽntexne'se(x)] *vt* to touch.
➠ **enternecer-se** *vp* to be touched.

enterrar [4] [ẽnte'xa(x)] *vt* **-1.** to bury. **-2.** *fig* [encerrar] to close. **-3.** *fig* [arruinar] to ruin. **-4.** [enfiar] **enterrou a estaca no coração do vampiro** he rammed the stake into the vampire's heart; **enterrou o chapéu na cabeça** he rammed his hat on his head.
➠ **enterrar-se** *vp* **-1.** [isolar-se] to hide o.s. away. **-2.** [arruinar-se] to ruin o.s.

enterro [ẽn'texul *m* **-1.** [sepultamento] burial. **-2.** [funeral] funeral.

entidade [ẽntʃi'dadʒil *f* entity.

entoação [ẽntwa'sãwl *f* chanting.

entoar [20] [ẽn'twa(x)] *vt* to chant.

entonação [ẽntona'sãwl *f* intonation.

entornar [4] [ẽntox'na(x)] <> *vt* **-1.** [derramar] to spill. **-2.** [despejar] to pour. <> *vi fig* [embriagar-se] to drink heavily.

entorpecente [ẽntoxpe'sẽntʃil *m* narcotic.

entorpecer [25] [ẽntoxpe'se(x)] *vt* **-1.** [causar torpor] to stupefy. **-2.** *fig* [insensibilizar] to numb.

entorpecido, da [ẽntoxpe'sidu, dal *adj* numb.

entorpecimento [ẽntoxpesi'mẽntul *m* **-1.** [paralisia] stupor. **-2.** *fig* [estagnação] numbness.

entorse [ẽn'toxsil *f* sprain.

entortar [4] [ẽntox'ta(x)] <> *vt* **-1.** [curvar] to bend. **-2.** [empenar] to jam. <> *vi* [empenar - porta] to warp; [- roda] to buckle.

entourage [ãntu'xaʒil *m* entourage.

entrada [ẽn'tradal *f* **-1.** [ger] entry; **'proibida a** ~' 'no entry'. **-2.** [lugar] entrance; ~ **de serviço** service entrance. **-3.** [admissão] admission. **-4.** [porta] doorway. **-5.** [corredor] hallway. **-6.** *CULIN* starter. **-7.** [calvície] receding hairline. **-8.** [pagamento inicial] down payment. **-9.** [ingresso] ticket; ~ **gratuita** *ou* **franca** free admission; **meia** ~ half price. **-10.** [abertura] opening. **-11.** *TEC* inlet. **-12.** *COMPUT* input. **-13.** [início]: **dar** ~ **em algo** to institute sthg.

entra-e-sai [ˌẽntri'sajl *m inv* coming and going.

entranhado, da [ẽntra'ɲadu, dal *adj* deep-seated.

entranhar [4] [ẽntra'ɲa(x)] *vi*: ~ **(em algo)** to penetrate (sthg).

entranhas [ẽn'traɲaʃl *fpl* **-1.** [vísceras] bowels. **-2.** *fig* [profundeza] depths.

entrar [4] [ẽn'tra(x)] *vi* **-1.** [adentrar]: ~ **(em)** to go/come (into). **-2.** [penetrar] to enter. **-3.** [começar a trabalhar] to begin. **-4.** [contribuir]: ~ **com algo** to contribute sthg. **- 5.** [começar]: ~ **de férias** to go on vacation. **- 6.** [aprofundar-se]: ~ **em algo** to go into sthg. **- 7.** [entabular]: ~ **em algo** to enter into sthg. **- 8.** [envolver-se]: ~ **em algo** to become involved in sthg. **- 9.** [caber]: ~ **em algo** to fit into sthg. **- 10.** [ser componente]: ~ **em algo** to be part of sthg. **- 11.** [ingressar]: ~ **para algo** [universidade] to go to sthg; [clube] to join sthg. **- 12.** *COMPUT*: ~ **com algo** to enter sthg. **- 13.** *loc*: ~ **bem** *fam* to get one's fingers burnt.

entrave [ẽn'travi] *m* obstacle.

entre ['ẽntri] *prep* between; **os dois dividiram o bolo** ~ **eles** the two shared the cake between them; **os alunos sempre conversavam** ~ **si** the schoolchildren always talked among themselves; **cá** ~ **nós** [confidencialmente] between you and me.

entreaberto, ta [ˌẽntrja'bɛxtu, ta] *adj* **-1.** [porta] ajar. **- 2.** [olho] half-open.

entreabrir [6] [ẽntrja'bri(x)] *vt* to half-open.
➤ **entreabrir-se** *vp* to open up.

entrecortado, da [ẽntrekox'tadu, da] *adj* intermittent.

entrecortar [ẽntre'koxta(x)] *vt* **-1.** [cortar] to cut off. **- 2.** [interromper] to interrupt.

entrega [ẽn'trɛga] *f* **-1.** [de carta, prêmio] delivery; ~ **em domicílio** home delivery; **pronta** ~ speedy delivery. **- 2.** [dedicação]: ~ **a algo/alguém** dedication to sthg/sb. **- 3.** [rendição] surrender.

entregador, ra [ẽntrega'do(x), ra] *m, f* [funcionário] delivery person.

entregar [14] [ẽntre'ga(x)] *vt* **-1.** [passar às mãos de - mercadoria, carta] to deliver; [- presente] to give; [- prêmio] to award. **- 2.** [delatar] to inform on. **- 3.** [devolver] to return. **- 4.** [confiar]: ~ **algo/alguém a alguém** to entrust sthg/sb to sb.
➤ **entregar-se** *vp* **-1.** [render-se - inimigo] to surrender; [- à dor *etc*]: ~**-se a algo** to surrender to sthg. **- 2.** [dedicar-se]: ~**-se a algo** to dedicate o.s. to sthg. **- 3.** [deixar-se seduzir]: ~**-se a alguém** to give o.s. to sb. **- 4.** *loc*: ~ **os pontos** to give up.

entregue [ẽn'trɛgi] *pp* ▷ **entregar**.

entreguismo [ẽntre'giʒmu] *m* selling-out, *policy of allowing exploitation of the country's natural resources by foreign entities.*

entreguista [ẽntre'giʃta] *adj supportive or typical of selling-out.*

entrelaçamento [ẽntrelasa'mẽntu] *m* [união] interlinking.

entrelaçar [13] [ẽntrela'sa(x)] *vt* to entwine.

entrelinha [ẽntre'liɲa] *f* [espaço] line space.
➤ **entrelinhas** *fpl*: **nas** ~**s** *fig* [subentendido] between the lines.

entremear [15] [ẽntre'mja(x)] *vt*: ~ **algo com algo** to mix sthg with sthg.

entreolhar-se [7] [ẽntrjo'ʎaxsi] *vp* to exchange glances.

entrepor [45] [ẽntre'po(x)] *vt* to insert.
➤ **entrepor-se** *vp*: ~**-se entre** to come between.

entreposto, ta [ẽntre'poʃtu, ta] *pp* ▷ **entrepor**.
➤ **entreposto** *m* warehouse.

entressafra [ẽntri'safra] *f* period between harvests.

entretanto [ẽntri'tãntu] *conj* however.

entretenimento [ẽntriteni'mẽntu] *m* **-1.** [passatempo] pastime. **- 2.** [diversão] entertainment.

entreter [1] [ẽntri'te(x)] *vt* **-1.** [ger] to entertain. **- 2.** [ocupar] to occupy.
➤ **entreter-se** *vp* **-1.** [divertir-se] to amuse o.s. **- 2.** [ocupar-se] to occupy o.s.

entretido, da [ẽntre'tʃidu, da] *adj* **-1.** [distraído] entertained. **- 2.** [ocupado] occupied.

entrevar [4] [ẽntre'va(x)] *vt* to cripple.

entrever [40] [ẽntre've(x)] *vt* **-1.** [ver] to glimpse. **- 2.** [prever] to foresee.

entrevero [ẽntre'vero] *m* mêlée *UK*, melee *US*.

entrevista [ẽntre'viʃta] *f* interview; ~ **coletiva** press conference.

entrevistado, da [ẽntre'viʃtadu, da] *m, f* interviewee.

entrevistador, ra [ẽntre'viʃtado(x), ra] (*mpl* **-es,** *fpl* **-s**) *m, f* interviewer.

entrevistar [4] [ẽntre'viʃ'ta(x)] *vt* to interview.

entristecedor, ra [ẽntriʃtese'do(x), ra] *adj* saddening.

entristecer [25] [ẽntriʃte'se(x)] ◇ *vt* to sadden. ◇ *vi* to become sad.
➤ **entristecer-se** *vp* to become sad.

entroncamento [ẽntrõɲka'mẽntu] *m* junction.

entrosado, da [ẽntro'zadu, da] *adj* [ambientado] integrated.

entrosamento [ẽntroza'mẽntu] *m* integration.

entrosar [4] [ẽntro'za(x)] *vt* **-1.** [endentar] to mesh. **- 2.** [ambientar]: ~ **alguém com alguém** to integrate sb with sb.
➤ **entrosar-se** *vp* [entender-se]: ~**-se (com alguém)** to get along (with sb).

entulhar [4] [ẽntu'ʎa(x)] *vt*: ~ **algo (de** *ou* **com)** to cram sthg with.

entulho [ẽn'tuʎu] *m* debris.

entupido, da [ẽntu'pidu, da] *adj* **-1.** [pia, nariz, ouvido] blocked. **- 2.** [de comida] stuffed. **- 3.** [de gente] packed.

entupimento [ẽntupi'mẽntu] *m* blockage.

entupir [60.61] [ẽntu'pi(x)] *vt* to block.
➤ **entupir-se** *vp*: ~**-se de comida** to stuff o.s. with food; ~**-se de bebida** to pump o.s. full of drink.

enturmar-se [7] [ẽntux'maxsi] *vp*: ~**-se (com)** to make friends (with).

entusiasmado, da [ẽntuzjaʒ'madu, da] *adj* enthusiastic.

entusiasmar [4] [ẽntuzjaʒ'ma(x)] *vt* to fill with enthusiasm.
➤ **entusiasmar-se** *vp* to get enthusiastic.

entusiasmo [ẽntu'zjaʒmu] *m* enthusiasm.

entusiasta [ẽntu'zjaʃta] ◇ *adj* enthusiastic. ◇ *mf* enthusiast.

entusiástico, ca [ẽntu'zjaʃtʃiku, ka] *adj* enthusiastic.

enumeração [enumera'sãw] (*pl* **-ões**) *f* enumeration.

enumerar [4] [enume'ra(x)] *vt* to enumerate.

enunciado, da [enũ'sjadu, da] <> *adj* stated. <> *m* statement.

enunciar [16] [enũ'sja(x)] *vt* to state.

envaidecer [25] [ẽnvajde'se(x)] *vt* to flatter.

◆ **envaidecer-se** *vp* to feel flattered.

envelhecer [25] [ẽnveʎe'se(x)] <> *vt* -**1.** [tornar velho] to age. -**2.** [fazer parecer velho]: ~ **alguém** to make sb look older. <> *vi* -**1.** [ficar velho] to grow old. -**2.** [fazer parecer velho] to age.

envelhecido, da [ẽnveʎe'sidu, da] *adj* aged.

envelhecimento [ẽnveʎesi'mẽntu] *m* ageing.

envelopar [ẽnve'lopa(x)] *vt* to put in an envelope.

envelope [ẽnve'lɔpi] *m* envelope.

envenenado, da [ẽnvene'nadu, da] *adj* -**1.** [ger] poisoned. -**2.** *fam fig* [carro] souped up.

envenenamento [ẽnvenena'mẽntu] *m* poisoning.

envenenar [4] [ẽnvene'na(x)] *vt* -**1.** [intoxicar] to poison. -**2.** [corromper] to corrupt. -**3.** AUTO to soup up.

◆ **envenenar-se** *vp* [intoxicar-se] to poison o.s.

enveredar [4] [ẽnvere'da(x)] *vi* to make one's way; ~ **por/para** to head for.

envergadura [ẽnvexga'dura] *f* -**1.** [dimensão] wingspan. -**2.** *fig* [importância] scope. -**3.** *fig* [capacidade]: **é um poeta de pouca** ~ he's a poet of little talent.

envergar [14] [ẽnvex'ga(x)] <> *vt* -**1.** [entortar] to bend. -**2.** [vestir] to wear. <> *vi* [arquear] to warp.

envergonhado, da [ẽnvexgo'nadu, da] *adj* -**1.** [tímido] shy. -**2.** [por má ação] ashamed.

envergonhar [4] [ẽnvexgo'na(x)] *vt* -**1.** [acanhar] to embarrass. -**2.** [com má ação] to disgrace.

◆ **envergonhar-se** *vp* -**1.** [acanhar-se] to be embarrassed. -**2.** [por má ação] to be ashamed.

envernizado, da [ẽnvexni'zadu, da] *adj* [com verniz] varnished.

envernizar [4] [ẽnvexni'za(x)] *vt* to varnish.

enviado, da [ẽn'vjadu, da] *m, f* envoy.

enviar [16] [ẽn'vja(x)] *vt*: ~ **algo a** ou **para alguém** to send sthg to sb.

envidar [4] [ẽnvi'da(x)] *vt* to endeavour *UK*, to endeavor *US*.

envidraçado, da [ẽnvidra'sadu, da] *adj* glazed.

envidraçar [13] [ẽnvidra'sa(x)] *vt* to glaze.

enviesado, da [ẽnvje'zadu, da] *adj* slanting.

enviesar [ẽnvje'za(x)] *vt* -**1.** [pôr obliquamente] to put at an angle. -**2.** [envesgar] to cross.

envio [ẽn'viu] *m* dispatch.

enviuvar [4] [ẽnvju'va(x)] *vi* to be widowed.

envolto, ta [ẽn'vowtu, ta] <> *pp* ▷ **envolver**. <> *adj* wrapped.

envoltório [ẽnvow'tɔrju] *m* wrapping.

envolvente [ẽnvow'vẽntʃi] *adj* compelling.

envolver [5] [ẽnvow've(x)] *vt* -**1.** [cobrir]: ~ **algo/alguém (em)** to wrap sthg/sb (in). -**2.** [comprometer]: ~ **alguém (em)** to involve sb (in). -**3.** [acarretar] to involve. -**4.** [abraçar] to embrace.

◆ **envolver-se** *vp* -**1.** [comprometer-se]: ~**-se em**

ou **com** to get involved in ou with. -**2.** [intrometer-se]: ~**-se em** to get involved in.

envolvimento [ẽnvowvi'mẽntu] *m* involvement.

enxada [ẽn'ʃada] *f* hoe.

enxadrista [ẽnʃa'driʃta] *mf* chess player.

enxaguada [ẽnʃa'gwada] *f* rinse.

enxaguar [22] [ẽnʃa'gwa(x)] *vt* to rinse.

enxágüe *m* = enxaguada.

enxame [ẽn'ʃami] *m* swarm.

enxaqueca [ẽnʃa'keka] *f* migraine.

enxergar [14] [ẽnʃex'ga(x)] <> *vt* -**1.** [ver] to catch sight of. -**2.** *fig* [perceber] to make out. <> *vi* [ver] to see.

◆ **enxergar-se** *vp*: **ele não se enxerga** he doesn't know his limitations.

enxerido, da [ẽnʃe'ridu, da] *adj* nosy.

enxertar [4] [ẽnʃex'ta(x)] *vt* -**1.** [planta] to graft. -**2.** *fig* [inserir] to insert.

enxerto [ẽn'ʃextu] *m* -**1.** [de planta] grafting. -**2.** MED graft. -**3.** *fig* [inserção] insertion.

enxofre [ẽn'ʃofri] *m* sulphur *UK*, sulfur *US*.

enxotar [4] [ẽnʃo'ta(x)] *vt* to drive away.

enxoval [ẽnʃo'vaw] (*pl* -**ais**) *m* [de noiva] trousseau.

enxugador [ẽnʃuga'do(x)] *m* clothes dryer.

enxugar [14] [ẽnʃu'ga(x)] *vt* -**1.** [secar] to dry. -**2.** *fig* [diminuir] to rationalize.

enxurrada [ẽnʃu'xada] *f* -**1.** [torrente] torrent. -**2.** *fig* [amontoado] flood.

enxuto, ta [ẽn'ʃutu, ta] *adj* -**1.** [seco] dry. -**2.** *fig* [bonito] good-looking.

enzima [ẽn'zima] *f* enzyme.

epicentro [epi'sẽntru] *m* epicentre *UK*, epicenter *US*.

épico, ca ['ɛpiku, ka] *adj* epic.

◆ **épico** *m* LITER epic.

epidemia [epide'mia] *f* -**1.** MED epidemic. -**2.** *fig* [modismo] mania.

epidêmico, ca [epi'demiku, ka] *adj* MED epidemic.

epiderme [epi'dexmi] *f* epidermis.

epidural [epidu'raw] *adj* epidural.

epifania [epifa'nia] *f* Epiphany.

epígrafe [e'pigrafi] *f* epigraph; **em** ~ in epigraph.

epigrama [epi'grama] *f* epigram.

epilepsia [epilep'sia] *f* epilepsy.

epiléptico, ca [epi'lɛptʃiku, ka] <> *adj* epileptic. <> *m, f* epileptic.

epílogo [e'pilugu] *m* epilogue.

episcopado [epiʃko'padu] *m* bishopric.

episcopal [epiʃko'paw] (*pl* -**ais**) *adj* episcopal.

episódico, ca [epi'zɔdiku, ka] *adj* episodic.

episódio [epi'zɔdju] *m* episode.

epistemologia *f* epistemology.

epístola [e'piʃtola] *f* -**1.** [bíblia] Epistle. -**2.** [carta] letter.

epistolar [epiʃto'la(x)] *adj* epistolary.

epistolário [epiʃto'larju] *m* collection of letters.

epitáfio [epi'tafju] *m* epitaph.

época ['ɛpoka] *f* -**1.** [período] age; **filme de** ~ period movie; **naquela** ~ at that time; **fazer** ~

to be epoch-making. **-2.** [estação] season.
epopéia [epo'pɛjal *f* epic.
equação [ekwa'sãw] (*pl* **-ões**) *f* equation.
equacionamento [ekwasiona'mẽ̄ntul *m* rationalizing.
equacionar [4] [ekwasjo'na(x)] *vt* to set out.
equador [ekwa'do(x)] *m* equator.
Equador [ekwa'do(x)] *n* Ecuador.
equânime [e'kwãnimil *adj* unbiased.
equatorial [ekwato'rjawl (*pl* **-ais**) *adj* equatorial.
equatoriano, na ⟨⟩ *adj* Ecuadorean. ⟨⟩ *m, f* Ecuadorean.
eqüestre [e'kwɛʃtril *adj* equestrian.
eqüidade [ekwi'dadʒil *f* equity.
eqüidistante [ekwidʒiʃ'tãntʃil *adj* equidistant.
eqüilátero, ra [ekwi'lateru, ral *adj* equilateral.
equilibrado, da [ekili'bradu, dal *adj* balanced.
equilibrar [4] [ekili'bra(x)l *vt* to balance.
⟡ **equilibrar-se** *vp* to balance.
equilíbrio [eki'libriwl *m* equilibrium.
equilibrista [ekili'briʃtal *mf* trapeze artist.
eqüino, na [e'kwinu, nal *adj* equine.
equinócio [eki'nɔsjul *m* equinox.
equipagem [ekipa'ʒẽl *f* crew.
equipamento [ekipa'mẽ̄ntul *m* equipment.
equipar [4] [eki'pa(x)l *vt:* ~ **algo/alguém (de)** to equip sthg/sb (with).
⟡ **equipar-se** *vp:* ~**-se (de)** to equip o.s. (with).
equiparação [ekipara'sãw] *m* parity.
equiparar [4] [ekipa'ra(x)l *vt:* ~ **algo (a** *ou* **com algo)** to compare sthg (against sthg).
⟡ **equiparar-se** *vp* **-1.** [igualar-se]: ~**-se (a** *ou* **com algo)** to compare o.s. (with sthg). **-2.** [comparar-se]: ~**-se (a** *ou* **com alguém)** to compare o.s. (with sb).
equiparável [ekipa'ravewl (*pl* **-eis**) *adj* comparable.
equipe [e'kipil *f* team; ~ **de socorros** rescue team.
equitação [ekita'sãw] *f* horse-riding.
eqüitativamente [ekwitatʃiva'mẽ̄ntʃil *adv* equitably.
eqüitativo, va [ekwita'tʃivu, val *adj* equitable.
equivalência [ekiva'lẽnsjal *f* equivalence.
equivalente [ekiva'lẽ̄ntʃil *adj* equivalent.
equivaler [43] [ekiva'le(x)l *vi:* ~ **a** to be equivalent to.
⟡ **equivaler-se** *vp* to be equal.
equivocado, da [ekivo'kadu, dal *adj* mistaken.
equivocar-se [12] [ekivo'kaxsil *vp* to make a mistake.
equívoco [e'kivokul *m* mistake.
era ['ɛral *f* era.
erário [e'rarjul *m* exchequer.
ereção [ere'sãwl (*pl* **-ões**) *f* erection.
eremita [ere'mital *mf* hermit.
ereto, ta [e'rɛtu, tal *adj* erect.
erguer [27] [ex'ge(x)l *vt* **-1.** [levantar] to raise. **-2.** [construir] to erect.
⟡ **erguer-se** *vp* [levantar-se] to get up.

eriçado, da [ēri'saɗu, dal *adj* standing on end.
eriçar [13] [eri'sa(x)l *vt* to make stand on end.
erigir [52] [eri'ʒi(x)l *vt* to erect.
ermo, ma ['exmu, mal *adj* deserted.
erodir [6] [ero'dʒi(x)l *vt* to erode.
erógeno, na [e'rɔʒenu, nal *adj* erogenous.
erosão [ero'zãwl *f* erosion.
erótico, ca [e'rɔtʃiku, kal *adj* erotic.
erotismo [ero'tʃiʒmul *m* eroticism.
erradicação [exadʒika'sãwl *f* eradication.
erradicar [12] [exadʒi'ka(x)l *vt* to eradicate.
errado, da [e'xadu, dal *adj* **-1.** [incorreto] wrong. **-2.** [inadequado] inappropriate. **-3.** *loc:* dar ~ to go wrong.
errante [e'xãntʃil *adj* wandering.
errar [4] [e'xa(x)l ⟨⟩ *vt* [não acertar - alvo] to miss; [- conta, resposta] to get wrong. ⟨⟩ *vi* **-1.** [enganar-se]: ~ **(em algo)** to be wrong (in sthg). **-2.** [proceder mal] to go wrong. **-3.** [vagar] to wander.
errata [e'xatal *f* erratum.
erro ['exul *m* [ger] error; ~ **de impressão** printing error; ~ **de pronúncia** mispronunciation.
errôneo, nea [e'xonju, njal *adj* erroneous.
erudição [erudʒi'sãwl *f* erudition.
erudito, ta [eru'dʒitu, ital ⟨⟩ *adj* erudite. ⟨⟩ *m, f* scholar.
erupção [erup'sãwl (*pl* **-ões**) *f* eruption.
erva ['ɛxval *f* **-1.** *BOT* herb; ~ **daninha** weed. **-2.** *fam* [maconha] grass.
erva-cidreira [ˌɛxva'sidrejral (*pl* **ervas-cidreiras**) *f* lemon verbena.
erva-doce [ˌɛxva'dosil (*pl* **ervas-doces**) *f* fennel.
erva-mate [ˌɛxva'matʃil (*pl* **ervas-mates**) *f* matte.
ervilha [ex'viʎal *f* pea.
ES (*abrev de* **Estado do Espírito Santo**) *m* state of Espírito Santo.
esbaforido, da [iʒbafo'ridu, dal *adj* breathless.
esbaldar-se [4] [iʒbaw'daxsil *vp* to have great fun.
esbanjador, ra [iʒbãnʒa'do(x), ral *adj* spendthrift.
esbanjamento [iʒbãnʒa'mẽ̄ntul *m* [de dinheiro] squandering.
esbanjar [4] [iʒbãn'ʒa(x)l *vt* **-1.** [dinheiro] to squander. **-2.** [saúde] to be bursting with.
esbarrão [iʒba'xãwl *m* bump.
esbarrar [4] [iʒba'xa(x)l *vi:* ~ **em algo/alguém** to bump into sthg/sb.
esbelto, ta [iʒ'bɛwtu, tal *adj* svelte.
esboçar [13] [iʒbo'sa(x)l *vt* **-1.** [ger] to sketch. **-2.** [sorriso] to trace.
esboço [iʒ'bosul *m* **-1.** [desenho] sketch. **-2.** [primeira versão] draft. **-3.** [tentativa] hint. **-4.** [resumo] outline.
esbodegado, da [ˌiʒbode'gadul *adj* **-1.** [estragado] worn out. **-2.** [exausto] exhausted.
esbodegar [iʒbode'ga(x)l ⟡ **esbodegar-se** *vp* *fam* [descuidar-se] to let o.s. go.
esbofetear [15] [iʒbofe'tʃja(x)l *vt* to slap.
esbórnia [iʒ'bɔxnjal *f* wild party.

esborrachar-se [4] liʒboxa'ʃaxsil *vp* **-1.** [arrebentar-se] to burst. **-2.** [cair] to fall sprawling.

esbranquiçado, da liʒbrãnki'sadu, dal *adj* whitish.

esbravejar [4] liʒbrave'ʒa(x)l *vi*: ~ **(com alguém)** to shout (at sb).

esbugalhado, da liʒbuga'ʎadu, dal *adj* bulging.

esbugalhar [4] liʒbuga'ʎa(x)l *vt* to bulge.

esburacado, da liʒbura'kadu, dal *adj* **-1.** [rua, jardim] potholed. **-2.** [rosto] pitted.

esburacar [12] liʒbura'ka(x)l *vt* to make holes in.

escabeche liʃka'beʃil *m* marinade.

escabroso, sa liʃka'brozu, zal *adj* **-1.** [difícil] tough. **-2.** [imoral] immoral.

escada liʃ'kadal *f* **-1.** [interna] stairs (*pl*), staircase. **-2.** [externa] steps (*pl*); ~ **de armar** ladder; ~ **de caracol** spiral staircase; ~ **de incêndio** fire escape; ~ **rolante** escalator. **-3.** *fig* [meio] ladder.

escadaria liʃkada'rial *f* staircase.

escafandrista liʃkafãn'driʃtal *mf* deep-sea diver.

escafandro liʃka'fãndrul *m* diving suit.

escafeder-se [5] liʃkafe'dexsil *vp* to slip off.

escala liʃ'kalal *f* **-1.** [ger] scale; **em grande** ~ on a grand scale. **-2.** [parada] stopover; **sem** ~ nonstop. **-3.** [turno] turn.

escalação liʃkala'sãwl *f* [designação] selection.

escalada liʃka'ladal *f* climbing.

escalão liʃka'lãwl (*pl* **-ões**) *m* level; **o alto** ~ **do governo** the upper echelon of government.

escalar [4] liʃka'la(x)l *vt* **-1.** [subir] to climb. **-2.** [designar] to select.

escaldado, da liʃkaw'dadu, dal *adj* **-1.** [fervido] scalded. **-2.** *fig* [experiente] wary.

escaldar [4] liʃkaw'da(x)l *vt* to scald.

escaler liʃka'lɛ(x)l *m* launch.

escalonamento liʃkalona'mẽntul *m* scheduling.

escalonar [4] liʃkalo'na(x)l *vt* to schedule.

escalope liʃka'lɔpil *m* escalope.

escalpelar liʃkawpe'la(x)l *vt* [escalpar] to scalp.

escalpelo liʃkaw'pelul *m* scalpel.

escama liʃ'kãmal *f* scale.

escamar [4] liʃka'ma(x)l <> *vt* [peixe] to scale. <> *vi* [pele] to flake.

escamotear [15] liʃkamo'tʃja(x)l *vt* to filch.

escancarado, da liʃkãŋka'radu, dal *adj* **-1.** [aberto] wide open. **-2.** [evidente] brazen. **-3.** [franco] open.

escancarar [4] liʃkãŋka'ra(x)l *vt* **-1.** [abrir] to open wide. **-2.** [exibir] to display openly.

escandalizar [4] liʃkãndali'za(x)l *vt* to scandalize.

◆ **escandalizar-se** *vp* to be shocked.

escândalo liʃ'kãndalul *m* **-1.** [fato] scandal. **-2.** [indignação] outrage. **-3.** [alvoroço]: **fazer** *ou* **dar um** ~ to make a scene.

escandaloso, sa liʃkãnda'lozu, ɔzal *adj* **-1.** [chocante] shocking. **-2.** [chamativo] outrageous.

Escandinávia liʃkãndʒi'navjal *n* Scandinavia.

escandinavo, va liʃkãndʒi'navu, val <> *adj* Scandinavian. <> *m, f* Scandinavian.

escanear [15] liʃkã'nea(x)l *vt* COMPUT to scan.

escangalhar [4] liʃkãŋga'ʎa(x)l *vt* **-1.** [ger] to break. **-2.** [sapatos] to fall apart.

escaninho liʃka'niɲul *m* pigeon-hole.

escanteio liʃkãn'tejul *m* corner.

escapada liʃka'padal *f* **-1.** [fuga] escape. **-2.** [ato leviano] escapade; **no meio da reunião, ele deu uma** ~ **para comprar flores para a mulher** in the middle of the meeting, he slipped out to buy flowers for his wife; **ele vive dando** ~**s com outras mulheres** he is always having affairs with other women; **a mulher sabe que ele dá umas** ~**s do casamento** his wife knows he has affairs outside marriage, his wife knows that he strays.

escapamento liʃkapa'mẽntul *m* **-1.** [de gás] leak. **-2.** [de veículo] exhaust.

escapar [4] liʃka'pa(x)l *vi* **-1.** [sobreviver]: ~ **(de algo)** to escape (from sthg). **-2.**: ~ **a alguém** to escape (from) sb. **-3.** [fugir] to escape from. **-4.** [esquivar-se] to avoid; ~ **de fazer algo** to get out of doing sthg. **-5.** [soltar-se, cair]: ~ **de algo** to run away from sthg. **-6.** *loc*: ~ **de boa** to have a close shave; **deixar** ~ [não aproveitar] to miss; [revelar por descuido] to let drop.

escapatória liʃkapa'tɔrjal *f* **-1.** [saída] way out. **-2.** [desculpa] excuse.

escape liʃ'kapil *m* [de veículo] exhaust pipe; **válvula de** ~ escape valve; **minha válvula de** ~ **é dançar todos os dias** *fig* my outlet is to dance every day.

escapismo liʃka'piʒmul *m* escapism.

escapulida liʃkapu'lidal *f* [saída] outing; **dar uma** ~ to slip away.

escapulir [61] liʃkapu'li(x)l *vi*: ~ **(de algo)** to escape (from sthg).

escarafunchar [4] liʃkarafũn'ʃa(x)l *vt* to rummage in.

escaramuça liʃkara'musal *f* skirmish.

escaravelho liʃkara'veʎul *m* beetle.

escarcéu liʃkax'sɛwl *m*: **fazer um** ~ to throw a fit.

escarlate liʃkax'latʃil *adj* scarlet.

escarlatina liʃkaxla'tʃinal *f* scarlet fever.

escarnecer [25] liʃkaxne'se(x)l *vi*: ~ **de algo/alguém** to mock sthg/sb, to make fun of sthg/sb.

escárnio liʃ'karnjul *m* **-1.** [desdém] scorn. **-2.** [zombaria] mockery.

escarpa liʃ'kaxpal *f* escarpment.

escarpado, da liʃkar'padu, dal *adj* steep.

escarrado, da liʃka'xadu, dal *adj*: **o menino é o avô** ~ the boy is the spitting image of his grandfather.

escarrapachar-se [4] liʃkaxapa'ʃaxsil *vp* to sprawl.

escarrar [4] liʃka'xa(x)l <> *vt* to spit. <> *vi* to hawk.

escarro liʃ'kaxul *m* phlegm.

escasseamento liʃkasja'mẽntul *m* shortage.

escassear [15] liʃka'sja(x)l *vi* to become scarce.

escassez liʃka'seʒl *f* shortage.

escasso, a [iʃ'kasu, sa] *adj* scarce.
escavação [iʃkava'sãw] (*pl* **-ões**) *f* excavation.
escavadeira [iʃkava'dejra] *f* digger.
escavar [12] [iʃka'va(x)] *vt* to dig.
esclarecedor, ra [iʃklarese'do(x), ra] *adj* illuminating.
esclarecer [25] [iʃklare'se(x)] *vt* **-1.** [explicar] to clarify. **-2.** [elucidar] to explain. **-3.** [informar] to inform.
  ◆ **esclarecer-se** *vp* [informar-se] to find out.
esclarecido, da [iʃklare'sidu, da] *adj* **-1.** [resolvido] solved. **-2.** [informado] well informed.
esclarecimento [iʃklaresi'mẽntu] *m* **-1.** [explicação] explanation. **-2.** [informação] (piece of) information.
esclerosado, da [iʃklero'zadu, da] *adj* senile.
esclerose [iʃkle'rɔzi] *f* sclerosis; ~ **múltipla** multiple sclerosis.
esclerótica [iʃkle'rɔtʃika] *f* white of the eye, sclera.
escoadouro [iʃkoa'doru] *m* drain.
escoar [20] [iʃ'kwa(x)] *vi*: ~ **(por)** to drain (through).
escocês, esa [iʃko'seʒ, eza] <> *adj* Scottish. <> *m, f* Scot.
  ◆ **escocês** *m* [língua] Gaelic.
Escócia [iʃ'kɔsja] *n* Scotland.
escoicear [15] [iʃkoj'sja(x)] *vt* & *vi* to kick.
escola [iʃ'kɔla] *f* [ger] school; ~ **particular/pública** private/public school *US*, private/state school *UK*; ~ **naval** naval college; ~ **de samba** *group of musicians and samba dancers who perform in street parades during carnival celebrations in Brazil.*
escolado, da [iʃko'ladu, da] *adj* experienced.
escola-modelo [iʃˌkɔlamo'delu] (*pl* **escolas-modelo**) *f* model school.
escolar [iʃko'la(x)] (*pl* **-es**) *adj* school *(antes de subst).*
escolaridade [iʃkolari'dadʒi] *f* schooling.
escolarização [iʃkolariza'sãw] *f* school education.
escolarizar [4] [iʃkolari'za(x)] *vt* to educate.
escolha [iʃ'kɔʎa] *f* choice.
escolher [5] [iʃko'ʎe(x)] *vt* to choose.
escolhido, da [iʃko'ʎidu, da] *adj* selected, chosen.
escoliose [iʃkoli'ɔzi] *f* MED curvature of the spine.
escolta [iʃkɔwta] *f* escort.
escoltar [4] [iʃkow'ta(x)] *vt* to escort.
escombros [iʃ'kõnbruʃ] *mpl* ruins.
esconder [5] [iʃkõn'de(x)] *vt* to hide.
  ◆ **esconder-se** *vp* to hide.
esconderijo [iʃkõnde'riʒu] *m* hiding place.
escondidas [iʃkõn'dʒidaʃ] ◆ **às escondidas** *loc adv* secretly.
esconjurar [4] [iʃkõnʒu'ra(x)] *vt* **-1.** [juramento] to swear. **-2.** [maldição] to curse.
escopeta [iʃko'peta] *f* shotgun.
escopo [iʃ'kopu] *m* purpose.
escora [iʃ'kɔra] *f* prop.

escorar [4] [iʃko'ra(x)] *vt* [pôr escoras] to support, to prop up.
  ◆ **escorar-se** *vp* **-1.** [encostar-se]: ~**-se (em)** to lean (on). **-2.** [fundamentar-se]: ~**-se em** to go by. **-3.** [amparar-se]: ~**-se em** to rely on.
escorbuto [iʃkox'butu] *m* scurvy.
escória [iʃ'kɔrja] *f* **-1.** [resíduo] slag. **-2.** *fig* [ralé] scum.
escoriação [iʃkorja'sãw] (*pl* **-ões**) *f* abrasion.
escorpiano, na [iʃkox'pãjanu, na] <> *adj* Scorpio. <> *m, f* Scorpio.
escorpião [iʃkox'pjãw] (*pl* **-ões**) *m* ZOOL scorpion.
  ◆ **Escorpião** *m* ASTRO Scorpio.
escorraçar [13] [iʃkoxa'sa(x)] *vt* to throw out.
escorredor [iʃkoxe'do(x)] *m* [para alimentos] colander; ~ **de pratos** dish drainer, draining board.
escorregadiço, dia [iʃkoxega'dʒisu, dʒia], **escorregadio, dia** [iʃkoxega'dʒiu, dʒia] *adj* slippery.
escorregador [iʃkoxega'do(x)] *m* slide.
escorregão [iʃkoxe'gãw] (*pl* **-ões**) *m* **-1.** [queda] slip. **-2.** *fig* [deslize] slip-up.
escorregar [14] [iʃkoxe'ga(x)] *vi* **-1.** [deslizar] to slip. **-2.** *fig* [errar]: ~ **em algo** to slip up on sthg.
escorrer [5] [iʃko'xe(x)] <> *vt* [tirar líquido de] to drain. <> *vi* [verter] to drip.
escorrido, da [iʃko'xidu, da] *adj* **-1.** [enxuto] dry. **-2.** [liso] straight, smooth.
escoteiro, ra [iʃko'tejru, ra] *m* scout.
escotilha [iʃko'tiʎa] *f* hatch, hatchway.
escova [iʃ'kova] *f* **-1.** [utensílio] brush; ~ **de dentes** toothbrush; ~ **de cabelo** hair brush. **-2.** [penteado]: **fazer uma** ~ [em si mesmo] to style one's hair.
escovar [4] [iʃko'va(x)] *vt* to brush.
escrachado, da [iʃkra'ʃadu, da] *adj fam* scruffy.
escrachar [iʃkra'ʃa(x)] *vt fam* **-1.** [desmascarar] to unmask. **-2.** [repreender] to tick off.
escracho [iʃ'kraʃu] *m fam* [bagunça] shambles.
escravatura [iʃkrava'tura] *f* slavery.
escravidão [iʃkravi'dãw] *f* slavery.
escravização [iʃkraviza'sãw] *f* enslavement.
escravizar [4] [iʃkravi'za(x)] *vt* **-1.** [tornar escravo] to enslave. **-2.** *fig* [subjugar] to dominate.
escravo, va [iʃ'kravu, va] <> *adj* **-1.** [ger] slave. **-2.** *fig* [dominado]: **ser** ~ **de alguém/algo** to be sb/sthg's slave. <> *m, f* slave.
escravocrata [iʃkravo'krata] <> *adj* slave-owning. <> *mf* slave-owner.
escrevente [iʃkre'vẽntʃi] *mf* clerk.
escrever [5] [iʃkre've(x)] *vt* & *vi* to write.
  ◆ **escrever-se** *vp* **-1.** [pessoas] to correspond. **-2.** [palavras] to spell; **esta palavra se escreve com x** this word is spelt with an 'x'.
escrevinhador, ra [iʃkreviɲa'do(x), ra] *m, f* hack (writer).
escrevinhar [4] [iʃkrevi'ɲa(x)] *vt* to scribble.
escrita [iʃ'krita] *f* **-1.** [letra] handwriting. **-2.** [tradição] tradition.
escrito, ta [iʃ'kritu, ta] <> *pp* ▷ **escrever**. <> *adj* written; **por** ~ in writing; **ser algo/alguém**

~ to be the spitting image of sthg/sb.

➡ **escrito** m text.

➡ **escritos** mpl [obra literária] manuscripts.

escritor, ra liʃkri'to(x), ral (mpl -es, fpl -s) m, f writer.

escritório liʃkri'tɔrjul m -1. COM office. -2. [em casa] study.

escritura liʃkri'tural f -1. JUR deed. -2. [na compra de imóvel] exchange of contracts.

escritura liʃkri'tural ➡ **Escrituras** fpl: as ~ the Scriptures.

escriturar [4] liʃkri'tura(x)l vt to draw up.

escriturário, ria liʃkritu'rarju, rjal m, f clerk.

escrivã liʃkri'vãl f ➣ **escrivão**.

escrivaninha liʃkriva'niɲal f desk.

escrivão, vã liʃkri'vãw, vãl (mpl -ões, fpl -s) m, f registrar.

escroto, ta liʃ'krotu, tal adj vulg [ordinário] shitty.

➡ **escroto** m ANAT scrotum.

escrúpulo liʃ'krupulul m -1. [ger] scruple; **sem** ~s unscrupulous. -2. [cuidado] care.

escrupuloso, osa liʃkrupu'lozu, ɔzal adj scrupulous.

escrutinar [4] liʃkrutʃi'na(x)l vt to scrutinize.

escrutínio liʃkru'tʃinjul m scrutiny.

escudar [4] liʃku'da(x)l vt [proteger] to shield.

➡ **escudar-se** vp -1. [proteger-se] to shield o.s. -2. fig [amparar-se]: ~-se em algo/alguém to shield o.s. with sthg/sb.

escudeiro liʃku'dejrol m squire.

escudo liʃkudul m -1. [proteção] shield. -2. [moeda] escudo.

esculachado, da liʃkula'ʃadu, dal adj fam messed up.

esculachar [4] liʃkula'ʃa(x)l fam vt -1. [avacalhar] to mess up. -2. [repreender] to tell off.

esculacho liʃku'laʃul m fam [repreensão] telling-off.

esculhambado, da liʃkuʎãn'badu, dal adj messed up.

esculhambar [4] liʃkuʎãn'ba(x)l fam vt -1. [repreender] to tell off. -2. [avacalhar] to trash. -3. [desarrumar] to mess up. -4. [quebrar] to screw up.

esculpir [6] liʃkuw'pi(x)l vt to sculpt.

escultor, ra liʃkuw'to(x), ral (mpl -es, fpl -s) m, f sculptor.

escultura liʃkuw'tural f sculpture.

escultural liʃkuwtu'rawl (pl -ais) adj statuesque.

escumadeira liʃkuma'dejral f skimmer.

escuna liʃ'kunal f schooner.

escuras liʃ'kuraʃl fpl ➣ **escuro**.

escurecer [25] liʃkure'se(x)l ⬦ vt [tornar escuro] to darken. ⬦ vi -1. [anoitecer] to go dark. -2. [ficar escuro] to get dark.

escuridão liʃkuri'dãwl f darkness.

escuro, ra liʃ'kuru, ral adj -1. [ger] dark. -2. [pessoa] dark-skinned.

➡ **escuro** m [escuridão] darkness; **fazer algo no** ~ fig to do sthg in the dark.

➡ **às escuras** loc adv -1. [sem luz] in the dark.

-2. fig [às escondidas] on the quiet.

escusa liʃ'kuzal f excuse.

escusado, da liʃku'zadu, dal adj unnecessary.

escusar [4] liʃku'za(x)l vt -1. [desculpar]: ~ alguém (de) to excuse sb (for). -2. [dispensar]: ~ alguém de to excuse sb from.

➡ **escusar-se** vp -1. [desculpar-se]: ~-se (de) to excuse o.s. (for). -2. [dispensar-se]: ~-se de to be excused from.

escusável liʃku'zavewl (pl -eis) adj excusable.

escuso, sa liʃ'kuzu, zal adj underhand.

escuta liʃ'kutal f listening; ~ **telefônica** phone tap.

➡ **à escuta** loc adv listening.

escutar [4] liʃku'ta(x)l ⬦ vt -1. [ouvir] to hear; [prestar atenção] to listen to. -2. [dar ouvidos a] to hear out. -3. [atender a] to heed. ⬦ vi [ouvir] to hear; [prestar atenção] to listen.

esdrúxulo, la liʒ'druʃulu, lal adj weird.

esfacelar [4] liʃfase'la(x)l vt to destroy.

➡ **esfacelar-se** vp to destroy o.s.

esfaimado, da liʃfaj'madu, dal adj famished.

esfaltar-se [4] liʃfaw'taxsil vp to tire o.s. out.

esfaquear [15] liʃfa'kja(x)l vt to stab.

esfarelar [4] liʃfare'la(x)l vt to crumble.

➡ **esfarelar-se** vp to crumble.

esfarrapado, da liʃfaxa'padu, dal adj -1. [roto] scruffy. -2. [não-convincente] unconvincing.

esfarrapar [4] liʃfaxa'pa(x)l vt to tear up.

esfera liʃ'feral f -1. [ger] sphere. -2. [globo] globe.

esférico, ca liʃ'feriku, kal adj spherical.

esferográfica liʃfero'grafikal f ballpoint pen.

esfiapar [4] liʃfja'pa(x)l vt & vi to fray.

esfinge liʃ'fĩʒil f sphinx.

esfolar [4] liʃfo'la(x)l vt -1. [tirar a pele] to skin. -2. [arranhar] to graze. -3. [cobrar caro] to rip off.

➡ **esfolar-se** vp to graze o.s.

esfomeado, da liʃfɔ'mjadu, dal adj starving.

esforçado, da liʃfox'sadu, dal adj committed.

esforçar-se [13] liʃfox'saxsil vp to make an effort.

esforço liʃ'foxsul m effort.

esfregação liʃfrega'sãwl f -1. [fricção] rubbing. -2. fam [bolinagem]: estar na ~ to pet.

esfregão liʃfre'gãwl (pl -ões) m mop.

esfregar [14] liʃfre'ga(x)l vt -1. [friccionar] to scrub. -2. [lavar] to scrub.

➡ **esfregar-se** vp -1. [friccionar-se] to rub o.s. -2. [lavar-se] to scrub o.s. -3. fam [bolinar-se] to fondle each other.

esfriamento liʃfrja'mẽntul m cooling.

esfriar [16] liʃfri'a(x)l ⬦ vt to cool. ⬦ vi -1. [perder o calor] to get cold. -2. fig [arrefecer] to cool.

esfumaçado, da liʃfuma'sadu, dal adj smoky.

esfumaçar [13] liʃfuma'sa(x)l vt to smoke out.

esfuziante liʃfu'zjãntʃil adj [alegre] effusive.

esganar [4] liʒga'na(x)l vt to strangle.

esganiçado, da liʒgani'sadu, dal adj shrill.

esgarçar [13] liʒgax'sa(x)l ⬦ vt to tear. ⬦ vi to wear thin.

esgoelar [4] liʒgwe'la(x)l vt [esganar] to strangle.

➡ **esgoelar-se** vp [gritar] to yell.

esgotado, da [izgo'tadu, da] *adj* **-1.** [exausto] exhausted. **-2.** [acabado - paciência, crédito] exhausted; [- reservas naturais] depleted; [- prazo] finished. **-3.** *fig* [esquadrinhado] scrutinized. **-4.** [totalmente vendido] sold out.

esgotamento [izgota'mẽtul] *m* [exaustão] exhaustion; ~ **nervoso** nervous breakdown.

esgotante [izgo'tãtʃi] *adj* exhausting.

esgotar [4] [izgo'ta(x)] *vt* **-1.** [ger] to exhaust. **-2.** [esquadrinhar] to scrutinize. **-3.** [esvaziar, secar] to drãin.

◆ **esgotar-se** *vp* **-1.** [ger] to be exhausted. **-2.** [ser vendido totalmente] to be sold out.

esgoto [iz'gotu] *m* drain.

esgrima [iz'grima] *f* fencing.

esgrimir [6] [izgri'mi(x)] *vi* to fence.

esgueirar-se [4] [izgej'raxsil] *vp* to slip away.

esguelha [iz'geʎa] *f* slant.

◆ **de esguelha** *loc adv* obliquely; **olhar de esguelha** to cast a sidelong glance.

esguichar [4] [izgi'ʃa(x)] ⟨⟩ *vt* to squirt. ⟨⟩ *vi* to gush.

esguicho [iz'giʃu] *m* squirt.

esguio, guia [iz'giu, gia] *adj* willowy.

eslavo, va [iz'lavu, va] ⟨⟩ *adj* Slav. ⟨⟩ *m, f* Slav.

◆ **eslavo** *m* [língua] Slavic.

eslovaco, ca [izlo'vaku, ka] ⟨⟩ *adj* Slovakian. ⟨⟩ *m, f* Slovak.

◆ **eslovaco** *m* [língua] Slovak.

Eslováquia [izlo'vakja] *n* Slovakia.

Eslovênia [izlo'venja] *n* Slovenia.

esloveno, na [izlo'venu, na] ⟨⟩ *adj* Slovene. ⟨⟩ *m, f* Slovene.

◆ **esloveno** *m* [língua] Slovene.

esmagador, ra [izmaga'do(x), ra] (*mpl* -es, *fpl* -s) *adj fig* overwhelming.

esmagar [14] [izma'ga(x)] *vt* **-1.** [esmigalhar] to crush. **-2.** *fig* [vencer] to overpower.

esmaltado, da [izmaw'tadu, da] *adj* enamelled.

esmaltar [4] [izmaw'ta(x)] *vt* to enamel.

esmalte [iz'mawtʃi] *m* enamel; ~ **de unha** nail polish *UK*, nail enamel *US*.

esmerado, da [izme'radu, da] *adj* **-1.** [cuidadoso] meticulous. **-2.** [bem acabado - produção] accomplished; [- trabalho] well finished.

esmeralda [izme'rawda] *f* emerald.

esmerar-se [4] [izme'raxsil] *vp:* ~-**se em algo/em fazer algo** to be meticulous about sthg/about doing sthg.

esmero ['izmeru] *m* meticulousness.

esmigalhar [4] [izmiga'ʎa(x)] *vt* **-1.** [fazer em migalhas] to crumble. **-2.** [despedaçar] to shatter. **-3.** [esmagar] to crush.

◆ **esmigalhar-se** *vp* **-1.** [fazer-se em migalhas] to crumble. **-2.** [despedaçar-se] to shatter.

esmiuçar [13] [izmju'sa(x)] *vt* **-1.** [explicar] to explain in great detail. **-2.** [investigar] to scrutinize.

esmo ['ezmu] ◆ **a esmo** *loc adv* at random.

esmola [iz'mɔla] *f* alms (*pl*).

esmolar [4] [izmo'la(x)] ⟨⟩ *vt* to beg for. ⟨⟩ *vi* to beg.

esmorecer [25] [izmore'se(x)] ⟨⟩ *vt* [pessoa] to discourage. ⟨⟩ *vi* **-1.** [pessoa] to lose heart. **-2.** [luz] to diminish.

esmorecimento [izmoresi'mẽtul] *m* discouragement.

esmurrar [4] [izmu'xa(x)] *vt* to punch.

esnobação [iznoba'sãw] *f* snobbery.

esnobar [4] [izno'ba(x)] ⟨⟩ *vt* to be snobbish towards. ⟨⟩ *vi* to be snobbish.

esnobe [iz'nɔbi] ⟨⟩ *adj* snobbish. ⟨⟩ *mf* snob.

esnobismo [izno'bizmul] *m* snobbishness.

esôfago le'zofagul *m* oesophagus *UK*, esophagus *US*.

esotérico, ca [ezo'tɛriku, ka] *adj* esoteric.

esoterismo [ezote'rifmul] *m* esotericism.

espaçado, da [ifpa'sadu, da] *adj* **-1.** [com intervalos] spaced out. **-2.** [esparso] scattered.

espaçar [13] [ifpa'sa(x)] *vt* to space out.

espacial [ifpa'sjaw] (*pl* -ais) *adj* space (*antes do subst*).

espaço [if'pasul] *m* **-1.** [ger] space; ~ **aéreo** air space. **-2.** [o universo] outer space. **-3.** [de tempo] space.

espaçoso, osa [ifpa'sozu, ɔza] *adj* spacious.

espada [if'pada] *f* [arma] sword.

◆ **espadas** *fpl* [naipe] spades.

espadachim [ifpada'ʃĩ] (*pl* -ns) *m* swordsman.

espádua [if'padwa] *f* shoulder blade.

espaguete [ifpa'getʃi] *m* spaghetti.

espairecer [25] [ifpajre'se(x)] *vt* & *vi* to relax.

espairecimento [ifpajresi'mẽtul] *m* relaxation.

espaldar [ifpaw'da(x)] *m* [de cadeira, sofá] back.

espalhafato [ifpaʎa'fatul] *m* commotion.

espalhafatoso, osa [ifpaʎafa'tozu, ɔza] *adj* **-1.** [roupa] gaudy. **-2.** [pessoa, jeito] loud.

espalhar [4] [ifpa'ʎa(x)] *vt* **-1.** [ger] to spread. **-2.** [dispersar - semente] to scatter; [- fumaça, odor] to spread. **-3.** [difundir] to diffuse.

◆ **espalhar-se** *vp* **-1.** [dissipar-se] to dissipate. **-2.** [propagar-se] to be spread.

espalmado, da [ifpaw'madu, da] *adj* splayed.

espalmar [4] [ifpaw'ma(x)] *vt* **-1.** [abrir] to splay. **-2.** [desviar] to deflect.

espanador [ifpana'do(x)] (*pl* -es) *m* duster.

espanar [4] [ifpa'na(x)] *vt* to dust.

espancamento [ifpãŋka'mẽtul] *m* beating.

espancar [12] [ifpãŋ'ka(x)] *vt* to beat.

Espanha [if'pãɲa] *n* Spain.

espanhol, la [ifpã'ɲɔw, la] (*mpl* -óis, *fpl* -s) ⟨⟩ *adj* Spanish. ⟨⟩ *m, f* Spaniard.

◆ **espanhol** *m* [língua] Spanish.

espantado, da [ifpãn'tadu, da] *adj* **-1.** [assustado] startled. **-2.** [surpreso] astonished.

espantalho [ifpãn'taʎul] *m* [boneco] scarecrow.

espantar [4] [ifpãn'ta(x)] ⟨⟩ *vt* **-1.** [assustar] to frighten. **-2.** [afugentar] to frighten (away). **-3.** [surpreender] to amaze. ⟨⟩ *vi* [surpreender] to be amazing.

◆ **espantar-se** *vp* **-1.** [assustar-se] to be frightened. **-2.** [surpreender-se] to be amazed.

espanto [if'pãntul] *m* **-1.** [susto] fright. **-2.** [assombro] amazement.

espantoso, osa [iʃpãn'tozu, ɔza] *adj* **-1.** [surpreendente] startling. **-2.** [admirável] astounding.

esparadrapo [iʃpara'drapu] *m* sticking plaster *UK*, Band-Aid® *US*.

espargir [52] [iʃpax'ʒi(x)] *vt* to spray.

esparramado, da [iʃpaxa'madu, da] *adj* **-1.** [espalhado] scattered. **-2.** [derramado] splashed. **-3.** [refastelado] sprawled.

esparramar [4] [iʃpaxa'ma(x)] *vt* **-1.** [espalhar] to scatter. **-2.** [derramar] to splash.

➡ esparramar-se *vp* [refastelar-se] to sprawl.

esparramo [iʃpa'xamul] *m* scattering.

esparso, sa [iʃ'paxsu, sa] *adj* **-1.** [espalhado] sparse. **-2.** [raro] scarce.

espartano, na [iʃpax'tãnu, na] *adj* spartan.

espartilho [iʃpax'tiʎu] *m* corset.

espasmo [iʃ'paʒmu] *m* spasm.

espasmódico, ca [iʃpaʒ'mɔdʒiku, ka] *adj* spasmodic.

espatifar [4] [iʃpatʃi'fa(x)] *vt & vi* to smash.

➡ espatifar-se *vp* to shatter.

espátula [iʃ'patula] *f* spatula.

espavento [iʃpa'vẽntu] *m* fright.

espavorido, da [iʃpavo'ridu, da] *adj* terrified.

especial [iʃpe'sjaw] (*pl* **-ais**) *adj* special; **em** ~ in particular.

especialidade [iʃpesjali'dadʒi] *f* speciality.

especialista [iʃpesja'liʃta] ⟨⟩ *adj* [perito]: ~ **em** expert in. ⟨⟩ *mf* **-1.** [profissional] expert. **-2.** [perito]: ~ **em** specialist in.

especialização [iʃpesjaliza'sãw] (*pl* **-ões**) *f* specialization.

especializado, da [iʃpesjali'zadu, da] *adj* **-1.** [treinado]: ~ **(em)** specialized (in). **-2.** [específico] specialized.

especializar-se [4] [iʃpesjali'zaxsi] *vp*: ~ **(em)** to specialize (in).

especiaria [iʃpesja'rial] *f* spice.

espécie [iʃ'pɛsjil] *f* **-1.** BIOL species. **-2.** [tipo] kind.

➡ em espécie *loc adv* FIN (in) cash.

especificação [iʃpesifika'sãw] (*pl* **-ões**) *f* specification.

especificar [12] [iʃpesifi'ka(x)] *vt* to specify.

específico, ca [iʃpe'sifiku, ka] *adj* specific.

espécime [iʃ'pɛsimi] (*pl* **-es**), **espécimen** (*pl* **-ns**) *m* specimen.

espectador, ra [iʃpekta'do(x), ra] (*mpl* **-res**, *fpl* **-ras**) *m, f* **-1.** [testemunha] witness. **-2.** [de espetáculo *etc*] spectator.

➡ espectadores *mpl* viewers.

espectro [iʃ'pɛktru] *m* **-1.** [fantasma] ghost. **-2.** FíSICA spectrum. **-3.** *fig* [pessoa esquálida] wretch.

especulação [iʃpekula'sãw] (*pl* **-ões**) *f* speculation.

especulador, ra [iʃpekula'do(x), ra] ⟨⟩ *adj* speculative. ⟨⟩ *m, f* BOLSA & COM speculator.

especular [4] [iʃpeku'la(x)] ⟨⟩ *vt* [averiguar] to speculate upon. ⟨⟩ *vi* **-1.** [informar-se]: ~ **sobre algo** to speculate about sthg. **-2.** [teorizar]: ~ **(sobre algo)** to speculate (about sthg). **-3.** BOLSA & COM: ~ **(em)** to speculate (in).

especulativo, va [iʃpekula'tʃivu, va] *adj* speculative.

espelhar [4] [iʃpe'ʎa(x)] *vt* [mostrar] to reflect.

➡ espelhar-se *vp* **-1.** [refletir-se] to be reflected. **-2.** [mirar-se] to reflect.

espelho [iʃ'peʎul] *m* mirror; ~ **retrovisor** rearview mirror.

espelunca [iʃpe'lũŋka] *f* dump.

espera [iʃ'pɛra] *f* **-1.** [ato] wait; à ~ **de** waiting for. **-2.** [tempo] delay. **-3.** [tocaia] ambush.

esperado, da [iʃpe'radu, da] *adj* **-1.** [aguardado] awaited. **-2.** [previsto] expected.

esperança [iʃpe'rãnsa] *f* **-1.** [expectativa] expectation. **-2.** [confiança] hope.

esperançoso, osa [iʃperãn'sozu, ɔza] *adj* hopeful.

esperanto [iʃpe'rãntul] *m* Esperanto.

esperar [13] [iʃpe'ra(x)] ⟨⟩ *vt* **-1.** [aguardar] to wait for. **-2.** [bebê] to expect. **-3.** [desejar]: ~ **que** to hope that; ~ **fazer algo** to hope to do sthg. **-4.** [supor] to expect. **-5.** [estar destinado a] to await. **-6.** [contar obter] to expect. ⟨⟩ *vi* [aguardar]: to hope; **fazer alguém** ~ to make sb wait; **espera (aí)!** wait (a moment)!

➡ esperar-se *vp*: **como era de se** ~ as was to be expected.

esperável [iʃpe'ravew] (*pl* **-eis**) *adj* probable.

esperma [iʃ'pɛxma] *m* sperm.

espermatozóide *m* spermatozoon, spermatozoa (*pl*).

espermicida [iʃpexmi'sidal] ⟨⟩ *adj* spermicidal. ⟨⟩ *m* spermicide.

espernear [15] [iʃpex'nja(x)] *vi* **-1.** [sacudir as pernas] to kick one's legs. **-2.** *fig* [protestar] to (put up a) protest.

espertalhão, ona [iʃpexta'ʎãw, ona] (*mpl* **-ões**, *fpl* **-s**) ⟨⟩ *adj* crafty. ⟨⟩ *m, f* smart operator.

esperteza [iʃpex'teza] *f* **-1.** [inteligência] intelligence. **-2.** [astúcia] shrewdness; **foi muita** ~ **dele fazer isso** it was very shrewd of him to do that.

esperto, ta [iʃ'pɛxtu, ta] *adj* **-1.** [inteligente] smart. **-2.** [ativo] lively. **-3.** [espertalhão] clever. **-4.** *fam* [bacana] groovy.

espesso, a [iʃ'pesu, sa] *adj* thick.

espessura [iʃpe'sural] *f* thickness.

espetacular [iʃpetaku'la(x)] (*pl* **-es**) *adj* amazing.

espetáculo [iʃpe'takulul] *m* **-1.** [show] show. **-2.** [maravilha]: **ser um** ~ to be amazing. **-3.** [cena ridícula] spectacle; **ele deu o maior** ~ **aqui por causa da bebedeira** he made a spectacle of himself here being so drunk.

espetada [iʃpe'tadal] *f* **-1.** [furada] prick. **-2.** [cul] kebab. **-3.** *fig* [implicância]: **dar** ~ **em alguém** to needle sb.

espetar [4] [iʃpe'ta(x)] *vt* to impale.

➡ espetar-se *vp* to prick o.s.

espeto [iʃ'petul] *m* **-1.** [utensílio de churrasco] (roasting) spit. **-2.** *fig* [pessoa magra] beanpole. **-3.** *fig* [situação difícil]: **ser um** ~ to be difficult.

espevitado, da [iʃpevi'tadu, da] *adj* lively.

espevitar [iʃpevi'ta(x)] ⟶ **espevitar-se** vp **-1.** [mostrar-se afetado] to show off. **-2.** [irritar-se] to fly off the handle.

espezinhar [4] [iʃpɛzi'ɲa(x)] vt **-1.** [implicar com] to put down. **-2.** [humilhar] to trample (on).

espiada [iʃ'pjada] f peep; **dar uma ~** to have a peep, to have a look-see.

espião, pia [iʃ'pjãw, pial (mpl -ões, fpl -s) m, f spy.

espiar [16] [iʃ'pja(x)] ⟨⟩ vt **-1.** [olhar] to watch. **-2.** [espionar] to spy on. ⟨⟩ vi **-1.** [olhar]: **~ (por)** [pela fechadura] to look (through); [pelo canto do olho] to glance. **-2.** [espionar] to spy.

espicaçar [13] [iʃpika'sa(x)] vt fig [torturar] to torment.

espichado, da [iʃpi'ʃadu, da] adj **-1.** [pessoa] stretched out. **-2.** [corda] tight.

espichar [4] [iʃpi'ʃa(x)] ⟨⟩ vt [esticar] to stretch out. ⟨⟩ vi [crescer] to shoot up.

⟶ **espichar-se** vp [espreguiçar-se] to stretch (out).

espiga [iʃ'piga] f ear.

espigão [iʃpi'gãw] (pl -ões) m **-1.** [pua] spike. **-2.** [pico] peak.

espinafrar [4] [iʃpina'fra(x)] vt **-1.** [repreender] to reprimand. **-2.** [criticar] to lambaste.

espinafre [iʃpi'nafri] m spinach.

espingarda [iʃpĩŋ'gaxda] f shotgun.

espinha [iʃ'piɲa] f **-1.** [na pele] pimple. **-2.** [de peixe] bone. **-3.** ANAT spine.

espinhento, ta [iʃpi'ɲẽntu, ta] adj **-1.** [planta] thorny. **-2.** [peixe] bony.

espinho [iʃ'piɲu] m **-1.** [de planta] thorn. **-2.** [de porco-espinho] quill. **-3.** [de ouriço] spine. **-4.** fig [dificuldade] snag.

espinhoso, osa [iʃpí'ɲozu, ɔza] adj thorny.

espionagem [iʃpio'naʒẽ] f espionage.

espionar [4] [iʃpio'na(x)] ⟨⟩ vt to spy on. ⟨⟩ vi to snoop.

espiral [iʃpi'raw] (pl -ais) ⟨⟩ adj spiral. ⟨⟩ f spiral; **em ~** in a spiral; **escada em ~** spiral staircase.

espírita [iʃ'pirital] ⟨⟩ adj spiritualistic. ⟨⟩ mf spiritualist.

espiritismo [iʃpiri'tʃiʒmul] m spiritualism.

espírito [iʃ'piritul] m **-1.** [ger] spirit. **-2.** [temperamento]: **~ esportivo** competitive spirit; **ter ~ forte/fraco** to be strong/weak willed; **ser ~ de porco** to be a busybody.

⟶ **Espírito Santo** m Holy Spirit.

espiritual [iʃpiri'twaw] (pl -ais) adj spiritual.

espiritualidade [iʃpiritwali'dadʒi] f spirituality.

espirituoso, osa [iʃpiri'twozu, ɔza] adj witty.

espirrar [4] [iʃpi'xa(x)] ⟨⟩ vi **-1.** [dar espirro] to sneeze. **-2.** [jorrar] to squirt out. ⟨⟩ vt [jorrar] to squirt.

espirro [iʃ'pixul] m sneeze.

esplanada [iʃpla'nadal] f esplanade.

esplêndido, da [iʃ'plẽndʒidu, da] adj splendid.

esplendor [iʃplẽn'do(x)] m splendour UK, splendor US.

espocar [12] [iʃpo'ka(x)] vi to explode.

espoleta [iʃpo'letal] f detonator.

espoliar [16] [iʃpo'lja(x)] vt to plunder.

espólio [iʃ'poljul] m **-1.** [herança] inheritance. **-2.** [restos] remains (pl).

esponja [iʃ'põnʒal] f **-1.** [ger] sponge. **-2.** fig [beberrão] soak.

esponjoso, osa [iʃpõn'ʒozu, ɔza] adj spongy.

espontaneidade [iʃpõntanej'dadʒil] f spontaneity.

espontâneo, nea [iʃpõn'tãnju, njal adj spontaneous.

espora [iʃ'poral] f spur.

esporádico, ca [iʃpo'radʒiku, kal adj sporadic.

esporão [iʃpo'rãwl] (pl -ões) m spur.

esporro [iʃ'poxul] m vulg **-1.** [barulho] racket. **-2.** [repreensão] tongue-lashing.

esporte [iʃ'poxtʃil] m sport.

ESPORTES

Although football is the absolute favourite sport of the Brazilian people, Brazil has excelled in other sports as well, including basketball, volleyball, sailing, swimming, judo, tennis and motor racing. Three Brazilian drivers have been Formula 1 world champions more than once: Emerson Fittipaldi ('72 and '74), Nelson Piquet ('81, '83 and '87) and Ayrton Senna ('88, '90 and '91).

esportista [iʃpox'tʃiʃtal] ⟨⟩ adj sporty. ⟨⟩ mf sportsman (f sportswoman).

esportividade [iʃpoxtʃivi'dadʒil] f sportsmanship.

esportivo, va [iʃpox'tʃivu, val adj sports (antes de subst).

⟶ **esportiva** f (sense of) fair play.

esposa [iʃpo'zal] f wife.

esposar [4] [iʃ'poza(x)] vt to marry.

esposo [iʃ'pozul] m husband.

espraiar [4] [iʃpraj'a(x)] ⟨⟩ vt to spread. ⟨⟩ vi to sprawl, to wash ashore.

espreguiçadeira [iʃpregisa'dejral] f deckchair.

espreguiçar-se [13] [iʃpregi'saxsil] vp to stretch.

espreita [iʃ'prejtal] loc: **à ~ (de)** on the lookout (for).

espreitar [4] [iʃprej'ta(x)] vt to peep at, to have a peep at.

espremedor [iʃpreme'do(x)] (pl -es) m masher; **~ de laranja** orange squeezer.

espremer [5] [iʃpre'me(x)] vt **-1.** [apertar] to squeeze. **-2.** [comprimir - fruta] to squeeze; [- toalha molhada] to wring out.

⟶ **espremer-se** vp [apertar-se] to press together.

espuma [iʃ'pumal] f foam.

espumante [iʃpu'mãntʃil] adj sparkling.

espumar [4] [iʃpu'ma(x)] vi to foam.

espumoso, osa [iʃpu'mozu, ɔzal adj foamy.

espúrio, ria [iʃ'purju, rjal adj spurious.

esquadra [iʃ'kwadral] f **-1.** NAÚT fleet. **-2.** MIL squadron.

esquadrão [iʃkwa'drãwl] (pl -ões) m squadron.

esquadria [iʃkwa'dria] f frame.
esquadrilha [iʃkwa'driʎa] f flotilla.
esquadrinhar [4] [iʃkwadri'ɲa(x)] vt -1. [procurar] to search. -2. [analisar] to examine.
esquadro [iʃ'kwadru] m set square.
esqualidez [iʃkwali'deʃ] f squalour.
esquálido, da [iʃ'kwalidu, da] adj squalid.
esquartejar [4] [iʃkwaxte'ʒa(x)] vt to quarter.
esquecer [25] [iʃke'se(x)] <> vt to forget; ~ que to forget that. <> vi: ~ (de algo/alguém) to forget (sthg/sb); ~ de fazer algo to forget to do sthg.
 ◆ **esquecer-se** vp: ~-se (de algo) to forget (about sthg); ~-se de fazer algo to forget to do sthg.
esquecido, da [iʃke'sidu, da] adj -1. [não lembrado] forgotten. -2. [distraído] forgetful.
esquecimento [iʃkesi'mẽntu] m forgetfulness; cair no ~ to become a thing of the past.
esqueitista [iʃkej'tʃiʃta] mf skateboarder.
esquelético, ca [iʃke'lɛtʃiku, ka] adj skeletal.
esqueleto [iʃke'letu] m -1. [ossatura] skeleton. -2. [estrutura] skeleton. -3. [esboço] rough draft. -4. fig [pessoa magra] bag of bones, skeleton.
esquema [iʃ'kema] m -1. [gráfico] diagram. -2. [plano] plan; ~ de segurança security plan. -3. [resumo] schema.
esquemático, ca [iʃke'matʃiku, ka] adj schematic.
esquematização [iʃkematʃiza'sãw] (pl -ões) f schematization.
esquematizar [4] [iʃkematʃi'za(x)] vt -1. [representar em desenho] to sketch. -2. [planejar] to plan. -3. [sintetizar] to plan.
esquentado, da [iʃkẽn'tadu, da] adj -1. [aquecido] heated. -2. fig [exaltado] irritable.
esquentar [4] [iʃkẽn'ta(x)] <> vt [aquecer] to heat up. <> vi -1. [aquecer] to get hot. -2. fig [exaltar-se] to become irritable.
 ◆ **esquentar-se** vp -1. [aquecer-se] to warm o.s. up. -2. fig [exaltar-se] to get annoyed.
esquerdista [iʃkex'dʒiʃta] <> adj leftist. <> mf leftist.
esquerdo, da [iʃ'kexdu, da] adj left.
 ◆ **esquerda** f -1. [lado] left; à ~ on the left. -2. POL left wing.
esquete [iʃ'kɛtʃi] m sketch.
esqui [iʃ'ki] m -1. [patim] ski. -2. [esporte] skiing; ~ aquático water-skiing.
esquiador, ra [iʃkja'do(x), ra] m, f skier.
esquiar [16] [iʃ'kja(x)] vi to ski.
esquife [iʃ'kifil] m coffin.
esquilo [iʃ'kilul] m squirrel.
esquimó [iʃki'mɔ] <> adj Eskimo. <> mf Eskimo.
 ◆ **esquimó** m [língua] Eskimo.
esquina [iʃ'kina] f corner; dobrar a ~ to turn the corner; minha rua faz ~ com a avenida principal my street goes off the main street.
esquisitice [iʃkizi'tʃisil] f -1. [qualidade] eccentricity. -2. [ato, dito] incongruity.

esquisito, ta [iʃki'zitu, ta] adj -1. [incomum] strange. -2. [pessoa] strange.
esquivar-se [4] [iʃki'vaxsi] vp: ~-se de algo to dodge sthg.
esquivo, va [iʃ'kivu, va] adj aloof.
 ◆ **esquiva** f dodge.
esquizofrenia [iʃkizofre'nia] f schizophrenia.
esquizofrênico, ca [iʃkizo'freniku, ka] <> adj schizophrenic. <> m, f schizophrenic.
esse, essa ['esi, 'ɛsa] <> adj that, those (pl). <> pron that (one), those (ones) (pl).
essência [e'sẽsja] f essence.
essencial [esẽn'sjaw] (pl -ais) <> adj -1. [ger] essential. -2. [preocupação, benefício, trecho] main. <> m: o ~ [o mais importante] the main thing.
essencialmente [esẽnsjaw'mẽntʃi] adv -1. [substancialmente] essentially. -2. [basicamente] essentially.
esta ['ɛʃta] ⊳ este.
estabanado, da [iʃtaba'nadu, da] adj careless.
estabelecer [25] [iʃtabele'se(x)] vt -1. [ger] to establish. -2. [instalar] to set up.
 ◆ **estabelecer-se** vp -1. [firmar-se] to establish o.s. -2. [instalar-se] to be established. -3. [em negócio] to become established. -4. [determinar-se]: ~-se (que) to be established (that).
estabelecimento [iʃtabelesi'mẽntu] m establishment.
estabilidade [iʃtabili'dadʒi] f stability; ~ financeira financial stability.
estabilização [iʃtabiliza'sãw] f stabilization.
estabilizador [iʃtabiliza'do(x)] (pl -es) m COMPUT transformer.
estabilizar [4] [iʃtabili'za(x)] vt to stabilize.
 ◆ **estabilizar-se** vp to become stable.
estábulo [iʃ'tabulul] m stable.
estaca [iʃ'taka] f -1. [para cravar] stake. -2. [de construção] support. -3. [de barraca] post. -4. loc: voltar à ~ zero to go back to square one.
estacada [iʃta'kada] f -1. [de proteção] stockade. -2. [fileira] fence.
estação [iʃta'sãw] (pl -ões) f -1. [de trem, metrô, ônibus] station. -2. [período]: ~ (do ano) season (of the year); ~ de chuvas rainy season; [de colheita]: frutas da ~ fruits of the season. -3. [estância]: ~ de águas spa. -4. [para fins científicos] station. -5. RÁDIO & TV station.
estacar [12] [iʃta'ka(x)] vi to stop short.
estacionamento [iʃtasjona'mẽntu] m -1. [ato] parking. -2. [lugar] car park.
estacionar [4] [iʃtasjo'na(x)] <> vt AUTO to park. <> vi -1. AUTO to park. -2. [não evoluir] to remain stationary.
estacionário, ria [iʃtasjo'narju, rja] adj -1. [parado] stationary. -2. ECON [estagnado] stagnant.
estada [iʃ'tadal], **estadia** [iʃ'tadʒa] f stay.
estádio [iʃ'tadʒjul] m stadium.
estadista [iʃta'dʒiʃta] mf statesman.
estado [iʃ'tadul] m -1. [ger] state; em bom/mau ~ in good/bad condition; ~ civil marital status; ~ de coisas state of affairs; ~ de espírito state of

mind; ~ **de saúde** (state of) health; **em** ~ **inte-ressante** in an interesting condition, pregnant; ~ **de sítio** state of siege; **em** ~ **de** in a state of; ~ **gasosa/líquido/sólido** gaseous/liquid/solid state. **-2.** *POL* state.

➡ **Estado** *m* [país] state.

estado-maior [iʃˌtaduma'jo(x)] (*pl* **estados-maiores**) *m MIL* general staff *UK*, army/air staff *US*.

Estados Unidos da América *n*: os ~ the United States of America.

estadual [iʃta'dwawl] (*pl* **-ais**) *adj* [receita, constituição] state (*antes de subst*).

estadunidense [iʃtaduni'dẽnsi] <> *adj* American. <> *mf* American.

estafa [iʃ'tafal] *f* **-1.** [esgotamento] exhaustion; **ter uma** ~ to be exhausted. **-2.** [fadiga] exhaustion.

estafado, da [iʃta'fadu, dal] *adj* exhausted.

estafante [iʃta'fãntʃil] *adj* exhausting.

estafar [4] [iʃta'fa(x)] *vt* to exhaust.

estafeta [iʃta'fetal] *m* courier.

estagflação [iʃtag'flasãwl] *f ECON* stagflation.

estagiar [16] [iʃta'ʒja(x)] *vi*: ~ **(em)** to train (in).

estagiário, ria [iʃta'ʒjarju, rjal] *m, f* trainee.

estágio [iʃ'taʒul] *m* **-1.** [fase] stage. **-2.** [treinamento] training period.

estagnação [iʃtagna'sãwl] *f* stagnation.

estagnado, da [iʃtag'nadu, dal] *adj* stagnant.

estagnar [4] [iʃtag'na(x)] <> *vt* to make stagnant. <> *vi* to stagnate.

➡ **estagnar-se** *vp* to be stagnant.

estalagem [iʃta'laʒẽl] (*pl* **-ns**) *f* inn.

estalar [4] [iʃta'la(x)] <> *vt* **-1.** [dedos] to snap. **-2.** [nozes, ovos] to crack. <> *vi* **-1.** [rachar] to crack. **-2.** [crepitar] to crackle.

estaleiro [iʃta'lejrul] *m* shipyard.

estalido [iʃta'lidul] *m* **-1.** [de dedos] snapping. **-2.** [de chicote, fogos] cracking.

estalo [iʃ'talul] *m* [de dedos] snap; [de chicote] crack; [de trovão] crash; [de foguete] bang; **dar um** ~ to crack; **me deu um** ~ *fig* I had a flash of inspiration; **de** ~ [de repente] suddenly.

estampa [iʃ'tãnpal] *f* **-1.** [ger] print. **-2.** [aparência] appearance.

estampado, da [iʃtãn'padu, dal] *adj* **-1.** [tecido] printed. **-2.** *fig* [evidente] etched.

➡ **estampado** *m* **-1.** [tecido] printed cloth. **-2.** [padrão impresso] print.

estampar [4] [iʃtãn'pa(x)] *vt* **-1.** [imprimir] to print. **-2.** [marcar] to imprint. **-3.** *fig* [mostrar]: **a mulher estampava no rosto seu desespero** the woman's despair was etched on her face.

estamparia [iʃtãnpa'rial] *f* **-1.** [oficina] print shop room. **-2.** [tecido] printed material.

estampido [iʃtãn'pidul] *m* bang.

estancar [12] [iʃtãn'ka(x)] *vt & vi* to stem *UK*, to staunch *US*.

estância [iʃ'tãnsja] *f* **-1.** [fazenda] estate. **-2.** [estação]: ~ **hidromineral** spa. **-3.** [estrofe] strophe, stanza.

estandarte [iʃtãn'daxtʃil] *m* standard.

estande [iʃ'tãndʒil] *m* stand.

estanho [iʃ'tãɲul] *m* tin.

estanque [iʃ'tãŋkil] *adj* **-1.** [estancado] tight, watertight **-2.** [vedado]: **compartimento** ~ airtight compartment.

estante [iʃ'tãntʃil] *f* **-1.** [móvel] bookcase. **-2.** [suporte] stand.

estapafúrdio, dia [iʃtapa'furdʒju, dʒjal] *adj* outlandish.

estar [10] [iʃ'ta(x)] *vi* **-1.** [com lugar] to be; [em casa] to be at home, to be in; **ela estará lá à hora certa** she'll be there on time; **estarei no emprego às dez** I'll be at work at ten. **-2.** [exprime estado] to be; **está quebrado** it's out of order; ~ **bem/mal de saúde** to be well/unwell; **está muito calor/frio** it's very hot/cold. **-3.** [manter-se] to be; **estive em casa toda a tarde** I was at home all afternoon; **estive esperando** I was waiting; **estive fora três anos** I lived abroad for three years; **deixe** ~ ... let it be ... **-4.** [em locuções]: **está bem** *OU* **certo!** OK!, all right!

➡ **estar a** *v + prep* [relativo a preço] to cost, to be; **o camarão está a 25 reais o quilo** shrimp cost *OU* are 25 reals a kilo.

➡ **estar de** *v + prep*: ~ **de baixa/férias** to be on sick leave/vacation; ~ **de saia** to be wearing a skirt; ~ **de vigia** to keep watch.

➡ **estar para** *v + prep*: ~ **para fazer algo** to be about to do sthg; **estou para sair** I'm about to go out, I'm on my way out; **ele está para chegar** he'll be here any minute now; **não estou para brincadeiras** I'm not in the mood for silly games.

➡ **estar perante** *v + prep* [frente a] to be facing; **você está perante um gênio** you're in the presence of a genius.

➡ **estar por** *v + prep* [apoiar] to support; [por realizar]: **a cama está por fazer** the bed hasn't been made yet; **a limpeza está por fazer** the cleaning hasn't been done yet.

➡ **estar sem** *v + prep*: **estou sem tempo** I don't have time; **estou sem dinheiro** I don't have any cash; **ele está sem comer há dois dias** he hasn't eaten for two days.

estardalhaço [iʃtaxda'ʎasul] *m* **-1.** [bulha] racket. **-2.** [ostentação] flamboyance.

estarrecer [25] [iʃtaxe'se(x)] <> *vt* to appal *UK*, to appall *US*. <> *vi* to be appalled.

estarrecido, da [iʃtaxe'sidu, dal] *adj* shaken.

estatal [iʃta'taw] (*pl* **-ais**) <> *adj* state (*antes de subst*). <> *f* [empresa] state-owned company.

estatelado, da [iʃtate'ladu, dal] *adj* [no chão] sprawled.

estatelar-se [4] [iʃtate'laxsil] *vp* [cair]: ~**-se (em)** to fall flat (on).

estática [iʃ'tatikal] *f FÍS* static.

estático, ca [iʃ'tatʃiku, kal] *adj* **-1.** [imóvel] still. **-2.** *FÍS* static.

estatístico, ca [iʃta'tʃiʃtʃiku, kal] <> *adj* statistical. <> *m, f* [profissional] statistician.

➡ **estatística** *f* statistics.

estatização [iʃtatʃiza'sãwl] (*pl* **-ões**) *f* nationalization.

estatizar [4] [iʃtatʃi'za(x)] *vt* to nationalize.
estátua [iʃ'tatwal *f* statue.
estatueta [iʃta'tweta] *f* statuette.
estatura [iʃta'tural *f* **-1.** [física] stature; ~ **alta /baixa/mediana** tall/short/medium stature. **-2.** [intelectual, moral] standing.
estatutário, ria [iʃtatu'tarju, rja] *adj* **-1.** [norma] statutory. **-2.** [funcionário]: **funcionário** ~ civil servant.
estatuto [iʃta'tutul *m* statute.
estável [iʃ'tavewl (*pl* **-eis**) *adj* **-1.** [ger] stable. **-2.** [cotação] fixed.
este¹ [ˈeʃtʃi] *m* east
este², esta [ˈeʃtʃi] <> *adj* this, these (*pl*). <> *pron* this (one), these ones (*pl*).
esteio [iʃ'teju] *m* **-1.** [escora] prop. **-2.** NÁUT chock. **-3.** *fig* [amparo] breadwinner.
esteira [iʃ'tejral *f* **-1.** [tecido] woven mat. **-2.** [usada na praia] reed mat. **-3.** [rolante] moving carpet. **-4.** *fig* [caminho] path; **na** ~ **de** in the course of.
estelionatário, ria [iʃteljona'tarju, rjal *m, f* swindler.
estelionato [iʃteljo'natul *m* swindle.
estêncil [iʃ'tẽsiwl (*pl* **-eis**) *m* stencil.
estender [5] [iʃtẽn'de(x)] *vt* **-1.** [ger] to spread. **-2.** [roupa] to hang out. **-3.** [corda, fio] to stretch out. **-4.** [massa] to roll out. **-5.** [pernas, braços, mãos] to stretch out. **-6.** [limites] to extend. **-7.** [oferecer]: ~ **algo para alguém** to give sthg to sb. **-8.** [prolongar] to prolong. **-9.** [fazer abranger]: ~ **algo a alguém/algo** to extend sthg to (include) sb/sthg.
➤ **estender-se** *vp* **-1.** [ocupar]: ~**-se por** to spread out over. **-2.** [durar]: ~**-se (por)** to last (for). **-3.** [alastrar-se]: ~**-se (por)** to spread (throughout). **-4.** [deitar-se]: ~**-se (em)** to lie down (on). **-5.** [falar, escrever muito]: ~**-se (sobre)** to enlarge (upon). **-6.** [abranger]: ~**-se a** to include.
estenodatilografia [iʃtenodatʃilogra'fial *f* shorthand typing.
estenodatilógrafo, fa [iʃtenodatʃi'lɔgrafu, fal *m, f* shorthand typist *UK*, stenographer *US*.
estenografar [4] [iʃtenogra'fa(x)] *vt* to write in shorthand.
estenografia [iʃtenogra'fial *f* shorthand *UK*, stenography *US*.
estenógrafo, fa [iʃte'nɔgrafu, fal *m, f* shorthand typist *UK*, stenographer *US*.
estepe [iʃ'tɛpil <> *m* [pneu] spare wheel. <> *f* [vegetação] steppe.
esterco [iʃ'texkul *m* manure.
estéreo [iʃ'tɛrju] *adj* stereo.
estereofônico, ca [iʃterjo'foniku, kal *adj* stereophonic.
estereotipado, da [iʃterjotʃi'padu, dal *adj* stereotypical.
estereotipar [4] [iʃterjotʃi'pa(x)] *vt* to stereotype.
estereótipo [iʃte'rjotʃipul *m* stereotype.
estéril [iʃ'tɛriwl (*pl* **-eis**) *adj* **-1.** [ger] sterile. **-2.** [terreno] barren. **-3.** *fig* [inútil, infrutífero] pointless.
esterilidade [iʃterili'dadʒil *f* **-1.** [infertilidade]

sterility. **-2.** [da terra] barrenness. **-3.** [escassez] dearth.
esterilização [iʃteriliza'sãwl (*pl* **-ões**) *f* sterilization.
esterilizado, da [iʃterili'zadu, dal *adj* sterilized.
esterilizador [iʃterili'do(x)l *m* sterilizer.
esterilizar [4] [iʃterili'za(x)] *vt* to sterilize.
esterlino, na [iʃtex'linu, nal <> *adj*: **libra** ~ pound sterling. <> *m* sterling.
esteróide [iʃte'rɔjdʒil *m* steroid.
esteta [iʃ'tɛtal *mf* aesthete *UK*, esthete *US*.
esteticista [iʃtetʃi'siʃtal *mf* beautician.
estético, ca [iʃ'tɛtʃiku, kal *adj* **-1.** [artístico] aesthetic *UK*, esthetic *US*. **-2.** [harmonioso] tasteful.
➤ **estética** *f* **-1.** FILOSOFIA aestheticism *UK*, estheticism *US*. **-2.** [beleza] beauty; [do corpo] physical beauty.
estetoscópio [iʃtɛtoʃ'kɔpjul *m* stethoscope.
estiagem [iʃ'tʃjaʒẽl (*pl* **-ns**) *f* **-1.** [período seco] dry spell. **-2.** [de rio, fonte] drying out.
estiar [16] [iʃ'tʃja(x)l *vi* **-1.** [parar de chover] to stop raining. **-2.** [faltar chuva] to be dry.
estibordo [iʃtʃi'bɔxdul *m* starboard; **a** ~ to starboard.
esticada [iʃtʃi'kadal <> *f*: **dar uma** ~ [espichar-se] to have a stretch. <> *f*: **dar uma** ~ **em** *fam* to procede to.
esticar [12] [iʃtʃi'ka(x)l <> *vt* to stretch. <> *vi* **-1.** [distender-se] to stretch. **-2.** *fam* [prolongar saída]: ~ **(em)** to go on (to).
➤ **esticar-se** *vp* [pessoa] to stretch.
estigma [iʃ'tʃigmal *m* **-1.** [ger] stigma. **-2.** [ferrete] mark; **a Inquisição o condenou a usar o** ~ **de cristão-novo** the Inquisition branded him a neo-Christian.
estigmatizar [4] [iʃtʃigmatʃi'za(x)l *vt* **-1.** [com infâmia] to stigmatize; **eles o estigmatizaram de traidor** they branded him a traitor. **-2.** [com preconceito] to revile.
estilete *m* [punhal] stiletto.
estilhaçar [13] [iʃtʃiʎa'sa(x)l *vt* to shatter.
➤ **estilhaçar-se** *vp* to be shattered.
estilhaço [iʃtʃi'ʎasul *m* **-1.** [de plástico, granada] splinter. **-2.** [de vidro] shard.
estilista [iʃtʃi'liʃtal *mf* **-1.** [escritor] stylist. **-2.** [de moda] fashion designer.
estilístico, ca [iʃtʃi'liʃtʃiku, kal *adj* **-1.** [talento, característica] stylish. **-2.** [análise] stylistic.
estilização [iʃtʃiliza'sãwl (*pl* **-ões**) *f* stylization.
estilizar [4] [iʃtʃili'za(x)l *vt* to stylize.
estilo [iʃ'tʃilul *m* style; ~ **de época** style of the period; **ter** ~ *fig* [ser autêntico] to have real style; **de** ~ [de época] fashionable; ~ **de vida** way of life; **em grande** ~ [com pompa] in grande style.
estima [iʃ'tʃimal *f* **-1.** [apreço] esteem. **-2.** [afeição] affection.
estimação [iʃtʃima'sãwl *f*: **de** ~ prized; **minha caneta de** ~ my favourite pen; **animal de** ~ (family) pet.
estimado, da [iʃtʃi'madu, dal *adj* **-1.** [avaliado] estimated. **-2.** [querido] esteemed.

estimar [4] [iʃtʃi'ma(x)] *vt* **-1.** [ger] to prize. **-2.** [avaliar]: ~ **algo (em)** to estimate sthg (at). **-3.** [desejar]: ~ **as melhoras de alguém** to hope sb gets better; ~ **que** to hope that.

estimativa [iʃtʃima'tʃiva] *f* estimation; ~ **de custo** estimate; **fazer uma** ~ **de algo** to make an appraisal of sthg.

estimável [iʃtʃi'mavew] (*pl* -eis) *adj* **-1.** [avaliável]: ~ **em** reckoned at. **-2.** [digno de respeito] respectable.

estimulação [iʃtʃimula'sãw] *f* stimulation.

estimulante [iʃtʃimu'lãntʃi] <> *adj* stimulating. <> *m* stimulant.

estimular [4] [iʃtʃimu'la(x)] *vt* **-1.** [excitar, ativar] to stimulate. **-2.** [instigar] to incite. **-3.** [incentivar]: ~ **alguém (a fazer algo)** to encourage sb (to do sthg).

estímulo [iʃ'tʃimulu] *m* **-1.** [ger] stimulus. **-2.** [excitação] stimulant. **-3.** [incentivo] motivation.

estio [iʃ'tʃiu] *m* summer.

estipêndio [iʃtʃi'pẽndʒu] *m* stipend.

estipular [4] [iʃtipu'la(x)] *vt* to stipulate.

estiramento [iʃtʃira'mẽntu] *m* MED [distensão] strain.

estirar [4] [iʃtʃi'ra(x)] *vt* **-1.** [alongar] to stretch. **-2.** [estender ao comprido] to stretch out.

• **estirar-se** *vp* [deitar-se] to stretch o.s out.

estirpe [iʃ'tʃixpi] *f* lineage.

estiva [iʃ'tʃiva] *f* NÁUT stowage.

estivador, ra [iʃtʃiva'do(x), ra] (*mpl* -es, *fpl* -s) *m, f* stevedore.

estocada [iʃto'kada] *f* stab.

estocagem [iʃto'kaʒẽ] *f* [provisão] stock.

estocar [12] [iʃto'ka(x)] *vt* **-1.** [armazenar] to stock. **-2.** [dar estocada em] to stab.

Estocolmo [iʃto'kowmu] *n* Stockholm.

estofado, da [iʃto'fadu, da] <> *adj* **-1.** [forrado] upholstered. **-2.** [acolchoado] padded. <> *m* suite.

estofador, ra [iʃtofa'do(x), ra] *m, f* upholsterer.

estofar [4] [iʃto'fa(x)] *vt* **-1.** [revestir] to upholster. **-2.** [acolchoar] to stuff.

estofo [iʃ'tofu] *m* **-1.** [revestimento] reupholstery. **-2.** [acolchoamento] stuffing.

estoicismo [iʃtoj'siʒmu] *m* stoicism.

estóico, ca [iʃ'tɔjku, ka] <> *adj* **-1.** FILOSOFIA stoical, stoic. **-2.** *fig* [austero] stoical. <> *m, f fig* [pessoa austera] stoic.

• **estóica** *f* FILOSOFIA stoicism.

estojo [iʃ'toʒu] *m* case; ~ **de unhas** manicure set.

estola [iʃ'tɔla] *f* stole.

estomacal [iʃtoma'kaw] (*pl* -ais) *adj* stomach (*antes de subst).*

estômago [iʃ'tomagu] *m* **-1.** ANAT stomach; **estar com o** ~ **embrulhado** to have an upset stomach; **forrar o** ~ to have a bite to eat. **-2.** *fig* [paciência]: **ter** ~ **para (fazer) algo** to have the stomach for (doing) sthg.

Estônia [iʃ'tonja] *n* Estonia.

estoniano, na [iʃto'njãnu, na] <> *adj* Estonian. <> *m, f* Estonian.

• **estoniano** *m* [língua] Estonian.

estonteante [iʃtõn'tʃãntʃi] *adj* stunning.

estopa [iʃ'tɔpa] *f* tow.

estopim (*pl* -ns) *m* **-1.** [de bomba] fuse. **-2.** *fig* [de crise, revolta] trigger.

estoque [iʃ'tɔki] *m* **-1.** [provisão] stock; **em** ~ in stock. **-2.** [local] store.

estória [iʃ'tɔrja] *f* story.

estorricar [12] [iʃtoxi'ka(x)] *vt & vi* to scorch.

estorvar [4] [iʃtox'va(x)] *vt* **-1.** [obstruir] to obstruct. **-2.** [importunar] to disturb.

estorvo [iʃ'toxvu] *m* **-1.** [obstáculo] obstacle; [pessoa] hindrance. **-2.** [incômodo] disturbance.

estourado, da [iʃto'radu, da] *adj* **-1.** [temperamental] boisterous. **-2.** *fam* [fatigado] knackered.

estourar [4] [iʃto'ra(x)] <> *vi* **-1.** [bomba] to explode. **-2.** [pneu] to blow up. **-3.** [guerra, revolução] to break out. **-4.** [escândalo] to become public. **-5.** *fig* [rebentar] to burst; **estar estourando de raiva/alegria** to be bursting with rage/joy. **-6.** [ralhar]: ~ **(com alguém)** to explode (at sb). **-7.** [no mais tardar]: **estourando cinco e meia** no later than five-thirty. <> *vt* **-1.** [bomba] to explode. **-2.** [boca-de-fumo] to bust up.

estouro [iʃ'toru] *m* **-1.** [ger] explosion. **-2.** *fam*: **ser um** ~ [filme, pessoa] to be a hit; [notícia, carro] to be a sensation.

estouvado, da [iʃto'vadu, da] *adj* [desajuizado] foolhardy.

estrábico, ca [iʃ'trabiku, ka] *adj* cross-eyed.

estrabismo [iʃtra'biʒmu] *m* squint, strabismus.

estraçalhar [4] [iʃtrasa'ʎa(x)] *vt* **-1.** [livro, objeto] to tear to shreds. **-2.** [pessoa] to kill.

• **estraçalhar-se** *vp* **-1.** [objeto] to smash. **-2.** [pessoa] to smash one another.

estrada [iʃ'trada] *m* **-1.** road; ~ **principal** main road *UK*, highway *US*; ~ **secundária** secondary road, B road; ~ **de ferro** railway track *UK*, railroad *US*; ~ **de rodagem** public road; ~ **vicinal** link road. **-2.** *fig* [carreira] work; **estar na** ~ to be in the field.

estrado [iʃ'tradu] *m* **-1.** [de cama] frame. **-2.** [tablado] platform.

estragado, da [iʃtra'gadu, da] *adj* **-1.** [podre] rotten. **-2.** [danificado] damaged. **-3.** [mimado] spoilt.

estragão [iʃtra'gãw] *m* tarragon.

estraga-prazeres [iʃ,tragapra'zeriʃ] *mf inv* killjoy, spoilsport.

estragar [14] [iʃtra'ga(x)] <> *vt* **-1.** [ger] to spoil. **-2.** [danificar] to damage. <> *vi* [apodrecer] to go off.

• **estragar-se** *vp* **-1.** [deteriorar-se] to be ruined. **-2.** [avariar-se] to go wrong. **-3.** [apodrecer] to go rotten.

estrago [iʃ'tragu] *m* **-1.** [dano] damage; **fazer um** ~ **em algo** to cause damage to sthg. **-2.** [desperdício] disaster.

estrangeiro, ra [iʃtrãn'ʒejru, ra] <> *adj* foreign. <> *m, f* [pessoa] foreigner.

• **estrangeiro** *m*: **no** ~ abroad.

estrangulador, ra [iʃtrãngula'do(x), ra] *m, f* strangler.

estrangulamento [iʃtrãŋgulaˈmẽntu] *m* -1. [de pessoa] strangulation. -2. [obstrução] blocking.

estrangular [4] [iʃtrãŋguˈla(x)] *vt* to strangle.

estranhamento [iʃtrãɲaˈmentu] *m* [espanto] surprise.

estranhar [4] [iʃtrãˈɲa(x)] <> *vt* -1. [achar fora do comum] to find strange. -2. [surpreender-se com] to be surprised by. -3. [não se habituar a] to be unaccustomed to. -4. [retrair-se diante de] to feel ill at ease with. -5. [hostilizar] to harass. <> *vi* [causar estranheza] to be strange.

➤ **estranhar-se** *vp* [hostilizar-se] to fall out with each other.

estranho, nha [iʃˈtrãɲu, ɲal *adj* -1. [diferente, estrangeiro] foreign. -2. [incomum, desconhecido] strange; **não ser ~ para alguém** to be familiar to sb.

estratagema [iʃtrataˈʒema] *m* stratagem.

estratégia [iʃtraˈtɛʒja] *f* strategy.

estratégico, ca [iʃtraˈtɛʒiku, ka] *adj* strategic.

estrategista [iʃtrateˈʒiʃtal *mf* strategist.

estratificar-se [12] [iʃtratʃifiˈkaxsil *vp* -1. [em camadas] to be stratified. -2. *fig* [cristalizar-se] to take shape.

estrato [iʃˈtratul *m* stratum.

estratosfera [iʃtratoʃˈfɛral *f* stratosphere.

estreante [iʃˈtrjãntʃil *adj* debut *(antes de subst)*.

estrear [15] [iʃtreˈa(x)] <> *vt* -1. [roupa, carro] to try out for the first time. -2. [filme, show] to premiere. -3. [carreira] to start. <> *vi* -1. [filme, show] to premiere. -2. [artista, jogador] to debut.

estrebaria [iʃtrebaˈrial *f* stable.

estrebuchar [4] [iʃtrebuˈʃa(x)] *vi* [em agonia] to writhe.

estréia [iʃˈtrɛjal *f* -1. [de filme, show] premiere. -2. [de artista, jogador] debut. -3. [de roupa, carro] first time out.

estreitamento [iʃtrejtaˈmẽntul *m* -1. [ger] narrowing. -2. [diminuição] shrinking. -3. [de relações] strengthening.

estreitar [4] [iʃtrejˈta(x)] <> *vt* -1. [diminuir] to shrink. -2. [apertar] to narrow. -3. [roupa] to constrict. -4. [relações, laços] to strengthen. -5. [tornar mais rigoroso] to tighten up. <> *vi* [estrada] to narrow.

➤ **estreitar-se** *vp* -1. [largura] to narrow. -2. [amizade, união] to strengthen.

estreiteza [iʃtrejˈtezal *f* narrowness.

estreito, ta [iʃˈtrejtu, ta] *adj* -1. [apertado] narrow. -2. [vestido, saia] straight. -3. [relação, amizade] strong.

➤ **estreito** *m* GEOGR strait.

estrela [iʃˈtrelal *f* -1. [ger] star; **~ de cinema** film star *UK*, movie star *US*; **~ cadente** shooting star. -2. [sorte] lucky star; **ter boa/má ~** to have good/bad luck.

estrela-de-davi [iʃˈtreladzidavil *(pl* estrelas-de-davi) *f* Star of David.

estrelado, da [iʃtreˈladu, dal *adj* -1. [céu, noite] starry. -2. [ovo] fried.

estrela-do-mar [iʃtreladuˈma(x)] *(pl* estrelas-do-mar) *f* starfish.

estrelar [4] [iʃtreˈla(x)] *vt* -1. [filme, peça] to star. -2. [ovos] to fry.

estrelato [iʃtreˈlatul *m*: **o ~** stardom.

estrelinha [iʃtreˈliɲal *f* [fogo de artifício] sparkler.

estrelismo [iʃtreˈliʒmul *m prima donna-ish behaviour.*

estremecer [25] [iʃtremeˈse(x)l <> *vt* to shake. <> *vi* -1. [tremer de espanto] to shiver. -2. [sacudir] to shudder. -3. [sofrer abalo] to be shaken.

estremecido, da [iʃtremeˈsidu, dal *adj* [amizade, união] shaken.

estremecimento [iʃtremesiˈmẽntul *m* shaking.

estrepar-se [4] [iʃtreˈpaxsil *vp* to come unstuck.

estrépito [iʃˈtrɛpitul *m* racket; **fazer ~** to make a racket; **com ~** noisily.

estrepitoso, osa [iʃtrepiˈtozu, ɔzal *adj* -1. [ruidoso] noisy. -2. *fig* [sensacional] resounding.

estressado, da [iʃtreˈsadu, dal *adj* stressed (out).

estressante [iʃtreˈsãntʃil *adj* stressful.

estressar [iʃtreˈsa(x)l *vt* to cause stress to.

➤ **estressar-se** *vp* to become stressed.

estresse [iʃˈtrɛsil *m* stress.

estria [iʃˈtrial *f* -1. [sulco] groove. -2. [na pele] stretch mark.

estribeira [iʃtriˈbejral *f*: **perder as ~s** *fam* to lose one's head.

estribilho [iʃtriˈbiʎul *m MÚS* chorus.

estribo [iʃˈtribul *m* -1. [de cavalo] stirrup. -2. [degrau] step.

estricnina [iʃtrikˈninal *f* strychnine.

estridente [iʃtriˈdẽntʃil *adj* strident.

estrilar [4] [iʃtriˈla(x)] *vi fam* -1. [vociferar] to make a shrill noise. -2. [reclamar] to clamour.

estrilo [iʃˈtrilul *m fam*: **dar um ~** to fly off the handle.

estripulia [iʃtripuˈlial *f* mischief.

estritamente [iʃtritaˈmẽntʃil *adv* [à risca] to the letter.

estrito, ta [iʃˈtritu, tal *adj* -1. [rigoroso] strict. -2. [exato] precise; **no sentido ~ da palavra** in the strict sense of the word.

estrofe [iʃˈtrɔfil *f* stanza.

estrogênio [iʃtroˈʒenjul *m* oestrogen.

estrogonofe [iʃtrogoˈnɔfil *m CULIN* stroganoff.

estrondo [iʃˈtrõndul *m* rumble.

estrondoso, osa [iʃtrõnˈdozu, ɔzal *adj* -1. [ruidoso] roaring. -2. [espetacular] spectacular.

estropiado, da [iʃtroˈpjadu, dal *adj* -1. [aleijado] crippled. -2. [exausto] worn out.

estropiar [16] [iʃtroˈpja(x)] *vt* -1. [aleijar] to cripple. -2. [cansar] to tire out. -3. *fig* [mutilar] to mutilate. -4. *fig* [pronunciar mal] to mispronounce.

estrume [iʃˈtrumil *m* manure.

estrupício *m fam pej* [pessoa estúpida]: **ser um ~** to be an idiot.

estrutura [iʃtruˈtural *f* -1. CONST structure. -2. [armação] frame.

estruturação [iʃtruturaˈsãw] *(pl* -ões) *f* structuring.

estrutural [iʃtrutuˈrawl *(pl* -ais) *adj* structural.

estruturalismo [iʃtrutura'liʒmul *m* structuralism.

estruturalista [iʃtrutura'liʃta] *adj* structuralist.

estruturar [4] [iʃtrutu'ra(x)] *vt* to structure.

estuário [iʃ'twarju] *m* estuary.

estudado, da [iʃtu'dadu, da] *adj* studied.

estudante [iʃtu'dãntʃi] *mf* student.

estudantil [iʃtudãn'tʃiw] (*pl* -**is**) *adj* student (*antes de subst*).

estudar [4] [iʃtu'da(x)] *vt & vi* to study.

estúdio [iʃ'tudʒju] *m* studio.

estudioso, osa [iʃtu'dʒjozu, ɔza] <> *adj* studious. <> *m*, *f* expert.

estudo [iʃ'tudul] *m* study; **ter muito** ~ to be very learned; ~ **de caso** case study; ~ **de viabilidade** feasibility study.

➡ **estudos** *mpl* [formação escolar] studies.

estufa [iʃ'tufal] *f* -**1.** [para plantas] greenhouse. -**2.** [aquecedor] stove.

estufar [4] [iʃtu'fa(x)] *vt* -**1.** [aquecer em estufa] to heat in the oven. -**2.** [encher] to stuff; **ele estufou o peito de orgulho** *fig* he puffed (his chest out) with pride; **o dinheiro estufava sua carteira** his wallet was stuffed with money. -**3.** *CULIN* [carne] to stew.

estupefação [iʃtupefa'sãw] *f* [espanto] amazement.

estupefato, ta [iʃtupe'fatu, ta] *adj* [espantado] amazed.

estupendo, da [iʃtu'pẽndu, da] *adj* -**1.** [maravilhoso] wonderful. -**2.** [espantoso] amazing.

estupidamente [iʃtupida'mẽntʃi] *adv* -**1.** [de maneira absurda] stupidly. -**2.** [extremamente] extremely; **uma cerveja estupidamente gelada, por favor** an extremely cold beer, please.

estupidez [iʃtupi'deʃ] *f* -**1.** [condição] stupidity. -**2.** [ato] stupid thing. -**3.** *fam* [grosseria]: **não é a primeira vez que ela me faz uma** ~ it is not the first time he has been rude to me.

estúpido, da [iʃ'tupidu, da] <> *adj* -**1.** [burro] stupid. -**2.** [grosseiro] rude; **um calor** ~ *fig* an unbearable heat. <> *m*, *f* -**1.** [pessoa burra] stupid person. -**2.** [pessoa grosseira] rude person.

estupor [iʃtu'po(x)] *m* -**1.** [estado] stupor. -**2.** [estarrecimento] amazement.

estuporado, da [iʃtupo'radu, da] *adj* -**1.** [paralisado] stupefied. -**2.** [estarrecido] stunned. -**3.** *fam* [estragado] messed up. -**4.** *fam* [cansado] wiped out. -**5.** *fam* [ferido] messed up.

estuporar [4] [iʃtupo'ra(x)] *vt* -**1.** [cair em estupor] to paralise. -**2.** [assustar] to shock. -**3.** [arruinar] to smash.

estuprador [iʃtupra'do(x)] *m* rapist.

estuprar [4] [iʃtu'pra(x)] *vt* to rape.

estupro [iʃ'tuprul] *m* rape.

estuque [iʃ'tukil] *m* stucco.

esturricado, da [iʃtuxi'kadu, da] *adj* dry.

esturricar [12] [iʃtuxi'ka(x)] <> *vt* to dry. <> *vi* to become dry.

esvair-se [68] [iʒva'ixsil] *vp* -**1.** [desaparecer] to disappear. -**2.** [desmaiar] to faint. -**3.** *loc*: ~ **em sangue** to bleed copiously; ~ **em lágrimas** to dissolve into tears.

esvaziamento [iʒvazja'mẽntul] *m* -**1.** [desocupação] emptying. -**2.** [evacuação] evacuation. -**3.** [perda de importância] nullification.

esvaziar [16] [iʒva'zja(x)] *vt* -**1.** [desocupar] to empty. -**2.** [beber de uma só vez] to drain. -**3.** [tirar a importância de] to nullify.

➡ **esvaziar-se** *vp* [tornar-se vazio] to empty.

esverdeado, da [iʒvex'dʒadu, da] *adj* greenish.

esvoaçante [iʒvwa'sãntʃil] *adj* fluttering.

esvoaçar [13] [iʒvwa'sa(x)] *vi* to flutter.

ET (*abrev de* Extra Terrestre) *m* ET.

eta [ˈetal] *interj* blast; ~ **ferro!** gee whiz!

ETA (*abrev de* Euskadi Ta Askatasuna) *m* ETA.

etapa [eˈtapal] *f* stage; **por** ~**s** in stages.

etário, ria [eˈtarju, rjal] *adj* aged.

etc. (*abrev de* et cetera) etc.

éter [ˈɛte(x)] *m* ether.

etéreo, rea [eˈtɛrju, rjal] *adj* ethereal.

eternidade [etexni'dadʒil] *f* eternity.

eternizar [4] [etexni'za(x)] *vt* -**1.** [tornar eterno] to eternalize. -**2.** [imortalizar] to immortalize. -**3.** *fam* [prolongar] to drag out.

➡ **eternizar-se** *vp* -**1.** [tornar-se eterno] to become eternal. -**2.** [imortalizar-se] to become immortal. -**3.** *fam* [prolongar-se] to drag on.

eterno, na [eˈtɛxnu, nal] *adj* eternal.

Ethernet [etex'netil] *f COMPUT* Ethernet®.

ético, ca [ˈɛtʃiku, kal] *adj* ethical.

➡ **ética** *f* ethics (*pl*).

etimologia [etʃimolo'ʒial] *f* etymology.

etíope [eˈtʃiopil] <> *adj* Ethiopian. <> *mf* Ethiopian.

Etiópia [eˈtʃiˈɔpjal] *n* Ethiopia.

etiqueta [etʃiˈketal] *f* -**1.** [ger] label; ~ **adesiva** sticky label. -**2.** [boas maneiras] etiquette. -**3.** [de preço] ticket; [de roupa] label.

etiquetar [4] [etʃike'ta(x)] *vt* to label.

etnia [etʃ'nial] *f* ethnic group.

étnico, ca [ˈɛtʃniku, kal] *adj* ethnic.

etnocentrismo [etʃnosẽn'triʒmul] *m* ethnocentrism.

etnografia [etʃnogra'fial] *f* ethnography.

etnologia [etʃnolo'ʒial] *f* ethnology.

etos [ˈɛtuʃ] *m inv* ethos.

eu [ˈewl] *pron* I; **e** ~ **?** what about me?; **sou** ~ it's me; ~ **mesmo** *ou* **próprio** (I) myself.

EUA (*abrev de* Estados Unidos da América) *n* USA.

eucalipto [ewka'liptul] *m* eucalyptus.

eucaristia [ewkariʃ'tʃial] *f* Eucharist.

eufemismo [ewfe'miʒmul] *m* euphemism.

eufonia [ewfo'nial] *f* euphony.

euforia [ewfo'rial] *f* euphoria.

eufórico, ca [ewˈfɔriku, kal] *adj* euphoric.

eunuco [ew'nukul] *m* eunuch.

euro [ˈewrul] *m* [moeda] euro.

eurodólar [ewro'dɔla(x)] *m* Eurodollar.

Europa [ew'rɔpal] *n* Europe.

europeizar [4,19] [ewropeji'za(x)] *vt* to Europeanize.

➤ **europeizar-se** *vp* to become Europeanized.

europeu, péia [ewro'pew, pɛja] ◇ *adj* European. ◇ *m, f* European.

eutanásia [ewta'naʒja] *f* euthanasia.

evacuação [evakwa'sãw] (*pl* -ões) *f* evacuation.

evacuar [4] [eva'kwa(x)] ◇ *vt* -1. [desocupar] to evacuate. -2. [expelir]: ~ **sangue** to bleed; ~ **fezes** to defecate. ◇ *vi* [defecar] to evacuate.

evadir [6] [eva'dʒi(x)] *vt* -1. [evitar] to avoid. -2. [eludir] to evade.

➤ **evadir-se** *vp* [escapar] to escape.

evanescente [evane'sẽtʃi] *adj* evanescent.

evangelho [evãn'ʒeʎu] *m* Gospel; **o ~ segundo Mateus** the Gospel according to Matthew.

evangélico, ca [evãn'ʒɛliku, ka] ◇ *adj* evangelical. ◇ *m, f* [pessoa] evangelist.

evangelização [evãnʒeliza'sãw] (*pl* -ões) *f* conversion (to Christianity).

evangelizar [evãnʒeli'za(x)] *vt* to convert (to Christianity).

evaporação [evapora'sãw] (*pl* -ões) *f* evaporation.

evaporar [4] [evapo'ra(x)] ◇ *vt* [vaporizar] to evaporate. ◇ *vi* to evaporate.

➤ **evaporar-se** *vp* to evaporate.

evasão [eva'zãw] (*pl* -ões) *f* -1. [fuga] escape. -2. *fig* [evasiva] evasion.

evasivo, va [eva'zivu, va] *adj* evasive.

➤ **evasiva** *f* evasion.

evento [e'vẽtu] *m* event.

eventual [evẽn'twaw] (*pl* -ais) *adj* chance *(antes de subst)*.

eventualidade [evẽntwali'dadʒi] *f* eventuality.

eventualmente [evẽntwal'mẽtʃi] *adv* [às vezes] occasionally.

Everest [eve'rɛstʃi] *n*: **o ~** (Mount) Everest.

evidência [evi'dẽsja] *f* evidence; **em ~** [destacado] obvious.

evidenciar [16] [evidẽn'sja(x)] *vt* -1. [comprovar] to prove. -2. [mostrar] to be evidence of. -3. [destacar] to show clearly.

➤ **evidenciar-se** *vp* -1. [comprovar-se] to be proven. -2. [destacar-se] to be shown clearly.

evidente [evi'dẽtʃi] *adj* obvious.

evidentemente [evidẽtʃi'mẽtʃi] *adv* clearly.

evitar [4] [evi'ta(x)] *vt* -1. [fugir a] to avoid; ~ **fazer algo** to avoid doing sthg. -2. [impedir] to prevent.

evitável [evi'tavew] (*pl* -eis) *adj* avoidable.

evocação [evoka'sãw] (*pl* -ões) *f* recollection.

evocar [12] [evo'ka(x)] *vt* [trazer à lembrança] to bring to mind.

evolução [evolu'sãw] (*pl* -ões) *f* -1. *BIOL* evolution. -2. [desenrolar] development. -3. [movimento] expansion. -4. *MIL* exercise.

evoluído, da [evo'lwidu, da] *adj* -1. [adiantado] advanced. -2. [aberto] open.

evoluir [74] [evo'lwi(x)] *vi* -1. [espécie] to evolve. -2. [adiantar-se] to progress.

ex. (*abrev de* **exemplo**) e.g.

exacerbação [ezaseba'sãw] *f* -1. [ger] exacerbation. -2. [irritação] provocation.

exacerbante [ezasex'bãtʃi] *adj* [intensificador] exacerbating.

exacerbar [4] [ezasex'ba(x)] *vt* -1. [intensificar] to exacerbate. -2. [irritar] to provoke.

➤ **exacerbar-se** *vp* -1. [intensificar-se] to be exacerbated. -2. [irritar-se] to be provoked.

exagerado, da [ezaʒe'radu, da] ◇ *adj* exaggerated. ◇ *m, f*: **o que ele diz é típico de um ~** what he says is typical of an exaggerator.

exagerar [4] [ezaʒe'ra(x)] *vt & vi* to exaggerate.

exagero [eza'ʒeru] *m* exaggeration.

exalação [ezala'sãw] (*pl* -ões) *f* exhalation.

exalar [4] [eza'la(x)] *vt* to exhale.

exaltação [ezawta'sãw] *f* -1. [engrandecimento] exaltation. -2. [irritação] irritation. -3. [excitação] excitement.

exaltado, da [ezaw'tadu, da] *adj* -1. [facilmente irritável] irritable. -2. [fanático] fanatical. -3. [exacerbado] irritated.

exaltar [4] [ezaw'ta(x)] *vt* -1. [engrandecer] to exalt. -2. [irritar] to irritate. -3. [excitar] to excite.

➤ **exaltar-se** *vp* [irritar-se] to become irritated.

exame [e'zãmi] *m* -1. [ger] examination; **fazer um ~** to have an examination; ~ **de sangue** blood test. -2. *EDUC* [teste] examination, exam; **fazer um ~** to sit an examination; ~ **de direção** driving test. -3. [inspeção] inspection.

examinador, ra [ezamina'do(x), ra] ◇ *adj* examining. ◇ *m, f* examiner.

examinar [4] [ezami'na(x)] *vt* -1. [ger] to examine. -2. [inspecionar] to inspect.

exasperação [ezaʃpera'sãw] *f* exasperation.

exasperado, da [ezaʃpe'radu, da] *adj* exasperated.

exasperador, ra [ezaʃpera'do(x), ra] *adj* exasperating.

exasperante [ezaʃpe'rãtʃi] *adj* exasperating.

exasperar [4] [ezaʃpe'ra(x)] *vt* to exasperate.

➤ **exasperar-se** *vp* to become exasperated.

exatamente [ezata'mẽtʃi] *adv* exactly.

exatidão [ezatʃi'dãw] *f* -1. [precisão] accuracy. -2. [perfeição] perfection.

exato, ta [e'zatu, ta] *adj* -1. [preciso] exact. -2. [correto] correct, right.

exaurir [6] [ezaw'ri(x)] *vt* [esgotar] to exhaust.

➤ **exaurir-se** *vp* to be exhausted.

exaustão [ezawʃ'tãw] *f* exhaustion.

exaustivo, va [ezawʃ'tʃivu, va] *adj* -1. [esgotante] exhausting. -2. [completo] exhaustive.

exausto, ta [e'zawʃtu, ta] ◇ *pp* ➤ **exaurir**. ◇ *adj* exhausted.

exaustor [ezawʃ'to(x)] (*pl* -es) *m* extractor fan.

exceção [ese'sãw] (*pl* -ões) *f*: **com ~ de** except for, with the exception of.

excedente [ese'dẽtʃi] ◇ *adj* excess *(antes de subst)*. ◇ *m* -1. *COM* surplus. -2. [aluno] student on waiting list.

exceder [5] [ese'de(x)] *vt* exceed.

➤ **exceder-se** *vp* [cometer excessos] to go too far.

excelência [ese'lẽnʒa] *f* **-1.** [primazia] excellence; **por ~ par** excellence. **-2.** [tratamento]: **(Vossa) Excelência** Your Excellency.

excelente [ese'lẽntʃi] *adj* excellent.

excelentíssimo, ma [eselẽn'tʃisimu, ma] *adj superl* [tratamento] most excellent; **~ Senhor** Your Excellence; **o ~ senhor presidente da república** His Excellency, the president of the republic.

excelso, sa [e'sɛwsu, sa] *adj* **-1.** [sublime] sublime. **-2.** [excelente] excellent.

excentricidade [esẽntrisi'dadʒi] *f* eccentricity.

excêntrico, ca [e'sẽntriku, ka] <> *adj* eccentric. <> *m, f* eccentric.

excepcional [esepsjo'naw] (*pl* **-ais**) <> *adj* **-1.** [extraordinário, excelente] exceptional. **-2.** MED disabled. <> *mf* MED [pessoa] person with special needs.

excepcionalidade [esepsjonali'dadʒi] *f* **-1.** [condição de extraordinário] exceptional nature. **-2.** [excelência] exceptional quality.

excepcionalmente [esepsjonaw'mẽntʃi] *adv* exceptionally.

excerto [e'sextul] *m* excerpt.

excessivamente [esesiva'mẽntʃi] *adv* excessively.

excessivo, va [ese'sivu, va] *adj* excessive.

excesso [e'sɛsu] *m* **-1.** [ger] excess; **~ de peso** [obesidade] excess weight; [em bagagem] excess baggage; **~ de velocidade** excessive speed. **-2.** COM surplus. **-3.** [desmando]: **cometer ~s** to go too far.

exceto [e'sɛtu] *prep* except.

excetuar [4] [ese'twa(x)] *vt* to except.

excitação [esita'sãw] *f* **-1.** [agitação] excitement. **-2.** [sexual] arousal.

excitamento [esita'mẽntu] *m* [agitação] excitement.

excitado, da [esi'tadu, da] *adj* **-1.** [agitado] excited. **-2.** [sexualmente] aroused.

excitante [esi'tãntʃi] *adj* **-1.** [ger] stimulating; **uma droga ~** a stimulant. **-2.** [filme] exciting.

excitar [4] [esi'ta(x)] *vt* **-1.** [agitar] to excite. **-2.** [sexualmente] to arouse. **-3.** [incitar] to incite.

➤ **excitar-se** *vp* **-1.** [agitar-se] to become excited. **-2.** [sexualmente] to become aroused.

exclamação [iʃklama'sãw] (*pl* **-ões**) *f* exclamation.

exclamar [4] [iʃkla'ma(x)] *vi* to exclaim.

exclamativo, va [iʃklama'tʃivu, va] *adj* exclamatory; **ponto de ~** exclamation mark.

excluir [74] [iʃklu'i(x)] *vt* **-1.** [eliminar] to exclude. **-2.** [omitir]: **~ algo/alguém de** to exclude sthg/sb from. **-3.** [privar]: **~ algo/alguém de** to leave sthg/sb out of. **-4.** [por incompatibilidade] to preclude.

exclusão [iʃklu'zãw] (*pl* **-ões**) *f* exclusion.

exclusividade [iʃkluzivi'dadʒi] *f* **-1.** [uso, posse] exclusivity. **-2.** COM [direito] sole rights.

exclusivista [iʃkluzi'viʃta] <> *adj* [individualista] self-centred. <> *mf* self-centred person.

exclusivo, va [iʃklu'zivu, va] *adj* exclusive.

excomungado, da [iʃkomũŋ'gadu, da] <> *adj* RELIG excommunicated. <> *m, f* excommunicated person.

excomungar [14] [iʃkomũŋ'ga(x)] *vt* to excommunicate.

excreção [iʃkre'sãw] (*pl* **-ões**) *f* **-1.** BIOL excretion. **-2.** [substância excretada] excreta.

excremento [iʃkre'mẽntu] *m* excrement.

excretar [iʃkre'ta(x)] *vt* [expelir] to excrete.

excruciante [iʃkru'sjãntʃi] *adj* excruciating.

excursão [iʃkux'sãw] (*pl* **-ões**) *f* **-1.** [ger] excursion. **-2.** [em caminhada] walk, ramble.

excursionar [4] [iʃkuxsjo'na(x)] *vi*: **~ (por)** to tour.

excursionista [iʃkuxsjo'niʃta] *mf* [turista] tourist; [por um dia] day-tripper; [em caminhada] walker, rambler.

execrar [4] [eze'kra(x)] *vt* to execrate.

execrável [eze'kravew] (*pl* **-eis**) *adj* execrable.

execução [ezeku'sãw] (*pl* **-ões**) *f* **-1.** [ger] execution. **-2.** [de peça musical] performance.

executante [ezeku'tãntʃi] <> *adj* [de peça musical] performing. <> *mf* **-1.** [músico] performer. **-2.** [jur] executor.

executar [4] [ezeku'ta(x)] *vt* **-1.** [ger] to execute. **-2.** [peça musical] to perform. **-3.** [cumprir] to carry out.

executivo, va [ezeku'tʃivu, va] <> *adj* executive. <> *m, f* executive.

executor, ra [ezeku'to(x), ra] *m, f* executor.

exemplar [ezẽn'pla(x)] (*pl* **-es**) <> *adj* [modelar] exemplary. <> *m* **-1.** [de livro, jornal] copy. **-2.** [peça] example. **-3.** [modelo] model. **-4.** BIOL [espécie] specimen.

exemplificação [ezẽnplifika'sãw] (*pl* **-ões**) *f* exemplification.

exemplificar [ezẽnplifi'ka(x)] *vt* to exemplify.

exemplo [e'zẽnplu] *m* **-1.** [ger] example; **por ~** for example; **bom/mau ~** good/bad example; **dar o ~** to set an example; **seguir o ~ de** to follow the example of; **ser um ~ de algo** to be a model of sthg; **a ~ de** just like. **-2.** [lição]: **servir de ~ a alguém** to serve as a warning to sb.

exéquias [eẽzɛkjaʃ] *fpl* funeral rites.

exequível [ezeẽkwivew] (*pl* **-eis**) *adj* feasible.

exercer [25] [ezex'se(x)] *vt* **-1.** [desempenhar] to carry out; [profissão] to practise UK, to practice US. **-2.** [fazer sentir]: **~ algo (sobre)** to exert sthg (on).

exercício [ezex'sisju] *m* **-1.** [ger] exercise; **fazer ~** to exercise; **em ~** [presidente, diretor] in office; [professor] in service; [de profissão] practising; [de direitos] exercising; **em pleno ~ de suas faculdades mentais** in full command of one's mental faculties. **-2.** EDUC exercise. **-3.** COM: **~ anterior /corrente** previous/current financial year.

exercitar [4] [ezexsi'ta(x)] *vt* **-1.** [ger] to exercise. **-2.** [praticar, treinar] to practise UK, to practice US.

➤ **exercitar-se** *vp* [adestrar-se] to take exercise.

exército [e'zɛxsitu] *m* army.

exibição [ezibi'sãw] (*pl* -**ões**) *f* - **1**. [demonstração] exhibition; **ser pura** ~ [ser falso] to be just for show. - **2**. [do corpo] exhibition. - **3**. [de filme, obra de arte] exhibition.

exibicionismo [ezibisjo'niʒmul] *m* - **1**. [ostentação] ostentation. - **2**. *PSIC* exhibitionism.

exibicionista [ezibisjo'niʃtal] <> *adj* [ostentativo] ostentatious. <> *mf* - **1**. [pessoa] show-off. - **2**. *PSIC* exhibitionist.

exibido, da [ezi'bidu, da] *fam* <> *adj* [exibicionista] flamboyant. <> *m, f* [pessoa] exhibitionist.

exibidor, ra [ezibi'do(x), ra] <> *adj* [que exibe] exhibiting. <> *mf* [dono de cinema] cinema owner.

exibir [6] [ezi'bi(x)] *vt* - **1**. [ger] to show. - **2**. [ostentar] to exhibit. - **3**. [expor] [obra de arte] to exhibit.
 ➡ **exibir-se** *vp* - **1**. [mostrar-se] to show off. - **2**. [indecentemente] to expose o.s.

exigência [ezi'ʒẽnsja] *f* - **1**. [imposição] demand. - **2**. [requisito] requirement. - **3**. [rigor] urgent request.

exigente [ezi'ʒẽntʃil] *adj* [rigoroso] demanding.

exigir [52] [ezi'ʒi(x)] *vt* - **1**. [reclamar] to demand; ~ **que alguém faça algo** to demand that sb do sthg. - **2**. [requerer] to require.

exíguo, gua [e'zigwu, gwa] *adj* - **1**. [diminuto] tiny. - **2**. [minguado] meagre.

exilado, da [ezi'ladu, da] <> *adj* [pessoa] exiled. <> *m, f* [pessoa] exile.

exilar [4] [ezi'la(x)] *vt* to exile.
 ➡ **exilar-se** *vp* to be exiled.

exílio [e'zilju] *m* - **1**. [ger] exile. - **2**. [expatriação] deportation.

exímio, mia [e'zimju, mja] *adj* [excelente] excellent.

eximir [6] [ezi'mi(x)] *vt*: ~ **alguém de algo** to exempt sb from sthg.
 ➡ **eximir-se** *vp*: ~-**se de algo** to excuse o.s. from sthg.

existência [eziʃ'tẽsja] *f* existence.

existencial [eziʃtẽ'sjãw] (*pl* -**ais**) *adj* existential.

existencialismo [eziʃtẽsja'liʒmul] *m* existentialism.

existente [eziʃ'tẽntʃil] *adj* - **1**. [que existe] existing. - **2**. [vivente] living.

existir [6] [eziʃ'tʃi(x)] *vi* - **1**. [haver] to be. - **2**. [viver] to exist. - **3**. *loc* [ser fantástico]: **não** ~ *fam* to be incredible; **este sorvete não existe!** this ice cream is incredible!

êxito ['ezitul] *m* - **1**. [sucesso] success; **ter/não ter** ~ **(em)** to be successful/unsuccessful (in). - **2**. [filme, música]: **ser um** ~ to be a success, to be a hit.

êxodo ['ezodul] *m* exodus; ~ **rural** rural exodus.

exoneração [ezonera'sãw] (*pl* -**ões**) *f* exoneration.

exonerar [4] [ezone'ra(x)] *vt* - **1**. [demitir]: ~ **alguém de algo** to exonerate sb from sthg. - **2**. [desobrigar]: ~ **alguém de algo** to exonerate sb from sthg.
 ➡ **exonerar-se** *vp* - **1**. [demitir-se]: ~-**se de algo** to exonerate o.s. from sthg. - **2**. [desobrigar-se]: ~-**se de algo** to release o.s. from sthg.

exorbitância [ezoxbi'tãnsja] *f* - **1**. [excesso] excess. - **2**. *fam* [preço excessivo] extortionate price.

exorcismo [ezox'siʒmul] *m* exorcism.

exorcista [ezox'siʃta] *mf* exorcist.

exorcizar [4] [ezoxsi'za(x)] *vt* to exorcize.

exortar [4] [ezox'ta(x)] *vt*: ~ **alguém a fazer algo** to exhort sb to do sthg.

exótico, ca [e'zɔtʃiku, kal] *f* exotic.

exotismo [ezo'tʃiʒmul] *m* exoticism.

expandir [6] [liʃpãn'dʒi(x)] *vt* [ger] to spread.
 ➡ **expandir-se** *vp* - **1**. [dilatar-se] to spread, to be spread. - **2**. [ser expansivo] to be expansive.

expansão [liʃpãn'sãw] (*pl* -**ões**) *f* - **1**. [ato] expansion. - **2**. [efusão] outpouring.

expansionista [liʃpãsjo'niʃtal] <> *adj* expansionist. <> *mf* expansionist.

expansividade [liʃpãnsivi'dadʒil] *f* expansiveness.

expansivo, va [liʃpã'sivu, val] *adj* expansive.

expatriação [liʃpatrja'sãw] (*pl* -**ões**) *f* expatriation.

expatriado, da [liʃpa'trjadu, dal] <> *adj* [pessoa] expatriated. <> *m, f* [pessoa] expatriate.

expatriar [16] [liʃpa'trja(x)] *vt* to expatriate.

expectativa [liʃpɛkta'tʃival] *f* expectation; **na** ~ **de** in the expectation of; ~ **de vida** life expectancy.

expectorante [liʃpɛkto'rãntʃil] <> *adj* expectorant. <> *m* expectorant.

expectorar [4] [liʃpɛkto'ra(x)] *vt* & *vi* to expectorate.

expedição [liʃpedʒi'sãw] (*pl* -**ões**) *f* - **1**. [de mercadorias] dispatch. - **2**. [por navio] shipment. - **3**. [por correio] dispatch. - **4**. [viagem] expedition. - **5**. [de documento] issue.

expedidor, ra [liʃpedʒi'do(x), ral] *adj* forwarding.

expediência [liʃpe'dʒjẽnsja] *f* [desembaraço, diligência] efficiency.

expediente [liʃpe'dʒjẽntʃil] <> *adj* [desembaraçado, diligente] efficient; **ser** ~ to be efficient. <> *m* - **1**. [horário] office hours; **durante o** ~ during office hours; **fora do** ~ out of office hours; ~ **administrativo/bancário** banking/business hours; **meio** ~ part-time. - **2**. [pessoal] resourceful. - **3**. [desembaraço, diligência]: **ter** ~ to be resourceful. - **4**. [meios, recursos] expedient. - **5**. [correspondência] correspondence.

expedir [70] [liʃpe'dʒi(x)] *vt* - **1**. [carta, mercadoria] to send. - **2**. [documento etc] to issue.

expedito, ta [liʃpe'dʒitu, tal] *adj* - **1**. [pessoa] efficient. - **2**. [trabalho, solução] expeditious.

expelir [57] [liʃpe'li(x)] *vt* to expel.

experiência [liʃpe'rjẽnsja] *f* experience; **em** ~ on trial.

experienciar [16] [liʃperjẽn'sja(x)] *vt* to experience.

experiente [liʃpe'rjẽntʃil] *adj* experienced.

experimentação [liʃperimẽnta'sãw] (*pl* -**ões**) *f* experimentation.

experimentado, da [liʃperimẽn'tadu, dal] *adj* - **1**.

[experimento] experienced. -**2.** [testado] tested. -**3.** [provado] tried.

experimental [iʃperimẽn'taw] (*pl* -**ais**) *adj* experimental.

experimentar [4] [iʃperimẽn'ta(x)] *vt* -**1.** [testar] to test. -**2.** [provar - comida, bebida] to try; [- roupa] to try on. -**3.** [sofrer] to go through. -**4.** [sentir] to experience.

experimento [iʃperi'mẽntu] *m* experiment.

expiação [iʃpja'sãw] (*pl* -**ões**) *f*: ~ **(de algo)** atonement (for sthg).

expiar [16] [iʃ'pja(x)] *vt* to atone for.

expiatório, ria [iʃpja'tɔrju, rja] *adj* ▷ **bode**.

expiração [iʃpira'sãw] (*pl* -**ões**) *f* -**1.** [de ar] exhalation. -**2.** [fim de prazo] expiry.

expirar [4] [iʃpi'ra(x)] <> *vt* [ar] to exhale. <> *vi* -**1.** [encerrar] to expire. -**2.** [morrer] to die.

explanação [iʃplana'sãw] (*pl* -**ões**) *f* explanation.

explanar [4] [iʃpla'na(x)] *vt* to explain.

explicação [iʃplika'sãw] (*pl* -**ões**) *f* explanation.

explicar [12] [iʃpli'ka(x)] *vt & vi* to explain.

➡ **explicar-se** *vp* [justificar-se] to explain o.s.

explicativo, va [iʃplika'tʃivu, va] *adj* explanatory.

explicável [iʃpli'kavew] (*pl* -**eis**) *adj* [justificável] explainable.

explicitar [4] [iʃplisi'ta(x)] *vt* to make explicit.

explícito, ta [iʃ'plisitu, ta] *adj* explicit.

explodir [6] [iʃplo'di(x)] <> *vi* -**1.** [bomba, avião, carro] to explode. -**2.** *fig* [não se conter] to burst; ~ **de** to be bursting with; ~ **em** to burst into. <> *vt* -**1.** [bomba] to detonate. -**2.** [edifício, avião] to blow up.

exploração [iʃplora'sãw] (*pl* -**ões**) *f* -**1.** [ger] exploration. -**2.** [emprego] use. -**3.** [de negócio] running. -**4.** [agrícola] cultivation, growing. -**5.** [abuso] exploitation. -**6.** [exorbitância]: **ser uma** ~ to be exorbitant.

explorador, ra [iʃplora'do(x), ra] <> *adj* -**1.** [pessoa, companhia] exploring, exploratory. -**2.** [aproveitador] exploitative. <> *m, f* -**1.** [desbravador] explorer. -**2.** [aproveitador] exploiter.

explorar [4] [iʃplo'ra(x)] *vt* -**1.** [ger] to exploit. -**2.** [empregar] to use. -**3.** [negócio] to run. -**4.** [desbravar] to explore.

exploratório, ria [iʃplora'tɔriu, ria] *adj* exploratory.

explosão [iʃplo'zãw] (*pl* -**ões**) *f* explosion.

explosivo, va [iʃplo'zivu, va] *adj* explosive.

➡ **explosivo** *m* [material] explosive.

EXPO (*abrev de* **Exposição**) *f* exhibition.

expoente [iʃ'pwẽntʃi] <> *mf* [figura ilustre] exponent. <> *m* MAT exponent.

expor [45] [iʃ'po(x)] *vt* -**1.** [mostrar] to display. -**2.** [explicar] to explain. -**3.** [exibir] to exhibit. -**4.** [revelar] to reveal. -**5.** [submeter]: ~ **algo (a algo)** to expose sthg (to sthg).

➡ **expor-se** *vp* -**1.** [submeter-se]: ~**-se a algo** to expose o.s. to sthg. -**2.** [exibir-se] to expose o.s.

exportação [iʃpoxta'sãw] (*pl* -**ões**) *f* -**1.** [ato] export. -**2.** [produtos] exports (*pl*).

exportador, ra [iʃpoxta'do(x), ra] <> *adj* -**1.** [país, companhia] exporting. -**2.** [política] export (*antes de subst*). <> *m, f* exporter.

exportar [4] [iʃpox'ta(x)] *vt* to export.

exposição [iʃpozi'sãw] (*pl* -**ões**) *f* -**1.** [mostra] display. -**2.** [explicação] explanation. -**3.** [narração] narrative. -**4.** FOTO exposure.

expositor, ra [iʃpozi'to(x), ra] *m, f* exhibitor.

exposto, osta [iʃ'poʃtu, oʃta] <> *pp* ▷ **expor**. <> *adj* [à vista - mercadoria] on show; [- corpo] exposed; [- fratura] compound.

expressão [iʃpre'sãw] (*pl* -**ões**) *f* -**1.** [ger] expression; ~ **escrita/oral** written/oral expression; ~ **artística** artistic expression; ~ **corporal** self-expression though movement. -**2.** [manifestação]: ~ **(de algo)** expression (of sthg). -**3.** [vivacidade] expressiveness.

expressar [4] [iʃpre'sa(x)] *vt* to express.

➡ **expressar-se** *vp* to express o.s.

expressionismo [iʃpresjo'niʒmul] *m* expressionism.

expressionista [iʃpresjo'niʃta] <> *adj* expressionist. <> *mf* expressionist.

expressividade [iʃpresivi'dadʒil] *f* expressiveness.

expressivo, va [iʃpre'sivu, va] *adj* expressive.

expresso, sa [iʃ'prɛsu, sa] <> *pp* ▷ **expressar**. <> *adj* express.

➡ **expresso** *m* express.

exprimir [6] [iʃpri'mi(x)] *vt* to express.

➡ **exprimir-se** *vp* to express o.s.

expropriação [iʃproprja'sãw] (*pl* -**ões**) *f* JUR expropriation.

expropriar [16] [iʃpropri'a(x)] *vt* JUR to expropriate.

expugnar [4] [iʃpugi'na(x)] *vt* to storm.

expulsão [iʃpuw'sãw] (*pl* -**ões**) *f* -**1.** [saída forçada] expulsion. -**2.** ESP sending-off.

expulsar [4] [iʃpuw'sa(x)] *vt* -**1.** [ger] to expel. -**2.** [inimigo] to drive out. -**3.** [deportar] to deport. -**4.** ESP to send off.

expulso, sa [iʃ'puwsu, sa] <> *pp* ▷ **expulsar**. <> *adj* expelled.

expurgar [14] [iʃpux'ga(x)] *vt* -**1.** [limpar] to clean. -**2.** [corrigir] to expurgate. -**3.** [livrar]: ~ **algo (de)** to purge sthg (of).

expurgo [iʃ'puxgu] *m* purge.

êxtase ['eʃtazil *m* -**1.** [enlevo] ecstasy. -**2.** [transe]: **estar em** ~ to be in ecstasy.

extasiado, da [iʃta'zjadu, da] *adj* -**1.** [enlevado] ecstatic. -**2.** [pasmado] astounded.

extasiar [16] [iʃta'zja(x)] *vt* to enrapture.

➡ **extasiar-se** *vp* to be entranced.

extemporâneo, nea [iʃtẽnpo'rãnju, ja] *adj* extemporary, extemporaneous.

extensão [iʃtẽn'sãw] (*pl* -**ões**) *f* -**1.** [ger] extent; **em toda a** ~ **da palavra** in the full meaning of the word. -**2.** [dimensão, área] area. -**3.** [comprimento] length; **a vegetação cobria toda a** ~ **da praia** the vegetation covered the whole length and breadth of the beach. -**4.** [duração] duration. **- 5.** [ampliação] scope. **- 6.** [ramal telefô-nico, fio elétrico] extension.

extensivo, va [iʃtẽn'sivu, va] *adj* **-1.** [extensível] extending. **- 2.** [amplo] extensive.

extenso, sa [iʃ'tẽnsu, sa] *adj* **-1.** [ger] long. **- 2.** [amplo, abrangente] extensive. **- 3.** *loc:* **por** ~ in full.

extenuado, da [iʃte'nwadu, da] *adj* worn out.

extenuante [iʃte'nwãntʃi] *adj* **-1.** [cansativo] exhausting. **- 2.** [debilitante] debilitating.

extenuar [4] [iʃtẽ'nwa(x)] *vt* **-1.** [cansar] to wear out. **- 2.** [debilitar] to debilitate.

➡ **extenuar-se** *vp* **-1.** [cansar-se] to wear o.s. out. **- 2.** [debilitar-se] to be debilitated.

exterior [iʃte'rjo(x)] (*pl* **-es**) <> *adj* **-1.** [externo] outer. **- 2.** [com outros países] external. **- 3.** [aparência] external. **- 4.** [o estrangeiro]: **o** ~ abroad; **estar no** ~ to be abroad; **ser do** ~ to be a foreigner. <> *m* [aparência] appearance.

exterioridade [iʃterjori'dadʒil *f* external nature; [aparências] (outward) appearances

exteriorização [iʃterjoriza'sãw] (*pl* **-ões**) *f* manifestation.

exteriorizar [4] [iʃterjori'za(x)] *vt* to externalize.

exteriormente [iʃterjox'mẽntʃil *adv* from the outside.

exterminação [iʃtexmina'sãw] (*pl* **-ões**) *f* extermination.

exterminar [4] [iʃtexmi'na(x)] *vt* **-1.** [aniquilar] to exterminate. **- 2.** [erradicar] to eradicate.

extermínio [iʃtex'minjul *m* extermination.

externa [iʃ'tɛxna] *f* ▷ **externo**.

externato [iʃtɛx'natul *m* day school.

externo, na [iʃtɛxnu, na] *adj* **-1.** [exterior- parede] exterior; [- lado] external. **- 2.** [aparente] exterior. **- 3.** [medicamento]: **uso** ~ external use.

extinção [iʃtʃĩn'sãw] *f* extinction; **em** ~ endangered.

extinguir [53] [iʃtʃĩŋ'gi(x)] *vt* **-1.** [fogo] to extinguish. **- 2.** [exterminar] to exterminate. **- 3.** [dissolver] to dissolve. **- 4.** ECOL to endanger.

➡ **extinguir-se** *vp* **-1.** [fogo] to go out. **- 2.** [desaparecer] to disappear. **- 3.** ECOL to become extinct.

extinto, ta [iʃ'tʃĩntu, tal *adj* **-1.** [ger] extinct. **- 2.** [fogo] extinguished. **- 3.** [associação] defunct.

extintor [iʃtʃĩn'to(x)] (*pl* **-res**) *m:* ~ **(de incêndio)** (fire) extinguisher.

extirpar [4] [iʃtix'pa(x)] *vt* **-1.** [arrancar] to pull out. **- 2.** [extrair- dente] to extract; [- tumor] to remove. **- 3.** [erradicar] to eradicate.

extorquir [79] [iʃtox'ki(x)] *vt:* ~ **algo (de alguém)** to extort sthg (from sb).

extorsão [iʃtox'sãw] (*pl* **-ões**) *f* extortion.

extorsivo, va [iʃtox'sivu, va] *adj* extortionate.

extra l'ɛʃtral <> *adj* [extraordinário] extra. <> *mf* extra.

extração [iʃtra'sãw] (*pl* **-ões**) *f* **-1.** [ger] extraction. **- 2.** [sorteio] draw.

extraconjugal [ɛʃtrakõnʒu'gawl (*pl* **-ais**) *adj* extramarital.

extracurricular [ɛʃtrakuxiku'la(x)] *adj* extracurricular.

extradição [eʃtradʒi'sãwl (*pl* **-ões**) *f* extradition.

extraditar [4] [iʃtradʒi'ta(x)] *vt* to extradite.

extrair [68] [iʃtra'i(x)] *vt* [tirar]: ~ **algo (de)** to extract sthg (from).

extrajudicial [ɛʃtraʒudʒi'sjawl (*pl* **-ais**) *adj* extrajudicial.

extranet [ejʃtra'netil *f* COMPUT extranet.

extra-oficial [ɛʃtraofi'sjawl (*pl* **-ais**) *adj* unofficial.

extraordinário, ria [iʃtraordʒi'narju, rjal *adj* extraordinary.

extrapolação [eʃtrapola'sãw] (*pl* **-ões**) *f* extrapolation.

extrapolar [4] [iʃtrapo'la(x)] *vt* to go beyond.

extraterreno, na [iʃtra'texenu, nal *adj* extraterrestrial.

extraterrestre [eʃtrate'xɛʃtril <> *adj* extraterrestrial. <> *mf* extraterrestrial.

extrato [iʃ'tratul *m* **-1.** [ger] extract; ~ **de tomate** tomato puree. **- 2.** [resumo] excerpt; ~ **bancário** bank statement.

extravagância [iʃtrava'gãnsjal *f* extravagance; **fazer uma** ~ to be extravagant.

extravagante [iʃtrava'gãntʃil <> *adj* [excêntrico] eccentric.

extravasar [4] [iʃtrava'sa(x)] <> *vt* [exteriorizar - sentimento, alegria] to show; [- raiva] to give vent to. <> *vi* **-1.** [expandir-se] to burst out. **- 2.** [transbordar] to spill over.

extraviado, da [iʃtra'vjadu, dal *adj* missing.

extraviar [16] [iʃtra'vja(x)] *vt* **-1.** [perder] to lose. **- 2.** [dinheiro] to embezzle. **- 3.** *fig* [perverter] to lead astray.

➡ **extraviar-se** *vp* **-1.** [carta] to go astray; [processo] to get lost. **- 2.** [pessoa - perder-se] to get lost; *fig* [perverter-se] to be led astray.

extravio [iʃtra'viwl *m* **-1.** [perda]: ~ **(de algo)** loss (of sthg). **- 2.** [roubo] embezzlement.

extremado, da [iʃtre'madu, dal *adj* extreme.

extremar-se [4] [iʃtre'maxsil *vp:* ~ **em esforços** to do one's utmost.

extrema-unção [iʃtremaũn'sãw] (*pl* **extrema-unções**) *f* extreme unction, sacrament of the sick.

extremidade [iʃtremi'dadʒil *f* **-1.** [fim, limite] end. **- 2.** [ponta] tip. **- 3.** [beira] edge.

➡ **extremidades** *fpl* ANAT extremities.

extremista [iʃtre'miʃtal <> *adj* extremist. <> *mf* extremist.

extremo, ma [iʃ'tremu, mal *adj* (*antes de subst*) **-1.** [ger] extreme; **o Extremo Oriente** the Far East. **- 2.** [derradeiro, exagerado] extreme.

➡ **extremo** *m* **-1.** [limite, ponta] extreme; **de um** ~ **ao outro** from one extreme to another. **- 2.** [máximo] utmost; **ao** ~ to the utmost.

➡ **extremos** *mpl* [exagero] extremes.

extroversão [iʃtrovex'sãwl *f* extroversion.

extroverter-se [5] [iʃtrovex'texsil *vp* to become (more) outgoing.

extrovertido, da [iʃtrɔvex'tʃidu, da] ⬦ *adj* extrovert. ⬦ *m*, *f* extrovert.

exu [e'ʃul] *m* devil *(in voodoo rituals)*.

exuberância [ezube'rãnsja] *f* exuberance.

exuberante [ezube'rãntʃi] *adj* exuberant.

exultação [ezuwta'sãw] *f* exultation.

exultante [ezuw'tãntʃi] *adj* exultant.

exultar [4] [ezuw'ta(x)] *vi*: ~ (de) to exult (in).

exumação [ezu'masãw] (*pl* -ões) *f* exhumation.

exumar [4] [ezu'ma(x)] *vt* -1. [corpo] to exhume. -2. *fig* [lembranças] to dig up.

ex-voto [ɛks'vɔtu] (*pl* ex-votos) *m* icon.

f, F [ˈɛfi] *m* [letra] f, F.

fá [fa] *m* MÚS F, fa(h).

fã [fã] (*pl* fãs) *mf* fan.

FAB (*abrev de* Força Aérea Brasileira) *m* Brazilian Air Force.

fábrica [ˈfabrika] *f* factory.

fabricação [fabrika'sãw] (*pl* -ões) *f* manufacture; **de ~ caseira** home-made.

fabricante [fabri'kãntʃi] *mf* manufacturer.

fabricar [12] [fabri'ka(x)] *vt* -1. [manufaturar] to manufacture. -2. [inventar] to fabricate.

fabril [fa'briw] (*pl* -is) *adj* manufacturing.

fábula [ˈfabula] *f* -1. [conto] fable. -2. *fam* [fortuna] fortune.

fabuloso, osa [fabu'lozu, ɔza] *adj* [ger] fabulous.

faca [ˈfaka] *f* knife; **entrar na ~** *fam* to go under the knife; **estar com a ~ e o queijo na mão** *fam* to have things in hand; **ser uma ~ de dois gumes** *fam* to be a double-edged sword.

facada [fa'kada] *f* -1. [golpe] stab; **ser uma ~ pelas costas** *fig* to be a stab in the back. -2. *fam* cut; **dar uma ~ em alguém** [pedir dinheiro a alguém] to cadge money off sb.

façanha [fa'saɲa] *f* exploit.

facão [fa'kãw] (*pl* -ões) *m* carving knife.

facção [fak'sãw] (*pl* -ões) *f* faction.

faccioso, sa [fak'sjozu, ɔza] *adj* factional.

face [ˈfasi] *f* -1. [ger] face; **fazer ~ a** *fig* [enfrentar] to face up to; [custear] to take on board; **~ a ~** face to face. -2. [lado] side. -3. [superfície]: **a ~ das águas** the surface of the water; **a ~ da terra** the face of the earth. -4. [aspecto] facet.

➤ **em face de** *loc prep* [diante de] faced with.

faceiro, ra [fa'sejru, ra] *adj* -1. [alegre - pessoa, sorriso] cheerful; [- dança] merry. -2. [elegante] smart.

fáceis [ˈfasejʃ] *pl* ➤ **fácil**.

faceta [fa'seta] *f* [aspecto] facet.

facetado, da [fase'tadu, da] *adj* [pedra] faceted.

fachada [fa'ʃada] *f* -1. [de prédio] façade. -2. *fig fam* [aparência] mug; **ser só ~** to be merely a façade.

facho [ˈfaʃu] *m* beam.

facial [fa'sjaw] (*pl* -ais) *adj* facial.

fácil [ˈfasiw] (*pl* -eis) *adj* -1. [simples] easy. -2. [dócil] easy(-going). -3. *pej* [mulher] easy.

➤ **fácil** *adv* easily.

facilidade [fasili'dadʒi] *f* -1. [ausência de dificuldade] ease; **com ~** easily. -2. [aptidão]: **ter ~ (para algo)** to have an aptitude (for sthg).

➤ **facilidades** *fpl* [meios] facilities.

facílimo, ma [fa'silimu, ma] *adj superl* ➤ **fácil**.

facilitação [fasilita'sãw] *f* -1. [ato] facilitation. -2. [fornecimento] provision.

facilitar [4] [fasili'ta(x)] ⬦ *vt* -1. [tornar fácil] to make easy. -2. [facultar] to facilitate. ⬦ *vi* [descuidar-se] to be careless.

facínora [fa'sinora] *m* criminal.

fã-clube [fãn'klubi] (*pl* fãs-clubes) *m* fan club.

facões [fa'kõjʃ] *pl* ➤ **facão**.

fac-símile [fak'simili] (*pl* fac-símiles) *m* -1. [cópia] facsimile. -2. [máquina] fax machine.

factível [fak'tʃivew] (*pl* -eis) *adj* feasible.

factótum [fak'tɔtũ] *m* factotum.

faculdade [fakuw'dadʒi] *f* -1. [capacidade] faculty. -2. [propriedade] property. -3. [escola superior] faculty.

facultar [4] [fakuw'ta(x)] *vt* -1. [conceder] to grant. -2. [permitir] to permit.

facultativo, va [fakuwta'tʃivu, va] ⬦ *adj* optional. ⬦ *m*, *f* [medical] doctor.

fada [ˈfada] *f* fairy.

fadado, da [fa'dadu, da] *adj*: **estar ~ a algo** to be fated to sthg.

fada-madrinha [ˌfadama'driɲa] (*pl* fadas-madrinhas) *f* fairy godmother.

fadiga [fa'dʒiga] *f* fatigue.

fado [ˈfadu] *m* -1. [destino] fate. -2. MÚS fado, *type of Portuguese folk song*.

fagueiro, ra [fa'gejru, ra] *adj* -1. [meigo] sweet. -2. [agradável] pleasant. -3. [contente] happy.

fagulha [fa'guʎa] *f* spark.

fahrenheit [fare'najtʃi] *adj* Fahrenheit.

faia [ˈfaja] *f* beech tree.

fair-play [fɛx'plej] *m* fair play.

faisão [faj'zãw] (*pl* -ões) *m* pheasant.

faísca [fa'iʃka] *f* spark.

faiscante [fajʃ'kãntʃi] *adj* -1. [fogo] flickering. -2. [olhos] sparkling.

faiscar [12] [fajʃ'ka(x)] *vi* -1. [fogo] to flicker. -2. [olhos] to flash.

faixa [ˈfajʃa] *f* -1. [tira] strip. -2. [para a cintura] belt. -3. [para o peito] sash; **~ de campeão/miss** champion's/beauty queen's sash; **~ presidencial** presidential sash. -4. [para pedestres]: **~ (de pedestres)** (pedestrian) crossing. -5. [pista] lane. -6. [atadura] bandage. -7. [de terra] strip.

- 8. [para mensagem] banner. **- 9.** [intervalo] interval; ~ **etária** age group; ~ **salarial** salary band. **-10.** [de disco] track.

faixa-título [ˌfajʃaˈtʃitulu] (*pl* **faixas-título**) *f* [de disco] title track.

fajuto, ta [faˈʒutu, ta] *adj fam* **- 1.** [de má qualidade - tecido, equipamento] shoddy; [- político] second-rate. **- 2.** [dinheiro] counterfeit.

fala [ˈfala] *f* **-1.** [ger] speech; **perder a** ~ to be struck dumb. **- 2.** [parte de diálogo] words *(pl)*.

falação [falaˈsãw] (*pl*-**ões**) *f fam* **- 1.** [ato] talk. **- 2.** [discurso] speech.

falácia [faˈlasja] *f* fallacy.

faladeira [falaˈdejra] *adj & f* ▻ **falador**.

falado, da [faˈladu, da] *adj* **- 1.** [comentado] much talked about. **- 2.** [famoso] well-known. **- 3.** *fam* [de má fama] notorious.

falador, deira [falaˈdo(x), dejra] (*mpl* -**es**, *fpl* -**s**) <> *adj* [pessoa] talkative. <> *m,f* [pessoa] chatterbox.

falange [faˈlãnʒi] *f* phalanx.

falante [faˈlãntʃi] *adj* talking.

falar [4] [faˈla(x)] <> *vi* **- 1.** [verbalmente] to speak; ~ **de** *ou* **em algo** to talk about sthg; ~ **com alguém** to speak to sb; ~ **alto/baixo** to speak loudly/softly; ~ **alto com alguém** *fig* to give sb a good talking-to; ~ **da boca para fora** *fam* not to mean a word one is saying; ~ **em inglês/espanhol** to speak in English/Spanish; ~ **mais alto** *fig* to win the day; ~ **para dentro** to mumble; ~ **pelos cotovelos** [falar muito] to talk one's head off; ~ **por alguém** to speak on behalf of sb; ~ **por** ~ to talk for the sake of talking; ~ **sozinho/dormindo** to talk to o.s./in one's sleep; **por** ~ **em** ... speaking *ou* talking of ...; **sem** ~ **de** *ou* **em** ... not to mention ...; **agora, falando sério,** ... but seriously, ...; **falou, está falado!** *fam* [OK] OK! **- 2.** [discursar] to make a speech. **- 3.** [tratar]: ~ **de** *ou* **sobre algo** to talk about sthg. **- 4.** [confessar] to talk. <> *vt* **-1.** [idioma]: ~ **inglês/espanhol** to speak English/Spanish. **- 2.** [dizer] to say; ~ **que** to say that; ~ **bem/mal de** to speak well/ill of; ~ **bobagem** to talk nonsense. **- 3.** [contar]: ~ **algo (a alguém)** to tell (sb) sthg **- 4.** *loc*: **dar o que** ~ [ser muito comentado] to cause a stir.

◆ **falar-se** *vp* **-1.** [dialogar] to talk. **- 2.** [estar em boas relações] to be talking to one another; **não se** ~ to not be talking to one another.

falatório [falaˈtɔrju] *m* **- 1.** [ruído] voices *(pl)*. **- 2.** [discurso] diatribe. **- 3.** [maledicência] slander.

falcão [fawˈkãw] (*pl*-**ões**) *m* falcon.

falcatrua [fawkaˈtrua] *f* fraud.

falecer [25] [faleˈse(x)] *vi* to pass away.

falecido, da [faleˈsidu, da] <> *adj* [pessoa] deceased. <> *m, f* [pessoa] deceased.

falecimento [falesiˈmẽntu] *m* decease.

falência [faˈlẽnsja] *f* bankruptcy; **abrir** ~ to declare o.s. bankrupt; **ir à** ~ to go bankrupt; **levar à** ~ to bankrupt.

falésia [faˈlɛzja] *f* cliff.

falha [ˈfaʎa] *f* **- 1.** [fenda] fault. **- 2.** [defeito] defect. **- 3.** [omissão] omission.

falhar [4] [faˈʎa(x)] <> *vt* **- 1.** [errar] to fail. **- 2.** [faltar com - promessa] to break; [- obrigação] to fail. <> *vi* **- 1.** [não funcionar, fracassar] to fail. **- 2.** [não acertar] to miss.

falho, lha [ˈfaʎu, ʎa] *adj* **- 1.** [defeituoso] faulty. **- 2.** [deficiente] flawed.

fálico, ca [ˈfaliku, ka] *adj* phallic.

falido, da [faˈlidu, da] <> *adj* bankrupt. <> *m, f* bankrupt.

falir [79] [faˈli(x)] *vi* **- 1.** [abrir falência] to go bankrupt. **- 2.** [fracassar] to fail.

falível [faˈlivew] (*pl*-**eis**) *adj* fallible.

falo [ˈfalu] *m* phallus.

falsário, ria [fawˈsarju, rja] *m* **- 1.** [falsificador] forger. **- 2.** [perjuro] perjurer.

falsear [15] [fawˈsja(x)] <> *vt* [falsificar] to falsify. <> *vi* [pisar em falso] to miss one's step.

falsete [fawˈsetʃi] *m* MÚS falsetto.

falsidade [fawsiˈdadʒi] *f* **- 1.** [fingimento] hypocrisy. **- 2.** [mentira] lie; ~ **ideológica** false declaration.

falsificação [fawsifikaˈsãw] (*pl*-**ões**) *f* forgery.

falsificador, ra [fawsifikaˈdo(x), ra] *m, f* [pessoa] forger.

falsificar [12] [fawsifiˈka(x)] *vt* **- 1.** [ger] to forge. **- 2.** [adulterar - alimento, remédio] to adulterate; [- documento] to falsify. **- 3.** [desvirtuar] to misrepresent.

falso, sa [ˈfawsu, sa] *adj* **- 1.** [ger] false. **- 2.** [falsificado] forged. **- 3.** [fingido] deceitful. **- 4.** [errôneo] erroneous. **- 5.** *loc*: **pisar em** ~ to miss one's step.

falso-testemunho [ˌfawsoteʃteˈmuɲul (*pl* **falsos-testemunhos**) *m* false witness.

falta [ˈfawta] *f* **-1.** [carência] lack; **ter** ~ **de** to be in need of; ~ **de água** water shortage; ~ **de ar** airlessness; ~ **de respeito** lack of respect; ~ **de responsabilidade** lack of responsibility. **- 2.** [ausência] absence; **sentir** ~ **de algo/alguém** to miss sthg/sb; **na** ~ **de** for lack of; **sem** ~ without fail. **- 3.** [erro, pecado] fault. **- 4.** *ESP* foul; **cobrar/cometer uma** ~ to commit a foul.

faltar [4] [fawˈta(x)] *vi* **-1.** [não haver]: **falta água/luz/comida** there's no water/electricity/food; **falta honestidade** there's a lack of honesty; ~ **sal/tempero** to need salt/seasoning. **- 2.** [estar ausente] to be absent; **ontem faltaram cinco alunos** yesterday five students were absent; **falta o Hélio** Hélio's not here, Hélio's missing. **- 3.** [ser escasso]: **falta-lhe dinheiro** he hasn't got enough money; **falta-lhe saúde** he's not too healthy; **faltou-lhe força de vontade** he lacked the willpower; **nada nos falta** we have everything we need, we want for nothing. **- 4.** [restar - por fazer]: **só falta fazermos o bolo** all that's left for us to do is make the cake; **falta pintarmos a casa** we've still got to paint the house; [- por acontecer]: **só me faltava essa!** *fam* that's all I needed!; [- por decorrer]: **faltam dois meses para o**

festival there are two months to go before the festival; **falta uma semana para irmos embora** it's a week until we go. **- 5.** [omitir-se]: **nunca faltou quando a família precisava** he was always there when the family needed him. **- 6.** [morrer] to die.

falto, ta ['fawtu, ta] adj: ~ **de** lacking in.

faltoso, osa [faw'tozu, ɔza] adj **-1.** [culpado] guilty. **- 2.** [que falta muito] frequently absent.

fama ['fãma] f **-1.** [celebridade] fame. **-2.** [reputação] reputation; **de** ~ by reputation; **de má** ~ of ill repute.

famigerado, da [famiʒe'radu, da] adj [célebre] famous.

família [fa'milja] <> f family; **de boa** ~ from a good family; **estar em** ~ to be one of the family; **ser de** ~ to run in the family. <> adj fam [decente]: **ser** ~ to be respectable.

familiar [fami'lja(x)] (pl **-es**) <> adj **-1.** [relativo à família] family (antes de subst). **- 2.** [conhecido] familiar. <> mf [pessoa da família]: **um** ~ a family member; **os** ~**es** the family (sg).

familiaridade [familjari'dadʒi] f **-1.** [intimidade] familiarity. **- 2.** [informalidade] informality.

familiarização [familjariza'sãw] f familiarization.

familiarizar [4] [familjari'za(x)] vt to familiarize.
◆ **familiarizar-se** vp: ~**-se com algo/alguém** to familiarize o.s. with sthg/sb.

faminto, ta [fa'mĩtu, ta] adj famished.

famoso, osa [fa'mozu, ɔza] adj famous.

fanático, ca [fa'natʃiku, ka] <> adj **-1.** POL & RELIG fanatical. **- 2.** [apaixonado]: ~ **(por)** crazy (about). <> m, f [pessoa] fanatic.

fanatismo [fana'tʃiʒmu] m fanaticism.

fanfarrão, ona [fãfa'xãw, ɔna] (mpl **-ões**, fpl **-s**) <> adj boastful. <> m, f braggart.

fanfarronice [fãnwfaxo'nisi] f [gabarolice] boasting.

fanho, nha ['faɲu, ɲal], **fanhoso, sa** [fã'ɲozu, za] adj **-1.** [voz] nasal. **- 2.** [pessoa] with a nasal-sounding voice.

faniquito [fani'kitu] m fam strop; **dar um** ~ to get into a strop.

fantasia [fãta'zia] f **-1.** [coisa imaginada] fantasy; **jóia de** ~ [bijuteria] costume jewellery. **- 2.** [imaginação] fancy. **-3.** [capricho] whim. **- 4.** [traje] fancy dress; ~ **de Carnaval** fancy dress; ~ **de árabe/pirata** Arab/pirate costume. **- 5.** MÚS fantasia.

fantasiar [16] [fãta'zja(x)] vt **-1.** [imaginar] to imagine. **- 2.** [pôr fantasia]: ~ **alguém de algo** to dress sb up as sthg. **-3.** [devanear] to daydream.
◆ **fantasiar-se** vp: ~**-se (de)** to dress up (as).

fantasioso, osa [fãta'zjozu, ɔza] adj fanciful.

fantasista [fãta'ziʃta] <> adj fanciful. <> mf whimsical person.

fantasma [fã'taʒma] m **-1.** [espectro] ghost. **-2.** [alucinação] phantom. **-3.** fig [coisa terrível] spectre.

fantasmagórico, ca [fãtazma'gɔriku, ka] adj phantasmagorical.

fantástico, ca [fãn'taʃtʃiku, ka] adj **-1.** [ger] fantastic. **- 2.** fam [ótimo] fantastic.
◆ **fantástico** m [fantasia]: **o** ~ the fantastic.

fantoche [fãn'tɔʃi] m puppet.

fanzoca [fãn'zɔka] mf mfam junkie.

FAQs (abrev de **Frequently Asked Questions**) fpl FAQs.

faqueiro [fa'kejru] m **-1.** [jogo de talheres] cutlery set. **- 2.** [pessoa] cutler.

faquir [fa'ki(x)] m fakir.

faraó [fara'ɔ] m pharaoh.

faraônico, ca [fara'oniku, ka] adj **-1.** [relativo aos faraós] pharaonic. **- 2.** fig [grandioso] grandiose.

FARC (abrev de **Forças Armadas Revolucionárias da Colômbia**) f FARC.

farda ['faxda] f [uniforme] uniform.

fardar [4] [fax'da(x)] vt to put in uniform.

fardo ['faxdu] m **-1.** [carga] load. **- 2.** fig [peso] burden.

farejar [4] [fare'ʒa(x)] <> vt to sniff. <> vi [tomar o faro] to pick up the scent.

farelento, ta [fare'lẽtu, ta] adj crumbly.

farelo [fa'relu] m **-1.** [de pão] crumb. **- 2.** [de cereal] husk; ~ **de trigo** wheat bran.

farfalhante [faxfa'ʎãntʃi] adj rustling.

farfalhar [4] [faxfa'ʎa(x)] vi to rustle.

farináceo, cea [fari'nasju, sja] adj farinaceous.
◆ **farináceos** mpl [alimentos] starchy foods.

faringe [fa'rĩʒi] f pharynx.

faringite [farĩ'ʒitʃi] f pharyngitis.

farinha [fa'riɲa] f: ~ **(de mesa ou de mandioca)** cassava flour; ~ **de rosca** toasted breadcrumbs; ~ **de trigo** wheat flour.

farinhento, ta [fari'ɲẽtu, ta] adj [que se esfarinha] floury.

farmacêutico, ca [farma'sewtiku, ka] <> adj pharmaceutical. <> m, f pharmacist.

farmácia [fax'masja] f **-1.** [ger] pharmacy. **- 2.** [coleção de medicamentos] first-aid box ou cabinet.

farmacologia [faxmakolo'ʒia] f pharmacology.

farnel [fax'nɛw] (pl **-éis**) m **-1.** [provisões] packed meal. **- 2.** [saco] lunch box.

faro ['faru] m **-1.** [olfato] sense of smell. **- 2.** fig [intuição] nose.

faroeste [fa'rwɛʃtʃi] m **-1.** [filme] western. **- 2.** [região] far west.

farofa [fa'rɔfa] f CULIN fried manioc flour

farofeiro, ra [faro'fejru, ra] m, f fam [de praia] beach bum.

farol [fa'rɔw] (pl **-óis**) m **-1.** [para navegantes] lighthouse. **- 2.** AUTO headlight; ~ **alto/baixo** full/low beam.

faroleiro [faro'lejru] m lighthouse keeper.

farolete [farɔ'letʃi] m AUTO indicator; ~ **dianteiro** sidelight; ~ **traseiro** rear light.

farpa ['faxpa] f **-1.** [de madeira] splinter. **- 2.** [metálica] shard. **- 3.** fam [crítica] barb.

farpado, da [fax'padu, da] adj ▷ **arame**.

farra ['faxa] f binge; **cair na** ~ to paint the town red; **fazer algo de ou por** ~ to do sthg as a joke.

farrapo [fa'xapu] m [trapo] rag; **estar um** ~ fig

[coisa] to be ragged; [pessoa] to be in rags; ~ **humano** failure.

farrear [15] [faˈxja(x)] *vi* to rave.

farrista [faˈxiʃta] <> *adj* fun-loving. <> *mf* raver.

farsa [ˈfaxsa] *f* -**1.** TEATRO farce. -**2.** *fig* [fraude] sham; **ser uma** ~ to be a sham.

farsante [faxˈsãntʃi] *mf* -**1.** [pessoa sem palavra] fraud. -**2.** [pessoa brincalhona] buffoon.

farsesco, ca [faxˈseʃku, ka] *adj* farsical.

fartar [4] [faxˈta(x)] *vt* -**1.** [saciar] to satiate; ~ **alguém com** to stuff sb with. -**2.** [cansar]: ~ **alguém (com)** to wear sb out (with).

➡ **fartar-se** *vp* -**1.** [saciar-se]: ~-**se (de algo)** to gorge (on sthg). -**2.** [cansar-se]: ~-**se (de algo/alguém)** to have had enough of sthg/sb.

farto, ta [ˈfaxtu, ta] *adj* -**1.** [saciado] replete. -**2.** [abundante] lavish. -**3.** [cansado]: **estar** ~ **(de algo/alguém)** to be fed up (with sthg/sb).

fartura [faxˈtura] *f* [abundância] abundance; ~ **de algo** abundance of sthg.

fascículo [faˈsikulu] *m* [de publicação] fascicle.

fascinação [fasinaˈsãw] *f* -**1.** [atração] fascination; **ter** ~ **por algo/alguém** to be fascinated by sthg/sb. -**2.** [deslumbramento] delight.

fascinante [fasiˈnãntʃi] *adj* -**1.** [cativante] fascinating. -**2.** [deslumbrante] amazing.

fascinar [4] [fasiˈna(x)] <> *vt* [cativar] to fascinate. <> *vi* [deslumbrar] to delight.

fascínio [faˈsinju] *m* [atração] fascination.

fascismo [faˈsiʒmu] *m* fascism.

fascista [faˈsiʃta] <> *adj* fascist. <> *mf* fascist.

fase [ˈfazi] *f* -**1.** [ger] phase; **ser só** ~ to be a passing phase. -**2.** ASTRON: **as** ~**s da Lua** the phases of the moon.

fastidioso, osa [faʃtʃiˈdʒjozu, ɔza] *adj* fastidious.

fastígio [faʃˈtʃiʒu] *m* apex.

fastio [faʃˈtʃiu] *m* -**1.** [falta de apetite] lack of appetite. -**2.** [tédio] boredom.

FAT (*abrev de* **Fundo de Amparo ao Trabalhador**) *m* *Brazilan fund for the support of workers*.

fatal [faˈtaw] (*pl* -**ais**) *adj* -**1.** [mortal] fatal. -**2.** [inevitável] inevitable.

fatalidade [fataliˈdadʒi] *f* -**1.** [destino] fate. -**2.** [desgraça] misfortune.

fatalista [fataˈliʃta] <> *adj* fatalistic. <> *mf* fatalist.

fatalmente [fatawˈmẽntʃi] *adv* -**1.** [mortalmente] fatally. -**2.** [certamente] surely. -**3.** [inevitavelmente] inevitably.

fatia [faˈtʃia] *f* slice.

fatiado, da [faˈtʃiadu, da] *adj* sliced.

fatiar [4] [faˈtʃja(x)] *vt* to slice.

fatídico, ca [faˈtʃidʒiku, ka] *adj* fateful.

fatigante [fatiˈgãntʃi] *adj* -**1.** [cansativo] tiresome. -**2.** [enfadonho] tedious.

fatigar [14] [fatiˈga(x)] *vt* -**1.** [cansar] to tire. -**2.** [enfadar] to bore.

➡ **fatigar-se** *vp* -**1.** [cansar-se] to tire. -**2.** [enfadar-se] to become bored.

fato [ˈfatu] *m* [ger] fact; ~ **consumado** fait accompli; **ser (um)** ~ to be a fact.

➡ **de fato** *loc adv* in fact.

fator [faˈto(x)] (*mpl* -**res**) *m* factor; ~ **Rh** rhesus factor.

fátuo, tua [ˈfatwu, twa] *adj* [vão] fatuous.

fatura [faˈtura] *f* invoice.

faturamento [faturaˈmẽntu] *m* -**1.** COM turnover. -**2.** [fatura] invoicing.

faturar [4] [fatuˈra(x)] <> *vt* -**1.** [mercadorias]: ~ **algo a alguém** to invoice sb for sthg. -**2.** [dinheiro]: **faturou um bom dinheiro** he got a good price. -**3.** *fam* [obter] to land. <> *vi fam* [ganhar dinheiro] to rake it in; ~ **alto** to make loads of dosh.

fauna [ˈfawna] *f* fauna.

fausto, ta [ˈfawʃtu, ta] *adj* fortunate.

➡ **fausto** *m* luxury.

faustoso, sa [fawʃˈtozu, ɔza] *adj* [luxuoso] sumptuous.

fava [ˈfava] *f*: **ser** ~**s contadas** to be a sure thing; **mandar alguém às** ~**s** to send sb on their way.

favela [faˈvɛla] *f* slum.

FAVELAS

Urban phenomenon common to all large cities of Brazil, *favelas* are nuclei of crude, improvised dwellings, found inside built-up areas or on the outskirts of the cities. Devoid of basic public amenities, such as water and sewerage, *favelas* are generally made up of conglomerations of dwellings known as *barracos*, built of various materials such as pieces of wood and pasteboard. In some cases, however, the houses can be made of masonry.

favelado, da [faveˈladu, da] *m, f* slum dweller.

favo [ˈfavu] *m* honeycomb.

favor [faˈvo(x)] (*pl* -**es**) *m* -**1.** [ger] favour *UK*, favor *US*; **fazer um** ~ **para alguém** to do sb a favour *UK*, to do sb a favor *US*; **pedir um** ~ **a alguém** to ask a favour of sb *UK*, to ask a favor of sb *US*; **por** ~ please; **por** ~**, que horas são?** excuse me, what time is it?; *fam* [em reprimenda] do me a favour!; **quer fazer o** ~ **de se calar?** would you kindly shut up! -**2.** [benefício]: **a** ~ **de** in favour of *UK*, in favor of *US*; **em** ~ **de** for; **ter algo a seu** ~ to have sthg in one's favour *UK ou* favor *US*.

favorável [favoˈravɛw] (*pl* -**eis**) *adj*: ~ **(a algo/a fazer algo)** favourable (to sthg/to doing sthg).

favorecer [25] [favoreˈse(x)] *vt* -**1.** [ger] to favour *UK*, to favor *US*. -**2.** [melhorar] to improve.

➡ **favorecer-se** *vp* [beneficiar-se] to take advantage of.

favorecido, da [favoreˈsidu, da] <> *adj* [protegido] favourite. <> *m, f* [beneficiário] beneficiary.

favoritismo [favoriˈtʃiʒmu] *m* favouritism *UK*, favoritism *US*.

favorito, ta [favoˈritu, ta] <> *adj* favourite *UK*, favorite *US*. <> *m, f* favourite *UK*, favorite *US*.

faxina [faˈʃina] *f* bundle of twigs; **fazer uma** ~ to have a spring clean.

faxineiro, ra [faʃiˈnejru, ra] *m, f* cleaner.

fax-modem (*pl* -dens) *m* fax-modem.
faz-de-conta [‚fajʒdʒi'kõntaI *m* make-believe.
fazenda [fa'zẽndaI *f* **-1.** [propriedade rural] fazenda.
-2. [de gado] cattle ranch. **-3.** [de café, cacau] plantation. **-4.** [tecido] cloth. **-5.** *ECON* revenue.
fazenda-modelo [fa‚zẽndamo'deluI (*pl* fazendas-modelos, fazendas-modelo) *f* model ranch.
fazendeiro, ra [fazẽ'dejru, raI *m, f* **-1.** [dono de fazenda] rancher. **-2.** [de café, cacau] planter. **-3.** [de gado] cattle rancher.
fazer [31] [fa'ze(x)I ◇ *vt* **-1.** [produzir] to make; ~ muito barulho to make a lot of noise; ~ planos/ um vestido to make plans/a dress; ~ uma pergunta to ask a question. **-2.** [comida] to cook. **-3.** [gerar] to produce. **-4.** [realizar]: estou fazendo um curso de computadores I'm taking a computer course; vamos ~ uma festa let's have a party. **-5.** [praticar] to do; você devia ~ mais exercício you should exercise more; faço jogging todas as manhãs I go jogging every morning. **-6.** [cama] to make; ~ a cama to make the bed. **-7.** [transformar] to make; ~ alguém feliz to make sb happy. **-8.** [anos]: faço anos amanhã it's my birthday tomorrow; fazemos cinco anos de casados we've been married (for) five years. **-9.** [obrigar] to make; ~ alguém fazer algo to make sb do sthg; ~ alguém rir/chorar to make sb laugh/cry. **-10.** [cálculo, conta] to do; faz a conta para ver quanto é work out the check to see what it comes to. ◇ *vi* **-1.** [causar]: ~ bem/mal a algo to be good/bad for sthg; ~ bem/mal a alguém [coisa] to be good/bad for sb; ~ mal a alguém [pessoa] to hurt sb. **-2.** [obrigar]: faça (com) que ele venha make him come; [imaginar]: ~ de conta que ... to pretend that ... ◇ *v impess* **-1.**: faz frio/calor it's cold/hot. **-2.** [tempo]: faz um ano que não o vejo it's been a year since I last saw him; faz tempo que estou à espera I've been waiting for a while; o Sérgio partiu faz três meses Sérgio left three months ago. **-3.** [importar]: não faz mal se está quebrado it doesn't matter if it's broken; tanto faz it doesn't matter.
◆ **fazer-se** *vp* [preparar-se] to be made; [ser correto]: é assim que se faz that's the way to do it; ~-se com [ser preparado com] to be made with.
◆ **fazer-se de** *vp + prep* [pretender ser]: ele gosta de ~-se de importante he likes to act important; ~-se de tolo to act stupid; ~-se de desentendido to feign ignorance.
faz-tudo [fajʒ'tuduI *mf inv* handyman.
FBI (*abrev de* Federal Bureau of Investigation) *m* FBI.
fé [ˈfɛI *f* [ger] faith; de boa ~ in good faith; de má ~ dishonestly; fazer ~ em to have faith in.
fealdade [feaw'dadʒiI *f* ugliness.
FEBEM (*abrev de* Fundação Estadual do Bem-Estar do Menor) *f* organization set up by individual states in Brazil for the rehabilitation of young offenders.
Febraban (*abrev de* Federação Brasileira de

Associações de Bancos) *f* Brazilian banking representative body.
febrão [fe'brãwI (*pl* -ões) *m* acute fever.
febre [ˈfɛbriI *f* **-1.** *MED* fever; ~ amarela yellow fever; ~ do feno hayfever. **-2.** *fig* [desejo]: ~ de fortuna/poder longing for fortune/power. **-3.** *fig* [mania] mania.
febril [fe'briwI (*pl* -is) *adj* feverish.
fecal [fe'kawI (*pl* -ais) *adj* faecal.
fechado, da [fe'ʃadu, daI *adj* **-1.** [ger] closed. **-2.** [pessoa] reticent. **-3.** *AUTO* [sinal] red light. **-4.** [tempo, céu] overcast. **-5.** [mato] dense. **-6.** [expressão] blank.
◆ **fechada** *f AUTO*: dar uma ~ em alguém to cut in front of sb; levei uma ~ de ele he cut in front of me.
fechadura [feʃa'duraI *f* flock.
fechamento [feʃa'mẽntuI *m* closure.
fechar [4] [fe'fa(x)I ◇ *vt* **-1.** [ger] to close. **-2.** *AUTO* to cut in front of. ◇ *vi* **-1.** [cicatrizar-se] to close. **-2.** [tempo] to turn close. **-3.** [sinal de trânsito] to turn red. **-4.** [parar de funcionar] to close down.
◆ **fechar-se** *vp* **-1.** [encerrar-se] to close o.s. off. **-2.** [retrair-se] to shut o.s. off.
fecho [ˈfeʃuI *m* **-1.** [de roupa] fastening; ~ ecler zip. **-2.** [de porta, bolsa] catch. **-3.** [término] end.
fécula [ˈfɛkulaI *f* starch.
fecundação [fekũnda'sãwI (*pl* -ões) *f* fertilization.
fecundar [4] [fekũn'da(x)I *vt* to fertilize.
fecundidade [fekũndʒi'dadʒiI *vt* fertility.
fecundo, da [fe'kũndu, daI *adj* **-1.** [ger] fertile. **-2.** *fig* [criador] creative.
fedelho, lha [fe'deʎu, ʎaI *m, f fam* brat.
fedentina [fedẽn'tʃinaI *f* stench.
feder [5] [fe'de(x)I *vi* to stink; não ~ nem cheirar to be wishy-washy.
federação [federa'sãwI (*pl* -ões) *f* federation.
federal [fede'rawI (*pl* -ais) *adj* **-1.** [da Federação] federal. **-2.** *fam* [enorme] huge.
federalismo [federa'liʒmuI *m* federalism.
federalizar [4] [federali'za(x)I *vt* to federalize.
federativo, va [federa'tʃivu, vaI *adj* federalist.
fedido, da [fe'ʒidu, daI *adj* stinking.
fedor [fe'do(x)I *m* stench.
fedorento, ta [fedo'rẽntu, taI *adj* stinking.
feedback [‚fidʒi'bɛkiI *m* feedback.
feição [fej'sãwI (*pl* -ões) *f* **-1.** [forma] shape. **-2.** [natureza] character à ~, de [ao jeito de] in the manner of.
◆ **feições** *fpl* [face] features.
feijão [fej'ʒãwI (*pl* -ões) *m* bean.
feijão-fradinho [fejʒãwfra'dʒiɲuI (*pl* feijões-fradinhos) *m* black-eyed bean.
feijão-mulatinho [fejʒãwmula'tʃiɲuI (*pl* feijões-mulatinhos) *m* kidney bean.
feijão-preto [fejʒãw'pretuI (*pl* feijões-pretos) *m* black bean.
feijão-tropeiro [fejʒãwtro'pejruI (*pl* feijões-tropeiros) *m* bean casserole.

feijoada [fej'ʒwadal] f *typical Brazilian dish made with black beans, pork, sausage and vegetables.*

FEIJOADA

A typical Brazilian dish, *feijoada* consists of black beans stewed with pork (dried meat, ribs, loin, tail, trotter, ear). It is generally served with chopped cabbage, *farofa* and orange. It is said that the *feijoada* was created by black slaves, who used up those parts of the pig disdained by their masters.

---

feijoeiro [fej'ʒwejrul] m bean.

feio, feia ['fejo, 'fejal] adj **-1.** [ger] ugly. **-2.** [tempo] nasty.
 ➡ **feio** adv: **fazer** ~ [dar vexame] to behave badly; **ficar** ~ [dar má impressão] to be rude; **perder** ~ ESP to lose badly.

feioso, osa [fe'jozu, ɔzal] adj plain.

feira ['fejral] f [ger] fair; ~ **livre** vegetable market.

feirante [fej'rãntʃil] mf stallholder.

feita ['fejtal] f: **certa** ~ once; **de uma** ~ once and for all.

feitiçaria [fejtʃisa'rial] f witchcraft.

feiticeiro, ra [fejtʃi'sejru, ral] ◇ adj [encantador] bewitching. ◇ m, f [pessoa] sorcerer (f witch).

feitiço [fej'tʃisul] m spell; **voltar-se o** ~ **contra o feiticeiro** to be hoist by one's own petard.

feitio [fej'tʃiwl] m **-1.** [forma] shape. **-2.** [natureza] make-up. **-3.** [de roupa] cut.

feito, ta ['fejtu, tal] ◇ pp ▷ **fazer**. ◇ adj **-1.** [concluído, pronto] finished. **-2.** [adulto]: **homem** ~/**mulher feita** grown man/woman.
 ➡ **feito** ◇ m [façanha] deed. ◇ conj [tal qual] just like.

feitor, ra [fej'to(x), ral] m, f **-1.** [administrador] manager. **-2.** [capataz] steward.

feitura [fej'tural] f make-up.

feiúra [fej'ural] f ugliness.

feixe ['fejʃi] m **-1.** [molho] bunch. **-2.** [de luz] beam.

fel ['fɛwl] m **-1.** [ger] bitterness. **-2.** [bílis] bile.

felação [fela'sãwl] (pl -ões) f fellatio.

felicidade [felisi'dadʒil] f **-1.** [ventura] happiness. **-2.** [êxito] success. **-3.** [boa sorte] good luck.
 ➡ **felicidades** fpl congratulations.

felicíssimo, ma [feli'sisimu, mal] superl ▷ feliz.

felicitação [felisita'sãwl] (pl -ões) f praise.
 ➡ **felicitações** fpl congratulations.

felicitar [4] [felisi'ta(x)] vt: ~ **alguém (por algo)** to congratulate sb (on sthg).

felino, na [fe'linu, nal] ◇ adj **-1.** [ger] feline. **-2.** fig [traiçoeiro] sly. ◇ m [animal] feline; **os** ~**s** the cat family (sg).

feliz [fe'liʒ] (pl -es) adj **-1.** [ger] happy; **ser** ~ **(em algo)** to be lucky (in sthg); **estar/ficar** ~ to be happy; ~ **aniversário** happy birthday; **Feliz Ano-Novo** happy new year; **Feliz Natal** happy Christmas UK, merry Christmas US; **ser** ~ to be happy. **-2.** [oportuno] good. **-3.** [bem-sucedido] successful.

felizardo, da [feli'zaxdu, dal] m, f very lucky person.

felizmente [feliʒ'mẽntʃi] adv **-1.** [por felicidade] luckily. **-2.** [de modo feliz] happily.

felonia [felo'nial] f felony.

felpa ['fewpal] f **-1.** [de tecido] nap. **-2.** [de animal] down.

felpudo, da [few'pudu, dal] adj downy.

feltro ['fewtrul] m felt.

fêmea ['femjal] f female.

feminilidade [feminili'dadʒil] f femininity.

feminino, na [femi'ninu, nal] adj feminine.
 ➡ **feminino** m GRAM feminine.

feminismo [femi'niʒmul] m feminism.

feminista [femi'niʃtal] ◇ adj feminist. ◇ mf feminist.

fêmur ['femu(x)l] m femur.

fenda ['fẽndal] f **-1.** [rachadura] crack. **-2.** GEOL crevice.

fender [5] [fẽn'de(x)l] vt to split.
 ➡ **fender-se** vp to split.

fenecer [25] [fene'se(x)l] vi **-1.** [extingüir-se] to die out. **-2.** [morrer] to die. **-3.** [murchar] to wilt.

feno ['fenul] m hay.

fenomenal [fenome'nawl] (pl -ais) adj **-1.** [maravilhoso] wonderful. **-2.** [surpreendente] phenomenal.

fenômeno [fe'nomenul] m phenomenon.

fenomenologia [fenomenolo'ʒial] f phenomenology.

fera ['fɛral] f **-1.** fig [ger] brute. **-2.** [animal] wild animal; **ficar uma** ~ **(com)** to be very angry (with). **-3.** fam fig [pessoa perita] ace; **ser (uma)** ~ **em algo** fam fig to be an ace at sthg.

féretro ['fɛretrul] m coffin.

feriado [fe'rjadul] m (public) holiday; ~ **bancário** bank holiday UK.

férias ['fɛrjaʃl] fpl holidays UK, vacation (sg) US; **de** ~ on holiday UK, on vacation US; **entrar/sair de** ~ to go on holiday UK, to go on vacation US; **passar as** ~ **em** to spend one's holiday in UK, to spend one's vacation in US; **tirar** ~ to take one's holidays UK, to take one's vacation US.

ferida [fe'ridal] f wound; **tocar na** ~ fig to re-open the wound.

ferido, da [fe'ridu, dal] ◇ adj **-1.** [machucado] wounded. **-2.** [magoado] wounded. ◇ m, f [pessoa] injured person; **os** ~**s** the injured.

ferimento [feri'mẽntul] m injury.

ferino, na [fe'rinu, nal] adj **-1.** [cruel] cruel. **-2.** fig [mordaz] biting.

ferir [57] [fe'ri(x)l] vt **-1.** [machucar] to wound. **-2.** fig [magoar] to wound.
 ➡ **ferir-se** vp **-1.** [machucar-se] to hurt o.s. **-2.** fig [magoar-se]: ~**-se com** to be wounded by.

fermentação [fexmẽnta'sãwl] (pl -ões) f fermentation.

fermentar [4] [fexmẽn'ta(x)l] ◇ vt to ferment. ◇ vi to ferment.

fermento [fex'mẽntul] m yeast; ~ **em pó** powdered yeast.

Fernando de Noronha *m National Marine Park situated off the coast of Rio Grande do Norte in Brazil.*

FERNANDO DE NORONHA

The archipelago Fernando de Noronha (PE) comprises 19 islands situated 345 km off the coast of Rio Grande do Norte, and totalling 26 km². The largest of these islands is the only inhabited one, and is also called Fernando de Noronha. Here is to be found the only urban centre of the islands, Vila dos Remédios. Because of its crystal-clear waters, dolphins, sharks and fifteen species of coral, Fernando de Noronha has been made into a National Marine Park.

ferocidade [fero'sidadʒi] *f* ferocity.
ferocíssimo, ma [fero'sisimu, ma] *superl* ▷ **feroz**.
feroz [fe'rɔʃ] (*pl* -es) *adj* fierce.
ferrado, da [fe'xadu, da] *adj* -1. [cavalo] shod. -2. *fam fig* [em mau estado] falling apart.
ferradura [fexa'dura] *f* horseshoe.
ferragem [fe'xaʒẽ] (*pl* -ns) *f* -1. [peças] hardware. -2. [guarnição] ironwork.
ferramenta [fexa'mẽnta] *f* tool.
ferramental [fexa'mẽntaw] (*pl* -ais) *m* tool kit.
ferrão [fe'xãw] (*pl* -ões) *m* -1. [de inseto] sting. -2. [aguilhão] barb.
ferrar [4] [fe'xa(x)] *vt* -1. [ornar de ferro] to decorate with ironwork. -2. [cavalgadura] to shoe. -3. [marcar a ferro] to brand. -4. *fam fig* [prejudicar] to damage.
    ◆ **ferrar-se** *vp* [sair-se mal] to do badly.
ferreiro [fe'xejru] *m* blacksmith.
ferrenho, nha [fe'xeɲu, ɲal] *adj* -1. [inflexível] iron. -2. [obstinado] passionate.
férreo, rrea ['fɛxju, xja] *adj* iron.
ferrete [fe'xetʃi] *m* branding iron.
ferro ['fɛxu] *m* -1. [material] iron; **a ~ e fogo** *fig* by hook or by crook; **de ~** *fig* [vontade, punhos] of iron; [pessoa] made of iron; **~ batido** wrought iron; **~ fundido** cast iron; **~ ondulado** corrugated iron; **~ velho** [sucata] scrap metal. -2. [aparelho]: **~ (de passar)** iron; **passar a ~** to iron. -3. *loc*: **levar ~** to fail.
    ◆ **ferros** *mpl* [grilhões] chains.
ferroada [fe'xwada] *f* sting.
ferroar [20] [fe'xwa(x)] ◇ *vt* -1. [picar] to sting. -2. [criticar] to criticize. ◇ *vi* -1. [picar] to sting. -2. [latejar, doer] to really hurt.
ferrões [fe'xõjʃ] *pl* ▷ **ferrão**.
ferrolho [fe'xoʎu] *m* bolt.
ferroso, sa [fe'xozu, ɔza] *adj* [ferruginoso] rust coloured.
ferro-velho [ˌfɛxu'vɛʎu] (*pl* ferros-velhos) *m* -1. [estabelecimento] scrapyard. -2. [sucata] scrap metal.
ferrovia [fexo'via] *f* railway *UK*, railroad *US*.
ferroviário, ria [fexo'vjarju, ja] ◇ *adj* railway *UK*, railroad *US*. ◇ *m, f* railway employee *UK*, railroad employee *US*.
ferrugem [fe'xuʒẽ] *f* rust.

fértil ['fɛxtiw] (*pl* -eis) *adj* -1. [terreno, período] fertile. -2. [pessoa] productive.
fertilidade [fextʃili'dadʒi] *f* -1. [de terra, pessoa] fertility. -2. [abundância] abundance.
fertilização [fextʃiliza'sãw] (*pl* -ões) *f* fertilization.
fertilizante [fextʃili'zãntʃi] ◇ *adj* fertilizing; **método ~** method of fertilization. ◇ *m* fertilizer.
fertilizar [4] [fextʃili'za(x)] *vt* to fertilize.
fervente [fex'vẽntʃi] *adj* boiling.
ferver [5] [fex've(x)] ◇ *vt* to boil; **~ algo em fogo baixo** to simmer on a low heat. ◇ *vi* to become excited; **~ de raiva** *fig* to be steaming with anger.
fervilhar [4] [fexvi'ʎa(x)] *vi* -1. [ferver] to boil. -2. *fig* [pulular]: **~ (de)** to swarm (with). -3. *fig* [de excitação] to bubble.
fervor [fex'vo(x)] *m* fervour *UK*, fervor *US*.
fervoroso, osa [fexvo'rozu, ɔza] *adj* -1. [ardoroso] fervent. -2. [dedicado] devoted.
fervura [fex'vura] *f* -1. [ebulição] boiling. -2. *fig* [efervescência] fervour *UK*, fervor *US*.
festa ['fɛʃta] *f* -1. [reunião] party; **~ de arromba** thrash. -2. [comemoração]: **~ da Independência** Independence Day party; **~s juninas** *traditional celebrations held in Brazil in June*. -3. [alegria] thrill. -4. [carinho]: **fazer ~ (s) (em)** to cuddle up to. -5. *loc*: **fazer a ~** to have a field day.
    ◆ **festas** *fpl* [Natal e Ano-Novo] festive season (*sg*).

FESTAS JUNINAS

Popular religious festivals during the month of June; these festivals of ancient origin came over with the Portuguese, and mostly celebrate the feast days of St Anthony (13th), St John (24th) and St Peter (29th). They are celebrated with music, typical drinks and dishes, always including fires and bonfires. Nowadays these festivities are held mainly in the north and northeast of the country.

festança [feʃ'tãnsa] *fam* thrash.
festeiro, ra [feʃ'tejru, ra] *adj* party-going.
festejar [4] [feʃte'ʒa(x)] *vt* to celebrate.
festejo [feʃ'teʒul] *m* celebration.
festim [feʃ'tʃĩ] (*pl* -ns) *m* -1. [festa] feast. -2. [cartucho sem bala]: **tiro de ~** blank shot.
festival [feʃtʃi'vaw] (*pl* -ais) *m* -1. [festa] festival. -2. *fig* [grande quantidade] load.
festividade [feʃtʃivi'dadʒi] *f* festivity.
festivo, va [feʃ'tʃivu, va] *adj* festive.
fetal [fe'taw] (*pl* -ais) *adj* foetal *UK*, fetal *US*.
fetiche [fe'tʃiʃi] *m* fetish.
fetichismo [fetʃi'ʃiʒmu] *m* fetishism.
fetichista [fetʃi'ʃiʃta] ◇ *adj* fetishistic. ◇ *m, f* fetishist.
fétido, da ['fɛtʃidu, da] *adj* fetid.
feto ['fɛtu] *m* foetus *UK*, fetus *US*.
feudal [few'daw] (*pl* -ais) *adj* feudal.

feudalismo [fewda'liʒmu] *m* feudalism.

fev. (*abrev de* **fevereiro**) Feb.

fevereiro [feve'rejru] *m* February; *veja também* **setembro**.

fezes ['fɛziʃ] *fpl* faeces *UK*, feces *US*.

FGTS (*abrev de* **Fundo de Garantia por Tempo de Serviço**) *m monthly contribution towards the support of sacked and unemployed workers in Brazil.*

FGV (*abrev de* **Fundação Getúlio Vargas**) *f Brazilian private educational organization for improvement in public administration.*

FIA (*abrev de* **Federação Internacional de Automobilismo**) *f* FIA.

fiação [fja'sãw] (*pl* **-ões**) *f* **-1.** *ELETR* wiring; **fazer a ~ (de)** to wire (sthg). **-2.** [fábrica] spinning mill.

fiado, da ['fjadu, da] *adj* **-1.** [vendido a crédito] sold on credit (*depois do subst*). **-2.** [conversa]: **isso é conversa fiada** that's far-fetched.

➡ **fiado** *adv* [a crédito] on credit.

fiador, ra [fja'do(x), ra] *m, f* guarantor.

fiambre ['fjãbri] *m* ham.

fiança ['fjãsa] *f* **-1.** [garantia] guarantee. **-2.** *JUR* bail; **sob ~** on bail; **pagar ~** to post bail.

fiapo ['fjapu] *m* thread.

fiar [16] ['fja(x)] *vt* [reduzir a fio] to spin.

➡ **fiar-se** *vp* [confiar em]: **~-se em alguém/algo** to trust sb/sthg.

fiasco ['fjaʃku] *m* fiasco.

fibra ['fibra] *f* [ger] fibre *UK*, fiber *US*; **mulher de ~** gutsy woman; **~ óptica** fibre optics (*pl*) *UK*, fiber optics (*pl*) *US*; **~ de vidro** fibreglass *UK*, fiberglass *US*.

fibroma [fi'broma] *m* fibroma.

fibroso, sa [fi'brozu, ɔza] *adj* fibrous.

ficar [12] [fi'ka(x)] *vi* **-1.** [ger] to remain; **só ficaram duas garrafas de refrigerante** there are only two bottles of soda left. **-2.** [permanecer] to stay; **~ sentado/de pé** to remain seated/standing; **~ por isso mesmo** to remain the same; **~ sem** not to have. **-3.** [estar situado] to be. **-4.** [tornar-se] to become; **~ com frio** to be cold; **~ feliz com algo** to be happy about sthg; **~ de bem/de mal (com alguém)** to get on well/badly (with sb); **~ bom** [de doença] to recover; [pintura etc] to be good. **-5.** [ser adiado]: **~ para** to leave until. **-6.** [combinar]: **~ de fazer algo** to agree to do sthg. **-7.** [persistir]: **~ fazendo algo** to go on doing sthg. **-8.** [prometer]: **~ de fazer algo** to promise to do sthg. **-9.** [custar]: **~ em** to come to. **-10.** [comprar]: **fico com a verde** I'll take the green. **-11.** [manter sob posse, tutela]: **~ com** to be left with. **-12.** [assumir função]: **~ de** to work as. **-13.** [ser]: **não fica bem** it's not right. **-14.** [assentar a]: **~ bem em** *ou* **para alguém** to look good on sb; **~ bem de algo** to look good in sthg. **-15.** [vir a]: **~ sabendo de algo** to get to know sthg. **-16.** *loc*: **~ atrás** [ser inferior] to be behind; **~ sobrando** [ser relegado] to be left out; **~ sujo** [no conceito alheio] to get a bad name.

ficção [fik'sãw] (*pl* **-ões**) *f* fiction.

ficcional [fik'sionaw] (*pl* **-ais**) *adj LITER* fictional.

ficcionista [fiksjo'niʃta] *mf* fiction writer.

ficha ['fiʃa] *f* **-1.** [ger] file; **ter ~ na polícia** to have a police record. **-2.** [de telefone] plug. **-3.** [de jogo] token. **-4.** *fam* [informação]: **dar a ~ de** to give information on; **ter ~ limpa** to have a clean record.

fichado, da [fi'ʃadu, da] *adj*: **ser ~ (na polícia)** to have a police record.

fichar [4] [fi'ʃa(x)] *vt* to file.

fichário [fi'ʃarju] *m* **-1.** [ger] file. **-2.** [móvel] filing cabinet.

fichinha [fi'ʃiɲa] *f fam* cinch.

fictício, cia [fik'tʃisju, sja] *adj* fictitious.

fidalgo, ga [fi'dawgu, ga] *m, f* noble.

fidalguia [fidaw'gia] *f* nobility.

fidedigno, na [fide'dʒignu, na] *adj* trustworthy.

fidelidade [fideli'dadʒi] *f* **-1.** [lealdade] faithfulness. **-2.** [conjugal] fidelity. **-3.** [precisão] precision; **com ~** faithfully.

fiduciário, ria [fidu'sjarju, rja] *adj* fiduciary.

➡ **fiduciário** *m JUR* trustee.

fiel ['fjɛw] (*pl* **-éis**) *adj* **-1.** [ger] faithful. **-2.** [constante] loyal.

➡ **fiéis** *mpl RELIG*: **os fiéis** the faithful (*pl inv*).

fielmente [fjew'mẽtʃi] *adv* faithfully.

FIFA (*abrev de* **Féderation Internationale de Football Association**) *f* FIFA.

figa ['figa] *f* charm.

➡ **de uma figa** *loc adj fam* effing.

fígado ['figadu] *m* liver; **desopilar o ~** *fig* to make one feel good.

figo ['figu] *m* fig.

figueira [fi'gejra] *f* fig tree.

figura [fi'gura] *f* **-1.** [ger] figure; **ser uma ~** *fam* to be a character; **mudar de ~** to change. **-2.** [em carta] picture card, court card. **-3.** *GRAM*: **~ de linguagem** figure of speech.

figura-chave [fi,gura'ʃavi] (*pl* **figuras-chave**) *f* key figure.

figurado, da [figu'radu, da] *adj* figurative.

figurante [figu'rãtʃi] *mf* extra.

figurão [figu'rãw] (*pl* **-ões**) *m* bigwig.

figurar [4] [figu'ra(x)] *vt* **-1.** [representar] to represent. **-2.** [ter a forma de] to look like. **-3.** [aparentar] to look. *vi* **-1.** [atuar]: **~ em** to act in. **-2.** [fazer parte]: **~ em/entre** to appear on/among.

figurinha [figu'riɲa] *f* **-1.** [cromo] sticker; **trocar ~s (com alguém)** *fig* to swap notes (with sb). **-2.** [pessoa]: **ele é uma ~ difícil** he's jumped up.

figurinista [figuri'niʃta] *mf* clothes designer.

figurino [figu'rinu] *m* **-1.** [molde] pattern. **-2.** [revista] fashion magazine. **-3.** *CINE, TEATRO & TV* [exemplo] model. **-4.** *fig*: **como manda o ~** as it should be.

Fiji ['fiʒi] *n* Fiji.

fila ['fila] *f* [fileira - de pessoas] queue *UK*, line *US*; [- de cadeiras] row; **em ~** in line; **fazer ~** to queue *UK*, to form a line *US*; **~ indiana** single file.

filamento [fila'mẽntu] *m* filament.
filantropia [filãntro'pia] *f* philanthropy.
filantrópico, ca [filãn'tropiku, ka] *adj* philanthropic.
filantropo, opa [filãn'tropu, ɔpa] *m, f* philanthropist.
filão [fi'lãw] (*pl* -ões) *m fig* [oportunidade] opportunity.
filar [16] [fi'la(x)] *vt fam* to cadge.
filarmônico, ca [filax'moniku, ka] *adj* philharmonic.
➨ **filarmônica** *f* philharmonic.
filatelia [filate'lia] *f* philately, stamp collecting.
filé [fi'lɛ] *m* fillet; ~ **mignon** filet mignon.
fileira [fi'lejra] *f* row.
➨ **fileiras** *fpl* MIL ranks.
filete [fi'lete] *m* fillet.
filha [ˈfiʎa] *f* ⊳ **filho**.
filharada [fiʎa'rada] *f* many sons and daughters.
filhinho, nha [fiˈʎiɲu, ɲal *m, f* young son; ~ **da mamãe** mummy's boy; ~ **de papai** spoilt brat.
filho, lha [ˈfiʎu, ˈfiʎa] *m, f* -**1.** [descendente] son; ~ **adotivo** adopted son; ~ **de criação** adopted son; ~ **único** only son; ~ **da mãe** *vulg* bastard; ~ **da puta** *vulg* son of a bitch. -**2.** *loc*: **ter um** ~ *fig* to have a turn, to have a fainting fit; **ser** ~ **único de mãe solteira** *fig* to be unique.
filhote [fiˈʎɔtʃi] *m* -**1.** [de animal - de leão, urso] cub; [- de cachorro] puppy. -**2.** [filho] young son.
filiação [filjaˈsãw] (*pl* -ões) *f* -**1.** [pais] filiation. -**2.** [admissão] affiliation.
filial [fi'ljaw] (*pl* -ais) ⟨⟩ *adj* [amor] filial. ⟨⟩ *f* [sucursal] branch.
filiar [16] [fi'ʎa(x)] *vt*: ~ **alguém a algo** to sign sb up to sthg.
➨ **filiar-se** *vp*: ~**-se a algo** to sign o.s. up to sthg.
filigrana [fili'grana] *f* filigree.
Filipinas [fili'pinaʃ] *npl*: **(as)** ~ the Philippines.
filipino, na [fili'pinu, na] ⟨⟩ *adj* Filipino. ⟨⟩ *m, f* Filipino.
➨ **filipino** *m* [língua] Filipino.
filmadora [fiwma'dora] *f* movie camera.
filmagem [fiw'maʒẽ] (*pl* -ns) *f* filming.
filmar [4] [fiw'ma(x)] ⟨⟩ *vt* to film. ⟨⟩ *vi* to film.
filme [ˈfiwmi] *m* -**1.** [obra cinematográfica] film *UK*, movie *US*; ~ **de bangue-bangue** Western; ~ **de época** period film *UK*, period movie *US*; ~ **mudo** silent film *UK*, silent movie *US*; ~ **de suspense** thriller. -**2.** *loc*: **queimar o** ~ to ruin one's image.
filmografia [fiwmogra'fia] *f* filmography.
filmoteca [fiwmo'tɛka] *f* film library.
filó [fi'lɔ] *m* voile.
filões [fi'lõjʃ] *mpl* ⊳ **filão**.
filologia [filolo'ʒia] *f* philology.
filólogo, ga [fi'lɔlogu, ga] *m, f* philologist.
filosofar [4] [filozo'fa(x)] *vi* to philosophize.
filosofia [filozo'fia] *f* philosophy.
filosófico, ca [filo'zɔfiku, ka] *adj* philosophical.
filósofo, fa [fiˈlɔzofu, fiˈlɔzofa] *m, f* philosopher.
filtragem [fiwtra'ʒẽ] (*pl* -ns) *f* [filtração] filtration.

filtrar [4] [fiw'tra(x)] *vt* -**1.** [purificar] to filter. -**2.** [selecionar] to select.
filtro [ˈfiwtru] *m* filter; ~ **de ar** air filter.
fim [ˈfĩ] (*pl* -ns) *m* [ger] end; ~ **de semana** weekend; ~ **de mundo, do mundo** [cafundó] middle of nowhere; **no** ~ **das contas** after all; **ser o** ~ **(da picada)** to be the last straw; **por** ~ finally.
➨ **a fim de** *loc prep* in order to; **estar a** ~ **de fazer algo** to be planning on doing sthg; **estar a** ~ **de alguém** to be attracted to sb.
fimose [fi'mɔzi] *f* phimosis.
finado, da [fi'nadu, da] ⟨⟩ *adj* dead. ⟨⟩ *m, f* dead person.
➨ **finados** *mpl* RELIG: **os** ~**s** All Souls.
final [fi'naw] (*pl* -ais) ⟨⟩ *adj* final; **minuto** ~ last minute; **ponto** ~ full stop. ⟨⟩ *m* end; ~ **feliz** happy ending. ⟨⟩ *f* ESP final.
finalidade [finali'dadʒi] *f* end.
finalista [fina'liʃta] *mf* finalist.
finalização [finaliza'sãw] (*pl* -ões) *f* conclusion.
finalizar [4] [finali'za(x)] ⟨⟩ *vt* [concluir] to conclude. ⟨⟩ *vi* FUT [fazer gol] to score.
finanças [fi'nãnsaʃ] *fpl* -**1.** [ciência] finance (*sg*). -**2.** [situação financeira] finances.
financeiro, ra [finãn'sejru, ra] *adj* financial.
➨ **financeira** *f* [firma] finance company.
financiamento [finãnsja'mẽntu] *m* financing.
financiar [16] [finãn'sja(x)] *vt* to finance.
financista [finãn'siʃta] *mf* financier.
fincar [12] [fĩ'ka(x)] *vt* [cravar] to stick.
findar [4] [fĩ'da(x)] *vt & vi* to end.
➨ **findar-se** *vp* to end.
findo, da [ˈfĩndu, da] *adj* finished.
fineza [fi'neza] *f* -**1.** [espessura] fineness. -**2.** [gentileza] politeness.
fingido, da [fĩ'ʒidu, da] ⟨⟩ *adj* fake. ⟨⟩ *m, f* dissembler.
fingimento [fĩʒi'mẽntu] *m* pretence *UK*, pretense *US*.
fingir [52] [fĩ'ʒi(x)] ⟨⟩ *vt* to fake. ⟨⟩ *vi* to pretend.
➨ **fingir-se** *vp*: ~**-se de algo** to pretend to be sthg.
finito, ta [fi'nitu, ta] *adj* finite.
finitude [fini'tudʒi] *f* [limitação] finite nature.
finlandês, esa [fĩlãn'dejʃ, eza] ⟨⟩ *adj* Finnish. ⟨⟩ *m, f* Finnish person, Finn.
➨ **finlandês** *m* [língua] Finnish.
Finlândia [fĩ'lãndʒia] *n* Finland.
fino, na [ˈfinu, na] *adj* -**1.** [ger] fine. -**2.** [agudo] shrill. -**3.** [refinado] elegant. -**4.** *loc*: **ser o** ~ to be the best; **tirar um** ~ **de** to come within a hair's breadth of.
fins [fĩʃ] *mpl* ⊳ **fim**.
finura [fi'nura] *f* -**1.** [espessura] fineness. -**2.** [refinamento] refinement.
fio [ˈfiw] *m* -**1.** [ger] thread. -**2.** ELETR wire. -**3.** [gume] blade. -**4.** [filete] trickle. -**5.** *loc*: **bater um** ~ *fam* to have a phone conversation.
➨ **a fio** *loc adj*: **dias/horas a** ~ days/hours on end.

por um fio *loc adv*: **o emprego dele está por um** ~ his job hangs by a thread; **escapou da morte por um** ~ he escaped death by a hair's breadth.

fiorde ['fjoxdʒil] *m* fjord.

firma ['fixma] *f* **-1.** COM firm. **-2.** [assinatura] signature.

firmamento [fixma'mēntul] *m* firmament.

firmar [4] [fix'ma(x)] <> *vt* **-1.** [fixar] to steady. **-2.** [assinar] to sign. **-3.** [estabelecer] to establish. **-4.** [basear]: ~ **algo em algo** to base sthg on sthg. <> *vi* [estabilizar-se] to settle.
firmar-se *vp* to settle.

firme ['fixmi] *adj* **-1.** [ger] firm. **-2.** [fixo] steady, stable. **-3.** [constante] settled. **-4.** [estável] stable.

firmeza [fix'meza] *f* **-1.** [ger] firmness. **-2.** [estabilidade] steadiness, stability. **-3.** [segurança] soundness.

fiscal [fiʃ'kaw] *(pl* **-ais)** <> *adj* [relativo ao fisco] fiscal. <> *mf* **-1.** [aduaneiro] customs officer. **-2.** [supervisor - de impostos] inspector; [- de prova] invigilator.

fiscalização [fiʃkaliza'sãw] *(pl* **-ões)** *f* overseeing.

fiscalizar [4] [fiʃkali'za(x)] *vt* **-1.** [estabelecimento, obras] to oversee. **-2.** [prova] to invigilate.

fisco ['fiʃku] *m*: **o** ~ the public purse.

fisgada [fiʒ'gada] *f* stabbing pain.

fisgar [14] [fiʒ'ga(x)] *vt* **-1.** [peixe] to harpoon. **-2.** [pessoa] to understand.

físico, ca ['fiziku, ka] <> *adj* [ger] physical; **educação física** physical education. <> *m, f* FÍSICA physicist.
físico *m* [corpo] physique.
física *f* [ciência] physics *(sg)*.

fisiologia [fizjolo'ʒia] *f* physiology.

fisiológico, ca [fizjo'lɔʒiku, ka] *adj* **-1.** MED physiological. **-2.** POL self-serving.

fisiologismo [fizjolo'ʒiʒmul] *m* POL self-interest.

fisionomia [fizjono'mia] *f* features *(pl)*, appearance; **ela está com boa** ~ she's looking well.

fisionomista [fizjono'miʃta] *mf* person who is good at remembering faces.

fisioterapeuta [fizjotera'pewta] *mf* physiotherapist.

fisioterapia [fizjotera'pia] *f* physiotherapy.

fissura [fi'sura] *f* **-1.** GEOL fissure. **-2.** *fam* [gana] hankering.

fissurado, da [fisu'radu, da] *adj* **-1.** [rachado] cracked. **-2.** *fam* [maluco por]: ~ **em** mad about.

fissurar [4] [fisu'ra(x)] *vt* to crack.

fístula ['fiʃtula] *f* fistula.

fita ['fita] *f* **-1.** [tira] ribbon; ~ **crepe** crêpe bandage; ~ **durex®** *ou* **colante** Sellotape® *UK;* Scotch tape® *US;* ~ **de impressora** typewriter ribbon; ~ **isolante** insulating tape; ~ **magnética** magnetic tape; ~ **métrica** tape measure, measuring tape. **-2.** [filme] tape. **-3.** [cassete]: ~ **de vídeo** videotape; ~ **virgem** blank tape. **-4.** [manha] play-acting.

fitar [4] [fi'ta(x)] *vt* to stare.
fitar-se *vp* to stare at one another.

fiteiro, ra [fi'tejru, ra] *adj* play-acting.

fito ['fitul] *m* target.

fivela [fi'vɛla] *f* **-1.** [fecho] buckle. **-2.** [de cabelo] hair clip.

fixação [fiksa'sãw] *(pl* **-ões)** *f* fixation.

fixador [fiksa'do(x)] *(pl* **-es)** *m* **-1.** [de cabelo] hairspray. **-2.** [de essência] fixing agent.

fixar [4] [fik'sa(x)] *vt* **-1.** [prender] to fix. **-2.** [apreender] to make stick. **-3.** [estabelecer] to set.
fixar-se *vp* **-1.** [estabilizar-se] to be fixed. **-2.** [estabelecer residência] to settle. **-3.** [fitar]: ~ **em** to stare at.

fixo, xa ['fiksu, ksa] *adj* fixed.

flacidez [flasi'deʒ] *f* flaccidity.

flácido, da ['flasidu, da] *adj* flaccid.

flagelado, da [flaʒe'ladu, da] *adj* flogged.

flagelante [flaʒe'lãntʃi] *adj* **-1.** [chicote] searing. **-2.** [isolamento] punishing.

flagelo [fla'ʒɛlul] *m* scourge.

flagrante [fla'grãntʃi] <> *adj* flagrant. <> *m*: **pegar em** ~ **(de algo)** to catch in the act (of sthg); **em** ~ red-handed, in flagrante.

flagrar [4] [fla'gra(x)] *vt* to catch in the act.

flama ['flãma] *f* flame.

flambar [4] [flã'ba(x)] *vt* to flambé.

flamejante [flame'ʒãntʃi] *adj* flaming.

flamejar [4] [flame'ʒa(x)] *vi* to flame.

flamenco, ca [fla'mẽŋku, ka] <> *adj* flamenco.
flamenco *m* flamenco.

flamengo, ga [fla'mẽŋgu, ga] *adj* Flemish.
flamengo *m* [língua] Flemish.

flamingo [fla'mĩŋgul] *m* flamingo.

flâmula ['flãmula] *f* pennant.

flanco ['flãŋkul] *m* flank.

flanela [fla'nɛla] *f* flannel.

flanelinha [flane'liɲa] *mf fam* unofficial car-park attendant.

flanquear [15] [flãŋ'kja(x)] *vt* **-1.** [atacar de flanco] to attack in the flank. **-2.** [ladear] to flank.

flash ['flɛʃi] *(pl* **-es)** *m* flash.

flash-back [flaʃ'baki] *(pl* **flash-backs)** *m* flash-back.

flatulência [flatu'lẽnsja] *f* flatulence.

flauta ['flawta] *f* flute; ~ **doce** tin whistle; ~ **transversa** transverse flute; **levar algo na** ~ to take sthg lightly.

flautim [flaw'tʃĩ] *(pl* **-ns)** *m* piccolo.

flautista [flaw'tʃiʃta] *mf* flautist.

flebite [fle'bitʃi] *f* phlebitis.

flecha ['flɛʃa] *f* arrow.

flechada [fle'ʃada] *f* **-1.** [arremesso] arrow shot. **-2.** [ferimento] arrow wound.

flertar [4] [flex'ta(x)] *vi*: ~ **(com alguém)** to flirt (with sb).

flerte ['flextʃi] *m* flirt.

fleuma ['flewma] *f* phlegm.

fleumático, ca [flew'matʃiku, ka] *adj* phlegmatic.

flexão [flek'sãw] *(pl* **-ões)** *f* **-1.** [movimento] flexing. **-2.** GRAM inflexion.

flexibilidade [fleksibili'dadʒil] *f* flexibility.

flexibilização [fleksibiliza'sãw] (*pl* -ões) *f* relaxation.

flexibilizar [fleksibili'za(x)] *vt* to relax.

flexionado, da [fleksio'nadu, da] *adj* LING inflected.

flexionar [4] [fleksjo'na(x)] <> *vt* -1. [joelho etc] to flex. -2. GRAM to inflect. <> *vi* GRAM to inflect.

flexível [flek'sivɛw] (*pl* -eis) *adj* flexible.

flexões [flek'sõjʃ] *fpl* ▷ **flexão**.

fliperama [flipe'rãma] *m* -1. [máquina] pinball machine. -2. [estabelecimento] amusement arcade.

floco ['flɔku] *m* flake; ~ **de milho** cornflake; ~ **de neve** snowflake.

➤ **flocos** *mpl*: **sorvete de** ~s chocolate chip ice-cream.

flor ['flo(x)] (*pl* -es) *f* -1. BOT flower. -2. [pessoa boa]: **ser uma** ~ to be a gem. -3. *loc*: **a fina** ~ **de** the flower of; **na** ~ **da idade** in the prime of life; **não ser** ~ **que se cheire** not to be trusted.

flora ['flɔra] *f* flora.

floral [flo'raw] (*pl* -ais) <> *adj* floral. <> *m* floral infusion; **florais de Bach** Bach flower remedies.

floreado, da [flo'rjadu, da] *adj* flowery.

florear [15] [flo'rja(x)] *vt* [rebuscar] to embellish.

floreio [flo'reju] *m* flourish.

Florença [flo'rẽsa] *n* Florence.

florescente [flore'sẽtʃi] *adj* -1. [BOT - árvore] blossoming; [- planta] flowering. -2. *fig* [próspero] flowering.

florescer [25] [flore'se(x)] *vi* -1. [BOT - árvore] to blossom; [- planta] to flower. -2. *fig* [prosperar] to flower.

floresta [flo'rɛʃta] *f* forest.

florestal [floreʃ'taw] (*pl* -ais) *adj* forest (*antes de subst).*

Florianópolis [florja'nɔpoliʃ] *n* Florianópolis.

floricultor, ra [florikuw'to(x), ra] *m, f* floriculturist.

floricultura [florikuw'tura] *f* floriculture.

florido, da [flo'ridu, da] *adj* flower-filled.

florir [79] [flo'ri(x)] *vi* -1. [árvore] to blossom. -2. [planta] to flower.

florista [flo'riʃta] *mf* florist.

flotilha [flo'tiʎa] *f* flotilla.

fluência [flu'ẽsja] *f* fluency.

fluente [flu'ẽtʃi] *adj* fluent.

fluidez [fluj'deʒ] *f* fluidity.

fluido, da [flu'idu, ida] *adj* -1. [substância] fluid. -2. *fig* [fácil] flowing; **tráfego** ~ smooth-flowing traffic.

➤ **fluido** *m* fluid.

fluir [74] [flwi(x)] *vi* -1. [ger] to flow. -2. [derivar]: ~ **de** to derive from.

flúor ['fluo(x)] *m* fluoride.

fluorescente [flworeʃ'sẽtʃi] *adj* fluorescent.

flutuação [flutwa'sãw] (*pl* -ões) *f* fluctuation.

flutuante [flu'twãtʃi] *adj* -1. [boiante] floating. -2. [oscilante] fluctuating.

flutuar [4] [flu'twa(x)] *vi* -1. [ger] to float. -2. [variar] to fluctuate.

fluvial [flu'vjaw] (*pl* -ais) *adj* river (*antes de subst).*

fluxo ['fluksu] *m* -1. [ger] flow. -2. COM: ~ **de caixa** cash flow. -3. MED: ~ **menstrual** menstrual flow. -4. FÍSICA: ~ **de massa** flow rate.

fluxograma [flukso'grama] *m* flow chart.

FM (*abrev de* **freqüencia modulada**) *m* FM.

FMI (*abrev de* **Fundo Monetário Internacional**) *m* IMF.

fobia [fo'bia] *f* phobia.

foca ['fɔka] <> *f* ZOOL seal. <> *mf* [jornalista] cub reporter.

focal [fo'kaw] (*pl* -ais) *adj* focal.

focalização [fokaliza'sãw] *f* focusing.

focalizar [4] [fokali'za(x)], **focar** [4] [fo'ka(x)] *vt* to focus.

focinho [fo'siɲu] *m* -1. [de suíno] snout. -2. [de cão] muzzle.

foco ['fɔku] *m* focus.

foder [5] ['fode(x)] *vulg* ~ <> *vt* [copular com] to fuck. <> *vi* [copular] to fuck.

➤ **foder-se** *vp vulg* [dar-se mal] to fuck up.

fodido, da [fo'dʒidu, da] *vulg adj* -1. [ferrado] fucked; ~ **e mal pago** up shit creek without a paddle. -2. [pobre] loser.

fofo, fa ['fofu, fa] *adj* -1. [macio] soft. -2. [gracioso] cute.

fofoca [fo'fɔka] *f* gossip; **fazer** ~ to spread gossip.

fofocar [12] [fofo'ka(x)] *vi* to gossip.

fofoqueiro, ra [fofo'kejru, ra] <> *adj* gossipy. <> *m, f* gossip.

fofura [fo'fura] *f* cuteness; **ser uma** ~ to be cute.

fogão [fo'gãw] (*pl* -ões) *m* stove, cooker.

fogareiro [foga'rejru] *m* (paraffin) cooker, coal pot.

fogaréu [foga'rɛw] *m* torch.

fogo ['fogu] (*pl* **fogos**) *m* -1. [ger] fire; **pegar** ~ to catch fire; **brincar com** ~ *fig* to play with fire; **ser** ~ **(na roupa)** to mean trouble. -2. [excitação] flame; ~ **de palha** hot air. -3. [desejo sexual] sex drive. -4. [disparo]: **abrir** ~ to open fire; **fogo!** fire!; **poder de** ~ firepower. -5. [pirotecnia]: ~(s) **de artifício** fireworks. -6. *loc*: **estar de** ~ [estar embriagado] to be plastered.

fogões [fo'gõjʃ] *mpl* ▷ **fogão**.

fogo-fátuo [ˌfogu'fatwu] (*pl* **fogos-fátuos**) *m* will-o'-the-wisp.

fogoso, osa [fo'gozu, ɔza] *adj* -1. [arrebatado] fiery. -2. [sexualmente] aroused.

fogueira [fo'gejra] *f* bonfire.

foguete [fo'getʃi] *m* rocket; **soltar** ~s **antes da hora** *fig* to count one's chickens before they're hatched.

fogueteiro, ra [foge'tejru, ra] *m, f* pyrotechnist.

foguetório [foge'tɔrju] *m* noise of fireworks.

foice ['fojsi] *f* scythe.

folclore [fow'klɔri] *m* folklore.

folclórico, ca [fow'klɔriku, ka] *adj* folk.

fole ['fɔli] *m* bellows (*pl*).

fôlego ['folegu] *m* -1. [respiração] breath; **perder o** ~ to lose one's breath; **tomar** ~ to take a breath. **-2.** *fig* [ânimo]: **recuperar o** ~ to recover one's breath.

folga [ˈfɔwgal] *f*-**1.** [descanso] break; **dia de** ~ day off. **-2.** [abuso]: **que** ~**!** what a cheek! **-3.** [sobra de espaço] space. **-4.** [sobra de tempo] gap.

folgado, da [fowˈgadu, dal] *adj* -**1.** [largo] loose. **-2.** [abusado] cocky. **-3.** [despreocupado] easy.
➡ **folgado** *adv* easily.

folgazão, zona [fowgaˈzãw, zɔnal] (*mpl* -**ões**, *fpl* -**s**) *adj* idler.

folha [ˈfoʎal] *f*-**1.** BOT leaf. **-2.** [página] page; ~ **de rosto** title page; ~ **de pagamento** pay sheet. **-3.** [chapa] plate. **-4.** [jornal] newspaper. **-5.** [lâmina] blade. **-6.** [pedaço de papel] sheet.
➡ **em folha** *loc adv*: **novo em** ~ brand new.

folhagem [foˈʎaʒẽl] (*pl* -**ns**) *f* foliage.

folha-seca [ˌfoʎaˈsekal] (*pl* **folhas-secas**) *f* FUT lob.

folheado, da [foˈʎadu, dal] *adj* -**1.** [revestido]: ~ **a ouro/prata** gold-/silver-plated. **-2.** CULIN: **massa folheada** puff pastry.

folhear [15] [foˈʎja(x)] *vt* to leaf through.

folhetim [foʎeˈtʃĩl] (*pl* -**ns**) *m* serialization.

folhetinesco, ca [foʎetʃiˈneʃku, kal] *adj* [de folhetim] *published daily in a newspaper or magazine*.

folheto [foˈʎetul] *m* pamphlet.

folhinha [foˈʎiɲal] *f* [calendário] calendar.

folia [foˈlial] *f* revelry.

folião, ona [foˈljãw, ɔnal] (*mpl* -**ões**, *fpl* -**s**) *m, f* reveller.

folículo [foˈlikulul] *m* follicle.

foliona [foˈljonal] *f* ➪ **folião**.

fome [ˈfɔmil] *f* [ger] hunger; **estar com** ~ to be hungry; **passar** ~ to go hungry.

fomentar [4] [fomẽˈta(x)] *vt* to foment.

fomento [foˈmẽtul] *m* -**1.** MED poultice. **-2.** [estímulo] fomentation.

fominha [foˈmiɲal] *adj* mean.

fonador, ra [fonaˈdo(x), ral] *adj* phonic; **aparelho** ~ speech apparatus.

fone [ˈfɔnil] (*abrev de* **telefone**) *m* phone.

fonema [foˈnemal] *m* phoneme.

fonético, ca [foˈnɛtʃiku, kal] *adj* phonetic.
➡ **fonética** *f* phonetics (*sg*).

fônico, ca [ˈfɔniku, kal] *adj* phonic.

fonoaudiologia [fonawdʒioloˈgial] *f* speech therapy.

fonoaudiólogo, ga [ˌfonawˈdʒjɔlogu, gal] *m, f* speech therapist.

fonologia [fonoloˈʒial] *f* phonology.

fonte [ˈfõtʃil] ◇ *f* -**1.** [ger] source; **de** ~ **limpa** from a reliable source; **imposto retido na** ~ taxed at source. **-2.** [chafariz] fountain. **-3.** COMPUT [tipo de caractere] font. ◇ *m* COMPUT source code.

fora [ˈfɔral] ◇ *m* -**1.** [gafe] gaffe; **dar um** ~ to commit a gaffe. **-2.** *fig* [dispensa]: **dar um** ~ **em alguém** to rebuff sb; **levar um** ~ **de alguém** to be rebuffed by sb; **fora!** get out! **-3.** *loc*: **dar o** ~ [partir] to skedaddle. ◇ *adv* -**1.** [na parte exterior]: **do lado de** ~ on the outside; **por** ~ outside. **-2.**

[ao ar livre]: **lá** ~ outside. **-3.** [em outro lugar] away, out; **fui para** ~ **a semana** I went away last week; **jantei** ~ **ontem** I went out to dinner yesterday; **a família está** ~ **no momento** the family is out *ou* away at the moment; [no estrangeiro] abroad. **-4.** *fig* [distanciado]: ~ **de** out of; **estar** ~ **de si** to be beside o.s. ◇ *prep* [exceto] except for, apart from.
➡ **de fora** *loc adv* -**1.** [nu] exposed; **ficar com as pernas de** ~ to have one's legs exposed. **-2.** [sem participar]: **ficar de** ~ to be left out.
➡ **para fora** *loc adv*: **ela costura para** ~ she takes sewing in.
➡ **por fora** *loc adv* -**1.** [cobrar, pagar]: **cobrar por** ~ to receive on the side; **pagar por** ~ to pay on the side. **-2.** [ignorante]: **estar por** ~ **(de)** to be unaware (of).
➡ **fora de série** *loc adj* [excepcional] exceptional.

fora-da-lei [ˌfɔradaˈlejl] *mf inv* outlaw.

fora-de-estrada [ˈfɔradʒiʃˈtradal] ◇ *adj* off-road. ◇ *m* all-terrain vehicle.

foragido, da [foraˈʒidu, dal] ◇ *adj* fugitive. ◇ *m, f* fugitive.

foragir-se [52] [foraˈʒixsil] *vp* to flee.

forasteiro, ra [foraʃˈtejru, ral] *m, f* foreigner.

forca [ˈfɔxkal] *f* gallows (*sg*).

força [ˈfɔxsal] *f* -**1.** [ger] power. **-2.** [energia física, moral] strength; **ter** ~ **para fazer algo** to have (the) strength to do sthg; ~ **de vontade** will power. **-3.** [violência] force; **à** ~ by force; **com** ~ violently. **-4.** [esforço]: **fazer** ~ to try hard. **-5.** MIL force; ~**s armadas** armed forces. **-6.** [causa]: **motivo de** ~ **maior** due to unavoidable circumstances; **por** ~ **de** by force of. **-7.** [ânimo, apoio]: **dar** ~ **a alguém** to give support to sb.
➡ **força de expressão** *f* understatement.

forcado [foxˈkadul] *m* pitchfork.

forçado, da [foxˈsadu, dal] *adj* -**1.** [ger] forced. **-2.** [interpretação] far-fetched.

forçar [13] [foxˈsa(x)] *vt* -**1.** [obrigar]: ~ **alguém (a algo/a fazer algo)** to force sb (to sthg/to do sthg). **-2.** [arrombar] to force. **-3.** [obter por força] to (obtain by) force. **-4.** [vista, voz] to strain. **-5.** [desvirtuar] to misinterpret. **-6.** *loc*: ~ **a barra** [insistir, pressionar] to force sb's hand.
➡ **forçar-se** *vp*: ~**-se a fazer algo** to force o.s. to do sthg, to make o.s. do sthg.

força-tarefa [ˌfoxsataˈrefal] (*pl* **forças-tarefa**) *f* task force.

fórceps [ˈfɔxsepiʃl] *m inv* forceps (*pl*).

forçosamente [foxsozaˈmẽtʃil] *adv* necessarily.

forçoso, osa [foxˈsozu, ɔzal] *adj* necessary.

forense [foˈrẽsil] *adj* judicial.

forja [ˈfɔxʒal] *f* forge.

forjado, da [foxˈʒadu, dal] *adj* -**1.** [utensílio, metal] forged. **-2.** [notícia] fabricated.

forjar [4] [foxˈsa(x)] *vt* to forge.

forma [ˈfɔxmal] *f* -**1.** [ger] form; **desta** ~ in this way, thus. **-2.** [estado físico, feitio] shape; **em** ~ **de** in the shape of; **estar em** ~ to be in shape; **estar**

fora de ~ to be out of shape. **-3.** [fila]: **entrar em** ~ to fall into line.
➡ **formas** *fpl* [silhueta] figure *(sg)*.
➡ **de forma que** *loc conj* so that.
➡ **da mesma forma** *loc adv* similarly.
➡ **de forma alguma** *loc adv* in no way.
➡ **de qualquer forma** *loc adv* all the same.
➡ **de tal forma** *loc adv* in such a way.
fôrma ['foxma] *f* **-1.** *CULIN* mould. **-2.** [molde] mould, cast. **-3.** [de sapato] last.
formação [foxma'sãw] *(pl* -ões) *f* **-1.** [ger] formation. **-2.** [educação] upbringing.
formado, da [fox'madu, da] *adj* **-1.** [constituído]: ~ **por** made up of. **-2.** [graduado]: **ser** ~ **por** to be educated by.
formador, ra [foxma'do(x), ra] *adj*: ~ **de vício** habit-forming, addictive; ~ **de opinião** opinion-making.
formal [fox'maw] *(pl* -ais) *adj* formal.
formalidade [foxmali'dadʒi] *f* formality; **com** ~ formally.
formalismo [foxma'liʒmu] *m* **-1.** [convencionalismo] formality. **-2.** *ARTE* formalism.
formalizar [4] [foxmali'za(x)] *vt* **-1.** [ger] to formalize. **-2.** [estruturar] to formulate.
formando, da [fox'mãndu, da] *m, f* finalist.
formão [fox'mãw] *(pl* -ões) *m* chisel.
formar [4] [fox'ma(x)] <> *vt* **-1.** [ger] to form. **-2.** [educar] to educate. <> *vi* *MIL* [entrar em fila] to fall in.
➡ **formar-se** *vp* **-1.** [constituir-se] to form. **-2.** [graduar-se] to graduate.
formatar [4] [foxma'ta(x)] *vt* *COMPUT* to format.
formativo, va [foxma'tʃivu, va] *adj* formative.
formato [fox'matu] *m* **-1.** [forma] shape. **-2.** [modelo] format.
formatura [foxma'tura] *f* *EDUC* graduation.
fórmica ['fɔxmika] *f* formica®.
formidável [foxmi'davew] *(pl* -eis) *adj* **-1.** [fantástico] fantastic. **-2.** [imenso] formidable.
formiga [fox'miga] *f* ant.
formigamento [foxmiga'mẽntu] *m* pins and needles.
formigar [14] [foxmi'ga(x)] *vi* **-1.** [coçar] to have pins and needles. **-2.** *fig* [abundar]: ~ **de** to swarm with.
formigueiro [foxmi'gejru] *m* **-1.** [de formigas] anthill. **-2.** *fig* [multidão] swarm.
formol [fox'mɔw] *(pl* -óis) *m* formaldehyde.
formoso, osa [fox'mozu, ɔza] *adj* beautiful.
formosura [foxmo'zura] *f* beauty.
fórmula ['fɔxmula] *f* **-1.** [ger] formula. **-2.** [modo] (polite) phrase, (politeness) formula. **-3.** *AUTO*: ~ **um** Formula One.
formulação [foxmula'sãw] *(pl* -ões) *f* formulation.
formular [4] [foxmu'la(x)] *vt* to formulate.
formulário [foxmu'larju] *m* form; ~ **contínuo** *COMPUT* continuous stationery.
fornalha [fox'naʎa] *f* furnace.
fornecedor, ra [foxnese'do(x), ra] *(mpl* -es, *fpl* -s)

<> *adj* supplying. <> *m, f* supplier.
fornecer [25] [foxne'se(x)] *vt* to supply.
fornecimento [foxnesi'mẽntu] *m* supply.
fornicar [12] [foxni'ka(x)] *vi* to fornicate.
forno ['foxnu] *m* **-1.** *CULIN* oven; ~ **de microondas** microwave (oven). **-2.** [fornalha] kiln. **-3.** *fig* [lugar quente]: **ser/estar um** ~ to be like an oven.
foro ['foru] *m* forum.
forquilha [fox'kiʎa] *f* pitchfork.
forra ['fɔxa] *f*: **ir à** ~ to take one's revenge.
forração [foxa'sãw] *(pl* -ões) *f* filling.
forragem [fo'xaʒẽ] *(pl* -ns) *f* forage.
forrar [4] [fo'xa(x)] *vt* **-1.** [ger] to line. **-2.** [sofá, chão] to cover. **-3.** [parede] to paper.
forro ['foxu] *m* **-1.** [interno] lining. **-2.** [externo] cover.
forró [fo'xɔ] *m* typical Brazilian dance of the north-east.
fortalecer [25] [foxtale'se(x)] *vt* to strengthen.
fortalecimento [foxtalesi'mẽntu] *m* strengthening.
fortaleza [foxta'leza] *f* **-1.** [forte] fortress. **-2.** *fig* [bastião] fortress.
Fortaleza [foxta'leza] *n* Fortaleza.
forte ['fɔxtʃi] <> *adj* **-1.** [ger] strong. **-2.** [piada, palavra, filme] crude. **-3.** [poderoso] powerful. **-4.** [versado]: **ser** ~ **em algo** to be strong at sthg. **-5.** [intenso - emoção, calor, dor] intense; [- chuva] heavy. **-6.** [violento] violent. <> *m* **-1.** [fortaleza] stronghold. **-2.** *fig* [ponto forte] strength. <> *adv* heavily.
fortificação [foxtʃifika'sãw] *(pl* -ões) *f* fortification.
fortificante [foxtʃifi'kãntʃi] <> *adj* fortifying. <> *m* fortifier.
fortificar [12] [foxtʃifi'ka(x)] *vt* to fortify.
➡ **fortificar-se** *vp* to fortify o.s.
fortuitamente [foxtwita'mẽntʃi] *adv* fortuitously.
fortuito, ta [fox'twitu, ta] *adj* fortuitous.
fortuna [fox'tuna] *f* fortune.
fosco, ca ['foʃku, ka] *adj* tarnished.
fosfato [foʃ'fatu] *m* phosphate.
fosforescente [foʃfore'sẽntʃi] *adj* phosphorescent.
fosforescer [25] [foʃfore'se(x)] *vi* to phosphoresce.
fósforo ['fɔʃforu] *m* **-1.** *QUÍM* phosphor. **-2.** [palito] matchstick.
fossa ['fɔsa] *f* **-1.** [buraco] hole; ~ **nasal** nostril; ~ **das Marianas** Mariana Trench. **-2.** [esgoto] ditch. **-3.** *fig* [depressão] slump; **estar/entrarna** ~ to be down in the dumps.
fóssil ['fɔsiw] *(pl* -eis) *m* fossil.
fosso ['fosu] *m* ditch.
foto ['fɔtu] *f* photo.
fotocomposição [fotokõmpozi'sãw] *(pl* -ões) *f* photocomposition, filmsetting.
fotocópia [foto'kɔpja] *f* photocopy.
fotocopiar [16] [fotoko'pja(x)] *vt* to photocopy.
fotofobia [fotofo'bia] *f* photophobia.

fotofóbico, ca [foto'fɔbiku, ka] adj photophobic.
fotogênico, ca [foto'ʒeniku, ka] adj photogenic.
fotografar [4] [fotogra'fa(x)] vt to photograph.
fotografia [fotogra'fia] f **-1.** [técnica] photography. **-2.** [foto] photograph.
fotográfico, ca [foto'grafiku, ka] adj photographic.
fotógrafo, fa [fo'tɔgrafu, fa] m, f photographer.
fotolito [foto'litu] m plate.
fotômetro [fo'tometru] m light meter.
fotomontagem [foto'mõntaʒẽ] (pl -ns) f photomontage.
fóton [fɔtõ] (pl -tons, -nes) m [fís] photon.
fotonovela [fotono'vɛla] f photo-strip story.
fotossíntese [foto'sĩtezi] f photosynthesis.
fototerapia [fototera'pia] f phototherapy.
foxtrote [fɔks'trɔtʃi] m foxtrot.
foyer [fwa'jel m foyer.
foz ['fɔʃ] f estuary.
fração [fra'sãw] (pl -ões) f **-1.** [pedaço] bit. **-2.** MAT fraction.
fracassar [4] [fraka'sa(x)] vi to fail.
fracasso [fra'kasu] m failure.
fracionar [4] [frasjo'na(x)] vt to fragment.
fracionário, ria [frasiona'riu, ria] adj MAT fractional.
fraco, ca ['fraku, ka] adj **-1.** [ger] weak. **-2.** [medíocre]: ~ **(em)** weak (at). **-3.** [não ativo - bebida] weak; [- cigarro] mild; [- perfume] delicate.
    ◆ **fraco** <> adv weakly. <> m **-1.** [ponto fraco] weak point. **-2.** [inclinação] weakness.
frade ['fradʒi] m friar.
fragata [fra'gata] f frigate.
frágil ['fraʒiw] (pl -eis) adj fragile.
fragilidade [fraʒili'dadʒi] f fragility.
fragilizar [4] [fraʒili'za(x)] vt to make vulnerable.
fragmentação [fragmẽnta'sãw] (pl -ões) f fragmentation.
fragmentar [4] [fragmẽn'ta(x)] vt to fragment.
    ◆ **fragmentar-se** vp to fragment.
fragmento [frag'mẽntu] m fragment.
fragrância [fra'grãnsja] f fragrance.
fragrante [fra'grãntʃi] adj fragrant.
fralda ['frawda] f **-1.** [cueiro] nappy UK, diaper US. **-2.** [de camisa] shirt tail.
framboesa [frãn'bweza] f raspberry.
frame ['frejmi] m COMPUT frame.
França ['frãnsa] n France.
francamente [ˌfrãŋka'mẽntʃi] adv frankly.
francês, esa [frã'seʃ, eza] (mpl -eses, fpl -s) <> adj French. <> m, f Frenchman (f Frenchwoman).
    ◆ **francês** m [língua] French.
franco, ca ['frãŋku, ka] adj **-1.** [ger] free. **-2.** [sincero] frank. **-3.** [clara] candid.
    ◆ **franco** m [moeda] franc.
franco-atirador, ra ['frãŋkuatriʃirado(x), ra] m, f sniper.
franco-brasileiro, ra [ˌfrãŋkobrazi'lejru, ra] (mpl franco-brasileiros, fpl franco-brasileiras) adj Franco-Brazilian.

francófono, na [frãn'kɔfonu, na] <> adj French-speaking. <> m, f French speaker.
franga ['frãnga] f pullet.
frangalho [frãŋ'gaʎu] m [farrapo] tatter; **em** ~**s** fig in tatters.
frango ['frãŋgu] <> m ZOOL chicken. <> m FUT easy goal.
franja ['frãnʒa] f fringe.
franjado, da [frãn'ʒadu, da] adj **-1.** [cabelo, xale] fringed. **-2.** [rebuscado] recherché.
franqueado, da [frãn'keadu, da] m franchise.
franquear [15] [frãŋ'kja(x)] vt **-1.** [liberar]: **a entrada foi franqueada, vamos à festa!** they've opened the doors, let's party! **-2.** [isentar de imposto] to exempt (from). **-3.** [pagar o transporte] to pay transport costs (for). **-4.** [ceder franquia] to franchise.
franqueza [frãŋ'keza] f frankness.
franquia [frãŋ'kia] f **-1.** COM franchise. **-2.** [isenção] exemption; ~ **de bagagem** baggage allowance; ~ **postal** postage.
franzido, da [frãn'zidu, da] adj **-1.** [saia] gathered, pleated. **-2.** [pele] wrinkled.
franzino, na [frã'zinu, na] adj delicate.
franzir [6] [frãn'zi(x)] vt **-1.** [preguear] to pleat. **-2.** [enrugar] to wrinkle; ~ **a sobrancelha** to frown.
fraque ['fraki] m frock coat.
fraquejar [4] [frake'ʒa(x)] vi to weaken.
fraqueza [fra'keza] f weakness.
frasco ['fraʃku] m flask.
frase ['frazi] f **-1.** [oração] sentence; ~ **feita** aphorism. **-2.** MÚS phrase.
fraseado [fra'zjadu] m phrasing.
fraseologia [frazjolo'gia] f phraseology.
frasqueira [fraʃ'kejra] f bottle rack.
fraternal [fratex'naw] (pl -ais) adj fraternal, brotherly.
fraternidade [fratexni'dadʒi] f fraternity.
fraterno, na [fra'tɛxnu, na] adj fraternal, brotherly.
fratricida [fratri'sida] mf fratricide.
fratura [fra'tura] f fracture.
fraturar [4] [fratu'ra(x)] vt to fracture.
fraudar [4] [fraw'da(x)] vt to defraud.
fraude ['frawdʒi] f fraud.
fraudulento, ta [frawdu'lẽntu, ta] adj fraudulent.
freada [fre'ada] f braking; **dar uma** ~ to brake.
frear [15] [fre'a(x)] <> vt **-1.** AUTO to brake. **-2.** fig [controlar] to curb. <> vi AUTO to brake.
freático, ca [fre'atʃiku, ka] adj: **lençol** ~ water table; **camada freática** aquifer.
freelance [fri'lãnsi] <> adj freelance. <> mf freelance, freelancer.
freeware [fri'wari] (pl freewares) m COMPUT freeware.
freezer ['frizɛx] (pl -res) m freezer.
frege ['frɛʒi] m quarrel.
freguês, esa [fre'geʃ, eza] (mpl -eses, fpl -s) m, f **-1.** [cliente] customer. **-2.** [paroquiano] parishioner.

freguesia [frege'zia] *f* **-1.** [clientela] clientele. **-2.** [paroquia] parish.

frei [frej] *m* friar.

freio ['freju] *m* **-1.** [cavalo] rein. **-2.** [carro] brake; ~ **de mão** handbrake; ~ **de pé** footbrake.

freira ['frejra] *f* nun.

freixo ['frejʃu] *m* ash.

fremir [6] [fre'mi(x)] *vi* **-1.** [rugir] to roar. **-2.** [tremer] to tremble.

frêmito ['fremitu] *m* shiver.

frenesi [frene'zi] *m* frenzy.

freneticamente [frenɛtʃika'mẽntʃi] *adv* frenetically.

frenético, ca [fre'nɛtʃiku, ka] *adj* frenetic.

frente ['frẽtʃi] *f* **-1.** [lado dianteiro]: **na** ~ **(de)** in front (of). **estar à** ~ **de** *fig* to be ahead of. **-2.** [avante]: **em** ~ ahead; **ir para a** ~ to move on; **levar algo à** ~ to make sthg succeed. **-3.** [resistência] front; ~ **de combate** frontline. **-4.** [presença] in front of; ~ **a** ~ face to face. **-5.** METEOR: ~ **fria/quente** cold/warm front.

frentista [frẽn'tʃiʃta] *mf* forecourt attendant.

freqüência [fre'kwẽnsja] *f* **-1.** [ger] frequency; **com** ~ frequently. **-2.** [pessoas] attendance.

freqüentador, ra [frekwẽnta'do(x), ra] *m, f* regular.

freqüentar [4] [frekwẽn'ta(x)] *vt* **-1.** [visitar] to frequent. **-2.** [cursar] to attend.

freqüente [fre'kwẽntʃi] *adj* recurrent.

freqüentemente [frekwẽntʃi'mẽntʃi] *adv* frequently.

fresa ['freza] *f* MEC milling cutter, drill.

fresca ['freʃka] *f* ⊳ **fresco**.

frescão [freʃ'kãw] (*pl* **-ões**) *m* de luxe coach.

fresco, ca ['freʃku, ka] *adj* **-1.** [ger] fresh. **-2.** [ameno] cool. **-3.** *fam* [luxento] posh. **-4.** *fam* [homossexual] camp.

 ➡ **fresca** *f* [aragem] breeze.

frescobol [freʃko'bɔw] (*pl* **-óis**) *m* beach tennis.

frescões [freʃ'kõjʃ] *mpl* ⊳ **frescão**.

frescor [freʃ'ko(x)] *m* [viço, vigor] freshness.

frescura [freʃ'kura] *f* **-1.** [frescor] freshness. **-2.** [afetação] affectation. **-3.** [formalidade] convention.

fresta ['frɛʃta] *f* slit.

fretado, da [fre'tadu, da] *adj* **-1.** [navio, caminhão] chartered. **-2.** [carro] hired.

fretar [4] [fre'ta(x)] *vt* to hire *UK*, to rent *US*.

frete ['frɛtʃi] *m* freight; **fazer** ~ to freight.

freudiano, na [frɔj'dʒanu, na] *adj* Freudian.

frevo ['frevu] *m* Brazilian carnival street-dance, where dancers improvise their own dances.

fria ['fria] *f fam* [apuros] fix; **entrar numa** ~ to be in a fix.

friagem ['frjaʒẽ] *f* cold.

fricção [frik'sãw] *f* friction.

friccionar [4] [friksjo'na(x)] *vt* to rub.

fricote [fri'kɔtʃi] *m*: **fazer** ~**s** to put on airs.

fricoteiro, ra [friko'tejru, ra] ⟨⟩ *adj* vain. ⟨⟩ *m, f* show-off.

frieira [fri'ejra] *f* chilblain.

frieza ['frjeza] *f* **-1.** [insensibilidade] cold-heartedness. **-2.** [desinteresse] off-handedness.

frigideira [friʒi'dejra] *f* frying pan.

frigidez [friʒi'deʒ] *f* frigidity.

frígido, da ['friʒidu, da] *adj* frigid.

frigir [63] [fri'ʒi(x)] *vt* to fry.

frigorífico [frigo'rifiku] *m* **-1.** [loja] cold store. **-2.** [aparelho] fridge, refrigerator.

frila ['frila] *mf fam* freelance.

frio, fria ['friu, 'fria] *adj* **-1.** [sem calor] cold. **-2.** [insensível] cold. **-3.** [falso] fake. **-4.** [cor] cold. **-5.** [luz] cold.

 ➡ **frio** *m* [baixa temperatura] cold; **estar com** ~ to be cold; **fazer** ~ to be cold.

 ➡ **frios** *mpl* [carne] cold meats.

friorento, ta [frjo'rẽntu, ta] *adj* chilly.

frisa ['friza] *f* TEATRO box.

frisar [4] [fri'za(x)] *vt* **-1.** [salientar] to highlight. **-2.** [enrolar] to curl.

friso ['frizu] *m* **-1.** [borda] border. **-2.** ARQUIT frieze.

fritada [fri'tada] *f* fried food.

fritar [4] [fri'ta(x)] *vt* to fry.

frito, ta ['fritu, ta] *adj* **-1.** CULIN fried. **-2.** *fam* [em apuros]: **estar** ~ to be in hot water.

 ➡ **fritas** *fpl* chips *UK*, (French) fries *US*.

fritura [fri'tura] *f* fried food, fry-up *UK*.

frivolidade [frivoli'dadʒi] *f* frivolity.

frívolo, la ['frivolu, la] *adj* frivolous.

frondoso, osa [frõn'dozu, ɔza] *adj* leafy.

fronha ['froɲa] *f* pillowcase.

front [frõ] *m* MIL front.

frontal [frõn'taw] (*pl* **-ais**) *adj* frontal.

fronte ['frõntʃi] *f* forehead.

fronteira [frõn'tejra] *f* ⊳ **fronteiro**.

fronteiriço, ça [frõntej'risu, sa] *adj* border (antes de subst).

fronteiro, ra [frõn'tejru, ra] *adj* facing.

 ➡ **fronteira** *f* **-1.** [extremidade] border. **-2.** *fig* [limite] border.

frontispício [frõntʃiʃ'pisju] *m* frontispiece.

frota ['frɔta] *f* fleet.

frouxo, xa ['froʃu, ʃa] *adj* **-1.** [folgado] loose. **-2.** [fraco, ineficiente] weak. **-3.** [condescendente]: **ser** ~ **com alguém** to be weak with sb. **-4.** [covarde] feeble.

frufru [fru'fru] *m* frill, frou-frou.

frugal [fru'gaw] (*pl* **-ais**) *adj* frugal.

frugalidade [frugali'dadʒi] *f* frugality.

fruição [frwi'sãw] *f* fruition.

fruir [74] ['frwi(x)] *vi*: ~ **de algo** to enjoy sthg.

frustração [fruʃtra'sãw] (*pl* **-ões**) *f* **-1.** [malogro] frustration. **-2.** [decepção] frustration.

frustrado, da [fruʃ'tradu, da] *adj* **-1.** [malogrado] frustrated. **-2.** [decepcionado] disappointed.

frustrante [fruʃ'trãntʃi] *adj* frustrating.

frustrar [4] [fruʃ'tra(x)] *vt* **-1.** [malograr] to frustrate. **-2.** [decepcionar] to cheat. **-3.** [privar]: ~ **alguém de algo** to deprive sb of sthg.

 ➡ **frustrar-se** *vp* **-1.** [malograr-se] to be frustrated. **-2.** [decepcionar-se] to be disappointed.

fruta [ˈfrutal] *f* fruit.

fruta-de-conde [ˌfrutadʒiˈkõndʒil] (*pl* **frutas-de-conde**) *f* custard apple.

fruta-pão [ˌfrutaˈpãwl] (*pl* **frutas-pães, frutas-pão**) *f* breadfruit.

fruteiro, ra [fruˈtejru, ral] *adj* fruit-loving.
➡ **fruteira** *f* fruit tree.

frutífero, ra [fruˈtʃiferu, ral] *adj* **-1.** [árvore] fruit-bearing. **-2.** [proveitoso] fruitful.

fruto [ˈfrutul] *m* **-1.** [fruta] fruit. **-2.** *fig* [resúltado] fruit.

FTP (*abrev de* File Transfer Protocol) *m* FTP.

fubá [fuˈbal] *m* **-1.** [de milho] maize flour. **-2.** [de arroz] rice flour.

fuça [ˈfusal] *f fam* [focinho] conk, nose; **nas ~s de** under the nose of.

fuçar [13] [fuˈsa(x)] *fam* ⬦ *vt* to meddle in. ⬦ *vi* to meddle.

fuga [ˈfugal] *f* **-1.** [escapada] escape. **-2.** *fig* [alívio] escape. **-3.** *MÚS* fugue.

fugaz [fuˈgaʒl] *adj* fleeting.

fugida [fuˈʒidal] *f* escape; **dar uma ~** to make one's escape.

fugidio, dia [fuˈʒidio, dial] *adj* **-1.** [animal] skittish. **-2.** [pessoa, personalidade] retiring.

fugir [62] [fuˈʒi(x)] *vi* **-1.** [escapar]: **~ (de)** to escape (from). **-2.** [evitar]: **~ de algo/alguém** to avoid sthg/sb.

fugitivo, va [fuʒiˈtʃivu, val] ⬦ *adj* fugitive. ⬦ *m, f* fugitive.

fulano, na [fuˈlanu, nal] *m, f* so-and-so; **~ de tal** some so-and-so; **~, beltrano e sicrano** Tom, Dick or Harry.

fuleiro, ra [fuˈlejru, ral] *adj* shabby.

fúlgido, da [ˈfuwʒidu, dal] *adj* dazzling.

fulgir [78] [fuwˈʒi(x)] *vi* to dazzle.

fulgor [fuwˈgo(x)] *m* brilliance.

fulgurante [fuwguˈrãntʃil] *adj* shining.

fuligem [fuˈliʒěl] *f* soot.

fulminante [fuwmiˈnãntʃil] *adj* **-1.** [mortal] deadly. **-2.** *fig* [irado] vicious.

fulminar [4] [fuwmiˈna(x)] *vt* **-1.** [matar] to kill. **-2.** [aniquilar] to annihilate.

fulo, la [ˈfulu, lal] *adj*: **estar** *ou* **ficar ~ da vida** to be totally fed up.

fumaça [fuˈmasal] *f* smoke; **e lá vai ~** something or other.

fumaceira [fumaˈsejral] *f* (cloud of) smoke.

fumante [fuˈmãntʃil] *mf* smoker; **não ~** non-smoker.

fumar [4] [fuˈma(x)] ⬦ *vt* to smoke. ⬦ *vi* to smoke.

fumê [fuˈmel] *adj inv* smoky.

fumegante [fumeˈgãntʃil] *adj* steaming.

fumegar [4] [fumeˈga(x)] *vi* **-1.** [fumaçar] to smoke. **-2.** *fig* [enfurecer-se] to blow up.

fumo [ˈfumul] *m* **-1.** [tabaco] tobacco. **-2.** [maconha] dope; **puxar ~** to draw (on a spliff). **-3.** [vício] smoking.

fumódromo [fuˈmɔdromul] *m fam* smoking area.

FUNAI (*abrev de* Fundação Nacional do Índio) *f* Brazilian government organization for the protection of the indigenous population.

FUNARTE (*abrev de* Fundação Nacional de Arte) *f* Brazilian government organization for the promotion of artistic activities.

FUNASA (*abrev de* Fundação Nacional de Saúde) *f* Brazilian government organization for health education and prevention of disease among indigenous peoples.

função [fũnˈsãwl] (*pl* **-ões**) *f* **-1.** [cargo] function. **-2.** [responsabilidade] function. **-3.** [utilidade] role. **-4.** [espetáculo] performance. **-5.** [papel] function. **-6.** [atribuição] function. **-7.** *GRAM* function. **-8.** *MAT* function.
➡ **em função de** *loc prep* due to.

funcional [fũnsjoˈnawl] (*pl* **-ais**) *adj* **-1.** [ger] functional.- **2.** [público] civil-service. **-3.** [de carreira] service-related.

funcionalidade [fũnsjonaliˈdadʒil] *f* functionality.

funcionalismo [fũnsjonaˈliʒmul] *m* **-1.** [praticidade] practicality. **-2.** [servidores]: **~ público** civil service.

funcionamento [fũnsjonaˈmẽntul] *m* functioning; **horário de ~** opening hours, working hours.

funcionar [4] [fũsjoˈna(x)] *vi* **-1.** [máquina *etc*] to work; **pôr algo para ~** to switch sthg on. **-2.** [loja *etc*] to be open. **-3.** [exercer função]: **~ como algo** to work as sthg. **-4.** [dar certo] to work.

funcionário, ria [fũsjoˈnarju, rjal] *m, f* employee; **~ público** civil servant.

funções [fũnˈsõjʃl] *fpl* ⬭ **função.**

fundação [fũndaˈsãwl] (*pl* **-ões**) *f* **-1.** [alicerce] foundation. **-2.** [instituição] foundation. **-3.** [criação] founding.

fundador, ra [fũndaˈdo(x), ral] ⬦ *adj* founding. ⬦ *m, f* founder.

fundamentação [fũndamẽntaˈsãwl] (*pl* **-ões**) *f* foundation.

fundamental [fũndamẽnˈtawl] (*pl* **-ais**) *adj* fundamental.

fundamentalismo [fũndamẽntaˈliʒmul] *m RELIG* fundamentalism.

fundamentalista [fũndamẽntaˈliʃtal] ⬦ *adj* fundamentalist. ⬦ *mf* fundamentalist.

fundamentar [4] [fũndamẽnˈta(x)] *vt* **-1.** [basear]: **~ algo em algo** to base sthg on sthg. **-2.** [justificar] to found.
➡ **fundamentar-se** *vp* [basear-se]: **~-se em algo** to be based on sthg.

fundamento [fũndaˈmẽntul] *m* fundament; **sem ~** unfounded.

FUNDAP (*abrev de* Fundação do Desenvolvimento Administrativo) *f* Brazilian organization for the coordination of training and educational programmes.

fundar [4] [fũnˈda(x)] *vt* **-1.** [instituir] to found. **-2.** [criar] to establish.

fundear [15] [fũnˈdʒja(x)] *vi* to drop anchor.

fundição [fũdʒiˈsãwl] (*pl* **-ões**) *f* melting down.

fundilho [fũn'dʒiʎul *m* seat, bottom.
fundir [6] [fũn'dʒi(x)] *vt* -**1.** [derreter] to melt. -**2.**
[moldar] to cast. -**3.** [incorporar] to merge. -**4.** *fam*
[perturbar]: ~ **a cuca de alguém** to do sb's head in.
➡ **fundir-se** *vp* -**1.** [derreter-se] to melt. -**2.**
[incorporar-se] to merge.
fundo, da [l'fũndu, da] *adj* -**1.** [profundo] deep.
-**2.** [reentrante] sunken. -**3.** *fam* [despreparado]: ~
(em algo) weak (at sthg).
➡ **fundo** ⟨⟩ *m* -**1.** [base] bottom. -**2.** [de local]
rear. -**3.** [segundo plano] background; **ao** ~ in the
distance. -**4.** [de tecido, papel] background. -**5.**
MÚS: ~ musical background music. -**6.** [íntimo]:
eu o perdoei do ~ **da alma** I forgave him from
the bottom of my heart. -**7.** *fig* [teor] element.
-**8.** *FIN* fund; ~ **de garantia** security; ~ **de inves-**
timento investment fund; **emprestei-lhe dinhei-**
ro a ~ **perdidos** I lent him some money
without expecting repayment. -**9.** *MED*: ~ **do**
olho back of the eye. ⟨⟩ *adv* [profundamente]
deeply; **a** ~ in depth.
➡ **fundos** *mpl* -**1.** [de casa] funds. -**2.** [capital]
capital; **cheque sem** ~ unsecured cheque.
➡ **no fundo** *loc adv* [intrinsecamente] basically.
fundura [fũn'dura] *f* depth.
fúnebre ['funebri] *adj* funereal.
funeral [fune'raw] (*pl* -**ais**) *m* funeral.
funerário, ria [fune'rarju, rja] *adj* funeral (antes
de subst).
➡ **funerária** *f* funeral parlour.
funesto, ta [fu'nɛʃtu, ta] *adj* dire.
fungar [14] [fũŋ'ga(x)] *vi* to sniff.
fungicida [fũnʒi'sida] *m* fungicide.
fungo ['fũŋgu] *m* fungus.
funicular [funiku'la(x)] ⟨⟩ *adj* funicular. ⟨⟩ *m*
-**1.** [sistema] funicular. -**2.** [veículo] cable car.
funil [fu'niw] (*pl* -**is**) *m* funnel.
funilaria [funi'laria] *f* panel beating.
funileiro [funi'lejru] *f* panel beater.
FUNRURAL (de abrev **Fundo de Assistência e**
Previdência ao Trabalhador Rural) *m* Brazilian
fund for the assistance and support of rural
workers.
furacão [fura'kãw] (*pl* -**ões**) *m* -**1.** [ciclone] cyclone.
-**2.** *fig* [turbilhão] maelstrom; **como um** ~ like a
whirlwind.
furadeira [fura'dejra] *f* drill.
furado, da [fu'radu, da] *adj* -**1.** [pneu] punctured.
-**2.** [orelha] pierced. -**3.** [sapato] holey. -**4.** *fam*
[infrutífero] unsuccessful.
fura-greve ['furagrevi] *mf* blackleg.
furão, rona [fu'rãw, rɔna] (*mpl* -**ões**, *fpl* -**s**) *adj* [ca-
vador] unreliable.
furar [4] [fu'ra(x)] ⟨⟩ *vt* -**1.** [pneu] to puncture.
-**2.** [orelha] to pierce. -**3.** [sapato] to make a hole
in. -**4.** [frustrar] to fail. -**5.** [não aderir a] to leave.
⟨⟩ *vi* -**1.** [perfurar] to puncture. -**2.** [sapato] to get
a hole. -**3.** [malograr] to fail.
furgão [fux'gãw] (*pl* -**ões**) *m* van.
fúria ['furja] *f* fury; **estar/ficar uma** ~ to be in a
fury.

furibundo, da [furi'bũndu, da] *adj* livid, in-
censed.
furioso, osa [fu'rjozu, ɔza] *adj* -**1.** [raivoso]
furious. -**2.** [violento] furious.
furo ['furul *m* -**1.** [buraco] puncture. -**2.** [orelha]
hole. -**3.** [sapato] hole. -**4.** *fig* [falha] mistake;
dar um ~ to put one's foot in it. -**5.** *JORN*: ~ **(de**
reportagem) scoop.
furões [fu'rõjʃ] *mpl* ▷ **furão**.
furona [fu'ronal *f* ▷ **furão**.
furor [fu'ro(x)] *m* -**1.** [fúria] fury. -**2.** [arrebatamen-
to]: **fazer algo com** ~ to do sthg furiously. -**3.** *loc*:
causar ~ to cause fury.
furreca [fu'xɛkal *adj fam* mean.
furta-cor [ˌfuxta'ko(x)] (*pl* **furta-cores**) *adj* iridescent.
furtar [4] [fux'ta(x)] ⟨⟩ *vt* [roubar] to steal. ⟨⟩ *vi*
[roubar] to steal.
➡ **furtar-se** *vp* [esquivar-se]: ~-**se a algo** to
dodge sthg.
furtivo, va [fux'tʃivu, va] *adj* -**1.** [às ocultas]
furtive. -**2.** [dissimulado] furtive.
furto ['fuxtul *m* theft.
furúnculo [fu'rũŋkulul *m* boil.
fusão [fu'zãwl (*pl* -**ões**) *f* -**1.** [ger] fusion. -**2.** *COM*
amalgamation. -**3.** [liga] amalgam.
fuseau [fu'zol *m* leggings (*pl*).
fuselagem [fuze'laʒẽl (*pl* -**ns**) *f* fuselage.
fusível [fu'zivewl (*pl* -**eis**) *m* fuse.
fuso ['fuzul *m* [peça] screw.
➡ **fuso horário** *m* time zone.
fusões [fu'zõjʃl *fpl* ▷ **fusão**.
fustigar [14] [fuʃtʃi'ga(x)] *vt* to whip.
futebol [futʃi'bɔwl *m* football; ~ **de salão** five-a-
side football.

FUTEBOL

Football is one of the great passions of the Brazilian
people, who have made an art form of their most
popular sport. Five times World Cup champions ('58,
'62, '70, '94 and 2002), the Brazilians export their star
players throughout the world, especially to Spain and
Italy. The pride of the nation, Pelé, is considered the
greatest football player of all time.

futebolismo [futʃibo'liʒmul *m* [paixão] football
mania.
futebolista [futʃibo'liʃtal *mf* -**1.** [jogador]
footballer. -**2.** [fã] football fan. -**3.** [conhecedor]
football expert.
futebolístico, ca [futʃibo'liʃtʃiku, kal *adj* football (antes de subst).
futevôlei [futʃi'volejl *m* ESP *sport practised on the*
beach and following the rules of volleyball but
in which the hands are not allowed to touch the
ball.
fútil ['futʃiwl (*pl* -**eis**) *adj* -**1.** [leviano] frivolous. -**2.**
[insignificante] trivial.
futilidade [futʃili'dadʒil *f* -**1.** [leviandade] frivolity.
-**2.** [insignificância] triviality. -**3.** [coisa fútil]
triviality.

futrica [fuˈtrika] f rag; **correr ~s (com)** to rag.
futurista [futuˈriʃta] adj futuristic.
futuro, ra [fuˈturu, ra] adj future.
➧ **futuro** m -1. [tempo] future. -2. [destino] future. -3. GRAM future.
FUVEST (abrev de **Fundação do Vestibular do Estado de São Paulo**) f organization regulating entrance examinations at some universities in São Paulo.
fuxicar [12] [fuʃiˈka(x)] vt to gossip.
fuxico [fuˈʃiku] m gossip.
fuxiqueiro, ra [fuʃiˈkejru, ra] <> adj gossipy. <> m, f gossip.
fuzil [fuˈziw] (pl -is) m rifle.
fuzilamento [fuzilaˈmẽntu] m shooting.
fuzilante [fuziˈlãntʃi] adj -1. [ameaçador] threatening. -2. [fatal] fatal.
fuzilar [4] [fuziˈla(x)] <> vt -1. [atirar] to shoot. -2. fig [ameaçar]: **~ alguém com os olhos** to look daggers at sb. <> vi fig: **~ (de ódio)** [pessoa] to radiate hatred; [olhos] to flash.
fuzileiro [fuziˈlejru] m rifleman; **~ naval** marine.
fuzuê [fuˈzwe] m party.

g¹, G [ʒe] m [letra] g, G.
g² (abrev de **grama**) m g.
gabar-se [4] [gabaxˈsi] vp: **~-se (de)** to boast (about).
gabardine [gabaxˈdʒini] m gaberdine.
gabaritado, da [gabariˈtadu, da] adj high-calibre.
gabaritar [4] [gabariˈta(x)] vt to enable.
➧ **gabaritar-se** vp to be able.
gabarito [gabaˈritu] m -1. [qualidade] high calibre. -2. [respostas] results (pl). -3. [limite] maximum size.
gabinete [gabiˈnetʃi] m -1. [escritório] study. -2. POL cabinet.
gado [ˈgadu] m cattle.
gaélico, ca [gaˈɛliku, ka] adj Gaelic.
➧ **gaélico** m [língua] Gaelic.
gafanhoto [gafãˈɲotu] m grasshopper.
gafe [ˈgafi] f gaffe.
gafieira [gaˈfjejra] f -1. [baile] ball. -2. [dança] dance.
gagá [gaˈga] adj gaga.
gago, ga [ˈgagu, ga] <> adj stammering. <> m, f stammerer.

gagueira [gaˈgejra] f stammer.
gaguejar [4] [gageˈʒa(x)] vt & vi to stammer.
gaiato, ta [gaˈjatu, ta] adj mischievous.
gaiola [gaˈjɔla] <> f -1. [clausura] cage. -2. fam [prisão] jail. <> m [vapor] steamboat.
gaita [ˈgajta] f -1. MÚS mouth organ; **~ de foles** bagpipe. -2. fam fig [dinheiro] dosh.
gaivota [gajˈvɔta] f seagull.
gala [ˈgala] f: **de ~** gala; **uniforme de ~** dress uniform.
galã [gaˈlã] m -1. [ator] lead. -2. [sedutor] playboy.
galáctico, ca [gaˈlaktʃiku, ka] adj galactic.
galante [gaˈlãntʃi] adj gallant.
galanteador [galãntʃjaˈdo(x)] adj gallant.
galantear [15] [galãnˈtʃja(x)] vt to play the gallant.
galanteio [galãnˈteju] m gallantry.
galão [gaˈlãw] (pl -ões) m -1. MIL stripe. -2. [enfeite] braid. -3. [medida] gallon.
Galápagos [gaˈlapaguʃ] npl: **as (ilhas) ~** the Galapagos (Islands).
galardão [galaxˈdãw] (pl -ões) m reward.
galáxia [gaˈlaksja] f galaxy.
galé [gaˈlɛ] f galley.
galera [gaˈlɛra] f -1. NÁUT galley. -2. fam [grupo] crowd.
galeria [galeˈria] f -1. TEATRO circle. -2. [coleção] collection. -3. [canalização] drainage. -4. [loja de arte] gallery. -5. [centro comercial] shopping centre.
Gales [ˈgaliʃ] n: **País de ~** Wales.
galês, esa [gaˈleʃ, eza] <> adj Welsh. <> m, f Welshman (f Welshwoman).
➧ **galês** m [língua] Welsh.
galeto [gaˈletu] m roast poussin.
galgar [14] [gawˈga(x)] vt -1. [saltar] to jump across. -2. [subir] to climb. -3. fig [ascender] to move up.
galhardia [gaʎaxˈdʒia] f -1. [elegância] smartness. -2. [bravura] bravery.
galhardo, da [gaˈʎaxdu, da] adj -1. [elegante] smart. -2. [bravo] gallant.
galheta [gaˈʎeta] f cruet.
galheteiro [gaʎeˈtejru] m cruet-stand.
galho [ˈgaʎu] m -1. BOT branch. -2. fam [problema] pickle; **dar ~** to cause a pickle; **quebrar um ~** to get out of a pickle.
Galícia [gaˈlisja] n Galicia.
galicismo [galiˈsiʒmu] m Gallicism.
galináceos [galiˈnasjuʃ] mpl Galliformes.
galinha [gaˈliɲa] <> f -1. [ave] hen. -2. CULIN chicken. -3. fam [namorador] easy lay. -4. loc: a **~ do vizinho é sempre mais gorda** the grass is always greener on the other side of the fence. <> m, f fam [covarde] chicken.
galinha-d'angola [ga.liɲadãŋˈgɔla] (pl galinhas-d'angola) f guinea-fowl.
galinhagem [galiˈɲaʒẽ] f fam [bolinação] touching up.
galinha-morta [ga.liɲaˈmɔxta] (pl galinhas-mortas) mf [covarde] chicken.

galinheiro [gali'ɲejru] *m* poulterer.

galo ['galu] *m* -**1.** [ave] cockerel, rooster; ~ **de briga** *ou* **de rinha** fighting cock. -**2.** [inchaço] bump.

galocha [ga'lɔʃa] *f* galosh; **chato de** ~ drag.

galopante [galo'pãntʃil] *adj fig* galloping.

galopar [4] [galo'pa(x)] *vi* to gallop.

galope [ga'lɔpi] *m* gallop.

galpão [gaw'pãw] (*pl* -**ões**) *m* hangar.

galvanizado, da [gawvani'zadu, da] *adj* [ferro, chapa] galvanized.

galvanizar [4] [gawvani'za(x)] *vt* to galvanize.

gama ['gãma] *f* -**1.** *MÚS* scale. -**2.** *fig* [série] range.

gamado, da [ga'madu, da] *adj:* **ser/estar** ~ **por alguém** to be hooked on sb.

gamão [ga'mãw] *m* backgammon.

gamar [4] [ga'ma(x)] *vi* to be hooked; ~ **por alguém/alguém** to fall for sthg/sb.

gambá [gãn'ba] *m ZOOL* opossum; **bêbado como um** ~ *fam* drunk as a skunk.

Gâmbia ['gãnbja] *n* Gambia.

gambito [gãn'bitul] *m* [xadrez] gambit.

gamela [ga'mɛla] *f* trough.

gana ['gãna] *f* -**1.** [desejo]: ~ **de algo/de fazer algo** desire for sthg/to do sthg. -**2.** [raiva]: **ter** ~ **de alguém** to be furious with sb.

Gana ['gãna] *n* Ghana.

ganância [ga'nãnsja] *f* greed.

ganancioso, osa [ganã'sjozu, ɔza] *adj* greedy.

gancho ['gãnʃu] *m* -**1.** [peça] hook. -**2.** *COST* hook. -**3.** *fig* [recurso] bait.

gandaia [gãn'daja] *f fig* dissipation; **ele passou a noite na** ~ he spent the night in dissipation; **ontem fomos para a** ~ yesterday we went on a binge, self-indulgence; **cair na** ~ to descend into a life of dissipation.

gandaiar [gãnda'ja(x)] *vi* -**1.** [farrear] to live it up, to party. -**2.** [vadiar] to idle about.

gânglio ['gãnglju] *m* ganglion.

gangorra [gãŋ'goxa] *f* seesaw.

gangrena [gãŋ'grena] *f* gangrene.

gangrenar [4] [gãŋgre'na(x)] *vi* to become gangrenous.

gângster ['gãŋgiʃte(x)] *m* gangster.

gangue ['gãŋgi] *f* gang.

ganhador, ra [gaɲa'do(x), ra] <> *adj* winning. <> *m, f* winner.

ganha-pão [ˌgãɲa'pãw] (*pl* **ganha-pães**) *m* -**1.** [trabalho] living, livelihood. -**2.** [objeto de trabalho] livelihood.

ganhar [4] [ga'ɲa(x)] <> *vt* -**1.** [ger] to win. -**2.** [receber] to get. -**3.** [salário] to earn. -**4.** [lucrar] to gain; ~ **tempo** to gain time; **ganhou o dia quando recebeu a notícia** it made his day when he got the news. -**5.** [atingir] to reach. <> *vi* -**1.** [vencer]: ~ **de alguém** to beat sb; ~ **de alguém em algo** to outdo sb at sthg. -**2.** [como remuneração] to earn. -**3.** [lucrar]: ~ **(com)** to profit (from); **sair ganhando** to come out on top.

ganho ['gãɲu] <> *pp* > **ganhar**. <> *m* -**1.** [salário] earnings (*pl*). -**2.** [lucro] profit. -**3.** *COM:* ~ **de**

capital capital gain. -**4.** *JUR:* ~ **de causa** successful lawsuit.

ganido [ga'nidu] *m* whine.

ganir [6] [ga'ni(x)] *vi* to whine.

ganso ['gãnsu] *m* goose.

GAPA (*abrev de* **Grupo de Apoio à Prevenção à Aids**) *m* Brazilian non-governmental organization working in AIDS prevention.

garagem [ga'raʒẽl] (*pl* -**ns**) *f* garage.

garagista [gara'ʒiʃta] *mf* -**1.** [manobrista] car jockey -**2.** [proprietário] garage owner.

garanhão [gara'ɲãw] (*pl* -**ões**) *m* -**1.** [cavalo] stallion. -**2.** *fig* [homem] stud.

garantia [garãn'tʃia] *f* -**1.** [ger] guarantee. -**2.** [de dívida] collateral.

garantir [6] [garãn'tʃi(x)] *vt* -**1.** [assegurar]: ~ **algo a alguém** to assure sb of sthg; ~ **que** to guarantee that. -**2.** [prometer]: ~ **algo a alguém** to promise sb sthg. -**3.** [asseverar] to guarantee.

> **garantir-se** *vp* [defender-se]: ~**-se contra algo** to protect o.s. against sthg.

garatuja [garatu'ʒa] *f* scribble.

garbo ['gaxbu] *m* -**1.** [elegância] elegance. -**2.** [distinção] distinction.

garboso, osa [gax'bozu, ɔza] *adj* -**1.** [elegante] elegant. -**2.** [distinto] distinguished.

garça ['gaxsa] *f* heron.

garçom [gax'sõ] (*pl* -**ns**) *m* waiter.

garçonete [garso'nɛtʃi] *f* waitress.

garçonnière [gaxso'njɛ(x)] *f* love nest.

garfada [gax'fada] *f* forkful.

garfo ['gaxfu] *m* fork; **ser um bom** ~ *fig* to be a gourmet.

gargalhada [gaxga'ʎada] *f* burst of laughter; **cair na** ~ to fall about laughing; **dar** *ou* **soltar uma** ~ to burst out laughing.

gargalhar [gaxga'ʎa(x)] *vi* to roar with laughter.

gargalo [gax'galu] *m* -**1.** [de garrafa] neck. -**2.** [obstáculo] *fig* bottleneck.

garganta [gax'gãnta] *f* -**1.** *ANAT* throat; **molhar a** ~ *fam* [beber] to wet one's whistle; **não passar pela** ~ to stick in one's throat; **ter boa** ~ [ter boa voz] to have a good voice. -**2.** [desfiladeiro] mountain pass.

gargantilha [gaxgãn'tʃiʎa] *f* choker.

gargarejar [4] [gaxgare'ʒa(x)] *vi* to gargle.

gargarejo [gaxga'reʒu] *m* -**1.** [ato] gargling. -**2.** [líquido] gargle.

gari [ga'ri] *mf* roadsweeper.

garimpar [4] [garĩ'pa(x)] *vi* to prospect (for precious metals or stones).

garimpeiro, ra [garĩ'pejru, ra] *m, f* prospector.

garimpo [ga'rĩpu] *m* [mina] mining deposit.

garoa [ga'roa] *f* drizzle.

garoar [20] [gar'rwa(x)] *vi* to drizzle.

garota [ga'rota] *f* > **garoto**.

garotada [garo'tada] *f:* **a** ~ the kids (*pl*).

garoto, ta [ga'rotu, ta] *m, f* -**1.** [menino] boy, kid. -**2.** [prostituto]: ~ **de programa** prostitute.

> **garoto** *m* [chope] small glass of draught beer.

> **garota** *f* [namorada] girlfriend.

garoto-propaganda, garota-propaganda [gar͵rotapropa'gãnda, gar͵rotapropa'gãnda] (*mpl* garotos-propaganda, *fpl* garotas-propaganda) *m* cover-boy (*f* cover-girl).

garoupa [ga'ropa] *f* grouper.

garra ['gaxa] *f* -1. [de animal] claw. -2. *fig* [entusiasmo] enthusiasm; **ter** ~ to be enthusiastic.

garrafa [ga'xafa] *f* bottle; ~ **térmica** Thermos flask® *UK*, Thermos bottle® *US*.

garrafada [gaxa'fada] *f* [pancada]: **dar uma** ~ **em alguém** to hit sb with a bottle.

garrafal [gaxa'faw] (*pl* -ais) *adj fig* [imenso - letra] large; [- aviso] severe.

garrafão [gaxa'fãw] *m* flagon.

garrancho [ga'xãnʃu] *m* scrawl.

garrote [ga'xɔtʃi] *m* -1. [de tortura] garrotte *UK*, garrote *US*. -2. [torniquete] tourniquet.

garupa [ga'rupa] *f* -1. [de cavalo] hindquarters, rump. -2. [de bicicleta, moto] pillion; **andar na** ~ to ride pillion.

gás ['gajʃ] (*pl* gases) *m* -1. [fluido] gas; ~ **encanado** piped gas; ~ **natural** natural gas; ~ **carbônico** carbon dioxide; ~ **lacrimogêneo** tear gas. -2. [do intestino] wind, flatulence. -3. *fam fig* [entusiasmo] go.

gaseificar [12] [gazejfi'ka(x)] *vt* to gasify.

◆ **gaseificar-se** *vp* to be gasified.

gasoduto [gazo'dutu] *m* gas pipeline.

gasóleo [ga'zɔlju] *m* diesel.

gasolina [gazo'lina] *f* petrol *UK*, gasoline *US*.

gasômetro [ga'zometru] *m* gasometer.

gasoso, osa [ga'zozu, ɔza] *adj* fizzy.

◆ **gasosa** *f* fizzy drink *UK*, soda *US*.

gastador, ra [gaʃta'do(x), ra] <> *adj* wasteful. <> *m, f* wasteful person.

gastar [4] [gaʃ'ta(x)] <> *vt* -1. [despender] to spend. -2. [consumir- energia, gasolina] to consume; [- tempo] to take up. -3. [usar - roupa, sapato] to wear; [- cosmético, produto] to use. -4. [desperdiçar] to waste. -5. [desgastar] to wear out. <> *vi* -1. [despender dinheiro] to spend money. -2. [desgastar-se] to wear out.

◆ **gastar-se** *vp* [desgastar-se] to wear out.

gasto, ta ['gaʃtu, ta] <> *pp* ⊳ **gastar**. <> *adj* -1. [ger] worn out. -2. [consumido - tempo] spent; [- energia] used up; [- electricidade] consumed. -3. [despendido] spent. -4. [produto, cosmético] used up. -5. [desperdiçado] wasted. -6. [envelhecido] worn.

◆ **gasto** *m* [despesa] expense.

◆ **gastos** *mpl* [despesas] expenses; ~s **públicos** public expenditure *(sg)*.

gástrico, ca ['gaʃtriku, ka] *adj* gastric.

gastrite [gaʃ'tritʃi] *f* gastritis *(inv)*.

gastroenterite [gaʃtrẽnte'ritʃi] *f* gastroenteritis *(inv)*.

gastronomia [gaʃtrono'mia] *f* gastronomy.

gastronômico, ca [gaʃtro'nomiku, ka] *adj* gastronomic.

gastrônomo, ma [gaʃ'tronomu, ma] *m, f* gastronome.

gata ['gata] *f* ⊳ **gato**.

gateway [gejtʃi'wej] (*pl* gateways) *m COMPUT* gateway.

gatilho [ga'tʃiʎu] *m* trigger.

gatinhas [ga'tʃinaʃ] *fpl*: **andar de** ~ to go on all fours, to crawl.

gato, ta ['gatu, ta] *m, f* -1. [animal] cat; ~ **montês** wild cat; ~ **escaldado tem medo de água fria** *prov* once bitten, twice shy; **vender** ~ **por lebre** to sell a pig in a poke. -2. *fam* [pessoa] sexy person.

◆ **gato** *m ELETR* illegal electrical connection; **fazer um** ~ to make an illegal electrical connection.

gato-pingado [͵gatupĩŋ'gadu] (*pl* gatos-pingados) *m*: **havia apenas uns gatos-pingados no cinema** there was hardly a soul in the cinema.

gato-sapato [͵gatusa'patu] (*pl* gatos-sapatos) *m*: **fazer** ~ **de alguém** to treat sb like a doormat.

gatuno, na [ga'tunu, na] <> *adj* thieving. <> *m, f* thief.

gaúcho, cha [ga'uʃu, ʃa] <> *adj* Rio Grande do Sul *(antes de subst)*. <> *m, f* person from Rio Grande do Sul.

gaveta [ga'veta] *f* drawer.

gavetão [gave'tãw] (*pl* -ões) *m* large drawer.

gaveteiro [gave'tejru] *m* drawer-runner.

gavião [ga'vjãw] (*pl* -ões) *m* hawk.

gaze ['gazi] *f* -1. [tecido] gauze. -2. [para curativo] antiseptic gauze.

gazela [ga'zɛla] *f* gazelle.

gazeta [ga'zeta] *f* -1. [jornal] gazette. -2. [vadiação]: **fazer** ~ to play truant.

gazua [ga'zua] *f* skeleton key.

GB (*abrev de* **Great Britain**) *n* GB.

geada ['ʒjada] *f* frost.

gear ['ʒia(x)] *vi* to freeze.

gel [ʒɛl] *f* gel.

geladeira [ʒela'dejra] *f* refrigerator, fridge.

gelado, da [ʒe'ladu, da] *adj* -1. [comida] frozen. -2. [bebida] chilled. -3. [mar, vento] icy.

gelar [4] [ʒe'la(x)] <> *vt* -1. [comida] to freeze. -2. [bebida] to chill. <> *vi* to be freezing.

gelatina [ʒela'tʃina] *f* -1. [gel] gelatine. -2. [sobremesa] jelly *UK*, Jell-O® *US*.

gelatinoso, osa [ʒelatʃi'nozu, ɔza] *adj* gelatinous.

geléia [ʒe'lɛja] *f* jam *UK*, jelly *US*.

geleira [ʒe'lejra] *f* glacier.

gélido, da ['ʒɛlidu, da] *adj* -1. [gelado] icy. -2. *fig* [imóvel] frozen.

gelo ['ʒelu] <> *adj inv* light grey *UK*, light gray *US*. <> *m* -1. [água solidificada] ice. -2. [cor] light grey *UK*, light gray *US*. -3. *fig* [indiferença]: **dar um** ~ **em alguém** to give sb the cold shoulder; **quebrar o** ~ to break the ice. -4. *loc*: **estar um** ~ to be freezing cold.

gelo-seco [͵ʒelu'seku] (*pl* gelos-secos) *m* dry ice.

gema ['ʒema] *f* -1. [do ovo] yolk. -2. [pedra preciosa] gem.

➠ **da gema** loc adv [autêntico]: **ela é carioca da ~** she is a true carioca.

gemada [ʒe'mada] f eggnog.

gêmeo, mea ['ʒemju, mja] ⬦ adj twin. ⬦ m, f twin.

➠ **Gêmeos** mpl ASTRO Gemini; **ser Gêmeos** to be Gemini.

gemer [5] [ʒe'me(x)] vi **-1.** [de dor] to groan. **-2.** [lastimar-se] to moan. **-3.** [ranger] to wail. **-4.** fig [vento] to howl.

gemido [ʒe'midu] m **-1.** [de dor] groan. **-2.** [de animal] howl. **-3.** [lamento] wail.

geminiano, na [ʒemi'nanu, na] ⬦ adj Gemini (antes de subst). ⬦ m, f Gemini.

gene ['ʒeni] m gene.

genealogia [ʒenjalo'ʒia] f genealogy.

genealógico, ca [ʒenja'lɔʒiku, ka] adj genealogical; **árvore genealógica** family tree.

Genebra [ʒe'nɛbra] n Geneva.

general [gene'raw] (pl **-ais**) m general.

generalidade [ʒenerali'dadʒi] f **-1.** [totalidade] generality. **-2.** [maioria] majority.

➠ **generalidades** fpl [assuntos gerais] general matters.

generalização [ʒeneraliza'sãw] (pl **-ões**) f generalization.

generalizar [4] [generali'za(x)] ⬦ vi [fazer generalizações] to generalize. ⬦ vt [difundir] to spread.

➠ **generalizar-se** vp [difundir-se] to spread.

genérico, ca [ʒe'nɛriku, ka] adj generic.

gênero ['ʒenerul] m **-1.** [ger] gender; **estudos de ~** gender studies. **-2.** [tipo] kind. **-3.** [estilo] style. **-4.** BIO genus. **-5.** loc: **fazer ~** to play up.

➠ **gêneros** mpl [mercadorias] goods; **~s alimentícios** foodstuffs; **~s de primeira necessidade** essentials.

generosidade [ʒenerozi'dadʒi] f generosity.

generoso, osa [ʒene'rozu, ɔza] adj generous.

gênese ['ʒenezi] f genesis (inv).

genética [ʒe'nɛtʃika] f genetics (sg).

genético, ca [ʒe'nɛtʃiku, ka] adj genetic.

gengibre [ʒēn'ʒibri] m ginger.

gengiva [ʒēn'ʒiva] f gum.

gengivite [ʒēnʒi'vitʃi] f gingivitis.

genial [ʒe'njaw] (pl **-ais**) adj **-1.** [extraordinário] inspired. **-2.** fam [formidável] terrific.

genialidade [ʒenjali'dadʒi] f genius.

gênio ['ʒenju] m **-1.** [ger] genius; **ser um ~ (em algo)** to be a genius (at sthg). **-2.** [temperamento] nature; **~ bom/ruim** good-/bad-tempered. **-3.** MITOL genie.

genioso, osa [ʒe'njozu, ɔza] adj ill-natured.

genital [ʒeni'taw] (pl **-ais**) adj genital.

genitália [ʒeni'talja] f genitalia.

genitivo [ʒeni'tʃivu] m LING genitive.

genitor, ra [ʒeni'to(x), ra] m, f progenitor.

genocídio [ʒeno'sidʒju] m genocide.

genoma [geno'ma] m genome.

GENOMA

Brazil has played a significant part in 'Projeto Genoma', dedicated to the genetic sequencing of the DNA of living beings. The success of Brazilian researchers has contributed greatly towards the scientific recognition of the country in the field of biotechnology.

Gênova ['ʒenova] n Genoa.

genro ['ʒēnxul] m son-in-law.

gentalha [ʒēn'taʎa], **gentinha** [ʒēn'tʃiɲa] f pleb.

gente ['ʒētʃi] ⬦ f **-1.** [pessoas] people; **~ bem** upper classes; **~ grande** grown-ups; **minha ~** my family; **toda a ~** everybody; fam [amigos, colegas] folks; **oi/tchau, ~** hi/bye, folks. **-2.** [alguém] somebody, someone. **-3.** fam [nós]: **a ~ vai viajar** we're going travelling; **você quer ir com a ~?** do you want to come with us?; **o carro da ~ está enguiçado** our car has broken down. ⬦ interj [exprimindo espanto] gosh!

gentil [ʒēn'tʃiw] (pl **-is**) adj kind.

gentileza [ʒētʃi'leza] f kindness; **por ~ poderia me ajudar?** would you be so kind as to help me?

gentinha [ʒēn'tʃiɲa] f = **gentalha**.

genuíno, na [ʒe'nwinu, na] adj genuine.

geofísica [ʒew'fizika] f geophysics (sg).

geografia [ʒjogra'fia] f geography.

geográfico, ca [ʒeo'grafiku, ka] adj geographical.

geógrafo, fa [ʒe'ɔgrafu, fa] m, f geographer.

geologia [ʒjolo'ʒia] f geology.

geológico, ca [geo'lɔʒiku, ka] adj geological.

geólogo, ga [ʒe'ɔlogu, ga] m, f geologist.

geometria [ʒjome'tria] f geometry.

geométrico, ca [ʒeo'mɛtriku, ka] adj geometric.

geopolítica [geo'politika] f geopolitics.

geopolítico, ca [ʒeopo'litʃiku, ka] adj geopolitical.

geração [ʒera'sãw] (pl **-ões**) f generation; **~ espontânea** [biol] spontaneous generation; **de última ~** COMPUT & TEC latest generation.

gerador [ʒera'do(x)] (pl **-res**) adj: **empresa ~ a de empregos** job-creating company; **grupo ~ de problemas** problem-causing group.

➠ **gerador** m TEC generator.

geral [ʒe'raw] (pl **-ais**) ⬦ adj [genérico] general; **de um modo ~** on the whole. ⬦ m [o normal] normal thing. ⬦ f **-1.** FUT & TEATRO gallery. **-2.** [revisão, arrumação] spring clean; **dar uma ~ em algo** to have a blitz on sthg.

➠ **em geral** loc adv in general.

geralmente [ʒeraw'mēntʃi] adv generally.

gerânio [ʒe'rãnju] m geranium.

gerar [4] [ʒe'ra(x)] vt **-1.** [ger] to generate. **-2.** [ter filhos] to beget. **-3.** [causar] to breed.

gerativo, va [ʒera'tʃivu, va] adj generative.

gerência [ʒe'rēnsja] f management.

gerenciador [ʒerēnsja'do(x)] m COMPUT manager.

gerencial [ʒerēn'sjaw] (pl **-ais**) adj management (antes do subst).

gerenciamento [ʒerẽnsja'mẽntu] *m* management.

gerenciar [16] [ʒerẽn'sja(x)] <> *vt* to manage. <> *vi* to manage.

gerente [ʒe'rẽntʃi] *mf* manager; ~ **de vendas** sales manager.

gergelim [ʒexʒe'lĩ] *m* sesame.

geriatra [ʒe'rjatra] *mf* geriatrician.

geriatria [ʒerja'tria] *f* geriatrics *(sg)*.

geriátrico, ca [ʒe'rjatriku, ka] *adj* geriatric.

geringonça [ʒerĩ'gõnsa] *f* contraption.

gerir [57] [ʒe'ri(x)] *vt* to manage.

germânico, ca [ʒex'maniku, ka] *adj* Germanic.

germanófono, na [gexma'nɔfonu, na] <> *adj* German-speaking. <> *m,f* German speaker.

germe ['ʒexmi] *m* germ; **ser o ~ de uma idéia** to be the germ of an idea.

germicida [ʒexmi'sida] *m* germicide.

germinação [ʒexmina'sãw] (*pl* -ões) *f* germination.

germinar [4] [ʒexmi'na(x)] *vi* to germinate.

gerúndio [ʒe'rũndʒju] *m* gerund.

gesso ['ʒesu] *m* -**1.** [nas artes plásticas] plaster of Paris. -**2.** [em parede] cast.

gestação [ʒeʃta'sãw] (*pl* -ões) *f* gestation.

gestante [ʒeʃ'tãntʃi] *f* pregnant woman.

gestão [ʒeʃ'tãw] (*pl* -ões) *f* -**1.** [administração] administration. -**2.** [gerência] management.

gesticulação [ʒeʃtʃikula'sãw] (*pl* -ões) *f* gesticulation.

gesticular [4] [ʒeʃtʃiku'la(x)] *vi* to gesticulate.

gesto ['ʒɛʃtu] *m* gesture; **fazer um ~** to make a gesture.

gestual [ʒeʃ'tuaw] (*pl* -ais) *adj* gestural.

gibi [ʒi'bi] *m* comic; **não estar no ~** *fam* to be no joke.

Gibraltar [ʒibraw'ta(x)] *n* Gibraltar.

GIF (*abrev de* **Graphics Interchange Format**) *m* GIF.

gigabyte [giga'bajtʃi] (*pl* **gigabytes**) *m* COMPUT gigabyte.

gigante [ʒi'gãntʃi] <> *adj* gigantic. <> *m* giant.

gigantesco, ca [ʒigãn'teʃku, ka] *adj* gigantic.

gigolô [ʒigo'lo] *m* gigolo.

gilete® [ʒi'lɛtʃi] <> *f* [lâmina] razor blade. <> *m* *vulg* [bissexual] AC/DC.

gim ['ʒĩ] (*pl* -ns) *m* gin.

ginasial [ʒina'ziaw] (*pl* -ais) <> *adj* [relativo a ginásio] secondary school *UK*, high school *US*. <> *m* [curso] *dated* primary education.

ginásio [ʒi'nazju] *m* -**1.** EDUC secondary school. -**2.** [para esportes] gymnasium.

ginasta [ʒi'naʃta] *mf* gymnast.

ginástica [ʒi'naʃtʃika] *f* -**1.** [esporte] gymnastics *(sg)*. -**2.** [aeróbica, corretiva] exercises *(pl)*.

gincana [ʒĩ'kãna] *f* gymkhana.

ginecologia [ˌʒinekolo'ʒia] *f* gynaecology.

ginecológico, ca [ʒineko'loʒiku, ka] *adj* gynaecological.

ginecologista [ˌʒinekolo'ʒiʃta] *mf* gynaecologist.

ginete [ʒi'netʃi] *m* thoroughbred.

ginga ['ʒĩga] *f* -**1.** [remo] oar. -**2.** [movimento]: **ter ~** to be nimble.

gingar [14] [ʒĩn'ga(x)] *vi* to sway.

girafa [ʒi'rafa] *f* giraffe.

girar [4] [ʒi'ra(x)] <> *vi* -**1.** [rodar] to rotate. -**2.** *fig* [funcionar]: ~ **em torno de** to revolve around. <> *vt* [fazer rodar] to turn.

girassol [ˌʒira'sɔw] (*pl* -óis) *m* sunflower.

giratório, ria [ʒira'tɔrju, rja] *adj* revolving; **cadeira giratória** swivel chair; **ponte giratória** swing bridge.

gíria ['ʒirja] *f* -**1.** [calão] slang. -**2.** [jargão] jargon.

giro, ra [ʒ'iru, ra] *m* -**1.** [volta] rotation. -**2.** *fam* [passeio] stroll; **dar um ~** to take a stroll.

giz ['ʒiʒ] *m* chalk.

glacê [gla'se] *m* icing.

glaciação [glasia'sãw] (*pl* -ões) *f* [período geológico] glaciation.

glacial [gla'sjaw] (*pl* -ais) *adj* glacial.

gladiador [gladʒja'do(x)] *m* gladiator.

glamour [gla'mu(x)] *m* glamour *UK*, glamor *US*.

glamouroso, osa [glamu'rozu, ɔza] *adj* glamorous.

glande ['glãndʒi] *f* -**1.** [do carvalho] acorn. -**2.** ANAT glans.

glândula ['glãndula] *f* gland.

glandular [glãndu'la(x)] *adj* glandular.

glaucoma [glaw'koma] *m* glaucoma.

gleba ['glɛba] *f* field.

glicerina [glise'rina] *f* glycerine.

glicose [gli'kɔzi] *f* glucose.

global [glo'baw] (*pl* -ais) *adj* -**1.** [total] total. -**2.** [relativo ao globo] global.

globalização [globaliza'sãw] (*pl* -ões) *f* globalization.

globalizado, da [globali'zadu, da] *adj* globalized.

globalizante [globali'zãntʃi] *adj* globalizing.

globalizar [globa'liza(x)] *vt* to globalize.

 ➤ **globalizar-se** *vp* to become globalized.

globo ['globu] *m* globe; ~ **ocular** eyeball; ~ **terrestre** terrestrial globe.

globular [globu'la(x)] *adj* globular.

glóbulo ['glɔbulu] *m* globule; ~ **s brancos/vermelhos** white/red blood corpuscles.

glória ['glɔrja] *f* glory.

glorificação [glorifika'sãw] (*pl* -ões) *f* glorification.

glorificar [12] [glorifi'ka(x)] *vt* -**1.** [honrar] to glorify. -**2.** [canonizar] to canonize.

glorioso, osa [glo'rjozu, ɔza] *adj* glorious.

glosa ['glɔza] *f* gloss.

glosar [4] [glo'za(x)] *vt* -**1.** [comentar] to gloss. -**2.** [conta] to scrap.

glossário [glo'sarju] *m* glossary.

glote ['glɔtʃi] *f* ANAT glottis.

GLP (*abrev de* **Gás Liquefeito de Petróleo**) *m* LPG.

glucose [glu'kɔzi] *f* glucose.

glutão, ona [glu'tãw, ɔna] (*mpl* -ões, *fpl* -s) <> *adj* [pessoa] greedy. <> *m, f* [pessoa] glutton.

glúten ['glutẽ] (*pl* -s) *m* gluten.

glúteo, tea ['glutew, tʃial <> *adj* ANAT gluteal. <> *m* gluteus.

glutões [glu'tõjʃ] *pl* ⊳ **glutão**.

glutona [glu'tonal *f* ⊳ **glutão**.

gnomo ['gnomul *m* gnome.

GO (*abrev de* **Estado de Goiás**) *n State of Goiás*.

Gobi ['gɔbi] *m*: **o deserto de** ~ the Gobi Desert.

godê [go'del *adj* flared.

goela ['gwɛlal *f* throat.

gogó [go'gol *m fam* [pomo-de-adão] Adam's apple.

goiaba [go'jabal *f* guava.

goiabada [goja'badal *f* guava jelly.

goiabeira [goja'bejral *f* guava tree.

Goiânia [go'jãnjal *n* Goiânia.

Goiás [go'jaʃl *n* Goiás.

gol ['gowl (*pl* **-es**) *m* goal; **marcar um** ~ to score a goal.

gola ['gɔlal *f* collar; ~ **rulê** polo neck.

golaço [go'lasul *m fam* FUT great goal.

gole ['gɔlil *m* gulp; **de um** ~ **só** in one gulp; **tomar um** ~ to take a sip.

goleada [go'ljadal *f* FUT hammering.

golear [15] [go'lja(x)] *vt* FUT to thrash.

goleiro [go'lejrul *m* goalkeeper.

golfada [gow'fadal *f* [jorro] spurt. •

golfar [4] [gow'fa(x)] <> *vt* **-1.** [vomitar] to cough up. **-2.** [expelir] to spurt out. <> *vi* [sair em golfadas] to spurt out.

golfe ['gowfil *m* golf.

golfinho [gow'fiɲul *m* dolphin.

golfista [gow'fiʃtal *mf* golfer.

golfo ['gowful *m* gulf.

Golfo Pérsico [ˌgowfu'pɛxsikul *n* Persian Gulf.

golinho [gɔ'liɲul *m* sip; **aos** ~**s** in sips.

golpe ['gowpil *m* **-1.** [ger] stroke; ~ **de sorte** stroke of luck; ~ **de vista** [olhar] glance; [no trânsito] knock; ~ **de mestre** master stroke; **dar o** ~ **do baú** to marry for money. **-2.** [pancada, abalo moral] blow; [soco] punch; [de faca] slash; [de chicote] lash; **dar um** ~ **em alguém** to hit sb; ~ **baixo** *fam fig* dirty trick; ~ **mortal** mortal blow; ~ **de vento** gust of wind. **-3.** POL coup; ~ **de Estado** coup d'état.

golpear [15] [gow'pja(x)] *vt* **-1.** [dar pancada em] to hit; [com soco] to punch; [com chicote] to lash; [com faca] to slash. **-2.** [moralmente] to wound.

golpista [gow'piʃtal <> *adj* [pessoa] tricky. <> *mf* [pessoa] trickster.

goma ['gomal *f* gum, glue; ~ **de mascar** chewing gum.

gomo ['gomul *m* slice.

gôndola ['gõdulal *f* gondola.

gondoleiro [gõdo'lejrul *m* gondolier.

gongo ['gõŋgul *m* **-1.** MÚS gong. **-2.** [sino] bell.

gonorréia [gono'xɛjal *f* gonorrhoea UK, gonorrhea US.

gorar [4] [go'ra(x)] <> *vt* [fracassar] to thwart. <> *vi* [fracassar] to fail.

gordo, da ['gordu, dal <> *adj* **-1.** [pessoa] fat; **nunca ter visto alguém mais** ~ [não conhecer] not have seen sb before. **-2.** [carne] fatty. **-3.** *fig* [quantia] considerable. <> *m, f* fat person.

gorducho, cha [gox'duʃu, ʃal <> *adj* plump. <> *m, f* plump person.

gordura [gox'dural *f* **-1.** [banha] fat. **-2.** [líquida] grease. **-3.** [obesidade] fatness.

gordurento, ta [goxdu'rẽntu, tal *adj* **-1.** [gordo] fatty. **-2.** [ensebado] greasy.

gorduroso, osa [goxdu'rozu, ɔzal *adj* **-1.** [ger] greasy. **-2.** [comida] fatty.

gorila [go'rilal *m* gorilla.

gorjear [15] [gox'ʒja(x)] *vi* to chirp.

gorjeio [gox'ʒejul *m* chirp.

gorjeta [gox'ʒetal *f* tip.

gororoba [goro'rɔbal *f fam* [comida] grub, nosh; [comida ruim] muck.

gorro ['goxul *m* cap.

gosma ['gɔʒmal *f* spittle.

gosmento, ta [goʒ'mẽntu, tal *adj* slimy.

gostar [4] [goʃ'ta(x)] *vi* **-1.** [ter prazer, gosto]: ~ **de** to enjoy; ~ **de fazer algo** to enjoy doing sthg; **eu** ~ **ia de ir** I would like to go; **gostei de vê-lo feliz** it was good to see him happy; ~ **mais de algo do que de** to prefer sthg to; ~ **de alguém** [simpatizar com] to like sb; [sentir afeição por] to be fond of sb. **-2.** [aproveitar]: ~ **de** to enjoy. **-3.** [ter costume]: ~ **de fazer algo** to like doing sthg. **-4.** [aprovar]: ~ **de** to like.

⬥ **gostar-se** *vp* [mutuamente] to be fond of each other *ou* one another.

gosto ['goʃtul *m* **-1.** [ger] taste; **ter** ~ **de** to taste of; **de bom/mau** ~ in good/bad taste; **a seu** ~ to one's taste; **com** ~ tastefully; **falta de** ~ lack of taste; **para o meu** ~ for my liking. **-2.** [prazer] pleasure; **ter** ~ **em fazer algo** to enjoy doing sthg; **tomar** ~ **por algo** to take a liking to sthg.

gostoso, osa [goʃ'tozu, ɔzal *adj* **-1.** [comida, bebida] tasty. **-2.** [cheiro] lovely. **-3.** [ambiente, música] pleasant. **-4.** [cama, cadeira] comfortable. **-5.** [risada] hearty. **-6.** *fam* [sensual, bonito] gorgeous.

gostosura [goʃto'zural *f fam*: **ser uma** ~ to be lovely.

gota ['gotal *f* **-1.** [ger] drop; **ser a** ~ **d'água** to be the last straw; **ser uma** ~ **de água no oceano** to be a drop in the ocean. **-2.** [de suor] bead. **-3.** MED gout.

goteira [go'tejral *f* [buraco no telhado] leak.

gotejante [gote'ʒãntʃil *adj* dripping.

gotejar [4] [gote'ʒa(x)] *vt & vi* to drip.

gótico, ca [ˈgetʃiku, kal *adj* Gothic.

⬥ **gótico** *m*: **o** ~ the Gothic style.

gotícula [go'tʃikulal *f* droplet.

gourmet [gux'mel (*pl* **-s**) *mf* gourmet.

governabilidade [govexnabili'dadʒil *f* governability.

governador, ra [govexna'do(x), ral *m, f* governor.

governamental [govexnamẽn'tawl (*pl* **-ais**) *adj* government (*antes de subst*), governmental.

governanta [govex'nãntal *f* **-1.** [de criança] governess. **-2.** [de casa] housekeeper.

governante [govex'nãntʃil <> *adj* [que governa] governing. <> *mf* [quem governa] governor.

governar [4] [govex'na(x)] ⟷ *vt* **-1.** POL to govern. **-2.** [embarcação] to steer. **-3.** [dominar] to dominate. ⟷ *vi* POL to govern.

governista [govex'niʃta] ⟷ *adj* pro-government. ⟷ *mf* government supporter.

governo [go'vexnu] *m* **-1.** POL government. **-2.** [controle]: **o carro estava sem ~** the car was out of control. **-3.** NÁUT steering. **-4.** *loc*: **para seu ~** for your information.

gozação [goza'sãw] (*pl* **-ões**) *f* teasing; **fazer uma ~ (com alguém)** to tease (sb).

gozado, da [go'zadu, da] *adj* **-1.** [engraçado] funny. **-2.** [estranho] strange.

◆ **gozada** *f fam*: **dar uma ~ em alguém** to pull sb's leg.

gozador, ra [goza'do(x), ra] ⟷ *adj* comical. ⟷ *m, f* joker.

gozar [4] [go'za(x)] ⟷ *vt* **-1.** [desfrutar] to enjoy. **-2.** *fam* [troçar de] to make fun of. ⟷ *vi* **-1.** [desfrutar]: **~ de** to enjoy. **-2.** *fam* [troçar] to mock; **~ da cara de alguém** to mock sb. **-3.** *fam* [ter orgasmo] to come.

gozo ['gozu] *m* **-1.** [prazer] pleasure. **-2.** [graça]: **ser um ~** to be a laugh. **-3.** [uso]: **~ de algo** use of sthg; **estar em pleno ~ das faculdades mentais** to be in full possession of one's mental faculties. **-4.** [orgasmo] orgasm.

GP (*abrev de* **Grande Prêmio**) *m* grand prix.

GPS (*abrev de* **Global Positioning System**) *m* GPS.

Grã-Bretanha [ˌgrãnbre'tãɲa] *n*: **(a) ~** Great Britain.

graça ['grasa] *f* **-1.** [ger] grace. **-2.** [humor] wit; **achar ~ em** OU **de algo** to find sthg funny; **fazer ~** [gracejar] to joke; **ter ~** to be funny. **-3.** [encanto] charm; **cheio de ~** full of charm; **não ter ~ nenhuma** [ser chato] to be boring; [estar errado] to be wrong; **sem ~** dull; **ver ~ em alguém/algo** to see sthg funny in sb/sthg; **não sei que ~ ela vê nele** I don't know what she sees in him. **-4.** [favor, proteção] favour; **cair nas ~s de** to be in favour with. **-5.** [nome] name. **-6.** *loc*: **ficar sem ~** to be embarrassed.

◆ **graças a** *loc prep* **-1.** [devido a] due to, thanks to. **-2.** [agradecimento]: **dar ~s a** to give thanks to; **~s a Deus!** thank goodness!

◆ **de graça** *loc adj* **-1.** [grátis] free. **-2.** [muito barato] given away.

gracejar [4] [grase'ʒa(x)] *vi* to joke.

gracejo [gra'seʒu] *m* joke.

gracinha [gra'siɲa] *f*: **ser uma ~** [criança, rosto] to be sweet; [cidade, desenho] to be attractive; **que ~!** how sweet!

gracioso, osa [gra'sjozu, ɔza] *adj* gracious.

gradação [grada'sãw] (*pl* **-ões**) *f* gradient.

gradativo, va [grada'tʃivu, va] *adj* gradual.

grade [gra'dʒi] *f* **-1.** [em janela] grille. **-2.** [no chão] grating. **-3.** *loc*: **atrás das ~s** *fam* [na cadeia] behind bars.

gradeado, da [gra'dʒiadu, da] *adj* [com grades - jardim] fenced; [- janela] with a grating (*antes de subst*).

◆ **gradeado** *m* [gradeamento] fencing.

gradear [15] [gra'dʒa(x)] *vt* **-1.** [janela] to put bars on. **-2.** [área] to fence off.

grado ['gradu] *m* [vontade]: **de bom/mau ~** willingly/unwillingly.

graduação [gradwa'sãw] (*pl* **-ões**) *f* **-1.** [classificação] grading. **-2.** MIL rank. **-3.** [EDUC - colação] graduation; [- curso]: **curso de ~** degree course.

graduado, da [gra'dwadu, da] *adj* **-1.** [dividido em graus] graduated. **-2.** [diplomado] graduate. **-3.** [conceituado] graded. **-4.** MIL ranked.

gradual [gra'dwaw] (*pl* **-ais**) *adj* gradual.

graduar [4] [gra'dwa(x)] *vt* **-1.** [regular] to regulate. **-2.** [classificar]: **~ em** to classify according to. **-3.** [marcar os graus] to graduate. **-4.** EDUC: **~ alguém em algo** to confer a degree on sb in sthg. **-5.** MIL: **~ alguém em general/ coronel** to promote sb to general/colonel.

◆ **graduar-se** *vp* EDUC: **~-se em algo** to graduate in sthg.

graduável [gra'dwavew] (*pl* **-eis**) *adj* adjustable.

grafar [4] [gra'fa(x)] *vt* [escrever] to write.

grafia [gra'fia] *f* **-1.** [escrita] writing. **-2.** [ortografia] spelling.

gráfico, ca ['grafiku, ka] ⟷ *adj* **-1.** [visual] graphic. **-2.** [tipográfico] typographic. ⟷ *m, f* [profissional] typesetter.

◆ **gráfico** *m* **-1.** [diagrama] diagram; **~ de barras** bar chart. **-2.** MAT graph.

◆ **gráfica** *f* [estabelecimento] graphics studio.

◆ **gráficos** *mpl* COMPUT graphics.

grã-finagem [grãfi'naʒẽ] (*pl* **grã-finagens**) *f* [classe]: **a ~** the upper class.

grã-fino, na [grã'finu, na] (*mpl* **grã-finos**, *fpl* **grã-finas**) ⟷ *adj* posh. ⟷ *m, f* toff.

grafite [gra'fitʃi] *f* **-1.** [material] graphite. **-2.** [de lápis] lead. **-3.** [pichação] graffiti.

grafologia [grafolo'ʒia] *f* graphology.

grama ['grãma] ⟷ *f* [relva] grass. ⟷ *m* [medida] gramme.

gramado [gra'madu] *m* **-1.** [de parque, jardim] lawn. **-2.** FUT pitch.

gramar [4] [gra'ma(x)] *vt* to sow with grass.

gramática [gra'matʃika] *f* ▷ **gramático**.

gramatical [gramatʃi'kãw] (*pl* **-ais**) *adj* grammatical.

gramático, ca [gra'matʃiku, ka] ⟷ *adj* grammatical. ⟷ *m, f* grammarian.

◆ **gramática** *f* **-1.** [disciplina] grammar. **-2.** [livro] grammar book.

gramofone [gramo'foni] *m* gramophone.

grampeador [grãnpja'do(x)] (*pl* **-es**) *m* stapler.

grampear [15] [grãm'pja(x)] *vt* **-1.** [prender com grampos] to staple. **-2.** [telefone] to tap.

grampo ['grãnpu] *m* **-1.** [para papel] staple. **-2.** [para cabelos] hairgrip. **-3.** [de chapéu] hatpin. **-4.** [de carpinteiro] clamp. **-5.** [de telefone] tap.

grana ['grãna] *f fam* dosh.

granada [gra'nada] *f* **-1.** [arma] projectile; **~ de mão** hand grenade. **-2.** [pedra] garnet.

Granada [gra'nada] *n* **-1.** [na Espanha] Granada. **-2.** [nas Antilhas] Grenada.

grandalhão, lhona [grãnda'ʎãw, ʎona] (*mpl* -lhões, *fpl* -s) *adj* large.

grandão, dona [grãn'dãw, dona] (*mpl* -ões, *fpl* -s) *adj* huge.

grande ['grãndʒi] *adj* **-1.** [em tamanho] large; **o Grande São Paulo** Greater São Paulo. **-2.** [em altura] tall. **-3.** [crescido] grown-up. **-4.** *(antes de subst)* [intenso] great. **-5.** *(antes de subst)* [excessivo] grand. **-6.** *(antes de subst)* [notável] great. **-7.** *(antes de subst)* [excepcional] great. **-8.** *(antes de subst)* [generoso] generous.

➡ **grandes** *mpl*: **os** ~**s** [os poderosos] the great.

grandeza [grãn'deza] *f* **-1.** [ger] greatness. **-2.** [ostentação] grandeur.

grandiloqüência [grãndʒilo'kwẽnsja] *f* grandiloquence.

grandiloqüente [grãndʒilo'kwẽntʃi] *adj* grandiloquent.

grandiosidade [grãndʒiozi'dadʒi] *f* magnificence.

grandioso, osa [grãn'dʒjozu, ɔza] *adj* grandiose.

granel [gra'nɛw] *m*: **a** ~ in bulk; **comprar/vender a** ~ to buy/sell in bulk.

granito [gra'nitu] *m* granite.

granizo [gra'nizu] *m* hailstone; **chover** ~ to hail; **chuva de** ~ hail.

granja ['grãnʒa] *f* farm.

granulado, da [granu'ladu, da] *adj* granulated.

grânulo ['grãnulu] *m* granule.

grão ['grãw] (*pl* grãos) *m* **-1.** [semente] seed; [de café] bean. **-2.** [de areia] grain.

➡ **grãos** *mpl* [cereais] cereal.

grão-de-bico [ˌgrãwdʒi'biku] (*pl* grãos-de-bico) *m* chick pea *UK*, garbanzo bean *US*.

grapefruit [ˌgreip'frutʃi] *m* grapefruit.

grasnar [4] [graʒ'na(x)] *vi* **-1.** [corvo] to caw. **-2.** [pato] to quack. **-3.** *fig* [gritar] to shout.

gratidão [gratʃi'dãw] *f* gratitude.

gratificação [gratʃifika'sãw] (*pl* -ões) *f* **-1.** [bônus] bonus. **-2.** [recompensa] reward. **-3.** [gorjeta] tip.

gratificante [gratʃifi'kãntʃi] *adj* gratifying.

gratificar [12] [gratʃifi'ka(x)] *vt* **-1.** [dar bônus] to give a bonus. **-2.** [dar gorjeta a] to tip. **-3.** [recompensar] to reward; **esse trabalho gratifica muito** this work is very rewarding.

gratinado, da [gratʃi'nadu, da] *adj* au gratin, gratiné.

➡ **gratinado** *m* **-1.** [prato] gratin. **-2.** [crosta] crust.

grátis ['gratʃiʃ] *adj* free.

grato, ta ['gratu, ta] *adj* **-1.** [agradecido]: **ficar** ~ **a alguém por algo/por fazer algo** to be grateful to sb for sthg/doing sthg. **-2.** *(antes de subst)* [agradável] pleasant.

gratuidade [gratwi'dadʒi] *f* gratuity.

gratuito, ta [gra'twitu, ta] *adj* **-1.** [grátis] free. **-2.** [sem fundamento] gratuitous.

grau ['graw] *m* **-1.** [ger] degree. **-2.** [nível, gradação] level.

graúdo, da [gra'udu, da] ◇ *adj* **-1.** [grande] large. **-2.** [influente] important. ◇ *m, f* [pessoa poderosa] bigwig.

gravação [grava'sãw] (*pl* -ões) *f* **-1.** [em fita, disco, telefone] recording. **-2.** [em madeira] carving.

gravador, ra [grava'do(x), ra] (*pl* -es) *m, f* [quem faz gravuras] engraver.

➡ **gravador** *m* [aparelho] tape recorder.

➡ **gravadora** *f* [empresa] record company.

gravar [4] [gra'va(x)] *vt* **-1.** [ger] to record. **-2.** [em pedra, metal, madeira] to carve. **-3.** [na memória] to memorize.

gravata [gra'vata] *f* **-1.** [adereço] tie. **-2.** [golpe] stranglehold; **dar uma** ~ **em alguém** to get sb in a stranglehold.

gravata-borboleta [graˌvataboxbo'leta] (*pl* gravatas-borboletas, gravatas-borboleta) *f* bow tie.

grave ['gravi] *adj* **-1.** [profundo] serious. **-2.** [sério] grave. **-3.** [rígido] grave. **-4.** *MÚS* deep. **-5.** *LING* [acento] grave.

gravemente [grave'mẽntʃi] *adv* seriously.

graveto [gra'vetu] *m* piece of kindling.

grávida ['gravida] *adj* pregnant.

gravidade [gravi'dadʒi] *f* gravity; **centro de** ~ centre of gravity.

gravidez [gravi'deʒ] *f* pregnancy; ~ **tubária** ectopic pregancy.

graviola [gra'vjola] *f* sweetsop.

gravitar [4] [gravi'ta(x)] *vi* **-1.** [orbitar] to gravitate. **-2.** *fig* [seguir]: ~ **em torno de** to gravitate around.

gravura [gra'vura] *f* **-1.** [estampa] print. **-2.** [em madeira, metal] engraving.

graxa ['graʃa] *f* **-1.** [para couro] polish; ~ **de sapatos** shoe polish. **-2.** [lubrificante] grease.

Grécia ['grɛsja] *f* Greece.

gregário, ria [gre'garju, rja] *adj* gregarious.

grego, ga ['gregu, 'ga] ◇ *adj* **-1.** [relativo à grécia] Greek. **-2.** *fig* [obscuro]: **isso para mim é** ~ that's Greek to me. ◇ *m, f* [pessoa] Greek.

➡ **grego** *m LING* Greek; **falar** ~ *fam* to speak a foreign language.

gregoriano, na [grego'rjanu, na] *adj* Gregorian.

grelha ['greʎa] *f* grill; **na** ~ cooked on the grill.

grelhado, da [gre'ʎadu, da] *adj* grilled.

➡ **grelhado** *m* grilled food.

grelhar [4] [gre'ʎa(x)] *vt* to grill.

grêmio ['gremju] *m* **-1.** [associação] guild. **-2.** [clube] club.

grená [gre'na] ◇ *adj* dark red. ◇ *m* dark red.

greta ['greta] *f* crack.

greve ['grɛvi] *f* strike; **fazer** ~ to strike; ~ **de fome** hunger strike.

grevista [gre'viʃta] *mf* striker.

grifado, da [gri'fadu, da] *adj* italicized.

grifar [4] [gri'fa(x)] *vt* **-1.** [compor em grifo] to italicize. **-2.** [sublinhar] to underline. **-3.** *fig* [enfatizar] to emphasize.

grife ['grifi] *f* label.

grifo ['grifu] *m* italics.

grilado, da [gri'ladu, da] *adj fam*: **estar/ficar ~ (com)** to be/get worked up (about).

grilagem [grila'ʒẽ] (*pl* **-ns**) *f* falsification of property deeds.

grilar [4] [gri'la(x)] *vt fam* [preocupar] to worry. ⬦ *vi fam* [chatear-se] to get annoyed.

➧ **grilar-se** *vp fam*: **~-se por** *ou* **com** to get worked up about.

grileiro, ra [gri'lejru, ra] *m, f* forger of property deeds.

grilhão [gri'ʎãw] (*pl* **-ões**) *m* chain.

grilo ['grilu] *m* **-1.** [inseto] cricket. **-2.** *fam* [problema] hiccup; **dar ~** to cause a hiccup.

grinalda [gri'nawda] *f* garland.

gringo, ga ['grĩgu, ga] *m, f fam pej* foreigner.

gripado, da [gri'padu, da] *adj*: **estar/ficar ~** to have/get flu.

gripar-se [4] [gri'paxsi] *vp* to catch flu.

gripe ['gripi] *f* flu; **pegar uma ~** to go down with flu.

grisalho, lha [gri'zaʎu, ʎa] *adj* greying *UK*, graying *US*.

gritante [gri'tãntʃi] *adj* **-1.** [evidente] glaring. **-2.** [de cor viva] dazzling.

gritar [4] [gri'ta(x)] *vt & vi* to shout; **~ com alguém** to shout at sb.

gritaria [grita'ria] *f* shouting.

grito ['gritu] *m* **-1.** [brado] shout; **falar aos ~s** to shout; **protestar aos ~s** to shout protests; **chegar aos ~s** to reach screaming point; **dar um ~** to give a shout. **-2.** [de animal] scream. **-3.** [de dor] scream. **-4.** [de pavor] scream.

➧ **no grito** *loc adv fam* by force.

Groenlândia [groẽ'lãndʒja] *n* Greenland.

grogue ['grɔgi] *adj* [pessoa] groggy.

grosa ['grɔza] *f* [doze dúzias] gross.

grosar [gro'za(x)] *vt* [limar, debastar] to file.

groselha [gro'zeʎa] *f* redcurrant.

grosseiro, ra [gro'sejru, ra] *adj* **-1.** [rude] rude. **-2.** [chulo] vulgar. **-3.** [ordinário] coarse.

grosseria [grose'ria] *f* rudeness; **dizer/fazer uma ~** to say/do something rude.

grosso, ssa ['grosu, sa] *adj* **-1.** [ger] thick. **-2.** [áspero] rough. **-3.** [rude] rude. **-4.** *fam* [abundante]: **dinheiro ~** a considerable sum of money.

➧ **grosso** *adv*: **falar ~ com alguém** to get tough with sb.

➧ **grosso modo** *loc adv* roughly.

grossura [gro'sura] *f* **-1.** [espessura] thickness. **-2.** *fam* [grosseria] rudeness.

grotão [gro'tãw] (*pl* **-ões**) *m* gorge.

grotesco, ca [gro'teʃku, ka] *adj* grotesque.

➧ **grotesco** *m*: **o ~** the grotesque.

grua ['grua] *f* crane.

grudado, da [gru'dadu, da] *adj fig*: **ser ~ com alguém** to be very attached to sb.

grudar [4] [gru'da(x)] ⬦ *vt*: **~ algo em algo** to stick sthg on sthg. ⬦ *vi* to stick.

grude ['grudʒi] *m* **-1.** [cola] glue. **-2.** *fam* [comida ruim] muck.

grudento, ta [gru'dẽntu, ta] *adj* sticky.

grumete [gru'mɛtʃi] *m* cabin boy.

grunhido [gru'ɲidu] *m* grunt.

grunhir [6] [gru'ɲi(x)] *vi* **-1.** [porco] to grunt. **-2.** *fig* [resmungar] to grumble.

grupo ['grupu] *m* group; **~ étnico** ethnic group; **~ sanguíneo** blood group; **~ de discussão** *COMPUT* newsgroup.

gruta ['gruta] *f* cave, grotto.

guache ['gwaʃi] *m* gouache.

guaraná [gwara'na] *m* guarana; **~ em pó** powdered guarana; **~ natural** natural guarana.

GUARANÁ

A small fruit borne by a very common bush in Amazonas and Pará; it is used to make one of the most popular national drinks, *guaraná*. High in caffeine, it is considered by alternative medicine as an excellent source of energy. It is sold as a soft drink and can also be obtained in the form of a powder.

guarani [gwara'ni] (*pl* **guaranis**) ⬦ *adj* Guarani (*antes de subst*). ⬦ *m, f* Guarani. ⬦ *m* **-1.** [língua] Guarani. **-2.** [moeda] guarani.

guarda ['gwaxda] ⬦ *f* **-1.** [proteção] care; **ficar de ~** to stand guard. **-2.** *MIL* guard. ⬦ *mf* [policial] police officer.

guarda-chuva [ˌgwaxda'ʃuva] (*pl* **guarda-chuvas**) *m* umbrella.

guarda-costas [ˌgwaxda'kɔʃtaʃ] *mf inv* **-1.** *NÁUT* coastguard. **-2.** *fig* [para defesa] bodyguard.

guardador, ra [gwaxda'do(x), ra] *m, f*: **~ (de automóveis)** (car) attendant.

guardados [gwax'daduʃ] *mpl* bits and pieces.

guarda-florestal [ˌgwaxdaflore'ʃ'taw] (*pl* **guardas-florestais**) *mf* forest ranger.

guarda-louça [ˌgwaxda'losa] (*pl* **guarda-louças**) *m* dresser.

guarda-mor [ˌgwaxda'mɔ(x)] (*pl* **guardas-mores**) *m* head customs-officer.

guarda-móveis [ˌgwaxda'mɔvejʃ] *m (inv)* furniture warehouse.

guardanapo [ˌgwaxda'napu] *m* (table) napkin.

guarda-noturno [ˌgwaxdano'tuxnu] (*pl* **guardas-noturnos**) *mf* nightwatchman.

guardar [4] [gwax'da(x)] *vt* **-1.** [ger] to keep; **~ segredo sobre algo** to keep quiet about sthg; **~ silêncio** to keep silent. **-2.** [pôr no lugar]: **~ algo (em)** to put sthg away (in). **-3.** [reservar]: **~ algo (para)** to keep sthg (for); **~ lugar para alguém** [em teatro, ônibus] to keep a seat for sb. **-4.** [gravar na memória] to remember. **-5.** [vigiar] to guard. **-6.** [cuidar de] to look after. **-7.** [observar] to keep; **guardadas as (devidas) proporções** to a certain extent.

➧ **guardar-se** *vp* **-1.** [proteger-se]: **~-se de** to steer clear of. **-2.** [prevenir-se]: **~-se de** to watch out for.

guarda-roupa [ˌgwaxda'xopa] (*pl* **guarda-roupas**) *m* wardrobe.

guarda-sol [ˌgwaxda'sɔw] (*pl* **guarda-sóis**) *m* parasol.

guarda-volumes [ˌgwaxdavoˈlumiʃ] *m (inv)* left-luggage office.
guardião, diã [gwaxˈdʒjãw, dʒjã] (*mpl* -ães, -ões, *fpl* -s) *m, f* guardian.
guarida [gwaˈridal] *f* -1. [refúgio] den. -2. [proteção]: **dar ~ a alguém** to harbour sb.
guarita [gwaˈrital] *f* -1. [torre] watchtower. -2. [casinha] sentry box.
guarnecer [25] [gwaxneˈse(x)] *vt* -1. [abastecer] to supply; **~ alguém de algo** to supply sb with sthg. -2. *MIL* to occupy. -3. *NÁUT* to crew.
guarnição [gwaxniˈsãw] (*pl* -ões) *f* -1. [ger] garnish. -2. *MIL* garrison. -3. *NAUT* crew.
Guatemala [gwateˈmalal] *n* Guatemala.
guatemalteco, ca [gwatemawˈtɛku, ka] <> *adj* Guatemalan. <> *m, f* Guatemalan.
gude [ˈgudʒil] *m* ▷ **bola.**
gueixa [ˈgejʃa] *f* geisha.
guelra [ˈgɛwxa] *f* gill.
guerra [ˈgɛxa] *f* -1. [ger] war; **declarar ~ a** to declare war on; **em ~** at war; **estar em pé de ~ (com)** to be ready for war (with); **~ civil** civil war; **~ fria** cold war; **~ mundial** world war; **~ nuclear** *ou* **atômica** nuclear war; **~ química** chemical warfare; **~ santa** holy war; **fazer ~ a** to do battle with; **~ de nervos** war of nerves. -2. *fig* [disputa] battle.
guerra-relâmpago [gɛxaˈxelãmpagul] (*pl* -guerras-relâmpago) *f* blitzkrieg.
guerrear [15] [geˈxja(x)] *vi*: **~ (com/contra)** to be at war (with/against).
guerreiro, ra [geˈxejru, ral] <> *adj* -1. [belicoso] warlike. -2. [espírito, índole] fighting. <> *m, f* [pessoa] warrior.
guerrilha [geˈxiʎa] *f* guerrilla warfare.
guerrilhar [4] [gexiˈʎa(x)] *vi* to engage in guerrilla warfare.
guerrilheiro, ra [gexiˈʎejru, ral] <> *adj* guerrilla (*antes de subst*). <> *m, f* guerrilla.
gueto [ˈgetul] *m* ghetto.
guia [ˈgial] <> *f* guide. <> *m* [manual - turístico, cultural] guide; [- de instruções] manual. <> *mf* [pessoa] guide; **~ turístico** tourist guide.
Guiana [gwiˈjãnal] *n* Guyana.
guianense [gwijaˈnɛnsil] <> *adj* Guyanese. <> *mf* Guyanese.
guiar [16] [ˈgja(x)] <> *vt* -1. [orientar] to guide. -2. [proteger] to watch over. -3. *AUTO* [dirigir] to drive. <> *vi AUTO* to drive.
 ◆ **guiar-se** *vp* [orientar-se] to orientate o.s.
guichê [giˈʃel] *m* -1. [no cinema, teatro] ticket office. -2. [em banco] counter.
guidom [giˈdõ] (*pl* -ns) *m* handlebars (*pl*).
guilhotina [giʎoˈtʃinal] *f* guillotine.
guilhotinar [4] [giʎotʃiˈna(x)] *vt* to guillotine.
guimba [ˈgĩbal] *f fam* [ponta de cigarro] stub.
guinada [giˈnadal] *f* -1. *NÁUT* yaw. -2. *AUTO* veer; **dar uma ~** to veer. -3. *fig* [virada] change of direction; **dar uma ~** to change direction.
guinchar [4] [gĩˈʃa(x)] <> *vt* [carro] to tow. <> *vi* [chiar] to squeal.

guincho [ˈgĩʃul] *m* -1. [reboque] tow. -2. [chiado] squeal.
guindar [4] [gĩˈda(x)] *vt* -1. [levantar] to raise. -2. *fig* [promover] to promote; **~ alguém a algo** to promote sb to sthg.
guindaste [gĩˈdaʃtʃil] *m* crane.
guineano, na [gineˈãnu, nal] <> *adj* Guinean. <> *m, f* Guinean.
Guiné-Bissau [giˌnɛbiˈsawl] *n* Guinea-Bissau.
Guiné Equatorial [giˌnɛkwatoˈrjawl] *n* Equatorial Guinea.
guirlanda [gixˈlãndal] *f* garland.
guisa [ˈgizal] *f*: **à ~ de** in the manner of.
guisado, da [giˈzadu, dal] *m CULIN* stew.
guisar [4] [giˈza(x)] *vt* to stew.
guitarra [giˈtaxal] *f*: **~ (elétrica)** electric guitar.
guitarrista [gitaˈxiʃtal] *mf* guitarist.
guizo [ˈgizul] *m* bell.
gula [ˈgulal] *f* gluttony.
gulodice [guloˈdʒisil] *f* greediness.
guloseima [guloˈzejmal] *f* titbit.
guloso, osa [guˈlozu, ɔzal] *adj* greedy.
gume [ˈgumil] *m* blade.
guri, ria [guˈri, rial] *m* kid.
gurizada [guriˈzadal] *f* [criançada] kids (*pl*).
guru [guˈrul] *m* guru.
gutural [gutuˈrawl] (*pl* -ais) *adj* guttural.

h¹, H [aˈgal] *m* [letra] h, H.
h² (*abrev de* **hora**) *f* hr., h.
ha (*abrev de* **hectare**) *m* ha.
hã [ãl] *interj* -1. [reflexão]: **hã! ah!** -2. [pergunta]: **hã?** sorry?
habeas-corpus [ˌabjasˈkɔxpuʃ] *m inv* habeas corpus.
hábil [ˈabiwl] (*pl* -eis) *adj* -1. [ger] skilful. -2. [sutil] subtle. -3. *loc*: **em tempo ~** in due course.
habilidade [abiliˈdadʒil] *f* -1. [aptidão] ability. -2. [competência] talent. -3. [astúcia] skill. -4. [sutileza] subtlety.
habilidoso, osa [abiliˈdozu, ɔzal] *adj* skilful *UK*, skillful *US*.
habilitação [abilitaˈsãwl] (*pl* -ões) *f* -1. [aptidão] aptitude. -2. [conhecimento formal] qualification. -3. *JUR* [documento] validation.
 ◆ **habilitações** *fpl* [qualificações] qualifications.
habilitado, da [abiliˈtadu, dal] *adj* -1. [profissional liberal] qualified. -2. [operário] skilled.

habilitar [4] [abili'ta(x)] *vt* -**1.** [capacitar] to enable. -**2.** [preparar] to prepare. -**3.** [dar direito a] to entitle to.

➤ **habilitar-se** *vp* [capacitar-se] to prepare o.s.

habitação [abita'sãw] (*pl* -ões) *f* -**1.** [casa] house. -**2.** POL [moradia] housing.

habitacional [abitasjo'naw] (*pl* -ais) *adj* housing *(antes de subst)*.

habitante [abi'tãntʃi] *mf* inhabitant.

habitar [4] [abi'ta(x)] <> *vt* -**1.** [morar em] to live in. -**2.** [povoar] to inhabit. <> *vi* [viver] to live.

hábitat ['abitatʃ] *m* habitat; ~ **natural** natural habitat.

habitável [abi'tavew] (*pl* -eis) *adj* inhabitable.

hábito ['abitu] *m* habit; **ter o** ~ **de fazer algo** to be used to doing sthg; **por força do** ~ through force of habit.

habituado, da [abi'twadu, da] *adj*: ~ **(a algo)** used (to sthg); ~ **a fazer algo** used to doing sthg.

habitual [abi'twaw] (*pl* -ais) *adj* habitual.

habituar [4] [abi'twa(x)] *vt* to accustom to; ~ **alguém a algo/a fazer algo** to get sb used to sthg/ to doing sthg.

➤ **habituar-se** *vp*: ~-**se a (fazer) algo** to get used to (doing) sthg.

habitué [abi'twe] *m* habitué.

hacker [xake(x)ʃ] (*pl* **hackers**) *m* COMPUT hacker.

hadoque [a'dɔki] *m* haddock.

Haia ['aja] *n* The Hague.

Haiti [aj'tʃi] *n* Haiti.

hálito ['alitu] *m* breath; **mau** ~ bad breath.

hall ['ɔw] *m* hall; ~ **de entrada** entrance hall.

halo ['alu] *m* halo.

haltere [aw'tɛri] *m* dumb-bell.

halterofilismo [awterofi'liʒmu] *m* weightlifting.

halterofilista [awterofi'liʃta] *mf* weight lifter.

hambúrguer [ãn'buxge(x)ʃ] (*pl* -es) *m* hamburger.

handicap [ãndʒi'kapi] *m* handicap.

hangar [ãŋ'ga(x)] (*pl* -es) *m* hangar.

Hanói [a'nɔj] *n* Hanoi.

Harare [a'rari] *n* Harare.

haras ['araʃ] *m inv* stud *(for racehorses)*.

hardware [ax'dwɛ(x)] *m* COMPUT hardware.

harém [a'rɛ̃] (*pl* -ns) *m* harem.

harmonia [axmo'nia] *f* harmony.

harmônico, ca [ax'moniku, ka] *adj* harmonic.

➤ **harmônica** *f* harmonica, mouth organ.

harmonioso, osa [axmo'njozu, jɔza] *adj* harmonious.

harmonizar [4] [axmoni'za(x)] *vt* -**1.** MÚS to harmonize. -**2.** [conciliar]: ~ **algo com algo** to reconcile sthg with sthg.

➤ **harmonizar-se** *vp*: ~-**se (com algo)** to be in harmony (with sthg).

harpa ['axpa] *f* harp.

harpista [ax'piʃta] *mf* harpist.

haste ['aʃtʃi] *f* -**1.** [de bandeira] pole. -**2.** [caule] stalk.

hasteamento [aʃtʃja'mẽntu] *m* hoisting.

hastear [15] [aʃ'tʃja(x)] *vt* to raise.

Havaí [ava'i] *n* Hawaii.

havaiano, na [ava'jãnu, na] <> *adj* Hawaiian. <> *m, f* Hawaiian.

havana [a'vãna] <> *adj* [cor] beige. <> *m* [charuto] Havana cigar.

Havana [a'vãna] *n* Havana.

havanês, esa [ava'neʃ, eza] <> *adj* Havana *(antes de subst)*. <> *m, f person from Havana*.

haver [2] [a've(x)] *v impess* -**1.** [existir, estar, ter lugar]: **há** there is, there are *pl*; **havia** there was, there were *pl*; **há um café muito bom ao fim da rua** there's a very good café at the end of the street; **não há nada aqui** there's nothing here; **não há correio amanhã** there's no mail tomorrow. -**2.** [exprime tempo]: **estou esperando há dez minutos** I've been waiting for ten minutes; **há séculos que não vou lá** I haven't been there for ages; **há três dias que não o vejo** I haven't seen him for três days. -**3.** [exprime obrigação]: **há que esperar três dias** you'll have to wait three days. -**4.** [em locuções]: **haja o que houver** come what may; **não há de quê!** don't mention it! <> *v aux* [em tempos compostos] to have; **ele havia chegado há pouco** he had just arrived; **como não havia comido estava com fome** I was hungry because I hadn't eaten; **havíamos reservado com antecedência** we'd reserved in advance.

➤ **haver de** *v* + *prep* [dever] to have; [exprime intenção]: **hei de ir** I'll go.

➤ **haver-se com** *vp* + *prep*: ~-**se com alguém** [prestar contas a] to answer to sb.

➤ **haveres** *mpl* [pertences] belongings; [bens] assets.

haxixe [a'ʃiʃi] *m* hashish.

HC (*abrev de* **Hospital das Clínicas**) *m famous teaching hospital in São Paulo.*

HD (*abrev de* **Hard Disk**) *m* HD.

hectare [ɛk'tari] *m* hectare.

hectograma [ɛkto'grãma] *m* hectogram, hectogramme.

hectolitro [ɛkto'litru] *m* hectolitre.

hedge [ɛdji] *m* ECON [proteção cambial] hedge.

hediondo, da [e'dʒõndu, da] *adj* hideous.

hedonista [edo'niʃta] <> *adj* hedonistic. <> *mf* hedonist.

hegemonia [eʒemo'nia] *f* hegemony.

hegemônico, ca [ege'moniku, ka] *adj* hegemonic.

hein [ẽj] *interj*: ~**?** what?; **aí,** ~**?** *fam* [muito bem] not bad, eh?

hélice ['ɛlisi] *f* propeller.

helicóptero [eli'kɔpterul] *m* helicopter.

heliporto [eli'pɔxtu] *m* heliport.

Helsinki [ɛw'sĩŋki] *n* Helsinki.

hematologia [ematolo'ʒia] *f* haematology UK, hematology US.

hematoma [ema'toma] *f* bruise, haematoma UK, hematoma US.

hemisférico, ca [emiʃ'feriku, ka] *adj* hemispherical.

hemisfério [emiʃ'fɛrjul *m* hemisphere.

hemodiálise [emo'dʒializi] *f* dialysis.

hemofilia [emofi'lial *f* haemophilia *UK*, hemophilia *US*.

hemofílico, ca [ɛmo'filiku, ka] <> *adj* haemophilic *UK*, hemophilic *US*. <> *m, f* haemophiliac *UK*, hemophiliac *US*.

hemoglobina [emoglo'binal *f* haemoglobin *UK*, hemoglobin *US*.

hemograma [emo'grãmal *m* full blood count.

hemorragia [emoxa'ʒia] *f* haemorrhage *UK*, hemorrhage *US*.

hemorrágico, ca [emo'xagiku, ka] *adj* haemorrhagic.

hemorróidas [emo'xɔjdaʃ] *fpl* haemorrhoid *UK*, hemorrhoid *US*.

henê [e'ne], **hena** ['ɛnal *f* henna.

hepatite [epa'tʃitʃil *f* hepatitis.

heptágono [ep'tagonul *m* heptagon.

hera ['ɛral *f* ivy.

heráldica [e'rawdʒikal *f* heraldry.

herança [e'rãnsal *f* inheritance.

herbáceo, cea [ex'basju, sjal *adj* herbaceous.

herbanário [exba'narjul *m* herbarium.

herbicida [exbi'sidal *m* herbicide.

herbívoro, ra [ex'bivoru, ral <> *adj* herbivorous. <> *m, f* herbivore.

hercúleo, lea [ex'kulju, ljal *adj fig* [muito forte] Herculean.

herdar [4] [ex'da(x)] *vt* -1. [ger]: ~ algo de alguém to inherit sthg from sb. -2. [legar]: ~ algo a alguém to pass sthg on to sb.

herdeiro, ra [ex'dejru, ral *m, f* heir.

hereditariedade [eredʒitarje'dadʒil *f* heredity.

hereditário, ria [eredʒi'tarju, rjal *adj* hereditary.

herege [e'rɛʒil *mf* heretic.

heresia [ere'zial *f* heresy.

herético, ca [e'rɛtʃiku, ka] <> *adj* heretical. <> *m, f* heretic.

hermafrodita [exmafro'dʒital <> *adj* hermaphrodite, hermaphroditic. <> *mf* hermaphrodite.

hermético, ca [ex'mɛtʃiku, ka] *adj* -1. [bem fechado] hermetic, airtight. -2. *fig* [obscuro] hermetic.

hérnia ['ɛxnjal *f* hernia; ~ de disco slipped disc.

herói [e'rɔjl *m* hero.

heróico, ca [e'rɔjku, ka] *adj* heroic.

heroína [e'rwinal *f* heroine.

heroísmo [e'rwiʒmul *m* heroism.

herpes ['ɛxpiʃl *m* herpes; ~ genital genital herpes.

hertz ['ɛxts] *m* hertz.

hesitação [ezita'sãwl (*pl* -ões) *f* hesitation.

hesitante [ezi'tãntʃil *adj* hesitant.

hesitar [4] [ezi'ta(x)] *vi*: ~ em fazer algo to hesitate to do sthg.

heterodoxo, xa [etero'dɔksu, ksal *adj* heterodox.

heterogêneo, nea [etero'ʒenju, njal *adj* heterogeneous.

heterônimo [ete'ronimul *m* pen-name, nom de plume.

heterossexual [eterosek'swawl (*pl* -ais) <> *adj* heterosexual. <> *mf* heterosexual.

hexagonal [ezago'nawl (*pl* -ais) *adj* hexagonal.

hexágono [e'zagonul *m* hexagon.

hiato ['jatul *m* hiatus.

hibernação [ibexna'sãwl (*pl* -ões) *f* hibernation.

hibernar [4] [ibex'na(x)] *vi* to hibernate.

hibisco [i'biʃkul *m* hibiscus.

híbrido, da ['ibridu, dal *adj* [mesclado] hybrid.
    ➡ **híbrido** *m* [animal ou vegetal]: ser um ~ (de) to be a hybrid (of).

hidramático, ca [idra'matʃiku, ka] *adj* Hydra-Matic®.

hidratante [idra'tãntʃil <> *adj* moisturizing. <> *m* moisturizer.

hidratar [4] [idra'ta(x)] *vt* -1. [pele] to moisturize. -2. *MED* to hydrate.

hidrato [i'dratul *m*: ~ de carbono carbohydrate.

hidráulico, ca [i'drawliku, ka] *adj* hydraulic.
    ➡ **hidráulica** *f* hydraulics (*sg*).

hidrelétrica [idre'lɛtrikal *f* -1. [usina] hydro-electric power station. -2. [empresa] hydro-electric company.

hidrelétrico, ca [idre'lɛtriku, ka] *adj* hydroelectric.

hidroavião [ˌidrwa'vjãwl (*pl* -ões) *m* seaplane.

hidrocarboneto [idrokaxbo'netul *m* hydrocarbon.

hidrodinâmica [idrodʒi'nãmikal *f* hydrodynamics (*sg*).

hidrófilo, la [i'drɔfilu, lal *adj* absorbent.

hidrofobia [idrofo'bial *f* hydrophobia, rabies.

hidrófobo, ba [i'drɔfobu, bal <> *adj* hydrophobic. <> *m, f* hydrophobic person.

hidrogênio [idro'ʒenjul *m* hydrogen.

hidrografia [idrogra'fial *f* hydrography.

hidromassagem [idruma'saʒẽl (*pl* -ns) *f* hydromassage.

hidroplano [idro'plãnul *m* hydroplane.

hidroterapia [idrotera'pial *f* hydrotherapy.

hidrovia [idro'vial *f* waterway.

hiena ['jenal *f* hyena.

hierarquia [jerar'kial *f* hierarchy.

hierárquico, ca [je'raxkiku, kal *adj* hierarchical.

hierarquizar [4] [jeraxki'za(x)] *vt* to organize into a hierarchy.

hieróglifo [je'rɔgliful *m* hieroglyph.

hífen ['ifɛl (*pl* -es) *m* hyphen.

hifenizar [4] [ifeni'za(x)] *vt* hyphenate.

Hi-Fi (*abrév de* High Fidelity) *m* hi-fi.

higiene [i'ʒjenil *f* hygiene.

higiênico, ca [i'ʒjeniku, ka] *adj* hygienic; papel ~ toilet paper.

higienizar [4] [ʒjeni'za(x)] *vt* to sterilize.

hilariante [ila'rjãntʃil *adj* hilarious.

hilário, ria [i'larju, rjal *adj* [hilariante] hilarious.

Himalaia [imaˈlajal *n*: **o** ~ the Himalayas *(pl)*.
hímen [ˈimẽl (*pl* **-ns**) *m* ANAT hymen.
hindi [ˈĩndʒil *m* Hindi.
hindu [ĩnˈdul (*pl* **hindus**) <> *adj* **-1.** [da Índia] Indian. **-2.** RELIG Hindu. <> *m, f* **-1.** [da Índia] Indian. **-2.** RELIG Hindu.
hinduísmo [ĩnˈdwiʒmul *m* Hinduism.
hino [ˈinul *m* hymn; ~ **nacional** national anthem.
hiper [ˈipe(x)l *prefixo* **-1.** [extremo, grande] hyper-. **-2.** *fam* [super] hyper-.
hipérbole [iˈpɛxbolil *f* **-1.** MAT hyperbola. **-2.** [exagero] hyperbole.
hiperinflação [iperĩnflaˈsãwl (*pl* **-ões**) *f* hyperinflation.
hiperlink [iperˈlinkil *m* COMPUT hyperlink.
hipermercado [ˌipexmexˈkadul *m* hypermarket.
hipermetropia [ipexmetroˈpial *f* hypermetropia, long-sightedness.
hipersensível [ipexsẽˈsivewl (*pl* **-eis**) *adj* hyper-.sensitive.
hipertensão [ˌipextẽˈsãwl (*pl* **-ões**) *f* high blood pressure, hypertension.
hipertenso, sa [ipexˈtẽsu, sal *adj* with high blood-pressure; **ser** ~ to have high blood pressure.
hipertexto [ipexˈtejʃtul *m* COMPUT hypertext.
hipertrofia [ipextroˈfial *f* **-1.** MED hypertrophy. **-2.** [fig] excessive increase.
hipertrofiar [ipextroˈfja(x)l *vt* to overstretch.
  ➡ **hipertrofiar-se** *vp* to become overdeveloped.
hípico, ca [ˈipiku, kal *adj* **-1.** [clube, competição] riding. **-2.** [sociedade] equestrian.
hipismo [iˈpiʒmul *m* horse riding, equestrianism.
hipnose [ipˈnɔzil *f* hypnosis.
hipnótico, ca [ipˈnɔtʃiku, kal *adj* hypnotic.
  ➡ **hipnótico** *m* [substância] hypnotic.
hipnotizado, da [ipnotʃiˈzadu, dal *adj* hypnotized.
hipnotizador, ra [ipnotʃizaˈdo(x), ral <> *adj* hypnotizing. <> *m, f* hypnotist.
hipnotizar [4] [ipnotʃiˈza(x)l *vt* to hypnotize.
hipocondria [ipokõnˈdrial *f* hypochondria.
hipocondríaco, ca [ˌipokõnˈdriaku, kal <> *adj* hypochondriac. <> *m, f* hypochondriac.
hipocrisia [ipokriˈzial *f* hypocrisy.
hipócrita [iˈpɔkrital <> *adj* hypocritical. <> *mf* hypocrite.
hipodérmico, ca [ipoˈdɛxmiku, kal *adj* hypodermic.
hipódromo [iˈpɔdrumul *m* racecourse.
hipófise [iˈpɔfizil *f* ANAT pituitary.
hipoglicemia [ipogliseˈmial *f* hypoglycaemia *UK*, hypoglycemia *US*.
hipopótamo [ipoˈpɔtamul *m* hippopotamus.
hipoteca [ipoˈtɛkal *f* mortgage.
hipotecar [12] [ipoteˈka(x)l *vt* to mortgage.
hipotecário, ria [ipoteˈkarju, rjal *adj* mortgage *(antes de subst)*.

hipotenusa [ipoteˈnuzal *f* hypotenuse.
hipotermia [ipotexˈmial *f* hypothermia.
hipótese [iˈpɔtezil *f* **-1.** [conjectura] hypothesis. **-2.** [possibilidade] eventuality; **não abandonaria meus filhos em** ~ **alguma** I wouldn't abandon my children under any circumstances, under no circumstance would I abandon my children; **na melhor/pior das** ~**s** at best/worst.
hipotético, ca [ipoˈtɛtʃiku, kal *adj* hypothetical.
hirsuto, ta [ixˈsutu, tal *adj* hairy.
hispânico, ca [iʃˈpaniku, kal <> *adj* Hispanic. <> *m, f* Hispanic.
hispano, na [iʃˈpãnu, nal <> *adj* Hispanic. <> *m, f* Hispanic.
hispano-americano, na [iʃˌpãnwameriˈkãnu, nal <> *adj* Spanish-American. <> *m, f* Spanish American.
histerectomia [iʃterektoˈmial *f* hysterectomy.
histeria [iʃteˈrial *f* hysteria.
histérico, ca [iʃˈtɛriku, kal *adj* hysterical.
histerismo [iʃteˈriʒmul *m* MED hysteria.
histologia [iʃtoloˈʒial *f* histology.
história [iʃˈtɔrjal *f* **-1.** [ger] history; ~ **antiga** ancient history; ~ **do Brasil** Brazilian history; ~ **natural** natural history. **-2.** [narração] story; ~ **do arco-da-velha** tall story; ~ **da carochinha** fairy tale; ~ **em quadrinhos** comic strip. **-3.** [lorota] nonsense; ~ **para boi dormir** empty talk. **-4.** [recato]: **deixa de** ~! come off it! **-5.** [explicação] excuse. **-6.** [idéia, proposta] suggestion. **-7.** [acontecimento] event; [caso amoroso] love affair. **-8.** [enredo] storyline. **-9.** [boato] rumour. **-10.** [tradição] tradition. **-11.** [problema] problem. **-12.** *fam* [abuso]: **que** ~ **é essa de ...?** what's the idea of ...?
historiador, ra [iʃtorjaˈdo(x), ral *m, f* historian.
historiar [16] [iʃtoˈrja(x)l *vt* to narrate.
historicidade [iʃtorisiˈdadʒil *f* historicity, historical authenticity.
histórico, ca [iʃˈtɔriku, kal *adj* **-1.** [ger] historical. **-2.** [importante] historic.
  ➡ **histórico** *m* history.
historieta [iʃtoˈrjetal *f* short story.
histrião [iʃtriˈãwl (*pl* **-ões**) *m* [comediante] comic.
histriônico, ca [iʃtriˈoniku, kal *adj* histrionic.
histrionismo [iʃrjoˈniʒmul *m* histrionics *(pl)*.
hit [ˈitil *m* COMPUT hit.
HIV (*abrev de* Human Immunodeficiency Virus) *m* HIV.
hobby [ˈɔbil *m* hobby.
hoje [ˈoʒil *adv* today; **ainda** ~ before the end of the day; **de** ~ **em diante** from today onwards, from this day forth; ~ **noite** tonight; ~ **em dia** nowadays; ~ **faz um mês** a month ago today.
Holanda [oˈlãndal *f* Holland, The Netherlands.
holandês, esa [olãnˈdeʃ, ezal (*mpl* **-eses** *fpl* **-s**) <> *adj* Dutch. <> *m, f* Dutchman (*f* Dutchwoman).
  ➡ **holandês** *m* [língua] Dutch.
holding [ˈxowdiŋl *f* holdings *(pl)*.
holocausto [oloˈkawʃtul *m* holocaust.
holofote [oloˈfɔtʃil *m* searchlight.

holograma [olo'grãmal *m* hologram.

hombridade [õnbri'dadʒil *f* decency.

home banking ['xomibãnkĩn] *m* COMPUT home banking.

homem ['ɔmẽl (*pl* -ns) *m* -1. [ger] man; ~ de negócios businessman; ~ do povo man of the people. -2. [humanidade]: o ~ mankind. -3. [chefe]: ser o ~ da casa to be the man of the house.

homem-feito [,omẽn'fejtul (*pl* homens-feitos) *m* grown man.

homem-rã [,omẽn'xãl (*pl* homens-rãs) *m* frogman.

homenageado, da [omena'ʒjadu, dal <> *adj* venerated. <> *m, f*: o ~ da festa é ... this party is being held in homage to ...

homenagear [15] [omena'ʒja(x)] *vt* to pay homage to.

homenagem [ome'naʒẽl (*pl* -ns) *f* homage; em ~ a algo/alguém in homage to sthg/sb.

homenzarrão [omẽnza'xãwl (*pl* -ões) *m* strapping man.

homeopata [omjo'patal <> *adj* homeopathic. <> *mf* homeopath.

homeopatia [omjopa'tʃial *f* homeopathy.

homeopático, ca [omjo'patʃiku, kal *adj* homeopathic.

homérico, ca [o'mɛriku, kal *adj fig* [extraordinário] epic.

homicida [omi'sidal <> *adj* homicidal. <> *mf* murderer.

homicídio [omi'sidʒjul *m* homicide; ~ culposo manslaughter.

homogeneidade [omoʒenej'dadʒil *f* homogeneity.

homogeneizado, da [omoʒenej'zadu, dal *adj* homogenized.

homogêneo, nea [omo'ʒenju, njal *adj* homogeneous.

homologação [omologa'sãwl (*pl* -ões) *f* ratification.

homologar [14] [omolo'ga(x)] *vt* -1. [lei, casamento] to ratify. -2. [sociedade] to grant official recognition to.

homólogo, ga [o'mɔlogu, gal <> *adj* -1. [ger] homologous. -2. [correspondente] equivalent. <> *m, f* [pessoa] counterpart, opposite number.

homônimo, ma [o'monimu, mal *adj* homonymous.
    ▸ **homônimo** *m* -1. [pessoa] namesake. -2. GRAM homonym.

homossexual [omosek'swawl (*pl* -ais) <> *adj* homosexual. <> *m, f* homosexual.

homossexualidade [omosekswali'dadʒil *f* homosexuality.

homossexualismo [omosekswa'liʒmul *m* homosexuality.

Honduras [õn'duraʃl *n* Honduras.

hondurenho, nha [õndu'reɲu, ɲal <> *adj* Honduran. <> *m, f* Honduran.

honestamente [oneʃta'mẽntʃil *adv* honestly.

honestidade [oneʃtʃi'dadʒil *f* honesty; com ~ honestly.

honesto, ta [o'nɛʃtu, tal *adj* honest.

Honolulu [onolu'lul *n* Honolulu.

honorário, ria [ono'rarju, rjal *adj* honorary.

honorários [ono'rarjuʃl *mpl* fee *(sg).*

honorífico, ca [ono'rifiku, kal *adj* honorific.

honra [ˈõnxal *f* -1. [ger] honour UK, honor US; em ~ de alguém in honour of sb UK, in honor of sb US. -2. [motivo de orgulho] credit.
    ▸ **honras** *fpl* honours UK, honors US; ~ militares military honours UK, military honors US; fazer as ~ da casa to do the honours UK, to do the honors US.

honradez [õnxa'deʒl *f* honesty.

honrado, da [õ'xadu, dal *adj* -1. [digno] worthy. -2. [respeitado] respectable.

honrar [4] [õ'xa(x)] *vt* [respeitar] to honour UK, to honor US.
    ▸ **honrar-se** *vp* [lisonjear-se]: ~-se com algo/em fazer algo to be honoured in sthg/to do sthg UK, to be honored in sthg/to do sthg US.

honraria [õnxa'rial *f* honour UK, honor US.

honroso, osa [õ'xozu, ɔzal *adj* honourable UK, honorable US.

hóquei ['ɔkejl *m* hockey; ~ sobre gelo ice hockey.

hora ['ɔral *f* -1. [do dia] hour; de ~ em ~ every hour. -2. [ger] time; altas ~s very late at night; dar as ~s to tell the time; ~ legal official time; que ~s são? what time is it?; ~ extra extra time; ~s vagas spare time; chegar a ~ to arrive on time; fazer algo fora de ~ to do sthg at the wrong time; em boa ~ opportunely; em má ~ inopportunely; estar na ~ de fazer algo to be time to do sthg; na ~ H on the dot; de última ~ last minute *(antes de subst)*; na última ~ at the last minute; não vejo a ~ de ir embora I can't wait for the time to leave; na ~ on time; em cima da ~ dead on time; perder a ~ to be late. -3. [compromisso]: marcar ~ com alguém to make an appointment with sb. -4. [brincadeira]: fazer ~ com alguém to play with sb. -5. *loc*: estar pela ~ da morte to cost the earth; fazer ~ to waste time.

horário, ria [o'rarju, rjal *adj* hourly.
    ▸ **horário** *m* -1. [tabela] timetable. -2. [hora prefixada] time; ~ nobre prime time; ~ de verão summer time.

horda ['ɔxdal *f* horde.

horista [o'riʃtal <> *adj* paid by the hour *(depois de subst).* <> *mf* employee paid by the hour.

horizontal [orizõn'tawl (*pl* -ais) <> *adj* horizontal. <> *f* [linha] horizontal.

horizonte [ori'zõntʃil *m* horizon.

hormonal [oxmo'nawl (*pl* -ais) *adj* hormonal.

hormônio [ox'monjul *m* hormone.

horóscopo [o'rɔʃkopul *m* horoscope.

horrendo, da [o'xẽndu, dal *adj* -1. [atemorizante] frightful. -2. [feio] horrendous.

horripilante [oxipi'lãntʃil *adj* horrifying.

horripilar [4] [oxipi'la(x)] *vt* to horrify.
➼ **horripilar-se** *vp* to be horrified.
horrível [o'xivɛwl (*pl* -eis) *adj* -1. [ger] terrible.
-2. [feio] horrible.
horror [o'xo(x)] (*pl* -es) *m* -1. [medo]: **ter ~ (de** *ou*
a algo) to have a horror (of sthg). -2. [repulsa]:
ter ~ a algo/a fazer algo to have a horror of
sthg/doing sthg. -3. [coisa feia]: **fiquei um ~ com**
essa roupa I looked a fright in those clothes. -4.
[atrocidade]: **que ~!** how awful! -5. [ruim]: **ser um**
~ to be terrible.
➼ **horrores** *mpl* -1. [palavras injuriosas]: **dizer ~**
de algo/alguém to say horrible things about
sthg/sb. -2. [ações terríveis]: **fazer ~** to do
horrible things. -3. [quantia vultuosa]: **ele está fa-**
turando ~ es he is raking it in. -4. [grande quan-
tidade]: **~ de algo** vast amounts of sthg.
horrorizar [4] [oxori'za(x)] *vt* to terrify.
➼ **horrorizar-se** *vp* to be terrified.
horroroso, osa [oxo'rozu, ɔza] *adj* -1. [ger]
terrible. -2. [feio] frightful.
horta ['ɔxta] *f* vegetable garden.
hortaliças [oxta'lisaʃ] *fpl* vegetables.
hortelã [oxte'lã] *f* mint.
hortelã-pimenta [oxte,lãpi'mẽnta] (*pl* **hortelãs-**
pimenta) *f* peppermint.
hortênsia [ox'tẽnsja] *f* hydrangea.
horticultor, ra [oxtʃikuw'to(x), ra] (*mpl* -es, *fpl* -s)
m, *f* horticulturist.
horticultura [oxtʃikuw'tural *f* horticulture.
hortifrutigranjeiro, ra [oxtʃiʃrutʃigrãn'ʒejru,
ra] *adj* relating to fruit, vegetable and small
farm production.
➼ **hortifrutigranjeiro** *m* smallholder (producing fruit and vegetables).
hortigranjeiros [oxtʃigrãn'ʒeiruʃ] *mpl* farm
produce.
horto ['ɔxtul *m* allotment.
hospedagem [oʃpe'daʒẽl (*pl* -ns) *f* -1. [acomoda-
ção] accommodation. -2. [diária] board and
lodging. -3. [pensão] inn.
hospedar [4] [oʃpe'da(x)] *vt* to lodge.
➼ **hospedar-se** *vp* to lodge.
hospedaria [oʃpeda'rial *f* guest house.
hóspede ['ɔʃpedʒil *mf* guest.
hospedeiro, ra [oʃpe'dejru, ra] *m*, *f* host.
hospício [oʃ'pisjul *m* hospice.
hospital [oʃpi'tawl (*pl* -ais) *m* hospital.
hospitalar [oʃpita'la(x)] *adj* hospital (antes de
subst).
hospitaleiro, ra [oʃpita'lejru, ra] *adj* hospitable.
hospital-escola [oʃpi,tawiʃ'kɔlal (*pl* **hospitais-**
escola, hospitais-escolas) *m* teaching hospital.
hospitalidade [oʃpitali'dadʒil *f* hospitality.
hospitalização [oʃpitaliza'sãwl *f* hospitaliza-
tion.
hospitalizar [4] [oʃpitali'za(x)] *vt* to hospitalize.
host ['xoʃtʃil *m* COMPUT host.
hostess ['ɔʃtesl *f* hostess.
hóstia ['ɔʃtʃial *f* Host.
hostil [oʃ'tiwl (*pl* -is) *adj* -1. [contrário]: **~ a algo/**

alguém hostile to sthg/sb. -2. [agressivo] hostile.
hostilidade [oʃtʃili'dadʒil *f* [sentimento] hostility.
➼ **hostilidades** *fpl* MIL hostilities.
hostilizar [4] [oʃtili'za(x)] *vt* to be hostile towards.
hotel [o'tɛwl (*pl* -éis) *m* hotel; **~ de alta rotativi-**
dade hotel of ill repute.
hotelaria [otela'rial *f* -1. COM hotel management.
-2. [conjunto de hotéis] hotels (pl).
hoteleiro, ra [ote'lejru, ra] ◇ *adj* hotel; **rede**
hoteleira chain of hotels. ◇ *m*, *f* hotelier.
hp (abrev de **horsepower**) *m* hp.
HTML (abrev de **Hypertext Markup Language**) *m*
HTML.
HTTP (abrev de **Hypertext Transfer Protocol**) *m*
HTTP.
hum [ũl *interj* hum!
humanamente [umãna'mẽntʃil *adv* humanly; **~**
impossível humanly impossible.
humanidade [umani'dadʒil *f* humanity.
humanismo [uma'niʒmul *m* humanism.
humanista [uma'niʃtal ◇ *adj* humanistic. ◇
mf humanist.
humanitário, ria [umani'tarju, rjal *adj* humanitarian.
humanizar [4] [umani'za(x)] *vt* to humanize.
➼ **humanizar-se** *vp* to become humanized.
humano, na [u'manu, nal *adj* -1. [da humanidade]
human; **ser ~** human being. -2. [bondoso]
human, understanding.
humanóide [uma'nɔjdʒil ◇ *adj* humanoid. ◇
mf humanoid.
humanos [u'mãnuʃ] *mpl* humans.
humildade [umiw'dadʒil *f* -1. [pobreza]
humbleness. -2. [modéstia] humility. -3. [submis-
são] humility; **com ~** humbly.
humilde [u'miwdʒil *adj* humble; **os ~s** the poor
(pl).
humildemente [umiwdʒi'mẽntʃil *adv* humbly.
humilhação [umiʎa'sãwl (*pl* -ões) *f* humiliation.
humilhante [umi'ʎãntʃil *adj* humiliating.
humilhar [4] [umi'ʎa(x)] *vt* to humiliate.
➼ **humilhar-se** *vp* to humble o.s.
humor [u'mo(x)] *m* -1. [ger] humour UK, humor
US; **de ~** humorous; **~ negro** black humour. -2.
[ânimo] mood; **estar de bom/mau ~** to be good-/
bad-tempered; **estar com ~ de cão** to be in a
foul mood. -3. [senso de humor] sense of humour
UK, sense of humor US.
humorismo [umo'riʒmul *m* humour UK, humor
US.
humorista [umo'riʃtal *mf* comedian.
humorístico, ca [umo'riʃtʃiku, kal *adj* comedy
(antes de subst).
húmus ['umuʃl *m inv* humus.
húngaro, ra ['ũŋgaru, ral ◇ *adj* Hungarian. ◇
m, *f* Hungarian.
➼ **húngaro** *m* [língua] Hungarian.
Hungria [ũŋ'grial *n* Hungary.
hurra ['uxal *interj* hooray, hurrah.
Hz (abrev de **hertz**) *m* Hz.

i, I [i] *m* [letra] i, I.

ianque [ʼjãŋkil] ◇ *adj* Yankee. ◇ *m*, *f* Yank.

iate [ʼjatʃil] *m* yacht.

iatismo [ja'tʃiʒmul] *m* yachting, sailing.

iatista [ja'tʃiʃtal] *mf* yachtsman (*f* yachtswoman).

IBAMA (*abrev de* **Instituto Brasileiro do Meio Ambiente e dos Recursos Naturais Renováveis**) *m Brazilian organization responsible for preserving the country's natural environment.*

Ibase (*abrev de* **Instituto Brasileiro de Análises Sociais e Econômicas**) *m Brazilian institute for social and economic analysis.*

IBDF (*abrev de* **Instituto Brasileiro de Desenvolvimento Florestal**) *m Brazilian institute for forestry development.*

IBGE (*abrev de* **Instituto Brasileiro de Geografia e Estatística**) *m Brazilian institute of geography and statistics.*

ibidem [i'bidɛl] *adv* ibid., ibidem.

Ibope (*abrev de* **Instituto Brasileiro de Opinião Pública e Estatística**) *m Brazilian opinion poll institute.*

IBP (*abrev de* **Instituto Brasileiro de Petróleo**) *m Brazilian petroleum institute.*

içar [13] [i'sa(x)] *vt* to hoist.

iceberg [ajs'bɛxgil] *m* iceberg.

ICMS (*abrev de* **Imposto sobre a Circulação de Mercadorias e Serviços**) *m government tax on goods and services*, ≃ VAT *UK*.

ícone [ʼikonil] *m* icon.

iconoclasta [ikono'klaʃtal] ◇ *adj* iconoclastic. ◇ *mf* iconoclast.

iconografia [ikonogra'fial] *f* iconography.

icterícia [ikte'risjal] *f* jaundice.

ida [ʼidal] *f* **-1.** [ato de ir] going; ~ **s e vindas** comings and goings. **-2.** [partida] departure. **-3.** [viagem] journey; **na** ~ on the outward journet; **(bilhete de)** ~ **e volta** return ticket. **-4.** [bilhete]: **só comprei a** ~ I only bought a single (ticket).

idade [i'dadʒil] *f* [ger] age; **de** ~ [idoso] elderly; **ser menor/maior de** ~ to be under/of age; **pessoa da terceira** ~ senior citizen; **estar na** ~ **de fazer algo** to be of an age to do sthg; ~ **adulta** adulthood; ~ **escolar** school age; **Idade Média**

Middle Ages *(pl)*; ~ **da pedra** Stone Age.

ideação [idea'sãwl] *f* ideation.

ideal [i'deawl] *(pl* **-ais**) ◇ *adj* ideal. ◇ *m* **-1.** [valores] ideal. **-2.** [perfeição] ideal thing.

idealismo [idea'liʒmul] *m* idealism.

idealista [idea'liʃtal] ◇ *adj* idealistic. ◇ *mf* idealist.

idealização [idealiza'sãwl] *(pl* **-ões**) *f* **-1.** [endeusamento] idealization. **-2.** [planejamento] planning.

idealizador [idealiza'do(x)l] *m*, *f* planner.

idealizar [4] [ideali'za(x)l] *vt* **-1.** [endeusar] to idealize. **-2.** [planejar] to plan.

idear [4] [ʼidea(x)l] *vt* [planejar] to plan.

ideário [ide'arjul] *m* ideas *(pl)*.

idéia [i'dɛjal] *f* **-1.** [ger] idea; ~ **de jerico** stupid idea; **estar com** ~ **de** to be thinking of; ~ **fixa** idée fixe, fixed idea; **fazer uma** ~ **errada de alguém** to misjudge sb; **ter uma** ~ **errada de algo** to have the wrong idea about sthg; **fazer** *ou* **ter** ~ **de algo** to have an idea of sthg. **-2.** [mente, opinião] mind; **mudar de** ~ to change one's mind.
　➡ **idéias** *fpl* [concepções] ideas; **trocar** ~ to exchange ideas.

idem [ʼidɛl] *pron* idem.

idêntico, ca [i'dʒẽtʃiku, kal] *adj* identical.

identidade [idẽtʃi'dadʒil] *f* identity; **(carteira de)** ~ identity card.

identificação [idẽtʃifika'sãwl] *(pl* **-ões**) *f* identification.

identificar [12] [idʒẽtʃifi'ka(x)l] *vt* to identify.
　➡ **identificar-se** *vp* **-1.** [revelar-se] to identify o.s. **-2.** [espelhar-se]: ~ **-se com algo/alguém** to identify o.s. with sthg/sb.

ideologia [ideolo'ʒial] *f* ideology.

ideológico, ca [ideo'lɔʒiku, kal] *adj* ideological.

ídiche [ʼidiʃil] *m* = **iídiche**.

idílico, ca [i'dʒiliku, kal] *adj* idyllic.

idílio [i'dʒiljul] *m* idyll.

idioma [i'dʒjomal] *m* language.

idiomático, ca [idʒo'matʃiku, kal] *adj* idiomatic; **expressão idiomática** idiomatic expression.

idiossincrasia [idʒjosĩŋkra'zial] *f* idiosyncrasy.

idiota [i'dʒɔtal] ◇ *adj* idiotic. ◇ *mf* idiot.

idiotia [idʒjo'tʃial] *f* idiocy.

idiotice [idʒo'tʃisil] *f* idiocy.

ido, ida [ʼidu, ʼidal *adj* past.

idólatra [i'dɔlatral] ◇ *adj* idolatrous. ◇ *mf* [de ídolos] idol worshipper.

idolatrar [4] [idola'tra(x)l] *vt* to idolize.

idolatria [idola'trial] *f* idolatry.

ídolo [ʼidulul] *m* idol.

idoneidade [idonej'dadʒil] *f* fitness.

idôneo, nea [i'donju, njal] *adj* **-1.** [pessoa, julgamento] fitting. **-2.** [empresa] suitable.

idos [ʼiduʃl] *mpl* bygone times.

idoso, osa [i'dozu, ɔzal *adj* aged.

Iemanjá [jemã'ʒal] *f goddess of the sea and water, in Afro-Brazilian lore.*

iene [ʼjenil] *m* yen.

Ierevan [jere'vãl] *n* Yerevan.

iglu [i'glul] *m* igloo.

ignaro, ra [igi'naru, ra] *adj* ignorant.

ignição [igni'sãw] *f* ignition.

ignóbil [ig'nɔbiw] (*pl* **-eis**) *adj* ignoble.

ignomínia [igno'minja] *f* ignominy.

ignominoso, osa [ignomi'nozu, ɔza] *adj* ignominious.

ignorado, da [igno'radu, da] *adj* unknown.

ignorância [igno'rãnsja] *f* **-1.** [desconhecimento] ignorance. **-2.** [grosseria] rudeness; **com** ~ rudely. **-3.** [violência]: **apelar para a** ~ to resort to violence.

ignorante [igno'rãntʃi] <> *adj* **-1.** [leigo]: ~ **(em)** ignorant (of). **-2.** [grosseiro] rude. <> *mf* **-1.** [leigo] lay person. **-2.** [grosseiro] rude person.

ignorar [4] [igno'ra(x)] *vt* **-1.** [desconhecer] not to know. **-2.** [desprezar] to ignore.

ignoto, ta [ig'nɔtu, ta] *adj* unknown.

IGP (*abrev de* **Índice Geral de Preços**) *m* general price index.

IGP-M (*abrev de* **Índice Geral de Preços de Mercado**) *m* general index of market prices.

igreja [i'greʒa] *f* church.

Iguaçu [igwa'su] *n*: **as cataratas do** ~ the Iguaçu Falls.

igual [i'gwaw] (*pl* **-ais**) <> *adj* **-1.** [idêntico] equal. **-2.** [uniforme] the same. <> *mf* equal; **de** ~ **para** ~ as equals; **por** ~ evenly. <> *adv* the same as.

igualar [4] [igwa'la(x)] *vt* **-1.** [tornar igual] to make equal. **-2.** [nivelar] to level.

➠ **igualar-se** *vp* **-1.** [tornar-se igual]: ~**-se a algo/alguém** to equal sthg/sb. **-2.** [nivelar-se]: ~**-se com algo** to equal sthg. **-3.** [comparar-se]: ~**-se a algo/alguém** to bear comparison with sthg/sb.

igualdade [igwaw'dadʒi] *f* **-1.** [ger] equality. **-2.** [constância] regularity.

igualitário, ria [igwali'tarju, rja] *adj* egalitarian.

igualmente [igwaw'mẽntʃi] *adv* equally.

iguana [i'gwãna] *m* iguana.

iguaria [igwa'ria] *f* delicacy.

ih [i] *interj* eek!

iídiche ['jidiʃi], **ídiche** ['idiʃi] *m* Yiddish.

ilação [ila'sãw] (*pl* **-ões**) *f* inference.

ilegal [ile'gaw] (*pl* **-ais**) *adj* illegal.

ilegalidade [ilegali'dadʒi] *f* illegality.

ilegítimo, ma [ile'ʒitʃimu, ma] *adj* illegitimate.

ilegível [ile'ʒivɛw] (*pl* **-eis**) *adj* illegible.

ileso, sa [i'lezu, za] *adj* unharmed.

iletrado, da [ile'tradu, da] *adj* **-1.** [inculto] unlettered. **-2.** [analfabeto] illiterate.

ilha ['iʎa] *f* island.

ILHAS

Two of the world's largest islands are part of Brazil. The island of Marajó, in the mouth of the Amazon river in Pará, has an area of 50,000 km²; it is both a fluvial island and a marine island, as to the north it is washed by the Atlantic ocean. The breeding of buffalo is the island's main economic activity. In the state of Tocantins, two branches of the river Araguaia form the largest fluvial island in the world, with an area of 20,000 km²: the island of Bananal. Its fauna is extremely abundant and the island of Bananal is home to the National Park of Araguaia and two indigenous reserves: Carajás and Javaés.

ilhar [4] [i'ʎa(x)] *vt* to isolate.

ilharga [i'ʎaxga] *f* ANAT flank.

ilhéu, ilhoa [i'ʎɛw, i'ʎoa] *m*, *f* islander.

ilhós [i'ʎɔʃ] (*pl* **ilhoses**) *m* eyelet.

ilhota [i'ʎɔta] *f* islet.

ilícito, ta [i'lisitu, ta] *adj* illicit.

ilimitado, da [ilemi'tadu, da] *adj* unlimited.

ilógico, ca [i'lɔʒiku, ka] *adj* illogical.

iludir [6] [ilu'di(x)] *vt* to delude.

➠ **iludir-se** *vp* to delude o.s.

iluminação [ilumina'sãw] (*pl* **-ões**) *f* **-1.** [luzes] lighting. **-2.** *fig* [insight] inspiration.

iluminado, da [ilumi'nadu, da] *adj* **-1.** [que recebe luz - sala] lit; [- palco, estádio] floodlit. **-2.** *fig* [esclarecido] enlightened.

iluminante [ilumi'nãntʃi] *adj* illuminating.

iluminar [4] [ilumi'na(x)] *vt* **-1.** [alumiar] to light up. **-2.** *fig* [esclarecer] to enlighten.

➠ **iluminar-se** *vp* to light up.

Iluminismo [ilumi'niʒmu] *m* Enlightenment.

iluminista [ilumi'niʃta] <> *adj* Enlightenment (*antes de subst*). <> *mf* member or follower of the Enlightenment.

ilusão [ilu'zãw] (*pl* **-ões**) *f* illusion; ~ **de ótica** optical illusion; **viver de ilusões** to delude o.s.

ilusionista [iluzjo'niʃta] *mf* illusionist.

ilusório, ria [ilu'zɔrju, rja] *adj* illusory.

ilustração [iluʃtra'sãw] (*pl* **-ões**) *f* illustration.

ilustrado, da [iluʃ'tradu, da] *adj* **-1.** [com figuras] illustrated. **-2.** [instruído] learned.

ilustrador, ra [iluʃtra'do(x), ra] <> *adj* illustrative. <> *m*, *f* illustrator.

ilustrar [4] [iluʃ'tra(x)] *vt* **-1.** [ger] to illustrate. **-2.** [instruir] to enlighten.

➠ **ilustrar-se** *vp* [instruir-se] to enlighten o.s.

ilustrativo, va [iluʃtra'tʃivu, va] *adj* illustrative.

ilustre [i'luʃtri] *adj* illustrious, distinguished; **um** ~ **desconhecido** a complete unknown.

ilustríssimo, ma [iluʃ'trisimu, ma] *superl* ⊳ ilustre; ~ **senhor** honourable gentleman *UK*, honorable gentleman *US*.

ímã ['imã] *m* magnet.

imaculado, da [imaku'ladu, da] *adj* immaculate.

imagem [i'maʒẽ] (*pl* **-ns**) *f* **-1.** [gen] image. **-2.** [TV] picture.

imagético, ca [ima'getiku, ka] *adj* fully illustrated.

imaginação [imaʒina'sãw] *f* imagination.

imaginar [4] [imaʒi'na(x)] <> *vt* **-1.** [fantasiar] to imagine. **-2.** [supor]: ~ **que** to imagine that. <> *vi* to daydream; **imagina!** just imagine!

➠ **imaginar-se** *vp* [supor-se] to imagine o.s.

imaginário, ria [imaʒi'narju, rja] *adj* imaginary.

imaginativo, va [imaʒina'tʃivu, va] *adj* imaginative.

imaginável [imaʒi'navewl] (pl -eis) adj imaginable.

imaginoso, osa [imaʒi'nozu, ɔza] adj fanciful.

imantar [4] [imãn'ta(x)] vt to magnetize.

imaturidade [imaturi'dadʒi] f immaturity.

imaturo, ra [ima'turu, ra] adj immature.

imbatível [ĩnba'tʃivɛw] (pl -eis) adj unbeatable.

imbecil [ĩnbe'siw] (pl -is) <> adj stupid, idiotic. <> mf imbecile.

imbecilidade [ĩnbesili'dadʒi] f stupidity.

imberbe [ĩn'bɛxbi] adj -1. [sem barba] beardless. -2. [juvenil] youthful.

imbricar [12] [ĩmbri'ka(x)] vt to overlap.

→ **imbricar-se** vp to overlap.

imbuído, da [ĩmbu'idu, da] adj imbued.

imbuir [74] [ĩm'bwi(x)] vt: ~ algo de algo to impregnate sthg with sthg; ~ alguém de algo to instil sthg in sb.

imediações [imedʒja'sõiʃ] fpl vicinity (sg); nas ~ de near, in the vicinity of.

imediatamente [ime,dʒjata'mẽntʃi] adv immediately.

imediatismo [imedʒja'tʃiʒmu] m immediacy.

imediatista [imedʒja'tʃiʃta] adj immediate.

imediato, ta [ime'dʒjatu, ta] adj immediate.

→ **imediato** m second in command.

→ **de imediato** loc adv at once.

imemorial [imemo'rjaw] (pl -ais) adj immemorial.

imensidão [imẽnsi'dãw], **imensidade** [imẽnsi'dadʒi] f immensity.

imenso, sa [i'mẽsu, sa] adj immense; sinto uma saudade imensa dele I miss him immensely.

imensurável [imẽnsu'ravew] (pl -eis) adj immeasurable.

imerecido, da [imere'sidu, da] adj undeserved.

imergir [78] [imex'ʒi(x)] <> vt to immerse. <> vi -1. [afundar] to sink. -2. fig [entrar]: ~ em algo to sink into sthg.

imersão [imex'sãw] (pl -ões) f immersion.

imerso, sa [i'mexsu, sa] adj immersed.

imigração [imigra'sãw] (pl -ões) f immigration.

imigrante [imi'grãntʃi] <> adj immigrant. <> mf immigrant.

imigrar [4] [imi'gra(x)] vi to immigrate.

iminência [imi'nẽnsja] f imminence; em ~ imminent; na ~ de fazer algo on the point of doing sthg.

iminente [imi'nẽntʃi] adj imminent.

imiscuir-se [74] [imiʃ'kwixsi] vp to become involved.

imitação [imita'sãw] (pl -ões) f imitation.

imitador, ra [imita'do(x), ra] <> adj imitation (antes de subst). <> m, f imitator.

imitar [4] [imi'ta(x)] vt -1. [arremedar] to imitate. -2. [falsificar] to forge.

imitativo, va [imita'tʃivu, va] adj imitative.

IML (abrev de Instituto Médico Legal) m Brazilian institute of forensic medicine.

imobiliário, ria [imobi'larju, rja] adj property (antes de subst).

→ **imobiliária** f estate agency.

imobilidade [imobili'dadʒi] f immobility.

imobilizar [4] [imobili'za(x)] vt to immobilize.

imoderação [imodera'sãw] f immoderation.

imoderado, da [imode'radu, da] adj immoderate.

imodéstia [imo'dɛʃtʃja] f immodesty.

imodesto, ta [imo'dɛʃtu, ta] adj immodest.

imolar [4] [imo'la(x)] vt -1. [sacrificar] to immolate. -2. [prejudicar] to damage.

imoral [imo'raw] (pl -ais) adj immoral.

imoralidade [imorali'dadʒi] f immorality.

imortal [imox'taw] (pl -ais) <> adj immortal. <> mf member of the Academia Brasileira de Letras.

imortalidade [imoxtali'dadʒi] f immortality.

imortalizar [4] [imoxtali'za(x)] vt to immortalize.

imóvel [i'mɔvɛw] (pl -eis) <> adj -1. [pessoa] immobile. -2. [olho, bem] fixed; bens imóveis real estate (U). <> m property.

impaciência [ĩnpa'sjẽnsja] f impatience.

impacientar [4] [ĩmpasjẽn'ta(x)] vt to be impatient.

→ **impacientar-se** vp to become impatient.

impaciente [ĩnpa'sjẽntʃi] adj -1. [sem paciência] impatient. -2. [ansioso] anxious.

impactante [ĩnpak'tãntʃi] adj [chocante] shattering.

impactar [4] [ĩnpak'ta(x)] <> vt -1. [impressionar, abalar] to shatter. -2. [colidir contra] to crash into. <> vi to have an impact.

impacto [ĩn'paktu] m impact.

impagável [ĩmpa'gavew] (pl -eis) adj priceless.

ímpar [ˈĩnpa(x)] (pl -es) adj -1. [número] odd. -2. [único] peerless; ele é um amigo ~ he's a friend in a million.

imparcial [ĩnpax'sjaw] (pl -ais) adj impartial.

imparcialidade [ĩnpaxsjali'dadʒi] f impartiality.

impasse [ĩn'pasi] m deadlock, impasse.

impassível [ĩnpa'sivew] (pl -eis) adj impassive.

impávido, da [ĩm'pavidu, da] adj undaunted.

impeachment [ĩnpitʃimẽnt] m impeachment.

impecável [ĩnpe'kavew] (pl -eis) adj impeccable.

impedido, da [ĩm'pedʒidu, da] adj -1. [bloqueado] blocked. -2. FUT off-side. -3. [impossibilitado]: ~ de fazer algo prevented from doing sthg.

impedimento [ĩnpedʒi'mẽntu] m -1. FUT off-side. -2. fig [obstáculo] impediment. -3. POL impeachment.

impedir [70] [ĩmpe'dʒi(x)] v -1. [obstruir] to obstruct. -2. [coibir] to prevent; ~ alguém de fazer algo to prevent sb from doing sthg.

impelir [57] [ĩmpe'li(x)] vt -1. [empurrar] to thrust. -2. [instigar]: ~ alguém a algo to drive sb to sthg; ~ alguém a fazer algo to impel sb to do sthg.

impenetrável [ĩnpene'travɛw] (pl -eis) adj impenetrable.

impenitente [ĩnpeni'tẽntʃi] adj unrepentant.

impensado, da [ĩnpẽn'sadu, da] adj -1. [não-pensado] thoughtless. -2. [imprevisto] unthought of.

impensável [ĩnpẽn'savɛwl] (pl -eis) adj unthinkable.

imperador [ĩnpera'do(x)] (mpl -es) m emperor (f empress).

imperar [4] [ĩmpe'ra(x)] vi -1. [reinar] to rule. -2. [prevalecer] to prevail.

imperativo, va [ĩmpera'tʃivu, va] adj -1. [urgente] imperative. -2. [autoritário] imperious.
➡ **imperativo** m imperative.

imperatriz [ĩnpera'triʃ] (mpl -zes) f ⊳ **imperador**.

imperceptível [ĩnpexsep'tʃivɛwl] (pl -eis) adj imperceptible.

imperdível [ĩnpex'dʒivɛwl] (pl -eis) adj -1. [show, filme, aula] unmissable. -2. [jogo, eleição, questão] impossible to lose (depois de verbo).

imperdoável [ĩnpex'dwavɛwl] (pl -eis) adj unforgivable.

imperecível [ĩnpere'sivewl] (pl -eis) adj imperishable.

imperfeição [ĩnpexfej'sãwl] (pl -ões) f [defeito] imperfection.

imperfeito, ta [ĩnpex'fejtu, ta] adj imperfect.
➡ **imperfeito** m GRAM imperfect.

imperial [ĩnpe'rjawl] (pl -ais) adj imperial.

imperialismo [ĩnperja'liʒmu] m imperialism.

imperialista [ĩnperja'liʃta] ⟨⟩ adj imperialist. ⟨⟩ mf imperialist.

imperícia [ĩnpe'risja] f -1. [inabilidade] incompetence. -2. [inexperiência] inexperience.

império [ĩn'pɛrju] m empire.

imperioso, osa [ĩmpe'rjozu, ɔza] adj -1. [ger] imperious. -2. [urgente] imperative.

impermeabilizante [ĩnpexmjabili'zãntʃil] ⟨⟩ adj waterproofing. ⟨⟩ m waterproofer.

impermeabilizar [4] [ĩmpexmjabili'za(x)] vt to waterproof.

impermeável [ĩnpex'mjavɛwl] (pl -eis) ⟨⟩ adj impermeable, waterproof. ⟨⟩ m [capa de chuva] raincoat.

impertinência [ĩnpextʃi'nẽnsja] f impertinence.

impertinente [ĩnpextʃi'nẽntʃil] adj impertinent.

imperturbável [ĩnpextux'bavɛwl] (pl -eis) adj imperturbable.

impessoal [ĩnpe'swawl] (pl -ais) adj -1. [objetivo] objective. -2. GRAM impersonal.

impessoalidade [ĩnpeswali'dadʒi] f [impersonalidade] impersonal nature.

ímpeto ['ĩnpetu] m -1. [movimento brusco] sudden movement; **ele se levantou num ~** he stood up with a start. -2. [impulso] urge, impulse; **sentir um ~ de fazer algo** to feel an urge to do sthg.

impetrar [4] [ĩmpe'tra(x)] vt JUR: **~ algo** to petition for sthg.

impetuosidade [ĩnpetwozi'dadʒi] f impetuosity.

impetuoso, osa [ĩmpe'twozu, ɔza] adj -1. [pessoa] impetuous. -2. [chuva] driving. -3. [rio] fast-flowing.

impiedade [ĩnpje'dadʒi] f [crueldade] cruelty.

impiedoso, osa [ĩmpje'dozu, ɔza] adj merciless.

impingir [52] [ĩmpĩn'ʒi(x)] vt: **~ algo a alguém** to fob sthg off on sb.

ímpio, pia ['ĩmpiu, pia] ⟨⟩ adj pitiless. ⟨⟩ m,f pitiless person.

implacável [ĩnpla'kavɛwl] (pl -eis) adj -1. [impiedoso] implacable. -2. [inexorável] unrelenting.

implantação [ĩnplãnta'sãwl] f -1. [introdução] establishing. -2. [implementação] implementation. -3. MED implant.

implantar [4] [ĩmplãn'ta(x)] vt -1. [introduzir] to establish. -2. [implementar] to implement. -3. MED to implant.

implante [ĩn'plãntʃil] m MED implant.

implementação [ĩnplemẽnta'sãwl] f implementation.

implementar [4] [ĩmplemẽn'ta(x)] vt to implement.

implemento [ĩnple'mẽntul] m implement.

implicação [ĩnplika'sãwl] (pl -ões) f -1. [conseqüência] implication. -2. [envolvimento] involvement.

implicância [ĩnpli'kãnsja] f -1. [provocação] provoking; **meus filhos passam o dia inteiro de ~ um com o outro** my children spend the whole day provoking each other. -2. [antipatia]: **ter uma ~ com alguém** to dislike sb.

implicante [ĩnpli'kãntʃil] adj provocative.

implicar [12] [ĩmpli'ka(x)] ⟨⟩ vt [envolver]: **~ alguém em algo** to involve sb in sthg. ⟨⟩ vi -1. [pressupor]: **~ em algo** to involve sthg. -2. [acarretar]: **~ em algo** to result in sthg. -3. [provocar]: **~ com alguém** to torment sb.

implícito, ta [ĩn'plisitu, ta] adj implicit.

implodir [78] [ĩmplo'dʒi(x)] ⟨⟩ vt to implode. ⟨⟩ vi to implode.

implorar [4] [ĩmplo'ra(x)] vt: **~ algo (a alguém)** to beg (sb) for sthg.

implosão [ĩnplo'zãwl] (pl -ões) f implosion.

impoluto, ta [ĩmpo'lutu, ta] adj unpolluted.

imponderado, da [ĩnpõnde'radu, da] adj rash.

imponderável [ĩnpõnde'ravewl] (pl -eis) adj imponderable.

imponência [ĩnpo'nẽnsja] f impressiveness.

imponente [ĩnpo'nẽntʃil] adj impressive, imposing.

impontual [ĩnpõn'twawl] (pl -ais) adj unpunctual.

impopular [ĩnpopu'la(x)] (pl -es) adj unpopular.

impopularidade [ĩnpopulari'dadʒil] f unpopularity.

impor [45] [ĩm'po(x)] vt to impose; **~ algo a alguém** to impose sthg on sb.
➡ **impor-se** vp [afirmar-se] to establish o.s.

importação [ĩnpoxta'sãwl] (pl -ões) f -1. [ato] importation. -2. [produtos] imports (pl).

importador, ra [ĩnpoxta'do(x), ra] ⟨⟩ adj importing (antes de subst). ⟨⟩ m, f importer.
➡ **importadora** f -1. [companhia] importer. -2. [loja] shop selling imported goods.

importância [ĩnpox'tãnsja] f -1. [mérito] importance; **não dar ~ a alguém/algo** to not care about sb/sthg; **ela não dá ~ ao que ele disse** she doesn't care about what he said; **isso não tem** ~ that doesn't matter. **-2.** [quantia] sum.

importante [ĩnpox'tãntʃi] *adj* important.

importar [4] [ĩmpox'ta(x)] ◇ *vt COM* to import. ◇ *vi* **-1.** [ser importante] to matter. **-2.** [resultar]: ~ **em** to result in. **-3.** [atingir]: ~ **em** to add up to.
➡ **importar-se** *vp* [fazer caso]: **não** ~-**se (com algo/de fazer algo)** not to mind sthg/about doing sthg.

importe [ĩn'pɔxtʃi] *m* **-1.** [soma] amount. **-2.** [preço] cost.

importunação [ĩnpoxtuna'sãw] *f* annoyance.

importunar [4] [ĩmpoxtu'na(x)] *vt* to annoy.

importuno, na [ĩnpox'tunu, na] *adj* annoying.

imposição [ĩnpozi'sãw] (*pl* -**ões**) *f* imposition.

impossibilidade [ĩnposibili'dadʒi] *f* impossibility.

impossibilitado, da [ĩnposibili'tadu, da] *adj*: ~ **de fazer algo** unable to do sthg.

impossibilitar [4] [ĩmposi'bili'ta(x)] *vt*: ~ **algo** to make sthg impossible; ~ **alguém de fazer algo** to prevent sb from doing sthg.

impossível [ĩnpo'sivew] (*pl* -**eis**) *adj* impossible.

impostação [ĩnpoʃta'sãw] *f* diction.

imposto, osta [ĩm'poʃtu, ɔsta] *pp* ▷ **impor**.
➡ **imposto** *m* tax; ~ **sobre Circulação de Mercadorias e Serviços** ≃ value added tax *UK*, ≃ sales tax *US*; ~ **predial** ≃ council tax *UK*; ~ **de renda** income tax.

impostor, ra [ĩnpoʃ'to(x), ra] (*mpl* -**es**, *fpl* -**s**) *m* impostor.

impostura [ĩnpoʃ'tura] *f* fraud.

impotência [ĩnpo'tẽnsja] *f* impotence.

impotente [ĩnpo'tẽntʃi] *adj* impotent.

impraticável [ĩnpratʃi'kavew] (*pl* -**eis**) *adj* **-1.** [impossível] impossible. **-2.** [inexequível] unworkable. **-3.** [intransitável] impassable.

imprecar [12] [ĩmpre'ka(x)] ◇ *vt* to curse. ◇ *vi* to curse.

imprecisão [ĩnpresi'zãw] (*pl* -**ões**) *f* imprecision.

impreciso, sa [ĩnpre'sizu, za] *adj* imprecise.

impregnar [4] [ĩmpreg'na(x)] ◇ *vt* to impregnate; ~ **algo de algo** to impregnate sthg with sthg. ◇ *vi*: ~ **en** to impregnate.

imprensa [ĩn'prẽnsa] *f* **-1.** [ger] press; ~ **marrom** gutter press. **-2.** [tipografia] printing press.

imprensar [ĩmprẽn'sa(x)] *vt* **-1.** [espremer] to crush. **-2.** [pressionar] to press.

imprescindível [ĩnpresĩn'dʒivew] (*pl* -**eis**) *adj* indispensable.

impressão [ĩnpre'sãw] (*pl* -**ões**) *f* **-1.** [marca] imprint; ~ **digital** fingerprint. **-2.** [reprodução] printing. **-3.** [sensação] feeling; **ter boa/má impressão de alguém/algo** to have a good/bad impression of sb/sthg.

impressionante [ĩnpresjo'nãntʃi] *adj* impressive.

impressionar [ĩmpresju'na(x)] ◇ *vt* to impress. ◇ *vi* to impress.
➡ **impressionar-se** *vp*: -**se com alguém/algo** [comover-se] to be moved by sb/sthg.

impressionável [ĩnpresjo'navew] (*pl* -**eis**) *adj* impressionable.

impressionismo [ĩnpresjo'niʒmu] *m* Impressionism.

impressionista [ĩnpresjo'niʃta] ◇ *adj* Impressionist. ◇ *m, f* Impressionist.

impresso, a [ĩn'prɛsu, sa] ◇ *pp* ▷ **imprimir**. ◇ *adj* printed.
➡ **impresso** *m* printed matter *(sg)*.

impressora [ĩnpre'soral] *f* printer; ~ **laser** laser printer; ~ **a jato de tinta** ink-jet printer; ~ **matricial** dot matrix printer.

imprestável [ĩnpreʃ'tavew] (*pl* -**eis**) *adj* **-1.** [inútil] unhelpful. **-2.** [estragado] useless.

impreterível [ĩnprete'rivew] (*pl* -**eis**) *adj* unavoidable.

imprevidente [ĩnprevi'dẽntʃi] *adj* **-1.** [imprudente] imprudent. **-2.** [que não soube prever] improvident.

imprevisão [ĩnprevi'zãw] *f* **-1.** [desleixo] carelessness. **-2.** [falta de previsão] improvidence.

imprevisível [ĩnprevi'zivew] (*pl* -**eis**) *adj* unforeseeable.

imprevisto, ta [ĩmpre'viʃtu, ta] *adj* unexpected.
➡ **imprevisto** *m*: **surgiu um** ~ **nos nossos planos** something unforeseen cropped up in our plans.

imprimir [ĩmpri'mi(x)] ◇ *vt* to print. ◇ *vi COMPUT* to print.

improbabilidade [ĩnprobabili'dadʒi] *f* improbability.

ímprobo, ba [ˈĩmprobu, ba] *adj* dishonest.

improcedente [ĩnprose'dẽntʃi] *adj* unjustified.

improdutivo, va [ĩnprodu'tʃivu, va] *adj* unproductive.

improfícuo, cua [ĩnpro'fikwu, kwa] *adj* useless.

impropério [ĩnpro'pɛrjul] *m* insult.

impróprio, pria [ĩn'prɔprju, prja] *adj* inappropriate.

improrrogável [ĩnproxo'gavew] (*pl* -**eis**) *adj* nonpostponable.

improvável [ĩnpro'vavew] (*pl* -**eis**) *adj* improbable.

improvisação [ĩnproviza'sãw] *f* improvisation.

improvisado, da [ĩnprovi'zadu, da] *adj* improvised.

improvisar [4] [ĩmprovi'za(x)] ◇ *vt* to improvise. ◇ *vi* **-1.** to improvise. **-2.** *TEATRO* to ad-lib.

improviso [ĩnpro'vizul] *m* **-1.** [repente]: **de** ~ [de repente] suddenly; [sem preparação] off the cuff; **falar de** ~ to speak off the cuff. **-2.** *TEATRO* improvisation.

imprudência [ĩnpru'dẽnsja] *f* [descuido] carelessness.

imprudente [ĩnpru'dẽntʃi] *adj* careless.

impudico, ca [ĩnpu'dʒiku, ka] *adj* shameless.

impugnação [ĩnpugna'sãw] (*pl* -**ões**) *f* [contestação] challenge.

impugnar [4] [ĩmpug'na(x)] *vt* **-1.** [refutar] to refute. **-2.** [opor-se a] to oppose.

impulsionar [4] [ĩmpuwsjuˈna(x)] vt - **1.** [impelir] to propel. - **2.** [estimular] to speed up.

impulsividade [ĩmpuwsiviˈdaʒi] f impulsiveness.

impulsivo, va [ĩmpuwˈsivu, va] adj impulsive.

impulso [ĩmˈpuwsu] m - **1.** [ger] impulse, urge; **dar un novo** ~ **a** to give a new impetus to; **tomar** ~ to gain strength; **por** ~ on impulse. - **2.** [força] thrust; **tomar** ~ to take a run.

impune [ĩˈpuni] adj unpunished.

impunemente [ĩmpuneˈmẽntʃi] adv with impunity.

impunidade [ĩpuniˈdaʒi] f impunity.

impureza [ĩpuˈreza] f impurity.

impuro, ra [ĩmˈpuru, ĩmˈpura] adj impure.

imputação [ĩmputaˈsãw] (pl -ões) f [acusação] accusation.

imputar [4] [ĩmpuˈta(x)] vt: ~ **algo a alguém** to attribute sthg to sb.

imundície [ĩmũnˈdʒisjil], **imundícia** [ĩmũnˈdʒisjal] f [falta de asseio] filthiness.

imundo, da [iˈmũndo, da] adj filthy.

imune [iˈmuni] adj: ~ **(a)** immune to.

imunidade [imuniˈdaʒi] f immunity.

imunização [imunizaˈsãw] f immunization.

imunizar [4] [imuniˈza(x)] vt to immunize.

imunologia [imunoloˈʒia] f immunology.

imutável [imuˈtavɛw] (pl -eis) adj immutable.

inabalável [inabaˈlavɛw] (pl -eis) adj unshakeable.

inábil [iˈnabiw] (pl -eis) adj - **1.** [desajeitado] clumsy. - **2.** [incapaz] incapable.

inabilidade [inabiliˈdaʒi] f inability.

inabilidoso, osa [inabiliˈdozu, ɔza] adj inept.

inabilitar [4] [inabiliˈta(x)] vt - **1.** [incapacitar] to disable. - **2.** [reprovar] to disqualify.
➡ **inabilitar-se** vp [reprovar-se] to fail.

inabitado, da [inabiˈtadu, da] adj uninhabited.

inabitável [inabiˈtavɛw] (pl -eis) adj uninhabitable.

inacabado, da [inakaˈbadu, da] adj unfinished.

inacabável [inakaˈbavɛw] (pl -eis) adj unending.

inação [inaˈsãw] f - **1.** [inércia] inaction. - **2.** [indecisão] indecision.

inaceitável [inasejˈtavɛw] (pl -eis) adj unacceptable.

inacessível [inaseˈsivɛw] (pl -eis) adj inaccessible.

inacreditável [inakredʒiˈtavɛw] (pl -eis) adj unbelievable.

inadaptado, da [inadapˈtadu, da] adj maladjusted.

inadiável [inaˈdjavɛw] (pl -eis) adj pressing.

inadimplência [inadʒĩˈplẽsja] f JUR non-compliance.

inadimplente [inadʒĩˈplẽntʃil] adj non-compliant.

inadmissível [inadʒimiˈsivɛw] (pl -eis) adj unacceptable.

inadvertência [inadʒivexˈtẽsja] f inadvertence; **por** ~ inadvertently.

inadvertidamente [inadʒivertʃidaˈmẽntʃil] adv inadvertently.

inadvertido, da [inadverˈtʃidu, da] adj inadvertent.

inalação [inalaˈsãw] (pl -ões) f inhalation.

inalar [4] [inaˈla(x)] vt to inhale.

inalcançável [inawkãˈsavɛw] (pl -eis) adj inaccessible.

inalterado, da [inawteˈradu, da] adj - **1.** [imudado] unaltered. - **2.** [calmo] composed.

inalterável [inawteˈravɛw] (pl -eis) adj - **1.** [imudável] immutable. - **2.** [imperturbável] imperturbable.

inanição [inaniˈsãw] f starvation.

inanimado, da [inaniˈmadu, da] adj inanimate.

inapetência [inapeˈtẽsja] f loss of appetite.

inapetente [inapeˈtẽntʃil] adj lacking appetite (depois de verbo).

inaplicável [inapliˈkavɛw] (pl -eis) adj inapplicable.

inaproveitável [inaprovejˈtavɛw] (pl -eis) adj useless.

inaptidão [inaptʃiˈdãw] f inability.

inapto, ta [iˈnaptu, ta] adj unsuitable.

inatacável [inataˈkavɛw] (pl -eis) adj unassailable.

inatenção [inatẽˈsãw] f inattention.

inatingível [inatʃĩˈʒivɛw] (pl -eis) adj unattainable.

inatividade [inatʃiviˈdaʒil] f - **1.** [ger] retirement. - **2.** [inércia] inactivity. - **3.** [desemprego] inactivity.

inativo, va [inaˈtʃivu, va] adj - **1.** [ger] retired. - **2.** [parado] idle.

inato, ta [iˈnatu, ta] adj innate.

inaudito, ta [inawˈdʒitu, ta] adj unheard of.

inaudível [inawˈdʒivɛw] (pl -eis) adj inaudible.

inauguração [inawguraˈsãw] (pl -ões) f inauguration.

inaugural [inawguˈraw] (pl -ais) adj inaugural.

inaugurar [4] [inawguˈra(x)] vt to open.

inca [ˈĩŋka] ◇ adj Inca. ◇ mf Inca.

incalculável [ĩŋkawkuˈlavɛw] (pl -eis) adj incalculable.

incandescente [ĩŋkãndeˈsẽntʃil] adj incandescent.

incansável [ĩŋkãˈsavɛw] (pl -eis) adj tireless.

incapacidade [ĩŋkapasiˈdaʒil] f - **1.** [deficiência] incapacity. - **2.** [incompetência] incompetence.

incapacitado, da [ĩŋkapasiˈtadu, da] ◇ adj - **1.** [inválido] disabled. - **2.** [impedido] unable; **estar** ~ **de fazer algo** to be unable to do sthg. ◇ m, f disabled person.

incapacitar [4] [ĩŋkapasiˈta(x)] vt to incapacitate.

incapaz [ĩŋkaˈpaʃ] (pl -es) adj - **1.** [incompetente]: ~ **(para)** incompetent (for). - **2.** JUR incompetent. - **3.** [imprestativo]: **ser** ~ **de fazer algo** [não se dignar a] to be incapable of doing sthg.

incauto, ta [ĩŋˈkawtu, ta] adj - **1.** [imprudente] reckless. - **2.** [ingênuo] naive.

incendiar [17] [ĩsẽnˈdʒia(x)] vt to set fire to.
➡ **incendiar-se** vp to catch fire.

incendiário, ria [ĩnsẽn'dʒjarju, rja] <> *adj* [bomba etc] incendiary. <> *m, f* arsonist.

incêndio [ĩn'sẽndʒjul] *m* fire; ~ **provocado** *ou* **criminoso** arson.

incenso [ĩn'sẽnsul] *m* incense.

incentivador, ra [ĩnsẽntʃiva'do(x), ra] *adj* -**1.** [olhar, atitude] motivating. -**2.** [consumo, negócio] stimulating.

incentivar [4] [ĩsẽntʒi'va(x)] *vt* to stimulate.

incentivo [ĩnsẽn'tʃivul] *m* incentive.

incerteza [ĩnsex'teza] *f* uncertainty.

incerto, ta [ĩ'sɛxtu, ta] *adj* uncertain.

incessante [ĩnse'sãntʃil] *adj* incessant.

incesto [ĩn'sɛʃtul] *m* incest.

incestuoso, osa [ĩnseʃ'twozu, ɔza] *adj* incestuous.

inchação [ĩnʃa'sãw] *f* swelling.

inchaço [ĩn'ʃasul] *m fam* swelling.

inchado, da [ĩ'ʃadu, da] *adj* swollen.

inchar [4] [ĩ'sa(x)] <> *vt* to swell. <> *vi* to swell.
➤ **inchar-se** *vp* [envaidecer-se] to be puffed up (with pride).

incidência [ĩnsi'dẽnsja] *f* incidence.

incidente [ĩnsi'dẽntʃil] *m* incident.

incidir [6] [ĩnsi'dʒi(x)] *vi* -**1.** [refletir]: ~ **em** *ou* **sobre** to reflect in. -**2.** [recair]: ~ **em** *ou* **sobre** to be placed on. -**3.** [incorrer]: ~ **em** to fall into.

incinerador, ra [ĩnsine'rado(x), ra] <> *adj* incineration *(antes de subst).* <> *m* incinerator.

incinerar [4] [ĩnsine'ra(x)] *vt* to incinerate.

incipiente [ĩnsi'pjẽntʃil] *adj* incipient.

incisão [insi'zãw] *(pl* -**ões)** *f* -**1.** [corte] cut. -**2.** MED incision.

incisivo, va [ĩsi'zivu, va] *adj* -**1.** [cortante] cutting. -**2.** [direto] incisive.

incitação [ĩnsita'sãw] *(pl* -**ões)** *f* incitement.

incitamento [ĩnsita'mẽntul] *m* incitement.

incitar [4] [ĩsi'ta(x)] *vt* -**1.** [instigar]: ~ **alguém a algo** to incite sb to sthg; ~ **alguém a fazer algo** to incite sb to do sthg. -**2.** [suj: ambição *etc*]: ~ **alguém (a algo/a fazer algo)** to drive sb to sthg/to do sthg. -**3.** [animal] to urge on.

incivil [ĩnsi'viw] *(pl* -**is)** *adj* discourteous.

incivilidade [ĩnsivili'dadʒi] *f* discourtesy.

inclemência [ĩnkle'mẽnsja] *f* -**1.** [impiedade] ruthlessness. -**2.** *fig* [rigor] mercilessness.

inclemente [ĩnkle'mẽntʃil] *adj* -**1.** [impiedoso] ruthless. -**2.** *fig* [rigoroso] merciless.

inclinação [ĩnklina'sãw] *(pl* -**ões)** *f* -**1.** [queda] inclination. -**2.** *fig* [propensão]: ~ **para** inclination towards. -**3.** [atração]: ~ **por** attraction towards.

inclinado, da [ĩnkli'nadu, da] *adj* -**1.** [oblíquo] inclined. -**2.** *fig* [propenso]: **estar** ~ **a algo/a fazer algo** to be inclined towards sthg/to do sthg.

inclinar [4] [ĩnkli'na(x)] *vt* -**1.** [fazer pender] to tilt. -**2.** [curvar] to bend.
➤ **inclinar-se** *vp* -**1.** [curvar-se] to bow. -**2.** [tender a]: ~-**se a** to tend towards.

incluir [74] [ĩnklu'i(x)] *vt* -**1.** [abranger] to include. -**2.** [inserir]: ~ **algo em algo** to insert sthg in sthg.

incluir-se *vp* to include o.s.

inclusão [ĩnklu'zãw] *f* inclusion.

inclusive [ĩnklu'zivil] *adv* -**1.** [com inclusão de] including; **de segunda a sábado** ~ from Monday to Saturday inclusive. -**2.** [até mesmo] even.

incluso, sa [ĩn'kluzo, za] *adj* included.

incoercível [ĩnkwex'sivewl] *(pl* -**eis)** *adj* uncontrollable.

incoerência [ĩnkwe'rẽnsja] *f* -**1.** [ilogicidade] incoherence. -**2.** [discordância]: **ser uma** ~ **com algo** to conflict with sthg.

incoerente [ĩnkwe'rẽntʃil] *adj* -**1.** [ilógico] illogical. -**2.** [discordante] conflicting. -**3.** [incompreensível] incoherent.

incógnito, ta [ĩŋ'kɔgnitu, ta] *adj* incognito *(depois de verbo).*
➤ **incógnita** *f* -**1.** MAT unknown quantity. -**2.** [mistério]: **ser uma** ~ to be a mystery.
➤ **incógnito** *adv* incognito.

incolor [ĩŋko'lo(x)] *(pl* -**es)** *adj* colourless.

incólume [ĩŋ'kolumil] *adj* safe and sound.

incomensurável [ĩŋkomẽnsu'ravewl] *(pl* -**eis)** *adj* unmeasurable.

incomodado, da [ĩŋkomo'dadu, da] *adj* [importunado] annoyed.
➤ **incomodada** *adj & f* [menstruada] having one's period.

incomodar [4] [ĩŋkomo'da(x)] <> *vt* to annoy. <> *vi* [irritar]: ~ **a** to annoy.
➤ **incomodar-se** *vp* -**1.** [irritar-se] to become annoyed. -**2.** [importar-se] to mind; **você se incomoda se eu fechar a porta?** would you mind if I closed the door?

incômodo, da [ĩŋ'komodu, da] *adj* -**1.** [ger] uncomfortable. -**2.** [enfadonho] boring.
➤ **incômodo** *m* -**1.** [embaraço] problem. -**2.** [menstruação] period, time of the month.

incomparável [ĩŋkõnpa'ravɛwl] *(pl* -**eis)** *adj* incomparable.

incompatibilidade [ĩŋkonpatʃibili'dadʒi] *f* incompatibility.

incompatibilizar [4] [ĩnkõmpatʃibili'za(x)] *vt*: ~ **alguém com alguém** to put sb in sb's bad books.
➤ **incompatibilizar-se** *vp*: ~-**se (com)** to clash (with).

incompatível [ĩŋkõnpa'tʃivɛwl] *(pl* -**eis)** *adj* incompatible.

incompetência [ĩŋkõnpe'tẽnsja] *f* incompetence.

incompetente [ĩŋkõnpe'tẽntʃil] <> *adj* incompetent. <> *mf* incompetent.

incompleto, ta [ĩŋkõn'plɛtu, ta] *adj* incomplete, unfinished.

incompreendido, da [ĩŋkõnprjẽn'dʒidu, da] *adj* misunderstood.

incompreensão [ĩŋkõnprjẽn'sãw] *f* incomprehension.

incompreensível [ĩŋkõnprjẽn'sivewl] *(pl* -**eis)** *adj* incomprehensible.

incompreensivo, va [ĩŋkõnprjẽn'sivu, va] *adj* uncomprehending.

incomum [ĩŋko'mũl (*pl* -ns) *adj* uncommon.
incomunicável [ĩŋkomuni'kavɛwl (*pl* -eis) *adj* -1. [sem comunicação] cut off. -2. [que não deve se comunicar] incommunicado. -3. *fig* [insociável] uncommunicative.
inconcebível [ĩŋkõnse'bivɛwl (*pl* -eis) *adj* inconceivable.
inconciliável [ĩŋkõnsi'ljavɛwl (*pl* -eis) *adj* irreconcilable.
inconcludente [ĩŋkõŋklu'dẽntʃil *adj* inconclusive.
inconcluso, sa [ĩŋkõŋ'kluzu, zal *adj* unfinished.
incondicional [ĩŋkõndʒisjo'nawl (*pl* -ais) *adj* -1. [total] unconditional. -2. [fiel] loyal.
inconfessável [ĩŋkõnfe'savɛwl (*pl* -eis) *adj* unconfessable.
inconfesso, ssa [ĩŋkõn'fɛsu, sal *adj* unconfessed.
inconfidência [ĩŋkõnfi'dẽnsjal *f* disloyalty.
inconfidente [ĩŋkõnfi'dẽntʃil ◇ *adj* disloyal. ◇ *mf* untrustworthy person.
inconformado, da [ĩŋkõnfox'madu, dal *adj*: **ela está ~** she has not come to terms with it.
inconfundível [ĩŋkõnfũn'dʒivɛwl (*pl* -eis) *adj* unmistakable.
incongruência [ĩŋkõŋ'grwẽnsjal *f* incongruity.
incongruente [ĩŋkõŋ'grwẽntʃil, **incôngruo, grua** [ĩn'kõŋgrwu, grwal *adj* incongruous.
inconsciência [ĩŋkõn'sjẽnsjal *f* -1. MED unconsciousness. -2. [leviandade] lack of awareness.
inconsciente [ĩŋkõn'sjẽntʃil ◇ *adj* -1. [ger] unconscious. -2. [leviano] thoughtless. ◇ *m* PSIC: **o ~** the unconscious.
inconscientemente [ĩŋkõnsjẽntʃi'mẽntʃil *adv* unconsciously.
inconseqüência [ĩŋkõnse'kwẽnsjal *f* -1. [incoerência] inconsistency. -2. [irresponsabilidade] irresponsibility.
inconseqüente [ĩŋkõnse̩'kwẽntʃil ◇ *adj* -1. [incoerente] inconsistent. -2. [irresponsável] irresponsible. ◇ *mf* irresponsible person.
inconsistência [ĩŋkõnsiʃ'tẽnsjal *f* -1. [fraqueza] inconsistency. -2. [fluidez] weakness.
inconsistente [ĩŋkõnsiʃ'tẽntʃil *adj* -1. [fraco] inconsistent. -2. [fluido] runny.
inconsolável [ĩŋkõnso'lavɛwl (*pl* -eis) *adj* inconsolable.
inconstância [ĩŋkõnʃ'tãnsjal *f* inconstancy.
inconstante [ĩŋkõnʃ'tãntʃil *adj* -1. [instável] unstable. -2. [volúvel] inconstant.
inconstitucional [ĩŋkõnʃtʃitusjo'nawl (*pl* -ais) *adj* unconstitutional.
inconstitucionalidade [ĩŋkõnʃtʃitusjonali'dadʒil *f* unconstitutionality.
incontável [ĩŋkõn'tavɛwl (*pl* -eis) *adj* countless.
incontestável [ĩŋkõnteʃ'tavɛwl (*pl* -eis) *adj* incontestable.
inconteste [ĩŋkõn'tɛtʃil *adj* undisputed.
incontinência [ĩŋkõntʃi'nẽnsjal *f* MED incontinence.

incontinente [ĩŋkõntʃi'nẽntʃil *adj* MED incontinent.
incontinênti [ĩŋkõutʃi'nẽntʃil *adv* at once.
incontrolável [ĩŋkõntro'lavɛwl (*pl* -eis) *adj* uncontrollable.
incontroverso, sa [ĩŋkõntro'vɛxsu, sal *adj* incontrovertible.
inconveniência [ĩŋkõnve'njẽnsjal *f* -1. [falta de conveniência] inconvenience. -2. [grosseria] rudeness.
inconveniente [ĩŋkõnve'njẽntʃil ◇ *adj* -1. [inoportuno] inconvenient. -2. [inadequado] unsuitable. -3. [incômodo] annoying. ◇ *m* -1. [desvantagem] disadvantage. -2. [obstáculo] obstacle.
INCOR (*abrev de* Instituto do Coração do Hospital das Clínicas) *m* institute of coronary diseases at the Hospital das Clínicas in São Paulo.
incorporação [ĩŋkoxpora'sãwl (*pl* -ões) *f* -1. COM incorporation. -2. [espirit] possession. -3. [inclusão] inclusion.
incorporado, da [ĩŋkoxpo'radu, dal *adj* -1. COM incorporated. -2. [espirit] possessed. -3. [embutido] incorporated.
incorporar [4] [ĩŋkoxpo'ra(x)l ◇ *vt* -1. COM to incorporate. -2. [espirit] to become possessed by. -3. [juntar]: **~ algo a algo** to include sthg in sthg. ◇ *vi* [espirit] to take possession of.
➡ **incorporar-se** *vp* [juntar-se] to join.
incorreção [ĩŋkoxe'sãwl (*pl* -ões) *f* inaccuracy.
incorrer [5] [ĩŋko'xe(x)l *vi*: **~ em algo** to fall into sthg.
incorreto, ta [ĩŋko'xɛtu, tal *adj* incorrect.
incorrigível [ĩŋkoxi'ʒivɛwl (*pl* -eis) *adj* incorrigible.
incorruptível [ĩŋkoxup'tʃivewl (*pl* -eis) *adj* incorruptible.
INCRA (*abrev de* Instituto Nacional de Colonização e Reforma Agrária) *m* Brazilian land reform institute.
incredulidade [ĩŋkreduli'dadʒil *f* incredulity.
incrédulo, la [ĩŋ'krɛdulu, lal *adj* incredulous.
incrementado, da [ĩŋkremẽn'tadu, dal *adj* -1. *fam* [melhorado - carro, computador] jazzed up; [- bebida, comida] fancy. -2. *fam* [moderno] trendy.
incrementar [4] [ĩŋkremẽn'ta(x)l *vt* -1. [aumentar] to increase. -2. [desenvolver] to develop. -3. *fam* [melhorar] to jazz up.
incremento [ĩŋkre'mẽntul *m* -1. [aumento] increment. -2. [desenvolvimento] development.
incriminar [4] [ĩŋkrimi'na(x)l *vt* to incriminate.
incrível [ĩŋ'krivɛwl (*pl* -eis) *adj* -1. [inacreditável] incredible. -2. *fam* [maravilhoso] incredible.
incrustação [ĩŋkruʃta'sãwl (*pl* -ões) *f* inlay.
incrustar [4] [ĩŋkruʃ'ta(x)l *vt* to inlay.
incubação [ĩŋkuba'sãwl *f* incubation.
incubadora [ĩŋkuba'doral *f* incubator.
incubar [4] [ĩŋku'ba(x)l *vt* & *vi* to incubate.
inculcar [12] [ĩŋkuw'ka(x)l *vt* to inculcate.
inculto, ta [ĩŋ'kuwtu, tal *adj* -1. [terreno] uncultivated. -2. [pessoa] coarse.

incumbência [ĩŋkũn'bẽnsja] f incumbency.
incumbir [6] [ĩŋkũm'bi(x)] <> vt: ~ alguém de algo to put sb in charge of sthg. <> vi: ~ a alguém fazer algo to be sb's responsibility to do sthg.
◆ **incumbir-se** vp: ~-se de algo to take charge of sthg.
incurável [ĩŋku'ravɛw] (pl -eis) adj incurable.
incursão [ĩŋkux'sãw] (pl -ões) f incursion.
incutir [6] [ĩŋku'tʃi(x)] vt: ~ algo (a ou em alguém) to inspire sthg (in sb).
indagação [ĩndaga'sãw] f inquiry.
indagar [14] [ĩnda'ga(x)] <> vt to ask for. <> vi to make inquiries.
indébito, ta [ĩn'dɛbitu, ta] adj unreasonable.
indecência [ĩnde'sẽnsja] f -1. [indecoro] indecency. -2. [obscenidade] obscenity.
indecente [ĩnde'sẽntʃi] adj -1. [obsceno] indecent. -2. [imoral] unscrupulous.
indecifrável [ĩndesi'fravɛw] (pl -eis) adj indecipherable.
indecisão [ĩndesi'zãw] (pl -ões) f indecision.
indeciso, sa [ĩnde'sizu, za] adj indecisive.
indeclinável [ĩndekli'navɛw] (pl -eis) adj that cannot be refused (depois de subst).
indecoroso, osa [ĩndeko'rozo, ɔza] adj indecent.
indefectível [ĩndefek'tʃivɛw] (pl -eis) adj that cannot fail (depois de subst).
indefensável [ĩndefẽn'savɛw] (pl -eis) adj indefensible; um pênalti ~ an unstoppable penalty.
indeferido, da [ĩndefe'ridu, da] adj rejected.
indeferir [57] [ĩndefe'ri(x)] vt to reject.
indefeso, sa [ĩnde'fezu, za] adj defenceless.
indefinição [ĩndefini'sãw] (pl -ões) f indecision.
indefinido, da [ĩndefi'nidu, da] adj -1. [ger] indefinite. -2. [vago] vague.
indefinível [ĩndefi'nivɛw] (pl -eis) adj indefinable.
indelével [ĩnde'lɛvɛw] (pl -eis) adj indelible.
indelicadeza [ĩndelika'dezal f -1. [grosseria] rudeness. -2. [desfeita] bad manners (pl).
indelicado, da [ĩndeli'kadu, da] adj indelicate.
indenização [ĩndeniza'sãw] (pl -ões) f indemnity, compensation.
indenizar [4] [ĩndeni'za(x)] vt: ~ alguém (por algo) to indemnify sb (for sthg), to compensate sb (for sthg).
independência [ĩndepẽn'dẽnsja] f independence.
independente [ĩndepẽn'dẽntʃi] adj -1. [ger] independent. -2. [separado, de livre acesso] separate. -3. [auto-suficiente] independent. -4. [financeiramente] of independent means, financially independent.
independer [5] [ĩndepẽn'de(x)] vi: ~ de algo to be independent of sthg.
indescritível [ĩndeʃkri'tʃivɛw] (pl -eis) adj indescribable.
indesculpável [ĩndʒiʃkuw'pavɛw] (pl -eis) adj unforgivable.

indesejável [ĩndeze'ʒavɛw] (pl -eis) adj undesirable.
indestrutível [ĩndeʃtru'tʃivɛw] (pl -eis) adj -1. [não destrutível] indestructible. -2. fig [inabalável] enduring.
indeterminado, da [ĩndetexmi'nadu, da] adj -1. [não fixado] indeterminate; por tempo ~ for an indefinite length of time. -2. [impreciso] imprecise.
indevassável [ĩndeva'savɛw] (pl -eis) adj impenetrable.
indevido, da [ĩnde'vidu, da] adj -1. [imerecido] undeserved. -2. [impróprio] inappropriate.
índex ['ĩndɛks] m index.
indexação [ĩndeksa'sãw] (pl -ões) f -1. ECON & COM index-linking. -2. COMPUT index.
indexar [4] [ĩndek'sa(x)] vt -1. [ger] to index. -2. ECON & COM to index-link.
Índia ['ĩndʒja] n India.
indiano, na [ĩn'dʒjanu, na] <> adj [da Índia] Indian. <> m, f [habitante da Índia] Indian.
indicação [ĩndʒika'sãw] (pl -ões) f -1. [denotação] sign. -2. [de caminho etc] sign. -3. [recomendação] recommendation; ~ de uso instructions for use. -4. [menção] indication.
indicado, da [ĩndʒi'kadu, da] adj -1. [recomendado] recommended. -2. [apropriado] appropriate.
indicador, ra [ĩndʒika'do(x), ra] (pl -es, fpl -s) adj [que indica]: ~ de indicator of.
◆ **indicador** m -1. [ger] indicator. -2. [dedo] index finger.
indicar [4] [ĩndʒi'ka(x)] vt -1. [ger] to indicate. -2. [apontar]: ~ algo com o dedo to point to sthg. -3. [recomendar] to recommend. -4. [mencionar] to indicate. -5. [designar] to name.
indicativo, va [ĩndʒika'tʃivu, va] adj -1. [que indica] indicative. -2. GRAM indicative.
◆ **indicativo** m GRAM indicative.
índice ['ĩndʒisil] m -1. [lista] index; ~ remissivo subject index; ~ onomástico name index. -2. [medida] level; ~ de audiência ratings; ~ do custo de vida cost of living index. -3. [dedo] index finger.
indiciado, da [ĩndʒi'sjadu, da] m, f accused, defendant.
indiciar [16] [ĩndʒi'sja(x)] vt -1. [acusar] to accuse. -2. [submeter a inquérito] to investigate.
indício [ĩn'dʒisju] m -1. [vestígio] sign. -2. JUR [prova] evidence (inv).
Índico n: o (Oceano) ~ the Indian Ocean.
indiferença [ĩndʒife'rẽnsa] f indifference.
indiferente [ĩndʒife'rẽntʃil] adj: ~ (a algo) indifferent (to sthg).
indígena [ĩn'dʒiʒena] <> adj indigenous. <> mf native.
indigência [ĩndʒi'ʒẽnsja] f -1. [miséria] poverty. -2. [indigentes]: a ~ do país the indigence of the country. -3. [falta] lack.
indigente [ĩndʒi'ʒẽntʃil] <> adj poverty-stricken. <> mf poor person.
indigestão [ĩndʒiʒeʃ'tãw] (pl -ões) f indigestion.

indigesto, ta [ĩndʒi'ʒɛʃtu, ta] *adj* indigestible.
indignação [ĩndʒigna'sãw] (*pl* -ões) *f* indignation.
indignado, da [ĩndʒig'nadu, da] *adj* indignant; ficar ~ **(com)** to be indignant (at).
indignar [4] [ĩndʒig'na(x)] *vt* to anger.
 ➣ **indignar-se** *vp*: ~-se **(com)** to be indignant (about).
indignidade [ĩndʒigni'dadʒi] *f* -1. [falta de dignidade] indignity. -2. [ultraje] outrage.
indigno, gna [ĩn'dʒignu, gna] *adj* -1. [não merecedor]: ~ **de algo** unworthy of sthg. -2. [vil] despicable.
índio, dia ['ĩndʒju, dʒja] ⬦ *adj* Indian. ⬦ *m,f* Indian; **programa de** ~ *fig* boring programme.
indireto, ta [ĩndʒi'rɛtu, ta] *adj* indirect.
 ➣ **indireta** *f* hint; **dar uma** ~ to make a hint.
indisciplina [ĩndʒisi'plina] *f* indiscipline.
indisciplinado, da [ĩndʒisipli'nadu, da] *adj* undisciplined.
indiscreto, ta [ĩndʒiʃ'krɛtu, ta] *adj* indiscreet.
indiscrição [ĩndʒiʃkri'sãw] (*pl* -ões) *f* indiscretion.
indiscriminado, da [ĩndʒiʃkrimi'nadu, da] *adj* indiscriminate.
indiscutível [ĩndʒiʃku'tʃivew] (*pl* -eis) *adj* incontestable.
indispensável [ĩndʒiʃpẽn'savew] (*pl* -eis) ⬦ *adj* indispensable, essential. ⬦ *m*: **o** ~ the essentials.
indisponível [ĩndʒiʃpo'nivew] (*pl* -eis) *adj* unavailable.
indispor [45] [ĩndʒiʃ'po(x)] *vt* -1. [adoecer] to make ill, to upset. -2. [inimizar] to set at odds.
 ➣ **indispor-se** *vp* [inimizar-se]: ~-se **com alguém** to fall out with sb.
indisposição [ĩndʒiʃpozi'sãw] (*pl* -ões) *f* [mal-estar] illness.
indisposto, osta [ĩndʒiʃ'poʃtu, oʃta] ⬦ *pp* ▷ indispor. ⬦ *adj* unwell.
indissolúvel [ĩndʒiso'luvew] (*pl* -eis) *adj* -1. [irrevogável] indissoluble. -2. [insolúvel] insoluble.
indistinguível [ĩndʒiʃtʃĩŋ'givew] (*pl* -eis) *adj* indistinguishable.
indistintamente [ĩndʒiʃtʃĩnta'mẽntʃi] *adv* -1. [vagamente] indistinctly. -2. [indiferentemente] without distinction.
indistinto, ta [ĩndʒiʃ'tʃĩntu, ta] *adj* indistinct.
individual [ĩndʒivi'dwaw] (*pl* -ais) *adj* individual.
individualidade [ĩndʒividwali'dadʒi] *f* individuality.
individualismo [ĩndʒividwa'liʒmu] *m* individualism.
individualista [ĩndʒividwa'liʃta] ⬦ *adj* individualistic. ⬦ *mf* individualist.
indivíduo [ĩndʒi'vidwu] *m* -1. [pessoa] individual. -2. *fam* [cara] person.
indivisível [ĩndʒivi'sivew] (*pl* -eis) *adj* indivisible.
indiviso, sa [ĩndʒi'vizu, za] *adj* undivided.
indizível [ĩndʒi'zivew] (*pl* -eis) *adj* -1. [inexprimível] inexpressible. -2. [extraordinário] extraordinary.

indócil [ĩn'dɔsiw] (*pl* -eis) *adj* -1. [rebelde] wayward. -2. [impaciente] restless.
indo-europeu, éia [ĩndwewro'pew, pɛja] *adj* Indo-European.
 ➣ **indo-europeu** *m* [língua] Indo-European.
índole ['ĩndoli] *f* -1. [temperamento] temperament. -2. [tipo] character.
indolência [ĩndo'lẽnsja] *f* indolence.
indolente [ĩndo'lẽntʃi] *adj* indolent.
indolor [ĩndo'lo(x)] (*pl* -es) *adj* painless.
indomável [ĩndo'mavew] (*pl* -eis) *adj* indomitable.
indômito, ta [ĩn'domitu, ta] *adj* indomitable, untamed.
Indonésia [ĩndo'nɛzja] *n* Indonesia.
indonésio, sia [ĩndo'nɛzju, zja] ⬦ *adj* Indonesian. ⬦ *m, f* Indonesian.
 ➣ **indonésio** *m* [língua] Indonesian.
indoor [ĩn'dɔ(x)] *adj inv* ESP indoor.
indubitável [ĩndubi'tavew] (*pl* -eis) *adj* indubitable; **é** ~ **que ...** it is beyond doubt that ...
indução [ĩndu'sãw] (*pl* -ões) *f* -1. [lógica] induction; **por** ~ by induction. -2. [persuasão] persuasion.
indulgência [ĩnduw'ʒẽnsja] *f* -1. [tolerância] leniency. -2. [perdão] indulgence. -3. *JUR* clemency.
indulgente [ĩnduw'ʒẽntʃi] *adj* lenient.
indultar [4] [ĩnduw'ta(x)] *vt JUR* to reprieve.
indulto [ĩn'duwtu] *m JUR* reprieve.
indumentária [ĩndumẽn'tarja] *f* attire.
indústria [ĩn'duʃtrja] *f* industry; ~ **automobilística** car industry *UK*, automobile industry *US*; ~ **fabril** manufacturing industry; ~ **leve** *ou* **de consumo** light industry; ~ **pesada** heavy industry; ~ **brasileira** made in Brazil.
industrial [ĩnduʃ'trjaw] (*pl* -ais) ⬦ *adj* industrial. ⬦ *mf* industrialist.
industrialização [ĩnduʃtrjaliza'sãw] *f* industrialization.
industrializado, da [ĩnduʃtrjali'zadu, da] *adj* industrialized; **produto** ~ manufactured product.
industrializar [4] [ĩnduʃtrjali'za(x)] *vt* -1. [ger] to industrialize. -2. [produto] to manufacture. -3. [usar na indústria] to put to industrial use.
 ➣ **industrializar-se** *vp* to become industrialized.
industrioso, osa [ĩnduʃ'trjozu, -ɔza] *adj* -1. [habilidoso] clever. -2. [diligente] industrious.
induzir [72] [ĩndu'zi(x)] *vt* -1. [levar]: ~ **alguém a algo** to lead sb to sthg; ~ **alguém a fazer algo** to persuade sb to do sthg. -2. [deduzir]: ~ **algo de algo** to deduce sthg from sthg.
inebriante [ine'brjãntʃi] *adj* intoxicating.
inebriado, da [inebri'adu, da] *adj* [extasiado] intoxicated.
inebriar [16] [ine'brja(x)] *vt* to intoxicate.
 ➣ **inebriar-se** *vp* to be intoxicated.
ineditismo [inedʒi'tʃiʒmu] *m*: **o** ~ **dos contos** the fact that the stories are unpublished.

inédito, ta [i'nɛdʒitu, ta] *adj* **-1.** [não publicado] unpublished. **-2.** [novo] novel.

inefável [ine'favɛw] (*pl* -**eis**) *adj* ineffable.

ineficácia [inefi'kasja] *f* **-1.** [ger] ineffectiveness. **-2.** [de pessoa] inefficience.

ineficaz [inefi'kaʃ] (*pl* -**es**) *adj* **-1.** [ger] ineffective. **-2.** [pessoa] inefficient.

ineficiência [inefi'sjẽnsja] *f* inefficiency.

ineficiente [inefi'sjẽntʃi] *adj* inefficient.

inegável [ine'gavɛw] (*pl* -**eis**) *adj* undeniable.

inegociável [inego'sjavɛw] (*pl* -**eis**) *adj* non-negotiable.

inelegível [inele'givɛw] (*pl* -**eis**) *adj* unelectable.

inenarrável [inena'xavɛw] (*pl* -**eis**) *adj* inexpressible.

inépcia [i'nɛpsja] *f* ineptitude.

inepto, ta [i'nɛptu, ta] *adj* inept.

inequívoco, ca [ine'kivoku, ka] *adj* unmistakable.

inércia [i'nɛxsja] *f* inertia.

inerente [ine'rẽntʃi] *adj* inherent.

inerte [i'nɛxtʃi] *adj* inert.

inescrupuloso, osa [ineʃkrupu'lozu, ɔza] *adj* unscrupulous.

inescrutável [ineʃkru'tavɛw] (*pl* -**eis**) *adj* inscrutable.

inesgotável [inezgo'tavɛw] (*pl* -**eis**) *adj* **-1.** [inacabável] inexhaustible. **-2.** [copioso] profuse.

inesperado, da [ineʃpe'radu, da] *adj* unexpected.

 inesperado *m* surprise.

inesquecível [ineʃke'sivɛw] (*pl* -**eis**) *adj* unforgettable.

inestimável [ineʃtʃi'mavɛw] (*pl* -**eis**) *adj* **-1.** [ger] priceless. **-2.** [prejuízo] incalculable.

inevitabilidade [inevitabili'dadʒi] *f* inevitability.

inevitável [inevi'tavɛw] (*pl* -**eis**) <> *adj* inevitable. <> *m*: o ~ the inevitable.

inexatidão [ineza'tʃidãw] (*pl* -**ões**) *f* inexactitude.

inexato, ta [ine'zatu, ta] *adj* inaccurate.

inexaurível [inezauw'rivɛw] (*pl* -**eis**) *adj* inexhaustible.

inexcedível [inese'dʒivɛw] (*pl* -**eis**) *adj* unsurpassable.

inexequível [ineze'kwivɛw] (*pl* -**eis**) *adj* unfeasible.

inexistência [ineziʃ'tẽnsja] *f* **-1.** [não existência] absence. **-2.** [carência] lack.

inexistente [ineziʃ'tẽntʃi] *adj* non-existent.

inexistir [6] [ineziʃ'ti(x)] *vi* not to exist.

inexorável [inezo'ravɛw] (*pl* -**eis**) *adj* inexorable.

inexperiência [ineʃpe'rjẽnsja] *f* inexperience.

inexperiente [ineʃpe'rjẽntʃi] *adj* inexperienced.

inexplicável [ineʃpli'kavɛw] (*pl* -**eis**) *adj* inexplicable.

inexplorado, da [ineʃplo'radu, da] *adj* unexplored.

inexpressivo, va [ineʃpre'sivu, va] *adj* **-1.** [rosto] expressionless. **-2.** [diferença] inexpressible.

inexpugnável [ineʃpug'navɛw] (*pl* -**eis**) *adj* **-1.**

[invencível] insuperable. **-2.** *fig* [firme] unassailable.

infalível [ĩnfa'livɛw] (*pl* -**eis**) *adj* infallible.

infame [ĩn'fãmi] *adj* **-1.** [vil] shameful. **-2.** [péssimo] dreadful.

infâmia [ĩn'fãmja] *f* **-1.** [calúnia] slander. **-2.** [desonra] discredit. **-3.** [vilania] infamy.

infância [ĩn'fãnsja] *f* childhood; **primeira** ~ early childhood, infancy.

infantaria [ĩnfãnta'ria] *f* infantry.

infante, ta [ĩ'fãntʃi, tʃa] *m, f* **-1.** [príncipe] infante (*f* infanta), prince (*f* princess). **-2.** [criança] infant.

 infante *m* [soldado] infantryman.

infanticida [ĩnfãntʃi'sida] <> *adj* infanticide. <> *m, f* infanticide, child-killer.

infantil [ĩnfãn'tiw] (*pl* -**is**) *adj* **-1.** [próprio da infância] childhood (*antes de subst*). **-2.** [para criança] children's (*antes de subst*). **-3.** *fig* [imaturo] childish.

infantilidade [ĩnfãntʃili'dadʒi] *f* childishness.

infanto-juvenil [ĩn,fãntuʒuve'niw] (*pl* **infanto-juvenis**) *adj* children's (*antes de subst*).

infarto [ĩn'faxtu] *m* = **enfarte**.

infatigável [ĩnfatʃi'gavɛw] (*pl* -**eis**) *adj* **-1.** [incansável] tireless. **-2.** [zeloso] untiring.

infecção [ĩnfek'sãw] (*pl* -**ões**) *f* infection.

infeccionar [4] [ĩfeksjo'na(x)] <> *vt* to infect. <> *vi* to become infected.

infeccioso, osa [ĩnfek'sjozu, ɔza] *adj* infectious.

infecto, ta [ĩ'fɛktu, ta] *adj* **-1.** [ger] contaminated. **-2.** *fig* [vil] sick.

infelicidade [ĩnfelisi'dadʒi] *f* **-1.** [tristeza] unhappiness. **-2.** [desgraça] misfortune. **-3.** [azar] bad luck; **por** ~ unfortunately.

infeliz [ĩnfe'liʒ] (*pl* -**es**) <> *adj* **-1.** [ger] unfortunate. **-2.** [triste] unhappy. **-3.** [desafortunado] wretched. <> *mf* **-1.** [triste] unfortunate person. **-2.** [desgraçado] wretch; **como um** ~ *fig* desperately.

infelizmente [ĩnfeliʒ'mẽntʃi] *adv* unfortunately.

infenso, sa [ĩ'fẽnsu, sa] *adj* adverse.

inferior [ĩnfe'rjo(x)] (*pl* -**es**) <> *adj* **-1.** [ger]: ~ **a** inferior to. **-2.** [que está mais baixo] lower. **-3.** [em valor]: ~ **(a)** lower (than). **-4.** [em quantidade]: ~ **(a)** fewer (than). **-5.** [em altura]: ~ **a** shorter (than). **-6.** [em qualidade]: ~ **(a)** inferior (to). <> *mf* [subalterno] inferior.

inferioridade [ĩnferjori'dadʒi] *f* **-1.** [condição, posição] inferiority. **-2.** *PSIC*: **complexo de** ~ inferiority complex.

inferiorizar-se [4] [ĩferjori'zaxsi] *vp* to degrade o.s.

inferir [57] [ĩfe'ri(x)] *vt*: ~ **algo (de)** to infer sthg (from).

infernal [ĩnfex'naw] (*pl* -**ais**) *adj* *fig* infernal.

inferninho [ĩnfex'nipu] *m* dive.

infernizar [4] [ĩfexni'za(x)] *vt* to render hellish; ~ **a vida de alguém** to make sb's life hell.

inferno [ĩn'fɛxnu] *m* hell; **vá para o** ~! go to hell!

infértil [i'fɛxtiw] *adj* infertile.

infertilidade [ĩnfextʃili'dadʒi] *f* infertility.
infestado, da [ĩnfeʃ'tadu, da] *adj* infested.
infestar [4] [ĩnfeʃ'ta(x)] *vt* to infest.
infidelidade [ĩnfideli'dadʒi] *f* infedility.
infiel [ĩn'fjɛwl] (*pl* -**éis**) <> *adj* -**1.** [desleal] unfaithful. -**2.** [inexato] inaccurate. <> *mf* RELIG non-believer.
infiltração [ĩnfiwtra'sãw] (*pl* -**ões**) *f* infiltration.
infiltrar [4] [ĩfiw'tra(x)] *vt* [parede] to penetrate.
➡ **infiltrar-se** *vp* to infiltrate; ~**-se em algo** to filter (into) sthg.
ínfimo, ma [ˈĩfimu, ma] *adj* insignificant; **preço** ~ rock-bottom price.
infindável [ĩnfĩn'davewl] (*pl* -**eis**) *adj* -**1.** [inacabável] interminable. -**2.** [permanente] unending. -**3.** [energia] boundless.
infinidade [ĩnfini'dadʒi] *f*: **uma** ~ **de vezes/roupas** countless times/clothes.
infinitamente [ĩnfinita'mẽntʃi] *adv* infinitely.
infinitesimal [ĩnfinitezi'mawl] (*pl* -**ais**) *adj* infinitesimal.
infinitivo, va [ĩnfini'tʃivu, va] GRAM *adj* infinitive.
➡ **infinitivo** *m* infinitive.
infinito, ta [ĩnfi'nitu, ta] *adj* -**1.** [ger] infinite. -**2.** [inumerável] countless.
➡ **infinito** *m* LING infinitive.
inflação [ĩnfla'sãw] *f* ECON inflation.
inflacionar [4] [ĩnflasjo'na(x)] *vt* ECON to inflate.
inflacionário, ria [ĩnflasjo'narju, rja] *adj* ECON inflationary.
inflamação [ĩnflama'sãw] (*pl* -**ões**) *f* MED inflammation.
inflamado, da [ĩnfla'madu, da] *adj* -**1.** MED inflamed. -**2.** *fig* [exaltado] heated.
inflamar [4] [ĩfla'ma(x)] <> *vt* to inflame. <> *vi* MED to become inflamed.
inflamatório, ria [ĩnflama'tɔrju, rja] *adj* inflammatory.
inflamável [ĩnfla'mavɛwl] (*pl* -**eis**) *adj* inflammable.
inflar [4] [ĩ'fla(x)] *vt* -**1.** [balão, bóia] to inflate. -**2.** [vela] to fill. -**3.** [peito] to puff out.
inflexível [ĩnflek'sivewl] (*pl* -**eis**) *adj* -**1.** [invergável] stiff. -**2.** *fig* [implacável] inflexible.
infligir [52] [ĩfli'ʒi(x)] *vt*: ~ **algo (a alguém)** to inflict sthg (on sb).
influência [ĩnflu'ẽnsja] *f* influence.
influenciar [16] [ĩflwẽn'sja(x)] <> *vt* to influence. <> *vi*: ~ **em algo** to influence sthg.
➡ **influenciar-se** *vp*: ~**-se (com algo)** to be influenced by sthg; ~**-se (por alguém/algo)** to be influenced (by sb/sthg).
influenciável [ĩnflwẽn'sjavewl] (*pl* -**eis**) *adj* easily influenced.
influente [ĩnflu'ẽntʃi] *adj* influential.
influir [74] [ĩnflu'i(x)] *vi* -**1.** [importar] to matter, to be important. -**2.** [atuar]: ~ **em algo** to interfere in sthg. -**3.** [influenciar]: ~ **para algo** to play a role in sthg.
influxo [ĩn'fluksu] *m* -**1.** [convergência] influx. -**2.** [maré alta] high tide.

infográfico, ca [ĩnfo'grafiku, ka] *adj* computer graphic *(antes de subst)*.
➡ **infográfico** *m* computer graphics designer.
informação [ĩnfoxma'sãw] (*pl* -**ões**) *f* -**1.** [ger] information. -**2.** [notícia] news. -**3.** MIL intelligence. -**4.** COMPUT data *(inv)*.
informado, da [ĩnfox'madu, da] *adj* -**1.** [esclarecido] well-informed. -**2.** [notificado]: ~ **de algo** informed of sthg.
informal [ĩnfox'mawl] (*pl* -**ais**) *adj* informal.
informalidade [ĩnfoxmali'dadʒi] *f* informality.
informante [ĩnfox'mãntʃi] *mf* informant.
informar [4] [ĩfox'ma(x)] <> *vt* -**1.** [esclarecer] to inform. -**2.** [notificar]: ~ **alguém de algo** to notify sb of sthg. <> *vi* [ser informativo] to inform.
➡ **informar-se** *vp* -**1.** [atualizar-se] to keep o.s. up to date. -**2.** [esclarecer-se]: ~**-se sobre algo** to make inquiries about sthg, to inquire about sthg.
informático, ca [ĩnfox'matʃiku, ka] <> *adj* computer *(antes de subst)*. <> *m, f* [pessoa] IT specialist.
➡ **informática** *f* -**1.** [ciência] computer science. -**2.** [atividade] computing.
informativo, va [ĩnfoxma'tʃivu, va] *adj* informative.
informatização [ĩnfoxmatʃiza'sãw] *f* COMPUT computerization.
informatizar [ĩnfurmati'za(x)] *vt* to computerize.
informe [ĩn'fɔxmi] <> *adj* shapeless. <> *m* -**1.** [informações] information. -**2.** MIL (piece of) intelligence.
infortúnio [ĩnfox'tunju] *m* misfortune.
infração [ĩnfra'sãw] (*pl* -**ões**) *f* -**1.** [de lei etc] infringement; ~ **de trânsito** driving offence *UK*, driving offense *US*. -**2.** ESP foul.
Infraero (*abrev de* **Empresa Brasileira de Infra-Estrutura Aeroportuária**) *f Brazilian company responsible for airport insfrastructure,* ≈ BAA *UK.*
infra-estrutura [ˌĩnfraʃtru'tura] (*pl* **infra-estruturas**) *f* infrastructure.
infrator, ra [ĩnfra'to(x), ra] (*mpl* -**es**, *fpl* -**s**) <> *adj* law-breaking. <> *m, f* infringer.
infravermelho, lha [ĩnfravex'meʎu, ʎa] *adj* infrared.
infreqüente [ĩnfre'kwẽntʃi] *adj* infrequent.
infringir [52] [ĩnfrĩ'ʒi(x)] *vt* to infringe.
infrutífero, ra [ĩnfru'tʃiferu, ra] *adj* fruitless.
infundado, da [ĩnfũn'dadu, da] *adj* unfounded, groundless.
infundir [6] [ĩnfũn'dʒi(x)] *vt* -**1.** [inspirar] to inspire. -**2.** [incutir] to instill.
infusão [ĩnfu'zãw] (*pl* -**ões**) *f* infusion.
ingenuidade [ĩnʒenwi'dadʒi] *f* ingenuousness, naivety.
ingênuo, nua [ĩn'ʒenwu, nwa] <> *adj* ingenuous, naive. <> *m, f* ingenuous person, naive person.
ingerência [ĩnʒe'rẽnsja] *f* intervention.

ingerir [57] [ĩnʒe'ri(x)] *vt* to ingest.

ingestão [ĩnʒeʃ'tãw] *f* ingestion.

Inglaterra [ĩ ɡla'tɛxal *n* England.

inglês, esa [ĩ ɡleʃ, ezal (*mpl* -eses, *fpl* -s) ◇ *adj* English. ◇ *mf* Englishman (*f* Englishwoman).
  ➡ **inglês** *m* [língua] English.

inglório, ria [ĩ ɡlɔrju, rjal *adj* inglorious.

ingovernabilidade [ĩ ɡovexnabili'dadʒi] *f* ungovernability.

ingovernável [ĩ ɡovex'navew] (*pl* -eis) *adj* -**1**. [rebelde] unruly. -**2**. [fora de controle] ungovernable.

ingratidão [ĩ ɡratʃi'dãw] *f* ingratitude.

ingrato, ta [ĩ 'ɡratu, tal *adj* -**1**. [sem gratidão] ungrateful. -**2**. [ruim] disagreeable.

ingrediente [ĩ ɡre'dʒẽntʃi] *m* ingredient.

íngreme ['ĩ ɡremil *adj* steep.

ingressar [ĩ ɡre'sa(x)] *vi*: ~ **em algo** to enter sthg.

ingresso [ĩ 'ɡresul *m* -**1**. [bilhete] (entrance) ticket. -**2**. [entrada] entry. -**3**. [admissão] entrance.

íngua ['ĩ ɡwal *f* bubo, *a swollen lymph node in the groin.*

inhame [i'ɲ amil *m* yam.

inibição [inibi'sãw] (*pl* -ões) *f* inhibition.

inibido, da [ini'bidu, ini'bidal *adj* inhibited.

inibidor, ra [inibi'do(x), ral *adj* inhibiting.

inibir [ini'bi(x)] *vt* -**1**. [embaraçar] to embarrass. -**2**. [dificultar] to inhibit. -**3**. [impedir]: ~ **alguém (de fazer algo)** to prevent sb (from doing sthg).
  ➡ **inibir-se** *vp* [ficar inibido] to become inhibited.

iniciação [inisja'sãw] (*pl* -ões) *f* initiation.

iniciado, da [ini'sjadu, dal ◇ *adj* [pessoa] initiated. ◇ *m*, *f* [pessoa] initiate.

inicial [ini'sjaw] (*pl* -ais) ◇ *adj* initial. ◇ *f* [letra] initial.
  ➡ **iniciais** *fpl* initials.

iniciante [ini'sjãntʃi] ◇ *adj* [pessoa] beginning. ◇ *mf* [pessoa] beginner.

iniciar [ini'sja(x)] *vt* -**1**. [começar] to initiate, to begin. -**2**. [introduzir]: ~ **alguém em algo** to introduce sb to sthg.
  ➡ **iniciar-se** *vp* [introduzir-se]: ~-**se em algo** to get into sthg.

iniciativa [inisja'tʃival *f* initiative; **não ter** ~ to have no initiative; **por** ~ **própria** on one's own initiative; **tomar a** ~ to take the initiative; ~ **privada** private initiative.

início [i'nisjul *m* beginning; **desde o** ~ from the outset; **no** ~ in the beginning.

inigualável [inigwa'lavew] (*pl* -eis) *adj* unequalled.

inimaginável [inimaʒi'navew] (*pl* -eis) *adj* unimaginable.

inimigo, ga [ini'migu, gal ◇ *adj* enemy *(antes de subst).* ◇ *m*, *f* enemy.

inimizade [inimi'zadʒi] *f* enmity.

ininteligível [inĩnteli'givew] (*pl* -eis) *adj* unintelligible.

ininterrupto, ta [inĩnte'xuptu, tal *adj* uninterrupted.

iniqüidade [inikwi'dadʒil *f* iniquity.

iníquo, qua [i'nikwu, kwal *adj* iniquitous.

injeção [ĩnʒe'sãw] (*pl* -ões) *f* injection.

injetado, da [ĩʒe'tadu, dal *adj* -**1**. [fluido] injected. -**2**. [corado de sangue]: **olhos** ~**s** bloodshot eyes.

injetar [4] [ĩʒe'ta(x)] *vt* to inject.

injunção [ĩnʒũn'sãw] (*pl* -ões) *f* -**1**. [ordem] injunction. -**2**. [pressão] pressure.

injúria [ĩn'ʒurjal *f* insult.

injuriado, da [ĩnʒu'rjadu, dal *adj* [pessoa] insulted.

injuriar [16] [ĩʒu'rja(x)] *vt* [insultar] to insult.
  ➡ **injuriar-se** *vp fam* [zangar-se] to get angry.

injurioso, osa [ĩnʒu'rjozu, ɔzal *adj* insulting.

injustiça [ĩnʒuʃ'tʃisal *f* injustice.

injustiçado, da [ĩnʒuʃtʃi'sadu, dal ◇ *adj* unjustly treated. ◇ *m*, *f* victim of injustice.

injustificável [ĩnʒuʃtʃifi'kavew] (*pl* -eis) *adj* unjustifiable.

injusto, ta [ĩ'ʒuʃtu, tal *adj* unfair.

INL (*abrev de* **Instituto Nacional do Livro**) *m* Brazilian national book institute.

INMETRO (*abrev de* **Instituto Nacional de Metrologia, Normalização e Qualidade Industrial**) *m* Brazilian national institute of industrial standards, ≃ TSI *UK*, ≃ NIST *US*.

inobservado, da [inobizex'vadu, dal *adj* unobserved.

inobservância [inobisex'vãnsjal *f* [violação] non-observance.

inobservante [inobisex'vãntʃil *adj* unobservant.

inocência [ino'sẽnsjal *f* innocence; **perder a** ~ to lose one's innocence.

inocentar [4] [inosẽn'ta(x)] *vt*: ~ **alguém de algo** to clear sb of sthg.
  ➡ **inocentar-se** *vp*: inocentou-se por sua sinceridade his sincerity showed that he was innocent.

inocente [ino'sẽntʃil ◇ *adj* innocent. ◇ *mf* innocent person.

inoculação [inokula'sãw] (*pl* -ões) *f* innoculation.

inocular [4] [inoku'la(x)] *vt* to innoculate.

inócuo, cua [i'nɔkwu, kwal *adj* innocuous.

inodoro, ra [ino'dɔru, ral *adj* odourless.

inofensivo, va [inofẽ'sivu, val *adj* inoffensive.

inolvidável [inowvi'davew] (*pl* -eis) *adj* unforgettable.

inominável [inomi'navew] (*pl* -eis) *adj fig* [vil] intolerable.

inoperante [inope'rãntʃil *adj* inoperative.

inopinado, da [inopi'nadu, dal *adj* -**1**. [imprevisto] unexpected. -**2**. [extraordinário] extraordinary.

inoportuno, na [inopox'tunu, nal *adj* inopportune.

inorgânico, ca [inox'ganiku, kal *adj* inorganic.

inóspito, ta [i'nɔʃpitu, tal *adj* inhospitable.

inovação [inova'sãw] (*pl* -ões) *f* innovation.

inovador, ra [inova'do(x), ra] <> *adj* innovative. <> *m, f* innovator.

inovar [4] [ino'va(x)] *vt* to innovate.

inoxidável [inoksi'davɛw] (*pl* -**eis**) *adj* ⊳ aço.

INPC (*abrev de* Índice Nacional de Preços ao Consumidor) *m national index of retail prices*, ≃ RPI *UK*.

inqualificável [iŋkwalifi'kavɛw] (*pl* -**eis**) *adj* indescribable.

inquebrantável [iŋkebrãn'tavɛw] (*pl* -**eis**) *adj* unbreakable.

inquérito [iŋ'kɛritul] *m* enquiry.

inquestionável [iŋkeʃtʃjo'navɛw] (*pl* -**eis**) *adj* unquestionable.

inquietação [iŋkjeta'sãw] (*pl* -**ões**) *f* anxiety.

inquietante [iŋkje'tãntʃi], **inquietador, ra** [iŋkjeta'do(x), ra] *adj* worrying.

inquietar [4] [iŋkje'ta(x)] *vt* to worry.

➡ **inquietar-se** *vp* to worry.

inquieto, ta [iŋ'kjɛtu, ta] *adj* -**1.** [apreensivo] worried. -**2.** [agitado] restless.

inquietude [iŋkje'tudʒi] *f* -**1.** [apreensão] worry. -**2.** [agitação] restlessness.

inquilino, na [iŋki'linu, na] *m, f* tenant.

inquirição [iŋkiri'sãw] (*pl* -**ões**) *f* inquiry.

inquirir [6] [iŋki'ri(x)] <> *vt* -**1.** [investigar] to enquire. -**2.** [interrogar] to question. -**3.** *JUR* to examine. <> *vi* [indagar] to investigate.

Inquisição [iŋkizi'sãw] *f*: a ~ the Inquisition.

inquisitivo, va [iŋkizi'tʃivu, va] *adj* inquisitive.

insaciável [insa'sjavɛw] (*pl* -**eis**) *adj* insatiable.

insalubre [insa'lubri] *adj* -**1.** [local, clima] unhealthy. -**2.** [trabalho] damaging to the health. -**3.** [água] unfit for drinking.

insanidade [insani'dadʒi] *f* insanity.

insano, na [i'sanu, na] <> *adj* -**1.** [demente] insane. -**2.** *fig* [incansável] relentless. <> *m, f* madman (madwoman).

insaciabilidade [insasjabili'dadʒi] *f* insatiable appetite.

insatisfação [insatʃiʃfa'sãw] (*pl* -**ões**) *f* dissatisfaction.

insatisfatório, ria [insatʃiʃfa'tɔrju, rja] *adj* unsatisfactory.

insatisfeito, ta [insatʃiʃ'fejtu, ta] *adj* dissatisfied.

inscrever [5] [iʃkre've(x)] *vt* -**1.** [gravar] to inscribe. -**2.** [pessoa]: ~ alguém (em algo) to register sb (for sthg).

➡ **inscrever-se** *vp* [pessoa]: ~-se (em algo) to register (for sthg).

inscrição [iʃkri'sãw] (*pl* -**ões**) *f* -**1.** [mensagem] inscription. -**2.** [matrícula, assentamento] registration; número de ~ registration number.

inscrito, ta [i'ʃkritu, ta] <> *pp* ⊳ inscrever. <> *adj* -**1.** [mensagem] inscribed. -**2.** [pessoa] registered.

insegurança [insegu'rãsa] *f* -**1.** [falta de segurança] lack of safety. -**2.** [de pessoa] insecurity.

inseguro, ra [inse'guru, ra] *adj* -**1.** [perigoso] unsafe. -**2.** [pessoa] insecure.

inseminação [insemina'sãw] (*pl* -**ões**) *f* insemination; ~ artificial artificial insemination.

inseminar [4] [isemi'na(x)] *vt* to inseminate.

insensatez [insẽnsa'teʒ] *f* foolishness.

insensato, ta [insẽn'satu, ta] *adj* foolish.

insensibilidade [insẽnsibili'dadʒi] *f* insensitivity.

insensibilizar [4] [isẽsibili'ta(x)] *vt* [tornar insensível] to desensitize.

➡ **insensibilizar-se** *vp* [emocionalmente] to harden o.s.

insensível [insẽn'sivɛw] (*pl* -**eis**) *adj* -**1.** [sem sensibilidade] numb. -**2.** [impassível] insensitive.

inseparável [insepa'ravɛw] (*pl* -**eis**) *adj* inseparable.

inserção [insex'sãw] (*pl* -**ões**) *f* -**1.** [introdução]: ~ (de algo em algo) insertion (of sthg into sthg). -**2.** *COMPUT* insertion.

inserir [57] [ise'ri(x)] *vt* -**1.**: ~ algo em algo to insert sthg into sthg. -**2.** *COMPUT* to insert.

➡ **inserir-se** *vp*: ~ -em algo to fit into sthg.

inseticida [insetʃi'sida] *m* insecticide.

inseto [in'sɛtul] *m* insect.

insídia [in'sidʒja] *f* ambush.

insidioso, osa [insi'dʒjozu, ɔza] *adj* insidious.

insight [in'sajtʃi] *m* insight; ter um ~ to have insight.

insigne [in'signi] *adj* celebrated.

insígnia [in'signja] *f* insignia.

insignificância [insignifi'kãnsja] *f* insignificance.

insignificante [insignifi'kãntʃi] *adj* insignificant.

insincero, ra [insĩ'sɛru, ra] *adj* insincere.

insinuação [insinwa'sãw] (*pl* -**ões**) *f* -**1.** [indireta, sugestão] insinuation. -**2.** [amorosa] advance.

insinuante [insi'nwãntʃi] *adj* [que se insinua] insinuating.

insinuar [4] [insi'nwa(x)] *vt* -**1.** [afirmar indiretamente] to hint at; ~ que to insinuate that. -**2.** [sugerir]: ~ que to suggest that.

➡ **insinuar-se** *vp* -**1.** [passar]: ~-se por *ou* entre to insinuate o.s. in *ou* among. -**2.** [amorosamente]: ~-se (para alguém) to make advances (to sb).

insípido, da [in'sipidu, da] *adj* -**1.** [sem sabor] insipid. -**2.** *fig* [sem graça] insipid.

insistência [insiʃ'tẽnsja] *f* insistence.

insistente [insiʃ'tẽntʃi] *adj* insistent.

insistir [6] [insiʃ'ti(x)] *vi* [perseverar]: ~ em (fazer algo) to insist on (doing sthg); ~ para alguém fazer algo to insist that sb do sthg.

insociável [inso'sjavɛw] (*pl* -**eis**) *adj* antisocial.

insolação [insola'sãw] (*pl* -**ões**) *f* sunstroke; ter uma ~ to have sunstroke.

insolência [inso'lẽnsja] *f* insolence.

insolente [inso'lẽntʃi] <> *adj* insolent. <> *mf* insolent person.

insólito, ta [in'sɔlitu, ta] *adj* unusual.

insolúvel [inso'luvɛw] (*pl* -**eis**) *adj* insoluble.

insolvência [insow'vẽnsja] *f* insolvency.

insolvente [ĩnsow'vẽntʃi] adj insolvent.
insondável [ĩnsõn'davew] (pl -eis) adj unfathomable. ◢
insone [ĩn'soni] adj -1. [pessoa] insomniac. -2. [noite] sleepless.
insônia [ĩn'sonja] f insomnia.
insosso, ssa [ĩn'sosu, sa] adj -1. [sem sal] unsalted. -2. [sem sabor] tasteless. -3. fig [sem graça] dull.
inspeção [ĩnʃpe'sãw] (pl -ões) f inspection.
inspecionar [4] [ĩʃpesjo'na(x)] vt to inspect.
inspetor, ra [ĩnʃpe'to(x), ra] (mpl -es, fpl -s) m, f inspector; ~ da alfândega customs officer.
inspetoria [ĩnʃpeto'rial f inspectorate.
inspiração [ĩnʃpira'sãw] (pl -ões) f -1. [estímulo] inspiration. -2. [na respiração] breathing in.
inspirador, ra [ĩnʃpira'do(x), ra] (mpl -es, fpl -s) adj inspiring.
inspirar [4] [ĩʃpi'ra(x)] vt -1. [estimular] to inspire. -2. [ar] to breathe in.
➡ **inspirar-se** vp [obter estímulo] to be inspired.
instabilidade [ĩnʃtabili'dadʒi] f instability.
instalação [ĩnʃtala'sãw] (pl -ões) f -1. [ger] installation. -2. [sistema]: ~ elétrica/hidráulica electric/hydraulic plant.
➡ **instalações** fpl -1. [para esporte, lazer] facilities. -2. [de indústria] plant.
instalador, ra [ĩnʃtala'do(x), ra] m, f fitter.
instalar [4] [ĩʃta'la(x)] vt -1. [ger] to install. -2. [estabelecer] to establish. -3. [num cargo]: ~ alguém em to install sb in.
➡ **instalar-se** vp -1. [alojar-se] to install o.s. -2. [em um cargo] to install o.s.
instância [ĩnʃ'tãnsja] f -1. [solicitação] demand; em última ~ as a last resort. -2. [jurisdição] jurisdiction. -3. JUR stages of a law suit; tribunal de segunda ~ court of second instance.
instantâneo, nea [ĩnʃtãn'tãnju, nja] adj instant.
➡ **instantâneo** m FOTsnap, snapshot.
instante [ĩnʃ'tãntʃi] ◇ m moment; a cada ~ at any moment; nesse ~ at that moment; num ~ in a moment. ◇ adj -1. [iminente] imminent. -2. [urgente] urgent.
instar [4] [ĩ'ta(x)] ◇ vt [pedir]: ~ que alguém faça algo to request that sb do sthg. ◇ vi [insistir]: ~ com alguém para que faça algo to urge sb to do sthg; ~ por algo to insist on sthg.
instauração [ĩnʃtawra'sãw] (pl -ões) f establishment.
instaurar [4] [ĩʃtaw'ra(x)] vt -1. [estabelecer] to establish. -2. [criar] to set up.
instável [ĩnʃ'tavew] (pl -eis) adj -1. [ger] unstable. -2. [sem equilíbrio] wobbly.
instigação [ĩʃtʃiga'sãw] (pl -ões) f instigation.
instigar [14] [ĩʃtʃi'ga(x)] vt -1. [incitar]: ~ alguém a fazer algo to encourage sb to do sthg. -2. [provocar]: ~ alguém contra alguém to rouse sb against sb.
instilar [4] [ĩʃtʃi'la(x)] vt to instil.
➡ **instilar-se** vp [infiltrar-se]: ~-se em to insinuate o.s. in.

instintivo, va [ĩnʃtʃĩn'tʃivu, va] adj instinctive.
instinto [ĩnʃ'tʃĩntu] m instinct; ~ de sobrevivência survival instinct.
institucional [ĩnʃtʃitusjo'naw] (pl -ais) adj institutional.
instituição [ĩnʃtʃitwi'sãw] (pl -ões) f institution; ~ de caridade charity, charitable institution.
instituir [74] [ĩʃtʃi'twi(x)] vt -1. [estabelecer] to institute. -2. [marcar] to set. -3. [nomear] to name.
instituto [ĩnʃtʃi'tutu] m institute; ~ de beleza beauty parlour.
instrução [ĩnʃtru'sãw] (pl -ões) f -1. [educação] education; ter/não ter ~ to be/not to be educated. -2. [ordem] instruction.
➡ **instruções** fpl instructions.
instruído, da [ĩʃ'trwidu, da] adj educated.
instruir [74] [ĩʃtru'i(x)] vt -1. [ger] to instruct. -2. [educar] to educate. -3. [informar]: ~ alguém sobre algo to instruct sb on sthg. -4. [adestrar] to train.
➡ **instruir-se** vp [educar-se] to become educated; ~-se em algo to train in sthg.
instrumentação [ĩnʃtrumẽnta'sãw] (pl -ões) f MÚS instrumentation.
instrumentador, ra [ĩnʃtrumẽnta'do(x), ra] m, f -1. MÚS score writer. -2. [em uma cirurgia] theatre nurse.
instrumental [ĩnʃtrumẽn'taw] (pl -ais) ◇ adj MÚS instrumental. ◇ m [equipamento] instrument; ~ cirúrgico surgical instrument.
instrumentar [47] [ĩnʃtrumẽn'ta(x)] vt MÚS to write scores.
instrumentista [ĩnʃtrumẽn'tʃiʃta] mf instrumentalist.
instrumento [ĩnʃtru'mẽntu] m -1. [ger] instrument; ~ de sopro wind instrument. -2. [ferramenta] tool; ~ de trabalho work tool.
instrutivo, va [ĩnʃtru'tʃivu, va] adj educational.
instrutor, ra [ĩnʃtru'to(x), ra] (mpl -es, fpl -s) m, f instructor.
insubordinação [ĩnsuboxdʒina'sãw] (pl -ões) f insubordination.
insubordinado, da [ĩnsuboxdʒi'nadu, da] adj insubordinate.
insubordinar-se [4] [ĩnsuboxdʒi'naxsi] vp to rebel.
insubstituível [ĩnsubʃtʃi'twivɛw] (pl -eis) adj irreplaceable.
insucesso [ĩnsu'sɛsu] m failure.
insuficiência [ĩnsufi'sjẽnsja] f -1. [carência] lack. -2. MED insufficiency.
insuficiente [ĩnsufi'sjẽntʃi] ◇ adj -1. [não-suficiente] insufficient. -2. [incompetente] inadequate. ◇ m [nota escolar] fail; tirar ~ to fail.
insuflar [4] [ĩsu'fla(x)] vt -1. [soprar] to blow into. -2. fig [incutir]: ~ algo em alguém to provoke sthg in sb.
insular [4] [ĩsu'la(x)] ◇ adj insular. ◇ vt to isolate.
insulina [ĩnsu'lina] f insulin.

insultar [4] [isuw'ta(x)] *vt* to insult.
insulto [ĩn'suwtu] *m* insult.
insultuoso, osa [ĩn'suw'twozu, ɔza] *adj* insulting.
insumo [ĩn'sumu] *m* input.
insuperável [ĩnsupe'ravεw] (*pl* -eis) *adj* -1. [invencível] insuperable. -2. [imbatível] unsurpassable.
insuportável [ĩnsupox'tavεw] (*pl* -eis) *adj* unbearable.
insurgente [ĩnsux'ʒẽntʃi] <> *adj* insurgent. <> *mf* insurgent.
insurgir-se [52] [ĩsux'ʒixsi] *vp* to revolt.
insurreição [ĩnsuxej'sãw] (*pl* -ões) *f* insurrection.
insurreto, ta [ĩnsu'xεtu, ta] <> *adj* insurgent. <> *m, f* insurgent.
insuspeito, ta [ĩnsuʃ'pejtu, ta] *adj* -1. [inocente] beyond suspicion. -2. [imparcial] impartial.
insustentável [ĩnsuʃtẽn'tavεw] (*pl* -eis) *adj* untenable.
intacto, ta [ĩn'ta(k)tu, ta] *adj* = intato.
intangibilidade [ĩntãnʒibili'dadʒi] *f* intangibility.
intangível [ĩntãn'ʒivew] (*pl* -eis) *adj* -1. [impalpável] intangible. -2. *fig* [intocável] irreproachable.
intato, ta [ĩn'tatu, ta] *adj* -1. [ileso] intact. -2. *fig* [puro] inviolate.
íntegra [ˈĩntegra] *f* entirety; **na** ~ in entirety.
integração [ĩntegra'sãw] (*pl* -ões) *f* integration.
integral [ĩnte'graw] (*pl* -ais) *adj* [total] whole; **leite** ~ full-cream milk; **cereal** ~ wholegrain cereal; **arroz** ~ brown rice; **pão** ~ wholemeal bread; **trigo** ~ wholewheat.
integralismo [ĩntegra'liʒmu] *m* Integralism, *Brazilian political movement of the 1930s*.
integralmente [ĩntegraw'mẽntʃi] *adv* fully.
integrante [ĩnte'grãntʃi] <> *adj* component. <> *mf* -1. [membro] constituent. -2. [parte] component. -3. *GRAM* conjunction.
integrar [4] [ĩnte'gra(x)] *vt* -1. [unir] to integrate. -2. [formar] to comprise. -3. [fazer parte] to be a member.
➤ **integrar-se** *vp* -1. [inteirar-se] to combine. -2. [juntar-se]: ~-se em *ou* a algo to join sthg.
integridade [ĩntegri'dadʒi] *f* integrity.
íntegro, gra [ˈĩntegru, gra] *adj* -1. [inteiro] entire. -2. [honesto] honest.
inteiramente [ĩnˌtejra'mẽntʃi] *adv* entirely.
inteirar [4] [ĩntej'ra(x)] *vt* -1. [completar] to make up. -2. [informar]: ~ alguém de algo to inform sb of sthg.
➤ **inteirar-se** *vp* [informar-se]: ~-se de algo to find out about sthg.
inteireza [ĩntej'reza] *f* -1. [totalidade] entirety. -2. *fig* [retidão] integrity.
inteiriço, ça [ĩntej'risu, sa] *adj* all-in-one.
inteiro, ra [ĩn'tejru, ra] *adj* -1. [todo] whole. -2. [intacto] intact. -3. [completo] entire. -4. [ileso] in one piece *(depois de verbo)*. -5. [inteiriço] all-in-one *(antes de subst)*; [total] complete. -6. *fam* [conservado] in good shape.
intelecto [ĩnte'lεktu] *m* intellect.

intelectual [ĩntelε'twaw] (*pl* -ais) <> *adj* intelectual. <> *mf* intellectual.
intelectualidade [ĩntelεktwali'dadʒi] *f* -1. [qualidade] intellect. -2. [o meio intelectual]: **a** ~ the intelligentsia.
inteligência [ĩnteli'ʒẽnsja] *f* -1. [destreza mental] intelligence. -2. [entendimento] comprehension. -3. [pessoa] brain. -4. *COMP*: ~ **artificial** artificial intelligence.
inteligente [ĩnteli'ʒẽntʃi] *adj* intelligent.
inteligível [ĩnteli'ʒivew] (*pl* -eis) *adj* intelligible.
intemperança [ĩntẽmpe'rãnsa] *f* intemperance.
intempérie [ĩntẽn'pεri] *f* bad weather.
intempestivo, va [ĩntẽmpeʃ'tʃivu, va] *adj* untimely.
intenção [ĩntẽn'sãw] (*pl* -ões) *f* intention; **com boa** ~ with good intentions, well meaning; **com má** ~ with bad intentions; **segundas intenções** ulterior motives; **ter a** ~ **de fazer algo** to intend to do sthg, to have the intention of doing sthg.
intencional [ĩntẽnsjo'naw] (*pl* -ais) *adj* intentional.
intencionar [4] [ĩntẽsjo'na(x)] *vt* to intend.
intendente [ĩntẽn'dẽntʃi] *mf* -1. [administrador] administrator. -2. *MIL* quartermaster.
intensidade [ĩntẽsi'dadʒi] *f* intensity.
intensificação [ĩntẽsifika'sãw] *f* intensification.
intensificar [12] [ĩntẽsifi'ka(x)] *vt* to intensify.
➤ **intensificar-se** *vp* to intensify.
intensivo, va [ĩntẽ'sivu, va] *adj* intensive.
intenso, sa [ĩn'tẽsu, sa] *adj* intense.
intentar [4] [ĩntẽn'ta(x)] *vt* -1. [tentar] to attempt. -2. [projetar] to plan. -3. [cometer] to commit. -4. *JUR*: ~ **uma ação contra alguém** to take sb to court.
intento [ĩn'tẽntu] *m* intent.
interação [ĩntera'sãw] (*pl* -ões) *f* interaction.
interagir [52] [ĩntera'ʒi(x)] *vi*: ~ **com algo/alguém** to interact with sthg/sb.
interatividade [ĩnteratʃivi'dadʒi] *f COMPUT* interactivity.
interativo, va [ĩntera'tʃivu, va] *adj COMPUT* interactive.
intercalar [4] [ĩntex'kala(x)] *vt* -1. [interpor]: ~ **algo em** *ou* **entre** to place sthg in *ou* between. -2. [inserir]: ~ **algo em** to insert sthg in(to).
➤ **intercalar-se** *vp* [interpor-se]: ~-se em *ou* entre to intervene in/between.
intercambiar [4] [ĩnterkãn'bia(x)] *vt* to interchange.
intercambiável [ĩnterkãn'bjavεw] (*pl* -eis) *adj* interchangeable.
intercâmbio [ˌĩnter'kãnbjul] *m* exchange.
interceder [5] [ĩntexse'de(x)] *vi*: ~ **por alguém** to intercede on behalf of sb.
interceptar [4] [ĩntexsεp'ta(x)] *vt* -1. [ger] to cut off. -2. [fazer parar] to stop. -3. [apoderar-se de] to intercept.
intercessão [ĩntexse'sãw] (*pl* -ões) *f* intercession.

interconexão [ĩntexkonek'sãw] (*pl* -ões) *f* interconnection.

intercontinental [ĩntexkõntʃinẽn'taw] (*pl* -ais) *adj* intercontinental.

interdependente [ĩntexdepẽn'dẽntʃi] *adj* interdependent.

interdição [ĩntexdʒi'sãw] (*pl* -ões) *f* -1. [proibição] ban. -2. [bloqueio] closure. -3. *JUR* injunction.

interdisciplinar [ĩntexdʒisipli'na(x)] *adj* interdisciplinary.

interdisciplinaridade [ĩntexdʒisiplinari'dadʒi] *f* interdisciplinary nature.

interditado, da [ĩntexdʒi'tadu, da] *adj* -1. [proibido] banned. -2. [bloqueado] closed.

interditar [4] [ĩntexdʒi'ta(x)] *vt* -1. [proibir] to ban. -2. [bloquear] to close. -3. *JUR* to interdict.

interessado, da [ĩntere'sadu, da] ◇ *adj* interested. ◇ *m, f* interested party.

interessante [ĩntere'sãntʃi] *adj* interesting.

interessar [4] [ĩntere'sa(x)] ◇ *vt* to interest. ◇ *vi* [despertar interesse] to be of interest; **a quem possa ~** *fml* to whom it may concern.

interessar-se *vp* [ter interesse]: **~-se em** *ou* **por** to take an interest in.

interesse [ĩnte'resi] *m* -1. [ger] interest. -2. [vantagem] benefit; **no ~ de** in the interest of; **por ~ próprio** out of self-interest.

interesseiro, ra [ĩntere'sejru, ra] ◇ *adj* self-seeking. ◇ *m, f* egotist.

interestadual [ĩntereʃta'dwaw] (*pl* -ais) *adj* interstate.

interface [ĩntex'fasi] *f* *COMPUT* interface.

interferência [ĩntexfe'rẽnsja] *f* interference.

interferir [57] [ĩntexfe'ri(x)] *vi* -1. [intervir]: **~ em algo** to interfere in sthg. -2. [em rádio, televisão] to cause interference.

interfonar [4] [ĩntexfo'na(x)] *vi*: **~ a alguém** to call sb on the internal phone.

interfone [ĩntex'foni] *m* intercom.

ínterim [ĩ'nterĩ] *m* interim; **nesse ~** meanwhile.

interior [ĩnte'rjo(x)] (*pl* -es) ◇ *adj* inner. ◇ *m* interior.

interiorano, na [ĩnterjo'rãnu, na] ◇ *adj* country (*antes de subst*). ◇ *m,f* country dweller.

interiorizar [ĩnterjori'za(x)] *vt* to internalize.

interjeição [ĩntexʒej'sãw] (*pl* -ões) *f* exclamation.

interligação [ĩntexliga'sãw] (*pl* -ões) *f* interconnection.

interligar [14] [ĩntexli'ga(x)] *vt* to interconnect.

interligar-se *vp* to be interconnected.

interlocutor, ra [ĩntexloku'to(x), ra] (*pl* -es, *fpl* -s) *m, f* interlocutor.

interlúdio [ĩntex'ludʒju] *m* interlude.

intermediar [17] [ĩntexme'dʒja(x)] *vt* -1. [servir como mediador] to mediate; **~ um debate entre** to chair a debate between. -2. [entremear, intercalar] to mix.

intermediário, ria [ĩntexme'dʒjarju, rja] ◇ *adj* intermediate. ◇ *m, f* -1. [mediador] mediator. -2. *COM* intermediary.

intermédio [ĩnter'mɛdʒu] *m*: **por ~ de** through.

interminável [ĩntexmi'navɛw] (*pl* -eis) *adj* endless.

intermitente [ĩntexmi'tẽntʃi] *adj* intermittent.

internação [ĩntexna'sãw] (*pl* -ões) *f* -1. [de doente] admission. -2. [de aluno] boarding.

internacional [ĩntexnasjo'naw] (*pl* -ais) *adj* international.

internacionalizar [4] [ĩntexnasjonali'za(x)] *vt* to internationalize.

internacionalizar-se *vp* to become international.

internamento [ĩntexna'mẽntu] *m* admission.

internar [4] [ĩntex'na(x)] *vt* -1. *MED* to admit. -2. [aluno] to board. -3. *POL* to intern.

internato [ĩntex'natu] *m* *EDUC* boarding school.

internauta [ĩntex'nawta] *mf* *COMPUT* Internet user *ou* surfer.

Internet [ĩntex'nɛtʃi] *f*: **a ~** the Internet.

interno, na [ĩn'tɛxnu, na] ◇ *adj* -1. [interior] inside; **de uso ~** for internal use. -2. *POL* internal. -3. [aluno] boarding. ◇ *m, f* -1. *MED* houseman *UK*, intern *US*. -2. [aluno] boarder.

interpelação [ĩntexpela'sãw] (*pl* -ões) *f* -1. [indagação] questioning. -2. *JUR* summons (*sg*).

interpelar [4] [ĩntexpe'la(x)] *vt* -1. [indagar]: **~ alguém sobre algo** to question sb about sthg. -2. [pedir explicações] to question. -3. *JUR* to summons.

interplanetário, ria [ĩntexplane'tarju, rja] *adj* interplanetary.

Interpol (*abrev de* **International Criminal Police Organization**) *f* Interpol.

interpolação [ĩntexpola'sãw] (*pl* -ões) *f* [inserção] insertion.

interpolar [4] [ĩntexpo'la(x)] *vt* -1. [texto, narrativa] to insert. -2. [intercalar] to interpolate.

interpor [45] [ĩntex'po(x)] *vt* -1. [entremeter] to put in. -2. [fazer intervir] to intervene with.

interpor-se *vp* -1. [pôr-se entre, mediar]: **~-se entre** to intervene between. -2. [contrapor-se]: **~-se a algo/alguém** to oppose sthg/sb.

interposto, ta [ĩntex'poʃtu, ta] ◇ *pp* ▷ interpor. ◇ *adj* interposing.

interpretação [ĩntexpreta'sãw] (*pl* -ões) *f* -1. [ger] interpretation. -2. [tradução] interpreting.

interpretar [4] [ĩntexpre'ta(x)] *vt* -1. [ger] to interpret. -2. [traduzir] to interpret.

interpretativo, va [ĩntexpreta'tʃivu, va] *adj* interpretative.

intérprete [ĩn'tɛxpretʃi] *mf* -1. *LING* interpreter. -2. *CINE, TEATRO & TV* performer.

interregno [ĩnte'xegnu] *m* [intervalo] interlude.

inter-racial [ĩntexa'sjaw] (*pl* -ais) *adj* interracial.

inter-relacionado, da [ĩntexelasjo'nadu, da] *adj* interrelated.

inter-relacionar [4] [ĩntexelasjo'na(x)] *vt* to interrelate.

interrogação [ĩntexoga'sãw] (*pl* -ões) *f* interrogation; **ponto de ~** question mark.

interrogador, ra [ĩntexoga'do(x), ra] *m, f* interrogator.

interrogar [14] [ĩntexu'ga(x)] *vt* -1. [indagar]: **~**

alguém **(sobre algo)** to interrogate sb (about sthg). **-2.** JUR to put questions to.

interrogativo, va [ĩntexoga'tʃivu, va] adj **-1.** [indagativo] questioning. **-2.** GRAM interrogative.

interrogatório [ĩntexoga'tɔrjul m interrogation.

interromper [5] [ĩntexõm'pe(x)] vt to interrupt.

interrompido, da [ĩntexõn'pidu, da] adj interrupted.

interrupção [ĩntexup'sãw] (pl -ões) f interruption.

interruptor [ĩntexup'to(x)] (pl -es) m switch.

interseção [ĩntexse'sãw] (pl -ões) f intersection.

interstício [ĩntexʃ'tʃisju] m interstice.

interurbano, na [ˌĩnterux'bãnu, na] adj **-1.** intercity UK, inter-urban US. **-2.** [telefonema] long distance.

➡ **interurbano** m [telefonema] long distance call.

intervalo [ĩntex'valul m **-1.** [ger] interval; a ~s at intervals; ~ **comercial** commercial break. **-2.** [no espaço] distance.

intervenção [ĩntexvẽn'sãw] (pl -ões) f **-1.** [interferência] intervention; ~ **cirúrgica** operation, surgical intervention. **-2.** JUR mediation.

intervencionismo [ĩntexvẽnsjo'niʒmul m interventionism.

intervencionista [ĩntervẽnsjo'niʃta] ⋄ adj interventionist. ⋄ mf interventionist.

interventor, ra [ĩntexvẽn'to(x), ra] m, f interim governor.

intervir [67] [ĩntex'vi(x)] vi to intervene.

intestinal [ĩnteʃtʃi'naw] (pl -ais) adj intestinal.

intestino [ĩnteʃ'tʃinu] m intestine; ~ **delgado** small intestine; ~ **grosso** large intestine.

intimação [ĩntʃima'sãw] (pl -ões) f **-1.** [ordem] order. **-2.** JUR summons (sg).

intimar [4] [ĩntʃi'ma(x)] vt **-1.** [ordenar]: ~ **alguém (a fazer algo)** to order sb (to do sthg). **-2.** JUR to summons.

intimidação [ĩntʃimida'sãw] (pl -ões) f intimidation.

intimidade [ĩntʃimi'dadʒi] f **-1.** [vida íntima] privacy. **-2.** [familiaridade] intimacy; **ter ~ com alguém** to be close to sb.

intimidar [4] [ĩntʃimi'da(x)] vt to intimidate.

➡ **intimidar-se** vp to be intimidated.

íntimo, ma ['ĩntʃimu, ma] ⋄ adj **-1.** [interior e profundo] intimate. **-2.** [privado] private. ⋄ m **-1.** [âmago]: **no ~, ela sabia que estava errada** deep down, she knew that she was wrong. **-2.** [amigo] close friend.

intitular [4] [ĩntʃitu'la(x)] vt **-1.** [dar título a] to title; ~ **algo de algo** to call sthg sthg. **-2.** [chamar]: ~ **alguém de algo** to call sb sthg.

➡ **intitular-se** vp [denominar-se] to call o.s.

intocável [ĩnto'kavew] (pl -eis) adj untouchable.

intolerância [ĩntole'rãnsja] f intolerance.

intolerante [ĩntole'rãntʃil adj intolerant.

intolerável [ĩntole'ravew] (pl -eis) adj intolerable.

intoxicação [ĩntoksika'sãw] (pl -ões) f poisoning;

~ **alimentar** food poisoning.

intoxicar [12] [ĩntoksi'ka(x)] vt to poison.

➡ **intoxicar-se** vp to poison o.s.

intraduzível [ĩntradu'zivew] (pl -eis) adj **-1.** [que não tem tradução] untranslatable. **-2.** [inexprimível] inexpressible.

intragável [ĩntra'gavew] (pl -eis) adj unpalatable.

intranet ['ĩntranetʃil f COMPUT intranet.

intranqüilidade [ĩntrãŋkwili'dadʒil f disquiet.

intranqüilo [ĩntrãn'kwilul adj restless.

intransferível [ĩntrãnʃfe'rivew] (pl -eis) adj **-1.** [bilhete, documento] non-transferable. **-2.** [inadiável] non-postponable.

intransigência [ĩntrãnsi'ʒẽnsja] f intransigence.

intransigente [ĩntrãnzi'ʒẽntʃil adj **-1.** [intolerante] intransigent. **-2.** fig [austero] uncompromising.

intransitável [ĩntrãnzi'tavew] (pl -eis) adj impassable.

intransitivo, va [ĩntrãnzi'tʃivu, va] adj intransitive.

intransponível [ĩntrãnʃpo'nivew] (pl -eis) adj **-1.** [rio, barreira] impassable. **-2.** [problema, obstáculo] insurmountable.

intratável [ĩntra'tavew] (pl -eis) adj [insociável] intractable.

intra-uterino, intra-uterina [ˌĩntrawte'rinu, na] (mpl intra-uterinos, fpl intra-uterinas) adj intrauterine.

intravenoso, osa [ĩntrave'nozu, ɔza] adj intravenous.

intrépido, da [ĩn'trɛpidu, da] adj intrepid.

intricado, da [ĩntri'kadu, da] adj **-1.** [emaranhado] tangled. **-2.** [confuso] intricate.

intriga [ĩn'triga] f **-1.** [trama] intrigue. **-2.** [cilada] conspiracy. **-3.** [enredo] plot.

➡ **intrigas** fpl [fofoca] gossip (sg).

intrigante [ĩntri'gãntʃil adj intriguing.

intrigar [14] [ĩntri'ga(x)] ⋄ vt [despertar curiosidade de] to intrigue. ⋄ vi [excitar a curiosidade] to intrigue.

intrínseco, ca [ĩn'trĩnseku, ka] adj intrinsic.

introdução [ĩntrodu'sãw] (pl -ões) f introduction.

introdutório, ria [ĩntrodu'tɔrju, rja] adj introductory.

introduzir [72] [ĩntrodu'zi(x)] vt **-1.** [inserir]: ~ **algo (em)** to introduce sthg (into). **-2.** [fazer adotar] to introduce.

➡ **introduzir-se** vp: ~ **(em)** to find one's way (into).

intróito [ĩn'trɔjtu] m **-1.** [início] beginning. **-2.** REL introit.

intrometer-se [5] [ĩntrome'texsil vp: ~**-se em algo** to meddle in sthg.

intrometido, da [ĩntrome'tʃidu, da] ⋄ adj meddlesome, interfering. ⋄ m, f meddler.

intromissão [ĩntromi'sãw] (pl -ões) f meddling.

introspecção [ĩntroʃpek'sãw] f introspection.

introspectivo, va [ĩntroʃpek'tʃivu, va] adj introspective.

introversão [ĩntrovex'sãw] *f* introversion.
introvertido, da [ĩntrovex'tʃidu, da] <> *adj* introverted. <> *m, f* introvert.
intruso, sa [ĩn'truzu, za] *m, f* intruder.
intuição [ĩntwi'sãw] (*pl* -ões) *f* intuition.
intuir [74] [ĩn'twi(x)] <> *vt* to intuit. <> *vi* to be intuitive.
intuitivo, va [ĩntwi'tʃivu, va] *adj* intuitive.
intuito [ĩn'twitu] *m* -**1.** [objetivo] purpose. -**2.** [intento] intention.
intumescência [ĩntume'sẽnsja] *f* swelling.
intumescer-se [25] [ĩntume'sɛxsi] *vp* to swell (up).
intumescido, da [ĩntume'sidu, da] *adj* swollen.
inumano, na [inu'manu, na] *adj* inhuman.
inúmeros, ras [i'numeruʃ, raʃ] *adj pl* [antes de subst] innumerable.
inundação [inũnda'sãw] (*pl* -ões) *f* flood.
inundado, da [inũn'dadu, da] *adj* -**1.** [de água] flooded. -**2.** *fig* covered.
inundar [4] [inũn'da(x)] <> *vt* [alagar] to flood. <> *vt fig* [encher] to swamp. <> *vi* [transbordar] to flood.
► inundar-se *vp* [alagar-se] to become flooded.
inusitado, da [inuzi'tadu, da] *adj* unusual.
inútil [i'nutʃiw] (*pl* -eis) *adj* -**1.** [imprestável] useless. -**2.** [desnecessário] needless. -**3.** [vão] pointless; **ser ~ fazer algo** to be pointless to do sthg.
inutilidade [inutʃili'dadʒi] *f* uselessness.
inutilizar [4] [inutʃili'za(x)] *vt* -**1.** [tornar inútil] to render useless. -**2.** [danificar] to ruin. -**3.** [frustrar] to thwart.
inutilizável [inutʃili'zavew] (*pl* -eis) *adj* [não-utilizável] unusable.
inutilmente [i,nutʃiwmẽntʃi] *adv* uselessly.
invadir [6] [ĩnva'di(x)] *vt* -**1.** [ger] to invade. -**2.** *fig* [dominar] to overwhelm.
invalidar [4] [ĩnvali'da(x)] *vt* -**1.** [anular] to invalidate. -**2.** [pessoa] to disable.
invalidez [ĩnvali'deʒ] *f* disability.
inválido, da [ĩnvalidu, da] <> *adj* -**1.** [nulo] invalid. -**2.** [pessoa] invalid, disabled. <> *m, f* [pessoa] invalid.
invariável [ĩnva'rjavɛw] (*pl* -eis) *adj* invariable.
invasão [ĩnva'zãw] (*pl* -ões) *f* invasion.
invasivo, va [ĩnva'zivu, va] *adj* -**1.** [agressivo] invasion (*antes de subst*). -**2.** MED invasive.
invasor, ra [ĩva'zo(x), ra] <> *adj* invading. <> *m, f* invader.
inveja [ĩn'vɛʒa] *f* envy.
invejar [4] [ĩnve'ʒa(x)] <> *vt* -**1.** [ter inveja de] to envy. -**2.** [cobiçar] to covet. <> *vi* [ter inveja] to be envious.
invejável [ĩnve'ʒavew] (*pl* -eis) *adj* enviable.
invejoso, osa [ĩnve'ʒozu, ɔza] <> *adj* [pessoa] envious. <> *m, f* [pessoa] envious person.
invenção [ĩnvẽn'sãw] (*pl* -ões) *f* -**1.** [ger] invention. -**2.** *fig* [mentira] fabrication.
invencibilidade [ĩnvẽnsibili'dadʒi] *f* invincibility.

invencionice [ĩnvẽnsjo'nisi] *f* [mentira, embuste] fabrication.
invencível [ĩnvẽn'sivew] (*pl* -eis) *adj* invincible.
inventar [4] [ĩnvẽn'ta(x)] <> *vt* to invent. <> *vi* [cismar]: **~ de fazer algo** to get it into one's head to do sthg.
inventariar [16] [ĩnvẽnta'rja(x)] *vt* to inventory.
inventário [ĩnvẽn'tarju] *m* inventory.
inventivo, va [ĩnvẽn'tʃivu, va] *adj* inventive.
inventor, ra [ĩnvẽn'to(x), ra] (*mpl* -es, *fpl* -s) *m, f* inventor.
inverdade [ĩnvex'dadʒi] *f* untruth.
invernada [ĩnvex'nada] *f* winter pasture.
invernal [ĩnvex'naw] (*pl* -ais) *adj* wintry.
inverno [ĩn'vɛxnu] *m* winter.
inverossímil [ĩnvero'simiw] (*pl* -eis) *adj* implausible.
inversão [ĩnvex'sãw] (*pl* -ões) *f* inversion.
inverso, sa [ĩn'vɛxsu, sa] *adj* -**1.** [invertido] inverse. -**2.** [oposto] opposite.
► inverso *m* [contrário] opposite.
invertebrado, da [ĩnvexte'bradu, da] <> *adj* [animal] invertebrate. <> *m* [animal] invertebrate.
inverter [5] [ĩnvex'te(x)] *vt* -**1.** [virar ao contrário] to reverse. -**2.** [trocar a ordem de] to invert. -**3.** [mudar] to alter.
invés [ĩn'vɛʃ] *m* inside out.
► ao invés de *loc prep* instead of.
investida [ĩnveʃ'tʃida] *f* -**1.** [ataque] attack. -**2.** *fig* [tentativa] attempt.
investidor, ra [ĩveʃtʃi'do(x), ra] *m, f* investor.
investidura [ĩnveʃtʃi'dura] *f* investiture.
investigação [ĩnveʃtʃiga'sãw] (*pl* -ões) *f* -**1.** [inquérito] investigation; **~ policial** police investigation. -**2.** [pesquisa] inquiry; **~ científica** scientific investigation.
investigador, ra [ĩnveʃtʃiga'do(x), ra] *m, f* [agente policial] detective.
investigar [14] [ĩnveʃtʃi'ga(x)] *vt* -**1.** [inquirir] to investigate. -**2.** [pesquisar] to research.
investimento [ĩnveʃtʃi'mẽntu] *m* investment.
investir [54] [ĩveʃ'tʃi(x)] <> *vt* -**1.** [dinheiro, verba] to invest. -**2.** [empossar]: **~ alguém diretor da empresa** to install sb as director of a company. <> *vi* -**1.** [aplicar dinheiro, verba]: **~ (em algo)** to invest (in sthg). -**2.** [atacar]: **~ contra algo** to storm sthg. -**3.** [atirar-se]: **~ para algo** to rush to sthg.
inveterado, da [ĩnvete'radu, da] *adj* [muito antigo] inveterate.
inviabilidade [ĩnvjabili'dadʒi] *f* impracticability.
inviabilizar [4] [ĩvjabili'za(x)] *vt* to make unviable.
► inviabilizar-se *vp* to become unviable.
inviável [ĩn'vjavew] (*pl* -eis) *adj* unviable.
invicto, ta [ĩn'viktu, ta] *adj* unbeaten.
inviolabilidade [ĩnviolabili'dadʒi] *f* inviolability.
inviolável [ĩnvjo'lavew] (*pl* -eis) *adj* inviolable.
invisível [ĩnvi'zivew] (*pl* -eis) *adj* invisible.
in vitro [,in'vitru] *loc adj* in vitro.

invocação [ĩvo'kasãw] (*pl* -ões) *f* invocation.

invocado, da [ĩvo'kadu, da] *adj fam* -**1.** [irritado] annoyed. -**2.** [cismado] preoccupied. -**3.** [incomum] bizarre. -**4.** [inconstante] inconsistent.

invocar [12] [ĩvo'ka(x)] <> *vt* -**1.** [chamar] to invoke. -**2.** *fam* [irritar] to wind up, to annoy. <> *vi fam* [antipatizar]: ~ **com alguém** to dislike sb.

invólucro [ĩn'vɔlukru] *m* -**1.** [envoltório] envelope. -**2.** [membrana] membrane. -**3.** [caixa] casing.

involuntário, ria [ĩnvolũn'tarju, rja] *adj* involuntary.

invulnerável [ĩvuwne'ravɛw] (*pl* -eis) *adj* invulnerable.

iodo ['jodu] *m* iodine.

IOF (*abrev de* **Imposto sobre Operações Financeiras**) *m* Brazilian tax on financial transactions.

ioga ['jɔga] *f* yoga.

iogue ['jɔgi] <> *adj* yoga (*antes de subst*). <> *mf* yogi.

iogurte [ju'guxtʃi] *m* yoghurt.

ioiô [jo'jo] *m* yo-yo.

íon ['iõ] (*pl* **íons**) *m* ion.

ionizar [joni'za(x)] *vt* to ionize.

IPC (*abrev de* **Índice de Preços ao Consumidor**) *m* consumer price index.

IPEM (*abrev de* **Instituto de Pesos e Medidas**) *m* Brazilian institute of weights and measures.

IPTU (*abrev de* **Imposto Predial e Territorial Urbano**) *m* annual tax based on the value of a house.

IPVA (*abrev de* **Imposto sobre Propriedade de Veículos Automotores**) *m* tax paid annually on the value of a car, ≃ road tax *UK*.

ir [66] ['i(x)] *vi* -**1.** [deslocar-se] to go; **fomos de ônibus** we went by bus; **iremos a pé** we'll go on foot, we'll walk; **vamos?** shall we go? -**2.** [assistir, freqüentar] to go; **ele nunca vai às reuniões** he never goes to the meetings; **você não vai à aula?** aren't you going to your class?; **vou ao cinema muitas vezes** I often go to the cinema. -**3.** [estender-se] to go; **o caminho vai até ao lago** the path leads to the lake. -**4.** [desenrolar-se] to go; **isto não vai nada bem** this isn't going at all well; **como vai você?** how are you?; **como vão as coisas?** how are things?; **os negócios vão mal** business is bad. -**5.** [exprime duração gradual]: ~ **fazendo algo** to continue doing sthg; **vá tentando!** keep trying! -**6.** [seguido de infinitivo]: **vou falar com ele** I'll speak to him; **você vai gostar** you'll like it; **não vou fazer nada** I'm not going to do anything. -**7.** [seguido de gerúndio]: **eu ia caindo** I almost fell. -**8.** [em locuções]: ~ **dar em** [desembocar] to lead to; ~ **ter com** [encontrar] to go and meet up with.

➤ **ir de** *v* + *prep* [disfarçado] to go as; [escolher]: **eu vou de filé com fritas, e você?** I'll have the steak and fries, what about you?

➤ **ir por** *v* + *prep* [auto-estrada, escadas] to take; ~ **pela esquerda/direita** to go (on the) left/right; ~ **pelo jardim** to go through the garden.

➤ **ir-se** *vp* [partir] to go; **ele já se foi** he's already left; ~-**se embora** to leave; **vai-te embora!** go away!

IR (*abrev de* **Imposto de Renda**) *m* income tax.

ira ['ira] *f* anger.

Irã [i'rã] *m*: (o) ~ Iran.

irado, da [i'radu, da] *adj* angry.

iraniano, na [ira'njãnu, na] <> *adj* Iranian. <> *m, f* Iranian.

Iraque [i'raki] *n*: (o) ~ Iraq.

iraquiano, na [ira'kjanu, na] <> *adj* Iraqi. <> *m, f* Iraqi.

irascível [ira'sivɛw] (*pl* -eis) *adj* irascible.

ir-e-vir [iri'vi(x)] (*pl* **ires-e-vires**) *m* coming and going.

iridescente [iride'sẽntʃi] *adj* iridescent.

íris ['iriʃ] *f inv* iris.

Irlanda [ix'lãnda] *n* Ireland; ~ **do Norte** Northern Ireland.

irlandês, esa [ixlãn'deʃ, eza] (*mpl* -eses, *fpl* -s) <> *adj* Irish. <> *m, f* Irishman (*f* Irishwoman).

➤ **irlandês** *m* [língua] Irish.

irmã [ix'mã] *f* ▷ **irmão**.

irmanar [4] [ixma'na(x)] *vt* to unite (as brothers).

➤ **irmanar-se** *vp*: ~-**se com algo/alguém** to join with sthg/sb.

irmandade [ixmãn'dadʒi] *f* -**1.** [RELIG - de irmãos] brotherhood; [- de irmãs] sisterhood. -**2.** [confraternidade] fraternity.

irmão, mã [ix'mãw, mã] *m, f* -**1.** [parente] brother (sister); ~ **de criação** stepbrother; ~ **gêmeo** twin brother; **irmãos siameses** siamese twins. -**2.** [afim] twin.

ironia [iro'nia] *f* irony.

irônico, ca [i'roniku, ka] *adj* ironic.

ironizar [4] [ironi'za(x)] *vt & vi* to mock.

IRPF (*abrev de* **Imposto de Renda de Pessoa Física**) *m* income tax paid by individuals.

IRPJ (*abrev de* **Imposto de Renda de Pessoa Jurídica**) *m* corporation tax.

irracional [ixasjo'naw] (*pl* -ais) *adj* irrational.

irracionalidade [ixasjonali'dadʒi] *f* irrationality.

irradiação [ixadʒja'sãw] (*pl* -ões) *f* -**1.** [transmissão] broadcast. -**2.** [propagação] diffusion. -**3.** *MED* irradiation.

irradiar [16] [ixa'dʒja(x)] *vt* -**1.** [transmitir] to broadcast. -**2.** [propagar] to spread. -**3.** *fig* [externar] to radiate.

➤ **irradiar-se** *vp* -**1.** [difundir-se] to be spread about. -**2.** [transmitir-se] to be broadcast.

irreal [i'xjaw] (*pl* -ais) *adj* unreal.

irrealizado, da [ixeali'zadu, da] *adj* unrealized.

irrealizável [ixeali'zavɛw] (*pl* -eis) *adj* unachievable.

irreconciliável [ixekõnsi'ljavɛw] (*pl* -eis) *adj* irreconcilable.

irreconhecível [ixekoɲe'sivɛw] (*pl* -eis) *adj* unrecognizable.

irrecorrível [ixeko'xivɛw] (*pl* -eis) *adj* [sentença] unappealable.

irrecuperável [ixekupe'ravɛwl (*pl* -**eis**) *adj* irrecoverable.

irrecusável [ixeku'zavewl (*pl* -**eis**) *adj* which cannot be refused.

irredutível [ixedu'tʃivewl (*pl* -**eis**) *adj* indomitable.

irrefletido, da [ixefle'tʃidu, dal *adj* rash.

irrefreável [ixefre'avewl (*pl* -**eis**) *adj* irrepressible.

irrefutável [ixefu'tavewl (*pl* -**eis**) *adj* irrefutable.

irregular [ixegu'la(x)] (*pl* -**es**) *adj* -**1.** [desigual] irregular. -**2.** [pouco convencional] unorthodox. -**3.** [irrecuperável] incurable.

irregularidade [ixegulari'dadʒi] *f* -**1.** [inconstância] unreliability. -**2.** [procedimento irregular] irregularity.

irrelevância [ixele'vãnsja] *f* irrelevance.

irrelevante [ixele'vãntʃi] *adj* irrelevant.

irremediável [ixeme'dʒjavɛwl (*pl* -**eis**) *adj* irreparable.

irremediavelmente [ixemedjavew'mẽntʃi] *adv* irremediably.

irremovível [ixemo'vivewl (*pl* -**eis**) *adj* immovable; **ser/estar ~ em algo** to be immovable in sthg.

irreparável [ixepa'ravewl (*pl* -**eis**) *adj* irreparable.

irrepreensível [ixeprjẽn'sivewl (*pl* -**eis**) *adj* irreproachable.

irreprimível [ixepri'mivewl (*pl* -**eis**) *adj* irrepressible.

irrequietação [ixikjeta'sãwl *f* restlessness.

irrequieto, ta [ixe'kjɛtu, tal *adj* [desassossegado] restless.

irresistível [ixezif'tʃivewl (*pl* -**eis**) *adj* irresistible.

irresoluto, ta [ixezo'lutu, tal *adj* irresolute.

irresponsabilidade [ixefpõnsabili'dadʒi] *f* irresponsibility.

irresponsável [ixefpõn'savɛwl (*pl* -**eis**) *adj* irresponsible. *mf* irresponsible person.

irrestrito, ta [ixeʃ'tritu, tal *adj* unlimited, limitless.

irreverência [ixeve'rẽnsja] *f* irreverence.

irreverente [ixeve'rẽntʃi] *adj* irreverent.

irreversível [ixevex'sivewl (*pl* -**eis**) *adj* irreversible.

irrevogável [ixevo'gavewl (*pl* -**eis**) *adj* irrevocable.

irrigação [ixiga'sãwl (*pl* -**ões**) *f* irrigation.

irrigar [14] [ixi'ga(x)] *vt* to irrigate.

irrisório, ria [ixi'zɔrju, rjal *adj* -**1.** [de zombaria] derisory. -**2.** *fig* [ínfimo] derisory.

irritabilidade [ixitabili'dadʒi] *f* irritability.

irritação [ixita'sãwl *f* irritation.

irritadiço, ça [ixita'dʒisu, sal *adj* irritable.

irritante [ixi'tãntʃi] *adj* irritating.

irritar [4] [ixi'ta(x)] *vt* to irritate.

➡ **irritar-se** *vp* [exasperar-se] to become irritated.

irritável [ixi'tavewl (*pl* -**eis**) *adj* irritable.

irromper [5] [ixõm'pe(x)] *vi* -**1.** [entrar]: ~ **em** to

burst into. -**2.** [surgir]: ~ **de** to surge from; ~ **em** to break out.

isca [ˈiʃkal *f* -**1.** [ger] bait. -**2.** *CULIN* morsel.

isenção [izẽn'sãwl (*pl* -**ões**) *f* -**1.** [dispensa] exemption. -**2.** [livramento] release. -**3.** [imparcialidade] impartiality.

isentar [4] [izẽn'ta(x)] *vt* -**1.** [dispensar]: ~ **alguém de algo/de fazer algo** to exempt sb from sthg/from doing sthg. -**2.** [livrar]: ~ **alguém de algo/fazer algo** to let sb off from sthg/from doing sthg.

➡ **isentar-se** *vp* to free o.s.

isento, ta [i'zẽntu, tal *adj* -**1.** [dispensado] exempt. -**2.** [livre] free. -**3.** [imparcial] unbiased.

Islã [iʒ'lãl *m* Islam.

Islamabad [iʒlama'badʒil *n* Islamabad.

islâmico, ca [iʒ'lamiku, kal *adj* Islamic.

islamismo [iʒla'miʒmul *m* Islam.

islamita [iʒla'mital ◇ *adj* Islamic. ◇ *mf* Islamist.

islandês, esa [iʒlãn'deʃ, ezal ◇ *adj* Icelandic. ◇ *m, f* Icelander.

➡ **islandês** *m* [língua] Icelandic.

Islândia [iʒ'lãndʒja] *f* Iceland.

ISO (*abrev de* **International Standards Organization**) *f* ISO.

isolacionismo [izolasjo'niʒmul *m* isolationism.

isolado, da [izo'ladu, dal *adj* -**1.** [separado] isolated. -**2.** [só] lone. -**3.** [afastado] remote. -**4.** *ELETR* insulated.

isolamento [izola'mẽntul *m* -**1.** [ger] isolation. -**2.** *ELETR* insulation.

isolante [izo'lãntʃi] ◇ *adj ELETR* insulating. ◇ *m* insulator.

isolar [4] [izo'la(x)] ◇ *vt* -**1.** [ger] to isolate; ~ **algo de algo** to isolate sthg from sthg. -**2.** *ELETR* to insulate. ◇ *vi* [afastar mau agouro]: **isola!** touch wood!

➡ **isolar-se** *vp* [afastar-se]: ~**-se de alguém/algo** to isolate o.s from sb/sthg.

isonomia [izono'mial *f* equality.

isopor [izo'poxl *m* polystyrene.

isqueiro [iʃ'kejrul *m* lighter.

Israel [iʒxa'ɛwl *n* Israel.

israelense [iʒxae'lẽnsil, **israelita** [iʒxae'lital ◇ *adj* Israeli. ◇ *mf* Israeli.

isso [ˈisul ◇ *pron* that; **é isso ai!** that's right!; **foi por isso que ele não veio** that's why he didn't come; **é por isso mesmo que en não vou!** that is exactly why I'm not going!; **isso não!** no way!; **não gosto disso** I don't like that; **não mexa nisso!** leave that alone!

➡ **por isso** *loc adv* therefore; **mem por ~** not really.

Istambul [iʃtãn'buwl *n* Istanbul.

istmo [ˈiʃtʃimul *m* isthmus.

isto [ˈiʃtul *pron* this; **disto eu não quero** I don't want any of this; **escreva nisto** write on this; **isto é** [quer dizer] that is (to say); **isto é que é vida!** this is the life!

Itália [i'taljal *n* Italy.

italiano, na [ita'ljanu, na] <> *adj* Italian. <> *m, f* Italian.
➡ **italiano** *m* [língua] Italian.
itálico, ca [i'taliku, ka] *adj* TIPO italic.
➡ **itálico** *m* TIPO italic.
Itamarati [itamara'tʃi] *m* Brazilian foreign ministry.
item ['itẽ] (*pl* **itens**) *m* - **1.** [ger] item. - **2.** JUR [artigo] point.
itinerante [itʃine'rãntʃi] <> *adj* itinerant. <> *mf* itinerant.
itinerário [itʃine'rarju] *m* - **1.** [roteiro] route. - **2.** [caminho] itinerary.
Iugoslávia [iwgo'ʒlavja] *f* Yugoslavia; **a ex-~** the ex-Yugoslavia.
iugoslavo, va [iwgoʒ'lavu, va] <> *adj* Yugoslav. <> *m, f* Yugoslav.

J

j, J ['ʒɔta] *m* [letra] j, J.
já ['ʒa] <> *adv* - **1.** [ger] already. - **2.** [agora] now. - **3.** [sem demora] just; **~ vou** just coming. - **4.** [até mesmo] even. - **5.** [daqui a pouco] soon; **até ~** see you soon. - **6.** [alguma vez] ever. <> *conj* however. <> *loc*: **~ era!** *fam* that's history!
➡ **desde já** *loc prep* from now on.
➡ **já que** *loc conj* since.
jabuti [ʒabu'tʃi] *m* jabuti, *indigenous Brazilian tortoise.*
jabuticaba [ʒabutʃi'kaba] *f* jaboticaba, *Brazilian evergreen tree or the fruit of this tree.*
jaca ['ʒaka] *f* jack fruit.
jacarandá [ʒakarãn'da] *f* jacaranda.
jacaré [ʒaka'rɛ] *m* - **1.** ZOOL Yacare caiman. - **2.** [surfe]: **pegar ~** to surf.
Jacarta [ʒa'kaxta] *n* Djakarta, Jakarta.
jacinto [ʒa'sĩntu] *m* hyacinth.
jactância [ʒak'tãnsja] *f* - **1.** [vaidade] boasting. - **2.** [arrogância] arrogance.
jactar-se [7] [ʒak'taxsi] *vp*: **~-se (de)** to boast (about).
jade ['ʒadʒi] *m* jade.
jaguar [ʒa'gwa(x)] (*pl* **-es**) *m* jaguar.
jaguatirica [ʒagwatʃi'rika] *f* leopard.
jagunço [ʒa'gũsu] *m* bodyguard.
jaleco [ʒa'lɛku] *m* coat.
Jamaica [ʒa'majka] *f* Jamaica.
jamais [ʒa'majʃ] *adv* never; (*com palavra negativa*) ever.

jamanta [ʒa'mãnta] *f* [caminhão] articulated truck.
jan. (*abrev de* **janeiro**) Jan.
janeiro [ʒa'nejru] *m* January; *veja também* **setembro**.
janela [ʒa'nɛla] *f* window.
janelão [ʒane'lãw] (*pl* **-ões**) *m* picture window.
jangada [ʒãŋ'gada] *f* raft.
jangadeiro, ra [ʒãŋga'dejru, ra] *m, f* raft owner.
janta ['ʒãnta] *f* dinner.
jantar [4] [ʒãn'ta(x)] (*pl* **-es**) <> *vt* to have for dinner. <> *vi* to have dinner. <> *m* dinner; **~ americano** buffet dinner.
Japão [ʒa'pãw] *n*: **(o) ~** Japan.
japona [ʒa'pona] *f* jacket.
japonês, esa [ʒapo'neʃ, eza] (*mpl* **-eses**, *fpl* **-s**) <> *adj* Japanese. <> *m, f* Japanese person.
➡ **japonês** *m* [língua] Japanese.
jaqueta [ʒa'keta] *f* jacket.
jaquetão [ʒake'tãw] (*pl* **-ões**) *m* double-breasted jacket.
jararaca [ʒara'raka] *f* - **1.** [cobra] viper. - **2.** *fig* [pessoa] harridan.
jarda ['ʒaxda] *f* yard.
jardim [ʒax'dʒĩ] (*pl* **-ns**) *m* garden; **~ botânico** botanical garden; **~ zoológico** zoo.
jardim-de-infância [ʒaxdʒĩndʒĩfãnsja] (*pl* **jardins-de-infância**) *m* kindergarten.
jardim-de-inverno [ʒaxdʒĩndʒĩvexnu] (*pl* **jardins-de-inverno**) *m* conservatory.
jardinagem [ʒaxdʒi'naʒẽ] *f* gardening.
jardineiro, ra [ʒaxdʒi'nejru, ra] *m, f* [pessoa] gardener.
➡ **jardineira** *f* - **1.** [móvel] jardinière. - **2.** [em parapeito] window box. - **3.** [roupa] overalls (*pl*).
jargão [ʒax'gãw] (*pl* **-ões**) *m* jargon.
jarra ['ʒaxa] *f* [pote] carafe; [vaso] vase.
jarro ['ʒaxu] *m* jug.
jasmim [ʒaʒ'mĩ] (*pl* **-ns**) *m* jasmine.
jato ['ʒatu] *m* - **1.** [raio] beam. - **2.** [avião] jet. - **3.** [propulsão]: **a ~** jet propelled. - **4.** [jorro] stream.
jaula ['ʒawla] *f* cage.
Java ['ʒava] *n* Java.
javali [ʒava'li] *m* wild boar.
jazer [33] [ʒa'ze(x)] *vi* - **1.** [estar sepultado] to lie. - **2.** [estar deitado] to be lying.
jazida [ʒa'zida] *f* seam.
jazigo [ʒa'zigu] *m* grave.
jazz ['ʒajʃ] *m* jazz.
jazzista [ʒa'ziʃta] *mf* jazz artist.
JC (*abrev de* **Jesus Cristo**) *m* JC.
jeans ['ʒĩnʃ] *m inv* jeans (*pl*).
jeca ['ʒɛka] *adj* rustic.
jeca-tatu ['ʒɛkatatu] (*pl* **-tus**) *m character from children's literature representing the village people of the Brazilian interior.*
jegue ['ʒɛgi] *m* ass.
jeitinho [ʒej'tʃinu] *m* touch; **dar um ~** to get something done one way or another.

JEITINHO BRASILEIRO

One of the more striking characteristics of the Brazilian people is their ability to rise to any occasion. Brazilians' adaptability to challenges and new situations is a cultural trait expressed in the famous *jeitinho brasileiro*, the belief that they will always have a special knack (*jeitinho*) for getting out of a tricky situation.

jeito ['ʒejtu] *m* **-1.** [modo] way; **ao ~ de** in the manner of; **de ~ algum!** no way!; **de qualquer ~** anyway; [sem cuidado] any old how. **-2.** [aspecto] air. **-3.** [índole] disposition. **-4.** [torção]: **dar um mau ~ em** to sprain. **-5.** [propensão]: **ter** *ou* **levar ~ para (fazer) algo** to be good at (doing) sthg. **-6.** [habilidade] aptitude; **falta de ~** clumsiness; **ter falta de ~ para (fazer) algo** to be bad at (doing) sthg. **-7.** [diplomacia] tact; **fazer algo com ~** to do sthg carefully. **-8.** [graça]: **ficar sem ~** to feel embarrassed. **-9.** [arrumação] clean up; **dar um ~ em algo** to tidy up. **-10.** [solução] solution; **dar um ~ em algo** to do something about sthg. **-11.** [corretivo]: **dar um ~ em alguém** to set sb straight. **-12.** [juízo]: **tomar ~** to grow up.

jeitoso, osa [ʒej'tozu, ɔza] *adj* **-1.** [habilidoso] dexterous. **-2.** [funcional] practical. **-3.** [diplomático] tactful.

jejuar [4] [ʒe'ʒwa(x)] *vi* to fast.

jejum [ʒe'ʒũ] (*pl* **-ns**) *m* fast; **em ~** fasting.

Jeová [ʒeo'val] *m*: **testemunha de ~** Jehovah's Witness.

jerico [ʒe'riku] *m* donkey; **idéia de ~** stupid idea.

jérsei ['ʒexsej] *m* jersey.

Jerusalém [ʒeruza'lẽ] *n* Jerusalem.

jesuíta [ʒe'zwita] <> *adj* Jesuit. <> *m* Jesuit.

jesuítico, ca [ʒezu'itʃiku, ka] *adj* [período, missão] Jesuitical.

jesus [ʒe'zuʃ] *interj* (good) heavens!

jetom [ʒe'tõ] (*pl* **-ns**) *m* **-1.** [remuneração] payment. **-2.** [ficha] jetton.

jet set [ʒet'sɛtʃi] *m* jet set.

jet ski [ʒɛtʃiʃ'ki] (*pl* **jet skis**) *m* jet ski.

jibóia [ʒi'bɔja] *f* [cobra] boa.

jiboiar [4] [ʒibo'ja(x)] *vi* to rest and digest after a big meal.

jiló [ʒi'lɔ] *m* type of Brazilian vegetable.

jingle ['ʒĩgow] *m* jingle.

jipe ['ʒipi] *m* jeep.

jiu-jitsu [ʒu'ʒitsu] *m* jiu-jitsu.

joalheiro, ra [ʒoaˈʎejru, ra] *m, f* jeweller *UK*, jeweler *US*.

joalheria [ʒwaʎe'ria] *f* jewellers *UK*, jewelers *US*.

joanete [ʒwa'netʃi] *m* bunion.

joaninha [ʒwa'niɲa] *f* **-1.** [inseto] ladybird. **-2.** [carro de polícia] patrol car.

joão-ninguém [ʒuãwˈnĩŋ'gẽ] (*pl* **joões-ninguém**) *m*: **um ~** a nobody, a nonentity.

joça ['ʒɔsa] *f fam* mess.

jocoso, sa [ʒoko'zu, za] *adj* [divertido, cômico] jocular.

joelheira [ʒweˈʎeira] *f ESP* knee-pad.

joelho ['ʒweʎu] *m* knee; **de ~s** kneeling, on one's knees; **ficar de ~s** to kneel down.

jogada [ʒo'gada] *f* **-1.** [ESP - tática] strategy; [- lance] shot. **-2.** *fam* [esquema] scam. **-3.** *fam* [intenção] intention. **-4.** *loc*: **tirar alguém da ~** to eliminate sb from the equation.

jogado, da [ʒo'gadu, da] *adj* thrown.

jogador, ra [ʒoga'do(x), ra] *m, f* **-1.** [atleta] player; **~ de futebol** football player. **-2.** [apostador] gambler.

jogar [14] [ʒo'ga(x)] <> *vt* **-1.** [tomar parte em jogo de] to play. **-2.** [atirar] to throw. **-3.** [apostar]: **~ algo em algo** to gamble sthg on sthg. **-4.** [desfazer-se de]: **~ algo fora** to throw sthg out. **-5.** [desperdiçar]: **~ algo fora** to throw around. <> *vi* **-1.** [divertir-se num jogo] to play. **-2.** [apostar]: **~ em algo** to bet on sthg. **-3.** [na Bolsa]: **~ em** to speculate on. **-4.** [manipular]: **~ com algo** to play around with sthg. **-5.** [balançar] to toss.

◆ **jogar-se** *vp* **-1.** [lançar-se] to throw o.s. **-2.** [paquerar]: **~-se para cima de alguém** to be all over sb.

jogatina [ʒoga'tʃinal *f* gambling.

jogging ['ʒɔgĩ] *m* **-1.** [corrida] jogging; **fazer ~** to go jogging. **-2.** [roupa] tracksuit.

jogo ['ʒogul (*pl* jogos) *m* **-1.** [ger] game; **~ limpo** clean game; **~ de azar** game of chance. **-2.** [partida] match. **-3.** [vício de jogar] gambling. **-4.** [conjunto] collection. **-5.** [aposta] bet. **-6.** *MEC* set. **-7.** *fig* [ardil] ruse. **-8.** [manipulação] play. **-9.** [movimentação] movement. **-10.** [balanço] tossing. **-11.** *AUTO* running. **-12.** *fam* [intenção] game. **-13.** *loc*: **abrir o ~** to lay one's cards on the table; **esconder o ~** to have a card up one's sleeve; **ter ~ de cintura para algo** to be quite capable of getting out of sthg.

jogo-da-velha [ˌʒoguda'veʎal (*pl* **jogos-da-velha**) *m* noughts and crosses *UK*, tic-tac-toe *US*.

joguete [ʒo'getʃil *m* plaything; **fazer alguém de ~** to make a laughing stock of sb.

jóia ['ʒɔjal <> *adj fam* delightful. <> *f* **-1.** [enfeite] jewel. **-2.** [taxa] fee.

joio ['ʒoju] *m* darnel; **separar o ~ do trigo** to separate the wheat from the chaff.

jojoba [ʒo'ʒɔbal *f* jojoba.

jóquei ['ʒɔkej], **jóquei-clube** *m* Jockey Club.

jornada [ʒox'nadal *f* **-1.** [ger] journey. **-2.** [período] duration; **~ de trabalho** working day.

jornal [ʒox'nawl (*pl* **-ais**) *m* **-1.** [gazeta] newspaper. **-2.** [noticiário] news.

jornaleiro, ra [ʒoxna'lejru, ra] *m, f* [pessoa] newspaper vendor.

◆ **jornaleiro** *m* [banca] news-stand.

jornalista [ʒoxna'liʃta] *mf* journalist.

jornalístico, ca [ʒoxna'liʃtʃiku, ka] *adj* journalistic.

jorrar [4] [ʒo'xa(x)] <> *vt* to spurt. <> *vi* to gush.

jorro ['ʒoxul *m* torrent.

jovem ['ʒovẽl (*pl* **-ns**) <> *adj* **-1.** [juvenil] youthful. **-2.** [para jovens] young. <> *mf* young person.

jovial [ʒo'vjawl (*pl* **-ais**) *adj* jovial.

jovialidade [ʒovjali'dadʒi] f joviality.
joystick [ʒɔj'ʃtʃik] (pl **joysticks**) m COMPUT joystick.
juazeiro [ʒwa'zejru] m jujube.
juba ['ʒuba] f mane.
jubilação [ʒubila'sãw] (pl **-ões**) UNIV f **-1.** [aposentadoria] retirement. **-2.** [desligamento] suspension.
jubilado, da [ʒubi'ladu, da] adj [aluno] barred (from a course for not having fulfilled the formal requirements).
jubilar [4] [ʒubi'la(x)] UNIV vt **-1.** [aposentar] to retire. **-2.** [desligar] to suspend.
jubileu [ʒubi'lew] m jubilee; ~ **de prata** silver jubilee.
júbilo ['ʒubilu] m elation.
jubiloso, osa [ʒubi'lozu, za] adj elated.
judaico, ca [ʒu'dajku, ka] adj Jewish.
judaísmo [ʒuda'iʒmu] m Judaism.
judas ['ʒudaʃ] m Judas, traitor.
judeu, dia [ʒu'dew, dʒia] <> adj Jewish. <> m, f Jewish person, Jew.
judiação [ʒudʒja'sãw] (pl **-ões**) f abuse, ill-treatment.
judiar [16] [ʒu'dʒja(x)] vi: ~ **de alguém** to abuse sb, to ill-treat sb.
judicial [ʒudʒi'sjaw] (pl **-ais**) adj judicial.
judiciário, ria [ʒudʒi'sjarju, rja] adj judicial.
➤ **Judiciário** m: o ~ the judiciary.
judicioso, osa [ʒudʒi'sjozu, ɔza] adj judicious.
judô [ʒu'do] m judo.
judoca [ʒu'dɔka] mf judoka.
jugo ['ʒugu] m: **sob o** ~ **de** under the yoke of.
juiz, íza ['ʒwiʃ, iza] (mpl **-es**, fpl **-s**) m, f **-1.** JUR judge; ~ **de direito** district judge; ~ **de menores** judge in a juvenile court; ~ **de paz** justice of the peace. **-2.** ESP referee.
juizado [ʒuj'zadu, da] m court; ~ **de menores** juvenile court; ~ **de pequenas causas** small claims court.
juízo ['ʒwizu] m **-1.** [julgamento] judgement. **-2.** [conceito] opinion. **-3.** [sensatez] prudence; **perder o** ~ to lose one's mind. **-4.** JUR [foro] tribunal.
Juízo Final [ˌʒwizufi'naw] m: o ~ Judgement Day.
jujuba [ʒu'ʒuba] f **-1.** BOT jujube. **-2.** [bala] jujube-flavoured boiled sweet.
jul. (abrev de julho) Jul.
julgador, ra [ʒuwga'do(x), ra] <> adj judging. <> m, f judge.
julgamento [ʒuwga'mẽntul m **-1.** [juízo] judgement. **-2.** [audiência] hearing. **-3.** [sentença] sentence.
julgar [14] [ʒuw'ga(x)] vt **-1.** [sentenciar sobre] to judge. **-2.** [avaliar]: ~ **algo/alguém por algo** to judge sthg/sb by sthg. **-3.** [supor] to think; ~ **que** to think that.
➤ **julgar-se** vp [supor-se] to consider o.s.
julho ['ʒuʎul m July; veja também **setembro**.
jumento [ʒu'mẽntul m donkey.
jun. (abrev de junho) Jun.

junção [ʒũn'sãw] (pl **-ões**) f **-1.** [união] union. **-2.** [ponto] junction.
junco ['ʒũŋkul m reed.
junho ['ʒuɲul m June; veja também **setembro**.
junino, na [ʒu'ninu, na] adj ▷ **festa**.
júnior ['ʒunjo(x)] (pl **juniores**) <> adj junior. <> mf ESP junior.
junta ['ʒũntal f **-1.** [comissão] council. **-2.** POL junta. **-3.** [articulação] joint. **-4.** [órgão]: ~ **comercial** chamber of commerce. **-5.** [parelha]: ~ **de bois** yoke of oxen.
juntamente [ʒũnta'mẽntʃil adv: ~ **com** together with.
juntar [4] [ʒũn'ta(x)] <> vt **-1.** [unir]: ~ **algo (a algo)** to mix sthg (with sthg). **-2.** [aproximar]: ~ **alguém (a alguém)** to unite sb (with sb). **-3.** [colocar junto] to mix (together). **-4.** [aglomerar] to assemble. **-5.** [recolher] to collect. <> vi [aglomerar-se] to cluster. <> vi [economizar]: ~ **(para)** to save (for).
➤ **juntar-se** vp [associar-se]: ~**-se a** to mix with; ~**-se com** to unite o.s. with.
junto, ta ['ʒũntu, tal <> adj together. <> adv at the same time; ~ **de** next to.
➤ **junto a, junto de** loc prep next to.
➤ **junto com** loc prep together.
jura ['ʒural f vow.
jurado, da [ʒu'radu, dal <> adj sworn. <> m, f juror.
juramentado, da [ʒuramẽn'tadu, dal adj under oath.
juramento [ʒura'mẽntul m oath; **fazer** ~ **a** to swear an oath to; **sob** ~ under oath.
jurar [4] [ʒu'ra(x)] <> vt **-1.** [prometer] to swear; **fazer algo** to swear to do sthg; ~ **que** to swear that. **-2.** [sob juramento]: ~ **fazer algo** to take an oath to do sthg. <> vi [prestar juramento]: ~ **(por/sobre)** to swear (by/on).
júri ['ʒuril m jury.
jurídico, ca [ʒu'ridʒiku, kal adj legal.
jurisconsulto, ta [ʒurʃkõn'suwtu, tal m, f legal expert UK, jurist US.
jurisdição [ʒuriʒdʒi'sãw] f jurisdiction.
jurisprudência [ʒuriʃpru'dẽnsjal f jurisprudence.
jurista [ʒu'riʃtal mf legal expert UK, jurist US.
juros ['ʒuruʃl mpl interest (sg); **empréstimo a** ~ **/ sem** ~ **s** loan with/without interest; ~ **acumulados** accumulated interest; ~ **fixos/variáveis** fixed/variable interest.
jururu [ʒuru'rul adj gloomy.
jus [ʒuʃl m: **fazer** ~ **a algo** to do justice to sthg.
jusante [ʒu'zãntʃil f: **a** ~ **de** downstream of.
justamente [ʒuʃta'mẽntʃil adv **-1.** [com justiça] rightly. **-2.** [precisamente] precisely.
justapor [45] [ʒuʃta'po(x)] vt: ~ **algo (a algo)** to juxtapose sthg (with sthg).
➤ **justapor-se** vp to be juxtaposed.
justaposição [ʒuʃtapozi'sãw] (pl **-ões**) f juxtaposition.
justaposto, osta [ʒuʃta'poʃtu, ɔʃtal pp ▷ **justapor**.

justeza [ʒuʃ'teza] *f* precision.
justiça [ʒuʃ'tʃisa] *f* **-1.** [virtude] fairness; **com** ~ justly; **fazer** ~ **a alguém/algo** to do justice to sb/sthg. **-2.** [eqüidade] equality; ~ **social** social justice. **-3.** [tribunal] justice; **ir à** ~ to go to court; **Justiça do Trabalho** Industrial Tribunal. **-4.** [poder judiciário]: **a Justiça** the judiciary.
justiceiro, ra [ʒuʃtʃi'sejru, ra] *adj* just.
justificação [ʒuʃtʃifika'sãw] (*pl* **-ões**) *f* justification.
justificar [12] [ʒuʃtʃifi'ka(x)] *vt* to justify.
   ➡ **justificar-se** *vp* [explicar-se]: ~**-se por algo** to excuse o.s for sthg.
justificativa [ʒuʃtʃifika'tʃiva] *f* justification.
justificável [ʒuʃtʃifi'kavew] (*pl* **-eis**) *adj* justifiable.
justo, ta ['ʒuʃtu, ta] ⟨⟩ *adj* **-1.** [ger] fair. **-2.** [apertado] tight. **-3.** [exato] precise. **-4.** [merecido] just. ⟨⟩ *adv* just.
juta ['ʒuta] *f* jute.
juvenil [ʒuve'niw] (*pl* **-is**) ⟨⟩ *adj* **-1.** [de jovens] youth, teenage. **-2.** *ESP* junior. ⟨⟩ *m ESP* [campeonato] junior.
juventude [ʒuvẽn'tudʒi] *f* youth.

k, K [ka] *m* [letra] k, K.
kafkiano, na [kaf'kianu, na] *adj* Kafkaesque.
Kalahari [kala'xari] *n*: **o deserto de** ~ the Kalahari Desert.
Kampala [kãn'pala] *n* Kampala.
karaokê [karaw'ke] *m* **-1.** [atividade] karaoke. **-2.** [casa noturna] karaoke bar.
kardecismo [kaxde'siʒmu] *m religious doctrine of the Frenchman Allan Kardec.*
kart ['kaxtʃi] *m* go-cart.
kartódromo [kax'tɔdromu] *m* go-kart track.
Katmandu [katʃimãn'du] *n* Kathmandu.
Kb (*abrev de* **kilobyte**) *m* Kb.
kg (*abrev de* **quilograma**) *m* kg.
ketchup [kɛ'tʃupi] *m* (tomato) ketchup.
Khartum [kax'tũ] *n* Khartoum.
Kíev ['kjɛvi] *n* Kiev.
Kingston ['kiŋgiʃtõ] *n* Kingston.
Kinshasa [kin'ʃaza] *n* Kinshasa.
kit ['kitʃi] *m* kit.
kitchenette [kitʃi'nɛtʃi] *f* kitchenette.
kitsch [kitʃi] *adj inv* kitsch.
kiwi ['kiwi] *m* [fruta] kiwi fruit.

kl (*abrev de* **quilolitro**) *m* kl.
km (*abrev de* **quilômetro**) *m* km.
km/h (*abrev de* **quilômetro por hora**) *m* km/h.
know-how [now'haw] *m* know-how.
Kuala Lumpur [kwalalãn'pu(x)] *n* Kuala Lumpur.
Kuwait [ku'ajtʃi] *n* Kuwait.
kW (*abrev de* **kilowatt**) *m* kW.

l, L ['ɛli] *m* [letra] l, L.
-la [la] *pron* **-1.** [pessoa] her; **-2.** [coisa] it; **-3.** [você] you.
lá ['la] *adv* there; **quero lá saber!** what do I care!; **sei lá!** how should I know; **para lá de** beyond.
lã ['lã] *f* wool; **calça de** ~ woollen trousers; **de pura** ~ pure wool; ~ **de camelo** camel hair.
labareda [laba'reda] *f* flame.
lábia ['labja] *f* [conversa] smooth talk; **ter** ~ to have the gift of the gab.
labial [la'bjaw] (*pl* **-ais**) *adj* labial.
lábio ['labju] *m* [ANAT- beiço] lip; [- genital] labium; ~ **leporino** harelip, cleft lip.
labirinto [labi'rĩntu] *m* labyrinth.
laborar [4] [labo'ra(x)] *vi*: ~ **em erro** to make a mistake.
laboratorial [laborato'riaw] (*pl* **-ais**) *adj* laboratory (antes de subst).
laboratório [labora'tɔrju] *m* laboratory; ~ **de línguas** language laboratory.
laborioso, osa [labo'rjozu, ɔza] *adj* **-1.** [trabalhador] hard-working. **-2.** [trabalhoso] laborious.
labuta [la'buta] *f* toil.
labutar [4] [labu'ta(x)] *vi* to toil.
laca ['laka] *f* lacquer; **de** ~ lacquered.
laçar [13] [la'sa(x)] *vt* [animal] to lasso.
laçarote [lasa'rɔtʃi] *m* large bow.
laço ['lasu] *m* **-1.** [nó] bow; **dar um** ~ **em algo** to tie a bow in sthg. **-2.** [para laçar animais] lasso. **-3.** *fig* [vínculo] tie; ~**s de família** family ties.
lacônico, ca [la'koniku, ka] *adj* laconic.
lacraia [la'kraja] *f* centipede.
lacrar [4] [la'kra(x)] *vt* to seal.
lacre ['lakri] *m* sealing wax.
lacrimal [lakri'maw] (*pl* **-ais**) *adj* lachrymal.
lacrimejante [lakrime'ʒãntʃi] *adj* tearful.
lacrimejar [4] [lakrime'ʒa(x)] *vi* **-1.** [olhos] to water. **-2.** [pessoa] to weep.

lacrimogêneo, nea [lakrimo'ʒenju, njal *adj* ▷ **gás**.

lacrimoso, osa [lakri'mozu, ɔzal *adj* [olhos] tearful.

lactação [lakta'sãw] (*pl* -ões) *f* [amamentação] lactation.

lactante [lak'tãntʃil] ◇ *adj* lactating. ◇ *f* nursing woman.

lácteo, tea ['laktju, tjal *adj* -1. [produto] milky. -2. ▷ **via**.

lactose [lak'tɔzil] *f* lactose.

lacuna [la'kunal *f* -1. [vão] gap. -2. [espaço em branco] blank. -3. [omissão] omission.

ladainha [lada'iɲal *f* -1. [oração] litany. -2. *fig* [lengalenga] rigmarole.

ladear [15] [la'dʒa(x)] *vt* -1. [ger] to flank. -2. [correr paralelo a] to run alongside. -3. *fig* [contornar] to skirt.

ladeira [la'dejral *f* -1. [rampa] slope. -2. [rua íngreme] steep road.

ladino, na [la'dʒinu, nal *adj* [esperto] sharp.

lado ['ladul *m* -1. [ger] side; **do ~ avesso** inside out; **estar do ~ de alguém** to be on sb's side; **por um ~ ... por outro ~** on the one hand ... on the other hand. -2. [direção, local] direction; **de todos os ~s** everywhere; **de um ~ para outro** from one side to the other; **do ~ de fora** outside.
➤ **ao lado** *loc adv* -1. [na casa adjacente] next door. -2. [próximo] close by.
➤ **ao lado de** *loc prep* next to.
➤ **de lado** *loc adv* [sentar, andar] on the side; **deixar algo de ~** [pôr de reserva] to put sthg aside; [desconsiderar] to drop sthg; **deixar alguém de ~** [ignorar] to ignore sb; **olhar alguém de ~** [desdenhar] to look down on sb.

ladrão, ladra [la'drãw, 'ladral (*mpl* -ões, *fpl* -s) ◇ *adj* thieving. ◇ *m*, *f* thief; **~ de loja** shoplifter.
➤ **ladrão** *m* [tubo] overflow pipe.

ladrar [4] [la'dra(x)] *vi* to bark.

ladrilhar [4] [ladri'ɲa(x)] *vt* to tile.

ladrilheiro, ra [ladri'ɲejru, ral *m*, *f* tiler.

ladrilho [la'driʎul *m* tile.

ladroagem [la'drwaʒẽl (*pl* -ns), **ladroeira** [la'drwejral *f* theft, robbery.

ladrões [la'drõjʃl *pl* ▷ **ladrão**.

lagarta [la'gaxtal *f* ZOOL caterpillar.

lagartixa [lagax'tʃiʃal *f* (small) lizard.

lagarto [la'gaxtul *m* ZOOL lizard.

lago ['lagul *m* -1. GEOGR lake. -2. [de jardim] pond. -3. *fig* [poça] puddle; **a cozinha está um ~** the kitchen is flooded.

lagoa [la'goal *f* lake.

lagosta [la'goʃtal *f* lobster.

lagostim [lagoʃ'tʃĩl (*pl* -ns) *m* crayfish.

lágrima ['lagrimal *f* tear; **derramar ~s** to cry.

laguna [la'gunal *f* lagoon.

laia ['lajal *f* kind, type.

laico, ca ['lajku, kal *adj* -1. [pessoa] lay. -2. [ensino] secular.

laje ['laʒil *f* -1. [pedra] flagstone. -2. CONSTR concrete flooring.

lajear [15] [la'ʒja(x)] *vt* to pave.

lajota [la'ʒɔtal *f* small flagstone.

lama ['lãmal *f* -1. [ger] mud. -2. *fig* [má situação]: **tirar alguém da ~** to help s.o. out of trouble.

lamaçal [lama'sawl (*pl* -ais), **lamaceiro** [lama'sejrul *m* muddy place.

lamacento, ta [lama'sẽntu, tal *adj* muddy.

lambada [lãn'badal *f* -1. [golpe] blow. -2. *fig* [descompostura] telling-off. -3. [dança] lambada.

lambança [lãn'bãnsal *f* mess.

lamber [5] [lãm'be(x)l *vt* to lick.

lambida [lãn'bidal *f* lick; **dar uma ~ em algo** to have a lick of sthg, to lick sthg.

lambido, da [lãm'bidu, dal *adj* -1. [cara] clean. -2. [cabelo] straight.

lambiscar [12] [lãmbiʃ'ka(x)l ◇ *vt* to nibble. ◇ *vi* to pick.

lambreta® [lãn'bretal *f* motor scooter.

lambri [lãn'bril (*pl* -bris) *m* panelling.

lambuja [lãn'buʒal *f* [vantagem] advantage.

lambuzar [4] [lãmbu'za(x)l *vt*: **~ alguém/algo (de com algo)** to cover sb/sthg (in sthg).

lambuzeira [lãnbu'zejral *f* mess.

lamentação [lamẽnta'sãw] (*pl* -ões) *f* complaint.

lamentar [4] [lamẽn'ta(x)l *vt* to regret; **lamento muito, mas ...** I am very sorry, but ...; **lamentamos comunicar-lhe ...** we regret to inform you ...
➤ **lamentar-se** *vp*: **~-se (de algo)** [lastimar-se] to feel sorry (about sthg).

lamentável [lamẽn'tavɛwl (*pl* -eis) *adj* -1. [lastimável] regrettable. -2. [deplorável] deplorable.

lamentavelmente [lamẽntavew'mẽntʃil *adv* unfortunately.

lamento [la'mẽntul *m* lament.

lâmina ['lãminal *f* -1. [ger] blade; **~ de barbear** razor blade. -2. [de vidro] slide.

laminado, da [lami'nadu, dal *adj* laminated.
➤ **laminado** *m* laminate.

laminar [4] [lami'na(x)l *vt* [reduzir a lâminas] to shave.

lâmpada ['lãnpadal *f* -1. [bulbo] light; **~ (elétrica)** (light) bulb; **~ fluorescente** fluorescent light bulb; **~ neon** neon light. -2. [aparelho] lamp; **~ de mesa** table lamp.

lamparina [lãnpa'rinal *f* [aparelho] blowlamp.

lampejar [4] [lãmpe'ʒa(x)l *vi* to flash.

lampejo [lãn'peʒul *m* flash.

lampião [lãn'pjãwl (*pl* -ões) *m* street light.

lamúria [la'murjal *f* lamentation.

lamuriante [lamu'rjãntʃil *adj* whining.

lamuriar-se [16] [lamu'rjaxsil *vp*: **~ (de algo)** to moan (about sthg).

LAN (*abrev de* **Local Area Network**) *f* LAN.

lança ['lãnsal *f* spear.

lançador, ra [lãnsa'do(x), ral *m*, *f* -1. ESP thrower. -2. [em leilão] bidder. -3. COM promoter.

lançamento [lãnsa'mẽntul *m* -1. [arremesso] throw. -2. ESP: **~ de dardos** to play darts; **~ de disco** discus throwing. -3. [ger] launch; **novo ~** [livro] new title. -4. [escrituração] entry. -5. [de impostos] rate.

lança-perfume [ˌlãnsapexˈfumi] (pl **lança-perfumes**) m canister of perfumed ethyl chloride used during carnival.

lançar [13] [lãˈsa(x)] vt **-1.** [ger] to launch. **-2.** [atirar] to throw. **-3.** [pôr em voga] to start. **-4.** [escriturar] to enter. **-5.** [impostos] to set. **-6.** [dirigir] to cast.

➡ **lançar-se** vp **-1.** [atirar-se] to throw o.s. **-2.** [iniciar-se]: ~-**se em algo** to take up sthg; ~-**se como algo** to set o.s. up as sthg.

lance [ˈlãnsi] m **-1.** [episódio, passagem] moment. **-2.** [fato] incident. **-3.** [em leilão] bid. **-4.** [no jogo - aposta] bet; [- jogada] play. **-5.** [de escada] staircase. **-6.** [de casas] terrace. **-7.** [rasgo] surge.

lancha [ˈlãnʃa] f **-1.** NÁUT launch; ~ **salva-vidas** lifeboat. **-2.** fam [pé] large foot. **-3.** fam [calçado] large shoe; **este sapato está uma** ~ this shoe is like a boat.

lanchar [4] [lãˈʃa(x)] ◇ vt to snack on. ◇ vi to have tea.

lanche [ˈlãnʃi] m [refeição ligeira] snack (in the afternoon).

lancheira [lãnˈʃejra] f lunch box.

lanchonete [lãnʃoˈnɛtʃi] f snack bar.

lancinante [lãnsiˈnãntʃi] adj piercing.

languidez [lãŋiˈdeʒ] f [debilitação] langour.

lânguido, da [ˈlãŋidu, da] adj languid.

lanhar [4] [laˈɲa(x)] vt [ferir] to scratch.

➡ **lanhar-se** vp [ferir-se] to scratch o.s.

lanho [ˈlãɲu] m scratch.

lanígero, ra [laˈniʒeru, ra] adj [animal] woolly.

lanolina [lãnoˈlina] f lanolin.

lantejoula [lãnteˈʒola] f sequin.

lanterna [lãnˈtɛxna] f **-1.** [aparelho] lantern; ~ **elétrica** torch UK, flashlight US. **-2.** AUTO light.

lanterninha [lãntexˈniɲa] mf usher.

laparoscopia [laparoʃkoˈpia] f laparoscopy.

La Paz [laˈpaʃ] n La Paz.

lapela [laˈpɛla] f lapel.

lapidar [4] [lapiˈda(x)] vt to polish.

lápide [ˈlapidʒi] f **-1.** [comemorativa] plaque. **-2.** [tumular] tombstone.

lápis [ˈlapiʃ] m inv pencil; ~ **de cera** wax crayon; ~ **de cor** colouring pencil; ~ **de olho** eye pencil.

lapiseira [lapiˈzejra] f pencil case.

lápis-lazúli [ˌlapiʃlaˈzuli] (pl **lápis-lazúlis**) m lapis-lazuli.

Lapônia [laˈponja] f Lapland.

lapso [ˈlapsu] m **-1.** [falta] mistake. **-2.** [espaço de tempo] lapse.

laptop [ˈlapitopi] (pl **laptops**) m COMPUT laptop.

laquê [laˈke] m hairspray.

laqueadura [lakjaˈdura] f MED tubal ligation.

laquear [15] [laˈkja(x)] vt **-1.** [com laca] to gloss. **-2.** MED to ligate.

lar [ˈla(x)] (pl **-es**) m home.

laranja [laˈrãnʒa] ◇ f [fruta] orange. ◇ m **-1.** [cor] orange. **-2.** fam [testa-de-ferro] scapegoat. ◇ adj (inv) [cor] orange.

laranjada [larãnˈʒada] f orangeade.

laranjal [larãnˈʒaw] (pl **-ais**) m orange grove.

laranjeira [larãnˈʒejra] f orange tree.

larápio [laˈrapju] m thief.

lareira [laˈrejra] f fireplace.

larga [ˈlaxga] f ▷ **largo**.

largada [laxˈgada] f [em corrida] start; **dar a** ~ to start.

largado, da [laxˈgadu, da] adj neglected.

largar [14] [laxˈga(x)] ◇ vt **-1.** [ger] to leave. **-2.** [soltar] to loosen. **-3.** [deixar cair] to drop. **-4.** [pôr em liberdade] to release. **-5.** [deixar em paz] to leave alone. **-6.** fam [dar] to give; ~ **a mão em alguém** to slap sb. ◇ vi **-1.** [deixar]: ~ **de algo/de ser algo** to stop doing sthg/being sthg. **-2.** NÁUT to set sail.

➡ **largar-se** vp **-1.** [desprender-se] to untie o.s. from. **-2.** [ir] to go.

largo, ga [ˈlaxgu, ga] adj **-1.** [grande de lado a lado] wide. **-2.** [folgado] loose. **-3.** (antes de subst) [extenso] great, large. **-4.** (antes de subst) [prolongado] long. **-5.** (antes de subst) [abundante] abundant.

➡ **largo** m [praça] square.

➡ **larga** f: **viver à larga** to live lavishly.

➡ **largas** fpl: **dar largas a algo** to give free rein to sthg.

➡ **ao largo** loc adv: **passar ao** ~ (**de**) to give a wide berth (to); **avistar algo ao** ~ to make something out in the distance; **ao** ~ **da costa brasileira** off the Brazilian coast; **fazer-se ao** ~ to head for the open sea.

largueza [laxˈgeza] f largesse; **com** ~ with largesse.

largura [laxˈgura] f width; **tem 3 metros de** ~ it is 3 metres wide; ~ **de banda** COMPUT bandwidth.

larica [laˈrika] f fam [fome] hunger.

laringe [laˈrĩʒi] f larynx.

laringite [larĩˈʒitʃi] f laryngitis.

larva [ˈlaxva] f larva.

lasanha [laˈzãɲa] f lasagne.

lasca [ˈlaʃka] f sliver.

lascado, da [laʃˈkadu, da] adj [rachado] cracked.

➡ **lascado** adv fam [a toda] full speed.

lascar [12] [laʃˈka(x)] ◇ vt **-1.** [rachar] to break. **-2.** fam [dar]: ~ **algo em alguém** suddenly to do sthg to sb. **-3.** fam [lançar]: ~ **algo em algo/alguém** to throw sthg at sthg/sb. ◇ vi [rachar] to crack.

➡ **de lascar** loc adj fam [terrível]: **ser/estar de** ~ to be nasty.

lascívia [laˈsivja] f lasciviousness.

lascivo, va [laˈsivu, va] adj lascivious.

laser [ˈlejze(x)] (pl **-es**) ◇ adj (inv) ▷ **raio**. ◇ m (inv) laser.

lassidão [lasiˈdãw], **lassitude** [lasiˈtudʒi] f [fadiga] lassitude.

lasso, ssa [ˈlasu, sa] adj **-1.** [fatigado] weary. **-2.** [bambo] weak.

lástima [ˈlaʃtʃima] f **-1.** [pessoa]: **ser/estar uma** ~ to be pathetic; [coisa] to be a disgrace. **-2.** [pena]: **é uma** ~ (**que**) it is a pity (that); **que** ~! what a pity!

lastimar [4] [laʃtʃiˈma(x)] vt **-1.** [lamentar] to

regret. **-2.** [ter pena de] to pity.

➤ **lastimar-se** *vp* [lamentar-se]: **~-se (de algo)** to moan (about sthg).

lastimável [laʃtʃi'mavɛw] (*pl* **-eis**) *adj* **-1.** [lamentável] regrettable. **-2.** [deplorável] disgraceful.

lastimoso, osa [laʃtʃi'mozu, ɔza] *adj* pitiful.

lastro ['laʃtru] *m* **-1.** NÁUT ballast. **-2.** FIN guaranty. **-3.** *fig* [base] grounding.

lastro ['laʃtro] *m* ECON standard.

lata ['lata] *f* **-1.** [material] tin. **-2.** [recipiente] can; **~ de conserva** tin; **~ de lixo** rubbish bin **-3.** *fam* **na ~** straight.

latada [la'tada] *f* [treliça] lattice.

latão [la'tãw] (*pl* **-ões**) *m* [material] brass.

lataria [lata'ria] *f* **-1.** AUTO bodywork. **-2.** [latas] large quantity of tins.

latejante [late'ʒãntʃi] *adj* throbbing.

latejar [4] [late'ʒa(x)] *vi* to throb.

latejo [la'teʒu] *m* throb.

latente [la'tẽntʃi] *adj* latent.

lateral [late'raw] (*pl* **-ais**) ◇ *adj* lateral. ◇ *m* FUT outfielder. ◇ *f* ESP [linha] sideline.

látex ['latɛks] *m inv* latex.

laticínio [latʃi'sinju] *m* dairy produce.

latido [la'tʃidu] *m* bark.

latifundiário, ria [latʃifũn'dʒjarju, rja] ◇ *adj* landed. ◇ *m, f* landowner.

latifúndio [latʃi'fũndʒju] *m* large property.

latim [la'tʃĩ] *m* Latin; **gastar o seu ~** to waste one's breath.

latino, na [la'tʃinu, na] ◇ *adj* Latin. ◇ *m, f* Latin.

latino-americano, latino-americana [la,tʃinwameri'kanu, la,tʃinwameri'kana] ◇ *adj* Latin American. ◇ *m, f* Latin American.

latir [6] [la'tʃi(x)] *vi* to bark.

latitude [latʃi'tudʒi] *f* **-1.** [ger] latitude. **-2.** [amplitude] capacity.

➤ **latitudes** *fpl* [região] latitudes.

lato, ta ['latu, ta] *adj* broad.

latrina [la'trina] *f* latrine.

latrocínio [latro'sinju] *m* larceny.

lauda ['lawda] *f* page.

laudatório, ria [lawda'tɔrju, rja] *adj* laudatory.

laudo ['lawdu] *m* **-1.** [parecer] verdict. **-2.** [documento] written verdict.

laureado, da [law'rjadu, da] *adj* laureate.

laurel [law'rɛw] (*pl* **-éis**) *m* award, prize.

lauto, ta ['lawtu, ta] *adj* [farto] sumptuous.

lava ['lava] *f* lava.

lavabo [la'vabu] *m* **-1.** [pia] washbasin. **-2.** [local] bathroom.

lavadeira [lava'dejra] *f* **-1.** [trabalhadora] washerwoman. **-2.** [libélula] dragonfly.

lavadora [lava'dora] *f* washing machine.

lavagem [la'vaʒẽ] (*pl* **-ns**) *f* **-1.** [limpeza] washing; **~ a seco** dry-cleaning. **-2.** MED washout. **-3.** PSIC: **~ cerebral** brainwashing. **-4.** FIN: **~ de dinheiro** money laundering. **-5.** *fam* ESP: **dar uma ~ num time** to wipe out a team. **-6.** [comida de porcos] swill.

La Valetta [lava'leta] *n* Valletta.

lavanda [la'vãnda] *f* **-1.** BOT lavender. **-2.** [colônia] lavender water. **-3.** [recipiente com água] finger bowl.

lavanderia [lavãnde'ria] *f* laundry.

lavar [4] [la'va(x)] *vt* to wash; **~ a seco** to dry-clean.

➤ **lavar-se** *vp* to wash o.s.

lavatório [lava'tɔrju] *m* **-1.** [pia] washbasin. **-2.** [toalete] cloakroom.

lavoura [la'vora] *f* cultivation.

lavrador, ra [lavra'do(x), ra] (*mpl* **-es**, *fpl* **-s**) *m, f* ploughman.

lavrar [4] [la'vra(x)] ◇ *vt* **-1.** [terra] to plough. **-2.** [sentença, escritura, contrato] to draw up. **-3.** [madeira] to plane. ◇ *vi* [alastrar-se] to rage.

laxante [la'ʃãntʃi] *adj* laxative.

lazer [la'ze(x)] *m* **-1.** [descanso] pleasure. **-2.** [tempo de folga] leisure.

LBV (*abrev de* **Legião da Boa Vontade**) *f Brazilian charitable organization for support of the needy.*

leal [le'aw] (*pl* **-ais**) *adj* loyal.

lealdade [leaw'dadʒi] *f* loyalty.

leão [le'ãw] (*pl* **-ões**) *m, f* lion.

➤ **Leão** *m* **-1.** ASTRO Leo. **-2.** *fig* [fisco]: **o Leão** the taxman.

leão-de-chácara [leãwdʒi'ʃakara] (*pl* **leões-de-chácara**) *m fam* bouncer.

leão-marinho [le,ãwma'riɲu] (*pl* **leões-marinhos**) *m* sea lion.

leasing ['lisĩ] *m* ECON leasing.

lebre ['lɛbri] *f* hare.

lecionar [4] [lesjo'na(x)] ◇ *vt* to teach. ◇ *vi* to teach.

legado [le'gadu] *m* **-1.** [herança] legacy. **-2.** [enviado] envoy.

legal [le'gaw] (*pl* **-ais**) ◇ *adj* **-1.** JUR legal. **-2.** *fam* [bom, bonito] cool. **-3.** [hora] official time. ◇ *adv fam* [bem] well.

legalidade [legali'dadʒi] *f* legality.

legalização [legaliza'sãw] (*pl* **-ões**) *f* legalization.

legalizar [4] [legali'za(x)] *vt* to legalize.

legar [14] [le'ga(x)] *vt* **-1.** JUR to bequeath. **-2.** [transmitir] to pass on.

legenda [le'ʒẽnda] *f* **-1.** [em foto, desenho *etc*] caption. **-2.** CINE subtitle. **-3.** POL *number identifying political party on ballot sheet*; **votar na ~** to vote for the party.

legendado, da [leʒẽn'dadu, da] *adj* **-1.** [filme] subtitled. **-2.** [fotos] captioned.

legendar [le'ʒẽnda(x)] *vt* **-1.** [filme] to subtitle. **-2.** [fotos] to caption.

legendário, ria [leʒẽn'darju, rja] *adj* legendary.

legião [le'ʒjãw] (*pl* **-ões**) *f* [de fãs, leitores] legion.

legislação [leʒiʒla'sãw] (*pl* **-ões**) *f* legislation.

legislador, ra [leʒiʒla'do(x), ra] *m, f* legislator.

legislar [4] [leʒiʒ'la(x)] ◇ *vi* to legislate. ◇ *vt* to legislate.

legislativo, va [leʒiʒla'tʃivu, va] *adj* legislative.

➤ **Legislativo** *m*: **o Legislativo** the legislature.

legislatura [leʒiʒla'tura] f -1. [corpo] legislature. -2. [período] term.

legista [le'ʒiʃta] mf -1. [jurista] legal expert. -2. [médico] forensic scientist.

legitimar [4] [leʒitʃi'ma(x)] vt [legalizar] to legitimize.

legitimidade [leʒitʃimi'dadʒi] f legitimacy.

legítimo, ma [le'ʒitʃimu, mal adj -1. [ger] legitimate; **em legítima defesa** in legitimate defense. -2. [autêntico] authentic.

legível [le'ʒivɛw] (pl -eis) adj -1. [nítido] legible. -2. [agradável de ler] readable.

légua [ˈlɛgwa] f [medida] league.

➤ **léguas** fpl fig [grande distância] miles.

legume [le'gume] m vegetable.

leguminosa [legumi'nɔza] f BOT leguminous plant.

➤ **leguminosas** fpl BOT leguminosae.

lei [lej] f -1. [ger] law; **ditar a ~** to lay down the law; **promulgar a ~** to uphold the law; **violar a ~** to break the law; **~ marcial** martial law; **~ trabalhista** industrial law; **~ da oferta e da procura** the laws of supply and demand. -2. [de um metal]: **prata de ~** hallmarked silver.

leiaute [lej'awtʃi] m layout.

leigo, ga [ˈlejgu, ga] ◇ adj -1. RELIG secular. -2. fig [imperito]: **ser ~ em algo** to be a layperson in sthg. ◇ m, f [pessoa imperita] layperson.

leilão [lej'lãw] (pl -ões) m auction.

leiloar [20] [lej'lwa(x)] vt to auction.

leiloeiro, ra [lej'lwejru, ra] m, f auctioneer.

leitão, toa [lej'tãw, toa] (pl -ões) m, f suckling pig.

leite [ˈlejtʃi] m milk; **~ em pó** powdered milk; **~ de côco** coconut milk; **~ condensado** condensed milk; **~ desnatado** ou **magro** skimmed milk; **~ integral** full-cream milk; **~ de magnésia** Milk of Magnesia; **~ de soja** soya milk.

leiteiro, ra [lej'tejru, ra] ◇ adj [que produz leite] dairy. ◇ m, f [pessoa] milkman (f milkwoman).

➤ **leiteira** f -1. [para ferver leite] milk pan. -2. [para servir leite] milk jug.

leiteria [lejte'ria] f -1. [em fazenda] dairy. -2. [lanchonete] milk bar.

leito [ˈlejtu] m bed.

leitor, ra [lej'to(x), ra] (mpl -es, fpl -s) m, f -1. [quem lê] reader. -2. UNIV visiting lecturer.

leitoso, osa [lej'tozu, ɔza] adj milky.

leitura [lej'tura] f reading; **ter muita ~** to be well-read; **~ dinâmica** speed reading.

lelé [le'lɛ] adj fam: **~ (da cuca)** bonkers.

lema [ˈlema] m -1. [norma] maxim. -2. [político] motto.

lembrança [lẽn'brãsa] f -1. [recordação] souvenir. -2. [presente] gift.

➤ **lembranças** fpl [cumprimentos]: **(dê) ~s minhas à sua família** (give) my regards to your family.

lembrar [4] [lẽm'bra(x)] ◇ vt -1. [recordar] to remember. -2. [parecer] to look like. -3. [trazer à memória]: **~ algo a alguém** to remind sb of sthg.

◇ vi -1. [recordar]: **~ (de alguém/algo)** to remember (sb/sthg). -2. [advertir]: **~ a alguém de algo/de fazer algo** to remind sb of sthg/to do sthg; **~ a alguém (de) que** to remind sb that.

➤ **lembrar-se** vp: **~-se (de alguém/algo)** to remember (sb/sthg); **~-se (de) que** to remember that.

lembrete [lẽn'bretʃi] m memo.

leme [ˈlemi] m -1. [ger] helm. -2. [dispositivo] rudder.

lenço [ˈlẽsu] m -1. [para limpar] handkerchief; **~ de papel** paper handkerchief, tissue. -2. [de cabeça] headscarf. -3. [de pescoço] neckerchief.

lençol [lẽ'sɔw] (pl -óis) m sheet; **~ d'água** water table; **estar em maus lençóis** fig to be in a fine mess.

lenda [ˈlẽda] f -1. [história] legend. -2. fig [mentira] tall story.

lendário, ria [lẽn'darju, rja] adj legendary.

lêndea [ˈlẽdʒja] f nit.

lengalenga [lẽnga'lẽnga] f rigmarole.

lenha [ˈleɲa] f [para queimar] firewood; **botar ~ na fogueira** fig to add fuel to the fire; **fazer uma ~** [criar caso] to make a fuss.

lenhador [leɲa'do(x)] m woodcutter.

lenho [ˈleɲu] m -1. [tora] log. -2. [madeira] timber.

leninismo [leni'niʒmu] m Leninism.

leninista [leni'niʃta] ◇ adj Leninist. ◇ mf Leninist.

lenitivo, va [leni'tʃivu, va] adj [remédio, terapia] soothing.

➤ **lenitivo** m relief.

lenocínio [leno'sinju] m procuring.

lente [ˈlẽtʃi] f lens; **~ de aumento** magnifying glass; **~s de contato** contact lenses.

lentidão [lẽntʃi'dãw] f slowness.

lentilha [lẽn'tʃiʎa] f lentil.

lento, ta [ˈlẽtu, ta] adj slow.

leoa [le'oa] f ▷ **leão**.

leões [le'õjʃ] pl ▷ **leão**.

leonino, na [leo'ninu, na] ◇ adj -1. [caráter] leonine ; [contrato] fraudulent. -2. ASTRO Leo. ◇ m, f ASTRO Leo.

leopardo [ljo'paxdu] m leopard.

lépido, da [ˈlɛpidu, da] adj -1. [ágil] nimble. -2. [contente] happy.

leporino, na [lepo'rinu, na] adj ▷ **lábio**.

lepra [ˈlɛpra] f leprosy.

leprosário [lepro'zarju] m leper colony.

leproso, osa [le'prozu, ɔza] ◇ adj leprous. ◇ m, f [pessoa] leper.

leque [ˈlɛki] m -1. [abano] fan. -2. fig [conjunto]: **um ~ de** a range of.

ler [42] [ˈle(x)] ◇ vt to read. ◇ vi to read.

lerdeza [lex'deza] f sluggishness.

lerdo, da [ˈlɛxdu, da] adj -1. [vagaroso] sluggish. -2. [idiota] slow.

lero-lero [lɛru'lɛru] m chit-chat.

lesado, da [le'zadu, da] adj [ferido] injured.

lesão [le'zãw] (pl -ões) f -1. MED lesion; **~ corporal** grievous bodily harm. -2. JUR [violação] violation.

lesar [4] [le'za(x)] *vt* -**1.** *fig* [prejudicar, enganar] to cheat. -**2.** *JUR* [violar] to violate.

lésbico, ca ['lɛʒbiku, ka] *adj* lesbian.
➡ **lésbica** *f* lesbian.

lesionar [4] [lezjo'na(x)] *vt* to injure.

lesivo, va [le'zivu, va] *adj* [prejudicial] harmful.

lesma ['leʒma] *f* -**1.** [animal] slug. -**2.** *fig* [pessoa] sluggard.

leso, sa [le'zu, za] *adj* [contundido] injured.

leste ['lɛʃtʃi] ⬦ *m (inv)* [ger] east; **a ~ (de)** to the east (of); **para ~** eastward. ⬦ *adj (inv)* easterly.

letal [le'taw] *(pl* -**ais)** *adj* lethal.

letão, tã [le'tãw, tã] ⬦ *adj* Latvian. ⬦ *m, f* Latvian.
➡ **letão** *m* [língua] Latvian.

letargia [letax'ʒial *f* lethargy.

letárgico, ca [le'taxʒiku, ka] *adj* lethargic.

letivo, va [le'tʃivu, va] *adj* school *(antes de subst)*; **ano ~** academic year, school year.

Letônia [le'tonja] *n* Latvia.

letra ['letra] *f* -**1.** [caractere] letter; **~ de fôrma** block capital *(pl)*; **~ de imprensa** print; **~ maiúscula/minúscula** capital/small letter; **com todas as ~ s** [explicitamente] in detail. -**2.** [caligrafia] handwriting; **~ de mão** handwriting; **~ de médico** *fig* scrawl. -**3.** [de música] lyrics *(pl)*. -**4.** *COM*: **~ de câmbio** bill of exchange.
➡ **letras** *fpl* -**1.** [curso] arts. -**2.** [literatura] literature.
➡ **à letra, ao pé da letra** *loc adv* -**1.** [literalmente] literally. -**2.** [rigorosamente] to the letter.
➡ **de letra** *loc adv*: **tirar algo de ~** to do sthg with one's eyes closed.

letrado, da [le'tradu, da] *adj* -**1.** [culto] lettered. -**2.** [versado em literatura] well read.

letreiro [le'trejru] *m* notice; **~ luminoso** neon sign.

léu ['lɛw] ➡ **ao léu** *loc adv* -**1.** [à toa] aimlessly. -**2.** [à mostra] uncovered.

leucemia [lewse'mia] *f* leukaemia *UK*, leukemia *US*.

leva ['lɛva] *f* [conjunto] batch.

levadiço [leva'dʒisu] *adj* ▷ **ponte**.

levado, da [le'vadu, da] *adj*: **~ (da breca)** unruly.

leva-e-traz [ˌlɛvi'traʃ] ⬦ *mf (inv)* [pessoa] gossip. ⬦ *m (inv)* [fofoca] gossip.

levantador, ra [levãnta'do(x), ra] *m, f ESP*: **~ de pesos** weightlifter.

levantamento [levãnta'mẽntul *m* -**1.** [pesquisa] survey. -**2.** [inventário] inventory. -**3.** *ESP*: **~ de pesos** weightlifting.

levantar [4] [levãn'ta(x)] ⬦ *vt* -**1.** [ger] to raise; **~ os olhos** to look up. -**2.** [do chão] to lift; **~ vôo** to take off. -**3.** [tornar mais alto] to lift up. -**4.** [coletar] to collect. -**5.** [inventariar] to count. ⬦ *vi* -**1.** [ficar de pé] to stand. -**2.** [sair da cama] to get up. -**3.** [avivar] to cheer.
➡ **levantar-se** *vp* -**1.** [ficar de pé] to stand up. -**2.** [sair da cama] to get up.

levante [le'vãntʃi] *m* -**1.** [revolta] uprising. -**2.** [leste] east.

levar [4] [le'va(x)] *vt* -**1.** [ger] to take; **isso leva algum tempo** that will take some time; **~ adiante** to carry on; **~ a cabo** to carry out. -**2.** [carregar] to carry. -**3.** [induzir] to lead; **~ alguém a algo/a fazer algo** to bring sb to sthg/to do sthg; **deixar-se ~ por algo** to let o.s. be led by sthg. -**4.** [retirar] to take away. -**5.** [lidar com] to deal with. -**6.** [vida]: **ele leva uma vida dura** he has a hard life; **~ a vida na flauta** to take life as it comes. -**7.** [susto, surra]: **~ um susto** to get a fright; **~ uma surra** to take a beating. -**8.** [ganhar] to win.

leve ['lɛvi] *adj* light; **de ~** lightly.

levedo [le'vedul *m*, **levedura** *f* [leve'dura] yeast.

levemente [levi'mẽntʃi] *adv* lightly.

leveza [le'veza] *f* lightness.

leviandade [levjãn'dadʒi] *f* -**1.** [imprudência] rashness. -**2.** [falta de seriedade] frivolity.

leviano, na [le'vjanu, na] *adj* -**1.** [imprudente] rash. -**2.** [sem seriedade] frivolous.

levitar [4] [levi'ta(x)] *vi* to levitate.

lexical [leksi'kaw] *(pl* -**ais)** *adj* [função, unidade] lexical.

léxico, ca ['lɛksiku, ka] *adj* [análise, família] lexical.
➡ **léxico** *m* [vocabulário] lexicon.

lexicografia [leksikogra'fia] *f* lexicography.

lexicógrafo, fa [leksi'kografu, fa] *m* lexicographer.

lexicologia [leksikolo'ʒia] *f* lexicology.

lexicólogo, ga [leksi'kɔlogu, ga] *m* lexicologist.

lhama ['ʎãma] *mf* llama.

lhe [ʎe] *(pl* **lhes)** *pron pess* -**1.** [a ele, ela] (to) him/her/it; **dei-~ um presente** I gave him/her a present; **Maria ~ contou um segredo** Maria told him/her a secret; **acertaram-~ um tiro** they shot him/her; **isto lhes custou caro** this cost them a lot of money -**2.** [a você] (to) you; **telefonei-~ ontem** I phoned you yesterday; **o que ~ aconteceu?** what's happened to you?; **ouçam bem o que lhes digo!** listen carefully to what I say! -**3.** [indicando posse - dele, dela] his *(f* her); **roubaram-~ o carro** they stole his/her car; **ardia-lhes a vista** their eyes were stinging; [- de você] your; **beijei-~ as faces** I kissed your cheeks; **não lhes pesa a consciência?** doesn't your conscience trouble you? -**4.** [para enfatizar - a ele, ela] his *(f* her); **não sei como ele agüenta as confusões que sua namorada ~ a pronta** I don't know how he puts up with his girlfriend's nonsense; [- a você] you; **não sei como você agüenta as confusões que sua namorada ~ apronta** I don't know how you put up with your girlfriend's nonsense.

lhufas ['ʎufaʃ] *pron indef fam* zilch.

lia ['lia] *f* sediment.

liame ['ljãmi] *m* tie.

libanês, esa [liba'neʃ, eza] ⬦ *adj* Lebanese. ⬦ *m, f* Lebanese.

Líbano ['libanul *n*: **o ~** Lebanon.

libelo [li'bɛlul *m* -**1.** [ger] lampoon. -**2.** *JUR* indictment.

libélula [li'bɛlula] *f* dragonfly.

liberação [libera'sãw] f **-1.** [ger] release. **-2.** [libertação] liberation. **-3.** [de preços, câmbio] freedom from controls. **-4.** [de cheque] clearing. **-5.** [do aborto] legalization.

liberal [libe'raw] (pl -ais) <> adj liberal. <> mf POL liberal.

liberalidade [liberali'dadʒi] f [generosidade] liberality.

liberalismo [libera'liʒmu] m liberalism.

liberalização [liberaliza'sãw] f freedom from controls.

liberalizar [4] [liberali'za(x)] vt [preços, mercado] to liberalize.

liberar [4] [libe'ra(x)] vt -**1.** [ger] to release; ~ alguém de algo to release sb from sthg. **-2.** [libertar] to release. **-3.** [preço, câmbio] to free from controls. **-4.** [cheque] to clear. **-5.** [aborto] to legalize.

liberdade [libex'dadʒi] f freedom; **dar** ~ **a alguém (para fazer algo)** to give sb the freedom (to do sthg); **estar em** ~ to be free; **pôr em** ~ to set free; **ter** ~ **para fazer algo** to be at liberty to do sthg; **tomar a** ~ **de fazer algo** to take the liberty of doing sthg; **estar em** ~ **condicional** to be on parole; ~ **de expressão** freedom of speech; ~ **de imprensa** freedom of press; ~ **de opinião** freedom of thought; ~ **sob fiança** release on bail.
➡ **liberdades** fpl liberties; **tomar** ~ **com alguém** to take liberties with sb.

Libéria [li'bɛrja] n Liberia.

líbero ['liberul] m FUT sweeper.

libertação [libex'tasãw] (pl -ões) f liberation.

libertador, ra [libexta'do(x), ra] <> adj liberating. <> m, f liberator.

libertar [4] [libex'ta(x)] vt [tornar livre] to liberate.

libertinagem [libextʃi'naʒẽ] f loose living.

libertino, na [libex'tʃinu, na] <> adj libertine. <> m, f libertine.

liberto, ta [li'bextu, ta] <> adj -**1.** [escravo] liberated. **-2.** [salvo] free. <> m,f [escravo] freedman (f freedwoman).

Líbia ['libja] n Libya.

libidinoso, osa [libidʒi'nozu, ɔza] adj libidinous.

libido [li'bidu] f libido.

líbio, bia ['libju, bja] <> adj Libyan. <> m, f Libyan.

libra ['libra] f pound; ~ **(esterlina)** pound (sterling).
➡ **Libra** m ASTRO Libra; **ser Libra** to be a Libran.

libreto [li'bretul] m libretto.

Libreville [,libre'vili] n Libreville.

libriano, na [li'brjanu, na] <> adj Libran. <> m, f Libran.

lição [li'sãw] (pl -ões) f -**1.** EDUC lesson. **-2.** fig [ensinamento] lesson; **dar uma** ~ **a alguém** to teach sb a lesson; **servir de** ~ **a alguém** to be a lesson to sb. **-3.** fig [repreensão]: **dar uma** ~ **em alguém** to teach sb a lesson.

licença [li'sẽsa] f **-1.** [permissão] permission; **dar**

~ **a alguém (para fazer algo)** to give sb permission (to do sthg); **com** ~ excuse me; ~ **poética** poetic licence. **-2.** [de trabalho] permit; **estar de** ~ to be on leave; **tirar** ~ to go on leave. **-3.** [documento] licence UK, license US.

licença-maternidade [li'sẽsa'matexni'dadʒi] (pl licenças-maternidade) f maternity leave.

licença-prêmio [li,sẽsa'premju] (pl licenças-prêmio) f six-months' leave from work, awarded every five years.

licenciado, da [lisẽ'sjadu, da] <> adj -**1.** UNIV graduated. **-2.** [do trabalho] on leave. <> m, f UNIV graduate.

licenciar [16] [lisẽn'sja(x)] vt [do trabalho] to allow time off work.
➡ **licenciar-se** vp -**1.** UNIV: ~-se (em algo) to obtain a degree (in sthg). **-2.** [do trabalho] to go on leave.

licenciatura [lisẽnsja'tura] f **-1.** [grau] degree. **-2.** [curso] degree course.

licencioso, osa [lisẽ'sjozu, ɔza] adj [obsceno] licentious.

licitação [lisita'sãw] (pl -ões) f -**1.** [em leilão] bid. **-2.** [concorrência] tender; **abrir uma** ~ to put a project out to tender; **vencer uma** ~ to win a tender.

licitante [lisi'tãntʃi] mf bidder.

lícito, ta ['lisitu, ta] adj -**1.** [legal] lawful. **-2.** [correto] licit.

lições [li'sõiʃ] pl ⊳ **lição**.

licor [li'ko(x)] (pl -es) m liqueur.

licoroso, osa [liko'rozu, ɔza] adj sweet and strong.

lida ['lida] f -**1.** [trabalho] toil. **-2.** [leitura] read; **dar uma** ~ **em algo** to have a read of sthg.

lidar [4] [li'da(x)] vi: ~ **com alguém/algo** [conviver com] to deal with sb/sthg; [tratar] to deal with sb/sthg; [trabalhar com] to deal with sb/sthg.

lide ['lidʒi] f -**1.** [combate] battle. **-2.** JUR case.

líder ['lide(x)] (pl -es) mf leader.

liderança [lide'rãnsa] f leadership.

liderar [4] [lide'ra(x)] vt to lead.

lido, da ['lidu, da] <> pp ⊳ **ler**. <> adj: **muito** ~ [culto] well read; [autor, obra] much read.

lifting ['liftĩŋ] m facelift.

liga ['liga] f -**1.** [associação] league. **-2.** [de meias] garter. **-3.** [de metais] alloy.

ligação [liga'sãw] (pl -ões) f -**1.** [ger] connection; **fazer a** ~ **entre algo e algo** to connect sthg with sthg. **-2.** TELEC [telephone] call; **a** ~ **caiu** we have been cut off; **completar a** ~ to get through (on the phone); **fazer uma** ~ **(para alguém)** to make a call (to sb). **-3.** [relacionamento - amoroso] liaison; [- profissional] relationship.

ligado, da [li'gadu, da] adj -**1.** [ger] connected. **-2.** [absorto] immersed; **ser** ~ **em algo** to be knowledgeable in sthg. **-3.** [afeiçoado] attached.
➡ **ligada** f TELEC phonecall; **dar uma** ~ **para alguém** to call sb.

ligadura [liga'dura] f -**1.** [atadura] bandage. **-2.** MÚS ligature.

ligamento [liga'mẽntu] *m* -**1.** ANAT ligament. -**2.** MED: ~ **de trompas** tubal ligation.

ligar [14] [li'ga(x)] <> *vt* -**1.** [ger] to connect. -**2.** [unir] to connect, to join. -**3.** [criar vínculos] to tie. -**4.** [dar importância a]: **não** ~ **a mínima (para alguém/algo)** to not pay the least bit of attention to sb/sthg. <> *vi* -**1.** [telefonar] to call; ~ **para alguém/algum lugar** to call sb/somewhere (on the phone). -**2.** [dar importância] to care; ~ **para alguém/algo** to care about sb/sthg. -**3.** [dar atenção] to notice; ~ **para alguém/algo** to notice sb/sthg.
 ligar-se *vp* -**1.** [unir-se] to unite; ~**-se a alguém/algo** to unite o.s. to sb/sthg. -**2.** [relacionar-se]: ~**-se a algo** to be connected to sthg. -**3.** [afeiçoar-se] to become attached.

ligeireza [liʒej'rezal *f* -**1.** [rapidez] lightness. -**2.** [agilidade] agility.

ligeiro, ra [li'ʒejru, ra] *adj* -**1.** [rápido] light. -**2.** [ágil] agile. -**3.** *(antes de subst) fig* [sutil] slight.
 ligeiro *adv* -**1.** [rapidamente] swiftly. -**2.** [com agilidade] nimbly.

lilás [li'laʃ] (*pl* -**lilases**) <> *adj* [cor] lilac. <> *m* lilac.

lima ['lima] *f* -**1.** [fruta] lime. -**2.** [ferramenta] file.

Lima ['lima] *n* Lima.

limão [li'mãw] (*pl* -**ões**) *m* lemon.

limbo ['lĩnbu] *m*: **estar no** ~ *fig* to be in limbo.

limenho, nha [li'meɲu, ɲal <> *adj* Lima (*antes de subst*). <> *m, f* person from Lima.

limiar [li'mja(x)] *m* threshold.

liminar [4] [li'mi'na(x)] *f* JUR preliminary verdict.

limitação [limita'sãw] (*pl* -**ões**) *f* limitation.

limitado, da [limi'tadu, dal *adj* limited.

limitar [4] [limi'ta(x)] *vt* [restringir] to limit.
 limitar-se *vp* -**1.** [restringir-se]: ~**-se a fazer algo** to limit o.s. to doing sthg. -**2.** [confinar-se]: ~**-se com algo** to border on sthg.

limite [li'mitʃi] *m* [ger] limit; ~ **de idade** age limit; **passar dos** ~**s** to go too far.

limítrofe [li'mitrofi] *adj* bordering.

limo ['limu] *m* BOT slime.

limoeiro [li'mwejru] *m* lemon tree.

limões [li'mõjʃ] *pl* > **limão**.

limonada [limo'nada] *f* lemonade *UK*, lemon soda *US*.

limpador [lĩnpa'do(x)] (*pl* -**es**) *m* cleaner; ~ **de chaminé** chimney sweep; ~ **de pára-brisas** windscreen wiper *UK*, windshield wiper *US*.

limpa-pés [ˌlĩnpa'pɛʃ] *m inv* boot scraper.

limpar [4] [lĩm'pa(x)] *vt* -**1.** [ger] to clean. -**2.** *fig* [elevar]: ~ **a imagem de alguém/algo** to clean up sb's/sthg's image. -**3.** [enxugar] to dry. -**4.** [esvaziar] to clean. -**5.** [roubar] to clean out. -**6.** *fig* [livrar] to rid.
 limpar-se *vp* -**1.** [assear-se] to wash o.s. -**2.** [moralmente] to make a clean start.

limpeza [lĩn'pezal *f* -**1.** [estado] cleanliness. -**2.** [ato] cleaning; **fazer uma** ~ **em algo** [livrar de excessos] to clear sthg out; [livrar de maus elemento] to clean sthg up; [roubar] to clean sthg out; ~ **de pele** skin cleansing; ~ **pública** refuse collection. -**3.** [esmero] neatness.

límpido, da ['lĩmpidu, dal *adj* -**1.** [translúcido] limpid. -**2.** [nítido] clear.

limpo, pa ['lĩnpu, pal <> *pp* > **limpar**. <> *adj* -**1.** [asseado] clean. -**2.** [esmerado] neat; **passar a** ~ to make a clean copy. -**3.** *fig* [honrado] blameless. -**4.** [desanuviado] clear. -**5.** [sem dinheiro] broke. -**6.** [sem descontos]: **recebi 100 mil** ~**s** I received 100,000 clear. -**7.** *loc*: **tirar a** ~ to get to the bottom of.
 limpa *f* -**1.** [limpeza]: **dar uma** ~ **em algo** to have a clean in sthg. -**2.** *fam fig* [roubo]: **fazer uma** ~ **(em algo)** to clean (sthg) out.

limusine [limu'zinil *f* limousine.

lince ['lĩnsil *m* lynx; **ter olhos de** ~ to have eyes like a hawk.

linchamento [lĩnʃa'mẽntul *m* lynching.

linchar [4] [lĩn'ʃa(x)] *vt* to lynch.

lindeza [lĩn'dezal *f* beauty.

lindo, da ['lĩndu, dal *adj* beautiful; **ser** ~ **de morrer** *fam* to be a knockout.

linear [li'nja(x)] *adj* linear.

linearidade [linja'ridadʒil *f* linearity.

linfático, ca [lĩn'fatʃiku, kal *adj* lymphatic.

lingerie [lãnʒe'xil *f* lingerie.

lingote [lĩn'gotʃil *m* ingot.

língua ['lĩngwal *f* -**1.** [órgão] tongue; **ter** ~ **presa** to be tongue-tied; **dar com a** ~ **nos dentes** to spill the beans; **ficar de** ~ **de fora** to be exhausted; **pagar pela** ~ to pay dearly; **estar na ponta da** ~ to be on the tip of one's tongue; **ter uma** ~ **comprida** to be a gossip; **dobrar a** ~ to mind what one says. -**2.** [idioma] language; ~ **materna** mother tongue; ~ **morta** dead language.

LÍNGUA PORTUGUESA

The Portuguese language is spoken in Europe (Portugal), South America (Brazil), Africa (Cape Verde, São Tomé and Príncipe, Angola, Mozambique, Guinea-Bissau) and Asia (East Timor, Goa, and Macao). It is the sixth most spoken language in the world, mostly through the 200 million speakers of Portuguese in Brazil. Brazilian Portuguese has acquired specific characteristics through the incorporation of many words mainly of African and indigenous origin. It has, therefore, many differences in pronunciation, spelling, vocabulary and even grammar, in relation to the Portuguese spoken in other parts of the world, although it remains essentially the same language.

linguado [lĩn'gwadul *m* [peixe] (Brazilian) flounder.

linguagem [lĩn'gwaʒẽl (*pl* -**ns**) *f* language; ~ **de máquina** machine language; ~ **de programação** programming language.

linguajar [lĩngwa'ʒa(x)] *m* language.

linguarudo, da [lĩngwa'rudu, dal <> *adj* gossipy. <> *m, f* gossip.

lingüeta [lĩn'gwetal *f* -**1.** [de fechadura] catch. -**2.** [balança] pointer.

lingüiça [liŋ'gwisa] f chorizo; **encher** ~ *fam* to waffle.

lingüista [liŋ'gwiʃta] mf linguist.

lingüístico, ca [liŋ'gwiʃtʃiku, ka] adj linguistic.
➤ **lingüística** f linguistics (pl).

linha ['liɲa] f -1. [ger] line; **as** ~s **gerais de algo** the general outlines of sthg; **em** ~s **gerais** in general terms; ~ **de mira** line of sight; ~ **de saque** service line; ~ **de crédito** credit line; ~s inimigas enemy lines; ~ **de fogo** firing line; ~ **de montagem** assembly line; ~ **cruzada** crossed line; **não dar** ~ to be dead; ~ **de conduta** code of conduct; **andar na** ~ fig to toe the line; **sair da** ~ fig to be out of line. -**2.** [fio de costura] thread. -**3.** [via] route; ~ **aérea** airline; ~ **férrea** railway line UK, railroad US. -**4.** [elegância] flair; **é um homem de** ~ he has a flair for things; **portar-se/vestir-se com muita** ~ to behave/dress o.s. with a lot of flair; **perder a** ~ to lose face. -**5.** COMPUT: ~ **de comando** command line; ~ **dedicada** dedicated line; ~ **discada** dial-up line.

linhaça [li'ɲasa] f linseed.

linha-dura [ˌliɲa'dura] (pl linhas-duras) ◇ mf hardliner. ◇ adj (inv) hard-line.

linhagem [li'ɲaʒẽ] f lineage.

linho ['liɲu] m -**1.** [tecido] linen. -**2.** [planta] flax.

link ['liɲkil] (pl links) m COMPUT link.

linóleo [li'nɔlju] m linoleum.

lipoaspiração [lipu'aʃpirasãw] (pl -ões) f liposuction.

liquefazer [31] [likefa'ze(x)] vt -**1.** [ger] to melt. -**2.** [tornar líquido] to liquefy.
➤ **liquefazer-se** vp to melt.

liquefeito, ta [like'fejtu, ta] ◇ pp ▷ **liquefazer**. ◇ adj molten.

líquen ['likẽ] m BOT lichen.

liquidação [likida'sãw] (pl -ões) f -**1.** [dissolução] settlement. -**2.** FIN liquidation. -**3.** COM clearance sale; **(estar) em** ~ (to be) in liquidation. -**4.** [destruição] elimination.

liquidar [4] [liki'da(x)] ◇ vt -**1.** [ger] to liquidate. -**2.** [dissolver] to settle. -**3.** [destruir] to eliminate. ◇ vi -**1.** COM to hold a clearance sale. -**2.**: ~ **com alguém/algo** [destruir] to destroy sb/sthg.

liquidez [liki'dejʃ] f ECON liquidity.

liqüidificador [likwidʒifika'do(x)] m liquidizer.

liqüidificar [likwidʒifi'ka(x)] vt to liquidize.

líquido, da ['likidu, 'likida] adj -**1.** [estado] liquid. -**2.** [valor] net; **peso** ~ COM net weight.
➤ **líquido** m [fluido] liquid.

lira ['lira] f -**1.** [instrumento] lyre. -**2.** fig [poesia] lyric poem. -**3.** [moeda] lira.

lírico, ca ['liriku, ka] adj -**1.** [gênero] lyrical. -**2.** fig [romântico] romantic.
➤ **lírica** f [coleção de poesia] lyrical poetry.

lírio ['lirju] m lily.

lírio-do-vale [ˌlirjudu'vali] (pl lírios-do-vale) m lily of the valley.

lirismo [li'riʒmu] m -**1.** [em poesia] lyricism. -**2.** fig [romantismo] romance.

Lisboa [liʒ'boa] n Lisbon.

lisboeta [liʒ'bweta] ◇ adj Lisbon (antes de subst). ◇ mf person from Lisbon.

liso, sa ['lizu, 'liza] adj -**1.** [superfície] smooth. -**2.** [cabelo] straight. -**3.** [tecido] plain. -**4.** fam [sem dinheiro] broke.

lisonja [li'zõʒa] f flattery.

lisonjeador, ra [lisõnʒja'do(x), ra] ◇ adj flattering. ◇ m, f flatterer.

lisonjear [15] [lizõn'ʒja(x)] vt to flatter.

lisonjeiro, ra [lizõn'ʒejru, ra] adj flattering.

lista ['liʃta] f -**1.** [relação] list; ~ **civil** civil list; ~ **negra** black list; ~ **de discussão** newsgroup; ~ **telefônica** telephone directory. -**2.** [listra] stripe.

listagem [liʃ'taʒẽ] (pl -ns) f listing.

listar [4] [liʃ'ta(x)] vt COMPUT to list.

listra ['liʃtra] f stripe.

listrado, da [liʃ'tradu, da], **listado, da** liʃ'tadu, da] adj striped.

lisura [li'zura] f [de superfície] smoothness.

literal [lite'raw] (pl -ais) adj literal.

literalmente [literaw'mẽtʃil] adv literally.

literário, ria [lite'rarju, lite'rarja] adj literary.

literato, ta [lite'ratu, ta] m writer.

literatura [litera'tural f literature; ~ **comparada** comparative literature; ~ **de cordel** popular fairground novelettes; ~ **de ficção** fiction writing; ~ **de vanguarda** avant-garde writing.

LITERATURA BRASILEIRA

Although not very widespread because of language difficulties, Brazilian literature has a wealth of good writers and poets. The great names of modern Brazilian poetry include Carlos Drummond de Andrade (1902-1987) from Minas Gerais and João Cabral de Melo Neto (1920-1999) from Pernambuco. Within prose writing, foremost are the novels of Machado de Assis (1839-1908) from Rio de Janeiro, the leading exponent of nineteenth century realism, those of Gumarães Rosa (1908-1967) from Minas Gerais, and those of Jorge Amado (1912-2001) from Bahia, the best known and most widely translated Brazilian author.

litigar [14] [litʃi'ga(x)] ◇ vt [pleitear] to litigate. ◇ vi [abrir processo] to litigate.

litígio [li'tʃiʒju] m -**1.** JUR [questão] litigation. -**2.** fig [disputa] quarrel.

litigioso, osa [litʃi'ʒozu, ɔza] adj JUR contentious.

litografia [litogra'fia] f -**1.** [técnica] lithography. -**2.** [gravura] lithograph.

litogravura [ˌlitogra'vural f [gravura] lithograph.

litoral [lito'raw] (pl -ais) ◇ adj [costeiro] coastal. ◇ m [beira-mar] coast.

litorâneo, nea [lito'ranju, nja] adj coastal.

litro ['litrul m [medida] litre UK, liter US.

Lituânia [li'twãnja] f Lithuania.

lituano, na [li'twãnu, na] ◇ adj Lithuanian. ◇ mf Lithuanian.
➤ **lituano** m [língua] Lithuanian.

liturgia [litux'ʒia] f liturgy.

lívido, da ['lividu, da] adj pallid.

livrar [4] [li'vra(x)] *vt* **-1.** [libertar] to free. **-2.** [salvar]: ~ **alguém/algo de algo** to save sb/sthg from sthg.
  ➡ **livrar-se** *vp* **-1.** [libertar-se]: ~**-se (de alguém/algo)** to free o.s. (from sb/sthg). **-2.** : ~ **-se de algo** [salvar-se] to escape from sthg; [evitar] to avoid sthg.

livraria [livra'rial *f* bookshop *UK*, bookstore *US*.

livre ['livril *adj* **-1.** [ger] free. **-2.** [independente] independent; **de** ~ **e espontânea vontade** of one's own free will. **-3.** [permitido] free. **-4.** [solto] free. **-5.** [isento]: ~ **de algo** free of sthg; ~ **de impostos** tax-free.

livre-arbítrio [ˌlivrjax'bitrjul (*pl* **livres-arbítrios**) *m* free will.

livre-docência [ˌlivrido'sẽnsja] (*pl* **livres-docências**) *f* [título universitário] *entitlement to teach and examine university lecturers.*

livre-docente ['livri'do'sẽntʃil (*pl* **-s**) *mf* ≃ research professor. ◇ *m* [título] ≃ research professor.

livre-iniciativa ['livri'inisja'tʃival (*pl* **-s**) *m* ECON free enterprise.

livreiro, ra [liv'rejru, ra] *m,f* bookseller.

livre-pensador, ra [ˌlivripẽnsa'do(x), ra] (*pl* **livres-pensadores** *m* freethinker.

livresco, ca [li'vreʃku, ka] *adj* book (*antes de subst*).

livro ['livrul *m* **-1.** [ger] book; ~ **de bolso** pocketbook; ~ **brochado** paperback; ~ **de capa dura** hardback; ~ **de cozinha** cookery book; ~ **didático** text book; ~ **de cabeceira** favourite reading. **-2.** *loc*: **ser um** ~ **aberto** to be an open book.

livro-caixa [ˌlivro'kajʃal (*pl* **livros-caixas**) *m* cash book.

lixa ['liʃal *f* **-1.** [papel] sandpaper. **-2.** [de ferro] file; ~ **de unhas** nail file.

lixadeira [liʃa'dejral *f* sander.

lixar [4] [li'ʃa(x)] *vt* **-1.** [madeira] to sand. **-2.** [unhas] to file.
  ➡ **lixar-se** *vp fam* [não se incomodar]: **ele está se lixando com a demissão** he couldn't care less about the resignation.

lixeira [li'ʃejra] *f* **-1.** [em prédio] rubbish chute *UK*, garbage chute *US*. **-2.** [local] rubbish dump *UK*, garbage dump *US*.

lixeiro [li'ʃejrul *m* refuse collector *UK*, dustman *UK*, garbage collector *US*.

lixo ['liʃul *m* **-1.** [restos] rubbish *UK*, garbage *US*; ~ **atômico** nuclear waste. **-2.** [coisa sem valor] rubbish *UK*, garbage *US*; **estar um** ~ [estar ruim, feio] to be rubbish.

-lo [lul *pron* [pessoa] him; [coisa] it; [você] you.

lobby ['lɔbil (*pl* **lobbies**) *m* POL lobby.

lobinho [lo'biɲul *m* [aprendiz de escoteiro] cub scout.

lobisomem [lobi'zomẽl (*pl* **-ns**) *m* werewolf.

lobista [lo'biʃtal *mf* lobbyist.

lobo ['lobul *m* wolf.

lobo-do-mar [ˌlobudu'ma(x)] (*pl* **lobos-do-mar**) *m* sea dog, old salt.

lobotomia [loboto'mial *f* lobotomy.

lóbulo ['lɔbulul *m* lobe; ~ **de orelha** ear lobe.

locação [loka'sãwl (*pl* **-ões**) *f* **-1.** [de carro, vídeo] hire, rental. **-2.** [de telefone, imóvel] rental. **-3.** CINE location.

locador, ra [loka'do(x), ra] *m* **-1.** [de imóvel] landlord. **-2.** [de carro] lessor.
  ➡ **locadora** *f* [agência] hire *ou* rental company; ~ **de vídeo** video hire *ou* rental shop.

local [lo'kawl (*pl* **-ais**) ◇ *adj* local. ◇ *m* place.

localidade [lokali'dadʒil *f* **-1.** [lugar] locality. **-2.** [povoado] town.

localização [lokaliza'sãwl (*pl* **-ões**) *f* **-1.** [ato] tracking down, localization. **-2.** [lugar] positioning.

localizar [4] [lokali'za(x)] *vt* **-1.** [encontrar] to find. **-2.** [limitar a certo local] to site.
  ➡ **localizar-se** *vp* [situar-se] to be sited.

loção [lo'sãwl (*pl* **-ões**) *f* lotion; ~ **após-barba** aftershave.

locatário, ria [loka'tarju, rja] *m* **-1.** [carro] lessee. **-2.** [imóvel] tenant.

locomoção [lokomo'sãwl (*pl* **-ões**) *f* locomotion.

locomotiva [lokomo'tʃival *f* locomotive.

locomover-se [5] [lokomo'vexsil *vp* to move.

locução [loku'sãwl (*pl* **-ões**) *f* **-1.** [expressão] expression. **-2.** [dicção] diction. **-3.** GRAM phrase.

locutor, ra [loku'to(x), ra] (*mpl* **-es**, *fpl* **-s**) *m,f* [profissional] presenter.

lodaçal [loda'sawl (*pl* **-ais**) *m* [lamaçal] mud.

lodacento, ta [loda'sẽntu, ta] *adj* muddy.

lodo ['lodul *m* mud.

lodoso, osa [lo'dozu, ɔza] *adj* = lodacento.

logaritmo [loga'ritʃimul *m* logarithm.

lógico, ca ['lɔʒiku, ka] *adj* logical; **(é)** ~! of course!
  ➡ **lógica** *f* **-1.** [ger] logic. **-2.** [raciocínio] reasoning.

log-in (*pl* **logins**) *m* COMPUT login.

logística [lo'ʒiʃtʃikal *f* logistics (*pl*).

logo ['lɔgul ◇ *adv* **-1.** [sem demora] at once; ~ **de saída** *ou* **de cara** straight away; **vem** ~! come at once! **-2.** [em breve] soon; **até** ~! see you later!; ~ **mais** in a while. **-3.** [exatamente]: ~ **agora** right now; ~ **ali** right there. **-4.** [pouco]: ~ **antes/depois** just before/after. ◇ *conj* [portanto] therefore.
  ➡ **logo que** *loc adv* as soon as.
  ➡ **tão logo** *loc adv* as soon as.

logomarca [logo'maxkal *f* logo.

logotipo [logo'tʃipul *m* logo.

logradouro [logra'dorul *m* public area.

lograr [4] [lo'gra(x)] *vt* **-1.** [conseguir] to achieve; ~ **fazer algo** to manage to do sthg. **-2.** [empurrar] to trick.

logro ['logrul *m* fraud.

loiro, ra ['lojru, ra] *adj* = louro.

loja ['lɔʒal *f* **-1.** COM shop *UK*, store *US*; ~ **de antiguidades** antique shop; ~ **de brinquedos** toy shop; ~ **de departamentos** department store; ~

de ferragens ironmonger's *UK*, hardware store *US*; ~ **de produtos naturais** health food store. **-2.** [maçônica] lodge.

lojista [lo'ʒiʃta] *mf* shopkeeper.

lombada [lõn'bada] *f* **-1.** [de livro] spine. **-2.** [de boi] fillet. **-3.** [no solo] ridge.

lombalgia [lõnbaw'ʒia] *f* backache.

lombar [lõn'ba(x)] *adj* lumbar.

lombinho [lõn'biɲu] *m* [carne de porco] pork fillet.

lombo ['lõnbu] *m* **-1.** [dorso] lower back. **-2.** [carne] loin. **-3.** [elevação] ridge.

lombriga [lõn'briga] *f* roundworm.

lona ['lona] *f* **-1.** [tecido] canvas. **-2.** [cobertura] tarpaulin. **-3.** [de pneu] layer. **-4.** *loc*: **estar na** ~ *fam* to be wiped out.

Londres ['lõndriʃ] *n* London.

londrino, na [lõn'drinu, na] ⟨⟩ *adj* London *(antes de subst).* ⟨⟩ *m, f* Londoner.

longamente [lõŋga'mẽntʃi] *adv* **-1.** [em grande extensão] for a long way. **-2.** [por muito tempo] for a long time.

longa-metragem [ˌlõŋgame'traʒẽ] *(pl* **longasmetragens)** *m*: **(filme de)** ~ feature-length film.

longe ['lõnʒi] ⟨⟩ *adv* far (away); **é ~?** is it far?; **ir** ~ **demais** *fig* [exceder-se] to go too far; **ver ~** *fig* [ter visão] to look far ahead. ⟨⟩ *adj* remote.
◆ **ao longe** *loc adv* **-1.** [no espaço] in the distance. **-2.** [no tempo] a long way.
◆ **de longe** *loc adv* **-1.** [no espaço] from far away. **-2.** [no tempo]: **vir de** ~ to be longstanding. **-3.** [sem comparação] by far.
◆ **longe de** ⟨⟩ *loc conj* far from; ~ **disso** far from it. ⟨⟩ *loc prep* far from.

longevidade [lõnʒevi'dadʒi] *f* longevity.

longevo, va [lõnʒe'vu, va] *adj* **-1.** [muito idoso] elderly. **-2.** [duradouro] long-lived.

longínquo, qua [lõ'ʒĩŋkwu, kwa] *adj* **-1.** [no espaço] distant, remote. **-2.** [no tempo] distant.

longitude [lõnʒi'tudʒi] *f* GEOGR longitude.

longitudinal [lõnʒitudʒi'naw] *(pl* **-ais)** *adj* longitudinal.

longo, ga ['lõŋgu, ga] *adj* **-1.** [ger] long. **-2.** *(antes de subst)* [duradouro] lasting.
◆ **longo** *m* [vestido] long dress.
◆ **ao longo de** *loc prep* **-1.** [no sentido longitudinal] along. **-2.** [à beira de] alongside. **-3.** [no tempo]: **ao ~ dos anos** over the years.

lontra ['lõntra] *f* otter.

loquacidade [lokwasi'dadʒi] *m* loquaciousness.

loquaz [lo'kwaʒ] *adj* **-1.** [falador] talkative. **-2.** [eloqüente] eloquent.

lorde ['lɔxdʒi] *m* **-1.** [título] Lord. **-2.** *fig* [homem refinado] refined gentleman.

lordose [lox'dɔzi] *f* MED lordosis, curvature of the spine.

lorota [lo'rɔta] *f fam* fib.

losango [lo'zãŋgu] *m* diamond, lozenge.

lotação [lota'sãw] *(pl* **-ões)** *f* **-1.** [capacidade] capacity; ~ **esgotada** [cinema, teatro] sold out, full house. **-2.** [quadro de pessoal] number of personnel. **-3.** [veículo] minibus.

lotado, da [lo'tadu, da] *adj* [cheio] full, crowded.

lotar [4] [lo'ta(x)] ⟨⟩ *vt* [encher] to fill. ⟨⟩ *vi* [encher]: ~ **(de)** to fill (with).

lote ['lɔtʃi] *m* **-1.** [parte] parcel. **-2.** [conjunto] set. **-3.** [terreno] plot.

loteamento [lotʃja'mẽntu] *m* division into plots.

lotear [15] [lo'tʃja(x)] *vt* to divide into plots.

loteca [lo'tɛka] *f fam* football pools *UK*, lottery *US*.

loteria [lote'ria] *f* lottery; **ganhar na** ~ to win the lottery; **jogar na** ~ to play the lottery; ~ **esportiva** (football) pools *UK*, lottery *US*.

loto ['lɔtu] *m* lottery.

louça ['losa] *f* china; **de** ~ china *(antes de subst)*; **lavar/secar a** ~ to wash/dry the dishes; ~ **de cerâmica** ceramics; ~ **de jantar** dinner service.

louco, ca ['loku, ka] ⟨⟩ *adj* **-1.** [ger] crazy. **-2.** [insano] mad. **-3.** [transtornado] crazed; **deixar alguém** ~ to drive sb mad; **ficar** ~ **com algo** to go mad with sthg; ~ **de fome** crazed with hunger. **-4.** [furioso]: ~ **(da vida com)** spitting mad (at). **-5.** [apaixonado]: **ser** ~ **por alguém/algo** to be crazy about sb/sthg. **-6.** [excêntrico] weird. **-7.** [intenso] extreme. **-8.** [extraordinário] unbelievable. ⟨⟩ *m, f* [insano] lunatic; ~ **varrido** *ou* **de pedra** *fam* stark raving mad.
◆ **louca** *f*: **dar a louca em alguém** to go mad.

loucura [lo'kura] *f* **-1.** [insanidade] insanity. **-2.** [imprudência] lunacy, madness; **ser (uma)** ~ **fazer algo** to be madness to do sthg. **-3.** [extravagância] antics *(pl)*; **fazer** ~**s** to get up to antics. **-4.** [paixão] passion; **ter** ~ **por alguém/algo** to be mad about sb/sthg.

louro, ra ['loru, ra] ⟨⟩ *adj* [cabelo, pessoa] fair. ⟨⟩ *m, f* [pessoa] fair-haired person.
◆ **louro** *m* **-1.** [cor] fair, blond. **-2.** [árvore] laurel. **-3.** CULIN bay leaf. **-4.** [papagaio] polly parrot.
◆ **louros** *mpl fig* [glórias] laurels.

lousa ['loza] *f* **-1.** [quadro-negro] blackboard. **-2.** [pedra] slate; ~ **tumular** tombstone.

louva-a-deus [ˌlova'dewʃ] *m inv* praying mantis.

louvação [lova'sãw] *(pl* **-ões)** *f* **-1.** [louvor] praise. **-2.** LITER popular poetry written for a special occasion, sometimes set to music.

louvar [4] [lo'va(x)] ⟨⟩ *vt* **-1.** [elogiar] to praise. **-2.** [glorificar] to exalt. ⟨⟩ *vi*: ~ **a Deus** to praise God.

louvável [lo'vavɛw] *(pl* **-eis)** *adj* praiseworthy.

louvor [lo'vo(x)] *m*: ~ **a alguém/algo** [elogio] praise for sb/sthg; [glorificação] glorification of sb/sthg.

Ltda *(abrev de* **Limitada)** *f* Ltd.

lua ['lua] *f* moon; ~ **cheia/nova** full/new moon; **estar no mundo da** ~ to be daydreaming; **ser de** ~ to have mood swings.

lua-de-mel [ˌluadʒi'mɛw] *(pl* **luas-de-mel)** *f* honeymoon.

Luanda ['lwãnda] *n* Luanda.

luar ['lwa(x)] *m* moonlight.

lubrificação [lubrifika'sãw] (*pl* -ões) *f* lubrication.

lubrificante [lubrifi'kãntʃi] ⬦ *adj* lubricating. ⬦ *m* lubricant.

lubrificar [12] [lubrifi'ka(x)] *vt* to lubricate.

lucidez [lusi'deʃ] *f* lucidity.

lúcido, da ['lusidu, da] *adj* lucid.

lucrar [4] [lu'kra(x)] ⬦ *vt*: ~ **algo com** *ou* **em algo** [financeiramente] to make a profit of sthg from sthg; [tirar vantagem de] to enjoy sthg through sthg; ~ **algo em fazer algo** to gain sthg by doing sthg. ⬦ *vi* [financeiramente] to make a profit; ~ **com algo** [tirar vantagem de] to benefit from sthg.

lucratividade [lukratʃivi'dadʒi] *f* profitability.

lucrativo, va [lukra'tʃivu, va] *adj* **-1.** [financeiramente] lucrative, profitable; **com/sem fins** ~**s** profit/non-profit-making. **-2.** [proveitoso] useful.

lucro ['lukru] *m* **-1.** [financeiro] profit; **ter** ~ to make a profit; ~ **bruto** gross profit; ~ **líquido** net profit; **participação nos** ~**s** profit-sharing. **-2.** [proveito] gain.

ludibriar [16] [ludʒi'brja(x)] *vt* to swindle.

lúdico, da ['ludʒiku, da] *adj* play *(antes de subst)*.

lufada [lu'fada] *f* gust.

lugar [lu'ga(x)] (*pl* -es) *m* **-1.** [ger] place; **em algum** ~ somewhere; **em** ~ **nenhum** nowhere; **em outro** ~ somewhere else; ~ **de nascimento** place of birth; **em primeiro** ~ [em competição] in first place; [em argumentação] in the first place; **tirar o primeiro/segundo** ~ to come first/second. **-2.** [espaço] room. **-3.** [assento] seat. **-4.** [função, ocupação] position; **colocar-se no** ~ **de alguém** to put o.s. in sb else's shoes. **-5.** [situação] **no seu** ~ **eu faria o mesmo** if I were you, I would do the same. **-6.** *loc*: **dar** ~ **a** to give rise to; **ter** ~ to take place.

➣ **em lugar de** *loc prep* instead of; **vá em meu** ~ go instead of me.

lugar-comum [lu,gaxku'mũ] (*pl* **lugares-comuns**) *m* commonplace.

lugarejo [luga'reʒu] *m* small village.

lugar-tenente [lu,ga(x)te'nẽntʃi] *m* deputy.

lúgubre ['lugubri] *adj* gloomy.

lula ['lula] *f* squid.

lumbago [lũn'bagu] *m* lumbago.

lume ['lumi] *m* **-1.** *ant* [fogo] fire. **-2.** [luz] light.

luminária [lumi'narja] *f* lamp.

luminosidade [luminozi'dadʒi] *f* brightness.

luminoso, osa [lumi'nozu, ɔza] *adj* **-1.** [que emite luz] luminous. **-2.** *fig* [raciocínio, idéia, talento] brilliant.

lunar [lu'na(x)] (*pl* -es) *adj* lunar.

lunático, ca [lu'natʃiku, ka] *adj* lunatic.

luneta [lu'neta] *f* telescope.

lupa ['lupa] *f* magnifying glass.

lúpulo ['lupulu] *m* BOT hop.

Lusaka [lu'zaka] *n* Lusaka.

lusco-fusco [,luʃku'fuʃku] *m* twilight.

lusitano, na [luzi'tanu, na] ⬦ *adj* Lusitanian. ⬦ *m, f* Lusitanian.

luso, sa [za, 'luzu] ⬦ *adj* Portuguese. ⬦ *m, f* Portuguese person.

luso-brasileiro, ra ['luzubrazi'lejru, ra] (*mpl* -ros, *fpl* -ras) ⬦ *adj* Luso-Brazilian. ⬦ *m, f* Luso-Brazilian.

lusófono, na [na, lu'zɔfonu, na] ⬦ *adj* Portuguese-speaking. ⬦ *m, f* Portuguese speaker.

lustra-móveis [,luʃtra'mɔvejʃ] *m inv* furniture polish.

lustrar [4] [luʃ'tra(x)] *vt* [móvel] to polish.

lustre ['luʃtri] *m* **-1.** [polimento] polish; **dar um** ~ **em algo** to give sthg a polish. **-2.** [luminária] chandelier.

lustroso, osa [luʃ'trozu, ɔza] *adj* shiny.

luta ['luta] *f* **-1.** [ger] struggle; ~ **de classes** class war; **ser uma** ~ **(fazer algo)** to be a struggle (to do sthg); **ir à** ~ to fight for it. **-2.** [combate] fight; ~ **armada** armed battle. **-3.** ESP: ~ **de boxe** boxing; ~ **livre** wrestling.

lutador, ra [luta'do(x), ra] ⬦ *adj* [esforçado] tough. ⬦ *m, f* **-1.** [ger] fighter. **-2.** BOXE boxer.

lutar [4] [lu'ta(x)] ⬦ *vi* **-1.** [combater]: ~ **(com/contra alguém)** to fight with/against sb; ~ **por algo** to fight for sthg. **-2.** *fig* [combater]: ~ **por/contra algo** to fight for/against sthg; ~ **com algo** [enfrentar] to battle with sthg. **-3.** [empenhar-se] to use all one's forces; ~ **(por algo/para fazer algo)** to fight (for sthg/to do sthg). **-4.** [resistir] to fight; ~ **contra algo** to fight against sthg. ⬦ *vt* [judô, caratê, capoeira, luta livre] to fight.

luterano, na [lute'ranu, na] ⬦ *adj* [pessoa, igreja, doutrina] Lutheran. ⬦ *m, f* [crente] Lutheran.

luto ['lutu] *m* mourning; **estar de** ~ **(por algo)** to be in mourning (over sthg); **estar de** ~ to be in mourning; **tirar o** ~ to come out of mourning; **pôr** ~ to go into mourning.

luva ['luva] *f* glove; **cair como uma** ~ to fit like a glove.

➣ **luvas** *fpl* [pagamento] payment.

luxação [luʃa'sãw] (*pl* -ões) *f* dislocation.

luxar [4] [lu'ʃa(x)] *vt* [deslocar] to dislocate.

Luxemburgo [luʃẽn'buxgu] *n* Luxemburg.

luxemburguês, esa [luʃẽnbux'geʃ, ezal] ⬦ *adj* Luxemburg *(antes de subst)*. ⬦ *m, f* person from Luxemburg.

luxo ['luʃu] *m* **-1.** [pompa] ostentation; **de** ~ luxury *(antes de subst)*. **-2.** [extravagância] luxury; **dar-se ao** ~ **de algo** to treat o.s. to sthg. **-3.** [afetação, cerimônia] ceremony; **cheio de** ~ full of airs and graces; **fazer** ~ to play hard to get.

luxuosidade [luʃwozi'dadʒi] *f* luxuriousness.

luxuoso, osa [lu'ʃwozu, ɔza] *adj* luxurious.

luxúria [lu'ʃurja] *f* [lascívia] lust.

luxuriante [luʃu'rjãntʃi] *adj* [vegetação] luxuriant.

luxurioso, osa [luʃu'rjozu, ɔza] *adj* = luxuriante.

luz ['luʃ] (*pl* -es) *f* **-1.** [claridade, fonte de luz] light; **acender a** ~ to turn on the light; **apagar a** ~ to turn off the light; ~ **do dia** daylight; ~ **(elétrica)** electric light; ~ **de freio** brake light; ~ **natural** natural light; **à** ~ **de vela** by candlelight. **-2.** [eletricidade] electricity; **corte de** ~ power cut;

falta ~ todos os dias aqui the electricity gets cut off here every day. **-3.** *fig* [discernimento]: **ter uma** ~ to see the light. **-4.** *loc*: **dar à** ~ to give birth.

luzidio, dia [luzi'dʒiu, dʒial *adj* gleaming.

luzir [72] [lu'zi(x)] *vi* to shine.

Lycra® ['lajkra] *f* Lycra®; **de** ~ Lycra®.

m, **M** ['emi] *m* [letra] m, M.

má [mal ▷ **mau**.

MA (*abrev de* **Estado do Maranhão**) *m* State of Maranhão.

maca ['maka] *f* MED trolley.

maçã [ma'sã] *f* apple; ~ **ácida** cooking apple; ~ **do rosto** cheek; ~ **do amor** toffee apple.

macabro, bra [ma'kabru, ma'kabra] *adj* macabre.

macacão [maka'kãw] (*pl* -ões) *m* overalls (*pl*) *UK*, coveralls (*pl*) *US*.

macaco, ca [ma'kaku, ka] *m* [animal] monkey; ~ **velho** *fig* [pessoa experiente] old hand.

◆ **macaco** *m* AUTO jack.

◆ **macaca** *f*: **estar/acordar com a macaca** *fam* to be/wake up in a foul mood.

maçada [ma'sada] *f* [situação enfadonha] bore.

macadame [maka'dãmi] *m inv* tarmac.

macambúzio, zia [makãm'buzju, zja] *adj* sullen.

maçaneta [masa'neta] *f* handle.

maçante [ma'sãntʃi] *adj* boring.

Macapá [maka'pa] *n* Macapá.

macaquear [15] [maka'kja(x)] <> *vt* [imitar] to ape, to imitate. <> *vi* to monkey about.

macaquice [maka'kisi] *f*: **fazer** ~**s** to monkey around.

maçarico [masa'riku] *m* blow torch.

maçaroca [masa'rɔka] *f* **-1.** [emaranhado] tangle. **-2.** [mixórdia] mess.

macarrão [maka'xãw] *m* **-1.** [massa] pasta. **-2.** [em tiras] spaghetti.

macarrônico, ca [maka'xoniku, ka] *adj fam* [idioma] broken.

Maceió [masej'ɔ] *n* Maceió.

macerado, da [mase'radu, da] *adj* **-1.** [esmagado] crushed. **-2.** [impregnado] marinated. **-3.** *fig* [macilento] emaciated.

macerar [4] [mase'ra(x)] *vt* **-1.** [esmagar] to crush. **-2.** [impregnar]: ~ **algo em algo** to marinate sthg in sthg. **-3.** *fig* [mortificar] to torment.

macete [ma'setʃi] *m* **-1.** [instrumento] mallet. **-2.** *fam* [truque] trick; **cheio de** ~**s** [sofisticado] full of gadgets.

machadada [maʃa'dadu] *f* axe blow.

machadinha [maʃa'dʒiɲa] *f* cleaver.

machado [ma'ʃadu] *m* axe.

machão, ona [ma'ʃãw, ɔna] (*mpl* -ões, *fpl* -s) *adj* **-1.** *pej* [ger] macho. **-2.** [corajoso] brave.

◆ **machão** *m* macho man.

◆ **machona** *f vulg* [lésbica] dyke.

machete [ma'ʃetʃi] *m* machete.

machismo [ma'ʃiʒmu] *m* machismo.

machista [ma'ʃiʃta] <> *adj* macho. <> *m* male chauvinist.

macho ['maʃu] <> *adj* **-1.** [ger] manly. **-2.** [gênero] male. <> *m* **-1.** [animal] male. **-2.** TEC tap. **-3.** [prega] box pleat.

machões [ma'ʃõjʃ] *pl* ▷ **machão**.

machona [ma'ʃona] *f* ▷ **machão**.

machucado, da [maʃu'kadu, da] *adj* **-1.** [ferido] hurt. **-2.** [contundido] injured. **-3.** [esmagado] bruised. **-4.** [lascado] scratched. **-5.** [magoado] hurt.

◆ **machucado** *m* [ferida] wound.

machucar [12] [maʃu'kax] <> *vt* **-1.** [ferir] to hurt. **-2.** [contundir] to injure. **-3.** [esmagar] to bruise. **-4.** [lascar] to scratch. **-5.** [magoar] to hurt. <> *vi* to hurt.

◆ **machucar-se** *vp* **-1.** [ferir-se] to injure o.s. **-2.** [contundir-se] to hurt o.s. **-3.** *fam* [sair-se mal]: ~**-se (com algo)** to get o.s. hurt (by sthg).

maciço, ça [ma'sisu, sa] *adj* **-1.** [sólido] massive. **-2.** [em quantidade] massive. **-3.** *fig* [sólido] solid.

◆ **maciço** *m* [cadeia montanhosa] massif.

macieira [ma'sjejra] *f* apple tree.

maciez [ma'sjeʒ] *f* softness.

macilento, ta [masi'lẽntu, ta] *adj* **-1.** [pálido] pale. **-2.** [sem brilho] dull.

macio, cia [ma'siu, sia] *adj* **-1.** [ger] smooth. **-2.** [fofo] soft.

maciota [ma'sjɔta] *f*: **na** ~ effortlessly.

maço ['masu] *m* **-1.** [de notas, folhas] bundle. **-2.** [de cartas] pack. **-3.** [de cigarros] packet.

maçom [ma'sõ] (*pl* -ns) *m* [membro da maçonaria] Freemason.

maçonaria [masona'ria] *f* freemasonry.

maconha [ma'koɲa] *f* **-1.** BOT hemp. **-2.** [droga] cannabis, to marijuana; **cigarro de** ~ spliff.

maconhado, da [mako'ɲadu, da] *adj* high (*on drugs*).

maconheiro, ra [mako'ɲejru, ra] <> *adj* [viciado] addicted. <> *m, f* **-1.** [viciado] addict. **-2.** [vendedor] pusher.

maçônico, ca [ma'soniku, ka] *adj* Masonic.

má-criação [makrja'sãw] *f* = **malcriação**.

macro ['makru] *f* COMPUT macro.

macrobiótico, ca [makro'bjɔtʃiku, ka] *adj* macrobiotic.

◆ **macrobiótica** *f* **-1.** [doutrina] macrobiotics. **-2.** [dieta] macrobiotic diet.

macrocosmo [makro'kɔʒmu] *m* macrocosm.

macroeconomia [makrwekono'mia] *f* macro-economics.

mácula ['makula] *f fig* [desonra, mancha] stain; **sem** ~ untarnished.

maculado, da [maku'ladu, da] *adj* **-1.** [manchado] stained. **-2.** [desonrado] tarnished.

macumba [ma'kũnba] *f* [espirit- religião] macumba, *Afro-Brazilian religion*; [- despacho] sacrificial offering; **fazer uma** ~ **contra alguém** to put a macumba curse on sb.

macumbeiro, ra [makũm'bejru, ra] <> *adj* [relativo à macumba] macumba *(antes de subst)*. <> *m, f* [adepto] macumba initiate.

Madagascar [madagaʃ'ka(x)] *n* Madagascar.

madame [ma'dãmi], **madama** [ma'dama] *f* **-1.** [senhora] Madam. **-2.** *irôn* [mulher rica] lady. **-3.** *irôn* [esposa] ladyship. **-4.** [cafetina] madam.

madeira [ma'dejrã] *f* wood; ~ **de lei** hardwood; **de** ~ wooden; **bater na** ~ to touch wood.

Madeira [ma'dejra] <> *n* Madeira <> *m* [vinho] Madeira (wine).

madeira-branca [ma,dejra'brãŋka] *(pl* **madeiras-brancas)** *f* softwood.

madeiramento [madejra'mẽntu] *m* [de casa, telhado] timber.

madeireiro, ra [madej'rejru, ra] <> *adj* timber *(antes de subst)*. <> *m, f* timber merchant.

➡ **madeireira** *f* [empresa] timber merchant's.

madeixa [ma'dejʃa] *f* [mecha] lock.

madona [ma'dona] *f* Madonna.

madrasta [ma'draʃta] *f* **-1.** [esposa do pai] stepmother. **-2.** *fig* [mãe má] unfit mother.

madre ['madri] *f* **-1.** [religiosa] nun. **-2.** [título] Mother; ~ **superiora** Mother Superior, Reverend Mother.

madrepérola [,madre'pɛrula] *f* mother-of-pearl.

madressilva [,madre'siwva] *f* BOT honeysuckle.

Madri [ma'dri] *n* Madrid.

madrileno, na [madri'lenu, na] <> *adj* Madrid *(antes de subst)*. <> *m & f* person from Madrid.

madrinha [ma'driŋa] *f* **-1.** [RELIG - de batismo] godmother; [- de crisma] sponsor; [- de casamento] chief bridesmaid. **-2.** *fig* [protetora, patrocinadora] patroness.

madrugada [madrù'gada] *f* early morning; **às três da** ~ at three in the morning; **de** ~ in the early hours.

madrugador, ra [madruga'do(x), ra] <> *adj* early rising. <> *m, f* early riser.

madrugar [14] [madru'ga(x)] *vi* **-1.** [acordar cedo] to wake up early. **-2.** [chegar cedo] to get in early.

maduro, ra [ma'duru, ra] *adj* **-1.** [fruto] ripe. **-2.** [pessoa, atitude, decisão] mature.

mãe ['mãj] *f* **-1.** [ger] mother; ~ **adotiva** adoptive mother; ~ **de criação** foster mother; ~ **de família** wife and mother; ~ **solteira** single mother. **-2.** [como forma de tratamento] mother. **-3.** [pessoa dedicada]: **ser uma** ~ **para alguém** to be a mother to sb.

mãe-benta [,mãj'bẽnta] *(pl* **mães-bentas)** *f* CULIN *small rice-flour cake.*

mãe-de-santo [,mãjʃdʒi'sãntu] *(pl* **mães-de-santo)** *f* [espirit] *high priestess in Afro-Brazilian religion.*

maestria [majʃ'tria] *f* mastery; **com** ~ masterfully.

maestro, trina [ma'ɛʃtru, trina] *m, f* maestro.

má-fé [,ma'fɛ] *f inv* bad faith; **agir de** ~ to act in bad faith.

máfia ['mafja] *f* **-1.** [bando do crime organizado] Mafia. **-2.** [grupo de corruptos] mafia.

mafioso, osa [ma'fjozu, ɔza] <> *adj* **-1.** [pessoa] Mafioso. **-2.** [ação] of the Mafia. <> *m, f* [membro da máfia] Mafioso.

má-formação [,mafoxma'sãw] *f* = **malformação**.

mafuá [ma'fwa] *m fam fig* [bagunça] shambles *(sg)*.

magazine [maga'zini] *m* **-1.** [loja] boutique. **-2.** [revista] magazine.

magérrimo, ma [ma'ʒɛximu, ma] *adj* [superl de magro] terribly thin, thinnest.

magia [ma'ʒia] *f* magic; ~ **negra** black magic.

mágico, ca ['maʒiku, ka] <> *adj* magic. <> *m, f* [prestidigitador] magician.

➡ **mágica** *f* **-1.** [prestidigitação] magic. **-2.** [truque] trick; **fazer mágica** to perform magic; *fig* to work miracles.

magistério [maʒiʃ'tɛrju] *m* **-1.** [profissão] teaching. **-2.** [classe dos professores] teaching profession. **-3.** [ensino] teaching.

magistrado, da [maʒiʃ'tradu, da] *m* magistrate.

magistral [maʒiʃ'traw] *(pl* **-ais)** *adj* [exemplar] masterly.

magistralmente [maʒiʃtraw'mẽntʃi] *adv* [com maestria] masterfully.

magistratura [maʒiʃtra'tura] *f* [os magistrados] magistracy.

magnanimidade [magnãnimi'dadʒi] *f* magnanimity.

magnânimo, ma [mag'nanimu, ma] *adj* magnanimous.

magnata [mag'nata] *m* magnate.

magnésia [mag'nɛzja] *f* magnesia.

magnésio [mag'nɛzju] *m* magnesium.

magnético, ca [mag'nɛtʃiku, ka] *adj* magnetic.

magnetismo [magne'tʃiʒmu] *m* magnetism.

magnetizar [4] [magnetʃi'za(x)] *vt* **-1.** [imantar] to magnetize. **-2.** *fig* [atrair] to fascinate.

magnificência [magnifi'sẽnsja] *f* [suntuosidade] magnificence.

magnífico, ca [mag'nifiku, ka] *adj* magnificent.

magnitude [magni'tudʒi] *f* [dimensão] magnitude.

magnólia [mag'nɔlja] *f* magnolia.

mago, ga ['magu, ga] <> *m, f* wizard *(f* witch). <> *adj*: **os reis** ~**s** the Three Kings.

mágoa ['magwa] *f* **-1.** [ressentimento] grief. **-2.** [tristeza] sorrow.

magoado, da [ma'gwadu, da] *adj*: **estar/ficar** ~ **(com algo)** [ressentido] to be/feel offended (by sthg); [triste] to be hurt (by sthg).

magoar [20] [ma'gwa(x)] <> *vt* [ferir] to hurt. <> *vi* [ferir] to hurt.

magrela [maˈgrɛla] *adj* skinny.

magreza [maˈgreza] *f* thinness.

magricela [magriˈsɛla] *adj* = **magrela**.

magro, gra [ˈmagru, ra] *adj* -**1.** [franzino] slim. -**2.** [sem gordura - carne, presunto] lean; [- leite] skimmed. -**3.** *(antes de subst)* *fig* [parco] meagre *UK*, meager *US*.

mai. *(abrev de maio)* May.

mail [mejo] *(pl mails)* *m COMPUT* e-mail.

mainframe [mẽjnˈfrejmi] *m COMPUT* mainframe.

maio [ˈmaju] *m* May; *veja também* **setembro**.

maiô [maˈjo] *m* swimming costume *UK*, swimsuit *US*.

maionese [majoˈnɛzi] *f* mayonnaise.

maior [maˈjɔ(x)] *(pl -es)* ◇ *adj* -**1.** [comparativo]: ~ **(do) que** [de tamanho] bigger than; [de importância] more important than; [de número] larger than. -**2.** [superlativo]: **o/a** ~ ... [de tamanho] the biggest ...; [de importância] the highest ...; [de número] the largest ...; **ser o** ~ **barato** [pessoa] to be really cool; [coisa] to be really great. -**3.** [adulto]: **ser** ~ **(de idade)** to be of age; **ser** ~ **de 21 anos** to be over 21. -**4.** *MÚS*: **em dó** ~ in C major. ◇ *mf* -**1.** [de tamanho]: **o/a** ~ the largest. -**2.** *fam* [superior]: **ser o/a** ~ to be the best. -**3.** [adulto] adult; **ser de** ~ to be an adult; **ser** ~ **e vacinado** *fam* to be grown up. ◇ *f* [notícia]: **você já soube da** ~? have you heard the latest?; **tenho a** ~ **para contar** have I got sthg to tell you!

maioral [majoˈraw] *(pl -ais)* *mf*: **o** ~ the boss; **ele se acha o** ~ he thinks he's the greatest.

maioria [majoˈria] *f* majority; **a** ~ **de** the majority of; ~ **absoluta** absolute majority; **a** ~ **das pessoas acha** ... the majority think ...

maioridade [majoriˈdadʒi] *f* age of majority; **atingir a** ~ to come of age.

mais [ˈmajʃ] ◇ *adv* -**1.** [em comparações] more; **a Ana é** ~ **alta/inteligente** Ana is taller/more intelligent; ~ **do que** more than; ~ ... **do que** ... more ... than ...; **bebeu um copo a** ~! he's had one too many!; **deram-me dinheiro a** ~ they gave me too much money; **é** ~ **alta do que eu** she's taller than me. -**2.** [como superlativo]: **o/a** ~ ... the most ...; **o** ~ **engraçado/inteligente** the funniest/most intelligent. -**3.** [indica adição] any more; **não necessito de** ~ **trabalho** I don't need any more work; **não necessito de** ~ **ninguém** I don't need anyone else. -**4.** [indica intensidade]: **que dia** ~ **feliz!** what a great day!; **que casa** ~ **feia!** what a horrible house! -**5.** [indica preferência]: **vale** ~ **a pena ficar em casa** it would be better to stay at home; **gosto** ~ **de comida chinesa** I prefer Chinese food. -**6.** [em locuções]: **de** ~ **a** ~ [ainda por cima] what's more; ~ **ou menos** more or less; **por** ~ **que se esforce** however hard he tries; **sem** ~ **nem menos** for no apparent reason; **uma vez** ~, ~ **uma vez** once *ou* yet again. ◇ *adj inv* -**1.** [em comparações] more; **eles têm** ~ **dinheiro** they have more money; **está** ~ **calor hoje** it's hotter today; ~ ... **do que** more ... than. -**2.** [como superlativo] (the)

most; **a pessoa que** ~ **discos vendeu** the person who sold (the) most records; **os que** ~ **dinheiro têm** those who have (the) most money. -**3.** [indica adição] more; ~ **água, por favor** I'd like some more water, please; ~ **alguma coisa?** anything else?; **tenho** ~ **três dias de férias** I have another three days of vacation left. ◇ *conj* and; **quero uma sopa** ~ **pão com manteiga** I'd like some soup and some bread and butter. ◇ *prep* [indica soma] plus; **dois** ~ **dois são quatro** two plus two is four.

maisena [majˈzena] *f*: **de** ~ cornflour *UK*, cornstarch *US*.

mais-valia [ˌmajʃvaˈlia] *(pl mais-valias)* *f ECON* surplus value.

maître [ˈmetri] *m* head waiter.

maiúsculo, la [maˈjuʃkulu, la] *adj*: **letra maiúscula** capitals *(pl)*.

➤ **maiúscula** *f* capital letter.

majestade [maʒeʃˈtadʒi] *f* majesty.

➤ **Majestade** *f*: **Sua Majestade** Your Majesty, His Majesty, Her Majesty.

majestoso, osa [maʒeʃˈtozu, ɔza] *adj* [grandioso] majestic.

major [maˈʒɔ(x)] *(pl -res)* *m MIL* major.

majoração [maʒoraˈsãw] *f* increase.

majorar [4] [maʒoˈra(x)] *vt* to increase.

majoritário, ria [maʒoriˈtarju, rja] *adj* majority *(antes de subst)*; **a opinião majoritária é que** ... the majority opinion is that ...

mal [ˈmaw] *(pl -es)* *m* -**1.** [ger] evil; **cortar o** ~ **pela raiz** to stop things going from bad to worse; **a luta entre o bem e o** ~ the fight between good and evil. -**2.** [dano] damage; **fazer** ~ **(a)** [à saúde] to damage; **o cigarro faz** ~ **à saúde** smoking damages your health; **fazer** ~ **a alguém** [afetar] to upset sb; [deflorar] to deflower sb; **você fez** ~ **em se divorciar** you did the wrong thing in getting divorced; **não faz** ~ it doesn't matter; **querer** ~ **a alguém** to wish sb ill. -**3.** [doença] illness. -**4.** [sofrimento] stress. -**5.** [inconveniente]: **o** ~ **é que** ... the problem is that ... -**6.** [opinião desfavorável]: **falar** ~ **de alguém/algo** to speak ill of sb/sthg.

➤ **mal** ◇ *adv* -**1.** [ger] badly; **dar-se** ~ **(em algo)** to do badly (in sthg); **de** ~ **a pior** from bad to worse; ~ **e porcamente** lousily. -**2.** [quase não]: **ele** ~ **consegue dormir** he barely manages to sleep. -**3.** [injustamente] wrongly. -**4.** [rudemente] rudely. -**5.** [de maneira desfavorável] unfavourably; **levar alguém/algo a** ~ to take sb/sthg badly; **não me leve a** ~, **mas** ... don't get me wrong, but ... -**6.** *PSIC* [doente] down; **estar** ~ to feel down; **passar** ~ to feel sick. ◇ *conj* just; ~ **cheguei, ele saiu** just as I arrived, he left.

mala [ˈmala] *f* -**1.** [recipiente] suitcase; **fazer as** ~**s** to pack one's bags; ~ **de mão** hand luggage. -**2.** *AUTO* boot *UK*, trunk *US*. -**3.** *COM*: ~ **direta** mail order. -**4.** [serviço]: ~ **aérea** air mail; ~ **postal** mail. -**5.** *fam pej* [pessoa chata]: **ser uma** ~ to be a pain.

malabarismo [malaba'riʒmu] *m* **-1.** [arte] juggling. **-2.** *fig* [habilidade] deftness; **fazer ~s** to juggle.

malabarista [malaba'riʃta] *mf* juggler.

mal-acabado, da [ˌmawaka'badu] *adj* **-1.** [construção, móvel] poorly finished. **-2.** [corpo] in poor shape.

mala-direta [ˌmaladʒi'rɛta] (*pl* **malas diretas**) *f* [marketing] direct marketing.

mal-afamado, da [mawafa'madu, da] *adj* notorious.

mal-agradecido, da [mawagrade'sidu, da] (*pl* **-s**) ⟨⟩ *adj* ungrateful. ⟨⟩ *m, f:* **o ~ nem sequer me agradeceu** he's so ungrateful he didn't even thank me.

malagueta [mala'geta] *m* chilli pepper.

malaio, ia [ma'laju, ja] ⟨⟩ *adj* Malay. ⟨⟩ *m, f* Malay.

➡ **malaio** *m* [língua] Malay.

mal-ajambrado, da [mawaʒãm'bradu, da] (*pl* **-s**) *adj* scruffy.

malandragem [malãn'draʒẽ] (*pl* **-ns**), **malandrice** [malãn'drisi] *f* **-1.** [patifaria] doubledealing. **-2.** [astúcia] cunning. **-3.** [vadiagem] vagrancy. **-4.** [preguiça] laziness.

malandro, dra [ma'lãndru, dra] ⟨⟩ *adj* **-1.** [patife] crooked. **-2.** [astuto] sharp. **-3.** [vadio] vagrant. **-4.** [preguiçoso] idle. ⟨⟩ *m, f* **-1.** [patife] crook. **-2.** [astuto] swindler. **-3.** [vadio] vagrant. **-4.** [preguiçoso] layabout.

mal-apanhado, da [mawapa'ɲadu, da] (*pl* **-s**) *adj* = mal-apessoado.

mal-apessoado, da [mawape'swadu, da] (*pl* **-s**) *adj* unpleasant-looking.

malária [ma'larja] *f* malaria.

mal-arrumado, da [mawaxu'madu, da] (*pl* **-s**) *adj* untidy.

mala-sem-alça ['malasẽ'sawa] (*pl* **malas-sem-alça**) *mf fam* bore.

Malásia [ma'lazja] *n* Malaysia.

mal-assombrado, da [mawasõm'bradu, da] (*pl* **-s**) *adj* haunted.

malbaratar [4] [mawbara'ta(x)] *vt* to squander.

malcheiroso, osa [mawʃej'rozu, ɔza] *adj* foulsmelling.

malcomportado, da [mawkõmpox'tadu, da] *adj* badly behaved.

malconceituado, da [mawkõnsej'twadu, da] *adj* badly thought of.

malcriação [mawkrja'sãw] (*pl* **-ões**), **má-criação** [makrja'sãw] (*pl* **-ões**) *f* bad manners; **respondeu com ~** he replied rudely; **fazer ~** to behave badly.

malcriado, da [mawkri'adu, da] ⟨⟩ *adj* illmannered. ⟨⟩ *m, f* yob.

maldade [maw'dadʒi] *f* **-1.** [ger] cruelty; **bater em criança é uma ~** it's cruel to hit children; **ser uma ~** to be cruel. **-2.** [malícia] malice.

maldição [mawdi'sãw] (*pl* **-ões**) *f* curse.

maldito, ta [maw'dʒitu, ta] ⟨⟩ *pp* ▷ maldizer. ⟨⟩ *adj* **-1.** [amaldiçoado] damned. **-2.** [funesto] tragic. **-3.** [cruel] cruel. **-4.** (*antes de subst) fam* [para enfatizar]: **essa chuva maldita** this bloody rain.

maldizer [29] [mawdʒi'ze(x)] ⟨⟩ *vt* to curse. ⟨⟩ *vi:* **~ de algo** to curse sthg.

maldoso, osa [maw'dozu, ɔza] *adj* **-1.** [malvado] nasty. **-2.** *fig* [mordaz] vicious.

maleável [ma'ljavew] (*pl* **-eis**) *adj* malleable.

maledicência [malidʒi'sẽnsja] *f* **-1.** [ação] slander. **-2.** [difamação] defamation.

maledicente [malidʒi'sẽntʃi] ⟨⟩ *adj* slanderous. ⟨⟩ *m, f* slanderer.

mal-educado, da [ˌmaledu'kadu, da] ⟨⟩ *adj* rude. ⟨⟩ *m, f:* **o ~** the rude man; **a malcriada** the rude woman.

malefício [male'fisju] *m* **-1.** [ação] wrong. **-2.** [dano] harm.

maléfico, ca [ma'lɛfiku, ka] *adj* harmful.

mal-e-mal ['mawimaw] *adv* extremely poorly.

mal-encarado, da [ˌmalẽŋka'radu, da] (*pl* **-s**) *adj* shady.

mal-entendido [ˌmawẽntẽn'dʒidul] (*pl* **mal-entendidos**) ⟨⟩ *adj* [mal interpretado] misunderstood. ⟨⟩ *m* misunderstanding.

males ['maliʃ] *pl* ▷ mal.

mal-estar [mawiʃ'ta(x)] (*pl* **mal-estares**) *m* **-1.** [indisposição] upset. **-2.** *fig* [embaraço] uneasiness.

maleta [ma'leta] *f* small suitcase.

malevolência [malevo'lẽnsja] *f* malevolence.

malevolente *adj* [malevo'lẽntʃi] malevolent.

malévolo, la [ma'lɛvolu, la] *adj* malevolent.

malfadado, da [mawfa'dadu, da] *adj* unlucky.

malfeito, ta [mal'fejtu, ta] *adj* **-1.** [mal-acabado] sloppy. **-2.** [deforme] misshapen. **-3.** *fig* [injusto] unjust.

malfeitor, ra [mawfej'to(x), ra] (*mpl* **-es**, *fpl* **-s**) *m* **-1.** [quem comete delito] wrongdoer. **-2.** [bandido] criminal.

malformação [mawfoxma'sãw] (*pl* **-ões**) *f* malformation.

malgrado [maw'gradu] *prep* despite.

malha ['maʎa] *f* **-1.** [tecido] jersey; **de ~** jersey; **roupas de ~** knitwear. **-2.** [de rede, tecido] mesh. **-3.** [de balé] leotard. **-4.** [suéter] sweatshirt.

mal-habituado, da [malabi'twadu, da] (*pl* **-s**) *adj* poorly trained.

malhação [maʎa'sãw] (*pl* **-ões**) *f fam* [crítica violenta] panning.

malhado, da [ma'ʎadu, ada] *adj* [animal] mottled.

malhar [4] [ma'ʎa(x)] ⟨⟩ *vt* **-1.** [ger] to beat. **-2.** [criticar] to knock. ⟨⟩ *vi* [fazer ginástica] *fam* to work out.

malharia [maʎa'ria] *f* **-1.** [loja] knitwear shop. **-2.** [fábrica] textile mill. **-3.** [artigos] knitted goods.

malho ['maʎu] *m* mallet.

mal-humorado, da [mawumo'radu, da] *adj* **-1.** [que tem mau humor] sullen. **-2.** [ranzinza] grumpy.

malícia [ma'lisja] *f* **-1.** [intenção maldosa] malice. **-2.** [intenção licenciosa] licentiousness; **pôr ~ em**

algo to misinterpret sthg. -**3.** [manha, marotice] cunning.

malicioso, osa [mali'sjozu, ɔza] adj -**1.** [maldoso] malicious. -**2.** [que vê licenciosidade] licentious. -**3.** [manhoso] sly.

malignidade [maligni'dadʒil f -**1.** MED malignancy. -**2.** [ação] malice.

maligno, gna [ma'lignu, gna] adj -**1.** [mau] malicious. -**2.** [nocivo] harmful. -**3.** MED malignant.

má-língua [,ma'lĩŋgwa] (pl **más-língua**) f scandalmonger; **dizem as más-línguas que** ... the scandalmongers are saying that ...

mal-intencionado, da [,mawĩntẽnsjo'nadu, da] (pl -**s**) adj malicious.

malmequer [mawmi'kɛ(x)] (pl -**es**) m marigold.

malnutrido, da [mawnu'tridu, da] adj malnourished.

maloca [ma'lɔka] f -**1.** [cabana] teepee. -**2.** [aldeia] encampment. -**3.** [esconderijo] hideout.

malogrado, da [malo'gradu, da] adj thwarted.

malograr [4] [malo'gra(x)] <> vt to thwart. <> vi to fall through.

malogro [ma'logru] m failure.

malote [ma'lɔtʃi] m -**1.** [bolsa] pouch. -**2.** [correspondência] mail. -**3.** [serviço] courier.

malpassado, da [mawpa'sadu, da] adj rare.

malproporcionado, da [mawpropoxsjo'nadu, da] adj out of proportion.

malquisto, ta [maw'kiʃtu, ta] adj disliked.

malsucedido, da [mawsuse'dʒidu, da] adj unsuccessful.

Malta ['mawta] n Malta.

malte ['mawtʃi] m malt.

maltês, esa [maw'teʃ, eza] <> adj Maltese. <> m, f Maltese.

maltrapilho, lha [mawtra'piʎu, ʎa] <> adj ragged. <> m, f -**1.** [mendigo] beggar. -**2.** [criança] urchin.

maltratar [4] [mawtra'ta(x)] vt -**1.** [fisicamente] to mistreat. -**2.** [verbalmente] to abuse. -**3.** [tratar com desleixo] to mishandle.

maluco, ca [ma'luku, ka] <> adj -**1.** PSIC crazy. -**2.** [adoidado] nuts. -**3.** [absurdo] mad. -**4.** [aficionado]: **ser ~ por algo** to be crazy about sthg. <> m, f PSIC insane.

maluquice [malu'kisi] f -**1.** PSIC madness. -**2.** [excentricidade]: **ser uma ~** to be madness.

malvadeza [mawva'deza], **malvadez** [mawva'deʒ] f wickedness.

malvado, da [maw'vadu, da] <> adj wicked. <> m, f thug.

malversação [mawvexsa'sãw] (pl -**ões**) f -**1.** [desvio]: **~ (de algo)** embezzlement (of sthg). -**2.** [mau gerenciamento] mismanagement.

Malvinas [maw'vinaʃ] npl: **as (ilhas) ~** the Falkland Islands, the Falklands.

malvisto, ta [maw'viʃtu, ta] adj -**1.** [malconceituado] badly thought of. -**2.** [antipatizado] disliked.

mama ['mãma] f breast.

mamadeira [mama'dejra] f baby's bottle.

mamãe [mã'mãj] f mummy, mum.

mamão [ma'mãw] (pl -**ões**) m papaya.

mamar [4] [ma'ma(x)] <> vt [sugar] to suck. <> vi -**1.** [alimentar-se] to feed; **dar de ~ a alguém** to breastfeed sb. -**2.** fig [tirar lucros ilícitos]: **ele está mamando nas tetas do governo** he's milking the government dry.

mamário, ria [ma'marju, rja] adj mammary.

mamata [ma'mata] f -**1.** fam [proveito ilícito] racket. -**2.** [facilidade] breeze; **ser uma ~** to be a piece of cake.

mambembe [mãn'bẽnbi] <> adj [circo, teatro] second-rate. <> m [grupo teatral ambulante] travelling theatre.

mameluco, ca [mame'luku, ka] m mixed race person of native Indian and European extraction.

mamífero, ra [ma'miferu, ra] adj mammalian.
➠ **mamífero** m mammal.

mamilo [ma'milu] m nipple.

maminha [ma'miɲa] f [carne] rump steak.

mamoeiro [ma'mwejru] m papaya tree.

mamões [ma'mõjʃ] pl ➠ **mamão**.

mamografia [mãmogra'fia] f mammography.

manada [ma'nada] f herd.

Manágua [ma'nagwa] n Managua.

manancial [manãn'sjaw] (pl -**ais**) m -**1.** [fonte] spring. -**2.** fig [origem] source.

Manaus [ma'nawʃ] n Manaus.

mancada [mãŋ'kada] f -**1.** [erro] mistake. -**2.** [gafe] gaffe; **dar uma ~** to make a gaffe.

mancar [12] [mãŋ'ka(x)] vi [coxear] to limp.
➠ **mancar-se** vp fam [desconfiar] to take a hint.

mancha ['mãnʃa] f -**1.** [ger] stain. -**2.** [em pintura] blotch. -**3.** [marca] mark.

manchado, da [mã'ʃadu, da] adj -**1.** [com manchas] stained. -**2.** [pintura] blotched. -**3.** [malhado] mottled.

manchar [4] [mã'ʃa(x)] vt -**1.** [ger] to stain. -**2.** [deixar marca] to mark.

manchete [mãn'ʃetʃil f headline; **o acidente virou ~ em todo o país** the accident hit the headlines nationwide.

manco, ca ['mãŋku, ka] <> adj lame. <> m, f disabled person.

mancomunado, da [mãŋkomu'nadu, da] adj hand in glove.

mancomunar [4] [mãŋkomu'na(x)] vt: **~ algo (com alguém)** to collude in sthg (with sb).
➠ **mancomunar-se** vp: **~-se (com alguém)** to collude (with sb).

mandachuva [mãnda'ʃuva] mf -**1.** [pessoa poderosa] boss. -**2.** [chefe, líder] chief.

mandado [mãn'dadu] m -**1.** [autorização] order. -**2.** JUR injunction; **~ de despejo** eviction order; **~ de prisão** arrest warrant; **~ de segurança** injunction.

mandamento [mãnda'mẽntul m -**1.** [preceito] order. -**2.** RELIG commandment.

mandante [mãn'dãntʃil mf -**1.** JUR person who grants a mandate. -**2.** [instigador] instigator.

mandão, ona [mãn'dãw, ɔna] (*mpl* -ões) *adj fam* [autoritário] bossy.

mandar [4] [mãn'da(x)] ⟨⟩ *vt* -**1.**: ~ alguém fazer *ou* que alguém faça algo [ordenar] to tell sb to do sthg; [recomendar] to order sb to do sthg; ~ chamar alguém to send for sb; ~ dizer que to send word that; ~ embora to send away. -**2.** [enviar] to send. ⟨⟩ *vi* -**1.** [chefiar, dominar]: ~ (em alguém/algo) to order (sb/sthg) around; no escritório, é ele quem manda he's the one who gives the orders in the office. -**2.** *fam* [noticiar]: o que é que você manda? what can I do for you?

➤ **mandar-se** *vp* -**1.** *fam* [ir-se embora] to get going. -**2.** [fugir] to take off.

mandarim [mãnda'rĩ] (*pl* -ns) *m* -**1.** [título] mandarin. -**2.** [dialeto] Mandarin.

mandatário, ria [mãnda'tarju, rja] *m* -**1.** [representante] deputy, representative. -**2.** [procurador] defence lawyer *UK*, defense lawyer *US*, counsel for the defence *UK*, defense attorney *US*.

mandato [mãn'datu] *m* -**1.** [procuração] mandate. -**2.** [missão] duty. -**3.** [ordem] order. -**4.** *POL* term of office.

mandíbula [mãn'dʒibula] *f* jaw.

mandinga [mãn'dʒĩga] *f* witchcraft.

mandioca [mãn'dʒɔka] *f* cassava, manioc.

mando ['mãndu] *m* -**1.** [autoridade] authority. -**2.** [ordem] order; a ~ de at the orders of.

mandões [mãn'dõjʃ] *mpl* ⊳ **mandão**.

mandona [mãn'dona] *f* ⊳ **mandão**.

maneira [4] [ma'nejra] *f* manner; à ~ (de) like; de ~ nenhuma *ou* alguma no way; não volto àquele clube de ~ alguma! no way am I going back to that club!; de ~ que so that; de qualquer ~ [sem cuidado] anyhow; [a qualquer preço] at whatever cost; [de todo modo] whatever; de qualquer ~ será útil it'll be useful, whatever.

➤ **maneiras** *fpl* manners; boas ~s good manners; ter boas ~s to have good manners.

maneirar [4] [manej'ra(x)] ⟨⟩ *vt* -**1.** *fam* [contornar] to sort out. -**2.** [controlar] to control. ⟨⟩ *vi* -**1.** [acomodar as coisas] to get sorted. -**2.** [controlar-se] to control o.s.

maneiro, ra [ma'nejru, ra] *adj* -**1.** [de fácil uso] simple. -**2.** [fácil] easy. -**3.** *fam* [legal] great.

manejar [4] [mane'ʒa(x)] *vt* -**1.** [ger] to control. -**2.** [manusear] to handle. -**3.** [administrar] to manage.

manejável [mane'ʒavɛw] (*pl* -eis) *adj* -**1.** [fácil de usar] simple. -**2.** [controlável] controllable.

manejo [ma'neʒu] *m* -**1.** [manuseio] handling. -**2.** [uso] use. -**3.** [administração] management.

manequim [mane'kĩ] (*pl* -ns) ⟨⟩ *m* [boneco] dummy. ⟨⟩ *mf* [pessoa] model.

maneta [ma'neta] *adj* one-handed.

manga ['mãga] *f* -**1.** [de roupa] sleeve; em ~s de camisa in shirt-sleeves. -**2.** [fruto] mango. -**3.** [filtro] filter. -**4.** *loc*: pôr as ~s de fora to show one's true self; arregaçar as ~s to roll up one's sleeves.

manganês [mãga'neʃ] *m* manganese.

mangue ['mãgi] *m* -**1.** [terreno] mangrove swamp. -**2.** [planta] mangrove.

mangueira [mãg'gejra] *f* -**1.** *BOT* mango tree. -**2.** [cano] hose.

manha ['mãɲa] *f* -**1.** [habilidade] skill. -**2.** [esperteza] shrewdness. -**3.** *fam* [choro, birra] tantrum; fazer ~ to throw a tantrum.

manhã [mã'ɲã] (*pl* -s) *f* morning; amanhã de ~ tomorrow morning; de ~ cedo in the early morning; de *ou* pela ~ in the morning; hoje de ~ this morning; seis horas da ~ six o'clock in the morning.

manhãzinha [mãɲã'ziɲa] *f*: de ~ early in the morning.

manhoso, osa [ma'ɲozu, ɔza] *adj* -**1.** [esperto] sly. -**2.** [chorão, birrento] whingeing.

mania [ma'nia] *f* -**1.** *PSIC* mania; ~ de perseguição persecution complex. -**2.** [gosto exagerado] obsession; ~ de algo obsession with sthg. -**3.** [hábito] habit; ter ~ de fazer algo to have a habit of doing sthg. -**4.** [mau hábito] bad habit. -**5.** [peculiaridade, excentricidade] quirk.

maníaco, ca [ma'niaku, ka] ⟨⟩ *adj* -**1.** *PSIC* maniacal. -**2.** [fanático]: ser ~ por algo to be manic about sthg. ⟨⟩ *m, f PSIC* maniac; ~ sexual sex maniac.

maníaco-depressivo, maníaca-depressiva [ma,niakudepre'sivu, ma,niakadepre'siva] ⟨⟩ *adj* manic-depressive. ⟨⟩ *m, f* manic-depressive.

manicômio [mani'komju] *m* lunatic asylum.

manicuro, ra [mani'kuru, ra] *m, f* manicurist.

manicure [mani'kuri] *f* manicure.

manifestação [manifeʃta'sãw] (*pl* -ões) *f* -**1.** [ger] manifestation. -**2.** [expressão] display.

manifestadamente [manifeʃtada'mẽntʃi] *adv* quite clearly.

manifestante [manifeʃ'tãntʃi] *mf* demonstrator.

manifestar [4] [manifeʃ'ta(x)] *vt* -**1.** [exprimir] to express. -**2.** [revelar] to display.

➤ **manifestar-se** *vp* -**1.** [revelar-se] to reveal o.s. -**2.** [pronunciar-se]: ~-se (sobre/a favor de/contra algo) to express an opinion (on/in favour of/against sthg).

manifesto, ta [mani'fɛʃtu, ta] *adj* manifest.

➤ **manifesto** *m* manifesto.

Manila [ma'nila] *n* Manila.

manilha [ma'niʎa] *f* [tubo] pipe.

manipulação [manipula'sãw] *f* -**1.** [com as mãos] handling. -**2.** [ger] manipulation. -**3.** *FARM* preparation.

manipulador, ra [manipula'do(x), ra] *adj* manipulative.

manipular [manipu'la(x)] *vt* -**1.** [ger] to manipulate. -**2.** [com as mãos] to handle. -**3.** *FARM* to prepare.

maniqueísmo [manike'iʒmu] *m* Manicheism.

maniqueísta [manike'iʃta] ⟨⟩ *adj* seeing things in black and white. ⟨⟩ *mf* Manichaean.

manivela [mani'vɛla] *f* crank.

manjado, da [mã'ʒadu, da] *adj fam* well-known.

manjar [4] [mã'ʒa(x)] ⬦ *m* [iguaria] delicacy. ⬦ *vt fam* **-1.** [compreender] to grasp. **-2.** [observar] to watch. ⬦ *vi* [conhecer]: ~ **de algo** to know about sthg.

manjar-branco [mãn,ʒax'brãŋku] (*pl* **manjares-brancos**) *m* blancmange.

manjedoura [mãnʒe'dora] *f* manger.

manjericão [mãnʒeri'kãw] *m* basil.

manjerona [mãnʒe'rona] *f* marjoram.

mano, na ['manu, na] *m,f fam* **-1.** [irmão] brother (sister). **-2.** *fam* [camarada, amigo] buddy.

manobra [ma'nɔbra] *f* **-1.** [ger] manoeuvre *UK*, maneuver *US*. **-2.** *fig* [manipulação] manipulation.

➥ **manobras** *fpl* MIL manoeuvres *UK*, maneuvers *US*.

manobrar [mano'bra(x)] ⬦ *vt* **-1.** [manejar] to manoeuvre *UK*, to maneuver *US*. **-2.** [dirigir] to direct. **-3.** *fig* [manipular] to manipulate. ⬦ *vi* MIL to manoeuvre *UK*, to maneuver *US*.

manobrista [mano'briʃta] *mf* **-1.** [de carro] valet *UK*, car jockey *US*. **-2.** [de trem] shunter.

mansão [mãn'sãw] (*pl* **-ões**) *f* mansion.

mansidão [mãnsi'dãw] *f* **-1.** [brandura] gentleness; **ele falava com** ~ he spoke gently. **-2.** [tranqüilidade] calmness.

mansinho, nha [mã'siɲu, ɲal] *adj* [diminutivo de manso] gentle.

➥ **de mansinho** *loc adv* **-1.** [de leve] gently. **-2.** [sorrateiramente]: **entrar/sair de** ~ to creep in/out.

manso, sa ['mãsu, sa] *adj* **-1.** [brando] gentle. **-2.** [tranqüilo] calm. **-3.** [domesticado] tame.

mansões [man'sõjʃ] *pl* ⊳ **mansão**.

manta ['mãnta] *f* **-1.** [cobertor] blanket. **-2.** [xale] shawl. **-3.** [de carne seca] cut.

manteiga [mãn'tejga] *f* butter; **passar** ~ **em algo** to spread butter on sthg; ~ **de cacau** cocoa butter; ~ **derretida** *fam fig* cry baby.

manteigueira [mãntej'gejra] *f* butter dish.

mantenedor, ra [mãntene'do(x), ra] *m, f* **-1.** [de filho, casa] supporter. **-2.** [de máquina] service engineer.

manter [4] [mãn'te(x)] *vt* **-1.** [ger] to keep. **-2.** [em bom estado - máquina] to service; [- casa, saúde] to keep. **-3.** [família] to support. **-4.** [opinião, posição] to hold. **-5.** [relações] to maintain; ~ **boas relações com alguém** to maintain a good relationship with sb.

➥ **manter-se** *vp* **-1.** [sustentar-se] to support o.s. **-2.** [permanecer] to remain; **~-se a par de algo** to keep abreast of sthg.

mantilha [mãn'tʃiʎa] *f* **-1.** [véu] veil. **-2.** [manta] shawl.

mantimentos [mãntʃi'mẽntuʃ] *m* provisions (*pl*).

manto ['mãntu] *m* **-1.** [vestimenta] cloak. **-2.** [de reis] robe. **-3.** *fig* [simulação] smokescreen.

mantô [mãn'to] *m* coat.

manual [ma'nwaw] (*pl* **-ais**) ⬦ *adj* manual; **ter habilidade** ~ to be good with one's hands. ⬦ *m* manual.

manufatura [manufa'tura] *f* [fabricação] manufacture.

manufaturado, da [manufatu'radu, da] *adj* manufactured.

manufaturar [manufatu'ra(x)] *vt* to manufacture.

manuscrito, ta [manuʃ'kritu] *adj* handwritten.

➥ **manuscrito** *m* manuscript.

manusear [manu'zea(x)] *vt* **-1.** [manejar] to handle. **-2.** [folhear] to thumb.

manuseio [manu'zeju] *m* handling.

manutenção [manutẽn'sãw] *f* **-1.** [ger] maintenance. **-2.** [da casa] upkeep. **-3.** [da família] support.

mão ['mãw] (*pl* **mãos**) *f* **-1.** [ger] hand; **à** ~ [perto] at hand; [com a mão] by hand; **feito à** ~ handmade; **à** ~ **armada** armed; **dar a** ~ **a alguém** to hold sb's hand; **de** ~**s dadas** hand in hand; **de primeira** ~ firsthand; **de segunda** ~ second-hand; **entregar algo em** ~**s** to deliver sthg by hand; ~**s ao alto!** hands up!; ~**s à obra!** let's get to work!; **pôr a** ~ **em algo** to lay one's hands on sthg; **ter a** ~ **pesada** to be clumsy; **ter algo em** ~ to have sthg to hand. **-2.** [no trânsito]: **esta rua dá** ~ **para a praia** this street takes you to the beach; **fora de** ~ out of the way; ~ **dupla** two-way; ~ **única** one-way; **uma rua de** ~ **dupla/única** a two-way/one-way street. **-3.** [de tinta] coat. **-4.** [habilidade]: **com** ~ **de mestre** with a master touch; **ter uma** ~ **boa para algo** to be good at sthg. **-5.** [poder, controle]: **estar nas** ~**s de alguém** to be in sb's hands; **estar em boas** ~**s** to be in good hands. **-6.** *loc*: **abrir** ~ **de algo** to give sthg up; **agüentar a** ~ *fam* [suportar] to hold out; [aguardar] to hang on; **dar a** ~ **à palmatória** to admit one's mistake; **ficar na** ~ to be duped; **forçar a** ~ to get nasty; **lançar** ~ **de algo** to make use of sthg; **largar a** ~ **em alguém** to hit sb; **largar alguém/algodo** ~ to wash one's hands of sb/ sthg; **pedir a** ~ **de alguém (em casamento)** to ask for sb's hand (in marriage); **passar a** ~ **em algo** [roubar] to nick sthg; **pôr a** ~ **no fogo por alguém** to stand up for sb; **ser uma** ~ **na roda** to be a great help; **de** ~ **beijada** bucksheet; **dar uma** ~ **a alguém** to give sb a hand; **preciso de uma** ~ I need a hand.

mão-aberta [ˌmãwa'bɛxta] (*pl* **mãos-abertas**) *adj* generous.

mão-boba [mãw'bɔba] (*pl* **-s**) ⬦ *f fam* [com propósito libidinoso]: **passar a** ~ **em alguém** to touch sb up. ⬦ *m* perv.

mão-cheia [ˌmãw'ʃeja] *f*: **de** ~ first-rate.

mão-de-obra [ˌmãw'dʒɔbra] (*pl* **mãos-de-obra**) *f* **-1.** [trabalho, custo] labour *UK*, labor *US*; **ser uma** ~ *fig* to be hard work. **-2.** [trabalhadores] workforce; ~ **especializada** skilled labour.

mão-de-vaca [mãwdʒi'vaka] (*pl* **-s**) *f fam* [avaro] skinflint.

mão-leve [ˌmãw'lɛvi] (*pl* **mãos-leves**) *mf* pilferer.

maoísta [maw'iʃta] ⬦ *adj* Maoist. ⬦ *mf* Maoist.

mapa ['mapa] *m* map; **sumir do** ~ *fam fig* to disappear off the face of the earth.

mapa-múndi [ˌmapaˈmũndʒil (*pl* **mapas-múndi**) *m* world map.
Maputo [maˈputul *n* Maputo.
maquete [maˈkɛtʃil *f* model.
maquiado, da [maˈkjadu, dal *adj* [com maquiagem] made-up.
maquiador, ra [makjaˈdo(x), ral, **maquilador, ra** [makilaˈdo(x), ral *m, f* make-up artist.
maquiagem [maˈkjaʒẽl (*pl* -ns) *f* -1. [ger] make-up; **ele se encarregou da** ~ he was in charge of make-up. -2. [disfarce]: ~ **financeira** financial cover-up.
maquiar [16] [maˈkjax] *vt* -1. [pintar] to make up. -2. *fig* [mascarar] to cover up.
➡ **maquiar-se** *vp* [pintar-se] to put on one's make-up.
maquiavélico, ca [makjaˈvɛliku, kal *adj* Machiavellian.
maquilador, ra [makilaˈdo(x), ral *m, f* = **maquiador.**
maquilagem [makiˈlaʒẽl *f* = **maquiagem.**
maquilar [4] [makiˈla(x)] *vt* [pintar] to make up.
➡ **maquilar-se** *vp* [pintar-se] to put on one's make-up.
máquina [ˈmakinal *f* -1. [ger] machine; **bater** *ou* **escrever à** ~ to type; **costurar à** ~ to machine-sew; **escrito à** ~ typewritten; **feito à** ~ machine-made; ~ **de calcular** calculator; ~ **de costura** sewing machine; ~ **de escrever** typewriter; ~ **fotográfica** camera; ~ **de lavar (roupa)** washing machine. -2. [locomotora] engine; ~ **a vapor** steam engine. -3. *fig* [de estado, partido *etc*] machinery.
➡ **máquinas** *fpl* machinery.
maquinação [makinaˈsãwl (*pl* -ões) *f* machination.
maquinar [4] [makiˈna(x)] ◇ *vt* to plot. ◇ *vi:* ~ **contra alguém/algo** to plot against sb/sthg.
maquinaria [makiˈnarjal, **maquinaria** [makiˈnarial *f* [máquinas] machinery.
maquinário [makiˈnarjul *m* = **maquinária.**
maquinista [makiˈniʃtal *mf* -1. *FERRO* engine driver. -2. *TEATRO* stagehand.
mar [ˈma(x)] (*pl* -es) *m* sea; **em pleno** ~ on the high seas; **fazer-se ao** ~ to set sail; ~ **aberto** open sea; **por** ~ by sea; ~ **Morto** Dead Sea; ~ **Negro** Black Sea; ~ **do Norte** North Sea; ~ **de rosas** [mar calmo] calm sea; *fig* bed of roses; **nem tanto ao** ~ **nem tanto à terra** neither one way nor the other.
mar. (*abrev de* março) Mar.
maraca [maˈrakal *f* maracas (*pl*).
maracujá [marakuˈʒal *m* passion fruit.
maracujazeiro [marakuʒaˈzejrul *m* passion fruit plant.
maracutaia [marakuˈtajal *f* dirty trick.
marajá [maraˈʒal *m* -1. [título] maharaja. -2. *fig* [servidor] a person who has uses their position, not necessarily honestly, in order to become very rich.
Maranhão [maraˈpãwl *n* Maranhão.

marasmo [maˈraʒmul *m* -1. [desânimo] lethargy. -2. [estagnação] stagnation.
maratona [maraˈtonal *m* marathon.
maratonista [maratoˈniʃtal *mf* marathon runner.
maravilha [maraˈviʎal *f* wonder; **às mil** ~ **s** wonderfully; **ser uma** ~ to be wonderful.
maravilhado, da [maraviˈʎadu, dal *adj:* ~ **(com)** amazed (at).
maravilhar [4] [maraviˈʎa(x)] *vt* to astonish.
➡ **maravilhar-se** *vp:* ~-**se (de algo)** to be amazed (at sthg).
maravilhoso, osa [maraviˈʎozu, ɔzal *adj* wonderful.
marca [ˈmaxkal *f* -1. [ger] mark. -2. [*COM* - de carro] make; [- de café, queijo] brand; ~ **comercial** *ou* **de fábrica** trademark; ~ **registrada** registered trademark. -3. [de prata] hallmark.
➡ **de marca maior** *loc adj pej* of the first order.
marcação [maxkaˈsãwl (*pl* -ões) *f* -1. [ato de marcar - enxoval] marking; [- gado] branding. -2. *ESP* marking. -3. [perseguição, vigilância] scrutiny; **estar de** ~ **com alguém** to pick on sb.
marcado, da [maxˈkadu, dal *adj* -1. [assinalado - roupa, texto] marked; [- gado] branded. -2. [reservado] booked. -3. [com marca, mancha] marked. -4. [pessoa - traumatizada] marked; [- em evidência] watched.
marcador [maxkaˈdo(x)] *m* -1. [de livro] bookmark. -2. [*ESP* - quadro] scoreboard; [- jogador] scorer.
marcante [maxˈkãtʃil *adj* marked.
marcapasso [maxkaˈpasul *m* *MED* pacemaker.
marcar [12] [maxˈka(x)] *vt* -1. [ger] to mark; ~ **época** to make history. -2. [pôr marca em - livro, roupa] to mark; [- animal] to brand. -3. [data, hora, prazo] to fix; ~ **o tempo de algo** to time sthg. -4. [almoço, encontro] to arrange; ~ **uma consulta** to make an appointment. -5. [*ESP* - jogador] to mark; [- gol] to score. -6. [suj: relógio] to say. -7. [suj: termômetro] to show. -8. [demarcar] to demarcate.
marcenaria [maxsenaˈrial *f* -1. [arte] marquetry. -2. [trabalho] cabinet-making. -3. [oficina] cabinet-maker's workshop.
marceneiro, ra [maxseˈnejru, ral *m, f* cabinet-maker.
marcha [ˈmaxʃal *f* -1. [ato] marching; **pôr-se em** ~ to set off. -2. [passo] pace. -3. [ger] march. -4. *AUTO* gear; **dar** ~ **à ré** to reverse; ~ **à ré** reverse. -5. [*MÚS* - tradicional] march; ~ **fúnebre** funeral march; [- popular] festive march. -6. *fig* [progressão] course.
marchar [4] [maxˈʃa(x)] *vi* -1. *MIL* to march; ~ **sobre** [avançar] to march into. -2. [ir]: ~ **para** to go to.
marchetar [4] [maxʃeˈta(x)] *vt* [incrustar]: ~ **algo (de algo)** to inlay sthg (with sthg).
marchinha [maxˈʃiɲal *f* *MÚS* *a satirical song in double time, in the main performed during carnival.*

marcial [max'sjaw] (pl -ais) adj martial; **corte ~** court martial.

marciano, na [max'sjanu, na] <> adj Martian. <> m, f Martian.

marco ['maxkul m -1. [ger] landmark. -2. [moeda] mark. -3. [da janela] frame.

março ['marsu] m March; veja também setembro.

maré [ma'rɛ] f -1. [do mar] tide; **~ alta/baixa** high/low tide; **remar contra a ~** fig to swim against the tide. -2. fig [ocasião] spell; **aproveitar a ~** to make the most of one's luck. -3. fig [tendência] tendency. -4. fig [humor]: **estar de ~ alta** to be in high spirits. -5. fig [multidão] sea.

mareado, da [ma'rjadu, da] adj -1. [enjoado] seasick. -2. [oxidado] tarnished.

marear [15] [ma'rja(x)] <> vt -1. [enjoar] to make seasick. -2. [oxidar] to tarnish. <> vi [enjoar] to be seasick.

marechal [mare'ʃaw] (pl -ais) m marshal.

maré-cheia [ma,rɛ'ʃeja] (pl marés-cheias) f high tide.

marejar [4] [mare'ʒa(x)] <> vt to shed. <> vi to flow.

◆ **marejar-se** vp: **~-se de lágrimas** to well up with tears.

maremoto [mare'mɔtu] m tidal wave.

maresia [mare'zia] f sea air.

marfim [max'fĩ] m ivory; **de ~** ivory (antes de subst).

margarida [maxga'rida] f BOT daisy.

margarina [maxga'rina] f margarine.

margear [15] [max'ʒja(x)] vt -1. [seguir pela margem de] to follow. -2. [estar à margem de] to border.

margem ['maxʒẽ] (pl -ns) f -1. [ger] margin; **~ de lucro** profit margin. -2. [beira - de estrada, lago] edge; **à ~ de** alongside; [- de rio] bank; [- litoral] shore. -3. [latitude] room; **~ de erro** margin of error; **~ de segurança** safety margin. -4. [limites] edge; **à ~ da sociedade/lei** on the fringes of society/the law; **manter-se à ~ de algo** to remain distant from sthg. -5. [ocasião]: **dar ~ a alguém para fazer algo** to give sb the chance to do sthg.

marginal [maxʒi'naw] (pl -ais) <> adj -1. [pessoa] delinquent. -2. [nota] marginal. <> mf [pessoa] delinquent.

marginalidade [maxʒinali'dadʒi] f delinquency.

marginalizar [4] [maxʒinali'za(x)] vt [excluir] to marginalize.

◆ **marginalizar-se** vp [tornar-se fora-da-lei] to marginalize o.s.

maria-fumaça [ma,riafu'masa] (pl marias-fumaças) m & f steam train.

maria-mijona [ma,riami'ʒona] adj inv unfashionably long.

maria-mole [ma,ria'mɔli] (pl -s) f CULIN marshmallow dessert covered with coconut.

maria-sem-vergonha [ma,riasẽvex'goɲa] (pl marias-sem-vergonha) f BOT busy lizzie.

maria-vai-com-as-outras [ma,riavajkwa'd zowtraʃ] mf inv sheep.

maricas [ma'rikaʃ] fam <> adj inv [medroso] chicken. <> m inv [efeminado] pretty boy.

marido [ma'ridu] m husband.

marimbondo [marĩ'bõdu] m hornet.

marina [ma'rina] f marina.

marinar [4] [mari'nax] vt to marinate.

marinha [ma'riɲa] f ▷ marinho.

marinheiro, ra [mari'ɲejru, ra] <> adj sailor's (antes de subst). <> m, f sailor; **~ de primeira viagem** fig greenhorn.

marinho, nha [ma'riɲu, ɲa] adj [do mar] marine.
◆ **marinho** <> adj inv [cor] navy. <> m [cor] navy blue.
◆ **marinha** f -1. [força] navy; **marinha (de guerra)** navy; **marinha mercante** merchant navy. -2. [pintura] seascape.

marionete [marjo'nɛtʃi] f puppet.

mariposa [mari'poza] f moth.

marisco [ma'riʃku] m shellfish.

marital [mari'taw] (pl -ais) adj marital.

maritalmente [maritaw'mẽtʃi] adv: **viver ~ (com alguém)** to live together (with sb).

marítimo, ma [ma'ritʃimu, ma] adj maritime.

marketing ['maxketʃĩ] m marketing.

marmanjo [max'mãʒu] m grown man.

marmelada [maxme'lada] f -1. [doce] quince jam. -2. fam [mamata] racket.

marmelo [max'mɛlu] m quince.

marmita [max'mita] f -1. [recipiente] casserole. -2. [refeição] packed lunch.

mármore ['maxmori] m marble; **de ~** marble (antes de subst).

marmóreo, rea [max'mɔriu, ria] adj marble.

marola [ma'rɔla] f small wave.

maroto, ta [ma'rotu, ta] adj -1. [esperto] crafty. -2. [malicioso] malicious.

marquês, quesa [max'keʃ, eza] (mpl -eses, fpl -esas) m, f marquis (f marchioness).

marquise [max'kizil f canopy.

marra ['maxa] f: **obedeceu na ~** he obeyed under pressure; **invadiram ~** they invaded in strength.

marreco [ma'xɛkul m wigeon.

Marrocos [ma'xɔkuʃ] n Morocco.

marrom [ma'xõ] (pl -ns) <> adj brown. <> m brown.

marrom-glacê [ma'xõ'gla'se] (pl -s) m marron glacé.

marroquino, na [maxo'kinu, na] <> adj Moroccan. <> m, f Morroccan.

Marte ['maxtʃi] m Mars.

martelada [maxte'lada] f -1. [pancada] blow. -2. [ruído] bang.

martelar [maxte'la(x)] <> vt -1. [com martelo] to hammer. -2. [afligir] to bother. -3. [repetir] to repeat. <> vi -1. [dar marteladas] to hammer. -2. [insistir]: **~ em algo** to keep on about sthg.

martelo [max'tɛlu] m hammer.

mártir ['maxti(x)] (pl -es) mf martyr.

martírio [max'tʃirju] m -1. [suplício] martyrdom.

-2. *fig* [tormento] torment; **ser um** ~ to be a torment.

martirizante [maxtʃiri'zãntʃi] *adj* agonizing.

martirizar [4] [maxtʃiri'za(x)] *vt* **-1.** [torturar] to torture. **-2.** *fig* [atormentar] to torment.

➤ **martirizar-se** *vp* [atormentar-se] to agonize.

marujo [ma'ruʒu] *m* sailor.

marulhar [4] [maru'ʎa(x)] *vi* **-1.** [mar] to surge. **-2.** [ondas] to lap. **-3.** [barulho das ondas] to crash.

marulho [ma'ruʎu] *m* **-1.** [do mar] surge. **-2.** [das ondas] lapping.

marxismo [max'ksiʒmu] *m* Marxism.

marxista [max'ksiʃta] <> *adj* Marxist. <> *mf* Marxist.

marzipã [maxzi'pã] *m* marzipan.

mas [ma(j)ʃ] <> *conj* but; ~ **que decepção!** how disappointing! <> *cont* = **me + as**.

➤ **mas também** *loc conj* but also; **não só ... ~ também** not only ... but also.

mascar [12] [maʃ'ka(x)] <> *vt* to chew. <> *vi* to chew.

máscara ['maʃkara] *f* **-1.** [ger] mask; **baile de** ~**s** masked ball; ~ **de oxigênio** oxygen mask; ~ **(de beleza)** face mask. **-2.** [fachada] disguise; **tirar a** ~ **de alguém** to unmask sb.

mascarado, da [maʃka'radu, da] *adj* **-1.** [fantasiado] masked. **-2.** *fig* [disfarçado]: ~ **de mendigo** disguised as a beggar.

mascarar [4] [maʃka'ra(x)] *vt* to mask.

mascate [maʃ'katʃi] *m* hawker.

Mascate [maʃ'katʃi] *n* Muscat.

mascavo [maʃ'kavu] *adj* ⊳ açúcar.

mascote [maʃ'kɔtʃi] *f* mascot.

masculinidade [maʃkulini'dadʒi] *f* masculinity.

masculinizado, da [maʃkulini'zadu, da] *adj* [mulher] masculine.

masculinizar [maʃkulini'za(x)] *vt* to masculinize.

masculino, na [maʃku'linu, na] *adj* **-1.** [sexo, população] male. **-2.** [modos, voz]: **esta foi uma reação tipicamente masculina** that was a typically male response. **-3.** GRAM masculine.

➤ **masculino** *m* GRAM masculine.

másculo, la ['maʃkulu, la] *adj* [viril] manly.

masmorra [maʒ'moxa] *f* **-1.** [calabouço] dungeon. **-2.** *fig* [aposento] hole.

masoquismo [mazo'kiʒmu] *m* masochism.

masoquista [mazo'kiʃta] <> *adj* masochistic. <> *mf* masochist.

massa ['masa] *f* **-1.** [ger] mass. **-2.** [culinária - de pão] dough; [- de bolo] mixture; [- de torta, empada] pastry; [- de tomate] paste. **-3.** [macarrão] pasta. **-4.** [grande quantidade]: **uma** ~ **de** a mass of. **-5.** CONSTR: ~ **de vidraceiro** putty. **-6.** [maioria]: **a** ~ **de** the majority of.

➤ **massas** *fpl*: **as** ~**s** the masses.

➤ **em massa** *loc adv* en masse.

massa-corrida ['masako'xida] (*pl* **-s**) *f plaster skim applied before painting*.

massacrante [masa'krãntʃi] *adj* annoying.

massacrar [4] [masa'kra(x)] *vt* **-1.** [ger] to

massacre. **-2.** [oprimir] to oppress. **-3.** *fig* [torturar] to torture.

massacre [ma'sakri] *m* massacre.

massagear [15] [masa'ʒea(x)] <> *vt* to massage. <> *vi* to do massage.

massagem [ma'saʒẽ] (*pl* **-ns**) *f* massage; ~ **facial** facial.

massagista [masa'ʒiʃta] *mf* masseur (masseuse).

massificação [masifika'sãw] (*pl* **-ões**) *f* popularization.

massificado, da [masifika'du, da] *adj* popular *(antes de subst)*.

massificar [12] [masifi'ka(x)] *vt* **-1.** [ensino universitário] to popularize. **-2.** [povo] to sell to the masses.

massinha [ma'siɲa] *f* **-1.** [para modelar] Plasticine®. **-2.** [comestível]: **sopa de** ~ minestrone.

massudo, da [ma'sudu, da] *adj* **-1.** [pão, torta] heavy. **-2.** [documentação, livro] bulky.

mastectomia [maʃtekto'mia] *f* mastectomy.

mastigado, da [maʃtʃi'gadu, da] *adj* **-1.** [triturado] chewed. **-2.** [facilitado] well-explained.

mastigar [14] [maʃtʃi'ga(x)] <> *vt* [triturar] to chew. <> *vi* [triturar] to chew.

mastim [maʃ'tʃĩ] (*pl* **-ns**) *m* mastiff.

mastite [mas'tʃitʃi] *f* mastitis.

mastodonte [maʃto'dõntʃi] *m* **-1.** [mamífero] mammoth. **-2.** *fam* [pessoa] hulk.

mastro ['maʃtru] *m* **-1.** NÁUT mast. **-2.** [para bandeira] flagpole.

masturbação [maʃtuxba'sãw] *f* masturbation.

masturbar [4] [maʃtux'ba(x)] *vt* to masturbate.

➤ **masturbar-se** *vp* to masturbate.

mata ['mata] *f* forest; ~ **virgem** virgin forest.

mata-baratas [mataba'rataʃ] *mpl* [inseticida] cockroach killer.

mata-borrão [,matabo'xãw] (*pl* **mata-borrões**) *m* **-1.** [papel] blotting paper. **-2.** [artefato] blotter.

matacão [mata'kãw] (*pl* **-ões**) *f*: **uma** ~ **de algo** a big lump of sthg.

matado, da [ma'tadu, da] *adj* [serviço] lousy.

matador, ra [mata'do(x), ra] *m, f* killer.

➤ **matador** *m* [tourada] matador.

matadouro [mata'doru] *m* slaughterhouse.

matagal [mata'gaw] (*pl* **-ais**) *m* **-1.** [terreno] bush. **-2.** [mata espessa] thicket.

mata-moscas [,mata'moʃkaʃ] *m (inv)* fly-swat.

mata-mosquito [,matamoʃ'kitu] (*pl* **mata-mosquitos**) *m* mosquito spray.

matança [ma'tãnsa] *f* **-1.** [de pessoas] massacre. **-2.** [de animais] slaughter.

matar [4] [ma'ta(x)] <> *vt* **-1.** [ger] to kill. **-2.** [saciar - fome] to satisfy; [- sede] to quench; [- curiosidade] to quell. **-3.** [gazetear] to skip. **-4.** [executar mal] to do badly. **-5.** [decifrar] to guess. **-6.** [fazer desaparecer] to crush. <> *vi* [causar morte] to kill.

➤ **matar-se** *vp* **-1.** [suicidar-se] to kill o.s. **-2.** [cansar-se]: ~**-se de algo/fazer algo** to kill o.s. with sthg/doing sthg.

de matar *loc adj fig* [terrível] terrible; **dor de** ~ excruciating pain; **ser de** ~ to be terrible.

mata-rato [ˌmataˈxatu] (*pl* **mata-ratos**) *m* -**1.** [veneno] rat poison. -**2.** *fam* [cigarro] cancer stick.

mate [ˈmatʃi] *m* [bebida] maté.

matelassê [matelaˈse] *adj* quilted.

matemático, ca [mateˈmatʃiku, ka] <> *adj* mathematical. <> *m, f* mathematician.

matemática *f* [ciência] mathematics *(sg).*

matéria [maˈtɛrja] *f* -**1.** [ger] matter; ~ **plástica** plastic. -**2.** [assunto] subject; **em** ~ **de política/esporte** in the area of politics/sports. -**3.** *EDUC* subject. -**4.** *JORN* article.

material [mateˈrjaw] (*pl* -**ais**) <> *adj* material. <> *m* -**1.** [substância] material. -**2.** [utensílios] materials *(pl)*; ~ **de escritório** office stationery; ~ **de limpeza** cleaning products *(pl)*. -**3.** [bélico] armaments *(pl)*. -**4.** [informativo, didático] teaching material.

materialismo [materjaˈliʒmu] *m* materialism.

materialista [materjaˈliʃta] <> *adj* materialistic. <> *mf* materialist.

materializar [4] [materjaliˈza(x)] *vt* to materialize.

materializar-se *vp* to materialize.

matéria-prima [maˌtɛrjaˈprima] (*pl* **matérias-primas**) *f* raw material.

maternal [matexˈnaw] (*pl* -**ais**) <> *adj* maternal. <> *m EDUC* nursery school.

maternidade [matexniˈdadʒi] *f* -**1.** [qualidade] motherhood. -**2.** [hospital] maternity hospital.

materno, na [maˈtɛxnu, na] *adj* -**1.** [ger] maternal. -**2.** [língua]: **língua** ~ mother tongue.

matilha [maˈtʃiʎa] *f* [cães] pack.·

matina [maˈtʃinal] *f fam* morning.

matinal [matʃiˈnaw] (*pl* -**ais**) *adj* morning *(antes de subst).*

matinê [matʃiˈne] *f* matinée.

matiz [maˈtʃiʒ] *m* -**1.** [tom] shade. -**2.** *fig* [traço] tinge.

matizar [4] [matʃiˈza(x)] *vt* -**1.** [dar nuances a] to tinge. -**2.** [colorir] to colour *UK*, to color *US.*

mato [ˈmatu] *m* -**1.** [área] scrubland. -**2.** [plantas] weeds *(pl)*. -**3.** [roça] countryside. -**4.** *loc:* **estar num** ~ **sem cachorro** *fam* to be up the creek without a paddle; **ser** ~ *fam* to be thick on the ground.

Mato Grosso do Sul [matuˌgrosuduˈsuw] *n* Mato Grosso do Sul.

matraca [maˈtraka] *f* -**1.** [instrumento] rattle; **falar como uma** ~ to talk the hind legs off a donkey. -**2.** *fig* [pessoa] chatterbox.

matraquear [15] [matraˈkja(x)] *vi* [tagarelar] to chatter.

matreiro, ra [maˈtrejru, ra] *adj fam* [astuto, ardiloso] crafty.

matriarca [maˈtrjaxka] *f* matriarch.

matriarcal [matrjaxˈkaw] (*pl* -**ais**) *adj* matriarchal.

matrícula [maˈtrikula] *f* -**1.** [inscrição] enrolment *UK*, enrollment *US*; **fazer (a)** ~ to enrol *UK*, to enroll *US*; **qual é o seu número de** ~ what's your registration number? -**2.** [taxa] fee.

matricular [4] [matrikuˈla(x)] *vt*: ~ **alguém (em algo)** to enrol sb (in sthg) *UK*, to enroll sb (in sthg) *US.*

matricular-se *vp*: ~-**se (em algo)** to enrol (in sthg) *UK*, to enroll (in sthg) *US.*

matrimonial [matrimoˈnjaw] (*pl* -**ais**) *adj* matrimonial.

matrimônio [matriˈmonju] *m* marriage; **contrair** ~ **(com alguém)** to be joined in marriage (to sb).

matriz [maˈtriʃ] (*pl* -**es**) <> *adj* -**1.** [igreja, língua] mother *(antes de subst).* -**2.** [idéia] original. <> *f* -**1.** [de empresa] head office. -**2.** [de igreja] mother church. -**3.** [molde] mould *UK*, mold *US.* -**4.** *MAT* matrix.

matrona [maˈtrona] *f pej* matron; **estar uma** ~ to look like an old cow.

maturação [maturaˈsãw] (*pl* -**ões**) *f* -**1.** [de fruta] ripening. -**2.** *fig* [amadurecimento] maturation.

maturar [4] [matuˈra(x)] <> *vt* to mature. <> *vi* to mature.

maturidade [maturiˈdadʒi] *f* maturity.

matusquela [matuʃˈkɛla] *mf fam* lunatic.

matutar [4] [matuˈta(x)] <> *vt* [planejar] to plan. <> *vi* [refletir] to think about; ~ **sobre algo** to turn sthg over in one's mind.

matutino, na [matuˈtʃinu, na] *adj* morning.

matutino *m* morning newspaper.

matuto, ta [maˈtutu, ta] <> *adj* -**1.** [da roça] country *(antes de subst).* -**2.** *fam* [sabido] shrewd. <> *m, f* -**1.** [pessoa da roça] country bumpkin. -**2.** [pessoa rude] peasant.

mau, má [ˈmaw, ˈma] <> *adj* -**1.** *(antes de subst)* [ger] bad. -**2.** *(antes de subst)* [incapaz] poor. <> *m, f* -**1.** [pessoa] bad person. -**2.** [em filme etc] baddy.

mau-caráter [ˌmawkaˈratex] (*pl* **maus-caráteres**) <> *adj* disreputable. <> *mf* bad character.

mau-olhado [ˌmawoˈʎadu] (*pl* **maus-olhados**) *m* evil eye.

mauricinho [mawriˈsiɲu] *m fam* posh kid.

Maurício [mawˈrisju] *n* Mauritius.

máuser® [ˈmawze(x)] *m* mauser.

mausoléu [mawzoˈlɛu] *m* mausoleum.

maus-tratos [mawʃˈtratuʃ] *mpl* abuse.

mavioso, osa [maˈvjozu, ɔza] *adj* affectionate.

maxidesvalorização [maksidʒiʒvalorizaˈsãw] (*pl* -**ões**) *f* steep devaluation.

maxilar [maksiˈla(x)] (*pl* -**es**) <> *m* jaw. <> *adj* maxillary.

máxima [ˈmasima] *f* [> **máximo.**

maximizar [4] [masimiˈza(x)] *vt* -**1.** [aumentar ao máximo] to maximize. -**2.** *MAT* to round up.

máximo, ma [ˈmasimu, ma] *adj* -**1.** [o maior possível] maximum. -**2.** [supremo] highest.

máximo *m* [o mais alto grau] maximum; **ao** ~ to the maximum; **chegar ao** ~ to reach the peak; **no** ~ at most; **ser o** ~ [ser maravilhoso] to be the best.

máxima f -1. [temperatura] maximum. -2. [sentença, princípio] maxim.

maxixe [ma'ʃiʃi] m -1. [legume] gourd. -2. [dança] *Brazilian dance, precursor of the samba*.

mazela [ma'zɛla] f -1. fam [doença]: **ela gosta de falar de suas ~s** she likes to talk about her aches and pains. -2. [infortúnio] misfortune.

MB (abrev de **Megabyte**) m MB.

MBA (abrev de **Master of Business Administration**) m MBA.

me [mi] pron [complemento direto] me; [complemento indireto] (to) me; [reflexo] myself; **eu nunca ~ engano** I'm never wrong; **eu ~ machuquei** I've hurt myself; **você já ~ contou essa história** you've already told me that story.

meado ['mjadu] m: **no ~ de** in the middle of; **em ~s de setembro** in mid-September.

meandro ['mjãndru] m meander.

meandros mpl meanderings.

MEC (abrev de **Ministério da Educação e Cultura**) m Brazilian ministry of education and culture.

Meca ['mɛka] n Mecca.

mecânico, ca [me'kãniku, ka] <> adj mechanical. <> m, f [profissional] mechanic.

mecânica f -1. [ger] mechanics (pl). -2. fig [mecanismo] workings (pl).

mecanismo [meka'niʒmu] m mechanism; **~ de defesa** defence mechanism; **~ de busca** COMPUT search engine.

mecanização [mekaniza'sãw] f mechanization.

mecanizar [4] [mekani'za(x)] vt to mechanize.

mecenas [me'senaʃ] m inv patron.

mecha ['mɛʃa] f -1. [de vela] wick. -2. [de explosivo] fuse. -3. [de cabelo] strand. -4. [cabelo tingido] streak; **fazer ~ (no cabelo)** to have one's hair streaked. -5. [em ferimento] wick.

medalha [me'daʎa] f medal.

medalhão [meda'ʎãw] (pl -ões) m -1. [jóia] medallion. -2. fig [figurão] high-flyer, big shot.

média ['mɛdʒja] f ⊳ **médio**.

mediação [medʒja'sãw] f mediation; **por ~ de** through the mediation of.

mediador, ra [medʒja'do(x), ra] m, f mediator.

mediano, na [me'dʒjãnu, na] adj -1. [ger] average. -2. [linha] median.

mediana f GEOM median.

mediante [me'dʒjãntʃi] prep -1. [por meio de] through; **~ ajuda de** with the help of; **~ a graça de Deus** by the grace of God. -2. [a troco de] in exchange for.

mediar [17] [me'dʒja(x)] <> vt [intervir em] to mediate; **~ um debate** to chair a debate. <> vi [intervir] to mediate; **~ entre/a favor de** to mediate between/in favour of.

medicação [medʒika'sãw] (pl -ões) f medication.

medicamento [medʒika'mẽntu] m medicine.

medição [medʒi'sãw] (pl -ões) f measurement.

medicar [12] [medʒi'ka(x)] <> vt to medicate. <> vi to practise medicine UK, to practice medicine US.

medicar-se vp to take medicine.

medicina [medʒi'sinal] f medicine; **~ alternativa** alternative medicine; **~ legal** forensic medicine.

medicinal [medʒisi'naw] (pl -ais) adj medicinal.

médico, ca ['mɛdʒiku, kal] <> adj medical. <> m, f doctor; **~ de família** family doctor, GP, general expert.

médico-hospitalar [ˌmɛdʒikwoʃpita'la(x)] (pl médico-hospitalares) adj hospital and medical (antes de subst).

médico-legal [ˌmedʒikule'gaw] (pl médico-legais) adj forensic.

médico-legista, médica-legista [ˌmedʒikule'ʒiʃta] (mpl médicos-legistas, fpl médicas-legistas) m, f forensic expert.

medida [me'dʒida] f -1. [ger] measurement; **~ de capacidade** measure of capacity. -2. [tamanho] size; **feito sob ~** made to measure; **tomar as ~s de alguém/algo** to take the measurements of sb/sthg. -3. [grau] degree; **na ~ do possível** as far as possible. -4. [providência] measure; **tomar ~s** to take measures; **~ provisória** JUR emergency measure; **~ de segurança** safety measure. -5. [limite]: **passar das ~s** to go beyond the limits.

à medida que loc conj as.

na medida em que loc conj in so far as.

medidor [medʒi'do(x)] m meter; **~ de pressão** pressure gauge.

medieval [medʒie'vaw] (pl -ais) adj medieval.

médio, dia ['mɛdʒju, dja] adj -1. [entre dois pontos - ger] middle; [- tamanho] medium. -2. [resultado de cálculo] average. -3. [ensino] secondary.

média f -1. MAT average; **em ~** on average. -2. EDUC secondary school. -3. [café com leite] white coffee. -4. loc: **fazer ~ com** to fawn over.

medíocre [me'dʒiwkri] <> adj mediocre. <> mf mediocrity.

mediocridade [medʒiwkri'dadʒi] f mediocrity.

medir [70] [me'dʒi(x)] vt -1. [ger] to measure; **~ alguém/algo por algo** to measure sb/sthg against sthg; **~ alguém/algo por alguém** to measure sb/sthg against sb. -2. [considerar, avaliar] to evaluate. -3. [moderar] to measure; **meça suas palavras!** watch what you say! -4. [olhar com desdém]: **~ alguém de alto a baixo** to look down on sb.

medir-se vp -1. [tomar as medidas] to measure o.s. -2. [igualar-se]: **~-se com alguém em algo** to equal sb at sthg.

meditação [medʒita'sãw] (pl -ões) f meditation.

meditar [4] [me'dʒita(x)] vi to meditate; **~ sobre algo** to meditate on sthg.

meditativo, va [medʒita'tʃivu, va] adj meditative.

mediterrâneo, nea [medʒite'xãnju, nja] adj Mediterranean.

Mediterrâneo n: **o (mar) ~** the Mediterranean (Sea).

médium ['mɛdʒjũ] (pl -ns) [espirit] mf medium.

mediúnico, ca [me'dʒuniku, ka] *adj* of a medium *(depois de subst)*.

mediunidade [medʒuni'dadʒil *f* spiritualism.

medo ['medul *m* -**1.** [pavor] fear; **dar ~** to frighten; **me dá ~ fazer algo** I am frightened of doing sthg; **estar com** *ou*ter **~ (de)** to be afraid (of); **estar com** *ou*ter **~ de fazer algo** to be afraid of doing sthg; **estar se cagando de ~** *vulg* to be shitting o.s. with fear; **feio de meter ~** as ugly as sin; **morrer de ~** to be frightened to death. -**2.** [receio]: **com ~ de/que** for fear of/that; **estar com** *ou*ter **~ de** to be afraid of.

medonho, nha [me'doɲu, ɲal *adj* -**1.** [assustador] terrifying. -**2.** [horrível] horrendous.

medrar [4] [me'dra(x)] *vi* -**1.** [planta] to grow. -**2.** *fam* [ficar com medo] to get scared.

medroso, osa [medrozu, ɔzal *adj* [temeroso] scared. *m, f* coward.

medula [me'dulal *f* ANAT marrow, medulla; **~ óssea** bone marrow.

megabyte [mɛga'bajtʃil *m* COMPUT megabyte.

megaevento [mɛgae'vẽntul *m* huge event.

megafone [mɛga'fonil *m* megaphone.

megahertz [mɛga'xɛxtʃiʃl *m (inv)* megahertz.

megalomania [megaloma'nial *f* megalomania.

megalomaníaco, ca [megaloma'njaku, kal *adj* megalomaniac. *m, f* megalomaniac.

megalópole [mega'lɔpolil *f* super-city.

megaton [mega'tõl *m* megaton.

megera [me'ʒɛral *f* shrew.

meia ['mejal *f* ⊳ **meio**.

meia-calça [ˌmeja'kawsal *(pl* **meias-calças)** *f* tights *(pl)* UK, pantyhose *(pl)* US.

meia-direita [ˌmejadʒi'rejtal *(pl* **meias-direitas)** FUT *f* inside right. *m* inside right.

meia-entrada [ˌmejaẽn'tradal *(pl* **meias-entradas)** *f* half-price ticket.

meia-esquerda [ˌmejaiʃ'kexdal *(pl* **meias-esquerdas)** FUT *f* inside left. *m* inside left.

meia-estação [ˌmejaiʃta'sãwl *(pl* **meias-estações)** *f* mid-season.

meia-idade [ˌmejej'dadʒil *(pl* **meias-idades)** *f* middle age; **mulher de ~** middle-aged woman.

meia-lua [ˌmeja'lual *f* -**1.** ASTRO half moon. -**2.** [semicírculo] semicircle.

meia-luz [ˌmeja'luʃl *(pl* meias-luzes) *f* half light; **à ~** in the gloom.

meia-noite [ˌmeja'nojtʃil *(pl* meias-noites) *f* midnight; **à ~** at midnight.

meia-volta [ˌmeja'vɔwtal *(pl* meias-voltas) *f* -**1.** [movimento] half turn. -**2.** MIL about-turn UK, about-face US; **fazer ~** to make an about-turn UK, to make an about-face US.

meigo, ga [ˈmejgu, gal *adj* gentle.

meiguice [mej'gisil *f* gentleness.

meio, meia ['meju, 'mejal *adj* half; **a ~ caminho** halfway; **meia dúzia** half a dozen; **meia hora** half an hour; **~ quilo** half a kilo; **são três e meia** it's half past three; **um quilo e ~** a kilo and a half.

meio *adv* half-; **~ cansado** rather tired.

m -**1.** [metade] half; **~ a ~** fifty-fifty; **veio ~ mundo à festa** *fig* half the world came to the party; **partir ao ~** to split *ou* break in half; **pelo ~** [inacabado] halfway through. -**2.** [centro] middle; **o filho do ~** the middle son; **no ~ (de)** in the middle (of). -**3.** [ambiente - social, profissional] circle; [- físico] milieu; **~ ambiente** environment. -**4.** [modo] way; **por ~ de** through, by means of;` **por todos os ~s** in every way.

meios *mpl* [recursos] means; **os ~s de comunicação** the media; **~s de transporte** means of transport.

meia *num* six. *f* -**1.** [meia - de seda] stocking; [- soquete] sock. -**2.** [entrada] half-price ticket. -**3.** [ponto]: **ponto de meia** stocking stitch.

meio-campo [ˌmeju'kãmpul *(pl* **meios-campo)** *m* -**1.** FUT [centro-médio] midfield player. -**2.** [zona] midfield.

meio-dia [ˌmeju'dʒial *(pl* **meios-dias)** *m* midday; **ao ~** at midday.

meio-fio [ˌmejo'fiwl *(pl* **meios-fios)** *m* kerb UK, curb US.

meio-tempo [ˌmeju'tẽnpul *(pl* **meios-tempos)** *m* -**1.** [ínterim]: **nesse ~** meanwhile. -**2.** ESP [período] half-time.

meio-termo [ˌmeju'texmul *(pl* **meios-termos)** *m* -**1.** [posição]: **~ (entre)** mid point (between). -**2.** *fig* [consenso] compromise.

meio-tom [ˌmeju'tõl *(pl* **meios-tons)** *m* -**1.** MÚS semitone. -**2.** [de cor] half-tone.

mel ['mɛwl *m* honey.

melado, da [me'ladu, dal *adj* [pegajoso] sticky.

melado *m* [doce] molasses.

melancia [melãn'sial *f* watermelon.

melancolia [melãnko'lial *f* melancholy.

melancólico, ca [melãn'kɔliku, kal *adj* melancholic.

melão [me'lãwl *(pl* -ões) *m* melon.

melar [4] [me'la(x)] *vt* [sujar] to get sticky. *vi fig* [falhar] to flop.

melar-se *vp* [sujar-se] to get sticky.

Melbourne [ˌmɛw'buxnil *n* Melbourne.

meleca [me'lɛkal *f* -**1.** *fam* [secreção] bogey; **ele está tirando ~ do nariz** he's picking his nose. -**2.** [coisa ruim]: **ser/ficar uma ~** to be rubbish. -**3.** *(enfático)*: **essa ~ dessa chuva** that dammed rain.

melhor [me'ʎɔ(x)] *(pl* -es) *adj* -**1.** *(comparativo de bom)*: **~ (do que)** better (than); **bem/muito ~** much better; **é ~ você ...** you had better ...; **quanto mais ~** the more the better. -**2.** *(superlativo de bom)*: **o/a ~** the best. *adv* -**1.** *(comparativo de bem)*: **~ (do que)** better (than); **estar ~** to be better; **estar ~ de vida** to be better off. -**2.** *(superlativo de bem)* best. *m, f*: **o/a ~** the best; **o ~ de todas** the best of all; **o ~ foi que ...** the best thing was that ...; **levar a ~** to come off best.

ou melhor *loc adv* or rather.

tanto melhor *loc adv* so much the better.

melhora [me'ʎɔral *f* improvement; **estimo suas**

~s I hope you get better soon.

melhorada [meʎoˈradɐ] *f fam*: **dar uma ~** to get better.

melhoramento [meʎoraˈmẽntu] *m* improvement.

melhorar [4] [meʎoˈra(x)] <> *vt* to improve. <> *vi* to improve; **~ de algo** to improve in sthg; **~ de vida** to get on in life.

melhoria [meʎoˈriɐ] *f* improvement; **fazer ~s (em algo)** to make improvements (in sthg).

meliante [meˈljãntʃi] *mf* **-1.** [marginal] vagabond. **-2.** [ladrão] thief. **-3.** [patife] scoundrel.

melífluo, flua [meˈliflwu, flwa] *adj fig* [suave] mellifluous.

Melilha [meˈliʎa] *n* Melilla.

melindrar [4] [melĩˈdra(x)] *vt* to offend.
◆ **melindrar-se** *vp* to feel hurt.

melindre [meˈlĩndri] *m* affection.
◆ **melindres** *mpl* [suscetibilidade] oversensitivity.

melindroso, osa [melĩˈdrɔza, ɔzu] *adj* **-1.** [suscetível, frágil] sensitive. **-2.** [difícil, arriscado] tricky.
◆ **melindrosa** *f* [dos anos vinte] flapper dress.

melodia [meloˈdʒiɐ] *f* melody.

melódico, ca [meˈlɔdʒiku, ka] *adj* melodic.

melodrama [meloˈdramɐ] *m* melodrama.

melodramático, ca [melodraˈmatʃiku, ka] *adj* melodramatic.

melões [meˈlõjʃ] *pl* ▷ **melão**.

meloso, osa [meˈlozu, ɔza] *adj* **-1.** *fig* [pessoa] sentimental. **-2.** [voz] honeyed.

melro [ˈmɛwxu] *m* blackbird.

membrana [mẽnˈbrãnɐ] *f* membrane.

membro [ˈmẽnbru] *m* **-1.** [ANAT - braços, pernas] limb; [- pênis] (male) member, penis. **-2.** [parte] member.

memorando [memoˈrãndu] *m* **-1.** [comunicação] memo. **-2.** [nota diplomática] memorandum.

memorável [memoˈravew] (*pl* -eis) *adj* memorable.

memória [meˈmɔrja] *f* **-1.** [ger] memory; **de ~** by heart; **~ de elefante** *fig* memory like an elephant; **~ visual** visual memory; **ter ~ fraca** to have a poor memory; **vir à ~** to come to mind; **~ RAM/ROM** RAM/ROM memory. **-2.** [recordação] recollection; **em ~ de** in memory of.
◆ **memórias** *fpl* memoirs.

memorial [memoˈrjaw] (*pl* -ais) *m* memorial.

memorização [ˈmemoriˈzasãw] (*pl* -ões) *f* memorizing.

memorizar [4] [memoriˈza(x)] *vt* to memorize.

menção [mẽnˈsãw] (*pl* -ões) *f* **-1.** [referência] mention; **fazer ~ a algo** to make mention of sthg; **digno de ~** worthy of mention. **-2.** [intento]: **fazer ~ de se levantar** to make as if to get up. **-3.** [distinção]: **~ honrosa** distinction.

mencionar [4] [mẽnsjoˈna(x)] *vt* to mention; **(isso) sem mencionar ...** not to mention ...

mendicância [mẽndʒiˈkãnsjɐ] *f* begging.

mendicante [mẽndʒiˈkãntʃi] <> *adj* begging. <> *mf* beggar.

mendigar [14] [mẽndʒiˈga(x)] <> *vt* **-1.** [esmola] to beg for. **-2.** [ajuda, favor] to beg. <> *vi* [pedir esmola] to beg.

mendigo, ga [mẽnˈdʒigu, ga] *m, f* beggar.

menear [15] [meˈnja(x)] *vt* to shake.

menina [meˈninɐ] *f* ▷ **menino**.

meninada [meniˈnadɐ] *f* kids *(pl)*.

meningite [menĩˈʒitʃi] *f* meningitis.

meninice [meniˈnisil] *f* **-1.** [período] childhood. **-2.** [criancice] childishness.

menino, na [meˈninu, na] <> *adj* young. <> *m, f* **-1.** [criança] child; **nasceu um ~** a boy was born; **os ~s** the children; **~ de rua** street child. **-2.** [jovem] youngster. **-3.** [como forma de tratamento] boy.
◆ **menina** *f*: **ser a menina dos olhos de alguém** to be the apple of sb's eye.

menopausa [menoˈpawzal *f* menopause.

menor [meˈnɔ(x)] (*pl* -es) <> *adj* **-1.** *(comparativo)*: **~ (do que)** [de tamanho] smaller (than); [de idade] younger (than); [de importância, número] less (than); **meu irmão ~** my younger brother. **-2.** *(superlativo)*: **o/a ~ ...** [ger] the least; [de tamanho] the smallest. **-3.** [jovem]: **ser ~ (de idade)** [para dirigir, votar] to be under age; JUR to be a minor, to be under age. **-4.** *(antes de subst)* [noção, paciência] slightest. **-5.** MÚS: **em dó ~** in C minor. <> *mf* **-1.** *(superlativo)*: **o/a ~** [de tamanho] the smallest; [de idade] the youngest; **proibido para ~es** prohibited to under 18s; **um ~ de 15 anos** a youth of 15. **-2.** [jovem] young person. **-3.** JUR minor.

menoridade [menoriˈdadʒil *f* minority.

menos [ˈmenuʃ] <> *adv* **-1.** [em comparações] less; **a Ana é ~ inteligente** Ana is less intelligent; **~ do que** less than; **~ ... do que ...** less ...than ...; **tenho ~ trabalho do que ele** I have less work than him; **tenho um livro a ~** I'm one book short; **deram-me 5 reais a ~** they gave me 5 reals too little, they short-changed me by 5 reals. **-2.** [como superlativo]: **o/a ~ ...** the least ...; **o ~ caro/interessante** the least expensive/interesting. **-3.** [em locuções]: **a ~ que** unless; **ao ~, pelo ~** at least; **isso é o de ~** that's the least of it; **pouco ~ de** just under. <> *adj inv* **-1.** [em comparações] less, fewer *pl*; **como ~ carne** I eat less meat; **eles têm ~ posses** they have fewer possessions; **está ~ frio do que ontem** it's less cold than it was yesterday; **~ ... do que** less ... than, fewer ... than *pl*. **-2.** [como superlativo] (the) least, (the) fewest *pl*; **as que ~ bolos comeram** those who ate (the) fewest cakes; **os que ~ dinheiro têm** those who have (the) least money. <> *prep* **-1.** [exceto] except (for); **todos gostaram ~ ele** they all liked it except (for) him; **tudo ~ isso** anything but that. **-2.** [indica subtração] minus; **três ~ dois é igual a um** three minus two equals one.

menosprezado, da [menoʃpreˈzadu, da] *adj* underestimated.

menosprezar [4] [menoʃpreˈza(x)] *vt* to disdain.

menosprezo [menoʃ'prezu] *m*: ~ **(por)** disdain (for).

mensageiro, ra [mēsa'ʒejru, ra] *m, f* messenger.

mensagem [mēnsa'ʒē] (*pl* -ns) *f* message.

mensal [mēn'saw] (*pl* -ais) *adj* monthly; **ganho 1.000 reais mensais** I earn 1,000 reals a month.

mensalidade [mēnsali'dadʒi] *f* monthly payment.

mensalmente [mēnsaw'mēntʃi] *adv* monthly.

menstruação [mēnʃtrwa'sãw] (*pl* -ões) *f* menstruation.

menstruada [mēnʃ'trwada] *adj f*: **estar/ficar ~** to be menstruating.

menstrual [mēnʃ'trwaw] (*pl* -ais) *adj* menstrual.

menstruar [4] [mēnʃ'trwa(x)] *vi* to menstruate.

mensurável [mēnsu'ravew] (*pl* -eis) *adj* measurable.

menta ['mēnta] *f* mint; **de ~** mint *(antes de subst)*.

mental [mēn'taw] (*pl* -ais) *adj* mental.

mentalidade [mēntali'dadʒi] *f* mentality.

mentalizar [4] [mēntali'za(x)] *vt* -**1.** [pensar em] to think. - **2.** [conceber] to imagine.

mente ['mēntʃi] *f* mind; **ter algo em ~** to have sthg in mind; **ter em ~ fazer algo** to have it in mind to do sthg; **vir à ~** to come to mind.

mentecapto, ta [mēnte'kaptu, ta] *m, f* insane, foolish.

mentir [56] [mēn'tʃi(x)] <> *vt*: ~ **que ...** to lie about ... <> *vi* to lie; ~ **a** *ou* **para alguém** to lie to sb.

mentira [mēn'tʃira] *f* -**1.** [falsidade] lie; **de ~** [como brincadeira] as a joke; [falso] fake; **embora pareça ~** although it seems unlikely; ~ **deslavada** downright lie; ~**!** [mostrando surpresa] you don't say!; **parece ~ que ...** it seems unbelievable that ... - **2.** [ato, hábito] lying.

mentiroso, osa [mēntʃi'rozu, ɔza] <> *adj* -**1.** [ger] untruthful. - **2.** [jornalista, artigo] lying. <> *m, f* [pessoa] liar.

mentol [mēn'tɔw] *m* menthol.

mentolado, da [mēnto'ladu, da] *adj* mentholated.

mentor, ra [mēn'to(x), ra] *m, f* -**1.** [orientador] mentor. - **2.** [autor intelectual]: **o/a ~** the brains.

menu [me'nu] *m* menu.

meramente [mɛra'mēntʃi] *adv* merely.

mercadinho [mexka'dʒiɲu] *m* local shop *UK*, local store *US*.

mercado [mex'kadu] *m* market; ~ **de capitais** investment market; ~ **financeiro** financial market; ~ **negro** black market; ~ **de trabalho** job market; ~ **das pulgas** flea market.
 Mercado Comum *m* Common Market.

mercadologia [mexkadolo'ʒia] *f* marketing.

mercadológico, ca [mexkado'lɔʒiku, ka] *adj* marketing *(antes de subst)*.

mercador [mexka'do(x)] *m* merchant.

mercadoria [mexkado'ria] *f* commodity.
 mercadorias *fpl* merchandise, goods *(pl)*.

mercante [mex'kãntʃi] *adj* merchant *(antes de subst)*.

mercantil [mexkãn'tʃiw] (*pl* -is) *adj* mercantile.

mercantilismo [mexkãntʃi'liʒmu] *m* mercantilism.

mercantilista [mexkãntʃi'liʃta] *adj* mercantilist.

mercê [mex'se] *f*: **estar/ficar à ~ de alguém/algo** to be at the mercy of sb/sthg.

mercearia [mexsja'ria] *f* grocery shop.

mercenário, ria [mexse'narju, rja] <> *adj* mercenary. <> *m, f* mercenary.

Mercosul [mexko'suw] (*abrev de* **Mercado do Cone Sul**) *m South American common market*.

mercúrio [mex'kurju] *m* mercury; ~ **cromo** merbromin, Mercurochrome®.

Mercúrio [mex'kurju] *m* Mercury.

merda ['mɛxda] *mfam* <> *f* -**1.** [ger] crap, shit; **essa ~ de ...** this crappy ...; **ser/estar uma ~** to be crap; **mandar alguém à ~** to tell sb to bugger off. - **2.** [excremento] shit. <> *mf* [pessoa] shit. <> *interj*: **(que) ~!** what crap!
 de merda *loc adj mfam*: **esta viagem de ~** this shitty journey.

merecedor, ra [merese'do(x), ra] *adj*: ~ **de** deserving of.

merecer [25] [mere'se(x)] <> *vt* to deserve. <> *vi*: **ele ganhou o prêmio, mas não merecia** he won the prize but he didn't deserve to.

merecido, da [mere'sidu, da] *adj* deserved; **foi um castigo bem ~** it was a well deserved punishment.

merecimento [meresi'mēntu] *m* [mérito, valor] merit.

merenda [me'rēnda] *f* snack; ~ **escolar** free school meal.

merendeira [merēn'dejra] *f* [lancheira] snack box.

merengue [me'rēngi] *m* meringue.

meretrício [mere'trisju] *m* prostitution.

meretriz [mere'triʒ] *f* prostitute.

mergulhador, ra [mexguʎa'do(x), ra] (*mpl* -es, *fpl* -s) <> *adj* diving. <> *m, f* diver.

mergulhar [4] [mexgu'ʎa(x)] <> *vt* [afundar]: ~ **algo (em algo)** to dip sthg (in sthg). <> *vi* -**1.**: ~ **(em algo)** [afundar] to dive (into sthg); [saltar] to spring (from sthg). - **2.**: ~ **em algo** [penetrar] to plunge into sthg; *fig* [concentrar-se] to plunge o.s. in sthg.

mergulho [mex'guʎu] *m* -**1.** [ger] dive; **dar um ~** [na praia] to take a dip; [de trampolim] to spring. - **2.** *ESP* diving.

meridiano, na [meri'dʒjãnu, na] *adj* meridian.
 meridiano *m GEOGR* meridian.

meridional [meridʒio'nawl] (*pl* **-ais**) *adj* southern.

meritíssimo, ma [meri'tʃisimu, ma] *adj* highly deserving.

mérito ['mɛritu] *m* merit; **julgar alguém por seus ~s** to judge sb by their merits.

meritório, ria [meri'tɔrju, rja] *adj* meritorious, deserving.

merluza [mex'luza] *f* hake.

mero, ra ['mɛru, ra] *adj* mere.

merreca [me'xɛka] *f*: **uma ~** a trifle; **custar/pagar uma ~** to cost/pay a trifle; **ser uma ~** [muito pequeno] to be a mere trifle.

mertiolate [mextʃjo'latʃil] *m* Merthiolate®, thiomersal.

mês ['meʃ] (*pl* **meses**) *m*: **de ~ em ~** monthly; **durante todo o ~ de setembro** throughout September; **no ~ que vem** next month; **recebo por ~** I am paid monthly; **uma vez por ~** once a month.

mesa ['meza] *f* **-1.** [móvel] table; **pôr/tirar a ~** to lay/clear the table; **~ de centro** centre table; **~ de jantar** dining table; **~ telefônica** switchboard. **-2.** [de uma assembléia etc] board; **~ eleitoral** polling station officials. **-3.** [apostas] **ganhar toda a ~** to sweep the table. **-4.** *loc*: **virar a ~** to turn the tables.

mesada [me'zada] *f* **-1.** [pagamento] monthly payment. **-2.** [de criança] pocket money *UK*, allowance *US*.

mesa-de-cabeceira [ˌmezadʒikabi'sejra] (*pl* **mesas-de-cabeceira**) *f* bedside table.

mesa-redonda [ˌmezaxe'dõnda] (*pl* **mesas-redondas**) *f* round table.

mesário, ria [me'zarju, rja] *m, f* **-1.** [de mesa eleitoral] polling officer. **-2.** [de associação etc] committee member.

mescla ['mɛʃkla] <> *adj (inv)* [tecido, paletó] blend. <> *f* **-1.** [mistura] mixture. **-2.** [tecido] blend.

mesclar [4] [meʃ'kla(x)] *vt* **-1.** [misturar]: **~ algo (com algo)** to mix sthg (with sthg). **-2.** [incorporar]: **~ algo a algo** to combine sthg with sthg.

mesmice [meʒ'misi] *f* sameness.

mesmo, ma ['meʒmu, ma] <> *adj* **-1.** [ger] same; **o ~ batom** the same lipstick; **na mesma hora** [imediatamente] at once. **-2.** [próprio]: **eu ~ fiz isso** I made that myself; **ele ~** himself; **ela mesma** herself; **eles mesmos** themselves. **-3.** [para enfatizar] very. <> *pron*: **o ~/a mesma** the same.

~ mesma <> *f*: **continuar na mesma** [não mudar] to be exactly the same; **ficar na mesma** [não entender] to be none the wiser. <> *m* [a mesma coisa]: **o mesma** the same; **dá no mesma** it's all the same.

~ mesmo *adv* **-1.** [precisamente]: **agora/aqui ~** right now/here; **é assim ~** that's just the way it is; **hoje/ontem ~** just today/yesterday; **por isso ~** for that very reason. **-2.** [realmente] really; **é ~?** really?; **só ~ você consegue fazer isso** only you can do it. **-3.** [até, ainda] even; **~ assim, assim ~** even so; **nem ~** not even.

~ mesmo que *loc conj* even though.

Mesopotâmia [mezopo'tãmja] *n* Mesopotamia.

mesquinharia [meʃkiɲa'ria] *f* meanness.

mesquinhez [meʃki'ɲeʃ] *f*[] meanness.

mesquinho, nha [meʃ'kiɲu, ɲa] *adj* mean.

mesquita [meʃ'kita] *f* mosque.

messias [me'siaʃ] *m fig* messiah.

~ Messias *m*: **o Messias** the Messiah.

mestiçagem [meʃtʃi'saʒẽ] (*pl* **-ns**) *f* **-1.** [cruzamento] cross-breeding. **-2.** [miscigenação] miscegenation.

mestiço, ça [meʃ'tʃisu, sa] <> *adj* mestizo. <> *m, f* mestizo.

mestra ['mɛʃtra] *f* ⊳ **mestre**.

mestrado [meʃ'tradu] *m* **-1.** [grau] masters (degree). **-2.** [curso] masters; **fazer ~** to study for a masters.

mestrando, da [meʃ'trãndu, da] *m student about to complete a master's degree.*

mestre, tra ['mɛʃtri, tra] <> *adj* **-1.** [extraordinário] fantastic. **-2.** [principal] master. <> *m, f* **-1.** [ger] master; **ser ~ em fazer algo** *irôn* to be a past master at doing sthg. **-2.** [fonte de ensinamento] teacher. **-3.** [músico] maestro.

mestre-cuca [ˌmɛʃtri'kuka] (*pl* **mestres-cucas**) *m fam* chef.

mestre-de-cerimônias [ˌmɛʃtridʒiseri'monjaʃ] (*pl* **mestres-de-cerimônias**) *m* master of ceremonies.

mestre-de-obras [ˌmɛʃtri'dʒɔbraʃ] (*pl* **mestres de-obras**) *m* foreman.

mestre-sala [ˌmɛʃtri'sala] (*pl* **mestres-sala**) *m* [em escola de samba] *leader of samba group display during carnival.*

mestria [meʃ'tria] *f* = **maestria**.

mesura [me'zura] *f* reverence; **cheio de ~s** kowtowing.

meta ['mɛta] *f* **-1.** [objetivo] aim, goal. **-2.** [gol] goal. **-3.** [na corrida] finishing line.

metabolismo [metabo'liʒmul] *m* metabolism.

metade [me'tadʒi] *f* half; **~ das pessoas** half the people; **cortar pela ~** to cut in half; **deixar pela ~** to leave halfway through; **na ~ do caminho** halfway; **na ~ do filme** halfway through the film; **pela ~ do preço** at half price.

metafísico, ca [meta'fiziku, ka] <> *adj* metaphysical. <> *m, f* [filósofo] metaphysicist.

~ metafísica *f* [disciplina] metaphysics *(pl)*.

metáfora [me'tafora] *f* metaphor.

metafórico, ca [meta'fɔriku, ka] *adj* metaphorical.

metal [me'taw] (*pl* **-ais**) *m* metal.

~ metais *mpl MÚS* brass instruments.

metálico, ca [me'taliku, ka] *adj* metallic.

metalinguagem [metalĩŋ'gwaʒẽ] (*pl* **-ns**) *f* metalanguage.

metalurgia [metalux'ʒia] *f* metallurgy.

metalúrgico, ca [meta'luxʒiku, ka] <> *adj* metallurgic. <> *m, f* [operário] metallurgist.

~ metalúrgica *f* [oficina] foundry.

metamorfose [metamox'fɔzi] *f* metamorphosis.

metamorfosear [15] [metamoxfo'zja(x)] *vt*: ~ alguém/algo (em) to change sb/sthg (into).

➡ **metamorfosear-se** *vp* **-1.** BIOL to metamorphose. **-2.** *fig* [mudar]: ~-se (em) to metamorphose (into).

metano [me'tãnu] *m* methane.

metástase [me'taʃtazi] *f* MED metastasis.

meteórico, ca [mete'ɔriku, ka] *adj* meteoric.

meteorito [metʃju'ritu] *m* meteorite.

meteoro [me'tjoru] *m* meteor.

meteorologia [metʃjorolo'ʒia] *f* meteorology.

meteorológico, ca [metʃjoro'lɔʒiku, ka] *adj* meteorological.

meteorologista [metʃjorolo'ʒiʃta] *mf* **-1.** [especialista] meteorologist. **-2.** RADIO & TV weather forecaster.

meter [5] [me'te(x)] *vt* **-1.** [ger] to put. **-2.** [enfiar]: ~ algo em OU dentro de algo to put sthg in/inside sthg. **-3.** [inspirar]: **ele me mete pena** he makes me feel sorry for him; **ele é feio de ~ medo** he's so ugly it's frightening. **-4.** [envolver]: ~ alguém em algo to involve sb in sthg.

➡ **meter-se** *vp* **-1.** [ir, esconder-se] to hide. **-2.** [recolher-se]: ~-se em algum lugar to shut o.s. in somewhere. **-3.** [intrometer-se]: ~-se (em algo) to stick one's nose (in sthg); **não se meta!** don't interfere! **-4.** [desafiar]: ~-se com alguém to provoke sb. **-5.** [associar-se]: ~-se com alguém to get mixed up with sb. **-6.** [fazer-se de]: ~-se a algo to play at being sthg; ~-se a valente to pretend to be brave. **-7.** [aventurar-se]: ~-se a fazer algo to start doing sthg. **-8.** [envolver-se]: ~-se em algo to get involved in sthg.

meticulosidade [metʃikulozi'dadʒi] *f* meticulousness.

meticuloso, osa [metʃiku'lozu, ɔza] *adj* meticulous.

metido, da [me'tʃidu, da] *adj* **-1.** [abelhudo] meddlesome, nosy. **-2.** [presumido]: ~ (a besta) full of o.s. **-3.** [cheio de intimidades] inquisitive. **-4.** [envolvido]: ~ com alguém involved with sb; ~ em algo involved in sthg. **-5.** [em roupa] dressed.

metódico, ca [me'tɔdʒiku, ka] *adj* methodical.

metodismo [meto'dʒiʒmu] *m* **-1.** RELIG Methodism. **-2.** [procedimento] method.

metodista [meto'dʒiʃta] RELIG <> *adj* Methodist. <> *mf* Methodist.

método ['mɛtodu] *m* method.

metodologia [metodolo'ʒia] *f* methodology.

metodológico, ca [metodo'lɔʒiku, ka] *adj* methodological.

metonímia [meto'nimja] *f* metonymy.

metragem [me'traʒẽ] *f* **-1.** [medida] length in metres UK OU meters US. **-2.** CINE: **filme de curta/ longa** ~ short/feature-length film.

metralhadora [metraʎa'dora] *f* machine gun.

metralhar [4] [metra'ʎa(x)] *vt* **-1.** [atirar em] to machine-gun. **-2.** *fig* [bombardear]: ~ alguém de perguntas to fire questions at sb.

métrico, ca ['mɛtriku, ka] *adj* **-1.** [do metro] metric; **fita métrica** tape measure. **-2.** LITER metrical.

➡ **métrica** *f* LITER metre UK, meter US.

metro ['mɛtru] *m* metre UK, meter US; ~ cúbico cubic metre; ~ quadrado square metre.

metrô [me'tro] *m* underground UK, subway US.

metrópole [me'trɔpoli] *f* **-1.** [cidade principal] capital. **-2.** [cidade grande] metropolis. **-3.** [nação] mother country.

metropolitano, na [metropoli'tãnu, na] *adj* metropolitan.

metroviário, ria [metro'vjarju, rja] <> *adj* underground UK (antes de subst), subway US (antes de subst). <> *m, f* [funcionário] underground worker UK, subway worker US.

meu, minha ['mew, 'miɲa] <> *adj* **-1.** [ger] my; **este é o** ~ **carro** this is my car; ~ **Deus!** my God!; **minha nossa!** oh me, oh my!, gosh! **-2.** [caro a mim] my; **como vai,** ~ **caro Affonso?** how are you, my dear Affonso?; ~ **irmão** *fam* [tratamento] my friend. <> *pron*: **o** ~ **/a minha** mine; **um amigo** ~ a friend of mine; **os** ~**s** [a minha família] my family; **este jeito de andar é bem** ~ this manner of walking is quite me.

mexer [5] [me'ʃe(x)] <> *vt* **-1.** [ger] to move. **-2.** [misturar] to mix. <> *vi* **-1.** [mover] to move. **-2.**: ~ **em alguém/algo** [tocar] to touch sb/sthg; [mudar de posição, remexer] to fiddle with sb/sthg. **-3.**: ~ **com alguém** [caçoar] to tease sb; [provocar] to provoke sb; [afetar] to affect sb. **-4.** [trabalhar]: ~ **com algo** to work with sthg.

➡ **mexer-se** *vp* **-1.** [mover-se] to move. **-2.** [apressar-se] to hurry; **mexam-se!** get a move on! **-3.** [agir] to move.

mexerica [meʃe'rika] *f* tangerine.

mexericar [12] [meʃeri'ka(x)] *vi* to gossip.

mexerico [meʃe'riku] *m* **-1.** [ato] gossip. **-2.** [intriga] intrigue.

mexeriqueiro, ra [meʃeri'kejru, ra] <> *adj* gossipy. <> *m, f* busybody, gossip.

mexicano, na [meʃi'kãnu, na] <> *adj* Mexican. <> *m, f* Mexican.

México ['mɛʃikul] *n* Mexico.

mexido, da [me'ʃidu, da] *adj* **-1.** [papéis] muddled. **-2.** [ovos] scrambled.

mexilhão [meʃi'ʎãw] (*pl* -ões) *m* mussel.

mezanino [meza'ninu] *m* mezzanine.

mg (*abrev de* miligrama) *m* mg.

MG (*abrev de* Estado de Minas Gerais) *n* State of Minas Gerais.

mi [mi] *m* MÚS E, mi.

miado ['mjadu] *m* miaow.

miar [16] ['mja(x)] *vi* to mew.

miasma ['mjaʒma] *m* **-1.** [emanação] miasma. **-2.** *fig*: ~ **social** social miasma.

miau ['mjaw] *m* miaow.

miçanga [mi'sãga] *f* **-1.** [conta] glass bead. **-2.** [ornato] beads (*pl*).

micção [mik'sãw] (*pl* -ões) *f* urination.

mico ['mikul] *m* ZOOL capuchin monkey.

mico-leão [miku'ljãw] (*pl* **micos-leão**) *m* ZOOL golden lion tamarin.

micose [mi'kɔzi] *f* fungal infection, mycosis.

micro ['mikru] *m* COMPUT computer, PC.

micro- [mikru-] *prefixo* micro-.

micróbio [mi'krɔbjul *m* microbe.

microbiologia [mikrobjolo'ʒia] *f* microbiology.

microcirurgia [mikrosirux'ʒia] *f* microsurgery.

microcomputador [mikrokõnputa'do(x)] *m* microcomputer.

microcosmo [mikro'kɔʒmu] *m* microcosm.

microempresa [mikrowẽn'preza] *f* small business.

microempresário, ria [mikrwẽnpre'zarju, ria] *m* small-business owner.

microfilme [mikro'fiwmi] *m* microfilm.

microfone [mikro'fɔni] *m* microphone.

microfonia [mikro'fonia] *f* ELETRON *vibrations in a sound system.*

microinformática [mikrwĩnfox'matʃika] *f* microcomputing.

microonda [mikro'õnda] *f* microwave.

➡ **microondas** *mpl* [forno] microwave oven (*sg*).

microônibus [mikro'onibuʃ] *m inv* minibus.

microorganismo [mikrwoxga'niʒmu] *m* microorganism.

microprocessador [mikruprosesa'do(x)] *m* microprocessor.

microscópico, ca [mikroʃ'kɔpiku, ka] *adj* microscopic.

microscópio [mikroʃ'kɔpju] *m* microscope.

mictório [mik'tɔrju] *m* urinal.

mídia ['midʒja] *f* media.

migalha [mi'gaʎa] *f* [de pão, bolo] crumb.

➡ **migalhas** *fpl* [sobras] leftovers.

migração [migra'sãw] (*pl* **-ões**) *f* migration.

migrante [mi'grãntʃi] ◇ *adj* **-1.** [pássaro] migratory. **- 2.** [população] migrant. ◇ *mf* migrant.

migrar [4] [mi'gra(x)] *vi* to migrate.

migratório, ria [migra'tɔrju, rja] *adj* migratory.

mijada [mi'ʒada] *f fam* pee; **dar uma** ~ to have a pee.

mijar [4] [mi'ʒa(x)] *vi fam* to pee.

➡ **mijar-se** *vp mfam* to piss o.s.; ~-**se de rir** to wet OU piss o.s. laughing.

mijo ['miʒu] *m fam* pee.

mil ['miw] *num* **-1.** [número] thousand; **três** ~ three thousand. **- 2.** [grande número] a thousand. **- 3.** *loc:* **estar a** ~ *fam* to be working flat out; **seis.**

milagre [mi'lagri] *m* miracle; **por** ~ miraculously.

milagroso, osa [mila'grozu, ɔza] *adj* miraculous.

milanesa [mila'neza] *f:* **à** ~ in breadcrumbs.

milenar [mile'na(x)] *adj* **-1.** [que tem um milênio] millenary. **- 2.** *fig* [antigo] age-old.

milênio [mi'lenju] *m* millennium.

milésimo, ma [mi'lɛzimu, ma] *num* thousandth; **a milésima parte** the thousandth part.

mil-folhas [miw'foʎaʃ] *f inv* millefeuille.

milha ['miʎa] *f* mile; ~ **marítima** nautical mile.

milhão [mi'ʎãw] (*pl* **-ões**) *num* million; **três milhões** three million.

milhar [mi'ʎa(x)] (*pl* **-es**) *m* thousand.

➡ **milhares** *mpl:* ~ **es de pessoas** thousands of people.

milharal [miʎa'raw] (*pl* **-ais**) *m* maize field *UK*, corn field *US*.

milho ['miʎu] *m* **-1.** [planta] maize *UK*, corn *US*. **- 2.** [grão] corn; ~ **de pipoca** popcorn. **- 3.** *loc:* **catar** ~ to type very slowly.

milhões [mi'ʎõjʃ] *pl* ➡ **milhão.**

miliardário, ria [miljax'darju, rja] ◇ *adj* multimillionaire. ◇ *m, f* multimillionaire.

milícia [mi'lisja] *f* militia.

milico [mi'liku] *m fam pej* military type; **os** ~**s** the military.

miligrama [mili'grãma] *m* milligram.

mililitro [mili'litru] *m* millilitre *UK*, milliliter *US*.

milímetro [mi'limetru] *m* millimetre *UK*, millimeter *US*.

milionário, ria [miljo'narju, rja] ◇ *adj* millionaire. ◇ *m, f* millionaire.

milionésimo, ma [miljo'nɛʒimu, ma] *num* millionth; **a milionésima parte** the millionth part.

militância [mili'tãnsja] *f* militancy.

militante [mili'tãntʃi] ◇ *adj* militant. ◇ *mf* militant.

militar [4] [mili'ta(x)] ◇ *adj* military. ◇ *mf* career soldier; **os** ~ **es** the military (*inv*). ◇ *vi* **-1.** [lutar]: ~ **(por/contra)** to fight for/against. **- 2.**: ~ **em** MIL to serve in; POL to be active in.

militarismo [mili'tariʒmu] *m* militarism.

militarista [mili'riʃta] ◇ *adj* militaristic. ◇ *mf* militarist.

militarizar [4] [militari'za(x)] *vt* to militarize.

mil-réis [miw'xɛj] *m inv early Brazilian and Portuguese monetary unit.*

mim ['mĩ] *pron* **-1.** [com preposição: complemento indireto] me; **ela comprou um presente para** ~ she bought a present for me, she bought me a present; **ele fez o serviço por** ~ he did the work for me; **a** ~ **ele não faria isto** he wouldn't do that to me; **falaram mal de** ~ they spoke ill of me; **o que você tem contra** ~**?** what have you got against me?; **eles foram embora sem** ~ they left without me; **para** ~**, este é o melhor quadro** [para expressar opinião] for me, this is the best painting; **por** ~**, você pode ficar aqui** [de minha parte] as far as I'm concerned, you can stay here. **- 2.** [com preposição: reflexo] myself; **a** ~**, você não engana** you don't fool me; **comprei-o para** ~ **(mesmo** OU **próprio)** I bought it for myself; **preciso cuidar mais de** ~ I need to look after myself a bit better; **de** ~ **para** ~ [comigo mesmo] to myself.

mimado, da [mi'madu, da] *adj* spoiled.

mimar [4] [mi'ma(x)] *vt* **-1.** [fazer todas as vontades de] to spoil. **- 2.** [tratar com carinho] to pamper.

mimeografar [4] [mimjogra'fa(x)] *vt* to mimeograph.

mimeógrafo [mi'mjɔgraful *m* mimeograph.

mímico, ca ['mimiku, ka] <> *adj* imitative. <> *m, f* -**1.** [pessoa] mimic. -**2.** [ator] mime artist.

mímica *f* mime; **fazer mímica** to mimic; **por mímica** in mime.

mimo ['mimul *m* -**1.** [carinho] affection; **fazer ~ s a alguém** to be affectionate towards sb. -**2.** [pessoa ou coisa graciosa]: **ser um ~** to be a delight.

mimoso, osa [mi'mozu, ɔza] *adj* -**1.** [carinhoso] affectionate. -**2.** [gracioso] delightful. -**3.** [delicado] delicate.

mina ['mina] *f* -**1.** [ger] mine; **~ de carvão/ouro** coal/gold mine. -**2.** *fig*: **ser uma ~** [de lucros] to be a goldmine; [preciosidade] to be precious; **ser uma ~ de informações** to be a mine of information. -**3.** *fam* [garota] girl.

minar [4] [mi'na(x)] <> *vt* -**1.** [pôr minas em] to mine. -**2.** [deteriorar, prejudicar] to undermine. <> *vi* [água]: **~ (de)** to stream (from).

minarete [mina'retʃi] *m* minaret.

Minas Gerais [,minaʒe'rajʃ] *n* Minas Gerais.

mindinho [mĩn'dʒiɲul *m fam* pinky.

mineiro, ra [mi'nejru, ra] <> *adj* -**1.** [relativo a mina] mining. -**2.** [de Minas Gerais] from Minas Gerais. <> *m, f* -**1.** [operário] miner. -**2.** [de Minas Gerais] *person from Minas Gerais*.

mineração [minera'sãw] *f* -**1.** [exploração] mining. -**2.** [depuração] purifying.

minerador, ra [minera'do(x),ra] <> *adj* mining *(antes de subst)*. <> *m, f* miner.

mineradora *f* mining company.

mineral [mine'raw] *(pl* -**ais**) <> *adj* mineral. <> *m* mineral.

mineralogia [mineralo'ʒia] *f* mineralogy.

minério [mi'nɛrjul *m* ore; **~ de ferro** iron ore.

mingau [mĩŋ'gawl *m* -**1.** [papa] porridge. -**2.** *fig* [coisa mole] mush.

míngua ['mĩŋgwal *f* lack; **estar à ~ de algo** to be short of sthg; **viver à ~ de algo** to live with a shortage of sthg.

minguado, da [mĩŋ'gwadu, da] *adj* -**1.** [escasso] scarce; **~ de algo** lacking sthg. -**2.** [pouco desenvolvido] flat.

minguante [mĩŋ'gwãntʃi] *m* ASTRON [moon] waning, last quarter.

minguar [4] [mĩŋ'gwa(x)] <> *vt* [reduzir] to reduce. <> *vi* [escassear] to dwindle.

minha ['miɲa] ⊳ **meu**.

minhoca [mi'ɲɔka] *f* earthworm; **com ~s na cabeça** with strange ideas.

míni ['mini] <> *adj inv* mini. <> *m* [vestido] minidress. <> *f* [saia] miniskirt.

miniatura [minja'tural *f* miniature; **em ~** in miniature.

mínima ['minimal *f* ⊳ **mínimo**.

minimalista [minima'liʃta] *adj* minimalist.

minimizar [4] [minimi'za(x)] *vt* -**1.** [tornar mínimo] to minimize. -**2.** [subestimar] to underestimate. -**3.** [fazer pouco caso de] to play down.

mínimo, ma ['minimu, ma] *adj* -**1.** [ger] minimal. -**2.** [muito pequeno] tiny. -**3.** [o menor possível] smallest. -**4.** *(antes de subst)* [nenhum] slightest.

mínimo *m* [limite] least; **o ~ que posso fazer** the least I can do; **no ~** at least.

mínima *f* -**1.** METEOR minimum (temperature). -**2.** MÚS minim. -**3.** *loc*: **não dar a mínima (para alguém/algo)** not to have the least concern (for sb/sthg).

minissaia [,mini'saja] *f* miniskirt.

minissérie [,mini'sɛrji] *f* miniseries.

ministerial [miniʃte'rjaw] *(pl* -**ais**) *adj* ministerial.

ministeriável [miniʃterj'avɛwl *(pl* -**eis**) *mf* ministerial candidate.

ministério [miniʃ'tɛrjul *m* -**1.** [ger] ministry; **Ministério da Fazenda** ≃ HM Treasury *UK*, ≃ the Treasury *US*; **Ministério do Interior** Home Office *UK*, Department of the Interior *US*; **Ministério Público** public prosecution; **Ministério das Relações Exteriores** ≃ Foreign (and Commonwealth) Office *UK*, ≃ State Department *US*; **Ministério do Trabalho** ≃ Department of Employment *UK*, ≃ Department of Labor *US*; **Ministério da Educação e Cultura** ≃ Department of Education; **Ministério dos Transportes** ≃ Department of Transport. -**2.** [gabinete] cabinet.

ministra [mi'niʃtra] *f* ⊳ **ministro**.

ministrar [4] [miniʃ'tra(x)] *vt* to administer.

ministro, tra [mi'niʃtru, tra] *m, f* minister; **~ sem pasta** minister without portfolio; **~ da Fazenda** ≃ Chancellor of the Exchequer *UK*, ≃ Secretary of the Treasury *US*; **~ do Interior** ≃ Home Secretary *UK*, ≃ Secretary of the Interior *US*; **~ das Relações Exteriores** ≃ Foreign Secretary *UK*, ≃ Secretary of State *US*; **~ da Educação e Cultura** ≃ Secretary for Education; **~ dos Transportes** ≃ Secretary for Transport.

minorar [4] [mino'ra(x)] *vt* to diminish.

minoria [mino'rial *f* minority.

minoritário, ria [minori'tarju, rja] *adj* minority *(antes de subst)*.

minúcia [mi'nusja] *f* -**1.** [detalhe] detail. -**2.** [coisa sem importância] minutiae *(pl)*.

minuciosidade [minusjozi'dadʒil *f* meticulousness.

minucioso, osa [minu'sjozu, ɔza] *adj* meticulous.

minúsculo, la [mi'nuʃkulu, la] *adj* -**1.** [tamanho] minuscule. -**2.** [letra] lower case *(antes de subst)*.

minúscula *f* [letra] lower case.

minuta [mi'nutal *f* -**1.** [rascunho] draft. -**2.** [prato] cooked to order.

minuteria [minute'rial *f* timing device.

minuto [mi'nutul *m* minute; **num ~** *fig* [rapidamente] in a minute; **um ~!** one minute!

miolo ['mjolul *m* -**1.** [pão] crumb. -**2.** [fruta] pulp.

miolos *mpl* -**1.** CULIN brains. -**2.** *fam* [cérebro] brains.

mioma ['mjomal *m* myoma.

míope ['mjupil <> *adj* short-sighted, myopic. <> *mf* short-sighted person, myope.

miopia [mju'pial *f* myopia.

miosótis [mjo'zɔtʃiʃ] *m inv BOT* forget-me-not.

mira ['mira] *f* -**1.** [ger] aim. -**2.** [de arma] sight.

mirabolante [mirabo'lãntʃi] *adj* -**1.** [surpreendente] incredible. -**2.** [espalhafatoso] gaudy.

miraculoso, osa [miraku'lozu, ɔza] *adj* [espantoso] miraculous.

mirada [mi'rada] *f* look.

miragem [mi'raʒẽ] (*pl* -ns) *f* -**1.** [efeito ótico] mirage. -**2.** *fig* [ilusão] illusion.

miramar [mira'ma(x)] *m* sea-view belvedere.

mirante [mi'rãntʃi] *m* belvedere.

mirar [4] [mi'ra(x)] <> *vt* -**1.** [fitar] to stare at. -**2.** [apontar para] to aim at. -**3.** [observar] to watch. <> *vi* [apontar]: ~ (**em algo**) to aim (at sthg).

➤ **mirar-se** *vp* -**1.** [olhar-se]: ~-**se** (**em algo**) to look at o.s. (in sthg). -**2.** [seguir o exemplo de]: ~ **se em alguém** to follow the example of sb.

miríade [mi'riadʒi] *f fig* myriad.

mirim [mi'rĩ] (*pl* -ns) *adj* little.

misantropo, pa [mizãn'tropu, pa] *m, f* misanthrope.

miscelânea [mise'lãnja] *f* -**1.** [coletânea] miscellany. -**2.** *fig* [mistura] assortment.

miscigenação [misiʒena'sãw] *f* interbreeding.

mise-en-plis [mizãn'pli] *m inv* shampoo and set.

miserável [mize'ravɛw] (*pl* -eis) <> *adj* -**1.** [ger] miserable. -**2.** [sovina] miserly. -**3.** [vil] despicable. -**4.** [terrível] dreadful. <> *mf* -**1.** [infeliz] miserable person. -**2.** [pessoa pobre] poor wretch. -**3.** [pessoa vil] despicable person.

miseravelmente [mizeravew'mẽntʃi] *adv* -**1.** [desgraçadamente] wretchedly. -**2.** [pobremente] in misery.

miséria [mi'zɛrja] *f* -**1.** [desgraça] misery. -**2.** [pobreza] poverty; **chorar** ~ to whinge. -**3.** [sovinice] meanness. -**4.** [ninharia]: **custar/ganha-ruma** ~ to cost/to earn a pittance.

➤ **misérias** *fpl*: **fazer** ~**s** to do wonders; **fazer** ~**s com alguém** to cause sb misery.

misericórdia [mizeri'kɔrdʒja] *f*: ~ (**de/com**) mercy (on/for).

misericordioso, osa [mizerikox'dʒjozu, ɔza] *adj* compassionate.

mísero, ra ['mizeru, ra] *adj fig* [escasso] miserly.

misoginia [mizoʒi'nia] *f* misogyny.

misógino, na [mi'zɔʒinu, na] <> *adj* misogynous. <> *m, f* mysoginist.

missa ['misa] *f* -**1.** *RELIG* mass; ~ **do galo** midnight mass. -**2.** *loc*: **não saber da** ~ **a metade** *fam* to not know the half of it.

missal [mi'saw] (*pl* -ais) *m* missal.

missão [mi'sãw] (*pl* -ões) *f* mission.

misse ['misi] *f* beauty queen.

míssil ['misiw] (*pl* -eis) *m* missile; ~ **de curto/médio/longo alcance** short-/medium-/long-range missile.

missionário, ria [misjo'narju, rja] <> *adj* missionary. <> *m, f* missionary.

Mississippi [misi'sipi] *n*: **o** ~ the Mississippi.

missiva [mi'siva] *f* missive.

missões [mi'sõjʃ] *pl* ▷ **missão**.

Missouri [mi'zuri] *n*: **o** ~ the Missouri.

mister [miʃ'te(x)] *m* -**1.** [ofício] office. -**2.** [necessidade] need; **ser** ~ **fazer algo** to be necessary to do sthg.

mistério [miʃ'tɛrju] *m* -**1.** [ger] mystery; **não ter** ~ to be straightforward. -**2.** [segredo] secret; **fazer** ~ to make a mystery.

misterioso, osa [miʃte'rjozu, ɔza] *adj* mysterious.

misticismo [miʃtʃi'siʒmu] *m* mysticism.

místico, ca ['miʃtʃiku, ka] <> *adj* mystic. <> *m, f* [pessoa] mystic.

mistificador, ra [miʃtʃifika'do(x), ra] <> *adj* mystifying (*antes de subst*). <> *m, f* deceiver.

mistificar [12] [miʃtʃifi'ka(x)] *vt* to mystify.

misto, ta ['miʃtu, ta] *adj* mixed.

➤ **misto** *m* mixture.

misto-quente [,miʃtu'kẽntʃi] (*pl* **mistos-quentes**) *m toasted cheese and ham sandwich.*

mistura [miʃ'tura] *f* mixture.

MISTURA DE RAÇAS

A large part of Brazil's cultural wealth is due to the many races that make up the Brazilian people. The Indians, Portuguese and Negroes of the colonial period were joined, from the mid-nineteenth century onwards, by millions of immigrants from, amongst many others, Italy, Germany, Spain, Syria, Lebanon and Japan.

misturar [4] [miʃtu'ra(x)] *vt* -**1.** [combinar, juntar] to mix. -**2.** [confundir] to mix up.

➤ **misturar-se** *vp* [socialmente]: ~-**se com alguém** to mix with sb.

mistureba [miʃtu'rɛba] *f fam* hotchpotch.

mítico, ca ['mitʃiku, ka] *adj* mythical.

mitificar [12] [mitʃifi'ka(x)] *vt* to mythicize.

mitigar [14] [mitʃi'ga(x)] *vt* to mitigate.

mito ['mitu] *m* -**1.** [ger] myth. -**2.** [pessoa] legend.

mitologia [mitolo'ʒia] *f* mythology.

mitológico, ca [mito'lɔʒiku, ka] *adj* mythological.

miudeza [mju'deza] *f* -**1.** [pormenor] detail. -**2.** [insignificância] trifle.

miudezas [mju'dezaʃ] *fpl* -**1.** [objetos pequenos] odds and ends. -**2.** [quinquilharia] trinkets.

miúdo, da ['mjudu, da] *adj* [pequeno] small.

➤ **miúdos** *mpl* -**1.** [dinheiro] small change. -**2.** [de animal] giblets. -**3.** *loc*: **trocar em** ~**s** to put it simply.

mixagem [mik'saʒẽ] *f CINE & RÁDIO* mixing.

mixar[1] [4] [mi'ʃa(x)] *vi fam* [gorar] to go down the drain.

mixar[2] [4] [mi'ʃa(x)] *vt CINE & RÁDIO* to mix.

mixaria [miʃa'ria] *f* -**1.** *fam* [soma insignificante]: **uma** ~ peanuts. -**2.** [coisa sem valor] rubbish.

mixórdia [mi'ʃɔxdʒia] *f* mess.

mixuruca [miʃu'ruka] *adj* -**1.** [presente] worthless. -**2.** [festa] lifeless.

ml (*abrev de mililitro*) *m* ml.

mm (*abrev de* **milímetro**) *m* mm.

mnemônico, ca [mneˈmoniku, ka] *adj* mnemonic.

mó [ˈmɔ] *f* -1. [de moinho] millstone. -2. [de afiar] whetstone.

moagem [ˈmwaʒẽ] *f* grinding.

móbile [ˈmɔbili] *m* mobile.

mobília [moˈbilja] *f* furniture; **sem ~** unfurnished.

mobiliar [16] [mobiˈlja(x)] *vt* to furnish.

mobiliário [mobiˈljarju] *m* furniture.

mobilidade [mobiliˈdadʒi] *f* mobility; **~ social** social mobility.

mobilização [mobilizaˈsãw] *f* mobilization.

mobilizar [14] [mobiliˈza(x)] *vt* to mobilize.

moça [ˈmosa] *f* ⊳ **moço**.

moçada [moˈsada] *f fam* group of young people.

Moçambique [mosãnˈbiki] *n* Mozambique.

moção [moˈsãw] *f* motion.

mocassim [mokaˈsĩ] (*pl* **-ns**) *m* moccasin.

mochila [moˈʃila] *f* rucksack.

mocidade [mosiˈdadʒi] *f* -1. [período] youth. -2. [os jovens]: **a ~** the young.

mocinho, nha [moˈsiɲu, ɲa] *m, f* -1. [jovem] boy. -2. [herói] hero.

moço, ça [ˈmosu, sa] ⟨⟩ *adj* [pessoa] young. ⟨⟩ *m, f* -1. [jovem] young person. -2. [adulto] young boy (young girl). -3. [como forma de tratamento]: **ei, ~!** hey, man!

moções [moˈsõjʃ] *pl* ⊳ **moção**.

moda [ˈmɔda] *f* -1. [ger] fashion; **cair** *ou* **sair de ~** to fall out of fashion; **estar na ~** to be in fashion, to be fashionable; **fora de ~** out of fashion; **lançar uma ~** to start a fashion. -2. [coqueluche] craze. -3. [maneira] way; **faço tudo à minha ~** I do everything my way; **à ~ portuguesa** Portuguese-style. -4. *loc:* **inventar ~** to create a new fad.

modalidade [modaliˈdadʒi] *f* -1. [tipo] mode. -2. *ESP* event.

modelador [modelaˈdo(x)] *m* [cinta] girdle.

modelagem [modeˈlaʒẽ] (*pl* **-ns**) *f* -1. [ato] modelling. -2. [produto] moulding *UK*, molding *US*. -3. [do corpo] shape.

modelar [4] [modeˈla(x)] *vt* -1. [ger] to mould *UK*, to mold *US*. -2. *fig* [moldar]: **~ algo por algo** to model sthg on sthg.

modelista [modeˈliʃta] *mf* designer.

modelo [moˈdelu] ⟨⟩ *m* model; **~ econômico** economic model; ⟨⟩ *mf* model; **~ vivo** live model.

modem [ˈmodẽ] (*pl* **-ns**) *m COMPUT* modem.

moderação [moderaˈsãw] *f* moderation.

moderado, da [modeˈradu, da] *adj* moderate.

moderar [4] [modeˈra(x)] *vt* to moderate.

⬤ **moderar-se** *vp* [comedir-se] to control o.s.

modernidade [modexniˈdadʒi] *f* modernity.

modernismo [modexˈniʒmu] *m* modernism.

modernização [modexnizaˈsãw] *f* modernization.

modernizar [4] [modexniˈza(x)] *vt* to modernize.

⬤ **modernizar-se** *vp* to keep o.s. up to date.

moderno, na [moˈdɛxnu, na] *adj* modern.

modernoso, osa [modexˈnozu, ɔza] *adj* newfangled.

modess® [ˈmɔdeʃ] *m inv* sanitary towel *UK*, sanitary napkin *US*.

modestamente [modeʃtaˈmẽntʃil] *adv* -1. [ger] modestly. -2. [sem pretensão] with modesty.

modéstia [moˈdɛʃtja] *f* modesty.

modesto, ta [moˈdɛʃtu, ta] *adj* modest.

módico, ca [ˈmɔdʒiku, ka] *adj* -1. [barato, parco] modest. -2. [moderado] moderate.

modificação [modʒifikaˈsãw] (*pl* **-ões**) *f* -1. [alteração] modification. -2. [transformação] transformation.

modificar [12] [modʒifiˈka(x)] *vt* -1. [ger] to modify. -2. [transformar] to change.

⬤ **modificar-se** *vp* to alter.

modinha [moˈdʒiɲa] *f popular Brazilian song.*

modismo [moˈdʒiʒmu] *m* -1. [tendência] trend. -2. [moda] fashion.

modista [moˈdʒiʃta] *mf* dressmaker.

modo [ˈmɔdu] *m* -1. [ger] way; **de ~ algum** in no way; **desse ~** that way; **de um ~ geral** in general; **~ de usar** directions for use. -2. [jeito] manner; **~ de andar** gait. -3. *GRAM* mood.

⬤ **modos** *mpl* manners.

⬤ **de modo que** *loc conj* -1. [de maneira que] so (that). -2. [assim sendo] so that.

modorra [moˈdoxa] *f* -1. [moleza] lethargy. -2. [sonolência] drowsiness.

modulação [modulaˈsãw] (*pl* **-ões**) *f* modulation; **~ de freqüência** frequency modulation.

modulado, da [moduˈladu, da] *adj* modular.

modular [4] [moduˈla(x)] ⟨⟩ *adj* modular. ⟨⟩ *vt* to modulate.

módulo [ˈmɔdulu] *m* -1. [unidade] module. -2. [veículo]: **~ lunar** lunar module.

moeda [ˈmwɛda] *f* -1. [peça] coin; **uma ~ de 10 centavos** a 10 cent coin; **uma ~ falsa** a counterfeit coin. -2. [dinheiro] money; **~ forte** hard currency; **pagar na mesma ~** to pay sb back in their own coin; ⊳ **casa**.

MOEDA

The monetary unit in Brazil has undergone many changes throughout history, due to the various periods of high inflation that the country has gone through. In the post-war period, Brazil has adopted, successively, the cruzeiro, the cruzeiro novo, the cruzado, the cruzado novo and the cruzado real. Since 1994, with the relative economic stability of the country, the real has become the Brazilian monetary unit.

---

moedor [mweˈdo(x)] *m* -1. [de café, pimenta] mill. -2. [de carne] mincer *UK*, grinder *US*.

moenda [ˈmwẽnda] *f* sugar mill.

moer [28] [ˈmwe(x)] ⟨⟩ *vt* -1. [café, pimenta] to grind. -2. [carne] to mince *UK*, to grind *US*. -3. [para extrair suco] to mill. ⟨⟩ *vi* [moinho] to grind.

mofado, da [mo'fadu, da] *adj* mouldy *UK*, moldy *US*.

mofar [4] [mo'fa(x)] <> *vt* [cobrir de mofo] to cover in mould *UK ou* mold *US*. <> *vi* -**1.** [criar mofo] to go mouldy *UK ou* moldy *US*. -**2.** *fig*: ~ **(em)** [ficar esperando] to kick one's heels (in); [permanecer] to gather moss (in).

mofo ['moful] *m* mould *UK*, mold *US*; **criar** ~ to go mouldy *UK ou* moldy *US*; **o pão está cheio de** ~ the bread is all mouldy *UK ou* moldy *US*; **esta camisa está com cheiro de** ~ this shirt smells musty.

Mogadício [moga'disju] *n* Mogadishu.

mogno ['mognu] *m* mahogany.

moído, da ['mwidu, da] *adj* -**1.** [café, pimenta] ground. -**2.** [carne] minced *UK*, ground *US*. -**3.** *fig* [doído]: ~ **de algo** hurting from sthg; ~ **de cansaço** shattered, tired out.

moinho ['mwiɲu] *m* mill; ~ **de vento** windmill.

moisés [moj'zɛʃ] *m inv* carrycot.

moita ['mojta] *f* thicket.
➡ **na moita** *loc adv* [às escondidas] in secret; **ficar na** ~ [fazer segredo] to keep quiet.

mola ['mɔla] *f* -**1.** [dispositivo] spring. -**2.** *fig* [impulsionador]: ~ **(mestra)** driving force.

molambento, ta [molãn'bẽntu, ta] *adj* ragged.

molambo [mo'lãnbu] *m* [roupa em mau estado] rags *(inv)*.

molar [mo'la(x)] *(pl* -**es)** <> *adj* [dente] molar. <> *m* molar.

moldar [4] [mow'da(x)] *vt* -**1.** [fazer o molde de] to make a mould *UK ou* mold *US* of. -**2.** [modelar] to mould *UK*, to mold *US*. -**3.** *fig* [dar forma a] to shape.
➡ **moldar-se** *vp fig* [orientar-se]: ~**-se por algo** to mould *UK ou* mold *US* o.s. on sthg.

Moldávia [mow'davja] *n* Moldova, Moldavia.

moldávio, via [mow'davju, vja] <> *adj* Moldovan, Moldavian. <> *m, f* Moldovan, Moldavian.

molde ['mɔwdʒi] *m* mould *UK*, mold *US*; ~ **(de vestido)** (dress) pattern.

moldura [mow'dura] *f* -**1.** [de quadro, espelho] frame. -**2.** *ARQUIT* moulding *UK*, molding *US*.

mole ['mɔli] <> *adj* -**1.** [ger] soft. -**2.** [flácido] flabby. -**3.** [lento] languid. -**4.** [fraco] limp. -**5.** [indolente] lazy. -**6.** [condescendente]: **ser** ~ **com alguém** to be lenient with sb. -**7.** *fam* [fácil] a piece of cake. <> *adv* -**1.** [lentamente]: **falar** ~ to speak languidly. -**2.** [facilmente] easily.

moleca [mo'lɛka] *f* ➪ **moleque**.

molecada [mole'kada] *f* bunch of kids.

molecagem [mole'kaʒẽ] *(pl* -**ns)** *f* -**1.** [travessura] prank. -**2.** [brincadeira] trick. -**3.** [patifaria]: **fazer uma** ~ **com alguém** to trick sb.

molécula [mo'lɛkula] *f* molecule.

molecular [moleku'la(x)] *adj* molecular.

moleira [mo'lejra] *f ANAT* fontanelle *UK*, fontanel *US*.

molejo [mo'leʒu] *m* -**1.** [de veículo] suspension. -**2.** *fam* [de pessoa, corpo] wiggle.

molenga [mo'lẽŋga] *adj* lazy.

moleque, leca [mo'lɛki, lɛka] <> *adj* -**1.** [travesso] wild. -**2.** [brincalhão] mischievous. <> *m, f* -**1.** [criança] youngster; ~ **(de rua)** (street) urchin. -**2.** [criança travessa] rascal. -**3.** [patife] scoundrel.

molestador [moleʃta'do(x)] *m* molester.

molestar [4] [moleʃ'ta(x)] *vt* -**1.** [importunar] to annoy. -**2.** [ofender] to offend. -**3.** [sexualmente] to molest.

moléstia [mo'lɛʃtʃja] *f* ailment.

moletom [mole'tõ] *m* brushed cotton; **de** ~ flannel *(antes de subst)*.

moleza [mo'leza] *f* -**1.** [maciez] softness. -**2.** [lentidão] slowness. -**3.** [fraqueza, falta de energia] limpness; **sentir** ~ to feel limp. -**4.** *fam* [coisa fácil]: **ser uma** ~ to be a piece of cake.

molhado, da [mo'ʎadu, da] *adj* wet.
➡ **molhado** *m* wet area.
➡ **molhada** *f*: **dar uma molhada em algo** to wet sthg.

molhar [4] [mo'ʎa(x)] *vt* -**1.** [banhar] to wet; ~ **algo em algo** to dip *ou* dunk sthg in sthg. -**2.** [umedecer] to dampen. -**3.** [regar] to water. -**4.** *fam* [urinar] to wet.
➡ **molhar-se** *vp* -**1.** [cobrir-se de líquido] to wet o.s. -**2.** *fam* [urinar] to get wet.

molhe ['mɔʎi] *m* -**1.** [de defesa] breakwater. -**2.** [de atracação] jetty.

molheira [mo'ʎejra] *f* sauce boat.

molho[1] ['mɔʎu] *m* sauce; ~ **de salada** salad dressing; ~ **branco** white sauce; ~ **inglês** Worcestershire sauce; ~ **pardo** *gravy made with chicken blood and vinegar*.
➡ **de molho** <> *loc adv*: **pôr/deixar de** ~ [roupa, feijão] to put/leave to soak. <> *loc adj*: **ficar de** ~ *fig* [pessoa] to stay in bed.

molho[2] ['mɔʎu] *m* bunch.

molinete [moli'netʃi] *m PESCA* fishing reel.

molusco [mo'luʃku] *m* mollusc.

momentaneamente [momẽntãnja'mẽntʃi] *adv* momentarily.

momentâneo, nea [momẽn'tãnju, nja] *adj* momentary.

momento [mo'mẽntu] *m* -**1.** moment; **de um para outro** from one moment to the next; **neste** ~ [agora mesmo] just now; **a qualquer** ~ any moment now; **(no)** ~ **oportuno** (at the) right moment. -**2.** [tempo presente]: **do** ~ of the moment; **no** ~ at the moment.

Mônaco ['monaku] *n*: **(o principado de)** ~ (the principality of) Monaco.

monarca [mo'naxka] *mf* monarch.

monarquia [monax'kia] *f* monarchy.

monarquista [monax'kiʃta] <> *adj* monarchic. <> *mf* monarchist.

monastério [monaʃ'tɛrju] *m* monastery.

monástico, ca [mo'naʃtʃiku, ka] *adj* monastic.

monção [mõn'sãw] *(pl* -**ões)** *f* [vento] monsoon.

monetário, ria [mone'tarju, rja] *adj* monetary;
➪ **correção**.

monetarismo [moneta'riʒmul *m* monetarism.
monetarista [moneta'riʃtal <> *adj* monetarist.
<> *mf* [partidário] monetarist.
monge, ja ['mõnʒi, ʒal *m, f* [monje] monk; [monja] nun.
mongol [mõŋ'gɔwl <> *adj* Mongol. <> *m* Mongol.
Mongólia [mõŋ'gɔljal *n* Mongolia.
mongolismo [mõŋgo'liʒmul *m* MED Down's syndrome.
mongolóide [mõŋgo'lɔjdʒil MED <> *adj* Down's syndrome *(antes de subst).* <> *mf* (person with) Down's syndrome.
monitor, ra [moni'to(x), ral *(mpl* -es, *fpl* -s) *m, f* EDUC monitor.
➧ **monitor** *m* -1. [ger] monitor. -2. TV screen.
monitorar [4] [monito'ra(x)l *vt* to monitor.
monja ['mõnʒal *f* ▷ **monge**.
monocromático, ca [monokro'matʃiku, kal *adj* monochromatic.
monóculo [mo'nɔkulul *m* monocle.
monocultura [monokuw'tural *f* monoculture.
monogamia [monoga'mial *f* monogamy.
monógamo, ma [mo'nɔgamu, mal *adj* monogamous.
monografia [monogra'fial *f* monograph.
monograma [mono'grãmal *m* monogram.
monolítico, ca [mono'litʃiku, kal *adj* monolithic.
monologar [14] [monolo'ga(x)l *vi* -1. [falar consigo mesmo] to talk to o.s. -2. TEATRO to give a monologue.
monólogo [mo'nɔlogul *m* monologue.
mononucleose [ˌmononukle'ɔzil *f* mononucleosis.
monopólio [mono'pɔljul *m* monopoly.
monopolista [monopo'liʃtal <> *adj* monopolistic. <> *mf* monopolist.
monopolizar [4] [monopoli'za(x)l *vt* to monopolize.
monossílabo, ba [mono'silabu, bal *adj* monosyllabic.
➧ **monossílabos** *mpl* monosyllables.
monotonia [monoto'nial *f* monotony.
monótono, na [mo'nɔtonu, nal *adj* monotonous.
monóxido [mo'nɔksidul *m* monoxide; ~ **de carbono** carbon monoxide.
monsenhor [mõnse'ɲo(x)l *m* Monsignor.
monstrengo, ga [mõnʃ'treŋgu, gal *m, f* [pessoa, coisa] monstrosity.
monstro ['mõnʃtrul <> *adj inv* [enorme] huge. <> *m* [criatura disforme] monster; **ser um** ~ [ser um prodígio] to be a wizard; [ser cruel, enorme, horrendo] to be monstrous.
monstruosidade [mõnʃtrwozi'dadʒil *f* monstrosity.
monstruoso, osa [mõnʃ'trwozu, ɔzal *adj* -1. [com conformação de monstro] deformed. -2. [enorme] enormous. -3. [horrendo] monstrous.
monta ['mõntal *f*: **de pouca** ~ of little importance.

montador, ra [mõnta'do(x), ral *m, f* CINE (film) editor.
montagem [mõn'taʒêl *(pl* -ns) *f* -1. [de equipamento, casa] assembly. -2. CINE (film) editing. -3. TEATRO (theatre) production.
montanha [mõn'tãɲal *f* mountain.
montanha-russa [mõnˌtãɲa'rusal *(pl* montanhas-russas) *f* roller coaster.
Montanhas Rochosas [mõnˌtãɲaʃxo'ʃɔzaʃl *n*: **as** ~ the Rocky Mountains, the Rockies.
montanhês, esa [mõnta'ɲeʃ, ezal *(pl* -eses) <> *adj* mountain *(antes de subst).* <> *m, f* highlander.
montanhismo [mõntã'ɲiʒmul *m* mountaineering.
montanhista [mõntã'niʃtal <> *adj* mountaineering. <> *mf* mountaineer.
montanhoso, osa [mõntã'ɲozu, ɔzal *adj* mountainous.
montante [mõn'tãntʃil *m* -1. [soma] amount, sum. -2. [direção]: **a** ~ **de** upstream of.
montão [mõn'tãwl *(pl* -ões) *m* pile.
montar [4] [mõn'ta(x)l <> *vt* -1. [armar] to prime. -2. [instalar] to ready. -3. [pôr sobre]: ~ **alguém em algo** to mount sb on sthg. -4. CINE to edit. -5. TEATRO to produce. <> *vi* -1. [cavalgar]: ~ **(a cavalo)** to ride (horseback). -2. [pôr-se sobre]: ~ **em algo** to mount sthg. -3. [atingir]: ~ **a algo** to amount to sthg.
montaria [mõnta'rial *f* [cavalo] mount.
monte ['mõntʃil *m* -1. [elevação] hill. -2. [pilha] pile. -3. *fig* [grande quantidade]: **um** ~ **de** a load of; **comida aos** ~s loads of food.
montepio [mõntʃi'piwl *m* trust fund.
montês [mõn'teʃl *adj* mountain *(antes de subst)*; **cabra** ~ mountain goat.
Montevidéu [mõntevi'dɛwl *n* Montevideo.
montoeira [mõn'twjral *f*: **uma** ~ **de** a heap of.
montões [mõn'tõjʃl *pl* ▷ **montão**.
monumental [monumẽn'tawl *(pl* -ais) *adj* -1. [enorme] monumental. -2. [magnífico] magnificent.
monumento [monu'mẽntul *m* monument.
moqueca [mo'kɛkal *f Brazilian fish or chicken stew made with coconut milk, onions and palm oil.*
moradia [mora'dʒial, **morada** [mo'radal *f* dwelling.
morador, ra [mora'do(x), ral *(mpl* -es, *fpl* -s) *m, f* resident.
moral [mo'rawl *(pl* -ais) <> *adj* moral. <> *m* [estado de espírito] morale; **levantar o** ~ **(de alguém)** to raise the morale (of sb). <> *f* -1. [ética] morals *(pl).* -2. [de história, fato] moral. -3. [estado de espírito]: **estar de** ~ **baixa** to be demoralized.
moralidade [morali'dadʒil *f* morality.
moralismo [mora'liʒmul *m* moralism.
moralista [mora'liʃtal <> *adj* moralistic. <> *mf* moralist.
moralização [moraliˈzasãwl *(pl* -ões) *f* moralization.
moralizar [4] [morali'za(x)l <> *vt* [tornar mais

moral] to moralize. <> *vi* [pregar moral]: ~ **(sobre)** to moralize (on).

morango [moˈrãŋgu] *m* strawberry.

morar [4] [moˈra(x)] *vi* **-1.** [habitar]: ~ **(em)** to live (in). **-2.** *fam* [entender] to catch on; **morou?** got it?

moratória [moraˈtɔrja] *f* moratorium.

morbidez [moxbiˈdeʒ] *f* morbidity.

mórbido, da [ˈmɔxbidu, da] *adj* morbid.

morcego [moxˈsegu] *m* bat.

mordaça [moxˈdasa] *f* **-1.** [de animal] muzzle. **-2.** *fig* [pano] gag.

mordaz [moxˈdaʒ] *adj* biting.

morder [5] [moxˈde(x)] <> *vt* & *vi* to bite.

mordida [moxˈdʒida] *f* bite; **dar uma** ~ **(em)** to bite (into).

mordomia [moxdoˈmia] *f* **-1.** [num emprego] perks *(pl)*. **-2.** [conforto, luxo] comfort.

mordomo [moxˈdomu] *m* butler.

morena [moˈrena] *f* ⊳ **moreno**.

morenaço, ça [moreˈnasu, sa] *m, f* dark-haired beauty.

moreno, na [moˈrenu, na] <> *adj* **-1.** [tipo - de pele] dark-skinned; [- de cabelo] dark-haired. **-2.** [bronzeado] tanned; **ficar** ~ to tan; **estar** ~ to be tanned. <> *m, f* **-1.** [de pele] dark-skinned person. **-2.** [de cabelo] dark-haired person. **-3.** [cor] tan.

morfina [moxˈfina] *f* morphine.

morfologia [moxfoloˈʒia] *f GRAM* morphology.

moribundo, da [moriˈbũdu, da] *adj* dying.

moringa [moˈrĩŋga] *f* water-cooler.

mormacento, ta [moxmaˈsẽtu, ta] *adj* sultry.

mormaço [moxˈmasu] *m* sultry weather.

mormente [moxˈmẽtʃi] *adv* especially.

mórmon [ˈmɔxmõ] *mf* Mormon.

morno, na [ˈmoxnu, na] *adj* lukewarm.

morosidade [moroziˈdadʒi] *f* slowness.

moroso, osa [moˈrozu, ɔza] *adj* slow.

morrer [5] [moˈxe(x)] *vi* **-1.** [ger] to die; ~ **afogado** to drown; **ele morreu atropelado** he was knocked down and killed. **-2.** [cair no esquecimento] to be dead. **-3.** *AUTO* to die. **-4.** *fig* [sentir intensamente]: **estou morrendo de calor/fome/frio** I'm dying of heat/hunger/cold; **morro de vontade de viajar** I'm dying to travel; **morri de medo** I was scared to death; **morri de rir** I died laughing. **-5.** *fam* [desembolsar]: ~ **em** to cough up.

morro [ˈmoxu] *m* **-1.** [monte] hill. **-2.** [favela] slum.

mortadela [moxtaˈdɛla] *f salami-type sausage*.

mortal [mox'taw] *(pl* **-ais***)* <> *adj* **-1.** [ger] mortal. **-2.** [terrível - dor] dreadful; [- pecado] deadly. <> *mf* mortal.

mortalha [moxˈtaʎa] *f* shroud.

mortalidade [moxtaliˈdadʒi] *f* mortality.

mortandade [moxtãˈdadʒi] *f* slaughter.

morte [ˈmɔxtʃi] *f* **-1.** [ger] death. **-2.** [fim] ending. **-3.** *fig*: **ser a** ~ **para alguém** [ser muito penoso] to be the end for sb. **-4.** *loc*: **pensar na** ~ **da bezerra** *fig* to daydream; **ser de** ~ *fam* to be impossible.

morteiro [moxˈtejru] *m* mortar.

mortífero, ra [moxˈtʃiferu, ra] *adj* lethal.

mortificar [12] [moxtʃifiˈka(x)] *vt* **-1.** [torturar] to torture. **-2.** [atormentar] to torment.

morto, ta [ˈmoxtu, ˈmɔxta] <> *pp* ⊳ **matar**. <> *adj* **-1.** [ger] dead; **nem** ~ no way; **não ter onde cair** ~ to have nowhere to lay one's head. **-2.** [sem atividades] deadly. **-3.** [desbotado] faded. **-4.** [sentindo intensamente]: ~ **de fome** dying of hunger; ~ **de raiva** seething with rage. <> *m, f* [falecido] deceased.

➧ **morto** *m* [biriba] *pile of overturned playing cards.*

mosaico [moˈzajku] *m* mosaic.

mosca [ˈmoʃka] *f* fly; **acertar na** ~ to hit the jackpot; **estar/viver às** ~s to be empty.

moscovita [moʃkoˈvita] <> *adj* Muscovite. <> *m, f* Muscovite.

Moscou [moʃˈkow] *n* Moscow.

mosquiteiro [moʃkiˈtejru] *m* mosquito net.

mosquito [moʃˈkitu] *m* mosquito.

mostarda [moʃˈtaxda] *f* mustard.

mosteiro [moʃˈtejru] *m* [de monges] monastery; [de monjas] convent.

mostra [ˈmoʃtra] *f* **-1.** [exposição] display. **-2.** [manifestação] sign; **dar** ~s **de algo** to show signs of sthg.

mostrador [moʃtraˈdo(x)] *(pl* **-es***) m* dial.

mostrar [4] [moʃˈtra(x)] *vt* **-1.** [ger] to show. **-2.** [apontar] to point out.

➧ **mostrar-se** *vp* **-1.** [revelar-se] to show o.s. to be. **-2.** [exibir-se] to show off.

mostruário [moʃˈtrwarju] *m* display case.

mote [ˈmotʃi] *m LITER* [tema] theme.

motel [moˈtɛw] *(pl* **-éis***) m* motel.

motim [moˈtʃĩ] *(pl* **-ns***) m* **-1.** [do povo] riot. **-2.** [de tropas] mutiny.

motivação [motʃivaˈsãw] *(pl* **-ões***) f* motivation.

motivado, da [motʃivaˈdu, da] *adj* [incentivado] motivated.

motivar [4] [motʃiˈva(x)] *vt* **-1.** [estimular] to motivate. **-2.** [provocar] to provoke. **-3.** [induzir]: ~ **alguém a fazer algo** to motivate sb to do sthg.

motivo [moˈtʃivu] *m* **-1.** [causa]: ~ **(de/para)** cause (of/for); **dar** ~ **a** to give rise to; **por** ~s **de força maior** for reasons beyond our control; **sem** ~ without reason; **ser** ~ **de** to be a cause for; **(não) ter** ~ **para** to have (no) reason to. **-2.** [justificativa] reason. **-3.** *ARTE, MÚS* motif.

moto¹ [ˈmotu] *m* [lema] motto.

➧ **de moto próprio** *loc adv* of one's own accord.

moto² [ˈmotu] *f* [motocicleta] motorbike.

motoca [moˈtɔka] *f fam* (motor)bike.

motocicleta [ˌmotosiˈklɛta] *f* motorcycle, motorbike.

motociclismo [motosiˈkliʒmu] *m* motorcycling.

motociclista [motosiˈkliʃta] *mf* motorcyclist, biker.

motoneta [motoˈneta] *f* motor scooter.

motoqueiro, ra [motoˈkejru, ra] *m, f* **-1.** *fam*

[motociclista] biker. **-2.** [entregador] deliveryman *(on a bike)*.

motor [ɪɲo'to(x)] *(pl* **-es**) ⟨⟩ *adj* **-1.** *TEC* driving. **-2.** *ANAT* motor. ⟨⟩ *m* engine; ~ **de arranque** starter (motor); ~ **diesel** diesel engine; ~ **de explosão** internal combustion engine; ~ **de popa** outboard motor.

motorista [moto'riʃta] *mf* driver.

motorizado, da [motori'zadu, da] *adj* motorized.

motorizar [4] [motori'za(x)] *vt* to motorize.
➠ **motorizar-se** *vp* [pessoa] to get one's own car.

motorneiro, ra [motox'nejru, ra] *m, f* tram driver *UK*, streetcar driver *US*.

motosserra [moto'sɛxa] *f* chainsaw.

motriz [mo'triʒ] *adj f* ⟼ **motor**.

mouco, ca ['moku, ka] *adj ant* deaf.

mountain bike [ˌmawntẽn'bajki] *f* mountain bike.

mourisco, ca [mo'riʃku, ka] *adj* Moorish.

mouro, ra ['moru, ra] ⟨⟩ *adj* Moorish. ⟨⟩ *m, f* Moor.

mouse [ˌmawzi] *m COMPUT* mouse.

movediço, ça [move'dʒisu, sa] *adj TEC* moving; **areia movediça** quicksand.

móvel ['mɔvɛw] *(pl* **-eis**) ⟨⟩ *adj* movable. ⟨⟩ *m* piece of furniture.
➠ **móveis** *mpl* furniture *(sg)*.

mover [5] [mo've(x)] *vt* **-1.** [ger] to move. **-2.** [começar] to set in motion.
➠ **mover-se** *vp* to move.

movido, da [mo'vidu, da] *adj* **-1.** [impelido]: ~ **a algo/a fazer algo** moved to sthg/ to do sthg; ~ **por algo** moved by sthg. **-2.** [promovido]: ~ **contra alguém/algo** started against sb/sthg. **-3.** [acionado]: ~ **a álcool/vapor** ethanol/steam-driven.

movimentação [movimẽnta'sãw] *(pl* **-ões**) *f* [ato] movement.

movimentado, da [movimẽn'tadu, da] *adj* **-1.** [bairro, loja, dia] busy. **-2.** [música, peça, show] lively.

movimentar [4] [movimẽn'ta(x)] *vt* **-1.** [ger] to move. **-2.** *fig* [animar] to liven up.

movimento [movi'mẽntu] *m* **-1.** [ger] movement. **-2.** [animação] bustle.

MP ⟨⟩ *m (abrev de* **Ministério Público**) *Brazilian state government.* ⟨⟩ *f (abrev de* **Medida Provisória**) *emergency law.*

MPB *(abrev de* **Música Popular Brasileira**) *f generic term for all popular Brazilian music.*

MS *(abrev de* **Estado do Mato Grosso do Sul**) *m State of Mato Grosso do Sul.*

MS-DOS *(abrev de* **Microsoft Disk Operating System**) *m* MS-DOS.

MST *(abrev de* **Movimento dos Trabalhadores Sem-Terra**) *m Brazilian movement for landless workers.*

MT *(abrev de* **Estado do Mato Grosso**) *m State of Mato Grosso.*

muamba ['mwãnba] *f* **-1.** *fam* [mercadoria contrabandeada] contraband. **-2.** [mercadoria roubada] loot.

muambeiro, ra [mwãn'bejru, ra] *m, f* **-1.** [contrabandista] smuggler. **-2.** [vendedor de objetos roubados] fence.

muco ['muku] *m* mucus.

mucosa [mu'kɔza] *f* mucous membrane.

muçulmano, na [musuw'mãnu, na] ⟨⟩ *adj* Muslim. ⟨⟩ *m, f* Muslim.

muda ['muda] *f* **-1.** *BOT* seedling. **-2.** *ZOOL* moult; **estar na** ~ to be moulting *UK*, to be molting *US*. **-3.** [vestuário]: ~ **(de roupa)** change (of clothes).

mudança [mu'dãnsa] *f* **-1.** [ger] move; **fazer a** ~ to move (house). **-2.** [modificação] change. **-3.** *AUTO* gear.

mudar [4] [mu'da(x)] ⟨⟩ *vt* to change. ⟨⟩ *vi* [modificar] to change; ~ **de algo** to change sthg; ~ **de casa** to move house; ~ **de roupa** to change clothes.

mudez [mu'deʒ] *f* muteness.

mudo, da ['mudu, da] ⟨⟩ *adj* **-1.** [ger] silent. **-2.** *MED* mute. **-3.** [telefone] dead. ⟨⟩ *m, f* mute.

mugido [mu'ʒidu] *m* moo.

mugir [52] [mu'ʒi(x)] *vi* [vaca] to moo.

muito, ta ['muĩntu, ta] ⟨⟩ *adj* **-1.** [grande quantidade - no sg] a lot of; ~ **problema** a lot of problems *(pl)*; **levou** ~ **tempo** it took a long time; **sinto muita fome** I'm very hungry; [- no pl] many; ~ **s dias** many days; [- em frases interrogativas e negativas] much, many; **não tenho** ~ **tempo/** ~ **s alunos** I haven't much time/many pupils. **-2.** *(no sg)* [demais] too much; ~ **calor** too hot; **muita gente** too many people. ⟨⟩ *pron (no sg)* much; *(no pl)* a lot; **tenho** ~ **que fazer** I've got a lot to do; ~ **s concordam comigo** many agree with me.
➠ **muito** *adv* **-1.** [intensamente] a lot; **gostei** ~ **de ir ao cinema** I enjoyed going to the cinema very much; **não gosto** ~ I don't like it very much; **feliz** very happy; ~ **mais** much more; **sinto** ~, **mas não posso** I'm very sorry, but I can't. **-2.** [muito tempo] a long time; ~ **antes/depois** a long time before/afterwards; ~ **mais tarde** much later. **-3.** [freqüentemente] often; **ela faz** ~ **isso** she often does that; **você vem** ~ **aqui?** do you come here often? **-4.** *loc*: **quando** ~ at most.
➠ **por muito que** *loc conj* however much.

mula ['mula] *f* mule.

mulato, ta [mu'latu, ta] ⟨⟩ *adj* mulatto. ⟨⟩ *m, f* mulatto.

muleta [mu'leta] *f* **-1.** [para andar] crutch. **-2.** *fig* [apoio] support.

mulher [mu'ʎɛ(x)] *(pl* **-es**) *f* **-1.** [ser] woman; ~ **-fatal** femme fatale; ~ **de negócios** businesswoman; ~ **da vida** prostitute. **-2.** [esposa] wife.

mulheraço [muʎe'rasu] *(pl* **-s**) **mulherão** [muʎe'rãw] *(pl* **-ões**) *f* fantastic woman.

mulherengo [muʎe'rẽngu] ⟨⟩ *adj* womanizing. ⟨⟩ *m* womanizer.

mulher-feita [muˌʎɛx'fejta] (*pl* **mulheres-feitas**) *f* grown woman.

mulherio [muʎe'riw] *m* **-1.** [grupo de mulheres] group of women. **-2.** [as mulheres] women.

mulher-objeto [muɲe(x)'obʒetu] (*pl* **mulheres-objeto**) *f* female sex object.

multa ['muwta] *f* fine; **levar uma** ~ to get fined; **dar uma** ~ to fine.

multar [4] [muw'ta(x)] *vt*: ~ **alguém (em R$ 100)** to fine sb (100 R$).

multicolor [muwtʃi'colo(x)] *adj* multicoloured *UK*, multicolored *US*.

multicultural [muwti'kuwturãw] (*pl* **-ais**) *adj* multicultural.

multidão [muwtʃi'dãw] (*pl* **-ões**) *f* **-1.** [de pessoas] crowd. **-2.** [grande quantidade] multitude; **uma** ~ **de** *fig* lots of.

multifacetado, da [muwtʃi'fasetadu, da] *adj* [personalidade, talento] multifaceted.

multiforme [muwtʃi'fɔxmi] *adj* multiform.

multilateral [muwtʃilate'raw] (*pl* **-ais**) *adj* multilateral.

multimilionário, ria [muwtʃimiljo'narju, rja] <> *adj* multimillionaire *(antes de subst)*. <> *m, f* multimillionaire.

multinacional [ˌmuwtʃinasjo'naw] (*pl* **-ais**) <> *adj* multinational. <> *f* multinational.

multiplicação [muwtʃiplika'sãw] (*pl* **-ões**) *f* **-1.** [ger] multiplication. **-2.** [aumento] increase.

multiplicar [12] [muwtʃipli'ka(x)] <> *vt* **-1.** MAT to multiply; **x multiplicado por y é igual a z** x times y equals z. **-2.** [aumentar] to increase. <> *vi* MAT to multiply.
   multiplicar-se *vp* **-1.** [aumentar] to increase. **-2.** BIOL to multiply.

multiplicidade [muwtʃiplisi'dadʒi] *f* multiplicity.

múltiplo, pla ['muwtʃiplu, pla] *adj* multiple.
   múltiplo *m* multiple.

multiprocessamento [muwtʃiprosesa'mẽntu] *m* COMPUT multiprocessing.

multirracial [muwtʃixa'sjaw] (*pl* **-ais**) *adj* multiracial.

multiuso [muwtʃi'uzu] *adj inv* multipurpose.

multiusuário, ria [muwtʃiuz'arju, rja] *adj* COMPUT multiuser.

múmia ['mumja] *f* **-1.** [cadáver] mummy. **-2.** *fig* [pessoa] moron.

mundano, na [mũn'dãnu, na] *adj* mundane.

mundial [mũn'dʒjaw] (*pl* **-ais**) <> *adj* **-1.** [política, guerra] world *(antes de subst)*. **-2.** [organização, fama] worldwide. <> *m* [campeonato] world championship; [de futebol] World Cup.

mundo ['mũndu] *m* **-1.** [ger] world; **o outro** ~ the next world; **vir ao** ~ to come into the world. **-2.** [pessoas]: **todo o** ~ everyone; **veio meio** ~ loads of people came. **-3.** [quantidade]: **um** ~ **de** loads of. **-4.** *loc*: **abarcar o** ~ **com as pernas** to take on too much; **estar no** ~ **da lua** to be miles away; **prometer** ~ **s e fundos** to promise the world; **como este** ~ **é pequeno** what a small world;

desde que o ~ **é** ~ since time immemorial.
   Mundo *m*: **Novo Mundo** New World; **Terceiro Mundo** Third World.

munguzá [mũŋgu'za] *m* corn meal.

munheca [mu'nɛka] *f* **-1.** *fam* [mão] hand. **-2.** [pulso] wrist.

munição [muni'sãw] (*pl* **-ões**) *f* ammunition.

municipal [munisi'paw] (*pl* **-ais**) *adj* municipal.

municipalidade [munisipali'dadʒi] *f* local authority.

municipalizar [munisipali'za(x)] *vt* [instituições, serviços] to municipalize.

município [muni'sipju] *m* **-1.** [divisão administrativa] local authority. **-2.** [território] town.

Munique [mu'niki] *n* Munich.

munir [6] [mu'ni(x)] *vt*: ~ **alguém de algo** to equip sb with sthg.
   munir-se *vp*: ~**-se de algo** to equip o.s. with sthg; ~**-se de coragem** to arm o.s. with courage; ~**-se de paciência** to arm o.s. with patience.

muque ['muki] *m* brute force.

mural [mu'raw] (*pl* **-ais**) <> *adj* wall *(antes de subst)*. <> *m* [pintura] mural.

muralha [mu'raʎa] *f* wall.

murchar [4] [mux'ʃa(x)] <> *vt* **-1.** [planta] to wither. **-2.** [sentimento] to fade. **-3.** *fig* [retrair] to shrink. <> *vi* **-1.** [planta] to wilt. **-2.** *fig* [pessoa] to droop.

murcho, cha ['muxʃu, ʃa] *adj* **-1.** [planta] wilting. **-2.** [bola] soft. **-3.** [pessoa - sem energia] languid; [- triste] droopy.

murmurante [muxmu'rãntʃi] *adj* murmuring.

murmurar [4] [muxmu'ra(x)] <> *vt* [sussurar] to whisper. <> *vi* **-1.** [sussurar] to murmur. **-2.** [falar mal]: ~ **a respeito de alguém** to complain about sb; ~ **contra alguém** to speak ill of sb.

murmurinho [muxmu'riɲu] *m* **-1.** [de vozes] murmuring. **-2.** [de folhas] rustling. **-3.** [som confuso] murmur.

murmúrio [mux'murju] *m* **-1.** [de vozes] murmuring. **-2.** [de folhas] rustling. **-3.** [de água] trickling.

muro ['muru] *m* wall.

murro ['muxu] *m* punch; **dar um** ~ **em alguém/algo** to punch sb/sthg; **dar** ~ **em ponta de faca** *fig* to bang one's head against a brick wall.

musa ['muza] *f* muse.

musculação [muʃkula'sãw] *f* bodybuilding.

muscular [muʃku'la(x)] *adj* muscular.

musculatura [muʃkula'tura] *f* musculature.

músculo ['muʃkulu] *m* **-1.** ANAT muscle. **-2.** CULIN sinewy meat.

musculoso, osa [muʃku'lozu, ɔza] *adj* **-1.** [cheio de músculo - costas, pernas] muscular; [- carne de comer] tough. **-2.** *fig* [forte] tough.

museu [mu'zew] *m* museum; ~ **de arte** art gallery.

musgo ['muʒgu] *m* moss.

musgoso, osa [muʒ'gozu, ɔza] *adj* mossy.

música ['muzika] *f* ▷ **músico**.

MÚSICA

The samba is, without doubt, the best known expression of Brazilian music. Yet it is far from being the only one. The size of a continent and with strong regional culture, Brazil has a huge variety of rhythms and dances, from the *baião* and *frevo* in the northeast to the gaucho *milonga*. Such a wealth of rhythms gives Brazil a prominent position in the international musical world, to which Brazil has contributed names that range from Heitor Villa-Lobos, in classical music, to Gilberto Gil and Milton Nascimento, in popular music, including famous musicians such as Egberto Gismonti, Toninho Horta and Naná Vasconcelos.

musicado, da [muzi'kadu, da] *adj* set to music.

musical [muzi'kaw] (*pl* -ais) <> *adj* musical. <> *m* musical.

musicalidade [muzikali'dadʒil] *f* musicality.

musicar [muzi'ka(x)] *vt* to set to music.

musicista [muzi'siʃta] *mf* -1. [músico] musician. -2. [especialista] musicologist.

músico, ca ['muziku, ka] <> *adj* [profissional] musical. <> *m, f* musician.

➡ **música** *f* -1. [ger] music; ~ **de câmara** chamber music; ~ **clássica** classical music; ~ **folclórica** folk music. -2. [canção] song.

musicologia [muzikolo'ʒia] *f* musicology.

musicólogo, ga [muzi'kɔlogu, ga] *m* musicologist.

musse ['musi] *f CULIN* mousse.

musselina [muse'lina] *f* muslin.

mutabilidade [mutabili'dadʒi] *f* mutability.

mutação [muta'sãw] (*pl* -ões) *f* -1. *BIOL* mutation. -2. *fig* [transformação] change.

mutável [mu'tavew] (*pl* -eis) *adj* changeable.

mutilação [mutʃila'sãw] *f* -1. [orgânico] mutilation. -2. [de texto] cutting.

mutilado, da [mutʃi'ladu, da] <> *adj* mutilated. <> *m, f* cripple.

mutilar [4] [mutʃi'la(x)] *vt* -1. [pessoa] to mutilate. -2. [texto] to cut.

mutirão [mutʃi'rãw] (*pl* -ões) *m* joint effort.

mutreta [mu'treta] *f fam* cheating; **fazer (uma)** ~ to cheat.

mutuamente [mutwa'mẽntʃi] *adv* mutually.

mútuo, tua ['mutwu, twa] *adj* mutual.

muxoxo [mu'ʃoʃu] *m* tutting; **fazer** ~ to tut.

n, N ['enil *m* -1. [letra] n, N. -2. [quantidade indeterminada] n; **contamos** ~ **vezes a mesma história** we told the story for the nth time.

na [na] = **em + a**.

-na [na] *pron* [pessoa] her; [coisa] it; [você] you.

nabo ['nabu] *m* turnip.

nação [na'sãw] (*pl* -ões) *f* nation.

nacional [nasjo'naw] (*pl* -ais) *adj* national.

nacionalidade [nasjonali'dadʒi] *f* nationality.

nacionalismo [nasjona'liʒmu] *m* nationalism.

nacionalista [nasjona'liʃta] <> *adj* nationalist. <> *mf* nationalist.

nacionalização [nasjonaliza'sãw] (*pl* -ões) *f* nationalization.

nacionalizar [4] [nasjonali'za(x)] *vt* -1. [estatizar] to nationalize. -2. [naturalizar] to naturalize.

naco ['naku] *m* [pedaço]: **um** ~ **(de)** a piece (of).

nações [na'sõjʃ] *fpl* ⊳ **nação**.

➡ **Nações Unidas** *fpl* United Nations.

nada ['nada] <> *pron indef* [coisa alguma] nothing; **não li** ~ **desse autor** I haven't read anything by this author; **ele fez a barba? – fez** ~ ! has he had a shave? – no, he hasn't!; **antes de mais** ~ first of all; **de** ~ ! [resposta a obrigado] not at all!, you're welcome!; **como se** ~ **tivesse acontecido** as if nothing had happened; **isso não é** ~ ! that's nothing!; ~ **disso!** not at all!; ~ **feito** nothing doing; ~ **de novo** nothing new; ~ **mais** nothing more; **não quero** ~ **mais com ele** I don't want anything more to do with him; ~ **mau** not bad; **não dizer** ~ to say nothing, not to say anything; **não foi** ~ [resposta a desculpa!] don't mention it; **por** ~ **neste mundo** for love nor money; **quase** ~ hardly anything, next to nothing; **que** ~ **!** nonsense! <> *adv* [de modo algum] not at all; **não gostei** ~ **do filme** I didn't enjoy the film at all; ~ **menos do que** nothing less than; **não é** ~ **difícil** it isn't at all difficult. <> *m* -1. [vazio]: **o** ~ the void. -2. [ninharia]: **um** ~ a trifle, nothing.

nada-consta [,nada'kõnʃta] *m inv* deed of indemnity.

nadadeira [nada'dejra] *f* -1. [de animal] fin. -2. [de mergulhador] flipper.

nadador, ra [nada'do(x), ra] (*mpl* -es, *fpl* -s) <> *adj* swimming. <> *m, f* swimmer.

nadar [4] [na'da(x)] *vi* -**1.** [em piscina, mar, rio] to swim. -**2.** [estar imerso] to be swimming; ~ **em dinheiro** *fig* to be rolling in money; **ficar nadando** *fig* to be out of one's depth.

nádegas ['nadegaʃ] *fpl* buttocks.

nado ['nadu] *m* swimming; **atravessar algo a** ~ to swim across sthg; ~ **borboleta** butterfly (stroke); ~ **cachorrinho** doggy paddle; ~ **de costas** backstroke; ~ **de peito** breaststroke; ~ **livre** freestyle.

NAFTA (*abrev de* **North American Free Trade Agreement**) *f* NAFTA.

naftalina [nafta'lina] *f* naphthaline.

náilon ['najlõ] *m* nylon.

naipe ['najpi] *m* -**1.** [cartas] suit. -**2.** *fig* [qualidade]: **de bom** ~ first class.

Nairóbi [naj'rɔbi] *n* Nairobi.

namoradeira [namora'dejra] *adj* flirtatious.

namorado, da [namo'radu, da] <> *adj* enamoured. <> *m, f* boyfriend (*f* girlfriend).

namorador, ra [namora'do(x), ra] *adj* flirtatious.

namorar [4] [namo'ra(x)] <> *vt* -**1.** [manter namoro] to be going out with. -**2.** [cobiçar] to covet. -**3.** [fitar] to stare longingly at. <> *vi* -**1.** [manter namoro] to be going out together. -**2.** [trocar carícias] to flirt.

namorico [na'moriku] *m* flirtation.

namoro [na'moru] *m* relationship.

nanico, ca [na'niku, ka] *adj* tiny.

nanquim [nãŋ'kĩ] *m* Indian ink.

não [nãw] <> *adv* -**1.** [resposta] no. -**2.** [negação] not; **ela** ~ **é fácil** she's not easy; **ela é médica,** ~ **é?** she's a doctor, isn't she?; **eu** ~ **tenho dinheiro** I haven't got any money; **agora** ~ not now; **como** ~**?** why not?; ~ **muito** not much; ~ **sei** I don't know; ~ **tem de quê** [resposta a obrigado] not at all, you're welcome; **pois** ~**!** [como interj] of course! <> *m* [recusa] refusal.

não-agressão [ˌnãwagre'sãw] *f*: **pacto de** ~ non-aggression pact.

não-alinhado, da [ˌnãwali'ɲadu, da] (*mpl* -s, *fpl*-s) *adj* non-aligned.

não-conformista [ˌnãwkõfox'miʃta] (*pl* -s) <> *adj* non-conformist. <> *mf* non-conformist.

não-governamental [nãwgovernemẽn'tawl] (*pl*-ais) *adj* non-governmental.

não-intervenção [ˌnãwĩntexvẽn'sãw] *f JUR* non-intervention.

napa ['napa] *f* nappa leather.

naquela [na'kɛla] = em + aquela.

naquele [na'keli] = em + aquele.

naquilo [na'kilu] = em + aquilo.

narcisismo [naxsi'ziʒmu] *m* narcissism.

narcisista [naxsi'ʒiʃta] *adj* narcissistic.

narciso [nax'sizu] *m* -**1.** *BOT* narcissus. -**2.** [pessoa] narcissist.

narcótico, ca [nax'kɔtʃiku, ka] *adj* narcotic.

➤ **narcótico** *m* narcotic.

narcotizar [4] [naxkotʃi'za(x)] *vt* to drug.

narcotráfico [naxko'trafiku] *m* drug traffic.

narigudo, da [nari'gudu, da] <> *adj* with a large nose; **ser** ~ to have a large nose. <> *m, f* large-nosed person.

narina [na'rina] *f* nostril.

nariz [na'riʃ] (*pl* -es) (*pl* -es [na'riziʃ]) *m* -**1.** [ger] nose. -**2.** *loc*: **dar com o** ~ **na porta** to find the doors closed; **meter o** ~ **em** to stick one's nose into; **torcer o** ~ **(para alguém/algo)** to turn up one's nose at sb/sthg; **sou dono do meu** ~ I know my own mind.

narração [naxa'sãw] (*pl* -ões) *f* -**1.** [conto] story. -**2.** [relato] narrative.

narrador, ra [naxa'do(x), ra] *m, f* narrator.

narrar [4] [na'xa(x)] *vt* -**1.** [contar] to describe. -**2.** [relatar] to recount.

narrativo, va [naxa'tʃivu, va] *adj* narrative.

➤ **narrativa** *f* = narração.

nas [naʃ] = em + as.

-nas [naʃ] *pron pl* [elas] them; [vocês] you.

NASA (*abrev de* **National Aeronautics and Space Administration**) *f* NASA.

nasal [na'zaw] (*pl* -ais) *adj* nasal.

nasalado, da [naza'ladu, da] *adj* nasal.

nascença [na'sẽnsa] *f* [nascimento] birth; **de** ~ from birth; **ela é surda de** ~ she has been deaf from birth; **marca de** ~ birthmark.

nascente [na'sẽntʃi] <> *adj* -**1.** [interesse, povo] emerging. -**2.** [planta] sprouting. <> *m* -**1.** [fonte] spring. -**2.** [nascer do sol] sunrise. -**3.** [leste] east.

nascer [25] [na'se(x)] *vi* -**1.** [vir ao mundo] to be born. -**2.** [brotar] to sprout. -**3.** [originar-se] to originate. -**4.** [surgir - sol, lua] to rise; [- dia] to dawn. -**5.** [formar-se] to be born. -**6.** [descender]: ~ **de** to be born into. -**7.** [ter aptidão]: **ele nasceu para o comércio** he is a born businessman. -**8.** [aparecer] to appear. -**9.** *loc*: ~ **em berço de ouro** to be born with a silver spoon in one's mouth; ~ **de novo** to take on a new lease of life; **eu não nasci ontem** I wasn't born yesterday.

nascido, da [na'sidu, da] *adj* [pessoa] born; **bem** ~ from a good family.

nascimento [nasi'mẽntul] *m* -**1.** [nascença] birth; **de** ~ since birth. -**2.** *fig* [origem] origin.

NASDAQ (*abrev de* **National Association of Securities Dealers Automated Quotation**) *f* NASDAQ.

Nassau [na'saw] *n* Nassau.

nata ['nata] *f* cream.

natação [nata'sãw] *f* swimming.

natal [na'taw] (*pl* -ais) *adj* native; **terra** ~ birthplace.

➤ **Natal** *m* Christmas; **Feliz Natal!** happy Christmas!, merry Christmas!

natalício, cia [nata'lisju, sja] *adj*: **aniversário** ~ birthday.

➤ **natalício** *m* birthday.

natalidade [natali'dadʒil] *f* birth rate; **índice de** ~ birth rate.

natalino, na [nata'linu, na] *adj* Christmas (*antes de subst*); **festas natalinas** Christmas celebrations.

natimorto, ta [natʃiˈmoxtu, ta] *m, f* stillborn baby.

natividade [natʃiviˈdadʒi] *f* nativity.

nativo, va [naˈtʃivu, va] ◇ *adj* native. ◇ *m, f* native.

nato, ta [ˈnatu, ta] *adj*: **ele é um escritor ~** he is a born writer.

natural [natuˈraw] (*pl* **-ais**) ◇ *adj* **-1.** [ger] natural; **ao ~** *CULIN* uncooked; **de tamanho ~** life-size. **- 2.** [nascido]: **ser ~ de** to be a native of. ◇ *mf* [nativo] native.

naturalidade [naturaliˈdadʒi] *f* **-1.** [espontaneidade] spontaneity; **agir com ~** to act naturally; **falar com ~** to speak naturally; **admiro sua ~** I admire your naturalness. **- 2.** [local de nascimento]: **ele é de ~ brasileira** he is Brazilian by birth.

naturalismo [naturaˈliʒmu] *m* *ARTE* naturalism.

naturalista [naturaˈliʃta] *mf* naturalist.

naturalização [naturalizaˈsãw] *f* naturalization.

naturalizado, da [naturaliˈzadu, da] ◇ *adj* naturalized. ◇ *m, f* naturalized citizen.

naturalizar-se [4] [naturaliˈzaxsi] *vp* to become naturalized.

naturalmente [naturawˈmẽntʃi] ◇ *adv* [evidentemente] naturally. ◇ *interj* of course!

natureba [natuˈrɛba] *mf* health freak.

natureza [natuˈreza] *f* **-1.** [ger] nature. **- 2.** [espécie] kind.

natureza-morta [natuˌrezaˈmoxta] (*pl* **naturezas-mortas**) *f* still life.

nau [ˈnaw] *f* *LITER* ship.

naufragar [4] [nawfraˈga(x)] *vi* **-1.** [embarcação] to be wrecked. **- 2.** [pessoa] to be shipwrecked. **- 3.** *fig* [fracassar] to fail.

naufrágio [nawˈfraʒju] *m* **-1.** [de embarcação, pessoa] shipwreck. **- 2.** *fig* [fracasso] failure.

náufrago, ga [ga, ˈnawfragu] *m* (shipwreck) survivor, castaway.

náusea [ˈnawzja] *f* nausea; **dar ~s a alguém** to make sb sick; **sentir ~s** to feel sick.

nauseabundo, da [nawzjaˈbũndu, da], **nauseante** [nawˈzjãntʃi] *adj* **-1.** [que produz náuseas] nauseating. **- 2.** *fig* [nojento] sickening.

nauseante [nawˈzjãntʃi] *adj* = nauseabundo.

nausear [15] [nawˈzja(x)] ◇ *vt* **-1.** [enjoar] to make sick. **- 2.** [repugnar] to nauseate. ◇ *vi* [sentir náusea] to feel sick.

náutico, ca [ˈnawtʃiku, ka] *adj* nautical.

◆ **náutica** *f* *ESP* seamanship.

naval [naˈvaw] (*pl* **-ais**) *adj* naval; **construção ~** shipbuilding.

navalha [naˈvaʎa] *f* **-1.** [de barba] razor blade. **- 2.** [faca] blade.

navalhada [navaˈʎada] *f* stab.

nave [ˈnavi] *f* **-1.** [de igreja] nave. **- 2.** *LITER* [embarcação] ship; **~ espacial** spaceship.

navegação [navegaˈsãw] (*pl* **-ões**) *f* voyage; **companhia de ~** shipping line; **~ costeira** coastal

shipping; **~ fluvial** river navigation.

navegador, ra [navegaˈdo(x), ra] *m, f* **-1.** [ger] navigator. **- 2.** *COMPUT* surfer.

navegante [naveˈgãntʃi] *mf* navigator.

navegar [14] [naveˈga(x)] ◇ *vt* to pilot. ◇ *vi* **-1.** [seguir viagem] to sail. **- 2.** *COMPUT* to surf; **~ na Internet** to surf the net.

navegável [naveˈgavew] (*pl* **-eis**) *adj* navigable.

navio [naˈviw] *m* ship; **~ cargueiro** cargo vessel; **~ de guerra** warship; **~ mercante** merchant ship; **ficar a ver ~s** to be left high and dry.

navio-petroleiro [naˌviwpetroˈlejru] (*pl* **navios-petroleiros**) *m* oil tanker.

navio-tanque [naˌviwˈtãŋki] (*pl* **navios-tanques**) *m* tanker.

nazismo [naˈziʒmu] *m* Nazism.

nazista [naˈziʃta] ◇ *adj* Nazi. ◇ *mf* Nazi.

NBA (*abrev de* **National Basketball Association**) *f* NBA.

NE (*abrev de* **Nordeste**) *m* NE.

neblina [neˈblina] *f* mist.

nebulizador [nebulizaˈdo(x)] *m* nebulizer.

nebulosa [nebuˈlɔza] *f* ▷ **nebuloso**.

nebulosidade [nebuloziˈdadʒi] *f* cloudiness.

nebuloso, osa [nebuˈlozu, ɔza] *adj* **-1.** [ger] cloudy. **- 2.** *fig* [sombrio] dark. **- 3.** *fig* [indefinido] nebulous. **- 4.** *fig* [obscuro] nebulous.

◆ **nebulosa** *f* *ASTRON* nebula.

nécessaire [neseˈsɛ(x)] *f* sponge bag.

necessariamente [nesesarjaˈmẽntʃi] *adv* necessarily.

necessário, ria [neseˈsarju, rja] ◇ *adj* necessary; **ser ~ fazer algo** to be necessary to do sthg; **se for ~** if necessary. ◇ *m* necessities (*pl*); **o ~** the necessities.

necessidade [nesesiˈdadʒi] *f* [o que se necessita] necessity; **gêneros de primeira ~** staple foods; **em caso de ~** in case of necessity, if need be; **não há ~ (de algo/fazer algo)** there is no need (for sthg/to do sthg).

◆ **necessidades** *fpl* **-1.** [privação] need (*sg*); **passar por muitas ~** to suffer many hardships. **- 2.**: **fazer suas ~** *fam* [defecar, urinar] to spend a penny.

necessitado, da [nesesiˈtadu, da] *adj*: **~ (de)** in need (of).

◆ **necessitados** *mpl*: **os ~** [miseráveis] the needy.

necessitar [4] [nesesiˈta(x)] ◇ *vt* to need. ◇ *vi* to be in need; **~ de** to need.

necrológio [nekroˈlɔʒul] *m* obituary.

necrópole [neˈkrɔpɔli] *f* cemetery.

necrotério [nekroˈtɛrju] *m* mortuary *UK*, morgue *US*.

néctar [ˈnɛkta(x)] (*pl* **-es**) *m* nectar.

nectarina [nektaˈrina] *f* nectarine.

nefando, da [neˈfãndu, da] *adj* **-1.** [abominável] nefarious. **- 2.** [sacrílego] iniquitous. **- 3.** [malvado] wicked.

nefasto, ta [neˈfaʃtu, ta] *adj* **-1.** [agourento] ominous. **- 2.** [trágico] tragic. **- 3.** [nocivo] harmful.

negação [nega'sãw] (*pl*-ões) *f*-**1.** [recusa] refusal.
-**2.** [inaptidão]: **ser uma ~ em algo** to be hopeless
at sthg. -**3.** [desmentido] denial.

negacear [15] [nega'sja(x)] *vt* -**1.** [menear] to
shake. -**2.** [seduzir] to deceive. -**3.** [recusar] to
refuse.

negar [14] [ne'ga(x)] *vt*-**1.** [ger] to deny.-**2.** [recusar,
não permitir] to refuse.

➨ **negar-se** *vp* [recusar-se] to refuse.

negativo, va [nega'tʃivu, va] <> *adj* negative.
<> *adv*: **negativo!** nope!

➨ **negativo** *m* FOT negative.

➨ **negativa** *f* [recusa] refusal.

negligê [negli'ge] *m* negligee.

negligência [negli'ʒẽnsjal *f* negligence.

negligenciar [16] [negli'ʒẽnsja(x)] *vt* to neglect.

negligente [negli'ʒẽntʃil *adj* negligent.

nego, ga ['negu, gal *m, f*-**1.** *fam* [negro] black.-**2.**
[colega] mate.

negociação [negosja'sãw] (*pl* -ões) *f* -**1.**
[transação] transaction. -**2.** [entendimento] negotiation.

negociador, ra [negosja'do(x), ral <> *adj* nego-
tiating. <> *m, f* negotiator.

negociante [nego'sjãntʃil *mf* businessman (*f*
businesswoman).

negociar [16] [nego'sja(x)] <> *vi* -**1.** COMM: **~ (com**
algo) to trade (in sthg); **~ com alguém/algo** to
negotiate with sb/sthg. -**2.** [discutir] to negotiate.
<> *vt*-**1.** [combinar] to negotiate. -**2.** COM to trade.

negociata [nego'sjatal *f* crooked deal.

negociável [nego'sjavewl (*pl*-eis) *adj inv* negotiable.

negócio [ne'gɔsjul *m*-**1.** COM business; **homem de**
~s businessman; **o mundo dos ~s** the business
world. -**2.** [transação] deal; **fazer um bom ~** to
get a good deal; **fechar um ~** to make a deal; **~**
da China very profitable deal; **~ fechado!** it's a
deal! -**3.** [caso] matter; **aconteceu um ~**
estranho something strange happened; **o ~ é**
o seguinte the deal is as follows. -**4.** *fam* [coisa]
thing; **o barco é um ~!** the boat is amazing!;
que ~ é esse? what's the big idea?

negra ['negral *f* ▷ **negro**.

negrito [ne'gritul *m* bold type.

negritude [negri'tudʒil *f* black awareness.

negro, gra ['negru, gral <> *adj* black. <> *m, f*
black.

➨ **negra** *f* ESP: **jogar a negra** to play a decider.

negrume [ne'grumil *m* darkness.

negrura [ne'grural *f* blackness.

nela ['nɛla] = **em + ela**.

nele ['nelil = **em + ele**.

nem [nẽl *conj* nor; **nem ... nem ...** neither ... nor ...;
eles ~ (sequer) me convidaram they didn't even
invite me; **~ bem ela tinha saído, ele chegou**
hardly had I that when someone else took my
place; **~ eu!** nor was I!; **ele foi agressivo mas ~**
por isso você deveria ter retrucado he was
aggressive but that was no reason for you to
retaliate; **~ sempre** not always; **~ tanto** not so

much; **~ todos** not all; **eles saíam sem ~ avisar**
they would go out even without warning.

➨ **nem que** *loc conj* even if.

nenê [ne'nel *m* [bebê] baby.

nenhum, ma [ne'ɲũ, mal (*mpl*-ns, *fpl*-s) <> *adj*
no; **ele não tomou nenhuma decisão** he has
made no decision; **em ~ momento** at no time.
<> *pron* none; **não comprei livro ~** I didn't buy a
single book; **não comprei ~** I didn't buy any; **não**
quero nenhuma bebida I don't want anything to
drink; **não tive problema ~** I didn't have a
single problem; **~ professor é perfeito** no
teacher is perfect; **todos os professores são pes-**
soas, ~ é perfeito all teachers are human; none
is/are perfect; **~ de** none of, not one of; **~ dos**
dois neither of them, neither of the two; **~ dos**
cinco none of the five, not one of the five.

neoclássico, ca [nɛw'klasiku, kal *adj* neoclassical.

➨ **Neoclássico** *m* neoclassical period.

neofascismo [nɛwfa'siʒmul *m* neo-fascism.

neofascista [nɛwfa'siʃtal <> *adj* neo-fascist.
<> *mf* neo-fascist.

neófito, ta [ne'ɔfitu, tal *adj* [principiante] beginner.

neolatino, na [nɛwla'tʃinu, nal *adj* Romance.

neoliberal [neo'liberawl (*pl*-ais) <> *adj* neoliberal. <> *mf* neoliberal.

neoliberalismo [nɛw'liberaliʒmul *m* neoliber-
alism.

neolítico, ca [neo'litʃiku, kal *adj* neolithic.

neologismo [nɛwlo'giʒmul *m* neologism.

néon ['nɛõl, **neônio** [ne'onjul *m* neon.

neonazismo [nɛw'naziʒmul *m* neo-Nazism.

neonazista [nɛw'naziʃtal <> *adj* neo-Nazi. <>
mf neo-Nazi.

neo-realismo [,nɛwxea'liʒmul *m* neo-realism.

neozelandês, esa [,nɛwzelãn'deʃ, ezal <> *adj*
New Zealand (*antes de subst*). <> *m, f* New
Zealander.

Nepal [ne'pawl *n* Nepal.

nepalês, esa [nepa'leʃ, ezal <> *adj* Nepalese,
Nepali. <> *m, f* Nepalese, Nepali.

➨ **nepalês** *m* [língua] Nepalese, Nepali.

nepotismo [nepo'tʃiʒmul *m* nepotism.

nervo [ne'nxvul *m* -**1.** ANAT nerve; **estar uma pilha**
de ~s to be a bag of nerves; **ter ~s de aço** to
have nerves of steel. -**2.** [na carne] sinew. -**3.** *fig*
[força] driving force.

nervosismo [nexvo'ziʒmul *m* -**1.** [ger] nervousness. -**2.** [irritabilidade] irritability.

nervoso, osa [nex'vozu, ɔzal *adj* -**1.** [ger] nervous. -**2.** [irritado] irritable; **isso me deixa ~!**
that gets on my nerves!

nervura [nex'vural *f*-**1.** [prega] rib. -**2.** BOT vein.

néscio, cia ['nɛʃju, ʃjal *adj* -**1.** [estúpido] stupid.
-**2.** [insensato] foolish.

nesga ['neʒgal *f* [pedaço, tira]: **uma ~ (de)** a piece
(of).

nessa ['nɛsal = **em + essa**.

nessas ['nɛsaʃl = **em + essas**.

nesse ['nesi] = **em** + **esse**.
nesses ['nɛsiʃ] = **em** + **esses**.
nesta ['nɛʃta] = **em** + **esta**.
nestas ['nɛstaʃ] = **em** + **estas**.
neste ['neʃtʃi] = **em** + **este**.
nestes ['nestʃiʃ] = **em** + **estes**.
net ['netʃi] *f COMPUT* net.
netiqueta [netʃi'keta] *f COMPUT* netiquette.
neto, ta ['nɛtu, ta] *m, f* grandson (*f* granddaughter).
  ◆ **netos** *mpl* grandchildren.
Netuno [ne'tunu] *n* Neptune.
neurastenia [newraʃte'nja] *f* -**1.** *PSIC* neurasthenia. -**2.** *fig* [mau humor] irritability.
neurastênico, ca [newraʃ'teniku, ka] ◇ *adj* -**1.** *PSIC* neurasthenic. -**2.** *fig* [irritado] irritated. ◇ *m, f* [pessoa irritadiça] irritable person.
neurocirurgião, giã [newrosirux'ʒjãw, ʒjã] (*mpl* -iões, *fpl* -s) *m, f* neurosurgeon.
neurolingüística [ˌnewroliŋ'gwiʃtʃika] *f* neurolinguistics.
neurologia [newrolo'ʒia] *f* neurology.
neurologista [newrolo'ʒiʃta] *mf* neurologist.
neurose [new'rɔzi] *f* neurosis.
neurótico, ca [new'rɔtʃiku, ka] ◇ *adj* neurotic. ◇ *m, f* neurotic.
neurovegetativo, va [newroveʒeta'tʃivu, va] *adj* neurovegetative.
neutralidade [newtrali'dadʒi] *f* neutrality.
neutralização [newtraliza'sãw] *f* neutralization.
neutralizar [4] ['newtrali'za(x)] *vt* to neutralize.
neutro, tra ['newtru, tra] *adj* neutral.
nêutron ['newtrõ] *m* neutron.
nevada [ne'vada] *f* snowfall.
nevado, da [ne'vadu, da] *adj* -**1.** [coberto de neve] snow-covered. -**2.** [branco] snow-white.
nevar [4] [ne'va(x)] *vi* to snow.
nevasca [ne'vaʃka] *f* snowstorm.
neve ['nɛvi] *f* snow; **branco feito** ~ as white as snow.
névoa ['nɛvwa] *f* fog.
nevoeiro [ne'vwejru] *m* thick fog.
nevoento, ta [ne'vwẽtu, ta] *adj* foggy.
nevralgia [nevraw'ʒia] *f* neuralgia.
nevrálgico, ca [ne'vrawʒiku, ka] *adj* neuralgic.
newsgroup [neuʃ'grupil] (*pl* -s) *m COMPUT* newsgroup.
nexo ['nɛksul] *m* -**1.** [ligação] connection. -**2.** [coerência] coherence; **sem** ~ incoherent.
nhenhenhém [ɲeɲe'ɲẽj] *m* -**1.** [resmungo] grumbling; **deixe de** ~! stop whinging! -**2.** [conversa] chattering.
nhoque ['nɔki] *m CULIN* gnocchi.
Niágara ['njagara] *n*: **as cataratas do** ~ the Niagara Falls.
Niamey [nja'mej] *n* Niamey.
Nicarágua [nika'ragwa] *n* Nicaragua.
nicaragüense [nikara'gwẽsi] ◇ *adj* Nicaraguan. ◇ *mf* Nicaraguan.
nicho ['niʃu] *m* niche.

nick (*abrev de* **nickname**) ['niki] *m COMPUT* nickname.
Nicósia [ni'kɔzja] *n* Nicosia.
nicotina [niko'tʃina] *f* nicotine.
Níger ['niʒe(x)] *n* Niger.
Nigéria [ni'ʒɛrja] *n* Nigeria.
niilista [nij'liʃta] ◇ *adj* nihilistic. ◇ *m,f* nihilist.
Nilo ['nilu] *n*: **o** ~ the Nile.
nimbo ['nĩbu] *m* -**1.** *METEOR* nimbus. -**2.** *fig* [auréola] halo.
ninar [4] [ni'na(x)] ◇ *vt* to sing to sleep. ◇ *vi* to fall asleep.
ninfeta [nĩ'feta] *f* nymphette.
ninfomaníaca [nĩfoma'njaka] *f* nymphomaniac.
ninguém [nĩ'gẽj] ◇ *pron indef* -**1.** [nenhuma pessoa] nobody; ~ **vai descobrir** nobody will find out; **não conte a** ~! don't tell anybody!, tell nobody!; ~ **respeita mais** ~ nobody respects anybody any more; ~ **mais** nobody else. -**2.** *fig* [pessoa desimportante]: **ser** ~ to be nobody. ◇ *m fig* [pessoa desimportante]: **esse (zé)** ~ that nobody.
ninhada [ni'ɲada] *f* brood.
ninharia [niɲa'ria] *f* trifle.
ninho ['niɲu] *m* nest; ~ **de rato** *fam* [bagunça] mess.
nipônico, ca [ni'poniku, ka] ◇ *adj* Nipponese. ◇ *m, f* Nipponese.
níquel ['nikew] (*pl* -**eis**) *m* nickel; **estar sem um** ~ to be penniless.
niquelar [nike'la(x)] *vt* to nickel-plate.
nirvana [nix'vãna] *m inv* nirvana.
nissei [ni'sej] *mf child of Japanese parents born in Brazil*.
nisso ['nisu] = **em** + **isso**.
nisto ['niʃtu] = **em** + **isto**.
nitidez [nitʃi'deʃ] *f* -**1.** [precisão] sharpness. -**2.** [clareza] clarity. -**3.** [brilho] brightness.
nítido, da ['nitʃidu, da] *f* -**1.** [preciso] distinct. -**2.** [claro] clear. -**3.** [brilhante] bright.
nitrato [ni'tratu] *m* nitrate.
nítrico, ca ['nitriku, ka] *adj* nitric.
nitrogênio [nitro'ʒenju] *m* nitrogen.
nitroglicerina [nitroglise'rina] *f* nitroglycerine.
nível ['nivew] (*pl* -**eis**) *m* -**1.** [ger] level; **em** ~ **de** level with; ~ **superior** *UNIV* higher education. -**2.** [condições] standard; **alto/baixo** ~ high/low standard; ~ **de vida** standard of living. -**3.** [ferramenta] spirit level.
nivelamento [nivela'mẽtu] *m* -**1.** [aplanamento] levelling *UK*, leveling *US*. -**2.** [equiparação] comparison.
nivelar [4] [nive'la(x)] ◇ *vt* -**1.** [aplanar] to level. -**2.** [equiparar] to compare; ~ **algo a** *ou* **por** *ou* **com algo** to put sthg on the same level as sthg. -**3.** [medir] to equal. ◇ *vi* [em altura]: ~ **com algo** to be level with sthg.
  ◆ **nivelar-se** *vp* [equiparar-se]: ~**-se a** *ou* **por** *ou* **com alguém** to measure up to sb; ~**-se a** *ou*

por *ou* com algo to measure up to sthg.

no [nul] = **em + o.**

NO (*abrev de* **Noroeste**) *m* NW.

nó [ˈnɔl] *m* -**1.** [laço] knot; **dar um** ~ to tie a knot; ~ **cego** fast knot; ~ **do dedo** knuckle; **ter um** ~ **na garganta** to have a lump in one's throat. -**2.** *fig* [dificuldade] knotty situation. -**3.** [ponto crucial] nub.

-no [nul] *pron* [pessoa] him; [coisa] it; [você] you.

nobilíssimo, ma [nobiˈlisimu, ma] *adj* [superl de nobre] most noble.

nobilitar [4] [nobiliˈta(x)] *vt* [dignificar] to ennoble.

nobre [ˈnɔbri] <> *adj* -**1.** [ger] noble; **bairro** ~ smart area. -**2.** *(antes de subst)* [ilustre] honourable. -**3.** ▷ **horário.** <> *m, f* nobleman (*f* noblewoman).

nobreza [noˈbreza] *f* nobility.

noção [noˈsãw] (*pl* -**ões**) *f* notion; **não ter a menor** ~ **de algo** not to have the slightest idea about sthg.

➤ **noções** *fpl* [rudimentos] basics.

nocaute [noˈkawtʃi] *m* -**1.** *BOXE* knockout; **levar alguém a** ~ / **pôr alguém em** ~ *BOXE* to knock sb out; *fig* [prostrar] to lay sb out; **perder/vencer por** ~ to lose/win by a knockout. -**2.** [soco] punch.

nocautear [15] [nokawˈtʃja(x)] *vt* to knock out.

nocivo, va [noˈsivu, va] *adj* harmful.

noções [noˈsõjʃ] *pl* ▷ **noção.**

noctívago [nokˈtʃivagu] *adj &* *n* = **notívago.**

nódoa [ˈnɔdwa] *f* stain.

nódulo [ˈnɔdulul] *m* *ANAT* nodule.

nogueira [noˈgejra] *f* walnut tree.

noitada [nojˈtada] *f* -**1.** [período] night. -**2.** [de diversão] night out. -**3.** : ~ **(de trabalho)** evening's work; **fazer uma** ~ to work at night. -**4.** [de insônia] sleepless night.

noite [ˈnojtʃi] *f* -**1.** [período] night; **à** *ou* **a** ~ at night; **a** ~ **passada** last night; **boa** ~! [cumprimento] good evening!; [despedida] good night!; **da** ~ **para o dia** from one day to the next, overnight; **esta** ~ [a noite passada] last night; [a próxima noite] this evening, tonight; **ontem/hoje/amanhã a** ~ yesterday/this/tomorrow evening; **passar a** ~ **em claro** to have a sleepless night; **tarde da** ~ late at night; ~ **de Natal** Christmas eve; **ao cair da** ~ at nightfall. -**2.** [vida noturna] nightlife.

noitinha [nojˈtʃiɲa] *f*: **à** *ou* **de** ~ at dusk.

noivado [nojˈvadul] *m* -**1.** [ger] engagement. -**2.** [festa] engagement party.

noivar [4] [nojˈva(x)] *vi* -**1.** [comprometer-se] to become engaged; ~ **com** to become engaged to. -**2.** [manter compromisso] to be engaged.

noivo, va [ˈnojvu, va] <> *adj* engaged. <> *m, f* -**1.** [comprometido]: **estar/ser** ~ **de alguém** to be sb's fiancé (*f* fiancée), to be engaged to sb. -**2.** [no altar] groom (*f* bride).

➤ **noivos** *mpl*: **os** ~**s** [no altar] the bride and groom; [na lua-de-mel] newly-weds.

nojeira [noˈʒejra] *f* filth; **estar/ficar uma** ~ [coisa] to be/turn out foul; [serviço] to be/turn out appalling.

nojento, ta [noˈʒẽntu, ta] *adj* -**1.** [que enoja] disgusting. -**2.** [antipático] loathsome.

nojo [ˈnoʒul] *m* -**1.** [náusea] nausea. -**2.** [repulsa] disgust; **estar um** ~ [estar sujo, ruim] to be filthy; **ser um** ~ [ser antipático] to be loathsome.

nômade [ˈnomadʒil] <> *adj* nomadic. <> *mf* nomad.

nome [ˈnɔmil] *m* -**1.** [designação] name; ~ **de batismo** Christian name; ~ **de família** surname; ~ **feio** swearword; ~ **de guerra** pseudonym; **de** ~ [renome] of renown; [reputação] well known. -**2.** [autoridade]: **em** ~ **de algo** in the name of sthg; **em** ~ **de alguém** on behalf of sb. -**3.** *loc*: **dar** ~ **aos bois** to name the culprit.

nomeação [nomjaˈsãw] (*pl* -**ões**) *f* -**1.** [denominação] naming. -**2.** [para cargo] nomination.

nomeadamente [no mjadaˈmẽntʃil] *adv* namely.

nomeado, da [nomeaˈdu, da] *adj* nominated.

nomear [15] [noˈmja(x)] *vt* -**1.** [proferir o nome, conferir o nome a] to name. -**2.** [conferir cargo a] to appoint.

nomenclatura [nomẽ̃klaˈtural] *f* nomenclature.

nominal [nomiˈnaw] (*pl* -**ais**) *adj* nominal.

nonagésimo, ma [nonaˈʒɛzimu, ma] *num* ninetieth; *veja também* **sexto.**

nono, na [ˈnonu, na] *num* ninth; *veja também* **sexto.**

nora [ˈnɔra] *f* daughter-in-law.

nordeste [nox'dɛʃtʃi] <> *adj* north-east. <> *m* northeast.

➤ **Nordeste** *m* north-east region of Brazil.

nordestino, na [na, noxdeʃˈtʃinu, na] <> *adj* -**1.** northeastern -**2.** *of north-eastern Brazil (depois de subst).*<> -**1.** Northeasterner *m, f* -**2.** *person from north-eastern Brazil.*

nórdico, ca [ˈnɔxdʒiku, ka] <> *adj* Nordic. <> *m, f* Nordic.

norma [ˈnɔxmal] *f* -**1.** [padrão] norm. -**2.** [regra] rule; **ter como** ~ to have as a norm.

normal [noxˈmaw] (*pl* -**ais**) *adj* -**1.** [ger] normal. -**2.** [no ensino]: **curso/escola** ~ teacher-training course/college *UK*, normal school *US*.

normalidade [noxmaliˈdadʒil] *f* normality.

normalização [noxmalizaˈsãw] *f* normalization.

normalizar [4] [noxmaliˈza(x)] *vt* to bring back to normal; ~ **relações** to normalize relations.

➤ **normalizar-se** *vp* to return to normal.

normalmente [noxmawˈmẽntʃil] *adv* -**1.** [regularmente] as expected. -**2.** [geralmente] usually.

normativo, va [noxmaˈtʃivu, va] *adj* normative.

noroeste [noˈrwɛʃtʃil] <> *adj* [relativo ao noroeste] north-west. <> *m* northwest.

norte [ˈnɔxtʃil] <> *adj* [relativo ao norte] north. <>

m -**1.** [direção] north; **ao ~ de** to the north of. -**2.** [região] North. -**3.** [guia] guide.

norte-americano, na [ˌnɔxtʃjameri'kãnu, na] <> *adj* North American. <> *m* & *f* North American.

nortear [15] [nox'tʃja(x)] *vt* -**1.** [guiar] to guide. -**2.** *fig* [orientar] to guide.

➡ **nortear-se** *vp:* **~-se para** [dirigir-se] to head towards; **~-se por** *fig* [orientar-se] to be guided by.

nortista [nox'tʃiʃta] <> *adj* [do norte] northern. <> *mf* [pessoa] northerner.

Noruega [no'rwɛgal *n* Norway.

norueguês, esa [norwe'geʃ, ezal <> *adj* Norwegian. <> *m, f* Norwegian.

➡ **norueguês** *m* [língua] Norwegian.

nos¹ [noʃl = **em + os.**

nos² [noʃl *pron pess* -**1.** (*objeto direto*) us; **convidaram-~ para a festa** they invited us to the party. -**2.** (*objeto indireto*) us; **ele ~ deu um presente** he gave us a present; **isto ~ saiu caro** that cost us a lot of money; [para enfatizar] us; **não ~ faça mais isto!** don't do that to us again! -**3.** (*reflexivo*) ourselves; **ontem ~ matriculamos na Universidade** yesterday we registered at University. -**4.** [reciprocamente] each other; **olhamo-~ com ternura** we looked lovingly at each other. -**5.** [indicando posse] us; **ela ~ beijou as faces** she kissed us on the cheeks; **ardia-~ a vista** our eyes were stinging. -**6.** [ao autor] us; **parece-~ ...** it seems to us ...; **neste caso, o que ~ chama a atenção é ...** in this case, what draws our attention is ...

nós [noʃl *pron pess* (*com + nós = conosco*) -**1.** [sujeito] we; **~ somos casados** we are married; **~, brasileiros/estudantes, somos ...** we Brazilians/students, are ...; **~, que gostamos de música, ...** we, who love music, ...; **não pude ver o jogo; ~ vencemos?** I couldn't watch the match; did we win?; **~ dois/quatro** the two/four of us, we two/four; **só ~ dois** just the two of us; **~ todos** all of us; **~ mesmos** *ou* **próprios** we ... ourselves; **~ mesmos pintaremos a casa** we shall paint the house ourselves. -**2.** (*depois de prep*) us; **chegou un convite para ~** an invitation arrived for us, we received an invitation; **o que ele tem contra ~?** what does he have against us?; **você fica para jantar conosco?** are you staying with us for dinner?; **alguns de ~serão premiados** some of us will be rewarded; **entre ~** [duas pessoas] between the two of us, between you and me; [mais de duas pessoas] among us. -**3.** [o autor] we; **neste capítulo, o que ~ pretendemos é ...** in this chapter, what we are attempting to do is ... -**4.** *loc:* **cá entre ~** between ourselves.

-nos [noʃl *pron pl* [eles] them; [vocês] you ▷ **nos²**.

nosso, a ['nosu, al <> *adj* our; **Nossa Senhora** Our Lady; **nossas coisas/brigas** our things/arguments; **um amigo ~** a friend of ours; **este iate é ~** this yacht is ours. <> *pron:* **o ~ /a nossa** ours; **um amigo ~** a friend of ours; **a nossa é maior** ours is bigger; **os ~s** [a nossa família] our

family; [do nosso time] ours; **ser um dos ~s** *fam* [estar do nosso lado] to be one of ours; **à nossa!** here's to us!

➡ **nossa** *interj* [exprimindo espanto] God; **~ mãe!**, **~ senhora!** God!, Holy Mary!

nostalgia [noʃtaw'ʒial *f* -**1.** [melancolia] nostalgia. -**2.** [da pátria] homesickness.

nostálgico, ca [noʃ'tawʒiku, kal *adj* nostalgic.

nota ['nɔtal *f* -**1.** [ger] note; **digno de ~** noteworthy; **tomar ~** to take note; **~ de rodapé** footnote; **cheio da ~** loaded; **uma ~ (preta)** a fortune. -**2.** *COM* bill; **~ fiscal** invoice; **~ promissória** promissory note, IOU. -**3.** *EDUC* mark. -**4.** [comunicado] notice; **~ oficial** official statement.

notabilizar [4] [notabili'za(x)] *vt* to distinguish.

➡ **notabilizar-se** *vp:* **~-se (em/por)** to distinguish o.s. in/through.

notação [nota'sãw] (*pl* -ões) *f* [sistema] notation; **~ musical** (scale of) notation.

notadamente [notada'mẽtʃil *adv* [em particular] in particular.

notar [4] [no'ta(x)] *vt* [reparar] to note; **fazer ~** to indicate.

➡ **notar-se** *vp:* **nota-se que ...** it is clear that ...; **é de se ~ que ...** it is noticeable that ...

notável [no'tavɛwl (*pl* -eis) *adj* notable.

notebook ['notʃibukil (*pl* -s) *m* *COMPUT* notebook.

notícia [no'tʃisjal *f* news (*sg*); **uma ~** a piece of news; **ter ~s** to have news; **ter ~s de alguém/algo** to have news of sb/sthg, to hear from sb/about sthg.

noticiar [16] [notʃi'sja(x)] *vt:* **~ algo a alguém** to inform sb of sthg; **~ algo** to report sthg; **~ a alguém que** to inform sb that.

noticiário [notʃi'sjarjul *m* -**1.** [de jornal] news section. -**2.** [rádio, tv] news bulletin. -**3.** [cinema] newsreel.

noticioso, osa [notʃi'sjozu, ɔzal *adj* news (*antes de subst*).

notificação [notʃifika'sãw] (*pl* -ões) *f* -**1.** [comunicado] notification. -**2.** *JUR* instruction.

notificar [12] [notʃifi'ka(x)] *vt* -**1.** [comunicar]: **~ algo a alguém** to notify sb of sthg. -**2.** *JUR* to instruct.

notívago, ga [no'tʃivagu, gal <> *adj* nocturnal. <> *m, f* [pessoa] sleepwalker.

notoriedade [notorje'dadʒil *f* -**1.** [fama] fame. -**2.** [evidência] blatancy.

notório, ria [no'tɔrju, rjal *adj* -**1.** [famoso] famous, well-known. -**2.** [evidente] blatant; **é público e ~ que ...** it is public knowledge and blatantly clear that ...

noturno, na [no'tuxnu, nal *adj* -**1.** [trem, aula] night (*antes de subst*); **vôo ~** night flight. -**2.** [animais, plantas] nocturnal.

➡ **noturno** *m* -**1.** *MÚS* nocturne. -**2.** [trem] night train.

noutro ['notrul = **em + outro.**

nov. (*abrev de* **novembro**) Nov.

nova ['nɔval *f* ▷ **novo.**

Nova Déli [ˌnɔva'dɛli] *n* New Delhi.

nova-iorquino, na [ˌnovajox'kinu, na] <> *adj* New York *(antes de subst)*.<> *m, f* New Yorker.

novamente [ˌnɔva'mẽntʃil *adv* **-1.** [outra vez] once again. **-2.** [recentemente] recently.

novato, ta [no'vatu, ta] <> *adj* inexperienced. <> *m, f* novice.

Nova York [ˌnɔva'jɔxki] *n* New York.

Nova Zelândia [ˌnɔvaze'lãndʒja] *n* New Zealand.

nove ['nɔvi] *num* nine; *veja também* **seis**.

novecentos, tas [nɔve'sẽntuʃ, taʃ] *num* nine hundred; *veja também* **seiscentos**.

nove-horas [nɔ'vjɔraʃ] *fpl fam:* **cheio de ~** [complicado] fussy; [sofisticado] fancy.

novela [no'vɛla] *f* **-1.** *RÁDIO* & *TV* soap opera. **-2.** *LITER* story.

novelesco, ca [nove'lɛsku, ka] *adj pej* soppy.

novelista [nove'liʃta] *mf* **-1.** [roteirista] script writer. **-2.** [escritor] novelist.

novelo [no'velu] *m* ball of yarn.

novembro [no'vẽnbru] *m* November; *veja também* **setembro**.

novena [no'vena] *f RELIG* novena.

noventa [no'vẽnta] *num* ninety; *veja também* **sessenta**.

noviciado [novi'sjadu] *m RELIG* novitiate.

noviço, ça [no'visu, sa] *m, f RELIG* novice.

novidade [novi'dadʒi] *f* **-1.** [ger] novelty. **-2.** [notícia] news *(sg)*.

novilho, lha [no'viʎu, ʎa] *m, f* calf.

novinho, nha [no'viɲu, ɲa] *adj* **-1.** [pessoa] young. **-2.** [objeto] new.

novo, nova ['novu, 'nɔva] <> *adj* **-1.** [ger] new; **~ em folha** brand new; **o que há de ~?** what's new? **-2.** [jovem] young. **-3.** [outro] different. <> *m, f:* **a nova/o novo** the new one.
➡ **de novo** *loc adv* again.
➡ **novo** *m* unknown.
➡ **nova** *f:* **boa nova** good news; **nova economia** new economy.

novo-rico [novu'xiku] *(pl* **novos-ricos**) *m,f* nouveau riche.

noz ['nɔʃ] *(pl* **-es**) *f* nut.

noz-moscada [ˌnɔʒmoʃ'kada] *(pl* **nozes-moscadas**) *f* nutmeg.

nu, nua ['nu, 'nual *adj* **-1.** [ger] bare. **-2.** [sem roupa] naked; **~ em pêlo** stark naked. **-3.** [sem rodeios]: **a verdade nua e crua** the naked truth; **a realidade nua e crua** the stark reality. **-4.** *loc:* **pôr algo a ~** *fig* to bring sthg out into the open.
➡ **nu** *m ARTE* nude.

nuança [nu'ãnsa], **nuance** [nu'ãsi] *f* nuance.

nublado, da [nu'bladu, da] *adj* cloudy.

nublar [4] [nu'bla(x)] *vt* to cloud.
➡ **nublar-se** *vp* to become cloudy.

nuca ['nuka] *f* nape.

nuclear [nukle'a(x)] *(pl* **-es**) *adj* **-1.** *TEC* nuclear. **-2.** *fig* [central] central.

núcleo ['nuklju] *m* nucleus.

nudez [nu'deʃ] *f* **-1.** [de pessoa] nudity. **-2.** [de coisas] bareness.

nudismo [nu'dʒiʒmu] *m* nudism.

nudista [nu'dʒiʃta] <> *adj* nudist. <> *mf* nudist.

nulidade [nuli'dadʒi] *f* insignificance; **ser uma ~** [coisa] to amount to nothing; [pessoa] to be a nonentity.

nulo, la ['nulu, la] *adj* **-1.** [sem valor] invalid. **-2.** [nenhum] non-existent. **-3.** [inepto] useless; **ser ~ em algo** to be useless at sthg.

num [nũ] = **em + um**.

núm. *(abrev de* **número**) *m* no.

numa ['numa] *cont* = **em + uma**.

numeração [numera'sãw] *(pl* **-ões**) *f* **-1.** [ato] numbering. **-2.** [sistema] numbers; **~ arábica/decimal** Arabic/decimal figures; **~ romana** Roman numerals. **-3.** [de calçados, roupas] size.

numerado, da [nume'radu, da] *adj* numbered.

numeral [nume'raw] *(pl* **-ais**) *m GRAM* numeral.

numerar [4] [nume'ra(x)] *vt* **-1.** [pôr número em] to number. **-2.** [pôr em ordem numérica] to place in numerical order.

numerário [nume'rarju] *m* cash.

numérico, ca [nu'mɛriku, ka] *adj* numerical.

número ['numerul *m* **-1.** [ger] number; **~ cardinal/ordinal** cardinal/ordinal number; **~ par/ímpar** even/odd number; **~ primo** prime number; **sem-~** countless; **um sem-~ de vezes** countless times; **~ de telefone/fax** telephone/fax number. **-2.** [tamanho]: **que ~ você calça?** what size shoe do you wear? **-3.** [edição] issue; **~ atrasado** back number. **-4.** [categoria]: **ser o ~ um** to be number one. **-5.** [quadro] act.

numeroso, osa [nume'rozu, ɔza] *adj* numerous.

nunca ['nũŋka] *adv* **-1.** [sentido negativo] never; **~ mais** never again; **ele quase ~ sorri** he hardly ever smiles. **-2.** [sentido afirmativo]: **como ~** as never before; **mais do que ~** more than ever.

núncio ['nũnsju] *m* nuncio.

nuns [nũʃ] = **em + uns**.

nupcial [nup'sjaw] *(pl* **-ais**) *adj* wedding *(antes de subst)*.

núpcias ['nupsjaʃ] *fpl* wedding.

nutrição [nutri'sãw] *f* nutrition.

nutricionista [nutrisjo'niʃta] *mf* nutritionist.

nutrido, da [nu'tridu, da] *adj* **-1.** [bem alimentado] well-fed. **-2.** [robusto] fit.

nutriente [nu'trjẽntʃi] <> *adj* nutritional. <> *m* nutrient.

nutrir [6] [nu'tri(x)] <> *vt* **-1.** [alimentar]: **~ (com/de)** to nourish (with). **-2.** *fig* [acalentar]: **~ algo por** to nurture sthg for. **-3.** *fig* [fornecer]: **~ algo de** to provide sthg with. <> *vi* to be nourishing; **~ de** to provide with.
➡ **nutrir-se** *vp* **-1.** [alimentar-se]: **~-se de** to obtain nourishment from; **~-se com** to feed on. **-2.** [prover-se] *fig*: **~-se de algo** to supply o.s. with.

nutritivo, va [nutri'tʃivu, va] *adj* nourishing; **valor ~** nutritional value.

nuvem ['nuvẽ] *(pl* **-ns**) *f* **-1.** [do céu] cloud. **-2.** *fig* [aglomeração - de pessoas] swarm; [- de insetos, gases, fumaça] cloud. **-3.** *loc:* **cair das nuvens** to come down to earth; **estar nas nuvens** to daydream; **passar em brancas nuvens** [data] to pass by unnoticed; **pôr nas nuvens** to praise to the skies.

O

o¹, O [ɔ] *m* [letra] o, O.

o², a [u, a] (*mpl* os, *fpl* as) <> *artigo definido* **-1.** [com substantivo genérico] the; **a casa** the house; **o hotel** the hotel; **os alunos** the students; **os noivos** the bride and groom. **- 2.** [com substantivo abstrato]: **a vida** life; **o amor** love. **-3.** [com adjetivo substantivado]: **o melhor/pior** the best/worst; **vou fazer o possível** I'll do what I can. **- 4.** [com nomes geográficos]: **a Inglaterra** England; **o Amazonas** the Amazon; **o Brasil** Brazil; **os Estados Unidos** the United States; **os Pirineus** the Pyrenees. **- 5.** [indicando posse]: **quebrei o nariz** I broke my nose; **estou com os pés frios** my feet are cold. **- 6.** [enfaticamente]: **ele pensa que é O gênio** he thinks he is THE genius; **ela é A supermãe** she is THE supermother; **Tentação, O perfume** Tentação, THE perfume. **- 7.** [com nome de pessoa]: **o Alexandre** Alexandre; **a Helena** Helena; **o Sr. Mendes** Mr. Mendes. **- 8.** [por cada] a, per; **3 reais a dúzia** 3 reals a dozen; **o linho é 5 reais o metro** linen is 5 reals per metre. **- 9.** [em datas, períodos] the; **o dois de Abril** the second of April *UK*, April second *US*; **o pós-guerra** the post-war years. **-10.** [em títulos] the; **Alexandre o Grande** Alexander the Great; **D. Maria a louca** Queen Mary the madwoman. <> *pron pess* **-1.** [pessoa] him (*f* her), them *pl*; **eu a deixei ali** I left her there; **ela o amava muito** she loved him very much; **não os vi** I didn't see them. **- 2.** [você, vocês] you; **eu o chamei, Dirceu, mas você não ouviu** I called you, Dirceu, but you didn't hear; **prazer em conhecê-los, meus senhores** pleased to meet you, gentlemen. **- 3.** [coisa] it, them *pl*; **onde estão as chaves? não consigo achá-los** where are the keys? I can't find them; **este paletó é novo, comprei-o no mês passado** this jacket is new, I bought it last month. **- 4.** [em locuções]: **o/a da esquerda** the one on the left; **os que desejarem vir terão de pagar** those who wish to come will have to pay; **o que (é que) ...?** what (is) ...?; **o que (é que) está acontecendo?** what's going on?; **era**

o que eu pensava it's just as I thought; **o quê?** what? <> *pron dem* **-1.** [especificativo - com substantivo] the one; **feche a porta da frente e a dos fundos** close the front door and the one at the back; **compre o que for mais barato** buy the one that's cheapest; **2.** [- com adjetivo] the; **destas balas, adoro as vermelhas** out of these sweets, I prefer the red ones **3.** [indicando posse] one; **minha casa e a de Teresa** my house and Teresa's, mine and Teresa's house; **minha casa é grande e a de Teresa é pequena** my house is big and Teresa's one is small.

ó [ɔ] *interj* oh!

ô [o] *interj* oh!

OAB (*abrev de* **Ordem dos Advogados do Brasil**) *f* Brazilian law society.

oásis [ɔ'aziʃ] *m inv* oasis.

oba [ˈoba] *interj* **-1.** [de alegria] great! **-2.** [cumprimento] hi!

obcecado, da [obiseˈkadu, da] *adj* obsessive.

obcecar [12] [obiseˈka(x)] *vt* to obsess.

◆ obcecar-se *vp:* ~ **(por/com)** to become obsessed by/with.

obedecer [25] [obedeˈse(x)] <> *vt* to obey. <> *vi:* ~ **a (alguém/algo)** to obey (sb/sthg).

obediência [obeˈdʒjẽnsja] *f* obedience.

obediente [obeˈdʒjẽntʃi] *adj* obedient.

obelisco [obeˈliʃku] *m* obelisk.

obesidade [obeziˈdadʒi] *f* obesity.

obeso, sa [oˈbezu, za] <> *adj* obese. <> *m, f* obese person.

óbice [ˈɔbisil] *m* obstacle.

óbito [ˈɔbitu] *m* death.

obituário [obiˈtwarju] *m* obituary.

objeção [obʒeˈsãw] (*pl* -ões) *f* **-1.** [contestação] objection. **-2.** [obstáculo] obstacle; **fazer** *ou* **pôr** ~ **a** to make an objection to.

objetar [4] [obʒeˈta(x)] <> *vt:* ~ **que** to contest (that). <> *vi:* ~ **(a)** to object (to).

objetiva [obʒeˈtʃiva] *f FOT* lens.

objetivar [4] [obʒetʃiˈva(x)] *vt* [visar a] to have as one's objective.

objetividade [obʒetʃiviˈdadʒil] *f* objectivity.

objetivo, va [obʒeˈtʃivu, va] *adj* objective.

◆ objetivo *m* objective, aim.

objeto [obˈʒɛtu] *m* **-1.** [coisa] object. **-2.** [de estudo] subject.

oblíquo, qua [oˈblikwu, kwa] *adj* **-1.** [diagonal - luz, chuva, traço] slanting; [- terreno, reta] sloping; [- ângulo] oblique. **-2.** *fig* [dissimulado] devious.

obliterar [4] [oblite'ra(x)] *vt* **-1.** [apagar] to obliterate. **-2.** *MED* to block.

oblongo, ga [obˈlõŋgu, ga] *adj* oblong.

oboé [oˈbwɛ] *m* oboe.

oboísta [oˈbwiʃta] *mf* oboist.

óbolo [ˈɔbulu] *m* [esmola] alms (*pl*).

obra [ˈɔbra] *f* **-1.** [trabalho] work; ~ **de arte** work of art; ~ **de caridade** charitable work; **ser** ~ **de alguém** *fig* to be the work of sb. **-2.** *CONSTR* works (*pl*); **em** ~**s** under repair.

obra-prima [ˌɔbraˈprima] (*pl* **obras-primas**) *f* **-1.**

[melhor obra] masterpiece. **-2.** [perfeição]: **ser/estar uma** ~ to be a work of art.

obrar [4] [o'bra(x)] <> vt [fazer] to perform. <> vi **-1.** [influir]: ~ **sobre** to work on. **-2.** [trabalhar]: ~ **(contra/a favor de)** to work (against/for).

obreiro, ra [o'brejru, ral m, f worker.

obrigação [obriga'sãw] (pl **-ões**) f **-1.** [dever] obligation; **cumprir (com) suas** ~**s** to fulfil one's obligations UK, to fulfill one's obligations US. **-2.** COM bond.

obrigado, da [obri'gadu, dal interj [agradecimento]: **(muito)** ~ **(por)** thank you (very much) (for).

obrigar [14] [obri'ga(x)] vt: ~ **alguém a fazer algo** [forçar] to force sb to do sthg; [impor] to require sb to do sthg; [induzir] to compel sb to do sthg.

➠ **obrigar-se** vp to take it upon o.s.

obrigatoriedade [obrigatorje'dadʒi] f obligatory nature.

obrigatório, ria [obriga'tɔrju, rjal adj obligatory.

obscenidade [obiseni'dadʒi] f obscenity; **ser uma** ~ to be a disgrace.

obsceno, na [obi'senu, nal adj obscene.

obscurecer [25] [obiʃkure'se(x)] vt **-1.** [escurecer] to darken. **-2.** fig [entristecer] to trouble. **-3.** fig [prejudicar] to damage; fig [perturbar] to unsettle.

➠ **obscurecer-se** vp to become dark.

obscuridade [obiʃkuri'dadʒi] f **-1.** [escuridão] darkness. **-2.** [anonimato] obscurity. **-3.** fig [esquecimento] obscurity.

obscuro, ra [obi'ʃkuru, ral adj **-1.** [escuro] dark. **-2.** fig [desconhecido, confuso] obscure.

obsequiar [16] [obize'kja(x)] vt **-1.** [fazer agrados a] to please. **-2.** [presentear]: ~ **alguém (com algo)** to make a present (of sthg) to sb.

obséquio [obi'zɛkjul m favour UK, favor US; **por** ~ please; **quer fazer o** ~ **de ...?** irôn would you kindly ...?

obsequioso, osa [obize'kjozu, ɔzal adj **-1.** [prestativo] obliging. **-2.** [respeitoso] respectful.

observação [obizexva'sãw] (pl **-ões**) f **-1.** [ato] observation. **-2.** [comentário] remark. **-3.** [cumprimento] observance.

observador, ra [obisexva'do(x), ral (pl **-es**, fpl **-s**) <> adj [perspicaz] observant. <> m, f observer.

observância [obisex'vãsja] f observance.

observar [4] [obisex'va(x)] vt **-1.** [ger] to observe. **-2.** [contemplar] to look at. **-3.**: ~ **que** [notar] to notice that; [comentar] to remark that.

observatório [obisexva'tɔrjul m observatory.

observável [obisex'vavew] (pl **-eis**) adj observable.

obsessão [obse'sãw] (pl **-ões**) f obsession.

obsessivo, va [obse'sivu, val adj obsessive.

obsoleto, ta [obso'letu, tal adj obsolete.

obstáculo [obiʃ'takulul m obstacle; **corrida de** ~**s** ESP obstacle race.

obstante [obiʃ'tãntʃil ➠ **não obstante** <> loc conj nevertheless. <> loc prep in spite of.

obstar [4] [obiʃ'ta(x)] vi: **nada obsta a que ele viaje**

there is nothing to prevent him from travelling.

obstetra [obiʃ'tɛtral mf obstetrician.

obstetrícia [obiʃte'trisjal f obstetrics (sg).

obstinação [obiʃtʃina'sãwl (pl **-ões**) f obstinacy.

obstinado, da [obiʃtʃi'nadu, dal adj **-1.** [perseverante] obdurate. **-2.** [teimoso] obstinate.

obstinar-se [4] [obiʃtʃi'naxsil vp: ~ **em algo** to persist in sthg.

obstrução [obiʃtru'sãwl (pl **-ões**) f **-1.** [entupimento] blockage. **-2.** [impedimento] obstruction.

obstruir [74] [obiʃ'trwi(x)] vt **-1.** [entupir] to block. **-2.** [impedir] to obstruct.

obtenção [obitẽ'sãwl (pl **-ões**) f **-1.** [aquisição] acquisition. **-2.** [consecução] achievement.

obtenível [obitẽ'nivewl (pl **-eis**) adj achievable.

obter [1] [obi'te(x)] vt **-1.** [diploma, verbas, absolvição] to obtain. **-2.** [desempenho, sucesso] to achieve.

obturação [obitura'sãwl (pl **-ões**) f [de dente] filling.

obturador [obitura'do(x)l (pl **-es**) m FOT shutter.

obturar [4] [obitu'ra(x)] vt [dente] to fill.

obtuso, sa [obi'tuzu, zal adj **-1.** [arredondado] blunt. **-2.** [bronco] obtuse. **-3.** [obscuro] obscure.

obviedade [ob'vjedadʒil f: **dizer** ~**s** to state the obvious.

óbvio, via ['ɔbvju, vjal adj obvious; **é** ~ **que** ... it's obvious that ...; **é** ~**!** of course!

➠ **óbvio** m: **o óbvio** the obvious; **ser o** ~ **ululante** to be blatantly obvious.

ocasião [oka'zjãwl (pl **-ões**) f **-1.** [ger] time; **em certas ocasiões** sometimes; **em duas ocasiões** twice; **certa** ~ ... once. **-2.** [oportunidade]: **aproveitar a** ~ to seize the moment; **ter** ~ **de fazer algo** to have the opportunity to do sthg.

ocasional [okazjo'nawl (pl **-ais**) adj chance (antes de subst).

ocasionar [4] [okazjo'na(x)] vt **-1.** [causar] to cause, to bring about. **-2.** [proporcionar]: ~ **algo a alguém** to afford sb sthg.

ocaso [o'kazul m **-1.** [do sol] sunset. **-2.** fig [fim] end. **-3.** fig [decadência] decline.

Oceania [osjã'nial n Oceania.

oceânico, ca [o'sjãniku, kal adj oceanic.

oceano [o'sjãnul m [mar] ocean; ~ **Antártico** Antarctic Ocean; ~ **Atlântico** Atlantic Ocean; ~ **Ártico** Arctic Ocean; ~ **Índico** Indian Ocean; ~ **Pacífico** Pacific Ocean.

oceanografia [osjanogra'fial f oceanography.

ocidental [osidẽ'tawl (pl **-ais**) <> adj western. <> m, f westerner.

ocidentalizar [osidẽtali'za(x)] vt to westernize.

➠ **ocidentalizar-se** vp to become westernized.

ocidente [osi'dẽntʃil m west.

➠ **Ocidente** m: **o Ocidente** the West.

ócio ['ɔsjul m **-1.** [tempo livre] free time. **-2.** [desocupação]: **estar no** ~ to be unoccupied. **-3.** [indolência] idleness.

ociosidade [osjozi'dadʒil f **-1.** [desocupação]:

estar na ~ to be unoccupied. **-2.** [indolência] idleness.

ocioso, sa [o'sjozu, za] *adj* **-1.** [desocupado] unoccupied. **-2.** [improdutivo] unproductive. **-3.** [indolente] idle. **-4.** [inútil] useless.

oco, oca ['oku, 'oka] *adj* **-1.** [vazio] hollow. **-2.** *fig* [fútil] empty.

ocorrência [oko'xěnsja] *f* **-1.** [acontecimento] event; ~ **policial** police matter. **-2.** [circunstância] circumstance.

ocorrer [5] [oko'xe(x)] *vi* **-1.** [acontecer] to occur. **-2.** [vir à memória]: ~ **a alguém** to occur to sb.

ocre ['okri] <> *adj* ochre *UK (antes de subst)*, ocher *US (antes de subst)*. <> *m* ochre.

octaedro [okta'εdru] *m* octahedron.

octogenário, ria [oktoʒe'narju, rja] <> *adj* octogenarian. <> *m, f* octogenarian.

octogonal [oktogo'naw] *(pl* -ais*) adj* octagonal.

octógono [ok'togonu] *m* octagon.

ocular [oku'la(x)] *adj* ocular.

oculista [oku'liʃta] *mf* oculist, ophthalmologist.

óculo ['okulu] *m* **-1.** [de navio] porthole. **-2.** *ARQUIT* oculus.

→ **óculos** *mpl* glasses *(pl);* ~**s escuros** sunglasses; ~**s de natação** goggles.

ocultar [4] [okuw'ta(x)] *vt* to conceal.

→ **ocultar-se** *vp* to hide.

ocultas [o'kuwtaʃ] → **às ocultas** *loc adv* secretly.

ocultismo [okuw'tʃiʒmul] *m* occultism.

oculto, ta [o'kuwtu, ta] *adj* **-1.** [secreto, desconhecido] hidden. **-2.** [sobrenatural] occult.

ocupação [okupa'sãw] *(pl* -ões*) f* **-1.** [ger] occupation. **-2.** [de um espaço] occupancy.

ocupacional [okupasjo'naw] *(pl* -ais*) adj* occupational.

ocupado, da [oku'padu, da] *adj* **-1.** [ger] occupied. **-2.** [atarefado] busy. **-3.** *TELEC* engaged *UK*, busy *US*; **dar (sinal de)** ~ to give the engaged tone *UK*, to give the busy signal *US*.

ocupante [oku'pãntʃi] *mf* occupant.

ocupar [4] [oku'pa(x)] *vt* **-1.** [ger] to occupy. **-2.** [atrair] to attract.

→ **ocupar-se** *vp* **-1.** [preencher tempo] to keep o.s. occupied. **-2.** [cuidar de]: ~**-se com alguém/ algo** to look after sb/sthg.

odalisca [oda'liʃka] *f* odalisque.

ode ['odʒi] *f* ode.

odiar [17] [o'dʒia(x)] <> *vt* to hate. <> *vi* to hate.

→ **odiar-se** *vp* **-1.** [a si mesmo] to hate o.s. **-2.** [um ao outro] to hate one another.

odiento, ta [o'dʒjẽntu, ta] *adj* hateful.

ódio ['odʒju] *m* hatred, hate; **ter** ~ **a/de alguém** to hate sb; **ter** ~ **a/de algo** to hate sthg.

odioso, osa [o'dʒjozu, ɔza] *adj* odious.

odisséia [odʒi'seja] *f* odyssey.

odontologia [odõntolo'ʒia] *f* odontology, dentistry.

odontologista [odõntolo'ʒiʃta] *mf* odontologist, dentist.

odor [o'do(x)] *(pl* -es*) m* odour.

OEA (*abrev de* **Organização dos Estados Americanos**) *f* OAS.

oeste ['wεʃtʃi] <> *adj inv* west. <> *m*: **a** ~ **de** west of; **em direção ao** ~ westwards.

ofegante [ofe'gãntʃi] *adj* **-1.** [arquejante] panting. **-2.** [cansado] breathless.

ofegar [12] [ofe'ga(x)] *vi* to pant.

ofender [5] [ofẽn'de(x)] *vt* to offend.

→ **ofender-se** *vp* [sentir-se insultado] to be offended.

ofensa [o'fẽnsa] *f* **-1.** [insulto] insult. **-2.** [desrespeito] offence *UK*, offense *US*.

ofensivo, va [ofẽn'sivu, va] *adj* offensive; ~ **à moral** morally offensive.

→ **ofensiva** *f* offensive; **estar/ficar na** ~ to be/get on the offensive; **tomar a** ~ *MIL* to take the offensive.

oferecer [25] [ofere'se(x)] *vt* to offer.

→ **oferecer-se** *vp* [propor seus serviços] to offer o.s.; ~**-se para fazer algo** to offer to do sthg.

oferecido, da [ofere'sidu, da] *adj pej* easy.

oferecimento [oferesi'mẽntu] *m* offer.

oferenda [ofe'rẽnda] *f RELIG* offering.

oferta [o'fεxta] *f* **-1.** [ger] offer; **em** ~ on offer. **-2.** *ECON* supply; **a** ~ **e a demanda** supply and demand.

ofertar [4] [ofex'ta(x)] *vt* to offer.

off-line ['oflajni] *adv COMPUT* off-line.

off-set [ɔfi'sɛtʃi] *m* offset printing.

oficial [ofi'sjaw] *(pl* -ais*)* <> *adj* official. <> *mf* **-1.** *MIL* officer. **-2.** [funcionário] official; ~ **de justiça** *JUR* bailiff.

oficializar [4] [ofisjali'za(x)] *vt* to officialize.

oficiar [16] [ofi'sja(x)] <> *vt* [endereçar ofício] to send officially; ~ **algo a alguém** to address sthg officially to sb. <> *vi RELIG* to officiate.

oficina [ofi'sina] *f* workshop; ~ **mecânica** garage.

ofício [o'fisju] *m* **-1.** [profissão] profession. **-2.** [incumbência] job. **-3.** *RELIG* office. **-4.** [correspondência] official letter. **-5.** [cartório]: ~ **de notas** notary public.

oficioso, osa [ofi'sjozu, ɔza] *adj* [não-oficial] unofficial; **de caráter** ~ unofficially.

oftalmologia [oftawmolo'ʒia] *f* ophthalmology.

oftalmológico, ca [oftawmo'lɔʒiku, ka] *adj* ophthalmological.

oftalmologista [oftawmolo'ʒiʃta] *mf* ophthalmologist.

ofuscante [ofuʃkãntʃi] *adj* dazzling.

ofuscar [12] [ofuʃ'ka(x)] <> *vt* **-1.** [encobrir] to conceal. **-2.** [suplantar em brilho] to outshine. **-3.** [olhos] to dazzle. **-4.** *fig* [apagar] to overshadow. <> *vi* [turvar a vista] to dazzle.

ogro ['ogru] *m* ogre.

ogum [o'gũ] *m god of war in Afro-Brazilian cults.*

oh [ɔ] *interj* oh!

oi ['oj] *interj* **-1.** [como saudação] hi! **-2.** [como resposta indagativa] mm?

oitava-de-final [oj,tavadʒifi'naw] *(pl* **oitavas-de-final***) f ESP round prior to quarter finals.*

oitavo, va [oj'tavu, va] <> *num* eighth; **a oitava parte** the eighth part. <> *m* eighth; *veja também* **sexto**.

oitenta [oj'tẽta] *num* eighty; *veja também* **sessenta**.

oito ['ojtu] *num* eight; *veja também* **seis**; **ou ~ ou oitenta** all or nothing.

oitocentos, tas [ojtu'sẽtuʃ] *num* eight hundred; *veja também* **seiscentos**.

ojeriza [oʒe'rizal f loathing; **ter ~ a alguém/algo** to have a loathing for sb/sthg.

ola ['ola] *f ESP* Mexican wave.

olá [o'la] *interj* hello.

olaria [ola'ria] *f* [fábrica] pottery.

oleado [o'ljadu] *m* tarpaulin.

oleiro, ra [o'lejru, ra] *m, f* potter.

óleo ['ɔlju] *m* oil; **~ de bronzear** sun-tan oil; **~ de cozinha** cooking oil; **~ diesel** diesel oil; **~ de fígado de bacalhau** cod liver oil; **~ de rícino** castor oil.

oleoduto [oljo'dutul *m* pipeline.

oleosidade [oljozi'dadʒi] *f* greasiness.

oleoso, osa [o'ljozu, ɔza] *adj* greasy.

olfato [ow'fatu] *m* smell.

olhada [o'ʎada] *f* look; **dar uma ~ (em)** to take a look (at).

olhadela [oʎa'dɛla] *f* glance.

olhar [4] [o'ʎa(x)] <> *vt* **-1.** [ger] to look at. **-2.** [cuidar de] to keep an eye on. **-3.** [ponderar] to look at. <> *vi* [ver] to look; **olha!** look!; **~ para alguém/algo** to look at sb/sthg; **~ por** [cuidar de] to keep an eye on. <> *m* look.
◆ olhar-se *vp* **-1.** [ver-se] to look at o.s. **-2.** [entreolhar-se] to look at each other.

olheiras [o'ʎejraʃ] *fpl* shadows under the eyes.

olho ['oʎu] *(pl* olhos) *m* **-1.** [ger] eye; **a ~ nu** to the naked eye; **de ~** [medir] by eye; **~ grande** *fig* envy; **pôr ~ grande em algo** to have one's eye on sthg; **~ de sogra** *CULIN Brazilian plum pudding with caramelized topping*; **ter ~ de peixe morto** to be glassy-eyed; **estar de ~ em alguém/algo** to have one's eye on sb/sthg. **-2.** [vista] glance; **dirigiu os ~s para todos durante o show** she cast her eyes over everyone during the show; **a ~s vistos** in front of one's very eyes; **passar os ~s por algo** to run one's eyes over sthg; **longe dos ~ s, longe do coração** out of sight, out of mind. **-3.** [de queijo] hole. **-4.** [de agulha] eye; **~ mágico** magic eye. **-5.** *loc*: **abrir os ~s** to open one's eyes; **abrir os ~s de alguém** to open sb's eyes; **custar/pagar os ~s da cara** to cost/pay an arm and a leg; **não pregar o ~** not to sleep a wink; **não ver com bons ~s** to take a dim view of; **pôr alguém no ~ da rua** to fire sb; **ter o ~ maior do que a barriga** to have eyes bigger than one's stomach.

olho-de-gato [oʎudʒi'gatul *(pl* olhos-de-gato) *m* reflector.

oligarquia [oligax'kia] *f* oligarchy.

oligárquico, ca [oli'gaxkiku, ka] *adj* oligarchical.

oligopólio [oligo'pɔljul *m* oligopoly.

olimpíada [olĩ'piada] *f* Olympiad; **as ~s** the Olympics.

olímpico, ca [o'lĩpiku, ka] *adj* Olympic.

olmo ['owmu] *m* elm.

OLP (Organização para Libertação da Palestina) *f* PLO.

olvidar [4] [owvi'da(x)] *vt* to forget.
◆ olvidar-se *vp*: **~-se (de)** to forget.

Omã [o'mã] *n* Oman.

ombreira [õn'brejra] *f* **-1.** [de roupa] shoulder pad. **-2.** [de porta] doorpost.

ombro ['õbrul *m ANAT* shoulder; **~ a ~** shoulder to shoulder; **encolher os ~s** to shrug.

OMC (*abrev de* Organização Mundial de Comércio) *f* WTO.

omelete [ome'lɛtʃi] *f* omelette *UK*, omelet *US*.

omissão [omi'sãw] *(pl* -ões) *f* omission.

omisso, ssa [o'misu, sa] *adj* **-1.** [negligente, ausente] negligent. **-2.** [faltando] omitted.

omitir [6] [omi'tʃi(x)] *vt* to omit.
◆ omitir-se *vp*: **~-se de algo** to refrain from sthg.

omoplata [omo'plata] *f* shoulder blade, scapula.

OMS (*abrev de* Organização Mundial de Saúde) *f* WHO.

onanismo [ona'niʒmul *m* onanism.

onça ['õsal *f* **-1.** [animal] jaguar; **estar/ficar uma ~** to be wild. **-2.** [peso] ounce.

onça-parda [õnsa'paxdal *(pl* onças-pardas) *f ZOOL* puma.

onça-pintada ['õnsapĩtadal *(pl* -s) *f ZOOL* jaguar.

oncologia [õŋkolo'ʒial *f* oncology.

oncologista [õŋkolo'ʒiʃtal *mf* oncologist.

onda ['õdal *f* **-1.** [ger] wave; **pegar ~** [surfar] to surf. **-2.** [moda] vogue; **estar na ~** to be in vogue. **-3.** *fam* [fingimento] lie. **-4.** *FÍSICA*: **~ curta/média/longa** short/medium/long wave; **~ sonora** sound wave. **-5.** *loc*: **deixar de ~** to stop messing about; **fazer ~** to make a fuss; **ir na ~ de alguém** to be taken in by sb.

onde ['õndʒil *(a + onde = aonde)* <> *adv (interrogativo)* **-1.** where; **~ fica o museu?** where is the museum?; **não sei ~ deixei meus óculos** I don't know where I've left my glasses; **aonde vamos esta noite?** where are we going tonight?; **por ~ vieram?** which way did you come?; **~ quer que** wherever; **carregue sua carteira por ~ você for** keep your wallet with you wherever you go. **-2.** *loc*: **fazer por ~** to do what's necessary. <> *pron* **-1.** *(relativo)* where; **a casa ~ moro** the house where I live; **o vale por ~ passa o rio** the valley where the river flows. **-2.** *(indefinido)* where; **eles não têm ~ morar** they have nowhere to live, they don't have anywhere to live; **pretendo voltar ~ estivemos ontem** I intend to go back to where we were yesterday; **até ~ eu sei** as far as I know.

ondeado, da [õn'dʒjadu, dal *adj* **-1.** [saia, desenho] flowing. **-2.** [cabelo] wavy.

ondear [15] [õn'dʒja(x)] vi to ripple.
ondulação [õndula'sãw] (pl -ões) f undulation.
ondulado, da [õndu'ladu, da] adj -1. [cabelo] wavy. -2. [folha] curled.
ondulante [õndu'lãntʃi] adj wavy.
onerar [4] [one'ra(x)] vt -1. [impor ônus a] to burden. -2. [sobrecarregar] to put a burden upon.
oneroso, osa [one'rozu, ɔza] adj -1. [dispendioso] costly. -2. [pesado] burdensome.
ONG (abrev de Organização Não-Governamental) f NGO.
ônibus ['onibuʃ] m inv bus.
onipotência [onipo'tẽsja] f omnipotence.
onipotente [,onipo'tẽntʃi] adj omnipotent.
onipresença [oni'prezẽsa] f omnipresence.
onipresente [onipre'zẽntʃi] adj omnipresent.
onírico, ca [o'niriku, ka] adj dreamlike.
onisciência [oni'sjẽsja] f omniscience.
onisciente [oni'sjẽntʃi] adj omniscient.
onívoro, ra [o'nivuru, ra] adj omnivorous.
ônix ['oniks] m (inv) onyx.
on-line ['õnlajni] adv COMPUT on-line.
onomástico, ca [ono'maʃtʃiku, ka] adj onomastic.
onomatopéia [onomato'pɛja] f onomatopoeia.
ontem ['õntẽ] adv yesterday; ~ **de manhã** yesterday morning; ~ **à noite/à tarde** yesterday evening/afternoon.
ONU ['ɔnu] (abrev de Organização das Nações Unidas) f UN.
ônus ['onuʃ] m -1. (inv) [peso] excess weight. -2. fig [encargo] obligation. -3. [imposto pesado] heavy tax.
onze ['õzi] num eleven; veja também **seis**.
opa ['opa] interj [de admiração] wow!; [de saudação] hi!
opacidade [opasi'dadʒi] f opacity.
opaco, ca [o'paku, ka] adj opaque.
opala [o'pala] f -1. [mineral] opal. -2. [tecido] fine cotton material.
opção [op'sãw] (pl -ões) f -1. [escolha] choice. -2. [preferência] preference.
opcional [opsjo'naw] (pl -ais) adj optional.
open market ['opẽn'maxkitʃ] m open market.
OPEP (abrev de Organização dos Países Exportadores de Petróleo) f OPEC.
ópera ['opera] f opera.
operação [opera'sãw] (pl -ões) f operation.
operacional [operasjo'naw] (pl -ais) adj operational.
operacionalidade [operasjionali'dadʒi] f operating efficiency.
operado, da [ope'radu, da] <> adj operated. <> m, f person or animal having had an operation.
operador, ra [opera'do(x), ra] (mpl -es, fpl -s) m, f operator.
operante [ope'rãntʃi] adj operative.
operar [4] [ope'ra(x)] <> vt -1. [fazer funcionar] to operate. -2. MED to operate on. -3. [realizar] to perform. <> vi -1. [ger] to operate. -2. MED to

operate. -3. [trabalhar]: ~ **com algo** to work with sthg.
◆ **operar-se** vp [ocorrer] to take place.
operária [ope'rarja] f ▷ **operário**.
operariado [opera'rjadu] m: o ~ the working class.
operário, ria [ope'rarju, rja] <> adj -1. [greve] workers' (antes de subst). -2. [classe] working. -3. [abelha] worker (antes de subst). <> m, f [trabalhador] worker.
opereta [ope'reta] f operetta.
opinar [4] [opi'na(x)] <> vi [emitir opinião]: ~ (sobre alguém/algo) to give one's opinion (on sb/sthg); ~ **a favor de/contra algo** to make a statement in favour of/against sthg. <> vt: ~ que to declare that.
opinião [opi'njãw] (pl -ões) f opinion; **a ~ pública** public opinion; **dar uma ~** to give an opinion; **mudar de ~** to change one's mind; **ser de ~ que** to be of the opinion that.
ópio ['opju] m opium.
oponente [opo'nẽntʃi] <> adj opposing. <> mf opponent.
opor [45] [o'po(x)] vt -1. [resistência, objeção] to oppose. -2. [argumento, razão] to set.
◆ **opor-se** vp -1. [ser contrário]: ~-se (a algo) to be opposed (to sthg). -2. [contradizer]: ~-se a algo to be in opposition to sthg.
oportunamente [opoxtuna'mẽntʃi] adv opportunely.
oportunidade [opoxtuni'dadʒi] f opportunity; **aproveitar a ~** to seize the opportunity; **na primeira ~** at the first opportunity.
oportunismo [opoxtu'niʒmu] m opportunism.
oportunista [opoxtu'niʃta] <> adj opportunistic. <> mf opportunist.
oportuno, na [opox'tunu, na] adj opportune; **momento ~** opportune moment.
oposição [opozi'sãw] (pl -ões) f -1. [objeção] opposition; **fazer ~ a** to oppose; **em ~ a** against. -2. POL: a ~ the opposition.
oposicionista [opozisjo'niʃta] <> adj opposition (antes de subst). <> mf member of the opposition.
oposto, ta [o'poʃtu, o'poʃta] adj -1. [contrário] opposite. -2. [em frente a] opposite.
◆ **oposto** m [inverso] opposite.
opressão [opre'sãw] (pl -ões) f -1. [ger] oppression. -2. [sufocação - no peito] tightness; [- no coração] oppression.
opressivo, va [opre'sivu, va] adj oppressive.
opressor, ra [opre'so(x), ra] m, f oppressor.
oprimido, da [opri'midu, da] adj oppressed.
oprimir [6] [opri'mi(x)] vt -1. [ger] to oppress. -2. [comprimir] to crush.
optar [4] [op'ta(x)] vi: ~ (por/entre) to opt (for/between); ~ **por fazer algo** to opt to do sthg, to choose to do sthg.
optativo, va [opta'tʃivu, va] adj optional.
óptico, ca ['optʃiku, ka] <> adj optical. <> mf optician.

óptica f-1. FÍS optics (sg). -2. [loja] optician's. -3. [ponto de vista] point of view.

opulência [opu'lẽsja] f opulence.

opulento, ta [opu'lẽtu, ta] adj opulent.

opúsculo [o'puʃkulul] m -1. [livreto] booklet. -2. [folheto] pamphlet.

ora ['ɔra] <> adv [agora] now; ela ~ quer uma coisa, ~ quer outra first she wants one thing, then she wants another; por ~ for now. <> conj now. <> interj: ~ bolas! oh hell!; ~ viva! hi there!

oração [ora'sãw] (pl -ões) f-1. [reza] prayer; fazer uma ~ to say a prayer. -2. GRAM clause.

oráculo [o'rakulul] m oracle.

orador, ra [ora'do(x), ra] (mpl -es, fpl -s) m, f orator.

oral [o'rawl] (pl -ais) <> adj oral. <> f oral (exam).

orangotango [orãŋgu'tãŋgu] m orang-utan.

orar [4] [o'ra(x)] vi: ~ (a/por) to pray (to/for).

oratório, ria [ora'tɔrju, rja] <> adj oratorial. <> m -1. RELIG oratory. -2. MÚS oratorio.

oratória f[arte de falar] oratory.

orbe ['ɔxbil] m orb.

órbita ['ɔxbita] f-1. ASTRON orbit; a lua está em ~ da Terra the moon orbits the Earth; o satélite entrou em ~ the satellite entered into orbit; entrar em ~ fam fig to be spaced out; estar fora de ~ fam fig to be out of one's mind. -2. [de olho] socket. -3. fig [área] orbit.

orbitar [oxbi'ta(x)] vi -1. [descrever órbita] to orbit. -2. fig [em torno de alguém] to revolve around.

orçamentário, ria [oxsamẽ'tarju, rja] adj budget (antes de subst).

orçamento [oxsa'mẽtul] m -1. [de família, governo] budget. -2. [de obra] estimate; ~ sem compromisso estimate without obligation, free estimate.

orçar [13] [ox'sa(x)] <> vt [calcular] to estimate. <> vi [avaliar] to make an estimate; ~ em to estimate at.

ordeiro, ra [ox'dejru, ra] adj orderly.

ordem ['ɔxdẽ] (pl -ns) f-1. [ger] order; dar uma ~ em algo to tidy sthg up; estar em ~ to be tidy; ~ do dia agenda; manter a ~ to maintain order; tudo em ~? everything OK?; ~ pública/social public/social order; às suas ordens at your service; até nova ~ until further notice; dar ~ a alguém para fazer algo to tell sb to do sthg; ~ de pagamento money order; ~ de prisão prison order. -2. [categoria]: foi um prejuízo da ~ de bilhões there was damage in the order of billions; de primeira/segunda ~ first/second rate; ~ dos Advogados Law Society; ~ de grandeza MAT order of magnitude.

ordenação [oxdena'sãw] (pl -ões) f -1. RELIG ordination. -2. [ordem] ordering.

ordenado, da [oxde'nadu, da] adj -1. [organizado] organized. -2. RELIG ordained.

ordenado m [salário] salary, wages (pl).

ordenança [oxde'nãsal] <> mf [soldado]

orderly. <> f MIL [regulamento] ordinance.

ordenar [4] [oxde'na(x)] vt to order.

ordenar-se vp -1. RELIG to be ordained. -2. [organizar-se] to organize o.s.

ordenhar [4] [oxde'ɲa(x)] vt to milk.

ordinal [oxdʒi'nawl] (pl -ais) adj ordinal.

ordinariamente [oxdʒinarja'mẽtʃil] adv usually.

ordinário, ria [oxdʒi'narju, rja] adj -1. [ger] ordinary. -2. [de má qualidade] poor. -3. [comum, freqüente] usual.

orégano [o'reganul] m oregano.

orelha [o'reʎa] f-1. ANAT ear; estar de ~ em pé fam fig to have one's wits about one; ~s de abano protruding ears; estar até as ~s com algo to be up to one's ears in sthg. -2. [aba] flap.

orelhada [ore'ʎada] f: de ~ by ear.

orelhão [ore'ʎãw] (pl -ões) m [cabine de telefone público] open telephone booth.

orelhudo, da [ore'ʎudu, da] adj -1. [de orelhas grandes] big-eared. -2. [estúpido] asinine. -3. [teimoso] stubborn.

orfanato [oxfa'natul] m orphanage.

orfandade [oxfãn'dadʒi] f orphanhood.

órfão, ã ['ɔxfãw, fã] <> adj orphaned; ~ de pai/mãe fatherless/motherless. <> m, f orphan.

orfeão [ox'fjãw] (pl -ões) m choir.

organdi [oxgãn'dʒil] m organdie UK, organdy US.

orgânico, ca [ox'gãniku, ka] adj organic.

organismo [oxga'niʒmul] m -1. [ger] organism. -2. fig [instituição] organization.

organista [oxga'niʃta] mf organist.

organização [oxganiza'sãwl] (pl -ões) f organization.

organizacional [oxganiza'sionawl] (pl -ais) adj organizational.

organizador, ra [oxganiza'do(x), ra] m, f organizer.

organizar [4] [oxgani'za(x)] vt to organize.

organizar-se vp to get organized.

organograma [oxgano'grãmal] m organization chart, organigram.

órgão ['ɔxgãw] (pl -s) m -1. [ger] organ. -2. [instituição] body; ~ de imprensa news publication.

orgasmo [ox'gaʒmul] m orgasm.

orgia [ox'ʒia] f orgy.

orgulhar [4] [oxgu'ʎa(x)] vt to make proud.

orgulhar-se vp: ~-se de to pride o.s. on.

orgulho [ox'guʎul] m -1. [ger] pride. -2. [arrogância] arrogance.

orgulhoso, osa [oxgu'ʎozu, ɔzal] adj -1. [brioso] self-satisfied. -2. [satisfeito] proud. -3. [arrogante] arrogant.

orientação [orjẽta'sãwl] (pl -ões) f -1. [ger] direction; ~ profissional careers guidance. -2. [supervisão] supervision. -3. fig [linha, tendência] orientation.

orientador, ra [orjẽta'do(x), ra] <> adj supervisory. <> m, f -1. [guia] adviser; ~ profissional careers counsellor. -2. [supervisor] supervisor.

oriental [orjēn'tawl] (*pl* -**ais**) <> *adj* oriental. <> *mf* oriental.

orientar [4] [orjēn'ta(x)] *vt* -**1.** [situar] to orient. -**2.** [nortear] to put in the right direction. -**3.** [supervisionar] to supervise. -**4.** *fig* [aconselhar] to advise.
→ **orientar-se** *vp* -**1.** [nortear-se] to orient o.s.; ~-**se por algo** to be guided by sthg. -**2.** [aconselhar-se, informar-se] to take advice.

oriente [o'rjēntʃil] *m* east.
→ **Oriente** *m*: **o Oriente** the East; **Extremo Oriente** Far East; **Oriente Médio** Middle East.

orifício [ori'fisjul] *m* orifice.

origem [o'riʒēl] (*pl* -**ns**) *f* -**1.** [início] origin; **ter** ~ **em** to originate from. -**2.** [ascendência] origin; **de** ~ **brasileira** of Brazilian descent; **país de** ~ country of origin. -**3.** [causa] cause; **dar** ~ **a** to give rise to.

original [oriʒi'nawl] (*pl* -**ais**) <> *adj* original. <> *m* [obra] original.

originalidade [oriʒinali'dadʒil] *f* -**1.** [origem] origin. -**2.** [excentricidade] originality.

originalmente [oriʒinaw'mēntʃil] *adv* originally.

originário, ria [oriʒi'narju, rja] *adj* [proveniente]: ~ **de** native of.

Orinoco [ori'nokul] *n*: **o** ~ the Orinoco.

oriundo, da [o'rjūndu, da] *adj*: ~ **de** from.

orixá [ori'ʃa] *m Orisha, a Yoruba divinity that symbolizes the forces of nature and acts as an intermediary between worshippers and the highest divinity.*

orla ['ɔxla] *f* [faixa] edge; ~ **marítima** coastline.

ornamentação [oxnamēnta'sãw] (*pl* -**ões**) *f* decoration.

ornamental [oxnamēn'tawl] (*pl* -**ais**) *adj* ornamental.

ornamento [oxna'mēntu] *m* ornament.

ornar [4] [ox'na(x)] *vt* to decorate.

ornato [ox'natul] *m* ornament.

ornitologia [oxnitolo'ʒial] *f* ornithology.

orquestra [ox'kɛʃtra] *f* orchestra; ~ **de câmara** chamber orchestra; ~ **sinfônica** symphony orchestra.

orquestração [oxkeʃtra'sãw] (*pl* -**ões**) *f* orchestration.

orquestrar [4] [oxkeʃ'tra(x)] *vt* to orchestrate.

orquídea [ox'kidʒja] *f* orchid.

ortodontista [oxtodōn'tʃiʃta] *mf* orthodontist.

ortodoxia [oxtodok'sia] *f* orthodoxy.

ortodoxo, xa [oxto'dɔksu, ksa] <> *adj* orthodox. <> *m, f* RELIG orthodox person.

ortografia [oxtogra'fia] *f* orthography, spelling.

ortográfico, ca [oxto'grafiku, ka] *adj* orthographic, spelling.

ortopedia [oxtope'dʒia] *f* orthopaedics (*pl*) UK, orthopedics (*pl*) US.

ortopédico, ca [oxto'pɛdʒiku, ka] *adj* orthopaedic UK, orthopedic US.

ortopedista [oxtope'dʒiʃta] *mf* orthopaedist UK, orthopedic US.

orvalhar [4] [oxva'ʎa(x)] *vi*: **orvalhou a noite inteira** the dew fell all night.

orvalho [ox'vaʎul] *m* dew.

os [uʃ] ⊳ **o**.

oscilação [osila'sãw] (*pl* -**ões**) *f* -**1.** [movimento] swinging. -**2.** [variação] swing. -**3.** *fig* [hesitação] hesitation.

oscilante [osi'lãntʃi] *adj* -**1.** *inv* [movimento] swinging. -**2.** [variável] variable. -**3.** *fig* [hesitante] hesitant.

oscilar [4] [osi'la(x)] *vi* -**1.** [ger] to swing. -**2.** *fig* [hesitar] to hesitate.

oscilatório, ria [osila'tɔrju, rja] *adj* swinging.

Oslo ['oʒlul *n* Oslo.

osmose [oʒ'mɔzil *f* osmosis.

ossatura [osa'tura] *f* -**1.** [esqueleto] skeletal structure. -**2.** [estrutura] framework.

ósseo, óssea ['ɔsju, 'ɔsja] *adj* bone (*antes de subst*).

ossificação [osifika'sãw] *f* ossification.

osso ['osu] (*pl* **ossos**) *m* -**1.** ANAT bone. -**2.** *fig* [dificuldade]: ~**s do ofício** occupational hazards; **ser um** ~ **duro de roer** to be a tough nut to crack.

ostensivo, va [oʃtēn'sivu, va] *adj* -**1.** [pessoa, luxo] ostentatious. -**2.** [policiamento] overt.

ostentação [oʃtēnta'sãw] (*pl* -**ões**) *f* ostentation.

ostentar [4] [oʃtēn'ta(x)] *vt* -**1.** [exibir] to show off. -**2.** [alardear] to display.

ostentoso, osa [oʃtēntozu, ɔza] *adj* ostentatious.

osteopata [oʃtʃjo'pata] *mf* osteopath.

osteoporose [oʃtʃjopo'rɔzi] *f* osteoporosis.

ostra ['oʃtra] *f* oyster.

ostracismo [oʃtra'siʒmu] *m* ostracism.

OTAN [o'tã] (*abrev de* **Organização do Tratado do Atlântico Norte**) *f* NATO.

otário, ria [o'tarju, rja] *m, f* sucker.

ótico, ca ['ɔtʃiku, ka] <> *adj* optic, optical. <> *m, f* [especialista] optician.
→ **ótica** *f* -**1.** [loja] optician's. -**2.** *fig* [ponto de vista] viewpoint. -**3.** FÍSICA optics (*sg*).

otimismo [otʃi'miʒmu] *m* optimism.

otimista [otʃi'miʃta] <> *adj* optimistic. <> *mf* optimist.

otimização [otʃimiza'sãw] (*pl* -**ões**) *f* optimization.

otimizar [otʃimi'za(x)] *vt* to optimize.

ótimo, ma ['ɔtʃimu, ma] <> *adj (superl de bom)* best. <> *interj* great!

otite [o'tʃitʃi] *f* otitis.

otorrinolaringologista [otoxinolarĩngolo'ʒiʃtal *mf* ear, nose and throat specialist.

Ottawa [o'tawa] *n* Ottawa.

ou [ow] *conj* or; ~ ..., ~ ... either ..., or ...; ~ **seja** in other words.

ouriçado, da [ori'sadu, da] *adj fam* prickly.

ouriçar [13] [ori'sa(x)] *vt* [pessoa] to bristle.
→ **ouriçar-se** *vp* to become excited.

ouriço [o'risul *m* -**1.** [casca espinhosa] burr. -**2.** ZOOL hedgehog.

ouriço-do-mar [o,risudu'ma(x)] (*pl* **ouriços-do-mar**) *m* sea urchin.

ourives [o'riviʃ] *mf inv* goldsmith.
ourivesaria [oriveza'ria] *f* -**1.** [arte] goldworking. -**2.** [oficina, loja] goldsmith's.
ouro ['oru] *m* -**1.** [metal] gold; **de** ~ *lit* gold; *fig* [coração] of gold; ~ **branco** white gold; **valer** ~ *fig* to be invaluable. -**2.** *fig* [dinheiro] money.
➡ **ouros** *mpl* [naipe] diamonds.

OURO PRETO

Ouro Preto is considered nowadays as a World Heritage Site; throughout the nineteenth century, it was the state capital of Minas Gerais. The city houses the masterpiece of Brazilian baroque: the church of St Francis of Assisi, created by Antônio Francisco Lisboa, the *Aleijadinho* (Cripple), who was also renowned for his soapstone sculptures.

ousadia [oza'dʒia] *f* daring; **ter a** ~ **de fazer algo** to have the audacity to do sthg.
ousado, da [o'zadu, da] *adj* -**1.** [audacioso] audacious. -**2.** [corajoso] daring.
ousar [4] [o'za(x)] ⇔ *vt* to dare. ⇔ *vi* to be daring.
out. (*abrev de* **outubro**) Oct.
outdoor [awtʃi'dɔr] *m* billboard, hoarding.
outeiro [o'tejru] *m* small hill.
outonal [oto'naw] (*pl* -**ais**) *adj* autumnal.
outono [o'tonu] *m* autumn.
outorgante [otox'gãntʃi] ⇔ *adj* granting. ⇔ *mf* grantor.
outorgar [14] [otox'ga(x)] *vt:* ~ **algo a alguém** to grant sthg to sb, to grant sb sthg.
outorgado, da [owtox'gadu, da] *adj* granted.
outra ['otra] *f* ➡ **outro**.
outrem [o'trẽ] *pron* -**1.** *inv* (*pl*) other people. -**2.** (*sg*) someone else.
outro, outra ['otru, 'otra] ⇔ *adj* -**1.** [ger] other; ~ **dia** the other day. -**2.** [diferente] another; **de** ~ **modo** in another way; **em** ~ **lugar** somewhere else; **entre outras coisas** among other things; **outra coisa** something else; ~**s tipos** other sorts. -**3.** [novo, adicional] another; **no** ~ **dia** the next day; **outra vez** again. ⇔ *pron* another; **o** ~ the other; **de um momento para o** ~ from one moment to the next; **tanto um quanto o** ~ both of them; **(um)** ~ another; **nem um, nem** ~ neither one nor the other, neither of them; **os** ~**s** [pessoas] others; [objetos] the others; **dos** ~**s** [pessoas] other people's.
➡ **outra** *f*: **a outra** [amante] the other woman; **estar em outra** *fam* to be into something else; **... e não deu outra** *fam* ... and that's precisely what happened.
outrora [o'trɔra] *adv* in the past.
outrossim [otro'sĩ] *adv* likewise.
outubro [o'tubru] *m* October; *veja também* **setembro**.

ouvido [o'vidu] *m* -**1.** *ANAT* ear; **entrar por um** ~ **e sair pelo outro** to go in one ear and out the other. -**2.** [audição] hearing; **dar** ~**s a algo/alguém** to listen to sthg/sb; **de** ~ by ear; **ser todo** ~**s** to be all ears; **ter bom** ~ **para algo** to have a good ear for sthg.
ouvinte [o'vĩntʃi] *mf* -**1.** *RÁDIO* listener. -**2.** *UNIV* auditor.
ouvir [71] [o'vi(x)] ⇔ *vt* -**1.** [pela audição] to hear. -**2.** [atentamente] to listen to. ⇔ *vi* -**1.** [pela audição] to hear; ~ **dizer que** to hear that; ~ **falar de algo/alguém** to hear of sthg/sb. -**2.** [atentamente] to listen. -**3.** [ser repreendido] to get a telling off.
ova ['ɔva] *f* roe; **uma** ~! *fam* no way!
ovação [ova'sãw] (*pl* -**ões**) *f* ovation.
ovacionar [4] [ovasjo'na(x)] *vt* to applaud.
oval [o'vaw] (*pl* -**ais**) *adj* oval.
ovalado, da [ova'ladu, da] *adj* oval.
ovariano, na [ova'rjãnu, na] *adj* ovarian.
ovário [o'varju] *m* ovary.
ovelha [o'veʎa] *f* sheep; ~ **negra** *fig* black sheep.
overdose [,ovex'dɔzi] *f* overdose.
ovni ['ɔvni] *m* (*abrev de* **Objeto Voador Não-Identificado**) UFO.
ovo ['ovu] (*pl* **ovos**) *m* *ANAT* egg; ~ **de codorna** quail egg; ~ **cozido** hard-boiled egg; ~ **estalado** *ou* **frito** fried egg; ~ **de granja** free-range egg; ~ **mexido** scrambled egg; ~ **de Páscoa** Easter egg; ~ **quente** boiled egg; **acordar/estar de** ~ **virado** *fam* to get out of bed on the wrong side; **pisar em** ~**s** to tread on egg shells; **ser um** ~ [quarto, apartamento] to be tiny.
ovóide [o'vɔjdʒi] *adj* ovoid.
ovulação [ovula'sãw] *f* ovulation.
ovular [ovu'la(x)] ⇔ *adj* oval. ⇔ *vi* to ovulate.
óvulo ['ɔvulu] *m* ovum.
oxalá [oʃa'la] ⇔ *interj* let's hope. ⇔ *m* *RELIG* highest Yoruba divinity in Afro-Brazilian cults.
oxidação [oksida'sãw] (*pl* -**ões**) *f* -**1.** *QUÍM* oxidation. -**2.** [ferrugem] rust.
oxidar [4] [oksi'da(x)] *vt* -**1.** *QUÍM* to oxidize. -**2.** [enferrujar] to rust.
➡ **oxidar-se** *vp* [enferrujar] to rust.
óxido ['ɔksidu] *m* oxide; ~ **de carbono** carbon monoxide.
oxigenado, da [oksiʒe'nadu, da] *adj* -**1.** [cabelo] bleached. -**2.** *QUÍM*: **água oxigenada** (hydrogen) peroxide.
oxigenar [4] [oksiʒe'na(x)] *vt* -**1.** [ger] to oxygenate. -**2.** [cabelo] to bleach.
oxum [o'ʃũ] *m Yoruba water goddess worshipped in Afro-Brazilian cults*.
ozônio [o'zonju] *m* ozone.
ozonizar [4] [ozoni'za(x)] *vt* to ozonize.

P

p, P [pe] *m* [letra] p, P.
pá ['pa] *f* -**1.** spade; ~ **de lixo** dustpan; ~ **mecânica** mechanical digger; ~ **para torta** cake slice. -**2.** [de hélice] blade. -**3.** *fam* [quantidade]: **uma** ~ **de** a mass of. -**4.** *loc*: **ser da** ~ **virada** to be of dubious character.
PA (*abrev de* **Estado do Pará**) *m State of Pará.*
PABX (*abrev de* **Private Automatic Branch Exchange**) *m* PABX.
paca ['paka] <> *mf ZOOL* paca. <> *adv fam* bloody; **isso está bom** ~ this is bloody good.
pacatez [paka'teʒ] *f* quietness.
pacato, ta [pa'katu, ta] *adj* quiet.
pachorra [pa'ʃoxa] *f* slowness.
pachorrento, ta [paʃo'xẽntu, ta] *adj* lumbering.
paciência [pa'sjẽnsja] *f* patience; **perder a** ~ to lose patience; **ter** ~ to be patient.
paciente [pa'sjẽntʃi] <> *adj* patient. <> *mf MED* patient.
pacificação [pasifika'sãw] *f* pacification.
pacificador, ra [pasifika'do(x), ra] <> *adj* pacifying. <> *m, f* peacemaker.
pacificar [12] [pasifi'ka(x)] *vt* to pacify.
pacífico, ca [pa'sifiku, ka] *adj* -**1.** [tranqüilo] tranquil. -**2.** [indiscutível] indisputable.
Pacífico [pa'sifiku] *n*: **o (oceano)** ~ the Pacific (Ocean).
pacifismo [pasi'fiʒmu] *m* pacifism.
pacifista [pasi'fiʃta] <> *adj* pacifist. <> *mf* pacifist.
paço ['pasu] *m* [palácio] palace.
paçoca [pa'sɔka] *f* -**1.** [doce] sweet made with peanuts and brown sugar. -**2.** *fig* [coisa amassada]: **estar uma** ~ to be all crumpled up.
pacote [pa'kɔtʃi] *m* -**1.** [embrulho] packet. -**2.** *ECON* package. -**3.** [turismo]: ~ **de viagem** package holiday.
pacto ['paktu] *m* [acordo] pact; ~ **social** social pact.
pactuante [pak'twãntʃi] *adj* cooperating.
pactuar [21] [pak'twa(x)] <> *vt* [combinar] to agree. <> *vi*: ~ **com alguém** to be in league with sb.
padaria [pada'ria] *f* bakery.

padecer [25] [pade'se(x)] <> *vt* to suffer. <> *vi*: ~ **de algo** to suffer from sthg.
padecimento [padesi'mẽntu] *m* suffering.
padeiro, ra [pa'dejru, ra] *m* baker.
padiola [pa'dʒjɔla] *f* stretcher.
padrão [pa'drãw] (*pl* -**ões**) <> *adj* [tamanho] standard. <> *m* -**1.** [ger] standard; ~ **de vida** standard of living. -**2.** [desenho] pattern.
padrasto [pa'draʃtu] *m* stepfather.
padre ['padri] *m* -**1.** [sacerdote] priest. -**2.** [como título] father.
➤ **Santo Padre** *m* Holy Father.
padrinho [pa'driɲu] *m* -**1.** [testemunha] godfather. -**2.** [paraninfo] guest of honour. -**3.** [protetor] protector.
➤ **padrinhos** *mpl* [padrinho e madrinha] godparents.
padroeiro, ra [pa'drwejru, ra] *m, f* patron saint.
padrões [pa'drõjʃ] *pl* ➤ **padrão**.
padronização [padroniza'sãw] (*pl* -**ões**) *f* standardization.
padronizado, da [padroni'zadu, da] *adj* [estandardizado] standardized.
padronizar [4] [padroni'za(x)] *vt* to standardize.
pães ['pãjʃ] *pl* ➤ **pão**.
paetê [pae'te] *m* sequin.
pág. (*abrev de* **página**) *f* p.
pagã [pa'gã] *f* ➤ **pagão**.
pagador, ra [paga'do(x), ra] <> *adj* paying. <> *m, f* payer; **ser bom/mau** ~ to be a good/bad payer.
pagamento [paga'mẽntu] *m* -**1.** [ger] payment. -**2.** [salário]: **dia de** ~ pay day. -**3.** *COM* [prestação, de dívida] repayment; ~ **contra entrega** cash on delivery; ~ **à vista** cash payment.
pagão, gã [pa'gãw, gã] (*mpl* -**s**, *fpl* -**s**) <> *adj* pagan. <> *m, f* pagan.
pagar [4] [pa'ga(x)] <> *vt* -**1.** [ger] to pay. -**2.** [compensar, reembolsar] to repay. <> *vi*: ~ **(a alguém)** to pay (sb); ~ **por algo** [desembolsar] to pay for sthg; *fig* [crime, pecado] to pay; **você me paga!** *fig* you'll pay for this!; ~ **caro** *fig* to pay dearly; ~ **para ver** *fig* to demand proof.
página ['paʒina] *f* page; ~ **de rosto** facing page.
paginação [paʒina'sãw] (*pl* -**ões**) *f* pagination.
paginar [4] [paʒi'na(x)] *vt* to paginate.
pago, ga ['pagu, ga] <> *pp* ➤ **pagar**. <> *adj* paid.
pagode [pa'gɔdʒi] *m* -**1.** [templo] pagoda. -**2.** *MÚS* type of samba. -**3.** [festa] party where pagode is danced.
pagodeiro, ra [pago'dejru, ra] [ra] *m pagode singer.*
págs. (*abrev de* **páginas**) *fpl* pp.
pai ['paj] *m* -**1.** [ger] father; ~ **adotivo** adoptive father; ~ **de criação** foster father; ~ **de família** paterfamilias. -**2.** [protetor] protector.
➤ **pais** *mpl* [pai e mãe] parents.
pai-de-santo [ˌpajdʒi'sãntu] (*pl* **pais-de-santo**) *m religious and spiritual candomblé leader.*

pai-dos-burros [ˌpajduʃˈbuxuʃ] (*pl* **pais-dos-burros**) *m fam* wordbook.

painel [pajˈnɛw] (*pl* **-éis**) *m* -**1**. [ger] panel. -**2**. [quadro, panorama] picture. -**3**. ARQUIT frame.

pai-nosso [ˌpajˈnɔsul] (*pl* **pais-nossos**) *m* Our Father, the Lord's Prayer.

paio [ˈpaju] *m salami-like pork sausage.*

paiol [paˈjɔw] (*pl* **-óis**) *m* -**1**. [celeiro] store. -**2**. [depósito] arsenal; ~ **de pólvora** *fig* powder keg.

pairar [4] [pajˈra(x)] *vi* -**1**. [sustentar-se]: ~ **em/ sobre** to hover in/over. -**2**. [ameaçar]: ~ **sobre** to hang over.

país [paˈiʃ] (*pl* **-es**) *m* country.

paisagem [pajˈzaʒẽ] (*pl* **-ns**) *f* -**1**. [vista] view. -**2**. [pintura] landscape.

paisagista [pajzaˈʒiʃta] <> *adj* landscape (*antes de subst*). <> *mf* -**1**. ARQUIT landscape architect. -**2**. ARTE landscape painter.

paisano, na [pajˈzãnu, na] *m, f* [civil] civilian.

➡ **à paisana** *loc adv* in mufti.

País Basco [paˌiʃˈbaʃku] *n*: **o** ~ the Basque Country.

Países Baixos [paˌiziʃˈbajʃuʃ] *n*: **os** ~ the Netherlands.

paixão [pajˈʃãw] (*pl* **-ões**) *f* passion.

paixonite [pajʃoˈnitʃi] *f fam*: **ter** ~ **aguda** to be madly in love.

pajé [paˈʒɛ] *m Amerindian priest and medicine man.*

pajear [15] [paˈʒja(x)] *vt* [tomar conta de] to look after.

pajem [ˈpaʒẽ] (*pl* **-ns**) <> *m* page. <> *f* nanny.

PAL (*abrev de* **Phase Alternate Line**) *m* PAL.

pala [ˈpala] *f* -**1**. [de roupa] yoke. -**2**. [de boné] peak. -**3**. [de sapato] tongue. -**4**. AUTO sun visor. -**5**. *fam* [dica] tip.

palacete [palaˈsetʃi] *m* stately home.

palácio [paˈlasju] *m* -**1**. [residência] palace. -**2**. [sede] headquarters (*pl*).

paladar [palaˈda(x)] (*pl* **-es**) *m* -**1**. [ger] taste. -**2**. ANAT palate.

palafita [palaˈfita] *f* -**1**. [habitação] house built on stilts. -**2**. [estacas] stilts (*pl*).

palanque [paˈlãŋki] *m* -**1**. [de comício] seating. -**2**. [para espectadores] stand.

palato [paˈlatu] *m* ANAT palate.

palavra [paˈlavra] *f* -**1**. [ger] word; ~**s cruzadas** crossword (puzzle) (*sg*); **medir as** ~**s** *fig* to measure one's words; **não dar uma** ~ not to say a word; ~ **de ordem** watchword; **pessoa sem** ~ person who cannot be trusted; **ter** ~ to keep one's word; ~ **de honra** word of honour. -**2**. [fala] speaking. -**3**. [direito de falar] right to speak; **dar a** ~ **a alguém** to hand the floor to sb; **pedir a** ~ to ask permission to speak.

palavra-chave [paˌlavraˈʃavi] (*pl* **palavras-chaves, palavras-chave**) *f* keyword.

palavrão [palaˈvrãw] (*pl* **-ões**) *m* swear word.

palavreado [palaˈvrjadu] *m* chatter, gabble.

palco [ˈpawku] *m* -**1**. TEATRO stage. -**2**. *fig* [cenário] scene.

paleolítico, ca [paljoˈlitʃiku, ka] *adj* paleolithic.

paleontologia [paljõntoloˈʒia] *f* paleontology.

palerma [paˈlɛxma] <> *adj* foolish. <> *mf* fool.

Palestina [paleʃˈtʃina] *n* Palestine.

palestino, na [paleʃˈtʃinu, na] <> *adj* Palestinian. <> *m, f* Palestinian.

palestra [paˈlɛʃtra] *f* [conferência] lecture, talk.

palestrante [paleʃtrãntʃi] *mf* speaker (*at conference*).

palestrar [4] [paleʃˈtra(x)] *vi* to give a talk.

paleta [paˈleta] *f* palette.

paletó [paleˈtɔ] *m* overcoat.

palha [ˈpaʎa] *f* straw; ~ **de aço** wire wool; **não mexer uma** ~ *fam fig* not to lift a finger.

palhaçada [paʎaˈsada] *f* -**1**. [brincadeira] clowning; **fazer** ~**s** to clown around. -**2**. [cena ridícula] ridiculous sight.

palhaço, ça [paˈʎasu, sa] *m, f* -**1**. [artista] clown. -**2**. *fam* [bobo] clown.

palheiro [paˈʎejru] *m* [celeiro] hayloft.

palheta [paˈʎeta] *f* -**1**. ARTE palette. -**2**. [lâmina - de veneziana] slat; [- de ventilador] blade. -**3**. [MÚS - para dedilhar] plectrum; [- embocadura] reed.

palhoça [paˈʎɔsa] *f* straw hut.

paliativo, va [paljaˈtʃivu, va] <> *adj* palliative. <> *m* palliative.

paliçada [paliˈsada] *f* -**1**. [tapume] palisade. -**2**. MIL stockade.

palidez [paliˈdeʒ] *f* -**1**. [de cor] paleness. -**2**. [de pessoa, rosto] pallor.

pálido, da [ˈpalidu, da] *adj* pale.

palitar [4] [paliˈta(x)] *vt*: ~ **os dentes** to pick one's teeth.

paliteiro [paliˈtejru] *m* toothpick holder.

palito [paˈlitu] *m* -**1**. [para os dentes] toothpick. -**2**. [biscoito] straw. -**3**. [fósforo] matchstick. -**4**. [pessoa magra] matchstick.

PAL-M (*abrev de* **Phase Alternate Line-Modified**) *m* PAL-M.

palma [ˈpawma] *f* palm.

➡ **palmas** *fpl* [aplauso]: **bater** ~ to clap.

palmada [pawˈmada] *f* smack; **dar/levar umas** ~**s** to smack/be smacked.

Palmas [ˈpawmaʃ] *n* Palmas.

palmatória [pawmaˈtɔrja] *f* ferule; ~ **do mundo** better than everyone else; **dar a mão à** ~ to climb down.

palmeira [pawˈmejra] *f* palm tree.

palmilha [pawˈmiʎa] *f* inner sole.

palmito [pawˈmitu] *m* Assai palm.

palmo [ˈpawmu] *m* handspan; **não enxergar um** ~ **adiante do nariz** not to be able to see past the end of one's nose; ~ **a** ~ inch by inch.

palmtop [ˈpawmitɔpi] (*pl* **palmtops**) *m* COMPUT palmtop.

palpável [pawˈpavew] (*pl* **-eis**) *adj* [tangível] palpable.

pálpebra [ˈpawpebra] *f* eyelid.

palpitação [pawpitaˈsãw] (*pl* **-ões**) *f* throbbing.

➡ **palpitações** *fpl* palpitations.

palpitar [4] [pawpiˈta(x)] *vi* -**1**. [pulsar] to throb. -**2**.

[agitar-se] to quiver. -**3.** [opinar] to speculate.

palpite [paw'pitʃi] *m* -**1.** [opinião] speculation. -**2.** [intuição]: **ter um** ~ to have a hunch. -**3.** [turfe] tip.

palpiteiro, ra [pawpi'tejru, ra] <> *adj* opinionated. <> *m, f* opinionated person.

paludismo [palu'dʒiʒmu] *m* malaria.

pamonha [pa'moɲa] <> *adj* sluggish, dull. <> *mf* sluggard, dullard.

pampa ['pãpa] *m* -**1.** GEOGR pampas. -**2.**: **às** ~**s** [com substantivo] loads of; [com adjetivo] extremely; [com advérbio] really.

panaca [pa'naka] <> *adj* dim-witted. <> *mf* dimwit.

panacéia [pana'sɛja] *f* panacea.

Panamá [pana'ma] *n* Panama.

panamenho, nha [pana'meɲu, ɲa] <> *adj* Panamanian. <> *m, f* Panamanian.

pan-americano, na [ˌpãnameri'kãnu, na] *adj* pan-American.

pança ['pãsa] *f fam* paunch.

pancada [pãŋ'kada] <> *adj fam* nuts. <> *f* -**1.** [golpe] blow; **dar uma** ~ **em alguém** to hit sb; **levar uma** ~ **de alguém** to be hit by sb. -**2.** [batida] hit. -**3.** [chuva]: ~ **d'água** downpour.

pancadaria [pãŋkada'ria] *f* brawl.

pâncreas ['pãŋkrjaʃ] *m* pancreas.

pançudo, da [pãn'sudu, da] *adj* paunchy.

panda ['pãda] *m* ZOOL panda.

pandarecos [pãda'rɛkuʃ] *mpl fam*: **em** ~ [exausto] shattered; [destruído] in pieces; [moralmente] thoroughly dejected.

pândego, ga ['pãdegu, ga] *adj* -**1.** [engraçado] funny. -**2.** [folião] reveller.

➡ **pândega** *f* [folia] revelry.

pandeiro [pãn'dejru] *m* MÚS tambourine.

pandemônio [pãde'monju] *m* pandemonium.

pane ['pãni] *f* breakdown.

panegírico [pane'ʒiriku] *m* panegyric.

panela [pa'nɛla] *f* -**1.** [recipiente] saucepan; ~ **de pressão** pressure cooker. -**2.** *fig* [conteúdo] saucepanful.

panelaço [pane'lasu] *m banging of pots and pans as a form of protest*.

panelinha [pane'liɲa] *f* clique.

panfletar [4] [pãfle'ta(x)] *vi* to hand out pamphlets.

panfleto [pãn'fletu] *m* pamphlet.

pangaré [pãŋga'rɛ] *m* nag.

pânico ['pãniku] *m* panic; **estar/entrar em** ~ to panic.

panificação [panifika'sãw] *f* -**1.** [padaria] bakery. -**2.** [fabrico] bread making.

pano ['pãnu] *m* -**1.** [tecido] cloth; ~ **de chão** floor cloth; ~ **de pó** duster; ~ **de prato** tea towel; **por baixo/debaixo do** ~ *fig* on the quiet; **dar** ~ **para mangas** *fig* to get people talking; **pôr** ~**s quentes em algo** *fig* to calm sthg down. -**2.** TEATRO curtain; ~ **de fundo** backdrop.

panorama [pano'rãma] *m* panorama.

panorâmico, ca [pano'rãmiku, ka] *adj* panoramic.

➡ **panorâmica** *f* [exposição] panorama.

panqueca [pãŋ'kɛka] *f* pancake.

pantalonas [pãta'lonaʃ] *fpl* -**1.** [calças] pantaloons. -**2.** [de bailarino] leggings.

pantanal [pãta'naw] (*pl* -**ais**) *m* large swamp.

PANTANAL

The *pantanal* (swamp) of Mato Grosso extends over the south-west of Mato Grosso, the west of Mato Grosso do Sul and part of Paraguay. The swamp is periodically flooded by the many lakes and gullies that crisscross it; it is the largest flood plain in the world and one of Brazil's finest natural features. Within it can be found 650 species of birds, 60 species of mammals, 260 species of fish and 50 species of reptiles.

pântano ['pãntanu] *m* swamp.

pantanoso, osa [pãta'nozu, ɔza] *adj* swampy.

panteão [pãn'tʃjãw] (*pl* -**ões**) *m* pantheon.

pantera [pãn'tɛra] *f* ZOOL panther.

pantomima [pãnto'mima] *f* TEATRO pantomime.

pantufa [pãn'tufa] *f* slipper.

pão ['pãw] (*pl* **pães**) *m* -**1.** [alimento] bread; ~ **de carne** meat loaf; ~ **de centeio** rye bread; ~ **de fôrma** tin loaf; ~ **de mel** honey bread; ~ **dormido** stale bread; ~ **francês** small baguette; ~ **integral** wholemeal bread; **comer o** ~ **que o diabo amassou** to go through a bad patch; **com ele é** ~, ~, **queijo, queijo** you know where you stand with him. -**2.** [sustento] daily bread; **ganhar o** ~ to earn a crust. -**3.** RELIG Eucharist.

pão-de-ló [ˌpãwdʒi'lɔ] (*pl* **pães-de-ló**) *m* sponge cake.

pão-durismo [ˌpãwdu'riʒmu] *m inv* stinginess.

pão-duro [ˌpãw'duru] (*pl* **pães-duros**) <> *adj* miserly. <> *m, f* miser.

pãozinho [pãw'ziɲu] *m* roll.

papa ['papa] *f* -**1.** [mingau] pap. -**2.** [pasta] mush; **não ter** ~**s na língua** to be outspoken.

➡ **Papa** *m* RELIG Pope.

papada [pa'pada] *f* ANAT double chin.

papagaiada [papaga'jada] *f fam* farce.

papagaio [papa'gaju] <> *m* -**1.** ZOOL parrot. -**2.** [pipa] soltar ~ to fly a kite. -**3.** COM promissory note. -**4.** AUTO provisional licence. <> *interj fam*: ~ **(s)!** golly!

papaguear [papa'gja(x)] <> *vt* [repetir] to parrot. <> *vi* [tagarelar] to chatter away.

papai [pa'paj] *m* daddy; **o** ~ **aqui** *fam* [eu] yours truly.

➡ **Papai Noel** *m*: **o Papai Noel** Father Christmas.

papaia [pa'paja] *m* papaya, pawpaw.

papal [pa'paw] (*pl* -**ais**) *adj* RELIG papal.

papar [4] [pa'pa(x)] *fam* <> *vt* -**1.** [comer] to gobble. -**2.** [conseguir] to win. <> *vi* to eat.

paparicar [12] [papari'ka(x)] *vt* to mollycoddle.

paparicos [papa'rikuʃ] *mpl* smotherings.

papear [15] [pa'pja(x)] *vi*: ~ **(com/sobre)** to chat (with/about).

papel [pa'pɛw] (*pl* -**éis**) *m* -**1.** [ger] role; **fazer o** ~

de to play the part of; **fazer ~ de bobo** *fig* to look like a fool. **- 2.** [folha] paper; **~ crepon** crepe paper; **~ de carta** notepaper; **~ de embrulho** wrapping paper; **~ de seda** tissue paper; **~ higiênico** toilet paper; **~ laminado** *ou* **de alumínio** aluminium foil; **~ machê** papier mâché; **~ ofício** headed paper; **~ pardo** brown wrapping paper; **ficar no ~** to remain on the drawing board. **- 3.** [documento] paper; **de ~ passado** officially. **- 4.** FIN paper money. **- 5.** *gír droga* twist.

papelada [pape'lada] *f* **- 1.** [papéis] pile of paper. **- 2.** [documentos] stack of papers.

papelão [pape'lãw] *m* **- 1.** [papel] cardboard. **- 2.** *fig* [fiasco] fiasco; **que ~!** what a fiasco!

papelaria [papela'ria] *f* stationer.

papel-bíblia [pa'pewbiblia] (*pl* **papéis-bíblia**) *m* India paper.

papel-carbono [pa,pɛwkax'bonu] (*pl* **papéis-carbono**) *m* carbon paper.

papel-manteiga [pa'pewmãntejga] (*pl* **papéis-manteiga**) *m* tracing paper.

papel-moeda [pa,pɛw'mwɛda] (*pl* **papéis-moeda**) *m* paper money.

papelote [pape'lotʃi] *m gír droga* twist.

➤ **papelotes** *mpl* [para o cabelo] curling paper.

papel-pergaminho [pa,pɛwpexga'miɲu] (*pl* **papéis-pergaminho**) *m* parchment.

papiro [pa'piru] *m* papyrus.

papo ['papu] *m* **- 1.** [de ave] crop. **- 2.** *fam* [de pessoa] double chin; **estar no ~** to be in the bag; **ficar de ~ para o ar** *fig* to sit on one's hands. **- 3.** *fam* [conversa] chat; **ser bom ~** to be good company; **~ furado** [mentira] hot air; **ficar de ~ furado** [conversa] to stay and have a chat; **bater (um) ~** to (have a) natter.

papo-de-anjo [,papu'dʒiãnʒu] (*pl* **papos-de-anjo**) *m* CULIN baked egg sweet.

papo-furado [,papufu'radu] (*pl* **papos-furados**) ⬦ *adj* full of hot air. ⬦ *mf:* **ser um ~** to be full of hot air.

papoula [pa'pola] *f* poppy.

páprica ['paprika] *f* paprika.

Papua-Nova Guiné [pa,puanɔvagi'ne] *n* Papua New Guinea.

papudo, da [pa'pudu, da] *adj* double-chinned.

paquera [pa'kera] ⬦ *f fam* [paqueração] casual affair. ⬦ *mf* pick-up.

paquerar [4] [pake'ra(x)] *fam* ⬦ *vt* to flirt with. ⬦ *vi* to pull.

paquete [pa'ketʃi] *m ant* & NÁUT steamship.

Paquistão [pakiʃ'tãw] *n* Pakistan.

paquistanês, esa [pakiʃta'neʃ, eza] ⬦ *adj* Pakistani. ⬦ *m, f* Pakistani.

par ['pa(x)] (*pl* **-es**) ⬦ *adj* **-1.** MAT even. **- 2.** [parelho] paired. ⬦ *m* **-1.** [dupla] pair; **de ~ em ~** wide (open); **~ a ~** side by side; **sem ~** peerless. **- 2.** [casal] couple. **- 3.** [em dança] partner. ⬦ *f* TELEC: **~ trançado** twisted pair.

➤ **a par** *loc adj:* **estar a ~ de algo** to be well informed about sthg.

para ['para] *prep* **-1.** [exprime finalidade, destinação] for; **um telefonema ~ o senhor** a phone call for the gentleman; **esta água não é boa ~ beber** this water is not good for drinking; **eu queria algo ~ comer** I would like something to eat; **~ que serve isto?** what's this for? **- 2.** [indica motivo, objetivo] (in order) to; **cheguei mais cedo ~ arranjar lugar** I arrived early (in order) to get a seat; **era só ~ lhe agradar** it was only to please you. **- 3.** [indica direção] towards; **ela apontou ~ cima/baixo** she pointed upwards/downwards; **olhei ~ ela** I looked at her; **ele seguiu ~ o aeroporto** he headed for the airport; **vá ~ casa!** go home! **- 4.** [relativo a tempo]: **de uma hora ~ a outra** from one hour to the next; **quero isso pronto ~ amanhã** I want it done by tomorrow; **estará pronto ~ a semana/o ano** it'll be ready next week/year; **são quinze ~ as três** it's a quarter of three *US*, it's a quarter to three *UK*. **- 5.** [em comparações]: **é caro demais ~ as minhas posses** it's too expensive for my budget; **~ o que come, está magro** he's thin, considering how much he eats. **- 6.** [relativo a opinião, sentimento]: **~ mim** as far as I'm concerned; **~ ele, você está errado** as far as he's concerned, you are wrong. **- 7.** [exprime a iminência]: **estar ~ fazer algo** to be about to do sthg; **o ônibus está ~ sair** the bus is about to leave; **ele está ~ chegar** he'll be here any minute now. **- 8.** [em locuções]: **~ com** towards; **~ mais de** well over; **~ que** so that; **é ~ já!** coming up!

Pará [pa'ra] *n* Pará.

parabenizar [4] [parabeni'za(x)] *vt:* **~ alguém por algo** to congratulate sb on sthg.

parabéns [para'bẽjʃ] *mpl* **-1.** [congratulações] congratulations; **dar ~ a alguém** to congratulate sb; **estar de ~ (por algo)** to be congratulated (on sthg); **meus ~!** congratulations! **- 2.** [por aniversário] congratulations; **cantar ~** to sing 'Happy Birthday'.

parábola [pa'rabola] *f* **-1.** [narrativa] parable. **- 2.** MAT parabola.

pára-brisa [,para'briza] (*pl* **pára-brisas**) *m* windscreen *UK*, windshield *US*.

pára-choque [,para'ʃoki] (*pl* **pára-choques**) *m* AUTO bumper.

paradeiro [para'dejru] *m* whereabouts.

paradigma [para'dʒigma] *m* paradigm.

paradisíaco, ca [paradʒi'ziaku, ka] *adj fig* idyllic.

parado, da [pa'radu, da] *adj* **-1.** [imóvel] motionless. **- 2.** [sem vida] dull. **- 3.** [desativado] stopped. **- 4.** [abandonado] axed. **- 5.** [em greve] on strike. **- 6.** [sem trabalhar] unemployed.

➤ **parada** *f* **-1.** [de ônibus, trem] stop. **- 2.** [pausa] break; **dar uma ~ (em algo)** to have a break (from sthg); **~ cardíaca** cardiac arrest. **- 3.** [desfile] parade. **- 4.** MÚS: **~ de sucessos** hit parade. **- 5.** *fam* [dificuldade] obstacle; **agüentar a ~** to take it. **- 6.** *loc:* **ser uma ~** *fam* [ser difícil] to be difficult; [ser bonito] *fam* to be a knockout; **topar qualquer ~** to be ready for anything.

paradoxal [paradok'saw] (*pl* **-ais**) *adj* paradoxical.

paradoxo [para'dɔksu] *m* paradox.

paraestatal [parajʃta'taw] (*pl* **-ais**) <> *adj* public. <> *f* public organization.

parafernália [parafɛx'naljа] *f* **-1.** [tralha] paraphernalia. **-2.** [equipamento] equipment.

parafina [para'fina] *f* paraffin.

paráfrase [pa'rafrazi] *f* paraphrase.

parafrasear [15] [parafra'zja(x)] *vt* to paraphrase.

parafusar [4] [parafu'za(x)] *vt* to screw.

parafuso [para'fuzu] *m* screw; **entrar em** ~ *fam* to be thrown off track; **ter um** ~ **de menos** *fam* to have a screw loose.

paragem [pa'raʒẽ] (*pl* **-ns**) *f*[local] stop; **em outras paragens** elsewhere.

parágrafo [pa'ragraful *m* paragraph.

Paraguai [para'gwaj] *n*: **(o)** ~ Paraguay.

paraguaio, ia [para'gwaju, ja] <> *adj* Paraguayan. <> *m, f* Paraguayan.

Paraíba [para'iba] *n* Paraíba.

paraíso [para'izu] *m* paradise; ~ **fiscal** *ECON fam* tax haven.

pára-lama [,para'lãma] (*pl* **pára-lamas**) *m* mudguard.

paralela [para'lɛla] *f* ⊳ **paralelo**.

paralelamente [paralela'mẽntʃi] *adv* **-1.** [em paralelo] in parallel. **-2.** [simultaneamente] as well as.

paralelepípedo [paralele'pipedu] *m* paving stone.

paralelo, la [para'lɛlu, la] *adj* parallel.
⬧ **paralelo** *m* parallel; **traçar um** ~ to draw a parallel.
⬧ **paralela** *f MAT* parallel (line).

paralisação [paraliza'sãw] (*pl* **-ões**) *f* **-1.** [interrupção] stoppage. **-2.** [greve] strike.

paralisar [4] [parali'za(x)] *vt* [fazer parar] to paralyse.
⬧ **paralisar-se** *vp* [obra] to be paralysed.

paralisia [parali'zia] *f* paralysis.

paralítico, ca [para'litʃiku, ka] <> *adj* paralytic. <> *m, f* paralytic.

Paramaribo [parama'ribu] *n* Paramaribo.

paramédico, ca [para'mɛdʒiku, ka] *adj* paramedic.

paramentado, da [paramẽn'tadu, da] *adj* dressed up.

paramentar [4] [paramẽn'ta(x)] *vt* [adornar] to decorate.
⬧ **paramentar-se** *vp* [adornar-se] to dress o.s up.

paramento [para'mẽntu] *m* ornament.
⬧ **paramentos** *mpl RELIG* vestments.

parâmetro [pa'rãmetru] *m* parameter.

paramilitar [paramili'ta(x)] *adj* paramilitary.

Paraná [para'na] *n* Paraná.

paraninfo [para'nĩfu] *m* sponsor.

paranóia [para'nɔja] *f* **-1.** *PSIC* paranoia. **-2.** *fig* [coletiva] fear.

paranóico, ca [para'nɔiku, ka] *adj* paranoid.

paranormal [paranox'maw] (*pl* **-ais**) <> *adj* paranormal. <> *mf* psychic.

paranormalidade [paranoxmali'dadʒi] *f* paranormal nature.

parapeito [para'pejtu] *m* **-1.** [de janela] window sill. **-2.** [muro] parapet.

parapente [para'pẽntʃi] *m ESP* paragliding.

paraplégico, ca [para'plɛʒiku, ka] <> *adj* paraplegic. <> *m, f* paraplegic.

pára-quedas [,para'kɛdaʃ] *m inv* parachute; **saltar de** ~ to parachute.

pára-quedista [,parake'dʒiʃta] (*pl* **pára-quedistas**) *mf* **-1.** [quem salta] parachutist. **-2.** *MIL* paratrooper.

parar [4] [pa'ra(x)] <> *vi* **-1.** [deter-se] to stop; ~ **de fazer algo** to stop doing sthg; **sem** ~ nonstop. **-2.** [permanecer] to stay. **-3.** [acabar]: **ir** ~ to end up. **-4.** [interromper-se] to stop. <> *vt* **-1.** [deter] to stop. **-2.** [paralisar] to bring to a standstill.

pára-raios [,para'xajuʃ] *m inv* lightning conductor *UK*, lightning rod *US*.

parasita [para'zita] <> *adj* parasitic. <> *mf* parasite.

parceiro, ra [pax'sejru, ra] *m, f* partner.

parcela [pax'sɛla] *f* **-1.** [parte] portion. **-2.** [de pagamento] instalment. **-3.** [de terreno] plot. **-4.** [do eleitorado] section. **-5.** *MAT* factor.

parcelado, da [paxse'ladu, da] *adj* [pagamento] in instalments.

parcelamento [paxsela'mẽntu] *m* **-1.** [de pagamento] payment by instalments. **-2.** [de terra] distribution.

parcelar [4] [paxse'la(x)] *vt* to divide into instalments.

parceria [paxse'ria] *f* partnership; **fazer algo em** ~ to do sthg in partnership.

parcial [pax'sjaw] (*pl* **-ais**) *adj* **-1.** [incompleto] partial. **-2.** [não-isento] biased.

parcialidade [paxsjali'dadʒil *f* bias.

parcimônia [parsi'monja] *f* [moderação] parsimony; **com** ~ frugally.

parcimonioso, osa [paxsimo'njozu, ɔza] *adj* parsimonious.

parco, ca ['paxku, ka] *adj* [escasso] scanty; ~ **de algo** lacking in sthg.

pardacento, ta [paxda'sẽntu, ta] *adj* brownish.

pardal [pax'daw] (*pl* **-ais**) *m* sparrow.

pardieiro [pax'dʒjejru] *m* ruin.

pardo, da ['paxdu, da] *adj* **-1.** [escuro] dark. **-2.** [mulato] coloured.

parecer [25] [pare'se(x)] <> *m* judgement, opinion. <> *vi* **-1.** [ger] to seem; ~ **a alguém** to seem to sb; ~ **a alguém que** to think that; ~ **(com) algo/alguém** to resemble sthg/sb. **-2.** [ser possível]: ~ **que** to look like. **-3.** [aparentar]: **ao que parece** apparently.
⬧ **parecer-se** *vp* [assemelhar-se] to resemble one another; ~**-se com algo/alguém** to resemble sthg/sb.

parecido, da [pare'sidu, da] *adj*: **ser ~ (com alguém/algo)** to be similar (to sb/sthg).

paredão [pare'dãw] (*pl*-ões) *m* -**1.** [encosta] steep face. -**2.** [muro] high wall.

parede [pa'redʒil] *f* wall; **~ divisória** dividing wall; **subir pelas ~s** to go up the wall.

parelha [pa'reʎa] *f* -**1.** [de cavalos] team. -**2.** [par] pair.

parente, ta [pa'rēntʃi, ta] ⬦ *m, f* relative. ⬦ *adj*: **ser ~ de alguém** to be related to sb.

parentela [parēn'tɛla] *f* relatives (*pl*).

parentesco [parēn'teʃku] *m* kinship.

parêntese [pa'rēntezi] *m* -**1.** [sinal] parenthesis; **abrir/fechar ~s** to open/close brackets. -**2.** [digressão] digression; **abrir um ~** to go off at a tangent.

páreo ['parju] *m* -**1.** [turfe] race. -**2.** [disputa] competition; **estar no ~** *fig* to be in the race; **um ~ duro** *fig* a hard nut to crack.

pária ['parja] *m* pariah.

paridade [pari'dadʒi] *f* parity; **abaixo/acima da ~** below/above par.

parir [6] [pa'ri(x)] ⬦ *vt* to give birth to. ⬦ *vi* to give birth.

Paris [pa'riʃ] *n* Paris.

parlamentar [4] [paxlamēn'ta(x)] ⬦ *adj* parliamentary. ⬦ *mf* member of parliament. ⬦ *vi* to discuss.

parlamentarismo [paxlamēnta'riʒmu] *m* parliamentarianism.

parlamentarista [paxlamēnta'riʃta] ⬦ *adj* parliamentarian. ⬦ *mf* parliamentarian.

parlamento [paxla'mēntu] *m POL* parliament.

parmegiana [parme'ʒjana] *f CULIN*: **à ~** cooked in the oven with a filling of tomato sauce and mozzarella cheese.

parmesão [paxme'zãw] *adj* parmesan.

pároco ['paroku] *m RELIG* parish priest.

paródia [pa'rodʒja] *f* parody.

parodiar [16] [paro'dʒja(x)] *vt* to parody.

paróquia [pa'rɔkja] *f* -**1.** *RELIG* parish. -**2.** *fig* [vizinhança] neighbourhood.

paroquial [paro'kjaw] (*pl*-ais) *adj RELIG* parochial, parish (*antes de subst*).

paroquiano, na [paro'kjãnu, na] *m, f* parishioner.

paroxismo [parok'siʒmu] *m* -**1.** *MED* paroxysm. -**2.** *fig* [culminância] brink.

parque ['paxki] *m* park; **~ de diversões** amusement park; **~ industrial** industrial park; **~ nacional** national park.

parquímetro [pax'kimetru] *m* parking meter.

parreira [pa'xejra] *f* grapevine.

parricida [paxi'sida] ⬦ *adj* parricidal. ⬦ *mf* parricide.

parrudo, da [pa'xudu, da] *adj* squat.

parte ['paxtʃi] *f* -**1.** [fração] part; **a maior ~ de** the majority of, most; **em grande ~** largely; **em ~** in parts; **fazer ~ de algo** to belong to sthg; **por ~s** in sections; **tomar ~ em** to take part in. -**2.** [lado] side; **~ interna** inside; **à ~** [separadamente]

separately; **à ~ de** [além de] apart from; **de ~ a ~** each other; **em alguma/qualquer ~** somewhere; **em ~ alguma** anywhere; **por toda (a) ~** everywhere. -**3.** [quinhão] share; **a ~ do leão** the lion's share. -**4.** *JUR* party. -**5.** [denúncia]: **dar ~ de algo/alguém** to report sthg/sb.
➡ **da parte de** *loc prep* from.

parteira [pax'tejra] *f* midwife.

partição [paxtʃi'sãw] *f COMPUT* partition.

participação [paxtʃisipa'sãw] (*pl*-ões) *f* -**1.** [atuação]: **~ em algo** participation in sthg. -**2.** [comunicação]: **fazer uma ~ (a alguém)sobre algo** to make a statement (to sb) about sthg. -**3.** *COM* share.

participante [paxtʃisi'pãntʃi] ⬦ *adj* participating. ⬦ *mf* participant.

participar [4] [paxtʃisi'pa(x)] ⬦ *vi* -**1.** [tomar parte]: **~ de algo** to take part in sthg. -**2.** [compartilhar]: **~ de algo** to share in sthg. ⬦ *vt* [anunciar]: **~ algo (a alguém)** to announce sthg (to sb).

participativo, va [paxtʃisipa'tʃivu, va] *adj* participatory; **orçamento ~** a public-spending budget agreed upon after organized public discussion with the local electorate.

particípio [paxtʃi'sipju] *m* participle; **~ passado/presente** past/present participle.

partícula [pax'tʃikula] *f* particle.

particular [paxtʃiku'la(x)] (*pl*-es) ⬦ *adj* -**1.** [privado] private. -**2.** [especial] particular. ⬦ *m* -**1.** [singularidade] detail. -**2.** *fam* [conversa] private talk.
➡ **em particular** *loc adv* in private.
➡ **particulares** *mpl fam* [detalhes íntimos] personal details.

particularidade [paxtʃikulari'dadʒil *f* detail.

particularizar [4] [paxtʃikulari'za(x)] *vt* -**1.** [especificar] to specify. -**2.** [detalhar] to go into the details of.

particularmente [paxtʃikulax'mēntʃil *adv* [especialmente] particularly.

partida [pax'tʃida] *f* -**1.** [saída] departure. -**2.** [*ESP* - largada] start; **dar a ~** to give the off; [- jogo] game. -**3.** [*COM* - quantidade] shipment; [- remessa] consignment. -**4.** *AUTO*: **dar ~** to start.

partidário, ria [partʃi'darju, rja] *adj* -**1.** [de partido] party (*antes de subst*). -**2.** [seguidor] follower.

partido, da [pax'tʃidu, da] *adj* [quebrado] broken.
➡ **partido** *m* -**1.** [político] party; **Partido dos Trabalhadores** Workers' Party. -**2.** [defesa]: **tomar o ~ de alguém** to take sb's side; **tomar ~ em algo** to take part in sthg. -**3.** [vantagem]: **tirar ~ de algo** to make the most of sthg. -**4.** [pretendente] catch.

partilha [pax'tʃiʎa] *f* sharing.

partilhar [4] [paxtʃi'ʎa(x)] ⬦ *vt* -**1.** [dividir] to share. -**2.** [distribuir] to share out. ⬦ *vi* [compartilhar]: **~ de algo** to share in sthg.

partir [6] [pax'tʃi(x)] ⬦ *vt* to break. ⬦ *vi* -**1.** [ir embora] to leave. -**2.**: **~ de** [originar-se em] to start from; [basear-se em] to take as one's starting point. - **3.** *fam* [recorrer]: ~ **para** to resort to; ~ **para outra** to change tack.

◆ **a partir de** *loc prep* -**1.** [desde] from. - **2.** [dali em diante]: **a ~ daquele momento** from that moment on; **a ~ de agora** from now on.

◆ **partir-se** *vp* to break.

partitura [paxtʃi'tural *f* score.

parto ['paxtu] *m* childbirth; **estar em trabalho de ~** to be in labour *UK*, to be in labor *US*; **ser um ~** *fig* [ser difícil] to be heavy going; ~ **prematuro** premature birth.

parturiente [paxtu'rjēntʃi] *f* woman giving birth, parturient.

parvo, va ['paxvu, va] <> *adj* stupid. <> *m, f* fool.

Páscoa ['paʃkwa] *f* -**1.** *RELIG* Easter. - **2.** *GEOG*: **a ilha de ~** Easter Island.

pasmaceira [paʒma'sejra] *f* apathy.

pasmado, da [paʒ'madu, da] *adj* amazed.

pasmar [4] [paʒ'ma(x)] <> *vt* to amaze. <> *vi* to be amazed.

◆ **pasmar-se** *vp* to be surprised.

pasmo, ma ['paʒmu, ma] *adj* amazed.

◆ **pasmo** *m* amazement.

paspalhão, lhona [paʃpa'ʎãw, ʎona] (*mpl* -**ões**, *fpl* -**s**) <> *adj* simple. <> *m, f* simpleton.

paspalho [paʃ'paʎu] *m* fool.

pasquim [paʃ'kĩ] (*pl* -**ns**) *m* [jornal] lampoon.

passa ['pasa] *f* raisin.

passada [pa'sada] *f*[passo] step; **dar uma ~ em** to drop by.

passadeira [pasa'dejra] *f*-**1.** [tapete] stair carpet. -**2.** [mulher] ironing woman.

passadiço [pasa'dʒisu] *m NÁUT* bridge.

passado, da [pa'sadu, da] *adj* -**1.** [que passou - tempo] past; [- semana, ano] last. - **2.** [ultrapassado]: **meio ~** dated. - **3.** [fruta] overripe. - **4.** [carne]: **bem ~** well done; **mal ~** rare. - **5.** [vexado] infuriated.

◆ **passado** *m* past.

passageiro, ra [pasa'ʒejru, ra] <> *adj* passing. <> *m, f* passenger.

passagem [pa'saʒē] (*pl* -**ns**) *f*-**1.** [caminho] way; ~ **de nível** level crossing; ~ **de pedestres** pedestrian crossing; ~ **subterrânea** underpass. - **2.** [condução - preço] fare; [- bilhete] ticket; ~ **de ida** one-way ticket; ~ **de ida e volta** return ticket. - **3.** [trecho] passage. - **4.** [transição] transition.

◆ **de passagem** *loc adv* in passing; **diga-se de ~ ...** I have to say ...; **estar de ~** to be passing through.

passamento [pasa'mēntu] *m* passing.

passaporte [pasa'poxtʃi] *m* passport.

passar [4] [pa'sa(x)] <> *vt* -**1.** [transpor] to cross. - **2.** [ultrapassar] to overtake; ~ **a frente de alguém** to get in front of sb; ~ **alguém para trás** *fig* [enganar] to dupe sb; [trair] to deceive sb. - **3.** [padecer] to endure. - **4.** [tarefa escolar] to set. - **5.** [reprimenda] to tell off. - **6.** [expedir] to send. - **7.** [entregar] to pass. - **8.** [deslizar]: ~ **algo em/por**

to run sthg over/through. - **9.** [tempo] to spend. -**10.** [espalhar] to spread. - **11.** [coar] to sieve. - **12.** [grelhar] to grill. - **13.** [a ferro] to iron. <> *vi* -**1.** [ger] to pass; ~ **por algo** to pass o.s. off as sthg *ou* as being sthg; ~ **(de ano)** to go up (a year); ~ **raspando** to scrape through. - **2.** [ir] to go past; ~ **em/por** to go in/through; ~ **pela cabeça de alguém** *fig* to cross one's mind; ~ **por cima de alguém** *fig* to go over sb's head. - **3.** [cruzar]: ~ **por alguém/algo** to go by sb/sthg. - **4.** [sentir-se] to feel; **como está passando?** [cumprimentando] how do you do? - **5.** [viver]: ~ **sem algo** to do without. - **6.** [sofrer]: ~ **por algo** to go through sthg. - **7.** [trocar de lado] to cross over. - **8.** [ser mais tarde que] to be past. - **9.** [ter mais de] to be over; **ela já passou dos 40** she's over 40 now; **aos cinco anos, o menino não passara dos 18 quilos** at five years of age, the boy still didn't weigh more than 18kg. - **10.** [ser apenas]: **não ~ de** *pej* to be no more than. - **11.** [ser aceitável] to be passable.

◆ **passar-se** *vp* -**1.** [suceder-se] to happen. - **2.** [transcorrer] to go by.

passarela [pasa'rεla] *f* -**1.** [para pedestre] footbridge. - **2.** [para manequim] catwalk.

passarinho [pasa'riɲu] *m* birdie.

pássaro ['pasaru] *m* bird.

passatempo [,pasa'tēnpu] *m* hobby; **como ~** as a hobby.

passável [pa'savew] (*pl* -**eis**) *adj* passable.

passe ['pasi] *m* -**1.** [licença] permit. - **2.** [*ESP* - de bola] pass; [- de jogador] transfer. - **3.** [lance]: ~ **de mágica** sleight of hand. - **4.** *REL* laying on of hands.

passear [15] [pa'sja(x)] *vi* -**1.** [ger] to go for a walk; **mandar alguém ir ~** *fig* to send sb packing. - **2.** [cavalo, carro] to ride.

passeata [pa'sjata] *f*[protesto] demonstration.

passeio [pa'seju] *m* -**1.** [a pé] walk; **dar** *ou* **fazer um ~** to go for a walk. - **2.** [a cavalo, de carro] ride; **fazer um ~** to go for a ride. - **3.** [calçada] pavement *UK*, sidewalk *US*; ~ **público** public footpath.

passional [pasjo'naw] (*pl* -**ais**) *adj* -**1.** [discurso, atitude, artista] passionate. - **2.** [crime] of passion.

passista [pa'siʃta] *mf* samba dancer.

passível [pa'sivεw] (*pl* -**eis**) *adj*: ~ **de algo** liable to sthg.

passividade [pasivi'dadʒi] *f*[condição] passivity.

passivo, va [pa'sivu, va] *adj* passive.

◆ **passivo** *m COM* liabilities (*pl*).

passo ['pasu] *m* -**1.** [ger] step; **seguir os ~s de alguém** *fig* to follow in sb's footsteps; **dar um mau ~** to go astray. - **2.** [medida]: **a uns seis ~s (de distância)** a short distance away; **a um ~ de** *fig* on the verge of. - **3.** [ruído de passos] footsteps. - **4.** [pegada] footprint. - **5.** [marcha] step; **apertar o ~** to quicken one's step; **a ~ de tartaruga** at a snail's pace. - **6.** [modo de andar] walk.

◆ **ao passo que** *loc adv* -**1.** [enquanto] whilst. - **2.** [contudo] whereas.

pasta ['paʃta] f-**1**. [creme] paste; ~ **de atum** tuna paste; ~ **de dentes** toothpaste. -**2**. *CULIN*: ~ **de atum/ricota** tuna/ricotta cheese spread. -**3**. [de couro] briefcase. -**4**. [de cartolina] folder. -**5**. *POL* portfolio.

pastagem [paʃ'taʒẽl (*pl* -ns) f pasture.

pastar [4] [paʃ'ta(x)] *vi* to graze; **vá** ~**!** *fig* & *pej* get lost!

pastel [paʃ'tɛwl (*pl* -**éis**) <> *adj* [cor] pastel. <> *m* -**1**. [ger] pastel. -**2**. [comida] pastie.

pastelão [paʃte'lãwl (*pl* -**ões**) *m* -**1**. *CULIN* [empadão] pie. -**2**. *CINE* slapstick.

pastelaria [paʃtela'rial f cake shop.

pasteurizado, da [paʃtewri'zadu, dal *adj* pasteurized.

pasteurizar [4] [paʃtewri'za(x)] *vt* to pasteurize.

pastiche [paʃ'tʃiʃil *m* pastiche.

pastilha [paʃ'tʃiʎal f-**1**. [bala] pastille. -**2**. *MED* pill; ~ **de garganta** throat lozenge. -**3**. *COMPUT* chip. -**4**. *CONSTR* mosaic piece.

pasto ['paʃtul *m* -**1**. [erva] grass. -**2**. [pastagem] pasture.

pastor, ra [paʃ'to(x), ral (*mpl* -**es**, *fpl* -**s**) *m*, f *AGR* shepherd (f shepherdess).
➤ **pastor** *m RELIG* pastor.

pastoral [paʃto'rawl (*pl* -**ais**) *RELIG* <> *adj* pastoral. <> f *church body providing care and support in the community*.

pastorear [15] [paʃto'rja(x)] <> *vt* to tend. <> *vi* to take animals to pasture.

pastoril [paʃto'riwl (*pl* -**is**) *adj* pastoral.

pastoso, osa [paʃ'tozu, ɔzal *adj* pasty.

pata ['patal f-**1**. [de animal - de cão, gato] paw; [- de cavalo] foot. -**2**. [ave] (female) duck.

patada [pa'tadal f kick; **dar/levar uma** ~ [de animal] to kick/to be kicked; *fig* [pessoa] to assault/be assaulted.

Patagônia [pata'gonjal *n*: **a** ~ Patagonia.

patamar [pata'ma(x)] (*pl* -**es**) *m* -**1**. [de escada] landing. -**2**. *fig* [nível] level.

patavina [pata'vinal *pron* nothing; **não entender/saber** ~ not to understand/know anything.

patê [pa'tel *m* pâté.

patente [pa'tẽntʃil <> *adj* obvious. <> f-**1**. *COM* patent. -**2**. *MIL* rank; **altas/baixas** ~**s** high/low ranks.

patentear [15] [patẽn'tʃja(x)] *vt COM* to patent.

paternal [patex'nawl (*pl* -**ais**) *adj* paternal, fatherly.

paternalista [patexna'liʃtal *adj* paternalistic.

paternidade [patexni'dadʒil f paternity.

paterno, na [pa'tɛxnu, nal *adj* paternal, father's (*antes de subst*).

pateta [pa'tɛtal <> *adj* foolish. <> *mf* fool.

patetice [pate'tʃisil f foolishness.

patético, ca [pa'tɛtʃiku, kal *adj* pathetic.

patíbulo [pa'tʃibulul *m* gallows (*pl*).

patifaria [patʃifa'rial f [ato] underhand trick.

patife [pa'tʃifil <> *adj* roguish. <> *m* scoundrel.

patim [pa'tĩl (*pl* -ns) *m* skate; **patins de rodas** roller skates.

patinação [patʃina'sãwl f skating; ~ **artística** figure skating; ~ **no gelo** ice skating.

patinador, ra [patʃina'do(x), ral *m*, f skater.

patinar [4] [patʃi'na(x)] *vi* -**1**. [de patins] to skate. -**2**. [carro] to skid.

patinete [patʃi'nɛtʃil f skateboard.

patinhar [4] [patʃi'ɲa(x)] *vi* [chafundar] to slosh about.

patinho [pa'tʃiɲul *m* -**1**. *ZOOL* duckling. -**2**. [carne] leg of beef. -**3**. [urinol] bedpan.

pátio ['patʃjul *m* patio.

pato ['patul *m* -**1**. *ZOOL* duck. -**2**. *fam* [otário] sucker; **cair como um** ~ to be a laughing stock. -**3**. *loc*: **pagar o** ~ to carry the can.·

patologia [patolo'ʒial f pathology.

patológico, ca [pato'lɔʒiku, kal *adj* pathological.

patologista [patolo'ʒiʃtal *mf* pathologist.

patota [pa'tɔtal f *fam* gang.

patrão, roa [pa'trãw, roal (*mpl* -**õe**, *fpl* -**oas**) *m*, f -**1**. [empregador] boss. -**2**. [de criados] master. -**3**. [como forma de tratamento] sir.
➤ **patroa** f-**1**. [mulher do patrão] master's/boss's wife. -**2**. *fam* [esposa] missus.

pátria ['patrjal f fatherland; **salvar a** ~ *fig* to save the day.

patriarca [pa'trjaxkal *m* patriarch.

patriarcal [patrjax'kawl (*pl* -**ais**) *adj* patriarchal.

patricinha [patri'siɲal f *pej* posh girl.

patrício, cia [pa'trisju, sjal *m*, f compatriot.

patrimonial [patrimo'njawl (*pl* -**ais**) *adj* patrimonial.

patrimônio [patri'monjul *m* -**1**. [bens] patrimony. -**2**. [herança] inheritance; ~ **histórico** historical heritage.

PATRIMÔNIOS CULTURAIS

Apart from historical centres such as Salvador (BA), Olinda (PE), São Luís (MA), Goiás (GO), Ouro Preto and Diamantina (MG), Brazil has at least another ten localities recognized by UNESCO as World Heritage Sites. In Piauí, for example, the National Park of Serra da Capivara contains one of the most important archaeological sites in the world, with around 30,000 cave paintings.

---

patriota [pa'trjɔtal *mf* patriot.

patriótico, ca [pa'trjɔtʃiku, kal *adj* patriotic.

patriotismo [patrjo'tʃiʒmul *m* patriotism.

patroa [pa'troal f ▷ **patrão**.

patrocinador, ra [patrosina'do(x), ral (*mpl* -**es**, *fpl* -**s**) <> *adj* sponsoring. <> *m*, f sponsor.

patrocinar [4] [patrosi'na(x)] *vt* -**1**. [ger] to support. -**2**. [financiar] to sponsor.

patrocínio [patro'sinjul *m* -**1**. [financiamento] sponsorship. -**2**. [apoio] support.

patrões [pa'trõjʃl *pl* ▷ **patrão**.

patrono [pa'tronul *m* patron.

patrulha [pa'truʎal f -**1**. [ronda] patrol. -**2**. [censura] censorship.

patrulhamento [patruʎa'mẽntu] *m* patrolling.
patrulhar [4] [patru'ʎa(x)] *vt* **-1.** [vigiar] to patrol. **-2.** [censurar] to censure.
patrulheiro [patru'ʎejru] *m* [navio] patrol boat.
pau ['paw] *m* **-1.** [bastão] stick. **-2.** [madeira]: **de ~** wooden. **-3.** [de bandeira] pole; **a meio ~** at half mast. **-4.** *fam* [briga] brawl; **o ~ comeu** all hell broke loose; **sair no ~** to start fighting. **-5.** *fam* [moeda] *slang for Brazilian currency*. **-6.** *mfam* [pênis] cock. **-7.** *loc fam*: **a dar com um ~** tons, loads; **meter o ~ em** [surrar] to beat up; [criticar] to run down; **ser ~ para toda obra** to be up for anything.
➤ **paus** *mpl* [naipe] clubs; **de ~s** of clubs.
➤ **pau a pau** *loc adj* on an equal footing.
pau-a-pique [ˌpawa'piki] *m*: **de ~** of wattle and daub.
pau-brasil [ˌpawbra'ziw] *m* Brazil wood.

PAU-BRASIL

Pau-brasil was a very common tree on the Brazilian shoreline, from Rio de Janeiro to Rio Grande do Norte. Much sought after during colonial times, it was through constant reference to the name of this red-wooded tree that the Portuguese named the country Brazil.

pau-d'água [ˌpaw'dagwa] (*pl* **paus-d'água**) *m* [beberrão] soak.
pau-de-arara [ˌpawdʒja'rara] (*pl* **paus-de-arara**) *mf* [retirante do Nordeste] *migrant from north-eastern Brazil*.
➤ **pau-de-arara** *m* [tortura] *form of torture where victim is suspended face down from a pole*.
pau-de-sebo [ˌpawdʒi'sebu] (*pl* **paus-de-sebo**) *m* [mastro de cocanha] greasy pole.
paulada [paw'lada] *f* blow (with a stick); **dar/levar uma ~** to hit/be hit with a stick.
paulatinamente [pawlatʃina'mẽntʃi] *adv* gradually.
paulatino, na [pawla'tʃinu, na] *adj* gradual.
Paulicéia [pawli'sɛja] *n* São Paulo.
paulista [paw'liʃta] <> *adj* São Paulo (*antes de subst*). <> *mf person from São Paulo*.
paupérrimo, ma [paw'pɛximu, ma] *adj* extremely poor.
pausa ['pawza] *f* **-1.** [interrupção, intervalo] break. **-2.** [descanso] rest.
pausadamente [pawzada'mẽntʃi] *adv* slowly and surely.
pausado, da [paw'zadu, da] *adj* **-1.** [lento] leisurely. **-2.** [cadenciado] rythmic.
➤ **pausado** *adv* unhurriedly.
pauta ['pawta] *f* **-1.** [linha] guideline; **sem ~** unruled. **-2.** [folha com linhas] ruled sheet. **-3.** [lista] list. **-4.** [ordem do dia] agenda; **em ~** on the agenda. **-5.** *MÚS* stave. **-6.** *JORN* issue, topic.
pautado, da [paw'tadu, da] *adj* ruled.
pautar [4] [paw'ta(x)] *vt* **-1.** [assuntos] to list. **-2.** *fig* [orientar]: **~ algo por algo** to guide sthg by sthg.
➤ **pautar-se** *vp fig* [orientar-se]: **~-se por algo** to guide o.s by sthg.

pauzinho [paw'ziɲu] *m fam*: **mexer os ~s** to pull strings.
pavão [pa'vãw] (*pl* **-ões**) *mf* peacock.
pavê [pa've] *m* *CULIN* *cream cake made of sponge soaked in liqueur*.
pavilhão [pavi'ʎãw] (*pl* **-ões**) *m* **-1.** [prédio] annex. **-2.** [de exposições] stand. **-3.** [tenda, abrigo] tent. **-4.** *fig* [bandeira] banner.
pavimentação [pavimẽnta'sãw] *f* paving.
pavimentar [4] [pavimẽn'ta(x)] *vt* to pave.
pavimento [pavi'mẽntu] *m* **-1.** [andar] storey *UK*, story *US*. **-2.** [chão] floor. **-3.** [de rua] pavement.
pavio [pa'viw] *m* wick; **ter o ~ curto** [ser de briga] to have a short fuse.
pavões [pa'võjʃ] *pl* ⮕ **pavão**.
pavonear [15] [pavo'nja(x)] <> *vt pej* [ostentar] to show off. <> *vi pej* [desfilar] to strut.
➤ **pavonear-se** *vp* **-1.** [assoberbar-se] to parade. **-2.** [enfeitar-se] to dress up.
pavor [pa'vo(x)] *m* fear; **ter ~ de alguém/algo** to dread sb/sthg.
pavoroso, osa [pavo'rozu, ɔza] *adj* **-1.** [repulsivo] appalling. **-2.** [muito ruim, feio] dreadful.
paz ['paʃ] (*pl* **-es**) *f* peace; **acordo de ~** peace treaty; **assinar a ~** to sign a peace treaty; **deixar alguém em ~** to leave sb in peace; **fazer as pazes** to make up; **~ de espírito** peace of mind.
PB (*abrev de* **Estado da Paraíba**) *n State of Paraíba*.
PBX (*abrev de* **Private Branch Exchange**) PBX.
PC (*abrev de* **Personal Computer**) *m* PC.
Pça. (*abrev de* **Praça**) *f* Sq.
PC do B (*abrev de* **Partido Comunista do Brasil**) *m Brazilian communist party*.
PCI (*abrev de* **Placa de Circuito Interno**) *f internal circuit board*.
PDT (*abrev de* **Partido Democrático Trabalhista**) *m* Democratic Labour Party, *the second largest left-wing party in Brazil*.
PDV (*abrev de* **Programa de Demissão Voluntária**) *m Brazilian voluntary redundancy scheme*.
pé ['pɛ] *m* **-1.** [ger] foot; **não arredar o ~** not to budge; **~ chato** flat foot; **a ~** on foot; **com um ~ nas costas** with the greatest of ease; **em ou de ~** standing; **~ ante ~** on tiptoe; **acordar com o ~ direito/esquerdo** to wake up in a good/bad mood; **dar no ~** *fam* [fugir] to do a runner; **cuidado que aquela parte da piscina não dá ~** be careful because you will be out of your depth in that part of the pool; *fig* [ser possível] to be viable; **estar de ~** *fam* to still be on; **ficar com o ~ atrás** to be on one's guard; **meter os ~s pelas mãos** to go haywire; **não chegar aos ~s de** to be nowhere near as good as; **não largar do ~ de alguém** to stick like glue to sb; **não ter ~ nem cabeça** not to make any sense; **pegar no ~ de alguém** *fig* [implicar] to leave sb alone; [brincar] to pull sb's leg; **ser ~ no chão** to have one's feet firmly on the ground. **-2.** [base - de monumento, morro] foot; **ao ~ de** at the foot of; **ao ~ do ouvido** in secret; [- de mesa] leg; [- de copo] stem. **-3.** *BOT* plant. **-4.** [de calçado, meia] sole. **-5.**

[situação] state of affairs; **em que ~ estão as coisas?** what's the state of play?; **em ~ de guerra/igualdade** on a war/equal footing.

➠ **ao pé da letra** *loc adv* to the letter.

PE (*abrev de* **Estado de Pernambuco**) *n* State of *Pernambuco*.

peão ['pjãw] (*pl* -ões) *m* -**1.** [trabalhador] labourer *UK*, laborer *US*. -**2.** [xadrez] pawn.

peça ['pɛsal *f* -**1.** [ger] piece; **~ fundamental** *fig* vital part; *MÚS* **~ de resistência** pièce de résistance; [o forte de alguém] strong point. -**2.** *MEC* part; **~ de reposição** *ou* **~ sobressalente** replacement *ou* spare part. -**3.** [cômodo] room. -**4.** [brincadeira] **pregar uma ~ em alguém** to play a practical joke on sb. -**5.** *TEATRO* play. -**6.** *JUR* document.

pecado [pe'kadu] *m* -**1.** *RELIG* sin; **~ capital** cardinal sin; **~ mortal** mortal sin; **~ original** original sin; **pagar os seus ~s** to pay for one's sins. -**2.** [pena] **que ~!** what a sin!

pecador, ra [peka'do(x), ra] *m, f* sinner.

pecaminoso, osa [pekami'nozu, ɔza] *adj* sinful.

pecar [12] [pe'ka(x)] *vi* -**1.** *RELIG* to sin. -**2.** [errar]: **~ por algo** to err on the side of sthg.

pechincha [pe'ʃĩʃa] *f* bargain; **ser uma ~** to be a bargain.

pechinchar [4] [pe'ʃĩʃa(x)] *vi* to haggle.

peçonha [pe'sona] *f* poison.

pecuário, ria [pe'kwarju, rja] *adj* cattle.

➠ **pecuária** *f* [criação] cattle-raising.

pecuarista [pekwa'riʃta] *mf* cattle dealer.

peculiar [peku'lja(x)] (*pl* -es) *adj* -**1.** [característico] particular. -**2.** [curioso] peculiar.

peculiaridade [pekuljari'dadʒi] *f* peculiarity.

pecúlio [pe'kulju] *m* -**1.** [economias] nest egg. -**2.** [bens] belongings (*pl*).

pedaço [pe'dasu] *m* -**1.** [parte] piece; **aos ~s** in pieces; **estar caindo aos ~s** to be falling to pieces. -**2.** [trecho] piece. -**3.** [lugar] area. -**4.** *fam* [beleza] **ser um ~ (de mau caminho)** to be a bit of all right.

pedágio [pe'daʒju] *m* toll.

pedagogia [pedago'ʒia] *f* -**1.** [prática] teaching method. -**2.** [curso] education.

pedagógico, ca [peda'gɔʒiku, ka] *adj* teaching (*antes de subst*).

pedagogo, ga [peda'gogu, ga] *m, f* educationalist.

pé-d'água [pɛ'dagwa] (*pl* **pés-d'água**) *m* deluge.

pedal [pe'daw] (*pl* -ais) *m* pedal.

pedalada [peda'lada] *f* pedalling; **dar uma ~** to go for a bike ride.

pedalar [4] [peda'la(x)] <> *vt* to pedal. <> *vi* to pedal.

pedalinho [peda'liɲu] *m* pedalo.

pedante [pe'dãntʃi] <> *adj* pedantic. <> *m, f* pedant.

pedantismo [pedãn'tʃiʒmu] *m* pedantry.

pé-de-atleta [pɛdʒja'tlɛta] *m* athlete's foot.

pé-de-cabra [pɛdʒi'kabra] (*pl* **pés-de-cabra**) *m* -**1.** [alavanca] crowbar. -**2.** *fam* [diabo] devil.

pé-de-galinha [pɛdʒiga'liɲa] (*pl* **pés-de-galinha**) *m* crow's foot.

pé-de-meia [pɛdʒi'meja] (*pl* **pés-de-meia**) *m* nest egg; **fazer um ~** to get some savings together.

pé-de-moleque [pɛdʒimu'lɛki] (*pl* **pés-de-moleque**) *m* -**1.** [doce] peanut brittle. -**2.** [calçamento] crazy paving.

pé-de-ouvido [pɛdʒio'vidul] (*pl* **pés-de-ouvido**) *m* [tapa] clip round the ear.

pé-de-pato [pɛdʒi'patu] (*pl* **pés-de-pato**) *m* -**1.** [nadadeira] flipper. -**2.** *fam* [diabo] Satan.

pedestal [pedeʃ'taw] (*pl* -ais) *m* pedestal.

pedestre [pe'dɛʃtri] *mf* pedestrian.

pé-de-valsa [pɛdʒi'vawsal] (*pl* **pés-de-valsas**) *m* expert dancer.

pé-de-vento [pɛdʒi'vẽntu] (*pl* **pés-de-vento**) *m* squall.

pediatra [pe'dʒjatra] *mf* paediatrician *UK*, pediatrician *US*.

pediatria [pedʒja'tria] *f* paediatrics *UK*, pediatrics *US*.

pedicuro, re [pedʒi'kuru, ri] *m, f* pedicure.

pedido [pe'dʒidu] *m* -**1.** [ger] order. -**2.** [solicitação] request; **a ~** to an encore; **a ~ de alguém** at sb's request; **~ de casamento** marriage proposal; **~ de demissão** resignation; **~ de divórcio** divorce petition.

➠ **pedida** *f fam* suggestion; **ser uma boa pedida** to be a good idea.

pedigree [pedʒi'gril] *m* pedigree.

pedinte [pe'dʒĩntʃil] *mf* beggar.

pedir [70] [pe'dʒi(x)] <> *vt* -**1.** [solicitar] to ask for; **~ algo a alguém** to ask sb for sthg; **~ a alguém que faça algo** to ask sb to do sthg; **~ algo emprestado** to borrow sthg; **~ alguém em casamento** to ask for sb's hand in marriage; **~ desculpas** *ou* **perdão (por algo)** to apologize (for sthg). -**2.** [cobrar] to charge. -**3.** [necessitar] to call for. -**4.** [encomendar] to order. -**5.** [exigir, requerer] to demand; **~ satisfações (a alguém)** to demand an apology (from sb). <> *vi* [fazer pedidos] to make demands; **~ por alguém** to pray for sb.

pé-direito [pɛdʒi'rejtul] (*pl* **pés-direitos**) *m* height of a room.

pedra ['pɛdra] *f* -**1.** [ger] stone. -**2.** [fragmento] pebble; **~ de amolar** grindstone; **~ de gelo** ice cube; **~ de toque** *fig* touchstone; **~ preciosa** precious stone; **dormir como uma ~** to sleep like a log; **pôr uma ~ em cima de** *fig* to bury; **ser de ~** to be made of stone; **vir com quatro ~s na mão** to jump down sb's throat. -**3.** [de açúcar] sugar lump.

pedrada [pe'drada] *f* -**1.** [com pedra] blow (with a stone). -**2.** *fig* [golpe] blow.

pedra-pomes [pɛdra'pomiʃ] (*pl* **pedras-pomes**) *f* pumice stone.

pedra-sabão [pɛdrasa'bãw] (*pl* **pedras-sabão**) *f* soapstone.

pedregoso, osa [pedre'gozu, ɔza] *adj* stony.

pedregulho [pedre'guʎul *m* boulder.
pedreira [pe'drejra] *f* stone quarry.
pedreiro [pe'drejru] *m CONSTR* mason.
pé-frio [ˌpɛ'friw] (*pl* **pés-frios**) *m*: **ser um** ~ to be jinxed.
pega [ˈpɛga] *m* **-1.** [briga] quarrel. **-2.** *fam* [corrida] illegal street race.
pegada [pe'gada] *f* footprint.
pegado, da [pe'gadu, da] *adj* **-1.** [contíguo] next door. **-2.** [unido] close.
pegajoso, osa [pega'ʒozu, ɔza] *adj* sticky.
pega-ladrão [ˌpegala'drãw] (*pl* **pega-ladrões**) *m* safety catch/switch.
pegar [14] [pe'ga(x)] ⬦ *vt* **-1.** [ger] to pick up. **-2.** [surpreender] to catch. **-3.** [embarcar em] to catch. **-4.** [seguir por] to take. **-5.** [compreender] to take in. **-6.** [vivenciar] to experience. **-7.** [aceitar fazer] to take on. ⬦ *vi* **-1.** [segurar] to catch; ~ **em algo** to hold on to sthg. **-2.** [grudar]: ~ **em algo** to stick to sthg. **-3.** [difundir-se - moda, mania] to catch on; [- doença] to be catching. **-4.** [fogo]: **a fogueira pega mais rápido com álcool** the fire lights quicker with alcohol; **ele pegou fogo na casa** he set fire to the house. **-5.** [planta] to take root. **-6.** *RÁDIO & TV*: ~ **(bem/mal)** to have good/poor reception. **-7.** [motor] to start. **-8.** [iniciar]: ~ **em algo** to start sthg. **-9.** [atitude]: ~ **bem/mal** to go down well/ badly; **não pega bem** it doesn't do. **-10.** [decidir-se]: ~ **a fazer algo** to make up one's mind and do sthg.
  ➤ **pegar-se** *vp* [brigar]: ~**-se (com)** to come to blows (with).
pega-rapaz [ˌpɛgaxa'paʒ] (*pl* **pega-rapazes**) *m* kiss-curl.
peia [ˈpeja] *f ant* & *fig* [estorvo] hindrance.
peidar [4] [pej'da(x)] *vi mfam* to fart.
peido [ˈpejdu] *m mfam* fart.
peitar [4] [pej'ta(x)] *vt* **-1.** [enfrentar] to face. **-2.** [subornar] to bribe.
peitilho [pej'tʃiʎu] *m* shirt front.
peito [ˈpejtu] *m* **-1.** *ANAT* chest; ~ **do pé** instep; **meter o** ~ *fam* to put one's heart into it. **-2.** [de mulher, ave] breast; **dar o** ~ to breastfeed. **-3.** *fig* [coragem] courage; **no** ~ **(e na raça)** fearlessly.
peitoril [pejto'riw] (*pl* **-is**) *m* windowsill.
peitudo, da [pej'tudu, da] *adj* **-1.** [de peito grande] big-chested. **-2.** [valente] plucky.
peixada [pej'ʃada] *f* fish stew.
peixaria [pejʃa'ria] *f* fishmonger.
peixe [ˈpejʃi] *m ZOOL* fish; **não ter nada com o** ~ *fam* to have nothing to do with it; **vender o seu** ~ [tratar de seus interesses] to look out for one's own interests; [opinar] to have one's say.
peixeira [pej'ʃejra] *f* [facão] *small, sharp knife.*
peixeiro, ra [pej'ʃejru, ra] *m, f* [vendedor] fishmonger.
Peixes [ˈpejʃiʃ] *mpl* [zodíaco] Pisces; **ser de** ~ to be Pisces.
pejorativo, va [peʒora'tʃivu, va] *adj* pejorative.
pela [ˈpela] = **por** + **a**.

pelada [pe'lada] *FUT f* **-1.** [jogo informal] (friendly) match. **-2.** [jogo ruim] wasted game.
pelado, da [pe'ladu, da] *adj* **-1.** [nu] naked. **-2.** [sem pêlos] shorn.
pelanca [pe'lãŋka] *f* **-1.** [em pessoa] flabby skin. **-2.** [de carne] poor quality meat.
pelancudo, da [pelãŋ'kudu, da] *adj* **-1.** [pessoa, braço] flabby. **-2.** [carne] flaccid.
pelar [4] [pe'la(x)] ⬦ *vt* **-1.** [animal] to skin. **-2.** [cabeça] to shave. ⬦ *vi*: **estar pelando** [estar quentíssimo] to be scalding.
  ➤ **pelar-se** *vp fam*: ~**-se de medo** to be scared stiff.
pelas [ˈpelaʃ] = **por** + **as**.
pele [ˈpɛli] *f* **-1.** [de pessoa] skin; ~ **e osso** skin and bone; **cair na** ~ **de** *fig fam* to pester; **salvar a** ~ **de alguém** *fig fam* to save sb's skin; **sentir algo na** ~ *fig* to experience sthg first hand. **-2.** [animal] hide; **de** ~ hide. **-3.** [couro] leather; ~ **leather. -4.** [agasalho] fur. **-5.** [de fruta, legume] skin, peel.
peleja [pe'leʒa] *f* battle.
pelejar [4] [pele'ʒa(x)] *vi* **-1.** [combater] to fight. **-2.** *fig* [lutar]: ~ **(por/para algo)** to fight (for sthg).
pelerine [pele'rini] *f* cape.
pelica [pe'lika] *f* kid leather.
pelicano [peli'kãnu] *m ZOOL* pelican.
película [pe'likula] *f* **-1.** *CINE* film. **-2.** [de pele] membrane. **-3.** [camada fina] layer.
pelo [ˈpelu] = **por** + **o**.
pêlo [ˈpelu] *m* **-1.** [em pessoa] hair; **nu em** ~ stark naked. **-2.** [de animal] fur.
pelos [ˈpeluʃ] = **por** + **os**.
pelota [pe'lɔta] *f* **-1.** [bola] ball; **dar** ~ **a alguém/ algo** *fig* to pay attention to sb/sthg. **-2.** [em molho, creme] lump. **-3.** [na pele] spot.
pelotão [pelo'tãw] (*pl* **-ões**) *m* platoon; ~ **de fuzilamento** firing squad.
pelúcia [pe'lusja] *f* plush.
peludo, da [pe'ludu, da] *adj* hairy.
pélvico, ca [ˈpɛwviku, ka] *adj* pelvic.
pélvis [ˈpɛwviʃ] *f (inv) ANAT* pelvis.
pena [ˈpena] *f* **-1.** [de ave] feather. **-2.** [pesar] sorrow; **que** ~! what a pity!; **ser uma** ~ to be a pity; **valer a** ~ *fig* [compensar] to be worthwhile; **a duras** ~**s** with great difficulty. **-3.** *JUR* punishment; ~ **capital** *ou* **de morte** capital punishment *ou* death penalty; **cumprir** ~ to serve a sentence; **sob** ~ **de** *fig* under penalty of. **-4.** [piedade] pity; **dar** ~ to arouse pity; **ter** ~ **de** to be sorry for. **-5.** *ant* [caneta] pen.
penacho [pe'naʃu] *m* **-1.** [de plumas] plume. **-2.** [crista] crest.
penal [pe'naw] (*pl* **-ais**) *adj JUR* penal.
penalidade [penali'dadʒi] *f* **-1.** *JUR* penalty. **-2.** [castigo] punishment. **-3.** *FUT*: ~ **máxima** penalty (kick).
penalizar [4] [penali'za(x)] *vt* **-1.** [dar pena a] to distress. **-2.** [castigar] to punish.
pênalti [pe'nawtʃi] *m FUT* penalty.

penar [4] [pe'na(x)] <> m [sofrimento] suffering. <> vt [sofrer] to hurt, to distress. <> vi [sofrer] to suffer.

penca ['pẽnka] f bunch; **uma ~ de algo** fig [quantidade] a bunch of sthg; **em ~** fig [quantidade] loads of.

pendão [pẽn'dãw] (pl -ões) m -1. [estandarte] pennant. -2. [bandeira] flag. -3. [de milho] tassel.

pendência [pẽn'dẽsja] f -1. [contenda] dispute. -2. [algo por decidir] pending matter.

pendente [pẽn'dẽtʃi] <> adj -1. [ger] hanging. -2. [por decidir] pending. <> m [de jóia] pendant.

pender [5] [pẽn'de(x)] vi -1. [estar pendurado] to hang. -2. [inclinar-se]: **~ para/sobre** to hang towards/over. -3. [tender] to have a leaning; **o jovem pende para as letras** the young man has a leaning towards literature.

pendões [pẽn'dõjʃ] pl |> **pendão**.

pendor [pẽn'do(x)] m tendency.

pêndulo ['pẽndulu] m pendulum.

pendurado, da [pẽndu'radu, da] adj -1. [pendente]: **~ (em)** hanging (on). -2. fig [conta] on tick.

pendurar [4] [pẽndu'ra(x)] vt -1. [colocar] to hang. -2. fig [conta] to pay on tick.

➤ **pendurar-se** vp [pessoa] to hang.

penduricalho [pẽnduri'kaʎu], **penduruca-lho** [pẽnduru'kaʎu] m trinket.

penedo [pe'nedu] m boulder.

peneira [pe'nejra] f -1. [para peneirar] sieve. -2. fig [seleção]: **passar na** ou **pela ~** to pass the selection.

peneirar [4] [penej'ra(x)] <> vt [na peneira] to sieve. <> vi fig [chuviscar] to drizzle.

penetra [pe'nɛtra] mf fam gatecrasher; **entrar de ~** to gatecrash.

penetração [penetra'sãw] (pl -ões) f -1. [ger] penetration. -2. fig [difusão] circulation.

penetrante [pene'trãtʃi] adj penetrating.

penetrar [4] [pene'tra(x)] <> vt to penetrate. <> vi -1. [entrar, infiltrar-se]: **~ em/por/entre** to penetrate. -2. fam [em festa] to gatecrash.

penhasco [pe'naʃku] m cliff.

penhoar [pe'nwa(x)] m dressing gown.

penhor [pe'ɲo(x)] m pawn; **fazer o ~ de algo** to pawn ou hock sthg, to leave sthg in pawn ou hock; **casa de ~ es** pawnshop; **dar em ~** to pawn, to hock.

penhora [pe'ɲɔra] f JUR confiscation.

penhorado, da [peɲo'radu, da] adj pawned, hocked.

penhorar [4] [peɲo'ra(x)] vt to pawn, to hock.

penicilina [penisi'lina] f penicillin.

penico [pe'niku] m chamber pot, potty; **pedir ~** fam fig to eat humble pie.

península [pe'nĩsula] f peninsula.

peninsular [penĩsu'la(x)] adj peninsular.

pênis ['peniʃ] m inv penis.

penitência [peni'tẽsja] f RELIG -1. [contrição] contrition. -2. [expiação] penance; **fazer ~** to do penance.

penitenciar [16] [penitẽn'sja(x)] vt RELIG -1. [impor penitência a] to give a penance to; **o arrependimento penitencia meu coração** my heart is mortified with remorse. -2. [expiar] to do penance.

➤ **penitenciar-se** vp: **~-se de/por** to punish o.s. for.

penitenciário, ria [penitẽn'sjarju, rja] <> adj penitentiary. <> m, f prisoner.

➤ **penitenciária** f penitentiary.

penitente [peni'tẽtʃi] <> adj penitent. <> inf penitent.

penoso, osa [pe'nozu, ɔza] adj -1. [assunto, trabalho] hard. -2. [tratamento, correção] harsh.

pensado, da [pẽn'sadu, da] adj considered; **de caso ~** on purpose.

pensador, ra [pẽnsa'do(x), ra] m, f thinker.

pensamento [pẽnsa'mẽntu] m -1. [ger] thought; **~ positivo** positive thinking; **fazer ~ positivo** to think positively. -2. [mente, opinião] mind. -3. [doutrina] thinking. -4. [idéia] idea.

pensante [pẽn'sãtʃi] adj thinking.

pensão [pẽn'sãw] (pl -ões) f -1. [pequeno hotel] boarding house. -2. [renda] pension; **~ alimentícia** maintenance allowance. -3. [restaurante] boarding house. -4. [refeição]: **dar ~** [hotel] to provide board; [cozinhar para fora] to provide meals; **~ completa** full board.

pensar [4] [pẽn'sa(x)] <> vt to think. <> vi -1. [ger] to think; **~ em/sobre algo** to think about sthg. -2. [tencionar] to intend.

pensativo, va [pẽnsa'tʃivu, va] adj thoughtful.

pênsil ['pẽnsiw] (pl -seis) adj [suspenso] hanging.

pensionato [pẽnsjo'natu] m hostel.

pensionista [pẽnsjo'niʃta] mf -1. [beneficiário] pensioner. -2. [morador] boarder.

penso, sa ['pẽnsu] adj hanging.

pentacampeão [ˌpẽntakãn'pjãw] (pl -ões) m five-times champion.

pentágono [pẽn'tagunu] m GEOM pentagon.

pentatlo [pẽn'tatlu] m pentathlon.

pente ['pẽtʃi] m -1. [de cabelo] comb. -2. [de pistola] cartridge.

penteadeira [pẽntʃja'dejra] f dressing table.

penteado, da [pẽn'tʃjadu] adj well groomed.

➤ **penteado** m hairstyle.

pentear [15] [pẽn'tʃja(x)] vt -1. [cabelo] to comb. -2. [fazer penteado] to style.

➤ **pentear-se** vp [pessoa] to do one's hair.

Pentecostes [pẽnte'kɔʃtʃiʃ] m RELIG Pentecost.

pente-fino [pẽntʃi'finu] (pl pentes-finos) m -1. [pente] fine-tooth comb. -2. fam fig [crivo] close scrutiny; **passar algo pelo ~** to go through sthg with a fine-tooth comb.

pentelhação [pẽnteʎa'sãw] (pl -ões) f [chateação] fam aggro, hassle.

pentelhar [4] [pẽnte'ʎa(x)] vt fam to aggravate.

pentelho, lha [pẽn'teʎu, ʎa] fam <> adj [chato] aggravating. <> m, f [pessoa chata] pain in the neck.

➤ **pentelho** m fam [pêlo] pubic hair.

penugem [pe'nuʒẽ] (pl -ns) f down.

penúltimo, ma [pe'nuwtʃimu, ma] *adj* penultimate, last but one.

penumbra [pe'nũbra] *f* **-1.** [meia-luz] half-light. **-2.** *fig* [obscuridade] obscurity.

penúria [pe'nurja] *f* penury; ~ **de algo** lack of sthg.

peões ['pjõjʃ] *pl* ▷ **peão**.

pepino [pe'pinu] *m* **-1.** [fruto] cucumber. **-2.** *fig* [problema] bit of a problem.

pepita [pe'pita] *f* [de ouro] nugget.

pequena [pe'kena] *f* ▷ **pequeno**.

pequenez [peke'neʒ] *f* **-1.** [de tamanho] smallness. **-2.** *fig* [mesquinhez] meanness.

pequenininho, nha [pekeni'ninu, ɲa] *adj* tiny.·

pequenino, na [peke'ninu, na] <> *adj* very small. <> *m, f* [criança] child.

➡ **pequeninos** *mpl*: **os** ~**s** [as crianças] the children; [os humildes] the little people.

pequeno, na [pe'kenu, na] <> *adj* **-1.** [tamanho] small. **-2.** [mesquinho] mean. <> *m, f* [criança] child.

➡ **pequena** *f* [namorada] girlfriend.

pequeno-burguês, pequeno-burguesa [pe,kenubux'geʃ, pe,kenabux'geza] (*pl* **pequenos-burgueses**) <> *adj* petit bourgeois. <> *m, f* petit bourgeois.

Pequim [pe'kĩ] *n* Beijing.

pequinês [peki'neʃ] *m* [cão] Pekinese.

pêra ['pera] (*pl* **pêras**) *f* pear.

peralta [pe'rawta] <> *adj* mischievous. <> *m, f* mischief-maker.

perambular [4] [perãbu'la(x)] *vi*: ~ **(por)** to wander (through).

perante [pe'rãtʃi] *prep* **-1.** [no espaço] before; **jurar** ~ **a Bíblia** to swear on the Bible. **-2.** [no sentido] faced with.

pé-rapado, da [,pɛxa'padu, da] (*mpl* **pés-rapados**, *fpl* **pés-rapadas**) *m, f* loser.

percalço [pex'kawsu] *m* pitfall.

per capita [pex'kapita] *loc adj* per capita.

perceber [5] [pexse'be(x)] *vt* **-1.** [através dos sentidos] to perceive. **-2.** [compreender] to realize. **-3.** [notar] to notice.

percentagem [pexsẽ'taʒẽ] (*pl* **-ns**) *f* percentage.

percentual [pexsẽ'twaw] (*pl* **-ais**) <> *adj* percentage. <> *m* [percentagem] percentage.

percepção [pexsep'sãw] *f* [dos sentidos] perception.

perceptível [pexsep'tʃivew] (*pl* **-eis**) *adj* perceptible.

perceptivo, va [pexsep'tʃivu, va] *adj* perceptive.

percevejo [pexse'veʒul] *m* **-1.** *ZOOL* bedbug. **-2.** [prego] drawing pin.

percorrer [5] [pexko'xe(x)] *vt* **-1.** [viajar] to travel through. **-2.** [passar por] to pass through. **-3.** [esquadrinhar] to search. **-4.** [consultar] to search through.

percurso [pex'kuxsu] *m* route.

percussão [pexku'sãw] (*pl* **-ões**) *f* percussion.

percussionista [pexkusjo'niʃta] *mf* drummer.

percutir [6] [pexku'tʃi(x)] *vt* to hit.

perda ['pexda] *f* **-1.** [ger] loss. **-2.** [desperdício]: ~ **de tempo** waste of time. **-3.** [prejuízo] damage; ~**s e danos** damages.

perdão [pex'dãw] (*pl* **-dões**) *m* [escusa] pardon; **pedir** ~ **a alguém** to apologize to sb; **perdão!** sorry!

perdedor, ra [pexde'do(x), ra] <> *adj* losing. <> *m, f* [de competição] loser.

perder [44] [pex'de(x)] <> *vt* **-1.** [ger] to lose. **-2.** [não chegar a tempo, não comparecer] to miss. **-3.** [desperdiçar] to waste; **pôr tudo a** ~ to ruin everything. <> *vi* [ser vencido] to lose; ~ **de oupara alguém** to lose to *ou* against sb; **saber** ~ to be a good loser.

➡ **perder-se** *vp* **-1.** [extraviar-se] to get lost; ~ **-se de alguém** to wander away from sb. **-2.** [arruinar-se] to waste one's life. **-3.** *ant* [mulher] to lose one's virginity. **-4.** [atrapalhar-se] to get bogged down. **-5.** [absorver-se] to lose o.s.

perdição [pexdʒi'sãw] *f* **-1.** [ruína] decay. **-2.** [mau caminho] evil; **ser uma** ~ *fig irôn* to be irresistible. **-3.** [desonra] fall from grace.

perdidamente [pexdʒida'mẽtʃi] *adv* desperately.

perdido, da [pex'dʒidu, da] <> *adj* **-1.** [ger] lost. **-2.** [amorosamente]: ~ **(de amor) por alguém** desperately in love with sb. **-3.** [arruinado]: **nem tudo está** ~ all is not lost; **meu pai descobriu que fui reprovado, estou** ~**!** my father's found out I've failed, I'm done for! <> *m, f* [pervertido] pervert.

perdigão [pexdʒi'gãw] (*pl* **-ões**) *m* [macho] male partridge.

perdigueiro [pexdʒi'gejru] *m* [cão] pointer.

perdiz [pex'dʒiʃ] (*pl* **-es**) *f* [fêmea] female partridge.

perdoar [20] [pex'dwa(x)] <> *vt* **-1.** [desculpar] to forgive; ~ **algo (a alguém)** to forgive (sb for) sthg. **-2.** [eximir de] to pardon. **-3.** *fig* [desperdiçar]: **não** ~ to make the most of. <> *vi* [desculpar] to forgive.

perdoável [pex'dwavew] (*pl* **-eis**) *adj* forgivable.

perdulário, ria [pexdu'larju, rja] *adj* wasteful.

perdurar [4] [pexdu'ra(x)] *vi* **-1.** [durar muito]: ~ **(por/através de)** to last (for/throughout). **-2.** [permanecer] to carry on.

pereba [pe'rɛba] *f* sore.

perebento, ta [pere'bẽtu, ta] *adj* covered in sores.

perecer [25] [pere'se(x)] *vi* **-1.** [extingüir-se] to perish. **-2.** [morrer] to die. **-3.** *ant* [frustrar-se] to come to nothing.

perecível [pere'sivew] (*pl* **-eis**) *adj* perishable.

peregrinação [peregrina'sãw] (*pl* **-ões**) *f* **-1.** [viagem] journey. **-2.** *RELIG* pilgrimage.

peregrinar [4] [peregri'na(x)] *vi* **-1.** [viajar] to travel. **-2.** *RELIG* to go on a pilgrimage.

peregrino, na [pere'grinu, na] *m, f* **-1.** [viajante] traveller. **-2.** *RELIG* pilgrim.

pereira [pe'rejra] *f* pear tree.

peremptório, ria [perẽp'tɔrju, rja] *adj* **-1.** [final]

decisive. **-2.** [taxativo] peremptory.

perene [pe'reni] *adj* **-1.** [eterno] eternal. **-2.** [incessante] unceasing. **-3.** *BOT* perennial.

perereca [pere'rɛka] *f* **-1.** *ZOOL* tree frog. **-2.** *mfam* [vulva] pussy.

perfazer [31] [pexfa'ze(x)] *vt* **-1.** [total] to reach. **-2.** [ação] to complete.

perfeccionismo [pexfeksjo'niʒmul *m* perfectionism.

perfeccionista [pexfeksjo'niʃta] <> *adj* perfectionist. <> *mf* perfectionist.

perfeição [pexfej'sãw] *f* perfection; **ser uma** ~ to be perfect; **à** ~ to perfection.

perfeitamente [pex,fejta'mẽntʃil <> *adv* perfectly. <> *interj* [de acordo] of course!

perfeito, ta [pex'fejtu, ta] *adj* **-1.** [ger] perfect. **-2.** *(antes de subst)* [completo] perfect.
➡ **perfeito** *m* *GRAM* perfect.

perfídia [pex'fidʒja] *f* [traição] treachery.

pérfido, da l'pɛxfidu, dal *adj* treacherous.

perfil [pex'fiwl *(pl* -is) *m* **-1.** [ger] profile; **de** ~ in profile. **-2.** *fig* [retrato] outline. **-3.** [caráter] personality.

perfilar [4] [pexfi'la(x)] *vt* **-1.** [alinhar] to line up. **-2.** [aprumar] to straighten up.
➡ **perfilar-se** *vp* **-1.** [alinhar-se] to line up. **-2.** [aprumar-se] to stand to attention.

performance [pex'fɔxmãnsil *f* performance.

perfumado, da [pexfu'madu, dal *adj* perfumed.

perfumar [4] [pexfu'ma(x)] *vt* to perfume.
➡ **perfumar-se** *vp* to put perfume on.

perfumaria [pexfuma'rial *f* **-1.** [loja] perfume shop. **-2.** *fig* & *pej* [bobagem] nonsense.

perfume [pex'fumil *m* perfume.

perfurado, da [pexfu'radu, dal *adj* perforated.

perfurar [4] [pexfu'ra(x)] *vt* to perforate.

perfuratriz [pexfura'triʒ] *f* drill.

pergaminho [pexga'miɲul *m* [documento] parchment.

pérgula l'pɛxgulal *f* pergola.

pergunta [pex'gũntal *f* question; **fazer uma** ~ **a alguém** to ask sb a question; ~ **capciosa** trick question.

perguntador, ra [pexgũnta'do(x), ral *adj* *pej* nosy.

perguntar [4] [pexgũn'ta(x)] <> *vt* **-1.** [indagar] to ask; ~ **algo a alguém** to ask sb sthg. **-2.** [interrogar] to question. <> *vi* [indagar] to ask questions; ~ **por alguém** to ask after sb.
➡ **perguntar-se** *vp* to wonder.

perícia [pe'risjal *f* **-1.** [ger] expertise. **-2.** [policial] investigation. **-3.** [examinadores] investigators.

pericial [peri'sjawl *(pl* -ais) *adj* expert.

periclitante [perikli'tãntʃil *adj* perilous.

periclitar [4] [perikli'ta(x)] *vi* to be in peril.

periculosidade [perikulozi'dadʒil *f* peril; **de alta** ~ highly perilous.

peridural [peridu'rawl *(pl* -ais) <> *adj* epidural. <> *f* epidural.

periferia [perife'rial *f* **-1.** [contorno] periphery. **-2.** *GEOM* circumference. **-3.** [subúrbio] outskirts *(pl).*

periférico, ca [peri'fɛriku, kal *adj* **-1.** [que contorna] peripheral. **-2.** *fig* [marginal] superficial.
➡ **periférico** *m* *COMPUT* peripheral.

perigar [14] [peri'ga(x)] *vi* to be in danger; ~ **com** to be endangered by; **periga ele ser morto** he may be dead; ~ **chover** to look like it's going to rain.

perigo [pe'rigul *m* danger; **correr** ~ to be in danger; **estar a** ~ *fam* *fig* [dinheiro] to be broke; *fig* [em dificuldade] to be in trouble; **estar em** ~ to be in danger; **pôr em** ~ to endanger; **fora de** ~ out of danger; **ser um** ~ [ser perigoso] to be dangerous; *fam* *fig* [ser uma tentação] to be tantalizing.

perigoso, osa [peri'gozu, ɔzal *adj* dangerous.

perímetro [pe'rimetrul *m* perimeter; ~ **urbano** city limits *(pl).*

periodicamente [perjɔdʒika'mẽntʃil *adv* periodically.

periódico, ca [pe'rjɔdʒiku, kal *adj* periodic.
➡ **periódico** *m* **-1.** [jornal] periodical (newspaper). **-2.** [revista] periodical (magazine).

período [pe'riwdul *m* **-1.** [ger] period; ~ **de carência** term. **-2.** *UNIV* semester; ~ **letivo** school term.

peripécia [peri'pɛsjal *f* **-1.** [aventura] adventure. **-2.** [incidente] incident.

periquito [peri'kitul *m* budgerigar.

periscópio [periʃ'kɔpjul *m* periscope.

perito, ta [pe'ritu, tal <> *adj* [experiente, especialista] expert; ~ **em algo** expert in sthg. <> *m, f* **-1.** [especialista] expert. **-2.** [quem faz perícia] investigator.

peritonite [perito'nitʃil *f* peritonitis.

perjúrio [pex'ʒurjul *m* perjury.

permanecer [25] [pexmane'se(x)] *vi* to remain.

permanência [pexma'nẽnsjal *f* **-1.** [continuação, constância] endurance. **-2.** [estada] stay.

permanente [pexma'nẽntʃil <> *adj* permanent. <> *m* [cartão] pass. <> *f* [penteado] perm; **fazer uma** ~ to have a perm.

permeável [pex'mjavewl *(pl* -eis) *adj* permeable; ~ **a algo** permeable to sthg.

permeio [pex'mejul *adv:* **de** ~ in between.

permissão [pexmi'sãwl *(pl* -ões) *f* permission; **ter** ~ **(para fazer algo)** to have permission (to do sthg).

permissível [pexmi'sivewl *(pl* -eis) *adj* permissible.

permissivo, va [pexmi'sivu, val *adj* permissive.

permitir [6] [pexmi'tʃi(x)] *vt* **-1.** [admitir] to allow; ~ **a alguém fazer algo** to allow sb to do sthg. **-2.** [conceder]: ~ **algo a alguém** to grant sb sthg.
➡ **permitir-se** *vp* [tomar a liberdade de] to allow o.s.

permuta [pex'mutal *f* exchange.

permutação [pexmuta'sãwl *(pl* -ões) *f* **-1.** *MAT* permutation. **-2.** [troca] exchange.

permutar [4] [pexmu'ta(x)] *vt:* ~ **algo (por algo)** to exchange sthg (for sthg).

perna l'pɛxnal *f* leg; ~ **de pau** wooden leg; **bater**

~ *fig* to wander; **passar a** ~ **em alguém** *fig* [enganar] to con sb; [trair] to cheat on sb; **trocar as** ~**s** *fam* [cambalear] to trip over one's feet.

perna-de-pau [ˌpɛxnadʒi'paw] (*pl* **pernas-de-pau**) *mf* **-1.** *fam pej* [perneta] one-legged man. **- 2.** *FUT* & *pej*: **aquele jogador é um** ~**!** that player has two left feet!

Pernambuco [pexnãn'bukul *n* Pernambuco.

perneta [pex'neta] *fam pej* <> *adj* one-legged. <> *mf* one-legged person.

pernicioso, osa [pexni'sjozu, ɔza] *adj* **-1.** [nocivo] destructive. **- 2.** *MED* pernicious.

pernil [pex'niw] (*pl* -**is**) *m* *CULIN* hock.

pernilongo [pexni'lõŋgu] *m* stilt.

pernoitar [4] [pexnoj'ta(x)] *vi* to spend the night.

pernoite [per'nojtʃil *m*: **após um** ~ **na minha casa** after spending the night at my house.

pernóstico, ca [pex'nɔʃtʃiku, ka] <> *adj* pretentious. <> *mf* pretentious person.

pérola [ˈpɛrolal *f* **-1.** [de ostra] pearl. **- 2.** *fig* [pessoa, peça rara] gem.

perpassar [4] [pexpa'sa(x)] *vt* *fig* [atravessar] to imbue.

perpendicular [pexpẽndʒiku'la(x)] (*pl* -**es**) <> *adj* perpendicular; **ser** ~ **a algo** to be at right angles to sthg. <> *f* perpendicular.

perpetrar [4] [pexpe'tra(x)] *vt* to perpetrate.

perpetuar [4] [pexpe'twa(x)] *vt* to prolong.

➠ **perpetuar-se** *vp* to survive.

perpétuo, tua [pex'pɛtwu, twa] *adj* **-1.** [eterno] eternal. **- 2.** [vitalício] permanent. **- 3.** *JUR*: **prisão perpétua** life imprisonment. **- 4.** *(antes de subst)* [freqüente] on-going.

perplexidade [pexpleksi'dadʒi] *f* perplexity.

perplexo, xa [pex'plɛksu, sa] *adj* perplexed; **estar/ficar** ~ to be perplexed.

perscrutar [4] [pexʃkru'ta(x)] *vt* [investigar] to scrutinize.

perseguição [pexsegi'sãw] (*pl* -**ões**) *f* **-1.** [ger] persecution. **- 2.** *fig* [de um objetivo] pursuit.

perseguidor, ra [pexsegi'do(x), ra] *m, f* **-1.** [que acossa] pursuer. **- 2.** *fig* [de um objetivo] seeker.

perseguir [55] [pexse'gi(x)] *vt* **-1.** [ger] to pursue. **- 2.** *POL* & *RELIG* to persecute.

perseverança [pexseve'rãnsa] *f* perseverance.

perseverante [pexseve'rãntʃi] *adj* persevering.

perseverar [4] [pexseve'ra(x)] *vi* **-1.** [persistir]: ~ (**em**) to persevere (with). **- 2.** [permanecer] to last.

Pérsia [ˈpɛxsja] *n* Persia.

persiana [pex'sjana] *f* blind.

persignar-se [7] [pexsig'naxsi] *vp* to cross o.s.

persistência [pexsiʃ'tẽnsja] *f* persistence.

persistente [pexsiʃ'tẽntʃi] *adj* persistent.

persistir [6] [pexsiʃ'tʃi(x)] *vi* [insistir]: ~ (**em algo**) to persist (in sthg).

personagem [pexso'naʒẽl (*pl* -**ns**) *m, f* **-1.** *CINE, LITER* & *TEATRO* character. **- 2.** [celebridade] celebrity.

personalidade [pexsonali'dadʒil *f* personality; **dupla** ~ split personality.

personalizado, da [pexsonali'zadu, da] *adj* personalized.

personalizar [412] [pexsonali'za(x)] *vt* [tonar pessoal] to personalize.

personificação [pexsonifika'sãw] (*pl* -**ões**) *f* personification.

personificar [12] [pexsonifi'ka(x)] *vt* personify.

perspectiva [pexʃpek'tʃival *f* **-1.** [ger] perspective. **- 2.** [probabilidade] prospect; **em** ~ [em vista] in prospect; [a distância] in perspective.

perspicácia [pexʃpi'kasja] *f* insight.

perspicaz [pexʃpi'kaʃ] (*pl* -**es**) *adj* insightful.

perspirar [4] [pexʃpi'ra(x)] *vi* to perspire, to sweat.

persuadir [6] [pexswa'dʒi(x)] <> *vt* **-1.** [convencer]: ~ **alguém (a fazer algo)** to persuade sb (to do sthg); **persuadiu a mulher de que tinha razão** he persuaded his wife that he was right. **- 2.** [induzir]: ~ **alguém a fazer algo** to persuade sb to do sthg. <> *vi* [induzir] to persuade.

➠ **persuadir-se** *vp* **-1.** [convencer-se]: ~**-se (de algo)** to be persuaded (of sthg). **- 2.** [resolver-se]: ~**-se (a fazer algo)** to make up one's mind (to do sthg).

persuasão [pexswa'zãw] *f* persuasion.

persuasivo, va [pexswa'zivu, va] *adj* persuasive.

pertencente [pextẽn'sẽntʃi] *adj*: ~ **a algo/alguém** belonging to sthg/sb.

pertencer [25] [pextẽn'se(x)] *vi*: ~ **a** [ger] to belong to; [concernir] to refer to.

pertences [pex'tẽnsiʃ] *mpl* [objetos pessoais] belongings.

pertinácia [pextʃi'nasja] *f* persistence.

pertinaz [pextʃi'najʃ] *adj* persistent.

pertinência [pextʃi'nẽnsja] *f* pertinence.

pertinente [pextʃi'nẽntʃi] *adj* **-1.** [ger] pertinent. **- 2.** [importante] relevant.

perto [ˈpɛxtul <> *adj* nearby. <> *adv* near; **de** ~ [a pouca distância] closely; *fig* [intimamente] first-hand; ~ **de** [ger] close to; [em comparação] next to.

perturbação [pextuxba'sãw] (*pl* -**ões**) *f* **-1.** [ger] disturbance; ~ **da ordem** breach of the peace. **- 2.** [transtorno] perturbation. **- 3.** *MED* trouble.

perturbado, da [pextux'badu, da] *adj* **-1.** [transtornado]: ~ (**com algo**) perturbed (by sthg). **- 2.** [desorientado] disorientated; **ser** ~ (**das idéias**) *irôn* to be addled.

perturbador, ra [pextuxba'do(x), ra] *adj* disturbing.

perturbar [4] [pextux'ba(x)] <> *vt* **-1.** [ger] to perturb. **- 2.** [atrapalhar] to disturb. **- 3.** [envergonhar] to embarass. <> *vi* [atordoar] to pester.

➠ **perturbar-se** *vp* **-1.** [atrapalhar-se] to be worried. **- 2.** [incomodar-se] to worry. **- 3.** [envergonhar-se] to be embarrassed.

peru, rua [pe'ru, rual *m, f* [ave] turkey.

➠ **peru** *n mfam* [pênis] cock.

➠ **perua** *f* **-1.** [caminhonete] estate car *UK*, station wagon *US*. **- 2.** *fam pej* [mulher] hussy.

Peru [pe'rul *n*: (**o**) ~ Peru.

peruada [pe'rwadal *f* **-1.** [palpite] tip. **- 2.** [espiada] look-see.

peruano, na [pe'rwãnu, na] <> *adj* Peruvian. <> *m, f* Peruvian.

peruar [4] [pe'rwa(x)] *vi* -**1.** [palpitar] to speculate. -**2.** [espiar] to size up.

peruca [pe'ruka] *f* wig.

perueiro, ra [pe'ruejru, ra] *m* [motorista de perua] minibus driver.

perversão [pexvex'sãw] (*pl* -ões) *f* -**1.** [depravação] perversion. -**2.** [alteração] alteration.

perversidade [pexvexsi'dadʒi] *f* perversity.

perverso, sa [pex'vɛxsu, sa] *adj* perverse.

perverter [5] [pexvex'te(x)] *vt* -**1.** [corromper] to pervert. -**2.** [alterar] to alter. -**3.** [deturpar] to distort.

- **perverter-se** *vp* [corromper-se] to become depraved.

pervertido, da [pexvex'tʃidu, da] <> *adj* [corrompido] depraved. <> *m, f* pervert.

pesadelo [peza'delu] *m* nightmare.

pesado, da [pe'zadu, da] *adj* -**1.** [ger] heavy. -**2.** [tenso] tense. -**3.** [grosseiro] coarse.

- **pesado** *m*: **pegar no** ~ to do hard work.

pesagem [pe'zaʒẽ] *f* weighing.

pêsames ['pezamiʃ] *mpl* condolences; **dar os** ~ **(a alguém)** to offer one's condolences (to sb).

pesar [4] [pe'za(x)] <> *m* sadness; **apesar dos** ~ **es** in spite of everything. <> *vt* to weigh. <> *vi* -**1.** [ger] to weigh. -**2.** [recair]: ~ **sobre alguém** to fall on sb. -**3.** [onerar] to be burdensome. -**4.** [influenciar]: ~ **em algo** to influence sthg. -**5.** [causar tristeza]: ~ **a alguém** to grieve sb. -**6.** [causar remorso] to weigh sb down.

- **pesar-se** *vp* [verificar o peso] to weigh o.s.

pesaroso, osa [peza'rozu, ɔza] *adj* -**1.** [triste] sorrowful. -**2.** [arrependido] sorry.

pesca ['pɛʃka] *f* -**1.** [ato] fishing; **ir à** ~ to go fishing; ~ **submarina** skin diving. -**2.** [o que se pescou] catch.

pescada [peʃ'kada] *f* whiting.

pescado [peʃ'kadu] *m* catch (*of fish*).

pescador, ra [peʃka'do(x), ra] (*mpl* -es, *fpl* -s) *m, f* fisherman (*f* fisherwoman).

pescar [12] [peʃ'ka(x)] <> *vt* -**1.** [apanhar] to fish. -**2.** *fig* [conseguir] to get. -**3.** *fig* [conquistar] to catch. <> *vi fam* [entender]: ~ **(de algo)** to catch on (to sthg).

pescoção [peʃko'sãw] (*pl* -ões) *m* -**1.** [pescoçada] blow on the neck; **levar um** ~ **de alguém** to be given a blow on the neck by sb. -**2.** [pescoço grande] large neck.

pescoço [peʃ'kosu] *m* neck; **até o** ~ *fig* up to one's neck; **torcer o** ~ **de alguém** *fig* to wring sb's neck.

pescoçudo, da [peʃko'sudu, da] *adj* thick-necked.

peso ['pezu] *m* -**1.** [ger] weight; ~ **bruto/líquido** gross/net weight; ~ **pesado** heavyweight; **ter dois** ~**s e duas medidas** *fig* to have double standards; **ele é um intelectual de** ~ he is a weighty intelectual. -**2.** [para papéis] paperweight. -**3.** [em atletismo] weights (*pl*). -**4.** [moeda]

peso. -**5.** *fig* [carga] burden.

- **em peso** *loc adj* en masse.

pespontar [4] [peʃpõn'ta(x)] *vt* COST to backstitch.

pesponto [peʃ'põntu] *m* backstitch.

pesqueiro, ra [peʃ'kejru, ra] *adj* fishing (*antes de subst*).

pesquisa [peʃ'kiza] *f* -**1.** [investigação] search. -**2.**: ~ **de mercado** market research; ~ **de opinião** opinion poll. -**3.** [estudo] research; ~ **de campo** field research; ~ **e desenvolvimento** research and development.

pesquisador, ra [peʃkiza'do(x), ra] <> *adj* research (*antes de subst*). <> *m, f* researcher.

pesquisar [4] [peʃki'za(x)] <> *vt* -**1.** [investigar] to investigate. -**2.** [estudar] to research. <> *vi* [estudar] to do research.

pêssego ['pesegu] *m* peach.

pessegueiro [pese'gejru] *m* peach tree.

pessimismo [pesi'miʒmu] *m* pessimism.

pessimista [pesi'miʃta] <> *adj* pessimistic. <> *mf* pessimist.

péssimo, ma ['pɛsimu, ma] *adj* (*superl de mau*) terrible; **ficou** ~ **com a notícia** the news made him feel terrible.

pessoa [pe'soal] *f* [ger] person; **em** ~ personally; ~ **física** JUR private individual; ~ **jurídica** JUR legal entity.

pessoal [pe'swaw] (*pl* -ais) <> *adj* personal. <> *m* -**1.** [empregados] personnel (*pl*), staff. -**2.** [grupo] people (*pl*).

pessoalmente [peswaw'mẽntʃi] *adv* personally.

pestana [peʃ'tãna] *f* -**1.** [cílio] eyelash; **queimar as** ~**s** *fig* [estudar] to swot; **tirar uma** ~ *fig* [dormir] to catch forty winks. -**2.** COST flap. -**3.** MÚS barré.

pestanejar [4] [peʃtane'ʒa(x)] *vi* to blink; **sem** ~ *fig* without batting an eyelid.

peste ['pɛʃtʃi] *f* -**1.** [ger] plague. -**2.** *fig* [pessoa] pest. -**3.** *fig* [coisa perniciosa] scourge.

pesticida [peʃtʃi'sida] *f* pesticide.

pestilência [peʃtʃi'lẽnsja] *f* [fedor] stench.

pestilento, ta [peʃtʃi'lẽntu, ta] *adj* -**1.** [fedorento] stinking. -**2.** [infectado] pestilent.

pétala ['pɛtala] *f* petal.

petardo [pe'taxdu] *m* FUT powerful kick.

peteca [pe'tɛka] *f* [brinquedo] shuttlecock; **não deixar a** ~ **cair** *fam fig* to keep the ball rolling.

peteleco [pete'lɛku] *m* flick.

petição [petʃi'sãw] (*pl* -ões) *f* -**1.** [requerimento] petition. -**2.** [súplica] plea. -**3.** [estado]: **em** ~ **de miséria** in a pitiful state.

peticionário, ria [petʃisjo'narju, rja] *m, f* JUR petitioner.

petiscar [12] [petʃiʃ'ka(x)] <> *vt* to pick at. <> *vi* to snack; **quem não arrisca não petisca** he who dares wins.

petisco [pe'tʃiʃku] *m* titbit UK, tidbit US.

petit-pois [petʃi'pwal *m inv* pea.

petrechos [pe'treʃuʃ] *mpl* -**1.** MIL munitions. -**2.** [utensílios] utensils.

petrificado, da [petrifi'kadu, da] *adj* petrified.

petrificar [12] [petrifi'ka(x)] *vt* -**1.** [tornar em pedra] to harden. **-2.** [insensibilizar] to numb. **-3.** [aterrorizar] to petrify.

Petrobras (*abrev de* **Petróleo Brasileiro S/A**) *f* *Brazilian state-owned petroleum company.*

petrodólar [petro'dɔla(x)] *m* petrodollar.

petroleiro, ra [petro'lejru] ⟨⟩ *adj*: **navio- ~** (oil) tanker. ⟨⟩ *m, f* [pessoa] oilman.

petróleo [pe'trɔljul *m* petroleum, oil; **~ bruto** crude oil.

petrolífero, ra [petro'liferu, ra] *adj* oil.

petroquímico, ca [petro'kimiku, ka] ⟨⟩ *adj* petrochemical. ⟨⟩ *m, f* petroleum chemist.

➡ **petroquímica** *f* [indústria] petrochemicals *(pl)*.

petulância [petu'lãnsja] *f* petulance.

petulante [petu'lãntʃi] *adj* petulant.

petúnia [pe'tunja] *f* petunia.

PFL (*abrev de* **Partido da Frente Liberal**) *m* Party of the Liberal Front, *the largest, very right-wing party in Brazil.*

Phnom Penh [fnõn'pẽ] *n* Phnom Penh.

pia ['pial *f* sink, washbasin; **~ batismal** baptismal font.

piaçaba [pia'saba] *f* BOT palm native to Brazil up to 15 meters in height producing a fibre used in the manufacture of brushes.

piada ['pjada] *f* joke.

piadista [pja'dʒiʃta] *mf* joker.

piamente [pja'mẽntʃi] *adv* earnestly.

pianista [pja'niʃta] *mf* pianist.

piano ['pjãnu] *m* piano; **~ de cauda** grand piano.

pianola [pja'nɔla] *f* pianola.

pião ['pjãw] (*pl* -ões) *m* spinning top.

piar [16] ['pja(x)] *vi* **-1.** [ave - pinto] to cheep; [- passarinho] to chirp; [- coruja] to hoot. **-2.** *fam* [falar]: **não ~** not to make a peep.

PIB (*abrev de* **Produto Interno Bruto**) *m* GDP.

picada [pi'kada] *f* ➡ **picado**.

picadeiro [pika'dejru] *m* (circus) ring.

picadinho [pika'dʒiɲul *m* CULIN **-1.** [de carne] minced meat. **-2.** [de legumes] vegetable stew.

picado, da [pi'kadu, da] *adj* **-1.** [ger] stung; **ser ~ por algo** to be bitten by sthg. **-2.** [em pedaços] chopped up. **-3.** [mar] choppy. **-4.** [vôo] nose-diving.

➡ **picada** *f* **-1.** [espetada] prick. **-2.** [mordida] bite. **-3.** [caminho] trail.

picanha [pi'kãɲa] *f* [carne bovina] rump.

picante [pi'kãntʃi] *adj* spicy.

pica-pau [,pika'paw] (*pl* **pica-paus**) *m* woodpecker.

picar [12] [pi'ka(x)] *vt* **-1.** [espetar] to prick. **-2.** [morder] to bite. **-3.** [cortar em pedaços] to chop. **-4.** [lascar] to splinter. **-5.** [bicar] to peck.

➡ **picar-se** *vp* **-1.** [espetar-se] to prick o.s. **-2.** [com droga] to inject o.s.

picardia [pikax'dʒia] *f* **-1.** [implicância] spitefulness. **-2.** [maldade] spite.

picaresco, ca [pika'reʃku, ka] *adj* [burlesco] burlesque.

picareta [pika'reta] ⟨⟩ *f* [instrumento] pickaxe

UK, pickax *US*. ⟨⟩ *mf* [mau-caráter] con artist.

picaretagem [pikare'taʒẽ] (*pl* -ns) *f* con.

pichação [piʃa'sãw] (*pl* -ões) *f* **-1.** [grafite] graffiti. **-2.** *fam* [crítica] smear.

pichar [4] [pi'ʃa(x)] *vt* **-1.** [grafitar] to graffitti. **-2.** *fam* [criticar] to smear. **-3.** [aplicar piche em] to pitch.

piche ['piʃil *m* pitch.

picles ['pikleʃ] *mpl* pickles.

pico ['pikul *m* **-1.** [cume] summit. **-2.** [de faca etc] point. **-3.** *fam* [de droga] shot.

picolé [piko'lɛl *m* ice lolly.

picotar [4] [piko'ta(x)] *vt* to perforate.

picote [pi'kɔtʃi] *m* [perfuração] perforation.

pictórico, ca [pik'tɔriku, ka] *adj* pictorial.

picuinha [pi'kwiɲa] *f* [implicância] dispute; **estar de ~ com alguém** to be at odds with sb.

piedade [pje'dadʒi] *f* **-1.** [compaixão] pity; **ter ~ de alguém** to have pity on sb. **-2.** [religiosidade] piety.

piedoso, osa [pje'dozu, ɔza] *adj* pious.

piegas ['pjɛgaʃ] *adj inv* soppy.

pieguice [pje'gisil *f* soppiness.

píer ['pie(x)] *m* pier.

pifado, da [pi'fadu, da] *fam adj* [enguiçado] broken down.

pifão [pi'fãw] (*pl* -ões) *m fam* drunk; **tomar um ~** to have a skinful.

pifar [4] [pi'fa(x)] *vi fam* **-1.** [enguiçar] to break down. **-2.** [gorar] to fall through.

pigarrear [15] [piga'xja(x)] *vi* to hawk.

pigarro [pi'gaxul *m* phlegm.

pigméia [pig'mɛja] *f* ➡ **pigmeu**.

pigmentação [pigmẽnta'sãw] *f* pigmentation.

pigmento [pig'mẽntul *m* pigment.

pigmeu, méia [pig'mew, mɛja] ⟨⟩ *adj* [pequeno] pygmy. ⟨⟩ *m, f* pygmy.

pijama [pi'ʒãma] *m* pyjamas *(pl)* UK, pajamas *(pl)* US.

pilantra [pi'lãntra] *mf* rogue.

pilantragem [pilãn'traʒẽ] (*pl* -ns) *f* roguishness.

pilão [pi'lãw] (*pl* -ões) *m* pestle.

pilar [4] [pi'la(x)] (*pl* -es) ⟨⟩ *m* [coluna] pillar. ⟨⟩ *vt* to grind.

pilastra [pi'laʃtra] *f* pilaster.

pileque [pi'lɛki] *m* skinful; **estar de ~** to be smashed; **tomar um ~** to have a skinful.

pilha ['piʎa] *f* **-1.** [monte] pile. **-2.** ELETR battery. **-3.** [pessoa]: **estar/ser uma ~ (de nervos)** to be a bundle of nerves. **-4.** COMPUT stack.

pilhagem [pi'ʎaʒẽ] (*pl* -ns) *f* **-1.** [saque] pillage. **-2.** [objetos] booty.

pilhar [4] [pi'ʎa(x)] *vt* **-1.** [saquear] to pillage. **-2.** [roubar] to rob.

pilhéria [pi'ʎɛrja] *f* jest.

pilheriar [16] [piʎe'rja(x)] *vi* to jest.

pilões [pi'lõjʃ] *pl* ➡ **pilão**.

pilotagem [pilo'taʒẽ] *f* flying.

pilotar [4] [pilo'ta(x)] ⟨⟩ *vt* to steer. ⟨⟩ *vi* to steer.

pilotis [pilo'tʃiʃ] *mpl* ARQUIT stilts.

piloto [pi'lotul ⟨⟩ *adj* [modelo] pilot. ⟨⟩ *m* **-1.** [ger] pilot; **~ automático** automatic pilot. **-2.**

[de corrida] driver; ~ **de prova** racing driver. **-3.** [bico de gás] pilot light.

pílula ['pilula] *f* pill; ~ **anticoncepcional** contraceptive pill.

pimenta [pi'mẽnta] *f* **-1.** CULIN pepper. **-2.** *fig* [malícia] spite.

pimenta-do-reino [pi,mẽntadu'xejnu] (*pl* pimentas-do-reino) *f* black pepper.

pimenta-malagueta [pi,mẽntamala'geta] (*pl* pimentas-malagueta) *f* chilli pepper UK, chili pepper US.

pimentão [pimẽn'tãw] (*pl* -ões) *m*: ~ **verde/vermelho** green/red pepper; **estar/ficar um** ~ *fig* to be/go as red as a beetroot.

pimenteira [pimẽn'tejra] *f* **-1.** BOT pepper tree. **-2.** [recipiente] pepper pot.

pimpolho [pĩ'poʎu] *m* [criança] kid.

pinacoteca [pinako'tɛka] *f* **-1.** [coleção] art collection. **-2.** [museu] art gallery.

pináculo [pi'nakulu] *m* pinnacle.

pinça ['pĩsa] *f* **-1.** MED forceps (*pl*). **-2.** [de sobrancelha] tweezers (*pl*).

pinçar [13] [pĩ'sa(x)] *vt* **-1.** [segurar] to grip (with pincers). **-2.** [sobrancelhas] to pluck. **-3.** *fig* [selecionar] to select.

píncaro ['pĩkaru] *m* **-1.** [cume] peak. **-2.** *fig* [apogeu] height.

pincel [pĩ'sɛw] (*pl* -éis) *m* brush; ~ **de barba** shaving brush.

pincelada [pĩse'lada] *f* (brush) stroke.

pincelar [4] [pĩse'la(x)] *vt* to paint.

pincenê [pĩse'ne] *m* pince-nez.

pindaíba [pĩda'iba] *f*: **estar na** ~ *fam* to be skint.

pinel [pi'nɛw] (*pl* -éis) *adj fam* crazy; **ficar** ~ to be driven crazy.

pinga ['pĩga] *f fam* [cachaça] booze.

pingado, da [pĩ'gadu, da] ◇ *adj* **-1.** [cheio de pingos]: ~ **de algo** splashed with sthg. **-2.** [leite] with a drop of coffee; [café] with a drop of milk. ◇ *m* [café] *coffee with a drop of milk*.

pingar [14] [pĩ'ga(x)] ◇ *vi* **-1.** [gotejar] to drip. **-2.** [chover] to spit. **-3.** [render] to trickle in. ◇ *vt* **-1.** [respingar] to spill. **-2.** [gotejar] to allow to drip through.

pingente [pĩ'ʒẽntʃi] *m* [objeto] pendant.

pingo ['pĩgu] *m* **-1.** [gota] drop. **-2.** [pequena quantidade]: **um** ~ **de** a little; ~ **de gente** [criança] little person. **-3.** [sinal ortográfico] dot; **pôr os** ~**s nos is** *fig* to dot the i's and cross the t's.

pingue-pongue [,pĩŋgi'põŋgi] (*pl* pingue-pongues) *m* ping-pong, table tennis.

pingüim [pĩ'gwĩ] (*pl* -ns) *m* penguin.

pinguinho [pĩ'giɲu] *m* **-1.** [pingo] droplet. **-2.** [pouquinho]: **um** ~ **(de)** a tiny bit (of).

pinha ['piɲa] *f* **-1.** [fruto do pinheiro] pine cone. **-2.** [fruta] pine nut.

pinhão [pi'ɲãw] (*pl* -ões) *m* pine nut.

pinheiral [piɲej'raw] (*pl* -ais) *m* pine forest.

pinheiro [pi'ɲejru] *m* pine tree.

pinho ['piɲu] *m* **-1.** BOT pine (tree). **-2.** [madeira]

pine wood. **-3.** *fam* [violão] fiddle.

pinicada [pini'kada] *f* **-1.** [de ave] peck. **-2.** [de agulha, espinho] stab.

pinicar [12] [pini'ka(x)] *vt* **-1.** [comichar] to be itchy. **-2.** [bicar] to peck. **-3.** [cutucar] to jab.

pinimba [pi'nĩba] *f fam* argument; **estar de** ~ **com alguém** to be at loggerheads with sb.

pino ['pinu] *m* **-1.** [peça] peg. **-2.** [AUTO - em motor] crankpin; [- tranca] lock; **bater** ~ to rattle; *fam fig* [estar mal] to fall apart. **-3.** [cume]: **a** ~ at the zenith; **sol a** ~ midday sun.

pinóia [pi'nɔja] *fam f* **-1.** [chatice]: **ser uma** ~ to be boring; **que** ~**!** what a bore! **-2.** [porcaria] junk. **-3.** [mentira]: **uma** ~**!** my foot!

pinote [pi'nɔtʃi] *m* buck; **dar** ~**s** to buck.

pinotear [15] [pino'tʃja(x)] *vi* to leap.

pinta ['pĩta] *f* **-1.** [sinal] mole. **-2.** *fam* [aparência]: **o rapaz é boa** ~ the boy is looking good; **essa comida está com boa** ~ that food looks good; **ter** ~ **de algo** to look like sthg. **-3.** *fam* [indício]: **estar com** ~ **de (ser) difícil** to look (like being) difficult; **ela deu na** ~ **que ia nos assaltar** [demonstrar] she looked like she was going to attack us.

pinta-brava [pĩta'brava] (*pl* pintas-bravas) *mf* [mau elemento] shady character.

pintado, da [pĩ'tadu, da] *adj* **-1.** [colorido - papel] coloured; [- parede, olhos, unhas] painted; [- face] painted, made-up; [- cabelo] dyed. **-2.** [sardento] freckled. **-3.** [idêntico]: **ser alguém** ~ to be the spitting image of sb.

pintar [4] [pĩ'ta(x)] ◇ *vt* **-1.** [ger] to paint. **-2.** [com tinta - ger] to paint; [- cabelo] to dye. **-3.** *fig* [conceber] to paint as. ◇ *vi* **-1.** ARTE to paint. **-2.** *fam* [aparecer] to turn up. **-3.** [exceder-se] to get overexcited; ~ **e bordar** *fig* to have a great time.
➤ **pintar-se** *vp* [maquilar-se] to make o.s. up.

pinto, ta ['pĩntu, ta] *m, f* **-1.** ZOOL chick; **ficar (molhado) como um** ~ to get soaked to the bone. **-2.** *mfam* [pênis] cock. **-3.** [coisa fácil]: **ser** ~ to be a pushover.

pintor, ra [pĩn'to(x), ra] (*mpl* -es, *fpl* -s) *m, f* painter.

pintura [pĩn'tura] *f* **-1.** ARTE painting; ~ **a óleo** oil painting. **-2.** [de casa etc] paintwork. **-3.** [maquiagem] make-up.

pio, pia ['piw, 'pia] *adj* **-1.** [devota] pious. **-2.** [caridoso] charitable.
➤ **pio** *m* [de ave] peep; **não dê um** ~, **senão atiro** not a peep, or else I'll shoot.

piões ['pjõjʃ] *pl* ▷ **pião**.

piolho ['pjoʎu] *m* louse.

pioneirismo [pjonej'riʒmu] *m* pioneering nature.

pioneiro, ra [pjo'nejru, ra] ◇ *adj* pioneering. ◇ *m, f* pioneer.

pior ['pjɔ(x)] (*pl* -es) ◇ *adj* **-1.** [comparativo]: ~ **(do que)** worse (than). **-2.** [superlativo]: **o/a** ~ ... the worst ... ◇ *m*: **o** ~ **(de)** [inferior] the worst (of); **o** ~ **é que** ... the worst of it is that ... ◇ *f*: **o/a** ~ **(de)** the worst (of); **estar na** ~ to be in a jam;

levar a ~ to lose. <> *adv* [comparativo]: ~ **(do que)** worse (than); **ela está** ~ **de saúde** her health is worse.

piora [ˈpjɔra] f deterioration.

piorar [4] [pjoˈra(x)] *vi* to deteriorate.

pipa [ˈpipa] f **-1.** [vasilhame] barrel. **-2.** [de papel] kite; **soltar** ~ to fly a kite.

piparote [pipaˈrɔtʃil] m flick.

pipi [piˈpi] m *fam* wee-wee *UK*, pee-pee *US*; **fazer** ~ to wee *UK*, to go pee-pee *US*.

pipilar [16] [pipiˈla(x)] *vi* to chirp.

pipoca [piˈpɔka] f **-1.** [de milho] popcorn. **-2.** [em pele] blister.

pipocar [12] [pipoˈka(x)] *vi* **-1.** [estourar] to burst out. **-2.** [espocar] to crackle. **-3.** [surgir] to sprout up.

pipoqueiro, ra [pipoˈkeiru, ra] m, f [vendedor] popcorn seller.

➡ **pipoqueira** f [panela] popcorn-making pan.

pique [ˈpiki] m **-1.** [brincadeira] catch. **-2.** [disposição] enthusiasm; **perder o** ~ to lose one's momentum; **ter** ~ to have what it takes. **-3.** [corte] notch. **-4.** *NÁUT:* **ir a** ~ to sink.

piquenique [ˌpikiˈnikil] m picnic.

piquete [piˈketʃil] m **-1.** [de greve] picket. **-2.** *MIL* squad.

pira [ˈpira] f *fam:* **dar o** ~ [ir-se embora] to scarper; [fugir] to abscond.

piração [piraˈsãw] (*pl* -ões) f *fam* **-1.** [doidice] madness. **-2.** [ser excelente]: **aquele filme é uma** ~ that film is really great.

pirado, da [piˈradu, da] *adj* crazy.

pirâmide [piˈramidʒi] f pyramid.

piranha [piˈraɲa] f **-1.** [peixe] piranha. **-2.** *mfam pej* [mulher] hussy. **-3.** [prendedor de cabelo] hair clasp.

pirão [piˈrãw] (*pl* -ões) m *CULIN* cassava porridge.

pirar [4] [piˈra(x)] *vi* **-1.** [endoidar] to go insane. **-2.** [fugir] to scarper.

pirata [piˈrata] <> *adj* pirate. <> *mf* pirate.

pirataria [pirataˈria] f [roubo] piracy.

piratear [piraˈtea(x)] *vt:* ~ **um programa** to pirate a program.

Pireneus [pireˈnewʃl] *n:* **os** ~ the Pyrenees.

pires [ˈpiriʃl] m *inv* saucer.

pirilampo [piriˈlãnpu] m glow-worm.

pirotecnia [pirotekˈnia] f **-1.** [arte] pyrotechnics (*sg*). **-2.** [fabricação] fireworks manufacturing.

pirotécnico, ca [piroˈtɛkniku, ka] <> *adj* [com fogos de artifício] firework (*antes de subst*). <> m, f [fabricante] firework manufacturer.

pirraça [piˈxasa] f: **fazer algo por** ~ to do sthg out of spite; **fazer** ~ **a alguém** [fazer desfeita] to spite sb.

pirracento, ta [pixaˈsẽntu, ta] *adj* spiteful.

pirralho, lha [piˈxaʎu, ʎa] m, f child.

pirueta [piˈrweta] f pirouette.

pirulito [piruˈlitu] m **-1.** [bala] lollipop. **-2.** *fam* [pênis] willy.

pisada [piˈzada] f **-1.** [passo] footstep; **dar uma** ~ **em algo/alguém** to tread on sthg/sb. **-2.** [pegada] footprint.

pisão [piˈsãw] (*pl* -ões) m [pisadela]: **dar um** ~ **no pé de alguém** to tread on sb's toes.

pisar [4] [piˈza(x)] <> *vt* **-1.** to tread on. **-2.** [esmagar] to crush. **-3.** [percorrer] to set foot on. <> *vi* **-1.** [andar]: ~ **(em)** to walk *ou* tread (on); **saber onde** ~ *fig* to know what one is getting into. **-2.:** ~ **em** [tocar com os pés] tơ step on; [ir, vir] to set foot in; [humilhar] to crush; ▷ **bola**, **ovos**.

piscadela [piʃkaˈdɛla] f **-1.** [ato reflexo] blink. **-2.** [sinal] wink; **dar uma** ~ to give a wink.

pisca-pisca [ˌpiʃkaˈpiʃka] (*pl* pisca-piscas) m *AUTO* indicator.

piscar [12] [piʃˈka(x)] <> *vt* [olho] to blink; ~ **o olho para alguém** [dar sinal] to wink at sb. <> *vi* **-1.** [pessoa, olho] to wink. **-2.** [trocar sinais]: ~ **para alguém** to wink at sb. **-3.** [tremeluzir] to twinkle. <> m twinkling; **num** ~ **de olhos** in a twinkling of an eye.

pisciano, na [piˈsjãnu, na] <> *adj:* **ser** ~ to be a Piscean. <> m, f Piscean.

piscicultura [pisikuwˈtura] f fish farming, pisciculture.

piscina [piˈsina] f swimming pool.

piso [ˈpizul] m **-1.** [ger] floor. **-2.** [revestimento] flooring. **-3.** [salário]: ~ **(salarial)** minimum (professional) wage.

pisotear [15] [pizoˈtʃja(x)] *vt* **-1.** [pisar] to trample (on). **-2.** [humilhar] to trample over.

píssico, ca [ˈpisiku, ka] <> *adj* crazy. <> m, f lunatic.

pista [ˈpiʃta] f **-1.** [vestígio] trace. **-2.** [encalço]: **na** ~ **de** in pursuit of, on the trail of. **-3.** *fig* [informação] clue. **-4.** [de rua, estrada] track. **-5.** *AERON* runway. **-6.** [*ESP*- de automobilismo, atletismo] track; [- de esqui] piste; [- de equitação] ring; [- de tênis] court. **-7.** [de dança] floor.

pistache [piʃˈtaʃil], **pistacho** [piʃˈtaʃul] m pistachio.

pistola [piʃˈtɔla] f **-1.** [arma] pistol. **-2.** [para pintar] (spray) gun.

pistolão [piʃtoˈlãw] (*pl* -ões) m **-1.** [pessoa] connection. **-2.** [recomendação] recommendation.

pistoleiro, ra [piʃtoˈlejru, ra] m, f [criminoso] gunman.

➡ **pistoleira** f *mfam* [vagabunda] tart.

pistom [piʃˈtõ] (*pl* -ns) m **-1.** [instrumento] trumpet. **-2.** [de motor] piston.

pitada [piˈtada] f pinch.

pitanga [piˈtãŋga] f [red Brazil] cherry.

pitar [4] [piˈta(x)] <> *vi* to smoke. <> *vt* to smoke.

piteira [piˈtejra] f cigarette-holder.

pito [ˈpitu] m **-1.** [cachimbo] pipe. **-2.** *fam* [repreensão] talking-to; **dar um** ~ **em alguém** to tell sb off; **levar um** ~ **de alguém** to be told off by sb. **-3.** *loc:* **sossegar o** ~ *fam* to calm down.

pitonisa [pitoˈniza] f fortune teller.

pitoresco, ca [pitoˈreʃku, ka] <> *adj* picturesque. <> m attraction.

pituitária [pitujˈtaria] f *ANAT* pituitary.

pivete [pi'vɛtʃi] *m* child thief.

pivô [pi'vo] *m* -**1.** [de dente] pivot. -**2.** *fig* [suporte] pivot. -**3.** *fig* [agente principal] central figure. -**4.** [jogador] centre.

pixaim [pi∫a'ĩ] (*pl* -ns) ◇ *adj* frizzy. ◇ *m* frizzy hair.

pixote [pi'∫ɔtʃi] *m* small child.

pizza ['pitsal *f* pizza.

pizzaria [pitsa'rial *f* pizzeria.

plá [plal *m*: **ter** *ou* **bater um** ~ **com alguém** to have a chat with sb.

placa ['plakal *f* -**1.** [ger] plaque. -**2.** [lâmina] sheet. -**3.** [aviso] sign; ~ **de sinalização** road sign. -**4.** AUTO number plate *UK*, license plate *US*; ~ **fria** false number plate. -**5.** COMPUT & ELECTRON board; ~ **de vídeo** video card. -**6.** [na pele] blotch.

placa-mãe ['plakamãj] (*pl* **placas-mãe** *ou* **placas-mães**) *f* COMPUT motherboard.

placar [pla'ka(x)] *m* -**1.** [escore] score. -**2.** [marcador] scoreboard.

placebo [pla'sebul *m* placebo.

placenta [pla'sẽntal *f* ANAT placenta.

placidez [plasi'deʒ] *f* quietness.

plácido, da ['plasidu, dal *adj* -**1.** [pessoa, olhar, semblante] placid. -**2.** [lugar, dia, vida] quiet.

plagiador, ra [plaʒja'do(x), ral *m, f* plagiarist.

plagiar [16] [pla'ʒja(x)] *vt* to plagiarize.

plagiário, ria [ju, pla'ʒjarju, rjal *m, f* plagiarist.

plágio ['plaʒjul *m* plagiarism.

plaina ['plãjnal *f* [ferramenta] plane.

planador [plana'do(x)] (*pl* -es) *m* glider.

planalto [pla'nawtul *m* plateau.

➤ **Planalto** *m* [palácio presidencial] president's office.

planar [4] [pla'na(x)] *vi* to glide.

planejador, ra [planeʒa'do(x), ral *m, f* planner.

planejamento [planeʒa'mẽntul *m* planning; ~ **familiar** family planning.

planejar [4] [plane'ʒa(x)] *vt* -**1.** [ger] to plan. -**2.** ARQUIT to design.

planeta [pla'netal *m* planet.

planetário, a [plane'tarjul *adj* planetary.

➤ **planetário** *m* planetarium.

plangente [plãn'ʒẽntʃil *adj* plaintive.

planície [pla'nisjil *f* plain.

planificar [12] [planifi'ka(x)] *vt* -**1.** [ger] to plan out. -**2.** [tornar plano] to level.

planilha [pla'niʎa] *f* -**1.** [formulário] table. -**2.** COMPUT spreadsheet.

plano, na ['plãnu, nal ◇ *adj* -**1.** [superfície] flat. -**2.** [liso] smooth. ◇ *m* -**1.** [ger] plan; ~ **piloto** outline plan. -**2.** [superfície plana] level surface. -**3.** [posição]: **em primeiro/segundo** ~ in the foreground/background; **para ela isso fica em segundo** ~ *fig* for her this takes second place. -**4.** [nível] level. -**5.** [seguro]: ~ **de saúde** health plan. -**6.** GEOM plane.

planta ['plãntal *f* -**1.** BIOL plant. -**2.** ANAT: ~ **do pé** sole of the foot. -**3.** ARQUIT plan.

plantação [plãnta'sãwl *m* -**1.** [ato] planting. -**2.** [terreno] plantation. -**3.** [produtos] crops (*pl*).

plantado, da [plãn'tadu, dal *adj* planted; **deixar alguém** ~ **em algum lugar** to leave sb standing somewhere.

plantão [plãn'tãwl (*pl* -ões) *m* -**1.** [serviço - diurno] duty; [- noturno] night duty; **estar de** ~ to be on duty; **médico de** ~ duty doctor. -**2.** [plantonista] person on duty.

plantar [4] [plãn'ta(x)] *vt* -**1.** [planta, árvore] to plant. -**2.** [semear] to sow. -**3.** [fincar] to drive in. -**4.** *fig* [estabelecer] to establish. -**5.** [incutir] to inspire. -**6.** [pôr] to set up.

➤ **plantar-se** *vp* [pôr-se] to remain.

plantões [plãn'tõj∫] *pl* ▷ plantão.

plantonista [plãnto'ni∫tal *mf* person on duty.

plaqueta [pla'ketal *f* -**1.** [placa pequena] small plaque, plaquette. -**2.** AUTO licensing badge. -**3.** COMPUT chip.

plasma ['plaʒmal *m* plasma.

plasmar [4] [plaʒ'ma(x)] *vt* to shape.

plástico, ca ['pla∫tʃiku, kal *adj* plastic.

➤ **plástico** *m* [matéria] plastic; **de** ~ plastic.

➤ **plástica** *f* -**1.** [cirurgia] plastic surgery; **fazer plástica** to have plastic surgery. -**2.** [corpo] build.

plastificado, da [pla∫tʃifi'kadu, dal *adj* laminated.

plastificar [12] [pla∫tʃifi'ka(x)] *vt* to laminate.

plataforma [plata'fɔxmal *f* -**1.** [ger] platform; ~ **de exploração de petróleo** oil rig; ~ **de lançamento** launch pad. -**2.** GEOGR shelf.

platéia [pla'tɛjal *f* -**1.** [espaço] stalls (*pl*) *UK*, orchestra *US*. -**2.** [público] audience.

platina [pla'tʃinal *f* [metal] platinum.

platinado, da [platʃi'nadu, dal *adj* platinum blond (antes de subst).

➤ **platinado** *m* AUTO contact point.

platô [pla'tol *m* plateau.

platônico, ca [pla'toniku, kal *adj* platonic.

plausível [plaw'zivɛwl (*pl* -eis) *adj* [aceitável] plausible.

playback [plej'bɛkil *m* MÚS playback.

playboy [plej'bɔjl *m* playboy.

playground [plej'grawndʒil *m* playground.

plebe ['plɛbil *f* common people.

plebeu, béia [ple'bew, bɛjal ◇ *adj* plebeian. ◇ *m, f* plebeian.

plebiscito [plebi'situl *m* plebiscite.

plêiade ['plejadʒil *f* [reunião] soirée.

pleitear [15] [plej'tʃja(x)] *vt* -**1.** [diligenciar] to strive for. -**2.** JUR to contest. -**3.** [concorrer a] to compete for.

pleito ['plejtul *m* -**1.** JUR legal dispute, lawsuit. -**2.** [eleição]: ~ **(eleitoral)** election.

plenamente [‚plena'mẽntʃil *adv* fully.

plenária [ple'narial *f* plenary (session).

plenário [ple'narjul *m* -**1.** [assembléia] plenary session. -**2.** [local] chamber.

plenipotenciário, ria [plenipotẽn'sjarju, rjal ◇ *adj* plenipotentiary. ◇ *m, f* plenipotentiary.

plenitude [pleni'tudʒil *f* fulfilment.

pleno, na ['plenu, nal *adj* -**1.** [cheio]: ~ **de** full of.

- **2.** [total] complete; **em plena luz do dia** in broad daylight; **em plena rua** smack in the middle of the street; **em plena forma** on top form; **em ~ verão** in high summer; **~s poderes** full powers.

pleonasmo [pljo'naʒmul] *m* pleonasm.

pletora [ple'tɔral] *f fig* plethora.

pleurisia [plewri'zial] *f* pleurisy.

plissado, da [pli'sadu, dal] *adj* pleated.

plugado, da [plu'gadu, dal] *adj* - **1.** [aparelho] plugged. - **2.** [pessoa]: **passar o dia ~ no computador** to spend the day glued to the computer.

plugar [plu'ga(x)l *vt* to plug.

plug-in ['plugĩn] *m* COMPUT plug-in.

plugue ['plugil *m* plug.

pluma ['plumal *f* - **1.** [de ave] feather. - **2.** [para escrever] quill. - **3.** [adorno] plume.

plumagem [plu'maʒẽl *f* plumage.

plural [plu'rawl (*pl* -ais) <> *adj* plural. <> *m* plural.

pluralidade [plurali'dadʒil *f* - **1.** [diversidade] diversity. - **2.** [maioria] majority.

pluralismo [plura'liʒmul *m* - **1.** [diversidade] diversity. - **2.** POL pluralism.

pluralista [plura'liʃtal *adj* - **1.** [diverso] diverse. - **2.** POL pluralist.

Plutão [plu'tãwl *n* Pluto.

plutocracia [plutokra'sial *f* plutocracy.

plutocrata [pluto'kratal *mf* plutocrat.

plutônio [plu'tonjul *m* plutonium.

pluvial [plu'vjawl (*pl* -ais) *adj* pluvial, rain (antes de subst).

pluviométrico, ca [pluvio'mɛtriku, kal *adj* rainfall (antes de subst).

PM (*abrev de* **Polícia Militar**) *f* military police.

PMDB (*abrev de* **Partido do Movimento Democrático Brasileiro**) *m* Brazilian Party for Democratic Movement, *the largest party of the centre*.

PNB (*abrev de* **Produto Nacional Bruto**) *m* GNP.

pneu [pi'newl *m* - **1.** AUTO tyre *UK*, tire *US*; **~ sobressalente** spare tyre *UK*, spare tire *US*. - **2.** *fam* [gordura] spare tyre *UK*, spare tire *US*.

pneumático, ca [pinew'matʃiku, kal *adj* pneumatic.

➡ **pneumático** *m* [pneu] tyre *UK*, tire *US*.

pneumonia [pinewmu'nial *f* pneumonia.

pó ['pɔl *m* - **1.** [poeira] dust; **tirar o ~ de algo** to dust sthg. - **2.** [substância pulverizada] powder; **em ~** powdered. - **3.** [pó-de-arroz] face powder. - **4.** *fam* [cocaína] snow.

pô [pol *interj* - **1.** *fam* [mostrando irritação] damn it! - **2.** [mostrando surpresa] blimey! *UK*, gee whiz! *US*.

pobre ['pɔbril <> *adj* - **1.** [ger] poor. - **2.** [escasso]: **~ de/em algo** lacking in sthg. - **3.** (antes do subst) [digno de pena] poor. <> *m* [pessoa] poor person; **os ~s** the poor.

pobre-diabo [,pɔbri'dʒjabul (*pl* **pobres-diabos**) *m* poor devil.

pobretão, tona [pobre'tãw, tonal (*mpl* -**ões**, *fpl* -**s**) *m*, *f* - **1.** [pessoa muito pobre] pauper. - **2.** *euf* poor thing.

pobreza [po'brezal *m* - **1.** [miséria] poverty. - **2.** [escassez]: **~ de** *ou* **em algo** lack of sthg; **~ de espírito** simplicity.

poça ['pɔsal *f*: **~ (d'água)** puddle; **~ de sangue** pool of blood.

poção [po'sãwl (*pl* -**ões**) *f* potion.

pocilga [po'siwgal *f* - **1.** [chiqueiro] pigsty. - **2.** *fig* [lugar imundo] hovel.

poço ['posul *f* - **1.** [cavidade] well; **~ de petróleo** oil well; **ir ao fundo do ~** *fig* to sink to the depths of despair. - **2.** [qualidade]: **ser um ~ de algo** *fig* to be a fount of sthg.

poda ['pɔdal *f* - **1.** [ato] pruning. - **2.** [época] pruning season.

podadeira [poda'dejral *f* pruning knife.

podar [4] [po'da(x)l *vt* to prune.

pó-de-arroz [,pɔdʒja'xoʃl (*pl* **pós-de-arroz**) *m* face powder.

poder [36] [po'de(x)l <> *m* - **1.** [político, influência] power; **estar no ~** to be in power; **~ de compra** purchasing power; **não tenho ~ nenhum** I'm powerless. - **2.** [possessão] power; **estar em ~ de alguém** to be in sb's power; **ter em seu ~ algo** to have sthg within one's power. <> *v aux* - **1.** [ser capaz de]: **~ fazer algo** to be able to do sthg; **posso fazê-lo** I can do it; **posso ajudar?** can I help?, may I help?; **você podia tê-lo feito antes** you could have done it earlier; **não posso mais!** [em relação a cansaço] I've had enough!; [em relação a comida] I'm full! - **2.** [estar autorizado para]: **~ fazer algo** to be allowed to do sthg; **posso fumar?** may I smoke?; **você não pode estacionar aqui** you can't park here; **não pude sair ontem** I wasn't allowed (to go) out yesterday. - **3.** [ser capaz moralmente] can; **não podemos magoar o gato** we can't hurt the cat. - **4.** [exprime possibilidade]: **você podia ter vindo de ônibus** you could have come by bus; **cuidado que você pode se machucar!** be careful, you might hurt yourself! - **5.** [exprime indignação, queixa]: **não pode ser!** this is outrageous!; **você podia ter nos avisado** you could have warned us!; **pudera!** I wish! <> *v impess* [ser possível]: **pode não ser verdade** it might not be true; **pode acontecer a qualquer um** it could happen to anybody; **pode ser que chova** it might rain.

➡ **poder com** *v* + *prep* - **1.** [suportar] to bear; **não posso com mentirosos** I cannot bear liars. - **2.** [rival, adversário] to bear. - **3.** [peso] to carry; **você não pode com tanto peso** you can't carry all that weight.

poderio [pode'riwl *m* power.

poderoso, sa [pode'rozu, sal *adj* - **1.** [influente] powerful. - **2.** [eficaz] powerful.

➡ **poderosos** *mpl*: **os ~** the powers that be.

pódio ['pɔdʒjul *m* podium.

podre ['podril <> *adj* - **1.** [ger] rotten. - **2.** *fig* [corrupto] corrupt. - **3.** *fig* [cheio]: **estou ~ (de cansaço)** I am dog-tired; **~ de gripe** full of flu; **~ de rico** filthy rich. <> *m* - **1.** [parte]: **o ~ da maçã** the bad part of the apple. - **2.** *fig* [defeito] dark secret.

podridão [podri'dãw] (*pl*-ões) *f*-**1.** [estado de podre] decay. -**2.** *fig* [corrupção] corruption.
poeira ['pwejra] *f* dust; ~ **radioativa** fallout.
poeirento, ta [pwej'rẽntu, ta] *adj* dusty.
poema ['pwema] *m* poem.
poente ['pwẽntʃi] <> *adj* [sol] setting. <> *m* -**1.** [ocidente] west. -**2.** [do sol] sunset.
poesia [pwi'zia] *f* -**1.** [arte] poetry. -**2.** [poema] poem. -**3.** [encanto] charm.
poeta, tisa ['pwɛta, tʃiza] *m*, *f* poet.
poético, ca ['pwɛtʃiku, ka] *adj* poetic.
 poética *f* ARTE poetics (*sg*).
poetizar [4] [pwetʃi'za(x)] <> *vi* [fazer versos] to write poetry. <> *vt* [tornar poético] to poeticize.
pogrom [po'grõ] *m* pogrom.
pois ['pojʃ] *conj* -**1.** [portanto] therefore. -**2.** [mas] well. -**3.** [porque] as.
 pois bem *loc adv* well then.
 pois então *loc adv* well then.
 pois é *loc adv* indeed.
 pois não <> *loc adv* [em loja, restaurante]: ~ não? can I help you? <> *interj* of course!
 pois sim *interj*: ~ **sim!** certainly not!, yeah right!
polaco, ca [po'laku, ka] <> *adj* Polish. <> *m*, *f* Pole.
 polaco *m* [língua] Polish.
polainas [po'lãjnaʃ] *fpl* gaiters.
polar [po'la(x)] *adj* polar.
polaridade [polari'dadʒi] *f* polarity.
polarizar [4] [polari'za(x)] *vt* to polarize.
polca ['powka] *f* polka.
polegada [pole'gada] *f* finch.
polegar [pole'ga(x)] (*pl*-es) *m* thumb.
poleiro [po'lejru] *m* perch.
polêmico, ca [po'lemiku, ka] *adj* controversial.
 polêmica *f* controversy.
polemista [pole'miʃta] *adj* argumentative.
polemizar [4] [polemi'za(x)] *vi*: ~ **sobre algo** to debate on sthg.
pólen ['polẽ] *m* pollen.
polenta [po'lẽnta] *f* polenta.
polia [po'lial] *f* pulley.
poliamida [polja'mida] *f* polyamide.
polichinelo [poliʃi'nɛlu] *m* Mr Punch.
polícia [po'lisja] <> *f* [corporação] police, police force; ~ **de choque** riot police; ~ **federal** federal police; ~ **militar** state police (force); ~ **rodoviária** traffic police. <> *mf* [policial] police officer.
policial [poli'sjaw] (*pl*-ais) <> *adj* police (*antes de subst*). <> *mf* police officer.
policiamento [polisja'mẽntu] *m* policing.
policiar [16] [poli'sja(x)] *vt* -**1.** [vigiar] to police. -**2.** [controlar] to control.
 policiar-se *vp* [controlar-se] to control o.s.
policlínica [poli'klinika] *f* general hospital.
policultura [polikuw'tural] *f* mixed farming.
polidez [poli'deʒ] *f* [cortesia] politeness.
polido, da [po'lidu, da] *adj* -**1.** [cortês] polite. -**2.** [liso] polished. -**3.** [lustroso] shiny.

poliéster [po'ljɛʃte(x)] *m* polyester.
poliestireno [poljeʃtʃi'renu] *m* polystyrene.
polietileno [poljetʃi'lenul] *m* polythene.
poligamia [poli'gamia] *f* polygamy.
polígamo, ma [po'ligamu, ma] *adj* polygamous.
poliglota [poli'glota] <> *adj* polyglot. <> *m* polyglot.
polígono [po'ligonul] *m* GEOM polygon.
polimento [poli'mẽntu] *m* -**1.** [lustração] polishing. -**2.** *fig* [finura] refinement.
polinização [poliniza'sãw] (*pl*-ões) *f* pollination.
polinizar [4] [polini'za(x)] <> *vt* to pollinate. <> *vi* to pollinate.
polinômio [poli'nomju] *m* MAT polynomial.
poliomielite [poljo'mjelitʃi] *f* MED polio(myelitis).
pólipo ['polipul] *m* MED polyp.
polir [60] [po'li(x)] *vt* -**1.** [ger] to polish. -**2.** *fig* [aprimorar - pessoa] to refine; [- linguagem] to polish up.
polissílabo [poli'silabul] (*f*-**ba**) [ba] *adj* polysyllabic.
 polissílabo *m* polysyllable.
politécnica [poli'teknika] *f* polytechnic.
política [po'litʃika] *f* => **político**.
politicagem [politʃi'kaʒẽl] *f* politicking.
político, ca [po'litʃiku, ka] *adj* -**1.** POL political. -**2.** *fig* [hábil] astute.
 político *m* politician.
 política *f* -**1.** [ciência] politics (*pl*). -**2.** [programa] policy; **política econômica** economic policy; **política de boa vizinhança** good neighbour policy *UK*, good neighbor policy *US*. -**3.** *fig* [habilidade] astuteness.
politiqueiro, ra [politʃi'kejru, ra] *pej* <> *adj* politicking. <> *m*, *f* political wheeler-dealer.
politização [politʃiza'sãw] (*pl*-ões) *f* politicization.
politizar [4] [politʃi'za(x)] *vt* to politicize.
 politizar-se *vp* to become politically aware.
polivalente [poliva'lẽntʃil] *adj* -**1.** [versátil] versatile. -**2.** MED polyvalent.
pólo ['polu] *m* -**1.** [ger] pole. -**2.** *fig* [extremo] side. -**3.** ASTRON: ~ **magnético** magnetic pole. -**4.** [concentração] hub; ~ **petroquímico** petrochemicals complex. -**5.** ESP polo; ~ **aquático** water polo.
Polônia [po'lonja] *n* Poland.
polpa ['powpa] *f* pulp.
polpudo, da [pow'pudu, da] *adj* -**1.** [fruta] fleshy. -**2.** [vultuoso] sizeable.
poltrão, ona [pow'trãw, ɔna] (*mpl*-ões, *fpl*-s) *m*, *f* coward.
poltrona [pow'trona] *f* armchair.
poluente [po'lwẽntʃil] <> *adj* pollutant. <> *m* pollutant.
poluição [poluj'sãw] *f* pollution.
poluidor, ra [poluj'do(x), ra] *adj* polluting.
poluir [74] [po'lwi(x)] *vt* -**1.** [sujar] to pollute. -**2.** *fig* [corromper] to corrupt.
polvilhar [4] [powvi'ʎa(x)] *vt* -**1.** [cobrir de pó] to powder. -**2.** [salpicar] to sprinkle.
polvilho [pow'viʎu] *m* -**1.** [pó] powder. -**2.** [farinha] manioc flour.

polvo [ˈpowvu] *m* octopus.

pólvora [ˈpɔwvora] *f* gunpowder; **descobrir a ~** *fig irôn* to do sthg highly original.

polvorosa [powvoˈrɔza] *f*: **em ~** [agitado] in a flap; [desarrumado] in a mess.

pomada [poˈmada] *f* ointment.

pomar [poˈma(x)] (*pl* -es) *m* orchard.

pombo, ba [ˈpõnbu, ba] *m*, *f* dove, pigeon.

➡ pomba *interj* for heaven's sake!

pombo-correio [ˌpõnbukoˈxeju] (*pl* **pombos-correios**) *m* -1. [ave] carrier pigeon. -2. *fig* [pessoa] go-between.

pomo [ˈpomu] *m* pome; **~ de discórdia** bone of contention.

pomo-de-Adão [ˌpomudʒjaˈdãw] (*pl* **pomos-de-Adão**) *m* Adam's apple.

pompa [ˈpõnpa] *f* splendour.

pomposo, osa [põnˈpozu, ɔza] *adj* ostentatious.

ponche [ˈpõnʃi] *m* punch.

poncheira [põnˈʃejra] *f* punchbowl.

poncho [ˈpõnʃu] *m* poncho.

ponderação [põnderaˈsãw] *f* -1. [reflexão] reflection. -2. [prudência] care.

ponderado, da [põnˈderadu, da] *adj* cautious.

ponderar [4] [põnˈdera(x)] <> *vi* -1. [refletir] to reflect. -2. [argumentar] to hold forth. <> *vt* -1. [avaliar] to weigh up. -2. [considerar] to consider.

pônei [ˈponej] *m* pony.

ponta [ˈpõnta] *f* -1. [extremidade] end; **na ~ do pé** on tiptoe; **na ~ do dedo** at one's fingertips. -2. [bico] point. -3. [canto] corner. -4. [vértice] apex. -5. *fig* [quantidade]: **estou com uma ~ de fome** I'm a touch hungry. -6. [de cigarro] cigarette end. -7. *CINE & TEATRO*: **fazer uma ~** to have a walk-on part. -8. *COM*: **~ de estoque** excess stock. -9. *GEOGR*: **~ de terra** point. -10. *loc*: **saber na ~ da língua** to have on the tip of one's tongue.

ponta-cabeça [ˌpõntakaˈbesa] *f*: **de ~** head first.

pontada [põnˈtada] *f* -1. [dor] twinge. -2. [ferroada] sting.

ponta-de-lança [ˌpõntadʒiˈlãnsa] (*pl* **pontas-de-lança**) *mf FUT* attacker.

ponta-direita [ˌpõntadʒiˈrejta] (*pl* **pontas-direitas**) *mf FUT* right-winger.

ponta-esquerda [ˌpõntajʃˈkexda] (*pl* **pontas-esquerdas**) *mf FUT* left-winger.

pontal [põnˈtaw] (*pl* -ais) *m* [de terra] promontory.

pontão [põnˈtãw] (*pl* -ões) *m* [plataforma] pontoon.

pontapé [põntaˈpɛ] *m* -1. [chute] kick; **dar um ~ em alguém** to kick sb. -2. *fig* [rejeição]: **ele levou um ~ da namorada** his girlfriend kicked him out.

pontaria [põntaˈria] *f* aim.

ponte [ˈpõntʃi] *f* -1. [ger] bridge; **~ levadiça** drawbridge; **~ suspensa** *ou* **pênsil** suspension bridge. -2. *AERON*: **~ aérea** air lift. -3. *MED*: **~ de safena** (heart) bypass operation.

pontear [15] [põnˈtʃja(x)] *vt* -1. [pontilhar] to dot. -2. [dar pontos] to sew.

ponteira [põnˈtejra] *f* tip.

ponteiro [põnˈtejru] *m* -1. [de velocímetro] pointer. -2. [de bússola] needle. -3. [de relógio] hand.

pontiagudo, da [põntʃjaˈgudu, da] *adj* pointed.

pontificar [12] [põntʃifiˈka(x)] *vi* to pontificate.

pontífice [põnˈtʃifisi] *m* pope.

pontilhado, da [põntʃiˈʎadu, da] <> *adj* dotted. <> *m* [conjunto de pontos] dotted line.

pontilhar [4] [põntʃiˈʎa(x)] *vt* to dot.

pontinha [põnˈtʃiɲa] *f*: **estar/ficar com uma ~ de inveja de algo/alguém** to feel a little envious of sthg/sb.

ponto [ˈpõntul] *m* -1. [ger] point; **~ final** terminus; **~ de ônibus** bus stop; **~ de táxi** taxi rank; **~ pacífico** established fact. -2. [costura, operação] stitch; **~ de meia** stocking stitch; **~ de tricô** garter stitch; **dar ~s** to put in stitches. -3. [sinal] spot. -4. [pontuação]: **~ (final)** full stop *UK*, period *US*; **dois ~s** colon; **~ de interrogação/exclamação** question/exclamation mark. -5. [mancha] mark. -6. [livro de presença] register; **assinar o ~** to sign in; **~ facultativo** optional day off. -7. [de calda] consistency. -8. [matéria escolar] topic. -9. *fig* [fim]: **pôr um ~ final em algo** to put and end to sthg. -10. *MÚS* (religious) chant. -11. *GEOGR*: **~ cardeal** cardinal point. -12. *AUTO*: **~ morto** neutral. -13. [espírit] spirit. -14. [boca-de-fumo] drugs den. -15. [traço]: **~ fraco** weak point. -16. *loc*: **dormir no ~** to miss the boat; **entregar os ~s** to give up; **não dar ~ sem nó** to look after number one.

➡ a ponto de *loc adv* on the point of.

pontocom [põntukõ] *adj ECON*: **empresa ~** dotcom company.

ponto-de-venda [ˌpõntudʒiˈvenda] (*pl* **pontos-de-venda**) *m COM* outlet.

pontões [põnˈtõjʃ] *pl* ⊳ **pontão**.

ponto-e-vírgula [ˌpontwiˈvixgula] (*pl* **ponto-e-vírgulas**) *m* semicolon.

pontuação [põntwaˈsãw] (*pl* -ões) *f* punctuation.

pontual [põnˈtwaw] (*pl* -ais) *adj* punctual.

pontualidade [põntwaliˈdadʒi] *f* punctuality.

pontuar [4] [põnˈtwa(x)] <> *vi* to punctuate. <> *vt* to punctuate.

pontudo, da [põnˈtudu, da] *adj* pointed.

poodle [ˈpudow] *m* poodle.

pool [puw] *m* pool.

POP (*abrev de* **Post Office Protocol**) *m* POP.

popa [ˈpopa] *f* stern.

população [populaˈsãw] (*pl* -ões) *f* population; **~ operária** working population; **~ escolar** school population.

populacional [populasjoˈnaw] (*pl* -ais) *adj* population (*antes de subst*).

popular [popuˈla(x)] (*pl* -es) <> *adj* popular. <> *m* [homem da rua] ordinary person.

popularidade [populariˈdadʒi] *f* popularity.

popularizar [4] [populariˈza(x)] *vt* to popularize.

➡ popularizar-se *vp* to become popular.

populismo [popuˈliʒmu] *m POL* populism.

populista [popuˈliʃta] *adj* populist.

populoso, osa [popuˈlozu, ɔza] *adj* populous.

pôquer ['poke(x)] *m* poker.

por [po(x)] *prep* **-1.** [indica causa] because of, due to; **foi ~ sua causa** it was your fault; **~ falta de fundos** due to lack of funds; **~ hábito** through force of habit. **-2.** [indica objetivo] for; **lutar ~ algo** to fight for sthg. **-3.** [indica meio, modo, agente] by; **foi escrito pela Cristina** it was written by Cristina; **~ correio/fax** by post/fax; **~ escrito** in writing; **~ avião** [carta] (by) air mail. **-4.** [relativo a tempo] for; **ele partiu ~ duas semanas** he went away for two weeks. **-5.** [relativo a lugar] through; **entramos no Brasil pelo Paraguai** we crossed into Brazil via Paraguay; **está ~ aí** it's around there somewhere; **~ onde você vai?** which way are you going?; **vamos ~ aqui** we're going this way. **-6.** [relativo a troca, preço] for; **paguei apenas 20 reais ~ este casaco** I only paid 20 reals for this coat; **troquei o carro velho ~ um novo** I exchanged my old car for a new one. **-7.** [indica distribuição] per; **25 ~ cento** 25 per cent; **são 100 reais ~ dia/mês** it's 100 reals per day/month. **-8.** [em locuções]: **~ que** why; **~ que (é que) ...?** why (is it that) ...?; **~ mim tudo bem!** that's fine by me!

pôr [45] ['po(x)] *vt* **-1.** [ger] to put; **~ a mesa** to set the table; **~ a roupa** to put on clothes; **~ defeito em tudo** to find fault with everything; **~ a culpa em alguém** to put the blame on sb; **~ o dedo na ferida** *fig* to touch a raw nerve. **-2.** [incutir]: **não lhe ponha medo!** don't frighten him! **-3.** [guardar] to keep. **-4.** [desovar] to lay.
◆ **pôr-se** *vp* **-1.** [colocar-se] to stand; **~-se de pé** to stand up. **-2.** [sol] to set. **-3.** [começar]: **~-se a fazer algo** to start doing sthg; **~-se a caminho** to set off.

porão [po'rãw] (*pl* -ões) *f* **-1.** [de navio] hold. **-2.** [de casa] basement.

porca ['poxka] *f* **-1.** *ZOOL* sow. **-2.** [parafuso] nut.

porcalhão, lhona [poxka'ʎãw, ʎona] (*mpl* -ões, *fpl* -s) <> *adj* **-1.** [imundo] filthy. **-2.** [que faz sujeira] messy. **-3.** [que trabalha mal] bungling. <> *m, f* **-1.** [imundo] filthy person. **-2.** [quem faz sujeira] messy person. **-3.** [quem trabalha mal] bungler.

porção [pox'sãw] (*pl* -ões) *f* [parte] portion; **uma ~ de** a portion of; [grande quantidade] a lot of.

porcaria [poxka'ria] <> *adj* [sem valor] rubbishy. <> *f* **-1.** [imundície] filth. **-2.** *fig* [coisa malfeita] piece of junk. **-3.** *fig* [coisa sem valor] rubbish.

porcelana [poxse'lãna] *f* porcelain.

porcentagem [poxsẽn'taʒẽ] (*pl* -ns) *f* percentage.

porco, ca ['poxku, ka] <> *adj* **-1.** [suja] dirty. **-2.** [grosseiro] coarse. **-3.** [malfeito] shoddy. <> *m, f* **-1.** *ZOOL* pig. **-2.** *CULIN* pork. **-3.** [pessoa] *fam* pig.

porções [pox'sõjʃ] *pl* ▷ **porção.**

pôr-do-sol [ˌpoxdu'sɔw] (*pl* pores-do-sol) *m* sunset.

porco-espinho [ˌpoxkwiʃ'piɲu] (*pl* porcos-espinhos) *m* porcupine.

porém [po'rẽj] <> *conj* [contudo] but, however. <> *m* [obstáculo] snag.

pormenor [poxme'nɔ(x)] (*pl* -es) *m* detail.

pormenorizar [4] [poxmenori'za(x)] *vt* to detail.

pornô [pox'no] <> *adj inv fam* porn. <> *m CINE* porn film.

pornochanchada [poxnoʃãn'ʃada] *m CINE* soft porn film *UK*, soft porn movie *US*.

pornografia [poxnogra'fia] *f* pornography.

pornográfico, ca [poxno'grafiku, ka] *adj* pornographic.

poro ['pɔru] *m* pore.

porões [po'rõjʃ] *pl* ▷ **porão.**

pororoca [poro'rɔka] *f* [onda] bore.

POROROCA

Word of Tupi origin, meaning 'thundering crash'; it describes the encounter of the waters of the Amazon with the Atlantic Ocean. Creating waves over 5m high and destroying everything in its passage, this phenomenon occurs mainly in March and is one of the main tourist attractions in Amazonia.

---

poroso, osa [po'rozu, ɔza] *adj* porous.

porquanto [pox'kwãntu] *conj* since.

porque [pux'ke] *conj* because; **ela trabalha ~ precisa** she works because she needs to; **~ sim** just because.

porquê [pux'ke] *m*: **o ~** the reason (for); **não entendo o ~ dessa atitude** I don't understand the reason for that attitude.

porquinho-da-Índia [pox.kiɲuda'ĩndʒja] (*pl* porquinhos-da-Índia) *m* guinea pig.

porra ['pɔxa] <> *f vulg* [esperma] spunk. <> *interj vulg* [exprime irritação] fucking hell!; **mas que ~!** fuck!

porrada [po'xada] *mfam* *f* **-1.** [pancada]: **ele deu uma ~ com o carro no muro** he smashed the car into the wall; **o garçom levou uma ~ do bêbado** the waiter took one hell of a beating from the drunkard. **-2.** [quantidade]: **uma ~ de loads of. -3.** *fig* [revés] fuck-up.

porra-louca [ˌpoxa'loka] (*pl* porras-loucas) *fam* <> *adj* crazy. <> *mf* nutter.

porre ['pɔxi] *fam m* **-1.** [bebedeira] booze-up; **estar/ficar de ~** to be plastered; **tomar um ~** to get a skinful. **-2.**: **ser um ~** [pessoa, festa] to be a drag.

porretada [poxe'tada] *m* beating.

porrete [po'xetʃi] *m* club.

porta ['pɔxta] *f* **-1.** [peça] door; **~ corrediça** sliding door; **~ dos fundos** back door; **~ da frente/da rua** front/street door; **~ giratória** revolving door. **-2.** *fig* [possibilidade, saída] opportunity. **-3.** *COMPUT*: **~ paralela** parallel port; **~ serial** serial port.

porta-aviões [ˌpɔxta'vjõjʃ] *m inv* aircraft carrier.

porta-bandeira [ˌpɔxtabãn'dejra] (*pl* porta-bandeiras) *mf* standard-bearer.

portador, ra [poxta'do(x), ra] (*mpl* -es, *fpl* -s) <> *adj* **-1.** [de vírus, doença] carrying. **-2.** [de notícias] bearing. <> *m, f* **-1.** [de bagagem, AIDS] carrier.

-2. [de títulos, letras de câmbio, notícias] bearer; **ao ~** [cheque, ação] to the bearer.

porta-estandarte [ˌpɔxtiʃtãn'daxtʃil] (pl **porta-estandartes**) mf standard-bearer.

porta-guardanapos [ˌpɔxtagwaxda'napuʃl m inv napkin holder.

porta-jóias [ˌpɔxta'ʒɔjaʃl m inv jewellery box.

portal [pox'tawl (pl **-ais**) m **-1.** [pórtico] doorway. **-2.** COMPUT portal.

porta-luvas [ˌpɔxta'luvaʃl m inv AUTO glove compartment.

porta-malas [ˌpɔxta'malaʃl m inv AUTO boot UK, trunk US.

porta-moedas [ˌpɔxta'mwɛdaʃl m inv [porta-níqueis] purse.

portanto [pox'tãntul conj therefore.

portão [pox'tãwl (pl **-ões**) m gate.

portar [4] [pox'ta(x)] vt [carregar] to carry.
➡ **portar-se** vp [comportar-se] to behave.

porta-retratos [ˌpɔxtaxe'tratuʃl m (inv) photo frame.

porta-revistas [ˌpɔxtaxe'viʃtaʃl m (inv) magazine rack.

portaria [poxta'rial f **-1.** [de edifício] entrance hall. **-2.** [documento oficial] order; **baixar uma ~** to issue a decree.

portátil [pox'tatʃiwl (pl **-eis**) adj portable.

porta-voz [ˌpɔxta'vɔjʃl (pl **porta-vozes**) mf spokesperson.

porte ['pɔrtʃil m **-1.** [transporte] carriage. **-2.** [preço] charge; **~ pago** post paid. **-3.** [postura] bearing. **-4.** [tamanho] scale; **de grande/médio/ pequeno ~** large/medium/small-sized. **-5.** [importância] stature; **de grande ~** of great stature. **-6.** [licença]: **~ de arma** gun permit.

porteiro, ra [pox'tejru, ral m, f[de edifício] caretaker UK, janitor US; **~ eletrônico** entryphone.
➡ **porteira** f[cancela] gate.

portento [pox'tẽntul m marvel.

portentoso, osa [poxtẽn'tozu, ɔzal adj marvellous.

portfolio [port'fɔljul m portfolio.

pórtico ['pɔxtʃikul m portico.

portinhola [poxtʃi'ɲɔlal f **-1.** [pequena porta] small door, trapdoor. **-2.** [postigo] window.

Port Louis [ˌpɔxtʃ'lujʃl n Port Louis.

Port Moresby [ˌpɔxtʃ'mɔreʒbil n Port Moresby.

porto ['poxtul m port; **~ de escala** port of call; **~ livre** freeport.

Porto Alegre [ˌpoxtwa'lɛgril n Porto Alegre.

portões [pox'tõjʃl pl ▷ **portão**.

Porto Príncipe [ˌpoxtu'prĩsipil n Port-au-Prince.

Porto Rico [ˌpoxtu'xikul n Puerto Rico.

Porto Velho [ˌpoxtu'vɛʎul n Porto Velho.

portuário, ria [pox'twarju, rjal <> adj port (antes de subst).<> m, f[funcionário] port official.

Portugal [poxtu'gawl n Portugal.

português, esa [poxtu'geʃ, ezal (mpl **-eses**, fpl **-s**) <> adj Portuguese. <> m, f Portuguese person.

➡ **português** m [língua] Portuguese.

portunhol [poxtu'ɲɔwl m mixture of Portuguese and Spanish.

porventura [poxvẽn'tural adv by chance; **se ~ você ...** if you happen to ...

porvir [pox'vi(x)l m future.

posar [4] [po'za(x)l vi **-1.** [fazer pose] to pose. **-2.** [bancar]: **~ de** to pose as.

pós-datado, da [ˌpɔjʃda'tadu, dal (mpl **-s**, fpl **-s**) adj post-dated.

pós-datar [ˌpɔjʃda'ta(x)l vt to postdate.

pose ['pɔzil f **-1.** [de modelo etc] pose. **-2.** pej [afetação] affectedness; **ela está com muita ~ desde sua promoção** she's full of airs and graces since being promoted; **fazer ~ de** to pretend to be.

pós-escrito [ˌpɔjʃiʃ'kritul (pl **pós-escritos**) m postscript, PS.

pós-graduação [ˌpɔjʃgradwa'sãwl (pl **pós-graduações**) f qualifying for a degree as a postgraduate UK or graduate US student.

pós-graduado, pós-graduada [ˌpɔjʃgra'-dwadu, dal (mpl **pós-graduados**, fpl **pós-graduadas**) <> adj postgraduate UK, graduate US. <> m, f postgraduate UK, graduate US.

pós-guerra [ˌpɔjʃ'gɛxal (pl **pós-guerras**) m post-war (antes de sust).

posição [pozi'sãwl (pl **-ões**) f **-1.** [ger] position; **tomar uma ~** to take a stand. **-2.** [arranjo] positioning.

posicionamento [pozisjona'mẽntul m **-1.** [maneira de colocar] positioning. **-2.** [opinião] position.

posicionar [4] [pozisjo'na(x)l vt **-1.** [ger] to position. **-2.** [funcionário] to place.
➡ **posicionar-se** vp **-1.** [ger] to take up position. **-2.** [opinar] to take a stand. **-3.** [tomar atitude] to make a stand.

positivista [pozitʃi'viʃtal <> adj positivist. <> mf positivist.

positivo, va [pozi'tʃivu, val adj positive.
➡ **positivo** <> m FOT positive. <> interj fam [sim] affirmative.

posologia [pozolo'ʒial f dosage.

pós-operatório, a [ˌpɔjʃopera'tɔrju, rjal (mpl **-s**, fpl **-s**) <> adj post-operative. <> m post-operative period.

pós-parto [ˌpɔjʃ'paxtul (pl **pós-partos**) m post-natal period.

pospor [45] [poʃ'po(x)l vt **-1.** [pôr depois] to put after. **-2.** [adiar] to postpone.

posposto, ta [poʃ'poʃtu, tal adj **-1.** [posto depois] put after. **-2.** [adiado] postponed.

possante [po'sãntʃil adj powerful.

posse ['pɔzil f **-1.** [de bens] ownership; **pessoa de ~s** person of means. **-2.** [ocupação] possession; **tomar ~ de** to take possession of. **-3.** [investidura] swearing-in; **cerimônia de ~** swearing-in ceremony; **tomar ~** to take office.
➡ **posses** fpl [bens] possessions.

posseiro, ra [po'sejru, ral m, f leaseholder.

possessão [pose'sãwl (pl **-ões**) f possession.

possessivo, va [pose'sivu, va] *adj* possessive.
➤ **possessivo** *m* GRAM possessive.
possesso, sa [po'sesu, sa] ◇ *adj* [furioso] enraged. ◇ *m, f* possessed person.
possibilidade [posibili'dadʒi] *f* -**1.** [gen] possibility. -**2.** [oportunidade] opportunity.
possibilitar [4] [posibili'ta(x)] *vt* to make possible.
possível [po'sivɛw] (*pl* -eis) ◇ *adj* possible. ◇ *m*: o ~ what is possible; **fazer o** ~ to do one's best.
possivelmente [posivew'mẽntʃi] *adv* possibly.
possuidor, ra [poswi'do(x), ra] *adj*: **ser** ~ **de** to be the owner of.
possuir [74] [po'swi(x)] *vt* [ter] to have.
posta ['pɔʃta] *f* [pedaço] piece; ~ **de peixe** piece of fish.
postal [poʃ'taw] (*pl* -ais) ◇ *adj* post, postage. ◇ *m* postcard.
postar [4] [poʃ'ta(x)] *vt* to post.
➤ **postar-se** *vp* to position o.s.
posta-restante [,poʃtaxeʃ'tãntʃi] (*pl* postas-restantes) *f* poste restante.
poste ['pɔʃtʃi] *m* -**1.** [haste] post. -**2.** ELECTR: ~ **de iluminação** lamp post; ~ **telegráfico** telegraph pole.
pôster ['poʃte(x)] (*pl* -es) *m* poster.
postergar [14] [poʃtex'ga(x)] *fml* *vt* -**1.** [adiar] to postpone. -**2.** [desprezar] to set aside.
posteridade [poʃteri'dadʒi] *f* posterity.
posterior [poʃte'rjo(x)] (*pl* -es) *adj* -**1.** [no tempo] later. -**2.** [traseiro] rear.
postiço, ça [poʃ'tʃisu, sa] *adj* false.
postigo [poʃ'tʃigu] *m* small door.
posto, ta ['poʃtu, 'pɔʃta] *pp* ⊳ **pôr**.
➤ **posto** *m* -**1.** [ger] post; ~ **de gasolina** petrol station *UK*, gas station *US*; ~ **de salvamento** first-aid post; ~ **de saúde** health centre *UK*, health center *US*. -**2.** [de polícia] station. -**3.** [diplomático] posting.
➤ **a postos** *loc adv* at the ready.
➤ **posto que** *loc conj* since.
posto-chave [,poʃtu'ʃavil] (*pl* postos-chave) *m* key position.
postulado [poʃtu'ladul] *m* assumption.
postulante [poʃtu'lãntʃi] ◇ *adj* candidate. ◇ *mf* applicant, candidate.
postular [4] [poʃtu'la(x)] *vt* -**1.** [pedir] to request. -**2.** [teorizar] to postulate. -**3.** JUR to apply for.
póstumo, ma ['pɔʃtumu, ma] *adj* posthumous.
postura [poʃ'tura] *f* -**1.** [ger] posture. -**2.** [municipal] position. -**3.** *fig* [atitude] point of view.
posudo, da [po'zudu, da] *adj* affected.
potássio [po'tasju] *m* potassium.
potável [po'tavɛw] (*pl* -eis) *adj*: **água** ~ drinking water.
pote ['pɔtʃi] *m* pot, jar.
potência [po'tẽnsja] *m* -**1.** [ger] power. -**2.** [sexual] potency.
potenciação [potẽnsia'sãw] (*pl* -ões) *f* [mat] exponentiation.

potencial [potẽn'sjaw] (*pl* -ais) ◇ *adj* potential. ◇ *m* potential; **o poder econômico em** ~ **do país é enorme** the country's potential economic power is great.
potencialidade [potẽnsjali'dadʒi] *f* [capacidade de realização] potencial.
potentado [potẽn'tadul] *m* potentate.
potente [po'tẽntʃi] *adj* powerful.
pot-pourri [pupu'xil] *m* pot-pourri.
potro ['potru] *m* colt.
pouca-vergonha [,pokavex'goɲa] (*pl* poucas-vergonhas) *f* -**1.** [ato] disgrace. -**2.** [falta de vergonha] shamelessness.
pouco, ca ['poku, ka] ◇ *adj* little; **de pouca importância** of little importance; **faz** ~ **tempo**, ~ **tempo (atrás)** a short time ago; (*pl*) few; **poucas pessoas** few people. ◇ *pron* little; (*pl*) few; **muito** ~**s** very few; ~**s** [pessoas] few; **dizer/ouvir poucas e boas** to tell/hear some home truths.
➤ **pouco** *m*: **um** ~ a little; **um** ~ **de** a little; **nem um** ~ **(de)** not at all; **aos** ~**s** gradually.
➤ **pouco** *adv* little; **dormi** ~ I hardly slept; **isso é** ~ **comum** that's uncommon, that's rare; **há** ~ a short time ago; **daqui a** ~, **dentro em** ~ shortly; **por** ~ **o carro não me atropelou** the car nearly ran me over; ~ **a** ~ little by little; **fazer** ~ **de** [zombar] to make fun of; [menosprezar] to belittle.
pouco-caso [,poku'kazul] *m* contempt; **ele fez** ~ **da minha história** he treated my story with contempt.
poupador, ra [popa'do(x), ra] *adj* thrifty.
poupança [po'pãnsa] *f* -**1.** [economia] saving. -**2.** [fundo]: **(caderneta de)** ~ savings account (book).
poupar [4] [po'pa(x)] ◇ *vt* -**1.** [economizar] to save. -**2.** [resguardar]: ~ **alguém (de algo)** to spare sb (from sthg). -**3.** [respeitar] to spare. ◇ *vi* [economizar] to save.
➤ **poupar-se** *vp* [eximir-se] to spare o.s.
pouquinho [po'kiɲu] *m*: **um** ~ **(de algo)** a little (sthg).
pouquíssimo, ma [po'kisimu, ma] *superl* ⊳ **pouco**.
pousada [po'zada] *f* -**1.** [hospedaria] inn. -**2.** [hospedagem] lodging.
pousar [4] [po'za(x)] ◇ *vi* -**1.** [aterrissar] to land. -**2.** [baixar] to settle. -**3.** [pernoitar] to spend the night. -**4.** [assentar] to rest. ◇ *vt* to put.
pouso ['pozul] *m* -**1.** [aterrissagem] landing; ~ **de emergência** emergency landing. -**2.** [lugar de descanso] bolt-hole.
povão [po'vãw] *m* hoi polloi (*pl*).
povaréu [pova'rɛw] *m* [multidão] crowd.
povo ['povul] *m* -**1.** [habitantes] people. -**2.** [multidão] crowd. -**3.** [família, amigos] family.
povoação [povwa'sãw] (*pl* -ões) *f* -**1.** settlement. -**2.** [aldeia] village. -**3.** [habitantes] population.
povoado, da [po'vwadu, da] ◇ *adj* populated. ◇ *m* [aldeia] village.
povoamento [povwa'mẽntul] *m* settlement.

povoar [20] [po'vwa(x)l *vt* to populate.

poxa ['poʃal *interj* gosh!

PPB (*abrev de* **Partido Progressista Brasileiro**) *m* Brazilian Progressive Party, *a right-wing party*.

PPS (*abrev de* **Partido Popular Socialista**) *m* Popular Socialist Party, *a centre-right party*.

PR (*abrev de* **Estado do Paraná**) *m State of Paraná*.

pra ['pral *fam* = **para, para a**.

praça ['prasal ⟨⟩ *f* -**1**. [largo] square. -**2**. [mercado financeiro] market. -**3**. *MIL*: ~ **de guerra** fortress. -**4**. [de touros] bull ring. ⟨⟩ *m MIL* [soldado] private (soldier).

pracinha [pra'siɲal *m Brazilian soldier in World War II*.

prado ['pradul *m* -**1**. [campo] meadow. -**2**. [hipódromo] racecourse.

pra-frente [ˌpra'frẽtʃil *adj inv fam* trendy.

praga ['pragal *f* -**1**. [ger] curse; **rogar uma** ~ **a alguém** to curse sb. -**2**. [doença] scourge. -**3**. *ZOOL* plague. -**4**. [pessoa chata] pest.

Praga ['pragal *n* Prague.

pragmático, ca [prag'matʃiku, kal *adj* pragmatic.

pragmatismo [pragma'tʃiʒmul *m* pragmatism.

praguejar [4] [prage'ʒa(x)l *vi*: ~ **(contra)** to curse (at).

praia ['prajal *f* beach.

prancha ['prãʃal *f* -**1**. [tábua] plank. -**2**. [de surfe] board. -**3**. *NÁUT* gangplank. -**4**. *FERRO* open wagon.

prancheta [prãˈʃetal *f* -**1**. [mesa de desenho] drawing board. -**2**. [suporte para escrever] board.

pranto ['prãtul *m* weeping.

prata ['pratal *f* -**1**. [metal] silver; **de** ~ silver (*antes de subst*); ~ **de lei** sterling silver. -**2**. *fam* [dinheiro] pennies (*pl*).

prataria [prata'rial *f* -**1**. [objetos de prata] silverware. -**2**. [pratos] crockery.

prateado, da [pra'tʃjadu, dal ⟨⟩ *adj* -**1**. [cor] silver (*antes de subst*). -**2**. *fig* [brilhante] silvery. ⟨⟩ *m* silver.

pratear [15] [pra'tʃja(x)l *vt* [com prata] to silver.

prateleira [pratʃi'lejral *f* shelf.

prática ['pratʃikal *f* ⊳ **prático**.

praticamente [pratʃika'mẽtʃil *adv* practically.

praticante [pratʃi'kãtʃil ⟨⟩ *adj* practising *UK*, practicing *US*. ⟨⟩ *mf* practitioner.

praticar [12] [pratʃi'ka(x)l ⟨⟩ *vt* -**1**. [cometer] to commit. -**2**. [exercer] to practise *UK*, to practice *US*. ⟨⟩ *vi* [exercitar] to practise *US*, to practice *US*.

praticável [pratʃi'kavɛwl (*pl* -eis) *adj* -**1**. [realizável] feasible. -**2**. [transitável] passable.

prático, ca ['pratʃiku, kal ⟨⟩ *adj* practical. ⟨⟩ *m, f NÁUT* pilot.
➡ **prática** *f* practice; **na** ~ in practice; **pôr em** ~ to put into practice.

prato ['pratul *m* -**1**. [louça] plate; ~ **fundo** soup plate; ~ **raso** dinner plate; ~ **de sobremesa** dessert plate. -**2**. [comida] dish; ~ **do dia** dish of the day; ~ **principal/segundo** ~ main/second course; ~ **de resistência** *fig* pièce de résistance.

-**3**. *MÚS* cymbal. -**4**. [de toca-disco] turntable. -**5**. [de balança] scale pan. -**6**. *loc*: **cuspir no** ~ **em que comeu** to bite the hand that feeds one; **vamos pôr isso em** ~**s limpos!** let's clear this up!; **ser um** ~ **cheio** to be manna from heaven.

praxe ['praʃil *f* habit; **ter como** ~ to be in the habit of; **ser de** ~ to be customary.

prazenteiro, ra [prazẽ'tejru, ral *adj* cheerful.

prazer [pra'ze(x)l (*pl* -es) *m* -**1**. pleasure. -**2**. [em apresentação]: **muito** ~ **(em conhecê-lo)** delighted (to meet you).

prazeroso, sa [prazeˈrozu, ɔzal *adj* pleasant.

prazo ['prazul *m* -**1**. [tempo] period; **tenho um** ~ **de trinta dias para pagá-lo** I have thirty days in which to pay him, I have to pay him within thirty days; **a** ~ on credit; **a curto/médio/longo** ~ in the short/medium/long term. -**2**. [vencimento] deadline; ~ **final** final deadline.

preamar [prea'ma(x)l *f* high tide.

preâmbulo [pre'ãbulul *m* -**1**. [prefácio] foreword. -**2**. [introdução] preamble.

preaquecer [25] [prjake'se(x)l *vt* to preheat.

pré-aviso [prɛa'vizul (*pl* **pré-avisos**) *m* (advance) notice.

precariedade [prekarje'dadʒil *m* precariousness.

precário, ria [pre'karju, rjal *adj* -**1**. [ger] precarious. -**2**. [escasso] scarce.

precatória [preka'tɔrjal *f JUR* writ.

precaução [prekaw'sãwl (*pl* -ões) *f* caution.

precaver-se [50] [preka'vexsil *vp* -**1**. [prevenir-se]: ~ **de** *ou* **contra algo** to be forearmed against sthg. -**2**. [preparar-se]: ~ **para algo** to prepare o.s. for sthg.

precavido, da [preka'vidu, dal *adj* cautious.

prece ['presil *f* -**1**. [oração] prayer. -**2**. [súplica] supplication.

precedência [presen'dẽsjal *f* precedence; **ter** ~ **sobre** to take precedence over.

precedente [prese'dẽtʃil ⟨⟩ *adj* precedent. ⟨⟩ *m* precedent; **sem** ~**s** unprecedented.

preceder [5] [prese'de(x)l ⟨⟩ *vt* to precede; ~ **algo de** to precede sthg with. ⟨⟩ *vi*: ~ **a** to precede.

preceito [pre'sejtul *m* precept.

preceptor [presep'to(x)l *m* tutor.

precificação [presifika'sãwl (*pl* -ões) *f* pricing policy.

precificar [presifi'ka(x)l *vt* to price.

preciosidade [presjozi'dadʒil *f* gem.

preciosismo [presjo'ziʒmul *m* preciosity.

precioso, osa [pre'sjozu, ɔzal *adj* -**1**. [ger] precious. -**2**. [importante] important. -**3**. [fino, rico] fine.

precipício [presi'pisjul *m* -**1**. [abismo] precipice. -**2**. *fig* [desgraça] hole.

precipitação [presipita'sãwl (*pl* -ões) *f* -**1**. [ger] haste. -**2**. *METEOR* precipitation.

precipitado, da [presipi'tadu, dal *adj* hasty.

precipitar [4] [presipi'ta(x)l ⟨⟩ *vt* [antecipar] to precipitate. ⟨⟩ *vi QUÍM* to precipitate.

precipitar-se *vp* -**1.** [ger] to rush. -**2.** [apressar-se] to hurry. -**3.** [despenhar-se] to drop.

precisado, da [presi'zadu, da] *adj*: ~ **de** in need of.

precisamente [pre,siza'mĕntʃi] *adv* precisely.

precisão [presi'zãw] *f* -**1.** [exatidão] precision, accuracy. -**2.** [necessidade]: **ter** ~ **de** to be in need of.

precisar [4] [presi'za(x)] <> *vt* -**1.** [ger] to need; ~ **fazer algo** to need to do sthg; **preciso que me ajudem** I need you to help me. -**2.** [indicar] to specify. <> *vi* -**1.** [necessitar] to be in need; ~ **de alguém/algo** to be in need of sb/sthg. -**2.** [ser necessário]: **não precisa** there is no need; **fiz isso sem precisar** I did this when there was no need; 'precisam-se vendedores' 'salespersons required'; **você precisa da chave para abrir a porta** you need a key to open the door.

preciso, sa [pre'sizu, za] *adj* -**1.** [ger] precise. -**2.** [necessário] necessary.

preço ['presu] *m* -**1.** [ger] price; ~ **de custo** cost price; ~ **à vista** [no comércio] cash price; [na bolsa] spot price; **vou comprar uma Ferrari por qualquer** ~ I am going to buy a Ferrari whatever the cost; **a** ~ **de banana** for peanuts; **não ter** ~ *fig* to be beyond price. -**2.** [importância] value.

precoce [pre'kɔsi] *adj* -**1.** [pessoa] precocious. -**2.** [fruto] early. -**3.** [calvície] premature.

precocidade [prekosi'dadʒi] *f* precociousness.

preconcebido, da [prɛkõnse'bidu, da] *adj* preconceived.

preconceito [prekõn'sejtu] *m* prejudice.

preconizar [4] [prekoni'za(x)] *vt* -**1.** [anunciar] to proclaim. -**2.** [propagar] to spread. -**3.** [elogiar] to praise.

precursor, ra [prekux'so(x), ra] (*mpl* -**es**, *fpl* -**s**) *m, f* precursor.

predador, ra [preda'do(x), ra] (*mpl* -**es**, *fpl* -**s**) <> *adj* predatory. <> *m, f* predator.

pré-datado, da [,prɛda'tadu, da] (*pl* -**s**) *adj* predated.

pré-datar [,prɛda'ta(x)] *vt* to predate.

predatório, ria [preda'tɔrju, rja] *adj* predatory.

predecessor, ra [predese'so(x), ra] (*mpl* -**es**, *fpl* -**s**) *m* predecessor.

predestinado, da [predeʃtʃi'nadu, da] *adj* predestined.

predestinar [4] [predeʃtʃi'na(x)] *vt* to predestine.

predeterminado, da [predetermi'nadu, da] *adj* predetermined.

predeterminar [predetermi'na(x)] *vt* to predetermine.

predial [pre'dʒjaw] (*pl* -**ais**) *adj* ⊳ **imposto**.

predicado [predʒi'kadu] *m* -**1.** [qualidade] quality. -**2.** GRAM predicate.

predição [predʒi'sãw] (*pl* -**ões**) *f* prediction.

predileção [predʒile'sãw] (*pl* -**ões**) *f*: ~ **(por)** predilection (for).

predileto, ta [predʒi'lɛtu, ta] <> *adj* favourite *UK*, favorite *US*. <> *m, f* favourite *UK*, favorite *US*.

prédio ['prɛdʒju] *m* building; ~ **de apartamentos** block of flats *UK*, apartment house *US*; ~ **comercial** commercial building.

predispor [45] [predʒiʃ'po(x)] <> *vt* to predispose. <> *vi*: ~ **a** to predispose to.

predispor-se *vp*: ~**-se a fazer algo** to be predisposed to do sthg.

predisposição [predʒiʃpozi'sãw] *f* predisposition.

predisposto, osta [predʒiʃ'poʃtu, ɔʃta] *adj* -**1.** [ger] predisposed. -**2.** [à doença] prone.

predizer [29] [predʒi'ze(x)] <> *vt* to predict, to forecast. <> *vi* [profetizar] to make predictions.

predominância [predomi'nãnsja] *f* predominance.

predominante [predomi'nãntʃil] *adj* predominant.

predominar [4] [predomi'na(x)] *vi* to predominate.

predomínio [predo'minju] *m* -**1.** [supremacia] supremacy. -**2.** [influência] predominance.

pré-eleitoral [,prɛelejto'raw] (*pl* -**ais**) *adj* pre-election (*antes de subst*).

preeminência [preemi'nĕnsja] *f* pre-eminence.

preeminente [preemi'nĕntʃi] *adj* pre-eminent.

preencher [5] [preĕn'ʃe(x)] *vt* -**1.** [completar - formulário, lacunas] to fill in; [- buracos] to fill. -**2.** [ocupar - tempo, férias] to spend; [- cargo, vaga] to fill. -**3.** [satisfazer] to fulfil *UK*, to fulfill *US*.

preenchimento [preĕnʃi'mĕntul] *m* -**1.** [de formulário, espaço em branco] filling in. -**2.** [de cargo, vaga, buraco] filling. -**3.** [de requisitos] fulfilment.

pré-escolar [,prɛiʃko'la(x)] (*pl* **pré-escolares**) *adj* pre-school (*antes de subst*).

preestabelecer [25] [,preeʃtabele'se(x)] *vt* to pre-establish.

pré-estréia [,prɛiʃ'trɛja] (*pl* -**s**) *f* preview.

preexistente [preeziʃ'tĕntʃi] *m* pre-existing.

preexistir [6] [preeziʃ'tʃi(x)] *vi* to pre-exist; ~ **a algo** to pre-exist sthg.

pré-fabricado, da [,prɛfabri'kadu, da] *adj* prefabricated.

prefaciar [16] [prefa'sja(x)] *vt* to preface.

prefácio [pre'fasjul] *m* preface.

prefeito, ta [pre'fejtu, ta] *m, f* mayor.

prefeitura [prefej'tural] *f* town hall.

preferência [prefe'rĕnsja] *f* -**1.** [precedência] priority; **dar** ~ **a** to give preference to. -**2.** AUTO: **ter** ~ to have priority. -**3.** [predileção] preference; **de** ~ preferably; **ter** ~ **por** to have a preference for.

preferencial [preferĕn'sjaw] (*pl* -**ais**) <> *adj* priority (*antes de subst*). <> *f* main road.

preferido, da [prefe'ridu, da] *adj* favourite *UK*, favorite *US*.

preferir [57] [prefe'ri(x)] *vt*: ~ **algo (a algo)** to prefer sthg (to sthg); **prefiro que você fique** I would prefer you to stay.

preferível [prefe'rivew] (*pl* -**eis**) *adj*: ~ **(a)** preferable (to).

prefigurar [4] [prefigu'ra(x)] *vt* to prefigure.

prefixo [pre'fiksu] *m* prefix.

prega ['prɛgal *f* -**1.** [dobra - em papel, pano] fold; [- na saia] pleat. -**2.** [ruga] wrinkle.

pregado, da [pre'gadu, da] *adj* -**1.** [fixado] nailed. -**2.** [olhos] glued. -**3.** [cansado] exhausted.

pregador [prega'do(x)] *m* -**1.** [orador] preacher. -**2.** [utensílio]: ~ **de roupa** clothes peg.

pregão [pre'gãw] (*pl* -ões) *m* -**1.** [proclamação] cry. -**2.** *BOLSA* trading. -**3.** [em leilão] bidding.

pregar [14] [pre'ga(x)] <> *vt* -**1.** [ger] to fix; ~ **os olhos em alguém/algo** to stare at sb/sthg; **não preguei os olhos a noite toda** I didn't sleep a wink all night. -**2.** [com prego] to nail. -**3.** [infligir]: ~ **algo em alguém** to inflict sthg on sb; ~ **um susto em alguém** to give sb a fright; ~ **uma mentira em alguém** to tell sb a lie; ~ **uma peça em alguém** to play a trick on sb. -**4.** *RELIG* [louvar] to preach. <> *vi* -**1.** [pronunciar sermão] to preach. -**2.** [clamar]: ~ **por/contra algo** to preach for/against sthg. -**3.** [cansar-se] to collapse.

prego ['prɛgu] *m* -**1.** [peça] nail. -**2.** [casa de penhor] pawn shop; **pôr algo no** ~ to pawn sthg. -**3.** [cansaço] exhaustion; **dar o** ~ to collapse.

pregões [pre'gõjʃ] *pl* ▷ **pregão**.

pré-gravado, da [ˌprɛgra'vadu, da] (*pl* -s) *adj* pre-recorded.

pregresso, sa [pre'grɛsu, sa] *adj* earlier.

preguear [15] [pre'gja(x)] *vt* -**1.** [saia] to pleat. -**2.** [calça] to put a crease in.

preguiça [pre'gisa] *f* -**1.** [indolência] laziness; **estar com** ~ **(de fazer algo)** to be too lazy (to do sthg). -**2.** [animal] sloth.

preguiçoso, osa [pregi'sozu, ɔza] <> *adj* lazy. <> *m, f* lazy person.

pré-história [ˌprɛiʃ'tɔrja] *f* prehistory.

pré-histórico, ca [prɛiʃ'tɔriku, ka] *adj* prehistoric.

preia ['prɛja] *f* prey.

preia-mar [ˌprɛja'ma(x)] (*pl* preia-mares) *f* high tide.

prejudicar [12] [preʒudʒi'ka(x)] *vt* -**1.** [afetar] to damage. -**2.** [transtornar] to disrupt. -**3.** [depreciar] to impair.

prejudicial [preʒudʒi'sjaw] (*pl* -ais) *adj* harmful.

prejuízo [pre'ʒwizu] *m* -**1.** [dano] damage. -**2.** [financeiro] loss.

prejulgar [14] [preʒuw'ga(x)] *vt* to prejudge.

prelado [pre'ladu] *m* prelate.

preleção [prele'sãw] (*pl* -ões) *f* lecture.

preliminar [prelimi'na(x)] <> *adj* preliminary. <> *f* [partida] preliminary.

prelo ['prɛlu] *m* (printing) press; **no** ~ in print.

prelúdio [pre'ludʒju] *m* prelude.

prematuro, ra [prema'turu, ra] *adj* -**1.** [bebê] premature. -**2.** [colheita, fruta] early.

pré-medicação [ˌprɛmedʒika'sãw] (*pl* -ões) *f* pre-medication.

premeditado, da [premedʒi'tadu, da] *adj* premeditated.

premeditar [4] [premedʒi'ta(x)] *vt* to premeditate.

premência [pre'mẽnsja] *f* urgency.

pré-menstrual [ˌprɛmẽnʃ'trwaw] (*pl* -ais) *adj* premenstrual.

premente [pre'mẽntʃi] *adj* urgent.

premiado, da [pre'mjadu, da] <> *adj* prize-winning. <> *m, f* prizewinner.

premiar [16] [pre'mja(x)] *vt* -**1.** [dar prêmio] to award a prize to. -**2.** [recompensar] to reward.

premiê [pre'mjel, **premier** [pre'mjel *m* premier.

prêmio ['premju] *m* -**1.** [em concurso, jogo] prize; ~ **de consolação** consolation prize. -**2.** [recompensa] reward. -**3.** [seguro] premium. -**4.** *ESP*: **Grande Prêmio** [de turfe, automobilismo] Grand Prix.

premissa [pre'misa] *f* premise.

pré-moldado, da [ˌprɛmow'dadu, da] (*pl* -s) *adj* precast.

◆ **pré-moldado** *m* [bloco] breeze block *UK*, cinder block *US*.

premonição [premuni'sãw] (*pl* -ões) *f* premonition.

premonitório, ria [premuni'tɔrju, rja] *adj* premonitory.

pré-natal [ˌprɛna'taw] (*pl* pré-natais) *adj* antenatal *UK*, prenatal *US*.

prenda ['prẽnda] *f* -**1.** [presente] present. -**2.** [em jogo] forfeit.

◆ **prendas** *fpl*: ~s domésticas housework (*inv*).

prendado, da [prẽn'dadu, da] *adj* gifted.

prendedor [prẽnde'do(x)] *m* peg; ~ **de papel** paper clip; ~ **de cabelo** hairgrip; ~ **de gravata** tie clip.

prender [5] [prẽn'de(x)] <> *vt* -**1.** [pregar] to fasten. -**2.** [amarrar] to tie. -**3.** [reter] to keep. -**4.** [capturar] to arrest. -**5.** [atrair] to capture. -**6.** [afetivamente] to unite. -**7.** [impedir] to restrict. <> *vi* [ficar preso]: ~ **em algo** to catch on sthg.

◆ **prender-se** *vp* -**1.**: ~**-se a alguém** [afeiçoar-se] to grow attached to sb; [em relacionamento] to tie o.s. down to sb. -**2.** [preocupar-se]: ~**-se a algo** to get caught up in sthg.

prenhe ['prẽ] *adj* pregnant.

prenome [pre'nɔmi] *m* forename.

prensa ['prẽnsa] *f* -**1.** [ger] press. -**2.** *fam*: dar uma ~ **em alguém** to tighten the screws on sb.

prensar [4] [prẽn'sa(x)] *vt* -**1.** [na prensa] to compress. -**2.** [fruta] to squeeze. -**3.** [pessoa]: ~ **alguém contra algo** to press sb against sthg.

prenunciar [16] [prenũn'sja(x)] *vt* to forewarn.

prenúncio [pre'nũnsjo] *m* harbinger; **essas nuvens são um** ~ **de chuva** clouds are a sign of rain.

preocupação [preokupa'sãw] (*pl* -ões) *f* concern.

preocupante [preoku'pãntʃi] *adj* worrying.

preocupar [4] [preoku'pa(x)] *vt* [inquietar] to worry.

◆ **preocupar-se** *vp*: ~**-se (com algo/alguém)** to worry (about sthg/sb).

preparação [prepara'sãw] (*pl* -ões) *f* [preparo] preparation.

preparado, da [prepa'radu, da] *adj* -**1.** [disposto] ready. -**2.** [instruído] well prepared.

◆ **preparado** *m* *FARM* preparation.

preparar [4] [prepa'ra(x)] *vt* to prepare.
◆ **preparar-se** *vp* -**1.** [aprontar-se] to get ready.
-**2.** [instruir-se]: ~**-se para algo** to train for sthg.
preparativos [prepara'tʃivuʃ] *mpl* preparations,
arrangements.
preparo [pre'paru] *m* -**1.** [preparação] preparation. -**2.** [condição]: ~ **físico** physical fitness.
preponderância [prepõnde'rãnsja] *f* preponderance.
preponderante [prepõnde'rãntʃi] *adj* prepon-
derant, predominant.
preponderar [4] [prepõnde'ra(x)] *vi* to prepon-
derate; ~ **sobre algo** to prevail over sthg.
preposição [prepozi'sãw] (*pl* -ões) *f* preposition.
preposto, ta [pre'poʃtu, ta] *m, f* [representante]
representative.
prepotência [prepo'tẽnsja] *f* -**1.** [grande poder]
forcefulness. -**2.** [despotismo] tyranny.
prepotente [prepo'tẽntʃi] *adj* -**1.** [poderoso]
forceful. -**2.** [despótico] overbearing.
prepúcio [pre'pusju] *m* prepuce.
prerrogativa [prexoga'tʃiva] *f* prerogative.
presa ['preza] *f* -**1.** [na guerra] spoils (*pl*). -**2.** [preia]
prey. -**3.** [dente] fang. -**4.** [garra] talon. -**5.** [vítima]
slave. -**6.** [mulher encarcerada] (female) prisoner.
presbiteriano, na [prezbite'rjãnu, na] <> *adj*
Presbyterian. <> *m, f* Presbyterian.
presbítero [preʃ'biʃterul] *m* [padre] priest.
presciência [pre'sjẽnsja] *f* [previsão] prescience.
presciente [pre'sjẽntʃi] *adj* prescient.
prescindir [6] [presĩn'dʒi(x)] *vi*: ~ **de algo** [dispen-
sar] to do without sthg; [abstrair] to disregard
sthg.
prescindível [presĩn'dʒivew] (*pl* -**eis**) *adj* dispensable.
prescrever [5] [preʃkre've(x)] <> *vt* -**1.** [ger] to
prescribe. -**2.** [determinar] to decide. <> *vi* -**1.** [ca-
ir em desuso] to fall into disuse. -**2.** *JUR* to lapse.
prescrição [preʃkri'sãw] (*pl* -ões) *f* -**1.** [ordem]
order. -**2.** *MED* prescription. -**3.** *JUR* lapse.
presença [pre'zẽnsa] *f* -**1.** [ger] presence; ~ **de**
espírito presence of mind; **marcar** ~ to be
present; **ter boa** ~ to be well turned out. -**2.**
[em curso etc] attendance.
presenciar [16] [prezẽn'sja(x)] *vt* to witness.
presente [pre'zẽntʃi] <> *adj* -**1.** [ger] present. -**2.**
[evidente] obvious. -**3.** [interessado] concerned. <>
m -**1.** [ger] present. -**2.** [pessoa]: **(entre) os** ~**s**
(among) those present. -**3.** [regalo] present, gift;
de ~ as a present; ~ **de grego** *fig* unwelcome
gift.
presentear [15] [prezẽn'tʃja(x)] *vt*: ~ **alguém (com**
algo) to give sb (sthg as) a present.
presentemente [prezẽntʃi'mẽntʃi] *adv* at present.
presepada [preze'pada] *f* nonsense.
presépio [pre'zɛpju] *m* crib, Nativity scene.
preservação [prezexva'sãw] (*pl* -ões) *f* preservation.
preservar [4] [prezex'va(x)] *vt* to preserve.
◆ **preservar-se** *vp* to protect o.s.

preservativo [prezexva'tʃivu] *m* -**1.** [substância]
preservative. -**2.** [camisinha] condom.
presidência [prezi'dẽnsja] *f* -**1.** [de país] presidency; **assumir a** ~ to assume the presidency.
-**2.** [de assembléia] chairmanship; **assumir a** ~ to
take the chair. -**3.** [tempo em excercício] time in
office.
presidencial [prezidẽn'sjaw] (*pl* -**ais**) *adj* presidential.
presidencialismo [prezidẽnsja'liʒmul] *m* presi-
dentialism.
presidenciável [prezidẽn'sjavewl] (*pl*-**eis**) <> *adj*
eligible to be president. <> *mf* presidential
candidate.
presidente, ta [prezi'dẽntʃi, ta] *m, f* -**1.** [de país]
president. -**2.** [de assembléia, empresa] chairman.
◆ **Presidente da República** *m* President of
the Republic.
presidiário, ria [prezi'dʒjarju, rja] <> *adj* prison
(*antes de subst*). <> *m, f* convict.
presídio [pre'zidʒju] *m* prison.
presidir [6] [prezi'dʒi(x)] <> *vt* -**1.** [dirigir] to lead.
-**2.** [reger] to rule. <> *vi*: ~ **a algo** [dirigir] to
preside over sthg; [reger] to rule sthg.
presilha [pre'ziʎa] *f* -**1.** [de suspensório, sapato]
strap. -**2.** [de cabelo] hairslide.
preso, sa ['prezu, zal] <> *adj* -**1.** [encarcerado]
imprisoned. -**2.** [detido] detained, under arrest.
-**3.** [atado] tied. -**4.** *fig* [em engarrafamento, casa]
stuck. -**5.** *fig* [ligado]: **ficar** ~ **a detalhes** to get
bogged down in detail. -**6.** *fig* [casado] spoken
for. -**7.** *fig* [língua, voz] tongue-tied; **ele está com a**
voz presa he has a catch in his voice. <> *m, f*
[prisioneiro] prisoner.
pressa ['presa] *f* -**1.** [velocidade] speed; **às** ~**s**
quickly; **com** ~ in a hurry; **sem** ~ unhurriedly;
vir sem ~ to take one's time. -**2.** [urgência] rush;
não ter ~ not to be urgent; **ter** ~ **de algo/de fa-**
zer algo to be in a hurry for sthg/to do sthg. -**3.**
[precipitação] hastiness.
pressagiar [16] [presa'ʒja(x)] *vt* to foretell.
presságio [pre'saʒjul] *m* -**1.** [indício] sign. -**2.** [pres-
sentimento] premonition.
pressão [pre'sãw] (*pl* -ões) *f* -**1.** [ger] pressure;
fazer ~ **sobre alguém** to put pressure on sb; ~
contra algo pressure against sthg. -**2.** [colchete]
press stud. -**3.** *MED*: ~ **alta/baixa** high/low
(blood) pressure; ~ **arterial** blood pressure.
-**4.** *FÍSICA*: ~ **atmosférica** atmospheric pressure.
pressentimento [presẽntʃi'mẽntul] *m* premonition.
pressentir [56] [presẽn'tʃi(x)] *vt* -**1.** [pressagiar] to
foresee. -**2.** [suspeitar] to suspect. -**3.** [perceber] to
sense.
pressionar [4] [presjo'na(x)] *vt* -**1.** [apertar] to
press. -**2.** *fig* [coagir]: ~ **alguém (a fazer algo)** to
pressurize sb (into doing sthg).
pressões [pre'sõjʃ] *pl* ▷ **pressão**.
pressupor [45] [presu'po(x)] *vt* to assume.
pressuposto, osta [presu'poʃtu, ʃtal] *pp* ▷
pressupor.

➡ **pressuposto** *m*: partir de um ~ to assume.

pressurização [presuriza'sãw] *f* pressurization.

pressurizado, da [presuri'zadu, da] *adj* pressurized.

prestação [preʃta'sãw] (*pl* -ões) *f* -1. [ger] instalment *UK*, installment *US*; ele só compra à ~ he only buys on hire purchase. -2. [acerto]: ~ de conta accounts rendered. -3. [trabalho]: ~ de serviço services rendered.

prestamista [preʃta'miʃta] *mf* moneylender.

prestar [4] [preʃ'ta(x)] ⟨⟩ *vt* -1. [conceder]: ~ algo (a alguém) [favores] to grant sthg (to sb); [informações] to provide (sb with) sthg. -2. [dispensar]: ~ algo (a alguém) to provide (sb with) sthg. -3. [apresentar]: ~ algo (a alguém) to present sthg (to sb). -4. [fazer]: ~ algo (a alguém/algo) to provide sthg to sb/sthg); ~ atenção to pay attention. -5. [dedicar]: ~ algo a alguém to pay sthg to sb. ⟨⟩ *vi* -1. [ser útil]: essa caneta não presta this pen isn't any good. -2. [ter bom caráter]: ele não presta! he's no good!

➡ **prestar-se** *vp* -1. [dispor-se]: ~-se a algo to accept sthg. -2. [servir]: ~-se a algo to be fit for sthg.

prestativo, va [preʃta'tʃivu, va] *adj* obliging.

prestes ['prɛʃtʃiʃ] *adj inv*: estar ~ a fazer algo to be about to do sthg.

presteza [preʃ'teza] *f* -1. [prontidão] promptness; com ~ promptly. -2. [agilidade] agility.

prestidigitação [preʃtʃidʒiʒita'sãw] *f* conjuring.

prestidigitador, ra [preʃtʃidʒiʒita'do(x), ra] (*mpl* -es, *fpl* -s) *m, f* conjurer.

prestigiar [16] [preʃtʃi'ʒja(x)] *vt* to honour *UK*, to honor *US*.

prestígio [preʃ'tʃiʒju] *m* prestige; é um escritor de ~ he is an eminent writer.

prestigioso, osa [preʃtʃi'ʒjozu, ɔza] *adj* prestigious.

préstimo ['prɛʃtʃimu] *m* [utilidade] use.

➡ **préstimos** *mpl* [favores]: oferecer ~s a alguém to offer one's services to sb.

presumido, da [prezu'midu, da] *adj* [presunçoso] presumptuous.

presumir [6] [prezu'mi(x)] *vt* [supor] to presume.

presunção [prezũn'sãw] (*pl* -ões) *f* presumption; ter a ~ de ser algo to believe o.s. to be sthg.

presunçoso, osa [prezũn'sozu, ɔza] *adj* presumptuous.

presunto [pre'zũntu] *m* -1. [de porco] ham. -2. *gír crime* [defunto] stiff.

prêt-à-porter [prɛtapox'te] *adj inv* ready-to-wear.

pretendente [pretẽn'dẽntʃi] ⟨⟩ *mf* [candidato]: ~ a algo applicant for sthg. ⟨⟩ *m* [de uma mulher] suitor.

pretender [5] [pretẽn'de(x)] *vt* -1. [desejar]: ~ fazer algo to want to do sthg. -2. [ter a intenção de]: ~ fazer algo to intend to do sthg; ~ que to intend (that).

pretensamente [pretẽnsa'mẽntʃi] *adv* supposedly.

pretensão [pretẽn'sãw] (*pl* -ões) *f* -1. [aspiração] pretension; ~ salarial proposed salary. -2. [arrogância] pretentions (*pl*). -3. [intenção] aim.

pretensioso, osa [pretẽn'sjozu, ɔza] *adj* pretentious.

pretenso, sa [pre'tẽsu, sa] *adj* [suposto] alleged.

preterir [prete'ri(x)] *vt* -1. [desprezar] to scorn. -2. [omitir] to omit. -3. [deixar de promover] to pass over. -4. [substituir] to replace.

pretérito, ta [pre'tɛritul] *adj* past.

➡ **pretérito** *m GRAM* preterite.

pretexto [pre'teʃtu] *m* [desculpa] pretext; a ~ de under the pretext of.

preto, ta ['pretu, ta] ⟨⟩ *adj* [cor] black; estar/andar ~ *fig* to be/look gloomy; ver as coisas pretas to look on the dark side. ⟨⟩ *m, f* [pessoa] black (person).

➡ **preto** *m* [cor] black.

preto-e-branco [,pretwi'brãŋku] *adj inv* black and white.

pretume [pre'tumi] *m* blackness.

prevalecente [prevale'sẽntʃi] *adj* prevailing.

prevalecer [25] [prevale'se(x)] *vi* -1. [predominar] to prevail. -2. [ter primazia]: ~ (a/sobre) to prevail (over).

➡ **prevalecer-se** *vp*: ~-se de algo [aproveitar-se] to avail o.s. of sthg.

prevaricação [prevarika'sãw] (*pl* -ões) *f JUR* prevarication.

prevaricar [12] [prevari'ka(x)] *vi* -1. [faltar ao dever] to fail to do one's duty. -2. [proceder mal] to do wrong. -3. [cometer adultério] to stray.

prevenção [prevẽn'sãw] (*pl* -ões) *f* -1. [precaução]: ~ (a/contra/de) prevention (against/of). -2. [implicância]: estar de ~ contra *ou* com alguém to pick on sb.

prevenido, da [previ'nidu, da] *adj* -1. [precavido] precautious. -2. [com dinheiro]: estar ~ to be in pocket.

prevenir [58] [previ'ni(x)] *vt* -1. [avisar] to warn. -2. [evitar] to avoid. -3. [proibir] to prohibit.

➡ **prevenir-se** *vp* -1. [precaver-se]: ~-se contra alguém/algo to protect o.s. against sb/sthg. -2. [equipar-se] ~-se de to equip o.s. with.

preventivo, va [prevẽn'tʃivu, va] *adj* preventive.

➡ **preventivo** *m* [teste]: (fazer um) ~ to have a check-up.

prever [40] [pre've(x)] *vt* -1. [conjeturar] to foresee; ~ que to foresee (that). -2. [profetizar] to predict.

pré-vestibular [,prevẽʃtʃibu'la(x)] (*pl* pré-vestibulares) ⟨⟩ *adj preparing for university entrance exam*. ⟨⟩ *m* [curso] *university entrance-exam preparatory course*.

prévia ['prɛvja] *f* ⊳ prévio.

previamente [,prɛvja'mẽntʃi] *adv* previously.

previdência [previ'dẽsja] *f* precaution; ~ social social security.

previdente [previ'dẽntʃi] *adj* -1. [que prevê] provident. -2. [cauteloso] cautious.

prévio, via ['prɛvju, vja] *adj* -1. [anterior] previous. -2. [preliminar] preliminary.

➤ **prévia** f -**1.** [pesquisa eleitoral] opinion poll. -**2.** [eleição interna de um partido] leadership elections.
previsão [previ'zãwl (pl -ões) f prediction; ~ **do tempo** weather forecast.
previsível [previ'zivɛwl (pl -eis) adj predictable.
previsto, ta [pre'viʃtu, tal ◇ pp ▷ **prever.** ◇ adj -**1.** [prognosticado] foreseen. -**2.** [calculado] predicted. -**3.** [em lei] prescribed.
prezado, da [pre'zadu, dal adj -**1.** [estimado] prized. -**2.** [em carta]: **Prezado Senhor** Dear Sir.
prezar [4] [pre'za(x)l vt -**1.** [gostar muito] to cherish. -**2.** [respeitar] to respect.
➤ **prezar-se** vp [respeitar-se] to have self-respect.
primado [pri'madul m [primazia] primacy.
prima-dona [,prima'donal (pl prima-donas) f prima donna.
primar [4] [pri'ma(x)l vi -**1.** [destacar-se] to excel. -**2.** [esmerar-se]: ~ **em** to excel in.
primário, ria [pri'marju, rjal adj -**1.** [ger] primary. -**2.** [primitivo] primitive.
➤ **primário** m [curso] primary education UK, elementary education US.
primata [pri'matal m primate.
primavera [prima'vɛral f -**1.** [estação] spring. -**2.** BOT primrose.
primaveril [primave'riwl (pl -is) adj spring (antes de subst).
primaz [pri'majʒl m primate.
primazia [prima'zial f -**1.** [prioridade] priority. -**2.** [superioridade] primacy.
primeira [pri'mejral f ▷ **primeiro.**
primeira-dama [pri,mejra'dãmal (pl primeiras-damas) f first lady.
primeiranista [primejra'niʃtal mf first-year student.
primeiro, ra [pri'mejru, ral ◇ num first. ◇ adj [inicial] first; ~ **grau** EDUC middle school; ~**s socorros** first aid; **à primeira vista** at first sight. ◇ m, f -**1.** [em ordem]: **ela foi o** ~ **a chegar** she was the first to arrive. -**2.** [o melhor]: **é o** ~ **na turma** he is the top of the class.
➤ **primeiro** ◇ adv [em primeiro lugar] first. ◇ m [andar] first.
➤ **primeira** f AUTO first; **passar a primeira** to get into first.
➤ **de primeira** ◇ loc adj -**1.** [hotel, restaurante] first-class. -**2.** [carne] prime. ◇ loc adv [viajar] first class.
primeiro-de-abril [pri,mejrudʒja'briwl (pl primeiros-de-abril) m April fool.
primeiro-ministro, primeira-ministra [pri,mejrumi'niʃtru, pri,mejrami'niʃtral (mpl primeiros-ministros, fpl primeiras-ministras) m, f prime minister.
primeiro time [pri,mejro'tʃimil adj inv: **de** ~ tip-top.
primitivo, va [primi'tʃivu, val adj primitive.
primo, ma ['primu, mal ◇ adj [número] prime. ◇ m, f [parente] cousin; ~ **em segundo grau** second cousin.

primogênito, ta [primo'ʒenitu, tal ◇ adj firstborn. ◇ m, f firstborn.
primo-irmão, prima-irmã [,primwix'mãw, ,primajx'mãl (mpl primos-irmãos, fpl primas-irmãs) m, f first cousin.
primor [pri'mo(x)l m -**1.** [excelência] excellence. -**2.** [beleza] beauty. -**3.** [esmero]: **com** ~ thoroughly.
primordial [primox'dʒjawl (pl -ais) adj -**1.** [primitivo] primordial. -**2.** [fundamental] fundamental.
primórdio [pri'mɔrdʒjul m [origem] origin.
primoroso, osa [primo'rozu, ɔzal adj perfect.
princesa [prĩn'sezal f princess.
principado [prĩnsi'padul m principality.
principal [prĩnsi'pawl (pl -ais) ◇ adj -**1.** [mais importante - ator] principal; [- rua, praça, entrada] main. -**2.** [fundamental] main. ◇ m principal.
principalmente [prĩnsipaw'mẽntʃil adv principally.
príncipe ['prĩnsipil m prince.
principesco, ca [prĩnsi'peʃku, kal adj princely.
principiante [prĩnsi'pjãntʃil ◇ adj budding. ◇ mf beginner.
principiar [16] [prĩnsi'pja(x)l ◇ vt to begin. ◇ vi to begin.
princípio [prĩn'sipjul m -**1.** [ger] beginning; **a** ~ at first; **desde o** ~ from the start; **do** ~ **ao fim** from beginning to end. -**2.** [lei, norma, elemento] principle. -**3.** [premissa]: **partir do** ~ to assume.
➤ **princípios** mpl [morais] principles.
➤ **em princípio** loc adv in principle.
prior ['prio(x)l m prior.
prioridade [prjori'dadʒil f [primazia] priority; **ter** ~ **sobre alguém/algo** to have priority over sb/sthg.
prioritário, ria [prjori'tarju, rjal adj priority (antes de subst).
priorizar [prjori'za(x)l vt [dar prioridade a] to prioritize.
prisão [prizãwl (pl -ões) f -**1.** [captura] arrest. -**2.** [encarceramento] imprisonment; ~ **perpétua** life imprisonment; ~ **preventiva** protective custody. -**3.** [cadeia] prison. -**4.** fig [sufoco] (holy) deadlock. -**5.** MED: ~ **de ventre** constipation.
prisioneiro, ra [prizjo'nejru, ral m, f prisoner.
prisma ['priʒmal m -**1.** [ger] prism. -**2.** fig [perspectiva]: **sob esse** ~ from that angle.
prisões [pri'zõjʃl pl ▷ **prisão.**
privação [priva'sãwl (pl -ões) f privation.
➤ **privações** fpl [penúria] hardship.
privacidade [privasi'dadʒil f privacy.
privada [pri'vadal f toilet.
privado, da [pri'vadu, dal adj -**1.** [particular] private. -**2.** [desprovido] deprived.
privar [4] [pri'va(x)l vt: ~ **alguém de algo** to deprive sb of sthg.
➤ **privar-se** vp: ~**-se de algo** to go without sthg.
privativo, va [priva'tʃivu, val adj [exclusivo] private.
privatização [privatʃiza'sãwl (pl -ões) f privatization.

privatizar [4] [privatʃi'za(x)] *vt* to privatize.
privilegiado, da [privile'ʒjadu, da] *adj* **-1.** [favorecido] privileged. **-2.** [excepcional] exceptional.
privilegiar [16] [privile'ʒja(x)] *vt* to favour *UK*, to favor *US*.
privilégio [privi'lɛʒju] *m* privilege.
pro [pru] = **para + o**.
pró [prɔ] ⟨⟩ *prep* [a favor de] pro. ⟨⟩ *m* [vantagem] pro; **os ~s e os contras** the pros and cons.
pró- [prɔ] *prefixo* pro-.
proa ['proa] *f* bow.
probabilidade [probabili'dadʒil] *f* probability, likelihood.
problema [pro'blema] *m* problem.
problemático, ca [proble'matʃiku, ka] *adj* problematic.
➧ **problemática** *f* problematic.
problematizar [problematʃi'za(x)] *vt* **-1.** [colocar em dúvida] to cast doubt on. **-2.** [dar forma de problema a] to find problems in. **-3.** [tornar difícil] to complicate.
probo, ba ['probu, ba] *adj* honest.
procedência [prose'dēnsja] *f* **-1.** [origem] origin. **-2.** [lugar de saída] point of departure. **-3.** [fundamento]: **não ter ~** to be unfounded.
procedente [prose'dēntʃi] *adj* **-1.** [oriundo] originating. **-2.** [lógico] logical.
proceder [5] [prose'de(x)] *vi* **-1.** [ger] to proceed. **-2.** [prosseguir] to continue. **-3.** [comportar-se] to behave; **~ mal/bem** to behave badly/well. **-4.** [ter fundamento] to have foundation.
procedimento [prosedʒi'mēntul] *m* **-1.** [comportamento] behaviour *UK*, behavior *US*. **-2.** [método] method. **-3.** *JUR* proceedings *(pl)*.
processador [prosesa'do(x)] *(pl -es) m COMPUT* processor; **~ de texto** word processor.
processamento [prosesa'mēntul] *m* processing; **~ de dados** data processing; **~ de texto** text processing.
processar [4] [prose'sa(x)] *vt* **-1.** *JUR* to sue, to prosecute. **-2.** *COMPUT* to process.
processo [pro'sɛsu] *m* **-1.** [*JUR* - ação] legal proceedings *(pl)*, lawsuit; **abrir** *ou* **mover um ~ contra** to instigate legal proceedings against, to file a lawsuit against; [- documentação] evidence. **-2.** [método] process. **-3.** [estágio] course.
procissão [prosi'sãw] *(pl -ões) f* procession.
proclamação [proklama'sãw] *(pl -ões) f* proclamation.
proclamar [4] [prokla'ma(x)] *vt* to proclaim.
Procon (*abrev de* **Fundação de Proteção e Defesa do Consumidor**) *m Brazilian organization for the protection of consumers' rights.*
procrastinar [4] [prokraʃtʃi'na(x)] ⟨⟩ *vt* to put off. ⟨⟩ *vi* to procrastinate.
procriação [prokrja'sãw] *f* procreation.
procriar [16] [pro'krja(x)] ⟨⟩ *vt* [gerar] to engender. ⟨⟩ *vi* [multiplicar] to procreate.
proctologia [proktolo'ʒia] *f* proctology.
procura [pro'kura] *f* **-1.** [busca] search; **estar à ~**

de to be searching for. **-2.** *COM* demand; **a ~ e a oferta** supply and demand.
procuração [prokura'sãw] *(pl -ões) f* power of attorney.
procurado, da [proku'radu, da] *adj* sought after; **ser ~ pela polícia** to be wanted by the police.
procurador, ra [prokura'do(x), ra] *(mpl -es, fpl -s) m, f*: **Procurador Geral da República** ≃ state prosecutor.
procurar [4] [proku'ra(x)] ⟨⟩ *vt* **-1.** [buscar - objeto, pessoa] to look for; [- verdade] to seek. **-2.** [requerer] to look for. **-3.** [esforçar-se por]: **~ fazer algo** to try to do sthg. **-4.** [contatar] to call on. ⟨⟩ *vi* [buscar]: **~ (por)** to search (for).
prodigalidade [prodʒigali'dadʒil] *f* **-1.** [abundância] abundance. **-2.** [generosidade] generosity.
prodígio [pro'dʒiʒju] *m* **-1.** [pessoa] prodigy. **-2.** [maravilha] feat.
prodigioso, osa [prodʒi'ʒozu, ɔza] *adj* prodigious.
pródigo, ga ['prɔdʒigu, ga] *adj* prodigal.
produção [produ'sãw] *(pl -ões) f* **-1.** [ger] production. **-2.** [volume, obra] output; **~ em massa** *ou* **em série** mass production.
produtividade [produtʃivi'dadʒil] *f* productivity.
produtivo, va [produ'tʃivu, va] *adj* **-1.** [fértil] productive. **-2.** [rendoso] profitable.
produto [pro'dutul *m* **-1.** [ger] product. **-2.** *AGR* produce. **-3.** *ECON*: **~ interno bruto** gross domestic product. **-4.** *fig* [consequência]: **ser ~ de** to be the product of.
produtor, ra [produ'to(x), ra] *(mpl -es, fpl -s)* ⟨⟩ *adj* producing; **país ~ de petróleo** oil-producing country. ⟨⟩ *m, f* producer.
➧ **produtora** *f* [empresa] production company.
produzido, da [produ'zidu, da] *adj* [esmerado] trendy.
proeminência [projmi'nēnsja] *f* prominence.
proeminente [projmi'nēntʃi] *adj* prominent.
proeza [pro'eza] *f* feat.
profanação [profana'sãw] *(pl -ões) f* profanity.
profanar [4] [profa'na(x)] *vt* to desecrate.
profano, na [pro'fânu, na] *adj* profane.
profecia [profe'sia] *f* prophecy.
proferir [57] [profe'ri(x)] *vt* **-1.** [dizer] to utter. **-2.** [decretar] to pronounce.
professar [4] [profe'sa(x)] ⟨⟩ *vt* **-1.** [exercer profissão] to practise *UK*, to practice *US*. **-2.** [propagar] to profess. ⟨⟩ *vi RELIG* to take holy orders.
professo, ssa [pro'fɛsu, sa] *adj* **-1.** *RELIG* avowed. **-2.** *fig* [perito] seasoned.
professor, ra [profe'so(x), ra] *(mpl -es, fpl -s) m, f* teacher; **~ titular** *ou* **catedrático** university professor.
professorado [profeso'radu] *m* **-1.** [magistério] professorship. **-2.** [conjunto de professores] teaching profession.
profeta, tisa [pro'fɛta, tʃiza] *m, f* prophet.
profético, ca [pro'fɛtʃiku, ka] *adj* prophetic.
profetisa [profe'tʃiza] *f* ▷ **profeta**.
profetizar [4] [profetʃi'za(x)] ⟨⟩ *vt* to prophesy.

⟨ *vi* to predict the future.

proficiência [profi'sjẽsja] *f* proficiency.

proficiente [profi'sjẽtʃil] *adj* [capaz] proficient.

profícuo, a [pro'fikwu, kwa] *adj* useful.

profissão [profi'sãw] (*pl* -ões) *f* -1. [ofício] profession. -2. [carreira] professional life. -3. [declaração] statement; ~ de fé *RELIG* profession of faith.

profissional [profisjo'naw] (*pl* -ais) ⟨⟩ *adj* professional. ⟨⟩ *mf* professional; ~ liberal *person in a liberal profession*.

profissionalizante [profisjonali'zãtʃil] *adj* [ensino] vocational.

profissionalizar [4] [profisjonali'za(x)] *vt* to professionalize.

◆ **profissionalizar-se** *vp* -1. [pessoa] to turn professional. -2. [atividade] to become professional.

profundamente [profũnda'mẽtʃil] *adv* deeply.

profundezas [profũn'dezaʃ] *fpl* depths.

profundidade [profũndʒi'dadʒi] *f* depth; o mar aqui tem 20 metros de ~ here the sea is 20 metres deep.

profundo, da [pro'fũndu, da] *adj* -1. [ger] deep. -2. *fig* [intenso - sono, respeito, amor] deep; [- dor] intense; [- ódio] profound.

profusão [profu'zãw] *f* profusion.

profuso, sa [pro'fuzu, za] *adj* profuse.

progenitor, ra [proʒeni'to(x), ra] *m, f* progenitor.

◆ **progenitores** *mpl* parents.

prognosticar [12] [prognoʃtʃi'ka(x)] ⟨⟩ *vt* [predizer] to forecast. ⟨⟩ *vi MED* to make a prognosis.

prognóstico [prog'nɔʃtʃikul *m* -1. [predição] prediction. -2. *MED* prognosis.

programa [pro'grãmal *m* -1. [plano] programme *UK*, program *US*; fazer um ~ to go out; ~ de índio *fam fig* boring activity. -2. *COMPUT* program.

programação [programa'sãw] (*pl*-ões) *f*-1. [ger] programming; ~ orientada a objetos object-orientated programming; ~ visual graphic design. -2. [organização] planning.

programador, ra [programa'do(x), ra] *m, f* -1. [de rádio, empresa] programme planner. -2. *COMPUT* programmer; ~ visual graphic designer.

programar [4] [progra'ma(x)] *vt* -1. [planejar] to plan. -2. *COMPUT* to program.

programável [progra'mavew] (*pl* -eis) *adj* programmable.

progredir [58] [progre'dʒi(x)] *vi* -1. [prosperar]: ~ (em algo) to progress (in sthg). -2. [agravar-se] to progress.

progressão [progre'sãw] (*pl*-ões) *f* progression.

progressista [progre'siʃta] ⟨⟩ *adj* progressive. ⟨⟩ *mf* progressive.

progressivo, va [progre'sivu, va] *adj* progressive.

progresso [pro'grɛsul *m* progress; fazer ~s em algo to make progress in sthg.

proibição [projbi'sãw] (*pl*-ões) *f* prohibition.

proibir [77] [proj'bi(x)] *vt*-1. [impedir]: ~ alguém (de fazer algo) to prohibit sb (from doing sthg).

-2. [interdizer] to ban. -3. [vedar] to prevent.

proibitivo, va [projbi'tʃivu, va] *adj* prohibitive.

projeção [proʒe'sãw] (*pl* -ões) *f* -1. [ger] projection; tempo de ~ running time. -2. *fig* [notoriedade] prominence.

projetar [4] [proʒe'ta(x)] *vt*-1. [ger] to project. -2. [planejar] to plan. -3. *ARQUIT* to design.

◆ **projetar-se** *vp* -1. [arremessar-se] to throw o.s. -2. [sombra] to be projected. -3. *fig* [ganhar notoriedade] to project o.s.

projétil [pro'ʒɛtʃiw] (*pl*-teis) *m* projectile.

projetista [proʒe'tʃiʃta] ⟨⟩ *adj* planning, design (*antes de subst*). ⟨⟩ *mf* planner, designer.

projeto [pro'ʒɛtul *m* -1. [ger] plan. -2. [empreendimento] project. -3. [esboço de texto] draft; ~ de lei bill.

projetor [proʒe'to(x)] (*pl*-es) *m* -1. [ger] projector. -2. [holofote] searchlight.

prol [prɔwl *m*: em ~ de in favour of.

pró-labore [ˌprɔla'boril (*pl* pró-labores) *m* remuneration.

prolapso [pro'lapsul *m MED* prolapse.

prole [ˈprɔlil *f* [filhos] offspring.

proletariado [proleta'rjadul *m* proletariat.

proletário, ria [prole'tarju, rja] ⟨⟩ *adj* proletarian. ⟨⟩ *m, f* proletarian.

proliferação [prolifera'sãw] (*pl*-ões) *f* proliferation.

proliferar [4] [prolife'ra(x)] *vi* to proliferate.

prolífico, ca [pro'lifiku, ka] *adj* prolific.

prolixo, xa [pro'liksu, ksal *adj* -1. [verboso] long-winded. -2. [muito longo] lengthy.

prólogo [ˈprɔlogul *m* prologue.

prolongado, da [prolõŋ'gadu, da] *adj* prolonged.

prolongamento [prolõŋga'mẽtul *m* extension.

prolongar [14] [prolõŋ'ga(x)] *vt* -1. [duração] to prolong. -2. [extensão] to extend. -3. [adiar] to put off.

◆ **prolongar-se** *vp* -1. [estender-se] to stretch. -2. [durar] to last.

promessa [pro'mɛsal *f* promise.

prometer [5] [prome'te(x)] ⟨⟩ *vt* -1. [ger] to promise. -2. [comprometer-se]: ~ algo a alguém to promise sb sthg; ~ fazer algo to promise to do sthg. -3. [assegurar]: ~ algo a alguém to promise sb sthg. ⟨⟩ *vi* -1. [fazer promessa] to promise. -2. [ter potencial] to be promising.

prometido, da [prome'tʃidu, da] *adj* promised.

◆ **prometido** *m*: aqui está o ~ here's what was promised; cumprir o ~ to keep one's promise.

promiscuidade [promiʃkwi'dadʒi] *f* promiscuity.

promiscuir-se [74] [promiʃ'kwixsil *vp* [misturar-se]: ~ (com) to mix (with).

promíscuo, cua [pro'miʃkwu, kwal *adj* -1. [sem ordem] disorderly. -2. [sexualmente] promiscuous.

promissor, ra [promi'so(x), ra] (*mpl*-es, *fpl*-s) *adj* promising.

promissória [promi'sɔrja] *f* [nota] promissory note.

promoção [promo'sãw] (pl-ões) f promotion; **em** ~ on special offer.

promocional [promo'sjonaw] (pl -ais) adj promotional.

promontório [promõn'tɔrju] m promontory.

promotor, ra [promo'to(x), ra] <> adj promoting. <> m, f promoter; ~ **público** public prosecutor.

promotoria [promoto'ria] f [Ministério Público] state prosecutor's office.

promover [5] [promo've(x)] vt -1. [ger] to promote. -2. [funcionário]: ~ **alguém (a)** to promote sb (to).

➤ **promover-se** vp [favorecer-se] to make o.s. look good.

promulgação [promuwga'sãw] f promulgation.

promulgar [14] [promuw'ga(x)] vt to promulgate.

pronome [pro'nɔmi] m pronoun; ~ **oblíquo** objective pronoun; ~ **pessoal** personal pronoun.

pronta-entrega [,prõntaẽn'trɛga] (pl **pronta-entregas**) f [departamento] immediate delivery department; **vocês têm** ~ do you do immediate delivery?, do you have an immediate delivery department?

prontidão [prõntʃi'dãw] f -1. [alerta] readiness; **estar de** ~ to be on the alert. -2. [rapidez] promptness.

prontificar-se [12] [prõntʃifi'kaxsi] vp: ~ **para algo/a fazer algo** to volunteer for sthg/to do sthg.

pronto, ta ['prõntu, ta] adj -1. [concluído, preparado] ready. -2. (antes de subst) [imediato] prompt. -3. [rápido] prompt. -4. [disposto]: ~ **a fazer algo** ready to do sthg. -5. fam [sem recursos] broke.

➤ **pronto** adv promptly; **de** ~ promptly.

pronto-socorro [,prõntuso'koxu] (pl **prontos-socorros**) m [hospital] casualty unit UK, emergency unit US.

prontuário [prõn'twarju] m -1. [ficha] file. -2. [manual] handbook.

pronúncia [pro'nũnsja] f -1. LING pronunciation. -2. JUR pronouncement.

pronunciamento [pronũnsja'mẽntu] m -1. [declaração] pronouncement. -2. JUR judgment.

pronunciar [16] [pronũn'sja(x)] vt to pronounce.

➤ **pronunciar-se** vp [emitir juízo]: ~-se **sobre/a favor de** to express an opinion about/in favour of.

propagação [propaga'sãw] (pl -ões) f -1. [ger] propagation. -2. [disseminação] spread.

propaganda [propa'gãnda] f -1. [COM - publicidade] advertising; [- anúncio] advert, advertisement; **fazer** ~ **de algo** to advertise sthg. -2. POL propaganda. -3. [divulgação] spreading.

propagar [14] [propa'ga(x)] vt -1. [disseminar] to spread. -2. BIOL to propagate.

➤ **propagar-se** vp -1. [ger] to propagate. -2. [disseminar-se] to spread.

propalado, da [propa'ladu, da] adj (antes de subst) known.

propalar [4] [propa'la(x)] vt to divulge.

propender [5] [propẽn'de(x)] vi: ~ **para** ou **a** to lean towards.

propensão [propẽn'sãw] (pl -ões) f inclination.

propenso, sa [pro'pẽnsu, sa] adj: ~ **a algo/a fazer algo** inclined to sthg/doing sthg.

propiciar [16] [propi'sja(x)] vt -1. [permitir, favorecer] to favour UK, to favor US. -2. [proporcionar]: ~ **algo a alguém** to allow sb sthg.

propício, cia [pro'pisju, sja] adj -1. [favorável]: ~ **a algo** propitious for sthg. -2. [oportuno] propitious.

propina [pro'pinaʃ] f -1. [gratificação] tip. -2. [ilegal] bribe.

propor [45] [pro'po(x)] vt -1. [ger] to propose; ~ **(a alguém) que** to propose (to sb) that. -2. JUR [ação] to move.

➤ **propor-se** vp: ~-se **a fazer algo** [visar] to aim to do sthg; [dispor-se] to offer to do sthg.

proporção [propox'sãw] (pl -ões) f proportion.

➤ **proporções** fpl -1. [tamanho] dimensions. -2. [importância] proportions.

➤ **à proporção que** loc adv as.

proporcionado, da [propoxsjo'nadu, da] adj proportionate.

proporcional [propoxsjo'naw] (pl -ais) adj proportional; ~ **a algo** proportional to sthg.

proporcionar [4] [propoxsjo'na(x)] vt -1. [propiciar] to provide. -2. [harmonizar]: ~ **algo com algo** to adjust sthg to sthg.

proporções [propox'sõjʃ] pl ➤ **proporção**.

proposição [propozi'sãw] (pl -ões) f -1. [proposta] proposal. -2. [enunciado] proposition.

propositadamente [propozitada'mẽntʃi] adv on purpose.

propositado, da [propozi'tadu, da] adj intentional.

proposital [propozi'taw] (pl -ais) adj intentional.

propósito [pro'pɔzitu] m intention; **de** ~ on purpose.

➤ **a propósito** loc adv [aliás] by the way.

➤ **a propósito de** loc prep concerning.

➤ **fora de propósito** loc adj unreasonable.

proposto, osta [pro'poʃtu, ɔʃta] <> pp ➤ **propor**. <> adj proposed.

➤ **proposta** f -1. [proposição] proposition. -2. [oferta] proposal.

propriamente [prɔprja'mẽntʃi] adv -1. [exatamente] exactly; ~ **dito** per se; **o Estado** ~ **dito** the actual State. -2. [adequadamente] suitably.

propriedade [proprje'dadʒi] f -1. [ger] property; ~ **pública** public property; ~ **privada** private property. -2. [direito de propriedade] ownership.

proprietário, ria [proprje'tarju, rja] m, f -1. [dono] owner. -2. [de imóvel de aluguel] landlord.

próprio, pria ['prɔprju, prja] adj -1. [ger] proper. -2. [particular] own; **meu** ~ **apartamento/carro** my own flat/car. -3. [apropriado]: ~ **(para)** suitable (for). -4. [peculiar] characteristic. -5. [mesmo] -self; **o** ~ **cliente do banco** the customer of the bank himself; **falei com o** ~ **presidente** I spoke to the president himself; **eu** ~ I myself; **é o** ~ [ser ele mesmo] speaking.

propulsão [propuw'sãw] *f* propulsion.

propulsor, ra [propuw'so(x), ra] *adj* propelling.

➡ **propulsor** *m* propellor.

prorrogação [proxoga'sãw] (*pl* -ões) *f* -**1.** [prolongação] deferment. -**2.** *FUT* extra time.

prorrogar [14] [proxo'ga(x)] *vt* to defer, to postpone.

prorrogável [proxo'gavew] (*pl* -eis) *adj* deferrable.

prorromper [5] [proxõn'pe(x)] *vi:* ~ **(de)** to burst (out of); ~ **em** to burst into.

prosa ['prɔza] <> *adj* [cheio de si] puffed up. <> *f* -**1.** *LITER* prose. -**2.** [conversa] chat. -**3.** [conversa fiada] chit-chat.

prosador, ra [proza'do(x), ra] *m, f* prose writer.

prosaico, ca [pro'zajku, ka] *adj* prosaic.

proscênio [pro'senju] *m* proscenium.

proscrever [5] [proʃkre've(x)] *vt* -**1.** [desterrar] to exile. -**2.** [expulsar] to ban. -**3.** [proibir] to prohibit. -**4.** [abolir] to do away with.

proscrito, ta [proʃ'kritu, ta] <> *pp* ▷ proscrever. <> *adj* -**1.** [desterrado] banished. -**2.** [expulso] outlawed. -**3.** [proibido] forbidden. <> *m, f* [exilado] exile.

prosear [15] [pro'zja(x)] *vi* to chat.

prosódia [pro'zodʒja] *f* *GRAM* prosody.

prosopopéia [prozopo'pɛja] *f* -**1.** [em retórica] prosopopoeia. -**2.** *fig* & *pej* [discurso] diatribe. -**3.** *fig* & *pej* [pose] airs and graces.

prospecção [proʃpek'sãw] (*pl* -ões) *f* *GEOL* prospecting; ~ **de petróleo** oil exploration.

prospecto [proʃ'pɛktu] *m* leaflet.

prospector, ra [proʃpek'to(x), ra] *m, f* *GEOL* prospector.

prosperar [4] [proʃpe'ra(x)] *vi* -**1.** [progredir]: ~ **(em algo)** [melhorar] to prosper (in sthg); [ter sucesso] to thrive (in sthg). -**2.** [enriquecer] to prosper.

prosperidade [proʃperi'dadʒi] *f* -**1.** [progresso] prosperity. -**2.** [sucesso] success.

próspero, ra ['prɔʃperu, ra] *adj* -**1.** [que progride] thriving. -**2.** [bem-sucedido] prosperous.

prosseguimento [prosegi'mẽntu] *m* continuation; **dar** ~ **a** to continue with.

prosseguir [55] [prose'gi(x)] <> *vt* to continue. <> *vi:* ~ **(em algo)** to continue (in sthg); ~ **fazendo algo** to continue doing sthg.

próstata ['prɔʃtata] *f* *ANAT* prostate.

prostíbulo [proʃ'tʃibulu] *m* brothel.

prostituição [proʃtʃitwi'sãw] *f* prostitution.

prostituir [74] [proʃtʃi'twi(x)] *vt* to prostitute.

➡ **prostituir-se** *vp* -**1.** [tornar-se prostituta] to turn to prostitution. -**2.** [ser prostituta] to be a prostitute. -**3.** *fig* [corromper-se] to prostitute o.s.

prostituta [proʃtʃi'tuta] *f* prostitute.

prostração [proʃtra'sãw] *f* prostration.

prostrado, da [proʃ'tradu, da] *adj* prostrate.

prostrar [4] [proʃ'tra(x)] *vt* -**1.** [ger] to prostrate. -**2.** [derrubar] to floor.

➡ **prostrar-se** *vp* [com reverência] to prostrate o.s.

protagonista [protago'niʃta] *mf* protagonist.

protagonizar [4] [protagoni'za(x)] *vt* -**1.** *CINE* & *TEATRO* to feature in. -**2.** [acontecimento] to be at the centre of *UK*, to be at the center of *US*.

proteção [prote'sãw] (*pl* -ões) *f* -**1.** [resguardo] protection. -**2.** [favorecimento] favour *UK*, favor *US*. -**3.** [dispositivo] defence *UK*, defense *US*.

protecionismo [protesjo'niʒmu] *m* [econômico] protectionism.

proteger [26] [prote'ʒe(x)] *vt* to protect; ~ **alguém de/contra algo** to protect sb from/against sthg.

➡ **proteger-se** *vp* [resguardar-se] to protect o.s.

protegido, da [prote'ʒidu, da] <> *adj* [resguardado] protected. <> *m, f* [favorito] protégé (*f* protégée).

proteína [prote'ina] *f* protein.

protelar [4] [prote'la(x)] *vt* to postpone.

prótese ['prɔtezi] *f* *MED* prosthesis.

protestante [proteʃ'tãntʃi] <> *adj* Protestant. <> *mf* Protestant.

protestantismo [proteʃtãn'tʃiʒmu] *m* Protestantism.

protestar [4] [proteʃ'ta(x)] <> *vt* -**1.** [título, promissória] to contest. -**2.** [declarar] to profess. <> *vi* -**1.** [reclamar]: ~ **(contra/em favor de algo)** to protest (against/in favour of sthg); **protesto!** *JUR* I protest! -**2.** [clamar]: ~ **por algo** to call for sthg.

protesto [pro'tɛʃtu] *m* -**1.** [ger] protest. -**2.** *fml* [declaração] declaration.

protetor, ra [prote'to(x), ra] *adj* (*mpl* -es, *fpl* -s) <> *adj* protective. <> *m, f* protector.

protocolar [4] [protoko'la(x)] <> *adj* formal. <> *vt* to register.

protocolo [proto'kɔlu] *m* -**1.** [ger] protocol; **quebrar o** ~ to break with protocol. -**2.** [registro] registration. -**3.** [recibo] record. -**4.** [setor] registry.

protocolo [proto'kɔlu] *m* *COMPUT* protocol.

protótipo [pro'tɔtʃipu] *m* -**1.** [modelo] prototype. -**2.** *fig* [exemplo]: **ser o** ~ **de algo** to be the epitome of sthg.

protuberância [protube'rãnsja] *f* protuberance.

protuberante [protube'rãntʃi] *adj* protuberant.

prova ['prɔval] *f* -**1.** [ger] proof; **tirar a** ~ **dos noves** to cast out 9s. -**2.** *EDUC* exam. -**3.** [teste] test; **à** ~ **de água** waterproof; **à** ~ **de bala** bulletproof; **à** ~ **de fogo** fireproof; **pôr algo à** ~ to put sthg to the test. -**4.** *ESP* event. -**5.** *COST* fitting. -**6.** [de comida, bebida] taster.

provação [prova'sãw] (*pl* -ões) *f* ordeal.

provado, da [pro'vadu, da] *adj* -**1.** [ger] proven. -**2.** [experimentado] tried.

provador [prova'do(x)] *m* -**1.** [em loja] fitting room. -**2.** [de café, vinho] taster.

provar [4] [pro'va(x)] <> *vt* -**1.** [demonstrar] to prove; ~ **algo por A mais B** to demonstrate sthg step by step. -**2.** [testar] to test. -**3.** [roupa] to try on. -**4.** [comida, bebida] to taste. <> *vi:* ~ **(de algo)**

[comida, bebida] to have a taste (of sthg).

provável [pro'vavɛw] (*pl* **-eis**) *adj* [possível] probable; **é ~ que chova** it looks like rain; **é ~ que ela não chegue hoje** she's not likely to come today.

provavelmente [provavew'mẽntʃil] *adv* probably.

provedor, ra [prove'do(x), ra] *m, f* provider; **~ de acesso** Internet service provider.

proveito [pro'vejtu] *m* advantage; **em ~ de** in favour of; **tirar ~ de algo** to benefit from sthg.

proveitoso, osa [provej'tozu, ɔzal *adj* **-1.** [vantajoso] advantageous. **- 2.** [lucrativo] profitable. **- 3.** [útil] useful.

proveniência [prove'njẽnsja] *f* origin.

proveniente [prove'njẽntʃil] *adj*: **~ de** [originário] originating from; [resultante] arising from; **esta uva é ~ da Itália** these grapes come from Italy.

proventos [pro'vẽntuʃ] *mpl* proceeds.

prover [41] [pro've(x)] <> *vt* **-1.** [ger]: **~ algo/alguém de algo** to provide sthg/sb with sthg. **- 2.** [providenciar] to provide. **- 3.** [vaga, cargo] to fill. <> *vi* [atender]: **~ a algo** to take care of sthg.

~ prover-se *vp* [abastecer-se]: **~-se de algo** to provide o.s. with sthg.

proverbial [provex'bjaw] *adj* proverbial.

provérbio [pro'vɛrbju] *m* proverb.

proveta [pro'veta] *f* test tube; **bebê de ~** test-tube baby.

providência [provi'dẽnsja] *f* [medida] measure; **tomar ~s** to take measures.

~ Providência *f*: **Divina Providência** (divine) Providence.

providencial [providẽn'sjaw] (*pl* **-ais**) *adj* providential.

providenciar [16] [providẽn'sja(x)] <> *vt* **-1.** [prover] to provide. **- 2.** [tomar providências para] to set into motion. <> *vi* **-1.** [cuidar]: **vamos ~ para que tudo dê certo** let's see to it that all works out. **- 2.** [tomar providências]: **~ contra/para algo** to take measures against/for sthg.

provido, da [pro'vidu, da] *adj* [abastecido]: **~ de algo** supplied with sthg; **bem ~** well stocked; **uma conta bancária bem provida** a fat bank account.

provimento [provi'mẽntul] *m* **-1.** [provisão] stocking up. **- 2.** *JUR* granting; **dar ~** to grant a petition.

província [pro'vĩnsja] *f* **-1.** [divisão administrativa] province. **- 2.** [interior] provinces (*pl*).

provincianismo [provĩnsja'niʒmul] *m* provincialism.

provinciano, na [provĩn'sjãnu, nal *adj pej* provincial.

provindo, da [pro'vĩndu, da] <> *pp* ⊳ **provir**. <> *adj*: **~ de** (coming) from.

provir [67] [pro'vi(x)] *vi*: **~ de** to come from.

provisão [provi'zãw] (*pl* **-ões**) *f* supply.

~ provisões *fpl* supplies.

provisoriamente [provizɔrja'mẽntʃil] *adv* provisionally.

provisório, ria [provi'zɔrju, rja] *adj* provisional.

provocação [provoka'sãw] (*pl* **-ões**) *f* **-1.** [implicância] provocation. **- 2.** [sensual] attraction.

provocador, ra [provoka'do(x), ra] (*mpl* **-es**, *fpl* **-s**) <> *adj* provocative. <> *m, f* provoker.

provocante [provo'kãntʃil] *adj* [sensualmente] provocative.

provocar [12] [provo'ka(x)] *vt* **-1.** [ger] to provoke. **- 2.** [incitar]: **~ alguém (a fazer algo)** to provoke sb (into doing sthg). **- 3.** [chamar a atenção, atrair sensualmente] to arouse. **- 4.** [promover] to cause.

provocativo, va [provoka'tʃivu, va] *adj* provocative.

proximidade [prosimi'dadʒi] *f* **-1.** [ger] proximity. **- 2.** [afinidade] closeness.

~ proximidades *fpl* [arredores] proximity (*sg*).

próximo, ma ['prɔsimu, mal <> *adj* **-1.** [no espaço]: **~ (a** *ou* **de)** close (to). **- 2.** [no tempo] recent; **futuro ~** near future. **- 3.** (*antes de subst*) [seguinte] next. **- 4.** [chegado] close. <> *m, f* [em fila] next (one).

~ próximo <> *m*: **o ~** [o semelhante] neighbour *UK*, neighbor *US*. <> *adv* close.

~ próxima *f* [a próxima vez]: **até a próxima!** [em despedida] see you soon!; **fica para a próxima** until some other time.

proxy ['prɔʃil (*pl* **proxies**) *m COMPUT* proxy.

prudência [pru'dẽnsja] *f* caution, prudence; **com ~** carefully.

prudente [pru'dẽntʃil *adj* **-1.** [comedido] prudent. **- 2.** [cauteloso] cautious.

prumo ['prumu] *m* **-1.** [instrumento] plumb line. **- 2.** *NÁUT* lead.

prurido [pru'ridul *m* **-1.** [comichão] itch. **- 2.** *fig* [desejo] urge.

PS *m* **-1.** (*abrev de* **Post Scriptum**) PS. **- 2.** (*abrev de* **Pronto Socorro**) *first aid*.

PSB (*abrev de* **Partido Socialista Brasileiro**) *m Brazilian socialist party*.

PSDB (*abrev de* **Partido da Social Democracia Brasileira**) *m Brazilian social democratic party, the second largest right-wing party in Brazil*.

pseudônimo [psew'donimul *m* pseudonym.

psicanálise [psika'nalizil *f* psychoanalysis.

psicanalista [psikana'liʃtal *mf* psychoanalyst.

psicanalítico, ca [psikana'litʃiku, kal *adj* psychoanalitical.

psicodélico, ca [psiko'dɛliku, kal *adj* psychedelic.

psicodrama [psiko'drãmal *m* psychodrama.

psicolingüístico, ca [ˌpsikolĩ'gwiʃtʃiku, kal *adj* psycholinguistic.

~ psicolingüística *f* psycholinguistics (*sg*).

psicologia [psikolo'ʒial *f* psychology.

psicológico, ca [psiko'lɔʒiku, kal *adj* psychological.

psicólogo, ga [psi'kɔlogu, gal *m, f* psychologist.

psicopata [psiko'patal *mf* psychopath.

psicose [psi'kɔzil *f* **-1.** *MED* psychosis. **- 2.** *fig* [obsessão]: **~ de algo** obsession with sthg.

psicossomático, ca [psikoso'matʃiku, kal *adj* psychosomatic.

psicotécnico, ca [psiko'tɛkniku, ka] *adj* response *(antes de subst)*.
→ **psicotécnico** *m* [exame] response test.
psicoterapeuta [psikotera'pewta] *mf* psychotherapist.
psicoterapia [psikotera'pia] *f* psychotherapy.
psicótico, ca [psi'kɔtʃiku, ka] *adj* psychotic.
psique [ˈpsiki] *f* psyche.
psiquiatra [psi'kjatra] *mf* psychiatrist.
psiquiatria [psikja'tria] *f* psychiatry.
psiquiátrico, ca [psi'kjatriku, ka] *adj* psychiatric.
psíquico, ca [ˈpsikiku, ka] *adj* psychic.
psiu [psiw] *interj* **-1.** [para chamar] hey! **-2.** [para calar] hush!
psoríase [pso'rjazil] *f* psoriasis.
PT *(abrev de* **Partido dos Trabalhadores**) *m Brazilian workers' party, the largest left-wing party in Brazil.*
PTB *(abrev de* **Partido Trabalhista Brasileiro**) *m Brazilian Workers' Party, a large party of the centre.*
pua [ˈpua] *f* [de broca] bit; **sentar a ~ em alguém** *fig* to put the pressure on sb.
puberdade [puber'dadʒi] *f* puberty.
púbere [ˈpuberi] *adj* pubescent.
púbico, ca [ˈpubiku, ka] *adj* pubic.
púbis [ˈpubiʃ] *m inv* pubis.
publicação [publika'sãw] *(pl* -ões) *f* publication.
publicar [12] [publiˈka(x)] *vt* **-1.** [ger] to publish. **-2.** [divulgar] to broadcast.
publicidade [publisi'dadʒi] *f* **-1.** [divulgação] publicity; **dar ~ a algo/alguém** to publicize sthg/sb. **-2.** COM advertising.
publicitário, ria [publisi'tarju, rja] <> *adj* advertising *(antes de subst).* <> *m, f* advertiser.
público, ca [ˈpubliku, ka] *adj* public.
→ **público** *m* **-1.** [o povo] public. **-2.** [plateia] audience; **o grande ~** general public; **em ~** in public.
PUC *(abrev de* **Pontifícia Universidade Católica**) *f Pontifical Catholic university.*
pudico, ca [puˈdʒiku, ka] *adj* **-1.** [recatado] bashful. **-2.** *pej* prudish.
pudim [puˈdʒĩ] *(pl* -ns) *m* pudding; **~ de leite** milk pudding; **~ de pão** bread pudding.
pudor [puˈdo(x)] *m* **-1.** [recato] modesty; **ter ~ de** [ter vergonha] to be ashamed of. **-2.** [decoro] decency; **atentado ao ~** indecent assault.
puericultura [pwerikuw'tural *f* childcare.
pueril [pweˈriwl] *adj* childish, puerile.
puerilidade [pwerili'dadʒi] *f* **-1.** [infantilidade] childishness, puerility. **-2.** *fig* [banalidade] foolish action.
pufe [ˈpufi] *m* pouffe.
pugilismo [puʒi'liʒmul *m* boxing.
pugilista [puʒi'liʃta] *m* boxer.
pugnaz [pug'najʒ] *adj* pugnacious.
puído, da [ˈpwidu, da] *adj* frayed.
puir [74] [pwi(x)] *vt* to fray.
pujança [pu'ʒãsa] *f* **-1.** [força, poderio] power. **-2.** [da vegetação] vitality.

pujante [pu'ʒãtʃil *adj* powerful.
pula-pula [ˌpula'pula] *(pl* pula-pulas) *m* **-1.** [brinquedo] pogo (stick). **-2.** [cama elástica] bouncy castle. **-3.** [ave] golden-crowned warbler.
pular [4] [pu'la(x)] <> *vt* **-1.** [saltar] to jump (over); **~ corda** to skip; **~ a cerca** *fig* [trair] to be unfaithful. **-2.** [páginas, trechos] to skip. **-3.:** **~ Carnaval** to celebrate carnival. <> *vi* **-1.** [saltar] to jump; **~ de alegria** to jump for joy. **-2.** [palpitar] to skip a beat.
pulga [ˈpuwga] *f* flea; **estar/ficar com a ~ atrás da orelha** to smell a rat.
pulgão [puw'gãw] *(pl* -ões) *m* aphid.
pulgueiro [puw'gejru] *m* [cinema] fleapit.
pulha [ˈpuʎa] *m* creep.
pulmão [puw'mãw] *(pl* -ões) *m* lung.
pulmonar [puwmo'na(x)] *adj* pulmonary.
pulo [ˈpulu] *m* leap; **a um ~ de** *fig* [perto de] just a hop away from; **dar um ~ em** *fig* [ir] to stop off at.
pulôver [pu'love(x)] *(pl* -es) *m* pullover.
púlpito [ˈpuwpitul *m* pulpit.
pulsação [puwsa'sãw] *(pl* -ões) *f* **-1.** [batimento] pulsation. **-2.** MED [pulso] pulse; **medir as pulsações (cardíacas)** to take the pulse.
pulsar [4] [puw'sa(x)] *vi* [palpitar] to beat, to throb.
pulular [4] [pulu'la(x)] *vi* **-1.** [multiplicar-se] to proliferate. **-2.** [abundar]: **~ de** to swarm with, to teem with.
pulverizador [puwveriza'do(x)] *m* [para líquidos] spray.
pulverizar [4] [puwveri'za(x)] *vt* **-1.** [ger] to spray. **-2.** [reduzir a pó] [destruir] to pulverize.
pum [pũl] *(pl* puns) <> *m mfam* [peido] fart; **soltar um ~** to pass wind. <> *interj* bang!
pumba [ˈpũbal *interj* [para ação rápida] whoosh!
punção [pũ'sãw] *(pl* -ões) <> *f* MED puncture. <> *m* [instrumento] stylus.
pungente [pũ'ʒẽtʃil *adj* poignant.
pungir [78] [pũ'ʒi(x)] *vt* ant & *fig* [afligir] to afflict.
punguista [pũ'giʃta] *m* pickpocket.
punhado [pu'ɲadul *m:* **um ~ de** a handful of.
punhal [pu'ɲawl *(pl* -ais) *m* dagger.
punhalada [puɲa'ladal *f* stab.
punheta [pu'ɲeta] *f vulg* [masturbação] jacking off, wanking *UK*; **bater** *ou* **tocar ~** to jack off, to wank *UK*.
punho [ˈpuɲul *m* **-1.** ANAT fist; **de próprio ~** in one's own handwriting. **-2.** [de manga] cuff. **-3.** [de espada, punhal] hilt.
punição [puni'sãw] *(pl* -ões) *f* punishment.
punir [6] [pu'ni(x)] *vt* to punish.
punitivo, va [puni'tʃivu, va] *adj* punitive.
puns [pũʃ] *mpl* ⊳ pum.
pupila [pu'pila] *f* ANAT pupil.
pupilo, la [pu'pilu, la] *m, f* **-1.** [aluno] pupil. **-2.** [tutelado] ward.
purê [pu'rel *m* purée, mash; **~ de batatas** mashed potato.
pureza [pu'reza] *f* purity.
purgação [puxga'sãw] *(pl* -ões) *f* **-1.** [expiação]

purge. -**2.** [de ferida] cleansing. -**3.** [purificação] purification.

purgante [pux'gãntʃi] m -**1.** [remédio] purgative. -**2.** fam [pessoa, trabalho] pain in the neck.

purgar [14] [pux'ga(x)] vt -**1.** [expiar] to purge. -**2.** [purificar]: ~ **algo (de algo)** to purge sthg (of sthg).

➡ **purgar-se** vp: ~-**se (de algo)** to purge o.s. (of sthg).

purgativo, va [puxga'tʃivu, va] adj purgative.

➡ **purgativo** m [remédio] purgative.

purgatório [puxga'tɔrju] m RELIG purgatory.

purificação [purifika'sãw] (pl -ões) f -**1.** [depuração] purification. -**2.** RELIG [ritual] cleansing.

purificar [12] [purifi'ka(x)] vt: ~ **algo (de algo)** [depurar] to cleanse sthg (of sthg).

➡ **purificar-se** vp to cleanse o.s.

purista [pu'riʃta] mf purist.

puritanismo [puritã'niʒmu] m puritanism.

puritano, na [puri'tãnu, na] ◇ adj puritanical. ◇ m, f puritan.

puro, ra ['puru, ra] adj -**1.** [ger] pure. -**2.** (antes de subst) [mero] pure. -**3.** (antes de subst) [absoluto] plain.

puro-sangue [ˌpuru'sãngi] (pl **puros-sangues**) mf thoroughbred.

púrpura ['puxpura] f [cor] purple.

purpúreo, rea [pux'purju, rja] adj crimson.

purpurina [puxpu'rina] f purpurin.

purulento, ta [puru'lẽntu, ta] adj purulent.

pus ['puʃ] m inv pus.

pusilânime [puzi'lãnimi] adj pusillanimous.

pústula ['puʃtula] f -**1.** [vesícula] pustule. -**2.** fig & pej [pessoa] rat.

puta ['putа] f ➡ **puto.**

putaria [puta'ria] f vulg [prostíbulo] knocking shop.

putativo, va [puta'tʃivu, va] adj putative.

puto, ta ['putu, ta] vulg adj -**1.** [devasso] rotten; **o** ~ **de ...** fam the bloody ... -**2.** [zangado] mad; **estar/ficar** ~ **(da vida)** to be/get furious.

➡ **puto** ◇ m vulg [dinheiro] penny UK, dime US ◇ adj [extraordinário]: **um** ~ **(de um)** ... a brilliant/hell of a ....

➡ **puta** vulg f [prostituta] whore; **filho da puta** son of a bitch; **puta que pariu!** fucking hell!; **mandar alguém para a puta que pariu** to tell sb to fuck off.

putrefação [putrefa'sãw] f putrefaction.

putrefato, ta [putre'fatu, ta] adj rotten.

putrefazer [31] [putrefa'ze(x)] vt to putrefy.

➡ **putrefazer-se** vp to rot.

pútrido, da ['putridu, da] adj rotten.

puxa ['puʃa] interj: ~ **(vida)!** goodness (me)!, gosh.

puxado, da [pu'ʃadu, da] adj -**1.** [cansativo] exhausting. -**2.** [difícil] testing. -**3.** [caro] steep. -**4.** [amendoado] almond-shaped.

➡ **puxada** f -**1.** [puxão] tug. -**2.** [esforço]: **dar uma puxada** [em corrida] to put on a spurt; [nos estudos] to make an effort.

puxador [puʃa'do(x)] (pl -**es**) mf -**1.** [de samba] the leading singer in an 'escola de samba', a group of musicians and samba dancers who perform in street parades during carnival celebrations in Brazil. -**2.** [de fumo] (marijuana) smoker. -**3.** [ladrão] thief. ◇ m handle.

puxão [pu'ʃãw] (pl -ões) m tug; **dar um** ~ **em alguém** to pull s.b.

puxa-puxa [ˌpuʃa'puʃa] (pl **puxa-puxas**) ◇ adj toffee (antes de subst). ◇ m toffee.

puxar [4] [pu'ʃa(x)] ◇ vt -**1.** [ger] to pull. -**2.** [arrancar, sacar] to pull out. -**3.** [iniciar - conversa] to start (up); [- briga] to break into; [- samba] to start (up), to break into; ~ **assunto** to bring up a subject. -**4.** [desencadear] to bring about; **uma coisa puxa a outra** one thing leads to another. -**5.** [adular]: ~ **o saco de alguém** fam fig to suck up to sb. -**6.** gír droga [fumo] to smoke. -**7.** gír crime [automóvel] to steal. ◇ vi -**1.** [impor esforço a]: ~ **por** to strain. -**2.** [ser parecido com]: ~ **a alguém** to take after sb. -**3.** [mancar]: ~ **de uma perna** to limp.

puxa-saco [ˌpuʃa'saku] (pl **puxa-sacos**) fam ◇ adj crawling. ◇ mf crawler.

puxões [pu'ʃõjʃ] pl ➡ **puxão.**

PV (abrev de **Partido Verde**) m Brazilian green party.

PVC (abrev de **Polyvinyl Chloride**) m PVC.

q, Q [ke] m [letra] q, Q.

Qatar [ka'ta(x)] n Qatar.

QG (abrev de Quartel General) m HQ.

QI (abrev de Quociente de Inteligência) m IQ.

QT (abrev de Qualidade Total) f TQM.

qua. (abrev de quarta-feira) f Wed.

quadra ['kwadra] f -**1.** [quarteirão] block; ~ **da praia** beachfront block. -**2.** [esportiva] court. -**3.** [em jogos] four. -**4.** [estrofe] quatrain. -**5.** AGR [medida] area of 48,400m².

quadrado, da [kwa'dradu, da] m: **dois ao** ~ two squared.

quadragésimo, ma [kwadra'ʒezimu, ma] num fortieth; veja também sexto.

quadrangular [kwadrãngu'la(x)] adj GEOM quadrangular.

quadrângulo [kwa'drãngulu] m quadrangle.

quadriculado, da [kwadriku'ladu, da] adj -**1.** [camisa, padrão] checked. -**2.** [papel] squared.

quadril [kwa'driw] (*pl* -**is**) *m* hip.

quadrilátero, ra [kwadri'lateru, ra] *adj* quadrilateral.
➡ **quadrilátero** *m* quadrilateral.

quadrilha [kwa'driʎa] *f* -**1.** [de ladrões etc] gang.
-**2.** [dança] quadrille.

quadrimestral [kwadrimeʃ'traw] (*pl* -**ais**) *adj* quarterly.

quadrimotor [kwadrimo'to(x)] ⬦ *adj* four-engined. ⬦ *m* [avião] four-engined plane.

quadrinho [kwa'driɲu] *m* [das tiras] (cartoon) drawing.
➡ **quadrinhos** *mpl*: **(história em)** ~**s** cartoon strip.

quadro ['kwadru] *m* -**1.** [ger] frame. -**2.** [pintura] painting. -**3.** [quadro-negro] blackboard. -**4.** [mural] board; ~ **de avisos** noticeboard. -**5.** [gráfico] chart. -**6.** *TEC* [painel] panel; ~ **de luz** light panel. -**7.** *TEATRO* & *TV* scene. -**8.** [situação] picture; ~ **clínico** clinical picture. -**9.** [de empresa, partido] staff. -**10.** *ESP* [equipe] team.

quadro-negro [ˌkwadru'negru] (*pl* **quadros-negros**) *m* blackboard.

quadrúpede [kwa'drupedʒi] ⬦ *adj* [animal] quadrupedal, four-footed. ⬦ *mf* -**1.** [animal] quadruped. -**2.** *mfam* [estúpido] clot *UK*, dumbhead *US*.

quadruplicar [12] [kwadrupli'ka(x)] ⬦ *vt* to quadruple. ⬦ *vi* to quadruple.

quádruplo, pla ['kwadruplu, pla] ⬦ *adj* quadruple. ⬦ *m, f* [quadrigêmeo] quad, quadruplet.
➡ **quádruplo** *m* quadruple.

quaisquer ▷ qualquer.

qual [kwaw] (*pl* **quais**) ⬦ *adj* which; ~ **perfume você prefere?** which perfume do you prefer?; **não sei** ~ **caminho devo seguir** I don't know which road I should follow. ⬦ *conj fml* [como] like; **(tal)** ~ exactly like. ⬦ *interj* what!; ~ ! [exprimindo espanto] what!; [exprimindo negação] no; ~ **nada!**, ~ **o quê!** yeah right! ⬦ *pron* -**1.** [em interrogativa] what; ~ **é o seu nome?** what's your name?; ~ **a cor dos seus cabelos?** what is the colour of your hair?; **quais são suas intenções?** what are your intentions? -**2.** [especificando] which (one); **perguntei** ~ **seria a melhor opção** I asked which (one) would be the better option; **o/a** ~ [suj: pessoa] who; [complemento: pessoa] whom; [suj, complemento: coisa] which; **ela teve três filhos, o mais velho dos quais tornou-se médico** she had three sons, the eldest of whom became a doctor; **este é o livro sobre o** ~ **lhe escrevi** this is the book (which/that) I wrote to you about; **cada** ~ each and every one; ~ **deles ...?** which one (of them) ...?

qualidade [kwali'dadʒi] *f* -**1.** [ger] quality; ~ **de vida** quality of life; **de** ~ good quality. -**2.** [tipo] grade. -**3.** *pej* [baixo nível] ilk. -**4.** [condição]: **na** ~ **de** in the capacity of.

qualificação [kwalifika'sãw] (*pl* -**ões**) *f* [avaliação] classification.
➡ **qualificações** *fpl* [formação, preparo] qualifications.

qualificado, da [kwalifi'kadu, da] *adj* -**1.** [preparado] qualified; **não** ~ unqualified. -**2.** *JUR* [caracterizado] aggravated.

qualificar [12] [kwalifi'ka(x)] *vt* -**1.** [classificar] to qualify. -**2.** [avaliar] to describe.
➡ **qualificar-se** *vp* [classificar-se] to qualify.

qualificativo, va [kwalifika'tʃivu, va] *adj* qualifying.
➡ **qualificativo** *m* label.

qualitativo, va [kwalita'tʃivu, va] *adj* qualitative.

qualquer [kwaw'kɛ(x)] (*pl* **quaisquer**) ⬦ *adj* -**1.** [algum]: **traga uma bebida** ~ bring me any old drink; **comprei um jornal** ~ I bought any old newspaper; **havia** ~ **coisa de errado** there was something wrong; **num ponto** ~ **da Sibéria** somewhere or other in Siberia; ~ **dia venha me visitar** come and see me some day; **a** ~ **momento** any minute now; **um outro** ~ [coisa] any other one; [pessoa] some; **ser** ~ **coisa** [ser ótimo, extraordinário] to be something else. -**2.** *(antes de subst)* [todo] any; **ele enfrenta quaisquer perigos** he braves all dangers; ~ **pessoa sabe fazer arroz** anybody can cook rice; ~ **que seja** whatever; ~ **um** anybody; **todo e** ~ each and every; **de** ~ **maneira** *ou* **jeito** [seja como for] somehow or other; [a todo custo] come what may. -**3.** *pej* [ordinário, sem importância]: **ele se contenta com** ~ **coisa** he's happy with any old thing; **de** ~ **maneira** *ou* **jeito** [sem cuidado] any (old) how. ⬦ *pron* -**1.** [algum]: ~ **(de)** any (of); **como não posso ter todas, terei de escolher** ~ as I can't have them all, I'll have to chose any one; **prove quaisquer destas balas** try any one of these sweets; **um** ~ *pej* [pessoa] a nobody. -**2.** [todo - coisa]: ~ **(de)** any (of); ~ **destas substâncias é perigosa** any of these substances is dangerous; [- pessoa] anyone; ~ **de nós faria o mesmo** anyone of us would do the same.

quando ['kwãdu] ⬦ *adv* when. ⬦ *conj* when; [ao passo que] while; **de** ~ **em** ~ from time to time; **de vez em** ~ from time to time; **desde** ~ how long; ~ **mais não seja** at least, if only; ~ **muito** at (the) most; ~ **quer que** whenever.

quanta ▷ quanto.

quantia [kwãn'tʃia] *f* sum.

quantidade [kwãntʃi'dadʒi] *f* -**1.** [medida] amount. -**2.** [número] number. -**3.** [abundância]: **uma** ~ **de** a number of; **em** ~ in large quantity.

quantificar [12] [kwãntʃifi'ka(x)] *vt* to quantify.

quantitativo, va [kwãntʃita'tʃivu, va] *adj* quantitative.

quanto, ta ['kwãntu, ta] ⬦ *adj* -**1.** *(interrogativo)* how; **quantas maçãs você quer?** how many apples do you want?; **há** ~ **tempo você está esperando?** how long have you been waiting? -**2.** *(exclamativo)* how; **quantos livros!** how many books!, so many books!; **quanta gente!** how many people!, so many people! ⬦ *pron* -**1.** *(interrogativo)* how; **quantos fugiram?** how many got away? -**2.** *(exclamativo)* how; **quantos não morrem antes de chegar à idade adulta!** how many died before reaching adulthood! **-3.** *(relativo)*: **tantos ... quantos ...** as many ... as ...; **faça tantas alterações quantas forem necessárias** make as many changes as necessary; **gosto de tudo** ~ **é verdura** I like all green vegetables; **tudo** ~ **é tipo de penteado** all kinds of hairstyles.

◆ **quanto** ⟷ *pron (interrogativo)* [quantia, preço] how; ~ **custa este casaco?** how much does this coat cost?; **a** ~ **está o dólar?** how much is the dollar?; [quantidade]: ~ **de maionese devo acrescentar?** how much mayonnaise should I add?; ~ **de combustível ainda temos?** how much fuel do we still have? ⟷ *adv* [indicando intensidade, proporção] much; **esforcei-me o** ~ **pude** I tried as much/hard as I could; **sei o** ~ **você me ama** I know how much you love me; **um tanto** ~ [meio] somewhat; **tanto** ~ as much as; **tanto um quanto o outro são incompetentes** [ambos] both are equally incompetent; **tão ...** ~ **... as ... as ...;** ~ **mais tem, mais quer** the more he has, the more he wants; ~ **mais rápido, melhor** the faster, the better; ~ **mais** [especialmente] especially; [muito menos] especially not.

◆ **quanto a** *loc prep* [com relação] as for, as far as; ~ **a mim** as for me, as far as I'm concerned.

◆ **quanto antes** *loc adv*: **o** ~ **antes** as soon as possible.

◆ **quantos** *pron pl fam*: **um certo Carlos não sei dos quantos** a certain Carlos something or other.

◆ **quantas** *pron pl fam*: **a quantas** [em que situação] at what stage; **não sei a quantas anda esse processo** I don't know what stage the trial is at.

quão [kwãw] *adv* how.

quarenta [kwa'rẽnta] *num* forty; *veja também* **sessenta**.

quarentão, tona [kwarẽn'tãw, tona] *(mpl -ões, fpl -s)* ⟷ *adj* in one's forties. ⟷ *m, f* person in their forties.

quarentena [kwarẽn'tena] *f* quarantine.

quarentona [kwarẽn'tona] *f* ⟼ **quarentão**.

quaresma [kwa'rɛʒma] *f* **-1.** RELIG Lent. **-2.** [flor] glory bush.

quarta ['kwaxta] *f* [quarta-feira] Wednesday; *veja também* **sábado**.

quarta-de-final [ˌkwaxtadʒifi'naw] *(pl quartas-de-final)* *f* quarter final.

quarta-feira [ˌkwaxta'fejra] *(pl quartas-feiras) f* Wednesday; ~ **de cinzas** Ash Wednesday; *veja também* **sábado**.

quarteirão [kwaxtej'rãw] *(pl -ões) m* block.

quartel [kwax'tɛw] *(pl -éis) m* MIL barracks *(pl)*.

quartel-general [kwaxˌtɛwʒene'raw] *(pl quartéis-generais) m* general headquarters *(pl)*.

quarteto [kwax'tetu] *m* **-1.** MÚS quartet; ~ **de cordas** string quartet. **-2.** LITER [em poesia] quatrain.

quarto, ta ['kwaxtu, ta] *num* fourth; **a quarta parte** a quarter; *veja também* **sexto**.

◆ **quarto** *m* **-1.** [a quarta parte] quarter; **passar um mau** ~ **de hora** *fig* to have a tough time (of it). **-2.** [aposento] bedroom; ~ **de casal** double room;

~ **de banho** bathroom; ~ **de despejo** store cupboard; ~ **de solteiro** single room. **-3.** MIL [plantão] watch; **estar/ficar de** ~ to be/remain on duty. **-4.** [de boi] haunch. **-5.** ASTRON [da lua]: ~ **crescente/minguante** first/last quarter.

◆ **quarta** *f* **-1.** [marcha] fourth; **passar a quarta** to shift into fourth. **-2.** MÚS perfect fourth. **-3.** [medida] quart.

quarto-e-sala [ˌkwaxtwi'sala] *(pl quarto-e-salas) m* studio apartment.

quarto-zagueiro [ˌkwaxtuza'gejru] *(pl -ros) m* FUT fullback.

quartzo ['kwaxtsu] *m* quartz.

quase ['kwazi] *adv* **-1.** [ger] nearly; **estou** ~, ~ **perdendo a paciência** I am on the verge of losing my temper; **tropecei e** ~ **caí** I tripped and almost fell. **-2.** [pouco mais, ou menos] almost, nearly; **ela tem** ~ **dez anos** she is almost *ou* nearly ten years old; ~ **não trabalhei hoje** I hardly worked today; ~ **nada/tudo** almost nothing/everything; ~ **nunca** almost never, hardly ever; ~ **sempre** nearly always.

quatro ['kwatru] *num* four; **de** ~ on all fours; **estar/ficar de** ~ [surpreso] to be astounded; **estar de** ~ **por alguém** [apaixonado] to be head over heels over sb; *veja também* **seis**.

quatrocentos, tas [ˌkwatru'sẽntuʃ, taʃ] *num* four hundred; *veja também* **seis**.

que [kil] ⟷ *adj inv* **-1.** [em interrogativas] what, which; ~ **livros você quer?** which books do you want?; ~ **dia é hoje?** what day is it today?; ~ **horas são?** what time is it? **-2.** [em exclamações]: **mas** ~ **belo dia!** what a beautiful day!; ~ **fome!** I'm starving!; ~ **maravilha!** how wonderful! ⟷ *pron* **-1.** [em interrogativas] what; ~ **é isso?** what's that?; **o** ~ **você quer?** what do you want?; **o** ~ **você vai comer?** what are you going to eat? **-2.** [uso relativo: sujeito-pessoa] who; **o homem** ~ **está correndo** the man who's running; [-coisa] which, that; **a guerra** ~ **começou em 1939** the war that started in 1939. **-3.** [uso relativo: complemento-pessoa] whom, that; **o homem** ~ **conheci** the man (whom) I met; [-coisa] which, that; **o bolo** ~ **comi era ótimo** the cake (that) I ate was great. ⟷ *conj* **-1.** [com complemento direto] that; **ele disse-me** ~ **ia de férias** he told me (that) he was going on holiday. **-2.** [em comparações]: **(do)** ~ **than**; **é mais caro (do)** ~ **o outro** it's more expensive than the other. **-3.** [exprime causa]: **leva o guarda-chuva** ~ **está chovendo** take an umbrella because it's raining; **vai depressa** ~ **você está atrasado** you'd better hurry because you're late. **-4.** [exprime consequência] that; **pediu-me tanto** ~ **acabei por lhe dar** he asked me for it so much that I ended up giving it to him. **-5.** [exprime tempo]: **há horas** ~ **estou à espera** I've been waiting for hours; **há muito** ~ **não voulá** I haven't been there for ages. **-6.** [indica desejo] that; **espero** ~ **você se divirta** I hope (that) you have fun; **quero** ~ **você o faça** I want you to do it; ~ **você seja feliz!** may you be happy! **-7.** [em locuções]: ~ **nem** like; **ele chorou**

~ **nem um bebê** he cried like a baby; **ele é feio ~ nem o irmão** he's as ugly as his brother.

quê [ˈkel◇ *m* [algo]: **um** ~ something; **um** ~ **de** [toque] a touch of; [sabor] slightly; **um não sei** ~ **a** je ne sais quoi; **sem** ~ **nem por** ~ [sem motivo] without rhyme or reason. ◇ *interj* [exprimindo espanto] what! ◇ *pron* ▷ **que**.

Quebec [keˈbɛkil *n*: (o) ~ Quebec.

quebra [ˈkɛbral *f* - **1.** [ger] break. - **2.** [despedaçamento] breakage. - **3.** [falência] bankruptcy. - **4.** *COMPUT*: ~ **de página** page break.

➡ **de quebra** *loc adv* what's more.

quebra-cabeça [ˌkɛbrakaˈbesal (*pl* **quebra-cabeças**) *m* - **1.** [jogo] puzzle. - **2.** *fig* [problema] dilemma.

quebradiço, ça [kebraˈdʒisu, sal *adj* fragile.

quebrado, da [keˈbradu, dal *adj* - **1.** [vaso, vidro, braço] broken. - **2.** [enguiçado - carro, máquina] broken down; [- telefone] out of order. - **3.** [cansado] worn out. - **4.** [falido] bankrupt. - **5.** *fam* [sem dinheiro] broke.

➡ **quebrados** *mpl* [trocados] change *(sg)*.

quebra-galho [ˌkɛbraˈgaʎul (*pl* **quebra-galhos**) *m* - **1.** [pessoa] Mr Fixit. - **2.** [objeto] contrivance.

quebra-gelos [ˌkɛbraˈʒeluʃ] *m inv* *NÁUT* icebreaker.

quebra-mar [ˌkɛbraˈma(x)l (*pl* **quebra-mares**) *m* breakwater.

quebra-molas [ˌkɛbraˈmɔlaʃl *m inv* speed bump *ou* hump, sleeping policeman.

quebra-nozes [ˌkɛbraˈnɔziʃl *m inv* nutcracker.

quebranto [keˈbrãntul *m* - **1.** [mau- olhado] evil eye. - **2.** [abatimento] run-down state.

quebra-pau [ˌkɛbraˈpawl (*pl* **quebra-paus**) *m fam* fisticuffs (*pl*).

quebra-quebra [ˌkɛbraˈkɛbral (*pl* **quebra-quebras**) *m* riot.

quebrar [4] [keˈbra(x)l ◇ *vt* - **1.** [ger] to break; ~ **algo ao meio** to split sthg in half. - **2.** [espancar] to beat up. - **3.** [enfraquecer] to weaken. - **4.** [interromper] to halt. - **5.** [desviar] to deflect. ◇ *vi* - **1.** [despedaçar-se] to break. - **2.** [enguiçar] to break down. - **3.** [falir] to go bankrupt. - **4.** *fam* [ficar sem dinheiro] to be broke.

➡ **quebrar-se** *vp* - **1.** [despedaçar-se] to break. - **2.** [desfazer-se] to be broken.

quebra-vento [ˌkɛbraˈvẽntul (*pl* **quebra-ventos**) *m AUTO* fanlight.

queda [ˈkɛdal *f* - **1.** [ger] fall; ~ **livre** free fall; ~ **de barreira** landslide; **em** ~ falling. - **2.** [declínio] fall; **estar em** ~ to be falling. - **3.** *fig* [inclinação]: **ter uma** ~ **para algo** to have a flair for sthg; **ter uma** ~ **por alguém** to have a soft spot for sb.

queda-d'água [ˌkɛdaˈdagwal (*pl* **quedas-d'água**) *f* waterfall.

queda-de-braço [kɛdadʒibrasul (*pl* **quedas-de-braço** [kɛdaʃibrasul) *f* - **1.** [jogo] arm-wrestling. - **2.** *fig* [disputa] dispute.

queijada [kejˈʒadal *f* cheesecake.

queijadinha [kejʒaˈdʒiɲal *f* coconut ice.

queijeira [kejˈʒejral *f* cheese cover.

queijo [ˈkejʒul *m* cheese; ~ **prato** (form of) processed cheese; ~ **ralado** grated cheese.

queima [ˈkejmal *f* - **1.** [queimada] burning fire; ~ **de fogos** fireworks display. - **2.** *COM & fig* [liquidação] clearance sale.

queimado, da [kejˈmadu, dal *adj* - **1.** [ger] burnt. - **2.** [de sol - bronzeado] tanned; [- ferido] sunburnt. - **3.** [plantas] scorched. - **4.** *fam fig* [malquisto] ruined.

➡ **queimado** *m* [coisa queimada]: **cheiro/gosto de** ~ smell of burning/taste burnt.

➡ **queimada** *f* slash-and-burn.

queimadura [kejmaˈdural *f* - **1.** [com fogo] burn; ~ **de primeiro/segundo grau** first-/second-degree burn. - **2.** [de sol] sunburn.

queimar [4] [kejˈma(x)l ◇ *vt* - **1.** [ger] to burn. - **2.** [atear fogo a] to set on fire. - **3.** [abrasar, ferir - fogo, choque, sol] to burn; [- líquido] to scald. - **4.** [bronzear] to tan. - **5.** *COM & fig* [liquidar] to liquidate. - **6.** *fam fig* [tornar malquisto] to ruin. - **7.** *fig* [dinheiro] to blow. ◇ *vi* - **1.** [abrasar] to be burning hot. - **2.** [arder em febre] to burn (up). - **3.** [lâmpada, fusível] to blow. - **4.** *ESP* to hit the net. - **5.** [comida] to burn.

➡ **queimar-se** *vp* - **1.** [ferir-se - ger] to burn o.s.; [- com líquido fervente] to scald o.s. - **2.** [bronzear-se] to sunbathe. - **3.** *fam fig* [enfezar-se] to take offence. - **4.** *fam fig* [tornar-se malquisto] to blow it.

queima-roupa [ˌkejmaˈxopal *f*: **à** ~ [disparo] at point-blank range; *fig* [sem rodeios] point-blank.

queixa [ˈkejʃal *f* - **1.** [reclamação] complaint; **dar** ~ **de algo/alguém** to complain about sthg/sb; **ter** ~ **de algo/alguém** to have a complaint against sthg/sb. - **2.** [lamento] grievance.

queixa-crime [ˌkejʃaˈkrimil (*pl* **queixas-crime(s)** *f JUR* citation.

queixada [kejˈʃadal *f* - **1.** [de animal] jaw. - **2.** [queixo grande] prominent jaw.

queixar-se [7] [kejˈʃaxsil *vp* - **1.** [reclamar]: ~ **-se** (**de algo/alguém**) to complain (about sthg/sb). - **2.** [lamentar-se] to moan.

queixo [ˈkejʃul *m* chin; **estava com tanto frio que chegava a bater o** ~ [de frio] I was so cold my teeth started chattering; **ele ficou de** ~ **caído** [ficar admirado] his jaw dropped in amazement.

queixoso, osa [kejˈʃozu, ɔzal *adj* - **1.** [agravado] querulous. - **2.** [magoado] aggrieved.

queixudo, da [kejˈʃudu, dal *adj* big-jawed.

queixume [kejˈʃumil *m* [lamentação] complaint.

quem [ˈkẽjl *pron* [interrogativo: sujeito] who; [interrogativo: complemento] who, whom; [indefinido] whoever; ~ **diria!** who would have thought it!; ~ **é?** [na porta] who's there?; ~ **fala?** [no telefone] who's calling?, who's speaking?; ~ **me dera ser rico!** if only I were rich!; ~ **quer que** whoever; **seja** ~ **for** no matter who it is, whoever it is it is.

quentão [kẽnˈtãwl *m* mulled wine.

quente [ˈkẽntʃil ◇ *adj* - **1.** [ger] hot. - **2.** [roupa] warm. - **3.** [animado] vibrant. - **4.** *gír jornalismo* [notícia] reliable. ◇ *m* [moda]: **o** ~ **agora é usar cabelo comprido** the in thing now is to wear one's hair long.

quentinha [kẽn'tʃiɲa] *f* -**1.** [embalagem] *insulated carton for food.* -**2.** [refeição] snack.
quentura [kẽn'tura] *f* warmth.
quepe ['kɛpi] *m* kepi.
quer [kɛ(x)] ◇ *conj*: ~ ..., ~ ... whether ... or ...; ~ você queira, ~ não whether you want to or not. ◇ *v* ⊳ **querer**.
➽ **onde quer que** *loc pron* wherever.
➽ **o que quer que** *loc pron* whatever.
➽ **quem quer que** *loc pron* whoever.
querela [ke'rɛla] *f* -**1.** [contenda] quarrel. -**2.** JUR charge.
querelar [4] [kere'la(x)] ◇ *vt* JUR to sue. ◇ *vi* [queixar-se]: ~ (contra/de) to quarrel (with/about).
querer [38] [ke're(x)] ◇ *m* -**1.** [vontade] wanting. -**2.** [amor] love. ◇ *vt* -**1.** [ger] to want; **como queira/quiser** as you wish; **como quem não quer nada** casually; **estar querendo fazer algo** [estar na iminência de] to be about to do sthg; **não ~ nada com** to want nothing to do with; ~ **dizer** to mean; **quer dizer** [em outras palavras] that is to say; **quer dizer que ...** [então] so that means ... -**2.** [ter a bondade de]: **queiram apertar seus cintos de segurança** please fasten your seatbelts; **quer me passar o vinho, por favor?** would you kindly pass me the wine, please? -**3.** [cobrar]: **quero dois mil pelo carro** I want two thousand for the car. -**4.** [ter afeição por] to love. -**5.** [conseguir]: **não ~ fazer algo** not to want to do sthg. ◇ *vi* -**1.** [desejar, ter vontade]: **não vou porque não quero** I am not going because I don't want to; ~ **é poder** *prov* where there's a will, there's a way; **por** ~ on purpose; **sem** ~ unintentionally. -**2.** [amar] to love; ~ **bem a alguém** to care about sb; ~ **mal a alguém** to wish sb ill.
➽ **querer-se** *vp* [amar-se] to love one another.
querido, da [ke'ridu, da] ◇ *adj* -**1.** [caro] dear; **ele é muito** ~ **na cidade** he is much liked in town. -**2.** [em carta]: **Querido ...** Dear ... ◇ *m, f* -**1.** [preferido] favourite *UK*, favorite *US*. -**2.** [como forma de tratamento] darling.
quermesse [kex'mɛsi] *f* fête *UK*, kermis *US*.
querosene [kero'zeni] *m* kerosene.
querubim [keru'bĩ] (*pl* -**ns**) *m* cherub.
quesito [ke'zitu] *m* -**1.** [ponto, questão] question. -**2.** [requisito] requirement.
questão [keʃ'tãw] (*pl* -**ões**) *f* -**1.** [ger] question; **isso ocorreu há** ~ **de cinco meses** that happened some five months ago; ~ **de honra** question of honour; ~ **de tempo** question of time; ~ **de vida ou morte** matter of life or death; **em** ~ in question; **fazer** ~ **(de algo)** *fig* [insistir em] to insist (on sthg). -**2.** JUR case.
questionamento [keʃtʃjona'mẽntu] *m* [pôr em dúvida] questioning.
questionar [4] [keʃtʃjo'na(x)] *vt* -**1.** [debater] to dispute. -**2.** [fazer perguntas] to question.
questionário [keʃtʃjo'narju] *m* questionnaire.
questionável [keʃtʃjo'navew] (*pl* -**eis**) *adj* questionable.

questões [keʃ'tõjʃ] *pl* ⊳ **questão**.
qui. (*abrev de* quinta-feira) *f* Thur.
quiabo ['kjabu] *m* okra.
quibe ['kibi] *m* deep-fried meat dish with mint and other spices.
quibebe [ki'bɛbi] *m* pumpkin purée.
quicar [12] [ki'ka(x)] ◇ *vt* [bola] to bounce. ◇ *vi* [bola] to bounce.
quiche ['kiʃi] *f* quiche.
quíchua ['kiʃwa] ◇ *adj* Quechuan. ◇ *m, f* Quechuan.
➽ **quíchua** *m* [língua] Quechuan.
quieto, ta ['kjɛtu, ta] *adj* -**1.** [em silêncio] quiet. -**2.** [tranqüilo] calm. -**3.** [imóvel] still.
quietude [kje'tudʒi] *f* tranquillity.
quilate [ki'latʃi] *m* -**1.** [de ouro] carat. -**2.** *fig* [excelência] calibre *UK*, caliber *US*.
quilha ['kiʎa] *f* keel.
quilo ['kilu] *m* kilo; **a** ~ by the kilo.
quilobyte [kilo'bajtʃi] *m* COMPUT kilobyte.
quilohertz [kilo'hɛxtʃis] *m* kilohertz.
quilombo [ki'lõnbu] *m* fortified village where runaway slaves lived.
quilometragem [kilome'traʒẽ] (*pl* -**ns**) *f* -**1.** [distância percorrida] distance in kilometres *UK* ou kilometers *US*, ≃ mileage. -**2.** [distância entre dois pontos] distance in kilometres *UK* ou kilometers *US*.
quilometrar [4] [kilome'tra(x)] *vt* to measure in kilometres *UK* ou kilometers *US*.
quilométrico, ca [kilo'mɛtriku, ka] *adj fig* [longo] mile (*antes de subst*).
quilômetro [ki'lometru] *m* kilometre *UK*, kilometer *US*.
quilowatt [kilo'vatʃi] *m* kilowatt.
quilowatt-hora [kilo,vatʃi'ɔra] (*pl* -**ras**) *m* ELETR kilowatt-hour.
quimbanda [kĩn'bãnda] *m* -**1.** [ritual] *macumba ritual*. -**2.** [feiticeiro] *priest of macumba*. -**3.** [terreiro] *place where macumba is practised*.
quimera [ki'mɛra] *f* [fantasia, ilusão] chimera.
químico, ca ['kimiku, ka] ◇ *adj* chemical. ◇ *m, f* [profissional] chemist.
➽ **química** *f* -**1.** [ger] chemistry. -**2.** [substância] chemical. -**3.** *fig* [segredo] secret.
quimioterapia [kimjotera'pia] *f* chemotherapy.
quimono [ki'monu] *m* kimono.
quina ['kina] *f* -**1.** [canto] corner; **de** ~ side on. -**2.** [de jogo] jackpot.
quindim [kĩn'dʒĩ] (*pl* -**ns**) *m* sweet made of egg, sugar and coconut.
quinhão [ki'ɲãw] (*pl* -**ões**) *m* share.
quinhentista [kiɲẽn'tʃiʃta] *adj* sixteenth century (*antes de subst*).
quinhentos, tas [ki'ɲẽntuʃ, taʃ] *num* five hundred; **ser outros** ~ to be a different kettle of fish; *veja também* **seis**.
quinhões [ki'ɲõjʃ] *pl* ⊳ **quinhão**.
quinina [ki'nina] *f* quinine.
qüinquagésimo, ma [kwiŋkwa'ʒɛzimu, ma] *num* fiftieth; *veja também* **sexto**.

qüinqüênio [kwiŋ'kwenju] *m* quinquennium.
quinquilharia [kĩŋkiʎa'ria] *f* **-1.** [bugiganga]
junk. **-2.** [ninharia] trinket.
  ➡ **quinquilharias** *fpl* [miudezas] odds and
ends.
quinta ['kĩta] *f* **-1.** [quinta-feira] Thursday. **-2.** [sítio] estate; *veja também* **sábado**.
quinta-essência [ˌkĩntae'sẽnsja] *f* **-1.** [essência]
quintessence. **-2.** [plenitude] epitome.
quinta-feira [ˌkĩnta'fejra] (*pl* **quintas-feiras**) *f*
Thursday; *veja também* **sábado**.
quintal [kĩn'taw] (*pl* **-ais**) *m* [de casa] backyard.
quinteto [kĩn'tetu] *m* MÚS quintet.
quinto, ta ['kĩntu, ta] *num* fifth; *veja também* **sexto**.
quintuplicar [kĩntupli'ka(x)] *vt*: **quintuplicou o
número de desempregados** the number of
unemployed has multiplied by five.
quíntuplo, pla ['kĩntuplu, pla] *adj* quintuple.
  ➡ **quíntuplo** *m* quintuple.
  ➡ **quíntuplos** *mpl* [gêmeos] quins, quintuplets.
quinze ['kĩnzi] *num* fifteen; *veja também* **seis**.
quinzena [kĩ'zena] *f* **-1.** [tempo] fortnight. **-2.**
[salário] fortnight's wages.
quinzenal [kĩnze'naw] (*pl* **-ais**) *adj* fortnightly.
quinzenalmente [kĩnzenaw'mẽntʃi] *adv* fortnightly.
quiosque ['kjɔʃki] *m* **-1.** [de jardim] gazebo. **-2.**
[banca] kiosk.
qüiprocó [kwipro'kɔ] *m* [confusão] mix-up.
quiromancia [kiromãn'sia] *f* palmistry, chiromancy.
quiromante [kiro'mãntʃi] *mf* palm reader.
quisto ['kiʃtu] *m* cyst.
quitação [kita'saw] (*pl* **-ões**) *f* **-1.** [remissão]
discharge. **-2.** [pagamento] settlement. **-3.** [recibo]
receipt.
quitanda [ki'tãnda] *f* grocer's shop *UK*, grocery
store *US*.
quitandeiro, ra [kitãn'dejru, ra] *m, f* greengrocer.
quitar [4] [ki'ta(x)] *vt* **-1.** [pagar] to settle. **-2.** [perdoar] to cancel. **-3.** [devedor] to release.
quite ['kitʃi] *adj* **-1.** [com credor]: **estar/ficar ~
(com alguém)** to be quits (with sb). **-2.** [livre]: **~
de algo** free of sthg. **-3.** [igualado] even.
quitenho, nha [ki'teɲu, ɲa] *adj* Quito (*antes
de subst*).*m, f* person from Quito.
Quito ['kitu] *n* Quito.
quitute [ki'tutʃi] *m* titbit *UK*, tidbit *US*.
quizumba [ki'zũba] *f fam* brawl.
quociente [kwo'sjẽntʃi] *m* MAT quotient; **~ de inteligência** intelligence quotient, IQ.

r, R ['ɛxi] *m* [letra] r, R.
rã ['xã] *f* frog.
rabada [xa'bada] *f* **-1.** [rabo] tail. **-2.** CULIN oxtail
stew. **-3.** *fam* [de corrida]: **ele chegou na ~** he
arrived at the tail end.
rabanada [xaba'nada] *f* **-1.** CULIN French toast. **-2.**
[golpe com rabo] whack with the tail.
rabanete [xaba'netʃi] *m* radish.
Rabat [xa'batʃi] *n* Rabat.
rabeca [xa'bɛka] *f* MÚS fiddle.
rabecão [xabe'kãw] (*pl* **-ões**) *m* [carro fúnebre]
hearse.
rabicho [xa'biʃu] *m* **-1.** [trança] pigtail. **-2.** *fam* [caso amoroso] passion.
rabino, na [xa'binu, na] *m* rabbi.
rabiscar [12] [xabiʃ'ka(x)] ⬦ *vt* **-1.** [encher com
rabiscos] to scribble over. **-2.** [riscos] to scribble.
-3. [escrever às pressas] to scrawl. **-4.** [desenhar] to
sketch. ⬦ *vi* [fazer rabiscos] to doodle.
rabisco [xa'biʃku] *m* **-1.** [risco] scribble. **-2.** [esboço] sketch.
  ➡ **rabiscos** *mpl* [caligrafia ruim] scrawl (*sg*).
rabo ['xabu] *m* **-1.** [cauda] tail; **~ de foguete** *fig*
can of worms; **com o ~ do olho** out of the corner
of one's eye; **meter o ~ entre as pernas** *fig* to be
left with one's tail between one's legs. **-2.** *vulg*
[nádegas] bum.
rabo-de-cavalo [ˌxabudʒika'valu] (*pl* **rabos-de-
cavalo**) *m* ponytail.
rabo-de-saia [ˌxabudʒi'saja] (*pl* **rabos-de-saia**)
m fam piece of skirt.
rabudo, da [xa'budu, da] *adj* [sortudo] lucky.
  ➡ **rabudo** *m fam* [diabo] devil.
rabugento, ta [xabu'ʒẽntu, ta] *adj* grumpy.
rabugice [xabu'ʒisi] *f* grumpiness.
raça ['xasa] *f* **-1.** [etnia] race. **-2.** [estirpe] lineage.
-3. *pej* [laia] breed; **acabar com a ~ de alguém**
[matar] to do away with sb. **-4.** *fig* [coragem, determinação] guts; **(no peito e) na ~** by sheer guts;
ter ~ (para algo) to have the guts (for sthg). **-5.**
[de animal] breed; **cão/cavalo de ~** pedigree dog/
thoroughbred horse.
ração [xa'saw] (*pl* **-ões**) *f* **-1.** [de alimento] ration. **-2.**
[para animal - para cão, gato] food; **~ para cachorro**

puppy food; [- para gado, cavalo] feed; ~ **para cavalo** horse feed.

racha ['xaʃa] m -1. fam [discórdia] split. -2. [em parede etc] crack.

rachadura [xaʃa'dura] f crack.

rachar [4] [xa'ʃa(x)] <> vt -1. [fender] to crack; **frio de** ~ bitterly cold; **ou vai ou racha** do or die; **sol de** ~ scorching sun. -2. [dividir]: ~ **algo (com alguém)** to split sthg (with sb). -3. fig [dividir] to split. -4. [cortar] to split. <> vi [fender-se] to crack.

racial [xa'sjaw] (pl -ais) adj racial.

raciocinar [4] [xasjosi'na(x)] vi to reason.

raciocínio [xasjo'sinju] m reasoning.

racional [xasjo'naw] (pl -ais) adj rational.

racionalidade [xasjonali'dadʒi] f rationality.

racionalização [xasjonaliza'sãw] f rationalization.

racionalizar [4] [xasjonali'za(x)] vt to rationalize.

racionalmente [xasjonaw'mẽntʃi] adv rationally, sensibly.

racionamento [xasjona'mẽntu] m rationing.

racionar [4] [xasjo'na(x)] vt to ration.

racismo [xa'siʒmu] m racism.

racista [xa'siʃta] <> adj racist. <> mf racist.

rack [xɛk] m rack.

rações [xa'sõjʃ] pl ▷ ração.

radar [xa'da(x)] (pl -es) m radar.

radiação [xadʒja'sãw] (pl -ões) f radiation.

radiador [xadʒja'do(x)] (pl -es) m AUTO radiator.

radialista [xadʒja'liʃta] mf -1. [apresentador] (radio) announcer. -2. [da produção] (radio) producer.

radiante [xa'dʒjãntʃi] adj -1. [objeto] radiant. -2. [de alegria] ecstatic.

radical [xadʒi'kaw] (pl -ais) <> adj radical. <> mf -1. [ger] root. -2. POL & QUÍM radical; ~ **livre** free radical.

radicalismo [xadʒika'liʒmu] m radicalism.

radicalizar [4] [xadʒikali'za(x)] <> vt [aprofundar] to radicalize. <> vi [tornar-se radical] to become radical.

➡ **radicalizar-se** vp [tornar-se radical] to become radical.

radicar-se [12] [xadʒi'kaxsi] vp to settle.

rádio ['xadʒju] <> m -1. [aparelho] radio. -2. QUÍM radium. -3. ANAT [osso] radius. <> f [emissora] radio station.

radioamador, ra [xadʒjwama'do(x), a] m, f radio ham.

radioatividade [xadʒwatʃivi'dadʒil f radioactivity.

radioativo, va [ˌxadʒwa'tʃivu, va] adj radioactive.

radiodifusão [xadʒodʒifu'zãw] f broadcasting.

radiodifusora [xadʒodʒifu'zora] f broadcasting station.

radioemissora [xadʒwemi'sora] f radio station.

radiografar [4] [xadʒogra'fa(x)] <> vt -1. MED to X-ray. -2. [notícia] to radio. <> vi [fazer contato] to radio.

radiografia [ˌxadʒjogra'fia] f -1. MED X-ray. -2. fig [análise] in-depth analysis.

radiograma [xadʒjo'grãma] m cablegram.

radiogravador [xadʒjugrava'do(x)] m radio-cassette player.

radiojornal [xadʒjuʒox'naw] (pl -ais) m radio news (sg).

radiologia [xadʒjolo'ʒia] f radiology.

radiologista [xadʒjolo'ʒiʃta] mf radiologist.

radionovela [xadʒjuno'vɛla] f radio soap.

radiooperador, ra [xadʒjoopera'do(x), ral m, f radio operator.

radiopatrulha [xadʒjupa'truʎa] f -1. [serviço] radio patrol. -2. [viatura] patrol car.

radiorepórter [xadʒjuxe'pɔxte(x)] mf radio reporter.

radioso, osa [xa'dʒjozu, ɔza] adj radiant.

radiotáxi [ˌxadʒjo'taksi] m radio cab.

radioterapia [xadʒjotera'pia] f radiotherapy.

radiouvinte [xadʒjo'vĩntʃi] mf (radio) listener.

ráfia ['xafja] f raffia.

ragu [xa'gu] m ragout.

raia ['xaja] f -1. [linha] line. -2. [limite] boundary; **às ~s de algo** to the limits of sthg. -3. [pista - de piscina] (lane) marker; [- de tiro] firing range. -4. [peixe] ray. -5. loc: **fugir da** ~ to cut and run.

raiado, da [xa'jadu, da] adj -1. [pista] marked. -2. [cano] rifled. -3. [piscina] divided into lanes. -4. [bandeira] striped.

raiar [4] [xa'ja(x)] <> vi -1. [brilhar] to shine. -2. [despontar] to dawn. <> vt [com raias - pista] to mark; [- cano] to rifle; [- piscina] to lane off; [- pintar] to mark with stripes.

rainha [xa'iɲa] f queen.

rainha-mãe [xaˌiɲa'mãj] (pl rainhas-mães) f queen mother.

raio ['xaju] m -1. [ger] ray; ~ **laser** laser beam; ~ **X** X-ray. -2. [de luz] beam. -3. METEOR bolt of lightening. -4. fam [como ênfase]: **perdi o ~ da carteira** I lost my blasted wallet. -5. GEOM radius. -6.: ~ **de ação** [alcance] range; fig [área de atuação] range.

raiva ['xajva] f -1. [fúria] rage; **com ~ (de)** angry (at); **dar ~** to drive mad; **morto de ~** absolutely furious; **ter/tomar ~ de** to hate. -2. [doença] rabies (sg).

raivoso, osa [xaj'vozu, ɔza] adj -1. [furioso] furious. -2. [doente] rabid.

raiz [xa'iʒ] (pl -es) f -1. [ger] root; **cortar o mal pela ~ fig** to root it out; **criar raízes fig** to put down roots; ~ **quadrada** square root. -2. [origem] roots (pl).

rajada [xa'ʒada] f -1. [de vento] gust. -2. [de tiros] volley.

ralado, da [xa'ladu, da] adj -1. [moído] grated. -2. [esfolado] grazed.

ralador [xala'do(x)] (pl -es) m grater.

ralar [4] [xa'la(x)] vt -1. [com ralador] to grate. -2. [esfolar] to graze.

ralé [xa'lɛ] f [escória] riff-raff.

ralhar [4] [xa'ʎa(x)] *vi*: ~ **(com alguém)** to tell (sb) off.

rali [xa'li] *m* rally.

ralo, la ['xalu, la] *adj* -**1.** [cabelo, café, sopa] thin. -**2.** [vegetação] sparse.
➡ **ralo** *m* drainpipe.

Ram. (*abrev de* ramal) *m* ext.

RAM (*abrev de* **Random Access Memory**) *f* RAM.

rama ['xãma] *f* foliage; **em** ~ raw; **pela** ~ *fig* [superficialmente] superficially.

ramadã [xama'dã] *m* Ramadan, Ramadhan.

ramagem [xa'maʒẽ] *f* BOT branches (*pl*).

ramal [xa'maw] (*pl* -**ais**) *m* -**1.** [de telefone] extension. -**2.** FERRO branch line. -**3.** [rodoviário] branch road.

ramalhete [xama'ʎetʃi] *m* [buquê] bunch.

rameira [xa'mejra] *f* *vulg* [prostituta] prostitute.

ramerrão [xame'xãw] *m* [rotina] grind.

ramificação [xamifika'sãw] (*pl* -**ões**) *f* [subdivisão] branch.

ramificar-se [12] [xamifi'kaxsi] *vp* -**1.** [subdividir-se] to be sub-divided. -**2.** [espalhar-se] to branch out.

ramo ['xãmu] *m* -**1.** [ger] branch. -**2.** [de flores] bouquet. -**3.** [área] field.

rampa ['xãnpa] *f* ramp.

rancheiro, ra [xãn'ʃejru, ra] *m, f* -**1.** [morador] farmer. -**2.** [zelador] tenant farmer. -**3.** [cozinheiro] cook.

rancho ['xãnʃu] *m* -**1.** [sítio] smallholding, farm. -**2.** [cabana] hut. -**3.** [refeição] mess. -**4.** MÚS [ritmo] carnival music.

ranço ['xãnsu] *m* -**1.** [sabor] rancid taste. -**2.** [cheiro] rank smell. -**3.** *fig* [atraso] age-old habit.

rancor [xãŋ'ko(x)] *m* -**1.** [ressentimento] resentment; **guardar** ~ **(de)** to be resentful (about). -**2.** [ódio] hatred.

rancoroso, osa [xãŋko'rozu, ɔza] *adj* resentful.

rançoso, osa [xãn'sozu, ɔza] *adj* rancid.

ranger [26] [xãn'ʒe(x)] <> *m* [ruído - de porta] creaking; [- de dentes] grinding. <> *vt* [os dentes] to grind. <> *vi* to creak.

rangido [xãn'ʒidu] *m* -**1.** [de porta] creak. -**2.** [de dente] grinding.

rango ['xãŋgu] *m* *fam* grub.

Rangun [xãŋ'gũ] *n* Rangoon.

ranheta [xã'ɲeta] *adj* surly.

ranhura [xã'ɲura] *f* -**1.** [entalhe] groove. -**2.** [canaleta] keyway. -**3.** [para moeda] slot.

ranzinza [xãn'zĩza] *adj* bolshy.

rapa ['xapa] *m* -**1.** [de comida] scrap. -**2.** *fam* [fiscal] *policeman dealing with illegal street traders.* -**3.** *fam* [carro] *police patrol on the look-out for illegal street traders.*

rapadura [xapa'dura] *f* raw cane sugar.

rapagão, gona [xapa'gãw, gona] (*mpl* -**ões**, *fpl* -**onas**) *m, f* burly person.

rapapé [xapa'pɛ] *m* [bajulação] fawning; **fazer** ~ **s a alguém** to kowtow to sb.

rapar [4] [xa'pa(x)] <> *vt* -**1.** [pelar] to shave. -**2.** *fam* [roubar] to nick. <> *vi fam* [ir embora] to scarper.

rapaz [xa'paʒ] (*pl* -**es**) *m* -**1.** [jovem] boy. -**2.** *fam* [cara] man.

rapaziada [xapa'zjada] *f* [rapazes] lads (*pl*).

rapé [xa'pɛ] *m* snuff.

rapidamente [xapida'mẽntʃi] *adv* rapidly.

rapidez [xapi'deʃ] *f* speed; **com** ~ quickly, at speed.

rápido, da ['xapidu, da] *adj* -**1.** [veloz] fast, quick. -**2.** [breve] brief.
➡ **rápido** <> *m* [trem] express. <> *adv* [ligeiro] quickly.

rapina [xa'pina] *f* violent robbery; ▷ **ave.**

raposa [xa'poza] *f* -**1.** ZOOL vixen (*f* vixen). -**2.** *fig* [pessoa astuta] sly old fox.

rapsódia [xap'zɔdʒja] *f* rhapsody.

raptado, da [xap'tadu, da] <> *adj* kidnapped. <> *m, f* kidnap victim.

raptar [4] [xap'ta(x)] *vt* to kidnap.

rapto ['xaptu] *m* kidnapping.

raptor, ra [xap'to(x), ra] *m, f* kidnapper.

raquete [xa'kɛtʃi] *f* -**1.** [de tênis, squash] racket. -**2.** [de pingue-pongue] bat.

raquidiana [xaki,dʒjãna] *f* [anestesia] epidural.

raquítico, ca [xa'kitʃiku, ka] *adj* -**1.** MED rachitic. -**2.** [magro] scrawny. -**3.** [escasso] sparse.

raquitismo [xaki'tʃiʒmu] *m* MED rickets (*sg or pl*).

raramente [,xara'mẽntʃi] *adv* rarely, seldom.

rarear [15] [xa'rja(x)] *vi* -**1.** [tornar-se raro] to become scarce. -**2.** [cabelos] to thin. -**3.** [vegetação, população] to thin out.

rarefazer [31] [xarefa'ze(x)] *vt* [tornar menos denso] to make thinner.
➡ **rarefazer-se** *vp* -**1.** [tornar-se menos denso] to get thinner. -**2.** [multidão] to disperse.

rarefeito, ta [xare'fejtu, ta] *adj* -**1.** [pouco denso] rarefied. -**2.** [disperso] dispersed.

raridade [xari'dadʒi] *f* -**1.** [qualidade] rareness. -**2.** [peça] rarity.

raro, ra ['xaru, ra] *adj* rare.
➡ **raro** *adv* [raramente] rarely; **não** ~ often.

rasante [xa'zãntʃi] <> *adj* low-flying. <> *adv*: **o avião passou** ~ the plane flew low.

rascunhar [4] [xaʃku'ɲa(x)] *vt* to draft.

rascunho [xaʃ'kuɲu] *m* draft.

rasgado, da [xaʒ'gadu, da] *adj* -**1.** [tecido, papel] torn. -**2.** *fig* [elogio, gesto] generous. -**3.** *fig* [ritmo, dança] flourishing.

rasgão [xaʒ'gãw] (*pl* -**ões**) *m* tear.

rasgar [14] [xaʒ'ga(x)] <> *vt* -**1.** [romper] to tear. -**2.** *fig* [elogios] to heap. <> *vi* [romper-se] to tear.
➡ **rasgar-se** *vp* -**1.** [romper-se] to be torn. -**2.** [pessoa] to be consumed.

rasgo ['xaʒgu] *m* -**1.** [rasgão] tear. -**2.** [traço] line. -**3.** *fig* [ação, ímpeto] burst.

rasgões [xaʒ'gõjʃ] *pl* ▷ **rasgão.**

raso, sa ['xazu, za] *adj* -**1.** [pouco fundo] shallow. -**2.** [colher etc] level. -**3.** [liso] even. -**4.** [rente] close-cropped. -**5.** [sapato] flat. -**6.** [soldado] private.
➡ **raso** *m* shallow end.

raspa ['xaʃpa] f -1. [lasca] shavings (pl). -2. [de panela] scrapings (pl).

raspadeira [xaʃpa'dejra] f scraper.

raspadinha [xaʃpa'dʒiɲa] f scratch card.

raspão [xaʃ'pãw] (pl -ões) m scratch; **o tiro pegou de ~** no braço the shot grazed his arm.

raspar [4] [xaʃ'pa(x)] <> vt -1. [alisar] to smooth down. -2. [pêlos] to shave. -3. [limpar] to scrape; **~ o tacho** fig [as economias] to scrape the bottom of the barrel. -4. [arranhar] to scratch. -5. [de raspão] to graze. <> vi [de raspão]: **~ em** to strike a glancing blow at.

raspões [xaʃ'põjʃ] pl ⊳ raspão.

rasteiro, ra [xaʃ'tejru, ra] adj -1. [vegetação] lowlying. -2. [vôo] low. -3. [que se arrasta] crawling. -4. fig [superficial] superficial.

➡ **rasteira** f trip; **dar uma ~ em alguém** [com pernada] to trip sb up; fig [trair] to double-cross sb.

rastejante [xaʃte'ʒãntʃi] adj -1. [que se arrasta - animal] crawling; [- planta] creeping. -2. fig [submisso] crawling.

rastejar [4] [xaʃte'ʒa(x)] <> vi -1. [arrastar-se - planta] to creep; [- animal] to crawl; [- cobra] to slide. -2. [andar de rastos] to crawl. -3. fig [rebaixar-se] to grovel. <> vt [rastrear] to track.

rastilho [xaʃ'tʃiʎu] m [de pólvora] fuse.

rasto ['xaʃtu] m -1. [pegada] track. -2. [de veículo] trail. -3. fig [vestígios] tracks (pl).

➡ **rastos** mpl: **de rastos** on all fours.

rastrear [15] [xaʃ'trja(x)] <> vt -1. [seguir o rasto de] to track. -2. [investigar] to search for. <> vi [seguir o rasto] to track.

rastro ['xaʃtru] m = rasto.

rasura [xa'zura] f crossing out.

rasurar [4] [xazu'ra(x)] <> vt to cross out. <> vi to cross out.

rata ['xata] f fam [mancada] blunder; **dar uma ~** to make a stupid mistake; **rato**.

ratazana [xata'zãna] f Norway rat.

ratear [15] [xa'tʃja(x)] <> vt [dividir] to share out. <> vi [motor] to stall.

rateio [xa'teju] m -1. [divisão] sharing. -2. [turfe] [quantia] payout.

ratificação [xatʃifika'sãw] (pl -ões) f -1. [confirmação] ratification. -2. [comprovação] confirmation.

ratificar [12] [xatʃifi'ka(x)] vt -1. [confirmar] to ratify. -2. [comprovar] to confirm.

rato, ta ['xatu, ta] m, f rat; **~ de biblioteca** fig bookworm; **~ de praia** fig thief (on the beach).

ratoeira [xa'twejra] f -1. [para ratos] mousetrap. -2. fig [armadilha] trap.

ravina [xa'vina] f ravine.

ravióli [xa'vjɔli] m ravioli.

razão [xa'zãw] (pl -ões) <> f -1. [faculdade] reason; **~ de ser** raison d'être; **de viver** reason for living; **~ de Estado** reasons of state; **em ~ de** on account of. -2. [bom senso] (common) sense. -3. [justiça]: **dar ~ a alguém** to side with sb; **estar coberto de ~** to be absolutely right; **perder a ~** to lose one's mind; **ter/não ter ~ (de)**

to be right/wrong (to); **com ~** with good reason; **sem ~** for no reason. -4. [MAT- proporção] ratio; [- quociente, fração] quotient; **à ~ de** at the rate of. -5. FIN account. <> m COM ledger.

➡ **razão social** f COM trade name.

razoável [xa'zwavew] (pl -eis) adj -1. [ger] reasonable. -2. [significativo] significant.

razoavelmente [xazwavew'mẽntʃil] adv reasonably.

ré ['xɛ] f AUTO reverse; **dar uma ~, dar marcha à ~** to reverse, to back up; ⊳ **réu**.

reabastecer [25] [xejabaʃte'se(x)] vt -1. [tanque, carro, avião] to refuel. -2. [despensa, cozinha] to restock. -3. [energias] to rebuild.

➡ **reabastecer-se** vp: **~-se de algo** to replenish one's supply of sthg.

reabastecimento [xeabaʃtesi'mẽntul] m -1. [carro] refuelling. -2. [cidade] resupplying. -3. [despensa] restocking. -4. [energias] rebuilding.

reabertura [xeabex'tura] f reopening.

reabilitação [xeabilita'sãw] (pl -ões) f -1. [regeneração] rehabilitation. -2. [recuperação] rehabilitation; **~ motora** physiotherapy; [da forma física] recovery.

reabilitar [4] [xeabili'ta(x)] vt -1. [regenerar] to rehabilitate. -2. [recuperar] to recover.

➡ **reabilitar-se** vp -1. [regenerar-se] to be rehabilitated. -2. [recuperar-se] to recover.

reabrir [6] [xea'bri(x)] <> vt to reopen. <> vi to reopen.

reabsorver [5] [xeabsox've(x)] vt to reabsorb.

reaça fam [xe'asa] <> adj reactionary. <> mf [pessoa] reactionary.

reação [xea'sãw] (pl -ões) f -1. [ger] reaction; **~ em cadeia** chain reaction. -2. [recuperação] recovery.

reacender [5] [xeasẽn'de(x)] vt -1. [fogo, forno] to relight. -2. fig [ânimo, nacionalismo] to rekindle.

reacionário, ria [xeasjo'narju, rja] <> adj reactionary. <> m, f [pessoa] reactionary.

readaptação [xeadapta'sãw] (pl -ões) f readjustment.

readaptar [4] [xeadap'ta(x)] vt to readapt.

➡ **readaptar-se** vp to readapt.

readmissão [xeadʒimi'sãw] f readmission.

readmitir [6] [xeadʒimi'tʃi(x)] vt to readmit.

readquirir [6] [xeadʒiki'ri(x)] vt to regain.

reafirmar [4] [xeafix'ma(x)] vt to reaffirm.

reagir [52] [xea'ʒi(x)] vi -1. [responder]: **~ (a)** to react (to). -2. [protestar, resistir]: **~ (a ou contra)** to resist. -3. [recuperar-se] to rally. -4. QUÍM: **~ com** to react with.

reajustar [4] [xeaʒuʃ'ta(x)] vt: **~ algo (a algo)** to readjust sthg (to sthg).

➡ **reajustar-se** vp: **~-se a algo** to readjust to sthg.

reajuste [xea'ʒuʃtʃil] m adjustment; **~ salarial** wage adjustment.

real [xe'aw] (pl -ais) <> adj -1. [verdadeiro] true. -2. [régio] royal. <> m [realidade] reality.

realçar [13] [xeaw'sa(x)] vt to highlight.

realce [xe'awsi] *m* **-1.** [destaque] emphasis; **dar ~ a** to emphasize. **-2.** [brilho] highlight.

realejo [xea'leʒu] *m* barrel organ.

realeza [xea'leza] *f* **-1.** [dignidade de rei] royalty. **-2.** [grandeza] *fig* grandeur.

realidade [xeali'dadʒil] *f* reality; **na ~** actually.

realismo [xea'liʒmu] *m* realism.

realista [xea'liʃta] <> *adj* realistic. <> *mf* **-1.** [pessoa] realist. **-2.** [adepto] royalist.

realização [xealiza'sãw] (*pl* **-ões**) *f* **-1.** [ger] realization. **-2.** [execução - de projeto, negócios] realization; [- de congresso, espetáculo] holding; [- de reforma] enactment. **-3.** [pessoal] fulfilment *UK*, fulfillment *US*.

realizado, da [xeali'zadu, da] *adj* **-1.** [pessoa] fulfilled. **-2.** [obra] carried out. **-3.** [sonho] realized.

realizador, ra [xealiza'do(x), ra] (*mpl* **-es**, *fpl* **-s**) <> *adj* enterprising. <> *m*, *f* [pessoa] producer.

realizar [4] [xeali'za(x)] *vt* **-1.** [ger] to realize. **-2.** [executar] to carry out; **ser realizado** [conferência, festa] to take place.

→ **realizar-se** *vp* **-1.** [concretizar-se] to be realized. **-2.** [ocorrer] to be carried out. **-3.** [alcançar seu ideal] to be fulfilled.

realizável [xeali'zavew] (*pl* **-eis**) *adj* achievable.

realmente [xeaw'mẽntʃil] <> *adv* **-1.** [de fato] in fact. **-2.** [muito] really. <> *interj* [expressando indignação] really!

reanimar [4] [xeani'ma(x)] *vt* **-1.** [fisicamente] to revive. **-2.** [moralmente] to cheer up. **-3.** *MED* to resuscitate.

→ **reanimar-se** *vp* **-1.** [fisicamente] to come to. **-2.** [moralmente] to rally.

reaparecer [25] [xeapare'se(x)] *vi* to reappear.

reaparecimento [xeaparesi'mẽntul] *m* [ressurgimento] reappearance.

reaprender [5] [xeaprẽn'de(x)] <> *vt* to relearn. <> *vi:* **~ a fazer algo** to learn to do sthg again.

reapresentar [4] [xeaprezẽn'ta(x)] *vt* to represent.

→ **reapresentar-se** *vp* to reappear.

reaproximação [xeaprosima'sãw] (*pl* **-ões**) *f* rapprochement.

reaproximar [4] [xeaprosi'ma(x)] *vt* to bring together again.

→ **reaproximar-se** *vp* to grow closer again.

reaquecer [25] [xeake'se(x)] *vt* **-1.** [sopa, café] to reheat. **-2.** [relações] to re-establish.

reaquecimento [xeakesi'mẽntul] *m* **-1.** reheating. **-2.** *ECON* revival.

reassumir [6] [xeasu'mi(x)] <> *vt* to regain. <> *vi* to take over again.

reatar [4] [xea'ta(x)] *vt* **-1.** [nó] to retie. **-2.** [amizade, conversa, negócios] to resume.

reativar [4] [xeatʃi'va(x)] *vt* to revive.

reator [xea'to(x)] *m* reactor; **~ nuclear** nuclear reactor.

reavaliação [xeavalja'sãw] *f* **-1.** [ger] re-evaluation. **-2.** [de jóia] revaluation.

reavaliar [xeava'lja(x)] *vt* to reappraise.

reaver [51] [xea've(x)] *vt* to recover.

reavivar [4] [xeavi'va(x)] *vt* **-1.** [cor] to revive. **-2.** [passado] to reawaken.

rebaixado, da [xebaj'ʃadu, da] *adj* **-1.** [teto, terreno] lowered. **-2.** [preço] cut. **-3.** *fig* [pessoa] discredited. **-4.** *FUT* relegated.

rebaixar [4] [xebaj'ʃa(x)] *vt* **-1.** [teto, terreno] to lower. **-2.** [preço] to cut. **-3.** [pessoa] to discredit. **-4.** *FUT* to relegate.

→ **rebaixar-se** *vp* [pessoa] to lower o.s.

rebanho [xe'baɲul *m* **-1.** [de bois, cabras] herd. **-2.** [de ovelhas] flock. **-3.** *fig* [de fiéis] flock.

rebater [5] [xeba'te(x)] <> *vt* **-1.** [bola] to kick back. **-2.** [golpe] to counter. **-3.** [argumentos, acusações] to rebut. **-4.** [à máquina] to retype. <> *vi* [chutar] to kick back.

rebelar-se [xebe'laxsil *vp:* **~-se (contra)** to rebel (against).

rebelde [xe'bɛwdʒil <> *adj* rebellious. <> *mf* rebel.

rebeldia [xebew'dʒial *f* **-1.** [qualidade] rebelliousness. **-2.** *fig* [oposição] defiance. **-3.** *fig* [obstinação] stubbornness.

rebelião [xebe'ljãw] (*pl* **-ões**) *f* [sublevação] rebellion.

rebentar [4] [xebẽn'ta(x)] <> *vi* **-1.** [ger] to break. **-2.** [não se conter]: **~ de** to burst with; **~ em** to burst into. **-3.** [surgir]: **~ (de/em)** to gush out (from/onto). **-4.** [guerra] to break out. <> *vt* **-1.** [romper] to tear. **-2.** [vidraça, louça] to smash.

rebento [xe'bẽntul *m* [filho] offspring.

rebite [xe'bitʃil *m* *TEC* rivet.

rebobinar [4] [xebobi'na(x)] *vt* [vídeo] to rewind.

rebocador [xeboka'do(x)] (*pl* **-es**) *m* *NÁUT* tug(-boat).

rebocar [12] [xebo'ka(x)] *vt* **-1.** [barco, carro] to tow. **-2.** [carro mal estacionado] to tow away. **-3.** *CONSTR* to plaster.

reboco [xe'bokul *m* *CONSTR* plaster.

rebolado [xebo'ladul *m* swing of the hips.

rebolar [4] [xebo'la(x)] <> *vt* [corpo, quadris] to swing. <> *vi* **-1.** [pessoa, corpo] to sway. **-2.** *fam fig* [empenhar-se] to fight hard.

reboque [xe'bɔkil *m* **-1.** [ger] tow; **a ~** in tow. **-2.** [carro-guincho] towtruck.

rebordosa [xebox'dɔzal *f* **-1.** [situação difícil] tough situation. **-2.** [reincidência de doença] recurrence (*of an illness*).

rebu [xe'bul *m fam* rumpus.

rebuliço [xebu'lisul *m* commotion.

rebuscado, da [xebuʃ'kadu, da] *adj* affected.

recado [xe'kadul *m* message; **dar conta do ~** *fig* to deliver the goods.

recaída [xeka'idal *f* relapse.

recair [68] [xeka'i(x)] *vi* **-1.** [tornar a fazer]: **~ em erro** to make the same mistake again. **-2.** [culpa, responsabilidade, suspeita]: **~ em** *ou* **sobre alguém** to fall (up)on sb. **-3.** [cair outra vez] to fall back.

recalcado, da [xekaw'kadu, da] *PSIC* <> *adj* repressed. <> *m*, *f* repressed person.

recalcar [12] [xekaw'ka(x)] *vt* **-1.** [comprimir] to

tread upon. **-2.** [reprimir] to repress. **-3.** *PSIC* to inhibit.

recalcitrante [xekawsi'trãntʃi] *adj* recalcitrant.

recalque [xe'kawki] *m PSIC* inhibition.

recanto [xe'kãntu] *m* nook.

recapitulação [xekapitula'sãw] *f* **-1.** [resumo] recapitulation. **-2.** [lembrança] recollection.

recapitular [4] [xekapitu'la(x)] *vt* **-1.** [resumir] to recap. **-2.** [relembrar] to recall.

recatado, da [xeka'tadu, da] *adj* **-1.** [pudico] modest. **-2.** [prudente] restrained.

recato [xe'katu] *m* **-1.** [pudor] modesty. **-2.** [prudência] restraint.

recauchutado, da [xekawʃu'tadu, da] *adj* [pneu] remoulded *UK*, remolded *US*.

recauchutagem [xekawʃu'taʒẽ] (*pl* **-ns**) *f* **-1.** [de pneu] remoulding *UK*, remolding *US*. **-2.** *fig* [em pessoa] plastic surgery; ~ **no rosto** facelift.

recauchutar [4] [xekawʃu'ta(x)] *vt* [pneu] to retread.

recear [15] [xe'sja(x)] ⟨⟩ *vt* **-1.** [temer] to fear; ~ **fazer algo** to be afraid to do sthg. **-2.** [preocupar-se com]: ~ **que** to be worried that. ⟨⟩ *vi* [preocupar-se]: ~ **por algo** to worry about sthg.

receber [5] [xese'be(x)] ⟨⟩ *vt* **-1.** [ger] to receive. **-2.** [recepcionar] to entertain. ⟨⟩ *vi* **-1.** [ser pago] to be paid; **a** ~ owing. **-2.** [recepcionar] to entertain.

recebimento [xesebi'mẽntu] *m* receipt; **acusar** ○ ~ **de** to acknowledge receipt of.

receio [xe'seju] *m* **-1.** [medo] fear. **-2.** [apreensão] concern; **ter** ~ **(de) que** to be afraid that.

receita [xe'sejta] *f* **-1.** [renda - pessoal] income; [- do Estado] tax revenue; ~ **pública** tax revenue. **-2.** *FIN* income. **-3.** *MED*: ~ **(médica)** prescription. **-4.** *CULIN* recipe. **-5.** *fig* [fórmula] way.

➽ **Receita** *f*: **a Receita (federal)** *Brazilian tax office,* ≃ Inland Revenue *UK,* ≃ Internal Revenue Service *US*.

receitar [4] [xesej'ta(x)] ⟨⟩ *vt* to prescribe. ⟨⟩ *vi* to issue prescriptions.

receituário [xesej'twarju] *m* prescription pad.

recém- [xesẽ] *prefixo* newly.

recém-casado, da [xe,sẽka'zadu, da] ⟨⟩ *adj* newly-wed. ⟨⟩ *m, f* newly-wed; **os** ~**s** the newly-weds.

recém-chegado, da [xe,sẽʃe'gadu, da] ⟨⟩ *adj* recently arrived. ⟨⟩ *m, f* newcomer.

recém-formado, da [xe,sẽfox'madu, da] (*pl* **-s**) ⟨⟩ *adj* newly qualified. ⟨⟩ *m,f* newly qualified person.

recém-nascido, da [xe,sẽna'sidu, da] ⟨⟩ *adj* newborn. ⟨⟩ *m, f* newborn child.

recém-publicado, da [xe,sẽpubli'kadu, da] (*pl* **-s**) *adj* recently published.

recender [5] [xesẽ'de(x)] *vi*: ~ **a algo** to smell of sthg.

recenseamento [xesẽsja'mẽntu] *m* census.

recensear [15] [xesẽ'sja(x)] *vt* to take a census of.

recente [xe'sẽntʃi] ⟨⟩ *adj* **-1.** [tempo] recent. **-2.** [novo] new; **este é o meu mais** ~ **hobby** this is my latest hobby. ⟨⟩ *adv* recently.

recentemente [xesẽntʃi'mẽntʃi] *adv* recently.

receoso, osa [xe'sjozu, ɔza] *adj* **-1.** [medroso] afraid. **-2.** [apreensivo] apprehensive; **estar** ~ **de algo/de fazer algo** to be worried about sthg/about doing sthg; **estar** ~ **de que** to be worried that.

recepção [xesep'sãw] (*pl* **-ões**) *f* reception.

recepcionar [4] [xesepsjo'na(x)] *vt* to entertain.

recepcionista [xesepsjo'niʃta] *mf* receptionist.

receptáculo [xesep'takulu] *m* receptacle.

receptador, ra [xesepta'do(x), ra] *m, f* fence.

receptar [4] [xesep'ta(x)] *vt* to fence.

receptividade [xeseptʃivi'dadʒi] *f* reception.

receptivo, va [xesep'tʃivu, va] *adj* receptive.

receptor [xesep'to(x)] (*pl* **-res**) *m* [aparelho] receiver.

recessão [xese'sãw] (*pl* **-ões**) *f* recession.

recesso [xe'sɛsu] *m* **-1.** [férias] recess. **-2.** [recanto] nook.

rechaçar [13] [xeʃa'sa(x)] *vt* **-1.** [opor-se a] to reject. **-2.** [repelir] to repel. **-3.** [negar] to decline.

recheado, da [xe'ʃjadu, da] *adj* **-1.** [comida]: ~ **(com** *ou* **de)** filled (with). **-2.** [repleto]: ~ **de algo** stuffed with sthg.

rechear [15] [xe'ʃja(x)] *vt* **-1.** [comida] to fill. **-2.** [encher muito]: ~ **algo de algo** to fill sthg with sthg.

recheio [xe'ʃeju] *m* **-1.** [de comida - de carne] stuffing; [- de bolo, pastel] filling. **-2.** *fig* [num texto] padding.

rechonchudo, da [xeʃõn'ʃudu, da] *adj* chubby.

recibo [xe'sibu] *m* receipt.

reciclagem [xesi'klaʒẽ] *f* **-1.** [de material] recycling. **-2.** [de pessoa] retraining.

reciclar [4] [xesi'kla(x)] *vt* **-1.** [material] to recycle. **-2.** [pessoa] to retrain.

recife [xe'sifi] *m* reef.

Recife [xe'sifi] *n* Recife.

recinto [xe'sĩntu] *m* area.

recipiente [xesi'pjẽntʃi] *m* recipient.

recíproca [xe'siproka] *f* ➽ **recíproco**.

reciprocar [12] [xesipro'ka(x)] *vt* to reciprocate.

reciprocidade [xesiprosi'dadʒi] *f* reciprocity.

recíproco, ca [xe'siproku, ka] *adj* reciprocal.
➽ **recíproca** *f*: **a recíproca** the reverse.

récita [ˈxɛsita] *f* performance.

recital [xesi'taw] (*pl* **-ais**) *m* recital.

recitar [4] [xesi'ta(x)] *vt* [declamar] to recite.

reclamação [xeklama'sãw] (*pl* **-ões**) *f* **-1.** [queixa] complaint. **-2.** *JUR* [petição] claim.

reclamante [xekla'mãntʃi] *mf JUR* claimant.

reclamar [4] [xekla'ma(x)] ⟨⟩ *vt* [exigir] to demand. ⟨⟩ *vi* **-1.** [protestar]: ~ **(de/contra)** to complain (about/against). **-2.** [exigir]: ~ **por** to demand.

reclame [xeklãmi] *m* advertisement.

reclinado, da [xekli'nadu, da] *adj* **-1.** [inclinado] bending over. **-2.** [recostado] lying back.

reclinar [4] [xekli'na(x)] *vt* [inclinar]: ~ **algo (em** *ou* **sobre)** to rest sthg (against *ou* on).
➽ **reclinar-se** *vp* [recostar-se] to lie back.

reclinável [xekli'navew] (*pl* **-eis**) *adj* reclining.

reclusão [xeklu'zãw] *f* -**1.** [isolamento] seclusion. -**2.** [em prisão] imprisonment. -**3.** [pena] solitary confinement.

recluso, sa [xe'kluzu, za] <> *adj* -**1.** [isolado] reclusive. -**2.** [preso] shut up. <> *m, f* -**1.** [pessoa que se isola] recluse. -**2.** [prisioneiro] prisoner.

recobrar [4] [xeko'bra(x)] *vt* to recover.

➡ **recobrar-se** *vp*: ~-**se de algo** to recover from sthg.

recolher [5] [xeko'ʎe(x)] *vt* -**1.** [ger] to collect. -**2.** [do chão] to pick up. -**3.** [juntar] to gather (together). -**4.** [pôr ao abrigo] to bring in. -**5.** [levar] to gather. -**6.** [tirar de circulação] to withdraw. -**7.** [coligir] to gather. -**8.** [encolher] to pull back.

➡ **recolher-se** *vp* -**1.** [ger] to retire. -**2.** [ir para casa] to go home. -**3.** [absorver-se] to become absorbed.

recolhido, da [xeko'ʎidu, da] *adj* -**1.** [lugar] secluded. -**2.** [absorvido] absorbed. -**3.** [dentro de casa] housebound.

recolhimento [xekoʎi'mẽntu] *m* -**1.** [ato de levar] reception. -**2.** [arrecadação] collection. -**3.** [de circulação] withdrawal. -**4.** [coleta] gathering. -**5.** [devido a doença] confinement. -**6.** [refúgio] refuge. -**7.** [retraimento] seclusion.

recomeçar [13] [xekome'sa(x)] <> *vt* to restart. <> *vi* to start again; ~ **a fazer algo** to start doing sthg again.

recomeço [xeko'mesu] *m* restart.

recomendação [xekomẽnda'sãw] (*pl* -**ões**) *f* [ger] recommendation; **por** ~ **de** on the recommendation of.

➡ **recomendações** *fpl* [saudações] regards.

recomendar [4] [xekomẽn'da(x)] *vt* -**1.** [ger] to recommend; **recomenda-se o uso de produtos naturais** the use of natural products is recommended. -**2.** [pedir] to ask. -**3.** [pedir proteção, favor]: ~ **alguém a alguém** to recommend sb to sb. -**4.** [enviar cumprimentos] to send one's regards.

recomendável [xekomẽn'davɛw] (*pl* -**eis**) *adj* advisable; **é** ~ **que ...** it's advisable that ...

recompensa [xekõn'pẽnsa] *f* reward.

recompensador, ra [xekõnpẽnsa'do(x), ra] *adj* rewarding.

recompensar [4] [xekõnpẽn'sa(x)] *vt* -**1.** [premiar] to reward. -**2.** [remunerar]: ~ **alguém de algo** to compensate sb for sthg.

recompor [45] [xekõn'po(x)] *vt* -**1.** [restabelecer] to reorganise. -**2.** [reordenar] to rearrange.

recôncavo [xe'kõŋkavu] *m* wide bay.

reconciliação [xekõnsilja'sãw] (*pl* -**ões**) *f* reconciliation.

reconciliar [16] [xekõnsi'lja(x)] *vt* to reconcile.

➡ **reconciliar-se** *vp*: ~-**se com** [pessoa] to be reconciled with; [situação] to become reconciled to.

recondicionado, da [xekõdisio'nadu, da] *adj* reconditioned.

recondicionar [4] [xekõndʒisjo'na(x)] *vt* to recondition.

recôndito, ta [xe'kõndʒitu, ta] *adj* -**1.** [retirado]

secluded. -**2.** [íntimo] innermost.

➡ **recôndito** *m fig* [âmago]: **no** ~ **da alma** in one's heart of hearts.

reconfortante [xekõnfox'tãntʃil] *adj* relaxing.

reconfortar [4] [xekõnfox'ta(x)] *vt* to comfort.

reconhecer [25] [xekoɲe'se(x)] *vt* -**1.** [ger] to recognize. -**2.** [mostrar-se agradecido por] [admitir] to acknowledge. -**3.** [constatar] to accept. -**4.** [autenticar] to authenticate; ~ **firma num documento** to authenticate officially the signature on a document. -**5.** [explorar] to reconnoitre UK, to reconnoiter US.

reconhecido, da [xekoɲe'sidu, da] *adj* -**1.** [grato] thankful. -**2.** [firma] authenticated.

reconhecimento [xekoɲesi'mẽntul] *m* -**1.** [ger] recognition. -**2.** [admissão] acknowledgement. -**3.** [autenticação] authentication. -**4.** [gratidão] gratitude. -**5.** [exploração] reconnaissance.

reconhecível [xekoɲe'sivɛw] (*pl* -**eis**) *adj* recognizable.

reconquista [xekõŋ'kiʃta] *f* reconquest.

reconquistar [4] [xekõŋkiʃ'ta(x)] *vt* -**1.** [território] to reconquer. -**2.** [pessoa, confiança] to regain.

reconsiderar [4] [xekõnside'ra(x)] *vt* to reconsider.

reconstituição [xekõnʃtʃitwi'sãw] (*pl* -**ões**) *f* reconstruction.

reconstituir [74] [xekõnʃtʃi'twi(r)] *vt* -**1.** [regime, grupo] to reconstitute. -**2.** [enfermo] to revive. -**3.** [crime] to reconstruct.

reconstrução [xekõnʃtru'sãw] *f* rebuilding, reconstruction.

reconstruir [xekõnʃ'trwi(x)] *vt* to rebuild, to reconstruct.

recontar [4] [xekõn'ta(x)] *vt* to recount.

recordação [xekoxda'sãw] (*pl* -**ões**) *f* -**1.** [ato, lembrança] memory. -**2.** [objeto] souvenir.

recordar [4] [xekox'da(x)] *vt* -**1.** [lembrar] to remember. -**2.** [por semelhança]: ~ **algo/alguém a alguém** to remind sb of sthg/sb. -**3.** [recapitular] to revise.

➡ **recordar-se** *vp* [lembrar]: ~-**se de alguém/algo** to remember sb/sthg; ~-**se (de) que** to remember that.

recorde [xe'kɔxdʒil] <> *adj inv* record (antes de subst); **em tempo** ~ in record time. <> *m* record; **bater/deter um** ~ to break/hold a record.

recordista [xekox'dʒiʃta] <> *adj* record-breaking. <> *mf* -**1.** [quem detém um recorde] record-holder. -**2.** [quem bate um recorde] record-breaker.

recorrente [xeko'xẽntʃil] <> *adj* [que se repete] recurring. <> *mf JUR* appellant.

recorrer [5] [xeko'xe(x)] *vi* -**1.**: ~ **a** to resort to. -**2.** JUR to appeal; ~ **de algo** to appeal against sthg.

recortado, da [xekox'tadu, da] *adj* -**1.** [papel, desenho] cut out. -**2.** [borda, litoral] ragged.

recortar [4] [xekox'ta(x)] *vt* to cut out.

recorte [xe'kɔxtʃil] *m* [de jornal etc] cutting.

recostar [4] [xekoʃ'ta(x)] *vt* -**1.** [encostar] to rest. -**2.** [pôr meio deitado] to recline.

recostar-se *vp* **-1.** [encostar-se] to lean against. **-2.** [pôr-se meio deitado] to lie back.

recreação [xekrja'sãw] *f* recreation.

recreativo, va [xekrja'tʃivu, va] *adj* recreational.

recreio [xe'kreju] *m* **-1.** [entretenimento] entertainment. **-2.** *EDUC* playtime *UK*, recess *US*; **hora do ~** breaktime.

recriação [xekrja'sãw] *(pl* **-ões)** *f* **-1.** [de história, mito] re-creation. **-2.** [de peça, ópera] new production. **-3.** [de filme] remake.

recriar [16] [xekri'a(x)] *vt* to recreate.

recriminação [xekrimina'sãw] *(pl* **-ões)** *f* recrimination.

recriminador, ra [xekrimina'do(x), ra] *adj* reproachful.

recriminar [4] [xekrimi'na(x)] *vt* to reproach.

recrudescer [25] [xekrude'se(x)] *vi* to intensify.

recrudescimento [xekrudesi'mẽntu] *m* intensification.

recruta [xe'kruta] *mf* recruit.

recrutamento [xekruta'mẽntu] *m* recruitment.

recrutar [4] [xekru'ta(x)] *vt* to recruit.

recuado, da [xe'kwadu, da] *adj* [edifício] set back.

recuar [4] [xe'kwa(x)] <> *vi* **-1.** [andar para trás] to step back. **-2.** [retirar-se] to retreat. **-3.** [voltar atrás - em intenção, decisão] to back out of; [- no tempo] to go back. **-4.** [canhão] to recoil. <> *vt* [mover para trás] to move back.

recuo [xe'kuw] *m* **-1.** [afastamento]: **com o ~, evitou ser atropelada** by stepping backwards, she avoided being run over; **o ~ do móvel, deu mais espaço na sala** moving this piece of furniture back has given the room more space. **-2.** [retirada] retreat. **-3.** [reconsideração - em intenção, decisão] reassessment; [- no tempo] going back. **-4.** [de canhão] recoil. **-5.** [em rua, terreno] setting back.

recuperação [xekupera'sãw] *f* **-1.** [reaquisição] recovery. **-2.** [restabelecimento] recuperation. **-3.** [reabilitação] rehabilitation. **-4.** [indenização] compensation.

recuperar [4] [xekupe'ra(x)] *vt* **-1.** [readquirir] to recover. **-2.** [restabelecer] to regain. **-3.** [reabilitar] to rehabilitate.

➤ **recuperar-se** *vp* [restabelecer-se] to recuperate.

recurso [xe'kuxsu] *m* **-1.** [ato]: **o ~ a algo** resorting to sthg. **-2.** [meio] recourse; **como** *ou* **em último ~** as a last resort. **-3.** [solução]: **~ contra algo** answer to sthg.

➤ **recursos** *mpl* [dinheiro] means.

recusa [xe'kuza] *f*: **~ (a/de algo)** refusal (to/ of sthg); **~ a** *ou* **em fazer algo** refusal to do sthg.

recusar [4] [xeku'za(x)] *vt* **-1.** [não aceitar] to refuse. **-2.** [não conceder]: **~ algo (a alguém)** to deny (sb) sthg. **-3.** [negar-se a]: **~ fazer algo** to refuse to do sthg.

➤ **recusar-se** *vp* [negar-se a]: **~-se (a fazer algo)** to refuse (to do sthg).

redação [xeda'sãw] *(pl* **-ões)** *f* **-1.** [ato] writing. **-2.** [modo de redigir] composition. **-3.** *EDUC* essay. **-4.** [redatores] editorial staff. **-5.** [seção] editorial office.

redargüir [xedax'gwi(x)] <> *vt*: **~ que** to retort that. <> *vi* to retort; **~ a alguém/algo** to respond to sb/sthg.

redator, ra [xeda'to(x), ra] *(mpl* **-es,** *fpl* **-s)** *m, f* **-1.** *JORN* writer. **-2.** [de obra de referência] editor, compiler.

redator-chefe, redatora-chefe [xedatoxʃɛfi, xedatoraʃɛfi] *(mpl* **redatores-chefes,** *fpl* **redatoras-chefes)** *m, f* editor in chief.

rede ['xedʒi] *f* **-1.** [ger] network; **comunicar-se em ~** to network. **-2.** [para pesca, caça & *ESP*] net. **-3.** [para cabelo] hairnet. **-4.** [leito] hammock.

rédea ['xɛdʒja] *f* **-1.** [correia] rein. **-2.** *fig* [direção]: **tomar as ~s de algo** to take the reins of sthg. **-3.** *loc*: **dar ~ larga a algo** to give free rein to sthg.

redemoinho [xedʒi'mwiɲu] *m* **-1.** [de água] whirlpool. **-2.** [de vento] whirlwind.

redenção [xedẽ'sãw] *f* redemption.

redentor, ra [xedẽ'to(x), ra] *m, f* [pessoa] redeemer.

➤ **Redentor** *m*: **o Redentor** *RELIG* the Redeemer.

redescobrir [59] [xedʒiʃko'bri(x)] *vt* to rediscover.

redigir [52] [xedʒi'ʒi(x)] <> *vt* to write. <> *vi* to write.

redimir [6] [xedʒi'mi(x)] *vt* **-1.** [*RELIG* - salvar] to redeem; [- expiar] to atone for. **-2.** [libertar] to set free.

➤ **redimir-se** *vp*: **~-se do castigo** to escape punishment; **redimiu-se dos seus erros da juventude** he made up for the errors of his youth.

redobrar [4] [xedo'bra(x)] <> *vt* **-1.** [dobrar de novo] to fold again. **-2.** [reduplicar, intensificar] to redouble. <> *vi* to intensify.

redoma [xe'doma] *f* bell jar.

redondamente [xe͜dõnda'mẽntʃi] *adv* [totalmente]: **me enganei ~** I was utterly wrong.

redondeza [xedõn'deza] *f* [qualidade] roundness.

➤ **redondezas** *fpl* [arredores] surroundings.

redondo, da [xe'dõndu, da] *adj* **-1.** [circular] round. **-2.** [rechonchudo] plump.

redor [xe'do(x)] *m*: **ao ~ de** around.

redução [xedu'sãw] *(pl* **-ões)** *f* **-1.** [ger] reduction. **-2.** [conversão] conversion.

redundância [xedũn'dãnsja] *f* redundancy.

redundante [xedũn'dãntʃi] *adj* redundant.

redundar [4] [xedũn'da(x)] *vi* [resultar]: **~ em algo** to result in sthg.

reduto [xe'dutu] *m* **-1.** [fortificação] fort. **-2.** *fig* [abrigo] shelter. **-3.** *fig* [lugar de reunião] meeting place.

reduzido, da [xedu'zidu, da] *adj* **-1.** [diminuído] reduced. **-2.** [pequeno] limited.

reduzir [72] [xedu'zi(x)] *vt* **-1.** [ger] to reduce. **-2.** [transformar]: **~ alguém/algo a algo** to reduce sb/ sthg to sthg. **-3.** [converter]: **~ algo a algo** to convert sthg to sthg. **-4.** [levar]: **~ alguém a algo** to reduce sb to sthg.

➡ **reduzir-se** *vp*: ~-**se a algo** [resumir-se] to be reduced to sthg.

reedição [xeedʒi'sãw] (*pl* -**ões**) *f* - **1.** [de obra] reprint. - **2.** [de medida] reissue.

reeditar [4] [xeedʒi'ta(x)] *vt* to republish.

reeducar [12] [xeedu'ca(x)] *vt* to re-educate.

reeleger [26] [xeele'ʒe(x)] *vt* to re-elect.

➡ **reeleger-se** *vp* to be re-elected.

reeleição [xeelej'sãw] *f* re-election.

reembolsar [4] [xeẽnbow'sa(x)] *vt* - **1.** [reaver] to recover. - **2.** [restituir]: ~ **alguém (de algo)** to refund sb (sthg). - **3.** [indenizar]: ~ **algo a alguém**, ~ **alguém de algo** to reimburse sthg to sb, to reimburse sb for sthg.

reembolso [xeẽnbowsu] *m* - **1.** [recuperação] recovery. - **2.** [restituição] refund. - **3.** [indenização] reimbursement.

reencarnação [xeẽnkaxna'sãw] *f* reincarnation.

reencarnar [4] [xeẽnkax'na(x)] *vi*: ~ **(em)** to reincarnate (as).

➡ **reencarnar-se** *vp*: ~-**se (em)** to be reincarnated (as).

reencontrar [4] [xeẽnkõn'tra(x)] *vt* to meet again.

➡ **reencontrar-se** *vp*: ~-**se (com alguém)** to meet (sb) again.

reencontro [xeẽŋ'kõntru] *m* reunion.

reentrância [xeẽn'trãnsja] *f* recess.

reescalonamento [xeeʃkalona'mẽntu] *m* [of a debt] rescheduling.

reescalonar [4] [xeeʃkalo'na(x)] *vt* [dívida] to reschedule.

reescrever [5] [xeeʃkre've(x)] *vt* to rewrite.

reexaminar [4] [xeezami'na(x)] *vt* to re-examine.

refazer [31] [xefa'ze(x)] *vt* - **1.** [fazer de novo] to redo. - **2.** [reconstruir] to rebuild. - **3.** [recuperar] to recover.

➡ **refazer-se** *vp* - **1.** [recuperar-se]: ~-**se (de algo)** to recover (from sthg). - **2.** [indenizar-se]: ~-**se de algo** to be compensated for sthg.

refeição [xefej'sãw] (*pl* -**ões**) *f* meal; **fazer uma** ~ to have a meal.

refeito, ta [ta, xe'fejtu] <> *pp* ➡ **refazer.** <> *adj* - **1.** [feito de novo] redone. - **2.** [reconstruído] rebuilt. - **3.** [recuperado] recovered.

refeitório [xefej'tɔrju] *m* dining hall.

refém [xe'fẽ] (*pl* -**ns**) *mf* hostage.

referência [xefe'rẽnsja] *f* reference; **fazer** ~ **a** to refer to.

➡ **referências** *fpl* [informação] references.

referencial [xefe'rẽnsjaw] (*pl* -**ais**) *adj* reference (*antes de subst*).

➡ **referencial** *m* [exemplo, modelo] yardstick.

referendar [457] [xeferẽn'da(x)] *vt* - **1.** [assinar] to countersign. - **2.** [validar] to endorse.

referendum [xefe'rẽndũ] *m* POL referendum.

referente [xefe'rẽntʃi] *adj*: ~ **a** concerning.

referido, da [xefe'ridu, da] *adj* - **1.** [mencionado] (afore)mentioned. - **2.** [referente]: ~ **a** in regard to.

referir [xefe'ri(x)] *vt* [narrar]: ~ **algo a alguém** to tell sb sthg.

➡ **referir-se** *vp*: ~-**se a** [aludir] to allude to; [dizer respeito] to refer to.

refestelado, da [xefeʃte'ladu, da] *adj* [estendido] sprawling.

refestelar-se [7] [xefeʃte'laxsi] *vp* [estender-se] to sprawl.

refil [xe'fiw] (*pl* -**is**) *m* refill.

refinado, da [xefi'nadu, da] *adj* refined.

refinamento [xefina'mẽntu] *m* - **1.** [ato] refining. - **2.** [requinte] refinement.

refinar [4] [xefi'na(x)] *vt* to refine.

refinaria [xefina'rial] *f* refinery.

refletido, da [xefle'tʃidu, da] *adj* - **1.** [espelhado] reflected. - **2.** [ponderado] considered.

refletir [65] [xefle'tʃi(x)] <> *vt* to reflect. <> *vi* - **1.** [luz]: ~ **de** to reflect off. - **2.** [pensar]: ~ **(em/sobre)** to reflect on/about. - **3.** [repercutir]: ~ **em** to reflect on.

➡ **refletir-se** *vp* - **1.** [espelhar-se] to be reflected. - **2.** [repercutir] to reflect on.

refletor [xefle'to(x)] (*pl* -**es**) *m* reflector.

reflexão [xeflek'sãw] (*pl* -**ões**) *f* reflection.

reflexivo, va [xeflek'sivu, va] *adj* reflective.

reflexo, xa [xe'flɛksu, sa] *adj* - **1.** [luz] reflected. - **2.** [movimento] reflex.

➡ **reflexo** *m* - **1.** [ger] reflection. - **2.** ANAT reflex.

➡ **reflexos** *mpl* [no cabelo] highlights.

reflorestamento [xefloreʃta'mẽntu] *m* reforestation.

reflorestar [4] [xefloreʃ'ta(x)] *vt* to reforest.

refluxo [xe'fluksu] *m* ebb.

refogado, da [xefo'gada, xefo'gadu] *adj* sautéed.

➡ **refogado** *m* - **1.** [molho] gravy. - **2.** [prato] stew.

refogar [14] [xefo'ga(x)] *vt* to sauté.

reforçado, da [xefox'sadu, da] *adj* - **1.** [ger] reinforced. - **2.** [refeição] hearty.

reforçar [13] [xefox'sa(x)] *vt* - **1.** [ger] to reinforce. - **2.** [ânimo] to invigorate.

reforço [xe'foxsu] *m* - **1.** [ger] reinforcement. - **2.** [a tropa, equipe] reinforcements (*pl*). - **3.** [de vacina] booster.

reforma [xe'fɔxma] *f* - **1.** [modificação] reform; ~ **ministerial** ministerial reshuffle; ~ **agrária** land reform. - **2.** ARQUIT renovation; **estar em** ~ to be under repair. - **3.** MIL regrouping.

➡ **Reforma** *f*: **a Reforma** RELIG the Reformation.

reformado, da [xefox'madu, da] *adj* - **1.** [modificado - ensino, instituição] reformed; [- leis] amended; [- sofá] repaired. - **2.** ARQUIT renovated. - **3.** MIL regrouped.

reformar [4] [xefox'ma(x)] *vt* - **1.** [modificar - ensino, constituição] to reform; [- sofá] to repair; [- lei] to amend; [- empresa] to restructure. - **2.** ARQUIT to renovate. - **3.** MIL to regroup. - **4.** JUR to amend.

➡ **reformar-se** *vp* - **1.** MIL to retire. - **2.** [regenerar-se] to be reformed.

reformatar [4] [xefoxma'ta(x)] *vt* COMPUT to reformat.

reformatório [xefoxma'tɔrju] *m* young offender institution *UK*, reformatory *US*.

refrão [xe'frãw] (*pl* -ões) *m* -**1.** [estribilho] chorus. -**2.** [provérbio] saying.

refratário, ria [xefra'tarju, rja] *adj* -**1.** [material] heat-resistant. -**2.** [rebelde]: **ser ~ a algo** to be impervious to sthg; [imune] to be immune to sthg.

refrear [15] [xefri'a(x)] *vt* [reprimir] to suppress.
➡ **refrear-se** *vp* [conter-se] to contain o.s.

refrega [xe'frɛga] *f* [briga] fight.

refrescante [xefreʃ'kãntʃi] *adj* refreshing.

refrescar [12] [xefreʃ'ka(x)] <> *vt* -**1.** [tornar menos quente] to cool. -**2.** [avivar] to refresh. -**3.** [tranqüilizar] to refresh. <> *vi* [tempo] to cool down.
➡ **refrescar-se** *vp* [pessoa] to refresh o.s.

refresco [xe'freʃku] *m* fruit squash.

refrigeração [xefriʒera'sãw] *m* [de alimentos] refrigeration; [de ambiente] air conditioning.

refrigerado, da [xefriʒe'radu, da] *adj* [alimento] chilled; [ambiente] air conditioned.

refrigerador [xefriʒera'do(x)] *m* -**1.** [de alimentos] refrigerator. -**2.** [de máquina] cooler.

refrigerante [xefriʒe'rãntʃi] *m* soft drink.

refrigerar [4] [xefriʒe'ra(x)] *vt* -**1.** [bebidas, alimentos] to chill. -**2.** [ambiente] to cool. -**3.** [máquina] to refrigerate.

refugar [14] [xefu'ga(x)] <> *vt* -**1.** [recusar] to refuse. -**2.** [menosprezar] to reject. <> *vi* [recusar-se] to refuse.

refugiado, da [xefu'ʒjadu, da] <> *adj* refugee. <> *m, f* refugee.

refugiar-se [16] [xefu'ʒjaxsi] *vp* [abrigar-se] to take refuge; **~ em** [abrigar-se] to take cover in; [asilar-se] to take refuge in; *fig* [amparar-se] to seek solace in.

refúgio [xe'fuʒju] *m* -**1.** [local] hideaway. -**2.** *fig* [apoio] refuge.

refugo [xe'fugu] *m* -**1.** [resto] waste. -**2.** [mercadoria] rubbish *UK*, garbage *US*.

refulgir [52] [xefuw'ʒi(x)] *vi* -**1.** [resplandecer] to shine. -**2.** *fig* [destacar-se] to stand out.

refutação [xefuta'sãw] (*pl* -ões) *f* -**1.** [desmentido] refutation. -**2.** [contestação] denial.

refutar [4] [xefu'ta(x)] *vt* to refute.

regaço [xe'gasu] *m* [colo] lap.

regador [xega'do(x)] (*pl* -es) *m* watering can.

regalia [xega'lia] *f* privilege.

regalo [xe'galu] *m* -**1.** [presente] gift. -**2.** [prazer]: **ser um ~** to be a pleasure.

regar [14] [xe'ga(x)] *vt* -**1.** [aguar] to water. -**2.** [banhar] to wash. -**3.** [acompanhar] to wash down.

regata [xe'gata] *f* regatta.

regatear [15] [xega'tʃja(x)] <> *vt* to haggle over. <> *vi* to haggle.

regato [xe'gatu] *m* stream.

regência [xe'ʒẽnsja] *f* -**1.** *MÚS* conducting. -**2.** *GRAM* government. -**3.** [administração] rule.

regeneração [xeʒenera'sãw] *f* -**1.** [recomposição] regeneration. -**2.** [moral] reform.

regenerar [4] [xeʒene'ra(x)] *vt* -**1.** [recompor] to regenerate. -**2.** [moralmente] to reform.
➡ **regenerar-se** *vp* -**1.** [recompor-se] to be

regenerated. -**2.** [moralmente] to be reformed.

regente [xe'ʒẽntʃi] *m* -**1.** *POL* regent. -**2.** *MÚS* conductor. -**3.** *UNIV* vice chancellor *UK*, president *US*.

reger [26] [xe'ʒe(x)] <> *vt* -**1.** [governar] to govern. -**2.** [regular] to rule. -**3.** *MÚS* to conduct. -**4.** *UNIV* to occupy. -**5.** *GRAM* to govern. <> *vi* -**1.** [governar] to rule. -**2.** *MÚS* to conduct.

região [xe'ʒjãw] (*pl* -ões) *f* -**1.** [território] region. -**2.** [de cidade, corpo] area.

regime [xe'ʒimi] *m* -**1.** [ger] system. -**2.** [dieta] diet; **estar de ~** to be on a diet; **fazer ~** to diet. -**3.** [regras] rules *(pl)*; **~ de vida** way of life.

regimento [xeʒi'mẽntu] *m* -**1.** [ger] regiment. -**2.** [normas] rules *(pl)*; **~ interno** [de escola] school rules; [de empresa] company rules.

regiões [xe'ʒjõjʃ] *mpl* ⊳ **região**.

regional [xeʒjo'naw] (*pl* -ais) *adj* regional.

regionalismo [xeʒjona'liʒmu] *m* regionalism.

regionalizar [xeʒjonali'za(x)] *vt* to regionalize.

registradora [xeʒiʃtra'doral] *f* [caixa] cash register.

registrar [4] [xeʒiʃ'tra(x)] *vt* -**1.** [ger] to register. -**2.** [anotar] to record. -**3.** [memorizar] to remember.

registro [xe'ʒiʃtru] *m* -**1.** [ger & *LING*] register. -**2.** [postal] registration. -**3.** [órgão]: **~ civil** registry office. -**4.** [torneira] tap *UK*, faucet *US*. -**5.** [relógio] meter. -**6.** *MÚS* range.

rego ['xegu] *m* -**1.** [valão] ditch. -**2.** [de arado] furrow. -**3.** *mfam ANAT* bum crack.

regozijar-se [4] [xegozi'ʒaxsi] *vp*: **~ com algo/por fazer algo** to be delighted with sthg/to do sthg.

regozijo [xego'ziʒul] *m* delight.

regra ['xɛgra] *f* -**1.** [norma] rule; **por via de ~** as a rule. -**2.** [rotina] routine; **sair da ~** to change one's routine. -**3.** [prudência]: **com ~** in moderation.

regrado, da [xe'gradu, da] *adj* sensible.

regrar [4] [xe'gra(x)] *vt* to regulate.
➡ **regrar-se** *vp*: **~-se por algo** to be guided by sthg.

regredir [57] [xegre'dʒi(x)] *vi*: **~ (a algo)** to regress (to sthg).

regressão [xegre'sãw] *f* -**1.** [retrocesso] regression. -**2.** *PSIC* relapse.

regressar [4] [xegre'sa(x)] *vi*: **~ (de/a)** to return from/to.

regressivo, va [xegre'sivu, va] *adj* regressive.

regresso [xe'gresul] *m* return.

régua ['xɛgwa] *f* ruler; **~ de cálculo** slide rule.

régua-tê [ˌxɛgwa'te] (*pl* réguas-tê) *f* *ARQUIT* T-square.

regulador, ra [xegula'do(x), ra] *adj* [força] regulating.
➡ **regulador** *m* [medicamento] regulator.

regulagem [xegu'laʒẽl] (*pl* -ns) *f* tuning.

regulamentação [xegulamẽnta'sãw] *f* -**1.** [ato] regulation. -**2.** [regras] regulations *(pl)*.

regulamentar [4] [xegula'mẽnta(x)] <> *adj* standardizing. <> *vt* to regulate.

regulamento [xegula'mẽntu] *m* rules *(pl)*.
regular [4] [xegu'la(x)] *(pl* **-es)** ⬦ *adj* **-1.** [ger]
regular. **-2.** [legal] legal. **-3.** [tamanho] medium.
-4. [razoável] reasonable. ⬦ *vt* **-1.** [ger] to
regulate. **-2.** [ajustar] to adjust. **-3.** [conformar]:
~ **algo por algo** to check sthg against sthg. ⬦
vi **-1.** [maquina]: ~ **bem/mal** to be well/badly
adjusted. **-2.** [pessoa]: **não ~ (bem)** to not be
quite right in the head. **-3.** [ter]: **ele ~ pelos 50**
he's about 50. **- 4.** [aproximar-se]: **meu filho regula
em idade com o seu** my son is about the same
age as yours.
➠ **regular-se por** *vp* [orientar-se] to be guided
by.
regularidade [xegulari'dadʒil *f* regularity.
regularizar [4] [xegulari'za(x)] *vt* **-1.** [legalizar] to
legalize. **-2.** [normalizar] to regularize.
➠ **regularizar-se** *vp* [normalizar-se] to return to
normal.
regurgitar [4] [xeguxʒi'ta(x)] *vt* & *vi* to regurgitate.
rei ['xej] *m* **-1.** [ger] king; **ser o ~ de algo** *fig* [da
música, do crime] to be the king of sthg; [da bagun-
ça] to be the world's worst for sthg. **-2.** *loc*: **ter o
~ na barriga** to be full of o.s.
Reikjavik [xejkʒa'vikil *n* Reykjavik.
reimpressão [xẽjnpre'sãw] *(pl* **-ões)** *f* reprint.
reimprimir [6] [xẽjnpri'mi(x)] *vt* to reprint.
reinado [xej'nadul *m* reign.
reinante [xej'nãntʃil *adj* prevailing.
reinar [4] [xej'na(x)] *vi* **-1.** [governar] to reign. **-2.**
fig [dominar] to dominate.
reincidência [xẽjnsi'dẽnsjal *f* **-1.** [de doença]
relapse. **-2.** [de crime] recidivism. **-3.** [de erro]
repetition. **-4.** [na bebida] backsliding.
reincidente [xẽjnsi'dẽntʃil ⬦ *adj*: ~ **em algo**
drawn back into sthg; **jamais perdoaremos os erros ~s** we shall never forgive repeated mistakes. ⬦ *mf* reoffender.
reincidir [6] [xẽjnsi'dʒi(x)] *vi* to recur; ~ **em algo**
to commit sthg again.
reingressar [4] [xẽjngre'sa(x)] *vt*: ~ **em** to re-
enter.
reiniciar [16] [xejni'sja(x)] *vt* to restart.
reino ['xejnul *m* **-1.** [ger] kingdom. **-2.** *fig* [âmbito]
realm.
reintegrar [4] [xẽjnte'gra(x)] *vt* **-1.** [em cargo etc] to
reinstate. **-2.** [reconduzir] to readmit.
reiterar [4] [xeite'ra(x)] *vt* to reiterate.
reitor, ra [xej'to(x), ral *m, f* vice chancellor *UK*,
president *US*.
reitoria [xejto'rial *f* **-1.** [cargo] vice-chancellor-
ship *UK*, presidency *US*. **-2.** [gabinete] vice
chancellor's office *UK*, president's office *US*.
reivindicação [xejvĩndʒika'sãw] *(pl* **-ões)** *f* claim.
reivindicar [12] [xejvĩndʒi'ka(x)] *vt* to claim.
rejeição [xeʒej'sãw] *(pl* **-ões)** *f* rejection.
rejeitar [4] [xeʒej'ta(x)] *vt* **-1.** [recusar] to reject.
-2. [vomitar] to vomit. **-3.** [desprezar] to ignore.
rejubilar-se [4] [xeʒubi'laxsil *vp* to rejoice.
rejuvenescer [25] [xeʒuvene'se(x)] ⬦ *vt* to

rejuvenate. ⬦ *vi* to be rejuvenating.
➠ **rejuvenescer-se** *vp* to be rejuvenated.
rejuvenescimento [xeʒuvenesi'mẽntu] *m* rejuvenation.
relação [xela'sãw] *(pl* **-ões)** *f* **-1.** [ligação] relationship; **em ~ a** in relation to; ~ **entre/com**
relationship between/with. **-2.** [listagem] list.
➠ **relações** *fpl* [relacionamento] relationship *(sg)*;
ele não é pessoa de minhas relações he's not sb I
have anything to do with; **cortar relações com
alguém** to break off with sb; **ter relações com alguém** [sexual] to sleep with sb; **relações públicas**
public relations; **relações sexuais** sex, sexual
intercourse.
relacionado, da [xelasjo'nadu, dal *adj* **-1.** [lista-
do] listed. **-2.** [ligado] related. **-3.** [pessoa]: **bem
~** well connected.
relacionamento [xelasjona'mẽntul *m* **-1.** [liga-
ção] relationship. **-2.** [trato]: **é uma garota de
fácil ~** she's a girl who's easy to get on with.
relacionar [4] [xelasjo'na(x)] *vt* **-1.** [listar] to list.
-2. [confrontar]: ~ **algo com algo** to compare sthg
with sthg. **-3.** [pessoa] to bring into contact with.
➠ **relacionar-se** *vp* **-1.** [ligar-se] to be related.
-2. [pessoa]: ~**-se com alguém** to mix with sb.
relações-públicas [xela‚sõjʃ'publikaʃl *mf inv*
[pessoa] PR officer.
relâmpago [xe'lãnpagul ⬦ *m METEOR* flash of
lightning; **num ~** [rapidamente] in a flash. ⬦ *adj*
[rápido] lightning *(antes de subst)*.
relampejar [4] [xelãnpe'ʒa(x)] *vi*: **relampejou esta
noite** there was lightening last night.
relance [xe'lãnsil *m*: **ver de ~** to glance at.
relapso, sa [xe'lapsu, sal ⬦ *adj* negligent. ⬦
m, f negligent person.
relatar [4] [xela'ta(x)] *vt* to relate.
relativamente [xelatʃiva'mẽntʃil *adv* relatively.
relatividade [xelatʃivi'dadʒil *f* relativity.
relativo, va [xela'tʃivu, val *adj* relative; ~ **a algo**
relative to sthg.
relato [xe'latul *m* account.
relator, ra [xela'to(x), ral *m, f* report writer.
relatório [xela'tɔrjul *m* report; ~ **anual** annual
report.
relax [xi'lɛkiʃl *m* relaxation.
relaxado, da [xela'ʃadu, dal *adj* **-1.** [desleixado]
careless. **-2.** [descansado] relaxed.
relaxamento [xelaʃa'mẽntul *m* **-1.** [desleixo]
carelessness. **-2.** [repouso] relaxation.
relaxante [xela'ʃãntʃil *adj* relaxing.
relaxar [4] [xela'ʃa(x)] ⬦ *vt* to relax. ⬦ *vi* **-1.**
[desleixar-se]: ~ **em algo** to become careless with
sthg. **-2.** [descansar] to relax. **-3.** [condescender]: ~
com algo/alguém to relent towards sthg/sb.
➠ **relaxar-se** *vp* **-1.** [desleixar-se]: ~**-se (com algo)** to be careless (with sthg). **-2.** [distender-se] to
be relaxed.
relegar [14] [xele'ga(x)] *vt* to relegate.
relembrar [4] [xelẽn'bra(x)] *vt* to recall.
relento [xe'lẽntul *m* dew; **ao ~** outdoors.
reler [42] [xe'le(x)] *vt* to reread.

reles ['xɛliʃ] *adj inv* **-1.** [desprezível] despicable. **-2.** [mero] mere.

relevância [xele'vãnsja] *f* **-1.** [saliência] prominence. **-2.** [importância] relevance; **ser de** ~ to be of importance, to be important.

relevante [xele'vãntʃi] *adj* **-1.** [saliente] prominent. **-2.** [importante] important.

relevar [4] [xele'va(x)] *vt* **-1.** [salientar] to emphasize. **-2.** [aliviar] to alleviate. **-3.** [perdoar] to forgive.

relevo [xe'levu] *m* **-1.** [em superfície] outstanding feature. **-2.** ARTE relief. **-3.** *fig* [destaque] importance; **pôr em** ~ to emphasize.

relicário [xeli'karju] *m* reliquary.

religião [xeli'ʒjãw] (*pl* -ões) *f* religion.

religiosidade [xeliʒjozi'dadʒi] *f* piety; **pagar as contas com** ~ to pay one's debts religiously.

religioso, osa [xeli'ʒozu, ɔza] ◇ *adj* religious. ◇ *m*, *f* [padre, freira] monk (*f* nun).
➤ **religioso** *m* [casamento] church wedding.

relinchar [4] [xelĩ'ʃa(x)] *vi* to neigh.

relincho [xe'lĩʃu] *m* neigh.

relíquia [xe'likja] *f* relic; ~ **de família** family heirloom.

relógio [xe'lɔʒju] *m* **-1.** [instrumento] clock; ~ **de pé** grandfather clock; ~ **de ponto** time clock; ~ **de pulso** wrist watch; ~ **de sol** sundial; **correr contra o** ~ to race against the clock. **-2.** [registro] meter.

relojoaria [xeloʒwa'ria] *f* **-1.** ARTE watchmaking. **-2.** [loja] watchmaker's.

relojoeiro, ra [xelo'ʒwejru, ra] *m*, *f* watchmaker.

relutância [xelu'tãnsja] *f* reluctance.

relutante [xelu'tãntʃi] *adj* reluctant.

relutar [4] [xelu'ta(x)] *vi*: ~ **(em fazer algo)** to be reluctant (to do sthg); ~ **(contra algo)** to be reluctant (to accept sthg).

reluzente [xelu'zẽntʃi] *adj* shining.

reluzir [72] [xelu'zi(x)] *vi* [brilhar] to shine.

relva ['xɛwva] *f* grass.

remador, ra [xema'do(x), ra] *m*, *f* rower.

remanescente [xemane'sẽntʃi] ◇ *adj* remaining; **isto é** ~ **de práticas antigas** this is what remains of ancient customs. ◇ *m* remainder.

remanescer [25] [xemane'se(x)] *vi* to remain.

remanso [xe'mãnsu] *m* backwater.

remar [4] [xe'ma(x)] ◇ *vt* to row. ◇ *vi* to row; ~ **contra a maré** *fig* to swim against the tide.

remarcação [xemaxka'sãw] (*pl* -ões) *f* adjustment.

remarcar [12] [xemax'ka(x)] *vt* to adjust.

rematado, da [xema'tadu, da] *adj* [concluído] completed.

rematar [4] [xema'ta(x)] *vt* **-1.** [concluir] to conclude. **-2.** [fazer o acabamento] to finish.

remate [xe'matʃi] *m* **-1.** [conclusão] end. **-2.** [acabamento] finishing touch. **-3.** [de piada] punchline.

remediado, da [xeme'dʒjadu, da] *adj* comfortably off.

remediar [17] [xeme'dʒja(x)] *vt* **-1.** [corrigir, solucionar] to put right. **-2.** [atenuar] to alleviate. **-3.** [evitar] to avoid.

remediável [xeme'dʒjavew] (*pl* -eis) *adj* rectifiable.

remédio [xe'mɛdʒju] *m* **-1.** [medicamento] remedy. **-2.** [solução] solution.

remela [xe'mɛla] *f* sleep.

remelento, ta [xeme'lẽntu, ta] *adj* bleary-eyed.

remelexo [xeme'leʃu] *m* swaying.

rememorar [4] [xememo'ra(x)] *vt* to remember.

remendar [4] [xemẽn'da(x)] *vt* **-1.** [roupa] to mend. **-2.** [erros] to rectify.

remendo [xe'mẽndu] *m* **-1.** [de pano] patch. **-2.** [de metal, couro] repair. **-3.** [emenda] correction.

remessa [xe'mɛsa] *f* **-1.** [ato] dispatch. **-2.** [de dinheiro] remittance; [de mercadorias] shipment.

remetente [xeme'tẽntʃi] *mf* [de carta] sender.

remeter [5] [xeme'te(x)] *vt* **-1.** [carta, encomenda] to send. **-2.** [dinheiro] to remit.
➤ **remeter-se** *vp* [referir-se] to refer to.

remexer [5] [xeme'ʃe(x)] ◇ *vt* **-1.** [mexer] to move. **-2.** [misturar] to mix. **-3.** [sacudir - braços] to shake; [- papéis, folhas] to shuffle. **-4.** [revolver] to stir up. **-5.** *fam* [rebolar] to roll. ◇ *vi* [mexer]: ~ **em algo** to rummage through sthg.
➤ **remexer-se** *vp* **-1.** [mover-se] to stir. **-2.** [rebolar-se] to roll.

remição [xemi'sãw] *f* **-1.** [libertação] release. **-2.** [expiação] redemption.

reminiscência [xemini'sẽnsja] *f* reminiscence.

remir [80] [xe'mi(x)] *vt* **-1.** [ger] to redeem. **-2.** [livrar]: ~ **alguém (de algo)** to free sb (from sthg). **-3.** [indenizar] to indemnify.
➤ **remir-se** *vp* [redimir-se] to redeem o.s.

remissão [xemi'sãw] (*pl* -ões) *f* **-1.** [ger] remission. **-2.** [em texto] cross-reference.

remo ['xemu] *m* **-1.** [instrumento] oar. **-2.** [esporte] rowing.

remoção [xemo'sãw] (*pl* -ões) *f* removal.

remoçar [13] [xemo'sa(x)] ◇ *vt* to rejuvenate. ◇ *vi* to be rejuvenated.

remoer [28] [xe'mwe(x)] *vt* **-1.** [moer novamente] to regrind. **-2.** [remastigar] to chew. **-3.** [refletir muito sobre] to chew over. **-4.** [afligir] to chew at.
➤ **remoer-se** *vp* [amofinar-se] to be consumed.

remontar [4] [xemõn'ta(x)] ◇ *vt* **-1.** [armar de novo] to reassemble. **-2.** TEATRO to restage. **-3.** [mobiliar] to refurnish. ◇ *vi* **-1.** [em cavalo] to remount. **-2.** [no tempo]: ~ **a** to date back to; ~ **ao passado** to return to the past.

remorso [xe'mɔxsu] *m* remorse.

remoto, ta [xe'mɔtu, ta] *adj* remote.

removedor [xemove'do(x)] *m* remover.

remover [5] [xemo've(x)] *vt* **-1.** [ger] to remove. **-2.** [transferir] to transfer. **-3.** [superar] to overcome.

remuneração [xemunera'sãw] (*pl* -ões) *f* remuneration.

remunerador, ra [xemunera'do(x), ra] *adj* [recompensador] remunerative.

remunerar [4] [xemune'ra(x)] *vt* to remunerate.

rena ['xɛna] *f* reindeer.

renal [xe'naw] (*pl* -ais) *adj* renal.

Renascença [xena'sɐ̃nsa] *f*: **a ~** the Renaissance.

renascentista [xenasɛ̃n'tʃiʃta] *adj* Renaissance (*antes de subst*).

renascer [25] [xena'se(x)] *vi* **-1.** [nascer de novo] to spring up again. **-2.** *fig* [recuperar-se, resurgir] to be reborn.

renascimento [xenasi'mɛ̃ntu] *m* rebirth.

➤ **Renascimento** *m*: **o Renascimento** the Renaissance.

renda ['xɛ̃da] *f* **-1.** [rendimento] income; **viver de ~** to have a private income; **~ bruta** gross income; **~ fixa** fixed yield; **~ líquida** net income. **-2.** [lucro] profit. **-3.** [tecido] lace.

rendado, da [xɛ̃'dadu, da] *adj* **-1.** [feito de renda] lace (*antes de subst*). **-2.** [como renda] lacy.

➤ **rendado** *m* lacework.

rendeiro, ra [xɛ̃'dejru, ra] *m, f* **-1.** [fabricante de renda] lacemaker. **-2.** [de terra] tenant farmer.

render [5] [xɛ̃'de(x)] <> *vt* **-1.** [dominar] to overpower. **-2.** [substituir] to relieve. **-3.** [lucrar] to yield. **-4.** [causar] to bring about. **-5.** [prestar] to render. <> *vi* **-1.** [dar lucro] to be profitable. **-2.** [trabalho] to be productive. **-3.** [comida]: **a comida rendeu para toda a semana** there was enough food for the whole week; **vamos fazer sopa porque rende mais** let's make soup because it goes further. **-4.** [durar] to last.

➤ **render-se** *vp* [entregar-se]: **~-se (a algo/alguém)** to surrender (to sb/sthg).

rendição [xɛ̃di'ʒãw] *f* **-1.** [capitulação] surrender. **-2.** [substituição] changing.

rendido, da [xɛ̃'dʒidu, da] *adj fig*: **~ a algo** overcome by sthg.

rendimento [xɛ̃dʒi'mɛ̃ntu] *m* **-1.** [renda] rental. **-2.** [lucro] profit. **-3.** [desempenho] performance. **-4.** [juro] interest.

rendoso, osa [xɛ̃'dozu, ɔza] *adj* **-1.** [lucrativo] profitable. **-2.** [proveitoso] productive.

renegado, da [xene'gadu, da] <> *adj* renegade. <> *m, f* renegade.

renegar [14] [xene'ga(x)] *vt* **-1.** [ger] to renounce. **-2.** [negar] to deny. **-3.** [desprezar] to reject.

renhido, da [xe'ɲidu, da] *adj* hard-fought.

renitente [xeni'tɛ̃ntʃi] *adj* persistent.

renomado, da [xeno'madu, da] *adj* renowned.

renome [xe'nɔmi] *m*: **de ~** renowned.

renovação [xenova'sãw] (*pl* -ões) *f* **-1.** [ger] renewal. **-2.** [de ensino, empresa] revamping. **-3.** ARQUIT renovation.

renovador, ra [xeno'vado(x), ra] <> *adj* reformist. <> *m, f* reformist.

renovar [4] [xeno'va(x)] *vt* **-1.** [ger] to renew. **-2.** [ensino, empresa] to revamp. **-3.** ARQUIT to renovate.

rentabilidade [xɛ̃tabili'dadʒi] *f* **-1.** [lucro] profitability. **-2.** [proveito] productiveness.

rentável [xɛ̃'tavɛw] (*pl* -eis) *adj* profitable.

rente ['xɛ̃tʃi] <> *adj* **-1.** [muito curto] close-cropped. **-2.** [junto]: **~ a** right next to. <> *adv* **-1.** [muito curto] very short. **-2.** [junto]: **ele caiu ~ ao chão** he fell flat on the floor; **ele foi esmagado ~ ao muro** he was crushed right up against the wall.

renúncia [xe'nũnsja] *f* renouncement.

renunciar [16] [xenũn'sja(x)] *vi*: **~ a algo** to renounce sthg.

reorganização [xeoxganiza'sãw] *f* reorganization.

reorganizar [4] [xeoxgani'za(x)] *vt* to reorganize.

reparação [xepara'sãw] (*pl* -ões) *f* **-1.** [conserto] repair. **-2.** [indenização] compensation. **-3.** [retratação] reparation.

reparar [4] [xepa'ra(x)] <> *vt* **-1.** [consertar] to repair. **-2.** [indenizar] to compensate. **-3.** [retratar-se de] to admit. **-4.** [notar] to notice. <> *vi* [notar]: **~ em algo/alguém** to notice sthg/sb; **não repare na bagunça** pay no attention to the mess.

reparo [xe'paru] *m* **-1.** [conserto] repair. **-2.** [crítica] criticism.

repartição [xepaxtʃi'sãw] (*pl* -ões) *f* **-1.** [partilha] distribution. **-2.** [órgão governamental] department; **~ pública** government department.

repartir [6] [xepax'tʃi(x)] *vt* **-1.** [dividir - em partes] to divide up; **~ o cabelo** to part one's hair; [- entre vários] to distribute. **-2.** [compartilhar] to share.

repassar [4] [xepa'sa(x)] *vt* **-1.** [passar de novo] to cross again. **-2.** [revisar] to revise. **-3.** [verbas] to transfer.

repasse [xe'pasi] *m* [de verba] transfer.

repatriação [xepatrja'sãw] (*pl* -ões) *f* repatriation.

repatriar [16] [xepa'trja(x)] *vt* to repatriate.

➤ **repatriar-se** *vp* to return home.

repelente [xepe'lɛ̃ntʃi] <> *adj* [repugnante] repellent. <> *m* [inseticida] repellent.

repelir [57] [xepe'li(x)] *vt* **-1.** [fazer regressar] to drive away. **-2.** [expulsar] to repel. **-3.** [rechaçar, impedir de entrar] to refuse admission to. **-4.** [recusar] to refuse. **-5.** [repudiar] to reject. **-6.** [desmentir] to refute.

repensar [4] [xepɛ̃'sa(x)] <> *vt* to reconsider. <> *vi*: **~ em algo** to reconsider sthg.

repente [xe'pɛ̃ntʃi] *m*: **num ~ tudo escureceu** all of a sudden everything went dark; **um ~ de carinho** a sudden show of affection.

➤ **de repente** *loc adv* **-1.** [repentinamente] suddenly. **-2.** *fam* [talvez] maybe.

repentinamente [xepɛ̃ntʃina'mɛ̃ntʃi] *adv* suddenly.

repentino, na [xepɛ̃n'tʃinu, na] *adj* sudden.

repercussão [xepexku'sãw] (*pl* -ões) *f* **-1.** *fig* [de som] reverberation. **-2.** [efeito] repercussion; **o CD teve boa ~ no exterior** the CD was very successful abroad.

repercutir [6] [xepexku'tʃi(x)] <> *vt* [som] to re-echo. <> *vi* **-1.** [som] to reverberate. **-2.** *fig* [afetar]: **~ em** to have repercussions on.

repertório [xepex'tɔrju] *m* **-1.** [conjunto] collection. **-2.** *MÚS* repertoire.

repetente [xepe'tẽntʃi] *EDUC* <> *adj* repeating. <> *mf* student who repeats a year.

repetição [xepetʃi'sãw] (*pl* -ões) *f* repetition.

repetido, da [xepe'tʃidu, da] *adj* repeated; **repetidas vezes** repeatedly.

repetir [57] [xepe'tʃi(x)] <> *vt* -**1.** [ger] to repeat. -**2.** [roupa] to wear again. -**3.** [refeição] to have a second helping of, to have seconds. -**4.** [tocar de novo]: ~ **uma música** to play an encore. <> *vi* to repeat.

◆ **repetir-se** *vp* -**1.** [fenômeno] to be repeated. -**2.** [pessoa] to repeat o.s.

repetitivo, va [xepetʃi'tʃivu, va] *adj* repetitive.

repicar [12] [xepi'ka(x)] *vt & vi* to ring.

repique [xe'piki] *m* -**1.** [de sino] peal. -**2.** *fig* [alarme] alarm bell; ~ **falso** false alarm.

replay [xi'plej] *m* replay.

repleto, ta [xe'plɛtu, ta] *adj* [cheio]: ~ **(de)** full (of).

réplica ['xɛplika] *f* -**1.** [cópia] replica. -**2.** [resposta] reply.

replicar [12] [xepli'ka(x)] <> *vt* -**1.** [responder] to reply. -**2.** [contestar] to answer. <> *vi* -**1.** [responder] to reply. -**2.** [contestar] to respond.

repolho [xe'poʎu] *m* cabbage.

repor [45] [xe'po(x)] *vt* -**1.** [recolocar] to replace. -**2.** [devolver] to repay.

◆ **repor-se** *vp* to recover.

reportagem [xepox'taʒẽ] (*pl* -ns) *f* -**1.** [ato] report. -**2.** [matéria]: ~ **(sobre)** report (on). -**3.** [repórteres] reporters (*pl*), the press.

reportar [4] [xepox'ta(x)] *vt* -**1.** [atribuir] to attribute. -**2.** [retroceder] to take back. -**3.** [relatar] to report.

◆ **reportar-se** *vp* [referir-se] to refer.

repórter [xe'pɔxte(x)] (*pl* -es) *mf* reporter.

repórter-fotográfico, ca [xe'pɔxte(x)foto'grafiku, ka] (*pl* -s) *m* press photographer.

reposição [xepozi'sãw] (*pl* -ões) *f* [restituição] return; ~ **salarial** wage adjustment.

repositório [xepozi'tɔrju] *m* repository.

repousante [xepo'zãntʃi] *adj* restful.

repousar [4] [xepo'za(x)] <> *vt* to rest. <> *vi* -**1.** [descansar] to rest. -**2.** [basear-se]: ~ **em/sobre algo** to be based on sthg. -**3.** [não produzir] to rest, to lie fallow.

repouso [xe'pozu] *m* [descanso] rest; **em** ~ at rest.

repreender [5] [xeprjẽn'de(x)] *vt* to reprimand.

repreensão [xeprjẽn'sãw] (*pl* -ões) *f* reprimand.

repreensível [xeprjẽn'sivew] (*pl* -eis) *adj* reprehensible.

represa [xe'preza] *f* dam.

represália [xepre'zalja] *f* reprisal; **em** ~ **in** reprisal.

representação [xeprezẽnta'sãw] (*pl* -ões) *f* -**1.** [reprodução] representation. -**2.** [queixa]: ~ **contra algo/alguém** complaint against sthg/sb. -**3.** [delegação] representatives (*pl*). -**4.** *TEATRO*

performance. -**5.** *COM*: **ter a** ~ **de algo** to display sthg. -**6.** *fig* [fingimento] pretence *UK*, pretense *US*.

representante [xeprezẽn'tãntʃi] <> *adj* representative. <> *mf* representative.

representar [4] [xeprezẽn'ta(x)] <> *vt* -**1.** [ger] to represent. -**2.** [*TEATRO* - encenar] to perform; [- interpretar] to play. <> *vi* *TEATRO* [interpretar] to perform.

representatividade [xeprezẽntatʃivi'dadʒi] *f* representation.

representativo, va [xeprezẽnta'tʃivu, va] *adj* representative; ~ **de algo** representative of sthg.

repressão [xepre'sãw] (*pl* -ões) *f* repression.

repressivo, va [xepre'sivu, va] *adj* repressive.

repressor, ra [xepre'so(x), ra] *adj* repressive.

reprimido, da [xepri'midu, da] *adj* repressed.

reprimir [6] [xepri'mi(x)] *vt* -**1.** [conter - paixão] to contain; [- pensamento] to suppress. -**2.** [dissimular] to suppress. -**3.** *PSIC* to repress. -**4.** [proibir] to prohibit.

◆ **reprimir-se** *vp* [conter-se] to control o.s.

reprisar [4] [xepri'za(x)] *vt* to repeat.

reprise [xe'prizi] *f* repeat.

réprobo, ba ['xɛprobu, ba] <> *adj* reprobate. <> *m, f* reprobate.

reprodução [xeprodu'sãw] (*pl* -ões) *f* reproduction.

reprodutivo, va [xeprodu'tʃivu, va] *adj* reproductive.

reprodutor, ra [xeprodu'to(x), ra] *adj* reproductive.

◆ **reprodutor** *m* breeding animal.

reproduzir [72] [xeprodu'zi(x)] *vt* -**1.** [copiar, repetir] to copy. -**2.** [procriar] to breed. -**3.** [reeditar] to republish.

◆ **reproduzir-se** *vp* -**1.** [procriar-se] to breed. -**2.** [repetir-se] to be repeated.

reprovação [xeprova'sãw] (*pl* -ões) *f* -**1.** [censura] disapproval. -**2.** [em exame, seleção] failure.

reprovado, da [xepro'vadu, da] <> *adj* failed. <> *m, f* failure.

reprovar [4] [xepro'va(x)] <> *vt* -**1.** [censurar] to disapprove of. -**2.** [rejeitar] to reject. -**3.** [em exame, seleção] to fail. <> *vi* [em exame, seleção] to fail.

réptil ['xɛptʃiw] (*pl* -eis) *m* reptile.

república [xe'publika] *f* -**1.** *POL* republic. -**2.** *EDUC* students' residence.

República Centro-Africana [xe,publikasẽntr'wafri'kãna] *n* Central African Republic.

República da África do Sul [xepublikada,africadu'suw] *n* Republic of South Africa.

República Dominicana [xe,publikadomini'kãna] *n* Dominican Republic.

republicano, na [xepubli'kãnu, na] <> *adj* republican. <> *m, f* republican.

República Tcheca [xe,publika'tʃɛka] *n* Czech Republic.

repudiar [16] [xepu'dʒjar] *vt* to repudiate.

repúdio [xe'pudʒju] *m* repudiation.

repugnância [xepug'nãsja] f -1. [ger] repugnance. -2. [oposição] opposition.

repugnante [xepug'nãntʃi] adj repugnant.

repugnar [4] [xepug'na(x)] ⬦ vt to disgust. ⬦ vi: ~ (a) to disgust, to be repugnant (to).

repulsa [xe'puwsa] f -1. [ato] repulsion. -2. [sentimento] repugnance. -3. [oposição] rejection.

repulsão [xepuw'sãw] (pl -ões) f -1. [repulsa] repulsion. -2. FÍSICA rejection.

repulsivo, va [xepuw'sivu, va] adj repulsive.

reputação [xeputa'sãw] (pl -ões) f reputation.

reputado, da [xepu'tadu, da] adj renowned.

reputar [4] [xepu'ta(x)] vt to consider, to regard as.

➡ **reputar-se** vp to consider o.s.

repuxado, da [xepu'ʃadu, da] adj -1. [esticado] tight; **cabelo** ~ pulled-back hair. -2. [amendoado] slanting.

repuxar [4] [xepu'ʃa(x)] ⬦ vt [esticar - roupa, pele] to stretch; [- cabelo] to pull back tight. ⬦ vi [retesar] to tense.

repuxo [xe'puʃu] m fountain.

requebrado [xeke'bradu] m swaying.

requebrar [4] [xeke'bra(x)] vt to wiggle.

➡ **requebrar-se** vp to wiggle one's hips.

requeijão [xekej'ʒãw] (pl -ões) m soft cheese.

requentado, da [xekẽn'tadu, da] adj reheated.

requentar [4] [xekẽn'ta(x)] vt to reheat.

requerente [xeke'rẽntʃi] mf JUR petitioner.

requerer [38] [xeke're(x)] ⬦ vt -1. [pedir] to request. -2. [exigir] to demand. -3. [merecer] to deserve. -4. JUR to petition for. ⬦ vi JUR to make a petition.

requerimento [xekeri'mẽntul m -1. [ato de requerer] application. -2. [petição] petition.

réquiem ['xɛkjẽ] (pl -ns) m requiem.

requintado, da [xekĩn'tadu, da] adj refined.

requintar [4] [xekĩn'ta(x)] ⬦ vt to refine. ⬦ vi: ~ em to be refined in.

➡ **requintar-se** vp to be refined.

requinte [xe'kĩntʃi] m -1. [refinamento] refinement. -2. [excesso] excess.

requisição [xekizi'sãw] (pl -ões) f requisition.

requisitado, da [xekizi'tadu, da] adj -1. [pedido] requested. -2. [muito procurado] in demand.

requisitar [4] [xekizi'ta(x)] vt to demand.

requisito [xeki'zitul m requirement.

rês [xeʃ] (pl reses) m head of cattle.

rescindir [6] [xesĩn'dʒi(x)] vt [contrato] to rescind.

rescrever [5] [xeʃkre've(x)] vt to rewrite.

resenha [xe'zaɲa] f -1. [de livro] review. -2. [relatório] report. -3. [resumo] summary.

resenhar [xeze'ɲa(x)] vt [sumariar] to write a summary of.

reserva [xe'zɛxva] ⬦ f -1. [ger] reserve; ~ internacionais foreign reserves; ~ natural nature reserve; ~ de mercado protected market. -2. [em hotel, avião etc] reservation; **fazer** ~ **de algo** to reserve sthg. -3. [restrição]: **ter** ~ **a** ou **para com** to have reservations about. -4. [discrição] discretion. ⬦ mf ESP reserve.

➡ **reservas** fpl [energia] reserves.

reservado, da [xezex'vadu, da] adj -1. [ger] reserved. -2. [íntimo] private.

➡ **reservado** m [privada] private room.

reservar [4] [xezex'va(x)] vt -1. [fazer reserva] to reserve. -2. [poupar] to save. -3. [destinar] to allow; **a vida lhe reserva muitas alegrias** life has much joy in store for him.

➡ **reservar-se** vp [preservar-se] to save o.s.

reservatório [xezexva'torju] m -1. [depósito] tank. -2. [de água] reservoir.

reservista [xezex'viʃta] mf reservist.

resfriado, da [xeʃfri'adu, da] adj -1. [pessoa] cold; **estar** ~ to have a cold; **ficar** ~ to catch cold. -2. [carne] chilled.

➡ **resfriado** m cold; **pegar um** ~ to catch a cold.

resfriar [16] [xeʃ'frja(x)] vt [esfriar] to cool.

➡ **resfriar-se** vp MED to catch a cold.

resgatar [4] [xeʒga'ta(x)] vt -1. [ger] to rescue. -2. [restituir] to recover. -3. [pagar] to pay off. -4. [recuperar] to recoup. -5. [expiar] to redeem.

resgate [xeʒ'gatʃi] m -1. [dinheiro] ransom. -2. [libertação] release. -3. [salvamento] rescue. -4. FIN [retirada] withdrawal; ~ **automático** automatic withdrawal. -5. COM redemption.

resguardar [4] [xeʒgwax'da(x)] vt -1. [proteger]: ~ **(de)** to protect (from). -2. [vigiar] to protect.

➡ **resguardar-se** vp [proteger-se]: ~-**se de** to protect o.s. from.

resguardo [xeʒ'gwaxdu] m -1. [proteção] protection. -2. [cuidado] care. -3. [repouso] rest; **estar/ficar de** ~ to take it easy.

residência [xezi'dẽnsja] f residence; **fixar** ~ **em** to take up residence in.

residencial [xezidẽn'sjaw] (pl -ais) adj residential.

residente [xezi'dẽntʃi] ⬦ adj resident. ⬦ mf -1. [morador] resident. -2. [médico] senior registrar UK, resident US.

residir [6] [xezi'dʒi(x)] vi to reside.

resíduo [xe'zidwu] m -1. [resto] residue. -2. [bancário] surplus.

resignação [xezigna'sãw] f: ~ **(a/com)** resignation to.

resignadamente [xezignada'mẽntʃi] adv resignedly, with resignation.

resignado, da [xezig'nadu, da] adj resigned.

resignar-se [4] [xezig'naxsi] vp to resign o.s.; ~ **com algo** to resign o.s. to sthg; ~ **a fazer algo** to resign o.s. to doing sthg.

resiliente [xezi'ljẽntʃi] adj resilient.

resina [xe'zina] f resin.

resistência [xeziʃ'tẽnsja] f -1. [ger] resistance; **o carro não teve** ~ **para subir a ladeira** the car did not have the power to go up the slope. -2. [moral] stamina. -3. fig [oposição]: ~ **a** resistance to.

resistente [xeziʃ'tẽntʃi] adj -1. [forte] strong; ~ **ao calor** heat-resistant. -2. [durável] durable. -3. [que se opõe a]: ~ **a** resistant to.

resistir [6] [xeziʃ'tʃi(x)] vi: ~ **a algo** to resist sthg.
resma ['xeʒma] f ream.
resmungão, ona [xeʒmũŋ'gãw, ɔna] (mpl -ões, fpl -nas) <> adj [rabugento] cantankerous. <> m,f grouch.
resmungar [14] [xeʒmũŋ'ga(x)] vt & vi to grumble.
resmungo [xeʒ'mũŋgu] m grumble.
resolução [xezolu'sãw] (pl -ões) f -1. [decisão] decision; **tomar uma** ~ to take a decision. -2. [solução] solution. -3. [firmeza] resolve. -4. [de imagem] resolution; **de alta** ~ high-resolution, hi-res.
resoluto, ta [xezo'lutu, ta] adj resolute; ~ **a fazer algo** resolved to do sthg.
resolver [5] [xezow've(x)] <> vt -1. [solucionar] to solve. -2. [decidir]: ~ **fazer algo** to decide to do sthg. <> vi -1. [adiantar]: **a violência não resolve** violence doesn't solve anything. -2. [decidir] to decide.
➡ **resolver-se** vp [decidir] to make up one's mind; ~-**se a fazer algo** to decide to do sthg; ~-**se sobre** ou **quanto a algo** to make a decision about sthg.
resolvido, da [xezow'vidu, da] adj -1. [pessoa] determined; ~ **a fazer algo** determined to do sthg. -2. [assunto, questão] resolved.
respaldar [4] [xeʃpaw'da(x)] vt [apoiar] to back.
respaldo [xeʃ'pawdu] m -1. [de cadeira] back. -2. fig [apoio] backing.
respectivamente [xeʃpektʃiva'mẽntʃi] adv respectively.
respectivo, va [xeʃpek'tʃivu, va] adj respective; ~ **a** in respect of.
respeitador, ra [xeʃpejtado(x), ra] adj respectful.
respeitar [4] [xeʃpej'ta(x)] vt to respect.
respeitável [xeʃpej'tavɛw] (pl -eis) adj -1. [digno de respeito] respectable. -2. [considerável] considerable.
respeito [xeʃ'pejtu] m -1. [deferência]: ~ **a** ou **por** respect for; **falta de** ~ lack of respect; **dar-se ao** ~ to command respect; **em** ~ **a** out of respect for; **faltar ao** ~ **com alguém** to be rude to sb; **impor** ~ **a** to command the respect of. -2. [relação] respect; **dizer** ~ **a** to concern; **a** ~ **de** [sobre] about; **com** ~ **a** [no tocante a] as regards.
respeitoso, osa [xeʃpej'tozu, ɔza] adj respectful.
respingar [14] [xeʃpĩŋ'ga(x)] vi to splash.
respingo [xeʃ'pĩŋgu] m splash.
respiração [xeʃpira'sãw] f breathing; ~ **artificial** artificial respiration.
respirador [xeʃpira'do(x)] m respirator.
respirar [4] [xeʃpi'ra(x)] <> vt [ar] to breathe. <> vi -1. [absorver o ar] to breathe. -2. fig [descansar] to have time to breathe; **não deixar alguém** ~ to not give sb breathing space. -3. fig [sentir alívio] to breathe freely again.
respiratório, ria [xeʃpira'tɔrju, rja] adj respiratory.
respiro [xeʃ'piru] m -1. [respiração] breath. -2. fig [descanso] rest. -3. [abertura] vent.

resplandecente [xeʃplãnde'sẽntʃil] adj -1. [jóia] resplendent. -2. [dia] splendid.
resplandecer [25] [xeʃplãnde'se(x)] vi -1. [brilhar] to shine. -2. [sobressair] to outshine.
resplendor [xeʃplẽn'do(x)] m brilliance.
respondão, dona [xeʃpõn'dãw, dona] (mpl -ões, fpl -s) m, f cheeky person.
responder [5] [xeʃpõn'de(x)] <> vt [dar resposta] to reply. <> vi -1. [dar resposta]: ~ **(a algo/alguém)** to reply to sthg/sb. -2. [replicar] to answer. -3. [ser respondão] to answer back. -4. [reagir]: ~ **a algo** to respond to sthg. -5. [responsabilizar-se]: ~ **por algo/alguém** to answer for sthg/sb. -6. [submeter-se a]: ~ **a algo** to undergo sthg.
responsabilidade [xeʃpõnsabili'dadʒi] f -1. [obrigação] responsibility. -2. JUR liability.
responsabilizar [4] [xeʃpõnsabili'za(x)] vt: ~ **algo/alguém (por algo)** to hold sthg/sb responsible for sthg.
➡ **responsabilizar-se** vp: ~-**se (por algo/alguém)** to hold o.s. responsible (for sthg/sb).
responsável [xeʃpõn'savɛw] (pl -eis) <> adj: ~ **(por)** responsible (for). <> mf -1. [encarregado] person in charge. -2. [culpado] person responsible.
resposta [xeʃ'pɔʃta] f -1. [de pergunta] answer; **em** ~ **a algo** in response to sthg. -2. fig [reação] response.
resquício [xeʃ'kisju] m -1. [vestígio] fragment. -2. [fragmento] fragment.
ressabiado, da [xesa'bjadu, da] adj -1. [desconfiado] suspicious. -2. [ressentido] resentful.
ressabiar [xesa'bja(x)] ➡ **ressabiar-se** vp -1. [ficar assustado] to be startled. -2. [magoar-se] to be offended.
ressaca [xe'saka] f -1. [do mar] rough sea; **estar de** ~ to be rough. -2. fig [de bebida] hangover; **estar/ficar de** ~ to have/to get a hangover.
ressaibo [xe'sajbu] m -1. [mau gosto] unpleasant taste. -2. fig [indício] sign. -3. [ressentimento] resentment.
ressaltar [4] [xesaw'ta(x)] vt to emphasize.
ressalva [xe'sawva] f -1. [emenda] correction. -2. [restrição] proviso; **fazer uma** ~ **a algo** to make an exception to sthg.
ressarcimento [xesaxsi'mẽntu] m [compensação] reparation.
ressarcir [79] [xesax'si(x)] vt [compensar]: ~ **algo (de)** to compensate for sthg (with); ~ **alguém (de)** to compensate sb (with).
➡ **ressarcir-se** vp [compensar-se]: ~-**se de** to be compensated for.
ressecado, da [xese'kadu, da] adj dried up.
ressecar [12] [xese'ka(x)] vt & vi to dry up.
ressentido, da [xesẽn'tʃidu, da] adj resentful.
ressentimento [xesẽntʃi'mẽntu] m resentment.
ressentir-se [56] [xesẽn'tʃixsi] vp -1. [magoar-se]: ~ **(de algo)** to resent (sthg). -2. [sofrer consequência]: ~ **de algo** to feel the effects of sthg.
ressequido, da [xese'kidu, da] adj dried up.

ressoar [20] [xe'swa(x)] *vi* to resound.

ressonância [xeso'nãnsja] *f* -**1.** [ger] resonance. -**2.** MED: ~ **magnética** magnetic resonance. -**3.** *fig* [repercussão]: **ter** ~ **em algo** to be a success in sthg.

ressonante [xeso'nãntʃi] *adj* resonant.

ressurgimento [xesuxʒi'mẽntul] *m* resurgence.

ressurgir [52] [xesux'zi(x)] *vi* -**1.** [reaparecer] to reappear. -**2.** [revitalizar-se] to revive. -**3.** [ressuscitar] to be resurrected.

ressurreição [xesuxej'sãw] (*pl* -**ões**) *f* resurrection.

ressuscitar [4] [xesusi'ta(x)] <> *vt* -**1.** [pessoa, animal] to resuscitate. -**2.** [costume, moda] to revive. <> *vi* -**1.** [pessoa, animal] to be resuscitated. -**2.** [costume, moda] to be revived.

restabelecer [25] [xeʃtabele'se(x)] *vt* to restore.
◆ **restabelecer-se** *vp* to recover.

restabelecimento [xeʃtabelesi'mẽntul] *m* -**1.** [de ordem, tradição] restoration. -**2.** [de doente] recovery.

restante [xeʃ'tãntʃi] <> *adj* remaining. <> *m* [resto] remainder.

restar [4] [xeʃ'ta(x)] *vi* -**1.** [sobrar] to be left over. -**2.** [sobreviver] to survive. -**3.** [subsistir] to remain; **não me resta dúvida de que ...** I no longer have any doubt that ... -**4.** [faltar]: **faltam duas páginas para terminar** there are two pages left to finish.

restauração [xeʃtawra'sãw] (*pl* -**ões**) *f* restoration.

restaurador, ra [xeʃtawra'do(x), ra] *m, f* restorer.

restaurante [xeʃtaw'rãntʃi] *m* restaurant.

restaurar [4] [xeʃtaw'ra(x)] *vt* -**1.** [ger] to restore. -**2.** [recuperar] to recuperate.

réstia [ˈxɛʃtʃja] *m* [de luz] ray.

restinga [xeʃ'tʃĩgal] *f* sandbank.

restituição [xeʃtʃitwi'sãw] (*pl* -**ões**) *f* -**1.** [devolução] return; ~ **do imposto de renda** refunding of income tax. -**2.** [pagamento] repayment.

restituir [74] [xeʃtʃi'twi(x)] *vt* -**1.** [devolver] to return. -**2.** [pagar] to repay. -**3.** [restabelecer] to restore.

resto [ˈxɛʃtu] *m* -**1.** [ger] remainder. -**2.** [restante] rest; **de** ~ [além disso] besides.
◆ **restos** *mpl* [de comida] leftovers.
◆ **restos mortais** *mpl* (mortal) remains.

restrição [xeʃtri'sãw] (*pl* -**ões**) *f* restriction.

restringir [52] [xeʃtrĩn'ʒi(x)] *vt* to restrict.
◆ **restringir-se** *vp* to restrict o.s.

restrito, ta [xeʃ'tritu, ta] *adj* restricted.

resultado [xezuw'tadul *m* -**1.** [ger] result. -**2.** [proveito]: **dar** ~ to be effective; **o filme deu bom** ~ **publicitário** the film was good publicity.

resultante [xezuw'tãntʃi] <> *adj* resulting; ~ **de algo** resulting from sthg. <> *f* -**1.** [consequência] outcome. -**2.** FÍSICA result.

resultar [46] [xezuw'ta(x)] *vi* -**1.** [originar-se]: ~ **de algo** to result from sthg. -**2.** [redundar] to turn out to be; ~ **em algo** to lead to sthg.

resumido, da [xezu'midu, da] *adj* concise.

resumir [xezu'mi(x)] *vt* to summarize.

resumir-se *vp*: ~-**se em** *ou* **a algo** to consist of sthg.

resumo [xe'zumul *m* summary; **em** ~ in short.

resvalar [4] [xeʒva'la(x)] *vi* -**1.** [deslizar]: ~ **(de/por algo)** to slip (from/through sthg). -**2.** *fig* [incidir]: ~ **em algo** to slide into sthg.

reta [ˈxɛtal *f* ▷ **reto**.

retaguarda [ˌxɛtaˈgwaxdal *f* -**1.** [posição] rear. -**2.** MIL rearguard.

retalhar [4] [xeta'ʎa(x)] *vt* -**1.** [cortar em pedaços] to cut up. -**2.** [golpear] to slash. -**3.** [dividir] to divide.

retalho [xe'taʎul *m* remnant; **colcha de** ~**s** patchwork quilt.

retaliação [xetalja'sãw] (*pl* -**ões**) *f* retaliation.

retaliar [16] [xeta'lja(x)] <> *vt* to repay. <> *vi* to retaliate.

retangular [xetãŋgu'la(x)] *adj* rectangular.

retângulo [xe'tãŋgulul *m* rectangle.

retardado, da [xetax'dadu, dal <> *adj* -**1.** [atrasado]: **fui** ~ **pelo trânsito** I was delayed by traffic. -**2.** PSIC retarded. <> *m, f* PSIC retarded person; ~ **mental** mentally retarded person.

retardar [4] [xetax'da(x)] *vt* -**1.** [atrasar] to delay. -**2.** [adiar] to postpone.
◆ **retardar-se** *vp* [atrasar-se] to be delayed.

retardatário, ria [xetaxda'tarju, rjal <> *adj* tardy. <> *m, f* latecomer.

retardo [xe'taxdul *m* -**1.** [atraso] delay. -**2.** PSIC retardedness.

retenção [xetẽn'sãw] *f* -**1.** [detenção] detention; **a** ~ **no trânsito é grande** there is a major traffic hold-up. -**2.** MED [de líquidos] retention.

reter [1] [xe'te(x)] *vt* -**1.** [ger] to retain. -**2.** [segurar, prender - rédeas, corda] to hold; [- ladrão, suspeito] to detain. -**3.** [guardar] to keep. -**4.** [reprimir, deter] to hold back.
◆ **reter-se** *vp* [reprimir-se] to restrain o.s.

retesado, da [xete'zadu, dal *adj* taut.

retesar [4] [xete'za(x)] *vt* to tense.
◆ **retesar-se** *vp* to tense.

reticência [xetʃi'sẽnsja] *f* reticence.
◆ **reticências** *fpl* [sinal] ellipsis *(sing)*, suspension points.

reticente [xetʃi'sẽntʃi] *adj* reticent.

retidão [xetʃi'dãwl *f* [lisura] rectitude.

retificar [12] [xetʃifi'ka(x)] *vt* -**1.** [corrigir] to rectify. -**2.** [purificar] to purify. -**3.** AUTO to repair.

retina [xe'tʃinal *f* ANAT retina.

retinir [6] [xetʃi'ni(x)] *vi* -**1.** [tinir] to clink. -**2.** [ressoar] to resound.

retinto, ta [xe'tʃĩtu, tal *adj* [muito escuro] inky.

retirado, da [xetʃi'radu, dal *adj* [pessoa] retiring; [vida] retired; [lugar, casa] isolated.
◆ **retirada** *f* -**1.** [ger] withdrawal; **bater em retirada** [fugir] to beat a retreat. -**2.** [migração] migration.

retirante [xetʃi'rãntʃil *mf* migrant.

retirar [4] [xetʃi'ra(x)] *vt* -**1.** [ger] to remove. -**2.** [retratar-se de] to take back. -**3.** [ganhar] to make. -**4.** [livrar, salvar] to get out.

➡ **retirar-se** *vp* **-1.** [ger] to leave. **-2.** [refugiar-se] to withdraw.

retiro [xe'tʃiru] *m* retreat.

reto, ta ['xɛtu, ta] *adj* **-1.** [ger] straight; **ângulo** ~ right angle. **-2.** *fig* [justo] straightforward. **-3.** *fig* [honesto] honest.

➡ **reto** *m* ANAT rectum.

➡ **reta** *f* **-1.** MAT straight line. **-2.** [de estrada, pista] straight; **reta de chegada**, **reta final** home straight.

retocar [12] [xeto'ka(x)] *vt* **-1.** [pintura] to touch up. **-2.** [texto] to tidy up.

retomada [xeto'mada] *f* [recuperação] recovery.

retomar [4] [xeto'ma(x)] *vt* **-1.** [continuar] to resume. **-2.** [reaver] to take back.

retoque [xe'tɔki] *m* finishing touch; **dar um** ~ to add a finishing touch.

retorcer [25] [xetox'se(x)] *vt* **-1.** [torcer de novo] to re-twist. **-2.** [contorcer-se] to twist.

➡ **retorcer-se** *vp* [contorcer-se] to writhe.

retorcido, da [xetox'sidu, da] *adj* **-1.** [muito torto] twisted. **-2.** [empolado] involved.

retórico, ca [xe'tɔriku, ka] *adj* **-1.** [sem conteúdo] rhetorical. **-2.** *fig* [afetado] affected.

➡ **retórico** *m* rhetorician.

➡ **retórica** *f* **-1.** [discurso] rhetoric. **-2.** *pej* [afetação] affectation.

retornar [4] [xetox'na(x)] *vi* [voltar] to return; ~ **de algo** to return from sthg.

retorno [xe'toxnu] *m* **-1.** [ger] return. **-2.** [resposta] response; **dar um** ~ (**sobre algo**) to give one's response (to sthg). **-3.** [em estrada] turning place; **fazer o** ~ to turn back.

retorquir [78] [xetox'ki(x)] <> *vt*: ~ **que** to retort that. <> *vi* to answer back.

retrabalhar [xetraba'ʎa(x)] *vt* [aprimorar] to re-condition.

retração [xetra'sãw] *f* **-1.** [de gengiva, de imagem] receding. **-2.** [em compras] contraction.

retraído, da [xetra'idu, da] *adj fig* [reservado, tímido] reserved.

retraimento [xetraj'mẽntul] *m* [reserva, timidez] reserve.

retrair [68] [xetra'i(x)] *vt* **-1.** [ger] to withdraw. **-2.** [tornar reservado] to make reserved.

➡ **retrair-se** *vp* **-1.** [afastar-se] to withdraw. **-2.** [tornar-se reservado] to become withdrawn.

retransmitir [6] [xetrãnʒmi'tʃi(x)] *vt* to show again.

retrasado, da [xetra'zadu, da] *adj* [ano, semana] before last.

retratar [4] [xetra'ta(x)] *vt* **-1.** [fazer retrato] to depict. **-2.** [descrever] to portray. **-3.** [desdizer] to retract. **-4.** [expressar] to express.

➡ **retratar-se** *vp* **-1.** [representar-se] to portray o.s. **-2.** [desdizer-se]: ~**-se de algo** to retract sthg. **-3.** [confessar erro] to admit one's mistake.

retrátil [xe'tratʃiw] (*pl* **-eis**) *adj* retractable.

retratista [xetra'tʃiʃta] *mf* portrait painter.

retrato [xe'tratu] *m* **-1.** [ger] portrait; ~ **falado** Identikit® picture; **ser o** ~ **de alguém** [parecer-se] to be the (spitting) image of sb. **-2.** *fig* [exemplo] picture.

retribuição [xetribwi'sãw] (*pl* **-ões**) *f* **-1.** [pagamento] remuneration. **-2.** [recompensa] reward. **-3.** [agradecimento] reciprocation.

retribuir [74] [xetri'bwi(x)] *vt* **-1.** [pagar] to pay. **-2.** [agradecer] to return. **-3.** [corresponder] to reciprocate.

retroagir [52] [xetrwa'ʒi(x)] *vi*: ~ **(a algo)** to be retroactive (on sthg).

retroativo, va [xetrwa'tʃivu, va] *adj* retroactive.

retroceder [5] [xetrose'de(x)] *vi* **-1.** [recuar] to step back. **-2.** [desistir]: ~ **(em algo)** to withdraw (from sthg). **-3.** [decair] to decline.

retrocesso [xetro'sɛsu] *m* **-1.** [retorno] return. **-2.** [declínio] step backwards. **-3.** [recaída] recurrence. **-4.** [tecla] backspace. **-5.** [na economia] slowdown.

retrógrado, da [xe'trɔgradu, da] *adj* **-1.** [idéia, movimento] retrograde, reactionary. **-2.** [pessoa] reactionary.

retroprojetor [ˌxɛtroproʒe'to(x)] *m* overhead projector.

retrós [xe'trɔʃ] *m* bobbin.

retrospectiva [xetroʃpek'tʃival] *f* retrospective.

retrospectivamente [xetroʃpektʃiva'mẽntʃi] *adv* retrospectively.

retrospecto [xetroʃ'pɛktu] *m* [retrospetiva] retrospect; **em** ~ in retrospect.

retrovisor [xetrovi'zo(x)] (*pl* **-es**) <> *adj* rearview. <> *m* rear-view mirror.

réu [xew], **ré** [xɛ] *m*, *f* accused.

reumático, ca [xewma'tʃiku, ka] <> *adj* rheumatic. <> *m*, *f* rheumatism sufferer.

reumatismo [xewma'tʃiʒmu] *m* rheumatism.

reumatologia [xewmatolo'ʒial] *f* rheumatology.

reumatologista [xewmatolo'ʒiʃta] *mf* rheumatologist.

reunião [xew'njãw] (*pl* **-ões**) *f* **-1.** [encontro] meeting; ~ **de cúpula** summit; ~ **de diretoria** board meeting. **-2.** [festa] party. **-3.** [coletânea] collection.

reunir [6] [xew'ni(x)] *vt* **-1.** [juntar] to gather. **-2.** [congregar] to join together. **-3.** [aliar] to combine. **-4.** [unir] to unite.

➡ **reunir-se** *vp* **-1.** [juntar-se] to gather. **-2.** [aliar-se] to be combined. **-3.** [realizar reunião] to meet. **-4.** [incorporar-se] to join together.

reutilizar [4] [xewtʃili'za(x)] *vt* to reuse.

revalorizar [4] [xevalori'za(x)] *vt* to revalue.

revanche [xe'vãnʃi] *f* **-1.** [desforra] revenge. **-2.** ESP return match.

revanchismo [xevãn'ʃiʒmu] *m* retaliation.

reveillon [xeve'jõn] *m* New Year's Eve.

revelação [xevela'sãw] (*pl* **-ões**) *f* **-1.** [ger] revelation. **-2.** FOT developing.

revelador, ra [xevela'do(x), ra] *adj* revealing.

revelar [4] [xeve'la(x)] *vt* **-1.** [ger] to reveal. **-2.** [mostrar, demonstrar] to show. **-3.** FOT to develop.

➡ **revelar-se** *vp* [dar-se a conhecer] to turn out to be.

revelia [xeve'lia] f default.
 ➤ **à revelia** loc adv **-1.** JUR in absentia. **-2.** [despercebidamente] without anybody knowing.
 ➤ **à revelia de** loc adv without the knowledge/consent of.
revenda [xe'vẽda] f resale.
revendedor, ra [xevẽde'do(x), ra] (mpl **-es**, fpl **-s**) <> adj resale (antes de subst). <> m, f [de automóveis] dealer.
revender [5] [xevẽn'de(x)] vt to resell.
rever [40] [xe've've(x)] vt **-1.** [tornar a ver] to see again. **-2.** [examinar] to check. **-3.** [revisar] to revise.
reverberação [xevexbera'sãw] (pl **-ões**) f **-1.** [de som] reverberation. **-2.** [de luz, calor] reflection.
reverberar [4] [xevexbe'ra(x)] vt [refletir] to reflect.
reverência [xeve'rẽsja] f **-1.** [respeito] reverence. **-2.** [saudação]: **fazer uma** ~ to bow.
reverenciar [16] [xeverẽ'sja(x)] vt **-1.** [respeitar] to respect. **-2.** [saudar] to salute.
reverendo [xeve'rẽdu] m priest.
reverente [xeve'rẽtʃi] adj reverent.
reversão [xevex'sãw] (pl **-ões**) f reversion.
reversível [xevex'sivew] (pl **-eis**) adj reversible.
reverso, sa [xe'vɛxsu, sa] <> adj reverse. <> m [lado contrário] reverse.
reverter [5] [xevex'te(x)] vi **-1.** [retroceder]: ~ **a** to return to. **-2.** [redundar]: ~ **em favor de alguém** to revert in s.o.'s favour; ~ **em benefício de** to benefit.
revertério [xevex'tɛrju] m fam turnabout.
revés [xe've∫] (pl **-eses**) m **-1.** [reverso] reverse; **ao** ~ [às avessas] inside out. **-2.** fig [infortúnio] setback.
 ➤ **de revés** loc adv [olhar, sorrir] askance.
revestimento [xeve∫tʃi'mẽtu] m covering.
revestir [54] [xeve∫'tʃi(x)] vt **-1.** [ger] to cover. **-2.** [munir]: ~ **alguém de algo** to invest sb with sthg. **-3.** [vestir] to don, to put on.
 ➤ **revestir-se** vp [munir-se] to summon up.
revezamento [xeveza'mẽtu] m **-1.** [ato]: **para cuidar do bebê, o casal fez um** ~ the couple took it in turns to look after the baby. **-2.** ESP relay.
revezar [4] [xeve'za(x)] <> vt to swap. <> vi: ~ **(com)** to take turns (with).
 ➤ **revezar-se** vp to alternate.
revidar [4] [xevi'da(x)] <> vt **-1.** [responder] to return. **-2.** [contestar] to answer. <> vi [responder] to answer back.
revide [xe'vidʒi] m response.
revigorar [4] [xevigo'ra(x)] vt to reinvigorate.
 ➤ **revigorar-se** vp to regain one's strength.
revirado, da [xevi'radu, da] adj **-1.** [casa] untidy. **-2.** [revolto] choppy.
revirar [4] [xevi'ra(x)] vt **-1.** [tornar a virar] to turn over. **-2.** [mudar] to change. **-3.** [os olhos] to roll. **-4.** [remexer em] to turn out.
 ➤ **revirar-se** vp [virar-se] to toss and turn.
reviravolta [xe,vira'vɔwta] f **-1.** [mudança] turnabout. **-2.** [pirueta] pirouette.
revisão [xevi'zãw] (pl **-ões**) f **-1.** [de texto] revision; ~ **de provas** proofreading. **-2.** [de máquina - ger]

overhaul; [- carro, motor de carro] service. **-3.** [os revisores] review board. **-4.** JUR review.
revisar [4] [xevi'za(x)] vt **-1.** [texto] to revise. **-2.** [máquina - ger] to overhaul; [- motor de carro] to service. **-3.** [recapitular] to review.
revisor, ra [xevi'zo(x), ra] (mpl **-es**, fpl **-s**) <> adj examining. <> m, f [de provas] proofreader.
revista [xe'vi∫ta] f **-1.** [publicação] magazine; ~ **feminina** women's magazine; ~ **em quadrinhos** comic. **-2.** [acadêmica] journal. **-3.** MIL [inspeção] review. **-4.** [busca] search. **-5.** TEATRO revue.
revistar [4] [xevi∫'ta(x)] vt to search.
revisto, ta [xe'vi∫tu, ta] <> pp ⊳ **rever.** <> adj checked.
revitalizar [4] [xevitali'za(x)] vt to revitalize.
reviver [5] [xevi've(x)] <> vi **-1.** [doente] to pick up. **-2.** [revigorar-se] to come back to life. <> vt [relembrar] to relive.
revocar [12] [xevo'ka(x)] vt **-1.** [lembrar] to recall. **-2.** [restituir]: ~ **alguém a algo** to bring sb back to sthg. **-3.** [tirar]: ~ **alguém de algo** to remove sb from sthg.
revogação [xevoga'sãw] (pl **-ões**) f repeal.
revogar [14] [xevo'ga(x)] vt to repeal.
revolta [xe'vɔwta] f **-1.** [ger] revolt. **-2.** [rebeldia]: ~ **(contra)** rebellion (against). **-3.** [indignação]: ~ **(diante de** ou **com)** indignation (at).
revolto, ta [xe'vowtu, ta] adj **-1.** [revirado] rough. **-2.** [conturbado] troubled. **-3.** [desarrumado] untidy.
revoltoso, osa [xevow'tozu, ɔza] adj rebellious.
 ➤ **revoltoso** m rebel.
revolução [xevolu'sãw] (pl **-ões**) f revolution.
revolucionar [4] [xevolusjo'na(x)] vt **-1.** [transformar] to revolutionize. **-2.** [sublevar] to stir up. **-3.** [agitar] to change completely.
revolucionário, ria [xevolusjo'narju, rja] <> adj revolutionary. <> m, f revolutionary.
revolver [5] [xevow've(x)] vt **-1.** [remexer] to rummage through. **-2.** [examinar, investigar] to search. **-3.** [revirar - olhos] to roll; [- corpo, terra] to turn over. **-4.** [agitar] to blow about. **-5.** [relembrar] to recall.
 ➤ **revolver-se** vp **-1.** [mexer-se] to roll over. **-2.** [agitar-se] to blow about.
revólver [xe'vɔwve(x)] (pl **-es**) m revolver.
reza ['xɛza] f prayer.
rezar [4] [xe'za(x)] <> vt **-1.** [orar] to pray. **-2.** [missa] to say mass. **-3.** [afirmar, preceituar] to state. <> vi [orar] to pray.
RG (abrev de **Registro Geral**) m Brazilian identity card, ≃ ID card.
RH (abrev de **Recursos Humanos**) m HR.
riacho ['xja∫u] m stream.
Riad ['xjadʒi] n Riyadh.
ribalta [xi'bawta] f **-1.** [luzes] footlights (pl). **-2.** fig [palco] boards (pl).
ribanceira [xibã'sejra] f **-1.** [margem elevada] steep river bank. **-2.** [despenhadeiro] ravine. **-3.** [rampa] steep slope.
ribeira [xi'bejra] f **-1.** [margem de rio] bank. **-2.** [riacho] stream.

ribeirão [xibej'rãw] (*pl* -ões) *m* stream.
ribeirinho, nha [xibej'riɲu, ɲal ⬦ *adj* river-side. ⬦ *m, f* riverside dweller.
ribombar [4] [xibõn'ba(x)] *vi* -1. [trovão] to rumble. -2. [canhão, granada] to boom.
ricaço, ça [xi'kasu, sa] *m, f* very rich person.
ricamente [xika'mẽntʃil *adv* richly.
rícino ['xisinul *m* castor-oil plant; **óleo de ~** castor oil.
rico, ca ['xiku, ka] ⬦ *adj* -1. [ger] rich. -2. [opulento] opulent. -3. [abundante]: **~ em algo** rich in sthg. -4. [esplêndido] splendid. -5. [valiosa] precious. ⬦ *m, f* [pessoa] rich person.
ricochetear [15] [xikoʃe'tʃja(x)] *vi* to ricochet.
ricota [xi'kɔta] *f* ricotta.
ridicularizar [4] [xidʒikulari'za(x)] *vt* to ridicule.
ridículo, la [xi'dʒikulu, la] *adj* ridiculous.
➡ **ridículo** *m* ridicule.
rifa ['xifa] *f* raffle.
rifar [4] [xi'fa(x)] *vt* to raffle.
rifle ['xifli] *m* rifle.
Riga ['xiga] *n* Riga.
rigidez [xiʒi'deʒ] *f* -1. [dureza - de metais, parede] rigidity; [- de músculo, corpo] stiffness. -2. *fig* [severidade] harshness. -3. *fig* [inflexibilidade] strictness.
rígido, da ['xiʒidu, da] *adj* -1. [hirto] stiff. -2. [resistente] strong. -3. [severo - pessoa, rosto] severe; [- disciplina] strict.
rigor [xi'go(x)] (*pl* -es) *m* -1. [rigidez] rigour *UK*, rigor *US*. -2. [severidade] severity. -3. [exatidão] rigour *UK*, rigor *US*. -4. [meticulosidade] thoroughness; **com ~** strictly. -5. [preceito] good manners (*pl*). -6. [auge] harshness.
➡ **a rigor** *loc adv* strictly speaking.
rigorosamente [xigoroza'mẽntʃil *adv* rigorously; **chega no trabalho ~ às 8 horas** he arrives at work at 8 o'clock sharp.
rigoroso, osa [xigo'rozu, ɔza] *adj* -1. [ger] strict. -2. [castigo] severe. -3. [exato] precise. -4. [meticuloso] meticulous. -5. *fig* [penoso] severe.
rijo, ja ['xiʒu, ʒa] *adj* -1. [rígido] firm. -2. [severo] severe.
rim ['xĩ] (*pl* -ns) *m ANAT* kidney.
➡ **rins** *mpl fam* [região lombar] lower back (*sg*).
rima ['xima] *f* rhyme.
rimar [4] [xi'ma(x)] ⬦ *vt* to set to rhyme. ⬦ *vi* to rhyme.
rímel® ['ximɛw] (*pl* -eis) *m* mascara.
rinçagem [xĩ'saʒẽl (*pl* -ns) *f* rinse.
rinçar [xĩ'sa(x)] *vt* to rinse.
ringue ['xĩgi] *m* ring.
rinha ['xiɲa] *f fam* [briga de galos] cockfight.
rinoceronte [xinose'rõntʃil *m* rhinoceros.
rinque ['xĩki] *m* rink.
rins [xĩʃ] *pl* ⬦ rim.
rio ['xiw] *m* river; **gastar ~s de dinheiro** to spend lots of money.
Rio Branco [xiw'brãŋku] *n* Rio Branco.
Rio de Janeiro [xiwdʒiʒa'nejru] *n* Rio de Janeiro.

RIO DE JANEIRO

Capital of the republic until the foundation of Brasília in 1960; Rio de Janeiro is one of the most beautiful and traditional icons of Brazil, thanks to its famous beaches, such as Copacabana and Ipanema, as well as the beauty of its natural landmarks, such as the Sugar Loaf Mountain and the Corcovado. In spite of its loss of political power following the move of the capital city, Rio de Janeiro still exerts a powerful influence on the culture of Brazil.

Rio da Prata [xiwda'prata] *n* River Plate.
Rio Grande do Norte [xiwgrãndʒidu'nɔxtʃil *n* Rio Grande do Norte.
Rio Grande do Sul [xiwgrãndʒidu'suwl *n* Rio Grande do Sul.
rio-platense [xiwpla'tẽnsi] ⬦ *adj* River Plate (*antes de subst*). ⬦ *mf* person from the River Plate region.
ripa ['xipa] *f* [de madeira] slat; **meter a ~ em alguém** *fig* [falar mal] to speak ill of sb.
riqueza [xi'keza] *f* -1. [ger] richness. -2. [fortuna, bens] wealth. -3. [beleza] beauty; **essa igreja é uma ~!** this church is beautiful!
rir [69] ['xi(x)] *vi* to laugh; **~ de algo/alguém** to laugh at sthg/sb; **~ para alguém** to smile at sb; **morrer de ~ (de algo/alguém)** to laugh one's head off (at sthg/sb), to laugh oneself silly (at sthg/sb).
risada [xi'zada] *f* -1. [riso] laughter. -2. [gargalhada] guffaw.
risca ['xiʃka] *f* -1. [listra] stripe. -2. [no cabelo] parting. -3. [traço] line.
➡ **à risca** *loc adv* to the letter.
riscar [12] [xiʃ'ka(x)] *vt* -1. [fazer riscas em - porta, parede] to scratch; [- papel] to draw lines on. -2. [esboçar] to sketch. -3. [marcar] to draw. -4. [apagar] to cross out. -5. [acender] to scratch. -6. [eliminar]: **~ alguém/algo de algo** to eliminate sb/sthg from sthg. -7. [atritar] to scrape.
risco ['xiʃku] *m* -1. [traço] scratch. -2. [esboço] sketch. -3. [perigo] risk; **correr ~ de** to run the risk of; **pôr algo/alguém em ~** to put sthg/sb at risk.
risco-país [xiʃkupa'jiʃ] *m ECON* country risk.
risível [xi'zivew] (*pl* -eis) *adj* laughable.
riso ['xizu] *m* laugh; **~ amarelo** forced laugh.
risonho, nha [xi'zoɲu, ɲal *adj* -1. [que sorri] smiling. -2. [alegre] cheerful.
risoto [xi'zotul *m* risotto.
rispidez [xiʃpi'deʒ] *f* harshness.
ríspido, da ['xiʃpidu, da] *adj* harsh.
rissole [xi'sɔlil *m* rissole.
riste ['xiʃtʃil *m*: **dedo em ~** pointing finger; **orelhas em ~** pointed ears.
rítmico, ca ['xitʃmiku, ka] *adj* rhythmic.
ritmo ['xitʃimul *m* rhythm.
rito ['xitul *m* rite.
ritual [xi'twawl (*pl* -ais [xi'twajʃl) ⬦ *adj* ritual. ⬦ *m* -1. [ger] ritual. -2. [livro] service book.
rival [xi'vawl (*pl* -ais) ⬦ *adj* rival. ⬦ *mf* rival.

rivalidade [xivali'dadʒi] *f* rivalry.

rivalizar [4] [xivali'za(x)] *vi*: ~ **com algo/alguém** to compete with sthg/sb; ~ **por algo/alguém** to compete for sthg/sb; ~ **em algo** to compete in sthg.

rixa ['xiʃa] *f* quarrel.

RJ (*abrev de* **Estado do Rio de Janeiro**) *n* State of Rio de Janeiro.

RN (*abrev de* **Estado do Rio Grande do Norte**) *n* State of Rio Grande do Norte.

RO (*abrev de* **Estado de Rondônia**) *n* State of Rondônia.

robalo [ro'balu] *m* sea bass.

robô [ro'bo] *m* robot.

robótica [xo'bɔtʃika] *f* robotics (*sg*).

robustecer [25] [xobuʃte'se(x)] <> *vt* to strengthen. <> *vi* to become stronger.

robustecer-se *vp* to become stronger.

robustez [xobuʃ'teʒ] *f* robustness.

robusto, ta [xo'buʃtu, ta] *adj* robust.

roça ['xɔsa] *f* **-1.** [plantação] plantation. **-2.** [campo] country. **-3.** [mato] clearing.

roçado [xo'sadu] *m* **-1.** [terreno] cleared land. **-2.** [clareira] clearing. **-3.** [plantação] plantation.

rocambole [xokãn'bɔli] *m* roll.

roçar [13] [xo'sa(x)] <> *vt* **-1.** [cortar] to clear. **-2.** [tocar de leve] to brush. **-3.** [atritar] to scrape. <> *vi* [tocar de leve]: ~ **em** to brush against.

roceiro, ra [xo'sejru, ra] *m, f* **-1.** [lavrador] country worker. **-2.** [caipira] yokel.

rocha ['xɔʃa] *f* **-1.** [pedra] rock. **-2.** [rochedo] crag.

rochedo [xo'ʃedu] *m* crag.

rock ['xɔki] *m* MÚS rock.

roda ['xɔda] *f* **-1.** [ger] wheel. **-2.** [círculo] circle; **alta** ~ high society; ~ **de samba** circle of samba dancers and musicians; **brincar de** ~ to play in a circle. **-3.** [de saia] hoop.

roda d'água [xɔdadagwa] *f* waterwheel.

rodado, da [xo'dadu, da] *adj* **-1.** [que tem roda] full. **-2.** [percorrido] on the clock.

rodada *f* **-1.** [giro] turn; **dar uma rodada** to turn round. **-2.** [de bebida] round. **-3.** ESP round.

rodagem [xo'daʒẽ] (*pl* **-ns**) *f* **-1.** [ato de rodar] driving. **-2.** [raio de roda] wheel ⊳ **estrada**.

roda-gigante [xɔdaʒi'gãntʃil] (*pl* **rodas-gigantes**) *f* big wheel, Ferris wheel.

rodamoinho [xɔda'mwiɲul] *m* **-1.** [de água] whirlpool. **-2.** [de cabelo] swirl.

rodapé [xɔda'pɛl] *m* **-1.** [de parede] skirting board. **-2.** [de página] foot; **nota de** ~ footnote. **-3.** [artigo] article.

rodar [4] [xo'da(x)] <> *vt* **-1.** [fazer girar] to turn. **-2.** [percorrer] to travel. **-3.** [imprimir] to print. **-4.** [filmar] to film. **-5.** AUTO to do. **-6.** COMPUT to run. <> *vi* **-1.** [girar] to turn. **-2.** [percorrer]: ~ **por** [a pé] to wander around; [de carro] to drive around. **-3.** [ser impresso] to be printed. **-4.** *fam* [ser reprovado]: ~ **(em algo)** to fail (in sthg). **-5.** *fam* [sair]: ~ **(de algo)** to leave (sthg). **-6.** [decorrer] to move on.

roda-viva [ˌxɔda'viva] (*pl* **rodas-vivas**) *f* commotion.

rodear [15] [xo'dʒja(x)] *vt* **-1.** [contornar] to go round. **-2.** [cercar] to surround.

rodear-se *vp* [cercar-se] to surround o.s.

rodeio [xo'deju] *m* **-1.** [circunlóquio] circumlocution. **-2.** [evasiva] evasiveness; **fazer** ~**s** to beat about the bush; **sem** ~**s** bluntly. **-3.** [de gado] rodeo.

rodela [xo'dɛla] *f* [pedaço] slice.

rodízio [xo'dʒizju] *m* **-1.** [revezamento] turn; **fazer** ~ to take turns. **-2.** [em restaurante] *type of service in a restaurant where you are served at your table as much meat or, sometimes, pizza as you can eat, and normally accompanied by a free buffet of salad, etc.*

rodo ['xodul] *m* **-1.** [para puxar água] brush. **-2.** [agrícola] rake.

a rodo *loc adv* a lot.

rodoanel [rodo'anewl] (*pl* **-éis**) *m* ring road UK, beltway US.

rododendro [xodo'dẽndrul] *m* rhododendron.

rodopiar [16] [xodo'pja(x)] *vi* to spin around.

rodopio [xodo'piwl] *m* spin.

rodovia [xodo'via] *f* motorway UK, highway US.

rodoviário, ria [xodo'vjarju, rja] *adj* road.

rodoviária *f* [estação de ônibus] bus station.

roedor, ra [xwe'do(x), ra] *adj* gnawing.

roedor *m* rodent.

roer [28] ['xwe(x)] *vt* **-1.** [com dentes] to gnaw; ~ **as unhas** to bite one's nails; **duro de** ~ *fam fig* a hard nut to crack. **-2.** [destruir] to eat away. **-3.** [corroer] to erode. **-4.** *fig* [atormentar] to eat away at, to gnaw at.

roer-se *vp fig* [atormentar-se]: ~**-se de algo** to be eaten up with sthg.

rogado, da [xo'gadu, da] *adj*: **fazer-se de** ~ to play hard to get.

rogar [14] [xo'ga(x)] <> *vt* to ask; ~ **pragas (contra algo/alguém)** to curse (sthg/sb). <> *vi* to pray; ~ **a alguém que faça algo** to beg sb to do sthg.

rogo ['xogul] *m* **-1.** [súplica] request; **a** ~ **de** [a pedido] at the request of. **-2.** [oração] prayer.

rojão [xo'ʒãwl] (*pl* **-ões**) *m* **-1.** [foguete] rocket. **-2.** *fig* [ritmo intenso] hectic pace; **aguentar o** ~ *fig* [resistir] to stand the pace.

rol [xɔwl] (*pl* **róis**) *m* list.

rolagem [xo'laʒẽl] (*pl* **-ns**) *f* [de dívida] postponement.

rolamento [xola'mẽntul] *m* MEC ball bearing.

rolar [4] [xo'la(x)] <> *vt* **-1.** [fazer girar] to roll. **-2.** *fig* [dívida] to run up. <> *vi* **-1.** [cair, deslizar] to roll; ~ **de/por/em algo** to roll off/down/on sthg. **-2.** [na cama] to toss and turn. **-3.** *fam* [estender-se] to roll on. **-4.** *fam* [ser servido] to be served. **-5.** *fam* [acontecer] to go on.

roldana [xow'dãnal] *f* pulley.

roleta [xo'letal] *f* **-1.** [jogo] roulette. **-2.** [borboleta] turnstile.

roleta-russa [xoˌleta'xusal] (*pl* **roletas-russas**) *f* Russian roulette.

rolha ['xoʎa] f-1. [peça] cork. -2. fam fig [censura] gag.

roliço, ça [xo'lisu, sa] adj -1. [redondo] round. -2. [gordo] chubby.

rolo ['xolu] m -1. [ger] roller; ~ **de pastel** rolling pin; ~ **compressor** steam roller. -2. [cilindro] roll. -3. [almofada] bolster. -4. fam [bafafá, confusão] brawl; **dar** ~ to cause trouble.

ROM (abrev de **Read Only Memory**) f ROM.

romã [xo'mã] f pomegranate.

Roma f 'xoma] n Rome.

romance [xo'mãnsi] m -1. LITER novel; ~ **policial** detective story. -2. fig [amoroso] romance. -3. fig [saga] saga. -4. fig [exageração]: **fazer um** ~ **de algo** to make a song and dance about sthg.

romanceado, da [xomãn'sjadu, da] adj -1. LITER novelized. -2. [fantasiado] romanticized.

romancear [15] [xomãn'sja(x)] vt -1. LITER to novelize. -2. [fantasiar] to romanticize.

romancista [xomãn'siʃta] mf novelist.

românico, ca [xo'mãniku, ka] adj -1. LING Romance. -2. ARQUIT & ARTE Romanesque.

romano, na [xo'mãnu, na] <> adj Roman. <> m, f Roman.

romântico, ca [xo'mãntʃiku, ka] <> adj -1. ARQUIT & LITER Romantic. -2. [poético, sentimental] romantic. <> m, f -1. ARQUIT & LITER Romantic. -2. [pessoa] romantic.

romantismo [xomãn'tʃiʒmu] m -1. ARQUIT & LITER Romanticism. -2. [sentimentalismo] romance.

romantizar [4] [xomãntʃi'za(x)] vt [fantasiar] to romanticize.

romaria [xoma'ria] f -1. [peregrinação] pilgrimage. -2. [festa] popular festival. -3. fig [muita gente] flock.

rombo ['xõnbu] m -1. [furo] hole. -2. fig [desfalque] embezzlement. -3. fig [prejuízo] deficit.

rombudo, da [xõn'budu, da] adj [faca, agulha] blunt.

romeiro, ra [xo'mejru, ra] m, f pilgrim.

Romênia [xo'menja] n Rumania.

romeno, na [xo'menu, na] <> adj Rumanian. <> m, f Rumanian.
→ **romeno** m [língua] Rumanian.

romeu-e-julieta [xo,mewiʒu'ljeta] m CULINguava preserve on cheese.

rompante [xõn'pãntʃi] m outburst.

romper [5] [xõn'pe(x)] <> vt to break. <> vi -1. [quebrar] to burst. -2. [rasgar] to tear. -3. [despontar] to break. -4. [relações]: ~ (**com alguém**) to break up (with sb); ~ **com algo** [tradição] to break from sthg. -5. [começar]: ~ **em algo** to break into sthg.
→ **romper-se** vp -1. [despedaçar-se] to break. -2. [interromper-se] to be broken off.

rompimento [xõnpi'mẽntu] m -1. [de cano, barragem] bursting. -2. [de contrato, relações] breaking.

roncar [12] [xõŋ'ka(x)] vi to snore.

ronco ['xõŋku] m -1. [no sono] snore. -2. MED rale. -3. [ruído] rumble. -4. [grunhido] grunt.

ronda ['xõnda] f beat; **fazer a** ~ to be on patrol.

rondar [4] [xõn'da(x)] <> vt -1. [andar vigiando] to patrol. -2. [espreitar] to prowl about. -3. [andar à volta de] to go round. -4. [cifra] to reach. <> vi: ~ (**por**) [andar vigiando] to be on patrol (throughout); [espreitar] to prowl (about).

Rondônia [xõn'donja] n Rondonia.

ronqueira [xõŋ'kejra] f wheeze.

ronrom [xõn'xõ] m purr.

ronronar [4] [xõnxo'na(x)] vi to purr.

roque ['xɔki] m -1. MÚSrock (and roll). -2. [dança] rock and roll.

roqueiro, ra [xo'kejru, ra] m, f -1. [músico] rock musician. -2. [cantor] rock singer.

Roraima [xo'rajma] n Roraima.

rosa ['xɔza] <> adj inv [cor] pink. <> f BOT rose. <> m [cor] pink.

rosado, da [xo'zadu, da] adj pink.

rosa-dos-ventos [,xɔzaduʃ'vẽntuʃ] f inv wind rose.

rosário [xo'zarju] m -1. [colar] string of beads. -2. [orações] rosary.

rosa-shocking [xɔza'ʃkĩŋ] adj inv shocking pink.

rosbife [xoʒ'bifi] m roast beef.

rosca ['xoʃka] f -1. [de parafuso, porca] thread. -2. [pão] twist. -3. [biscoito] biscuit.

roseira [xo'zejra] f rose bush.

róseo, sea ['xɔzju, zja] adj rosy.

roseta [xo'zeta] f -1. [ger] rosette. -2. [de espora] rowel.

rosnar [4] [xoʒ'na(x)] <> vi [cão] to growl. <> m [de cão] growl.

rosto ['xoʃtu] m face.

rota ['xɔta] f route.

ROTA (abrev de **Rondas Ostensivas Tobias de Aguiar**) f shock police force of São Paulo.

rotação [xota'sãw] (pl -ões) f rotation.

rotativa [xota'tʃiva] f ▷ **rotativo**.

rotatividade [xotatʃivi'dadʒi] f -1. [movimento] turning. -2. [rodízio] rotation ▷ **hotel**.

rotativo, va [xota'tʃivu, va] adj -1. [giratório] rotary. -2. [alternativo] rotating.
→ **rotativa** f TIP rotary press.

roteador, ra [rotea'do(x),ra] m COMPUTrouter.

roteirista [xotej'riʃta] mf script writer.

roteiro [xo'tejru] m -1. [ger] script. -2. [de viagem] guide book. -3. [de trabalho] schedule.

rotina [xo'tʃina] f routine.

rotineiro, ra [xotʃi'nejru, ra] adj routine.

roto, ta ['xotu, ta] adj -1. [rasgado] torn. -2. [maltrapilho] ragged.

rótula ['xɔtula] f ANATkneecap.

rotular [4] [xotu'la(x)] <> adj ANAT patellar. <> vt -1. [etiquetar] to label. -2. fig [qualificar]: ~ **alguém/algo (de algo)** to label sb/sthg (as sthg).

rótulo ['xɔtulu] m label.

rotundo, da [xo'tũndu, da] adj -1. [redondo] round. -2. [gordo] rotund.
→ **rotunda** f ARQUITrotunda.

roubada [xo'bada] f FUT[de bola] tackle.

roubalheira [xoba'ʎejra] f (outright) robbery.

roubar [4] [xo'ba(x)] <> vt **-1.** [ger] to steal. **-2.** [furtar] to rob. <> vi **-1.** [furtar] to steal. **-2.** [enganar] to cheat.

roubo ['xobu] m **-1.** [ato] theft. **-2.** [produto roubado] stolen goods (pl). **-3.** fig [preço extorsivo]: **ser um ~** to be exorbitant.

rouco, ca ['xoku, ka] adj hoarse.

round ['xawndʒil] m ESP round.

roupa ['xopa] f clothes (pl); **~ de baixo** underwear; **~ de cama/mesa** bed/table linen; **~ suja se lava em casa** fig don't wash your dirty linen in public.

roupagem [xo'paʒel] f clothing.

roupão [xo'pãw] (pl -ões) m dressing gown; **~ de banho** bathrobe.

rouparia [xopa'ria] f **-1.** [roupas] clothes (pl). **-2.** [local] linen room.

rouquidão [xoki'dãw] f hoarseness.

rouxinol [xoʃi'nɔw] (pl -óis) m nightingale.

roxo, xa ['xoʃu, ʃa] adj **-1.** [cor] violet; **~ de inveja** fig green with envy; **estar ~ de saudades** fig to have the blues. **-2.** MED purple. **-3.** [apaixonado]: **ser ~ por** to be passionate about.
  ◆ **roxo** m [cor] violet.

royalty ['xɔjawtʃi] (pl royalties) m royalty.

RP (abrev de Relações Públicas) f PR.

RPM (abrev de Rotações por Minuto) f RPM.

RR (abrev de Estado de Roraima) n State of Roraima.

RS (abrev de Estado do Rio Grande do Sul) n State of Rio Grande do Sul.

RSVP (abrev de répondez s'il vous plaît) RSVP.

rua ['xua] f **-1.** [ger] street; **~ de mão única** one way street; **~ principal** main street; **~ sem saída** dead end. **-2.** loc: **ir para a ~** [sair] to go out; **pôr alguém na ~** [expulsar] to kick sb out; [demitir] to fire sb; **viver na ~** fig to go out a lot.

rubéola [xu'bɛwla] f German measles, rubella.

rubi [xu'bi] m ruby.

rubor [xu'bo(x)] (pl -es) m **-1.** [na face] flush. **-2.** [vergonha] blush.

ruborizar [4] [xubori'za(x)] vt [envergonhar] to embarrass.
  ◆ **ruborizar-se** vp to blush.

rubrica [xu'brika] f **-1.** [assinatura] initials (pl). **-2.** [indicação de assunto etc] rubric.

rubricar [12] [xubri'ka(x)] vt to initial.

rubro, bra ['xubru, bra] adj **-1.** [ger] bright red. **-2.** [faces] ruddy.

ruço, ça ['xusu, sa] adj **-1.** [desbotado, surrado] faded. **-2.** fam [difícil] tricky.

rúcula ['xukula] f rocket (salad).

rude ['xudʒi] adj **-1.** [descortês] rude. **-2.** [primitivo] crude.

rudeza [xu'deza] f **-1.** [descortesia] rudeness. **-2.** [primitivismo] crudeness.

rudimentar [xudʒimẽn'ta(x)] adj rudimentary.

rudimentos [xudʒi'mẽntuʃ] mpl rudiments.

rueiro, ra ['xwejru, ra] adj: **ser ~** to be a gadabout.

ruela ['xwɛla] f alleyway.

rufar [4] [xu'fa(x)] <> vt [tambor] to beat. <> vi to drum.

rufião, fiona [xu'fjãw, fjona] (mpl -ões, fpl -s) m, f [gigolô] gigolo.

ruga ['xuga] f **-1.** [na pele] wrinkle; **cheio de ~s** covered in wrinkles. **-2.** [na roupa] crease.

rúgbi ['xugbi] m rugby.

ruge ['xuʒi] m rouge.

rugido [xu'ʒidu] m roar.

rugir [52] [xu'ʒi(x)] vi to roar.

ruído ['xwidu] m noise.

ruidoso, osa [xwi'dozu, ɔza] adj noisy.

ruim ['xuĩ] (pl -ns) adj **-1.** [nocivo] vile. **-2.** [malvado] wicked. **-3.** [imprestável, ineficiente] useless. **-4.** [podre] rotten. **-5.** [defeituoso] faulty. **-6.** [ordinário] poor. **-7.** [desagradável] bad; **achar ~** [zangar-se] to get upset.

ruína [xwina] f **-1.** [ger] ruin; **levar alguém à ~** to ruin sb; **estar em ~s** to be in ruins. **-2.** [causa de destruição, queda] ruination. **-3.** [decadência] downfall.
  ◆ **ruínas** fpl [escombros] ruins.

ruindade [xwĩn'dadʒi] f **-1.** [qualidade] wickedness. **-2.** [ação] sin.

ruins [xu'ĩʃ] pl ▷ ruim.

ruir [74] ['xwi(x)] vi to collapse.

ruivo, va ['xuivu, va] <> adj **-1.** [pessoa] redheaded. **-2.** [cabelo, barba] red. <> m, f redhead.

rulê [xu'le] adj ▷ gola.

rum ['xũ] m rum.

rumar [4] [xu'ma(x)] <> vt: **~ algo para** to steer sthg towards. <> vi: **~ para** to head for.

rumba ['xũba] f rumba.

ruminante [xumi'nãntʃi] <> adj ruminant. <> m ruminant.

ruminar [4] [xumi'na(x)] <> vt to think over. <> vi to ruminate.

rumo ['xumu] m **-1.** [direção] course; **ir ~ a** to head for. **-2.** fig [destino] fate; **sem ~** lit adrift; fig aimless.

rumor [xu'mo(x)] (pl -es) m **-1.** [ruído] noise. **-2.** [boato] rumour.

rumorejante [xumore'ʒãntʃi] adj whispering.

ruptura [xup'tura] f **-1.** [ger] rupture. **-2.** [de fiação] break. **-3.** [de relações, negociações] break-up. **-4.** [de contrato] breach.

rural [xu'raw] (pl -ais) adj rural.

ruralista [xura'liʃta] <> adj rural. <> mf landowner who protects the interests of rural life, and especially those of landowners themselves.

rusga ['xuʒga] f brawl.

rush ['xãʃi] m heavy traffic; **a hora do ~** rush hour.

Rússia ['xusja] n Russia.

russo, sa ['xusu, sa] <> adj Russian. <> m, f Russian.
  ◆ **russo** m [língua] Russian.

rústico, ca ['xuʃtʃiku, ka] adj rustic.

S

s, S [ˈɛsi] *m* [letra] s, S.
sã [sã] *f* ⊳ **são**.
S.A. (*abrev de* **Sociedade Anônima**) *f limited company*, ≃ Ltd.
Saara [saˈara] *n*: **o (deserto do)** ~ the Sahara (Desert).
saariano, na [saaˈrjãnu, na] ◇ *adj* Saharan. ◇ *m, f* Saharan.
sáb. (*abrev de* **sábado**) *m* Sat.
sábado [ˈsabadu] *m* Saturday; **aos** ~**s** on Saturdays; **cair num** ~ to fall on a Saturday; **esse** ~ **agora** [próximo] next Saturday; **(no)** ~ (on) Saturday; **(no)** ~ **que vem/no próximo** ~ (on) the coming, next Saturday; ~ **de manhã** Saturday morning; ~ **de** *ou* **á tarde/noite** Saturday afternoon/evening; ~ **passado** *ou* **retrasado** last Saturday, Saturday just gone; ~ **sim,** ~ **não** every other Saturday; **todos os** ~**s** every Saturday; ~ **de aleluia** Easter Saturday.
sabão [saˈbãw] (*pl*-ões) *m* **- 1.** [produto] soap; ~ **de coco** coconut soap; ~ **em pó** soap powder. **- 2.** [repreensão]: **passar um** ~ **em alguém** to tell sb off.
sabatina [sabaˈtʃina] *f* revision test.
sabedoria [sabedoˈria] *f* wisdom; ~ **popular** popular wisdom.
saber [35] [saˈbe(x)] ◇ *m* knowledge. ◇ *vt* to know. ◇ *vt* to know; ~ **de cor** to know (off) by heart; ~ **(como) fazer algo** to know how to do sthg; **que eu saiba** as far as I know; **sei lá!** *fam* who knows!; **você que sabe** *fam* it's up to you. ◇ *vi* **-1.** [ter erudição] to know. **- 2.** [estar a par de]: ~ **(de algo)** to know (sthg). **- 3.** [ter notícia]: ~ **de alguém** to hear from sb.
➠ **a saber** *loc adv* namely.
sabiá [saˈbja] *m* song thrush.
sabichão, chona [sabiˈʃãw, ʃona] (*mpl* **-chões**, *fpl* **-s**) *adj irôn* know-all.
sabido, da [saˈbidu, da] *adj* **-1.** [astuto] wise. **- 2.** [conhecedor] knowledgeable. **- 3.** [conhecido]: **como é** ~ as is generally known; **é** ~ **que ...** it is known that ...
sábio, bia [ˈsabju, bja] ◇ *adj* wise. ◇ *m, f* wise person.

sabões [saˈbõjʃ] *pl* ⊳ **sabão**.
sabonete [saboˈnetʃi] *m* toilet soap.
saboneteira [saboneˈtejra] *f* soap dish.
sabor [saˈbo(x)] (*pl* -es) *m* taste; **ao** ~ **de** at the mercy of.
saborear [15] [saboˈrja(x)] *vt* to savour.
saboroso, osa [saboˈrozu, ɔza] *adj* tasty.
sabotador, ra [sabotaˈdo(x), ra] *m, f* saboteur.
sabotagem [saboˈtaʒẽ] (*pl* -**ns**) *f* sabotage.
sabotar [4] [saboˈta(x)] *vt* to sabotage.
sabugo [saˈbugo] *m* ANAT nail root.
SAC (*abrev de* **Serviço de Atendimento ao Consumidor**) *m* Brazilian consumer telephone service.
saca [ˈsaka] *f* [saco largo] sack.
sacação [sakaˈsãw] (*pl* -**ões**) *f fam* **- 1.** [achado] find. **- 2.** [invenção] clever idea.
sacada [saˈkada] *f* ARQUIT balcony.
sacado, da [saˈkadu, da] *m, f* COM drawee.
sacador, ra [sakaˈdo(x), ra] *m, f* COM drawer.
sacal [saˈkaw] (*pl* -**ais**) *adj* boring; **ser** ~ to be boring.
sacana [saˈkana] *adj mfam* **- 1.** [sujo]: **ser** ~ to be a bastard. **- 2.** [esperto] sharp. **- 3.** [libidinoso] randy. **- 4.** [brincalhão] raffish.
sacanagem [sakaˈnaʒẽ] (*pl* -**ns**) *f mfam* **- 1.** [sujeira] dirty trick. **- 2.** [libidinagem] screwing. **- 3.** [brincadeira] joke.
sacanear [15] [sakaˈnja(x)] *vt* **- 1.** [amolar] to pester. **- 2.** [fazer sujeira com] to screw.
sacar [12] [saˈka(x)] ◇ *vt* **- 1.** [arma, carteira] to pull out; ~ **algo de algo** to draw sthg from sthg. **- 2.** [em banco] to draw. **- 3.** *fam* [compreender] to twig. ◇ *vi* **- 1.** [de arma]: ~ **de algo** to whip out sthg. **- 2.** [em banco]: ~ **(contra/sobre)** to draw (against/from). **- 3.** *ESP* to serve. **- 4.** *fam* [compreender] to twig. **- 5.** *fam* [mentir] to fib. **- 6.** *fam* [falar sem saber] to talk through one's hat.
sacarina [sakaˈrina] *f* saccharin.
saca-rolha [ˌsakaˈxoʎa] (*pl* **saca-rolhas**) *m* corkscrew.
sacerdócio [sasexˈdɔsju] *m* priesthood.
sacerdote, tisa [sasexˈdɔtʃi, tʃizal] *m, f* [pagão] priest (*f* priestess).
➠ **sacerdote** *m* RELIG priest.
sachê [saˈʃe] *m* sachet.
saci-pererê [saˌsiperˈere] *m* figure of Brazilian folklore who typically ambushes travellers.
saciar [16] [saˈsja(x)] *vt* to satisfy.
saciedade [sasjeˈdadʒi] *f* [satisfação plena] satisfaction.
saco [ˈsaku] *m* **- 1.** [recipiente] bag. **- 2.** [utensílio]: ~ **de água quente** hot-water bottle; ~ **de café** coffee filter; ~ **de dormir** sleeping bag. **- 3.** [enseada] cove. **- 4.** *vulg* [testículos] balls. **- 5.** *fam* [amolação]: **encher o** ~ **(de alguém)** to get one's goat; **estar de** ~ **cheio (de alguém/algo)** to have a bellyful (of sb/sthg); **que** ~**!** what a bore!; **ser/estar um** ~ to be boring. **- 6.** *fam* [paciência]: **haja** ~**!** keep your knickers on!, don't get your knickers in a twist!; **ter** ~ **(com alguém)** to be cool (with sb). **- 7.** *fam* [disposição]: **estar com/sem**

~ **de fazer algo** to give/not to give a hoot about doing sthg.

sacola [sa'kɔla] f saddlebag.

sacolão [sako'lãw] m greengrocer's.

sacoleiro, ra [sako'lejru, ra] m,f pedlar *UK*, peddler *US*.

sacolejar [4] [sakole'ʒa(x)] vt **-1.** [sacudir] to shake. **-2.** [rebolar] to sway.

sacolejo [sako'leʒu] m fam jerk.

sacramentar [4] [sakramẽn'ta(x)] vt **-1.** *RELIG* to bless. **-2.** [ultimar] to close.

sacramento [sakra'mẽntu] m *RELIG* sacrament.

sacrificar [12] [sakrifi'ka(x)] vt **-1.** [ger] to sacrifice. **-2.** [prejudicar] to damage. **-3.** [matar] to put down.

➠ **sacrificar-se** vp **-1.** [ger] to sacrifice o.s. **-2.** [sujeitar-se] to give in to.

sacrifício [sakri'fisju] m sacrifice.

sacrilégio [sakri'lɛʒu] m sacrilege.

sacrílego, ga [sa'krilegu, ga] adj sacrilegious.

sacristão [sakriʃ'tãw] (pl -ões) m sacristan.

sacristia [sakriʃ'tʃia] f sacristy.

sacro, cra ['sakru, kra] adj **-1.** [sagrado] sacred. **-2.** *ANAT* sacral.

➠ **sacro** m *ANAT* sacrum.

sacrossanto, ta [sakro'sãntu, ta] adj sacrosanct.

sacudida [saku'dʒida] f shake.

sacudido, da [saku'dʒidu, da] adj [sacolejado] shaken.

sacudir [41] [saku'dʒi(x)] vt to shake.

➠ **sacudir-se** vp **-1.** [tremer] to shake. **-2.** [saracotear] to waggle.

sádico, ca ['sadʒiku, ka] ⬦ adj sadistic. ⬦ m, f sadist.

sadio, dia [sa'dʒiu, dʒia] adj healthy.

sadismo [sa'dʒiʒmu] m sadism.

sadomasoquismo [sadomazo'kiʒmu] m sadomasochism.

sadomasoquista [sadomazo'kiʃta] ⬦ adj sadomasochistic. ⬦ mf sadomasochist.

safadeza [safa'deza] f **-1.** [ger] mischief. **-2.** [devassidão] debauchery.

safado, da [sa'fadu, da] adj **-1.** [ger] mischievous. **-2.** [devasso] debauched. **-3.** [com raiva]: ~ **(da vida)** fed up to the back teeth.

safanão [safa'nãw] (pl -ões) m fam **-1.** [tranco, puxão] tug. **-2.** [cascudo] box (on the ears).

safári [sa'fari] m safari.

safena [sa'fena] f *ANAT* saphena; **ponte de** ~ coronary bypass.

safira [sa'fira] f sapphire.

safra ['safra] f **-1.** *AGR* harvest. **-2.** fig [de cantores etc] crop.

saga ['saga] f saga.

sagacidade [sagasi'dadʒil] f shrewdness.

sagaz [sa'gajʒ] adj shrewd.

sagitariano, na [saʒita'rjãnu, na] ⬦ adj Sagittarian. ⬦ m, f Sagittarian.

Sagitário [saʒi'tarju] ⬦ m [zodíaco] Sagittarius; **ser** ~ to be a Sagittarian. ⬦ mf [pessoa] Sagittarian.

sagrado, da [sa'gradu, da] adj sacred.

saguão [sa'gwãw] (pl -ões) m **-1.** [entrada] lobby. **-2.** [pátio] courtyard.

saia ['saja] f **-1.** [roupa] skirt; ~ **escocesa** kilt. **-2.** [de mesa] (floor-length) tablecloth. **-3.** fam fig [mulher] skirt; ~ **justa** tight spot.

saia-calça [,saja'kawsa] (pl saias-calça) f culottes (pl).

saibro ['sajbru] m gravel.

saída [sa'ida] f **-1.** [ger] way out; **de** ~ straight away; ~ **de emergência** emergency exit. **-2.** [ato] leaving; **dar uma** ~ to pop out. **-3.** *COM*: **ter muita** ~ to sell well. **-4.** [dito]: **ter boas** ~**s** to be witty. **-5.** [*COMPUT* - de programa] exit; [- de dados] output.

saída-de-praia [sa,idadʒi'praja] (pl saídas-de-praia) f beach wrap.

saideira [saj'dejra] f one for the road.

saiote [sa'jɔtʃi] m petticoat.

sair [68] [sa'i(x)] vi **-1.** [gen] to come out; ~ **do armário** fig to come out (as being homosexual). **-2.** [ir para fora - de ônibus, trem, avião] to get off; [- de carro] to get out of. **-3.** [ir para a rua] to go out. **-4.** [ir embora, deixar] to leave; ~ **de fininho** to sneak off. **-5.** [fugir] to get out. **-6.** [escapar]: ~ **de** to get out of. **-7.** [aparecer] to appear. **-8.** [desaparecer]: ~ **de moda** to go out of fashion. **-9.** [parecer-se]: ~ **a alguém** to take after sb. **-10.** [resultar] to turn out; ~ **ganhando/perdendo** to end up winning/losing. **-11.** [custar]: ~ **(a** ou **por)** to come to; ~ **caro** to be expensive. **-12.** *COMPUT* to exit.

➠ **sair-se** vp **-1.** [obter resultado]: ~**-se bem/mal** to come out well/badly. **-2.** [dizer]: ~**-se com** to come out with.

sal ['saw] (pl sais) m salt; **sem** ~ [manteiga etc] unsalted; [precisando de mais sal] bland; ~ **de banho** bath salts (pl); ~ **de cozinha** kitchen salt; ~ **grosso** rock salt.

sala ['sala] f **-1.** [aposento] room; ~ **de embarque** departure lounge; ~ **de espera** waiting room; ~ **de estar** living room; ~ **de operações** operating theatre; ~ **de parto** delivery room. **-2.** [de espetáculos] concert hall. **-3.** *EDUC*: ~ **(de aula)** classroom; [alunos] class. **-4.** fig: **fazer** ~ **a alguém** [entreter] to entertain sb.

salada [sa'lada] f **-1.** *CULIN* salad; ~ **de frutas** fruit salad. **-2.** fig [confusão]: **fazer uma** ~ **de algo** to make a muddle of sthg.

saladeira [sala'dejra] f salad bowl.

sala-e-quarto [,salaj'kwaxtu] (pl sala-e-quartos) m studio (flat).

salafrário, ria [sala'frarju, rja] m, f fam scoundrel.

salamaleque [salama'lɛki] m exaggerated greeting.

salame [sa'lãmi] m salami.

salaminho [salã'miɲu] m small salami.

salão [sa'lãw] (pl -ões) m **-1.** [aposento] lounge. **-2.** [estabelecimento]: ~ **de beleza** beauty salon; ~ **de chá** tea room. **-3.** [exposição] exhibition hall.

➠ **de salão** loc adj **-1.** [piada] tasteful. **-2.** [jogo]

indoor. **-3.** [dança] dance hall *(antes de subst)*.
salarial [sala'rjaw] *(pl* **-ais)** *adj* pay *(antes de subst)*.
salário [sa'larju] *m* wage; ~ **de fome** miserly wage; **décimo terceiro** ~ *Christmas bonus equal to one month's wages;* ~ **mínimo** minimum wage; ~ **líquido** net salary.
salário-base [sa‚larju'bazil] *(pl* **salários-base)** *m* basic wage.
salário-família [sa‚larjufa'milja] *(pl* **salários-família)** *m extra pro rata pay for employees with dependants.*
saldão [saw'dãw] *(pl* **-ões)** *m* [saldo] sale.
saldar [4] [saw'da(x)] *vt* to settle.
saldo ['sawdul] *m* **-1.** [ger] balance; ~ **credor/devedor** credit/debit balance; ~ **negativo/positivo** debit/credit balance; ~ **a receber/pagar** balance due/to pay. **-2.** *fig* [resultado] outcome.
saleiro [sa'lejru] *m* **-1.** [recipiente] salt cellar. **-2.** [moedor] salt mill.
saleta [sa'leta] *f* small living room.
salgadinho [sawga'dʒiɲul] *m* canapé.
salgado, da [saw'gadu, da] *adj* **-1.** [comida - com sal] salted; [- com excesso de sal] salty. **-2.** [anedota] salty. **-3.** [preço] steep.
salgar [14] [saw'ga(x)] *vt* to salt.
salgueiro [saw'gejrul] *m* willow.
saliência [sa'ljẽnsjal] *f* **-1.** [proeminência] projection. **-2.** *fig* [espevitamento] eagerness.
salientar [4] [saljẽn'ta(x)] *vt* **-1.** [ressaltar] to highlight. **-2.** [enfatizar] to stress.
➤ **salientar-se** *vp* [distinguir-se] to distinguish o.s.
saliente [sa'ljẽntʃil] *adj* **-1.** [ressaltado] salient. **-2.** *fig* [espevitado] eager.
salino, na [sa'linu, na] *adj* saline.
➤ **salina** *f* **-1.** [terreno] salt bed. **-2.** [empresa] salt works.
salitre [sa'litril] *m* saltpetre.
saliva [sa'lival] *f* saliva; **gastar** ~ to waste one's breath.
salivar [4] [sa'liva(x)] *vi* to salivate.
salmão [saw'mãw] *(pl* **-ões)** <> *m* [peixe] salmon. <> *m inv* [cor] salmon. <> *adj inv* [cor] salmon-pink.
salmo ['sawmul] *m* psalm.
salmões [saw'mõjʃl] *pl* ▷ **salmão**.
salmonela [sawmo'nɛla] *f* salmonella.
salmoura [saw'moral] *f* brine.
salobro, bra [sa'lobru, bra] *adj* brackish.
salões [sa'lõjʃl] *pl* ▷ **salão**.
salpicão [sawpi'kãw] *(pl* **-ões)** *m* **-1.** [paio] smoked sausage. **-2.** [prato]: ~ **(de galinha)** *cold shredded chicken and vegetable dish.*
salpicar [12] [sawpi'ka(x)] *vt* **-1.**: ~ **algo em algo**, ~ **algo de algo** [temperar] to season sthg with sthg; [sarapintar, sujar] to splash; ~ **alguém de algo** [sujar] to splash sb with sthg. **-2.** [entremear]: ~ **algo com** *ou* **de algo** to pepper sthg with sthg.
salsa ['sawsal] *f* **-1.** [erva] parsley. **-2.** *MÚS* salsa.
salsicha [saw'siʃal] *f* sausage.

salsichão [sawsi'ʃãw] *(pl* **-chões)** *m* large sausage.
saltado, da [saw'tadu, da] *adj* prominent.
saltar [4] [saw'ta(x)] <> *vt* **-1.** [ger] to jump. **-2.** *fam* [fazer vir] to send for. <> *vi* **-1.** [pular]: ~ **(de/sobre)** to jump (from/on). **-2.** [de ônibus, trem, cavalo]: ~ **(de)** to jump (from). **-3.** [brotar]: ~ **de** to pour from. **-4.** [rolha] to pop.
salteado, da [saw'tʃjadu, da] *adj* [alternado] alternate; **saber de cor e** ~ to know off by heart.
salteador, ra [sawtʃja'do(x), ral *m, f* mugger.
saltimbanco [sawtʃĩn'bãŋkul] *m* travelling acrobat.
saltitante [sawtʃi'tãntʃil] *adj* [ave, criança] hopping; ~ **de alegria** jumping for joy.
saltitar [4] [sawtʃi'ta(x)] *vi* **-1.** [pular] to hop. **-2.** *fig* [divagar]: ~ **de ... para ...** to jump from ... to ...
salto ['sawtu] *m* **-1.** [pulo] jump; **dar um** ~ to leap; **dar** ~**s de alegria** to leap for joy. **-2.** *ESP*: ~ **em altura** high jump; ~ **em distância** long jump; ~ **de vara** pole vault. **-3.** [de sapato] heel; ~ **alto/baixo** high/low heel.
salto-mortal [‚sawtumox'tawl] *(pl* **saltos-mortais)** *m* somersault.
salubre [sa'lubril] *adj* salubrious.
salutar [salu'ta(x)] *(pl* **-es)** *adj* **-1.** [saudável] healthy. **-2.** *fig* [moralizador] salutary.
salva ['sawva] *f* **-1.** *MIL*: ~ **(de tiros)** salvo (of gunshots). **-2.** *fig*: **uma** ~ **de palmas** a round of applause. **-3.** [bandeja] tray.
salvação [sawva'sãw] *f* salvation; **não ter** ~ to be without hope; **ser a** ~ **da pátria** *fam fig* to be one's salvation.
salvador, ra [sawva'do(x), ral *m, f* [pessoa] saviour.
Salvador [sawva'do(x)l *n* Salvador.
salvadorenho, nha [sawvado'reɲu, ɲal <> *adj* Salvadorean. <> *m, f* Salvadorean.
salvados [saw'vaduʃl *mpl* salvage *(sg)*.
salvaguarda [sawva'gwaxdal] *f* safeguard.
salvaguardar [4] [‚sawvagwax'da(x)] *vt* to safeguard.
salvamento [sawva'mẽntul] *m* rescue; **equipe de** ~ rescue team.
salvar [4] [saw'va(x)] *vt* to save.
➤ **salvar-se** *vp* [escapar] to escape.
salva-vidas [‚salva'vidaʃl <> *adj inv* lifeguard; **lancha** ~ life boat. <> *m* **-1.** *inv* [bóia] lifebelt. **-2.** [pessoa] lifeguard. **-3.** [jaqueta] life jacket.
salve ['sawvil] *interj* cheers!
sálvia ['sawvjal] *f* *BOT* sage.
salvo, va ['sawvu, val <> *adj* safe; **estar a** ~ to be safe. <> *prep* except.
salvo-conduto [‚sawvukõn'dutul] *(pl* **salvo-condutos, salvos-condutos)** *m* safe conduct.
samambaia [samãn'bajal] *f* fern.
samaritano [samari'tãnul] *m*: **bom** ~ *RELIG* good Samaritan; *fig & pej* do-gooder.
samba ['sãnbal] *m* samba.

SAMBA

Through its catchy rhythm and vitality, samba has become synonymous with Brazilian music. Afro-Brazilian in origin, it developed mainly in Bahia, Rio de Janeiro and São Paulo. It is characterized by a syncopated beat and is generally performed on percussion instruments, guitars and *cavaquinho* (small four-stringed guitar). There are many kinds of samba. One of the more traditional forms is the 'samba-de-roda' from Bahia; another very popular form is the 'sambas-enredo' of the carnival in Rio de Janeiro, which express the theme of each samba school's parade; finally, there is a fairly characteristic form of samba, known as the 'samba de breque', with a generally satirical content.

samba-canção [ˌsãnbakãn'sãw] (*pl* **sambas-canções**) <> *m MÚS type of samba.* <> *adj inv:* **cueca** ~ shorts *(pl)*.

samba-de-roda ['sãnbadʒi'xɔda] (*pl* **sambas-de-roda**) *m samba in which the dancers form a circle and each dances in turn.*

samba-enredo [ˌsãnbên'xedu] (*pl* **sambas-enredo**) *m samba describing the theme chosen by a samba school for the carnival.*

sambar [4] [sãn'ba(x)] *vi* to samba.

sambista [sãn'biʃta] *mf* **-1.** [dançarino] samba dancer. **-2.** [compositor] composer of sambas.

sambódromo [sãn'bɔdromu] *m track along which samba schools parade.*

samovar [samo'va(x)] *m* samovar.

Sana ['sana] *n* San'a.

sanar [4] [sa'na(x)] *vt* **-1.** [curar] to cure. **-2.** [remediar] to remedy.

sanatório [sana'tɔrju] *m* sanatorium.

sanável [sa'navew] (*pl* **-eis**) *adj* **-1.** [curável] curable. **-2.** [remediável] remediable.

sanção [sãn'sãw] (*pl* **-ões**) *f* **-1.** [ger] sanction. **-2.** [punição] ~ **(contra)** sanction (against).

sancionar [4] [sãnsjo'na(x)] *vt* [aprovar] to sanction.

sanções [sãn'sõjʃ] *pl* ⊳ **sanção**.

sandália [sãn'dalja] *f* sandal.

sândalo ['sãndalu] *m* sandalwood.

sanduíche [sãn'dwiʃi] *m* sandwich; ~ **americano** double-decker sandwich; ~ **misto** cheese and ham sandwich.

saneamento [sanja'mẽntu] *m* **-1.** [limpeza] sanitization. **-2.** *fig* [correção] purge.

sanear [15] [sa'nja(x)] *vt* **-1.** [tornar salubre] to sanitize. **-2.** *fig* [corrigir] to purge.

sanfona [sãn'fona] *f* **-1.** *MÚS* concertina. **-2.** [em suéter] ribbing.

sanfonado, da [sãnfo'nadu, da] *adj* **-1.** [porta] folding *(antes de subst)*. **-2.** [suéter] ribbed.

sangramento [sãngra'mẽntu] *m* **-1.** [de ferida] bleeding. **-2.** [de açude, represa] overflow.

sangrar [4] [sãn'gra(x)] <> *vi* [verter sangue] to bleed. <> *vt* **-1.** [ger] to bleed. **-2.** [açude, represa] to drain.

sangrento, ta [sãŋ'grẽntu, ta] *adj* **-1.** [ger]

bloody. **-2.** *CULIN* [carne] rare.

sangria [sãŋ'gria] *f* **-1.** [bebida] sangria. **-2.** *MED* blood-letting. **-3.** *fig* [extorsão] extortion.

sangue ['sãŋgi] *m* **-1.** [ger] blood; **de** ~ [exame, transfusão] blood; **começou a sair muito** ~ **do corte** the cut started to bleed a lot; **tirar** ~ to take blood. **-2.** *fig* [raça]: **puro** ~ thoroughbred.

⇒ **a sangue frio** *loc adv* in cold blood.

sangue-frio [ˌsãŋgi'friw] *m* sangfroid.

sanguessuga [ˌsãŋgi'suga] *f* leech.

sanguinário, ria [sãŋgi'narju, rja] *adj* bloodthirsty.

sanguíneo, nea [sãŋ'g(w)inju, nja] *adj* **-1.** [relativo ao sangue] blood *(antes de subst)*. **-2.** [pessoa] ruddy.

sanha ['sãɲa] *f*: ~ **(contra)** anger (against).

sanidade [sani'dadʒi] *f* [mental] sanity.

sanitário, ria [sani'tarju, rja] *adj* **-1.** [ger] sanitary. **-2.** [banheiro] bath *(antes de subst)*.

San José [ˌsãnxo'se] *n* San José.

San Marino [ˌsãnma'rinu] *n* San Marino.

San Salvador [ˌsãnsawva'do(x)] *n* San Salvador.

Santa Catarina [ˌsãntakata'rina] *n* Santa Catarina.

santidade [sãntʃi'dadʒi] *f* sanctity.

⇒ **Santidade** *f* [Vossa Santidade] Holiness.

santificar [12] [sãntʃifi'ka(x)] *vt* to sanctify.

Santiago de Cuba [ˌsãnˌtʃjagudʒi'kuba] *n* Santiago de Cuba.

Santiago do Chile [sãnˌtʃagudu'ʃili] *n* Santiago de Chile.

santinho [sãn'tʃiɲu] *m* **-1.** [figura] religious figurine. **-2.** *fam* [pessoa] goody-goody.

santo, ta ['sãntu, ta] <> *adj* **-1.** [sagrado] holy; **todo o** ~ **dia** *fam fig* the whole blessed day long. **-2.** *(antes de subst)* [caridoso] kind. **-3.** [eficaz]: **um** ~ **remédio** an effective medicine. <> *m, f* **-1.** [ger] saint. **-2.** *loc*: ~ **de casa não faz milagre** a prophet is not without honour save in his own country; **ter** ~ **forte** *fam* to have the gods smiling on you.

SANTOS-DUMONT

Aviator and inventor from Minas Gerais; Alberto Santos-Dumont (1873-1832) invented the airship in 1901, with which he flew round the Eiffel Tower. In 1906, he built the 14-Bis, the first plane officially to fly over 25m above ground. Santos-Dumont also invented the wristwatch and is considered by Brazilians to be the inventor of the airplane.

Santo Domingo [ˌsãntudo'mĩŋgu] *n* Santo Domingo.

santuário [sãn'twarju] *m* sanctuary.

são, sã ['sãw, 'sã] *adj* **-1.** [ger] healthy. **-2.** *PSIC* sane. **-3.** [curado] well. **-4.** [ileso]: ~ **e salvo** safe and sound. **-5.** [sensato] sensible.

São [sãw] *m* Saint.

SÃO FRANCISCO

'Old Chico' is the nickname given to the largest river in Brazilian territory; its source is in Minas Gerais and it crosses the states of Bahia, Pernambuco, Alagoas and Sergipe, covering a total of 3,160 km. It is fundamental to the economy of the region, providing significant opportunities for hydroelectric output, fluvial access to certain areas, allowing agricultural activity on its banks and irrigation to distant areas.

São Luís [ˌsãwluˈiʒ] n São Luis.
São Paulo [ˌsãwˈpawlu] n São Paulo.
São Tomé [ˌsãwtoˈmɛ] n São Tomé.
São Tomé e Príncipe [sãwtoˌmɛjˈprĩsipi] n São Tomé and Príncipe.
sapata [saˈpata] f -**1.** [suporte] prop. -**2.** [de freio] shoe.
sapatão [sapaˈtãw] m mfam pej dyke.
sapataria [sapataˈria] f -**1.** [ofício] shoe trade. -**2.** [loja] shoe shop.
sapateado [sapaˈtʃjadu] m tap dance.
sapateador, ra [sapatʃjaˈdo(x), ra] m, f tap dancer.
sapatear [15] [sapaˈtʃja(x)] vi -**1.** [dançar] to tap-dance. -**2.** [bater com os pés] to stamp.
sapateiro, ra [sapaˈtejru, ra] m, f -**1.** [fabricante] shoemaker. -**2.** [quem conserta] cobbler.
◆ **sapateiro** m [loja] shoe shop.
◆ **sapateira** f [móvel] shoe cupboard.
sapatilha [sapaˈtʃiʎa] f -**1.** [de balé] ballet shoe. -**2.** [sapato baixo] slipper.
sapato [saˈpatu] m shoe.
sapê, sapé [saˈpe] m thatch; **telhado de ~** thatched roof.
sapeca [saˈpɛka] adj -**1.** [levado] mischievous. -**2.** [assanhado] irritable.
sapecar [15] [sapeˈka(x)] vt [tapa, soco etc]: **~ algo em alguém** to hit sb with sthg.
sapiência [saˈpjẽsja] f -**1.** [erudição] knowledge. -**2.** [bom julgamento] wisdom.
sapiente [saˈpjẽtʃi] adj [erudito] knowledgeable.
sapinho [saˈpiɲu] m MED thrush.
sapo [ˈsapu] m toad; **engolir ~** fig to take the flak.
saque [ˈsaki] m -**1.** FIN [withdrawal]; **~ a descoberto** overdraft. -**2.** ESP serve. -**3.** [de cidade, loja] ransacking. -**4.** fam [mentira] fib.
saquê [saˈke] m sake.
saquear [15] [saˈkja(x)] vt to ransack.
saracotear [15] [sarakoˈtʃja(x)] vt to sway.
saraivada [sarajˈvada] f hail storm; **uma ~ de** fig a shower of.
saraivar [4] [sarajˈva(x)] vi to hail.
sarampo [saˈrãnpu] m measles.
sarapintado, da [sarapĩˈtadu, da] adj dotted.
sarar [4] [saˈra(x)] ◇ vt [pessoa, doença, ferida] to heal. ◇ vi -**1.** [pessoa] to get better. -**2.** [ferida] to heal.
sarau [saˈraw] m soirée.
sarcasmo [saxˈkaʒmu] m sarcasm.
sarcástico, ca [saxˈkaʃtʃiku, ka] adj sarcastic.
sarcófago [saxˈkɔfagu] m sarcophagus.

sarda [ˈsaxda] f freckle.
Sardenha [saxˈdeɲa] n Sardinia.
sardento, ta [saxˈdẽtu, ta] adj freckly.
sardinha [saxˈdʒiɲa] f sardine.
sardônico, ca [saxˈdoniku, ka] adj sardonic.
sargento [saxˈʒẽtu] mf sergeant.
sári [ˈsari] m sari.
sarjeta [saxˈʒeta] f gutter.
sarna [ˈsaxna] f scabies; **procurar ~ para se coçar** to look for trouble.
sarnento, ta [saxˈnẽtu, ta] adj [com sarna] mangy.
sarrafo [saˈxafu] m batten; **baixar o ~ em alguém** fam to batter sb.
sarro [ˈsaxu] m -**1.** [borra] residue. -**2.** [de nicotina] tartar. -**3.** [na língua] fur. -**4.** fam [pessoa, coisa]: **ser um ~** to be fun. -**5.** mfam [bolinagem]: **tirar um ~ (de alguém)** to grope (sb).
Satã [saˈtã], **Satanás** [sataˈnaʃ] m Satan.
satânico, ca [saˈtãniku, ka] adj -**1.** [culto] satanic. -**2.** fig [diabólico] devilish.
satélite [saˈtɛlitʃi] ◇ m satellite. ◇ adj [cidade, país] satellite (antes de subst).
sátira [ˈsatʃira] f satire.
satírico, ca [saˈtʃiriku, ka] adj satirical.
satirizar [4] [satʃiriˈza(x)] vt to satirize.
satisfação [satʃiʃfaˈsãw] (pl -ões) f -**1.** [alegria, prazer] pleasure; **dar ~ a alguém** to give sb pleasure; **ter ~ em fazer algo** to to be pleased to do sthg. -**2.** [de desejos, necessidades] satisfaction. -**3.** [explicação] explanation; **dar uma ~ a alguém** to give sb an explanation; **não dar satisfações a ninguém** to owe an explanation to nobody; **tomar satisfações de alguém** to get an explanation from sb.
satisfatório, ria [satʃiʃfaˈtɔrju, rja] adj satisfactory.
satisfazer [31] [satʃiʃfaˈze(x)] ◇ vt to satisfy. ◇ vi -**1.** [ser satisfatório] to be satisfactory. -**2.** [contentar, convir]: **~ a** to satisfy.
◆ **satisfazer-se** vp: **~-se (com)** to be satisfied (with).
satisfeito, ta [satʃiʃˈfejtu, ta] ◇ pp ⊳ satisfazer. ◇ adj -**1.** [ger] satisfied. -**2.** [alegre] pleased.
saturação [saturaˈsãw] f saturation.
saturado, da [satuˈradu, da] adj -**1.**: **~ de algo** saturated with sthg. -**2.** fig [enfastiado]: **~ (de algo/alguém)** fed up (with sthg/sb).
saturar [4] [satuˈra(x)] vt -**1.**: **~ algo (de algo)** to saturate sthg (with sthg). -**2.** fig [enfastiar]: **~ alguém de algo** to wear sb out with sthg. -**3.** [saciar] to fill.
Saturno [saˈtuxnu] m Saturn.
saudação [sawdaˈsãw] (pl -ões) f -**1.** [cumprimento] greeting. -**2.** [homenagem] homage.
saudade [sawˈdadʒi] f -**1.** [de pessoa, país, família] pining. -**2.** [do passado, de época] nostalgia; **estar morrendo de ~ (s) de alguém** to be pining for sb; **matar as ~s de alguém** to catch up with sb; **estava louco para as ~s da minha cama** I was dying to sleep in my own bed again; **sentir ~(s) de alguém/algo** to pine for sb/sthg.

saudar [19] [saw'da(x)] *vt* to greet.

saudável [saw'davɛwl] (*pl* **-eis**) *adj* healthy.

saúde [sa'udʒi] ◇ *f* health; **estado de** ~ state of health; **estar bem/mal de** ~ to be in good/bad health; **não ter** ~ **para fazer algo** *fam fig* to not be fit to do sthg; **brindar à** ~ **de alguém** to drink to sb's health; ~ **pública** public health; [órgão] health service. ◇ *interj* [para brindar] cheers!; [depois de um espirro] bless you!

saudita [saw'dʒita] (*pl* **sauditas**) ◇ *adj* Saudi. ◇ *mf* Saudi.

saudosismo [sawdo'ziʒmu] *m* nostalgia.

saudoso, osa [saw'dozu, ɔza] *adj* **-1.** [que causa saudades] dearly missed. **-2.** [que sente saudades]: **estar** ~ **de alguém/algo** to miss sb/sthg. **-3.** [que denota saudades] grieving.

sauna ['sawna] *f* **-1.** [ger] sauna; **fazer** ~ to have a sauna. **-2.** *fig*: **estar uma** ~ [estar muito quente] to be like a sauna.

saveiro [sa'vejru] *m* fishing boat.

saxão, xã [sak'sãw, sãl] ◇ *adj* Saxon. ◇ *mf* Saxon.

saxofone [sakso'foni] *m* saxophone.

saxofonista [saksofo'niʃta] *mf* saxophonist.

sazonado, da [sazo'nadu, da] *adj* ripe.

sazonal [sazo'naw] (*pl* **-ais**) *adj* seasonal.

sazonalidade [sazonali'dadʒi] *f* seasonal variation.

SBT (*abrev de* **Sistema Brasileiro de Televisão**) *m* the second most popular Brazilian television station.

SC (*abrev de* **Estado de Santa Catarina**) *n* State of Santa Catarina.

scanner [liʃka'ne(x)] (*pl* **-s**) *m* COMPUT scanner.

script [liʃkriptji] (*pl* **-s**) *m* script.

se [si] ◇ *pron* **-1.** [reflexo: pessoa] himself (*f* herself); [você, vocês] yourself, yourselves *pl*; [impessoal] oneself; **lavar-**~ to wash (oneself); **eles** ~ **perderam** they got lost; **vocês se perderam** you got lost. **-2.** [reflexo: coisa, animal] itself; **o vidro partiu-**~ the glass broke. **-3.** [recíproco] each other; **escrevem-**~ **regularmente** they write to each other regularly. **-4.** [com sujeito indeterminado]: **'aluga-**~ **quarto'** 'room to let'; **'vende-**~**'** 'for sale'; **come-**~ **bem aqui** the food here is very good. ◇ *conj* **-1.** [indica condição] if; ~ **tiver tempo, escrevo** I'll write if I have time; ~ **fizer sol, iremos à praia** if it's sunny, we'll go to the beach. **-2.** [indica causa] if; ~ **você está com fome, coma alguma coisa** if you're hungry, have something to eat; ~ **..., então ...** if ..., then ...; ~ **diminui a oferta, então aumenta o preço** if demand diminishes, the cost goes up. **-3.** [indica comparação] if; ~ **um é feio, o outro ainda é pior** if you think he's ugly, you should see the other one. **-4.** [em interrogativas]: **que tal** ~ **fôssemos ao cinema?** how about going to the movies?; **e** ~ **ela não vier?** and what if she doesn't come? **-5.** [exprime desejo] if; ~ **pelo menos tivesse dinheiro!** if only I had the money! **-6.** [em interrogativa indireta] if, whether; **avisem-me** ~ **quiserem ir** let me know if you'd like to go; **perguntei-lhe** ~ **gostou** I asked him if he liked it. **-7.** [em locuções]: ~ **bem que** even though, although.

sé ['sɛl *f* cathedral.

➤ **Santa Sé** *f*: **a Santa Sé** the Holy See.

SE (*abrev de* **Estado de Sergipe**) *n State of Sergipe*.

seara ['sjara] *f* **-1.** [terra] sown field. **-2.** [de cereais] corn field.

sebáceo, cea [se'basju, sja] *adj* sebaceous.

sebento, ta [se'bẽntu, ta] *adj* [sujo] filthy.

sebo ['sebu] *m* **-1.** [substância] sebum. **-2.** [livraria] second-hand bookshop.

seborréia [sebo'xɛja] *f* seborrhoea *UK*, seborrhea *US*.

seboso, osa [se'bozu, ɔza] *adj* **-1.** [ger] greasy. **-2.** *fam fig* [pessoa] conceited.

SEBRAE (*abrev de* **Serviço de Apoio às Micro e Pequenas Empresas**) *m Brazilian support body for small and very small businesses*.

seca ['seka] *f* ➤ **seco**.

secador [seka'do(x)] (*pl* **-es**) *m* dryer; ~ (**de cabelo**) hairdryer; ~ **de pratos** drainer; ~ **de roupa** [varal] clothes line.

secadora [seka'dora] *f* tumble-dryer.

secagem [se'kaʒẽ] *f* drying.

seção [se'sãw] (*pl* **-ões**) *f* section.

secar [12] [se'ka(x)] ◇ *vt & vi* to dry.

seccionar [4] [seksjo'na(x)] *vt* **-1.** [cortar] to cut into sections. **-2.** [dividir] to divide.

secessão [sese'sãw] *f* secession.

seco, ca ['seku, ka] *adj* **-1.** [ger] dry. **-2.** [magro] thin. **-3.** *fam* [ávido]: **estar** ~ **por algo/para fazer algo** to be dying for sthg/to do sthg.

➤ **seca** *f* drought.

SECA

Drought is one of the most long-standing and critical problems afflicting the Brazilian north-east. The semi-arid region known as the *sertão nordestino* covers parts of the states of Bahia, Pernambuco, Paraíba, Ceará, Piauí, Rio Grande do Norte, Sergipe and Alagoas. Its population suffers periodically from the lack of rain, and is forced to migrate to other states of the country in search of better conditions for survival.

seções [se'sõjʃ] *pl* ➤ **seção**.

secreção [sekre'sãw] (*pl* **-ões**) *f* secretion.

secretaria [sekreta'ria] *f* secretariat.

secretária [sekre'tarja] *f* ➤ **secretário**.

secretariado [sekreta'rjadu] *m* [cargo, curso] secretarial course.

secretariar [16] [sekreta'rja(x)] ◇ *vt* to take minutes of. ◇ *vi* to work as a secretary.

secretário, ria [sekre'tarju, rja] *m, f* [ger] secretary; ~ **de Estado** Secretary of State.

➤ **secretária** *f* **-1.** [mesa] desk. **-2.** [aparelho]: ~ **eletrônica** answering machine.

secretário-geral, secretária-geral [sekre,tarjuʒe'raw, sekre,tarjaʒe'raw] (*mpl* **secretários-gerais**, *fpl* **secretárias-gerais**) *m, f* secretary general.

secreto, ta [se'krɛtu, ta] *adj* secret.
sectário, ria [sɛk'tarju, rja] <> *adj* sectarian. <> *m, f* [seguidor] sectarian.
sectarismo [sɛkta'riʒmu] *m* sectarianism.
secular [seku'la(x)] (*pl* -es) *adj* -1. [ger] secular. -2. [antigo] age-old.
secularizar [4] [sekulari'za(x)] *vt* to secularize.
século [ʹsɛkulu] *m* century; **do** ~ [descoberta, romance] of the century.
  ➤ **séculos** *mpl* *fig* [longo tempo] ages; **há** ~**s** for ages; **há** ~**s que não viajava** it's ages since I travelled, I haven't travelled for ages; ~**s atrás** ages ago.
secundar [4] [sekũn'da(x)] *vt* -1. [auxiliar] to help. -2. [reforçar] to reinforce.
secundário, ria [sekũn'darju, rja] *adj* secondary.
secura [se'kura] *f* -1. [ger] dryness. -2. *fam* [desejo]: ~ **por algo** longing for sthg.
seda [ʹseda] *f* -1. [material] silk; **de** ~ silk; ~ **crua/pura** raw/pure silk. -2. *fig* [pessoa]: **estar uma** ~ to be very friendly.
sedã [se'dã] *m* sedan.
sedar [4] [se'da(x)] *vt* to sedate.
sedativo, va [seda'tʃivu, va] *adj* MED sedative; *fig* [música, balanço, silêncio] soothing.
  ➤ **sedativo** *m* MED sedative.
sede¹ [ʹsedʒi] *f* -1. [secura] thirst; **estar com** ~ to be thirsty; **matar a** ~ to quench one's thirst. -2. *fig* [desejo]: ~ **de algo** thirst for sthg.
sede² [ʹsedʒi] *f* -1. [estabelecimento] headquarters. -2. [de governo] seat. -3. [centro, local] venue.
sedentário, ria [sedẽn'tarju, rja] *adj* sedentary.
sedento, ta [se'dẽntu, ta] *adj* -1. [de água] thirsty. -2. *fig* [ávido]: ~ **de algo** thirsty for sthg.
SEDEX (*abrev de* Serviço de Encomenda Expressa) *m Brazilian express mail delivery service.*
sediar [15] [se'dʒja(x)] *vt* to base.
sedição [sedʒi'sãw] (*pl* -ões) *f* sedition.
sedicioso, osa [sedʒi'sjozu, ɔza] *adj* seditious.
sedimentação [sedʒimẽnta'sãw] (*pl* -ões) *f* sedimentation.
sedimentar [4] [sedʒimẽn'ta(x)] *vi* to sediment.
sedimento [sedʒi'mẽntu] *m* sediment.
sedoso, osa [se'dozu, ɔza] *adj* silky.
sedução [sedu'sãw] (*pl* -ões) *f* -1. [ato] seduction. -2. [atração]: ~ **por algo/alguém** attraction towards sthg/sb.
sedutor, ra [sedu'to(x), ra] (*mpl* -es, *fpl* -s) <> *adj* seductive. <> *m, f* [sexualmente] seducer.
seduzir [72] [sedu'zi(x)] *vt* -1. [ger] to seduce. -2. [induzir] to encourage.
seg. (*abrev de* segunda-feira) *f* Mon.
segmentação [segmẽnta'sãw] (*pl* -ões) *f* segmentation.
segmentar [4] [segmẽn'ta(x)] *vt* to segment.
segmento [seg'mẽntu] *m* segment.
segredar [4] [segre'da(x)] *vt* &*vi* to whisper.
segredo [se'gredu] *m* -1. [ger] secret; **guardar** ~ to keep secret; ~ **de Estado** state secret. -2. [discrição] secrecy; **em** ~ in secret. -3. [dispositivo] secret lock.

segregação [segrega'sãw] *f* segregation.
segregar [14] [segre'ga(x)] *vt* -1. [ger] to segregate. -2. [expelir] to secrete.
seguidamente [se,gida'mẽntʃi] *adv* -1. [com frequência] often. -2. [continuamente] continuously.
seguido, da [se'gidu, da] *adj* -1. [consecutivo] consecutive; **cinco dias** ~**s** five days running; **horas seguidas** hours on end. -2. [adotado] widely adopted. -3. [que se segue]: ~ **a** following. -4. [acompanhado]: ~ **de/por** followed by.
  ➤ **em seguida** *loc adv* -1. [consecutivamente] shortly after. -2. [imediatamente] straight away, at once.
seguidor, ra [segi'do(x), ra] *m, f* follower.
seguimento [segi'mẽntu] *m* continuation; **dar** ~ **a algo** to continue with sthg.
seguinte [se'gĩntʃi] <> *adj* -1. [subseqüente] following, next; ~ **a** following. -2. (*antes de subst*) [citando, explicando] following. <> *mf*: **o/a** ~ [numa fila, ordem] the next; [citando, explicando] as follows; **o negócio é o** ~ *fam* the matter is as follows; **pelo** ~ for the following reason.
seguir [55] [se'gi(x)] <> *vt* -1. [ger] to follow. -2. [perseguir] to chase. -3. [continuar] to continue. <> *vi* -1. [ger] to follow. -2. [continuar] to carry on, to keep going. -3. [direção] to continue; ~ **reto** to go straight ahead.
  ➤ **seguir-se** *vp* -1. [suceder]: ~**-se (a algo)** to follow on (from sthg); **seguiram-se dias de euforia** there followed days of euphoria. -2. [em citações] to follow.
segunda [se'gũnda] *f* ▷ **segundo**.
segunda-feira [se,gũnda'fejra] (*pl* **segundas-feiras**) *f* Monday; *veja também* **sábado**.
segundanista [segũndã'niʃta] *mf* second year (*university*) *student*.
segundo, da [se'gũndu, da] <> *num adj* second; ~ **grau** EDUC secondary education; ~ **tempo** FUT second half. <> *num m, f* second. <> *adj* -1. [outro] second; **segundas intenções** ulterior motives; **de segunda mão** second-hand. -2. [inferior]: **de** ~ **time** second-rate.
  ➤ **segundo** <> *m* [medida de tempo] second; **(só) um** ~! *fig* just a second!, (just) one second! <> *prep* according to. <> *conj* [conforme] according to.
  ➤ **segunda** *f* -1. AUTO second (gear). -2. [segunda-feira] Monday.
  ➤ **de segunda** *loc adj* second class. <> *loc adv* [viajar] second class.
segurado, da [segu'radu, da] <> *adj* insured. <> *m, f* person insured.
segurador, ra [segura'do(x), ra] *m, f* [agente] insurance broker.
  ➤ **seguradora** *f* [companhia] insurance company.
seguramente [se,gura'mẽntʃi] *adv* -1. [com certeza] certainly. -2. [muito provavelmente] surely.
segurança [segu'rãnsa] <> *f* -1. [proteção, estabilidade] security; **de** ~ security; **cinto de** ~ safety

belt; ~ **nacional** national security. **-2.** [ausência de perigo] safety. **-3.** [certeza, confiança] assurance. <> *mf* [pessoa] security guard.

segurar [4] [segu'ra(x)] <> *vt* **-1.** [pegar] to hold. **-2.** [firmar] to fix. **-3.** [sustentar] to hold up. **-4.** [pôr no seguro]: ~ **algo/alguém (contra)** to insure sthg/sb (against). <> *vi* [apoiar-se]: ~ **(em)** to hold on (to).

➡ **segurar-se** *vp* **-1.** [apoiar-se]: ~**-se em** to hold on to. **-2.** [fazer seguro] to steady o.s. **-3.** [controlar-se] to control o.s.

seguro, ra [se'guru, ra] *adj* **-1.** [ger] safe. **-2.** [certo] sure; **estar** ~ **de algo** to be sure of sthg. **-3.** [confiante, firme] secure; ~ **de si** self-assured. **-4.** [infalível] foolproof.

➡ **seguro** <> *m* [contrato] insurance policy; **fazer** ~ to take out an insurance policy; ~ **de automóvel** car insurance; ~ **contra incêndio** fire insurance; ~ **de vida** life insurance. <> *adv* steadily.

seguro-desemprego [se,gurudesẽn'pregu] (*pl* **seguros-desemprego**) *m* unemployment benefit *UK*, unemployment compensation *US*.

seguro-saúde [se,gurusa'udʒi] (*pl* **seguros-saúde**) *m* health insurance.

seio ['seju] *m* **-1.** *ANAT* breast. **-2.** *fig* [meio] heart.

seis ['sejʃ] *num* **-1.** [ger] six; **o (número)** ~ the (number) six; **duzentos e** ~ two hundred and six; **trinta e** ~ thirty-six; **Rua das Acácias, (número)** ~ number six, Rua das Acácias; **pacotes de** ~ packets of six; ~ **de cada vez** six at a time; **somos** ~ we are six, there are six of us; **vieram os** ~ the six of them came; **tirar** ~ [nos estudos] to get (a) six. **-2.** [hora]: **às** ~ **(horas)** at six o'clock; **são** ~ **horas** it is six o'clock; **são** ~ **e meia** it is half past six. **-3.** [data] sixth; **hoje é dia** ~ today is the sixth; **(no) dia** ~ **de janeiro** (on the) sixth of January. **-4.** [idade]: **ele tem** ~ **anos (de idade)** he is six years old. **-5.** [temperatura]: ~ **graus abaixo de zero** six degrees below freezing. **-6.** *ESP* [jogador]: **o número** ~ number six. **-7.** *ESP* [resultado]: **empatar de** ~ **a** ~ to draw six all; ~ **a zero** six nil. **-8.** [em naipes]: ~ **de espadas** six of spades.

seiscentos, tas [sejʃ'sẽntuʃ, taʃ] *num* six hundred; *veja também* **seis**.

seita ['sejta] *f* sect.

seiva ['sejva] *f* sap.

seixo ['sejʃu] *m* pebble.

seja ['seʒa] *conj* whether it be; **ou** ~ that is.

sela ['sɛla] *f* saddle.

selagem [se'laʒẽ] *f* [de carta] postage.

selar [4] [se'la(x)] *vt* **-1.** [ger] to seal. **-2.** [cavalo] to saddle. **-3.** [carta] to stamp.

seleção [sele'sãw] (*pl* **-ões**) *f* **-1.** [escolha] selection. **-2.** [equipe] team; **a** ~ **brasileira** the Brazilian team.

selecionado, da [selesjo'nadu, da] *adj* [escolhido] chosen.

➡ **selecionado** *m* [equipe] team.

selecionar [4] [selesjo'na(x)] *vt* to select.

seleta [se'lɛta] *f* ⊳ **seleto**.

seletivo, va [sele'tʃivu, va] *adj* selective.

seleto, ta [se'lɛtu, ta] *adj* select.

➡ **seleta** *f* selection.

selim [se'lĩ] (*pl* **-ns**) *m* saddle.

selo ['selu] *m* **-1.** [carimbo, sinete] seal. **-2.** [postal] stamp. **-3.** *fig* [cunho] seal of approval.

selva ['sɛwva] *f* jungle.

selvagem [sew'vaʒẽ] (*pl* **-ns**) *adj* **-1.** [ger] wild. **-2.** [bárbaro] savage. **-3.** [ermo] desolate. **-4.** *fig* [grosseiro] rude.

selvageria [sewvaʒe'ria] *f* savagery.

sem [sẽ] *prep* without; ~ **algo/fazer algo** without sthg/doing sthg; ~ **ajuda** without help; ~ **dúvida** without doubt; **passar** ~ **algo** to go without sthg.

➡ **sem que** *loc conj* without.

semáforo [se'maforu] *m* **-1.** *AUTO* traffic lights (*pl*). **-2.** *FERRO* signal.

semana [se'mãna] *f* week; **há uma** ~ a week ago; **uma** ~ **atrás** a week ago; **a** ~ **passada** last week; **a** ~ **retrasada** the week before last; **por** ~ [número de vezes] per week; [ser pago] weekly.

➡ **Semana Santa** *f* Holy Week.

semanal [sema'naw] (*pl* **-ais**) *adj* weekly.

semanalmente [semanaw'mẽntʃi] *adv* weekly.

semanário [sema'narju] *m* weekly.

semântico, ca [se'mãntʃiku, ka] *adj* semantic.

➡ **semântica** *f* semantics (*pl*).

semblante [sẽn'blãntʃi] *m* [rosto] countenance.

sem-cerimônia [sẽnseri'monja] (*pl* **-s**) *f* **-1.** [informalidade] informality. **-2.** [grosseria] rudeness.

semeadura [semja'dura] *f* [semeação] sowing; **começaram a** ~ **do trigo** they began sowing the wheat.

semear [15] [se'mja(x)] *vt* **-1.** [ger] to sow. **-2.** *fig* [espalhar] to spread.

semelhança [seme'ʎãnsa] *f* resemblance; **ter** ~ **com** to resemble.

semelhante [seme'ʎãntʃi] <> *adj* **-1.** [parecido]: ~ **(a)** similar (to). **-2.** [tal] such. <> *m* (*ger pl*) [próximo] fellow man.

semelhar [4] [seme'ʎa(x)] *vt* to resemble.

sêmen ['semẽ] *m* semen.

semente [se'mẽntʃi] *f* seed.

semestral [semeʃ'traw] (*pl* **-ais**) *adj* half-yearly.

semestralmente [semeʃtraw'mẽntʃi] *adv* every semester, every six months.

semestre [se'mɛʃtri] *m* semester; **todo** ~ every six months; **todo o** ~ the whole semester.

sem-fim [ˌsẽn'fĩ] *m*: **um** ~ **de** an endless amount of.

semi-aberto, ta [semja'bɛxtu, ta] (*mpl* **-s**, *fpl* **-s**) *adj* **-1.** [ger] half-opened. **-2.** [porta] ajar.

semi-analfabeto, ta [semjanawfa'bɛtu, ta] (*mpl* **-s**, *fpl* **-s**) *adj* semi-literate.

semibreve [semi'brɛvi] *f* *MÚS* semibreve.

semicerrar [semi'sexa(x)] *vt* to half-close.

semicírculo [semi'sixkulu] *m* semicircle.

semicolcheia [semikow'ʃeja] *f* *MÚS* semiquaver.

semiconsciente [semikõn'sjẽntʃi] *adj* semiconscious.

semifinal [semifi'naw] (*pl* -**ais**) *f* semi-final.
semifinalista [semifina'liʃta] <> *adj* semi-final (*antes de subst*). <> *mf* semi-finalist.
semi-internato [semiĩntex'natu] (*pl* **semi-internatos**) *m* day school.
seminal [semi'naw] (*pl* -**ais**) *adj* seminal.
seminário [semi'narju] *m* -**1.** *RELIG* seminary. -**2.** *EDUC* seminar.
seminarista [semina'riʃta] *mf* seminarist.
seminu, nua [semi'nu, nua] *adj* half-naked.
semiótica [se'mjɔtʃika] *f* semiotics.
semiprecioso, osa [sempre'sjozu, ɔza] *adj* semi-precious.
semita [se'mita] <> *adj* Semitic. <> *mf* Semite.
semítico, ca [se'mitʃiku, ka] *adj* Semitic.
semitom [semi'tõ] (*pl* -**ns**) *m* MÚS semitone.
sem-número [sẽn'numeru] *m*: **um ~ de** a countless number of.
semolina [semo'lina] *f* semolina.
sem-par [sẽn'pa(x)] *adj inv* peerless.
sempre ['sẽnpri] *adv* always; **como ~** as always; **de ~** usual; **para ~** for ever; **quase ~** nearly always.
   • **sempre que** *loc conj* whenever.
sem-terra [sẽn'tɛxa] *mf inv* landless farm worker.
sem-teto [sẽn'tɛtu] *mf inv* homeless person.
sem-vergonha [sẽnvex'goɲa] <> *adj inv* shameless. <> *mf inv* shameless person.
SENAC (*abrev de* Serviço Nacional de Aprendizagem Comercial) *m Brazilian training body for people working in the general business sector*.
senado [se'nadu] *m* senate.
senador, ra [sena'do(x), ra] *m, f* senator.
SENAI (*abrev de* Serviço Nacional de Aprendizagem Industrial) *m Brazilian training body for people working in industry*.
senão [se'nãw] (*pl* -**ões**) <> *prep* [exceto] apart from. <> *conj* [caso contrário] or else. <> *m* hiccup.
senda ['sẽnda] *f* path.
Senegal [sene'gaw] *n*: **(o) ~** Senegal.
senhor, ra [se'ɲo(x), ɔra] (*mpl* -**es**, *fpl* -**s**) *adj* grand; **uma senhora indigestão** a bad case of indigestion.
   • **senhor** *m* -**1.** [tratamento - antes de nome, cargo]: **~ X** Mr X; **o Senhor Ministro** (the) Minister; [- você]: **o ~** you; [mais formal] sir; [- em cartas]: **Prezado Senhor** Dear Sir. -**2.** [homem] man. -**3.** [cavalheiro] gentleman. -**4.** [homem idoso]: **~ (de idade)** elderly man. -**5.** [dono] master; **ser ~ de seu nariz** to be one's own master. -**6.** [patrão] boss. -**7.** *RELIG*: **o Senhor** the Lord.
   • **senhora** *f* -**1.** [tratamento - antes de nome, cargo]: **senhora X** Mrs X; [- você]: **a senhora** you; [mais formal] madam; **senhoras e ~ es!** ladies and gentlemen!; [- em cartas]: **Prezada Senhora** Dear Madam. -**2.** [mulher] woman. -**3.** [dama] lady. -**4.** [mulher idosa]: **senhora (de idade)** elderly woman. -**5.** [esposa] wife. -**6.** *RELIG*: **Nossa Senhora** Our Lady; **(Minha) Nossa (Senhora)!** *fam* Heavens (above)!, (My/Dear) Lord!

senhoria [seɲo'ria] *f* ⊳ **senhorio**.
senhoril [seɲo'riw] (*pl* -**is**) *adj* distinguished.
senhorio, ria [seɲo'riu, rial *m, f* [proprietário] landlord (*f* landlady).
   • **Senhoria** *f* [em carta]: **Vossa Senhoria** Your Honour.
senhorita [seɲo'rita] *f* -**1.** [tratamento - antes de nome]: **~ X** Miss X; [- você]: **a ~** you. -**2.** [moça] young lady.
senil [se'niw] (*pl* -**is**) *adj* senile.
senilidade [senili'dadʒi] *f* senility.
sênior ['sẽnjo(x)] (*pl* -**s**) <> *adj* senior. <> *m* [desportista] senior.
senões [se'nõjʃ] *mpl* ⊳ **senão**.
sensação [sẽnsa'sãw] (*pl* -**ões**) *f* -**1.** [ger] feeling; **ter a ~ de que** to have the feeling that. -**2.** [surpresa, agitação]: **causar ~** to cause a sensation.
sensacional [sẽnsasjo'naw] (*pl* -**ais**) *adj* sensational.
sensacionalismo [sẽnsasjona'liʒmu] *m* sensationalism.
sensacionalista [sẽnsasjona'liʃta] *adj* sensationalist.
sensatez [sẽnsa'teʒ] *f* common sense.
sensato, ta [sẽn'satu, ta] *adj* sensible.
sensibilidade [sẽnsibili'dadʒi] *f* sensitivity.
sensibilizar [4] [sẽnsibili'za(x)] *vt* -**1.** [comover] to move. -**2.** [impressionar] to sensitize.
   • **sensibilizar-se** *vp* [comover-se] to be touched.
sensitivo, va [sẽnsi'tʃivu, va] *adj* sensitive.
sensível [sẽn'sivew] (*pl* -**eis**) *adj* -**1.** [ger] sensitive. -**2.** [evidente, considerável] marked.
sensivelmente [sẽnsivew'mẽntʃi] *adv* markedly.
senso ['sẽnsu] *m* [juízo] sense; **~ de humor** sense of humour; **bom ~**, good sense; **~ comum** common sense; **~ de responsabilidade** sense of responsibility.
sensor [sẽn'so(x)] *m* sensor.
sensorial [sẽnso'rjaw] (*pl* -**ais**) *adj* sensory.
sensual [sẽn'swaw] (*pl* -**ais**) *adj* sensual.
sensualidade [sẽnswali'dadʒi] *f* sensuality.
sentado, da [sẽn'tadu, da] *adj* -**1.** [pessoa] sitting. -**2.** [jantar] sit-down.
sentar [4] [sẽn'ta(x)] *vt & vi* to sit.
   • **sentar-se** *vp* to sit down.
sentença [sẽn'tẽnsa] *f* JUR sentence; **~ de morte** death sentence.
sentenciar [sẽntẽn'sia(x)] <> *vt* [condenar] to sentence. <> *vi* [decidir] to decide.
sentencioso, sa [sẽntẽ'sjosu, sa] *adj* sententious.
sentido, da [sẽn'tʃidu, da] *adj* -**1.** [ressentido] offended. -**2.** [triste] hurt. -**3.** [lamentoso] sorrowful.
   • **sentido** *m* -**1.** [ger] sense; **sexto ~** sixth sense. -**2.** [significado] meaning; **sem ~** meaningless; **duplo ~** double meaning; **~ figurado** figurative sense; **fazer ~** to make sense; **ter/ não ter ~** to make/not make sense. -**3.** [direção] direction; **~ horário/anti-horário** clockwise/

anticlockwise. **-4.** [aspecto] way. **-5.** [atenção]: **estar com o ~ em algo/alguém** to have one's attention on sthg/sb. **-6.** [propósito] aim; **no ~ de** towards.

→ **sentidos** *mpl* [consciência] senses; **perder/recobrar os ~s** to lose/regain consciousness.

sentimental [sẽntʃimẽ'tawl *(pl* -ais) <> *adj* **-1.** [ger] sentimental. **-2.** [amoroso] love *(antes de subst).* <> *mf* sentimental person.

sentimentalismo [sẽntʃimẽta'liʒmul *m* sentimentality.

sentimentalóide [sẽntʃimẽta'lɔidʒil *adj* oversentimental.

sentimento [sẽntʃi'mẽntul *m* **-1.** [ger] feeling. **-2.** [emoção]: **com ~** with feeling. **-3.** [senso] sense.

→ **sentimentos** *mpl* **-1.** [pêsames] condolences. **-2.** [índole]: **uma pessoa de bons ~s** a well-meaning person.

sentinela [sẽntʃi'nɛla] *f* guard.

sentir [56] [sẽn'tʃi(x)] <> *vt* **-1.** [ger] to feel. **-2.** [pelos sentidos] to sense. **-3.** [sofrer com] to be upset by. **-4.** [melindrar-se com] to resent. **-5.** [lamentar] to regret. <> *vi* **-1.** [sofrer] to suffer. **-2.** [lamentar] to regret; **sinto muito** I am very sorry. **-3.** [perceber]: **sem ~** without realizing.

→ **sentir-se** *vp* to feel.

senzala [sẽn'zala] *f* slave quarters *(pl).*

separação [separa'sãw] *(pl* -ões) *f* separation; **~ de bens** *(contract of)* separation of property *(prior to marriage).*

separado, da [sepa'radu, da] *adj* **-1.** [apartado] separate. **-2.** [do cônjuge] separated.

separar [4] [sepa'ra(x)] *vt* **-1.** [ger] to separate. **-2.** [isolar] to isolate. **-3.** [reservar] to set aside.

→ **separar-se** *vp* **-1.** [ger] to separate. **-2.** [cônjuges]: **~-se (de alguém)** to separate (from s.o.). **-3.** [estrada, rio]: **~-se em** to divide into.

separata [sepa'rata] *f* offprint.

separatismo [separa'tʃiʒmul *m* separatism.

separatista [separa'tʃiʃta] <> *adj* separatist. <> *mf* separatist.

septicemia [septʃise'mia] *f* septicaemia *UK*, septicemia *US*.

séptico, ca ['sɛptʃiku, ka] *adj* septic.

septuagésimo, ma [septwa'ʒɛzimu, ma] *num* seventieth.

sepulcro [se'puwkru] *m* tomb.

sepultamento [sepuwta'mẽntul *m* burial.

sepultar [4] [sepuw'ta(x)] *vt* to bury.

sepultura [sepuw'tura] *f* tomb, grave.

seqüela [se'kwɛla] *f* **-1.** [seqüência] sequel. **-2.** [conseqüência] consequence. **-3.** *MED* sequela.

seqüência [se'kwẽsja] *f* sequence.

seqüenciador [sekwẽsia'do(x)] *m* sequencer.

sequer [se'kɛ(x)] *adv* at least; **nem ~** not even; **não sabia ~ o nome de seus pais** he didn't even know his parents' name.

seqüestrador, ra [sekweʃtra'do(x), ra] *(mpl* -res, *fpl* -s) *m, f* **-1.** [de pessoa] kidnapper. **-2.** [de avião] hijacker.

seqüestrar [sekweʃ'tra(x)] *vt* **-1.** [pessoa] to kidnap. **-2.** [avião] to hijack. **-3.** *JUR* [bens] to sequestrate.

seqüestro [se'kwɛʃtrul *m* **-1.** [de pessoa] kidnapping. **-2.** [de avião] hijacking. **-3.** *JUR* [de bens] sequestration.

seqüestro-relâmpago [se,kweʃtruxe'lãpagul *(pl* -gos) *m kidnapping in which a person is held for a few hours while the kidnappers, having extracted passwords, use his bank cards to withdraw cash.*

sequioso, osa [se'kjozu, ɔza] *adj* thirsty.

séquito ['sɛkitul *m* retinue.

ser [3] ['se(x)] *(pl* -res) <> *m* [criatura] being; **~ humano** human being. <> *vi* **-1.** [para descrever] to be; **é longo demais** it's too long; **são bonitos** they're pretty; **sou médico** I'm a doctor. **-2.** [para designar lugar, origem] to be; **ele é do Brasil** he's from Brazil; **é em São Paulo** it's in São Paulo; **sou brasileira** I'm Brazilian. **-3.** [custar] to be; **quanto é? - são 100 reais** how much is it? - (it's) 100 reais. **-4.** [com data, dia, hora] to be; **hoje é sexta** it's Friday today; **que horas são?** what time is it?; **são seis horas** it's six o'clock. **-5.** [exprime possessão] to be; **é do Ricardo** it's Ricardo's; **este carro é seu?** is this your car? **-6.** [em locuções]: **a não ~ que** unless; **que foi?** what's wrong?; **ou seja** in other words; **será que ele vem?** will he be coming? <> *v aux* [forma a voz passiva] to be; **ele foi visto na saída do cinema** he was seen on his way out of the cinema. <> *v impess* **-1.** [exprime tempo] to be; **é de dia/noite** it's daytime/night-time; **é tarde/cedo** it's late/early. **-2.** [com adjetivo] to be; **é difícil dizer** it's difficult to say; **é fácil de ver** it's easy to see; **eles são Fluminense** they're Fluminense fans.

→ **ser de** *v + prep* [matéria] to be made of; [ser adepto de] to be a fan of.

→ **ser para** *v + prep* to be for; **isto não é para comer** this isn't for eating.

serão [se'rãw] *(pl* -ões) *m* [trabalho noturno] night duty; **fazer ~** to work late.

sereia [se'reja] *f* mermaid.

serelepe [sere'lɛpil *adj* lively.

serenar [4] [sere'na(x)] <> *vt* **-1.** [acalmar] to calm down. **-2.** [suavizar] to relieve. <> *vi* [acalmar] to calm down.

serenata [sere'nata] *f* serenade.

serenidade [sereni'dadʒil *f* serenity.

sereno, na [se'renu, na] *adj* **-1.** [tranqüilo] serene. **-2.** [límpido] clear.

→ **sereno** *m* night air; **apanhar ~** to get a chill; **no ~** in the open air.

seresta [se'rɛʃta] *f* serenade.

Sergipe [sex'ʒipil *n* Sergipe.

seriado, da [se'rjadu, da] *adj* serialized.

→ **seriado** *m TV* series.

serial [se'rjawl *(pl* -ais) *adj COMPUT* serial.

série ['sɛrjil *f* **-1.** [ger] series; **uma ~ de** a series of; **número de ~** serial number. **-2.** *EDUC* year.

em série *loc adv*: **fabricar em ~** to mass-produce.

fora de série *loc adj* [excepcional] exceptional.

seriedade [serje'dadʒil *f* -**1.** [ger] seriousness. -**2.** [circunspecção] sobriety. -**3.** [honestidade] integrity.

seringa [se'rĩŋgal *f* syringe.

seringal [serĩŋ'gawl (*pl* -**ais**) *m* rubber-tree plantation.

seringueiro, ra [serĩŋ'gejru, ral *m, f* rubber tapper.

seringueira *f* rubber tree.

sério, ria ['sɛrju, rjal ⬦ *adj* -**1.** [ger] serious. -**2.** [sóbrio] sober. -**3.** [sem rir] straight-faced. ⬦ *adv* really; **falando ~** seriously.

a sério *loc adv* seriously; **levar a ~** [dedicar-se] to take seriously; [magoar-se com] to take seriously.

sermão [sex'mãwl (*pl* -**ões**) *m* sermon; **levar um ~ de alguém** to be given a sermon by sb; **passar um ~ em alguém** to give sb a sermon.

serpente [sex'pẽntʃil *f* -**1.** *ZOOL* serpent, snake. -**2.** *fig* [pessoa] snake (in the grass).

serpentear [15] [sexpẽn'tʃja(x)l *vi* -**1.** [rio, caminho] to meander. -**2.** [cobra] to snake.

serpentina [serpẽn'tʃinal *f* -**1.** [de papel] streamer. -**2.** [conduto] coil.

SERPRO (*abrev de* Serviço Federal de Processamento de Dados) *m Brazilian federal data-processing agency.*

serra ['sɛxal *f* -**1.** [ferramenta] saw; **~ circular** circular saw. -**2.** [lâmina] serrated blade. -**3.** [montanhas] mountain range, sierra.

serrado, da [se'xadu, dal *adj* -**1.** [madeira] sawn. -**2.** [folha] serrated.

serragem [se'xaʒẽl *f* [resíduo] sawdust.

Serra Leoa [ˌsexale'oal *n* Sierra Leone.

serralheiro, ra [sexa'ʎejru, ral *m, f* blacksmith.

serralheria [sexaʎe'rial *f* -**1.** [ofício] smithery. -**2.** [oficina] smithy.

serrano, na [se'xãnu, nal ⬦ *adj* mountain (*antes de subst*). ⬦ *m, f* mountain dweller.

serrar [4] [se'xa(x)l *vt* to saw.

serraria [sexa'rial *f* sawmill.

serrote [se'xɔtʃil *m* saw.

sertanejo, ja [sextane'ʒu, ʒal ⬦ *adj of the sertão.* ⬦ *m, f* person who lives in the sertão.

sertão [sex'tãwl *m* -**1.** [o interior do país] bush. -**2.** [região agreste] wilderness.

servente [sex'vẽntʃil *mf* -**1.** [faxineiro] caretaker *UK,* janitor *US.* -**2.** [operário] labourer; **~ de pedreiro** bricklayer's labourer.

Sérvia ['sɛxvjal *n* Serbia.

serviçal [sexvi'sawl (*pl* -**ais**) ⬦ *adj* [prestativo] obliging. ⬦ *mf* [criado] servant.

serviço [sex'visul *m* -**1.** [ger] service; **~ de bordo** ship's roster; **~ militar** military service; **~ de informações** information service; **Serviço Nacional de Saúde** National Health Service; **Serviço Público** Civil Service; **~s públicos** public

services. -**2.** [trabalho, local de trabalho] work; **prestar ~ s** [trabalhar] to render services; [fazer favores] to help out; **prestação de ~s** services rendered; **~ social** social services (*pl*). -**3.** [iguarias] catering. -**4.** *loc:* **dar o ~** *fam* to spill the beans; **fazer um ~** *gír crime* to carry out a contract; **não brincar em ~** [ser eficiente] to be a stickler; [não desperdiçar oportunidade] to not miss an opportunity.

de serviço *loc adj* [entrada, elevador] tradesmen's (*antes de subst*).

servidão [sexvi'dãwl *f* -**1.** [escravidão] servitude. -**2.** *JUR* [de passagem] right of way.

servido, da [sex'vidu, dal *adj* -**1.** [que se serve] served. -**2.** [provido]: **bem ~ de** well-supplied with.

servidor, ra [sexvi'do(x), ral ⬦ *m, f* [funcionário] official; **~ público** civil servant.

servidor *m COMPUT* server.

servil [sex'viwl (*pl* -**is**) *adj* [subserviente]: **~ (a)** servile (to).

servir [54] [sex'vi(x)l ⬦ *vt* -**1.** [jantar, bebida] to serve; **pedi para o garçom nos ~ duas cervejas** I asked the waiter to bring us a couple of beers; **~ algo a alguém, ~ alguém de algo** to serve sthg to sb, to serve sb with sthg. -**2.** [ajudar] to help. ⬦ *vi* -**1.** [ger] to serve. -**2.** [prestar serviço]: **~ a** to serve. -**3.** [prestar, ser útil] to be of use. -**4.** [ser adequado] to be good; **qualquer trem serve** any train will do; **não ~ para algo** to be no good for. -**5.** [caber] to fit. -**6.** [fazer as vezes de]: **~ de algo** to act as. -**7.** [ser apto] to be fit.

servir-se *vp* -**1.** [de comida, bebida]: **~-se (de)** to help o.s. to. -**2.** [usar]: **~-se de** to use.

servo, va ['sɛxvu, val *m, f* -**1.** [escravo] slave. -**2.** [criado] servant.

SESC (*abrev de* Serviço Social do Comércio) *m Brazilian body providing social, sport and cultural facilities to people working in the general business sector.*

sessão [se'sãwl (*pl* -**ões**) *f* -**1.** [ger] session. -**2.** *CINE* performance; **primeira ~** first performance; **~ da tarde** matinée.

sessenta [se'sẽntal *num* sixty; **os anos ~** the sixties; *veja também* **seis**.

sessões [se'sõjʃl *pl* ⬥ **sessão**.

sesta ['sɛʃtal *f* siesta, afternoon nap.

set. (*abrev de* setembro) Sept.

set ['sɛtʃil *m ESP* set.

seta ['sɛtal *f* arrow.

sete ['sɛtʃil *num* seven; **pintar o ~** *fig* to get up to mischief; *veja também* **seis**.

setecentos, tas [sɛtʃi'sẽntuʃ, taʃl *num* seven hundred; *veja também* **seis**.

sete-e-meio [sɛtʃi'mejul (*pl* **sete-e-meios**) *m* [jogo] *kind of card game.*

setembro [se'tẽnbrul *m* September; **em ~, no mês de ~** in September/in the month of September; **em ~ do ano que vem/do ano passado** in September next year/last year; **em meados de ~** in mid-September; **dia primeiro/dois/**

seis de ~ first/second/sixth of September; **no dia três de** ~ on the third of September; **no início/fim de** ~ at the beginning/end of September; **todo ano em** ~ every year in September.

setenta [se'tẽnta] *num* seventy; **os anos** ~ the seventies; *veja também* **seis**.

setentrional [setẽntrjo'naw] (*pl* -ais) *adj* northern.

sétimo, ma ['sɛtʃimu, ma] *num* seventh; **a sétima parte** the seventh part.
 ➡ **sétima** *f* MÚS seventh.

setor [se'to(x)] (*pl* -es) *m* -1. [ger] sector. -2. [de repartição, estabelecimento] section.

setorial [seto'riaw] (*pl* -ais) [raijʃ] *adj* sector.

setorizar [setori'za(x)] *vt* to divide into sectors.

setuagésimo, ma [setwa'ʒɛsimu, ma] *num* seventieth.

seu, sua ['sew, 'sua] <> *adj* -1. [dele] his; [dela] her; [de você, vocês] your; [deles, delas] their; **ela trouxe o** ~ **carro** she brought her car; **onde estacionou a sua moto?** where did you park your motorcycle? -2. [de coisa, animal: singular] its; **o cachorro foi para o seu canil** the dog went into its kennel -3. [de coisa, animal: plural] their. <> *pron*: **o** ~/**a sua** [dele] his; [dela] hers; [deles, delas] theirs; [de coisa, animal: singular] its; [de coisa, animal: plural] theirs; **um amigo** ~ a friend of his/hers; **os** ~**s** [a família de cada um] his/her etc. family. <> *m, f* -1. *pej*: **como vai,** ~ **Pedro?** how are you, mister Pedro?; ~ **estúpido!** you fool!; ~**s irresponsáveis!** you irresponsible lot! -2. [com malícia]: ~ **malandro!** you cheeky one!, cheeky thing!; **sua danadinha!** you rotter!, rotten thing!

Seul [se'uw] *n* Seoul.

seus [sewʃ] ➡ **seu**.

severidade [severi'dadʒi] *f* -1. [ger] severity. -2. [com filho] strictness.

severo, ra [se'vɛru, ra] *adj* -1. [castigo] severe. -2. [pessoa] strict.

sex. (*abrev de* **sexta-feira**) *f* Fri.

sexagenário, ria [seksaʒe'narjo, rja] <> *adj*: **ser** ~ to be a sexagenarian, to be in one's sixties. <> *m, f* sexagenarian.

sexagésimo, ma [seksa'ʒɛzimu, ma] *num* sixtieth.

sexo ['sɛksu] *m* sex.

sexólogo, ga [sek'sɔlogu, ga] *m, f* sexologist.

sexta ['seʃta] *f* ➡ **sexto**.

sexta-feira [,seʃta'fejra] (*pl* **sextas-feiras**) *f* Friday; *veja também* **sábado**.
 ➡ **Sexta-feira Santa** *f* Good Friday.

sexto, ta ['seʃtu, ta] *num* sixth; **a sexta parte** the sixth part.
 ➡ **sexta** *f* [sexta-feira] Friday.

sêxtuplos ['seʃtupluʃ] *mpl* sextuplets.

sexual [sek'swaw] (*pl* -ais) *adj* -1. [ger] sexual. -2. [educação, vida] sex (*antes de subst*).

sexualidade [sekswali'dadʒi] *f* sexuality.

sexualmente [seksuaw'mẽntʃi] *adv* sexually.

sexy ['sɛksi] *adj* sexy.

Seychelles [sej'ʃɛliʃ] *npl*: **as (ilhas)** ~ the Seychelles.

SFH (*abrev de* **Sistema Financeiro de Habitação**) *m Brazilian housing credit advisory service*.

shareware [ʃari'waril (*pl* -s) *m* COMPUT shareware.

shopping ['ʃopĩŋ] *m* shopping centre *UK*, shopping mall *US*.

short ['ʃɔxtʃil *m* shorts (*pl*).

show ['ʃow] *m* -1. [espetáculo] show; **ser/estar um** ~ *fig* to be spectacular. -2. *fig* [atuação brilhante]: **dar um** ~ **(de algo)** to give a brilliant performance (of sthg). -3. *fig* [escândalo]: **dar um** ~ to create a scene.

showroom [ʃow'xũl *m* showroom.

Sibéria [si'bɛrja] *n*: **(a)** ~ Siberia.

siberiano, na [sibe'rjãnu, na] <> *adj* Siberian. <> *m, f* Siberian.

sibilante [sibi'lãntʃi] *adj* sibilant.

sibilar [sibi'la(x)] *vi* [silvar] to whistle; [zumbir] to buzz.

sicário [si'karju] *m* paid assassin.

Sicília [si'silja] *n* Sicily.

sicrano, na [si'krãnu, na] *m, f*: **fulano e** ~ so-and-so.

sideral [side'raw] (*pl* -ais) *adj* sidereal.

siderurgia [si'derux'ʒia] *f* iron and steel industry.

siderúrgico, ca [side'ruxʒiku, ka] *adj* iron and steel (*antes de sust*).
 ➡ **siderúrgica** *f* [usina] steelworks (*sg*).

sidra ['sidra] *f* cider.

sifão [si'fãw] (*pl* -ões) *m* -1. [tubo] siphon. -2. [de aparelho sanitário] U-bend. -3. [garrafa] soda siphon.

sífilis ['sifiliʃ] *f inv* syphilis.

sifilítico, ca [sifi'litʃiku, ka] <> *adj* syphilitic. <> *m, f* syphilitic.

sifões [si'fõjʃ] *pl* ➡ **sifão**.

sigilo [si'ʒilu] *m* secrecy; ~ **bancário** bank confidentiality.

sigiloso, osa [siʒi'lozu, ɔza] *adj* secret.

sigla ['sigla] *f* -1. [abreviatura] acronym. -2. [sinal] initial.

signatário, ria [signa'tarju, rja] *m, f* signatory.

significação [signifika'sãw] *f* -1. [significado] meaning. -2. [importância] significance.

significado [signifi'kadu, da] *m* -1. [sentido] meaning. -2. LING signified.

significante [signifi'kãntʃi] *adj* -1. [significativo] significant. -2. LING signifying.

significar [12] [signifi'ka(x)] <> *vt* -1. [ger] to mean. -2. [indicar] to signify. <> *vi* [ter importância] to mean.

significativo, va [signifika'tʃivu, va] *adj* significant.

signo ['signu] *m* sign; ~ **do zodíaco** sign of the zodiac, star sign.

sílaba ['silaba] *f* syllable.

silenciador [silẽnsja'do(x)] *m* [de arma] silencer.

silenciar [16] [silẽn'sja(x)] <> *vt* -1. [calar] to silence. -2. [omitir] to conceal. <> *vi* -1. [calar-se] to be quiet. -**2.** [omitir-se]: ~ **sobre** to keep quiet about.

silêncio [si'lẽsju] *m* silence; **ficar em** ~ to remain silent.

silencioso, osa [silẽ'sjozu, ɔza] *adj* silent.

silhueta [si'ʎweta] *f* -**1.** [ger] silhouette. -**2.** [corpo] outline.

silício [si'lisju] *m* silicon.

silicone [sili'koni] *m* silicone.

silo ['silu] *m* silo.

silvar [4] [siw'va(x)] *vi* -**1.** [ger] to hiss. -**2.** [vento] to whistle.

silvestre [siw'vɛʃtri] *adj* wild.

silvícola [siw'vikola] *mf* forest dweller.

silvo ['siwvu] *m* -**1.** [ger] hiss. -**2.** [ventania] whistle.

sim ['sĩ] <> *adv* yes; **acho** *ou* **creio que** ~ I think *ou* believe so; **dizer que** ~ to say yes; **pelo** ~, **pelo não** just in case; **quero**, ~ yes, I'd like to; **vou**, ~ yes, I'm going. <> *m*: **dar o** ~ to consent.

simbiose [sĩ'bjɔzi] *f* symbiosis.

simbiótico, ca [sĩbi'ɔtiku, ca] *adj* symbiotic.

simbólico, ca [sĩ'bɔliku, ka] *adj* symbolic.

simbolismo [sĩbo'liʒmu] *m* -**1.** [representação] symbolism. -**2.** ARTE & LITER Symbolism.

simbolizar [4] [sĩboli'za(x)] *vt* to symbolize.

símbolo ['sĩbolu] *m* -**1.** [ger] symbol. -**2.** [insígnia] emblem.

simbologia [sĩbolo'ʒia] *f* symbology.

simetria [sime'tria] *f* symmetry.

simétrico, ca [si'mɛtriku, ka] *adj* symmetrical.

similar [simi'la(x)] (*pl* -**es**) *adj*: ~ **(a)** similar (to).

similaridade [similari'dadʒi] *f* similarity.

símile ['simili] *m* -**1.** [de objeto] copy. -**2.** [de palavra] analogy, simile.

similitude [simili'tudʒi] *f* similitude.

simpatia [sĩpa'tʃia] *f* -**1.** [qualidade] warmth. -**2.** [atração - por outrem, lugar] liking; **sentir** ~ **por alguém** to like sb. -**3.** [pessoa]: **ser uma** ~ to be friendly. -**4.** [solidariedade] sympathy. -**5.** [espirit] charm.

simpático, ca [sĩ'patʃiku, ka] *adj* -**1.** [pessoa - atraente] pleasant; [- amável] nice. -**2.** [agradável] pleasant. -**3.** [favorável]: ~ **a algo/alguém** favourable towards sthg/sb. -**4.** ANAT sympathetic.

simpatizante [sĩpatʃi'zãntʃi] *adj*: ~ **com** sympathetic towards.

simpatizar [4] [sĩpatʃi'za(x)] *vi*: ~ **com alguém/algo** to like sb/sthg; ~ **com uma causa** to sympathize with a cause.

simples ['sĩpliʃ] <> *adj* -**1.** [ger] simple. -**2.** (*antes de subst*) [mero] mere; [único] single. <> *adv* simply.

simplesmente [sĩpliʃ'mẽntʃi] *adv* simply.

simplicidade [sĩplisi'dadʒi] *f* simplicity.

simplificação [sĩplifika'sãw] *f* simplification.

simplificar [12] [sĩplifi'ka(x)] *vt* to simplify.

simplista [sĩ'pliʃta] *adj* simplistic.

simplório, ria [sĩ'plɔrju, rja] *adj* simple.

simpósio [sĩ'pɔzju] *m* symposium.

simulação [simula'sãw] (*pl* -**ões**) *f* -**1.** [de combate, salvamento] simulation. -**2.** [de sentimento, desmaio] pretence. -**3.** [de animal, voz] imitation.

simulacro [simu'lakru] *m* -**1.** [ger] pretence. -**2.** [de exame] mock. -**3.** [de bosque] imitation.

simulador [simula'do(x)] *m* simulator.

simular [4] [simu'la(x)] *vt* -**1.** [combate, salvamento] to simulate. -**2.** [sentimento, desmaio] to feign. -**3.** [animal, vozes] to imitate.

simultaneamente [simuwtãnja'mẽntʃi] *adv* simultaneously.

simultâneo, nea [simuw'tãnju, nja] *adj*: ~ **(a** *ou* **com)** simultaneous (with).

sina ['sina] *f* fate.

sinagoga [sina'gɔga] *f* synagogue.

Sinai [si'naj] *n*: o ~ Sinai.

sinal [si'naw] (*pl* -**ais**) *m* -**1.** [ger] sign; **fazer um** ~ **(para alguém)** to signal (to sb); **dar** ~ **de vida** to give sign of life; **em** ~ **de** as a sign of. -**2.** [símbolo] signal; ~ **de pontuação** punctuation mark; ~ **de mais/menos** plus/minus sign. -**3.** [aviso]: **dar o** ~ ESP [para partida] to give the off; ~ **de alarme** alarm bell. -**4.** TELEC tone; ~ **de chamada** ringing tone; ~ **de discar** dialling tone; **dar** ~ **(de discar)** to give the (dialling) tone; **dar** ~ **de ocupado** to give the engaged tone. -**5.** AUTO: ~ **(luminoso de tráfego)** traffic lights (*pl*); ~ **verde** green light; **avançar o** ~ to jump the lights. -**6.** [pinta] mole; [de nascença] birthmark. -**7.** COM deposit; **de** ~ as a deposit.

➥ **por sinal** *loc adv* -**1.** [a propósito] by the way. -**2.** [aliás] besides.

sinal-da-cruz [si,nawda'kruʒ] (*pl* sinais-da-cruz) *m* sign of the cross.

sinaleiro [sina'lejru] *m* NÁUT signalman.

sinalização [sinaliza'sãw] *f* -**1.** [sinais de tráfego - AUTO] traffic signs (*pl*); [- FERRO] signals (*pl*). -**2.** [indicação em estrada *etc*] road sign.

sinalizar [4] [sinali'za(x)] <> *vt* [avenida, estrada] to signpost. <> *vi* [pessoa] to signal.

sinceramente [sĩsera'mẽntʃi] *adv* sincerely.

sinceridade [sĩseri'dadʒi] *f* sincerity; **com toda** ~ in all sincerity.

sincero, ra [sĩ'sɛru, ra] *adj* sincere.

sincopado, da [sĩko'padu, da] *adj* MÚS syncopated.

síncope ['sĩkopi] *f* MED syncope.

sincronia [sĩkro'nia] *f* synchrony.

sincronizar [4] [sĩkroni'za(x)] *vt* -**1.** [combinar] to synchronize. -**2.** CINE to sync.

sindical [sĩdʒi'kaw] (*pl* -**ais**) *adj* trade union (*antes de subst*).

sindicalismo [sĩdʒika'liʒmu] *m* trade unionism.

sindicalista [sĩdʒika'liʃta] <> *adj* trade union (*antes de subst*). <> *mf* trade unionist.

sindicalizado, da [sĩdʒikali'zadu, da] *adj* unionized.

sindicalizar-se [4] [sĩdʒikali'zaxsi] *vp* to join a trade union.

sindicância [sĩdʒi'kãnsja] f[inquérito]: ~ **(de/so-bre)** enquiry (into).

sindicato [sĩdʒi'katu] m -**1.** [de profissionais] trade union. -**2.** [financeiro] syndicate.

síndico, ca ['sĩdʒiku, ka] m,f -**1.** [de prédio] residents' representative. -**2.** [de falência] receiver. -**3.** [de inquérito] leader.

síndrome ['sĩdromi] f syndrome; ~ **de absti-nência** withdrawal symptoms (pl).

sinecura [sine'kura] f sinecure.

sineta [si'neta] f small bell.

sinfonia [sĩfo'nia] f symphony.

sinfônico, ca [sĩ'foniku, ka] adj symphonic.

➡ **sinfônica** f [orquestra] symphonic orchestra.

singeleza [sĩʒe'leza] f simplicity.

singelo, la [sĩ'ʒɛlu, la] adj simple.

singular [sĩgu'la(x)] (pl -es) ⟷ adj -**1.** [ger] singular. -**2.** [peculiar] strange. ⟷ m GRAM singular.

singularidade [sĩgulari'dadʒi] f -**1.** [raridade] singularity. -**2.** [peculiaridade] oddness.

singularizar [4] [sĩgulari'za(x)] vt -**1.** [distinguir] to single out. -**2.** [detalhar] to list.

➡ **singularizar-se** vp [distinguir-se] to distin-guish o.s.

sinistro, tra [si'niʃtru, tra] adj sinister.

➡ **sinistro** m -**1.** [acidente] disaster. -**2.** [dano] damage.

sino ['sinu] m bell.

sinônimo, ma [si'nonimu, ma] adj synonymous.

➡ **sinônimo** m synonym.

sinopse [si'nɔpsi] f synopsis.

sintagma [sĩ'tagma] m syntagma.

sintático, ca [sĩ'tatʃiku, ka] adj syntactic.

sintaxe [sĩ'tasi] f syntax.

síntese ['sĩtezi] f -**1.** [ger] synthesis. -**2.** [resumo] summary; **em** ~ in short.

sintético, ca [sĩ'tɛtʃiku, ka] adj -**1.** [artificial] synthetic. -**2.** [conciso] concise.

sintetizador [sĩtetʃiza'do(x)] m synthesizer.

sintetizar [4] [sĩtetʃi'za(x)] vt -**1.** [resumir] to summarize. -**2.** QUÍM to synthesize.

sintoma [sĩ'toma] m -**1.** MED symptom. -**2.** fig [indício] sign.

sintomático, ca [sĩto'matʃiku, ka] adj sympto-matic.

sintonia [sĩto'nia] f -**1.** ELETRON tuning. -**2.** fig [entrosamento] harmony.

sintonizador [sĩtoniza'do(x)] m tuner.

sintonizar [4] [sĩtoni'za(x)] ⟷ vt ELETRON to tune. ⟷ vi -**1.** ELETRON: ~ **com** to tune into. -**2.** fig [en-trosar-se]: ~ **(com)** to harmonise (with).

➡ **sintonizar-se** vp [harmonizar-se]: ~ **com** to be in tune with.

sinuca [si'nuka] f -**1.** ESP snooker. -**2.** [situação difí-cil]: **estar numa** ~ **(de bico)** to be snookered.

sinuosidade [sinwozi'dadʒi] f [tortuosidade]: **a** ~ **da estrada** the twistiness of the road.

sinuoso, osa [si'nwozu, ɔza] adj -**1.** [linha] wavy. -**2.** [estrada, rio] meandering. -**3.** [recorte] wavy.

sinusite [sinu'zitʃi] f sinusitis.

sionismo [sjo'niʒmu] m Zionism.

sionista [sjo'niʃta] ⟷ adj Zionist. ⟷ mf Zionist.

sirene [si'reni] f siren.

siri [si'ri] m crab; **casquinha de** ~ CULIN stuffed crab shells.

Síria ['sirja] n Syria.

sirigaita [siri'gajta] f fam shrew.

sírio, ria ['sirju, rja] ⟷ adj Syrian. ⟷ m, f Syrian.

sísmico, ca ['siʒmiku, ka] adj seismic.

sismógrafo [siʒ'mɔgraful m seismograph.

siso ['sizul m -**1.** [juízo] wisdom. -**2.** [dente]: **(dente de)** ~ wisdom tooth.

sistema [siʃ'tema] m -**1.** [ger] system; ~ **nervoso** nervous system; ~ **solar** solar system; ~ **fiscal** tax system; ~ **operacional** COMPUT operating system. -**2.** [maneira] method.

sistemática [siʃte'matʃika] f -**1.** [sistematização] systematization. -**2.** [ciência] systematics (sg).

sistemático, ca [siʃte'matʃiku, ka] adj systema-tic.

sistematização [siʃte'matʃiza'sãw] (pl -ões) f systematization.

sistematizar [4] [siʃtematʃi'za(x)] vt to system-atize.

sisudo, da [si'zudu, da] adj wise.

site ['sajtʃi] (pl -s) m COMPUT site.

sitiante [si'tʃiãntʃi] mf settler.

sitiar [16] [si'tʃja(x)] vt -**1.** [cercar] to besiege. -**2.** [assediar] to harrass.

sítio ['sitʃju] m -**1.** [propriedade] farm. -**2.** MIL siege; **estado de** ~ state of siege; **em estado de** ~ under siege.

situação [sitwa'sãw] (pl -ões) f -**1.** [ger] situation. -**2.** [localização] position.

situacionista [sitwasjo'niʃta] ⟷ adj ruling party. ⟷ mf member of the ruling party.

situado, da [si'twadu, da] adj situated; **estar** OU **ficar** ~ to be situated.

situar [4] [si'twa(x)] vt to place.

➡ **situar-se** vp -**1.** [localizar-se - casa, filme] to be located; [- pessoa] to place o.s.; **tenho que me** ~ **para saber que rua seguir** I have to get my bearings in order to know which street to take. -**2.** [classificar-se] to be placed. -**3.** [em assunto, questão] to take a position.

skate [iʃ'kejtʃi] m -**1.** [esporte] skateboarding. -**2.** [prancha] skateboard.

slide [iʒ'lajdʒi] m slide, transparency.

slogan [iʒ'logãn] m slogan.

smart card [iʒimaxtʃi'kaxdʒi] (pl smart cards) m COMPUT smart card.

smoking [iʒ'mokĩŋ] m dinner jacket.

SNI (abrev de **Serviço Nacional de Informações**) m Brazilian information service concerned parti-cularly with state security, ≃ MI5 UK, ≃ CIA US.

só ['sɔ] ⟷ adj -**1.** [sozinho] alone; **a** ~**s** alone. -**2.** [solitário] lonely. -**3.** [único] single. ⟷ adv [so-mente] only; **é** ~**?** is that all?; **é** ~**!** that's all!

SO (abrev de **Sudoeste**) m SW.

soalho ['swaʎu] *m* = **assoalho**.
soar [20] ['swa(x)] ⟨⟩ *vi* -**1**. [ger] to sound; ~ **a algo (a alguém)** to sound like sthg (to s.o.). -**2**. [ser pronunciado] to be voiced. -**3**. [hora] to strike. ⟨⟩ *vt* [suj: horas] to strike.
sob ['sobi] *prep* under; ~ **esse aspecto** from that perspective.
soberania [sobera'nia] *f* -**1**. [de nação] sovereignty. -**2**. *fig* [superioridade] supremacy.
soberano, na [sobe'rãnu, na] ⟨⟩ *adj* -**1**. [independente] sovereign. -**2**. [poderoso] powerful. -**3**. [supremo] supreme. -**4**. [altivo] haughty. ⟨⟩ *m, f* [monarca] sovereign.
soberba [so'bexba] *f* [altivez] arrogance.
soberbo, ba [so'bexbu, ba] *adj* -**1**. [arrogante] arrogant. -**2**. [magnífico] magnificent.
sobra ['sɔbra] *f* leftover; **dar de** ~ to be more than enough; **ter algo de** ~ to have sthg spare.
➻ **sobras** *fpl* leftovers.
sobraçar [13] [sobra'sa(x)] *vt* to carry under one's arm.
sobrado [so'bradu] *m* floor.
sobranceiro, ra [sobrãn'sejru, ra] *adj* -**1**. [que está acima]: ~ **a** above. -**2**. [arrogante] supercilious.
sobrancelha [sobrãn'seʎa] *f* eyebrow.
sobrar [4] [so'bra(x)] *vi* -**1**. [ger]: ~ to be left over; **me sobra tempo para ir ao cinema** I have some free time to go to the cinema; **o médico examinou duas crianças, sobrou uma** the doctor examined two children, there was one still left; **isso dá e sobra** that is more than enough. -**2**. [ficar de fora] to be left out.
sobre ['sobri] *prep* -**1**. [ger] on. -**2**. [por cima de] over. -**3**. [a respeito de] about.
sobreaviso [sobrja'vizu] *m*: **estar/ficar de** ~ to be on the alert.
sobrecapa [sobre'kapa] *f* dust jacket.
sobrecarga [sobre'kaxga] *f* overload.
sobrecarregar [4] [sobrekaxe'ga(x)] *vt* -**1**. [com carga] to overload. -**2**. [pessoa] to overburden.
sobre-humano, na [sobrju'mãnu, na] (*mpl* -**s**, *fpl* -**s**) *adj* superhuman.
sobreloja [sobre'lɔʒa] *f* mezzanine.
sobremaneira [sobrema'nejra] *adv* excessively.
sobremesa [sobre'meza] *f* dessert; **de** ~ for dessert.
sobrenatural [ˌsobrenatu'rawl] (*pl* -**ais**) *adj* supernatural.
sobrenome [ˌsobri'nɔmi] *m* surname.
sobrepor [45] [sobre'po(x)] *vt* -**1**. [pôr em cima]: ~ **algo a algo** to put sthg on top of sthg. -**2**. *fig* [antepor]: ~ **algo a algo** to put sthg before sthg.
➻ **sobrepor-se** *vp* -**1**. [pôr-se em cima] to be put on top. -**2**. *fig* [antepor-se] to come before. -**3**. *fig* [a críticas] to overcome.
sobreposição [ˌsobrepozi'sãw] (*pl* -**ões**) *f* [de objetos] superimposition.
sobreposto, ta [sobre'poʃtu, ta] ⟨⟩ *pp* ▷ **sobrepor**. ⟨⟩ *adj* [posto em cima]: ~ **a** placed on top of.

sobrepujar [4] [sobrepu'ʒa(x)] *vt* -**1**. [ger] to overcome. -**2**. [ser superior a]: ~ **algo/alguém (em algo)** to outdo sthg/s.o. (in sthg).
sobrescrito [ˌsobreʃ'kritu] *m* address.
sobressair [68] [sobresa'i(x)] *vi* to stand out.
➻ **sobressair-se** *vp* to stand out.
sobressalente [sobresa'lẽntʃi] ⟨⟩ *adj* spare. ⟨⟩ *m* spare.
sobressaltado, da [sobresaw'tadu, da] *adj* -**1**. [assustado] startled; **acordar** ~ to wake up with a start. -**2**. [apreensivo] worried.
sobressaltar [4] [sobresaw'ta(x)] *vt* -**1**. [assustar] to startle. -**2**. [inquietar] to worry.
➻ **sobressaltar-se** *vp* -**1**. [assustar-se] to be startled. -**2**. [inquietar-se] to worry.
sobressalto [sobre'sawtu] *m* -**1**. [ger] start. -**2**. [inquietação] concern.
sobretaxa [ˌsobre'taʃa] *f* surcharge.
sobretudo [sobre'tudu] ⟨⟩ *m* overcoat. ⟨⟩ *adv* especially.
sobrevida [sobre'vida] *f*: **após o transplante, teve uma** ~ **de dez anos** after the transplant, he survived for another ten years.
sobrevir [67] [sobre'vi(x)] *vi*: ~ **(a algo)** to survive (sthg).
sobrevivência [sobrevi'vẽnsja] *f*: ~ **(a)** survival (from).
sobrevivente [sobrevi'vẽntʃi] ⟨⟩ *adj* surviving. ⟨⟩ *mf* survivor.
sobreviver [5] [sobrevi've(x)] *vi*: ~ **(a algo/alguém)** to survive (sthg/s.o.).
sobrevoar [20] [sobre'vwa(x)] *vt* to fly over.
sobrevôo [sobre'vow] *m* overflying.
sobriedade [sobrje'dadʒi] *f* -**1**. [moderação] moderation. -**2**. [ausência de embriaguez] sobriety.
sobrinho, nha [so'briɲu, ɲa] *m, f* nephew (*f* niece).
sóbrio, bria ['sɔbrju, brja] *adj* -**1**. [ger] sober. -**2**. [moderado]: ~ **(em)** moderate (in).
socado, da [so'kadu, da] *adj* -**1**. [esmagado] crushed. -**2**. [metido] stuck. -**3**. [pessoa] squat.
socador [soka'do(x)] *m* pestle; ~ **de alho** garlic crusher.
soçaite [so'sajtʃi] *m fam* high society.
socar [12] [so'ka(x)] *vt* -**1**. [dar socos em] to punch. -**2**. [esmagar] to crush. -**3**. [calcar] to grind. -**4**. [amassar] to knead. -**5**. [meter] to chuck.
sociabilidade [sosjabili'dadʒi] *f* sociability.
sociabilizar [4] [sosjabili'za(x)] *vt* to socialize.
social [so'sjaw] (*pl* -**ais**) *adj* -**1**. [ger] social. -**2**. [relativo a sócios] members' *(antes de subst)*. -**3**. [via de acesso] front *(antes de subst)*. -**4**. [banheiro] guest *(antes de subst)*. -**5**. [camisa] dress. -**6**. *COM*: **razão** ~ trade name.
➻ **sociais** *fpl* [em hipódromo *etc* - área] members' enclosure; [- cadeiras] members' seats.
socialdemocracia [soˌsjawdemokra'sia] *f* social democracy.
socialdemocrata [soˌsjawdemo'krata] ⟨⟩ *adj* social democratic. ⟨⟩ *mf* social democrat.
socialismo [sosja'liʒmu] *m* socialism.

socialista [sosjaˈliʃta] <> *adj* socialist. <> *mf* socialist.

socialite [sosjaˈlajtʃil *mf* socialite.

socializar [4] [sosjaliˈza(x)] *vt* to socialize.

sociável [soˈsjavew] (*pl* -**eis**) *adj* sociable.

sociedade [sosjeˈdadʒi] *f* -**1**. [ger] society; ~ **de consumo** consumer society; **a alta** ~ high society; **uma mulher da** ~ a woman of the world; **Sociedade Protetora dos Animais** *society for the protection of animals*, ≃ RSPCA *UK*. -**2**. [COM-empresa] company; [- entre sócios] partnership; ~ **anônima** limited company; ~ (**de responsabilidade**) **limitada** limited (liability) company. -**3**. [parceria] patnership; **em** ~ **com** in partnership with.

sócio, cia [ˈsɔsju, sja] *m*, *f* -**1**. [ger] partner. -**2**. [membro] member.

sociocultural [ˈsɔsjokuwtuˈraw] (*pl* -**ais**) *adj* sociocultural.

sócio-econômico, ca [sosjoekoˈnomiku, ka] (*mpl* -**s**, *fpl* -**s**) *adj* socio-economic.

sociolingüística [ˌsɔsjoliŋˈgwiʃtʃikal *f* sociolinguistics (*sg*).

sociologia [sosjoloˈʒia] *f* sociology.

sociológico, ca [sosjoˈlɔʒiku, ka] *adj* sociological.

sociólogo, ga [soˈsjɔlogu, ga] *m*, *f* sociologist.

sóciopolítico, ca [sosjopoˈlitʃiku, ka] (*mpl* -**s**, *fpl* -**s**) *adj* socio-political.

soco [ˈsoku] *m* punch; **dar um** ~ **em algo/alguém** to punch sthg/sb.

soco-inglês [sokwĩˈgleʃ] (*pl* **socos-ingleses**) *m* knuckleduster.

socorrer [5] [sokoˈxe(x)] *vt* to rescue.

socorro [soˈkoxul *m* rescue; **equipe de** ~ rescue team; **pedir** ~ to ask for help; **socorro!** help!; **primeiros** ~**s** first aid (*sg*).

soda [ˈsɔda] *f* -**1**. [bebida] soda. -**2**. [substância]: ~ **cáustica** caustic soda.

sódio [ˈsɔdʒju] *m* sodium.

sodomia [sodoˈmia] *f* sodomy.

sodomizar [sodomiˈza(x)] *vt* to sodomize.

sofá [soˈfa] *m* sofa.

sofá-cama [soˌfaˈkama] (*pl* **sofás-camas**) *m* sofa bed.

Sófia [ˈsɔfja] *n* Sofia.

sofisma [soˈfiʒma] *m* -**1**. [em filosofia] sophism. -**2**. [falsidade] false statement.

sofista [soˈfiʃta] <> *adj* sophist. <> *mf* sophist.

sofisticação [sofiʃtʃikaˈsãw] (*pl* -**ões**) *f* -**1**. [requinte] sophistication. -**2**. [aprimoramento] refinement.

sofisticado, da [sofiʃtʃiˈkadu, da] *adj* -**1**. [requintado] sophisticated. -**2**. [aprimorado] fancy. -**3**. [afetado] refined.

sofisticar [12] [sofiʃtʃiˈka(x)] *vt* to refine.

sofredor, ra [sofreˈdo(x), ra] <> *adj* suffering. <> *m*, *f* [pessoa] sufferer.

sôfrego, ga [ˈsofregu, ga] *adj* -**1**. [ávido] eager. -**2**. [ao comer, beber] greedy. -**3**. [impaciente] impatient; **o pai aguardava** ~ **notícias sobre o filho** the father waited impatiently for news of his son.

sofreguidão [sofregiˈdãw] *f* -**1**. [avidez] eagerness. -**2**. [ao comer, beber] greed. -**3**. [impaciência] impatience.

sofrer [5] [soˈfre(x)] <> *vt* -**1**. [ger] to suffer. -**2**. [suportar] to bear. -**3**. [receber] to undergo. <> *vi* [padecer] to suffer; ~ **de** MED to suffer from.

sofrido, da [soˈfridu, da] *adj* long-suffering.

sofrimento [sofriˈmẽntul *m* suffering.

sofrível [soˈfrivew] (*pl* -**eis**) *adj* bearable.

soft [ˈsoftʃil, **software** [sofˈtwe(x)] *m* COMPUT software.

sogro, gra [sogru, gra] *m*, *f* father-in-law (*f* mother-in-law).

sóis [sɔjʃ] *pl* [> **sol**.

soja [ˈsɔʒal *f* soya.

sol [ˈsow] (*pl* **sóis**) *m* -**1**. [ger] sun; **fazer** ~ to be sunny; ~ **a pino** mid-day sun; **tomar (banho de)** ~ to sunbathe; **ao** ~ in the sun; **tapar o** ~ **com a peneira** to hide the truth. -**2**. MÚS [nota] soh, sol.

sola [ˈsɔla] *f* -**1**. [de sapato] sole. -**2**. ANAT: ~ **do pé** sole of the foot. -**3**. *loc*: **entrar de** ~ FUT to make an illegal tackle; [com garra] to enter aggressively.

solado, da [soˈladu, da] *adj* flat.

➡ **solado** *m* [de calçado] sole.

solão [soˈlãw] *m* [sol quente] very hot sun.

solapar [4] [solaˈpa(x)] *vt* -**1**. [minar] to undermine. -**2**. [abalar] to shake. -**3**. *fig* [arruinar] destroy.

solar [4] [soˈla(x)] (*pl* -**es**) <> *adj* solar. <> *m* [moradia] manor house. <> *vt* [sapato] to sole. <> *vi* -**1**. [bolo] to fail to rise. -**2**. MÚS to perform a solo.

solavanco [solaˈvãŋku] *m* jolt.

solda [ˈsowda] *f* -**1**. [substância] solder. -**2**. [soldadura] weld.

soldado [sowˈdadu] *mf* -**1**. MIL soldier; ~ **de chumbo** tin soldier; ~ **raso** private (soldier). -**2**. [defensor] defender.

soldador, ra [sowdaˈdo(x), ra] *m*, *f* welder.

soldadura [sowdaˈdura] *f* -**1**. [ato] welding. -**2**. [junta] weld.

soldagem [sowˈdaʒẽl *f* welding.

soldar [4] [sowˈda(x)] *vt* to weld.

soldo [ˈsowdul *m* MIL pay.

soleira [soˈlejra] *f* -**1**. [de porta] threshold. -**2**. [de ponte] foundation.

solene [soˈleni] *adj* solemn.

solenemente [soleniˈmẽntʃil *adv* solemnly.

solenidade [soleniˈdadʒi] *f* -**1**. [qualidade] solemnity. -**2**. [cerimônia] ceremony.

soletrar [4] [soleˈtra(x)] *vt* -**1**. [letras] to spell. -**2**. [ler devagar] to read out slowly.

solicitação [solisitaˈsãw] (*pl* -**ões**) *f* [pedido] request.

➡ **solicitações** *fpl* [apelo] appeal (*sg*).

solicitar [4] [solisiˈta(x)] *vt* -**1**. [pedir] to request; ~ **algo a alguém** to ask sb for sthg. -**2**. [requerer] to apply for. -**3**. [atenção, amizade] to seek.

solícito, ta [soˈlisitu, ta] *adj* helpful.

solicitude [solisi'tudʒi] f -**1.** [zelo] care. -**2.** [boa-vontade] concern. -**3.** [empenho] commitment.

solidão [soli'dãw] f -**1.** [isolamento] solitude. -**2.** [ermo] desolation. -**3.** [sentimento] loneliness.

solidariedade [solidarje'dadʒi] f solidarity.

solidário, ria [soli'darju, rja] adj -**1.** [na dor] united; **mostrar-se** ~ to show one's solidarity; **ser** ~ **com** to stand by. -**2.** [simpático]: **ser** ~ **a** to be sympathetic to.

solidarizar-se [4] [solidari'zaxsi] vp: ~**-se com** to sympathise with.

solidez [soli'deʒ] f -**1.** [ger] strength. -**2.** [física] solidity. -**3.** [estabilidade] stability.

solidificar [12] [solidʒifi'ka(x)] vt -**1.** [fisicamente] to solidify. -**2.** fig [laços, amizade] to strengthen.

  ▸ **solidificar-se** vp -**1.** [fisicamente] to set. -**2.** fig [laços, amizade] to become strong.

sólido, da ['sɔlidu, da] adj -**1.** [ger] solid. -**2.** [moralmente] strong. -**3.** fig [firme - ger] strong; [- conhecimento] firm; [- argumento] sound.

  ▸ **sólido** m MAT solid.

solilóquio [soli'lɔkju] m soliloquy.

solista [so'liʃta] m MÚS soloist.

solitário, ria [soli'tarju, rja] <> adj solitary. <> m, f [eremita] solitary person.

  ▸ **solitário** m [diamante] solitaire.

  ▸ **solitária** f -**1.** [cela] solitary (confinement) cell. -**2.** [verme] tapeworm.

solo ['sɔlu] m -**1.** [chão] ground. -**2.** MÚS solo.

solstício [sowʃ'tʃisju] m ASTRON solstice; ~ **de inverno/verão** winter/summer solstice.

soltar [4] [sow'ta(x)] vt -**1.** [libertar] to release; ~ **os cachorros** fig to lash out. -**2.** [desatar] to untie. -**3.** [afrouxar] to loosen. -**4.** [largar] to let go. -**5.** [deixar cair (das mãos)] to drop. -**6.** [emitir] to let out. -**7.** [pronunciar] to utter; ~ **um palavrão** to swear; ~ **o verbo** fig to blow one's top. -**8.** [lançar] to let off; ~ **pipa** to fly a kite.

  ▸ **soltar-se** vp [desprender-se]: ~**-se (de algo)** to free o.s. (from sthg).

solteira [sow'tejra] f ⊳ **solteiro**.

solteirão, rona [sowtej'rãw, rona] (mpl **-ões**, fpl **-s**) m, f bachelor (f spinster).

solteiro, ra [sow'tejru, ra] adj unmarried, single.

solteirona [sowtej'rona] f ⊳ **solteirão**.

solto, ta ['sowtu, ta] <> pp ⊳ **soltar**. <> adj [ger] loose; **ter a língua solta** fam fig to have a loose tongue.

  ▸ **à solta** loc adv on the loose.

soltura [sow'tura] f -**1.** [libertação] release. -**2.** [desregramento] looseness.

solução [solu'sãw] (pl **-ões**) f solution; ~ **de continuidade** interruption; **sem** ~ **de continuidade** without interruption.

soluçar [13] [solu'sa(x)] vi -**1.** [chorar] to sob. -**2.** MED to hiccup.

solucionar [13] [solusjo'na(x)] vt to resolve.

soluço [su'lusu] m -**1.** [choro] sob; **aos** ~**s** sobbing. -**2.** MED hiccup.

solúvel [so'luvɛw] (pl **-eis**) adj soluble.

solvência [sow'vẽsja] f -**1.** FIN [de dívida] solvency. -**2.** [dissolução] solubility.

solvente [sow'vẽtʃi] <> adj -**1.** [substância] soluble. -**2.** FIN [devedor] solvent. <> m [substância] solvent.

solver [5] [sow've(x)] vt -**1.** FIN [dívida] to pay. -**2.** [dissolver] to dissolve.

som ['sõ] (pl **-ns**) m -**1.** [ger] sound; **fazer um** ~ fam to make music; **ao** ~ **de** to the sound of. -**2.** [aparelho] hi-fi.

soma ['soma] f -**1.** [ger] sum. -**2.** fig [conjunto] combination.

Somália [so'malja] n Somalia.

somar [4] [so'ma(x)] <> vt -**1.** [adicionar] to add; ~ **algo a algo** to add sthg to sthg. -**2.** [totalizar] to add up to. <> vi to add (up).

  ▸ **somar-se** vp to gather together.

somatório [soma'tɔrju] m -**1.** [soma] sum total. -**2.** fig [total] total. -**3.** fig [conjunto] series.

sombra ['sõbra] f -**1.** [projeção] shadow; **fazer** ~ **a alguém** fig to put sb in the shade; **ser a** ~ **de alguém** fig to shadow sb. -**2.** [área] shade; **à** ~ **de** in the shade of; fig [sob a proteção de] under the protection of; **querer** ~ **e água fresca** fig to want an easy life. -**3.** fig [sinal] shadow; **sem** ~ **de dúvida** without a shadow of a doubt. -**4.** fig [anonimato] in the shade.

sombreado, da [sõ'brjadu, da] adj shaded.

  ▸ **sombreado** m ARTE shading.

sombrear [15] [sõ'brja(x)] <> vt [com sombra] to shade; **a nuvem sombreou a praia** the cloud cast a shadow over the beach. <> vi ARTE to shade (in).

sombreiro [sõ'brejru] m hat.

sombrinha [sõ'brijna] f umbrella.

sombrio, bria [sõ'briw, bria] adj -**1.** [escuro] dark. -**2.** [triste] gloomy. -**3.** [carrancudo] grim.

somente [sɔ'mẽtʃi] adv only.

sonambulismo [sonãbu'liʒmu] m sleepwalking.

sonâmbulo, la [so'nãbulu, la] <> adj sleepwalking. <> m, f sleepwalker.

sonata [so'nata] f sonata.

sonda ['sõda] f -**1.** MED probe. -**2.** MED [de alimentação] drip. -**3.** NÁUT depth finder. -**4.** TEC [para mineiração] bore. -**5.** TEC [petrolífera] drill. -**6.** METEOR weather balloon.

  ▸ **sonda espacial** f space probe.

sondagem [sõ'daʒẽ] (pl **-ns**) f -**1.** [com sonda - biliar] exploration; [- marítima, meteorológica] sounding; [- petrolífera] drilling. -**2.** [de opinião] survey.

sondar [4] [sõ'da(x)] vt -**1.** [ger] to probe. -**2.** NÁUT to sound. -**3.** TEC [terreno] to bore. -**4.** TEC [petróleo] to drill. -**5.** METEOR [atmosfera] to take soundings of. -**6.** [opinião] to survey. -**7.** fig [investigar] to fathom.

soneca [so'nɛka] f nap; **tirar uma** ~ to take a nap.

sonegação [sonega'sãw] f -**1.** [ocultação] withholding; ~ **de impostos** ou fiscal tax evasion. -**2.** [roubo] theft.

sonegador, ra [sonega'do(x), ra] <> *adj* [de impostos] fraudulent. <> *m, f* [de impostos] tax dodger.

sonegar [14] [sone'ga(x)] *vt* -1. [dinheiro, bens] to conceal. -2. [impostos] to dodge. -3. [roubar] to steal. -4. [informações] to withhold.

soneto [so'netu] *m* sonnet.

sonhador, ra [soɲa'do(x), ra] (*mpl* -es, *fpl* -s) <> *adj* dreaming. <> *m, f* dreamer.

sonhar [4] [so'ɲa(x)] <> *vt* [ter sonho com] to dream. <> *vi* -1. [ter sonho] to dream; ~ **com algo/alguém** to dream about sthg/sb; **nem sonhando!** in your dreams!; ~ **acordado** to daydream. -2. [desejar]: ~ **com algo** to dream of sthg; ~ **em fazer algo** to dream of doing sthg.

sonho ['soɲu] *m* -1. [ger] dream. -2. CULIN doughnut.

sono ['sonu] *m* -1. [período] sleep; ~ **leve/pesado** light sleep/heavy sleep; **pegar no** ~ to fall asleep. -2. [vontade de dormir]: **estar caindo** *ou* **morrendo de** ~ to be dead on one's feet; **estar com** *ou* **sentir** ~ to be *ou* feel sleepy; **estar sem** ~ not to be sleepy.

sonolência [sono'lẽnsja] *f* drowsiness.

sonolento, ta [sono'lẽntu, ta] *adj* sleepy.

sonoridade [sonori'dadʒi] *f* -1. [timbre, altura] sound quality. -2. [ressonância] resonance.

sonorizar [sonori'za(x)] *vt* -1. [filme] to make the soundtrack for. -2. [sala] to set up the sound for.

sonoro, ra [so'noru, ra] *adj* -1. [de som] resonant. -2. GRAM voiced.

sonoterapia [sonotera'pia] *f* sleep therapy.

sons [sõʃ] *pl* ▷ **som**.

sonso, sa ['sõsu, sa] *adj* sly.

sopa ['sopa] *f* -1. CULIN soup; ~ **de lentilhas** lentil soup. -2. *fam* [facilidade] easy life; **ser** ~ to be a piece of cake. -3. *loc:* **dar** ~ [descuidar-se] to be careless; [estar disponível] to be going spare; [abundar] to be in abundance.

sopapo [so'papu] *m* slap; **dar um** ~ **em alguém** to slap sb.

sopé [so'pɛ] *m* foot.

sopeira [so'pejra] *f* (soup) tureen.

soporífero, ra [sopo'riferu, ra] *adj* -1. [que faz dormir] soporific. -2. *fig* [chato] boring.

▶ **soporífero** *m* [substância] soporific.

soporífico [sopo'rifiku] = **soporífero**

soprano [so'prãnu] <> *adj* soprano (*antes de subst*). <> *mf* soprano.

soprar [4] [so'pra(x)] <> *vt* -1. [com sopro] to blow. -2. *fig* [segredar] to whisper. <> *vi* [vento] to blow.

sopro ['sopru] *m* -1. [ar] puff. -2. [som - de vento] sigh; [- de fole] puff; [- de saxofone] soft sound; **instrumento de** ~ wind instrument. -3. [aragem] breeze. -4. *fig* [ânimo] breath. -5. MED murmur; ~ **cardíaco** heart murmur.

soquete [so'kɛtʃi] *f* [meia] ankle sock.

sordidez [soxdʒi'deʒ] *f* -1. [imundície] squalor. -2. [torpeza] sordidness.

sórdido, da ['sɔrdʒidu, da] *adj* -1. [imundo] squalid. -2. [torpe] sordid.

soro ['soru] *m* -1. MED serum. -2. [de leite] whey.

soropositivo, va [soropozi'tʃivu, va] <> *adj* seropositive. <> *m, f* seropositive person.

sóror ['soro(x)] *f* RELIG sister.

sorrateiramente [soxatejra'mẽntʃi] *adv* stealthily.

sorrateiro, ra [soxa'tejru, ra] *adj* stealthy.

sorridente [soxi'dẽntʃi] *adj* smiling.

sorrir [69] [so'xi(x)] *vi* to smile; ~ **(para)** to smile (at); [destino, fortuna *etc*] to smile on.

sorriso [so'xizu] *m* smile; **dar um** ~ **(para alguém)** to smile (at sb); ~ **amarelo** wry smile.

sorte ['sɔxtʃi] *f* -1. [ventura] luck; **boa** ~! good luck!; **dar** ~ [ter sorte] to be lucky; **dar** ~ **(para alguém)** to bring (sb) luck; **estar com** *ou* **ter** ~ to be lucky; **má** ~ bad luck; **que** ~! what luck!; **de** ~ [sortudo] lucky; **tirar a** ~ to draw lots; **tirar a** ~ **grande** [na loteria] to hit the jackpot; [enriquecer] to become rich; [ser afortunado] to do the right thing. -2. [acaso] chance; **tentar a** ~ to try one's luck; **por** ~ by chance. -3. [sina] fate. -4. [situação] lot. -5. [maneira]: **desta** ~ in this way; **de** ~ **que** in such a way that. -6. [espécie] sort; **toda** ~ **de iguarias** all sorts of delicacies.

sorteado, da [sox'tʃjadu, da] *adj* winning.

sortear [15] [sox'tʃja(x)] *vt* -1. [pessoa, bilhete] to draw lots for. -2. [rifar] to raffle.

sorteio [sox'teju] *m* -1. [de pessoa, bilhete] draw. -2. [rifa] raffle.

sortido, da [sox'tʃidu, da] *adj* -1. [abastecido] stocked. -2. [variado] assorted.

sortilégio [soxtʃi'lɛʒu] *m* -1. [bruxaria] sorcery. -2. [encantamento] enchantment.

sortimento [soxtʃi'mẽntu] *m* [provisão] stock.

sortir [60] [sox'tʃi(x)] *vt* -1. [abastecer]: ~ **algo com** *ou* **de** to supply sthg with. -2. [variar] to vary.

▶ **sortir-se** *vp* [abastecer-se]: ~**-se com** *ou* **de** to supply o.s. with.

sortudo, da [sox'tudu, da] <> *adj* lucky. <> *m, f* lucky person.

sorumbático, ca [sorũn'batʃiku, ka] *adj* gloomy.

sorvedouro [soxve'doru] *m* -1. [redemoinho] whirlpool; ~ **de dinheiro** *fig* a drain on resources. -2. [abismo] chasm.

sorver [5] [sox've(x)] *vt* -1. [ger] to inhale. -2. [beber] to sip. -3. [absorver] to absorb.

sorvete [sox'vetʃi] *m* -1. [com leite] ice cream. -2. [sem leite] sorbet.

sorveteiro, ra [soxve'tejru, ra] *m, f* ice-cream man.

sorveteria [soxvete'ria] *f* ice-cream parlour.

sósia ['sɔzja] *mf* double.

soslaio [soʒ'laju] ▶ **de soslaio** *loc adv* sideways.

sossegado, da [sose'gadu, da] *adj* quiet.

sossegar [14] [sose'ga(x)] *vt & vi* to calm down.

sossego [so'segu] *m* peace (and quiet).

sotaina [so'tãjna] *f* cassock.

sótão ['sɔtãw] (*pl* -ãos) *m* attic.

sotaque [so'taki] *m* accent.

sotavento [sɔta'vẽntu] *m* NÁUT lee; **a** ~ leeward.

soterrar [4] [sote'xa(x)] *vt* to bury.

soturno, na [so'tuxnu, na] *adj* -**1**. [triste] sad. -**2**. [amedrontador] frightening.

soutien [su'tʃjã] *m* = sutiã.

sova ['sɔva] *f* -**1**. [amassamento - uva, cacau] crushing; [- de massa] keading. -**2**. [surra] beating; **dar uma ~ em alguém** to beat sb up; **levar uma ~ (de alguém)** to take a beating (from sb).

sovaco [so'vaku] *m* armpit.

sovado, da [so'vadu, da] *adj* -**1**. [trabalhado] kneaded. -**2**. [espancado] beaten. -**3**. [usado, fatigado] worn out.

sovar [4] [so'va(x)] *vt* -**1**. [amassar - uva, cacau] to crush; [- massa] to knead. -**2**. [surrar] to beat up. -**3**. *fig* [roupa, couro] to tan.

sovina [so'vina] <> *adj* miserly. <> *mf* miser.

sovinice [sovi'nisi] *f* meanness; **ser pura ~** to be utterly mean.

sozinho, nha [sɔ'ziɲu, ɲa] *adj* -**1**. [desacompanhado] alone. -**2**. [solitário] all alone. -**3**. [único] by itself. -**4**. [por si só] by myself/yourself/himself etc.

SP (*abrev de* Estado de São Paulo) *n* State of São Paulo.

spam ['ijpãm] (*pl* -**s**) *m COMPUT* spam.

SPC (*abrev de* Serviço de Proteção ao Crédito) *m* Brazilian service providing information on credit credit rating.

spot [iʃ'pɔtʃi] *m* spotlight.

spray [iʃ'prej] *m* spray.

SQL (*abrev de* Structured Query Language) *f* SQL.

Sr. (*abrev de* senhor) *m* ≃ Mr.

Sra. (*abrev de* senhora) *f* ≃ Mrs.

SRF (*abrev de* Secretaria da Receita Federal) *f* department of the Brazilian ministry of finance responsible for taxes and customs and excise.

Sri Lanka [ˌsri'lãŋka] *n* Sri Lanka.

Srs. (*abrev de* senhores) *mpl* Messrs, Mr and Mrs.

srta (*abrev de* senhorita) *f* ≃ Miss.

staff [iʃ'tafi] *m* staff.

standard [iʃ'tãndaxdʒi] *adj inv* standard.

status [iʃ'tatus] *m* status; **~ quo** status quo.

STF (*abrev de* Supremo Tribunal Federal) *m* Brazilian supreme federal tribunal responsible for the enforcement of the constitution and also heading the judiciary.

STJ (*abrev de* Superior Tribunal de Justiça) *m* Brazilian higher court of justice.

strip-tease [iʃˌtripi'tʃizil] *m* striptease; **fazer um ~** to do a striptease.

sua ['sua] > seu.

suado, da ['swadu, da] *adj* -**1**. [da suor] sweaty. -**2**. *fam fig* [difícil de obter] hard-earned.

suador, ra [swa'do(x), ra] *m* -**1**. [sudorífero] sudorific. -**2**. [dificuldade, esforço] sweat, hard job.

suar [4] ['swa(x)] <> *vt* -**1**. [transpirar] to sweat. -**2**. [roupa] to make sweaty. <> *vi* -**1**. [transpirar] to sweat; **~ em bicas** to sweat buckets; **~ frio** to come out in a cold sweat. -**2**. [verter umidade] to sweat. -**3**. *fam fig* [esforçar-se]: **~ por algo/para fazer algo** to sweat blood for sthg/to do sthg;

ela suou por esse emprego she had to work hard for that job.

suas ['suaʃ] > seu.

suástica ['swaʃtʃika] *f* swastika.

suave ['swavi] *adj* -**1**. [ger] mild. -**2**. [vinho, pele, cabelos] smooth. -**3**. [brisa, ritmo] gentle. -**4**. [cor] delicate. -**5**. [música, tecido] soft. -**6**. [terno - pessoa] charming; [- carícia] gentle; [- voz] soft. -**7**. [leve - trabalho] light; [- vida] easy; **em ~s prestações** in easy instalments.

suavidade [swavi'dadʒi] *f* -**1**. [ger] mildness. -**2**. [de pele, cabelos] smoothness. -**3**. [de brisa, música, ritmo] gentleness. -**4**. [de tecido, cor, brisa, música] softness. -**5**. [ternura] charm.

suavizar [4] [swavi'za(x)] *vt* -**1**. [abrandar] to tone down. -**2**. [amenizar] to ease. -**3**. [amaciar - pele, cabelo] to smooth; [- tecido] to soften.

 suavizar-se *vp* [amenizar-se] to ease.

subalimentado, da [subalimẽ'tadu, da] *adj* undernourished.

subalterno, na [subaw'tɛxnu, na] <> *adj* subordinate. <> *m, f* subordinate.

subchefe [sub'ʃɛfi] *mf* assistant director.

subconsciente [subkõn'sjẽtʃi] <> *adj* subconscious. <> *m* subconscious.

subcutâneo, nea [subku'tãnju, nja] *adj* subcutaneous.

subdesenvolvido, da [subdʒizĩnvow'vidu, da] <> *adj* -**1**. [não-desenvolvido] underdeveloped. -**2**. *pej* [atrasado] moronic. <> *m, f pej* [pessoa] moron.

subdesenvolvimento [subdizĩnvowvi'mẽtu] *m* underdevelopment.

subdividir [6] [subdʒivi'dʒi(x)] *vt*: **~ algo (em)** to subdivide sthg (into).

 subdividir-se *vp*: **~-se (em)** to be subdivided (into).

subemprego [subẽn'pregu] *m* -**1**. [trabalho] underpaid job. -**2**. [condição] underpaid work.

subentender [5] [subẽtẽn'de(x)] *vt* to infer.

 subentender-se *vp* to be inferred; **subentende-se que ...** it can be inferred that ...

subentendido, da [subẽtẽn'dʒidu, da] *adj* inferred.

 subentendido *m* innuendo.

subestimar [4] [subeʃtʃi'ma(x)] *vt* to underestimate.

subida [su'bida] *f* -**1**. [ato] climb. -**2**. [ladeira] slope. -**3**. [de preços] rise.

subir [61] [su'bi(x)] <> *vt* -**1**. [galgar] to climb (up). -**2**. [ir para cima, percorrer] to go up. -**3**. [escalar] to climb, to scale. -**4**. [aumentar] to raise. -**5**. [ascender] to climb. -**6**. [voz] to raise. <> *vi* -**1**. [ger] to go up; **~ a** *ou* **até** to go up to; **~ em** [árvore] to climb (up); [telhado, cadeira] to climb onto; **~ por** to go up; **~ à cabeça** *fig* to go to one's head. -**2**. [ascender - balão, neblina, fumaça] to rise; [- elevador, teleférico] to go up; [- em ônibus] to get on. -**3**. [socialmente] to go up in the world; **~ a/de** to rise from; **~ na vida** to get on in life. -**4**. [aumentar] to rise.

súbito, ta ['subitu, ta] *adj* sudden.
➤ **súbito** *adv* suddenly; **de** ~ suddenly.
subjacente [subʒa'sẽtʃi] *adj* underlying.
subjazer [subʒa'ze(x)] *vi*: **as tramas políticas que subjaziam** the underlying political plots.
subjetividade [subʒetʃivi'dadʒi] *f* subjectivity.
subjetivo, va [subʒɛ'tʃivu, va] *adj* subjective.
subjugar [14] [subʒu'ga(x)] *vt* -**1.** [derrotar] to overpower. -**2.** [dominar] to dominate. -**3.** [impor-se a] to supplant. -**4.** [moralmente] to subdue.
subjuntivo [subʒũn'tʃivu] *m* subjunctive.
sublevação [subleva'sãw] (*pl* -ões) *f* uprising.
sublevar [4] [suble'va(x)] *vt*: ~ **alguém (contra algo)** to stir up sb (against sthg).
➤ **sublevar-se** *vp*: ~-**se (contra algo)** to rebel (against sthg).
sublimação [sublima'sãw] (*pl* -ões) *f* -**1.** [engrandecimento] exaltation. -**2.** [de desejos] sublimation.
sublimar [4] [subli'ma(x)] *vt* -**1.** [engrandecer] to exalt. -**2.** [desejos] to sublimate.
sublime [su'blimi] *adj* sublime.
sublinhar [4] [subli'ɲa(x)] *vt* -**1.** [palavras] to underline. -**2.** [enfatizar] to emphasize.
sublocar [12] [sublo'ka(x)] *vt* to sublet.
sublocatário, ria [subloka'tarju, rja] *m, f* subtenant.
submarino, na [subma'rinu, na] *adj* underwater.
➤ **submarino** *m* submarine.
submergir [78] [submex'ʒi(x)] *vt & vi* to submerge.
submersão [submex'sãw] (*pl* -ões) *f* submersion.
submeter [5] [subme'te(x)] *vt* -**1.** [dominar] to subdue. -**2.** [para apreciação]: ~ **algo a** to submit sthg to. -**3.** [sujeitar]: ~ **alguém/algo a algo** to subject sb/sthg to sthg.
➤ **submeter-se** *vp* -**1.** [render-se] to surrender. -**2.** [sujeitar-se]: ~ **a algo** to undergo sthg; ~ **a alguém** to submit to sb.
submissão [submi'sãw] *f* -**1.** [sujeição, obediência] submission. -**2.** [apatia] lack of determination.
submisso, sa [sub'misu, sa] *adj* submissive.
submundo [sub'mũndu] *m* underworld.
subnutrição [subnutri'sãw] *f* malnutrition.
subnutrido, da [subnu'tridu, da] *adj* malnourished.
subordinado, da [suboxdʒi'nadu, da] <> *adj* subordinate. <> *m,f* [subalterno] subordinate.
subordinar [4] [suboxdʒi'na(x)] *vt* -**1.** [ger] to subordinate. -**2.** [sujeitar] to subject.
➤ **subordinar-se** *vp* [sujeitar-se]: ~-**se a algo/alguém** to subject o.s. to sthg/sb.
subornar [4] [subox'na(x)] *vt* to bribe.
suborno [su'boxnu] *m* bribe.
subproduto [subpro'dutu] *m* by-product.
sub-reptício, cia [subxrep'tʃisju, sja] *adj* surreptitious.
subscrever [5] [subʃkre've(x)] <> *vt* -**1.** [assinar] to sign. -**2.** [aprovar] to subscribe to. -**3.** [arrecadar] to collect. <> *vi* -**1.** [aceder]: ~ **a** to endorse *UK*, to indorse *US*. -**2.** [contribuir]: ~ **(com algo)**

para algo to contribute (sthg) to sthg.
➤ **subscrever-se** *vp* [assinar] to sign; **subscrevemo-nos** *fml* & *COM* we remain; **atenciosamente, subscrevemo-nos** *fml* & *COM* we remain, yours sincerely.
subscrição [subʃkri'sãw] (*pl* -ões) *f* -**1.** [ato de assinatura] signing. -**2.** [contribuição] contribution.
subscrito, ta [subʃ'kritu, ta] <> *pp* ▷ **subscrever**. <> *adj* undersigned. <> *m, f* undersigned.
subsecretário, ria [subsekre'tarju, rja] *m, f* undersecretary.
subseqüente [subse'kwẽtʃi] *adj* subsequent; ~ **(a)** subsequent (to).
subserviência [subsexvjẽsja] *f* subservience.
subserviente [subsex'vjẽtʃi] *adj* subservient, servile; ~ **(a)** subservient (towards).
subsidiar [15] [subzi'dʒja(x)] *vt* to subsidize.
subsidiário, ria [subzi'dʒjarju, rja] *adj* subsidiary.
➤ **subsidiária** *f* [empresa] subsidiary.
subsídio [sub'zidʒjul *m* -**1.** [contribuição] contribution. -**2.** [estatal] subsidy.
➤ **subsídios** *mpl* [dados, contribuições] information *(sg)*.
subsistência [subziʃ'tẽsja] *f* [sustento, sobrevivência] subsistence; **de** ~ subsistence *(antes de subst)*.
subsistir [6] [subziʃ'tʃi(x)] *vi* -**1.** [existir] to exist. -**2.** [persistir] to remain. -**3.** [sobreviver] to survive.
subsolo [sub'solu] *m* -**1.** [da terra] subsoil. -**2.** [de prédio] basement.
substância [subʃ'tãnsja] *f* substance; **em** ~ in essence.
substancial [subʃtãn'sjaw] (*pl* -ais) <> *adj* substantial. <> *m* [essência] essence.
substantivo, va [subʃtãn'tʃivu, va] *adj* -**1.** [essencial] essential. -**2.** *GRAM* substantive.
➤ **substantivo** *m* *GRAM* noun.
substituição [subʃtʃitwi'sãw] (*pl* -ões) *f* substitution, replacement.
substituir [74] [subʃtʃi'twi(x)] *vt* to substitute, to replace.
substituto, ta [subʃtʃi'tutu, ta] <> *adj* substitute *(antes de subst)*, replacement *(antes de subst)*. <> *m, f* substitute, replacement.
subterfúgio [subtex'fuʒju] *m* subterfuge.
subterrâneo, nea [subte'xãnju, nja] *adj* underground.
➤ **subterrâneos** *mpl* underground movements.
subtítulo [sub'tʃitulu] *m* subtitle.
subtotal [subto'taw] (*pl* -ais) *m* subtotal.
subtração [subtra'sãw] (*pl* -ões) *f* -**1.** [furto] theft. -**2.** [dedução] deduction. -**3.** *MAT* subtraction.
subtrair [68] [subtra'i(x)] <> *vt* -**1.** [furtar] to steal. -**2.** [deduzir] to deduct. -**3.** *MAT* to subtract. <> *vi* *MAT* to subtract.
➤ **subtrair-se** *vp* [esquivar-se]: ~-**se a algo** to dodge sthg.
subumano, na [subju'mãnu, na] *adj* subhuman.
suburbano, na [subux'bãnu, na] <> *adj* -**1.** [do subúrbio] suburban. -**2.** *pej* [atrasado] backward.

◇ m, f-1. [morador] suburbanite. -2. pej [atrasado] moron.

suburbio [su'buxbju] m suburb.

subvenção [subvẽn'sãw] (pl -ões) f subsidy.

subvencionar [4] [subvẽnsjo'na(x)] vt to subsidize.

subversão [subvex'sãw] f subversion.

subversivo, va [subvex'sivu, va] ◇ adj subversive. ◇ m, f [pessoa] subversive.

subverter [5] [subvex'te(x)] vt -1. [desordenar] to subvert. -2. [agitar] to incite. -3. [arruinar] to upset.

sucata [su'kata] f scrap metal.

sucção [suk'sãw] f suction.

sucedâneo, nea [suse'dãnju, nja] ◇ adj substitute. ◇ m, f substitute.

suceder [5] [suse'de(x)] vi -1. [acontecer] to happen. -2. [seguir-se a]: ~ a algo/alguém to follow (on from) sthg/sb.

➤ **suceder-se** vp -1. [seguir-se]: **sucedem-se os governantes, mas nada muda** rulers come and go but nothing changes. -2. [repetir-se]: **os dias se sucediam e ele não regressava** day followed day and still he didn't return.

sucedido, da [suse'dʒidu, da] m: **vou lhe contar o ~** I'll tell you what happened.

sucessão [suse'sãw] (pl -ões) f succession.

sucessivo, va [suse'sivu, va] adj successive; **crimes ~s** a succession of crimes.

sucesso [su'sɛsu] m -1. [êxito] success; **fazer** ou**ter ~** to be successful; **com/sem ~** successfully/unsuccessfully; **de ~** successful. -2. [música, filme] hit; **ser um ~** to be a hit.

sucessor, ra [suse'so(x), ra] m, f successor.

sucinto, ta [su'sĩntu, ta] adj succinct.

suco ['suku] m juice.

suculento, ta [suku'lẽntu, ta] adj succulent.

sucumbir [6] [sukũn'bi(x)] vi -1. [vergar]: ~ a algo to yield to sthg. -2. [ceder]: ~ a algo to succumb to sthg. -3. [morrer]: ~ (a algo) to succumb (to sthg).

sucursal [sukux'saw] (pl -ais) f -1. [de empresa, loja] branch. -2. [de jornal, emissora] subsidiary.

SUDAM (**Superintendência do Desenvolvimento da Amazônia**) f body overseeing the use of resources for the development of the Amazon region.

sudanês, esa [suda'neʃ, eza] ◇ adj Sudanese. ◇ m, f Sudanese.

Sudão [su'dãw] n Sudan.

SUDENE (abrev de **Superintendência do Desenvolvimento do Nordeste**) f body responsible for overseeing economic and financial incentives in northeastern Brazil.

sudeste [su'dɛʃtʃi] ◇ adj south-east. ◇ m south-east.

súdito, ta ['sudʒitu, ta] m, f subject.

sudoeste [su'dwɛʃtʃi] ◇ adj south-west. ◇ m south-west.

Suécia ['swɛsja] n Sweden.

sueco, ca ['swɛku, ka] ◇ adj Swedish. ◇ m, f Swede.

➤ **sueco** m [língua] Swedish.

suéter ['swɛtɛ(x)] (pl -es) m ou f sweater.

suficiência [sufi'sjẽnsja] f sufficiency.

suficiente [sufi'sjẽntʃi] ◇ adj sufficient. ◇ m: **tenho o ~ até amanhã** I have enough until tomorrow.

sufixo [su'fiksu] m suffix.

suflê [su'fle] m soufflé.

sufocação [sufoka'sãw] (pl -ões) f -1. [ger] suffocation. -2. fig [opressão] oppression.

sufocante [sufo'kãntʃi] adj -1. [ger] suffocating. -2. fig [opressivo] oppressive.

sufocar [12] [sufo'ka(x)] ◇ vt -1. [asfixiar] to suffocate. -2. fig [oprimir] to oppress. -3. fig [debelar] to crush. ◇ vi [asfixiar-se] to be stifled.

➤ **sufocar-se** vp [asfixiar-se] to be suffocated.

sufoco [su'foku] m -1. [aflição] dread; **que ~!** how dreadful!; **ser um ~** to be dreadful. -2. [dificuldade] hassle; **deixar alguém no ~** to leave sb in the lurch; **passar (por) um ~** to have a hard time.

sufrágio [su'fraʒju] m -1. [voto] vote; **~ universal** universal suffrage. -2. [apoio] support.

sugar [14] [su'ga(x)] vt -1. [por sucção] to suck. -2. fig [extorquir] to extort; **~ o sangue de alguém** to get every last drop of blood out of sb.

sugerir [57] [suʒe'ri(x)] vt to suggest; **~ algo a alguém** to suggest sthg to sb.

sugestão [suʒeʃ'tãw] (pl -ões) f -1. [ger] suggestion; **dar uma ~** to make a suggestion. -2. [evocação, insinuação] hint.

sugestionar [4] [suʒeʃtʃjo'na(x)] vt: **~ algo a alguém** to inspire sb with sthg.

➤ **sugestionar-se** vp: **~ se con algo** to experience sthg.

sugestionável [suʒeʃtʃjo'navew] (pl -eis) adj impressionable.

sugestivo, va [suʒeʃ'tʃivu, va] adj -1. [evocativo] evocative. -2. [insinuante] suggestive.

Suíça ['swisa] n Switzerland.

suíças ['swisaʃ] fpl sideburns.

suicida [swi'sida] ◇ adj suicidal. ◇ mf [pessoa] suicidal person.

suicidar-se [7] [swisi'daxsi] vp to commit suicide.

suicídio [swi'sidʒju] m suicide; **ser ~** fig [ser arriscado] to be suicide.

suíço, ça ['swisu, sa] ◇ adj Swiss. ◇ m, f Swiss.

sui generis [swi'ʒeneris] adj inv unique, sui generis.

suingar [swĩŋ'ga(x)] vi to dance the swing.

suingue ['swĩŋgi] m swing.

suíno, na ['swinu, na] adj pig (antes de subst).

➤ **suíno** m [porco] pig.

suíte ['switʃi] f suite.

sujar [4] [su'ʒa(x)] ◇ vt -1. [tornar sujo] to dirty. -2. fig [macular] to disgrace. ◇ vi fam [dar errado] to go wrong.

➤ **sujar-se** vp -1. [tornar-se sujo] to get dirty. -2. fig [macular-se] to disgrace o.s.

sujeição [suʒej'sãw] f -1. [subordinação] subordination. -2. [submissão] submission.

sujeira [su'ʒejra] *f* **-1.** [coisa suja] dirt. **-2.** [estado] dirtiness; **a sala estava uma ~ quando cheguei** the room was a dirty mess when I arrived. **-3.** *fam* [bandalheira] dirty trick; **fazer uma ~ com alguém** to play a dirty trick on sb.

sujeitar [4] [suʒej'ta(x)] *vt* **-1.** [submeter]: **~ algo/ alguém a algo** to subject sthg/sb to sthg. **-2.** [apresentar]: **~ algo a algo** to submit sthg to sthg.
➤ **sujeitar-se** *vp* [submeter-se]: **~-se a algo** to subject o.s. to sthg.

sujeito, ta [su'ʒejtu, ta] ⬦ *adj*: **~ a** subject to. ⬦ *m, f* person.
➤ **sujeito** *m* GRAM subject.

sujo, ja ['suʒu, ʒa] ⬦ *adj* **-1.** [imundo] dirty; **estar/ficar ~ com alguém** *fig* to be/fall out of favour with sb, to be in sb's bad books. **-2.** *fig* [mau-caráter] dishonest. ⬦ *m, f fig* [pessoa] dishonest person.

sul ['suw] ⬦ *adj* southern. ⬦ *m* [região] south; **ao ~ de** to the south of.

sulcar [12] [suw'ka(x)] *vt* **-1.** [abrir sulcos em] to plough *UK*, to plow *US*. **-2.** [rosto] to line. **-3.** [singrar] to cut through.

sulco [suw'ku] *m* furrow.

sulfato [suw'fatu] *m* sulphate.

sulfúrico, ca [suw'furiku, ka] *adj* sulphuric.

sulista [su'liʃta] ⬦ *adj* southern. ⬦ *mf* southerner.

sultão, tana [suw'tãw, tãna] (*pl* **-ões**) *m, f* sultan (*f* sultana).

suma ['suma] ➤ **em suma** *loc adv* in short.

sumamente [suma'mẽtʃi] *adv* [extremamente] extremely.

sumário, ria [su'marju, rja] *adj* **-1.** [breve] brief. **-2.** [julgamento] summary. **-3.** [traje] skimpy.
➤ **sumário** *m* **-1.** [resumo] summary. **-2.** [no início de livro] table of contents. **-3.** JUR: **~ de culpa** indictment.

sumiço [su'misu] *m* disappearance; **dar (um) ~ em** to do away with.

sumidade [sumi'dadʒi] *f*: **~ (em algo)** authority (in sthg).

sumido, da [su'midu, da] *adj* **-1.** [desaparecido] vanished; **andar ~** to have disappeared. **-2.** [voz] low. **-3.** [apagado] faint.

sumir [61] [su'mi(x)] *vi* to disappear; **~ com algo** to disappear with sthg.

sumo, ma ['sumu, ma] *adj* extreme; **~ sacerdote** high priest.
➤ **sumo** *m* [suco] juice.

sundae ['sãdej] *m* sundae.

sunga ['sũga] *f* [de banho] (swimming) trunks.

suntuoso, osa [sũn'twozu, ɔza] *adj* sumptuous.

suor ['swɔ(x)] (*pl* **-es**) *m* **-1.** [transpiração] sweat. **-2.** *fig* [trabalho]: **fiz esta casa com o meu próprio ~** I built this house by the sweat of my brow.

super ['supe(x)] *fam* ⬦ *adj* [ótimo] super. ⬦ *interj* super!

superabundante [ˌsuperabũn'dãntʃi] *adj* excessive.

superação [supera'sãw] (*pl* **-ões**) *f* overcoming; é

fundamental para a **~ do estresse** it's essential for overcoming stress.

superado, da [supe'radu, da] *adj* **-1.** [ultrapassado] outmoded, old-fashioned. **-2.** [resolvido] overcome.

superalimentar [4] [4] [ˌsuperalimẽn'ta(x)] *vt* **-1.** [animais, pacientes] to overfeed. **-2.** [indústria, sistema] to supercharge.

superaquecer [25] [ˌsuperake'se(x)] *vt* & *vi* to overheat.

superaquecimento [ˌsuperakesi'mẽntu] *m* overheating.

superar [4] [supe'ra(x)] *vt* **-1.** [sobrepujar]: **~ alguém (em algo)** to outdo sb (in sthg); **~ o inimigo** to defeat an enemy; **superou a todos em velocidade** he surpassed everyone in terms of speed. **-2.** [recorde] to beat. **-3.** [expectativa, objetivos *etc*] to exceed. **-4.** [ultrapassar] to surpass. **-5.** [resolver] to overcome.
➤ **superar-se** *vp* **-1.** [melhorar]: **~-se (em algo)** to excel o.s. (in sthg). **-2.** [exceder-se] to excel o.s.

superávit [supe'ravitʃi] *m* COM surplus.

supercílio [super'silju] *m* eyebrow.

superdotado, da [ˌsupexdo'tadu, da] ⬦ *adj* **-1.** [em inteligência] (exceptionally) gifted. **-2.** *fam* [sexualmente] well endowed. ⬦ *m, f* [em inteligência] (exceptionally) gifted person.

superestimar [4] [ˌsupereʃtʃi'ma(x)] *vt* to overestimate.

superestrutura [ˌsupereʃtru'tura] *f* superstructure.

superficial [supexfi'sjaw] (*pl* **-ais**) *adj* superficial.

superficialidade [supexfisjali'dadʒil] *f* superficiality.

superfície [supex'fisji] *f* **-1.** [parte externa] surface. **-2.** [extensão] area.

supérfluo, lua [su'pɛxflu, lua] *adj* superfluous.
➤ **supérfluo** *m* [gasto]: **vamos cortar o ~** we're going to cut out what is superfluous.

super-homem [ˌsuper'ɔmẽl] (*pl* **-ns**) *m* superman.

superintendência [ˌsuperĩntẽn'dẽnsja] *f* [órgão] management.

superintendente [ˌsuperĩntẽn'dẽntʃil] *mf* manager.

superior [supe'rjo(x)] (*pl* **-es**) ⬦ *adj* RELIG superior. ⬦ *m, f* [em hierarquia] superior.
➤ **superior** *adj* **-1.** [de cima] upper. **-2.** [mais alto] higher. **-3.** [maior] greater. **-4.** [melhor] better; **~ a** better than. **-5.** [excelente] first class. **-6.** EDUC higher; **escola ~** senior school; **curso ~** degree course.

superioridade [superjori'dadʒil] *f* superiority.

superlativo, va [supexla'tʃivul] *adj* superlative.
➤ **superlativo** *m* GRAM superlative.

superlotado, da [ˌsupexlo'tadu, da] *adj*: **~ (de)** overcrowded (with).

superlotar [ˌsupexlo'ta(x)] *vt* to pack.

supermercado [ˌsupexmex'kadul] *m* supermarket.

superpotência [ˌsupexpoˈtẽnsja] f superpower.

superpovoado, da [ˌsupexpoˈvwadu, da] adj overpopulated.

superprodução [ˌsupexproduˈsãw] (pl -ões) f -1. ECON overproduction. -2. CINE mega-production.

superproteger [26] [ˌsupexproteˈʒe(x)] vt to over-protect.

supersensível [ˌsupexsẽnˈsivew] (pl -eis) adj hypersensitive.

supersônico, ca [ˌsupexˈsoniku, ka] adj supersonic.

superstição [supexʃtʃiˈsãw] (pl -ões) f superstition.

supersticioso, osa [supexʃtʃiˈsjozu, ɔza] <> adj superstitious. <> m, f superstitious person.

supervisão [ˌsupexviˈzãw] (pl -ões) f -1. [ato] supervision. -2. [instância] supervisory authority.

supervisionar [4] [ˌsupexvizjoˈna(x)] vt to supervise.

supervisor, ra [ˌsupexviˈzo(x), ra] m, f supervisor.

supetão [supeˈtãw] ◆ de supetão loc adv all of a sudden.

suplantar [4] [suplãnˈta(x)] vt [sobrepujar]: ~ algo/alguém (em algo) to supplant sthg/sb (in sthg).

suplementar [4] [suplemẽnˈta(x)] <> adj extra. <> vt -1. [fornecer] to provide. -2. [servir de suplemento a] to supplement.

suplemento [supleˈmẽntu] m -1. [suprimento] supply. -2. [complemento] supplement; ~ policial police reinforcement. -3. JORN supplement.

suplente [suˈplẽntʃi] mf substitute.

súplica [ˈsuplika] f plea.

suplicar [12] [supliˈka(x)] <> vt to beg for; ~ algo a/de alguém to beg sb for sthg. <> vi to plead.

suplício [suˈplisju] m torture.

supor [45] [suˈpo(x)] vt -1. [ger] to suppose; suponho que sim I suppose so; suponhamos que let's suppose (that), supposing. -2. [pressupor] to presuppose.
◆ supor-se vp to be assumed.

suportar [4] [supoxˈta(x)] vt -1. [sustentar] to support. -2. [resistir a] to withstand. -3. [tolerar] to bear.

suportável [supoxˈtavew] (pl -eis) adj bearable.

suporte [suˈpɔxtʃi] m support.

suposição [supoziˈsãw] (pl -ões) f [conjetura] assumption.

supositório [supoziˈtɔrju] m suppository.

supostamente [supoʃtaˈmẽntʃi] adv supposedly.

suposto, osta [suˈpoʃtu, oʃta] <> pp ▷ supor. <> adj supposed.
◆ suposto m [pressuposto] assumption.

supracitado, da [suprasiˈtadu, da] <> adj aforementioned. <> m, f: o ~ the abovementioned.

supra-sumo [ˌsupraˈsumu] m: o ~ de algo [máximo] the culmination of sthg; [irôn] the height of sthg.

supremacia [supremaˈsia] f supremacy.

supremo, ma [suˈpremu, ma] adj -1. [amor, perdão, tribunal] supreme. -2. [qualidade] superior.
◆ Supremo m: o Supremo the Supreme Court.

supressão [supreˈsãw] (pl -ões) f -1. [corte] cutback. -2. [eliminação] deletion. -3. [abolição] abolition. -4. [omissão] suppression.

suprimento [supriˈmẽntu] m supply.

suprimir [6] [supriˈmi(x)] vt -1. [cortar] to cut back. -2. [eliminar] to delete. -3. [abolir] to abolish. -4. [omitir] to suppress.

suprir [6] [suˈpri(x)] <> vt -1. [prover]: ~ alguém de ou com algo to supply sb with sthg. -2. [substituir]: ~ algo por algo to substitute sthg with sthg. -3. [fazer as vezes de] to replace. -4. [preencher] to meet; ~ a falta de algo to make up for the lack of sthg; ~ a falta de alguém to make up for sb's absence. -5. [perfazer] to make up. <> vi -1. [fazer as vezes de]: ~ por to stand in for. -2. [preencher]: ~ a to meet; ~ a falta to make up for the lack.

supurar [4] [supuˈra(x)] vi to suppurate, to fester.

surdez [suxˈdeʒ] f deafness.

surdina [suxˈdʒina] f MÚS mute.
◆ em surdina loc adv on the quiet.

surdo, da [ˈsuxdu, da] <> adj -1. MED deaf. -2. [som] muffled. -3. [consoante] voiceless. <> m, f [pessoa] deaf person.
◆ surdo m MÚS [de bateria] kind of drum.

surdo-mudo, surda-muda [ˈsuxduˈmudu, ˈsuxdaˈmuda] (mpl surdos-mudos, fpl surdas-mudas) <> adj [pessoa] deaf and dumb. <> m, f [pessoa] deaf mute.

surfar [4] [suxˈfa(x)] vi to surf.

surfe [ˈsuxfi] m surfing.

surfista [suxˈfiʃta] mf surfer.

surgimento [suxʒiˈmẽntu] m emergence.

surgir [52] [suxˈʒi(x)] vi -1. [aparecer] to appear. -2. [sobrevir] to arise; ~ de to come from.

Suriname [suriˈnãmi] n Surinam.

surpreendente [surprjẽnˈdẽntʃi] adj surprising.

surpreender [5] [surprjẽnˈde(x)] <> vt -1. [ger] to surprise. -2. [apanhar em flagrante]: ~ alguém (fazendo algo) to catch sb (doing sthg). -3. [vislumbrar]: ~ algo em algo to glimpse sthg in sthg. <> vi [causar espanto] to be surprising.
◆ surpreender-se vp [espantar-se]: ~-se de/com algo to be amazed by/at sthg.

surpreso, sa [suxˈprezu, za] <> pp ▷ surpreender. <> adj surprised.
◆ surpresa f -1. [espanto] amazement. -2. [imprevisto] surprise; fazer uma surpresa para alguém to give sb a surprise; que surpresa! [em encontro casual] what a surprise!; ser uma surpresa to be a surprise; de surpresa by surprise. -3. [presente] surprise.

surra [ˈsuxa] f thrashing; dar uma ~ em alguém to give sb a thrashing; levar uma ~ (de alguém) to get a thrashing (from sb).

surrado, da [suˈxadu, da] adj -1. [espancado] beaten. -2. [muito usado] worn out.

surrar [4] [su'xa(x)] *vt* -**1.** [espancar] to beat up. -**2.** *ESP* to thrash. -**3.** [usar muito] to wear out.

surrealismo [suxea'liʒmu] *m* surrealism.

surrealista [suxea'liʃta] <> *adj* -**1.** *ARTE* surrealist. -**2.** *fig* [fora do normal] surreal. <> *mf ARTE* surrealist.

surrupiar [16] [suxu'pja(x)] *vt* to steal.

sursis [sux'si] *m (inv) JUR* suspended sentence.

surtar [sur'ta(x)] *vi fam* to go berserk.

surtir [6] [sux'tʃi(x)] <> *vt* [produzir] to bring about; ~ **efeito** to be effective. <> *vi* [funcionar] to work out.

surto ['suxtu] *m* -**1.** [irrupção] outburst. -**2.** [de doença] outbreak. -**3.** [de progresso, industrialização] surge.

suscetibilidade [susetʃibili'dadʒi] *f* -**1.** [melindre] touchiness. -**2.** [propensão] susceptibility.

suscetível [suse'tʃivɛw] (*pl* -**eis**) *adj* -**1.** [melindroso] sensitive. -**2.** [propenso]: ~ **a** susceptible to; ~ **de** liable to.

suscitar [4] [susi'ta(x)] *vt* -**1.** [provocar] to provoke. -**2.** [fazer surgir] to arouse. -**3.** [despertar] to awaken.

suspeição [suʃpej'sãw] (*pl* -**ões**) *f* suspicion.

suspeita [suʃ'pejta] *f* ▷ **suspeito**.

suspeitar [4] [suʃpej'ta(x)] <> *vt* [crer, supor]: ~ **que** to suspect (that). <> *vi* [desconfiar]: ~ **de alguém** to suspect sb; ~ **de que** to suspect that.

suspeito, ta [suʃ'pejtu, ta] <> *adj* -**1.** [que desperta suspeita] suspicious. -**2.** [de ser tendencioso]: **sou ~ para falar, mas ...** I'm biased in saying this but ... <> *m, f* [pessoa]: ~ **(de algo)** suspect (of sthg).

➡ **suspeita** *f* suspicion; **estar com suspeita de algo** to be suspected of having sthg.

suspender [6] [suʃpẽn'de(x)] *vt* -**1.** [ger] to suspend. -**2.** [levantar] to lift up. -**3.** [adiar] to postpone. -**4.** [encomenda] to cancel.

suspensão [suʃpẽn'sãw] (*pl* -**ões**) *f* -**1.** [ger] suspension. -**2.** [adiamento] postponement. -**3.** [de encomenda] cancellation. -**4.** [de sanções] lifting.

suspense [suʃ'pẽnsil] *m* suspense; **estamos assistindo um (filme de)** ~ we are watching a thriller; **fazer** ~ to create suspense.

suspenso, sa [suʃ'pẽnsu, sa] <> *pp* ▷ **suspender**. <> *adj* -**1.** [ger] suspended. -**2.** [levantado] held up. -**3.** [adiado] postponed. -**4.** [encomenda] cancelled. -**5.** [sanções] lifted.

suspensórios [suʃpẽn'sɔrjuʃ] *mpl* braces *UK*, suspenders *US*.

suspirar [4] [suʃpi'ra(x)] *vi* to sigh; ~ **de alívio** to sigh with relief; ~ **por algo** to long for sthg.

suspiro [suʃ'pirul] *m* -**1.** [aspiração] sigh; **dar um** ~ to give a sigh. -**2.** *CULIN* meringue.

sussurrar [4] [susu'xa(x)] <> *vt & vi* to whisper.

sussurro [su'suxul] *m* whisper.

sustância [suʃ'tãnsjal] *f* -**1.** [vigor] strength. -**2.** [de comida] sustenance.

sustar [4] [suʃ'ta(x)] *vt & vi* [deter-se] to stop.

sustentáculo [suʃtẽn'takulul] *m* -**1.** [base]

support. -**2.** *fig* [base] mainstay.

sustentar [4] [suʃtẽn'ta(x)] *vt* -**1.** [ger] to support. -**2.** [afirmar]: ~ **que** to maintain (that). -**3.** [defender] to uphold.

➡ **sustentar-se** *vp* -**1.** [ger] to support o.s.; ~ -**se no ar** to hover. -**2.** [alimentar-se] to sustain o.s.

sustento [suʃ'tẽntul] *m* -**1.** [alimento] sustenance. -**2.** [manutenção] support.

suster [1] [suʃ'te(x)] *vt* -**1.** [sustentar] to hold up. -**2.** [conter] to keep in check.

➡ **suster-se** *vp* -**1.** [sustentar-se] to be supported. -**2.** [conter-se] tó contain o.s. -**3.** [de pé] to hold o.s. up.

susto ['suʃtul] *m* fright; **dar um** ~ **em alguém** to give sb a fright; **levar** *ou* **tomar um** ~ to get a fright; **que** ~! what a fright!

sutiã [su'tʃjãl] *m* bra.

sutil [su'tʃiwl] (*pl* -**is**) *adj* subtle.

sutileza [sutʃi'lezal] *f* subtlety.

sutilmente [sutʃiw'mẽntʃil] *adv* subtly.

Suva ['suval] *n* Suva.

suvenir [suve'ni(x)] *m* souvenir.

t, T *m* [letra] t, T.

tá ['tal *fam* = **está**.

tabacaria [tabaka'rial] *f* tobacconist's.

tabaco [ta'bakul] *m* tobacco.

tabagismo [taba'ʒiʒmul] *m* -**1.** [uso do tabaco] nicotine addiction. -**2.** [intoxicação] nicotine poisoning.

tabefe [ta'bɛfil] *m fam* slap; **dar um** ~ **em alguém** to slap sb; **levar um** ~ **de alguém** to be slapped by sb.

tabela [ta'bɛlal] *f* -**1.** [quadro] table. -**2.** [lista] list; ~ **de preços** price list. -**3.:** **por** ~ [indiretamente] indirectly. -**4.** *loc*: **estar caindo pelas** ~ **s** [estar fatigado, adoentado] to feel out of sorts; [estar em más condições] to be in a bad way.

tabelado, da [tabe'ladu, dal] *adj* -**1.** [produtos] price-controlled. -**2.** [preços] controlled. -**3.** [dados] listed.

tabelamento [tabela'mẽntul] *m* [controle de preços]: ~ **de preços** price control.

tabelar [4] [tabe'la(x)] *vt* -**1.** [fixar o preço de] to set the price of. -**2.** [dados] to list.

tabelião, liã [tabe'ljãw, ljãl] (*mpl* -**ães**, *fpl* -**s**) *m, f* notary public.

taberna [ta'bɛxna] f public house *UK*, tavern *US*.

tabique [ta'biki] m [parede divisória] dividing wall.

tablado [ta'bladu] m **-1.** [palco] stage. **-2.** [palanque] stand. **-3.** [estrado] dais.

tablete [ta'blɛtʃi] m **-1.** [de chocolate] bar. **-2.** [de manteiga] pat. **-3.** [medicamento] tablet.

tablóide [ta'blɔjdʒi] m tabloid.

tabu [ta'bu] <> adj taboo. <> m taboo.

tábua ['tabwa] f **-1.** [de madeira] board; ~ **corrida** ARQUIT wooden floor; ~ **de passar roupa** ironing board; ~ **de salvação** *fig* last resort. **-2.** [de mesa] leaf. **-3.** MAT table.

tabuada [ta'bwada] f **-1.** [tabela] multiplication table, times table. **-2.** [livro] book of tables.

tabulador [tabula'do(x)] m tab key.

tabular [4] [tabu'la(x)] vt to tabulate.

tabuleiro [tabu'lejru] m **-1.** [bandeja] tray. **-2.** CU-LIN baking tray. **-3.** [de jogo] board.

tabuleta [tabu'leta] f notice board.

taça ['tasa] f **-1.** [copo] glass. **-2.** [troféu] cup.

tacada [ta'kada] f **-1.** ESP strike. **-2.** *fig*: **de uma** ~ **só** [de uma só vez] in one go.

tacanho, nha [ta'kãɲu, ɲal adj **-1.** [baixo] short. **-2.** [mesquinho] mean. **-3.** *fig* [sem visão] obtuse.

tacar [12] [ta'ka(x)] vt **-1.** ESP to strike. **-2.** [atirar] to hurl; ~ **um soco em alguém** to throw a punch at sb.

tacha ['taʃa] f **-1.** [prego] tack. **-2.** [em roupa, cadeira] stud.

tachar [4] [ta'ʃa(x)] vt: ~ **alguém/algo de algo** to brand sb/sth as sthg.

tacheado, da [ta'ʃjadu, da] adj studded.

tachinha [ta'ʃiɲa] f drawing pin *UK*, thumbtack *US*.

tacho [ta'ʃu] m [recipiente] pan, dish.

tácito, ta ['tasitu, ta] adj [implícito] tacit.

taciturno, na [tasi'tuxnu, na] adj [introverso, sério] taciturn.

taco ['taku] m **-1.** [ESP - bilhar] cue; [- golfe] club; [- hóquei] stick; [- pólo] mallet. **-2.** [de assoalho] block.

tadinho, nha [ta'dʒiɲu, ɲa] *interj fam* ⊳ **coitado.**

tafetá [tafe'ta] m taffeta.

tagarela [taga'rɛla] <> adj prattling, chattering. <> mf chatterbox.

tagarelar [4] [tagare'la(x)] vi to prattle, to chatter.

tagarelice [tagare'lisi] f prattle, chatter.

tailandês, esa [tajlãn'deʃ, ezal <> adj Thai. <> m, f Thai.

⇒ **tailandês** m [língua] Thai.

Tailândia [taj'lãndʒja] n Thailand.

tailleur [taj'ɛ(x)] m (woman's) suit.

tainha [ta'iɲa] f mullet.

taipa ['tajpa] f: **casa de** ~ mud hut; **parede de** ~ mud wall.

Taipei [taj'pej] n Taipei.

tais [tajʃ] pl ⊳ **tal.**

Taiti [taj'tʃi] n Tahiti.

Taiwan [taj'wãl n Taiwan.

taiwanês, esa [tajwãneʃ, ezal <> adj Taiwanese. <> m, f Taiwanese.

tal ['tawl (pl **tais**) <> adj **-1.** [ger] such; **eu nunca diria** ~ **coisa** I would never say such a thing; **não me misturo com tais pessoas** I don't mix with such people; **isso nunca teve** ~ **repercussão** this never had such an effect; **a dor foi** ~, **que desmaiei** the pain was such that I fainted. **-2.** [este, aquele]: **não existe** ~ **hotel** there is no such hotel; **a** ~ **respeito** on that subject; **o** ~ **vizinho** that neighbour. **-3.** [valor indeterminado]: **na avenida** ~ in such and such street. **-4.** [introduz um exemplo ou uma enumeração]: ~ **como** such as. **-5.** [introduz uma comparação]: ~ **qual** just like; ~ **pai,** ~ **filho** like father, like son. <> *pron indef* [isto, aquilo]: **por** ~ for that reason; **fulano de** ~ Joe Bloggs. <> mf: **ele se acha o** ~ he thinks he's it.

➡ **que tal** *loc* [pedindo opinião]: **que** ~? what do you think?; **que** ~ **(tomarmos) um drinque?** what about (us having) a drink?

➡ **e tal** *loc*: **ele é simpático e** ~, **mas ineficiente** he's nice and all that, but inefficient; **ela tem trinta e** ~ **anos** she's thirty something.

➡ **um tal de** *loc*: **um** ~ **de João** John what's-his-name; **foi um** ~ **de gente reclamar** there were loads of people complaining.

➡ **a tal ponto que** *loc conj* such a point that.

➡ **de tal maneira que** *loc conj* in such a way that.

tala ['tala] f MED splint.

talão [ta'lãw] (pl **-ões**) m **-1.** [bloco] book; ~ **de cheques** cheque book *UK*, check book *US*. **-2.** [canhoto] stub.

talco ['tawku] m **-1.** [material] talc. **-2.** [produto de higiene] talcum powder.

talento [ta'lẽntu] m **-1.** [aptidão] ability; **uma pessoa de** ~ a very able person. **-2.** [pessoa talentosa] talented person.

talentoso, osa [talẽn'tozu, ɔza] adj talented.

talhado, da [ta'ʎadu, da] adj **-1.** [leite] curdled. **-2.** [madeira] carved. **-3.** [apropriado] appropriate. **-4.** [cortado]: **um terno bem** ~ a well-cut suit.

talhar [4] [ta'ʎa(x)] <> vt [madeira] to carve. <> vi [leite] to curdle.

talharim [taʎa'rĩ] (pl **-ns**) m tagliatelle.

talhe [ta'ʎi] m [de roupa] cut.

talher [ta'ʎɛ(x)] (pl **-es**) m place setting; ~ **es** cutlery (sg).

talho [ta'ʎu] m [corte] cut.

talismã [taliʒ'mã] m talisman.

talo ['talu] m BOT stalk, stem.

talude [ta'ludʒi] m slope.

taludo, da [ta'ludu, da] adj **-1.** [corpulento - adulto] stout; [- criança] plump. **-2.** [de talo resistente] strong-stalked, thick-stemmed.

talvez [taw've3] adv maybe, perhaps; ~ **ele esteja certo** maybe he is right.

tamanco [ta'mãŋku] m clog.

tamanduá [tamãn'dwa] m anteater.

tamanho, nha [ta'mãɲu, ɲa] adj **-1.** [tão grande]: **seu erro foi** ~ **que ele pediu desculpas** his mistake was so great he apologized. **-2.** [tão notável]: **ele é um ~ escritor** he is such a great author.

➤ **tamanho** _m_ size; **de que ~ é?** what size is it?; **em ~ natural** life-size, life-sized; **um prédio que não tem ~ ou do ~ de um bonde** _fam_ an enormous building.

tamanho-família [ta͵mãŋufa'milja] _adj inv_ **-1.** [garrafa, caixa] family-size. **-2.** _fig_ [casa, carro] family _(antes de subst)._

tâmara ['tãmara] _f_ date.

tamarindo [tama'rĩndu] _m_ tamarind.

também [tãn'bẽ] <> _adv_ **-1.** [igualmente] too; **ele ~ é inteligente** he's intelligent, too, he too is intelligent; **quero um café – eu ~** I want a coffee – so do I _ou_ me too; **sou do Rio, e ele ~ é** I'm from Rio, and so is he; **ela não viajou, e eu ~ não** she didn't go, and neither did I; **ele não fala inglês, e eu ~ não** he doesn't speak English, and neither do I. **-2.** [além disso] too. <> _interj_ [não é de surpreender] hardly surprising!

tambor [tãn'bo(x)] _(pl_ **-es)** _m_ drum.

tamborete [tãnbo'retʃi] _m_ [banco] stool.

tamborilar [4] [tãnbori'la(x)] _vi_ [tocar] to drum.

tamborim [tãnbo'rĩ] _(pl_ **-ns)** _m_ tambourine.

Tâmisa ['tãmiza] _n_: **o (rio) ~** the (river) Thames.

tampa ['tãnpa] _f_ **-1.** [de caixa, privada, panela] lid. **-2.** [de garrafa] cap.

tampado, da [tãn'padu, da] _adj_: **a panela está tampada** the saucepan is covered.

tampão [tãn'pãw] _(pl_ **-ões)** _m_ **-1.** [de pia, banheira] plug. **-2.** _MED_ compress. **-3.** [vaginal] tampon. **-4.** [de poço, esgoto] bung.

tampar [4] [tãn'pa(x)] _vt_ **-1.** [com tampa - ger] to put a lid on; [- em garrafa] to put a top on. **-2.** [tapar] to cover.

tampinha [tãn'piɲa] <> _f_ [tampa pequena] bottle top. <> _mf fam_ [pessoa baixa] dumpy person.

tampo ['tãnpu] _m_ **-1.** [de privada] seat, lid. **-2.** [de mesa] top.

tampouco [͵tãn'poku] _adv_: **não foi à reunião e ~ justificou sua ausência** he didn't turn up at the meeting, nor did he justify his absence.

Tananarive [tanana'rivi] _n_ Antananarivo.

tanga ['tãŋa] _f_ **-1.** [roupa indígena] loincloth. **-2.** [biquíni] G-string.

Tanganica [tãŋa'nika] _n_: **o (lago) ~** Lake Tanganyika.

tangente [tãn'ʒẽntʃi] _f_ tangent; **escapar pela ~** _fig_ to narrowly escape.

tanger [26] [tãn'ʒe(x)] <> _vt_ [instrumento] to play; [sinos] to ring. <> _vi_ **-1.** [sinos] to ring. **-2.** [dizer respeito]: **no que tange a** with regard to, as regards.

tangerina [tãnʒe'rina] _f_ tangerine.

tangível [tãn'ʒivew] _(pl_ **-eis)** _adj fig_ **-1.** [alcançável] attainable. **-2.** [real] tangible.

tango ['tãŋgu] _m_ tango.

tanque ['tãŋki] _m_ **-1.** _MIL_ tank. **-2.** [de lavar roupa] washtub. **-3.** [reservatório] reservoir.

tantã [tãn'tã] _adj fam_ [maluco] crazy.

tanto, ta ['tãntu, ta] <> _adj_ **-1.** [tão grande] so much; **~ tempo** so much time. **-2.** [tão numeroso] so many; **ela tem trinta e ~s anos** he is thirty something; **~ ... quanto** as many ... as; **tanta gente** so many people. <> _pron_ so much; **pode ficar com o lápis, já tenho ~s** you can keep the pencil, I already have so many.

➤ **tanto** <> _m_: **um ~ de** some. <> _adv_ so much; **ela trabalha ~** she works so much; **~ quanto** as much as; **~ ... como** both ... and; **nem ~ assim** not that much; **~ melhor** all the better; **se ~** if that.

➤ **tantas** _fpl_: **às tantas** the early hours of the morning.

➤ **e tanto** _loc adj_: **é um professor e ~** he's an amazing teacher.

➤ **tanto que** _loc conj_ so much so that.

➤ **tanto faz** _loc adv_ it's all the same.

➤ **um tanto (ou quanto)** _loc adv_: **uma pessoa um ~ (ou quanto) difícil** a somewhat difficult person.

Tanzânia [tãn'zãnja] _n_ Tanzania.

tão [tãw] _adv_ so; **~ ... quanto** as... as; **~ logo** as soon as.

tão-só [tãw'sɔ] _adv_ only.

tão-somente [tãoso'mẽntʃi] _adv_ only.

tapa ['tapa] _m_ [tabefe] slap; **dar um ~ em alguém** to slap sb; **levar um ~ de alguém** to be slapped by sb; **no ~** by force.

tapado, da [ta'padu, da] _adj_ **-1.** [ger] covered. **-2.** _fam_ [pessoa] thick.

tapar [4] [ta'pa(x)] _vt_ **-1.** [ger] to cover. **-2.** [garrafa] to put the lid back on.

tapeação [tapja'sãw] _(pl_ **-ões)** _f_ **-1.** [engano] hoax. **-2.** [reparo, limpeza malfeitos] quick going-over.

tapear [15] [ta'pja(x)] _vt_ [enganar] to fool.

tapeçaria [tapesa'ria] _f_ **-1.** [tapete - de chão] rug; [- de parede] tapestry, wall hanging. **-2.** [loja] carpet shop. **-3.** [arte - de chão] rug-making; [- de parede] tapestry.

tapeceiro, ra [tape'sejru, ra] _m, f_ **-1.** [vendedor] seller of carpets and soft furnishings. **-2.** [fabricante] manufacturer of carpets and soft furnishings.

tapete [ta'petʃi] _m_ **-1.** [solto] rug; **~ de banheiro** bathmat. **-2.** [fixo] carpet.

tapioca [ta'pjɔka] _f_ tapioca.

tapume [ta'pumi] _m_ **-1.** [cerca de sebe] hedge. **-2.** [anteparo de madeira] fence. **-3.** [parede divisória] partition.

taquara [ta'kwara] _f BOT_ bamboo; **voz de ~ rachada** gravelly voice.

taquicardia [takikax'dʒia] _f_ palpitations _(pl)_, tachycardia.

taquigrafar [4] [takigra'fa(x)] <> _vt_ to take shorthand. <> _vi_ to write in shorthand.

taquigrafia [takigra'fia] _f_ shorthand _UK_, stenography _US_.

taquígrafo, fa [ta'kigrafu, fa] _m, f_ shorthand typist _UK_, stenographer _US_.

tara ['tara] _f PSIC_ mania.

tarado, da [taˈradu, da] <> *adj* **-1.** [desequilibrado] unbalanced. **-2.** [sexualmente] depraved. **-3.** *fam fig* [fascinado]: **ser ~ por** to be mad about. <> *m, f* [desequilibrado] maniac; **~ (sexual)** (sexual) pervert.

tarar [4] [taˈra(x)] *vi fam*: **~ por alguém/algo** to fall madly in love with sb/sthg.

tardar [4] [taxˈda(x)] <> *vt* [retardar] to put off. <> *vi* [demorar-se, vir tarde] to delay; **~ a fazer algo** to take a long time to do sthg; **o mais ~** at the latest; **sem mais ~** without further delay.

tarde [ˈtaxdʒi] <> *f* afternoon; **às cinco da ~** at five in the afternoon; **boa ~!** good afternoon!; **de ou à ~** in the afternoon; **hoje à ~** this afternoon; **ontem à ~** yesterday afternoon. <> *adv* late; **~ demais** too late; **mais ~** later; **antes ~ do que nunca** better late than never; **~ da noite** late at night.

tardinha [taxˈdʒiɲa] *f* late afternoon; **à ou de ~** late in the afternoon.

tardio, dia [taxˈdʒiu, dʒia] *adj* late.

tarefa [taˈrɛfa] *f* **-1.** [trabalho em geral] task. **-2.** [empreitada] job.

tarifa [taˈrifa] *f* **-1.** [preço - de gás, água] tariff; **~ alfandegária** customs duty; [- de transporte] fare. **-2.** [tabela de preços] price list.

tarifar [4] [tariˈfa(x)] *vt* to price.

tarifaço [tariˈfasu] *m general price rise in publicly-owned utilities.*

tarimba [taˈrĩba] *f fig* [experiência] experience; **ter ~ (em/como algo)** to be an old hand at/as sthg.

tarimbado, da [tarĩˈbadu, da] *adj*: **~ (em)** highly-experienced (in).

tarô [taˈro] *m* tarot.

tarrafa [taˈxafa] *f* fishing net.

tarraxa [taˈxaʃa] *f* [rosca] screw.

tartaruga [taxtaˈruga] *f* **-1.** [grande] turtle. **-2.** [pequena] tortoise; **pente de ~** tortoiseshell comb.

tascar [12] [taʃˈka(x)] *vt fam*: **~ algo em alguém** to plant sthg on sb.

tasco [ˈtaʃku] *m fam* bit.

Tasmânia [taʒˈmãnja] *n* Tasmania.

tataraneto, ta [tataraˈnɛtu] *m* great-great-great-grandson (*f* -granddaughter).

tataravô, vó [tataraˈvo, vɔ] *m, f* great-great grandfather (*f* -grandmother).

tatear [15] [taˈtʃja(x)] <> *vt* to feel. <> *vi* to feel one's way.

táteis [ˈtatejʃ] *pl* |> **tátil**.

tatibitate [tatʃibiˈtatʃi] *adj* [que troca consoantes - devido à idade] stumbling; [- por defeito] stammering.

tático, ca [ˈtatʃiku, ka] *adj* tactical.
  ➤ tática *f* **-1.** *MIL* tactic. **-2.** [ciência] tactics *(sg)*. **-3.** *fam* [plano de ação] strategy.

tátil [ˈtatʃiw] (*pl* -eis) *adj* tactile.

tato [ˈtatu] *m* **-1.** [ger] touch. **-2.** *fig* [cautela]: **ter ~** to be tactful.

tatu [taˈtu] *m* armadillo.

tatuador, ra [tatwaˈdo(x), ra] *m, f* tattooist.

tatuagem [taˈtwaʒẽ] (*pl* -ns) *f* **-1.** [desenho] tattoo. **-2.** [técnica] tattooing.

tatuar [4] [taˈtwa(x)] *vt* to tattoo.

taurino, na [tawriˈnu, na] <> *adj* *ASTRO* Taurus. <> *m, f* *ASTRO* Taurus.

tautologia [tawtoloˈʒia] *f* tautology.

taxa [ˈtaʃa] *f* **-1.** [ger] rate; **~ de natalidade/crescimento** birth/growth rate; **~ de câmbio** exchange rate; **~ de conversão** *COM* conversion rate; **~ de juros** interest rate; **~ de retorno** *COM* rate of return; **~ bancária** bank rate; **~ fixa** *COM* flat rate; **~ de inscrição** registration fee; **~ de matrícula** enrolment fee. **-2.** [imposto] tax; **~ de embarque** airport tax; **~ de exportação** *COM* export duty; **~ rodoviária** road tax.

taxação [taʃaˈsãw] *f* **-1.** [de impostos] taxation. **-2.** [de preços] fixing.

taxar [4] [taˈʃa(x)] *vt* **-1.** [onerar com imposto] to tax. **-2.** [fixar o preço de] to fix.

taxativo, va [taʃaˈtʃivu, va] *adj* [categórico] categorical; **ser ~ (em algo)** to be categorical (about sthg).

táxi [ˈtaksil] *m* taxi *UK*, cab *US*; **~ aéreo** air taxi.

taxiar [takˈsja(x)] *vi* to taxi.

taxímetro [takˈsimetru] *m* taxi meter.

taxinomia [taksinoˈmia] *f* taxonomy.

taxista [takˈsiʃta] *mf* taxi driver *UK*, cab driver *US*.

tchã [ˈtʃã] *m fam* [charme] charm.

tchau [ˈtʃaw] *interj fam* bye, ciao.

tcheco, ca [ˈtʃɛku, ka] <> *adj* Czech. <> *m, f* Czech.
  ➤ tcheco *m* [língua] Czech.

tchecoslovaco, ca [tʃɛkoʒloˈvaku, ka] <> *adj* Czechoslovakian. <> *m, f* Czechoslovak.

Tchecoslováquia [tʃɛkoʒloˈvakja] *n* Czechoslovakia.

te [ˈtʃi] *pron pess* **-1.** [você] you. **-2.** [a, para, em você]: **~ mandei duas cartas** I sent you two letters.

tear [teˈa(x)] (*pl* -es) *m* loom.

teatral [tʃjaˈtraw] (*pl* -ais) *adj* **-1.** [ger] theatre (antes de subst) *UK*, theater (antes de subst) *US*. **-2.** *fig* [pessoa, comportamento] theatrical.

teatro [ˈtʃjatru] *m* **-1.** [ger] theatre *UK*, theater *US*; **~ de arena** theatre in the round; **~ de bolso** small theatre; **peça de ~** stage play; **~ de marionetes** puppet theatre; **~ rebolado** burlesque; **~ de variedades** variety show. **-2.** [LITER - gênero] playwriting; [- obras de um autor] plays *(pl)*. **-3.** [curso] drama. **-4.** *MIL*: **~ de operações** theatre of war *UK*. **-5.** *fig* [palco] scene. **-6.** *fig*: **fazer ~** [exagerar] to dramatize.

teatrólogo, ga [tʃjaˈtrɔlogu, ga] *m, f* dramatist.

teatro-revista [ˌtʃjatruˈxe] *viʃta] (*pl* teatros-revista) *m* theatre review *UK*, theater review *US*.

tecelagem [teseˈlaʒẽ] (*pl* -ns) *f* weaving.

tecelão, lã [teseˈlãw, lã] (*mpl* -ões, *fpl* -s) *m, f* weaver.

tecer [25] [te'se(x)] *vt* -**1.** [ger] to weave. -**2.** *fig* [fazer]: ~ **elogios a alguém/algo** to praise sb/ sthg; ~ **intrigas sobre/contra alguém** to create conspiracies about/against sb.

tecido [te'sidu] *m* -**1.** [têxtil] material. -**2.** BIOL & ANAT tissue.

tecla ['tɛkla] *f* -**1.** [ger] key; ~ **de função** function key; ~ **de saída** exit key; ~ **de tabulação** tab key. -**2.** [de máquina de calcular, de gravador] button. -**3.** *loc*: **bater na mesma** ~ *fig* to harp on about sthg.

tecladista [tekla'dʒiʃta] *mf* MÚS keyboard player.

teclado [te'kladu] *m* keyboard.

teclar [4] ['tekla(x)] <> *vt* to key (in) <> *vi* COMPUT: ~ **(com alguém)** to chat (with sb); **você quer** ~? do you want to chat?

técnica ['tɛknika] *f* ➪ **técnico**.

tecnicamente [tɛknika'mẽntʃi] *adv* technically.

técnico, ca ['tɛkniku, ka] <> *adj* technical. <> *m, f* -**1.** [profissional] technician. -**2.** [especialista] expert. -**3.** ESP coach.

➪ **técnica** *f* -**1.** [procedimentos, métodos] technique. -**2.** [conhecimento prático] skill.

tecnicolor [tekni'kɔlo(x)] *adj*: **em** ~ **(in)** techni- colour UK, **(in)** technicolor US.

tecnocrata [tekno'krata] *mf* technocrat.

tecnologia [tɛknolo'ʒia] *f* technology; ~ **de pon- ta** latest technology.

tecnológico, ca [tɛkno'lɔʒiku, ka] *adj* technolo- gical.

teco ['tɛku] *m* [batida de uma bola em outra] hit; **dar um** ~ **em** [em bola] to hit; *fig* [em pessoa] to be angry with.

teco-teco [ˌtɛku'tɛku] (*pl* teco-tecos) *m* light aircraft.

tectônico, ca [katek'toniku, ka] *adj* tectonic.

➪ **tectônica** *f* GEOL tectonics (*sg*).

tédio ['tɛdʒiu] *m* tedium.

tedioso, osa [te'dʒiozu, ɔza] *adj* tedious.

Teerã [tee'rã] *n* Teheran.

Tegucigalpa [tegusi'kawpa] *n* Tegucigalpa.

teia ['teja] *f* -**1.** [ger] web; ~ **de aranha** spider's web, cobweb. -**2.** *fig* [organização]: ~ **de espiona- gem** espionage network.

teima ['tejma] *f* obstinacy.

teimar [4] [tej'ma(x)] <> *vt*: ~ **que** to insist that. <> *vi* [insistir] to persist; ~ **em fazer algo** to persist in doing sthg.

teimosia [tejmo'zia] *f* stubborness; ~ **em fazer algo** obstinacy in doing sthg.

teimoso, osa [tej'mozu, ɔza] *adj* -**1.** [adulto] obstinate. -**2.** [criança] stubborn.

teipe ['tejpil] *m* magnetic tape.

Tejo ['tɛʒul] *n*: **o (rio)** ~ the (river) Tagus.

tel. [tell] (*abrev de* telefone) *m* tel.

tela ['tɛla] *f* -**1.** [ger] canvas. -**2.** [de arame] wire netting. -**3.** CINE, COMPUT & TV screen.

telão [te'lãw] (*pl* -ões) *m* big screen.

tele ['tɛle] *pref* tele.

telecomandar [4] [tɛlekomãn'da(x)] *vt* to ope- rate by remote control.

telecomando [tɛleko'mãndul] *m* remote control.

telecomunicação [tɛlekomunika'sawl] (*pl* -ões) *f* telecommunication.

➪ **telecomunicações** *fpl* telecommunica- tions.

teleconferência [telekõnferẽnsja] *f* teleconfe- rence.

telecurso [tɛle'kuxsul] *m* television course.

teleférico [tele'fɛriku] *m* -**1.** [de esqui] ski lift. -**2.** [bondinho] cable car.

telefonar [4] [telefo'na(x)] *vi* to (tele)phone, to call; ~ **para alguém** to (tele)phone sb, to call sb.

telefone [tele'fonil] *m* -**1.** [aparelho, linha] (tele)- phone; **estar/falar ao** ~ to be on the phone; ~ **celular** mobile phone UK, cellphone US; ~ **sem fio** cordless phone; ~ **público** public (tele)phone. -**2.** [número] (tele)phone number.

telefonema [telefo'nemal] *m* (tele)phone call; **dar um** ~ **para alguém/algum lugar** to make a call to sb/somewhere.

telefonia [telefo'nial] *f* [sistema] telephone sys- tem.

telefônico, ca [tele'foniku, ka] *adj* telephone (*an- tes de subst*); **chamada telefônica** (tele)phone call.

telefonista [telefo'niʃta] *mf* telephonist.

telefoto [tele'fɔtul] *f* telephoto.

telegrafar [4] [telegra'fa(x)] <> *vt* to telegraph. <> *vi* to telegraph; ~ **a alguém** to telegraph sb.

telegrafia [telegra'fial] *f* telegraphy.

telegráfico, ca [tele'grafiku, ka] *adj* telegraphic.

telegrafista [telegra'fiʃta] *mf* telegraphist.

telégrafo [te'lɛgraful] *m* -**1.** [aparelho] telegraph. -**2.** [local] telegraph office.

telegrama [tele'grãma] *m* telegram; **passar um** ~ to send a telegram; ~ **fonado** telemessage.

teleguiado, da [tɛle'gjadu, dal] *adj* -**1.** [guiado a distância] remote-controlled; **míssil** ~ **guided missile**. -**2.** *fig* [influenciado] (easily) led.

teleguiar [16] [tɛle'gja(x)] *vt* to operate by remote control.

telejornal [ˌtɛleʒox'nawl] (*pl* -ais) *m* TV television news (*sg*).

telejornalismo [tɛleʒoxna'liʒmul] *m* television journalism.

telenovela [ˌtɛleno'vɛla] *f* TV soap opera.

TELENOVELA

Telenovelas are very popular; episodes of these dramatized stories are broadcast daily on prime-time television. Although the main plot usually revolves around a love interest, the *telenovelas*, shown nationwide, often address important social issues. Having reached high technical standards, Brazilian *telenovelas* are currently exported to around 120 countries.

---

teleobjetiva [ˌtɛljobʒe'tʃival] *f* telephoto lens.

telepatia [telepa'tʃial] *f* telepathy; **por** ~ by telepathy.

telepático, ca [tele'patʃiku, ka] *adj* telepathic.

teleprocessamento [tɛleprosesa'mẽntul] *m* te- leprocessing.

telescópico, ca [teleʃ'kɔpiku, ka] *adj* telescopic.

telescópio [teleʃ'kɔpju] *m* telescope.

telespectador, ra [teleʃpekta'do(x), ra] <> *adj* viewing. <> *m, f* viewer.

teletexto [tɛle'teʃtu] *m* teletext.

teletipo [tɛle'tʃipu] *m* teletype.

televisão [televi'zãw] (*pl* **-ões**) *f* **-1.** [ger] television; ~ a cabo cable television; ~ a cores colour television. **-2.** [empresa] television company.

televisionar [4] [televizjo'na(x)] *vt* to televise.

televisivo, va [televi'zivu, va] *adj* television *(antes de subst)*.

televisor [televi'zo(x)] (*pl* **-es**) *m* television.

telex [tɛ'lɛkiʃ] (*pl* **-es**) *m* telex; **passar um** ~ to send a telex.

telha [ˈteʎa] *f* **-1.** [de casa *etc*] tile. **-2.** *fam fig* [mente]: **dar na** ~ **de alguém fazer algo** to get it into sb's head to do sthg; **ter uma** ~ **de menos** to have a screw loose.

telhado [te'ʎadu] *m* roof.

telha-vã [ˌteʎa'vã] (*pl* **telhas-vãs**) *f* unlined roof.

telnet [tel'netji] (*pl* **-s**) *f* COMPUT telnet.

telões [tɛ'lõjʃ] *pl* = **telão**.

tema [ˈtema] *m* **-1.** [assunto - de redação, romance] theme; [- de palestra] subject. **-2.** MÚS theme. **-3.** [dever de casa] homework.

temático, ca [te'matʃiku, ka] *adj* thematic.

temática *f* thematics *(sg)*.

temer [5] [te'me(x)] <> *vt* to fear; ~ **que** to fear that; ~ **fazer algo** to be afraid to do sthg, to be afraid of doing sthg. <> *vi* to be afraid; ~ **por alguém/algo** to fear for sb/sthg.

temerário, ria [teme'rarju, rja] *adj* **-1.** [audacioso, destemido] fearless. **-2.** [perigoso, arriscado] reckless.

temeridade [temeri'dadʒi] *f*: **ser uma** ~ [ser arriscado, perigoso] to be a foolhardy act; [ser atemorizador] to be terrifying.

temeroso, osa [teme'rozu, ɔza] *adj* **-1.** [medroso, receoso] afraid. **-2.** [amedrontador] dreadful.

temido, da [te'midu, da] *adj* [assustador] frightening.

temível [te'mivew] (*pl* **-eis**) *adj* fearsome.

temor [te'mo(x)] (*pl* **-es**) *m* fear.

tempão [tẽn'pãw] *m fam*: **um** ~ ages.

têmpera [ˈtẽnpera] *f* **-1.** [ger] tempera. **-2.** [de metais] tempering.

temperado, da [tẽnpe'radu, da] *adj* **-1.** [ferro, aço] hardened. **-2.** [clima] temperate. **-3.** [CULIN - condimentado] seasoned; [- marinado] marinated.

temperamental [tẽnperamẽn'taw] (*pl* **-ais**) <> *adj* temperamental. <> *mf* temperamental person.

temperamento [tẽnpera'mẽntu] *m* temperament.

temperança [tẽnpe'rãnsa] *f* temperance.

temperar [4] [tẽnpe'ra(x)] *vt* **-1.** [metal] to temper. **-2.** [CULIN - condimentar] to season; [- marinar] to marinate.

temperatura [tẽnpera'tural] *f* temperature; ~

ambiente room temperature.

tempero [tẽn'peru] *m* **-1.** [condimento] seasoning. **-2.** [vinha d'alho] marinade. **-3.** [sabor] flavour *UK*, flavor *US*.

tempestade [tẽnpeʃ'tadʒi] *f* storm; ~ **de areia** sandstorm; **fazer uma** ~ **em copo d'água** to make a mountain out of a molehill.

tempestuoso, osa [tẽnpeʃ'twozu, ɔza] *adj* [dia, tempo] stormy.

templo [ˈtẽnplu] *m* **-1.** [pagão] temple. **-2.** [cristão] church.

tempo [ˈtẽnpu] *m* **-1.** [ger] time; **o** ~ **todo** the whole time; **quanto** ~? how long?; **há quanto** ~ **você mora aqui?** how long have you been living here?; **não a vejo há muito** ~ it's a long time since I saw her; **há muito** ~ a long time ago; **não dá** ~ there isn't (enough) time; ~ **integral** fulltime; **dar** ~ **ao** ~ to give things time; **ganhar/perder** ~ to gain/lose time; **em seu devido** ~ in due course; **em** ~ **hábil** in reasonable time; **a** ~ on time; **a** ~ **e a hora** at the appropriate time; **nos bons** ~**s** in the good times; **nesse meio** ~ in the meanwhile; **ao mesmo** ~ at the same time; **de** ~**s em** ~**s** from time to time; **esse vestido é do** ~ **do Onça** that dress went out with the ark. **-2.** METEOR weather; **previsão do** ~ weather forecast. **-3.** GRAM tense. **-4.** ESP: **primeiro/segundo** ~ first/second half. **-5.** [MÚS - divisão de compasso] time; [- velocidade de execução] timing.

tempo-quente [ˌtẽnpu'kẽntʃi] *m* [briga, discussão] heated words *(pl)*.

têmpora [ˈtẽnpora] *f* ANAT temple.

temporada [tẽnpo'rada] *f* **-1.** [ger] season; **baixa/alta** ~ high/low season. **-2.** [espaço de tempo] time.

temporal [tẽnpo'raw] (*pl* **-ais**) <> *adj* **-1.** [temporário] temporary. **-2.** [não-espiritual] temporal. <> *m* storm.

temporão, rã [tẽnpo'rãw, rã] *adj* [filho] premature.

temporário, ria [tẽnpo'rarju, rja] *adj* temporary.

tenacidade [tenasi'dadʒi] *f* tenacity.

tenaz [te'najʒ] <> *adj* [pessoa] tenacious. <> *f* [ferramenta] tongs *(pl)*.

tencionar [4] [tẽnsjo'na(x)] *vt*: ~ **algo/fazer algo** to be planning sthg/to do sthg.

tenda [ˈtẽnda] *f* tent; ~ **de oxigênio** oxygen tent.

tendão [tẽn'dãw] (*pl* **-ões**) *m* tendon.

tendência [tẽn'dẽnsja] *f* **-1.** [propensão] tendency; ~ **a** *ou* **paraalgo** tendency to *ou* towards sthg; ~ **a fazer algo** tendency to do sthg. **-2.** [vocação] inclination; ~ **a** *ou* **para algo** inclination towards sthg; ~ **a fazer algo** inclination to do sthg. **-3.** [da moda, música] trend.

tendencioso, osa [tẽndẽn'sjozu, ɔza] *adj* tendentious.

tendente [tẽn'dẽntʃi] *adj*: **ser** ~ **a fazer algo** to tend to do sthg.

tender [5] [tẽn'de(x)] *vt* **-1.** [ter tendência]: ~ **a** *ou* **para algo** to be inclined to *ou* towards sthg; ~

a fazer algo to tend to do sthg. **-2.** [ter vocação]: ~ a ou para algo to be inclined towards sthg; ~ a fazer algo to intend to do sthg. **-3.** [encaminhar-se]: ~ a ou para algo to move towards sthg; ~ a fazer algo to be closer to doing sthg.

tênder [ˈtẽnde(x)] *m* NÁUT tender.

tendinite [tẽndʒiˈnitʃi] *f* MED tendinitis.

tenebroso, sa [teneˈbrozu, zal *adj* **-1.** [ger] dark. **-2.** *fig* [terrível, horrível] horrendous.

tenente [teˈnẽntʃi] *mf* lieutenant.

tenho [ˈtɐɲu] ⊳ ter.

tênis [ˈtenif] *m* **-1.** *inv* ESP tennis; ~ de mesa table tennis. **-2.** [calçado] trainer *UK*, sneaker *US*.

tenista [teˈniʃta] *mf* tennis player.

tenor [teˈno(x)] ⋄ *m* tenor. ⋄ *adj inv* [instrumento] tenor *(antes de subst).*

tenro, ra [ˈtẽnxu, xal *adj* **-1.** [ger] tender. **-2.** [recente, novo] new.

tensão [tẽnˈsãwl *(pl -ões) f* **-1.** [ger] tension; ~ pré-menstrual pre-menstrual tension, PMT. **-2.** [pressão] pressure. **-3.** [voltagem] voltage.

tenso, sa [ˈtẽnsu, sal *adj* **-1.** [ger] taut. **-2.** [pessoa, ambiente] tense.

tentação [tẽntaˈsãwl *(pl -ões) f* temptation; ~ de fazer algo temptation to do sthg.

tentáculo [tẽnˈtakulul *m* tentacle.

tentado, da [tẽnˈtadu, dal *adj* **-1.** [atraído, seduzido] tempted; estar ~ a fazer algo to be tempted to do sthg. **-2.** [experimentado] attempted.

tentador, ra [tẽntaˈdo(x), ral *(mpl -es, fpl -s) adj* tempting.

tentar [4] [tẽnˈta(x)] *vt* **-1.** [experimentar] to try. **-2.** [usar de meios para] to attempt; ~ fazer algo to try to do sthg. **-3.** [atrair] to tempt.

tentativa [tẽntaˈtʃival *f* attempt; ~ de fazer algo attempt at doing sthg; ~ de roubo attempted robbery.

tênue [ˈtenwil *adj* **-1.** [fraco - luz, voz, desejo] faint; [- sentimento] slight; [- argumento] tenuous. **-2.** [fino] flimsy. **-3.** [leve] slight.

teologia [tʃoloˈʒial *f* theology.

teológico, ca [tʃjoˈlɔʒiku, kal *adj* theological.

teólogo, ga [ˈtʃjologu, gal *m, f* theologian.

teor [ˈtʃjo(x)] *m* **-1.** [conteúdo, significado] tenor. **-2.** [proporção de uma substância] content; baixo ~ de nicotina low nicotine content; ~ alcoólico alcohol content.

teorema [teoˈremal *m* theorem.

teoria [teoˈrial *f* theory.

teoricamente [ˌtjorikaˈmẽntʃil *adv* theoretically.

teórico, ca [teˈɔriku, kal ⋄ *adj* theoretical. ⋄ *m, f* theorist.

teorizar [4] [teoriˈza(x)] ⋄ *vt* to theorize. ⋄ *vi* **-1.** [expor teorias] to expound theories. **-2.** [discorrer teoricamente] to theorize; ~ sobre algo to theorize about sthg.

tépido, da [ˈtɛpidu, dal *adj* tepid, lukewarm.

ter [1] [ˈte(x)] *vt* **-1.** [ger] to have; ~ razão to be right. **-2.** [obter]: ~ sucesso em algo to be successful in sthg. **-3.** [sentir] to be; ~ fome/pressa/calor to be hungry/hurried/hot; o que é

que você tem? what's wrong with you? **-4.** [contar]: 'quantos anos você tem?' - 'tenho 30 anos' [idade] 'how old are you?' - 'I'm 30'; ele tem 2 metros de altura [medida] he is 2 metres tall. **-5.** [proceder com]: ~ cuidado to be careful; tenha calma! calm down! **-6.** [considerar]: ~ alguém por ou como algo to consider sb as sthg. ⋄ *v impess* [haver]: tem algo/alguém there is sthg/sb; não tem problema (it's) no problem; não tem de quê you're welcome; tem três meses que não chove it hasn't rained for three months; tem três meses que cheguei it's three months since I arrived. ⋄ *v aux*: ~ que ou de fazer algo to have to do sthg; ~ como fazer algo to be able to do sthg; ~ a ver com to have sthg to do with; não tenho nada a ver com isso I have nothing to do with it; não ~ onde cair morto to have nowhere to turn.

ter. *(abrev de* terça-feira*) f* Tue.

terabyte [texaˈbajtʃil *(pl* terabytes*) m* terabyte.

terapeuta [teraˈpewtal *mf* therapist.

terapêutico, ca [teraˈpewtʃiku, kal *adj* therapeutic.

➡ **terapêutica** *f* **-1.** [parte da medicina] therapeutics *(pl)*. **-2.** [tratamento] therapy.

terapia [teraˈpial *f* **-1.** [ger] therapy. **-2.**: ~ de casal marriage guidance.

terça [ˈtexsal, **terça-feira** [texsaˈfejral *(pl* terças-feiras [texsaʃˈfejraʃ]*) f* Tuesday; ~ gorda Shrove Tuesday, Pancake Day; *veja também* sexta-feira.

terceirização [texsejriʒaˈsãwl *f* outsourcing.

terceirizar [4] [texsejriˈza(x)] *vt* to outsource.

terceiro, ra [texˈsejru, ral ⋄ *num* third; o Terceiro Mundo the Third World; *veja também* sexto. ⋄ *m, f* **-1.** [ger] third party. **-2.** [aquele ou aquilo em terceiro lugar] third.

➡ **terceira** *f* AUTO third (gear).

➡ **terceiros** *mpl* [outras pessoas] others.

terciário, ria [texˈsjarju, rjal *adj* tertiary.

terço, ça [ˈtexsu, sal *num*: a terça parte the third part.

➡ **terço** *m* [rosário] rosary.

terçol [texˈsɔwl *(pl -óis) m* stye.

Tergal® [texˈgawl *m* Terylene®.

tergiversar [4] [texʒivexˈsa(x)] *vi* [usar de subterfúgios ou evasivas] to avoid the issue.

termas [ˈtɛxmaʃl *fpl* spa *(sg)*.

termelétrica [texmeˈlɛtrikal *f* thermoelectric plant.

térmico, ca [texˈmiku, kal *adj* thermal.

terminação [texminaˈsãwl *(pl -ões) f* **-1.** [ger] end. **-2.** [ato] termination. **-3.** GRAM ending.

terminal [texmiˈnawl *(pl -ais)* ⋄ *adj* terminal; em estado ~ terminally ill. ⋄ *m* **-1.** [ger] terminal. **-2.** [fim da linha] terminus; ~ marítimo sea terminal.

terminante [texmiˈnãntʃil *adj* **-1.** [categórico] categorical. **-2.** [decisivo, inapelável] final. **-3.** [concludente] concluding.

terminantemente [texminãntʃiˈmẽntʃil *adv* categorically.

terminar [4] [texmi'na(x)] <> *vt* to finish. <> *aux*: ~ **de fazer algo** [finalmente] to finish doing sthg; [há pouco tempo] to have just done sthg. <> *vi* to finish; ~ **em algo** [em local, forma] to end in sthg.

término ['tɛxminu] *m* end.

terminologia [texminolo'ʒia] *f* terminology.

terminológico, ca [texmino'lɔʒiku, ka] *adj* terminological.

termo ['texmu] *m* - **1.** [ger] term. - **2.** [fim] end; **pôr** ~ **a algo** to put an end to sthg; **a longo** ~ in the long term; **meio** ~ compromise.

  ➠ **termos** *mpl* terms; **em** ~ **s de** in terms of; **em** ~ **s gerais** in general terms; **em** ~ **s** on terms; **estar em bons/maus** ~ **s** to be on good/bad terms.

termodinâmica [texmodʒi'nãmika] *f* thermodynamics *(sg)*.

termômetro [ter'mɔmetru] *m* [instrumento] thermometer.

termonuclear [tɛxmonukle'a(x)] <> *adj* thermonuclear. <> *f* [usina termonuclear] nuclear power station.

termostato [tɛxmoʃ'tatu] *m* thermostat.

terninho [tɛx'niɲu] *m* trouser suit *UK*, pantsuit *US*.

terno, na ['tɛxnu, na] *adj* tender.

  ➠ **terno** *m* [traje] suit.

ternura [tex'nura] *f* tenderness.

terra ['tɛxa] *f* - **1.** [ger] earth; ~ **vegetal** compost; **chão de** ~ **batida** earth floor. - **2.** [por oposição ao mar] [terreno] land; ~ **firme** terra firma. - **3.** [região, país]: **já me habituei a viver nesta** ~ I've got used to living in this area; ~ **de ninguém** no-man's-land; **a** ~ **prometida** the promised land; **a Terra Santa** the Holy Land. - **4.** [pátria] homeland; ~ **natal** birthplace.

terraço [te'xasu] *m* - **1.** [varanda] terrace. - **2.** [cobertura plana de um edifício] roof terrace.

terracota [texa'kɔta] *f* [argila] terracotta.

Terra do Fogo [ˌtɛxadu'fogu] *n* Tierra del Fuego.

Terra Nova [ˌtɛxa'nɔva] *n* Newfoundland.

terraplenagem [texaple'naʒẽ] *f* site levelling *UK*, site leveling *US*.

terraplenar [texaple'na(x)] *vt* to level.

terreiro [te'xejru] *m* - **1.** [espaço de terra] yard. - **2.** [espírit] *place where Afro-Brazilian rites are performed*.

terremoto [texe'mɔtu] *m* earthquake.

terreno, na [te'xenu, na] *adj* [material, mundano] material.

  ➠ **terreno** *m* - **1.** [extensão de terra] land. - **2.** [para construção, plantação] site; ~ **baldio** wasteland. - **3.** GEOL terrain. - **4.** *loc*: **ganhar/perder** ~ to lose/gain ground; **sondar o** ~ to check the lie of the land.

térreo, ea ['tɛxju, ja] *adj* [andar, casa] ground level *(antes de subst)*.

  ➠ **térreo** *m* [andar térreo] ground floor *UK*, first floor *US*.

terrestre [te'xɛʃtri] *adj* - **1.** [relativo ou pertencente à Terra - globo, crosta] earth's, of the earth; [- seres,

fenômenos] earthly. - **2.** [por oposição a aquático] land *(antes de subst)*.

terrificante [texifi'kãntʃi], **terrífico, ca** [te'xifiku, ka] *adj* terrifying.

terrina [te'xinal *f* tureen.

territorial [texito'rjaw] *adj* territorial.

território [texi'tɔrju] *m* - **1.** [ger] territory. - **2.** [parte de uma federação] district.

terrível [te'xivɛw] *(pl* -**eis)** *adj* - **1.** [ger] terrible. - **2.** [muito forte, enorme] dreadful.

terror [te'xo(x)] *(pl* -**es)** *m* [medo] terror; **ser um** ~ [ser amedrontador] to be terrifying; [ser horrível] to be awful.

terrorismo [texo'riʒmu] *m* terrorism.

terrorista [texo'riʃta] <> *adj* terrorist *(antes de subst)*. <> *mf* [pessoa] terrorist.

tesão [te'sãw] *(pl* -**ões)** *m* - **1.** *mfam* [desejo sexual] hots *(pl)*; **estar com** ~ to have the hots, to be horny; **sentir** ~ **por alguém** to have the hots for sb; **ser um** ~ [pessoa] to be sexy; [coisa] to be fantastic. - **2.** [ereção] stiffy, hard-on; **estar com** ~ to have a hard-on.

tese ['tɛzi] *f* thesis.

  ➠ **em tese** *loc adv* in theory.

teso, sa ['tezu, za] *adj* - **1.** [esticado] taut. - **2.** [ereto] stiff. - **3.** *fam* [sem dinheiro] skint.

tesões [te'zõjʃ] *pl* ⊳ **tesão**.

tesoura [te'zoral *f* scissors *(pl)*.

tesourar [4] [tezo'ra(x)] *vt* - **1.** [cortar] to cut with scissors. - **2.** *fam* [falar mal de] to slag off.

tesouraria [tezora'ria] *f* - **1.** [departamento] finance department. - **2.** [cargo] finance director.

tesoureiro, ra [tezo'rejru, ra] *m, f* - **1.** [de banco] treasurer. - **2.** [de empresa] financial director.

tesouro [te'zoru] *m* - **1.** [ger] treasure. - **2.** [lugar onde são guardadas as riquezas] treasury.

  ➠ **Tesouro** *m*: **o Tesouro Nacional** the Treasury.

testa ['tɛʃta] *f* forehead; **à** ~ **de** at the head of.

testa-de-ferro [ˌtɛʃtadʒi'fɛxu] *(pl* **testas-de-ferro)** *mf* figurehead.

testamentário, ria [tɛʃtamẽntarju, rja] *adj* of a will.

testamento [teʃta'mẽntu] *m* will.

  ➠ **Novo Testamento** *m* New Testament.

  ➠ **Velho Testamento** *m* Old Testament.

testar [4] [teʃ'ta(x)] *vt* - **1.** [submeter a teste] to test. - **2.** [deixar em testamento] to bequeath.

teste ['tɛʃtʃi] *m* test.

testemunha [teʃte'muɲa] *f* witness; ~ **ocular** eye witness; ~ **de acusação** witness for the prosecution.

testemunha-de-Jeová [teʃte'muɲadʒiʒeo'va] *mf* Jehovah's Witness.

testemunhar [4] [teʃte'muɲa(x)] <> *vt* - **1.** [ger] to witness. - **2.** JUR [depor sobre] to testify to. - **3.** [comprovar] to prove. - **4.** [manifestar] to display. <> *vi* JUR to testify; ~ **sobre/a favor de/contra algo** to give evidence about/for/against sthg; ~ **sobre/a favor de/contra alguém** to act as witness regarding/for/against sb.

testemunho [teʃte'muɲu] *m* testimony; **dar** ~

(sobre algo) to give evidence (about sthg).
testículo [teʃ'tʃikulu] *m* testicle.
testudo, da [teʃ'tudu, da] *adj* with a wide forehead.
teta ['teta] *f* [ANAT- de mulher] breast; [- de animal] teat; [- de vaca] udder.
tétano ['tɛtanu] *m* tetanus.
tête-à-tête [ˌtɛtʃja'tɛtʃi] *m* tête-à-tête.
tetéia [te'tɛja] *f fam* [pessoa] dish.
teto ['tɛtu] *m* -**1.** [ger] ceiling. -**2.** [de peça da casa] roof; ~ **solar** AUTO sunroof. -**3.** [habitação]: **sem** ~ homeless person.
tetracampeão, peã [tetrakãn'pjãw, pjã] *m, f* four times champion.
tetraplégico, ca [tetra'plɛʒiku, ka] ◇ *adj* quadriplegic. ◇ *m, f* quadriplegic.
tétrico, ca ['tɛtriku, ka] *adj* -**1.** [medonho, horrível] grim. -**2.** [triste, fúnebre] gloomy.
teu, tua ['tew, 'tua] ◇ *adj poss* your. ◇ *pron poss* yours.
tevê [te've] *f* = **televisão**.
têxtil ['teʃtʃiw] (*pl* -**teis**) *adj* textile.
texto ['teʃtu] *m* text.
textual [teʃ'twaw] *adj* -**1.** [relativo ao texto] textual. -**2.** *fig* [exato]: **foram estas minhas palavras textuais** those were my precise words.
textualmente [teʃtwaw'mẽntʃi] *adv* [exatamente, literalmente] verbatim.
textura [teʃ'tura] *f* texture.
texugo [te'ʃugul] *m* ZOOL badger.
tez ['teʃ] *f* [cútis] complexion.
ti ['tʃi] *pron pess* you; **trouxe este presente para** ~ I brought this present for you.
tia ['tʃia] *f* aunt.
tia-avó [ˌtʃia'vɔ] (*pl* tias-avós) *f* great-aunt.
tiara ['tʃjara] *f* tiara.
tibetano, na [tʃibe'tanu, na] ◇ *adj* Tibetan. ◇ *m, f* Tibetan.
   ➡ **tibetano** *m* [língua] Tibetan.
Tibete [tʃi'bɛtʃi] *n* Tibet.
tíbia ['tʃibja] *f* ANAT tibia.
tíbio, bia ['tʃibju, bja] *adj* lukewarm.
tição [tʃi'sãw] (*pl* -**ões**) *m* -**1.** [lenha] ember. -**2.** [negro] *fig & pej* nigger.
ticar [4] [tʃi'ka(x)] *vt* to tick.
tico ['tʃiku] *m*: **um** ~ **(de)** a bit (of).
tico-tico [ˌtʃiku'tʃiku] (*pl* -**s**) *m* ZOOL ruffous-collared sparrow.
tido, da ['tʃidu, da] *adj* [considerado]: ~ **como** considered.
   ➡ **tido** *pp* ▷ **ter**.
tietagem [tʃje'taʒẽ] (*pl* -**ns**) *f fam*: **fazer** ~ **para** to show admiration towards.
tiete ['tʃjɛtʃi] *mf fam* fan.
tifo ['tʃifu] *m* typhus.
tigela [tʃi'ʒɛla] *f* [vasilha] bowl.
tigre [tʃigril] *m* ZOOL tiger.
tigresa [tʃi'greza] *f* ZOOL tigress.
tijolo [tʃi'ʒolu] *m* brick; **de** ~ **aparente** brick-faced; ~ **refratário** firebrick.
til ['tʃiw] *m* tilde.

tilintar [4] [tʃilĩn'ta(x)] ◇ *vt* [sino, chocalho] to jingle. ◇ *vi* [sino, moeda] to jingle. ◇ *m* jingle.
timaço [tʃi'masul] *m fam* [grande time] great team.
timão [tʃi'mãw] (*pl* -**ões**) *m* NÁUT helm, tiller.
timbrado, da [tʃĩn'bradu, da] *adj*: **papel** ~ headed paper.
timbre ['tʃĩnbri] *m* -**1.** [em papel de correspondência] heading. -**2.** [de voz] tone. -**3.** MÚS [tom] timbre. -**4.** [de vogal] sound.
time ['tʃimi] *m* -**1.** [ger] team. -**2.** *fig*: **de segundo** ~ second-rate. -**3.** *fam loc*: **tirar o** ~ **de campo** to pull out.
timer ['tajme(x)] *m* timer.
timidez [tʃimi'deʃ] *f* timidity.
tímido, da ['tʃimidu, da] *adj* -**1.** [avanço, governo] timid. -**2.** [pessoa, temperamento] timid, shy.
timões [tʃi'mõjʃ] *pl* ▷ **timão**.
timoneiro, ra [tʃimo'nejru, ra] *m, f* NÁUT helmsman.
tímpano ['tʃĩnpanu] *m* -**1.** ANAT eardrum. -**2.** [em campainha] bell.
tina ['tʃina] *f* -**1.** [para lavar roupa] trough. -**2.** [para banho] bathtub. -**3.** [para uso industrial] vat.
tíner ['tʃine(x)] *m* thinner.
tingido, da [tʃĩn'ʒidu, da] *adj* [tinto] dyed.
tingimento [tʃĩnʒi'mẽntul] *m* dyeing.
tingir [52] [tʃĩn'ʒi(x)] *vt* -**1.** [ger] to dye. -**2.** [parede, corpo] to paint.
tinha ['tʃiɲa] ▷ **ter**.
tinhoso, osa [tʃi'ɲozu, ɔza] *adj* -**1.** [teimoso] obstinate. -**2.** [persistente] stubborn.
tinido [tʃi'nidu] *m* ring.
tinir [6] [tʃi'ni(x)] *vi* -**1.** [ger] to ring. -**2.** *loc*: **estar tinindo** [estar em ótimo estado de limpeza] to be sparkling; [estar bem preparado] to be well-primed; [estar em ótimas condições] to be in excellent order; ~ **de fome/raiva** to be extremely hungry/furious.
tinjo ['tʃĩnʒul] *vb* ▷ **tingir**.
tino ['tʃinul] *m* -**1.** [juízo] common sense; **perder o** ~ to lose one's common sense. -**2.** [prudência] care. -**3.**: **ter** ~ **para algo** [ter queda para] to have a gift for sthg.
tinta ['tʃĩnta] *f* -**1.** [para imprimir, escrever] ink. -**2.** [para tingir] dye. -**3.** [para pintar] paint; ~ **a óleo** oil paint; ~ **plástica** emulsion.
tinteiro [tʃĩn'tejrul] *m* inkwell.
tintim [tʃĩn'tʃĩ] *m*: **tintim!** cheers!
   ➡ **tintim por tintim** *loc adv* word for word.
tinto ['tʃĩntul] *adj* -**1.** [cabelos] dyed. -**2.**: **vinho** ~ red wine.
tintura [tʃĩn'tura] *f* -**1.** [tinta] dye. -**2.** [ato] dyeing.
tinturaria [tʃĩntura'ria] *f* -**1.** [ramo] dyeing. -**2.** [lavanderia] dry-cleaner's. -**3.** [onde se faz tingimento] dyer's.
tintureiro, ra [tʃĩntu'rejru, ra] *m, f* [profissional - que lava a seco] dry-cleaner; [- que tinge] dyer.
tio ['tʃiw] *m* uncle; **os meus** ~**s** [casal] my aunt and uncle.
tio-avô ['tʃiwa'vo] (*pl* tios-avôs) *m* great-uncle.

tipão [tʃi'pãw] *m* stunner.

tipicamente [tʃipika'mẽntʃil] *adv* typically.

típico, ca ['tʃipiku, ka] *adj* typical.

tipificar [12] [tʃipifi'ka(x)] *vt* to typify.

tipo, pa ['tʃipu, pal] *m* -1. [espécie] type; ~ **sangüí-neo** blood group. -2. [pessoa] sort. -3. *fam* [sujei-to] guy (*f* girl). -4. [TIP- peça] type; [- letra] font.

tipografia [tʃipogra'fial] *f* -1. [arte] typography. -2. [estabelecimento] printer's.

tipográfico, ca [tʃipo'grafiku, ka] *adj* typographical; **erro** ~ typo.

tipógrafo, fa [tʃi'pɔgrafu, fal] *m, f* [profissional - que imprime] printer; [- que compõe] typesetter.

tipóia [tʃi'pɔjal] *f* [tira de pano] sling.

tique ['tʃikil] *m* tick; ~ **nervoso** nervous tic.

tique-taque [,tʃiki'takil] (*pl* **tique-taques**) *m* tick-tock.

tíquete [tʃi'ketʃil] *m* ticket, voucher.

tíquete-restaurante [tʃiketʃixeʃtaw'rãntʃil] (*pl* **tíquetes-restaurante**) *m* [vale-refeição] luncheon voucher.

tiquinho [tʃi'kiɲul] *m*: **um** ~ (**de**) a shred (of).

tira ['tʃiral] <> *f* [ger] strip. <> *m gír* [agente de polícia] cop.

tiracolo [tʃira'kɔlul] *m*: **a** ~ across the shoulder; **com os filhos a** ~ with the children in tow.

tirada [tʃi'radal] *f* [dito] tirade.

tiragem [tʃi'raʒẽl] (*pl* -ns) *f* -1. [operação de imprimir] print run. -2. [número de exemplares] circulation.

tira-gosto ['tʃira'goʃtul] (*pl* **tira-gostos**) *m* savoury *UK*, savory *US*.

tira-manchas [,tʃira'mãnʃaʃl] *m inv* stain remover.

Tirana [tʃi'rãnal] *n* Tirana.

tirania [tʃira'nial] *f* tyranny.

tirânico, ca [tʃi'rãniku, ka] *adj* tyrannical.

tiranizar [4] [tʃirani'za(x)] *vt* to tyrannize.

tirano, na [tʃi'rãnu, nal] <> *adj* [cruel, injusto] tyrannical. <> *m, f* tyrant.

tirante [tʃi'rãntʃil] <> *adj*: ~ **dois ou três problemas, o resto deu certo** except for a couple of problems, the rest worked out well; **uma cor** ~ **a verde** a greenish colour *UK*, a greenish color *US*. <> *m* -1. [correia] harness. -2. [viga] tie beam. -3. *MEC* connecting rod.

tirar [4] [tʃi'ra(x)] *vt* -1. [ger] to take. -2. [retirar] to take away. -3. [de cima] [despir, descalçar] to take off. -4. [de dentro] [sacar] to take out, to withdraw. -5. [trazer abaixo] to take down. -6. [extrair] to extract. -7. [eliminar] to remove. -8. [obter] to get; ~ **proveito de** to make use of. -9. [mesa] to clear. -10. [para dançar] to ask. -11. *MÚS* to take down. -12. *TIP* [imprimir] to print. -13.: ~ **algo/alguém de algo** [afastar, fazer sair] to take sthg/sb away from sthg; -14. [loc]: **sem** ~ **nem pôr** exactly like; **ele é o pai sem** ~ **nem pôr** he's the spitting image of his father.

tiririca [tʃiri'rikal] *adj fam*: **estar/ficar** ~ to be hopping mad.

tiritar [4] [tʃiri'ta(x)] *vi* to shiver; ~ **de frio** to shiver with cold.

tiro ['tʃirul] *m* -1. [ger] shot; **dar um** ~ (**em**) to fire a shot (at); **trocar** ~**s** to exchange fire; ~ **ao alvo** target practice; **o** ~ **saiu pela culatra** *fig* it backfired. -2. [loc]: **ser** ~ **e queda** to be sure-fire.

tiro-de-guerra [tʃirudʒi'gɛxal] (*pl* **tiros-de-guerra**) *m army reserve training centre*.

tiroteio [tʃiro'tejul] *m* -1. [tiros amiudados] shooting. -2. [troca de tiros] shootout.

tis [tʃiʃl] *pl* ▷ **til**.

tísico, ca ['tʃiziku, ka] <> *adj* consumptive. <> *m, f* consumptive.

titânio [tʃi'tãnjul] *m* titanium.

títere ['tʃiteril] *m* [marionete] puppet.

titia [tʃi'tʃial] *f fam* aunty; **ficar para** ~ to become an old maid.

Titicaca [tʃitʃi'kakal] *n*: **o** (**lago**) ~ Lake Titicaca.

titio [tʃi'tʃiwl] *m fam* uncle.

titititi [tʃitʃitʃi'tʃil] *m* -1. *gír* [falatório] tittle-tattle. -2. [badalação] hubbub. -3. [discussão, briga] brawl.

titubeante [tʃitu'bjãntʃil] *adj* -1. [cambaleante] lurching. -2. [hesitante] hesitant.

titubear [15] [tʃitu'bja(x)] *vi* -1. [hesitar] to hesitate; ~ **em algo/em fazer algo** to hesitate in sthg/at doing sthg. -2. [cambalear] to lurch.

titular [tʃitu'la(x)] <> *adj* [efetivo - juiz] incumbent; [- professor] tenured; [- oficial] official. <> *mf* -1. [ocupante efetivo de função ou cargo] incumbent. -2. *POL* [de ministério]: **o** ~ **do Ministério da Saúde** the Health Minister. -3. [possuidor] holder.

título ['tʃitulul] *m* -1. [ger] title. -2. [documento] (title) deed; ~ **ao portador** *COM* bearer bond *ou* certificate; ~ **de crédito** *COM* bond; ~ **de propriedade** *JUR* title deed. -3. [motivo]: **a** ~ **de** by way of; **a** ~ **de curiosidade** out of curiosity; **a** ~ **de quê?** what for?

tive ['tʃivil] *v* ▷ **ter**.

tlintlim [tlĩn'tlĩl] *m* tinkle.

TM (*abrev de* Trademark) *f* TM.

TO (*abrev de* Estado de Tocantins) *n State of Tocantins*.

toa ['toal] *f NÁUT* towline.
    ▸ **à toa** *loc adv* -1. [ger] for no reason; **não é à** ~ **que** it's not by chance that. -2. [inutilmente] in vain. -3. [desocupado] at a loose end. -4. [sem rumo] aimlessly.

toada ['twadal] *f MÚS* tune, melody.

toalete [twa'letʃil] <> *m* [banheiro] toilet. <> *f* -1. [ato]: **fazer a** ~ to get washed and dressed. -2. [traje] outfit.

toalha ['twaʎal] *f* towel; ~ **de banho/rosto/praia** bath/hand/beach towel; ~ **de mesa** tablecloth.

toalheiro [twa'ʎejrul] *m* [utensílio] towel rail.

tobogã [tobo'gãl] *m* -1. [trenó] toboggan. -2. [pista] slide.

toca ['tɔkal] *f* -1. [covil] den. -2. *fig* [refúgio] bolthole.

toca-discos [,tɔka'dʒiskuʃl] *m inv* record player.

tocado, da [to'kadu, dal] *adj* -1. *fam* [meio embriagado] tipsy. -2. [expulso] turfed out.

toca-fitas [,tɔka'fitaʃl] *m inv* cassette player.

tocaia [to'kaja] f ambush.

tocante [to'kãtʃi] adj inv [comovente] touching.

➤ **no tocante a** loc prep when it comes to.

Tocantins [tokãn'tʃĩn] npl Tocantins.

tocar [12] [to'ka(x)] ⋄ vt -**1.** [ger] to touch. -**2.** MÚS to play. -**3.** [campainha, sino] to ring. -**4.** [buzina] to hoot. -**5.** [conduzir] to drive. -**6.** [fazer progredir]: ~ **algo (para frente)** to move (sthg) forward. -**7.** [expulsar]: ~ **alguém/algo de algum lugar** to throw sb/sthg out of somewhere. ⋄ vi -**1.** [ger] to ring. -**2.** [apalpar, encostar]: ~ **(em) algo/alguém** to touch sthg/sb.

➤ **tocar a** vi [dizer respeito a]: **no** ou **pelo que me toca** as far as I am concerned.

➤ **tocar em** vi -**1.** [referir-se a] to touch (up)on. -**2.** [fazer escala em] to stop off in. -**3.** [caber a]: **toca a você fazer isso** it's up to you to do it.

➤ **tocar para** vi [telefonar] to ring.

➤ **tocar-se** vp -**1.** [pôr-se em contato] to touch. -**2.** [perceber] to notice. -**3.** [ofender-se] to be provoked.

tocha ['tɔʃa] f [facho] torch.

toco ['toku] m -**1.** [de árvore] stump. -**2.** [de cigarro, charuto] butt(-end), stub.

todavia [toda'via] conj however.

todo, da ['todu, da] ⋄ adj indef [inteiro] all; **a Europa toda** the whole of Europe; **a equipe toda** the entire team; **o dia** ~, **o dia** the whole day (long). ⋄ adv [completamente] completely. ⋄ pron indef [qualquer, cada] every; ~ **dia**, ~**s os dias** every day; **em** ou **por toda parte** everywhere; ~ **mundo** everyone; **em** ~ **caso** in any case; **de** ~ **jeito** all the same.

➤ **todo** m whole; **ao** ~ in all; **de** ~ entirely.

➤ **todos** pron pl [todas as pessoas] everyone (sg).

➤ **a toda (velocidade)** loc adv at top speed.

todo-poderoso, osa [,todupode'rozu, ɔza] adj all-powerful.

➤ **Todo-Poderoso** m: **o Todo Poderoso** the Almighty.

toga ['tɔga] f -**1.** HIST toga. -**2.** [jur] gown.

toicinho [toj'siɲu] m = **toucinho**.

toldo ['towdu] m awning.

tolerância [tole'rãnsja] f tolerance.

tolerante [tole'rãntʃi] adj tolerant.

tolerar [4] [tole'ra(x)] vt -**1.** [ger] to tolerate. -**2.** [suportar] to bear.

tolerável [tole'ravew] (pl -eis) adj -**1.** [aceitável] tolerable. -**2.** [suportável] bearable.

tolher [5] [to'ʎe(x)] vt -**1.** [dificultar] to impede. -**2.** [impedir]: ~ **alguém de algo/de fazer algo** to prevent sb from sthg/from doing sthg.

tolice [to'lisi] f -**1.** [ato] stupid thing. -**2.** [qualidade] idiocy. -**3.** [dito] rubbish.

tolo, la ['tolu, la] ⋄ adj -**1.** [ger] stupid. -**2.** [pessoa - idiota] idiotic; [- ingênuo] foolish. ⋄ m, f [pessoa] idiot.

tom ['tõ] (pl -ns) m -**1.** [ger] tone. -**2.** [altura de um som] pitch; ~ **agudo/grave** high/low pitch. -**3.** [matiz] shade. -**4.** [MÚS - intervalo entre duas notas] tone; [- escala] key; ~ **maior/menor** major/minor

key. -**5.** loc: **ser de bom** ~ to be polite.

tomada [to'mada] f -**1.** [ato] taking; ~ **de decisão** decision making; ~ **de preços** tender; ~ **de posse** [de presidente] investiture; ~ **de posto oficial** taking office. -**2.** [ELETR - plugue] plug; [- na parede] socket. -**3.** [ocupação] taking. -**4.** CINE take.

tomar [4] [to'ma(x)] vt -**1.** [ger] to take; ~ **alguém em/por algo** to take sb in/by sthg; ~ **emprestado** to borrow; **toma!** there you are!; ~ **um susto** to get a fright. -**2.** [ocupar] to take. -**3.** [beber] to have. -**4.** [ocupar aspecto] to take up. -**5.** [satisfação]: ~ **satisfação de alguém** to get an explanation from sb. -**6.** [considerar]: ~ **algo como algo** to take sthg as sthg; ~ **alguém por algo** to take sb for sthg.

➤ **tomar-se** vp: ~-**se de algo (por)** [ser invadido por] to be full of sthg (for ou towards); ~-**se (de) horror a** to be filled with horror at.

tomara [to'mara] interj let's hope so!; ~ **que chova!** let's hope it rains!

tomara-que-caia [to,maraki'kaja] ⋄ adj inv strapless. ⋄ m inv strapless dress.

tomate [to'matʃi] m tomato.

tomateiro [toma'tejru] m tomato plant.

tombadilho [tõnba'dʒiʎu] m (poop) deck.

tombar [4] [tõn'ba(x)] ⋄ vt -**1.** [derrubar] to knock down. -**2.** [para preservar] to list (for the preservation of buildings). ⋄ vi: ~ **(em/de/para)** [cair] to fall on/off/towards; [cair rolando] to tumble on/off/towards.

tombo ['tõnbu] m [queda] fall; **levar um** ~ to take a tumble.

tomilho [to'miʎu] m thyme.

tomo ['tomu] m -**1.** [parte] tome. -**2.** [volume] volume.

tomografia [tomogra'fia] f MED tomography; ~ **computadorizada** computerized axial tomography, CAT scanning.

tona ['tona] f: **à** ~ to the surface; **vir/trazer à** ~ fig [vir à baila] to come/bring up.

tonal [to'naw] (pl -ais) adj MÚS tonal.

tonalidade [tonali'dadʒi] f -**1.** [ger] shade. -**2.** [mus] tonality.

tonel [to'nɛw] (pl -éis) m [recipiente] cask.

tonelada [tone'lada] f -**1.** [medida] ton. -**2.** fig [grande quantidade de]: **uma** ~ **de** tons of.

tonelagem [tone'laʒẽ] f tonnage.

toner ['tone(x)] m TEC toner.

tônico, ca ['toniku, ka] adj tonic.

➤ **tônico** m [cosmético] tonic; ~ **para o cabelo** hair tonic.

➤ **tonica** f -**1.** [água tônica] tonic water. -**2.** MÚS tonic. -**3.** fig [idéia, assunto principal] keynote.

tonificante [tonifi'kãntʃi] adj invigorating.

tonificar [12] [tonifi'ka(x)] vt to tone.

tons [tõʃ] pl ▷ **tom**.

tontas ['tõntaʃ] fpl: **às** ~ [atarantadamente] in a fluster.

tontear [15] [tõn'tʃja(x)] ⋄ vt -**1.** [suj: bebida, perfume] to make giddy. -**2.** [suj: pessoa, notícia, revelação] to stun. -**3.** [suj: barulho, confusão] to

drive mad. ◇ *vi* **-1.** [bebida, perfume] to be
intoxicating. **-2.** [notícia, revelação] to be
shocking. **-3.** [barulho, confusão] to be
maddening. **-4.** [pessoa - ficar tonto] to become
dizzy; [- perturbar-se] to be stunned; [- ficar ator-
doado] to be maddened.

tonteira [tõn'tejra] *f* [vertigem] giddiness, dizziness; **ter** ~ to suffer a dizzy spell.

tonto, ta ['tõntu, ta] *adj* **-1.** [zonzo] dizzy. **-2.**
[perturbado, atordoado] giddy. **-3.** [tolo] giddy.

tontura [tõn'tura] *f* = **tonteira.**

tônus ['tonuʃ] *m inv:* ~ **muscular** muscle tone.

top ['tɔpil] *m* **-1.** [bustiê] bodice. **-2.** [o melhor]: ~
de linha top-of-the-range.

topada [to'pada] *f* trip; **dar uma** ~ **em algo** to trip
over sthg.

topar [4] [to'pa(x)] ◇ *vt* [aceitar, concordar com]: ~
algo/fazer algo to agree to sthg/to do sthg; **você
topa ir à praia?** do you feel like going to the
beach? ◇ *vi* [aceitar, concordar] to agree.

➡ **topar com** *vi* [encontrar] to come across.

➡ **topar em** *vi* [tropeçar em] to trip over.

➡ **topar-se** *vp* [deparar-se]: ~ **com algo/alguém**
to come across sthg/sb.

topázio [to'pazju] *m* topaz.

topete [to'petʃi] *m* [cabelo levantado] quiff; **ter o** ~
de fazer algo to have the nerve to do sthg.

topetudo, da [topetu'du, da] *adj* **-1.** [que usa to-
pete] with a quiff *(depois de subst)*. **-2.** [destemido]
daring.

tópico, ca ['tɔpiku, ka] *adj* [questão, assunto]
topical.

➡ **tópico** *m* [tema, assunto] topic.

topless [tɔpi'lɛʃ] ◇ *adj inv* topless. ◇ *m inv*
topless bikini.

topo ['topu] *m* top.

topografia [topogra'fia] *f* topography.

topográfico, ca [topo'grafiku, ka] *adj* topogra-
phical.

topônimo [to'ponimul *m* toponym, place name.

toque ['tɔki] ◇ *v* ▷ **tocar.** ◇ *m* **-1.** [ger] touch.
-2. [de campainha] ring. **-3.** [de corneta] blast. **-4.**
MED palpation. **-5.** [pequeno teor ou quantidade]: **um**
~ **de** a touch of. **-6.** [retoque] finishing touch. **-7.**
fam : **dar um** ~ **em alguém** to have a word with
sb. **-8.** MIL: ~ **de recolher** curfew. **-9.** *loc*: **a** ~ **de
caixa** hurriedly.

Tóquio ['tɔkju] *n* Tokyo.

tora ['tɔra] *f* **-1.** [de madeira] log. **-2.** [pedaço] piece;
tirar uma ~ [cochilar] to take a nap.

tórax ['tɔrakiʃ] *m inv* thorax.

torção [tox'sãw] *f* **-1.** [ato de torcer] twist(ing). **-2.**
MED sprain.

torcedor, ra [toxse'do(x), ra] *(mpl* -es, *fpl* -s) *m, f*
ESP supporter; **sou** ~ **do Flamengo** I am a
Flamengo supporter.

torcedura [toxse'dura] *f* MED sprain.

torcer [25] [tox'se(x)] ◇ *vt* **-1.** [ger] to twist. **-2.**
[espremer] to wring. **-3.** MED to sprain. ◇ *vi* **-1.**
[ger] to twist **-2.** [num jogo] to do one's bit as a
supporter.

➡ **torcer por** *vi* ESP [ser aficionado de] to be a
supporter of.

➡ **torcer para, torcer por** *vi* [desejar o êxito de]
to back.

torcicolo [toxsi'kɔlu] *m* MED stiff neck, wryneck;
estar com ~ to have a stiff neck.

torcida [tox'sida] *f* [ESP- ato] support; [- torcedores]
supporters *(pl)*.

tormenta [tox'mẽnta] *f* **-1.** METEOR storm. **-2.** *fig*
[transtorno] upheaval.

tormento [tox'mẽntu] *m* torment.

tormentoso, sa [toxmẽn'tozu, za] *adj* stormy.

tornado [tox'nadu] *m* tornado.

tornar [4] [tox'na(x)] ◇ *vt* [fazer ser] to make; ~
algo em algo to turn sthg into sthg. ◇ *vi*: ~ **a
fazer algo** to do sthg again; **ela tornou a insistir**
she again insisted.

➡ **tornar-se** *vp* [vir a ser] to become.

torneado, da [tox'njadu, da] *adj* [arredondado]
turned; **bem** ~ *fig* [corpo, pernas] well-turned,
shapely.

tornear [15] [tox'nja(x)] *vt* to turn.

torneio [tox'neju] *m* [competição] tournament.

torneira [tox'nejra] *f* tap UK, faucet US.

torniquete [toxni'ketʃi] *m* MED tourniquet.

torno ['toxnul *m* TEC lathe.

➡ **en torno de** *loc prep* around.

tornozeleira [toxnoze'lejra] *f* ankle strap.

tornozelo [toxnu'zelu] *m* ankle.

toró [to'rɔ] *m* METEOR downpour; **caiu um** ~ there
was a heavy downpour.

torpe ['toxpi] *adj* **-1.** [vil] foul. **-2.** [desonesto]
shameful. **-3.** [obsceno] disgraceful.

torpedear [15] [toxpe'dʒja(x)] *vt* to torpedo.

torpedo [tox'pedul *m* torpedo.

torpeza [tox'peza] *f* **-1.** [vileza] foulness. **-2.** [de-
sonestidade] shamefulness. **-3.** [obscenidade] disgrace.

torpor [tox'po(x)] *m* **-1.** [entorpecimento] torpor.
-2. [indiferença] inertia. **-3.** MED unresponsive-
ness.

torquês [tox'keʃ] *f* [pair of] pliers.

torrada [to'xada] *f* toast.

torradeira [toxa'dejra] *f* toaster.

torrão [to'xãw] *(pl* -ões) *m* **-1.** [de terra endurecida]
clod. **-2.** [de açúcar] lump. **-3.** : ~ **natal** birthplace.

torrar [4] [to'xa(x)] ◇ *vt* **-1.** [tostar] to toast. **-2.**
[ressecar] to parch. **-3.** *fig* [mercadorias] to dump.
-4. *fig* [dinheiro] to burn. **-5.** *fam fig* [irritar] to
annoy; ~ **a paciência de alguém** to try sb's
patience. ◇ *vi* to be irritating.

torre ['toxi] *f* **-1.** [construção] tower; ~ **de controle**
AERON control tower; ~ **de vigia** watchtower. **-2.**
ELETR pylon. **-3.** RÁDIO & TV mast. **-4.** [xadrez] castle,
rook.

torrefação [toxefa'sãw] *(pl* -oes) *f* **-1.** [de café, ca-
cau] roast(ing). **-2.** [estabelecimento] roasting
house.

torrencial [toxẽn'sjaw] *adj* torrential.

torrente [to'xẽntʃi] *f* torrent.

torresmo [to'xeʒmu] *m CULIN* crackling, pork scratchings (pl).

tórrido, da ['tɔxidu, da] *adj* torrid.

torrone [to'xɔnil *m* nougat.

torso ['tɔxsu] *m* torso.

torta ['tɔxtal *f*[empadão, doce] pie; ~ **de limão/ma-çã** lemon/apple pie/tart.

torto, ta ['tɔxtu, ta] *adj* -**1.** [ger] crooked. -**2.** *loc*: **a ~ e a direito** left, right and centre; **cometer erros a ~ e a direito** to make mistakes left, right and centre.

tortuoso, osa [tox'twozu, ɔza] *adj* -**1.** [sinuoso] winding. -**2.** *(fig)* [que não segue uma linha reta] convoluted.

tortura [tox'tura] *f*[ger] torture; [lance difícil]: **ser uma ~** to be torture.

torturador, ra [toxtura'do(x), ra] *m, f* torturer.

torturante [toxtu'rãntʃi] *adj* -**1.** [dor] excruciating. -**2.** [espera] agonizing. -**3.** [viagem] harrowing.

torturar [4] [toxtu'ra(x)] *vt*[ger] to torment; [inco-modar fisicamente] to kill.

torvelinho [toxve'liɲu] *m* [confusão] turmoil.

tosa ['tɔza] *f* -**1.** [de pêlo] trimming. -**2.** [de lã] shearing.

tosar [4] [to'za(x)] *vt* -**1.** [pêlo] to clip. -**2.** [cabelo] to crop.

tosco, ca ['toʃku, ka] *adj* crude.

tosquiar [16] [toʃ'kja(x)] *vt* [ovelha] to shear.

tosse ['tɔsi] *f* cough; ~ **de cachorro** *ou* **comprida** whooping cough; ~ **seca** dry cough.

tossir [59] [to'si(x)] *vi* -**1.** [ger] to cough. -**2.** [expe-lir] to cough up.

tostado, da [toʃ'tadu, da] *adj* -**1.** [levemente quei-mado] browned. -**2.** [moreno] tanned.

tostão [toʃ'tãw] (*pl* -ões) *m* [dinheiro] cash; **estava sem um ~** I didn't have a penny; **fiquei sem um ~** I was left penniless.

tostar [4] [toʃ'ta(x)] *vt* -**1.** [ger] to brown. -**2.** [pele] to tan.

total [to'taw] (*pl* -ais) <> *adj* total. <> *m* total; **no ~** in total.

totalidade [totali'dadʒi] *f* entirety; **a ~ da popu-lação** the entire population; **a ~ dos alunos** all the students; **em sua ~** in its/their entirety.

totalitário, ria [totali'tarju, rja] *adj* totalitarian.

totalitarismo [totalita'riʒmu] *m* totalitarianism.

totalizar [4] [totali'za(x)] *vt* -**1.** [calcular o total de] to total up. -**2.** [atingir o total de] to total.

totalmente [totaw'mẽntʃi] *adv* entirely, totally.

touca ['toka] *f* [de lã, malha] bonnet; ~ **de banho/natação** bathing/swimming cap.

toucador [toka'do(x)] (*mpl* -es) *m* [cômoda] dres-sing table.

toucinho [to'siɲu] *m* uncured bacon; ~ **defuma-do** smoked bacon.

toupeira [to'pejra] *f* -**1.** *ZOOL* mole. -**2.** *fig* [igno-rante] dimwit.

tourada [to'rada] *f* bullfight.

tourear [15] [to'rja(x)] <> *vt* to fight *(bulls)*. <> *vi* to be a bullfighter.

toureiro, ra [to'rejru, ra] *m, f* bullfighter.

touro ['toru] *m* -**1.** *ZOOL* bull. -**2.** *fig*: **ser um ~** [ser robusto] to be as strong as an ox.
➡ **Touro** *m ASTRO* Taurus.

toxemia [tokse'mia] *f* toxaemia *UK*, toxemia *US*.

tóxico, ca ['tɔksiku, ka] *adj* toxic.
➡ **tóxico** *m* -**1.** [veneno] poison. -**2.** [droga] drug.

toxicômano, na [toksi'komanu, na] *m, f* drug addict.

toxina [tok'sina] *f* toxin.

TPM (*abrev de* **Tensão Pré-Menstrual**) *f* PMT.

trabalhadeira [trabaʎa'dejra] *f* ▷ **trabalhador**.

trabalhado, da [traba'ʎadu, da] *adj* worked.

trabalhador, ra [trabaʎa'do(x), ra] (*mpl* -es, *fpl* -s) <> *adj* [laborioso] hard-working; **classe traba-lhadora** *POL* working class. <> *m, f* worker; (~) **autônomo** freelance (worker); ~ **braçal** manual worker.

trabalhão [traba'ʎãw] *m* = **trabalheira**.

trabalhar [4] [traba'ʎa(x)] <> *vt* -**1.** [ger] to work. -**2.** [aprimorar] to work on. -**3.** [elaborar] to develop. <> *vi* to work; ~ **em algo** [em projeto] to work at sthg; *TEATRO* to perform in sthg; ~ **com algo** [num ramo] to work in sthg; [comerciar com] to deal in; ~ **como algo** [exercer a profissão de] to work as sthg.

trabalheira [traba'ʎejra] *f* hard work; **ser** *ou* **dar uma ~** to be a lot of work.

trabalhista [traba'ʎiʃta] <> *adj* -**1.** [ger] labour *UK*, labor *US*; **Partido Trabalhista** Labour Party. -**2.** [que é especialista em direito do trabalho] employ-ment (*antes de subst*). <> *mf*[*POL* - partidário] Labour Party supporter; [- membro] Labour Party member.

trabalho [tra'baʎu] *m* -**1.** [ger] work; ~ **braçal** manual work; ~ **de campo** fieldwork; ~ **domés-tico** domestic work; ~**s forçados** forced labour *UK*, forced labor *US*; ~ **de parto** labour *UK*, labor *US*; ~ **artesanal** craftwork. -**2.** [tarefa] job. -**3.** *ECON* labour *UK*, labor *US*. -**4.** *EDUC* homework. -**5.** [espírit] spell; **fazer um ~** to cast a spell. -**6.**: **dar ~ (a alguém)** [exigir esforço] to be a lot of work (for sb); [causar transtorno] to be a bother (to sb).

trabalhoso, osa [traba'ʎozu, ɔza] *adj* arduous.

traça ['trasa] *f* -**1.** [de roupa] moth. -**2.** [de livro] bookworm.

traçado [tra'sadu] *m* -**1.** [conjunto de traços] sketch. -**2.** [planta] plan.

tração [tra'sãw] *f* traction; ~ **nas quatro rodas** four-wheel drive.

traçar [13] [tra'sa(x)] *vt* -**1.** [fazer com traços] to sketch. -**2.** [planejar] to draw up. -**3.** [demarcar] to mark out. -**4.** *fam* [devorar] to devour.

traço ['trasu] *m* -**1.** [linha] line. -**2.** [sinal de pontua-ção] (en) dash. -**3.** [modo de desenhar] style. -**4.** [característica] trait.
➡ **traços** *mpl* -**1.** [feições] features. -**2.** *fig* [vestí-gio] traces. -**3.** *fig* [laivos] traces. -**4.** [pequena quantidade de substância] traces.

tradição [tradʒi'sãw] (*pl* -ões) *f* tradition.

tradicional [tradʒisjo'naw] (*pl* **-ais**) *adj* traditional.

tradicionalista [tradʒisjona'liʃtal] ⟨⟩ *adj* traditionalist. ⟨⟩ *mf* traditionalist.

tradicionalmente [tradʒisjonaw'mẽntʃil] *adv* traditionally.

tradução [tradu'sãw] (*pl* **-ões**) *f* **-1.** [ger] translation. **-2.** *COMPUT*: ~ **eletrônica** machine translation, automatic translation.

tradutor, ra [tradu'to(x), ra] (*mpl* **-es**, *fpl* **-s**) ⟨⟩ *adj* translating. ⟨⟩ *m, f* translator; ~ **juramentado** accredited translator.

traduzir [72] [tradu'zi(x)] ⟨⟩ *vt* **-1.** [texto, código] to translate; ~ **algo do português para o inglês** to translate sthg from Portuguese into English. **-2.** [sentimento, pensamento] to express. ⟨⟩ *vi* **-1.** [saber traduzir] to translate. **-2.** [ser tradutor] to work as a translator.

➡ **traduzir-se** *vp* [manifestar-se]**: sua tristeza se traduz em agressão** her grief is expressed through aggression.

traduzível [tradu'zivew] (*pl* **-eis**) *adj* translatable.

trafegar [14] [trafe'ga(x)] *vi* [transitar] to be driven.

trafegável [trafe'gavew] (*pl* **-eis**) *adj* passable.

tráfego ['trafegu] *m* traffic; ~ **engarrafado** traffic jam; ~ **aéreo** air traffic.

traficante [trafi'kãntʃi] *mf* trafficker; ~ **de drogas** drug trafficker *ou* dealer.

traficar [12] [trafi'ka(x)] ⟨⟩ *vt* to traffic in. ⟨⟩ *vi* to traffic; ~ **com** to deal in.

tráfico ['trafiku] *m* traffic; ~ **de drogas** drug trafficking; ~ **de influência** backscratching.

tragada [tra'gada] *f* [em cigarro] drag.

tragar [14] [tra'ga(x)] ⟨⟩ *vt* **-1.** [engolir] to swallow. **-2.** [inalar] to inhale. **-3.** *fam* [tolerar] to tolerate. ⟨⟩ *vi* [inalar] to inhale.

tragédia [tra'ʒɛdʒja] *f* tragedy.

trágico, ca ['traʒiku, ka] ⟨⟩ *adj* **-1.** [ger] tragic. **-2.** *fig* [dado a fazer drama] over-dramatic. ⟨⟩ *m, f* [ator] tragic actor (*f* actress).

tragicomédia [traʒiko'mɛdʒja] *f* tragicomedy.

tragicômico, ca [traʒi'komiku, ka] *adj* tragicomic.

trago ['tragu] ⟨⟩ *v* ⊳ **trazer**. ⟨⟩ *m* **-1.** [gole] mouthful; **de um só** ~ in one gulp. **-2.** [dose pequena] drop. **-3.** [em cigarro] puff; **dar um** ~ **(em)** to take a puff (of).

traguei [tra'gejl *v* ⊳ **tragar**.

traição [traj'sãw] (*pl* **-ões**) *f* **-1.** [deslealdade] disloyalty. **-2.** [infidelidade] infidelity. **-3.** *POL* treason.

traiçoeiro, ra [traj'swejru, ra] *adj* **-1.** [pessoa] disloyal. **-2.** [ação] treacherous. **-3.** [mar, passagem] treacherous.

traidor, ra [traj'do(x), ra] (*mpl* **-es**, *fpl* **-s**) ⟨⟩ *adj* **-1.** [infiel] unfaithful. **-2.** [comprometedor] betraying. ⟨⟩ *m, f* [pessoa] traitor.

trailer ['trejle(x)] *m* **-1.** [ger] trailer. **-2.** [tipo casa] caravan *UK*, trailer *US*.

traineira [traj'nejra] *f NÁUT* trawler.

training ['trejnĩŋ] *m* tracksuit.

trair [68] [tra'i(x)] *vt* **-1.** [atraiçoar] to betray. **-2.** [ser infiel a] to be unfaithful to. **-3.** [não cumprir - promessa] to break; [- dever] to fail in. **-4.** [revelar] to betray.

➡ **trair-se** *vp*: ~**-se por algo/fazendo algo** [denunciar-se] to give o.s. away by sthg/doing sthg.

trajar [4] [tra'ʒa(x)] *vt* to wear.

➡ **trajar-se** *vp*: ~**-se de** to be dressed in.

traje ['traʒi] *m* dress; ~ **de banho** swimsuit; ~ **de passeio** smart dress; ~ **a rigor** evening dress; ~**s menores** underwear (*sg*).

trajeto [tra'ʒɛtu] *m* distance, journey.

trajetória [traʒe'tɔrja] *f* **-1.** [trajeto] path. **-2.** *fig* [caminho] course.

tralha ['traʎa] *f* [traste] junk.

trama ['trãma] *f* **-1.** [ger] plot. **-2.** [de tecido] weft.

tramar [4] [tra'ma(x)] ⟨⟩ *vt* **-1.** [tecer] to weave. **-2.** [maquinar] to plot. ⟨⟩ *vi* [conspirar]**:** ~ **contra** to plot against.

trambique [trãn'biki] *m fam* [negócio fraudulento] con; **dar um** ~ **em** [burlar] to con.

trambiqueiro, ra [trãnbi'kejru, ra] ⟨⟩ *adj* slippery. ⟨⟩ *m, f* con artist.

trambolhão [tranbo'ʎãw] (*pl* **-ões**) *m* tumble; **levar um** ~ to be knocked down; **desceu as escadas aos trambolhões** he stumbled down the stairs; **abrir caminho aos trambolhões** to push one's way through.

trambolho [tran'boʎu] *m* [objeto grande e incômodo] encumbrance.

tramitar [4] [trami'ta(x)] *vi* to be dealt with.

trâmites ['trãmitʃiʃ] *mpl fig* [vias] procedures.

tramóia [tra'mɔja] *f* **-1.** [trama] scheme. **-2.** [trapaça] swindle.

trampolim [trãnpo'lĩ] (*pl* **-ns**) *m* **-1.** *ESP* diving board. **-2.** *fig* [meio] springboard.

tranca ['trãnka] *f* **-1.** [de porta] bolt; **passar a** ~ **em** to bolt. **-2.** [de carro] lock; **passar a** ~ **em** to lock.

trança ['trãnsa] *f* **-1.** [ger] plaited bread. **-2.** [trançado] braid.

trançado, da [trãn'sadu, da] *adj* **-1.** [cabelo] plaited. **-2.** [cinto, galão, fita] braided. **-3.** [cesto] woven.

trancado, da [trãnka'du, da] *adj* [fechado] firmly shut.

trancafiar [16] [trãnka'fja(x)] *vt* to lock up.

trancar [12] [trãn'ka(x)] *vt* **-1.** [chavear] to lock. **-2.** [prender] to lock up. **-3.** *EDUC & UNIV* [matrícula] to suspend. **-4.** *FUT* to shove (to one side).

➡ **trancar-se** *vp* **-1.** [fechar-se] to shut o.s. away. **-2.** [não se manifestar] to clam up.

trançar [13] [trãn'sa(x)] ⟨⟩ *vt* **-1.** [cabelo] to plait. **-2.** [palha, fita] to weave. ⟨⟩ *vi fam* [zanzar] to mope.

tranco ['trãŋku] *m* **-1.** [andadura de cavalo] trot. **-2.** [esbarrão] shove. **-3.** [solavanco] jolt. **-4.** *fam* [advertência] jolt.

➡ **aos trancos** *loc adv* [aos solavancos] jolting.

➡ **aos trancos e barrancos** *loc adv* [com dificuldade] with great difficulty.

tranqüilamente [trãŋkwila'mẽntʃil] *adv* **-1.** [com

calma] calmly. **-2.** [sossegadamente] peacefully. **-3.** [com facilidade, seguramente] easily.

tranqüilidade [trãŋkwili'dadʒi] *f* tranquillity; **preciso de ~ para fazer isso** I need peace and quiet to do this.

tranqüilizador, ra [trãŋkwiliza'do(x), ral *adj* **-1.** [música] soothing. **-2.** [pessoa, notícia] reassuring.

tranqüilizante [trãŋkwili'zãntʃil <> *adj* soothing. <> *m* MED tranquillizer.

tranqüilizar [trãŋkwili'za(x)] *vt* **-1.** [acalmar] to calm (down). **-2.** [despreocupar] to reassure.
➤ **tranqüilizar-se** *vp* to calm down.

tranqüilo, la [trãŋ'kwilu, lal *adj* **-1.** [mulher, criança] calm. **-2.** [lugar, sono] peaceful. **-3.** [consciência] clear. **-4.** [sem dificuldades] easy. **-5.** [certo] certain.

transa ['trãnzal *f fam* **-1.** [combinação] arrangement. **-2.** [relação] relationship. **-3.** [relação sexual] sex. **-4.** [assunto] matter. **-5.** [negócios] business.

transação [trãnza'sãwl (*pl* -ões) *f* **-1.** [combinação, acordo] agreement. **-2.** [negociação] deal. **-3.** COM business.

transamazônico, ca [trãnzama'zoniku, kal *adj* trans-Amazonian.

transar [4] [trãn'za(x)] <> *vt* **-1.** *fam* [combinar] to arrange. **-2.** [arranjar] to obtain. **-3.** [drogas - tomar] to take; [- negociar] to deal in. <> *vi* **-1.** [ter relação sexual] to have sex; **~ com** to have sex with. **-2.** [relacionar-se]: **~ com** to hang out with. **-3.** [negociar, trabalhar]: **~ com** to deal in.

transatlântico, ca [trãnza'tlãntʃiku, kal *adj* transatlantic.
➤ **transatlântico** *m* liner.

transbordamento [trãnʒboxda'mẽntul *m* overflow.

transbordar [4] [trãnʒbox'da(x)] *vi*: **~ (de)** to overflow (from); **~ de felicidade** to be overjoyed.

transbordo [trãnʒ'bɔxdul *m* NÁUT transfer.

transcendência [trãnsẽn'dẽnsjal *f* transcendence.

transcendental [trãnsẽndẽn'tawl (*pl* -ais) *adj* transcendental.

transcender [5] [trãnsẽn'de(x)] *vt*: **~ (a) algo** to transcend sthg.

transcodificar [5] [trãnʒkodʒifi'ka(x)] *vt* [videoteipe] to transcode.

transcorrer [trãnʃko'xe(x)] *vi* **-1.** [decorrer] to go by. **-2.** [decorrer em certo estado ou condição] to pass off.

transcrever [5] [trãnʃkre've(x)] *vt* **-1.** [ger] to transcribe. **-2.** [copiar] to copy.

transcrição [trãnʃkri'sãwl (*pl* -ões) *f* **-1.** [ato] transcription. **-2.** [texto transcrito] transcript; **~ fonética** phonetic transcription.

transcrito, ta [trãnʃ'kritu, tal <> *pp* ➤ transcrever.
➤ **transcrito** *m* transcript.

transcurso [trãnʃ'kuxsul *m* course.

transe ['trãnzil *m* **-1.** [espirit] anguish. **-2.** [situação difícil] ordeal. **-3.** [hipnótico] trance.

transeunte [trãn'zeũntʃil *mf* passer-by.

transferência [trãnʃfe'rẽnsjal *f* **-1.** [ger] transfer. **-2.** PSIC transference. **-3.** [adiamento] postponement.

transferir [57] [trãnʃfe'ri(x)] *vt* **-1.** [deslocar]: **~ algo/alguém para algum lugar** to transfer sthg/sb somewhere. **-2.** [transmitir]: **~ algo para alguém** to transfer sthg to sb; PSIC to transfer sthg onto sb. **-3.** [adiar] to postpone.
➤ **transferir-se** *vp* [mudar-se] to move.

transfigurar [4] [trãnʃfigu'ra(x)] *vt* [pessoa, rosto] to transfigure.
➤ **transfigurar-se** *vp* [pessoa, rosto] to be transfigured.

transformação [trãnʃfoxma'sãwl (*pl* -ões) *f* transformation.

transformador, ra [trãnʃfoxma'do(x), ral (*mpl* -es, *fpl* -s) *m* ELETR transformer.

transformar [4] [trãnʃfox'ma(x)] *vt* **-1.** [dar nova forma, modificar] to transform. **-2.** [converter]: **~ algo/alguém em** to turn sthg/sb into.
➤ **transformar-se** *vp* **-1.** [mudar, transfigurar-se] to be transformed. **-2.** [converter-se]: **~-se em** to turn into, to become. **-3.** [disfarçar-se]: **~-se em** to disguise o.s. as.

transformista [trãnʃfox'miʃtal *m* [travesti] transvestite.

transfusão [trãnʃfu'zãwl (*pl* -ões) *f* transfusion; **~ de sangue** blood transfusion.

transgredir [57] [trãnʒgre'dʒi(x)] *vt* [infringir] to transgress.

transgressão [trãnʒgre'sãwl (*pl* -ões) *f* transgression.

transgressor, ra [trãʒgre'so(x), ral <> *adj* offending. <> *m*, *f* offender; **~ da lei** offender.

transição [trãnzi'sãwl (*pl* -ões) *f* [passagem de um estado a outro] transition; **fase de ~** transition stage.

transigente [trãnzi'ʒẽntʃil *adj* compliant.

transigir [52] [trãnzi'ʒi(x)] *vi* **-1.** [ceder] to compromise; **~ com alguém** to meet sb halfway. **-2.** [condescender] to condescend; **~ com algo** to yield to sthg.

transitar [4] [trãnzi'ta(x)] *vi*: **~ (por)** [pessoa, carro] to travel (through); [documentos] to work one's way (through).

transitável [trãnzi'tavewl (*pl* -eis) *adj* passable.

transitivo, va [trãnzi'tʃivu, val *adj* GRAM transitive.

trânsito ['trãnzitul *m* **-1.** [ger] passage; **passageiro em ~** transit passenger. **-2.** [tráfego] traffic; **~ impedido** no entry. **-3.** [boa aceitação] acceptance; **ter bom ~ em** to be well-accepted in.

transitório, ria [trãnzi'tɔrju, rjal *adj* transitory.

transladar [4] [trãnʒla'da(x)] *vt* = trasladar.

translado [trãnʒ'ladul *m* = traslado.

translúcido, da [trãnʒ'lusidu, dal *adj* **-1.** [que deixa passar a luz] translucent. **-2.** *fig* [claro] clear.

transmissão [trãnʒmi'sãwl (*pl* -ões) *f* **-1.** [ger]

transmission. -2. [de ordem, notícia, recado] sending; ~ **de pensamento** mind-reading. **-3.** [de bens, cargo] transfer. **-4.** [*RÁDIO & TV* - programa] broadcast; [- ato de transmitir] broadcasting; ~ **ao vivo** live broadcast.

transmissível [trãnʒmi'sivew] (*pl* -**eis**) *adj* [doença] transmittable.

transmissor, ra [trãnʒmi'so(x), ra] *adj* transmitting.
◆ **transmissor** *m* **-1.** [ger] transmitter. **-2.** [de doença] carrier.

transmitir [6] [trãnʒmi'tʃi(x)] *vt* **-1.** [ger] to transmit. **-2.** [comunicar] to send. **-3.** [transferir] to transfer. **-4.** *RÁDIO & TV* to broadcast.

transparecer [25] [trãnʃpare'se(x)] *vi* **-1.** [aparecer]: ~ **através/por trás de** to be visible through/behind. **-2.** *fig* [revelar-se]: ~ **(em)** to show through (in).

transparência [trãnʃpa'rẽnʒa] *f* **-1.** [ger] transparency. **-2.** [usada em projetor] slide.

transparente [trãnʃpa'rẽntʃi] *adj* **-1.** [ger] transparent. **-2.** [roupa] see-through. **-3.** *fig* [claro, evidente - sentimentos, intenções] clear; **o livro é de um moralismo** ~ the book is clearly moralistic; [- pessoa] transparent.

transpassar [4] [trãnʃpa'sa(x)] *vt* **-1.** [atravessar] to cross. **-2.** [penetrar, furar] to pierce. **-3.** [peça de vestuário] to overlap.

transpiração [trãnʃpira'sãw] *f* **-1.** [ato] perspiration. **-2.** [suor] perspiration.

transpirar [4] [trãnʃpi'ra(x)] ◇ *vt* **-1.** [suar] to perspire. **-2.** [exprimir] to exude. ◇ *vi* **-1.** [suar] to perspire. **-2.** [revelar-se] to transpire. **-3.** [divulgar-se] to become known.

transplantar [4] [trãnʃplãn'ta(x)] *vt*: ~ **algo (de/para)** to transplant sthg (from/to).

transplante [trãnʃ'plãntʃi] *m* transplant.

transpor [45] [trãnʃ'po(x)] *vt* **-1.** [ger] to transpose. **-2.** [atravessar] to cross. **-3.** *fig* [obstáculos] to overcome. **-4.** [mudar de lugar] to change the position of.

transportadora [trãnʃpoxta'dora] *f* haulage company.

transportar [trãnʃpox'ta(x)] *vt* **-1.** [levar] to transport. **-2.** *fig* [remontar mentalmente]: ~ **alguém a algum lugar/tempo** to take sb back to some place/time.

transporte [trãnʃ'pɔxtʃi] *m* **-1.** [ato] transport. **-2.** [condução] haulage; ~ **coletivo** public transport. **-3.** [soma] amount carried forward.

transposto, osta [trãnʃ'postu, ɔʃta] *pp* ▷ transpor.

transtornado, da [trãnʃtox'nadu, da] *adj* upset.

transtornar [4] [trãnʃtox'na(x)] *vt* **-1.** [abalar] to upset. **-2.** [alterar] to disrupt.
◆ **transtornar-se** *vp* to get upset.

transtorno [trãnʃ'toxnu] *m* **-1.** [perturbação] confusion. **-2.** [desordem, alteração] disruption. **-3.** [contrariedade, contratempo] upset.

transversal [trãnʒvex'saw] (*pl* -**ais**) ◇ *adj* **-1.** [corte, linha] transverse. **-2.** [rua]: **esta rua é** ~ **à**

avenida principal this street crosses the main avenue. ◇ *f* [rua transversal] cross street.

transverso, sa [trãnʒ'vɛxsu, sa] *adj* transverse.

transviado, da [trãnʒ'vjadu, da] *adj* wayward.

transviar [16] [trãnʒ'vja(x)] *vt* to lead astray.
◆ **transviar-se** *vp* **-1.** [perder-se] to go astray. **-2.** [corromper-se] to become corrupted.

trapaça [tra'pasa] *f* cheating; **fazer** ~ **s no jogo** to cheat during the game.

trapacear [15] [trapa'sja(x)] *vt & vi* to cheat.

trapaceiro, ra [trapa'sejru, ra] ◇ *adj* cheating. ◇ *m, f* cheat.

trapalhada [trapa'ʎada] *f* [confusão] confusion.

trapalhão, ona [trapa'ʎãw, ʎona] (*mpl* -**ões**, *fpl* -**s**) *adj* clumsy.

trapeiro, ra [tra'pejru, ra] *m, f* **-1.** [quem cata trapos] rag-and-bone-man. **-2.** [quem cata papéis] scavenger.

trapézio [tra'pɛzju] *m* **-1.** [aparelho] trapeze. **-2.** *GEOM* trapezium. **-3.** [*ANAT* - no pescoço] trapezius; [- do carpo] trapezium.

trapezista [trape'ziʃta] *mf* trapeze artist.

trapezoidal [trapezoj'daw] (*pl* -**ais**) *adj* trapezoidal.

trapo ['trapu] *m* **-1.** [pedaço de pano] rag. **-2.** *fig*: **estar um** ~ [estar mal física ou moralmente] to be down and out; [estar muito cansado] to be washed out.
◆ **trapos** *mpl* [roupa surrada] rags.

traquéia [tra'kɛja] *f* trachea, windpipe.

traquejo [tra'keʒu] *m* experience.

traqueotomia [trakjoto'mia] *f* tracheotomy.

traquinas [tra'kinaʃ] *adj inv* mischievous.

trarei [tra'rej] *v* ▷ trazer.

traria [tra'ria] *v* ▷ trazer.

trás ['trajʃ] *adv & prep* behind; **de** ~ **para frente** back to front; **andar para** ~ to walk backwards; **ficar para** ~ to fall behind; **de** ~ back; **por** ~ **de** behind; **dar para** ~ to back out.

traseira [tra'zejra] *f* **-1.** [parte posterior] rear. **-2.** *fam* [nádegas] bottom.

traseiro, ra [tra'zejru, ra] *adj* rear.
◆ **traseiro** *m fam* [nádegas] bottom.

trasladar [4] [traʒla'da(x)] *vt* **-1.** *JUR* to transfer. **-2.** [transferir]: ~ **algo (de ...) para** to transfer sthg (from ...) to.

traslado [traʒ'ladu] *m* **-1.** *JUR* transcript. **-2.** [transferência] transfer.

traspassar [trazpa'sa(x)] *vt* = transpassar.

traste ['traʃtʃi] *m* **-1.** [objeto de pouco valor] bauble. **-2.** [pessoa - inútil] no-hoper; [- de mau caráter] rogue; **estar um** ~ [estar mal fisicamente] to be a wreck.

tratado, da [tra'tadu, da] *m* **-1.** [acordo] treaty; ~ **de paz** peace treaty. **-2.** [obra] treatise.

tratador, ra [trata'do(x), ra] *m, f*: ~ **de cavalos** groom.

tratamento [trata'mẽntu] *m* **-1.** [ger] treatment; **forma de** ~ form of address; ~ **médico** medical treatment; ~ **de choque** shock treatment. **-2.** [de problema, tema] handling.

tratante [traˈtãntʃi] *mf* rogue.

tratar [4] [traˈta(x)] *vt* **-1.** [ger] to treat. **-2.** [combinar] to deal with. **-3.** MED: ~ **(de) alguém/algo** to treat sb/sthg. **-4.** [negociar] to organize. **-5.** [abordar] to deal with. **-6.** [forma de tratamento]: ~ **alguém de** ou **por algo** to address sb as ou by sthg.
◆ **tratar com** *vi* [lidar com] to deal with.
◆ **tratar de** *vi* **-1.** [cuidar de - pessoa, planta] to care for; [- caso, negócio] to look after. **-2.** [organizar] to organize. **-3.** [discorrer, versar sobre] to deal with. **-4.** [empenhar-se]: ~ **de fazer algo** to try to do sthg.
◆ **tratar-se** *vp* **-1.** [cuidar-se] to look after o.s. **-2.** MED: ~**-se com alguém** to be under sb's care. **-3.** *loc*: **trata-se de ...** it's a matter of ...; **trata-se de uma moça de origem muito humilde** she happens to be a girl from a very humble background; **de que se trata?** what's it about?

tratável [traˈtavew] (*pl* **-eis**) *adj* **-1.** [pessoa] approachable. **-2.** [doença] treatable.

trato [ˈtratu] *m* **-1.** [tratamento] treatment. **-2.** [convivência, contato] dealings (*pl*). **-3.** [acordo, combinação] agreement. **-4.** [modo]: **mulher de fino** ~ a refined woman.

trator [traˈto(x)] (*pl* **-es**) *m* tractor.

trauma [ˈtrawma] *m* **-1.** MED injury. **-2.** PSIC trauma.

traumático, ca [trawˈmatʃiku, ka] *adj* traumatic.

traumatismo [trawmaˈtʃiʒmu] *m* MED injury.

traumatizante [trawmatʃiˈzãntʃi] *adj* traumatizing.

traumatizar [4] [trawmatʃiˈza(x)] *vt* **-1.** MED to injure. **-2.** PSIC to traumatize. **-3.** *fig* [afetar] to affect.

trava [ˈtrava] *f* [peça] stop.

travada [traˈvada] *f* [freada] braking; **dar uma** ~ **em algo** [frear] to put on the breaks; *fig* [interromper] to put the brakes on sthg.

travado, da [traˈvadu, da] *adj* **-1.** [preso] locked. **-2.** [freado] stopped.

travar [4] [traˈva(x)] <> *vt* **-1.** [fazer parar] to stop. **-2.** [frear] to brake. **-3.** [iniciar, desencadear - conversa, amizade] to strike up; [- luta] to start. **-4.** [movimento] to hinder. **-5.** [segurar] to take hold of. <> *vi* to stop.

trave [ˈtravi] *f* **-1.** CONSTR beam. **-2.** ESP crossbar.

través [traˈvɛʃ] *m*: **olhar de** ~ **(para)** to look sideways (at).

travessa [traˈvɛsa] *f* **-1.** [rua] alleyway. **-2.** [prato] serving dish. **-3.** [prendedor de cabelo] slide.

travessão [traveˈsãw] (*pl* **-ões**) *m* GRAM (em) dash.

travesseiro [traveˈsejru] *m* pillow.

travessia [traveˈsia] *f* **-1.** [ato] crossing. **-2.** [viagem] journey.

travesso, ssa [traˈvesu, sa] *adj* [criança] naughty.

travessura [traveˈsura] *f* **-1.** [de criança] mischief; **fazer** ~**s** to get up to mischief. **-2.** [brincadeira] prank.

travesti [traveʃˈtʃi] *m* **-1.** [homossexual] transvestite. **-2.** [artista] drag artist.

trazer [30] [traˈze(x)] *vt* **-1.** [ger] to bring; ~ **de volta** to bring back. **-2.** [ter] to have. **-3.** [usar, trajar] to wear. **-4.** *loc*: ~ **algo à baila** to air sthg.

TRE (*abrev de* **Tribunal Regional Eleitoral**) *m* Regional Electoral Court.

trecho [ˈtreʃu] *m* **-1.** [parte do espaço de um lugar] stretch. **-2.** LITER & MÚS passage.

treco [ˈtrɛku] *m fam* [coisa] thing; **ter um** ~ [sentir-se mal] to have a nasty turn; [zangar-se] to have a fit.

trégua [ˈtrɛgwa] *f* **-1.** MIL truce. **-2.** *fig* [descanso] rest.

treinado, da [trejˈnadu, da] *adj* **-1.** [animal] trained. **-2.** [atleta] fit. **-3.** [acostumado] practised UK, practiced US.

treinador, ra [trejnaˈdo(x), ra] (*mpl* **-es**, *fpl* **-s**) *m, f* trainer.

treinamento [trejnaˈmẽntu] *m* training.

treinar [4] [trejˈna(x)] <> *vt* **-1.** [ger] to train. **-2.** [praticar] to practise UK, to practice US. <> *vi* [praticar] to train.

treino [ˈtrejnu] *m* **-1.** [ger] training. **-2.** [destreza] skill.

trejeito [treˈʒejtu] *m* **-1.** [gesto] gesture. **-2.** [gesto cômico] funny face.

trela [ˈtrɛla] *f*: **dar** ~ **a** ou **para alguém** [conversar com] to keep chatting to sb; [dar confiança a] to encourage sb.

treliça [treˈlisa] *f* [para porta, planta] trellis.

trem [ˈtrẽ] (*pl* **-ns**) *m* **-1.** FERRO train; **ir de** ~ to go by train; **pegar um** ~ to take a train; ~ **de carga** goods train; ~ **expresso** express train. **-2.** AÉRON: ~ **de aterrissagem** landing gear, undercarriage. **-3.** *loc*: ~ **da alegria** [nepotismo] jobs for the boys.

trema [ˈtrema] *m* diaeresis UK, dieresis US.

trem-bala [ˌtrẽˈbala] (*pl* **trens-bala**) *m* high-speed train.

tremedeira [tremeˈdejra] *f* [tremor] trembling.

tremelicante [tremeliˈkãntʃi] *adj* **-1.** [pessoa] shivering. **-2.** [bandeira] fluttering.

tremelicar [12] [tremeliˈka(x)] *vi* to tremble; ~ **de frio** to shiver with cold.

tremelique [tremeˈliki] *m* trembling.

tremendo, da [treˈmẽndu, da] *adj* **-1.** [imenso] enormous. **-2.** [terrível] terrible. **-3.** [fantástico] amazing.

tremer [5] [treˈme(x)] *vi* to shake; ~ **de frio/medo** to shake with cold/fear.

tremor [treˈmo(x)] (*pl* **-es**) *m* tremor; ~ **de terra** earthquake.

tremular [4] [tremuˈla(x)] *vi* **-1.** [bandeira] to flutter. **-2.** [luz] to flicker.

trêmulo, la [ˈtremulu, la] *adj* **-1.** [pessoa, mão] trembling. **-2.** [passo, voz] faltering.

trena [ˈtrena] *f* [fita métrica] tape measure.

trenó [treˈnɔ] *m* sledge UK, sled US.

trepada [treˈpada] *f fam* leg-over; **dar uma** ~ to get laid.

trepadeira [trepaˈdejra] *f* creeper.

trepar [4] [treˈpa(x)] *vi* **-1.** [subir]: ~ **(em algo)** to climb (up sthg). **-2.** *mfam* [ter relações sexuais]: ~ **(com alguém)** to get laid.

trepidação [trepida'sãw] *f* shaking.

trepidante [trepi'dãntʃil *adj* **-1.** [que trepida] shaking. **-2.** *fig* [agitado] restless.

trepidar [4] [trepi'da(x)] *vi* to shake.

três ['trejʃ] <> *num* three. <> *m* three; *veja também* seis.

➤ **a três por dois** *loc adv* often.

tresloucado, da [treʒlo'kadu, da] *adj* crazy.

Três-Marias [,trejʃma'riaʃ] *fpl* **-1.** ASTRON Orion's Belt. **-2.** BOT bougainvillea.

três-quartos [trejʃ'kwaxtuʃ] <> *adj inv* [manga, saia] three-quarter length. <> *m* [apartamento] three-room flat *UK ou* apartment *US.*

trevas ['trɛvaʃ] *fpl* [escuridão] darkness *(sg).*

trevo ['trevul *m* **-1.** BOT clover. **-2.** [de vias] intersection.

treze ['trezil <> *num* thirteen. <> *m* [algarismo] thirteen; *veja também* seis.

trezentos, tas [tre'zẽntuʃ, taʃ] <> *num* three hundred. <> *m* [algarismo] three hundred; *veja também* seis.

triagem ['trjaʒẽl *f* **-1.** [seleção] selection; **fazer uma** ~ to make a selection. **-2.** [separação] sorting; **fazer uma** ~ to sort out.

triangular [trjãŋgu'la(x)] *adj* triangular.

triângulo ['trjãŋgulul *m* triangle.

triathlon ['trjatlul *m* triathlon.

tribal [tri'baw] *adj* tribal.

tribo [tri'bul *m* tribe.

tribulação [tribula'sãw] *(pl* **-ões)** *f* tribulation.

tribuna [tri'bunal *f* **-1.** [de orador] rostrum. **-2.** [em espetáculos públicos] platform; ~ **da imprensa** press gallery; ~ **de honra** rostrum.

tribunal [tribu'naw] *(pl* **-ais)** *m* **-1.** [instituição] court; **Tribunal de Contas** Court of Accounts; **Tribunal do Júri** trial by jury; **Tribunal de Justiça** Court of Justice; **Tribunal do Trabalho** Industrial Tribunal. **-2.** [os magistrados] bench.

tributação [tributa'sãw] *f* taxation.

tributar [4] [tribu'ta(x)] *vt* **-1.** [ger] to tax. **-2.** [pagar como tributo] to pay tax on. **-3.** *fig* [render, prestar] to pay.

tributário, ria [tribu'tarju, rja] *adj* **-1.** [relativo a tributo] tax *(antes de subst).* **-2.** [rio] tributary *(antes de subst).*

➤ **tributário** *m* [afluente] tributary.

tributável [tribu'tavew] *(pl* **-eis)** *adj* taxable.

tributo [tri'butul *m* **-1.** [imposto] tax. **-2.** *fig* [ônus] duty.

tricampeão, peã [trikãn'pjãw, pjã] *m, f* three-times champion.

triciclo [tri'siklul *m* **-1.** [de criança] tricycle. **-2.** [usado para a entrega de mercadorias] (delivery) tricycle.

tricô [tri'kol *m* knitting; **fazer** ~ to knit; **de** ~ knitted.

tricolor [triko'lo(x)] *adj* **-1.** [desenho, bandeira] three-coloured *UK,* three-colored *US.* **-2.** FUT tricolour *UK,* tricolor *US.*

tricotar [4] [triko'ta(x)] *vt & vi* to knit.

tridimensional [tridʒimẽnsjo'naw] *(pl* **-ais)** *adj* three-dimensional.

trienal [trje'naw] <> *adj* triennial. <> *f* [exposição] triennial.

triênio ['trjenjul *m* three-year period.

trigal [tri'gawl *m* wheat field.

trigêmeo, mea [tri'ʒemju, mja] <> *adj* [criança] triplet *(antes de subst).* <> *m, f* triplet.

trigésimo, ma [tri'ʒɛzimu, mal <> *num* thirtieth. <> *m* thirtieth; *veja também* sexto.

trigo ['trigul *m* wheat.

trigonometria [trigonome'trial *f* trigonometry.

trilha ['triʎal *f* **-1.** [caminho] path. **-2.** [rasto] trail. **-3.** *fig* [exemplo]: **seguir a** ~ **de alguém** to follow in sb's footsteps. **-4.** COMPUT track. **-5.** CINE: ~ **sonora** soundtrack.

trilhado, da [tri'ʎadu, da] *adj* [percorrido] well-trodden.

trilhão [tri'ʎãw] *(pl* **-ões)** *num* trillion.

trilhar [4] [tri'ʎa(x)] *vt* [percorrer] to tread.

trilho ['triʎul *m* **-1.** FERRO rail. **-2.** [caminho] track.

trilíngüe [tri'liŋgwel *adj* trilingual.

trilogia [trilo'ʒial *f* trilogy.

trimestral [trimeʃ'trawl *(pl* **-ais)** *adj* quarterly.

trimestralidade [trimeʃtrawi'dadʒil *f* quarterly payment.

trimestralmente [trimeʃtraw'mẽntʃil *adv* quarterly.

trimestre [tri'mɛʃtril *m* quarter.

trinca [tri'ŋkal *f* **-1.** [de cartas] set of three. **-2.** *fam* [de pessoas] threesome.

trincar [12] [tri'ŋka(x)] <> *vt* **-1.** [cortar com os dentes] to crunch. **-2.** [cerrar] to grit. **-3.** [rachar] to crack. <> *vi* [rachar] to crack.

trinchar [4] [tri'ŋʃa(x)] *vt* [carne] to carve.

trincheira [tri'ŋʃejral *f* MIL trench.

trinco ['triŋkul *m* **-1.** [ferrolho] latch. **-2.** [lingüeta] catch; **passar o** ~ **na porta** to put the door on the latch.

trindade [tri'ŋdadʒil *f:* **a Santíssima Trindade** the Holy Trinity.

➤ **trindades** *fpl* angelus *(sg).*

Trinidad e Tobago [trini,dadʒito'bagul *n* Trinidad and Tobago.

trinta ['trintal <> *num* thirty. <> *m* thirty; *veja também* sessenta.

trio ['triwl *m* trio; ~ **elétrico** music float.

tripa [tri'pal *f* **-1.** [intestino] intestine. **-2.** CULIN tripe *(inv).* **-3.** *loc:* **fazer das** ~**s coração** to work one's guts out.

tripartir [6] [tripax'tʃi(x)] *vt* to divide into three parts.

tripé [tri'pɛl *m* [suporte] tripod.

tríplex ['tripleks] <> *adj inv* three-storey *UK,* three-story *US.* <> *m inv* three-storey flat *UK,* three-storey apartment *US.*

triplicar [12] [tripli'ka(x)] <> *vt* **-1.** MAT to treble. **-2.** [aumentar muito] to triple. <> *vi* **-1.** [tornar-se triplo] to treble. **-2.** [aumentar muito] to triple.

tríplice ['triplisil *adj* triple.

triplo, pla ['triplu, pla] adj triple.
* **triplo** m: **27 é o ~ de 9** 27 is three times 9; **este sofá é o ~ daquele** this sofa is three times the size of that one.
Trípoli ['tripoli] n Tripoli.
tripulação [tripula'sãw] (pl -ões) f crew.
tripulado, da [tripula'du, da] adj -1. [nave] manned. -2. [barco] crewed.
tripulante [tripu'lãntʃi] mf crew member.
tripular [4] [tripu'la(x)] vt -1. [prover·de tripulação] to man. -2. [governar] to crew.
trisavô, vó [triza'vo, vɔl m, f great-great-grand-father (f great-great-grandmother); **os ~s** great-great-grandparents.
triste ['trisʃti] adj -1. [ger] sad. -2. [entristecedor] depressing. -3. [sombrio, lúgubre] sombre. -4. fam [pessoa] sad.
tristeza [tris'teza] f -1. [de pessoa] sadness. -2. [de lugar] gloominess. -3.: **ser uma ~** [ser terrível] to be appalling.
tristonho, nha [tris'toɲu, ɲa] adj [pessoa, rosto, ar] melancholy.
triturar [4] [tritu'ra(x)] vt -1. [reduzir a fragmentos] to grind. -2. fig [afligir] to crush.
triunfal [trjũn'faw] (pl -ais) adj triumphal.
triunfante [trjũn'fãntʃi] adj triumphant.
triunfar [4] [trjũn'fa(x)] vi [vencer] to triumph.
triunfo ['trjũnfu] m triumph.
trivial [tri'vjaw] (pl -ais) <> adj -1. [comida] ordinary. -2. [assunto, preocupações] trivial. <> m [comida cotidiana] everyday food.
trivialidade [trivjali'dadʒi] f triviality.
triz ['triʃ] m: **por um ~** by a whisker; **escapar por um ~** to escape by the skin of one's teeth.
troca ['trɔka] f exchange; **em ~ de** in exchange for.
troça ['trɔsa] f [zombaria] ridicule; **fazer ~ de alguém** to make fun of sb.
trocadilho [troka'dʒiʎu] m pun.
trocado, da [tro'kadu, da] adj -1. [errado] wrong. -2. [dinheiro] in coins.
* **trocado** m small change.
trocador, ra [troka'do(x), ra] m, f [em ônibus] conductor.
trocar [12] [tro'ka(x)] <> vt -1. [ger] to change; **~ alguém/algo de lugar** to change the place of sb/sthg; **~ dinheiro** to change money. -2. [permutar] to swap. -3. [confundir] to mix up. -4. [cheque] to cash. -5. [reciprocar] to exchange. -6. [permutar]: **~ algo/alguém por algo, ~ algo/alguém por alguém** to change sthg/sb for sthg, to change sthg/sb for sb; **~ o dia pela noite** to live at night. -7. [dar preferência]: **~ algo por algo** to exchange sthg for sthg. -8. loc: **~ as pernas** fig to trip over one's (own) feet. <> vi: **~ de algo** to change sthg; **~ de bem/mal** to make up/fall out.
* **trocar-se** vp [mudar de roupa] to get changed.
troçar [tro'sa(x)] vt to ridicule.
troca-troca [ˌtroka'trɔka] m swap.
troco ['trokul m -1. [dinheiro] change. -2. fig [revide] retort, rejoinder; **dar o ~ a alguém** to get one's own back; **a ~ de que ela fez isso?** [por quê, para quê] what on earth did she do that for?; **a ~ de algo/de fazer algo** [por causa de] by way of sthg/of doing sthg; [por meio de] by means of sthg/of doing sthg; **em ~ de** [em recompensa a] in exchange for.
troço ['trɔsul m -1. fam [coisa] thing; **ter um ~** [sentir-se mal] to feel a pang; [ficar chocado, danado] to get a shock; **ser ~ em algum lugar/em algo** [ser influente] to have influence somewhere/in sthg; **ser um ~** [ser muito bonito, bom] to be amazing.
troféu [tro'fɛw] m trophy.
tromba ['trõnba] f -1. [de elefante] trunk. -2. fam [cara amarrada] long face; **estar de ~** to sulk.
trombada [trõn'bada] f crash; **dar uma ~** to crash.
tromba-d'água [ˌtrõnba'dagwa] (pl trombas-d'água) f [chuva] downpour; **caiu uma ~** there was a huge downpour.
trombadinha [trõnba'dʒiɲa] mf gír [pivete] very young thief.
trombeta [trõn'beta] f MÚS [instrumento] trumpet.
trombone [trõn'boni] m -1. MÚS trombone. -2.: **botar a boca no ~** fam fig to tell the whole world.
trombose [trõn'bɔzi] f thrombosis.
trombudo, da [trõn'budu, da] adj fig [emburrado] sulky.
trompa ['trõnpa] f -1. MÚS horn. -2. ANAT: **~ de Falópio** Fallopian tube; **ligar as ~s** to have one's tubes tied, to undergo tubal ligation.
troncho, cha ['trõnʃu, ʃa] adj -1. [torto] crooked. -2. [desajeitado] clumsy. -3. [mutilado]: **~ de uma perna** one-legged.
tronco ['trõnkul m -1. [BOT- caule] trunk; [- ramo] branch. -2. ANAT trunk. -3. TELEC trunkline. -4. [de família, raça] lineage.
troncudo, da [trõn'kudu, da] adj stocky.
trono ['tronul m -1. [cadeira] throne. -2. fig [poder] driving seat. -3. fam [latrina] throne.
tropa ['trɔpa] f -1. MIL army. -2. [conjunto de pessoas] troop. -3. [polícia]: **~ de choque** riot squad.
tropeção [trope'sãw] (pl -ões) m trip; **dar um ~ em algo** to trip over sthg.
tropeçar [13] [trope'sa(x)] vi to trip; **~ em algo** [dar topada em] to trip over sthg; fig [esbarrar em] to stumble on sthg.
tropeço [tro'pesul m fig [obstáculo] setback.
tropeções [trope'sõjʃ] pl |> tropeção.
trôpego, ga ['tropegu, ga] adj unsteady; **estar ~ de sono** to be asleep on one's feet.
tropel [tro'pɛw] m -1. [multidão desordenada] mob. -2. [de animais] herd. -3. [ruído] clattering. -4. [grande confusão] hubbub.
tropical [tropi'kaw] (pl -ais) adj tropical.
tropicalismo [tropika'lizmu] m Brazilian musical movement.

TROPICALISMO

Tropicalismo was a musical movement that renewed the so-called MPB (*Música Popular Brasileira*) in the midst of the cultural and political effervescence of the late 60s; it incorporated elements of the international cultural scene into the Brazilian music tradition. The movement also had an important influence on theatre and the arts. Two of its main exponents were Caetano Veloso and Gilberto Gil.

trópico ['trɔpikul] *m* tropic; **Trópico de Câncer/Capricórnio** Tropic of Cancer/Capricorn.

troquei [tro'kej] *v* ⊳ **trocar.**

trotar [4] [tro'ta(x)] *vi* to trot.

trote ['trɔtʃi] *m* -**1.** [de cavalo] trot. -**2.** [por telefone] hoax; **passar um ~ em alguém** to play a hoax on sb. -**3.** [em calouro] trick; **dar um ~ em alguém** to play a trick on sb.

trottoir [tro'twa(x)] *m*: **fazer ~** to walk the streets.

trouxa ['troʃa] <> *adj fam* [bobo] foolish. <> *mf fam* [bobo] fool. <> *f* bundle.

trouxe ['trosi] *v* ⊳ **trazer.**

trova ['trɔva] *f* -**1.** [cantiga] folksong. -**2.** [poesia] ballad.

trovador [trova'do(x)] *m* troubadour.

trovão [tro'vãw] (*pl* -ões) *m* thunder.

trovejar [4] [trove'ʒa(x)] *vi METEOR* to thunder.

trovoada [tro'vwada] *f* thunderstorm.

trucidar [trusi'da(x)] *vt* to slaughter, to massacre.

truculência [truku'lẽnsja] *f* horror.

truculento, ta [truku'lẽntu, ta] *adj* gruesome.

trufa ['trufa] *f* truffle.

truísmo [tru'iʒmu] *m* truism.

truncar [trũŋ'ka(x)] *vt* -**1.** [texto] to shorten. -**2.** [discurso] to cut off.

trunfo ['trũnfu] *m* trump card.

trupe ['trupi] *f* -**1.** [de artistas] troop. -**2.** *pej* [grupo] buch.

truque ['truki] *m* trick.

truste ['truʃtʃi] *m* -**1.** [organização financeira] trust. -**2.** [grupo de empresas] corporation.

truta ['truta] *f* trout.

TSE [te 'ɛsi ɛ] (*abrev de* **Tribunal Superior Eleitoral**) *m* Brazilian higher electoral tribunal.

TST [te 'ɛsi te] (*abrev de* **Tribunal Superior do Trabalho**) *m* Brazilian higher employment tribunal.

tu ['tu] *pron pess* you.

tua ['tua] *f* ⊳ **teu.**

tuba ['tuba] *f MÚS* tuba.

tubarão [tuba'rãw] (*pl* -ões) *m* shark.

tubário, ria [tu'barju, rja] *adj* [MED - gravidez] ectopic; [- infecção] tubal.

tuberculose [tubexku'lɔzi] *f* tuberculosis, TB.

tuberculoso, osa [tubexku'lozu, ɔza] <> *adj* tubercular. <> *m, f* person with TB.

tubinho [tu'biɲu] *m* -**1.** [tubo pequeno] small tube. -**2.** [vestido] tube dress.

tubo ['tubu] *m* -**1.** [ger] tube; **~ de ensaio** test tube. -**2.** [canal] pipe. -**3.** *ANAT*: **~ digestivo** digestive tract.

➡ **tubos** *mpl*: **gastar/custar os ~s** to spend/cost a bomb.

tubulação [tubula'sãw] *f* -**1.** [conjunto de tubos] pipework. -**2.** [colocação de tubos] plumbing.

tubular [tubu'la(x)] *adj* tubular.

TUCA (*abrev de* **Teatro da Universidade Católica**) *m* theatre of the Catholic university in São Paulo.

tucano [tu'kãnu] *m* -**1.** *ZOOL* toucan. -**2.** *POL* member of Brazilian Social Democratic Party.

tudo ['tudu] *pron indef* -**1.** [todas as coisas, a totalidade] everything; **~ (o) que** *ou* **quanto** everything that; **é ~** that's all; **~ isso** all that; **~ quanto é tipo de gente** all kinds of people. -**2.** [a coisa fundamental]: **ser ~** to be everything.

➡ **acima de tudo** *loc adv* above all.

➡ **antes de tudo** *loc adv* first of all.

➡ **apesar de tudo** *loc prep* despite everything.

➡ **depois de tudo** *loc adv* after all.

tufão [tu'fãw] (*pl* -ões) *m* typhoon.

tufo ['tufu] *m* -**1.** [de planta] shoot. -**2.** [de cabelo] lock. -**3.** [de terra, pedra] mound.

tulipa [tu'lipa] *f* -**1.** *BOT* tulip. -**2.** [chope servido em copo alto] tall glass of draught beer.

tumba ['tũnba] *f* [sepultura] tomb.

tumefação [tumefa'sãw] *f* swelling.

tumor [tu'mo(x)] (*pl* -es) *m* tumour *UK*, tumor *US*; **~ cerebral** brain tumour; **~ maligno/benigno** malignant/benign tumour.

túmulo ['tumulu] *m* -**1.** [monumento] tomb. -**2.** [cova] grave. -**3.** *fig*: **ser um ~** [ser lúgubre] to be like a tomb; [ser discreto] to be very discreet.

tumulto [tu'muwtu] *m* -**1.** [grande movimento] commotion. -**2.** [confusão, balbúrdia] hubbub. -**3.** [motim] riot.

tumultuado, da [tumuw'twadu, da] *adj* -**1.** [vida] turbulent. -**2.** [rua] noisy.

tumultuar [4] [tumuw'twa(x)] <> *vt* [desordenar, agitar] to disrupt. <> *vi* -**1.** [fazer barulho] to make a noise. -**2.** [amotinar-se] to rise up.

túnel ['tunɛwl] (*pl* -eis) *m* tunnel.

túnica ['tunika] *f* [vestimenta] tunic.

Túnis ['tuniʃ] *n* Tunis.

Tunísia [tu'nizja] *f* Tunisia.

tunisino, na [tuni'zinu, na] <> *adj* Tunisian. <> *m, f* Tunisian.

tupi [tu'pi] <> *adj* Tupi. <> *mf* Tupi Indian. <> *m* [língua] Tupi.

TUPI

The Tupi were an indigenous people in the north and central-west of the country and their language had a marked influence on Brazilian Portuguese. Many place-names derive from Tupi, such as the famous 'Ipanema', which, in Tupi, means 'thick-barked tree'. Other words have even reached the English language, such as 'cashew' (*caju* in Portuguese) and 'jaguar'.

tupi-guarani [tu,pigwara'ni] (*pl* -**is**) ◇ *adj* Tupi. ◇ *mf* [indígena] Tupi (Indian). ◇ *m* Tupi.

tupiniquim [tupini'kĩ] ◇ *adj* -**1.** [relativo aos tupiniquins] Brazilian Indian. -**2.** *pej* [brasileiro] Brazilian. ◇ *mf* Brazilian Indian.

turba ['tuxba] *f* -**1.** [multidão em desordem] mob. -**2.** [multidão] mass.

turbante [tux'bãntʃi] *m* turban.

turbar [4] [tux'ba(x)] *vt* [perturbar] to trouble.
➡ **turbar-se** *vp* [tornar-se sombrio] to darken.

turbilhão [tuxbi'ʎãw] (*pl* -**ões**) *m* -**1.** [de água] whirlpool. -**2.** [de ar] whirlwind. -**3.** *fig* [agitação] whirl.

turbina [tux'bina] *f* turbine.

turbinado, da [tuxbina'du, da] *adj fam* [motor, processador] turbocharged.

turbulência [tuxbu'lẽnsia] *f* -**1.** METEOR turbulence. -**2.** [desordem, inquietação] unrest.

turbulento, ta [tuxbu'lẽntu, ta] *adj* -**1.** METEOR stormy. -**2.** [tumultuoso] turbulent. -**3.** [que cria desordem] disorderly.

turco, ca ['tuxku, ka] ◇ *adj* Turkish. ◇ *m, f* Turk.
➡ **turco** *m* [língua] Turkish.

turfa ['tuxfa] *f* peat.

turfe ['tuxfi] *m* ESP horse-racing.

túrgido, da ['tuxʒidu, da] *adj* swollen, turgid.

turíbulo [tu'ribulu] *m* incense-burner.

turismo [tu'riʒmu] *m* tourism; **fazer** ~ to go sightseeing.

turista [tu'riʃta] *mf* -**1.** [quem faz turismo] tourist. -**2.** [aluno] persistent absentee.

turístico, ca [tu'riʃtʃiku, ka] *adj* tourist *(antes de subst)*.

turma ['tuxma] *f* -**1.** [grupo] group. -**2.** [grupo de trabalhadores] shift. -**3.** EDUC class. -**4.** *fam* [grupo de amigos] gang.

turmalina [tuxma'lina] *f* tourmaline.

turnê [tux'ne] *f* tour.

turno ['tuxnu] *m* -**1.** [turma] group. -**2.** [horário de trabalho] shift; [- de escola] class; ~ **da noite** night shift; ~ **da manhã** morning shift. -**3.** ESP round. -**4.** [de eleição] round. -**5.** [vez] turn; **por** ~**s** in turns; **por seu** ~ in turn.

turquesa [tux'keza] ◇ *adj inv* turquoise. ◇ *m* [cor] turquoise. ◇ *f* [pedra] turquoise.

Turquia [tux'kia] *n* Turkey.

turra ['tuxa] *f*: **viver às** ~**s** to argue all the time.

turrão, ona [tu'xãw, ɔna] *adj fam* [teimoso, pertinaz] stubborn.

turvar [4] [tux'va(x)] ◇ *vt* -**1.** [água, rio] to stir up. -**2.** [vista] to cloud. ◇ *vi* -**1.** [água, rio] to grow rough. -**2.** [vista] to become cloudy. -**3.** [vinho] to become cloudy.

turvo, va ['tuxvu, va] *adj* cloudy.

tusso ['tusu] *v* ▷ **tossir.**

tutano [tu'tãnu] *m* ANAT marrow.

tutela [tu'tɛla] *f* -**1.** JUR guardianship; **estar sob** ~ to be in care. -**2.** [proteção] protection. -**3.** [supervisão] supervision.

tutelar [4] [tute'la(x)] ◇ *adj* protective. ◇ *vt* -**1.**

JUR to act as guardian to. -**2.** [proteger] to protect.

tutor, ra [tu'to(x), ra] (*mpl* -**es**, *fpl* -**s**) *m, f* guardian.

tutu [tu'tu] *m* -**1.** CULIN Brazilian dish consisting of beans, bacon and cassava flour. -**2.** *fam* [dinheiro] cash.

TV [te' ve] (*abrev de* **televisão**) *f* TV.

tweed ['twidʒi] *m* tweed.

u, U *m* [letra] u, U.

uai ['waj] *interj* -**1.** [espanto, surpresa, terror] oh! -**2.** [reforço, confirmação] yeah!

úbere ['uberi] ◇ *adj* [solo] fertile. ◇ *m* [mama] udder.

Ubes (*abrev de* **União Brasileira dos Estudantes Secundaristas**) *f* Brazilian union of secondary students.

ubiqüidade [ubikwi'dadʒi] *f* ubiquity.

ubíquo, qua [u'bikwu, kwa] *adj* ubiquitous.

Ucrânia [u'krãnja] *n* Ukraine.

ué ['wɛ] *interj* -**1.** [exprimindo surpresa] what? -**2.** [exprimindo ironia] hey!

UE (*abrev de* **União Européia**) *f* EU.

UEM (*abrev de* **União Econômica e Monetária**) *f* EMU.

UERJ (*abrev de* **Universidade Estadual do Rio de Janeiro**) *f* state university of Rio de Janeiro.

UF (*abrev de* **Unidade Federativa**) *f* state.

ufa ['ufa] *interj* phew!

ufanar-se [4] [ufa'naxsi] *vp*: ~ **de** to take inordinate pride in.

ufanismo [ufa'niʒmu] *m* -**1.** [por feitos pessoais] vainglory. -**2.** [pela pátria] national pride.

UFBA (*abrev de* **Universidade Federal da Bahia**) *f* federal university of Bahia.

UFMG (*abrev de* **Universidade Federal de Minas Gerais**) *f* federal university of Minas Gerais.

UFRGS (*abrev de* **Universidade Federal do Rio Grande do Sul**) *f* federal university of Rio Grande do Sul.

UFRJ (*abrev de* **Universidade Federal do Rio de Janeiro**) *f* federal university of Rio de Janeiro.

Uganda [u'gãnda] *n* Uganda.

UHF (*abrev de* **Ultra High Frequency**) *f* UHF.

ui ['uj] *interj* -**1.** [exprimindo dor] ouch! -**2.** [exprimindo surpresa] hey!

uísque ['wiʃki] *m* whisky.

uivada [uj'vada] *f* howl.

uivante [uj'vãntʃi] *adj* howling.

uivar [4] [uj'va(x)] *vi* [ger] to howl; ~ **(de)** to howl (with).

uivo ['ujvu] *m* howl.

UK (*abrev de* **United Kingdom**) *m* UK.

Ulan Bator [u‚lãnba'to(x)] *n* Ulan Bator.

úlcera ['uwsera] *f* ulcer; ~ **de estômago** gastric ulcer.

ulcerar [4] [uwse'ra(x)] <> *vt* to ulcerate. <> *vi* to develop an ulcer.

ulterior [uwte'rjo(x)] *adj* [que ocorre depois] subsequent.

ulteriormente [uwterjox'mẽntʃi] *adv* subsequently.

última ['uwtʃima] *f* ▷ **último**.

ultimamente [‚uwtʃima'mẽntʃi] *adv* lately.

ultimar [4] [uwtʃi'ma(x)] *vt* to conclude.

últimas ['uwtʃimaʃ] *fpl* ▷ **último**.

ultimato [uwtʃi'matu], **ultimátum** [uwtʃi'matũ] *m* ultimatum.

último, ma ['uwtʃimu, ma] <> *adj* **-1.** [ger] last; **por** ~ [em último lugar] last; [finalmente] lastly. **-2.** [mais recente] latest. **-3.** [o pior] worst. **-4.** [gravíssimo] final. **-5.** [máximo] ultimate. <> *m, f* [em fila, competição] last.

  ◆ **última** *f* **-1.** [novidade] latest. **-2.** [asneira] latest blunder.

  ◆ **últimas** *fpl*: **dizer as últimas a alguém** to vilify sb; **estar nas últimas** [estar moribundo] to be on one's last legs; [estar na miséria] to be down and out.

ultrajante [uwtra'ʒãntʃi] *adj* outrageous.

ultrajar [4] [uwtra'ʒa(x)] *vt* to outrage.

ultraje [uw'traʒi] *m* outrage.

ultraleve [‚uwtra'lɛvi] <> *adj* ultralight. <> *m* microlight.

ultramar [‚uwtra'ma(x)] *m* overseas.

ultramarino, na [‚uwtrama'rinu, na] *adj* overseas (antes de subst).

ultramoderno, na [‚uwtramo'dɛxnu, na] *adj* state-of-the-art.

ultrapassado, da [‚uwtrapa'sadu, da] *adj* out-of-date.

ultrapassagem [‚uwtrapa'saʒẽ] (*pl* **-ns**) *f* overtaking UK, passing US.

ultrapassar [4] [‚uwtrapa'sa(x)] <> *vt* **-1.** [passar à frente de] to overtake UK, to pass US. **-2.** [transpor] to cross. **-3.** [em qualidade]: ~ **alguém (em algo)** to surpass sb (in sthg). **-4.** [exceder] to exceed. <> *vi* [passar à frente] to overtake UK, to pass US.

ultra-romântico, ca [‚uwtraxo'mãntʃiku, ka] (*pl* **-s**) *adj* highly romantic.

ultra-secreto, ta [‚uwtrase'krɛtu, ta] (*pl* **-s**) *adj* top secret.

ultra-sensível [‚uwtrasẽn'sivew] (*pl* **-eis**) *adj* hypersensitive.

ultra-som [‚uwtra'sõ] (*pl* **-s**) *m* ultrasound.

ultra-sônico, ca [‚uwtra'soniku, ka] (*pl* **-s**) *adj* **-1.** [onda sonora] ultrasonic. **-2.** MED ultrasound (antes de subst).

ultra-sonografia [‚uwtrasonogra'fia] (*pl* **-s**) *f* ultrasound scanning.

ultravioleta [‚uwtravjo'leta] *adj* ultraviolet.

ululante [ulu'lãntʃi] *adj* **-1.** [multidão] screaming. **-2.** *fig* [gritante] blatant; **o óbvio** ~ the glaring truth.

ulular [4] [ulu'la(x)] <> *vt* [protestos, insultos] to scream. <> *vi* **-1.** [vento] to howl. **-2.** [multidão] to scream.

um, uma [ũ, 'uma] (*mpl* **uns**, *fpl* **umas**) <> *artigo indefinido* a, an (antes de vogal ou h mudo); ~ **homem** a man; **uma casa** a house; **uma mulher** a woman; **uma hora** an hour; **uma maçã** an apple. <> *adj* **-1.** [exprime quantidade, data indefinida] one, some *pl*; **comprei uns livros** I bought some books; ~ **dia voltarei** I'll be back one day; **estou saindo umas semanas de férias** I'm going on holidays for a few weeks. **-2.** [para indicar quantidades] one; **trinta e** ~ **dias** thirty-one days; ~ **litro/metro/quilo** one litre/metre/kilo. **-3.** [aproximadamente] about, around; **esperei uns dez minutos** I waited for about ten minutes; **estavam lá umas cinqüenta pessoas** there were about fifty people there. **-4.** [para enfatizar]: **está** ~ **frio/calor** it's so cold/hot; **estou com uma sede** I'm so thirsty; **foi** ~ **daqueles dias!** it's been one of those days! <> *pron* [indefinido] one, some *pl*; **me dê** ~ give me one; **pede mais uma** ask for another one; ~ **deles** one of them; ~ **a** ~, ~ **por** ~ one by one; **uns e outros** some/other people. <> *num* one ▷ **veja também seis.**

umbanda [ũn'bãnda] *f* [espirit] Afro-Brazilian cult.

umbigo [ũn'bigu] *m* navel.

umbilical [ũnbili'kaw] (*pl* **-ais**) *adj* ▷ **cordão.**

umbral [ũn'braw] (*pl* **-ais**) *m* **-1.** [de porta] doorway. **-2.** [limiar] threshold.

umedecer [25] [umide'se(x)] *vt* to dampen.

  ◆ **umedecer-se** *vp* to mist over.

umedecido, da [umide'sidu, da] *adj* damp.

umidade [umi'dadʒi] *f* **-1.** [de clima, ar] humidity. **-2.** [de parede, terra] damp.

úmido, da ['umidu, da] *adj* damp.

UN (*abrev de* **United Nations**) *f* UN.

UnB (*abrev de* **Universidade de Brasília**) *f* university of Brasilia.

unânime [u'nãnimi] *adj* unanimous.

unanimidade [unãnimi'dadʒi] *f* unanimity.

unção [ũn'sãw] *f* RELIG unction.

undécimo, ma [ũn'dɛsimu, ma] *num* eleventh.

UNE (*abrev de* **União Nacional dos Estudantes**) *f* Brazilian national union of students, ≃ NUS UK.

UNESCO (*abrev de* **United Nations Educational, Scientific and Cultural Organization**) *f* UNESCO.

ungir [78] [ũn'ʒi(x)] *vt* RELIG to anoint.

ungüento [ũn'gwẽntu] *m* ointment.

unha ['uɲa] *f* nail; **fazer as** ~**s** [com manicure] to do one's nails; ~ **encravada** ingrowing nail; **ser** ~ **e carne (com alguém)** to be hand in glove (with sb).

unhada [uˈɲada] f scratch.
unha-de-fome [ˌuɲadʒiˈfɔmi] (pl **unhas-de-fome**) <> adj miserly. <> mf miser.
unhar [4] [uˈɲa(x)] vt to scratch.
união [uˈnjãw] (pl -ões) f -1. [ger] union. -2. [junção] joining.
 União f -1. [o governo federal]: **a União** the Union. -2. [confederação]: **a União Européia** the European Union.
unicamente [ˌunikaˈmẽntʃi] adv -1. [exclusivamente] exclusively. -2. [somente] only.
Unicamp (abrev de **Universidade Estadual de Campinas**) f university of Campinas.
UNICEF (abrev de **United Nations International Children's Emergency Fund**) m UNICEF.
único, ca [ˈuniku, ka] adj -1. [ger] unique. -2. [só] single; **ser filho** ~ to be an only child; **ser o** ~ **que ...** to be the only one to ...
unicórnio [uniˈkɔxnju] m unicorn.
unidade [uniˈdadʒi] f -1. [ger] unit; ~ **central de processamento** central processing unit; ~ **de CD-ROM** CD-ROM drive; ~ **de disco** disc drive. -2. [uniformidade, união, coesão] unity.
unidimensional [unidʒimẽnsjoˈnaw] (pl -ais) adj one-dimensional.
unido, da [uˈnidu, da] adj -1. [ligado] joined. -2. fig [pessoas] united.
UNIFESP (abrev de **Universidade Federal de São Paulo**) f federal university of São Paulo.
unificação [unifikaˈsãw] f unification.
unificar [12] [unifiˈka(x)] vt -1. [unir] to unite. -2. [uniformizar] to unify.
uniforme [uniˈfɔxmi] <> adj -1. [que só tem uma forma, semelhante] uniform. -2. [que não varia] regular. <> m [roupa] uniform; **de** ~ in uniform.
uniformidade [unifoxmiˈdadʒi] f uniformity.
uniformizado, da [unifoxmiˈzadu, da] adj -1. [de uniforme] uniformed. -2. [uniforme] uniform.
uniformizar [4] [unifoxmiˈza(x)] vt -1. [unificar] to standardize. -2. [pessoa] to put into uniform.
 uniformizar-se vp [vestir uniforme] to wear one's uniform.
unilateral [unilateˈraw] (pl -ais) adj unilateral.
unir [6] [uˈni(x)] vt -1. [ger] to unite. -2. [juntar] [comunicar cidades] to join (together). -3. [combinar] to combine; ~ **o útil ao agradável** to mix business with pleasure.
 unir-se vp -1. [juntar-se] to unite; ~**-se a algo/alguém** to join sthg/sb. -2. [afetivamente] to be united. -3. [conciliar-se] to be reconciled. -4. [casar]: ~**-se em matrimônio** to unite in marriage, to join in matrimony.
unissex [uniˈsɛkiʃ] adj inv unisex.
uníssono, na [uˈnisonu, na] adj unison; **em** ~ in unison.
unitário, ria [uniˈtarju, rja] adj -1. [preço] unit (antes de subst). -2. POL unitary.
universal [univexˈsaw] (pl -ais) adj universal.
universalidade [univexsaliˈdadʒi] f universality.
universalizar [4] [univexsaliˈza(x)] vt to universalize.

universidade [univexsiˈdadʒi] f -1. [ger] university. -2. [pessoal] faculty.
universitário, ria [univexsiˈtarju, rja] <> adj university (antes de subst). <> m, f -1. [professor] faculty member, university lecturer. -2. [aluno] university student.
universo [uniˈvɛxsu] m -1. ASTRON universe. -2. fig [mundo] world.
uno, una [ˈunu, ˈuna] adj single.
uns [ũnʃ] ⊳ **um**.
untar [4] [ũnˈta(x)] vt: ~ **algo (com)** [fôrma] to grease sthg (with); [corpo] to oil sthg (with).
upa [ˈupa] interj [numa caída] oops!; [para pessoa se levantar] upsy-daisy!; [para incentivar animal] gee up!
update [ˈapdejtʃi] m COMPUT update.
upgrade [ˈapgrejdʒi] m COMPUT: **fazer um** ~ to upgrade.
upload [ˈaplodʒi] m COMPUT: **fazer um** ~ to upload.
Urais [uˈrajʃ] npl: **os** ~ the Urals.
urânio [uˈrãnju] m uranium.
Urano [uˈrãnu] n Uranus.
urbanismo [uxbaˈniʒmu] m town planning.
urbanista [uxbaˈniʃta] mf town planner.
urbanístico, ca [uxbaˈniʃtʃiku, ka] adj town planning (antes de subst).
urbanização [uxbanizaˈsãw] f urbanization.
urbanizado, da [uxbaniˈzadu, da] adj [área] built-up.
urbanizar [4] [uxbaniˈza(x)] vt -1. [área] to urbanize. -2. [pessoa] to refine.
urbano, na [uxˈbãnu, na] adj -1. [da cidade] urban. -2. [pessoa - com hábitos citadinos] urban; [- cortês] urbane.
urbe [ˈuxbil] f city.
urdidura [uxdʒiˈdura] f -1. [conjunto de fios] warp. -2. [enredo] plot.
urdir [6] [uxˈdʒi(x)] vt fig [tramar] to plot.
urdu [uxˈdu] m [língua] Urdu.
uretra [uˈrɛtra] f urethra.
urgência [uxˈʒẽnsja] f urgency; **com** ~ urgently.
urgente [uxˈʒẽntʃi] adj urgent.
urgentemente [uxʒẽntʃiˈmẽntʃi] adv urgently.
urgir [52] [uxˈʒi(x)] <> vt -1. [pressionar]: ~ **alguém (a/para) que** to urge sb to. -2. [exigir] to demand. <> vi -1. [tempo, circunstâncias] to press on. -2. [ser urgente] to be pressing; ~ **fazer algo** to have to do sthg; **urge resolver a situação** the situation must be resolved; **uma situação que urge ser contornada** a situation that urgently needs to be turned around.
úrico, ca [ˈuriku, ka] adj [ácido] uric.
urina [uˈrina] f urine.
urinar [4] [uriˈna(x)] <> vt -1. [sangue] to pass. -2. [cama] to wet. <> vi [expelir urina] to urinate; ~ **em** to wet.
 urinar-se vp [com urina] to wet o.s.
urinário, ria [uriˈnarju, rja] adj urinary.
urinol [uriˈnɔw] (pl -óis) m chamber pot.
URL (abrev de **Universal Resources Locator**) f URL.
urna [ˈuxna] f [caixa] urn; ~ **eleitoral** ballot box; ~ **eletrônica** computerized vote.

urnas *fpl fig* [pleito eleitoral] polls.
urologia [urolo'ʒial *f* urology.
urologista [urolo'ʒiʃta] *mf* urologist.
urrar [4] [u'xa(x)] <> *vt* [gritar] to scream. <> *vi* -1. [animal] to roar. -2. [gritar]: ~ **de dor** to scream with pain.
urro ['uxu] *m* -1. [de animal] roar. -2. [grito] scream.
ursa ['uxsa] *f* ⊳ **urso.**
ursada [ux'sada] *f fam*: **fazer uma** ~ **com alguém** to be disloyal to sb.
urso, sa ['uxsu, sa] *m, f* bear.
Ursa *f*: **Ursa Maior/Menor** Ursa Major/Minor.
urso-branco [ˌuxsu'brãŋku] *m* polar bear.
urso-polar [ˌuxsu'pola(x)] *(pl* **ursos-polares)** *m* polar bear.
urticária [uxtʃi'karja] *f* (nettle) rash, urticaria.
urtiga [ux'tʃiga] *f* nettle.
urubu [uru'bu] *m* black vulture.
urubuzar [urubu'za(x)] *vt fam* [com o olhar] to watch like a hawk.
urucubaca [uruku'baka] *f* bad luck; **estar com** ~ to be unlucky.
Uruguai [uru'gwaj] *n*: **(o)** ~ Uruguay.
uruguaio, ia [uru'gwaju, ja] <> *adj* Uruguayan. <> *m, f* Uruguayan.
urze ['uxzi] *f* heather.
usado, da [u'zadu, da] *adj* -1. [utilizado] used; **muito/pouco** ~ much/little used. -2. [comum] usual. -3. [na moda] fashionable. -4. [gasto] worn out.
usar [4] [u'za(x)] <> *vt* -1. [ger] to use. -2. [gastar] to wear out. -3. [vestir, ter] to wear. -4. [costumar]: ~ **fazer algo** to be in the habit of doing sthg. <> *vi* [servir-se de]: ~ **de algo** to use sthg; **modo de** ~ [em medicamento] directions for use.
Usenet *(abrev de* **Users Network)** [uze'ntʃil *f* Usenet.
username [uzex'nejml *(pl* **usernames)** *m COMPUT* username.
usina [u'zina] *f* -1. [industrial] factory; ~ **de aço** steelworks *(pl).* -2. [agrícola]: ~ **de açúcar** sugar mill. -3. [de energia elétrica]: ~ **hidrelétrica** hydroelectric power station; ~ **termonuclear** nuclear power station.
usineiro, ra [uzi'nejru, ra] <> *adj* plant *(antes de subst).* <> *m, f* sugar mill owner.
uso ['uzu] *m* -1. [ger] use; **objetos de** ~ **pessoal** personal belongings; **de** ~ **fácil** easy to use; **fazer** ~ **de** to make use of; **para** ~ **externo/interno** *FARM* for external/internal use. -2. [vestir] wearing. -3. [costume] common practice. -4. [desgaste] wear. -5. *LING* usage.
USP *(abrev de* **Universidade de São Paulo)** *f university of São Paulo.*
usual [u'zwaw] *(pl* -**ais)** *adj* usual.
usualmente [uzwaw'mẽntʃi] *adv* usually.
usuário, ria [u'zwarju, rja] *m, f* user.
usucapião [uzuka'pjãw] *m JUR* prescription.
usufruir [74] [uzufru'i(x)] <> *vt* -1. [desfrutar] to enjoy. -2. *JUR* to hold in usufruct. <> *vi*: ~ **de** [desfrutar] to enjoy.
usufruto [uzu'frutu] *m JUR* usufruct.
usura [u'zura] *f* -1. [avareza] avarice. -2. [cobrança alta] usury. -3. [desgaste] wear.
usurário, ria [uzu'rarju, rja] <> *adj* [avaro] avaricious. <> *m, f* [agiota] usurer.
usurpação [uzuxpa'sãw] *(pl* -**ões)** *f* usurpation.
usurpar [4] [uzux'pa(x)] *vt* to usurp.
úteis ['utejʃ] *pl* ⊳ **útil.**
utensílio [utẽ'silju] *m* -1. [instrumento] tool. -2. [de cozinha, doméstico] utensil.
uterino, na [ute'rinu, na] *adj* uterine.
útero ['uteru] *m* uterus, womb.
UTI *(abrev de* **Unidade de Terapia Intensiva)** *f* ICU.
útil ['utʃiw] *(pl* -**eis)** *adj* -1. [ger] useful. -2. [reservado ao trabalho]: **dia** ~ working day.
utilidade [utʃili'dadʒi] *f* -1. [ger] usefulness; **de muita/pouca** ~ of great/little use. -2. [utensílio]: ~**s domésticas** domestic appliances.
utilitário, ria [utʃili'tarju, rja] *adj* -1. [objetivo, peça *etc*] practical. -2. *AUTO & COMPUT* utility.
utilitário *m COMPUT* utility.
utilização [utʃiliza'sãw] *(pl* -**ões)** *f* use.
utilizar [4] [utʃili'za(x)] *vt* to use.
utilizar-se *vp*: ~-**se de** to make use of.
utilizável [utʃili'zavew] *(pl* -**eis)** *adj* -1. [máquina, instrumento] utilizable. -2. [sugestão] practical.
utopia [uto'pia] *f* Utopia.
utópico, ca [u'tɔpiku, ka] *adj* Utopian.
UV *(abrev de* **Ultravioleta)** *m* UV.
uva ['uva] *f* -1. [fruta] grape. -2. *fam* [pessoa, coisa: **que** ~ **de ...!** what a delightful ...!; **uma** ~ a delight; **uma** ~ **de criança** a delightful child.
úvula ['uvula] *f* uvula.

v, V *m* [letra] v, V.
vã [vã] *f* ⊳ **vão.**
vaca ['vaka] *f* -1. *ZOOL* cow; **carne de** ~ beef; **couro de** ~ cowhide; ~ **leiteira** dairy cow; **a** ~ **foi para o brejo** it went out the window. -2. *fam pej* [pessoa] lump. -3. *loc*: **no tempo das** ~**s gordas** in times of plenty; **no tempo das** ~**s magras** during lean times.
vaca-fria [ˌvaka'fria] *f*: **voltar à** ~ to get back to the point in question.
vacância [va'kãnsja] *f* vacancy.
vacante [va'kãntʃi] *adj* vacant.

vaca-preta [ˌvaka'preta] (*pl* **vacas-pretas**) *f* Coca-Cola® float.
vacilação [vasila'sãw] (*pl* -**ões**) *f* -**1**. [hesitação] hesitation. -**2**. [oscilação] swaying.
vacilada [vasi'lada] *f* slip-up; **dar uma** ~ to slip up.
vacilante [vasi'lãntʃi] *adj* -**1**. [hesitante] hesitant. -**2**. [pouco firme] wobbly. -**3**. [luz] flickering.
vacilar [4] [vasi'la(x)] *vi* -**1**. [hesitar] to hesitate; ~ **em algo/em fazer algo** to hesitate in sthg/in doing sthg. -**2**. [oscilar] to sway. -**3**. [cambalear] to totter. -**4**. [luz] to flicker.
vacilo [va'silu] *m fam* -**1**. [hesitação] havering, shilly-shallying. -**2**. [erro, falha] howler, blunder.
vacina [va'sina] *f* vaccine.
vacinação [vasina'sãw] (*pl* -**ões**) *f* vaccination.
vacinar [4] [vasi'na(x)] *vt* -**1**. MED: ~ **alguém (contra)** to vaccinate sb (against). -**2**. *fig* [imunizar]: ~ **alguém contra** to protect sb from.
➡ **vacinar-se** *vp* -**1**. MED: ~-**se (contra)** to be vaccinated (against). -**2**. *fig* [imunizar-se]: ~-**se contra** to be immune to.
vacum [va'kũ] *adj*: **gado** ~ cattle.
vácuo [ˈvakwu] *m* -**1**. FÍSICA vacuum; **embalhado a** ~ vacuum-packed. -**2**. METEOR low. -**3**. [espaço] space. -**4**. *fig* [vazio] void.
vadiagem [va'dʒiaʒẽ], **vadiação** [vadʒia'sãw] *f* vagrancy.
vadiar [16] [va'dʒia(x)] *vi* -**1**. [viver na ociosidade] to lounge about. -**2**. [suj: aluno, professional] to skive. -**3**. [perambular] to roam.
vadio, dia [va'dʒiu, ʒia] *adj* -**1**. [ocioso] idle. -**2**. [aluno, professional] skiving. -**3**. [vagabundo] vagrant.
vaga [ˈvaga] *f* ➡ **vago**.
vagabundagem [vagabũn'daʒẽ] *f* -**1**. [vagabundismo] roaming. -**2**. [vadiagem] loafing.
vagabundear [15] [vagabũn'dʒia(x)] *vi* -**1**. [vadiar] to drift. -**2**. [vaguear] to roam.
vagabundo, da [vaga'bũndu, da] <> *adj* -**1**. [errante] vagabond. -**2**. [vadio] idle. -**3**. [safado] shameless. -**4**. [mulher] easy. -**5**. [produto] shoddy. <> *m, f* -**1**. [pessoa errante] tramp. -**2**. [vadio] idler. -**3**. [safado] rogue.
vagalhão [vaga'ʎãw] (*pl* -**ões**) *m* breaker.
vaga-lume [ˌvaga'lumi] (*pl* **vaga-lumes**) *m* -**1**. ZOOL glow-worm. -**2**. [cine] usher.
vagão [va'gãw] (*pl* -**ões**) *m* -**1**. [de passageiros] carriage. -**2**. [de carga] wagon.
vagão-leito [va.gãw'lejtu] (*pl* **vagões-leito**) *m* sleeping car.
vagão-restaurante [va.gãwxeʃtaw'rãntʃi] (*pl* **vagões-restaurante**) *m* buffet car.
vagar [14] [va'ga(x)] <> *vi* -**1**. [ficar desocupado] to be vacant. -**2**. [vaguear] to drift. <> *m* [lentidão] slowness; **com mais** ~ at greater leisure.
vagareza [vaga'reza] *f* slowness.
vagaroso, osa [vaga'rozu, ɔza] *adj* slow.
vagem [ˈvaʒẽ] (*pl* -**ns**) *f* green bean.
vagina [va'ʒina] *f* vagina.
vaginal [vaʒi'naw] (*pl* -**ais**) *adj* vaginal.

vago, ga [ˈvagu, ga] *adj* -**1**. [impreciso] vague. -**2**. [desocupado] vacant; **horas vagas** spare time. -**3**. [desabitado] empty.
➡ **vaga** *f* -**1**. [em hotel] vacancy. -**2**. [em empresa *etc*] vacancy; **abriu uma vaga para gerente** an opening has appeared for manager. -**3**. [para carro] space. -**4**. [onda] wave.
vagões [va'gõjʃ] *pl* ➡ **vagão**.
vaguear [15] [va'gja(x)] *vi* -**1**. [perambular] to drift. -**2**. [passear] to ramble.
vaia [ˈvaja] *f* boo.
vaiar [4] [va'ja(x)] *vt & vi* to boo.
vaidade [vaj'dadʒi] *f* -**1**. [orgulho] vanity. -**2**. [futilidade] futility.
vaidoso, osa [vaj'dozu, ɔza] *adj* vain; **ser** ~ **de alguém/algo** to be proud of sb/sthg.
vai-não-vai [vajnãw'vaj] *m inv* shilly-shallying.
vaivém [vaj'vẽ] (*pl* -**ns**) *m* -**1**. [de pessoas] to and fro. -**2**. [de pêndulo] swinging. -**3**. [de barco] rocking.
vala [ˈvala] *f* -**1**. [escavação] ditch. -**2**. [sepultura]: ~ **comum** common grave.
vale [ˈvali] *m* -**1**. GEOGR valley. -**2**. [documento] receipt. -**3**. [postal] ~ **postal** postal order.
valentão, ona [valẽn'tãw, ona] (*mpl* -**ões**, *fpl* -**s**) <> *adj* burly. <> *m, f* burly person.
valente [va'lẽntʃi] *adj* brave.
valentia [valẽn'tʃia] *f* -**1**. [coragem] courage. -**2**. [ação] feat.
valentona [valẽn'tona] *f* ➡ **valentão**.
valer [43] [va'le(x)] <> *vt* -**1**. [ger] to be worth; ~ **a pena** to be worthwhile. -**2**. [acarretar]: ~ **algo a alguém** to bring sb sthg. <> *vi* -**1**. [ger] to be worth; **mais vale ... (do que)** it is better to ... (than to); **valeu!** *fam* cheers! -**2**. [equivaler]: ~ **por** to be worth the same as; **ou coisa que o valha** or something similar. -**3**. [ser válido] to be valid; [em jogos] to be fair; **assim não vale!** that's unfair!; **fazer** ~ **os direitos** to assert one's rights; **ser para ra** ~ to be the real thing. -**4**. [vigorar] to be in force.
➡ **para valer** *loc adv* [muito]: **me diverti para** ~ I had a really good time.
➡ **valer-se** *vp* [servir-se]: ~-**se de** to make use of.
vale-refeição [ˌvalixefej'sãw] (*pl* **vales-refeição**) *m* [tíquete-refeição] meal ticket.
valeta [va'leta] *f* gutter.
valete [va'lɛtʃi] *m* [carta] jack.
vale-transporte [ˌvalitrãnʃ'pɔxtʃi] (*pl* **vales-transporte**) *m* travel voucher.
vale-tudo [ˌvali'tudu] *m inv* free-for-all.
valia [va'lia] *f* value; **de grande** ~ [de grande valor] very valuable; [de grande utilidade] very useful.
validação [valida'sãw] *f* validation.
validade [vali'dadʒi] *f* validity; **prazo de** ~ [em comida] expiry date.
validar [4] [vali'da(x)] *vt* to validate.
válido, da [ˈvalidu, da] *adj* valid.
valioso, osa [va'ljozu, ɔza] *adj* valuable.
valise [va'lizi] *f* case.

valor [va'lo(x)] (*pl* **-es**) *m* value; **de (grande)** ~ of (great) value; **objetos de** ~ valuables; **sem** ~ worthless; **ter** ~ to be valuable; ~ **de mercado** market value; ~ **nominal** *ECON* face value; **no** ~ **de** to the value of; **dar** ~ **a algo/alguém** to value sthg/sb.
➡ **valores** *mpl* **-1.** [princípios] values. **-2.** *BOLSA* securities.

valorização [valoriza'sãw] *f* appreciation.

valorizar [4] [valori'za(x)] *vt* **-1.** [imóvel, moeda] to push up the value of. **-2.** [pessoa, trabalho] to appreciate.
➡ **valorizar-se** *vp* to appreciate.

valoroso, osa [valo'rozu, ɔza] *adj* courageous.

valsa ['vawsa] *f* waltz.

valsar [4] [vaw'sa(x)] *vi* to waltz.

válvula ['vawvula] *f* valve; ~ **de escape** *fig* safety valve; ~ **de segurança** safety valve.

vampe ['vãnpi] *f* vamp.

vampiro [vãm'piru] *m* **-1.** [personagem] vampire. **-2.** *ZOOL* vampire bat.

vandalismo [vãnda'liʒmu] *m* vandalism.

vândalo, la ['vãndalu, la] *m, f* vandal.

vangloriar-se [16] [vãŋglo'rjaxsi] *vp*: ~**-se (de)** to boast (about).

vanguarda [vãŋ'gwaxda] *f* **-1.** *MIL* front line. **-2.** [cultural] avant-garde; **de** ~ avant-garde *(antes de subst)*.

vantagem [vãn'taʒẽ] (*pl* **-ns**) *f* **-1.** [ger] advantage; **levar** ~ **(em)** to get the upper hand (in); **tirar** ~ **de** to take advantage from. **-2.** [superioridade]: ~ **(sobre)** advantage (over); **contar** ~ to brag; **levar** ~ **(sobre)** to have an advantage (over).

vantajoso, osa [vãnta'ʒozu, ɔza] *adj* **-1.** [benéfico] advantageous. **-2.** [lucrativo] profitable.

vão, vã ['vãw, 'vã] *adj* **-1.** [frívolo] empty. **-2.** [inútil] vain; **em** ~ in vain. **-3.** [irreal] futile.
➡ **vão** *m* **-1.** [espaço] space. **-2.** [de porta *etc*] opening.

vapor [va'po(x)] (*pl* **-es**) *m* **-1.** [de água] steam; **a** ~ [máquina, ferro] steam *(antes de subst)*; **cozinhar no** ~ to steam. **-2.** *FÍSICA* vapour *UK*, vapor *US*.
➡ **a todo o vapor** *loc adv* at full speed.

vaporização [vaporiza'sãw] *f* **-1.** [nebulização] spray. **-2.** *FÍSICA* vaporization.

vaporizador [vaporiza'do(x)] (*pl* **-es**) *m* **-1.** [de perfume *etc*] spray. **-2.** *MED* vaporizer.

vaporizar [4] [vapori'za(x)] *vt* **-1.** [nebulizar] to spray. **-2.** *FÍSICA* to vaporize.

vaporoso, osa [vapo'rozu, ɔza] *adj* **-1.** [tecido, cortina] see-through, diaphanous. **-2.** [com vapor] steamy.

vapt-vupt [,vapt∫i'vupt∫i] <> *interj* zap! <> *m* [lençol] fitted sheet.

vaqueiro [va'kejru] *m* cowherd *UK*, cowboy *US*.

vaquinha [va'kiɲa] *f*: **fazer uma** ~ to have a whip-round.

vara ['vara] *f* **-1.** [pau] stick; ~ **de condão** magic wand. **-2.** [para salto] pole. **-3.** *TEC* rod. **-4.** [de trombone] slide. **-5.** *JUR* jurisdiction. **-6.** [de porcos] herd.

varal [va'raw] (*pl* **-ais**) *m* [de roupas] clothes line.

varanda [va'rãnda] *f* **-1.** [sacada] verandah. **-2.** [balcão] balcony.

varão [va'rãw] (*pl* **-ões**) <> *adj* male. <> *m* male.

varapau [vara'paw] *mf fam* [pessoa] beanpole.

varar [4] [va'ra(x)] <> *vt* **-1.** [furar] to pierce. **-2.** [passar por] to cross. <> *vi*: ~ **por** [passar por] to pass through; [atravessar] to go through.

varejeira [vare'ʒejra] *f* [mosca] bluebottle.

varejista [vare'ʒi∫ta] <> *adj* retail *(antes de subst)*. <> *mf* [vendedor] retailer.

varejo [va'reʒu] *m* *COM* retail trade; **preço no** ~ retail price; **a loja vende a** ~ the shop sells retail.

variação [varja'sãw] (*pl* **-ões**) *f* [alteração] change, variation; ~ **cambial** *ECON* exchange-rate fluctuation.

variado, da [va'rjadu, da] *adj* **-1.** [diverso] varied. **-2.** [sortido] assorted.

variante [va'rjãnt∫i] <> *adj* different. <> *f* **-1.** [variação] change. **-2.** [versão] variant.

variar [16] [va'rja(x)] <> *vt* [diversificar] to vary. <> *vi* **-1.** [ger] to vary; ~ **em algo** to vary in sthg. **-2.** [diversificar] to make changes; ~ **de** to change; **para** ~ [para diversificar] for a change; *irôn* and just for a change. **-3.** *fam* [delirar] to unhinge.

variável [va'rjavew] (*pl* **-eis**) <> *adj* changeable, variable. <> *f* *MAT* variable.

varicela [vari'sɛla] *f* chickenpox.

variedade [varje'dadʒi] *f* **-1.** [diversidade] variety. **-2.** [tipo] type.
➡ **variedades** *fpl* variety *(sg)*; **espetáculo/teatro de** ~**s** variety show *ou* theatre *UK ou* theater *US*.

varinha [va'riɲa] *f* stick; ~ **de condão** magic wand.

vário, ria ['varju, rja] *adj* [variado] diverse.
➡ **vários** <> *adj pl* several. <> *pron pl* several.

varíola [va'riwla] *f* smallpox.

varizes [va'rizi∫] *fpl* varicose veins.

varões [va'rõj∫] *pl* ⇨ **varão**.

varonil [varo'niw] (*pl* **-is**) *adj* virile.

varredor, ra [vaxe'do(x), ra] (*mpl* **-es**, *fpl* **-s**) *m, f* sweeper; ~ **de rua** road sweeper.

varredura [vaxe'dura] *f* **-1.** [ato] sweep. **-2.** *COMPUT* scan.

varrer [5] [va'xe(x)] *vt* **-1.** [com vassoura] to sweep. **-2.** [arrastar] to sweep away. **-3.** *fig* [devastar] to raze. **-4.** *fig* [livrar]: ~ **algo de** to sweep sthg from.

varrido, da [va'xidu, da] *adj*: **doido** ~ raving lunatic.

Varsóvia [vax'sɔvja] *n* Warsaw.

várzea ['vaxzja] *f* [vale] low, flat valley.

vascular [va∫ku'la(x)] (*pl* **-es**) *adj* vascular.

vasculhar [4] [va∫ku'ʎa(x)] *vt* **-1.** [pesquisar] to research. **-2.** [revirar] to rummage through.

vasectomia [vazekto'mia] *f* vasectomy.

vaselina® [vaze'lina] <> *f* [substância] vaseline. <> *mf fam pej* [pessoa]: **ser um** ~ to be smooth talker.

vasilha [va'ziʎa] f vessel.

vasilhame [vazi'ʎãmi] m -**1**. [para alimentos] storage jars (pl). -**2**. [garrafa vazia] empties (pl).

vaso ['vazu] m -**1**. [para plantas] pot; ~ **de flores** flower vase. -**2**. [privada] toilet; ~ **sanitário** toilet bowl. -**3**. ANAT vessel; ~ **sanguíneo** blood vessel.

vassalo, la [va'salu, la] m, f vassal.

vassoura [va'sora] f broom.

vastidão [vaʃtʃi'dãw] f vastness.

vasto, ta ['vaʃtu, ta] adj -**1**. [extenso] vast. -**2**. fig [considerável] wide.

vatapá [vata'pa] m CULIN a very spicy Bahian dish made with fish, coconut milk, prawns, peanuts and cashew nuts, vatapá.

vaticano, na [vatʃi'kãnu, na] adj Vatican (antes de subst).
➤ **Vaticano** m: o **Vaticano** the Vatican.

vaticinar [4] [vatʃisi'na(x)] vt to foretell.

vaticínio [vatʃi'sinju] m prophecy.

vau [vaw] m -**1**. [de rio] ford. -**2**. NÁUT beam.

vazado, da [va'zadu, da] adj -**1**. [letra] outlined. -**2**. [círculo] hollow. -**3**. [moeda] embossed. -**4**. [olhos] sunken.

vazamento [vaza'mẽntu] m leakage.

vazante [va'zãntʃi] <> adj ebbing. <> f [maré] ebb tide.

vazão [va'zaw] (pl -**ões**) f -**1**. [vazamento] leak. -**2**. [escoamento] flow. -**3**. COM [venda] sale. -**4**. loc: dar ~ a [liberar] to give vent to; [atender a] to deal with; [solucionar] to sort out; COM to clear.

vazar [4] [va'za(x)] <> vi -**1**. [ger] to leak. -**2**. [maré] to go out. -**3**. fig [informação] to leak out. <> vt -**1**. [esvaziar] to empty. -**2**. [olhos] to gouge out. -**3**. [derramar]: ~ **algo (em)** to spill sthg (on). -**4**. fig [moldar] to model.

vazio, zia [va'ziu, zia] adj -**1**. [ger] empty. -**2**. [com pouca gente] deserted.
➤ **vazio** m -**1**. [vácuo] vacuum. -**2**. [lacuna] blank space. -**3**. fig [sentimento] void.

vazões [va'zõjʃ] pl ➤ **vazão**.

veado ['vjadu] m -**1**. [animal] deer; **carne de** ~ venison. -**2**. vulg pej [homossexual] poof(ter) UK, fag(got) US.

vedado, da [ve'dadu, da] adj -**1**. [proibido, impedido] barred; ~ **a** prohibited to. -**2**. [hermeticamente fechado] sealed.

vedar [4] [ve'da(x)] vt -**1**. [proibir, impedir] to prohibit, to bar. -**2**. [sangue]: **vedou o sangramento com um lenço** he stopped the flow of blood with a handkerchief. -**3**. [hermeticamente] to seal.

vedete [ve'dɛtʃi] f -**1**. [de teatro] star. -**2**. fam fig [destaque] star.

veemência [veje'mẽnsja] f vehemence; **com** ~ vehemently.

veemente [veje'mẽntʃi] adj vehement.

vegetação [veʒeta'sãw] (pl -**ões**) f vegetation.

vegetal [veʒe'taw] (pl -**ais**) <> adj plant (antes de subst). <> m plant.

vegetar [4] [veʒe'ta(x)] vi -**1**. [planta] to grow. -**2**. fig [pessoa] to vegetate.

vegetarianismo [veʒetarjã'niʒmu] m vegetarianism.

vegetariano, na [veʒeta'rjãnu, na] <> adj vegetarian. <> m, f vegetarian.

vegetativo, va [veʒeta'tʃivu, va] adj fig vegetative.

veia ['veja] f -**1**. [ger] vein. -**2**. fig [tendência] streak.

veiculação [vejkula'sãw] (pl -**ões**) f -**1**. [de mercadorias, visitantes] transport UK, transportation US. -**2**. [de doença] transmission. -**3**. [de idéias, mensagens, doutrinas] spreading.

veicular [4] [vejku'la(x)] vt -**1**. [publicar, divulgar] to spread. -**2**. [anúncios] to distribute.

veículo [ve'ikulu] m -**1**. [de locomoção] vehicle. -**2**. [de informação] means (sg).

veio ['veju] m -**1**. [de rocha] vein. -**2**. [de madeira] grain. -**3**. [em mina] seam.

vela ['vɛla] f -**1**. [de cera] candle; **segurar** ~ fam fig to play gooseberry. -**2**. NÁUT sail; **à** ~ sailing; **fazer-se à** ou **de vela** to set sail; ~ **mestra** mainsail. -**3**. [embarcação] yacht.

velame [ve'lãmi] m NÁUT sails (pl).

velar [4] [ve'la(x)] <> adj LING velar. <> f LING velar. <> vt -**1**. [cobrir]: ~ **algo (com algo)** to cover sthg (with sthg). -**2**. [ocultar] to hide. -**3**. [dissimular] to disguise. -**4**. [doente, sono] to watch over. -**5**. [defunto] to keep vigil for, to hold a wake for. <> vi -**1**. [cuidar]: ~ **por algo/alguém** to watch over sthg/sb. -**2**. FOT [filme] to be damaged by exposure to light.
➤ **velar-se** vp -**1**. [cobrir-se] to keep o.s. covered. -**2**. [ocultar-se] to hide.

veleidade [velej'dadʒi] f -**1**. [capricho] whim. -**2**. [inconstância] fickleness.

veleiro [ve'lejru] m NÁUT sailing boat.

velejar [4] [vele'ʒa(x)] vi to sail.

velhaco, ca [ve'ʎaku, ka] <> adj dishonest. <> m, f crook.

velha-guarda [ˌveʎa'gwaxda] f old guard.

velharia [veʎa'ria] f -**1**. pej [grupo de idosos] old people (pl). -**2**. [velhos objetos, trastes]: ~ **(s)** old stuff (sg).

velhice [vε'ʎisi] f old age.

velho, lha ['vεʎu, ʎa] <> adj old; **nos** ~ **s tempos** in the old days. <> m, f -**1**. [pessoa] old person. -**2**. fam [pai] old man; **os** ~ **s** [pai e mãe] one's folks. -**3**. fam [amigo]: **meu** ~ old chap.

velhote, ta [ve'ʎotʃi, ta] <> adj old. <> m, f old person.

velocidade [velosi'dadʒi] f [ger] speed; **aumentar/diminuir a** ~ to increase/reduce one's speed; ~ **de processamento** COMPUT processing speed; ~ **máxima** maximum speed; **a toda** ~ at full speed; **em alta** ~ at high speed.

velocímetro [velo'simetru] m speedometer.

velocípede [velo'sipedʒi] m velocipede.

velocíssimo, ma [velo'sisimu, ma] adj superl ➤ **veloz**.

velocista [velo'siʃta] mf sprinter.

velódromo [ve'lɔdrumu] m cycle track.

velório [ve'lɔrju] *m* wake.

veloz [ve'lɔʃ] (*pl* **-es**) *adj* **-1.** [ger] fast. **-2.** [movimento] quick.

velozmente [veloz'mẽntʃi] *adv* quickly.

veludo [ve'ludu] *m* [tecido] velvet; ~ **cotelê** corduroy.

venal [ve'naw] (*pl* **-ais**) *adj* **-1.** [subornável] corrupt. **-2.:** **valor** ~ selling price.

vencedor, ra [vẽse'do(x), ra] (*pl* **-es**, *fpl* **-s**) <> *adj* winning. <> *m, f* winner.

vencer [25] [vẽ'se(x)] <> *vt* **-1.** [ger] to win. **-2.** [superar, dominar, resistir a] to overcome. **-3.** [derrotar] to defeat. **-4.** [exceder]: ~ **algo/alguém (em algo)** to outdo sthg/sb (in sthg). **-5.** [conter] to contain. **-6.** [percorrer] to cross. <> *vi* **-1.** [ganhar] to win. **-2.** [expirar - prazo, garantia, contrato, validade] to expire; [- pagamento, conta, promissória] to become due.

vencido, da [vẽ'sidu, da] *adj* **-1.** [derrotado] beaten; **dar-se por** ~ to give up. **-2.** [expirado] expired.

vencimento [vẽsi'mẽntu] *m* **-1.** [expiração] expiry. **-2.** [data] due date.

▸ **vencimentos** *mpl* [salário] earnings.

venda ['vẽda] *f* **-1.** [vendagem] sale; **à** ~ on *ou* for sale; **pôr algo à** ~ to put sthg up for sale; **preço de** ~ selling price; ~ **a crédito** credit sale; ~ **a prazo** *ou* **prestação** sale in instalments. **-2.** [mercearia] general store. **-3.** [nos olhos] blindfold.

▸ **vendas** *fpl* [vendagem] sales.

vendagem [vẽ'daʒẽ] *f* [venda] sale.

vendar [4] [vẽ'da(x)] *vt*: ~ **(os olhos de) alguém** to blindfold sb.

vendaval [vẽda'vaw] (*pl* **-ais**) *m* **-1.** [ventania] gale. **-2.** *fig* [turbilhão] whirlwind.

vendável [vẽ'davew] (*pl* **-eis**) *adj* saleable.

vendedor, ra [vẽde'do(x), ra] (*mpl* **-es**, *fpl* **-s**) *m, f* **-1.** [dono] seller. **-2.** [em loja] sales assistant; ~ **ambulante** street vendor. **-3.** [de seguros] salesperson.

vender [5] [vẽ'de(x)] <> *vt* **-1.** [pôr à venda] to sell; ~ **no varejo** to sell retail; ~ **no/por atacado** to sell wholesale; **estar vendendo saúde** *fig* to be bursting with health. **-2.** [entregar em venda] to sell off; ~ **algo a/para alguém (por)** to sell sb sthg (for); ~ **algo a prazo** *ou* **prestação** to sell sthg on credit/in instalments; ~ **fiado** to give credit. <> *vi* to sell.

▸ **vender-se** *vp* **-1.** [estar à venda]: **vendem-se picolés** ice lollies for sale. **-2.** [deixar-se subornar]: **ele se vendeu por 30 mil dólares** he accepted a bribe of 30 thousand dollars.

vendeta [vẽ'deta] *f* vendetta.

vendido, da [vẽ'dʒidu, da] *pej* <> *adj* bribed. <> *m, f* grafter.

vendinha [vẽ'dʒiŋa] *f* corner shop.

veneno [ve'nenu] *m* **-1.** [peçonha] poison; **o cigarro é um** ~ **para a saúde** smoking is a health hazard. **-2.** [de cobra, inseto] venom. **-3.** *fig* [malícia] venom.

venenoso, osa [vene'nozu, ɔza] *adj* **-1.** [ger]

poisonous. **-2.** *fig* [malicioso] venomous.

veneração [venera'sãw] *f*: ~ **(por)** veneration (for).

venerar [4] [vene'ra(x)] *vt* **-1.** [adorar] to revere. **-2.** *RELIG* to worship.

venéreo, rea [ve'nɛrju, rja] *adj* venereal.

veneta [ve'neta] *f*: **me deu na** ~ **que ...** [idéia] I took it into my head that ...; [impulso] I had a sudden impulse to ...; **fazer algo de** ~ to do sthg on impulse.

Veneza [ve'neza] *n* Venice.

veneziana [vene'zjana] *f* **-1.** [porta] louvred door *UK*, louvered door *US*. **-2.** [janela] louvred window *UK*, louvered window *US*.

veneziano, na [vene'zjãnu, na] <> *adj* Venetian. <> *m, f* Venetian.

Venezuela [vene'zwɛla] *n* Venezuela.

venezuelano, na [venezwɛ'lanu, na] <> *adj* Venezuelan. <> *m, f* Venezuelan.

vênia ['venja] *f* **-1.** [permissão] permission. **-2.** *JUR* [desculpa] pardon.

venial [ve'njaw] (*pl* **-ais**) *adj* **-1.** [desculpável] forgiveable. **-2.** *RELIG* [pecado] venial.

venta ['vẽta] *f* [narina] nostril.

▸ **ventas** *fpl* [nariz] nose (*sg*).

ventania [vẽta'nia] *f* gale.

ventar [4] [vẽ'ta(x)] *vi*: **venta muito aqui** it is very windy here; **estar ventando** to be windy.

ventarola [vẽta'rɔla] *f* fan.

ventilação [vẽntʃila'sãw] *f* **-1.** [de ambiente] ventilation. **-2.** *AUTO* [de motor] cooling.

ventilador [vẽntʃila'do(x)] (*pl* **-es**) *m* [elétrico] fan.

ventilar [4] [vẽntʃi'la(x)] *vt* [arejar] to air.

vento ['vẽtu] *m* **-1.** [ar] air. **-2.** [brisa] wind. **-3.** *loc*: **ir de** ~ **em popa** to go very well.

ventoinha [vẽ'twiɲa] *f* **-1.** [catavento] windmill. **-2.** [grimpa] weather vane. **-3.** *AUTO* fan.

ventoso, osa [vẽ'tozu, ɔza] *adj* windy.

▸ **ventosa** *f* **-1.** *MED* ventouse. **-2.** *ZOOL* sucker.

ventre ['vẽtri] *m* **-1.** *ANAT* belly. **-2.** *euf* [útero] womb.

ventríloquo, qua [vẽ'trilokwu, kwa] *m, f* ventriloquist.

ventura [vẽ'tura] *f* **-1.** [destino] fate; **por** ~ by chance. **-2.** [sorte] good fortune; **boa** ~ good luck.

venturoso, osa [vẽntu'rozu, ɔza] *adj* [feliz] happy.

Vênus ['venuʃ] *n* Venus.

ver [40] ['ve(x)] <> *vt* **-1.** [ger] to see; **já volto, viu?** I'll be back soon, OK? **-2.** [assistir] to watch. **-3.** [resolver] to see to. **-4.** [tomar cuidado em] to watch. **-5.** [em remissiva]: **veja ...** look ... <> *vi* **-1.** [enxergar] to see; **ela é bonita que só vendo** you wouldn't believe how pretty she is; ~ **em** *fig* [em situação, pessoa] to see in. **-2.** [pensar]: **deixa eu** ~ ... let me see ... **-3.** [ger]: **ter a** *ou* **que** ~ **com** to have to do with; [ter envolvimento com] to be involved with; **são pessoas muito diferentes, não têm nada a** ~ **uma com a outra** they are two very different people, they are not at all alike; **este trabalho tem muito a** ~ **com você** that work is right up

your street. <> *m*: **a meu** ~ in my opinion.
 ◆ **ver-se** *vp* -**1.** [ger] to see o.s. -**2.** [avistar-se] to see one another. -**3.** [ter contato]: **há anos que não nos víamos** it's years since we saw each other, we hadn't seen each other for years. -**4.** [em dificuldade, lugar] to find o.s. -**5.** [entender-se]: **bem se vê que ...** it's obvious that ...; ~**-se com alguém** to pay sb back.
 ◆ **pelo visto** *loc adv* by the look of it.
 ◆ **vai ver que** *loc adv* [talvez] perhaps.

veracidade [verasi'dadʒi] *f* truthfulness.
veranear [vera'nja(x)] *vi* to spend the summer.
veraneio [vera'neju] *m* summer holidays *(pl)* UK, summer vacation US; **cidade de** ~ holiday resort.
veranista [vera'niʃta] *mf* summer holidaymaker UK, summer vacationer US.
verão [ve'rãw] *(pl* -**ões)** *m* summer.
veraz [ve'rajʒ] *adj* truthful.
verba ['vɛxba] *f* funding.
verbal [vex'baw] *(pl* -**ais)** *adj* verbal.
verbalizar [4] [vexbali'za(x)] *vt & vi* to verbalize.
verbalmente [vexbaw'mẽntʃi] *adv* verbally.
verbete [vex'betʃi] *m* [em dicionário] entry.
verbo ['vɛxbu] *m* -**1.** GRAM verb; **deitar o** ~ *fam* to make a speech; **soltar o** ~ *fam* to shoot one's mouth off. -**2.** RELIG: **o Verbo** the Word.
verborragia [vexboxa'ʒial] *f* waffle.
verborrágico, ca [vexbo'xaʒiku, ka] *adj* verbose.
verdade [vex'dadʒi] *f* truth; **a** ~ **nua e crua** the naked truth; **não é** ~? isn't that right?; **na** ~ in fact; **para falar a** ~ to tell the truth; ~? *fam* really?
 ◆ **verdades** *fpl* home truths; **dizer umas** ~**s a alguém** *fam* to tell sb a few home truths.
 ◆ **de verdade** <> *loc adv* -**1.** [realmente]: **tudo o que relato aconteceu de** ~ everything I'm describing really happened. -**2.** [a sério] seriously. <> *loc adj* [autêntico]: **é um vencedor de** ~ he's a true winner.
verdadeiramente [vexdadejra'mẽntʃi] *adv* truly.
verdadeiro, ra [vexda'dejru, ra] *adj* -**1.** [ger] true. -**2.** [autêntico] real.
verde ['vexdʒi] <> *adj* -**1.** [cor] green; ~ **de fome** weak with hunger; ~ **de raiva** livid. -**2.** [fruta] unripe, green. <> *m* -**1.** [cor] green. -**2.** [natureza] country. -**3.** *loc*: **jogar (um)** ~ **(para colher maduro)** to get at the truth.
verde-abacate [ˌvexdʒjaba'katʃi] *adj (inv)* avocado-green.
verde-claro, ra ['vexdʒi'klaru, ra] *(pl* -**s)** <> *adj* light green. <> *m* light green.
verde-escuro, ra ['vexdʒiiʃ'kuru, ra] *(pl* -**s)** <> *adj* dark green. <> *m* dark green.
verdejante [vexde'ʒãntʃi] *adj* verdant.
verdejar [4] [vexde'ʒa(x)] *vi* to become green.
verde-oliva ['vexdʒjo'liva] <> *adj inv* olive green. <> *m* olive green.
verdor [vex'do(x)] *m* -**1.** [cor verde] greenness. -**2.** [as plantas verdes] greenery. -**3.** *fig* [exuberância]: **o**

~ **da mocidade** the vigour of youth. -**4.** *fig* [inexperiência] inexperience.
verdugo [vex'dugu] *m* -**1.** [carrasco] executioner. -**2.** *fig* [pessoa cruel] beast.
verdura [vex'dura] *f* [hortaliça] greens *(pl)*.
verdureiro, ra [vexdu'rejru, ral *m*, *f* greengrocer.
vereador, ra [verja'do(x), ra] *m*, *f* councillor UK, councilor US.
vereda [ve'reda] *f* path.
veredicto [vere'dʒiktu] *m* verdict.
verga ['vexga] *f* -**1.** [vara] stick. -**2.** [metálica] rod.
vergão [vex'gãw] *(pl* -**ões)** *m* [marca] weal.
vergar [14] [vex'ga(x)] <> *vt* [dobrar] to bend. <> *vi* -**1.** [dobrar] to bend. -**2.** [com peso] to sag.
vergões [vex'gõjʃ] *pl* ⊳ **vergão**.
vergonha [vex'goɲa] *f* -**1.** [acanhamento] shyness; **me dá** ~ **falar em público** I feel shy about speaking in public; **perder a** ~ to overcome one's shyness; **que** ~! how embarrassing!; **sentir** ~ to feel embarrassed; **ter** ~ **de fazer algo** to feel shy about doing sthg. -**2.** [brio, pudor] shame; **que falta de** ~! how disgraceful!; **ter** ~ **na cara** to be shameless; **tomar** ~ to swallow one's pride. -**3.** [desonra] shame. -**4.** [vexame] outrage; **passar por uma** ~ to be outraged.
vergonhoso, osa [vexgo'nozu, ɔza] *adj* -**1.** [indigno] disgraceful. -**2.** [indecoroso] indecent. -**3.** [que dá vergonha] shameful.
verídico, ca [ve'ridʒiku, ka] *adj* true.
verificação [verifika'sãw] *(pl* -**ões)** *f* -**1.** [averiguação] checking. -**2.** [comprovação] verification.
verificar [12] [verifi'ka(x)] *vt* -**1.** [averiguar] to check. -**2.** [comprovar] to confirm.
 ◆ **verificar-se** *vp*: **verifica-se um aumento na inflação** an increase in inflation has been confirmed.
verme ['vɛxmi] *m* worm.
vermelhidão [vexmeʎi'dãw] *f* redness.
vermelho, lha [vex'meʎu, ʎa] *adj* -**1.** [ger] red; **ficar** ~ **de raiva/vergonha** to flush with anger/ embarrassment. -**2.** [ao chorar]: **olhos** ~**s** red eyes.
 ◆ **vermelho** *m* -**1.** [cor] red. -**2.** [déficit]: **estar no** ~ to be in the red.
vermicida [vexmi'sida], **vermífugo** [vex'mifugu] *m* vermicide.
vermute [vex'mutʃi] *m* vermouth.
vernáculo, la [vex'nakulu, la] *adj* vernacular.
 ◆ **vernáculo** *m* vernacular.
vernissage [vexni'saʒi] *f* opening.
verniz [vex'niʃ] *(pl* -**es)** *m* -**1.** [solução] varnish. -**2.** [couro] patent leather; **de** ~ [bolsa, sapatos] patent leather *(antes de subst)*. -**3.** *fig* [polidez] veneer.
verões [ve'rõjʃ] *pl* ⊳ **verão**.
verossímil [vero'simiw] *(pl* -**eis)** *adj* -**1.** [crível] credible. -**2.** [provável] likely.
verossimilhança [verosimi'ʎãnsa] *f* -**1.** [credibilidade] credibility. -**2.** [probabilidade] likelihood.
verruga [ve'xuga] *f* wart.

versado, da [vex'sadu, da] *adj*: ~ **em** versed in.

versão [vex'sãw] *(pl* **-ões)** *f* **-1.** [interpretação] version. **-2.** [tradução]: ~ **(para)** translation (into).

versar [4] [vex'sa(x)] *vi*: ~ **sobre** to be about.

versátil [vex'satʃiw] *(pl* **-eis)** *adj* versatile.

versatilidade [vexsatʃili'dadʒi] *f* versatility.

versejar [4] [vexse'ʒa(x)] <> *vt* to versify. <> *vi* to write in verse.

versículo [vex'sikulu] *m* **-1.** [de artigo] paragraph. **-2.** RELIG verse.

verso ['vɛxsu] *m* **-1.** [gênero] verse; **~s brancos** blank verse *(sg).* **-2.** [linha de poema] line. **-3.** [poema] poem. **-4.** [de página] verso; **vide** ~ see over(leaf).

versões [vex'sõjʃ] *pl* ⊳ **versão.**

versus ['vɛxsuʃ] *prep* versus.

vértebra ['vɛxtebra] *f* vertebra.

vertebrado, da [vexte'bradu, da] *adj* vertebrate. ⬝ **vertebrado** *m* vertebrate.

vertebral [vexte'braw] *(pl* **-ais)** *adj* vertebral.

vertente [vex'tẽtʃil] *f* **-1.** [declive] slope. **-2.** *fig* [aspecto] angle.

verter [5] [vex'te(x)] <> *vt* **-1.** [despejar - líquido] to pour; [- recipiente] to tip. **-2.** [derramar] to spill. **-3.** [lágrimas, sangue] to shed. **-4.** [traduzir]: ~ **(para)** to translate (into). <> *vi* [brotar]: ~ **de** [água] to spring from; [rio] to rise from.

vertical [vextʃi'kaw] *(pl* **-ais)** <> *adj* vertical. <> *f* vertical.

vértice ['vɛxtʃisil] *m* **-1.** GEOM vertex. **-2.** [de montanha *etc*] summit.

vertigem [vex'tʃiʒẽl] *(pl* **-ns)** *f* **-1.** MED vertigo. **-2.** [tonteira] giddiness, dizziness; **dar** ~ to make dizzy; **ter** ~ to feel giddy, to feel dizzy.

vertiginoso, osa [vextʃiʒi'nozu, ɔza] *adj* vertiginous.

verve ['vɛxvi] *f* verve.

vesgo, ga ['veʒgu, ga] *adj* cross-eyed.

vesícula [ve'zikula] *f*: ~ **(biliar)** gall bladder.

vespa ['veʃpa] *f* wasp.

véspera ['vɛʃpera] *f*: **na** ~ **de** the day before; ~ **de Natal** Christmas Eve. ⬝ **vésperas** *fpl* [um tempo antes]: **nas ~s de** on the eve of; **estar nas ~s de** to be about to.

vesperal [veʃpe'raw] *(pl* **-ais)** <> *adj* evening *(antes de subst).* <> *f* matinee.

vespertino, na [veʃpex'tʃinu, na] *adj* evening *(antes de subst).* ⬝ **vespertino** *m* evening paper.

veste ['veʃtʃil] *f* **-1.** [vestido] dress. **-2.** [eclesiástica] vestment.

vestiário [veʃ'tʃjarju] *m* **-1.** [onde se troca roupa] changing room. **-2.** [onde se deixa casacos *etc*] cloakroom.

vestibulando, da [veʃtʃibu'lãndu, da] *m, f* university candidate.

vestibular [veʃtʃibu'la(x)] *m* university entrance exam.

vestíbulo [veʃ'tʃibulu] *m* **-1.** [de casa] hall. **-2.** [de teatro] foyer.

vestido, da [veʃ'tʃidu, da] *adj* **-1.** [com roupa]: ~ **(com/de)** dressed in. **-2.** [fantasiado]: ~ **de** dressed as. ⬝ **vestido** *m* dress; ~ **de noiva** wedding dress.

vestígio [veʃ'tʃiʒju] *m* **-1.** [pegada] trail. **-2.** *fig* [indício] trace.

vestimenta [veʃtʃi'mẽtal] *f* **-1.** [roupa] garment. **-2.** RELIG vestment.

vestir [54] [veʃ'tʃi(x)] <> *vt* **-1.** [pôr sobre alguém] to put on. **-2.** [usar] to wear. **-3.** [costurar para] to make clothes for. **-4.** [dar vestuário para] to dress. **-5.** [fantasiar]: ~ **alguém de** to dress sb as. **-6.** [fronha] to cover. <> *vi* [ter caimento]: ~ **bem/mal** to dress well/badly. ⬝ **vestir-se** *vp* **-1.** [usar]: **ela só se veste de branco** she only wears white. **-2.** [aprontar-se] to get dressed. **-3.** [comprar roupa]: **~-se em** to buy clothes in. **-4.** [fantasiar-se]: **vestiu-se de pirata** he was dressed (up) as a pirate.

vestuário [veʃ'twarju] *m* **-1.** [roupas] clothing. **-2.** TEATRO costumes *(pl).*

vetar [4] [ve'ta(x)] *vt* **-1.** [lei, proposta, candidato] to veto. **-2.** [acesso] to forbid.

veterano, na [vete'rãnu, na] <> *adj* veteran *(antes de subst).* <> *m, f* veteran.

veterinário, ria [veteri'narju, rja] <> *adj* veterinary. <> *m, f* vet, veterinary surgeon.

veto ['vetu] *m* veto.

véu ['vɛu] *m* **-1.** [pano] veil. **-2.** ANAT: ~ **do paladar** soft palate.

vexame [ve'ʃãmi] *m* **-1.** [vergonha] shame; **dar um** ~ to make a fool of o.s.; **passar um** ~ to be disgraced. **-2.** [humilhação] humiliation. **-3.** [ultraje] outrage.

vexaminoso, sia [veʃami'nozu, za] *adj* **-1.** [vergonhoso] disgraceful. **-2.** [humilhante] humiliating. **-3.** [ultrajante] outrageous.

vexar [4] [ve'ʃa(x)] *vt* **-1.** [envergonhar] to embarrass. **-2.** [humilhar] to humiliate. **-3.** [ultrajar] to outrage. ⬝ **vexar-se** *vp* [envergonhar-se] to be ashamed.

vexatório [veʃa'torju] *adj* = **vexaminoso.**

vez ['veʃ] *(pl* **-es)** *f* **-1.** [freqüência, quantidade] time; **uma** ~ once; **duas** ~ **es** twice; **três** ~ **es** three times; **algumas** ~ **es** a few times; **às** ~ **es** sometimes; **cada** ~ **mais** more and more; **cada** ~ **mais alto** higher and higher; **cada** ~ **menos** less and less; **de** ~ **em quando** from time to time; **mais** ~ **es** more often; **mais uma** ~, **outra** ~ (once) again; **raras** ~ **es** seldom; **uma** ~ **ou outra** once in a while; **uma** ~ **na vida e outra na morte** once in a blue moon; **várias** ~ **es** several times. **-2.** [ocasião] time; **você já sentiu isso alguma** ~**?** have you ever felt that?; **cada** ~ **que**, **toda** ~ **que** every time; **desta** ~ this time; **de uma** ~ **por todas** once and for all; **de uma** ~ **só** once only; **de** ~ once and for all; **era uma** ~ **...** once upon a time ...; **na maioria das** ~ **es** on most occasions, most times. **-3.** [turno] turn; **ter** ~ to have a chance. **-4.** [multiplicação] times; **2** ~ **es 4** 2 times 4.

➡ **vezes** *fpl* [função]**: fazer as** ~ **es de** to stand in for.

➡ **em vez de** *loc prep* instead of.

➡ **uma vez que** *loc conj* **-1.** [já que] since. **-2.** [se] if.

VHF (*abrev de* **Very High Frequency**) *f* VHF.
VHS (*abrev de* **Video Home System**) *m* VHS.
via ['via] ◇ *f* **-1.** [caminho, estrada] road; ~ **de acesso** access road; ~ **férrea** railway; ~ **pública** thoroughfare. **-2.** [transporte]**: por** ~ **aérea** by air; [postal] by airmail; **por** ~ **terrestre** by land, overland. **-3.** [meio] route; **por** ~ **de** through (means of); **por** ~ **oficial** through official means. **-4.** [processo]**: em** ~ **(s) de** on the way to. **-5.** [de documento] copy; **primeira/segunda** ~ original/ duplicate (copy). **-6.** [de drenagem *etc*] channel. **-7.** ANAT tract; **por** ~ **oral** by mouth. **-8.** *loc*: **chegar às** ~**s de fato** to come to blows. ◇ *prep* via.

➡ **Via Láctea** *f* Milky Way.

➡ **por via das dúvidas** *loc adv* just in case.

➡ **via de regra** *loc adv*: **(por)** ~ **de regra** as a general rule.

viabilidade [vjabili'dadʒil] *f* feasibility, viability.
viabilizar [vjabili'za(x)] *vt* to make possible.
viação [vja'sãw] (*pl* -ões) *f* **-1.** [conjunto de estradas] highways, roads (*pl*). **-2.** [companhia] bus company.
viaduto [vja'dutu] *m* viaduct.
viagem ['vjaʒẽl] (*pl* -ns) *f* **-1.** [ger] journey; **boa** ~**!** have a good journey!; ~ **de ida e volta** return trip; ~ **inaugural** NÁUT maiden voyage; ~ **de negócios** business trip. **-2.** *fig* [sob efeito de droga] trip.

➡ **viagens** *fpl* travels.

viajado, da [vja'ʒadu, da] *adj* [pessoa] well-travelled *UK*, well-traveled *US*.
viajante [vja'ʒãntʃi] ◇ *adj* travelling *UK*, traveling *US*. ◇ *mf* traveller *UK*, traveler *US*.
viajar [4] [vja'ʒa(x)] *vi*: ~ **(por)** to travel (across/ through).
viário, ria ['vjarju, rja] *adj* road (*antes de subst*).
viatura [vja'tura] *f* vehicle.
viável ['vjavɛw] (*pl* -eis) *adj* viable, feasible.
víbora ['viboral] *f* **-1.** ZOOL viper. **-2.** *fig* [pessoa] snake in the grass.
vibração [vibra'sãw] (*pl* -ões) *f* **-1.** [tremor] vibration. **-2.** *fig* [entusiasmo] thrill.

vibrador, ra [vibra'do(x),ra] *adj* [vibratório] vibrating.

➡ **vibrador** *m* [estimulador] vibrator.

vibrante [vi'brãntʃil] *adj fig* [entusiasmado] vibrant.
vibrar [4] [vi'bra(x)] ◇ *vt* **-1.** [fazer tremer] to shake. **-2.** [dedilhar] to vibrate. ◇ *vi* **-1.** [tremer] to shake. **-2.** *fig* [entusiasmar-se] to be thrilled.
vibrião [vi'brjãw] (*pl* -ões) *m* vibrio.
vice ['visil] *mf* deputy.
vice- [visil] *prefixo* vice-.
vice-campeão, peã [,visikãn'pjãw, pjã] (*mpl* -ões, *fpl* -s) *m*, *f* runner-up.
vicejante [vise'ʒãntʃil] *adj* **-1.** [horta, pomar] lush. **-2.** [estilo, poesia] flowery.
vicejar [4] [vise'ʒa(x)] ◇ *vi* [vegetar] to flourish. ◇ *vt* [dar viço a] to cause to flourish.
vice-presidente, ta [,visiprezi'dẽntʃi, ta] (*mpl* -s, *fpl* -s) *m*, *f* **-1.** POL vice-president. **-2.** [de comitê, empresa] deputy chairman.
vice-rei [,visi'xejl] (*pl* vice-reis) *m* viceroy.
vice-reitor, ra [,visixej'to(x), ral] (*mpl* -es, *fpl* -s) *m*, *f* deputy head.
vice-versa [,visi'vɛxsa] *adv* vice versa.
viciado, da [vi'sjadu, da] *adj* **-1.** [em droga *etc*]**: (em)** addicted (to); **ser** ~ **em drogas** to be hooked on drugs. **-2.** [adulterado] vitiated.
viciante [vi'sjãntʃil] *adj* addictive.
viciar [16] [vi'sja(x)] ◇ *vt* **-1.** [dar vício a] to addict. **-2.** [adulterar] to vitiate. ◇ *vi* [criar vício] to be addictive.

➡ **viciar-se** *vp* [tornar-se viciado]**:** ~**-se (em)** to become addicted (to).

vicinal [visi'naw] (*pl* -ais) *adj*: **estrada** ~ local route.
vício ['visju] *m* **-1.** [devassidão] vice. **-2.** [em droga, bebida] addiction. **-3.** [mau hábito] bad habit; ~ **de linguagem** barbarism.
vicioso, osa [vi'sjozu, ɔza] *adj* **-1.** [sistema, hábito] corrupt. **-2.** [círculo] vicious.
vicissitude [visisi'tudʒil] *f* vicissitude; **as** ~**s da vida** the ups and downs of life.
viço ['visul] *m* **-1.** [de planta] vigour *UK*, vigor *US*. **-2.** [de pele] freshness.
viçoso, osa [vi'sozu, ɔzal] *adj* **-1.** [planta] luxuriant. **-2.** [pele] glowing.
Victoria [vik'torjal] *n*: **o lago** ~ Lake Victoria.
vida ['vidal] *f* **-1.** [ger] life; **a outra** ~ the life beyond; **dar a** ~ **por** *fig* to give anything for; **em** ~ [doar *etc*] alive; **estar entre a** ~ **e a morte** to be at death's door; **estilo de** ~ lifestyle; **feliz da** ~ delighted; **para toda a** ~ forever; **padrão de** ~ standard of living; **que** ~**!** what a life!; **tratar da** ~ to get on with one's life; ~ **de cão** dog's life; ~ **conjugal** married life; ~ **doméstica** home life; ~ **sentimental** love life; ~ **útil** [de máquina *etc*] useful life. **-2.** [subsistência]**: custo de** ~ cost of living; **estar bem de** ~ to be well off; **ganhar a** ~ to earn one's living; **meio de** ~ means of living; **cheio de** ~ full of life; **dar** ~ **a algo** to liven sthg up; **sem** ~ lifeless. **-3.** [direção]**: seguir (reto) toda a** ~ to continue straight on as far as you can go. **-4.**

[prostituição]: **cair na** ~ to go on the game; **mulher da** ~ prostitute.

vidão [vi'dãw] *m fam* life of Riley.

vide ['vidʒi] *vt* see; ~ **verso** see over(leaf).

videira [vi'dejra] *f* grapevine.

vidente [vi'dãntʃi] *mf* seer.

vídeo ['vidʒju] *m* -**1.** [ger] video. -**2.** [tela] screen.

videocâmara [vidʒju'kãmara] *f* video camera.

videocassete [ˌvidʒjuka'sɛtʃi] *m* -**1.** [aparelho] video cassette recorder, VCR. -**2.** [fita] video-tape.

videoclipe [ˌvidʒju'klipi] *m* music video.

videoclube [ˌvidʒju'klubi] *m* video club.

videoconferência ['vidʒjukõnʃe'rẽnsja] *f* TELEC video-conference.

vídeo game ['vidʒju'gejmi] *m* video game.

videolocadora [ˌvidʒjuloka'dora] *f* video rental.

videoteca [ˌvidʒju'tɛka] *f* video library.

videoteipe [ˌvidʒju'tejpi] *m* -**1.** [fita] videotape. -**2.** [processo] videotaping.

videotexto [ˌvidʒju'teʃtul] *m* teletext, video-tex(t).

vidraça [vi'drasa] *f* window pane.

vidraçaria [vidrasa'ria] *f* -**1.** [loja] glazier's. -**2.** [fábrica] glass factory. -**3.** [vidraças] glazing.

vidraceiro [vidra'sejru] *m* glazier.

vidrado, da [vi'dradu, da] *adj* -**1.** [ger] glazed. -**2.** *fam* [encantado]: ~ **em** crazy about.

vidrar [4] [vi'dra(x)] <> *vt* [cerâmica *etc*] to glaze. <> *vi fam* [encantar-se]: ~ **(em)** to fall in love (with).

vidreiro, ra [vi'drejru, ra] *m, f* glass-maker.

vidro ['vidru] *m* -**1.** [material] glass; ~ **aramado** reinforced glass; ~ **fosco** frosted glass; ~ **fumê** smoked glass. -**2.** [frasco] bottle.

viela ['vjɛla] *f* alley(way).

Viena ['vjena] *n* Vienna.

viés [vjɛʃ] *m* COST bias.

◆ **de viés** *loc adv* sideways.

Vietnã [vjɛt'nã] *n*: **(o)** ~ Vietnam.

vietnamita [vjɛtna'mita] <> *adj* Vietnamese. <> *mf* Vietnamese.

◆ **vietnamita** *m* [língua] Vietnamese.

viga ['viga] *f* -**1.** [de madeira] beam. -**2.** [de concreto, ferro] girder.

vigamento [viga'mẽntu] *m* rafters *(pl)*.

vigarice [viga'risi] *f* swindle.

vigário [vi'garju] *m* vicar.

vigarista [viga'riʃta] *mf* swindler.

vigência [vi'ʒẽnsja] *f* validity; **estar em** ~ to be in force.

vigente [vi'ʒẽntʃi] *adj* -**1.** [lei, contrato, norma] in force. -**2.** [situação política, costume] current.

viger [26] [vi'ʒe(x)] *vi* to be in force.

vigésimo, ma [vi'ʒɛzimu, ma] *num* twentieth; *veja também* sexto.

vigia [vi'ʒia] <> *f* -**1.** [vigilância] surveillance. -**2.** NÁUT porthole. <> *mf* [pessoa] nightwatchman.

vigiar [16] [vi'ʒja(x)] <> *vt* -**1.** [banco, presos] to guard. -**2.** [mala, criança] to keep an eye on. -**3.** [espreitar] to watch. <> *vi* to be on the lookout.

vigilância [viʒi'lãnsja] *f* surveillance.

vigilante [vi'ʒilãntʃi] <> *adj* alert. <> *mf* guard.

vigília [vi'ʒilja] *f* -**1.** [privação de sono]: **fez-se uma** ~ **para evitar ataques** a watch was kept in order to avoid attack. -**2.** [prática religiosa] vigil.

vigor [vi'go(x)] *m* -**1.** [energia - de corpo, espírito] vigour; [- para o trabalho] energy. -**2.** [veemência] vigour. -**3.** [vigência]: **em** ~ in force; **entrar em** ~ to come into force.

vigorar [4] [vigo'ra(x)] *vi* to be in force.

vigoroso, osa [vigo'rozu, ɔza] *adj* vigorous.

vil ['viw] *(pl* vis) *adj* vile.

vila ['vila] *f* -**1.** [povoação] town. -**2.** [conjunto residencial] residential block. -**3.** [casa] villa.

vilã [vi'lã] *f* ▷ **vilão**.

vilania [vila'nia] *f* villainy.

vilão, lã [vi'lãw, lã] *(mpl* -**ãos, -ães,** *fpl* -**s)** *m, f* villain.

vilarejo [vila'reʒu] *m* hamlet.

vileza [vi'leza] *f* -**1.** [ato] vileness. -**2.** [qualidade] meanness.

vilipendiar [vilipẽn'dʒja(x)] *vt* to belittle.

vime ['vimi] *m* osier, withy; **de** ~ wicker.

vinagre [vi'nagri] *m* vinegar.

vinagreira [vina'grejra] *f* vinegar cruet.

vinagrete [vina'grɛtʃi] *m* vinaigrette.

vincar [12] [vĩn'ka(x)] *vt* -**1.** [roupa, papel] to crease. -**2.** [rosto] to wrinkle. -**3.** [terra] to furrow.

vinco ['vĩŋku] *m* -**1.** [em roupa, papel] crease. -**2.** [no rosto] wrinkle. -**3.** [sulco] furrow.

vinculação [vĩŋkula'sãw] *f* link, linking; **ele não quer a** ~ **do seu nome aos escândalos** he doesn't want his name to be linked to the scandals.

vincular [4] [vĩŋku'la(x)] *vt* -**1.** [ligar] to tie. -**2.** [por obrigação] to bind.

vínculo ['vĩŋkulu] *m* -**1.** [pessoal, familiar] bond. -**2.** [profissional, entre países] tie; ~ **empregatício** work contract.

vinda ['vĩnda] *f* ▷ **vindo**.

vindicar [12] [vĩndʒi'ka(x)] *vt* -**1.** [vingar] to avenge. -**2.** [defender] to vindicate. -**3.** [reivindicar] to claim.

vindima [vĩn'dʒima] *f* grape harvest.

vindo, da ['vĩndu, da] <> *pp* ▷ **vir**. <> *adj*: ~ **(de)** originating (in).

◆ **vinda** *f* -**1.** [ger] arrival (in). -**2.** [regresso] return.

vindouro, ra [vĩn'doru, ra] *adj* -**1.** [ano, década] coming. -**2.** [geração] future.

vingador, ra [vĩnga'do(x), ra] <> *adj* avenging. <> *m, f* avenger.

vingança [vĩŋ'gãnsa] *f* revenge.

vingar [4] [vĩŋ'ga(x)] <> *vt* [tirar desforra de] to avenge. <> *vi* -**1.** [medrar] to thrive. -**2.** [dar certo] to be successful.

◆ **vingar-se** *vp* [tirar desforra]: ~**-se (de)** to take revenge (on/for).

vingativo, va [vĩŋga'tʃivu, va] *adj* vindictive.

vinha ['viɲa] *f* -**1.** [vinhedo] vineyard. -**2.** [planta] vine.

vinhedo [vi'ɲedu] *m* vineyard.

vinheta [vi'ɲeta] *f* vignette.
vinho ['viɲul] ◇ *adj inv* [cor] burgundy. ◇ *m* **-1.** [cor] burgundy. **-2.** [bebida] wine; ~ **branco** white wine; ~ **espumante** sparkling wine; ~ **de mesa** table wine; ~ **do Porto** port; ~ **rosado** rosé (wine); ~ **tinto** red wine.
vinícola [vi'nikula] *adj* wine-producing.
vinicultor, ra [ˌvinikuw'to(x), ra] (*mpl* **-es**, *fpl* **-s**) *m, f* wine producer.
vinicultura [vinikuw'tura] *f* winemaking.
vinil [vi'niw] *m* vinyl.
vinte ['vĩtʃi] *num* twenty; *veja também* **seis.**
vintém [vĩ'tẽ] (*pl* **-ns**) *m* **-1.** [moeda antiga] *old Brazilian coin.* **-2.** [dinheiro]: **estar sem um** ~ to be penniless.
vintena [vĩ'tena] *f*: **uma** ~ **de** a score of.
viola ['vjɔla] *f* viola.
violação [vjola'sãw] (*pl* **-ões**) *f* **-1.** [de lei, pacto, direitos] violation. **-2.** [invasão]: ~ **de domicílio** housebreaking. **-3.** [de pessoa] violation, rape. **-4.** [de correspondência] interference. **-5.** [de local sagrado] violation, desecration.
violão [vjo'lãw] (*pl* **-ões**) *m* guitar.
violar [4] [vjo'la(x)] *vt* **-1.** [lei, pacto, direitos] to violate. **-2.** [domicílio] to break in. **-3.** [pessoa] to violate, to rape. **-4.** [correspondência] to interfere with. **-5.** [local sagrado] to violate. **-6.** [segredo] to breach.
violeiro, ra [vjo'lejru, ra] *m, f* guitarist.
violência [vjo'lẽsja] *f* **-1.** [ato] violence. **-2.** [agressividade] vehemence. **-3.** [força - de vendaval] force; [- de paixões] violence.
violentar [4] [vjolẽ'ta(x)] *vt* **-1.** [mulher] to violate, to rape. **-2.** [deturpar] to distort.
violento, ta [vjo'lẽtu, ta] *adj* violent.
violeta [vjo'leta] ◇ *f* [flor] violet. ◇ *adj inv* [cor] violet.
violinista [vjoli'niʃta] *mf* violinist.
violino [vjo'linu] *m* violin.
violoncelista [vjolõse'liʃta] *mf* cellist.
violoncelo [vjolõ'sɛlu] *m* cello.
violonista [vjolo'niʃta] *mf* guitarist.
VIP (*abrev de* **Very Important Person**) [vipil] ◇ *adj* [pessoa, local] VIP. ◇ *mf* VIP.
vir [67] ['vi(x)] *vi* **-1.** [apresentar-se] to come; **veio me ver** he came to see me; **venho visitá-lo amanhã** I'll come and see you tomorrow. **-2.** [chegar] to arrive; **ele veio atrasado/adiantado** he arrived late/early; **ela veio no ônibus das onze** she came on the eleven o'clock bus. **-3.** [a seguir no tempo] to come; **a semana/o ano que vem** next week/year, the coming week/year. **-4.** [estar] to be; **vem escrito em português** it's written in Portuguese; **vinha embalado** it came in a package. **-5.** [regressar] to come back; **eles vêm de férias amanhã** they're coming back from holidays tomorrow; **hoje, venho mais tarde** today, I'll be coming later than usual. **-6.** [surgir] to come; **o carro veio não sei de onde** the car came out of nowhere; **veio-me uma idéia** I've got an idea. **-7.** [provir]: ~ **de** to come from; **venho agora mesmo**

de lá I've just come from there. **-8.** [em locuções]: ~ **a ser** to become; **que vem a ser isto?** what's the meaning of this?; ~ **abaixo** [edifício, construção] to collapse; ~ **ao mundo** [nascer] to come into the world, to be born; ~ **a saber (de algo)** to find out (about sthg); ~ **sobre** [arremeter contra] to lunge at; ~ **a tempo de algo** to arrive in time for sthg; ~ **a tempo de fazer algo** to arrive in time to do sthg.
viração [vira'sãw] (*pl* **-ões**) *f* breeze.
vira-casaca [ˌviraka'zaka] (*pl* **vira-casacas**) *mf* turncoat.
virado, da [vi'radu, da] *adj* [voltado]: ~ **para** facing.
 virado *m* CULIN: ~ **de feijão** *sautéed beans with fried egg and sausage.*
 virada *f* **-1.** [viradela] turning. **-2.** [guinada] swerve. **-3.** *ESP* sudden turnaround. **-4.** [esforço]: **dar uma virada** to make a last effort.
vira-lata [ˌvira'lata] (*pl* **vira-latas**) *m* **-1.** [cachorro] mongrel. **-2.** [pessoa] down-and-out.
virar [4] [vi'ra(x)] ◇ *vt* **-1.** [volver]: ~ **algo (para)** to turn sthg (towards); ~ **as costas** to turn one's back. **-2.** [mostrar pelo verso] to turn over. **-3.** [entornar] to tip. **-4.** [emborcar] to capsize. **-5.** [contornar] to turn. **-6.** [apontar]: ~ **algo contra alguém** to turn sthg on sb. **-7.** [meter]: ~ **a mão em alguém** to attack sb. **-8.** [fazer mudar de opinião] to change. **-9.** [transformar-se] to turn into. ◇ *vi* **-1.** [volver] to turn; ~ **para** to turn towards; ~ **de bruços** to turn on to one's tummy; ~ **de costas** to turn on to one's back; ~ **do avesso** to turn inside out. **-2.** [emborcar] to capsize. **-3.** [contornar]: ~ **(em)** to turn (into); ~ **à direita/esquerda** to turn (to the) right/left. **-4.** [mudar] to change. **-5.** [mudar de direção] to change direction. **-6.** [rebelar-se, voltar-se]: ~ **contra** to turn against.
 virar-se *vp* **-1.** [volver-se] to turn around. **-2.** [rebelar-se] to rebel; ~-**se contra** to turn against. **-3.** [defender-se] to stand up for o.s. **-4.** [empenhar-se] to struggle.
viravolta [ˌvira'vɔwta] *f* **-1.** [volta inteira] spin. **-2.** [sobre si mesmo] somersault. **-3.** *fig* [mudança] turnabout.
virgem ['vixʒẽ] (*pl* **-ns**) ◇ *adj* **-1.** [ger] virgin. **-2.** [fita, filme] blank. **-3.** [mel] pure. **-4.** [isento]: ~ **de algo** lacking sthg. ◇ *f* [pessoa] virgin.
 Virgem *f* **-1.** *RELIG* Virgin. **-2.** *ARTE* madonna. **-3.** [zodíaco] Virgo; **ser Virgem** to be a Virgo.
virginal [vixʒi'naw] (*pl* **-ais**) *adj* virginal.
virgindade [vixʒĩ'dadʒil] *f* virginity.
virginiano, na [vixʒi'njãnu, na] ◇ *adj* Virgo (*antes de subst*). ◇ *m, f* Virgo.
vírgula ['vixgula] *f* **-1.** [entre palavras] comma. **-2.** [entre números] (decimal) point. **-3.** [mecha] curl. **-4.** [objetando-se]: **uma** ~! *fam* my foot!
viril [vi'riw] (*pl* **-is**) *adj* virile.
virilha [vi'riʎa] *f* groin.
virilidade [virili'dadʒil] *f* virility.
virose [vi'rɔzi] *f* viral infection.
virótico, ca [vi'rɔtʃiku, ka] *adj* viral.

virtual [vix'twaw] (pl -ais) adj -1. [possível] potential. -2. COMPUT virtual; **realidade** ~ virtual reality.

virtualmente [vixtwaw'mẽntʃil] adv virtually.

virtude [vix'tudʒi] f-1. [qualidade] virtue. -2. [capacidade] knack. -3. [razão]: **em** ~ **de** due to.

virtuose [vix'twɔzi] mf virtuoso.

virtuosidade [vixtwozi'dadʒi] f virtuosity.

virtuosismo [vixtwo'ziʒmu] m virtuosity.

virtuoso, osa [vix'twozu, ɔza] <> adj [íntegro] virtuous. <> m, f [gênio] virtuoso.

virulência [viru'lẽnsja] f virulence.

virulento, ta [viru'lẽntu, ta] adj virulent.

vírus ['viruʃ] m inv virus.

vis [viʃ] pl ⊳ vil.

visado, da [vi'zadu, da] adj -1. [cheque] valid. -2. [pessoa] watched.

visão [vi'zãw] (pl -ões) f-1. [sentido] vision, sight. -2. [o que se vê] sight; ~ **de conjunto** overall impression. -3. [alucinação] vision; **ter visões** to have visions. -4. [percepção, ponto de vista]: ~ **(de/sobre)** view (on/about). -5. [revelação] vision.

visar [4] [vi'za(x)] <> vt -1. [cheque, passaporte] to stamp. -2. [objetivar] to look for; ~ **(a) fazer algo** to aim to do sthg. <> vi [objetivar]: ~ **a algo/a fazer algo** to aim for sthg/to aim to do sthg.

vis-à-vis [viza'viʃ] adv vis-à-vis.

víscera ['visera] f viscus.

➡ **vísceras** fpl viscera, bowels.

visceral [vise'raw] (pl -ais) adj -1. [ger] visceral. -2. [arraigado] deep-rooted.

visconde, dessa [viʃ'kõndʒi, desa] m, f viscount.

viscoso, osa [viʃ'kozu, ɔza] adj viscous.

viseira [vi'zejra] f visor.

visibilidade [vizibili'dadʒi] f visibility.

visionário, ria [vizjo'narju, rja] <> adj visionary. <> m, f visionary.

visita [vi'zita] f-1. [ato] visit; **fazer uma** ~ **a alguém** to pay sb a visit; ~ **de médico** fig flying visit. -2. [visitante] visitor; **ter** ~**s** to have visitors; ~ **de cerimônia** official visit. -3. [vistoria] inspection.

visitação [vizita'sãw] (pl -ões) f [visita] visit; **aberto à** ~ **pública** open to the public.

➡ **Visitação** f RELIG Visitation.

visitante [vizi'tãntʃi] mf visitor.

visitar [4] [vizi'ta(x)] vt -1. [fazer visita a] to visit. -2. [vistoriar] to inspect.

➡ **visitar-se** vp [fazer visitas mútuas] to visit one another.

visível [vi'zivɛw] (pl -eis) adj visible.

visivelmente [vizivew'mẽntʃil] adv visibly.

vislumbrar [viʒlũm'bra(x)] vt to glimpse.

vislumbre [viʒ'lũnbri] m glimpse.

visões [vi'zõjʃ] pl ⊳ visão.

visom [vi'zõ] (pl -s) m mink; **casaco de** ~ mink coat.

visor [vi'zo(x)] (pl -es) m viewfinder.

vista ['viʃta] f ⊳ visto.

vista-d'olhos [ˌviʃta'dɔʎuʃ] (pl vistas-d'olhos) f glance; **passar uma** ~ **(em)** to glance (at).

visto, ta ['viʃtu, ta] <> pp ⊳ ver. <> adj -1. [olhado]: ~ **(de)** seen (from). -2. [considerado] thought of. -3. [estudado] looked at.

➡ **visto** m -1. [em documento] stamp. -2. [em passaporte] visa.

➡ **vista** f-1. [ger] view; **com vista para o mar** with sea view. -2. [sentido] sight. -3. [olhos, olhar] eyesight; **a perder de vista** as far as the eye can see; [pagamento] long-term; **à primeira vista** at first sight; **à vista** [visível] visible; [pagamento] in cash; **pôr à vista** to put on display; **até a vista!** see you later!; **conhecer de vista** to know by sight; **perder de vista** to lose sight of; **vista cansada** tired eyes. -4. [propósito]: **com vista a** with a view to; **ter em vista** to have in mind. -5. loc: **dar na vista** to be obvious; **fazer vista grossa (a)** to turn a blind eye (to); **saltar à vista** to be glaringly obvious, to stand out a mile.

➡ **em vista de** loc prep in view of.

➡ **pelo visto** loc adv by the look of it.

➡ **visto que** loc conj seeing.

vistoria [viʃto'ria] f inspection.

vistoriar [viʃto'rja(x)] vt to inspect.

vistoso, osa [viʃ'tozu, ɔza] adj eye-catching.

visual [vi'zwaw] (pl -ais) <> adj visual. <> m fam -1. [aspecto] appearance, look. -2. [vista] view.

visualizar [4] [vizwali'za(x)] vt to visualize.

visualmente [vizuaw'mẽntʃil] adv visually; ~ **incapacitado** visually impaired.

vital [vi'taw] (pl -ais) adj vital.

vitalício, cia [vita'lisju, sja] adj lifelong (antes de subst).

vitalidade [vitali'dadʒil] f vitality.

vitalizar [4] [vitali'za(x)] vt to vitalize.

vitamina [vita'mina] f vitamin.

vitaminado, da [vitami'nadu, da] adj with added vitamins.

vitamínico, ca [vita'miniku, ka] adj vitamin (antes de subst).

vitela [vi'tɛla] f-1. ZOOL calf. -2. [carne] veal.

vítima ['vitʃima] f [pessoa] victim; **fazer-se de** ~ to play the victim; **ser** ~ **de** to be the victim of.

vitimar [4] [vitʃi'ma(x)] vt -1. [matar] to claim the life of. -2. [sacrificar] to sacrifice. -3. [danificar] to destroy.

vitória [vi'tɔrja] f victory.

Vitória [vi'tɔrja] n Vitória.

vitória-régia [viˌtɔrja'xɛʒja] (pl vitórias-régias) f giant water lily.

vitorioso, osa [vito'rjozu, ɔza] adj victorious.

vitral [vi'traw] (pl -ais) m stained-glass window.

vítreo, trea ['vitrju, trja] adj -1. [de vidro] glass (antes de subst). -2. [aspecto] glassy.

vitrificar [12] [vitrifi'ka(x)] <> vt -1. [converter em vidro] to vitrify. -2. [fazer tomar aparência de vidro] to make as smooth as glass. <> vi -1. [converter-se em vidro] to turn into glass. -2. [tomar aparência de vidro] to become as smooth as glass.

vitrine [vi'trini], **vitrina** [vi'trina] f-1. [de loja] shop window. -2. [armário] display case.

vitrinista [vitri'niʃta] mf window dresser.

vitrola [vi'trɔla] *mf fig fam* gossip.
➤ **vitrola** *f* gramophone.
viuvez [vju'veʒ] *f* widowhood.
viúvo, va ['vjuvu, va] ◇ *adj* widowed. ◇ *m, f* widower (*f* widow).
viva ['viva] ◇ *m* cheer. ◇ *interj* hooray!; ~ **a rainha!** long live the Queen!
vivacidade [vivasi'dadʒi] *f* vivacity.
vivalma [vi'vawma] *f*: **não tinha** ~ there wasn't a living soul about.
vivamente [viva'mẽntʃi] *adv* - **1.** [descrever, sentir] vividly. - **2.** [debater, discursar, protestar] vigorously.
vivaz [vi'vajʒ] *adj* lively.
viveiro [vi'vejru] *m* - **1.** [de plantas] nursery. - **2.** [de pássaros] aviary. - **3.** [de peixes] fish farm.
vivência [vi'vẽnsja] *f* - **1.** [existência] existence. - **2.** [experiência] experience; **ter** ~ **em algo** to have experience in sthg.
vivenciar [18] [vivẽn'sja(x)] *vt* to live through.
vivenda [vi'vẽnda] *f* (detached) house.
vivente [vi'vẽntʃi] ◇ *adj* living. ◇ *mf* living being.
viver [5] [vi've(x)] ◇ *vt* - **1.** [vida] to live. - **2.** [fase, situação] to experience. ◇ *vi* - **1.** [ger] to live; ~ **bem** [economicamente] to live comfortably; [em harmonia] to live happily. - **2.** [estar vivo] to be alive. - **3.** [perdurar] to last. - **4.** [sustentar-se]: ~ **de** to live off; ~ **à custa de** to live off. - **5.** [conviver]: ~ **com** to mingle with; [maritalmente] to live with. - **6.** [dedicar-se completamente]: ~ **para** to live for. - **7.** [residir]: ~ **(em)** to live (in). - **8.** [freqüentar muito]: ~ **(em)** to live (in). - **9.** [estar sempre] to always be; ~ **doente/gripado** to always be ill/have a cold; ~ **trabalhando** to do nothing but work. ◇ *m* life.
víveres ['viveriʃ] *mpl* provisions.
vivido, da [vi'vidu, da] *adj* [pessoa] experienced.
vívido, da ['vividu, da] *adj* - **1.** [ger] vivid. - **2.** [expressivo] vivacious.
vivificar [12] [vivifi'ka(x)] *vt* to revive.
vivo, va ['vivu, va] *adj* - **1.** [ger] bright. - **2.** [existente] living; **estar** ~ to be alive. - **3.** [animado, buliçoso] lively. - **4.** [ardente] fervent.
➤ **vivos** *mpl*: **os** ~**s** the living.
➤ **ao vivo** *loc adv* live.
vizinhança [vizi'ɲãnsa] *f* neighbourhood *UK*, neighborhood *US*.
vizinho, nha [vi'ziɲu, ɲa] ◇ *adj* neighbouring *UK*, neighboring *US*. ◇ *m, f* neighbour *UK*, neighbor *US*.
voador, ra [vwa'do(x), ra] *adj* flying.
voar [20] ['vwa(x)] *vi* - **1.** [ger] to fly; ~ **em algo** to fly in sthg; **fazer algo voando** *fig* to do sthg quickly. - **2.** [explodir]: ~ **pelos ares** to explode; **fazer** ~ **pelos ares** to blow up. - **3.** *loc*: **estar/ficar voando** *fam* [ficar sem entender] to be thrown; ~ **alto** *fig* to aim high; ~ **para cima de alguém** [assediar] to mob sb; [atacar] to fly at sb.
vocabulário [vokabu'larju] *m* vocabulary.
vocábulo [vo'kabulu] *m* word.
vocação [voka'sãw] (*pl* -ões) *f* vocation.

vocacional [vokasjo'naw] (*pl* -ais) *adj* vocational.
vocal [vo'kaw] (*pl* -ais) *adj* vocal.
vocálico, ca [vo'kaliku, ka] *adj* vocal.
vocalista [voka'liʃta] *mf* vocalist.
você [vo'se] (*pl* **vocês**) *pron pess* - **1.** [tratamento] you; ~ **é médico?** are you a doctor?; ~ **está muito elegante** you're looking very elegant; **vocês precisam estudar** you need to study; ~ **mesmo** *ou* **próprio** you yourself. - **2.** [depois de prep]: **isto pertence a** ~? is this yours?; **quero ir com vocês** I want to go with you; **penso muito em** ~ I think about you a lot; **esta carta é para** ~ this letter is for you. - **3.** [em anúncios]: **'o novo Fiat Regatta** ~ **vai adorar'** 'the new Fiat Regatta - you'll love it'; **'o melhor para** ~**'** 'the best thing for you'. - **4.** [alguém qualquer um] one; **na Universidade,** ~ **tem que estudar muito** at university, one has to study a lot.
vocês [vo'seʃ] ▷ **você**.
vociferar [4] [vosife'ra(x)] ◇ *vt* [bradar] to shout. ◇ *vi* [reclamar]: ~ **(contra)** to complain (about).
vodca ['vɔdʒka] *f* vodka.
voga ['vɔga] ◇ *f* - **1.** [ger] fashion; **estar em** ~ to be in vogue. - **2.** *NÁUT* [cadência] rowing. ◇ *m* [remador] oarsman.
vogal [vo'gaw] (*pl* -ais) *f* LING vowel.
vogar [14] [vo'ga(x)] *vi* - **1.** [navegar] to sail. - **2.** [circular] to circulate. - **3.** [estar em moda] to be in vogue. - **4.** [vigorar] to be in force.
voile ['vwaw] (*pl* **voiles**) *m* voile; **cortina de** ~ net curtain.
volante [vo'lãntʃi] *m* - **1.** *AUTO* steering wheel; **estar no** ~ to be at the wheel. - **2.** [motorista, piloto] driver. - **3.** [para apostas] betting slip. - **4.** [de máquina] flywheel.
volátil [vo'latʃiw] (*pl* -eis) *adj* volatile.
volatilidade [volatʃili'dadʒi] *f* ECON volatility.
vôlei ['volej], **voleibol** [volei'bow] *m* volleyball.
voleio [vo'leju] *m* volley.
volt ['vɔwtʃil] *m* volt.
volta ['vɔwta] *f* - **1.** [giro] turn; **dar a** ~ **(a algo)** to go around (sthg); **dar uma** ~ [sobre si mesmo] to turn round. - **2.** [retorno] return; **de** ~ back; **estar de** ~ to be back; **na** ~ [voltando] on the way back; [ao chegar] on arrival. - **3.** [passeio]: **dar uma** ~ [a pé] to go for a walk; [de carro] to go for a drive. - **4.** *ESP* lap. - **5.** *MIL*: **dar meia** ~ to about-turn *UK*, to about-face *US*. - **6.** *AUTO*: **fazer a** ~ to make a U-turn, to turn back. - **7.** [mudança]: **dar** ~**s** [vida *etc*] to go round in circles. - **8.** [de espiral] twist. - **9.** [contorno] edge. - **10.** [curva] curve. - **11.** *fig* [troco] comeback. - **12.** *loc*: **dar a** ~ **por cima** *fig* to get over (it).
➤ **às voltas com** *loc prep*: **estar/andar às** ~**s com** to be struggling with.
➤ **em volta de** *loc prep* around.
➤ **por volta de** *loc prep* around.
➤ **volta e meia** *loc adv* every now and again.
voltado, da [vow'tadu, da] *adj* - **1.** [de frente para] facing. - **2.** [concentrado]: **estar** ~ **para** to be focussed on.

voltagem [vow'taʒẽ] *f* voltage.

voltar [4] [vow'ta(x)] ⟨⟩ *vt* - **1.** [dirigir]: ~ **algo para** to turn sthg towards. - **2.** [mudar a posição de] to turn. - **3.** [mostrar pelo verso] to turn over. ⟨⟩ *vi* - **1.** [ger] to return; ~ **a si** to come to; ~ **atrás** *fig* to back out. - **2.** [mudar de direção]: ~ **a** *ou* **para** to turn towards. - **3.** [repetir-se] to come back. - **4.** [tratar novamente]: ~ **a algo** to return to sthg. - **5.** [recomeçar]: ~ **a fazer algo** to do sthg again.
➤ **voltar-se** *vp* - **1.** [virar-se] to turn round. - **2.** [recorrer]: ~-**se para** to turn to. - **3.** [rebelar-se]: ~ -**se contra** to turn against.

voltear [15] [vow'tʃja(x)] ⟨⟩ *vt* - **1.** [contornar] to go round. - **2.** [fazer girar] to turn. ⟨⟩ *vi* - **1.** [girar] to revolve. - **2.** [esvoaçar] to flutter.

volteio [vow'teju] *m* - **1.** [rodopio] spin. - **2.** [volta] bend. - **3.** [de equilibrista] movement.

voltímetro [vowt'ʃi'metru] *m* ELETR voltmeter.

volubilidade [volubili'dadʒil] *f* fickleness.

volume [vo'lumi] *m* - **1.** [ger] volume; **aumentar/ diminuir o** ~ to turn the volume up/down. - **2.** [pacote] package.

volumoso, osa [volu'mozu, ɔza] *adj* bulky.

voluntário, ria [volũn'tarju, rja] ⟨⟩ *adj* voluntary. ⟨⟩ *m, f* volunteer.

voluntarioso, osa [volũnta'rjozu, ɔza] *adj* headstrong.

volúpia [vo'lupja] *f* - **1.** [sexual] pleasure. - **2.** [ambição] desire.

voluptuoso, osa [volup'twozu, ɔza] *adj* voluptuous.

volúvel [vo'luvew] (*pl* -**eis**) *adj* changeable.

volver [5] [vow've(x)] ⟨⟩ *vt* to turn. ⟨⟩ *vi*: ~ **a** to return to.

vomitar [4] [vomi'ta(x)] ⟨⟩ *vt* - **1.** [expelir] to vomit, to throw up. - **2.** [sujar com vômito] to vomit on, to be sick on. - **3.** *fig* [proferir] to spew out. ⟨⟩ *vi* [expelir vômito] to vomit, to be sick.

vômito ['vomitu] *m* - **1.** [ato] vomiting, throwing up. - **2.** [substância] vomit, sick.

vontade [võn'tadʒi] *f* - **1.** [determinação] will; **força de** ~ will power; **por** ~ **própria** of one's own accord; ~ **de ferro** iron will. - **2.** [desejo] wish; **dar** ~ **a alguém de fazer algo** to make sb feel like doing sthg; **me deu vontade de sair** I felt like going out; **o filme me deu vontade de viajar** the film made me feel like travelling; **fazer a** ~ **de alguém** to do what sb wants; **ter** ~ **de fazer algo** to feel like doing sthg; **contra a** ~ unwillingly; **sem** ~ reluctantly. - **3.** [necessidade] need. - **4.** [empenho, interesse]: **boa/má** ~ good/ill will; **de boa/má** ~ gladly/grudgingly.
➤ **vontades** *fpl* [caprichos]: **cheio de** ~**s** wilful; **fazer todas as** ~**s de alguém** to pander to sb.
➤ **à vontade** *loc adv* - **1.** [sem cerimônia]: **ficar à** ~ to feel at ease; **fique à** ~ make yourself at home. - **2.** [em quantidade] loads. - **3.** [quanto se quiser] as much as one wants.
➤ **com vontade** *loc adv* [comer *etc*] heartily.

vôo ['vow] *m* flight; **levantar** ~ to take off; ~ **cego** flying blind; ~ **livre** ESP hang-gliding.

voragem [vo'raʒẽ] (*pl* -**s**) *f* - **1.** [abismo] chasm. - **2.** [de águas] maelstrom. - **3.** *fig* [de paixão, ambição] confusion.

voraz [vo'raʃ] (*pl* -**es**) *adj* - **1.** [pessoa, apetite] voracious. - **2.** *fig* [fogo *etc*] devastating.

vos [vuʃ] *pron pl* [complemento direto] you; [complemento indireto] (to) you; *fml* [reflexo] yourselves; *fml* [recíproco] each other, one another.

vós ['vɔʃ] *pron pess* [sujeito, complemento direto] you; [complemento indireto] (to) you; ~ **mesmos** *ou* **próprios** you, yourselves.

vosso, vossa ['vɔsu, 'vɔsa] ⟨⟩ *adj* your. ⟨⟩ *pron*: **o** ~/**a vossa** yours; **um amigo** ~ a friend of yours; **os** ~**s** [a vossa família] your family.

votação [vota'sãw] (*pl* -**ões**) *f* [ato] voting; [voto] vote; **decidir algo por** ~ to decide sthg by ballot.

votado, da [vo'tadu, da] *adj*: **o mais** ~ [chapa, senador etc] the one with the highest vote.

votante [vo'tãntʃi] *mf* voter.

votar [4] [vo'ta(x)] ⟨⟩ *vt* - **1.** [eleger] to vote. - **2.** [submeter a votação] to take a vote on. - **3.** [aprovar] to pass. ⟨⟩ *vi* - **1.** [dar voto] to vote; ~ **em/contra/ por** to vote on/against/for; ~ **em branco** to abstain. - **2.** [ter direito a voto] to have a vote.

voto ['vɔtu] *m* - **1.** [votação] voting; ~ **nulo/em branco** invalid/blank vote; ~ **secreto** secret ballot. - **2.** [promessa] vow; ~ **de castidade/pobreza** vow of chastity/poverty. - **3.** [desejo] wish; **fazer** ~**s por** to wish for; **fazer** ~**s que** to hope that; ~**s de felicidade** best wishes.

vovó [vo'vɔ] *f* granny.

vovô [vo'vo] *m* grandpa.

voyeur [voj'ɛ(x)] (*pl* -**s**) *mf* voyeur.

voyeurismo [voje'riʒmu] *m* voyeurism.

voz ['vɔʃ] (*pl* -**es**) *f* - **1.** [ger] voice; **de viva** ~ orally, **viva** (voce); ~ **arrastada** drawling voice; **a meia** ~ softly; **em** ~ **alta/baixa** in a loud/low voice; **levantar a** ~ **para alguém** to raise one's voice at sb; ~ **de cana rachada** rasping voice. - **2.** [poder decisório, autoridade]: **ter** ~ **(ativa) em** to have a say in; **dar** ~ **de prisão** to announce an arrest. - **3.** *fig* [conselho]: **a** ~ **da experiência** the voice of experience. - **4.** MIL: ~ **de comando** command. - **5.** GRAM: ~ **ativa/passiva** active/passive voice.

vozeirão [vozej'rãw] (*pl* -**ões**) *m* thundering voice.

vozerio [voze'riw] *m* uproar.

vulcânico, ca [vuw'kãniku, ka] *adj* volcanic.

vulcão [vuw'kãw] (*pl* -**ões**) *m* volcano.

vulgar [vuw'ga(x)] (*pl* -**es**) *adj* - **1.** [comum] common. - **2.** [baixo, grosseiro] vulgar. - **3.** [medíocre] mediocre.

vulgaridade [vuwgari'dadʒi] *f* vulgarity.

vulgarizar [4] [vuwgari'za(x)] *vt* [popularizar] to popularize.
➤ **vulgarizar-se** *vp* - **1.** [popularizar-se] to become commonplace. - **2.** [tornar-se reles] to coarsen.

vulgarmente [vuwgax'mẽntʃil] *adv* commonly.

vulgo ['vuwgu] <> *m* common people. <> *adv* otherwise known as.
vulnerabilidade [vuwnerabili'dadʒi] *f* vulnerability.
vulnerável [vuwne'ravεw] (*pl*-eis) *adj* vulnerable.
vulto ['vuwtu] *m* -**1.** [figura, sombra] figure. -**2.** [semblante] face. -**3.** *fig* [importância] stature; **de** ~ important. -**4.: tomar** ~ [desenvolver-se] to take shape.
vultoso, osa [vuw'tozu, ɔza] *adj* -**1.** [volumoso] bulky. -**2.** [obra, negócio] weighty. -**3.** [quantia] considerable.
vulva ['vuwva] *f* vulva.

w, W *m* [letra] w, W.
walkie-talkie [ˌwɔki'tɔki] (*pl* walkie-talkies) *m* walkie-talkie.
walkman® ['wɔkm] *m* Walkman.
WAN (*abrev de* **Wide Area Network**) *f* WAN.
Washington ['wɔʃintõ] *n* Washington.
watt ['wɔtʃi] *m* watt.
WC (*abrev de* **water closet**) *m* WC.
Web [web] (**world wide web**) *f* COMPUT web.
webcam ['uɛbikã] (*pl* webcams) *f* COMPUT webcam.
webmail ['uɛbimejo] (*pl* webmails) *m* COMPUT webmail.
webmaster ['uɛbimaʃtɛ(x)] (*pl* webmasters) *mf* COMPUT webmaster.
webpage ['uɛbipeʒi] (*pl* webpages) *f* COMPUT webpage.
western ['wɛʃtexn] *m* western.
windsurfe [wĩdʒi'suxfi] *m* windsurfing.
windsurfista [wĩdʒisux'fiʃta] *mf* windsurfer.
workshop [woxki'ʃɔpi] *m* workshop.
WWW (*abrev de* **World Wide Web**) *f* WWW.

x, X *m* [letra] x, X.
xá [ʃa] *m* shah.
xadrez [ʃa'dreʃ] <> *m* -**1.** [jogo] chess. -**2.** [desenho] check. -**3.** [tecido] checked cloth; **de** ~ checked. -**4.** *fam* [prisão] clink. <> *adj inv* checked.
xale ['ʃali] *m* shawl.
xampu [ʃãn'pu] *m* shampoo.
xará [ʃa'ra] *mf* namesake.
xaropada [ʃaro'pada] *f fam* drag.
xarope [ʃa'rɔpi] *m* syrup.
xaveco [ʃa'vεku] *m fig* [objeto sem valor] piece of junk.
xaxim [ʃa'ʃĩ] *m* fibrous-stemmed plant.
xeique ['ʃejki] *m* sheikh.
xelim [ʃe'lĩ] (*pl*-s) *m* shilling.
xenofobia [ʃenofo'bia] *f* xenophobia.
xepa ['ʃepa] *f fam* [de feira] scraps (*pl*).
xeque ['ʃɛki] *m* -**1.** [xadrez] check. -**2.** [xeique] sheikh. -**3.** *loc*: pôr em ~ to threaten.
xeque-mate [ˌʃɛki'matʃi] (*pl* xeque-mates) *m* checkmate.
xereta [ʃe'reta] *adj fam* [bisbilhoteiro] busybody.
xeretar [4] [ʃere'ta(x)] <> *vt* to snoop into. <> *vi*: ~ **(em/sobre)** to snoop (into/on).
xerez [ʃe'reʃ] *m* sherry.
xerife [ʃe'rifi] *m* sheriff.
xerocar [12] [ʃero'ka(x)], *vt* to photocopy.
xerocópia [ʃero'kɔpja] *f* photocopy.
xerocopiar [16] [ʃeroko'pja(x)] *vt* = xerocar.
xérox® [ʃe'rɔks] *m* -**1.** [cópia] photocopy. -**2.** [máquina] photocopier.
xexelento, ta [ʃeʃe'lẽtu, ta] *adj fam* gross.
xexéu [ʃe'ʃew] *m fam* pong.
xi [ʃi] *interj* -**1.** [exprimindo espanto] oh no! -**2.** [exprimindo inquietação] oh no!
xícara ['ʃikara] *f* cup; ~ **de chá** cup of tea.
xiita [ʃi'ita] <> *adj* [muçulmano] Shiite. <> *mf* -**1.** [muçulmano] Shiite. -**2.** *fig* [radical] extremist.
xifópago, ga [ʃi'fɔpagu, ga] *adj* conjoined.
xilofone [ʃilo'foni] *m* xylophone.
xilografia [ʃilogra'fia] *f* -**1.** [técnica] wood engraving. -**2.** [gravura] woodcut.
xilogravura [ʃilogra'vura] *f* wood engraving.

xingação [ʃĩŋa'sãw] (*pl* -ões) *f* swearing.

xingamento [ʃĩŋa'mẽntu] *m* swearing.

xingar [14] [ʃĩŋ'ga(x)] ⬦ *vt* to swear at; ~ alguém de algo to call sb sthg. ⬦ *vi* to swear.

xinxim [ʃĩn'ʃĩ] (*pl* -ns) *m*: ~ de galinha chicken casserole.

xixi [ʃi'ʃi] *m fam* pee; fazer ~ to pee.

xodó [ʃo'dɔ] *m* -1. [pessoa querida] sweetheart. -2. [estima]: ter ~ por alguém/algo to be passionate about sb/sthg. -3. [flerte, namoro]: estar de ~ com alguém to be soft on sb.

xota ['ʃɔta] *f vulg* [vulva] pussy.

xoxota [ʃo'ʃɔta] *f vulg* [vulva] pussy.

xucro, cra ['ʃukru, kra] *adj* -1. [animal] untamed. -2. [grosseiro] coarse. -3. [ignorante] thick.

Z

z, Z *m* [letra] z, Ź.

zabumba [za'bũnba] *m* [bombo] (big) bass drum.

zaga ['zaga] *f FUT* fullback.

zagueiro [za'gejru] *m FUT* fullback.

zaino ['zãjnu] *adj* [cavalo] dark brown.

Zaire ['zajri] *n* Zaire.

Zâmbia ['zãnbja] *m* Zambia.

zanga ['zãŋga] *f* -1. [irritação] annoyance. -2. [briga] anger.

zangado, da [zãŋ'gadu, da] *adj* -1. [aborrecido] angry; estar ~ com alguém [sem falar] to be angry with sb. -2. [irritado] annoyed. -3. [malhumorado] cross.

zangão ['zãŋgãw] (*pl* -ões) *m ZOOL* drone.

zangar [14] [zãŋ'ga(x)] ⬦ *vt* [irritar] to annoy. ⬦ *vi* -1. [irritar-se] to get angry. -2. [ralhar] to scold; ~ com alguém to tell sb off.

➤ **zangar-se** *vp* -1. [aborrecer-se] to get angry. -2. [irritar-se] to get annoyed.

zangões [zãŋ'gõjʃ] *pl* ➳ zangão.

zanzar [4] [zan'za(x)] *vi* to wander about.

zarcão [zar'kãw] *m* [tinta] red lead.

zarolho, lha [za'roʎu, ʎa] *adj* one-eyed.

zarpar [4] [zax'pa(x)] *vi* -1. [embarcação] to weigh anchor. -2. [partir] to set off. -3. [fugir] to run away.

zebra ['zebra] *f* -1. *ZOOL* zebra. -2. [faixa para pedestres] zebra crossing. -3. *fam pej* [pessoa] dunce. -4. *loc*: dar ~ to turn out badly.

zebu [ze'bu] *m ZOOL* zebu.

zelador, ra [zela'do(x), ra] (*pl* -es, *fpl* -s) *m, f* [de prédio] caretaker *UK*, janitor *US*.

zelar [4] [ze'la(x)] *vi*: ~ por to care for.

zelo ['zelu] *m* -1. [cuidado] care. -2. [empenho] zeal.

zeloso, osa [ze'lozu, za] *adj* -1. [cuidadoso]: ~ (de/por) caring (for), careful (of). -2. [diligente]: ~ em zealous in.

zé-mané [ˌzɛma'nɛ] (*pl* -s) *m fam* [otário, bobalhão] idiot, airhead.

zen [zẽ] *adj inv* zen.

zen-budismo [zẽn bu'dʒiʒmu] *m* Zen Buddhism.

zé-ninguém [ˌzɛnĩŋ'gẽ] (*pl* zés-ninguém) *m*: um ~ a nobody.

zênite ['zenitʃi] *m* zenith.

zepelim [ze'pelĩ] (*pl* -ns) *m* [balão] zeppelin.

zé-povinho [ˌzɛpo'viɲu] (*pl* -s) *m* -1. [homem comum] Joe Public, Joe Bloggs. -2. [povo] common people.

zerar [4] [ze'ra(x)] *vt* -1. [reduzir a zero] to reduce to zero. -2. [liquidar] to wipe out.

zerinho, nha [ze'riɲu, ɲa] *adj fam* spanking new.

zero ['zɛru] *num* -1. [ger] zero; ~ erros no mistakes; abaixo/acima de ~ below/above zero. -2. *ESP* nil; [em tênis] love. -3. *loc*: começar do ~ to start from scratch; ser um ~ à esquerda to be a nothing.

➤ **a zero** *loc adv*: estar com a moral a ~ to be at rock bottom; ficar a ~ to end up broke; *veja também* seis.

zero-quilômetro [ˌzɛruki'lɔmetru] ⬦ *adj inv* brand new. ⬦ *m inv* brand new car.

ziguezague [ˌzigi'zagi] *m* zigzag.

ziguezagueante [zigiza'gjãntʃi] *adj* zigzagging.

ziguezaguear [zigiza'gja(x)] *vi* to zigzag.

Zimbábue [zĩn'babwe] *n* Zimbabwe.

zinco ['zĩŋku] *m* zinc; folha de ~ corrugated iron.

zipar [4] [zi'pa(x)] *vt COMPUT* to zip.

zíper ['zipe(x)] (*pl* -es) *m* [fecho ecler] zip *UK*, zipper *US*.

ziquizira [ziki'zira] *f fam* bug.

zircônio [zix'konju] *m* zirconium.

zoada ['zwada] *f* = zoeira.

zoar ['zwa(x)] ⬦ *vt* [caçoar] to make fun of. ⬦ *vi* -1. [fazer grande ruído] to make a din. -2. [zumbir] to buzz. -3. [fazer troça] to make fun. -4. [promover confusão] to cause trouble.

zodiacal [zodʒia'kaw] *adj* of the zodiac (*depois de subst*).

zodíaco [zo'dʒiaku] *m* zodiac.

zoeira ['zwejra] *f* din.

zombador, ra [zõnba'do(x), ra] *adj* mocking.

zombar [4] [zõm'ba(x)] *vi* -1. [debochar]: ~ de alguém/algo to make fun of sb/sthg. -2. [desdenhar]: ~ de algo to sneer at sthg.

zombaria [zõnba'ria] *f* [deboche] ridicule.

zombeteiro, ra [zõnbe'tejru, ra] ⬦ *adj* [zombador] joking. ⬦ *m, f* joker.

zona ['zona] *f* -1. [ger] zone; ~ eleitoral electoral district; ~ franca free trade area. -2. *fam* [bagunça, confusão] mess; fazer ~ to make a mess.

zoneamento [zonja'mẽntu] *m* [divisão em zonas] zoning.

zonear [15] [zo'nja(x)] <> *vt* -**1.** *fam* [bagunçar] to mess up. -**2.** [dividir em zonas] to zone. <> *vi fam* [bagunçar] to mess up.

zonzeira [zõn'zejra] *f* dizziness, giddiness; **dar ~ em alguém** to make sb giddy; **sentir ~** to feel giddy.

zonzo, za ['zõnzu, za] *adj* -**1.** [tonto] dizzy. -**2.** [atordoado, confuso] giddy.

zôo ['zow] *m* zoo.

zoologia [zwolo'ʒia] *f* zoology.

zoológico, ca [zo'lɔʒiku, ka] *adj* zoological.
 ➡ **zoológico** *m* zoo.

zoólogo, ga ['zwɔlogu, ga] *m, f* zoologist.

zoom [zũ] *m* zoom.

zorra ['zoxa] *f fam* mess.

zum [zũ] *m* zoom.

zumbido [zũn'bidu] *m* -**1.** [de inseto] buzz. -**2.** [de motor, vozes *etc*] hum. -**3.** [no ouvido] ringing.

zumbir [6] [zũm'bi(x)] *vi* -**1,** [inseto] to buzz. -**2.** [motor, vozes] to hum. -**3.** [bala, vento] to whistle. -**4.** [ouvido] to ring.

zunido [zu'nidu] *m* -**1.** [de inseto] buzz. -**2.** [de motor] hum. -**3.** [de vento] whistle.

zunir [6] [zu'ni(x)] *vi* -**1.** [inseto] to buzz. -**2.** [motor] to hum. -**3.** [vento *etc*] to whistle.

zunzum [zũn'zũ] (*pl* -**ns**) *m* -**1.** [ruído] humming. -**2.** [boato] rumour.

zureta [zu'reta] *mf* halfwit.

zurrar [4] [zu'xa(x)] *vi* to bray.

zurro ['zuxu] *m* bray.

Vivendo no Reino Unido e nos Estados Unidos

ÍNDICE

Reino Unido

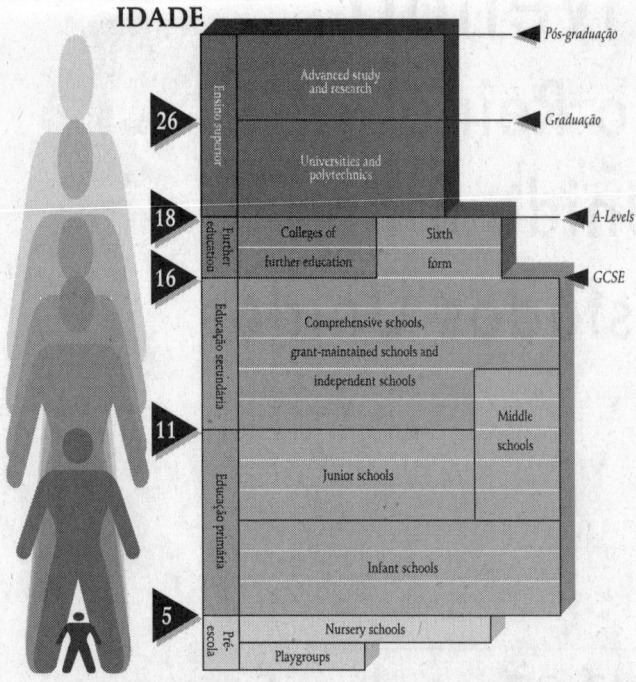

No Reino Unido, a educação é obrigatória dos 5 aos 16 anos de idade. O sistema educacional é, em grande parte, descentralizado, ou seja, de responsabilidade regional, e estrutura-se da seguinte maneira:

Educação pré-escolar (até 5 anos) Não é obrigatória, embora as crianças possam, a partir de dois anos de idade, matricular-se em escolas maternais (*nursery schools*). Muitas crianças em idade pré-escolar freqüentam grupos de atividades lúdico-educativas (*playgroups*), organizados pelos próprios pais.

Educação primária (dos 5 aos 11 anos) A educação primária subdivide-se em escolas para crianças dos 5 aos 7 anos (*infant schools*) e para aquelas dos 7 aos 11 anos (*junior schools*). Certas regiões optam por oferecer escolas para alunos dos 8 aos 14 anos (*middle schools*), que, depois, ingressam diretamente no nível secundário (*upper secondary schools*). Alguns institutos particulares de educação primária são chamados *prep* (*preparatory*) *schools*.

Educação secundária (dos 11 aos 16/18 anos) É ministrada tanto em escolas públicas quanto nas escolas privadas.

▸ As **comprehensive schools**, financiadas pelo Estado, oferecem educação genérica e gratuita para todos. Elas são freqüentadas pela maioria dos estudantes britânicos.

▸ As **independent schools** são instituições privadas, financiadas mediante semestralidade paga pelos pais. Elas também são chamadas *private schools* ou *public schools*, e

congregam apenas 16% das crianças em idade escolar. Dentre essas escolas, algumas são famosas, como *Eton* ou *Harrow*.

▶ As **grant-maintained schools** são escolas de administração autônoma, não sujeitas a autoridade regional, mas subvencionadas diretamente pelo Estado.

Currículo Durante os primeiros cinco anos da educação secundária, a maioria dos alunos segue um currículo comum, o chamado *national curriculum*, definido pelo governo central. Aos 16 anos, o aluno presta um exame chamado *General Certificate of Secondary Education* (*GCSE*). Cerca de 50% dos estudantes concluem nesse ponto seus estudos, independentemente de seu desempenho no exame.

▶ **A-Levels** Aqueles que desejarem ingressar na universidade devem prosseguir os estudos por mais dois anos, ao longo dos quais se preparam para prestar um exame chamado *GCE Advanced Level*. Em geral, desse exame constam três disciplinas. Os *A-Levels* são prestados na Inglaterra, no País de Gales e na Irlanda do Norte. Na Escócia, que possui sistema educacional próprio, os alunos concluem seus estudos prestando os chamados *Highers*, que são exames de várias disciplinas.

Educação secundária não-obrigatória (*Further Education, dos 16 aos 18 anos*)

Futher Education designa os estudos que se seguem ao ensino obrigatório. Os alunos que prosseguem seus estudos visando à obtenção de *A-Levels* costumam cursar na mesma escola os dois anos adicionais, também chamados *sixth form*. Mas podem ainda cursá-los nos *sixth-form colleges*. Cursos de orientação profissional são ministrados por instituições tais como os *colleges of further education*, que incluem escolas de arte, escolas agrícolas etc.

Ensino superior (dos 18 aos 26 anos)

O ensino superior é ministrado pelas universidades. O acesso à universidade depende de uma quantidade mínima de *A-Levels* obtidos com boas notas, e a disputa por vagas é acirrada. Bolsas de estudo são oferecidas pelas autoridades regionais, mas, em geral, precisam ser complementadas, seja pelo auxílio financeiro dos pais ou por empréstimos bancários para estudantes, a juros menores. Normalmente, os cursos universitários estendem-se por três anos, conduzindo ao *undergraduate degree*. A partir daí, aqueles que desejarem prosseguir com seus estudos o fazem na qualidade de *post-graduates*, podendo concluí-los com o *higher degree* ou com um *doctorate*.

> **Oxbridge**
>
> *Oxbridge* é uma expressão utilizada para designar conjuntamente as famosas universidades de Oxford e Cambridge. Fundadas no século XIII, elas se distinguem tanto das universidades fundadas no Reino Unido na década de 60 - as *redbrick universities*, que visavam à expansão do número de vagas universitárias -, quanto das ex-escolas politécnicas, transformadas em universidades apenas na década de 1990. Ainda hoje, embora 50% dos alunos de Oxford e Cambridge provenham da escola pública, persiste a crença de que seus estudantes gozam de situação econômica privilegiada. Isso de deve à grande quantidade de graduados em *Oxbridge* que exercem cargos importantes em áreas como economia, política e direito.

Educação de adultos A educação de adultos é proporcionada por centros de educação pós-escolar e por departamentos especiais de algumas universidades. Os adultos podem, ainda, realizar seus estudos na *Open University*, instituição de ensino a distância, fundada em 1969, que oferece cursos universitários de graduação e pós-graduação por correspondência. Para tanto, não existem pré-requisitos, e os estudos baseiam-se em livros e programas de rádio e televisão.

A sigla UK, *United Kingdom* (Reino Unido), é uma forma abreviada de Reino Unido da Grã-Bretanha e Irlanda do Norte. A Grã-Bretanha compõe-se de Inglaterra, País de Gales e Escócia. As chamadas Ilhas Britânicas, por sua vez, são formadas pela Grã-Bretanha, Irlanda e pelas ilhas adjacentes, como as do Canal da Mancha e a Ilha de Man. Os quatro países que integram o Reino Unido têm um governo comum, embora o parlamento escocês e a assembléia galesa cuidem dos assuntos internos da Escócia e do País de Gales, respectivamente. Cada uma dessas nações tem identidade cultural própria. No País de Gales, fala-se também o galês, língua de origem celta (há um canal de televisão que transmite em galês - ver **meios de comunicação** - e a maioria dos sinais de trânsito se vale dessa língua), mas o inglês é o idioma mais utilizado. A Escócia goza de maior autonomia do que o País de Gales, tendo também seu próprio sistema legal e educacional. O gaélico, língua celta da Escócia, tem uso menos generalizado do que o galês, mas é idioma corrente nas Terras Altas (*Highlands*) e nas ilhas escocesas. A Irlanda subdivide-se politicamente em Irlanda do Norte, de maioria protestante, e República da Irlanda (ou *Eire*, em gaélico irlandês), de maioria católica. A República da Irlanda é independente desde 1921.

País	Área (km²)	População
■ Inglaterra	130.400	46.161.000
■ País de Gales	20.800	2.798.000
■ Escócia	78.800	4.957.000
■ Irlanda do Norte	5.452	1.583.000

Geografia Cerca de mil quilômetros separam a costa sul da Inglaterra do extremo norte da Escócia; de leste a oeste do Reino Unido, a distância máxima atinge cerca de quinhentos quilômetros. Na Grã-Bretanha, nunca se está a mais de 120 km do mar. O interior da Inglaterra compõe-se de planícies, à exceção do norte e do sudoeste, ao passo que grande parte da Escócia e do País de Gales apresenta terreno montanhoso. A paisagem da Irlanda do Norte é formada de montanhas baixas e campos ondulados por colinas. Bem no centro, encontra-se Lough Neagh, o maior lago de água doce do Reino Unido, com cerca de 390 km². Nas áreas urbanas entre Londres e Manchester concentra-se 90% da população britânica.

Administração local O Reino Unido divide-se em condados (ou regiões, na Escócia), que, por sua vez, subdividem-se em distritos.

❏ A Inglaterra e o País de Gales têm seis condados metropolitanos (Grande Manchester, Merseyside, South Yorkshire, Tyne and Wear, West Midlands e West Yorkshire), os quais se subdividem em 36 distritos metropolitanos; há, ainda, 39 condados não-metropolitanos, que se subdividem em outros 296 distritos não-metropolitanos.

❏ A Grande Londres é uma área à parte, composta de 32 municípios (*boroughs*) e da *Corporation of the City of London*, o centro financeiro londrino.

❏ A Escócia possui 29 autoridades locais (*unitary authorities*) e três conselhos de ilhas (Órcadas, Shetland e Hébridas).

❏ A Irlanda do Norte subdivide-se em 26 conselhos distritais (*district councils*).

A maioria dos condados, regiões, distritos e municípios possui conselhos próprios. Em geral, seus representantes são eleitos a cada quatro anos. As autoridades metropolitanas, municipais e as dos condados respondem pelos serviços mais importantes: segurança, educação e transporte. As autoridades distritais ocupam-se de questões como habitação e coleta de lixo. Os serviços públicos são subvencionados por impostos municipais que taxam a propriedade de imóveis para habitação (*council tax*) e comércio (*non-domestic rates*).

r ao restaurante, ao cinema ou a um *pub* são as atividades preferidas da maioria dos britânicos, no que se refere ao lazer. O teatro e as danceterias são também populares, assim como assistir à televisão, praticar jardinagem ou dedicar-se a trabalhos manuais. Em anos mais recentes, a ginástica aeróbica e os exercícios físicos têm atraído uma maior quantidade de adeptos.

Festas populares A Grã-Bretanha tem poucas festas nacionais, que são também chamadas *bank holidays*, porque, nessas ocasiões, os bancos permanecem fechados, assim como as escolas e boa parte do comércio.

▸ **A Semana Santa e o Natal** são as únicas festas religiosas nacionais. No domingo de Páscoa, é comum presentear amigos e familiares com ovos de chocolate. Como ocorre em outros países europeus, a segunda-feira que sucede à Páscoa também é feriado no Reino Unido, à exceção da Escócia. O Natal é a festa popular mais importante. Costuma-se enviar cartões a parentes e amigos e decorar a árvore de Natal com bolas, fitas e luzes coloridas. A troca de presentes, depositados ao pé da árvore, acontece na

Feriados	
1º de janeiro	Dia de Ano-Novo
2 de janeiro	Feriado de Ano-Novo (somente na Escócia)
17 de março	Dia de São Patrício (somente na Irlanda do Norte)
Março ou abril	Sexta-feira Santa e Páscoa
	Segunda-feira de Páscoa (exceto na Escócia)
Primeira segunda-feira de maio	Dia do trabalho
Última segunda-feira de maio	Feriado de primavera (*Spring Bank Holiday*, exceto na Escócia)
12 de julho	Batalha de Boyne (somente na Irlanda do Norte)
Primeira segunda-feira de agosto	Feriado de verão (*Summer Bank Holiday*, sòmente na Escócia)
Última segunda-feira de agosto	Feriado de verão (*Summer Bank Holiday*, exceto na Escócia)
25 de dezembro	Dia de Natal
26 de dezembro	*Boxing Day*

manhã de 25 de dezembro, seguindo-se o almoço de Natal, que tradicionalmente consiste em peru recheado ao forno, batatas assadas e legumes. O dia 26, chamado *Boxing Day*, é feriado, e é costume passá-lo em casa, descansando, ou em visita a parentes ou amigos.

▸ **A véspera de Ano-Novo** (*Silvester* ou *Hogmanay*, na Escócia) caracteriza-se pelas festas que atravessam a noite. À meia-noite, é costume cantar uma canção chamada *Auld Lang Syne* ("Os velhos tempos").

Pubs Os *pubs* (forma abreviada de *public house*), os famosos bares da Grã-Bretanha, são parte importante da vida social do país. Em geral, dividem-se em uma área com mesas e cadeiras (*lounge bar*) e outra, em que se bebe em pé (*public bar*). Costuma-se pedir a bebida no balcão e pagar por ela de imediato. Nos *pubs*, não é hábito dar gorjetas. Em muitos deles, pode-se jogar dardos ou bilhar; karaokê e música ao vivo estão também entre as atrações oferecidas.

Off-licenses Bebidas alcoólicas em lata ou garrafa, como cerveja e vinho, podem ser compradas em lojas chamadas *off-licenses*. A maioria delas abre de segunda a sábado, das 10 horas da manhã às 10 horas da noite, ou mesmo aos domingos, em algumas regiões.

Restaurantes Na Grã-Bretanha, é grande a oferta de restaurantes e cafés dotados de excelente cozinha, tanto nacional quanto internacional. As lanchonetes de *fast food* são populares, mas o tradicional *fish and chips*, peixe frito com batatas fritas, continua sendo a opção preferida da maioria. A comida indiana também é muito popular, e são numerosos os restaurantes hindus existentes na Grã-Bretanha. De modo geral, os *pubs* também servem almoço barato e de boa qualidade. Nos restaurantes, o vinho pode custar o triplo do que se paga por ele nas lojas de bebidas, e a conta pode incluir um acréscimo de 10%, cobrado pelo serviço. Quando esse acréscimo não é cobrado, é costume deixar gorjeta correspondente a 10% ou 15% da conta.

Nas horas vagas, ver televisão é a atividade preferida dos britânicos. Em geral, rádio e televisão desfrutam de sólida reputação de imparcialidade política na Grã-Bretanha.

Canais de televisão São cinco os canais nacionais de televisão:

▸ A **BBC** (*British Broadcasting Corporation*) transmite em dois canais para toda a Grã-Bretanha, BBC1 e BBC2, ambos financiados por um imposto anual, pago por todos os proprietários de aparelhos de televisão. A BBC1 oferece uma programação de alta qualidade, dirigida a um amplo público, que inclui filmes, notícias, esportes e programas humorísticos. A BBC2 atinge um público mais restrito, com programação voltada para a educação e a cultura, incluindo-se aí os programas relacionados à *Open University* (ver **educação**).

▸ A **ITV** (*Independent Television* ou canal 3) transmite programas de 15 emissoras regionais independentes, financiadas por publicidade. Em linhas gerais, sua programação se assemelha à da BBC1. Os dois canais travam feroz batalha por audiência.

▸ O **Channel 4**, um canal comercial independente e de alcance nacional (à exceção do País de Gales), apresenta programas especializados para públicos específicos, buscando cobrir temas não explorados pela ITV. Em lugar do *Channel 4*, o País de Gales recebe o *S4C Welsh Fourth Channel*, que transmite seus programas em galês.

▸ O **Channel 5** é um canal comercial com um apelo jovem e descontraído, transmitindo programas culturais e informativos de caráter mais popular do que os de seus concorrentes.

TV por satélite e a cabo A *British Sky Broadcasting* (*BSkyB*) domina as transmissões por satélite, oferecendo programas esportivos, filmes, notícias, serviços de telecompras e concursos televisivos. Ela compete com diversos canais a cabo e companhias cuja programação apresenta atrações similares, além de filmes pelo sistema *pay-per-view*, televisão interativa e acesso à internet. Em 1998, foi introduzida na Grã-Bretanha a televisão digital, que oferece qualidade superior de imagem e de som.

Rádio A BBC tem cinco emissoras nacionais de rádio (ver quadro), além de estações na Escócia, País de Gales e Irlanda do Norte.

A Grã-Bretanha possui duas emissoras independentes: a *Classic FM* e a *Virgin Radio 1215 AM*. A Inglaterra conta ainda com 39 emissoras regionais da BBC, além de mais de uma centena de estações regionais independentes.

Jornais Cerca de 56% dos adultos lêem jornal na Grã-Bretanha. Além dos jornais diários nacionais e das edições dominicais (ver quadro), algumas cidades publicam periódicos vespertinos, e há diversos jornais regionais, como o *Yorkshire Post* (de Leeds), o *Herald* (de Glasgow), *The Scotsman* (de Edimburgo), o *South Wales Echo* (de Cardiff) e *The Belfast Telegraph*.

Existem também centenas de jornais semanais e numerosas publicações distribuídas

---

Radio nacional: BBC

■ **Rádio 1** (1053/1089 kHz MW; 97.6-99.8 MHz FM) Música pop, rock, notícias e informação sobre o trânsito.

■ **Rádio 2** (88-90.2 MHz FM) Música popular, entretenimento, comédias, programas culturais e notícias.

■ **Rádio 3** (1215 kHz MW; 90.2-92.4 MHz FM) Música clássica, radioteatro e documentários.

■ **Rádio 4** (198 kHz LW; 92.4-94.6 MHz FM) Notícias, documentários, atualidades, radioteatro, entretenimento e críquete.

■ **Rádio 5** Live (693/909 kHz OM) Notícias e esportes 24 horas por dia.

gratuitamente. Os jornais podem ser entregues em domicílio ou podem ser adquiridos nos diversos postos de vendas, em pequenas lojas de bairro, nos supermercados e nos quiosques.

Os jornais britânicos podem ser classificados pelo formato grande ou pequeno. Em geral, os jornais de qualidade têm formato grande (*broadsheet*), embora alguns, como *The Guardian* e *The Times*, tragam suplementos com formato pequeno ou tablóide. Os jornais populares, sempre em formato tablóide, preferem trocar a seriedade das análises por notícias sobre a vida pessoal de personalidades públicas, crimes mórbidos, boatos sobre os famosos e cobertura obsessiva da vida da família real britânica.

▶ Em geral, não há espaço para questões políticas nos tablóides, cujas tiragens são bem maiores do que as da grande imprensa. Pode-se afirmar, contudo, que a maioria dos jornais britânicos situa-se à direita do espectro político.

▶ Os **jornais dominicais** são mais grossos do que os diários e, com freqüência, trazem dois ou mais suplementos, além de uma revista em cores.

Principais jornais britânicos

Jornais populares (diários)
The Sun (1964) D 3 502.923 P
Daily Mail (1896) D 2 489.264 P
Daily Mirror (1903) E 2 164.576 P
Daily Express (1900)D 991.560 P
Daily Star (1978) D 706.554 P
Daily Record (1895) C/E 584.290 P

Jornais populares (dominicais)
News of the World (1843) D 4.086.621 P
The Mail on Sunday (1982)D 2.342.860 P
The Sunday Mirror (1963) D 1.845.860 P
The People (1881) D 1.389.778 P
The Sunday Express (1918) D 834,999 G
Sunday Sport (1988) D 301.000 P

Grande imprensa (diários)
Daily Telegraph (1855) D 1.013.653 G
The Times (1785) D 711,295 G
Financial Times (1888) C 475.475 G
The Guardian (1821) E 411.386 G
The Independent (1985) C/E 224,655 G

Grande imprensa (dominicais)
The Sunday Times (1822) D 1.405.430 G
Sunday Telegraph (1961) D 784.069 G
The Observer (1791) E 449.806 G
The Independent on Sunday (1990)
C/E 231.869 G

Os números indicam circulação. Entre parênteses: ano de fundação. Orientação política:
E = esquerda, D = direita, C = centro. Fomato: G = grande; P = pequeno (tablóide)

Revistas Os pontos de venda de jornais oferecem também uma ampla gama de revistas, que vão desde os semanários de análise político-econômica, como *The Economist*, até revistas de conteúdo satírico, como *Viz*. Milhares de publicações atendem a todo tipo de interesse. As revistas de maior vendagem são os guias da programação da televisão e publicações como *Reader's Digest, Computer Shopper, What Car* e *National Geographic*. Revistas femininas como *Woman's Own, Bella, Best* e *Prima* também vendem milhões de exemplares.

O uso da internet vem se ampliando cada vez mais no Reino Unido. Os domicílios conectados à rede já ultrapassam os 10 milhões, número superior à média européia, ainda que inferior àquele verificado na Escandinávia. Os britânicos passam, em média, mais tempo na rede do que a maioria dos europeus - mais de sete horas semanais. O Reino Unido encontra-se também entre os primeiros países da Europa no tocante às compras pela internet, embora muitos usuários ainda temam usar o cartão de crédito na rede.

Cerca de 74% dos internautas britânicos têm acesso à internet a partir de suas casas. O acesso desde o local de trabalho se dá também em proporções consideráveis, sendo menor o número daqueles que se valem de bibliotecas, centros educacionais ou cafés para o acesso à rede. Os principais provedores de acesso no Reino Unido são Freeserve, AOL, BT Internet, NTL, LineOne e VirginNet. A maioria das conexões se faz ainda por linha discada, mas os serviços de banda larga vêm se difundindo cada vez mais no mercado.

Embora o número de internautas do sexo masculino seja ainda superior ao de mulheres na rede, essa desproporção vem diminuindo progressivamente. No Reino Unido, o usuário típico da internet é do sexo masculino, jovem ou de meia-idade e de alto poder aquisitivo.

Uma grande porcentagem das empresas britânicas está conectada à rede (86%). Muitas fazem uso constante da internet em seus negócios, para envio e recebimento de mensagens de correio eletrônico, nas atividades relacionadas a marketing e publicidade, e nos setores de compras, vendas, administração e formação de pessoal.

Na indústria manufatureira, a semana de trabalho oscila entre 38 e 40 horas, ao passo que, nos escritórios, a carga horária semanal é de 35 a 38 horas. Funcionários de hospitais, restaurantes e hotéis chegam a trabalhar cem horas por semana, embora a média esteja em torno de cinqüenta ou sessenta horas.

▸ Muitas empresas utilizam o sistema de **horário móvel**, sobretudo em escritórios. Seus empregados devem estar presentes em certos horários de maior demanda, o chamado *core time*: das 9 às 11.30 e das 13.30 às 16 horas, por exemplo. As pausas e os horários de entrada, saída e de almoço são flexíveis, podendo-se, assim, chegar mais tarde ao trabalho, desde que a diferença seja compensada ao final do expediente.

Férias A maioria dos britânicos dispõe de férias anuais remuneradas por um período de quatro a seis semanas. Em geral, as férias anuais são gozadas dentro do período correspondente, mas algumas empresas permitem que seus funcionários acumulem férias para o ano seguinte. Além das férias, há também os diversos feriados ao longo do ano (ver **lazer**).

Salários Os trabalhadores britânicos recebem o salário mensal depositado diretamente em suas contas bancárias. O pagamento é acompanhado de um contracheque (*wage slip*), detalhando o salário bruto e eventuais deduções, como o imposto retido, o desconto relativo à previdência social, aos fundos de pensão das empresas e à contribuição sindical. Trabalhadores manuais e temporários costumam receber por semana e em dinheiro. Em geral, o pagamento é realizado às sextas-feiras, também acompanhado de um demonstrativo, contendo os valores da remuneração e dos descontos.

Ausência por doença Em caso de ausência no trabalho por um período inferior a sete dias, basta ao trabalhador preencher um formulário (*self-certification form*) ao retornar, explicando o motivo da ausência. Períodos de tempo maiores, porém, demandam apresentação de atestado médico.

Imposto de renda O imposto é recolhido pelas autoridades fiscais (o *Inland Revenue*) e cobrado sobre o total dos ganhos anuais. O ano fiscal britânico começa em 6 de abril, estendendo-se até 5 de abril do ano seguinte. A maioria das pessoas não faz declaração de renda, uma vez que o imposto é recolhido na fonte pelas empresas, sistema que, no Reino Unido, chama-se *Pay-As-You-Earn* (*PAYE*). Os trabalhadores autônomos pagam seus impostos ao final do ano fiscal. O montante a pagar é definido com base nas informações contidas na declaração de renda, que devem ser devidamente documentadas.

Previdência social A assistência social pública é parcialmente financiada pelas contribuições à previdência social: a chamada *National Insurance* ou *NI*. Essas contribuições dão direito a aposentadoria, seguro-desemprego e outros benefícios. Elas são obrigatórias para a maioria dos residentes na Grã-Bretanha e, em geral, as empresas as deduzem diretamente dos salários.

Seguro-desemprego Para ter direito ao seguro-desemprego, o trabalhador precisa ter contribuído para a previdência social por determinado período de tempo. O benefício é pago a cada duas semanas, mediante cheque postal. Os requerentes devem renovar sua solicitação a cada duas semanas, comprovando sua situação. Aqueles que não são beneficiados pelo seguro-desemprego podem solicitar outros benefícios sociais destinados a pessoas de baixa renda, como o chamado *Income Support*. Centrais de trabalho (*job centres*) congregam ofertas de emprego, assessoram o desempregado em sua busca por uma nova colocação e orientam-no na solicitação dos benefícios.

O Reino Unido é visitado por mais de 25 milhões de pessoas por ano, que procuram seu patrimônio histórico-cultural, seus castelos, as cidades antigas e ruínas históricas, os museus e as galerias de arte, bem como sua beleza natural. A maior parte desses turistas - cerca de 12 milhões ao ano - dirige-se para Londres, atraída pelo caráter cosmopolita da cidade e por seus famosos monumentos. Londres oferece também muitas atrações culturais, como museus, teatros e espetáculos musicais. Muita gente aproveita a estada na capital inglesa para visitar as tradicionais cidades universitárias de Oxford e Cambridge. O interior da Inglaterra oferece muitos outros atrativos: cidades medievais, como York, as termas romanas e a elegância georgiana de Bath; Stratford-upon-Avon - a cidade-natal de William Shakespeare; Stonehenge e seu famoso monumento de pedras pré-históricas; ou a beleza natural de Lake District, a 160 km ao norte de Manchester, que serviu de cenário e inspiração a numerosos pintores e escritores.

Muitos turistas visitam também a Escócia, para desfrutar de sua beleza natural, da fauna e flora locais e, sobretudo, da sensação de amplidão e tranqüilidade propiciada pelas vastas paisagens. Numerosas atividades podem ser praticadas ao ar livre, como golfe, montanhismo, esqui, pesca e esportes aquáticos. Também o País de Gales atrai os que buscam atividade física e a prática de esportes, tais como o *tracking*, o montanhismo e o ciclismo pelas montanhas dos parques naturais de Snowdonia ou Breacon Beacons.

Uma importante categoria de visitantes compõem os estudantes de inglês. Todos os anos, milhares de jovens e adultos dirigem-se a diferentes pontos do Reino Unido com o intuito de fazer cursos de inglês e praticar o idioma. As cidades mais procuradas por esses estudantes de língua são Londres, Oxford, Cambridge, Bristol, Bath, Brighton e Edimburgo.

Boa parte dos visitantes chega ao Reino Unido de avião, embora o Eurostar tenha, nos últimos anos, popularizado o acesso por trem, a partir da França. Muitos ainda preferem cruzar o Canal da Mancha de balsa, sobretudo aqueles que viajam de carro, com suas famílias ou num grupo de pessoas.

Além dos hotéis, os turistas costumam hospedar-se também nos *bed & breakfast* - quartos em casas particulares, com café da manhã. Os *bed & breakfast* oferecem um ambiente mais íntimo e aconchegante do que os hotéis, além de maior economia. Essas acomodações estão sujeitas a inspeção por parte das autoridades responsáveis pelo turismo e por associações como a *AA* (*Automobile Association*, o automóvel-clube britânico). Elas são avaliadas pelo seu conforto, limpeza e qualidade dos serviços e recebem uma classificação, expressa em número de estrelas ou diamantes. Além disso, estão presentes em toda parte, até mesmo em áreas remotas do país.

Outra opção, bastante popular entre as famílias ou grupos que viajam para o campo, é o aluguel de *cottages*. Os *cottages* são, em geral, casas no campo - por vezes moinhos ou silos. Com freqüência, são construções antigas que foram reformadas para esse fim. Pode-se também optar pelo aluguel de uma casa flutuante, quando se deseja viajar pelos muitos rios e canais da Inglaterra.

Estados Unidos

Os Estados Unidos da América ocupam uma área de 9.809.155 km², sendo o quarto país do mundo em extensão territorial. Com 286.488.000 de habitantes, são também o terceiro país mais populoso do mundo, depois de China e Índia. Sua superfície cobre toda a faixa intermediária do continente norte-americano, estendendo-se por cerca de 4 mil quilômetros do Atlântico ao Pacífico, e por quase 2 mil quilômetros de norte a sul, desde a fronteira canadense até o Golfo do México. Fazem parte dos Estados Unidos o Alasca, situado a noroeste do Canadá, e o Havaí, no Pacífico central. Sob administração americana encontram-se, ainda, várias ilhas do Pacífico e do Caribe, incluindo-se aí Porto Rico, Guam, as Ilhas Virgens e a Samoa norte-americana.

As 10 maiores áreas metropolitanas dos EUA		
Cidade	População	Estado
Nova York	20.124.000	Nova York
Los Angeles	15.781.000	Califórnia
Chicago	8.810.000	Illinois
Washington DC-Baltimore	6.726.000	DC/Maryland
São Francisco	6.278.000	Califórnia
Filadélfia	5.893.000	Pensilvânia
Boston	5.455.000	Massachusetts
Detroit	5.187.000	Michigan
Dallas	4.037.000	Texas
Houston	3.731.000	Texas

[Fonte: World Almanac]

Regiões Os EUA dividem-se em quatro regiões geográficas:

- ❏ Nordeste - Nova Inglaterra (formada pelos estados de Connecticut, New Hampshire, Maine, Massachusetts, Rhode Island e Vermont), Nova Jersey, Nova York, Pensilvânia, Maryland, Delaware e Washington DC.

- ❏ Centro-oeste (*Midwest*) - Illinois, Indiana, Iowa, Kansas, Michigan, Minnesota, Missouri, Nebraska, Dakota do Norte, Ohio, Dakota do Sul e Wisconsin.

- ❏ Sul - Alabama, Arkansas, Flórida, Georgia, Kentucky, Louisiana, Mississippi, Carolina do Norte, Oklahoma, Carolina do Sul, Tennessee, Texas, Virgínia e Virgínia Ocidental.

- ❏ Oeste - Alasca, Arizona, Califórnia, Colorado, Havaí, Idaho, Montana, Nevada, Novo México, Oregon, Utah, Washington e Wyoming.

Governos federal e estadual Os EUA são uma república federativa, formada por cinqüenta estados e o Distrito de Colúmbia, território situado no estado de Maryland, que abriga a capital do país, Washington DC. O poder se divide entre os governos federal, estadual e municipal.

- ❏ O governo federal constitui-se do presidente da República, do Congresso (formado pela Câmara de Representantes e pelo Senado) e da Corte Suprema. Sob seu controle estão áreas como defesa, relações exteriores, emissão de moeda e regulamentação do comércio.

- ❏ O poder estadual compõe-se do governador e de um congresso bicameral (*State Congress*). Estão sob sua responsabilidade a cobrança de impostos, a saúde pública, a educação e a legislação civil e penal.

☐ Os estados se dividem em condados, que, por sua vez, subdividem-se em municípios, cada um deles com administração própria. A maioria das cidades é governada por um prefeito e uma Câmara municipal (*city council*). As autoridades locais encarregam-se da administração de escolas, hospitais, serviços de emergência, da limpeza pública, do sistema viário e das leis que regulam a atividade comercial.

Estados Unidos

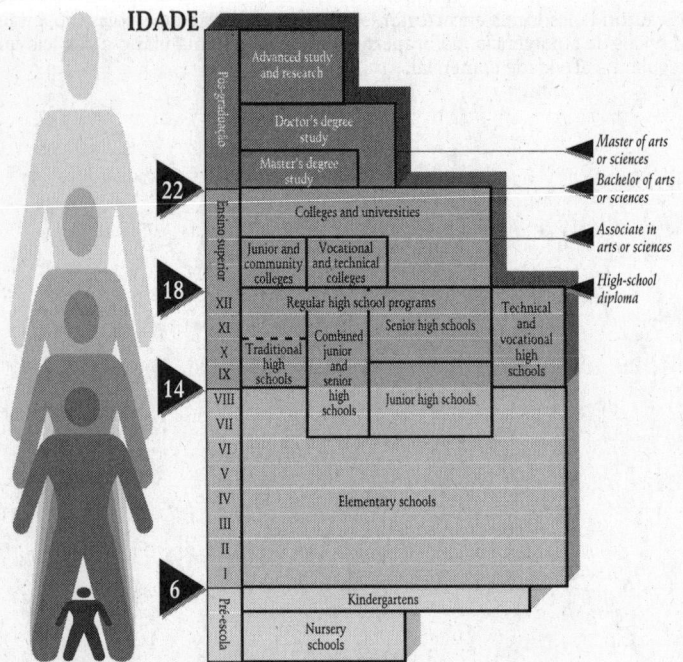

O governo central dos EUA exerce pouco controle direto sobre a educação. O sistema educacional varia de uma região para outra. A maioria das instituições de ensino compõe-se de escolas estaduais, mas cerca de 25% dessas escolas e 45% das faculdades estão nas mãos de grupos privados ou religiosos. O ensino é, em geral, obrigatório, e se estende dos 5 ou 6 anos até por volta dos 16 ou 18 anos de idade.

Educação pré-escolar (até 5 anos) Cerca de 35% das crianças de 3 e 4 anos freqüentam escolas maternais (*nursery schools*), e quase todas entre 4 e 5 vão ao jardim da infância.

Escola primária (dos 6 aos 13 anos) e escola secundária (até 18 anos) Nos dois casos, o número de anos de estudo varia de um estado para outro. Os modelos mais comuns são os seguintes:

- ❏ seis anos de escola primária, seguidos por três anos de *junior high school* (ensino fundamental) e três anos de *senior high school* (ensino médio).
- ❏ oito anos de escola primária (ensino fundamental), seguidos por quatro anos de escola secundária (ensino médio).
- ❏ quatro ou cinco anos de escola primária, seguidos por três ou quatro anos de *middle school* (ensino fundamental), e quatro anos de escola secundária ou *high school* (ensino médio).

OS ANOS ESCOLARES

	Escola Secundária		Faculdade
	Idade	Série	Idade
■ estudante de primeiro ano *(freshman)*	14-15	9ª	18
■ estudante de segundo ano *(sophomore)*	15-16	10ª	19
■ estudante de terceiro ano *(junior)*	16-17	11ª	20
■ estudante de último ano *(senior)*	17-18	12ª	21

Currículo Não há um currículo nacional nos EUA. A maioria dos estudantes das escolas secundárias (*high schools*) deve cursar algumas disciplinas obrigatórias, podendo, nas últimas séries, cursar matérias optativas.

Exames Os estudantes fazem provas ao final de cada curso semestral, mas, ao contrário do que ocorre em outros países, inexiste um exame nacional ao término do ensino secundário. As avaliações são contínuas, ao longo dos anos escolares, e o desempenho dos alunos é determinado pela média dessas avaliações, chamada *Grades Point Average* (GPA). Aqueles que desejarem ingressar na universidade fazem exames nacionais, tais como o *American College Test* (ACT) e o *Scholastic Aptitude Test* (SAT).

Escolas privadas Cerca de 12% dos estudantes estadunidenses freqüentam escolas privadas. Seus cursos organizam-se de forma idêntica ao das escolas públicas, mas o currículo tem por alvo prioritário assegurar o ingresso dos alunos nas melhores universidades e faculdades, como as que integram as chamadas *Ivy League* e *Seven Sisters* (ver quadro).

Ensino superior (dos 18 aos 26 anos)

Mais de 50% dos graduados na escola secundária dão prosseguimento aos estudos em nível superior, onde podem obter os seguintes graus: *undergraduate, graduate* e *postgraduate*. Cursos superiores são oferecidos por *state colleges*, *community* ou *junior colleges* (que oferecem cursos de dois anos), *undergraduate colleges* (com cursos universitários de quatro anos de duração), escolas técnicas e as prestigiosas universidades e *graduate schools*. Os cursos são pagos pelos estudantes (ou por seus pais), mas cerca de 50% dos alunos conseguem ajuda econômica.

Instituições mais respeitadas de ensino superior

Universidades	Faculdades
Ivy League	*Seven Sisters*
Brown	Barnard
Columbia	Bryn Mawr
Cornell	Mount Holyoke
Dartmouth	Radcliffe
Harvard	Smith
Univ. of Pennsylvania	Vassar
Princeton	Wellesley
Yale	

Educação de adultos Nos EUA, milhões de adultos freqüentam universidades e outras instituições de ensino superior, seja em cursos de tempo integral ou de um único período. Cerca de 40% dos estudantes universitários têm mais de 25 anos.

Os Estados Unidos têm a mais alta porcentagem *per capita* de televisores do mundo. Na prática, todos os lares americanos possuem pelo menos um aparelho de TV, e 70% deles possuem dois ou mais. Uma típica família americana vê sete horas de televisão por dia, e a média por pessoa é de trinta horas semanais.

Canais de televisão

Existem quatro redes comerciais nacionais nos EUA:

- ❏ American Broadcasting Company (ABC)
- ❏ Columbia Broadcasting Service (CBS)
- ❏ National Broadcasting Company (NBC)
- ❏ Fox TV

Essas quatro redes respondem por 70% da audiência nos horários de maior demanda. Existem cerca de 1.300 canais comerciais, bem como por volta de quatrocentos canais estatais não-comerciais e canais educativos. A maioria dos canais comerciais é afiliada a uma rede nacional, porém existem mais de quatrocentos canais comerciais independentes, oferecendo uma programação especializada, composta, por exemplo, de filmes antigos.

Programação das redes

A programação das tevês baseia-se quase exclusivamente no entretenimento, como competições televisivas, programas de entrevistas, comédias de costumes e filmes. De modo geral, apenas o noticiário local e os grandes eventos esportivos são transmitidos ao vivo.

Os índices de audiência e a publicidade

O motor das grandes redes de televisão é sobretudo a publicidade, permitida à razão de 15 minutos por hora. Os índices de audiência são, portanto, o fator mais importante na televisão norte-americana. Índice baixo significa receita publicitária menor, o que pode fazer com que mesmo programas de relativa popularidade sejam tirados do ar, se assim exigirem as estatísticas.

TV a cabo e por satélite

Cerca de 60% dos lares americanos possuem TV a cabo. Nas grandes cidades, há uma média de 35 canais disponíveis, além das redes nacionais e do *Public Broadcasting System* (PBS), a rede pública de televisão (ver abaixo). Ao contrário do que ocorre com as redes, a televisão a cabo não está sujeita às leis federais, razão pela qual pode, eventualmente, veicular material considerado impróprio. Em geral, cada canal especializa-se em determinado tema, como esportes, filmes, religião, notícias (como é o caso da CNN), compras, música (como a MTV), saúde, pornografia ou programas em língua estrangeira. Muitos hotéis, bares e clubes oferecem TV a cabo em seus estabelecimentos, um atrativo sobretudo quando da transmissão ao vivo de eventos esportivos.

Rede pública de televisão (*Public Broadcasting System*, PBS)

O PBS compõe-se de uma rede de canais não-comerciais, financiada por fundos federais, pelo patrocínio de empresas e por doações de particulares. Suas transmissões oferecem programas de conteúdo educativo e cultural.

Rádio Há mais de 10 mil estações de rádio nos EUA, sendo que as principais cidades chegam a ter de cinqüenta a cem estações. Muitas delas são afiliadas a redes nacionais como a ABC, a NBC e a CBS, mas há também cerca de 100 redes regionais. Programas de conteúdo diferenciado podem ser encontrados na *National Public Radio* (NPR), especializada em notícias e em temas da atualidade, e na *American Public Radio* (APR), cuja especialidade são os programas de entretenimento. Assim como o PBS, a NPR e a APR sobrevivem com a ajuda de subsídios governamentais e do patrocínio privado.

Jornais Existem por volta de 1.700 jornais diários e 850 jornais dominicais nos EUA, perfazendo uma tiragem total superior a 68 milhões de exemplares. Jornais semanais e quinzenais somam cerca de 7.500 títulos. Os principais grupos étnicos têm também seus próprios jornais, e todas as regiões distribuem jornais gratuitos, contendo notícias das comunidades locais.

> **Identificação das estações de rádio**
>
> As estações de rádio são identificadas por um prefixo de quatro letras, KLMN ou WBNS, por exemplo. As estações a leste do Mississippi e das Montanhas Rochosas têm por primeira letra o "W", e aquelas situadas a oeste, o "K". Em geral, a indicação AM ou FM sucede ao prefixo, como em WBNS FM.

▸ **Imprensa nacional?** A maioria dos jornais americanos possui caráter regional. *Christian Science Monitor, USA Today* e *Wall Street Journal* são os únicos com circulação nacional, embora alguns jornais de prestígio, como o *New York Times*, o *Washington Post* e o *Los Angeles Times* publiquem edições nacionais. O *USA Today* destaca-se entre os jornais populares, com uma vendagem superior a 5 milhões de exemplares por dia. O *Wall Street Journal*, a mais importante publicação sobre negócios, é impresso em diversas cidades e tem quatro edições regionais, sendo o jornal de maior circulação nos EUA. Outras publicações regionais de qualidade, sobretudo em formato grande, são o *Boston Globe*, o *Chicago Tribune*, o *Denver Post*, o *Miami Herald* e o *San Francisco Herald*.

> **A compra do jornal**
>
> Um terço dos norte-americanos recebe seu jornal na porta de casa. Jornais são vendidos também em quiosques e máquinas. Nas máquinas, introduz-se o valor correspondente e retira-se o exemplar pelo qual se pagou.

▸ Os leitores podem optar entre jornais de formato grande ou pequeno. Assim como no Reino Unido, os jornais de conteúdo mais diferenciado são aqueles de formato grande, ao passo que os tablóides se concentram em temas como sexo, escândalos e esportes. A maioria das cidades publica seus próprios tablóides. Exemplos disso são o *Herald* (Boston), o *Sun Times* (Chicago) e o *Daily News* (Nova York). Os semanários mais escandalosos são o *National Enquirer*, o *Globe* e o *Star*.

▸ A maioria dos diários publica uma edição dominical, normalmente com diversas seções. Os jornais dominicais podem ser adquiridos no sábado à tarde (à exceção da seção de notícias), chegando a custar o triplo dos diários, embora, de modo geral, os jornais sejam baratos.

As revistas semanais de notícias, como *Newsweek, Time* e *US News and World Report*, são bastante populares e oferecem boa cobertura jornalística. Contudo, as revistas mais populares são as que tratam de moda, delinqüência, guerras e pessoas famosas.

Internet Nos EUA, muitas pessoas se conectam diariamente à internet, de suas casas, do trabalho ou da escola, enviando e recebendo milhões de mensagens de correio eletrônico - o serviço mais utilizado. Há centenas de provedores de acesso, dentre os quais destacam-se a *America Online* (AOL) e a MSN, que proporcionam aos usuários notícias de política, economia, finanças ou esportes, além de informações sobre os espetáculos em cartaz. Boa parte dos internautas conecta-se à rede por linha discada, mas é cada vez maior o número de usuários que se valem de modalidades mais rápidas de conexão, como ADSL e cabo. Bastante populares são os programas de troca de mensagens em tempo real, como o ICQ e o Instant Messenger, que permitem a comunicação rápida, por intermédio de texto ou de voz, além de possibilitar a transferência de arquivos em geral.

A semana de trabalho nos EUA tem de quarenta a 45 horas, embora os trabalhadores industriais cheguem a trabalhar 53 horas semanais. O horário típico de expediente vai das 8 às 17 horas, com uma hora para almoço.

▸ O sistema de horário móvel é menos utilizado nos EUA do que na Grã-Bretanha.

Férias Nos EUA, é comum ter apenas uma ou duas semanas de férias remuneradas ao ano, e muitos trabalhadores não têm direito a férias remuneradas durante o primeiro ano de trabalho. Cada ano de permanência num mesmo posto resulta num acréscimo do tempo de férias.

Imposto de renda Existem dois tipos de impostos: o federal e o estadual. Os impostos são recolhidos pelo *Internal Revenue Service* (IRS). O sistema baseia-se em cálculo individual (*self-assessment*), de responsabilidade exclusiva dos contribuintes. Às empresas, cabe deduzir o imposto do salário de seus empregados. Esse sistema de retenção do imposto na fonte chama-se *withholding*. Todos aqueles que recebem salário sujeito a retenção devem preencher uma declaração de renda relativa ao ano fiscal anterior (de janeiro a dezembro) e apresentá-la antes de 15 de abril. O imposto de renda recolhido pelos estados é, em geral, menor do que o imposto federal e varia de um estado a outro. Alguns estados não recolhem impostos.

> ### Green Card
> Todos os estrangeiros que desejem permanecer nos EUA necessitam de um visto. Em linhas gerais, existem dois tipos de visto: os concedidos para imigrantes (residência permanente) e os concedidos para não-imigrantes (residência temporária). Os imigrantes recebem um documento chamado *Alien Registration Receipt Card*, mais conhecido como *Green Card*, embora sua cor atual seja rosa. O trâmite para obtenção do *Green Card* é demorado e complicado. Para consegui-lo, o solicitante deve ser parente próximo de um cidadão americano ou funcionário de uma empresa sediada nos EUA. Do contrário, terá de comprovar que possui recursos suficientes para investir significativa importância em dinheiro na economia do país.

Previdência social A previdência norte-americana cobre a aposentadoria, compulsória ou por doença, pensões por invalidez e viuvez, e o programa de assistência chamado *Medicare*. Todos os cidadãos estadunidenses, bem como residentes estrangeiros, recebem uma carteira da chamada *social security*, contendo um número de identificação composto de nove dígitos. O pré-requisito para o direito à assistência consiste num número mínimo de anos de trabalho, que, em geral, é de cerca de dez anos.

As contribuições à previdência social são feitas por empregados e empresas, cada qual destinando ao sistema certa porcentagem do salário bruto. A contribuição dos trabalhadores é descontada diretamente pela empresa. Trabalhadores autônomos contribuem anualmente.

Desemprego Um fundo administrado conjuntamente pelo governo federal e pelos governos estaduais garante uma renda semanal por tempo limitado (em geral, 26 semanas) aos desempregados, que, para recebê-la, precisam se inscrever no órgão competente. O montante do auxílio depende da renda anterior do trabalhador, mas procura-se proporcionar-lhe uma renda equivalente à metade de seu salário semanal prévio.

O tempo livre de que desfrutam os norte-americanos é relativamente pequeno (ver **trabalho**).

Festas nacionais Além das festas nacionais, muitos estados têm suas próprias datas comemorativas.

▶ **Natal e Ano-Novo** No Natal, costuma-se enviar cartões a parentes e amigos e decorar a árvore de Natal com bolas, fitas e luzes coloridas. A troca de presentes, depositados ao pé da árvore, acontece na manhã de 25 de dezembro, seguindo-se o almoço de Natal, que tradicionalmente consiste em peru recheado ao forno, batatas assadas e legumes. A véspera de Ano-Novo (*Silvester*) caracteriza-se pelas festas que atravessam a noite.

▶ **Semana Santa** Nos EUA, as crianças associam a data ao coelho da Páscoa, que entrega cestas de doces e ovos de chocolate (*Easter baskets*) na manhã do domingo de Páscoa.

Feriados nacionais	
1° de janeiro	Dia de Ano-Novo
Terceira segunda-feira de janeiro	Dia de Martin Luther King
Terceira segunda-feira de fevereiro	Dia dos presidentes (comemoram-se os aniversários de nascimento de Lincoln e Washington
Última segunda-feira de maio	*Memorial Day* (comemoração dos mortos na guerra)
4 de julho	Dia da independência
Primeira segunda-feira de setembro	Dia do trabalho
Segunda segunda-feira de outubro	Dia da hispanidade (Cristóvão Colombo)
11 de novembro	Dia do armistício
Quarta quinta-feira de novembro	Dia de ação de graças
25 de dezembro	Dia de Natal

▶ O **dia de ação de graças** comemora, em sua origem, a colheita na colônia de Plymouth no ano de 1621, após um inverno de grandes privações. Hoje em dia, toda a família se reúne para compartilhar um almoço tradicional, que consiste, entre outros pratos, em peru recheado, purê de batatas e tortas de abóbora e maçã.

Bares O melhor lugar para uma conversa tranqüila são os bares onde se servem coquetéis (*cocktail lounge*). A bebida é servida nas mesas e a conta pode ser paga a cada rodada ou ao final. Nos EUA, a prática mais comum é cada um pagar o que consumiu, e costuma-se deixar gorjeta, algo entre 15% a 20% do valor total da conta.

Restaurantes Os norte-americanos comem fora com bastante freqüência: cerca de 40% do orçamento de uma família típica americana são gastos em restaurantes. Os pratos são servidos em porções generosas e é bem ampla a oferta de comidas de diversos países. Em geral, a conta não inclui o serviço, sendo hábito deixar gorjeta equivalente a 15% ou 20% do valor total.

Esportes Os esportes individuais de maior popularidade são a natação, o ciclismo, o esqui, a pesca, a corrida para manter a forma, o *tracking* e a ginástica aeróbica. Os esportes coletivos que atraem maior público são o beisebol (o esporte nacional), o futebol americano e o basquetebol.

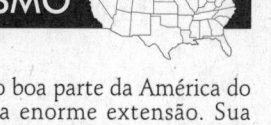
Desde o trópico de Câncer até o Ártico, abrangendo boa parte da América do Norte, os Estados Unidos se destacam por sua enorme extensão. Sua topografia caracteriza-se por grandes espaços abertos e pela diversidade da paisagem, que apresenta desde áridos desertos até os bosques mais densos, das imponentes montanhas às vastas pradarias.

Esse país gigantesco divide-se em cinqüenta estados, e viajar por eles significa apreciar as diferenças geográficas e culturais que os distinguem, cada um com seu sabor individual, mas todos contribuindo para o amálgama vital e dinâmico que deu forma ao país ao longo de sua história.

O turismo concentra-se sobretudo nos estados da Flórida, Califórnia e Havaí, nos centros de esqui em meio às montanhas e nas metrópoles. Mas são também bastante visitados os parques nacionais, como Yosemite e Yellowstone, os Grandes Lagos, e a impressionante paisagem dos cânions no Colorado e em Monument Valley. Entre as cidades norte-americanas destacam-se Nova York, com seus imponentes arranha-céus e suas muitas atrações culturais, além da energia e do dinamismo de sua gente; Nova Orleans, onde se pode desfrutar da típica cultura sulista e ouvir o jazz em sua terra-natal; e Las Vegas, um oásis no meio do deserto, com seus palácios de neon dedicados ao jogo e ao divertimento.

Viajar pelos Estados Unidos é fácil, ainda que as distâncias sejam grandes. A maneira mais simples de percorrer o país é por avião, sobretudo quando se deseja atravessar grandes extensões. Ônibus e trens são uma boa opção para aqueles que pretendem percorrer sem pressa uma área menor, como o noroeste do país, entre Boston e Washington. Mas o melhor meio de transporte para viajar pelo território americano é o carro, porque permite explorar as cidades pequenas e conhecer os locais de menor afluência turística. Além disso, o aluguel de veículos é simples, com preços bastante acessíveis, e o custo da gasolina é barato.

Não é difícil encontrar hospedagem, disponível em todos os níveis, desde pequenos motéis ao longo das estradas e nas cercanias das cidades até as grandes cadeias de hotéis. Outra opção de hospedagem são os *bed & breakfast*, ou *b&b*, normalmente situados em casas antigas transformadas em hospedarias. Muitos desses *b&b* são famosos pelos esplêndidos cafés-da-manhã que servem a seus hóspedes.

Living in Brazil

CONTENTS

Brazil is a country the size of a continent, with an area of 8,514,205 km². Situated in South America, it is the largest country in the southern hemisphere. With the Atlantic Ocean on its east coast, Brazil shares borders with Argentina, Paraguay, Bolivia, Peru and Colombia in the west, Uruguay in the south and Venezuela, Guyana, Suriname and French Guyana in the north. The official language is Portuguese and its 170 million inhabitants make it the fifth most populous country in the world, after China, India, the USA and Indonesia.

Brazil is world famous for its natural beauty and talented football players; it is also becoming a valuable contributor to the world's scientific knowledge, supplying important research into agriculture, space, engineering, geosciences and physics. In addition, it has one of the most powerful economies in the world due to the size and strength of its industries, agriculture and cattle ranching.

The population of Brazil is characterized by its great ethnic and cultural diversity. It has developed from three basic ethnic groups: the indigenous, the White and the African (Black). The intensive intermarriage between these groups resulted in a large mixed-race population, and was added to in turn by various immigrant peoples, thus further broadening and diversifying the ethnic composition of the Brazilian population. Since independence from Portugal in 1822 there has been a huge influx of immigrants, coming mainly from Italy, Spain, Germany, Poland, Ukraine and Japan.

Indians In 1500, the indigenous population, speaking around one thousand different languages, exceeded 3 million. By the 1950s, this figure had been reduced to less than 100,000; this has since risen so that by 2001 there were 358,000 Indians, accounting for 0.21% of the Brazilian population. They live in 561 government-acknowledged reservations, which cover 1 million km², that is 12.26% of the entire country. These are spread throughout the country except for the states of Piauí and Rio Grande do Norte. Most of the indigenous people live in so-called Constitutional Amazonia (*Amazônia Legal*), comprising the states of Amazonas, Acre, Amapá, Pará, Rondônia, Roraima, Tocantins, Mato Grosso and part of Maranhão. Some tribes, such as the Ticuna, the Guarani and the Ianomâmi, are still quite large; others however, such as the Juma, the Xeta, the Caripuna and the Avá-canoeiro, are greatly reduced in number.

Black population In 1800, 47% of the Brazilian population was black, 30% mixed-race and 23% white. By 1880 this had changed: 20% were black, 38% white and 42% mixed-race. The ethnic composition of the Brazilian people was profoundly affected by a number of factors, including the end of the slave trade (slavery in Brazil was only abolished in 1888), the high mortality rate among the Black population, intense European immigration during the growth of the coffee industry, and the intense intermarrying between Whites and Blacks. The data from 2000 show that Blacks and mixed-race people make up 45.3% of the population in a proportion of 6.2% Black and 39.1 % mixed-race.

Immigration In 1808 the king of Portugal, Dom Joāo VI, passed a decree permitting non-Portuguese to own land in Brazil. The first to take advantage of this were the Swiss, who founded the city of Nova Friburgo in the state of Rio de Janeiro in 1818. Throughout the 19th century, waves of immigrants entered the country. The Germans headed towards the states of Santa Catarina and Espírito Santo; the Italians went to São Paulo. The Japanese arrived in 1908, along with significant contingents of Swiss, Spaniards, Poles and Syrian-Lebanese. Over half these immigrants settled in the state of São Paulo, to work in the coffee plantations, replacing slave labour. In other areas of Brazil, immigration was characterized by the settling of the colonists in

> **Black Awareness Day**
> During the time Brazil was a colony, there were many conflicts between black slaves and whites. Rebellious slaves gathered in quilombos, fortified settlements. The most noteworthy quilombo was Palmares, situated in lands belonging to the states of Pernambuco and Alagoas. It contained up to eleven settlements, spread over an area of around 350 km². In the seventeenth century, Macaco, the most important centre of Palmares, comprised 1,500 dwellings and approximately 8,000 inhabitants. The chief of this quilombo, Zumbi, was killed in 1695 and became a symbol of the Black struggle against racial oppression; the date of his death – 20th November – is now Black Awareness Day.

small properties, as opposed to the vast fazendas of São Paulo. Nowadays, immigrants, for the most part Koreans and Bolivians, seek out the big cities, where they work illegally. There is also a significant number of highly qualified workers who are settling in Brazil in order to work for multinational firms.

Total population growth and proportion by sex				
	1980	1990	1996	2000
Total Population	119,002,706	146,825,475	157,070,163	169,799,170
% Men	49.68	49.36	49.30	49.22
% Women	50.31	50.63	50.69	50.78

Source: IBGE (Instituto Brasileiro de Geografia e Estatística)

The majority of the Brazilian population is Roman Catholic. There are indicators, however, that show a decline in the number of practising Catholics, with a significant drift towards other Christian Protestant or free churches. Between 1970 and 1990, the number of Protestants increased by 10%; other free-church Christians, by 9%; and the number of Catholics by a mere 2%. One of the striking characteristics of Brazilian society is its religious syncretism. A large number of people not only profess the Christian faith, but also believe in spiritualism and the worship of Afro-Brazilian deities.

Religions in Brazil	
Religion/Doctrine	Number of adherents (% of total population)
■ Roman Catholicism	73.60
■ Evangelical	15.41
■ Spiritualist (espírita)	1.38
■ Spiritualist (espiritualista)	0.02
■ Umbanda	0.25
■ Candomblé	0.08
■ Judaism	0.06
■ Buddhism	0.14
■ Other oriental religions	0.11
■ Islam	0.01
■ Hindu	--
■ Esoteric traditions	0.04
■ Indigenous traditions	0.01
■ Other religions	1.17
■ No religion	7.26
■ Indeterminate	0.23

Source: IBGE, Demographic Census 2000

The Regions of Brazil Brazil is divided into five regions, according to the physical, population and economic features of the states that make up the country:

▸ *Região Norte (Northern Region)*: Rondônia, Acre, Amazonas, Roraima, Pará, Amapá and Tocantins

▸ *Região Nordeste (North-Eastern Region)*: Maranhão, Piauí, Ceará, Rio Grande do Norte, Paraíba, Pernambuco, Alagoas, Sergipe and Bahia

▸ *Região Centro-Oeste (Central-Western Region)*: Mato Grosso do Sul, Mato Grosso, Goiás, and Distrito Federal

▸ *Região Sudeste (South-Eastern Region)*: Minas Gerais, Espírito Santo, Rio de Janeiro and São Paulo

▸ *Região Sul (Southern Region)*: Paraná, Santa Catarina and Rio Grande do Sul

Norte The Northern Region has an area of 3,852,968 km^2 and a population of 12,893,561 (2000). The climate is equatorial, hot and humid, providing the ideal conditions for the survival of the Amazon forest, which covers nearly the whole region. The rubber boom, begun in the mid-nineteenth century, drew waves of people from the North-Eastern Region who settled along the region's rivers, which, until then, had remained practically undiscovered. In the 1970s, with the opening up of roadways and new projects in agriculture, livestock production and mineral exploitation, the population was enticed into the south of Pará, the north of Tocantins, the west of Amazonia, Rondônia and Acre. The economy of the region is based on plant produce such as latex, the Assai palm, various woods and cashew nuts, and on the extraction of minerals – most of the iron ore exported from Brazil comes from Carajás, in the state of Pará.

Nordeste The North-Eastern Region covers 1,553,918 km^2 and has a population of 47,693,253 (2000). This region is subdivided into four distinct areas, according to their geo-economic features: the *zona da mata*, *agreste*, the *sertão* and the *meio-norte*. The *zona da mata* corresponds to the coastal strip that stretches from the state of Rio Grande do Norte to the south of Bahia; most of the region's population is concentrated in this area, where the main urban centres of the *Nordeste* are to be found. The soil is fertile, due to the large rainfall, and it is here that the great sugarcane plantations are located, as well as the oil fields, the production of cocoa and the region's main industrial centres. The *agreste* is a narrow strip of land situated between the *zona da mata* and the *sertão*, stretching from Rio Grande do Norte to the north-east of Bahia. Although it is an area of lower rainfall, it is nevertheless very fertile. The *sertão*, on the other hand, is characterized by its semi-arid climate, with scarce and irregular rainfall; the harshness of this climate adversely affects the economic activities in the area, especially agriculture. The *sertão* covers a large part of the *Nordeste* region, forming a significant part of Piauí and almost the whole of Ceará. In spite of a greater vitality of the *Nordeste* economy over the past few years, the region still struggles with poverty and high infant mortality rates.

Centro-Oeste The Central-Western Region covers an area of 1,606,445 km^2 and has a population of 11,616,745 (2000). It includes most of the Central Plateau (*Planalto Central*), with extensive areas of wooded grassland and a tropical climate with a clearly-defined dry season. The vast plain of Pantanal is situated in Mato Grosso do Sul and provides natural pasture land, which is flooded by the river Paraguay and its tributaries during the rainy season. Part of the region is covered in equatorial forest, and shares features with the Amazon Rainforest. The main economy is agriculture, and the area produces vast quantities of soya, sorghum, cotton, sunflower, rice and corn. Beef farming is also an important endeavour here, with the ...

country's largest herd, 57 million head of cattle, based mainly in the Mato Grosso do Sul. There are large mineral resources too, particularly manganese. The region is developing a growing tourist trade, encouraging interest in picturesque historic towns like Goiás and Pirenópolis, as well as the capital of Brazil, modern Brasilia.

Sudeste The South-Eastern Region is the most populous of the five Brazilian regions, with 72,297,351 inhabitants (2000). Its 924,574 km² are home to the largest cities of the country: São Paulo, Rio de Janeiro and Belo Horizonte. Interest in the area was first stimulated by the gold rush in Minas Gerais during the 18th century. The end of the mining boom saw the development of livestock production and agriculture, especially the cultivation of coffee, which spread from the *Baixada Fluminense* (the alluvial plain in the state of Rio de Janeiro), through the valley of Paraíba (which runs between the states of São Paulo and Rio de Janeiro), expanding then throughout the south of Minas Gerais, Espírito Santo and finally into the interior of São Paulo. Brazilian industrialization started at the turn of the 19th century in the Sudeste region, mainly in São Paulo, where the largest concentration of industries in the country is to be found. The *Sudeste* is considered the economic heart of Brazil, with its diverse industrial production, productive agriculture intensive, modern cattle farming and numerous mineral deposits. These deposits are concentrated in the Serra do Espinhaço (MG), where there is iron and manganese, and in the basin of Campos (RJ), where there is oil. The region has always attracted immigrants, especially from the *Nordeste*, although the influx has slowed recently.

Sul The Southern Region covers 576,300 km² and has a population of 25,089,783 (2000). The climate is colder than the rest of the country, with occasional frosts and snow in some parts of Rio Grande do Norte and Santa Catarina. The region was first settled by Portuguese missionaries, who remained only at certain isolated points along the coast and in the interior. European immigrants started to establish small farms in the region in the 19th century, and agriculture and livestock production formed the basis of its economy until the development of a car industry in Curitiba and Porto Alegre in the 1990s. However, agriculture and beef production remain important for the local economy, and Sul has some of the country's highest indices in health and education.

The Brazilian states and their capital cities

State	Abbr.	Capital City
ACRE	AC	Rio Branco
ALAGOAS	AL	Maceió
AMAPÁ	AP	Macapá
AMAZONAS	AM	Manaus
BAHIA	BA	Salvador
CEARÁ	CE	Fortaleza
DISTRITO FEDERAL	DF	Brasília
ESPÍRITO SANTO	ES	Vitória
GOIÁS	GO	Goiânia
MARANHÃO	MA	São Luís
MATO GROSSO	MT	Cuiabá
MATO GROSSO DO SUL	MS	Campo Grande
MINAS GERAIS	MG	Belo Horizonte
PARÁ	PA	Belém
PARAÍBA	PB	João Pessoa
PARANÁ	PR	Curitiba
PERNAMBUCO	PE	Recife
PIAUÍ	PI	Teresina
RIO DE JANEIRO	RJ	Rio de Janeiro
RIO GRANDE DO NORTE	RN	Natal
RIO GRANDE DO SUL	RS	Porto Alegre
RONDÔNIA	RO	Porto Velho
RORAIMA	RR	Boa Vista
SANTA CATARINA	SC	Florianópolis
SÃO PAULO	SP	São Paulo
SERGIPE	SE	Aracaju
TOCANTINS	TO	Palmas

Main cities of Brazil by population

São Paulo	10,405,867
Rio de Janeiro	5, 851,914
Salvador	2,440,828
Belo Horizonte	2,232,747
Fortaleza	2,138,234
Brasília	2,043,169
Curitiba	1,586,848
Recife	1,421,993
Manaus	1,403,796
Porto Alegre	1,360,033

Source: Almanaque Abril, data from 2000

Environment Between 15% and 20% of the earth's biological diversity is found in Brazil. It is estimated that, from a world total of 250,000 plant species, 55,000 can be found in Brazil, as can the world's greatest variety of primates, amphibians and vertebrates. This natural wealth could be exploited by the pharmaceutical or cosmetic industries, which represents a huge economic potential. However, these resources also attract plant and animal trafficking. Every year, 38 million animals are captured illegally in the country and 10% of international animal trafficking targets the fauna of Brazil.

In an effort to protect Brazilian fauna and flora the government has established so-called 'conservation units'. According to official figures, 5.05% of national territory is environmentally protected by these federal conservation units, which include national parks and biological reservations, as well as ecological stations and reserves.

Brazil's varied natural landscapes – the forests, bush, *caatinga*, the *Pantanal* (swamps) of Mato Grosso, fields, mangroves, sandbanks, coconut and pine plantations – are essential for the survival of its abundant flora. Some of the following areas form part of the greatest concentration of biodiversity in the world and deserve special mention:

Amazon Rainforest The largest tropical rainforest in the world, it has an area of 4.9 million km^2 and covers 54.4% of the country. Large projects such as the building of roads and hydroelectric plants have already resulted in the destruction of around 13.9% of its original area. Government organizations and the Brazilian scientific community have developed plans for the conservation and sustainable exploitation of species, in an attempt to broaden knowledge of the forest's biodiversity and how to protect it.

Atlantic woods Another important forested region, the Atlantic woods are now reduced to 7% of the area they occupied at the time the Portuguese arrived in Brazil. This is due to the fact that this area has been settled and populated the longest, and holds the greatest concentration of inhabitants in the country – from the coastline of the *Nordeste* to the interior of Rio Grande do Sul, stretching westwards through the states of São Paulo and Paraná. Once rich in rare woods such as Brazilian copal, peroba and tauari, the depletion of the region's riches began with the deforestation of Brazilwood, which is nowadays all but extinct. However, the Atlantic woods are still home to significant numbers of animal and plant species.

Pantanal The Pantanal, or swamp, is the largest floodplain in the world and has a wealth of relatively heterogeneous fauna and flora, with 650 species of birds, 80 species of mammals, 260 species of fish and 50 species of reptiles. Its rivers are thought to be the richest in fish in the world. In 2001, the Pantanal was declared a site of natural heritage for humanity by Unesco.

Cerrado This wooded grassland is a form of savannah, with abundant grasses and small, twisted, thick-barked trees. Around 20% of Brazilian territory is covered by this form of vegetation, which covers the whole of the country's central plateau (*Planalto Central*); it can also be found, less strikingly, in Amazônia, Minas Gerais, parts of São Paulo, Bahia, Maranhão and Piauí. An estimated 10,000 plant species, over 800 species of birds and 161 species of mammals are thought to live in the *cerrado*. Nowadays, extensive beef production, monocultures and road-building present the main threats to this environment.

Caatinga The *caatinga* has been reduced to half its original size and covers a mere 10% of the national territory. It is characteristic of the Brazilian *Nordeste*, and its vegetation is particularly adapted to a dry climate and poor, stony soil. The long peri-

ods of drought and the irregular rainfall in-between make life extremely hard for the *sertanejos*, as the inhabitants of the *sertão* (or *caatinga*) are known.

Apart from this wealth of vegetation, Brazil also has one of the world's largest river networks, due to its size, flatness and high rainfall in most regions. The more important water systems are the Amazon basin, with 3,904,393 km^2 in national territory (from a total of 7,050,000 km^2). The Amazon river is 6,868 km long and has around 7,000 tributaries; it is the largest river in the world in terms of water flow, and second only to the Nile in length. Other important water systems are formed by the basins of the rivers Paraná, Paraguai, Uruguai, São Francisco, Parnaíba and Tocantins-Araguaia. The São Francisco river is the longest river entirely within Brazilian territory.

Political administration The Federal Republic of Brazil comprises 26 states, 1 federal district and 5,561 municipalities; it has a presidential government. The political organization in Brazil is based on three independent bodies: the executive, the legislative and the judicial.

Executive body Within the federal framework, the executive body's leader is the President of the Republic, who has a four-year mandate, with a right to stand for re-election. Within the states, governors centralize executive power and, in the municipalities, this power is held by mayors (*prefeitos*). The President must be Brazilian-born and over 35 years of age to be eligible for election; he or she is elected through direct voting. If no candidate gets an absolute majority in the first round, a second round is held. The Vice-President is elected at the same time as the President.

Legislative body Responsible for making the laws that govern the country, the legislative body is formed at federal level by the National Congress, made up of the Chamber of Deputies and the Senate. At state level, it consists of Legislative Assemblies, led by state deputies. In the municipalities, it consists of Municipal Chambers, or town halls, led by councillors. The Chamber of Deputies is made up of 513 representatives elected by direct vote and proportional representation, for four-year mandates. Three Senators per state are elected to the Senate, with eight-year mandates. The Senate alternates the representation by one- and two-thirds every four years.

Judicial body At federal level, judicial power is exercised by the Supreme Federal Tribunal (the highest court in the country), the High Court of Justice, Regional Federal Tribunals, the Labour High Court, the Electoral High Court, the Military High Court and the Union Accounts Court. At regional level, there are Regional Labour Courts, Regional Electoral Courts and Military Courts.

Armed forces The Brazilian Armed Forces are made up of the Navy, the Army and the Air Force. Military service is compulsory for all male citizens. Young men are called up during the year of their eighteenth birthday. Nowadays, the three forces allow the voluntary enrolment of women in auxiliary roles.

The Brazilian economy In the past, the Brazilian economy was characterized by monoculture for exportation (Brazilwood, sugarcane, cotton, coffee, cocoa, rubber). Beef production and ore extraction have also been of great economic significance, being directly responsible for the development of Brazil's interior and for building up a transport network between its various regions. The cultivation of coffee was developed after independence and brought about the first stages of industrialization in the country during the nineteenth century. The crisis that followed the Wall Street Crash of 1929 saw the price of coffee plummet, yet it promoted industrialization by forcing the Brazilian government to take measures that were to accelerate the country's development. Since then, industry has continued to expand to such an extent that it overtook agriculture in terms of economic importance in the mid-1950s. Today, Brazil's GDP places the country amongst the top ten economies in the world, with the largest industrial park amongst so-called emergent countries.

GDP:	US$ 529.3 billion (1999)
GDP per sector:	Services 55.1%
	Industry 37.1%
	Agriculture 7.8%

Source: Banco Central do Brasil

Inflation Inflation has been a constant subject for debate in Brazilian economy, especially since the 1940s. Between 1915 and 1940, the rates of inflation varied greatly, though rarely reaching two figures, something that subsequently became a regular occurrence. In the 1960s, for the first time in history, the inflation index came very close to 100% per year. After the military coup in 1964 measures to fight inflation were implemented, especially wage control, which caused inflation indices to drop. In 1973, Brazilian inflation was 13.7% per year. However, international crises led to an increase in this rate, until it reached 76% per year in 1979. In the 1980s, rates of inflation increased dramatically, reaching three figures – in 1981, Brazilian inflation was 100% per year. In an attempt to contain the instability of the monetary system, there followed a number of governmental plans – the 'Cruzado' plan, the 'Collor 1' plan and the 'Collor 2' plan – but these were only partially successful. Finally, the 'Real' plan, implemented in July 1994, managed to contain inflation and provided the country with relative economic stability.

Income distribution In 2000, UN data relating to 174 nations placed Brazil amongst the countries of greatest income concentration in the world. The average income of the wealthiest 20% is 25.5 times greater than the average income of the poorest 20%. The first group receives 63.8% of national income, whereas the second receives a mere 2.5% of the total. This strong concentration of the country's wealth means that around 15% of Brazilians live in conditions of extreme poverty, a condition that affects mainly the Black and rural populations. Regional differences also have to be taken into consideration when looking at poverty in the country: the *Nordeste* region, with 30% of the national population, is home to 62% of the poorest people in Brazil. In spite of the social programmes that have been implemented, poverty in Brazil in 2002 has similar indices to those of the 1970s. One of the main factors in this unequal distribution of the country's wealth is the difficulty in gaining access to adequate education. In spite of the progress made in education in recent times, only a small proportion of the population can attend good schools and universities, thereby getting better jobs and higher income.

Work and employment Most labour relations in Brazil are ruled by the CLT ('Consolidation of Labour Laws'), created during the government of Getúlio Vargas (1930-1945). Since 1940, there has also been a minimum national wage, whose value is set by the federal government. The working day must not exceed 8 hours, or 44 hours a week. Data from 1999 shows an economically active population of 79.3 million people, and an unemployment figure of 9.6%. The Brazilian workplace has seen a dramatic fall in formal employment between 1989 and 1999: in 1999, there were around 38.9 million casual workers.

Women's social position There have been significant changes in the profile of the Brazilian woman and the family model. The census in 2000 and other studies have shown an increase in the number of women as principal earners in the family: in 1991, the proportion was 8.5%; by 2000, the number had increased to 13%. There has also been a dramatic fall in the birth rate and this coincides with the greater presence of women in the workplace. In spite of the continued difference in wages between men and women, women are increasingly active in the Brazilian workplace.

The Brazilian education system is divided into basic education and higher education. The former includes infant, primary and intermediate education. Higher education includes undergraduate and post-graduate studies, other university courses and further studies. These 'further studies', implemented in 1999, lead to earlier qualification than an undergraduate degree, but do not give access to post-graduate studies. Ongoing education for young people and adults, including professional and special training, are also supplied. Education is provided by both the public sector (municipal, state or federal) and by private schools and universities.

Infant education (*up to age 6*) This includes day-care nurseries for children from birth up to 3, and pre-school for children aged 4 to 6. Since 1996, infant education is no longer seen as a social service, being now considered part of basic education and, in the case of public schools, the responsibility of the municipalities. Nevertheless, infant education is not compulsory, and it remains a weak spot in the Brazilian education system: it provides for the needs of only a third of all children aged 6 or under. The Southern region has the highest proportion of pre-school attendance (99%), while the South-Eastern region has the most children in nurseries (78%). According to the schools' census of 2001, 6 million children aged 6 and under have access to infant education.

Basic education (*from age 7 to 14*) Basic education lasts eight academic years, or *series* – 1st to 4th *series* for children aged between 7 and 10, and 5th to 8th *series* for children between 11 and 14. According to the constitution of 1988, it is the duty of the state to provide free and compulsory basic education. There is a core curriculum common to the whole of Brazil, which is determined by the Federal Education Council of Brazil and takes regional differences into account, in order to make allowances for local characteristics. Many children fail to pass their final school exams, and many are forced to stay away from school. These problems have been addressed with some success by the educational policies of recent years. Data from 2000 shows that 94.9% of children aged between 7 and 14 attend school.

Intermediate education (*from age 15 to 17*) This takes place over three academic years, and most of those who attend go to public-sector schools. Figures from Unesco show that only 33.4% of the relevant age group attend school at this level in Brazil, though there has been some increase over the last decade.

Higher education (*from age 18 to 24*) There are 1,097 institutions for higher education in Brazil, provided by both private organisations and municipal, state and federal universities. In contrast to the other tiers of education, the public sector accounts for the majority of places – 65%. University candidates are selected primarily through an entrance exam, the *vestibular*, which is taken at the end of intermediate education.

Public Universities of Brazil

The Faculties of Law in São Paulo (1827) and Recife (1854), the Mining School of Ouro Preto (1854) and the Polytechnic of Rio de Janeiro (1870) developed from institutions that have existed in the country since 1808, and were the first universities in Brazil. Nowadays, with the exception of Tocantins, all Brazilian states have a public federal university. The more prominent of these are:

- Federal University of Bahia (UFBA)
- University of Brasília (UnB)
- Federal University of Minas Gerais (UFMG)
- Federal University of Rio de Janeiro (UFRJ)
- Federal University of Rio Grande do Sul (UFRGS)

The state of São Paulo also has three state public universities, which are among the most respected higher-education institutions in the country:

- São Paulo University (USP)
- Campinas State University (UNICAMP)
- São Paulo State University (UNESP)

Young people and adult education There are also courses and exams available for both young people and adults who did not finish their basic or intermediate education during their school years. The Brazilian education system thus enables these people to attend adult classes and resume their studies, so affording them greater professional possibilities.

Professional education Courses leading to professional qualifications are provided mainly by SENAC ('National Service for Commercial Training') and SENAI ('National Service for Industrial Training'), as well as by companies who are willing to take on trainees. These courses are geared towards employment. In 1999, there were 33,000 professional training courses in the whole country.

Special education Special education is intended for young people and adults with special needs; it is officially part of government policy, but its practical implementation is, as yet, in its early stages.

Illiteracy The 1999 data indicate 22.8 million illiterates in Brazil, that is, 13.8% of the population aged 15 or over. The country also has a rate of 30.5% functional illiterates, namely people aged 15 or over who have had less than four years of schooling, and who therefore read and write well below standard.

Schooling in Brazil				
Illiteracy rates	**1996**	**1997**	**1998**	**1999**
People aged 10 & over	13.7	13.9	12.9	12.3
People between 10 & 14	8.3	8.7	6.9	5.5
Years at school (people aged 10 or over) (% in 1999)	**Total**	**Men**	**Women**	
No education or less than 1 year	13.4	13.6	13.2	
1 to 3 years	18.3	19.4	17.2	
4 to 7 years	34.2	34.5	34.0	
8 to 10 years	14.8	14.7	14.9	
11 and over	19.0	17.5	20.4	

Source: IBGE

School curriculum The national curriculum includes: Portuguese, social studies (history and geography), mathematics, physics, biology and physical education. From the age of 11 (fifth *serie*), it is obligatory to learn at least one foreign language. In 1997, the Ministry of Education established educational guidelines ('National Curriculum Parameters', or PCNs), in an effort to redefine teaching in Brazil. They aim to encourage the critical and creative spirit of the pupil, stimulate ethical awareness and develop concern for health, the environment and multiculturalism, as well as to provide sex education.

Education versus work In Brazil, many young people are forced to leave school in order to work and help support the family. In the 1990s, however, there was a drop in the number of pupils forced to study part-time, or leave school altogether. Amongst 15 to 17 year-olds, the percentage of students who do not need to work as well rose from 38.9% in 1992 to 55.7% in 1999. Amongst young people aged between 20 and 24, the percentage of those who study full-time rose from 6.9% in 1992 to 10.9% in 1999.

Television In Brazil, the most popular means of communication, and the most far-reaching, is television; most advertising funds are channelled into this medium. The first televised broadcast took place in 1950, made by São Paulo's *TV Tupi*. In 1956, Brazilians watched their first football match on television and in 1972, colour television arrived. In 1996, subscription television was introduced, and now includes cable and satellite transmissions. Studies made in 2001 show that 97% of the population over the age of 10 watch television at least once a week. The biggest broadcasting station, *Rede Globo*, reaches most Brazilian municipalities (99.77%), and is famous for the quality of its soaps, which are exported to several countries worldwide. Other national commercial networks are *Rede Bandeirantes, Rede Record, SBT (Sistema Brasileiro de Televisão)* and *Rede TV!* Apart from these open-signal commercial stations, the country also has a public network of educational stations such as *TV Cultura* (in São Paulo) and *TVE* (in Rio de Janeiro).

Radio Much has changed since Brazil's first radio transmission, on September 7th 1922, when the speech of the then President of the Republic was broadcast over the airwaves while the country celebrated its first 100 years of Independence. Since then, radio has become the second most wide-reaching medium in the country after television, and it has evolved with the market, being also transmitted on the Brazilian internet. According to the Ministry of Communication, there are currently around 2,965 radio stations in the country.

Main Brazilian newspapers

The *Correio Braziliense* was the first Portuguese language newspaper to be distributed in Brazil; it was first published in London by Hipólito José da Costa between June 1808 and December 1822. The newspaper went against the interests of the Portuguese Crown. Free from censorship, it openly criticized Portuguese policies in Brazil and greatly influenced political journalism around Independence. Hipólito José da Costa was also the first famous Brazilian to defend the abolition of slavery.

Among the main present-day Brazilian newspapers are the following:

▸ *Folha de São Paulo* (SP)
▸ *O Estado de São Paulo* (SP)
▸ *O Globo* (RJ)
▸ *Jornal do Brasil* (RJ)
▸ *O Estado de Minas* (MG)
▸ *Correio Braziliense* (DF)
▸ *Zero Hora* (RS)

The press The history of the press in Brazil dates only from the nineteenth century, as Portugal would not allow it to exist in its colony. When the Portuguese Court moved to Brazil in 1808, it brought a printing plant with it; in the same year, the Royal Press was created. Editorial censorship was brought along too, and only came to an end in 1821. With the end of censorship, important newspapers emerged in opposition to the Portuguese Crown. During the reign of Dom Pedro II (1831-1889), there came a period of freedom and prosperity for the press; abolitionist and republican newspapers were printed, as were more humorous publications. Since the beginning of the 20th century the Brazilian press has gone from strength to strength; in 2000, there were around 500 daily newspapers being printed, with an average circulation in excess of 7 million, while weekly news and information magazines represent 32% of market: *Veja*, *Época* and *IstoÉ* being the three most widely-distributed. There are also specialized publications dedicated to a wide variety of subjects, which account for 22% of the market.

Telephone In 1877, just one year after Alexander Graham Bell's invention, some telephones were made in Rio de Janeiro by the Western and Brazilian Telegraph Company; one was installed in the residence of Emperor Dom Pedro II. Two years later the first grant to establish a telephone network was conceded, in Rio de Janeiro and Niterói (RJ). Phone networks in Brazil were managed by private foreign concession until 1970, and the service was unreliable; however, in 1972 the Ministry of Communication created *Telebrás* to manage the planning of public telecommunications services. By the 1990s, *Telebrás* had installed 10 million phone outlets in the country. Since 1995 the telecommunications network has been gradually privatized and in 1998 the *Telebrás* system, by then divided into 12 regional holdings for fixed and mobile telephony, was taken over by private enterprise. According to 2001 figures, Brazil now has 43.77 million land lines, around 26 million mobile phones and 1.3 million public telephones.

Internet Until 1994, the internet in Brazil was restricted to universities. However, once it became available to the general public, in 1996, and once the telephone lines had been improved, the internet grew rapidly. The country is already in the leading position in Latin America, both in terms of providers and of users, and is ninth in the world ranking of internet users. In 2001, 11.9 million people owned a home computer with access to the net, although these people belong mainly to the more affluent classes of the population – classes A (34%) and B (50%). The installation of broadband services, especially from 2000 onwards, has allowed faster navigation and file transfer. It is estimated that by the end of 2002, the number of users of this kind of service will have reached 634,000. At present, a huge effort is being made to take the internet into public-sector schools, in order to avoid so-called digital exclusion, namely the marginalizing of the poorer social layers in relation to access to information and technology. Brazil is also the third Latin American country to have access to Internet 2, a project that allows communication amongst the international scientific community via a high-tech network.

The Internet in South America		
	Country	No. of hosts
1st	**Brazil (.br)**	**1,644,575**
2nd	Argentina (.ar)	465,359
3rd	Chile (.cl)	122,727
4th	Uruguay (.uy)	70,892
5th	Columbia (.co)	57,419
6th	Venezuela (.ve)	22,614
7th	Peru (.pe)	13,504
8th	Ecuador (.ec)	3,383
9th	Paraguay (.py)	2,704
10th	Bolivia (.bo)	1,522

Source: Network Wizards, January 2002

The calendar of Brazilian feast days is intimately linked to Christianity and, more especially, to Roman Catholicism. The celebrations of Easter, Christmas and the feast days in June (*festas juninas*) are popular. There are also secular celebrations such as Carnival, the greatest of all feasts in Brazil, and other civic feast days. The religious syncretism that characterizes the country becomes quite apparent during many religious feast days, when both Catholic saints and their Afro-Brazilian counterparts are honoured at the same time.

Carnival This is without doubt the most famous of all Brazilian celebrations. It was probably introduced into the country in the 17th century under the name of *entrudo*. This was a form of merrymaking where people pelted each other with water, dust, chalk and anything else that was to hand. However, the rel-

> **Groups and troupes: the birth of the samba schools**
>
> Groups (or *blocos*) were the most democratic way of celebrating Carnival. They were neither planned nor choreographed, and brought together friends, family and neighbours. Troupes (or *ranchos*) formed a much more organized parade, with a greater number of women and more instruments such as *cavaquinhos*, guitars, clarinets and flutes that played music especially composed for the occasion. The troupes also contained an element that was to become a feature of the samba schools: the standard-bearer. These groups and troupes were later to give rise to the samba schools. In 1899, the first *marcha-rancho* – a musical genre typical of carnival celebrations – to be recorded in the history of Brazilian carnivals was composed: *Ó abre alas*, by Chiquinha Gonzaga.

ative violence of this activity soon encountered strong opposition. Little by little, the missiles were replaced by more harmless ones, such as paper streamers and confetti. In 1840, in Rio de Janeiro, the first documented fancy-dress ball took place, inspired by similar events in European cities. In 1846, *Zé Pereira* emerged, a group of jesters that took to the streets, banging on *bumbos* and drums. Since then, Carnival has become a tradition in Rio de Janeiro. Its popularity helped it to spread throughout the various regions of the country. It officially takes place during the four days preceding Ash Wednesday (Saturday until Shrove Tuesday).

> **National Bank Holidays**
>
> ■ January 1st - *New Year's Day*
> ■ Moveable Date - *Good Friday*
> ■ April 21st - *Tiradentes**
> ■ May 1st - *Labour Day*
> ■ September 7th - *Independence Day*
> ■ October 12th - *Nossa Senhora Aparecida***
> ■ November 15th - *Proclamation of the Republic*
> ■ December 25th - *Christmas Day*
> * national hero, freedom fighter
> ** Patron saint of Brazil

Festas Juninas The *festas juninas* are also celebrated throughout the country, in commemoration of Saints Anthony, John and Peter. Originally these feast days were called *joaninas*, having reached Brazil through the Jesuits in the hope of luring the natives they intended to convert. The feast days occurred during the same period that the indigenous people celebrated their fertility rituals, namely the harvest season. The *festas juninas* became quite popular and the tradition spread. During these days, it is customary to have bonfires, fireworks, dancing and bunting, as well as traditional food and drink.

Feast of the Divine This feast is of Portuguese origin and was introduced into

Brazil during the 16th century; it celebrates the descent of the divine Holy Spirit to the apostles of Jesus Christ. It takes place on Whit Sunday, 50 days after Easter. The way it is celebrated varies very much from region to region, but all festivities have as a high point the crowning of the Emperor of the Divine. In the city of Pirenópolis (GO), where it is celebrated with great pomp, jousts are held as well, representing the battles between Christians and Moors. Some commemorations are accompanied by music and dances typical of the day, along with a glut of food for all.

Optional Bank Holidays

- Moveable Date - *Carnival*
- Moveable Date - *Ash Wednesday*
- Moveable Date - *Corpus Christi*
- November 2nd - *All Souls' Day*
- December 24th - *Christmas Eve*
- December 31st - *New Year's Eve*

Círio de Nazaré Our Lady of Nazareth is the patron saint of the city of Belém (Bethlehem), in Pará. Her feast day is one of the most important in the region and brings together thousands of locals and people from other regions as well. The procession of the Círio (candle) wends through the streets of Belém to the sound of prayers and chants, starting from the city's baroque cathedral and ending up at the basilica of Nazaré (Nazareth).

Christian Celebrations

The Epiphany: January 6th
Ash Wednesday
Palm Sunday
Holy Saturday
Easter Sunday
Ascension Day
Pentecost
Corpus Christi
St John: June 24th
St Peter: June 29th
Nossa Senhora Aparecida: October 12th; patron saint of Brazil
All Souls' Day: November 2nd
Christmas Day: December 25th

Bom Jesus dos Navegantes This celebration takes place on the São Francisco river in Alagoas and Salvador (BA). In Salvador, the statue of *Bom Jesus dos Navegantes* is taken by boat across the Baía de Todos os Santos accompanied by thousands of other highly-decorated sailing vessels, to the beach of Boa Viagem. A similar celebration takes place in Aracaju (SE). In Porto Alegre (RS), the celebration is held in honour of *Nossa Senhora dos Navegantes*.

Afro-Brazilian Celebrations

January 1st: *Day of Oxalá*
January 20th: *Day of Oxóssi (St Sebastian)*
February 2nd: *Day of Iemanjá*
April 23rd: *Ogum (St George)*
September 27th: *Ibeji (SS Cosmas and Damian)*

Manual de comunicação em inglês

Cartas

Início e término

A fórmula de despedida, utilizada ao término de uma carta, depende da saudação empregada em seu início.

Quando se sabe o nome do destinatário:
Dear Sir
Dear Madam

Quando não se sabe se o destinatário é homem ou mulher:
Dear Sir or Madam
ou
Dear Sir/Madam

Assim se conclui uma carta, quando não se sabe o nome do destinatário:
Yours faithfully (UK)

Quando o destinatário é uma empresa ou organização:
Dear Sirs (UK)
Gentlemen (US)

No inglês americano, a ordem das palavras é a inversa:
Faithfully yours (US)

Quando se sabe o nome do destinatário:
Dear Mr Robertson
Dear Mrs Dent
Dear Miss Carrington
Dear Ms Paton

Yours sincerely (UK)
Sincerely yours (US)
Sincerely (US)

Se o destinatário é uma mulher, a abreviatura *Ms* é cada vez mais utilizada, porque não especifica se ela é casada (*Mrs*) ou solteira (*Miss*).

Mais amigável:
Yours very sincerely (UK)

Dear Dr Howells

Menos formal:
With best wishes
With kind regards
K indest regards

Nos Estados Unidos, a abreviatura é normalmente seguida de um ponto: Mr., Mrs., Ms., Dr.

Essas frases podem encerrar a carta ou preceder qualquer uma das fórmulas de despedida acima.

Quando o destinatário é um amigo ou parente:
Dear Bob
Dear Jane
Dear Martin and Kathryn
Dear All
Dear Mum and Dad
Dear Uncle John/Auntie Annie
My dear Chris
Dearest/My dearest Ruth

With love
Love
Love from
Love and best wishes

Mais afetuoso:
With all my/our love
Much love

Mais informal:
Lots of love

Mais formal:
Yours
All the best (UK)
Best wishes
Regards

Ao se escrever para o editor de um jornal:
Sir

Quando não se sabe o nome do destinatário:
Yours faithfully (UK)
Faithfully yours (US)

Para um membro do parlamento britânico:
Dear Mr/Mrs Brown

Quando se sabe o nome do destinatário:
Yours sincerely (UK)
Sincerely yours (US)
Sincerely (US)

Para um membro da Câmara ou do Senado americano:
Sir/Madam
Dear Congressman/
Congresswoman Fox
Dear Senator Mitcham

Menos comum:
Yours respectfully (UK)
Respectfully yours (US)
Respectfully (US)

Carta impressa formal

Os parágrafos não têm margem e são separados por um espaço.

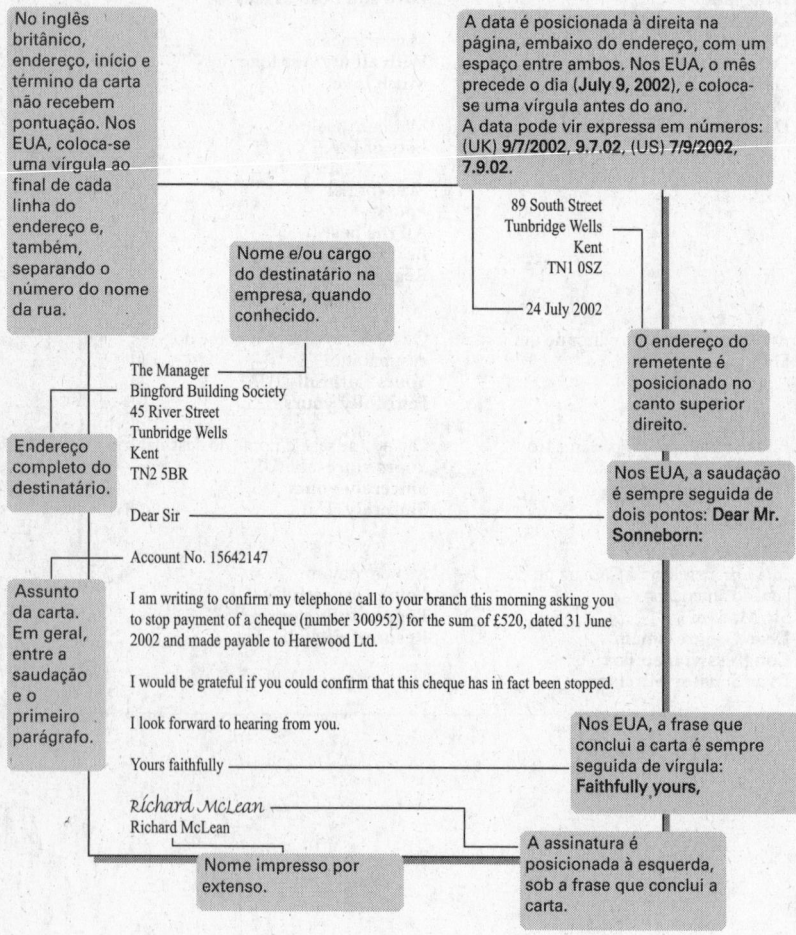

No inglês britânico, endereço, início e término da carta não recebem pontuação. Nos EUA, coloca-se uma vírgula ao final de cada linha do endereço e, também, separando o número do nome da rua.

A data é posicionada à direita na página, embaixo do endereço, com um espaço entre ambos. Nos EUA, o mês precede o dia (**July 9, 2002**), e coloca-se uma vírgula antes do ano.
A data pode vir expressa em números: (UK) **9/7/2002, 9.7.02,** (US) **7/9/2002, 7.9.02.**

Nome e/ou cargo do destinatário na empresa, quando conhecido.

89 South Street
Tunbridge Wells
Kent
TN1 0SZ

24 July 2002

O endereço do remetente é posicionado no canto superior direito.

The Manager
Bingford Building Society
45 River Street
Tunbridge Wells
Kent
TN2 5BR

Endereço completo do destinatário.

Dear Sir

Nos EUA, a saudação é sempre seguida de dois pontos: **Dear Mr. Sonneborn:**

Account No. 15642147

Assunto da carta. Em geral, entre a saudação e o primeiro parágrafo.

I am writing to confirm my telephone call to your branch this morning asking you to stop payment of a cheque (number 300952) for the sum of £520, dated 31 June 2002 and made payable to Harewood Ltd.

I would be grateful if you could confirm that this cheque has in fact been stopped.

I look forward to hearing from you.

Yours faithfully

Nos EUA, a frase que conclui a carta é sempre seguida de vírgula: **Faithfully yours,**

Richard McLean
Richard McLean

Nome impresso por extenso.

A assinatura é posicionada à esquerda, sob a frase que conclui a carta.

Carta para um amigo

Deixa-se uma margem no início de cada parágrafo.

Os nomes de meses com mais de duas sílabas são, em geral, abreviados: Jan, Feb, Aug, Sept, Oct, Nov, Dec.

Saudação inicial e fórmula de despedida são seguidos de vírgula.

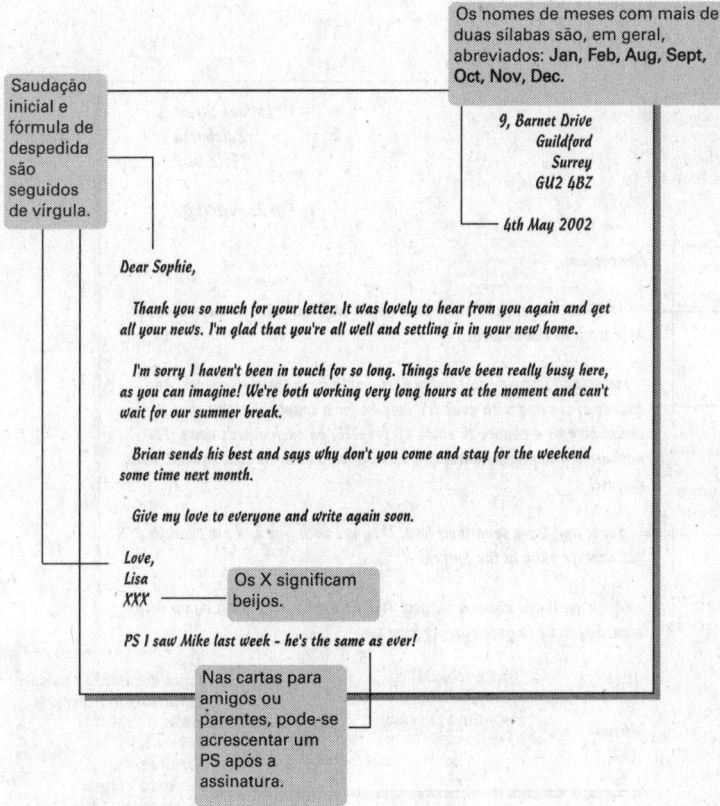

9, Barnet Drive
Guildford
Surrey
GU2 4BZ

4th May 2002

Dear Sophie,

Thank you so much for your letter. It was lovely to hear from you again and get all your news. I'm glad that you're all well and settling in in your new home.

I'm sorry I haven't been in touch for so long. Things have been really busy here, as you can imagine! We're both working very long hours at the moment and can't wait for our summer break.

Brian sends his best and says why don't you come and stay for the weekend some time next month.

Give my love to everyone and write again soon.

Love,
Lisa
XXX

Os X significam beijos.

PS I saw Mike last week - he's the same as ever!

Nas cartas para amigos ou parentes, pode-se acrescentar um PS após a assinatura.

Outro exemplo de carta para um amigo

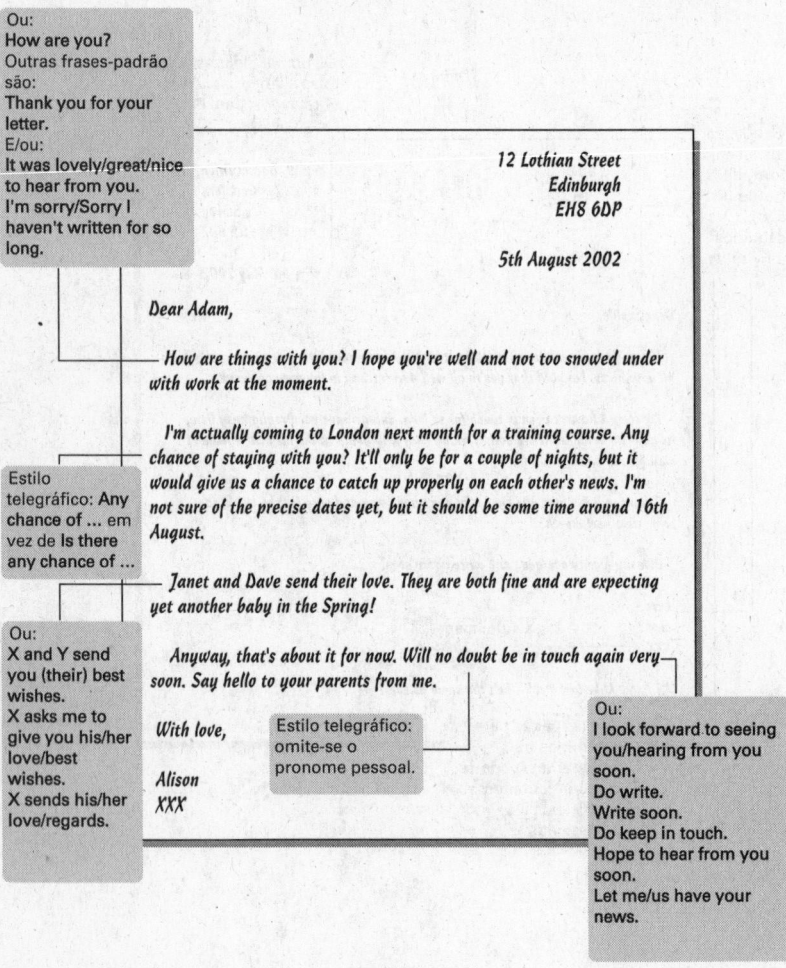

Ou:
How are you?
Outras frases-padrão são:
Thank you for your letter.
E/ou:
It was lovely/great/nice to hear from you.
I'm sorry/Sorry I haven't written for so long.

Estilo telegráfico: **Any chance of ...** em vez de **Is there any chance of ...**

Ou:
X and Y send you (their) best wishes.
X asks me to give you his/her love/best wishes.
X sends his/her love/regards.

12 Lothian Street
Edinburgh
EH8 6DP

5th August 2002

Dear Adam,

How are things with you? I hope you're well and not too snowed under with work at the moment.

I'm actually coming to London next month for a training course. Any chance of staying with you? It'll only be for a couple of nights, but it would give us a chance to catch up properly on each other's news. I'm not sure of the precise dates yet, but it should be some time around 16th August.

Janet and Dave send their love. They are both fine and are expecting yet another baby in the Spring!

Anyway, that's about it for now. Will no doubt be in touch again very soon. Say hello to your parents from me.

With love,

Alison
XXX

Estilo telegráfico: omite-se o pronome pessoal.

Ou:
I look forward to seeing you/hearing from you soon.
Do write.
Write soon.
Do keep in touch.
Hope to hear from you soon.
Let me/us have your news.

Convite de casamento

Modelo de convite

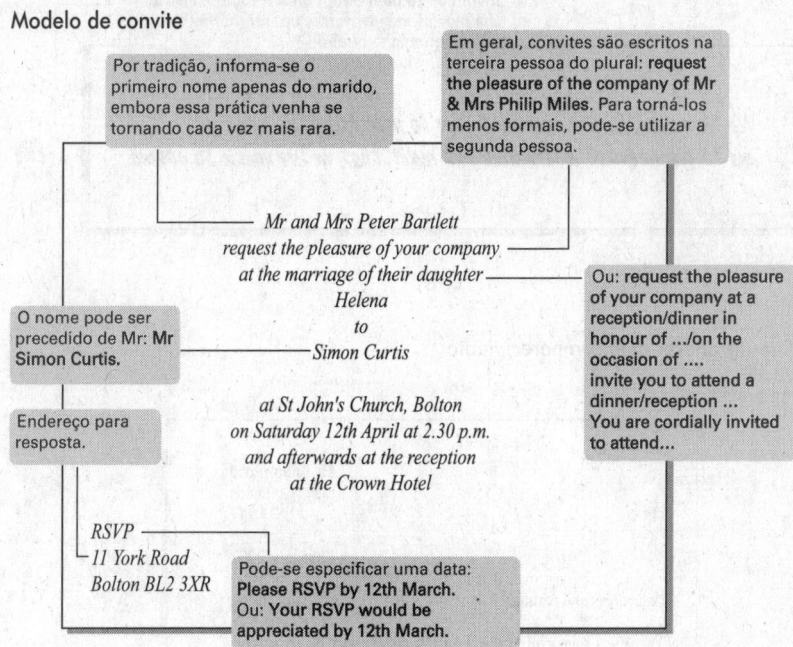

Por tradição, informa-se o primeiro nome apenas do marido, embora essa prática venha se tornando cada vez mais rara.

Em geral, convites são escritos na terceira pessoa do plural: **request the pleasure of the company of Mr & Mrs Philip Miles**. Para torná-los menos formais, pode-se utilizar a segunda pessoa.

Mr and Mrs Peter Bartlett
request the pleasure of your company
at the marriage of their daughter
Helena
to
Simon Curtis

at St John's Church, Bolton
on Saturday 12th April at 2.30 p.m.
and afterwards at the reception
at the Crown Hotel

O nome pode ser precedido de Mr: **Mr Simon Curtis.**

Ou: **request the pleasure of your company at a reception/dinner in honour of .../on the occasion of ....
invite you to attend a dinner/reception ...
You are cordially invited to attend...**

Endereço para resposta.

RSVP
11 York Road
Bolton BL2 3XR

Pode-se especificar uma data: **Please RSVP by 12th March.** Ou: **Your RSVP would be appreciated by 12th March.**

Para aceitar o convite

Não é necessário datar ou assinar a resposta. Se o convite estiver na terceira pessoa do plural, a resposta também deve empregar a terceira pessoa: **Mr & Mrs Mark Payne thank Mr & Mrs Peter Bartlett for their kind invitation to the marriage of their daughter Helena on 12th April, and to the reception afterwards. They have great pleasure in accepting.**

A resposta deve ser escrita à mão.

We thank you for your kind invitation to the marriage of your daughter Helena on 12th April, and to the reception afterwards. We have great pleasure in accepting.

Ou: **It is with great/much pleasure that we/they accept.**

Para declinar do convite

Ou, na terceira pessoa do plural: **Mr and Mrs Crosbie thank Mr and Mrs Bartlett for their kind invitation to their daughter's wedding, and to the reception afterwards, but regret that they will be unable to attend.**

We thank you for the kind invitation to your daughter's wedding, and to the reception afterwards, but regret that we are unable to attend.

Para agradecer pelo comparecimento

45 Talbot Road
Leeds
LS11 9KY

1st February 2002

Dear Chris and Natalie,

Ou: **bought us ...**

Thank you so much for the beautiful coffee set you sent us as a wedding present. You must come and visit next week so that you can be the first to enjoy them.

Ou: **We were both delighted you could come...; It was really nice to see you at the wedding.**

I was so glad that you could come to the wedding. It was nice to have all our friends and family there, even Uncle George! Give my thanks to Tom for the catering: he did us proud.

Ou: **Say thank you to ...**

We had a wonderful honeymoon in the Maldives and are now trying to settle down to work again. Let us known when is good for you to come to dinner.

Many thanks once again!

With much love,

Sheila & Sam

XXX

Reservas

Cada vez mais, reservas de passagens ou hotel são feitas pela internet e por e-mail. Toda reserva feita por telefone precisa ser confirmada por escrito.

Para fazer uma reserva

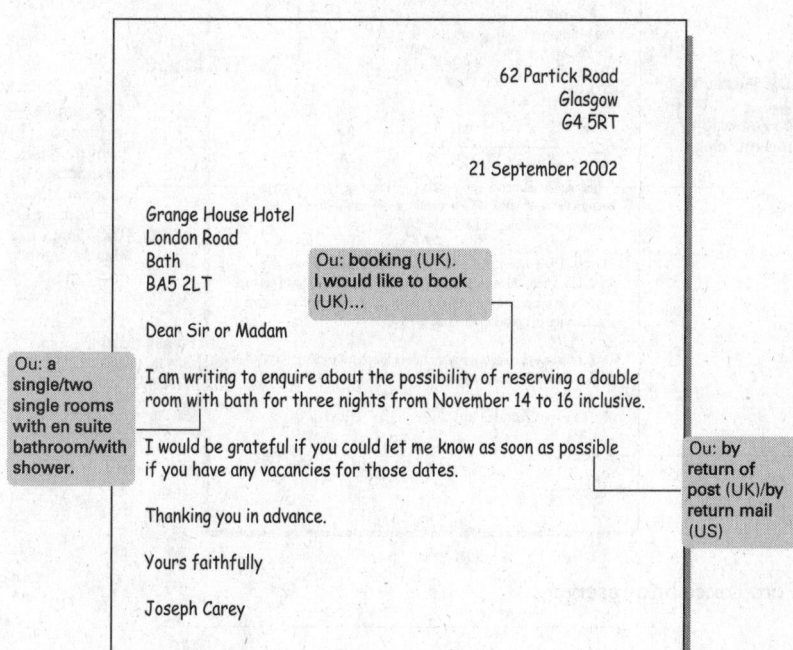

62 Partick Road
Glasgow
G4 5RT

21 September 2002

Grange House Hotel
London Road
Bath
BA5 2LT

Ou: **booking** (UK).
I would like to book (UK)...

Dear Sir or Madam

Ou: **a single/two single rooms with en suite bathroom/with shower.**

I am writing to enquire about the possibility of reserving a double room with bath for three nights from November 14 to 16 inclusive.

I would be grateful if you could let me know as soon as possible if you have any vacancies for those dates.

Ou: **by return of post** (UK)/**by return mail** (US)

Thanking you in advance.

Yours faithfully

Joseph Carey

Para confirmar a reserva

622 Monroe Street
Philadelphia
PA 19145
USA

Tel: 215.617.1439

May 11, 2002

> Nos EUA, a saudação é seguida de dois pontos, e a fórmula de despedida, de vírgula.

> Ou: 11 May 2002 (UK)

The Manager
The Pines Hotel
Denver
CO 80348
USA

> Ou: Further to our conversation this morning, ...

Dear Sir:

Following our telephone conversation this morning, I am writing to confirm the reservation of your restaurant and bar facilities for the afternoon and evening of June 22.

There will be a total of 300 guests requiring a four-course meal with wine. I look forward to receiving copies of your menus and will get back to you with our choices as soon as possible. I would appreciate written confirmation of the price which we agreed.

Do not hesitate to contact me at the above telephone number, if you need to discuss any further details.

Thanking you in advance.

Sincerely yours,

Joel Stein

> Ou: I am writing to confirm the telephone reservation (ou booking UK) I made this morning for...

> Ou: Please do not hesitate to get in touch (with me/us) ...

Para cancelar a reserva

62 Partick Road
Glasgow
G4 5RT

27th September 2002

Grange House Hotel
London Road
Bath
BA5 2LT

Dear Sir or Madam

I am afraid I must cancel the reservation I made with you for a double room with bath for three nights from November 14th to 16th 2002.

I apologise for any inconvenience caused.

Yours faithfully

Joseph Carey

> Ou: Unfortunately I must/have to cancel ...
> I regret I must cancel ...

> Ou: Please accept my apologies for any inconvenience this may have caused.

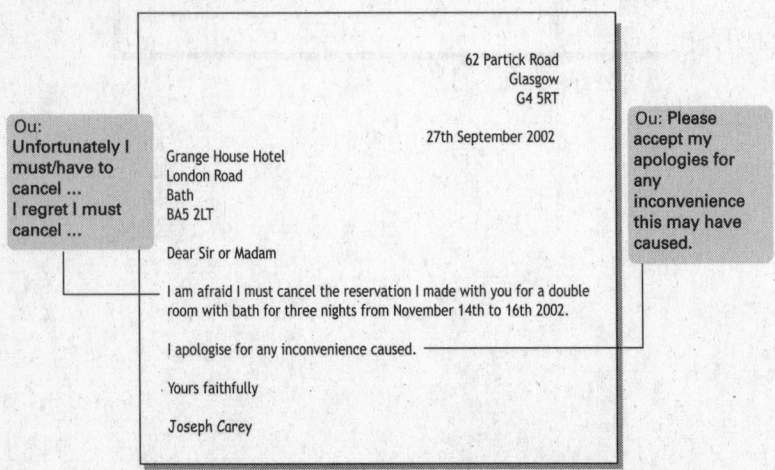

Para solicitar informação

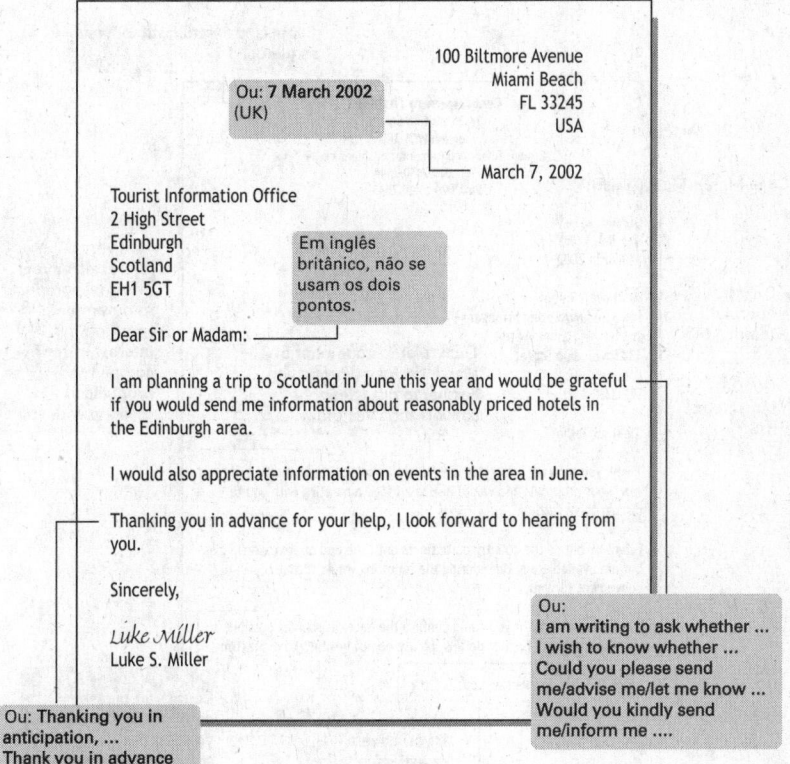

100 Biltmore Avenue
Miami Beach
FL 33245
USA

Ou: **7 March 2002** (UK)

March 7, 2002

Tourist Information Office
2 High Street
Edinburgh
Scotland
EH1 5GT

Em inglês britânico, não se usam os dois pontos.

Dear Sir or Madam:

I am planning a trip to Scotland in June this year and would be grateful if you would send me information about reasonably priced hotels in the Edinburgh area.

I would also appreciate information on events in the area in June.

Thanking you in advance for your help, I look forward to hearing from you.

Sincerely,

Luke Miller
Luke S. Miller

Ou: Thanking you in anticipation, ...
Thank you in advance for your help, ...

Ou:
I am writing to ask whether ...
I wish to know whether ...
Could you please send me/advise me/let me know ...
Would you kindly send me/inform me ....

Correspondência comercial

Para marcar reunião

Cabeçalho centralizado ou à esquerda.

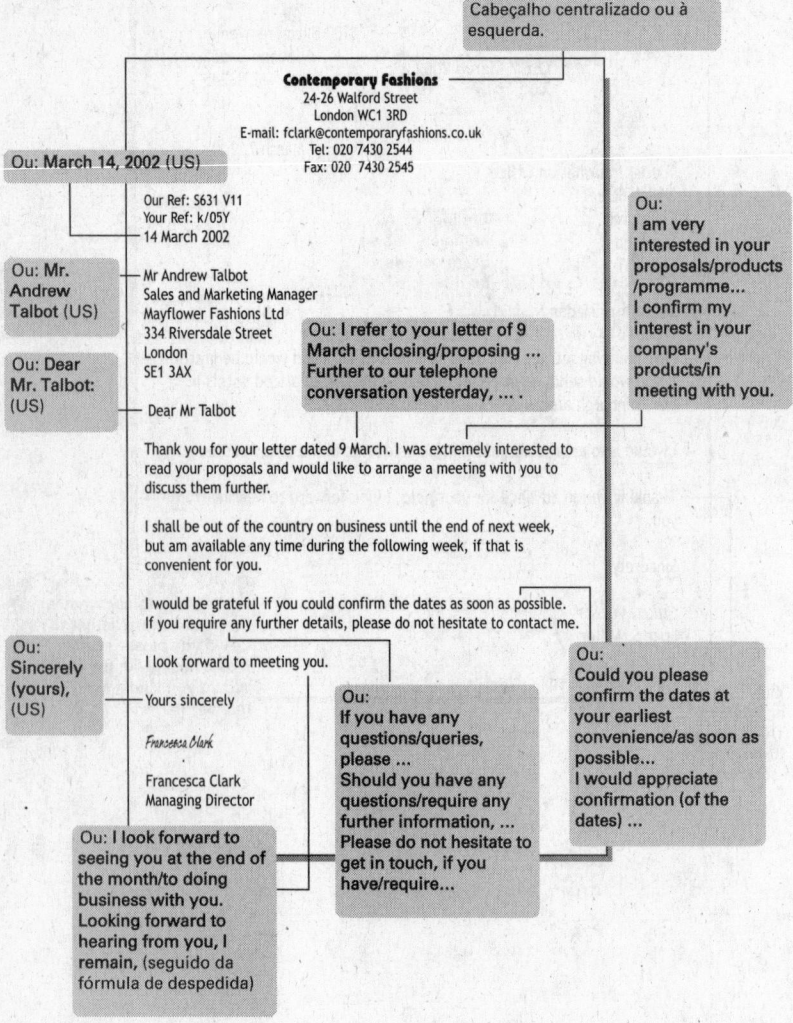

Contemporary Fashions
24-26 Walford Street
London WC1 3RD
E-mail: fclark@contemporaryfashions.co.uk
Tel: 020 7430 2544
Fax: 020 7430 2545

Ou: March 14, 2002 (US)

Our Ref: S631 V11
Your Ref: k/05Y
14 March 2002

Ou: Mr. Andrew Talbot (US)

Mr Andrew Talbot
Sales and Marketing Manager
Mayflower Fashions Ltd
334 Riversdale Street
London
SE1 3AX

Ou: I refer to your letter of 9 March enclosing/proposing ... Further to our telephone conversation yesterday, ...

Ou: Dear Mr. Talbot: (US)

Dear Mr Talbot

Ou:
I am very interested in your proposals/products /programme... I confirm my interest in your company's products/in meeting with you.

Thank you for your letter dated 9 March. I was extremely interested to read your proposals and would like to arrange a meeting with you to discuss them further.

I shall be out of the country on business until the end of next week, but am available any time during the following week, if that is convenient for you.

I would be grateful if you could confirm the dates as soon as possible. If you require any further details, please do not hesitate to contact me.

I look forward to meeting you.

Ou: Sincerely (yours), (US)

Yours sincerely

Francesca Clark

Francesca Clark
Managing Director

Ou:
If you have any questions/queries, please ... Should you have any questions/require any further information, ... Please do not hesitate to get in touch, if you have/require...

Ou:
Could you please confirm the dates at your earliest convenience/as soon as possible... I would appreciate confirmation (of the dates) ...

Ou: I look forward to seeing you at the end of the month/to doing business with you. Looking forward to hearing from you, I remain, (seguido da fórmula de despedida)

Para responder a um pedido de informação

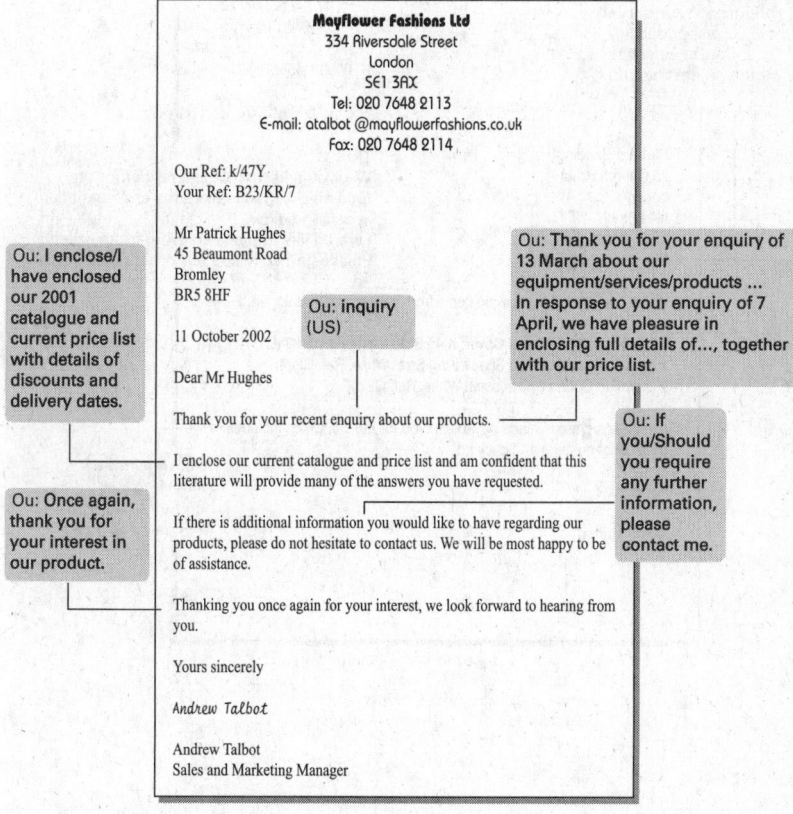

Mayflower Fashions Ltd
334 Riversdale Street
London
SE1 3AX
Tel: 020 7648 2113
E-mail: atalbot @mayflowerfashions.co.uk
Fax: 020 7648 2114

Our Ref: k/47Y
Your Ref: B23/KR/7

Mr Patrick Hughes
45 Beaumont Road
Bromley
BR5 8HF

11 October 2002

Dear Mr Hughes

Thank you for your recent enquiry about our products.

I enclose our current catalogue and price list and am confident that this literature will provide many of the answers you have requested.

If there is additional information you would like to have regarding our products, please do not hesitate to contact us. We will be most happy to be of assistance.

Thanking you once again for your interest, we look forward to hearing from you.

Yours sincerely

Andrew Talbot

Andrew Talbot
Sales and Marketing Manager

Ou: I enclose/I have enclosed our 2001 catalogue and current price list with details of discounts and delivery dates.

Ou: Once again, thank you for your interest in our product.

Ou: inquiry (US)

Ou: Thank you for your enquiry of 13 March about our equipment/services/products ... In response to your enquiry of 7 April, we have pleasure in enclosing full details of..., together with our price list.

Ou: If you/Should you require any further information, please contact me.

Para fazer um pedido de compra

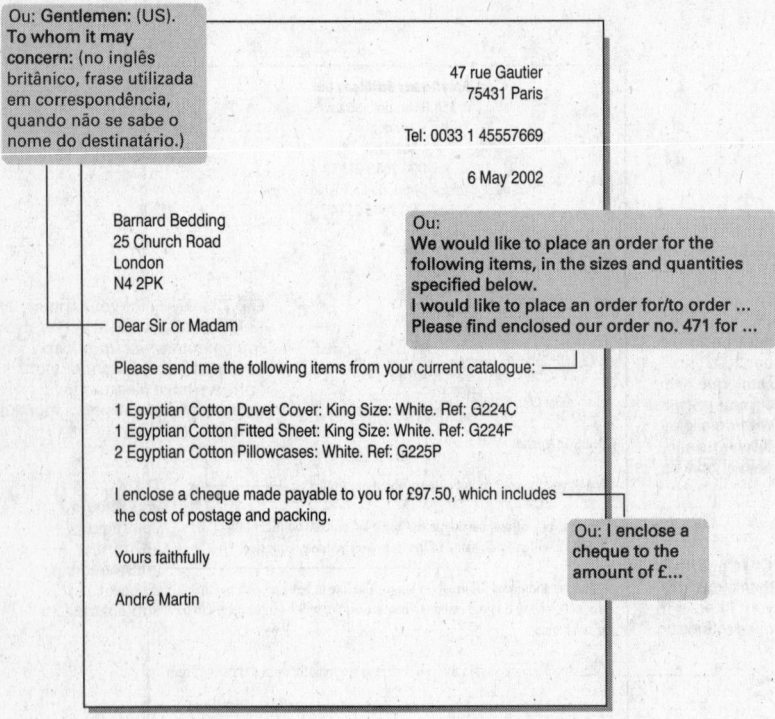

Ou: **Gentlemen: (US).**
To whom it may
concern: (no inglês
britânico, frase utilizada
em correspondência,
quando não se sabe o
nome do destinatário.)

47 rue Gautier
75431 Paris

Tel: 0033 1 45557669

6 May 2002

Barnard Bedding
25 Church Road
London
N4 2PK

Ou:
We would like to place an order for the
following items, in the sizes and quantities
specified below.
I would like to place an order for/to order ...
Please find enclosed our order no. 471 for ...

Dear Sir or Madam

Please send me the following items from your current catalogue:

1 Egyptian Cotton Duvet Cover: King Size: White. Ref: G224C
1 Egyptian Cotton Fitted Sheet: King Size: White. Ref: G224F
2 Egyptian Cotton Pillowcases: White. Ref: G225P

I enclose a cheque made payable to you for £97.50, which includes
the cost of postage and packing.

Ou: **I enclose a**
cheque to the
amount of £...

Yours faithfully

André Martin

Emprego

Nos países de língua inglesa, cartas escritas com o intuito de candidatar-se a um emprego devem ser datilografadas ou impressas, a não ser quando em resposta a um anúnico solicitando que sejam escritas à mão.

Para candidatar-se a um estágio

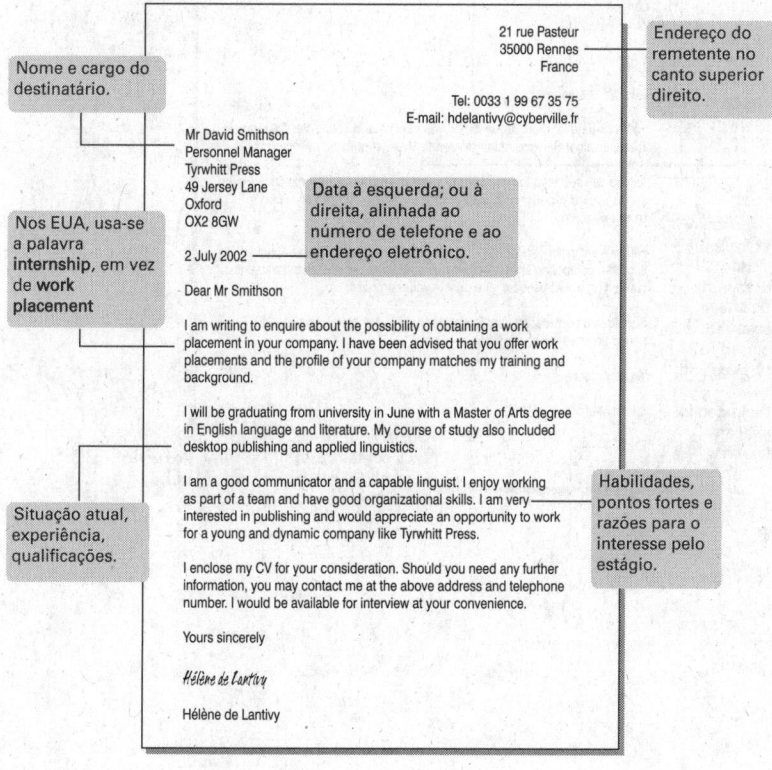

Endereço do remetente no canto superior direito.

21 rue Pasteur
35000 Rennes
France

Tel: 0033 1 99 67 35 75
E-mail: hdelantivy@cyberville.fr

Nome e cargo do destinatário.

Mr David Smithson
Personnel Manager
Tyrwhitt Press
49 Jersey Lane
Oxford
OX2 8GW

Data à esquerda; ou à direita, alinhada ao número de telefone e ao endereço eletrônico.

Nos EUA, usa-se a palavra **internship**, em vez de **work placement**

2 July 2002

Dear Mr Smithson

I am writing to enquire about the possibility of obtaining a work placement in your company. I have been advised that you offer work placements and the profile of your company matches my training and background.

I will be graduating from university in June with a Master of Arts degree in English language and literature. My course of study also included desktop publishing and applied linguistics.

Situação atual, experiência, qualificações.

I am a good communicator and a capable linguist. I enjoy working as part of a team and have good organizational skills. I am very interested in publishing and would appreciate an opportunity to work for a young and dynamic company like Tyrwhitt Press.

Habilidades, pontos fortes e razões para o interesse pelo estágio.

I enclose my CV for your consideration. Should you need any further information, you may contact me at the above address and telephone number. I would be available for interview at your convenience.

Yours sincerely

Hélène de Lantivy

Hélène de Lantivy

Para saber sobre vagas

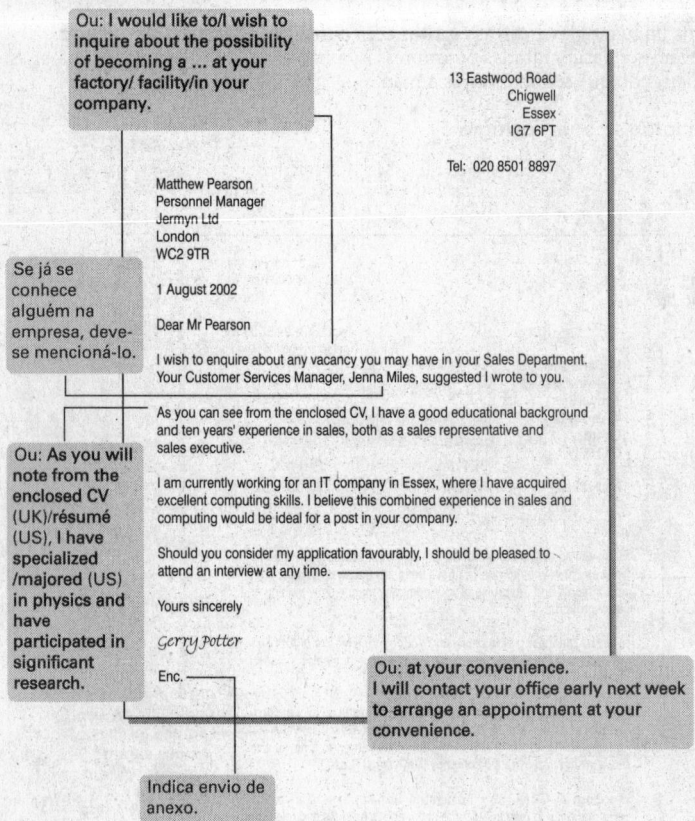

Ou: I would like to/I wish to inquire about the possibility of becoming a ... at your factory/ facility/in your company.

13 Eastwood Road
Chigwell
Essex
IG7 6PT

Tel: 020 8501 8897

Matthew Pearson
Personnel Manager
Jermyn Ltd
London
WC2 9TR

1 August 2002

Dear Mr Pearson

Se já se conhece alguém na empresa, deve-se mencioná-lo.

I wish to enquire about any vacancy you may have in your Sales Department. Your Customer Services Manager, Jenna Miles, suggested I wrote to you.

As you can see from the enclosed CV, I have a good educational background and ten years' experience in sales, both as a sales representative and sales executive.

Ou: As you will note from the enclosed CV (UK)/résumé (US), I have specialized /majored (US) in physics and have participated in significant research.

I am currently working for an IT company in Essex, where I have acquired excellent computing skills. I believe this combined experience in sales and computing would be ideal for a post in your company.

Should you consider my application favourably, I should be pleased to attend an interview at any time.

Yours sincerely

Gerry Potter

Enc.

Ou: at your convenience.
I will contact your office early next week to arrange an appointment at your convenience.

Indica envio de anexo.

Para responder a um anúncio de jornal

12 Beaconsfield Street
London
W1 9JB

Tel: 020 7580 7095

Mr Nathan Richards
Chief Analyst
Pritchard Investments
Albert Street
London EC1 2KM

31 May 2002

Dear Mr Richards

Financial Analyst

> Ou: I would like to apply for the above post as recently advertised in the July issue of.../which was advertised in today's "Daily Post".
> I am writing to apply for the above post/for the post of ... (as) advertised in ....
> I am writing in response to your advertisement in ... for ...
> I would like to be considered for the above post which your company advertised in ...

> Assunto da carta: função ou cargo.

> Ou: and (I) enclose my (current) CV (UK)/résumé (US) for your consideration.

I would like to apply for the above post as advertised in "The Financial Times" of 25 May, and I enclose my CV for your attention.

As you can see from my CV, I am an experienced financial analyst and consultant, having worked extensively in this sector in both London and Frankfurt. I am currently looking for a position that will allow me to develop my skills and experience in a dynamic environment such as Pritchard Investments.

I believe that my financial and academic background would be of benefit to your company. Should you consider me suitable for the post, I can provide the names of three referees.

I thank you for your consideration and remain at your disposal for any further information. I look forward to meeting you in the near future.

Your sincerely

Michael Griffin

Michael Griffin

Enc.

> Ou:
> Thank you for considering my application. If you would like to schedule an interview, please call me at .... I will be available at your convenience.
> I would appreciate the chance to meet you (UK)/meet with you (US).
> You may reach me at the above telephone number or e-mail address.

> Ou: I look forward to talking with you/to discussing matters with you (at a future interview).

Frases úteis:

I know how to/I can operate a cash register/computer/power equipment.
I am computer literate/a good communicator/a good organizer.
I am a capable linguist/can speak fluent English and German.
I have good computer/IT/language/editing/communication/organisational skills.
I can learn new tasks and enjoy/can accept a challenge.
I enjoy working/can work with a variety of people.
I work well in team, and can also work under pressure.
I perform well under stress/am good with difficult customers.
I can handle multiple tasks simultaneously.

Curriculum Vitae

Recém-formado, com alguma experiência (UK)

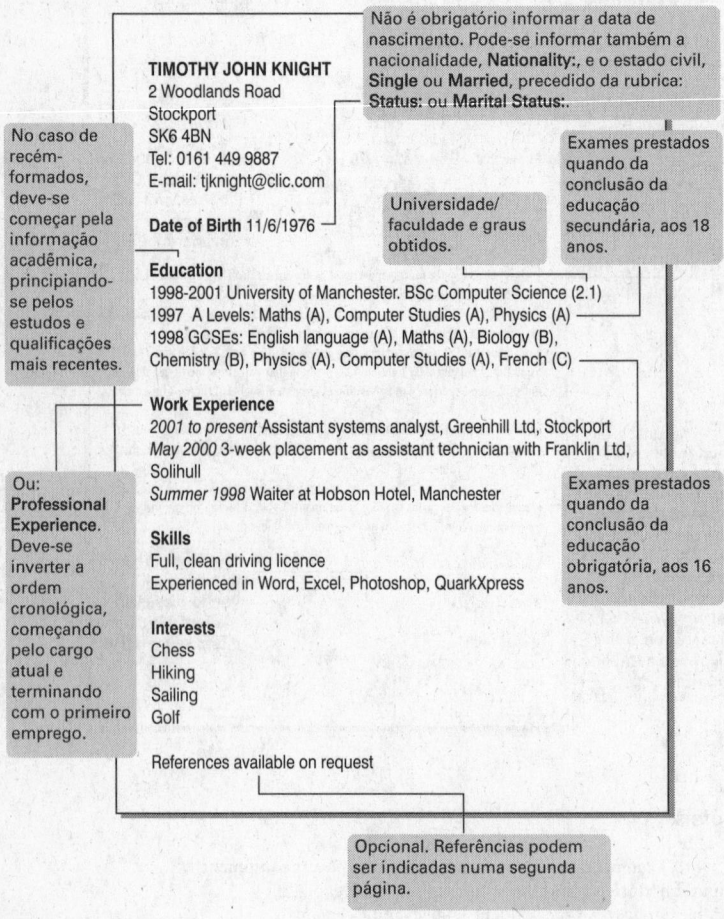

No caso de recém-formados, deve-se começar pela informação acadêmica, principiando-se pelos estudos e qualificações mais recentes.

TIMOTHY JOHN KNIGHT
2 Woodlands Road
Stockport
SK6 4BN
Tel: 0161 449 9887
E-mail: tjknight@clic.com

Date of Birth 11/6/1976

Não é obrigatório informar a data de nascimento. Pode-se informar também a nacionalidade, **Nationality:**, e o estado civil, **Single** ou **Married**, precedido da rubrica: **Status:** ou **Marital Status:**.

Universidade/ faculdade e graus obtidos.

Exames prestados quando da conclusão da educação secundária, aos 18 anos.

Education
1998-2001 University of Manchester. BSc Computer Science (2.1)
1997 A Levels: Maths (A), Computer Studies (A), Physics (A)
1998 GCSEs: English language (A), Maths (A), Biology (B), Chemistry (B), Physics (A), Computer Studies (A), French (C)

Work Experience
2001 to present Assistant systems analyst, Greenhill Ltd, Stockport
May 2000 3-week placement as assistant technician with Franklin Ltd, Solihull
Summer 1998 Waiter at Hobson Hotel, Manchester

Ou:
Professional Experience. Deve-se inverter a ordem cronológica, começando pelo cargo atual e terminando com o primeiro emprego.

Exames prestados quando da conclusão da educação obrigatória, aos 16 anos.

Skills
Full, clean driving licence
Experienced in Word, Excel, Photoshop, QuarkXpress

Interests
Chess
Hiking
Sailing
Golf

References available on request

Opcional. Referências podem ser indicadas numa segunda página.

Cargo de gerência (UK)

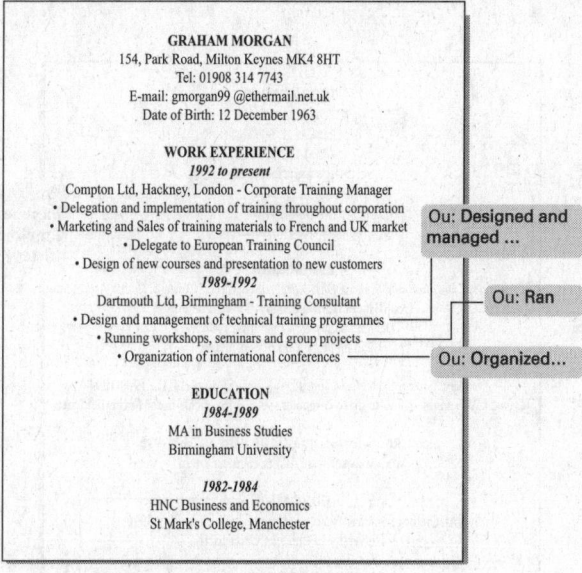

GRAHAM MORGAN
154, Park Road, Milton Keynes MK4 8HT
Tel: 01908 314 7743
E-mail: gmorgan99 @ethermail.net.uk
Date of Birth: 12 December 1963

WORK EXPERIENCE
1992 to present
Compton Ltd, Hackney, London - Corporate Training Manager
• Delegation and implementation of training throughout corporation
• Marketing and Sales of training materials to French and UK market
• Delegate to European Training Council
• Design of new courses and presentation to new customers
1989-1992
Dartmouth Ltd, Birmingham - Training Consultant
• Design and management of technical training programmes
• Running workshops, seminars and group projects
• Organization of international conferences

EDUCATION
1984-1989
MA in Business Studies
Birmingham University

1982-1984
HNC Business and Economics
St Mark's College, Manchester

Ou: Designed and managed ...

Ou: Ran

Ou: Organized...

Recém-formado, com alguma experiência (US)

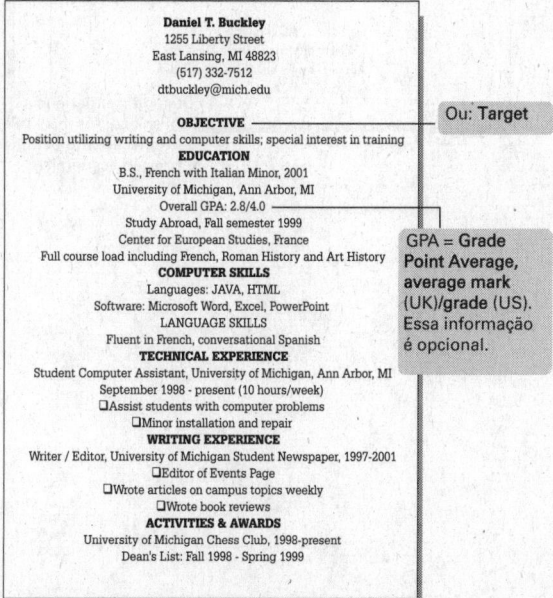

Daniel T. Buckley
1255 Liberty Street
East Lansing, MI 48823
(517) 332-7512
dtbuckley@mich.edu

OBJECTIVE
Position utilizing writing and computer skills; special interest in training
EDUCATION
B.S., French with Italian Minor, 2001
University of Michigan, Ann Arbor, MI
Overall GPA: 2.8/4.0
Study Abroad, Fall semester 1999
Center for European Studies, France
Full course load including French, Roman History and Art History
COMPUTER SKILLS
Languages: JAVA, HTML
Software: Microsoft Word, Excel, PowerPoint
LANGUAGE SKILLS
Fluent in French, conversational Spanish
TECHNICAL EXPERIENCE
Student Computer Assistant, University of Michigan, Ann Arbor, MI
September 1998 - present (10 hours/week)
❑Assist students with computer problems
❑Minor installation and repair
WRITING EXPERIENCE
Writer / Editor, University of Michigan Student Newspaper, 1997-2001
❑Editor of Events Page
❑Wrote articles on campus topics weekly
❑Wrote book reviews
ACTIVITIES & AWARDS
University of Michigan Chess Club, 1998-present
Dean's List: Fall 1998 - Spring 1999

Ou: Target

GPA = Grade Point Average, average mark (UK)/grade (US). Essa informação é opcional.

Cargo de gerência (US)

TESSA PARKS
437 West 94th Street,
Chicago, IL 60637
(733) 702-1336
tessaparks@chicol.com

OBJECTIVE
Product Designer/Manager

Ou: **Work Experience Employment History.**

EXPERIENCE
Computer Consultant and Systems Designer, Oakwood Inc., Chicago, IL, 1994-present
Troubleshoot hardware and software problems
Design and test new operating systems
Head up large team of consultants

Assistant Systems Consultant, Jones Davis Inc., Springfield, IL, 1990-1994
Created Web pages and customized computer systems for clients in the Springfield area

Intern, Roseberry Inc., Chicago, IL, June - August 1990
Worked as software design engineer intern.

EDUCATION
Bachelor of Science Degree in Computer Science, May 1990
University of Chicago, Chicago, IL

COMPUTER SKILLS
Languagues and Software : B, CC, Java, HTML, Excel, Word
Operating Systems : Unix, Windows, Mac OS

ACTIVITIES
Society of Manufacturing Engineers
Aircraft Owners and Pilots Association

Quando a experiência profissional for mais relevante, não é necessário detalhar a formação acadêmica.

E-mail

Como o e-mail é uma forma bastante rápida de comunicação, o estilo das mensagens é, em geral, informal e telegráfico, contendo muitas abreviações e acrônimos.

As convenções que regem a comunicação pela internet - a chamada netiqueta - recomendam que não se escrevam mensagens em letras maiúsculas, pois isso é entendido como sinal de raiva.

Em geral, não se empregam as formas tradicionais de saudação (**Dear ...**). Quando se conhece bem o destinatário da mensagem, pode-se iniciá-la com uma saudação informal, **Hello** ou **Hi**, seguida do primeiro nome da pessoa em questão.

Na empresa

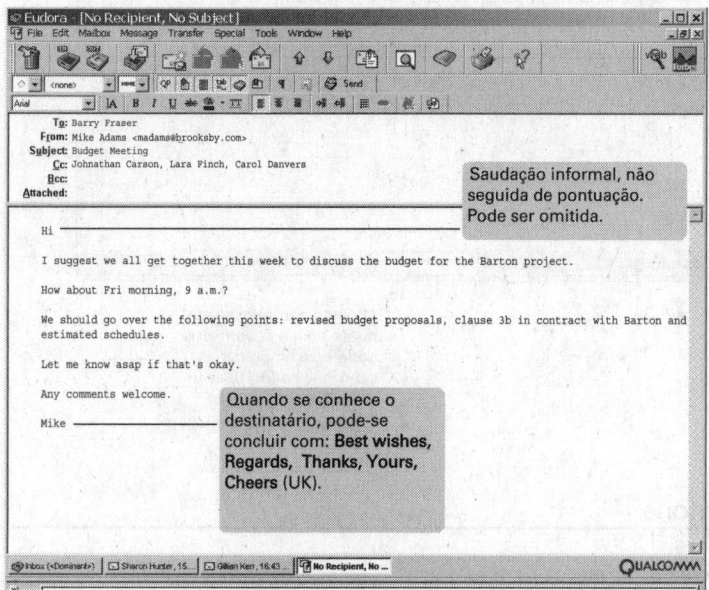

Entre empresas

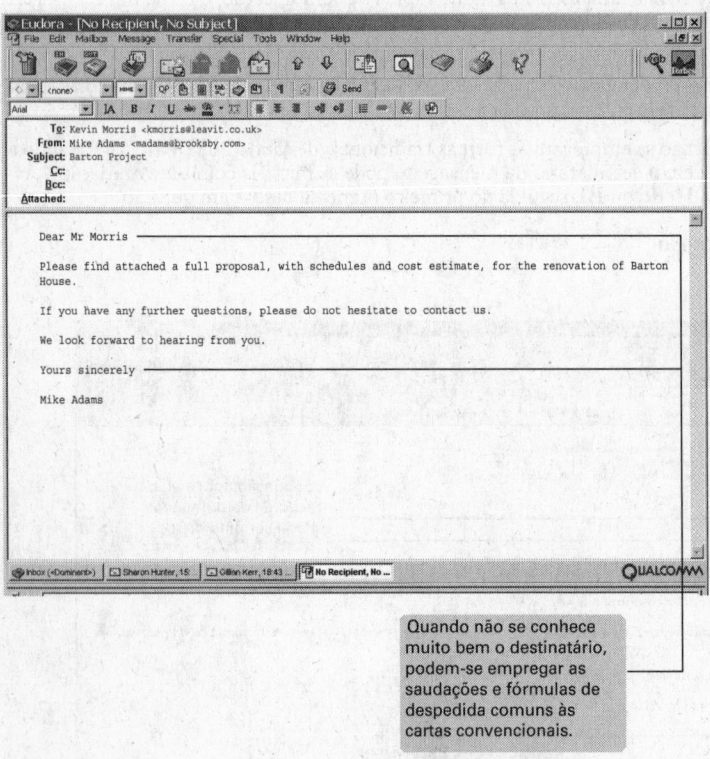

Quando não se conhece muito bem o destinatário, podem-se empregar as saudações e fórmulas de despedida comuns às cartas convencionais.

Ao telefone

Pronúncia dos números de telefone:
20995 = Two oh double nine five (UK)
Two zero double nine five (US)

Frases típicas

Para pedir informação à telefonista:
- Can I have directory enquiries (UK)/directory assistance (US) please?
- I'm trying to get through to a London number.
- What is the (country) code for Canada?
- How do I get an outside line?

Para chamar alguém:
Hello,
- could I speak to ...?
- can I speak to ...?
- I'd like to speak to ...
- (could I have) extension 593 please?

Para atender a uma chamada:
- Robert McQueen speaking, can I help you?
- Hello, this is ...
- Yes, speaking *(confirmando que se é a pessoa chamada)*
- Hold on/hold please, I'll (just) get him/her.
- I'm sorry, he's/she's not here. Can I take a message?
- I'm afraid he's away on business/out of the office/off sick/on holiday/on vacation (US)

Para deixar um recado
Na secretária eletrônica:
- I'm returning your call...
- I'll be in London next week, perhaps we can...
- I'd like to talk to you about...
- Could you call me back, so we can discuss...?

Com outra pessoa:
- Could you ask him/her to call me on ...?
- Could you tell him/her I won't be able to...?
- I'll call back later.
- I need to speak to ... urgently
- Please ask him/her to confirm... . Thank you.

Para entender melhor:
- Could you spell that please?
- Could you speak a bit more slowly please?
- I'm sorry I didn't catch that. Could you repeat that please?
- Let me check, 11 a.m. Wednesday 10th ... Yes, that's fine.

Para concluir a chamada:
- Thank you, I look forward to seeing you on Wednesday. Goodbye.
- Thank you for your help.

Mensagem de secretária eletrônica:
- We are unable to take your call at the moment/I am not here at the moment. Please leave a message after the tone.

Portuguese Communication Guide

Letters

In Portuguese, informal letters to friends or relatives do not follow a very rigid pattern. But commercial letters and letters that require more formality are written according to given formats and rules, depending on their purpose. There are also specific ways for heading correspondence and addressing envelopes to given posts and authorities, as well as specific modes of address for a specific authority.

Beginnings and endings of formal letters

When you know the name of the person you are writing to:	*Endings:*
Prezado sr. Antonio Prezada sra. Carmem	Atenciosamente Muito atenciosa- mente Cordialmente Cordiais saudações Respeitosamente
When you do not know whether it is a man or woman that you are writing to:	
Prezado sr(a).	This is the abbreviation for **senhor(a)**. In Portuguese, pronouns agree with gender (masculine or feminine) and number (singular and plural).
When you are writing to a company or organization:	
Prezados senhores	

Letters to authorities

In the case of authorities, letters should be headed and addressed according to the following conventions:

Presidents, governors, mayors, senators, deputies, councillors, ministers, ambassadors, judges, high-ranking military (general, admiral, marshal), university rectors:	*Pronouns of address:*
Exmo. Sr. Exmo. Sr. Governador Exmo. Sr. Deputado Exmo. Sr. Marechal Exmo. Sr. Ministro	V. Exa. (Vossa Excelência), *with verbs and pronouns inflected in the third person*
Other authorities: Ilmo. Sr. Ilma. Sra.	V.Sa. (Vossa Senhoria), senhor, senhora, *with verbs and pronouns inflected in the third person*

Informal letters

To friends and relatives, letters may start as follows:	And end as follows:
Querido Pedro	Um abraço
Meu querido Pedro	Um grande abraço
Querida Laura	Seu sobrinho/sua sobrinha
Minha querida Laura	
Queridos Pedro e Laura	*More affectionately:*
Meus queridos	Um beijo
Minha cara	Um grande beijo
Querido irmão/querida irmã	Muitos beijos
Querida mamãe/querido papai	Abraços e beijos
Queridos pais	Com muito carinho
Querido tio/querida tia	Com saudades
Queridos tios	Seu/sua
Caro/cara	
	More formally:
Or simply:	Com votos de
Pedro	Sinceramente
Laura	

Letters to friends

Below are two examples of letters to friends:

The date is usually preceded by the name of the place where the letter is being written, and can be placed either on the left or on the right. The date can also be abbreviated to 5/7/02 or 5.7.02.

Both here and at the end, the comma is required.

The first line of paragraphs is indented.

Dê lembranças and Mande lembranças are also commonly used.

In letters to friends or relatives, a PS may be added.

Você is the most common pronoun of address in Brazil; it is informal.

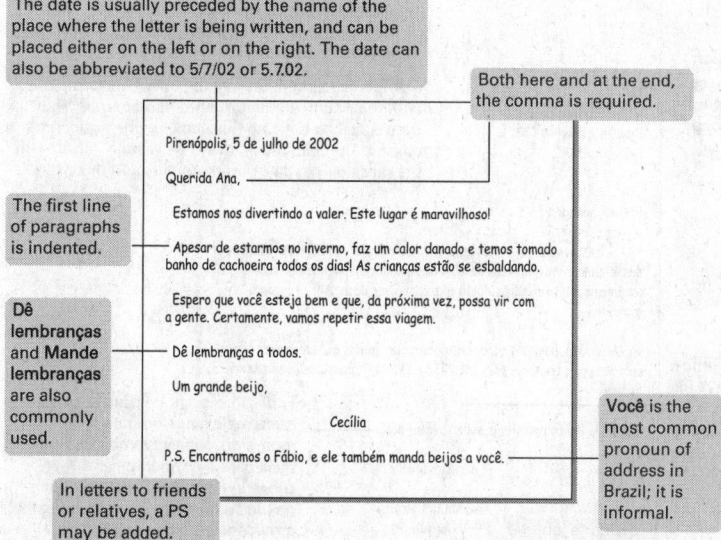

Pirenópolis, 5 de julho de 2002

Querida Ana,

Estamos nos divertindo a valer. Este lugar é maravilhoso!

Apesar de estarmos no inverno, faz um calor danado e temos tomado banho de cachoeira todos os dias! As crianças estão se esbaldando.

Espero que você esteja bem e que, da próxima vez, possa vir com a gente. Certamente, vamos repetir essa viagem.

Dê lembranças a todos.

Um grande beijo,

Cecília

P.S. Encontramos o Fábio, e ele também manda beijos a você.

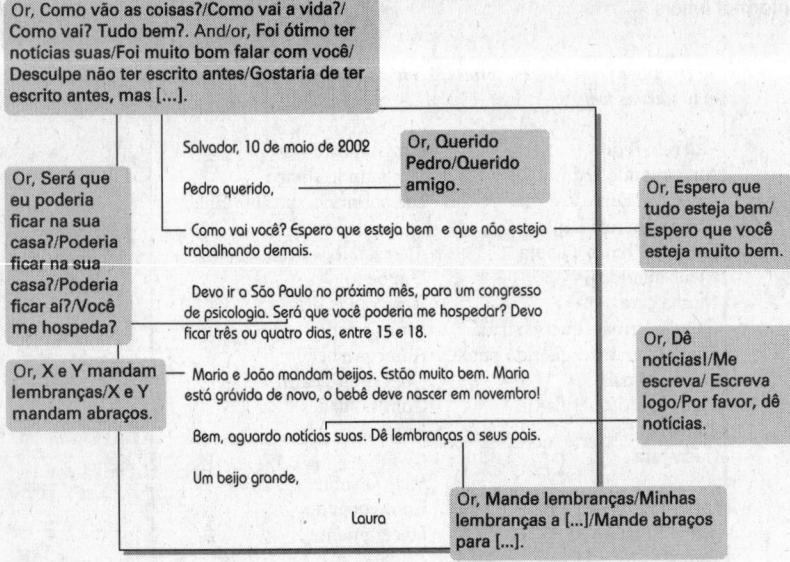

Or, Como vão as coisas?/Como vai a vida?/ Como vai? Tudo bem?. And/or, Foi ótimo ter notícias suas/Foi muito bom falar com você/ Desculpe não ter escrito antes/Gostaria de ter escrito antes, mas [...].

Salvador, 10 de maio de 2002

Pedro querido,

Or, Querido Pedro/Querido amigo.

Como vai você? Espero que esteja bem e que não esteja trabalhando demais.

Devo ir a São Paulo no próximo mês, para um congresso de psicologia. Será que você poderia me hospedar? Devo ficar três ou quatro dias, entre 15 e 18.

Maria e João mandam beijos. Estão muito bem. Maria está grávida de novo, o bebê deve nascer em novembro!

Bem, aguardo notícias suas. Dê lembranças a seus pais.

Um beijo grande,

Laura

Or, Será que eu poderia ficar na sua casa?/Poderia ficar na sua casa?/Poderia ficar aí?/Você me hospeda?

Or, X e Y mandam lembranças/X e Y mandam abraços.

Or, Espero que tudo esteja bem/ Espero que você esteja muito bem.

Or, Dê notícias!/Me escreva/ Escreva logo/Por favor, dê notícias.

Or, Mande lembranças/Minhas lembranças a [...]/Mande abraços para [...].

Commercial letters: format and language

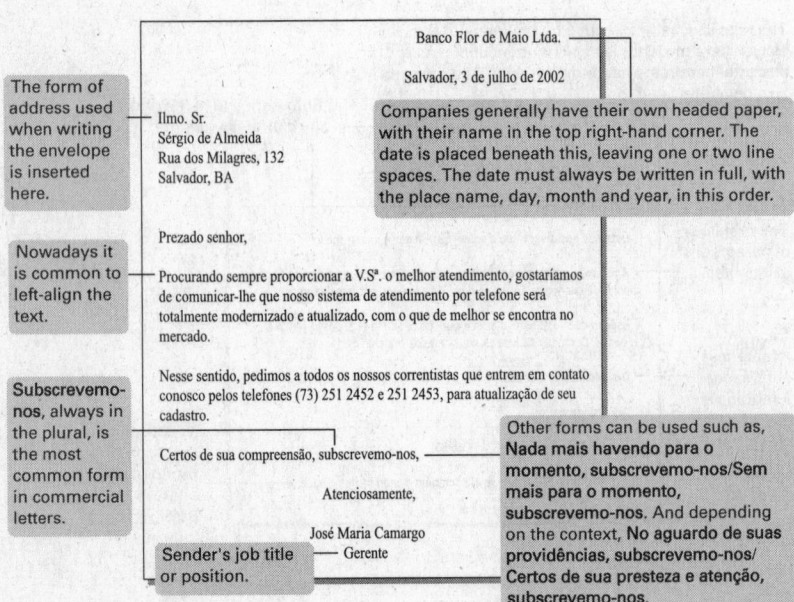

Banco Flor de Maio Ltda.

Salvador, 3 de julho de 2002

The form of address used when writing the envelope is inserted here.

Ilmo. Sr.
Sérgio de Almeida
Rua dos Milagres, 132
Salvador, BA

Companies generally have their own headed paper, with their name in the top right-hand corner. The date is placed beneath this, leaving one or two line spaces. The date must always be written in full, with the place name, day, month and year, in this order.

Prezado senhor,

Nowadays it is common to left-align the text.

Procurando sempre proporcionar a V.Sª. o melhor atendimento, gostaríamos de comunicar-lhe que nosso sistema de atendimento por telefone será totalmente modernizado e atualizado, com o que de melhor se encontra no mercado.

Nesse sentido, pedimos a todos os nossos correntistas que entrem em contato conosco pelos telefones (73) 251 2452 e 251 2453, para atualização de seu cadastro.

Subscrevemo-nos, always in the plural, is the most common form in commercial letters.

Certos de sua compreensão, subscrevemo-nos,

Atenciosamente,

José Maria Camargo
Gerente

Sender's job title or position.

Other forms can be used such as, Nada mais havendo para o momento, subscrevemo-nos/Sem mais para o momento, subscrevemo-nos. And depending on the context, No aguardo de suas providências, subscrevemo-nos/ Certos de sua presteza e atenção, subscrevemo-nos.

Requerimentos

A *requerimento* is a letter of petition to an authority. This also follows more rigid rules in terms of the structure and layout of the text.

> This is the more commonly used form of address to people in this position; it is followed by the name of the institution. It could be, for instance, **Ilmo. Sr. Secretário da Saúde da Prefeitura do Município de São Paulo,** or **Ilmo. Sr. Diretor da Eletropaulo.**

Exmo. Sr. Reitor da Universidade Padre Manoel da Nóbrega

Mônica Batista, estudante do 3º ano da Faculdade de Economia desta Universidade, encontrando-se em sérias dificuldades financeiras, vem respeitosamente requerer a V. Exa. uma bolsa de estudo para que possa terminar seu curso.

Nestes termos,
pede deferimento.

Belo Horizonte, 5 de janeiro de 2002.

_____
(Assinatura)

Wedding invitation

Sample invitation

> Or a more formal, somewhat pompous expression, **enlace matrimonial.**

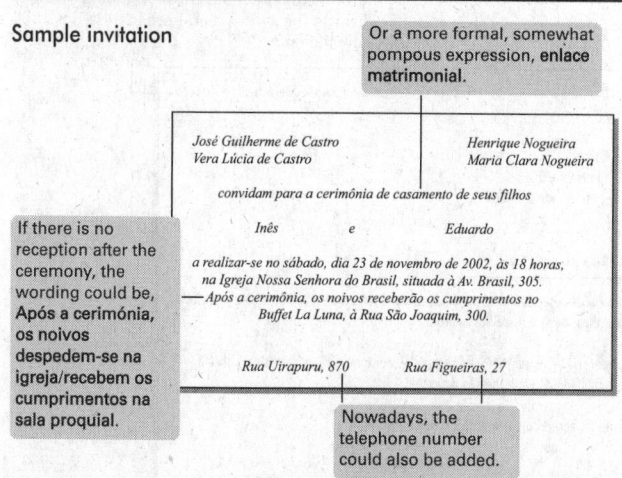

José Guilherme de Castro   Henrique Nogueira
Vera Lúcia de Castro   Maria Clara Nogueira

convidam para a cerimônia de casamento de seus filhos

Inês   e   Eduardo

a realizar-se no sábado, dia 23 de novembro de 2002, às 18 horas, na Igreja Nossa Senhora do Brasil, situada à Av. Brasil, 305.
Após a cerimônia, os noivos receberão os cumprimentos no Buffet La Luna, à Rua São Joaquim, 300.

Rua Uirapuru, 870   Rua Figueiras, 27

> If there is no reception after the ceremony, the wording could be, **Após a cerimônia, os noivos despedem-se na igreja/recebem os cumprimentos na sala proquial.**

> Nowadays, the telephone number could also be added.

To thank someone for coming

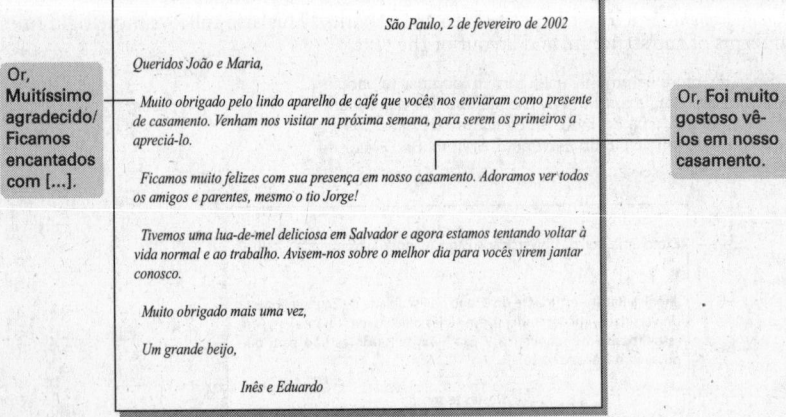

Or,
Muitíssimo agradecido/ Ficamos encantados com [...].

São Paulo, 2 de fevereiro de 2002

Queridos João e Maria,

Muito obrigado pelo lindo aparelho de café que vocês nos enviaram como presente de casamento. Venham nos visitar na próxima semana, para serem os primeiros a apreciá-lo.

Ficamos muito felizes com sua presença em nosso casamento. Adoramos ver todos os amigos e parentes, mesmo o tio Jorge!

Tivemos uma lua-de-mel deliciosa em Salvador e agora estamos tentando voltar à vida normal e ao trabalho. Avisem-nos sobre o melhor dia para vocês virem jantar conosco.

Muito obrigado mais uma vez,

Um grande beijo,

Inês e Eduardo

Or, **Foi muito gostoso vê-los em nosso casamento.**

Reservations

Travel and hotel reservations are increasingly being made by email or via the internet. However, reservations made by phone need to be confirmed in writing.

Making a reservation

Companies usually have their own headed notepaper, with their name or logo in the top right-hand corner. It is not common practice to write the sender's address in this spot; only the date.

São Paulo, 21 de setembro de 2002

Hotel Pitanga
Av. Ponta Negra, 450
Natal - Rio Grande do Norte

Or, **com cama de casal/um apartamento de solteiro/dois apartamentos de solteiro/uma suíte para casal/uma suíte para solteiro.**

Prezados senhores,

Gostaria de reservar um apartamento para casal, com banheiro, para um período de três dias, de 14 a 16 de novembro.

Agradeceria se os senhores me respondessem o mais rápido possível sobre a disponibilidade de vagas nessas datas.

Desde já, agradeço sua atenção e subscrevo-me,

Atenciosamente,

Paula Moraes

Confirming a reservation

São Paulo, 3 de julho de 2002

Ilmo. Sr.
Mário Loureiro
Gerente
Hotel Pinheiro

Prezado senhor,

De acordo com nossa conversa ao telefone esta manhã, escrevo para confirmar a reserva de seu restaurante para o dia 24 julho. Serão 300 pessoas, para três refeições. Assim que recebermos cópias de seu cardápio, entraremos em contato novamente para informá-lo de nossas escolhas. Gostaria que o senhor confirmasse por escrito o orçamento combinado.

Em caso de necessidade, queira entrar em contato comigo pelo telefone 7905643.

Desde já agradeço sua atenção,

Atenciosamente,

Miriam Muniz

> Or, **Não deixe de entrar em contato comigo pelo telefone [...] caso necessário.**

> Or, **Certa(o) de sua atenção e pronto atendimento, subscrevo-me [...].**

Cancelling a reservation

São Paulo, 29 de setembro de 2002

Hotel Pitanga
Av. Ponta Negra, 450
Natal - Rio Grande do Norte

Prezados senhores,

Infelizmente, gostaria de cancelar a reserva que havia feito de um apartamento de casal, para os dias 14 a 16 de novembro.

Queiram me desculpar pelo aborrecimento.

Sinceramente,

Paula Moraes

> Or, **Lamento informar que devo cancelar/ Lamentavelmente/sou obrigada(o) a cancelar[...]**

> Or, **Por favor, aceitem minhas sinceras desculpas.**

Requesting information

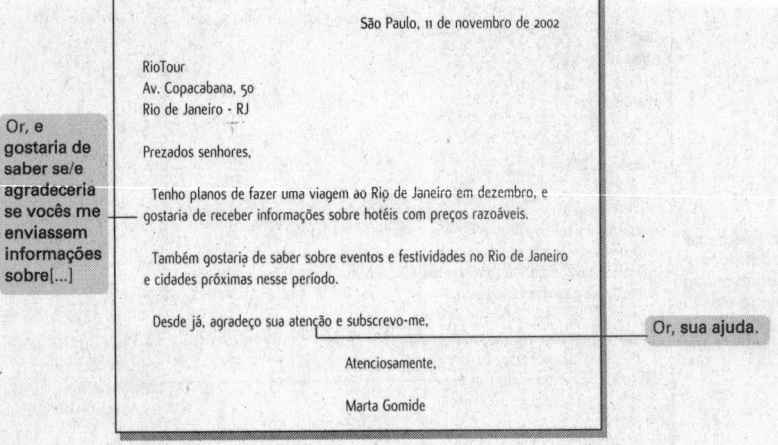

São Paulo, 11 de novembro de 2002

RioTour
Av. Copacabana, 50
Rio de Janeiro - RJ

Prezados senhores,

Or, e gostaria de saber se/e agradeceria se vocês me enviassem informações sobre[...]

Tenho planos de fazer uma viagem ao Rio de Janeiro em dezembro, e gostaria de receber informações sobre hotéis com preços razoáveis.

Também gostaria de saber sobre eventos e festividades no Rio de Janeiro e cidades próximas nesse período.

Desde já, agradeço sua atenção e subscrevo-me,

Or, sua ajuda.

Atenciosamente,

Marta Gomide

Business correspondence

Arranging a meeting

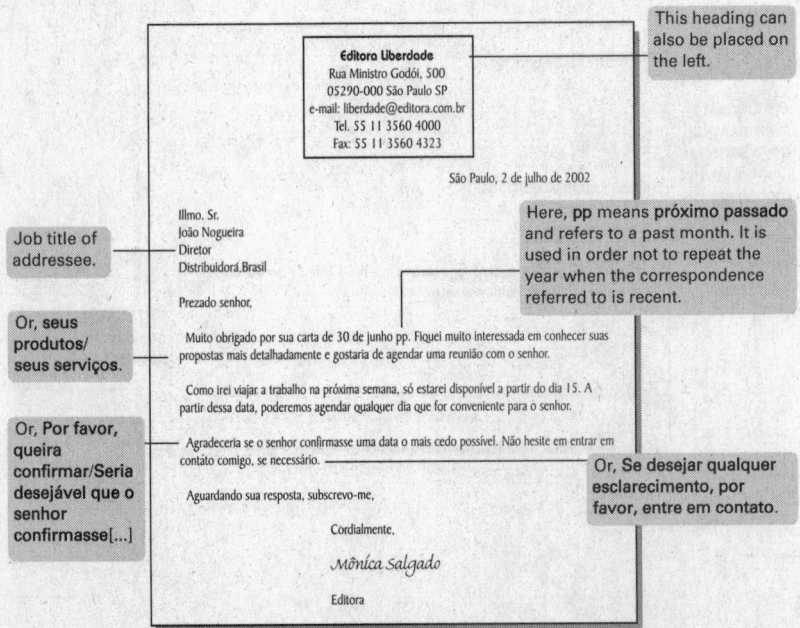

This heading can also be placed on the left.

Editora Liberdade
Rua Ministro Godói, 500
05290-000 São Paulo SP
e-mail: liberdade@editora.com.br
Tel. 55 11 3560 4000
Fax: 55 11 3560 4323

São Paulo, 2 de julho de 2002

Job title of addressee.

Illmo. Sr.
João Nogueira
Diretor
Distribuidora Brasil

Prezado senhor,

Here, pp means próximo passado and refers to a past month. It is used in order not to repeat the year when the correspondence referred to is recent.

Or, seus produtos/ seus serviços.

Muito obrigado por sua carta de 30 de junho pp. Fiquei muito interessada em conhecer suas propostas mais detalhadamente e gostaria de agendar uma reunião com o senhor.

Como irei viajar a trabalho na próxima semana, só estarei disponível a partir do dia 15. A partir dessa data, poderemos agendar qualquer dia que for conveniente para o senhor.

Or, Por favor, queira confirmar/Seria desejável que o senhor confirmasse[...]

Agradeceria se o senhor confirmasse uma data o mais cedo possível. Não hesite em entrar em contato comigo, se necessário.

Or, Se desejar qualquer esclarecimento, por favor, entre em contato.

Aguardando sua resposta, subscrevo-me,

Cordialmente,

Mônica Salgado

Editora

Placing an order

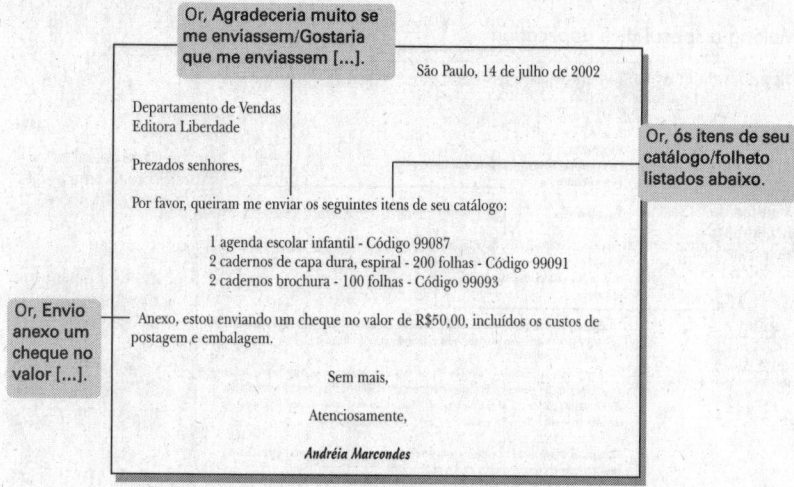

Or, Agradeceria muito se me enviassem/Gostaria que me enviassem [...].

São Paulo, 14 de julho de 2002

Departamento de Vendas
Editora Liberdade

Prezados senhores,

Por favor, queiram me enviar os seguintes itens de seu catálogo:

Or, ós itens de seu catálogo/folheto listados abaixo.

    1 agenda escolar infantil - Código 99087
    2 cadernos de capa dura, espiral - 200 folhas - Código 99091
    2 cadernos brochura - 100 folhas - Código 99093

Or, Envio anexo um cheque no valor [...].

Anexo, estou enviando um cheque no valor de R$50,00, incluídos os custos de postagem e embalagem.

Sem mais,

Atenciosamente,

Andréia Marcondes

Replying to a request for information

Milflores Moda Ltda.
Rua Fiandeiras, 300
03090-000 São Paulo SP
tel. 6790 4321
fax: 6790 4322
e-mail: moreira@milflores.com.br

São Paulo, 12 de julho de 2002

Ilmo. Sr.
Patrício Moraes

Or, por ter entrado em contato conosco em junho pp./19 de junho pp.

Or, nossos serviços/nossos equipamentos.

Prezado senhor,

Gostaríamos de agradecer por ter entrado em contato conosco e solicitado informações sobre nossos produtos.

Em anexo, enviamos nosso catálogo e lista de preços, na certeza de que eles atenderão a suas necessidades.

Or, Por favor, entre em contato conosco sempre que desejar.

Para mais detalhes e informações referentes a nossos produtos, não deixe de entrar em contato conosco. Teremos enorme prazer em atendê-lo.

Or, Será um prazer atendê-lo/Teremos grande satisfação em atendê-lo.

Agradecemos seu interesse, e ficamos à sua disposição para qualquer esclarecimento,

Muito atenciosamente,

José Batísta
Gerente de Marketing e Vendas

Or, Mais uma vez, agradecemos seu interesse.

Employment

Making a speculative application

Department in which the addressee works, or job title, if known.

Or, de Vendas/de Marketing/ de Arte.

Less formally, Soube que[...]

Or, Gostaria de saber sobre/Escrevo para pedir-lhe informações sobre[...]

Current position, experience and education.

Personal qualities and reasons for the application.

Or, Contando com sua compreensão e atenção[...]

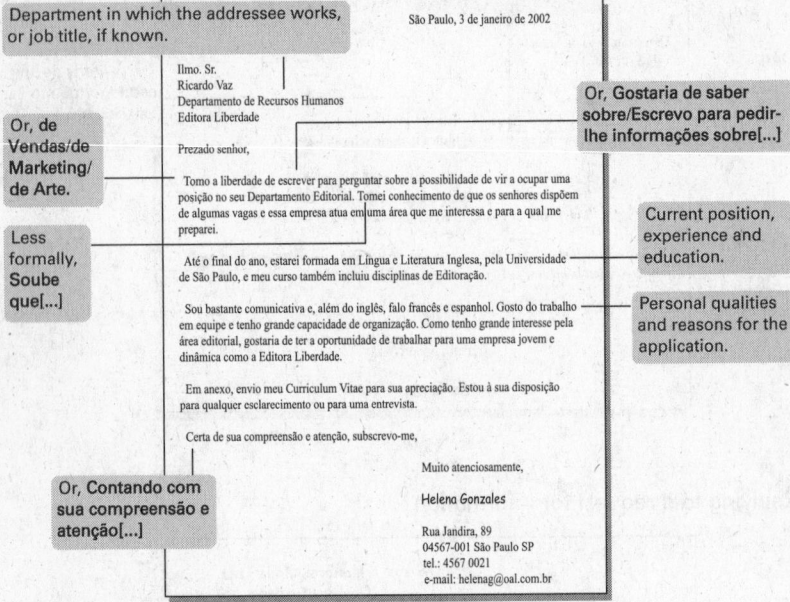

São Paulo, 3 de janeiro de 2002

Ilmo. Sr.
Ricardo Vaz
Departamento de Recursos Humanos
Editora Liberdade

Prezado senhor,

Tomo a liberdade de escrever para perguntar sobre a possibilidade de vir a ocupar uma posição no seu Departamento Editorial. Tomei conhecimento de que os senhores dispõem de algumas vagas e essa empresa atua em uma área que me interessa e para a qual me preparei.

Até o final do ano, estarei formada em Língua e Literatura Inglesa, pela Universidade de São Paulo, e meu curso também incluiu disciplinas de Editoração.

Sou bastante comunicativa e, além do inglês, falo francês e espanhol. Gosto do trabalho em equipe e tenho grande capacidade de organização. Como tenho grande interesse pela área editorial, gostaria de ter a oportunidade de trabalhar para uma empresa jovem e dinâmica como a Editora Liberdade.

Em anexo, envio meu Curriculum Vitae para sua apreciação. Estou à sua disposição para qualquer esclarecimento ou para uma entrevista.

Certa de sua compreensão e atenção, subscrevo-me,

Muito atenciosamente,

Helena Gonzales

Rua Jandira, 89
04567-001 São Paulo SP
tel.: 4567 0021
e-mail: helenag@oal.com.br

Enquiring about vacancies

Or, para solicitar informações sobre[...]

Or, Sou muito qualificado e tenho mais de dez/cinco anos/muitos anos de[...]

Or, à sua inteira disposição.

Or, O sr. (name), (job title) nessa empresa, sugeriu-me que lhe escrevesse sobre/para[...]

Or, para uma entrevista, quando melhor lhe convier.

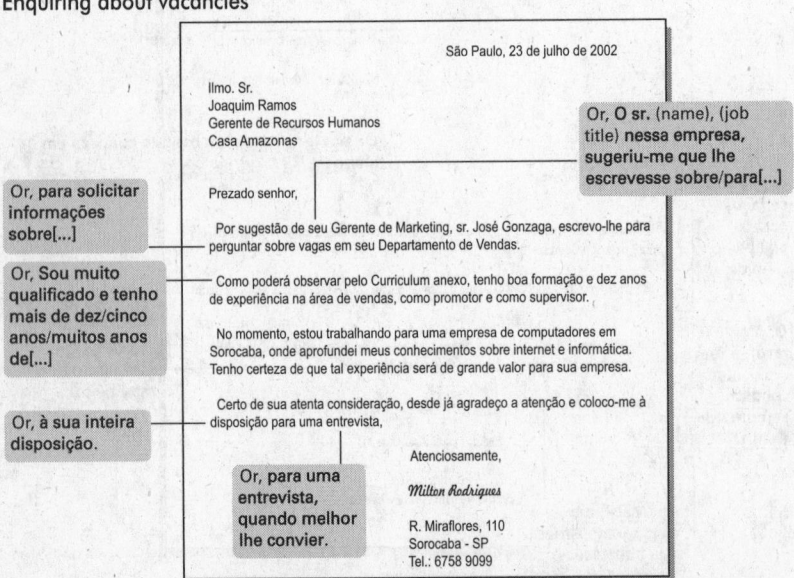

São Paulo, 23 de julho de 2002

Ilmo. Sr.
Joaquim Ramos
Gerente de Recursos Humanos
Casa Amazonas

Prezado senhor,

Por sugestão de seu Gerente de Marketing, sr. José Gonzaga, escrevo-lhe para perguntar sobre vagas em seu Departamento de Vendas.

Como poderá observar pelo Curriculum anexo, tenho boa formação e dez anos de experiência na área de vendas, como promotor e como supervisor.

No momento, estou trabalhando para uma empresa de computadores em Sorocaba, onde aprofundei meus conhecimentos sobre internet e informática. Tenho certeza de que tal experiência será de grande valor para sua empresa.

Certo de sua atenta consideração, desde já agradeço a atenção e coloco-me à disposição para uma entrevista,

Atenciosamente,

Milton Rodrigues

R. Miraflores, 110
Sorocaba - SP
Tel.: 6758 9099

Replying to a job advertisement

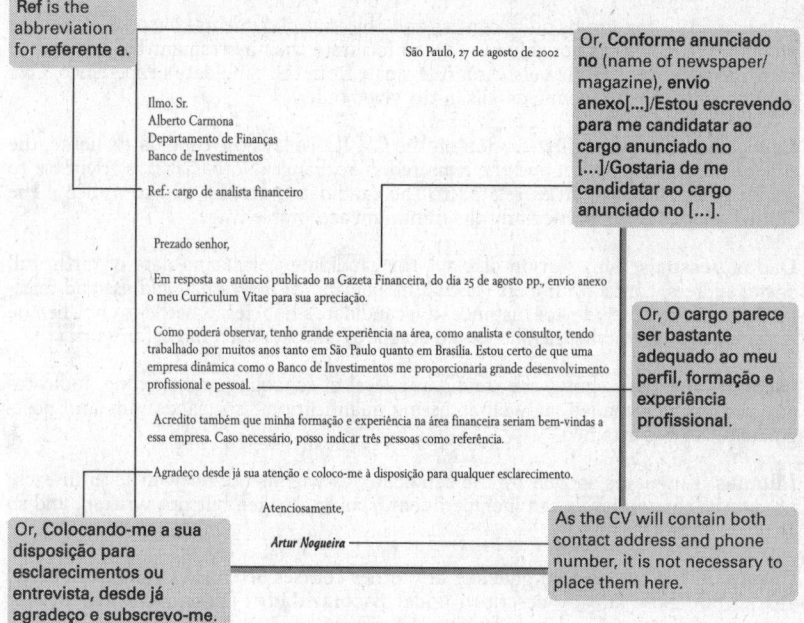

Ref is the abbreviation for referente a.

São Paulo, 27 de agosto de 2002

Ilmo. Sr.
Alberto Carmona
Departamento de Finanças
Banco de Investimentos

Ref.: cargo de analista financeiro

Prezado senhor,

Em resposta ao anúncio publicado na Gazeta Financeira, do dia 25 de agosto pp., envio anexo o meu Curriculum Vitae para sua apreciação.

Como poderá observar, tenho grande experiência na área, como analista e consultor, tendo trabalhado por muitos anos tanto em São Paulo quanto em Brasília. Estou certo de que uma empresa dinâmica como o Banco de Investimentos me proporcionaria grande desenvolvimento profissional e pessoal.

Acredito também que minha formação e experiência na área financeira seriam bem-vindas a essa empresa. Caso necessário, posso indicar três pessoas como referência.

Agradeço desde já sua atenção e coloco-me à disposição para qualquer esclarecimento.

Atenciosamente,

Artur Nogueira

Or, Conforme anunciado no (name of newspaper/magazine), **envio anexo[...]/Estou escrevendo para me candidatar ao cargo anunciado no [...]/Gostaria de me candidatar ao cargo anunciado no [...].**

Or, O cargo parece ser bastante adequado ao meu perfil, formação e experiência profissional.

Or, Colocando-me a sua disposição para esclarecimentos ou entrevista, desde já agradeço e subscrevo-me.

As the CV will contain both contact address and phone number, it is not necessary to place them here.

Useful phrases:

Tenho experiência em/no/na/com [...].
Sou bastante comunicativo(a)/muito organizado(a).
Sou fluente/Tenho fluência em inglês/espanhol/alemão/francês.
Tenho bons conhecimentos de informática/editoração/telecomunicações.
Estou apto a aprender novas tarefas/aceitar novos desafios.
Gosto de trabalhar em equipe/com pessoas diferentes.
Sou competente em [...].
Tenho competência para lidar com várias tarefas simultaneamente.
Meus pontos fortes são [...].
Tenho grande capacidade de organização/planejamento.

Currículum Vitae or *Currículo*

CVs nowadays tend to be quite concise and objective documents. Personal details are presented as clearly as possible in order to facilitate their assessment by prospective employers and/or interviewers. As a rule, apart from the candidate's experience, CVs should include the following details in the given order.

Cabeçalho: This is the first section on the CV. It displays the candidate's name, the title of the job applied for and the expected salary range. Note that it is advisable to insert up to three job titles related to the candidate's profile, and to indicate the desired salary, noting particularly the minimum acceptable wage.

Dados pessoais: This section displays the candidate's place and date of birth, full postal address, contact numbers (phone, mobile and/or fax), email address and marital status. It can include, for instance, the candidate's hobbies, whether or not he/she is a smoker, and whether he/she would accept to travel or even move for work.

Escolaridade: This shows the candidate's level of schooling and training, indicates any university attended, as well as listing qualifications, specializations and post-graduate degrees attained.

Idiomas: Languages spoken by the candidate, as well as the relevant level in each, need to be shown; levels can include fluent, spoken, spoken but not written, and so on.

Cursos: A list can also be given of any other courses attended by the candidate, apart from those already described under **Escolaridade**. These could include, for instance, professional and/or redeployment courses.

Experiência profissional: This section lists the posts held previously by the candidate, from the latest to the earliest, mentioning one or two past jobs or responsibilities of interest or relevance to the post applied for.

Habilidades/qualificações: This section describes the areas in which the candidate has the most aptitude and ability, and indicates the time spent acquiring each.

Capacitação profissional: A brief description is given here of the length of time the candidate has been working, the field he/she is currently working in, knowledge acquired, previously held posts, as well as training programmes and courses attended that are of relevance to his/her career.

Sample CV

It is important to date the CV or to indicate an update, such as **atualização: 15/07/02**, to show when the CV was either written or updated.

BERENICE BUENO

15/07/2002

Analista de cobrança
Analista de orçamentos

Mínimo aceitável: R$ 1.500,00/mês
Salário pretendido: R$ 2.000,00/mês

Dados pessoais

Data de nascimento: 21 de janeiro de 1970
Experiência profissional: 10 anos
Atualmente empregado
Hobbies: teatro, cinema e leitura
Não fumante

> This is not obligatory, but nowadays this piece of information can be important for the prospective employer.

Endereço: R. José Vicente, 700
06543-000 São Paulo-SP
Tel. (11) 899-7766
e-mail: berebueno@oal.com.br

Aceita: transferência de cidade, de estado; viajar a trabalho
Informática: Word, Excel, Power Point, Access

> Here you can indicate the level of knowledge of or proficiency in (**bom/ótimo/médio**) such programs.

Escolaridade

Pós-graduação incompleta – Contabilidade e Finanças – Unifesp - 2001/2003 – São Paulo
Superior completo – Ciências Contábeis – Universidade São Judas – 1991/1995 – São Paulo

Idiomas

Inglês: fluente
Espanhol: fluente

Cursos

Análise de risco – Universidade do Paraná – 1998 – 1 semana
Contabilidade Avançada – Senac – 1993 – 1 mês
Inglês - Cultura Inglesa – 1990 – 2 anos

> You can list as many details as you want, provided they are relevant.

Experiência profissional

	Empresa	Cargo ocupado	Período
Emprego atual	Banco DBC	Consultor financeiro	De 1999 até hoje
Anterior	Cia. VVV	Analista financeiro	De 1995 a 1999
Outros:	Banco Finans	Analista financeiro	De 1990 a 1995

Habilidades/Qualificações

Área fiscal (ótimo) – última atualização: 1999 – Experiência: 9 anos
Área contábil (ótimo) – última atualização: 2001 – Experiência: 10 anos

Capacitação profissional

Profissional com 10 anos de experiência no mercado, sempre atuando na área financeira e contábil em empresas de médio e grande porte. Bons conhecimentos na área fiscal: ativo imobilizado, tesouraria, logística e expedição. Atuação na área contábil de contas patrimoniais, classificação e reclassificação contábil, participação em processos de diligências, fusões e aquisições.

Email

As emailing is a rapid and concise means of communication, the style of the messages themselves tends to be informal and telegraphic. According to internet conventions (netiquette), messages should never be written in capital letters, as this is interpreted as a sign of anger. Formal methods of address, such as, **Prezado(a) senhor(a)** are not normally used. If you are sending an email to someone you know well, the message can begin with a simple **Ola** or **Oi**, followed by the recipient's first name.

Within a company

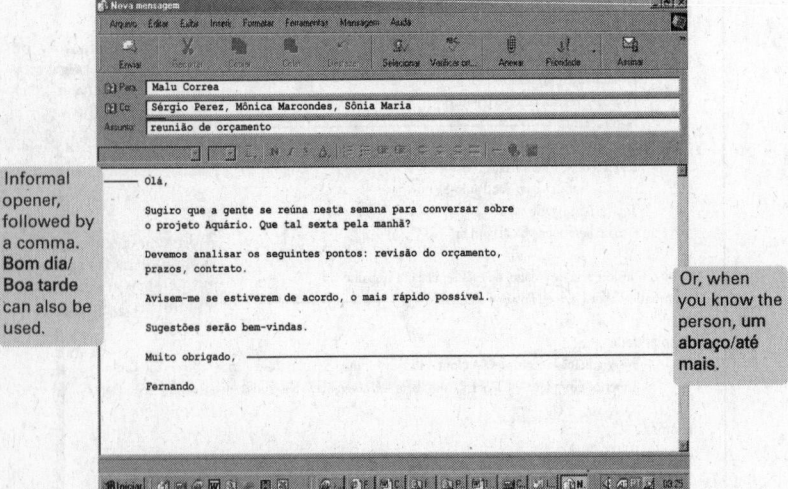

Informal opener, followed by a comma. **Bom dia/ Boa tarde** can also be used.

Or, when you know the person, **um abraço/até mais.**

Business to business

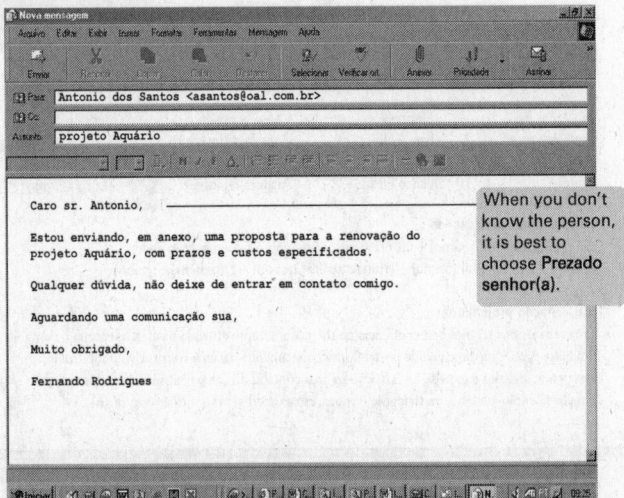

When you don't know the person, it is best to choose **Prezado senhor(a)**.

Between friends

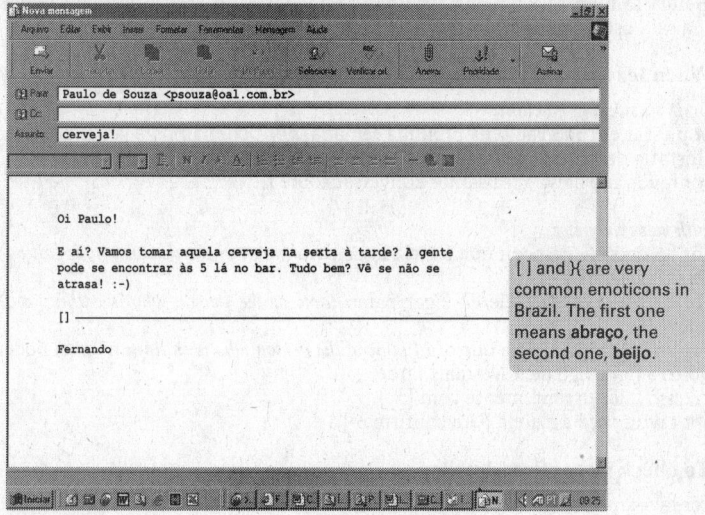

[ ] and)(are very common emoticons in Brazil. The first one means **abraço**, the second one, **beijo**.

Telephone calls

This is how to say a telephone number in Brazil:

3719 4465
três-sete-um-nove, quatro-quatro-meia-cinco

In Brazil, when giving a telephone number, you normally say **meia** (from **meia dúzia**, or 'half a dozen') instead of **seis**.

Useful phrases

Asking the operator for information:

Por favor, telefonista, quero falar com [...].
Por favor, telefonista, estou tentando falar com [...].
Por favor, qual é o código do DDD/o código para [...](*long-distance calls*).
Por favor, qual é o código do DDI/o código para [...] (*international calls*).

When asking to speak to someone:

Alô!
        Poderia falar com [...]?
        Gostaria de falar com [...].
        Ana Maria, por favor.
        Ramal 257, por favor.

When answering a call:

Alô! Aqui é [...] (*confirming who you are*)
Alô, quem fala? Alô, com quem deseja falar? (*to find out who the person wants to speak to*)
Marco Aurélio, pois não?/o que deseja?
Um minuto, por favor./Um instante, por favor.

Desculpe, ele/ela não está. Deseja/Quer deixar um recado?
Ele/ela saiu da sala um instante/não se encontra no escritório/não se encontra em sua sala/está viajando.

When leaving a message:

on an answering machine:
Vou estar em São Paulo na próxima semana, nós poderíamos/a gente poderia [...]
Gostaria de/Queria falar com você sobre [...]
Por favor, me ligue. Precisamos conversar sobre [...]

with somebody else:
Por favor, poderia pedir que ele/ela ligue para (*name of the person who is calling*) no telefone (*number*)[...]?
Por favor, peça para ele/ela ligar para (*name of the person who is calling*) no telefone (*number*)[...].
Por favor, diga a ele/ela que o/a (*name of the person who is calling*) não vai poder [...]
Volto a ligar/ligo de novo mais tarde.
Preciso falar urgentemente com [...].
Por favor, peça a ele/ela para confirmar [...].

To check or confirm details:

Por favor, poderia soletrar?
Por favor, poderia falar mais/um pouco mais devagar?
Desculpe, não entendi. Poderia repetir, por favor?
Confirmando: 11 horas, quarta-feira, dia 10... Certo? Ótimo.

To end a telephone conversation:

Men say obrigado; women say obrigada.

Obrigado(a). Vejo você na quarta. Até lá.
Obrigado(a) pela ajuda.

Or, Até quarta, então. Tchau.

Message left on an answering machine:

Não posso/podemos atendê-lo agora. Por favor, deixe seu recado após/logo após o sinal.

ENGLISH-PORTUGUESE
INGLÊS - PORTUGUÊS

a¹ (*pl* as *OR* a's), **A** (*pl* As *OR* A's) [eɪ] *n* [letter] a, A *m*; **to get from A to B** ir de um lugar para outro; **from A to Z** de A a Z, de cabo a rabo.
➨ **A** *n* **-1.** *MUS* [note] lá *m* **-2.** *SCH* [mark] A *m*.

a² [stressed eɪ, unstressed ə] (*before vowel or silent 'h' an*) [stressed æn, unstressed ən] *indef art* **-1.** [non-specific] um *m*, uma *f*; **~ boy** um garoto; **~ table** uma mesa; **an orange** uma laranja **-2.** [referring to occupation]: **she's ~ teacher/actress** ela é professora/atriz **-3.** [one] um, uma; **~ hundred/thousand pounds** cem/mil libras **-4.** [to express prices, ratios etc] por; **£10 ~ day/person** £10 por dia/pessoa; **twice ~ week/month** duas vezes por semana/mês; **50 km an hour** 50 km por hora **-5.** [to express prices, ratios etc]: **20 cents ~ kilo** 20 centavos o quilo **-6.** [preceding person's name]: **~ Mr Smith phoned** um certo senhor Smith ligou; **do you know ~ Miss Costa?** você conhece alguma senhora Costa?

a. acre.

A-1 *adj inf* de primeira.

A4 *n UK* A4.

AA ◇ *adj* (*abbr of* **anti-aircraft**) antiaéreo(rea). ◇ *n* **-1.** (*abbr of* **Automobile Association**) *associação britânica que presta serviço de emergência a seus filiados em situações de problemas e acidentes automobilísticos*, ≃ Touring *m* Club do Brasil. **-2.** (*abbr of* **Associate in Arts**) *(titular de) diploma em ciências humanas nos Estados Unidos*. **-3.** (*abbr of* **Alcoholics Anonymous**) AA *mpl*.

AAA *n* **-1.** (*abbr of* **Amateur Athletic Association**) *federação britânica de atletas amadores*. **-2.** (*abbr of* **American Automobile Association**) *associação automobilística americana*.

AAU *n* (*abbr of* **Amateur Athletic Union**) *confederação norte-americana de atletas amadores*.

AAUP (*abbr of* **American Association of University Professors**) *n associação norte-americana de professores universitários*, ≃ ANDES *f*.

AB ◇ *n* (*abbr of* **Bachelor of Arts**) *(titular de) graduação em ciências humanas nos Estados Unidos*. ◇ *abbr of* **Alberta**.

aback [əˈbæk] *adv*: **to be taken ~ (by sthg)** ficar surpreso(sa) (com algo), ser surpreendido(da) (por algo).

abacus [ˈæbəkəs] (*pl* **-cuses** *OR* **-ci** [-saɪ]) *n* ábaco *m*.

abandon [əˈbændən] ◇ *vt* **-1.** [leave, desert] abandonar **-2.** [give up] desistir de. ◇ *n (U)*: **with ~** sem inibição, desenfreado(da).

abandoned [əˈbændənd] *adj* [deserted] abandonado(da).

abashed [əˈbæʃt] *adj* envergonhado(da).

abate [əˈbeɪt] *vi fml* [storm, noise, wind] abrandar; [pain, fear, anxiety] diminuir.

abattoir [ˈæbətwɑː'] *n* matadouro *m*.

abbess [ˈæbes] *n* abadessa *f*.

abbey [ˈæbɪ] *n* abadia *f*.

abbot [ˈæbət] *n* abade *m*.

abbreviate [əˈbriːvɪeɪt] *vt* abreviar.

abbreviation [ə,briːvɪˈeɪʃn] *n* [short form] abreviatura *f*.

ABC *n* **-1.** [alphabet] abc *m*. **-2.** *fig* [basics]: **the ~ of** o abc de. **-3.** (*abbr of* **American Broadcasting Company**) *rede de televisão norte-americana*, ABC *f*.

abdicate [ˈæbdɪkeɪt] ◇ *vi* abdicar. ◇ *vt* [responsibility] abrir mão de.

abdication [,æbdɪˈkeɪʃn] *n* [of throne] abdicação *f*.

abdomen [ˈæbdəmen] *n* abdome *m*.

abdominal [æbˈdɒmɪnl] *adj* abdominal.

abduct [əbˈdʌkt] *vt* raptar.

abduction [əbˈdʌkʃn] *n* rapto *m*.

aberration [,æbəˈreɪʃn] *n* aberração *f*; **a mental ~** um desatino.

abet [əˈbet] (*pt & pp* **-ted**, *cont* **-ting**) *vt* ▷ **aid**.

abeyance [əˈbeɪəns] *n fml*: **in ~** em estado jacente.

abhor [əbˈhɔː'] (*pt & pp* **-red**, *cont* **-ring**) *vt* abominar.

abhorrent [əbˈhɒrənt] *adj* abominável.

abide [əˈbaɪd] *vt* suportar.
➨ **abide by** *vt fus* sujeitar-se a.

abiding [əˈbaɪdɪŋ] *adj* duradouro(ra).

ability [əˈbɪlətɪ] (*pl* **-ies**) *n* **-1.** (*U*) [capacity, level of capability] capacidade *f*; **to do sthg to the best of one's** ~ fazer algo da melhor maneira possível **-2.** [skill, talent] habilidade *f*.

abject [ˈæbdʒektl] *adj* **-1.** [miserable, depressing] abjeto(ta) **-2.** [humble] servil.

ablaze [əˈbleɪz] *adj* **-1.** [on fire] em chamas **-2.** *fig* [bright]: **to be** ~ **with** estar iluminado(da) com.

able [ˈeɪbl] *adj* **-1.** [capable] capaz; **to be** ~ **to do sthg** ser capaz de fazer algo; [in a position to] poder fazer algo; [manage to] conseguir fazer algo **-2.** [accomplished, talented] competente.

able-bodied [-ˌbɒdɪd] *adj* **-1.** robusto(ta) **-2.** MIL (fisicamente) apto(ta).

ablutions [əˈbluːʃnz] *npl fml* abluções *fpl*.

ably [ˈeɪblɪ] *adv* competentemente, habilmente.

abnormal [æbˈnɔːml] *adj* anormal.

abnormality [ˌæbnɔːˈmælətɪ] (*pl* **-ies**) *n* anormalidade *f*.

abnormally [æbˈnɔːməlɪ] *adv* **-1.** [behave, develop, grow] irregularmente, de modo anormal **-2.** [cold, wide, loud]: **it's** ~ **cold for this time of the year** não é normal este frio nesta época do ano.

aboard [əˈbɔːd] <> *adv* [on ship, plane] a bordo. <> *prep* [ship, plane] a bordo de; [bus, train] em.

abode [əˈbəʊd] *n fml*: **of no fixed** ~ sem domicílio fixo.

abolish [əˈbɒlɪʃ] *vt* abolir.

abolition [ˌæbəˈlɪʃn] *n* abolição *f*.

A-bomb (*abbr of* atom bomb) *n* bomba *f* atômica.

abominable [əˈbɒmɪnəbl] *adj* abominável.

abominable snowman *n*: **the** ~ o abominável homem das neves.

abominably [əˈbɒmɪnəblɪ] *adv* abominavelmente.

aborigine [ˌæbəˈrɪdʒənɪ] *n* aborígine *mf*.

abort [əˈbɔːt] *vt & vi* abortar.

abortion [əˈbɔːʃn] *n* [of pregnancy] aborto *m*; **to have an** ~ abortar.

abortive [əˈbɔːtɪv] *adj* fracassado(da).

abound [əˈbaʊnd] *vi* **-1.** [be plentiful] existir em abundância, abundar **-2.** [be full]: **to** ~ **with** OR **in sthg** ser rico(ca) em algo, ser cheio(cheia) de algo.

about [əˈbaʊt] <> *adv* **-1.** [approximately] cerca de; ~ **fifty/a hundred/a thousand** quase OR cerca de cinqüenta/cem/mil; **to be just** ~ **ready** estar quase pronto(ta); **at** ~ **five o'clock** por volta das cinco horas **-2.** [referring to place] por perto; **to walk** ~ andar por perto; **to jump** ~ saltitar **-3.** [on the point of]: **to be** ~ **to do sthg** estar prestes a fazer algo. <> *prep* **-1.** [relating to, concerning] sobre; **a film** ~ **Paris** um filme sobre Paris; **what is it** ~ ? de que se trata?; **to talk** ~ **sthg** falar sobre algo **-2.** [referring to place] por; **to wander** ~ **the streets** vagar pelas ruas.

about-turn *esp UK*, **about-face** *esp US n* **-1.** MIL meia-volta *f* **-2.** *fig* [change of attitude] guinada *f* de 180 graus.

above [əˈbʌv] <> *adv* **-1.** [on top, higher up] de cima **-2.** [in text] acima; **the items mentioned** ~ os itens acima mencionados **-3.** [more, over] acima de; **children aged five and** ~ crianças de cinco anos ou mais. <> *prep* acima de.

~ **above all** *adv* acima de tudo.

aboveboard [əˌbʌvˈbɔːd] *adj* **-1.** legítimo(ma) **-2.** limpo(pa).

abracadabra [ˌæbrəkəˈdæbrə] *excl* abracadabra!

abrasion [əˈbreɪʒn] *n fml* [graze] esfolamento *m*.

abrasive [əˈbreɪsɪv] <> *adj* **-1.** [cleaner, cloth] abrasivo(va) **-2.** *fig* [person, manner] mordaz. <> *n* abrasivo *m*.

abreast [əˈbrest] *adv* lado a lado.

~ **abreast of** *prep*: **to keep** ~ **of sthg** estar a par de algo.

abridged [əˈbrɪdʒd] *adj* resumido(da), compacto(ta).

abroad [əˈbrɔːd] *adv* [overseas]: **to live** ~ viver/ morar no exterior; **to go** ~ ir para o exterior.

abrupt [əˈbrʌpt] *adj* **-1.** [sudden] repentino(na) **-2.** [brusque, rude] brusco(ca).

abruptly [əˈbrʌptlɪ] *adv* **-1.** [suddenly] repentinamente **-2.** [brusquely, rudely] bruscamente.

ABS (*abbr of* anti-lock breaking system) *n* ABS *m*.

abscess [ˈæbsɪs] *n* abcesso *m*.

abscond [əbˈskɒnd] *vi* esconder-se; **to** ~ **with sthg** sumir com algo.

abseil [ˈæbseɪl] *vi* praticar rappel; **to** ~ **down a rock** praticar rappel numa rocha.

absence [ˈæbsəns] *n* **-1.** [of person] ausência *f*; **in sb's** ~ na ausência de alguém **-2.** [lack] falta *f*; **in the** ~ **of sthg** na falta de algo.

absent [ˈæbsənt] *adj* **-1.** [not present]: ~ **(from)** ausente (de); **to be** ~ **without leave** MIL estar ausente sem autorização **-2.** [absent-minded] desatento(ta).

absentee [ˌæbsənˈtiː] *n* ausente *mf*.

absenteeism [ˌæbsənˈtiːɪzm] *n* absenteísmo *m*.

absent-minded [-ˈmaɪndɪd] *adj* distraído(da).

absent-mindedness *n* distração *f*.

absent-mindedly [-ˈmaɪndɪdlɪ] *adv* distraidamente.

absinth(e) [ˈæbsɪnθ] *n* absinto *m*.

absolute [ˈæbsəluːt] *adj* **-1.** [complete, utter] absoluto(ta) **-2.** [totalitarian] arbitrário(ria).

absolutely [ˈæbsəluːtlɪ] <> *adv* [completely, utterly] absolutamente. <> *excl* [expressing agreement] sem dúvida.

absolute majority *n* maioria *f* absoluta.

absolution [ˌæbsəˈluːʃn] *n* RELIG absolvição *f*.

absolve [əbˈzɒlv] *vt* [free, clear]: **to** ~ **sb (of sthg)** absolver alguém (de algo).

absorb [əbˈsɔːb] *vt* **-1.** [soak up] absorver **-2.** *fig* [learn] assimilar **-3.** [interest] absorver; **to be** ~ **ed in sthg** estar absorvido(da) em algo **-4.** [take over] incorporar.

absorbent [əbˈsɔːbənt] *adj* absorvente.

absorbing [əbˈsɔːbɪŋ] *adj* cativante.

absorption [əbˈsɔːpʃn] *n* **-1.** [soaking up] absorção *f* **-2.** [interest] concentração *f* **-3.** [taking over] incorporação *f*.

abstain [əbˈsteɪn] *vi* **-1.** [refrain]: **to** ~ **from sthg** abster-se de algo **-2.** [in vote] abster-se.

abstemious [æbˈstiːmjəs] *adj fml* abstêmio(mia).

abstention [əbˈstenʃn] *n* [in vote] abstenção *f*.

abstinence [ˈæbstɪnəns] *n*: ~ **(from sthg)** abstinência *f* (de algo).

abstract [adj & n 'æbstrækt, vb æb'strækt] <> adj abstrato(ta). <> n [summary] resumo m. <> vt [summarize] resumir.

abstraction [æb'strækʃn] n -1. (U) [distractedness] distração f - 2. [abstract idea] abstração f.

abstruse [æb'stru:s] adj confuso(sa).

absurd [əb'sɜ:d] adj absurdo(da).

absurdity [əb'sɜ:dətɪ] (pl -ies) n absurdo m.

absurdly [əb'sɜ:dlɪ] adv incrivelmente.

ABTA (abbr of Association of British Travel Agents) n associação britânica de agentes de viagens, ≃ ABAV f.

Abu Dhabi [,æbu:'dɑ:bɪ] n Abu Dabi.

abundance [ə'bʌndəns] n abundância f.

abundant [ə'bʌndənt] adj abundante.

abundantly [ə'bʌndəntlɪ] adv -1. [manifestly] suficientemente; it is ~ clear that ... está suficientemente claro que ...; he made it ~ clear that ... ele deixou mais do que claro que ... - 2. [in large amounts] em abundância.

abuse [n ə'bju:s, vb ə'bju:z] <> n -1. [offensive remarks] insultos mpl - 2. [maltreatment, misuse] abuso m. <> vt -1. [insult] insultar - 2. [maltreat] maltratar - 3. [misuse] abusar de.

abusive [ə'bju:sɪv] adj abusivo(va).

abut [ə'bʌt] (pt & pp -ted, cont -ting) vi: to ~ on to ser limítrofe a.

abysmal [ə'bɪzml] adj abismal.

abysmally [ə'bɪzməlɪ] adv terrivelmente.

abyss [ə'bɪs] n -1. abismo m - 2. fig [gap] abismo m.

Abyssinia [,æbɪ'sɪnɪə] n Abissínia; in/to ~ na/à Abissínia.

Abyssinian adj & n abissínio(nia).

a/c (abbr of account (current)) c.c. f.

AC (abbr of alternating current) n CA f.

acacia [ə'keɪʃə] n acácia f.

academic [,ækə'demɪk] <> adj -1. [of college, university] acadêmico(ca) - 2. [studious] intelectual - 3. [hypothetical] conjetural. <> n [teacher, researcher] acadêmico m, -ca f.

academic year n ano m letivo.

academy [ə'kædəmɪ] (pl -ies) n -1. [school, college] academia f, escola f - 2. [institution, society] academia f.

ACAS (abbr of Advisory Conciliation and Arbitration Service) n organização britânica para conciliação entre sindicatos e empregadores.

accede [æk'si:d] vi -1. fml [agree]: to ~ to sthg aceder a algo - 2. [monarch]: to ~ to the throne subir ao trono.

accelerate [ək'seləreɪt] <> vt apressar. <> vi -1. [car, driver] acelerar - 2. [inflation, growth] disparar.

acceleration [ək,selə'reɪʃn] n -1. [of car] aceleração f - 2. [of inflation, growth] disparada f.

accelerator [ək'seləreɪtə'] n acelerador m.

accent ['æksent] n -1. [when speaking] sotaque m - 2. [in writing] acento m - 3. fig [emphasis] ênfase f.

accentuate [æk'sentjʊeɪt] vt [emphasize, stress] acentuar.

accept [ək'sept] vt -1. [agree to take, receive] aceitar - 2. [agree to follow] assentir - 3. [recognize as satisfactory] aprovar - 4. [get used to] reconhecer - 5. [admit, recognize as one's own] assumir - 6. [person - as

part of group] acolher; [- for job, as member of club] aceitar - 7. [agree, believe]: to ~ that aceitar que - 8. [process] aceitar.

acceptable [ək'septəbl] adj -1. [permissible] aceitável - 2. [passable] admissível.

acceptably [ək'septəblɪ] adv apropriadamente.

acceptance [ək'septəns] n -1. [gen] aceitação f - 2. [recognizing as satisfactory] aprovação f.

accepted [ək'septɪd] adj [recognized as correct, true] aceito(ta).

access ['ækses] <> n -1. [entry, way in] acesso m; to gain ~ to [place, building] obter acesso a - 2. [opportunity to use, see]: to have ~ to sthg ter acesso a algo. <> vt COMPUT acessar.

accessibility [ək,sesə'bɪlətɪ] n -1. [of place] acessibilidade f - 2. [availability] acesso m.

accessible [ək'sesəbl] adj -1. [reachable, understandable] acessível - 2. [available] disponível.

accession [æk'seʃn] n [of monarch] ascensão f.

accessory [ək'sesərɪ] (pl -ies) n -1. [extra part, device] acessório m - 2. JUR cúmplice mf.

➠ **accessories** npl [to outfit] acessórios mpl.

access road n -1. [gen] rua f de acesso - 2. UK [to motorway] via f de acesso.

access time n COMPUT tempo m de acesso.

accident ['æksɪdənt] n -1. acidente m; to have an ~ sofrer um acidente - 2. (U) [chance]: by ~ por acaso; it was an ~ foi sem querer.

accidental [,æksɪ'dentl] adj acidental.

accidentally [,æksɪ'dentəlɪ] adv -1. [drop, break] sem querer - 2. [meet, find, discover] acidentalmente.

accident-prone adj propenso(sa) a acidentes.

acclaim [ə'kleɪm] <> n (U) aclamação f. <> vt aclamar.

acclamation [,æklə'meɪʃn] n aclamação f.

acclimatize, -ise [ə'klaɪmətaɪz], **acclimate** US ['æklɪmeɪt] vi: to ~ (to sthg) aclimatar-se (a algo).

accolade ['ækəleɪd] n honra f.

accommodate [ə'kɒmədeɪt] vt -1. [provide room for] acomodar - 2. [oblige] comprazer a.

accommodating [ə'kɒmədeɪtɪŋ] adj complacente.

accommodation UK [ə,kɒmə'deɪʃn] n, **accommodations** US [ə,kɒmə'deɪʃnz] npl -1. [lodging] alojamento m, acomodação f - 2. [work space] instalações fpl.

accompaniment [ə'kʌmpənɪmənt] n MUS acompanhamento m.

accompanist [ə'kʌmpənɪst] n MUS pessoa que canta ou toca junto com alguém.

accompany [ə'kʌmpənɪ] (pt & pp -ied) vt -1. acompanhar - 2. MUS [with instrument]: to ~ sb (on sthg) acompanhar alguém (em algo).

accomplice [ə'kʌmplɪs] n cúmplice m.

accomplish [ə'kʌmplɪʃ] vt [achieve, manage] conseguir; [carry out, effect] realizar; [reach, attain] alcançar.

accomplished [ə'kʌmplɪʃt] adj [skilled] excelente, competente.

accomplishment [ə'kʌmplɪʃmənt] n -1. [achievement, finishing] realização f, conclusão f - 2. [feat, deed] feito m.

➠ **accomplishments** npl [skills] habilidades fpl.

accord [əˈkɔːd] n -1. [settlement] acordo m -2. [agreement, harmony]: **to be in ~ (with sb/sthg)** estar de acordo com alguém algo; **with one ~** unanimamente; **to do sthg of one's own ~** fazer algo por iniciativa própria.

accordance [əˈkɔːdəns] n: **in ~ with sthg** de acordo com algo.

according to prep -1. [as stated or shown by] segundo; **to go ~ to plan** sair conforme o planejado -2. [with regard to, depending on] conforme.

accordingly [əˈkɔːdɪŋlɪ] adv -1. [appropriately] de modo apropriado -2. [consequently] conseqüentemente.

accordion [əˈkɔːdjən] n acordeão m, sanfona f.

accordionist [əˈkɔːdjənɪst] n acordeonista mf, sanfoneiro m, -ra f.

accost [əˈkɒst] vt abordar.

account [əˈkaʊnt] n -1. [with bank, company] conta f -2. [with shop]: **I have an ~ at the butcher's** tenho conta no açougue -3. [report]: **to give an~ of sthg** fazer um relato de algo -4. phr: **to call sb to ~** fazer alguém se explicar; **to give a good ~ of o.s.** causar boa impressão; **to take ~ of sthg, to take sthg into ~** levar algo em consideração; **to be of no ~** não ter importância; **on no ~** de modo algum.
  ➡ **accounts** npl [of business] contabilidade f.
  ➡ **by all accounts** adv de acordo com a opinião geral.
  ➡ **on account of** prep devido a; **on my ~** por minha causa.
  ➡ **account for** vt fus -1. [explain] justificar; **a theory that ~s for all the facts** uma teoria que justifique os fatos -2. [represent] representar.

accountability [ə,kaʊntəˈbɪlətɪ] n responsabilidade f.

accountable [əˈkaʊntəbl] adj [responsible]: **to be held ~ for sthg** ser responsabilizado(da) por algo; **~ to sb** [answerable] obrigado(da) a prestar contas a alguém.

accountancy [əˈkaʊntənsɪ] n [profession, business] contabilidade f.

accountant [əˈkaʊntənt] n contador m, -ra f.

accounting [əˈkaʊntɪŋ] n [skill, practice of accountancy] contabilidade f.

accounts department n setor m de contabilidade.

accoutrements UK [əˈkuːtrəmənts], **accouterments** US [əˈkuːtərmənts] npl hum [baggage] parafernália f.

accredited [əˈkredɪtd] adj [authorized, recognized] acreditado(da).

accrue [əˈkruː] vt & vi FIN render.

accumulate [əˈkjuːmjʊleɪt] ◇ vt acumular. ◇ vi acumular-se.

accumulation [ə,kjuːmjʊˈleɪʃn] n -1. (U) [accumulating] acumulação f -2. [group of things] monte m.

accuracy [ˈækjʊrəsɪ] n -1. [truth, correctness] exatidão f -2. [precision - of weapon, marksman] precisão f; [- of typing, figures, estimate] exatidão f.

accurate [ˈækjʊrət] adj -1. [true, correct] exato(ta) -2. [precise - shot, marksman] preciso(sa); [- typist, figures, estimate] exato(ta).

accurately [ˈækjʊrətlɪ] adv -1. [truthfully, correctly] com exatidão -2. [precisely - aim] com precisão; [- type, estimate] com exatidão.

accusation [,ækjuːˈzeɪʃn] n -1. [charge, criticism] acusação f -2. JUR [formal charge] incriminação f.

accuse [əˈkjuːz] vt -1. [charge, criticize]: **to ~ sb of sthg/of doing sthg** acusar alguém de algo/de fazer algo -2. JUR: **to ~ sb of sthg/of doing sthg** incriminar alguém por algo/por fazer algo.

accused [əˈkjuːzd] n JUR: **the ~** [defendant] o réu(a ré).

accusing [əˈkjuːzɪŋ] adj acusador(ra).

accusingly [əˈkjuːzɪŋlɪ] adv acusatoriamente.

accustomed [əˈkʌstəmd] adj: **to be ~ to sthg/to doing sthg** estar acostumado(da) a algo/a fazer algo.

ace [eɪs] ◇ n -1. [playing card] ás m -2. TENNIS ace m -3. phr: **to be within an ~ of victory** estar a um passo da vitória. ◇ adj [top-class]: **he's an ~ tennis player** ele é um tenista de primeira.

acerbic [əˈsɜːbɪk] adj acerbo(ba).

acetate [ˈæsɪteɪt] n acetato m.

acetic acid [əˈsiːtɪk-] n (U) ácido m acético.

acetone [ˈæsɪtəʊn] n (U) acetona f.

acetylene [əˈsetɪliːn] n (U) acetileno m.

ache [eɪk] ◇ n [dull pain] dor f. ◇ vi -1. [be painful] doer -2. fig [want]: **to be aching for sthg/to do sthg** estar morrendo de vontade de algo/de fazer algo.

achieve [əˈtʃiːv] vt [success] conseguir ; [goal, ambition] realizar ; [victory, fame] conquistar.

achievement [əˈtʃiːvmənt] n -1. [feat, deed] conquista f -2. [process of achieving] realização f.

Achilles' heel [əˈkɪliːz-] n calcanhar m de Aquiles.

Achilles' tendon n tendão m de Aquiles.

acid [ˈæsɪd] ◇ adj -1. ácido(da) -2. fig [remark, tone] áspero(ra). ◇ n -1. ácido m -2. inf [LSD] ácido m.

acidic [əˈsɪdɪk] adj CHEM acidífero(ra).

acidity [əˈsɪdətɪ] n -1. CHEM acidez f -2. fig [of remark, tone] aspereza f.

acid rain n chuva f ácida.

acid test n fig [test of worth] prova f dos nove.

acknowledge [əkˈnɒlɪdʒ] vt -1. [accept, recognize] reconhecer; **to ~ sb as sthg** reconhecer alguém como algo -2. [letter]: **to ~ (receipt of) sthg** acusar (o recebimento de algo) -3. [greet] cumprimentar.

acknowledg(e)ment [əkˈnɒlɪdʒmənt] n -1. [acceptance, recognition] reconhecimento m -2. [of letter] aviso m de recebimento -3. [thanks, gratitude] retribuição f.
  ➡ **acknowledg(e)ments** npl [in book] agradecimentos mpl.

ACLU (abbr of **American Civil Liberties Union**) n associação norte-americana para a defesa das liberdades civis.

acme [ˈækmɪ] n apogeu m.

acne [ˈæknɪ] n acne f.

acorn [ˈeɪkɔːn] n bolota f, glande m.

acoustic [əˈkuːstɪk] adj acústico(ca).
  ➡ **acoustics** npl [of room, auditorium] acústica f.

acoustic guitar n violão m acústico.

acquaint [əˈkweɪnt] *vt*: **to ~ sb with sthg** [information] informar alguém sobre algo; **to be ~ed with sthg** [method, technique] estar por dentro de algo; **to be ~ed with sb** *fml* conhecer alguém.

acquaintance [əˈkweɪntəns] *n* **- 1.** [personal associate] conhecido *m*, -da *f* **- 2.** (U) *fml*: **to make sb's ~** conhecer alguém.

acquiesce [ˌækwɪˈes] *vi*: **to ~ (to OR in sthg)** aquiescer-se (a algo).

acquiescence [ˌækwɪˈesns] *n* aquiescência *f*.

acquire [əˈkwaɪəʳ] *vt* **- 1.** [obtain] [property, company, object] adquirir **- 2.** [information, document] obter **- 3.** [skill, knowledge, habit] adquirir.

acquired taste [əˈkwaɪəd-] *n* gosto *m* adquirido.

acquisition [ˌækwɪˈzɪʃn] *n* **- 1.** [of property, company, object] aquisição *f* **- 2.** (U) [of information, document] obtenção *f* **- 3.** (U) [of skill, knowlege, habit] aquisição *f*.

acquisitive [əˈkwɪzɪtɪv] *adj* ambicioso(sa), consumista.

acquit [əˈkwɪt] (*pt & pp* -ted, *cont* -ting) *vt* **- 1.** JUR: **to ~ sb of sthg** absolver alguém de algo **- 2.** [conduct]: **to ~ o.s. well/badly** desempenhar-se bem/mal.

acquittal [əˈkwɪtl] *n* JUR absolvição *f*.

acre [ˈeɪkəʳ] *n* [unit of measurement] acre *m (4046,9 m²)*.

acreage *n* [size in acres] área *f* medida em acres.

acrid [ˈækrɪd] *adj* **- 1.** [smoke, smell, taste] acre **- 2.** *fig* [remark] mordaz.

acrimonious [ˌækrɪˈməʊnjəs] *adj* acrimonioso(sa).

acrobat [ˈækrəbæt] *n* [circus performer] acrobata *mf*.

acrobatic [ˌækrəˈbætɪk] *adj* **- 1.** [somersault, display] acrobático(ca) **- 2.** [person] astuto(ta).

➡ **acrobatics** *npl* acrobacias *fpl*.

acronym [ˈækrənɪm] *n* acrônimo *m*.

across [əˈkrɒs] ◇ *adv* **- 1.** [from one side to the other]: **they came ~ in a small boat** eles atravessaram num barco pequeno **- 2.** [in the direction of]: **she looked ~ at me** ela olhou em minha direção; **he went ~ to speak to her** ele foi em sua direção para lhe falar **- 3.** [in measurements] de um lado a outro **- 4.** [in crosswords] cruzado(da) **- 5.** *fig*: **to get sthg ~ (to sb)** fazer-se entender (por alguém). ◇ *prep* **- 1.** [from one side to the other] de um lado a outro; **he drew a line ~ the page** ele traçou uma linha de um lado a outro da página; **there is a bridge ~ the river** há uma ponte sobre o rio; **she walked/ran ~ the road** ela atravessou a estrada caminhando/correndo; **he looked ~ the street** ele olhou pela rua **- 2.** [on the other side of] no outro lado de.

➡ **across from** *prep* na frente de.

acrylic [əˈkrɪlɪk] ◇ *adj* [fibre, jumper, paint] acrílico(-ca). ◇ *n* (U) [fibre] acrílico *m*.

act [ækt] ◇ *n* **- 1.** [action, deed] ato *m*; **to catch sb in the ~** pegar alguém em flagrante **- 2.** JUR lei *f* **- 3.** [of play, opera] ato *m*; [in cabaret etc] número *m* **- 4.** *fig* [pretence] fingimento *m*; **to put on an ~** agir com fingimento **- 5.** *phr*: **to get in on the ~** aproveitar-se de algo iniciado por outrem; **to get one's ~ together** organizar-se. ◇ *vi* **- 1.** [gen] agir; **to ~ as if/like** agir como se/como **- 2.** [in play, film] representar, atuar **- 3.** *fig* [pretend] fingir **- 4.** [fulfil function]: **to ~ as sthg** atuar como algo; **to ~ for OR**

on behalf of sb representar alguém. ◇ *vt* [role] desempenhar; **to ~ the fool/innocent** fazer-se de bobo/inocente.

➡ **act out** *vt sep* **- 1.** [feeling] expressar **- 2.** [event] representar.

➡ **act up** *vi inf* **- 1.** [machine] emperrar **- 2.** [person] comportar-se mal.

ACT (*abbr of* **American College Test**) *n exame realizado ao final do ensino médio em escolas norte-americanas.*

acting [ˈæktɪŋ] ◇ *adj* [interim] interino(na). ◇ *n* (U) [in play, film] atuação *f*; **to enjoy ~** gostar de atuar.

action [ˈækʃn] *n* **- 1.** (U) [fact of doing sthg] ação *f*; **to take ~** agir; **to put sthg into ~** pôr algo em ação; **in ~** [person, machine] em atividade; **out of ~** [person] fora de combate; [machine] desativado(da) **- 2.** [deed] atividade *f* **- 3.** (U) [in battle, war] ação *f*; **to be killed in ~** ser morto(ta) em ação **- 4.** JUR ação *f* judicial; **to bring an ~ against sb** entrar com uma ação judicial contra alguém **- 5.** [in play, book, film] história *f* **- 6.** [effect] efeito *m*.

action group *n* [lobby] grupo *m* de ação.

action replay *n* replay *m*.

activate [ˈæktɪveɪt] *vt* [set off] ativar.

active [ˈæktɪv] *adj* **- 1.** [lively, energetic] ativo(va) **- 2.** [involved, hardworking] dinâmico(ca) **- 3.** [positive] incessante **- 4.** [volcano] ativo(va).

actively [ˈæktɪvlɪ] *adv* **- 1.** [promote] ativamente **- 2.** [seek, encourage] incessantemente.

active service *n* (U) MIL serviço *m* ativo; **to be killed on ~** ser morto(ta) em serviço.

activist [ˈæktɪvɪst] *n* [political campaigner] ativista *mf*.

activity [ækˈtɪvətɪ] (*pl* -ies) *n* (U) atividade *f*.

➡ **activities** *npl* [actions, doings] ações *fpl*.

act of God *n* força *f* maior.

actor [ˈæktəʳ] *n* ator *m*.

actress [ˈæktrɪs] *n* atriz *f*.

actual [ˈæktʃʊəl] *adj* real; **in ~ fact** na verdade.

actuality [ˌæktʃʊˈælətɪ] *n*: **in ~** de fato.

actually [ˈæktʃʊəlɪ] *adv* **- 1.** [really, in truth] na verdade, realmente **- 2.** [by the way] a propósito **- 3.** [contradicting sb] pensando bem, de fato; **that's not true, ~** pensando bem, aquilo não é verdade.

actuary [ˈæktjʊərɪ] (*pl* -ies) *n* [statistician] estatístico *m*, -ca *f*.

actuate [ˈæktjʊeɪt] *vt* [activate] acionar.

acuity [əˈkjuːətɪ] *n fml* acuidade *f*.

acumen [ˈækjʊmen] *n* (U): **business ~** tino para os negócios.

acupuncture [ˈækjʊpʌŋktʃəʳ] *n* (U) acupuntura *f*.

acute [əˈkjuːt] *adj* **- 1.** [severe, extreme] agudo(da) **- 2.** [perceptive, intelligent] engenhoso(sa) **- 3.** [keen, sensitive] aguçado(da) **- 4.** LING: **e ~** e agudo **- 5.** MATH agudo(da).

acute accent *n* acento *m* agudo.

acutely [əˈkjuːtlɪ] *adv* [extremely] acentuadamente.

ad (*abbr of* **advertisement**) *n fam* **- 1.** [in newspaper] anúncio *m*. **- 2.** [on TV] propaganda *f*.

AD (*abbr of* **Anno Domini**) d.C.

adage [ˈædɪdʒ] *n* adágio *m*.

adamant [ˈædəmənt] *adj* [determined]: **to be ~**

(about sthg/that) estar inflexível (em relação a algo).

Adam's apple ['ædəmz-] *n* pomo-de-adão *m*.

adapt [ə'dæpt] ⬦ *vt* adaptar. ⬦ *vi*: **to ~ to sthg** adaptar-se a algo.

adaptability [ə,dæptə'bɪlətɪ] *n* adaptabilidade *f*.

adaptable [ə'dæptəbl] *adj* [person] maleável.

adaptation [,ædæp'teɪʃn] *n* [of book, play] adaptação *f*.

adapter, adaptor [ə'dæptə'] *n* ELEC adaptador *m*.

ADAS (*abbr of* Agricultural Development and Advisory Service) *n organização britânica de pesquisa e consultoria para as indústrias do setor agrícola.*

ADC (*abbr of* analogue to digital converter) *n* ADC *m*, conversor *m* analógico-digital.

add [æd] *vt* -1.: **to ~ sthg to sthg** adicionar algo a algo -2. [total] somar; **6 ~ 3 equals 9** *US* 6 mais 3 é igual a 9 -3. [say as an afterthought] acrescentar.
➤ **add in** *vt sep* [include] incluir.
➤ **add on** *vt sep*: **to ~ sthg on (to sthg)** [to building] anexar algo (a algo); [to bill, total] incluir algo (em algo).
➤ **add to** *vt fus* [increase] aumentar.
➤ **add up** ⬦ *vt sep* [total up] adicionar. ⬦ *vi* -1. [make sense] fazer sentido -2. [accumulate] acumular.
➤ **add up to** *vt fus* [represent] representar.

addendum [ə'dendəm] (*pl* -da) *n* [additional section] adendo *m*.

adder ['ædə'] *n* [snake] víbora *f*.

addict ['ædɪkt] *n* -1. [to drug, harmful substance] viciado *m*, -da *f*, dependente *mf* -2. [exercise, TV etc.] fanático *m*, -ca *f*.

addicted [ə'dɪktɪd] *adj* -1. [to drug, harmful substance]: **~ (to sthg)** viciado(da) (em algo), dependente de algo -2. *fig* [to exercise, TV] fanático(ca) (por algo).

addiction [ə'dɪkʃn] *n* (*U*) -1. [to drug, harmful substance] vício *m*, dependência *f*; **~ to sthg** vício em algo, dependência de algo -2. *fig* [to exercise, food, TV] fanatismo *m*; **~ to sthg** fanatismo por algo.

addictive [ə'dɪktɪv] *adj* -1. [drug, harmful substance] que vicia -2. *fig* [exercise, food, TV] que vicia.

Addis Ababa ['ædɪs 'æbəbə] *n* Adis-Abeba; **in/to ~** em/para Adis-Abeba.

addition [ə'dɪʃn] *n* -1. (*U*) MATH adição *f* -2. [extra thing] acréscimo *m* -3. (*U*) [act of adding] adicionamento *m*; **in ~** além disso; **in ~ to** além de.

additional [ə'dɪʃənl] *adj* [extra] adicional.

additive ['ædɪtɪv] *n* aditivo *m*.

addled ['ædld] *adj* -1. [rotten] podre -2. *inf* [confused] confuso(sa).

add-on COMPUT ⬦ *adj* adicional. ⬦ *n* add-on *m*, *software ou hardware acrescentado a um computador para melhorar seu desempenho.*

address [ə'dres] ⬦ *n* -1. [location] endereço *m* -2. [speech] discurso *m*. ⬦ *vt* -1. [letter, parcel] endereçar -2. [give a speech to] discursar -3. [speak to, accost]: **to ~ sb as** dirigir-se a alguém como -4. [deal with] tratar; **to ~ o.s. to sthg** interessar-se por algo.

address book *n* agenda *f* de endereços.

addressee [,ædre'si:] *n* [of letter, parcel] destinatário *m*, -ria *f*.

Aden ['eɪdn] *n* Áden; **in/to ~** em/à Áden.

adenoids ['ædɪnɔɪdz] *npl* adenóides *fpl*.

adept ['ædept] *adj*: **to be ~ at sthg/at doing sthg** ser perito(ta) em algo/em fazer algo.

adequacy ['ædɪkwəsɪ] *n* (*U*) -1. [sufficiency] suficiência *f* -2. [competence] adequação *f*.

adequate ['ædɪkwət] *adj* -1. [sufficient] suficiente -2. [competent] adequado(da).

adequately ['ædɪkwətlɪ] *adv* -1. [sufficiently] suficientemente -2. [competently] adequadamente.

adhere [əd'hɪə'] *vi* -1. [to surface, principle]: **to ~ (to sthg)** aderir (a algo) -2. [to regulation, decision]: **to ~ to sthg** respeitar algo.

adherence [əd'hɪərəns] *n*: **~ (to sthg)** [surface] aderência *f* (a algo); [principle] adesão *f* (a algo); [regulation, decision] respeito *m* (a algo).

adhesive [əd'hi:sɪv] ⬦ *adj* [sticky] adesivo(va). ⬦ *n* [glue] cola *f*.

adhesive tape *n* fita *f* adesiva.

ad hoc [,æd'hɒk] *adj* ad hoc.

ad infinitum [,ædɪnfɪ'naɪtəm] *adv* ad infinitum.

adjacent [ə'dʒeɪsənt] *adj* adjacente; **~ to sthg** adjacente a algo.

adjective ['ædʒɪktɪv] *n* adjetivo *m*.

adjoin [ə'dʒɔɪn] *vt* unir.

adjoining [ə'dʒɔɪnɪŋ] ⬦ *adj* [next-door] vizinho(-nha). ⬦ *prep* ao lado de.

adjourn [ə'dʒɜ:n] ⬦ *vt* [postpone] adiar. ⬦ *vi* -1. [come to a temporary close] ser/estar suspenso(sa) -2. *hum* [go]: **to ~ (to)** ir para.

adjournment [ə'dʒɜ:nmənt] *n* adiamento *m*, suspensão *f*.

Adjt (*abbr of* adjutant) *assistente administrativo de oficial do exército.*

adjudge [ə'dʒʌdʒ] *vt* -1. [declare] decretar -2. JUR sentenciar.

adjudicate [ə'dʒu:dɪkeɪt] ⬦ *vt* [contest, claim] adjudicar. ⬦ *vi* [serve as judge, arbiter in contest] julgar; **to ~ on** OR **upon sthg** deliberar sobre algo.

adjudication [ə,dʒu:dɪ'keɪʃn] *n* adjudicação *f*.

adjunct ['ædʒʌŋkt] *n* [something added] acessório *m*.

adjust [ə'dʒʌst] ⬦ *vt* [alter, correct] ajustar. ⬦ *vi*: **to ~ (to sthg)** adaptar-se (a algo).

adjustable [ə'dʒʌstəbl] *adj* [machine, chair] regulável.

adjustable spanner *n* chave *f* inglesa.

adjusted [ə'dʒʌstɪd] *adj* [emotionally stable]: **to be well ~** estar equilibrado(da).

adjustment [ə'dʒʌstmənt] *n* -1. [to heat, speed, machine] ajuste *m*; **to make an ~ to sthg** fazer um ajuste em algo -2. (*U*) [change of attitude] mudança *f*; **~ to sthg** adaptação a algo.

adjutant ['ædʒʊtənt] *n* ajudante *mf*.

ad lib [,æd'lɪb] (*pt* & *pp* ad-libbed, *cont* ad-libbing) ⬦ *adj* [improvised] espontâneo(nea). ⬦ *adv* [freely] de improviso. ⬦ *n* [improvised joke, remark] improviso *m*.
➤ **ad-lib** *vi* [improvise] improvisar.

adman ['ædmæn] (*pl* admen ['ædmen]) *n* anunciante *m*.

admin ['ædmɪn] *n* UK *inf* administração *f*.

administer [əd'mɪnɪstə'] *vt* -1. [company, business]

administrar - 2. [justice, punishment] aplicar **- 3.** [drug, medication] ministrar.

administration [ədˌmɪnɪˈstreɪʃn] n **-1.** *(U)* [of company, business] administração f **- 2.** *(U)* [of justice, punishment] aplicação f.

➤ **Administration** n US [government]: **the Administration** o Governo.

administrative [ədˈmɪnɪstrətɪv] adj [job, work, staff] administrativo(va).

administrator [ədˈmɪnɪstreɪtəʳ] n administrador m, -ra f.

admirable [ˈædmərəbl] adj admirável.

admirably [ˈædmərəblɪ] adv admiravelmente.

admiral [ˈædmərəl] n almirante mf.

Admiralty [ˈædmərəltɪ] n UK: **the** ~ o Ministério da Marinha.

admiration [ˌædməˈreɪʃn] n admiração f.

admire [ədˈmaɪəʳ] vt **-1.** [respect, like] admirar; **to** ~ **sb for sthg** admirar alguém por algo **- 2.** [look at with pleasure] apreciar.

admirer [ədˈmaɪərəʳ] n **-1.** [suitor] pretendente mf **- 2.** [enthusiast, fan] fã mf.

admiring [ədˈmaɪərɪŋ] adj [look] de admiração.

admiringly [ədˈmaɪərɪŋlɪ] adv [gaze] com admiração.

admissible [ədˈmɪsəbl] adj JUR [evidence] aceitável.

admission [ədˈmɪʃn] n **-1.** [permission to enter] admissão f **- 2.** [cost of entrance] entrada f **- 3.** [confession] confissão f; **by his/her own** ~ conforme ele/ela mesmo(ma) admitiu.

admit [ədˈmɪt] (pt & pp **-ted**, cont **-ting**) ⬦ vt **-1.** [acknowledge, confess] confessar, admitir; **to** ~ **that** admitir que; **to** ~ **doing sthg** admitir/confessar ter feito algo; **to** ~ **defeat** fig dar-se por vencido(da) **- 2.** [allow to enter] admitir; **to be admitted to hospital.** UK OR **to the hospital** US dar entrada no hospital **- 3.** [allow to join] admitir; **to** ~ **sb to sthg** admitir alguém em algo. ⬦ vi: **to** ~ **to sthg/to doing sthg** admitir algo/fazer algo.

admittance [ədˈmɪtəns] n [right to enter, entrance]: **to gain** ~ **to sthg** ser admitido(da) em algo; **'no** ~' 'entrada proibida'.

admittedly [ədˈmɪtɪdlɪ] adv reconhecidamente.

admixture n fml mistura f.

admonish [ədˈmɒnɪʃ] vt fml [tell off] repreender.

ad nauseam [ˌædˈnɔːzɪæm] adv exaustivamente.

ado [əˈduː] n: **without further** OR **more** ~ sem mais delongas OR preâmbulos.

adolescence [ˌædəˈlesns] n adolescência f.

adolescent [ˌædəˈlesnt] ⬦ adj **-1.** [teenage] adolescente **- 2.** pej [immature] imaturo(ra). ⬦ n [teenager] adolescente mf.

adopt [əˈdɒpt] ⬦ vt [recommendation, suggestion] aceitar. ⬦ vi [give a home to a child] adotar.

adoption [əˈdɒpʃn] n *(U)* adoção f.

adoptive [əˈdɒptɪv] adj adotivo(va).

adorable [əˈdɔːrəbl] adj adorável.

adoration [ˌædəˈreɪʃn] n adoração f.

adore [əˈdɔːʳ] vt adorar.

adoring [əˈdɔːrɪŋ] adj **-1.** [look] de admiração **- 2.** [smile, person] encantador(ra).

adorn [əˈdɔːn] vt [decorate] adornar.

adornment [əˈdɔːnmənt] n [decoration] adorno m.

ADP (abbr of **automatic data processing**) n PAD m, processamento m automático de dados.

adrenalin [əˈdrenəlɪn] n *(U)* adrenalina f.

Adriatic [ˌeɪdrɪˈætɪk] n: **the** ~ **(Sea)** o (Mar) Adriático.

adrift [əˈdrɪft] ⬦ adj [boat, ship] à deriva. ⬦ adv: **to go** ~ fig [go wrong] ir por água abaixo.

adroit [əˈdrɔɪt] adj hábil.

ADT (abbr of **Atlantic Daylight Time**) n horário de verão na costa leste dos Estados Unidos.

adulation [ˌædjʊˈleɪʃn] n *(U)* adulação f.

adult [ˈædʌlt] ⬦ adj **-1.** [mature, responsible] adulto(ta) **- 2.** [for adults] para adultos, para maiores. ⬦ n [person, animal] adulto m, -ta f.

adult education n *(U)* educação f para adultos.

adulterate [əˈdʌltəreɪt] vt adulterar.

adulteration [əˌdʌltəˈreɪʃn] n *(U)* adulteração f.

adulterer [əˈdʌltərəʳ] n adúltero m, -ra f.

adultery [əˈdʌltərɪ] n *(U)* adultério m.

adulthood [ˈædʌlthʊd] n maioridade f.

advance [ədˈvɑːns] ⬦ n **-1.** [gen] avanço m **- 2.** [money] adiantamento m. ⬦ comp **-1.** [early] antecipado(da) **- 2.** [prior]: ~ **warning** aviso prévio. ⬦ vt **-1.** [improve] progredir **- 2.** [bring forward in time] adiantar **- 3.** [money]: **to** ~ **sb sthg** adiantar algo a alguém. ⬦ vi **-1.** [go forward] avançar; **to** ~ **on sb** avançar em alguém **- 2.** [improve] progredir.

➤ **advances** npl: **to make** ~ **s to sb** [sexual] assediar alguém; [business] propor um bom negócio para alguém.

➤ **in advance** adv com antecedência; **to book in** ~ reservar antecipadamente; **to know in** ~ saber de antemão; **half an hour in** ~ meia hora antes.

➤ **in advance of** prep **-1.** [superior to] superior a **- 2.** [prior to] antes de.

advanced [ədˈvɑːnst] adj avançado(da); ~ **in years** euph [elderly] em idade avançada.

advancement [ədˈvɑːnsmənt] n **-1.** *(U)* [promotion in job] promoção f **- 2.** [improvement] avanço m.

advantage [ədˈvɑːntɪdʒ] n **-1.** vantagem f; **to be to one's** ~ ser conveniente para alguém; **to have** OR **hold the** ~ **(over sb)** ter OR levar vantagem (sobre alguém) **- 2.** phr: **to take** ~ **of sthg/sb** aproveitar-se de algo/alguém.

advantageous [ˌædvənˈteɪdʒəs] adj vantajoso (sa).

advent [ˈædvənt] n [of invention, person, period] advento m.

➤ **Advent** n RELIG Advento m.

Advent calendar n calendário com figuras decorativas em cada dia das quatro semanas antecedentes ao Natal, marcando o período do Advento.

adventure [ədˈventʃəʳ] n aventura f; **to have no sense of** ~ não ter espírito de aventura.

adventure holiday n férias fpl de aventura.

adventure playground n área de lazer para crianças que oferece materiais diversos para montar e brincar.

adventurer [ədˈventʃərəʳ] n **-1.** [adventurous person] aventureiro m, -ra f **- 2.** [unscrupulous person] inescrupuloso m, -sa f.

adventurous [əd'ventʃərəs] adj -1. [person] intrépido(da) -2. [life, project] aventureiro(ra) -3. [menu, programme etc.] atraente, interessante.

adverb ['ædvɜ:b] n advérbio m.

adverbial ◇ adj adverbial. ◇ n adjunto m adverbial.

adversary ['ædvəsərɪ] (pl -ies) n adversário m, -ria f.

adverse ['ædvɜ:s] adj adverso(sa).

adversely ['ædvɜ:slɪ] adv negativamente.

adversity [əd'vɜ:sətɪ] n (U) adversidade f.

advert ['ædvɜ:t] n UK = advertisement.

advertise ['ædvətaɪz] ◇ vt [job, car, product] anunciar. ◇ vi [in newspaper, on TV, in shop window]: they're advertising for sales representatives estão anunciando vaga para representantes comerciais.

advertisement [əd'vɜ:tɪsmənt] n -1. [in newspaper, on TV, in shop window] anúncio m -2. fig [recommendation] propaganda f.

advertiser ['ædvətaɪzəʳ] n anunciante mf.

advertising ['ædvətaɪzɪŋ] n (U) -1. [advertisements] propaganda f-2. [industry] publicidade f.

advertising agency n agência f de publicidade.

advertising campaign n campanha f publicitária.

advice [əd'vaɪs] n (U) conselho m; to give sb ~ dar conselhos a alguém; to take sb's ~ aceitar conselhos de alguém; a piece of ~ um conselho.

advice note n aviso m de envio.

advisability [əd,vaɪzə'bɪlətɪ] n (U) conveniência f.

advisable [əd'vaɪzəbl] adj aconselhável.

advise [əd'vaɪz] ◇ vt -1. [give advice to]: to ~ sb to do sthg/not to do sthg aconselhar alguém a fazer algo/a não fazer algo -2. [professionally]: to ~ sb on sthg assessorar alguém em algo -3. fml [inform] avisar; to ~ sb of sthg avisar alguém sobre algo. ◇ vi -1. [give advice]: to ~ against sthg/against doing sthg desaconselhar algo/a fazer algo -2. [act as adviser]: to ~ on sthg assessorar em algo.

advisedly [əd'vaɪzɪdlɪ] adv deliberadamente.

adviser UK, **advisor** US [əd'vaɪzəʳ] n assessor m, -ra f.

advisory [əd'vaɪzərɪ] adj [group, organization] de assessoria; **in an ~ capacity** OR **role** com função OR no papel de assessor(ra).

advocacy ['ædvəkəsɪ] n (U) [support] defesa f.

advocate [n 'ædvəkət, vb 'ædvəkeɪt] ◇ n -1. Scot JUR advogado m, -da f -2. [supporter] defensor m, -ra f. ◇ vt fml [recommend] defender.

AEC (abbr of Atomic Energy Commission) n organismo norte-americano de energia nuclear, ≃ CNEN f.

Aegean [i:'dʒi:ən] n: the ~ (Sea) o (Mar) Egeu; in the ~ no Egeu.

aegis ['i:dʒɪs] n: under the ~ of sob a égide de.

aeon UK, **eon** US ['i:ən] n -1. GEOL éon m -2. fig [very long time] século m.

aerial ['eərɪəl] ◇ adj [of, from, in the air] aéreo(rea). ◇ n UK [antenna] antena f.

aerobatics [,eərəʊ'bætɪks] n (U) acrobacias fpl aéreas.

aerobics [eə'rəʊbɪks] n (U) aeróbica f, ginástica f aeróbica.

aerodrome ['eərədrəʊm] n esp UK aeródromo m.

aerodynamic [,eərəʊdaɪ'næmɪk] adj aerodinâmico(ca).

◆ **aerodynamics** ◇ n (U) SCIENCE aerodinâmica f. ◇ npl [aerodynamic qualities] aerodinâmicas f.

aerogramme ['eərəgræm] n aerograma m.

aeronautics [,eərə'nɔ:tɪks] n (U) aeronáutica f.

aeroplane UK ['eərəpleɪn], **airplane** ['eəpleɪn] US n avião m.

aerosol ['eərəsɒl] n aerossol m.

aerospace ['eərəʊspeɪs] n: the ~ industry a indústria aeroespacial.

aesthete, esthete US ['i:sθi:t] n esteta mf.

aesthetic, esthetic US [i:s'θetɪk] adj estético(ca).

aesthetically, esthetically US [i:s'θetɪklɪ] adv esteticamente.

aesthetics, esthetics US [i:s'θetɪks] n (U) estética f.

afar [ə'fɑ:ʳ] adv: from ~ à distância.

AFC (abbr of Association Football Club) n futebol clube britânico, FC f.

AFDC (abbr of Aid to Families with Dependent Children) n associação norte-americana para auxílio a famílias com crianças portadoras de necessidades especiais, ≃ APAE f.

affable ['æfəbl] adj [pleasant] afável.

affair [ə'feəʳ] n -1. [event] acontecimento m -2. [concern] assunto m -3. [extramarital relationship] caso m.

◆ **affairs** npl -1. [business, personal interests] negócios mpl -2. [matters] questões fpl.

affect [ə'fekt] vt -1. [influence, act upon] afetar -2. [imitate, put on] imitar -3. [feign] fingir.

affectation [,æfek'teɪʃn] n -1. [mannerism] afetação f -2. [pretence] fingimento m.

affected [ə'fektɪd] adj [mannered] afetado(da).

affection [ə'fekʃn] n afeição f.

affectionate [ə'fekʃnət] adj afetuoso(osa).

affectionately [ə'fekʃnətlɪ] adv afetuosamente.

affidavit [,æfɪ'deɪvɪt] n juramento m.

affiliate [n ə'fɪlɪət, vb ə'fɪlɪeɪt] ◇ n filiado m, -da f. ◇ vt: to be ~d to OR with sthg ser filiado(da) a algo.

affiliation [ə,fɪlɪ'eɪʃn] n afiliação f.

affinity [ə'fɪnətɪ] (pl -ies) n -1. (U) [attraction] atração f; to have an ~ with sb/sthg sentir atração por alguém/algo -2. [connection, similarity] afinidade f; to have an ~ with sb/sthg ter afinidade com alguém/algo.

affirm [ə'fɜ:m] vt afirmar.

affirmation [,æfə'meɪʃn] n afirmação f.

affirmative [ə'fɜ:mətɪv] ◇ adj afirmativo(va). ◇ n afirmativa f; **to reply in the ~** responder que sim/positivamente.

affix [ə'fɪks] vt [stamp] afixar.

afflict [ə'flɪkt] vt afligir; **to be ~ed with sthg** sofrer de algo.

affliction [ə'flɪkʃn] n -1. [distress] aflição f -2. [physical] doença f.

affluence ['æflʊəns] n (U) riqueza f.

affluent ['æfluəntl *adj* rico(ca).
affluent society *n* sociedade *f* afluente.
afford [ə'fɔːd] *vt* -**1.** [have enough money for]: **to be able to** ~ **sthg** poder pagar por algo - **2.** [time, energy]: **to be able to** ~ **the time (to do sthg)** ter tempo (para fazer algo) - **3.** [allow]: **we can't** ~ **to let this happen** não podemos nos dar ao luxo de deixar que isto aconteça - **4.** *fml* [provide, give] oferecer.
affordable [ə'fɔːdəbl] *adj* acessível.
afforestation [æˌfɒrɪ'steɪʃn] *n (U)* florestamento *m*.
affray [ə'freɪ] *n UK fml* [disturbance] desordem *f*.
affront [ə'frʌnt] <> *n* afronta *f*. <> *vt* ofender.
Afghan ['æfgæn], **Afghani** [æf'gænɪ] <> *adj* afegão(gã) <> *n* afegão *m*, -gã *f*, afegane *mf*.
Afghan hound *n* Afghan hound *mf*.
Afghani *adj* & *n* = **Afghan**.
Afghanistan [æf'gænɪstæn] *n* Afeganistão; **in** ~ no Afeganistão.
afield [ə'fiːld] *adv*: **far** ~ longe.
AFL-CIO (*abbr of* American Federation of Labor and Congress of Industrial Organizations) *n* federação norte-americana de sindicatos da indústria.
afloat [ə'fləʊt] *adj* -**1.** [above water] flutuante - **2.** *fig* [out of debt] em dia.
afoot [ə'fʊt] *adj* [present, happening] em ação.
aforementioned [əˌfɔː'menʃənd], **aforesaid** [ə'fɔːsed] *adj fml* acima mencionado(da).
afraid [ə'freɪd] *adj* -**1.** [frightened] assustado(da); **to be** ~ **(of sb/sth)** ter medo (de alguém/algo); **to be** ~ **of doing** *OR* **to do sthg** ter medo de fazer algo - **2.** [reluctant, apprehensive] apreensivo(va); **to be** ~ **(that)** ter medo (que); **to be** ~ **of sthg** ter medo de algo; **he was** ~ **of losing his job** tinha medo de perder seu emprego - **3.** [in apologies]: **to be** ~ **(that)** ter receio (que); **I'm** ~ **so/not** receio que sim/não.
afresh [ə'freʃ] *adv* novamente.
Africa ['æfrɪkə] *n* África; **in** ~ na África.
African ['æfrɪkən] <> *adj* africano(na). <> *n* africano *m*, -na *f*.
African American <> *adj* afro-americano(na). <> *n* afro-americano *m*, -na *f*.
African violet *n* violeta *f* africana.
Afrikaans [ˌæfrɪ'kɑːns] *n* africâner *m*.
Afrikaner [ˌæfrɪ'kɑːnəʳ] *n* africâner *mf*.
aft [ɑːft] *adv* à popa *OR* ré.
after ['ɑːftəʳ] <> *prep* -**1.** [following - in time] após; [- in order] após; ~ **you!** atrás de você! - **2.** [as a result of] depois - **3.** [in spite of] apesar de - **4.** *inf* [in search of, looking for] atrás de - **5.** [with the name of] em homenagem a - **6.** [directed at sb moving away] atrás de - **7.** *ART* à moda de - **8.** *US* [telling the time]: **it's twenty** ~ **three** são três e vinte. <> *adv* em seguida, depois. <> *conj* depois que/de; ~ **she left university ...** depois que deixou/de deixar a universidade, ela ...
➣ **afters** *npl UK* sobremesa *f*.
➣ **after all** *adv* -**1.** [in spite of everything] apesar de tudo - **2.** [it should be remembered] afinal.
afterbirth ['ɑːftəbɜːθ] *n* placenta *f*.

aftercare ['ɑːftəkeəʳ] *n (U)* ajuda oficial para quem acabou de sair do hospital ou da prisão.
after-effects *npl* efeitos *mpl* secundários, conseqüências *fpl*.
afterlife ['ɑːftəlaɪf] (*pl* -lives [-laɪvz]) *n* vida *f* após a morte.
aftermath ['ɑːftəmæθ] *n* conseqüências *fpl*.
afternoon [ˌɑːftə'nuːn] *n* tarde *f*; **good** ~ boa tarde.
➣ **afternoons** *adv esp US* à tarde.
after-sales service *n* serviço *m* pós-venda.
aftershave ['ɑːftəʃeɪv] *n* loção *f* após-barba.
aftershock ['ɑːftəʃɒk] *n* pequenos tremores *mpl* (após terremoto).
aftersun (lotion) *n* creme *m* hidratante após-sol.
aftertaste ['ɑːftəteɪst] *n* [of food, drink] ressaibo *m*, mau sabor *m*.
afterthought ['ɑːftəθɔːt] *n* pensamento *m* a posteriori.
afterwards, afterward *US* ['ɑːftəwəd(z)] *adv* posteriormente, depois.
again [ə'gen] *adv* -**1.** [one more time] outra vez; ~ **and** ~ repetidas vezes; **all over** ~ tudo de novo; **time and** ~ mil vezes - **2.** [once more as before] de novo - **3.** [asking for information to be repeated]: **what was that** ~? o que foi mesmo que você disse? - **4.** *phr*: **half as much** ~ cinqüenta por cento a mais; **(twice) as much** ~ (duas) vezes mais; **come** ~? *inf* o que?; **then** *OR* **there** ~ por outro lado.
against [ə'genst] <> *prep* -**1.** [gen] contra - **2.** [in contrast to]: **as** ~ em comparação com, em vez de. <> *adv* contra.
age [eɪdʒ] (*cont* ageing *OR* aging) <> *n* -**1.** [of person, animal, thing] idade *f*; **what** ~ **are you?** quantos anos você tem?; **to be of** ~ *US* ser maior de idade; **to come of** ~ atingir à maioridade; **to be under** ~ ser menor de idade; **act your** ~! pare de agir como criança! - **2.** *(U)* [state or process of ageing - of person] idade *f*; [- of object, cheese, wine] tempo *m*; **wine improves with** ~ o vinho melhora com o tempo - **3.** [stage - of person's life] idade *f*, hora *f*; [- of history] era *f*. <> *vt* envelhecer. <> *vi* envelhecer.
➣ **ages** *npl* [a long time]: ~**s ago** séculos atrás; **for** ~**s** há séculos.
aged [*adj sense 1* eɪdʒd, *adj sense 2 & npl* 'eɪdʒɪd] <> *adj* -**1.** [of the stated age] da idade de; **a person** ~ **30** uma pessoa de 30 anos; **to be** ~ **20** ter 20 anos (de idade) - **2.** [very old] envelhecido(da), antigo(ga). <> *npl*: **the** ~ [the elderly] os idosos.
age group *n* grupo *m* etário.
ageing ['eɪdʒɪŋ] <> *adj* -**1.** [getting old - person] idoso(sa); **the** ~ **population** a população de idosos; [- thing] velho(lha), ultrapassado(da) - **2.** [thing] velho(lha), ultrapassado(da). <> *n (U)* [process of getting old] envelhecimento *m*.
ageless ['eɪdʒlɪs] *adj* [person, thing] imutável, eterno(na).
agency ['eɪdʒənsɪ] (*pl* -ies) *n* -**1.** [gen] agência *f* - **2.** [government organisation] órgão *m*.
agenda [ə'dʒendə] (*pl* -s) *n* pauta *f*, agenda *f*.
agent ['eɪdʒənt] *n* -**1.** [person] agente *mf* - **2.** [substance] reagente *m*.
age-old *adj* [very old] antigo(ga).

aggravate [ˈægrəveɪt] *vt* -**1.** [make worse] agravar -**2.** [annoy] irritar.

aggravating [ˈægrəveɪtɪŋ] *adj* [person, behaviour, problem] agravante, irritante.

aggravation [ˌægrəˈveɪʃn] *n (U)* [irritation] agravo *m*, irritação *f*.

aggregate [ˈægrɪgət] <> *adj* total. <> *n* -**1.** [total] total *m* -**2.** [material] agregado *m*.

aggression [əˈgreʃn] *n (U)* agressão *f*.

aggressive [əˈgresɪv] *adj* -**1.** [belligerent] agressivo(-va) -**2.** [forceful - campaign] agressivo(va); [- person] audaz, empreendedor(ra).

aggressively [əˈgresɪvlɪ] *adv* [belligerently] agressivamente.

aggressor [əˈgresəʳ] *n* agressor *m*, -ra *f*.

aggrieved [əˈgriːvd] *adj* [upset, hurt] magoado(da).

aggro [ˈægrəʊ] *n UK inf* arruaça *f*.

aghast [əˈgɑːst] *adj* [horrified] espantado(da); ~ **at sthg** espantado(da) (com algo).

agile [*UK* ˈædʒaɪl, *US* ˈædʒəl] *adj* [body, person, mind] ágil.

agility [əˈdʒɪlətɪ] *n (U)* agilidade *f*.

aging *adj* & *n* = ageing.

agitate [ˈædʒɪteɪt] <> *vt* -**1.** [disturb, worry] perturbar -**2.** [shake] agitar. <> *vi* [campaign actively]: **to ~ for/against sthg** fazer campanha pró/contra algo.

agitated [ˈædʒɪteɪtɪd] *adj* [disturbed, anxious] agitado(-da).

agitation [ˌædʒɪˈteɪʃn] *n* [anxiety] agitação *f*.

agitator [ˈædʒɪteɪtəʳ] *n* [political activist] agitador *m*, -ra *f*.

AGM (*abbr of* **annual general meeting**) *n UK* assembléia *f* geral anual (*de clube, empresa etc*).

agnostic [ægˈnɒstɪk] <> *adj* agnóstico(ca). <> *n* agnóstico *m*, -ca *f*.

ago [əˈgəʊ] *adv* atrás; **three days ~** três dias atrás; **years/long ~** anos/tempos atrás.

agog [əˈgɒg] *adj* ansioso(osa), impaciente; **to be all ~ (with)** estar ansioso(sa) (com).

agonize, -ise [ˈægənaɪz] *vi* agonizar; **to ~ (over** *OR* **about sth)** atormentar-se (com algo).

agonized [ˈægənaɪzd] *adj* [faces, screams] agoniado(-da).

agonizing [ˈægənaɪzɪŋ] *adj* -**1.** [decision, wait] angustiante -**2.** [pain] agonizante.

agonizingly [ˈægənaɪzɪŋlɪ] *adv* [difficult, painful] angustiosamente, dolorosamente.

agony [ˈægənɪ] (*pl* -ies) *n* -**1.** [physical pain] dores *fpl*, agonia *f*; **to be in ~** estar morrendo de dor -**2.** [mental pain] angústia *f*; **to be in ~** estar angustiado(da).

agony aunt *n UK inf* conselheira *f* sentimental.

agony column *n UK inf* consultório *m* sentimental.

agoraphobia [ˌægərəˈfəʊbjəl] *n* agorafobia *f*.

agree [əˈgriː] <> *vi* -**1.** [concur] concordar; **to ~ with sb/sthg** concordar com alguém/algo; **to ~ on sthg** chegar a um acordo sobre algo; **to ~ about sthg** concordar sobre algo -**2.** [consent] concordar; **to ~ to sthg** concordar com algo -**3.** [statements] conferir -**4.** [food]: **to ~ with sb** combinar com alguém -**5.** *GRAMM*: **to ~ (with)** concordar (com). <> *vt* -**1.** [price, terms] concordar -**2.** [concur]: **to ~ that** concordar que -**3.** [arrange]: **to ~ to do sthg** combinar para fazer algo -**4.** [concede]: **to ~ (that)** concordar (que).

agreeable [əˈgriːəbl] *adj* -**1.** [weather, experience] agradável -**2.** [willing]: **to be ~ to sthg** ser favorável a algo.

agreeably [əˈgriːəblɪ] *adv* [pleasantly] agradavelmente.

agreed [əˈgriːd] <> *adj*: **to be ~ on sthg** estar de acordo sobre algo. <> *adv* -**1.** [decided] de acordo -**2.** [admittedly]: **~ (that)** sem dúvida (que).

agreement [əˈgriːmənt] *n* -**1.** [accord] acordo *m*; **to be in ~ with sb/sthg** estar de acordo com alguém/algo -**2.** [settlement, contract] acordo *m*; **to reach an ~** chegar a um acordo -**3.** [consent] aceitação *f* -**4.** *GRAMM* concordância *f*.

agricultural [ˌægrɪˈkʌltʃərəl] *adj* agrícola.

agriculture [ˈægrɪkʌltʃəʳ] *n* [farming] agricultura *f*.

aground [əˈgraʊnd] *adv*: **to run ~** encalhar.

ah [ɑː] *excl* ah!

aha [ɑːˈhɑː] *excl* ah! ah!

ahead [əˈhed] *adv* -**1.** [in front] à frente; **right** *OR* **straight ~** direto em frente -**2.** [forwards] em frente; **to go on ~** ir na frente; **to be sent on ~** ser mandado(da) antes *OR* primeiro -**3.** [in competition, game] à frente -**4.** [indicating success]: **to get ~** ir adiante, prosperar -**5.** [in time] à frente.
➡ **ahead of** *prep* -**1.** [gen] à frente de -**2.** [in time] antes de; **~ of schedule** adiantado(da).

ahoy [əˈhɔɪ] *excl NAUT* à vista!; **land/ship ~!** terra/barco à vista!

AI *n* -**1.** (*abbr of* **Amnesty International**) AI *f*. -**2.** (*abbr of* **artificial intelligence**) IA *f*. -**3.** (*abbr of* **artificial insemination**) IA *f*.

aid [eɪd] <> *n* -**1.** [help] socorro *m*, assistência *f*; **to go to the ~ of sb** socorrer alguém; **in ~ of sb/sthg** em benefício de alguém/algo; **with the ~ of sb/sthg** com a ajuda de alguém/algo -**2.** [device - for teaching, learning] ferramenta *f*; [- for walking, hearing etc] aparelho *m*. <> *vt* -**1.** [help] socorrer -**2.** *JUR*: **to ~ and abet** ser cúmplice de.

aide [eɪd] *n POL* assistente *mf*.

aide-de-camp [eɪdːdəˈkɑː] (*pl* **aides-de-camp**) *n* ajudante-de-ordens *mf*.

AIDS, Aids (*abbr of* **acquired immune deficiency syndrome**) <> *n* AIDS *f*. <> *comp*: **~ specialist** médico *mf* especialista em AIDS; **~ patient** aidético *m*, -ca *f*.

aid worker *n* pessoa que presta assistência em áreas atingidas por catástrofes ou guerras.

AIH (*abbr of* **artificial insemination by husband**) *n* inseminação artificial com sêmen do marido.

ail [eɪl] *vi* [be ill] estar doente.

ailing [ˈeɪlɪŋ] *adj* -**1.** [ill] doente -**2.** *fig* [economy] debilitado(da).

ailment [ˈeɪlmənt] *n* [illness] doença *f*.

AIM (*abbr of* **alternative investment market**) *n* mercado financeiro britânico de investimentos alternativos.

aim [eɪm] <> *n* -**1.** [objective] objetivo *m* -**2.** [in firing gun, arrow] mira *f*; **to take ~ at sthg** apontar para algo. <> *vt* -**1.** [gun, camera]: **to ~ sthg at sb/sthg** mirar algo em alguém/algo -**2.** [plan, programme]:

to be ~ed at doing sthg ser *or* estar voltado(da) para algo **-3.** [remark, criticism]**: to be ~ed at sb** ser *or* estar direcionado(da) para alguém. ⬦ *vi* **-1.** [point weapon] mirar; **to ~ at sthg** mirar em algo **-2.** [intend]**: to ~ at** *or* **for sthg** visar a algo; **to ~ to do sthg** pretender fazer algo.

aimless [ˈeɪmlɪs] *adj* [person, life, work] sem objetivo.

aimlessly [ˈeɪmlɪslɪ] *adv* [wander, look] a esmo, sem rumo.

ain't [eɪnt] *inf* = am not, are not, is not, have not, has not.

air [eəʳ] ⬦ *n* **-1.** [for breathing] ar *m* **-2.** [sky]**: to be seen from the ~** ser visto(ta) do alto *or* de cima; **to throw sthg into the ~** mandar algo pelos ares; **by ~** [travel] de avião; **to be (up) in the ~** *fig* ser avoado(da) **-3.** [distinctive quality] ar *m* **-4.** *literary* [tune] melodia *f* **-5.** RADIO & TV**: to be on the ~** estar no ar **-6.** *phr*: **to clear the ~** *fig* esclarecer as coisas. ⬦ *comp* aéreo(rea). ⬦ *vt* **-1.** [washing, room, bed] arejar **-2.** [feelings, opinions] manifestar **-3.** [broadcast] anunciar. ⬦ *vi* [washing] arejar.
➡ **airs** *npl*: **~s and graces** ares *mpl*; **to give o.s. ~s, to put on ~s** fazer pose.

airbag [ˈeəbæg] *n* AUT airbag *m*.

airbase [ˈeəbeɪs] *n* base *f* aérea.

airbed [ˈeəbed] *n UK* [inflatable mattress] colchão *m* inflável.

airborne [ˈeəbɔ:n] *adj* **-1.** [troops, regiment] transportado(da) por via aérea **-2.** [plane] em vôo.

airbrake [ˈeəbreɪk] *n* freio *m* de ar comprimido.

airbrush [ˈeəbrʌʃ] ⬦ *n* ART aerógrafo *m*. ⬦ *vt* **-1.** ART pintar com aerógrafo **-2.** PHOT retocar com aerógrafo **-3.** *fig*: **an ~ed version** uma versão melhorada.

airbus [ˈeəbʌs] *n* airbus *m*.

air-conditioned [-kənˈdɪʃnd] *adj* climatizado(-da).

air-conditioning [-kənˈdɪʃnɪŋ] *n* ar *m* condicionado.

aircraft [ˈeəkrɑ:ft] (*pl inv*) *n* aeronave *f*, avião *m*.

aircraft carrier *n* porta-aviões *m inv*.

air cushion *n* **-1.** [inflatable cushion] almofada *f* inflável **-2.** [of hovercraft etc] colchão *m* de ar.

airfield [ˈeəfi:ld] *n* aeródromo *m*.

air force ⬦ *n* força *f* aérea. ⬦ *comp* da força aérea.

air freight *n* frete *m* aérea.

air freshener [-ˈfreʃnəʳ] *n* purificador *m* de ar.

airgun [ˈeəgʌn] *n* pistola *f* de ar comprimido.

air hostess *n UK* aeromoça *f*.

airily [ˈeərɪlɪ] *adv* [light-heartedly, casually] despreocupadamente, alegremente.

airing [ˈeərɪŋ] *n*: **to give sthg an ~** [clothes] dar uma arejada em algo; [room] ventilar algo; *fig* [opinion] refrescar algo.

airing cupboard *n UK* armário *m* para secar roupa.

air lane *n* rota *f* aérea.

airless [ˈeəlɪs] *adj* abafado(da).

air letter *n* aerograma *m*.

airlift [ˈeəlɪft] ⬦ *n* transporte *m* aéreo. ⬦ *vt* transportar por via aérea.

airline [ˈeəlaɪn] *n* companhia *f* aérea.

airliner [ˈeəlaɪnəʳ] *n* avião *m* de passageiros.

airlock [ˈeəlɒk] *n* **-1.** [in tube, pipe] retentor *m* de ar **-2.** [airtight chamber] câmara *f* de compressão.

airmail [ˈeəmeɪl] *n* correio *m* aéreo; **by ~** por via aérea.

airman [ˈeəmən] (*pl* **-men** [-mən]) *n* [aviator] aviador *m*.

air mattress *n* colchão *m* de ar.

air miles *npl* milhas *fpl* aéreas.

airplane [ˈeəpleɪn] *n US* = aeroplane.

airplay [ˈeəpleɪ] *n* [on radio] divulgação *m*.

air pocket *n* bolsa *f* de ar.

airport [ˈeəpɔ:t] ⬦ *n* aeroporto *m*. ⬦ *comp* de aeroporto.

air raid *n* ataque *m* aéreo.

air-raid shelter *n* abrigo *m* antiaéreo.

air rifle *n* espingarda *f* de ar comprimido.

airship [ˈeəʃɪp] *n* dirigível *m*.

airsick [ˈeəsɪk] *adj*: **to be ~** estar enjoado(da).

airspace [ˈeəspeɪs] *n* espaço *m* aéreo.

airspeed [ˈeəspi:d] *n* velocidade *f* no ar.

air steward *n* comissário *m* de bordo.

air stewardess *n* aeromoça *f*.

air strike *n* MIL ataque *m* aéreo.

airstrip [ˈeəstrɪp] *n* campo *m* de pouso.

air terminal *n* terminal *m* aéreo.

airtight [ˈeətaɪt] *adj* hermético(ca).

airtime [ˈeətaɪm] *n* [on radio] tempo *m* de transmissão.

air-to-air *adj* [missile] do ar para o ar.

air-traffic control *n* controle *m* de tráfego aéreo.

air-traffic controller *n* controlador *m* de tráfego aéreo.

air travel *n* viagem *f* aérea; **~ is cheaper now** viajar de avião é mais barato agora.

airwaves [ˈeəweɪvz] *npl* ondas *fpl* de rádio.

airy [ˈeərɪ] (*compar* **-ier**, *superl* **-iest**) *adj* **-1.** [room] arejado(da) **-2.** [notions, promises] leviano(na) **-3.** [nonchalant] indiferente.

aisle [aɪl] *n* **-1.** [in church] nave *f* lateral **-2.** [in plane, theatre, shop] corredor *m*.

ajar [əˈdʒɑ:ʳ] *adj* [door] entreaberto(ta).

AK *abbr of* Alaska.

aka (*abbr of* also known as) também conhecido(da) como.

akin [əˈkɪn] *adj* semelhante.

AL *abbr of* Alabama.

Alabama [ˌæləˈbæmə] *n* Alabama.

alabaster [ˌæləˈbɑːstəʳ] *n* alabastro *m*.

à la carte *adj & adv* à la carte.

alacrity [əˈlækrɪtɪ] *n fml* [eagerness] prontidão *f*.

alarm [əˈlɑːm] ⬦ *n* **-1.** [fear] susto *m* **-2.** [device] alarme *m*; **to raise** *or* **sound the ~** dar *or* soar o alarme. ⬦ *vt* [scare] alarmar.

alarm clock *n* despertador *m*.

alarming [əˈlɑːmɪŋ] *adj* alarmante.

alarmingly [əˈlɑːmɪŋlɪ] *adv* [worryingly] de forma alarmante.

alarmist [əˈlɑːmɪst] *adj* [person, ideas] alarmista.

alas [əˈlæs] *excl literary* ai!

Alaska [əˈlæskə] *n* Alasca.

Albania [æl'beɪnjəl] n Albânia; **in ~** na Albânia.
Albanian [æl'beɪnjən] <> adj albanês(nesa). <> n
-1. [person] albanês m, -sa f - 2. [language] albanês m.
albatross ['ælbətrɒs] (pl inv OR -es) n albatroz m.
albeit [ɔ:l'bi:ɪt] conj fml embora.
Alberta [æl'bɜ:tə] n Alberta.
Albert Hall n: **the ~** o Albert Hall.
alderman ['ɔ:ldəmən] (pl -men [-mənl]) n vereador
m.
ale [eɪl] n cerveja f.
alert [ə'lɜ:t] <> adj - 1. [vigilant, aware] alerta; **to be
~ to sthg** estar alerta para algo - 2. [perceptive]
atento(ta). <> n [warning] alerta f; **on the ~**
[watchful] em estado de alerta; **on ~** MIL em estado
de alerta; **to give the ~** dar o sinal de alerta.
<> vt - 1. [warn] alertar, avisar - 2. [make aware]: **to
~ sb to sthg** alertar alguém sobre algo.
Aleutian Islands [ə'lu:ʃjən-] npl: **the ~** as Ilhas
Aleutas.
A level (abbr of Advanced level) n SCH exame feito
ao final do ensino médio na Grã-Bretanha

A LEVEL

Na Grã-Bretanha (à exceção da Escócia), os A-Levels são
exames prestados por aqueles que desejam dar
prosseguimento a seus estudos, após a conclusão do
ensino secundário. Em geral, o estudante faz os A-Levels
aos 18 anos, após dois anos de curso preparatório, e pode
escolher as disciplinas em que prestará seus exames.
Normalmente, são necessários três A-Levels para
ingressar na universidade, embora muita gente preste os
exames apenas para melhorar seu currículo.

Alexander technique n: **the ~** a técnica de
Alexander.
Alexandria [ˌælɪg'zɑ:ndrɪə] n Alexandria; **in ~** em
Alexandria.
alfalfa [æl'fælfə] n alfalfa f.
alfresco [æl'freskəʊ] adj, adv [meal, eat] ao ar livre.
algae ['ældʒi:] npl algas fpl.
Algarve [æl'gɑ:v] n: **the ~** o Algarve; **in the ~** no
Algarve.
algebra ['ældʒɪbrə] n álgebra f.
Algeria [æl'dʒɪərɪə] n Argélia; **in ~** na Argélia.
Algerian [æl'dʒɪərɪən] <> adj argelino(na). <> n
argelino m, -na f.
Algiers [æl'dʒɪəz] n Argel; **in ~** em Argel.
algorithm ['ælgərɪðml] n algoritmo m.
alias ['eɪlɪəs] (pl -es) <> adv vulgo. <> n nome m
falso.
alibi ['ælɪbaɪ] n álibi m.
alien ['eɪlɪən] <> adj - 1. [foreign] estrangeiro(ra) - 2.
[from outer space] alienígena - 3. [unfamiliar] estra-
nho(nha). <> n - 1. [from outer space] alienígena mf
- 2. JUR [foreigner] estrangeiro m, -ra f.
alienate ['eɪljəneɪt] vt [estrange] alienar.
alienation [ˌeɪljə'neɪʃn] n - 1. [estrangement] afastamento m - 2. [feeling of not belonging] alienação f.
alight [ə'laɪt] (pt & pp -ed OR alit) <> adj [on fire] em
chamas. <> vi fml - 1. [land] pousar - 2. [from train,
bus] descer; **to ~ from sthg** descer de algo.
align [ə'laɪn] vt - 1. [line up] alinhar - 2. [ally]: **to ~ o.s.
with sb** aliar-se a alguém.

alignment [ə'laɪnmənt] n - 1. [of car wheels, brakes,
books] alinhamento m - 2. [with an ally] aliança f.
alike [ə'laɪk] <> adj [two people, things] semelhante,
parecido(da). <> adv [in a similar way] de forma
semelhante; **they look ~** eles são parecidos.
alimentary canal [ˌælɪ'mentərɪ-] n tubo m digestivo.
alimony ['ælɪmənɪ] n pensão f (alimentícia).
A-line adj evasê.
alive [ə'laɪv] adj - 1. [living] vivo(va); **to come ~**
ganhar vida - 2. [aware]: **to be ~ to sthg** estar
consciente de algo - 3. [full]: **to be ~ with sthg**
estar cheio(cheia) de algo, fervilhar de algo.
alkali ['ælkəlaɪ] (pl -s OR -es) n álcali m.
alkaline ['ælkəlaɪn] adj alcalino(na).
all [ɔ:l] <> adj - 1. [with singular noun] todo(da); **~ the
money** o dinheiro todo; **~ the time** sempre; **we
were out ~ day** estivemos fora o dia inteiro. - 2.
[with plural noun] todos(das); **~ the houses** todas as
casas; **~ trains stop at Trenton** todos os trens
param em Trenton. <> adv - 1. [completely]
completamente; **~ alone** completamente só. - 2.
[in scores]: **it's two ~** dois a dois (empate). - 3. [in
phrases]: **~ but empty** quase vazio(zia); **~ over**
[finished] terminado(da). <> pron - 1. [everything]
tudo; [people, things] todos mpl, -das fpl; **is that ~?**
[in store] mais alguma coisa?; **the best of ~** o
melhor de todos. - 2. [everybody] todos, todo o
mundo; **~ of us went** fomos todos. - 3. [in
phrases]: **can I help you at ~** posso ajudar em
alguma coisa?; **in ~** [in total] ao todo; **in ~ it was a
great success** resumindo, foi um grande êxito.
Allah ['ælə] n Alá m.
all-around adj US = all-round.
allay [ə'leɪ] vt fml - 1. [calm] abrandar - 2. [solve, settle]
dirimir.
all clear n - 1. [signal] sinal de fim de estado de
alerta - 2. fig [go-ahead] permissão f para prosseguir.
allegation [ˌælɪ'geɪʃn] n alegação f; **to make ~s
(about sb/sthg)** fazer alegações (sobre alguém/
algo).
allege [ə'ledʒ] vt [claim] alegar; **to ~ that** alegar
que.
alleged [ə'ledʒd] adj suposto(ta).
allegedly [ə'ledʒɪdlɪ] adv supostamente.
allegiance [ə'li:dʒəns] n: **~ (to sb/sthg)** lealdade
(a alguém/algo).
allegorical [ˌælɪ'gɒrɪkl] adj alegórico(ca).
allegory ['ælɪgərɪ] (pl -ies) n alegoria f.
alleluia [ˌælɪ'lu:jə] excl aleluia!
allergic [ə'lɜ:dʒɪk] adj alérgico(ca); **~ to sthg** lit &
fig alérgico(ca) a algo.
allergy ['ælədʒɪ] (pl -ies) n alergia f; **to have an ~
to sthg** ter alergia a algo.
alleviate [ə'li:vɪeɪt] vt [ease] aliviar.
alley(way) ['ælɪ(weɪ)] n [narrow path] beco m.
alliance [ə'laɪəns] n - 1. [agreement] acordo m - 2. [un-
ion] aliança f.
allied ['ælaɪd] adj - 1. [powers, troops] aliado(da) - 2.
[related] relacionado(da).
alligator ['ælɪgeɪtəʳ] (pl inv OR -s) n aligátor m.
all-important adj [crucial] crucial.

all-in *adj UK* [price] tudo incluído.
  all in *adj inf* [tired] exausto(ta). *adv UK* [inclusive] com extras incluído.
all-in-one *n* [garment - underwear or for cycling] macaquinho *m*; [- top and trousers] macacão *m*.
all-in wrestling *n* luta *f* livre.
alliteration [ə,lɪtə'reɪʃn] *n* aliteração *f*.
all-night *adj* [party, vigil, session] que dura toda a noite; [chemist's, shop] 24 horas.
allocate ['æləkeɪt] *vt*: **to ~ sthg to sb/sthg** [money, resources, items] alocar algo para alguém/algo; [task] atribuir algo para alguém/algo.
allocation [,ælə'keɪʃn] *n* -**1.** [sharing out - of money, resources, items] alocação *f*; [- of task, responsibility] atribuição *f* -**2.** [share - of money, resources] alocação *f*; [- of tickets, seats, places] atribuição *f*.
allot [ə'lɒt] (*pt* & *pp* -**ted**, *cont* -**ting**) *vt* [allocate - task] distribuir; [- money, resources] repartir; [- time] dedicar.
allotment [ə'lɒtmənt] *n* -**1.** *UK* [garden] lote *m* -**2.** [sharing out - of tasks, resources] distribuição *f*; [- of money] partilha *f*; [- of time] dedicação *f* -**3.** [share - of money, resources] cota *f*; [- of time] alocação *f*.
all-out *adj* [effort] supremo(ma) ; [war] total ; [attack] resoluto(ta).
allow [ə'laʊ] *vt* -**1.** [permit] permitir; **to ~ sb to do sthg** permitir *or* deixar alguém fazer algo; **~ me** permita-me, deixe-me -**2.** [allocate] destinar -**3.** [admit]: **to ~ (that)** admitir que.
  allow for *vt fus* levar em conta *or* consideração.
allowable [ə'laʊəbl] *adj* [acceptable] aceitável, permitido(da).
allowance [ə'laʊəns] *n* -**1.** [grant] subsídio *m*, auxílio *m* -**2.** *Am* [pocket money] mesada *f* -**3.** *FIN* [tax exemption] isenção *f* -**4.** [excuse]: **to make ~ s for sb/sthg** fazer concessões para alguém *or* algo.
alloy ['ælɔɪ] *n* [metal] liga *f*.
all-powerful *adj* onipotente, todo-poderoso(sa).
all right *adv* -**1.** [gen] bem -**2.** [indicating agreement] sim, o.k. -**3.** [do you understand?]: **all right?** certo? -**4.** [now then] certo, o.k. *adj* -**1.** [healthy, unharmed]: **to be ~** estar bem -**2.** *inf* [acceptable, satisfactory]: **how was the film? - ~ , I suppose** como foi o filme? - legal, imagino; **sorry I'm late - that's ~** desculpe, estou atrasada - não tem importância -**3.** [permitted]: **is it ~ if ...?** tudo bem se ...?, posso ...?
all-round *UK*, **all-around** *US adj* -**1.** [athlete, worker] versátil -**2.** [improvement] global.
all-rounder [-'raʊndə^r] *n* -**1.** [versatile person] pessoa *f* versátil -**2.** *SPORT*: **he is an ~ at football** no futebol, ele se destaca em várias posições.
all-terrain vehicle *n* (veículo) *m* fora-de-estrada *m*.
all-time *adj* [record, best]: **it was an ~ record** foi um recorde insuperável; **one of the ~ greatest songs** uma das melhores canções de todos os tempos.
allude [ə'luːd] *vi*: **to ~ to sthg** aludir a algo.
allure [ə'ljʊə^r] *n* [attraction] fascinação *f*, encanto *m*.
alluring [ə'ljʊərɪŋ] *adj* [attractive] fascinante, encantador(ra).
allusion [ə'luːʒn] *n* [reference] alusão *f*.

ally [*n* 'ælaɪ, *vb* ə'laɪ] (*pl* -**ies**, *pt* & *pp* -**ied**) *n* -**1.** *MIL* & *POL* aliado *m*, -da *f* -**2.** [associate, helper] associado *m*, -da *f*. *vt*: **to ~ o.s. with sb** aliar-se a alguém.
almanac ['ɔːlmənæk] *n* [book] almanaque *m*.
almighty [ɔːl'maɪtɪ] *adj inf* [enormous] enorme.
  Almighty *adj* onipotente. *n*: **the Almighty** o Todo-Poderoso.
almond ['ɑːmənd] *n* -**1.** [nut] amêndoa *f* -**2.** [tree] amendoeira *f*.
almond paste *n* pasta *f* de amêndoas.
almost ['ɔːlməʊst] *adv* quase, praticamente.
alms [ɑːmz] *npl dated* esmola *f*.
aloft [ə'lɒft] *adv* -**1.** [in the air] no ar, nas alturas -**2.** *NAUT* no topo do mastro.
alone [ə'ləʊn] *adj* [without others] só, sozinho(nha); **to be ~ with sb** estar a sós com alguém. *adv* -**1.** [without others] só; **to go it ~** fazer algo por conta própria -**2.** [only] somente, só; **he ~ knows the answer** só *or* somente ele sabe a resposta -**3.** [untouched, unchanged]: **to leave sthg ~** deixar algo em paz, parar de mexer em algo; **leave me ~!** deixe-me em paz!
  let alone *conj* sem falar em.
along [ə'lɒŋ] *adv*: **they went ~ to the demonstration** eles foram *or* se dirigiram para a demonstração; **she insisted on coming ~** ela insistiu em vir junto *or* também; **I took her ~ to the concert** levei-a comigo ao concerto. *prep* -**1.** [from one end to the other] ao longo de -**2.** [beside] ao lado de, junto de -**3.** [in] em.
  all along *adv* o tempo todo.
  along with *prep* junto com.
alongside [ə,lɒŋ'saɪd] *prep* [next to] junto a; [beside] ao lado de. *adv* lado a lado.
aloof [ə'luːf] *adj* [reserved] reservado(da). *adv* [distant]: **to remain ~ (from sthg)** ficar indiferente (a algo).
aloud [ə'laʊd] *adv* alto, em voz alta.
alpaca [æl'pækə] *n* -**1.** [animal] alpaca *f* -**2.** [material] lã *f* de alpaca.
alphabet ['ælfəbet] *n* alfabeto *m*.
alphabetical [,ælfə'betɪkl] *adj* alfabético(ca); **in ~ order** em ordem alfabética.
alphabetically [,ælfə'betɪklɪ] *adv* alfabeticamente, em ordem alfabética.
alphabetize, -ise ['ælfəbətaɪz] *vt* alfabetizar.
alphanumeric key *n* *COMPUT* tecla *f* alfanumérica.
alpine ['ælpaɪn] *adj* alpino(na).
Alps [ælps] *npl*: **the ~** os Alpes; **in the ~** nos Alpes.
already [ɔːl'redɪ] *adv* já.
alright [,ɔːl'raɪt] *adv* & *adj* = **all right**.
Alsace [æl'sæs] *n* Alsácia; **in ~** na Alsácia.
Alsatian [æl'seɪʃn] *adj* alsaciano(na). *n* -**1.** [person] alsaciano *m*, -na *f* -**2.** [dog] pastor *m* alemão.
also ['ɔːlsəʊ] *adv* [as well] também.
also-ran *n* -**1.** [gen] perdedor *m*, -ra *f* -**2.** [horseracing] *cavalo que não chega entre os três primeiros.*
Alta *abbr of* Alberta.
altar ['ɔːltə^r] *n* altar *m*.

alter [ˈɔːltəʳ] ⬦ *vt* [change, modify] alterar. ⬦ *vi* alterar-se.

alteration [ˌɔːltəˈreɪʃn] *n* -**1.** [act of changing] alteração *f*, modificação *f* -**2.** [change] alteração *f*, mudança *f*; **to make an** ~ *OR* ~**s to sthg** fazer uma alteração *OR* alterações em algo.

altercation [ˌɔːltəˈkeɪʃn] *n fml* altercação *f*.

alter ego (*pl* -**s**) *n* alter ego *m*.

alternate [*adj UK* ɔːlˈtɜːnət, *US* ˈɔːltərnət, *vb* ˈɔːltərneɪt] ⬦ *adj* alternado(da). ⬦ *vt* alternar. ⬦ *vi:* **to ~ (with)** alternar(com); **to ~ between sthg and sthg** alternar entre uma coisa e outra.

alternately [ɔːlˈtɜːnətlɪ] *adv* [by turns] alternadamente.

alternating current [ˈɔːltəneɪtɪŋ-] *n ELEC* corrente *f* alternada.

alternation [ˌɔːltəˈneɪʃn] *n* alternação *f*, alternância *f*.

alternative [ɔːlˈtɜːnətɪv] ⬦ *adj* alternativo(va). ⬦ *n* alternativa *f*; **an ~ to sb/sthg** uma alternativa a alguém/algo; **to have no ~ (but to do sthg)** não ter alternativa (a não ser fazer algo).

alternatively [ɔːlˈtɜːnətɪvlɪ] *adv* por outro lado, de outro modo.

alternative medicine *n* medicina *f* alternativa.

alternator [ˈɔːltəneɪtəʳ] *n ELEC* alternador *m*.

although [ɔːlˈðəʊl] *conj* embora, apesar de.

altitude [ˈæltɪtjuːd] *n* altitude *f*.

alto [ˈæltəʊ] (*pl* -**s**) ⬦ *n* contralto *m*. ⬦ *comp* [flute, saxophone] alto.

altogether [ˌɔːltəˈgeðəʳ] *adv* -**1.** [completely] completamente, totalmente -**2.** [in general] de modo geral, no geral -**3.** [in total] ao todo, no total.

altruism [ˈæltruːɪzm] *n* altruismo *m*.

altruistic [ˌæltrʊˈɪstɪk] *adj* altruista.

aluminium *UK* [ˌæljʊˈmɪnɪəm], **aluminum** *US* [əˈluːmɪnəm] ⬦ *n* alumínio *m*. ⬦ *comp* de alumínio; ~ **foil** papel-alumínio *m*.

alumnus [əˈlʌmnəs] (*pl* -**ni** [-naɪ]) *n* ex-aluno *m*, -na *f*.

always [ˈɔːlweɪz] *adv* sempre.

am [æm] *vb* ▷ **be**.

a.m. (ante meridiem): **at three** ~ às três da manhã.

AM (*abbr of* amplitude modulation) *n* -**1.** AM *f*. -**2.** (*abbr of* Master of Arts) (*titular de*) *diploma de mestre em ciências humanas nos Estados Unidos.*

AMA (*abbr of* American Medical Association) *n associação norte-americana de médicos,* ≃ AMB *f*.

amalgam [əˈmælgəm] *n* -**1.** *fml* [combination] amálgama *m OR f* -**2.** *TECH* [of metals] amálgama *m OR f*.

amalgamate [əˈmælgəmeɪt] ⬦ *vt* [unite] amalgamar, misturar. ⬦ *vi* [unite] unir-se.

amalgamation [əˌmælgəˈmeɪʃn] *n* [process] amalgamação *f*.

amass [əˈmæs] *vt* [fortune, power, information] acumular.

amateur [ˈæmətəʳ] ⬦ *adj* amador(ra). ⬦ *n* amador *m*, -ra *f*.

amateurish [ˌæməˈtɜːrɪʃ] *adj pej* [unprofessional]

malfeito(ta), mal-acabado(da).

amaze [əˈmeɪz] *vt* [astonish] surpreender, assombrar.

amazed [əˈmeɪzd] *adj* surpreso(sa), assombrado(da).

amazement [əˈmeɪzmənt] *n* surpresa *f*, assombro *m*.

amazing [əˈmeɪzɪŋ] *adj* [incredible] incrível, surpreendente.

amazingly [əˈmeɪzɪŋlɪ] *adv* [very] surpreendentemente.

Amazon [ˈæməzn] *n* -**1.** [river]: **the** ~ o Amazonas -**2.** [region]: **in the** ~ na Amazônia; **the ~ (Basin)** a bacia amazônica; **the ~ rainforest** a floresta amazônica -**3.** [woman] amazona *f*.

Amazonian [ˌæməˈzəʊnjən] *adj* amazônico(ca).

ambassador [æmˈbæsədəʳ] *n* embaixador *m*, -ra *f*.

amber [ˈæmbəʳ] ⬦ *adj* -**1.** [amber-coloured] ambárico(ca), ambariano(na) -**2.** *UK* [traffic light] amarelo(la). ⬦ *n* -**1.** [substance] âmbar *m* -**2.** *UK* [colour of traffic light] amarelo *m*. ⬦ *comp* [made of amber] de âmbar.

ambiance [ˈæmbɪəns] *n* = ambience.

ambidextrous [ˌæmbɪˈdekstrəs] *adj* ambidestro(tra).

ambience [ˈæmbɪəns] *n* [atmosphere] ambiente *m*, atmosfera *f*.

ambiguity [ˌæmbɪˈgjuːətɪ] (*pl* -**ies**) *n* ambigüidade *f*.

ambiguous [æmˈbɪgjʊəs] *adj* ambíguo(gua).

ambiguously [æmˈbɪgjʊəslɪ] *adv* de modo ambíguo.

ambition [æmˈbɪʃn] *n* ambição *f*.

ambitious [æmˈbɪʃəs] *adj* ambicioso(sa).

ambivalence [æmˈbɪvələns] *n* -**1.** [uncertainty] incerteza *f* -**2.** [ambiguity] ambivalência *f*.

ambivalent [æmˈbɪvələnt] *adj* -**1.** [uncertain] incerto(ta) -**2.** [ambiguous] ambivalente.

amble [ˈæmbl] *vi* [walk] passear.

ambulance [ˈæmbjʊləns] ⬦ *n* ambulância *f*. ⬦ *comp* [service, driver] de ambulância.

ambush [ˈæmbʊʃ] ⬦ *n* emboscada *f*. ⬦ *vt* [attack] emboscar.

ameba *n US* = amoeba.

ameliorate [əˈmiːljəreɪt] *vt & vi fml* melhorar.

amen [ˌɑːˈmen] *excl* [at end of prayer] amém!

amenable [əˈmiːnəbl] *adj:* ~ **(to sthg)** receptivo(va) (a algo).

amend [əˈmend] *vt* [change] emendar, corrigir.
➡ **amends** *npl:* **to make** ~**s (for sthg)** compensar (por algo).

amendment [əˈmendmənt] *n* -**1.** [change] correção *f* -**2.** [act of changing] emenda *f*.

amenities [əˈmiːnətɪz] *npl* comodidades *fpl*, conforto *m*.

America [əˈmerɪkə] *n* América, Estados Unidos (da América); **in ~** na América, nos Estados Unidos (da América).
➡ **Americas** *npl:* **the ~s** as Américas, a América.

American [əˈmerɪkn] ⬦ *adj* americano(na), estadunidense. ⬦ *n* americano *m*, -na *f*, estadunidense *mf*.

American football n UK futebol m americano.
American Indian n ameríndio m.
Americanism [ə'merɪkənɪzm] n [word, phrase] americanismo m.
americanize, -ise [ə'merɪkənaɪz] vt americanizar.
amethyst ['æmɪθɪst] n ametista f.
Amex n (abbr of American Stock Exchange) segunda maior bolsa de valores dos Estados Unidos.
amiable ['eɪmjəbl] adj [pleasant, likable] amável.
amiably ['eɪmjəblɪ] adv amavelmente.
amicable ['æmɪkəbl] adj [friendly] amigável.
amicably ['æmɪkəblɪ] adv amigavelmente.
amid(st) [ə'mɪd(st)] prep fml [among] entre, no meio de.
amino acid [ə'mi:nəʊ-] n aminoácido m.
amiss [ə'mɪs] <> adj [wrong] errado(da). <> adv [wrongly]: **to take sthg ~** levar algo a mal.
Amman n Amã; **in ~** em Amã.
ammo ['æməʊ] n inf MIL munição f.
ammonia [ə'məʊnjə] n [liquid] amônia f; [gas] amoníaco m.
ammunition [ˌæmjʊ'nɪʃn] n **-1.** [bombs, bullets] munição f **-2.** fig [information, argument] argumento m.
ammunition dump n paiol m, depósito m de munição.
amnesia [æm'ni:zjə] n amnésia f.
amnesty ['æmnəstɪ] (pl -ies) n anistia f.
Amnesty International n Anistia f Internacional.
amniocentesis n amniocentese f.
amoeba UK (pl -bas OR -bae [-bi:]), **ameba** US (pl - bas OR -bae [-bi:]) [ə'mi:bə] n ameba f.
amok [ə'mɒk] adv: **to run ~** correr cega e furiosamente com o intuito de matar.
among(st) [ə'mʌŋ(st)] prep **-1.** [surrounded by, in middle of] no meio de, entre **-2.** [within, between, included in] entre.
amoral [ˌeɪ'mɒrəl] adj [person, behaviour] amoral.
amorous ['æmərəs] adj amoroso(sa).
amorphous [ə'mɔ:fəs] adj amorfo(fa).
amortize [ə'mɔ:taɪz] vt fɪn amortizar.
amount [ə'maʊnt] n **-1.** [quantity] quantidade f, volume m **-2.** [sum of money] quantia f.
◆ **amount to** vt fus **-1.** [total] totalizar, atingir a quantia de **-2.** [be equivalent to] equivaler.
amp n **-1.** (abbr of ampere) A. **-2.** fam (abbr of amplifier) amplificador m.
amperage ['æmpərɪdʒ] n ELEC amperagem f.
ampere ['æmpeə'] n ampère m.
ampersand ['æmpəsænd] n ampersand m (nome do sinal gráfico '&')
amphetamine [æm'fetəmi:n] n anfetamina f.
amphibian [æm'fɪbɪən] n anfíbio m.
amphibious [æm'fɪbɪəs] adj [animal, vehicle] anfíbio(bia).
amphitheatre UK, **amphitheater** US ['æmfɪˌθɪətə'] n anfiteatro m.
ample ['æmpl] adj **-1.** [enough] suficiente **-2.** [large] amplo(pla).
amplification [ˌæmplɪfɪ'keɪʃn] n **-1.** [of sound] amplificação f **-2.** [of idea, statement] ampliação f.

amplifier ['æmplɪfaɪə'] n [for radio, stereo] amplificador m.
amplify ['æmplɪfaɪ] (pt & pp -ied) <> vt **-1.** [sound] amplificar **-2.** [idea, statement] ampliar. <> vi [expand]: **to ~ (on sthg)** complementar (algo).
amply ['æmplɪ] adv **-1.** [sufficiently] amplamente **-2.** [considerably] consideravelmente.
ampoule UK, **ampule** US ['æmpu:l] n ampola f.
amputate ['æmpjʊteɪt] <> vt [limb] amputar. <> vi [perform amputation] amputar.
amputation [ˌæmpjʊ'teɪʃn] n amputação f.
Amsterdam [ˌæmstə'dæm] n Amsterdã; **in ~** em Amsterdã.
Amtrak ['æmtræk] n empresa pública de trens mais importante dos Estados Unidos no transporte de passageiros.
amuck [ə'mʌk] adv = amok.
amulet ['æmjʊlɪt] n amuleto m.
amuse [ə'mju:z] vt **-1.** [cause to laugh, smile] divertir **-2.** [entertain] entreter; **to ~ o.s. (by doing sthg)** entreter-se (fazendo algo).
amused [ə'mju:zd] adj **-1.** [entertained, delighted] divertido(da), entretido(da); **to be ~ at OR by sthg** estar entretido(da) com algo **-2.** [entertained]: **to keep o.s. ~** entreter-se.
amusement [ə'mju:zmənt] n **-1.** [enjoyment] divertimento m **-2.** [diversion, game] diversão f, entretenimento m.
amusement arcade n fliperama m.
amusement park n parque m de diversões.
amusing [ə'mju:zɪŋ] adj [funny] divertido(da).
an [stressed æn, unstressed ən] indef art ⊳ a².
anabolic steroid [ˌænə'bɒlɪk-] n esteróide m anabólico OR anabolizante.
anachronism [ə'nækrənɪzm] n anacronismo m.
anachronistic [əˌnækrə'nɪstɪk] adj anacrônico(ca).
anaemia UK, **anemia** US [ə'ni:mjə] n anemia f.
anaemic UK, **anemic** US [ə'ni:mɪk] adj [suffering from anaemia] anêmico(ca).
anaesthesia UK, **anesthesia** US [ˌænɪs'θi:zjə] n anestesia f.
anaesthetic UK, **anesthetic** US [ˌænɪs'θetɪk] n anestésico m; **under ~** anestesiado(da).
anaesthetist UK, **anesthetist** US [æ'ni:sθətɪst] n anestesista mf.
anaesthetize UK, **-ise** UK, **anesthetize** US [æ'ni:sθətaɪz] vt anestesiar.
anagram ['ænəgræm] n anagrama m.
anal ['eɪnl] adj anal.
analgesic [ˌænæl'dʒi:sɪk] <> adj analgésico(ca). <> n analgésico m.
analog adj & n US = analogue.
analogous [ə'næləgəs] adj fml [comparable]: **~ (to sthg)** análogo OR semelhante (a algo).
analogue, analog US ['ænəlɒg] <> adj [watch, clock] analógico(ca). <> n fml [similar object, device] análogo m.
analogy [ə'nælədʒɪ] (pl -ies) n [similarity] analogia f; **to draw an ~ with/between** fazer uma analogia com/entre; **by ~** por analogia.
analyse UK, **analyze** US ['ænəlaɪz] vt [examine] analisar.

analysis [ə'næləsɪs] (*pl* **analyses** [ə'næləsi:z]) *n* **-1.** análise *f* **-2.** *phr:* **in the final** *OR* **last** ~ afinal de contas.

analyst ['ænəlɪst] *n* **-1.** [political, computer, statistics] analista *mf* **-2.** [psychoanalyst] psicanalista *mf*.

analytic(al) [,ænə'lɪtɪk(l)] *adj* [person, study, approach] analítico(ca).

analyze *vt US* = **analyse**.

anarchic [æ'nɑ:kɪk] *adj* [lacking control] anárquico(-ca).

anarchist ['ænəkɪst] *n* *POL* anarquista *mf*.

anarchy ['ænəkɪ] *n* [lawlessness, disorder] anarquia *f*.

anathema [ə'næθəməl] *n* [object of dislike, disapproval] anátema *m*.

anatomical [,ænə'tɒmɪkl] *adj* anatômico(ca).

anatomy [ə'nætəmɪ] (*pl* **-ies**) *n* anatomia *f*.

ANC (*abbr of* **African National Congress**) *n* Congresso *m* Nacional Africano.

ancestor ['ænsestə'] *n* **-1.** [person] ancestral *mf*, antepassado *m*, -da *f* **-2.** *fig* [of machine, vehicle] antecessor *m*, -ra *f*.

ancestral home [æn'sestrəl-] *n* casa *f* dos antepassados.

ancestry ['ænsestrɪ] (*pl* **-ies**) *n* linhagem *f*.

anchor ['æŋkə'] <> *n* **-1.** *NAUT* âncora *f*; **to drop/ weigh** ~ lançar/içar âncora **-2.** *TV* [presenter] âncora *mf*. <> *vt* **-1.** [secure] assegurar **-2.** *TV* [present] apresentar. <> *vi NAUT* ancorar.

anchorage ['æŋkərɪdʒ] *n* **-1.** *NAUT* ancoradouro *m* **-2.** [means of securing] ancoragem *f*.

anchorman ['æŋkəmæn] (*pl* **-men** [-menl]) *n* *TV* âncora *m*.

anchorwoman ['æŋkə,wʊmən] (*pl* **women** [-,wɪmɪn]) *n* *TV* âncora *f*.

anchovy ['æntʃəvɪ] (*pl inv OR* **-ies**) *n* anchova *f*.

ancient ['eɪnʃənt] *adj* **-1.** [dating from distant past] antigo(ga) **-2.** *hum* [very old] pré-histórico(ca).

ancillary [æn'sɪlərɪ] *adj* [staff, workers, device] auxiliar.

and [strong form ænd, weak form ənd, ənl *conj* **-1.** [as well as, in addition to] e **-2.** [in numbers] e **-3.** *(with infinitive)* [in order to]: **come** ~ **see!** venha ver!; **try** ~ **come!** tente vir!; **to wait** ~ **see** esperar para ver.
➡ **and all that** *adv* e (todas) essas coisas.
➡ **and so on, and so forth** *adv* e assim por diante.

Andes ['ændi:z] *n:* **the** ~ os Andes; **in** ~ nos Andes.

Andorra [æn'dɔ:rə] *n* Andorra; **in** ~ em Andorra.

androgynous [æn'drɒdʒɪnəs] *adj* andrógino(na).

android ['ændrɔɪd] *n* andróide *mf*.

anecdote ['ænɪkdəʊt] *n* anedota *f*.

anemia *n US* = **anaemia**.

anemic *adj US* = **anaemic**.

anemone [ə'nemənɪ] *n* anêmona *f*.

anesthetic *etc* *n US* = **anaesthetic** etc.

anew [ə'nju:] *adv* novamente.

angel ['eɪndʒəl] *n* **-1.** *RELIG* anjo *m* **-2.** *fig inf* [delightful person] anjo *m*.

Angeleno [,ændʒə'li:nəʊ] *n* *habitante de ou nascido em Los Angeles*.

angelic [æn'dʒelɪk] *adj* angélico(ca).

anger ['æŋgə'] <> *n* raiva *f*. <> *vt* irritar, zangar.

angina [æn'dʒaɪnə] *n* angina *f*.

angle ['æŋgl] <> *n* **-1.** *MATH* ângulo *m* **-2.** [corner] canto *m*, ângulo *m* **-3.** [point of view] ângulo *m* **-4.** [slope] ladeira *f*; **at an** ~ [aslant] em ângulo. <> *vt* [slant] apresentar tendenciosamente. <> *vi* **-1.** [fish] pescar **-2.** [manoeuvre]: **to** ~ **for sthg** tramar para obter algo.

Anglepoise (lamp)® ['æŋglpɔɪz-] *n* luminária *f* de mesa *(flexível)*.

angler ['æŋglə'] *n* pescador *m*, -ra *f* (de linha e anzol).

Anglican ['æŋglɪkən] <> *adj* anglicano(na). <> *n* anglicano *m*, -na *f*.

anglicism ['æŋglɪsɪzm] *n* anglicismo *m*.

angling ['æŋglɪŋ] *n* [fishing] pesca *f* (com linha e anzol).

Anglo- *prefix* anglo-.

Anglo-Saxon [,æŋgləʊ'sæksn] <> *adj* anglo-saxão(ônica). <> *n* **-1.** [person] anglo-saxão *m*, -ônica *f* **-2.** [language] anglo-saxão *m*.

Angola [æŋ'gəʊlə] *n* Angola; **in** ~ em Angola.

Angolan [æŋ'gəʊlən] <> *adj* angolano(na). <> *n* angolano *m*, -na *f*.

angora [æŋ'gɔ:rə] *n* **-1.** [goat] angorá *f*; [rabbit] angorá *mf* **-2.** [material] angorá *m*.

angrily ['æŋgrəlɪ] *adv* com irritação *OR* raiva.

angry ['æŋgrɪ] (*compar* **-ier**, *superl* **-iest**) *adj* zangado(da), furioso(sa); **to be** ~ **(with sb)** estar zangado(da) (com alguém); **to get** ~ **(with sb)** zangar-se (com alguém).

angst [æŋst] *n* ânsia *f*.

anguish ['æŋgwɪʃ] *n* angústia *f*.

anguished ['æŋgwɪʃt] *adj* angustiado(da).

angular ['æŋgjʊlə'] *adj* [face, jaw, body] angular.

animal ['ænɪml] <> *adj* animal. <> *n* **-1.** [living creature] animal *m* **-2.** *inf pej* [brutal person] animal *m*.

animate ['ænɪmət] *adj* animado(da).

animated ['ænɪmeɪtɪd] *adj* animado(da).

animated cartoon *n* desenho *m* animado.

animation [,ænɪ'meɪʃn] *n* animação *f*.

animosity [,ænɪ'mɒsətɪ] (*pl* **-ies**) *n* animosidade *f*.

aniseed ['ænɪsi:d] *n* semente *f* de anis.

ankle ['æŋkl] <> *n* tornozelo *m*. <> *comp:* ~ **deep** até o tornozelo.

annals ['ænlz] *npl fml* anais *mpl*.

annex ['æneks] *vt* anexar.

annexation [,ænek'seɪʃn] *n* anexação *f*.

annexe ['æneks] *n* [building] anexo *m*.

annihilate [ə'naɪəleɪt] *vt* [destroy] aniquilar.

annihilation [ə,naɪə'leɪʃn] *n* [destruction] aniquilação *f*.

anniversary [,ænɪ'vɜ:sərɪ] (*pl* **-ies**) *n* aniversário *m* *(de casamento, de independência, etc.)*.

annotate ['ænəteɪt] *vt fml* comentar.

annotated *adj:* ~ **edition** edição *f* comentada.

announce [ə'naʊns] *vt* anunciar.

announcement [ə'naʊnsmənt] *n* [public statement] anúncio *m*.

announcer [ə'naʊnsə'] *n:* **television/radio** ~ locutor de televisão/rádio.

annoy [ə'nɔɪ] *vt* [irritate] irritar, amolar.

annoyance [ə'nɔɪəns] *n* irritação *f*, aborrecimento *m*.

annoyed [ə'nɔɪd] *adj* irritado(da); **to be** ~ **at sthg**

estar irritado(da) com algo; **to be** ~ **with sb** estar irritado(da) com alguém; **to get** ~ irritar-se.

annoying [ə'nɔɪɪŋ] *adj* irritante.

annual ['ænjʊəl] <> *adj* anual. <> *n* -**1.** [plant] planta *f* sazonal -**2.** [book] anuário *m*, publicação *f* anual.

annual general meeting *n* reunião *f* geral anual.

annually ['ænjʊəlɪ] *adv* anualmente.

annuity [ə'nju:ɪtɪ] (*pl* -**ies**) *n FIN* anuidade *m*.

annul [ə'nʌl] (*pt* & *pp* -**led**, *cont* -**ling**) *vt* anular, invalidar.

annulment [ə'nʌlmənt] *n* anulação *f*.

annum ['ænəm] *n*: **per** ~ por ano.

Annunciation [ə,nʌnsɪ'eɪʃn] *n*: **the** ~ a Anunciação.

anode ['ænəʊd] *n TECH* ânodo *m*.

anoint [ə'nɔɪnt] *vt RELIG* ungir.

anomalous [ə'nɒmələs] *adj fml* anômalo(la).

anomaly [ə'nɒməlɪ] (*pl* -**ies**) *n* [different thing, person] anomalia *f*.

anon. (*abbr of* **anonymous**) anônimo(ma).

anonymity [,ænə'nɪmətɪ] *n* anonimato *m*, anonímia *f*.

anonymous [ə'nɒnɪməs] *adj* anônimo(ma).

anonymously [ə'nɒnɪməslɪ] *adv* anonimamente.

anorak ['ænəræk] *n esp UK* anoraque *m*.

anorexia (nervosa) [,ænə'reksɪə(nɜ:'vəʊsə)] *n* anorexia *f* nervosa.

anorexic [,ænə'reksɪk] <> *adj* anoréxico(ca). <> *n* anoréxico *m*, -ca *f*.

another [ə'nʌðəʳ] <> *adj* -**1.** [additional] outro(tra); **in** ~ **few minutes ...** dentro de alguns minutos ... -**2.** [different] outro(tra). <> *pron* -**1.** [an additional one] outro *m*, -tra *f*; **one after** ~ um(a) depois do(da) outro(tra) -**2.** [a different one] outro *m*, -tra *f*; **to argue with one** ~ discutir um com o outro/ uma com a outra; **to love one** ~ amar-se.

ANSI (*abbr of* **American National Standards Institute**) *n instituto norte-americano de padronização*, ≃ ABNT *f*.

answer ['ɑ:nsəʳ] <> *n* [reply] resposta *f*; **in** ~ **to** sthg em resposta a algo. <> *vt* -**1.** responder -**2.** [respond to]: **to** ~ **the door/phone** atender a porta/o telefone. <> *vi* [reply] responder.
◆ **answer back** <> *vt sep* retrucar. <> *vi* retrucar.
◆ **answer for** *vt fus* responder por.

answerable ['ɑ:nsərəbl] *adj* [accountable] responsável; ~ **to sb** adequado(da) a alguém; ~ **for sthg** responsável por algo.

answering machine, answerphone ['ɑ:nsərɪŋ-] *n* secretária *f* eletrônica.

ant [ænt] *n* formiga *f*.

antacid [,ænt'æsɪd] *n* antiácido *m*.

antagonism [æn'tægənɪzm] *n* antagonismo *m*.

antagonist [æn'tægənɪst] *n* antagonista *mf*.

antagonistic [æn,tægə'nɪstɪk] *adj* antagônico(ca).

antagonize, -ise [æn'tægənaɪz] *vt* hostilizar.

Antarctic [æn'tɑ:ktɪk] <> *n*: **the** ~ o Antártico; **in the** ~ no Antártico. <> *adj* antártico(ca).

Antarctica [æn'tɑ:ktɪkə] *n* Antártica *f*.

Antarctic Circle *n*: **the** ~ o Círculo Polar Antártico.

Antarctic Ocean *n*: **the** ~ o Oceano Antártico.

ante ['æntɪ] *n inf fig inf*: **to up** OR **raise the** ~ jogar alto.

anteater ['ænt,i:təʳ] *n* tamanduá *m*.

antecedent [,æntɪ'si:dənt] *n fml* [earlier event] antecedente *m*.

antediluvian [,æntɪdɪ'lu:vjən] *adj hum* [outdated] antidiluviano(na).

antelope ['æntɪləʊp] (*pl inv* OR -**s**) *n* antílope *m*.

antenatal [,æntɪ'neɪtl] *adj* pré-natal.

antenatal clinic *n* clínica *f* pré-natal.

antenna [æn'tenə] (*pl sense 1* -**nae** [-ni:], *pl sense 2* -**s**) *n* -**1.** [of insect, lobster] antena *f* -**2.** US [aerial] antena *f*.

anteroom ['æntɪrʊm] *n* -**1.** [antechamber] ante-sala *f* -**2.** [waiting room] sala *f* de espera.

anthem ['ænθəm] *n* [song, hymn] hino *m*.

anthill ['ænthɪl] *n* formigueiro *m*.

anthology [æn'θɒlədʒɪ] (*pl* -**ies**) *n* antologia *f*.

anthrax ['ænθræks] *n* antraz *m*.

anthropologist [,ænθrə'pɒlədʒɪst] *n* antropólogo *m*, -ga *f*.

anthropology [,ænθrə'pɒlədʒɪ] *n* antropologia *f*.

anti- ['æntɪ] *prefix* anti.

anti-aircraft [,æntɪ'eəkrɑ:ft] *adj* antiaéreo(a).

antiapartheid *adj* antiapartheid.

antiballistic missile [,æntɪbə'lɪstɪk-] *n* míssil *m* antibalístico.

antibiotic [,æntɪbaɪ'ɒtɪk] *n* [medicine] antibiótico *m*.

antibody ['æntɪ,bɒdɪ] (*pl* -**ies**) *n BIOL* anticorpo *m*.

anticipate [æn'tɪsɪpeɪt] *vt* -**1.** [expect, experience prematurely] prever -**2.** [preempt] antecipar-se a.

anticipation [æn,tɪsɪ'peɪʃn] *n* -**1.** [advance action] antecipação *f*; **thanking you in** ~ antecipadamente grato(ta) -**2.** [expectation] expectativa *f*; **in** ~ **of** na expectativa de -**3.** [foresight] pressentimento *m*.

anticlimax [,æntɪ'klaɪmæks] *n* [disappointment] anticlímax *m*.

anticlockwise UK [,æntɪ'klɒkwaɪz] <> *adj* [direction] em sentido anti-horário. <> *adv* em sentido anti-horário.

antics ['æntɪks] *npl* -**1.** [of children, animals] palhaçadas *fpl* -**2.** *pej* [of politician etc] trapaças *fpl*.

anticyclone [,æntɪ'saɪkləʊn] *n METEOR* anticiclone *m*.

antidepressant [,æntɪdɪ'presnt] <> *adj* antidepressivo(va). <> *n* [drug] antidepressivo *m*.

antidote ['æntɪdəʊt] *n* -**1.** [drug, medicine] antídoto *m*; ~ **to sthg** antídoto contra algo -**2.** *fig* [relief] antídoto.

antifreeze ['æntɪfri:z] *n* anticongelante *m*.

Antigua [æn'ti:gə] *n* Antígua *f*; **in** ~ em Antígua.

antihero ['æntɪ,hɪərəʊ] (*pl* -**es**) *n* [in literature] anti-herói *m*.

antihistamine [,æntɪ'hɪstəmɪn] <> *adj* anti-histamínico(ca). <> *n* anti-histamínico *m*.

antinuclear *adj* antinuclear.

antipathy [æn'tɪpəθɪ] *n* antipatia *f*; ~ **to** OR **towards sb/sthg** antipatia por alguém/algo.

antipersonnel ['æntɪ,pɜ:sə'nell] *adj* MIL contra pessoas.

antiperspirant [ˌæntɪ'pɜːspərənt] n desodorante m.

Antipodes [æn'tɪpədiːz] npl: **the ~** as Antípodas (Austrália e Nova Zelândia).

antiquarian [ˌæntɪ'kweərɪən] <> adj [bookshop, bookseller] de antiguidades. <> n [antique collector] antiquário m.

antiquated ['æntɪkweɪtɪd] adj antiquado(da).

antique [æn'tiːk] <> adj [furniture, object] antigo(-ga). <> n [pece·of furniture, object] antiguidade f.

antique dealer n antiquário m.

antique shop n loja f de antiguidades.

antiquity [æn'tɪkwətɪ] (pl -ies) n antiguidade f.

anti-Semitic [-sɪ'mɪtɪk] adj anti-semita.

anti-Semitism [ˌæntɪ'semɪtɪzm] n anti-semitismo m.

antiseptic [ˌæntɪ'septɪk] <> adj anti-séptico(ca). <> n anti-séptico m.

antisocial [ˌæntɪ'səʊʃl] adj anti-social.

antistatic [ˌæntɪ'stætɪk] adj antiestático(ca).

anti-tank adj MIL antitanque.

antithesis [æn'tɪθɪsɪs] (pl -theses [-θɪsiːz]) n fml [direct opposite] antítese f.

antlers ['æntləz] npl cornos mpl.

antonym ['æntənɪm] n antônimo m.

Antrim n [county] Antrim; **in ~** em Antrim.

Antwerp ['æntwɜːp] n Antuérpia; **in ~** em Antuérpia.

anus ['eɪnəs] n ânus m.

anvil ['ænvɪl] n bigorna f.

anxiety [æŋ'zaɪətɪ] (pl -ies) n -1. [worry] ansiedade f -2. [cause of worry] angústia f -3. [keenness] anseio m.

anxious ['æŋkʃəs] adj -1. [worried] preocupado(da); **to be ~ about sb/sthg** estar preocupado(da) com alguém/algo -2. [keen]: **to be ~ to do sthg** estar ansioso(sa) por fazer algo; **to be ~ that** estar ansioso(sa) para que.

anxiously ['æŋkʃəslɪ] adv -1. [nervously] nervosamente -2. [eagerly] ansiosamente.

any ['enɪ] <> adj -1. (with negative) nenhum(ma); **I haven't got ~ money** não tenho dinheiro nenhum; **he never does ~ work** ele nunca faz trabalho algum -2. [some] (with sg n) algum(ma) ; (with pl n) alguns(mas); **can I be of ~ help?** posso ajudar (em algo)?; **have you got ~ money?** você tem algum dinheiro? -3. [no matter which] qualquer; **~ box will do** qualquer caixa serve. <> pron -1. (with negative) nenhum(ma); **I didn't buy ~ of them** não comprei nenhum deles -2. [some] algum(ma); **do you have ~?** você tem (algum)?; **if ~** se é que algum -3. [no matter which one or ones] qualquer um (uma); **take ~ you like** pegue qualquer um que você queira. <> adv -1. (with negative): **I don't want it ~ more** não quero mais isto; **I can't stand it ~ longer** não agüento mais isto -2. [some, a little] um pouco; **is that ~ better/different?** está um pouco melhor/diferente?

anybody ['enɪˌbɒdɪ] pron = anyone.

anyhow ['enɪhaʊ] adv -1. [in spite of that] assim mesmo -2. [carelessly] de qualquer jeito -3. [returning to topic in conversation] seja como for.

anyone ['enɪwʌn] pron -1. (in negative statements) ninguém -2. (in questions) alguém -3. [someone]

alguém -4. [any person] qualquer pessoa.

anyplace adv US = anywhere.

anything ['enɪθɪŋ] pron -1. (in negative statements) nada -2. (in questions) algo -3. [something] algo, qualquer coisa -4. [any object, event] qualquer coisa.

➤ **anything but** adv: **he wasn't friendly when I saw him, ~ but** ele não foi amigável quando o vi, muito pelo contrário; **she was ~ but complimentary about my painting** ela não foi nada elogiosa sobre meus quadros.

anyway ['enɪweɪ] adv [in any case] de qualquer forma.

anywhere ['enɪweə'], **anyplace** US ['enɪpleɪs] adv -1. (in negative statements) nenhum lugar -2. (in questions) em/a algum lugar -3. [any place] (em) qualquer lugar -4. [unspecified amount, number] aproximadamente; **to last ~ from three weeks to two months** durar algo entre três semanas e dois meses.

Anzac (abbr of Australia–New Zealand Army Corps) n corporação de soldados australianos ou neozelandeses.

AOB, a.o.b. (abbr of any other business) questão que não foi incluída na pauta principal de uma reunião.

Apache [ə'pætʃɪ] n [native American] apache m.

apart [ə'pɑːt] adv -1. [separated in space] à parte, separadamente, distante; **we're living ~** estamos vivendo separados; **the houses were only a few yards ~ from each other** as casas ficavam a apenas algumas jardas de distância uma da outra; **I had to keep them ~** eu tinha que mantê-los à distância -2. [to pieces] em pedaços -3. [aside, excepted] à parte.

➤ **apart from** <> prep [except for] exceto, a não ser (por). <> conj [in addition to] além de.

apartheid [ə'pɑːθeɪt] n apartheid m.

apartment [ə'pɑːtmənt] n apartamento m.

apartment building n prédio m de apartamentos.

apathetic [ˌæpə'θetɪk] adj apático(ca).

apathy ['æpəθɪ] n apatia f.

APB (abbr of all points bulletin) n US mensagem de rádio da polícia sobre pessoa que está sendo procurada.

ape [eɪp] <> n [animal] macaco m, -ca f. <> vt pej [imitate] imitar.

Apennines ['æpɪnaɪnz] npl: **the ~** os Apeninos.

aperitif [əperə'tiːf] n aperitivo m.

aperture ['æpəˌtjʊə'] n abertura f.

apex ['eɪpeks] (pl -es OR apices) n [top] ápice m.

Apex (abbr of advance purchase excursion) n UK passagem comprada com antecedência e que oferece descontos.

aphid ['eɪfɪd] n pulgão m.

aphorism ['æfərɪzm] n aforismo m.

aphrodisiac [ˌæfrə'dɪzɪæk] <> adj afrodisíaco(ca). <> n afrodisíaco m.

apices ['eɪpɪsiːz] pl ➤ apex.

apiece [ə'piːs] adv [each] cada.

aplomb [ə'plɒm] n [composure] compostura f.

apocalypse [ə'pɒkəlɪps] n apocalípse m.

apocalyptic [ə‚pɒkə'lɪptɪk] *adj* apocalíptico(ca).
apogee ['æpədʒiː] *n fig* & *fml* [peak] apogeu *m*.
apolitical [‚eɪpə'lɪtɪkəl] *adj* [non-political] apolítico (ca).
apologetic [ə‚pɒlə'dʒetɪk] *adj* arrependido(da); **to be ~ about sthg** estar arrependido(da) em relação a algo, desculpar-se por algo.
apologetically [ə‚pɒlə'dʒetɪklɪ] *adv* em tom de desculpas.
apologize, -ise [ə'pɒlədʒaɪz] *vi* [say sorry]: **to ~ to sb for sthg** pedir desculpas a alguém por algo.
apology [ə'pɒlədʒɪ] (*pl* **-ies**) *n* [spoken, written] desculpa *f*.
apoplectic [‚æpə'plektɪk] *adj* **-1.** MED apoplético(ca) **-2.** *inf* [very angry] furioso(sa).
apoplexy ['æpəpleksɪ] *n* MED apoplexia *f*.
apostle [ə'pɒsl] *n* RELIG apóstolo *m*.
apostrophe [ə'pɒstrəfɪ] *n* GRAMM apóstrofe *f*.
appal (*UK pt* & *pp* **-led**, *cont* **-ling**), **appall** US [ə'pɔːl] *vt* [shock deeply] horrorizar.
Appalachian [‚æpə'leɪtʃən] *n*: **the ~s** os Apalaches; **the ~ Mountains** os Montes Apalache.
appall *vt US* = **appal**.
appalled [ə'pɔːld] *adj* horrorizado(da).
appalling [ə'pɔːlɪŋ] *adj* **-1.** [shocking] espantoso(sa) **-2.** *inf* [very bad] terrível.
appallingly [ə'pɔːlɪŋlɪ] *adv* **-1.** [shockingly] espanto-samente **-2.** *inf* [very badly] terrivelmente.
apparatus [‚æpə'reɪtəs] (*pl inv OR* **-es**) *n* **-1.** [equipment] aparelho *m* **-2.** [system, organization] organiza-ção *f*.
apparel [ə'pærəl] *n US* traje *m*.
apparent [ə'pærənt] *adj* aparente; **for no ~ reason** sem nenhuma razão aparente.
apparently [ə'pærəntlɪ] *adv* aparentemente.
apparition [‚æpə'rɪʃn] *n fml* [ghost] aparição *f*.
appeal [ə'piːl] ⟨> *vi* **-1.** [request] apelar; **to ~ to sb for sthg** apelar a alguém por algo **-2.** [to sb's hon-our, common sense]: **to ~ to sthg** apelar para algo **-3.** [contest a decision or verdict] recorrer; **to ~ against sthg** recorrer contra algo **-4.** [attract, inter-est]: **to ~ (to sb)** agradar a alguém. ⟨> *n* **-1.** [re-quest] apelo *m* **-2.** [contesting a decision or verdict] apelação *m* **-3.** [charm, interest] encanto *m*.
appealing [ə'piːlɪŋ] *adj* [attractive] encantador(ra).
appear [ə'pɪəʳ] ⟨> *vi* **-1.** [gen] aparecer **-2.** [act] atuar **-3.** JUR comparecer. ⟨> *vt* [seem]: **to ~ to be/do sthg** aparentar ser/fazer algo; **it would ~ that ...** parecería que.
appearance [ə'pɪərəns] *n* **-1.** [arrival] chegada *f* **-2.** [becoming visible - of person] aparecimento *m*; [- of object] chegada *f*; [- of rash etc. on skin] surgimento *m*; **to make an ~** aparecer; **to put in an ~** marcar presença **-3.** [outward aspect] aparência *f*; **to keep up ~s** manter as aparências; **by OR to all ~s** a julgar pelas aparências **-4.** [bodily features] aspec-to *m* **-5.** [in play, film, on TV] participação *f*.
appease [ə'piːz] *vt* **-1.** [placate] apaziguar **-2.** [satis-fy] saciar.
appeasement [ə'piːzmənt] *n* **-1.** [placating, pol] apaziguamento *m*, conciliação *f* **-2.** [satisfaction] satisfação *f*.

append [ə'pend] *vt fml* [add]: **to ~ sthg (to sthg)** anexar algo a algo.
appendage [ə'pendɪdʒ] *n* anexo *m*.
appendices [ə'pendɪsiːz] *pl* ▷ **appendix**.
appendicitis [ə‚pendɪ'saɪtɪs] *n* apendicite *f*.
appendix [ə'pendɪks] (*pl* **-dixes** OR **-dices**) *n* apên-dice *m*; **to have one's ~ out** OR **removed** sofrer a remoção do apêndice.
appertain *vi fml*: **to ~ to sthg** ser pertinente a algo.
appetite ['æpɪtaɪt] *n* **-1.** [for food] apetite *m*; **~ for sthg** desejo por algo **-2.** *fig* [enthusiasm]: **~ for sthg** gosto por algo.
appetizer, -iser ['æpɪtaɪzəʳ] *n* [food] entrada *f*; [drink] aperitivo *m*.
appetizing, -ising ['æpɪtaɪzɪŋ] *adj* [food] apetito-so(sa).
applaud [ə'plɔːd] ⟨> *vt* **-1.** [clap for] aplaudir **-2.** *fig* [approve] aplaudir. ⟨> *vi* [clap] aplaudir.
applause [ə'plɔːz] *n* aplauso *m*.
apple ['æpl] *n* maçã *f*; **to be the ~ of sb's eye** ser a menina dos olhos de alguém.
apple pie *n* torta *f* de maçã.
apple tree *n* macieira *f*.
appliance [ə'plaɪəns] *n* [device] utensílio *m*.
applicable [ə'plɪkəbl] *adj* apropriado(da); **~ to sb/sthg** apropriado(da) a alguém/algo.
applicant ['æplɪkənt] *n* candidato *m*, -ta *f*; **~ for sthg** [job] candidato(ta) a algo; [state benefit] pre-tendente a algo *m*.
application [‚æplɪ'keɪʃn] *n* **-1.** [gen] aplicação *f* **-2.** [for job, college, club] inscrição *f*; **~ for sthg** inscrição para algo **-3.** COMPUT aplicativo *m*.
application form *n* ficha *f* de inscrição.
applicator ['æplɪkeɪtəʳ] *n* aplicador *m*.
applied [ə'plaɪd] *adj* [science] aplicado(da).
appliqué [ə'pliːkeɪ] *n* SEWING aplique *m*.
apply [ə'plaɪ] (*pt* & *pp* **-ied**) ⟨> *vt* **-1.** [rule, skill] aplicar; **to ~ o.s. (to sthg)** dedicar-se a algo; **to ~ one's mind to sthg** concentrar-se em algo **-2.** [paint, ointment] aplicar **-3.** [brakes] usar. ⟨> *vi* **-1.** [for work, grant] candidatar-se; **to ~ for sthg** candidatar-se a algo; **to ~ to sb for sthg** recorrer a alguém por algo **-2.** [be relevant] aplicar-se; **to ~ to sb/sthg** aplicar-se a alguém/algo.
appoint [ə'pɔɪnt] *vt* **-1.** [to job, position] nomear; **to ~ sb to/as sthg** nomear alguém para/como algo **-2.** *fml* [time, place] marcar.
appointment [ə'pɔɪntmənt] *n* **-1.** (U) [to job, posi-tion] nomeação *f*; **'by ~ to Her Majesty the Queen'** 'por indicação de Sua Majestade, a Rainha' **-2.** [job, position] posição *f* **-3.** [with doctor, hairdresser, in business] hora *f* marcada; **to have an ~** ter uma hora marcada; **to make an ~** marcar uma hora; **by ~** com hora marcada; **the doctor only sees patients by ~** o médico só atende (pacientes) com hora marcada.
apportion [ə'pɔːʃn] *vt* [money, blame] dividir.
apposite ['æpəzɪt] *adj fml* apropriado(da).
appraisal [ə'preɪzl] *n* [report, opinion] apreciação *f*.
appraise [ə'preɪz] *vt fml* [evaluate] apreciar.
appreciable [ə'priːʃəbl] *adj* [noticeable] apreciável.

appreciably [ə'pri:ʃəblɪ] *adv* [noticeably] visivelmente.

appreciate [ə'pri:ʃɪeɪt] ⬦ *vt* **-1.** [value] valorizar **-2.** [recognize, understand] reconhecer **-3.** [be grateful for] reconhecer. ⬦ *vi* FIN [increase in value] valorizar.

appreciation [ə,pri:ʃɪ'eɪʃn] *n* **-1.** (U) [liking] apreciação *m* **-2.** (U) [recognition, understanding] reconhecimento *f* **-3.** (U) [gratitude] gratidão *m* **-4.** FIN [increase in value] valorização *f* **-5.** [assessment] avaliação *f*.

appreciative [ə'pri:ʃjətɪv] *adj* apreciativo(va).

apprehend [,æprɪ'hend] *vt fml* [arrest] deter.

apprehension [,æprɪ'henʃn] *n* [anxiety] apreensão *f*.

apprehensive [,æprɪ'hensɪv] *adj* [anxious]: ~ **(about sthg)** apreensivo(va) com algo.

apprehensively [,æprɪ'hensɪvlɪ] *adv* apreensivamente.

apprentice [ə'prentɪs] ⬦ *n* [trainee] aprendiz *mf*, estagiário(ria). ⬦ *vt*: **to be ~d to sb** tornar-se aprendiz de alguém.

apprenticeship [ə'prentɪʃɪp] *n* estágio *m*.

appro. (*abbr of* **approval**) *n fam*: **on ~** sujeito(ta) à aprovação.

approach [ə'prəʊtʃ] ⬦ *n* **-1.** [arrival] chegada *f* **-2.** [way in, access] acesso *m* **-3.** [method] abordagem *m* **-4.** [proposal]: **to make an ~ to sb** fazer uma proposta a alguém. ⬦ *vt* **-1.** [come near to] aproximar-se de **-2.** [speak to]: **to ~ sb about sthg** abordar alguém sobre algo; COMM sondar alguém sobre algo **-3.** [deal with] abordar **-4.** [approximate, reach] alcançar. ⬦ *vi* aproximar-se.

approachable [ə'prəʊtʃəbl] *adj* acessível.

approaching [ə'prəʊtʃɪŋ] *adj* [in time] próximo(ma); [in space] que se aproxima.

approbation [,æprə'beɪʃn] *n fml* [approval] sanção *f*.

appropriate [*adj* ə'prəʊprɪət, *vb* ə'prəʊprɪeɪt] ⬦ *adj* [suitable] apropriado(da). ⬦ *vt* **-1.** [steal] apropriar-se de **-2.** [allocate] destinar.

appropriately [ə'prəʊprɪətlɪ] *adv* adequadamente.

appropriation [ə,prəʊprɪ'eɪʃn] *n* **-1.** [stealing] apropriação *f* **-2.** [allocation] alocação *f*.

approval [ə'pru:vl] *n* **-1.** [liking, admiration] aprovação *f* **-2.** [official agreement] sanção *f* **-3.** COMM: **on ~** sob condição.

approve [ə'pru:v] ⬦ *vi*: **to ~ (of sb/sthg)** ser a favor de alguém/algo. ⬦ *vt* [ratify] aprovar.

approved [ə'pru:vd] *adj* aprovado(da).

approving [ə'pru:vɪŋ] *adj* [favourable] favorável.

approx. (*abbr of* **approximately**) aprox.

approximate [*adj* ə'prɒksɪmət, *vb* ə'prɒksɪmeɪt] ⬦ *adj* aproximado(da). ⬦ *vi*: **to ~ to sthg** aproximar-se de algo.

approximately [ə'prɒksɪmətlɪ] *adv* aproximadamente.

approximation [ə,prɒksɪ'meɪʃn] *n* **-1.** [estimate] aproximação *f* **-2.** [similar thing]: ~ **(to sthg)** semelhança com algo.

Apr. (*abbr of* **April**) abr.

APR *n* **-1.** (*abbr of* **annualized percentage rate**) taxa *f* de juros anual. **-2.** (*abbr of* **annual purchase rate**) taxa *f* de aquisição anual.

après-ski [,æpreɪ'ski:] *n* après-ski *m*, entretenimento noturno e atividades sociais que ocorrem nos lugares em que se costuma ir esquiar.

apricot ['eɪprɪkɒt] ⬦ *n* **-1.** [fruit] damasco *m* **-2.** [colour] laranja claro *m*. ⬦ *comp* de damasco.

apricot tree *n* damasqueiro *m*.

April ['eɪprəl] *n* abril *m*; *see also* **September**.

April Fools' Day *n* primeiro *m* de abril.

APRIL FOOLS' DAY

Assim como no Brasil, também na Grã-Bretanha e nos Estados Unidos é costume pregar peças em amigos e conhecidos no 1° de abril. Nessa data, até mesmo os jornais mais sérios e as estações de rádio e TV brincam com seus leitores, ouvintes e espectadores, divulgando notícias falsas.

---

apron ['eɪprən] *n* **-1.** [clothing] avental *m*; **to be tied to sb's ~ strings** *inf* estar preso(sa) à saia de alguém **-2.** AERON pátio *m* de manobras.

apropos ['æprəpəʊ] *fml* ⬦ *adj* [pertinent] concernente. ⬦ *prep*: ~ **(of)** a propósito de.

apt [æpt] *adj* **-1.** [pertinent] adequado(da) **-2.** [likely]: **to be ~ to do sthg** costumar fazer algo.

Apt. (*abbr of* **apartment**) apto.

aptitude ['æptɪtju:d] *n* [skill] aptidão *f*; **to have an ~ for sthg** ter aptidão para algo.

aptitude test *n* teste *m* de aptidão.

aptly ['æptlɪ] *adv* [suitably] apropriadamente.

aqualung ['ækwəlʌŋ] *n* aqualung *m*.

aquamarine [,ækwəmə'ri:n] *n* [colour] azul-turquesa *m*.

aquaplane ['ækwəpleɪn] *vi* UK AUT aquaplanar.

aquarium [ə'kweərɪəm] (*pl* **-riums** OR **-ria** [-rɪə]) *n* aquário *m*.

Aquarius [ə'kweərɪəs] *n* **-1.** [sign] Aquário *m* **-2.** [person] aquariano *m*, -na *f*.

aquatic [ə'kwætɪk] *adj* aquático(ca).

aqueduct ['ækwɪdʌkt] *n* aqueduto *m*.

AR *abbr of* **Arkansas**.

ARA (*abbr of* **Associate of the Royal Academy**) *n* membro associado da Royal Academy, academia real britânica de artes.

Arab ['ærəb] ⬦ *adj* árabe. ⬦ *n* [person, horse] árabe *mf*.

Arabia [ə'reɪbjə] *n* Arábia *f*; **in ~** na Arábia.

Arabian [ə'reɪbjən] ⬦ *adj* árabe. ⬦ *n* [person] árabe *mf*.

Arabian desert *n*: **the ~** o deserto da Arábia.

Arabian Peninsula *n*: **the ~** a Península Arábica.

Arabian Sea *n*: **the ~** o Mar das Arábias.

Arabic ['ærəbɪk] ⬦ *adj* arábico(ca). ⬦ *n* [language] arábico *m*.

Arabic numeral *n* algarismo *m* arábico.

arable ['ærəbl] *adj* cultivável.

Arab League *n*: **the ~** a Liga Árabe.

arbiter ['ɑ:bɪtəʳ] *n fml* [judge] árbitro *m*.

arbitrary ['ɑ:bɪtrərɪ] *adj* [random] arbitrário(ria).

arbitrate ['ɑ:bɪtreɪt] *vi* arbitrar.

arbitration [,ɑ:bɪ'treɪʃn] *n* arbitragem *f*; **to go to ~** ir à arbitragem.

arc [ɑ:k] *n* [curve] arco *m*.

ARC (*abbr of* **AIDS-related complex**) *n* ARC *m*, complexo *m* relacionado à AIDS.

arcade [ɑ:'keɪd] *n* arcada *f*.

arch [ɑ:tʃ] <> *adj* [knowing] travesso(sa). <> *n* arco *m*. <> *vt* [back, eyebrow] arquear. <> *vi* arquear-se.

arch- [ɑ:tʃ] *prefix* [chief] arqui.

archaeological [,ɑ:kɪə'lɒdʒɪkl] *adj* arqueológico(-ca).

archaeologist [,ɑ:kɪ'ɒlədʒɪst] *n* arqueólogo *m*, -ga *f*.

archaeology [,ɑ:kɪ'ɒlədʒɪ] *n* arqueologia *f*.

archaic [ɑ:'keɪɪk] *adj* **-1.** [ancient] arcaico(ca) **-2.** [old-fashioned] antiquado(da).

archangel ['ɑ:k,eɪndʒəl] *n* arcanjo *m*.

archbishop [,ɑ:tʃ'bɪʃəp] *n* arcebispo *m*.

archduchess [,ɑ:tʃ'dʌtʃɪs] *n* arquiduquesa *f*.

archduke [,ɑ:tʃ'dju:k] *n* arquiduque *m*.

arched [ɑ:tʃt] *adj* **-1.** ARCHIT em arco **-2.** [curved] arqueado(da).

archenemy [,ɑ:tʃ'enmɪ] (*pl* **-ies**) *n* arqui-inimigo *m*, -ga *f*.

archeology etc [,ɑ:kɪ'ɒlədʒɪ] *n* = **archaeology etc**.

archer ['ɑ:tʃəʳ] *n* arqueiro *m*.

archery ['ɑ:tʃərɪ] *n* arco-e-flecha *m*.

archetypal [,ɑ:kɪ'taɪpl] *adj* [typical] arquetípico(ca).

archetype ['ɑ:kɪtaɪp] *n* arquétipo *m*.

archipelago [,ɑ:kɪ'pelɪgəʊ] (*pl* **-es** OR **-s**) *n* arquipélago *m*.

architect ['ɑ:kɪtekt] *n* **-1.** [of buildings] arquiteto *m*, -ta *f* **-2.** *fig* [of plan, event] idealizador *m*, -ra *f*.

architectural [,ɑ:kɪ'tektʃərəl] *adj* arquitetônico(-ca).

architecture ['ɑ:kɪtektʃəʳ] *n* arquitetura *f*.

archive file ['ɑ:kaɪv-] *n* COMPUT arquivo *m* armazenado.

archives ['ɑ:kaɪvz] *npl* [of documents] arquivo *m*.

archivist ['ɑ:kɪvɪst] *n* arquivista *mf*.

archway ['ɑ:tʃweɪ] *n* passagem *f* em arco.

Arctic ['ɑ:ktɪk] <> *adj* **-1.** GEOGR ártico(ca) **-2.** *inf* [very cold] gélido(da). <> *n*: **the ~** o Ártico; **in the ~** no Ártico.

Arctic Circle *n*: **the ~** o Círculo Polar Ártico.

Arctic Ocean *n*: **the ~** o Oceano Ártico.

ardent ['ɑ:dənt] *adj* [passionate] ardente.

ardour UK, **ardor** US ['ɑ:dəʳ] *n* [zeal] ardor *m*.

arduous ['ɑ:djʊəs] *adj* [difficult] árduo(a).

are [stressed ɑ:ʳ, unstressed əʳ] (cf **a**, **an**) *vb* ▷ **be**.

area ['eərɪə] *n* **-1.** [gen] área *f*; **in the ~** na área **-2.** *fig* [approximate size, number]: **in the ~ of** ao redor de.

area code *n* US código *m* de área.

arena [ə'ri:nə] *n* **-1.** SPORT estádio *m* **-2.** *fig* [area of activity] área *f*.

aren't [ɑ:nt] = **are not**.

Argentina [,ɑ:dʒən'ti:nə] *n* Argentina; **in ~** na Argentina.

Argentine ['ɑ:dʒəntaɪn], **Argentinian** <> *adj* argentino(na). <> *n* [person] argentino *m*, -na *f*.

arguable ['ɑ:gjʊəbl] *adj* [questionable] questionável.

arguably ['ɑ:gjʊəblɪ] *adv* indubitavelmente.

argue ['ɑ:gju:] <> *vi* **-1.** [quarrel] discutir; **to ~ (with sb about sthg)** discutir (com alguém sobre algo) **-2.** [reason] argumentar; **to ~ for/against sthg** argumentar a favor/contra algo. <> *vt* [case, point] afirmar; **to ~ that** afirmar que.

argument ['ɑ:gjʊmənt] *n* **-1.** [quarrel] discussão *f*; **to have an ~ (with sb)** ter uma discussão (com alguém) **-2.** [reason] argumento *m* **-3.** [reasoning] argumentação *f*.

argumentative [,ɑ:gjʊ'mentətɪv] *adj* questionador(ra).

aria ['ɑ:rɪə] *n* ária *f*.

arid ['ærɪd] *adj* **-1.** [land] árido(da) **-2.** *fig* [subject, writing] árido(da).

Aries ['eəri:z] *n* **-1.** [sign] Áries *f* **-2.** [person] ariano(-na).

arise [ə'raɪz] (*pt* **arose**, *pp* **arisen** [ə'rɪzn]) *vi* [appear] surgir; **to ~ from sthg** surgir de algo; **if the need ~s** se houver necessidade.

aristocracy [,ærɪ'stɒkrəsɪ] (*pl* **-ies**) *n* aristocracia *f*.

aristocrat [UK 'ærɪstəkræt, US ə'rɪstəkræt] *n* aristocrata *mf*.

aristocratic [UK ,ærɪstə'krætɪk, US ə,rɪstə'krætɪk] *adj* aristocrático(ca).

arithmetic [ə'rɪθmətɪk] <> *adj* aritmético(ca). <> *n* aritmética *f*.

Arizona [,ærɪ'zəʊnə] *n* Arizona; **in ~** no Arizona.

ark [ɑ:k] *n* [ship] arca *f*.

Arkansas ['ɑ:kənsɔ:] *n* Arkansas; **in ~** no Arkansas.

arm [ɑ:m] <> *n* **-1.** [of person] braço *m*; **~ in ~** de braços dados; **to keep sb at ~'s length** *fig* manter alguém à distância; **to welcome sb/sthg with open ~s** *fig* receber alguém/algo de braços abertos; **to twist sb's ~** *fig* forçar alguém a fazer algo; **to cost an ~ and a leg** *fig* custar os olhos da cara **-2.** [of garment] manga *f* **-3.** [of chair] braço *m* **-4.** [of organization] ramo *m*. <> *vt* [with weapons] armar.
◆ **arms** *npl* [weapons] armas *fpl*; **to take up ~s** pegar em armas; **to be up in ~s (about sthg)** estar furioso(sa) em relação a algo.

armada [ɑ:'mɑ:də] *n* [fleet of boats, ships] armada *f*.

armadillo [,ɑ:mə'dɪləʊ] (*pl* **-s**) *n* tatu *m*.

Armageddon [,ɑ:mə'gedn] *n* armagedom *m*.

armaments ['ɑ:məmənts] *npl* [weapons] armamento *m*.

armband ['ɑ:mbænd] *n* braçadeira *f*.

armchair ['ɑ:mtʃeəʳ] *n* poltrona *f*.

armed [ɑ:md] *adj* **-1.** [with weapon] armado(da) **-2.** *fig* [with information]: **~ with sthg** munido(da) de algo.

armed forces *npl* forças *fpl* armadas.

armed robbery *n* roubo *m* a mão armada.

Armenia [ɑ:'mi:njə] *n* Armênia; **in ~** na Armênia.

Armenian [ɑ:'mi:njən] <> *adj* armênio(a). <> *n* **-1.** [person] armênio *m*, -a *f* **-2.** [language] armênio *m*.

armhole ['ɑ:mhəʊl] *n* cava *f*.

armistice ['ɑ:mɪstɪs] *n* armistício *m*.

armour UK, **armor** US ['ɑ:məʳ] *n* **-1.** [for person] armadura *f* **-2.** [for military vehicle] blindagem *f*.

armoured UK, **armored** US ['ɑ:məd] adj MIL blindado(da).

armoured car [ɑ:məd-] n MIL carro m blindado.

armour-plated [-'pleɪtɪd] adj MIL blindado(da).

armoury UK (pl -ies), **armory** US (pl -ies) ['ɑ:mərɪ] n arsenal m.

armpit ['ɑ:mpɪt] n axila f.

armrest ['ɑ:mrest] n braço m.

arms control ['ɑ:mz-] n controle m armamentista.

army ['ɑ:mɪ] (pl -ies) n **-1.** MIL exército m **-2.** fig [large group] exército m.

A road n UK rodovia principal.

aroma [ə'rəʊmə] n [smell] aroma m.

aromatherapy [ərəʊmə'θerəpɪ] n aromaterapia f.

aromatic [ˌærə'mætɪk] adj aromático(ca).

arose [ə'rəʊz] pt ▷ arise.

around [ə'raʊnd] ◇ adv **-1.** [about, around] por aí **-2.** [on all sides] ao redor **-3.** [in circular movement] ao redor **- 4.** phr: **to have been ~** inf ter experiência. ◇ prep **-1.** [encircling] ao redor de **-2.** [through, throughout] por todo(da) **-3.** [near] perto **- 4.** [approximately] cerca de.

arousal [ə'raʊzl] n (U) [of feelings, emotions] despertar m.

arouse [ə'raʊz] vt **-1.** [excite - feeling] provocar; [- person] estimular **-2.** [wake] despertar.

arrange [ə'reɪndʒ] vt **-1.** [flowers, books, furniture] arrumar **-2.** [event, meeting, party] organizar; **to ~ to do sthg** combinar para fazer algo; **to ~ sthg for sb** arranjar algo para alguém; **to ~ for sb to do sthg** combinar com alguém para que faça algo **- 3.** MUS fazer um arranjo.

arranged marriage [ə'reɪndʒd-] n casamento m arranjado.

arrangement [ə'reɪndʒmənt] n **-1.** [agreement] acordo m; **to come to an ~** chegar a um acordo **- 2.** [of objects] arranjo m; **flower ~** arranjo de flores **- 3.** MUS arranjo m.

➧ **arrangements** npl providências fpl; **to make ~s** tomar providências.

array [ə'reɪ] ◇ n **-1.** [of objects, people, ornaments] série f **- 2.** COMPUT array m. ◇ vt [ornaments] enfeitar.

arrears [ə'rɪəz] npl [money owed] dívida f; **in ~** [retrospectively] retroativamente; [late] em atraso.

arrest [ə'rest] ◇ n [by police] prisão f; **under ~** preso(sa). ◇ vt **-1.** [subj: police] prender **-2.** fml [sb's attention] prender **- 3.** fml [stop] deter.

arresting [ə'restɪŋ] adj [striking] impressionante.

arrival [ə'raɪvl] n [gen] chegada f; **late ~** [of train, bus, mail] chegada atrasada; **new ~** [person] recém-chegado(da); [baby] recém-nascido(da).

arrive [ə'raɪv] vi **-1.** [gen] chegar; **to ~ at a conclusion/decision** chegar a uma conclusão/decisão **- 2.** [baby] nascer.

arrogance ['ærəgəns] n arrogância f.

arrogant ['ærəgənt] adj arrogante.

arrogantly ['ærəgəntlɪ] adv presunçosamente.

arrow ['ærəʊ] n **-1.** [weapon] flecha f **-2.** [symbol] seta f.

arrowroot n araruta f.

arse [UK ɑ:s], **ass** [US æs] n vulg [bottom] bunda f.

arsenal ['ɑ:sənl] n [of weapons] arsenal m.

arsenic ['ɑ:snɪk] n arsênico m.

arson ['ɑ:sn] n incêndio m premeditado.

arsonist ['ɑ:sənɪst] n incendiário m, -ria f.

art [ɑ:t] ◇ n (U) arte f. ◇ comp de artes.

➧ **arts** ◇ npl **- 1.** SCH & UNIV [humanities] artes fpl **- 2.** [fine arts]: **the ~s** as belas artes. ◇ comp SCH & UNIV de belas artes.

➧ **arts and crafts** n [school subject] artes fpl.

art deco [-'dekəʊ] n arte f deco.

artefact ['ɑ:tɪfækt] n = artifact.

arterial [ɑ:'tɪərɪəl] adj **-1.** [blood] arterial **-2.** [road] principal.

arteriosclerosis [ɑ:ˌtɪərɪəʊsklɪ'rəʊsɪs] n arteriosclerose f.

artery ['ɑ:tərɪ] (pl -ies) n artéria f.

artful ['ɑ:tfʊl] adj [cunning] astuto(ta).

art gallery n **-1.** [public] museu m de arte **-2.** [for selling paintings] galeria f de arte.

arthritic [ɑ:'θrɪtɪk] adj artrítico(ca).

arthritis [ɑ:'θraɪtɪs] n artrite f.

artic [ɑ:'tɪk] n UK inf = articulated lorry.

artichoke ['ɑ:tɪtʃəʊk] n alcachofra f.

article ['ɑ:tɪkl] n artigo m.

articled clerk ['ɑ:tɪkld-] n UK estagiário m de advocacia.

articles of association ['ɑ:tɪklz-] npl estatutos mpl.

articulate [adj ɑ:'tɪkjʊlət, vb ɑ:'tɪkjʊleɪt] ◇ adj [eloquent - person] articulado(da); [- speech] claro(ra). ◇ vt [give clear expression to] articular.

articulated lorry [ɑ:'tɪkjʊleɪtɪd-] n UK caminhão m articulado.

articulation [ɑ:ˌtɪkjʊ'leɪʃn] n **-1.** [enunciation] articulação f **-2.** [expression in words] expressão f.

artifact ['ɑ:tɪfækt] n artefato m.

artifice ['ɑ:tɪfɪs] n artifício m.

artificial [ˌɑ:tɪ'fɪʃl] adj artificial.

artificial insemination n inseminação f artificial.

artificial intelligence n inteligência f artificial.

artificially [ˌɑ:tɪ'fɪʃəlɪ] adv artificialmente.

artificial respiration n respiração f artificial.

artillery [ɑ:'tɪlərɪ] n [guns] artilharia f.

artisan [ˌɑ:tɪ'zæn] n artesão m, -sã f.

artist ['ɑ:tɪst] n artista mf.

artiste [ɑ:'ti:st] n artista mf.

artistic [ɑ:'tɪstɪk] adj artístico(ca).

artistically [ɑ:'tɪstɪklɪ] adv artisticamente.

artistry ['ɑ:tɪstrɪ] n [creative skill] talento m artístico.

artless ['ɑ:tlɪs] adj [naive, simple] ingênuo(nua), simples.

art nouveau [ˌɑ:nu:'vəʊ] n art nouveau m.

as [stressed æz, unstressed əz] ◇ conj **-1.** [referring to time] enquanto; **she rang (just) ~ I was leaving** ela ligou (bem) na hora em que eu estava saindo; **~ time goes by** com o passar do tempo **-2.** [referring to manner, way] como; **do ~ I say** faça como eu digo; **~ it is** como está; **~ it turns/turned out** no final; **~ things stand** pelo jeito **-3.** [introducing a statement] como; **~ you see, ...** como você pode ver; **~ you know, ...** como você sabe **-4.** [because]

como. <> *prep* **-1.** [referring to function, characteristic]: **he lived in Africa** ~ **a boy** ele viveu na África quando garoto; **he made his name** ~ **an actor** ele fez seu nome como ator; **she works** ~ **a nurse** ela trabalha como enfermeira **- 2.** [referring to attitude, reaction] como; **she treats it** ~ **a game** ela trata isto como um jogo. <> *adv (in comparisons)*: ~ ... ~ tão ... quanto; ~ **red** ~ **a tomato** tão vermelho quanto um tomate; **he's** ~ **tall** ~ **I am** ele é tão alto quanto eu; ~ **much/many** ~ tanto ... quanto; ~ **much wine/chocolate** ~ **you want** tanto vinho/chocolate quanto você queira.
➤ **as it were** *adv* por assim dizer.
➤ **as for, as to** *prep* quanto a.
➤ **as from, as of** *prep* a partir de.
➤ **as if, as though** *conj* como se.
➤ **as to** *prep* sobre.

AS <> *n* (*abbr of* **Associate in Science**) *(titular de) graduação em ciências em universidade norte-americana*. <> *abbr of* **American Samoa**.

ASA (*abbr of* **American Standards Association**) *n* **-1.** *associação norte-americana de padronização*, ≃ ABNT *f*. **- 2.** (*abbr of* **Advertising Standards Authority**) *órgão britânico que regula a propaganda*, ≃ CONAR *m*. **- 3.** (*abbr of* **Amateur Swimming Association**) *associação britânica de nadadores amadores*.

asap (*abbr of* **as soon as possible**) o mais rápido possível.

asbestos [æs'bestəs] *n* asbesto *m*.

asbestosis [ˌæsbes'təʊsɪs] *n* asbestose *f*.

ascend [ə'send] <> *vt fml* [hill, staircase, ladder] subir; **to** ~ **the throne** ascender ao trono. <> *vi* [climb] subir, elevar-se.

ascendancy [ə'sendənsɪ] *n* [dominance] domínio *m*.

ascendant [ə'sendənt] *n*: **to be in the** ~ [rising in power] estar em ascensão.

ascendency [ə'sendənsɪ] *n* = **ascendancy**.

ascending [ə'sendɪŋ] *adj* [increasing] ascendente; **in** ~ **order** em ordem ascendente.

ascension [ə'senʃn] *n* [to throne] ascensão *f*.
➤ **Ascension** *n RELIG* Ascensão *f*.

Ascension Island *n* Ilha *f* da Ascensão.

ascent [ə'sent] *n* **-1.** [climb] escalada *f* **- 2.** [upward slope] subida *f* **- 3.** (*U*) *fig* [progress] escalada *f*.

ascertain [ˌæsə'teɪn] *vt* averiguar.

ascetic [ə'setɪk] <> *adj* ascético(ca). <> *n* asceta *mf*.

ASCII (*abbr of* **American Standard Code for Information Interchange**) *n* ASCII *m*.

ascorbic acid [ə'skɔːbɪk-] *n* ácido *m* ascórbico.

ascribe [ə'skraɪb] *vt* [attribute]: **to** ~ **sthg to sthg/sb** atribuir algo a algo/alguém.

aseptic [ˌeɪ'septɪk] *adj* [germ-free] asséptico(ca).

asexual [ˌeɪ'sekʃʊəl] *adj BIOL* assexuado(da).

ash [æʃ] *n* **-1.** [from cigarette, fire] cinza *f* **- 2.** [tree] freixo *m*.
➤ **ashes** *npl* [from cremation] cinzas *fpl*.

ASH (*abbr of* **Action on Smoking and Health**) *n grupo britânico de combate ao tabagismo*.

ashamed [ə'ʃeɪmd] *adj* [embarrassed] envergonhado(da); **to be** ~ **of sb/sthg** estar envergonhado(da) por alguém/algo; **to be** ~ **to do sthg** estar com vergonha de fazer algo.

ashcan ['æʃkæn] *n US* lixeira *f*.

ashen-faced ['æʃnˌfeɪst] *adj* pálido(da).

ashore [ə'ʃɔːʳ] *adv* [go, swim] em direção à costa.

ashtray ['æʃtreɪ] *n* cinzeiro *m*.

Ash Wednesday *n* Quarta-feira *f* de Cinzas.

Asia ['eɪʒə] *n* Ásia; **in** ~ na Ásia.

Asia Minor *n* Ásia Menor.

Asian ['eɪʒn] <> *adj* asiático(ca). <> *n* [person] asiático *m*, -ca *f*.

Asiatic [UK ˌeɪʃɪ'ætɪk, US ˌeɪʒɪ'ætɪk] *adj* asiático(ca).

aside [ə'saɪd] <> *adv* **-1.** [to one side] para o lado; **to take sb** ~ chamar alguém à parte; **to brush** OR **sweep sthg** ~ ignorar algo **-2.** [apart] à parte; ~ **from** com exceção de. <> *n* **-1.** [in play] aparte *m* **-2.** [remark] observação *f*.

ask [ɑːsk] <> *vt* **-1.** [question] perguntar; **to** ~ **sb sthg** perguntar algo a alguém; **if you** ~ **me ...** se você quer saber ... **-2.** [enquire] perguntar; **to** ~ **a question** fazer uma pergunta **-3.** [request] pedir; **to** ~ **sb for sthg** pedir algo a alguém; **to** ~ **sb to do sthg** pedir a alguém para fazer algo **-4.** [invite] convidar **-5.** [set a price of]: **how much are they asking?** quanto estão pedindo? <> *vi* **-1.** [enquire] perguntar **-2.** [request] pedir.
➤ **ask after** *vt fus*: **to** ~ **sb** perguntar por alguém.
➤ **ask for** *vt fus* **-1.** [person] pedir por, chamar por **-2.** [thing] pedir por.

askance [ə'skæns] *adv* [disapprovingly]: **to look** ~ **at sb/sthg** olhar alguém/algo com desconfiança, olhar de soslaio para alguém/algo.

askew [ə'skjuː] *adj* [not straight] torto(ta).

asking price ['ɑːskɪŋ-] *n* [for house, car, item in sale] preço *m* estipulado.

asleep [ə'sliːp] *adj* [sleeping] adormecido(da); **to fall** ~ pegar no sono; **to be fast** OR **sound** ~ estar em sono profundo.

ASM (*abbr of* **air-to-surface missile**) *n* ASM *m*, míssil *m* ar-superfície.

asparagus [ə'spærəgəs] *n* aspargo *m*.

ASPCA (*abbr of* **American Society for the Prevention of Cruelty to Animals**) *n sociedade norte-americana protetora dos animais*, ≃ SUIPA *f*.

aspect ['æspekt] *n* **-1.** aspecto *m* **-2.** ARCHIT posição *f*.

aspen ['æspən] *n* álamo *m*.

aspersions [ə'spɜːʃnz] *npl*: **to cast** ~ **(on sb)** levantar calúnias (sobre alguém); **to cast** ~ **(on sthg)** levantar suspeitas (sobre algo).

asphalt ['æsfælt] *n* asfalto *m*.

asphyxiate [əs'fiksɪeɪt] *vt* asfixiar.

aspic ['æspɪk] *n* geléia *f* (*de carne ou peixe*).

aspidistra *n* aspidistra *f*.

aspirate ['æspərət] <> *adj* LING aspirado(da). <> *vt MED, LING* aspirar.

aspiration [ˌæspə'reɪʃn] *n* aspiração *f*.

aspire [ə'spaɪəʳ] *vi*: **to** ~ **to sthg/to do sthg** aspirar algo, aspirar fazer algo.

aspirin ['æsprɪn] *n* aspirina *f*.

aspiring [ə'spaɪrɪŋ] *adj* aspirante.

ass [æs] *n* **-1.** [donkey] jumento *m* **-2.** UK *inf* [idiot] burro *m*, -ra *f* **-3.** US *vulg* = **arse**.

assail [ə'seɪl] *vt* **-1.** [attack physically] atacar **-2.** *fig* [beset] acometer.

assailant [əˈseɪlənt] n [attacker] agressor m, -ra f.
assassin [əˈsæsɪn] n assassino m, -na f.
assassinate [əˈsæsɪneɪt] vt assassinar; **to be ~ed** ser assassinado(da).
assassination [əˌsæsɪˈneɪʃn] n assassinato m.
assault [əˈsɔːlt] <> n **-1.** MIL ataque m; **~ on sthg** ataque a algo **- 2.** [physical attack] agressão f; **~ on sb** agressão a alguém; **~ and battery** JUR agressão f seguida de lesões. <> vt [attack - physically] agredir; [- sexually] violentar, estuprar.
assault course n pista f de combate.
assemble [əˈsembl] <> vt **-1.** [gather] reunir **- 2.** [fit together] montar. <> vi [gather] reunir.
assembler language n = assembly language.
assembly [əˈsemblɪ] (pl -ies) n **-1.** [meeting] reunião f **- 2.** [law-making body] assembléia f, parlamento m **- 3.** (U) [gathering together] assembléia f **- 4.** (U) [fitting together] montagem f.
assembly language n COMPUT linguagem f assembly, linguagem f assembler.
assembly line n linha f de montagem.
assent [əˈsent] <> n [agreement] acordo m, aprovação f. <> vi concordar; **to ~ to sthg** aceitar algo.
assert [əˈsɜːt] vt **-1.** [fact, belief] afirmar **- 2.** [authority] impor; **to ~ o.s.** firmar-se.
assertion [əˈsɜːʃn] n [claim] afirmação f.
assertive [əˈsɜːtɪv] adj positivo(va).
assess [əˈses] vt **-1.** [judge] avaliar **- 2.** [estimate] estimar.
assessment [əˈsesmənt] n **-1.** [judgment] avaliação f **- 2.** [estimate] estimativa f.
assessor [əˈsesəʳ] n FIN analista mf.
asset [ˈæset] n ativo m.
◆ **assets** npl COMM ativos mpl; **~s and liabilities** ativo m e passivo.
asset-stripping [-ˌstrɪpɪŋ] n compra de uma empresa em baixa e venda lucrativa de seu capital, seguida de seu fechamento.
assiduous [əˈsɪdjʊəs] adj [diligent] assíduo(dua).
assiduously [əˈsɪdjʊəslɪ] adv [diligently] com assiduidade.
assign [əˈsaɪn] vt **-1.** [allot, allocate]: **to ~ sthg (to sb/sthg)** designar algo (a alguém/algo) **- 2.** [appoint]: **to ~ sb (to sthg/to do sthg)** designar alguém (para algo/fazer algo).
assignation [ˌæsɪgˈneɪʃn] n fml [secret meeting] encontro m amoroso.
assignment [əˈsaɪnmənt] n **-1.** [task] tarefa f **- 2.** (U) [act of appointing] designação f **- 3.** [law] partilha f, transferência f de bens.
assimilate [əˈsɪmɪleɪt] vt **-1.** [ideas, facts] assimilar **- 2.** [people]: **to ~ sb (into sthg)** absorver alguém (em algo) **- 3.** [nutrients, food] absorver.
assimilation [əˌsɪmɪˈleɪʃn] n **-1.** [of ideas, facts] assimilação f **- 2.** [of people, food] absorção f.
assist [əˈsɪst] vt [help] auxiliar; **to ~ sb with sthg/in doing sthg** auxiliar alguém em algo/a fazer algo.
assistance [əˈsɪstəns] n [help] auxílio m, ajuda f; **to be of ~ (to sb)** ser de alguma ajuda (para alguém).
assistant [əˈsɪstənt] <> n **-1.** [helper] assistente mf **- 2.** [in shop] balconista mf, atendente mf. <> comp assistente mf; **~ manager** gerente adjunto.

assistant referee n árbitro m assistente, -tra assistente f.
associate [adj & n əˈsəʊʃɪət, vb əˈsəʊʃɪeɪt] <> adj [member] associado(da). <> n [business partner] sócio m, -cia f. <> vt [connect] associar-se; **to ~ o.s. with sb/sthg** associar-se a alguém/algo; **to ~ sthg with sb/sthg** associar algo a alguém/algo; **to be ~d with sb/sthg** ser associado a alguém/algo. <> vi: **to ~ with sb** relacionar-se com alguém.
association [əˌsəʊsɪˈeɪʃn] n **-1.** [organization] associação f **- 2.** (U) [relationship, of ideas] associação f; **in ~ with sb/sthg** em associação com alguém/algo.
assonance [ˈæsənəns] n assonância f.
assorted [əˈsɔːtɪd] adj [of various types] sortido(da), variado(da).
assortment [əˈsɔːtmənt] n [mixture] diversidade f.
Asst (abbr of assistant) assistente mf.
assuage [əˈsweɪdʒ] vt fml [relieve] minorar.
assume [əˈsjuːm] vt **-1.** [suppose] supor **- 2.** [take on] assumir.
assumed name [əˈsjuːmd-] n nome m falso.
assuming [əˈsjuːmɪŋ] conj: **~ that** supondo que.
assumption [əˈsʌmpʃn] n **-1.** [supposition] suposição f **- 2.** [of power] tomada f.
◆ **Assumption** n RELIG: **the Assumption** a Ascensão f.
assurance [əˈʃʊərəns] n **-1.** [promise] promessa f **- 2.** (U) [confidence] segurança f **- 3.** (U) FIN [insurance] seguro m.
assure [əˈʃʊəʳ] vt [reassure] assegurar; **to ~ sb of sthg** assegurar alguém de algo; **to be ~d of sthg** [be certain] estar seguro(ra de algo).
assured [əˈʃʊəd] adj [confident] autoconfiante.
AST (abbr of Atlantic Standard Time) n horário de inverno na costa leste dos Estados Unidos.
asterisk [ˈæstərɪsk] n asterisco m.
astern [əˈstɜːn] adv NAUT à popa.
asteroid [ˈæstərɔɪd] n asteróide m.
asthma [ˈæsmə] n asma f.
asthmatic [æsˈmætɪk] <> adj asmático(ca). <> n asmático m, -ca f.
astigmatism [əˈstɪgmətɪzm] n astigmatismo m.
astonish [əˈstɒnɪʃ] vt [amaze] surpreender.
astonished adj surpreso(sa).
astonishing [əˈstɒnɪʃɪŋ] adj extraordinário(ria), surpreendente.
astonishment [əˈstɒnɪʃmənt] n espanto m, surpresa f.
astound [əˈstaʊnd] vt [amaze] pasmar.
astounded adj pasmado(da).
astounding [əˈstaʊndɪŋ] adj espantoso(sa).
astrakhan [ˌæstrəˈkæn] n astracã m.
astray [əˈstreɪ] adv: **to go ~** [become lost] extraviar-se; **to lead sb ~** fig [into bad ways] levar alguém para o mal caminho.
astride [əˈstraɪd] prep: **sitting ~ a horse** montado(da) em um cavalo; **sitting ~ a chair** sentado(da) numa cadeira com uma perna de cada lado.
astringent [əˈstrɪndʒənt] <> adj **-1.** [cosmetic lotion] adstringente **- 2.** [criticism] severo(ra). <> n [cosmetic] adstringente m.
astrologer [əˈstrɒlədʒəʳ] n astrólogo m, -ga f.
astrological [ˌæstrəˈlɒdʒɪkl] adj astrológico(ca).

astrologist [ə'strɒlədʒɪst] *n* = **astrologer**.
astrology [ə'strɒlədʒɪ] *n* astrologia *f*.
astronaut ['æstrənɔːt] *n* astronauta *mf*.
astronomer [ə'strɒnəmə[r]] *n* astrônomo *m*, -ma *f*.
astronomical [ˌæstrə'nɒmɪkl] *adj* **-1.** ASTRON astronômico(ca) **-2.** *inf fig* [very large] astronômico(ca).
astronomy [ə'strɒnəmɪ] *n* astronomia *f*.
astrophysics [ˌæstrəʊ'fɪzɪks] *n* astrofísica *f*.
astute [ə'stjuːt] *adj* [shrewd] perspicaz.
asunder [ə'sʌndə[r]] *adv literary* [apart]: **to tear** ~ dilacerar.
ASV (*abbr of* **American Standard Version**) *n* tradução da Bíblia adotada nos Estados Unidos.
asylum [ə'saɪləm] *n* **-1.** *dated* [mental hospital] hospício *m* **-2.** (U) [protection] asilo *m*.
asymmetrical [ˌeɪsɪ'metrɪkl] *adj* assimétrico(ca).
at [*stressed* æt, *unstressed* ət] *prep* **-1.** [indicating place, position] em; ~ **work** no trabalho; ~ **my father's** na casa do meu pai; ~ **home** em casa; ~ **the top of the house** em cima de casa; ~ **the bottom of the hill** ao pé da colina **-2.** [indicating direction] para, em direção a; **to smile** ~ **sb** sorrir para alguém; **to stare** ~ **sb/sthg** olhar para alguém/algo; **to shoot** ~ **sb/sthg** atirar em (direção a) alguém/algo **-3.** [indicating a particular time] em; ~ **midnight/noon** à meia-noite, ao meio-dia; ~ **eleven o'clock** às onze horas; ~ **Christmas** no Natal; ~ **night** à noite **-4.** [indicating age, speed, rate] a, em; ~ **your age** na sua idade; ~ **high speed** em alta velocidade; ~ **52 (years of age)** aos 52 anos (de idade); ~ **100 mph** a 100 milhas por hora **-5.** [indicating price] a; ~ **£50 a** *OR* **por 50 libras -6.** [indicating particular state, condition] a, em; ~ **liberty** em liberdade; ~ **my invitation** a meu convite; ~ **peace/war** em paz/guerra; ~ **lunch/dinner** no almoço/jantar **-7.** [indicating tentativeness, noncompletion] em; **to snatch** ~ **sthg** tentar pegar algo; **to nibble** ~ **sthg** beliscar/mordiscar algo **-8.** (*after adjectives*) com; **amused/appalled/puzzled** ~ **sthg** entretido(da)/apavorado(da)/embaraçado(da) com algo; **to be bad/good** ~ **sthg** ser ruim/bom(boa) em algo.
➤ **at all** *adv* **-1.** (*with negative*): **not** ~ **all** [when thanked] não há de que; [when answering a question] de forma alguma; **she's not** ~ **all happy** ela não está nem um pouco feliz **-2.** [in the slightest]: **anything** ~ **all will do** qualquer coisa está bem; **do you know her** ~ **all?** você a conhece de algum lugar?
ATC (*abbr of* **Air Training Corps**) *n* unidade de formação e treinamento das forças aéreas britânicas.
ate [*UK* et, *US* eɪt] *pt* ⊳ **eat**.
atheism ['eɪθɪɪzm] *n* ateísmo *m*.
atheist ['eɪθɪɪst] *n* ateu *m*, -téia *f*.
Athenian [ə'θiːnjən] ⇔ *adj* ateniense *mf*. ⇔ *n* ateniense *mf*.
Athens ['æθɪnz] *n* Atenas; **in** ~ em Atenas.
athlete ['æθliːt] *n* atleta *mf*.
athlete's foot *n* MED pé-de-atleta *f*.
athletic [æθ'letɪk] *adj* atlético(ca).
➤ **athletics** *npl* atletismo *m*.
Atlantic [ət'læntɪk] ⇔ *adj* atlântico(ca). ⇔ *n*: **the** ~ **(Ocean)** o (Oceano) Atlântico.

Atlantis [ət'læntɪs] *n* Atlântida.
atlas ['ætləs] *n* atlas *m inv*.
Atlas ['ætləs] *n*: **the** ~ **Mountains** os Montes Atlas.
atm. (*abbr of* **atmosphere**) atm.
ATM (*abbr of* **automated teller machine**) *n* caixa *m* automático.
atmosphere ['ætmə,sfɪə[r]] *n* atmosfera *f*.
atmospheric [ˌætməs'ferɪk] *adj* **-1.** [relating to the atmosphere] atmosférico(ca) **-2.** [attractive, mysterious] envolvente.
ATOL (*abbr of* **Air Travel Organisers' Licence**) *n* organização britânica mantida pela CAA que defende os interesses das pessoas que utilizam a aviação comercial no Reino Unido.
atoll ['ætɒl] *n* atol *m*.
atom ['ætəm] *n* **-1.** TECH átomo *m* **-2.** *fig* [tiny amount] ponta *f* pingo *m*.
atom bomb *n* bomba *f* atômica.
atomic [ə'tɒmɪk] *adj* atômico(ca).
atomic bomb *n* = **atom bomb**.
atomic energy *n* energia *f* atômica.
atomic number *n* PHYS número *m* atômico.
atomizer, -iser ['ætəmaɪzə[r]] *n* vaporizador *m*.
atone [ə'təʊn] *vi*: **to** ~ **for sthg** redimir-se por algo.
atonement [ə'təʊnmənt] *n* remissão *f*; ~ **for sthg** punição por algo.
A to Z *n* A a Z *m*.
ATP (*abbr of* **automatic train protection**) *n* **-1.** sistema britânico para frear automaticamente um trem. **-2.** (*abbr of* **Association of Tennis Professionals**) ATP *f*.
atrocious [ə'trəʊʃəs] *adj* **-1.** [cruel] desumano(na), atroz **-2.** [very bad] atroz.
atrocity [ə'trɒsətɪ] (*pl* **-ies**) *n* [terrible act] atrocidade *f*.
attach [ə'tætʃ] *vt* **-1.** [fasten] prender; **to** ~ **sthg to sthg** prender algo em algo **-2.** [to document] anexar; **to** ~ **sthg to sthg** anexar algo a algo **-3.** [importance, blame] atribuir; **to** ~ **sthg to sthg** atribuir algo a algo **-4.** COMPUT atachar, anexar.
attaché [ə'tæʃeɪ] *n* adido *m*.
attaché case [ə'tæʃeɪ-] *n* pasta *f*.
attached [ə'tætʃt] *adj* **-1.** [included] anexado(da) **-2.** [fastened]: ~ **to sthg** preso(sa) a *OR* em algo **-3.** [assigned]: ~ **to sthg** designado(da) para algo **-4.** [fond]: ~ **to sb/sthg** apegado(da) a alguém/algo.
attachment [ə'tætʃmənt] *n* **-1.** [device] dispositivo *m* **-2.** [fondness]: ~ **(to sb/sthg)** apego (a alguém/algo) **-3.** COMPUT anexo *m*.
attack [ə'tæk] ⇔ *n* **-1.** [gen] ataque *f*; ~ **on sb** sthg ataque contra *OR* a alguém/algo **-2.** [physical, verbal] agressão *f*; ~ **on sb** agressão a alguém ⇔ *vt* **-1.** [gen] atacar **-2.** [physically, verbally] agredir. ⇔ *vi* atacar.
attacker [ə'tækə[r]] *n* **-1.** [assailant] agressor *m*, -ra *f* **-2.** SPORT atacante *mf*.
attain [ə'teɪn] *vt* [reach] atingir.
attainment [ə'teɪnmənt] *n* **-1.** (U) [act of achieving] conquista *f* **-2.** [skill] capacitação *f*, qualificação *f*.
attempt [ə'tempt] ⇔ *n* [try] tentativa *m*; ~ **at sthg** tentativa de fazer algo; ~ **on sb's life** atentado

contra a vida de alguém. ⬦ *vt* [try] tentar; **to ~ to do sthg** tentar fazer algo.

attend [ə'tend] ⬦ *vt* -**1.** [meeting, party] comparecer -**2.** [school, church] freqüentar. ⬦ *vi* -**1.** [be present] comparecer -**2.** [pay attention]: **to ~ (to sthg)** prestar atenção (a algo).
➡ **attend to** *vt fus* -**1.** [deal with] cuidar de -**2.** [look after] atender a.

attendance [ə'tendəns] *n* -**1.** [number of people present] audiência *f* -**2.** *(U)* [presence] presença *f.*

attendant [ə'tendənt] ⬦ *adj* [accompanying] relacionado(da). ⬦ *n* [at museum, petrol station] atendente *mf.*

attention [ə'tenʃn] ⬦ *n* -**1.** [gen] atenção *f*; **to attract sb's ~** atrair a atenção de alguém; **to bring sthg to sb's ~**, **to draw sb's ~ to sthg** chamar a tenção de alguém para algo; **to pay ~ to sb/sthg** prestar atenção a alguém/algo; **to pay no ~ to sb/sthg** não prestar atenção a alguém/algo -**2.** [care] atenção *f*, cuidados *mpl* -**3.** *COMM:* **for the ~ of** aos cuidados de -**4.** *MIL:* **to stand to ~** ficar em posição de sentido. ⬦ *excl MIL* sentido!

attentive [ə'tentɪv] *adj* -**1.** [paying attention] atento(ta) -**2.** [politely helpful] atencioso(sa).

attentively [ə'tentɪvlɪ] *adv* -**1.** [with attention] atentamente -**2.** [helpfully] cuidadosamente.

attenuate [ə'tenjʊeɪt] *fml* ⬦ *vt* atenuar. ⬦ *vi* atenuar.

attest [ə'test] ⬦ *vt* [affirm] atestar. ⬦ *vi:* **to ~ to sthg** [prove] dar testemunho de algo.

attic ['ætɪk] *n* sótão *m.*

attire [ə'taɪəʳ] *n fml* [clothing] traje *m.*

attitude ['ætɪtjuːd] *n* -**1.** [way of thinking/acting] atitude *f*; **~ to(wards) sb/sthg** atitude frente a alguém/algo -**2.** [posture] postura *f.*

attn *(abbr of* **for the attention of)** a/c.

attorney [ə'tɜːnɪ] *n US* [lawyer] advogado *m*, -da *f.*

attorney general *(pl* **attorneys general)** *n* procurador *m*, -ra *f* público, -ca *f.*

attract [ə'trækt] *vt* atrair; **to be ~ed to sb/sthg** ser atraído(da) por alguém/algo.

attraction [ə'trækʃn] *n* -**1.** *(U)* [liking] atração *f*; **~ to sb** atração por alguém -**2.** *(U)* [appeal, charm] graça *f* -**3.** [attractive feature, event] atração *f.*

attractive [ə'træktɪv] *adj* atraente.

attractively [ə'træktɪvlɪ] *adv* de modo atraente.

attributable [ə'trɪbjʊtəbl] *adj:* **~ to sb/sthg** atribuível a alguém/algo.

attribute [*vb* ə'trɪbjuːt, *n* 'ætrɪbjuːt] ⬦ *vt:* **to ~ sthg to sb/sthg** atribuir algo a alguém/algo. ⬦ *n* [quality] atributo *m.*

attribution *n* atribuição *f*; **~ to sb/sthg** atribuição a alguém/algo.

attrition [ə'trɪʃn] *n* desgaste *m*; **war of ~** guerra de desgaste.

attuned [ə'tjuːnd] *adj* -**1.** [accustomed] acostumado(da); **~ to sthg** familiarizado(da) a algo -**2.** [tuned in] sintonizado(da); **~ to sthg** ligado(da) em algo.

ATV *n (abbr of* **all-terrain vehicle)** off-road *m.*

atypical [ˌeɪ'tɪpɪkl] *adj* atípico(ca).

atypically [ˌeɪ'tɪpɪklɪ] *adv* atipicamente.

aubergine ['əʊbəʒiːn] *n UK* beringela *f.*

auburn ['ɔːbən] *adj* [hair] castanho avermelhado(-da).

auction ['ɔːkʃn] ⬦ *n* [sale] leilão *m*; **at** *OR* **by ~** em leilão; **to put sthg up for ~** pôr algo em leilão. ⬦ *vt* leiloar.
➡ **auction off** *vt sep* leiloar.

auctioneer [ˌɔːkʃə'nɪəʳ] *n* leiloeiro *m*, -ra *f.*

audacious [ɔː'deɪʃəs] *adj* [daring, impudent] audacioso(sa).

audacity [ɔː'dæsətɪ] *n* audácia *f.*

audible ['ɔːdəbl] *adj* audível.

audience ['ɔːdjəns] *n* -**1.** [of play, film, TV programme] platéia *f* -**2.** [formal meeting] audiência *f.*

audio ['ɔːdɪəʊ] *adj* áudio, auditivo(va).

audio frequency *n* freqüência *f* auditiva.

audiotyping *n* transcrição *f* de fitas de áudio.

audiotypist ['ɔːdɪəʊˌtaɪpɪst] *n* transcritor *m*, -ra *f* de fitas (de áudio).

audio-visual ['ɔːdɪəʊ-] *adj* audiovisual.

audit ['ɔːdɪt] ⬦ *n* [of accounts] auditoria *f.* ⬦ *vt* [accounts] auditorar.

audition [ɔː'dɪʃn] ⬦ *n* audição *f.* ⬦ *vi:* **she is ~ing for a part in a film** ela está fazendo um teste para um papel num filme.

auditor ['ɔːdɪtəʳ] *n* [of accounts] auditor *m*, -ra *f.*

auditorium [ˌɔːdɪ'tɔːriəm] *(pl* -**riums** *OR* -**ria** [-riə]*) n* auditório *m.*

au fait [ˌəʊ'feɪ] *adj:* **~ with sthg** estar a par de algo.

Aug. *(abbr of* **August)** ago.

augment [ɔːg'ment] *vt* [increase] aumentar.

augur ['ɔːgəʳ] *vi:* **to ~ well/badly** ser um bom/mau sinal.

august [ɔː'gʌst] *adj literary* [dignified] augusto(ta).

August ['ɔːgəst] *n* agosto *m*; *see also* **September.**

Auld Lang Syne [ˌɔːldlæŋ'saɪn] *n* canção escocesa tradicionalmente cantada no ano-novo.

aunt [ɑːnt] *n* tia *f.*

auntie, aunty ['ɑːntɪ] *(pl* -**ies)** *n inf* titia *f.*

au pair [ˌəʊ'peəʳ] *n* au pair *mf.*

aura ['ɔːrə] *n* aura *f.*

aural ['ɔːrəl] *adj* auditivo(va), auricular.

aurally ['ɔːrəlɪ] *adv* auditivamente.

auspices ['ɔːspɪsɪz] *npl:* **under the ~ of** sob o patrocínio de.

auspicious [ɔː'spɪʃəs] *adj* [promising] promissor(ra).

Aussie ['ɒzɪ] *inf* ⬦ *adj* australiano(na). ⬦ *n* australiano *m*, -na *f.*

austere [ɒ'stɪəʳ] *adj* -**1.** [person, life] duro(ra), austero(ra) -**2.** [room, building] austero(ra).

austerity [ɒ'sterətɪ] *n* austeridade *f.*

austerity measures *npl* medidas *fpl* austeras.

Australasia [ˌɒstrə'leɪʒə] *n* Australásia *f.*

Australia [ɒ'streɪljə] *n* Austrália *f*; **in ~** na Austrália.

Australian [ɒ'streɪljən] ⬦ *adj* australiano(na). ⬦ *n* australiano *m*, -na *f.*

Austria ['ɒstrɪə] *n* Áustria *f*; **in ~** na Áustria.

Austrian ['ɒstrɪən] ⬦ *adj* austríaco(ca). ⬦ *n* austríaco *m*, -ca *f.*

authentic [ɔː'θentɪk] *adj* -**1.** [genuine] autêntico(ca) -**2.** [accurate] fidedigno(na).

authenticate [ɔːˈθentɪkeɪt] *vt* autenticar.

authentication [ɔːˌθentɪˈkeɪʃn] *n* autenticação *f.*

authenticity [ˌɔːθenˈtɪsətɪ] *n* autenticidade *f.*

author [ˈɔːθəʳ] *n* autor *m,* -ra *f.*

authoritarian [ɔːˌθɒrɪˈteərɪən] *adj* autoritário(ria).

authoritative [ɔːˈθɒrɪtətɪv]* *adj* **-1.** [person, voice] autoritário(ria) **-2.** [report] oficial.

authority [ɔːˈθɒrətɪl] (*pl* **-ies**) *n* **-1.** [gen] autoridade *f;* ~ **on** sthg autoridade em algo **-2.** *(U)* [power] autoridade *f;* **in** ~ com autoridade **-3.** *(U)* [permission] autorização *f* **-4.** *phr:* **to have it on good** ~ receber de fonte segura.

  ➠ **authorities** *npl* [people in power]: **the authorities** as autoridades.

authorize, -ise [ˈɔːθəraɪz] *vt* autorizar; **to** ~ **sb to** do sthg autorizar alguém a fazer algo.

Authorized Version [ˈɔːθəraɪzd-] *n:* **the** ~ **a** Versão Autorizada *(da Bíblia).*

authorship [ˈɔːθəʃɪp] *n* autoria *f.*

autistic [ɔːˈtɪstɪk] *adj* autista.

auto [ˈɔːtəʊl] (*pl* **-s**) *n US* [car] auto *m.*

autobiographical [ˈɔːtəˌbaɪəˈgræfɪkl] *adj* autobiográfico(ca).

autobiography [ˌɔːtəbaɪˈɒgrəfɪl] (*pl* **-ies**) *n* autobiografia *f.*

autocrat [ˈɔːtəkræt] *n* autocrata *mf.*

autocratic [ˌɔːtəˈkrætɪk] *adj* autocrático(ca).

autocross [ˈɔːtəʊkrɒsl] *n UK* autocross *m.*

Autocue® [ˈɔːtəʊkjuː] *n UK* teleprompter *m.*

autofocus *n* autofoco *m.*

autograph [ˈɔːtəgrɑːfl] <> *n* autógrafo *m.* <> *vt* autografar.

Automat® *n* [restaurant] *tipo de restaurante americano comum nos anos 50 e 60, onde a comida era vendida em máquinas com a inserção de moedas.*

automata [ɔːˈtɒmətə] *pl* ⊳ **automaton.**

automate [ˈɔːtəmeɪt] *vt* automatizar.

automatic [ˌɔːtəˈmætɪk] <> *adj* **-1.** [gen] automático(ca) **-2.** [fine, right of appeal] imediato(ta). <> *n* **-1.** [car] carro *n* automático **-2.** [gun] pistola *f* automática **-3.** [washing machine] máquina *f* de lavar automática.

automatically [ˌɔːtəˈmætɪklɪ] *adv* automaticamente.

automatic pilot *n AERON* & *NAUT* piloto *m* automático; **on** ~ *fig* no automático.

automation [ˌɔːtəˈmeɪʃn] *n* [of process] automação *f,* automatização *f.*

automaton [ɔːˈtɒmətən] (*pl* **-tons** OR **-ta**) *n* **-1.** [robot] autômata *mf,* robô *m* **-2.** *pej* [person] robô *m.*

automobile [ˈɔːtəməbiːl] *n US* [car] automóvel *m.*

automotive [ˌɔːtəˈməʊtɪv] *adj* [relating to automobiles] automotivo(va).

autonomous [ɔːˈtɒnəməsl] *adj* autônomo(ma).

autonomy [ɔːˈtɒnəmɪ] *n* autonomia *f.*

autopilot [ˈɔːtəʊpaɪlɒt] *n* = **automatic pilot.**

autopsy [ˈɔːtɒpsɪ] (*pl* **-ies**) *n* autópsia *f.*

autumn [ˈɔːtəm] <> *n* outono *m;* **in** ~ no outono. <> *comp* de outono, outonal.

autumnal [ɔːˈtʌmnəl] *adj* outonal, de outono.

auxiliary [ɔːgˈzɪljərɪ] (*pl* **-ies**) <> *adj* auxiliar. <> *n* [person] auxiliar *mf.*

AV <> *n* (*abbr of* **Authorized Version**) versão *f* autorizada. <> (*abbr of* **audio-visual**) audiovisual.

avail [əˈveɪl] <> *n:* **to no** ~ em vão. <> *vt:* **to** ~ **o.s. of** sthg aproveitar-se de algo.

availability [əˌveɪləˈbɪlətɪ] *n* disponibilidade *f.*

available [əˈveɪləbl] *adj* disponível.

avalanche [ˈævəlɑːnʃ] *n* avalanche *f.*

avant-garde [ˌævɒŋˈgɑːd] <> *n* vanguarda *f.* <> *adj* de vanguarda.

avarice [ˈævərɪs] *n* avareza *f.*

avaricious [ˌævəˈrɪʃəs] *adj* avarento(ta).

avdp. (*abbr of* **avoirdupois**) *sistema inglês de pesos baseado na libra.*

Ave. (*abbr of* **avenue**) Av.

avenge [əˈvendʒ] *vt* vingar.

avenue [ˈævənjuː] *n* [wide road] avenida *f.*

average [ˈævərɪdʒ] <> *adj* **-1.** [mean] média(dio) **-2.** [typical] comum **-3.** *pej* [mediocre] mediano(na). <> *n* [mean] média *f;* **on** ~ em média. <> *vt* [speed, distance, quantity]: **they** ~ **300 cars a day** eles atingem uma média de 300 carros por dia.

  ➠ **average out** <> *vt sep* calcular a média. <> *vi:* **to** ~ **out at** chegar à média de.

averse [əˈvɜːs] *adj:* **to be** ~ **to** sthg/**to doing** sthg ser contrário(ria) a algo/fazer algo.

aversion [əˈvɜːʃn] *n* **-1.** [dislike] aversão *f;* ~ **to** sthg aversão a algo **-2.** [object of dislike] aversão *f.*

avert [əˈvɜːt] *vt* [avoid] evitar.

aviary [ˈeɪvjərɪ] (*pl* **-ies**) *n* aviário *m.*

aviation [ˌeɪvɪˈeɪʃn] *n* aviação *f.*

aviator [ˈeɪvɪeɪtəʳ] *n dated* aviador *m,* -ra *f.*

avid [ˈævɪd] *adj* [keen] ávido(da); ~ **for** sthg ávido (da) de/por algo.

avocado [ˌævəˈkɑːdəʊ] (*pl* **-s** OR **-es**) *n:* ~ **(pear)** abacate *m.*

avoid [əˈvɔɪd] *vt* evitar; **to** ~ **doing** sthg evitar fazer algo.

avoidable [əˈvɔɪdəbl] *adj* evitável.

avoidance [əˈvɔɪdəns] *n* ⊳ **tax avoidance.**

avowed [əˈvaʊd] *adj* declarado(da).

AWACS (*abbr of* **airborne warning and control system**) *n sistema aéreo de monitoramento terrestre por radar;* ~ **planes** aviões *mpl* AWACS.

await [əˈweɪt] *vt* **-1.** [wait for] esperar **-2.** [be ready for] estar pronto(ta) para.

awake [əˈweɪk] (*pt* awoke OR awaked, *pp* awoken) <> *adj* [not sleeping] acordado(da); **to be wide** ~ estar totalmente desperto(ta). <> *vt* **-1.** [wake up] acordar **-2.** *fig* [provoke] despertar. <> *vi* [wake up] acordar.

awakening [əˈweɪknɪŋ] *n* **-1.** [from sleep] despertar *m* **-2.** *fig* [of feeling] despertar *m.*

award [əˈwɔːd] <> *n* **-1.** [prize] prêmio *m* **-2.** [compensation] recompensa *f.* <> *vt* [give] premiar; **to** ~ **sb** sthg, **to** ~ sthg **to sb** conceder algo a alguém.

aware [əˈweəʳ] *adj* **-1.** [conscious]: ~ **of** sthg consciente de algo; ~ **that** ciente de que **-2.** [informed, sensitive] consciente; ~ **of** sthg informado(da) sobre algo.

awareness [əˈweənɪs] *n* consciência *f.*

awash [əˈwɒʃ] *adj:* ~ **(with** sthg**)** cheio(a) (de algo).

away [əˈweɪ] <> *adv* **-1.** [indicating movement] embora; ~ **from** longe de; **to look/turn** ~

virar-se **- 2.** [at a distance - in space]: **she lives 3 miles** ~ ela mora a três milhas daqui; **we live 4 miles** ~ **from the city centre** moramos a 4 milhas do centro da cidade; [- in time]: **the exams were only two days** ~ faltavam apenas dois dias para os exames **- 3.** [separate from]: **to be kept** ~ **from** sthg ser mantido(da) afastado(da) de algo; **to give sthg** ~ dar algo; **to take sthg** ~ levar algo **- 4.** [absent]: **to be** ~ estar fora **- 5.** [in a safe place]: **to put sthg** ~ guardar algo **- 6.** [indicating disappearance, cessation]: **the stain has faded** ~ a mancha desapareceu; **the wood had rotted** ~ a madeira tinha apodrecido **-7.** [continuously]: **to sing/work** ~ cantar/trabalhar sem parar. <> *adj SPORT* : ~ **team** time *m* visitante; ~ **game** jogo fora de casa.

awe [ɔːl] *n* temor *m*; **to be in** ~ **of sb** estar intimidado(da) por alguém.

awesome ['ɔːsəm] *adj* [impressive] terrível.

awestruck ['ɔːstrʌk] *adj* aterrorizado(da).

awful ['ɔːfʊl] *adj* **-1.** [terrible] horrível **- 2.** *inf* [very great]: **to have an** ~ **lot of work to do** ter um bocado de coisas para fazer.

awfully ['ɔːflɪ] *adv inf* [very] pra caramba; **to be** ~ **difficult** ser difícil pra caramba.

awhile [ə'waɪl] *adv literary* durante um tempo.

awkward ['ɔːkwəd] *adj* **-1.** [clumsy] desajeitado(da) **- 2.** [embarrassing] embaraçoso(sa) **- 3.** [embarrassed]: **to feel** ~ sentir-se embaraçado(da) **- 4.** [difficult to deal with] complicado(da) **- 5.** [inconvenient] inadequado(da).

awkwardly ['ɔːkwədlɪ] *adv* **-1.** [clumsily] desajeitadamente **- 2.** [in an embarrassed way] embaraçosamente **- 3.** [inconveniently] inconvenientemente.

awkwardness ['ɔːkwədnɪs] *n* **-1.** [clumsiness - of movement, position] falta *f* de jeito; [- of person] indelicadeza *f* **- 2.** [unease] dificuldade *f* **- 3.** [inconvenience] embaraço *m*.

awl [ɔːl] *n* furador *m*.

awning ['ɔːnɪŋ] *n* **-1.** [of tent] cobertura *f* **- 2.** [of shop] toldo *m*.

awoke [ə'wəʊk] *pt* ▷ **awake**.

awoken [ə'wəʊkn] *pp* ▷ **awake**.

AWOL (*abbr of* absent without leave): **to go** ~ *MIL* sair sem permissão; **the cat has gone** ~ *hum* o gato sumiu.

awry [ə'raɪ] <> *adj* [twisted] desajeitado(da). <> *adv* : **to go** ~ [wrong] dar errado.

axe *UK*, **ax** *US* [æks] <> *n* machado *m*; **to have an** ~ **to grind** ter um interesse pessoal. <> *vt* [project, jobs] cortar.

axes ['æksiːz] *pl* ▷ **axis**.

axiom ['æksɪəm] *n* axioma *m*.

axis ['æksɪs] (*pl* **axes**) *n* eixo *m*.

axle ['æksl] *n* [shaft] eixo *m*.

ayatollah [ˌaɪə'tɒlə] *n* aiatolá *m*.

aye [aɪ] <> *adv* [yes] sim. <> *n* [affirmative vote] sim *m*.

AYH (*abbr of* American Youth Hostels) *n* Albergues *mpl* da Juventude *(nos Estados Unidos).*

A-Z *n* guia que contém mapas de ruas das cidades britânicas.

AZ *abbr of* Arizona.

---

azalea [ə'zeɪljə] *n* azaléia *f*.

Azerbaijan [ˌæzəbaɪ'dʒɑːn] *n* Azerbaijão; **in** ~ **no** Azerbaijão.

Azerbaijani [ˌæzəbaɪ'dʒɑːnɪ] <> *adj* azerbaijano(na). <> *n* azerbaijano *m*, -na *f*.

Azeri [ə'zerɪ] <> *adj* azeri. <> *n* azeri *mf*.

Azores [ə'zɔːz] *npl*: **the** ~ os Açores; **in the** ~ nos Açores.

AZT (*abbr of* azidothymidine) *n* AZT® *m*.

Aztec ['æztek] <> *adj* asteca. <> *n* asteca *mf*.

azure ['æʒəʳ] *adj* [bright blue] azul-celeste.

B

b (*pl* **b's** *OR* **bs**), **B** (*pl* **B's** *OR* **Bs**) [biː] *n* [letter] b, B *m*.
▶ **B** *n* **-1.** *MUS* si *m* **- 2.** *SCH* [mark] B *m*.

b. (*abbr of* born) n.

BA *n* **-1.** (*abbr of* Bachelor of Arts) *titular de graduação em ciências humanas.* **- 2.** (*abbr of* British Academy) *organismo público britânico para fomento de pesquisa em ciências humanas.*

BAA (*abbr of* British Airports Authority) *n organismo independente que controla os aeroportos britânicos,* ≃ INFRAERO *f.*

babble ['bæbl] <> *n* [noise] balbucio *m*. <> *vi* [person] balbuciar.

babe [beɪb] *n* **-1.** *literary* [baby] nenê *mf* **-2.** *inf* [term of affection] garota *f* **- 3.** *inf* [beautiful woman] boneca *f*.

baboon [bə'buːn] *n* [animal] babuíno *m*.

baby ['beɪbɪ] (*pl* **-ies**) *n* **-1.** [child] bebê *mf*, nenê *mf* **-2.** *pej* [feeble person]: **don't be such a** ~! não seja tão criança! **- 3.** *esp US inf* [term of affection] pequeno(na).

baby boomer [-ˌbuːməʳ] *n US pessoa nascida num período de explosão demográfica nos Estados Unidos, especialmente entre 1946 e 1954.*

baby buggy *UK*, **baby carriage** *UK n* [foldable pushchair] carrinho *m* de bebê

baby food *n* comida *f* de nenê.

babyish ['beɪbɪʃ] *adj pej* infantil.

baby-sit *vi* tomar conta de crianças, trabalhar como babá.

baby-sitter [-ˌsɪtəʳ] *n* babá *f*, baby-sitter *f*.

bachelor ['bætʃələʳ] *n* [unmarried man] solteirão *m*; **confirmed** ~ solteirão convicto.

Bachelor of Arts *n* [person]; [degree] *bacharelado em Artes, Ciências Humanas ou Sociais.*

Bachelor of Science *n* [person] Bacharel *m* em Ciências ; [degree] bacharelado *m* em ciências.

bachelor's degree *n* grau *m* de bacharel.

back [bæk] <> *adj* (in compounds) **-1.** [rear] traseiro (ra); ~ **legs** patas traseiras **-2.** [at the back] de trás, dos fundos; ~ **seat** assento de trás; ~ **garden** jardim dos fundos **-3.** [overdue] atrasado(da). <> *adv* **-1.** [backwards] para trás **-2.** [indicating return to former position or state] de volta; **is he** ~ **yet?** ele já está de volta?, ele já voltou?; **to go** ~ **to sleep** voltar a dormir; **to go** ~ **and forth** ficar indo e vindo **-3.** [earlier]: ~ **in January** em janeiro passado **-4.** [in reply, in return] de volta; **to phone** ~ ligar de volta; **to pay** ~ reembolsar; **to write** ~ responder **-5.** [in fashion again]: **to be** ~ **(in fashion)** estar de volta (à moda). <> *n* **-1.** [of person, animal] costas *fpl*; **to break the** ~ **of sthg** *fig* conseguir terminar algo; **to do sthg behind sb's** ~ fazer algo pelas costas de alguém; **to know somewhere like the** ~ **of one's hand** conhecer um lugar como a palma da mão; **to put sb's** ~ **up** encher o saco de alguém; **to stab sb in the** ~ apunhalar pelas costas; **to turn one's** ~ **on sb/ sthg** virar as costas para alguém/algo **-2.** [reverse side - of page, envelope] verso *m*; [- of head] parte *f* de trás, parte *f* anterior **-3.** [furthest point away from front - of room] fundos *mpl*; [- of cupboard, fridge]: **in the** ~ **of the fridge** na parte de trás geladeira; [- of car] traseira *f*; [- of chair] encosto *m*; **at the** ~ **of, in the** ~ **of** *US* atrás de; **in the** ~ **of beyond** *UK* no fim do mundo **-4.** *SPORT* [player] zagueiro(ra). <> *vt* **-1.** [reverse] recuar **-2.** [support] apoiar **-3.** [bet on] apostar **-4.** [provide lining for] forrar. <> *vi* [reverse] retornar; **to** ~ **into sthg** [walking] voltar-se para algo; [in vehicle] entrar de ré em algo.

➤ **back to back** *adv* [with backs touching]: **to stand** ~ **to** ~ ficar costas com costas.
➤ **back to front** *adv* [the wrong way round] de trás para frente, ao contrário.
➤ **back away** *vi* afastar-se.
➤ **back down** *vi* voltar atrás.
➤ **back off** *vi* afastar-se.
➤ **back onto** *vt fus* *UK* dar (com os fundos) para.
➤ **back out** *vi* [of promise, arrangement] dar para trás.
➤ **back up** <> *vt sep* **-1.** [support] apoiar **-2.** [reverse] dar marcha à ré **-3.** *COMPUT* fazer cópia de segurança de. <> *vi* **-1.** [reverse] dar marcha à ré **-2.** *COMPUT* fazer cópia de segurança.

backache ['bækeɪk] *n* dor *f* nas costas.
backbencher [ˌbæk'bentʃəʳ] *n* *UK* *POL* membro do Parlamento Britânico, sem cargo oficial no governo ou na oposição.
backbenches [ˌbæk'bentʃɪz] *npl* *UK* *POL*: **the** ~ as cadeiras reservadas aos membros do Parlamento Britânico, sem cargo oficial no governo ou na oposição.
backbiting ['bækbaɪtɪŋ] *n* (U) falar *m* pelas costas.
backbone ['bækbəʊn] *n* **-1.** [spine] coluna *f* vertebral **-2.** (U) *fig* [courage, force] tutano *m* **-3.** *fig* [main support]: **the** ~ **of** a espinha dorsal de.
backbreaking ['bækˌbreɪkɪŋ] *adj* [exhausting] estafante.
back burner *n*: **to put sthg on the** ~ *fig* deixar algo em segundo plano.
backchat *UK* ['bæktʃæt], **backtalk** *US* ['bæktɔːk] *n* (U) *inf* contestações *fpl*.

backcloth ['bækklɒθ] *n* *UK* = backdrop.
backcomb ['bækkəʊm] *vt* *UK* pentear o cabelo em direção ao couro cabeludo para fazê-lo parecer mais volumoso.
back copy *n* = back number.
backdate [ˌbæk'deɪt] *vt* antedatar.
back door *n* porta *f* dos fundos; **to get in through** *OR* **by the** ~ *fig* conseguir algo por baixo do pano.
backdrop ['bækdrɒp] *n* **-1.** *THEATRE* pano *m* de fundo **-2.** *fig* [background] pano *m* de fundo.
backer ['bækəʳ] *n* *FIN* avalista *mf*.
backfire [ˌbæk'faɪəʳ] *vi* **-1.** [motor vehicle] engasgar **-2.** [go wrong] dar errado; **his plans** ~**d (on him)** seus planos não deram o resultado esperado.
backgammon ['bækˌgæmən] *n* (U) gamão *m*.
background ['bækgraʊnd] <> *n* **-1.** [in picture, view] fundo *m*; **in the** ~ *lit* ao fundo; *fig* [unnoticeable] em segundo plano **-2.** [of event, situation] cenário *m* **-3.** [upbringing] background *m*. <> *comp* **-1.** [music, noise] de fundo **-2.** [reading, information] preliminar.
backhand ['bækhænd] *n* backhand *m*.
backhanded ['bækhændɪd] *adj* *fig* [equivocal] falso(-sa).
backhander ['bækhændəʳ] *n* *UK* *inf* [bribe] suborno *m*.
backing ['bækɪŋ] *n* **-1.** (U) [support] suporte *m* **-2.** [lining] forro *m* **-3.** *MUS* acompanhamento *m*.
backing group *n* *MUS* grupo *m* de acompanhamento.
back issue *n* = back number.
backlash ['bæklæʃ] *n* [adverse reaction] revolta *f*.
backless ['bæklɪs] *adj* frente-única.
backlog ['bæklɒg] *n* acúmulo *m*.
back number *n* número *m* atrasado.
backpack ['bækpæk] *n* mochila *f*.
backpacker ['bækpækəʳ] *n* mochileiro *m*, -ra *f*.
backpacking ['bækpækɪŋ] *n*: **to go** ~ viajar com a mochila nas costas.
back passage *n* *euphemism* reto *m*.
back pay *n* (U) salário *m* atrasado.
backpedal [ˌbæk'pedl] (*UK* *pt* & *pp* -**led**, *cont* -**ling**, *US* *pt* & *pp* -**ed**, *cont* -**ing**) *vi* *fig* [change one's mind]: **to** ~ **(on sthg)** dar pra trás (em algo).
back seat *n* [in car] banco *m* de trás; **to take a** ~ *fig* desempenhar um papel secundário.
back-seat driver *n* carona que fica dizendo ao motorista como dirigir.
backside [ˌbæk'saɪd] *n* *inf* traseiro *m*.
backslapping *n* (U) *inf* [congratulations] saudações *mpl*.
backslash ['bækslæʃ] *n* *COMPUT* barra *f* invertida.
backslide [ˌbæk'slaɪd] (*pt* & *pp* -**slid** [-'slɪd]) *vi* ter uma recaída.
backspace ['bækspeɪs] <> *n* [key] tecla *f* de retorno. <> *vi* [in typing] clicar o retorno, retornar.
backstage [ˌbæk'steɪdʒ] *adv* nos bastidores.
back street *n* *UK* ruela *f*.
back-street abortion *n* *UK* aborto *m* clandestino.
backstroke ['bækstrəʊk] *n* [in swimming] nado *m* (de) costas.
backtalk *n* *US* = backchat.

backtrack ['bæktræk] *vi* = backpedal.

backup ['bækʌp] <> *adj* -1. [reserve] de reserva - 2. COMPUT de segurança. <> *n* -1. [support] suporte *m* -2. COMPUT backup *m*, cópia *f* de segurança.

backward ['bækwəd] <> *adj* -1. [directed towards the rear] para trás - 2. *pej* [late in development - person] retardado(da); [- society, ideas] atrasado(da). <> *adv US* = backwards.

backward-looking [-ˌlʊkɪŋ] *adj pej* retrógrado(-da).

backwards ['bækwədz], **backward** *US* ['bækwəd] *adv* -1. [towards the rear] de trás para a frente; ~ **and forwards** de um lado para outro - 2. [back to front] de trás para a frente, ao contrário.

backwash ['bækwɒʃ] *n* [of event, situation] repercussão *f*.

backwater ['bækˌwɔːtəʳ] *n fig & pej* [place behind the times] lugar *m* atrasado; **cultural** ~ atraso *m* cultural.

backwoods ['bækwʊdz] *npl* [remote place] confins *mpl*.

backyard [ˌbækˈjɑːd] *n* -1. *UK* [yard] pátio *m*, quintal *m* - 2. *US* [garden] jardim *m*.

bacon ['beɪkən] *n (U)* bacon *m*.

bacteria [bækˈtɪərɪə] *npl* bactérias *fpl*.

bacteriology [bækˌtɪərɪˈɒlədʒɪ] *n (U)* bacteriologia *f*.

bad [bæd] (*compar* **worse**, *superl* **worst**) <> *adj* -1. [gen] ruim; **not** ~ nada mal; **too** ~ uma pena; **to be** ~ **at sthg** ser ruim em algo - 2. [unfavourable] mau (má); **to go from** ~ **to worse** ir de mal a pior - 3. [severe] grave, severo(ra) - 4. [inadequate] ruim - 5. [guilty]: **to feel** ~ **about sthg** sentir-se mal por algum motivo - 6. [food, milk, meat] mal; **to go** ~ ir mal. <> *adv US* = badly.

bad blood *n (U)* [anger] ódio *m*.

bad cheque *UK*, **bad check** *US n* cheque *m* sem fundo.

bad debt *n* dívida *f* perdida.

baddy (*pl* -ies) *n inf* vilão *m*, vilã *f*.

bade [bæd] *pt* ⊳ bid.

bad feeling *n (U)* [resentment] rancor *m*, ressentimento *m*.

badge [bædʒ] *n* -1. [metal, plastic] crachá *m* - 2. [sewn on] distintivo *m* - 3. [on car] selo *m*.

badger ['bædʒəʳ] <> *n* [animal] texugo *m*. <> *vt* [pester]: **to** ~ **sb (to do sthg)** convencer alguém (a fazer algo).

badly ['bædlɪ] (*compar* **worse**, *superl* **worst**) *adv* -1. [poorly] mal; **to think** ~ **of sb** pensar mal de alguém - 2. [severely] gravemente - 3. [improperly] indevidamente - 4. [cruelly] mal - 5. [very much]: **to be** ~ **in need of sthg** precisar muito de algo.

badly-off *adj* -1. [poor] carente - 2. [lacking]: **to be** ~ **for sthg** estar carente de algo.

bad-mannered [-ˈmænəd] *adj* mal-educado(da).

badminton ['bædmɪntən] *n (U)* badminton *m*.

bad-mouth *vt esp US inf* falar mal de.

badness ['bædnɪs] *n (U)* maldade *f*.

bad-tempered [-ˈtempəd] *adj* -1. [by nature] genioso(sa) - 2. [in a bad mood] mal-humorado(da).

baffle ['bæfl] *vt* [puzzle] desnortear.

baffling ['bæflɪŋ] *adj* [puzzling] desnorteante.

BAFTA (*abbr of* British Academy of Film and Television Arts) *n* organização britânica que promove e premia os melhores em filmes, televisão e outras mídias interativas.

bag [bæg] (*pt & pp* -ged, *cont* -ging) <> *n* -1. [container] saco *m*; ~ **of bones** saco de ossos; **in the** ~ *inf* no papo; **to pack one's** ~**s** *fig* [leave] fazer as malas - 2. [handbag] bolsa *f*; [when travelling] mala *f* - 3. [bagful] sacola *f*. <> *vt* -1. [put into bags] ensacar - 2. *UK inf* [get] pegar - 3. *UK inf* [reserve] marcar.
bags *npl* -1. [under eyes] bolsas *fpl* - 2. [lots]: ~**s of sthg** *inf* um montão de algo.

bagel ['beɪgəl] *n* pão *m* enrolado.

baggage ['bægɪdʒ] *n (U)* bagagem *f*.

baggage car *n US* vagão *m* de bagagens.

baggage reclaim *n* esteira *f* de bagagem.

baggage room *n US* guarda-volumes *m inv*.

baggy ['bægɪ] (*compar* -ier, *superl* -iest) *adj* largo(ga).

Baghdad [bægˈdæd] *n* Bagdá; **in** ~ em Bagdá.

bag lady *n inf* mulher *f* de rua.

bagpipes ['bægpaɪps] *npl* gaita *f* de foles.

bagsnatcher ['bægsnætʃəʳ] *n* batedor *m* de carteira.

baguette [bəˈget] *n* [loaf] baguete *f*.

bah [bɑː] *excl* bah!

Bahamas [bəˈhɑːməz] *npl*: **the** ~ as Bahamas; **in the** ~ nas Bahamas.

Bahrain, Bahrein [bɑːˈreɪn] *n* Barein; **in** ~ em Barein.

Bahraini, Bahreini [bɑːˈreɪnɪ] <> *adj & n* baraini. <> *n* baraini *mf*.

bail [beɪl] *n (U)* JUR fiança *f*; **on** ~ sob fiança.
bail out <> *vt sep* -1. JUR [pay bail for] afiançar - 2. [rescue] resgatar - 3. [boat] tirar água. <> *vi* [from plane] saltar de pára-quedas.

bailiff ['beɪlɪf] *n* -1. [in court] oficial *mf* de justiça - 2. [in charge of repossession] administrador *m*, -ra *f* de propriedades.

bait [beɪt] <> *n (U)* [food] isca *f*; **to rise to** OR **take the** ~ *fig* morder a isca. <> *vt* -1. [hook] pôr isca em - 2. [mousetrap] armar - 3. [tease, torment - person] atormentar; [- bear, badger] provocar.

baize [beɪz] *n (U)* feltro *m*.

bake [beɪk] <> *vt* -1. [cook] assar - 2. [dry, harden] queimar. <> *vi* [food] assar.

baked beans [beɪkt-] *npl* feijão *cozido em molho de tomate*.

baked potato [beɪkt-] *n* batata grande assada *com casca e servida com recheio*.

Bakelite® ['beɪkəlaɪt] *n* baquelita *f*.

baker ['beɪkəʳ] *n* padeiro *m*; ~'**s (shop)** padaria *f*.

bakery ['beɪkərɪ] (*pl* -ies) *n* padaria *f*.

baking ['beɪkɪŋ] <> *adj inf* [hot] escaldante. <> *n* [process] cozimento *m*.

baking powder *n (U)* fermento *m* em pó.

baking tin *n* fôrma *f*.

baking tray *n* assadeira *f*.

balaclava (helmet) [bæləˈklɑːvə-] *n UK* balaclava *f*.

balance ['bæləns] <> *n* -1. [equilibrium] equilíbrio *m*; **to keep/lose one's** ~ manter/perder o equilíbrio; **off** ~ desequilibrado(da) - 2. *fig* [counterweight] contra-peso *m* - 3. *fig* [weight, force]: ~ **of evidence**

peso *m* da evidência **- 4.** [scales] balança *f*; **to be** OR **hang in the** ~ estar na balança **- 5.** [remainder] restante *m* **- 6.** [of bank account] saldo *m*. <> *vt* **-1.** [keep in balance] balancear **- 2.** [compare]: **to** ~ **sthg against sthg** contrabalançar algo em relação a algo **- 3.** [in accounting]: **to** ~ **the books/a budget** fazer o balanço dos livros/do orçamento. <> *vi* **- 1.** [maintain equilibrium] equilibrar-se **- 2.** [in accounting] fechar, bater.

◆ **on balance** *adv* de um modo geral.

balanced ['bælənst] *adj* equilibrado(da).

balanced diet ['bælənst-] *n* dieta *f* equilibrada.

balance of payments *n* balança *f* de pagamentos.

balance of power *n* equilíbrio *m* de forças.

balance of trade *n* balança *f* comercial.

balance sheet *n* balancete *m*.

balancing act ['bælənsɪŋ-] *n fig* [careful manoeuvre] malabarismo *m*.

balcony ['bælkənɪ] (*pl*-ies) *n* **-1.** [on building] sacada *f* **- 2.** [in theatre] balcão *m*, galeria *f*.

bald [bɔːld] *adj* **-1.** [head, man, tyre] careca **- 2.** *fig* [unadorned] curto(ta) e grosso(sa).

bald eagle *n* águia *f* americana (*símbolo dos Estados Unidos que aparece em todos os emblemas oficiais*).

balding ['bɔːldɪŋ] *adj* careca, calvo(va).

baldness ['bɔːldnɪs] *n* (*U*) calvície *f*.

bale [beɪl] *n* fardo *m*.

◆ **bale out** *UK vt sep* = **bail out.**

Balearic Islands [ˌbælɪˈærɪk-], **Balearics** [ˌbælɪˈærɪks] *npl*: **the** ~ as Ilhas Baleares; **in the** ~ nas Ilhas Baleares.

baleful ['beɪlfʊl] *adj* fulminante.

Bali ['bɑːlɪ] *n* Bali; **in** ~ em Bali.

balk [bɔːk] *vi* [recoil]: **to** ~ **(at sthg)** [person] recusar-se (a fazer algo).

Balkan [bɔːlkən] *adj* balcânico(ca).

Balkans ['bɔːlkənz], **Balkan States** *npl*: **the** ~ os Balcãs; **in the** ~ nos Balcãs.

ball [bɔːl] *n* **-1.** [in game] bola *f*; **to start/keep the** ~ **rolling** *fig* pôr/manter a bola em jogo; **to be on the** ~ *fig* estar ligado(da) em tudo; **to play** ~ **with sb** *fig* colaborar (com alguém) **- 2.** [sphere] novelo *m* **- 3.** [dance] baile *m*; **to have a** ~ *fig* divertir-se.

◆ **balls** *vulg* <> *n* [nonsense] merda *f*. <> *npl* [testicles] saco *m*; *fig* [courage]: **to have** ~ ter colhões. <> *excl* caralho!

ballad ['bæləd] *n* balada *f*.

ball-and-socket joint *n* junta *f* articulada (*bola-e-soquete*).

ballast ['bæləst] *n* (*U*) lastro *m*.

ball bearing *n* rolamento *m*.

ball boy *n* gandula *m*.

ballcock ['bɔːlkɒk] *n* bóia *f*.

ballerina [ˌbæləˈriːnə] *n* bailarina *f*.

ballet ['bæleɪ] *n* (*U*) balé *m*.

ballet dancer *n* bailarino(na).

ball game *n* **- 1.** *US* [baseball match] jogo *m* de beisebol **- 2.** *fig* [situation]: **it's a whole new** ~ *inf* é outra história.

ball girl *n* gandula *f*.

ballistic missile *n* míssil *m* balístico.

ballistics [bəˈlɪstɪks] *n* (*U*) balística *f*.

balloon [bəˈluːn] <> *n* balão *m*. <> *vi* [swell] inflar.

ballooning [bəˈluːnɪŋ] *n* (*U*) balonismo *m*.

ballot ['bælət] <> *n* **- 1.** [voting paper] voto *m* **- 2.** [voting process] votação *f*. <> *vt* [canvass] caçar votos. <> *vi* [vote]: **to** ~ **for sthg** votar para algo.

ballot box *n* **- 1.** [container] urna *f* **- 2.** [voting process] urnas *fpl*.

ballot paper *n* cédula *f* de votação.

ball park *n US* estádio *m* de beisebal.

ball-park figure *n inf* [estimate] valor *m* estimado.

ballpoint (pen) ['bɔːlpɔɪnt-] *n* caneta *f* esferográfica.

ballroom ['bɔːlrʊm] *n* salão *m* de baile.

ballroom dancing *n* (*U*) dança *f* de salão.

balls-up *UK*, **ball-up** *US n v inf* cagada *f*.

balm [bɑːm] *n* bálsamo *m*.

balmy ['bɑːmɪ] (*compar*-ier, *superl*-iest) *adj* suave.

baloney [bəˈləʊnɪ] *n* **- 1.** *inf* [rubbish] asneira *f* **- 2.** *US* [sausage] mortadela *f*.

balsa ['bɒlsə] *n* = **balsawood.**

balsam ['bɔːlsəm] *n* (*U*) [substance] bálsamo *m*.

balsawood ['bɒlsəwʊd] *n* balsa *f*.

Baltic ['bɔːltɪk] <> *adj* [port, coast] báltico(ca). <> *n*: **the** ~ **(Sea)** o (mar) Báltico.

Baltic Republic *n*: **the** ~ **s** as Repúblicas Bálticas.

Baltic State *n*: **the** ~ **s** os Estados Bálticos.

balustrade [ˌbæləsˈtreɪd] *n* balaustrada *f*.

bamboo [bæmˈbuː] *n* bambu *m*.

bamboozle [bæmˈbuːzl] *vt inf* lograr.

ban [bæn] (*pt* & *pp*-ned, *cont*-ning) <> *n* proibição *f*; ~ **on sthg** proibição de algo. <> *vt* banir; **to** ~ **sb from doing sthg** proibir alguém de fazer algo.

banal [bəˈnɑːl] *adj pej* banal.

banana [bəˈnɑːnə] *n* banana *f*.

banana republic *n* república *f* das bananas.

banana split *n* banana *f* split.

band [bænd] *n* **- 1.** [musical group] banda *f* **- 2.** [gang] bando *m* **- 3.** [long strip] correia *f* **- 4.** [broad stripe, range] faixa *f*.

◆ **band together** *vi* unir-se.

bandage ['bændɪdʒ] <> *n* faixa *f*. <> *vt* enfaixar.

Band-Aid® *n* band-aid *m*.

bandan(n)a [bænˈdænə] *n* bandana *f*.

b and b, B and B (*abbr of* bed and breakfast) *n* tipo de acomodação típica da Grã-Bretanha em que residências privadas oferecem serviço de quarto e café da manhã.

bandit ['bændɪt] *n* bandido *m*.

bandmaster ['bændˌmɑːstəʳ] *n* maestro *m*, -trina *f*.

band saw *n* serra *f* de fita.

bandsman ['bændzmən] (*pl*-men [-mən]) *n* músico *m*.

bandstand ['bændstænd] *n* palanque *m*.

bandwagon ['bændˌwægən] *n*: **to jump on the** ~ pegar carona na idéia.

bandy ['bændɪ] (*compar*-ier, *superl*-iest, *pt* & *pp*-ied) *adj* [bandy-legged] cambaio(a).

◆ **bandy about, bandy around** *vt sep* ficar repetindo.

bandy-legged [-ˌlegd] *adj* = bandy.

bane [beɪn] *n*: the ~ of sb's life a cruz da vida de alguém.

bang [bæŋ] <> *adv* -**1.** [right]: ~ in the middle bem no meio; ~ on certeiro(ra) -**2.** *phr*: ~ goes/go ... *inf* lá se vai/vão ... <> *n* -**1.** [blow] golpe *m* -**2.** [loud noise] estrondo *m*; to go with a ~ *inf fig* ser um estouro. <> *vt* -**1.** [hit] bater -**2.** [move noisily] bater. <> *vi* -**1.** [knock]: to ~ on sthg dar pancadas -**2.** [make a loud noise] bater -**3.** [crash]: to ~ into sb/ sthg bater em alguém/algo. <> *excl* bum.

 bangs *npl US* franjas *fpl*.

 bang down *vt sep*: to ~ sthg down on bater algo com força em.

banger [ˈbæŋəʳ] *n UK*-**1.** *inf* [sausage] salsicha *f*-**2.** *inf* [old car] carroça *f*-**3.** [firework] rojão *m*.

Bangkok [bæŋˈkɒk] *n* Bangkok; in ~ em Bangkok.

Bangladesh [ˌbæŋgləˈdeʃ] *n* Bangladesh; in ~ em Bangladesh.

Bangladeshi [ˌbæŋgləˈdeʃi] <> *adj* bangladeshiano(na). <> *n* bangladeshiano *m*, -na *f*.

bangle [ˈbæŋgl] *n* pulseira *f*.

banish [ˈbænɪʃ] *vt* -**1.** [gen, fig] banir -**2.** *literary* [dismiss] afugentar.

banister [ˈbænɪstəʳ] *n*, **banisters** [ˈbænɪstəz] *npl* corrimão *m*.

banjo [ˈbændʒəʊ] (*pl* -s OR -es) *n* banjo *m*.

bank [bæŋk] <> *n* -**1.** [gen & FIN] banco *m*; blood/ data ~ banco *m* de sangue/dados -**2.** [alongside river, lake] margem *m* -**3.** [slope] monte *m* -**4.** [of clouds, fog] massa *f*. <> *vt FIN* depositar. <> *vi* -**1.** *FIN*: to ~ with sb ser correntista de -**2.** [plane] inclinar lateralmente.

 bank on *vt fus* contar com.

bank account *n* conta *f* corrente.

bank balance *n* saldo *m* bancário.

bankbook [ˈbæŋkbʊk] *n* extrato *m* bancário.

bank card *n* cartão *m* de garantia de cheque.

bank charges *npl* tarifas *fpl* bancárias.

bank draft *n* ordem *f* bancária.

banker [ˈbæŋkəʳ] *n FIN* banqueiro *m*, -ra *f*.

banker's order *n UK* débito *m* em conta.

bank holiday *n UK* feriado *m* bancário.

banking [ˈbæŋkɪŋ] *n (U)* serviços *mpl* bancários.

bank loan *n* empréstimo *m* bancário.

bank manager *n* gerente *mf* de banco.

bank note *n* cédula *f*.

bank rate *n* taxa *f* referencial de juros.

bankrupt [ˈbæŋkrʌpt] <> *adj* [financially] falido(da); to go ~ ir à falência; to be morally ~ *fig* estar desmoralizado(da). <> *n* falido *m*, -da *f*. <> *vt* falir.

bankruptcy [ˈbæŋkrəptsɪ] (*pl* -ies) *n* falência *f*; moral ~ *fig* desmoralização *f*.

bank statement *n* extrato *m* bancário.

banner [ˈbænəʳ] *n* [made of cloth] faixa *f*.

bannister [ˈbænɪstəʳ] *n*, **bannisters** [ˈbænɪstəz] *npl* = banister.

banns [bænz] *npl*: to publish the ~ proclamar os votos.

banquet [ˈbæŋkwɪt] *n* banquete *m*.

bantam [ˈbæntəm] *n* garnisé *m*.

bantamweight [ˈbæntəmweɪt] *n* peso-galo *m*.

banter [ˈbæntəʳ] <> *n (U)* brincadeiras *fpl*. <> *vi* brincar.

bap [bæp] *n UK* bisnaguinha *f*.

baptism [ˈbæptɪzm] *n* batismo *m*; ~ of fire *fig* batismo de fogo.

Baptist [ˈbæptɪst] *n* batista *mf*.

baptize, -ise [*UK* bæpˈtaɪz, *US* ˈbæptaɪz] *vt* batizar.

bar [baːʳ] (*pt* & *pp* -red, *cont* -ring) <> *n* -**1.** [of wood, metal, chocolate, soap etc] barra *f*; to be behind ~s estar atrás das grades -**2.** *fig* [obstacle] barreira *f* -**3.** [drinking place] bar *m* -**4.** [counter] balcão *m* -**5.** *MUS* compasso *m*. <> *vt* -**1.** [bolt] trancar -**2.** [block off] bloquear; to ~ sb's way bloquear a passagem de alguém -**3.** [ban] barrar; to ~ sb (from somewhere/from doing sthg) impedir alguém (de entrar em algum lugar/fazer algo). <> *prep* [except] exceto; ~ none sem exceção.

 Bar *n* -**1.** *UK*: the Bar [barristers] o Magistrado; [profession] a Magistratura -**2.** *US*: the Bar [lawyers] advogados(das); [profession] a Advocacia.

Barbados [baːˈbeɪdɒs] *n* Barbados; in ~ em Barbados.

barbarian [baːˈbeərɪən] *n* -**1.** *HIST* bárbaro *m* -**2.** *pej* & *fig* [uncultured person] bárbaro *m*, -ra *f*.

barbaric [baːˈbærɪk] *adj pej* bárbaro(ra).

barbarous [ˈbaːbərəs] *adj pej* bárbaro(ra).

barbecue [ˈbaːbɪkjuː] <> *n* -**1.** [grill] churrasqueira *f* -**2.** [party] churrasco *m*. <> *vt* assar (*na churrasqueira*).

barbed [baːbd] *adj* -**1.** [pointed, spiked] farpado(da) -**2.** [unkind] espinhento(ta).

barbed wire [baːbd-] *n UK* (*U*) arame *m* farpado.

barber [ˈbaːbəʳ] *n* barbeiro *m*; ~ 's (shop) barbearia *f*.

barbiturate [baːˈbɪtjʊrət] *n* barbitúrico *m*.

Barcelona [ˌbaːsəˈləʊnə] *n* Barcelona; in ~ em Barcelona.

bar chart, bar graph *US n* gráfico *m* de barras.

bar code *n* código *m* de barras.

bare [beəʳ] <> *adj* -**1.** [without covering] descoberto(ta) -**2.** [basic] mínimo(ma); the ~ essentials o mínimo necessário -**3.** [empty] vazio(a) <> *vt* [reveal - chest, limbs] exibir, mostrar; to ~ one's teeth mostrar os dentes to ~ one's head tirar o chapéu.

bareback [ˈbeəbæk] <> *adj* em pêlo. <> *adv* em pêlo.

barefaced [ˈbeəfeɪst] *adj* deslavado(da).

barefoot(ed) [ˌbeəˈfʊt(ɪd)] <> *adj* descalço(ça). <> *adv* descalço.

bareheaded [ˌbeəˈhedɪd] <> *adj* sem chapéu. <> *adv* sem chapéu.

barelegged [ˌbeəˈlegd] <> *adj* de pernas de fora. <> *adv* de pernas de fora.

barely [ˈbeəlɪ] *adv* [scarcely] mal.

bargain [ˈbaːgɪn] <> *n* -**1.** [agreement] barganha *f*; into the ~ ainda por cima -**2.** [good buy] pechincha *f*. <> *vi* barganhar; to ~ with sb for sthg pechinchar com alguém por algo.

 bargain for, bargain on *vt fus* esperar.

bargaining [ˈbaːgɪnɪŋ] *n (U)* barganha *f*.

bargaining power *n (U)* poder *m* de barganha.

barge [baːdʒ] <> *n* barca *f*. <> *vi inf* to ~ into sb/

sthg esbarrar em alguém/algo; **to ~ past sb/ sthg** passar empurrando alguém/algo.
barge in *vi*: **to ~ in (on sb/sthg)** interromper (alguém/algo).

barge pole *n inf*: **I wouldn't touch it with a ~** não quero nem de graça.

bar graph *n US* = **bar chart**.

baritone ['bærɪtəʊn] *n* barítono *m*.

barium meal ['beərɪəm-] *n UK* (líquido de) contraste *m*.

bark [bɑːk] ◇ *n* -**1.** [of dog] latido *m*; **his ~ is worse than his bite** *inf* cão que late não morde -**2.** [on tree] casca *f.* ◇ *vt* [order] gritar. ◇ *vi* [dog] latir; **to ~ at sb/sthg** xingar alguém/algo.

barking ['bɑːkɪŋ] ◇ *n* (*U*) latidos *mpl.* ◇ *adj & adv*: **to be ~ (mad)** *UK inf* ser/estar completamente louco(ca); **to go ~ mad** *UK inf* pirar de vez.

barley ['bɑːlɪ] *n* (*U*) cevada *f.*

barley sugar *n UK* bala feita com caramelo e cevada.

barley water *n UK* (*U*) bebida à base de cevada e suco de fruta.

barmaid ['bɑːmeɪd] *n* garçonete *f.*

barman ['bɑːmən] (*pl* **-men** [-mən]) *n* barman *m.*

barmy ['bɑːmɪ] (*compar* **-ier,** *superl* **-iest**) *adj UK inf* doido(da).

barn [bɑːn] *n* celeiro *m.*

barnacle ['bɑːnəkl] *n* cirrípede *m.*

barn dance *n* -**1.** [occasion] ≃ baile *m* caipira -**2.** *UK* [type of dance] ≃ dança *f* caipira.

barn owl *n* coruja *f* branca.

barnstorm *US vi* -**1.** [politician] viajar em campanha (pelo país) -**2.** [performer] sair em turnê.

barnstorming *UK adj* vigoroso(sa).

barometer [bə'rɒmɪtər] *n* -**1.** [instrument] barômetro *m* -**2.** *fig* [way of measuring] ≃ termômetro *m.*

baron ['bærən] *n* barão *m*; **oil/press ~** *fig* magnata da imprensa/do petróleo.

baroness ['bærənɪs] *n* baronesa *f.*

baronet ['bærənɪt] *n* baronete *m.*

baroque [bə'rɒk] *adj* barroco(ca).

barrack ['bærək] *vt UK* interromper com gritos.
barracks *npl* quartel *m.*

barracking ['bærəkɪŋ] *n* (*U*) *UK* gritaria *f.*

barracuda [ˌbærə'kuːdə] *n* barracuda *f.*

barrage ['bærɑːʒ] *n* -**1.** [of firing] bombardeio *m* -**2.** [of questions] bombardeio *m* -**3.** *UK* [dam] barragem *f.*

barred [bɑːd] *adj* [window, door] trancado(da).

barrel ['bærəl] *n* -**1.** [container] barril *m* -**2.** [of gun] cano *m.*

barrel organ *n* realejo *m.*

barren ['bærən] *adj* -**1.** [unable to have children] estéril -**2.** [unable to produce crops] improdutivo(va) -**3.** [dull] enfadonho(nha).

barrette [bə'ret] *n US* [for hair] fivela *f* passador *m.*

barricade [ˌbærɪ'keɪd] ◇ *n* barricada *f.* ◇ *vt* bloquear, obstruir com barricadas; **to ~ o.s. in** entrincheirar-se em.

barrier ['bærɪər] *n* -**1.** [fence, wall] barreira *f* -**2.** *fig* [obstacle] obstáculo *m.*

barrier cream *n UK* loção *f* protetora.

barring ['bɑːrɪŋ] *prep*: **~ accidents** a menos que

haja imprevistos; **~ further complications** se não houver complicações.

barrister ['bærɪstər] *n UK* advogado *m*, -da *f.*

barroom ['bɑːrʊm] *n US* sala *f* de bar.

barrow ['bærəʊ] *n* [market stall] carrinho *m* de frutas/verduras.

bar stool *n* tamborete *m* de bar.

bartender ['bɑːtendər] *n US* garçom *m*, -nete *f.*

barter ['bɑːtər] ◇ *n* barganha *f*, troca *f.* ◇ *vt* trocar; **to ~ sthg for sthg** trocar algo por algo. ◇ *vi* barganhar.

base [beɪs] ◇ *n* base *f.* ◇ *vt* -**1.** [use as starting point]: **to ~ sthg (up)on sthg** basear algo em algo -**2.** [locate] estabelecer; **to be ~d in** viver/trabalhar em; **a New York-based company** uma empresa sediada em Nova York. ◇ *adj pej* [dishonourable] desprezível.

baseball ['beɪsbɔːl] *n* (*U*) beisebol *m.*

baseball cap *n* boné *m* de beisebol.

base camp *n* acampamento *m* de base.

baseless ['beɪslɪs] *adj* infundado(da).

baseline ['beɪslaɪn] *n SPORT* linha *f* de base.

basement ['beɪsmənt] *n* porão *m.*

base metal *n dated* metal *m* não-precioso.

base rate *n* taxa *f* de base.

bases ['beɪsiːz] *pl* ⊳ **basis**.

bash [bæʃ] *inf* ◇ *n* -**1.** [painful blow] pancada *f* -**2.** [attempt]: **to have a ~ (at sthg)** tentar fazer (algo) -**3.** [party] farra *f.* ◇ *vt* -**1.** [hit] bater -**2.** [criticize] xingar.

bashful ['bæʃfʊl] *adj* tímido(da).

basic ['beɪsɪk] *adj* [fundamental] básico(ca).
basics *npl* -**1.** [rudiments] princípios *mpl* básicos -**2.** [essential foodstuffs] ≃ cesta *f* básica.

BASIC (*abbr of* Beginners' All-purpose Symbolic Instruction Code) *n* BASIC *m.*

basically ['beɪsɪklɪ] *adv* [essentially] basicamente, no fundo.

basic rate *n UK* taxa *f* básica.

basic wage *n* salário *m* base.

basil ['bæzl] *n* (*U*) manjericão *m.*

basin ['beɪsn] *n* -**1.** *UK* [bowl, container] tigela *f*; [for washing] pia *f* -**2.** *GEOGR* bacia *f.*

basis ['beɪsɪs] (*pl* **-ses**) *n* -**1.** [gen] base *f*; **on the ~ that** com base no fato de que, considerando que -**2.** [arrangement]: **on a weekly/monthly ~** numa base semanal/mensal; **on the ~ of** com base em.

bask [bɑːsk] *vi* -**1.** [sunbathe]: **to ~ in the sun** tomar banho de sol -**2.** *fig* [take pleasure]: **to ~ in sb's praise/approval** gozar do elogio/da aprovação de alguém.

basket ['bɑːskɪt] *n* [container - for rubbish] cesto *m*; [- for shopping] cesta *f.*

basketball ['bɑːskɪtbɔːl] ◇ *n* (*U*) basquete *m.* ◇ *comp* de basquete.

basket case *n inf* -**1.** [person] bagaço *m* -**2.** [failure] ruína *f.*

basketwork ['bɑːskɪtwɜːk] *n* -**1.** (*U*) [craft, activity] trabalho *m* em vime -**2.** (*U*) [articles] artigos *mpl* de vime.

basking shark ['bɑːskɪŋ-] *n* tubarão-frade *m.*

Basle [bɑːl] *n* Basiléia; **in ~** na Basiléia.

Basque [bɑːsk] ◇ adj basco(ca). ◇ n -1. [person] basco m, -ca f -2. [language] basco m.

bass¹ [beɪs] ◇ adj [part, singer] baixo(xa). ◇ n -1. [singer] baixo m, -xa f -2. [double bass] duplo baixo m -3. = bass guitar.

bass² [bæs] (pl inv OR -es) n [fish] perca f.

bass clef [beɪs-] n MUS clave f de fá.

bass drum [beɪs-] n MUS tambor m baixo.

basset (hound) [ˈbæsɪt-] n cão m bassê.

bass guitar [beɪs-] n MUS baixo m.

bassoon [bəˈsuːn] n MUS fagote m.

bassoonist n MUS fagotista mf.

bastard [ˈbɑːstəd] n -1. [illegitimate child] bastardo m, -da f -2. v inf pej [person] canalha mf, filho m da mãe.

baste [beɪst] vt CULIN regar.

bastion [ˈbæstɪən] n fig bastião m.

bat [bæt] (pt & pp -ted, cont -ting) ◇ n -1. [animal] morcego m -2. [SPORT - for cricket] pá f; [- for baseball] bastão m; [- for table tennis] raquete f -3. phr: to do sthg off one's own ~ fazer algo sem auxílio. ◇ vt & vi rebater.

batch [bætʃ] n -1. [of papers, letters] pilha f -2. [of work] porção f -3. [of products] lote m -4. [of people] grupo m -5. [of bread, cakes etc] fornada f.

batch file n COMPUT arquivo m em lote.

batch processing n (U) COMPUT processamento m em lote.

bated [ˈbeɪtɪd] adj: with ~ breath [expectantly] segurando a respiração.

bath [bɑːθ] ◇ n -1. [bathtub] banheira f -2. [act of washing] banho m; to have OR take a bath tomar (um) banho. ◇ vt dar banho em.

➠ **baths** npl UK [public] banhos mpl públicos.

bath chair n cadeira f de banho.

bath cube n cubos mpl de sais de banho.

bathe [beɪð] ◇ vt -1. [wound] lavar -2. [in light, sweat] banhar; to be ~d in sthg estar coberto(ta) de algo. ◇ vi -1. [swim] nadar -2. US [take a bath] tomar (um) banho.

bather [ˈbeɪðəʳ] n [swimmer] banhista m.

bathing [ˈbeɪðɪŋ] n (U) banho m; safe for ~ próprio(pria) para banho; to go ~ dar um mergulho.

bathing cap n touca f de banho.

bathing costume, bathing suit n maiô m.

bathing trunks npl calção m de banho.

bath mat n tapete m de banheiro.

bath oil n óleo m de banho.

bathrobe [ˈbɑːθrəʊb] n -1. [made of towelling] roupão m de banho -2. [dressing gown] US chambre m.

bathroom [ˈbɑːθrʊm] n UK banheiro m.

bath salts npl sais mpl de banho.

bath towel n toalha f de banho.

bathtub [ˈbɑːθtʌb] n banheira f.

batik [bəˈtiːk] n batique m.

baton [ˈbætən] n -1. [of conductor] batuta f -2. [in relay race] bastão m -3. UK [of policeman] cassetete m.

baton charge n UK [by police] investida f policial.

batsman [ˈbætsmən] (pl -men [-mən]) n CRICKET batedor m.

battalion [bəˈtæljən] n batalhão m.

batten [ˈbætn] n [piece of wood] tábua f.

➠ **batten down** vt fus fig: to ~ down the hatches preparar-se para momentos difíceis/ enfrentar uma crise.

batter [ˈbætəʳ] ◇ n -1. CULIN massa f (mole) -2. SPORT batedor m, -ra f. ◇ vt [child, woman] surrar. ◇ vi [beat] bater.

➠ **batter down** vt sep botar abaixo.

battered [ˈbætəd] adj -1. [child, woman] maltratado(-da) -2. [old, worn-out - car] arruinado(da); [- hat] surrado(da) -3. CULIN misturado(da).

battering [ˈbætərɪŋ] n: to take a ~ sofrer uma derrota.

battering ram n aríete m.

battery [ˈbætərɪ] (pl -ies) n -1. [gen] bateria f -2. [ELEC - of car] bateria f; [- of radio, torch etc] pilha f -3. [group - of people] grupo m; [- of things] série f, conjunto m.

battery charger n carregador m de bateria.

battery hen n frango m de granja.

battle [ˈbætl] ◇ n batalha f; ~ for/against/with sthg batalha por/contra/com algo; ~ of wits disputa de intelectos; to be half the ~ ser a metade do caminho; to be fighting a losing ~ estar lutando em vão. ◇ vi [fight] lutar; to ~ for/ against/with sthg lutar por/contra/com algo.

battledress [ˈbætldres] n UK uniforme m de combate.

battlefield [ˈbætlfiːld], **battleground** [ˈbætl-graʊnd] n MIL & fig campo m de batalha.

battlements [ˈbætlmənts] npl [of castle] ameias fpl.

battleship [ˈbætlʃɪp] n couraçado m.

bauble [ˈbɔːbl] n bugiganga f.

baud [bɔːd] n COMPUT baud m.

baud rate n COMPUT baud rate m, taxa f de bauds.

baulk [bɔːk] vi = balk.

Bavaria [bəˈveərɪə] n Baviera f; in ~ na Baviera.

Bavarian [bəˈveərɪən] ◇ adj bávaro(ra). ◇ n bávaro m, -ra f.

bawdy [ˈbɔːdɪ] (compar -ier, superl -iest) adj obsceno(na).

bawl [bɔːl] ◇ vt [shout] gritar. ◇ vi -1. [shout] gritar -2. [weep] berrar.

bay [beɪ] n -1. GEOGR baía f -2. [for loading] zona m de carga e descarga -3. [for parking] vaga f -4. [horse] baio m -5. phr: to keep sb/sthg at ~ manter alguém/algo à distância. ◇ vi [dog, wolf] latir.

bay leaf n folha f de louro.

Bay of Biscay n: the ~ o Golfo de Biscaia.

bayonet [ˈbeɪənɪt] n baioneta f.

bay tree n loureiro m.

bay window n bay window f janela f saliente.

bazaar [bəˈzɑːʳ] n -1. [market] bazar m -2. UK [charity sale] bazar m beneficente.

bazooka [bəˈzuːkə] n bazuca f.

B & B n abbr of bed and breakfast

BBC (abbr of British Broadcasting Corporation) n companhia estatal britânica de rádio e televisão, BBC f.

BC -1. (abbr of before Christ) a.C. **-2.** abbr of British Columbia.

BCG (abbr of Bacillus Calmette-Guérin) n BCG f.

BD (abbr of Bachelor of Divinity) n (titular de) graduação em teologia cristã protestante.

BDS (abbr of Bachelor of Dental Science) n (titular de) gradução em odontologia.

be [bi:] (*pt* was OR were, *pp* been) <> *aux vb* -**1.** (*in combination with ppr: to form cont tense*) estar; **what is he doing?** o que ele está fazendo?; **it's snowing** está nevando -**2.** (*in combination with pp: to form passive*) ser; **to ~ loved** ser amado(da) -**3.** (*in question tags*) ser, estar; **the meal was delicious, wasn't it?** a comida estava deliciosa, não estava? -**4.** (*followed by to + infin*) dever; **I'm to ~ promoted** devo ser promovido(da); **you're not to tell anyone** você não deve contar a ninguém. <> *copulative vb* -**1.** (*with adj, n*) ser, estar; **to ~ a doctor/lawyer/plumber** ser médico/advogado/bombeiro; **she's intelligent/attractive** ela é inteligente/atraente; **~ quiet!** fique quieto!; **1 and 1 are 2** 1 e 1 são 2 -**2.** [referring to health] estar; **how are you?** como vai você? -**3.** [referring to age] ter; **how old are you?** quantos anos você tem? -**4.** [cost] custar; **how much was it?** quanto custou?; **that will ~ £10, please** são £10, por favor. <> *vi* -**1.** [exist] existir, haver, ser; **~ that as it may** seja como for -**2.** [referring to place] estar; **Toulouse is in France** Toulouse fica na França; **he will ~ here tomorrow** ele estará aqui amanhã -**3.** [referring to movement] estar; **I've been to the cinema/to France/to the butcher's** fui ao cinema/para a França/ao açougue. <> *v impers* -**1.** [referring to time, dates] ser; **it's two o'clock** são duas horas -**2.** [referring to distance] ser; **it's 3 km to the next town** são 3 quilômetros até a próxima cidade -**3.** [referring to the weather] estar; **it's hot/cold/windy** está quente OR frio OR ventando -**4.** [for emphasis] ser; **it's me** sou eu; **it's the milkman** é o leiteiro.

beach [bi:tʃ] <> *n* praia *f*. <> *vt* [boat, whale] encalhar.

beach ball *n* bola *f* de praia.

beach buggy *n* buggy *m*.

beachcomber [ˈbi:tʃˌkəʊməʳ] *n* pessoa que ganha a vida catando e vendendo artigos deixados na praia.

beachhead [ˈbi:tʃhed] *n* MIL cabeça-de-ponte *f*.

beachwear [ˈbi:tʃweəʳ] *n* (U) roupa *f* de praia.

beacon [ˈbi:kən] *n* -**1.** [warning fire] fogaréu *m* -**2.** [lighthouse] farol *m* -**3.** [radio beacon] radiofarol *m*.

bead [bi:d] *n* -**1.** [of wood, glass] conta *f* -**2.** [of sweat] gota *f*.

beaded *adj* [decorated with beads] enfeitado(da) com contas.

beading [ˈbi:dɪŋ] *n* [wood] moldura *f*.

beady [ˈbi:dɪ] (*compar* -ier, *superl* -iest) *adj* [eyes] pequeno(na) e brilhante; **to keep a ~ eye on sb/sthg** *fig* ficar de olho em alguém/algo.

beagle [ˈbi:gl] *n* bigle *m*.

beak [bi:k] *n* [of bird] bico *m*.

beaker [ˈbi:kəʳ] *n* copo *m* (de plástico).

be-all *n*: the ~ **and end-all** a razão de ser.

beam [bi:m] <> *n* -**1.** [of wood, concrete] viga *f* -**2.** [of light] raio *m*, feixe *m* -**3.** US AUT: **high/low ~s** luz alta/baixa. <> *vt* [signal, news] transmitir. <> *vi* -**1.** [smile] irradiar-se -**2.** [shine] irradiar.

beaming [ˈbi:mɪŋ] *adj* radiante.

bean [bi:n] *n* CULIN feijão *m*, grão *m*; **to be full of ~s** *inf* estar cheio (cheia) de vida; **to spill the ~s** *inf* dar com a língua nos dentes.

beanbag [ˈbi:nbæg] *n* [seat] almofada grande e redonda, feita de flocos de espuma que se adapta ao corpo de quem senta.

beanshoot [ˈbi:nʃu:t], **beansprout** [ˈbi:nspraʊt] *n* broto *m* de feijão.

bear [beəʳ] (*pt* bore, *pp* borne) <> *n* -**1.** [animal] urso *m*, -sa *f* -**2.** ST EX baixista *mf*. <> *vt* -**1.** [carry] carregar -**2.** [sustain] suportar -**3.** [accept] aceitar -**4.** [show] exibir -**5.** [produce, interest] produzir -**6.** [give birth to] parir -**7.** [feeling] guardar. . <> *vi* -**1.** [turn] virar -**2.** [have effect]: **to bring pressure/influence to ~ on sb** exercer pressão/influência sobre alguém.

➤ **bear down** *vi*: **to ~ down on sb/sthg** abater-se sobre algo/alguém.

➤ **bear out** *vt sep* confirmar.

➤ **bear up** *vi* resistir.

➤ **bear with** *vt fus* tolerar.

bearable [ˈbeərəbl] *adj* [tolerable] suportável.

beard [bɪəd] *n* [of man] barba *f*.

bearded *adj* [man, face] com barba.

bearer [ˈbeərəʳ] *n* -**1.** [of stretcher, coffin] carregador *m*, -ra *f* -**2.** [of news, document] portador *m*, -ra *f* -**3.** [of name, title] detentor *m*, -ra *f*.

bear hug *n inf* abraço *m* forte.

bearing [ˈbeərɪŋ] *n* -**1.** [connection] relação *f*; **~ on sthg** relação com algo -**2.** [deportment] conduta *f* -**3.** TECH mancal *m* -**4.** [on compass] direção *f*; **to get/lose one's ~s** *fig* achar/perder o rumo.

bear market *n* ST EX mercado *m* em baixa.

bearskin [ˈbeəskɪn] *n* -**1.** [fur] pele *f* de urso -**2.** [hat] barretina *f* (de pele).

beast [bi:st] *n* -**1.** [animal] besta *m* -**2.** *inf pej* [person] besta *f*.

beastly [ˈbi:stlɪ] (*compar* -ier, *superl* -iest) *adj dated* abominável.

beat [bi:t] (*pt* beat, *pp* beaten) <> *n* -**1.** [gen] batida *f* -**2.** [of heart, pulse] batimento -**3.** MUS [rhythm] ritmo *m* -**4.** [of policeman] ronda *f*. <> *adj inf* [exhausted] nocauteado(da). <> *vt* -**1.** [hit] bater em -**2.** [defeat] derrotar; **it ~s me** *inf* isto acaba comigo -**3.** [arrive ahead of] chegar antes; **she ~ me to it** ela me venceu -**4.** [be better than] superar -**5.** [eggs, wings] bater -**6.** MUS [time] marcar -**7.** *phr*: **~ it!** *inf* [go away] caia fora! <> *vi* -**1.** [rain] cair -**2.** [heart, pulse] bater.

➤ **beat down** <> *vi* -**1.** [sun] bater -**2.** [rain] cair uma pancada. <> *vt sep* [force to lower price] fazer baixar.

➤ **beat off** *vt sep* [resist] repelir.

➤ **beat up** *vt sep inf* [person] espancar.

beaten *adj* -**1.** [metal] forjado(da) -**2.** [path] batido(da).

beater [ˈbi:təʳ] *n* -**1.** [for eggs, cream etc] batedeira *f* -**2.** [for carpet] batedor *m* -**3.** [of woman, child] agressor *m*, -ra *f*.

beat generation *n* geração *f* beat.

beating [ˈbi:tɪŋ] *n* [defeat, punishment] surra *f*; **to take a ~** levar uma surra; **to take some ~** *inf* ser difícil de superar.

beating up (*pl* beatings up) *n inf* [thrashing] espancamento *m*.

beatnik [ˈbi:tnɪk] *n* beatnik *m*.

beat-up *adj inf* [shabby] caindo aos pedaços.

beautician [bju:ˈtɪʃn] *n* esteticista *mf*.

beautiful ['bjuːtɪfʊl] adj **-1.** [gen] bonito(ta) **-2.** [well executed] belo(la).

beautifully ['bjuːtəflɪ] adv **-1.** [attractively] belamente **-2.** inf [very well] esplendidamente.

beauty ['bjuːtɪ] (pl **-ies**) <> n **-1.** (U) [attractiveness] beleza f **-2.** [beautiful woman] beldade f **-3.** inf [very good thing] maravilha f. <> comp [product] de beleza.

beauty contest n concurso m de beleza.

beauty parlour n salão m de beleza.

beauty queen n miss f.

beauty salon n = beauty parlour.

beauty spot n **-1.** [place] recanto m **-2.** [on skin] sinal m.

beaver ['biːvəᵊ] n castor m.
- **beaver away** vi: to ~ away (at sthg) dar duro (em algo).

becalmed [bɪˈkɑːmd] adj [ship] parado(da) por falta de vento.

became [bɪˈkeɪm] pt ⊳ **become**.

because [bɪˈkɒz] conj porque.
- **because of** prep por causa de.

béchamel sauce [ˌbeɪʃəˈmel-] n molho m bechamel OR branco.

beck [bek] n: to be at sb's ~ and call estar sempre à disposição de alguém.

beckon ['bekən] <> vt **-1.** [make a signal to] acenar **-2.** fig [call] chamar. <> vi [signal]: to ~ to sb acenar para alguém.

become [bɪˈkʌm] (pt became, pp become) vt **-1.** [grow] ficar; **what has** ~ **of ...?** o que foi feito de ...? **-2.** [acquire post of] tornar-se **-3.** [suit, be appropriate to] combinar com, ficar bem em; **sarcasm doesn't** ~ **you** o sarcasmo não combina com você.

becoming [bɪˈkʌmɪŋ] adj **-1.** [attractive] elegante **-2.** [appropriate] adequado(da).

bed [bed] (pt & pp **-ded**, cont **-ding**) n **-1.** [to sleep on] cama f; **to go to** ~ ir para a cama; **to make the** ~ arrumar a cama; **to make one's (own)** ~ fig fazer a própria cama; **to go to** ~ **with sb** euphemism ir para a cama com alguém **-2.** [flowerbed] canteiro m; **a** ~ **of roses** fig [easy, pleasant] um mar de rosas **-3.** [bottom - of sea] fundo m; [- of river] leito m.
- **bed down** vt & vi acolher.

BEd (abbr of Bachelor of Education) n (titular de) graduação que habilita para o magistério.

bed and breakfast n **-1.** [service] hospedagem f com café da manhã **-2.** [hotel] bed and breakfast m, acomodação típica da Grã-Bretanha (geralmente em casa de família) acompanhada de café da manhã.

bed-bath n banho m na cama.

bedbug ['bedbʌg] n percevejo m.

bedclothes ['bedkləʊðz] npl roupa f de cama.

bedcover ['bedˌkʌvəᵊ] n colcha f.

bedding ['bedɪŋ] n = bedclothes.

bedding plant n planta f de canteiro.

bedeck [bɪˈdek] vt: to ~ sthg with sthg decorar algo com algo.

bedevil [bɪˈdevl] (UK pt & pp **-led**, cont **-ling**, US pt & pp **-ed**, cont **-ing**) vt: to be bedevilled with sthg estar atormentado(da) com algo.

bedfellow ['bedˌfeləʊ] n fig [colleague] aliado m, -da f.

bedlam ['bedləm] n [chaos] tumulto m.

bed linen n roupa f de cama.

Bedouin, Beduin ['beduɪn] <> adj beduíno(na). <> n beduíno m, -na f.

bedpan ['bedpæn] n comadre f.

bedraggled [bɪˈdrægld] adj enlameado(da).

bedridden ['bedˌrɪdn] adj acamado(da).

bedrock ['bedrɒk] n (U) **-1.** GEOL leito m de rocha firme **-2.** fig [solid foundation] alicerce m.

bedroom ['bedrʊm] n quarto m.

bedside ['bedsaɪd] <> n beira f da cama. <> comp [lamp, table] de cabeceira.

bedside manner n [of doctor] jeito m para lidar com doentes.

bedside table n mesa f de cabeceira, criado-mudo m.

bed-sit(ter) n UK conjugado m.

bedsore ['bedsɔːᵊ] n assadura f.

bedspread ['bedspred] n colcha f.

bedtime ['bedtaɪm] n hora f de dormir.

Beduin adj & n = Bedouin.

bed-wetting [-ˌwetɪŋ] n incontinência f urinária.

bee [biː] n abelha f; **to have a** ~ **in one's bonnet about sthg** fig estar obcecado(da) por algo.

Beeb [biːb] n UK inf: **the** ~ a BBC.

beech [biːtʃ] n faia f.

beef [biːf] <> n (U) [meat] carne f de vaca. <> vi inf [complain]: to ~ about sthg reclamar de algo.
- **beef up** vt sep inf [strengthen] reforçar.

beefburger ['biːfˌbɜːɡəᵊ] n hambúrguer m bovino.

Beefeater ['biːfˌiːtəᵊ] n guarda da Torre de Londres.

beefsteak ['biːfˌsteɪk] n bife m.

beehive ['biːhaɪv] n r **1.** [for bees] colméia f **-2.** [hairstyle] ≃ pixaim m.

beekeeper ['biːˌkiːpəᵊ] n apicultor m, -ra f.

beeline ['biːlaɪn] n: to make a ~ for sb/sthg inf ir direto a alguém/algo.

been [biːn] pp ⊳ be.

beep [biːp] inf <> n bipe m. <> vi bipar.

beeper ['biːpəᵊ] n [device] bipe m.

beer [bɪəᵊ] n cerveja f.

beer garden n terraço de um bar em que geralmente se admite a presença de crianças.

beer mat n bolacha f.

beeswax ['biːzwæks] n (U) cera f de abelha.

beet [biːt] n **-1.** [sugar beet] acelga f **-2.** US [beetroot] beterraba f.

beetle ['biːtl] n besouro m.

beetroot ['biːtruːt] n beterraba f.

befall [bɪˈfɔːl] (pt **-fell** [-ˈfel], pp **-fallen** [-ˈfɔːlən]) literary <> vt suceder. <> vi acontecer.

befit [bɪˈfɪt] (pt & pp **-ted**, cont **-ting**) vt fml convir a.

before [bɪˈfɔːᵊ] <> adv [previously] antes. <> prep **-1.** [preceding in time] antes de **-2.** [in front of]: **the road stretched out** ~ **them** a estrada se abria diante OR à frente deles; ~ **my very eyes** diante de meus próprios olhos; **standing** ~ **the door** parado(da) em frente à porta **-3.** [confronting] perante **-4.** [in the presence of] diante de, perante a. <>

conj: ~ **leaving the country** antes de deixar o país; ~ **he entered the house** antes de entrar na casa.

beforehand [bɪ'fɔːhænd] *adv* [in advance] de antemão.

befriend [bɪ'frend] *vt* -1. [make friends with] fazer amizade com -2. [support] favorecer.

befuddled [bɪ'fʌdld] *adj* [confused] atordoado(da).

beg [beg] (*pt* & *pp* -ged, *cont* -ging) <> *vt* -1. [money, food] mendigar, pedir -2. [favour, forgiveness, mercy] pedir; I ~ **your pardon** desculpe-me; **to** ~ **sb for sthg** pedir algo a alguém ; **to** ~ **sb to do sthg** pedir a alguém para fazer algo. <> *vi* -1. [for money, food] mendigar, pedir; **to** ~ **for sthg** mendigar *OR* pedir algo -2. [for favour, forgiveness, mercy] pedir; **to** ~ **for sthg** pedir algo.

began [bɪ'gæn] *pt* ⊏ **begin**.

beggar ['begə'] *n* mendigo *m*, -ga *f*.

begin [bɪ'gɪn] (*pt* **began**, *pp* **begun**, *cont* -ning) <> *vt* -1. [start] começar; **to** ~ **doing** *OR* **to do sthg** começar a fazer algo -2. [initiate] começar. <> *vi* [start] começar; **to** ~ **with, ...** para começar, ...

beginner [bɪ'gɪnə'] *n* [learner] principiante *mf*, aprendiz *mf*.

beginning [bɪ'gɪnɪŋ] *n* -1. [start] começo *m*; **in the** ~ no começo -2. [origin] início *m*, origem *f*.

begonia [bɪ'gəʊnjə] *n* begônia *f*.

begrudge [bɪ'grʌdʒ] *vt* -1. [envy]: **to** ~ **sb sthg** invejar algo de alguém -2. [give, do unwillingly]: **to** ~ **doing sthg** fazer algo de má vontade.

beguile [bɪ'gaɪl] *vt* [charm] encantar.

beguiling [bɪ'gaɪlɪŋ] *adj* [charming] encantador(ra).

begun [bɪ'gʌn] *pp* ⊏ **begin**.

behalf [bɪ'hɑːf] *n*: **on** ~ **of sb** *UK*, **in** ~ **of sb** *US* em nome de alguém.

behave [bɪ'heɪv] <> *v refl*: **to** ~ **o.s.** comportar-se bem. <> *vi* -1. [in a particular way] comportar-se -2. [in an acceptable way] comportar-se bem.

behaviour *UK*, **behavior** *US* [bɪ'heɪvjə'] *n* comportamento *m*.

behaviourism *UK*, **behaviorism** *US* [bɪ'ḋ heɪvjərɪzm] *n* behaviorismo *m*.

behead [bɪ'hed] *vt* degolar.

beheld [bɪ'held] *pt* & *pp* ⊏ **behold**.

behind [bɪ'haɪnd] <> *prep* -1. [at the back of] atrás de -2. [causing, responsible for] por trás de -3. [supporting]: **to be** ~ **sb** apoiar alguém, estar com alguém -4. [indicating deficiency, delay] atrás de; **to run** ~ **schedule** estar atrasado(da). <> *adv* -1. [at, in the back] atrás -2. [late] para trás; ~ **with sthg** com atraso em algo. <> *n inf* [buttocks] traseiro *m*.

behold [bɪ'həʊld] (*pt* & *pp* **beheld**) *vt literary* contemplar.

beige [beɪʒ] <> *adj* bege. <> *n* bege *m*; **in** ~ em bege.

Beijing [,beɪ'dʒɪŋ] *n* Beijing; **in** ~ em Beijing.

being ['biːɪŋ] *n* -1. [creature] ser *m* -2. (U) [state of existing]: **in** ~ em vigor; **to come into** ~ nascer; **for the time** ~ por enquanto.

Beirut [,beɪ'ruːt] *n* Beirute; **in** ~ em Beirute.

belated [bɪ'leɪtɪd] *adj* tardio(dia).

belatedly [bɪ'leɪtɪdlɪ] *adv* tardiamente.

belch [beltʃ] <> *n* arroto *m*. <> *vt* [smoke, fire] expelir. <> *vi* [person] arrotar.

beleaguered [bɪ'liːgəd] *adj* -1. [MIL - city] sitiado (da); [- troops] cercado(da) -2. *fig* [harassed] assediado(da).

belfry ['belfrɪ] (*pl* -ies) *n* campanário *m*.

Belgian ['beldʒən] <> *adj* belga. <> *n* belga *mf*.

Belgium ['beldʒəm] *n* Bélgica; **in** ~ na Bélgica.

Belgrade [,bel'greɪd] *n* Belgrado; **in** ~ em Belgrado.

belie [bɪ'laɪ] (*cont* **belying**) *vt* -1. [disprove] desmentir -2. [give false idea of] esconder, disfarçar.

belief [bɪ'liːf] *n* -1. (U) [opinion] opinião *f*; **in the** ~ **that** na certeza de que.

believable [bɪ'liːvəbl] *adj* -1. [creditable] crível -2. [possible] possível.

believe [bɪ'liːv] <> *vt* -1. [think] achar; **I** ~ **so** acho que sim -2. [person, statement] acreditar em; ~ **it or not** acredite ou não. <> *vi* -1. [be religious] crer -2. [know to exist]: **to** ~ **in sb/sthg** acreditar em alguém/algo.

believer [bɪ'liːvə'] *n* -1. *RELIG* crente *mf* -2. [supporter]: ~ **in sthg** partidário(ria) de algo.

Belisha beacon [bɪ'liːʃə-] *n* *UK* sinal *laranja intermitente identificando local de travessia de pedestres.*

belittle [bɪ'lɪtl] *vt* [disparage] depreciar.

Belize [be'liːz] *n* Belize; **in** ~ em Belize.

bell [bel] *n* -1. [of church] sino *m* -2. [on door, bicycle] campainha *f*; **to ring a** ~ *fig* trazer à lembrança.

bell-bottoms *npl* calça *f* boca-de-sino.

bellhop ['belhɒp] *n* *US* mensageiro *m*, -ra *f* (de hotel).

belligerence [bɪ'lɪdʒərəns] *n* [aggression] agressividade *f*.

belligerent [bɪ'lɪdʒərənt] *adj* -1. [at war] beligerante -2. [aggressive] agressivo(va).

bellow ['beləʊ] <> *vt* [order] gritar. <> *vi* -1. [person] gritar -2. [bull] mugir.

bellows ['beləʊz] *npl* fole *m*.

bell push *n* *UK* campainha *f*.

bell-ringer *n* sineiro *m*, -ra *f*.

belly ['belɪ] (*pl* -ies) *n* barriga *f*.

bellyache ['belɪeɪk] <> *n* [stomachache] dor *f* de estômago. <> *vi inf* [complain] reclamar.

belly button *n inf* [navel] umbigo *m*.

belly dancer *n* dançarina *f* do ventre.

belly dancing *n* dança *f* do ventre.

belong [bɪ'lɒŋ] *vi* -1. [be property]: **to** ~ **to sb** pertencer a alguém -2. [be a member]: **to** ~ **to sthg** fazer parte *OR* ser membro de algo -3. [be situated in right place] encaixar-se.

belongings [bɪ'lɒŋɪŋz] *npl* pertences *mpl*.

Belorussia [,beləʊ'rʌʃə] *n* Bielo-Rússia; **in** ~ na Bielo-Rússia.

beloved [bɪ'lʌvd] <> *adj* amado(da), querido(da). <> *n* amado *m*, -da *f*.

below [bɪ'ləʊ] <> *adv* -1. [in a lower position] de baixo -2. [in text or with numbers, quantities] abaixo -3. *NAUT*: **to go** ~ descer. <> *prep* abaixo de.

belt [belt] <> *n* -1. [for clothing] cinto *m*; **to be below the** ~ *fig* ser cruel, ser um golpe baixo; **to have sthg under one's** ~ [as experience] ter algo como experiência; [qualification] ter algo no currículo; **to tighten one's ~** apertar o cinto **- 2.** TECH correia f **- 3.** [of land, sea] faixa f, cinturão m. <> vt **- 1.** inf [hit with a belt] dar uma surra de cinto em **- 2.** inf [punch, beat] meter o couro em. <> vi UK inf [move at speed]: **to ~ along/down sthg** ir à toda por.

➡ **belt out** vt sep inf cantar a plenos pulmões.

➡ **belt up** vi UK inf [be quiet] botar zíper na boca, calar o bico.

beltway ['belt,weɪ] n US anel m viário, rodoanel m.

bemused [bɪ'mjuːzd] adj bestificado(da).

bench [bentʃ] n **- 1.** [seat] banco m **- 2.** [in laboratory, workshop] bancada f **- 3.** UK JUR magistratura f.

benchmark n **- 1.** [standard] referência f **- 2.** COMPUT padrão m de desempenho **- 3.** ECON benchmark m, indicador m.

bend [bend] (pt & pp bent) <> n **- 1.** curva f **- 2.** phr: **round the ~** inf pirado(da), maluco(ca); **to drive sb round the ~** deixar alguém maluco(ca). <> vt dobrar. <> vi **- 1.** [arm, leg] dobrar-se ; [tree, person] inclinar-se **- 2.** [river, road] fazer uma curva.

➡ **bends** npl MED : **the ~s** o mal da descompressão.

➡ **bend down** vi curvar-se.

➡ **bend over** vi inclinar-se; **to ~ over backwards for sb** fig fazer todo o possível por alguém.

bendy ['bendɪ] (compar -ier, superl -iest) adj UK flexível.

beneath [bɪ'niːθ] <> adv [below] debaixo. <> prep **- 1.** [under] debaixo de, sob **- 2.** [unworthy of]: **he felt the job was ~** him ele sentia que o emprego estava aquém dele; **to be ~ sthg** não ser digno(na) de algo.

benediction [,benɪ'dɪkʃn] n RELIG bênção f.

benefactor ['benɪfæktə'] n benfeitor m.

benefactress ['benɪfæktrɪs] n benfeitora f.

beneficial [,benɪ'fɪʃl] adj benéfico(ca); **~ to sb/sthg** benéfico(ca) para alguém/algo.

beneficiary [,benɪ'fɪʃərɪ] (pl -ies) n JUR beneficiário m, -ria f.

benefit ['benɪfɪt] <> n **- 1.** [advantage] benefício m; **to be to sb's ~**, **to be of ~ to sb** ser benéfico(ca) para alguém; **for the ~ of** em benefício OR prol de **- 2.** [good point] vantagem f **- 3.** ADMIN [allowance of money] auxílio m. <> comp [concert, match, performance] beneficente. <> vt beneficiar. <> vi: **to ~ from sthg** beneficiar-se de algo.

Benelux ['benɪlʌks] n Benelux; **the ~ countries** os países Benelux.

benevolent [bɪ'nevələnt] adj [kind, generous] benevolente.

BEng [,biː'eŋ] (abbr of Bachelor of Engineering) n (titular de) graduação em engenharia.

Bengal [beŋ'gɔːl] n Bengala; **in ~** em Bengala; **the Bay of ~** a Baía de Bengala.

benign [bɪ'naɪn] adj **- 1.** [gen] benévolo(la) **- 2.** [influence, conditions] agradável, propício(cia) **- 3.** MED benigno(na).

Benin [be'nɪn] n Benim; **in ~** em Benim.

bent [bent] <> pt & pp [➤ bend. <> adj **- 1.** [wire, bar] torto(ta) **- 2.** [person, body] curvado(da) **- 3.** UK inf [dishonest] corrupto(ta) **- 4.** [determined]: **to be ~ on sthg/on doing sthg** ter inclinação para algo/

fazer algo. <> n [natural aptitude] inclinação f; **to have a ~ for sthg** ter uma inclinação para algo.

bequeath [bɪ'kwiːð] vt **- 1.** [money, property] deixar; **to ~ sb sthg**, **to ~ sthg to sb** deixar algo para alguém **- 2.** fig [idea, system] passar; **to ~ sb sthg**, **to ~ sthg to sb** passar algo para alguém.

bequest [bɪ'kwest] n [in will] herança f.

berate [bɪ'reɪt] vt [rebuke] repreender.

Berber ['bɜːbə'] <> adj berbere. <> n **- 1.** [person] berbere mf **- 2.** [language] berbere m.

bereaved [bɪ'riːvd] (pl inv) <> adj enlutado(da). <> npl: **the ~** os enlutados.

bereavement [bɪ'riːvmənt] n luto m.

bereft [bɪ'reft] adj literary desolado(da); **~ of sthg** privado(da) de algo.

beret ['bereɪ] n boina f.

Bering Sea ['berɪŋ-] n: **the ~** o Mar de Bering.

Bering Strait ['berɪŋ-] n: **the ~** o Estreito de Bering.

berk [bɜːk] n UK inf palhaço m, -ça f.

Berlin [bɜː'lɪn] n Berlim; **in ~** em Berlim; **in East/ West ~** na Berlim Oriental/Ocidental; **the ~ Wall** o Muro de Berlim.

Berliner [bɜː'lɪnə'] n berlinense mf.

berm [bɜːm] n US berma f.

Bermuda [bə'mjuːdə] n (Ilhas) Bermudas fpl.

Bermuda shorts npl bermuda f.

Bern [bɜːn] n Berna; **in ~** em Berna.

berry ['berɪ] (pl -ies) n baga f.

berserk [bə'zɜːk] adj: **to go ~** ficar furioso(sa).

berth [bɜːθ] <> n **- 1.** [in harbour] ancoradouro m **- 2.** [in ship, train] beliche m **- 3.** phr: **to give sb a wide ~** fig manter distância de alguém. <> vt NAUT ancorar, atracar. <> vi [ship] ancorar, atracar.

beseech [bɪ'siːtʃ] (pt & pp besought OR beseeched) vt literary [implore] suplicar; **to ~ sb to do sthg** suplicar a alguém para que faça algo.

beset [bɪ'set] (pt & pp beset, cont -ting) <> adj: **~ with OR by sthg** cercado (cercada) de algo. <> vt envolver.

beside [bɪ'saɪd] prep **- 1.** [next to] ao lado de **- 2.** [compared with] comparado(da) com **- 3.** phr: **to be ~ o.s. with sthg** estar louco(ca) de algo.

besides [bɪ'saɪdz] <> adv além disso. <> prep [in addition to] além de.

besiege [bɪ'siːdʒ] vt **- 1.** [town, fortress] sitiar **- 2.** fig: **to be ~d by people** ser/estar assediado(da) de pessoas; **to be ~d with calls/complaints** ser bombardeado(da) com ligações/reclamações.

besotted [bɪ'sɒtɪd] adj: **~ (with sb)** obcecado(da) (por alguém).

besought [bɪ'sɔːt] pt & pp [➤ beseech.

bespectacled [bɪ'spektəkld] adj com óculos.

bespoke [bɪ'spəʊk] adj UK dated **- 1.** [clothes] feito (feita) sob medida **- 2.** [tailor] que costura sob medida.

best [best] <> adj [in quality] melhor. <> adv **- 1.** [better than all the others] melhor; **whoever does ~ in the exam** quem se sair melhor no exame **- 2.** [more than all the others] mais; **which one did you like ~?** de qual deles você gostou mais? <> n **- 1.** [highest standard possible] melhor m; **to do one's ~** fazer o melhor possível; **he is the ~ of friends**

ele é o melhor amigo do mundo **-2.** [utmost] máximo *m*; **she tried her best** ~ ela fez o tudo o que podia **-3.** [most outstanding person, thing etc] melhor *mf* **-4.** *phr*: **to make the** ~ **of sthg** tirar o máximo de proveito de algo; **to be for the** ~ ser melhor; **all the** ~! um abraço!; **the** ~ **of both worlds** o melhor de ambas as partes.
at best *adv* na melhor das hipóteses.

bestial [ˈbestjəl] *adj* [disgusting] bestial.

best man *n* padrinho *m* de casamento.

bestow [bɪˈstəʊ] *vt fml*: **to** ~ **sthg on sb** outorgar OR conceder algo a alguém.

best-seller *n* **-1.** [article sold] mais vendido *m*, -da *f* **-2.** [book] best-seller *m*.

best-selling *adj* mais vendido(da).

bet [bet] (*pt & pp* bet OR -ted, *cont* -ting) <> *n* **-1.** [wager] aposta *f*; **a** ~ **on sthg** uma aposta em algo; **to hedge one's** ~**s** resguardar-se **-2.** *fig* [prediction] aposta *f*; **it's a safe** ~ **that ...** é certo que ...; **your best** ~ **is to ...** o melhor a se fazer é ... <> *vt* apostar. <> *vi* apostar; **to** ~ **on sthg** apostar em algo; **you** ~! *inf* pode apostar!, com certeza!

beta-blocker [ˈbiːtəˌblɒkəʳ] *n* bloqueador-beta *m*.

Bethlehem [ˈbeθlɪhem] *n* Belém; **in** ~ em Belém.

betray [bɪˈtreɪ] *vt* **-1.** [person, principles] trair **-2.** [secret, emotion] revelar.

betrayal [bɪˈtreɪəl] *n* **-1.** [of person, principles] traição *f* **-2.** [of secret, emotion] revelação *f*.

betrothed [bɪˈtrəʊðd] *adj dated* [engaged to be married] prometido(da); ~ **to sb** prometido(da) para alguém.

better [ˈbetəʳ] <> *adj* melhor; **to get** ~ melhorar; **to get** ~ **and** ~ ficar cada vez melhor. <> *adv* **-1.** [gen] melhor **-2.** [when giving advice, stating intention]: **you'd** ~ **phone her** é melhor você ligar para ela; **I'd** ~ **go now** é melhor eu ir embora. <> *n* [best one] melhor *mf*; **to get the** ~ **of sb** apoderar-se OR tomar conta de alguém; **her emotions got the** ~ **of her** suas emoções tomaram conta dela. <> *vt* [improve] melhorar; **to** ~ **o.s.** melhorar de vida, aprimorar-se.

better half *n inf* cara-metade *mf*.

better off *adj* **-1.** [financially] melhor de vida **-2.** [in a better situation] melhor; **you're** ~ **taking a taxi** será melhor você pegar um táxi.

betting [ˈbetɪŋ] *n* **-1.** [bets] apostar *m* **-2.** [odds] chance *f*.

betting shop *n UK* casa *f* de apostas.

between [bɪˈtwiːn] <> *prep* entre. <> *adv*: **(in)** ~ entre.

bevelled *UK*, **beveled** *US* [ˈbevld] *adj* chanfrado(da).

beverage [ˈbevərɪdʒ] *n fml* [drink] bebida *f*.

bevy [ˈbevɪ] (*pl* -ies) *n* [group] bando *m*.

beware [bɪˈweəʳ] *vi* tomar cuidado, ter cautela; **to** ~ **of sthg** tomar cuidado com algo.

bewildered [bɪˈwɪldəd] *adj* [confused] confuso(sa), desnorteado(da).

bewildering [bɪˈwɪldərɪŋ] *adj* [confusing] desnorteante, desconcertante.

bewitched [bɪˈwɪtʃt] *adj* encantado(da).

bewitching [bɪˈwɪtʃɪŋ] *adj* encantador(ra).

beyond [bɪˈjɒnd] <> *prep* **-1.** além de; **it is** ~ **my**

responsibility vai além de minha responsabilidade **-2.** [outside the range of] fora de; **it is** ~ **my control** está fora de meu controle; **the town has changed** ~ **all recognition** a cidade ficou irreconhecível. <> *adv* **-1.** [in space] mais além, mais adiante **-2.** [in time] mais além, mais um pouco.

b.f. (*abbr of* brought forward) cont.

BFPO (*abbr of* British Forces Post Office) *n* código utilizado em cartas escritas para membros das forças britânicas.

b.h.p. (*abbr of* brake horsepower) b.h.p.

bi- [baɪ] *prefix* bi.

biannual [baɪˈænjʊəl] *adj* semestral.

bias [ˈbaɪəs] *n* **-1.** [prejudice] preconceito *m* **-2.** [tendency] propensão *f*, tendência *f*.

biased [ˈbaɪəst] *adj* **-1.** [prejudiced] preconceituoso(sa); **to be** ~ **against sthg/sb** ser preconceituoso(sa) em relação a algo/alguém **-2.** [tendentious] tendencioso(sa); **to be** ~ **towards sthg** ser tendencioso(sa) em relação a algo; **to be** ~ **towards sb** pender para o lado de alguém.

bib [bɪb] *n* [for baby] babador *m*.

Bible [ˈbaɪbl] *n*: **the** ~ a Bíblia.
bible *n* [copy of the Bible] bíblia *f*.

biblical [ˈbɪblɪkl] *adj* bíblico(ca).

bibliography [ˌbɪblɪˈɒgrəfɪ] (*pl* -ies) *n* [list of books] bibliografia *f*.

bicarbonate of soda [baɪˈkɑːbənət-] *n* bicarbonato *m* de sódio.

bicentenary *UK* [ˌbaɪsenˈtiːnərɪ] (*pl* -ies), **bicentennial** *US* [ˌbaɪsenˈtenjəl] *n* bicentenário *m*.

biceps [ˈbaɪseps] (*pl inv*) *n* bíceps *m*.

bicker [ˈbɪkəʳ] *vi* [quarrel] brigar.

bickering [ˈbɪkərɪŋ] *n* (U) [quarrelling] briga *f*.

bicycle [ˈbaɪsɪkl] <> *n* bicicleta *f*. <> *vi* andar de bicicleta.

bicycle path *n* ciclovia *f*.

bicycle pump *n* bomba *f* de ar *(para bicicleta)*.

bid [bɪd] (*pt & pp vt sense 1 & vi* bid, *cont* bidding, *pt vt senses 2 & 3* bade, *pp vt senses 2 & 3* bid OR bidden [ˈbɪdn], *cont* bidding) <> *n* **-1.** [attempt] tentativa *f*, intento *m*; **a** ~ **for power** uma busca pelo poder **-2.** [at auction] licitação *f* **-3.** COMM proposta *f*. <> *vt* **-1.** [at auction] licitar **-2.** *literary* [request]: **to** ~ **sb do sthg** convidar alguém a fazer algo **-3.** *fml* [say]: **to** ~ **sb good morning/farewell** dizer bom dia/adeus a alguém. <> *vi* **-1.** [at auction]: **to** ~ **(for sthg)** abrir licitação (para algo) **-2.** [attempt]: **to** ~ **for sthg** tentar algo.

bidder [ˈbɪdəʳ] *n* [at auction] licitante *mf*.

bidding [ˈbɪdɪŋ] *n* [at auction] licitação *f*.

bide [baɪd] *vt*: **to** ~ **one's time** esperar a vez.

bidet [ˈbiːdeɪ] *n* bidê *m*.

biennial [baɪˈenɪəl] <> *adj* [every two years] bienal. <> *n* **-1.** [plant] planta *f* bienal **-2.** [festival] bienal *f*.

bier [bɪəʳ] *n* caixão *m*.

bifocals [ˌbaɪˈfəʊklz] *npl* lentes *fpl* bifocais.

big [bɪg] (*compar* -ger, *superl* -gest) *adj* **-1.** [gen] grande **-2.** [older] mais velho(lha) **-3.** [successful] importante **-4.** *phr*: **in a** ~ **way** em grande estilo.

bigamist *n* bígamo *m*, -ma *f*.

bigamy ['bɪgəmɪ] *n (U)* bigamia *f.*
Big Apple *n*: the ~ a Big Apple, Nova York.
Big Bang *n*: the ~ theory a teoria do big-bang.
Big Ben *n* Big Ben *m.*
big business *n (U)* [large companies] grandes negócios *mpl.*
big cat *n* animal grande da família dos felinos.
big deal *inf* <> *n* grande coisa *f*; **it's no** ~ não é nada de mais; **what's the** ~? e daí? <> *excl* grande coisa!
Big Dipper [-'dɪpəˀ] *n* -1. *UK* [rollercoaster] montanha-russa *f* -2. *US ASTRON*: the ~ a Ursa Maior.
big end *n AUT* cabeça *f* de biela.
big fish *n inf* [important person] peixe *m* grande.
big game *n (U)* animais *mpl* de grande porte.
big hand *n* -1. [on clock] ponteiro *m* dos minutos -2. *inf* [applause] salva *f* de palmas.
bighead ['bɪghed] *n inf* metido *m* a besta.
big-headed *adj inf* metido(da).
big-hearted [-'hɑːtɪd] *adj* gentil, generoso(sa).
big money *n (U) inf* bolada *f*; **to make** ~ ganhar um dinheirão *ou* uma bolada.
big mouth *n inf* -1. [tendency to gossip] língua *f* solta -2. [person] linguarudo *m*, -da *f.*
big name *n inf* grande figura *f.*
bigot ['bɪgət] *n* fanático *m*, -ca *f.*
bigoted ['bɪgətɪd] *adj* fanático(ca).
bigotry ['bɪgətrɪ] *n (U)* fanatismo *m.*
big shot *n inf* figurão *m*, costa-larga *m.*
big time *n inf*: the ~ o auge.
big toe *n* dedão *m* do pé.
big top *n* (lona do) circo *m.*
big wheel *n* -1. *UK* [at fairground] roda-gigante *f* -2. *inf* [big shot] peixe *m* grande.
bigwig ['bɪgwɪg] *n inf pej* figurão *m*, -rona *f.*
bike [baɪk] *n inf* -1. [cycle] bike *f*, bicicleta *f* -2. [motorcycle] moto *f.*
bikeway ['baɪkweɪ] *n US* ciclovia *f.*
bikini [bɪ'kiːnɪ] *n* biquíni *m.*
bilateral [ˌbaɪ'lætərəl] *adj* [talks] bilateral.
bilberry ['bɪlbərɪ] *(pl -ies)* *n* uva-do-monte *f*, mirtilo *m.*
bile [baɪl] *n* -1. [fluid] bílis *f* -2. [anger] irritação *f.*
bilingual [baɪ'lɪŋgwəl] *adj* bilíngüe.
bilious ['bɪljəs] *adj* -1. [sickening] bilioso(sa) -2. [nauseous] nauseado(da).
bill [bɪl] <> *n* -1. [statement of cost] conta *f*; ~ **for** sthg conta de algo -2. [in parliament] projeto *m* de lei -3. [of show, concert] programa *m* -4. *US* [banknote] nota *f* -5. [poster]: **'post** *OR* **stick no** ~ **s'** 'proibido colar cartazes' -6. [beak] bico *m* -7. *phr*: **to be given a clean** ~ **of health** *MED* obter um atestado de boa saúde. <> *vt* [send a bill to]: **to** ~ **sb (for sthg)** cobrar (algo) de alguém.
billboard ['bɪlbɔːd] *n* quadro *m* de anúncios.
billet ['bɪlɪt] <> *n* boleto *m*, alojamento *m.* <> *vt* aboletar, alojar.
billfold ['bɪlfəʊld] *n US* carteira *f.*
billiards ['bɪljədz] *n (U)* bilhar *m.*
billion ['bɪljən] *num* -1. [thousand million] bilhão *m* -2. *UK dated* [million million] trilhão *m.*
billionaire [ˌbɪljə'neəˀ] *n* bilionário *m*, -ria *f.*

bill of exchange *n* letra *f* de câmbio.
bill of lading [-'leɪdɪŋ] *n* conhecimento *m* de embarque marítimo.
Bill of Rights *n*: the ~ *as dez primeiras emendas da Constituição norte-americana.*

BILL OF RIGHTS ▪▪▪▪▪▪▪▪▪▪

É o nome que se dá às dez primeiras emendas da Constituição norte-americana, as quais garantem direitos fundamentais, tais como a liberdade de expressão, de credo e de reunião.

bill of sale *n* contrato *m* de venda.
billow ['bɪləʊ] <> *n* [of smoke] nuvem *f.* <> *vi* -1. [smoke, steam] formar nuvens -2. [skirt, sail] ondular.
billposter *n* -1. pessoa *f* que cola cartazes -2. [unauthorised] pichador *m*, -ra *f.*
billycan ['bɪlɪkæn] *n* caldeirão *m.*
billy goat ['bɪlɪ-] *n* bode *m.*
BIM (*abbr of* **British Institute of Management**) *n* instituto britânico de administração.
bimbo ['bɪmbəʊ] *(pl -s OR -es)* *n inf pej* ≃ burra gostosa.
bimonthly [ˌbaɪ'mʌnθlɪ] <> *adj* -1. [every two months] bimestral -2. [twice a month] bimensal. <> *adv* -1. [every two months] bimestralmente -2. [twice a month] bimensalmente.
bin [bɪn] *(pt & pp -ned, cont -ning)* <> *n* -1. *UK* [for rubbish] lixeira *f* -2. [for storage] lata *f.* <> *vt inf* [discard] descartar.
binary ['baɪnərɪ] *adj* [system, code] binário(ria).
bind [baɪnd] *(pt & pp bound)* <> *vt* -1. [tie up] amarrar -2. [unite] ligar -3. [bandage] atar -4. [book] encadernar -5. [constrain] comprometer. <> *n inf* -1. *UK* [nuisance] saco *m* -2. [difficult situation] aperto *m.*
➡ **bind over** *vt sep JUR* obrigar legalmente.
binder ['baɪndəˀ] *n* -1. [machine] encadernadora *f* -2. [person] encadernador *m*, -ra *f* -3. [cover] encadernação *f.*
binding ['baɪndɪŋ] <> *adj* comprometedor(ra), obrigatório(ria). <> *n* -1. [of book - process] encadernação *f*; [- cover] capa *f* -2. [on dress, tablecloth] laço *m.*
binge [bɪndʒ] *inf* <> *n*: **to go on a** ~ ir à farra. <> *vi*: **to** ~ **on sthg** empanturrar-se de algo.
bingo ['bɪŋgəʊ] *n* bingo *m.*
bin-liner *n UK* saco *m* de lixo.
binoculars [bɪ'nɒkjʊləz] *npl* binóculo *m.*
biochemistry [ˌbaɪəʊ'kemɪstrɪ] *n (U)* bioquímica *f.*
biodegradable [ˌbaɪəʊdɪ'greɪdəbl] *adj* biodegradável.
biodiversity [ˌbaɪəʊdaɪ'vɜːsətɪ] *n (U)* biodiversidade *f.*
bioethics [ˌbaɪəʊ'eθɪks] *n (U)* bioética *f.*
biographer [baɪ'ɒgrəfəˀ] *n* biógrafo *m*, -fa *f.*
biographic(al) [ˌbaɪə'græfɪk(l)] *adj* biográfico(ca).
biography [baɪ'ɒgrəfɪ] *(pl -ies)* *n* biografia *f.*
biofuel ['baɪəʊfjʊəl] *n* biocombustível *m.*
biological [ˌbaɪə'lɒdʒɪkl] *adj* biológico(ca); ~ **washing powder** sabão em pó com enzimas.
biological clock *n* relógio *m* biológico.

biological warfare n guerra f biológica.
biological weapon n arma f biológica.
biologist [baɪˈɒlədʒɪst] n biólogo m, -ga f.
biology [baɪˈɒlədʒɪ] n (U) biologia f.
biopic [ˈbaɪəʊpɪk] n inf filme m biográfico.
biopsy [ˈbaɪɒpsɪ] (pl -ies) n biópsia f.
biosphere [ˈbaɪəʊˌsfɪəʳ] n biosfera f.
biotech company [ˈbaɪəʊtek-] n empresa f de biotecnologia.
biotechnology [ˌbaɪəʊtekˈnɒlədʒɪ] n (U) biotecnologia f.
bioterrorism [ˌbaɪəʊˈterərɪzm] n bioterrorismo m.
bipartite [ˌbaɪˈpɑːtaɪt] adj [treaty] bipartido(da).
biplane [ˈbaɪpleɪn] n biplano m.
birch [bɜːtʃ] n -1. [tree] bétula f -2. [for punishment]: the ~ a vara.
bird [bɜːd] n -1. [creature] pássaro m, ave f; to kill two ~s with one stone ≃ matar dois coelhos com uma cajadada só -2. inf [woman] perua f.
birdcage [ˈbɜːdkeɪdʒ] n gaiola f.
birdie [ˈbɜːdɪ] n -1. [bird] passarinho m -2. [in golf] birdie m.
bird of paradise n ave-do-paraíso f.
bird of prey n ave f de rapina.
birdseed [ˈbɜːdsiːd] n (U) alpiste m.
bird's-eye view n vista f panorâmica.
birdwatcher n observador m, -ra f de pássaros.
biro® n caneta f esferográfica.
birth [bɜːθ] n nascimento m; to give ~ (to) dar à luz (a); fig [of idea, system, country] dar origem(a).
birth certificate n certidão f de nascimento.
birth control n (U) controle m de natalidade.
birthday [ˈbɜːθdeɪ] ⟨⟩ n aniversário m. ⟨⟩ comp de aniversário.
birthmark [ˈbɜːθmɑːk] n sinal m de nascença.
birthplace [ˈbɜːθpleɪs] n local m de nascimento.
birthrate [ˈbɜːθreɪt] n taxa f de natalidade.
birthright [ˈbɜːθraɪt] n direito m inato.
Biscay [ˈbɪskɪ] n: the Bay of ~ a Baía de Biscaia.
biscuit [ˈbɪskɪt] n -1. UK [crisp] biscoito m, bolacha f -2. US [bread-like cake] bolacha f.
bisect [baɪˈsekt] vt -1. GEOM cortar ao meio -2. [cut in two] dividir em duas partes.
bisexual [ˌbaɪˈsekʃʊəl] ⟨⟩ adj bissexual. ⟨⟩ n bissexual mf.
bishop [ˈbɪʃəp] n bispo m.
bison [ˈbaɪsn] (pl inv OR -s) n búfalo f.
bistro [ˈbɪstrəʊ] (pl -s) n bistrô m.
bit [bɪt] ⟨⟩ pt ⟨⟩ bite. ⟨⟩ n -1. [small piece] pedaço m; ~s and pieces UK inf bugigangas; to ~s aos pedaços -2. [unspecified amount]: a ~ of um pouco de; quite a ~ of um bocado de -3. [short time]: for a ~ por um instante/momento -4. [of drill] broca f -5. [of bridle] freio m -6. COMPUT bit m -7. phr: to do one's ~ UK fazer a sua parte; every ~ as ... as exatamente tão ... quanto; it's a ~ much [overwhelming] é um pouco demais; not a ~ nem um pouco.
➡ **a bit** adv um pouco.
➡ **bit by bit** adv pouco a pouco.
bitch [bɪtʃ] ⟨⟩ n -1. [female dog] cadela f -2. v inf pej

[unpleasant woman] vaca f. ⟨⟩ vi inf -1. [complain] emputecer-se -2. [talk unpleasantly]: to ~ about sb falar mal de alguém.
bitchy [ˈbɪtʃɪ] (compar -ier, superl -iest) adj inf malicioso(sa).
bite [baɪt] (pt bit, pp bitten) ⟨⟩ n -1. [act of biting] mordida f, dentada f -2. inf [food]: a ~ (to eat) algo (para beliscar) -3. [wound] picada f -4. UK [sharp flavour] sabor m picante. ⟨⟩ vt -1. [subj: person, animal] morder; to ~ one's nails roer as unhas -2. [subj: insect, snake] picar. ⟨⟩ vi -1. [animal, person] morder; to ~ into sthg morder algo; to ~ off sthg abocanhar algo; to ~ off more than one can chew ≃ dar um passo maior que a perna; to ~ the hand that feeds one ≃ cuspir no prato em que comeu -2. [insect, snake] picar -3. [tyres, clutch] furar -4. fig [sanction, law] morder.
biting [ˈbaɪtɪŋ] adj -1. [very cold] cortante -2. [caustic] mordaz.
bitmap n COMPUT bitmap m.
bit part n ponta f.
bitten [ˈbɪtn] pp ⟷ bite.
bitter [ˈbɪtəʳ] ⟨⟩ adj -1. [gen] amargo(ga); to the ~ end até o fim -2. [acrimonious] pungente -3. [resentful] amargurado(da) -4. [icy] gelado(da). ⟨⟩ n UK [beer] cerveja f amarga.
bitter lemon n batida f de limão.
bitterly [ˈbɪtəlɪ] adv -1. [cold] amargamente -2. [intensely] duramente.
bitterness [ˈbɪtənɪs] n (U) -1. [gen] amargor m -2. [of wind, weather] rigor m.
bittersweet [ˈbɪtəswiːt] adj agridoce.
bitty [ˈbɪtɪ] (compar -ier, superl -iest) adj UK inf sem pé nem cabeça.
bitumen [ˈbɪtjʊmɪn] n (U) betume m.
bivouac [ˈbɪvʊæk] (pt & pp -ked, cont -king) ⟨⟩ n acampamento m sem barracas. ⟨⟩ vi dormir ao relento (acampado).
biweekly [ˌbaɪˈwiːklɪ] ⟨⟩ adj -1. [every two weeks] quinzenal -2. [twice a week]: ~ magazine revista publicada duas vezes por semana. ⟨⟩ adv -1. [every two weeks] quinzenalmente -2. [twice a week] duas vezes por semana.
bizarre [bɪˈzɑːʳ] adj bizarro(ra), estranho(nha).
BL n -1. (abbr of Bachelor of Law(s)) (titular de) graduação em direito. -2. (abbr of Bill of Lading) conhecimento de embarque marítimo.
blab [blæb] (pt & pp -bed, cont -bing) vi inf fazer fofoca.
black [blæk] ⟨⟩ adj -1. [in colour] preto(ta); to be beaten ~ and blue ficar roxo(xa) de pancada; ~ and white [films, photos] preto-e-branco -2. [person, skin] negro(gra) -3. [without milk] puro(ra), preto(ta) -4. [grim] sombrio(a); ~ humour humor negro -5. [angry] furioso(sa). ⟨⟩ n -1. (U) [colour] preto m; in ~ and white [in writing] o preto no branco, por escrito; in the ~ [solvent] sem dívidas -2. [person] negro m, -gra f. ⟨⟩ vt UK [boycott] boicotar.
➡ **black out** ⟨⟩ vt sep -1. [put out lights] ficar no escuro -2. [suppress] tirar do ar. ⟨⟩ vi [faint] desmaiar.
blackball [ˈblækbɔːl] vt votar contra (para excluir alguém de um clube).

black belt n faixa-preta mf.
blackberry ['blækbərı] (pl -ies) n amora f.
blackbird ['blækbɜːd] n melro m.
blackboard ['blækbɔːd] n quadro-negro m, lousa f.
black box n [flight recorder] caixa-preta f.
black comedy n tragicomédia f, comédia f de humor negro.
blackcurrant [ˌblæk'kʌrənt] n groselha-preta f.
black economy n economia f informal.
blacken ['blækn] <> vt -1. pretejar -2. fig [reputation, name] denegrir. <> vi [sky] escurecer.
black eye n olho m roxo.
Black Forest n: the ~ a Floresta Negra.
blackhead ['blækhed] n cravo m.
black hole n ASTRON buraco m negro.
black ice n (U) camada fina e transparente de gelo sobre as ruas que dificulta a passagem de carros.
blackjack ['blækdʒæk] n -1. (U) [card game] blackjack m -2. Am [weapon] cassetete m.
blackleg ['blækleg] n pej fura-greve mf.
blacklist ['blæklɪst] <> n lista f negra. <> vt incluir na lista negra.
black magic n (U) magia f negra.
blackmail ['blækmeɪl] <> n lit & fig chantagem f. <> vt chantagear.
blackmailer ['blækmeɪlə'] n chantagista mf.
Black Maria [-mə'raɪə] n inf camburão m.
black mark n mancha f negra.
black market n mercado m negro.
blackout ['blækaʊt] n -1. [in wartime] blecaute m -2. [power cut] blecaute m, apagão m -3. [suppression of news] censura f -4. [fainting fit] desmaio m.
Black Power n movimento que marcou a luta dos negros norte-americanos pelo direito à igualdade e liberdade.
black pudding n UK morcela f preta.
Black Sea n: the ~ o Mar Negro.
black sheep n fig ovelha f negra.
blacksmith ['blæksmɪθ] n ferreiro m.
black spot n ponto m cego.
black-tie adj black-tie, de gala.
bladder ['blædə'] n ANAT bexiga f.
blade [bleɪd] n -1. [of knife, saw] lâmina f -2. [of propeller] pá f -3. [of grass] folha f.
blame [bleɪm] <> n (U) [responsibility] culpa f; to take the ~ for sthg assumir a culpa por algo. <> vt culpar; to ~ sthg on sb/sthg, to ~ sb/sthg for sthg culpar alguém/algo de alguma coisa; to be to ~ for sthg ser culpado(da por algo).
blameless ['bleɪmlɪs] adj [innocent] inocente, irrepreensível.
blanch [blɑːntʃ] <> vt CULIN escaldar. <> vi [go white] empalidecer.
blancmange [blə'mɒndʒ] n manjar-branco m.
bland [blænd] adj -1. [person] agradável, meigo(ga) -2. [food] insosso(sa) -3. [music, style] suave.
blank [blæŋk] <> adj -1. em branco -2. fig [look] vazio(a). <> n -1. [empty space] espaço m em branco -2. MIL [cartridge] cartucho m -3. phr: to draw a ~ tirar leite de pedra.
blank cheque n -1. cheque m em branco

-2. fig [free hand] carta f branca.
blanket ['blæŋkɪt] <> adj [comprehensive] na íntegra, completo(ta). <> n -1. [bed cover] cobertor m, colcha f -2. [layer] camada f. <> vt [cover] cobrir.
blanket bath n UK MED banho m na cama.
blankly ['blæŋklɪ] adv [stare] inexpressivamente.
blank verse n (U) verso m branco.
blare [bleə'] vi soar.
➡ **blare out** vi soar.
blasé [UK 'blɑːzeɪ, US ˌblɑː'zeɪ] adj [unconcerned] indiferente.
blasphemous ['blæsfəməs] adj blasfemo(ma).
blasphemy ['blæsfəmɪ] (pl -ies) n blasfêmia f.
blast [blɑːst] <> n -1. [of bomb] explosão f -2. [of air] corrente f -3. US inf [celebration] farra f. <> vt [hole, tunnel] dinamitar. <> excl UK inf diabos!
➡ **(at) full blast** adv -1. [maximum volume] a todo volume -2. [maximum effort, speed] a todo vapor.
➡ **blast off** vi SPACE decolar.
blasted ['blɑːstɪd] adj inf [for emphasis] maldito(ta).
blast furnace n alto-forno m.
blast-off n (U) SPACE decolagem f.
blatant ['bleɪtənt] adj [shameless] descarado(da).
blatantly ['bleɪtəntlɪ] adv descaradamente.
blaze [bleɪz] <> n -1. [fire] incêndio m -2. fig [of colour, light] explosão f; a ~ of publicity uma grande onda de publicidade. <> vi -1. [fire] arder -2. fig [with colour, emotion] resplandecer.
blazer ['bleɪzə'] n [jacket] blazer m.
blazing ['bleɪzɪŋ] adj -1. [sun, heat] abrasador(ra); it was ~ hot fazia um calor infernal -2. [row] acalorado(da).
bleach [bliːtʃ] <> n [chemical] alvejante m. <> vt -1. [hair] clarear -2. [clothes] alvejar. <> vi desbotar.
bleached [bliːtʃt] adj -1. [hair] descolorido(da), clareado(da) -2. [jeans] desbotado(da).
bleachers ['bliːtʃəz] npl US SPORT arquibancadas fpl.
bleak [bliːk] adj -1. [future] sombrio(a) -2. [place] escuro(ra) -3. [weather] gélido(da) -4. [face, person] triste.
bleary ['blɪərɪ] (compar -ier, superl -iest) adj [eyes] turvo(va).
bleary-eyed [ˌblɪərɪ'aɪd] adj com os olhos turvos.
bleat [bliːt] <> n [of sheep, goat] balido m. <> vi -1. [sheep, goat] balir -2. fig [person - speak] tagarelar; [- complain] balbuciar.
bleed [bliːd] (pt & pp bled) <> vt [drain] esvaziar. <> vi sangrar.
bleep [bliːp] <> n apito m. <> vt & vi apitar.
bleeper ['bliːpə'] n bipe m.
blemish ['blemɪʃ] <> n -1. [flaw] mancha f -2. [pimple, scar] cicatriz f -3. fig [on name, reputation] mancha f. <> vt [reputation] manchar.
blend [blend] <> n mistura f. <> vt [mix] misturar; to ~ sthg with sthg misturar algo com algo. <> vi [colours, sounds] misturar-se; to ~ with sthg misturar com algo.
➡ **blend in** vi -1. [person] confundir-se -2. [colours, sounds] confundir-se.
➡ **blend into** vt fus confundir-se com.
blender ['blendə'] n [food mixer] liquidificador m.
bless [bles] (pt & pp -ed OR blest) vt RELIG & fig

abençoar; **to be ~ed with sthg** ser abençoado(-da) com algo; **~ you!** [after sneezing] saúde!; [thank you] obrigado(da)!

blessed ['blesɪd] *adj* -**1.** *RELIG & fig* abençoado(da) -**2.** *inf* [for emphasis] bendito(ta).

blessing ['blesɪŋ] *n* benção *f*; **to count one's ~s** dar graças a Deus pelo que se tem; **a ~ in disguise** um mal que vem para bem; **to be a mixed ~** ter seus prós e contras.

blest [blest] *pt & pp* ▷ **bless**.

blew [blu:] *pt* ▷ **blow**.

blight [blaɪt] ◇ *n* -**1.** [plant disease] ferrugem *f* -**2.** *fig* [curse] desgraça *f* -**3.** *(U) fig* [decay] declínio *m*. ◇ *vt* arruinar.

blimey ['blaɪmɪ] *excl UK inf* minha nossa!, caramba!

blind [blaɪnd] ◇ *adj* -**1.** [gen] cego(ga) -**2.** *fig* [unaware]: **~ to sthg** cego(ga) para algo -**3.** *UK inf* [for emphasis]: **it doesn't make a ~ bit of difference to me** isso não faz a menor diferença para mim. ◇ *adv*: **~ drunk** completamente bêbado. ◇ *n* [for window] persiana *f*. ◇ *npl*: **the ~s** os cegos. ◇ *vt* -**1.** cegar -**2.** *fig* [make unobservant] ofuscar; **to ~ sb to sthg** impedir alguém de ver algo.

blind alley *n* -**1.** [street] beco *m* -**2.** *fig* [dead end] beco *m* sem saída.

blind corner *n* curva *f* sem visibilidade.

blind date *n* encontro *m* às cegas.

blinders ['blaɪndəz] *npl US* antolhos *mpl*.

blindfold ['blaɪndfəʊld] ◇ *adv* de olhos vendados. ◇ *n* venda *f*. ◇ *vt* vendar.

blinding ['blaɪndɪŋ] *adj* -**1.** [light] ofuscante -**2.** [severe]: **~ headache** dor de cabeça de matar.

blindingly ['blaɪndɪŋlɪ] *adv* [clearly]: **~ obvious** totalmente óbvio(via).

blindly ['blaɪndlɪ] *adv* -**1.** [without seeing] às cegas -**2.** *fig* [without knowing] sem saber.

blindness ['blaɪndnɪs] *n (U)* cegueira *f*; **~ to sthg** falta *f* de visão para algo.

blind spot *n* [when driving] ponto *m* cego.

blink [blɪŋk] ◇ *n* -**1.** piscar *m*; **in the ~ of an eye** num piscar de olhos -**2.** *inf* [machine]: **on the ~** enguiçado(da). ◇ *vt* -**1.** [eyes] piscar -**2.** *Am AUT*: **to ~ one's lights** dar farol alto *OR* luz alta. ◇ *vi* -**1.** [person] piscar -**2.** [light] cintilar.

blinkered ['blɪŋkəd] *adj fig* [view, attitude] bitolado(-da).

blinkers ['blɪŋkəz] *npl UK* [for horse] antolhos *mpl*.

blinking ['blɪŋkɪŋ] *adj UK inf* [for emphasis]: **that ~ phone!** que droga de telefone!

blip [blɪp] *n* -**1.** [sound] bipe *m* -**2.** [on radar] luz *f* intermitente -**3.** *fig* [temporary problem] problema *m* temporário.

bliss [blɪs] *n* êxtase *m*, bem-aventurança *f*.

blissful ['blɪsfʊl] *adj* abençoado(da); **~ ignorance** santa ignorância.

blissfully ['blɪsfʊlɪ] *adv* -**1.** [contentedly] maravilhosamente -**2.** [unknowingly]: **~ unaware** *OR* **ignorant** totalmente sem saber.

blister ['blɪstəʳ] ◇ *n* [on skin] bolha *f*. ◇ *vi* formar bolhas.

blistering ['blɪstərɪŋ] *adj* -**1.** [very hot] abrasador(ra) -**2.** [scathing] mordaz.

blister pack *n* blíster *m*.

blithe [blaɪð] *adj* -**1.** [unworried] despreocupado(da) -**2.** *dated* [cheerful] alegre.

blithely ['blaɪðlɪ] *adv* -**1.** [without a care] despreocupadamente -**2.** [casually] tranqüilamente.

BLitt (*abbr of* **Bachelor of Letters (Baccalaureus Litterarum)**) *n* (*titular de*) *graduação em letras*.

blitz [blɪts] *n* -**1.** *MIL* bombardeio *m* aéreo -**2.** *UK fig* [attack]: **to have a ~ on sthg** dar uma geral em algo.

blizzard ['blɪzəd] *n* nevasca *f*.

BLM (*abbr of* **Bureau of Land Management**) *n* *instituto norte-americano de gestão territorial*, ≃ INCRA *m*.

bloated ['bləʊtɪd] *adj* -**1.** [swollen] inchado(da) -**2.** [having eaten too much] empanturrado(da).

blob [blɒb] *n* -**1.** [drop] pingo *m* -**2.** [shapeless thing] borrão *m*, mancha *f*.

bloc [blɒk] *n POL* bloco *m*.

block [blɒk] ◇ *n* -**1.** [gen] bloco *m* -**2.** [of buildings] quadra *f*, quarteirão *m* -**3.** [obstruction] bloqueio *m* -**4.** *TECH*: **~ and tackle** talha *f* patente. ◇ *vt* -**1.** bloquear -**2.** [hinder] barrar.
➤ **block off** *vt sep* bloquear.
➤ **block out** *vt sep* bloquear.
➤ **block up** ◇ *vt sep* [obstruct] entupir. ◇ *vi* entupir.

blockade [blɒ'keɪd] ◇ *n* bloqueio *m*. ◇ *vt* bloquear.

blockage ['blɒkɪdʒ] *n* [obstruction] obstrução *f*.

block booking *n* reserva *f* conjunta.

blockbuster ['blɒkbʌstəʳ] *n inf* [book, film] estouro *m*.

block capitals *npl* maiúsculas *fpl*.

blockhead ['blɒkhed] *n inf* cabeça-dura *mf*.

block letters *npl* maiúsculas *fpl*.

block release *n UK na Inglaterra, liberação de estagiários de fábricas do trabalho para que possam estudar numa faculdade durante várias semanas*.

block vote *n UK* voto *m* em bloco.

bloke [bləʊk] *n UK inf* cara *m*.

blond [blɒnd] *adj* [hair, man] loiro(ra), claro(ra).

blonde [blɒnd] ◇ *adj* [hair, woman] loiro(ra), claro(ra). ◇ *n* [woman] loira *f*.

blood [blʌd] *n* sangue *m*; **new** *OR* **fresh ~** sangue novo; **in cold ~** a sangue frio; **it's in his ~** está em seu sangue; **to make one's ~ boil** deixar alguém danado(da) da vida; **to make sb's ~ run cold** gelar a alma de alguém.

blood bank *n* banco *m* de sangue.

bloodbath ['blʌdbɑːθ] *n* banho *m* de sangue.

blood brother *n* irmão *m* de sangue.

blood cell *n* glóbulo *m* sangüíneo.

blood count *n* contagem *f* de glóbulos sangüíneos.

blood-curdling *adj* de gelar o sangue.

blood donor *n* doador *m*, -ra *f* de sangue.

blood group *n* grupo *m* sangüíneo.

bloodhound ['blʌdhaʊnd] *n* cão *m* de Santo Humberto.

bloodless ['blʌdlɪs] *adj* -**1.** [face, lips] pálido(da) -**2.** [coup, victory] sem derramamento de sangue.

bloodletting ['blʌdˌletɪŋ] *n* [killing] matança *f*.

blood money n [money paid to killer] *dinheiro pago a um assassino*.

blood orange n laranja f sangüínea.

blood poisoning n septicemia f.

blood pressure n pressão f sangüínea OR arterial.

blood relation, blood relative n parente mf consangüíneo, -nea.

bloodshed [ˈblʌdʃed] n derramamento m de sangue.

bloodshot [ˈblʌdʃɒt] adj [eyes] injetado(da).

blood sports npl *esportes que envolvem a matança de animais*.

bloodstained [ˈblʌdsteɪnd] adj manchado(da) de sangue.

bloodstream [ˈblʌdstriːm] n corrente f sangüínea.

blood test n exame m de sangue.

bloodthirsty [ˈblʌdˌθɜːstɪ] adj sanguinário(ria).

blood transfusion n transfusão f de sangue.

blood type n tipo m sangüíneo.

blood vessel n vaso m sangüíneo.

bloody [ˈblʌdɪ] (compar -ier, superl -iest) ◇ adj -1. [war, conflict] sangrento(ta) -2. [face, hands] ensangüentado(da) -3. UK v inf [for emphasis]: **that** ~ ... essa droga de ...; **you** ~ **idiot!** seu imbecil! ◇ adv UK v inf: ~ **good** bom pra caramba; ~ **difficult** difícil para burro.

bloody-minded [-ˈmaɪndɪd] adj UK inf do contra.

bloom [bluːm] ◇ n [flower] flor f. ◇ vi [plant, tree] florir.

blooming [ˈbluːmɪŋ] ◇ adj -1. UK inf [for emphasis]: ~ **heck!** esse inferno miserável! -2. [healthy, attractive] radiante. ◇ adv UK inf pra caramba.

blossom [ˈblɒsəm] ◇ n [of tree] flor f; **in** ~ em flor. ◇ vi -1. [tree] florescer -2. fig [person] desabrochar.

blot [blɒt] (pt & pp -ted, cont -ting) ◇ n -1. [of ink etc] borrão m -2. fig [- on character, reputation] mancha f; [- on landscape] estrago m. ◇ vt -1. [dry] secar -2. [stain with ink] borrar.

➤ **blot out** vt sep -1. [obscure] ocultar -2. [erase] apagar.

blotch n mancha f.

blotchy [ˈblɒtʃɪ] (compar -ier, superl -iest) adj manchado(da).

blotting paper [ˈblɒtɪŋ-] n papel m mata-borrão.

blouse [blaʊz] n blusa f.

blouson [ˈbluːzɒn] n UK blusão m.

blow [bləʊ] (pt blew, pp blown) ◇ vi -1. [wind] ventar -2. [through mouth] soprar -3. [fuse] estourar -4. [whistle] assoviar. ◇ vt -1. [subj: wind] soprar -2. [whistle, horn, trumpet] soar -3. inf [money] torrar -4. [clear]: **to** ~ **one's nose** assoar o nariz -5. phr: **to** ~ **bubbles** fazer bolas OR bolhas. ◇ n -1. [hit] golpe m; **to come to** ~**s** começar a brigar; **to strike a** ~ **for sthg** fig lutar por algo -2. [shock] choque m; **to soften the** ~ amortecer o golpe.

➤ **blow away** vi [in wind] voar longe, sair voando.

➤ **blow out** ◇ vt sep apagar. ◇ vi -1. [candle] apagar -2. [tyre] estourar.

➤ **blow over** vi -1. [storm] cessar -2. [argument] esquecer-se.

➤ **blow up** ◇ vt sep -1. [inflate] encher -2. [with bomb] explodir -3. [enlarge] ampliar. ◇ vi [explode] explodir.

blow-by-blow adj detalhado(da).

blow-dry ◇ n secagem f. ◇ vt secar.

blowfly [ˈbləʊflaɪ] (pl -flies) n mosca-varejeira f.

blowgun n US = blowpipe.

blowlamp UK [ˈbləʊlæmp], **blowtorch** [ˈbləʊtɔːtʃ] n maçarico m.

blown [bləʊn] pp ▷ blow.

blowout [ˈbləʊaʊt] n -1. [of tyre] furo m -2. inf [big meal] comilança f.

blowpipe UK [ˈbləʊpaɪp], **blowgun** US [ˈbləʊɡʌn] n zarabatana f.

blowtorch n = blowlamp.

blowzy [ˈblaʊzɪ] (compar -ier, superl -iest) adj Br: a ~ **woman** uma mulher desalinhada.

BLS (abbr of Bureau of Labor Statistics) n *instituto norte-americano de economia e estatística do trabalho*.

BLT (abbr of bacon, lettuce and tomato) n fam *sanduíche de bacon, alface e tomate*.

blubber [ˈblʌbəʳ] ◇ n [of whale] gordura f. ◇ vi pej [weep] choramingar.

bludgeon [ˈblʌdʒən] vt espancar; **to** ~ **sb into doing sthg** fig ameaçar alguém para que faça algo.

blue [bluː] ◇ adj -1. [in colour] azul -2. inf [sad] triste -3. [pornographic - film, movie] pornográfico(-ca); [- joke] obsceno(na). ◇ n azul m; **dressed in** ~ vestido(da) de azul; **out of the** ~ inesperadamente.

➤ **blues** npl **the** ~**s** MUS o blues; inf [sad feeling] a melancolia.

blue baby n MED bebê m cianótico.

bluebell [ˈbluːbel] n campainha f (azul).

blueberry [ˈbluːbərɪ] (pl -ies) n mirtilo m.

bluebird [ˈbluːbɜːd] n azulão m norte-americano.

blue-black adj azul-ferrete.

blue-blooded [-ˈblʌdɪd] adj de sangue azul.

bluebottle [ˈbluːˌbɒtl] n mosca-varejeira f.

blue channel n: **the** ~ *acesso direto utilizado pelos membros da Comunidade Européia ao passar pelo controle de passaportes*.

blue cheese n queijo m azul.

blue chip n ST EX blue chip f, ação f de primeira ordem.

➤ **blue-chip** comp ST EX de primeira ordem.

blue-collar adj operário(ria).

blue-eyed boy [-aɪd-] n inf queridinho m.

blue jeans npl US jeans m, calça f jeans.

blue moon n inf: **once in a** ~ uma vez a cada século.

blueprint [ˈbluːprɪnt] n -1. CONSTR planta f -2. fig [plan, programme] projeto m.

bluestocking [ˈbluːˌstɒkɪŋ] n pej sabichona f.

blue tit n UK chapim-azul m.

blue whale n baleia f azul.

bluff [blʌf] ◇ adj [person, manner] expansivo(va). ◇ n -1. [deception] blefe m; **to call sb's** ~ pagar para ver (o que alguém está ameaçando fazer)

-2. [cliff] penhasco *m.* <> *vt:* **to ~ one's way into/ out of sthg** *trapacear para entrar em/sair de algo.* <> *vi* blefar.

blunder ['blʌndəʳ] <> *n* gafe *f.* <> *vi* **-1.** [make mistake] cometer um grande equívoco **-2.** [move clumsily] cambalear ; [stumble] tropeçar.

blundering ['blʌndərɪŋ] *adj* [stupid] desajeitado(-da).

blunt [blʌnt] <> *adj* **-1.** [gen] obtuso(sa) **-2.** [pencil] sem ponta **-3.** [knife] cego(ga) **-4.** [forthright] direto(ta). <> *vt* **-1.** [knife] cegar **-2.** *fig* [enthusiam, interest etc] murchar **-3.** [impact] amortecer.

bluntly ['blʌntlɪ] *adv* [say, reply] com franqueza, sem rodeios.

bluntness ['blʌntnɪs] *n* [forthrightness] franqueza *f.*

blur [blɜːʳ] (*pt* & *pp* **-red**, *cont* **-ring**) <> *n* borrão *m*, névoa *f.* <> *vt* **-1.** [outline, photograph] desfocar **-2.** [distinction, memory, vision] embaçar **-3.** [confuse] obscurecer.

blurb [blɜːb] *n inf* [on book] sinopse *f.*

blurred [blɜːd] *adj* **-1.** [outline, photograph] desfocado(da) **-2.** [distinction, memory, vision] obscuro(ra).

blurt [blɜːt] ◆ **blurt out** *vt sep* falar sem pensar.

blush [blʌʃ] <> *n* rubor *m.* <> *vi* corar.

blusher ['blʌʃəʳ] *n* ruge *m.*

bluster ['blʌstəʳ] <> *n* **-1.** [angry talk] discussão *f* **-2.** [boasting] bazófia *f.* <> *vi* **-1.** [speak angrily] vociferar **-2.** [boast] fanfarronar.

blustery ['blʌstərɪ] *adj* ventoso(sa).

BM *n* **-1.** (*abbr of* **Bachelor of Medicine**) (*titular de*) *graduação em medicina.* **- 2.** (*abbr of* **British Museum**) Museu *m* Britânico.

BMA (*abbr of* **British Medical Association**) *n* associação britânica de medicina, ≃ AMB *f.*

BMJ (*abbr of* **British Medical Journal**) *n* publicação da associação britânica de medicina.

BMus (*abbr of* **Bachelor of Music**) *n* (*titular de*) *graduação em música.*

BNP (*abbr of* **British National Party**) *n* partido britânico de extrema direita.

BO (*abbr of* **body odour**) *n* cê-cê *m.*

boa constrictor ['bəʊəkən'strɪktəʳ] *n* jibóia *f.*

boar [bɔːʳ] *n* **-1.** [male pig] barrão *m* **-2.** [wild pig] javali *m.*

board [bɔːd] <> *n* **-1.** [plank] tábua *f* **-2.** [for notices] quadro *m* (de avisos) **-3.** [for games] tabuleiro *m* **-4.** [blackboard] quadro-negro *m* **-5.** ADMIN direção *f*; **~ of directors** conselho *m* de diretores; **examining ~** banca *f* examinadora; **~ of enquiry** comissão *f* de inquérito **-6.** *UK* [at hotel, guesthouse] pensão *f*; **~ and lodging** casa e comida; **full ~** pensão completa; **half ~** meia pensão **-7.** *phr:* **above ~** honesto(ta); **to go by the ~** ir por água abaixo; **to sweep the ~** ganhar todas. <> *vt* [get onto] embarcar em.

◆ **across the board** <> *adj* generalizado(da). <> *adv* de forma generalizada.

◆ **on board** <> *adj* a bordo. <> *adv* a bordo; **to take sthg on ~** aceitar algo.

◆ **board up** *vt sep* fechar com tábuas.

boarder ['bɔːdəʳ] *n* **-1.** [lodger] pensionista *mf* **-2.** [at school] interno *m*, -na *f.*

board game *n* jogo *m* de tabuleiro.

boarding card ['bɔːdɪŋ-] *n* cartão *m* de embarque.

boarding house *n* hospedaria *f.*

boarding school ['bɔːdɪŋ-] *n* colégio *m* interno.

board meeting *n* reunião *f* de conselho.

Board of Trade *n* *UK*: **the ~** ≃ Câmara *f* do Comércio, *na Inglaterra, comissão governamental responsável pela supervisão do comércio e pelo estímulo às exportações.*

boardroom ['bɔːdrʊm] *n* sala *f* da diretoria.

boardwalk ['bɔːdwɔːk] *n* *US* passeio *m* de tábuas.

boast [bəʊst] <> *n* alarde *m.* <> *vt* [special feature] ostentar. <> *vi* [show off] vangloriar-se; **to ~ about sthg** gabar-se de algo.

boastful ['bəʊstfʊl] *adj* presunçoso(sa).

boasting *n* presunção *f*, ostentação *f.*

boat [bəʊt] *n* [ship] barco *m*; [for rowing] bote *m*; [for sailing] veleiro *m*; **by ~** de barco; **in the same ~** *fig* no mesmo barco; **to rock the ~** *fig* complicar as coisas.

boater ['bəʊtəʳ] *n* [hat] chapéu *m* de palha.

boating ['bəʊtɪŋ] *n* passeio *m* de barco.

boat people *npl* *refugiados que escapam de seu país de barco.*

boatswain ['bəʊsn] *n* NAUT contramestre *m.*

boat train *n* *trem que leva as pessoas para embarcar num navio ou que recolhe as que desembarcaram.*

bob [bɒb] (*pt* & *pp* **-bed**, *cont* **-bing**) <> *n* **-1.** [hairstyle] corte *m* chanel **-2.** *UK inf dated* [shilling] xelim *m* **-3.** = **bobsleigh**. <> *vi* [boat, ship] balouçar-se.

bobbin ['bɒbɪn] *n* [spool] bobina *f.*

bobble ['bɒbl] *n* [fluffy ball] pompom *m.*

bobby ['bɒbɪ] (*pl* **-ies**) *n* *UK inf* [policeman] tira *m.*

bobby pin *n* *US* grampo *m* (de cabelo).

bobby socks, bobby sox *npl* *US* meias *fpl* soquete.

bobsleigh ['bɒbsleɪ] *n* trenó *m* de esporte.

bode [bəʊd] *vi literary*: **to ~ ill/well (for sb/ sthg)** ser de mau/bom agouro (para alguém/ algo).

bodice ['bɒdɪs] *n* [of dress] corpete *f.*

bodily ['bɒdɪlɪ] <> *adj* [needs] físico(ca). <> *adv* [carry, lift] em peso.

body ['bɒdɪ] (*pl* **-ies**) *n* **-1.** [gen] corpo *m*; **to keep ~ and soul together** ganhar o suficiente só para pagar as contas **-2.** [corpse] cadáver *m*; **over my dead ~!** só por cima do meu cadáver! **-3.** [organization] entidade *f* **-4.** [of car] carroceria *f* **-5.** [of plane] fuselagem *f* **-6.** (*U*) [of wine] corpo *m* **-7.** [garment] body *m.*

body bag *n* saco *m* mortuário.

body building *n* fisiculturismo *m.*

bodyguard ['bɒdɪgɑːd] *n* guarda-costas *mf inv.*

body odour *UK*, **body odor** *US* *n* odor *m* corporal.

body search *n* revista *f* corporal.

body shop *n* **-1.** [garage] oficina *f* mecânica **-2.** *Am inf* [gym] academia *f* (de ginástica).

body stocking *n* macaquinho *m* colante (*para ginástica, dança*).

bodywork ['bɒdɪwɜːk] *n* [of car] carroceria *f.*

boffin ['bɒfɪn] *n* *UK inf* cientista *mf.*

bog [bɒg] *n* -1. [marsh] lodaçal *m* -2. *UK v inf* [toilet] privada *f.*

bogey ['bəʊgɪ] *n* -1. [spectre]: **the ~ of recession** o fantasma da recessão -2. *inf* [in nose] meleca *f.*

bogeyman *n* ≃ bicho-papão *m.*

bogged down [ˌbɒgd-] *adj* atolado(da).

boggle ['bɒgl] *vi*: **the mind ~s!** não dá para acreditar!

boggy ['bɒgɪ] (*compar* -ier, *superl* -iest) *adj* lamacento(ta), pantanoso(sa).

bogie *n* RAIL truque *m.*

Bogotá [ˌbɒgə'tɑː] *n* Bogotá; **in ~** em Bogotá.

bog-standard *adj inf* comum.

bogus ['bəʊgəs] *adj* falso(sa).

Bohemia [bəʊ'hiːmjə] *n* Boêmia; **in ~** na Boêmia.

bohemian [bəʊ'hiːmɪən] ◇ *adj* boêmio(mia). ◇ *n* boêmio *m,* -mia *f.*
    ◆ **Bohemian** ◇ *adj* boêmio(mia). ◇ *n* boêmio *m,* -mia *f.*

boil [bɔɪl] ◇ *n* -1. MED [on skin] furúnculo *m* -2. [boiling point]: **to bring sthg to the ~** deixar algo ferver; **to come to the ~** começar a ferver. ◇ *vt* -1. [water, kettle] ferver -2. [food] cozinhar. ◇ *vi* [water, kettle] ferver.
    ◆ **boil away** *vi* [evaporate] evaporar.
    ◆ **boil down to** *vt fus fig* reduzir-se a.
    ◆ **boil over** *vi* -1. [liquid] derramar -2. *fig* [feelings] descontrolar-se.

boiled [bɔɪld] *adj* cozido(da); **~ sweet** *UK* caramelo *m;* **~ egg** ovo *m* cozido.

boiler ['bɔɪlə'] *n* boiler *m.*

boiler suit *n UK* macacão *m.*

boiling ['bɔɪlɪŋ] *adj* -1. [liquid] fervente -2. *inf* [hot - person] morto(ta) de calor; [- weather] abrasador(ra) -3. [angry]: **~ with rage** fervendo de raiva.

boiling point *n* ponto *m* de ebulição.

boisterous ['bɔɪstərəs] *adj* [child, behaviour] irriquieto(ta).

bold [bəʊld] *adj* -1. [confident] audacioso(sa) -2. [brave] corajoso(sa) -3. ART [lines, design] arrojado(da) -4. [colour] nítido(da) -5. TYPO: **in ~ type** OR **print** em negrito.

boldly ['bəʊldlɪ] *adv* corajosamente.

Bolivia [bə'lɪvɪə] *n* Bolívia; **in ~** na Bolívia.

Bolivian [bə'lɪvɪən] ◇ *adj* boliviano(na). ◇ *n* boliviano *m,* -na *f.*

bollard ['bɒlɑːd] *n* [on road] poste *m* de sinalização.

bollocks ['bɒləks] *UK vulg* ◇ *npl* saco *m.* ◇ *excl* saco!

Bolshevik ['bɒlʃɪvɪk] ◇ *adj* bolchevique. ◇ *n* bolchevique *mf.*

bolster ['bəʊlstə'] ◇ *n* [pillow] travesseiro *m* longo. ◇ *vt* [encourage] alentar.
    ◆ **bolster up** *vt fus* [support] sustentar.

bolt [bəʊlt] ◇ *n* -1. [on door, window] ferrolho *m,* trinco *m* -2. [type of screw] parafuso *m.* ◇ *adv*: **to sit ~ upright** sentar direito. ◇ *vt* -1. [fasten together] aparafusar -2. [close] trancar -3. [food] devorar. ◇ *vi* [run] disparar.

bomb [bɒm] ◇ *n* [explosive device] bomba *f.* ◇ *vt* bombardear.

bombard [bɒm'bɑːd] *vt* MIL & *fig* bombardear, **to ~ sb with sthg** bombardear alguém com algo.

bombardment [bɒm'bɑːdmənt] *n* bombardeio *m.*

bombastic [bɒm'bæstɪk] *adj* bombástico(ca).

bomb disposal squad *n* esquadrão *m* antibombas.

bomber ['bɒmə'] *n* -1. [plane] bombardeiro *m* -2. [person] pessoa que pratica atentados a bomba.

bomber jacket *n* jaqueta curta ajustada ao peito e aos quadris.

bombing ['bɒmɪŋ] *n* bombardeio *m.*

bombproof *adj* [shelter] à prova de bombas.

bombshell ['bɒmʃell] *n fig* [unpleasant surprise] bomba *f;* **to come as a ~** cair como uma bomba.

bombsite *n* área *f* bombardeada.

bona fide ['bəʊnə'faɪdɪ] *adj* [genuine] legítimo(ma).

bonanza [bə'nænzə] *n* fonte, muitas vezes repentina ou inesperada, de sorte ou riqueza.

bond [bɒnd] ◇ *n* -1. [emotional link] laço *m* -2. [binding promise] compromisso *m* -3. FIN título *m.* ◇ *vt* -1. [glue]: **to ~ sthg to sthg** colar algo a algo -2. *fig* [people] unir. ◇ *vi* -1. [stick together]: **to ~ (together)** colar -2. *fig* [people] unir-se.

bondage *n literary* [servitude] servidão *f.*

bonded warehouse ['bɒndɪd-] *n* depósito *m* da alfândega.

bone [bəʊn] ◇ *n* -1. [of body, material] osso *m;* **~ of contention** pomo *m* da discórdia; **to feel sthg in one's ~s** sentir algo na pele; **to know sthg in one's ~s** saber algo intuitivamente; **to make no ~s about sthg** não fazer cerimônia sobre algo -2. [of fish] espinha *f.* ◇ *vt* [fish, meat] desossar.

bone china *n* porcelana fina e branca feita com cinzas de ossos.

bone-dry *adj* completamente seco(ca).

bone-idle *adj inf* encostado(da).

boneless ['bəʊnlɪs] *adj* sem osso.

bone marrow *n* tutano *m.*

bonfire ['bɒnˌfaɪə'] *n* fogueira *f* ao ar livre.

bonfire night *n UK* noite de 5 de novembro, quando os ingleses lançam fogos de artifício e queimam a figura de Guy Fawkes numa fogueira ao ar livre.

bongo ['bɒŋgəʊ] (*pl* -s OR -es) *n*: **~ (drum)** bongô *m.*

bonk [bɒŋk] *inf* ◇ *vt* [have sex with] transar com. ◇ *vi* [have sex] transar.

Bonn [bɒn] *n* Bonn; **in ~** em Bonn.

bonnet ['bɒnɪt] *n* -1. *UK* [of car] capô *m* -2. [hat] touca *f.*

bonus ['bəʊnəs] (*pl* -es) *n* -1. [extra money] bônus *m inv* -2. *fig* [added treat] vantagem *f* adicional.

bonus issue *n UK* FIN emissão *f* de títulos de bonificação.

bony ['bəʊnɪ] (*compar* -ier, *superl* -iest) *adj* -1. [person, hand, face] ossudo(da) -2. [meat] com osso; [fish] cheio (cheia) de espinhas.

boo [buː] (*pl* -s) ◇ *excl* bu! ◇ *n* vaia *f.* ◇ *vt & vi* vaiar.

boob [buːb] *n inf* [mistake] gafe *f.*
    ◆ **boobs** *npl UK inf* [breasts] tetas *fpl.*

boob tube *n* -1. *UK* [garment] tomara-que-caia *m inv* -2. *US inf* [TV] telinha *f.*

booby prize ['buːbɪ-] *n* prêmio *m* de consolação.

booby trap ['buːbɪ-] *n* -1. [bomb] bomba *f* camuflada -2. [prank] armadilha *f.*

➡ **booby-trap** *vt* [car, building] colocar explosivos em.

boogie ['buːgɪ] *inf* ◇ *n* [dance]: **let's have a ~** vamos sacudir. ◇ *vi* [dance] sacudir.

book [bʊk] ◇ *n* **-1.** [for reading] livro *m*; **to do sthg by the ~** fazer algo como manda o figurino; **to throw the ~ at sb** fazer todas as acusações possíveis a alguém **-2.** [pack - of stamps] bloco *m*; [- of matches] caixa *f*; [- of cheques, tickets] talão *m*. ◇ *vt* **-1.** [reserve] reservar; **to be fully ~ed** estar totalmente cheio (cheia) OR esgotado(da) **-2.** *inf* [subj: police] autuar **-3.** *UK FTBL* dar cartão amarelo OR vermelho a. ◇ *vi* reservar, fazer uma reserva.

➡ **books** *npl* COMM registros *mpl*; **to do the ~s** escriturar, fazer a contabilidade; **to be in sb's good/bad ~s** ser bem/mal visto por alguém.

➡ **book in** ◇ *vt sep* registrar-se. ◇ *vi* [at hotel] registrar-se.

➡ **book up** *vt sep*: **to be ~ed up** [fully booked] estar completamente cheio (cheia); **the hotel is ~ed up** o hotel está lotado.

bookable ['bʊkəbl] *adj* **-1.** [seats, tickets] a ser reservado(da) **-2.** FTBL: **a ~ offence** uma falta digna de cartão.

book bag *n US* = **booksack**.

bookbinding ['bʊk,baɪndɪŋ] *n* encadernação *f*.

bookcase ['bʊkkeɪs] *n* estante *f* (para livros).

book club *n* clube *m* do livro.

bookends *npl* prateleiras *fpl*.

bookie ['bʊkɪ] *n inf* bookmaker *m*.

booking ['bʊkɪŋ] *n* **-1.** *esp UK* [reservation] reserva *f* **-2.** *esp UK* FTBL cartão *m* amarelo OR vermelho.

booking clerk *n esp UK* vendedor *m*, -ra *f* de ingressos.

booking office *n esp UK* bilheteria *f*.

bookish ['bʊkɪʃ] *adj* [person] aficionado(da) pelos livros.

bookkeeper ['bʊk,kiːpəʳ] *n* COMM contador *m*, -ra *f*.

bookkeeping ['bʊk,kiːpɪŋ] *n* COMM contabilidade *f*.

booklet ['bʊklɪt] *n* [pamphlet] folheto *m*.

bookmaker ['bʊk,meɪkəʳ] *n* bookmaker *m*.

bookmark ['bʊkmɑːk] *n* marcador *m* de páginas.

booksack *n US* mochila *f*.

bookseller ['bʊk,seləʳ] *n* vendedor *m*, -ra *f* de livros.

bookshelf ['bʊkʃelf] (*pl* **-shelves** [-ʃelvz]) *n* prateleira *f* OR estante *f* (para livros).

bookshop *UK* ['bʊkʃɒp], **bookstore** *US* ['bʊkstɔːʳ] *n* livraria *f*.

bookstall ['bʊkstɔːl] *n UK* banca *f* de jornal.

bookstore *n US* = **bookshop**.

book token *n esp UK* vale-livro *m*.

bookworm ['bʊkwɜːm] *n fig* [person] rato *m* de biblioteca.

boom [buːm] ◇ *n* **-1.** [loud noise] estrondo *m* **-2.** [increase] boom *m*, crescimento *m* **-3.** NAUT retranca *f* **-4.** [for TV camera, microphone] bum *m*. ◇ *vi* **-1.** [make noise] ribombar **-2.** ECON [grow] crescer rapidamente.

boomerang ['buːməræŋ] *n* bumerangue *m*.

boon [buːn] *n* [help, advantage] ajuda *f*.

boor [bʊəʳ] *n* pessoa *f* rude.

boorish ['bʊərɪʃ] *adj* rude.

boost [buːst] ◇ *n* **-1.** [increase] incremento *m*; **to give a ~ to sthg** dar um empurrão em algo **-2.** [improvement] impulso *m*. ◇ *vt* **-1.** [increase] incrementar **-2.** [improve] levantar **-3.** *US inf* [steal] afanar.

booster ['buːstəʳ] *n* MED [vaccine] reforço *m*.

booster seat *n* cadeirinha *f* para automóvel, bebê-conforto *m*.

boot [buːt] ◇ *n* **-1.** [footwear] bota *f* **-2.** *UK* [of car] porta-bagagem *m*. ◇ *vt* **-1.** *inf* [kick] dar um pé na bunda de **-2.** COMPUT inicializar, dar boot em.

➡ **to boot** *adv* também.

➡ **boot out** *vt sep inf* mandar às favas.

➡ **boot up** *vi* COMPUT inicializar, dar boot.

booth [buːð] *n* **-1.** [at fair] barraca *f* **-2.** [telephone booth] cabine *f* (telefônica) **-3.** [voting booth] cabine *f* eleitoral.

bootleg ['buːtleg] *adj* [alcohol] de contrabando; [recording] pirata.

bootlegger ['buːt,legəʳ] *n inf* contrabandista *mf*.

booty ['buːtɪ] *n literary* butim *m*.

booze [buːz] *inf* ◇ *n* [alcohol] trago *m*. ◇ *vi* [drink alcohol] tomar umas e outras.

boozer ['buːzəʳ] *n inf* **-1.** [person] bebum *mf* **-2.** *UK* [pub] bar *m*.

bop [bɒp] (*pt & pp* **-ped**, *cont* **-ping**) *inf* ◇ *n* **-1.** [hit] batida *f* **-2.** [disco, dance] festa *f* dançante. ◇ *vt* [hit] bater. ◇ *vi* [dance] dançar.

border ['bɔːdəʳ] ◇ *n* **-1.** [between countries] fronteira *f* **-2.** [edge] borda *f* **-3.** [hem] orla *f* **-4.** [outer boundary] limite *m* **-5.** [bank, shore] margem *f* **-6.** [for flowers] bordadura *f*. ◇ *vt* **-1.** [country] limitar-se com **-2.** [surround] cercar.

➡ **border on** *vt fus* [verge on] beirar em.

border collie *n* border collie *m*.

borderline ['bɔːdəlaɪn] ◇ *adj*: **~ case** caso-limite *m*. ◇ *n fig* [division] limite *m*.

bore [bɔːʳ] ◇ *pt* ▷ **bear**. ◇ *n* **-1.** *pej* [tedious person] chato *m*, -ta *f*; [tedious situation, event] chatice *f* **-2.** [of gun] calibre *m*. ◇ *vt* **-1.** [not interest] entediar; **to ~ sb stiff** OR **to tears** OR **to death** *inf* matar alguém de tédio **-2.** [drill] furar.

bored [bɔːd] *adj* entediado(da); **to be ~ with sthg** estar entediado(da) com algo.

boredom ['bɔːdəm] *n* tédio *m*.

boring ['bɔːrɪŋ] *adj* chato(ta).

born [bɔːn] *adj* **-1.** [given life] nascido(da); **to be ~** nascer; **~ and bred (in)** nascido e criado (em), nascida e criada (em) **-2.** [for emphasis] nato(ta).

born-again *adj* **-1.** [Christian] convertido(da) **-2.** *fig* [earnestly enthusiastic] fanático(ca).

borne [bɔːn] *pp* ▷ **bear**.

Borneo ['bɔːnɪəʊ] *n* Bornéu *f*; **in ~** em Bornéu.

borough ['bʌrə] *n* município *m*, distrito *m*.

borrow ['bɒrəʊ] *vt* [property, money] tomar emprestado(da); **to ~ sthg from sb** pegar algo emprestado de alguém.

borrower ['bɒrəʊəʳ] *n* [of money] tomador *m*, -ra *f* de empréstimo.

borrowing ['bɒrəʊɪŋ] *n* [of money] empréstimo *m*.

borstal ['bɔ:stll *n UK* instituto *m* correcional para jovens.

Bosnia ['bɒznɪə] *n* Bósnia; **in** ~ na Bósnia.

Bosnia-Herzegovina [-ˌhɜ:tsəgə'vi:nə] *n* Bósnia-Herzegovina.

Bosnian ['bɒznɪən] ◇ *adj* bósnio(nia). ◇ *n* bósnio *m*, -nia *f.*

bosom ['bʊzəm] *n* -1. [of woman] peito *m* -2. *fig* [centre] seio *m*; ~ **friend** amigo *m*, -ga *f* do peito.

Bosporus ['bɒspərəs], **Bosphorus** ['bɒsfərəs] *n*: **the** ~ o Bósforo.

boss [bɒs] ◇ *n* -1. [of company, department, organization] chefe *mf*; **to be one's own** ~ trabalhar por conta própria -2. *fig* [of gang] chefão *m*; **you're the** ~! você é quem manda! ◇ *vt pej* [give orders to] mandar.
➤ **boss about, boss around** *vt sep* mandar em.

bossy ['bɒsɪ] (*compar* -**ier**, *superl* -**iest**) *adj* mandão(o-na).

bosun ['bəʊsn] *n* = boatswain.

botanic(al) [bə'tænɪk(l)] *adj* botânico(ca).

botanical garden *n* jardim *m* botânico.

botanist ['bɒtənɪst] *n* botânico *m*, -ca *f.*

botany ['bɒtənɪ] *n* botânica *f.*

botch [bɒtʃ] ➤ **botch up** *vt sep inf* fazer nas coxas.

both [bəʊθ] ◇ *adj* ambos(bas), os dois, as duas; **we** ~ **left** nós dois (duas) saímos, ambos saímos; ~ **my brother and myself will be there** tanto meu irmão quanto eu estaremos lá, nós dois estaremos lá. ◇ *adv* não apenas ... como; **she is** ~ **witty and intelligent** ela não só é espirituosa, como também inteligente. ◇ *pron* ambos *mpl*, -bas *fpl*; ~ **of us** nós dois (duas).

bother ['bɒðər] ◇ *vt* -1. [worry] preocupar; **I can't be** ~**ed to do that** não me disponho a fazer isso -2. [irritate, annoy] incomodar. ◇ *vi* [trouble o.s.] incomodar-se; **to** ~ **about sthg** incomodar-se com algo; **to** ~ **doing** *OR* **to do sthg** incomodar-se em fazer algo. ◇ *n* -1. (*U*) [inconvenience] aborrecimento *m* -2. [nuisance] incômodo *m* -3. [difficulty] dificuldade *f* -4. [obstacle] estorvo *m*. ◇ *excl* (que) droga!

bothered ['bɒðəd] *adj* -1. [worried] preocupado(da) -2. [annoyed] chateado(da).

Botswana [bɒ'tswɑ:nə] *n* Botsuana; **in** ~ em Botsuana.

bottle ['bɒtl] ◇ *n* -1. [gen] garrafa *f* -2. [of medicine] frasco *m* -3. [of perfume] vidro *m* -4. [for baby] mamadeira *f* -5. (*U*) *UK inf* [courage]: **he didn't have the** ~ **to do it** ele não teve coragem de fazer isso. ◇ *vt* -1. [wine] engarrafar -2. [fruit] enfrascar.
➤ **bottle out** *vi UK inf* dar para trás.
➤ **bottle up** *vt sep* [feelings] reprimir.

bottle bank *n* contêiner no qual se recolhem garrafas de vidro vazias para reciclagem.

bottled ['bɒtld] *adj* engarrafado(da).

bottle-feed *vt* [baby] dar mamadeira para.

bottleneck ['bɒtlnek] *n* -1. [in traffic] engarrafamento *m* -2. [in production] gargalo *m*.

bottle-opener *n* abridor *m* (de garrafa).

bottle party *n festa informal em que cada convidado leva bebida.*

bottom ['bɒtəm] ◇ *adj* -1. [lowest] de baixo -2. [least successful] último(ma). ◇ *n* -1. [lowest part - of glass, bag, lake] fundo *m*; [- of page] fim *m*, final *m*; [- of mountain, hill] sopé *m*; **at the** ~ embaixo; **at the** ~ **of** no fundo de -2. [far end] fim *m*, final *m* -3. [least successful level] nível *m* mais baixo -4. [buttocks] traseiro *m* -5. *fig* [root, cause]: **at the** ~ **of** por trás de; **to get to the** ~ **of sthg** ir até o fundo de algo.
➤ **bottom out** *vi* [prices, recession] estabilizar-se.

bottomless ['bɒtəmlɪs] *adj* -1. [very deep] sem fundo -2. [endless] infinito(ta).

bottom line *n fig*: **the** ~ **is that ...** a questão toda é que ...

botulism *n* (*U*) botulismo *m.*

bough [baʊ] *n* [of tree] galho *m.*

bought [bɔ:t] *pt & pp* ▷ **buy.**

boulder ['bəʊldər] *n* pedregulho *m.*

boulevard ['bu:ləvɑ:d] *n* alameda *f.*

bounce [baʊns] ◇ *vi* -1. [ball] quicar -2. [light, sound] refletir -3. [person - with energy, enthusiasm]: **she was bouncing with energy/enthusiasm** ela estava pulando de alegria/entusiasmo; **she bounced into the room, singing** ela entrou na sala radiante, cantando; [- jump up and down]: **to** ~ **on sthg** saltar sobre algo -4. *inf* [cheque] ser devolvido(da). ◇ *vt* [ball] bater. ◇ *n* -1. [of ball] pulo *m* -2. *fig* [vigour] vigor *m*, vivacidade *f.*
➤ **bounce back** *vi* [after illness, setback] recuperar-se.

bouncer ['baʊnsər] *n inf* [at club etc] leão-de-chácara *m.*

bouncy ['baʊnsɪ] (*compar* -**ier**, *superl* -**iest**) *adj* -1. [lively] vivaz -2. [bed, trampoline] com bom molejo -3. [ball] saltitante.

bound [baʊnd] ◇ *pt & pp* ▷ **bind.** ◇ *adj* -1. [certain]: **to be** ~ **to do sthg** fazer algo na certa -2. [forced, morally obliged]: ~ **by sthg/to do sthg** obrigado(da) por algo/fazer algo; **I'm** ~ **to say/admit** devo dizer/admitir -3. [en route]: **to be** ~ **for** estar a caminho de. ◇ *n* [leap] salto *m*. ◇ *vt* [border]: **to be** ~**ed by** ser limitado(a) por. ◇ *vi* [leap] correr aos pulos.
➤ **bound up with** *prep* [connected] estreitamente ligado a.
➤ **bounds** *npl* [limits] limites *mpl*; **out of** ~**s** interditado(da).

boundary ['baʊndərɪ] (*pl* -**ies**) *n* -1. [of area of land] fronteira *f* -2. *fig* [of science, knowledge] fronteiras *fpl.*

boundless ['baʊndlɪs] *adj* ilimitado(da).

bountiful ['baʊntɪfʊl] *adj literary* [ample] abundante.

bounty ['baʊntɪ] *n* (*U*) *literary* [generosity] generosidade *f.*

bouquet [bəʊ'keɪ] *n* -1. [bunch] buquê *m* -2. [smell] buquê *m.*

bouquet garni ['bu:keɪgɑ:'ni:] *n* bouquet garni *m* (*ervas para tempero*).

bourbon ['bɜ:bən] *n* bourbon *m* (*uísque norte-americano*).

bourgeois ['bɔ:ʒwɑ:] *adj pej* burguês(esa).

bourgeoisie [ˌbɔ:ʒwɑ:'zi:] *n pej*: **the** ~ a burguesia.

bout [baʊt] n -1. [attack] ataque m -2. [session] período m -3. [boxing match] assalto m.

boutique [buːˈtiːk] n butique f.

bow¹ [baʊ] ◇ n -1. [act of bowing] reverência f -2. [of ship] proa f. ◇ vt [lower] inclinar. ◇ vi -1. [make a bow] inclinar-se -2. [defer]: **to ~ to** sthg submeter-se a algo.
  ➡ **bow down** vi [give in]: **to ~ down (to** sb) render-se(a alguém).
  ➡ **bow out** vi afastar-se.

bow² [baʊ] n -1. [gen & MUS] arco m -2. [knot] laço m.

bowels [ˈbaʊəlz] npl -1. [intestines] intestinos mpl -2. fig [deepest part] entranhas fpl.

bowl [baʊl] ◇ n -1. [container - gen] tigela f; [- for sugar] açucareiro m; [- for fruit] fruteira f -2. [bowl-shaped part - of toilet, sink] bacia f; [- of pipe] fornilho m -3. [bowlful] prato m. ◇ vt & vi [in cricket] atirar.
  ➡ **bowls** n (U) jogo m de bocha.
  ➡ **bowl over** vt sep -1. [knock over] derrubar -2. fig [surprise, impress] surpreender.

bow-legged [ˌbəʊˈlegɪd] adj cambota.

bowler [ˈbəʊləʳ] n -1. [in cricket, bowls] lançador m -2. [headgear]: **~ (hat)** chapéu-coco m.

bowling [ˈbəʊlɪŋ] n: **(tenpin) ~** jogo m de boliche.

bowling alley n -1. [building] boliche m -2. [alley] pista f de boliche.

bowling green n cancha m de bocha.

bow tie [bəʊ-] n gravata-borboleta f.

bow window [bəʊ-] n janela f em arco.

box [bɒks] ◇ n -1. [gen] caixa f -2. [in theatre] camarote m -3. [in car races] box m -4. UK inf [television]: **the ~** a TV -5. [shrub, tree] buxo m. ◇ vt -1. [punch] esmurrar -2. [put in boxes] colocar em caixas. ◇ vi [fight] lutar.
  ➡ **box in** vt sep -1. [hem in]: **to get ~ed in** ficar espremido(da) -2. [build a box around] encaixotar, encaixar.

boxed [bɒkst] adj empacotado(da).

boxer [ˈbɒksəʳ] n -1. [fighter] boxeador m, -ra f -2. [dog] boxer mf.

boxer shorts npl cuecas fpl samba-canção.

boxing [ˈbɒksɪŋ] n (U) boxe m.

Boxing Day n dia seguinte ao Natal em que é feriado nacional no Reino Unido. Tradicionalmente, era o dia em que os empregados recebiam os presentes dos patrões, geralmente uma caixinha em dinheiro.

boxing glove n luva f de boxe.

boxing ring n ringue m de boxe.

box junction n UK cruzamento de ruas demarcado com faixas amarelas sobre o qual um veículo não pode avançar a menos que seu caminho esteja livre.

box number n caixa f postal.

box office n bilheteria f.

boxroom [ˈbɒksrʊm] n UK quarto m de despejo.

boy [bɔɪ] ◇ n -1. [young male] menino m -2. [adult male] rapaz m -3. [son] filho m -4. [male friend]: **the ~s** os caras. ◇ excl: **(oh) ~!** inf nossa!

boycott [ˈbɔɪkɒt] ◇ n boicote m. ◇ vt boicotar.

boyfriend [ˈbɔɪfrend] n namorado m.

boyish [ˈbɔɪɪʃ] adj juvenil.

boy scout n escoteiro m.

Bp (abbr of **Bishop**) bispo m.

Br (abbr of **Brother**) RELIG Ir.

bra [brɑː] n sutiã f.

brace [breɪs] (pl sense 3 inv) ◇ n -1. MED aparelho m -2. [pair] par m. ◇ vt lit & fig **to ~ o.s. (for** sthg): preparar-se (para algo).
  ➡ **braces** npl UK [for trousers] suspensórios mpl.

bracelet [ˈbreɪslɪt] n bracelete m.

bracing [ˈbreɪsɪŋ] adj revigorante.

bracken [ˈbrækn] n (U) samambaia f.

bracket [ˈbrækɪt] ◇ n -1. [support] suporte m, mão-francesa f -2. [parenthesis] parêntese m; **in ~s** entre parênteses -3. [group] faixa f. ◇ vt -1. [enclose in brackets] colocar entre parênteses -2. [group]: **to ~ sb/sth (together) with** sb/sthg equiparar alguém/algo a alguém/algo.

brackish [ˈbrækɪʃ] adj salobre.

brag [bræg] (pt & pp -ged, cont -ging) vi [boast] gabar-se.

braid [breɪd] ◇ n -1. [on uniform] galão m -2. US [hairstyle] trança f. ◇ vt US trançar.

braille [breɪl] n (U) braile m.

brain [breɪn] n -1. [organ] cérebro m -2. [mind] cabeça f; **to have sthg on the ~** estar com algo na cabeça -3. inf [clever person] gênio m.
  ➡ **brains** npl [intelligence] sabedoria f; **to pick sb's ~s** recorrer à sabedoria de alguém; **to rack** UK OR **cudgel** US **one's ~s** fig queimar OR gastar os neurônios.

brainchild [ˈbreɪntʃaɪld] n invenção f.

brain death n (U) morte f cerebral.

brain drain n evasão f de cérebros.

brainless [ˈbreɪnlɪs] adj idiota, tolo(la).

brainstorm [ˈbreɪnstɔːm] n -1. UK [moment of aberration] bobeira f -2. US [brilliant idea] idéia f luminosa.

brainstorming [ˈbreɪnˌstɔːmɪŋ] n (U) brainstorming m.

brainteaser [ˈbreɪnˌtiːzəʳ] n quebra-cabeça m.

brainwash [ˈbreɪnwɒʃ] vt fazer lavagem cerebral em.

brainwave [ˈbreɪnweɪv] n idéia f luminosa.

brainy [ˈbreɪnɪ] (compar -ier, superl -iest) adj inf sabichão(chona).

braise [breɪz] vt refogar.

brake [breɪk] ◇ n -1. [on vehicle] freio m -2. fig [restraint] freio m. ◇ vi frear.

brake fluid n (U) líquido m de freio.

brake light n luz f de freio.

brake lining n lona f de freio.

brake pedal n pedal m do freio.

brake shoe n sapata f de freio.

bramble [ˈbræmbl] n [bush] amoreira f silvestre; [fruit] amora f silvestre.

bran [bræn] n (U) farelo m.

branch [brɑːntʃ] ◇ n -1. [of tree] galho m -2. [of river] braço m -3. [of railway] ramal m -4. [of company, bank, organization] sucursal f -5. [of subject] ramo m. ◇ vi [road] bifurcar-se.
  ➡ **branch off** vi [road, track] ramificar-se.
  ➡ **branch out** vi [person, company] expandir-se em nova direção.

branch line n [railway] ramal m secundário.

brand [brænd] ◇ n -1. COMM marca f -2. fig [type]

tipo *m* -**3.** [mark on cattle] marca *f* de ferro em brasa. <> *vt* -**1.** [cattle] marcar com ferro em brasa -**2.** *fig* [classify]: **to ~ sb (as) sthg** rotular alguém de algo.

brandish ['brændɪʃ] *vt* brandir.

brand leader *n* marca *f* dominante.

brand name *n* marca *f* registrada.

brand-new *adj* novo(va) em folha.

brandy ['brændɪ] (*pl* -**ies**) *n* conhaque *m*.

brash [bræʃ] *adj pej* atrevido(da).

Brasilia [brə'zɪljə] *n* Brasília; **in ~** em Brasília.

brass [brɑːs] *n* -**1.** (*U*) [type of metal] latão *m* -**2.** *MUS*: **the ~** os metais.

    ◆ **brasses** *npl* [ornaments] objetos *mpl* decorativos em latão.

brass band *n* fanfarra *f*.

brasserie ['bræsərɪ] *n* *restaurante simples e barato que serve comida em estilo francês*.

brassiere [*UK* 'bræsɪə^r, *US* brə'zɪr] *n* sutiã *m*.

brass knuckles *npl Am* soco-inglês *m*.

brass rubbing *n* [picture] gravura *f* em latão.

brass tacks *npl inf*: **to get down to ~** ir direto ao assunto.

brat [bræt] *n inf pej* capeta *m*.

bravado [brə'vɑːdəʊ] *n* (*U*) bravata *f*.

brave [breɪv] <> *adj* corajoso(sa). <> *n* [warrior] guerreiro *m* índio, bravo *m*. <> *vt* enfrentar.

bravely ['breɪvlɪ] *adv* bravamente.

bravery ['breɪvərɪ] *n* (*U*) bravura *f*.

bravo [ˌbrɑːˈvəʊ] *excl* bravo!

brawl [brɔːl] *n* briga *f*.

brawn [brɔːn] *n* (*U*) [muscle] músculo *m*

brawny ['brɔːnɪ] (*compar* -**ier**, *superl* -**iest**) *adj* musculoso(sa).

bray [breɪ] *vi* [donkey] zurrar.

brazen ['breɪzn] *adj* descarado(da).

    ◆ **brazen out** *vt sep*: **to ~ it out** encarar.

brazier ['breɪzjə^r] *n* braseiro *m*.

Brazil [brə'zɪl] *n* Brasil; **in ~** no Brasil.

Brazilian [brə'zɪljən] <> *adj* brasileiro(ra). <> *n* brasileiro *m*, -ra *f*.

brazil nut *n* castanha-do-pará *f*.

breach [briːtʃ] <> *n* -**1.** [act of disobedience] quebra *f*; **a ~ of an agreement** o rompimento de um acordo; **a ~ of the law** uma transgressão da lei; **to be in ~ of sthg** estar transgredindo algo; **~ of contract** quebra de contrato -**2.** [opening, gap] brecha *f*; **to step into the ~** *fig* ficar no lugar de alguém temporariamente -**3.** *fig* [in friendship, marriage] rompimento *m*. <> *vt* -**1.** [disobey] romper -**2.** [make hole in] abrir uma brecha em.

breach of the peace *n* atentado *m* à ordem pública.

bread [bred] *n* -**1.** [food] pão *m*; **~ and butter** [food] pão com manteiga; *fig* [main income] sustento *m* -**2.** *inf* [money] ganha-pão *m*.

bread bin *UK*, **bread box** *US n* caixa *f* para pão.

breadboard ['bredbɔːd] *n* tábua *f* de pão.

breadcrumbs ['bredkrʌmz] *npl* farinha *f* de rosca.

breaded ['bredɪd] *adj* empanado(da).

breadline ['bredlaɪn] *n*: **to be on the ~** estar no limite da pobreza.

breadth [bretθ] *n* -**1.** [in measurements] largura *f* -**2.** *fig* [scope] alcance *f*.

breadwinner ['bredˌwɪnə^r] *n* arrimo *m* (de família).

break [breɪk] (*pt* broke, *pp* broken) <> *n* -**1.** [interruption] interrupção *f*; **a ~ in transmission** uma queda na transmissão -**2.** [gap] brecha *f* -**3.** [fracture] fratura *f* -**4.** [change] rompimento *m*; **~ with sthg** rompimento *m* com algo -**5.** [pause] pausa *f*; **tea/coffee/lunch ~** pausa para o chá/café/almoço; [rest] descanso *m*; **a weekend ~** um feriado curto; **give me a ~!** me dá um tempo/uma trégua!; **to have a ~ from sthg** dar uma parada em algo; **without a ~** sem parar -**6.** *SCOL* recreio *m* -**7.** *inf* [luck, chance] chance *f*; **lucky ~** golpe de sorte -**8.** *literary* [of day]: **at ~ of day** alvorecer, ao raiar do dia -**9.** *COMPUT* [key] tecla *f* break. <> *vt* -**1.** [gen] quebrar -**2.** [fracture] fraturar -**3.** [cause to malfunction] danificar -**4.** [burst through] romper; **to ~ sb's hold** esquivar-se de alguém -**5.** [interrupt] interromper -**6.** [destroy, cause to fail] arruinar -**7.** [undermine, cause to fail] furar -**8.** [announce]: **to ~ the news (of sthg to sb)** dar a notícia (de algo a alguém) -**9.** *TENNIS*: **to ~ sb's serve** quebrar o serviço de alguém. <> *vi* -**1.** [gen] quebrar -**2.** [split] partir-se -**3.** [burst through] romper -**4.** [pause] parar -**5.** [day] raiar -**6.** [weather] mudar -**7.** [escape]: **to ~ loose OR free** escapar -**8.** [voice - with emotion] perturbar-se; [- at puberty] mudar -**9.** [become known] ser divulgado(da) -**10.** *phr*: **to ~ even** ficar em ponto de equilíbrio.

    ◆ **break away** *vi* -**1.** [escape] escapar -**2.** [end relationship]: **to ~ away (from sb)** romper (com alguém).

    ◆ **break down** <> *vt sep* -**1.** [destroy, demolish] derrubar -**2.** [analyse] analisar -**3.** [bring to an end] acabar com. <> *vi* -**1.** [stop working] estragar -**2.** [end unsuccessfully] concluir sem sucesso -**3.** [collapse, disintegrate] terminar -**4.** [*MED*: collapse] sofrer um colapso; **to ~ down in tears** romper em lágrimas -**5.** [decompose] decompor-se.

    ◆ **break in** <> *vi* -**1.** [enter by force] arrombar -**2.** [interrupt] interromper; **to ~ in on sb/sthg** interromper alguém/algo. <> *vt sep* -**1.** [horse] domar -**2.** [person] acostumar -**3.** [shoes] amaciar.

    ◆ **break into** *vt fus* -**1.** [enter by force] arrombar -**2.** [begin suddenly] romper em -**3.** [become involved in] entrar em.

    ◆ **break off** <> *vt sep* -**1.** [detach] quebrar -**2.** [put an end to] acabar. <> *vi* -**1.** [become detached] quebrar-se -**2.** [stop talking] deter-se -**3.** [stop working] parar-se.

    ◆ **break out** *vi* -**1.** [begin suddenly] rebentar -**2.** [become covered]: **to ~ out in spots/a rash** aparecer com manchas/uma erupção; **to ~ out in a cold sweat** começar a suar frio -**3.** [escape]: **to ~ out (of)** fugir (de).

    ◆ **break through** <> *vt fus* [force a way through] abrir caminho por. <> *vi* [force a way through] romper.

    ◆ **break up** <> *vt sep* -**1.** [separate into smaller pieces - ice] partir; [- soil] repartir; [- car] desmontar -**2.** [bring to an end] acabar. <> *vi* -**1.** [separate into smaller pieces] partir-se -**2.** [come to an end] acabar-se; **to ~ up with sb** acabar com alguém -**3.**

[disperse] dispersar-se **- 4.** [for school holiday] terminar.
➤ **break with** *vt fus* romper com.
breakable [ˈbreɪkəbl] *adj* quebradiço(ça).
breakage [ˈbreɪkɪdʒ] *n* quebra *f*.
breakaway [ˈbreɪkəweɪl] *adj* dissidente.
break dancing *n (U)* break *m*.
breakdown [ˈbreɪkdaʊn] *n* **- 1.** [failure, ending] quebra *f* **- 2.** [analysis] detalhamento *m* **- 3.** MED nervous ~ colapso *m* nervoso.
breaker [ˈbreɪkəʳ] *n* [wave] rebentação *f*.
breakeven *n (U)* ponto *m* de equilíbrio.
breakfast [ˈbrekfəst] ◇ *n* café *m* da manhã. ◇ *vi*: **to ~ (on sthg)** tomar (algo no) café da manhã.
breakfast cereal *n* cereal *m* matinal.
breakfast television *n* UK programa *m* de tv matutino.
break-in *n* arrombamento *m*.
breaking [ˈbreɪkɪŋ] *n (U)*: ~ **and entering** JUR invasão *m* de domicílio.
breaking point *n* limite *m*.
breakneck [ˈbreɪknek] *adj*: **at ~ speed** em altíssima velocidade.
breakthrough [ˈbreɪkθruː] *n* avanço *m*.
breakup [ˈbreɪkʌp] *n* **- 1.** [of system, group] dissociação *f* **- 2.** [of relationship] rompimento *m*.
breakup value *n* COMM valor *m* de liquidação.
bream [briːm] (*pl inv* OR **-s**) *n* brema *f*; **sea ~** pargo *m*.
breast [brest] *n* **- 1.** [gen] peito *m* **- 2.** [of woman] seio *m* **- 3.** *fig*: **to make a clean ~ of it** desabafar.
breast-feed ◇ *vt & vi* amamentar.
breast pocket *n* bolso *m* superior.
breaststroke [ˈbreststrəʊk] *n (U)* nado *m* de peito.
breath [breθ] *n* **- 1.** *(U)* [air taken into lungs] respiração *f*; **out of ~** sem fôlego; **to get one's ~ back** retomar o fôlego; **to hold one's ~** [stop breathing] prender o fôlego; *fig* [wait anxiously] ficar apreensivo(va); **to save one's ~** poupar seu fôlego; **to say sthg under one's ~** dizer algo ao pé do ouvido; **to take one's ~ away** ser surpreendente; **to waste one's ~** gastar sua saliva; **to go out for a ~ of (fresh) air** sair para tomar ar (fresco) **- 2.** [air breathed out] hálito *m*; **bad ~** mau hálito.
breathalyse UK, **-yze** US [ˈbreθəlaɪz] *vt* aplicar o teste do bafômetro em.
Breathalyser® UK, **-yzer®** US [ˈbreθəlaɪzəʳ] *n* bafômetro *m*.
breathe [briːð] ◇ *vi* respirar; **to ~ more easily** *fig* respirar aliviado(da). ◇ *vt* **- 1.** [inhale] inalar **- 2.** [whisper] murmurar.
➤ **breathe in** ◇ *vi* [inhale] respirar. ◇ *vt sep* [inhale] inalar.
➤ **breathe out** *vi* [exhale] exalar.
breather [ˈbriːðəʳ] *n inf* respirada *f*, descanso *m*.
breathing [ˈbriːðɪŋ] *n (U)* respiração *f*.
breathing space *n fig* pausa *f*.
breathless [ˈbreθlɪs] *adj* **- 1.** [physically] ofegante **- 2.** [with excitement] radiante.
breathtaking [ˈbreθˌteɪkɪŋ] *adj* **- 1.** [beautiful] surpreendente **- 2.** [extreme] incrível.
breath test *n* teste *m* de bafômetro.
breed [briːd] (*pt & pp* **bred** [bred]) ◇ *n* **- 1.** [of

animal] ráça *f* **- 2.** *fig* [sort, style] tipo *m*. ◇ *vt* **- 1.** [cultivate] criar **- 2.** *fig* [provoke] gerar. ◇ *vi* [produce young] procriar.
breeder [ˈbriːdəʳ] *n* [of animals] criador *m*.
breeder reactor *n* reator *m* regenerador.
breeding [ˈbriːdɪŋ] *n (U)* **- 1.** [raising animals, plants] criação *f* **- 2.** [manners] boa educação *f*; **a person of good ~** uma pessoa de berço.
breeding-ground *n fig* [of ideas, activity] fonte *f*.
breeze [briːz] ◇ *n* [light wind] brisa *f*. ◇ *vi*: **to ~ in/out** entrar/sair calmamente.
breezeblock [ˈbriːzblɒk] *n* UK tijolo *m* leve.
breezy [ˈbriːzɪ] (*compar* **-ier**, *superl* **-iest**) *adj* **- 1.** [windy] ventoso(sa) **- 2.** [cheerful] alegre.
Breton [ˈbretn] ◇ *adj* bretão(tã). ◇ *n* **- 1.** [person] bretão *m*, -tã *f* **- 2.** [language] bretão *m*.
brevity [ˈbrevɪtɪ] *n* **- 1.** [shortness] brevidade *f* **- 2.** [conciseness] concisão *f*.
brew [bruː] ◇ *vt* [beer] fermentar; [tea] preparar. ◇ *vi* **- 1.** [infuse] preparar-se **- 2.** *fig* [develop - crisis, trouble] armar-se; [- storm] formar-se.
brewer [ˈbruːəʳ] *n* fabricante *mf* de cerveja.
brewery [ˈbrʊərɪ] (*pl* **-ies**) *n* cervejaria *f*.
briar [braɪəʳ] *n* BOT urze *f* branca.
bribe [braɪb] ◇ *n* suborno *m*. ◇ *vt* subornar; **to ~ sb to do sthg** subornar alguém para fazer algo.
bribery [ˈbraɪbərɪ] *n (U)* suborno *m*.
bric-a-brac [ˈbrɪkəbræk] *n (U)* bugiganga *f*.
brick [brɪk] *n* [for building] tijolo *m*.
➤ **brick up** *vt sep* fechar com tijolos.
bricklayer [ˈbrɪkˌleɪəʳ] *n* pedreiro *m*.
brickwork [ˈbrɪkwɜːk] *n (U)* alvenaria *f*.
bridal [ˈbraɪdl] *adj* de noiva.
bride [braɪd] *n* noiva *f*.
bridegroom [ˈbraɪdgrʊm] *n* noivo *m*.
bridesmaid [ˈbraɪdzmeɪd] *n* dama *f* de honra.
bridge [brɪdʒ] ◇ *n* **- 1.** [gen] ponte *f*; **I'll cross that ~ when I come to it** *fig* só vou me preocupar quando chegar a hora **- 2.** [on ship] ponte *f* de comando **- 3.** [of nose] cavalete *m* **- 4.** [card game] bridge *m* **- 5.** [for teeth] ponte *f*. ◇ *vt* [gap] transpor.
bridging loan [ˈbrɪdʒɪŋ-] *n* UK empréstimo *m* bancário (*a curto prazo*).
bridle [ˈbraɪdl] ◇ *n* [of horse] cabresto *m*. ◇ *vt* [put a bridle on] colocar cabresto em. ◇ *vi*: **to ~ (at sthg)** indignar-se (diante de algo).
bridle path *n* trilha *f*.
brief [briːf] ◇ *adj* **- 1.** [short, concise] breve; **in ~** em suma **- 2.** [revealing, skimpy] reduzido(da). ◇ *n* **- 1.** JUR [statement] declaração *f* **- 2.** UK [instructions] instrução *f*. ◇ *vt* informar; **to ~ sb on sthg** [bring up to date] pôr alguém a par de algo; [instruct] treinar alguém sobre/em algo.
➤ **briefs** *npl* [underwear] cuecas *fpl*.
briefcase [ˈbriːfkeɪs] *n* pasta *f* executiva.
briefing [ˈbriːfɪŋ] *n* instruções *fpl*.
briefly [ˈbriːflɪ] *adv* **- 1.** [for a short time] brevemente **- 2.** [concisely] rapidamente.
Brig. (*abbr of* **brigadier**) brig..
brigade [brɪˈgeɪd] *n* brigada *f*.
brigadier [ˌbrɪgəˈdɪəʳ] *n* brigadeiro *m*.
bright [braɪt] *adj* **- 1.** [full of light] claro(ra) **- 2.** [colour] vivo(va) **- 3.** [lively, cheerful] alegre **- 4.** [intelligent]

brighten

inteligente **- 5.** [hopeful, promising] radioso(sa).
➤ **brights** *npl US inf* AUT luz *f* alta.
➤ **bright and early** *adv* de manhã cedo.
brighten ['braɪtn] *vi* **-1.** [become lighter] iluminar-se **- 2.** [become more cheerful] alegrar-se.
➤ **brighten up** <> *vt sep* alegrar. <> *vi* **-1.** [become more cheerful] alegrar-se **- 2.** [weather] melhorar.
brightly ['braɪtlɪ] *adv* **-1.** [shine] fortemente **- 2.** [cheerfully] alegremente **- 3.** [coloured] em cores vivas.
brightness ['braɪtnɪs] *n (U)* brilho *m*.
brilliance ['brɪljəns] *n* **-1.** [cleverness] inteligência *f* **- 2.** [of light, colour] brilho *m*.
brilliant ['brɪljənt] *adj* **-1.** [clever, successful] brilhante **- 2.** [colour] vivo(va) **-3.** [light] brilhante **- 4.** *inf* [wonderful, enjoyable] genial.
brilliantly ['brɪljəntlɪ] *adv* **-1.** [cleverly] inteligentemente, de forma brilhante **- 2.** [coloured] em cores vivas **- 3.** [shine] fortemente.
Brillo pad ['brɪləʊ-] *n* esfregão *m (de aço com sabão)*.
brim [brɪm] (*pt* & *pp* **-med**, *cont* **-ming**) <> *n* **-1.** [edge] borda *f* **- 2.** [of hat] aba *f*. <> *vi*: **to ~ with enthusiasm** transbordar de entusiasmo.
➤ **brim over** *vi*: **to ~ over (with sthg)** transbordar (de algo).
brine [braɪn] *n (U)* salmoura *f*.
bring [brɪŋ] (*pt* & *pp* **brought**) *vt* **-1.** [gen] trazer; **to ~ sthg to an end** acabar com algo **- 2.** JUR: **to ~ charges against sb** acusar alguém; **to be brought to trial** ser levado(da) a julgamento **- 3.** *phr*: **I couldn't ~ myself to do it** não tive coragem de fazê-lo.
➤ **bring about** *vt sep* produzir.
➤ **bring along** *vt sep* trazer.
➤ **bring around** *vt sep* [make conscious]: **to bring sb around** fazer alguém recuperar os sentidos.
➤ **bring back** *vt sep* **-1.** [hand over] devolver **- 2.** [carry, transport] trazer de volta **- 3.** [recall] relembrar **- 4.** [reinstate] trazer de volta.
➤ **bring down** *vt sep* **-1.** [cause to fall] derrubar **- 2.** [reduce] baixar.
➤ **bring forward** *vt sep* **-1.** [in time] adiantar **- 2.** [in bookkeeping] transportar.
➤ **bring in** *vt sep* **-1.** [introduce] apresentar **- 2.** [earn] render **- 3.** JUR [verdict] apresentar.
➤ **bring off** *vt sep* conseguir.
➤ **bring on** *vt sep* [cause] causar; **to ~ sthg on o.s.** causar algo a si próprio(pria).
➤ **bring out** *vt sep* **-1.** [produce and sell] lançar **- 2.** [reveal] ressaltar.
➤ **bring round, bring to** *vt sep* = **bring around**.
➤ **bring up** *vt sep* **-1.** [educate] educar **- 2.** [mention] mencionar **- 3.** [vomit] vomitar.
brink [brɪŋk] *n*: **on the ~ of** à beira de.
brisk [brɪsk] *adj* **-1.** [walk, swim] rápido(da) **- 2.** [business, trading] ativo(va) **-3.** [manner, tone] enérgico(ca) **- 4.** [wind, weather] forte.
brisket ['brɪskɪt] *n* carne *f* de peito.
briskly ['brɪsklɪ] *adv* **-1.** [walk] rapidamente **- 2.** [speak, act] desembaraçadamente.

bristle ['brɪsl] <> *n* **-1.** [hair] pêlo *m* **- 2.** [on brush] cerda *f*. <> *vi* **-1.** [stand up] ficar em pé **- 2.** [react angrily]: **to ~ (at sthg)** eriçar-se (diante de algo).
➤ **bristle with** *vt fus* estar apinhado(da) de.
bristly ['brɪslɪ] (*compar* **-ier**, *superl* **-iest**) *adj* [hairy] cabeludo(da).
Brit (*abbr of* Briton) *n fam* britânico *m*, -ca *f*.
Britain ['brɪtn] *n* Grã-Bretanha; **in ~** na Grã-Bretanha.
British ['brɪtɪʃ] <> *adj* britânico(ca). <> *npl*: **the ~** os britânicos.
British Columbia *n* Colúmbia Britânica.
British Council *n*: **the ~** o British Council, o Conselho Britânico.
British Isles *npl*: **the ~** as Ilhas Britânicas.
British Summer Time *n (U)* horário *m* britânico de verão.
British Telecom *n principal empresa britânica de telecomunicações*.
Briton ['brɪtn] *n* britânico *m*, -ca *f*.
Britpop ['brɪtpɒp] *n (U) tipo de música pop tocada por bandas britânicas, muito popular em meados dos anos 90*.
Brittany ['brɪtənɪ] *n* Bretanha; **in ~** na Bretanha.
brittle ['brɪtl] *adj* [easily broken] quebradiço(ça).
Bro = Br.
broach [brəʊtʃ] *vt* [subject] abordar.
broad [brɔːd] <> *adj* **-1.** [physically wide] largo(ga) **- 2.** [wide-ranging, extensive] amplo(pla) **- 3.** [general, unspecific] geral **- 4.** [hint] explícito(ta) **- 5.** [accent] forte. <> *n US inf* [woman] sujeita *f*.
➤ **in broad daylight** *adv* em plena luz do dia.
B road *n UK* estrada *f* secundária.
broad bean *n* fava *f*.
broadcast ['brɔːdkɑːst] (*pt* & *pp* **broadcast**) <> *n* transmissão *f*. <> *vt* transmitir.
broadcaster ['brɔːdkɑːstəʳ] *n* locutor *m*, -ra *f*.
broadcasting ['brɔːdkɑːstɪŋ] *n (U)* transmissão *f*.
broaden ['brɔːdn] <> *vt* **-1.** [make physically wider] alargar **- 2.** [make more general, wide-ranging] ampliar. <> *vi* [become physically wider] alargar-se.
➤ **broaden out** *vi* ampliar-se.
broadly ['brɔːdlɪ] *adv* **-1.** [generally] em geral; **~ speaking** em termos gerais **- 2.** [smile] abertamente.
broadly-based [-'beɪst] *adj* de bases amplas.
broadminded [ˌbrɔːd'maɪndɪd] *adj* tolerante.
broadsheet ['brɔːdʃiːt] *n* jornal *m (de tamanho grande)*.

BROADSHEET/BROADSIDE

Broadsheet, na Grã-Bretanha, e *broadside*, nos Estados Unidos, são os termos empregados para designar os jornais de maior reputação e prestígio. Trata-se de dois jornais impressos em formato grande, que apresentam as notícias com seriedade e oferecem seções importantes sobre cultura, esportes e finanças. De modo geral, esses jornais gozam de maior respeito do que os tablóides, que tendem a usar uma linguagem mais simples e direta, e são publicados em formato pequeno.

---

brocade [brə'keɪd] *n (U)* brocado *m*.
broccoli ['brɒkəlɪ] *n* brócolis *mpl*.

brochure ['brəʊʃəʳ] *n* folheto *m*.

brogue *n* -1. [accent] sotaque *m* -2. [shoe] chanca *f*.

broil [brɔɪl] *vt US* grelhar.

broiler ['brɔɪləʳ] *n* -1. [chicken for broiling] galeto *m* -2. *Am* [pan] grelha *f*.

broke [brəʊk] ◇ *pt* ▷ **break**. ◇ *adj inf* [penniless] falido(da); **to go** ~ ir à falência; **to go for** ~ arriscar tudo.

broken ['brəʊkn] ◇ *pp* ▷ **break**. ◇ *adj* -1. [damaged, in pieces] quebrado(da) -2. [fractured] fraturado(da) -3. [not working] estragado(da) -4. [interrupted] interrompido(da) -5. [unfulfilled] rompido(da) -6. [marriage, home] desfeito(ta) -7. [hesitant, inaccurate] incorreto(ta).

broken-down *adj* -1. [not working] avariado(da) -2. [dilapidated] arruinado(da).

broker ['brəʊkəʳ] *n* corretor *m*, -ra *f*.

brokerage ['brəʊkərɪdʒ] *n (U)* -1. [business] corretora *f* -2. [fee] corretagem *f*.

brolly ['brɒlɪ] *(pl -ies) n UK inf* guarda-chuva *m*.

bromine *n* bromo *m*.

bronchitis [brɒŋ'kaɪtɪs] *n (U)* bronquite *f*.

bronze [brɒnz] ◇ *n* -1. *(U)* [metal] bronze *m* -2. [sculpture] escultura *f* em bronze -3. = **bronze medal**. ◇ *comp* [made of bronze] em bronze. ◇ *adj* [bronze-coloured] bronzeado(da).

bronzed *adj* bronzeado(da).

bronze medal *n* medalha *f* de bronze.

brooch [brəʊtʃ] *n* broche *m*.

brood [bru:d] ◇ *n* -1. [of animals] ninhada *f* -2. *inf* [of children] penca *f*. ◇ *vi*: **to** ~ **(over** *or* **about sthg)** matutar (sobre algo).

broody ['bru:dɪ] *(compar -ier, superl -iest) adj* -1. [sad] pensativo(va) -2. [bird] choco(ca).

brook [brʊk] ◇ *n* riacho *m*. ◇ *vt fml* tolerar.

broom [bru:m] *n* -1. [brush] vassoura *f* -2. [shrub] giesta *f*.

broomstick ['bru:mstɪk] *n* cabo *m* de vassoura.

Bros, bros *(abbr of* **brothers)** irmãos.

broth [brɒθ] *n (U)* caldo *m*.

brothel ['brɒθl] *n* bordel *m*.

brother ['brʌðəʳ] ◇ *n* -1. [gen & *RELIG*] irmão *m* -2. *fig* [associate, comrade] irmão *m*. ◇ *excl US inf* puxa vida!

brotherhood ['brʌðəhʊd] *n* -1. *(U)* [companionship] fraternidade *f* -2. [organization] irmandade *f*.

brother-in-law *(pl* **brothers-in-law)** *n* cunhado *m*.

brotherly ['brʌðəlɪ] *adj* fraternal.

brought [brɔːt] *pt & pp* ▷ **bring**.

brow [braʊ] *n* -1. [forehead] testa *f* -2. [eyebrow] sobrancelha *f*; **to knit one's** ~**s** franzir a testa -3. [of hill] topo *m*.

browbeat ['braʊbiːt] *(pt* **browbeat**, *pp* **-en)** *vt* intimidar.

browbeaten ['braʊbiːtn] *adj* intimidado(da).

brown [braʊn] ◇ *adj* -1. [colour - hair, eyes] castanho(nha); [- object] marrom; ~ **bread** pão *m* integral -2. [tanned] bronzeado(da). ◇ *n* [colour] marrom *m*; **in** ~ em marrom. ◇ *vt* [food] tostar.

Brownie (Guide) *n* escoteira junior de sete a dez anos.

brownie point *n fig*: **to earn** ~**s** fazer média.

brown paper *n (U)* papel *m* pardo.

brown rice *n (U)* arroz *m* integral.

brown sugar *n (U)* açúcar *m* mascavo.

browse [braʊz] ◇ *vt COMPUT*: **to** ~ **the Web** navegar na Web. ◇ *vi* -1. [in shop] dar uma olhada -2. [read]: **to** ~ **through sthg** dar uma olhada em algo -3. [graze] pastar.

browser ['braʊzəʳ] *n COMPUT* navegador *m*.

bruise [bru:z] ◇ *n* equimose *f*. ◇ *vt* -1. [leave a bruise on] machucar -2. *fig* [hurt, offend] ferir. ◇ *vi* machucar-se.

bruised [bru:zd] *adj* -1. [having bruise] machucado(-da) -2. *fig* [hurt, offended] ferido(da).

Brummie, Brummy ['brʌmɪ] *UK inf* ◇ *adj* de Birmingham. ◇ *n* habitante *mf* de Birmingham.

brunch [brʌntʃ] *n* brunch *m, combinação de café da manhã e almoço servido ao meio-dia.*

Brunei ['bru:naɪ] *n* Brunei; **in** ~ em Brunei.

brunette [bru:'net] *n* morena *f*.

brunt [brʌnt] *n*: **to bear** *or* **take the** ~ **of sthg** suportar *or* sofrer a força de algo.

brush [brʌʃ] ◇ *n* -1. [for hair] escova *f* -2. [of artist, for shaving, paint] pincel *m* -3. [encounter] atrito *m*. ◇ *vt* -1. [clean with brush] escovar -2. [move with hand] sacudir -3. [touch lightly] roçar.

➡ **brush aside** *vt sep* desprezar.

➡ **brush off** *vt sep* [dismiss] desprezar.

➡ **brush up** ◇ *vt sep* [revise] recapitular. ◇ *vi*: **to** ~ **up on sthg** treinar *or* praticar algo.

brushed [brʌʃt] *adj* [fabric]: ~ **cotton** fio *m* de algodão penteado.

brush-off *n inf*: **to give sb the** ~ dar um chega pra lá em alguém, botar alguém de escanteio.

brush-up *n (U) inf*: **to have a wash and** ~ dar uma geral.

brushwood ['brʌʃwʊd] *n (U)* graveto *m*.

brushwork ['brʌʃwɜːk] *n (U)* pincelada *f*.

brusque [bru:sk] *adj* brusco(ca).

Brussels ['brʌslz] *n* Bruxelas; **in** ~ em Bruxelas.

brussels sprout *n* couve-de-bruxelas *f*.

brutal ['bru:tl] *adj* brutal.

brutality [bru:'tælətɪ] *(pl -ies) n* -1. *(U)* [cruelty] brutalidade *f* -2. [cruel act] brutalidade *f*.

brutalize, -ise ['bru:təlaɪz] *vt* -1. [make brutal] brutalizar -2. [treat brutally] maltratar.

brute [bru:t] ◇ *adj* bruto(ta). ◇ *n* -1. [large animal] besta *f* -2. [bully] animal *mf*.

BS *(abbr of* Bachelor of Science) *n (titular de)* graduação em ciências nos Estados Unidos.

BSA *(abbr of* Boy Scouts of America) *n* associação de escoteiros norte-americanos, ≃ UEB *f*.

BSc *(abbr of* Bachelor of Science) *n (titular de)* graduação em ciências.

BSE *(abbr of* bovine spongiform encephalopathy) *n* EEB *f*.

BSI *(abbr of* British Standards Institution) *n* instituto britânico de normatização, ≃ ABNT *f*.

B-side *n* lado-B *m*.

BST *(abbr of* British Summer Time) *n* horário de verão britânico.

BT *(abbr of* British Telecom) *n* empresa de telefonia britânica.

Btu (*abbr of* **British thermal unit**) *n* unidade de calor britânica, btu *m*.

bubble ['bʌbl] ⟨⟩ *n* bolha *f*. ⟨⟩ *vi* borbulhar.

bubble bath *n* **- 1.** [liquid] espuma *f* de banho **- 2.** [bath] banho *m* de espuma.

bubble gum *n* (*U*) chiclete *m* de bola.

bubblejet printer ['bʌbldʒet-] *n* impressora *f* a jato de tinta.

bubbly ['bʌblɪ] (*compar* **-ier**, *superl* **-iest**) ⟨⟩ *adj* [person] efervescente. ⟨⟩ *n inf* champanhe *m*.

Bucharest [ˌbuːkə'rest] *n* Bucareste; **in** ~ em Bucareste.

buck [bʌk] (*pl sense 1 inv OR* **-s**) ⟨⟩ *n* **- 1.** [male animal] macho *m* **- 2.** *US inf* [dollar] pila *mf*; **to make a fast** ~ fazer grana fácil *OR* rápido **- 3.** *inf* [responsibility]: **the** ~ **stops here** a responsabilidade pára aqui; **to pass the** ~ passar *OR* transferir a responsabilidade. ⟨⟩ *vt* **- 1.** [subj: horse] derrubar **- 2.** *inf* [oppose] ir contra. ⟨⟩ *vi* [horse] corcovear.
 ➡ **buck up** *inf* ⟨⟩ *vt sep* **- 1.** [make more positive] avivar **- 2.** [cheer up] animar. ⟨⟩ *vi* **- 1.** [hurry up] apressar-se **- 2.** [cheer up, become more positive] animar-se.

bucket ['bʌkɪt] *n* **- 1.** [container] balde *m* **- 2.** [bucketful] balde *m*.
 ➡ **buckets** *npl inf fig* [large quantity]: ~**s of sthg** baldes de algo.

Buckingham Palace ['bʌkɪŋəm-] *n* Palácio *m* de Buckingham.

buckle ['bʌkl] ⟨⟩ *n* fivela *f*. ⟨⟩ *vt* **- 1.** [fasten] afivelar **- 2.** [bend] arquear. ⟨⟩ *vi* [bend] arquear-se, vergar-se.
 ➡ **buckle down** *vi* [work harder]: **to** ~ **down (to sthg)** empenhar-se (em algo).

buckshot ['bʌkʃɒt] *n* (*U*) chumbo *m* (de espingarda).

buckskin ['bʌkskɪn] *n* (*U*) pele *f* de cervo.

buckteeth [bʌk'tiːθ] *npl* dentes *mpl* salientes.

buckthorn *n* escambroeiro *m*, espinheiro *m*.

buckwheat ['bʌkwiːt] *n* (*U*) fagopiro *m*, trigo-mouro *m*.

bud [bʌd] (*pt & pp* **-ded**, *cont* **-ding**) ⟨⟩ *n* botão *m*; **to nip sthg in the** ~ *fig* cortar algo pela raiz. ⟨⟩ *vi* florescer.

Budapest [ˌbjuːdə'pest] *n* Budapeste; **in** ~ em Budapeste.

Buddha ['bʊdə] *n* Buda *m*.

Buddhism ['bʊdɪzm] *n* (*U*) budismo *m*.

Buddhist ['bʊdɪst] ⟨⟩ *adj* budista. ⟨⟩ *n* budista *mf*.

budding ['bʌdɪŋ] *adj* [aspiring] principiante.

buddy ['bʌdɪ] (*pl* **-ies**) *n US inf* [friend] camarada *mf*.

budge [bʌdʒ] ⟨⟩ *vt* **- 1.** [move] mexer **- 2.** [change mind of] dissuadir. ⟨⟩ *vi* **- 1.** [move - object] mover-se; [- person] mudar-se **- 2.** [change mind] mudar de opinião.

budgerigar ['bʌdʒərɪgaːʳ] *n* periquito *m* (australiano).

budget ['bʌdʒɪt] ⟨⟩ *adj* [cheap] econômico(ca). ⟨⟩ *n* orçamento *m*; **the Budget** *UK POL* o Orçamento. ⟨⟩ *vt* estimar. ⟨⟩ *vi* calcular.
 ➡ **budget for** *vt fus* planejar os gastos com.

budget account *n* **- 1.** [with shop] conta *f* (crediário) **- 2.** [at bank] conta *f* orçamentária.

budgetary ['bʌdʒɪtrɪ] *adj* orçamentário(ria).

budgie ['bʌdʒɪ] *n inf* periquito *m* (australiano).

Buenos Aires [ˌbwenəs'aɪrɪz] *n* Buenos Aires; **in** ~ em Buenos Aires.

buff [bʌf] ⟨⟩ *adj* [brown] pardo(da). ⟨⟩ *n inf* [expert] expert *mf*.

buffalo ['bʌfələʊ] (*pl inv OR* **-es** *OR* **-s**) *n* búfalo *m*.

buffer ['bʌfəʳ] *n* **- 1.** [for trains] pára-choque *m* **- 2.** [protection] proteção *f* **- 3.** *COMPUT* buffer *m*.

buffer state *n* estado-tampão *m*.

buffet¹ [*UK* 'bʊfeɪ, *US* bə'feɪ] *n* **- 1.** [meal] bufê *m* **- 2.** [cafeteria] cantina *f*.

buffet² ['bʌfɪt] *vt* [physically] bater.

buffet car ['bʊfeɪ-] *n* vagão-restaurante *m*.

buffoon [bə'fuːn] *n* palhaço *m*.

bug [bʌg] (*pt & pp* **-ged**, *cont* **-ging**) ⟨⟩ *n* **- 1.** *US* [small insect] inseto *m* **- 2.** *inf* [germ] vírus *m* **- 3.** *inf* [listening device] grampo *m* **- 4.** *COMPUT* [fault in program] bug *m* **- 5.** [enthusiasm]: **the travel** ~ a febre de viajar. ⟨⟩ *vt inf* **- 1.** [spy on] grampear **- 2.** *Am* [annoy] chatear.

bugbear ['bʌgbeəʳ] *n* bicho-papão *m*.

bugger ['bʌgəʳ] *UK v inf* ⟨⟩ *n* **- 1.** [unpleasant person, task] porre *mf* **- 2.** [particular type of person] infeliz *mf*. ⟨⟩ *excl* merda! ⟨⟩ *vt*: ~ **it!** dane-se!
 ➡ **bugger off** *vi*: ~ **off!** vá à merda!

buggy ['bʌgɪ] (*pl* **-ies**) *n* [pushchair, stroller] carrinho *m* de bebê.

bugle ['bjuːgl] *n* trombeta *f*.

build [bɪld] (*pt & pp* **built**) ⟨⟩ *vt* construir. ⟨⟩ *n* corpo *m*, constituição *f* física.
 ➡ **build into** *vt sep* embutir em.
 ➡ **build on** ⟨⟩ *vt fus* [further] ampliar. ⟨⟩ *vt sep* [base on] alicerçar.
 ➡ **build up** ⟨⟩ *vt sep* [strengthen] fortalecer. ⟨⟩ *vi* [increase] intensificar.
 ➡ **build upon** *vt fus* & *vt sep* = **build on**.

builder ['bɪldəʳ] *n* construtor *m*.

building ['bɪldɪŋ] *n* **- 1.** [structure] edifício *m*, prédio *m* **- 2.** (*U*) [profession] construção *f*.

building and loan association *n US* associação *f* de financiamento imobiliário, ≃ sistema *m* financeiro de habitação.

building block *n* **- 1.** [toy] bloco *m* para montar **- 2.** *fig* [element] alicerce *f*.

building contractor *n* construtor *m*, -ra *f*.

building site *n* canteiro *m* de obras.

building society *n UK* sociedade *f* de financiamento imobiliário.

BUILDING SOCIETY

As *building societies* funcionam como bancos, embora não possuam um sistema de compensação. Elas se dedicam a conceder financiamentos imobiliários e, no passado, desempenharam papel muito importante na Grã-Bretanha. Hoje, muitas delas converteram-se em bancos.

build-up *n* [increase] intensificação *f*.

built [bɪlt] ⟨⟩ *pt & pp* ▷ **build**. ⟨⟩ *adj* [person]: **heavily** ~ de forte constituição; ~ **for sthg** de constituição apropriada para algo.

built-in *adj* **-1.** *CONSTR* embutido(da) **-2.** [inherent] embutido(da).

built-up *adj*: ~ **area** área *f* urbanizada.

bulb [bʌlb] *n* **-1.** [for lamp] lâmpada *f* **-2.** [of plant] bulbo *m*.

bulbous ['bʌlbəs] *adj* bulboso(sa).

Bulgaria [bʌl'geərɪə] *n* Bulgária; **in** ~ na Bulgária.

Bulgarian [bʌl'geərɪən] <> *adj* búlgaro(ra). <> *n* **-1.** [person] búlgaro *m*, -ra *f* **-2.** [language] búlgaro *m*.

bulge [bʌldʒ] <> *n* **-1.** [lump] protuberância *f* **-2.** [sudden increase] aumento *m*. <> *vi*: **to** ~ **(with sthg)** estar estourando(de algo).

bulging ['bʌldʒɪŋ] *adj* **-1.** abarrotado(da) **-2.** musculoso(sa).

bulimia (nervosa) [bjʊ'lɪmɪə-] *n (U)* bulimia *f* nervosa.

bulk [bʌlk] <> *n* **-1.** [mass] volume *m* **-2.** [of person] massa *f* **-3.** *COMM*: **in** ~ a granel **-4.** [majority, most of]: **the** ~ **of** a maior parte de. <> *adj* a granel.

bulk buying [-'baɪŋ] *n (U)* compra *f* a granel.

bulkhead ['bʌlkhed] *n* biombo *m*.

bulky ['bʌlkɪ] (*compar* **-ier**, *superl* **-iest**) *adj* volumoso(osa).

bull [bʊl] *n* **-1.** [male cow] touro *m* **-2.** [male animal] macho *m* **-3.** *STEX* especulador *m*, -ra *f* **-4.** *(U) v inf US* [nonsense] tolice *f*.

bulldog ['bʊldɒg] *n* buldogue *m*.

bulldog clip *n* prendedor *m* de papel, clipe *m* buldogue.

bulldoze ['bʊldəʊz] *vt* **-1.** [with bulldozer] aplainar **-2.** *fig* [force]: **to** ~ **one's way** forçar sua passagem; **to** ~ **sb into sthg/into doing sthg** obrigar alguém a algo/a fazer algo.

bulldozer ['bʊldəʊzə'] *n* escavadeira *f*.

bullet ['bʊlɪt] *n* **-1.** [for gun] bala *f* **-2.** [in text] marcador *m*.

bulletin ['bʊlətɪn] *n* **-1.** [brief report] boletim *m* **-2.** [regular publication] boletim *m*.

bulletin board *n* **-1.** *US* quadro *m* de avisos **-2.** *COMPUT* sistema *m* BBS.

bullet-proof *adj* à prova de bala.

bullfight ['bʊlfaɪt] *n* tourada *f*.

bullfighter ['bʊl,faɪtə'] *n* toureiro *m*.

bullfighting ['bʊl,faɪtɪŋ] *n* touradas *fpl*.

bullion ['bʊljən] *n (U)* barras *fpl* de ouro ou prata.

bullish ['bʊlɪʃ] *adj* **-1.** *STEX*: ~ **market** mercado em alta **-2.** [optimistic] otimista.

bull market *n* mercado *m* em alta.

bullock ['bʊlək] *n* boi *m*.

bullring ['bʊlrɪŋ] *n* arena *f* de touros.

bullrush ['bʊlrʌʃ] *n* = bulrush.

bull's-eye *n* **-1.** [target] mosca *f* **-2.** [shot] mosca *f*.

bullshit ['bʊlʃɪt] (*pt* & *pp* **-ted**, *cont* **-ting**) *vulg* <> *n* papo *m* furado. <> *vi* falar abobrinhas.

bull terrier *n* bull terrier *mf*.

bully ['bʊlɪ] (*pl* **-ies**, *pt* & *pp* **-ied**) <> *n* brigão *m*, -gona *f*. <> *vt* amedrontar; **to** ~ **sb into doing sthg** amedrontar alguém para que faça algo.

bullying ['bʊlɪŋ] *n (U)* maus-tratos *mpl*.

bulrush ['bʊlrʌʃ] *n* papiro *m*.

bum [bʌm] (*pt* & *pp* **-med**, *cont* **-ming**) *n* **-1.** *esp UK v inf* [bottom] traseiro *m* **-2.** *US inf pej* [tramp] vagabundo *m* **-3.** *US inf pej* [idler] desocupado *m*, -da *f*.

bum around *esp US vi inf* **-1.** [waste time] vadiar **-2.** [travel aimlessly] perambular.

bum bag *n inf* pochete *f*.

bumblebee ['bʌmblbi:] *n* abelhão *m*.

bumbling ['bʌmblɪŋ] *adj inf* inútil; ~ **incompetence** incompetência extraordinária.

bumf [bʌmf] *n UK inf* papelada *f*.

bump [bʌmp] <> *n* **-1.** [road] elevação *f* **-2.** [head] galo *m* **-3.** [leg] inchaço *m* **-4.** [knock, blow] batida *f* **-5.** [noise] pancada *f*. <> *vt* [knock, damage] bater. <> *vi* **-1.** [move unevenly] solavancar **-2.** [knock, hit]: **to** ~ **into sthg** topar em algo.

bump into *vt fus* [meet by chance]: **to** ~ **into sb** topar com alguém.

bump off *vt sep inf* apagar.

bump up *vt sep inf* aumentar.

bumper ['bʌmpə'] <> *adj* super-. <> *n* **-1.** [on car] pára-choque *m* **-2.** *US RAIL* pára-choque *m*.

bumper-to-bumper *adj*: ~ **traffic** trânsito congestionado e lento.

bumph [bʌmf] *n* = bumf.

bumptious ['bʌmpʃəs] *adj pej* presunçoso(sa).

bumpy ['bʌmpɪ] (*compar* **-ier**, *superl* **-iest**) *adj* **-1.** [surface] esburacado(da) **-2.** [ride, journey] turbulento(-ta).

bun [bʌn] *n* **-1.** [cake] bolo *m* doce (*pequeno e com passas*) **-2.** [bread roll] pãozinho *m* **-3.** [hairstyle] coque *m*.

bunch [bʌntʃ] <> *n* [group - of people] grupo *m*; [- of flowers] ramalhete *m*; [- of fruit] cacho *m*; [- of keys] molho *m*. <> *vt* agrupar. <> *vi* unir.

bunches *npl* [hairstyle] maria-chiquinha *f*.

bundle ['bʌndl] <> *n* **-1.** [clothes] trouxa **-2.** [paper] maço **-3.** [wood] feixe. <> *vt* socar.

bundle off *vt sep* mandar, enviar.

bundle up *vt sep* **-1.** [put into bundles] entrouxar **-2.** [dress warmly] agasalhar(-se).

bundled software ['bʌndld-] *n COMPUT* software *m* incluído.

bung [bʌŋ] <> *n* tampo *m*. <> *vt UK inf* **-1.** [give] passar **-2.** [put] deixar **-3.** [toss] jogar.

bungalow ['bʌŋgələʊ] *n* [single-storey house] casa *f* térrea.

bunged up [bʌŋd-] *adj* **-1.** [nose] congestionado -(da) **-2.** [sink, drains] entupido(da).

bungee jump *n* bungee jump *m*.

bungee-jumping ['bʌndʒɪ-] *n* bungee jumping *m*.

bungle ['bʌŋgl] *vt* fracassar.

bunion ['bʌnjən] *n* joanete *m*.

bunk [bʌŋk] *n* **-1.** [bed] beliche *m* **-2.** *inf* [nonsense] besteira *f* **-3.** *phr*: **to do a** ~ *inf* dar no pé.

bunk bed *n* beliche *m*.

bunker ['bʌŋkə'] *n* **-1.** *MIL* [shelter] abrigo *m* **-2.** [for coal] carvoeira *f* **-3.** [in golf] bunker *m*.

bunkhouse *n* alojamento *m*.

bunny ['bʌnɪ] (*pl* **-ies**) *n*: ~ **(rabbit)** coelhinho *m*.

bunny hill *n US SKIING* morro baixo e sem obstáculos utilizado como pista para a prática de esqui na neve.

Bunsen burner ['bʌnsn-] *n* bico *m* de Bunsen.

bunting ['bʌntɪŋ] *n* [flags] bandeirolas *fpl*.

buoy [*UK* bɔɪ, *US* 'bu:ɪ] *n* [float] bóia *f*.

buoy up *vt sep* [encourage] animar.
buoyancy ['bɔɪənsɪ] *n (U)* **-1.** [ability to float] capacidade *f* de flutuar **-2.** [optimism] otimismo *m*.
buoyant ['bɔɪənt] *adj* **-1.** [able to float] capaz de flutuar, flutuante **-2.** [optimistic] otimista.
BUPA (*abbr of* **British United Provident Association**) *n plano de saúde privado existente na Grã-Bretanha*.
burden ['bɜːdn] <> *n* **-1.** [physical load] carga *f* **-2.** *fig* [heavy responsibility] fardo *m*; **to be a ~ on sb** ser um peso para alguém; **to relieve the ~ on sb** aliviar a carga sobre alguém. <> *vt*: **to ~ sb with sthg** sobrecarregar alguém com algo.
bureau ['bjʊərəʊ] (*pl* **-x**) *n* **-1.** *US* [government department] departamento *m* **-2.** [office, branch] agência *f*, escritório *m* **-3.** *UK* [desk] escrivaninha *f* **-4.** *US* [chest of drawers] cômoda *f*.
bureaucracy [bjʊə'rɒkrəsɪ] (*pl* **-ies**) *n* **-1.** [system] burocracia *f* **-2.** *(U) pej* [rules] burocracia *f*.
bureaucrat ['bjʊərəkræt] *n pej* burocrata *mf*.
bureaucratic [ˌbjʊərə'krætɪk] *adj pej* burocrático(ca).
bureau de change [ˌbjʊərəʊdə'ʃɒndʒ] (*pl* **bureaux de change** [ˌbjʊərəʊdə'ʃɒndʒ]) *n* casa *f* de câmbio.
bureaux ['bjʊərəʊz] *pl* ⊳ **bureau**.
burger ['bɜːɡəʳ] *n* [hamburger] hambúrguer *m*.
burglar ['bɜːɡləʳ] *n* ladrão *m*, -dra *f*.
burglar alarm *n* alarme *m* anti-roubo.
burglarize *vt US* = **burgle**.
burglary ['bɜːɡlərɪ] (*pl* **-ies**) *n* **-1.** [event] roubo *m* (*de casa*), arrombamento *m* (*de casa*) **-2.** [activity] roubo *m* (*de casa*), arrombamento *m* (*de casa*).
burgle ['bɜːɡl], **burglarize** ['bɜːɡləraɪz] *US vt* roubar (*casa*), arrombar (*casa*).
Burgundy *n* Borgonha.
burial ['berɪəl] *n* enterro *m*.
burial ground *n* cemitério *m*.
burk [bɜːk] *n UK inf* idiota *mf*.
Burkina Faso [bɜːˌkiːnə'fæsəʊ] *n* Burquina Faso; **in ~** em Burquina Faso.
burly ['bɜːlɪ] (*compar* **-ier**, *superl* **-iest**) *adj* robusto(ta).
Burma ['bɜːmə] *n* Birmânia.
Burmese [ˌbɜː'miːz] <> *adj* birmanês(esa). <> *n* **-1.** [person] birmanês *m*, -esa *f* **-2.** [language] birmanês *m*.
burn [bɜːn] (*pt & pp* **burnt** *OR* **-ed**) <> *vt* **-1.** [gen] queimar; **to ~ o.s.** queimar-se **-2.** [destroy by fire] incendiar <> *vi* **-1.** [gen] queimar **-2.** [be on fire] incendiar-se **-3.** *fig* [feel strong emotion]: **to ~ with sthg** arder de algo. <> *n* **-1.** [wound, injury] queimadura *f* **-2.** [mark] queimadura *f*.
➡ **burn down** <> *vt sep* [destroy by fire] incendiar. <> *vi* **-1.** [be destroyed by fire] incendiar-se **-2.** [burn less brightly] extinguir-se.
➡ **burn out** <> *vt sep* [exhaust]: **to ~ o.s. out** esgotar-se. <> *vi* [die down] extinguir-se.
➡ **burn up** <> *vt sep* [use up] queimar. <> *vi* [be destroyed by fire, heat] carbonizar.
burner ['bɜːnəʳ] *n* [on cooker] queimador *m*.
burning ['bɜːnɪŋ] *adj* **-1.** [on fire] em chamas **-2.** [very hot] escaldante; **to be ~ hot** estar ardendo

OR derretendo de calor **-3.** [very red] em brasa **-4.** [intense] ardente.
burnish ['bɜːnɪʃ] *vt* lustrar.
burnout *n* **-1.** *TECH* combustão *f* **-2.** *fig* [of person] exaustão *f*.
Burns Night *n festa celebrada na Escócia em 25 de janeiro para comemorar o aniversário do poeta Robert Burns.*
burnt [bɜːnt] *pt & pp* ⊳ **burn**.
burnt-out *adj* **-1.** [by fire] carbonizado(da) **-2.** *fig* [exhausted] esgotado(da).
burp [bɜːp] *inf* <> *n* arroto *m*. <> *vi* arrotar.
burrow ['bʌrəʊ] <> *n* toca *f*. <> *vi* **-1.** [dig] entocar-se **-2.** *fig* [in order to search] remexer.
bursar ['bɜːsəʳ] *n* tesoureiro *m*, -ra *f*.
bursary ['bɜːsərɪ] (*pl* **-ies**) *n UK* [scholarship, grant] bolsa *f* (*de estudos*).
burst [bɜːst] (*pt & pp* **burst**) <> *vi* **-1.** [break open] estourar **-2.** [explode] explodir **-3.** [door, lid]: **to ~ open** abrir-se de repente **-4.** [go suddenly] irromper. <> *vt* [break open] estourar. <> *n* [bout] estouro *m*.
➡ **burst into** *vt fus* **-1.** [gen] irromper em **-2.** [flower, leaf, blossom] desabrochar.
➡ **burst out** *vt fus* **-1.** [say suddenly] exclamar **-2.** [begin suddenly]: **to ~ out laughing/crying** começar a gargalhar/chorar.
bursting ['bɜːstɪŋ] *adj* **-1.** [full] repleto(ta) **-2.** [with emotion]: **~ with sthg** repleto(ta) de algo **-3.** [eager]: **to be ~ to do sthg** estar morrendo de vontade de fazer algo.
Burundi [bʊ'rʊndɪ] *n* Burundi; **in ~** em Burundi.
bury ['berɪ] (*pt & pp* **-ied**) *vt* **-1.** [gen] enterrar **-2.** [hide - face, hands] esconder **-3.** *fig* [immerse]: **to ~ o.s. in sthg** enterrar-se em algo.
bus [bʌs] *n* ônibus *m*; **by ~** de ônibus.
bus conductor *n* cobrador *m*, -ra *f* de ônibus.
bus driver *n* motorista *mf* de ônibus.
bush [bʊʃ] *n* **-1.** [plant] arbusto *m* **-2.** [open country]: **the ~** a selva **-3.** *phr*: **to beat about the ~** fazer rodeios.
bushel ['bʊʃl] *n* alqueire *m*.
bushy ['bʊʃɪ] (*compar* **-ier**, *superl* **-iest**) *adj* espesso(sa).
business ['bɪznɪs] <> *n* **-1.** *(U)* [commerce] negócios *mpl*; **on ~** a negócios; **to mean ~** *inf* falar sério; **to go out of ~** ir à falência **-2.** [company] negócio *m* **-3.** *(U)* [concern, duty] assunto *m*; **to have no ~ doing** *OR* **to do sthg** não ter o direito de fazer algo; **mind your own ~!** *inf* meta-se com sua vida! **-4.** [affair, matter] negócio *m*, assunto *m*. <> *comp* comercial *mf*.
business address *n* endereço *m* comercial.
business card *n* cartão *m* de visita.
business class *n (U)* classe *f* executiva.
businesslike ['bɪznɪslaɪk] *adj* profissional.
businessman ['bɪznɪsmæn] (*pl* **-men** [-men]) *n* [occupation] empresário *m*, homem *m* de negócios.
business school *n* escola *f* de comércio.
business trip *n* viagem *f* de negócios.
businesswoman ['bɪznɪsˌwʊmən] (*pl* **-women** [-ˌwɪmɪn]) *n* [occupation] empresária *f*, mulher *f* de negócios.
busker ['bʌskəʳ] *n UK* artista *mf* de rua.

bus lane *n* faixa *f* exclusiva para ônibus.
bus shelter *n* abrigo *m* de ônibus.
bus station *n* estação *f* rodoviária.
bus stop *n* parada *f* OR ponto *m* de ônibus.
bust [bʌst] (*pt* & *pp* bust OR -ed) <> *adj inf* -1. [broken] quebrado(da) -2. [bankrupt]: **to go ~** quebrar. <> *n* -1. [gen] busto *m* -2. *police sl* [raid] batida *f*. <> *vt inf* -1. [break] quebrar -2. [arrest] prender -3. *police sl* [raid] revistar. <> *vi inf* quebrar.
bustle [bʌsl] <> *n* [activity] movimento *m*. <> *vi* apressar-se.
bustling [bʌslɪŋ] *adj* movimentado(da).
bust-up *n inf* -1. [quarrel, fight] quebra-pau *m* -2. [breakup] rompimento *m*.
busy [bɪzɪ] (*compar* -ier, *superl* -iest) <> *adj* -1. [gen & TELEC] ocupado(da); **to be ~** doing sthg estar ocupado(da) fazendo algo -2. [hectic - time] agitado(da); [- place] movimentado(da) <> *vt*: **to ~ o.s.** (doing sthg) ocupar-se fazendo algo.
busybody [bɪzɪˌbɒdɪ] (*pl* -ies) *n pej* intrometido *m*, -da *f*.
busy lizzie *n* maria-sem-vergonha *f*.
busy signal *n* US TELEC sinal *m* de ocupado.
but [bʌt] <> *conj* mas <> *prep* senão, a não ser; **you've been nothing ~ trouble** você só tem me dado trabalho; **the last ~ one** o penúltimo (a penúltima).
➦ **but for** *prep* se não fosse.
butane [bju:teɪn] *n* (U) butano *m*.
butch [bʊtʃ] *adj* UK *inf* [woman] sapatão.
butcher [bʊtʃəʳ] <> *n* -1. [shopkeeper] açougueiro *m*, -ra *f*; **~'s (shop)** açougue *m* -2. *fig* [indiscriminate killer] carniceiro *m*, -ra *f*. <> *vt* -1. [kill for meat] abater -2. *fig* [kill indiscriminately] exterminar, fazer uma carnificina com.
butchery [bʊtʃərɪ] *n* (U) *fig* [indiscriminate killing] carnificina *f*.
butler [bʌtləʳ] *n* mordomo *m*.
butt [bʌt] <> *n* -1. [of cigarette, cigar] bagana *f* -2. [of rifle] coronha *f* -3. [for water] tina *m* -4. [target] alvo *m* -5. *esp* US *inf* [bottom] traseiro *m*. <> *vt* [hit with head] dar cabeçada em.
➦ **butt in** *vi* [interrupt] atrapalhar, interromper; **to ~ in on sb/sthg** atrapalhar OR interromper alguém/algo.
butter [bʌtəʳ] <> *n* (U) manteiga *f*; **~ wouldn't melt in her mouth** *inf* parece uma mosca morta. <> *vt* passar manteiga em.
➦ **butter up** *vt sep inf* bajular.
butter bean *n* feijão-manteiga *m*, feijão-de-lima *m*.
buttercup [bʌtəkʌp] *n* botão-de-ouro *m*.
butter dish *n* manteigueira *f*.
buttered [bʌtəd] *adj* com manteiga.
butterfingers [bʌtəˌfɪŋgəz] (*pl inv*) *n inf* estabanado *m*, -da *f*.
butterfly [bʌtəflaɪ] (*pl* -ies) *n* -1. [insect] borboleta *f*; **to have butterflies in one's stomach** *inf* estar com frio na barriga -2. (U) [swimming style] nado *m* borboleta.
buttermilk [bʌtəmɪlk] *n* (U) soro *m* (*do leite*).
butterscotch [bʌtəskɒtʃ] *n* (U) doce *m* de manteiga.

buttocks [bʌtəks] *npl* nádegas *fpl*.
button [bʌtn] <> *n* -1. [on clothes] botão *m* -2. [on machine] botão *m* -3. US [badge] button *m*. <> *vt* = button up.
➦ **button up** *vt sep* [fasten] abotoar.
button-down *adj* abotoado(da). <> *n*.
buttonhole [bʌtnhəʊl] <> *n* -1. [hole] casa *f* (*de botão*) -2. UK [flower] flor *f* (*de lapela*). <> *vt inf* pegar para conversar.
button mushroom *n* cogumelo *m* de Paris.
buttress [bʌtrɪs] <> *n* contraforte *m*. <> *vt* [wall] reforçar.
buxom [bʌksəm] *adj* de corpo e seios grandes.
buy [baɪ] (*pt* & *pp* bought) <> *vt* -1. *lit* & *fig* comprar; **to ~ sthg from sb** comprar algo de alguém <> *n* compra *f*, aquisição *f*.
➦ **buy in** *vt sep* UK provisionar.
➦ **buy into** *vt fus* investir em.
➦ **buy off** *vt sep* subornar.
➦ **buy out** *vt sep* -1. [in business] comprar a parte de -2. [from army] pagar para sair; **he bought himself out** ele comprou sua saída do exército.
➦ **buy up** *vt sep* comprar a totalidade de.
buyer [baɪəʳ] *n* -1. [purchaser] comprador *m*, -ra *f* -2. [profession] gerente *mf* de compras.
buyout [baɪaʊt] *n* compra *f* majoritária de ações.
buzz [bʌz] <> *n* [noise - of insect, machinery] zumbido *m*; [- of conversation] murmúrio *m*; **to give sb a ~** *inf* [on phone] dar uma ligada para alguém. <> *vi* -1. zunir; *lit* & *fig* **to ~ (with sthg)** zunir (de algo) <> *vt* [on intercom] ligar, chamar.
➦ **buzz off** *vi* UK *inf*: **~ off!** dê o fora!
buzzard [bʌzəd] *n* -1. UK [hawk] gavião *m* -2. US [vulture] abutre *m*.
buzzer [bʌzəʳ] *n* campainha *f*.
buzzing [bʌzɪŋ] *n* zumbido *m*.
buzzword [bʌzwɜ:d] *n inf* palavra *f* da moda.
by [baɪ] <> *prep* -1. [expressing cause, agent] por; **he's worried ~ her absence** está preocupado com a sua ausência; **he was hit ~ a car** ele foi atropelado por um carro; **a book ~ Stephen King** um livro de Stephen King; **funded ~ the government** financiado pelo governo. -2. [expressing method, means]: **~ car/bus/plane** de carro/ônibus/avião; **~ phone/mail** pelo telefone/correio; **to pay ~ credit card/check** pagar com cartão de crédito/cheque; **to win ~ cheating** ganhar trapaceando. -3. [near to, beside] junto a; **~ the sea** à beira-mar, junto ao mar. -4. [past] por; **a car went ~ the house** um carro passou pela casa. -5. [via] por; **exit ~ the door on the left** saia pela porta do lado esquerdo. -6. [with time]: **be there ~ nine** esteja lá às nove horas; **~ day** de dia; **it should be ready ~ now** já deve estar pronto. -7. [expressing quantity] a; **sold ~ the dozen** vende-se à dúzia; **prices fell ~ 20%** os preços baixaram 20%; **we charge ~ the hour** cobramos por hora. -8. [expressing meaning] com; **what do you mean ~ that?** que quer dizer com isso? -9. [in division, multiplication] por; **about six feet ~ fifteen** aproximadamente dois metros por cinco. -10. [according to] segundo; **~ law** segundo a lei; **it's fine ~ me** por mim tudo bem. -11. [expressing gradual process] a; **one ~ one** um a

um; **day** ~ **day** dia a dia. **-12.** [in phrases]: ~ **mistake** por engano; ~ **oneself** sozinho; ~ **profession** por profissão. <> *adv* [past]: **to go/drive** ~ passar.

bye (-bye) [baɪ(baɪ)] *excl inf* tchau!

bye-election *n* = **by-election**.

byelaw [ˈbaɪlɔː] *n* = **bylaw**.

by-election *n* eleição suplementar realizada para substituir um político que renunciou ao cargo parlamentar ou morreu.

Byelorussia [bɪ‚eləʊˈrʌʃə] *n* = **Belorussia**.

bygone [ˈbaɪgɒn] *adj* decorrido(da).
 ◆ **bygones** *npl*: **to let** ~s **be** ~s deixar o que passou para trás.

bylaw [ˈbaɪlɔː] *n* estatuto *m*.

by-line *n* linha no início de um artigo de jornal ou revista dando o nome do autor.

BYOB (*abbr of* bring your own bottle) traga sua própria bebida.

bypass [ˈbaɪpɑːs] <> *n* **-1.** [road] rodoanel *m* **-2.** *MED:* ~ **(operation)** (cirurgia de) ponte *f* de safena. <> *vt* **-1.** [place] passar ao redor de **-2.** [issue, person] passar por cima de.

by-product *n* **-1.** [product] subproduto *m* **-2.** *fig* [consequence] subproduto *m*.

bystander [ˈbaɪ‚stændəʳ] *n* espectador *m*, -ra *f*.

byte [baɪt] *n* COMPUT byte *m*.

byword [ˈbaɪwɜːd] *n* [symbol]: **to be a** ~ **for sthg** ser um exemplo de algo.

c¹ (*pl* c's *OR* cs), **C** (*pl* C's *OR* Cs) [siː] *n* [letter] c, C *m*.
 ◆ **C** *n* **-1.** MUS dó *m* **-2.** SCH [mark] C *m*, regular *m* **-3.** (*abbr of* celsius, centigrade) C.

c² **-1.** (*abbr of* century) séc. **-2.** (*abbr of* cent(s)) cent.

c., ca. (*abbr of* circa) c.

C/A -1. (*abbr of* capital account) *conta de empréstimos e investimentos.* **-2.** (*abbr of* credit account) conta *f* de crédito. **-3.** (*abbr of* current account) c/c *f.*

CA <> *n* (*abbr of* chartered accountant) *contador com certificado de qualificação profissional na Escócia e no Canadá.* <> **-1.** (*abbr of* Central America) América *f* Central. **-2.** *abbr of* California.

CAA *n* **-1.** (*abbr of* Civil Aviation Authority) *organismo regulador da aviação civil na Grã-Bretanha.* **-2.** (*abbr of* Civil Aeronautics Authority) *autoridade de aviação civil nos Estados Unidos.*

cab [kæb] *n* **-1.** [taxi] táxi *m* **-2.** [of lorry] cabine *f.*

CAB (*abbr of* Citizens' Advice Bureau) *n centro*

britânico de informação e assistência ao cidadão.

cabaret [ˈkæbəreɪ] *n* cabaré *m.*

cabbage [ˈkæbɪdʒ] *n* [vegetable] repolho *m.*

cabbie, cabby [ˈkæbɪ] *n inf* taxista *mf.*

caber [ˈkeɪbəʳ] *n*: **tossing the** ~ *esporte praticado na Escócia no qual o vencedor é aquele que arremessa um tronco de pinheiro à maior distância.*

cabin [ˈkæbɪn] *n* **-1.** [on ship] camarote *m* **-2.** [in aircraft] cabine *f* **-3.** [house] cabana *f.*

cabin class *n* classe *f* cabina.

cabin crew *n* tripulação *f.*

cabin cruiser *n* iate *m.*

cabinet [ˈkæbɪnɪt] *n* **-1.** [cupboard] armário *m* **-2.** POL gabinete *m.*

cabinet-maker *n* marceneiro *m*, -ra *f.*

cabinet minister *n* ministro *m*, -tra *f* de gabinete.

cable [ˈkeɪbl] <> *n* **-1.** [rope] cabo *m* **-2.** [telegram] telegrama *m* **-3.** ELEC cabo *m* **-4.** TV = **cable television.** <> *vt* [telegraph] telegrafar.

cable car *n* teleférico *m.*

cablegram *n* cabograma *m.*

cable railway *n* ferrovia *f* funicular.

cable television, cable TV *n (U)* televisão *f* a cabo.

caboodle [kəˈbuːdl] *n inf*: **the whole (kit and)** ~ a tralha toda.

cabriolet [ˈkæbrɪəʊleɪ] *n* [car] conversível *m.*

cache [kæʃ] <> *n* **-1.** [store] esconderijo *m* **-2.** COMPUT cache *f.* <> *vt* COMPUT armazenar em cache.

cachet [ˈkæʃeɪ] *n fml* prestígio *m.*

cackle [ˈkækl] <> *n* **-1.** [of hen] cacarejo *m* **-2.** [of person] gargalhada *f.* <> *vi* **-1.** [hen] cacarejar **-2.** [person] gargalhar.

cacophony [kæˈkɒfənɪ] *n* balbúrdia *f.*

cactus [ˈkæktəs] (*pl* -tuses *OR* -ti [-taɪ]) *n* cacto *m.*

CAD (*abbr of* computer-aided design) *n* CAD *m.*

caddie [ˈkædɪ] <> *n* carregador *m*, -ra *f* de tacos. <> *vi*: **to** ~ **for sb** carregar os tacos de golfe para alguém.

caddy [ˈkædɪ] (*pl* -ies) *n* porta-chá *m.*

cadence [ˈkeɪdəns] *n* [of voice] cadência *f.*

cadet [kəˈdet] *n* [in police] cadete *m.*

cadge [kædʒ] *UK inf* <> *vt*: **to** ~ **sthg** (off *OR* from sb) filar algo (de alguém). <> *vi*: **to** ~ **off** *OR* from sb pedir esmolas a *OR* para alguém.

Cadiz [kəˈdɪz] *n* Cádiz.

Caesar [ˈsiːzəʳ] *n* César *m.*

caesarean (section) UK, **cesarean (section)** US [sɪˈzeərɪən-] *n* cesariana *f*; **she had a** ~ ela fez uma cesariana.

CAF (*abbr of* cost and freight) custo *m* e frete.

cafe, café [ˈkæfeɪ] *n* café *m.*

cafeteria [‚kæfɪˈtɪərɪə] *n* cantina *f.*

caffeine [ˈkæfiːn] *n (U)* cafeína *f.*

cage [keɪdʒ] *n* **-1.** [for animals] jaula *f* **-2.** [for birds] gaiola *f.*

caged [keɪdʒd] *adj* **-1.** [animals] enjaulado(da) **-2.** [birds] engaiolado(da).

cagey [ˈkeɪdʒɪ] (*compar* -ier, *superl* -iest) *adj inf* cauteloso(sa), cuidadoso(sa).

cagoule [kə'gu:l] *n UK* capa *f* de chuva.

cahoots [kə'hu:ts] *n inf*: **to be in ~ with/against** sb estar de armação com/contra alguém.

CAI (*abbr of* **computer-aided instruction**) *n* CAI *f*, instrução *f* assistida por computador.

cairn [keən] *n* [heap of stones] marco *m* de pedras.

Cairo ['kaɪərəʊ] *n* Cairo.

cajole [kə'dʒəʊl] *vt*: **to ~ sb out of sthg** persuadir alguém a desistir de algo; **to ~ sb into doing sthg** persuadir alguém a fazer algo.

cake [keɪk] *n* -**1.** [type of sweet food] bolo *m*; **to sell like hot ~s** vender como água; **you can't have your ~ and eat it** não dá para assobiar e chupar cana ao mesmo tempo; **a piece of ~** *inf* uma moleza *OR* barbada -**2.** [of fish, potato] bolinho *m* (*achatado*) -**3.** [of soap] sabonete *m*.

caked [keɪkt] *adj*: **~ with sthg** empastado(da) de algo, coberto(ta) de algo.

cake pan *n US* fôrma *f* (*de bolo*).

cake tin *n UK* [for baking] fôrma *f* (*de bolo*); [for storing] pote *m*.

cal (*abbr of* **calorie**) *n* cal.

CAL (*abbr of* **computer-assisted learning**) *n* CAL *f*, aprendizagem *f* assistida por computador.

calamine lotion [kæləməm-] *n* (U) loção *f* de calamina.

calamitous [kə'læmɪtəs] *adj fml* calamitoso(sa).

calamity [kə'læmɪtɪ] (*pl* -**ies**) *n fml* calamidade *f*.

calcium ['kælsɪəm] *n* (U) cálcio *m*.

calculate ['kælkjʊleɪt] *vt* -**1.** [work out - figures, result etc] calcular; [- consequences, risk etc] medir -**2.** [plan, intend]: **to be ~d to do sthg** ter o intuito de fazer algo.

calculate on *vi*: **to ~ on sthg** contar com algo; **to ~ on sb doing sthg** contar com que alguém faça algo.

calculated ['kælkjʊleɪtɪd] *adj* [planned, intentional - risk] calculado(da); [- crime, deception] premeditado(da); [- insult] intencional.

calculating ['kælkjʊleɪtɪŋ] *adj pej* calculista.

calculation [ˌkælkjʊ'leɪʃn] *n MATH* cálculo *m*.

calculator ['kælkjʊleɪtə'] *n* calculadora *f*.

calculus [ˌkælkjʊləs] *n* (U) *MATH* cálculo *m*.

calendar ['kælɪndə'] *n* calendário *m*.

calendar month *n* mês *m* civil.

calendar year *n* ano *m* civil.

calf [ka:f] (*pl* **calves**) *n* -**1.** [young animal - cow] bezerro *m*, -ra *f*; [- elephant, whale] filhote *m* -**2.** (U) [leather] couro *m* de bezerro -**3.** [of leg] panturrilha *f*, barriga *f* da perna.

calf-length *adj* três-quartos.

calfskin *n* couro *m* de bezerro.

caliber *n US* = **calibre** *m*.

calibrate ['kælɪbreɪt] *vt* -**1.** [mark out] graduar -**2.** [adjust] calibrar.

calibre, caliber *US* ['kælɪbə'] *n* -**1.** [quality] nível *m* -**2.** [size] calibre *m*.

calico ['kælɪkəʊ] *n* (U) morim *m*.

California [ˌkælɪ'fɔ:njə] *n* Califórnia.

Californian [ˌkælɪ'fɔ:njən] <> *adj* californiano (na). <> *n* californiano *m*, -na *f*.

calipers *npl US* = **callipers**.

call [kɔ:l] <> *n* -**1.** [cry - of person] grito *m*; [- of animal,

bird] canto *m* -**2.** [visit] visita *f*; **to pay a ~ on sb** fazer uma visita a alguém -**3.** [for flight] chamada *f*; **final ~** última chamada -**4.** [demand] pedido *m*; **~ for sthg** solicitação por algo; **there's no ~ for that** não há razão para isso -**5.** [summons] chamado *m* -**6.** [standby]: **on ~** de plantão -**7.** [telephone call] telefonema *m*, ligação *f*; **long-distance ~** chamada de longa distância; **to give sb a ~** telefonar para alguém, dar uma ligada para alguém -**8.** [lure, fascination] encanto *m*. <> *vt* -**1.** [gen] chamar; **disgraceful, I'd ~ it!** uma vergonha, eu diria!; **would you ~ what he does art?** você chamaria o que ele faz de arte?; **he ~ed me a liar** ele me chamou de mentiroso; **let's ~ it £10** a gente faz por £10 -**2.** [telephone] ligar para. <> *vi* -**1.** [shout] chamar -**2.** [animal, bird] cantar -**3.** [by telephone] ligar -**4.** [visit] visitar.

call back <> *vt sep* -**1.** [on telephone] ligar de volta -**2.** [ask to return] chamar de volta. <> *vi* -**1.** [on phone] ligar de volta -**2.** [visit again] voltar outra vez.

call by *vi inf* dar uma passada.

call for *vt fus* -**1.** [collect] ir buscar -**2.** [demand] exigir.

call in <> *vt sep* -**1.** [send for] chamar -**2.** *COMM* [goods] fazer um recall de; *FIN* [loan] resgatar. <> *vi*: **could you ~ in at the butcher's on your way home?** você pode passar no açougue ao voltar para casa?

call off *vt sep* -**1.** [cancel] cancelar -**2.** [order not to attack] mandar voltar.

call on *vt fus* -**1.** [visit] visitar -**2.** [ask]: **to ~ on sb to do sthg** convocar alguém para fazer algo.

call out <> *vt sep* -**1.** [gen] convocar -**2.** [cry out] gritar. <> *vi* [cry out] gritar.

call round *vi* dar uma passada.

call up *vt sep* -**1.** *MIL* convocar -**2.** [on telephone] dar uma ligada -**3.** *COMPUT* chamar, buscar.

call box *n UK* cabine *f* telefônica, ≃ orelhão *m*.

caller ['kɔ:lə'] *n* -**1.** [visitor] visita *f* -**2.** [on telephone]: **I'm sorry ~, the number is engaged** sinto muito, senhor(ra), a linha está ocupada.

caller (ID) display *n* [on telephone] identificador *m* de chamadas.

call girl *n* garota *f* de programa.

calligraphy [kə'lɪgrəfɪ] *n* (U) caligrafia *f*.

call-in *n US RADIO & TV* programa com participação por telefone de ouvintes ou telespectadores.

calling ['kɔ:lɪŋ] *n* -**1.** [profession, trade] profissão *f* -**2.** [vocation] vocação *f*.

calling card *n US* cartão *m* de visita.

callipers *UK*, **calipers** *US* ['kælɪpəz] *npl* -**1.** *MATH* compasso *m* de calibre -**2.** *MED* aparelho *m* ortopédico.

callous ['kæləs] *adj* insensível.

callously ['kæləslɪ] *adv* insensivelmente.

callousness ['kæləsnɪs] *n* (U) insensibilidade *f*.

call-up *n UK* convocação *f*.

callus ['kæləs] (*pl* -**es**) *n* calo *m*.

calm [ka:m] <> *adj* [person, voice, weather] calmo(ma), tranqüilo(la). <> *n* (U) [peaceful state] tranqüilidade *f*, calmaria *f*. <> *vt* acalmar, tranqüilizar.

calm down ⟨> *vt sep* acalmar, tranqüilizar. ⟨> *vi* acalmar-se, tranqüilizar-se.

calmly ['kɑ:mlɪ] *adv* calmamente, tranqüilamente.

calmness ['kɑ:mnɪs] *n (U)* tranqüilidade *f*.

Calor gas® ['kælə'-] *n UK (U)* ≃ butano *m*.

calorie ['kælərɪ] *n* [in food] caloria *f*.

calorific [ˌkælə'rɪfɪk] *adj* [fattening] calórico(ca).

calumny *adj fml* calúnia *f*.

calve [kɑ:v] *vi* [cow] dar cria.

calves [kɑ:vz] *pl* ▷ **calf**.

cam [kæm] *n* came *f*.

CAM (*abbr of* **computer-aided manufacturing**) *n* CAM *f*, produção *f* assistida por computador.

camaraderie [ˌkæmə'rɑ:dərɪ] *n (U)* camaradagem *f*.

camber ['kæmbə'] *n* inclinação *f*.

Cambodia [kæm'bəʊdjə] *n* Camboja; **in** ~ no Camboja.

Cambodian [kæm'bəʊdjən] ⟨> *adj* cambojano(-na). ⟨> *n* cambojano *m*, -na *f*.

camcorder ['kæmˌkɔ:də'] *n* filmadora *f*.

came [keɪm] *pt* ▷ **come**.

camel ['kæml] ⟨> *adj*: ~-coloured da cor de camelo; **a** ~ **coat** um casaco de pele de camelo. ⟨> *n* [animal] camelo *m*.

camellia [kə'mi:ljə] *n* camélia *f*.

cameo ['kæmɪəʊ] (*pl* -s) *n* -**1.** [piece of jewellery] camafeu *m* -**2.** [in writing] descrição *f* breve e inteligente -**3.** [in acting] ponta *f*.

camera ['kæmərə] *n* câmera *f*.
⟐ **in camera** *adv fml* em câmara.

cameraman ['kæmərəmæn] (*pl* -men [-men]) *n* cameraman *m*, câmera *m*.

Cameroon [ˌkæmə'ru:n] *n* Camarões; **in** ~ nos Camarões.

Cameroonian [ˌkæmə'ru:nɪən] ⟨> *adj* camaronês(esa). ⟨> *n* camaronês *m*, -esa *f*.

camisole ['kæmɪsəʊl] *n* camisola *f*.

camomile ['kæməmaɪl] ⟨> *n* [plant, herb] camomila *f*. ⟨> *comp*: ~ **tea** chá de camomila.

camouflage ['kæməflɑ:ʒ] ⟨> *n* comuflagem *f* ⟨> *vt* camuflar.

camp [kæmp] ⟨> *n* -**1.** [gen] acampamento *m*; **holiday** ~ acampamento de férias; **training** ~ campo *m* de treinamento; **concentration/refugee** ~ campo de concentração/refugiados -**2.** *fig* [faction] facção *f*. ⟨> *vi* acampar.
⟐ **camp out** *vi* acampar.

campaign [kæm'peɪn] ⟨> *n* campanha *f*. ⟨> *vi*: **to** ~ **(for/against sthg)** fazer campanha (a favor de/contra algo).

campaigner [kæm'peɪnə'] *n* [activist] ativista *mf*; **old** ~ veterano *m*, -na *f*.

camp bed *n* cama *f* de armar.

camper ['kæmpə'] *n* -**1.** [person] campista *mf* -**2.** [vehicle]: ~ **(van)** trailer *m*.

campground ['kæmpgraʊnd] *n US* camping *m*.

camphor ['kæmfə'] *n (U)* cânfora *f*.

camping ['kæmpɪŋ] *n (U)* acampamento *m*; **to go** ~ ir acampar.

camping site, campsite ['kæmpsaɪt] *n* camping *m*.

campus ['kæmpəs] (*pl* -es) *n* campus *m*.

camshaft ['kæmʃɑ:ft] *n* eixo *m* de came.

can¹ [kæn] *n* [container] lata *f*. ⟨> *vt* enlatar.

can² [weak form kən, strong form kæn] (*pt* **was, were**, *pt & conditional* **could**) *aux vb* -**1.** [be able to] poder; ~ **you help me?** pode me ajudar?; **I** ~ **see the mountains** posso ver as montanhas -**2.** [know how to] saber; ~ **you drive?** você sabe dirigir?; **I** ~ **speak Portuguese** eu sei falar português -**3.** [be allowed to] poder; **you can't smoke here** você não pode fumar aqui -**4.** [in polite requests] poder; ~ **you tell me the time?** pode me dizer as horas?; ~ **I speak to the manager?** posso falar com o gerente? -**5.** [expressing occasional occurrence] poder; **it** ~ **get cold at night** às vezes a temperatura diminui bastante à noite -**6.** [expressing possibility] poder; **they could be lost** eles podem estar perdidos.

Canada ['kænədə] *n* Canadá; **in** ~ no Canadá.

Canadian [kə'neɪdjən] ⟨> *adj* canadense. ⟨> *n* canadense *mf*.

canal [kə'næl] *n* [waterway] canal *m*.

Canaries *npl*: **the** ~ as Canárias.

canary [kə'neərɪ] (*pl* -ies) *n* canário *m*.

Canary Islands, Canaries [kə'neərɪz] *npl*: **the** ~ as Ilhas Canárias; **in the** ~ nas Ilhas Canárias.

Canberra *n* Canberra; **em** ~ em Camberra.

cancel ['kænsl] (*UK pt & pp* -**led**, *cont* -**ling**, *US pt & pp* -**ed**, *cont* -**ing**) *vt* [call off, invalidate] cancelar.
⟐ **cancel out** *vt sep* anular.

cancellation [ˌkænsə'leɪʃn] *n* cancelamento *m*.

cancer ['kænsə'] ⟨> *n* [disease] câncer *m*. ⟨> *comp*: ~ **cell** célula cancerosa; ~ **research** pesquisa sobre câncer; ~ **specialist** especialista em câncer.
⟐ **Cancer** *n* -**1.** [sign] Câncer *m* -**2.** [person] canceriano *m*, -na *f*; **I'm** ~ sou de Câncer.

cancerous ['kænsərəs] *adj* canceroso(sa).

candelabra [ˌkændɪ'lɑ:brə] *n* candelabro *m*.

candid ['kændɪd] *adj* [frank] sincero(ra), franco(ca).

candidacy ['kændɪdəsɪ] *n (U)* candidatura *f*.

candidate ['kændɪdət] *n* -**1.** [for job]: ~ **for sthg** candidato(ta) a algo -**2.** [taking exam] candidato *m*, -ta *f*.

candidature ['kændɪdətʃə'] *n* candidatura *f*.

candidly ['kændɪdlɪ] *adv* sinceramente, francamente.

candidness ['kændɪdnɪs] *n* = **candour**.

candied ['kændɪd] *adj* cristalizado(da).

candle ['kændl] *n* vela *f*; **to burn the** ~ **at both ends** *inf* dar duro dia e noite.

candlelight ['kændllaɪt] *n (U)* luz *f* de vela.

candlelit ['kændllɪt] *adj* à luz de velas.

candlestick ['kændlstɪk] *n* castiçal *m*.

candour *UK*, **candor** *US* ['kændə'] *n (U)* sinceridade *f*, franqueza *f*.

candy ['kændɪ] (*pl* -ies) *n esp US (U)* [confectionery] doce *m*, guloseima *f*.

candy bar *n US* barra *f* de doce.

candy box *n US* caixa *f* de doces.

candyfloss *UK* ['kændɪflɒs], **cotton candy** *US* *n (U)* algodão-doce *m*.

candy store *n US* confeitaria *f*.

cane [keın] ◇ n - 1. (U) [for making furniture] palhinha f - 2. [walking stick] bengala f - 3. [for punishment]: **the ~** ≃ a palmatória - 4. [for supporting plant] vara f. ◇ comp de palhinha. ◇ vt bater com vara em.

cane sugar n (U) cana-de-açúcar f.

canine ['keınaın] ◇ adj canino(na). ◇ n: ~ **(tooth)** (dente m) canino m.

canister ['kænıstə'] n lata f de metal; **a ~ of tear gas** uma bomba de gás lacrimogênio; **a smoke ~** uma bomba de fumaça.

cannabis ['kænəbıs] n (U) maconha f.

canned [kænd] adj - 1. [tinned - food] enlatado(da); [- drink] em lata, de latinha - 2. inf fig [music] gravado(da).

cannelloni [,kænı'ləʊnı] n (U) canelone m.

cannery (pl -ies) n fábrica f de enlatados.

cannibal ['kænıbl] n canibal mf.

cannibalize, -ise ['kænıbəlaız] vt [vehicle, machine] desmanchar.

cannon ['kænən] (pl inv OR -s) n - 1. [on ground] canhão m - 2. [on aircraft] canhão m.

➤ **cannon into** vt fus UK esbarrar.

cannonball ['kænənbɔːl] n bala f de canhão.

cannot ['kænɒt] vb fml ⊳ can².

canny ['kænı] (compar -ier, superl -iest) adj [shrewd] astuto(ta).

canoe [kə'nuː] ◇ n canoa f. ◇ vi andar de canoa.

canoeing [kə'nuːıŋ] n (U): **to go ~** praticar canoagem.

canon ['kænən] n - 1. [clergyman] cônego m - 2. [general principle] cânone m.

➤ **Canon** n [of Mass]: **the Canon** o cânon.

canonize, -ise ['kænənaız] vt canonizar.

canoodle [kə'nuːdl] vi UK inf amassar-se.

can opener n abridor m de lata.

canopy ['kænəpı] (pl -ies) n - 1. [over bed, seat] dossel m - 2. [of trees, branches] cobertura f.

cant [kænt] n pej [insincere talk] papo-furado m.

can't [kɑːnt] = cannot.

Cantab (abbr of **Cantabrigiensis**) da Universidade de Cambridge.

Cantabrian Mountains [kæn'teıbrıən-] npl: **the ~** as Montanhas Cantábricas.

cantaloup UK, **cantaloupe** US ['kæntəluːp] n cantalupo m.

cantankerous [kæn'tæŋkərəs] adj rabugento(ta).

canteen [kæn'tiːn] n - 1. [restaurant] cantina f - 2. [box of cutlery] faqueiro m.

canter ['kæntə'] ◇ n meio m galope. ◇ vi andar a meio galope.

cantilever ['kæntıliːvə'] n viga f em balanço, cantiléver.

Canton [kæn'tɒn] n Cantão.

Cantonese [,kæntə'niːz] ◇ adj cantonês(esa). ◇ n [language] cantonês m. ◇ npl: **the ~** os cantoneses.

canvas ['kænvəs] n - 1. (U) [cloth] lona f; **under ~** [in a tent] em uma barraca - 2. ART tela f.

canvass ['kænvəs] ◇ vt - 1. POL pedir - 2. [investigate] sondar. ◇ vi POL [campaign] pedir votos.

canvasser ['kænvəsə'] n - 1. POL [campaigner] cabo mf eleitoral - 2. [investigator] pesquisador m, -ra f.

canvassing ['kænvəsıŋ] n - 1. POL [campaigning] angariação f de votos - 2. [investigation] pesquisa f.

canyon ['kænjən] n desfiladeiro m.

cap [kæp] (pt & pp -ped, cont -ping) ◇ n - 1. [hat] boné m - 2. [swimming, shower] touca f; **to go ~ in hand to sb** fig dirigir-se a alguém com o chapéu na mão - 3. [lid, top] tampa f - 4. UK [contraceptive device] diafragma m. ◇ vt - 1. [cover top of] cobrir - 2. [improve on]: **to ~ it all** para arrematar.

CAP (abbr of Common Agricultural Policy) n política que permite que todos os países da União Européia organizem e controlem sua produção agrícola conjuntamente.

capability [,keıpə'bılətı] (pl -ies) n - 1. [ability] capacidade f - 2. MIL poderio m.

capable ['keıpəbl] adj - 1. [able, having capacity]: **to be ~ of sthg/of doing sthg** ser capaz de algo/de fazer algo - 2. [competent, skilful] competente, hábil.

capably ['keıpəblı] adv habilmente.

capacious [kə'peıʃəs] adj fml espaçoso(sa).

capacitor [kə'pæsıtə'] n capacitor m.

capacity [kə'pæsıtı] (pl -ies) ◇ n - 1. (U) [limit, ability] capacidade f; **to be filled to ~** estar com a lotação esgotada; **~ for sthg** capacidade para algo; **~ for doing** OR **to do sthg** capacidade para OR de fazer algo - 2. [position] qualidade f; **in my ~ as** ... na qualidade de ...; **in a ... ~** na condição de ... ◇ comp máximo(ma).

cape [keıp] n - 1. GEOGR cabo m - 2. [cloak] capa f.

Cape Canaveral [-kə'nævərəl] n Cabo m Canaveral.

Cape of Good Hope n: **the ~** o Cabo da Boa Esperança.

caper ['keıpə'] ◇ n - 1. [for flavouring food] alcaparra f - 2. inf [escapade] mutreta f. ◇ vi fazer travessuras, pular.

Cape Town n Cidade f do Cabo.

Cape Verde [-vɜːd] n: **the ~ Islands** as Ilhas de Cabo Verde; **in ~** em Cabo Verde.

capillary [kə'pılərı] (pl -ies) n capilar m.

capita ⊳ **per capita**.

capital ['kæpıtl] ◇ adj - 1. [letter] maiúsculo(la) - 2. [punishable by death] capital. ◇ n - 1. [of country]: **(city)** capital f - 2. fig [centre] capital f - 3. TYPO : ~ **(letter)** (letra) maiúscula; **in ~s** em letras maiúsculas - 4. [money] capital m; **to make ~ (out) of sthg** fig aproveitar-se de algo.

capital allowance n margem f fiscal para investimentos.

capital assets npl ativos mpl fixos.

capital expenditure n (U) dispêndio m com ativos fixos.

capital gains tax n imposto m sobre lucros de capital.

capital goods npl bens mpl de capital.

capital-intensive adj de capital intensivo.

capitalism ['kæpıtəlızm] n (U) capitalismo m.

capitalist ['kæpıtəlıst] ◇ adj capitalista. ◇ n capitalista mf.

capitalize, -ise ['kæpıtəlaız] vi: **to ~ on sthg** [make most of] tirar proveito de algo, capitalizar algo.

capital punishment *n (U)* pena *f* de morte.
capital stock *n* estoque *m* de capital.
capital transfer tax *n* imposto *m* sobre transferência de capital.
Capitol ['kæpɪtl] *n*: the ~ o Capitólio.
Capitol Hill ['kæpɪtl-] *n congresso norte-americano*.
capitulate [kə'pɪtjʊleɪt] *vi*: to ~ (to sthg) render-se (a algo), ceder (frente a algo).
capitulation [kə,pɪtjʊ'leɪʃn] *n (U)* capitulação *f*.
cappuccino [,kæpʊ'tʃiːnəʊ] *(pl* -s) *n* cappuccino *m*.
capricious [kə'prɪʃəs] *adj* inconstante.
Capricorn ['kæprɪkɔːn] *n* -1. [sign] Capricórnio *m* -2. [person]: I'm ~ sou de Capricórnio.
caps *(abbr of* **capital letters)** *npl* maiúsc.
capsicum ['kæpsɪkəm] *n* pimentão *m*.
capsize [kæp'saɪz] <> *vt* emborcar. <> *vi* emborcar-se.
capsule ['kæpsjuːl] *n* cápsula *f*.
Capt. *(abbr of* **captain)** cap.
captain ['kæptɪn] <> *n* -1. [gen] capitão *m* -2. [of airliner] comandante *mf*. <> *vt* [ship] comandar.
caption ['kæpʃn] *n* legenda *f*.
captivate ['kæptɪveɪt] *vt* cativar.
captivating ['kæptɪveɪtɪŋ] *adj* cativante.
captive ['kæptɪv] <> *adj* -1. [imprisoned] de cativeiro -2. *fig* [unable to leave] cativo(va); ~ **audience** audiência cativa. <> *n* prisioneiro *m*, -ra *f*.
captivity [kæp'tɪvətɪ] *n*: in ~ em cativeiro.
captor ['kæptə'] *n* capturador *m*, -ra *f*.
capture ['kæptʃə'] <> *vt* -1. [gen] capturar -2. [gain, take control of] conquistar. <> *n (U)* captura *f*.
car [kɑː'] <> *n* -1. [motor car] carro *m* -2. [on train] vagão *m*. <> *comp* de automóvel.
Caracas [kə'rækəs] *n* Caracas; **em** ~ em Caracas.
carafe [kə'ræf] *n* garrafa *f* de mesa.
car alarm *n* alarme *m* de carro.
caramel ['kærəmel] *n* -1. *(U)* [burnt sugar] caramelo *m* -2. [sweet] caramelo *m*.
carat ['kærət] *n UK* quilate *m*.
caravan ['kærəvæn] <> *n* -1. *UK* [vehicle - towed by car] trailer *m*; [- towed by horse] carruagem *m* -2. [travelling group] caravana *f*. <> *comp* de trailer; ~ **holiday** férias de trailer.
caravanning ['kærəvænɪŋ] *n UK* viagem *f* de trailer.
caravan site *n UK* área *f* para trailers.
caraway seed ['kærəweɪ-] *n* semente *f* de alcaravia.
carbohydrate [,kɑːbəʊ'haɪdreɪt] *n (U)* [chemical substance] carboidrato *m*.
◆ **carbohydrates** *npl* [food] carboidratos *mpl*.
carbon ['kɑːbən] *n* -1. *(U)* [element] carbono *m* -2. = **carbon copy** -3. = **carbon paper**.
carbonated ['kɑːbəneɪtɪd] *adj* com gás.
carbon copy *n* -1. [document] cópia *f* em papel carbono -2. *fig* [exact copy] cópia *f* perfeita.
carbon dating [-'deɪtɪŋ] *n (U)* datação *f* por carbono 14.
carbon dioxide [-daɪ'ɒksaɪd] *n (U)* dióxido *m* de carbono.
carbon fibre *n (U)* fibra *f* de carbono.

carbon monoxide [-mɒ'nɒksaɪd] *n* monóxido *m* de carbono.
carbon paper *n* papel-carbono *m*.
car-boot sale *n UK* feira em que objetos usados são vendidos no porta-malas de um carro.
carburettor *UK*, **carburetor** *US* [,kɑːbə'retə'] *n* carburador *m*.
carcass ['kɑːkəs] *n* [of animal] carcaça *f*.
carcinogenic [,kɑːsɪnə'dʒenɪk] *adj* cancerígeno(na).
card [kɑːd] *n* -1. [playing card] carta *f*; to play one's ~s **right** *fig* agir de forma inteligente; to put *or* lay one's ~s on the table *fig* pôr as cartas na mesa -2. [for information, greetings] cartão *m* -4. [postcard] postal *m*, cartão *m* postal -5. *(U)* [cardboard] papelão *m*.
◆ **cards** *npl* [game] cartas *fpl*.
◆ **on the cards** *UK*, **in the cards** *US adv inf*: to be on the ~ estar na cara.
cardamom ['kɑːdəməm] *n* cardamomo *m*.
cardboard ['kɑːdbɔːd] <> *n (U)* papelão *m*. <> *comp* [made of cardboard] de papelão *m*.
cardboard box *n* caixa *f* de papelão.
card-carrying [-'kæriŋ] *adj* ativo(va).
card catalog *n US* fichário *m*.
cardiac ['kɑːdiæk] *adj* cardíaco(ca), do coração.
cardiac arrest *n* ataque *m* cardíaco.
cardigan ['kɑːdɪgən] *n* cardigã *m*.
cardinal ['kɑːdɪnl] <> *adj* primordial. <> *n RELIG* cardeal *m*.
cardinal number, cardinal numeral *n* número *m* cardinal.
card index *n UK* fichário *m*.
cardiograph ['kɑːdɪəgrɑːf] *n* cardiógrafo *m*.
cardiology [,kɑːdɪ'ɒlədʒɪ] *n (U)* cardiologia *f*.
cardiovascular [,kɑːdɪəʊ'væskjʊlə'] *adj* cardiovascular.
cardphone ['kɑːdfəʊn] *n* telefone *m* (público) de cartão.
cardsharp ['kɑːd,ʃɑːp] *n* trapaceiro *m*, -ra *f*.
card table *n* mesa *f* de jogo.
card vote *n UK* voto *m* representativo da classe.
care [keə'] <> *n* -1. *(U)* [protection, looking after] cuidado *m*; to be taken into ~ ser entregue aos cuidados de uma instituição social; to take ~ of **sb** [look after] cuidar de alguém; to take ~ of **sthg** [deal with] cuidar de algo; take ~! *inf* [when saying goodbye] cuide-se! -2. *(U)* [caution, carefulness] cuidado *m*; to take ~ to do **sthg** ter o cuidado de fazer algo; take ~! [be careful] tenha cuidado! -3. [cause of worry] preocupação *f*. <> *vi* -1. [be concerned] preocupar-se; to ~ **about sb/sthg** preocupar-se com alguém/algo -2. [mind] importar-se; I couldn't ~ less *inf* não dou a mínima.
◆ **care of** *prep* aos cuidados de.
◆ **care for** *vt fus* [like] gostar de.
CARE *(abbr of* **Cooperative for American Relief Everywhere)** *n organização humanitária norte-americana*.
career [kə'rɪə'] <> *n* carreira *f*. <> *comp* [professional] de carreira *f*. <> *vi* desgovernar-se; to ~ **into sthg** ir desgovernado(da) em direção a algo.
careerist [kə'rɪərɪst] *n pej* carreirista *mf*.

careers [kə'rıəz] *comp* de orientação vocacional.

careers adviser *n* orientador *m*, -ra *f* vocacional.

career woman *n* mulher *f* de carreira.

carefree ['keəfriː] *adj* despreocupado(da).

careful ['keəfʊl] *adj* -**1.** [cautious] cuidadoso(sa); ~ **with sthg** cuidadoso(sa) com algo; **to be** ~ **to do sthg** ter o cuidado de fazer algo -**2.** [thorough] cuidadoso(sa).

carefully ['keəflɪ] *adv* -**1.** [cautiously] cuidadosamente, com cuidado -**2.** [thoroughly] cuidadosamente.

careless ['keəlɪs] *adj* -**1.** [inattentive] desatento(ta), descuidado(da) -**2.** [unconcerned] despreocupado(da).

carelessly ['keəlɪslɪ] *adv* -**1.** [inattentively] sem atenção, descuidadamente -**2.** [unconcernedly] despreocupadamente.

carelessness ['keəlɪsnɪs] *n* (U) -**1.** [inattention] desatenção *f* -**2.** [lack of concern] descuido *m*.

carer ['keərəl *n pessoa que cuida de um familiar incapacitado ou doente*.

caress [kə'res] <> *n* carícia *f*. <> *vt* acariciar.

caretaker ['keəˌteɪkəʳ] *n UK* zelador *m*, -ra *f*.

caretaker government *n* governo *m* de transição.

car ferry *n* balsa *f*.

cargo ['kɑːgəʊ] (*pl* -**es** OR -**s**) <> *n* carregamento *m*. <> *comp* de carga.

car hire *n UK* (U) aluguel *m* de carros.

Carib ['kærɪb] *n* Caribe *m*.

Caribbean [*UK* kærɪ'bɪən, *US* kə'rɪbɪən] <> *adj* caribenho(nha). <> *n* -**1.** [sea]: **the** ~ **(Sea)** o (Mar do) Caribe -**2.** [region]: **the** ~ o Caribe; **in the** ~ no Caribe.

caribou ['kærɪbuː] (*pl inv* OR -**s**) *n* caribu *m*.

caricature ['kærɪkəˌtjʊəʳ] <> *n* [cartoon, travesty] caricatura *f*. <> *vt* fazer caricatura de.

caries ['keərɪːz] *n* (U) cárie *f*.

caring ['keərɪŋ] *adj* afetuoso(sa).

caring professions *npl*: **the** ~ as profissões humanitárias.

carnage ['kɑːnɪdʒ] *n* (U) carnificina *f*.

carnal ['kɑːnl] *adj literary* carnal.

carnation [kɑː'neɪʃn] *n* craveiro *m*.

carnival ['kɑːnɪvl] *n* -**1.** [festive occasion] carnaval *m* -**2.** [fair] parque *m* de diversões.

carnivore ['kɑːnɪvɔː] *n* carnívoro *m*, -ra *f*.

carnivorous [kɑː'nɪvərəs] *adj* carnívoro(ra).

carol ['kærəl] *n*: **(Christmas)** ~ cântico *m* de Natal.

carouse [kə'raʊz] *vi* farrear.

carousel [ˌkærə'sel] *n* -**1.** *esp US* [at fair] carrossel *m* -**2.** [at airport] esteira *f*.

carp [kɑːp] (*pl inv* OR -**s**) <> *n* carpa *f*. <> *vi* queixar-se; **to** ~ **about sthg** queixar-se de algo.

car park *n UK* estacionamento *m*.

Carpathians [kɑː'peɪθɪənz] *npl*: **the** ~ os Cárpatos.

carpenter ['kɑːpəntəʳ] *n* carpinteiro *m*, -ra *f*.

carpentry ['kɑːpəntrɪ] *n* (U) carpintaria *f*.

carpet ['kɑːpɪt] <> *n* -**1.** [floor covering] carpete *m*; **to sweep sthg under the** ~ *fig* varrer algo para baixo do tapete -**2.** *fig* [of flowers, snow] tapete *m*.

<> *vt* -**1.** [fit with floor covering] acarpetar -**2.** *fig* [with flowers, snow] cobrir.

carpet slipper *n* pantufas *fpl*.

carpet sweeper [-'swiːpəʳ] *n* limpador *m* de carpete, feiticeira *f*.

car phone *n* telefone *m* para automóvel.

car pool *n UK* [fleet of cars] frota *f*.

carport ['kɑːˌpɔːt] *n* garagem *f*.

car radio *n* rádio *m* de carro.

car rental *n Am* aluguel *m* de carro.

carriage ['kærɪdʒ] *n* -**1.** [horsedrawn vehicle] carruagem *f* -**2.** *UK* [railway coach] vagão -**3.** (U) [transport of goods] carregamento *m*; ~ **paid** OR **free** *UK* frete pago; ~ **forward** *UK* frete ao portador -**4.** [on typewriter] carro *m* -**5.** (U) *literary* [deportment] postura *f*.

carriage clock *n* relógio *m* com alça.

carriageway ['kærɪdʒweɪ] *n UK* pista *f* simples.

carrier ['kærɪəʳ] *n* -**1.** COMM transportador *m*, -ra *f* -**2.** [of disease] portador *m*, -ra *f* -**3.** MIL: **(aircraft)** ~ porta-aviões *m inv* -**4.** [on bicycle] cestinha *f* -**5.** = **carrier bag**.

carrier bag *n* sacola *f*.

carrier pigeon *n* pombo-correio *m*.

carrion ['kærɪən] *n* (U) carniça *f*.

carrot ['kærət] *n* -**1.** [vegetable] cenoura *f* -**2.** *inf fig* [incentive] incentivo *m*.

carry ['kærɪ] (*pt & pp* -**ied**) <> *vt* -**1.** [transport - subj: person, animal] carregar; [- subj: water, wind, vehicle] levar -**2.** [be equipped with] dispor de; **all planes** ~ **lifejackets** todos os aviões dispõem de coletes salva-vidas -**3.** [weapon] portar -**4.** [disease] transmitir -**5.** [involve as a consequence] implicar; **the job carries considerable responsibility** o emprego implica em responsabilidades consideráveis -**6.** [motion, proposal] aprovar -**7.** [be pregnant with] carregar -**8.** MATH sobrar. <> *vi* [sound] projetar-se.

➡ **carry away** *vt sep*: **to get carried away** entrar no embalo.

➡ **carry forward** *vt sep* transportar.

➡ **carry off** *vt sep* -**1.** [make a success of] tornar um sucesso -**2.** [win] sair-se bem.

➡ **carry on** <> *vt fus* [continue] continuar; **to** ~ **on doing sthg** continuar a fazer algo. <> *vi* -**1.** [continue] continuar; **to** ~ **on with sthg** continuar algo -**2.** *inf* [make a fuss] criar caso -**3.** *inf* [have an affair]: **to** ~ **on with sb** estar de caso com alguém.

➡ **carry out** *vt fus* -**1.** [task, plan, experiment] levar a cabo -**2.** [promise, order, threat] cumprir.

➡ **carry through** *vt sep* [accomplish] completar.

carryall ['kærɪɔːl] *n US* bolsa *f* de viagem.

carrycot ['kærɪkɒt] *n esp UK* moisés *m inv*.

carry-on *n UK inf* bagunça *f*.

carryout *n US & Scot* -**1.** [food] comida *f* para viagem OR para levar -**2.** [drink] bebida *f* para viagem OR para levar.

carsick ['kɑːˌsɪk] *adj* enjoado(da) *(em carro)*.

cart [kɑːt] <> *n* -**1.** [vehicle] carroça *f* -**2.** (*abbr of* **cartridge**) COMPUT cartucho *m* -**3.** *US* [for shopping]: **(shopping** OR **grocery)** ~ carrinho *m* (de compras). <> *vt inf* carregar.

carte blanche ['kɑːtblɑ̃ʃ] *n* (U) carta *f* branca.

cartel [ka:'tel] *n* cartel *m*.
cartilage ['ka:tɪlɪdʒ] *n (U)* cartilagem *f*.
carton ['ka:tn] *n* -1. [brick-shaped] caixa *f* -2. [plastic] frasco *m*.
cartoon [ka:'tu:n] *n* -1. [satirical drawing] cartum *m* -2. [comic strip] tira *f*, tirinha *f* -3. [film] desenho *m* animado.
cartoonist [ka:'tu:nɪst] *n* cartunista *mf*.
cartridge ['ka:trɪdʒ] *n* -1. [for gun] cartucho *m* -2. [for pen] recarga *f* -3. [for camera] rolo *m* de filme -4. [for record player] cápsula *f*.
cartridge paper *n (U)* papel-manilha *m*.
cartwheel ['ka:twi:l] *n* [movement] pirueta *f*.
car valeting *n* lavagem *f* completa.
carve [ka:v] ⬦ *vt* -1. [shape, sculpt] esculpir -2. [slice] fatiar -3. [cut into surface] gravar. ⬦ *vi* [slice joint] fatiar a carne.
➤ **carve out** *vt sep* [create, obtain] criar.
➤ **carve up** *vt sep* [divide] dividir.
carving ['ka:vɪŋ] *n* [art, work, object] entalhe *m*.
carving knife *n* faca *f* de trinchar.
car wash *n* -1. [process] lavagem *f* de carro -2. [place] lava-rápido *m*.
cascade [kæ'skeɪd] ⬦ *n* -1. [waterfall] cascata *f* -2. [of blossom, information] chuva *f*. ⬦ *vi* [flow downwards] cair em cascatas.
case [keɪs] *n* -1. [gen] caso *m*; **a** ~ **in point** um exemplo típico; **to be the** ~ ser o caso; **in that** ~ nesse caso; **he may still come, in which** ~ **we can all leave together** pode ser que ele ainda venha, e neste caso todos podemos partir juntos; **as** *OR* **whatever the** ~ **may be** seja qual for o caso; **in** ~ **of** em caso de -2. [argument] razões *fpl*; ~ **for/against sthg** razões a favor de/contra algo -3. *JUR* [trial, inquiry] causa *f* -4. [container, holder] estojo *m* -5. *UK* [suitcase] mala *f*.
➤ **in any case** *adv* seja como for.
➤ **in case** ⬦ *conj* caso. ⬦ *adv*: (just) in ~ só por precaução.
case-hardened *adj* [person] calejado(da).
case history *n* prontuário *m*.
casement window *n* janela *f* de batente.
case study *n* estudo *m* de caso.
cash [kæʃ] ⬦ *n (U)* -1. [notes and coins] dinheiro *m*; **to pay (in)** ~ pagar em dinheiro -2. *inf* [money] dinheiro *m* -3. [payment]: ~ **in advance** pagamento *m* adiantado/antecipado; ~ **on delivery** pagamento contra entrega. ⬦ *vt* descontar.
➤ **cash in** *vi*: **to** ~ **in on sthg** *inf* tirar proveito de algo.
cash and carry *n* sistema *f* pague e leve.
cashbook ['kæʃbʊk] *n* livro-caixa *m*.
cash box *n* cofre *m*.
cash card *n* cartão *m* de saque.
cash crop *n* plantação *f* para venda direta.
cash desk *n UK* caixa *m*.
cash discount *n* desconto *m* no pagamento à vista.
cash dispenser [-dɪ'spensə'] *n* = cashpoint
cashew (nut) ['kæʃu:-] *n* castanha *f* de caju.
cash flow *n* fluxo *m* de caixa.
cashier [kæ'ʃɪə'] *n* caixa *mf*.
cash machine *n* = cash point.

cashmere [kæʃ'mɪə'] ⬦ *n (U)* caxemira *f*. ⬦ *comp* de caxemira.
cashpoint ['kæʃpɔɪnt] *n* caixa *m* automático.
cash price *n* preço *m* à vista.
cash register *n* caixa *f* registradora.
cash sale *n* venda *f* à vista.
casing ['keɪsɪŋ] *n* [protective cover] invólucro *m*.
casino [kə'si:nəʊ] (*pl* -s) *n* cassino *m*.
cask [ka:sk] *n* barril *m*.
casket ['ka:skɪt] *n* -1. [for jewels] porta-jóias *m inv* -2. *US* [coffin] caixão *m*.
Caspian Sea ['kæspɪən-] *n*: **the** ~ o mar Cáspio.
casserole ['kæsərəʊl] *n* -1. [stew] ensopado *m* (no forno) -2. [pot] prato *f* de ir ao forno.
cassette [kæ'set] *n* cassete *f*.
cassette deck *n* deck *m*.
cassette player *n* toca-fitas *m inv*.
cassette recorder *n* gravador *m*.
cassock ['kæsək] *n* batina *f*.
cast [ka:st] (*pt* & *pp* cast) ⬦ *n* -1. [of play, film] elenco *m* -2. *MED* gesso *m*. ⬦ *vt* -1. [turn, direct] dar uma espiada em; **to** ~ **doubt on sthg** pôr algo em dúvida; **to** ~ **a spell (on sb)** lançar um feitiço (sobre alguém) -2. [light, shadow] lançar -3. [throw] arremessar -4. [choose for play, film] dar o papel a; **she** ~ **him in the role of Hamlet** ela deu-lhe o papel de Hamlet -5. *POL*: **to** ~ **one's vote** votar -6. [metal] moldar -7. [lose, shed] trocar. ⬦ *vi* [in fishing] lançar.
➤ **cast about, cast around** *vi*: **to** ~ **about for sthg** procurar algo.
➤ **cast aside** *vt sep* rejeitar.
➤ **cast down** *vt sep fml* [make sad] deixar deprimido(da).
➤ **cast off** ⬦ *vt* -1. *fml* [old practices, habits, burden] livrar-se de -2. [in knitting] arrematar. ⬦ *vi* -1. *NAUT* soltar as amarras -2. [in knitting] arrematar os pontos.
➤ **cast on** ⬦ *vt* [in knitting] montar. ⬦ *vi* [in knitting] montar os pontos.
castanets [,kæstə'nets] *npl* castanholas *fpl*.
castaway ['ka:stəweɪ] *n* náufrago *m*, -ga *f*.
caste [ka:st] *n* [class] casta *f*.
caster ['ka:stə'] *n* [wheel] rodízio *m*.
caster sugar *n (U) UK* açúcar *m* refinado.
castigate ['kæstɪgeɪt] *vt fml* [punish] castigar; [criticize severely] criticar severamente.
casting ['ka:stɪŋ] *n* [object] peça *f* fundida.
casting vote ['ka:stɪŋ-] *n* voto *m* de minerva.
cast iron *n (U)* ferro *m* fundido.
➤ **cast-iron** *adj* -1. [made of cast iron] de ferro fundido -2. *fig* [indisputable] incontestável.
castle ['ka:sl] *n* -1. [building] castelo *m* -2. [in chess] torre *f*.
castoff *n*: **to wears sb's** ~ **s** usar as roupas velhas de alguém.
castor ['ka:stə'] *n* = caster.
castor oil *n (U)* óleo *m* de rícino.
castor sugar *n* = caster sugar.
castrate [kæ'streɪt] *vt* castrar.
castration [kæ'streɪʃn] *n (U)* castração *f*.
casual ['kæʒʊəl] *adj* -1. [relaxed, uninterested] despreocupado(da) -2. *pej* [offhand] deselegante, informal

- 3. [chance] ocasional **- 4.** [clothes] informal **- 5.** [irregular] temporário(ria).

casually [ˈkæʒʊəlɪ] adv **- 1.** [in a relaxed manner, without interest] casualmente **- 2.** [dress] informalmente.

casualty [ˈkæʒjʊəltɪ] (pl -ies) n **- 1.** [dead or injured person] vítima mf; MIL baixa f **- 2.** MED = **casualty department - 3.** fig [of change, policy, system] vítima f.

casualty department n pronto-socorro m.

cat [kæt] n **- 1.** [domestic animal] gato m, -ta f; **to let the ~ out of the bag** abrir o bico; **to be like a ~ on hot bricks** UK OR **on a hot tin roof** US não estar à vontade; **to put the ~ among the pigeons** UK criar confusão; **to rain ~s and dogs** chover canivetes; **to think one is the ~'s whiskers** UK achar-se muito especial; **there's no room to swing a ~** não há espaço nem para respirar; **to play ~ and mouse** brincar de gato e rato **- 2.** [wild animal] felino m, -na f **- 3.** (abbr of **catalytic converter**) AUT catalisador m.

CAT (abbr of **computer-assisted testing**) n **- 1.** CAT f, verificação f assistida por computador. **- 2.** (abbr of **computer-assisted translation**) tradução f assistida por computador. **- 3.** (abbr of **computerized axial tomography**) tomografia f axial computadorizada.

cataclysmic [ˌkætəˈklɪzmɪk] adj cataclísmico(ca).

catacombs [ˈkætəkuːmz] npl catacumbas fpl.

Catalan [ˈkætəˌlæn] <> adj catalão(lã). <> n **- 1.** [person] catalão m, -lã f **- 2.** [language] catalão m.

catalogue UK, **catolog** US [ˈkætəlɒg] <> n **- 1.** [of items for sale] catálogo m **- 2.** [in library, museum] catálogo m **- 3.** fig [list] lista f. <> vt catalogar.

Catalonia [ˌkætəˈləʊnɪə] n Catalunha; **in ~** na Catalunha.

Catalonian [ˌkætəˈləʊnɪən] <> adj catalão(lã). <> n [person] catalão m, -lã f.

catalyst [ˈkætəlɪst] n **- 1.** CHEM catalisador m **- 2.** fig [cause] motivo m.

catalytic converter n conversor m catalítico.

catamaran [ˌkætəməˈræn] n catamarã f.

catapult UK [ˈkætəpʊlt] <> n **- 1.** [hand-held] atiradeira f, estilingue m **- 2.** HIST [machine] catapulta f. <> vt **- 1.** [hurl] catapultar **- 2.** fig [promote] projetar.

cataract [ˈkætərækt] n catarata f.

catarrh [kəˈtɑː] n (U) catarro m.

catastrophe [kəˈtæstrəfi] n catástrofe f.

catastrophic [ˌkætəˈstrɒfɪk] adj catastrófico(ca).

catatonic adj catatônico(ca).

cat burglar n UK gatuno que entra e sai pela janela ou telhado.

catcall [ˈkætkɔːl] n vaia f.

catch [kætʃ] (pt & pp caught) <> vt **- 1.** [gen] pegar **- 2.** [ball etc] apanhar **- 3.** [discover, surprise] flagrar; **to ~ sb doing sthg** flagrar alguém fazendo algo; **to ~ sb unawares** pegar alguém desprevenido(da) **- 4.** [hear clearly] compreender **- 5.** [interest, imagination, attention] despertar **- 6.** [sight]: **to ~ sight of sb/sthg, to ~ a glimpse of sb/sthg** conseguir avistar alguém/algo **- 7.** [on hook, in door, in trap] prender **- 8.** [strike] atingir. <> vi **- 1.** [become hooked, get stuck] ficar preso(sa) em **- 2.** [start to burn] pegar. <> n **- 1.** [of ball etc] pegada f **- 2.** [thing or amount caught] pesca f **- 3.** [fastener] trinco m **- 4.** [snag] armadilha f.

→ **catch at** vt fus tentar agarrar.

→ **catch on** vi **- 1.** [become popular] pegar **- 2.** inf [understand] entender; **to ~ on to sthg** dar-se conta de algo.

→ **catch out** vt sep [trick] apanhar em erro.

→ **catch up** <> vt sep **- 1.** [come level with] alcançar **- 2.** [involve]: **to get caught up in sthg** ser envolvido(da) em algo. <> vi alcançar; **to ~ up on sthg** por algo em dia.

→ **catch up with** vt fus **- 1.** [get to same point as] alcançar **- 2.** [catch, find] pegar.

catch-22 n (U): **it's a ~ situation** é um beco sem saída.

catch-all adj que engloba tudo.

catching [ˈkætʃɪŋ] adj [infectious] contagioso(sa).

catchment area [ˈkætʃmənt-] n região atendida por uma escola ou um hospital.

catchphrase [ˈkætʃfreɪz] n [of entertainer] bordão m.

catchword [ˈkætʃwɜːd] n [slogan] slogan m.

catchy [ˈkætʃɪ] (compar -ier, superl -iest) adj que pega com facilidade.

catechism [ˈkætəkɪzm] n catecismo m.

categorical [ˌkætɪˈgɒrɪkl] adj categórico(ca).

categorically [ˌkætɪˈgɒrɪklɪ] adv categoricamente.

categorize, -ise [ˈkætəgəraɪz] vt [classify]: **to ~ sb (as sthg)** classificar alguém (como algo).

category [ˈkætəgərɪ] (pl -ies) n categoria f.

cater [ˈkeɪtə] vi [provide food] fornecer comida.

→ **cater for** vt fus UK **- 1.** [provide for] satisfazer; **the magazine ~s for independent working women** a revista se destina a mulheres autônomas **- 2.** [anticipate] contar com.

→ **cater to** vt fus servir de instrumento a.

caterer [ˈkeɪtərə] n [serviço m de] bufê m.

catering [ˈkeɪtərɪŋ] n bufê m; **a ~ college** uma escola de culinária.

caterpillar [ˈkætəpɪlə] n [insect] lagarta f.

catfish (pl inv OR -es) n peixe-gato m.

cat flap n UK portinhola f para gatos.

catgut n (U) categute m.

catharsis [kəˈθɑːsɪs] (pl catharses [kəˈθɑːsiːz]) n fml [relief of tension] catarse f.

cathedral [kəˈθiːdrəl] n catedral f.

catheter [ˈkæθɪtə] n catéter m.

cathode ray tube [ˈkæθəʊd-] n tubo m de raios catódicos.

Catholic [ˈkæθlɪk] <> adj católico(ca). <> n católico m, -ca f.

→ **catholic** adj [broad] eclético(ca).

Catholicism [kəˈθɒlɪsɪzm] n (U) catolicismo m.

catkin [ˈkætkɪn] n amento m.

cat litter n granulado m higiênico (para gatos).

Catseyes® [ˈkætsaɪz] npl UK olhos-de-gato mpl.

catsuit [ˈkætsuːt] n UK colante m feminino (de corpo inteiro).

catsup [ˈkætsəp] n US ketchup m.

cattle [ˈkætl] npl gado m.

cattle grid n UK mata-burro m.

catty [ˈkætɪ] (compar -ier, superl -iest) adj inf pej [spiteful] rancoroso(sa).

catwalk [ˈkætwɔːk] n passarela f.

Caucasian [kɔːˈkeɪzjən] <> adj caucásio(sia). <> n **- 1.** GEOGR caucásio m, -sia f **- 2.** [white person] pessoa f de raça branca.

Caucasus ['kɔːkəsəs] n: the ~ o Cáucaso.
caucus ['kɔːkəs] n POL **-1.** US [meeting] cáucus m **-2.** [interest group] ala f.
caught [kɔːt] pt & pp ▷ **catch**.
cauldron n caldeirão m.
cauliflower ['kɒlɪ,flaʊəʳ] n couve-flor f.
causal ['kɔːzl] adj causal.
cause [kɔːz] ◇ n **-1.** [gen] causa f **-2.** [grounds] razão f; **to have** ~ **for** sthg ter razão para algo; **to have** ~ **to do** sthg ter razão para fazer algo ◇ vt causar; **to** ~ **sb to do** sthg fazer com que alguém faça algo; **to** ~ sthg **to be done** fazer com que algo seja feito.
causeway ['kɔːzweɪ] n caminho m elevado (sobre a água).
caustic ['kɔːstɪk] adj **-1.** CHEM cáustico(ca) **-2.** fig [comment] mordaz.
caustic soda n soda f cáustica.
cauterize, -ise ['kɔːtəraɪz] vt cauterizar.
caution ['kɔːʃn] ◇ n **-1.** (U) [care] cuidado m; **to do** sthg **with** ~ fazer algo com cautela **-2.** [warning] aviso m **-3.** UK JUR injunção f. ◇ vt **-1.** [warn]: **to** ~ sb **against doing** sthg prevenir alguém para não fazer algo **-2.** UK JUR advertir; **to** ~ sb **for** sthg advertir alguém por algo.
cautionary ['kɔːʃənərɪ] adj preventivo(va).
cautious ['kɔːʃəs] adj cauteloso(sa).
cautiously ['kɔːʃəslɪ] adv com cautela.
cautiousness ['kɔːʃəsnɪs] n (U) cautela f.
cavalier [,kævə'lɪəʳ] adj [offhand] arrogante.
cavalry ['kævlrɪ] n (U) **-1.** [on horseback] cavalaria f **-2.** [in armoured vehicles] cavalaria f.
cave [keɪv] n gruta f, caverna f.
◆ **cave in** vi **-1.** [physically collapse] desabar **-2.** [yield, stop arguing]: **to** ~ **in (to** sthg) ceder (a algo).
caveman ['keɪvmæn] (pl -men [-menl] n troglodita mf.
cavern ['kævən] n caverna f.
cavernous ['kævənəs] adj imenso(sa).
caviar(e) ['kævɪɑːʳ] n (U) caviar m.
caving ['keɪvɪŋ] n (U) UK espeleologia f; **to go** ~ ir explorar cavernas.
cavity ['kævətɪ] (pl -ies) n **-1.** [in object, structure, body] cavidade f; **buccal** ~ cavidade bucal; **nasal** ~ fossas fpl nasais **-2.** [in tooth] cárie f.
cavort [kə'vɔːt] vi saracotear.
cayenne (pepper) [keɪ'en-] n (U) pimenta-de-caiena f.
CB n **-1.** (abbr of Citizens' Band) CB, faixa f do cidadão. **-2.** (abbr of Companion of (the Order of) the Bath) (titular de) distinção britânica de honra.
CBC (abbr of Canadian Broadcasting Corporation) n rede canadense de rádio e televisão.
CBE (abbr of Companion of (the Order of) the British Empire) n (beneficiário de) distinção britânica de honra.
CBI (abbr of Confederation of British Industry) n confederação britânica de empresários, ≃ CNI f.
CBS (abbr of Columbia Broadcasting System) n rede norte-americana de rádio e televisão, CBS f.
cc ◇ n (abbr of cubic centimetre) cm. ◇ (abbr of carbon copy) cópia f carbono.

CC (abbr of County Council) n **-1.** autoridade de estados administrativos britânicos. **- 2.** (abbr of City Council) corpo administrativo de cidade britânica.
CCTV (abbr of closed-circuit television) n CFT m.
CD ◇ n (abbr of compact disc) CD m. ◇ (abbr of Corps Diplomatique) corpo m diplomático.
CD-I (abbr of compact disc (interactive)) n CD-I m.
CD player n tocador m de CD.
Cdr. (abbr of commander) n com.
CD-R (abbr of compact disc (rewritable)) n CD-R m.
CD-R drive n unidade f de CD-R.
CD rewriter ['siːdiːˈiːˌraɪtə] = **CD-RW drive**.
CD-ROM (abbr of compact disc read-only memory) n CD-ROM m.
CD-RW (abbr of compact disc rewritable) n CD-RW m.
CD-RW drive n gravador m de CD.
CDT (abbr of Central Daylight Time) ◇ n horário de verão na região central dos Estados Unidos. ◇ (abbr of craft, design and technology) disciplina de artes, desenho e tecnologia ensinada em escolas britânicas.
CD tower n torre f para CDs.
CDV (abbr of compact disc video) n CDV m.
CE (abbr of Church of England) igreja anglicana.
cease [siːs] fml ◇ vt cessar; **to** ~ **doing** OR **to do** sthg parar de fazer algo; ~ **fire!** cessar fogo! ◇ vi parar.
ceasefire n cessar-fogo m.
ceaseless ['siːslɪs] adj fml incessante.
ceaselessly ['siːslɪslɪ] adv fml incessantemente.
cedar n cedro m.
cede [siːd] vt [yield] ceder; **to** ~ sthg **to** sb ceder algo a alguém.
cedilla n cedilha f.
CEEB (abbr of College Entry Examination Board) n organismo responsável pelo acesso ao ensino superior nos Estados Unidos.
Ceefax® ['siːfæks] n UK serviço de teletexto da BBC.
ceilidh ['keɪlɪ] n festa realizada na Escócia e na Irlanda na qual as pessoas cantam e dançam músicas regionais e contam histórias.
ceiling ['siːlɪŋ] n **-1.** [of room] teto m **-2.** fig [limit] teto m máximo.
celebrate ['selɪbreɪt] ◇ vt celebrar. ◇ vi comemorar.
celebrated ['selɪbreɪtɪd] adj célebre, famoso(sa).
celebration [,selɪ'breɪʃn] n **-1.** (U) [activity, feeling] celebração f **-2.** [event] comemoração f.
celebrity [sɪ'lebrətɪ] (pl -ies) n [star] celebridade f.
celeriac [sɪ'lerɪæk] n aipo-rábano m.
celery ['selərɪ] n (U) aipo m.
celestial [sɪ'lestɪəl] adj celestial.
celibacy ['selɪbəsɪ] n (U) celibato m.
celibate ['selɪbət] adj celibatário(ria).
cell [sel] n **-1.** BIOL & COMPUT célula f **-2.** [small room] cela f **-3.** [secret group] unidade f.
cellar ['seləʳ] n **-1.** [basement] porão m **-2.** [stock of wine] adega f.
cellist ['tʃelɪst] n violoncelista mf.
cello ['tʃeləʊ] (pl -s) n [instrument] violoncelo m.

Cellophane® ['seləfeɪn] *n (U)* celofane *m.*

cellphone ['selfəʊn], **cellular phone** ['səljʊlə'-] *n* (telefone *m*) celular *m.*

cellulite ['seljʊlaɪt] *n* celulite *f.*

celluloid *n (U)* [plastic] celulóide *m.*

cellulose ['seljʊləʊs] *n (U)* celulose *f.*

Celsius ['selsɪəs] *adj* Célsius.

Celt [kelt] *n* celta *mf.*

Celtic ['keltɪk] <> *adj* celta. <> *n* [language] celta *m.*

cement [sɪ'ment] <> *n (U)* -**1.** [for concrete] cimento *m*, argamassa *f* -**2.** [glue] cola *f.* <> *vt* -**1.** [cover with cement] cimentar -**2.** [glue] colar -**3.** *fig* [reinforce] fortalecer.

cement mixer *n* betoneira *f.*

cemetery ['semɪtrɪ] (*pl* -**ies**) *n* cemitério *m.*

cenotaph ['senɑ:fl] *n* cenotáfio *m.*

censor ['sensə'] <> *n* [of films, books, letters] censor *m*, -ra *f.* <> *vt* [film, book, letter] censurar.

censorship ['sensəʃɪp] *n (U)* censura *f.*

censure ['senʃə'] <> *n (U)* repreensão *f.* <> *vt* repreender.

census ['sensəs] (*pl* **censuses**) *n* [population survey] censo *m.*

cent [sent] *n* centavo *m.*

centenary *UK* [sen'ti:nərɪ] (*pl* -**ies**), **centennial** *US* [sen'tenjəl] *n* centenário *m.*

center *n, adj & vt US* = **centre**.

centigrade ['sentɪgreɪd] *adj* centígrado(da).

centigram(me) ['sentɪgræm] *n* centigrama *m.*

centilitre *UK*, **centiliter** *US* ['sentɪˌli:tə'] *n* centilitro *m.*

centimetre *UK*, **centimeter** *US* ['sentɪˌmi:tə'] *n* centímetro *m.*

centipede ['sentɪpi:d] *n* centopéia *f.*

central ['sentrəl] *adj* central; ~ **to sthg** [crucial] essencial para algo.

Central African <> *adj* centro-africano(na). <> *n* centro-africano *m*, -na *f.*

Central African Republic *n*: **the** ~ a República Centro-Africana; **in the** ~ na República Centro-Africana.

Central America *n* América Central.

Central American <> *adj* centro-americano(na). <> *n* centro-americano *m*, -na *f.*

Central Asia *n* Ásia Central.

Central Europe *n* Europa Central.

central government *n (U)* governo *m* central.

central heating *n (U)* aquecimento *m* central.

centralization [ˌsentrəlaɪˈzeɪʃn] *n (U)* centralização *f.*

centralize, -ise ['sentrəlaɪz] *vt* centralizar.

centralized ['sentrəlaɪzd] *adj* centralizado(da).

central locking [-'lɒkɪŋ] *n* travamento *f* central (das portas).

centrally ['sentrəlɪ] *adv* no centro.

centrally heated *adj* com aquecimento *f* central.

central nervous system *n* sistema *f* nervoso central.

central processing unit *n* COMPUT unidade *f* central de processamento.

central reservation *n UK* canteiro *m* central.

centre *UK*, **center** *US* ['sentə'] <> *n* -**1.** [gen] centro *m*; **health/leisure** ~ centro de saúde/lazer; ~ **of attention** centro das atenções; ~ **of gravity** centro de gravidade; **the** ~ *POL* o centro -**2.** *SPORT* [player] pivô. <> *adj* -**1.** [middle] central, do meio -**2.** *POL* de centro. <> *vt* [place centrally] centralizar.

⬟ **centre around**, **centre on** *vt fus* centrar em.

centre back *n SPORT* centromédio *m.*

centrefold *n* página *f* central.

centre forward *n SPORT* centroavante *m.*

centre half *n* = centre back.

centrepiece *UK*, **centerpiece** *US* ['sentəpi:s] *n* -**1.** [decoration] centro *m* de mesa -**2.** [principal element] peça-chave *f.*

centre spread *n* = centrefold.

centrifugal force [sentrɪˈfju:gl-] *n* força *f* centrífuga.

century ['sentʃʊrɪ] (*pl* -**ies**) *n* -**1.** [one hundred years] século *m* -**2.** *CRICKET:* **to score a** ~ marcar cem pontos.

CEO (*abbr of* chief executive officer) *n* executivo *m*, -va *f* -chefe.

ceramic [sɪ'ræmɪk] *adj* de cerâmica, cerâmico(ca).

⬟ **ceramics** *n* [craft, objects] cerâmica *f.*

cereal ['sɪərɪəl] *n* [crop, breakfast food] cereal *m.*

cerebral ['serɪbrəl] *adj* cerebral.

cerebral palsy *n (U)* MED paralisia *f* cerebral.

ceremonial [ˌserɪ'məʊnjəl] <> *adj* cerimonial, de cerimônia. <> *n* -**1.** [event] cerimônia *f OR m* -**2.** [pomp, formality] cerimonial *m.*

ceremonious [ˌserɪ'məʊnjəs] *adj* cerimonioso(sa).

ceremony ['serɪmənɪ] (*pl* -**ies**) *n* -**1.** [event] cerimônia *f*; **degree** ~ cerimônia *f* de colação de grau -**2.** *(U)* [pomp, formality] formalidade *f*; **without** ~ sem cerimônia; **to stand on** ~ fazer cerimônia.

cert [sɜ:t] *n UK inf* [certainty] barbada *f.*

cert. (*abbr of* certificate) certificado *m.*

certain ['sɜ:tn] *adj* -**1.** [gen] certo(ta); **she is** ~ **to be late** ela certamente vai se atrasar; **to be** ~ **of sthg/of doing sthg** ter a certeza de algo/fazer algo; **to make** ~ **of sthg/of doing sthg** assegurar-se de algo/fazer algo; **for** ~ com certeza; **to a** ~ **extent** até certo ponto -**2.** [named person]: **a** ~ ... um certo ... (uma certa ...).

certainly ['sɜ:tnlɪ] *adv* com certeza; **do you agree?- I** ~ **do** com certeza (que sim); ~ **not!** de modo algum.

certainty ['sɜ:tntɪ] (*pl* -**ies**) *n (U)* certeza *f.*

CertEd (*abbr of* Certificate in Education) *n diploma universitário em educação.*

certifiable [ˌsɜ:tɪ'faɪəbl] *adj* [insane] demente.

certificate [sə'tɪfɪkət] *n* -**1.** [gen] certificado *m* -**2.** [of birth, marriage] certidão *f*; **death** ~ atestado *m* de óbito.

certification [ˌsɜ:tɪfɪ'keɪʃn] *n* certificação *f.*

certified ['sɜ:tɪfaɪd] *adj* -**1.** [professional person] habilitado(da) -**2.** [document] autenticado(da).

certified mail *n US* postagem *f* registrada.

certified public accountant *n US* perito-contador *m*, -ra *f.*

certify ['sɜ:tɪfaɪ] (*pt & pp* -**ied**) *vt* -**1.** [declare true]: **to** ~ **that** certificar *OR* atestar que -**2.** [give certificate of qualification to]: **to be certified as** receber certificado de **-3.** [declare insane]: **to be certified** ser declarado(da) incapacitado(da).

cervical [sə'vaɪkl] *adj* cervical; ~ **cancer** câncer *m* de colo de útero.

cervical smear *n* exame *f* de lâmina.

cervix ['sɜːvɪks] (*pl* **-ices** [-ɪsiːz]) *n* colo *m* do útero.

cesarean (section) *n US* = **caesarean (section)**.

cessation [se'seɪʃn] *n fml* [stopping] suspensão *f*.

cesspit ['sespɪt], **cesspool** ['sespuːl] *n* fossa *f*.

CET (*abbr of* Central European Time) *n* horário da Europa Central.

cf. (*abbr of* confer) cf., cfr.

CFC (*abbr of* chlorofluorocarbon) *n* CFC *m*.

cg (*abbr of* centigram) cg.

CGT (*abbr of* capital gains tax) *n imposto sobre ganhos de capital.*

ch (*abbr of* central heating) aquecimento *m* central.

ch. (*abbr of* chapter) cap.

CH (*abbr of* Companion of Honour) *n (beneficiário de) distinção de honra britânica.*

Chad [tʃæd] *n* Chade.

chafe [tʃeɪf] ⬦ *vt* [rub] roçar. ⬦ *vi* **-1.** [be sore] esfolar **-2.** *fig* [be annoyed]: **to** ~ **at sthg** irritar--se com algo.

chaff [tʃɑːf] *n* [husks] palhiço *m*.

chaffinch ['tʃæfɪntʃ] *n* tentilhão *m*.

chain [tʃeɪn] ⬦ *n* **-1.** [metal] corrente *f*; ~ **of office** *condecoração usada por oficiais em cerimônias* **-2.** [of islands] série *f*; ~ **of events** rede *f* de acontecimentos **-3.** [of mountains] cadeia *f* **-4.** [of shops, hotels] cadeia *f*, rede *f*. ⬦ *vt* **-1.** [prisoner, bicycle] acorrentar **-2.** [hands] algemar **-3.** [dog] amarrar.

chain letter *n* carta *f* de corrente.

chain reaction *n* reação *f* em cadeia.

chainsaw *n* serra *f* articulada.

chain-smoke *vi* fumar um cigarro atrás do outro.

chain-smoker *n* fumante *mf* inveterado, -da.

chain store *n* filial *f*.

chair [tʃeəʳ] ⬦ *n* **-1.** [for sitting in] cadeira *f* **-2.** [university post] cátedra *f* **-3.** [of meeting, organization - position] presidência *f*; **to take the** ~ presidir; [- person] presidente *mf*. ⬦ *vt* [meeting, discussion] presidir.

chairlift *n* teleférico *m*.

chairman ['tʃeəmən] (*pl* **-men** [-mən]) *n* presidente *m*.

chairmanship ['tʃeəmənʃɪp] *n* presidência *f*.

chairperson ['tʃeə,pɜːsn] (*pl* **-s**) *n* presidente *mf*.

chairwoman ['tʃeə,wʊmən] (*pl* **-women** [,wɪmɪn]) *n* presidenta *f*.

chaise longue [ʃeɪz'lɒŋ] (*pl* **chaises longues** [ʃeɪz'lɒŋ]) *n* espreguiçadeira *f*.

chalet ['ʃæleɪ] *n* chalé *f*.

chalice ['tʃælɪs] *n* cálice *m*.

chalk [tʃɔːk] *n* **-1.** (*U*) [mineral] greda *f* **-2.** [for drawing] giz *m*.

➡ **by a long chalk** *adv* de longe.

➡ **not by a long chalk** *adv* nem de longe.

➡ **chalk up** *vt sep* [attain] obter.

chalkboard ['tʃɔːkbɔːd] *n UK* quadro-negro *m*.

challenge ['tʃælɪndʒ] ⬦ *n* desafio *m*. ⬦ *vt* **-1.** [to fight, competition]: **to** ~ **sb (to sthg)** desafiar alguém (para algo); **to** ~ **sb to do sthg** desafiar alguém a fazer algo **-2.** [question] questionar.

challenger ['tʃælɪndʒəʳ] *n* competidor *m*, -ra *f*.

challenging ['tʃælɪndʒɪŋ] *adj* **-1.** [difficult] desafiador(ra) **-2.** [aggressive] provocador(ra).

chamber ['tʃeɪmbəʳ] *n* **-1.** [room] gabinete *m*; **the council** ~ o gabinete do conselho **-2.** [body] câmara *f* **-3.** [of gun] tambor *m*.

➡ **chambers** *npl* [of barrister] sala *f* de audiências.

chambermaid ['tʃeɪmbəmeɪd] *n* camareira *f*.

chamber music *n (U)* música *f* de câmara.

chamber of commerce *n* câmara *f* de comércio.

chamber orchestra *n* orquestra *f* de câmara.

chameleon [kə'miːljən] *n* [animal] camaleão *m*, -oa *f*.

chamois¹ ['ʃæmɪ] (*pl inv*) *n* [animal] cabra *f* montês.

chamois² ['ʃæmɪ] *n*: ~ **(leather)** camurça *f*.

champ [tʃæmp] ⬦ *n inf* [champion] campeão *m*, -ã *f*. ⬦ *vi* [horse] mascar.

champagne [,ʃæm'peɪn] *n (U)* champanha *m*.

champion ['tʃæmpjən] *n* **-1.** [of competition] campeão *m*, -ã *f* **-2.** [of cause] defensor *m*, -ra *f*.

championship ['tʃæmpjənʃɪp] *n* campeonato *m*.

chance [tʃɑːns] ⬦ *n* **-1.** (*U*) [luck] acaso *m*, sorte *f*; **by** ~ por acaso; **by any** ~ por acaso **-2.** [likelihood, opportunity] chance *f*; **not to stand a** ~ **(of doing sthg)** não ter a menor chance (de fazer algo); **on the off-**~ **(that)** na esperança de que **-3.** [risk] risco *m*; **to take a** ~ **(on sthg/on doing sthg)** arriscar-se (em algo/a fazer algo). ⬦ *adj* acidental. ⬦ *vt* **-1.** [risk] arriscar **-2.** [happen]: **to** ~ **to do sthg** acontecer algo por acaso.

chancellor ['tʃɑːnsələʳ] *n* **-1.** [chief minister] chanceler *m* **-2.** *UNIV* reitor *m*, -ra *f*.

Chancellor of the Exchequer *n UK* ≃ Ministro *m*, -tra *f* da Fazenda.

chancy ['tʃɑːnsɪ] (*compar* **-ier**, *superl* **-iest**) *adj inf* [risky] arriscado(da).

chandelier [,ʃændə'lɪəʳ] *n* lustre *m*.

change [tʃeɪndʒ] ⬦ *n* **-1.** [alteration, difference] mudança *f*, alteração *f*; ~ **in sb/sthg** mudança em alguém/algo **-2.** [contrast, for variety] diferença *f*; **to make a** ~ fazer diferença; **Peter arriving on time? That makes a** ~! Peter chegando na hora?! Que mudança!; **for a** ~ para variar **-3.** [switch, replacement] mudança *f*; ~ **of clothes** muda *f* de roupa **-4.** (*U*) [money returned after payment, smaller units of money] troco *m* **-5.** (*U*) [coins] trocado *m*. ⬦ *vt* **-1.** [gen] mudar; **to** ~ **sthg into sthg** transformar algo em algo; **to** ~ **one's mind** mudar de idéia; **to get** ~ **d** mudar de roupa; **to** ~ **hands** *COMM* mudar de dono **-2.** [replace, exchange] trocar. ⬦ *vi* **-1.** [gen] mudar; **to** ~ **into sthg** transformar-se em algo **-2.** [put on different clothes] trocar-se; **to** ~ **into sthg** trocar algo **-3.** [move to different train, bus] fazer conexão.

➡ **change over** *vi* [convert] trocar para; **to** ~ **over to sthg** trocar para algo.

➡ **change round** *vt sep* trocar.

changeable ['tʃeɪndʒəbl] *adj* -**1.** [mood] inconstante -**2.** [weather] instável.

changed [tʃeɪndʒd] *adj* [person] mudado(da); **to be a ~ person** ser uma outra pessoa.

change machine *n* máquina *f* de troco.

change of life *n*: **the ~** a menopausa.

changeover ['tʃeɪndʒ,əʊvə'] *n*: **~ (to sthg)** mudança *f* (para algo).

change purse *n US* porta-níqueis *m inv*, niqueleira *f*.

changing ['tʃeɪndʒɪŋ] *adj* variável, instável.

changing room *n* vestiário *m*.

channel ['tʃænl] (*UK pt* & *pp* -**led**, *cont* -**ling**, *US pt* & *pp* -**ed**, *cont* -**ing**) ⬦ *n* canal *m*. ⬦ *vt* canalizar.
 ➡ **Channel** *n*: **the (English) Channel** o Canal da Mancha.
 ➡ **channels** *npl*: **to go through the proper ~ s** seguir os trâmites legais.

channel-hopping *n TV* troca *f* rápida de canal, zapping *m*.

Channel Islands *npl*: **the ~** as Ilhas Normandas.

Channel Tunnel *n*: **the ~** o Túnel do Canal da Mancha.

chant [tʃɑːnl] ⬦ *n* -**1.** *RELIG* [song] canto *m* -**2.** [repeated words] coro *m*. ⬦ *vt* -**1.** *RELIG* cantar, entoar -**2.** [words] entoar. ⬦ *vi* -**1.** *RELIG* [sing] cantar -**2.** [repeat words] entoar.

chaos ['keɪɒs] *n* caos *m*.

chaotic [keɪ'ɒtɪk] *adj* caótico(ca).

chap [tʃæp] *n UK inf* [man] cara *m*, chapa *m*.

chapat(t)i [tʃə'pætɪ] *n* pão indiano feito de farinha, água e sal, de formato arrendondado.

chapel ['tʃæpl] *n* capela *f*.

chaperon(e) ['ʃæpərəʊn] ⬦ *n* acompanhante *mf*. ⬦ *vt* acompanhar.

chaplain ['tʃæplɪn] *n* capelão *m*.

chapped [tʃæpt] *adj* rachado(da).

chapter ['tʃæptə'] *n* -**1.** capítulo *m* -**2.** *phr*: **to give sb ~ and verse on sthg** falar tudo a alguém sobre algo.

char [tʃɑː'] (*pt* & *pp* -**red**, *cont* -**ring**) ⬦ *vt* [burn] carbonizar, torrar. ⬦ *vi* [work as cleaner] trabalhar como diarista.

character ['kærəktə'] *n* -**1.** [nature - of place] jeito *m*; [- of person] caráter *m*; **out of ~** atípico; **in ~** típico -**2.** (*U*) [unusual quality, style] estilo *m* -**3.** [in film, book, play] personagem *mf* -**4.** *inf* [unusual person] tipo *m* -**5.** [letter, symbol] caractere *m*.

character code *n COMPUT* código *m* de caracteres.

characteristic [,kærəktə'rɪstɪk] ⬦ *adj* [typical] característico(ca). ⬦ *n* [attribute] característica *f*.

characteristically [,kærəktə'rɪstɪklɪ] *adv* [typically] caracteristicamente.

characterization [,kærəktəraɪ'zeɪʃn] *n* caracterização *f*.

characterize, -ise ['kærəktəraɪz] *vt* -**1.** [typify] caracterizar -**2.** [portray]: **to ~ sthg as** caracterizar algo como.

charade [ʃə'rɑːd] *n* charada *f*.
 ➡ **charades** *n* (*U*) mímica *f*.

charcoal ['tʃɑːkəʊl] *n* carvão *m* (vegetal).

charge [tʃɑːdʒ] ⬦ *n* -**1.** [cost] preço *m*; **admission ~ entrada** *f*; **telephone ~ s** tarifas *fpl* telefônicas; **delivery ~** taxa *f* de entrega; **free of ~** grátis -**2.** [command, control] responsabilidade *f*; **to have ~ of sthg** estar no comando de algo; **to take ~ (of sthg)** tomar conta (de algo); **in ~** encarregado(-da); **in ~ of** no comando de -**3.** *JUR* acusação *f* -**4.** *ELEC* & *MIL* carga *f*. ⬦ *vt* -**1.** [sum of money] cobrar; **to ~ sthg to sb/sthg** debitar algo de alguém/algo -**2.** [suspect, criminal] acusar; **to ~ sb with sthg** acusar alguém de algo -**3.** [attack] investir contra -**4.** *ELEC* carregar. ⬦ *vi* -**1.** [ask for payment]: **to ~ (for sthg)** cobrar (por algo) -**2.** [rush] correr -**3.** [attack] investir.

chargeable ['tʃɑːdʒəbl] *adj* -**1.** [costs]: **~ (to sb/ sthg)** debitável (de alguém/algo) -**2.** [offence] imputável.

charge account *n* conta *f* aberta.

charge card *n* cartão de crédito de um estabelecimento comercial.

charged [tʃɑːdʒd] *adj* [tense] carregado(da).

chargé d'affaires [,ʃɑːzeɪdæ'feəl] (*pl* **chargés d'affaires** [,ʃɑːzeɪdæ'feəl]) *n* encarregado *m*, -da *f* de negócios.

charge hand *n UK* capataz *m*.

charge nurse *n UK* enfermeiro *m*, -ra *f*-chefe.

charger ['tʃɑːdʒə'] *n* -**1.** [for batteries] carregador *m* -**2.** *literary* [soldier's horse] cavalo *m* de batalha.

charge sheet *n UK* boletim *m* de ocorrência.

chariot ['tʃærɪət] *n* biga *f*.

charisma [kə'rɪzmə] *n* carisma *m*.

charismatic [,kærɪz'mætɪk] *adj* [charming] carismático(ca).

charitable ['tʃærətəbl] *adj* -**1.** [person, remark] generoso(sa) -**2.** [organization] de caridade, beneficente.

charity ['tʃærətɪ] (*pl* -**ies**) *n* -**1.** (*U*) [gifts, money] caridade *f*-**2.** [organization] instituição *f* de caridade -**3.** [kindness] simpatia *f*.

charity shop *n* loja *f* beneficente.

charlatan ['ʃɑːlətən] *n* charlatão *m*, -tona *f*.

charm [tʃɑːm] ⬦ *n* -**1.** (*U*) [appeal, attractiveness] charme *m*, encanto *m* -**2.** [spell] feitiço *m* -**3.** [on bracelet] amuleto *m*. ⬦ *vt* encantar.

charm bracelet *n* pulseira *f* com berloques.

charmer ['tʃɑːmə'] *n* [charming person] sedutor *m*, -ra *f*.

charming ['tʃɑːmɪŋ] *adj* encantador(ra).

charmingly ['tʃɑːmɪŋlɪ] *adv* encantadoramente.

charred [tʃɑːd] *adj* carbonizado(da).

chart [tʃɑːt] ⬦ *n* -**1.** [diagram] gráfico *m* -**2.** [map] mapa *m*, carta *f*; **a star/sea ~** uma carta celeste/marítima. ⬦ *vt* -**1.** [plot, map] cartografar -**2.** *fig* [record] registrar.
 ➡ **charts** *npl*: **the ~ s** as paradas de sucesso.

charter ['tʃɑːtə'] ⬦ *n* [document] carta *f*. ⬦ *vt* [plane, boat] fretar.

chartered accountant ['tʃɑːtəd-] *n UK* contador *m* diplomado, contadora *f* diplomada.

charter flight *n* vôo *m* fretado.

charter plane *n* avião *m* fretado.

chary ['tʃeərɪ] (*compar* -**ier**, *superl* -**iest**) *adj*: **to be ~ of doing sthg** ser cuidadoso(sa) ao fazer algo.

chase [tʃeɪs] ⬦ *n* -**1.** [pursuit] perseguição *f*; **to give ~** dar perseguição -**2.** [hunt] caça *f*. ⬦ *vt*

-1. [pursue] perseguir **-2.** [drive away] enxotar **-3.** [money, jobs] correr atrás de. <> *vi*: **to** ~ **after sb/sthg** correr atrás de alguém/algo.

■ **chase up** *vt sep UK* [person, information] correr OR sair atrás de.

chaser ['tʃeɪsəʳ] *n* [drink] *bebida suave tomada após uma bebida alcoólica mais forte ou mais fraca.*

chasm ['kæzm] *n* abismo *m*.

chassis ['ʃæsɪ] (*pl inv*) *n* [of vehicle] chassi *m*.

chaste [tʃeɪst] *adj* casto(ta).

chasten ['tʃeɪsnl] *vt* disciplinar.

chastise [tʃæ'staɪz] *vt fml* [scold] repreender.

chastity ['tʃæstətɪ] *n* castidade *f*.

chat [tʃætl] (*pt & pp* **-ted**, *cont* **-ting**) <> *n* bate-papo *m*, conversa *f*; **to have a** ~ bater papo. <> *vi* bater papo, conversar.

■ **chat up** *vt sep UK inf* bater papo.

chatiquette ['tʃætɪket] *n COMPUT* etiqueta *f* no bate-papo, chatiqueta *f*.

chat room *n COMPUT* sala *f* de bate-papo.

chat show *n UK* programa *m* de entrevistas.

chatter ['tʃætəʳ] <> *n* **-1.** [of person] tagarelice *f* **-2.** [of animal, bird] chilro *m*. <> *vi* **-1.** [person] tagarelar **-2.** [animal, bird] chilrar **-3.** [teeth] bater.

chatterbox ['tʃætəbɒks] *n inf* tagarela *mf*.

chattering classes *npl UK*: **the** ~ os pseudo-formadores de opinião.

chatty ['tʃætɪ] (*compar* **-ier**, *superl* **-iest**) *adj* **-1.** [person] tagarela **-2.** [letter] informal.

chauffeur ['ʃəʊfəʳ] <> *n* chofer *m*. <> *vt* trabalhar como chofer.

chauvinist ['ʃəʊvɪnɪst] *n* chauvinista *mf*.

chauvinistic ['ʃəʊvɪ'nɪstɪk] *adj* chauvinista.

cheap [tʃiːp] <> *adj* **-1.** [gen] barato(ta) **-2.** [despicable, vulgar] de mau gosto. <> *adv* barato. <> *n*: **on the** ~ por uma ninharia.

cheapen ['tʃiːpn] *vt* [degrade] rebaixar; **to** ~ **o.s.** rebaixar-se.

cheaply ['tʃiːplɪ] *adv* [at a low price] barato.

cheapness ['tʃiːpnɪs] *n* **-1.** [low cost] baixo preço *m* **-2.** [vulgarity] mau gosto *m*.

cheapskate ['tʃiːpskeɪt] *n inf pej* pão-duro *m*.

cheat [tʃiːt] <> *n* trapaceiro *m*, -ra *f*. <> *vt* trapacear; **to** ~ **sb out of sthg** passar alguém para trás em algo; **to feel** ~**ed** sentir-se passado(da) para trás. <> *vi* [be dishonest] trapacear.

■ **cheat on** *vt fus inf* [be unfaithful to] trair.

cheating ['tʃiːtɪŋ] *n* **-1.** [at cards] blefe *m* **-2.** [in exam] cola *f*.

check [tʃek] <> *n* **-1.** [gen]: ~ **(on sthg)** checagem *f* (de algo) **-2.** [restraint]: ~ **(on sthg)** controle *m* (sobre algo); **in** ~ sob controle **-3.** *US* [bill] conta *f* **-4.** [pattern] xadrez *m* **-5.** [in chess] xeque *m*. <> *vt* **-1.** [test, verify] verificar, conferir **-2.** [restrain, stop] conter. <> *vi* verificar; **to** ~ **for sthg** verificar se há algo, procurar por algo; **to** ~ **on sthg** examinar algo.

■ **check in** <> *vt sep* [luggage, coat] despachar. <> *vi* **-1.** [at hotel] registrar-se **-2.** [at airport] fazer check-in.

■ **check off** *vt sep* [names on a list] marcar.

■ **check out** <> *vt sep* **-1.** [luggage, coat] dar

baixa em **-2.** [investigate] averiguar. <> *vi* [from hotel] fechar a conta e sair.

■ **check up** *vi* informar-se; **to** ~ **up on sb/sthg** informar-se sobre alguém/algo.

checkbook *n US* = chequebook.

checked [tʃekt] *adj* [patterned] quadriculado(da).

checkered *adj US* = chequered.

checkers ['tʃekəz] *n US* (jogo *m* de) damas *fpl*.

check guarantee card *n US* cartão *m* de garantia de cheque.

check-in *n* check-in *m*.

checking account ['tʃekɪŋ-] *n US* conta *f* corrente.

checklist ['tʃeklɪst] *n* lista *f* de verificação.

checkmate ['tʃekmeɪt] *n* [in chess] xeque-mate *m*.

checkout ['tʃekaʊt] *n* **-1.** [in supermarket] caixa *m* **-2.** [in hotel] saída *f*, checkout *m*.

checkpoint ['tʃekpɔɪnt] *n* [place] posto *m* de controle.

check-up *n* check-up *m*.

Cheddar (cheese) ['tʃedəʳ-] *n* queijo *m* Cheddar.

cheek [tʃiːk] <> *n* **-1.** [of face] bochecha *f* **-2.** [buttock] nádega *f* **-3.** *inf* [impudence] audácia *f*. <> *vt inf* atrever-se a.

cheekbone ['tʃiːkbəʊn] *n* osso *m* malar, maçã *f* do rosto.

cheekily ['tʃiːkɪlɪ] *adv* descaradamente.

cheekiness ['tʃiːkɪnɪs] *n* descaramento *m*.

cheeky ['tʃiːkɪ] (*compar* **-ier**, *superl* **-iest**) *adj* descarado(da).

cheep *vi* piar.

cheer [tʃɪəʳ] <> *n* [shout] vivas *fpl*. <> *vt* **-1.** [shout approval, encouragement at] ovacionar **-2.** [gladden] animar. <> *vi* aclamar, aplaudir.

■ **cheers** *excl* **-1.** [said before drinking] saúde! **-2.** *UK inf* [goodbye] tchau! **-3.** *UK inf* [thank you] valeu!

■ **cheer on** *vt sep* torcer por.

■ **cheer up** <> *vt sep* animar. <> *vi* animar-se.

cheerful ['tʃɪəfʊl] *adj* alegre.

cheerfully ['tʃɪəfʊlɪ] *adv* **-1.** [happily] alegremente **-2.** [willingly] de boa vontade.

cheerfulness ['tʃɪəfʊlnɪs] *n* [happiness] alegria *f*.

cheering ['tʃɪərɪŋ] <> *adj* [gladdening] animado(-da). <> *n* animação *f*.

cheerio [,tʃɪərɪ'əʊ] *excl UK inf* tchau!

cheerleader ['tʃɪə,liːdəʳ] *n* animador *m*, -ra *f* de torcida.

cheerless ['tʃɪəlɪs] *adj* triste.

cheery ['tʃɪərɪ] (*compar* **-ier**, *superl* **-iest**) *adj* cordial.

cheese [tʃiːz] *n* queijo *m*.

cheeseboard ['tʃiːzbɔːd] *n* **-1.** [board] tábua *f* de queijos **-2.** [on menu] variedade *f* de queijos.

cheeseburger ['tʃiːz,bɜːgəʳ] *n* xisburguer *m*.

cheesecake ['tʃiːzkeɪk] *n CULIN* torta *f* de queijo.

cheesed off *adj inf* chateado(da).

cheesy ['tʃiːzɪ] (*compar* **-ier**, *superl* **-iest**) *adj* **-1.** [tasting of cheese] de queijo **-2.** [grin] de chulé **-3.** *inf* [cheap, unpleasant] cafona.

cheetah ['tʃiːtə] *n* guepardo *m*.

chef [ʃef] *n* cozinheiro *m*, -ra *f*-chefe.

chemical ['kemɪkl] <> *adj* químico(ca). <> *n* substância *f* química.

chemically ['kemɪklɪ] *adv* quimicamente.

chemical weapons *npl* armas *fpl* químicas.

chemist ['kemɪst] *n* -**1.** *UK* [pharmacist] farmacêutico *m*, -ca *f*; ~ 's (shop) farmácia *f* -**2.** [scientist] químico *m*, -ca *f*.

chemistry ['kemɪstrɪ] *n* química *f*.

chemotherapy [ˌkiːməʊ'θerəpɪ] *n* quimioterapia *f*.

cheque *UK*, **check** *US* [tʃek] *n* cheque *m*; **to pay by** ~ pagar com cheque.

cheque account *n* [at bank, building society] conta *f* corrente.

chequebook *UK*, **checkbook** *US* ['tʃekbʊk] *n* talão *m* de cheques.

cheque (guarantee) card *n UK* cartão *m* de garantia de cheque.

chequered *UK* ['tʃekəd], **checkered** *US* ['tʃekerd] *adj* -**1.** [patterned] xadrez -**2.** *fig* [varied] cheio (cheia) de altos e baixos.

cherish ['tʃerɪʃ] *vt* [treasure - hope, memory] acalentar; [- privilege, right] apreciar; [- person, thing] acariciar.

cherished ['tʃerɪʃt] *adj* [dear] precioso(sa).

cherry ['tʃerɪ] (*pl* -**ies**) *n* -**1.** [fruit] cereja *f* -**2.**: ~ **(tree)** cerejeira *f*.

cherry-pick *vt* adquirir as empresas mais lucrativas durante a privatização de um setor da economia.

cherub ['tʃerəb] (*pl* -**s** *OR* -**im** [-ɪm]) *n* -**1.** [angel] querubim *m* -**2.** [child] anjinho *m*, -nha *f*.

chervil ['tʃɜːvɪl] *n (U)* [herb] cerefólio *m*.

chess [tʃes] *n* xadrez *m*.

chessboard ['tʃesbɔːd] *n* tabuleiro *m* de xadrez.

chessman ['tʃesmæn] (*pl* -**men** [-men]), **chess piece** *n* peça *f* do jogo de xadrez.

chest [tʃest] *n* -**1.** *ANAT* peito *m*; **to get sthg off one's** ~ *inf* desabafar -**2.** [box, trunk] caixa *f* -**3.** [coffer] baú *m*.

chestnut ['tʃesnʌt] <> *adj* [colour] castanho(nha). <> *n* -**1.** [nut] castanha *f* -**2.**: ~ **(tree)** castanheiro *m*.

chest of drawers (*pl* **chests of drawers**) *n* [piece of furniture] cômoda *f*.

chesty ['tʃestɪ] (*compar* -**ier**, *superl* -**iest**) *adj* [cough] com catarro.

chevron ['ʃevrən] *n* -**1.** [on road] placa *f* de sinalização -**2.** [on uniform] divisa *f*.

chew [tʃuː] <> *n* [biting] mastigação *f*. <> *vt* -**1.** [food] mastigar -**2.** [nails, carpet] roer.

➤ **chew over** *vt sep fig* [think over] ponderar, refletir sobre.

➤ **chew up** *vt sep* [food, slippers] roer.

chewing gum ['tʃuːɪŋ-] *n* chiclete *m*.

chewy [tʃuːɪ] (*compar* -**ier**, *superl* -**iest**) *adj* [food] duro(ra).

chic [ʃiːk] <> *adj* chique. <> *n* elegância *f*.

chicanery [ʃɪ'keɪnərɪ] *n* [trickery] tramóia *f*; [deception] ilusão *f*.

chick [tʃɪk] *n* -**1.** [baby bird] filhote *m* (de pássaro) -**2.** *inf* [woman] garota *f*.

chicken ['tʃɪkɪn] <> *adj inf* [cowardly] galinha. <> *n* -**1.** [bird] galinha *f*; **it's a** ~ **and egg situation** é a história do ovo e da galinha -**2.** *(U)* [food] frango *m* -**3.** *inf* [coward] galinha *m*.

➤ **chicken out** *vi inf*: **to** ~ **out (of sthg/of**

doing sthg) acovardar-se (de algo/de fazer algo).

chicken feed *n fig* [small sum of money] ninharia *f*.

chickenpox ['tʃɪkɪnpɒks] *n* catapora *f*.

chicken wire *n* tela *f* de arame *(para galinheiros)*.

chickpea ['tʃɪkpiː] *n* grão-de-bico *m*.

chicory ['tʃɪkərɪ] *n* [vegetable] chicória *f*.

chide [tʃaɪd] (*pt* **chided** *OR* **chid** [tʃɪd], *pp* **chid** *OR* **chidden** ['tʃɪdn]) *vt literary* repreender.

chief [tʃiːf] <> *adj* -**1.** [most important] principal -**2.** [head] chefe; ~ **accountant** contador *m*, -ra *f* chefe. <> *n* -**1.** [of organization] chefe *mf* -**2.** [of tribe] chefe *m*, cacique *m*.

chief constable *n UK* chefe *mf* de polícia.

chief executive *n* [head of company] presidente *mf* executivo, -va.

➤ **Chief Executive** *n US* [US president]: **the Chief Executive** o (a) Chefe de Governo.

chief justice *n Am* ≃ presidente *mf* do Supremo Tribunal.

chiefly ['tʃiːflɪ] *adv* [mainly] principalmente.

chief of staff *n* chefe *mf* do estado-maior.

chieftain ['tʃiːftən] *n* líder *m*, chefe *m*.

chiffon ['ʃɪfɒn] *n* chiffon *m*.

chihuahua [tʃɪ'wɑːwə] *n* chihuahua *m*.

chilblain ['tʃɪlbleɪn] *n* frieira *f*.

child [tʃaɪld] (*pl* **children**) *n* -**1.** [boy, girl] criança *f* -**2.** [son, daughter] filho *m*, -lha *f*.

childbearing ['tʃaɪldˌbeərɪŋ] *n (U)* parto *m*.

child benefit *n UK* benefício pago pelo governo britânico a todas as famílias de acordo com o número de filhos.

childbirth ['tʃaɪldbɜːθ] *n (U)* parto *m*.

childcare ['tʃaɪldkeəʳ] *n* assistência *f* à infância; **they share the** ~ eles dividem as responsabilidades relativas às crianças.

childhood ['tʃaɪldhʊd] *n* infância *f*.

childish ['tʃaɪldɪʃ] *adj pej* infantil.

childishly ['tʃaɪldɪʃlɪ] *adv pej* de modo infantil.

childless ['tʃaɪldlɪs] *adj* sem filhos.

childlike ['tʃaɪldlaɪk] *adj* ingênuo(nua).

childminder ['tʃaɪldˌmaɪndəʳ] *n UK* babá *mf*.

child prodigy *n* criança *f* prodígio.

childproof ['tʃaɪldpruːf] *adj* seguro(ra) para crianças, à prova de crianças.

children ['tʃɪldrən] *pl* ➳ **child**.

Chile ['tʃɪlɪ] *n* Chile; **in** ~ no Chile.

Chilean ['tʃɪlɪən] <> *adj* chileno(na). <> *n* chileno *m*, -na *f*.

chili ['tʃɪlɪ] *n* = **chilli**.

chill [tʃɪl] <> *adj* glacial. <> *n* -**1.** [illness] resfriado *m* -**2.** [in temperature]: **a** ~ **in the air** uma friagem -**3.** [feeling of fear] calafrio *m*. <> *vt* -**1.** [drink, food] gelar -**2.** [person] arrepiar-se de. <> *vi* [drink, food] esfriar.

chilli ['tʃɪlɪ] (*pl* -**ies**) *n* [vegetable] pimenta-malagueta *f*.

chilling ['tʃɪlɪŋ] *adj* -**1.** [very cold] gelado(da) -**2.** [frightening] arrepiante.

chilli powder *n* pimenta *f* em pó.

chilly ['tʃɪlɪ] (*compar* -**ier**, *superl* -**iest**) *adj* frio(fria).

chime [tʃaɪm] <> *n* [of bell, clock] batida *f*. <> *vt* [time] bater. <> *vi* [bell, clock] tocar.

➧ **chime in** *vi* concordar.

chimney ['tʃɪmnɪ] *n* chaminé *f*.

chimneypot ['tʃɪmnɪpɒt] *n* cano *m* de chaminé.

chimneysweep ['tʃɪmnɪswi:p] *n* limpador *m*, -ra *f* de chaminé.

chimp [tʃɪmp] *inf*, **chimpanzee** [ˌtʃɪmpən'zi:] *n* chimpanzé *mf*.

chin [tʃɪn] *n* queixo *m*.

china ['tʃaɪnə] <> *n (U)* **-1.** [substance] porcelana *f* **-2.** [crockery] louças *fpl* de porcelana. <> *comp* de porcelana.

China ['tʃaɪnə] *n* China; **in** ~ na China; **the People's Republic of** ~ a República Popular da China.

china clay *n (U)* caulim *m*.

China Sea *n*: **the** ~ o Mar da China.

Chinatown ['tʃaɪnətaʊn] *n* bairro *m* chinês.

chinchilla [tʃɪn'tʃɪlə] *n* chinchila *f*.

Chinese [ˌtʃaɪ'ni:z] <> *adj* chinês(esa). <> *n* [language] chinês *m*. <> *npl*: **the** ~ os chineses.

Chinese cabbage *n* repolho *m* chinês.

Chinese lantern *n* [light] lanterna *f* chinesa.

Chinese leaf *n UK* = **Chinese cabbage**.

chink [tʃɪŋk] <> *n* **-1.** [narrow opening] fresta *f* **-2.** [sound] tinido *m*. <> *vi* tilintar.

chinos ['tʃi:nəʊz] *npl* calça *f* de algodão grosso.

chintz [tʃɪnts] <> *n (U)* tecido *m* de algodão estampado, chita *f*. <> *comp* de algodão estampado, de chita.

chinwag ['tʃɪnwæg] *n inf*: **to have a** ~ bater um papo.

chip [tʃɪp] (*pt & pp* -ped, *cont* -ping) <> *n* **-1.** *UK* [hot, fried potato strip] batata *f* frita em palito **-2.** *US* [snack] batata *f* frita de pacote **-3.** [fragment] lasca *f* **-4.** [flaw] defeito *m* **-5.** *COMPUT* chip *m* **-6.** [token] ficha *f*; **when the** ~**s are down** quando chega a hora da verdade **-7.** *SPORT* tacada *f* **-8.** *phr*: **to have a** ~ **on one's shoulder** ficar ressentido(da). <> *vt* [damage] lascar.

➧ **chip in** *inf* <> *vt fus* [contribute] contribuir com. <> *vi* **-1.** [contribute] fazer uma vaquinha **-2.** [interrupt] interromper.

➧ **chip off** *vt sep* lascar.

chipboard ['tʃɪpbɔ:d] *n (U)* compensado *m*.

chipmunk ['tʃɪpmʌŋk] *n* tâmia *m*.

chipped ['tʃɪpt] *adj* [flawed] lascado(da).

chippings ['tʃɪpɪŋz] *npl* cavacos *mpl*; **'loose** ~' 'cascalho solto'.

chip shop *n UK* loja onde se compram peixe com batatas fritas.

chiropodist [kɪ'rɒpədɪst] *n* quiropodista *mf*.

chiropody [kɪ'rɒpədɪ] *n (U)* quiropodia *f*.

chiropractor *n* quiroprático *m*, -ca *f*.

chirp [tʃɜ:p] *vi* chilrar, piar.

chirpy ['tʃɜ:pɪ] (*compar* -ier, *superl* -iest) *adj esp UK inf* [cheerful] animado(da).

chisel ['tʃɪzl] (*UK pt & pp* -led, *cont* -ling, *US pt & pp* -ed, *cont* -ing) <> *n* **-1.** [for wood] formão *m* **-2.** [for stone] cinzel *m*. <> *vt* **-1.** [wood] esculpir com formão **-2.** [stone] cinzelar.

chit [tʃɪt] *n* [note] vale *m*.

chit-chat *n (U) inf* bate-papo *m*.

chivalrous ['ʃɪvlrəs] *adj* cavalheiresco(ca).

chivalry ['ʃɪvlrɪ] *n* **-1.** *literary* [of knights] cavalaria *f*

-2. [courtesy] cavalheirismo *m*.

chives [tʃaɪvz] *npl* cebolinha *f*.

chivy (*pt & pp* -ied), **chivvy** (*pt & pp* -ied) ['tʃɪvɪ] *vt inf*: **to** ~ **sb along** dar uma apressada em alguém.

chloride ['klɔ:raɪd] *n* cloreto *m*.

chlorinated ['klɔ:rɪneɪtɪd] *adj* clorado(da).

chlorine ['klɔ:ri:n] *n (U)* cloro *m*.

chlorofluorocarbon ['klɔ:rəʊˌfluərəʊ'kɑ:bən] *n* clorofluorcarbono *m*.

chloroform ['klɒrəfɔ:m] *n (U)* clorofórmio *m*.

chlorophyll *n* clorofila *f*.

choc-ice ['tʃɒkaɪs] *n UK* bola de sorvete com cobertura de chocolate.

chock [tʃɒk] *n* calço *m (para roda de veículo)*.

chock-a-block, chock-full *adj inf*: ~ **(with)** [people] apinhado(da) (de); [things] entupido(da) (de).

chocolate ['tʃɒkələt] <> *n (U)* chocolate *m*; **plain/ milk** ~ chocolate amargo/ao leite; **a box of** ~**s** uma caixa de bombons. <> *comp* [biscuit, cake, mousse] de chocolate.

choice [tʃɔɪs] <> *n* **-1.** [gen] escolha *f*, opção *f*; **to have no** ~ **but to do sthg** não ter outra escolha a não fazer algo; **it was my first** ~ foi a minha primeira opção; **to do sthg by** ~ fazer algo por vontade própria **-2.** [variety, selection] variedade *f*. <> *adj* selecionado(da).

choir ['kwaɪə'] *n* [singers] coro *m*.

choirboy ['kwaɪəbɔɪ] *n* menino *m* de coro.

choke [tʃəʊk] <> *n AUT* afogador *m*. <> *vt* **-1.** [subj: person] estrangular **-2.** [subj: smoke, fumes] asfixiar, sufocar **-3.** [block] entupir, obstruir. <> *vi* [on food, water] engasgar.

➧ **choke back** *vt fus* segurar, controlar.

choker *n* gargantilha *f*.

cholera ['kɒlərə] *n (U)* cólera *f*.

cholesterol [kə'lestərɒl] *n (U)* colesterol *m*.

choose [tʃu:z] (*pt* chose, *pp* chosen) <> *vt* **-1.** [select] escolher; **there's little** *OR* **not much to** ~ **between them** não há muito o que escolher entre eles (elas) **-2.** [opt]: **to** ~ **to do sthg** optar por fazer algo. <> *vi* [select]: **to** ~ **(from sthg)** escolher (entre algo).

choos(e)y ['tʃu:zɪ] (*compar* -ier, *superl* -iest) *adj* exigente.

chop [tʃɒp] (*pt & pp* -ped, *cont* -ping) <> *n* **-1.** [meat] costeleta *f* **-2.** [blow] pancada *f*; **to be for the** ~ [person] estar para ser demitido(da); [project] estar para ser cancelado(da). <> *vt* **-1.** [wood] retalhar **-2.** [vegetables, apple] picar **-3.** *inf* [funding, budget] cortar **-4.** *phr*: **to** ~ **and change** ser inconstante.

➧ **chop down** *vt sep* derrubar.

➧ **chop up** *vt sep* **-1.** [vegetables, fruit] picar **-2.** [wood, meat] cortar.

chopper ['tʃɒpə'] *n* **-1.** [axe] machadinha *f* **-2.** *inf* [helicopter] helicóptero *m*.

chopping board ['tʃɒpɪŋ-] *n* tábua *f* de cozinha.

choppy ['tʃɒpɪ] (*compar* -ier, *superl* -iest) *adj* [sea] agitado(da).

chopsticks ['tʃɒpstɪks] *npl* hashi *mpl*.

choral ['kɔ:rəl] *adj* de coral.

chord [kɔːd] *n MUS* acorde *m*; **to strike a ~ (with sb)** tocar fundo (em alguém).

chore [tʃɔːˤ] *n* afazeres *mpl*; **household ~s** afazeres domésticos.

choreographer [ˌkɒrɪˈɒɡrəfəˤ] *n* coreógrafo *m*, -fa *f*.

choreography [ˌkɒrɪˈɒɡrəfɪ] *n (U)* coreografia *f*.

chortle [ˈtʃɔːtl] *vi* dar gargalhadas.

chorus [ˈkɔːrəs] *n* **-1.** [gen] coro *m* **-2.** [part of song] refrão *m*.

chose [tʃəʊz] *pt* ⊳ **choose**.

chosen [ˈtʃəʊzn] *pp* ⊳ **choose**.

choux pastry [ʃuː-] *n (U)* doce feito com ovos e em cujo interior se acrescenta creme.

chow [tʃaʊ] *n* [dog] chow-chow *m inv*.

chowder [ˈtʃaʊdəˤ] *n (U)* sopa *f (de frutos do mar)*; **clam ~** sopa de mariscos.

Christ [kraɪst] ⇔ *n* Cristo *m*. ⇔ *excl* Jesus Cristo!, Minha Nossa!

christen [ˈkrɪsn] *vt* batizar.

christening [ˈkrɪsnɪŋ] ⇔ *n* batizado *m*. ⇔ *comp* de batismo.

Christian [ˈkrɪstʃən] ⇔ *adj* cristão(tã). ⇔ *n* cristão *m*, -tã *f*.

Christian Democrat *n POL* democrata *mf* cristão, -tã.

Christianity [ˌkrɪstɪˈænətɪ] *n (U)* cristianismo *m*.

Christian name *n* nome *m* de batismo.

Christmas [ˈkrɪsməs] ⇔ *n* Natal *m*; **Happy OR Merry ~!** Feliz Natal! ⇔ *comp* de Natal.

Christmas cake *n UK* bolo escuro e decorado que contém muitas frutas secas e que é coberto com marzipã e glacê e servido no Natal.

Christmas card *n* cartão *m* de Natal.

Christmas carol *n* cântico *m* de Natal.

Christmas cracker *n UK* cilindro de papel que produz um estalido ao ser aberto e que contém dentro um presente de Natal.

Christmas Day *n* dia *m* de Natal.

Christmas Eve *n* noite *f* de Natal.

Christmas Island *n* Ilha de Natal.

Christmas pudding *n UK* pudim rico e escuro feito com frutas secas, condimentos e gordura animal, servido no Natal.

Christmas stocking *n* meias *fpl* de Natal *(penduradas na lareira)*.

Christmas tree *n* árvore *f* de Natal.

chrome [krəʊm], **chromium** [ˈkrəʊmɪəm] ⇔ *n (U)* cromo *m*. ⇔ *comp* de cromo, cromado(da).

chrome-plated *adj* cromado(da).

chromosome [ˈkrəʊməsəʊm] *n* cromossomo *m*.

chronic [ˈkrɒnɪk] *adj* **-1.** [long-lasting] crônico(ca) **-2.** [habitual] inveterado(da).

chronically [ˈkrɒnɪklɪ] *adv* [ill] cronicamente.

chronicle [ˈkrɒnɪkl] ⇔ *n* crônica *f*. ⇔ *vt* narrar.

chronological [ˌkrɒnəˈlɒdʒɪkl] *adj* cronológico(-ca).

chronologically [ˌkrɒnəˈlɒdʒɪklɪ] *adv* cronologicamente.

chronology [krəˈnɒlədʒɪ] *n* [sequence] cronologia *f*.

chrysalis [ˈkrɪsəlɪs] *(pl* **-lises** [-lɪsiːz]*) n* [insect] crisálida *f*.

chrysanthemum [krɪˈsænθəməm] *(pl* **-s**) *n* crisântemo *m*.

chub *(pl inv OR* **-s**) *n* espécie de carpa.

chubbiness *n (U)* fofice *f*.

chubby [ˈtʃʌbɪ] *(compar* **-ier**, *superl* **-iest**) *adj* rechonchudo(da).

chuck [tʃʌk] *vt inf* **-1.** [throw] jogar, atirar **-2.** *inf* : **to ~ sb** dar o fora em alguém; **to ~ sthg** largar algo.

◆ **chuck away, chuck out** *vt sep inf* jogar fora; **to ~ sthg out** botar algo fora; **to ~ sb out** botar alguém para fora.

chuckle [ˈtʃʌkl] ⇔ *n* risadinha *f*. ⇔ *vi* rir discretamente.

chuffed [tʃʌft] *adj UK inf*: **~ (with sthg/to do sthg)** muito contente (com algo/por fazer algo).

chug [tʃʌg] *(pt & pp* **-ged**, *cont* **-ging**) *vi* ratear.

chum [tʃʌm] *n inf* camarada *mf*, companheiro *m*, -ra *f*.

chummy [ˈtʃʌmɪ] *(compar* **-ier**, *superl* **-iest**) *adj inf*: **to be ~ (with sb)** ser legal (com alguém).

chump [tʃʌmp] *n inf* [fool] tonto *m*, -ta *f*.

chunk [tʃʌŋk] *n* **-1.** [piece] pedaço *m* **-2.** *inf* [large amount] grande parte *f*.

chunky [ˈtʃʌŋkɪ] *(compar* **-ier**, *superl* **-iest**) *adj* **-1.** [person] parrudo(da) **-2.** [jewellery, furniture] maciço(-ça) **-3.** [cardigan] grosso(sa).

church [tʃɜːtʃ] *n* **-1.** [building] igreja *f*;. **to go to ~** freqüentar a igreja **-2.** [organization]: **the Church** a Igreja.

churchgoer [ˈtʃɜːtʃˌgəʊəˤ] *n* fiel *m*, devoto *m*, -ta *f*.

churchman [ˈtʃɜːtʃmən] *(pl* **-men** [-mən]*) n* clérigo *m*, eclesiástico *m*.

Church of England *n*: **the ~** a Igreja Anglicana.

CHURCH OF ENGLAND

A Igreja Anglicana originou-se da disputa entre o rei Henrique VIII, que desejava divorciar-se, e a Igreja Católica, que lhe negou o divórcio, em meados do século XVI. Autoproclamando-se chefe da Igreja Anglicana, Henrique VIII separou-a da Igreja Católica. O chefe laico da Igreja Anglicana é o monarca, e seu chefe espiritual, o arcebispo de Canterbury.

Church of Scotland *n*: **the ~** a Igreja Presbiteriana da Escócia.

churchyard [ˈtʃɜːtʃjɑːd] *n* cemitério ao redor de uma igreja.

churlish [ˈtʃɜːlɪʃ] *adj* indelicado(da).

churn [tʃɜːn] ⇔ *n* **-1.** [for making butter] batedeira *f* de manteiga **-2.** [for transporting milk] latão *m*. ⇔ *vt* [stir up] agitar. ⇔ *vi* revolver-se.

◆ **churn out** *vt sep inf* produzir em larga escala.

◆ **churn up** *vt sep* **-1.** [mud] agitar **-2.** [water] revolver.

chute [ʃuːt] *n* **-1.** [waterfall] queda *f* d'água, cachoeira *f* **-2.** [for escape] rampa *f* **-3.** [for rubbish] calha *f* **-4.** [in a pool] tobogã *m*.

chutney [ˈtʃʌtnɪ] *n (U)* molho feito à base de frutas, sementes picantes e açúcar que se come com carne ou queijo.

CI *abbr of* **Channel Islands.**
CIA (*abbr of* **Central Intelligence Agency**) *n* CIA *f.*
cicada [sɪ'kɑːdə] *n* cigarra *f.*
CID (*abbr of* **Criminal Investigation Department**) *n departamento de investigação criminal da polícia britânica.*
cider ['saɪdəʳ] *n* sidra *f.*
c.i.f. (*abbr of* **cost, insurance and freight**) c.i.f., custo, seguro e frete.
cigar [sɪ'gɑːʳ] *n* charuto *m.*
cigarette [ˌsɪgə'ret] *n* cigarro *m.*
cigarette butt, cigarette end *UK n* bagana *f.*
cigarette holder *n* piteira *f.*
cigarette lighter *n* isqueiro *m.*
cigarette paper *n* mortalha *f.*
C-in-C (*abbr of* **commander in chief**) *n* comandante-em-chefe *m.*
cinch [sɪntʃ] *n inf*: **it's a** ~ é sopa *OR* canja.
cinder ['sɪndəʳ] *n* cinza *f.*
cinderblock ['sɪndəblɒk] *n US* bloco *m* de cimento e cinzas.
Cinderella [ˌsɪndə'relə] *n* Cinderela *f* gata-borralheira *f.*
cine camera *n* filmadora *f.*
cine film *n* filme *m*, película *f.*
cinema ['sɪnəmə] *n* [place, art] cinema *m.*
cinematic [ˌsɪnɪ'mætɪk] *adj* cinematográfico(ca).
cinnamon ['sɪnəmən] *n (U)* canela *f.*
cipher ['saɪfəʳ] *n* **-1.** [secret writing system] cifra *f* **-2.** *fig* [person] nulidade *f.*
circa ['sɜːkə] *prep* cerca de, aproximadamente.
circle ['sɜːkl] ◇ *n* **-1.** [gen] círculo *m*; **to come full** ~ voltar ao ponto de partida; **to go round in** ~**s** andar em círculos **-2.** [seats in theatre, cinema] galeria *f.* ◇ *vt* **-1.** [draw a circle round] marcar com círculo **-2.** [move round] circundar. ◇ *vi* mover-se em círculos.
circuit ['sɜːkɪt] *n* **-1.** [gen] circuito *m* **-2.** [lap, movement round] volta *f.*
circuit board *n* placa *f* de circuito.
circuit breaker *n* disjuntor *m.*
circuitous [sə'kjuːɪtəs] *adj* tortuoso(sa).
circular ['sɜːkjʊləʳ] ◇ *adj* **-1.** [shape, object] redondo(da) **-2.** [argument] circular. ◇ *n* circular *f.*
circulate ['sɜːkjʊleɪt] ◇ *vi* circular. ◇ *vt* circular.
circulation [ˌsɜːkjʊ'leɪʃn] *n* circulação *f*; **in** ~ em circulação.
circumcise ['sɜːkəmsaɪz] *vt* circuncidar.
circumcision [ˌsɜːkəm'sɪʒn] *n* circuncisão *f.*
circumference [sə'kʌmfərəns] *n* circunferência *f.*
circumflex ['sɜːkəmfleks] *n*: ~ **(accent)** (acento) *m* circunflexo *m.*
circumnavigate [ˌsɜːkəm'nævɪgeɪt] *vt* circunavegar.
circumscribe ['sɜːkəmskraɪb] *vt fml* [restrict] circunscrever.
circumspect ['sɜːkəmspekt] *adj* circunspecto(ta).
circumstances *npl* circunstâncias *fpl*; **under** *OR* **in no** ~ sob *OR* em nenhuma circunstância; **under** *OR* **in the** ~ nas *OR* nestas circunstâncias.
circumstantial [ˌsɜːkəm'stænʃl] *adj fml*: ~ evidence evidência *f* circunstancial.
circumvent [ˌsɜːkəm'vent] *vt fml* burlar.
circus ['sɜːkəs] *n* **-1.** [for entertainment] circo *m* **-2.** [in place names] *no Reino Unido, praça circular à qual convergem várias ruas.*
cirrhosis [sɪ'rəʊsɪs] *n (U)* cirrose *f.*
CIS (*abbr of* **Commonwealth of Independent States**) *n* CEI *f.*
cissy ['sɪsɪ] (*pl* **-ies**) *n UK inf* maricas *m inv.*
cistern ['sɪstən] *n* **-1.** *UK* [in roof] cisterna *f* **-2.** [on lavatory] caixa *f* de descarga.
citation [saɪ'teɪʃn] *n* **-1.** [quotation] citação *f* **-2.** [official praise]: ~ **(for sthg)** menção *f* honrosa (por algo).
cite [saɪt] *vt* citar.
citizen ['sɪtɪzn] *n* [of country, of town] cidadão *m*, -dã *f.*
Citizens' Advice Bureau *n* Centro *m* de Apoio ao Cidadão.
Citizens' Band *n (U)* banda *f* do cidadão.
citizenship ['sɪtɪznʃɪp] *n (U)* cidadania *f.*
citric acid ['sɪtrɪk-] *n (U)* ácido *m* cítrico.
citrus fruit ['sɪtrəs-] *n* fruta *f* cítrica.
city ['sɪtɪ] (*pl* **-ies**) *n* cidade *f.*
➤ **City** *n UK*: **the City** *o bairro financeiro de Londres.*

THE CITY

A *City*, o bairro financeiro de Londres, compõe uma unidade administrativa autônoma da capital inglesa, dotada inclusive de sua própria polícia. É o bairro mais antigo da cidade, conhecido também como *Square Mile*, pelo fato de sua área total ter uma milha quadrada (ou 2,6 km²). Por extensão, *the City* é hoje termo empregado para designar o mundo financeiro britânico.

---

city centre *n* centro *m* da cidade.
city hall *n US* prefeitura *f.*
city technology college *n UK centro de formação técnica profissional custeada por indústrias.*
civic ['sɪvɪk] *adj* cívico(ca).
civic centre *n UK* centro *m* cívico.
civil ['sɪvl] *adj* **-1.** [involving ordinary citizens] civil **-2.** [polite] educado(da).
civil defence *n (U)* defesa *f* civil.
civil disobedience *n (U)* desobediência *f* civil.
civil engineer *n* engenheiro *m*, -ra *f* civil.
civil engineering *n (U)* engenharia *f* civil.
civilian [sɪ'vɪljən] ◇ *n* civil *mf.* ◇ *comp* civil.
civility [sɪ'vɪlətɪ] *n (U)* civilidade *f.*
civilization [ˌsɪvɪlaɪ'zeɪʃn] *n (U)* civilização *f.*
civilize, -ise ['sɪvɪlaɪz] *vt* civilizar.
civilized ['sɪvɪlaɪzd] *adj* civilizado(da).
civil law *n (U)* [relating to private case] direito *m* civil.
civil liberties *npl* liberdades *fpl* civis.
Civil List *n UK verba anual designada pelo Parlamento inglês à Família Real.*
civil rights *npl* direitos *mpl* civis.
civil servant *n* funcionário *m* público, funcionária *f* pública.
civil service *n* serviço *m* público.
civil war *n* guerra *f* civil.

CJD (*abbr of* **Creutzfeldt-Jakob disease**) *n forma humana da doença da vaca louca*, doença f de Creutzfeldt-Jakob.

cl (*abbr of* **centilitre**) *n* cl.

clad [klæd] *adj literary* [dressed]: ~ **in** sthg vestido(da) de algo.

cladding ['klædɪŋ] *n (U) UK* revestimento *m*.

claim [kleɪm] <> *n* -**1.** [assertion] alegação f- **2.** [demand] reivindicação f- **3.** [rightful]: **to have a** ~ **on sb** ter direitos sobre alguém; **to have a** ~ **on sb's attention** reivindicar a atenção de alguém; **to lay** ~ **to sthg** reivindicar algo - **4.** [financial] reclamação f. <> *vt* -**1.** [assert, maintain] alegar; **to** ~ **(that)** alegar que - **2.** [apply for, assert one's rights to] reivindicar - **3.** [take] levar. <> *vi*: **to** ~ **on one's insurance** acionar o seguro; **to** ~ **for sthg** reclamar algo.

claimant ['kleɪmənt] *n* -**1.** [to the throne] pretendente *mf*- **2.** [of benefit, in law case] requerente *mf*.

claim form *n* formulário *m* de reclamação.

clairvoyant [kleə'vɔɪənt] <> *adj* clarividente. <> *n* vidente *mf*.

clam [klæm] (*pt & pp* -**med**, *cont* -**ming**) *n* marisco *m*.

➤ **clam up** *vi inf* fechar a boca.

clamber ['klæmbə[r]] *vi* subir com dificuldade.

clammy ['klæmɪ] (*compar* -**ier**, *superl* -**iest**) *adj inf* melado(da).

clamor *n & vi US* = clamour.

clamorous ['klæmərəs] *adj* clamoroso(sa).

clamour *UK*, **clamor** *US* ['klæmə[r]] <> *n* (U) -**1.** [noise] clamor *m* - **2.** [demand]: ~ **for sthg** queixa f por algo. <> *vi*: **to** ~ **for sthg** queixar-se por algo.

clamp [klæmp] <> *n* -**1.** [fastener] presilha f, braçadeira f- **2.** MED & TECH grampo *m*. <> *vt* -**1.** [with fastener] apertar - **2.** [parked car] pôr travas em.

➤ **clamp down** *vi*: **to** ~ **down (on** sthg**)** impor restrições (a algo).

clampdown ['klæmpdaʊn] *n*: ~ **(on** sthg**)** restrição f (sobre algo).

clan [klæn] *n* clã *m*.

clandestine [klæn'destɪn] *adj* clandestino(na).

clang [klæŋ] <> *n* som *m* metálico, tinido *m*. <> *vi* tinir.

clanger ['klæŋə[r]] *n UK inf* mancada f; **to drop a** ~ dar uma mancada.

clank [klæŋk] <> *n* ruído *m* metálico grave. <> *vi* retinir.

clap [klæp] (*pt & pp* -**ped**, *cont* -**ping**) <> *n* -**1.** [of hands] palmas fpl - **2.** [of thunder] estrondo *m*. <> *vt* -**1.**: **to** ~ **one's hands** bater palmas - **2.** *inf*: **to** ~ **eyes on** sb/sthg botar os olhos em alguém/algo. <> *vi* aplaudir.

clapboard ['klæpbɔːd] *n US* tábua *para revestimento externo da casa ou do edifício*.

clapped-out [klæpt-] *adj UK inf* [machine] caindo aos pedaços.

clapperboard ['klæpəbɔːd] *n* indicador *m* de cenas.

clapping ['klæpɪŋ] *n (U)* aplauso *m*.

claptrap ['klæptræp] *n (U) inf* conversa f mole.

claret ['klærət] *n* -**1.** [wine] clarete *m* - **2.** [colour] cor-de-vinho f.

clarification [ˌklærɪfɪ'keɪʃn] *n* [explanation] esclarecimento *m*.

clarify ['klærɪfaɪ] (*pt & pp* -**ied**) *vt* [explain, expand on] esclarecer.

clarinet [ˌklærə'net] *n* clarinete *m*.

clarity ['klærətɪ] *n (U)* clareza f.

clash [klæʃ] <> *n* -**1.** [of interests, personality] choque *m*; ~ **with sb** choque com alguém - **2.** [disagreement] divergência f; ~ **with sb** divergência com alguém - **3.** [noise] estrépito *m*. <> *vi* -**1.** [be incompatible - ideas, beliefs] chocar-se; [- colours] destoar; **to** ~ **with sthg** destoar de algo - **2.** [fight] chocar-se; **to** ~ **with sb** chocar-se com alguém - **3.** [disagree] divergir; **to** ~ **with sb** divergir de alguém - **4.** [coincide] coincidir; **to** ~ **with sthg** coincidir com algo - **5.** [make noise] soar.

clasp [klɑːsp] <> *n* [fastener] fecho *m*. <> *vt* [hold tight] apertar.

class [klɑːs] <> *n* -**1.** [gen] classe f- **2.** [lesson] aula f - **3.** [category] espécie f; **to be in a** ~ **of one's own** ser excelente. <> *comp* [relating to social groups] de classes. <> *vt* classificar; **to** ~ **sb as** sthg classificar alguém como algo.

class-conscious *adj pej* esnobe.

classic ['klæsɪk] <> *adj* clássico(ca). <> *n* clássico *m*.

➤ **classics** *npl*: **the** ~ os clássicos.

classical ['klæsɪkl] *adj* clássico(ca).

classical music *n (U)* música f clássica.

classicism *n (U)* classicismo *m*.

classicist *n (U)* classicista *mf*.

classification [ˌklæsɪfɪ'keɪʃn] *n* classificação f.

classified ['klæsɪfaɪd] *adj* [secret] confidencial.

classified ad *n* (anúncio *m*) classificado *m*.

classify ['klæsɪfaɪ] (*pt & pp* -**ied**) *vt* classificar.

classless ['klɑːslɪs] *adj* sem classes.

classmate ['klɑːsmeɪt] *n* colega *mf* de classe.

classroom ['klɑːsrʊm] *n* sala f de aula.

classy ['klɑːsɪ] (*compar* -**ier**, *superl* -**iest**) *adj inf* bacana, chique.

clatter ['klætə[r]] <> *n* -**1.** [of pans, dishes] tinido *m* - **2.** [of hooves] repique *m*. <> *vi* -**1.** [pans, dishes] retinir - **2.** [hooves] repicar - **3.** [person]: **to** ~ **in/out/down** entrar/sair/descer fazendo barulho.

clause [klɔːz] *n* -**1.** [in legal document] cláusula f- **2.** GRAMM oração f.

claustrophobia [ˌklɔːstrə'fəʊbjə] *n (U)* claustrofobia f.

claustrophobic [ˌklɔːstrə'fəʊbɪk] *adj* claustrofóbico(ca).

claw [klɔː] <> *n* -**1.** [of wild animal, bird] garra f- **2.** [of cat, dog] unha f- **3.** [of sea creature] pinça f- **4.** [of insect] ferrão f. <> *vt* arranhar; **to** ~ **one's way to** galgar seu caminho para. <> *vi*: **to** ~ **at** sthg agarrar-se a algo.

➤ **claw back** *vt sep UK* recuperar.

clay [kleɪ] *n* argila f, barro *m*.

clay pigeon shooting *n (U)* tiro *m* ao prato.

clean [kliːn] <> *adj* -**1.** [gen] limpo(pa); **to come** ~ **about** sthg *inf* confessar algo - **2.** [blank] em branco - **3.** [inoffensive] inofensivo(va) - **4.** [cut, break] preciso(sa). ⬦ *adv* [completely] completamente. ⬦ *vt* [make clean] limpar; **to ~ one's teeth** *UK* escovar os dentes. ⬦ *vi* fazer faxina. ⬦ *n* faxina *f*; **to give sthg a ~** dar uma limpada em algo.

➤ **clean out** *vt sep* **-1.** [clear out] fazer uma limpeza (em) **-2.** *inf fig* [leave penniless] deixar sem um centavo **-3.** *inf* [take everything from] depenar.

➤ **clean up** ⬦ *vt sep* [clear up] arrumar. ⬦ *vi inf* [win] limpar.

cleaner ['kliːnəʳ] *n* **-1.** [person] faxineiro *m*, -ra *f* **-2.** [substance] produto *m* de limpeza **-3.** [shop]: **~'s** lavanderia *f*.

cleaning ['kliːnɪŋ] *n* (U) limpeza *f*, faxina *f*.

cleaning lady *n* faxineira *f*.

cleanliness ['klenlɪnɪs] *n* (U) limpeza *f*, asseio *m*.

clean-living *adj* de vida limpa.

cleanly ['kliːnlɪ] *adv* com precisão.

cleanness ['kliːnnɪs] *n* (U) limpeza *f*, asseio *m*.

cleanse [klenz] *vt* **-1.** [make clean] limpar **-2.** [make pure] purificar; **to ~ sb/sthg of sthg** livrar alguém/algo de algo.

cleanser ['klenzəʳ] *n* **-1.** [for skin] creme *m* de limpeza **-2.** [detergent] detergente *m*.

clean-shaven [-'ʃevn] *adj* de barba feita.

cleanup ['kliːnʌp] *n* limpeza *f*.

clear [klɪəʳ] ⬦ *adj* **-1.** [gen] claro(ra); **to make sthg ~ (to sb)** tornar algo claro (para alguém); **to make it ~ that** deixar claro que; **to make o.s. ~** fazer-se entender; **to be ~ about sthg** [understand] entender algo com clareza; [explain clearly] fazer-se entender sobre algo; **~ head** mente *f* lúcida **-2.** [obvious, unmistakable] óbvio(via) **-3.** [transparent] transparente **-4.** [water] límpido(da) **-5.** [unobstructed, free] livre **-6.** [conscience] tranqüilo(la) **-7.** [profit] líquido(da). ⬦ *adv* [out of the way]: **to step ~** ficar fora do caminho; **stand ~!** afaste-se!; **to stay** *OR* **steer ~ of sb/sthg** afastar-se de alguém/algo. ⬦ *n*: **in the ~** [out of danger] fora de perigo; [free from suspicion] acima de qualquer suspeita. ⬦ *vt* **-1.** [remove obstacles from - way, path] desimpedir; [- pipe] limpar; [- table] tirar **-2.**: **to ~ one's throat** limpar a garganta **-3.** [take out of the way] retirar **-4.** [jump] transpor **-5.** [pay] saldar **-6.** [authorize] autorizar **-7.** [prove not guilty] livrar de culpa; **to be ~ed of sthg** ser declarado(da) inocente de algo **-8.** [accept for payment] liberar **-9.** [customs] desembaraçar. ⬦ *vi* **-1.** [disperse, diminish - fog, smoke] dissipar-se; [- headache] passar **-2.** [brighten up] clarear.

➤ **clear away** *vt sep* arrumar.

➤ **clear off** *vi UK inf* dar o fora.

➤ **clear out** ⬦ *vt sep* [tidy up] arrumar. ⬦ *vi inf* [leave] dar o fora.

➤ **clear up** ⬦ *vt sep* **-1.** [tidy] arrumar **-2.** [solve, settle] resolver. ⬦ *vi* **-1.** [weather] clarear **-2.** [illness] desaparecer **-3.** [tidy up] arrumar.

clearance ['klɪərəns] *n* (U) **-1.** [removal] retirada *f*; **the ~ of mines** a remoção de minas terrestres; **land ~** a limpeza da terra **-2.** [of contents of house] desocupação *f* **-3.** [permission] autorização *f*; **customs ~** desembaraço *m* alfandegário **-5.** [free space] vão *m* livre; **the bridge has a 12m ~** a ponte tem um vão livre de 12m.

clearance sale *n* liquidação *f*.

clear-cut *adj* bem definido(da).

clear-headed [-'hedɪd] *adj* esperto(ta).

clearing ['klɪərɪŋ] *n* [in forest] clareira *f*.

clearing bank *n UK* banco *m* compensador.

clearing house *n* **-1.** [organization] central *f* de informações **-2.** [bank] carteira *f* de compensação.

clearing up *n* (U) limpeza *f*, arrumação *f*.

clearly ['klɪəlɪ] *adv* **-1.** [distinctly, lucidly] claramente **-2.** [obviously] evidentemente.

clearout ['klɪəraʊt] *n esp UK inf* faxina *f* geral.

clear-sighted [-'saɪtɪd] *adj* [person] perspicaz.

clearway ['klɪəweɪ] *n UK AUT* via *f* expressa.

cleavage ['kliːvɪdʒ] *n* **-1.** [between breasts] decote *m* **-2.** [division] rachadura *f*.

cleave *literary* ⬦ *vt* [split] rachar. ⬦ *vi* [be very attached to]: **to ~ to sb/sthg** ser fiel a alguém/algo.

cleaver ['kliːvəʳ] *n* cutelo *m* de açougueiro.

clef [klef] *n* clave *f*.

cleft [kleft] *n* fenda *f*, rachadura *f*.

cleft palate *n* fenda *f* palatina.

clematis ['klemətɪs] *n* clematite *f*.

clemency ['klemənsɪ] *n* (U) *fml* [mercy] clemência *f*.

clementine ['kleməntaɪn] *n* clementina *f*.

clench [klentʃ] *vt* cerrar; **to have sthg ~ed between one's teeth** ter algo preso entre os dentes.

clergy ['klɜːdʒɪ] *npl*: **the ~** o clero.

clergyman ['klɜːdʒɪmən] (*pl* -men [-mən]) *n* clérigo *m*.

cleric ['klerɪk] *n* clérigo *m*.

clerical ['klerɪkl] *adj* **-1.** [in office] de escritório **-2.** [in church] clerical.

clerk [*UK* klɑːk, *US* klɜːrk] *n* **-1.** [in office] auxiliar *mf* de escritório **-2.** [in court] escriturário *m*, -ria *f*, escrevente *mf* **-3.** *US* [shop assistant] balconista *mf*.

clever ['klevəʳ] *adj* **-1.** [intelligent] inteligente **-2.** [ingenious] engenhoso(sa); **that's ~!** que engenhoso! **-3.** [skilful] hábil.

cleverly ['klevəlɪ] *adv* **-1.** [intelligently] inteligentemente **-2.** [ingeniously] engenhosamente **-3.** [skilfully] habilmente.

cleverness ['klevənɪs] *n* **-1.** [intelligence] esperteza *f*, inteligência *f* **-2.** [ingenuity] engenhosidade *f* **-3.** [skill] habilidade *f*.

cliché ['kliːʃeɪ] *n* clichê *m*.

click [klɪk] ⬦ *n* **-1.** [gen] clique *m* **-2.** [of tongue] estalo *m*. ⬦ *vt* estalar. ⬦ *vi* **-1.** [gen] estalar; **the door ~ed shut** a porta se fechou com um clique **-2.** *inf* [fall into place] cair a ficha **-3.** *COMPUT* clicar.

client ['klaɪənt] *n* cliente *mf*.

clientele [ˌkliːən'tel] *n* (U) clientela *f*, freguesia *f*.

cliff [klɪf] *n* penhasco *m*.

cliffhanger ['klɪfˌhæŋəʳ] *n inf* suspense *m*.

climactic [klaɪ'mæktɪk] *adj* culminante.

climate ['klaɪmɪt] *n* clima *m*.

climatic [klaɪ'mætɪk] *adj* climático(ca).

climate change *n* mudança *f* climática.

climax ['klaɪmæks] *n* clímax *m*.

climb [klaɪm] <> n [ascent] escalada f. <> vt [go up - tree, ladder] subir em; [- hill, mountain] escalar; [- fence] transpor. <> vi -1. [person]: **to ~ up/ down/over** sthg subir em/decer de/transpor algo; **to ~ into/out of** sthg subir em/descer de algo -2. [plant] trepar -3. [road, plane, prices] subir.
◆ **climb down** vi [back down] admitir o erro.
climb-down n retratação f.
climber ['klaɪmə'] n -1. [person] alpinista mf -2. [plant] trepadeira f.
climbing ['klaɪmɪŋ] <> adj [plant] trepadeira. <> n (U) alpinismo m.
climbing frame n UK estrutura feita de metal, madeira ou corda na qual as crianças sobem para brincar.
climes [klaɪmz] npl literary clima m.
clinch [klɪntʃ] vt [settle] fechar.
cling [klɪŋ] (pt & pp clung) vi -1. [person]: **to ~ to** sb/ sthg [physically] agarrar-se a alguém/algo; fig [emotionally: to person] apegar-se a alguém/algo; [to beliefs, ideas, principles] aferrar-se a alguém/algo -2. [clothes]: **to ~ (to** sb) ajustar-se bem (a alguém) -3. [smell] impregnar.
clingfilm ['klɪŋfɪlm] n (U) UK filme m de PVC transparente.
clinging ['klɪŋɪŋ] adj -1. [person, child] apegado(da) -2. [clothes] colado(da).
clinic ['klɪnɪk] n [building] clínica f.
clinical ['klɪnɪkl] adj -1. MED clínico(ca) -2. pej [coldly rational] analítico(ca) -3. [functional] impessoal.
clinically ['klɪnɪklɪ] adv -1. MED clinicamente -2. pej [coldly] analiticamente.
clink [klɪŋk] <> n tilintar m. <> vi tilintar.
clip [klɪp] (pt & pp -ped, cont -ping) <> n -1. [fastener - for paper] clipe m; [- for hair] grampo m; [- for earring] fecho m -2. TV & CINEMA videoclipe m -3. inf [smack]: **to give sb a ~ around the ear** dar um tapa na orelha de alguém. <> vt -1. [fasten] prender -2. [cut - lawn, hedge, nails] cortar; [- newspaper cutting] recortar -3. inf [hit - person] dar um tapa em; [- car] bater em.
◆ **clip on** vi [fasten] segurar, prender.
clipboard ['klɪpbɔːd] n prancheta f com prendedor.
clip-on adj de prender; ~ **earrings** brincos mpl de pressão; ~ **badge** button m; ~ **bow tie** gravata-borboleta f.
clipped [klɪpt] adj [speech] entrecortado(da).
clippers ['klɪpəz] npl -1. [for hair] máquina f de cortar cabelo -2. [for nails] cortador m de unhas -3. [for plants, hedges] tesoura f de podar.
clipping ['klɪpɪŋ] n [newspaper cutting] recorte m.
◆ **clippings** npl [small pieces] fragmentos mpl; **grass/nail ~ s** restos mpl de grama/unha cortada.
clique [kliːk] n pej panelinha f.
clitoris n clitóris m inv.
cloak [kləʊk] <> n -1. [garment] capa f -2. fig [cover for secret] disfarce m. <> vt [hide, disguise] ocultar; **to be ~ ed in** estar envolto(ta) em.
cloak-and-dagger adj misterioso(sa).
cloakroom ['kləʊkrʊm] n -1. [for clothes] guarda-volumes m inv -2. UK [toilet - in public place] banheiro m; [- in house] lavabo m.

clobber ['klɒbə'] inf <> n -1. (U) [things] tralhas fpl -2. (U) [clothes] trapos mpl. <> vt inf -1. [hit] bater -2. [defeat] massacrar -3. [affect very badly] afetar.
clock [klɒk] <> n -1. [timepiece] relógio m; **round the ~** dia e noite; **to put the ~ back** lit atrasar o relógio; fig fazer de conta que nada mudou; **to put the ~ forward** adiantar o relógio -2. [in vehicle - mileometer] hodômetro m; [- speedometer] velocí-metro m. <> vt [reach time or speed] marcar.
◆ **clock in, clock on** vi UK [at work] bater o ponto OR cartão-de-ponto na entrada.
◆ **clock off, clock out** vi UK [at work] bater o ponto OR cartão-de-ponto na saída.
◆ **clock up** vt fus [amass] acumular.
clock radio n rádio-relógio m.
clockwise ['klɒkwaɪz] <> adj em sentido horário. <> adv em sentido horário.
clockwork ['klɒkwɜːk] <> n (U): **to go like ~** funcionar como um relógio. <> comp de corda.
clod [klɒd] n [of earth] torrão m.
clog [klɒg] (pt & pp -ged, cont -ging) vt entupir, bloquear.
◆ **clogs** npl tamancos mpl.
◆ **clog up** <> vt sep -1. [drains] entupir -2. [nose] congestionar. <> vi [drains] entupir; [roads] bloquear; [pores] fechar.
clogged [klɒgd] adj [drains] entupido(da); [roads] bloqueado(da); [pores] fechado(da).
cloister ['klɔɪstə'] n ARCHIT claustro m.
cloistered adj literary [secluded] enclausurado(da), recluso(sa).
clone [kləʊn] <> n clone m. <> vt BIOL clonar.
close¹ [kləʊs] <> adj -1. [near] próximo(ma), perto; ~ **to** sb/sthg perto de alguém/algo; ~ **to tears** à beira das lágrimas; **it was a ~ shave** foi por um fio OR triz; ~ **up**, ~ **to** de perto; ~ **by**, ~ **at hand** bem perto -2. [in relationship] íntimo(ma); ~ **to** sb apegado(da) a alguém -3. [in degree of connection - resemblance, family] próximo(ma); [- link, connection] estreito(ta) -4. [careful]: **a ~ watch** um olhar atento; **to pay ~ attention** prestar muita atenção; ~ **questioning** uma pergunta detalhada; **a ~ r look** um olhar mais de perto; **a ~ r examination** um exame minucioso -5. [oppressive] carregado(-da) -6. [almost equal] com uma pequena margem de diferença. <> adv perto. <> n [street] rua f sem saída.
◆ **close on, close to** prep [almost] cerca de.
close² [kləʊz] <> vt -1. [shut, shut down] fechar -2. [bring to an end] encerrar, concluir. <> vi -1. [shut] fechar -2. [heal] cicatrizar -3. [end] terminar. <> n [end] fim m, final m.
◆ **close down** <> vt sep [shut] fechar. <> vi -1. [shut down] fechar -2. [end] terminar.
◆ **close in** vi -1. [night, fog] fechar -2. [person] cercar; **to ~ in on** sb/sthg cercar alguém/algo.
◆ **close off** vt sep interditar.
close-cropped [kləʊs-] adj rente.
closed [kləʊzd] adj fechado(da).
closed circuit television n televisão f em circuito fechado.
closedown ['kləʊzdaʊn] n -1. UK [of TV, radio station] encerramento m da programação -2. [of factory, mine] fechamento m.

closed shop *n estabelecimento em que todos os trabalhadores devem pertencer a um determinado sindicato.*

close-fitting [ˌkləʊs-] *adj* justo(ta).

close-knit [ˌkləʊs-] *adj* muito unido(da).

closely ['kləʊslɪ] *adv* **-1.** [in degree of connection] intimamente; **to resemble sb/sthg** ~ parecer muito com alguém/algo **-2.** [carefully] atentamente.

closeness ['kləʊsnɪs] *n* (U) **-1.** [of shops, facilities] proximidade *f* **-2.** [of relationship] intimidade *f.*

closeout ['kləʊzaʊt] *n US* liquidação *f.*

close quarters [ˌkləʊs-] *npl*: **at** ~ [very close] muito próximo(ma); *MIL* em contato direto (com o inimigo).

close season ['kləʊs-] *n UK* temporada *f* de caça proibida.

closet ['klɒzɪt] <> *adj inf* inconfesso(sa). <> *n* **-1.** *Am* closet *m*, armário *m* **-2.** *fig*: **to come out of the** ~ sair do armário. <> *vt*: **to be** ~**ed with sb** ficar trancado(da) com alguém.

close-up ['kləʊs-] *n* primeiro plano *m.*

closing ['kləʊzɪŋ] *adj* [final] final, de encerramento.

closing price *n* preço *m OR* cotação *f* de fechamento.

closing time *n* horário *m* de fechamento.

closure ['kləʊʒə'] *n* **-1.** [of business, company] fechamento *m* **-2.** [of road, railway line: temporarily] interdição *f.*

clot [klɒt] (*pt & pp* **-ted**, *cont* **-ting**) <> *n* **-1.** [of blood] coágulo *m* **-2.** *UK inf* [fool] idiota *mf.* <> *vi* [blood] coagular.

cloth [klɒθ] *n* **-1.** (U) [fabric] tecido *m* **-2.** [for cleaning] pano *m* **-3.** [tablecloth] toalha *f.*

clothe [kləʊð] *vt fml* [dress] vestir; ~ **d in** vestido(da) de.

clothes [kləʊðz] *npl* roupa *f*; **to put one's** ~ **on** vestir-se; **to take one's** ~ **off** tirar a roupa.

clothes basket *n* cesto *m* de roupa.

clothes brush *n* escova *f* de roupa.

clothes horse *n* **-1.** [for drying clothes] estendedor *m* de roupa **-2.** *pej* [person] *pessoa que só se preocupa em andar na moda, pouco inteligente e sem habilidades.*

clothesline ['kləʊðzlaɪn] *n* varal *m.*

clothes peg *UK*, **clothespin** *US* ['kləʊðzpɪn] *n* prendedor *m* de roupa.

clothing ['kləʊðɪŋ] *n* (U) roupa *f*; ~ **allowance** auxílio-vestuário *m.*

clotted cream [ˌklɒtɪd-] *n* (U) *UK* creme feito de nata muito espesso, típico da Cornualha.

cloud [klaʊd] <> *n* [gen] nuvem *f*; **to be under a** ~ ter má fama. <> *vt* **-1.** [mist up] embaçar **-2.** [make less pleasant] estragar **-3.** [make less clear]: **to** ~ **the issue** obscurecer a questão.

◆ **cloud over** *vi* **-1.** [sky] encobrir-se **-2.** [face] entristecer-se.

cloudburst ['klaʊdbɜːst] *n* temporal *m* repentino.

cloudless ['klaʊdlɪs] *adj* limpo(pa), sem nuvens.

cloudy ['klaʊdɪ] (*compar* **-ier**, *superl* **-iest**) *adj* **-1.** [sky] nublado(da) **-2.** [liquid] turvo(va).

clout [klaʊt] *inf* <> *n* **-1.** [blow] bofetão *m* **-2.** (U)

[influence] influência *f.* <> *vt* [hit] dar um bofetão em.

clove [kləʊv] *n*: **a** ~ **of garlic** um dente de alho.

◆ **cloves** *npl* [spice] cravo-da-índia *m.*

clover ['kləʊvə'] *n* (U) trevo *m.*

clown [klaʊn] <> *n* **-1.** [performer] palhaço *m* **-2.** [fool] palhaço *m*, -ça *f.* <> *vi* fazer palhaçadas.

cloying ['klɔɪɪŋ] *adj* enjoativo(va).

club [klʌb] (*pt & pp* **-bed**, *cont* **-bing**) <> *n* **-1.** [association] clube *m* **-2.** [nightclub] boate *f*, casa *f* noturna **-3.** [weapon] bastão *m* **-4.** *SPORT* [equipment]: **(golf)** ~ taco *m* (de golfe). <> *comp* do clube. <> *vt* [hit] espancar.

◆ **clubs** *npl* [playing cards] paus *mpl.*

◆ **club together** *vi UK* fazer vaquinha.

club car *n US RAIL* vagão-restaurante *m.*

clubhouse ['klʌbhaʊs] *n* clube *m.*

cluck [klʌk] *vi* [hen, person] cacarejar.

clue [kluː] *n* **-1.** [in crime] pista *f*, vestígio *m*; **I haven't (got) a** ~ não tenho (a menor) idéia **-2.** [hint] dica *f* **-3.** [key to problem]: **the** ~ **(to sthg)** a chave (para algo) **-4.** [in crossword] pista *f.*

clued-up [kluːd-] *adj UK inf* antenado(da).

clueless ['kluːlɪs] *adj UK inf* tapado(da); **she's completely** ~ ela é completamente tapada; **to be** ~ **about sth** não ter a menor idéia sobre algo.

clump [klʌmp] <> *n* [group - of trees] arvoredo *m*; [- of bushes] moita *m*; [- of flowers] ramalhete *m.* <> *vi* [move heavily] mover-se pesadamente.

clumsily ['klʌmzɪlɪ] *adv* **-1.** [move, express o.s.] desajeitadamente **-2.** [designed, executed] grosseiramente.

clumsy ['klʌmzɪ] (*compar* **-ier**, *superl* **-iest**) *adj* **-1.** [gen] desajeitado(da) **-2.** [unwieldy] tosco(ca).

clung [klʌŋ] *pt & pp* ⊳ **cling**.

cluster ['klʌstə'] <> *n* [group - of people, houses, trees] grupo *m*; [- of grapes] cacho *m*; [- of flowers] ramalhete *m.* <> *vi* **-1.** [people] agrupar-se, reunir-se **-2.** [things] amontoar-se.

clutch [klʌtʃ] <> *n AUT* embreagem *f.* <> *vt* [with hands - object] agarrar; [- part of body] apertar. <> *vi*: **to** ~ **at sb/sthg** agarrar-se a alguém/algo.

◆ **clutches** *npl*: **in the** ~**es of** nas garras de.

clutch bag *n* bolsa *f* feminina.

clutter ['klʌtə'] <> *n* bagunça *f.* <> *vt* bagunçar.

cm (*abbr of* centimetre) *n* cm.

CNAA (*abbr of* **Council for National Academic Awards**) *n organismo britânico que outorga diplomas de cursos superiores de instituições que não possuem status de universidade.*

CND (*abbr of* **Campaign for Nuclear Disarmament**) *n organização britânica que realiza campanhas contra o armamento nuclear.*

c/o (*abbr of* care of) a/c.

co- [kəʊ] *prefix* co.

Co. -1. (*abbr of* **Company**) Cia. **- 2.** (*abbr of* **County**) *área administrativa britânica, usada, em alguns casos, na representação de endereços.*

CO <> *n* **-1.** (*abbr of* commanding officer) com. **- 2.** (*abbr of* **Commonwealth Office**) *ministério para as relações com o Commonwealth britânico.* **-3.** (*abbr of* **conscientious objector**) *aquele que não é voluntário para entrar nas forças armadas por* *razões morais.* <> *abbr of* Colorado.

coach [kəʊtʃ] <> *n* -1. *UK* [bus] ônibus *m inv* -2. *RAIL* vagão *m* -3. [horsedrawn] carruagem *f* -4. *SPORT* treinador *m*, -ra *f* -5. [tutor] professor *m*, -ra *f* particular. <> *vt* -1. *SPORT* treinar -2. [tutor] preparar; **to ~ sb in sthg** preparar alguém em algo.

coaching [ˈkəʊtʃɪŋ] *n (U)* -1. *SPORT* treinamento *m* -2. [tutoring] preparação, *f*.

coach station *n UK* (estação *f*) rodoviária *f*.

coach trip *n UK* passeio *m* de ônibus.

coagulate [kəʊˈægjʊleɪt] *vi* coagular.

coal [kəʊl] *n (U)* carvão *m*.

coalesce [ˌkəʊəˈles] *vi fml* fundir-se.

coalface [ˈkəʊlfeɪs] *n* veio *m* de carvão.

coalfield [ˈkəʊlfiːld] *n* jazida *f* de carvão.

coal gas *n (U)* gás *m* de carvão.

coalition [ˌkəʊəˈlɪʃn] *n POL* coalizão *f*.

coal mine *n* mina *f* de carvão.

coal miner *n* minerador *m*, -ra *f* de carvão.

coal mining *n (U)* mineração *f* de carvão.

coarse [kɔːs] *adj* -1. [rough] áspero(ra) -2. [vulgar] grosseiro(ra).

coarsen [ˈkɔːsn] <> *vt* -1. [make vulgar] deixar grosso(sa) -2. [make rough] deixar áspero(ra). <> *vi* -1. [become vulgar] vulgarizar-se -2. [become rough] tornar-se áspero(ra).

coast [kəʊst] <> *n* costa *f*. <> *vi* -1. [car] ir em ponto morto -2. *fig* [through life, exam] passar; **to ~ through life** deixar a vida passar; **to be ~ing happily along** estar curtindo o momento.

coastal [ˈkəʊstl] *adj* costeiro(ra); **a ~ town** uma cidade litorânea.

coaster [ˈkəʊstə^r] *n* -1. [small mat] descanso *m* para copos -2. *UK* [ship] navio *m* costeiro.

coastguard [ˈkəʊstgɑːd] *n* -1. [person] guarda *mf* costeiro, -ra -2. [organization]: **the ~** a guarda costeira.

coastline [ˈkəʊstlaɪn] *n* litoral *m*.

coat [kəʊt] <> *n* -1. [garment] casaco *m* -2. [of animal] pêlo *m* -3. [of paint, varnish] demão *f*. <> *vt*: **to ~ sthg (with sthg)** revestir algo (com algo).

coat hanger *n* cabide *m*.

coating [ˈkəʊtɪŋ] *n* [covering - of chocolate, icing] cobertura *f*; [- of dust] camada *f*.

coat of arms *(pl* coats of arms) *n* brasão *m*.

coat stand *n* cabide *m*.

coat-tails *npl* -1. abas *fpl* (de casaca); **on sb's ~ fig** na esteira de alguém.

co-author <> *n* co-autor *m*, -ra *f*. <> *vt*: **to ~** ser co-autor(ra) de.

coax [kəʊks] *vt*: **to ~ sb (to do OR into doing sthg)** persuadir alguém (a fazer algo); **to ~ sthg out of sb** conseguir algo de alguém com jeitinho.

coaxial cable [kəʊˈæksɪəl-] *n COMPUT* cabo *m* coaxial.

cobalt [ˈkəʊbɔːlt] *n* cobalto *m*.

cobble ◆ **cobble together** *vt sep* deixar alinhavado(da).

cobbled [ˈkɒbld] *adj* de pedras arredondadas.

cobbler [ˈkɒblə^r] *n* sapateiro *m*, -ra *f*.

cobbles [ˈkɒblz], **cobblestones** [ˈkɒblstəʊnz] *npl* pedras arredondadas (para pavimentação).

COBOL (*abbr of* Common Business Oriented Language) *n (U) COMPUT* COBOL.

cobra [ˈkəʊbrə] *n* naja *f*.

cobweb [ˈkɒbweb] *n* teia *f* de aranha.

Coca-Cola® [ˌkəʊkəˈkəʊlə] *n* Coca-Cola® *f*.

cocaine [kəʊˈkeɪn] *n (U)* cocaína *f*.

cock [kɒk] <> *n* -1. *UK* [male chicken] galo *m* -2. [male bird] pássaro *m* macho -3. *vulg* [penis] pinto *m*. <> *vt* -1. [gun] engatilhar -2. [head] virar.

◆ **cock up** *vt sep UK vulg*: **the project was going fine, but they ~ed it up** o projeto estava indo bem, mas eles acabaram fodendo tudo.

cock-a-hoop *adj inf* [delighted] exultante.

cock-and-bull story *n inf* história *f* para boi dormir.

cockatoo [ˌkɒkəˈtuː] *(pl* -s) *n* cacatua *f*.

cockerel [ˈkɒkrəl] *n* frango *m*.

cocker spaniel [ˌkɒkə-] *n* cocker spaniel *mf*.

cockeyed [ˈkɒkaɪd] *adj inf* -1. [not straight] torto(ta) -2. [unlikely to succeed] absurdo(da).

cockfight [ˈkɒkfaɪt] *n* rinha *f*.

cockle [ˈkɒkl] *n* [shellfish] berbigão *m*.

Cockney [ˈkɒknɪ] *(pl* Cockneys) <> *n* -1. [person] pessoa vinda da área leste de Londres, em geral da classe trabalhadora -2. [accent] cockney *m*. <> *comp* de cockney.

cockpit [ˈkɒkpɪt] *n* -1. [in plane] cabine *f* de comando -2. [in F1 car] cockpit *m*.

cockroach [ˈkɒkrəʊtʃ] *n* barata *f*.

cocksure [ˌkɒkˈʃʊə^r] *adj* convencido(da).

cocktail [ˈkɒkteɪl] *n* [drink] coquetel *m*.

cocktail party *n* coquetel *m*.

cocktail shaker [-ˌʃeɪkə^r] *n* coqueteleira *f*.

cocktail stick *n* garfo *m* para coquetéis.

cock-up *n vinf* cagada *f*.

cocky [ˈkɒkɪ] *(compar* -ier, *superl* -iest) *adj inf* petulante.

cocoa [ˈkəʊkəʊ] *n (U)* -1. [powder] cacau *m* -2. [drink] chocolate *m*.

coconut [ˈkəʊkənʌt] *n* coco *m*.

cocoon [kəˈkuːn] <> *n* casulo *m*. <> *vt* [protect from reality] preservar.

cod [kɒd] *(pl inv OR* -s) *n* bacalhau *m*.

COD -1. (*abbr of* cash on delivery) entrega contra pagamento. -2. (*abbr of* collect on delivery) entrega contra pagamento.

code [kəʊd] <> *n* código *m*. <> *vt* -1. [encode] codificar -2. [give identifier to] identificar como.

coded [ˈkəʊdɪd] *adj* [written in code] em código.

codeine [ˈkəʊdiːn] *n (U)* codeína *f*.

code name *n* pseudônimo *m*.

code of practice *n* código *m* de conduta.

cod-liver oil *n (U)* óleo *m* de fígado de bacalhau.

codswallop [ˈkɒdzˌwɒləp] *n (U) UK inf* asneira *f*.

coed <> *adj* (*abbr of* co-educational) relativo à escola mista. <> *n* -1. (*abbr of* co-educational student) aluno de escola mista nos Estados Unidos. -2. (*abbr of* co-educational school) escola mista na Grã-Bretanha.

coeducational [ˌkəʊedjuːˈkeɪʃənl] *adj* [school] misto(ta).

coefficient [ˌkəʊɪˈfɪʃnt] *n* coeficiente *m*.

coerce [kəʊˈɜːs] *vt*: **to ~ sb (into doing sthg)**

coagir alguém(a fazer algo).

coercion [kəʊ'ɜ:ʃn] n (U) coerção f.

coexist [ˌkəʊɪg'zɪst] vi coexistir.

coexistence [ˌkəʊɪg'zɪstəns] n (U) coexistência f.

C. of E. (abbr of Church of England) n igreja anglicana.

coffee ['kɒfɪ] n [drink] café m.

coffee bar n UK lanchonete f.

coffee beans npl grãos mpl de café.

coffee break n intervalo m para o café, coffee break m.

coffee cup n xícara f de café.

coffee-maker n cafeteira f.

coffee mill n moedor m de café.

coffee morning n UK evento social, realizado durante o café da manhã, cuja finalidade é arrecadar dinheiro para organizações beneficentes.

coffee pot n bule m para café.

coffee shop n - 1. UK [café] café m - 2. US [restaurant] cafeteria f - 3. [shop selling coffee] cafeteria f.

coffee table n mesinha f de centro.

coffee-table book n livro m de gravuras.

coffers ['kɒfəz] npl fundos mpl, quantia f disponível.

coffin ['kɒfɪn] n caixão m.

cog [kɒg] n [tooth on wheel] dente m de engrenagem; [wheel] roda f dentada; **a ~ in the machine** fig uma peça secundária.

cogent ['kəʊdʒənt] adj irrefutável.

cogitate ['kɒdʒɪteɪt] vi fml cogitar.

cognac ['kɒnjæk] n conhaque m.

cognitive ['kɒgnɪtɪv] adj cognitivo(va).

cogwheel ['kɒgwi:l] n roda f dentada.

cohabit [ˌkəʊ'hæbɪt] vi: to ~ (with sb) coabitar (com alguém).

coherent [kəʊ'hɪərənt] adj coerente.

coherently [kəʊ'hɪərəntlɪ] adv coerentemente.

cohesion [kəʊ'hi:ʒn] n (U) [unity] coesão f.

cohesive [kəʊ'hi:sɪv] adj [united] coeso(sa).

cohort ['kəʊhɔ:t] n - 1. pej [companion] bando m - 2. [in statistics] grupo m.

COI (abbr of Central Office of Information) n serviço de informação do governo britânico.

coil [kɔɪl] <> n - 1. [of rope, wire] rolo m - 2. [of smoke] espiral f - 3. ELEC bobina f - 4. UK [contraceptive device] DIU m. <> vt enrolar. <> vi enrolar-se, enroscar-se.

→ **coil up** vt sep enrolar-se.

coiled [kɔɪld] adj enrolado(da).

coin [kɔɪn] <> n moeda f. <> vt [invent] criar; **to ~ a phrase** como se pode dizer.

coinage ['kɔɪnɪdʒ] n - 1. (U) [currency] moeda f - 2. (U) [system] sistema m monetário - 3. [invented word, phrase] invenção f.

coincide [ˌkəʊɪn'saɪd] vi - 1. [occur simultaneously]: to ~ (with sthg) coincidir (com algo) - 2. [be in agreement] coincidir.

coincidence [kəʊ'ɪnsɪdəns] n [chance event] coincidência f.

coincidental [kəʊˌɪnsɪ'dentl] adj coincidente.

coincidentally [kəʊˌɪnsɪ'dentəlɪ] adv coincidentemente.

coin-operated [-'ɒpəˌreɪtɪd] adj que funciona com moedas.

coitus ['kɔɪtəs] n (U) fml coito m.

coke [kəʊk] n - 1. [fuel] coque m - 2. inf [cocaine] coca f.

Coke® [kəʊk] n Coca® f.

Col. (abbr of colonel) cel.

cola ['kəʊlə] n refrigerante m de cola.

COLA (abbr of cost-of-living adjustment) n na Grã-Bretanha, atualização salarial feita de acordo com o custo de vida.

colander ['kʌləndəˈ] n coador m.

cold [kəʊld] <> adj frio (fria); **to feel ~** [person] sentir frio; **to be ~** [person] estar com frio; **it's ~ today** está frio hoje; **to get ~** [person] ficar com frio; [food] esfriar. <> n - 1. [illness] resfriado m; **to catch (a) ~** pegar um resfriado - 2. (U) [low temperature]: **the ~** o frio.

cold-blooded [-'blʌdɪd] adj - 1. BIOL de sangue frio - 2. [unfeeling] frio (fria) - 3. [ruthless - killer, murderer] de sangue frio; [- killing, murder] a sangue frio.

cold cream n (U) creme m para a pele.

cold cuts npl US frios mpl.

cold feet npl: **to have** OR **get ~** inf amarelar.

cold-hearted [-'hɑ:tɪd] adj insensível.

coldly ['kəʊldlɪ] adv friamente.

coldness ['kəʊldnɪs] n (U) - 1. [low temperature] friagem f - 2. [attitude, response] frieza f.

cold shoulder n: **to give sb the ~** inf dar um gelo em alguém.

cold sore n herpes m inv bucal.

cold storage n (U) [of food] refrigeração f.

cold sweat n suor m frio; **to be in a ~ about sthg** suar frio por causa de algo.

cold war n: **the ~** a guerra fria.

coleslaw ['kəʊlslɔ:] n (U) salada f de repolho.

colic ['kɒlɪk] n (U) cólica f.

collaborate [kə'læbəreɪt] vi - 1. [work together] colaborar; **to ~ with sb** colaborar com alguém - 2. pej [with enemy] conspirar; **to ~ with sb** conspirar com alguém.

collaboration [kəˌlæbə'reɪʃn] n - 1. (U) [teamwork] colaboração f; **~ with sb** colaboração com alguém - 2. pej [with enemy] conspiração f; **~ with sb** conspiração com alguém.

collaborative [kə'læbərətɪv] adj conjunto(ta).

collaborator [kə'læbəreɪtəˈ] n - 1. [colleague] colaborador m, -ra f - 2. pej [traitor] traidor m, -ra f.

collage ['kɒlɑ:ʒ] n colagem f.

collagen ['kɒlədʒən] n (U) colágeno m.

collapse [kə'læps] <> n (U) - 1. [gen] colapso m - 2. [of building, roof] desmoronamento m. <> vi - 1. [gen] desmoronar - 2. [fail] fracassar - 3. [person] ter um colapso; **his lung ~d** o pulmão dele entrou em falência; **to ~ with a heart attack** ter um ataque do coração; **I ~d into bed** desfaleci na cama - 4. [folding table, chair] desmontar-se.

collapsible [kə'læpsəbl] adj desmontável.

collar ['kɒləˈ] <> n - 1. [on garment - shirt] colarinho m; [- dress, jacket] gola f - 2. [for dog] coleira f - 3. TECH anel m. <> vt inf [detain] segurar.

collarbone ['kɒləbəʊn] n clavícula f.

collate [kə'leɪt] vt - 1. [compare] confrontar - 2. [put in order] ordenar.

collateral [kɒ'lætərəl] *n (U)* garantia *f* de empréstimo, caução *f*.

collation [kə'leɪʃn] *n (U)* **-1.** [comparison] confrontação *f* **-2.** [ordering] ordenação *f*.

colleague ['kɒliːg] *n* colega *mf*.

collect [kə'lekt] <> *vt* **-1.** [gather together - wood, bottles, belongings] juntar; [- material for book] colher, coletar: **to ~ o.s.** *OR* **one's thoughts** recompor-se **-2.** [as a hobby] colecionar **-3.** [fetch, pick up] buscar **-4.** [money, taxes] cobrar; **~ on delivery** *US* cobrar na entrega. <> *vi* **-1.** [crowd, people] reunir-se **-2.** [dust, dirt] juntar **-3.** [for charity, gift] arrecadar. <> *adv US TELEC*: **to call (sb) ~** ligar (para alguém) a cobrar.

   collect up *vt sep* juntar.

collectable [kə'lektəbl] <> *adj* [desirable to collectors] de coleção. <> *n* [desirable object] colecionável *m*.

collected [kə'lektɪd] *adj* **-1.** [person] controlado(da) **-2.** [works, poems] completo(ta).

collecting [kə'lektɪŋ] *n (U)* [hobby] coleção *f*; **stamp ~** colecionar selos.

collection [kə'lekʃn] *n* **-1.** [of objects] coleção *f* **-2.** [anthology] antologia *f* **-3.** *(U)* [act of collecting] coleta *f* **-4.** [of money] arrecadação *f*, vaquinha *f*; **they made a ~ to buy flowers for her** fizeram uma vaquinha para comprar flores para ela.

collective [kə'lektɪv] <> *adj* coletivo(va). <> *n* cooperativa *f*.

collective bargaining *n (U)* negociações *fpl* *(entre empregadores e sindicatos)*.

collectively [kə'lektɪvlɪ] *adv* coletivamente.

collective ownership *n (U)* propriedade *f* conjunta.

collector [kə'lektəʳ] *n* **-1.** [as a hobby] colecionador *m*, -ra *f* **-2.** [of taxes] coletor *m*, -ra *f* **-3.** [of debts, rent] cobrador *m*, -ra *f*.

collector's item *n* peça *f* de coleção.

college ['kɒlɪdʒ] *n* **-1.** [for further education] escola *f*; **a ~ of technology** um instituto de tecnologia; **art ~** escola de artes; **community ~** *US* escola politécnica **-2.** *UK* [of university] *instituição dentro de certas universidades britânicas que possui corpo docente, instalações e estudantes próprios* **-3.** [organized body] colégio *m*; **electoral ~** colégio eleitoral.

college of education *n* faculdade *f* de educação.

collide [kə'laɪd] *vi*: **to ~ (with sb/sthg)** colidir (com alguém/algo).

collie ['kɒlɪ] *n* collie *m*.

colliery ['kɒljərɪ] *(pl* -ies*)* *n UK* mina *f* de carvão *(incluindo suas instalações)*.

collision [kə'lɪʒn] *n* **-1.** [crash]: **~ (with sb/sthg)** colisão *f* (com alguém/algo); **~ between** colisão de **-2.** *fig* [conflict] conflito *m*; **head-on ~** colisão *f* frontal.

collision course *n*: **to be on a ~** estar em rota de colisão.

colloquial [kə'ləʊkwɪəl] *adj* coloquial.

colloquialism [ka'ləʊkwɪəlɪzm] *n* coloquialismo *m*.

collude [kə'luːd] *vi*: **to ~ with sb** entrar em conluio com alguém.

collusion [kə'luːʒn] *n*: **in ~ with** em conluio com.

cologne [kə'ləʊn] *n (U)* água-de-colônia *f*.

Colombia [kə'lɒmbɪə] *n* Colômbia; **in ~** na Colômbia.

Colombian [kə'lɒmbɪən] <> *adj* colombiano(na). <> *n* colombiano *m*, -na *f*.

colon ['kəʊlən] *n* **-1.** *ANAT* cólon *m* **-2.** [punctuation mark] dois-pontos *mpl*.

colonel ['kɜːnl] *n* coronel *m*.

colonial [kə'ləʊnjəl] *adj* [rule, power] colonial.

colonialism [kə'ləʊnjəlɪzm] *n (U)* colonialismo *m*.

colonist ['kɒlənɪst] *n* colonizador *m*, -ra *f*.

colonize, -ise ['kɒlənaɪz] *vt* colonizar.

colonnade [ˌkɒlə'neɪd] *n* colunata *f*.

colony ['kɒlənɪ] *(pl* -ies*)* *n* **-1.** [gen] colônia *f* **-2.** [of artists] retiro *m*.

color etc *US* = **colour etc**.

colorado beetle *n* doríforo *m*.

colossal [kə'lɒsl] *adj* colossal.

colostomy [kə'lɒstəmɪ] *(pl* -ies*)* *n* colostomia *f*.

colour *UK*, **color** *US* ['kʌləʳ] <> *n* cor *f*; **red/blue in ~** na cor vermelha/azul; **the photos are in ~** as fotos são coloridas. <> *adj* colorido(da); **~ television/diagram** televisão/diagrama em cores. <> *vt* **-1.** [food, liquid] tingir; [with pen, crayon] pintar, colorir **-2.** [dye] tingir **-3.** *fig* [affect] influenciar. <> *vi* [blush] corar.

   colours *npl* **-1.** [of school, team] cores *fpl* **-2.** [flag] bandeira *f*.

   colour in *vt sep* colorir.

colour bar *n* discriminação *f* racial.

colour blind *adj* **-1.** daltônico(ca) **-2.** *fig* [racially unprejudiced] que não faz discriminação racial.

colour-coded *adj* identificado(da) *OR* codificado(da) por cores.

coloured *UK*, **colored** *US* ['kʌləd] *adj* **-1.** [having colour] colorido(da) **-2.** [having stated colour]: **a cream-~ ed jacket** uma jaqueta cor de creme; **a brightly ~ed shirt** uma camisa de cores vivas.

colourfast *UK*, **colorfast** *US* ['kʌləfɑːstl] *adj* de cores firmes.

colourful *UK*, **colorful** *US* ['kʌləfʊl] *adj* **-1.** [brightly coloured] colorido(da) **-2.** [story] vivo(va) **-3.** [person] animado(da).

colouring *UK*, **coloring** *US* ['kʌlərɪŋ] *n* **-1.** [dye] corante *m* **-2.** *(U)* [complexion, hair] tonalidade *f* **-3.** [colours] cor *m*.

colourless *UK*, **colorless** *US* ['kʌləlɪs] *adj* **-1.** [not coloured] incolor **-2.** *fig* [uninteresting] sem graça.

colour scheme *n* distribuição *f* de cores.

colour supplement *n UK* suplemento *m* em cores.

colt [kəʊlt] *n* [young horse] pôtro *m*.

column ['kɒləm] *n* **-1.** [gen] coluna *f* **-2.** [of people, vehicles] fila *f*.

columnist ['kɒləmnɪst] *n* colunista *mf*.

coma ['kəʊmə] *n* coma *m*.

comatose ['kəʊmətəʊs] *adj* [in a coma] em coma.

comb [kəʊm] <> *n* [for hair] pente *m*. <> *vt* **-1.** [hair] pentear **-2.** *fig* [search] vasculhar.

combat ['kɒmbæt] <> *n* combate *m*. <> *vt* [fight] combater.

combative ['kɒmbətɪv] *adj* combativo(va).

combination [ˌkɒmbɪ'neɪʃn] n combinação f.
combination lock n fechadura f com segredo.
combine [vb kəm'baɪn, n 'kɒmbaɪn] <> vt [join together] agrupar; **to ~ sthg with sthg** [two substances] combinar algo com algo; [two qualities] reunir; [two activities] conjugar. <> vi [businesses, political parties]: **to ~ (with sb/sthg)** aliar-se (a alguém/algo). <> n -1. [group] associação f -2. = **combine harvester**.
combined adj: **~ (with sb/sthg)** conjunto(ta) (com alguém/algo).
combine harvester [-'hɑːvɪstəʳ] n colheitadeira f.
combustible [kəm'bʌstəbl] adj [substance] combustível.
combustion [kəm'bʌstʃn] n (U) combustão f.
come [kʌm] (pt came, pp come) vi -1. [move] vir; [arrive] chegar; **the news came as a shock** a notícia foi um choque; **coming!** estou indo; **the time has ~** chegou a hora; **he doesn't know whether he's coming or going** fig ele não sabe o que fazer -2. [reach]: **to ~ up/down to** chegar a -3. [happen] chegar a; **how did you ~ to fail your exam?** como que você foi rodar no exame?; **~ what may** haja o que houver -4. [become]: **to ~ true** tornar-se realidade; **to ~ undone/unstuck** se desfazer/soltar -5. [begin gradually]: **to ~ to do sthg** passar a fazer algo -6. [be placed in order] classificar-se; **P ~s before Q** o P vem antes do Q; **she came second in the exam** ela se classificou em segundo lugar no exame -7. v inf [sexually] gozar -8. phr: **~ to think of it** pensando bem.
➤ **to come** adv vindouro(ra); **in (the) days/years to ~** nos dias/anos vindouros.
➤ **come about** vi [happen] acontecer.
➤ **come across** <> vt fus [find] encontrar. <> vi [speaker, message] apresentar-se; **to ~ across as** parecer.
➤ **come along** vi -1. [arrive by chance] aparecer -2. [improve] desenvolver-se; **the project is coming along nicely** o projeto está se desenvolvendo bem -3. phr: **~ along!** [expressing encouragement] anda!; [hurry up] anda logo!
➤ **come apart** vi -1. [fall to pieces] desfazer-se -2. [come off] cair.
➤ **come at** vt fus [attack] avançar para.
➤ **come back** vi -1. [in talk, writing]: **to ~ back to sthg** voltar a algo -2. [memory]: **to ~ back (to sb)** lembrar(-se) de -3. [become fashionable again] voltar.
➤ **come by** vt fus -1. [get, obtain] conseguir -2. US [visit, drop in on] dar uma chegada.
➤ **come down** vi -1. [unemployment, prices] baixar -2. [aeroplane, parachutist] descer -3. [rain] cair.
➤ **come down to** vt fus resumir-se a.
➤ **come down with** vt fus [cold, flu] apanhar.
➤ **come forward** vi [witnesses, volunteers] apresentar-se.
➤ **come from** vt fus vir de.
➤ **come in** vi -1. [enter] entrar -2. [arrive, be received] chegar -3. [be involved] entrar.
➤ **come in for** vt fus [criticism] receber.
➤ **come into** vt fus -1. [inherit] receber -2. [begin to be]: **to ~ into being** surgir; **to ~ into sight** aparecer.

➤ **come of** vt fus [result from] dar em; **no good will ~ of it** isso não vai acabar bem.
➤ **come off** vi -1. [button, label, lid] abrir -2. [attempt, joke] dar certo -3. [finish]: **to ~ off well/badly** sair-se bem/mal -4. [stain] sair -5. phr: **~ off it!** inf deixa disso!
➤ **come on** vi -1. [start] começar -2. [light, heating] ligar-se -3. [progress, improve] ir; **how's the work coming on?** como está indo o trabalho? -4. phr: **~ on!** [expressing encouragement] vamos lá!; [hurry up] vamos; [expressing disbelief] que é isso.
➤ **come out** vi -1. [truth, fact] revelar-se -2. [product, book, film] ser lançado -3. [finish] acabar; **to ~ out well/badly** sair(-se) bem/mal -4. [go on strike] entrar em greve -5. [declare publicly]: **to ~ out for/against sthg** manifestar-se a favor/contra algo -6. [photograph] sair -7. [sun, moon, stars] aparecer.
➤ **come out in** vt fus: **to ~ out in spots** ficar com manchas.
➤ **come out with** vt fus [remark] sair com.
➤ **come over** vt fus [subj: sensation, emotion] tomar conta de.
➤ **come round** vi -1. [change opinion]: **to ~ round (to sthg)** concordar (com algo) -2. [regain consciousness] voltar a si -3. [Christmas, birthday, summer] chegar.
➤ **come through** <> vt fus [survive] sobreviver a. <> vi -1. [news, reports, results] chegar -2. [survive] sobreviver.
➤ **come to** <> vt fus -1. [reach]: **to ~ to an end** chegar ao fim; **to ~ to power** chegar ao poder; **to ~ to a decision** chegar a uma decisão -2. [amount to] chegar a. <> vi [regain consciousness] voltar a si.
➤ **come under** vt fus -1. [be governed by] ser de competência de -2. [heading] aparecer em -3. [suffer]: **to ~ under attack (from)** sofrer ataque (de).
➤ **come up** vi -1. [gen] surgir -2. [be imminent] estar próximo.
➤ **come up against** vt fus [opposition, difficulties] enfrentar.
➤ **come upon** vt fus [find] encontrar.
➤ **come up to** vt fus -1. [in space] chegar até; [in time] estar chegando -2. [equal] comparar-se.
➤ **come up with** vt fus [answer, idea, solution] aparecer com.
comeback ['kʌmbæk] n [return] reaparecimento m; **to make a ~** reaparecer.
comedian [kə'miːdjən] n [comic] comediante m.
comedienne [kəˌmiːdɪ'en] n [comic] comediante f.
comedown ['kʌmdaʊn] n inf [anticlimax] retrocesso m.
comedy ['kɒmədɪ] (pl -ies) n comédia f.
comely ['kʌmlɪ] adj literary atraente.
come-on n inf: **to give sb the ~** estar a fim de alguém.
comet ['kɒmɪt] n cometa m.
come-uppance [ˌkʌm'ʌpəns] n inf: **to get one's ~** levar o troco.
comfort ['kʌmfət] <> n -1. (U) [ease] conforto m;

too close for ~ desconfortável devido à proximidade -**2.** [luxury] luxo *m* -**3.** [solace] consolo *m*. <> *vt* consolar.

comfortable [ˈkʌmftəbl] *adj* -**1.** [chair, room] confortável -**2.** [at ease] à vontade -**3.** [financially secure] bem de vida -**4.** [after operation, accident] bem -**5.** [ample] amplo(pla).

comfortably [ˈkʌmftəblɪ] *adv* -**1.** [sit, sleep] confortavelmente -**2.** [without financial difficulty] bem; **I can manage** ~ **on £50 a week** posso me virar bem com 50 libras por semana; ~ **off** em boa situação -**3.** [win] com facilidade.

comforter [ˈkʌmfətəʳ] *n* -**1.** [person] consolador *m*, -ra *f* -**2.** *US* [quilt] edredon *m*.

comforting [ˈkʌmfətɪŋ] *adj* [thought, words] consolador(ra), confortante.

comfort station *n US euph* banheiro *m* público.

comfy [ˈkʌmfɪ] (*compar* -**ier**, *superl* -**iest**) *adj inf* -**1.** [chair, room] confortável -**2.** [person] à vontade.

comic [ˈkɒmɪk] <> *adj* [amusing] engraçado(da). <> *n* -**1.** [comedian] comediante *mf* -**2.** [magazine] história *f* em quadrinhos, gibi *m*.
↪ **comics** *npl US* [in newspaper] tira *f* em quadrinhos.

comical [ˈkɒmɪkl] *adj* [amusing] engraçado(da).

comic strip *n* tira *f* em quadrinhos.

coming [ˈkʌmɪŋ] <> *adj* [future] próximo(ma). <> *n*: ~ **s and goings** idas *fpl* e vindas.

comma [ˈkɒmə] *n* vírgula *f*.

command [kəˈmɑːnd] <> *n* -**1.** [order] comando *m* -**2.** (*U*) [control] comando *m*; **in** ~ **of sthg** no comando de algo -**3.** [mastery] domínio *m*; **at one's** ~ à disposição; **she has four languages at her** ~ ela domina quatro idiomas -**4.** *COMPUT* comando *m*. <> *vt* -**1.** [order] mandar; **to** ~ **sb to do sthg** mandar alguém fazer algo -**2.** *MIL* [control] comandar -**3.** [deserve] merecer.

commandant [ˌkɒmənˈdænt] *n* comandante *mf*.

commandeer [ˌkɒmənˈdɪəʳ] *vt* confiscar.

commander [kəˈmɑːndəʳ] *n* -**1.** [in army] comandante *mf* -**2.** [in navy] capitão *m*, -tã *f*.

commander in chief (*pl* **commanders in chief**) *n* comandante-chefe *m*.

commanding [kəˈmɑːndɪŋ] *adj* -**1.** [lead, position] de comando -**2.** [voice, manner] autoritário(ria) -**3.** [view] dominante.

commanding officer *n* comandante *mf*.

commandment [kəˈmɑːndmənt] *n* RELIG mandamento *m*.

command module *n* módulo *m* de comando.

commando [kəˈmɑːndəʊ] (*pl* -**s** OR -**es**) *n* -**1.** [unit] unidade *f* de assalto -**2.** [soldier] soldado *m* da unidade de assalto.

command performance *n* no *Reino Unido, espetáculo feito por ordem superior.*

commemorate [kəˈmeməreɪt] *vt* homenagear.

commemoration [kəˌmeməˈreɪʃn] *n*: **in** ~ **of** em homenagem a.

commemorative [kəˈmemərətɪv] *adj* comemorativo(va).

commence [kəˈmens] *fml* <> *vt* principiar; **to** ~ **doing sthg** principiar algo. <> *vi* principiar.

commencement [kəˈmensmənt] *n fml* [beginning] princípio *m*.

commend [kəˈmend] *vt* -**1.** [praise]: **to** ~ **sb (on** OR **for sthg)** elogiar alguém (por algo) -**2.** [recommend]: **to** ~ **sthg (to sb)** recomendar algo (a alguém); **we** ~ **our souls to God** encomendamos nossas almas a Deus.

commendable [kəˈmendəbl] *adj* louvável.

commendation [ˌkɒmenˈdeɪʃn] *n* [special award] condecoração *f*.

commensurate [kəˈmenʃərət] *adj fml*: ~ **with** sthg proporcional a algo.

comment [ˈkɒment] <> *n* comentário *m*; **no** ~ sem comentários. <> *vt*: **to** ~ **that** comentar que. <> *vi* comentar; **to** ~ **on** sthg comentar algo.

commentary [ˈkɒməntrɪ] (*pl* -**ies**) *n* -**1.** RADIO & TV comentário *m* -**2.** [written explanation, comment] crítica *f*.

commentate [ˈkɒmənteɪt] *vi* RADIO & TV: **to** ~ **(on** sthg) narrar (algo).

commentator [ˈkɒmənteɪtəʳ] *n* -**1.** [RADIO & TV - making comments] comentarista *mf*; [- describing] narrador *m*, -ra *f* -**2.** [expert] analista *mf*; **political** ~ analista político.

commerce [ˈkɒmɜːs] *n* (*U*) comércio *m*.

commercial [kəˈmɜːʃl] <> *adj* comercial. <> *n* [advertisement] comercial *m*.

commercial bank *n* banco *m* comercial.

commercial break *n* (intervalo *m*) comercial *m*.

commercialism [kəˈmɜːʃəlɪzm] *n* (*U*) *pej* mercantilismo *m*.

commercialize, -ise [kəˈmɜːʃəlaɪz] *vt* comercializar.

commercialized [kəˈmɜːʃəlaɪzd] *adj pej* comercializado(da).

commercially [kəˈmɜːʃəlɪ] *adv* comercialmente.

commercial vehicle *n UK* veículo *m* comercial.

commie [ˈkɒmɪ] *inf pej* <> *adj* comuna. <> *n* comuna *mf*.

commiserate [kəˈmɪzəreɪt] *vi*: **to** ~ **(with sb)** compadecer-se (de alguém).

commiseration [kəˌmɪzəˈreɪʃn] *n* compadecimento *m*, comiseração *f*.

commission [kəˈmɪʃn] <> *n* -**1.** [gen] comissão *f* -**2.** [piece of work] encomenda *f*. <> *vt* [work] encomendar; **to** ~ **sb (to do sthg)** encarregar alguém (de fazer algo).

commissionaire [kəˌmɪʃəˈneəʳ] *n UK* porteiro *m*, -ra *f*.

commissioner [kəˈmɪʃnəʳ] *n* -**1.** [high-ranking public official] comissário *m*, -ria *f* -**2.** [member of commission] membro *m* de uma comissão, delegado *m*, -da *f*.

commit [kəˈmɪt] (*pt* & *pp* -**ted**, *cont* -**ting**) *vt* -**1.** [carry out] cometer -**2.** [promise] comprometer; **to** ~ **o.s. (to sthg/to doing sthg)** comprometer-se (a algo/a fazer algo) -**3.** [person to institution] confinar -**4.**: **to** ~ **sthg to memory** confiar algo à memória.

commitment [kəˈmɪtmənt] *n* -**1.** (*U*) [dedication] dedicação *f* -**2.** [responsibility] compromisso *m*.

committed [kəˈmɪtɪd] *adj* [writer, artist, Christian] comprometido(da); ~ **to sb/sthg** comprometido(da) com alguém/algo.

committee [kəˈmɪtɪ] *n* comitê *m*.

commode [kə'məʊd] n comadre f.

commodity [kə'mɒdətɪ] (pl -ies) n -1. [gen] mercadoria f -2. ECON commodity f.

commodity exchange n bolsa f de mercadorias.

common ['kɒmən] <> adj -1. [gen] comum; ~ to comum a -2. UK pej [vulgar] vulgar. <> n [land] área f pública.

 ➡ **in common** adv em comum.

common denominator n -1. MATH denominador m comum -2. [characteristic in common] característica f em comum.

commoner ['kɒmənə'] n plebeu m, -béia f.

common good n: for the ~ pelo bem comum.

common ground n (U) ponto m pacífico.

common knowledge n (U) conhecimento m geral.

common land n (U) área f pública.

common law n direito m consuetudinário, lei f comum.

 ➡ **common-law** adj concubinário(ria).

commonly ['kɒmənlɪ] adv [generally] geralmente.

commonplace ['kɒmənpleɪs] <> adj [everyday] trivial. <> n [frequent phenomenon] lugar-comum m.

common room n [in school, college] sala f de recreação.

Commons ['kɒmənz] npl UK: the ~ a Câmara dos Comuns.

common sense n (U) senso m comum.

Commonwealth ['kɒmənwelθ] n [former British colonies]: the ~ a Comunidade Britânica.

Commonwealth of Independent States n: the ~ a Comunidade dos Estados Independentes.

commotion [kə'məʊʃn] n comoção f.

communal ['kɒmjʊnl] adj comum.

commune [n 'kɒ'mjuːn, vb kə'mjuːn] <> n [group of people] comuna f. <> vi: to ~ with comungar com.

communicate [kə'mjuːnɪkeɪt] <> vt comunicar. <> vi comunicar-se, relacionar-se; to ~ with comunicar-se com.

communicating [kə'mjuːnɪkeɪtɪŋ] adj [doors, rooms] com comunicação.

communication [kə,mjuːnɪ'keɪʃn] n (U) comunicação f.

 ➡ **communications** npl comunicações fpl.

communications satellite n satélite m de comunicações.

communications technology n tecnologia f de comunicação.

communicative [kə'mjuːnɪkətɪv] adj [talkative] comunicativo(va).

communicator [kə'mjuːnɪkeɪtə'] n: a good/bad ~ um bom/mau comunicador, uma boa/má comunicadora.

communion [kə'mjuːnjən] n (U) [communication] comunhão f.

 ➡ **Communion** n (U) RELIG comunhão f.

communiqué ['kɒmjuːnɪkeɪ] n comunicado m.

communism n (U) comunismo m.

communist <> adj comunista. <> n comunista mf.

community [kə'mjuːnətɪ] (pl -ies) n [group] comunidade f; the ~ a comunidade.

community centre n centro m comunitário.

community home n UK ≃ Febem f.

community policing n (U) policiamento m comunitário.

community service n (U) -1. [imposed on offender] prestação m de serviços à comunidade -2. UK [voluntary] trabalho m voluntário.

community spirit n (U) espírito m comunitário.

commutable [kə'mjuːtəbl] adj JUR [sentence] comutável.

commutation ticket [,kɒmjuː'teɪʃn-] n US passagem f integrada.

commute [kə'mjuːt] <> vt JUR comutar. <> vi [to work] viajar regularmente entre a casa e o trabalho, especialmente de trem.

commuter [kə'mjuːtə'] n pessoa que viaja regularmente entre a casa e o trabalho, especialmente de trem.

commy ['kɒmɪ] (pl -ies) adj & n = commie.

Comoro Islands npl: the ~ as Ilhas de Comoro.

compact [adj & vb kəm'pækt, n 'kɒmpækt] <> adj [small and neat] compacto(ta). <> n -1. [for face powder] estojo m -2. US AUT: ~ (car) carro m de médio porte. <> vt compactar.

compact disc n disco m compacto, CD m.

compact disc player n CD-player m, toca-CD m.

companion [kəm'pænjən] n -1. [gen] companheiro m, -ra f -2. [book] compêndio m.

companionable [kəm'pænjənəbl] adj amigável.

companionship [kəm'pænjənʃɪp] n (U) camaradagem f.

company ['kʌmpənɪ] (pl -ies) n -1. [gen] companhia f; to keep sb ~ fazer companhia a alguém; to part ~ (with sb) romper relações (com alguém) -2. [business] companhia f, empresa f.

company car n carro m da empresa.

company director n diretor m, -ra f de empresa OR companhia.

company secretary n secretário m, -ria f geral da empresa OR companhia.

comparable ['kɒmprəbl] adj comparável; ~ to OR with comparável a OR com.

comparative [kəm'pærətɪv] adj -1. [relative] relativo(va) -2. [study, literature] comparado(da) -3. GRAM comparativo(va).

comparatively [kəm'pærətɪvlɪ] adv [relatively] relativamente.

compare [kəm'peə'] <> vt comparar; to ~ sb/sth with OR to comparar alguém/algo com OR a; ~ d with OR to comparado com OR a. <> vi: to ~ (with sb/sth) comparar-se (com alguém/algo); to ~ favourably/unfavourably with sthg ser melhor/pior que algo.

comparison [kəm'pærɪsn] n comparação f; in ~ (with OR to) em comparação (com OR a).

compartment [kəm'pɑːtmənt] n compartimento m.

compartmentalize, -ise [,kɒmpɑː'mentəlaɪz] vt compartimentar.

compass ['kʌmpəs] n -1. [for finding direction] bússola

f -2. fml [scope] alcance *f*; **within the ~ of sb/sthg** ao alcance de alguém/algo.
➣ **compasses** *npl* compasso *m*; **a pair of ~es** um compasso.
compassion [kəm'pæʃn] *n (U)* compaixão *f*.
compassionate [kəm'pæʃənət] *adj* compassível.
compassionate leave *n tempo que o empregador permite que o funcionário se ausente do trabalho por razões pessoais*.
compatibility [kəm,pætə'bɪlətɪ] *n (U)* **~ (with)** compatibilidade *f* (com).
compatible [kəm'pætəbl] *adj* **~ (with)** compatível (com).
compatriot [kəm'pætrɪət] *n* compatriota *mf*.
compel [kəm'pel] (*pt* & *pp* -led, *cont* -ling) *vt* -1. [force] compelir; **to ~ sb to do sthg** compelir alguém a fazer algo -2. [demand] impelir.
compelling [kəm'pelɪŋ] *adj* -1. [argument, reason] convincente -2. [book, film, performance] envolvente.
compendium [kəm'pendɪəm] (*pl* -diums OR -dia [-dɪəl) *n* [book] compêndio *m*.
compensate ['kɒmpenseɪt] *vt*: **to ~ sb for sthg** [financially] compensar alguém por algo. *vi*: **to ~ for sthg** compensar algo.
compensation [,kɒmpen'seɪʃn] *n*: **~ (for sthg)** compensação *f* (por algo).
compere ['kɒmpeəʳ] *UK* *n* apresentador *m*, -ra *f*. *vt* apresentar.
compete [kəm'pi:t] *vi* -1. [vie]: **to ~ (for sthg)** competir (por algo); **to ~ with** OR **against sb (for sthg)** competir com OR contra alguém (por algo) -2. COMM: **to ~ (with sb/sthg)** concorrer (com alguém/algo); **to ~ for sthg** disputar algo -3. [take part]: **to ~ (in sthg)** participar (de algo).
competence ['kɒmpɪtəns] *n (U)* [proficiency] competência *f*.
competent ['kɒmpɪtənt] *adj* competente.
competently ['kɒmpɪtəntlɪ] *adv* competentemente.
competing [kəm'pi:tɪŋ] *adj* [conflicting] conflitante.
competition [,kɒmpɪ'tɪʃn] *n* -1. [gen] competição *f* -2. (U) COMM concorrência *f*.
competitive [kəm'petətɪv] *adj* competitivo(va).
competitively [kəm'petətɪvlɪ] *adv* competitivamente.
competitor [kəm'petɪtəʳ] *n* -1. [in business] concorrente *mf* -2. [in race, contest] competidor *m*, -ra *f*.
compilation [,kɒmpɪ'leɪʃn] *n* compilação *f*.
compile [kəm'paɪl] *vt* compilar.
complacency [kəm'pleɪsnsɪ] *n (U)* complacência *f*.
complacent [kəm'pleɪsnt] *adj* complacente.
complacently [kəm'pleɪsntlɪ] *adv* com complacência.
complain [kəm'pleɪn] *vi* [moan] queixar-se; **to ~ about sthg** queixar-se de algo.
complaining [kəm'pleɪnɪŋ] *adj* que reclama.
complaint [kəm'pleɪnt] *n* queixa *f*.
complement [*n* 'kɒmplɪmənt, *vb* 'kɒmplɪment] *n* -1. [gen & GRAM] complemento *m* -2. [accompaniment] acompanhamento *m* -3. [number]: **a full ~ of** a totalidade de. *vt* -1. [gen] complementar -2. [accompany] acompanhar.

complementary [,kɒmplɪ'mentərɪ] *adj* complementar.
complete [kəm'pli:t] *adj* -1. [total, thorough] completo(ta); **~ with** completo(ta) com -2. [finished, ended] concluído(da). *vt* -1. [collection, set, form] completar -2. [work, painting, book] concluir.
completely [kəm'pli:tlɪ] *adv* [totally] completamente.
completion [kəm'pli:ʃn] *n (U)* [of work] conclusão *f*.
complex ['kɒmpleks] *adj* complexo(xa). *n* complexo *m*.
complexion [kəm'plekʃn] *n* -1. [of face] aparência *f* -2. [aspect] caráter *m*.
complexity [kəm'pleksətɪ] (*pl* -ies) *n* complexidade *f*.
compliance [kəm'plaɪəns] *n (U)* [obedience] cumprimento *m*; **~ with sthg** de acordo com algo.
compliant [kəm'plaɪənt] *adj* obediente.
complicate ['kɒmplɪkeɪt] *vt* complicar.
complicated ['kɒmplɪkeɪtɪd] *adj* complicado(da).
complication [,kɒmplɪ'keɪʃn] *n* complicação *f*.
complicity [kəm'plɪsətɪ] *n (U)*: **~ (in sthg)** cumplicidade *f* (em algo).
compliment [*n* 'kɒmplɪmənt, *vb* 'kɒmplɪment] *n* cumprimento *m*, elogio *m*. *vt*: **to ~ sb (on sthg)** cumprimentar alguém (por algo).
➣ **compliments** *npl fml* cumprimentos *mpl*.
complimentary [,kɒmplɪ'mentərɪ] *adj* -1. [admiring] lisonjeiro(ra) -2. [free] gratuito(ta).
complimentary ticket *n* bilhete *m* gratuito.
compliments slip *n* bilhete *m* de saudação.
comply [kəm'plaɪ] (*pt* & *pp* -ied) *vi*: **to ~ with sthg** cumprir algo.
component [kəm'pəʊnənt] *n* componente *m*.
compose [kəm'pəʊz] *vt* -1. [constitute] compor; **to be ~d of sthg** ser composto(ta) por algo -2. [write, create] escrever -3. [make calm]: **to ~ o.s.** recompor-se.
composed [kəm'pəʊzd] *adj* [calm] tranqüilo(la).
composer [kəm'pəʊzəʳ] *n* compositor *m*, -ra *f*.
composite ['kɒmpəzɪt] *adj* composto(ta). *n* composto *m*.
composition [,kɒmpə'zɪʃn] *n* composição *f*.
compost [*UK* 'kɒmpɒst, *US* 'kɒmpəʊst] *n (U)* adubo *m*.
composure [kəm'pəʊʒəʳ] *n (U)* compostura *f*.
compound [*adj* & *n* 'kɒmpaʊnd, *vb* kəm'paʊnd] *adj* composto(ta). *n* -1. [gen] composto *m* -2. [enclosed area] complexo *m*. *vt* -1. [exacerbate] agravar -2. [mixture, substance]: **to be ~ed of sthg** ser composto(ta) por algo.
compound fracture *n* MED fratura *f* exposta.
compound interest *n (U)* juros *mpl* compostos.
comprehend [,kɒmprɪ'hend] *vt* [understand] compreender.
comprehension [,kɒmprɪ'henʃn] *n* -1. (U) [understanding] compreensão *f* -2. SCH [exercise] interpretação *f*.
comprehensive [,kɒmprɪ'hensɪv] *adj* -1. [wide-ranging] abrangente -2. [insurance] total. *n UK* [school] = **comprehensive school**.

comprehensively [ˌkɒmprɪ'hensɪvlɪ] *adv* completamente.

comprehensive school *n* escola estadual de ensino médio que abrange todas as habilidades.

compress [kəm'pres] ◇ *n* MED compressa *f.* ◇ *vt* -1. [squeeze, press] comprimir -2. [condense] sintetizar.

compression [kəm'preʃn] *n* (U) -1. [of air] compressão *f* -2. [of text] redução *f.*

comprise [kəm'praɪz] *vt* -1. [consist of]: **to be ~d of** ser constituído(da) de -2. [constitute] constituir.

compromise ['kɒmprəmaɪz] ◇ *n* [concession, agreement] meio-termo *m.* ◇ *vt* [undermine integrity of] comprometer; **to ~ o.s.** comprometer-se. ◇ *vi* [make concessions] fazer concessões.

compromising ['kɒmprəmaɪzɪŋ] *adj* [embarrassing] comprometedor(ra).

compulsion [kəm'pʌlʃn] *n* -1. [strong desire] compulsão *f* -2. (U) [force] coação *f.*

compulsive [kəm'pʌlsɪv] *adj* -1. [behaviour, gambler, liar] compulsivo(va) -2. [compelling] envolvente.

compulsory [kəm'pʌlsərɪ] *adj* compulsório(ria).

compulsory purchase *n* UK desapropriação *f.*

compunction [kəm'pʌŋkʃn] *n* (U) compunção *f.*

computation [ˌkɒmpju:'teɪʃn] *n* cômputo *m.*

compute [kəm'pju:t] *vt* computar.

computational linguistics *n* (U) lingüística *f* computacional.

computer [kəm'pju:təʳ] ◇ *n* computador *m.* ◇ *comp* de computador.

computer dating [-'deɪtɪŋ] *n* agência *f* de namoro por computador.

computer game *n* jogo *m* de computador.

computer graphics *npl* infografia *f.*

computerization [kəmˌpju:təraɪ'zeɪʃn] *n* (U) informatização *f.*

computerize, -ise [kəm'pju:təraɪz] *vt* informatizar.

computerized [kəm'pju:təraɪzd] *adj* informatizado(da).

computer-literate *adj* com conhecimentos de informática.

computer science *n* ciência *f* da computação.

computing [kəm'pju:tɪŋ] *n* (U) computação *f,* informática *f.*

comrade ['kɒmreɪd] *n* companheiro *m,* -ra *f.*

comradeship ['kɒmreɪdʃɪp] *n* (U) companheirismo *m,* camaradagem *f.*

con (*pt & pp* -ned, *cont* -ning) *fam n* (*abbr of* convict) *fam* presidiário *m,* -a *f.*

concave [ˌkɒn'keɪv] *adj* côncavo(va).

conceal [kən'si:l] *vt* [hide - object, substance] esconder; [- information, feelings] ocultar; **to ~ sthg from sb** esconder algo de alguém.

concede [kən'si:d] ◇ *vt* [admit] conceder. ◇ *vi* aceitar.

conceit [kən'si:t] *n* (U) [arrogance] presunção *f.*

conceited [kən'si:tɪd] *adj* presunçoso(sa).

conceivable [kən'si:vəbl] *adj* concebível.

conceivably [kən'si:vəblɪ] *adv* possivelmente.

conceive [kən'si:v] ◇ *vt* conceber. ◇ *vi* -1. MED conceber -2. [imagine]: **to ~ of sthg** conceber algo.

concentrate ['kɒnsəntreɪt] ◇ *vt* concentrar. ◇ *vi* concentrar-se; **to ~ on sthg** concentrar-se em algo.

concentrated ['kɒnsəntreɪtɪd] *adj* concentrado(da).

concentration [ˌkɒnsən'treɪʃn] *n* concentração *f.*

concentration camp *n* campo *m* de concentração.

concentric [kən'sentrɪk] *adj* concêntrico(ca).

concept ['kɒnsept] *n* conceito *m.*

conception [kən'sepʃn] *n* concepção *f.*

conceptual art *n* arte *f* conceitual.

conceptualize, -ise [kən'septʃʊəlaɪz] *vt* conceituar.

concern [kən'sɜ:n] ◇ *n* -1. [worry, anxiety] preocupação *f* -2. [matter of interest] assunto *m;* **it's no ~ of mine!** não é da minha conta! -3. COMM [company] negócio *m.* ◇ *vt* -1. [worry]: **to be ~ed (about sb/ sthg)** estar preocupado(da) (com alguém/ algo) -2. [involve] dizer respeito(a); **to be ~ed with sthg** [subj: person] estar envolvido(da) com algo; **to ~ o.s. with sthg** preocupar-se com algo; **as far as ... is ~ed** no que diz respeito a ... -3. [subj: book, report, film] tratar de.

concerning [kən'sɜ:nɪŋ] *prep* acerca de, sobre.

concert ['kɒnsət] *n* concerto *m.*

➤ **in concert** *adv* -1. MUS em concerto -2. *fml* [acting as one] conjuntamente.

concerted [kən'sɜ:tɪd] *adj* [effort] conjunto(ta).

concertgoer ['kɒnsətˌɡəʊəʳ] *n* freqüentador *m,* -ra *f* de concertos.

concert hall *n* casa *f* de concertos.

concertina [ˌkɒnsə'ti:nə] (*pt & pp* -ed, *cont* -ing) ◇ *n* concertina *f.* ◇ *vi* engavetar-se.

concerto [kən'tʃeətəʊ] (*pl* -s) *n* concerto *m.*

concession [kən'seʃn] *n* -1. [allowance, point won] concessão *f* -2. COMM [franchise] franquia *f* -3. [special price] desconto *m.*

concessionaire *n* concessionário *m,* -ria *f.*

concessionary [kən'seʃnərɪ] *adj* [fare, price] com desconto.

conciliation [kənˌsɪlɪ'eɪʃn] *n* (U) conciliação *f.*

conciliatory [kən'sɪlɪətrɪ] *adj* conciliatório(ria).

concise [kən'saɪs] *adj* conciso(sa).

concisely [kən'saɪslɪ] *adv* concisamente.

conclave ['kɒŋkleɪv] *n* conclave *m.*

conclude [kən'klu:d] ◇ *vt* -1. [bring to an end] concluir -2. [deduce]: **to ~ (that)** concluir (que) -3. [agree on] firmar. ◇ *vi* [finish] concluir.

conclusion [kən'klu:ʒn] *n* [ending, decision] conclusão *f;* **to jump to the wrong ~** chegar à conclusão errada; **a foregone ~** uma conclusão previsível.

conclusive [kən'klu:sɪv] *adj* conclusivo(va).

concoct [kən'kɒkt] *vt* -1. [story, excuse, alibi] forjar -2. [mixture, drink] preparar.

concoction [kən'kɒkʃn] *n* [mixture, drink] mistura *f.*

concord ['kɒŋkɔ:d] *n* (U) [peaceful agreement] acordo *m.*

concourse ['kɒŋkɔ:s] *n* [hall] hall *m.*

concrete ['kɒŋkri:t] ◇ *adj* concreto(ta). ◇ *n* (U) [building material] concreto *m.* ◇ *comp* [made of concrete] de concreto. ◇ *vt* [path, garden] concretar.

concrete mixer *n* betoneira *f.*
concur [kən'kɜ:ʳ] (*pt* & *pp* -red, *cont* -ring) *vi* [agree]: to ~ (with sthg) concordar (com algo).
concurrent *adj* simultâneo(nea).
concurrently [kən'kʌrəntlɪ] *adv* simultaneamente, concomitantemente.
concussed [kən'kʌst] *adj* que sofreu concussão.
concussion [kən'kʌʃn] *n* (U) concussão *f.*
condemn [kən'dem] *vt* -1. condenar; to ~ sb for sthg condenar alguém por algo - 2. [force]: to ~ sb to sthg/to do sthg condenar alguém a algo/a fazer algo - 3. *JUR* [sentence]: to ~ sb to sthg condenar alguém a algo.
condemnation [ˌkɒndem'neɪʃn] *n* (U) condenação *f.*
condemned [kən'demd] *adj* condenado(da).
condensation [ˌkɒnden'seɪʃn] *n* (U) condensação *f.*
condense [kən'dens] <> *vt* condensar. <> *vi* [gas, liquid] condensar-se.
condensed milk [kən'denst-] *n* (U) leite *m* condensado.
condescend [ˌkɒndɪ'send] *vi* -1. [behave patronizingly]: to ~ to sb condescender-se a alguém - 2. [lower o.s.]: to ~ to do sthg condescender em fazer algo.
condescending [ˌkɒndɪ'sendɪŋ] *adj* condescendente.
condiments ['kɒndɪmənts] *npl* *fml* condimentos *mpl.*
condition [kən'dɪʃn] <> *n* -1. [of person] forma *f*; out of ~ fora de forma - 2. [of car] estado *m*; in good/bad ~ em bom/mau estado - 3. *MED* [disease, complaint] problema *m* - 4. [provision] condição *f*; on one ~ sob *OR* com uma condição; on ~ that desde que; to agree to do sthg on one ~ concordar em fazer algo sob *OR* com uma condição. <> *vt* -1. condicionar - 2. [hair] hidratar.
◆ **conditions** *npl* [circumstances] condições *fpl.*
conditional [kən'dɪʃənl] <> *adj* condicional; ~ (up)on sthg condicionado(da) a algo. <> *n* *GRAM* condicional *m.*
conditionally [kən'dɪʃnəlɪ] *adv* condicionalmente.
conditioner [kən'dɪʃnəʳ] *n* -1. [for hair] condicionador *m* - 2. [for clothes] amaciante *m.*
conditioning [kən'dɪʃnɪŋ] *n* (U) *PSYCH* condicionamento *m.*
condolences [kən'dəʊlənsɪz] *npl* condolências *fpl*, pêsames *mpl.* •
condom ['kɒndəm] *n* camisinha *f*, preservativo *m.*
condominium [ˌkɒndə'mɪnɪəm] *n* *US* [apartment, building] condomínio *m.*
condone [kən'dəʊn] *vt* tolerar.
condor ['kɒndɔ:ʳ] *n* condor *m.*
conducive [kən'dju:sɪv] *adj*: ~ to sthg/to doing sthg conducente a algo/a fazer algo.
conduct [*n* 'kɒndʌkt, *vb* kən'dʌkt] <> *n* (U) conduta *f.* <> *vt* -1. [research, survey & *PHYS*] conduzir - 2. [behave]: to ~ o.s. well/badly comportar-se bem/mal - 3. *MUS* reger. <> *vi* *MUS* reger.
conducted tour [kən'dʌktɪd-] *n* excursão *f* guiada.

conductor [kən'dʌktəʳ] *n* -1. [on bus] cobrador *m* - 2. [on train] *US* condutor *m* - 3. *PHYS* condutor *m* - 4. *MUS* maestro *m*, -trina *f.*
conductress [kən'dʌktrɪs] *n* [on bus] cobradora *f.*
conduit ['kɒndɪt] *n* conduto *m.*
cone [kəʊn] *n* -1. [gen] cone *m* - 2. [for ice cream] casquinha *f* - 3. [from tree] pinha *f.*
◆ **cone off** *vt* *sep* *UK* bloquear com cones (*uma estrada*).
confectioner [kən'fekʃnəʳ] *n* confeiteiro *m*, -ra *f*; ~ 's (shop) confeitaria *f.*
confectionery [kən'fekʃnərɪ] *n* (U) confeito *m.*
confederacy *n* confederação *f.*
confederate *n* cúmplice *mf.*
confederation [kənˌfedə'reɪʃn] *n* [group] confederação *f.*
Confederation of British Industry *n*: the ~ a Confederação das Indústrias Britânicas.
confer [kən'fɜ:ʳ] (*pt* & *pp* -red, *cont* -ring) <> *vt* *fml*: to ~ sthg (on sb) conferir algo (a alguém). <> *vi*: to ~ (with sb on *OR* about sthg) confabular (com alguém sobre *OR* a respeito de algo).
conference ['kɒnfərəns] *n* conferência *f*; in ~ em reunião.
conference call *n* teleconferência *f.*
conference centre *n* centro *m* de conferências.
conference hall *n* salão *m* de conferências.
conferencing ['kɒnfərənsɪŋ] *n* (U) (sistema *m* de) teleconferência *f.*
confess [kən'fes] <> *vt* confessar; to ~ (that) confessar que. <> *vi* [gen] confessar; to ~ to sthg confessar *OR* admitir algo.
confession [kən'feʃn] *n* confissão *f.*
confessional [kən'feʃənl] *n* confessionário *m.*
confetti [kən'fetɪ] *n* (U) confete *m.*
confidant [ˌkɒnfɪ'dænt] *n* confidente *m.*
confidante [ˌkɒnfɪ'dænt] *n* confidente *f.*
confide [kən'faɪd] <> *vt* confiar <> *vi*: to ~ in sb confiar em alguém.
confidence ['kɒnfɪdəns] *n* -1. (U) [assurance] autoconfiança *f* - 2. (U) [trust] confiança *f*; to have ~ in sb ter confiança em alguém - 3. [secrecy]: in ~ em segredo - 4. [secret] confidência *f.*
confidence trick *n* conto-do-vigário *m.*
confident ['kɒnfɪdənt] *adj* -1. [assured] autoconfiante - 2. [sure] confiante; ~ of sthg confiante em algo.
confidential [ˌkɒnfɪ'denʃl] *adj* confidencial.
confidentiality ['kɒnfɪˌdenʃɪ'ælətɪ] *n* (U) sigilo *m*; a breach of ~ uma quebra de sigilo.
confidentially [ˌkɒnfɪ'denʃəlɪ] *adv* -1. [in confidence] confidencialmente - 2. [in private] em particular.
confidently ['kɒnfɪdəntlɪ] *adv* -1. [with assurance] com autoconfiança - 2. [with certainty] com confiança.
configuration [kənˌfɪgə'reɪʃn] *n* configuração *f.*
confine [kən'faɪn] *vt* confinar; to be ~d to estar confinado(da) a; to ~ o.s. to sthg/to doing sthg confinar-se a algo/a fazer algo.
◆ **confines** *npl* confins *mpl.*
confined [kən'faɪnd] *adj* [space, area] confinado(da).

confinement [kənˈfaɪnmənt] *n* -**1.** (*U*) [imprisonment] confinamento *m* -**2.** *dated* & *MED* (trabalho *m* de) parto *m*.
confirm [kənˈfɜːm] *vt* -**1.** [gen] confirmar -**2.** *RELIG* crismar.
confirmation [ˌkɒnfəˈmeɪʃn] *n* -**1.** [gen] confirmação *f* -**2.** *RELIG* crisma *f*.
confirmed [kənˈfɜːmd] *adj* [habitual] convicto(ta).
confiscate [ˈkɒnfɪskeɪt] *vt* confiscar.
confiscation [ˌkɒnfɪˈskeɪʃn] *n* (*U*) confisco *m*.
conflagration [ˌkɒnfləˈɡreɪʃn] *n* *fml* conflagração *f*.
conflate *vt* *fml* fundir.
conflict [*n* ˈkɒnflɪkt, *vb* kənˈflɪkt] ⟨⟩ *n* [fighting, clash] conflito *m*; ~ **of interest** conflito de interesses. ⟨⟩ *vi* [clash] entrar em conflito; **to** ~ **with sb/sthg** entrar em conflito com alguém/algo.
conflicting [kənˈflɪktɪŋ] *adj* [contradictory] conflitante.
confluence *n* [of rivers] confluência *f*.
conform [kənˈfɔːm] *vi* -**1.** [behave as expected] conformar-se -**2.** [be in accordance]: **to** ~ **(to** *OR* **with sthg)** conformar-se (com algo).
conformist [kənˈfɔːmɪst] *pej* ⟨⟩ *adj* conformista. ⟨⟩ *n* conformista *mf*.
conformity [kənˈfɔːmətɪ] *n* (*U*) conformidade *f*; ~ **to** *OR* **with sthg** conformidade com algo.
confound [kənˈfaʊnd] *vt* [confuse, defeat] confundir.
confounded [kənˈfaʊndɪd] *adj* *inf* [for emphasis] maldito(ta).
confront [kənˈfrʌnt] *vt* -**1.** [person] defrontar-se com -**2.** [task, problem] enfrentar -**3.** [present]: **to** ~ **sb (with sthg)** confrontar alguém (com algo).
confrontation [ˌkɒnfrʌnˈteɪʃn] *n* confrontação *f*.
confrontational *adj* de confrontamento.
confuse [kənˈfjuːz] *vt* -**1.** [bewilder] confundir -**2.** [mix up]: **to** ~ **sb/sthg (with)** confundir alguém/algo (com) -**3.** [complicate, make less clear] complicar.
confused [kənˈfjuːzd] *adj* confuso(sa).
confusing [kənˈfjuːzɪŋ] *adj* confuso(sa).
confusion [kənˈfjuːʒn] *n* confusão *f*.
conga [ˈkɒŋɡə] *n*: **the** ~ a conga.
congeal [kənˈdʒiːl] *vi* -**1.** [blood] coagular -**2.** [food] congelar.
congenial [kənˈdʒiːnjəl] *adj* agradável.
congenital [kənˈdʒenɪtl] *adj* *MED* congênito(ta).
conger eel [ˈkɒŋɡəˈ-] *n* enguia *f* marinha.
congested [kənˈdʒestɪd] *adj* congestionado(da).
congestion [kənˈdʒestʃn] *n* (*U*) -**1.** [overcrowding] congestionamento *m* -**2.** *MED* congestão *f*.
conglomerate [kənˈɡlɒmərət] *n* *COMM* conglomerado *m*.
conglomeration [kənˌɡlɒməˈreɪʃn] *n* *fml* conglomeração *f*.
Congo [ˈkɒŋɡəʊ] *n* -**1.** [country]: **the** ~ o Congo; **in the** ~ no Congo -**2.** [river]: **the** ~ o Congo.
Congolese [ˌkɒŋɡəˈliːz] ⟨⟩ *adj* congolês(esa). ⟨⟩ *n* congolês *m*, -esa *f*.
congratulate [kənˈɡrætʃʊleɪt] *vt*: **to** ~ **sb (on)** felicitar alguém (por); **to** ~ **o.s. (on)** congratular-se (por).
congratulations [kənˌɡrætʃʊˈleɪʃənz] ⟨⟩ *npl* felicitações *fpl*. ⟨⟩ *excl* parabéns!

congratulatory [kənˈɡrætʃʊlətrɪ] *adj* de felicitações.
congregate [ˈkɒŋɡrɪɡeɪt] *vi* congregar-se.
congregation [ˌkɒŋɡrɪˈɡeɪʃn] *n* *RELIG* congregação *f*.
congress [ˈkɒŋɡres] *n* [meeting] congresso *m*.
➤ **Congress** *n* *US* *POL* Congresso *m*.

CONGRESS

O órgão legislativo estadunidense compõe-se do Senado (*Senate*) e da Câmara de Representantes (*House of Representatives*). Os senadores são em número de 100; a Câmara conta hoje com 435 membros. Todo projeto de lei deve ser, obrigatoriamente, aprovado pelas duas casas, para que a lei possa entrar em vigor.

congressional [kənˈɡreʃənl] *adj* *US* *POL* parlamentar.
congressman [ˈkɒŋɡresmən] (*pl* -men [-mən]) *n* *US* *POL* congressista *m*.
congresswoman [ˈkɒŋɡresˌwʊmən] (*pl* -women [-ˌwɪmɪn]) *n* *US* *POL* congressista *f*.
conical [ˈkɒnɪkl] *adj* cônico(ca).
conifer [ˈkɒnɪfəʳ] *n* conífera *f*.
coniferous [kəˈnɪfərəs] *adj* conífero(ra).
conjecture [kənˈdʒektʃəʳ] ⟨⟩ *n* conjectura *f*. ⟨⟩ *vt*: **to** ~ **(that)** prever (que). ⟨⟩ *vi* conjecturar.
conjugal [ˈkɒndʒʊɡl] *adj* *fml* conjugal.
conjugate [ˈkɒndʒʊɡeɪt] *vt* conjugar.
conjugation [ˌkɒndʒʊˈɡeɪʃn] *n* conjugação *f*.
conjunction [kənˈdʒʌŋkʃn] *n* -**1.** *GRAM* conjunção *f* -**2.** [combination] combinação *f*; **in** ~ **with** em conjunto com.
conjunctivitis [kənˌdʒʌŋktɪˈvaɪtɪs] *n* (*U*) conjuntivite *f*.
conjure [ˈkʌndʒəʳ] ⟨⟩ *vt* [by magic] fazer aparecer. ⟨⟩ *vi* [by magic] fazer truques.
➤ **conjure up** *vt* *sep* [evoke] evocar.
conjurer [ˈkʌndʒərəʳ] *n* [magician] mágico *m*, -ca *f*.
conjuring trick [ˈkʌndʒərɪŋ-] *n* [magic trick] truque *m* de mágica.
conjuror [ˈkʌndʒərəʳ] *n* = **conjurer**.
conk [kɒŋk] *n* *inf* [nose] narigão *m*.
➤ **conk out** *vi* *inf* -**1.** [person] estar em frangalhos -**2.** [car, machine] escangalhar-se.
conker [ˈkɒŋkəʳ] *n* *UK* castanha-da-índia *f*.
con man (*pl* -men) *n* vigarista *m*.
connect [kəˈnekt] ⟨⟩ *vt* -**1.** [gen] ligar, conectar; **to** ~ **sthg (to sthg)** ligar algo (a algo); **I'm just** ~ **ing you** [on telephone] estou completando sua ligação -**2.** [associate]: **to** ~ **sb/sthg to** *OR* **with** relacionar alguém/algo a *OR* com -**3.** *ELEC* [to power supply]: **to** ~ **sthg to** conectar algo a. ⟨⟩ *vi* [train, plane, bus]: **to** ~ **(with)** conectar com.
connected [kəˈnektɪd] *adj* [related, associated] relacionado(da); ~ **with** conectado(da) com.
Connecticut [kəˈnetɪkət] *n* Connecticut.
connecting [kəˈnektɪŋ] *adj* [flight, train] de conexão.
connecting rod *n* *AUT* biela *f*.
connection [kəˈnekʃn] *n* -**1.** [relationship] conexão *f*, relação *f*; ~ **between/with sthg** relação entre /com algo; **in** ~ **with** em relação a -**2.** [plane, train,

bus & *ELEC*] conexão *f* - **3**. [on telephone] ligação *f* - **4**. [influential contact] contato *m*.

connective tissue [kə'nektɪv-] *n* tecido *m* conjuntivo.

connexion [kə'nekʃn] *n UK* = **connection**.

connive [kə'naɪv] *vi* - **1**. [plot] conspirar; **to ~ with sb** tramar com alguém - **2**. [allow to happen]: **to ~ at sthg** ser conivente em algo.

conniving [kə'naɪvɪŋ] *adj pej* traidor(ra).

connoisseur [ˌkɒnə'sɜː'] *n* conhecedor *m*, -ra *f*, especialista *mf*.

connotation [ˌkɒnə'teɪʃn] *n* conotação *f*.

conquer ['kɒŋkə'] *vt* - **1**. [take by force] conquistar - **2**. *fig* [overcome] dominar.

conqueror ['kɒŋkərə'] *n* conquistador *m*, -ra *f*.

conquest ['kɒŋkwest] *n* conquista *f*.

cons *npl* - **1**. *Br fam* (*abbr of* **conveniences**): **all mod ~** com todas as comodidades. - **2**. ⊳ **pro**.

Cons. (*abbr of* **Conservative**) *partido político britânico de centro-direita.*

conscience ['kɒnʃəns] *n* consciência *f*; **to have a guilty ~** ter a consciência pesada; **in all ~** em sã consciência.

conscientious [ˌkɒnʃɪ'enʃəs] *adj* consciencioso(sa).

conscientiously [ˌkɒnʃɪ'enʃəslɪ] *adv* conscienciosamente.

conscientiousness *n* (*U*) consciência *f*, escrúpulo *m*.

conscientious objector *n pessoa que, por razões morais ou religiosas, recusa-se a servir nas forças armadas.*

conscious ['kɒnʃəs] *adj* consciente; **~ of sthg** consciente de algo; **fashion-~** conhecedor(ra) da moda.

consciously ['kɒnʃəslɪ] *adv* [intentionally] deliberadamente.

consciousness ['kɒnʃəsnɪs] *n* (*U*) consciência *f*; **to lose/regain ~** perder/recobrar os sentidos.

conscript [*n* 'kɒnskrɪpt, *vb* kən'skrɪpt] *MIL* ⋄ *n* recruta *mf*. ⋄ *vt* recrutar.

conscription [kən'skrɪpʃn] *n* (*U*) serviço *m* militar obrigatório.

consecrate ['kɒnsɪkreɪt] *vt* - **1**. *RELIG* [make holy] consagrar - **2**. *fig* [dedicate] dedicar.

consecration [ˌkɒnsɪ'kreɪʃn] *n RELIG* consagração *f*.

consecutive [kən'sekjʊtɪv] *adj* consecutivo(va).

consecutively [kən'sekjʊtɪvlɪ] *adv* consecutivamente.

consensus [kən'sensəs] *n* consenso *m*.

consent [kən'sent] ⋄ *n* (*U*) consentimento *m*. ⋄ *vi*: **to ~ (to sthg)** consentir (em algo).

consenting [kən'sentɪŋ] *adj*: **~ adults** *adultos que aceitam ter relações sexuais.*

consequence ['kɒnsɪkwəns] *n* - **1**. [result] conseqüência *f*; **to face the ~s** encarar as conseqüências; **in ~** em conseqüência - **2**. [importance] importância *f*; **to be of little ~** não ter importância.

consequent ['kɒnsɪkwənt] *adj* conseqüente.

consequently ['kɒnsɪkwəntlɪ] *adv* conseqüentemente.

conservation [ˌkɒnsə'veɪʃn] *n* conservação *f*.

conservation area *n* área *f* de preservação permanente.

conservationist [ˌkɒnsə'veɪʃənɪst] *n* conservacionista *mf*.

conservatism [kən'sɜːvətɪzm] *n* (*U*) conservadorismo *m*.

➡ **Conservatism** *n* (*U*) *UK POL* Conservadorismo *m*.

conservative [kən'sɜːvətɪv] ⋄ *adj* - **1**. [traditional] conservador(ra) - **2**. [cautious] cauteloso(sa). ⋄ *n* conservador *m*, -ra *f*.

➡ **Conservative** *POL UK* ⋄ *adj* conservador(ra). ⋄ *n* conservador *m*, -ra *f*.

Conservative Party *n UK*: **the ~** o Partido Conservador.

conservatory [kən'sɜːvətrɪ] (*pl* -ies) *n* estufa *f*.

conserve [*n* 'kɒnsɜːv, *vb* kən'sɜːv] ⋄ *n* conserva *f*. ⋄ *vt* conservar.

consider [kən'sɪdə'] *vt* - **1**. [gen] considerar; **all things ~ed** considerando tudo - **2**. [believe] achar.

considerable [kən'sɪdrəbl] *adj* considerável.

considerably [kən'sɪdrəblɪ] *adv* consideravelmente.

considerate [kən'sɪdərət] *adj* [thoughtful] atencioso(sa); **that's very ~ of you** é muita consideração de sua parte.

consideration [kənˌsɪdə'reɪʃn] *n* - **1**. (*U*) [gen] consideração *f*; **to take sthg into ~** levar algo em consideração; **to show no ~ for others** não mostrar consideração pelos outros - **2**. [factor] fator *m* - **3**. [discussion]: **under ~** em consideração; **your proposal is under ~** sua proposta está sendo considerada.

considered [kən'sɪdəd] *adj*: **~ opinion** opinião *f* sincera.

considering [kən'sɪdərɪŋ] ⋄ *prep* considerando, em vista de. ⋄ *conj* considerando que. ⋄ *adv* apesar de tudo, pensando bem.

consign [kən'saɪn] *vt* [relegate]: **to ~ sb/sthg to sthg** consignar alguém/algo a algo.

consignee [ˌkɒnsaɪ'niː] *n* consignatário *m*, -ria *f*.

consignment [ˌkən'saɪnmənt] *n* [load] remessa *f*, despacho *m*.

consignment note *n* nota *f* de expedição.

consist [kən'sɪst] ➡ **consist in** *vt fus*: **to ~ in sthg/in doing sthg** consistir em algo/em fazer algo.

➡ **consist of** *vt fus* consistir em.

consistency [kən'sɪstənsɪ] (*pl* -ies) *n* - **1**. (*U*) [coherence] consistência *f*, coerência *f* - **2**. [texture] consistência *f*.

consistent [kən'sɪstənt] *adj* - **1**. [gen] constante - **2**. [growth, improvement] consistente - **3**. [argument, facts, position]: **~ (with)** coerente (com).

consistently [kən'sɪstəntlɪ] *adv* - **1**. [gen] constantemente - **2**. [argue, reason] coerentemente.

consolation [ˌkɒnsə'leɪʃn] *n* consolação *f*.

consolation prize *n* [in competition] prêmio *m* de consolação.

console [*n* 'kɒnsəʊl, *vt* kən'səʊl] ⋄ *n* [control panel] console *m*. ⋄ *vt* consolar; **to ~ o.s. with sthg** contentar-se com algo.

consolidate [kən'sɒlɪdeɪt] ⋄ *vt* - **1**. [strengthen]

consolidar **-2.** *COMM* [merge] fundir-se. ⬦ *vi COMM* fundir-se.

consolidation [kən͵sɒlɪ'deɪʃn] *n (U)* **-1.** [strengthening] consolidação *f* **-2.** *COMM* [merging] fusão *f*.

consommé [*UK* kən'sɒmeɪ, *US* ͵kɒnsə'meɪ] *n (U)* consomê *m*.

consonant ['kɒnsənənt] *n* consoante *f*.

consort [*vb* kən'sɔ:t, *n* 'kɒnsɔ:t] ⬦ *n* **-1.** [spouse] consorte *mf* **-2.** *MUS* grupo *m*. ⬦ *vi fml*: **to ~ with sb** ter ligações com alguém.

consortium [kən'sɔ:tjəm] (*pl* **-tiums** *OR* **-tia** [-tjəl] *n* consórcio *m*.

conspicuous [kən'spɪkjʊəs] *adj* conspícuo(cua).

conspicuously [kən'spɪkjʊəslɪ] *adv* conspicuamente.

conspiracy [kən'spɪrəsɪ] (*pl* **-ies**) *n* conspiração *f*.

conspirator [kən'spɪrətər] *n* conspirador *m*, -ra *f*.

conspiratorial [kən͵spɪrə'tɔ:rɪəl] *adj* conspiratório(ria).

conspire [kən'spaɪər] ⬦ *vt*: **to ~ to do sthg** conspirar para fazer algo. ⬦ *vi* **-1.** [plan secretly]: **to ~ against/with sb** conspirar contra/com alguém **-2.** [combine] cooperar.

constable ['kʌnstəbl] *n UK* [policeman] guarda *m*.

constabulary [kən'stæbjʊlərɪ] (*pl* **-ies**) *n UK* força *f* policial.

constancy ['kɒnstənsɪ] *n (U)* **-1.** [continuity] constância *f* **-2.** *literary* [faithfulness] fidelidade *f*.

constant ['kɒnstənt] *adj* **-1.** [gen] constante **-2.** *literary* [faithful] fiel.

constantly ['kɒnstəntlɪ] *adv* constantemente.

constellation [͵kɒnstə'leɪʃn] *n ASTRON* constelação *f*.

consternation [͵kɒnstə'neɪʃn] *n (U)* consternação *f*.

constipated ['kɒnstɪpeɪtɪd] *adj* constipado(da).

constipation [͵kɒnstɪ'peɪʃn] *n (U)* constipação *f*, prisão *f* de ventre.

constituency [kən'stɪtjʊənsɪ] (*pl* **-ies**) *n* **-1.** [area] distrito *m* eleitoral **-2.** [group] eleitorado *m*.

constituency party *n UK* partido *m* local.

constituent [kən'stɪtjʊənt] ⬦ *adj* constituinte. ⬦ *n* **-1.** [voter] eleitor *m*, -ra *f* **-2.** [element] constituinte *m*.

constitute ['kɒnstɪtju:t] *vt* constituir.

constitution [͵kɒnstɪ'tju:ʃn] *n* **-1.** [health] constituição *f* (física) **-2.** [composition] constituição *f*.
➠ **Constitution** *n*: **the (United States) Constitution** a Constituição (dos Estados Unidos).

CONSTITUTION

Ao contrário da Constituição norte-americana, expressa num texto escrito e definitivo, à Constituição britânica não é um documento propriamente dito, mas resulta do conjunto das leis ao longo da história, tendo por base o princípio da jurisprudência.

constitutional [͵kɒnstɪ'tju:ʃənl] *adj* constitucional.

constrain [kən'streɪn] *vt* **-1.** [person] coagir; **to ~ sb to do sthg** forçar alguém a fazer algo **-2.** [process, development] impedir, restringir.

constrained [kən'streɪnd] *adj* [inhibited] constrangido(da), contido(da).

constraint [kən'streɪnt] *n* **-1.** [restriction] restrição *f*; **~ on sthg** restrição a algo **-2.** *(U)* [control] força *f* **-3.** [coercion] coação *f*.

constrict [kən'strɪkt] *vt* **-1.** [part of body] apertar **-2.** [person] restringir.

constricting [kən'strɪktɪŋ] *adj* **-1.** [clothes] apertado(da) **-2.** [circumstances, lifestyle] limitado(da).

construct [*vb* kən'strʌkt, *n* 'kɒnstrʌkt] ⬦ *vt* **-1.** [edifice, object] construir **-2.** [sentence, argument] formar. ⬦ *n fml* [concept] constructo *m*.

construction [kən'strʌkʃn] ⬦ *n* **-1.** [gen] construção *f* **-2.** *(U)* [building industry] construção *f* (civil). ⬦ *comp* de construção.

construction industry *n* setor *m* da construção civil.

constructive [kən'strʌktɪv] *adj* construtivo(va).

constructively [kən'strʌktɪvlɪ] *adv* construtivamente.

construe [kən'stru:] *vt fml* [interpret]: **to ~ sthg as** interpretar algo como.

consul ['kɒnsəl] *n* [envoy] cônsul *m*, consulesa *f*.

consular ['kɒnsjʊlər] *adj* consular.

consulate ['kɒnsjʊlət] *n* [building] consulado *m*.

consult [kən'sʌlt] ⬦ *vt* consultar. ⬦ *vi*: **to ~ with sb** consultar-se com alguém.

consultancy [kən'sʌltənsɪ] (*pl* **-ies**) *n* [company] empresa *f* de consultoria.

consultancy fee *n* taxa *f* de consultoria.

consultant [kən'sʌltənt] *n* **-1.** [expert] consultor *m*, -ra *f* **-2.** *UK* [medical specialist] especialista *mf*.

consultation [͵kɒnsəl'teɪʃn] *n* **-1.** [gen] consulta *f* **-2.** [of book, map] orientação *f*.

consulting room [kən'sʌltɪŋ-] *n* consultório *m*.

consume [kən'sju:m] *vt* consumir.

consumer [kən'sju:mər] ⬦ *n* consumidor *m*, -ra *f*. ⬦ *comp* do consumidor.

consumer credit *n (U)* crédito *m* ao consumidor.

consumer durables *npl* bens *mpl* duráveis.

consumer goods *npl* bens *mpl* de consumo.

consumerism [kən'sju:mərɪzm] *n (U) pej* [theory] consumismo *m*.

consumer society *n (U)* sociedade *f* de consumo.

consumer spending *n (U)* gastos *mpl* com bens de consumo.

consuming *adj* profundo(da); **a ~ passion** uma paixão ardente.

consummate [*adj* kən'sʌmət, *vb* 'kɒnsəmeɪt] ⬦ *adj* **-1.** [perfect] consumado(da) **-2.** [highly skilled] perfeito(ta). ⬦ *vt* consumar.

consummation [͵kɒnsə'meɪʃn] *n (U)* consumação *f*.

consumption [kən'sʌmpʃn] *n (U)* **-1.** [use] consumo *m* **-2.** *dated* [tuberculosis] tuberculose *f*.

cont. (*abbr of* continued): **~ on page 10** continua na página 10.

contact ['kɒntækt] ⬦ *n* **-1.** *(U)* [physical, eye, communication] contato *m*; **to lose ~ with sb** perder contato com alguém; **to make ~ with sb** fazer contato com alguém; **in ~** em contato; **in ~ with**

sb em contato com alguém **- 2.** [person] contato *m*. ◇ *vt* contatar, entrar em contato com.
contact lens *n* lente *f* de contato.
contact number *n* telefone *m* para contato.
contagion *n* contágio *m*.
contagious [kən'teɪdʒəs] *adj* **- 1.** MED contagioso(sa) **- 2.** *fig* [laughter, good humour] contagiante.
contain [kən'teɪn] *vt* conter; **to ~ o.s.** conter-se.
contained [kən'teɪnd] *adj* [unemotional] contido(da).
container [kən'teɪnə'] *n* **- 1.** [box, bottle etc] recipiente *m* **- 2.** COMM [for transporting goods] contêiner *m*.
containerize, -ise [kən'teɪnəraɪz] *vt* COMM **- 1.** [transport] transportar em contêiner **- 2.** [pack] acondicionar em contêiner.
container ship *n* navio *m* de carga.
containment [kən'teɪnmənt] *n* contenção *f*.
contaminate [kən'tæmɪneɪt] *vt* contaminar.
contaminated [kən'tæmɪneɪtɪd] *adj* contaminado(da).
contamination [kən,tæmɪ'neɪʃn] *n (U)* contaminação *f*.
cont'd (*abbr of* continued) cont.
contemplate ['kɒntempleɪt] ◇ *vt* **- 1.** [scheme, idea, proposal] considerar; **to ~ doing sthg** pensar em fazer algo **- 2.** *literary* [sunset, flower] contemplar. ◇ *vi* [meditate] contemplar.
contemplation [,kɒntem'pleɪʃn] *n (U)* contemplação *f*.
contemplative [kən'templətɪv] *adj* contemplativo(va).
contemporary [kən'tempərərɪ] (*pl* -ies) ◇ *adj* contemporâneo(nea). ◇ *n* contemporâneo *m*, -nea *f*.
contempt [kən'tempt] *n (U)* **- 1.** [gen] desprezo *m*; **~ for sb/sthg** desprezo por alguém/algo; **to hold sb in ~** menosprezar alguém **- 2.** JUR: **~ (of court)** desacato *m* (à autoridade do tribunal).
contemptible [kən'temptəbl] *adj* vil.
contemptuous [kən'temptʃʊəs] *adj* desdenhoso(sa); **to be ~ of sthg** fazer pouco caso de algo.
contend [kən'tend] ◇ *vt* **- 1.** [deal]: **to ~ with sthg** lidar com algo; **to have enough to ~ with** ter muitos problemas para resolver **- 2.** [compete]: **to ~ for sthg** disputar algo; **to ~ against sb** disputar com alguém. ◇ *vt fml* [claim]: **to ~ that** sustentar que.
contender [kən'tendə'] *n* **- 1.** [in fight, race] oponente *mf* **- 2.** [for political office] candidato *m*, -ta *f*.
content [*n* 'kɒntent, *adj & vb* kən'tent] ◇ *adj* contente; **~ with sthg** contente com algo; **to be ~ to do sthg** estar a fim de fazer algo. ◇ *n* **- 1.** [amount contained] teor *m* **- 2.** [subject matter] conteúdo *m*. ◇ *vt*: **to ~ o.s. with sthg/with doing sthg** contentar-se com algo/em fazer algo.
 ◆ **contents** *npl* **- 1.** [of container, document] conteúdo *m* **- 2.** [at front of book] sumário *m*.
contented [kən'tentɪd] *adj* satisfeito(ta).
contentedly [kən'tentɪdlɪ] *adv* com satisfação.
contention [kən'tenʃn] *n* **- 1.** [argument, assertion] argumentação *f* **- 2.** *(U)* [disagreement] discussão *f* **- 3.** *(U)* [competition]: **to be in ~** estar em discussão; **the bone of ~** o pomo da discórdia.
contentious [kən'tenʃəs] *adj fml* contencioso(sa).

contentment [kən'tentmənt] *n (U)* contentamento *m*.
contest [*n* 'kɒntest, *vb* kən'test] ◇ *n* **- 1.** [competition] concurso *m* **- 2.** [for power, control] disputa *f*. ◇ *vt* **- 1.** [compete for] concorrer **- 2.** [dispute] questionar.
contestant [kən'testənt] *n* concorrente *mf*.
context ['kɒntekst] *n* contexto *m*; **out of ~** fora de contexto.
continent ['kɒntɪnənt] *n* GEOGR continente *m*.
 ◆ **Continent** *n* UK: **the Continent** o *Continente Europeu (excluindo-se a Grã-Bretanha)*.
continental [,kɒntɪ'nentl] ◇ *adj* **- 1.** GEOGR continental **- 2.** UK [European] europeu(péia) (do continente). ◇ *n* UK *inf* europeu *m*, -péia *f* (do continente).
continental breakfast *n* café *m* da manhã continental.
contingency [kən'tɪndʒənsɪ] (*pl* -ies) *n* contingência *f*.
contingency plan *n* plano *m* de contingência.
contingent [kən'tɪndʒənt] ◇ *adj fml*: **~ (up)on sthg** dependente de algo. ◇ *n* contingente *m*.
continual [kən'tɪnjʊəl] *adj* contínuo(nua).
continually [kən'tɪnjʊəlɪ] *adv* continuamente.
continuation [kən,tɪnjʊ'eɪʃn] *n* **- 1.** *(U)* [act of extending] prolongamento *m* **- 2.** [sequel] continuação *f*.
continue [kən'tɪnju:] ◇ *vt* **- 1.** [carry on] continuar, prosseguir; **to ~ doing** OR **to do sthg** continuar a fazer algo **- 2.** [begin again] recomeçar **- 3.** [resume speaking] prosseguir. ◇ *vi* **- 1.** [carry on] continuar; **to ~ with sthg** continuar com algo **- 2.** [begin again] recomeçar **- 3.** [resume speaking, travelling] prosseguir.
continuity [,kɒntɪ'nju:ətɪ] *n (U)* [gen] continuidade *f*; **~ announcer** anunciante *m (que oferece um programa)*; **~ boy/girl** continuísta *mf*.
continuous [kən'tɪnjʊəs] *adj* [uninterrupted] contínuo(nua).
continuous assessment *n (U)* avaliação *f* contínua.
continuously [kən'tɪnjʊəslɪ] *adv* [without interruption] continuamente.
contort [kən'tɔ:t] *vt* contorcer.
contortion [kən'tɔ:ʃn] *n* contorção *f*.
contour ['kɒn,tʊə'] ◇ *n* **- 1.** [outline] contorno *m* **- 2.** [on map] relevo *m*. ◇ *comp* de relevo.
contraband ['kɒntrəbænd] ◇ *adj* contrabandeado(da). ◇ *n (U)* contrabando *m*.
contraception [,kɒntrə'sepʃn] *n (U)* contracepção *f*.
contraceptive [,kɒntrə'septɪv] ◇ *adj* anticoncepcional. ◇ *n* anticoncepcional *m*.
contraceptive pill *n* pílula *f* anticoncepcional.
contract [*n* 'kɒntrækt, *vb* kən'trækt] ◇ *n* contrato *m*. ◇ *vt* **- 1.** [through legal agreement] contratar; **to ~ to do sthg** contratar para fazer algo **- 2.** COMM: **to ~ sb (to do sthg)** contratar alguém (para fazer algo) **- 3.** *fml* [illness, disease] contrair **- 4.** [word] abreviar. ◇ *vi* [metal, plastic] contrair-se.
 ◆ **contract in** *vi esp* UK comprometer-se *(por contrato)*.

contract out <> *vt sep* terceirizar. <> *vi esp UK*: **to ~ out (of sthg)** desmanchar (algo).

contraction [kən'trækʃn] *n* contração *f.*

contractor [kən'træktə^r] *n* contratante *mf.*

contractual [kən'træktʃʊəl] *adj* contratual.

contradict [ˌkɒntrə'dɪkt] *vt* -**1.** [challenge] contradizer -**2.** [conflict with]: **to ~ each other** contradizer-se.

contradiction [ˌkɒntrə'dɪkʃn] *n* contradição *f*; **~ in terms** contradição em termos.

contradictory [ˌkɒntrə'dɪktərɪ] *adj* contraditório(-ria).

contraflow ['kɒntrəfləʊ] *n* contrafluxo *m.*

contralto [kən'træltəʊ] (*pl* -s) *n* contralto *m.*

contraption [kən'træpʃn] *n* geringonça *f.*

contrary ['kɒntrərɪ, *adj sense 2* kən'treərɪ] <> *adj* [opposing] contrário(ria); **~ to sthg** contrário(ria) a algo. <> *n* contrário *m*; **on the ~** pelo contrário; **to the ~** em contrário.

contrary to *prep* contrário à.

contrast [*n* 'kɒntrɑːst, *vb* kən'trɑːst] <> *n* -**1.** [difference]: **~ (between/with)** contraste *m* (entre/com); **by** *or* **in ~** em comparação, por outro lado; **in ~ with** *or* **to sthg** em comparação com algo -**2.** [something different]: **~ (to sb/sthg)** oposto *m*, -ta *f* (a alguém/algo). <> *vt*: **to ~ sthg with sthg** contrastar algo com algo. <> *vi*: **to ~ (with sthg)** contrastar *or* dar contraste (com algo).

contrasting [kən'trɑːstɪŋ] *adj* contrastante.

contravene [ˌkɒntrə'viːn] *vt* violar.

contravention [ˌkɒntrə'venʃn] *n* violação *f.*

contribute [kən'trɪbjuːt] <> *vt* -**1.** [give] contribuir com -**2.** [to magazine, newspaper] colaborar com. <> *vi* -**1.** [give money]: **to ~ (to sthg)** contribuir (para algo) -**2.** [be part of cause]: **to ~ to sthg** contribuir para algo -**3.** [write material]: **to ~ to sthg** colaborar com algo.

contributing [kən'trɪbjuːtɪŋ] *adj* [factor] contribuinte.

contribution [ˌkɒntrɪ'bjuːʃn] *n* -**1.** [gen]: **~ (to sthg)** contribuição *f* (para algo) -**2.** [written article] colaboração *f.*

contributor [kən'trɪbjʊtə^r] *n* -**1.** [of money] contribuinte *mf* -**2.** [to magazine, newspaper] colaborador *m*, -ra *f.*

contributory [kən'trɪbjʊtərɪ] *adj* [factor] contribuinte.

contrite ['kɒntraɪt] *adj literary* contrito(ta).

contrivance [kən'traɪvns] *n* -**1.** [contraption] dispositivo *m* -**2.** [ploy] manobra *f*, artimanha *f.*

contrive [kən'traɪv] *fml vt* -**1.** [manoeuvre to put in place] manipular -**2.** [manage]: **to ~ to do sthg** dar um jeito de fazer algo -**3.** [invent, construct] improvisar.

contrived [kən'traɪvd] *adj pej* arranjado(da).

control [kən'trəʊl] (*pt* & *pp* -**led**, *cont*-**ling**) <> *n* -**1.** [gen] controle *m*; **to gain ~ (of sthg)** obter o controle (de algo); **to take ~ (of sthg)** tomar o controle (de algo); **beyond** *or* **outside one's ~** fora do controle de alguém; **in ~ of** no controle de, no comando de; **out of ~** fora de controle; **under ~** sob controle; **to lose ~** [of emotions] perder o controle -**2.** *COMPUT* comando *m.* <> *vt*

controlar. <> *comp* de controle.

controls *npl* [of machine, vehicle] controles *mpl.*

control code *n COMPUT* código *m* de controle.

control group *n* [in experiment, survey] grupo *m* de controle.

control key *n COMPUT* tecla *f* control.

controlled [kən'trəʊld] *adj* controlado(da).

controller [kən'trəʊlə^r] *n* [person responsible] controller *mf*, diretor *m*, -ra *f*; **financial ~** contador *m*, -ra *f.*

controlling *adj* [factor] de controle.

controlling interest *n* controle *m* acionário.

control panel *n* painel *m* de controle.

control room *n* sala *f* de controle.

control tower *n* torre *f* de controle.

controversial [ˌkɒntrə'vɜːʃl] *adj* controverso(sa), polêmico(ca).

controversy ['kɒntrəvɜːsɪ, *UK* kən'trɒvəsɪ] (*pl* -ies) *n* controvérsia *f*, polêmica *f.*

conundrum [kə'nʌndrəm] (*pl* -s) *n fml* [problem] enigma *m.*

conurbation [ˌkɒnɜː'beɪʃn] *n* conurbação *f.*

convalesce [ˌkɒnvə'les] *vi* convalescer.

convalescence [ˌkɒnvə'lesns] *n (U)* convalescença *f.*

convalescent [ˌkɒnvə'lesnt] <> *adj* convalescente. <> *n* convalescente *mf.*

convection [kən'vekʃn] *n (U)* convecção *f.*

convector *n*: **~ heater** aquecedor *m* de convecção.

convene [kən'viːn] <> *vt* [meeting, conference] convocar. <> *vi* [court, parliament] reunir-se.

convenience [kən'viːnjəns] *n* -**1.** *(U)* [gen] conveniência *f*; **at your earliest ~** assim que possível -**2.** [facility] comodidade *f.*

convenience food *n* alimentos *mpl* pré-prontos.

convenience store *n US* loja *f* de conveniências.

convenient [kən'viːnjənt] *adj* -**1.** [suitable] conveniente -**2.** [handy] cômodo(da); **~ for sthg** conveniente para algo.

conveniently [kən'viːnjəntlɪ] *adv* convenientemente.

convent ['kɒnvənt] *n* [building] convento *m.*

convention [kən'venʃn] *n* convenção *f.*

conventional [kən'venʃənl] *adj* convencional; **~ person** *pej* pessoa *f* sem graça; **~ weapons** armas *fpl* não-nucleares.

conventionally [kən'venʃnəlɪ] *adv* de maneira convencional.

convent school *n* colégio *m* de freiras.

converge [kən'vɜːdʒ] *vi* convergir; **to ~ on sb/sthg** [to move towards] dirigir-se para alguém/algo.

convergence [kən'vɜːdʒəns] *n* [in EU] convergência *f*; **~ criteria** critérios *mpl* de convergência.

conversant [kən'vɜːsənt] *adj fml*: **~ with sthg** familiarizado(da) com algo.

conversation [ˌkɒnvə'seɪʃn] *n* conversação *f*, conversa *f*; **to make ~** puxar conversa.

conversational [ˌkɒnvə'seɪʃənl] *adj* [chatty] conversador(ra).

conversationalist [ˌkɒnvəˈseɪʃnəlɪst] *n* conversador *m*, -ra *f*.

converse [*n* & *adj* ˈkɒnvɜːs, *vb* kənˈvɜːs] ⟨⟩ *adj fml* [opposing] inverso(sa). ⟨⟩ *n* [opposite]: **the** ~ o inverso. ⟨⟩ *vi fml* [talk] conversar; **to** ~ **with sb** conversar com alguém.

conversely [kənˈvɜːslɪ] *adv fml* inversamente.

conversion [kənˈvɜːʃn] *n* -**1.** [gen] conversão *f* -**2.** [converted building, room] reforma *f*.

conversion table *n* tabela *f* de conversão.

convert [*vb* kənˈvɜːt, *n* ˈkɒnvɜːt] ⟨⟩ *vt*: **to** ~ **sthg (in)to sthg** converter algo em algo; **to** ~ **sb (to sthg)** converter alguém (para algo); **I didn't like jazz much but she** ~**ed me to it** eu não gostava muito de jazz, mas ela me converteu. ⟨⟩ *vi* -**1.** [change]: **she's** ~**ed to Catholicism** ela se converteu ao catolicismo; **the seating** ~**s to a double bed** o sofá se transforma numa cama de casal -**2.** *SPORT* converter. ⟨⟩ *n* convertido *m*, -da *f*.

converted [kənˈvɜːtɪd] *adj* -**1.** [building, room, ship] transformado(da), adaptado(da) -**2.** *RELIG* [person] convertido(da).

convertible [kənˈvɜːtəbl] ⟨⟩ *adj* -**1.** [car, currency] conversível -**2.** [bed, sofa] dobrável. ⟨⟩ *n* [car] conversível *m*.

convex [kɒnˈveks] *adj* convexo(xa).

convey [kənˈveɪ] *vt* -**1.** *fml* [people, cargo] conduzir -**2.** [feelings, ideas, thoughts] expressar; **to** ~ **sthg to sb** transmitir algo a alguém.

conveyancing [kənˈveɪənsɪŋ] *n (U)* transferência *f* de posse.

conveyer belt [kənˈveɪəʳ-], **conveyor belt** *n* esteira *f* transportadora.

convict [*n* ˈkɒnvɪkt, *vb* kənˈvɪkt] ⟨⟩ *n* condenado *m*, -da *f*. ⟨⟩ *vt JUR*: **to** ~ **sb of sthg** condenar alguém por algo.

convicted [kənˈvɪktɪd] *adj JUR* condenado(da).

conviction [kənˈvɪkʃn] *n* -**1.** [gen] convicção *f* -**2.** *JUR* condenação *f*.

convince [kənˈvɪns] *vt* [persuade] convencer; **to** ~ **sb of sthg** convencer alguém de algo; **to** ~ **sb to do sthg** convencer alguém a fazer algo.

convinced [kənˈvɪnst] *adj*: ~ **(of sthg)** convencido(da) (de algo).

convincing [kənˈvɪnsɪŋ] *adj* convincente.

convivial [kənˈvɪvɪəl] *adj* alegre, festivo(va).

convoluted [ˈkɒnvəluːtɪd] *adj* [tortuous] enrolado(da).

convoy [ˈkɒnvɔɪ] *n* [group] comboio *m*; **in** ~ em comboio.

convulse [kənˈvʌls] *vt*: **to be** ~**d with** [laughter, pain] dobrar-se de.

convulsion [kənˈvʌlʃn] *n MED* convulsão *f*.

convulsive [kənˈvʌlsɪv] *adj* convulsivo(va).

coo [kuː] *vi* -**1.** [bird] arrulhar -**2.** [person] sussurrar.

cook [kʊk] ⟨⟩ *n* cozinheiro *m*, -ra *f*. ⟨⟩ *vt* -**1.** [food, meal] cozinhar; **I'll** ~ **dinner** vou preparar o jantar -**2.** *inf* [books, accounts] falsificar. ⟨⟩ *vi* cozinhar.

◆ **cook up** *vt sep* [plan, scheme, excuse] inventar.

cookbook [ˈkʊkˌbʊk] *n* = **cookery book**.

cooked [kʊkt] *adj* [food] cozido(da).

cooker [ˈkʊkəʳ] *n esp UK* [stove] fogão *m*.

cookery [ˈkʊkərɪ] *n (U)* culinária *f*.

cookery book *n* livro *m* de receitas.

cookie [ˈkʊkɪ] *n* -**1.** *esp US* [biscuit] biscoito *m* -**2.** *COMPUT* cookie *m*.

cooking [ˈkʊkɪŋ] ⟨⟩ *n (U)* -**1.** [activity] culinária *f*; **do you like** ~? você gosta de cozinhar? -**2.** [food] cozinha *f*; **her** ~ **is awful!** ela cozinha mal pra caramba! ⟨⟩ *comp* -**1.** [oil, utensils, salt] de cozinha -**2.** [sherry, chocolate] para cozinhar.

cooking apple *n* maçã *f* para cozinhar.

cookout [ˈkʊkaʊt] *n US* refeição *f* ao ar livre.

cool [kuːl] ⟨⟩ *adj* -**1.** [not warm] frio (fria) -**2.** [calm] tranqüilo(la) -**3.** [unfriendly] frio (fria) -**4.** *inf* [excellent] legal -**5.** *inf* [trendy] bacana. ⟨⟩ *vt* esfriar. ⟨⟩ *vi* -**1.** [food, liquid, room] esfriar -**2.** [enthusiasm, ardour] arrefecer. ⟨⟩ *n inf* [calm]: **to keep/lose one's** ~ manter/perder a calma.

◆ **cool down** ⟨⟩ *vt sep* -**1.** [make less warm] esfriar -**2.** [make less angry] acalmar-se. ⟨⟩ *vi* -**1.** [become less warm] esfriar -**2.** [become less angry] acalmar-se.

◆ **cool off** *vi* -**1.** [become less warm] esfriar -**2.** [become less angry] acalmar-se.

coolant [ˈkuːlənt] *n* líquido *m* refrigerante.

cool bag *n* bolsa *f* térmica.

cool box *UK*, **cooler** *US n* caixa *f* de gelo.

cool-headed [-ˈhedɪd] *adj* calmo(ma), de sangue-frio.

cooling-off period [ˈkuːlɪŋ-] *n* período *m* de calmaria.

cooling tower [ˈkuːlɪŋ-] *n* torre *f* de resfriamento.

coolly [ˈkuːlɪ] *adv* -**1.** [calmly] calmamente -**2.** [coldly] friamente.

coolness [ˈkuːlnɪs] *n (U)* -**1.** [in temperature] friagem *f* -**2.** [unfriendliness] frieza *f*.

coop [kuːp] *n* gaiola *f*; **chicken** ~ galinheiro *m*.

◆ **coop up** *vt sep inf* trancafiar.

co-op (*abbr of* **cooperative**) *n fam* coop.

cooperate [kəʊˈɒpəreɪt] *vi* cooperar; **to** ~ **with sb/sthg** cooperar com alguém/algo.

cooperation [kəʊˌɒpəˈreɪʃn] *n (U)* cooperação *f*.

cooperative [kəʊˈɒpərətɪv] ⟨⟩ *adj* cooperativo(va). ⟨⟩ *n* [enterprise] cooperativa *f*.

co-opt *vt*: **to** ~ **sb (into/onto sthg)** cooptar alguém (em algo).

coordinate [*n* kəʊˈɔːdɪnət, *vt* kəʊˈɔːdɪneɪt] ⟨⟩ *n* [on map, graph] coordenada *f*. ⟨⟩ *vt* coordenar.

◆ **coordinates** *npl* [clothes] conjuntos *mpl*.

coordination [kəʊˌɔːdɪˈneɪʃn] *n (U)* coordenação *f*.

coot *n* [bird] galeirão *m*.

co-ownership *n (U)* co-propriedade *f*.

cop [kɒp] (*pt* & *pp* -**ped**, *cont* -**ping**) *n inf* [policeman] tira *m*.

◆ **cop out** *vi inf*: **to** ~ **out (of sthg)** cair fora (de algo).

cope [kəʊp] *vi* suportar; **to** ~ **with sthg** lidar com algo.

Copenhagen [ˌkəʊpənˈheɪgən] *n* Copenhague *f*.

copier [ˈkɒpɪəʳ] *n* [photocopier] copiadora *f*.

copilot [ˈkəʊˌpaɪlət] *n* co-piloto *m*, -ta *f*.

copious [ˈkəʊpjəs] *adj* copioso(sa).

cop-out *n inf* desculpa *f* furada.

copper ['kɒpə'] n -**1.** (U) [metal] cobre m -**2.** UK inf [policeman] tira m.

coppice ['kɒpɪs], **copse** [kɒps] n capão m.

copulate ['kɒpjʊleɪt] vi fml: to ~(with) copular (com).

copulation [,kɒpjʊ'leɪʃn] n (U) cópula f.

copy ['kɒpɪ] (pt & pp -ied) <> n cópia f. <> vt copiar. <> vi [cheat] colar.
◆ **copy down** vt sep anotar.
◆ **copy out** vt sep copiar.

copycat ['kɒpɪkæt] <> n inf maria-vai-com-as-outras mf inv. <> comp [crime, killing] idêntico(ca) a outro mais famoso.

copy protect vt COMPUT proteger contra cópias.

copyright ['kɒpɪraɪt] n (U) direitos mpl autorais, copyright m.

copy typist n UK digitador m, -ra f.

copywriter ['kɒpɪ,raɪtə'] n redator m, -ra f de material publicitário.

coral ['kɒrəl] <> n (U) coral m. <> comp de coral; a ~ pink uma rosa coral.

coral reef n recife m de corais.

Coral Sea n: the ~ o Mar de Coral.

cord [kɔːd] <> n -**1.** [string] cordão m -**2.** [wire] fio m -**3.** [fabric] veludo m cotelê. <> comp de veludo cotelê.
◆ **cords** npl inf calça f de veludo cotelê.

cordial ['kɔːdjəl] <> adj cordial. <> n cordial m.

cordially ['kɔːdɪəlɪ] adv cordialmente.

cordless adj sem-fio.

cordon ['kɔːdn] n [barrier] cordão m de isolamento.
◆ **cordon off** vt sep isolar (com cordão).

cordon bleu [-'blɜː] adj: a ~ cook cozinheiro m, -ra f de alto nível.

corduroy ['kɔːdərɔɪ] <> n veludo m cotelê. <> comp de veludo cotelê.

core [kɔː'] <> n -**1.** [gen] centro m -**2.** [of apple, pear] caroço m -**3.** [of argument, policy] âmago m -**4.** phr: to be English/royalist to the ~ ser inglês(esa)/monarquista até morrer; to be shaken to the ~ ficar muito comovido(da). <> vt [fruit] descaroçar.

CORE (abbr of Congress on Racial Equality) n organização norte-americana contra o racismo.

corer ['kɔːrə'] n [for fruit] descaroçador m.

co-respondent n JUR co-responsável mf (em caso de divórcio por adultério).

Corfu [kɔː'fuː] n Corfu; in ~ em Corfu.

corgi ['kɔːgɪ] (pl -s) n pequeno cão do País de Gales de nariz alongado e pernas curtas.

coriander [,kɒrɪ'ændə'] n (U) -**1.** [herb] coriandro m -**2.** [spice] coentro m.

cork [kɔːk] n -**1.** (U) [material] cortiça f -**2.** [stopper] rolha f.

corkage ['kɔːkɪdʒ] n (U) taxa cobrada num restaurante pela abertura das garrafas trazidas pelos clientes.

corked [kɔːkt] adj com gosto de rolha.

corkscrew ['kɔːkskruː] n saca-rolhas m.

cormorant ['kɔːmərənt] n cormorão m.

corn [kɔːn] n -**1.** (U) UK [wheat, barley, oats] cereais mpl -**2.** (U) esp Am [maize] milho m -**3.** [callus] calo m.

corn bread n broa f de milho.

cornea ['kɔːnɪə] (pl -s) n córnea f.

corned beef [kɔːnd-] n (U) carne f bovina enlatada.

corner ['kɔːnə'] <> n -**1.** [gen] canto m; to cut ~s fig pular etapas -**2.** [in street, road] esquina f -**3.** FTBL escanteio m. <> vt -**1.** [trap] encurralar -**2.** [monopolize] monopolizar.

corner flag n FTBL bandeirinha f de escanteio.

corner kick n FTBL cobrança f de escanteio.

corner shop n pequeno armazém de esquina que vende comida e artigos de limpeza.

cornerstone ['kɔːnəstəʊn] n fig [basis] fundamento m.

cornet ['kɔːnɪt] n -**1.** [instrument] corneta f -**2.** UK [ice-cream cone] casquinha f.

cornfield ['kɔːnfiːld] n -**1.** UK [of wheat] campo m de trigo -**2.** esp US [of maize] milharal m.

cornflakes ['kɔːnfleɪks] npl flocos mpl de cereais.

cornflour UK ['kɔːnflaʊə'], **cornstarch** US ['kɔːnstɑːtʃ] n (U) amido m de milho.

cornice ['kɔːnɪs] n cornija f.

Cornish ['kɔːnɪʃ] <> adj da Cornualha.

corn oil n óleo m de milho.

corn on the cob n milho m cozido.

cornstarch n US = cornflour.

cornucopia [,kɔːnjʊ'kəʊpjə] n literary cornucópia f.

Cornwall ['kɔːnwɔːl] n Cornualha f; in ~ na Cornualha.

corny ['kɔːnɪ] (compar -ier, superl -iest) adj inf batido(da).

corollary [kə'rɒlərɪ] (pl -ies) n corolário m.

coronary ['kɒrənrɪ] (pl -ies), **coronary thrombosis** [-θrɒm'bəʊsɪs] (pl coronary thromboses [-θrɒm'bəʊsiːz]) n trombose f coronária.

coronation [,kɒrə'neɪʃn] n coroação f.

coroner ['kɒrənə'] n oficial responsável por investigar as mortes das pessoas que morreram de forma violenta, brusca ou incomum.

Corp. (abbr of corporation) Corp.

corpora ['kɔːpərə] pl ▷ corpus.

corporal ['kɔːpərəl] n cabo m.

corporal punishment n (U) castigo m corporal.

corporate ['kɔːpərət] adj -**1.** [business] corporativo(va) -**2.** [collective] coletivo(va).

corporate hospitality n diversão proporcionada por uma empresa a seus clientes, como refeições especiais ou drinks em locais agradáveis.

corporate identity, corporate image n imagem f da empresa.

corporation [,kɔːpə'reɪʃn] n -**1.** [council] associação f -**2.** [large company] corporação f.

corporation tax n UK imposto m sobre renda de corporações.

corps [kɔː'] (pl inv) n -**1.** MIL unidade f -**2.** [group] corpo m.

corpse [kɔːps] n cadáver m.

corpulent ['kɔːpjʊlənt] adj fml corpulento(ta).

corpus ['kɔːpəs] (pl -pora OR -puses) n [collection of writings] corpus m.

corpuscle ['kɔːpʌsl] n corpúsculo m.

corral [kɒ'rɑːl] *n esp US* curral *m*.
correct [kə'rekt] ⟨⟩ *adj* -**1.** [right, accurate] certo(ta) -**2.** [appropriate, suitable] adequado(da). ⟨⟩ *vt* corrigir.
correction [kə'rekʃn] *n* -**1.** (U) [act of correcting] correção *f* -**2.** [change] emenda *f*.
correctly [kə'rektlɪ] *adv* -**1.** [accurately] corretamente -**2.** [appropriately, suitably] adequadamente.
correlate ['kɒrəleɪt] ⟨⟩ *vt* correlacionar. ⟨⟩ *vi*: to ~ (with sthg) corresponder (a algo).
correlation [ˌkɒrə'leɪʃn] *n*: ~ (between) correlação (entre).
correspond [ˌkɒrɪ'spɒnd] *vi* -**1.** [be equivalent]: to ~ (with OR to sthg) corresponder (com OR a algo) -**2.** [tally]: to ~ (with OR to sthg) ajustar-se (a algo) -**3.** [write letters]: to ~ (with sb) corresponder-se (com alguém).
correspondence [ˌkɒrɪ'spɒndəns] *n* -**1.** [letters] correspondência *f* -**2.** [letter-writing]: ~ with/between sb correspondência com/entre alguém -**3.** [relationship, similarity]: ~ with sthg relação com algo.
correspondence course *n* curso *m* por correspondência.
correspondent [ˌkɒrɪ'spɒndənt] *n* [reporter] correspondente *mf*.
corresponding [ˌkɒrɪ'spɒndɪŋ] *adj* [relevant] correspondente.
corridor ['kɒrɪdɔː'] *n* [in building] corredor *m*.
corroborate [kə'rɒbəreɪt] *vt* corroborar.
corroboration [kəˌrɒbə'reɪʃn] *n* (U) corroboração *f*.
corrode [kə'rəʊd] ⟨⟩ *vt* corroer. ⟨⟩ *vi* corroer-se.
corrosion [kə'rəʊʒn] *n* (U) [of metal] corrosão *f*.
corrosive [kə'rəʊsɪv] *adj* [poison, substance] corrosivo(sa).
corrugated ['kɒrəgeɪtɪd] *adj* ondulado(da).
corrugated iron *n* (U) ferro *m* corrugado.
corrupt [kə'rʌpt] ⟨⟩ *adj* -**1.** [dishonest] corrupto(ta) -**2.** [depraved] depravado(da) -**3.** COMPUT [damaged] corrompido(da). ⟨⟩ *vt* corromper.
corruption [kə'rʌpʃn] *n* (U) -**1.** [gen] corrupção *f* -**2.** [depravity] depravação *f*.
corsage [kɔː'sɑːʒ] *n* [flowers] *pequeno buquê utilizado pelas mulheres à altura dos ombros.*
corset ['kɔːsɪt] *n* [undergarment] espartilho *m*.
Corsica ['kɔːsɪkə] *n* Córsega; in ~ na Córsega.
Corsican ['kɔːsɪkən] ⟨⟩ *adj* córsico(ca). ⟨⟩ *n* -**1.** [person] córsico *m*, -ca *f*, -**2.** [language] córsico *m*.
cortege, cortège [kɔː'teɪʒ] *n* séquito *m*.
cortisone ['kɔːtɪzəʊn] *n* (U) cortisona *f*.
cos¹ [kɒz] *conj UK inf* = because.
cos² [kɒs] *n* = cos lettuce.
cosh [kɒʃ] ⟨⟩ *n* cacete *m*. ⟨⟩ *vt* dar cacetadas.
cosignatory [ˌkəʊ'sɪgnətrɪ] (*pl* -ies) *n* co-signatário(ria).
cosine ['kəʊsaɪn] *n* co-seno *m*.
cos lettuce [kɒs-] *n UK* alface *f* romana.
cosmetic [kɒz'metɪk] ⟨⟩ *adj fig* [superficial] superficial. ⟨⟩ *n* cosmético *m*.
cosmetic surgery *n* (U) cirurgia *f* estética.
cosmic ['kɒzmɪk] *adj* cósmico(ca).

cosmonaut ['kɒzmənɔːt] *n* cosmonauta *mf*.
cosmopolitan [kɒzmə'pɒlɪtn] *adj* cosmopolita.
cosmos ['kɒzmɒs] *n*: the ~ o cosmos.
Cossack ['kɒsæk] *n* cossaco *m*.
cosset ['kɒsɪt] *vt* acarinhar.
cost [kɒst] (*pt* & *pp senses 1* & *3* cost, *pt* & *pp sense 2* - ed) ⟨⟩ *n* -**1.** custo *m*; at all ~s a qualquer custo -**2.** *vt* -**1.** [in financial transactions - sum of money] custar; [- person] custar a -**2.** COMM [estimate price of] orçar; to ~ a product orçar um produto; the work was ~ed at £65 o trabalho foi orçado em £65.
 ➤ **costs** *npl* JUR custas *fpl*.
cost accountant *n* contador *m*, -ra *f* de custos.
co-star ['kəʊ-] ⟨⟩ *n* coadjuvante *mf*. ⟨⟩ *vt* atuar como coadjuvante. ⟨⟩ *vi*: to ~ (with) contracenar (com).
Costa Rica [ˌkɒstə'riːkə] *n* Costa Rica; in ~ na Costa Rica.
Costa Rican [ˌkɒstə'riːkən] ⟨⟩ *adj* costarriquenho(nha). ⟨⟩ *n* costarriquenho *m*, -nha *f*.
cost-benefit analysis *n* (U) análise *f* de custo-benefício.
cost-effective *adj* rentável, lucrativo(va).
cost-effectiveness *n* (U) rentabilidade *f*.
costing ['kɒstɪŋ] *n* estimativa *f* de custos.
costly ['kɒstlɪ] (*compar*-ier, *superl*-iest) *adj* -**1.** [expensive] oneroso(sa) -**2.** *fig* [involving loss, damage] dispendioso(sa).
cost of living *n*: the ~ o custo de vida.
cost-of-living index *n* ≃ índice *m* de preços ao consumidor.
cost price *n* preço *m* de custo.
costume ['kɒstjuːm] *n* -**1.** THEATRE roupa *f*; lion ~ fantasia de leão; in ~ and make-up vestido(da) e maquiado(da) -**2.** (U) [dress] traje *m*; swimming ~ maiô *m*.
costume jewellery *n* (U) bijuteria *f*.
cosy UK, **cozy** US ['kəʊzɪ] (*compar*-ier, *superl*-iest, *pl*-ies) ⟨⟩ *adj* -**1.** [clothes] confortável -**2.** [person] aconchegado(da); to feel ~ sentir-se aconchegado(da) -**3.** [chat, atmosphere] aconchegante. ⟨⟩ *n* [for teapot] abafador *m*.
cot [kɒt] *n* -**1.** UK [for child] berço *m* -**2.** US [folding bed] cama *f* de campanha.
cot death *n* morte *f* no berço.
cottage ['kɒtɪdʒ] *n* cabana *f*, chalé *m*; a country ~ uma casa de campo.
cottage cheese *n* (U) requeijão *m*.
cottage hospital *n* UK hospital *m* pequeno no campo.
cottage industry *n* indústria *f* caseira.
cottage pie *n* UK *bolo de carne picada coberto com purê de batata.*
cotton ['kɒtn] ⟨⟩ *n* (U) -**1.** [fabric, plants] algodão *m* -**2.** [thread] linha *f*. ⟨⟩ *comp* de algodão.
 ➤ **cotton on** *vi inf*: to ~ on (to sthg) sacar (algo).
cotton bud UK, **cotton swab** US *n* cotonete *m*.
cotton candy *n* US = candyfloss.
cotton swab *n* US = cotton bud.
cotton wool *n* (U) chumaço *m* de algodão.
couch [kaʊtʃ] ⟨⟩ *n* -**1.** [gen] sofá *m* -**2.** [psychiatrist's]

divã m. ⟨⟩ vt fig: **to ~ sthg in** [express] formular algo em.

couchette [ku:'ʃet] n UK cama f (em trem ou navio).

couch potato n inf folgado m, -da f.

cougar ['ku:gəʳ] (pl inv OR -s) n puma m.

cough [kɒf] ⟨⟩ n -**1.** [noise] tossida f -**2.** [illness] tosse f. ⟨⟩ vi tossir. ⟨⟩ vt expelir tossindo.
➻ **cough up** vt sep -**1.** [bring up] expelir tossindo -**2.** v inf [pay up] desembolsar.

coughing ['kɒfɪŋ] n tosse f.

cough mixture n UK xarope m para a tosse.

cough sweet n UK pastilha f para tosse.

cough syrup n = cough mixture.

could [kʊd] pt ⟨⟩ can².

couldn't ['kʊdnt] = could not.

could've ['kʊdəv] = could have.

council ['kaʊnsl] ⟨⟩ n -**1.** [local authority] câmara f municipal -**2.** [group, organization] conselho m -**3.** [meeting] assembléia f. ⟨⟩ comp [of local authority] de conselho.

council estate n UK conjunto de casas de propriedade do município destinado à locação.

council flat n UK apartamento de propriedade do município para ser alugado a baixo custo.

council house n UK casa de propriedade do município para ser alugada a baixo custo.

councillor ['kaʊnsələʳ] n vereador m, -ra f.

Council of Europe n Conselho m da Europa.

council of war n conselho m de guerra.

council tax n UK ≃ imposto m territorial urbano.

counsel ['kaʊnsəl] (UK pt & pp -led, cont -ling, US pt & pp -ed, cont -ing) ⟨⟩ n -**1.** (U) fml [advice] parecer m -**2.** [lawyer] conselheiro m, -ra f, advogado m, -da f. ⟨⟩ vt aconselhar; **to ~ sb to do sthg** fml aconselhar alguém a fazer algo.

counselling UK, **counseling** US ['kaʊnsəlɪŋ] n (U) aconselhamento m, orientação f.

counsellor UK, **counselor** US ['kaʊnsələʳ] n -**1.** [adviser, helper] conselheiro m, -ra f, orientador(ra) ra -**2.** US [lawyer] advogado m, -da f.

count [kaʊnt] ⟨⟩ n -**1.** [total] conta f; **to keep ~ of sthg** registrar algo; **to lose ~ of sthg** perder a conta de algo -**2.** [point] ponto m -**3.** JUR [charge] enquadramento m -**4.** [aristocrat] conde m. ⟨⟩ vt -**1.** [add up] contar -**2.** [consider, include]: **to ~ sb/sthg as sthg** considerar alguém/algo como algo. ⟨⟩ vi contar; **to ~ for** contar (para); **to ~ (up) to** contar até; **to ~ as sthg** contar como algo.
➻ **count against** vt fus pesar contra.
➻ **count in** vt sep inf incluir.
➻ **count on** vt fus [rely on, expect] contar com.
➻ **count out** vt sep -**1.** [money] contar um a um -**2.** inf [leave out] excluir.
➻ **count up** vt fus contar.
➻ **count upon** vt fus = count on.

countdown ['kaʊntdaʊn] n contagem f regressiva.

countenance ['kaʊntənəns] ⟨⟩ n literary [face] semblante m. ⟨⟩ vt [approve of] aprovar.

counter ['kaʊntəʳ] ⟨⟩ n -**1.** [in shop, kitchen] balcão m -**2.** [in board game] ficha f -**3.** [in post office, bank]

guichê m. ⟨⟩ vt: **to ~ sthg with sthg** [respond to] responder algo com algo; **to ~ sthg by doing sthg** responder algo fazendo algo. ⟨⟩ vi: **to ~ with sthg/by doing sthg** responder com/fazendo algo.
➻ **counter to** adv ao contrário de; **to run ~ to sthg** ir contra algo/ser contrário a algo.

counteract [,kaʊntə'rækt] vt neutralizar.

counter-attack ⟨⟩ n contra-ataque m. ⟨⟩ vt & vi contra-atacar.

counterbalance [,kaʊntə'bæləns] vt fig [correct, balance] contrapeso m.

counterclaim ['kaʊntəkleɪm] n reivindicação f.

counterclockwise US [,kaʊntə'klɒkwaɪz] ⟨⟩ adj anti-horário(ria). ⟨⟩ adv em sentido anti-horário.

counter-espionage n (U) contra-espionagem f.

counterfeit ['kaʊntəfɪt] ⟨⟩ adj falsificado(da). ⟨⟩ vt falsificar.

counterfoil ['kaʊntəfɔɪl] n canhoto m.

counter-intelligence n (U) contra-espionagem f.

countermand [,kaʊntə'mɑ:nd] vt revogar.

counter-measure n contramedida f.

counter-offensive n contra-ofensiva f.

counterpane ['kaʊntəpeɪn] n colcha f.

counterpart ['kaʊntəpɑ:t] n contraparte f.

counterpoint ['kaʊntəpɔɪnt] n (U) MUS contraponto m.

counter-productive adj contraproducente.

counter-revolution n contra-revolução f.

countersank ['kaʊntəsæŋk] pt ⟨⟩ countersink.

countersign ['kaʊntəsaɪn] vt [document] -**1.** referendar -**2.** [cheque] endossar.

countersink ['kaʊntəsɪŋk] (pt -sank, pp -sunk [-sʌŋk]) vt escarear.

countess ['kaʊntɪs] n condessa f.

countless ['kaʊntlɪs] adj inúmero(ra).

countrified ['kʌntrɪfaɪd] adj pej rústico(ca).

country ['kʌntrɪ] (pl -ies) ⟨⟩ n -**1.** [nation] país m; **to go to the ~** UK POL fazer uma eleição -**2.** [countryside]: **the ~** o campo -**3.** [area of land, region] região f. ⟨⟩ comp do campo.

country and western ⟨⟩ n (U) música f country. ⟨⟩ comp country inv.

country club n clube m de campo, country club m.

country dancing n (U) dança f tradicional.

country house n casa f de campo.

countryman ['kʌntrɪmən] (pl -men [-mən]) n [from same country] compatriota m.

country music n & comp = country and western.

country park n UK parque m regional.

countryside ['kʌntrɪsaɪd] n (U) campo m.

countrywoman ['kʌntrɪˌwʊmən] (pl -women [-ˌwɪmɪn]) n [from same country] compatriota f.

county ['kaʊntɪ] (pl -ies) n condado m.

county council n UK conselho m regional.

county court n UK tribunal m regional.

county town UK, **county seat** US n capital de um condado.

coup [ku:] n -**1.** [rebellion]: **~ (d'état)** golpe de estado - **2.** [masterstroke] golpe *m* de mestre.

coupé [ˈkuːpeɪ] *n AUT* cupê *m*.

couple [ˈkʌpl] ◇ *n* - **1.** [in relationship] casal *m* - **2.** [small number]: **a** ~ alguns, algumas; **a** ~ **of** dois, duas. ◇ *vt* - **1.** [join]: **to** ~ **sthg (to sthg)** unir algo (a algo) - **2.** *fig* [associate]: **to** ~ **sthg with sthg** associar algo a algo; ~ **d with** aliado(da) a.

couplet [ˈkʌplɪt] *n* dístico *m*.

coupling [ˈkʌplɪŋ] *n RAIL* engate *m*.

coupon [ˈkuːpɒn] *n* - **1.** [voucher] vale *m* - **2.** [form] cupom *m*.

courage [ˈkʌrɪdʒ] *n (U)* coragem *f*; **to take** ~ **(from sthg)** tirar coragem (de algo); **to have the** ~ **of one's convictions** ter coragem de manter suas opiniões.

courageous [kəˈreɪdʒəs] *adj* corajoso(sa).

courageously [kəˈreɪdʒəslɪ] *adv* corajosamente.

courgette [kɔːˈʒet] *n UK* abobrinha *f*.

courier [ˈkʊrɪəʳ] *n* - **1.** [on holiday tour] *representante de uma agência de viagens que cuida das pessoas que estão a passeio* - **2.** [delivering letters, packages] mensageiro *m*, -ra *f*, courier *m*.

course [kɔːs] ◇ *n* - **1.** [gen] curso *m* - **2.** *MED* [of treatment] tratamento *m* - **3.** [path, route] rota *f*; **to run** OR **take its** ~ seguir OR tomar o curso natural; **to be on** ~ **for** [ship, plane] estar rumando para; *fig* [on target] em curso; **off** ~ fora de curso - **4.** [plan]: ~ **(of action)** curso (de ação) - **5.** [of time]: **in due** ~ no tempo devido; **in the** ~ **of** no decorrer de - **6.** [in meal] prato *m* - **7.** *SPORT* campo *m*. ◇ *vi literary* [flow] correr.

➤ **of course** *adv* - **1.** [inevitably, not surprisingly] evidentemente - **2.** [certainly] claro que sim; **of** ~ **you can!** claro que pode!; '**do you want the job?'** - '**of** ~ **I do!**' 'você quer o trabalho?' - 'claro que quero!'; **of** ~ **not** claro que não.

coursebook [ˈkɔːsbʊk] *n* livro *m* de curso.

coursework [ˈkɔːswɜːk] *n (U)* trabalho *m* de curso.

court [kɔːt] ◇ *n* - **1.** *JUR* tribunal *m*; **to appear in** ~ comparecer perante um tribunal; **to settle out of** ~ resolver fora dos tribunais; **to go to** ~ processar; **to take sb to** ~ levar alguém a julgamento; **the** ~ o tribunal - **2.** *SPORT* quadra *f*; **on** ~ na quadra - **3.** [courtyard] pátio *m* - **4.** [of king, queen etc] corte *f*. ◇ *vt* [seek] procurar. ◇ *vi dated* [go out together] cortejar.

court circular *n UK* ≃ diário *m* da corte.

courteous [ˈkɜːtjəs] *adj* cortês.

courtesan [ˌkɔːtɪˈzæn] *n* cortesã *f*.

courtesy [ˈkɜːtɪsɪ] *n (U)* [polite behaviour] cortesia *f*.

➤ **(by) courtesy of** *prep* [thanks to] por cortesia de.

courtesy car *n* carro *m* de cortesia.

courtesy coach *n* ônibus *m* de cortesia.

courthouse [ˈkɔːthaʊs] *n US* palácio *m* da justiça.

courtier [ˈkɔːtjəʳ] *n* cortesão *m*.

court-martial (*pl* **court-martials** OR **courts-martial**, *UK pt* & *pp* -**led**, *cont* -**ling**, *US pt* & *pp* -**ed**, *cont* -**ing**) ◇ *n* corte *m* marcial. ◇ *vt* submeter a uma corte marcial.

court of appeal *UK*, **court of appeals** *US n* tribunal *m* de apelação.

court of inquiry *n* - **1.** [investigation] tribunal *m*

de investigação - **2.** [investigating group] comissão *f* de inquérito.

court of law *n* tribunal *m*.

courtroom [ˈkɔːtrʊm] *n* sala *f* de tribunal.

courtship [ˈkɔːtʃɪp] *n (U)* - **1.** [of people] galanteio *m* - **2.** [of animals] requesta *f*.

court shoe *n* escarpim *m*.

courtyard [ˈkɔːtjɑːd] *n* pátio *m*.

cousin [ˈkʌzn] *n* primo *m*, -ma *f*.

couture [kuːˈtʊəʳ] *n*: **haute** ~ alta-costura *f*.

cove [kəʊv] *n* [bay] enseada *f*.

coven [ˈkʌvn] *n* grupo *m* de bruxas.

covenant [ˈkʌvənənt] *n* - **1.** [promise of money] convênio *m* - **2.** [pact] pacto *m*.

Covent Garden [ˌkɒvnt-] *n área comercial e artística coberta no centro de Londres, que também inclui o Royal Opera House.*

Coventry [ˈkɒvəntrɪ] *n*: **to send sb to** ~ pôr alguém no ostracismo.

cover [ˈkʌvəʳ] ◇ *n* - **1.** [covering] capa *f* - **2.** [lid] tampa *f* - **3.** [blanket] coberta *f* - **4.** [protection, shelter] abrigo *m*; **to take** ~ [from weather] abrigar-se; [from gunfire] proteger-se; **under** ~ [from weather] abrigado(da); **under** ~ **of darkness** sob o manto da escuridão; **to break** ~ sair do esconderijo - **5.** [disguise, front or insurance] cobertura *f*. ◇ *vt* cobrir; **to** ~ **sthg with sthg** cobrir algo com algo; **to** ~ **sb against sthg** [give insurance] cobrir alguém contra algo.

➤ **cover up** *vt sep* - **1.** [person, animal] cobrir - **2.** *fig* [story, scandal] encobrir.

coverage [ˈkʌvərɪdʒ] *n (U)* [of news] cobertura *f*.

coveralls [ˈkʌvərɔːlz] *npl US* macacão *m*.

cover charge *n* couvert *m*.

cover girl *n* garota *f* da capa.

covering [ˈkʌvərɪŋ] *n* cobertura *f*.

covering letter *UK*, **cover letter** *US n* carta *ou nota contendo explicações ou informações adicionais que acompanha uma encomenda ou outra carta.*

cover note *n UK* nota *f* de cobertura.

cover price *n* [of book, magazine] preço *m* de capa.

covert [ˈkʌvət] *adj* secreto(ta), oculto(ta).

cover-up *n* encobrimento *m*.

cover version *n* regravação *f* de música.

covet [ˈkʌvɪt] *vt fml* ambicionar.

cow [kaʊ] ◇ *n* - **1.** [female type of cattle] vaca *f* - **2.** [female elephant, whale, seal] fêmea *f* - **3.** *UK inf pej* [woman] vaca *f*. ◇ *vt* intimidar.

coward [ˈkaʊəd] *n* covarde *mf*.

cowardice [ˈkaʊədɪs] *n (U)* covardia *f*.

cowardly [ˈkaʊədlɪ] *adj* covarde.

cowboy [ˈkaʊbɔɪ] ◇ *n* - **1.** [cattlehand] vaqueiro - **2.** *UK inf* [dishonest workman] patife *m*. ◇ *comp* [western] caubói *m*.

cower [ˈkaʊəʳ] *vi* encolher-se de medo.

cowhide [ˈkaʊhaɪd] *n (U)* couro *m* de vaca.

cowl neck *n* capuz *m*.

co-worker *n* colega *mf* de trabalho.

cowpat [ˈkaʊpæt] *n* estrume *m* de vaca.

cowshed [ˈkaʊʃed] *n* estábulo *m*.

cox [kɒks], **coxswain** [ˈkɒksən] *n* timoneiro *m*, -ra *f*.

coy [kɔɪ] *adj* recatado(da).

coyly ['kɔɪlɪ] *adv* recatadamente.

coyote [kɔɪ'əʊtɪ] *n* coiote *m*.

cozy *adj* & *n US* = cosy.

CP (*abbr of* Communist Party) *n* partido *m* comunista.

CPA (*abbr of* certified public accountant) *n* contador público certificado nos Estados Unidos.

Cpl. (*abbr of* corporal) corporal.

cps (*abbr of* characters per second) cps.

CPS (*abbr of* Crown Prosecution Service) *n* organismo britânico que decide quais casos policiais devem ser levados ao tribunal.

CPU (*abbr of* central processing unit) *n COMPUT* CPU *f*.

Cr - 1. *abbr of* Councillor. **- 2.** *abbr of* credit.

crab [kræb] *n* **- 1.** [sea creature] caranguejo *m* **- 2.** [food] siri *m*.

crab apple *n* **- 1.** [fruit] maçã *f* silvestre **- 2.** [tree] macieira *f* silvestre.

crabby (*compar* -ier, *superl* -iest) *adj* mal-humorado(da).

crack [kræk] <> *n* **- 1.** [fault - in cup, glass, mirror] trinca *f*; [- in wall, ceiling] rachadura *f*; [- in skin] arranhão *m* **- 2.** [small opening, gap] fresta *f*; **at the ~ of dawn** no raiar do dia **- 3.** [sharp noise] estalo *m* **- 4.** [joke] piada *f* **- 5.** *inf* [attempt]: **to have a ~ at sthg** tentar (fazer) algo **- 6.** [cocaine] crack *m*. <> *adj* de primeira. <> *vt* **- 1.** [damage - gen] arranhar; [- cup, glass] trincar; [- wall, ceiling] rachar **- 2.** [open - egg] quebrar; [- bottle] abrir; [- safe] arrombar **- 3.** [cause to make sharp noise] estalar **- 4.** [bang, hit] bater **- 5.** [solve - problem] resolver; [- code] decifrar **- 6.** *inf* [make]: **to ~ a joke** soltar uma piada. <> *vi* **- 1.** [split, be damaged - gen] arranhar; [- cup, glass] trincar; [- wall, ceiling,] rachar **- 2.** [make sharp noise] estalar **- 3.** [give way, collapse] ruir **- 4.** *UK inf* [act quickly]: **to get ~ing** pôr mãos à obra.

➡ **crack down** *vi*: **to ~ down (on sb/sthg)** fazer linha dura (contra alguém/algo).

➡ **crack up** *vi* ter um colapso nervoso.

crackdown ['krækdaʊn] *n*: **~ (on sthg)** endurecimento *m* (em relação a algo).

cracked ['krækt] *adj* **- 1.** [damaged - cup, glass, skin] arranhado(da); [- wall, ceiling] rachado(da) **- 2.** *inf* [mad] doido(da).

cracker ['krækə'] *n* **- 1.** [biscuit] biscoito *m* **- 2.** *UK* [for Christmas] tubo colorido que faz barulho ao abrir e contém um presente surpresa.

crackers ['krækəz] *adj UK inf* [mad] doido(da).

cracking ['krækɪŋ] *adj inf*: **to walk at a ~ pace** andar a passos largos.

crackle ['krækl] <> *n* **- 1.** [of fire, cooking] crepitação *f* **- 2.** [of phone, radio] interferência *f*. <> *vi* **- 1.** [fire, cooking] crepitar **- 2.** [phone, radio] estar com interferência.

crackling ['kræklɪŋ] *n* (U) **- 1.** [noise - on phone] tilintar *m*; [- on radio] interferência *f* **- 2.** [pork skin] torresmo *m*.

crackpot ['krækpɒt] *inf* <> *adj* maluco(ca). <> *n* excêntrico *m*, -ca *f*.

cradle ['kreɪdl] <> *n* **- 1.** [baby's bed, birthplace] berço *m* **- 2.** [hoist] pedestal *m*. <> *vt* **- 1.** [person] embalar **- 2.** [object] segurar cuidadosamente.

craft [krɑːft] (*pl sense 2 inv*) *n* **- 1.** [trade, skill] arte *f* **- 2.** [boat] barco *m*.

craftsman ['krɑːftsmən] (*pl* -men [-mən]) *n* artesão *m*.

craftsmanship ['krɑːftsmənʃɪp] *n* destreza *f*, habilidade *f*.

craftsmen *pl* ➡ craftsman.

crafty ['krɑːftɪ] (*compar* -ier, *superl* -iest) *adj* astuto(-ta).

crag [kræg] *n* penhasco *m*.

craggy ['krægɪ] (*compar* -ier, *superl* -iest) *adj* **- 1.** [rock] escarpado(da) **- 2.** [face] de traços fortes.

Crakow ['krækaʊ] *n* Cracóvia; **in ~** em Cracóvia.

cram [kræm] (*pt* & *pp* -med, *cont* -ming) <> *vt* abarrotar; **to ~ sthg with sthg** abarrotar algo com algo; **to be crammed (with sthg)** estar abarrotado(da) (de algo). <> *vi* [study hard] rachar de estudar.

cramp [kræmp] <> *n* **- 1.** [in leg, arm] cãibra *f* **- 2.** [in stomach] cólica *f*. <> *vt* [restrict, hinder] limitar.

cramped [kræmpt] *adj* [confined] apertado(da).

crampon ['kræmpən] *n* ganho *m* de ferro.

cranberry ['krænbərɪ] (*pl* -ies) *n* uva-do-monte *f*.

crane [kreɪn] <> *n* **- 1.** [machine] guindaste *m* **- 2.** [bird] grou *m*. <> *vt* espichar. <> *vi* espichar-se.

crane fly *n* mosquito-berne *m*.

cranium ['kreɪnjəm] (*pl* -niums *OR* -nia [-njə]) *n* crânio *m*.

crank [kræŋk] <> *n* **- 1.** *TECH* manivela *f* **- 2.** *inf* [eccentric] extravagante *mf*. <> *vt* **- 1.** [gen] dar manivela em **- 2.** *AUT* dar partida em.

crankshaft ['kræŋkʃɑːft] *n* virabrequim *m*.

cranky ['kræŋkɪ] (*compar* -ier, *superl* -iest) *adj inf* **- 1.** [odd] esquisito(ta) **- 2.** [bad-tempered] irritadiço(ça).

cranny ['krænɪ] (*pl* -ies) *n* ➡ nook.

crap [kræp] *n* (U) *vulg* **- 1.** [excrement] bosta *f* **- 2.** *fig* [rubbish] asneira *f*.

crappy ['kræpɪ] (*compar* -ier, *superl* -iest) *adj vulg* de péssima qualidade.

crash [kræʃ] <> *n* **- 1.** [accident] acidente *m* **- 2.** [loud noise] estrépito *m* **- 3.** *FIN* crash *m*. <> *vt* [cause to collide] bater com. <> *vi* **- 1.** [collide] colidir; **to ~ into sthg** colidir em algo **- 2.** [make loud noise - drums] soar; [- cymbals] retinir; [- waves] quebrar; [- china] espatifar **- 3.** *FIN* [collapse] entrar em colapso **- 4.** *COMPUT* dar pane.

crash barrier *n* cerca *f* de proteção.

crash course *n* curso *m* intensivo.

crash diet *n* dieta *f* rigorosa.

crash-dive *vi* submersão *f* súbita.

crash helmet *n* elmo *m*.

crash-land <> *vt* aterrisar forçosamente. <> *vi* aterrisar forçosamente.

crash-landing *n* aterrissagem *f* forçada.

crass [kræs] *adj* crasso(sa).

crate [kreɪt] *n* **- 1.** [for carrying things] caixote *m* **- 2.** [crateful] engradado *m*.

crater ['kreɪtə'] *n* cratera *f*.

cravat [krə'væt] *n* cachecol *m*.

crave [kreɪv] <> *vt* ansiar. <> *vi*: **to ~ for sthg** ansiar por algo.

craving ['kreɪvɪŋ] *n*: **~ (for sthg/to do sthg)** desejo incontrolável (por algo/fazer algo).

crawl [krɔːl] ⋄ *vi* -**1.** [on hands and knees] engatinhar - **2.** [move slowly - insect] rastejar; [- vehicle, traffic] arrastar-se -**3.** *inf*: **to be** ~**ing with sthg** estar infestado(da) de algo - **4.** *inf* [grovel]: **to** ~ **(to sb)** rastejar (aos pés de alguém). ⋄ *n* -**1.** [slow pace]: **at a** ~ vagarosamente -**2.** *(U)* [swimming stroke]: **the** ~ o crawl.

crawler lane [ˈkrɔːlə⁻] *n UK* faixa *f* para veículos lentos.

crayfish [ˈkreɪfɪʃ] *(pl inv OR* -**es**) *n* -**1.** [fish] lagostim *m* - **2.** [food] camarão-d'água-doce *m*.

crayon [ˈkreɪɒn] *n* lápis *m* de cera.

craze [kreɪz] *n* [fashion] moda *f.*

crazed [kreɪzd] *adj* enlouquecido(da); ~ **with** louco(ca) de.

crazy [ˈkreɪzɪ] (*compar* -**ier**, *superl* -**iest**) *adj inf* [mad, enthusiastic] louco(ca); **to be** ~ **about sthg/sb** ser/ estar louco(ca) por algo/alguém.

crazy paving *n UK* pavimento *m* irregular.

CRC (*abbr of* **camera-ready copy**) *PRINT n* versão pronta para impressão.

CRE (*abbr of* **Commission for Racial Equality**) *n* comissão para combater a desigualdade racial.

creak [kriːk] ⋄ *n* rangido *m.* ⋄ *vi* ranger.

creaky [ˈkriːkɪ] (*compar* -**ier**, *superl* -**iest**) *adj* que range.

cream [kriːm] ⋄ *adj* [in colour] creme. ⋄ *n* -**1.** creme *m* -**2.** [elite] **the** ~ a nata. ⋄ *vt* [puree] fazer purê com.
➡ **cream off** *vt sep* tirar o melhor de.

cream cake *n UK* bolo *m* de creme.

cream cheese *n (U)* queijo *m* cremoso.

cream cracker *n UK* bolacha *f* cream cracker.

cream of tartar *n (U)* cremor *m* de tártaro.

cream tea *n UK* chá acompanhado de bolinhos com presunto, geléia e creme, comum na Inglaterra.

creamy [ˈkriːmɪ] (*compar* -**ier**, *superl* -**iest**) *adj* -**1.** [texture, taste] cremoso(sa) -**2.** [colour] creme.

crease [kriːs] ⋄ *n* [in fabric - deliberate] friso *m*; [- accidental] dobra *f.* ⋄ *vt* [deliberately] amassar; [accidentally] amarrotar. ⋄ *vi* -**1.** [fabric] amassar -**2.** [face, forehead] franzir-se.

creased [kriːst] *adj* -**1.** [fabric] amarrotado(da) -**2.** [face] franzido(da).

crease-resistant *adj*: ~ **fabric** tecido *m* que não amassa.

create [kriːˈeɪt] *vt* -**1.** [gen] criar -**2.** [noise, fuss, impression] causar.

creation [kriːˈeɪʃn] *n* criação *f.*

creative [kriːˈeɪtɪv] *adj* criativo(va); ~ **writing** produção *f* literária.

creativity [ˌkriːeɪˈtɪvətɪ] *n (U)* criatividade *f.*

creator [kriːˈeɪtə⁻] *n* [person] criador *m*, -ra *f.*

creature [ˈkriːtʃə⁻] *n* -**1.** [animal] criatura *f* -**2.** *literary* [person] ser *m.*

crèche [kreʃ] *n UK* creche *f.*

credence [ˈkriːdns] *n (U)* credibilidade *f*; **to give** *OR* **lend** ~ **to sthg** conferir credibilidade a algo.

credentials [krɪˈdenʃlz] *npl* -**1.** [papers] credenciais *fpl* - **2.** *fig* [qualifications] credenciais *fpl* -**3.** [references] referências *fpl.*

credibility [ˌkredəˈbɪlətɪ] *n (U)* credibilidade *f.*

credible [ˈkredəbl] *adj* crível.

credit [ˈkredɪt] ⋄ *n* -**1.** *(U)* [financial aid] crédito *m*; **in** ~ com saldo positivo; **on** ~ a prazo -**2.** *(U)* [praise] honras *fpl*; **to his/her** ~ [successfully completed] a seu favor; [in his/her favour] para o seu próprio bem; **to do sb** ~ dizer muito em favor de alguém; **to give sb** ~ **for sthg** crer que alguém seja capaz de algo -**3.** *SCH & UNIV* crédito *m* -**4.** *FIN* [money credited] saldo *m* positivo. ⋄ *vt* -**1.** *FIN* creditar -**2.** *inf* [believe] acreditar -**3.** [attribute]: **to** ~ **sb with sthg** atribuir a alguém o mérito por algo.
➡ **credits** *npl CINEMA* créditos *mpl.*

creditable [ˈkredɪtəbl] *adj* louvável.

credit account *n UK* conta *f* de crédito.

credit broker *n* intermediário *m* financeiro, intermediária *f* financeira.

credit card *n* cartão *m* de crédito.

credit control *n (U)* controle *m* de crédito.

credit facilities *npl* facilidades *fpl* de crédito.

credit limit *UK*, **credit line** *US n* limite *m* de crédito.

credit note *n* -**1.** *COMM* nota *f* promissória -**2.** *FIN* letra *f* de câmbio.

creditor [ˈkredɪtə⁻] *n* credor *m*, -ra *f.*

credit rating *n* índice *f* de crédito.

credit squeeze *n* contenção *f* de crédito.

credit transfer *n* transferência *f* bancária.

creditworthy [ˈkredɪtˌwɜːðɪ] *adj* merecedor(ra) de crédito.

credulity [krɪˈdjuːlətɪ] *n (U) fml* credulidade *f.*

credulous [ˈkredjʊləs] *adj* crédulo(la).

creed [kriːd] *n* -**1.** [political] doutrina *f* -**2.** *RELIG* credo *m.*

creek [kriːk] *n* -**1.** [inlet] enseada *f* -**2.** *US* [stream] riacho *m.*

creep [kriːp] (*pt & pp* **crept**) ⋄ *vi* -**1.** [move slowly] arrastar-se -**2.** [move stealthily] andar furtivamente - **3.** [grovel]: **to** ~ **(to sb)** rastejar-se (diante de alguém). ⋄ *n inf* [person] pegajoso *m*, -sa *f.*
➡ **creeps** *npl*: **to give sb the** ~**s** *inf* dar arrepios *mpl* em alguém.
➡ **creep in** *vi* [mistakes, doubts] surgir.
➡ **creep up on** *vt* -**1.** [subj: person, animal] aproximar-se furtivamente -**2.** [subj: feeling, state] aproximar-se.

creeper [ˈkriːpə⁻] *n* [plant] trepadeira *f.*

creeping *adj* [gradual] gradual.

creepy [ˈkriːpɪ] (*compar* -**ier**, *superl* -**iest**) *adj inf* horripilante.

creepy-crawly [-ˈkrɔːlɪ] (*pl* **creepy-crawlies**) *n inf* bicho *m* rastejante.

cremate [krɪˈmeɪt] *vt* cremar.

cremation [krɪˈmeɪʃn] *n (U)* cremação *f.*

crematorium *UK* [ˌkreməˈtɔːrɪəm] (*pl* -**riums** *OR* -**ria** [-rɪə]), **crematory** *US* [ˈkremətrɪ] (*pl* -**ies**) *n* crematório *m.*

creosote [ˈkrɪəsəʊt] ⋄ *n (U)* creosoto *m.* ⋄ *vt* aplicar creosoto em.

crepe [kreɪp] *n* crepe *m.*

crepe bandage *n UK* atadura *f.*

crepe paper *n (U)* papel *m* crepom.

crepe-soled shoes [-səʊld-] *npl UK* calçado *m* com sola emborrachada.

crept [krept] *pt & pp* ▷ **creep**.

Cres. *abbr of* **Crescent**.

crescendo [krɪˈʃendəʊ] (*pl* -s) *n* crescendo *m*.

crescent [ˈkresnt] ◇ *adj* [shaped] crescente. ◇ *n* -1. [shape] crescente *mf* -2. [street] rua *f* em forma de arco.

cress [kres] *n (U)* agrião *m*.

crest [krest] *n* -1. [on bird's head, of wave] crista *f* -2. [of hill] cume *m* -3. [on coat of arms] brasão *m*.

crestfallen [ˈkrestˌfɔːln] *adj* desanimado(da).

Crete [kriːt] *n* Creta; **in** ~ em Creta.

cretin [ˈkretɪn] *n inf offensive* [idiot] cretino *m*, -na *f*.

crevasse [krɪˈvæs] *n* fissura *f*, fenda *f*.

crevice [ˈkrevɪs] *n* fenda *f*, rachadura *f*.

crew [kruː] *n* -1. [of ship, plane, ambulance] tripulação *f* -2. *CINEMA & TV* equipe *f* -3. *inf* [gang] bando *m*.

crew cut *n* corte *m* de cabelo à escovinha.

crewman [ˈkruːmæn] (*pl* -men [-men]) *n* -1. [of aircraft] tripulante *mf* -2. [of film set] membro *m* da equipe.

crew neck *n* [on sweater] gola *f* redonda.

crew-neck(ed) [-nek(t)] *adj* de gola redonda.

crib [krɪb] (*pt & pp* -bed, *cont* -bing) ◇ *n* berço *m*. ◇ *vt inf* [copy]: **to** ~ **sthg off** *OR* **from sb** copiar algo de alguém.

cribbage [ˈkrɪbɪdʒ] *n (U)* jogo de cartas em que a pontuação é marcada com madeira num tabuleiro.

crick [krɪk] ◇ *n* [in neck] torcicolo *m*. ◇ *vt* dar mau jeito em.

cricket [ˈkrɪkɪt] ◇ *n* -1. *(U)* [game] críquete *m* -2. [insect] grilo *m*. ◇ *comp* de críquete.

cricketer [ˈkrɪkɪtəʳ] *n* jogador *m*, -ra *f* de críquete.

crikey [ˈkraɪkɪ] *excl UK inf dated* caramba!

crime [kraɪm] ◇ *n* crime *m*. ◇ *comp*: ~ **prevention** prevenção *f* contra o crime; ~ **novel** novela *f* policial.

Crimea *n*: **the** ~ a Criméia; **in the** ~ na Criméia.

crime wave *n* onda *f* de criminalidade.

criminal [ˈkrɪmɪnl] ◇ *adj* -1. [*JUR* - act] criminal; [- lawyer] criminalista; [offence] penal -2. *inf* [shameful] vergonhoso(sa). ◇ *n* criminoso *m*, -sa *f*.

criminalize, -ise [ˈkrɪmɪnəlaɪz] *vt* criminalizar.

criminal law *n (U)* direito *m* penal.

criminology [ˌkrɪmɪˈnɒlədʒɪ] *n (U)* criminologia *f*.

crimped *adj* ondulado(da).

crimson [ˈkrɪmzn] ◇ *adj* -1. [in colour] carmesim -2. [with embarrassment] vermelho(lha). ◇ *n* carmesim *mf*.

cringe [krɪndʒ] *vi* -1. [out of fear] encolher-se -2. *inf* [with embarrassment]: **to** ~ **(at sthg)** encolher-se de vergonha (por algo).

crinkle [ˈkrɪŋkl] ◇ *n* ruga *f*. ◇ *vt* enrugar. ◇ *vi* enrugar-se.

cripple [ˈkrɪpl] ◇ *n offensive* aleijado *m*, -da *f*. ◇ *vt* -1. *MED* [disable] aleijar -2. [put out of action] inutilizar -3. *fig* [bring to a halt] paralisar.

crippling [ˈkrɪplɪŋ] *adj* -1. *MED* [disease] devastador(ra) -2. [taxes, prices, debts] excessivo(va).

crisis [ˈkraɪsɪs] (*pl* crises [ˈkraɪsiːz]) *n* crise *f*.

crisp [krɪsp] *adj* -1. [pastry, bacon] crocante; [fruit,

vegetables] fresco(ca); [banknote] liso(sa); [snow] quebradiço(ça) -2. [weather] revigorante -3. [manner, toner] seco(ca).

◆ **crisps** *npl UK* batatas *fpl* fritas *(em pacote)*.

crispbread [ˈkrɪspbred] *n (U)* biscoito de centeio ou trigo, que substitui o pão para quem está de dieta.

crispy [ˈkrɪspɪ] (*compar* -ier, *superl* -iest) *adj* [pastry, bacon] crocante; [fruit, vegetables] fresco(ca).

criss-cross ◇ *adj* [pattern] xadrez. ◇ *vt* [subj: roads] entrecruzar. ◇ *vi* [lines, pattern] entrecruzar-se.

criterion [kraɪˈtɪərɪən] (*pl* -ria [-rɪə], -rions) *n* critério *m*.

critic [ˈkrɪtɪk] *n* crítico *m*, -ca *f*.

critical [ˈkrɪtɪkl] *adj* -1. [serious] crítico(ca), grave -2. [crucial] fundamental -3. [analytical, disparaging] crítico(ca); **to be** ~ **of sb/sthg** criticar alguém/algo.

critically [ˈkrɪtɪklɪ] *adv* -1. [seriously] criticamente, gravemente -2. [crucially] fundamentalmente -3. [analytically, disparagingly] criticamente.

criticism [ˈkrɪtɪsɪzm] *n* crítica *f*.

criticize, -ise [ˈkrɪtɪsaɪz] ◇ *vt* [judge unfavourably] criticar. ◇ *vi* [make unfavourable comments] criticar.

critique [krɪˈtiːk] *n* crítica *f*.

croak [krəʊk] ◇ *n* -1. [of frog] coaxo *m* -2. [of bird] grasnido *m* -3. [hoarse voice] rouquidão *f*. ◇ *vt* grunhir. ◇ *vi* -1. [animal] coaxar -2. [bird] granir -3. [person] ter rouquidão.

Croat [ˈkrəʊæt], **Croatian** [krəʊˈeɪʃn] ◇ *adj* croata. ◇ *n* -1. [person] croata *mf* -2. [language] croata *m*.

Croatia [krəʊˈeɪʃn] *n* Croácia; **in** ~ na Croácia.

crochet [ˈkrəʊʃeɪ] ◇ *n (U)* crochê *m*. ◇ *vt* fazer de crochê.

crockery [ˈkrɒkərɪ] *n (U)* louça *f (de barro)*.

crocodile [ˈkrɒkədaɪl] (*pl inv OR* -s) *n* [animal] crocodilo *m*.

crocus [ˈkrəʊkəs] (*pl* -cuses) *n* açafrão *m*.

croft [krɒft] *n UK* sítio *m*.

croissant [ˈkrwæsã] *n* croissant *m*.

crony [ˈkrəʊnɪ] (*pl* -ies) *n inf* [friend] camarada *mf*.

crook [krʊk] ◇ *n* -1. [criminal] vigarista *mf* -2. *inf* [dishonest person] trapaceiro *m*, -ra *f* -3. [angle] curvatura *f* -4. [shepherd's staff] cajado *m*. ◇ *vt* entortar, dobrar.

crooked [ˈkrʊkɪd] *adj* -1. [not straight - back] arqueado(da); [- teeth, smile] torto(ta); [- path] sinuoso(sa) -2. *inf* [dishonest] desonesto(ta).

croon [kruːn] ◇ *vt* [sing softly] cantarolar. ◇ *vi* [sing softly] cantarolar.

crop [krɒp] (*pt & pp* -ped, *cont* -ping) ◇ *n* -1. [kind of plant] cultura *f* -2. [harvested produce] colheita *f* -3. *inf fig* [group]: **a** ~ **of books** uma coleção de livros; **a** ~ **of graduates** um grupo de formandos -4. [whip] chicote *m* -5. [of bird] papo *m* -6. [haircut] cabelo *m* curto. ◇ *vt* -1. [cut short] tosar -2. [eat] mascar.

◆ **crop up** *vi* surgir.

cropper [ˈkrɒpəʳ] *n inf*: **to come a** ~ [fall] levar um tombo; [fail] entrar pelo cano.

crop spraying [-ˌspreɪɪŋ] *n (U)* pulverização *f*.

croquet [ˈkrəʊkeɪ] *n (U)* croqué *m*.

croquette [krɒˈket] *n* croquete *m*.

cross [krɒs] ◇ *adj* zangado(da). ◇ *n* -**1**. [gen] cruz *f* -**2**. [mixture] cruzamento *m*; **a Labrador ~** um cruzamento de labrador; **a ~ between two things** uma mistura de duas coisas. ◇ *vt* -**1**. [gen] cruzar -**2**. [move across - street, room] atravessar; [- subj: expression] trespassar; **a look of distaste ~ed her face** um olhar de desagrado trespassou-lhe o rosto -**3**. *RELIG* : **to ~ o.s.** fazer o sinal da cruz -**4**. *UK* [cheque] cruzar -**5**. [thwart] frustrar, impedir. ◇ *vi* -**1**. [intersect] cruzar-se -**2**. [traverse] fazer uma travessia.
  ➞ **cross off, cross out** *vt sep* riscar.

crossbar [ˈkrɒsbɑ:ʳ] *n* -**1**. [of goal] trave *f* -**2**. [of bicycle] barra *f* transversal.

crossbow [ˈkrɒsbəʊ] *n* besta *f*.

crossbreed [ˈkrɒsbri:d] *n* cruza *f*.

cross-Channel *adj* [ferry, route] do Canal da Mancha; **~ travel** viagem pelo Canal da Mancha.

cross-check ◇ *n* verificação *f* cruzada. ◇ *vt* verificar de forma cruzada.

cross-country ◇ *adj* & *adv* através do campo. ◇ *n* [race, running] esporte praticado através dos campos.

cross-cultural *adj* intercultural.

cross-dress *vi* -**1**. [man] vestir-se de mulher -**2**. [woman] vestir-se de homem.

crossed line [krɒst-] *n* linha *f* cruzada.

cross-examination *n* -**1**. *JUR* interrogatório *m* (para confirmar veracidade) -**2**. *fig* [close questioning] interrogatório *m*.

cross-examine *vt* -**1**. *JUR* interrogar (para confirmar veracidade) -**2**. *fig* [question closely] interrogar.

cross-eyed [ˈkrɒsaɪd] *adj* vesgo(ga).

cross-fertilize *vt* [plant] fecundar por cruzamento.

crossfire [ˈkrɒsˌfaɪəʳ] *n (U)* fogo *m* cruzado.

crosshead [ˈkrɒsˌhed] *adj* [screw] com cabeça Philips®; **~ screwdriver** chave *f* de fenda Philips®.

crossing [ˈkrɒsɪŋ] *n* -**1**. [place to cross] faixa *f* de segurança -**2**. [sea journey] travessia *f*. ʄ

cross-legged [ˈkrɒslegd] *adv* de pernas cruzadas.

crossly [ˈkrɒslɪ] *adv* com irritação.

cross-ply (*pl* -ies) *adj* [tyre] de carcaça diagonal.

cross-purposes *npl* mal-entendido *m*; **to be at ~** não se entender.

cross-question *vt* interrogar novamente.

cross-refer ◇ *vt* remeter. ◇ *vi* fazer uma referência.

cross-reference *n* referência *f* cruzada.

crossroads [ˈkrɒsrəʊdz] (*pl inv*) *n* cruzamento *m*, encruzilhada *f*; **to be at a ~** *fig* estar numa encruzilhada.

cross-section *n* -**1**. [drawing] corte *m* transversal -**2**. [of population] amostra *f* representativa.

crosswalk [ˈkrɒswɔ:k] *n US* faixa *f* de segurança.

crossways [ˈkrɒsweɪz] *adv* = **crosswise**.

crosswind [ˈkrɒswɪnd] *n* vento *m* contrário.

crosswise [ˈkrɒswaɪz] *adv* em diagonal, transversalmente.

crossword (puzzle) [ˈkrɒswɜ:d-] *n* palavras *fpl* cruzadas.

crotch [krɒtʃ] *n* -**1**. [of person] entreperna *f* -**2**. [of garment] gancho *m*.

crotchet [ˈkrɒtʃɪt] *n* semínima *f*.

crotchety [ˈkrɒtʃɪtɪ] *adj UK inf* rabugento(ta).

crouch [kraʊtʃ] *vi* -**1**. [person] agachar-se -**2**. [animal] armar o bote.

croup [kru:p] *n* -**1**. [illness] crupe *m* -**2**. [of horse] garupa *f*.

croupier [ˈkru:pɪəʳ] *n* crupiê *mf*.

crouton [ˈkru:tɒn] *n* pão torrado cortado em cubos que acompanha a sopa.

crow [krəʊ] ◇ *n* corvo *m*; **as the ~ flies** em linha reta. ◇ *vi* -**1**. [cock] cantar -**2**. *inf* [gloat] gabar-se.

crowbar [ˈkrəʊbɑ:ʳ] *n* pé-de-cabra *m*.

crowd [kraʊd] ◇ *n* -**1**. [mass of people] multidão *f* -**2**. [social group] turma *f*. ◇ *vi* aglomerar-se. ◇ *vt* -**1**. [fill] lotar -**2**. [force into small space] empurrar; **to ~ everyone in** colocar todo mundo para dentro.

crowded [ˈkraʊdɪd] *adj* cheio (cheia), lotado(da); **~ with** cheio (cheia) de, repleto(ta) de.

crown [kraʊn] ◇ *n* -**1**. [gen] coroa *f* -**2**. [top - of hat] copa *f*; [- of head] topo *m*; [- of hill] cume *m*. ◇ *vt* -**1**. [monarch] coroar -**2**. [tooth] pôr uma coroa em -**3**. [cover top of] cobrir.
  ➞ **Crown** ◇ *n*: **the Crown** [monarchy] a Coroa. ◇ *comp* da Coroa.

crown court *n* tribunal *m* (com júri).

crowning [ˈkraʊnɪŋ] *adj* supremo(ma).

Crown Jewels *npl*: **the ~** as jóias da Coroa.

crown prince *n* príncipe *m* herdeiro.

crow's feet *npl* pés-de-galinha *mpl*.

crow's nest *n* cesto *m* de gávea.

crucial [ˈkru:ʃl] *adj* [vital] crucial.

crucially [ˈkru:ʃlɪ] *adv* [vitally] crucialmente; **~ important** de vital importância.

crucible [ˈkru:sɪbl] *n* [container] cadinho *m*.

crucifix [ˈkru:sɪfɪks] *n* crucifixo *m*.

Crucifixion [ˌkru:sɪˈfɪkʃn] *n*: **the ~** a Crucificação.

crucify [ˈkru:sɪfaɪ] (*pt* & *pp* -**ied**) *vt lit* & *fig* crucificar.

crude [kru:d] ◇ *adj* -**1**. [commodity] cru (crua) -**2**. [joke, person] grosseiro(ra) -**3**. [sketch] tosco(ca) -**4**. [method, shelter] primitivo(va). ◇ *n* = **crude oil**.

crudely [ˈkru:dlɪ] *adj* -**1**. [vulgarly] de maneira grosseira -**2**. [clumsily] toscamente.

crude oil *n (U)* petróleo *m* bruto.

cruel [krʊəl] (*compar* -**ler**, *superl* -**lest**) *adj* -**1**. [sadistic] cruel -**2**. [painful, harsh - disappointment] doloroso(sa); [- winter] rigoroso(sa).

cruelly [ˈkrʊəlɪ] *adv* -**1**. [sadistically] cruelmente -**2**. [painfully, harshly] dolorosamente.

cruelty [ˈkrʊəltɪ] *n (U)* crueldade *f*.

cruet [ˈkru:ɪt] *n* galheta *f*.

cruise [kru:z] ◇ *n* cruzeiro *m*. ◇ *vi* -**1**. [sail] fazer um cruzeiro -**2**. [drive] ir à velocidade de cruzeiro -**3**. [fly] voar.

cruise missile *n* míssil *m* de cruzeiro.

cruiser [ˈkru:zəʳ] *n* -**1**. [warship] cruzador *m* -**2**. [cabin cruiser] iate *m*.

crumb [krʌm] *n* -**1.** [of food] migalha *f* -**2.** [of information] fragmento *m*.

crumble ['krʌmbl] <> *n doce de frutas coberto com uma mistura de farinha, manteiga e açúcar e cozido no forno.* <> *vt* esmigalhar. <> *vi* -**1.** [disintegrate - bread, cheese] esmigalhar-se; [- building, cliff] desmoronar -**2.** *fig* [collapse] desmoronar.

crumbly ['krʌmblɪ] (*compar* -**ier**, *superl* -**iest**) *adj* farelento(ta).

crummy ['krʌmɪ] (*compar* -**ier**, *superl* -**iest**) *adj inf* [bad] fajuto(ta).

crumpet ['krʌmpɪt] *n* -**1.** [food] *fatias de bolo tostadas que se come com manteiga* -**2.** (*U*) *inf offensive* [women] gostosona *f*.

crumple ['krʌmpl] <> *vt* amassar. <> *vi* -**1.** [crease, dent] amassar -**2.** [collapse] desmoronar.
➤ **crumple up** *vt sep* amassar.

crunch [krʌntʃ] <> *n* [sound] mastigação *f* barulhenta; **if/when it comes to the ~** *inf* se/quando chegar a hora da verdade. <> *vt* -**1.** [with teeth] mastigar ruidosamente -**2.** [underfoot] esmagar com o pé ao caminhar. <> *vi* [snow, gravel] estalar.

crunchy ['krʌntʃɪ] (*compar* -**ier**, *superl* -**iest**) *adj* -**1.** [food] crocante -**2.** [snow, gravel] que estala.

crusade [kru:'seɪd] <> *n* -**1.** [war] cruzada *f* -**2.** *fig* [campaign] campanha *f*. <> *vi*: **to ~ for/against sthg** fazer campanha em favor de/contra algo.

crusader [kru:'seɪdə^r] *n* -**1.** *HIST* cavaleiro *m* das cruzadas -**2.** *fig* [campaigner] defensor *m*, -ra *f*.

crush [krʌʃ] <> *n* -**1.** [crowd] aglomeração *f* -**2.** *inf* [infatuation]: **to have a ~ on sb** estar obcecado(da) por alguém -**3.** *UK* [drink] batida *f*. <> *vt* -**1.** [squash, press, smash] esmagar -**2.** *fig* [destroy] acabar com.

crush barrier *n UK* barreira *f*.

crushing ['krʌʃɪŋ] *adj* esmagador(ra).

crust [krʌst] *n* -**1.** [on bread] casca *f* -**2.** [on pie] crosta *f* torrada -**3.** [hard covering] crosta *f*.

crustacean [krʌ'steɪʃn] *n* crustáceo *m*.

crusty ['krʌstɪ] (*compar* -**ier**, *superl* -**iest**) *adj* -**1.** [food] crocante -**2.** [person] ríspido(da).

crutch [krʌtʃ] *n* -**1.** [stick] muleta *f* -**2.** *fig* [support] apoio *m* -**3.** [crotch] gancho *m*.

crux [krʌks] *n* ponto *m* crucial.

cry [kraɪ] (*pl* **cries**, *pt* & *pp* **cried**) <> *n* -**1.** [weep] choro *m* -**2.** [shout] grito *m*; **to be a far ~ from** não se parecer em nada com -**3.** [of bird] canto *m*. <> *vt* -**1.** [weep] chorar -**2.** [shout] gritar. <> *vi* -**1.** [weep] chorar -**2.** [shout] gritar.
➤ **cry off** *vi* desistir de.
➤ **cry out** <> *vt* gritar. <> *vi* [call out] gritar.
➤ **cry out for** *vt fus* [be in need of]: **to be ~ing out for sthg** precisar de algo.

crybaby ['kraɪ,beɪbɪ] (*pl* -**ies**) *n inf pej* chorão *m*, -rona *f*.

crying ['kraɪɪŋ] <> *adj inf*: **it's a ~ shame** é uma vergonha enorme; **a ~ need for sthg** uma necessidade evidente de algo. <> *n* (*U*) choro *m*.

crypt [krɪpt] *n* cripta *f*.

cryptic ['krɪptɪk] *adj* [mysterious] enigmático(ca).

crypto- *prefix*: **a ~-communist** um comunista enrustido.

crystal ['krɪstl] <> *n* cristal *m*. <> *comp* [glass] de cristal.

crystal ball *n* bola *f* de cristal.

crystal clear *adj* -**1.** [water, voice] cristalino(na) -**2.** [motive, meaning] claro(ra).

crystallize, -ise ['krɪstəlaɪz] <> *vi* -**1.** [substance] cristalizar -**2.** [idea, plan] clarear. <> *vt* -**1.** [idea, plan] clarear -**2.** [fruit] cristalizar.

CSA (*abbr of* **Child Support Agency**) *n agência britânica responsável pela coleta de doações para auxílio a crianças carentes.*

CSC (*abbr of* **Civil Service Commission**) *n organização britânica responsável pela contratação de funcionários públicos.*

CSE (*abbr of* **Certificate of Secondary Education**) *n antigo certificado de conclusão de ensino médio na Grã-Bretanha.*

CS gas *n* gás *m* lacrimogêneo.

CST (*abbr of* **Central Standard Time**) *n horário oficial no centro dos Estados Unidos e do Canadá.*

ct (*abbr of* **carat**) ql.

CT *abbr of* **Connecticut**.

CTC (*abbr of* **city technology college**) *n escola de ensino médio que tem parceria com empresas e com o governo para ensino de tecnologia na Grã-Bretanha.*

cu. (*abbr of* **cubic**) cúbico(ca).

cub [kʌb] *n* -**1.** [young animal] filhote *m* -**2.** [boy scout] lobinho *m*.

Cuba ['kju:bə] *n* Cuba; **in ~** em Cuba.

Cuban ['kju:bən] <> *adj* cubano(na). <> *n* cubano *m*, -na *f*.

cubbyhole ['kʌbɪhəʊl] *n* cubículo *m*.

cube [kju:b] <> *n* cubo *m*. <> *vt MATH* elevar ao cubo.

cube root *n* raiz *f* cúbica.

cubic ['kju:bɪk] *adj* cúbico(ca).

cubicle ['kju:bɪkl] *n* -**1.** [shower] boxe *m* -**2.** [in shop] provador *m*.

cubism ['kju:bɪzm] *n* (*U*) cubismo *m*.

cubist ['kju:bɪst] *n* cubista *mf*.

cub reporter *n* jornalista *mf* novato, -ta.

Cub Scout *n* lobinho *m*.

cuckoo ['kʊku:] *n* cuco *m*.

cuckoo clock *n* [relógio *m* de] cuco *m*.

cucumber ['kju:kʌmbə^r] *n* pepino *m*.

cud [kʌd] *n*: **to chew the ~** *lit* & *fig* ruminar.

cuddle ['kʌdl] <> *n* abraço *m*. <> *vt* abraçar. <> *vi* abraçar-se.
➤ **cuddle up** *vi*: **to ~ up (to sb)** aconchegar-se (em alguém).

cuddly ['kʌdlɪ] (*compar* -**ier**, *superl* -**iest**) *adj* [person] mimoso(sa).

cuddly toy ['kʌdlɪ-] *n* bicho *m* de pelúcia.

cudgel ['kʌdʒəl] (*UK pt* & *pp* -**led**, *cont* -**ling**, *US pt* & *pp* -**ed**, *cont* -**ing**) <> *n* cacete *m*; **to take up the ~s for sb/sthg** sair em defesa de alguém/algo. <> *vt* dar cacetadas.

cue [kju:] *n* -**1.** *RADIO*, *THEATRE* & *TV* deixa *f*; **on ~** no momento certo; **to take one's ~ from sb** seguir o exemplo de alguém -**2.** *fig* [stimulus, signal] sinal *f* -**3.** [in snooker, pool] taco *m*.

cuff [kʌf] <> *n* -**1.** [of sleeve] punho *m* -**2.** *US* [of trouser] barra *f* **-3.** [blow] tapa *m.* <> *vt* [hit] bater.

cufflink *n* abotoadura *f.*

cu. in. *abbr of* cubic inch(es).

cuisine [kwɪ'zi:n] *n (U)* arte *f* culinária.

cul-de-sac ['kʌldəsæk] *n* beco *m* sem saída.

culinary ['kʌlɪnərɪ] *adj* culinária.

cull [kʌl] <> *n* [kill] extermínio *m.* <> *vt* **-1.** [kill] exterminar **-2.** *fml* [gather] reunir.

culminate ['kʌlmɪneɪt] *vi*: **to ~ in sthg** culminar em algo.

culmination [,kʌlmɪ'neɪʃn] *n* culminação *f.*

culottes [kju:'lɒts] *npl* saia-calça *f.*

culpable ['kʌlpəbl] *adj fml* culpável; **~ homicide** homicídio *m* culposo.

culprit ['kʌlprɪt] *n* culpado *m*, -da *f.*

cult [kʌlt] <> *n* **-1.** REUG culto *m* **-2.** [book, film] objeto *m* de culto. <> *comp* [book, film] de culto.

cultivate ['kʌltɪveɪt] *vt* **-1.** [gen] cultivar **-2.** [get to know] fazer amizade com.

cultivated ['kʌltɪveɪtɪd] *adj* **-1.** [land] cultivado(da) **-2.** [person, accent] culto(ta).

cultivation [,kʌltɪ'veɪʃn] *n (U)* [farming] cultivo *m.*

cultural ['kʌltʃərəl] *adj* cultural.

culture ['kʌltʃə'] *n* cultura *f.*

cultured ['kʌltʃəd] *adj* [educated] culto(ta).

cultured pearl *n* pérola *f* cultivada.

culture shock *n* choque *m* cultural.

culture vulture *n inf* amante *mf* da cultura.

culvert ['kʌlvət] *n* bueiro *m.*

cumbersome ['kʌmbəsəm] *adj* **-1.** [object] de difícil manejo **-2.** [system] ineficiente.

Cumbria *n* Cúmbria.

cumin ['kʌmɪn] *n (U)* cominho *m.*

cumulative ['kju:mjʊlətɪv] *adj* cumulativo(va).

cunning ['kʌnɪŋ] <> *adj* **-1.** [person] astuto(ta) **-2.** [method, idea] engenhoso(sa). <> *n (U)* astúcia *f.*

cup [kʌp] (*pt & pp* -**ped**, *cont* -**ping**) <> *n* **-1.** [gen] xícara *f*; **it's not my ~ of tea** *inf* não faz o meu gênero **-2.** [as prize, of bra] taça *f* **-3.** [competition] copa *f.* <> *vt* dispor (as mãos) em forma de concha.

cupboard ['kʌbəd] *n* armário *m.*

cupcake ['kʌpkeɪk] *n* bolinho *m* coberto com glacê.

Cup Final *n*: **the ~** o jogo final da copa.

cup holder *n* SPORT atual campeão *m*, -ã *f* da copa.

cupid ['kju:pɪd] *n* [figure] cupido *m.*

cupola ['kju:pələ] (*pl* -**s**) *n* ARCHIT cúpula *f.*

cup tie *n UK* jogo *m* eliminatório.

curable ['kjʊərəbl] *adj* curável.

curate ['kjʊərət] <> *n* RELIG coadjutor *m*, -ra *f.* <> *vt* [exhibition] organizar.

curator [,kjʊə'reɪtə'] *n* [of museum] curador *m*, -ra *f.*

curb [kɜ:b] <> *n* **-1.** [control]: **~ (on sthg)** controle *m* (sobre algo) **-2.** *US* [of road] meio-fio *m.* <> *vt* controlar.

curd cheese [kɜ:d-] *n (U) UK* requeijão *m.*

curdle ['kɜ:dl] *vi* **-1.** [milk] coalhar **-2.** [blood] coagular.

cure [kjʊə'] <> *n* **-1.** MED : **~ (for sthg)** cura *f* (de algo) **-2.** [solution]: **~ (for sthg)** solução *f* (para algo). <> *vt* **-1.** MED curar *f* **-2.** [solve] remediar **-3.**

[rid]: **to ~ sb of sthg** *fig* livrar alguém de algo **-4.** [preserve] curtir.

cure-all *n* panacéia *f.*

curfew ['kɜ:fju:] *n* toque *m* de recolher.

curio ['kjʊərɪəʊ] (*pl* -**s**) *n* raridade *f*, curiosidade *f.*

curiosity [,kjʊərɪ'ɒsətɪ] *n* **-1.** (*U*) [inquisitiveness] curiosidade *f* **-2.** [rarity] raridade *f.*

curious ['kjʊərɪəs] *adj* curioso(sa); **~ about sb/ sthg** curioso(sa) sobre alguém/algo.

curiously ['kjʊərɪəslɪ] *adv* curiosamente.

curl [kɜ:l] <> *n* **-1.** [of hair] cacho *m* **-2.** [of smoke] onda *f.* <> *vt* **-1.** [hair] encrespar, encaracolar **-2.** [tail, ribbon] enrolar. <> *vi* **-1.** [hair] encrespar, encaracolar **-2.** [paper, leaf, road, smoke, snake] enrolar; **to ~ into a ball** enrolar-se numa bola.

⮞ **curl up** *vi* [person, animal] enrolar-se.

curler ['kɜ:lə'] *n* rolo *m.*

curling ['kɜ:lɪŋ] *n* SPORT jogo *escocês que consiste em deslizar pedras sobre o gelo.*

curling tongs *npl* ferros *mpl* de frisar.

curly ['kɜ:lɪ] (*compar* -**ier**, *superl* -**iest**) *adj* [hair] encaracolado(da).

currant ['kʌrənt] *n* [dried grape] uva *f* passa.

currency ['kʌrənsɪ] (*pl* -**ies**) *n* **-1.** [money] moeda *f* corrente; **foreign ~** moeda *f* estrangeira **-2.** *fml* [acceptability]: **to gain ~** ganhar aceitação.

current ['kʌrənt] <> *adj* atual; **in ~ use** de uso corrente. <> *n* corrente *f.*

current account *n UK* conta *f* corrente.

current affairs *npl* atualidades *fpl.*

current assets *npl* ativo *m* corrente.

current liabilities *npl* passivo *m* circulante.

currently ['kʌrəntlɪ] *adv* atualmente.

curricular *adj* curricular.

curriculum [kə'rɪkjələm] (*pl* -**lums** OR -**la** [-lə]) *n* [course of study] currículo *m.*

curriculum vitae [-'vi:taɪ] (*pl* curricula vitae) *n* currículo *m*, curriculum *m* (vitae).

curried ['kʌrɪd] *adj* com molho de caril.

curry ['kʌrɪ] (*pl* -**ies**) *n* caril *m.*

curry powder *n (U)* caril *m* em pó.

curse [kɜ:s] <> *n* **-1.** [evil charm]: **~ (on sb/sthg)** maldição *f* OR praga *f* (sobre alguém/algo) **-2.** [swearword] palavrão *m* **-3.** [source of problems] desgraça *f.* <> *vt* **-1.** [wish misfortune on] maldizer **-2.** [complain about] xingar. <> *vi* [swear] praguejar.

cursor ['kɜ:sə'] *n* COMPUT cursor *m.*

cursory ['kɜ:sərɪ] *adj* apressado(da); **a ~ glance** um olhada por cima.

curt [kɜ:t] *adj* brusco(ca).

curtail [kɜ:'teɪl] *vt* **-1.** [cut short] encurtar **-2.** [restrict, reduce] reduzir.

curtailment [kɜ:'teɪlmənt] *n (U) fml* [reduction] redução *f.*

curtain ['kɜ:tn] *n* cortina *f.*

⮞ **curtain off** *vt sep* separar com uma cortina.

curtain call *n* chamada *à frente do palco para receber aplausos.*

curtain raiser *n fig* [warm-up] preâmbulo *m*, prelúdio *m.*

curts(e)y ['kɜ:tsɪ] (*pt & pp* curtsied) <> *n* reverência *f* (feita por mulher). <> *vi* fazer reverência.

curvaceous [kɜːˈveɪʃəs] *adj inf* bom (boa) de curvas.

curvature [ˈkɜːvətʃəʳ] *n (U)* curvatura *f.*

curve [kɜːv] ◇ *n* curva *f.* ◇ *vi* fazer uma curva.

curved [kɜːvd] *adj* curvo(va).

curvy [ˈkɜːvɪ] (*compar*-ier, *superl*-iest) *adj*: a ~ blond uma loira cheia de curvas.

cushion [ˈkʊʃn] ◇ *n* -1. [for sitting on] almofada *f* -2. [protective layer] colchão *m.* ◇ *vt* amortecer; **to be ~ed against sthg** estar protegido(da) de algo.

cushy [ˈkʊʃɪ] (*compar*-ier, *superl*-iest) *adj inf* mole.

custard [ˈkʌstəd] *n* [sauce] creme *m (para doces).*

custard pie *n* torta *f* de creme.

custard powder *n (U)* pó desidratado que se mistura ao leite e ao açúcar para fazer creme.

custodial *adj* [sentence] custódio(dia).

custodian [kʌˈstəʊdjən] *n* [of building, museum] guarda *m.*

custody [ˈkʌstədɪ] *n (U)* -1. [of child] custódia *f* -2. [of suspect]: **in ~** sob custódia.

custom [ˈkʌstəm] *n* -1. [tradition, habit] costume *m*, hábito *m* -2. *(U)* COMM [trade] preferência *f*; **thank you for your ~** agradecemos a preferência.

➤ **customs** *n (U)* [place, organization] alfândega *f*; **to go through ~** passar pela alfândega.

customary [ˈkʌstəmrɪ] *adj* costumeiro(ra), habitual.

custom-built *adj* personalizado(da).

customer [ˈkʌstəməʳ] *n* -1. [client] cliente *mf* -2. *inf* [person] tipo *m*; **an awkward ~** um tipo complicado.

customer services *npl* serviço *m* de atendimento ao consumidor.

customize, -ise [ˈkʌstəmaɪz] *vt* -1. [gen] personalizar -2. COMPUT customizar.

custom-made *adj* feito(ta) sob medida.

Customs and Excise *n (U)* UK *departamento do governo britânico responsável por coletar impostos sobre a compra e venda de bens e serviços ou sobre bens importados.*

customs duty *n (U)* imposto *m* alfandegário.

customs officer *n* fiscal *mf* de alfândega.

cut [kʌt] (*pt* & *pp* cut, *cont*-ting) ◇ *n* -1. [gen] corte *m*; ~ **(in sthg)** corte (em algo) -2. *inf* [share] parte *f* -3. *phr*: **a ~ above (the rest)** melhor que os outros. ◇ *vt* -1. [gen] cortar -2. [tooth] romper -3. *inf* [miss] matar -4. *phr*: **to ~ sb dead** fazer que não se vê alguém; ~ **and dried** definitivo(va). ◇ *vi* -1. cortar -2. *phr*: **to ~ both ways** ser uma faca de dois gumes.

➤ **cut across** *vt fus* -1. [as short cut] cortar caminho por -2. [transcend] transcender, estar acima de.

➤ **cut back** ◇ *vt sep* -1. [tree, bush] podar -2. [expenditure, budget] reduzir, diminuir. ◇ *vi*: **to ~ back (on sthg)** reduzir (algo).

➤ **cut down** ◇ *vt sep* -1. [chop down] cortar, derrubar -2. [reduce] reduzir, diminuir. ◇ *vi*: **to ~ down on sthg** reduzir algo.

➤ **cut in** *vi* -1. [interrupt]: **to ~ in (on sb)** interromper (alguém) -2. [in car] cortar (a frente de), fechar.

➤ **cut off** *vt sep* -1. [sever] cortar fora -2. [sever supply of] cortar; **I got ~ off** [on telephone] cortaram

meu telefone -3. [isolate]: **to be ~ off (from sb/ sthg)** ficar isolado(da) (de alguém/algo).

➤ **cut out** ◇ *vt sep* -1. [gen] cortar; **to ~ out the light** cortar a entrada de luz; ~ **it out!** pare com isso! -2.: **to be ~ out for sthg** *fig* ser feito(ta) para algo. ◇ *vi* [stall] morrer.

➤ **cut up** *vt sep* [chop up] picar.

cut and paste COMPUT ◇ *vt* recortar e colar. ◇ *vi* recortar e colar.

cutback [ˈkʌtbæk] *n*: ~ **(in sthg)** corte *m* (em algo).

cute [kjuːt] *adj esp* US [appealing] bonitinho(nha).

cut glass ◇ *n (U)* vidro *m* lapidado. ◇ *comp* de vidro lapidado.

cuticle [ˈkjuːtɪkl] *n* cutícula *f.*

cutlery [ˈkʌtlərɪ] *n (U)* talheres *mpl.*

cutlet [ˈkʌtlɪt] *n* costeleta *f.*

cut-off (point) *n* [limit] (ponto *m*) limite *m.*

cut-out *n* -1. [on machine] disjuntor *m* -2. [shape] figura *f* para recortar.

cut-price, cut-rate US *adj* com desconto.

cutter [ˈkʌtəʳ] *n* [tool] cortador *m.*

cut-throat *adj* [ruthless] acirrado(da).

cutting [ˈkʌtɪŋ] ◇ *adj* [sarcastic] mordaz. ◇ *n* -1. [of plant] chantão *m* -2. [from newspaper] recorte *m* -3. *UK* [for road, railway] corte *m.*

cutting edge *n* centro *m.*

cutting room *n* CINEMA sala *f* de edição.

cuttlefish [ˈkʌtlfɪʃ] (*pl inv*) *n* siba *m.*

cut up *adj* UK *inf* [upset] chateado(da).

CV (*abbr of* curriculum vitae) *n* UK CV *m.*

c.w.o. (*abbr of* cash with order) *pagamento no ato da ordem de compra.*

cwt. *abbr of* hundredweight.

cyanide [ˈsaɪənaɪd] *n (U)* cianeto *m*, cianureto *m.*

cybercafé *n* COMPUT cibercafé *m.*

cybernetics [ˌsaɪbəˈnetɪks] *n (U)* cibernética *f.*

cyberspace [ˈsaɪbəspeɪs] *n* COMPUT ciberespaço *m.*

cyclamen [ˈsɪkləmən] (*pl inv*) *n* ciclâmen *m.*

cycle [ˈsaɪkl] ◇ *n* -1. [process] ciclo *m* -2. [bicycle] bicicleta *f.* ◇ *comp*: ~ **path** ciclovia *f*; ~ **track** pista *f* para ciclismo; ~ **race** corrida *f* de bicicletas. ◇ *vi* andar de bicicleta.

cyclic(al) [ˈsaɪklɪk(l)] *adj* cíclico(ca).

cycling [ˈsaɪklɪŋ] *n (U)* ciclismo *m*; **to go ~** andar de bicicleta.

cycling helmet *n* capacete *m* de ciclismo.

cyclist [ˈsaɪklɪst] *n* ciclista *mf.*

cyclone [ˈsaɪkləʊn] *n* ciclone *m.*

cygnet [ˈsɪgnɪt] *n* filhote *m* de cisne.

cylinder [ˈsɪlɪndəʳ] *n* -1. [gen] cilindro *m* -2. [container] tambor *m.*

cylinder block *n* bloco *m* de cilindros.

cylinder head *n* cabeça *f* de cilindro, culatra *f.*

cylindrical [sɪˈlɪndrɪkl] *adj* cilíndrico(ca).

cymbals [ˈsɪmblz] *npl* címbalos *mpl.*

cynic [ˈsɪnɪk] *n* cético *m*, -ca *f.*

cynical [ˈsɪnɪkl] *adj* cético(ca).

cynically [ˈsɪnɪklɪ] *adv* ceticamente.

cynicism [ˈsɪnɪsɪzm] *n (U)* ceticismo *m.*

cypher [ˈsaɪfəʳ] *n* = cipher.

cypress [ˈsaɪprəs] *n* cipreste *m.*

Cypriot [ˈsɪprɪət] ◇ *adj* cipriota. ◇ *n* cipriota

dancing

mf; **Greek** ~ cipriota grego(ga); **Turkish** ~ cipriota turco(ca).
Cyprus ['saɪprəs] *n* Chipre; **in** ~ em Chipre.
cyst [sɪst] *n* cisto *m*.
cystic fibrosis [ˌsɪstɪkfaɪ'brəʊsɪs] *n (U)* fibrose *f* cística.
cystitis [sɪs'taɪtɪs] *n (U)* cistite *f*.
cytology [saɪ'tɒlədʒɪ] *n (U)* citologia *f*.
czar [zɑ:'] *n* czar *m*.
Czech [tʃek] <> *adj* tcheco(ca). <> *n* **- 1.** [person] tcheco *m*, -ca *f* **- 2.** [language] tcheco *m*.
Czechoslovak *adj* & *n* = **Czechoslovakian**.
Czechoslovakia [ˌtʃekəslə'vækɪə] *n* Tchecoslováquia; **in** ~ na Tchecoslováquia.
Czechoslovakian [ˌtʃekəslə'vækɪən] <> *adj* tchecoslovaco(ca). <> *n* tchecoslovaco *m*, -ca *f*.
Czech Republic *n*: **the** ~ a República Tcheca.

d (*pl* **d's** *OR* **ds**), **D** (*pl* **D's** *OR* **Ds**) [di:] *n* [letter] d , D *m*.
 D <> *n* **- 1.** *MUS* ré *m* **- 2.** *SCH* [mark] D *m*. <> *US abbr of* **Democrat(ic)**.
d. (*abbr of* **died**) m.
DA (*abbr of* **district attorney**) *n* promotor nos Estados Unidos.
D/A (*abbr of* **digital to analogue**) *adj* D/A.
dab [dæb] (*pt* & *pp* -**bed**, *cont* -**bing**) <> *n* [small amount - of powder, ointment] pitada *f*; [- of paint] pincelada *f*. <> *vt* **- 1.** [skin, wound] aplicar de leve **- 2.** [eyes] tocar de leve **- 3.** [cream, ointment]: **to** ~ **sthg on(to) sthg** aplicar algo em algo.
dabble ['dæbl] <> *vt* agitar (*com as mãos ou os pés*). <> *vi*: **to** ~ **(in sthg)** atuar como amador (em algo).
dab hand *n UK inf*: **to be a** ~ **(at sthg)** ser um craque (em algo).
Dacca ['dækə] *n* Dacca.
dachshund ['dækshʊnd] *n* dachshund *m*.
dad [dæd] *n inf* pai *m*.
daddy ['dædɪ] (*pl* -**ies**) *n inf* papai *m*.
daddy longlegs [-'lɒŋlegz] (*pl inv*) *n* pernilongo *m*.
daffodil ['dæfədɪl] *n* narciso *m*.
daft [dɑ:ft] *adj UK inf* bobo(ba).
dagger ['dægə'] *n* adaga *f*.
dahlia ['deɪljə] *n* dália *f*.
daily ['deɪlɪ] (*pl* -**ies**) <> *adj* diário(ria). <> *adv* diariamente; **twice** ~ duas vezes por dia. <> *n* **- 1.** [newspaper] diário *m* **- 2.** *esp UK* [cleaning woman] diarista *f*.

daintily ['deɪntɪlɪ] *adv* delicadamente, suavemente; **to eat** ~ comer com delicadeza.
dainty ['deɪntɪ] (*compar* -**ier**, *superl* -**iest**) *adj* delicado(da).
dairy ['deərɪ] (*pl* -**ies**) *n* leiteria *f*.
dairy cattle *npl* gado *m* leiteiro.
dairy farm *n* fazenda *f* de gado leiteiro.
dairy products *npl* lacticínios *mpl*.
dais ['deɪs] *n* estrado *m*.
daisy ['deɪzɪ] (*pl* -**ies**) *n* margarida *f*.
daisy wheel *n* margarida *f* (de impressão).
daisy-wheel printer *n* impressora *f* de margarida.
Dakar ['dækɑ:] *n* Dacar.
dale [deɪl] *n literary* vale *m*.
dalmatian [dæl'meɪʃn] *n* [dog] dálmata *m*.
dam [dæm] (*pt* & *pp* -**med**, *cont* -**ming**) <> *n* [across river] represa *f*, barragem *f*. <> *vt* [river] represar.
 dam up *vt sep* **- 1.** [river] represar **- 2.** [feelings] conter.
damage ['dæmɪdʒ] <> *n*: ~ **(to sthg)** [gen] dano *m* (a algo); [to health, skin] mal *m* (a algo). <> *vt* **- 1.** [object] danificar **- 2.** [person] machucar **- 3.** *fig* [chances, reputation] prejudicar.
 damages *npl JUR* danos *mpl*.
damaging ['dæmɪdʒɪŋ] *adj fig* prejudicial, danoso(sa); ~ **to sthg** prejudicial a algo.
Damascus [də'mæskəs] *n* Damasco.
Dame [deɪm] *n UK título honorífico concedido a uma mulher pelos serviços prestados à sociedade.*
damn [dæm] <> *adj inf* maldito(ta). <> *adv inf* muito. <> *n inf*: **not to give** *OR* **care a** ~ **(about sthg)** não estar nem aí (para algo). <> *vt* **- 1.** *RELIG* [condemn] condenar **- 2.** *inf* [curse] amaldiçoar; ~ **you!** maldito seja! <> *excl inf* droga!
damnable ['dæmnəbl] *adj dated* [appalling] execrável.
damnation [dæm'neɪʃn] *n (U) RELIG* danação *f*.
damned [dæmd] *inf* <> *adj* maldito(ta); **I'm** ~ **if I'll do it** bem capaz que eu vou fazer isso; **well I'll be** *OR* **I'm** ~ ! ora veja só! <> *adv* muito.
damning ['dæmɪŋ] *adj* condenatório(ria), incriminatório(ria).
damp [dæmp] <> *adj* úmido(da). <> *n (U)* umidade *f*. <> *vt* [make wet] umedecer.
 damp down *vt sep* [restrain] controlar.
damp course *n UK* impermeabilização *f*.
dampen ['dæmpən] *vt* **- 1.** [make wet] umedecer **- 2.** *fig* [emotion] esfriar.
damper ['dæmpə'] *n* [for fire] abafador *m*; **to put a** ~ **on sthg** *inf* jogar um balde de água fria em algo.
dampness ['dæmpnɪs] *n* umidade *f*.
damp-proof course *n* = **damp course**.
damson ['dæmzn] *n* abrunheiro *m*.
dance [dɑ:ns] <> *n* **- 1.** [gen] dança *f*; **shall we have a** ~? vamos dançar? **- 2.** [social event] baile *m*. <> *vt* dançar. <> *vi* dançar.
dance floor *n* pista *f* de dança.
dance hall *n* salão *m* de baile.
dancer ['dɑ:nsə'] *n* dançarino *m*, -na *f*.
dancing ['dɑ:nsɪŋ] *n (U)* dança *f*; **to go** ~ ir dançar.

D & C (*abbr of* dilation and curettage) *n* D&C.

dandelion ['dændɪlaɪən] *n* dente-de-leão *m*.

dandruff ['dændrʌf] *n (U)* caspa *f*.

dandy ['dændɪ] (*pl* -ies) *n* almofadinha *m*.

Dane [deɪn] *n* dinamarquês *m*, -esa *f*.

danger ['deɪndʒə'] *n* perigo *m*; **in** ~ em perigo; **out of** ~ fora de perigo; ~ **to sb/sthg** perigo para alguém/algo; **to be in** ~ **of doing sthg** perigar fazer algo.

danger list *n UK*: **to be on the** ~ estar em estado grave:

danger money *n (U) UK* adicional *m* por periculosidade.

dangerous ['deɪndʒərəs] *adj* perigoso(sa).

dangerous driving *n (U) JUR* direção *f* perigosa.

dangerously ['deɪndʒərəslɪ] *adv* -**1.** [riskily] perigosamente -**2.** *MED*: ~ **ill** em estado grave.

danger zone *n* zona *f* de perigo.

dangle ['dæŋgl] *vt, vi* balançar.

Danish ['deɪnɪʃ] <> *adj* dinamarquês(quesa). <> *n* -**1.** [language] dinamarquês *m* -**2.** *US* = Danish pastry. <> *npl*: **the** ~ os dinamarqueses.

Danish blue *n* tipo de queijo azul.

Danish pastry, Danish *US n* torta recheada com maçãs, glacê e marzipã.

dank [dæŋk] *adj* úmido e frio, úmida e fria.

Danube ['dænju:b] *n*: **the** ~ o Danúbio.

dapper ['dæpə'] *adj* garboso(sa).

dappled ['dæpld] *adj* -**1.** [animal] pintado(da), malhado(da) -**2.** [shade] pintado(da).

Dardanelles *npl*: **the** ~ o estreito de Dardanelos.

dare [deə'] <> *vt* -**1.** [be brave enough]: **to** ~ **to do sthg** ousar fazer algo -**2.** [challenge]: **to** ~ **sb to do sthg** desafiar alguém a fazer algo -**3.** *phr*: **I** ~ **say** ouso dizer (que). <> *vi* atrever-se; **how** ~ **you!** como se atreve! <> *n* desafio *m*.

daredevil ['deə,devl] *n* intrépido *m*, -da *f*.

daren't [deənt] = dare not.

Dar es-Salaam [,dɑ:ressə'lɑ:m] *n* Dar es-Salaam.

daring ['deərɪŋ] <> *adj* ousado(da). <> *n (U)* ousadia *f*.

dark [dɑ:k] <> *adj* -**1.** [gen] escuro(ra) -**2.** [gloomy] obscuro(ra) -**3.** [sinister] sombrio(bria). <> *n* -**1.** *(U)* [darkness]: **the** ~ a escuridão, o escuro; **to be in the** ~ **about sthg** estar às escuras sobre algo -**2.** [night]: **before/after** ~ antes/depois de escurecer.

Dark Ages *npl*: **the** ~ a baixa Idade Média.

darken ['dɑ:kn] <> *vt* escurecer. <> *vi* -**1.** escurecer -**2.** *fig* [face] anuviar-se.

dark glasses *npl* óculos *m inv* escuros.

dark horse *n fig* [person] pessoa *f* enigmática.

darkness ['dɑ:knɪs] *n (U)* escuridão *f*, trevas *fpl*.

darkroom ['dɑ:krʊm] *n* câmara *f* escura.

darling ['dɑ:lɪŋ] <> *adj* -**1.** [dear] querido(da) -**2.** *inf* [cute] adorável. <> *n* -**1.** [loved person] querido *m*; -da *f*; **she's a little** ~ é uma graça de criança -**2.** [favourite] preferido *m*, -da *f*.

darn [dɑ:n] <> *adj inf* maldito(ta). <> *adv inf* pra caramba. <> *n* remendo *m*. <> *vt* [repair] remendar, cerzir. <> *excl inf* [damn] que droga!

darning ['dɑ:nɪŋ] *n (U)* [work] remendagem *f*,

cerzidura *f*; **I hate** ~ odeio cerzir.

darning needle *n* agulha *f* de cerzir.

dart [dɑ:t] <> *n* -**1.** [arrow] dardo *m* -**2.** *SEWING* pence *f*. <> *vt* lançar. <> *vi* [move quickly] lançar-se.

➡ **darts** *n (U)* [game] dardos *mpl*.

dartboard ['dɑ:tbɔ:d] *n* alvo *m* para dardos.

dash [dæʃ] <> *n* -**1.** [of liquid] pingo *m* -**2.** [in punctuation] travessão *m* -**3.** *AUT* painel *m* (de instrumentos) -**4.** [rush]: **to make a** ~ **for sthg** sair em disparada por algo. <> *vt* -**1.** *literary* [hurl] arremessar -**2.** [hopes] frustar. <> *vi* correr; **I must** ~! preciso correr!

➡ **dash off** *vt sep* [write quickly] rabiscar. <> *vi* [rush off] chispar.

dashboard ['dæʃbɔ:d] *n* painel *m* de instrumentos.

dashing ['dæʃɪŋ] *adj* [handsome, energetic] atraente.

dastardly ['dæstədlɪ] *adj dated* cruel.

DAT [dæt] (*abbr of* digital audio tape) *n* DAT *m*.

data ['deɪtə] *n* dados *mpl*.

databank ['deɪtəbæŋk] *n* banco *m* de dados.

database ['deɪtəbeɪs] *n* base *f* de dados.

data capture *n (U)* captura *f* de dados.

data management *n COMPUT* gerenciamento *m* de dados.

data processing *n (U)* processamento *m* de dados.

data protection *n COMPUT* proteção *f* de dados.

data recovery *n COMPUT* recuperação *f* de dados.

data transmission *n (U)* transmissão *f* de dados.

date [deɪt] <> *n* -**1.** [in time] data *f*; **what's today's** ~? que dia é hoje?; **at a later** ~ um outro dia; **to bring sb/sthg up to** ~ atualizar alguém/algo; **to keep sb/sthg up to** ~ manter alguém/algo atualizado(da); **to be out of** ~ [dictionary, database] estar desatualizado(da); [passport] estar vencido(da); **to** ~ até agora -**2.** [appointment] encontro *m* -**3.** [person] par *m* -**4.** [fruit] tâmara *f*, datil *m*. <> *vt* -**1.** [put a date on] datar -**2.** [go out with] sair com. <> *vi* [go out of fashion] cair de moda.

➡ **date back to, date from** *vt fus* datar de.

datebook *n US* agenda *f*.

dated ['deɪtɪd] *adj* antiquado(da).

date of birth *n* data *f* de nascimento.

date rape *n* estupro realizado por um homem após ter se relacionado socialmente com uma mulher.

date stamp *n* -**1.** [device] carimbo *m* datador -**2.** [mark] data *f* carimbada.

daub [dɔ:b] *vt*: **to** ~ **sthg with sthg** manchar algo.

daughter ['dɔ:tə'] *n* filha *f*.

daughter-in-law (*pl* daughters-in-law) *n* nora *f*.

daunt [dɔ:nt] *vt* desalentar.

daunting ['dɔ:ntɪŋ] *adj* desalentador(ra).

dawdle ['dɔ:dl] *vi* fazer cera.

dawn [dɔ:n] <> *n* -**1.** [of day] amanhecer *m*, alvorada *f*; **at** ~ ao amanhecer; **from** ~ **to dusk** do amanhecer ao pôr-do-sol -**2.** *fig* [of era, period] aurora *f*. <> *vi* -**1.** [day] amanhecer -**2.** *fig* [era, period] despertar.

➡ **dawn (up)on** *vt fus* dar-se conta de; **it finally**

~ed on me that ... finalmente me dei conta de que ...

dawn chorus n canto m dos pássaros ao amanhecer.

day [deɪ] n -**1.** [gen] dia m; **the** ~ **before** a véspera; **the** ~ **after** o dia seguinte; **the** ~ **before Christmas** a véspera de Natal; **the** ~ **before yesterday** anteontem; **the** ~ **after tomorrow** depois de amanhã; **any** ~ **now** qualquer dia destes; **let's call it a** ~ por hoje chega; **to make sb's** ~ ganhar o dia, guardar algo para dias mais difíceis; **it's early** ~**s yet: to save sthg for a rainy** ~ é cedo para saber; **his** ~**s are numbered** seus dias estão contados; ~ **and night** dia e noite -**2.** [age, era] tempo m; **in this** ~ **and age** hoje em dia; **one** ~, **some** ~, **one of these** ~**s** um dia (desses).
➡ **days** adv [work] durante o dia.

dayboy ['deɪbɔɪ] n UK SCH aluno m de semi-internato.

daybreak ['deɪbreɪk] n romper m do dia; **at** ~ ao romper do dia.

day care n assistência diurna proporcionada a idosos e/ou portadores de deficiência.

day centre n UK centro assistencial que proporciona cuidados e recreação durante o dia a idosos e/ou portadores de deficiência.

daydream ['deɪdriːm] <> n devaneio m. <> vi devanear, sonhar acordado(da).

daygirl ['deɪgɜːl] n UK SCH aluna f de semi-internato.

Day-Glo® ['deɪgləʊ] adj fluorescente.

daylight ['deɪlaɪt] n -**1.** (U) [light] luz f do dia -**2.** [dawn] amanhecer m -**3.** phr inf: **to scare the (living)** ~**s out of sb** quase matar alguém de susto.

daylight robbery n (U) inf: **50 pounds? that's** ~! 50 libras? isso é um roubo!

daylight saving time n esp US horário m de verão.

day nursery n creche f.

day off (pl days off) n dia m de folga.

day pupil n UK aluno m, -na f de semi-internato.

day release n UK sistema na Inglaterra que permite que os trabalhadores se ausentem um dia por semana do serviço para estudar.

day return n UK passagem f de ida e volta (no mesmo dia).

day room n sala f de estar (em hospital, asilo).

day school n escola f diurna (particular).

day shift n turno m do dia.

daytime ['deɪtaɪm] <> n dia m; **in the** ~ durante o dia. <> comp de dia; ~ **flight** vôo m diurno.

day-to-day adj diário(ria).

daytrader ['deɪtreɪdə'] n STEX day-trader mf.

day trip n viagem f de um dia.

day-tripper n UK pessoa que sai em viagem de um dia.

daze [deɪz] <> n: **in a** ~ atordoado(da). <> vt atordoar.

dazed [deɪzd] adj [lit & fig] atordoado(da).

dazzle ['dæzl] vt -**1.** [blind] ofuscar -**2.** [impress] deslumbrar.

dazzling ['dæzlɪŋ] adj -**1.** [blinding] ofuscante -**2.** [impressive] deslumbrante.

DBE (abbr of Dame Commander of the Order of the British Empire) n (beneficiária de) distinção de honra britânica.

DBS n -**1.** (abbr of direct broadcasting by satellite) transmissão f direta via satélite. -**2.** (abbr of direct-broadcast satellite) satélite f de transmissão direta.

DC <> n (abbr of direct current) CC f. <> abbr of District of Columbia.

DD (abbr of Doctor of Divinity) n (titular de) doutorado em teologia.

D-day ['diːdeɪ] n dia m D.

DDT (abbr of dichlorodiphenyltrichloroethane) n DDT m.

DE abbr of Delaware.

DEA (abbr of Drug Enforcement Administration) n departamento da polícia norte-americana encarregado do controle de questões relacionadas a drogas, ≃ DENARC m.

deacon ['diːkn] n -**1.** [minister] diácono m -**2.** [lay assistant] acólito m.

deaconess [ˌdiːkə'nes] n diaconisa f.

deactivate [ˌdiː'æktɪveɪt] vt desativar.

dead [ded] <> adj -**1.** [not alive] morto(ta); **to shoot sb** ~ matar alguém com um tiro; **he wouldn't be seen** ~ **doing that** inf nunca seria visto fazendo aquilo -**2.** [numb] dormente, adormecido(da) -**3.** [ELEC - battery] descarregado(da); [- radio, TV] quebrado(da); [- telephone line] mudo(da) -**4.** [complete]: ~ **silence** silêncio m mortal; ~ **stop** parada f repentina -**5.** [not lively] morto(ta). <> adv -**1.** [directly, precisely] diretamente; ~ **on time** bem na hora -**2.** inf [completely, very] totalmente; **to be** ~ **set on doing sthg** estar totalmente determinado(da) a fazer algo; **to be** ~ **against sthg/doing sthg** ser totalmente contra algo/fazer algo -**3.** [suddenly]: **to stop** ~ parar repentinamente. <> n: **at** ~ **of night** na calada da noite. <> npl: **the** ~ os mortos.

deadbeat ['dedbiːt] n US inf malandro m, -dra f.

dead-beat adj inf morto(ta).

dead centre n ponto m morto.

dead duck n inf fracasso m.

deaden ['dedn] vt -**1.** [noise] amortecer -**2.** [feeling] abrandar.

dead end n -**1.** [street] rua f sem saída -**2.** fig [course of action] impasse m.

dead-end job n emprego m sem perspectivas.

deadhead ['dedhed] vt podar.

dead heat n empate m.

dead letter n fig [rule, law] letra f morta.

deadline ['dedlaɪn] n prazo m final.

deadlock ['dedlɒk] n impasse m.

deadlocked ['dedlɒkt] adj paralisado(da).

dead loss n inf -**1.** [person] traste m -**2.** [thing] porcaria f.

deadly ['dedlɪ] (compar -ier, superl -iest) <> adj -**1.** [lethal] letal -**2.** [mortal] mortal -**3.** [fatally precise] fatal. <> adv [extremely] terrivelmente.

deadly nightshade [-'naɪtʃeɪd] n (U) beladona f.

deadpan ['dedpæn] <> adj supostamente sério(ria). <> adv afetadamente sério(ria).

Dead Sea n: **the** ~ o Mar Morto.

dead wood UK, **deadwood** US ['dedwʊd] n (U) fig estorvo m.

deaf [def] <> adj -1. [unable to hear] surdo(da) -2. fig [unwilling to hear]: **to be ~ to sthg** ser surdo(da) a algo. <> npl: **the ~** os surdos.

deaf-aid n UK aparelho m de surdez.

deafen ['defn] vt ensurdecer.

deafening ['defnɪŋ] adj ensurdecedor(ra).

deaf mute <> adj surdo-mudo(da). <> n surdo-mudo m, -da f.

deafness ['defnɪs] n (U) surdez f.

deal [di:l] (pt & pp dealt) <> n -1. [business agreement] transação f, acordo m; **to do** OR **strike a ~ with sb** fazer um acordo com alguém -2. inf [treatment] tratamento m; **big ~!** iron grande coisa! -3. [quantity]: **a good** OR **great ~** muito; **a good** OR **great ~ of work** muito trabalho. <> vt -1. [strike]: **to ~ sb/sthg a blow** dar um golpe em alguém/algo; **to ~ a blow to sthg** fig ser um golpe em/para algo -2. [cards] repartir. <> vi -1. [in cards] repartir -2. [trade] negociar.

➡ **deal in** vt fus COMM negociar.

➡ **deal out** vt sep repartir.

➡ **deal with** vt fus -1. [handle, cope with, be faced with] lidar com -2. [be concerned with] tratar de.

dealer ['di:lə'] n -1. [trader] negociante m -2. [in cards] carteador m, -ra f.

dealership ['di:ləʃɪp] n revendedor m, -ra f.

dealings npl [relations]: **~s with sb** relações mpl com alguém.

dealt [delt] pt & pp ⊳ **deal**.

dean [di:n] n -1. [of church, cathedral] deão m -2. [of university] decano m, -na f.

dear [dɪə'] <> adj -1. [loved] querido(da); **to be ~ to sb** ser precioso(sa) para alguém -2. [in letter]: **Dear Sir/Madam** Prezado Senhor/Prezada Senhora -3. esp UK [expensive] caro(ra). <> n: **my ~** meu querido, minha querida. <> excl: **oh ~!** oh céus!

dearly ['dɪəlɪ] adv -1.: **to love sb ~** amar muito alguém -2. [very much] muito; **I would ~ love to know ...** eu adoraria saber ... -3. [pay, cost] caro.

dearth [dɜ:θ] n carência f.

death [deθ] n morte f; **to frighten/worry sb to ~** quase matar alguém de susto/preocupação; **to be bored to ~ with sthg** inf morrer de tédio com algo; **to be sick to ~ of sthg/of doing sthg** inf estar de saco cheio de algo/de fazer algo; **to be put to ~** ser morto(ta); **to be at ~'s door** estar à beira da morte.

deathbed ['deθbed] n leito m de morte.

death certificate n certidão f de óbito.

death duty UK, **death tax** US n imposto m de transmissão causa mortis.

death knell n fig: **to sound the ~ for sb/sthg** soar o alarme para alguém/algo.

deathly ['deθlɪ] (compar -ier, superl -iest) <> adj [silence, hush] mortal. <> adv [pale, cold] mortalmente.

death penalty n pena f de morte.

death rate n taxa f de mortalidade.

death row n US corredor m da morte.

death sentence n sentença f de morte.

death squad n esquadrão m da morte.

death tax n US = **death duty**.

death toll n número m de mortos.

death trap n inf: **this car is a ~** este carro é um perigo.

Death Valley n Vale m da Morte.

deathwatch beetle ['deθwɒtʃ-] n caruncho f.

death wish n desejo m de morrer.

deb [deb] n UK inf debutante mf.

debacle n fracasso m.

debar [di:'bɑ:'] (pt & pp -red, cont -ring) vt: **to ~ sb (from somewhere/from doing sthg)** privar alguém (do acesso a algum lugar/de fazer algo).

debase [dɪ'beɪs] vt [person, sport] degradar; **to ~ o.s.** degradar-se.

debasement [dɪ'beɪsmənt] n [of person, sport] degradação f.

debatable [dɪ'beɪtəbl] adj contestável, controverso(sa).

debate [dɪ'beɪt] <> n (U) debate m; **open to ~** aberto(ta) ao debate. <> vt [issue] debater; **to ~ whether to do sthg** discutir sobre o que fazer. <> vi debater.

debating society [dɪ'beɪtɪŋ-] n grupo m de discussão.

debauched [dɪ'bɔ:tʃt] adj devasso(sa), depravado(da).

debauchery [dɪ'bɔ:tʃərɪ] n (U) depravação f.

debenture [dɪ'bentʃə'] n debênture f.

debilitate [dɪ'bɪlɪteɪt] vt enfraquecer.

debilitating [dɪ'bɪlɪteɪtɪŋ] adj enfraquecedor(ra).

debility [dɪ'bɪlətɪ] n (U) fraqueza f.

debit ['debɪt] <> n débito m. <> vt [account, sum of money] debitar.

debit card n cartão m de débito.

debonair [ˌdebə'neə'] adj garboso(sa).

debrief [ˌdi:'bri:f] vt interrogar (ao se terminar uma missão).

debriefing [ˌdi:'bri:fɪŋ] n interrogatório m (após o término de uma missão).

debris ['deɪbri:] n -1. escombros mpl -2. GEOL fragmento m de rocha.

debt [det] n -1. dívida f; **to be in ~** estar endividado(da) -2. [feeling of gratitude] dívida f; **to be in sb's ~** estar em débito com alguém.

debt collector n cobrador m, -ra f de dívidas.

debtor ['detə'] n devedor m, -ra f.

debug [ˌdi:'bʌg] (pt & pp -ged, cont -ging) vt -1. [room] tirar microfones escondidos de -2. COMPUT [program] depurar.

debunk [ˌdi:'bʌŋk] vt derrubar.

debut ['deɪbju:] n debute m.

debutante ['debjʊtɑ:nt] n debutante mf.

dec. (abbr of deceased) m.

Dec. (abbr of December) dez.

decade ['dekeɪd] n década f.

decadence ['dekədəns] n decadência f.

decadent ['dekədənt] adj decadente.

decaf n inf café m descafeinado.

decaffeinated [dɪ'kæfɪneɪtɪd] adj descafeinado(da).

decal ['di:kæl] n US adesivo m, decalque m.

decamp [dɪ'kæmp] vi inf safar-se.

decant [dɪ'kænt] *vt* decantar.

decanter [dɪ'kæntə^r] *n* [container] licoreira *f.*

decapitate [dɪ'kæpɪteɪt] *vt* decapitar.

decathlete [dɪ'kæθliːt] *n* decatleta *mf.*

decathlon [dɪ'kæθlɒn] *n* decatlo *m.*

decay [dɪ'keɪ] <> *n* **-1.** [of tooth] cárie *f*-**2.** [of body, plant] decomposição *f*-**3.** *fig* [of building, society]: **to fall into** ~ [building] cair em ruínas; [system] entrar em decadência; [society] entrar em declínio; **urban** ~ decadência *f* urbana. <> *vi* **-1.** [tooth] criar cáries - **2.** [body, plant] decompor-se - **3.** *fig* [building, society] entrar em declínio.

deceased [dɪ'siːst] (*pl inv*) *fml* <> *adj* falecido(da). <> *n*: **the** ~ o falecido, a falecida. <> *npl*: **the** ~ os mortos.

deceit [dɪ'siːt] *n* engano *m.*

deceitful [dɪ'siːtfʊl] *adj* enganoso(sa).

deceive [dɪ'siːv] *vt* enganar; **to** ~ **o.s.** enganar-se.

decelerate [ˌdiː'seləreɪt] *vi* desacelerar.

December [dɪ'sembə^r] *n* dezembro; *see also* **September.**

decency ['diːsnsɪ] *n* **-1.** [respectability] decência *f*-**2.** [consideration]: **to have the** ~ **to do sthg** ter a decência de fazer algo.

decent ['diːsnt] *adj* decente.

decently ['diːsntlɪ] *adv* decentemente.

decentralization [diːˌsentrəlaɪ'zeɪʃn] *n* descentralização *f.*

decentralize, -ise [ˌdiː'sentrəlaɪz] *vt* descentralizar.

deception [dɪ'sepʃn] *n* **-1.** [lie, pretence] engano *m* - **2.** [act of lying, pretending] embuste *m.*

deceptive [dɪ'septɪv] *adj* enganoso(sa).

deceptively [dɪ'septɪvlɪ] *adv* enganosamente.

decibel ['desɪbel] *n* decibel *m.*

decide [dɪ'saɪd] <> *vt* - **1.** [resolve, determine] decidir; **to** ~ **to do sthg** decidir fazer algo; **to** ~ **that** decidir que - **2.** [settle] decidir, resolver. <> *vi* [make up one's mind] decidir-se.

    decide (up)on *vt fus* decidir-se por.

decided [dɪ'saɪdɪd] *adj* **-1.** [distinct] evidente - **2.** [resolute] decidido(da).

decidedly [dɪ'saɪdɪdlɪ] *adv* decididamente.

deciding [dɪ'saɪdɪŋ] *adj*: ~ **vote** voto *m* de Minerva.

deciduous [dɪ'sɪdjʊəs] *adj* decíduo(dua).

decimal ['desɪml] <> *adj* decimal. <> *n* (número *m*) decimal *m.*

decimal currency *n* moeda *f* de sistema decimal.

decimalize, -ise ['desɪməlaɪz] *vt* converter em decimal.

decimal place *n* casa *f* decimal.

decimal point *n* vírgula *f* decimal.

decimate ['desɪmeɪt] *vt* dizimar.

decipher [dɪ'saɪfə^r] *vt* decifrar.

decision [dɪ'sɪʒn] *n* - **1.** [gen] decisão *f*; **to make a** ~ tomar uma decisão - **2.** [decisiveness] determinação *f.*

decision-maker *n* tomador *m*, -ra *f* de decisões.

decision-making *n* tomada *f* de decisão.

decisive [dɪ'saɪsɪv] *adj* **-1.** [person] decidido(da)

- **2.** [factor, event] decisivo(va).

decisively [dɪ'saɪsɪvlɪ] *adv* - **1.** [confidently] decididamente - **2.** [conclusively] claramente.

decisiveness [dɪ'saɪsɪvnɪs] *n* [of person] determinação *f.*

deck [dek] <> *n* - **1.** [of ship] convés *m* - **2.** [of bus] piso *m* - **3.** [of cards] baralho *m* - **4.** *US* [of house] *área com piso e sem telhado junto a uma casa.* <> *vt* [decorate]: **to** ~ **sthg with** decorar algo com.

    deck out *vt sep* enfeitar.

deckchair ['dektʃeə^r] *n* espreguiçadeira *f.*

deckhand ['dekhænd] *n* taifeiro *m.*

declaration [ˌdeklə'reɪʃn] *n* declaração *f.*

Declaration of Independence *n*: **the** ~ *a declaração da independência norte-americana em 1776.*

declare [dɪ'kleə^r] *vt* declarar.

declared [dɪ'kleəd] *adj* [intention] declarado(da).

declassify [ˌdiː'klæsɪfaɪ] (*pt* & *pp* -**ied**) *vt* revelar, tornar público(ca).

decline [dɪ'klaɪn] <> *n* declínio *m*; **to be in** ~ estar em declínio; **on the** ~ em declínio. <> *vt* [refuse] recusar, declinar; **to** ~ **to do sthg** recusar-se a fazer algo. <> *vi* - **1.** [deteriorate] decair - **2.** [refuse] recusar-se.

declutch [dɪ'klʌtʃ] *vi* AUT soltar a embreagem.

decode [ˌdiː'kəʊd] *vt* decodificar.

decoder [ˌdiː'kəʊdə^r] *n* decodificador *m.*

decommission [ˌdiːkə'mɪʃn] *vt* desmontar.

decompose [ˌdiːkəm'pəʊz] *vi* [decay] decompor.

decomposition [ˌdiːkɒmpə'zɪʃn] *n* [decay] decomposição *f.*

decompression chamber [ˌdiːkəm'preʃn-] *n* câmara *f* de descompressão.

decompression sickness [ˌdiːkəm'preʃn-] *n* mal *m* da descompressão.

decongestant [ˌdiːkən'dʒestənt] *n* descongestionante *m.*

decontaminate [ˌdiːkən'tæmɪneɪt] *vt* descontaminar.

décor ['deɪkɔː^r] *n* decoração *f.*

decorate ['dekəreɪt] *vt* - **1.** [gen] decorar; **to** ~ **sthg with** decorar algo com - **2.** [with medal] condecorar.

decoration [ˌdekə'reɪʃn] *n* - **1.** [ornament] enfeite *m* - **2.** [activity, appearance] decoração *f*-**3.** [medal] condecoração *f.*

decorative ['dekərətɪv] *adj* decorativo(va).

decorator ['dekəreɪtə^r] *n* decorador *m*, -ra *f.*

decorous ['dekərəs] *adj fml* decoroso(sa).

decorum [dɪ'kɔːrəm] *n* (*U*) decoro *m.*

decoy [*n* 'diːkɔɪ, *vb* dɪ'kɔɪ] <> *n* chamariz *m*, isca *f.* <> *vt* atrair.

decrease [*n* 'diːkriːs, *vb* dɪ'kriːs] <> *n* diminuição *f*; ~ **in sthg** diminuição de algo. <> *vt* diminuir. <> *vi* diminuir.

decreasing [diː'kriːsɪŋ] *adj* decrescente.

decree [dɪ'kriː] <> *n* - **1.** [order, decision] decreto *m* - **2.** *US* [judgment] sentença *f.* <> *vt* decretar; **to** ~ **that** decretar que.

decree absolute (*pl* **decrees absolute**) *n* UK JUR sentença *f* definitiva de divórcio.

decree nisi [-'naɪsaɪ] (*pl* **decrees nisi**) *n* UK JUR sentença *f* provisória de divórcio.

decrepit [dɪ'krepɪt] *adj* decrépito(ta).

decry [dɪ'kraɪ] (*pt* & *pp* **-ied**) *vt fml* depreciar, censurar.

dedicate ['dedɪkeɪt] *vt* **-1.** [book, song, poem]: **to ~ sthg to sb** dedicar algo a alguém **-2.** [life, career] dedicar; **to ~ o.s. to sthg** dedicar-se a algo.

dedicated ['dedɪkeɪtɪd] *adj* [gen & COMPUT] dedicado(da).

dedication [ˌdedɪ'keɪʃn] *n* dedicação *f*.

deduce [dɪ'dju:s] *vt* deduzir; **to ~ sthg from sthg** deduzir algo de algo.

deduct [dɪ'dʌkt] *vt* deduzir; **to ~ sthg from sthg** descontar OR deduzir algo de algo.

deduction [dɪ'dʌkʃn] *n* **-1.** [conclusion] dedução *f* **-2.** [sum deducted] desconto *m*.

deed [di:d] *n* **-1.** [action] ação *f*, feito *m* **-2.** JUR escritura *f*.

deed poll (*pl* **deed polls** OR **deeds poll**) *n UK*: **to change one's name by ~** trocar oficialmente de nome.

deem [di:m] *vt fml* julgar; **the building was ~ed to be unsafe** o edifício foi considerado inseguro; **to ~ it wise to do sthg** julgar sensato fazer algo.

deep [di:p] ◇ *adj* **-1.** [gen] profundo(da); **to be thrown in at the ~ end** *fig* ser posto(ta) numa situação nova sem preparação **-2.** [in measurements] de profundidade **-3.** [colour] intenso(sa) **-4.** [sound, voice] grave. ◇ *adv* fundo; **to go ~ into the forest** embrenhar-se floresta adentro; **to be ~ in thought** estar imerso(sa) em pensamentos; **to know ~ down** *fig* saber bem no fundo.

deepen ['di:pn] ◇ *vt* [hole, channel] aprofundar. ◇ *vi* **-1.** [river, sea] aprofundar-se **-2.** [crisis, recession, feeling] agravar-se **-3.** [darkness] tornar-se mais profundo(da).

deepening ['di:pnɪŋ] *adj* [crisis, recession] cada vez mais grave.

deep-fat fryer *n* fritadeira *f* por imersão.

deep freeze *n* freezer *m*.
 ➡ **deep-freeze** *vt* congelar.

deep-fry *vt* fritar *(com muito óleo)*.

deeply ['di:plɪ] *adv* **-1.** [dig, sigh] fundo **-2.** [profoundly, sincerely] profundamente.

deep-rooted *adj* arraigado(da).

deep-sea *adj* submarino(na).

deep-seated *adj* [belief, fear] profundamente arraigado(da).

deep-set *adj* [eyes] encovado(da).

deer [dɪə'] (*pl inv*) *n* veado *m*, cervo *m*.

deerstalker ['dɪəˌstɔ:kə'] *n* [hat] boné *m* com abas.

de-escalate [ˌdi:'eskəleɪt] ◇ *vt* suavizar. ◇ *vi* suavizar.

deface [dɪ'feɪs] *vt* danificar.

defamation [ˌdefə'meɪʃn] *n fml* difamação *f*.

defamatory [dɪ'fæmətrɪ] *adj fml* difamatório(ria).

default [dɪ'fɔ:lt] ◇ *n* **-1.** JUR falta *f*; **to declare s.o. in ~** declarar alguém inadimplente; **by ~** à revelia **-2.** COMPUT default *m*, padrão *m*. ◇ *adj* COMPUT default, OR padrão ◇ *vi* FIN, JUR: **to ~ on sthg** estar/ficar inadimplente com algo.

defaulter [dɪ'fɔ:ltə'] *n* [on payment] inadimplente *mf*.

default value *n* COMPUT valor-padrão *m*, valor *m* default.

defeat [dɪ'fi:t] ◇ *n* [gen] derrota *f*; **to admit ~** admitir a derrota. ◇ *vt* **-1.** [team, opponent] derrotar **-2.** [motion, proposal] rechaçar **-3.** [plans] frustrar.

defeatism [dɪ'fi:tɪzm] *n* derrotismo *m*.

defeatist [dɪ'fi:tɪst] ◇ *adj* derrotista. ◇ *n* derrotista *mf*.

defecate ['defəkeɪt] *vi fml* defecar.

defect [*n* 'di:fekt, *vb* dɪ'fekt] ◇ *n* [fault] defeito *m*. ◇ *vi* POL: **to ~ to the other side** ≃ passar para o outro lado, virar a casaca.

defection [dɪ'fekʃn] *n* deserção *f*. ·

defective [dɪ'fektɪv] *adj* defeituoso(sa).

defector [dɪ'fektə'] *n* desertor *m*, -ra *f*.

defence *UK*, **defense** *US* [dɪ'fens] *n* **-1.** [gen & SPORT] defesa *f*; **~ against sb/sthg** defesa contra alguém/algo **-2.** [protective device, system] proteção *f*; **~ against sb/sthg** proteção *f* contra alguém/algo **-3.** [JUR - lawyers]: **the ~** a defesa; [- denial of charge] defesa *f*; **in sb's ~** em defesa de alguém.
 ➡ **defences** *npl* [of country] defesas *fpl*.

defenceless *UK*, **defenseless** *US* [dɪ'fenslɪs] *adj* indefeso(sa).

defend [dɪ'fend] ◇ *vt* defender; **to ~ sb/sthg against sb/sthg** defender alguém/algo de alguém/algo; **to ~ o.s.** defender-se. ◇ *vi* SPORT defender-se.

defendant [dɪ'fendənt] *n* réu *m*, ré *f*.

defender [dɪ'fendə'] *n* **-1.** [gen] defensor *m*, -ra *f* **-2.** [SPORT - player] zagueiro *m*, -ra *f*; [- of title] defensor *m*, -ra *f*.

defense *n US* = **defence**.

defenseless *adj US* = **defenceless**.

defensive [dɪ'fensɪv] ◇ *adj* **-1.** [weapons, tactics] defensivo(va) **-2.** [person] receoso(sa). ◇ *n*: **on the ~** na defensiva.

defer [dɪ'fɜ:'] (*pt* & *pp* **-red**, *cont* **-ring**) ◇ *vt* adiar, protelar. ◇ *vi*: **to ~ to sb** deferir a alguém.

deference ['defərəns] *n* deferência *f*.

deferential [ˌdefə'renʃl] *adj* deferente.

defiance [dɪ'faɪəns] *n* desafio *m*; **in ~ of sb/sthg** a despeito de alguém/algo.

defiant [dɪ'faɪənt] *adj* desafiador(ra).

defiantly [dɪ'faɪəntlɪ] *adv* desafiadoramente.

deficiency [dɪ'fɪʃnsɪ] (*pl* **-ies**) *n* **-1.** [lack] deficiência *f* **-2.** [inadequacy] deficiência *f*, imperfeição *f*.

deficient [dɪ'fɪʃnt] *adj* **-1.** [lacking]: **~ in sthg** deficiente em algo **-2.** [inadequate] deficiente.

deficit ['defɪsɪt] *n* déficit *m*.

defile [dɪ'faɪl] *vt* **-1.** [grave, church] profanar **-2.** [mind, purity] corromper.

define [dɪ'faɪn] *vt* definir.

definite ['defɪnɪt] *adj* **-1.** [date, plan] definido(da) **-2.** [improvement, difference] claro(ra) **-3.** [person] seguro(ra).

definitely ['defɪnɪtlɪ] *adv* sem dúvida.

definition [ˌdefɪ'nɪʃn] *n* **-1.** [of word, expression, concept] definição *f*; **by ~** por definição **-2.** [of problem, function] explicação *f* **-3.** [clarity] nitidez *f*.

definitive [dɪ'fɪnɪtɪv] *adj* definitivo(va).

deflate [dɪ'fleɪt] ◇ *vt* **-1.** [balloon, tyre] esvaziar **-2.**

fig [person] diminuir **-3.** *ECON* deflacionar. ◇ *vi* [balloon, tyre] esvaziar-se.

deflation [dɪˈfleɪʃn] *n* *ECON* deflação *f*.

deflationary [dɪˈfleɪʃnərɪ] *adj* *ECON* deflacionário(-ria).

deflect [dɪˈflekt] *vt* desviar.

deflection [dɪˈflekʃn] *n* desvio *m*.

defog [ˌdiːˈfɒg] *vt* *US* *AUT* desembaçar.

defogger [ˌdiːˈfɒgəʳ] *n* *US* *AUT* desembaçador *m*.

deforest [ˌdiːˈfɒrɪst] *vt* desflorestar.

deforestation [diːˌfɒrɪˈsteɪʃn] *n* desflorestamento *m*.

deform [diːˈfɔːm] *vt* deformar.

deformed [dɪˈfɔːmd] *adj* deformado(da).

deformity [dɪˈfɔːmətɪ] (*pl* -ies) *n* **-1.** [state of being deformed] deformidade *f* **-2.** [deformed part] máformação *f* (congênita).

DEFRA (*abbr of* **Department for the Environment, Food and Rural Affairs**) *n* *divisão do governo britânico que trata de questões agrárias e do meio ambiente*.

defraud [dɪˈfrɔːd] *vt* fraudar.

defray [dɪˈfreɪ] *vt* custear.

defrost [ˌdiːˈfrɒst] ◇ *vt* **-1.** [fridge] degelar **-2.** [frozen food] descongelar **-3.** *US* [AUT- de-ice] descongelar. ◇ *vi* **-1.** [fridge] degelar **-2.** [frozen food] descongelar.

deft [deft] *adj* **-1.** [movement, fingers] ágil **-2.** [handling of situation] hábil.

deftly [ˈdeftlɪ] *adv* **-1.** [move] agilmente **-2.** [deal with situation] habilmente.

defunct [dɪˈfʌŋkt] *adj* extinto(ta).

defuse [ˌdiːˈfjuːz] *vt* *UK* **-1.** [bomb] desativar **-2.** *fig* [situation] acalmar.

defy [dɪˈfaɪ] (*pt & pp* -ied) *vt* **-1.** [disobey] desafiar **-2.** [challenge]: **to ~ sb to do sthg** desafiar alguém a fazer algo **-3.** *fig* [elude - description] impossibilitar; [- efforts] tornar inútil.

degenerate [*adj & n* dɪˈdʒenərət, *vb* dɪˈdʒenəreɪt] ◇ *adj* degenerado(da). ◇ *n* degenerado *m*, -da *f*. ◇ *vi* degenerar; **to ~ into** degenerar para.

degradation [ˌdegrəˈdeɪʃn] *n* degradação *f*.

degrade [dɪˈgreɪd] *vt* [debase] degradar.

degrading [dɪˈgreɪdɪŋ] *adj* [debasing] degradante.

degree [dɪˈgriː] *n* **-1.** [unit of measurement, amount] grau *m*; **by ~s** gradualmente **-2.** [qualification] título *m* universitário; **to have/take a ~ (in sthg)** ter/obter graduação (em algo).

dehumanize, -ise [diːˈhjuːmənaɪz] *vt* desumanizar.

dehydrated [ˌdiːhaɪˈdreɪtɪd] *adj* desidratado(da).

dehydration [ˌdiːhaɪˈdreɪʃn] *n* desidratação *f*.

de-ice [diːˈaɪs] *vt* descongelar.

de-icer [diːˈaɪsəʳ] *n* substância *f* descongelante.

deign [deɪn] *vi*: **to ~ to do sthg** dignar-se a fazer algo.

deity [ˈdiːɪtɪ] (*pl* -ies) *n* divindade *f*, deidade *f*.

déjà vu [ˌdeʒɑːˈvjuː] *n* déjà vu *m*.

dejected [dɪˈdʒektɪd] *adj* abatido(da), desanimado(da).

dejection [dɪˈdʒekʃn] *n* abatimento *m*, desânimo *m*.

Del. *abbr of* **Delaware**.

Delaware [ˈdeləweəʳ] *n* Delaware; **in ~** em Delaware.

delay [dɪˈleɪ] ◇ *n* atraso *m*; **without ~** sem demora. ◇ *vt* **-1.** [cause to be late] atrasar **-2.** [postpone] adiar; **to ~ doing sthg** adiar (fazer) algo. ◇ *vi* demorar-se; **to ~ in doing sthg** demorar-se para fazer algo.

delayed [dɪˈleɪd] *adj* atrasado(da).

delayed-action [dɪˈleɪd-] *adj* de ação retardada; **~ shutter** *PHOT* obturador *m* automático.

delectable [dɪˈlektəbl] *adj* **-1.** [food] delicioso(sa) **-2.** [person] fabuloso(sa).

delegate [*n* ˈdelɪgət, *vb* ˈdelɪgeɪt] ◇ *n* delegado *m*, -da *f*. ◇ *vt* **-1.** [appoint to do job] delegar; **to ~ sb to do sthg** delegar alguém para fazer algo **-2.** [hand over responsibility for] delegar; **to ~ sthg to sb** delegar algo a alguém. ◇ *vi* delegar responsabilidades.

delegation [ˌdelɪˈgeɪʃn] *n* delegação *f*.

delete [dɪˈliːt] *vt* **-1.** [remove] apagar **-2.** *COMPUT* deletar.

deletion [dɪˈliːʃn] *n* exclusão *f*.

Delhi [ˈdelɪ] *n* Delhi.

deli [ˈdelɪ] (*abbr of* **delicatessen**) *n* *fam* loja onde se vendem bebidas, frios, conservas e pães.

deliberate [*adj* dɪˈlɪbərət, *vb* dɪˈlɪbəreɪt] ◇ *adj* **-1.** [intentional] deliberado(da) **-2.** [slow] pausado(da). ◇ *vi* *fml* deliberar.

deliberately [dɪˈlɪbərətlɪ] *adv* **-1.** [on purpose] deliberadamente **-2.** [slowly] pausadamente.

deliberation [dɪˌlɪbəˈreɪʃn] *n* **-1.** [careful consideration] deliberação *f* **-2.** [slowness] morosidade *f*.
　◆ **deliberations** *npl* deliberações *fpl*.

delicacy [ˈdelɪkəsɪ] (*pl* -ies) *n* **-1.** (*U*) [gracefulness, tact] delicadeza *f* **-2.** [food] iguaria *f*.

delicate [ˈdelɪkət] *adj* **-1.** [gen] delicado(da) **-2.** [flavour, colour] suave **-3.** [instrument] delicado(da), sensível.

delicately [ˈdelɪkətlɪ] *adv* **-1.** [made, drawn] com delicadeza **-2.** [flavoured, coloured] suavemente **-3.** [hint, suggest] delicadamente.

delicatessen [ˌdelɪkəˈtesn] *n* delicatessen *f*.

delicious [dɪˈlɪʃəs] *adj* **-1.** [tasty] delicioso(sa) **-2.** *fig* [delightful] encantador(ra).

delight [dɪˈlaɪt] ◇ *n* **-1.** [great pleasure] prazer *m*, deleite *m*; **to take ~ in doing sthg** ter prazer em fazer algo **-2.** [wonderful thing, person] encanto *m*. ◇ *vt* encantar. ◇ *vi*: **to ~ in sthg/in doing sthg** encantar-se em algo/em fazer algo.

delighted [dɪˈlaɪtɪd] *adj* muito contente; **~ by** *OR* **with sthg** encantado(da) com algo; **to be ~ to do sthg** estar muito feliz por fazer algo; **to be ~ that** ficar contente que.

delightful [dɪˈlaɪtfʊl] *adj* encantador(ra).

delightfully [dɪˈlaɪtfʊlɪ] *adv* encantadoramente.

delimit [diːˈlɪmɪt] *vt* *fml* delimitar.

delineate [dɪˈlɪnɪeɪt] *vt* *fml* delinear.

delinquency [dɪˈlɪŋkwənsɪ] *n* delinqüência *f*.

delinquent [dɪˈlɪŋkwənt] ◇ *adj* delinqüente. ◇ *n* delinqüente *mf*.

delirious [dɪˈlɪrɪəs] *adj* delirante; **to be ~** estar delirando.

delirium [dɪˈlɪrɪəm] *n* delírio *m*.

deliver [dɪ'lɪvə^r] ⟨> vt -**1.** [distribute]: **to ~ sthg (to sb)** entregar algo (a alguém) - **2.** [give - speech, lecture] proferir; [- message] entregar; [- warning, ultimatum] dar - **3.** [blow] desferir - **4.** [baby] trazer ao mundo - **5.** *fml* [liberate]: **to ~ sb (from sthg)** libertar alguém (de algo) - **6.** *US POL* [votes] captar. ⟨> vi -**1.** *COMM* repartir - **2.** [fulfil promise] cumprir (o prometido).

deliverance [dɪ'lɪvərəns] *n fml* libertação *f.*

delivery [dɪ'lɪvərɪ] (*pl* -**ies**) *n* - **1.** [of goods, letters] entrega *f* - **2.** [goods delivered] remessa *f* - **3.** [way of speaking] elocução *f* - **4.** [birth] parto *m.*

delivery note *n* guia *f* de remessa.

delivery van *UK,* **delivery truck** *US n* camionete *f* de entrega.

delphinium [del'fɪnɪəm] (*pl* -**s**) *n* espora *f* de jardim.

delta ['deltə] (*pl* -**s**) *n GEOGR* delta *m.*

delude [dɪ'lu:d] *vt* enganar; **to ~ o.s.** enganar-se.

deluge ['delju:dʒ] ⟨> *n* -**1.** [flood] dilúvio *m* - **2.** *fig* [huge number] mar *m.* ⟨> *vt*: **to be ~d with sthg** ser inundado(da) por algo.

delusion [dɪ'lu:ʒn] *n* ilusão *f*; **~s of grandeur** delírios *mpl* de grandeza.

de luxe [də'lʌks] *adj* de luxo.

delve [delv] *vi* - **1.** [into mystery] pesquisar; **to ~ into sthg** investigar algo - **2.** [in bag, cupboard] remexer; **to ~ into** *OR* **inside sthg** revolver dentro de algo.

Dem. - **1.** (*abbr of* **Democrat**) Democrata *mf.* - **2.** (*abbr of* **Democratic**) Democrático(ca).

demagogue *UK,* **demagog** *US* ['deməgɒg] *n* demagogo *m,* -ga *f.*

demand [dɪ'mɑ:nd] ⟨> *n* -**1.** [gen] exigência *f*; **wage ~** reivindicação *f* salarial; **on ~** [gen] a pedido; *COMM* sob demanda - **2.** [need & *COMM*]: **~ for sthg** demanda *f* por algo; **in ~** solicitado(da). ⟨> *vt* -**1.** [gen] exigir; **to ~ to do sthg** exigir fazer algo - **2.** [enquire forcefully] inquirir.

demanding [dɪ'mɑ:ndɪŋ] *adj* -**1.** [exhausting] que exige muito esforço - **2.** [not easily satisfied] exigente.

demarcation [ˌdi:mɑ:'keɪʃn] *n* demarcação *f.*

demarcation dispute *n disputa entre sindicatos sobre as funções a serem realizadas por seus membros.*

dematerialize, -ise [di:mə'tɪərɪəlaɪz] *vi* desmaterializar-se.

demean [dɪ'mi:n] *vt* rebaixar; **to ~ o.s.** rebaixar-se, humilhar-se.

demeaning [dɪ'mi:nɪŋ] *adj* humilhante.

demeanour *UK,* **demeanor** *US* [dɪ'mi:nə^r] *n fml* comportamento *m.*

demented [dɪ'mentɪd] *adj* demente.

dementia [dɪ'menʃə] *n* demência *f.*

demerara sugar [ˌdemə'reərə-] *n UK* açúcar *m* mascavo.

demigod ['demɪgɒd] *n* semideus *m.*

demijohn ['demɪdʒɒn] *n* garrafão *m.*

demilitarized zone, demilitarised zone [ˌdi:'mɪlɪtəraɪzd-] *n* zona *f* desmilitarizada.

demise [dɪ'maɪz] *n fml* -**1.** [death] falecimento *m* - **2.** *fig* [end] fim *m.*

demist [ˌdi:'mɪst] *vt UK AUT* desembaçar *m.*

demister [ˌdi:'mɪstə^r] *n UK AUT* desembaçador *m.*

demo ['deməʊ] (*pl* -**s**) (*abbr of* **demonstration**) *n* -**1.** *fam* [protest] manifestação *f.* - **2.** [tape, video] demo *f.*

demobilize, -ise [ˌdi:'məʊbɪlaɪz] *vt fml* desmobilizar.

democracy [dɪ'mɒkrəsɪ] (*pl* -**ies**) *n* democracia *f.*

democrat ['deməkræt] *n* democrata *mf.*

➡ Democrat *n US* democrata *mf.*

democratic [demə'krætɪk] *adj* democrático(ca).

➡ Democratic *adj US* democrata.

democratically [ˌdemə'krætɪklɪ] *adv* democraticamente.

Democratic Party *n US*: **the ~** o Partido Democrata (*dos Estados Unidos*).

democratize, -ise [dɪ'mɒkrətaɪz] *vt* democratizar.

demographic [ˌdemə'græfɪk] *adj* demográfico(ca).

demolish [dɪ'mɒlɪʃ] *vt* -**1.** [knock down] demolir - **2.** [prove wrong] destruir, acabar com - **3.** *inf* [eat] acabar com.

demolition [ˌdemə'lɪʃn] *n* -**1.** [knocking down] demolição *f* - **2.** [proving wrong] destruição *f.*

demon ['di:mən] ⟨> *n* [evil spirit] demônio *m.* ⟨> *comp inf* [skilled] fantástico(ca).

demonstrable [dɪ'mɒnstrəbl] *adj* demonstrável.

demonstrably [dɪ'mɒnstrəblɪ] *adv* decididamente.

demonstrate ['demənstreɪt] ⟨> *vt* -**1.** [gen] demonstrar - **2.** [appliance, machine] mostrar o funcionamento de. ⟨> *vi* manifestar-se; **to ~ for/against sthg** manifestar-se a favor de/contra algo.

demonstration [demən'streɪʃn] *n* -**1.** [gen] demonstração *f* - **2.** [protest gathering, march] manifestação *f.*

demonstrative [dɪ'mɒnstrətɪv] *adj* efusivo(va).

demonstrator ['demənstreɪtə^r] *n* - **1.** [of machine, product] demonstrador *m,* -ra *f* - **2.** [protester] manifestante *mf.*

demoralize, -ise [dɪ'mɒrəlaɪz] *vt* desmoralizar.

demoralized [dɪ'mɒrəlaɪzd] *adj* desmoralizado(da).

demote [ˌdi:'məʊt] *vt* rebaixar (*na carreira profissional*).

demotion [ˌdi:'məʊʃn] *n* rebaixamento *m* (*na carreira profissional*).

demotivate [ˌdi:'məʊtɪveɪt] *vt* desmotivar.

demure [dɪ'mjʊə^r] *adj* recatado(da).

demystify [ˌdi:'mɪstɪfaɪ] (*pt* & *pp* -**ied**) *vt* desmistificar.

den [den] *n* [lair] toca *f.*

denationalization ['di:ˌnæʃnəlaɪ'zeɪʃn] *n* desnacionalização *f.*

denationalize, -ise [ˌdi:'næʃnəlaɪz] *vt* desnacionalizar.

denial [dɪ'naɪəl] *n* -**1.** [refutation] contestação *f* - **2.** (*U*) [refusal] negação *f.*

denier ['denɪə^r] *n* [of stockings, tights] denier *m, medida da espessura do fio de náilon ou de seda usado na fabricação de roupas.*

denigrate ['denɪgreɪt] *vt fml* difamar, denegrir.

denim ['denɪm] *n* brim *m.*

➡ denims *npl* jeans *m inv.*

denim jacket *n* jaqueta *f* jeans.

denizen ['denizn] *n literary or hum* habitante *mf*.

Denmark ['denmɑːk] *n* Dinamarca; **in ~** na Dinamarca.

denomination [dɪˌnɒmɪ'neɪʃn] *n* -**1**. *RELIG* denominação *f*, seita *f* -**2**. *FIN* valor *m*.

denominator [dɪ'nɒmɪneɪtə'] *n* denominador *m*.

denote [dɪ'nəʊt] *vt fml* denotar.

denouement [deɪ'nuːmɒn] *n* desfecho *m*.

denounce [dɪ'naʊns] *vt* denunciar.

dense [dens] *adj* -**1**. [thick - trees, undergrowth] denso(sa); [- mist, fog] espesso(sa) -**2**. *inf* [stupid] estúpido(da).

densely ['densli] *adv* [thickly] densamente.

density ['densətɪ] (*pl* -ies) *n* densidade *f*.

dent [dent] <> *n* amassado *m*. <> *vt* [surface] amassar.

dental ['dentl] *adj* dentário(ria); **a ~ problem** um problema nos dentes.

dental floss *n* (*U*) fio *m* dental.

dental plate *n* dentadura *f* postiça, chapa *f*.

dental surgeon *n* cirurgião-dentista *m*, cirurgiã-dentista *f*.

dental surgery *n* cirurgia *f* dentária.

dental treatment *n* (*U*) tratamento *m* dentário.

dented ['dentɪd] *adj* amassado(da).

dentist ['dentɪst] *n* dentista *mf*; **to go to the ~'s** ir ao dentista.

dentistry ['dentɪstrɪ] *n* (*U*) odontologia *f*.

dentures ['dentʃəz] *npl* dentadura *f*.

denude *vt fml*: **to ~ sthg (of sthg)** despojar algo (de algo).

denunciation [dɪˌnʌnsɪ'eɪʃn] *n* denúncia *f*.

deny [dɪ'naɪ] (*pt* & *pp* -ied) *vt* negar; **to ~ sb sthg** negar algo a alguém.

deodorant [diː'əʊdərənt] *n* desodorante *m*.

depart [dɪ'pɑːt] *vi fml* -**1**. [leave] partir; **to ~ from** partir de -**2**. [differ]: **to ~ from sthg** afastar-se de algo.

department [dɪ'pɑːtmənt] *n* -**1**. [gen] departamento -**2**. [of government] ministério *m*.

departmental [ˌdiːpɑːt'mentl] *adj* de departamento.

department store *n* loja *f* de departamentos.

departure [dɪ'pɑːtʃə'] *n* -**1**. [leaving] partida *f* -**2**. [variation]: **~ (from sthg)** abandono *m* (de algo) -**3**. [orientation] início *m*.

departure lounge *n* sala *f* de embarque.

depend [dɪ'pend] *vi* -**1**. [rely - financially]: **to ~ on sb/ sthg** depender de alguém/algo; [- emotionally]: **to ~ on sb** confiar em alguém -**2**. [be determined]: **it ~s** depende; **it ~s on** depende de; **~ing on** dependendo de.

dependable [dɪ'pendəbl] *adj* confiável.

dependant [dɪ'pendənt] *n* dependente *mf*.

dependence [dɪ'pendəns] *n* -**1**. [reliance]: **~ (on sb/sthg)** dependência *f* (de alguém/algo) -**2**. [addiction]: **~ (on sthg)** dependência (de algo).

dependent [dɪ'pendənt] *adj* -**1**. [reliant]: **to be ~ (on sb/sthg)** ser dependente (de alguém/algo) -**2**. [addicted] dependente -**3**. [determined by]: **to be ~ on sb/sthg** depender de alguém/algo.

depict [dɪ'pɪkt] *vt* -**1**. [show in picture] retratar -**2**.

[describe]: **to ~ sb/sthg as sthg** retratar alguém/algo como algo.

depilatory [dɪ'pɪlətrɪ] *adj* depilatório(ria).

deplete [dɪ'pliːt] *vt* reduzir.

depletion [dɪ'pliːʃn] *n* (*U*) redução *f*.

deplorable [dɪ'plɔːrəbl] *adj* deplorável.

deplore [dɪ'plɔː'] *vt* deplorar.

deploy [dɪ'plɔɪ] *vt* dispor.

deployment [dɪ'plɔɪmənt] *n* (*U*) disposição *f*.

depopulated [ˌdiː'pɒpjʊleɪtɪd] *adj* despovoado(da).

depopulation [diːˌpɒpjʊ'leɪʃn] *n* (*U*) despovoamento *m*.

deport [dɪ'pɔːt] *vt* deportar.

deportation [ˌdiːpɔː'teɪʃn] *n* deportação *f*.

deportation order *n* ordem *f* de deportação.

depose [dɪ'pəʊz] *vt* [king, ruler] depor.

deposit [dɪ'pɒzɪt] <> *n* -**1**. *GEOL* [of gold, oil] jazida *f* -**2**. [of sediment, silt] depósito *m* -**3**. [fin] depósito *m*; **make a ~** fazer um depósito -**4**. [down payment - on house, car] entrada *f*; [- on hotel room] depósito *m* -**5**. [returnable payment - on hired goods] caução *f*; [- on bottle, container] depósito *m*. <> *vt* -**1**. [gen] depositar -**2**. [bag, case, shopping] colocar.

deposit account *n UK* conta *f* remunerada.

depositor [də'pɒzɪtə'] *n* depositante *mf*.

depot ['depəʊ] *n* -**1**. [storage facility - for goods] armazém *m*; [- for vehicles] garagem *f* -**2**. *US* [bus or train terminus] terminal *m*.

depraved [dɪ'preɪvd] *adj* depravado(da).

depravity [dɪ'prævətɪ] *n* (*U*) depravação *f*.

deprecate ['deprɪkeɪt] *vt fml* censurar.

deprecating ['deprɪkeɪtɪŋ] *adj* desaprovador(ra).

depreciate [dɪ'priːʃɪeɪt] *vi* depreciar.

depreciation [dɪˌpriːʃɪ'eɪʃn] *n* (*U*) depreciação *f*.

depress [dɪ'pres] *vt* -**1**. [sadden, discourage] deprimir -**2**. *ECON* depreciar -**3**. [slow down, reduce] reduzir.

depressant [dɪ'presənt] *n MED* sedativo *m*.

depressed [dɪ'prest] *adj* -**1**. [person] deprimido(da) -**2**. *ECON* em depressão -**3**. [area]: **~ point** ponto inferior.

depressing [dɪ'presɪŋ] *adj* deprimente.

depression [dɪ'preʃn] *n* depressão *f*.

  ➡ **Depression** *n*: **the (Great) Depression** a Grande Depressão.

depressive [dɪ'presɪv] *adj* depressivo(va).

deprivation [ˌdeprɪ'veɪʃn] *n* [privation] privação *f*.

deprive [dɪ'praɪv] *vt*: **to ~ sb of sthg** privar alguém de algo.

deprived [dɪ'praɪvd] *adj* necessitado(da).

Dept. (*abbr of* **department**) Dep.

depth [depθ] *n* -**1**. profundidade *f*; **to be out of one's ~** [lit & fig] não dar pé para alguém; **in ~** em profundidade -**2**. [severity] gravidade *f*; **the ~ of sthg** a gravidade de algo.

  ➡ **depths** *npl*: **the ~s** [of sea, memory] as profundezas; [of winter] o auge; **to be in the ~s of despair** estar no auge do desespero.

depth charge *n* carga *f* de profundidade.

deputation [ˌdepjʊ'teɪʃn] *n* delegação *f*.

deputize, -ise ['depjʊtaɪz] *vi*: **to ~ (for sb)** substituir oficialmente (alguém).

deputy ['depjʊtɪ] (*pl* -ies) <> *adj* adjunto(ta); **~**

head subdiretor *m*, -ra *f*; ~ **chairman** vice-presidente *m*. ◇ *n* **-1.** [second-in-command] suplente *mf* **-2.** *US* [deputy sheriff] ajudante *mf* do delegado.

derail [dɪ'reɪl] *vt* [train] descarrilhar.

derailment [dɪ'reɪlmənt] *n* descarrilhamento *m*.

deranged [dɪ'reɪndʒd] *adj* perturbado(da), transtornado(da).

derby [*UK* 'dɑːbɪ, *US* 'dɜːbɪ] (*pl* **-ies**) *n* **-1.** [sports event] jogo *m* local **-2.** *US* [hat] chapéu-coco *m*.

deregulate [ˌdiː'regjʊleɪt] *vt* desregulamentar.

deregulation [ˌdiː'regjʊ'leɪʃn] *n (U)* desregulamentação *f*.

derelict ['derəlɪkt] *adj* abandonado(da).

deride [dɪ'raɪd] *vt* escarnecer de, zombar de.

derision [dɪ'rɪʒn] *n (U)* escárnio *m*, zombaria *f*.

derisive [dɪ'raɪsɪv] *adj* zombeteiro(ra).

derisory [də'raɪzərɪ] *adj* **-1.** [ridiculous] irrisório(ria) **-2.** [scornful] zombeteiro(ra).

derivation [ˌderɪ'veɪʃn] *n* [of word] origem *f*.

derivative [dɪ'rɪvətɪv] ◇ *adj pej* pouco original. ◇ *n* derivado *m*.

derive [dɪ'raɪv] ◇ *vt* **-1.** [pleasure]: **to ~ sthg from sthg** encontrar algo em algo **-2.** [word, expression]: **to be ~d from sthg** derivar de algo. ◇ *vi* [word, expression]: **to ~ from sthg** derivar-se de algo.

dermatitis [ˌdɜːmə'taɪtɪs] *n (U)* dermatite *f*.

dermatologist [ˌdɜːmə'tɒlədʒɪst] *n* dermatologista *mf*.

dermatology [ˌdɜːmə'tɒlədʒɪ] *n (U)* dermatologia *f*.

derogatory [dɪ'rɒgətrɪ] *adj* depreciativo(va).

derrick ['derɪk] *n* **-1.** [crane] guindaste *m* **-2.** [over oil well] torre *f* de perfuração.

derv [dɜːv] *n UK* gasóleo *m*.

desalination [diːˌsælɪ'neɪʃn] *n (U)* dessalinização *f*.

descant ['deskænt] *n* [tune] contraponto *m*.

descend [dɪ'send] ◇ *vi* **-1.** *fml* [go down] descer **-2.** [fall]: **to ~ (on sb/sthg)** recair (sobre alguém/algo) **-3.** [invade]: **to ~ on** invadir **-4.** [stoop, lower o.s.]: **to ~ to sthg/to doing sthg** rebaixar-se a algo/a fazer algo. ◇ *vt fml* [go down] descer.

descendant [dɪ'sendənt] *n* [family member] descendente *mf*.

descended [dɪ'sendɪd] *adj*: **to be ~ from sb** ser descendente *OR* descender de alguém.

descending [dɪ'sendɪŋ] *adj*: **in ~ order** em ordem decrescente.

descent [dɪ'sent] *n* **-1.** [downwards movement] descida *f* **-2.** *(U)* [origin] ascendência *f*.

describe [dɪ'skraɪb] *vt* [recount] descrever.

description [dɪ'skrɪpʃn] *n* **-1.** [account] descrição *f* **-2.** [type] tipo *m*.

descriptive [dɪ'skrɪptɪv] *adj* descritivo(va).

desecrate ['desɪkreɪt] *vt* profanar.

desecration [ˌdesɪ'kreɪʃn] *n (U)* profanação *f*.

desegregate [ˌdiː'segrɪgeɪt] *vt* dessegregar.

deselect [ˌdiːsɪ'lekt] *vt UK POL* [rejeitar (uma candidatura].

desert [*n* 'dezət, *vb* & *npl* dɪ'zɜːt] ◇ *n* **-1.** GEOGR deserto *m* **-2.** *fig* [boring place] deserto *m*; **a cultural** ~ um deserto cultural. ◇ *vt* abandonar. ◇ *vi* MIL desertar.

➤ **deserts** *npl*: **to get one's just ~s** receber aquilo que se merece.

deserted [dɪ'zɜːtɪd] *adj* [place] deserto(ta), abandonado(da).

deserter [dɪ'zɜːtəʳ] *n* desertor *m*, -ra *f*.

desertion [dɪ'zɜːʃn] *n* **-1.** *(U)* MIL deserção *f* **-2.** [of person] abandono *m*.

desert island ['dezət-] *n* ilha *f* deserta.

deserve [dɪ'zɜːv] *vt* merecer; **to ~ sthg** merecer algo; **we ~ to win** merecemos vencer.

deserved [dɪ'zɜːvd] *adj* merecido(da).

deservedly [dɪ'zɜːvɪdlɪ] *adv* merecidamente.

deserving [dɪ'zɜːvɪŋ] *adj* merecedor(ra); **~ of sthg** *fml* merecedor(ra) de algo.

desiccated ['desɪkeɪtɪd] *adj* desidratado(da).

design [dɪ'zaɪn] ◇ *n* **-1.** [plan, drawing] projeto *m* **-2.** *(U)* [art] design *m* **-3.** [pattern, motif] padrão *m* **-4.** [structure, shape] modelo *m* **-5.** *fml* [intention] intenção *f*; **by ~** por intenção; **to have ~s on sb/sthg** ter más intenções com relação a alguém/algo. ◇ *vt* **-1.** [building, car] projetar **-2.** [clothes, costumes] desenhar **-3.** [plan, system, test] projetar, criar; **to be ~ed for sthg/to do sthg** ser projetado(da) para algo/para fazer algo.

designate [*adj* 'dezɪgnət, *vb* 'dezɪgneɪt] ◇ *adj* designado(da). ◇ *vt* [appoint] designar; **to ~ sb as sthg/to do sthg** designar alguém como algo/para fazer algo.

designation [ˌdezɪg'neɪʃn] *n fml* [name] designação *f*.

designer [dɪ'zaɪnəʳ] ◇ *adj* [jeans, glasses, stubble] de marca. ◇ *n* **-1.** [of building, machine] projetista *mf* **-2.** [of theatre set] cenógrafo *m*, -fa *f* **-3.** [of clothes] estilista *mf*.

desirable [dɪ'zaɪərəbl] *adj* **-1.** *fml* [appropriate] apropriado(da) **-2.** [attractive] agradável **-3.** [sexually attractive] desejável.

desire [dɪ'zaɪəʳ] ◇ *n* **-1.** [wish] desejo *m*, vontade *f*; **~ for sthg/to do sthg** desejo por algo/de fazer algo, vontade de algo/de fazer algo **-2.** *(U)* [sexual longing] desejo *m*. ◇ *vt* desejar; **it leaves a lot to be ~d** isso deixa muito a desejar.

desirous [dɪ'zaɪərəs] *adj fml*: **~ of sthg/of doing sthg** desejoso(sa) de algo/de fazer algo.

desist [dɪ'zɪst] *vi fml*: **to ~ (from doing sthg)** desistir (de fazer algo).

desk [desk] *n* **-1.** [piece of furniture - in office, study] escrivaninha *f*; [- in school] carteira *f* **-2.** [service point] balcão *m*.

desk clerk *n US* recepcionista *mf (de hotel)*.

desk diary *n* agenda *f (de mesa)*.

desk lamp *n* luminária *f (de mesa)*.

desktop ['desk‚tɒp] *adj* [computer]: **a ~ computer** um computador de mesa *OR* desktop.

desktop publishing *n (U)* editoração *f* eletrônica.

desolate ['desələt] *adj* desolado(da).

desolation [ˌdesə'leɪʃn] *n* **-1.** [gen] desolação *f* **-2.** [despair] aflição *f*.

despair [dɪ'speəʳ] ◇ *n (U)* desespero *m*; **in ~** desesperado(da). ◇ *vi* desesperar-se; **to ~ of**

sb/sthg perder a esperança com alguém/algo; **to ~ of doing sthg** perder a esperança de fazer algo.

despairing [dɪ'speərɪŋ] *adj* desesperador(ra).

despairingly [dɪ'speərɪŋlɪ] *adv* desesperadamente.

despatch [dɪ'spætʃ] *n* & *vt* = **dispatch**.

desperate ['desprət] *adj* - **1.** [gen] desesperado(da); **to feel ~** sentir-se desesperado(da) - **2.** [situation, problem] desesperador(ra) - **3.** [criminal] implacável - **4.** [in great need]: **to be ~ for sthg** estar louco(ca) por algo.

desperately ['desprətlɪ] *adv* - **1.** [gen] desesperadamente - **2.** [busy, sorry, in love] muito.

desperation [ˌdespə'reɪʃn] *n* (U) desespero *m*; **in ~ em** desespero.

despicable [dɪ'spɪkəbl] *adj* desprezível.

despise [dɪ'spaɪz] *vt* desprezar.

despite [dɪ'spaɪt] *prep* apesar de.

despondent [dɪ'spɒndənt] *adj* desanimado(da).

despot ['despɒt] *n* déspota *mf*.

despotic [de'spɒtɪk] *adj* despótico(ca).

dessert [dɪ'zɜ:t] *n* sobremesa *f*.

dessertspoon [dɪ'zɜ:tspu:n] *n* - **1.** [spoon] colher *f* de sobremesa - **2.** [spoonful] colherada *f* de sobremesa.

dessert wine *n* vinho *m* doce *(servido com a sobremesa)*.

destabilize, -ise [ˌdi:'steɪbɪlaɪz] *vt* desestabilizar.

destination [ˌdestɪ'neɪʃn] *n* destino *m*.

destined ['destɪnd] *adj* - **1.** [intended]: **~ for sthg/to do sthg** predestinado(da) a algo/a fazer algo - **2.** [bound]: **to be ~ for** estar indo para.

destiny ['destɪnɪ] *(pl* -**ies***)* *n* destino *m*.

destitute ['destɪtju:t] *adj* [extremely poor] necessitado(da), miserável.

destroy [dɪ'strɔɪ] *vt* - **1.** [gen] destruir - **2.** [animal] acabar com.

destroyer [dɪ'strɔɪə[r]] *n* - **1.** [ship] contratorpedeiro *m* - **2.** [person, thing] destruidor *m*, -ra *f*.

destruction [dɪ'strʌkʃn] *n* (U) destruição *f*.

destructive [dɪ'strʌktɪv] *adj* [harmful] destrutivo(va).

destructively [dɪ'strʌktɪvlɪ] *adv* destrutivamente.

desultory ['desəltrɪ] *adj fml* sem propósito, desinteressado(da).

Det. *(abbr of* **Detective***)* detetive *mf*.

detach [dɪ'tætʃ] *vt* - **1.** [remove] tirar; **to ~ sthg from sthg** tirar algo de algo ; [tear off] destacar - **2.** [dissociate]: **to ~ o.s. from sthg** afastar-se de algo.

detachable [dɪ'tætʃəbl] *adj* removível.

detached [dɪ'tætʃt] *adj* [unemotional] imparcial.

detached house *n* casa *f* separada.

detachment [dɪ'tætʃmənt] *n* - **1.** (U) [aloofness] desinteresse *m*, desapego *m* - **2.** MIL destacamento *m*.

detail ['di:teɪl] *<> n* - **1.** [small point] detalhe *m* - **2.** (U) [collection of facts, points] detalhe *m*, particularidade *f*; **to go into ~** entrar em detalhes; **in ~** detalhadamente - **3.** MIL destacamento *m*. *<> vt* [list] detalhar.

➡ details *npl* - **1.** [information] dados *mpl* - **2.** [personal information] dados *mpl* (pessoais).

detailed ['di:teɪld] *adj* detalhado(da).

detain [dɪ'teɪn] *vt* - **1.** [in hospital, police station] deter - **2.** [delay] retardar.

detainee [ˌdi:teɪ'ni:] *n* detento *m*, -ta *f*.

detect [dɪ'tekt] *vt* - **1.** [subj: person] perceber - **2.** [subj: device] detectar.

detection [dɪ'tekʃn] *n* - **1.** (U) [discovery] detecção *f* - **2.** [investigation] investigação *f*.

detective [dɪ'tektɪv] *n* detetive *mf*.

detective novel *n* romance *m* policial.

detector [dɪ'tektə[r]] *n* detector *m*.

détente [deɪ'tɒnt] *n* POL détente *f*.

detention [dɪ'tenʃn] *n* - **1.** (U) [of suspect, criminal] detenção *f*; **in ~** em detenção - **2.** [at school] castigo *m* *(depois da aula)*; **to be in ~** ficar de castigo.

detention centre *n* UK centro *m* de detenção.

deter [dɪ'tɜ:[r]] *(pt* & *pp* -**red**, *cont* -**ring***)* *vt* dissuadir; **to ~ sb from doing sthg** dissuadir alguém de fazer algo.

detergent [dɪ'tɜ:dʒənt] *n* detergente *m*.

deteriorate [dɪ'tɪərɪəreɪt] *vi* piorar.

deterioration [dɪˌtɪərɪə'reɪʃn] *n* - **1.** (U) [in health, economic situation] agravamento *f* - **2.** (U) [in weather] piora *f*.

determination [dɪˌtɜ:mɪ'neɪʃn] *n* - **1.** (U) [resolve] determinação *f* - **2.** [establishing, fixing] definição *f*.

determine [dɪ'tɜ:mɪn] *vt* - **1.** [gen] determinar - **2.** *fml* [resolve]: **to ~ to do sthg** determinar-se a fazer algo - **3.** [fix, settle] definir.

determined [dɪ'tɜ:mɪnd] *adj* [person, effort] determinado(da); **~ to do sthg** determinado(da) a fazer algo.

deterrent [dɪ'terənt] *<> adj* dissuasivo(va). *<> n* dissuasão *f*.

detest [dɪ'test] *vt* detestar.

detestable [dɪ'testəbl] *adj* detestável.

dethrone [dɪ'θrəʊn] *vt* destronar.

detonate ['detəneɪt] *<> vt* detonar. *<> vi* detonar.

detonator ['detəneɪtə[r]] *n* detonador *m*.

detour ['di:ˌtʊə[r]] *n* desvio *m*.

detox ['di:tɒks] *n inf* desintoxicação *f*.

detoxification *n* desintoxicação *f*.

detract [dɪ'trækt] *vi*: **to ~ from** [quality, achievement] depreciar; [enjoyment] perturbar.

detractor [dɪ'træktə[r]] *n* detrator *m*, -ra *f*.

detrain *vi* desembarcar *(de trem)*.

detriment ['detrɪmənt] *n*: **to the ~ of sb/sthg** em detrimento de alguém/algo.

detrimental [ˌdetrɪ'mentl] *adj* prejudicial.

detritus [dɪ'traɪtəs] *n* (U) detrito *m*.

deuce [dju:s] *n* TENNIS empate *m*.

Deutschmark ['dɔɪtʃˌmɑːk] *n* marco *m* alemão.

devaluation [ˌdi:væljʊ'eɪʃn] *n* FIN desvalorização *f*.

devalue [ˌdi:'vælju:] *vt* desvalorizar.

devastate ['devəsteɪt] *vt* - **1.** [place] devastar - **2.** *fig* [person] arrasar.

devastated ['devəsteɪtɪd] *adj* - **1.** [place] devastado(da) - **2.** *fig* [person] arrasado(da).

devastating ['devəsteɪtɪŋ] *adj* - **1.** [disastrous] devastador(ra) - **2.** [very effective, attractive] avassalador(ra).

devastation [ˌdevə'steɪʃn] n (U) [destruction] devastação f.

develop [dɪ'veləp] <> vt -1. [gen] desenvolver -2. [land, area, resources] explorar -3. [illness] contrair -4. PHOT revelar. <> vi -1. [gen] desenvolver -2. [problem, illness] aparecer.

developer [dɪ'veləpəʳ] n -1. [of land] empreendedor m imobiliário, empreendedora f imobiliária -2. [person]: **an early/a late~** criança f com desenvolvimento precoce/tardio -3. PHOT [chemical] revelador m.

developing country [dɪ'veləpɪŋ-] n país m em desenvolvimento.

development [dɪ'veləpmənt] n -1. (U) [expansion, growth, conception - gen] desenvolvimento m; [- of business, company] crescimento m -2. (U) [of land, area] exploração f -3. [developed land] loteamento m -4. [further incident] acontecimento m -5. (U) [of illness, fault, habit] desenvolvimento m -6. PHOT revelação f.

development area n UK zona f de desenvolvimento urbano.

deviant ['di:vjənt] <> adj anormal, pervertido(-da). <> n pervertido m, -da f.

deviate ['di:vɪeɪt] vi: **to ~ (from sthg)** desviar-se (de algo).

deviation [ˌdi:vɪ'eɪʃn] n desvio m; **sexual ~** perversão f sexual.

device [dɪ'vaɪs] n -1. [apparatus] dispositivo m, aparelho m -2. [plan, method] artifício m; **to leave sb to their own ~s** deixar alguém à própria sorte -3. [bomb]: **(incendiary) ~** bomba f incendiária.

devil ['devl] n -1. [evil spirit] demônio m -2. inf [person] diabo m, -ba f; **poor ~!** pobre diabo! -3. [for emphasis]: **who/where/why the ~ ...?** que/onde/por que diabos ...?
◆ **Devil** n [Satan]: **the Devil** o Diabo.

devilish ['devlɪʃ] adj [fiendish] diabólico(ca).

devil-may-care adj inconseqüente, imprudente.

devil's advocate n advogado m do diabo.

devious ['di:vjəs] adj -1. [gen] desonesto(ta) -2. [route] sinuoso(sa).

deviousness n (U) [dishonesty] desonestidade f.

devise [dɪ'vaɪz] vt conceber.

devoid [dɪ'vɔɪd] adj fml: **~ of sthg** desprovido(da) de algo.

devolution [ˌdi:və'lu:ʃn] n (U) POL descentralização f.

devolve [dɪ'vɒlv] vi fml: **to ~ (up)on sb** ser incumbência de alguém.

devote [dɪ'vəʊt] vt: **to ~ sthg to sthg** dedicar algo a algo; **to ~ o.s. to sthg** dedicar-se a algo.

devoted [dɪ'vəʊtɪd] adj [person] dedicado(da); **~ to sb/sthg** dedicado(da) a alguém/algo.

devotee [ˌdevə'ti:] n -1. [disciple] devoto m, -ta f -2. [fan] fã mf -3. [enthusiast] entusiasta mf.

devotion [dɪ'vəʊʃn] n -1. (U) [commitment]: **~ to sb/sthg** dedicação f a alguém/algo -2. RELIG devoção f.

devour [dɪ'vaʊəʳ] vt -1. [eat, read avidly] devorar -2. fig [subj: fire] consumir.

devout [dɪ'vaʊt] adj RELIG devoto(ta).

dew [dju:] n (U) orvalho m.

dexterity [dek'sterətɪ] n (U) agilidade f, destreza f.

dexterous ['dekstrəs] adj ágil.

dextrose ['dekstrəʊs] n (U) dextrose f.

dextrous ['dekstrəs] adj = **dexterous**.

diabetes [ˌdaɪə'bi:ti:z] n (U) diabete f.

diabetic [ˌdaɪə'betɪk] <> adj -1. [person] diabético(ca) -2. [jam, chocolate] para diabéticos. <> n diabético m, -ca f.

diabolic(al) [ˌdaɪə'bɒlɪk(l)] adj -1. [evil] diabólico(-ca) -2. inf [very bad] horroroso(sa).

diaeresis UK, **dieresis** US (pl -eses) [daɪ'erɪsɪs] n diérese f.

diagnose ['daɪəgnəʊz] vt diagnosticar.

diagnosis [ˌdaɪəg'nəʊsɪs] (pl -oses [-əʊsi:z]) n diagnóstico m.

diagnostic [ˌdaɪəg'nɒstɪk] adj MED diagnóstico(ca).

diagonal [daɪ'ægənl] <> adj [line] diagonal. <> n diagonal f.

diagonally [daɪ'ægənəlɪ] adv diagonalmente.

diagram ['daɪəgræm] n diagrama m.

diagrammatic [ˌdaɪəgrə'mætɪk] adj diagramático(ca).

dial ['daɪəl] (UK pt & pp -led, cont -ling, US pt & pp -ed, cont -ing) <> n -1. [of watch, clock, meter] mostrador m -2. [of radio] dial m -3. [of telephone] teclado m. <> vt [number] discar.

dialect ['daɪəlekt] n dialeto m.

dialling code UK, **dialing code** US ['daɪəlɪŋ-] n código m de discagem.

dialling tone UK ['daɪəlɪŋ-], **dial tone** US n linha f (no telefone).

dialogue UK, **dialog** US ['daɪəlɒg] n diálogo m.

dial tone n US = **dialling tone**.

dialysis [daɪ'ælɪsɪs] n (U) diálise f.

diamanté adj de vidrilhos.

diameter [daɪ'æmɪtəʳ] n diâmetro m.

diametrically [ˌdaɪə'metrɪklɪ] adv: **~ opposed** diametralmente oposto(ta).

diamond ['daɪəmənd] n -1. [gem] diamante m -2. [shape] losango m.
◆ **diamonds** npl [cards] ouros mpl.

diamond wedding n bodas fpl de diamante.

diaper ['daɪpəʳ] n US fralda f.

diaphanous [daɪ'æfənəs] adj transparente.

diaphragm ['daɪəfræm] n diafragma m.

diarrh(o)ea [ˌdaɪə'rɪə] n (U) diarréia f.

diary ['daɪərɪ] (pl -ies) n -1. [appointment book] agenda f -2. [personal record] diário m.

diatribe ['daɪətraɪb] n crítica f violenta.

dice [daɪs] (pl inv) <> n [for games] dado m; **no ~** US inf de jeito nenhum. <> vt cortar em cubinhos.

dicey ['daɪsɪ] (compar -ier, superl -iest) adj UK inf incerto(ta).

dichotomy [daɪ'kɒtəmɪ] (pl -ies) n fml dicotomia f.

Dictaphone® ['dɪktəfəʊn] n dictafone® m.

dictate [vb dɪk'teɪt, n 'dɪkteɪt] <> vt -1. [letter] ditar; **to ~ sthg to sb** ditar algo para alguém -2. [conditions, terms] ditar, impor. <> vi: **to ~ to sb** [read aloud] ditar para alguém; [give orders] impor a alguém. <> n ditado m.

dictation [dɪk'teɪʃn] n ditado m.

dictator [dɪkˈteɪtəʳ] n POL ditador m, -ra f.
dictatorship [dɪkˈteɪtəʃɪp] n ditadura f.
diction [ˈdɪkʃn] n (U) [pronunciation] dicção f.
dictionary [ˈdɪkʃənrɪ] (pl -ies) n dicionário m.
did [dɪd] pt ⊳ **do**.
didactic [dɪˈdæktɪk] adj didático(ca).
diddle [ˈdɪdl] vt UK inf passar a perna em.
didn't [ˈdɪdnt] = **did not**.
die [daɪ] (pt & pp died, cont dying, pl sense 2 only dice)
◇ vi -1. [person, animal, plant] morrer; to be dying
estar morrendo; to be dying for sthg/to do sthg inf
estar morrendo de vontade de algo/de fazer algo
-2. fig [love, anger, memory] morrer. ◇ n -1. [for
shaping metal] molde m -2. [dice] dado m.
➔ **die away** vi [sound, wind] desvanecer-se.
➔ **die down** vi -1. [fire] arrefecer -2. [sound,
wind] abrandar.
➔ **die out** vi -1. [family, custom] desaparecer -2.
[species] ser extinto(ta).
diehard [ˈdaɪhɑːd] n teimoso(sa).
dieresis n US = **diaeresis**.
diesel [ˈdiːzl] n -1. (U) [fuel, oil] diesel m -2. [vehicle]
veículo m a diesel.
diesel engine n motor m a diesel.
diesel fuel, diesel oil n óleo m diesel.
diet [ˈdaɪət] ◇ n -1. [gen] dieta f -2. [in order to lose
weight] dieta f, regime m; to be/go on a ~ estar
de/entrar em dieta. ◇ comp [low-calorie] de
baixa caloria; a ~ Coke® uma Coca® light. ◇ vi
[in order to lose weight] fazer regime.
dietary [ˈdaɪətrɪ] adj alimentar.
dietary fibre n (U) fibra f alimentar.
dieter [ˈdaɪətəʳ] n pessoa f de regime.
dietician [ˌdaɪəˈtɪʃn] n nutricionista mf.
differ [ˈdɪfəʳ] vi -1. [be different] diferir; to ~ from sb/
sthg diferir/distinguir-se de alguém/algo -2. [dis-
agree]: to ~ with sb (about sthg) discordar de
alguém (sobre algo); to agree to ~ parar de
discutir.
difference [ˈdɪfrəns] n diferença f; it doesn't make
any ~ não faz a menor diferença; to make all the
~ fazer toda a diferença.
different [ˈdɪfrənt] adj diferente; ~ from diferente
de.
differential [ˌdɪfəˈrenʃl] ◇ adj diferencial. ◇ n
diferencial m.
differentiate [ˌdɪfəˈrenʃɪeɪt] ◇ vt: to ~ sthg
from sthg diferenciar algo de algo. ◇ vi: to ~
(between) diferenciar (entre).
differently [ˈdɪfrəntlɪ] adv diferentemente.
difficult [ˈdɪfɪkəlt] adj difícil.
difficulty [ˈdɪfɪkəltɪ] (pl -ies) n dificuldade f; to
have ~ in doing sthg ter dificuldade em fazer
algo; with ~ com dificuldade.
diffidence [ˈdɪfɪdəns] n (U) acanhamento m.
diffident [ˈdɪfɪdənt] adj acanhado(da).
diffuse [adj dɪˈfjuːs, vb dɪˈfjuːz] ◇ adj difuso(sa).
◇ vt -1. [light] difundir -2. [information] divulgar.
◇ vi difundir-se.
diffusion [dɪˈfjuːʒn] n (U) -1. [of light] difusão f -2. [of
information] divulgação f.
dig [dɪg] (pt & pp dug, cont digging) ◇ n -1. fig
[unkind remark] zombaria f -2. ARCHAEOL escavação f.

◇ vt -1. [in ground] cavar -2. [press, jab]: to ~ sthg
into sb/sthg fincar algo em alguém/algo; to ~ sb
in the ribs cutucar alguém. ◇ vi -1. [in ground]
enterrar-se -2. [press, jab]: to ~ into sthg cravar-
se em algo; my strap's ~ging into me a alça do
vestido está me apertando.
➔ **dig out** vt sep -1. [car, accident victims] resgatar
-2. inf [letter, document] desencavar.
➔ **dig up** vt sep -1. [from ground] desenterrar -2.
inf [information] desencavar.
digest [n ˈdaɪdʒest, vb dɪˈdʒest] ◇ n [book] resenha
f. ◇ vt [food, information] digerir.
digestible [dɪˈdʒestəbl] adj digerível.
digestion [dɪˈdʒestʃn] n digestão f.
digestive [dɪˈdʒestɪv] adj digestivo(va).
digestive biscuit [dɪˈdʒestɪv-] n UK biscoito liso
levemente adocicado muito comum na Grã-
Bretanha.
digestive system n sistema m digestivo.
digger n [machine] escavadeira f.
digit [ˈdɪdʒɪt] n -1. [figure] dígito m -2. [finger, toe]
dedo m.
digital [ˈdɪdʒɪtl] adj [watch, readout] digital.
digital camera n câmera f digital.
digital recording n gravação f digital.
digital television, digital TV n televisão f
digital.
digital watch n relógio m digital.
digitize, -ise [ˈdɪdʒɪtaɪz] vt digitalizar.
dignified [ˈdɪgnɪfaɪd] adj digno(na).
dignify [ˈdɪgnɪfaɪ] (pt & pp -ied) vt honrar.
dignitary [ˈdɪgnɪtrɪ] (pl -ies) n dignitário m, -ria f.
dignity [ˈdɪgnətɪ] n dignidade f.
digress [daɪˈgres] vi fugir do assunto, divagar; to ~
(from sthg) desviar-se (de algo).
digression [daɪˈgreʃn] n digressão f.
digs [dɪgz] npl UK inf quarto m alugado.
dike [daɪk] n -1. [wall, bank] dique m -2. inf pej [lesbian]
sapatão m.
diktat n [pol] imposição f.
dilapidated [dɪˈlæpɪdeɪtɪd] adj em ruínas.
dilate [daɪˈleɪt] ◇ vt dilatar. ◇ vi dilatar-se.
dilated [daɪˈleɪtɪd] adj dilatado(da).
dilemma [dɪˈlemə] n dilema m.
dilettante [ˌdɪlɪˈtæntɪ] (pl -tes OR -ti [-tɪ]) n pej
amador m, -ra f.
diligence [ˈdɪlɪdʒəns] n (U) [hard work] diligência f.
diligent [ˈdɪlɪdʒənt] adj diligente, aplicado(da).
dill [dɪl] n (U) aneto m.
dillydally [ˈdɪlɪdælɪ] (pt & pp -ied) vi inf dated
embromar-se.
dilute [daɪˈluːt] ◇ adj diluído(da). ◇ vt: to ~
sthg (with sthg) diluir algo(com algo).
dilution [daɪˈluːʃn] n: ~ (with sthg) diluição
f (com algo).
dim [dɪm] (compar -mer, superl -mest, pt & pp -med,
cont -ming) ◇ adj -1. [dark] sombrio(bria) -2. [indis-
tinct - shape] indistinto(ta); [- sight, sound] fraco(ca); [-
memory] vago(ga) -3. [weak] fraco(ca) -4. [gloomy]: to
take a ~ view of sthg não levar fé em algo -5. inf
[stupid] idiota. ◇ vt [light] diminuir. ◇ vi [beauty,
hope, memory] extinguir-se.
dime [daɪm] n US moeda de 10 centavos de dólar;

cars are a ~ a dozen in the world today [common] hoje tem carros a dar com pau no mundo.

dimension [dɪˈmenʃn] n dimensão f.
  ➡ **dimensions** pl [of room, object] dimensões fpl.
-dimensional [dɪˈmenʃnl] suffix dimensional.
diminish [dɪˈmɪnɪʃ] ⟨⟩ vt [make less important] diminuir. ⟨⟩ vi diminuir.
diminished [dɪˈmɪnɪʃt] adj -1. [profits, budget] reduzido(da) -2. [reputation] em baixa -3. [person] menosprezado(da).
diminished responsibility n (U) JUR responsabilidade f diminuída.
diminishing returns [dɪˈmɪnɪʃɪŋ] npl rendimentos mpl decrescentes.
diminutive [dɪˈmɪnjʊtɪv] ⟨⟩ adj fml [tiny] diminuto(ta). ⟨⟩ n GRAMM diminutivo m.
dimly [ˈdɪmlɪ] adv -1. [shine] fracamente -2. [see, remember] vagamente.
dimmer [ˈdɪmə̯ʳ] n [switch] dimmer m.
  ➡ **dimmers** npl US -1. [dipped headlights] faróis mpl baixos -2. [parking lights] pisca-alerta m.
dimmer switch n = dimmer.
dimple [ˈdɪmpl] n covinha f (no rosto).
dimwit [ˈdɪmwɪt] n inf estúpido m, -da f, anta mf.
dim-witted [-ˈwɪtɪd] adj inf estúpido(da).
din [dɪn] n inf zoeira f.
dine [daɪn] vi fml jantar.
  ➡ **dine out** vi jantar fora.
diner [ˈdaɪnə̯ʳ] n -1. [person] cliente mf (de restaurante) -2. US [restaurant] lanchonete f (em beira de estrada).
dingdong [ˌdɪŋˈdɒŋ] ⟨⟩ adj inf [battle, argument] tumultuado(da). ⟨⟩ n [of bell] badalada f.
dinghy [ˈdɪŋɡɪ] (pl -ies) n [for sailing] barco m a vela (pequeno); [for rowing] bote m a remo.
dingo [ˈdɪŋɡəʊ] (pl -es) n dingo m.
dingy [ˈdɪndʒɪ] (compar -ier, superl -iest) adj [dirty, drab] sujo(ja).
dining car [ˈdaɪnɪŋ-] n vagão-restaurante m.
dining room [ˈdaɪnɪŋ-] n sala f de jantar.
dining table [ˈdaɪnɪŋ-] n mesa f de jantar.
dinner [ˈdɪnə̯ʳ] n -1. [meal - in evening] jantar m; [- at midday] almoço m -2. [formal event] jantar m.
dinner dance n jantar m dançante.
dinner jacket n UK smoking m.
dinner party n jantar m (para poucas pessoas).
dinner service n aparelho m de jantar.
dinner table n: the ~ a mesa de jantar.
dinnertime [ˈdɪnətaɪm] n hora f do jantar.
dinosaur [ˈdaɪnəsɔːʳ] n [reptile] dinossauro m.
dint [dɪnt] n fml: by ~ of por meio de.
diocese [ˈdaɪəsɪs] n diocese f.
diode [ˈdaɪəʊd] n diodo m.
dip [dɪp] (pt & pp -ped, cont -ping) ⟨⟩ n -1. [in road, ground] depressão f -2. [sauce] molho m cremoso -3. [swim]: to go for a ~ dar um mergulho. ⟨⟩ vt -1. [into liquid]: to ~ sthg in (to) sthg mergulhar algo em algo -2. UK [headlights] baixar. ⟨⟩ vi -1. [sun, wing] baixar -2. [road, ground] descer -3. [temperature, price] cair.
Dip. UK abbr of diploma.
Dip. Ed. (abbr of Diploma in Education) (titular de)

diploma em educação na Grã-Bretanha.
diphtheria [dɪfˈθɪərɪə] n (U) difteria f.
diphthong [ˈdɪfθɒŋ] n LING ditongo m.
diploma [dɪˈpləʊmə] (pl -s) n diploma m.
diplomacy [dɪˈpləʊməsɪ] n diplomacia f.
diplomat [ˈdɪpləmæt] n diplomata mf.
diplomatic [ˌdɪpləˈmætɪk] adj diplomático(ca).
diplomatic bag n mala f diplomática.
diplomatic corps n corpo m diplomático.
diplomatic immunity n imunidade f diplomática.
diplomatic relations npl relações fpl diplomáticas.
dipsomaniac [ˌdɪpsəˈmeɪnɪæk] n dipsomaníaco m, -ca f.
dipstick [ˈdɪpstɪk] n AUT vareta f do nível do óleo.
dipswitch [ˈdɪpswɪtʃ] n UK AUT chave f de luz alta e baixa.
dire [ˈdaɪəʳ] adj [serious] terrível.
direct [dɪˈrekt] ⟨⟩ adj -1. [gen] direto(ta) -2. [insurance] sem intermediários. ⟨⟩ vt -1. [aim]: to ~ sthg at sb dirigir algo a alguém -2. [person to place] guiar -3. [group, project, film, play] dirigir -4. [order]: to ~ sb to do sthg mandar alguém fazer algo. ⟨⟩ adv direto.
direct action n ação f direta.
direct current n corrente f contínua.
direct debit n UK débito m automático (em conta corrente).
direct dialling [-ˈdaɪəlɪŋ] n discagem f direta.
direct hit n: to score a ~ on the target acertar em cheio no alvo.
direction [dɪˈrekʃn] n -1. [spatial] direção f -2. fig [orientation] rumo m -3. [of group, project, play, film] direção f; under the ~ of sob a direção de.
  ➡ **directions** npl -1. [instructions to place] indicações fpl -2. [instructions for use] instruções fpl.
directive [dɪˈrektɪv] n diretriz f.
directly [dɪˈrektlɪ] adv -1. [in straight line] diretamente, direto -2. [frankly, openly] diretamente -3. [exactly] logo, bem -4. [very soon] imediatamente.
direct mail n mala-direta f.
director [dɪˈrektəʳ] n diretor m, -ra f.
directorate [dɪˈrektərət] n [board of directors] diretoria f.
director-general (pl directors-general OR director-generals) n diretor-geral m, diretora-geral f.
Director of Public Prosecutions n UK ≃ Procurador m, -ra f da República.
directorship [dɪˈrektəʃɪp] n -1. [position] cargo m de diretor, -ra f -2. [period] diretorado m.
directory [dɪˈrektərɪ] (pl -ies) n -1. [book, list] lista f -2. COMPUT diretório m.
directory enquiries n UK (serviço m de) auxílio m à lista.
direct rule n governo m central.
direct selling n vendas f diretas.
direct speech n discurso m direto.
direct taxation n imposto m direto.
dire straits npl: in ~ em apuros.
dirge [dɜːdʒ] n música m fúnebre.
dirt [dɜːt] n -1. [mud, dust] sujeira f -2. [earth] terra f.

dirt cheap *inf* ◇ *adj* bem barato(ta). ◇ *adv* bem barato; **this was** ~ isso foi uma ninharia.

dirt track *n* estrada *f* de terra.

dirty ['dɜːtɪ] (*compar* -**ier**, *superl* -**iest**, *pt* & *pp* -**ied**) ◇ *adj* - **1.** [not clean] sujo(ja) - **2.** [unfair] baixo(xa); ~ **trick** golpe *m* baixo - **3.** [smutty] obsceno(na); ~ **joke** piada *f* suja. ◇ *vt* sujar.

disability [ˌdɪsə'bɪlətɪ] (*pl* -**ies**) *n* deficiência *f*.

disable [dɪs'eɪbl] *vt* [injure] incapacitar.

disabled [dɪs'eɪbld] ◇ *adj* [person] incapacitado(-da). ◇ *npl*: **the** ~ os deficientes.

disablement [dɪs'eɪblmənt] *n* [of person] incapacidade *f*, deficiência *f*.

disabuse [ˌdɪsə'bjuːz] *vt fml*: **to** ~ **sb (of sthg)** desiludir alguém (sobre algo).

disadvantage [ˌdɪsəd'vɑːntɪdʒ] *n* desvantagem *f*; **to be at a** ~ estar em desvantagem; **to be to one's** ~ pesar contra alguém.

disadvantaged [ˌdɪsəd'vɑːntɪdʒd] *adj* desfavorecido(da).

disadvantageous [ˌdɪsædvɑːn'teɪdʒəs] *adj* desvantajoso(sa).

disaffected [ˌdɪsə'fektɪd] *adj* insatisfeito(ta).

disaffection [ˌdɪsə'fekʃn] *n (U)* insatisfação *f*.

disagree [ˌdɪsə'griː] *vi* - **1.** [have different opinions] discordar, não estar de acordo; **to** ~ **with sb** discordar de alguém; **to** ~ **with sthg** discordar de algo - **2.** [differ] divergir - **3.** [subj: food, drink]: **to** ~ **with sb** fazer mal a alguém.

disagreeable [ˌdɪsə'griːəbl] *adj* desagradável.

disagreement [ˌdɪsə'griːmənt] *n* - **1.** [of opinions, records] divergência *f* - **2.** [argument] discussão *f*.

disallow [ˌdɪsə'laʊ] *vt* - **1.** *fml* [appeal, claim] rejeitar - **2.** [goal] anular.

disappear [ˌdɪsə'pɪəʳ] *vi* desaparecer.

disappearance [ˌdɪsə'pɪərəns] *n* - **1.** [of person, object] desaparecimento *m* - **2.** [of species, civilization] extinção *f*.

disappoint [ˌdɪsə'pɔɪnt] *vt* [fail to satisfy] desapontar, decepcionar.

disappointed [ˌdɪsə'pɔɪntɪd] *adj* desapontado(da), decepcionado(da); ~ **in** OR **with sthg** decepcionado(da) com algo.

disappointing [ˌdɪsə'pɔɪntɪŋ] *adj* desapontador(-ra), decepcionante.

disappointment [ˌdɪsə'pɔɪntmənt] *n* - **1.** *(U)* [feeling] desapontamento *m* - **2.** [letdown] decepção *f*.

disapproval [ˌdɪsə'pruːvl] *n (U)* desaprovação *f*.

disapprove [ˌdɪsə'pruːv] *vi*: **to** ~ **(of sb/sthg)** desaprovar (algo/alguém).

disapproving [ˌdɪsə'pruːvɪŋ] *adj* desaprovador(-ra).

disarm [dɪs'ɑːm] *vt & vi* desarmar.

disarmament [dɪs'ɑːməmənt] *n (U)* desarmamento *m*.

disarming [dɪs'ɑːmɪŋ] *adj* [smile, person] que desarma, irresistível.

disarray [ˌdɪsə'reɪ] *n (U)*: **in** ~ *fml* [clothes, hair] em desalinho; [room] em desordem; POL em desacordo.

disassociate [ˌdɪsə'səʊʃɪeɪt] *vt*: **to** ~ **o.s. from sb/sthg** desligar-se de alguém/algo.

disaster [dɪ'zɑːstəʳ] *n* - **1.** [gen] desastre *m*; **natural** ~ desastre *m* natural - **2.** *(U)* [misfortune] azar *m*; **to court** ~ procurar encrenca.

disaster area *n* [after natural disaster] área *f* de calamidade pública.

disastrous [dɪ'zɑːstrəs] *adj* [catastrophic] desastroso(sa).

disastrously [dɪ'zɑːstrəslɪ] *adv* [catastrophically] desastrosamente.

disband [dɪs'bænd] ◇ *vt* dispersar. ◇ *vi* dispersar-se.

disbelief [ˌdɪsbɪ'liːf] *n (U)*: **in** OR **with** ~ com descrença.

disbelieve [ˌdɪsbɪ'liːv] *vt* [person, words] não acreditar em. .

disc UK, **disk** US [dɪsk] *n* disco *m*.

discard [dɪ'skɑːd] *vt* desfazer-se de, pôr fora.

discarded [dɪ'skɑːdɪd] *adj* posto(ta) fora.

disc brake *n* freio *m* a disco.

discern [dɪ'sɜːn] *vt* - **1.** [see] discernir - **2.** [detect] perceber.

discernible [dɪ'sɜːnəbl] *adj* - **1.** [visible] discernível - **2.** [detectable] perceptível.

discerning [dɪ'sɜːnɪŋ] *adj* perspicaz.

discharge [*n* 'dɪstʃɑːdʒ, *vb* dɪs'tʃɑːdʒ] ◇ *n* - **1.** [of patient] alta *f*; [of prisoner, defendant] libertação *f*; [from armed forces] dispensa *f* - **2.** *fml* [fulfilment] cumprimento *m* - **3.** [toxic emission] descarga *f* - **4.** MED [from nose, wound] secreção *f* - **5.** [payment] quitação *f*. ◇ *vt* - **1.** [allow to leave - patient] dar alta para; [- prisoner, defendant] libertar; [- from armed forces] dispensar - **2.** *fml* [fulfil] cumprir - **3.** [emit] emitir - **4.** [pay] quitar.

discharged bankrupt [dɪs'tʃɑːdʒd-] *n* pessoa falida que cumpriu as disposições legais e pode retornar aos negócios.

disciple [dɪ'saɪpl] *n* - **1.** RELIG apóstolo *m* - **2.** *fig* [follower] discípulo *m*, -la *f*.

disciplinarian [ˌdɪsɪplɪ'neərɪən] *n* disciplinador *m*, -ra *f*.

disciplinary ['dɪsɪplɪnərɪ] *adj* disciplinar; **to take** ~ **action against sb** tomar ações disciplinares contra alguém.

discipline ['dɪsɪplɪn] ◇ *n* disciplina *f*. ◇ *vt* - **1.** [train] disciplinar - **2.** [punish] punir.

disciplined ['dɪsɪplɪnd] *adj* [controlled] disciplinado(da).

disc jockey *n* disc-jóquei *mf*.

disclaim [dɪs'kleɪm] *vt fml* negar.

disclaimer [dɪs'kleɪməʳ] *n* negação *f*.

disclose [dɪs'kləʊz] *vt* divulgar.

disclosure [dɪs'kləʊʒəʳ] *n* - **1.** *(U)* [act of disclosing] divulgação *f* - **2.** [revealed fact] revelação *f*.

disco ['dɪskəʊ] (*pl* -**s**) (*abbr of* **discotheque**) *n* casa *f* noturna.

discoloration [dɪsˌkʌlə'reɪʃn] *n* [fading, staining] descoloração *f*.

discolour UK, **discolor** US [dɪs'kʌləʳ] *vt & vi* descolorir.

discoloured UK, **discolored** US [dɪs'kʌləd] *adj* descolorido(da).

discomfort [dɪs'kʌmfət] *n* - **1.** [gen] desconforto *m* - **2.** *(U)* [physical pain] mal-estar *m*.

disconcert [ˌdɪskən'sɜːt] *vt* desconcertar.

disconcerting [,dıskən'sɜ:tıŋ] adj desconcertante.
disconnect [,dıskə'nekt] vt -1. [detach] desconectar
-2. [from gas, electricity - appliance] desconectar,
desligar; [- house, building] cortar -3. [on phone]
cortar.
disconnected [,dıskə'nektıd] adj -1. [remarks,
thoughts, events] desconexo(xa) -2. [telephone, wire]
desconectado(da).
disconsolate [dıs'kɒnsələt] adj inconsolável.
discontent [,dıskən'tent] n (U): ~ (with sthg)
descontentamento m (com algo).
discontented [,dıskən'tentıd] adj: ~ (with sthg)
descontente (com algo).
discontentment [,dıskən'tentmənt] n (U): ~
(with sthg) descontentamento m (com algo).
discontinue [,dıskən'tınju:] vt suspender.
discontinued line [,dıskən'tınju:d-] n COMM (produto m) fora f de linha.
discord ['dıskɔ:d] n -1. (U) fml [conflict] discórdia f -2.
MUS dissonância f.
discordant [dı'skɔ:dənt] adj -1. [conflicting] discordante -2. MUS dissonante.
discotheque ['dıskəutek] n discoteca f.
discount [n 'dıskaunt, vb UK dıs'kaunt, US 'dıskaunt]
◇ n [price reduction] desconto m. ◇ vt -1. [disre-
gard] desconsiderar -2. COMM [offer at lower price]
dar desconto em; [price] abater.
discount house n -1. FIN casa f de câmbio -2.
COMM [store] loja f que vende com descontos.
discount rate n taxa f de desconto.
discount store n COMM loja f que vende com
descontos.
discourage [dı'skʌrıdʒ] vt -1. [dishearten] desencorajar -2. [dissuade] dissuadir; to ~ sb from doing
sthg desestimular alguém de fazer algo.
discouraging [dı'skʌrıdʒıŋ] adj desencorajador(-
ra).
discourse ['dıskɔ:s] n: ~ (on sthg) discurso m
(sobre algo).
discourteous [dıs'kɜ:tjəs] adj fml descortês.
discourtesy [dıs'kɜ:tısı] n (U) descortesia f.
discover [dı'skʌvə'] vt -1. [gen] descobrir -2.
[realize] perceber, dar-se conta de.
discoverer [dı'skʌvərə'] n descobridor m, -ra f.
discovery [dı'skʌvərı] (pl -ies) n -1. [gen] descoberta
f; the ~ of America o descobrimento da América
-2. [realization] compreensão f.
discredit [dıs'kredıt] ◇ n (U) [shame] descrédito
m. ◇ vt -1. [person] desonrar -2. [idea, belief,
theory] desacreditar.
discredited [dıskredıtıd] adj desacreditado(da).
discreet [dı'skri:t] adj discreto(ta).
discreetly [dı'skri:tlı] adv discretamente.
discrepancy [dı'skrepənsı] (pl -ies) n: ~ (in/be-
tween) discrepância f (em/entre).
discrete [dıs'kri:t] adj fml distinto(ta).
discretion [dı'skreʃn] n -1. [tact] discrição f
-2. [judgment] ponderação f; at the ~ of a critério
de.
discretionary [dı'skreʃənərı] adj discricionário(-
ria).
discriminate [dı'skrımıneıt] vi -1. [distinguish] discriminar; to ~ between fazer distinção entre -2.

[treat unfairly]: to ~ against sb discriminar alguém.
discriminating [dı'skrımıneıtıŋ] adj [discerning] cri-
terioso(sa).
discrimination [dı,skrımı'neıʃn] n (U) -1. [prejudice]
discriminação f -2. [good judgment] discernimento
m.
discus ['dıskəs] (pl -es) n [sport] disco m.
discuss [dı'skʌs] vt discutir; to ~ sthg with sb
discutir algo com alguém.
discussion [dı'skʌʃn] n -1. (U) [act of discussing]
discussão f; under ~ em discussão -2. [talk]
debate f.
disdain [dıs'deın] fml ◇ n (U) desdém m; ~ for
sb/sthg desprezo m por alguém/algo. ◇ vt
desdenhar. ◇ vi: to ~ to do sthg não se dar
ao trabalho de fazer algo.
disdainful [dıs'deınful] adj desdenhoso(sa).
disease [dı'zi:z] n doença f.
diseased [dı'zi:zd] adj doente.
disembark [,dısım'bɑ:k] vi desembarcar.
disembarkation [,dısembɑ:'keıʃn] n (U) desembarque m.
disembodied [,dısım'bɒdıd] adj -1. [spirit] desen-
carnado(da) -2. [voice] desincorporado(da).
disembowel [,dısım'bauəl] (UK pt & pp -led, cont
-ling, US pt & pp -ed, cont -ing) vt estripar.
disenchanted [,dısın'tʃɑ:ntıd] adj: ~ (with sthg)
desencantado(da) (com algo).
disenchantment [,dısın'tʃɑ:ntmənt] n (U) desen-
cantamento m.
disenfranchise [,dısın'fræntʃaız] vt = disfranchise.
disengage [,dısın'geıdʒ] vt -1. [release]: to ~ sthg
(from sthg) desprender algo (de algo); to ~ o.s.
(from sthg) soltar-se (de algo) -2. TECH [gears, me-
chanism] desengatar.
disengagement n desligamento m.
disentangle [,dısın'tæŋgl] vt: to ~ sthg from
sthg desemaranhar algo de algo; to ~ o.s. from
sthg desenredar-se de algo.
disfavour UK, **disfavor** US [dıs'feıvə'] n: to look
on sthg with ~ olhar para algo com desaprovação; to fall into ~ with sb cair em desgraça com
alguém.
disfigure [dıs'fıgə'] vt desfigurar.
disfranchise [,dıs'fræntʃaız] vt caçar o direito de
voto de.
disgorge [dıs'gɔ:dʒ] vt despejar.
disgrace [dıs'greıs] ◇ n -1. (U) [shame] desgraça f;
in ~ com vergonha -2. [cause for shame - thing]
desgraça f; [- person] vergonha f. ◇ vt envergonhar; to ~ o.s. envergonhar-se.
disgraceful [dıs'greısful] adj vergonhoso(sa).
disgruntled [dıs'grʌntld] adj decepcionado(da).
disguise [dıs'gaız] ◇ n disfarce m; in ~ disfar-
çado(da). ◇ vt disfarçar; to ~ o.s. as sb/sthg
disfarçar-se de alguém/algo.
disgust [dıs'gʌst] ◇ n nojo m; ~ at sthg nojo de
algo; in ~ com nojo. ◇ vt enojar.
disgusting [dıs'gʌstıŋ] adj [very unpleasant] nojento(-
ta).
dish [dıʃ] n [container, food] prato m.
➡ **dishes** npl louça f; to do OR wash the ~es
lavar a louça.

dish out *vt sep inf* distribuir.
dish up *vt sep inf* pôr na mesa.
dish aerial *UK*, **dish antenna** *US n* antena *f* parabólica.
disharmony [ˌdɪsˈhɑːmənɪ] *n (U)* desarmonia *f*.
dishcloth [ˈdɪʃklɒθ] *n* pano *m* de prato.
disheartened [dɪsˈhɑːtnd] *adj* desanimado(da).
disheartening [dɪsˈhɑːtnɪŋ] *adj* desanimador(ra).
dishevelled *UK*, **disheveled** *US* [dɪˈʃevəld] *adj* desalinhado(da).
dishonest [dɪsˈɒnɪst] *adj* desonesto(ta).
dishonesty [dɪsˈɒnɪstɪ] *n (U)* desonestidade *f*.
dishonor *n* & *vt US* = dishonour.
dishonorable *adj US* = dishonourable.
dishonour *UK*, **dishonor** *US* [dɪsˈɒnəʳ] *fml* ⋄ *n* desonra *f*. ⋄ *vt* desonrar.
dishonourable *UK*, **dishonorable** *US* [dɪsˈɒnərəbl] *adj* desonroso(sa).
dish soap *n US* detergente *m (para lavar louça)*.
dish towel *n US* pano *m* de prato.
dishwasher [ˈdɪʃˌwɒʃəʳ] *n* [machine] lava-louças *fpl inv*.
dishy [ˈdɪʃɪ] *(compar*-ier, *superl* -iest) *adj UK inf* [attractive] gato *m*, -ta *f*.
disillusioned [ˌdɪsɪˈluːʒnd] *adj* desiludido(da); ~ with sb/sthg desiludido(da) com alguém/algo.
disillusionment [ˌdɪsɪˈluːʒnmənt] *n (U)*: ~ (with sb/sthg) desilusão *f* (com alguém/algo).
disincentive [ˌdɪsɪnˈsentɪv] *n* desestímulo *m*.
disinclined [ˌdɪsɪnˈklaɪnd] *adj*: to be ~ to do sthg estar pouco disposto(ta) a fazer algo.
disinfect [ˌdɪsɪnˈfekt] *vt* desinfetar.
disinfectant [ˌdɪsɪnˈfektənt] *n* desinfetante *m*.
disinformation [ˌdɪsɪnfəˈmeɪʃn] *n (U)* desinformação *f*.
disingenuous [ˌdɪsɪnˈdʒenjʊəs] *adj* dissimulado(da).
disinherit [ˌdɪsɪnˈherɪt] *vt* deserdar.
disintegrate [dɪsˈɪntɪɡreɪt] *vi* -1. [object] desintegrar-se -2. *fig* [project, marriage] desmoronar.
disintegration [dɪsˌɪntɪˈɡreɪʃn] *n (U)* -1. [of object] desintegração *f* -2. *fig* [of project, marriage] desmoronamento *m*.
disinterested [ˌdɪsˈɪntrəstɪd] *adj* -1. [objective] neutro(tra) -2. [uninterested]: ~ (in sb/sthg) desinteressado(da) (em alguém/algo).
disinvestment [ˌdɪsɪnˈvestmənt] *n (U)* desinvestimento *m*.
disjointed [dɪsˈdʒɔɪntɪd] *adj* desconjuntado(da).
disk [dɪsk] *n COMPUT*: floppy ~ disquete *m*; hard ~ disco *m* rígido.
disk drive *UK*, **diskette drive** *US n COMPUT* drive *m*, unidade *f* de disco.
diskette [dɪskˈet] *n COMPUT* disquete *m*.
diskette drive *n US* = disk drive.
disk operating system [-ˈɒpəreɪtɪŋ-] *n COMPUT* sistema *m* operacional de disco.
dislike [dɪsˈlaɪk] ⋄ *n* -1. *(U)* [feeling] aversão *f*; ~ of sb/sthg aversão a alguém/algo; to take a ~ to sb não simpatizar com alguém; to take a ~ to sthg ter aversão a algo -2. [thing not liked] desgosto *m*. ⋄ *vt* não gostar de.

dislocate [ˈdɪsləkeɪt] *vt* -1. *MED* deslocar -2. [disrupt] desorganizar.
dislodge [dɪsˈlɒdʒ] *vt* [remove - person]: to ~ sb (from) desalojar alguém (de); [- thing]: to ~ sthg (from) remover algo (de).
disloyal [ˌdɪsˈlɔɪəl] *adj*: ~ (to sb) desleal (a alguém).
dismal [ˈdɪzml] *adj* -1. [gloomy, depressing] sombrio(bria), deprimente -2. [unsuccessful] frustrante.
dismantle [dɪsˈmæntl] *vt* [machine, structure] desmantelar.
dismay [dɪsˈmeɪ] ⋄ *n (U)* consternação *f*; to sb's ~ para desespero de alguém. ⋄ *vt* consternar.
dismember [dɪsˈmembəʳ] *vt* desmembrar.
dismiss [dɪsˈmɪs] *vt* -1. [from job]: to ~ sb (from sthg) despedir alguém (de algo) -2. [refuse to take seriously] descartar -3. [allow to leave] dispensar -4. [JUR - case] encerrar; [- jury] dispensar.
dismissal [dɪsˈmɪsl] *n* -1. [from job] demissão *f* -2. [refusal to take seriously] descartamento *m* -3. [JUR - of case] encerramento *m*; [- of jury] dispensa *f*.
dismissive [dɪsˈmɪsɪv] *adj* [attitude, tone] de menosprezo; to be ~ of sb/sthg menosprezar algo/alguém.
dismount [ˌdɪsˈmaʊnt] *vi*: to ~ (from sthg) descer (de algo).
disobedience [ˌdɪsəˈbiːdjəns] *n* desobediência *f*.
disobedient [ˌdɪsəˈbiːdjənt] *adj* desobediente.
disobey [ˌdɪsəˈbeɪ] ⋄ *vt* [person, rule] desobedecer a. ⋄ *vi* desobedecer.
disorder [dɪsˈɔːdəʳ] *n* -1. [disarray]: in ~ em desordem -2. [rioting] tumulto *m* -3. *MED* distúrbio *m*.
disordered [dɪsˈɔːdəd] *adj* -1. [in disarray] desordenado(da) -2. *MED*: mentally ~ mentalmente perturbado(da).
disorderly [dɪsˈɔːdəlɪ] *adj* -1. [untidy] desordenado(da) -2. [unruly] indisciplinado(da).
disorderly conduct *n JUR* perturbação *f* da ordem.
disorganized, -ised [dɪsˈɔːɡənaɪzd] *adj* desorganizado(da).
disorientated *UK* [dɪsˈɔːrɪəntertɪd], **disoriented** *US* [dɪsˈɔːrɪəntɪd] *adj* desorientado(da).
disown [dɪsˈəʊn] *vt* renegar.
disparage [dɪˈspærɪdʒ] *vt* depreciar.
disparaging [dɪˈspærɪdʒɪŋ] *adj* depreciativo(va).
disparate [ˈdɪspərət] *adj fml* diverso(sa).
disparity [dɪˈspærətɪ] *(pl* -ies) *n*: ~ (between/in) disparidade *f* (entre/em).
dispassionate [dɪˈspæʃnət] *adj* imparcial.
dispatch [dɪˈspætʃ] ⋄ *n* [message] envio *m*. ⋄ *vt* [send] enviar, despachar.
dispatch box *n UK POL* -1. [box] *caixa na qual se transporta documentos oficiais* -2. [in House of Commons]: the ~ *local onde os parlamentares mais importantes fazem seus discursos*.
dispatch rider *n* emissário *m*, -ria *f*.
dispel [dɪˈspel] *(pt* & *pp* -led, *cont* -ling) *vt* [feeling] dissipar.
dispensable [dɪˈspensəbl] *adj* dispensável.
dispensary [dɪˈspensərɪ] *(pl* -ies) *n* dispensário *m*.
dispensation [ˌdɪspenˈseɪʃn] *n* [permission] dispensa *f*.

dispense [dɪ'spens] *vt* **-1.** [justice] administrar **-2.** [advice] oferecer **-3.** [drugs, medicine] preparar.
 ◆ **dispense with** *vt fus* dispensar.

dispenser [dɪ'spensəʳ] *n* [machine, container] máquina *f* automática; **cash** ~ caixa *m* automático; **soap** ~ sabão *m* líquido *(em banheiro público)*.

dispensing chemist *UK*, **dispensing pharmacist** *US* [dɪ'spensɪŋ-] *n* farmacêutico *m*, -ca *f*.

dispersal [dɪ'spɜːsl] *n* dispersão *f*.

disperse [dɪ'spɜːs] ⟨⟩ *vt* **-1.** [crowd] dispersar **-2.** [knowledge, news] disseminar **-3.** [substance, gas, oil slick] dispersar. ⟨⟩ *vi* [crowd] dispersar-se.

dispirited [dɪ'spɪrɪtɪd] *adj* desalentado(da).

dispiriting [dɪ'spɪrɪtɪŋ] *adj* desalentador(ra).

displace [dɪs'pleɪs] *vt* **-1.** [supplant] substituir **-2.** *CHEM & PHYS* deslocar.

displaced person [dɪs'pleɪst-] *n* exilado *m*, -da *f*.

displacement [dɪs'pleɪsmənt] *n* deslocamento *m*.

display [dɪ'spleɪ] ⟨⟩ *n* **-1.** [of goods, merchandise, ornaments] exposição *f*; **on** ~ em exposição; **window** ~ vitrine *f*- **2.** [of feeling, courage, skill] demonstração *f*- **3.** [performance] exibição *f*- **4.** *COMPUT* exibição *f*. ⟨⟩ *vt* **-1.** [gen] expor **-2.** [feeling, courage, skill] demonstrar.

display advertising *n* propaganda *f* artística.

displease [dɪs'pliːz] *vt* descontentar.

displeasure [dɪs'pleʒəʳ] *n (U)* descontentamento *m*.

disposable [dɪ'spəʊzəbl] *adj* **-1.** [to be thrown away after use] descartável; ~ **nappy** *UK*, ~ **diaper** *US* fralda *f* descartável **-2.** [available] disponível.

disposal [dɪ'spəʊzl] *n (U)* **-1.** [getting rid] descarte *f* **-2.** [availability]: **at sb's** ~ à disposição de alguém.

dispose ◆ **dispose of** *vt fus* [get rid of - rubbish, nuclear waste] descartar-se de; [- problem] livrar-se de.

disposed [dɪ'spəʊzd] *adj* **-1.** [willing]: **to be** ~ **to do sthg** estar disposto(a) a fazer algo **-2.** [positive]: **to be well-** ~ **to** *OR* **towards sb** estar bem-intencionado(da) com/em relação a alguém.

disposition [ˌdɪspə'zɪʃn] *n* **-1.** [temperament] temperamento *m*- **2.** [willingness, tendency]: ~ **to do sthg** disposição *f* para fazer algo.

dispossess [ˌdɪspə'zes] *vt* *fml*: **to** ~ **sb of sthg** despojar alguém de algo.

disproportion [ˌdɪsprə'pɔːʃn] *n* desproporção *f*.

disproportionate [ˌdɪsprə'pɔːʃnət] *adj* desproporcional; ~ **to sthg** desproporcional a algo.

disprove [ˌdɪs'pruːv] *vt* [theory, idea]: **to** ~ **sthg** mostrar que algo está errado.

dispute [dɪ'spjuːt] ⟨⟩ *n* **-1.** [quarrel] disputa *f*- **2.** *(U)* [disagreement] discussão *f*; **in** ~ em discussão. ⟨⟩ *vt* **-1.** [question, challenge] discutir **-2.** [fight for] disputar.

disqualification [dɪsˌkwɒlɪfɪ'keɪʃn] *n*: ~ **(from sthg)** desqualificação *f* (de algo); ~ **from a sporting event** desqualificação de um evento esportivo; ~ **from standing for election** ineligibilidade *f* para uma eleição; ~ **from driving** *UK* proibição *f* para dirigir.

disqualify [ˌdɪs'kwɒlɪfaɪ] *(pt & pp -ied) vt* **-1.** [subj: authority, illness, criminal record]: **to** ~ **sb (from doing sthg)** desqualificar alguém (para fazer algo) **-2.**

SPORT desqualificar **-3.** *UK* [from driving] ser proibido de.

disquiet [dɪs'kwaɪət] *n (U)* inquietação *f*.

disregard [ˌdɪsrɪ'gɑːd] ⟨⟩ *n*: ~ **(for sthg)** desconsideração *f* *OR* indiferença *f* (por algo). ⟨⟩ *vt* desconsiderar.

disrepair [ˌdɪsrɪ'peəʳ] *n (U)* mau estado *m* de conservação; **to fall into** ~ estar caindo aos pedaços.

disreputable [dɪs'repjʊtəbl] *adj* desacreditado(-da).

disrepute [ˌdɪsrɪ'pjuːt] *n*: **to bring sthg into** ~ desacreditar algo; **to fall into** ~ cair em descrédito.

disrespectful [ˌdɪsrɪ'spektfʊl] *adj* desrespeitoso(-sa).

disrupt [dɪs'rʌpt] *vt* transtornar.

disruption [dɪs'rʌpʃn] *n* transtorno *m*.

disruptive [dɪs'rʌptɪv] *adj* perturbador(ra).

dissatisfaction ['dɪsˌsætɪs'fækʃn] *n (U)* insatisfação *f*.

dissatisfied [ˌdɪs'sætɪsfaɪd] *adj* insatisfeito(ta); ~ **with sthg** insatisfeito(ta) com algo.

dissect [dɪ'sekt] *vt* dissecar.

dissection [dɪ'sekʃn] *n* dissecação *f*.

disseminate [dɪ'semɪneɪt] *vt* [information] disseminar.

dissemination [dɪˌsemɪ'neɪʃn] *n (U)* [of information] disseminação *f*.

dissension [dɪ'senʃn] *n* divergência *f*.

dissent [dɪ'sent] ⟨⟩ *n (U)* [disagreement] divergência *f*. ⟨⟩ *vi*: **to** ~ **(from sthg)** divergir (de algo).

dissenter [dɪ'sentəʳ] *n* [protester] dissidente *mf*.

dissenting [dɪ'sentɪŋ] *adj* [not in agreement] dissidente.

dissertation [ˌdɪsə'teɪʃn] *n* dissertação *f*.

disservice [ˌdɪs'sɜːvɪs] *n*: **to do sb a** ~ fazer um desserviço a alguém.

dissident ['dɪsɪdənt] *n* dissidente *mf*.

dissimilar [ˌdɪ'sɪmɪləʳ] *adj* diferente; ~ **to** diferente de.

dissipate ['dɪsɪpeɪt] ⟨⟩ *vt* **-1.** [heat] dissipar **-2.** [efforts, money] dispersar. ⟨⟩ *vi* [heat, crowd] dissipar-se.

dissipated ['dɪsɪpeɪtɪd] *adj* [person, life] desregrado(-da).

dissociate [dɪ'səʊʃɪeɪt] *vt* dissociar; **to** ~ **o.s. from sthg** dissociar-se de algo.

dissolute ['dɪsəluːt] *adj* dissoluto(ta).

dissolution [ˌdɪsə'luːʃn] *n (U)* [of organization, relationship] dissolução *f*.

dissolve [dɪ'zɒlv] ⟨⟩ *vt* dissolver. ⟨⟩ *vi* **-1.** [substance] dissolver-se **-2.** *fig* [disappear] desaparecer.
 ◆ **dissolve in(to)** *vt fus* [tears, laughter] dissolver-se em.

dissuade [dɪ'sweɪd] *vt*: **to** ~ **sb (from doing sthg)** dissuadir alguém (de fazer algo).

distance ['dɪstəns] ⟨⟩ *n* **-1.** [between two places] distância *f* **-2.** [distant point]: **a** ~ à distância; **from a** ~ de longe; **in the** ~ ao longe. ⟨⟩ *vt*: **to** ~ **o.s. from sb/sthg** distanciar-se de alguém/algo.

distant ['dɪstənt] *adj* distante; ~ **from** distante de.

distaste [dɪs'teɪst] *n (U)* repugnância *f*; ~ **for sthg** repugnância a algo.

distasteful [dɪs'teɪstful] *adj* [unpleasant] desagradável, repugnante.

distemper [dɪ'stempəʳ] *n (U)* -**1.** [paint] pintura *f* à têmpera -**2.** [disease] cinomose *f*.

distended [dɪ'stendɪd] *adj* dilatado(da).

distil *UK* (*pt* & *pp* -**led**, *cont* -**ling**), **distill** *US* [dɪ'stɪl] *vt* destilar.

distiller [dɪ'stɪləʳ] *n* destilador *m*.

distillery [dɪ'stɪlərɪ] (*pl* -**ies**) *n* destilaria *f*.

distinct [dɪ'stɪŋkt] *adj* -**1.** [different] distinto(ta); ~ **from** distinto(ta de); **as** ~ **from** em oposição a -**2.** [clear] nítido(da).

distinction [dɪ'stɪŋkʃn] *n* -**1.** [difference, excellence] distinção *f*; **to draw** *OR* **make a** ~ **between** fazer uma distinção entre -**2.** [in exam result] destaque *m*.

distinctive [dɪ'stɪŋktɪv] *adj* [flavour, voice] característico(ca).

distinctly [dɪ'stɪŋktlɪ] *adv* -**1.** [clearly] claramente -**2.** [considerably] excessivamente.

distinguish [dɪ'stɪŋgwɪʃ] <> *vt* -**1.** [tell apart]: **to** ~ **sthg from sthg** distinguir algo de algo -**2.** [discern, perceive, make different] distinguir; **to** ~ **o.s.** [perform well] distinguir-se. <> *vi*: **to** ~ **between** distinguir-se entre.

distinguished [dɪ'stɪŋgwɪʃt] *adj* ilustre.

distinguishing [dɪ'stɪŋgwɪʃɪŋ] *adj* [feature, mark] peculiar.

distort [dɪ'stɔːt] *vt* distorcer.

distorted [dɪ'stɔːtɪd] *adj* distorcido(da).

distortion [dɪ'stɔːʃn] *n* distorção *f*.

distract [dɪ'strækt] *vt* [person, attention]: **to** ~ **sb (from sthg)** distrair alguém(de algo).

distracted [dɪ'stræktɪd] *adj* [preoccupied] atordoado(da).

distraction [dɪ'strækʃn] *n* -**1.** [gen] distração *f* -**2.** (*U*): **to drive sb to** ~ levar alguém à loucura.

distraught [dɪ'strɔːt] *adj* transtornado(da).

distress [dɪ'stres] <> *n* -**1.** [suffering - mental] aflição *f*; [- physical] agonia *f*, dor *f*; **to be in** ~ estar em agonia -**2.** [danger]: **in** ~ em perigo. <> *vt* [upset] afligir.

distressed [dɪ'strest] *adj* [anxious, upset] angustiado(da).

distressing [dɪ'stresɪŋ] *adj* [news, account, image] angustiante.

distress signal *n* pedido *m* de socorro.

distribute [dɪ'strɪbjuːt] *vt* distribuir.

distribution [ˌdɪstrɪ'bjuːʃn] *n* distribuição *f*.

distributor [dɪ'strɪbjʊtəʳ] *n* -**1.** *COMM* distribuidor *m*, -ra *f* -**2.** *AUT* distribuidor *m*.

district ['dɪstrɪkt] *n* -**1.** [of country] distrito *m* -**2.** [of town] bairro *m*.

district attorney *n US JUR* promotor *m* público, promotora *f* pública.

district council *n UK ADMIN* conselho *m* de bairro.

district nurse *n UK* enfermeira encarregada de atender a domicílio os pacientes de uma área.

District of Columbia *n* Distrito *m* de Colúmbia.

distrust [dɪs'trʌst] <> *n* desconfiança *f*. <> *vt* desconfiar.

distrustful [dɪs'trʌstful] *adj* desconfiado(da).

disturb [dɪ'stɜːb] *vt* -**1.** [interrupt] incomodar -**2.** [upset, worry] preocupar -**3.** [cause to change] mexer em.

disturbance [dɪ'stɜːbəns] *n* -**1.** [fight] distúrbio *m* -**2.** [interruption, disruption]: ~ **of the peace** *JUR* perturbação *f* da ordem -**3.** [distress, upset] perturbação *f*.

disturbed [dɪ'stɜːbd] *adj* perturbado(da).

disturbing [dɪ'stɜːbɪŋ] *adj* [news, image] perturbador(ra).

disunity *n (U)* desunião *f*.

disuse [ˌdɪs'juːs] *n*: **to fall into** ~ cair em desuso.

disused [ˌdɪs'juːzd] *adj* [factory, railway line] abandonado(da).

ditch [dɪtʃ] <> *n* fosso *m*. <> *vt inf* -**1.** [boyfriend, girlfriend] livrar-se de -**2.** [plan] descartar -**3.** [old car, clothes] desfazer-se de.

dither ['dɪðəʳ] *vi* [be indecisive] hesitar.

ditto ['dɪtəʊ] *adv* idem.

diuretic [ˌdaɪjʊ'retɪk] *n* diurético *m*.

diva ['diːvə] (*pl* -**s**) *n* diva *f*.

divan [dɪ'væn] *n* divã *m*.

divan bed *n* divã *m*.

dive [daɪv] (*UK pt* & *pp* -**d**, *US pt* & *pp* -**d** *OR* **dove**) <> *vi* -**1.** [gen] mergulhar; **to** ~ **(into sthg)** mergulhar (em algo) -**2.** [as sport] mergulhar, saltar -**3.** [into pocket, bag]: **to** ~ **into sthg** enfiar a mão em algo. <> *n* -**1.** [gen] mergulho *m* -**2.** [sudden movement] movimento *m* brusco -**3.** *inf pej* [bar, restaurant] espelunca *f*.

dive-bomb *vt* bombardear com caça de mergulho.

diver ['daɪvəʳ] *n* mergulhador *m*, -ra *f*.

diverge [daɪ'vɜːdʒ] *vi* -**1.** [opinions, interests] divergir; **to** ~ **from sthg** divergir de algo -**2.** [roads, paths] separar-se.

divergence [daɪ'vɜːdʒəns] *n* [of opinions, interests] divergência *f*.

divergent [daɪ'vɜːdʒənt] *adj* [opinions, interests] divergente.

diverse [daɪ'vɜːs] *adj* diferente.

diversification [daɪˌvɜːsɪfɪ'keɪʃn] *n (U)* [in industry] diversificação *f*.

diversify [daɪ'vɜːsɪfaɪ] (*pt* & *pp* -**ied**) <> *vt* [products] diversificar. <> *vi* [in industry] diversificar-se.

diversion [daɪ'vɜːʃn] *n* -**1.** (*U*) [gen] desvio *m* -**2.** [distraction] diversão *f*.

diversionary [daɪ'vɜːʃnrɪ] *adj* [tactics] diversivo(va).

diversity [daɪ'vɜːsətɪ] *n (U)* diversidade *f*.

divert [daɪ'vɜːt] *vt* -**1.** [gen] desviar -**2.** [distract] distrair.

divest [daɪ'vest] *vt fml*: **to** ~ **sb of sthg** [take away] privar alguém de algo; **to** ~ **o.s. of sthg** [get rid of] livrar-se de algo.

divide [dɪ'vaɪd] <> *vt* -**1.** dividir; **to** ~ **sthg between** *OR* **among** dividir algo entre -**2.** [split up]: **to** ~ **sthg into** dividir algo em -**3.** *MATH*: **to** ~ **sthg by** dividir algo por. <> *vi* [split into two] dividir-se. <> *n* [difference] divisão *f*.

➡ **divide up** *vt sep* dividir.

divided [dɪ'vaɪdɪd] *adj* [disunited] dividido(da).

dividend ['dıvıdend] *n* [profit] dividendo *m*; **to pay ~s** trazer benefícios.

dividers [dı'vaıdəz] *npl* compasso *m*.

dividing line [dı'vaıdıŋ-] *n* linha *f* divisória.

divine [dı'vaın] ◇ *adj* divino(na). ◇ *vt* **-1.** [gen] adivinhar **-2.** [water] descobrir.

diving ['daıvıŋ] *n* [from board] salto *m (de trampolim)*; [underwater] mergulho *m*.

diving board *n* trampolim *m*.

diving suit *n* escafandro *m*.

divinity [dı'vınətı] (*pl* **-ies**) *n* **-1.** (U) [godliness] divindade *f*- **2.** (U) [study] teologia *f*- **3.** [god, goddess] deidade *f*.

divisible [dı'vızəbl] *adj* MATH divisível; **~ by** divisível por.

division [dı'vıʒn] *n* **-1.** [gen] divisão *f*- **2.** (U) [sharing out, distribution] repartição *f*- **3.** [disagreement] discórdia *f*.

division sign *n* sinal *m* de divisão.

divisive [dı'vaısıv] *adj* que causa divisão.

divorce [dı'vɔːs] ◇ *n* JUR divórcio *m*. ◇ *vt* **-1.** JUR [husband, wife] divorciar-se de **-2.** [separate]: **to ~ sthg from sthg** separar algo de algo.

divorced [dı'vɔːst] *adj* **-1.** JUR divorciado(da) **-2.** *fig* [separated]: **to be ~ from sthg** estar distante de algo.

divorcee [dıvɔː'siː] *n* divorciado *m*, **-da** *f*.

divulge [daı'vʌldʒ] *vt* [information, secret] divulgar.

DIY (*abbr of* **do-it-yourself**) *n UK conceito utilizado para atividades do tipo faça-você-mesmo, como montar objetos ou fazer reparos em casa.*

dizziness ['dızınıs] *n* (U) vertigem *f*, tontura *f*.

dizzy ['dızı] (*compar* **-ier**, *superl* **-iest**) *adj* **-1.** [giddy] tonto(ta) **-2.** *fig* [height, speed] vertiginoso(sa).

DJ *n* **-1.** (*abbr of* **disc jockey**) DJ *mf*- **2.** (*abbr of* **dinner jacket**) smoking *m*.

Djakarta [dʒə'kɑːtə] *n* Jacarta; **in ~** em Jacarta.

Djibouti [dʒı'buːtı] *n* Djibouti; **in ~** no Djibouti.

dl (*abbr of* **decilitre**) dl.

DLit(t) [ˌdiː'lıt] (*abbr of* **Doctor of Letters**) *n (titular de) doutorado em letras.*

dm (*abbr of* **decimetre**) dm.

DM (*abbr of* **Deutschmark**) marco *m* alemão.

DMA (*abbr of* **direct memory access**) *n* DMA *m*.

DMus [ˌdiː'mjuːz] (*abbr of* **Doctor of Music**) *n (titular de) doutorado em música.*

DMZ (*abbr of* **demilitarized zone**) *n US* zona *f* desmilitarizada.

DNA (*abbr of* **deoxyribonucleic acid**) *n* DNA *m*.

D-notice *n UK pedido oficial à imprensa para que uma determinada informação não se torne pública por razões de segurança nacional.*

DNS (*abbr of* **Domain Name System**) *n* COMPUT DNS *m*.

do¹ [duː] (*pt* **did**, *pp* **done**) *aux vb* **-1.** [in negatives]: **don't ~ that!** não faça isso!; **she didn't see it** ela não o viu. **-2.** [in questions]: **~ you like it?** você gosta?; **how ~ you do it?** como é que se faz? **-3.** [referring to previous verb]: **~ you smoke? - yes, I ~ / no, I don't** você fuma? sim/não; **I eat more than you ~** eu como mais do que você; **no, I didn't do it!** não fiz, não!; **so ~ I** eu também. **-4.** [in question tags]: **so, you like Scotland, ~ you?** então você gosta da Escócia, não gosta?; **the train leaves at five o'clock, doesn't it?** o trem sai às cinco, não é (verdade)? **-5.** [for emphasis]: **I ~ like this bedroom** eu realmente gosto deste quarto; **~ come in!** faça o favor de entrar!

☛ *vt* **-1.** [perform] fazer; **to ~ one's homework** fazer o dever de casa; **what is she doing?** o que ela está fazendo?; **what can I ~ for you?** em que posso ajudá-lo? **-2.** [clean, brush, etc]: **to ~ one's hair** pentear-se; **to ~ one's make-up** maquiar-se; **to ~ one's teeth** escovar os dentes. **-3.** [cause] fazer; **to ~ damage** fazer estragos; **to ~ sb good** fazer bem a alguém. **-4.** [have as job]: **what do you ~?** o que você faz? **-5.** [provide, offer] fazer; **we ~ pizzas for under $5** vendemos pizzas por menos de 5 dólares. **-6.** [subj: vehicle] ir a; **the car was ~ing 50mph** o carro ia a 80 km/h. **-7.** *inf* [visit] visitar; **we're doing Scotland next week** para a semana vamos visitar a Escócia.

☛ *vi* **-1.** [behave, act] fazer; **~ as I say** faça como eu lhe digo. **-2.** [progress]: **he did badly/well on his test** ele foi mal/bem no exame; **how did you ~?** como é que foi? **-3.** [be sufficient] chegar; **will $10 ~?** 10 dólares chega? **-4.** [in phrases]: **how ~ you ~?** [greeting] (muito) prazer (em conhecê-lo); **how are you ~ing?** como é que vão as coisas?; **what does that have to ~ with it?** o que é que isso tem a ver?

☛ *n* [party] festa *f*; **~s and don'ts** o que fazer e não fazer.

☛ **do up** *vt sep* [coat, shirt] abotoar; [shoes, laces] apertar, atar; [zip] fechar; [decorate] renovar.

☛ **do with** *vt fus* [need]: **I could ~ with a drink** eu bem que beberia alguma coisa.

☛ **do without** *vt fus* passar sem.

do² (*abbr of* **ditto**) ditto *m*.

DOA (*abbr of* **dead on arrival**) *adj diz-se do corpo que chega sem vida ao hospital.*

doable ['duːəbl] *adj* inf exequível.

d.o.b. (*abbr of* **date of birth**) data *f* de nascimento.

Doberman ['dəʊbəmən] (*pl* **-s**) *n*: **~ (pinscher)** dobermann *m* pinscher.

docile [*UK* 'dəʊsaıl, *US* 'dɒsəl] *adj* dócil.

dock [dɒk] ◇ *n* **-1.** [in harbour] doca *f*- **2.** [in court] banco *m* dos réus. ◇ *vt* [wages] descontar. ◇ *vi* **-1.** [ship] atracar **-2.** [passengers] chegar.

docker ['dɒkəʳ] *n* estivador *m*, -ra *f*.

docket ['dɒkıt] *n* **-1.** *UK documento que descreve o conteúdo de algo sendo entregue ou transportado* **-2.** *US* JUR lista *f* das sentenças.

docklands ['dɒkləndz] *npl UK* região *f* das docas.

dock worker *n* = **docker**.

dockyard ['dɒkjɑːd] *n* estaleiro *m*.

doctor ['dɒktəʳ] ◇ *n* **-1.** [of medicine] médico *m*, -ca *f*; **to go to the ~'s** ir ao médico **-2.** [holder of PhD] doutor *m*, -ra *f*. ◇ *vt* **-1.** [change, tamper with] adulterar **-2.** *UK* [neuter] castrar.

doctorate ['dɒktərət], **doctor's degree** *n* doutorado *m*.

Doctor of Medicine *n* doutor *m*, -ra *f* em medicina.

doctrinaire [ˌdɒktrı'neəʳ] *adj* doutrinário(ria).

doctrine ['dɒktrın] *n* doutrina *f*.

docudrama [ˌdɒkjʊ'drɑːmə] (*pl* **-s**) *n* TV dramatização *f*.

document [n 'dɒkjʊmənt, vb dɒkjʊ'ment] ⬦ n documento m. ⬦ vt [record, detail] documentar.
documentary [ˌdɒkjʊ'mentərɪ] (pl -ies) ⬦ adj [evidence] documental. ⬦ n documentário m.
documentation [ˌdɒkjʊmen'teɪʃn] n (U) [evidence] documentação f.
DOD (abbr of **Department of Defense**) n departamento m de defesa (norte-americano).
doddering ['dɒdərɪŋ], **doddery** ['dɒdərɪ] adj inf senil.
doddle ['dɒdl] n UK inf barbada f.
Dodecanese [ˌdəʊdɪkə'niːz] npl: the ~ o Dodecaneso.
dodge [dɒdʒ] ⬦ n inf mutreta f; a tax ~ uma mutreta para não pagar impostos. ⬦ vt [avoid] fugir de. ⬦ vi esquivar-se.
Dodgems® ['dɒdʒəmz] npl UK carros m de batida (em parques de diversão).
dodgy ['dɒdʒɪ] adj UK inf -1. [dishonest] desonesto(ta) -2. [risky, unreliable] arriscado(da) -3. [weak, unhealthy] fraco(ca).
doe [dəʊ] n -1. [female deer] corça f -2. [female rabbit] coelha f.
doer ['duːəʳ] n inf: he's a ~! ele põe a mão na massa!
does [weak form dəz, strong form dʌz] vb ⊳ **do**.
doesn't ['dʌznt] = does not.
dog [dɒg] (pt & pp -ged, cont -ging) ⬦ n -1. [animal] cão m, cachorro m; it's a ~'s life é uma vida de cão; to go to the ~s inf entrar pelo cano; let sleeping ~s lie não mexa em casa de marimbondo -2. UK [sport]: the ~s corrida f de cachorros -3. US [hot dog] cachorro-quente m. ⬦ vt -1. [follow closely] seguir -2. [subj: problems, bad luck] atormentar.
dog biscuit n biscoito m canino.
dog collar n -1. [of dog] coleira f de cachorro -2. [of clergyman] gola f de padre.
dog-eared [-ɪəd] adj [book, page] com orelhas.
dog-eat-dog adj muito competitivo(va).
dog-end n inf [of cigarette] guimba f, bagana f.
dogfight ['dɒgfaɪt] n -1. [between dogs] briga f de cachorro -2. [between aircraft] combate m aéreo.
dogfish (pl inv) n cação m.
dog food n ração f para cachorro.
dogged ['dɒgɪd] adj [resistance, perseverance] persistente.
doggone ['dɒgɒn], **doggoned** ['dɒgɒnd] adj US inf maldito(ta).
doggy ['dɒgɪ] (pl -ies) n inf cachorrinho m.
doggy bag n ≃ quentinha f, pequena sacola que os restaurantes oferecem para o cliente levar a comida que sobrou.
dogma ['dɒgmə] n dogma m.
dogmatic [dɒg'mætɪk] adj dogmático(ca).
do-gooder [-'gʊdəʳ] n pej pessoa bem-intencionada, mas que acaba atrapalhando.
dog paddle n nado m cachorrinho.
dogsbody ['dɒgzˌbɒdɪ] (pl -ies) n UK inf faz-tudo mf, burro m de carga.
dog tag n US placa de identificação usada no pescoço de um soldado.
doing ['duːɪŋ] n: is this your ~? foi você que fez isso?

doings npl [activities] atividades fpl.
do-it-yourself n (U) sistema m faça-você-mesmo.
doldrums ['dɒldrəmz] npl: to be in the ~ fig estar estagnado(da).
dole [dəʊl] n UK [unemployment benefit] ≃ seguro-desemprego m; to be on the ~ estar recebendo seguro-desemprego.
➡ **dole out** vt sep [food, money] repartir.
doleful ['dəʊlfʊl] adj lúgubre.
doll [dɒl] n [toy] boneca f.
dollar ['dɒləʳ] n dólar m.
dolled up [dɒld-] adj inf enfeitado(da), produzido(da).
dollhouse n US = doll's house.
dollop ['dɒləp] n inf monte m.
doll's house UK, **dollhouse** US ['dɒlhaʊs] n casa f de bonecas.
dolly ['dɒlɪ] (pl -ies) n -1. [doll] bonequinha f -2. TECH [for TV or film camera] plataforma f móvel.
Dolomites ['dɒləmaɪts] npl: the ~ os Dolomíticos.
dolphin ['dɒlfɪn] n golfinho m.
domain [də'meɪn] n [sphere of interest, land] domínio m.
domain name n COMPUT nome m de domínio.
dome [dəʊm] n ARCHIT domo m.
domestic [də'mestɪk] ⬦ adj -1. [gen - flight] doméstico(ca); [- production] nacional -2. [person] caseiro(ra). ⬦ n doméstico m, -ca f.
domestic appliance n eletrodoméstico m.
domesticated [də'mestɪkeɪtɪd] adj -1. [animal] domesticado(da) -2. hum [person] caseiro(ra).
domesticity [ˌdəʊme'stɪsətɪ] n (U) [home life] vida f caseira.
domicile ['dɒmɪsaɪl] n fml domicílio m.
dominance ['dɒmɪnəns] n (U) -1. [control, power] dominância f -2. [importance] predominância f.
dominant ['dɒmɪnənt] adj -1. [colour] predominante -2. [personality, group] influente.
dominate ['dɒmɪneɪt] vt dominar.
dominating ['dɒmɪneɪtɪŋ] adj [person] dominador(-ra).
domination [ˌdɒmɪ'neɪʃn] n (U) domínio m.
domineering [ˌdɒmɪ'nɪərɪŋ] adj [person, personality] dominador(ra).
Dominica [də'mɪnɪkə] n Domínica; in ~ na Domínica.
Dominican Republic [də'mɪnɪkən-] n: the ~ a República Dominicana; in the ~ na República Dominicana.
dominion [də'mɪnjən] n -1. (U) [power] dominação f -2. [land] domínio m.
domino ['dɒmɪnəʊ] (pl -es) n peça f de dominó.
➡ **dominoes** npl [game] dominó m.
domino effect n efeito m dominó.
don [dɒn] (pt & pp -ned, cont -ning) ⬦ n UK UNIV professor m, -ra f universitário, -ria f. ⬦ vt fml [clothing] vestir.
donate [də'neɪt] vt [give] doar.
donation [də'neɪʃn] n doação f.
done [dʌn] ⬦ pp ⊳ **do**. ⬦ adj -1. [finished] pronto(ta) -2. [cooked] assado(da) -3. [socially acceptable] socialmente aceito(ta); it's not ~ to insult

your host não é de bom tom insultar seu anfitrião; **it's the ~ thing to thank your host when leaving** é de bom tom agradecer seu anfitrião ao partir. ⟨⟩ *excl* [to conclude deal] combinado!

donkey ['dɒŋkɪ] (*pl* **donkeys**) *n* burro *m*, -ra *f*.

donkey jacket *n UK jaqueta feita de material resistente.*

donkey work *n UK inf* maçada *f*; **to do the ~** fazer a pior parte.

donor ['dəʊnəʳ] *n* doador *m*, -ra *f*.

donor card *n* carteira *f* de doador.

don't [dəʊnt] = **do not.**

doodle ['du:dl] ⟨⟩ *n* rabisco *m*. ⟨⟩ *vi* rabiscar.

doom [du:m] *n* destino *m*.

doomed [du:md] *adj* [plan, mission] condenado(da); **to be ~ to sthg/to do sthg** estar destinado(da) a algo/a fazer algo; **to be ~ to failure** estar fadado(da) ao fracasso.

door [dɔ:ʳ] *n* porta *f*; **the next ~ neighbour** o vizinho do lado; **the house next ~** a casa ao lado; **she showed him the ~** ela pediu para que ele saísse; **out of ~ s** ao ar livre; **it's three miles ~ to ~** são três milhas de um ponto a outro; **as one ~ closes another one opens** quando se fecha uma porta, se abre uma janela; **to open the ~ to sthg** *fig* abrir as portas para algo.

doorbell ['dɔ:bell] *n* campainha *f*.

doorhandle ['dɔ:hændl] *n* maçaneta *f*.

doorknob ['dɔ:nɒb] *n* maçaneta *f*.

doorknocker ['dɔ:nɒkəʳ] *n* aldrava *f*.

doorman ['dɔ:mən] (*pl* **-men** [-mən]) *n* porteiro *m*.

doormat ['dɔ:mæt] *n* **-1.** [mat] capacho *m* **-2.** *fig* [person] capacho *m*.

doorstep ['dɔ:step] *n* [step] degrau *m*; **there's a cinema right on the ~** há um cinema bem próximo de casa.

doorstop ['dɔ:stɒp] *n* encosto *m* para porta.

door-to-door *adj* [salesman, selling] de porta em porta.

doorway ['dɔ:weɪ] *n* vão *m* da porta.

dope [dəʊp] ⟨⟩ *n* **-1.** *drugs sl* [cannabis] maconha *f* **-2.** [for athlete, horse] estimulante *m* **-3.** *inf* [fool] babaca *mf*. ⟨⟩ *vt* [drug] dopar.

dope test *n SPORT* exame *m* antidoping.

dopey ['dəʊpɪ] (*compar* **-ier**, *superl* **-iest**) *adj inf* **-1.** [groggy] grogue **-2.** [stupid] tonto(ta).

dormant ['dɔ:mənt] *adj* inativo(va).

dormer (window) ['dɔ:məʳ-] *n* água-furtada *f*.

dormice ['dɔ:maɪs] *pl* ⊳ **dormouse.**

dormitory ['dɔ:mətrɪ] (*pl* **-ies**) *n* **-1.** [room] dormitório *m* **-2.** *US* [in university] casa *f* de estudante.

Dormobile® ['dɔ:mə‚bi:l] *n* motocasa *f*.

dormouse ['dɔ:maʊs] (*pl* **-mice**) *n* rato-silvestre *m*, rata-silvestre *f*.

DOS [dɒs] (*abbr of* **disk operating system**) *n* DOS *m*.

dosage ['dəʊsɪdʒ] *n* **-1.** [amount] dosagem *f* **-2.** [on label] posologia *f*.

dose [dəʊs] ⟨⟩ *n* **-1.** [of medicine, drug] dose *f* **-2.** [of illness] ataque *f*. ⟨⟩ *vt* [person]: **to ~ sb (with sthg)** medicar alguém (com algo).

doss [dɒs] ⊸ **doss down** *vi UK inf* ajeitar-se para dormir *(num lugar qualquer).*

dosser ['dɒsəʳ] *n UK inf* pessoa que não tem onde

morar e dorme na rua ou em pensões baratas.

dosshouse ['dɒshaʊs, *pl* -haʊzɪz] *n UK inf* pensão *f* barata *(para os sem-teto).*

dossier ['dɒsɪeɪ] *n* dossiê *m*.

dot [dɒt] (*pt* & *pp* **-ted**, *cont* **-ting**) ⟨⟩ *n* **-1.** [on material] mancha *f* **-2.** [in punctuation] ponto *m*; **since the year ~** desde que o mundo é mundo. ⟨⟩ *vt* [scatter - over surface] salpicar; [- over town, area, country] espalhar.

⊸ **on the dot** *adv* em ponto.

DOT (*abbr of* **Department of Transportation**) *n departamento de transportes do governo norte-americano.*

dotage ['dəʊtɪdʒ] *n*: **to be in one's ~** estar fraco(ca) da cabeça.

dotcom ['dɒtkɒm] *adj* ponto-com.

dote ⊸ **dote on** *vt fus* adorar; **to ~ on sb/sthg** babar por alguém/algo.

doting ['dəʊtɪŋ] *adj* babão(ona).

dot-matrix printer *n* impressora *f* matricial.

dotted line ['dɒtɪd-] *n* linha *f* pontilhada; **to sign on the ~** *fig* assinar na linha pontilhada.

dotty ['dɒtɪ] (*compar* **-ier**, *superl* **-iest**) *adj inf* [mad] doido(da).

double ['dʌbl] ⟨⟩ *adj* duplo(pla). ⟨⟩ *adv* **-1.** [twice] dobro **-2.** [two of the same] em dobro **-3.** [in two] em dois; **to bend ~** dobrar ao meio. ⟨⟩ *n* **-1.** [twice the amount] dobro *m* **-2.** [of alcohol] duplo *m*, -pla *f* **-3.** [look-alike] cópia *f* **-4.** *CINEMA* dublê *mf*. ⟨⟩ *vt* [increase twofold] dobrar. ⟨⟩ *vi* **-1.** [increase twofold] duplicar **-2.** [serve two purposes]: **to ~ as** fazer as vezes de.

⊸ **doubles** *npl TENNIS* dupla *f*.

⊸ **double up** ⟨⟩ *vt sep*: **to be ~d up with laughter** rachar de tanto rir; **to be ~d up in pain** dobrar-se de dor. ⟨⟩ *vi* [bend over] curvar-se, dobrar-se.

double act *n* dupla *f* cômica.

double agent *n* agente *mf* duplo.

double-barrelled *UK*, **double-barreled** *US* [-'bærəld] *adj* **-1.** [shotgun] de dois canos **-2.** [plan, question] de duplo sentido **-3.** [name]: **a ~ surname** um sobrenome composto.

double bass [-beɪs] *n* contrabaixo *m*.

double bed *n* cama *f* de casal.

double-breasted [-'brestɪd] *adj* [jacket] trespassado(da).

double-check ⟨⟩ *vt* verificar duas vezes. ⟨⟩ *vi* verificar duas vezes.

double chin *n* papada *f*.

double-click *COMPUT* ⟨⟩ *n* duplo clique *m*. ⟨⟩ *vt* dar um duplo clique em. ⟨⟩ *vi* dar um duplo clique.

double cream *n UK* creme *m* muito espesso.

double-cross *vt* passar para trás.

double-dealer *n* hipócrita *mf*.

double-decker [-'dekəʳ] *n* [bus] ônibus *m inv* de dois andares.

double-density *adj COMPUT* [disk] de dupla densidade.

double-dutch *n UK hum*: **to talk ~** falar grego.

double-edged *adj* **-1.** [blade] de dois gumes **-2.** *fig* [remark, compliment] ambíguo(gua).

double entendre [ˌduːblɑːˈtɑːndr] *n* duplo sentido *m*.

double fault *n* TENNIS falta *f* dupla.

double figures *npl* números *mpl* de dois algarismos.

double-glazing [-ˈgleɪzɪŋ] *n* vidros *mpl* duplos.

double-jointed [-ˈdʒɔɪntɪd] *adj* [person, joint] de articulações flexíveis.

double-park *vi* AUT estacionar em fila dupla.

double-quick *inf* ⬦ *adj* acelerado(da). ⬦ *adv* de forma acelerada.

double room *n* quarto *m* de casal.

double-sided *adj* COMPUT [disk] de dupla face.

double standards *npl* critérios *mpl* tendenciosos; **to have** ~ não medir as coisas segundo os mesmos critérios.

double take *n*: **to do a** ~ dar uma segunda olhada.

double-talk *n* linguagem *f* confusa, algaravia *f*.

double time *n* pagamento *m* em dobro.

double vision *n* visão *f* dupla.

double whammy [-ˈwæmɪ] *n* golpe *m* duplo.

doubly [ˈdʌblɪ] *adv* duplamente.

doubt [daʊt] ⬦ *n* dúvida *f*; **there is no** ~ **that** não há dúvida de que; **to cast** ~ **on sthg** lançar dúvida sobre algo; **no** ~ sem dúvida; **without (a)** ~ sem dúvida; **beyond (all)** ~ sem dúvida alguma; **in** ~ em dúvida. ⬦ *vt* **-1.** [distrust] desconfiar de **-2.** [consider unlikely] duvidar; **to** ~ **whether** OR **if** duvidar se.

doubtful [ˈdaʊtfʊl] *adj* **-1.** [unlikely] improvável **-2.** [uncertain] incerto(ta); **to be** ~ **about** OR **of sthg** estar em dúvida sobre algo **-3.** [dubious] duvidoso(sa).

doubtless [ˈdaʊtlɪs] *adv* sem dúvida.

dough [dəʊ] *n* (U) **-1.** [for baking] massa *f* **-2.** *inf* [money] grana *f*.

doughnut [ˈdəʊnʌt] *n* **-1.** [without hole] sonho *m* **-2.** [with hole] rosca *f*.

dour [dʊəˈ] *adj* austero(ra).

douse [daʊs] *vt* **-1.** [put out] jogar água em **-2.** [drench] encharcar.

dove¹ [dʌv] *n* [bird] pomba *f*.

dove² [dəʊv] *pt US* ⊳ **dive.**

dovecot(e) [ˈdʌvkɒt] *n* pombal *m*.

dovetail [ˈdʌvteɪl] ⬦ *vt* combinar com. ⬦ *vi* combinar.

dovetail joint *n* ensambladura *f* em cauda de andorinha.

dowager [ˈdaʊədʒəˈ] *n literary* [old lady] senhora *f* digna.

dowdy [ˈdaʊdɪ] (*compar* **-ier**, *superl* **-iest**) *adj* deselegante.

Dow-Jones average [ˌdaʊˈdʒəʊnz-] *n*: **the** ~ o índice Dow Jones.

down [daʊn] ⬦ *adv* **-1.** [downwards] para baixo; **to fall** ~ cair; ~ **here/there** aqui/ali em baixo **-2.** [along]: **I'm going** ~ **to the shops** estou indo fazer compras; **we walked** ~ **to the park** fomos até o parque **-3.** [southwards]: **we flew** ~ **from Recife to Rio** viajamos para o sul, do Recife até o Rio **-4.** [reduced, lower] baixo; **prices are coming** ~ os preços estão baixando; ~ **to the last detail** até o último detalhe **-5.** [as deposit]: **to pay £5** ~·pagar £5 de entrada **-6.** [in written form]: **get sthg** ~ **in writing** conseguir algo por escrito; **write it** ~ tome nota. ⬦ *prep* **-1.** [downwards] para baixo; **they ran** ~ **the hill** eles correram morro abaixo **-2.** [along]: **we walked** ~ **the street** caminhamos pela rua. ⬦ *adj* **-1.** *inf* [depressed] desanimado(da) **-2.** [behind] por trás **-3.** [lower in amount] mais baixo(xa) **-4.** [not in operation] fora de operação. ⬦ *n* **-1.** (U) [feathers, hair] penugem *f* **-2.** US SPORT tempo *m*. ⬦ *vt* **-1.** [knock over] abater **-2.** [swallow] engolir.

➡ **Downs** *npl* UK: **the Downs** chapada ao sul da Inglaterra.

➡ **down with** *excl*: ~ **with the king!** abaixo o rei!

down-and-out ⬦ *adj* sem futuro• ⬦ *n* mendigo *m*, -ga *f*.

down-at-heel *adj esp* UK desleixado(da).

downbeat [ˈdaʊnbiːt] *adj inf* [gloomy] sombrio(bria).

downcast [ˈdaʊnkɑːst] *adj fml* **-1.** [person] abatido(da) **-2.** [eyes] cabisbaixo(xa).

downer [ˈdaʊnəˈ] *n inf* **-1.** [drug] calmante *m* **-2.** [depressing event or situation] droga *f*; **to be on a** ~ estar de baixo-astral.

downfall [ˈdaʊnfɔːl] *n* **-1.** (U) [ruin] queda *f* **-2.** [cause of ruin] ruína *f*.

downgrade [ˈdaʊngreɪd] *vt* rebaixar.

downhearted [ˌdaʊnˈhɑːtɪd] *adj* desacorçoado(da).

downhill [ˌdaʊnˈhɪl] ⬦ *adj* **-1.** [path] íngreme **-2.** *fig* [easy] canja; **it's** ~ **all the way now** daqui pra frente, é canja **-3.** [skier]: **he's a** ~ **skier** ele esquia morro abaixo. ⬦ *adv* **-1.** [downwards] para baixo **-2.** *fig* [from bad to worse] de mau a pior. ⬦ *n* SKIING descida *f*.

Downing Street [ˈdaʊnɪŋ-] *n* rua no centro de Londres onde fica a residência oficial do primeiro-ministro inglês, governo *m* britânico.

DOWNING STREET

Situada no centro de Londres, e fechada ao público, a *Downing Street* abriga, no número 10, a residência oficial do primeiro-ministro britânico, e, no número 11, a do ministro das finanças. Por isso, a expressão é utilizada com freqüência para designar o governo britânico como um todo.

download [ˌdaʊnˈləʊd] *vt* COMPUT baixar, fazer download.

downmarket ⬦ *adj* barato(ta), de baixa qualidade. ⬦ *adv*: **to go** ~ produzir mais barato com qualidade inferior.

down payment *n* entrada *f*.

downplay [ˈdaʊnpleɪ] *vt* minimizar.

downpour [ˈdaʊnpɔːˈ] *n* aguaceiro *m*.

downright [ˈdaʊnraɪt] ⬦ *adj* [lie, fool] inequívoco(ca). ⬦ *adv* completamente.

downside [ˈdaʊnsaɪd] *n* [disadvantage] desvantagem *f*.

downsize ⬦ *vt* [workforce] reduzir o número

de. ⇔ *vi* [subj: company] reduzir o número de empregados.

Down's syndrome *n (U)* síndrome *f* de Down.

downstairs [ˌdaʊnˈsteəz] ⇔ *adj* do andar de baixo. ⇔ *adv*: **to come** ~ vir para *OR* andar de baixo; **to go** ~ ir para *OR* andar de baixo; **to live** ~ morar no andar de baixo.

downstream [ˌdaʊnˈstriːm] *adv* a jusante, rio abaixo.

downtime [ˈdaʊntaɪm] *n* tempo *m* ocioso.

down-to-earth *adj* realista.

downtown [ˌdaʊnˈtaʊn] *esp US* ⇔ *adj* do centro; ~ New York Nova York central. ⇔ *adv*: **to go** ~ ir ao centro; **to live** ~ viver no centro.

downtrodden [ˈdaʊnˌtrɒdn] *adj* oprimido(da).

downturn [ˈdaʊntɜːn] *n* decréscimo *m*; ~ **in sthg** queda em algo.

down under *adv* na *OR* para Austrália/Nova Zelândia.

downward [ˈdaʊnwəd] ⇔ *adj* **-1.** [towards ground] para baixo **-2.** [decreasing] descendente. ⇔ *adv* *US* = downwards.

downwards [ˈdaʊnwədz] *adv* **-1.** [look, move] para baixo; **the overall trend is** ~ a tendência geral é de baixa **-2.** [in hierarchy] para baixo.

downwind [ˌdaʊnˈwɪnd] *adv* a favor do vento.

dowry [ˈdaʊərɪ] (*pl* -ies) *n* dote *m*.

doz. (*abbr of* **dozen**) dz.

doze [dəʊz] ⇔ *n* soneca *f*; **to have a** ~ tirar uma soneca. ⇔ *vi* dormitar.
> ◆ **doze off** *vi* cochilar.

dozen [ˈdʌzn] ⇔ *num adj* dúzia *f*. ⇔ *n* [twelve] dúzia *f*; **50p a** ~ 50p a dúzia.
> ◆ **dozens** *npl inf*: ~s of um montão de.

dozy [ˈdəʊzɪ] (*compar* -ier, *superl* -iest) *adj* **-1.** [sleepy] sonolento(ta) **-2.** *UK inf* [stupid] retardado(da).

DP (*abbr of* **data processing**) *n* PD *m*.

DPhil [ˌdiːˈfɪl] (*abbr of* **Doctor of Philosophy**) *n* (*titular de*) doutorado em ciências humanas.

DPP (*abbr of* **Director of Public Prosecutions**) *n* fiscal geral do estado na Grã-Bretanha.

DPT (*abbr of* **diphtheria, pertussis, tetanus**) *n* (vacina *f*) tríplice *f*.

Dr (*abbr of* **Doctor**) Dr. (Dra.).

Dr. (*abbr of* **Drive**) usado em nomes de rua na Grã-Bretanha.

drab [dræb] (*compar* -ber, *superl* -best) *adj* **-1.** [buildings] sombrio(bria) **-2.** [colour, garment] apagado(da) **-3.** [life] monótono(na).

draconian [drəˈkəʊnjən] *adj fml* draconiano(na).

draft [drɑːft] ⇔ *n* **-1.** [early version] rascunho *m* **-2.** [money order] ordem *f* de pagamento **-3.** *US MIL*: **the** ~ o destacamento **-4.** *US* = draught. ⇔ *vt* **-1.** [write] rascunhar, fazer um rascunho de **-2.** *US MIL* recrutar **-3.** [transfer] deslocar.

draft dodger [-ˈdɒdzər] *n US* o que tenta fugir do serviço militar.

draftee [ˌdrɑːfˈtiː] *n US* recruta *m*.

draftsman *n US* = draughtsman.

draftsmanship *n US* = draughtsmanship.

drafty *adj US* = draughty.

drag [dræg] (*pt* & *pp* -ged, *cont* -ging) ⇔ *vt* **-1.** [gen] arrastar **-2.** [search] dragar. ⇔ *vi* **-1.** [trail] arrastar

-2. [pass slowly] arrastar-se. ⇔ *n* **-1.** *inf* [bore] chatice *f*; **what a** ~! que pé no saco! **-2.** *inf* [on cigarette] tragada *f* **-3.** [air resistance] resistência *f* aerodinâmica **-4.** *(U)* [cross-dressing]: **in** ~ vestido como mulher.
> ◆ **drag down** *vt sep fig* [debase]: **to** ~ **sb down** levar alguém para o buraco.
> ◆ **drag in(to)** *vt sep* [involve] meter em; **don't** ~ **me into this!** não me meta nisso!
> ◆ **drag on** *vi* arrastar-se.
> ◆ **drag out** *vt sep* **-1.** [protract] prolongar-se em demasia **-2.** [extract]: **to** ~ **sthg out of sb** arrancar algo de alguém.

dragnet [ˈdrægnet] *n* **-1.** [net] rede *f* de arrasto **-2.** *fig* [to catch criminal] batida *f*.

dragon [ˈdrægən] *n* **-1.** [beast] dragão *m* **-2.** *inf* [woman] bruxa *f*.

dragonfly [ˈdrægnflaɪ] (*pl* -ies) *n* libélula *f*.

dragoon [drəˈguːn] ⇔ *n* dragão *m*. ⇔ *vt*: **to** ~ **sb into doing sthg** forçar alguém a fazer algo.

drag racing *n (U)* corrida *f* de carros envenenados.

dragster [ˈdrægstəʳ] *n* carro *m* envenenado.

drain [dreɪn] ⇔ *n* **-1.** [pipe] cano *m* de esgoto; **to go down the** ~ ir para o brejo; [grating in street] bueiro *m* **-2.** [depletion]: ~ **on sthg** sorvedouro de algo; **it's a** ~ **on my energy** esgota todas as minhas forças. ⇔ *vt* **-1.** [remove water from] drenar **-2.** [deplete] esgotar, exaurir **-3.** [drink, glass] beber até o fim. ⇔ *vi* **-1.** [dry] escoar **-2.** [disappear] desaparecer.

drainage [ˈdreɪnɪdʒ] *n* **-1.** [pipes, ditches] esgoto *m* **-2.** [draining] drenagem *f*.

draining board *UK* [ˈdreɪnɪŋ-], **drainboard** *US* [ˈdreɪnbɔːrd] *n* escorredor *m* de louça.

drainpipe [ˈdreɪnpaɪp] *n* cano *m* de esgoto.

drake [dreɪk] *n* pato *m* (macho).

dram [dræm] *n* [of whisky] trago *m*.

drama [ˈdrɑːmə] ⇔ *n* **-1.** [play, excitement] drama *f* **-2.** *(U)* [art] teatro *m*. ⇔ *comp* de teatro.

dramatic [drəˈmætɪk] *adj* **-1.** [concerned with theatre] teatral **-2.** [exciting] dramático(ca) **-3.** [sudden, noticeable] drástico(ca).

dramatically [drəˈmætɪklɪ] *adv* **-1.** [noticeably] drasticamente **-2.** [theatrically] teatralmente.

dramatist [ˈdræmətɪst] *n* dramaturgo *m*, -ga *f*.

dramatization [ˌdræmətaɪˈzeɪʃn] *n* [for theatre, film, television] dramatização *f*.

dramatize, -ise [ˈdræmətaɪz] *vt* **-1.** [rewrite as play] dramatizar **-2.** *pej* [make exciting] tornar dramático(ca).

drank [dræŋk] *pt* ⊳ drink.

drape [dreɪp] *vt* colocar suavemente; **to be** ~ **d with** *OR* **in sthg** estar/ser coberto(ta) com algo.
> ◆ **drapes** *npl US* cortinas *fpl*.

draper [ˈdreɪpəʳ] *n*: ~**'s (shop)** loja *f* de cortinas e tecidos.

drastic [ˈdræstɪk] *adj* drástico(ca).

drastically [ˈdræstɪklɪ] *adv* drasticamente.

draught *UK*, **draft** *US* [drɑːft] *n* **-1.** [air current] corrente *f* **-2.** *literary* [gulp] golfada *f* **-3.** [from barrel]: **on** ~ [beer] de barril.
> ◆ **draughts** *n UK* damas *fpl*.

draught beer *n UK* chope *m*.

draughtboard ['drɑːftbɔːd] *n UK* tabuleiro *m* de damas.

draughtsman *UK*, **draftsman** *US* ['drɑːftsmən] (*pl* **-men** [-mən]) *n* [of technical drawings] desenhista *m* industrial.

draughtsmanship *UK*, **draftsmanship** *US* ['drɑːftsmənʃɪp] *n* **-1.** [of artist] habilidade *f* para o desenho **-2.** [of work] desenho *m* industrial.

draughtswoman *UK*, **draftswoman** *US* (*pl* **-women** [-wɪmɪn]) *n* [of technical drawings] desenhista *f* industrial.

draughty *UK* (*compar* **-ier**, *superl* **-iest**), **drafty** *US* (*compar* **-ier**, *superl* **-iest**) ['drɑːftɪ] *adj* pouco protegido(da) do frio.

draw [drɔː] (*pt* **drew**, *pp* **drawn**) <> *vt* **-1.** [sketch] desenhar **-2.** [pull] puxar; **to ~ the curtains** [open] abrir as cortinas; [close] fechar as cortinas **-3.** [breath] inalar **-4.** [pull out] sacar **-5.** [arrive at, form] chegar a **-6.** [formulate] estabelecer **-7.** [attract] atrair; **to be** *OR* **feel drawn to** ser/sentir-se atraído(da) por; **to ~ sb's attention to sthg** chamar a atenção de alguém para algo. <> *vi* **-1.** [sketch] esboçar **-2.** [move]: **to ~ near** aproximar-se; **to ~ away** afastar-se; **to ~ to an end** *OR* **a close** tender para um final **-3.** *SPORT* empatar; **to ~ with sb** empatar com alguém. <> *n* **-1.** *SPORT* [result] empate *m* **-2.** [lottery] sorteio *m* **-3.** [attraction] atração *f*.

  draw in *vi* [days] declinar.

  draw into *vt sep*: **to ~ sb into sthg** envolver alguém em algo.

  draw on *vt fus* **-1.** = draw upon **-2.** [smoke] tragar.

  draw out *vt sep* **-1.** [encourage] desinibir **-2.** [prolong] prolongar **-3.** [withdraw] sacar.

  draw up <> *vt sep* [draft] redigir, preparar. <> *vi* [stop] parar.

  draw upon *vt fus* recorrer a.

drawback ['drɔːbæk] *n* inconveniente *m*.

drawbridge ['drɔːbrɪdʒ] *n* ponte *f* levadiça.

drawer [drɔːʳ] *n* [in desk, chest] gaveta *f*.

drawing ['drɔːɪŋ] *n* **-1.** [picture] desenho *m*, croqui *m* **-2.** (*U*) [skill, act] ato *m* de desenhar.

drawing board *n* prancheta *f* de desenho; **back to the ~!** *inf* de volta ao ponto de partida!

drawing pin *n UK* percevejo *m*.

drawing room *n* [living room] sala-de-estar *f*.

drawl [drɔːl] <> *n* fala *f* arrastada. <> *vt* arrastar. <> *vi* falar de forma arrastada.

drawn [drɔːn] <> *pp* ▷ **draw**. <> *adj* **-1.** [curtain, blind] fechado(da) **-2.** [face, person] abatido(da).

drawn-out *adj* esticado(da).

drawstring ['drɔːstrɪŋ] *n* cordão *m*.

dread [dred] <> *n* (*U*) medo *m*, pavor *m*. <> *vt* temer; **to ~ doing sthg** ter medo de fazer algo; **I ~ to think** tenho medo de pensar.

dreaded ['dredɪd] *adj* [feared] temido(da).

dreadful ['dredfʊl] *adj* **-1.** [terrible] terrível **-2.** [unpleasant] desagradável **-3.** [ill] horrível **-4.** [embarrassed] envergonhado(da) **-5.** [poor] fraco(ca) **-6.** [for emphasis] horroroso(sa).

dreadfully ['dredfʊlɪ] *adv* **-1.** [badly] terrivelmente **-2.** [extremely] extremamente.

dreadlocks ['dredlɒks] *npl* cabelo *m* rastafári.

dream [driːm] (*pt & pp* **-ed** *OR* **dreamt**) <> *n* **-1.** [during sleep] sonho *m*; **bad ~** pesadelo *m* **-2.** [aspiration] sonho *m*; **to be beyond one's wildest ~s** ser muito melhor do que o esperado. <> *adj* almejado(da). <> *vt* [during sleep]: **to ~ (that)** sonhar que; **I never ~ed this would happen** jamais imaginei que isso pudesse acontecer. <> *vi* **-1.** [during sleep] sonhar; **to ~ of** *OR* **about sthg** sonhar com algo; **I wouldn't ~ of it** *fig* nem pensar, de maneira nenhuma **-2.** [aspire]: **to ~ of sthg/of doing sthg** sonhar com algo/em fazer algo.

  dream up *vt sep* bolar.

dreamer ['driːməʳ] *n* [unrealistic person] sonhador *m*, -ra *f*.

dreamily ['driːmɪlɪ] *adv* como em sonhos.

dreamlike ['driːmlaɪk] *adj* de sonho.

dreamt [dremt] *pt & pp* ▷ **dream**.

dream world *n* mundo *m* de sonhos.

dreamy ['driːmɪ] (*compar* **-ier**, *superl* **-iest**) *adj* **-1.** [look, smile] distraído(da), sonhador(ra) **-2.** [music, feeling] sentimental.

dreary ['drɪərɪ] (*compar* **-ier**, *superl* **-iest**) *adj* **-1.** [gloomy, depressing] sombrio(a) **-2.** [dull, boring] chato(-ta).

dredge [dredʒ] *vt* [lake, harbour, river] dragar.

  dredge up *vt sep* **-1.** [with dredger] dragar **-2.** *fig* [from past] trazer à tona.

dredger ['dredʒəʳ] *n* [ship, machine] draga *f*.

dregs [dregz] *npl* **-1.** [of liquid] borra *f* **-2.** *fig* [of society] ralé *f*.

drench [drentʃ] *vt* encharcar; **to be ~ed in** *OR* **with sthg** estar encharcado(da) de algo.

Dresden ['drezdən] *n* Dresden; **in ~** em Dresden.

dress [dres] <> *n* **-1.** [frock] vestido *m* **-2.** [type of clothing] roupa *f*. <> *vt* **-1.** [clothe] vestir; **to be ~ed** estar vestido(da); **to be ~ed in** estar vestido(da) de; **to get ~ed** vestir-se **-2.** [bandage] fazer curativo em **-3.** *CULIN* temperar. <> *vi* vestir-se.

  dress up <> *vt sep* **-1.** [in costume] disfarçar-se **-2.** [in best clothes] vestir-se elegantemente **-3.** [in formal clothes] vestir-se a rigor **-4.** *fig* [embellish] enfeitar. <> *vi* **-1.** [in costume] fantasiar-se **-2.** [in best clothes] vestir-se elegantemente **-3.** [in formal clothes] vestir-se a rigor.

dressage ['dresɑːʒ] *n* (*U*) adestramento *m*.

dress circle *n THEATRE* balcão *m* nobre.

dresser ['dresəʳ] *n* **-1.** [for dishes] aparador *m* **-2.** *US* [chest of drawers] cômoda *f* **-3.** [person]: **to be a smart ~** vestir-se bem **-4.** *THEATRE* camareiro *m*, -ra *f*.

dressing ['dresɪŋ] *n* **-1.** [bandage] curativo *m* **-2.** [for salad] tempero *m*, molho *m* **-3.** *US* [for turkey etc] molho *m*.

dressing gown *n* **-1.** [man's] roupão *m* **-2.** [woman's] robe *f*.

dressing room *n* **-1.** *SPORT* vestiário *m* **-2.** *THEATRE* camarim *m*.

dressing table *n* penteadeira *f*.

dressmaker ['dres,meɪkəʳ] *n* costureiro *m*, -ra *f*.

dressmaking ['dres,meɪkɪŋ] *n* (*U*) costura *f*.

dress rehearsal *n THEATRE* ensaio *m* geral.

dress shirt *n* camisa *f* social.

dressy ['dresɪ] (*compar* -ier, *superl* -iest) *adj* [smart] chique.

drew [dru:] *pt* ▷ draw.

dribble ['drɪbl] ◇ *n* -1. *(U)* [of saliva] filete *m* -2. [of other liquid] gota *f.* ◇ *vt* -1. *SPORT* [ball] driblar -2. [liquid] pingar. ◇ *vi* -1. [drool] babar -2. [trickle] derramar.

dribs [drɪbz] *npl*: **in ~ and drabs** aos poucos.

dried [draɪd] ◇ *pt & pp* ▷ dry. ◇ *adj* -1. [powdered] em pó -2. [fruit, herbs, flowers] seco(ca).

dried fruit *n (U)* fruta *f* seca.

dried-up *adj* seco(ca).

drier ['draɪə'] *n* = dryer.

drift [drɪft] ◇ *n* -1. [movement, trend] tendência *f* -2. [of current] fluxo *m* -3. [geol] pressão *f* -4. [of people] curso *m* -5. [of snow, leaves, sand] monte *m* -6. [meaning] sentido *m*; **to get the general ~** pegar a idéia geral. ◇ *vi* -1. [boat] estar à deriva -2. [snow, sand, leaves] acumular-se -3. [person]: **they're ~ing towards bankruptcy** eles estão indo a caminho da falência; **to ~ into marriage** acabar se casando; **to ~ apart** acabar se afastando.

◆ **drift off** *vi* [fall asleep] cair de sono.

drifter ['drɪftə'] *n* [person] nômade *mf.*

driftwood ['drɪftwʊd] *n (U)* madeira *f* flutuante.

drill [drɪl] ◇ *n* -1. [tool] furadeira *f* -2. [industrial] perfuradora *f* -3. [dentist's] broca *f* -4. [exercise, training] treinamento *m.* ◇ *vt* -1. [metal, wood, hole] perfurar -2. [instruct] instruir; **to ~ sthg into sb** ensinar algo a alguém *(repetindo a lição regularmente).* ◇ *vi* furar; **to ~ into sthg** penetrar em algo; **to ~ for sthg** procurar algo *(perfurando com broca).*

drilling platform ['drɪlɪŋ-] *n* plataforma *f* de perfuração.

drily ['draɪlɪ] *adv* = dryly.

drink [drɪŋk] (*pt* drank, *pp* drunk) ◇ *n* -1. [non-alcoholic beverage] bebida *f* -2. [alcoholic beverage] bebida *f* alcoólica; **to have a ~** tomar um drinque -3. *(U)* [alcohol] bebida *f.* ◇ *vt* beber. ◇ *vi* beber; **to ~ to sb/sb's success** brindar a alguém/ao sucesso de alguém.

drinkable ['drɪŋkəbl] *adj* -1. [safe to drink] potável -2. [tasty] saboroso(sa).

drink-driving *UK,* **drunk-driving** *US n (U)* ato *m* de dirigir bêbado, -da *f.*

drinker ['drɪŋkə'] *n* -1. [of alcohol] beberrão *m,* -rona *f* -2. [of tea, coffee]: **he's a great tea/coffee ~** ele gosta muito de tomar chá/café.

drinking ['drɪŋkɪŋ] ◇ *adj*: **I'm not a ~ man** não sou um homem que bebe; **~ laws** leis de consumo de bebida alcoólica. ◇ *n*: **to go ~** ir beber; **heavy ~** embriagamento.

drinking companion *n* companheiro *m,* -ra *f* de bebida.

drinking fountain *n* bebedouro *m.*

drinking-up time *n UK inf tempo concedido nos bares para acabar os drinks antes de fechar.*

drinking water ['drɪŋkɪŋ-] *n (U)* água *f* potável.

drip [drɪp] (*pt & pp* -ped, *cont* -ping) ◇ *n* -1. [drop] gota *f* -2. *MED* aparelho *m* de soro -3. *inf* [wimp] sonso *m,* -sa *f.* ◇ *vt* pingar. ◇ *vi* -1. [gen] pingar

-2. [nose] escorrer -3. [person]: **to be ~ping with** [sweat, blood] estar encharcado(da) de; [diamonds, furs] *fig* estar coberto(ta) de.

drip-dry *adj* que não amarrota ao secar.

drip-feed ◇ *n* alimentação *f* por conta-gotas. ◇ *vt* alimentar por conta-gotas.

dripping ['drɪpɪŋ] ◇ *adj* -1. [person, clothes, hair]: **~ (wet)** encharcado(da) -2. [tap] que pinga. ◇ *n CULIN* [from meat] banha *f (de carne).*

drive [draɪv] (*pt* drove, *pp* driven) ◇ *n* -1. [journey] passeio *m,* volta *f* de carro -2. [urge] ímpulso *m* -3. [campaign] campanha *f* -4. *(U)* [energy] ímpeto *m* -5. [road to house] caminho *m (de entrada)* -6. *SPORT* [stroke] tacada *f* -7. *US AUT* [in automatic car] transmissão *f* automática. ◇ *vt* -1. [vehicle] dirigir; [passenger] levar *(de carro)* -2. *TECH* [operate] operar -3. [chase] seguir -4. [motivate] motivar -5. [force]: **to ~ sb to sthg/to do sthg** levar alguém a algo/a fazer algo; **to ~ sb mad** *OR* **crazy** [make insane] deixar alguém louco(ca) *OR* maluco(ca); [irritate] deixar alguém furioso(sa) -6. [hammer] bater -7. *SPORT* [hit] rebater. ◇ *vi AUT* -1. [driver] dirigir -2. [travel by car] viajar.

◆ **drive at** *vt fus* querer dizer, insinuar.

◆ **drive out** *vt sep* fazer sair.

drive-in *esp US* ◇ *adj* drive-in. ◇ *n* -1. [restaurant] drive-in *m* -2. [cinema] autocine *m.*

drivel ['drɪvl] *n inf* bobagem *f.*

driven ['drɪvn] *pp* ▷ drive.

driver ['draɪvə'] *n* -1. [of vehicle] motorista *mf* -2. *COMPUT* driver *m.*

driver's license *n US* = driving licence.

drive shaft *n* eixo *m* de transmissão.

driveway ['draɪvweɪl] *n* acesso *m.*

driving ['draɪvɪŋ] ◇ *adj* [rain, wind] forte; **~ rain** chuva *f* torrencial. ◇ *n (U)* direção *f.*

driving force *n* força *f* motriz.

driving instructor *n* instrutor *m,* -ra *f* de direção.

driving lesson *n* aula *f* de direção.

driving licence *UK,* **driver's license** *US n* carteira *f* de motorista.

driving mirror *n* [espelho *m*] retrovisor *m.*

driving school *n* auto-escola *f.*

driving test *n* exame *m* de direção.

drizzle ['drɪzl] ◇ *n* garoa *f,* chuvisco *m.* ◇ *v impers* garoar, chuviscar.

drizzly ['drɪzlɪ] (*compar* -ier, *superl* -iest) *adj* chuvoso(sa); **~ rain** garoa *f* fina.

droll [drəʊl] *adj* engraçado(da).

dromedary ['drɒmədrɪ] (*pl* -ies) *n* dromedário *m.*

drone [drəʊn] ◇ *n* -1. [sound] zunido *m* -2. [bee] zangão *m.* ◇ *vi* zunir.

◆ **drone on** *vi* falar de forma monótona; **to ~ on about sthg** falar de forma monótona sobre algo.

drool [dru:l] *vi* -1. [dribble] babar -2. *fig* [admire]: **to ~ over sb/sthg** babar por alguém/algo.

droop [dru:p] *vi* -1. [hang down - shoulders] encurvarse; [- head] inclinar-se; [- eyelids] fechar-se; [- flowers] murchar-se -2. *fig* [weaken, flag] desanimar-se.

drop [drɒp] (*pt & pp* -ped, *cont* -ping) ◇ *n* -1. [of liquid - water, blood, rain] gota *f;* [- tea, coffee, milk] gole *m*; [- alcohol] dose *f* **- 2.** [sweet] bala *f* **- 3.** [decrease] queda *f*; ~ **in sthg** queda de algo **- 4.** [vertical distance] descida *f*. <> **vt - 1.** [let fall - gen] deixar cair; [- bombs] lançar; [- stitch]: **she ~ped a stitch** escapou um ponto **- 2.** [decrease, lower] reduzir **- 3.** [voice] baixar **- 4.** [leave, abandon] deixar **- 5.** [leave out] excluir **- 6.** [hint, remark] lançar **- 7.** *TENNIS* [lose] perder **- 8.** [write]: **to ~ sb a line** *OR* **note** escrever a alguém umas linhas *OR* um bilhete. <> **vi - 1.** [fall] cair; **to ~ to one's knees** ajoelhar-se; ~ **dead!** vai tomar banho! **- 2.** [fall] baixar **- 3.** [wind, attendance] diminuir.

➡ **drops** *npl MED* gotas *fpl*.
➡ **drop by** *vi inf* dar um pulo *(como visita)*.
➡ **drop in** *vi inf* passar na casa de; **to ~ in on sb** passar na casa de alguém.
➡ **drop off** <> *vt sep* deixar. <> *vi* **- 1.** [fall asleep] cair no sono **- 2.** [grow less] diminuir.
➡ **drop out** *vi* [withdraw] retirar-se; **to ~ out of** *OR* **from sthg** desligar-se de algo.

drop-in centre *n* centro mantido pelos serviços sociais, pela igreja, etc., que as pessoas podem freqüentar se desejarem.
droplet ['drɒplɪt] *n* gotícula *f*.
dropout ['drɒpaʊt] *n* **- 1.** [from society] marginalizado *m*, -da *f* **- 2.** [from university] pessoa *f* que largou os estudos.
dropper ['drɒpəʳ] *n* conta-gotas *m inv*.
droppings ['drɒpɪŋz] *npl* excremento *m* (de animais).
drop shot *n TENNIS* deixada *f*.
dross [drɒs] *n* **- 1.** *TECH* [waste material] refugo *m* **- 2.** *fig* [rubbish] porcaria *f*.
drought [draʊt] *n* seca *f*.
drove [drəʊv] <> *pt* ▷ **drive**. <> *n* [of people] multidão *f*.
drown [draʊn] <> *vt* **- 1.** [kill] afogar **- 2.** [sound]: **to ~ sb/sthg (out)** abafar alguém/algo. <> *vi* afogar-se.
drowsy ['draʊzɪ] (*compar* -ier, *superl* -iest) *adj* [person] sonolento(ta).
drudge [drʌdʒ] *n* escravo *m*, -va *f* do trabalho.
drudgery ['drʌdʒərɪ] *n (U)* trabalho *m* pesado.
drug [drʌg] (*pt* & *pp* -ged, *cont* -ging) <> *n* **- 1.** [medication] remédio *m* **- 2.** [illegal substance] droga *f*. <> *vt* **- 1.** [person, animal] drogar **- 2.** [food, drink] adicionar droga a.
drug abuse *n (U)* abuso *m* de drogas.
drug addict *n* drogado *m*, -da *f*, viciado *m*, -da *f* em drogas.
drug addiction *n (U)* vício *m* em drogas, toxicomania *f*.
drug dealer *n* traficante *mf* de drogas.
druggist ['drʌgɪst] *n US* farmacêutico *m*, -ca *f*.
drugstore ['drʌgstɔːʳ] *n US* farmácia *f*, drogaria *f*.
druid ['druːɪd] *n* druida *m*.
drum [drʌm] (*pt* & *pp* -med, *cont* -ming) <> *n* **- 1.** [instrument] tambor *m* **- 2.** [container, cylinder] barril *m*. <> *vt* [fingers] tamborilar. <> *vi* **- 1.** [on drums] tocar **- 2.** [rain, fingers] tamborilar **- 3.** [hooves] bater.
➡ **drums** *npl* [set of drums] bateria *f*.
➡ **drum into** *vt sep*: **to ~ sthg into sb** incutir algo em alguém.
➡ **drum up** *vt sep* angariar.

drumbeat ['drʌmbiːt] *n* rufo *m* (de tambores).
drum brake *n* freio *m* de tambor.
drummer ['drʌməʳ] *n* baterista *mf*.
drumming ['drʌmɪŋ] *n* **- 1.** [of drums] rufar *m* **- 2.** [of rain, fingers] tamborilo *m* **- 3.** [of hooves] batida *f*.
drum roll *n* rufar *m* de tambor.
drumstick ['drʌmstɪk] *n* **- 1.** [for drum] baqueta *f* **- 2.** [food] coxa *f*.
drunk [drʌŋk] <> *pp* ▷ **drink**. <> *adj* **- 1.** [on alcohol] bêbado(da); **to get ~** embebedar-se; **to be charged with being ~ and disorderly** *JUR* ser acusado(da) de estar embriagado(do) **- 2.** *fig* [excited, carried away]: **to be ~ with** *OR* **on sthg** estar encantado(da) com algo. <> *n* bêbado *m*, -da *f*.
drunkard ['drʌŋkəd] *n* beberrão *m*, -rona *f*.
drunk-driving *n US* = **drink-driving**.
drunken ['drʌŋkn] *adj* **- 1.** [person] bêbado(da) **- 2.** [state, event] = **de bêbado**.
drunken driving *n* = **drink-driving**.
drunkenness ['drʌŋkənnɪs] *n (U)* embriaguez *f*.
dry [draɪ] (*compar* -ier, *superl* -iest, *pt* & *pp* dried) <> *adj* **- 1.** [gen] seco(ca) **- 2.** [climate] árido(da) **- 3.** [sense of humour] sarcástico(ca) **- 4.** [tedious] monótono(na). <> *vt* & *vi* secar.
➡ **dry out** <> *vt sep* secar completamente. <> *vi* [get dry - gen] secar; [- person] secar-se.
➡ **dry up** <> *vt sep* [dishes] secar. <> *vi* **- 1.** [gen] secar **- 2.** [supplies, inspiration] esgotar-se **- 3.** [actor, speaker] calar-se.
dry-clean *vt* lavar a seco.
dry cleaner *n*: ~ **'s** tinturaria *f*.
dry cleaning *n* [work, service] lavagem *f* a seco.
dry dock *n* dique *m* seco.
dryer ['draɪəʳ] *n* [for clothes] secadora *f*.
dry ginger *n (U)* ginger ale *m*.
dry goods *npl* artigos *mpl* de armarinho.
dry ice *n (U)* gelo-seco *m*.
dry land *n* terra *f* firme.
dryly ['draɪlɪ] *adv* [wryly] secamente.
dryness ['draɪnɪs] *n (U)* **- 1.** [lack of water] aridez *f* **- 2.** [wryness] secura *f* **- 3.** [tedium] monotonia *f*.
dry rot *n (U)* apodrecimento *m* da madeira (de casa).
dry run *n* [practice] ensaio *m*.
dry ski slope *n* rampa *f* de esqui artificial.
dry-stone wall *n* parede *f* de pedra.
DSc (*abbr of* Doctor of Science) *n (titular de)* doutorado em ciências.
DST (*abbr of* daylight saving time) *horário de verão nos Estados Unidos*.
DTI (*abbr of* Department of Trade and Industry) *n* ministério britânico da indústria e do comércio, ≈ MDIC *m*.
DTLR (*abbr of* Department for Transport, Local Government and the Regions) *n* departamento dos transportes do governo britânico e dos governos locais.
DTP (*abbr of* desktop publishing) *n* DTP *f*.
DTs [ˌdiːˈtiːz] (*abbr of* delirium tremens) *npl fam*: **to have the ~** estar em crise de abstinência.
dual ['djuːəl] *adj* duplo(pla).
dual carriageway *n UK* pista *f* dupla.

dual control n controle m duplo.

dual nationality n dupla nacionalidade f.

dual-purpose adj que tem dupla finalidade.

Dubai [ˌduːˈbaɪ] n Dubai.

dubbed [dʌbd] adj **-1.** CINEMA dublado(da) **-2.** [nicknamed] apelidado(da).

dubious [ˈdjuːbjəs] adj **-1.** [suspect, questionable] duvidoso(sa) **-2.** [uncertain, undecided]: **to be ~ about doing sthg** estar indeciso(sa) sobre fazer algo.

Dublin [ˈdʌblɪn] n Dublin; **in ~** em Dublin.

Dublin Bay prawn n camarão m à Dublin Bay.

Dubliner [ˈdʌblɪnər] n dublinense mf.

duchess [ˈdʌtʃɪs] n duquesa f.

duchy [ˈdʌtʃɪ] (pl -ies) n ducado m.

duck [dʌk] <> n **-1.** [bird] pato m, -ta f; **to take to sthg like a ~ to water** tirar algo de letra; **like water off a ~'s back** sem nenhum efeito **-2.** (U) [food] pato m. <> vt **-1.** [lower] curvar **-2.** [try to avoid] esquivar-se de; **to ~ the issue** evitar a questão **-3.** [submerge] mergulhar. <> vi **-1.** [lower head] curvar-se **-2.** [move down quickly] abaixar-se.

➡ **duck out** vi: **to ~ out (of sthg/of doing sthg)** safar-se (de algo/de fazer algo).

duckling [ˈdʌklɪŋ] n **-1.** [animal] patinho m, -nha f **-2.** [food] pato m novo.

duct [dʌkt] n **-1.** [pipe - heating] tubo m; [- water] canal m **-2.** ANAT ducto m.

dud [dʌd] <> adj **-1.** [banknote, coin, cheque] falso(sa) **-2.** [machine, idea] imprestável **-3.** [bomb, shell, bullet] que falhou. <> n negação f; **to be a ~ at sthg** [person] ser uma negação em algo; **to be a ~** [banknote, cheque] não ter fundos; [bomb, shell, bullet] não prestar.

dude [djuːd] n US inf [man] cara m.

dude ranch n US rancho m para turistas.

due [djuː] <> adj **-1.** [expected] previsto(ta); **she's ~ back shortly** espera-se que ela volte logo; **when is the next train ~?** quando chega o próximo trem? **-2.** [proper] devido(da); **in ~ course** no tempo devido **-3.** [owed, owing]: **the rent is ~** o aluguel venceu; **she's ~ a pay rise** ela deve ganhar um aumento de salário; **how much are you ~?** quanto te devem? <> n [deserts] direito m; **to give him his ~, ...** para lhe fazer justiça, ... <> adv exatamente; **~ north** bem ao norte.

➡ **dues** npl direitos mpl.

➡ **due to** prep devido a.

due date n (data f de) vencimento m.

duel [ˈdjuːəl] n duelo m.

duet [djuːˈet] n dueto m.

duff [dʌf] adj UK inf inútil.

➡ **duff up** vt sep UK inf dar uma surra em.

duffel bag [ˈdʌfl-] n mochila f.

duffel coat [ˈdʌfl-] n casaco m grosso (com capuz).

duffle bag [ˈdʌfl-] n = **duffel bag**.

duffle coat [ˈdʌfl-] n = **duffel coat**.

dug [dʌg] pt & pp ▷ **dig**.

dugout [ˈdʌgaʊt] n **-1.** [canoe] canoa f **-2.** SPORT fosso m.

duke [djuːk] n duque m.

dull [dʌl] <> adj **-1.** [boring] entediante **-2.** [colour,

light] opaco(ca) **-3.** [day, weather] nublado(da) **-4.** [thud, boom] surdo(da) **-5.** [ache, pain] incômodo(da). <> vt **-1.** [deaden - pain] aliviar; [- senses, memory] enfraquecer; [- pleasure] diminuir **-2.** [make less bright] embaciar.

duly [ˈdjuːlɪ] adv **-1.** [properly] devidamente **-2.** [as expected] como era de se esperar.

dumb [dʌm] adj **-1.** [unable to speak] mudo(da) **-2.** esp US inf [stupid] estúpido(da).

dumbbell [ˈdʌmbell] n [weight] haltere m.

dumbfound [dʌmˈfaʊnd] vt pasmar; **to be ~ed** ficar pasmado(da).

dumbstruck [ˈdʌmstrʌk] adj chocado(da), pasmado(da).

dumbwaiter [ˌdʌmˈweɪtəʳ] n [lift] elevador m de comida.

dumdum (bullet) [ˈdʌmdʌm-] n bala f dundum.

dummy [ˈdʌmɪ] (pl -ies) <> adj [fake] falso(sa). <> n **-1.** [model of human figure - tailor's] manequim m; [- ventriloquist's] boneco m **-2.** [copy, fake object] imitação f **-3.** (U) [for baby] chupeta f **-4.** SPORT drible m. <> vt SPORT driblar.

dummy run n prova f, ensaio m.

dump [dʌmp] <> n **-1.** [for rubbish] lixeira f **-2.** [for ammunition] depósito m **-3.** inf pej [ugly place] espelunca f. <> vt **-1.** [put down] deixar cair **-2.** [dispose of] descarregar **-3.** COMM liquidar **-4.** COMPUT mover de um dispositivo para outro **-5.** inf [jilt] romper com.

➡ **dumps** npl: **to be (down) in the ~s** estar na fossa.

dumper (truck) [ˈdʌmpəʳ-] UK, **dump truck** US n caminhão m basculante.

dumping [ˈdʌmpɪŋ] n (U) descarregamento m; **'no ~'** 'proibido jogar lixo'.

dumping ground n depósito m.

dumpling [ˈdʌmplɪŋ] n CULIN bolinho m de massa de pão.

dumpster n US caçamba f de lixo.

dump truck n US = **dumper (truck)**.

dumpy [ˈdʌmpɪ] (compar -ier, superl -iest) adj inf atarracado(da).

dunce [dʌns] n burro m, -ra f, ignorante mf.

dune [djuːn] n duna f.

dung [dʌŋ] n (U) esterco m.

dungarees [ˌdʌŋgəˈriːz] npl UK macacão m.

dungeon [ˈdʌndʒən] n masmorra f.

dunk [dʌŋk] vt inf molhar.

Dunkirk [dʌnˈkɜːk] n Dunquerque.

duo [ˈdjuːəʊ] n **-1.** MUS dueto m **-2.** [couple] casal m.

duodenal ulcer [ˈdjuːəʊˈdiːnl-] n úlcera f duodenal.

dupe [djuːp] <> n [person] otário m, -ria f. <> vt [trick]: **to ~ sb (into doing sthg)** iludir alguém (a fazer algo).

duplex [ˈdjuːpleks] n US dúplex m inv.

duplicate [adj & n ˈdjuːplɪkət, vb ˈdjuːplɪkeɪt] <> adj [document] duplicado(da); **~ key** cópia f de chave. <> n [of document] cópia f; **in ~** em duplicata. <> vt **-1.** [document] copiar **-2.** [double, repeat] repetir.

duplication [ˌdjuːplɪˈkeɪʃn] n (U) **-1.** [copying] duplicação f **-2.** [doubling, repetition] repetição f.

duplicity [dju:'plɪsətɪ] *n (U) fml* [deceit] duplicidade *f*.

durability [ˌdjʊərə'bɪlətɪ] *n (U)* durabilidade *f*.

durable ['djʊərəbl] *adj* durável, duradouro(ra).

duration [djʊ'reɪʃn] *n (U)* duração *f*; **for the ~ of** durante.

duress [djʊ'res] *n (U)*: **under ~** sob coerção.

Durex® ['djʊəreks] *n* [condom] preservativo *m*, camisinha *f*.

during ['djʊərɪŋ] *prep* durante.

dusk [dʌsk] *n (U)* crepúsculo *m*, anoitecer *m*.

dusky ['dʌskɪ] *(compar* **-ier,** *superl* **-iest)** *adj literary* [skin] moreno(na).

dust [dʌst] ◇ *n (U)* **-1.** [gen] pó *m*; **to gather ~** [get dusty] pegar pó; *fig* [be ignored] ser privado(da); **to let the ~ settle** deixar a poeira baixar; **to have bitten the ~** ser derrubado(da) por terra **-2.** [earth, sand] poeira *f*, pó *m*. ◇ *vt* **-1.** [clean] tirar o pó de **-2.** [cover]: **to ~ sthg with sthg** polvilhar algo com algo.
   dust off *vt sep* **-1.** [clean] sacudir a poeira de **-2.** *fig* [re-use] reaproveitar.

dustbin ['dʌstbɪn] *n UK* lata *f* de lixo.

dustbowl ['dʌstbəʊl] *n* zona *f* de desertificação.

dustcart ['dʌstkɑːt] *n UK* caminhão *m* de lixo.

dust cover *n* **-1.** [for book] = **dust jacket -2.** [for furniture] = **dust sheet**.

duster ['dʌstə'] *n* **-1.** [cloth] espanador *m* de pó **-2.** *US* [overall] guarda-pó *m*.

dust jacket, dust cover *n* [on book] sobrecapa *f*.

dustman ['dʌstmən] *(pl* **-men** [-mən]) *n UK* lixeiro *m*.

dust mite *n* ácaro *m (da poeira doméstica)*.

dustpan ['dʌstpæn] *n* pá *f* de lixo.

dust sheet, dust cover *n UK* capa *f (para os móveis)*.

dust storm *n* tempestade *f* de poeira.

dust-up *n inf* briga *f*, rinha *f*.

dusty ['dʌstɪ] *(compar* **-ier,** *superl* **-iest)** *adj* [covered in dust] empoeirado(da).

Dutch [dʌtʃ] ◇ *adj* holandês(esa). ◇ *n* [language] holandês *m*. ◇ *npl*: **the ~** os holandeses. ◇ *adv*: **let's go ~** cada um paga a sua parte.

Dutch auction *n UK* leilão *no qual vai se baixando o preço de venda até que haja um comprador*.

Dutch barn *n UK* celeiro *m* holandês.

Dutch cap *n UK* diafragma *m*.

Dutch courage *n* coragem *f (produzida pela embriaguez)*.

Dutch elm disease *n (U)* doença *f do olmo holandês*.

Dutchman ['dʌtʃmən] *(pl* **-men** [-mən]) *n* holandês *m*.

Dutchwoman ['dʌtʃˌwʊmən] *(pl* **-women** [-ˌwɪm-ɪn]) *n* holandesa *f*.

dutiable ['dju:tjəbl] *adj* tributável.

dutiful ['dju:tɪfʊl] *adj* zeloso(sa).

duty ['dju:tɪ] *(pl* **-ies)** *n* **-1.** *(U)* [moral, legal responsibility] dever *m*; **to do one's ~** cumprir um dever **-2.** *(U)* [work] obrigação *f*; **to be on/off ~** estar de plantão/folga **-3.** [tax] imposto *m*.
   duties *npl* [tasks, part of job] funções *fpl*.

duty bound *adj* [obliged] obrigado(da); **to be ~ to do sthg** ser obrigado(da) a fazer algo.

duty-free ◇ *n* **-1.** [goods] artigo *m* isento de impostos **-2.** [shop] loja *f* duty-free. ◇ *adj* [whisky, cigarettes] isento(ta) de impostos.

duty-free shop *n* loja *f* duty-free.

duty officer *n* oficial *mf* em serviço.

duvet ['du:veɪ] *n UK* edredom *m*, acolchoado *m*.

duvet cover *n UK* capa *f* do edredom.

DVD *(abbr of* Digital Versatile Disk) *n* DVD *m*.

DVD player *n* (reprodutor *m* de) DVD *m*.

DVD ROM *(abbr of* Digital Versatile Disk read only memory) *n* DVD-ROM *m*.

DVLA *(abbr of* Driver and Vehicle Licensing Agency) *n* órgão britânico responsável pelo registro de automóveis e emissão de carteiras de motorista, ≃ DENATRAN *m*.

DVM *(abbr of* Doctor of Veterinary Medicine) *n (titular de)* doutorado em medicina veterinária.

dwarf [dwɔ:f] *(pl* **-s** OR **dwarves** [dwɔ:vz]) ◇ *adj* [plant, animal] anão (anã). ◇ *n* anão *m*, anã *f*. ◇ *vt* [tower over] sobrepujar.

dwell [dwel] *(pt & pp* **dwelt** OR **-ed)** *vi literary* [live] morar.
   dwell on *vt fus* [past, problem] ficar dando voltas com.

-dweller ['dwelə'] *suffix* [inhabitant] habitante *mf*; **city-~** habitante *mf* da cidade.

dwelling ['dwelɪŋ] *n literary* morada *f*.

dwelt [dwelt] *pt & pp* ⊳ **dwell**.

dwindle ['dwɪndl] *vi* [decrease, grow smaller] ir diminuindo.

dwindling ['dwɪndlɪŋ] *adj* [decreasing, growing smaller] decrescente.

DWP *(abbr of* Department for Work and Pensions) *n* departamento britânico para administração de trabalhadores e pensionistas.

dye [daɪ] ◇ *n* [colouring] tintura *f*. ◇ *vt* [change colour of] tingir.

dyed [daɪd] *adj* tingido(da).

dying ['daɪŋ] ◇ *cont* ⊳ **die**. ◇ *adj* **-1.** [about to die - person] agonizante; [- species] em vias de extinção **-2.** *fig* [declining] que está desaparecendo. ◇ *npl*: **the ~** os moribundos.

dyke [daɪk] *n* = **dike**.

dynamic [daɪ'næmɪk] *adj* [energetic] dinâmico(ca).
   dynamics *npl* [forces of change] dinâmica *f*.

dynamism ['daɪnəmɪzm] *n (U)* [energy] dinamismo *m*.

dynamite ['daɪnəmaɪt] ◇ *n (U)* **-1.** [explosive] dinamite *f* **-2.** *inf fig* [person, story, news]: **to be ~** ser uma bomba **-3.** *inf fig* [excellent] excelente. ◇ *vt* [blow up] dinamitar.

dynamo ['daɪnəməʊ] *(pl* **-s)** *n TECH* dínamo *m*.

dynasty [*UK* 'dɪnəstɪ, *US* 'daɪnəstɪ] *(pl* **-ies)** *n* [ruling family] dinastia *f*.

dysentery ['dɪsntrɪ] *n (U)* disenteria *f*.

dyslexia [dɪs'leksɪə] *n (U)* dislexia *f*.

dyslexic [dɪs'leksɪk] *adj* disléxico(ca).

dyspepsia [dɪs'pepsɪə] *n (U) MED* dispepsia *f*.

dystrophy ['dɪstrəfɪ] *n* ⊳ **muscular dystrophy**.

e (pl **e's** OR **es**), **E** (pl **E's** OR **Es**) [i:] n [letter] e, E m.
➤ **E** n **-1.** MUS mi m **-2.** (abbr of **east**) l **-3.** (abbr of **ecstasy**) ecstasy m.

E111 n formulário que garante seguro saúde a cidadãos britânicos em estadas temporárias em outros países da União Européia.

ea. (abbr of **each**) cada.

each [i:tʃ] ⟨⟩ adj [every] cada. ⟨⟩ pron [every one] cada um (uma); **two of** ~ dois de cada; ~ **other** um ao outro; **we know** ~ **other** nós nos conhecemos.

eager ['i:gəʳ] adj [keen, enthusiastic] animado(da); **to be** ~ **for sthg/to do sthg** estar ansioso(sa) por algo/para fazer algo.

eagerly ['i:gəlɪ] adv [talk, plan] animadamente.

eagle ['i:gl] n [bird] águia f.

eagle-eyed [-'aɪd] adj [person] com olhos de lince.

eaglet ['i:glɪt] n águia f nova.

E and OE (abbr of **errors and omissions excepted**) ≃ SEO, salvo erro ou omissão.

ear [ɪəʳ] n **-1.** [of person, animal] orelha f; **by** ~ MUS de ouvido; **to go in one** ~ **and out the other** inf entrar por um ouvido e sair pelo outro; **to have** OR **keep one's** ~ **to the ground** inf estar/manter-se atento(ta) aos últimos acontecimentos; **to have sb's** ~ ter a atenção de alguém; **to have an** ~ **for sthg** ter ouvido para algo; **to play it by** ~ fig nadar de acordo com a maré **-2.** [of corn] espiga f.

earache ['ɪəreɪk] n dor f de ouvido.

eardrum ['ɪədrʌm] n tímpano m.

earl [ɜːl] n conde m.

earlier ['ɜːlɪəʳ] ⟨⟩ adj **-1.** [previous] anterior **-2.** [according to clock]: **let's take the** ~ **train** vamos pegar o trem que tem antes. ⟨⟩ adv antes; ~ **on** antes; ~ **that day** mais cedo naquele dia; **they arrived** ~ **than expected** eles chegaram antes do esperado.

earliest ['ɜːlɪəst] ⟨⟩ adj **-1.** [first] primeiro(ra); **at your** ~ **convenience** assim que puder **-2.** [according to clock] primeiro(ra). ⟨⟩ adv: **at the** ~ no mínimo.

earlobe ['ɪələʊb] n lóbulo m da orelha.

early ['ɜːlɪ] (compar **-ier**, superl **-iest**) ⟨⟩ adj **-1.** [gen] adiantado(da); **the** ~ **train** o primeiro trem; **to make an** ~ **start** começar na primeira hora **-2.** [of the beginning of a period of time - old] antigo(ga);

[- period]: **this chair is** ~ **Victorian** esta cadeira é do início da era Vitoriana; [- in career, life] os primeiros anos de; [- in time] no começo de; ~**-morning** da madrugada; **the** ~ **chapters** os primeiros capítulos. ⟨⟩ adv **-1.** [before expected time] antes da hora **-2.** [in the morning, in a period of time] cedo; **to get up** ~ madrugar; **as** ~ **as 1950** já em 1950; ~ **on** cedo.

early closing n meio-feriado m (para as lojas).

early retirement n aposentadoria f antecipada.

early warning system n MIL sistema m de alerta imediato.

earmark ['ɪəmɑːk] vt: **to be** ~ **ed for sthg** ser destinado(da) para algo.

earn [ɜːn] vt **-1.** [as salary] ganhar **-2.** COMM gerar **-3.** fig [respect, praise] merecer.

earned income [ɜːnd-] n rendimento m do trabalho.

earner ['ɜːnəʳ] n **-1.** [person] assalariado m, -da f **-2.** [product] fonte f de recursos **-3.** UK inf [business]: **a nice little** ~ um negócio da China.

earnest ['ɜːnɪst] adj [serious, sincere] sério(ria), sincero(ra).
➤ **in earnest** ⟨⟩ adj convicto(ta). ⟨⟩ adv para valer.

earnestly ['ɜːnɪstlɪ] adv **-1.** [talk] seriamente **-2.** [wish] de todo o coração.

earnings ['ɜːnɪŋz] npl [of person, business] rendimentos mpl.

earnings-related adj [pension, payment, benefit] proporcional aos rendimentos.

ear, nose and throat specialist n otorrinolaringologista mf.

earphones ['ɪəfəʊnz] npl [headset] fones mpl de ouvido.

earpiece n audiofone m.

earplugs ['ɪəplʌgz] npl protetores mpl de ouvido.

earring ['ɪərɪŋ] n brinco m.

earshot ['ɪəʃɒt] n: **within/out of** ~ dentro/fora do alcance do ouvido.

ear-splitting adj ensurdecedor(ra).

earth [ɜːθ] ⟨⟩ n **-1.** [gen] terra f; **how/what on** ~ ...? como/o que é que ...?; **where/why on** ~ ...? onde/por que diabos ...?; **to cost the** ~ UK custar uma fortuna **-2.** (U) [soil] solo m **-3.** UK [in electric plug, appliance] terra m. ⟨⟩ vt UK: **to be** ~ **ed** estar aterrado(da).

earthenware ['ɜːθnweəʳ] ⟨⟩ adj de barro, de louça. ⟨⟩ n (U) cerâmica f.

earthling ['ɜːθlɪŋ] n habitante mf da terra.

earthly ['ɜːθlɪ] adj **-1.** [of material world] terreno(na) **-2.** inf [possible] concreto(ta).

earthquake ['ɜːθkweɪk] n terremoto m.

earth-shattering adj UK inf surpreendente.

earth tremor n tremor m de terra.

earthward(s) ['ɜːθwəd(z)] adv em direção à terra.

earthworm ['ɜːθwɜːm] n minhoca f.

earthy ['ɜːθɪ] (compar **-ier**, superl **-iest**) adj **-1.** [humour, person] direto(ta) **-2.** [taste, smell] de terra.

earwax ['ɪəwæks] n (U) cera f de ouvido.

earwig ['ɪəwɪg] n lacraia f.

ease [i:z] <> *n (U)* **-1.** [lack of difficulty] facilidade *f*; **to do sthg with** ~ fazer algo com facilidade **-2.** [comfort] comodidade *f*; **at** ~ à vontade; **ill at** ~ pouco(ca) à vontade. <> *vt* **-1.** [make less severe - pain, restrictions] aliviar; [- problems] atenuar **-2.** [move carefully] ajeitar; **to** ~ **sthg open** abrir algo com cuidado. <> *vi* [become less severe] aliviar; **to show signs of easing** mostrar sinais de alívio.
➤ **ease off** *vi* diminuir.
➤ **ease up** *vi* **-1.** [rain] acalmar **-2.** [relax] relaxar; **to** ~ **up on sb** *inf* ser menos duro(ra) com alguém.

easel ['i:zl] *n* cavalete *m*.

easily ['i:zɪlɪ] *adv* **-1.** [without difficulty] facilmente **-2.** [undoubtedly] sem sombra de dúvida **-3.** [in a relaxed manner] tranqüilamente.

easiness ['i:zɪnɪs] *n* [lack of difficulty] facilidade *f*.

east [i:st] <> *adj* **-1.** [in the east, facing the east] oriental **-2.** [from the east] leste. <> *adv* a leste; ~ **of** ao leste de. <> *n* **-1.** [direction] leste *m* **-2.** [region]: **the** ~ o leste.
➤ **East** *n*: **the East** [of country] o leste; [Asia, Eastern bloc] o Oriente.

eastbound ['i:stbaʊnd] *adj* em direção ao leste.

East End *n*: **the** ~ o leste de *Londres*.

Easter ['i:stə'] *n* Páscoa *f*.

Easter egg *n* ovo *m* de Páscoa.

Easter Island *n* Ilha da Páscoa.

easterly ['i:stəlɪ] *adj* **-1.** [towards the east, in the east] a leste **-2.** [from the east] do leste.

eastern ['i:stən] *adj* [part of country, continent] oriental, do leste.
➤ **Eastern** *adj* oriental.

Eastern bloc [-'blɒk] *n*: **the** ~ o bloco Oriental.

Easter Sunday *n* Domingo *m* de Páscoa.

East German <> *adj* da Alemanha Oriental. <> *n* [person] alemão *m*, -mã *f* oriental.

East Germany *n*: **(the former)** ~ (a antiga) Alemanha Oriental; **in** ~ na Alemanha Oriental.

eastward ['i:stwəd] <> *adj* ao leste. <> *adv* = **eastwards**.

eastwards ['i:stwədz] *adv* em direção ao leste.

easy ['i:zɪ] (*compar* **-ier**, *superl* **-iest**) <> *adj* **-1.** [not difficult] fácil **-2.** [comfortable] cômodo(da) **-3.** [relaxed] sossegado(da). <> *adv*: **to go** ~ **on sb/sthg** *inf* [treat more kindly] ir com calma com alguém/algo; **to take it** *OR* **things** ~ *inf* levar isso *OR* as coisas com calma.

easy-care *adj UK* [clothes] que não precisa ser passado(da).

easy chair *n* [armchair] poltrona *f*.

easygoing [ˌi:zɪ'gəʊɪŋ] *adj* [person, manner] descontraído(da).

eat [i:t] (*pt* ate, *pp* eaten) <> *vt & vi* comer.
➤ **eat away** *vt sep*, **eat into** *vt fus* **-1.** [corrode away] corroer **-2.** [deplete] destruir.
➤ **eat out** *vi* [at restaurant] comer fora.
➤ **eat up** *vt sep* **-1.** [food] comer tudo **-2.** *fig* [money, time] consumir um monte de.

eatable ['i:təbll] *adj* [palatable] comestível.

eaten ['i:tn] *pp* ⊳ **eat**.

eater ['i:tə'] *n* comedor *m*, -ra *f*.

eatery ['i:tərɪ] (*pl* **-ies**) *n* restaurante *m*.

eating apple ['i:tɪŋ-] *n* maçã *f (para a sobremesa)*.

eau de cologne [ˌəʊdəkə'ləʊn] *n* água-de-colônia *f*, colônia *f*.

eaves ['i:vz] *npl* [of house] beirado *m*.

eavesdrop ['i:vzdrɒp] (*pt & pp* **-ped**, *cont* **-ping**) *vi* [listen, spy] bisbilhotar; **to** ~ **on sb** bisbilhotar alguém.

ebb [eb] <> *n (U)* [of tide, sea] vazante *f*; **the** ~ **and flow of sthg** *fig* os altos e baixos de algo; **to be at a low** ~ *fig* estar cabisbaixo(xa). <> *vi* **-1.** [tide, sea] baixar **-2.** *literary* [strength, pain, feeling]: **to** ~ **(away)** desaparecer.

ebb tide *n* maré *f* baixa.

ebony ['ebənɪ] <> *adj literary* [colour] da cor do ébano. <> *n (U)* [wood] ébano *m*.

ebullient [ɪ'bʊljənt] *adj* [lively] entusiasmado(da).

e-business *n* **-1.** [company] empresa *f* de e-business **-2.** [electronic commerce] e-business *m*.

EC (*abbr of* **European Community**) *n* CE *f*.

e-cash *n COMPUT* dinheiro *m* eletrônico.

ECB (*abbr of* **European Central Bank**) *n* BCE *m*.

eccentric [ɪk'sentrɪk] <> *adj* [odd] excêntrico(ca). <> *n* [person] excêntrico *m*, -ca *f*.

eccentricity [ˌeksen'trɪsətɪ] (*pl* **-ies**) *n* excentricidade *f*.

ecclesiastic(al) [ɪˌkli:zɪ'æstɪ(l)] *adj* [of Christian church] eclesiástico(ca).

ECG *n* **-1.** (*abbr of* **electrocardiogram**) ECG *m*. **- 2.** (*abbr of* **electrocardiograph**) eletrocardiógrafo *m*.

ECH (*abbr of* **electric central heating**) *n* aquecimento *m* central elétrico.

echelon ['eʃəlɒn] *n fml* [level in organization] escalão *m*.

echo ['ekəʊ] (*pl* **-es**, *pt & pp* **-ed**, *cont* **-ing**) <> *n* eco *m*. <> *vt* [repeat - words] repetir; [- opinion] repercurtir. <> *vi* ecoar.

éclair [eɪ'kleə'] *n* [cake] bomba *f*.

eclectic [ɪ'klektɪk] *adj* eclético(ca).

eclipse [ɪ'klɪps] <> *n* **-1.** [of sun, moon] eclipse *m*; **total/partial** ~ eclipse total/parcial **-2.** *fig* [decline] declínio *m*. <> *vt fig* [overshadow] eclipsar.

ECM (*abbr of* **European Common Market**) *n US* MCE *m*.

eco-friendly ['i:kəʊ'frendlɪ] *adj* ecológico(ca).

ecological [ˌi:kə'lɒdʒɪkl] *adj* ecológico(ca).

ecologically [ˌi:kə'lɒdʒɪklɪ] *adv* [from ecological point of view] ecologicamente.

ecologist [ɪ'kɒlədʒɪst] *n* ecologista *mf*.

ecology [ɪ'kɒlədʒɪ] *n (U)* ecologia *f*.

e-commerce *n* comércio *m* eletrônico.

economic [ˌi:kə'nɒmɪk] *adj* econômico(ca).

economical [ˌi:kə'nɒmɪkl] *adj* econômico(ca).

Economic and Monetary Union *n* União *f* Monetária e Econômica.

economics [ˌi:kə'nɒmɪks] <> *n (U)* [study] economia *f*. <> *npl* [of plan, business, trade] aspectos *mpl* econômicos.

economist [ɪ'kɒnəmɪst] *n* [expert] economista *mf*.

economize, -ise [ɪ'kɒnəmaɪz] *vi* [save money, resources] economizar; **to** ~ **on sthg** economizar em algo.

economy [ɪ'kɒnəmɪ] (*pl* -ies) *n* economia *f*; **economies of scale** economias de escala.

economy class *n* classe *f* econômica.

economy-size(d) *adj* [pack, jar] de tamanho econômico.

ecosystem ['i:kəʊˌsɪstəm] *n* ecossistema *m*.

ecotax ['i:kəʊtæks] *n* ecotaxa *f*.

ecotourism [i:kəʊ'tʊərɪzm] *n* ecoturismo *m*.

ecstasy ['ekstəsɪ] (*pl* -ies) *n* -1. (*U*) [great happiness] êxtase *m* -2. [feeling of happiness]: **to go into ecstasies about sthg** entrar em êxtase por algo -3. [drug] ecstasy *m*.

ecstatic [ek'stætɪk] *adj* extasiado(da).

ecstatically [ek'stætɪklɪ] *adv* em êxtase.

ECT (*abbr of* **electroconvulsive therapy**) *n* terapia *f* de eletrochoque.

ectoplasm ['ektəplæzm] *n* (*U*) [of cell] ectoplasma *m*.

ECU, Ecu ['ekju:] (*abbr of* **European Currency Unit**) *n* Unidade *f* Monetária Européia.

Ecuador ['ekwədɔ:ʳ] *n* Equador; **in** ~ no Equador.

Ecuadoran [ˌekwə'dɔ:rən], **Ecuadorian** [ˌekwə'dɔ:rɪən] <> *adj* equatoriano(na). <> *n* equatoriano *m*, -na *f*.

ecumenical [i:kju'menɪkl] *adj* RELIG ecumênico(ca).

eczema ['eksmə] *n* (*U*) eczema *m*.

ed. -1. (*abbr of* **edited**) ed. -2. (*abbr of* **edition**) Ed. -3. (*abbr of* **editor**) ed.

eddy ['edɪ] (*pl* -ies, *pt* & *pp* -ied) <> *n* redemoinho *m*. <> *vi* redemoinhar.

Eden ['i:dn] *n*: **(the Garden of)** ~ (o Jardim do) Éden.

edge [edʒ] <> *n* -1. [outer limit] borda *f*; **to be on the** ~ **of sthg** estar à beira de algo -2. [of blade] fio *m* -3. [advantage]: **to have an** ~ **over sb/sth, to have the** ~ **on sb/sthg** levar ligeira vantagem sobre alguém/algo -4. (*U*) *fig* [in voice] rispidez *f*. <> *vi* [move slowly] avançar lentamente.
 on edge *adj* -1. [person] nervoso(sa) -2. [nerves] à flor da pele.

edged [edʒd] *adj*: ~ **with sthg** orlado(da) por algo.

edgeways ['edʒweɪz], **edgewise** ['edʒwaɪz] *adv* [sideways] de lado.

edging ['edʒɪŋ] *n* borda *f*.

edgy ['edʒɪ] (*compar* -ier, *superl* -iest) *adj* impaciente.

edible ['edɪbl] *adj* [safe to eat] comestível.

edict ['i:dɪkt] *n* [decree] edital *m*.

edifice ['edɪfɪs] *n fml* [building] edifício *m*.

edify ['edɪfaɪ] (*pt* & *pp* -ied) *vt fml* edificar.

edifying ['edɪfaɪŋ] *adj fml* edificante.

Edinburgh ['edɪmbrə] *n* Edimburgo.

Edinburgh Festival *n*: **the** ~ o Festival de Edimburgo.

edit ['edɪt] *vt* -1. [gen] editar -2. [correct] revisar; **to need** ~ **ing** precisar de revisão.
 edit out *vt sep* [word, sentence, passage] cortar.

edition [ɪ'dɪʃn] *n* edição *f*.

editor ['edɪtəʳ] *n* -1. [gen] editor *m*, -ra *f* -2. [copy editor] revisor *m*, -ra *f* -3. COMPUT editor *m* (de texto).

editorial [ˌedɪ'tɔ:rɪəl] <> *adj* editorial. <> *n* editorial *m*.

EDP (*abbr of* **electronic data processing**) *n* PED *m*.

EDT (*abbr of* **Eastern Daylight Time**) *n* horário de verão na zona leste dos Estados Unidos.

educate ['edʒʊkeɪt] *vt* -1. SCH & UNIV educar -2. [inform] informar.

educated ['edʒʊkeɪtd] *adj* [cultured] educado(da), culto(ta).

education [ˌedʒʊ'keɪʃn] *n* (*U*) -1. [activity, sector] educação *f*, ensino *m* -2. [process or result of teaching] educação *f*.

educational [ˌedʒʊ'keɪʃənl] *adj* -1. [establishment, policy] educacional -2. [toy, experience] educativo(-va).

educationalist [ˌedʒʊ'keɪʃnəlɪst] *n* especialista *mf* em educação.

educator ['edʒʊkeɪtəʳ] *n* US *fml* [teacher] educador *m*, -ra *f*.

Edwardian [ed'wɔ:dɪən] *adj* eduardiano(na), da época do rei Eduardo VII.

EEC (*abbr of* **European Economic Community**) *n* CEE *f*.

EEG *n* -1. (*abbr of* **electroencephalogram**) EEG *m*. -2. (*abbr of* **electroencephalograph**) eletrencefaló-grafo *m*.

eel [i:l] *n* enguia *f*.

EEOC (*abbr of* **Equal Employment Opportunity Commission**) *n* comissão norte-americana para a prevenção da discriminação no trabalho.

eerie ['ɪərɪ] *adj* lúgubre, sinistro(tra).

EET (*abbr of* **Eastern European Time**) *n* horário da Europa Oriental.

efface [ɪ'feɪs] *vt* apagar.

effect [ɪ'fekt] <> *n* -1. [gen] efeito *m*; **to have an** ~ **on sb/sthg** ter um efeito sobre alguém/algo; **to take** ~ [law, rule] entrar em vigor; [drug] fazer efeito; **to put sthg into** ~ pôr algo em prática; **for** ~ para impressionar -2. [meaning]: **to the** ~ **that** no sentido de que; **to that** ~ neste sentido. <> *vt* -1. [recovery, change] causar -2. [reconciliton, come-back, repairs] fazer.
 effects *npl* -1. : **(special)** ~ **s** efeitos (especiais) -2. [property] bens *mpl*.
 in effect *adv* na prática; **the law is in** ~ a lei está em vigor.

effective [ɪ'fektɪv] *adj* -1. [successful] eficaz -2. [actual, real] efetivo(va) -3. [in operation] em vigor.

effectively [ɪ'fektɪvlɪ] *adv* -1. [well, successfully] eficazmente -2. [in fact] efetivamente.

effectiveness [ɪ'fektɪvnɪs] *n* (*U*) [success, efficiency] eficácia *f*.

effeminate [ɪ'femɪnət] *adj pej* efeminado(da).

effervesce [ˌefə'ves] *vi* efervescer.

effervescent [ˌefə'vesənt] *adj* [liquid] efervescente.

effete [ɪ'fi:t] *adj pej* [weak, effeminate] efeminado(da).

efficacious [efɪ'keɪʃəs] *adj fml* eficaz.

efficacy ['efɪkəsɪ] *n* (*U*) [effectiveness] eficácia *f*.

efficiency [ɪ'fɪʃənsɪ] *n* (*U*) eficiência *f*.

efficient [ɪ'fɪʃənt] *adj* eficiente.

efficiently [ɪ'fɪʃəntlɪ] *adv* [competently] eficientemente.

effigy ['efɪdʒɪ] (*pl* -ies) *n* efígie *f*.

effluent ['efluənt] *n* efluente *m*.

effort ['efət] *n* -1. (*U*) [physical or mental exertion] esforço *m*; **to be worth the** ~ valer o esforço; **to make the** ~ **to do sthg** esforçar-se para fazer algo; **with** ~ com esforço -2. [attempt] esforço *m*, tentativa *f*; **to make an/no ~ to do sthg** empenhar-se/não se empenhar em fazer algo.

effortless ['efətlɪs] *adj* fácil, com desenvoltura.

effortlessly ['efətlɪslɪ] *adv* facilmente, sem esforço.

effrontery [ɪ'frʌntərɪ] *n (U)* atrevimento *m*.

effusive [ɪ'fju:sɪv] *adj* efusivo(va).

effusively [ɪ'fju:sɪvlɪ] *adv* efusivamente.

EFL (*abbr of* English as a Foreign Language) *n* inglês para estrangeiros.

EFTA ['eftə] (*abbr of* European Free Trade Association) *n* associação para o livre comércio europeu.

EFTS (*abbr of* electronic funds transfer system) *n* sistema que processa transferência eletrônica de fundos de uma conta para a outra.

e.g. (*abbr of* exempli gratia) *adv* e.g.

egalitarian [ɪ,gælɪ'teərɪən] *adj* igualitário(ria).

egg [eg] *n* **- 1.** [gen] ovo *m* **- 2.** [of woman] óvulo *m*.
➡ **egg on** *vt sep* instigar.

eggcup ['egkʌp] *n* oveiro *m*.

eggplant ['egplɑ:nt] *n US* berinjela *f*.

eggshell ['egʃel] *n* casca *f* de ovo.

egg timer *n* ampulheta *f (para marcar tempo de cozimento de um ovo)*.

egg whisk *n* batedor *m* de ovos.

egg white *n* clara *f* de ovo.

egg yolk [-jəʊk] *n* gema *f* de ovo.

EGM (*abbr of* extraordinary general meeting) *n* assembléia geral extraordinária, AGE *f*.

ego ['i:gəʊ] (*pl* -s) *n* [opinion of self] ego *m*.

egocentric [,i:gəʊ'sentrɪk] *adj fml & pej* [selfish] egocêntrico(ca).

egoism ['i:gəʊɪzm] *n (U)* [self-interest] egoísmo *m*.

egoist ['i:gəʊɪst] *n* [self-centred person] egoísta *mf*.

egoistic [,i:gəʊ'ɪstɪk] *adj* [self-centred] egoísta.

egotism ['i:gətɪzm] *n (U)* egotismo *m*, egoísmo *m*.

egotist ['i:gətɪst] *n* egotista *mf*, egoísta *mf*.

egotistic(al) [,i:gə'tɪstɪk(l)] *adj* egotista, egoísta.

ego trip *n inf* massagem *f* no ego.

Egypt ['i:dʒɪpt] *n* Egito; **in ~** no Egito.

Egyptian [ɪ'dʒɪpʃn] *adj* egípcio(cia). *n* [person] egípcio *m*, -cia *f*.

eh [eɪ] *excl UK inf* **- 1.** [inviting reply, agreement] ahã! **- 2.** [what did you say?] hmm? **- 3.** [expressing astonishment] ah!

eiderdown ['aɪdədaʊn] *n UK* [bed cover] edredom *m*.

eight [eɪt] *num* oito; *see also* **six**.

eighteen [,eɪ'ti:n] *num* dezoito; *see also* **six**.

eighteenth [,eɪ'ti:nθ] *num* décimo oitavo, décima oitava; *see also* **sixth**.

eighth [eɪtθ] *num* oitavo(va); *see also* **sixth**.

eightieth ['eɪtɪθ] *num* octagésimo(ma); *see also* **sixth**.

eighty ['eɪtɪ] (*pl* -ies) *num* oitenta; *see also* **sixty**.

Eire ['eərə] *n* (República da) Irlanda.

either ['aɪðər, 'i:ðər] *adj* **- 1.** [one or the other] qualquer; **~ side could win** qualquer um dos lados poderia ganhar; **she couldn't find ~ jumper** ela não conseguiu achar nenhuma das blusas; **~ way** de qualquer jeito; **I don't mind ~ way** por mim tanto faz **- 2.** [each] cada; **on ~ side** de cada

lado. *pron*: **~ (of them) will do** qualquer um (deles) serve; **I don't like ~ (of them)** não gosto de nenhum (dos dois). *adv (after negative)* também não; **they don't smoke ~** eles também não fumam. *conj*: **~ ... or ...** [in positive sentence] ou ...ou ...; [in negative sentence] nem ...nem ...; **~ he leaves or I do** ou ele sai ou saio eu; **you are not being ~ clever or funny** você não está sendo nem inteligente nem engraçado.

ejaculate [ɪ'dʒækjʊleɪt] *vt* [exclaim] exclamar. *vi* [have orgasm] ejacular.

eject [ɪ'dʒekt] *vt* **- 1.** [object] ejetar **- 2.** [person]: **to ~ sb (from)** expulsar alguém (de).

ejector seat *UK* [ɪ'dʒektər-], **ejection seat** *US* [ɪ'dʒekʃn-] *n* assento *m* ejetor.

eke [i:k] ➡ **eke out** *vt sep* [save - money] esticar; [- food, supply] racionar. *vt fus*: **to ~ out a living** ganhar a vida com dificuldade.

EKG (*abbr of* electrocardiogram) *n US* ECG *m*.

el (*abbr of* elevated railroad) *n US fam* elevado *m* férreo.

elaborate [*adj* ɪ'læbrət, *vb* ɪ'læbəreɪt] *adj* [complicated, detailed] elaborado(da). *vi*: **to ~ (on sthg)** detalhar (algo).

elaborately [ɪ'læbərətlɪ] *adv* [in detail] detalhadamente.

elapse [ɪ'læps] *vi* [time] transcorrer.

elastic [ɪ'læstɪk] *adj* **- 1.** [material, skin] elástico(ca) **- 2.** *fig* [plan, timetable] elástico(ca). *n (U)* [material] elástico *m*.

elasticated [ɪ'læstɪkeɪtɪd] *adj* [waistband] elástico(ca).

elastic band *n UK* elástico *m*.

elasticity [,elæ'stɪsətɪ] *n (U)* [stretchiness] elasticidade *f*.

elated [ɪ'leɪtɪd] *adj* exultante.

elation [ɪ'leɪʃn] *n (U)* exultação *f*.

elbow ['elbəʊ] *n* cotovelo *m*. *vt*: **to ~ sb aside** empurrar alguém com os cotovelos.

elbow grease *n (U) inf* duro *m* danado.

elbowroom ['elbəʊrʊm] *n inf* [physical space] espaço *m (para trabalhar)*.

elder ['eldər] *adj* [older] mais velho(lha), primogênito(ta). *n* **- 1.** [older person] velho *m*, -lha *f* **- 2.** [of tribe] ancião *m*, -ã *f* **- 3.** [of church] presbítero *m* **- 4.** *BOT*: **~ (tree)** sabugueiro *m*.

elderberry ['eldə,berɪ] (*pl* -ies) *n* **- 1.** [fruit] fruto *m* do sabugueiro **- 2.** [tree] sabugueiro *m*.

elderly ['eldəlɪ] *adj* [old - person] idoso(sa); [- thing] velho(lha), antigo(ga). *npl*: **the ~** os idosos.

elder statesman *n* estadista *mf* experiente.

eldest ['eldɪst] *adj* [oldest] mais velho(lha).

El Dorado *n* El Dorado.

elect [ɪ'lekt] *adj* eleito(ta). *vt* **- 1.** [by voting] eleger; **to ~ sb (as) sthg** eleger alguém (como) algo **- 2.** *fml* [choose]: **to ~ to do sthg** escolher fazer algo.

elected [ɪ'lektɪd] *adj* [president, chairperson] eleito(ta).

election [ɪ'lekʃn] *n* eleição *f*; **to have** *OR* **hold an ~** ter *OR* fazer uma eleição; **local ~s** eleições locais.

Nos EUA, as eleições presidenciais realizam-se a cada quatro anos. Por lei, o presidente não pode permanecer no cargo por mais de dois mandatos consecutivos. As eleições gerais britânicas realizam-se a cada cinco anos, mas o primeiro-ministro pode convocar eleições a qualquer momento. Tanto nos Estados Unidos como na Grã-Bretanha, o voto não é obrigatório.

election campaign n campanha f eleitoral.
electioneering [ɪˌlekʃə'nɪərɪŋ] n (U) **pej** propaganda f eleitoral, eleitoralismo m.
elective [ɪ'lektɪv] n **SCH** & **UNIV** disciplina f opcional.
elector [ɪ'lektə^r] n [voter] eleitor m, -ra f.
electoral [ɪ'lektərəl] adj eleitoral.
electoral college n **POL** colégio m eleitoral.
electoral register, electoral roll n: the ~ o registro dos eleitores.
electorate [ɪ'lektərət] n: the ~ o eleitorado.
electric [ɪ'lektrɪk] adj - **1.** [using or producing electricity] elétrico(ca) - **2.** fig [exciting] eletrizante.
◆ **electrics** npl **UK** inf [in car, machine] partes fpl elétricas.
electrical [ɪ'lektrɪkl] adj elétrico(ca).
electrical engineer n engenheiro m, -ra f eletricista.
electrical engineering n (U) engenharia f elétrica.
electrically [ɪ'lektrɪklɪ] adv [by electricity] eletricamente.
electrical shock n **US** = electric shock.
electric blanket n cobertor m elétrico.
electric chair n: the ~ a cadeira elétrica.
electric cooker n fogão m elétrico.
electric current n corrente f elétrica.
electric drill n furadeira f elétrica.
electric fence n cerca f elétrica.
electric fire n estufa f elétrica.
electric guitar n guitarra f elétrica.
electrician [ˌɪlek'trɪʃn] n eletricista mf.
electricity [ˌɪlek'trɪsətɪ] n - **1.** **ELEC** eletricidade f - **2.** fig [excitement] excitação f.
electric light n (U) luz f elétrica.
electric shock **UK**, **electrical shock** **US** n choque m elétrico.
electric storm n tempestade f elétrica.
electrify [ɪ'lektrɪfaɪ] (pt & pp -ied) vt - **1.** [convert to electric power] eletrificar - **2.** fig [excite] deixar eletrizado(da).
electrifying [ɪ'lektrɪfaɪŋ] adj fig [exciting] eletrizante.
electro- [ɪ'lektrəʊ] prefix eletro-.
electrocardiogram n **MED** eletrocardiograma m.
electrocardiograph [ɪˌlektrəʊ'kɑːdɪəgrɑːf] n **MED** eletrocardiógrafo m.
electrocardiography n **MED** eletrocardiografia f.
electrocute [ɪ'lektrəkjuːt] vt eletrocutar; to ~ o.s eletrocutar-se.
electrode [ɪ'lektrəʊd] n eletrodo m.

electroencephalogram n **MED** eletrencefalograma m.
electroencephalograph [ɪˌlektrəʊen'sefələgrɑːf] n **MED** eletrencefalógrafo m.
electroencephalography n **MED** eletrencefalografia f.
electrolysis [ˌɪlek'trɒləsɪs] n (U) eletrólise f.
electromagnet n eletroímã m.
electromagnetic [ɪˌlektrəʊmæg'netɪk] adj eletromagnético(ca).
electron [ɪ'lektrɒn] n elétron m.
electronic [ˌɪlek'trɒnɪk] adj eletrônico(ca).
◆ **electronics** <> n (U) [technology] eletrônica f. <> npl [equipment] componentes mpl eletrônicos.
electronic banking n serviço m bancário via internet.
electronic data processing n (U) processamento m eletrônico de dados.
electronic mail n (U) correio m eletrônico.
electronic organizer n agenda f eletrônica.
electron microscope n microscópio m eletrônico.
electroplated [ɪ'lektrəʊˌpleɪtɪd] adj galvanizado(da).
elegance ['elɪgəns] n (U) elegância f.
elegant ['elɪgənt] adj - **1.** [stylish, beautiful] elegante - **2.** [clever, neat] brilhante.
elegantly ['elɪgəntlɪ] adv - **1.** [stylishly, beautifully] elegantemente - **2.** [cleverly, neatly] brilhantemente.
elegy ['elɪdʒɪ] (pl -ies) n elegia f.
element ['elɪmənt] n - **1.** **SCIENCE** elemento m - **2.** [small amount, proportion] parcela f - **3.** [in heater, kettle] resistência f - **4.** pej [in society, group] elemento m - **5.** phr: to be in one's ~ estar em seu meio.
◆ **elements** npl - **1.** [basics] conhecimentos mpl básicos - **2.** [weather]: the ~ s os fenômenos atmosféricos.
elementary [ˌelɪ'mentərɪ] adj elementar.
elementary school n **US** escola f primária.
elephant ['elɪfənt] (pl inv **OR** -s) n elefante m
elevate ['elɪveɪt] vt - **1.** [give importance to, promote]: to ~ sb/sthg to sthg, to ~ sb/sthg into sthg elevar alguém/algo a algo - **2.** [raise physically] levantar.
elevated ['elɪveɪtɪd] adj fml - **1.** [person, situation] digno(na) - **2.** [idea, sentiment] elevado(da) - **3.** [platform, position] alto(ta).
elevated railway n ferrovia f elevada.
elevation [ˌelɪ'veɪʃn] n fml - **1.** (U) [promotion, raising of person] promoção f; [- of standards] elevação f - **2.** [of hill, land] altitude f.
elevator ['elɪveɪtə^r] n **US** elevador m.
eleven [ɪ'levn] num onze; see also **six**.
elevenses [ɪ'levnzɪz] n (U) **UK** lanche m rápido (às 11 da manhã).
eleventh [ɪ'levnθ] num décimo primeiro, décima primeira; see also **sixth**.
eleventh hour n fig: the ~ a última hora.
elf [elf] (pl **elves**) n elfo m.
elicit [ɪ'lɪsɪt] vt fml - **1.** [response, reaction]: to ~ sthg (from sb) obter algo (de alguém) - **2.** [information]: to ~ sthg (from sb) extrair algo (de alguém).

eligibility [ˌelɪdʒəˈbɪlətɪ] *n (U)* **- 1.** [suitability] eligibilidade *f* **- 2.** *dated* [of bachelor] aptidão *f (para o casamento)*.

eligible [ˈelɪdʒəbl] *adj* **- 1.** [suitable, qualified] elegível; **to be ~ for sthg/to do sthg** estar habilitado(da) a algo/a fazer algo **- 2.** *dated* [marriageable]: **to be ~** ser um bom partido.

eliminate [ɪˈlɪmɪneɪt] *vt* **- 1.** [remove]: **to ~ sb/sthg (from)** eliminar alguém/algo (de) **- 2.** [in sport, competition]: **to be ~ d from sthg** ser eliminado(da) de algo.

elimination [ɪˌlɪmɪˈneɪʃn] *n (U)* eliminação *f*.

elite [ɪˈliːt] ◇ *adj* de elite. ◇ *n* elite *f*.

elitism [ɪˈliːtɪzm] *n (U) pej* elitismo *m*.

elitist [ɪˈliːtɪst] *pej* ◇ *adj* elitista. ◇ *n* elitista *mf*.

elixir [ɪˈlɪksəʳ] *n literary* **- 1.** [magic drink] elixir *m* **- 2.** *fig* [magic cure] poção *f* mágica.

Elizabethan [ɪˌlɪzəˈbiːθn] ◇ *adj* elizabetano(na). ◇ *n* elizabetano *m*, -na *f*.

elk [elk] (*pl inv OR* **-s**) *n* alce *m*.

ellipse [ɪˈlɪps] *n* elipse *f*.

elliptical [ɪˈlɪptɪkl] *adj* **- 1.** [in shape] elíptico(ca) **- 2.** *fml* [phrase, remark] obscuro(ra).

elm [elm] *n*: **~ (tree)** olmo *m*.

elocution [ˌeləˈkjuːʃn] *n (U)* elocução *f*.

elongated [ˈiːlɒŋgeɪtɪd] *adj* alongado(da).

elope [ɪˈləʊp] *vi*: **to ~ (with sb)** fugir para casar (com alguém).

elopement [ɪˈləʊpmənt] *n* fuga *f (com o namorado)*.

eloquence [ˈeləkwənsl] *n (U)* eloqüência *f*.

eloquent [ˈeləkwənt] *adj* eloqüente.

eloquently [ˈeləkwəntlɪ] *adv* eloqüentemente.

El Salvador [ˌelˈsælvədɔːʳ] *n* El Salvador; **in ~** em El Salvador.

else [els] *adv*: **anything ~** mais alguma coisa; **he doesn't need anything ~** ele não precisa de nada mais; **everyone ~** todos os outros, todas as outras; **nothing ~** nada mais; **someone ~** alguma outra pessoa; **something ~** outra coisa; **somewhere ~** outro lugar; **who/what/where ~?** quem/que/onde mais?
⇢ **or else** *conj* **- 1.** [or if not] ou então, senão **- 2.** [as threat] senão.

elsewhere [elsˈweəʳ] *adv* em outro lugar.

ELT (*abbr of* **English Language Teaching**) *n.* ensino *m* de língua inglese

elucidate [ɪˈluːsɪdeɪt] *fml* ◇ *vt* elucidar. ◇ *vi* elucidar.

elude [ɪˈluːd] *vt* escapar de; **his name ~ s me completely** o nome dele me escapa totalmente.

elusive [ɪˈluːsɪv] *adj* esquivo(va), evasivo(va).

elves [elvz] *pl* ⊳ **elf**.

'em [əm] *cont inf* = **them**.

emaciated [ɪˈmeɪʃɪeɪtɪd] *adj* emagrecido (da).

e-mail *n COMPUT* e-mail *m*, correio *m* eletrônico.

e-mail address *n* endereço *m* (de correio) eletrônico, e-mail *m*.

e-mail phone *n* telefone *m* com correio eletrônico.

emanate [ˈeməneɪt] *fml* ◇ *vt* emanar. ◇ *vi*: **to ~ from** emanar de.

emancipate [ɪˈmænsɪpeɪt] *vt*: **to ~ sb (from sthg)** emancipar alguém (de algo).

emancipation [ɪˌmænsɪˈpeɪʃn] *n (U)*: **~ (from sthg)** emancipação *f* (de algo).

emasculate [ɪˈmæskjʊleɪt] *vt fml* [weaken] enfraquecer.

emasculation [ɪˌmæskjʊˈleɪʃn] *n (U) fml* [weakening] enfraquecimento *m*.

embalm [ɪmˈbaːm] *vt* [body] embalsamar.

embankment [ɪmˈbæŋkmənt] *n* **- 1.** [along road, railway] barreira *f* **- 2.** [along river] margem *f*.

embargo [emˈbaːgəʊ] (*pl* **-es**, *pt & pp* **-ed**, *cont* **-ing**) ◇ *n* **- 1.** [gen]: **~ (on sthg)** embargo *m* (de algo) **- 2.** *fig* [ban]: **~ (on sthg)** proibição *f* (de algo). ◇ *vt* **- 1.** *COMM & POL* embargar **- 2.** *fig* [ban] proibir.

embark [ɪmˈbaːk] *vi* **- 1.** [board ship]: **to ~ (on)** embarcar(em) **- 2.** [start]: **to ~ (up)on sthg** dar início (a algo).

embarkation [ˌembaːˈkeɪʃn] *n* embarque *m*.

embarkation card *n UK* cartão *m* de embarque.

embarrass [ɪmˈbærəs] *vt* [shame] envergonhar.

embarrassed [ɪmˈbærəst] *adj* [self-conscious] envergonhado(da).

embarrassing [ɪmˈbærəsɪŋ] *adj* [shameful] embaraçoso(sa).

embarrassment [ɪmˈbærəsmənt] *n* vergonha *f*.

embassy [ˈembəsɪ] (*pl* **-ies**) *n* embaixada *f*.

embattled [ɪmˈbætld] *adj* [troubled] em dificuldade.

embedded [ɪmˈbedɪd] *adj* **- 1.** [buried]: **~ in sthg** enterrado(da) em algo **- 2.** *COMPUT*: **~ in sthg** embutido(da) em algo **- 3.** *fig* [ingrained] enraizado(da).

embellish [ɪmˈbelɪʃ] *vt* **- 1.** [room, garment]: **to ~ sthg with sthg** embelezar algo com algo **- 2.** *fig* [story, account] enfeitar.

embers [ˈembəz] *npl* brasa *f*.

embezzle [ɪmˈbezl] *vt* [money] desviar.

embezzlement [ɪmˈbezlmənt] *n (U)* desvio *m (de dinheiro)*.

embezzler [ɪmˈbezləʳ] *n* defraudador *m*, -ra *f*.

embittered [ɪmˈbɪtəd] *adj* amargurado(da).

emblazoned [ɪmˈbleɪzndl] *adj*: **~ (on sthg)** gravado(da) (em algo); **~ (with sthg)** ornado(da) (com algo).

emblem [ˈembləm] *n* [symbolic design] emblema *m*.

embodiment [ɪmˈbɒdɪmənt] *n* [epitome] personificação *f*.

embody [ɪmˈbɒdɪ] (*pt & pp* **-ied**) *vt* **- 1.** [epitomize] personificar **- 2.** [include]: **to be embodied in sthg** estar incorporado(da) em algo.

embolism [ˈembəlɪzml] *n* embolia *f*.

embossed [ɪmˈbɒst] *adj* **- 1.** [material] em relevo **- 2.** [design, lettering]: **~ (on sthg)** em relevo (sobre algo).

embrace [ɪmˈbreɪs] ◇ *n* abraço *m*. ◇ *vt* **- 1.** [person] abraçar **- 2.** *fml* [religion, way of life] converter-se a **- 3.** *fml* [aspects, elements] conter. ◇ *vi* abraçar-se.

embrocation [ˌembrəˈkeɪʃn] *n (U) fml* [liquid] embrocação *f*.

embroider [ɪmˈbrɔɪdəʳ] ◇ *vt* **- 1.** *SEWING* bordar **- 2.** *pej* [embellish] enfeitar. ◇ *vi SEWING* bordar.

embroidered [ɪmˈbrɔɪdəd] *adj SEWING* bordado(da).

embroidery [ɪm'brɔɪdərɪ] *n (U)* bordado *m*.
embroil [ɪm'brɔɪl] *vt*: **to get/be** ~**ed (in sthg)** envolver-se/ser envolvido(da) (em algo).
embryo ['embrɪəʊ] (*pl* **-s**) *n* **-1.** *BIOL* embrião *m* **-2.** *fig* [beginnings]: **in** ~ em estado embrionário.
embryonic [,embrɪ'ɒnɪk] *adj fig* [emergent] embrionário(ria).
emcee (*abbr of* master of ceremonies) *n US* mestre *mf* de cerimônias.
emend [ɪ'mend] *vt* corrigir.
emerald ['emərəld] ◇ *adj* [colour] esmeralda. ◇ *n* [stone] esmeralda *f*.
emerge [ɪ'mɜːdʒ] ◇ *vi* **-1.** [come out] aparecer; **to** ~ **from sthg** surgir de algo **-2.** [from experience, situation]: **to** ~ **from** surgir de **-3.** [become known - facts, truth] vir à tona; [- writer, movement] surgir. ◇ *vt*: **it** ~**s that** vem à tona que.
emergence [ɪ'mɜːdʒəns] *n (U)* surgimento *m*, aparecimento *m*.
emergency [ɪ'mɜːdʒənsɪ] (*pl* **-ies**) ◇ *adj* de emergência. ◇ *n* emergência *f*.
emergency brake *n US* [of car] freio *m* de mão.
emergency exit *n* saída *f* de emergência.
emergency landing *n* pouso *m* de emergência.
emergency number *n* número *m* de emergência.
emergency room *n US* [in hospital] sala *f* de emergência.
emergency services *npl* serviços *mpl* de emergência.
emergency stop *n* parada *f* de emergência.
emergent [ɪ'mɜːdʒənt] *adj* emergente.
emery board ['emərɪ-] *n* lixa *f (de unhas)*.
emetic [ɪ'metɪk] ◇ *adj* que provoca vômitos. ◇ *n* vomitório *m*.
emigrant ['emɪɡrənt] *n* emigrante *mf*.
emigrate ['emɪɡreɪt] *vi* emigrar; **to** ~ **to/from** emigrar para/de.
emigration [,emɪ'ɡreɪʃn] *n (U)* emigração *f*.
émigré ['emɪɡreɪ] *n fml* exilado *m* político, exilada *f* política.
eminence ['emɪnəns] *n (U)* [prominence] eminência *f*.
eminent ['emɪnənt] *adj* [distinguished] eminente.
eminently ['emɪnəntlɪ] *adv fml* [extremely] eminentemente.
emir [e'mɪəʳ] *n* emir *m*.
emissary ['emɪsərɪ] (*pl* **-ies**) *n fml* emissário *m*, -ria *f*.
emission [ɪ'mɪʃn] *n fml* emissão *f*.
emit [ɪ'mɪt] (*pt & pp* **-ted**, *cont* **-ting**) *vt fml* emitir.
emollient [ɪ'mɒlɪənt] *n fml* emoliente *m*.
emolument [ɪ'mɒljʊmənt] *n fml* [payment fee] honorários *mpl*; [salary] remuneração *f*.
emoticon [ɪ'məʊtɪkɒn] *n COMPUT* emoticon *m*.
emotion [ɪ'məʊʃn] *n* emoção *f*.
emotional [ɪ'məʊʃənl] *adj* **-1.** [easily moved] emotivo(va) **-2.** [charged with emotion] emocionado(da) **-3.** [appealing to the emotions] comovente.
emotionally [ɪ'məʊʃnəlɪ] *adv* emocionalmente.
emotionless [ɪ'məʊʃnlɪs] *adj* sem emoção.
emotive [ɪ'məʊtɪv] *adj* emotivo(va), emocionante.
empathy ['empəθɪ] *n (U)*: ~ **(with sb)** empatia *f* (com alguém).

emperor ['empərəʳ] *n* imperador *m*.
emphasis ['emfəsɪs] (*pl* **-ases** [-əsiːz]) *n*: ~ **(on sthg)** ênfase *f* (em algo); **to lay** OR **place** ~ **on sthg** dar ênfase a algo.
emphasize, -ise ['emfəsaɪz] *vt* enfatizar.
emphatic [ɪm'fætɪk] *adj* [forceful] enfático(ca).
emphatically [ɪm'fætɪklɪ] *adv* **-1.** [with emphasis] enfaticamente **-2.** [definitely] terminantemente.
emphysema [,emfɪ'siːmə] *n (U)* enfisema *m*.
empire ['empaɪəʳ] *n* império *m*.
empire building *n* desenvolvimento *m* de impérios econômicos.
empirical [ɪm'pɪrɪkl] *adj* empírico(ca).
empiricism [ɪm'pɪrɪsɪzm] *n (U)* empirismo *m*.
employ [ɪm'plɔɪ] *vt* **-1.** [give work to] empregar; **to be** ~**ed as sthg** estar empregado(da) como algo **-2.** *fml* [use] empregar; **to** ~ **sthg as sthg/to do sthg** empregar algo como algo/para fazer algo.
employable [ɪm'plɔɪəbl] *adj* empregável.
employee [ɪm'plɔɪiː] *n* empregado *m*, -da *f*.
employer [ɪm'plɔɪəʳ] *n* empregador *m*, -ra *f*.
employment [ɪm'plɔɪmənt] *n* **-1.** [being in work] emprego *m*; **to be in** ~ estar empregado(da) **-2.** [work] trabalho *m*.
employment agency *n* agência *f* de empregos.
employment office *n* agência *m* de empregos.
emporium [em'pɔːrɪəm] *n* empório *m*.
empower [ɪm'paʊəʳ] *vt fml*: **to be** ~**ed to do sthg** receber autoridade para fazer algo.
empress ['emprɪs] *n* imperatriz *f*.
emptiness ['emptɪnɪs] *n (U)* vazio *m*.
empty ['emptɪ] (*compar* **-ier**, *superl* **-iest**, *pt & pp* **-ied**, *pl* **-ies**) ◇ *adj* vazio(zia). ◇ *vt* esvaziar; **to** ~ **sthg into/out of sthg** despejar algo em/de dentro de algo. ◇ *vi* [become empty] esvaziar. ◇ *n inf* casco *m*.
empty-handed [-'hændɪd] *adv* de mãos vazias.
empty-headed [-'hedɪd] *adj pej* de cabeça vazia.
EMS (*abbr of* European Monetary System) *n* SMT *m*.
emu ['iːmjuː] (*pl inv* OR **-s**) *n* emu *f*.
EMU (*abbr of* Economic and Monetary Union) *n* UME *f*.
emulate ['emjʊleɪt] *vt* **-1.** [gen] imitar **-2.** *COMPUT* emular.
emulsion [ɪ'mʌlʃn] ◇ *n* **-1.**: ~ **(paint)** tinta *f* plástica **-2.** *PHOT* emulsão *f*. ◇ *vt UK* [paint] pintar *(com tinta plástica)*.
enable [ɪ'neɪbl] *vt*: **to** ~ **sb to do sthg** permitir que alguém faça algo.
enact [ɪ'nækt] *vt* **-1.** *JUR* promulgar **-2.** [act] representar.
enactment [ɪ'næktmənt] *n* **-1.** *JUR* promulgação *f* **-2.** [of scene, play] representação *f*.
enamel [ɪ'næml] *n (U)* esmalte *m*.
enamelled *UK*, **enameled** *US* [ɪ'næmld] *adj* esmaltado(da).
enamel paint *n (U)* tinta *f* esmalte.
enamoured *UK*, **enamored** *US* [ɪ'næməd] *adj*: ~ **of sb/sthg** encantado(da) por alguém/algo.
en bloc [ɑːˈblɒk] *adv fml* em bloco.

enc. -1. (*abbr of* **enclosure**) anexo *m*. **-2.** (*abbr of* **enclosed**) anexo(xa).

encamp *vi* acampar, acampar-se.

encampment [ɪnˈkæmpmənt] *n* [of soldiers, gipsies] acampamento *m*.

encapsulate [ɪnˈkæpsjʊleɪt] *vt* *fig* [philosophy, idea]: **to ~ sthg (in)** resumir algo (em).

encase [ɪnˈkeɪs] *vt*: **~d in sthg** envolvido(da) em algo.

encash [ɪnˈkæʃ] *vt* *UK* [cheque] descontar.

enchanted [ɪnˈtʃɑːntɪd] *adj* **-1.** [delighted]: **~ (by** *or* **with sthg)** encantado(da) (por *or* com algo) **-2.** [under a spell] encantado(da).

enchanting [ɪnˈtʃɑːntɪŋ] *adj* encantador(ra).

encircle [ɪnˈsɜːkl] *vt* cercar.

enclave [ˈenkleɪv] *n* [of country] enclave *m*.

enclose [ɪnˈkləʊz] *vt* **-1.** [surround, contain] cercar; **~d by** *or* **with sthg** cercado(da) por *or* com algo **-2.** [put in envelope] anexar; **please find ~d ...** segue anexo(xa) ...

enclosure [ɪnˈkləʊʒəʳ] *n* **-1.** [place] cercado *m* **-2.** [in letter] anexo *m*.

encompass [ɪnˈkʌmpəs] *vt* *fml* **-1.** [include] abranger **-2.** [surround] cercar.

encore [ˈɒŋkɔːʳ] ⬦ *n* [by singer, performer] bis *m*. ⬦ *excl* bis!

encounter [ɪnˈkaʊntəʳ] ⬦ *n* encontro *m*. ⬦ *vt* *fml* **-1.** [person] encontrar, encontrar-se com **-2.** [problem, difficulty etc.] deparar-se com.

encourage [ɪnˈkʌrɪdʒ] *vt* **-1.** [give confidence to]: **to ~ sb (to do sthg)** incentivar alguém (a fazer algo) **-2.** [foster] incentivar, estimular.

encouragement [ɪnˈkʌrɪdʒmənt] *n* (*U*) incentivo *m*, estímulo *m*.

encouraging [ɪnˈkʌrɪdʒɪŋ] *adj* incentivador(ra).

encroach [ɪnˈkrəʊtʃ] *vi*: **to ~ (up)on sthg** apossar-se de algo; [rights] abusar de algo; [privacy] invadir algo.

encrusted [ɪnˈkrʌstɪd] *adj*: **~ with sthg** incrustado(da) de algo.

encrypt [ɪnˈkrɪpt] *vt* *COMPUT* criptografar.

encumber [ɪnˈkʌmbəʳ] *vt* *fml*: **to be ~ed with sthg** estar carregado(da) de algo; [debts] estar sobrecarregado(da) de algo.

encyclop(a)edia [ɪnˌsaɪkləˈpiːdjə] *n* enciclopédia *f*.

encyclop(a)edic [ɪnˌsaɪkləʊˈpiːdɪk] *adj* enciclopédico(ca).

end [end] ⬦ *n* **-1.** [last part, finish] fim *m*, final *m*; **to be at an ~** estar no fim; **to come to an ~** acabar, chegar ao fim; **to put an ~ to sthg** pôr fim a algo; **at the ~ of the day** *fig* no final das contas; **in the ~** [finally] finalmente **-2.** [tip, edge] extremidade *f* **-3.** [point, final section] ponta *f*; **from ~ to ~** de ponta a ponta **-4.** [side, one of two ends, of phone line] lado *m*; **which ~ does it open?** de que lado abre?; **to make ~s meet** conseguir que o dinheiro chegue **-5.** *fml* [purpose] fim *m*, objetivo *m*; **an ~ in itself** um fim em si mesmo **-6.** *literary* [death] fim *m*. ⬦ *vt* acabar, terminar; **to ~ sthg with** acabar *or* terminar algo com. ⬦ *vi* [finish] acabar, terminar; **to ~ in** acabar em; **to ~ with** acabar *or* terminar com.

on end *adv* **-1.** [upright] em pé **-2.** [continuously] a fio.

no end *adv* *inf*: **it cheered me up no ~** me alegrou o tempo inteirinho.

no end of *prep* *inf* um mar de.

end up *vi* acabar, terminar; **to ~ up doing sthg** acabar fazendo algo.

endanger [ɪnˈdeɪndʒəʳ] *vt* pôr em perigo.

endangered species [ɪnˈdeɪndʒəd-] *n* espécie *f* em perigo de extinção.

endear [ɪnˈdɪəʳ] *vt*: **to ~ sb to sb** fazer com que alguém conquiste alguém; **to ~ o.s. to sb** conquistar a afeição de alguém.

endearing [ɪnˈdɪərɪŋ] *adj* simpático(ca).

endearment [ɪnˈdɪəmənt] *n* *fml* palavra *f* carinhosa.

endeavour *UK*, **endeavor** *US* [ɪnˈdevəʳ] *fml* ⬦ *n* tentativa *f*, esforço *m*. ⬦ *vt*: **to ~ to do sthg** tentar fazer algo.

endemic [enˈdemɪk] *adj* endêmico(ca).

ending [ˈendɪŋ] *n* **-1.** [gen] final *m* **-2.** *GRAM* terminação *f*.

endive [ˈendaɪv] *n* **-1.** [salad vegetable] endívia *f* **-2.** [chicory] chicória *f*.

endless [ˈendlɪs] *adj* **-1.** [unending] interminável **-2.** [inexhaustible] inesgotável **-3.** [vast] sem fim.

endlessly [ˈendlɪslɪ] *adv* **-1.** [in time] interminavelmente **-2.** [in amount, degree] infinitamente.

endorse [ɪnˈdɔːs] *vt* **-1.** [approve] endossar **-2.** *UK* [driving licence]: **to have one's licence ~d** receber pontos na carteira.

endorsement [ɪnˈdɔːsmənt] *n* **-1.** (*U*) [gen] endosso *m* **-2.** *UK* [on driving licence] pontos *mpl*.

endow [ɪnˈdaʊ] *vt* **-1.** [equip]: **to be ~ed with sthg** ser dotado(da) de algo **-2.** [donate money to] dotar.

endowment [ɪnˈdaʊmənt] *n* dote *m*.

endowment insurance *n* seguro *m* dotal.

endowment mortgage *n* *UK* hipoteca *f* dotal.

end product *n* produto *m* final.

end result *n* resultado *m* final.

endurable [ɪnˈdjʊərəbl] *adj* suportável.

endurance [ɪnˈdjʊərəns] *n* (*U*) resistência *f*.

endurance test *n* teste *m* de resistência.

endure [ɪnˈdjʊəʳ] ⬦ *vt* resistir, suportar. ⬦ *vi* *fml* perdurar.

enduring [ɪnˈdjʊərɪŋ] *adj* *fml* perdurável.

end user *n* usuário *m*, -ria *f* final.

endways *UK* [ˈendweɪz], **endwise** *US* [ˈendwaɪz] *adv* **-1.** [lengthways] de frente **-2.** [end to end] ponta a ponta.

enema [ˈenəmə] *n* *MED* enema *m*.

enemy [ˈenɪmɪ] (*pl* -ies) ⬦ *n* **-1.** [person] inimigo *m*, -ga *f* **-2.** *MIL*: **the ~** o inimigo. ⬦ *comp* inimigo(ga).

energetic [ˌenəˈdʒetɪk] *adj* **-1.** [lively] ativo(va) **-2.** [physically taxing] vigoroso(sa) **-3.** [enthusiastic] ativo(va).

energy [ˈenədʒɪ] (*pl* -ies) *n* (*U*) energia *f*.

energy-saving *adj* [device] que poupa energia.

enervating [ˈenəveɪtɪŋ] *adj* *fml* desgastante.

enfold [ɪnˈfəʊld] *vt* *literary* **-1.** [engulf] envolver **-2.** [embrace]: **to ~ sb (in sthg)** envolver alguém (em algo).

enforce [ɪn'fɔːs] *vt* **-1.** [law] fazer cumprir, aplicar **-2.** [standards, discipline] impor.
enforceable [ɪn'fɔːsəbl] *adj* aplicável.
enforced [ɪn'fɔːst] *adj* **-1.** [obligatory] compulsório(ria) **-2.** [unavoidable] inevitável.
enforcement [ɪn'fɔːsmənt] *n (U)* aplicação *f*.
enfranchise [ɪn'fræntʃaɪz] *vt* **-1.** [give vote to] conferir o direito de voto a **-2.** [set free] emancipar.
engage [ɪn'geɪdʒ] ⟨⟩ *vt* **-1.** [attract] atrair; **to ~ sb in conversation** travar conversa com alguém **-2.** *TECH* engrenar **-3.** *fml* [employ] contratar; **to be ~d in** *OR* **on sthg** dedicar-se a algo; [busy with] estar ocupado(da) em algo. ⟨⟩ *vi* [be involved]: **to ~ in** envolver-se em.
engaged [ɪn'geɪdʒd] *adj* **-1.** [couple] noivo(va); **~ to sb** noivo(va) de alguém; **to get ~** noivar **-2.** [busy, occupied] ocupado(da); **~ in sthg** envolvido(da) em algo **-3.** [phone, toilet] ocupado(da).
engaged tone *n UK* sinal *m* de ocupado.
engagement [ɪn'geɪdʒmənt] *n* **-1.** [of couple] noivado *m* **-2.** [appointment] compromisso *m*.
engagement ring *n* anel *m* de noivado.
engaging [ɪn'geɪdʒɪŋ] *adj* atraente.
engender [ɪn'dʒendəʳ] *vt fml* gerar.
engine ['endʒɪn] *n* **-1.** [of car, plane, ship] motor *m* **-2.** *RAIL* locomotiva *f*.
engine driver *n UK* maquinista *mf*.
engineer [ˌendʒɪ'nɪəʳ] ⟨⟩ *n* **-1.** [of roads, machines, bridges] engenheiro *m*, -ra *f* **-2.** [on ship] técnico *m*, -ca *f* **-3.** *US* [engine driver] maquinista *mf*. ⟨⟩ *vt* **-1.** [construct] construir **-2.** [contrive] tramar.
engineering [ˌendʒɪ'nɪərɪŋ] *n* engenharia *f*.
England ['ɪŋglənd] *n* Inglaterra; **in ~** na Inglaterra.
English ['ɪŋglɪʃ] ⟨⟩ *adj* inglês(esa). ⟨⟩ *n* [language] inglês *m*. ⟨⟩ *npl*: **the ~** os ingleses.
English breakfast *n* café *m* da manhã inglês.

English Channel *n*: **the ~** o Canal da Mancha.
Englishman ['ɪŋglɪʃmən] (*pl* **-men** [-mən]) *n* inglês *m*.
English muffin *n US* pãozinho redondo e chato que se costuma torrar antes de comer.
Englishwoman ['ɪŋglɪʃˌwʊmən] (*pl* **-women** [-ˌwɪmɪn]) *n* inglesa *f*.
engrave [ɪn'greɪv] *vt* **-1.** [metal, glass] gravar **-2.** [design]: **to ~ sthg (on sthg)** gravar algo (em algo) **-3.** *fig* [on memory] gravar.
engraver [ɪn'greɪvəʳ] *n* gravador *m*, -ra *f*.
engraving [ɪn'greɪvɪŋ] *n* **-1.** [design] gravura *f* **-2.** *(U)* [skill] gravação *f*.
engrossed [ɪn'grəʊst] *adj*: **to be ~ (in sthg)** estar absorto(ta) (em algo).
engrossing [ɪn'grəʊsɪŋ] *adj* absorvente.

engulf [ɪn'gʌlf] *vt* **-1.** [cover, surround - subj: fire] devorar; [- subj: water] tragar **-2.** *fig* [overwhelm] tomar conta de.
enhance [ɪn'hɑːns] *vt* **-1.** [increase] aumentar **-2.** [improve] melhorar **-3.** [heighten: beauty, graphics] realçar.
enhancement [ɪn'hɑːnsmənt] *n* **-1.** *(U)* [increase] aumento *m* **-2.** [improvement] melhoria *f* **-3.** *COMPUT* realçamento *m*.
enigma [ɪ'nɪgmə] *n* enigma *m*.
enigmatic [ˌenɪg'mætɪk] *adj* enigmático(ca).
enjoy [ɪn'dʒɔɪ] ⟨⟩ *vt* **-1.** [like] gostar de; **to ~ doing sthg** gostar de fazer algo; **to ~ o.s.** divertir-se **-2.** *fml* [possess] desfrutar de. ⟨⟩ *vi US*: **~ !** [enjoy yourself] divirta-se!; [before meal] bom apetite!
enjoyable [ɪn'dʒɔɪəbl] *adj* agradável.
enjoyment [ɪn'dʒɔɪmənt] *n* **-1.** *(U)* prazer *m* **-2.** *(U) fml* [possession] gozo *m*, desfrute *m*.
enlarge [ɪn'lɑːdʒ] *vt* ampliar.
    ◆ **enlarge (up)on** *vt fus* desenvolver.
enlargement [ɪn'lɑːdʒmənt] *n* **-1.** *(U)* [gen] ampliação *f* **-2.** *MED* dilatação *f*.
enlighten [ɪn'laɪtn] *vt fml* esclarecer.
enlightened [ɪn'laɪtnd] *adj* esclarecido(da).
enlightening [ɪn'laɪtnɪŋ] *adj* esclarecedor(ra).
enlightenment [ɪn'laɪtnmənt] *n (U)* esclarecimento *m*.
    ◆ **Enlightenment** *n*: **the Enlightenment** o Iluminismo.
enlist [ɪn'lɪst] ⟨⟩ *vt* **-1.** *MIL* [recruit] recrutar **-2.** [support, help] angariar. ⟨⟩ *vi MIL*: **to ~ (in)** alistar-se(em).
enlisted man [ɪn'lɪstɪd-] *n US* recruta *m*.
enliven [ɪn'laɪvn] *vt* animar.
en masse [ˌɒn'mæs] *adv* em massa.
enmeshed [ɪn'meʃt] *adj*: **to be ~ in sthg** estar enredado(da) em algo.
enmity ['enmətɪ] (*pl* **-ies**) *n (U)* inimizade *f*.
ennoble [ɪ'nəʊbl] *vt* **-1.** [elevate to nobility] nobilitar **-2.** [dignify] enobrecer.
enormity [ɪ'nɔːmətɪ] *n (U)* enormidade *f*.
enormous [ɪ'nɔːməs] *adj* enorme.
enormously [ɪ'nɔːməslɪ] *adv* enormemente.
enough [ɪ'nʌf] ⟨⟩ *adj* suficiente. ⟨⟩ *pron* suficiente; **to have had ~ (of sthg)** [expressing annoyance] estar farto(ta) (de algo); **more than ~** mais que suficiente; **~ is ~** já chega; **that's ~ (of that)!** chega! ⟨⟩ *adv* **-1.** [sufficiently] suficientemente, bastante; **to suffer ~** sofrer o bastante; **he hasn't tried hard ~** ele ainda não tentou o suficiente; **to be good ~ to do sthg** *fml* ter a bondade de fazer algo **-2.** [rather] bastante; **strangely ~** curiosamente.
enquire [ɪn'kwaɪəʳ] *vt* & *vi* = inquire.
enquiry [ɪn'kwaɪərɪ] (*pl* **-ies**) *n* = inquiry.
enraged [ɪn'reɪdʒd] *adj* enfurecido(da).
enrich [ɪn'rɪtʃ] *vt* enriquecer.
enrol *UK* (*pt* & *pp* **-led**, *cont* **-ling**), **enroll** *US* [ɪn'rəʊl] ⟨⟩ *vt* matricular. ⟨⟩ *vi*: **to ~ (on** *OR* **in sthg)** matricular-se (em algo).
enrolment *UK*, **enrollment** *US* [ɪn'rəʊlmənt] *n* **-1.** *(U)* [act of registering] inscrição *f* **-2.** [entry in register] matrícula *f*.

en route [ˌɒnˈruːt] *adv*: ~ **(from)** vindo de: ~ **(to)** a caminho de.

ensconced [ɪnˈskɒnst] *adj fml* [in chair] acomodado(-da).

enshrine [ɪnˈʃraɪn] *vt*: **to be** ~**d in sthg** estar amparado(da) em algo, ser garantido(da) por algo.

ensign [ˈensaɪn] *n* -**1.** [flag] bandeira *f* -**2.** *US* [sailor] guarda-marinha *mf*.

enslave [ɪnˈsleɪv] *vt* escravizar.

ensue [ɪnˈsjuː] *vi fml* resultar.

ensuing [ɪnˈsjuːɪŋ] *adj fml* subseqüente.

ensure [ɪnˈʃʊəʳ] *vt* assegurar; **to** ~ **(that)** assegurar que.

ENT (*abbr of* **ear, nose and throat**) *n* otorrino *mf*.

entail [ɪnˈteɪl] *vt* [involve] implicar.

entangled [ɪnˈtæŋgld] *adj* -**1.** [ensnared]: **to be** ~ **in sthg** estar emaranhado(da) em algo -**2.** [involved]: **to be** ~ **in sthg** estar envolvido(da) em algo; **to be** ~ **with sb** estar envolvido(da) com alguém.

entanglement [ɪnˈtæŋglmənt] *n* [involvement] envolvimento *m*.

enter [ˈentəʳ] <> *vt* -**1.** [come or go into] entrar em -**2.** [join - competition, race, the church] entrar em; [- school, politics, parliament] ingressar em; [- armed forces] alistar-se em; [- university] matricular-se em -**3.** [register]: **to** ~ **sb/sthg for sthg** inscrever alguém/algo em algo -**4.** [write down] registrar -**5.** *COMPUT* inserir; ~ **your name, please** insira seu nome. <> *vi* -**1.** [come or go in] entrar -**2.** [register]: **to** ~ **(for sthg)** inscrever-se (para algo).

 ◆ **enter into** *vt fus* -**1.** [begin] iniciar -**2.** [become involved in] comprometer-se em -**3.** [affect]: **money shouldn't** ~ **into it** o dinheiro não deveria contar aqui.

enteritis [ˌentəˈraɪtɪs] *n* (*U*) enterite *f*.

enter key *n* *COMPUT* tecla *f* enter.

enterprise [ˈentəpraɪz] *n* -**1.** [company, business] empresa *f* -**2.** [venture] aventura *f* -**3.** (*U*) [initiative] empreendimento *m*.

enterprise culture *n* cultura *f* empresarial.

enterprise zone *n* *UK* zona do Reino Unido na qual se fomenta a atividade cultural e empresarial.

enterprising [ˈentəpraɪzɪŋ] *adj* empreendedor(-ra).

entertain [ˌentəˈteɪn] <> *vt* -**1.** [amuse] entreter -**2.** [have as guest] receber -**3.** *fml* [consider] considerar -**4.** *fml* [harbour] nutrir. <> *vi* -**1.** [amuse] divertir -**2.** [have guests] receber.

entertainer [ˌentəˈteɪnəʳ] *n* animador *m*, -ra *f*.

entertaining [ˌentəˈteɪnɪŋ] <> *adj* divertido(da). <> *n* (*U*) [receiving guests]: **she does a lot of** ~ ela sempre recebe muitos convidados.

entertainment [ˌentəˈteɪnmənt] <> *n* -**1.** (*U*) [amusement] divertimento *m*, entretenimento *m* -**2.** [show] espetáculo *m*. <> *comp* do espetáculo.

entertainment allowance *n* verba *f* de representação.

enthral (*pt* & *pp* -**led**, *cont* -**ling**), **enthrall** *US* [ɪnˈθrɔːl] *vt* fascinar.

enthralling [ɪnˈθrɔːlɪŋ] *adj* fascinante.

enthrone [ɪnˈθrəʊn] *vt fml* entronizar.

enthuse [ɪnˈθjuːz] *vi*: **to** ~ **(about sthg)** entusiasmar-se (com algo).

enthusiasm [ɪnˈθjuːzɪæzm] *n* -**1.** (*U*) [passion, eagerness] entusiasmo *m*; ~ **for sthg** entusiasmo por algo -**2.** [interest, hobby] paixão *f*, interesse *m*.

enthusiast [ɪnˈθjuːzɪæst] *n* [fan] entusiasta *mf*.

enthusiastic [ɪnˌθjuːzɪˈæstɪk] *adj* entusiástico(ca).

enthusiastically [ɪnˌθjuːzɪˈæstɪklɪ] *adv* entusiasticamente.

entice [ɪnˈtaɪs] *vt* atrair; **to** ~ **sb away from sthg** desviar alguém de algo; **to** ~ **sb into sthg** instigar alguém a algo.

enticing [ɪnˈtaɪsɪŋ] *adj* tentador(ra).

entire [ɪnˈtaɪəʳ] *adj* inteiro(ra).

entirely [ɪnˈtaɪəlɪ] *adv* inteiramente; **that's** ~ **different** isso é completamente diferente.

entirety [ɪnˈtaɪrətɪ] *n* (*U*) *fml*: **in its** ~ em sua totalidade.

entitle [ɪnˈtaɪtl] *vt* [allow]: **to** ~ **sb to sthg** dar a alguém o direito a algo; **to** ~ **sb to do sthg** autorizar alguém a fazer algo.

entitled [ɪnˈtaɪtld] *adj* -**1.** [having a right to]: **to be** ~ **to sthg/to do sthg** ter direito a algo/a fazer algo -**2.** [called] intitulado(da).

entitlement [ɪnˈtaɪtlmənt] *n* direito *m*.

entity [ˈentətɪ] (*pl* -**ies**) *n* entidade *f*.

entomology [ˌentəˈmɒlədʒɪ] *n* (*U*) entomologia *f*.

entourage [ˌɒntʊˈrɑːʒ] *n* [of politician, popstar] séquito *m*.

entrails [ˈentreɪlz] *npl* entranhas *fpl*.

entrance [*n* ˈentrəns, *vb* ɪnˈtrɑːns] <> *n* -**1.** [arrival] entrada *f* -**2.** [way in]: ~ **(to sthg)** entrada (para *OR* de algo) -**3.** (*U*) [entry]: **to gain** ~ **to sthg** *fml* [to building] obter acesso a algo; [to society, university] ingressar em algo. <> *vt* [delight] encantar.

entrance examination *n* [for school, profession] exame *m* de admissão ; [for university] ≃ vestibular *m*.

entrance fee *n* -**1.** [gen] (preço *m* do) ingresso *m* -**2.** [to club] taxa *f* de admissão.

entrancing [ɪnˈtrɑːnsɪŋ] *adj* encantador(ra).

entrant [ˈentrənt] *n* -**1.** [gen] participante *mf* -**2.** [to profession] novato *m*, -ta *f* -**3.** [to university] calouro *m*, -ra *f*.

entreat [ɪnˈtriːt] *vt*: **to** ~ **sb (to do sthg)** suplicar a alguém (para que faça algo).

entreaty [ɪnˈtriːtɪ] (*pl* -**ies**) *n* súplica *f*.

entrenched *adj* [firm] arraigado(da).

entrepreneur [ˌɒntrəprəˈnɜːʳ] *n* empresário *m*, -ria *f*.

entrepreneurial [ˌɒntrəprəˈnɜːrɪəl] *adj* empresarial.

entrust [ɪnˈtrʌst] *vt*: **to** ~ **sthg to sb**, **to** ~ **sb with sthg** confiar algo a alguém.

entry [ˈentrɪ] (*pl* -**ies**) *n* -**1.** [gen] entrada *f*; ~ **(into)** entrada (em) -**2.** (*U*) [admission]: ~ **(to)** acesso *m* (a); **to gain** ~ **to** conseguir acesso a; **'no** ~**'** [to room, building] 'proibida a entrada'; *AUT* 'não entre' -**3.** [in competition] inscrição *f* -**4.** [in diary] anotação *f* -**5.** [in ledger] lançamento *m* -**6.** *fig* [joining] ingresso *m*.

entry fee *n* ingresso *m*.

entry form *n* ficha *f* de inscrição.

entry phone *n* porteiro *m* eletrônico.

entryway ['entrɪˌweɪ] *n US* passagem *f* de entrada.
entwine [ɪn'twaɪn] ⟨⟩ *vt* entrelaçar. ⟨⟩ *vi* entrelaçar-se.
E number *n* na Europa, *número que representa a substância química adicionada a um alimento.*
enumerate [ɪ'njuːməreɪt] *vt* enumerar.
enunciate [ɪ'nʌnsɪeɪt] ⟨⟩ *vt* - **1.** [pronounce clearly] pronunciar - **2.** [express clearly] expor, enunciar. ⟨⟩ *vi* [speak clearly] enunciar.
envelop [ɪn'veləp] *vt* : **to ~ sb/sthg in sthg** envolver alguém/algo em algo.
envelope ['envələʊp] *n* [for letter] envelope *m*.
enviable ['envɪəbl] *adj* invejável.
envious ['envɪəs] *adj* invejoso(sa); **~ (of sb/ sthg)** invejoso(sa) (de alguém/algo).
enviously ['envɪəslɪ] *adv* com inveja.
environment [ɪn'vaɪərənmənt] *n* - **1.** [gen] ambiente *m* - **2.** [natural world]: **the ~** o meio ambiente; **Department of the Environment** *UK* ≃ Ministério *m* do Meio Ambiente.
environmental [ɪnˌvaɪərən'mentl] *adj* ambiental.
environmentalist [ɪnˌvaɪərən'mentəlɪst] *n* ambientalista *mf*.
environmentally [ɪnˌvaɪərən'mentəlɪ] *adv* ecologicamente; **~ friendly** que não prejudica o meio ambiente, ecológico(ca).
Environmental Protection Agency *n US*: **the ~** a Secretaria Especial do Meio Ambiente.
environs [ɪn'vaɪərənz] *npl* [of town, place] arredores *mpl*.
envisage [ɪn'vɪzɪdʒ], **envision** *US* [ɪn'vɪʒn] *vt* prever.
envoy ['envɔɪ] *n* enviado *m*, -da *f*.
envy ['envɪ] (*pt* & *pp* -**ied**) ⟨⟩ *n (U)* inveja *f*; **to be the ~ of** ser objeto de inveja de; **to be green with ~** estar morrendo de inveja. ⟨⟩ *vt* invejar; **to ~ sb sthg** invejar algo a alguém.
enzyme ['enzaɪm] *n* enzima *f*.
EOC (*abbr of* **Equal Opportunities Commission**) *n organismo do governo britânico que trata da discriminação sexual.*
eon *n US* = aeon.
EPA (*abbr of* **Environmental Protection Agency**) *n agência norte-americana de proteção ambiental,* ≃ APA *f*.
epaulet(te) ['epəˈlet] *n* dragona *f*.
ephemeral [ɪ'femərəl] *adj* efêmero(ra).
epic ['epɪk] ⟨⟩ *adj* épico(ca). ⟨⟩ *n* [book, film] épico *m*.
epicentre *UK*, **epicenter** *US* ['epɪsentə'] *n* epicentro *m*.
epidemic [ˌepɪ'demɪk] *n* [of disease] epidemia *f*.
epidural [ˌepɪ'djʊərəl] *n* [injection] epidural *f*.
epigram ['epɪgræm] *n* epigrama *f*.
epilepsy ['epɪlepsɪ] *n (U)* epilepsia *f*.
epileptic [ˌepɪ'leptɪk] ⟨⟩ *adj* [fit, person] epilético(ca). ⟨⟩ *n* epilético *m*, -ca *f*.
epilogue *UK*, **epilog** *US* ['epɪlɒg] *n* [to play, book] epílogo *m*.
Epiphany [ɪ'pɪfənɪ] *n*: **(the) ~ (a)** Epifania *f*.
episcopal [ɪ'pɪskəpl] *adj* [of bishop] episcopal.
episode ['epɪsəʊd] *n* episódio *m*.

episodic [ˌepɪ'sɒdɪk] *adj* episódico(ca).
epistle [ɪ'pɪsl] *n literary* [letter] epístola *f*.
epitaph ['epɪtɑːf] *n* epitáfio *m*.
epithet ['epɪθet] *n* epíteto *m*.
epitome [ɪ'pɪtəmɪ] *n*: **the ~ of sb/sthg** [person] o exemplo vivo de alguém/algo, a personificação de alguém/algo; **this hotel is the ~ of luxury** este hotel é o número um em termos de luxo.
epitomize, -ise [ɪ'pɪtəmaɪz] *vt* personificar, representar o paradigma de.
epoch ['iːpɒk] *n* época *f*.
epoch-making *adj* que marcou época.
eponymous [ɪ'pɒnɪməs] *adj* epônimo(ma).
EPOS (*abbr of* **electronic point of sale**) *n* ponto *m* eletrônico de venda, EPOS *m*.
equable ['ekwəbl] *adj* [calm, reasonable] calmo(ma).
equal ['iːkwəl] (*UK* & *pp* -**led**, *cont* -**ling**, *US pt* & *pp* -**ed**, *cont* -**ing**) ⟨⟩ *adj* - **1.** igual; **~ to sthg** [sum] igual a algo; **on ~ terms** em igualdade de condições - **2.** [capable]: **to be ~ to sthg** estar à altura de algo. ⟨⟩ *n* [person] igual *mf*; **he's her ~ in everything** ele é igual a ela em tudo. ⟨⟩ *vt* - **1.** *MATH* ser igual a - **2.** [in standard] igualar-se a.
equality [iː'kwɒlətɪ] *n (U)* igualdade *f*.
equalize, -ise ['iːkwəlaɪz] ⟨⟩ *vt* igualar. ⟨⟩ *vi* *SPORT* empatar.
equalizer ['iːkwəlaɪzə'] *n* *SPORT* gol *m* de empate.
equally ['iːkwəlɪ] *adv* - **1.** [to the same extent] igualmente - **2.** [in equal amounts] por igual - **3.** [by the same token] da mesma forma.
equal opportunities *npl* oportunidades *fpl* iguais.
Equal Opportunities Commission *n*: **the ~** *organismo do governo britânico que trata da discriminação sexual.*
equal(s) sign *n* sinal *m* de igual.
equanimity [ˌekwə'nɪmətɪ] *n (U)* equanimidade *f*.
equate [ɪ'kweɪt] *vt* : **to ~ sthg with sthg** equiparar algo com algo.
equation [ɪ'kweɪʒn] *n* *MATH* equação *f*.
equator [ɪ'kweɪtə'] *n*: **the ~** o equador.
equatorial [ˌekwə'tɔːrɪəl] *adj* equatorial.
Equatorial Guinea *n* Guiné Equatorial.
equestrian [ɪ'kwestrɪən] *adj* equestre.
equidistant [ˌiːkwɪ'dɪstənt] *adj* : **~ (from)** eqüidistante (de).
equilateral triangle [ˌiːkwɪ'lætərəl-] *n* triângulo *m* equilátero.
equilibrium [ˌiːkwɪ'lɪbrɪəm] *n* equilíbrio *m*.
equine ['ekwaɪn] *adj* eqüino(na).
equinox ['iːkwɪnɒks] *n* equinócio *m*.
equip [ɪ'kwɪp] (*pt* & *pp* -**ped**, *cont* -**ping**) *vt* - **1.** [provide with equipment] equipar; **to ~ sb/sthg with sthg** equipar alguém/algo com algo - **2.** [prepare mentally]: **to ~ sb for sthg** preparar alguém psicologicamente para algo.
equipment [ɪ'kwɪpmənt] *n (U)* equipamento *m*.
equitable ['ekwɪtəbl] *adj* eqüitativo(va).
equity ['ekwətɪ] *n* *FIN* [market value] patrimônio *m* líquido.
⬥ **equities** *npl* *ST EX* ações *fpl* ordinárias.
equivalent [ɪ'kwɪvələnt] ⟨⟩ *adj* equivalente; **to be**

~ **to sthg** ser equivalente a algo. <> *n* equivalente *m*.

equivocal [ɪˈkwɪvəkl] *adj* **-1.** [statement, remark] ambíguo(gua) **-2.** [behaviour, event] duvidoso(sa).

equivocate [ɪˈkwɪvəkeɪt] *vi* usar expressões ambíguas.

er [ɜːʳ] *excl* **-1.** [in hesitation] ãhn! **-2.** [to attract attention] ei!

ER -1. (*abbr of* Elizabeth Regina) *emblema da rainha Elizabete* **-2.** *n US* (*abbr of* emergency room) MED pronto-socorro *m*.

era [ˈɪərə] (*pl* -s) *n* era *f*.

ERA (*abbr of* Equal Rights Amendment) *n lei norteamericana de igualdade de direitos para as mulheres.*

eradicate [ɪˈrædɪkeɪt] *vt* erradicar.

eradication [ɪˌrædɪˈkeɪʃn] *n* (*U*) erradicação *f*.

erase [ɪˈreɪz] *vt* **-1.** [rub out] apagar **-2.** *fig* [drive away, eliminate] eliminar, extinguir.

eraser [ɪˈreɪzəʳ] *n US* borracha *f*.

erect [ɪˈrekt] <> *adj* ereto(ta). <> *vt* **-1.** [building, statue] erigir **-2.** [tent, roadblock] montar.

erection [ɪˈrekʃn] *n* **-1.** (*U*) [of building, statue] construção *f* **-2.** [erect penis] ereção *f*; **to get/have an** ~ conseguir/ter uma ereção.

ergonomic [ˌɜːgəˈnɒmɪk] *adj* ergonômico(ca).

ergonomics [ˌɜːgəˈnɒmɪks] *n* (*U*) ergonomia *f*.

ERISA (*abbr of* Employee Retirement Income Security Act) *n lei norte-americana que trata de questões de aposentadoria.*

Eritrea [ˌerɪˈtreɪə] *n* Eritréia; **in** ~ na Eritréia.

Eritrean [ˌerɪˈtreɪən] <> *adj* eritreu(tréia). <> *n* eritreu *m*, -tréia *f*.

ERM (*abbr of* Exchange Rate Mechanism) *n* MTC *m*.

ermine [ˈɜːmɪn] *n* (*U*) [fur] arminho *m*.

erode [ɪˈrəʊd] <> *vt* **-1.** GEOL causar erosão em **-2.** *fig* [destroy] destruir. <> *vi* **-1.** GEOL sofrer erosão **-2.** *fig* [be destroyed] ser destruído(da).

erogenous zone [ɪˈrɒdʒɪnəs-] *n* zona *f* erógena.

erosion [ɪˈrəʊʒn] *n* **-1.** GEOL erosão *f* **-2.** *fig* [destruction] destruição *f*.

erotic [ɪˈrɒtɪk] *adj* erótico(ca).

eroticism [ɪˈrɒtɪsɪzm] *n* (*U*) erotismo *m*.

err [ɜːʳ] *vi* errar; **to** ~ **on the side of caution** pecar por excesso de cautela; **to** ~ **is human** errar é humano.

errand [ˈerənd] *n* **-1.** [task] tarefa *f*; **to go on** OR **run an** ~ **(for sb)** encarregar-se de alguma tarefa (para alguém) **-2.** [message] recado *m*.

errand boy *n* menino *m* de recados.

erratic [ɪˈrætɪk] *adj* irregular.

erroneous [ɪˈrəʊnjəs] *adj fml* errôneo(nea).

error [ˈerəʳ] *n* **-1.** [mistake] erro *m*; ~ **of judgment** erro de julgamento; **in** ~ por engano **-2.** FIN: ~ **s and omissions excepted** salvo erro ou omissão.

error message *n* COMPUT mensagem *f* de erro.

erstwhile [ˈɜːstwaɪl] *adj literary* anterior, antigo(ga).

erudite [ˈeruːdaɪt] *adj* erudito(ta).

erupt [ɪˈrʌpt] *vi* **-1.** [volcano] entrar em erupção **-2.** *fig* [violence, war] explodir.

eruption [ɪˈrʌpʃn] *n* **-1.** [of volcano] erupção *f* **-2.** [of violence, war] explosão *f*.

ESA (*abbr of* European Space Agency) *n agência espacial européia.*

escalate [ˈeskəleɪt] *vi* **-1.** [conflict, violence] intensificar-se **-2.** [costs, prices] aumentar.

escalation [ˌeskəˈleɪʃn] *n* **-1.** [of conflict, violence] intensificação *f* **-2.** [of costs, prices] aumento *m*.

escalator [ˈeskəleɪtəʳ] *n* escada *f* rolante.

escalator clause *n* cláusula *f* de indexação.

escapade [ˌeskəˈpeɪd] *n* escapada *f*.

escape [ɪˈskeɪp] <> *n* **-1.** [gen] fuga *f*; ~ **(from sb/sthg)** fuga (de alguém/algo); **to make an** OR **one's** ~ **(from)** fugir (de); **we had a narrow** ~ escapamos por um triz **-2.** [leakage] escapamento *m* **-3.** COMPUT tecla *f* Esc. <> *vt* **-1.** [gen] fugir de **-2.** [death, injury] escapar a; **to** ~ **notice** passar desapercebido(da) **-3.** [subj: fact, name] escapar. <> *vi* **-1.** [from person, place, situation]: **to** ~ **(from sb/sthg)** fugir (de alguém/algo) **-2.** [from danger] escapar **-3.** [leak] vazar.

escape clause *n* cláusula *f* de exceção, *cláusula que permite revogação de um contrato.*

escape key *n* COMPUT tecla *f* Esc.

escape route *n* **-1.** [from prison] rota *f* de fuga **-2.** [from fire] saída *f* de emergência.

escapism [ɪˈskeɪpɪzm] *n* (*U*) escapismo *m*.

escapist [ɪˈskeɪpɪst] *adj* escapista.

escapologist [ˌeskəˈpɒlədʒɪst] *n* ilusionista *mf*.

escarpment [ɪˈskɑːpmənt] *n* escarpa *f*.

eschew [ɪsˈtʃuː] *vt fml* evitar.

escort [*n* ˈeskɔːt, *vb* ɪˈskɔːtl] <> *n* **-1.** [guard] escolta *f*; **under** ~ sob escolta **-2.** [companion] acompanhante *mf*. <> *vt* [accompany] acompanhar.

escort agency *n* agência *f* de acompanhantes.

Eskimo [ˈeskɪməʊl] (*pl* -s) <> *adj* esquimó. <> *n* **-1.** [person] esquimó *mf* **-2.** [language] esquimó *m*.

ESL (*abbr of* English as a Second Language) *n inglês para imigrantes que vivem permanentemente no Reino Unido e obtiveram cidadania britânica.*

esophagus *n US* = oesophagus.

esoteric [ˌesəˈterɪk] *adj* esotérico(ca).

esp. (*abbr of* especially) espec.

ESP *n* **-1.** (*abbr of* extrasensory perception) percepção *f* extrasensorial. **-2.** (*abbr of* English for Special Purposes) *inglês para fins específicos.*

espadrille [ˌespəˈdrɪl] *n* alpargata *f*.

especial *adj* especial.

especially [ɪˈspeʃəlɪ] *adv* **-1.** [in particular, specifically] especialmente **-2.** [more than usually] excepcionalmente.

Esperanto [ˌespəˈræntəʊ] *n* esperanto *m*.

espionage [ˈespɪəˌnɑːʒ] *n* (*U*) espionagem *f*.

esplanade [ˌespləˈneɪd] *n* esplanada *f*.

espouse [ɪˈspaʊz] *vt fml* abraçar.

espresso [eˈspresəʊ] (*pl* -s) *n* café *m* expresso.

Esq. (*abbr of* esquire) *n título formal utilizado após um nome masculino, especialmente se ele não tiver nenhum outro título.*

Esquire [ɪˈskwaɪəʳ] *n*: **James Smith,** ~ Sr. James Smith.

essay [ˈeseɪ] *n* **-1.** SCH & UNIV trabalho *m* **-2.** LITERATURE ensaio *m*.

essayist [ˈeseɪɪst] *n* ensaísta *mf*.

essence [ˈesns] *n* essência *f*; **in** ~ em essência.

essential [ɪ'senʃl] *adj* essencial; ~ **(to** OR **for sthg)** essencial (para algo).
 ◆ **essentials** *npl* **-1.** [basic commodities] o essencial **-2.** [most important elements] fundamentos *mpl*, elementos *mpl* essenciais.

essentially [ɪ'senʃəlɪ] *adv* [basically] essencialmente, basicamente.

essential oil *n* óleo *m* essencial.

est. -1. (*abbr of* **established**) estabelecido(da). **-2.** (*abbr of* **estimated**) estimado(da).

EST (*abbr of* **Eastern Standard Time**) *n* horário oficial na zona oriental dos Estados Unidos.

establish [ɪ'stæblɪʃ] *vt* **-1.** [create, found] criar, estabelecer **-2.** [initiate]: **to** ~ **contact with sb** estabelecer contato com alguém **-3.** [ascertain] provar **-4.** [cause to be accepted] firmar; **to** ~ **o.s. (as)** estabelecer-se (como).

established [ɪ'stæblɪʃt] *adj* **-1.** [accepted] aceito(ta) **-2.** [founded] fundado(da).

establishment [ɪ'stæblɪʃmənt] *n* **-1.** (*U*) [creation, foundation] fundação *f*, criação *f* **-2.** [shop, business] estabelecimento *m*.
 ◆ **Establishment** *n* [status quo]: **the Establishment** a classe governante.

estate [ɪ'steɪt] *n* **-1.** [land, property] propriedade *f* **-2.**: **housing** ~ loteamento *m* **-3.**: **industrial** ~ zona *f* industrial **-4.** JUR [inheritance] herança *f*.

estate agency *n* UK agência *f* imobiliária.

estate agent *n* UK corretor *m*, -ra *f* de imóveis; ~'s agência *f* imobiliária.

estate car *n* UK van *f*, perua *f*.

estd., est'd. (*abbr of* **established**) estabelecido(-da).

esteem [ɪ'stiːm] ◇ *n* estima *f*; **to hold sb/sthg in high** ~ ter alguém/algo em alta estima. ◇ *vt* [respect] estimar.

esthetic etc US = **aesthetic etc**.

estimate [*n* 'estɪmət, *vb* 'estɪmeɪt] ◇ *n* **-1.** [calculation, reckoning] cálculo *m*, estimativa *f* **-2.** COMM orçamento *m*. ◇ *vt* calcular, estimar. ◇ *vi* COMM: **to** ~ **for sthg** fazer um orçamento de algo.

estimated ['estɪmeɪtɪd] *adj* estimado(da); **an** ~ **5,000 people died** estima-se que 5.000 pessoas morreram.

estimation [ˌestɪ'meɪʃn] *n* **-1.** [opinion] opinião *f* **-2.** [calculation] cálculo *m*, estimativa *f*.

Estonia [e'stəʊnɪə] *n* Estônia; **in** ~ na Estônia.

Estonian [e'stəʊnɪən] ◇ *adj* estoniano(na). ◇ *n* **-1.** [person] estoniano *m*, -na *f* **-2.** [language] estoniano *m*.

estranged [ɪ'streɪndʒd] *adj* separado(da); **his** ~ **son** o filho com o qual ele não fala.

estrogen *n* US = **oestrogen**.

estuary ['estjʊərɪ] (*pl* **-ies**) *n* estuário *m*.

ETA (*abbr of* **estimated time of arrival**) *n* hora *f* prevista de chegada.

e-tailer ['iːteɪləʳ] *n* varejista *mf* eletrônico(ca), e-tailer *mf*.

et al. [ˌet'æl] (*abbr of* **et alii**) et al.

etc. (*abbr of* **etcetera**) etc.

etcetera [ɪt'setərə] *adv* et cetera.

etch [etʃ] *vt* **-1.** [engrave] gravar com água-forte **-2.** *fig* [imprint]: **to be** ~**ed on sb's memory** estar gravado(da) na memória de alguém.

etching ['etʃɪŋ] *n* gravura *f* de água-forte.

ETD (*abbr of* **estimated time of departure**) *n* hora *f* prevista de partida.

eternal [ɪ'tɜːnl] *adj* **-1.** [gen] eterno(na) **-2.** [truth, value] absoluto(ta).

eternally [ɪ'tɜːnəlɪ] *adv* [forever] eternamente.

eternity [ɪ'tɜːnətɪ] *n* (*U*) eternidade *f*.

eternity ring *n* UK aliança que simboliza o amor eterno.

ether ['iːθəʳ] *n* (*U*) [solvent, anaesthetic] éter *m*.

ethereal [ɪ'θɪərɪəl] *adj literary* [unearthly] etéreo(rea).

ethic ['eθɪk] *n* ética *f*.
 ◆ **ethics** ◇ *n* (*U*) [study] ética *f*. ◇ *npl* [morals] moral *f*.

ethical ['eθɪkl] *adj* [morally right] ético(ca).

Ethiopia [ˌiːθɪ'əʊpɪə] *n* Etiópia; **in** ~ na Etiópia.

Ethiopian [ˌiːθɪ'əʊpɪən] ◇ *adj* etíope. ◇ *n* etíope *mf*.

ethnic ['eθnɪk] *adj* **-1.** [traditions, groups, conflict] étnico(ca) **-2.** [clothes, food] folclórico(ca).

ethnic cleansing [-'klensɪŋ] *n* limpeza *f* étnica.

ethnic minority *n* minoria *f* étnica.

ethnology [eθ'nɒlədʒɪ] *n* (*U*) etnologia *f*.

ethos ['iːθɒs] *n* sistema *m* de valores.

etiquette ['etɪket] *n* etiqueta *f*.

ETV (*abbr of* **Educational Television**) *n* rede norte-americana de televisão especializada em programas culturais e educacionais.

etymology [ˌetɪ'mɒlədʒɪ] (*pl* **-ies**) *n* etimologia *f*.

EU (*abbr of* **European Union**) *n* UE *f*.

eucalyptus [ˌjuːkə'lɪptəs] (*pl* **-tuses**) *n* eucalipto *m*.

eulogize, -ise ['juːlədʒaɪz] *vt fml* elogiar, louvar.

eulogy ['juːlədʒɪ] (*pl* **-ies**) *n fml* elogio *m*.

eunuch ['juːnək] *n* eunuco *m*.

euphemism ['juːfəmɪzml] *n* eufemismo *m*.

euphemistic [ˌjuːfə'mɪstɪk] *adj* eufemístico(ca).

euphoria [juː'fɔːrɪə] *n* euforia *f*.

euphoric [juː'fɒrɪk] *adj* eufórico(ca).

Eurasia [jʊə'reɪʒə] *n* Eurásia; **in** ~ na Eurásia.

Eurasian [jʊə'reɪʒən] ◇ *adj* **-1.** [of Europe and Asia] eurásico(ca) **-2.** [of mixed European and Asian descent] eurasiático(ca). ◇ *n* eurasiático *m*, -ca *f*.

eureka [jʊə'riːkə] *excl* heureca!

Euro- ['jʊərəʊ] *prefix* euro-.

Eurocheque ['jʊərəʊˌtʃek] *n* eurocheque *m*.

Eurocrat ['jʊərəˌkræt] *n* eurocrata *mf*.

Eurocurrency ['juːrəʊˌkʌrənsɪl] (*pl* **-ies**) *n* moeda *f* européia.

Eurodollar ['jʊərəʊˌdɒləʳ] *n* eurodólar *m*.

Euro-elections *npl* eleições *fpl* do Parlamento Europeu.

Euro MP *n* membro *m* do Parlamento Europeu.

Europe ['jʊərəp] *n* Europa; **in** ~ na Europa.

European [ˌjʊərə'piːən] ◇ *adj* europeu(péia). ◇ *n* europeu *m*, -péia *f*.

European Central Bank *n*: **the** ~ o Banco Central Europeu.

European Community *n*: **the** ~ a Comunidade Européia.

European Court of Human Rights *n*: **the** ~ o Tribunal Europeu de Direitos Humanos.

European Court of Justice *n*: the ~ o Tribunal Europeu de Justiça.

European Currency Unit *n* Unidade *f* Monetária Européia.

Europeanism [jʊərə'piːənɪzm] *n* europeísmo *m*.

Europeanize, -ise [jʊərə'piːənaɪz] *vt* europeizar.

European Monetary System *n*: the ~ o Sistema Monetário Europeu.

European Parliament *n*: the ~ o Parlamento Europeu.

European Union *n*: the ~ a União Européia.

Eurosceptic ['ʊərəʊˌskeptɪk] <> *adj* eurocético(-ca). <> *n* eurocético *m*, -ca *f*.

Eurostar ['ʊərəʊstɑː'] *n* Eurostar *m*, *trem de alta velocidade que vai da Inglaterra à França passando sob o Canal da Mancha.*

euthanasia [juːθə'neɪzjəl *n* eutanásia *f*.

evacuate [ɪ'vækjʊeɪtl *vt* evacuar.

evacuation [ɪˌvækjʊ'eɪʃn] *n* evacuação *f*.

evacuee [ɪˌvækjuː'iː] *n* evacuado *m*, -da *f* (*devido a uma guerra*).

evade [ɪ'veɪd] *vt* -**1.** [pursuers, capture] fugir a -**2.** [issue, question] fugir de -**3.** [subj: love, success] escapar de.

evaluate [ɪ'væljʊeɪtl *vt* avaliar.

evaluation [ɪˌvæljʊ'eɪʃn] *n* avaliação *f*.

evangelical [ˌiːvæn'dʒelɪkl] *adj* evangélico(ca).

evangelism [ɪ'vændʒəlɪzm] *n* (*U*) evangelismo *m*.

evangelist [ɪ'vændʒəlɪst] *n* evangelista *mf*.

evangelize, -ise [ɪ'vændʒəlaɪz] *vt* evangelizar.

evaporate [ɪ'væpəreɪt] *vi* -**1.** [liquid] evaporar -**2.** *fig* [feeling] evaporar-se, dissipar-se.

evaporated milk [ɪ'væpəreɪtɪd-] *n tipo de leite condensado por evaporação que não contém açucar.*

evaporation [ɪˌvæpə'reɪʃn] *n* -**1.** [of liquid] evaporação *f*-**2.** *fig* [of feeling] dissipação *f*.

evasion [ɪ'veɪʒn] *n* -**1.** (*U*) [of responsibility, payment etc] evasão *f*-**2.** [lie] evasiva *f*.

evasive [ɪ'veɪsɪv] *adj* -**1.** [to avoid question, subject] evasivo(va) -**2.** [to avoid being hit]**: to take ~ action** tomar uma ação defensiva.

evasiveness [ɪ'veɪsɪvnɪs] *n* (*U*) atitude *f* evasiva.

eve [iːv] *n* [day before] véspera *f*.

even ['iːvn] <> *adj* -**1.** [regular] regular -**2.** [calm] equilibrado(da) -**3.** [flat, level] plano(na) -**4.** [equal] igual; **to get ~ with sb** ficar quite com alguém -**5.** : ~ **number** número par. <> *adv* -**1.** [for emphasis] mesmo; ~ **I** mesmo eu; ~ **now** mesmo agora; ~ **then** [at that time] mesmo então; [in spite of that] mesmo assim -**2.** [in comparisons] ainda -**3.** [indeed] até.

➡ **even as** *conj* [while] enquanto.

➡ **even if** *conj* mesmo se.

➡ **even so** *adv* [in spite of that] mesmo assim.

➡ **even though** *conj* ainda que.

➡ **even out** <> *vt sep* nivelar. <> *vi* nivelar-se.

even-handed [-'hændɪd] *adj* justo(ta).

evening ['iːvnɪŋ] *n* -**1.** [end of day - from 5 pm until 8 pm] tardinha *f*; **good ~** boa tarde; **in the ~** à tarde; [- from 8 pm onwards] noite *f*; **good ~** boa noite; **in the ~** à noite, ao anoitecer -**2.** [event, entertainment] noite *f*.

➡ **evenings** *adv US* à noite.

evening class *n* aula *f* noturna.

evening dress *n* -**1.** (*U*) [formal clothes] traje *m* a rigor -**2.** [woman's garment] vestido *m* de gala.

evening star *n*: the ~ a estrela vespertina.

evenly ['iːvnlɪ] *adv* -**1.** [regularly] regularmente -**2.** [equally] igualmente -**3.** [calmly] tranqüilamente.

evenness ['iːvnnɪs] *n* -**1.** [regularity] regularidade *f* -**2.** [equality] igualdade *f*.

evensong ['iːvnsɒŋ] *n* culto *m* da tarde.

event [ɪ'vent] *n* -**1.** [happening] acontecimento *m*; social -**2.** *SPORT* evento *m* -**3.** [case] caso *m*; **in the ~ of** em caso de; **in the ~ that the train is cancelled** na eventualidade de o trem ser cancelado.

➡ **in any event** *adv* [all the same] em todo o caso.

➡ **in the event** *adv UK* na realidade.

even-tempered [-'tempəd] *adj* equilibrado(da).

eventful [ɪ'ventfʊl] *adj* movimentado(da), agitado(da).

eventide home ['iːvntaɪd-] *n UK euphemism* lar *m* de idosos.

eventing [ɪ'ventɪŋ] *n UK* [horseriding]**: (three-day) ~** concurso *m* hípico (de três dias).

eventual [ɪ'ventʃʊəl] *adj* final.

eventuality [ɪˌventʃʊ'ælətɪ] (*pl* -**ies**) *n* eventualidade *f*.

eventually [ɪ'ventʃʊəlɪ] *adv* finalmente, no fim.

ever ['evə'] *adv* -**1.** [already, at some time] já, alguma vez; **have you ~ been to Scotland?** você já/alguma vez foi para a Escócia?; **the worst film I've ~ seen** o pior filme que eu já vi; **if ~** se por acaso -**2.** [with negative - gen] nunca; **no one ~ calls these days** ninguém nunca telefona por esses dias; **hardly ~** quase nunca; [- emphatic] jamais; **don't ~ speak to me like that!** jamais fale comigo desse jeito -**3.** [all the time] sempre; **as ~** como sempre; **for ~** para sempre -**4.** [for emphasis]: **why ~ did you do that?** por que cargas d'água você fez isso?; **how ~ did he get back?** como será que ele voltou?; ~ **so kind** tão gentil; ~ **such a mess** tamanha bagunça.

➡ **ever since** <> *adv* desde então. <> *conj* desde que. <> *prep* desde.

Everest ['evərɪst] *n*: **Mount ~** o Monte Everest.

Everglades ['evəˌgleɪdz] *npl*: **the ~** região pantanosa da Flórida.

evergreen ['evəgriːn] <> *adj* sempre-verde. <> *n* sempre-verde *m*.

everlasting [ˌevə'lɑːstɪŋ] *adj* [lasting forever] eterno(-na).

every ['evrɪ] *adj* -**1.** [each] cada -**2.** [to express frequency]: ~ **three hours** a cada três horas; ~ **day** cada dia -**3.** [all] todo (da); ~ **day** todos os dias.

➡ **every now and then, every so often** *adv* de vez em quando.

➡ **every other** *adj* [every alternate]: ~ **other day** dia sim, dia não; ~ **other week** cada duas semanas.

➡ **every which way** *adv US* para todos os lados.

everybody ['evrɪˌbɒdɪ] *pron* = **everyone**.

everyday ['evrɪdeɪ] *adj* diário(ria).

everyone ['evrɪwʌn] *pron* todo mundo, todos *mpl* -das *fpl*.

everyplace *adv US* = everywhere.

everything ['evrɪθɪŋ] *pron* tudo.

everywhere ['evrɪweə'], **everyplace** *US* ['evrɪ,pleɪs] *adv* por todo o lado; [with verbs of motion] para todo o lado; **~ you go it's the same** onde quer que se vá é o mesmo.

evict [ɪ'vɪkt] *vt*: **to ~ sb (from)** despejar alguém (de).

eviction [ɪ'vɪkʃn] *n* despejo *m*.

eviction notice *n* aviso *m* de despejo.

evidence ['evɪdəns] *n* -1. [proof] evidência *f* -2. JUR prova *f*; **to give ~** prestar depoimento.
➡ **in evidence** *adj* [noticeable] em evidência.

evident ['evɪdənt] *adj* evidente.

evidently ['evɪdəntlɪ] *adv* evidentemente.

evil ['iːvl] <> *adj* [morally bad] mau(má). <> *n* -1. (U) [wicked behaviour] maldade *f* -2. [wicked thing] mal *m*.

evildoer *n* malfeitor *m*, -ra *f*.

evil-minded [-'maɪndɪd] *adj* malvado(da).

evince [ɪ'vɪns] *vt fml* evidenciar.

evocation [,evəʊ'keɪʃn] *n* evocação *f*.

evocative [ɪ'vɒkətɪv] *adj* evocativo(va).

evoke [ɪ'vəʊk] *vt* -1. [call up, summon] chamar -2. [elicit, provoke] evocar.

evolution [,iːvə'luːʃn] *n* evolução *f*.

evolve [ɪ'vɒlv] <> *vt* [develop] desenvolver. <> *vi* -1. BIOL: **to ~ (into/from)** evoluir (para/de) -2. [develop] desenvolver-se.

ewe [juː] *n* ovelha *f*.

ex- [eks] *prefix* ex-.

exacerbate [ɪg'zæsəbeɪt] *vt* exacerbar.

exact [ɪg'zækt] <> *adj* [precise] exato(ta); **to be ~** para ser exato(ta). <> *vt*: **to ~ sthg (from sb)** exigir algo (de alguém).

exacting [ɪg'zæktɪŋ] *adj* [demanding, rigorous] exigente.

exactitude [ɪg'zæktɪtjuːd] *n* (U) *fml* exatidão *f*.

exactly [ɪg'zæktlɪ] <> *adv* [precisely] exatamente; **not ~** [not really] não exatamente. <> *excl* exatamente!

exaggerate [ɪg'zædʒəreɪt] <> *vt* exagerar. <> *vi* exagerar.

exaggerated [ɪg'zædʒəreɪtɪd] *adj* exagerado(da).

exaggeration [ɪg,zædʒə'reɪʃn] *n* exagero *m*.

exalted [ɪg'zɔːltɪd] *adj* [important] sublime.

exam [ɪg'zæm] (*abbr of* examination) *n* -1. SCH prova *f*; **to take** *OR* **sit an ~** fazer uma prova. -2. MED US exame *m*.

examination [ɪg,zæmɪ'neɪʃn] *n* -1. [gen] exame *m* -2. [inspection] investigação *f* -3. [consideration] análise *f* -4. JUR [of witness, suspect] interrogatório *m*.

examination board *n* banca *f* examinadora.

examination paper *n UK* [test] prova *f*, exame *m*.

examine [ɪg'zæmɪn] *vt* -1. [gen] examinar -2. [consider] estudar -3. JUR interrogar.

examiner [ɪg'zæmɪnə'] *n* examinador *m*, -ra *f*; **internal/external ~** examinador externo/interno, examinadora externa/interna.

example [ɪg'zɑːmpl] *n* exemplo *m*; **for ~** por exemplo; **to follow sb's ~** seguir o exemplo de

alguém; **to make an ~ of sb** fazer exemplo de alguém.

exasperate [ɪg'zæspəreɪt] *vt* exasperar.

exasperating [ɪg'zæspəreɪtɪŋ] *adj* exasperador(-ra), irritante.

exasperation [ɪg,zæspə'reɪʃn] *n* (U) exasperação *f*.

excavate ['ekskəveɪt] *vt* escavar.

excavation [,ekskə'veɪʃn] *n* escavação *f*.

excavator ['ekskə,veɪtə'] *n UK* [machine] escavadeira *f*.

exceed [ɪk'siːd] *vt* -1. [be bigger than] exceder -2. [go beyond, go over - limit] ultrapassar; [- expectations] superar.

exceedingly [ɪk'siːdɪŋlɪ] *adv* extremamente.

excel [ɪk'sel] (*pt* & *pp* **-led**, *cont* **-ling**) <> *vi*: **to ~ (in** *OR* **at sthg)** sobressair-se (em algo). <> *vt*: **to ~ o.s.** *UK* superar-se.

excellence ['eksələns] *n* (U) excelência *f*.

Excellency ['eksələnsɪ] (*pl* **-ies**) *n*: **Your/His ~** Sua Excelência.

excellent ['eksələnt] <> *adj* excelente. <> *excl* excelente!

except [ɪk'sept] <> *prep* exceto. <> *conj* exceto. <> *vt*: **to ~ sb (from sthg)** excluir alguém (de algo).
➡ **except for** <> *prep* com exceção de. <> *conj* exceto.

excepted [ɪk'septɪd] *prep*: **Jenny ~, everyone agreed** com a exceção de Jenny, todos concordaram.

excepting [ɪk'septɪŋ] *prep* & *conj* = except.

exception [ɪk'sepʃn] *n* -1. [exclusion] exceção *f*; **to ~ sthg** exceção a algo; **with the ~ of** com a exceção de; **without ~** sem exceção -2. [offence]: **to take ~ to sthg** ofender-se com algo.

exceptional [ɪk'sepʃənl] *adj* [unusually clever, talented] excepcional.

exceptionally [ɪk'sepʃnəlɪ] *adv* [unusually] excepcionalmente.

excerpt ['eksɜːpt] *n*: **~ (from sthg)** excerto *m* (de algo).

excess [ɪk'ses, *before nouns* 'ekses] <> *adj* excessivo(va). <> *n* excesso *m*; **to ~** em excesso; **debts in ~ of £200,000** débitos de mais de £200.000. <> *vt* RAIL sobretaxar.

excess baggage *n* excesso *m* de bagagem.

excess fare *n UK* sobretaxa *f*.

excessive [ɪk'sesɪv] *adj* excessivo(va).

excess luggage *n* = excess baggage.

exchange [ɪks'tʃeɪndʒ] <> *n* -1. (U) [act of swapping] troca *f*, intercâmbio *m*; **in ~** em troca; **in ~ for** em troca de -2. [swap] troca *f* -3. FIN: **stock ~** bolsa *f* (de valores) -4. FIN: **(foreign) ~** câmbio *m*, divisas *fpl* -5. TELEC: **(telephone) ~** central *f* telefônica -6. [educational visit] intercâmbio *m* -7. *fml* [conversation] diálogo *m*. <> *vt* [swap] trocar; **to ~ sthg for sthg** trocar algo por algo; **to ~ sthg with sb** trocar algo com alguém.

exchange rate *n* FIN taxa *f* de câmbio.

Exchequer [ɪks'tʃekə'] *n UK*: **the ~** o Ministério da Fazenda britânico.

excise ['eksaɪz] <> *n* (U) imposto *m*; **Customs and Excise** ≃ a Receita Federal. <> *vt fml* extrair.

excise duties *npl* impostos *mpl* indiretos *OR* de consumo.

excitable [ɪk'saɪtəbl] *adj* excitável.

excite [ɪk'saɪt] *vt* **-1.** [person] entusiasmar **-2.** [nerves, heart] agitar **-3.** [interest, suspicion] despertar.

excited [ɪk'saɪtɪd] *adj* **-1.** [enthused] entusiasmado(-da) **-2.** [agitated] agitado(da).

excitement [ɪk'saɪtmənt] *n* **-1.** (U) [state - enthusiasm] entusiasmo *m*; [- agitation] agitação *f* **-2.** [exciting thing] emoção *f*.

exciting [ɪk'saɪtɪŋ] *adj* emocionante.

excl. (*abbr of* excluding) exc.

exclaim [ɪk'skleɪm] <> *vt & vi* exclamar.

exclamation [,eksklə'meɪʃn] *n* exclamação *f*.

exclamation mark *UK*, **exclamation point** *US n* ponto *m* de exclamação.

exclude [ɪk'sklu:d] *vt* excluir; to ~ sb/sthg (from sthg) excluir alguém/algo (de algo).

excluding [ɪk'sklu:dɪŋ] *prep* excluindo.

exclusion [ɪk'sklu:ʒn] *n* (U) exclusão *f*; ~ (from) exclusão (de); to the ~ of a ponto de excluir.

exclusion clause *n COMM* cláusula *f* de exclusão.

exclusive [ɪk'sklu:sɪv] <> *adj* exclusivo(va). <> *n PRESS* artigo *m* exclusivo.

◆ **exclusive of** *prep:* ~ of sales tax imposto sobre vendas não-incluído.

exclusively [ɪk'sklu:sɪvlɪ] *adv* exclusivamente.

excommunicate [,ekskə'mju:nɪkeɪt] *vt* excomungar.

excommunication ['ekskə,mju:nɪ'keɪʃn] *n* excomungação *f*.

excrement ['ekskrɪmənt] *n fml* excremento *m*.

excrete [ɪk'skri:t] *vt* excretar.

excruciating [ɪk'skru:ʃɪeɪtɪŋ] *adj* **-1.** [pain] insuportável **-2.** [emotion, performance] terrível.

excursion [ɪk'skɜ:ʃn] *n* [trip] excursão *f*.

excusable [ɪk'skju:zəbl] *adj* desculpável.

excuse [*n* ɪk'skju:s, *vb* ɪk'skju:z] <> *n* **-1.** [reason, explanation] desculpa *f* **-2.** [justification]: ~ (for sthg) desculpa (para algo). <> *vt* **-1.** desculpar; to ~ sb for sthg/for doing sthg desculpar alguém por algo/por fazer algo **-2.** [let off, free] dispensar; to ~ sb from sthg dispensar alguém de algo **-3.** [allow to leave] dar licença **-4.** *phr:* ~ me [to attract attention] com licença; [forgive me] desculpe; *US* [sorry] perdão.

ex-directory *adj UK* que não consta na lista telefônica.

exec [ɪg'zek] (*abbr of* executive) executivo(va).

execrable ['eksɪkrəbl] *adj fml* execrável.

execute ['eksɪkju:t] *vt* executar.

execution [,eksɪ'kju:ʃn] *n* execução *f*.

executioner [,eksɪ'kju:ʃnəʳ] *n* carrasco *m*, -ca *f*.

executive [ɪg'zekjʊtɪv] <> *adj* executivo(va). <> *n* **-1.** *COMM* executivo *m*, -va *f* **-2.** [of government] executivo *m* **-3.** [of political party] executiva *f*.

executive director *n* diretor *m* executivo, diretora *f* executiva.

executive toy *n brinquedo usado por executivos para ajudar na concentração.*

executor [ɪg'zekjʊtəʳ] *n* [of will] testamenteiro *m*, -ra *f*.

exemplary [ɪg'zemplərɪ] *adj* [perfect] exemplar.

exemplify [ɪg'zemplɪfaɪ] (*pt & pp* -ied) *vt* **-1.** [typify] ilustrar **-2.** [give example of] exemplificar.

exempt [ɪg'zempt] <> *adj:* to be ~ (from sthg) [tax] estar isento(ta) (de algo); [duty, rules] estar livre (de algo); [military service] estar dispensado(-da) (de algo). <> *vt:* to ~ sb/sthg (from sthg) [tax] isentar alguém/algo (de algo); [duty, rules, military service] dispensar alguém/algo (de algo).

exemption [ɪg'zempʃn] *n* **-1.** [from tax] isenção *f* **-2.** [from military service] dispensa *f*.

exercise ['eksəsaɪz] <> *n* exercício *m*; to take ~ fazer exercício; an ~ in sthg um exercício de algo. <> *vt* **-1.** exercitar; to ~ sb's mind exercer a mente de alguém **-2.** *fml* [use, practise] exercer. <> *vi* exercitar-se.

exercise bike *n* bicicleta *f* ergométrica.

exercise book *n* **-1.** [for notes] caderno *m (de anotações)* **-2.** [published book] livro *m* de exercícios.

exert [ɪg'zɜ:t] *vt* exercer; to ~ o.s. esforçar-se.

exertion [ɪg'zɜ:ʃn] *n* **-1.** [physical effort] esforço *m* **-2.** *fig* [committed effort] empenho *m* **-3.** (U) [of power, influence] exercício *m*.

ex gratia [eks'greɪʃə] *adj UK:* ~ payment gratificação *f*.

exhale [eks'heɪl] <> *vt* exalar. <> *vi* exalar.

exhaust [ɪg'zɔ:st] <> *n* **-1.** [fumes] descarga *f*, escapamento *m* **-2.** [tube]: ~ (pipe) (cano *m* de) descarga *f*. <> *vt* **-1.** [person, patience, subject] esgotar **-2.** [supply, money] usar.

exhausted [ɪg'zɔ:stɪd] *adj* exausto(ta).

exhausting [ɪg'zɔ:stɪŋ] *adj* exaustivo(va).

exhaustion [ɪg'zɔ:stʃn] *n* (U) exaustão *f*.

exhaustive [ɪg'zɔ:stɪv] *adj* exaustivo(va).

exhibit [ɪg'zɪbɪt] <> *n* **-1.** *ART* objeto *m* exposto **-2.** *JUR* [piece of evidence] prova *f*, evidência *f*. <> *vt* **-1.** *fml* [demonstrate] demonstrar **-2.** *ART* expor. <> *vi ART* expor.

exhibition [,eksɪ'bɪʃn] *n* **-1.** *ART* exposição *f* **-2.** [demonstration] demonstração *f* **-3.** *phr:* to make an ~ of o.s. *UK* fazer um escândalo.

exhibitionist [,eksɪ'bɪʃnɪst] *n* exibicionista *mf*.

exhibitor [ɪg'zɪbɪtəʳ] *n* expositor *m*, -ra *f*.

exhilarating [ɪg'zɪləreɪtɪŋ] *adj* estimulante.

exhort [ɪg'zɔ:t] *vt fml:* to ~ sb to do sthg exortar alguém a fazer algo.

exhume [eks'hju:m] *vt fml* exumar.

exile ['eksaɪl] <> *n* **-1.** [condition] exílio *m*; in ~ no exílio **-2.** [person] exilado *m*, -da *f*. <> *vt:* to ~ sb (from/to) exilar alguém (de/para).

exiled ['eksaɪld] *adj* exilado(da).

exist [ɪg'zɪst] *vi* existir.

existence [ɪg'zɪstəns] *n* (U) existência *f*; to come into ~ entrar em vigor; to be in ~ existir.

existentialism [,egzɪ'stenʃəlɪzm] *n* (U) existencialismo *m*.

existentialist [,egzɪ'stenʃəlɪst] <> *adj* existencialista. <> *n* existencialista *mf*.

existing [ɪg'zɪstɪŋ] *adj* existente, atual.

exit ['eksɪt] <> *n* saída *f*. <> *vi* sair.

exit poll *n UK POL* pesquisa *f* de boca-de-urna.

exit visa *n* visto *m* de saída.

exodus ['eksədəs] *n* êxodo *m*.

ex officio [eksə'fɪʃɪəʊ] *fml* <> *adj* ex officio. <> *adv* em ex officio.

exonerate [ɪg'zɒnəreɪtl] *vt*: to ~ sb (from sthg) exonerar alguém (de algo).

exorbitant [ɪg'zɔ:bɪtəntl] *adj* exorbitante.

exorcism *n* exorcismo *m*.

exorcist ['eksɔ:sɪstl] *n* exorcista *mf*.

exorcize, -ise ['eksɔ:saɪz] *vt* exorcizar.

exotic [ɪg'zɒtɪk] *adj* exótico(ca).

expand [ɪk'spænd] <> *vt* **-1.** [gen] expandir **-2.** [department, area] ampliar **-3.** [influence] aumentar. <> *vi* **-1.** [gen] expandir-se **-2.** [influence] aumentar **-3.** PHYS dilatar.

➡ **expand (up)on** *vt fus* entrar em detalhes.

expanse [ɪk'spæns] *n* vastidão *f*.

expansion [ɪk'spænʃn] *n* **-1.** (U) [gen] expansão *f* **-2.** [of department, area] ampliação *f* **-3.** [of influence] aumento *m* **-4.** PHYS dilatação *f*.

expansion card *n* COMPUT cartão *m* de expansão.

expansionism *n* (U) expansionismo *m*.

expansionist [ɪk'spænʃənɪstl] *adj* expansionista.

expansion slot *n* COMPUT slot *m* de expansão.

expansive [ɪk'spænsɪv] *adj* [relaxed, talkative] expansivo(va).

expatriate [eks'pætrɪətl] <> *adj* expatriado(da). <> *n* expatriado *m*, -da *f*.

expect [ɪk'spekt] <> *vt* **-1.** [gen] esperar; to ~ to do sthg esperar fazer algo; to ~ sb to do sthg esperar que alguém faça algo; to ~ sthg from sb esperar algo de alguém **-2.** [suppose]: to ~ (that) supor que; I ~ so suponho que sim; what do you ~? e o que você queria? <> *vi* [be pregnant]: to be ~ing estar esperando bebê.

expectancy *n* ▷ life expectancy.

expectant [ɪk'spektəntl] *adj* [crowd, person] ansioso(-sa).

expectantly [ɪk'spektəntlɪ] *adv* ansiosamente.

expectant mother *n* gestante *f*.

expectation [ˌekspek'teɪʃn] *n* **-1.** [hope] expectativa *f* **-2.** [belief] convicção *f*; against OR contrary to all ~(s) ao contrário de todas as expectativas.

expectorant [ɪk'spektərəntl] *n* expectorante *m*.

expedient [ɪk'spi:dʒənt] *fml* <> *adj* pertinente, conveniente. <> *n* expediente *m*.

expedite ['ekspɪdaɪt] *vt fml* expedir.

expedition [ˌekspɪ'dɪʃn] *n* **-1.** [organized journey] expedição *f* **-2.** [short trip, outing] passeio *m*.

expeditionary force [ˌekspɪ'dɪʃnərɪ-] *n* força *f* expedicionária.

expel [ɪk'spell] (*pt* & *pp* **-led**, *cont* **-ling**) *vt* **-1.** [from school, country]: to ~ sb (from) expulsar alguém (de) **-2.** [from container]: to ~ sthg (from) expelir algo (de).

expend [ɪk'spendl] *vt*: to ~ sthg (on sthg) gastar algo (com/em algo).

expendable [ɪk'spendəbll] *adj* **-1.** [person] dispensável **-2.** [resources] consumível.

expenditure [ɪk'spendɪtʃəˡ] *n* **-1.** [of money] gastos *mpl* **-2.** [of energy, resource] gasto *m*.

expense [ɪk'spens] *n* **-1.** [amount spent] despesa *f*, gasto *m* **-2.** (U) [cost] custo *m*; to go to great ~ (to do sthg) ter uma grande despesa (para fazer algo); at the ~ of em detrimento de, à custa de; at his/her own ~ [financial] do seu próprio bolso; at sb's ~ *fig* [in order to mock] às custas de alguém.

➡ **expenses** *npl* COMM despesas *fpl*; on ~s nas despesas.

expense account *n* relatório *m* de despesas.

expensive [ɪk'spensɪv] *adj* [financially] caro(ra).

experience [ɪk'spɪərɪəns] <> *n* experiência *f*. <> *vt* experimentar.

experienced [ɪk'spɪərɪənstl] *adj* [well-practised] experiente; ~ at OR in sthg experiente em algo.

experiment [ɪk'sperɪmənt] <> *n* **-1.** SCIENCE experimento *m*; to carry out an ~ conduzir um experimento **-2.** [exploratory attempt] tentativa *f*. <> *vi* SCIENCE fazer experiências; to ~ with sthg fazer experiências com algo; to ~ on sb/sthg fazer experiências em alguém/algo.

experimental [ɪkˌsperɪ'mentl] *adj* SCIENCE experimental.

expert ['ekspɜ:t] <> *adj* especializado(da), perito(ta); ~ at sthg/at doing sthg perito(ta) em algo/em fazer algo. <> *n* especialista *mf*, perito *m*, -ta *f*.

expertise [ˌekspɜ:'ti:z] *n* (U) excelência *f*, perícia *f*.

expert system *n* COMPUT sistema *m* especialista.

expiate *vt fml* expiar.

expire [ɪk'spaɪəˡ] *vi* [run out] vencer.

expiry [ɪk'spaɪərɪ] *n* (U) vencimento *m*.

expiry date *n* data *f* de vencimento.

explain [ɪk'spleɪn] <> *vt* **-1.** [describe, clarify] explicar; to ~ sthg to sb explicar algo a alguém **-2.** [account for] justificar. <> *vi* explicar-se; to ~ to sb (about sthg) justificar-se (para alguém) sobre algo.

➡ **explain away** *vt sep* justificar.

explanation [ˌeksplə'neɪʃn] *n* **-1.** (U) [act of explaining] explicação *f* **-2.** [account]: ~ (for sthg) justificativa *f* (por algo) **-3.** [description, clarification] explanação *f*.

explanatory [ɪk'splænətrɪ] *adj* explicativo(va).

expletive [ɪk'spli:tɪv] *n fml* imprecação *f*.

explicit [ɪk'splɪsɪtl] *adj* [clearly expressed] explícito(ta).

explode [ɪk'spləʊdl] <> *vt* **-1.** [set off] explodir **-2.** *fig* [disprove] derrubar. <> *vi* **-1.** [blow up] explodir **-2.** *fig* [with feeling] explodir.

exploit [*n* 'eksplɔɪt, *vb* ɪk'splɔɪtl] <> *n* façanha *f*. <> *vt* explorar.

exploitation [ˌeksplɔɪ'teɪʃn] *n* (U) [of workers, resources] exploração *f*.

exploration [ˌeksplə'reɪʃn] *n* [of space, countries] exploração *f*.

exploratory [ɪk'splɒrətrɪ] *adj* exploratório(ria).

explore [ɪk'splɔ:ˡ] <> *vt* explorar. <> *vi* explorar.

explorer [ɪk'splɔ:rəˡ] *n* explorador *m*, -ra *f*.

explosion [ɪk'spləʊʒn] *n* explosão *f*.

explosive [ɪk'spləʊsɪv] <> *adj* **-1.** [gen] explosivo(-va) **-2.** [controversial] controverso(sa). <> *n* explosivo *m*.

explosive device *n* dispositivo *m* explosivo.

exponent [ɪk'spəʊnəntl] *n* **-1.** [gen] expoente *mf* **-2.** [supporter] defensor *m*, -ra *f*.

exponential [ˌekspə'nenʃll] *adj fml* [growth] exponencial.

export [n & comp 'ekspɔːt, vb ɪk'spɔːt] ◇ n (U) exportação f. ◇ comp de exportação. ◇ vt exportar.
  ➡ **exports** npl [goods] exportações fpl.
exportable [ɪk'spɔːtəbl] adj exportável.
exportation [ˌekspɔː'teɪʃn] n (U) exportação f.
exporter [ek'spɔːtə'] n exportador m, -ra f.
export licence n UK COMM licença f de exportação.
expose [ɪk'spəʊz] vt -1. [gen] expor; **to be ~d to** sthg estar exposto(ta) a algo; **to ~ o.s.** mostrar-se -2. [unmask] desmascarar.
exposé [eks'pəʊzeɪ] n exposição f (de fatos reveladores).
exposed [ɪk'spəʊzd] adj [unsheltered] desprotegido(-da).
exposition [ˌekspə'zɪʃn] n fml exposição f.
exposure [ɪk'spəʊʒə'] n -1. [gen] exposição f -2. MED [hypothermia]: **to die from ~** morrer de frio -3. [unmasking - of person] desmascaramento m; [- of corruption] descoberta f -4. [PHOT - time] exposição f; [- photograph] pose f.
exposure meter n fotômetro m.
expound [ɪk'spaʊnd] fml ◇ vt expor. ◇ vi: **to ~ on** sthg explanar sobre algo.
express [ɪk'spres] ◇ adj -1. UK [urgent letter, parcel] expresso(sa) -2. [transport] expresso(sa) -3. fml [specific] explícito(ta). ◇ adv por correio expresso. ◇ n: ~ (train) (trem m) expresso m. ◇ vt -1. [show, state] expressar, exprimir; **to ~ o.s.** expressar-se -2. MATH representar.
expression [ɪk'spreʃn] n expressão f.
expressionism [ɪk'spreʃənɪzml] n (U) expressionismo m.
expressionist [ɪk'spreʃənɪst] ◇ adj expressionista. ◇ n expressionista mf.
expressionless [ɪk'spreʃənlɪs] adj sem expressão, inexpressivo(va).
expressive [ɪk'spresɪv] adj [full of feeling] expressivo(va).
expressively [ɪk'spresɪvlɪ] adv expressivamente.
expressly [ɪk'spreslɪ] adv [specifically] expressamente.
expressway [ɪk'spresweɪ] n via f expressa.
expropriate [eks'prəʊprɪeɪt] vt fml expropriar.
expropriation [eks,prəʊprɪ'eɪʃn] n fml expropriação f.
expulsion [ɪk'spʌlʃn] n expulsão f; ~ **(from)** expulsão (de).
exquisite [ɪk'skwɪzɪt] adj -1. [beautiful] fino(na) -2. [very pleasing] delicado(da).
exquisitely [ɪk'skwɪzɪtlɪ] adv [beautifully] finamente.
ex-serviceman n UK ex-combatente m.
ex-servicewoman n UK ex-combatente f.
ext., extn. (abbr of extension) extens.
extant [ek'stænt] adj existente.
extemporize, -ise [ɪk'stempəraɪz] vi fml improvisar.
extend [ɪk'stend] ◇ vt -1. [make bigger] ampliar -2. [make longer - in space] estender; [- in time] prolongar -3. [postpone] prorrogar -4. [make more wide-ranging] estender -5. fml [stretch out] esticar -6. [offer - welcome, help] estender; [- credit] conceder. ◇ vi

-1. [stretch, reach] extender-se -2. [rule, law]: **to ~ to sb/sthg** extender-se a alguém/algo -3. [protrude] extender-se.
extendable [ɪk'stendəbl] adj -1. [in time] prorrogável -2. [in space] expansível.
extended-play [ɪk'stendɪd-] adj de grande duração.
extension [ɪk'stenʃn] n -1. [gen] aumento m -2. [longer time limit] prorrogação f -3. [development, growth] expansão f -4. TELEC & ELEC extensão f -5. COMPUT: **filename ~** extensão do arquivo.
extension cable, extension lead n ELEC extensão f.
extensive [ɪk'stensɪv] adj -1. [in amount] amplo(pla) -2. [in area, range] extenso(sa).
extensively [ɪk'stensɪvlɪ] adv -1. [in amount] amplamente -2. [in range] extensivamente.
extent [ɪk'stent] n -1. [gen] extensão f -2. [degree]: **to what ~ ...?** até que ponto ...?; **to the ~ that** [in that, in so far as] na medida em que; [to the point where] até o ponto em que; **to a certain ~** até um certo ponto; **to a large** OR **great ~** em grande parte; **to some ~** até certo ponto.
extenuating circumstances [ɪk'stenjʊeɪtɪŋ-] npl circunstâncias fpl atenuantes.
exterior [ɪk'stɪərɪə'] ◇ adj externo(na). ◇ n exterior m.
exterminate [ɪk'stɜːmɪneɪt] vt exterminar.
extermination [ɪkˌstɜːmɪ'neɪʃn] n (U) extermínação f.
external [ɪk'stɜːnl] adj -1. [outside] externo(na) -2. [foreign] exterior(ra).
  ➡ **externals** npl aparências fpl.
externally [ɪk'stɜːnəlɪ] adv externamente.
extinct [ɪk'stɪŋkt] adj extinto(ta).
extinction [ɪk'stɪŋkʃn] n (U) [of species] extinção f.
extinguish [ɪk'stɪŋgwɪʃ] vt -1. fml [put out] apagar -2. fig [eliminate] extinguir.
extinguisher [ɪk'stɪŋgwɪʃə'] n: **(fire) ~** extintor m (de incêndio).
extol (pt & pp -led, cont -ling), **extoll** US [ɪk'stəʊl] vt enaltecer.
extort [ɪk'stɔːt] vt: **to ~** sthg **from** sb extorquir algo de alguém.
extortion [ɪk'stɔːʃn] n extorção f.
extortionate [ɪk'stɔːʃnət] adj extorsivo(va).
extra ['ekstrə] ◇ adj [additional] extra; ~ **charge** sobrecarga f. ◇ n -1. [addition] acessório m -2. CINEMA & THEATRE extra mf. ◇ adv extra.
  ➡ **extras** npl [in price] extras mpl.
extra- ['ekstrə] prefix extra.
extract [n 'ekstrækt, vb ɪk'strækt] ◇ n -1. [excerpt] trecho m -2. CHEM & CULIN extrato m. ◇ vt -1. [take out]: **to ~** sthg **(from** sthg) extrair algo (de algo) -2. [obtain, elicit]: **to ~** sthg **(from** sb) arrancar algo (de alguém).
extraction [ɪk'strækʃn] n -1. [origin, descent] origem f -2. [removal] extração f.
extractor (fan) [ɪk'stræktə'] n UK exaustor m.
extracurricular [ˌekstrəkə'rɪkjʊlə'] adj extracurricular.
extradite ['ekstrədaɪt] vt: **to ~** sb **(from/to)** extraditar alguém (de/para).

extradition [ˌekstrə'dɪʃn] <> n extradição f. <> comp de extradição.

extramarital [ˌekstrə'mærɪtl] adj extraconjugal.

extramural [ˌekstrə'mjʊərəl] adj UNIV de extensão universitária.

extraneous [ɪk'streɪnjəs] adj -1. [irrelevant] irrelevante -2. [outside] externo(na).

extraordinary [ɪk'strɔ:dnrɪ] adj -1. [special] extraordinário(ria) -2. [strange] exquisito(ta).

extraordinary general meeting n assembléia f geral extraordinária.

extrapolate [ɪk'stræpəleɪt] <> vt -1. MATH: to ~ sthg from sthg extrapolar algo a partir de algo -2. [deduce]: to ~ sthg from sthg inferir algo de algo. <> vi -1. MATH: to ~ from sthg extrapolar a partir de algo -2. [deduce]: to ~ from sthg inferir de algo.

extrasensory perception [ˌekstrə'sensərɪ-] n (U) percepção f extrasensorial.

extraterrestrial [ˌekstrətə'restrɪəl] adj extraterrestre.

extra time n UK SPORT prorrogação f.

extravagance [ɪk'strævəgəns] n -1. [luxury] extravagância f -2. (U) [excessive spending] gasto m excessivo.

extravagant [ɪk'strævəgənt] adj -1. [excessive] extravagante -2. [elaborate] caprichado(da).

extravaganza [ɪkˌstrævə'gænzə] n espetáculo público de pompa.

extreme [ɪk'stri:ml] <> adj extremo(ma). <> n [furthest limit] extremo m; **in the** ~ ao extremo; **to** ~s aos extremos.

extremely [ɪk'stri:mlɪ] adv [very] extremamente.

extreme sports npl esportes mpl radicais.

extremism [ɪk'stri:mɪzm] n (U) extremismo m.

extremist [ɪk'stri:mɪst] <> adj extremista. <> n extremista mf.

extremity [ɪk'stremətɪ] (pl -ies) n -1. (U) fml [extreme adversity] suma gravidade f -2. (U) [extremeness] extremismo m -3. fml [end] extremidade f.

➡ **extremities** npl [of body] extremidades fpl.

extricate ['ekstrɪkeɪt] vt: **to** ~ sthg (from) soltar algo (de); **to** ~ o.s. (from) livrar-se (de).

extrovert ['ekstrəvɜ:t] <> adj extrovertido(da). <> n extrovertido m, -da f.

extruded [ɪk'stru:dɪd] adj TECH prensado(da).

exuberance [ɪg'zju:bərəns] n (U) exuberância f.

exuberant [ɪg'zju:bərənt] adj exuberante.

exude [ɪg'zju:d] <> vt -1. [ooze, give off] exsudar -2. fig [be full of] exalar. <> vi exsudar.

exult [ɪg'zʌlt] vi: **to** ~ (at OR in sthg) alegrar-se (com algo).

exultant [ɪg'zʌltənt] adj exultante.

eye [aɪ] (cont eyeing OR eying) <> n -1. [gen & ANAT] olho m; **before my (very)** ~s bem debaixo dos meus olhos; **in my** ~s a meu ver; **to cast** OR **run one's** ~ **over sthg** passar os olhos em algo; **to catch sb's** ~ chamar a atenção de alguém; **to clap** OR **lay** OR **set** ~s **on sb** pôr os olhos em alguém; **to cry one's** ~s **out** inf chorar muito; **to feast one's** ~s **on sthg** alimentar os olhos com algo; **to have an** ~ **for sthg** ter bons olhos para algo; **to have one's** ~ **on sb/sthg** ter os olhos sobre

alguém/algo; **to keep one's** ~s **open (for)**, **to keep an** ~ **out (for)** ficar de olhos abertos (em); **to keep an** ~ **on sb/sthg** dar uma olhada em alguém/algo; **there is more to this than meets the** ~ a coisa é mais complicada do que parece; **to open sb's** ~s **(to sthg)** abrir os olhos de alguém (em relação a algo); **not to see** ~ **to** ~ **with sb** não ver as coisas com os mesmos olhos de alguém; **to close** OR **shut one's** ~s **to sthg** fechar os olhos para algo; **to turn a blind** ~ **(to sthg)** fazer vista grossa (para algo); **to be up to one's** ~s **in sthg** UK inf estar até aqui de algo -2. [of needle] buraco m. <> vt olhar.

➡ **eye up** vt sep UK encarar, comer com os olhos.

eyeball ['aɪbɔ:ll] <> n globo m ocular. <> vt US inf encarar.

eyebath ['aɪbɑ:θ] n copinho m para lavar os olhos.

eyebrow ['aɪbraʊ] n sobrancelha f; **to raise one's** ~s **(at sthg)** fig ficar surpreendido(da) (com algo).

eyebrow pencil n lápis m inv de sobrancelha.

eye-catching adj chamativo(va).

eye contact n (U): **to make/avoid** ~ **(with sb)** fazer/evitar contato direto (com alguém).

eyedrops ['aɪdrɒps] npl colírio m.

eyeglasses ['aɪglɑ:sɪz] npl US óculos m inv.

eyelash ['aɪlæʃ] n cílio m.

eyelet ['aɪlɪt] n ilhó m.

eye-level adj à altura dos olhos.

eyelid ['aɪlɪd] n pálpebra f; **not to bat an** ~ inf não dar a mínima.

eyeliner ['aɪˌlaɪnəʳ] n delineador m (para os olhos).

eye-opener n inf revelação f.

eyepatch ['aɪpætʃ] n tapa-olho m.

eye shadow n sombra f (para os olhos).

eyesight ['aɪsaɪt] n visão f.

eyesore ['aɪsɔ:ʳ] n horror m, monstruosidade f.

eyestrain ['aɪstreɪn] n vista f cansada.

eyetooth ['aɪtu:θ] (pl -teeth) n: **to give one's eyeteeth for sthg/to do sthg** dar tudo por algo/para fazer algo.

eyewash ['aɪwɒʃ] n (U) inf [nonsense] disparates mpl.

eyewitness [ˌaɪ'wɪtnɪs] n testemunha mf ocular.

eyrie ['ɪərɪ] n ninho m de águia.

e-zine ['i:zi:n] n revista f eletrônica.

f (pl f's OR fs), **F** (pl F's OR Fs) [ef] n [letter] f, F m.

➡ **F** n -1. MUS fá m -2. (abbr of **Fahrenheit**) F.

FA (abbr of **Football Association**) n confederação de

futebol da Inglaterra e do País de Gales, ≃ CBF f.

FAA (*abbr of* **Federal Aviation Administration**) *n* órgão federal norte-americano de aviação civil.

fable ['feɪbl] *n* [traditional story] fábula f.

fabled ['feɪbld] *adj* lendário(ria).

fabric ['fæbrɪk] *n* - **1.** [cloth] tecido *m* - **2.** *fig* [of building, society] estrutura f.

fabricate ['fæbrɪkeɪt] *vt* - **1.** [invent] inventar - **2.** [manufacture] fabricar.

fabrication [,fæbrɪ'keɪʃn] *n* - **1.** [lie, lying] invenção f - **2.** (U) [manufacture] fabricação f.

fabulous ['fæbjʊləs] *adj* fabuloso(sa).

fabulously ['fæbjʊləslɪ] *adv* fabulosamente.

facade [fə'sɑːd] *n* fachada f.

face [feɪs] ◇ *n* - **1.** [of person] rosto *m*, cara f; ~ **to** ~ cara a cara; **to fall flat on one's** ~ cair de cara no chão; **to look sb in the** ~ olhar alguém na cara; **to say sthg to sb's** ~ dizer algo na cara de alguém; **to show one's** ~ mostrar a cara; **it was staring me in the** ~ saltava aos meus olhos - **2.** [expression] expressão f; **to make** *OR* **pull a** ~ fazer careta - **3.** [of building] fachada f - **4.** [of coin] lado *m* - **5.** [of clock, watch] mostrador *m* - **6.** [appearance, nature] cara f - **7.** [surface] face f; **on the** ~ **of it** à primeira vista - **8.** [respect]: **to lose** ~ perder a reputação; **to save** ~ livrar a cara - **9.** *phr*: **to fly in the** ~ **of sthg** ir de encontro a algo. ◇ *vt* - **1.** [gen] encarar - **2.** [look on to, point towards] dar para - **3.** [confront] enfrentar.

➥ **face down** *adv* [person] de bruços; [object] para baixo.

➥ **face up** *adv* [person] de costas; [object] para cima.

➥ **in the face of** *prep* [confronted with] diante de.

➥ **face up to** *vt fus* enfrentar.

facecloth ['feɪsklɒθ] *n UK* toalhinha f de rosto.

face cream *n* (U) creme *m* para o rosto.

faceless ['feɪslɪs] *adj* sem rosto, anônimo(ma).

facelift *n* - **1.** [on face] lifting *m* - **2.** *fig*: **to give sthg a** ~ dar uma cara nova para algo.

face pack *n* máscara f facial.

face powder *n* (U) pó-de-arroz *m*.

face-saving [-'seɪvɪŋ] *adj* para salvar as aparências.

facet ['fæsɪt] *n* faceta f.

facetious [fə'si:ʃəs] *adj* brincalhão(lhona).

facetiously *adv* de forma brincalhona.

face-to-face *adj* cara a cara.

face value *n* [of coin, stamp] valor *m* nominal; **to take sthg at** ~ *fig* levar algo ao pé da letra.

facial ['feɪʃl] ◇ *adj* facial. ◇ *n* limpeza f de pele.

facile [*UK* 'fæsaɪl, *US* 'fæsl] *adj pej* [trivial] trivial.

facilitate [fə'sɪlɪteɪt] *vt fml* facilitar.

facility [fə'sɪlətɪ] (*pl* -ies) *n* - **1.** [ability]: **to have a** ~ **for sthg** ter facilidade para algo - **2.** [feature] recurso *m*.

➥ **facilities** *npl* - **1.** [amenities] instalações *fpl* - **2.** [services] serviços *mpl*.

facing ['feɪsɪŋ] *adj* [opposite] oposto(ta).

facsimile [fæk'sɪmɪlɪ] *n* fac-símile *m*; **a** ~ **edition** uma edição fac-similar.

facsimile machine *n fml* aparelho *m* de fax.

fact [fækt] *n* fato *m*; **the** ~ **is, ...** o fato é que ...; **the** ~ **remains that ...** a verdade que fica é que ...; **to know sthg for a** ~ ter certeza de algo.

➥ **in fact** ◇ *conj* na verdade. ◇ *adv* na verdade.

fact-finding [-'faɪndɪŋ] *adj* de investigação.

faction ['fækʃn] *n* facção f.

factional ['fækʃənl] *adj* [dispute] faccional.

fact of life *n* fato *m* consumado.

➥ **facts of life** *npl euphemism*: **to tell sb (about) the** ~**s of life** contar a alguém como nascem as crianças.

factor ['fæktə'] *n* fator *m*.

factory ['fæktərɪ] (*pl* -ies) *n* fábrica f.

factory farming *n* (U) criação f intensiva.

factory ship *n* navio-fábrica *m*.

factotum [fæk'təʊtəm] (*pl* -s) *n* factótum *m*.

fact sheet *n UK* informativo *m*.

factual ['fæktʃʊəl] *adj* real, concreto(ta).

faculty ['fækltɪ] (*pl* -ies) *n* - **1.** [gen] faculdade f - **2.** *US* [in college]: **the** ~ o corpo docente.

fad [fæd] *n* mania f, capricho *m*.

faddy ['fædɪ] (*compar* -ier, *superl* -iest) *adj inf pej* chato(ta).

fade [feɪd] ◇ *vt* [remove colour] desbotar. ◇ *vi* - **1.** [colour] desbotar - **2.** [sound] diminuir - **3.** [hope, memory, feeling] esvaecer - **4.** [smile, flower] murchar.

➥ **fade away, fade out** *vi* esvaecer.

faded ['feɪdɪd] *adj* desbotado(da).

faeces *UK*, **feces** *US* ['fi:si:z] *npl* fezes *fpl*.

Faeroe, Faroe ['feərəʊ] *n*: **the** ~ **Islands, the** ~**s** as Ilhas Feroé; **in the** ~ **Islands** nas Ilhas Feroé.

faff [fæf] ➥ **faff about, faff around** *vi UK inf* enrolar.

fag [fæg] *n* - **1.** *UK inf* [cigarette] cigarro *m* - **2.** *UK inf* [chore] tarefa f chata - **3.** *US inf pej* [homosexual] bicha f.

fag end *n UK inf* bagana f.

fagged out [fægd-] *adj UK inf* acabado(da), moído(da).

faggot, fagot *US* ['fægət] *n* - **1.** *UK CULIN* almôndega f - **2.** *US inf pej* [homosexual] bicha f.

Fahrenheit ['færənhaɪt] *adj* Fahrenheit *inv*.

fail [feɪl] ◇ *vt* - **1.** [not succeed in]: **to** ~ **to do sthg** não conseguir fazer algo - **2.** [*SCH & UNIV*- exam, test] não passar em; [- candidate] rodar - **3.** [neglect]: **to** ~ **to do sthg** deixar de fazer algo - **4.** [let down] falhar. ◇ *vi* - **1.** [not succeed] não conseguir - **2.** *SCH & UNIV* rodar - **3.** [stop functioning] falhar - **4.** [weaken] enfraquecer.

failed [feɪld] *adj* [singer, writer etc] fracassado(da).

failing ['feɪlɪŋ] ◇ *n* [weakness] fraqueza f. ◇ *prep* na falta de; **or,** ~ **that, ...** ou, caso contrário, ...

fail-safe *adj* [device, system] protegido(da) contra falhas.

failure ['feɪljə'] *n* - **1.** fracasso *m* - **2.** [to attend, appear, act]: **I was surprised by her** ~ **to attend the meeting** fiquei surpreso pelo fato de ela não ter comparecido à reunião - **3.** [breakdown, malfunction] falha f - **4.** *MED*: **heart** ~ falência f do coração.

faint [feɪnt] ◇ *adj* **-1.** [slight] vago(ga) **-2.** [half-hearted] desmaiado(da) **-3.** [dizzy] fraco(ca). ◇ *vi* desmaiar.

faint-hearted [-'hɑːtɪd] *adj* covarde.

faintly ['feɪntlɪ] *adv* **-1.** [gen] tenuamente **-2.** [slightly] levemente.

faintness ['feɪntnɪs] *n* (U) **-1.** [dizziness] fraqueza *f* **-2.** [dimness - of image] imprecisão *f*; [- of sound, hope, memory] debilidade *f*.

fair [feəʳ] ◇ *adj* **-1.** [just] justo(ta); **it's not** ~ **!** não é justo!; **to be** ~, **...** para ser franco(ca), **... -2.** [quite large] considerável **-3.** [quite good] bom (boa) **-4.** [hair, person] loiro(ra) **-5.** [skin, complexion] claro(ra) **-6.** [weather] claro(ra), bom (boa). ◇ *n* **-1.** *UK* [funfair] parque *m* de diversões **-2.** [trade fair] feira *f*. ◇ *adv* [fairly] limpo.

➤ **fair enough** *excl UK inf* tudo bem.

fair copy *n* cópia *f* passada a limpo.

fair game *n* (U) alvo *m* fácil; ~ **for sb/sthg** alvo fácil para alguém/algo.

fairground ['feəɡraʊnd] *n* parque *m* de exposições.

fair-haired [-'heəd] *adj* [person] loiro(ra).

fairly ['feəlɪ] *adv* **-1.** [rather] bastante **-2.** [justly] justamente.

fair-minded [-'maɪndɪd] *adj* justo(ta).

fairness ['feənɪs] *n* (U) [justness] imparcialidade *f*, justiça *f*; **in** ~ **to sb** para ser justo(ta) com alguém.

fair play *n* (U) jogo *m* limpo.

fairway ['feəweɪ] *n* [on golf course] *parte lisa do campo de golfe entre os buracos*.

fairy ['feərɪ] (*pl* -ies) *n* [imaginary creature] fada *f*.

fairy lights *npl UK* lâmpadas *fpl* decorativas.

fairy tale *n* conto *m* de fadas.

fait accompli [ˌfeɪtə'kɒmplɪ] (*pl* **faits accomplis** [ˌfeɪtə'kɒmplɪ]) *n* fato *m* consumado.

faith [feɪθ] *n* **-1.** (U) [trust] fé *f*; ~ **in sb/sthg** fé em alguém/algo; **in good/bad** ~ de boa/má fé **-2.** [religion] crença *f*, fé *f*.

faithful ['feɪθfʊl] ◇ *adj* fiel. ◇ *npl RELIG*: **the** ~ os fiéis.

faithfully ['feɪθfʊlɪ] *adv* [loyally] fielmente; **Yours** ~ *UK* [in letter] atenciosamente, cordialmente.

faithfulness ['feɪθfʊlnɪs] *n* (U) fidelidade *f*.

faith healer *n* curandeiro *m*, -ra *f*.

faithless ['feɪθlɪs] *adj* [disloyal] infiel.

fake [feɪk] ◇ *adj* falso(sa). ◇ *n* **-1.** [object, painting] falsificação *f* **-2.** [person] falsário *m*, -ria *f*. ◇ *vt* **-1.** [falsify] falsificar **-2.** [simulate] fingir. ◇ *vi* [pretend] fingir.

falcon ['fɔːlkən] *n* falcão *m*.

Falkland Islands ['fɔːklənd-], **Falklands** ['fɔːkləndz] *npl*: **the** ~ as (Ilhas) Malvinas; **in the** ~ nas (Ilhas) Malvinas.

fall [fɔːl] (*pt* fell, *pp* fallen) ◇ *vi* **-1.** [gen] cair; **to** ~ **flat** [joke] não surtir efeito **-2.** [become] ficar; **to** ~ **in love** apaixonar-se; **to** ~ **open** cair aberto(ta) **-3.** [be classified]: **to** ~ **into/under** pertencer a **-4.** [disintegrate]: **to** ~ **to bits** *OR* **pieces** cair aos pedaços **-5.** [city, country]: **to** ~ **(to sb)** cair (nas mãos de alguém) **-6.** [occur]: **to** ~ **on** cair em **-7.** *UK POL* [constituency]: **to** ~ **to sb** passar ao controle de alguém **-8.** [light, shadow] bater. ◇ *n* **-1.** [accident] tombo *m*, caída *f* **-2.** [of snow] nevasca *f* **-3.** [from power] queda *f* **-4.** [decrease] queda *f*; ~ **in sthg** queda de algo **-5.** *US* [autumn] outono *m*.

➤ **falls** *npl* [waterfall] cataratas *fpl*.

➤ **fall about** *vi UK inf*: **to** ~ **about (laughing)** cair na risada.

➤ **fall apart** *vi* **-1.** [book, chair] cair aos pedaços **-2.** *fig* [country, person] desmoronar.

➤ **fall away** *vi* **-1.** [plaster, paint] descolar **-2.** [land, slope] descer.

➤ **fall back** *vi* **-1.** [retreat, recede] retroceder **-2.** [lag behind] recuar.

➤ **fall back on** *vt fus* [resort to] recorrer a.

➤ **fall behind** *vi* **-1.** [in race] ficar para trás **-2.** [with rent, with work] atrasar-se.

➤ **fall down** *vi* **-1.** [person, picture, building] desabar **-2.** [fail] falhar.

➤ **fall for** *vt fus* **-1.** *inf* [fall in love with] ficar caído(da) por **-2.** [be deceived by] deixar-se enganar por.

➤ **fall in** *vi* **-1.** [roof, ceiling] desabar **-2.** *MIL* entrar em forma.

➤ **fall in with** *vt fus* [go along with] concordar com.

➤ **fall off** *vi* **-1.** [drop off] desprender-se **-2.** [diminish] diminuir.

➤ **fall on** *vt fus* **-1.** [subj: eyes, gaze] dirigir-se para **-2.** [attack] atacar, lançar-se sobre.

➤ **fall out** *vi* **-1.** [drop out] cair **-2.** [quarrel]: **to** ~ **out (with sb)** brigar (com alguém) **-3.** *MIL* sair de forma.

➤ **fall over** ◇ *vt fus* tropeçar em; **to be** ~ **ing over o.s. to do sthg** *inf* desdobrar-se para fazer algo. ◇ *vi* [lose balance] cair.

➤ **fall through** *vi* [plan, deal] fracassar.

➤ **fall to** *vt fus* [devolve upon] recair; **it** ~ **s to me to make a speech** toca para mim fazer o discurso.

fallacious [fə'leɪʃəs] *adj fml* falacioso(sa).

fallacy ['fæləsɪ] (*pl* -ies) *n* [misconception] falácia *f*.

fallen ['fɔːln] *pp* ▷ **fall**.

fall guy *n US inf* [scapegoat] bode *m* expiatório.

fallible ['fæləbl] *adj* falível.

falling ['fɔːlɪŋ] *adj* [decreasing] em declínio.

fallopian tube [fə'ləʊpɪən-] *n* trompa *f* de Falópio.

fallout ['fɔːlaʊt] *n* (U) [radiation] chuva *f* radioativa.

fallout shelter *n* abrigo *m* antinuclear.

fallow ['fæləʊ] *adj* [land] alqueivado(da); **to lie** ~ ficar sem cultivo.

false [fɔːls] *adj* **-1.** [gen] falso(sa) **-2.** [artificial] postiço(ça).

false alarm *n* alarme *m* falso.

falsehood ['fɔːlshʊd] *n fml* **-1.** [lie] mentira *f* **-2.** (U) [lack of truth] falsidade *f*.

falsely ['fɔːlslɪ] *adv* **-1.** [wrongly] erroneamente **-2.** [insincerely] falsamente.

false start *n* tentativa *f* frustrada.

false teeth *npl* dentadura *f* postiça.

falsetto [fɔːl'setəʊ] (*pl* -s) *n MUS* falsete *m*. ◇ *adv* [sing] em falsete.

falsify ['fɔːlsɪfaɪ] (*pt* & *pp* -ied) *vt* [facts, accounts] falsificar.

falter ['fɔːltə'] vi -**1.** [gen] vacilar -**2.** [hesitate, lose confidence] hesitar.

faltering ['fɔːltərɪŋ] adj [steps, voice] vacilante.

fame [feɪm] n (U) fama f.

familiar [fə'mɪljə'] adj -**1.** [known] familiar; ~ **to sb** familiar para alguém -**2.** [conversant]: ~ **with sthg** familiarizado(da) com algo; **to be on** ~ **terms with sb** ter relações amigáveis com alguém -**3.** pej [overly informal - person] que se dá muitas liberdades; [- tone, manner] amigável em excesso.

familiarity [fə,mɪlɪ'ærətɪ] n -**1.** [with book, rules, subject]: ~ **with sthg** conhecimento m de algo -**2.** [of place, face] familiaridade f -**3.** pej [excessive informality] liberdades fpl.

familiarize, -ise [fə'mɪljəraɪz] vt: **to** ~ **o.s. with sthg** familiarizar-se com algo; **to** ~ **sb with sthg** familiarizar alguém com algo.

family ['fæmlɪ] (pl -**ies**) <> n família f. <> comp -**1.** [belonging to family] familiar; ~ **car** carro da família -**2.** [suitable for all ages] para toda a família.

family business n negócio m familiar.

family credit n (U) UK auxílio-família m.

family doctor n médico m, -ca f de família.

family life n (U) vida f familiar.

family planning n (U) planejamento m familiar.

family tree n árvore f genealógica.

famine ['fæmɪn] n fome f extrema e coletiva.

famished ['fæmɪʃt] adj inf [very hungry] faminto(ta), morto(ta) de fome.

famous ['feɪməs] adj famoso(sa); ~ **for sthg** famoso(sa) por algo.

famously ['feɪməslɪ] adv dated: **to get on** OR **along** ~ **with sb** ficar íntimo(ma) de alguém.

fan [fæn] (pt & pp -**ned**, cont -**ning**) <> n -**1.** [of paper, silk] leque m -**2.** [electric or mechanical] ventilador m -**3.** [enthusiast] fã mf, admirador m, -ra f. <> vt -**1.** [cool] abanar; **to** ~ **o.s.** abanar-se -**2.** [stimulate] atiçar.

  fan out vi [army, search party] espalhar-se.

fanatic [fə'nætɪk] n fanático m, -ca f.

fanatical [fə'nætɪkl] adj fanático(ca).

fanaticism [fə'nætɪsɪzm] n (U) fanatismo m.

fan belt n correia f do ventilador.

fanciful ['fænsɪfʊl] adj -**1.** [odd] estapafúrdio(dia) -**2.** [elaborate] extravagante.

fan club n fã-clube m.

fancy ['fænsɪ] (compar -**ier**, superl -**iest**, pl -**ies**, pt & pp -**ied**) <> adj -**1.** [elaborate] caprichado(da) -**2.** [expensive] extravagante. <> n -**1.** [liking] gosto m; **to take a** ~ **to sb/sthg** ter simpatia por alguém/ algo; **to take sb's** ~ cair nas graças de alguém -**2.** [whim] capricho m -**3.** [fantasy] fantasia f. <> vt -**1.** inf [want] querer; **I** ~ **going to the cinema** me agrada a idéia de ir ao cinema -**2.** [like] agradar-se de; **to** ~ **o.s.** estar cheio (cheia) de si -**3.** [imagine] imaginar; ~ **meeting you here!** imagina só, te encontrar por aqui!; **to** ~ **o.s. as sthg** imaginar-se como alguém; ~ **that!** imagina só!, quem diria!

fancy dress n (U) fantasia f.

fancy-dress party n festa f à fantasia.

fancy goods npl artigos mpl de luxo.

fanfare ['fænfeə'] n MUS fanfarra f.

fang [fæŋ] n -**1.** [of snake] presa f -**2.** [of carnivore] colmilho m.

fan heater n aquecedor m de ventoinha.

fanlight ['fænlaɪt] n UK clarabóia f.

fan mail n (U) cartas fpl de fãs.

fanny ['fænɪ] n US inf [backside] bunda f.

fanny pack n US pochete f.

fantasize, -ise ['fæntəsaɪz] vi fantasiar; **to** ~ **about sthg/about doing sthg** fantasiar sobre algo/sobre fazer algo.

fantastic [fæn'tæstɪk] adj -**1.** inf [gen] fantástico(ca) -**2.** [bizarre, strange] exótico(ca).

fantastically [fæn'tæstɪklɪ] adv -**1.** [extremely] extremamente -**2.** [bizarrely, strangely] exoticamente.

fantasy ['fæntəsɪ] (pl -**ies**) <> n fantasia f. <> comp de sonhos, imaginário(ria).

fanzine ['fænziːn] n fanzine m.

fao (abbr of for the attention of) a/c.

FAO (abbr of Food and Agriculture Organization) n FAO f.

FAQ (abbr of frequently asked questions) n perguntas fpl mais freqüentes, FAQ f.

far [fɑː'] (compar **farther** OR **further**, superl **farthest** OR **furthest**) <> adv -**1.** [in distance] longe; **how** ~ **is it?** a que distância fica?; **how** ~ **have you come?** até onde você veio?; **is it** ~? é longe?; ~ **away** OR **off** muito longe; ~ **and wide** por todo o lugar; **as** ~ **as** até; **we walked as** ~ **as the river** caminhamos até o rio -**2.** [in time]: ~ **away** OR **off** muito longe; **as** ~ **back as 1900** já em 1900; **so** ~ até agora -**3.** [in degree or extent] muito; **how** ~ **have you got with your novel?** até onde você já foi no romance?; **he's not** ~ **wrong** OR **out** OR **off** ele não está tão errado; **as** ~ **as I know** até onde eu sei; **as** ~ **as I'm concerned** no que me diz respeito; **as** ~ **as possible** até onde é possível; ~ **and away, by** ~ de longe; ~ **from it** pelo contrário; **so** ~ até este ponto; **so** ~ **so good** até agora tudo bem; **to go so** ~ **as to do sthg** chegar ao ponto de fazer algo; **to go too** ~ ir longe demais. <> adj -**1.** [distant, extreme] extremo(ma) -**2.** [remote] distante, remoto(ta).

faraway ['fɑːrəweɪ] adj -**1.** [distant] distante -**2.** [dreamy] ausente.

farce [fɑːs] n farsa f.

farcical ['fɑːsɪkl] adj ridículo(la).

fare [feə'] <> n -**1.** [payment, rate] tarifa f -**2.** [price of ticket] preço m -**3.** [person] passageiro m, -ra f -**4.** fml [food] comida f. <> vi [manage]: **to** ~ **well/badly** passar bem/mal.

Far East n: **the** ~ o Extremo Oriente.

fare stage n UK parada na qual aumenta o preço da passagem.

farewell [,feə'wel] <> n despedida f, adeus m. <> excl literary adeus!

farfetched [,fɑː'fetʃt] adj forçado(da).

far-flung adj -**1.** [remote] longínquo(qua) -**2.** [extensive] vasto(ta).

farm [fɑːm] <> n fazenda f. <> vt cultivar. <> vi cultivar a terra.

  farm out vt sep mandar fazer.

farmer ['fɑːmə'] n fazendeiro m, -ra f.

farmhand ['fɑːmhænd] n peão m, -oa f.

farmhouse ['fɑ:mhaʊs, *pl* -haʊzɪz] *n* granja *f*, quinta *f*.

farming ['fɑ:mɪŋ] *n (U)* **- 1.** [activity] agricultura *f* **- 2.** [of animals] criação *f* **- 3.** [of crops] cultivo *m*.

farmland ['fɑ:mlænd] *n (U)* terra *f* cultivada.

farmstead ['fɑ:msted] *n US* granja *f*.

farmyard ['fɑ:mjɑ:d] *n* terreiro *m (de fazenda)*.

Faroe *n* = Faeroe.

far-off *adj* distante.

far-reaching [-'ri:tʃɪŋ] *adj* **- 1.** [implications] de longo alcance **- 2.** [changes] abrangente.

farrier ['færɪə'] *n* ferrador *m*, -ra *f*.

far-sighted *adj* **- 1.** [person] prudente; [plan] perspicaz **- 2.** *US* [longsighted] hipermetrope.

fart [fɑ:t] *vulg* ◇ *n* **- 1.** [wind] peido *m* **- 2.** [person] pé-no-saco *m*. ◇ *vi* peidar.

farther ['fɑ:ðə'] *compar* ▷ **far**.

farthest ['fɑ:ðəst] *superl* ▷ **far**.

fascia ['feɪʃə] *n* **- 1.** [on shop] fachada *m* **- 2.** *AUT* painel *m* **- 3.** [for mobile phone] frente *f*.

fascinate ['fæsɪneɪt] *vt* fascinar.

fascinating ['fæsɪneɪtɪŋ] *adj* fascinante.

fascination [ˌfæsɪ'neɪʃn] *n (U)* fascinação *f*.

fascism ['fæʃɪzm] *n (U)* fascismo *m*.

fascist ['fæʃɪst] ◇ *adj* fascista. ◇ *n* fascista *mf*.

fashion ['fæʃn] ◇ *n* **- 1.** [current style] moda *f*; ~ **model** modelo *mf* (de passarela); **in/out of** ~ [vogue] na/fora de moda **- 2.** [manner] maneira *f*; **after a** ~ até certo ponto. ◇ *vt fml* [shape] moldar.

fashionable ['fæʃnəbl] *adj* [in vogue] da moda.

fashion-conscious *adj* atento(ta) às tendências da moda.

fashion designer *n* estilista *mf*.

fashion show *n* desfile *m* de modas.

fast [fɑ:st] ◇ *adj* **- 1.** [rapid] rápido(da); **she's in the** ~ **track** ela está indo pelo caminho mais rápido; **to pull a** ~ **one on sb** *inf* passar a perna em alguém **- 2.** [clock, watch] adiantado(da) **- 3.** [dye] permanente. ◇ *adv* **- 1.** [rapidly] depressa; **how** ~ **does this car go?** a que velocidade este carro chega?; **I need help** ~ preciso de ajuda rápido **- 2.** [firmly] firmemente; **to hold** ~ **to sthg** [grip firmly] segurar firme algo; *fig* [stick to] manter-se firme em algo; **to be** ~ **asleep** dormir profundamente. ◇ *n* jejum *m*. ◇ *vi* jejuar.

fast breeder reactor *n* reator *m* super-regenerador.

fasten ['fɑ:sn] ◇ *vt* **- 1.** [close - jacket, bag] fechar; [- seat belt] apertar **- 2.** [attach]: **to** ~ **sthg to sthg** fixar algo em algo **- 3.** [grasp] prender. ◇ *vi*: **to** ~ **on to sb/sthg** agarrar-se a alguém/algo.

fastener ['fɑ:snə'] *n* **- 1.** [dress, bag] fecho *m* **- 2.** [necklace] presilha *f* **- 3.** [door] fechadura *f*.

fastening ['fɑ:snɪŋ] *n* **- 1.** [gen] fechadura *f* **- 2.** [on window] trinco *m*.

fast food *n (U)* fast-food *m*.

fast-forward ◇ *n* avanço *m* rápido. ◇ *vt* avançar rapidamente. ◇ *vi* avançar rapidamente.

fastidious [fə'stɪdɪəs] *adj* [fussy] meticuloso(sa).

fast lane *n* **- 1.** [on motorway] pista *f* de alta velocidade **- 2.** *fig* [exciting lifestyle]: **life in the** ~ vida *f* excitante.

fat [fæt] (*compar* -ter, *superl* -test) ◇ *adj* **- 1.** [person, animal, face, legs, meat] gordo(da); **to get** ~ engordar **- 2.** [volume, file, wallet] pesado(da) **- 3.** [FIN - profit, fee] avultado(da); [- cheque, bank account] gordo(da) **- 4.** *iro* [small]: **that was a** ~ **lot of good** *OR* **use** não foi nada bom o que você fez!; ~ **chance!** nem pensar! ◇ *n* **- 1.** *(U)* *ANAT* gordura *f* **- 2.** *(U)* [in food - raw] banha *f*; [- cooked] sebo *m*; [- in cooking, diet] gordura *f*.

fatal ['feɪtl] *adj* **- 1.** [ruinous] fatal **- 2.** [mortal] mortal.

fatalism ['feɪtəlɪzm] *n (U)* fatalismo *m*.

fatalistic [ˌfeɪtə'lɪstɪk] *adj* fatalista.

fatality [fə'tælətɪ] (*pl* -ies) *n* [accident victim] fatalidade *f*; [fatalism] fatalismo *m*.

fatally ['feɪtəlɪ] *adv* **- 1.** [ruinously] fatalmente **- 2.** [mortally] mortalmente.

fate [feɪt] *n* **- 1.** *(U)* [destiny] destino *m*; **to tempt** ~ brincar com a sorte **- 2.** [of person, thing] sina *f*.

fated ['feɪtɪd] *adj* **- 1.** [destined] predestinado(da); **to be** ~ **to do sthg** estar fadado(da) a fazer algo **- 2.** [doomed] condenado(da).

fateful ['feɪtfʊl] *adj* [decisive] fatídico(ca).

fathead *n inf* estúpido *m*, -da *f*.

father ['fɑ:ðə'] ◇ *n lit, fig* pai *m*. ◇ *vt* ser o pai de.

➧ **Father** *n* **- 1.** [priest] padre *m* **- 2.** [God]: **our Father** nosso Pai.

Father Christmas *n UK* Papai *m* Noel.

fatherhood ['fɑ:ðəhʊd] *n (U)* paternidade *f*.

father-in-law (*pl* **father-in-laws** *OR* **fathers-in-law**) *n* sogro *m*.

fatherly ['fɑ:ðəlɪ] *adj* paternal.

Father's Day *n* Dia *f* dos Pais.

fathom ['fæðəm] ◇ *n* braça *f*. ◇ *vt*: **to** ~ **sthg (out)** desvendar algo; **to** ~ **sb (out)** compreender alguém.

fatigue [fə'ti:g] ◇ *n (U)* fadiga *f*. ◇ *vt* [weary] fatigar.

➧ **fatigues** *npl* farda *f* de serviço.

fatless *adj* sem gordura.

fatness ['fætnɪs] *n (U)* [of person] gordura *f*.

fatten ['fætn] *vt* engordar.

➧ **fatten up** *vt sep* engordar.

fattening ['fætnɪŋ] *adj* que engorda; **to be very** ~ engordar muito.

fatty ['fætɪ] (*compar* -ier, *superl* -iest, *pl* -ies) ◇ *adj* **- 1.** [food] gorduroso(sa) **- 2.** *BIOL* [tissue] adiposo(sa). ◇ *n inf pej* gorducho *m*, -cha *f*.

fatuous ['fætjʊəs] *adj* fátuo(tua).

fatuously *adv* tolamente.

fatwa ['fætwə] *n* mandado *m* religioso islâmico.

faucet ['fɔ:sɪt] *n US* torneira *f*.

fault [fɔ:lt] ◇ *n* **- 1.** [responsibility] culpa *f* **- 2.** [defect] defeito *m* **- 3.** [mistake, imperfection] falha *f*; **to find** ~ **with sb/sthg** criticar algo/alguém; **to be at** ~ equivocar-se; **through no** ~ **of my own I missed the train** perdi o trem, mas não foi culpa minha **- 4.** *GEOL* falha *f* **- 5.** [in tennis] falta *f*. ◇ *vt*: **to** ~ **sb (on sthg)** criticar alguém (em algo).

faultless ['fɔ:ltlɪs] *adj* impecável.

faulty ['fɔ:ltɪ] (*compar* -ier, *superl* -iest) *adj* **- 1.** [machine, system] defeituoso(sa) **- 2.** [reasoning, logic] falho(lha).

fauna ['fɔːnə] *n* fauna *f.*

faux pas [ˌfəʊ'pɑː] (*pl inv*) *n* gafe *f.*

favour *UK*, **favor** *US* ['feɪvə'] <> *n* **-1.** (*U*) [approval] aprovação *f*; **in sb's** ~ em favor de alguém; **to be in** ~ **(with sb)** contar com o apoio (de alguém); **to be out of** ~ **(with sb)** não contar com o apoio (de alguém); **to curry** ~ **with sb** puxar o saco de alguém **-2.** [kind act] favor *m*; **to do sb a** ~ fazer um favor a alguém **-3.** (*U*) [favouritism] favoritismo *m* **-4.** [advantage]: **to rule in sb's** ~ decidir a favor de alguém. <> *vt* **-1.** [gen] favorecer **-2.** *iro* [honour]: **to** ~ **sb with sthg** honrar alguém com algo.
  in favour *adv* [in agreement] a favor.
  in favour of *prep* **-1.** [in preference to] em favor de **-2.** [in agreement with]: **to be in** ~ **of sthg/ of doing sthg** estar a favor de algo/de fazer algo.

favourable *UK*, **favorable** *US* ['feɪvrəbl] *adj* favorável.

favourably *UK*, **favorably** *US* ['feɪvrəblɪ] *adv* [well] favoralmente.

favoured *UK*, **favored** *US* ['feɪvəd] *adj* [with special advantages] favorecido(da).

favourite *UK*, **favorite** *US* ['feɪvrɪt] <> *adj* [preferred] favorito(ta). <> *n* favorito(ta).

favouritism *UK*, **favoritism** *US* ['feɪvrɪtɪzm] *n* (*U*) favoritismo *m.*

fawn [fɔːn] <> *adj* castanho(nha) claro(ra). <> *n* [animal] cervato *m.* <> *vi*: **to** ~ **on sb** bajular alguém.

fax [fæks] <> *n* fax *m.* <> *vt* **-1.** [send fax to] enviar um fax para **-2.** [send by fax] enviar por fax.

fax machine *n* (máquina *f* de) fax *m.*

fax number *n* número *m* de fax.

faze [feɪz] *vt inf* grilar.

FBI (*abbr of* Federal Bureau of Investigation) *n* FBI *m.*

FC (*abbr of* Football Club) *n* FC.

FCC (*abbr of* Federal Communications Commission) *n* comissão federal norte-americana de comunicação audiovisual.

FCO (*abbr of* Foreign and Commonwealth Office) *n* ministério britânico de relações exteriores e com o Commonwealth, ≃ MRE *m.*

FDA *n* (*abbr of* Food and Drug Administration) órgão norte-americano que controla os medicamentos e produtos alimentícios.

FE (*abbr of* Further Education) *n* estudos de educação continuada após o término do ensino superior na Grã-Bretanha.

fear [fɪə'] <> *n* **-1.** [gen] medo *m* **-2.** [risk] risco *m*, perigo *m*; **for** ~ **of** por medo de. <> *vt* **-1.** [be afraid of] ter medo de, temer **-2.** [anticipate] temer, recear; **to** ~ **(that)** recear que. <> *vi* [be afraid]: **to** ~ **for sb/sthg** temer por alguém/algo.

fearful ['fɪəfʊl] *adj* **-1.** *fml* [frightened] temeroso(sa); ~ **of sthg/of doing sthg** temeroso(sa) de algo/de fazer algo **-2.** [frightening] terrível, pavoroso(sa).

fearless ['fɪəlɪs] *adj* sem medo, destemido(da).

fearlessly ['fɪəlɪslɪ] *adv* destemidamente, sem medo.

fearsome ['fɪəsəm] *adj* terrível.

feasibility [ˌfiːzə'bɪlətɪ] *n* (*U*) [of plan] viabilidade *f.*

feasibility study *n* estudo *m* de viabilidade.

feasible ['fiːzəbl] *adj* [plan] viável.

feast [fiːst] <> *n* [meal] banquete *m.* <> *vi*: **to** ~ **on** *OR* **off sthg** banquetear-se com algo.

feat [fiːt] *n* façanha *f.*

feather ['feðə'] *n* pena *f*; **a** ~ **in one's cap** motivo de muito orgulho.

feather bed *n* cama *f* de penas.

feather-brained *adj* disparatado(da); **a** ~ **person** um cabeça-de-vento.

featherweight ['feðəweɪt] *n* [boxer] peso-pena *m.*

feature ['fiːtʃə'] <> *n* **-1.** [characteristic - of house] característica *f*; [- of machine] recurso *m*; [- of style, landscape] aspecto *m*; [- of face, personality] traço *m* **-2.** [article] reportagem *f* especial **-3.** *RADIO* & *TV* [programme] especial *m* **-4.** *CINEMA* longa-metragem *m.* <> *vt* [subj: film, exhibition] ter como atração principal; **a film featuring Juliette Binoche** um filme estrelando Juliette Binoche. <> *vi*: **to** ~ **(in sthg)** [appear, figure] figurar (em algo).

feature film *n* longa-metragem *m.*

featureless ['fiːtʃəlɪs] *adj* sem traços característicos.

Feb. [feb] (*abbr of* February) fev.

February ['februərɪ] *n* fevereiro *m*; *see also* September.

feces *npl US* = faeces.

feckless ['feklɪs] *adj* displicente.

fed [fed] *pt* & *pp* ⊳ feed.

Fed [fed] <> *n* **-1.** *fam* (*abbr of* Federal agent/official) oficial ou agente oficial norte-americano, especialmente do FBI. **-2.** *fam* (*abbr of* Federal Reserve Board) órgão de controle do banco central norte-americano. <> **-1.** (*abbr of* federal) fed. **-2.** (*abbr of* federation) Fed.

federal ['fedrəl] *adj* federal.

Federal Bureau of Investigation *n* polícia federal americana, FBI *m.*

federalism ['fedrəlɪzm] *n* (*U*) federalismo *m.*

federation [ˌfedə'reɪʃn] *n* **-1.** [country] federação *f* **-2.** [association] liga *f.*

fed up *adj* farto(ta), cheio(a); **to be** ~ **with sb/ sthg** estar cheio de alguém/algo.

fee [fiː] *n* [payment - school] (taxa *f* de) matrícula *f*; [- doctor] preço *m* da consulta; [- lawyer] honorários *mpl*; [- monthly membership] mensalidade *f*; [- annual membership] anuidade *f*; [- entrance] taxa *f* de admissão.

feeble ['fiːbl] *adj* **-1.** [weak] fraco(ca) **-2.** [lacking conviction] débil.

feeble-minded *adj* [stupid] imbecil, de idéias curtas.

feebleness ['fiːblnɪs] *n* (*U*) **-1.** [weakness] fraqueza *f* **-2.** [lack of conviction] debilidade *f.*

feebly ['fiːblɪ] *adv* **-1.** [weakly] fracamente **-2.** [without conviction] sem convicção.

feed [fiːd] (*pt* & *pp* fed) <> *vt* **-1.** [give food to] alimentar **-2.** *fig* [fuel] alimentar **-3.** [put, insert]: **to** ~ **sthg into sthg** inserir algo em algo. <> *vi* **-1.** [take food] alimentar-se; **to** ~ **on** *OR* **off sthg** alimentar-se de algo **-2.** *fig* [be fuelled]: **to** ~ **on** *OR* **off sthg** crescer com algo. <> *n* **-1.** [meal] comida *f* **-2.** (*U*) [animal food] ração *f.*

feedback ['fiːdbæk] *n* (*U*) **-1.** [reaction] reação *f* **-2.** *ELEC* feedback *m.*

feedbag ['fi:dbæg] n US embornal m.
feeder road n via f de alimentação.
feeding bottle ['fi:dɪŋ-] n UK mamadeira f.
feel [fi:l] (pt & pp felt) ⬦ vt -1. [touch] tocar -2. [believe, think] achar, acreditar; to ~ (that) achar que -3. [experience, be aware of] sentir; to ~ o.s. doing sthg sentir-se fazendo algo -4. phr: I'm not ~ing myself today não estou me sentindo bem hoje. ⬦ vi -1. [have sensation, emotion] sentir--se; to ~ like sthg/like doing sthg [be in mood for] ter vontade de algo/de fazer algo -2. [seem] parecer -3. [by touch]: to ~ for sthg procurar algo com as mãos. ⬦ n -1. [sensation, touch] sensação f-2. [atmosphere] clima m -3. phr: to get/have a ~ for sthg acostumar-se a algo.
feeler ['fi:lə'] n -1. [of insect, snail] antena f -2. [of octopus] tentáculo m.
feeling ['fi:lɪŋ] n -1. [emotion] sensação f; bad ~ mau pressentimento -2. [physical - of nausea, vertigo etc] sensação f; [- sensation] sensibilidade f -3. [awareness, impression] impressão f -4. [understanding] disposição f; to have a ~ for sthg levar jeito para algo.
⬥ **feelings** npl sentimentos mpl; to hurt sb's ~s magoar alguém, magoar os sentimentos de alguém; no hard ~s! sem ressentimentos!
fee-paying [-'peɪŋ] adj UK pago(ga).
feet [fi:t] pl ⬥ foot.
feign [feɪn] vt fml fingir.
feint [feɪnt] ⬦ n finta f. ⬦ vi fintar.
feisty ['faɪstɪ] (compar -ier, superl -iest) adj esp US inf determinado(da).
felicitous [fɪ'lɪsɪtəs] adj fml [fortunate] oportuno(na).
feline ['fi:laɪn] ⬦ adj felino(na). ⬦ n fml felino m, -na f.
fell [fel] ⬦ pt ⬥ fall. ⬦ vt -1. [tree] cortar -2. [person] derrubar.
⬥ **fells** npl GEOGR charneca f.
fellow ['feləʊ] ⬦ adj companheiro m, -ra f. ⬦ n -1. dated [man] cara mf -2. [comrade, peer] camarada mf -3. [of society or college] membro m honorário.
fellowship ['feləʊʃɪp] n -1. (U) [comradeship] companheirismo m -2. [organization] sociedade f -3. [in university - grant] bolsa f de pesquisa; [- post] pesquisador m, -ra f.
felony ['felənɪ] (pl -ies) n JUR delito m grave.
felt [felt] ⬦ pt & pp ⬥ feel. ⬦ n (U) [textile] feltro m.
felt-tip pen n pincel m atômico.
female ['fi:meɪl] ⬦ adj -1. [gen] feminino(na) -2. [plant] fêmeo(mea). ⬦ n -1. [female animal] fêmea f -2. inf pej [woman] fêmea f.
feminine ['femɪnɪn] ⬦ adj feminino(na). ⬦ n GRAMM feminino m.
femininity [femɪ'nɪnətɪ] n (U) feminilidade f.
feminism ['femɪnɪzm] n (U) feminismo m.
feminist ['femɪnɪst] n feminista f.
fence [fens] ⬦ n [barrier] cerca f; to sit on the ~ fig ficar em cima do muro. ⬦ vt cercar.
⬥ **fence in** vt sep -1. [garden] cercar -2. fig [person] prender; she feels completely ~d in ela se sente totalmente presa.
⬥ **fence off** vt sep isolar.

fencing ['fensɪŋ] n (U) -1. SPORT esgrima f -2. [fences] cerca f -3. [material] material m para fazer cerca.
fend [fend] vi: to ~ for o.s. saber se virar.
⬥ **fend off** vt sep rechaçar.
fender ['fendə'] n -1. [round fireplace] guarda-fogo m -2. [on boat] proteção f -3. US [on car] pára-lama f.
fennel ['fenl] n (U) erva-doce f.
fens [fenz] npl UK pântano m.
feral ['fɪərəl] adj selvagem.
ferment [n 'fɜ:ment, vb fə'ment] ⬦ n (U) [unrest] grande agitação f, polvorosa f; in ~ em polvorosa. ⬦ vi [change chemically] fermentar.
fermentation [fɜ:mən'teɪʃn] n (U) fermentação f.
fermented [fə'mentɪd] adj fermentado(da).
fern [fɜ:n] n samambaia f.
ferocious [fə'rəʊʃəs] adj feroz.
ferociously [fə'rəʊʃəslɪ] adv ferozmente.
ferocity [fə'rɒsətɪ] n (U) ferocidade f.
ferret ['ferɪt] n [animal] furão m.
⬥ **ferret about, ferret around** vi inf vasculhar.
⬥ **ferret out** vt sep inf desenterrar.
ferris wheel ['ferɪs-] n esp US roda-gigante f.
ferry ['ferɪ] (pl -ies, pt & pp -ied) ⬦ n balsa f. ⬦ vt transportar.
ferryboat ['ferɪbəʊt] n = ferry.
ferryman ['ferɪmən] (pl -men [-mən]) n balseiro m.
fertile ['fɜ:taɪl] adj fértil.
fertility [fə'tɪlətɪ] n (U) fertilidade f.
fertility drug n remédio f para infertilidade.
fertilization [fɜ:tɪlaɪ'zeɪʃn] n (U) -1. [enrichment] fertilização f -2. [insemination] fecundação f.
fertilize, -ise ['fɜ:tɪlaɪz] vt -1. [enrich] fertilizar -2. [inseminate] fecundar.
fertilizer ['fɜ:tɪlaɪzə'] n fertilizante m.
fervent ['fɜ:vənt] adj -1. [admirer, believer] fervoroso(-sa) -2. [belief, desire, hope] ardente.
fervour UK, **fervor** US ['fɜ:və'] n (U) fervor m.
fester ['festə'] vi -1. [wound] inflamar, inflamar-se -2. fig [situation, problem, feeling] inflamar.
festival ['festəvl] n -1. [series of organized events] festival m -2. [holiday] feriado m, dia m festivo.
festive ['festɪv] adj festivo(va).
festive season n: the ~ a época do Natal.
festivities [fes'tɪvətɪz] npl festividades fpl.
festoon [fe'stu:n] vt enfeitar; to be ~ed with sthg estar enfeitado(da) com algo.
fetal ['fi:tl] adj = foetal.
fetch [fetʃ] vt -1. [go and get] ir buscar -2. [sell for] alcançar.
fetching ['fetʃɪŋ] adj atraente.
fete, fête [feɪt] ⬦ n festa f beneficente. ⬦ vt festejar (em honra de alguém).
fetid ['fetɪd] adj fétido(da).
fetish ['fetɪʃ] n -1. [sexual obsession] fetiche m -2. [mania] mania f -3. [object] amuleto m.
fetishism ['fetɪʃɪzm] n (U) fetichismo m.
fetlock ['fetlɒk] n machinho m.
fetter ['fetə'] vt restringir.
⬥ **fetters** npl fig [constraints] restrição f.
fettle ['fetl] n (U): in fine ~ [person] em forma.
fetus ['fi:təs] n = foetus.

feud [fjuːd] ⬦ *n* contenda *f.* ⬦ *vi* brigar.

feudal ['fjuːdl] *adj* feudal.

fever ['fiːvəʳ] *n* **-1.** MED febre *f* **-2.** *fig* [frenzy] frenesi *m.*

fevered ['fiːvəd] *adj* **-1.** [hot] febril **-2.** [wild, excited] exaltado(da).

feverish ['fiːvərɪʃ] *adj* **-1.** MED febril **-2.** [frenzied] frenético(ca).

fever pitch *n (U)* ponto *m* máximo.

few [fjuː] ⬦ *adj* [not many] pouco(ca); a ~ alguns(mas); a ~ **more** mais alguns(mas); **quite a** ~, **a good** ~ bastante; ~ **and far between** pouquíssimos(mas). ⬦ *pron* poucos *mpl,* -cas *fpl;* a ~ poucos(cas); **quite a** ~, **a good** ~ bastante.

fewer ['fjuːəʳ] ⬦ *adj* menos; **no** ~ **than** não menos do que. ⬦ *pron* menos.

fewest ['fjuːəst] *adj* o menos possível.

FHA (*abbr of* **Federal Housing Administration**) *n* órgão norte-americano que controla a habitação social.

fiancé [fɪˈɒnseɪ] *n* noivo *m.*

fiancée [fɪˈɒnseɪ] *n* noiva *f.*

fiasco [fɪˈæskəʊ] (*UK pl* -s, *US pl* -s OR -es) *n* fiasco *m.*

fib [fɪb] (*pt* & *pp* -**bed,** *cont* -**bing**) *inf* ⬦ *n* lorota *f.* ⬦ *vi* contar lorotas.

fibber ['fɪbəʳ] *n inf* mentiroso(sa).

fibre UK, **fiber** US ['faɪbəʳ] *n* **-1.** *(U)* [material, substance] fibra *f* **-2.** [thread] filamento *m* **-3.** *(U)* [strength] força *f.*

fibreboard UK, **fiberboard** US ['faɪbəbɔːdl] *n (U)* madeira *f* compensada.

fibreglass UK, **fiberglass** US ['faɪbəglɑːs] ⬦ *n (U)* fibra *f* de vidro. ⬦ *comp* de fibra de vidro.

fibre optics *n (U)* fibra *f* óptica.

fibrositis [ˌfaɪbrəˈsaɪtɪs] *n (U)* fibrosite *f.*

FICA (*abbr of* **Federal Insurance Contributions Act**) *n lei norte-americana que regulamenta o pagamento obrigatório de contribuição social mensal por parte dos trabalhadores.*

fickle ['fɪkl] *adj* inconstante, volúvel.

fiction ['fɪkʃn] *n* **-1.** *(U)* [literature] ficção *f* **-2.** [fabrication, lie] invenção *f.*

fictional ['fɪkʃənl] *adj* **-1.** [literary] ficcional **-2.** [invented] imaginário(ria).

fictionalize, -ise ['fɪkʃənəlaɪz] *vt* romancear.

fictitious [fɪkˈtɪʃəs] *adj* [false] fictício(cia).

fiddle ['fɪdl] ⬦ *n* **-1.** [violin] rabeca *f;* **(as) fit as a** ~ em excelente forma; **to play second** ~ **(to sb)** estar em segundo plano (para alguém) **-2.** *UK inf* [fraud] embuste *m.* ⬦ *vt UK inf* falsificar. ⬦ *vi* **-1.** [fidget]: **to** ~ **(about** OR **around)** enrolar; **to** ~ **(about** OR **around) with sthg** mexer em algo **-2.** [waste time]: **to** ~ **about** OR **around** perder tempo.

fiddler ['fɪdləʳ] *n* [violinist] violinista *mf.*

fiddly ['fɪdlɪ] (*compar* -**ier,** *superl* -**iest**) *adj UK inf* trabalhoso(sa).

fidelity [fɪˈdelətɪ] *n (U)* **-1.** [loyalty] fidelidade *f* **-2.** [accuracy] veracidade *f.*

fidget ['fɪdʒɪt] *vi* estar irrequieto(ta), mover-se sem parar.

fidgety ['fɪdʒɪtɪ] *adj inf* inquieto(ta).

fiduciary [fɪˈduːʃjərɪ] (*pl* -**ies**) ⬦ *adj* fiduciário

(ria). ⬦ *n* fiduciário *m,* -ria *f.*

field [fiːld] ⬦ *n* **-1.** [gen] campo *m* **-2.** [of knowledge] área *f* **-3.** [real environment]: **in the** ~ no campo de batalha **-4.** : ~ **of vision** campo visual. ⬦ *vt* [avoid answering] responder. ⬦ *vi* SPORT interceptar.

field day *n* [for study, sport] dia *m* de atividades externas; **to have a** ~ *fig* fazer a festa.

fielder ['fiːldəʳ] *n* **-1.** [in baseball] jardineiro *m* **-2.** [in cricket] interceptador *m.*

field event *n* esporte *m* de campo.

field glasses *npl* binóculos *mpl.*

field marshal *n* marechal-de-campo *m.*

field mouse *n* ratazana *f.*

field trip *n* viagem *f* de estudos.

fieldwork ['fiːldwɜːk] *n (U)* pesquisa *f* de campo.

fieldworker ['fiːldwɜːkəʳ] *n* pesquisador *m,* -ra *f* de campo.

fiend [fiːnd] *n* **-1.** [cruel person] demônio *m* **-2.** *inf* [fanatic] fanático *m,* -ca *f.*

fiendish ['fiːndɪʃ] *adj* **-1.** [evil] diabólico(ca) **-2.** *inf* [very difficult] cabeludo(da).

fierce [fɪəs] *adj* **-1.** [aggressive, ferocious] feroz **-2.** [wild, uncontrolled] violento(ta) **-3.** [intense - competition, battle] árduo(a); [- heat] intenso(sa); [- criticism] ferrenho(nha).

fiercely ['fɪəslɪ] *adv* **-1.** [aggressively, ferociously] ferozmente **-2.** [wildly] violentamente **-3.** [intensely] arduamente.

fiery ['faɪərɪ] (*compar* -**ier,** *superl* -**iest**) *adj* **-1.** [burning] ardente **-2.** [spicy] picante **-3.** [volatile] explosivo(va) **-4.** [bright red] cor-de-fogo.

FIFA (*abbr of* **Fédération Internationale de Football Association**) *n* FIFA *f.*

fifteen [fɪfˈtiːn] *num* quinze; *see also* **six.**

fifteenth [fɪfˈtiːnθ] *num* décimo quinto, décima quinta; *see also* **sixth.**

fifth [fɪfθ] *num* quinto, quinta; *see also* **sixth.**

Fifth Amendment *n:* **the** ~ a Quinta Emenda, *emenda constitucional americana que estabelece direitos civis aos criminosos.*

fifth column *n* quinta-coluna *f.*

fiftieth ['fɪftɪəθ] *num* qüinquagésimo, qüinquagésima; *see also* **sixth.**

fifty ['fɪftɪ] (*pl* -**ies**) *num* cinqüenta; *see also* **sixty.**

fifty-fifty ⬦ *adj:* **to have a** ~ **chance** ter cinqüenta por cento de chance. ⬦ *adv:* **to split sthg** ~ dividir algo meio a meio.

fig [fɪg] *n* figo *m.*

fight [faɪt] (*pt* & *pp* **fought**) ⬦ *n* **-1.** [physical] briga *f,* luta *f;* **to have a** ~ **(with sb)** ter uma briga (com alguém); **to put up a** ~ desencadear uma luta **-2.** *fig* [battle, struggle] luta *f,* batalha *f* **-3.** [argument] discussão *f;* **to have a** ~ **(with sb)** ter uma discussão (com alguém). ⬦ *vt* **-1.** [gen] lutar (com), combater; [physically] brigar com **-2.** [combat, struggle against] lutar contra. ⬦ *vi* **-1.** [physically, in war] lutar **-2.** *fig* [battle, struggle]: **to** ~ **for/against sthg** lutar por/contra algo **-3.** [argue] discutir sobre; **to** ~ **about** OR **over sthg** discutir sobre algo.

➤ **fight back** ⬦ *vt fus* segurar. ⬦ *vi* revidar.

➤ **fight off** *vt sep* **-1.** [deter physically] rechaçar **-2.** *fig* [overcome] superar.

fight out *vt sep*: **to ~ it out** resolver a questão.

fighter ['faɪtə'] *n* **-1.** [plane] caça *m* **-2.** [soldier] guerreiro *m*, -ra *f* **-3.** [combative person] lutador *m*, -ra *f*.

fighting ['faɪtɪŋ] *n (U)* [in war, punch-up] luta *f*.

fighting chance *n*: **to have a ~** ter uma boa chance.

figment ['fɪgmənt] *n*: **a ~ of sb's imagination** um produto da imaginação de alguém.

figurative ['fɪgərətɪv] *adj* [language, art] figurado(da).

figuratively ['fɪgərətɪvlɪ] *adv* metaforicamente.

figure [*UK* 'fɪgə', *US* 'fɪgjər] <> *n* **-1.** [statistic] índice *m*; **to put a ~ on sthg** declarar o valor total de algo **-2.** [symbol of number] número *m*; **in single/double ~s** em valores até dez/acima de dez **-3.** [human shape, outline] silhueta *f* **-4.** [diagram, representative personality] figura *f* **-5.** [famous person] personalidade *f* **-6.** [aesthetic shape of body] forma *f* **-7.** <> *vt esp US* [suppose] supor. <> *vi* **-1.** [feature] figurar **-2.** *US* [make sense]: **that ~s!** faz sentido!

figure out *vt sep* compreender.

figure eight *n US* = figure of eight.

figurehead ['fɪgəhed] *n* **-1.** [on ship] carranca *f* de proa **-2.** [leader without real power] testa-de-ferro *m*.

figure of eight *UK*, **figure eight** *US n* forma *f* de oito.

figure of speech *n* figura *f* de linguagem.

figure-skating *n (U)* patinação *f* artística.

figurine [*UK* 'fɪgəriːn, *US* ˌfɪgjə'riːn] *n* estatueta *f (de metal ou cerâmica)*.

Fiji ['fiːdʒiː] *n* Fiji; **in ~** em Fiji.

Fijian [ˌfiː'dʒiːən] <> *adj* fijiano(na). <> *n* fijiano *m*, -na *f*.

filament ['fɪləmənt] *n* [in light bulb] filamento *m*.

filch [fɪltʃ] *vt inf* surrupiar.

file [faɪl] <> *n* **-1.** [folder] pasta *f* **-2.** [report] relatório *m*; **on ~**, **on the ~s** em arquivo, arquivado(da) **-3.** *COMPUT* arquivo *m* **-4.** [tool] lixa *f* **-5.** [line]: **in single ~** em fila indiana. <> *vt* **-1.** [put in folder] pôr na pasta **-2.** *JUR* dar entrada em **-3.** [shape, smooth] lixar. <> *vi* **-1.** [walk in single file] andar em fila única **-2.** *JUR*: **to ~ for divorce** dar entrada no divórcio.

file clerk *n US* = filing clerk.

filename ['faɪlˌneɪm] *n COMPUT* nome *m* de arquivo.

filet *n US* = fillet.

filibuster ['fɪlɪbʌstə'] *vi esp US POL* fazer discursos obstrucionistas.

filigree ['fɪlɪgriː] <> *adj* filigranado(da). <> *n (U)* filigrana *f*.

filing cabinet ['faɪlɪŋ-] *n* fichário *m*.

filing clerk *UK* ['faɪlɪŋ-], **file clerk** *US n* arquivista *mf*.

Filipino [ˌfɪlɪ'piːnəʊ] *(pl -s)* <> *adj* filipino(na). <> *n* filipino *m*, -na *f*.

fill [fɪl] <> *vt* **-1.** [make full - container] encher; [- room, street] ocupar; **to ~ sthg (with sthg)** encher algo com algo **-2.** [fulfill] preencher **-3.** [tooth] obturar. <> *vi* encher-se. <> *n*: **to have had one's ~ of sthg** estar até o pescoço de algo; **to eat one's ~** fartar-se.

fill in <> *vt sep* **-1.** [form] preencher **-2.** [hole]

tapar **-3.** [inform]: **to ~ sb in (on sthg)** informar alguém (sobre algo). <> *vt fus*: **to be ~ing in time** fazer tempo. <> *vi* [substitute]: **to ~ in (for sb)** substituir alguém.

fill out <> *vt sep* [complete] completar. <> *vi* [get fatter] engordar.

fill up <> *vt sep* encher. <> *vi* lotar.

filled [fɪld] *adj* **-1.** [with sandwich filling] recheado(da) **-2.** [with emotion]: **~ (with sthg)** cheio(a) (de algo).

filler ['fɪlə'] *n (U)* [for cracks] enchimento *m*.

filler cap *n UK* tampa *f* do tanque de combustível.

fillet *UK*, **filet** *US* ['fɪlɪt] *n* **-1.** [piece of meat] filé *m* **-2.** *(U)* [type of meat] lombo *m*.

fillet steak *n* filé *m*.

fill-in *n inf* [stopgap] tapa-buraco *m*.

filling ['fɪlɪŋ] <> *adj* [satisfying] que satisfaz. <> *n* **-1.** [in tooth] obturação *f* **-2.** [in cake, sandwich] recheio *m*.

filling station *n* posto *m* de gasolina.

fillip ['fɪlɪp] *n* estímulo *m*.

filly ['fɪlɪ] *(pl -ies)* *n* potranca *f*.

film [fɪlm] <> *n* **-1.** [cinema, TV, photographic] filme *m* **-2.** *(U)* [footage] cobertura *f* **-3.** [layer] película *f*. <> *vt* filmar. <> *vi* filmar.

filming ['fɪlmɪŋ] *n (U)* filmagem *f*.

film-maker *n* cineasta *mf*.

film star *n* astro *m* de cinema, estrela *f* de cinema.

filmstrip ['fɪlmˌstrɪp] *n* diafilme *m*.

film studio *n* estúdio *m* de cinema.

Filofax® ['faɪləʊfæks] *n* agenda *f (de folhas descartáveis)*.

filter ['fɪltə'] <> *n* filtro *m*. <> *vt* **-1.** [water, petrol] filtrar **-2.** [coffee] coar. <> *vi* [people] infiltrar-se.

filter out *vt sep* [remove by filtering] filtrar.

filter through *vi* infiltrar-se.

filter coffee *n* café *m* coado.

filter lane *n UK* faixa *f* de conversão *(à direita ou esquerda)*.

filter paper *n* filtro *m* de papel *(para café)*.

filter-tipped [-'tɪpt] *adj* com filtro.

filth [fɪlθ] *n (U)* **-1.** [dirt] sujeira *f* **-2.** [obscenity] obscenidade *f*.

filthy ['fɪlθɪ] *(compar* -ier, *superl* -iest) *adj* **-1.** [very dirty] imundo(da) **-2.** [obscene] obsceno(na).

filtration plant [fɪl'treɪʃn-] *n* unidade *f* de filtragem.

fin [fɪn] *n* **-1.** [on fish] barbatana *f* **-2.** *US* [for swimmer] nadadeira *f*.

final ['faɪnl] <> *adj* **-1.** [last in order] último(ma) **-2.** [at end, definitive] final. <> *n* final *f*.

finals *npl UNIV* exames *mpl* finais; **to sit one's ~s** prestar os exames finais.

final demand *n* último aviso *m*.

finale [fɪ'nɑːlɪ] *n* final *m*.

finalist ['faɪnəlɪst] *n* finalista *mf*.

finalize, -ise ['faɪnəlaɪz] *vt* finalizar.

finally ['faɪnəlɪ] *adv* **-1.** [at last] finalmente **-2.** [lastly] finalmente, por fim.

finance [*n* 'faɪnæns, *vb* faɪ'næns] <> *n (U)* **-1.** [money] financiamento *m* **-2.** [money management] finanças *fpl*. <> *vt* financiar.

finances *npl* finanças *fpl*.

financial [fɪˈnænʃl] adj financeiro(ra).

financial adviser n assessor m financeiro, assessora f financeira.

financially [fɪˈnænʃəlɪ] adv financeiramente.

financial services npl serviços mpl financeiros.

financial year UK, **fiscal year** US n ano m fiscal.

financier [fɪˈnænsɪəʳ] n UK financista mf.

finch [fɪntʃ] n tentilhão m.

find [faɪnd] (pt & pp **found**) <> vt **-1.** [gen] encontrar, achar; **to ~ one's way** achar o caminho **- 2.** [realize, discover]: **to ~ (that)** descobrir que **-3.** JUR: **to be found guilty/not guilty of sthg** ser declarado(da) culpado(da)/inocente de algo. <> n descoberta f.

  ➡ **find out** <> vi descobrir. <> vt fus **-1.** [information] informar-se **-2.** [truth] desmascarar. <> vt sep [person] descobrir.

findings [ˈfaɪndɪŋz] npl constatações fpl.

fine [faɪn] <> adj **-1.** [good, high-quality] excelente **- 2.** [perfectly satisfactory] ótimo(ma) **-3.** [healthy] bem **- 4.** [not rainy] bom(boa) **-5.** [thin, smooth] fino(na) **-6.** [minute, exact] sutil. <> adv [quite well] bem. <> n multa f. <> vt multar.

fine arts npl belas-artes fpl.

finely [ˈfaɪnlɪ] adv **-1.** [thinly, smoothly]: **to cut ~** cortar fino(na) **-2.** [tuned, balanced] com precisão.

fineness [ˈfaɪnnɪs] n (U) **-1.** [high quality] excelência f **-2.** [thinness, smoothness] finura f **-3.** [precision] minúcia f.

finery [ˈfaɪnərɪ] n (U) refinamento m.

finesse [fɪˈnes] n (U) finura f, delicadeza f.

fine-tooth comb [ˈfaɪntuːθ-] n: **to go over sthg with a ~** passar o pente fino em algo.

fine-tune [faɪntjuːn] vt ajustar.

finger [ˈfɪŋgəʳ] <> n dedo m; **to keep one's ~s crossed** manter os dedos cruzados; **she didn't lay a ~ on him** ela não encostou um dedo nele; **he didn't lift a ~ to help** ele não levantou um dedo para ajudar; **to point a** OR **the ~ at sb** apontar um OR o dedo para alguém; **to put one's ~ on sthg** colocar o dedo na ferida de algo, identificar algo corretamente; **to slip through one's ~s** escorrer pelos dedos; **to twist sb round one's little ~** fazer alguém de gato e sapato. <> vt [feel] tocar com os dedos.

fingermark [ˈfɪŋgəmɑːk] n marca f de dedo.

fingernail [ˈfɪŋgəneɪl] n unha f (dos dedos da mão).

fingerprint [ˈfɪŋgəprɪnt] n impressão f digital; **to take sb's ~s** tirar as impressões digitais de alguém.

fingertip [ˈfɪŋgətɪp] n ponta f do dedo; **at one's ~s** ao alcance da mão.

finicky [ˈfɪnɪkɪ] adj pej [- person] meticuloso(sa); [- task] minucioso(sa).

finish [ˈfɪnɪʃ] <> n **-1.** [end] final m **-2.** [texture] acabamento m. <> vt **-1.** [conclude, complete] terminar; **to ~ doing sthg** terminar de fazer algo **-2.** [consume] acabar **-3.** [leave] terminar, acabar. <> vi **-1.** [gen] terminar **-2.** [complete task] terminar, acabar.

  ➡ **finish off** vt sep [conclude, complete, consume] terminar.

  ➡ **finish up** vi acabar, terminar.

  ➡ **finish with** vt fus [break off with] terminar com.

finished [ˈfɪnɪʃt] adj **-1.** [ready, completed] terminado(da), pronto(ta) **-2.** [no longer interested]: **to be ~ with sthg** não estar mais interessado(da) em algo **- 3.** [over, no longer in existence] liquidado(da) **- 4.** inf [done for] acabado(da).

finishing line [ˈfɪnɪʃɪŋ-] n linha f de chegada.

finishing school [ˈfɪnɪʃɪŋ-] n ≃ colégio privado no qual se preparam as alunas da alta classe para entrar na sociedade.

finite [ˈfaɪnaɪt] adj **-1.** [limited] finito(ta) **-2.** GRAMM conjugado(da).

Finland [ˈfɪnlənd] n Finlândia; **in ~** na Finlândia.

Finn [fɪn] n [inhabitant of Finland] finlandês m, -esa f.

Finnish [ˈfɪnɪʃ] <> adj [of or relating to Finland] finlandês(esa). <> n [language] finlandês m.

fiord [fjɔːd] n = **fjord**.

fir [fɜːʳ] n abeto m.

fire [faɪəʳ] <> n **-1.** (U) [flames, burning] fogo m; **on ~** em chamas; **to catch ~** pegar fogo; **to set ~ to sthg** pôr fogo em algo **-2.** [for warmth, cooking] fogueira f **-3.** [blaze, conflagration] incêndio m **-4.** UK [heater, apparatus] aquecedor m, estufa f **-5.** (U) [shooting] fogo m; **to open ~ (on sb)** abrir fogo (contra alguém). <> vt **-1.** [shoot] disparar **-2.** [rap out] lançar **-3.** esp US [dismiss] demitir, despedir. <> vi: **to ~ (on** OR **at)** atirar em.

fire alarm n alarme m contra incêndio.

firearm [ˈfaɪərɑːm] n arma f de fogo.

fireball [ˈfaɪəbɔːl] n bola f de fogo.

firebomb [ˈfaɪəbɒm] <> n bomba f incendiária. <> vt lançar bombas incendiárias em.

firebreak [ˈfaɪəbreɪk] n aceiro m.

fire brigade UK, **fire department** US n corpo m de bombeiros.

fire chief n US = **fire master**.

firecracker [ˈfaɪəˌkrækəʳ] n rojão m.

fire-damaged adj deteriorado(da) por incêndio.

fire department n US = **fire brigade**.

fire door n porta f corta-fogo.

fire drill n simulação f de incêndio.

fire-eater n [performer] engolidor m, -ra f de fogo.

fire engine n carro m de bombeiros.

fire escape n escada f de incêndio.

fire extinguisher n extintor m de incêndio.

fire fighter n bombeiro m, -ra f.

fireguard [ˈfaɪəgɑːd] n guarda-fogo m.

fire hazard n risco m de incêndio.

fire hydrant [-ˈhaɪdrənt], **fireplug** US [ˈfaɪəplʌg] n hidrante m.

firelight [ˈfaɪəlaɪt] n (U) luz f de fogo.

firelighter [ˈfaɪəlaɪtəʳ] n acendedor m de fogo.

fireman [ˈfaɪəmən] (pl -men [-mən]) n bombeiro m.

fire master UK, **fire chief** US n chefe mf do corpo de bombeiros.

fireplace [ˈfaɪəpleɪs] n lareira f.

fireplug n US = **fire hydrant**.

firepower [ˈfaɪəˌpaʊəʳ] n (U) potência f de fogo.

fireproof [ˈfaɪəpruːf] adj à prova de fogo.

fire-raiser [-ˌreɪzəʳ] n UK incendiário m, -ria f.

fire regulations *npl* medidas *fpl* contra incêndio.

fire service *n UK* corpo *m* de bombeiros.

fireside ['faɪəsaɪd] *n*: **by the** ~ ao calor da lareira.

fire station *n* posto *m* de bombeiros.

firewood ['faɪəwʊd] *n (U)* lenha *f.*

firework ['faɪəwɜːk] *n* fogo *m* de artifício.

➡ **fireworks** *npl fig* [outburst of anger] fogos *mpl* de artifício.

firework display *n* espetáculo *m* pirotécnico.

firing ['faɪərɪŋ] *n (U)* MIL tiroteio *m.*

firing squad *n* pelotão *m* de fuzilamento.

firm [fɜːm] ◇ *adj* -1. [gen] firme; **to stand** ~ manter-se firme -2. [definite] claro(ra) -3. [investment, rate] estável. ◇ *n* empresa *f.*

➡ **firm up** ◇ *vt sep* [make clearer, finalize] firmar. ◇ *vi* firmar.

firmly ['fɜːmlɪ] *adv* firmemente.

firmness ['fɜːmnɪs] *n (U)* firmeza *f.*

first [fɜːst] ◇ *adj* primeiro(ra); **for the** ~ **time** pela primeira vez; ~ **thing (in the morning)** à primeira hora (da manhã); ~ **things** ~ primeiro o mais importante; **I don't know the** ~ **thing about it** não tenho a mais remota idéia sobre isso. ◇ *adv* -1. [before anyone, anything else] primeiro; ~ **of all** antes de mais nada, em primeiro lugar -2. [for the first time] pela primeira vez -3. [firstly, in list of points] primeiramente. ◇ *n* -1. [person] primeiro *m*, -ra *f* -2. [unprecedented event] acontecimento *m* sem precedentes -3. *UK* UNIV diploma *m* universitário -4. AUT: ~ **(gear)** primeira *f* (marcha).

➡ **at first** *adv* no princípio.

➡ **at first hand** *adv* em primeira mão.

first aid *n (U)* primeiros socorros *mpl.*

first-aider [-'eɪdəʳ] *n* socorrista *mf.*

first-aid kit *n* kit *m* de primeiros socorros.

first-class *adj* -1. [excellent] de primeira -2. *UK* UNIV com louvor -3. [letter, ticket] de primeira classe.

first-class mail *n (U)* correio *m* de primeira classe.

first course *n* entrada *f.*

first cousin *n* primo-irmão *m*, prima-irmã *f.*

first-day cover *n* envelope com carimbo comemorativo de lançamento de um selo.

first-degree *adj* -1. MED: ~ **burn** queimadura *f* de primeiro grau -2. *US* JUR: ~ **murder** homicídio *m* em primeiro grau.

first floor *n* -1. *UK* [above ground level] primeiro andar *m* -2. *US* [at ground level] andar *m* térreo.

firsthand [ˌfɜːst'hænd] ◇ *adj* de primeira mão. ◇ *adv* em primeira mão.

first lady *n* POL primeira-dama *f.*

first language *n* língua *f* materna.

first lieutenant *n* primeiro-tenente *m.*

firstly ['fɜːstlɪ] *adv* primeiramente.

first mate *n* primeiro piloto *m*, imediato *m.*

first name *n* nome *m* de batismo, nome *m.*

➡ **first-name** *adj*: **to be on first-name terms (with sb)** relacionar-se intimamente (com alguém).

first night *n* noite *f* de estréia.

first offender *n* delinqüente *mf* primário, -ria.

first officer *n* = first mate.

first-past-the-post system *n UK* sistema *m* de eleição por voto majoritário.

first-rate *adj* de primeira.

first refusal *n* primeira opção *f* de compra.

First World War *n*: **the** ~ a Primeira Guerra Mundial.

firtree ['fɜːtriː] *n* = fir.

fiscal ['fɪskl] *adj* fiscal.

fiscal year *n US* = financial year.

fish [fɪʃ] *(pl inv)* ◇ *n* peixe *m.* ◇ *vt* pescar em. ◇ *vi* -1. [try to catch fish] pescar; **to** ~ **for sthg** pescar algo -2. [try to obtain]: **to** ~ **for sthg** buscar algo.

➡ **fish out** *vt sep inf* [bring out] sacar.

fish and chips *npl UK* peixe *m* frito com batatas fritas.

fish and chip shop *n UK* barraca *f* de peixe frito com batatas fritas.

fishbowl ['fɪʃbəʊl] *n* aquário *m.*

fishcake ['fɪʃkeɪk] *n* bolinho *m* de peixe.

fisherman ['fɪʃəmən] *(pl* -men [-mən]*)* *n* pescador *m.*

fishery ['fɪʃərɪ] *(pl* -ies*)* *n* pescaria *f.*

fish-eye lens *n* lente *f* objetiva *(na câmera).*

fish farm *n* viveiro *m* de peixes.

fish fingers *UK*, **fish sticks** *US npl* porções *fpl* de peixe empanado.

fishhook ['fɪʃhʊk] *n* anzol *m.*

fishing ['fɪʃɪŋ] *n (U)* pesca *f*; **to go** ~ ir pescar.

fishing boat *n* barco *m* de pesca.

fishing line *n* linha *f* de pesca.

fishing rod *n* vara *f* de pescar.

fishmonger ['fɪʃˌmʌŋgəʳ] *n esp UK* peixeiro *m*; ~ **'s (shop)** peixaria *f.*

fishnet ['fɪʃnet] *n* -1. [for fishing] rede *f* de pesca -2. *(U)* [material]: ~ **stockings/tights** malhas *fpl*/meias *fpl* de malha.

fish pond *n* lagoa *f* de peixe.

fish shop *n* peixaria *f.*

fish slice *n UK* escumadeira *f.*

fish sticks *npl US* = fish fingers.

fish tank *n* aquário *m (usado como viveiro).*

fishwife ['fɪʃwaɪf] *(pl* -wives [-waɪvz]*)* *n pej*: **to behave like a** ~ comportar-se como uma lavadeira.

fishy ['fɪʃɪ] *(compar* -ier, *superl* -iest*)* *adj* -1. [like fish] de peixe -2. *fig* [suspicious] duvidoso(sa).

fission ['fɪʃn] *n (U)* fissão *f.*

fissure ['fɪʃəʳ] *n* fissura *f.*

fist [fɪst] *n* punho *m.*

fit [fɪt] *(pt & pp* -ted, *cont* -ting*)* ◇ *adj* -1. [suitable] adequado(da); **to be** ~ **for sthg** estar apto(ta) para algo; **to be** ~ **to do sthg** estar apto(ta) a fazer algo; **to see** OR **think** ~ **(to do sthg)** julgar OR achar conveniente (fazer algo); **do as you think** ~ faça como você achar melhor -2. [healthy] em forma; **to keep** ~ manter-se em forma. ◇ *n* -1. [of clothes, shoes etc.] tamanho *m*; **it's a good** ~ fica bem; **it's a tight** ~ fica justo -2. [epileptic seizure] ataque *m*; **to have a** ~ MED ter um ataque; *fig* [be angry] ter um ataque (de fúria) -3. [bout - of crying, depression] crise *f*; [- of rage, sneezing, giggles] acesso *m*; **in** ~**s and starts** aos trancos e barrancos. ◇

vt **-1.** [be correct size for] servir **-2.** [place]: **to ~ sthg into sthg** encaixar algo em algo **-3.** [provide]: **to ~ sthg with sthg** equipar algo com algo; **to have sthg ~ted** instalar algo **-4.** [be suitable for] adequar-se. <> *vi* **-1.** [be correct size] servir **-2.** [go] encaixar **-3.** [into container] caber.

➡ **fit in** <> *vt sep* [accommodate] arranjar tempo para. <> *vi* adaptar-se; **to ~ in with sb/sthg** adaptar-se com alguém/algo; **that ~s in with what she told me** isso vem ao encontro do que ela me contou.

➡ **fit out** *vt sep* equipar.

➡ **fit together** *vt sep* **-1.** [assemble] unir-se **-2.** [make sense] fazer sentido.

fitful ['fitful] *adj* intermitente.

fitment ['fitmənt] *n* móvel *m (da casa)*.

fitness ['fitnɪs] *n (U)* **-1.** [health] bom estado *m* físico **-2.** [suitability] aptidão *f*; **~ for sthg** aptidão para algo.

fitted ['fitəd] *adj* **-1.** [suited]: **~ for** OR **to sthg** adequado(da) para algo; **to be ~ to do sthg** ser adequado(da) para fazer algo **-2.** [tailored] na medida **-3.** UK [built-in] embutido(da).

fitted carpet ['fitəd-] *n* carpete *m*.

fitted kitchen ['fitəd-] *n* UK cozinha *f* de módulos.

fitted sheet *n* lençol *m* com elástico.

fitter ['fitə'] *n* [mechanic] mecânico *m*, -ca *f*.

fitting ['fitɪŋ] <> *adj fml* apropriado(da). <> *n* **-1.** [part] acessório *m* **-2.** [for clothing] prova *f*.

➡ **fittings** *npl* acessórios *mpl*.

fitting room *n* provador *m*.

five [faɪv] *num* cinco; *see also* **six**.

five-day week *n* semana *f* de cinco dias.

fiver ['faɪvə'] *n inf* **-1.** UK [amount] *cinco libras*; [note] *cédula de cinco libras* **-2.** US [amount] *cinco dólares*; [note] *cédula de cinco dólares*.

five-star *adj* [of highest standard]: **~ hotel** hotel cinco estrelas; **~ treatment** tratamento de primeira.

fix [fiks] <> *vt* **-1.** [attach, concentrate] fixar; **to ~ sthg to sthg** fixar algo em algo **-2.** [set, arrange] arranjar **-3.** [repair] consertar **-4.** *inf* [rig] manipular **-5.** *esp* US [food, drink] preparar. <> *n* **-1.** *inf* [difficult situation]: **to be in a ~** estar em apuro **-2.** *drugs sl* dose *f* de entorpecente.

➡ **fix up** *vt sep* **-1.** [provide]: **to ~ sb up with sthg** arranjar algo para alguém **-2.** [arrange] organizar, preparar.

fixation [fik'seɪʃn] *n* fixação *f*; **~ on** OR **about sb/sthg**, **~** fixação em OR por alguém/algo.

fixed [fikst] *adj* fixado(da).

fixed assets *npl* ativo *m* fixo.

fixture ['fikstʃə'] *n* **-1.** [in building] instalação *f* **-2.** *fig* [permanent feature] figura *f* constante **-3.** [sports event] encontro *m*.

fizz [fiz] <> *vi* **-1.** [drink] espumar **-2.** [firework] crepitar. <> *n* **-1.** [sound] chiado *m* **-2.** *(U)* [of drinks] efervescência *f*.

fizzle ['fizl] ➡ **fizzle out** *vi* **-1.** [firework] falhar **-2.** *fig* [interest] sumir.

fizzy ['fizi] *(compar* -ier, *superl* -iest) *adj* gasoso(sa).

fjord [fjɔːd] *n* fiorde *m*.

FL *abbr of* Florida.

flab [flæb] *n (U)* flacidez *f (do corpo)*.

flabbergasted ['flæbəgɑːstɪd] *adj* estarrecido(da), pasmado(da).

flabby ['flæbɪ] *(compar* -ier, *superl* -iest) *adj* flácido(-da), gordo(da).

flaccid ['flæsɪd] *adj* flácido(da).

flag [flæg] *(pt & pp* -ged, *cont* -ging) <> *n* [banner] bandeira *f*. <> *vi* **-1.** [person] desanimar **-2.** [spirts] decair **-3.** [conversation] acabar.

➡ **flag down** *vt sep* fazer sinal para.

Flag Day *n 14 de junho, dia da bandeira nos Estados Unidos*.

flag of convenience *n* bandeira *f* de conveniência.

flagon ['flægən] *n* **-1.** [bottle] garrafão *m* **-2.** [jug] jarro *m*.

flagpole ['flægpəʊl] *n* mastro *m* de bandeira.

flagrant ['fleɪgrənt] *adj* flagrante.

flagship ['flægʃɪp] *n* **-1.** [ship] nau *f* capitânia **-2.** [main asset] carro-chefe *m*.

flagstone ['flægstəʊn] *n* laje *f*.

flail [fleɪl] <> *vt* agitar. <> *vi* agitar-se.

flair [fleə'] *n* **-1.** [talent] dom *m*; **to have a ~ for sthg** ter um dom para algo **-2.** *(U)* [stylishness] habilidade *f*.

flak [flæk] *n (U)* **-1.** [gunfire] fogo *m* antiaéreo **-2.** *inf* [criticism] críticas *fpl*.

flake [fleɪk] <> *n* [small piece - of snow] floco *m*; [- of paint, plaster] lasca *f*; [- of skin] pedaço *m*. <> *vi* descascar.

➡ **flake out** *vi inf* desfalecer.

flaky ['fleɪkɪ] *(compar* -ier, *superl* -iest) *adj* **-1.** [flaking - skin] com escamas; [- paintwork] lascado(da); [- texture] folhado(da) **-2.** *US inf* [person, idea] extravagante.

flaky pastry *n (U)* massa *f* folhada, mil-folhas *m inv*.

flambé ['flɑːmbeɪ] *(pt & pp* -ed, *cont* -ing) <> *adj* flambado(da). <> *vt* flambar.

flamboyant [flæm'bɔɪənt] *adj* **-1.** [person, behaviour] extravagante **-2.** [clothes, design] chamativo(va).

flame [fleɪm] <> *n* chama *f*; **in ~s** em chamas; **to burst into ~s** irromper em chamas. <> *vi* **-1.** [be on fire] estar queimando **-2.** [redden] inflamar-se.

flameproof ['fleɪmpruːf] *adj* à prova de fogo.

flame-retardant [-rɪ'tɑːdənt] *adj* resistente ao fogo.

flame-thrower [-'θrəʊə'] *n* lança-chamas *m inv*.

flaming ['fleɪmɪŋ] *adj* **-1.** [fire-coloured] em cor de fogo **-2.** UK [very angry] acalorado(da) **-3.** UK *inf* [for emphasis] maldito(ta).

flamingo [flə'mɪŋgəʊ] *(pl* -s OR -es) *n* flamingo *m*.

flammable ['flæməbl] *adj* inflamável.

flan [flæn] *n* torta *f*.

Flanders ['flɑːndəz] *n* Flanders; **in ~** em Flanders.

flange [flændʒ] *n* rebordo *m*.

flank [flæŋk] <> *n* **-1.** [of animal] lado *m* **-2.** [of army] flanco *m*. <> *vt*: **to be ~ed by sb/sthg** ser ladeado(da) por alguém/algo.

flannel ['flænl] *n* **-1.** *(U)* [fabric] flanela *f* **-2.** UK [face-cloth] luva *f* de banho.

flannels *npl* calças *fpl* de flanela.

flannelette [ˌflænəˈlet] *n (U)* baetilha *f.*

flap [flæp] (*pt* & *pp* -ped, *cont* -ping) ⋄ *n* -**1.** [piece] dobra *f* -**2.** *inf* [state of panic]: **to get in a ~** ficar estérico(ca). ⋄ *vt* -**1.** [wings] bater -**2.** [arms] agitar, mexer. ⋄ *vi* -**1.** [wave - skirt, jacket] ondear, agitar-se; [- wings, bird] bater -**2.** *inf* [panic] estar estérico(ca).

flapjack [ˈflæpdʒæk] *n* -**1.** *UK* [biscuit] biscoito *m* de aveia -**2.** *US* [pancake] panqueca *f.*

flare [fleəʳ] ⋄ *n* [distress signal] sinal *m* luminoso. ⋄ *vi* -**1.**: **to ~ (up)** [fire] chamejar; [person] enfurecer-se; [war, revolution, disease] deflagrar-se -**2.** [trousers, skirt] alargar-se -**3.** [nostrils] abrir-se.

flares *npl* *UK* [trousers] calças *fpl* boca-de-sino.

flared [fleəd] *adj* [trousers, skirt] boca-de-sino.

flash [flæʃ] ⋄ *adj* -**1.** PHOT com flash -**2.** *inf* [expensive-looking] ostentoso(sa). ⋄ *n* -**1.** [of light, colour] brilho *m* -**2.** PHOT flash *m* -**3.** [sudden moment] instante *m*; **in a ~** num instante; **quick as a ~** rápido(da) **como um raio.** ⋄ *vt* -**1.** [light, torch] brilhar (*numa direção específica*) -**2.** [look, smile]: **she flashed a smile at him** ela sorriu rapidamente para ele -**3.** [show on screen] projetar -**4.** [show briefly] mostrar rapidamente. ⋄ *vi* -**1.** [gen] reluzir -**2.** [move fast] irromper; **it ~ed through his mind that ...** imediatamente lhe ocorreu que ...; **to ~ past** passar feito um raio.

flashback [ˈflæʃbæk] *n* flashback *m.*

flashbulb [ˈflæʃbʌlb] *n* [lâmpada *f* de) flash *m.*

flash card *n* cartão no qual se aparecem uma palavra ou um desejo e que se utiliza como material didático.

flashcube [ˈflæʃkjuːb] *n* flash *m* de cubo.

flasher [ˈflæʃəʳ] *n* *UK* -**1.** [light] pisca-pisca *m* -**2.** *inf* [man] exibicionista *m.*

flash flood *n* enchente *f.*

flashgun [ˈflæʃgʌn] *n* disparador *m* de flash.

flashlight [ˈflæʃlaɪt] *n* [torch] lanterna *f* (elétrica).

flashpoint *n* -**1.** [moment] ponto *m* de fulgor -**2.** [place] zona *f* de conflito.

flashy [ˈflæʃɪ] (*compar* -ier, *superl* -iest) *adj inf* ostentoso(sa).

flask [flɑːsk] *n* -**1.** [to keep drinks hot] garrafa *f* térmica -**2.** [used in chemistry] frasco *m* -**3.** [hip flask] cantil *m.*

flat [flæt] (*compar* -ter, *superl* -test) ⋄ *adj* -**1.** [level] plano(na); **~ feet** pés *mpl* chatos -**2.** [shoes] sem salto -**3.** [punctured] vazio(zia) -**4.** [categorical] categórico(ca) -**5.** [business, trade] estagnado(da) -**6.** [monotonous - voice] monótono(na); [- performance, writing] uniforme -**7.** [MUS - lower than correct note] abaixo do tom; [- lower than stated note] abemolado(da) -**8.** COMM [fare, fee] único(ca) -**9.** [no longer fizzy - beer] choco(ca); [- lemonade] que passou do ponto -**10.** [battery] descarregado(da). ⋄ *adv* -**1.** [level] horizontalmente -**2.** [absolutely]: **~ broke** completamente quebrado(da) -**3.** [categorically] terminantemente -**4.** [exactly] precisamente -**5.** MUS abaixo do tom. ⋄ *n* -**1.** *UK* [apartment] flat *m* -**2.** MUS bemol *m.*

flat out *adv* a todo vapor.

flat cap *n* *UK* gorro *m.*

flat-chested [-ˈtʃestɪd] *adj* de seios pequenos.

flatfish [ˈflætfɪʃ] (*pl inv*) *n* linguado *m.*

flat-footed [-ˈfʊtɪd] *adj* [with flat feet] de pés chatos.

flatlet *n* *UK* flat *m.*

flatly [ˈflætlɪ] *adv* -**1.** [absolutely] categoricamente -**2.** [dully] de forma monótona.

flatmate [ˈflætmeɪt] *n* *UK* colega *mf* que divide o apartamento com outro.

flat-packed *adj* [furniture] para montar.

flat racing *n (U)* corrida *f* de cavalos sem obstáculos.

flat rate *n* preço *m* único.

flatscreen television, flatscreen TV [ˈflæt,-skriːn] *n* tv *f* de tela plana.

flatten [ˈflætn] *vt* -**1.** [make flat - steel, bumps] aplanar; [- wrinkles] esticar; [- paper] alisar; **to ~ o.s. against sthg** prensar-se contra algo -**2.** [building] demolir -**3.** *inf* [opponent] esmagar.

flatten out ⋄ *vi* aplanar-se, nivelar-se. ⋄ *vt sep* [wrinkles] esticar ; [lumps, bumps] aplanar.

flatter [ˈflætəʳ] *vt* -**1.** [compliment] adular, bajular; **I'm ~ed** sinto-me lisonjeado(da); **to ~ o.s. (that)** congratular-se de que -**2.** [suit] cair bem.

flatterer [ˈflætərəʳ] *n* bajulador *m*, -ra *f.*

flattering [ˈflætərɪŋ] *adj* [remark, offer] lisonjeiro(ra); [dress, colour, neckline] que cai bem.

flattery [ˈflætərɪ] *n (U)* bajulação *f.*

flatulence [ˈflætjʊləns] *n (U)* flatulência *f.*

flatware [ˈflætweəʳ] *n* *US* talheres *mpl.*

flaunt [flɔːnt] *vt* ostentar.

flautist *UK* [ˈflaʊtɪst], **flutist** *US* [ˈfluːtɪst] *n* flautista *mf.*

flavour *UK*, **flavor** *US* [ˈfleɪvəʳ] ⋄ *n* -**1.** [taste] sabor *m* -**2.** *fig* [atmosphere] ar *m*, toque *m.* ⋄ *vt* [food, drink] condimentar.

flavouring *UK*, **flavoring** *US* [ˈfleɪvərɪŋ] *n (U)* condimento *m.*

flaw [flɔː] *n* [fault] imperfeição *f*; **~ in sthg** imperfeição em algo.

flawed [flɔːd] *adj* imperfeito(ta), defeituoso(sa).

flawless [ˈflɔːlɪs] *adj* impecável.

flax [flæks] *n* linho *m.*

flay [fleɪ] *vt* [skin] pelar.

flea [fliː] *n* pulga *f*; **to send sb away with a ~ in his/her ear** mandar alguém embora com forte reprovação.

flea market *n* mercado *m* das pulgas.

fleck [flek] ⋄ *n* mancha *f.* ⋄ *vt* : **~ed with sthg** manchado(da) com algo.

fled [fled] *pt* & *pp* ⊳ **flee.**

fledg(e)ling [ˈfledʒlɪŋ] ⋄ *adj* [new, young] novato(ta). ⋄ *n* ave *f* recém-emplumada.

flee [fliː] (*pt* & *pp* fled) ⋄ *vt* [country, enemy] fugir de. ⋄ *vi* fugir.

fleece [fliːs] ⋄ *n* -**1.** [material, of sheep] velo *m* -**2.** [garment] sobretudo *m* de lã. ⋄ *vt inf* [cheat] trapacear.

fleet [fliːt] *n* frota *f.*

fleeting [ˈfliːtɪŋ] *adj* fugaz.

Fleet Street *n* Fleet Street *f.*

Fleming ['flemɪŋ] *n* flamengo *m*, -ga *f.*

Flemish ['flemɪʃ] ◇ *adj* flamengo(ga). ◇ *n* [language] flamengo *m.* ◇ *npl*: **the** ~ os flamengos.

flesh [fleʃ] *n* **-1.** [of body] carne *f*; **to be only** ~ **and blood** ser de carne e osso; **to be sb's own** ~ **and blood** ser sangue do sangue de alguém; **in the** ~ em carne e osso **-2.** [of fruit, vegetable] polpa *f.*
➥ **flesh out** *vt sep* detalhar.

flesh wound *n* ferimento *m* superficial.

fleshy ['fleʃɪ] (*compar* -ier, *superl* -iest) *adj* [fat] carnudo(da).

flew [flu:] *pt* ⊳ **fly.**

flex [fleks] ◇ *n* ELEC fio *m*, cabo *m.* ◇ *vt* [bend] flexionar.

flexibility [ˌfleksəˈbɪlətɪ] *n (U)* flexibilidade *f.*

flexible ['fleksəbl] *adj* flexível.

flexitime ['fleksɪtaɪm] *n (U)* horário *m* flexível.

flick [flɪk] ◇ *n* **-1.** [of whip, towel] pancada leve **-2.** [with finger] peteleco *m.* ◇ *vt* **-1.** [whip, towel] dar uma pancada leve em **-2.** [with finger] dar um peteleco em **-3.** [switch - turn on] ligar; [- turn off] desligar.
➥ **flicks** *npl inf*: **the** ~ **s** o cinema.
➥ **flick through** *vt fus* folhear.

flicker ['flɪkəʳ] ◇ *n* **-1.** [of light, candle] oscilação *f* **-2.** *fig* [of hope, interest] centelha *f.* ◇ *vi* **-1.** [candle, light] tremeluzir **-2.** [shadow, eyelids] tremer.

flick knife *n UK* canivete *f* de mola.

flier ['flaɪəʳ] *n* **-1.** [pilot] aviador *m* **-2.** [advertising leaflet] folheto *m* publicitário.

flight [flaɪt] *n* **-1.** [gen] vôo *m*; ~ **of fancy** OR **of the imagination** *fig* vôo da imaginação **-2.** [of steps, stairs] lance *m* **-3.** [escape] fuga *f.*

flight attendant *n* comissário *m*, -ria *f* de bordo.

flight crew *n* tripulação *f* de vôo.

flight deck *n* **-1.** [of aircraft carrier] pista *f* de aterrissagem **-2.** [of aircraft] cabine *f* de comando.

flight path *n* trajetória *f* de vôo.

flight recorder *n* caixa-preta *f.*

flighty ['flaɪtɪ] (*compar* -ier, *superl* -iest) *adj* volúvel.

flimsy ['flɪmzɪ] (*compar* -ier, *superl* -iest) *adj* **-1.** [fabric, structure] frágil **-2.** [excuse, argument] furado(da).

flinch [flɪntʃ] *vi* encolher-se; **to** ~ **from sthg/from doing sthg** vacilar diante de algo/em fazer algo; **without** ~ **ing** sem pestanejar.

fling [flɪŋ] (*pt* & *pp* **flung**) ◇ *n* [affair] caso *m.* ◇ *vt* [throw] atirar; **to** ~ **o.s. into an armchair/onto the ground** atirar-se numa poltrona/no chão.

flint [flɪnt] *n* **-1.** *(U)* [rock] sílex *m* **-2.** [in lighter] pedra *f.*

flip [flɪp] (*pt* & *pp* -**ped**, *cont* -**ping**) ◇ *vt* **-1.** [move with a flick] mover rapidamente, sacudir; **to** ~ **a coin** tirar cara ou coroa; **to** ~ **sthg open** abrir algo de supetão; **to** ~ **sthg over** virar algo bruscamente; **to** ~ **through sthg** folhear algo **-2.** [switch]: **to** ~ **on** ligar; **to** ~ **off** desligar **-3.** [throw]

atirar, jogar. ◇ *vi inf* [become angry] perder o controle. ◇ *n* **-1.** [of coin] arremesso *m* rápido **-2.** [somersault] piparote *m* **-3.** *phr*: **at the** ~ **of a switch** ao toque de um interruptor.

flipchart *n* quadro *m* de folhas móveis.

flip-flop *n UK* [shoe] sandália *f* de dedo.

flippant ['flɪpənt] *adj* leviano(na).

flippantly ['flɪpəntlɪ] *adv* levianamente.

flipper ['flɪpəʳ] *n* **-1.** [of animal] barbatana *f* **-2.** [for swimmer, diver] pé-de-pato *m.*

flipping ['flɪpɪŋ] *UK inf* ◇ *adj* maldito(ta). ◇ *adv* absolutamente.

flip side *n* [of record] lado *m* B.

flirt [flɜ:t] ◇ *n* [person] paquerador *m*, -ra *f.* ◇ *vi* **-1.** [with person] flertar; **to** ~ **with sb** flertar com alguém **-2.** [with idea] interessar-se por; **to** ~ **with sthg** interessar-se por algo.

flirtation [flɜ:ˈteɪʃn] *n* **-1.** *(U)* [flirting] flerte *m* **-2.** [love affair] caso *m* **-3.** [brief interest]: ~ **with sthg** interesse *m* em algo.

flirtatious [flɜ:ˈteɪʃəs] *adj* galanteador(ra).

flit [flɪt] (*pt* & *pp* -**ted**, *cont* -**ting**) *vi* [move quickly - bird] esvoaçar; [- expression, idea] passar rapidamente.

float [fləʊt] ◇ *n* **-1.** [on fishing line, net] bóia *f* **-2.** [in procession] carro *m* alegórico **-3.** [money] caixa *m.* ◇ *vt* **-1.** [on water] fazer boiar **-2.** [idea, project] lançar. ◇ *vi* **-1.** [on water] boiar **-2.** [through air] flutuar.

floating ['fləʊtɪŋ] *adj* flutuante.

floating voter *n UK* eleitor *m* indeciso, eleitora *f* indecisa.

flock [flɒk] ◇ *n* **-1.** [of birds, people] bando *m* **-2.** [of sheep] rebanho *m.* ◇ *vi*: **to** ~ **to** ir em massa para.

floe [fləʊ] *n* banquisa *f.*

flog [flɒg] (*pt* & *pp* -**ged**, *cont* -**ging**) *vt* **-1.** [whip] chicotear **-2.** *UK inf* [sell] pôr no prego.

flood [flʌd] ◇ *n* **-1.** [of water] enchente *f* **-2.** *fig* [great amount] dilúvio *m.* ◇ *vt* **-1.** [with water] inundar **-2.** *fig* [overwhelm]: **to** ~ **sthg (with)** inundar algo (com); **to** ~ **the market** inundar o mercado **-3.** [with light] encher **-4.** AUT [engine] afogar. ◇ *vi* **-1.** [river] transbordar **-2.** [street, land] inundar-se **-3.** *fig* [arrive in great amounts] chegar aos montes; **to** ~ **back** retornar.
➥ **floods** *npl* **-1.** [from river, rain] enchentes *fpl* **-2.** *fig* [of tears] torrente *f.*

floodgates ['flʌdgeɪts] *npl*: **to open the** ~ *fig* abrir caminho.

flooding ['flʌdɪŋ] *n (U)* [from river, rain] enchente *f*, inundação *f.*

floodlight ['flʌdlaɪt] *n* holofote *m.*

floodlit ['flʌdlɪt] *adj* iluminado(da) por holofotes.

flood tide *n* preamar *f*, maré *f* alta.

floor [flɔ:ʳ] ◇ *n* **-1.** [of room] piso *m*, chão *m* **-2.** [bottom] fundo *m* **-3.** [storey] andar *m*; **first** *US* OR **ground** *UK* ~ andar térreo **-4.** [at meeting, debate]: **from the** ~ da platéia; **to have/give the** ~ ter/dar a palavra **-5.** [for dancing] pista *f* **-6.** [of stock exchange] sala *f* de pregões; **to go through the** ~ [share prices] atingir a cotação mais baixa. ◇ *vt* **-1.** [knock down] nocautear **-2.** [baffle] confundir.

floorboard ['flɔ:bɔ:d] *n* tábua *f* de assoalho.

floor cloth n UK pano m de chão.

flooring ['flɔ:rɪŋ] n (U) pavimentação f.

floor lamp n US abajur m de pé.

floor show n espetáculo m noturno (em bar, restaurante, cabaré).

floorwalker ['flɔːˌwɔːkə^r] n esp US supervisor m, -ra f de seção (em lojas).

floozy ['flu:zɪ] (pl -ies) n dated & pej mulher f promíscua.

flop [flɒp] (pt & pp -ped, cont -ping) inf <> n [failure] fracasso m. <> vi -1. [fail] fracassar -2. [fall] esparramar-se; **the book ~ed open at page 20** o livro caiu aberto na página 20.

floppy ['flɒpɪ] (compar -ier, superl -iest) adj desengonçado(da).

floppy (disk) n disquete m.

flora ['flɔ:rə] n flora f; **~ and fauna** flora e fauna.

floral ['flɔːrəl] adj -1. [made of flowers] floral -2. [patterned with flowers] florido(da), de flores.

Florence ['florəns] n Florença; **in ~** em Florença.

floret ['florɪt] n florzinha f.

florid ['florɪd] adj -1. [face, complexion] corado(da) -2. [style] florido(da).

Florida ['floridə] n Flórida; **in ~** na Flórida.

florist ['florɪst] n florista mf; **~'s (shop)** floricultura f.

floss [flɒs] <> n (U) -1. [dental floss] fio-dental m -2. [for embroidery] seda f crua. <> vt limpar com fio-dental. <> vi limpar os dentes com fio-dental.

flotation [fləʊ'teɪʃn] n ST EX levantamento m de capital.

flotilla [flə'tɪlə] n flotilha f.

flotsam ['flotsəm] n (U): **~ and jetsam** [debris] entulho m; [people] gente f desocupada.

flounce [flaʊns] <> n [in cloth] babado m. <> vi [move] mover-se com ar de indignação; **he ~d out of the room** ele saiu indignado.

flounder ['flaʊndə^r] (pl inv OR -s) <> n [fish] linguado m. <> vi -1. [in water, mud] debater-se -2. [in conversation, speech] atrapalhar-se.

flour ['flaʊə^r] n (U) farinha f.

flourish ['flʌrɪʃ] <> vi -1. [grow healthily - plants, garden] florescer; [- child] crescer -2. [be successful] prosperar. <> vt movimentar. <> n -1. [movement]: **to do sthg with a ~** fazer algo de maneira a ser notado(da) -2. [of trumpets] fanfarra f.

flourishing ['flʌrɪʃɪŋ] adj -1. [growing healthily] viçoso(sa) -2. [successful] próspero(ra).

flout [flaʊt] vt desrespeitar.

flow [fləʊ] <> n fluxo m. <> vi -1. [liquid, electricity, air] correr f -2. [traffic, words, ideas] fluir -3. [tide] baixar -4. [hair, dress] ondear -5. [result]: **to ~ from** sthg brotar de algo.

flow chart, flow diagram n fluxograma m.

flower ['flaʊə^r] <> n BOT flor f; **in ~** em flor. <> comp de flores. <> vi florescer.

flowerbed ['flaʊəbed] n canteiro m de flores.

flowered adj florido(da).

flowering ['flaʊərɪŋ] <> adj BOT florido(da). <> n fig [of artistic movement, talents] florescência f.

flowerpot ['flaʊəpɒt] n vaso m de flores.

flowery ['flaʊərɪ] (compar -ier, superl -iest) adj -1. [patterned] florido(da) -2. pej [elaborate] floreado(da)

-3. [sweet-smelling] com odor de flores.

flowing ['fləʊɪŋ] adj -1. fig [writing, style] fluente -2. fig [hair, robes] esvoaçante.

flown [fləʊn] pp ⊳ fly.

fl. oz. abbr of fluid ounce.

flu [flu:] n (U) gripe m; **to have ~** estar com gripe.

fluctuate ['flʌktʃʊeɪt] vi oscilar, flutuar.

fluctuation [ˌflʌktʃʊ'eɪʃn] n [act of fluctuating] oscilação f, flutuação f.

flue [flu:] n fumeiro m.

fluency ['flu:ənsɪ] n (U) [in a foreign language] fluência f.

fluent ['flu:ənt] adj fluente; **he speaks ~ Spanish** ele fala espanhol fluentemente; **to be ~ in sthg** ser fluente em algo.

fluently ['flu:əntlɪ] adv fluentemente.

fluff [flʌf] <> n (U) -1. [down] felpa f -2. [dust] penugem f. <> vt -1. [puff up]: **to ~ sthg (up)** afofar -2. inf [do badly] fazer mal, não acertar.

fluffy ['flʌfɪ] (compar -ier, superl -iest) adj [downy] macio(cia).

fluid ['flu:ɪd] <> n fluido m. <> adj -1. [flowing] fluido(da) -2. [unfixed] mutável.

fluid ounce n onça f fluida (0,028 litro).

fluke [flu:k] n inf [chance] obra f do acaso.

flummox ['flʌməks] vt esp UK inf bestificar.

flung [flʌŋ] pt & pp ⊳ fling.

flunk [flʌŋk] esp US inf <> vt [SCH & UNIV - exam, test] não passar em; [- student] reprovar. <> vi levar pau, ser reprovado(da).

fluorescent [fluə'resnt] adj [colour] fluorescente.

fluorescent light n luz f fluorescente.

fluoridate vt adicionar flúor a.

fluoride ['fluəraɪd] n fluoreto m.

fluorine ['fluəri:n] n (U) flúor m.

flurry ['flʌrɪ] (pl -ies) n -1. [shower] lufada f -2. [sudden burst] erupção f.

flush [flʌʃ] <> adj -1. [level]: **~ with sthg** nivelado(da) com -2. inf [not short of money]: **to be ~ with money** estar sentado(da) no dinheiro. <> n -1. [in toilet] descarga f -2. [blush] rubor m -3. [sudden feeling] acesso m; **in the first ~ of sthg** literary no primeiro afluxo de algo. <> vt -1. [with water]: **to ~ the toilet** dar a descarga na privada; **to ~ sthg down the toilet** deixar algo cair na privada -2. fig [force out of hiding]: **to ~ sb out** fazer alguém sair. <> vi -1. [toilet] dar a descarga -2. [blush] ruborizar.

flushed [flʌʃt] adj -1. [red-faced] ruborizado(da) -2. [excited]: **~ with sthg** empolgado(da) com algo.

fluster ['flʌstə^r] <> n atrapalhação f. <> vt atrapalhar.

flustered ['flʌstəd] adj atrapalhado(da).

flute [flu:t] n MUS flauta f.

fluted ['flu:tɪd] adj ARCHIT acanalado(da).

flutist n US = flautist.

flutter ['flʌtə^r] <> n -1. [of wings] bater m -2. [of eyelashes] pestanejo m -3. [of heart] pulso m -4. inf [sudden feeling] agito m -5. inf [bet] aposta f. <> vt -1. [wings] bater, agitar -2. [eyelashes] pestanejar. <> vi -1. [bird, insect, wings] agitar -2. [flag] tremular -3. [dress] esvoaçar -4. [heart, pulse] pulsar.

flux [flʌks] n -1. (U) [change] fluxo m; **to be in a state of** ~ mudar continuamente -2. TECH fundente m.

fly [flaɪ] (pl **flies**, pt **flew**, pp **flown**) ◇ n -1. [insect] mosca f; **a** ~ **in the ointment** fig ≃ um pequeno problema -2. [of trousers] braguilha f. ◇ vt -1. [cause to fly] fazer voar -2. [transport by air] transportar em avião -3. [flag] tremular. ◇ vi -1. [bird, insect, plane] voar -2. [pilot] pilotar -3. [travel by plane] ir de avião -4. [move fast] voar; **time flies** o tempo voa -5. [attack]: **to** ~ **at sb** voar para cima de alguém.- 6. [flag] tremular.

➡ **fly away** vi ir-se embora.

➡ **fly in** ◇ vt sep trazer em avião. ◇ vi chegar.

➡ **fly into** vt fus: **to** ~ **into a rage/temper** enfurecer-se.

➡ **fly out** ◇ vt sep levar de avião. ◇ vi sair de avião.

flyby n US = flypast.

fly-fishing n (U) pesca f com iscas artificiais.

fly half n UK no rúgbi, jogador rápido cujo objetivo é passar a bola para uma linha de jogadores.

flying [ˈflaɪɪŋ] ◇ adj -1. [able to fly] voador(ra) -2. [running] veloz. ◇ n [in plane]: **I hate** ~ odeio viajar de avião.

flying colours npl: **to pass (sthg) with** ~ passar (em algo) com louvor.

flying doctor n médico que utiliza o avião para visitar seus pacientes em áreas mais isoladas.

flying officer n UK tenente-aviador m.

flying saucer n disco m voador.

flying squad n UK radiopatrulha f.

flying start n: **to get off to a** ~ começar muito bem.

flying visit n visita f rápida.

flyleaf [ˈflaɪliːf] (pl **-leaves**) n guarda f.

flyover [ˈflaɪˌəʊvəʳ] n UK viaduto m.

flypast UK [ˈflaɪˌpɑːst], **flyby** US [ˈflaɪˌbaɪ] n apresentação f aérea.

flysheet [ˈflaɪʃiːt] n [on tent] teto m duplo.

fly spray n inseticida f.

flyweight [ˈflaɪweɪt] n peso-mosca m.

flywheel [ˈflaɪwiːl] n TECH volante m.

FM -1. (abbr of **frequency modulation**) FM f. - 2. (abbr of **field marshal**) mestre-de-campo m.

FMCS (abbr of **Federal Mediation and Conciliation Services**) n serviço federal norte-americano que oferece serviços de conciliação entre empregadores e sindicatos em disputas industriais.

FO (abbr of **Foreign Office**) n ≃ MRE m.

foal [fəʊl] n potro m.

foam [fəʊm] ◇ n -1. [bubbles] espuma f -2. [material]: ~ **rubber** espuma de borracha. ◇ vi espumar.

foamy [ˈfəʊmɪ] (compar **-ier**, superl **-iest**) adj [with bubbles] espumoso(sa), espumante.

fob [fɒb] (pt & pp **-bed**, cont **-bing**) ➡ **fob off** vt sep: **to** ~ **sthg off on sb** empurrar algo para alguém; **to** ~ **sb off with sthg** enrolar alguém com algo.

FOB, f.o.b. (abbr of **free on board**) FOB m.

fob watch n relógio m de corrente.

focal [ˈfəʊkl] adj focal.

focal point [ˈfəʊkl-] n -1. [of view, room] ponto m central -2. fig [of report, study] foco m.

focus [ˈfəʊkəs] (pl **-cuses** OR **-ci** [-saɪ]) ◇ n [gen] foco m; **out of/in** ~ fora de/em foco; ~ **of attention** foco de atenção. ◇ vt -1. [lens, camera] focar; **to** ~ **sthg on sb/sthg** [lens, camera, eyes] focar algo em alguém/algo -2. [mentally]: **to** ~ **one's attention on sb/sthg** concentrar a atenção em alguém/algo. ◇ vi -1.: **to** ~ **on sb/sthg** enfocar alguém/algo -2. [mentally]: **to** ~ **on sthg** concentrar-se em algo.

focussed adj [mentally] concentrado(da).

fodder [ˈfɒdəʳ] n [feed] forragem f.

foe [fəʊ] n literary inimigo m, -ga f, antagonista mf.

FOE n (abbr of **Friends of the Earth**) ≃ NAT f.

foetal [ˈfiːtl] adj fetal.

foetus [ˈfiːtəs] n feto m.

fog [fɒg] n [mist] nevoeiro m, neblina f.

fogbound [ˈfɒgbaʊnd] adj fechado(da) por causa de nevoeiro.

fogey [ˈfəʊgɪ] n = fogy.

foggiest [ˈfɒgɪəst] n inf: **I haven't the** ~ não tenho a menor idéia.

foggy [ˈfɒgɪ] (compar **-ier**, superl **-iest**) adj [misty] nevoento(ta).

foghorn [ˈfɒghɔːn] n buzina f de nevoeiro.

fog lamp n farol m de neblina.

fogy [ˈfəʊgɪ] (pl **-ies**) n inf: **old** ~ raposa mf velha.

foible [ˈfɔɪbl] n ponto m fraco.

foil [fɔɪl] ◇ n -1. (U) [metal sheet] papel m alumínio -2. [contrast]: **to act as a** ~ **to** OR **for sb/sthg** complementar alguém/algo, ser um complemento de alguém/algo. ◇ vt frustrar.

foist [fɔɪst] vt: **to** ~ **sthg on sb** impingir algo a alguém.

fold [fəʊld] ◇ vt -1. [gen] dobrar; **to** ~ **one's arms** cruzar os braços -2. [wrap] abraçar. ◇ vi -1. [bed, chair] dobrar -2. inf [newspaper, play] fracassar -3. inf [business] falir. ◇ n -1. [in material, paper] dobra f -2. [for animals] curral m -3. fig [group of people]: **the** ~ o grupo.

➡ **fold up** ◇ vt sep dobrar. ◇ vi -1. dobrar -2. inf [newspaper, play] fracassar -3. inf [business] falir.

foldaway [ˈfəʊldəˌweɪl] adj dobrável.

folder [ˈfəʊldəʳ] n -1. [gen & COMPUT] pasta f -2. [binder] fichário f -3. [brochure] folheto f.

folding [ˈfəʊldɪŋ] adj [chair, table] dobrável.

foliage [ˈfəʊlɪdʒ] n (U) folhagem f.

folk [fəʊk] ◇ adj popular. ◇ n [music] música f folk. ◇ npl [people] gente f.

➡ **folks** npl inf -1. [relatives] parentes mpl -2. [everyone] pessoal m.

folklore [ˈfəʊklɔːʳ] n (U) folclore m.

folk music n (U) música m folk.

folk singer n cantor m, -ra f folk.

folk song n canção f folk.

folksy [ˈfəʊksɪ] (compar **-ier**, superl **-iest**) adj US inf amigável.

follicle [ˈfɒlɪkl] n folículo m.

follow [ˈfɒləʊ] ◇ vt -1. [gen] seguir; ~ **that taxi!** siga aquele táxi!; **(to be)** ~**ed by sthg** ser/vir acompanhado(da) por algo, ser seguido(da) de algo - **2.** [pursue] perseguir - **3.** [go along with, understand] acompanhar. ◇ *vi* - **1.** [come after] seguir-se; **as ~s** conforme segue, da seguinte forma - **2.** [happen as logical result] vir em seguida - **3.** [be logical] proceder; **it ~s that** isso quer dizer que - **4.** [understand] acompanhar.

➤ **follow up** *vt sep* - **1.** [pursue] acompanhar - **2.** [supplement]: **to ~ sthg up with** responder a algo com.

follower ['fɒləʊə'] *n* [disciple, believer] seguidor *m*, -ra *f*.

following ['fɒləʊɪŋ] ◇ *adj* seguinte. ◇ *n* [group of supporters, fans] séquito *m*. ◇ *prep* [after] depois de.

follow-up ◇ *adj* complementar. ◇ *n* [to visit, treatment, programme] continuação *f*.

folly ['fɒlɪ] *n (U)* [foolishness] loucura *f*.

foment [fəʊ'ment] *vt fml* fomentar.

fond [fɒnd] *adj* - **1.** [affectionate] carinhoso(sa); **to be ~ of sb** gostar muito de alguém; **to be ~ of sthg/of doing sthg** gostar muito de algo/de fazer algo - **2.** *fml* [hope, wish] ingênuo(nua).

fondle ['fɒndl] *vt* acariciar.

fondly ['fɒndlɪ] *adv* - **1.** [affectionately] carinhosamente - **2.** [naively] ingenuamente.

fondness ['fɒndnɪs] *n (U)* afeição *f*, carinho *m*; **~ for sb/sthg** gosto por alguém/algo.

fondue ['fɒndju:] *n* CULIN fondue *m*.

font [fɒnt] *n* - **1.** [in church] pia *f* batismal - **2.** COMPUT & TYPO fonte *f*.

food [fu:d] *n* comida *f*; **~ for thought** assunto para reflexão.

food chain *n* cadeia *f* alimentar.

food mill *n* processador *m* de alimentos.

food mixer *n* batedeira *f*.

food poisoning [-'pɔɪznɪŋ] *n (U)* intoxicação *f* alimentar.

food processor [-ˌprəʊsesə'] *n* multiprocessador *m*.

food stamp *n US* vale-alimentação *m (fornecido pelo governo)*.

foodstuffs ['fu:dstʌfs] *npl* gêneros *mpl* alimentícios.

fool [fu:l] ◇ *n* - **1.** [idiot] idiota *mf*; **to make a ~ of sb** fazer alguém de bobo; **to make a ~ of o.s.** fazer papel de bobo; **to act** OR **play the ~** bancar o bobo - **2.** *UK* [dessert] musse *f*. ◇ *vt* enganar; **to ~ sb into doing sthg** enrolar alguém para que faça algo. ◇ *vi* brincar.

➤ **fool about, fool around** *vi* - **1.** [behave foolishly]: **to ~ about (with sthg)** fazer-se de bobo (em relação a algo) - **2.** [be unfaithful]: **to ~ about (with sb)** pular a cerca (com alguém) - **3.** *US* [tamper]: **to ~ around with sthg** brincar com algo.

foolhardy ['fu:lˌhɑ:dɪ] *adj* temerário(ria).

foolish ['fu:lɪʃ] *adj* - **1.** [unwise, silly] bobo(ba), idiota - **2.** [laughable, undignified] tolo(la).

foolishly ['fu:lɪʃlɪ] *adv* - **1.** [unwisely, in a silly manner] de maneira idiota - **2.** [laughably, in an undignified manner] estupidamente.

foolishness ['fu:lɪʃnɪs] *n (U)* idiotice *f*.

foolproof ['fu:lpru:f] *adj* infalível.

foolscap ['fu:lzkæp] *n (U)* papel *m* ofício.

foot [fʊt] (*pl senses 1 and 2* feet, *pl sense 3 inv* OR feet) ◇ *n* - **1.** [of animal] pata *f* - **2.** [of person] pé *m*; **on ~** a pé; **to be on one's feet, to get to one's feet** ficar de pé; **to be back on one's feet** estar logo de pé; **to have/get cold feet** não ter coragem suficiente; **to have itchy feet** ter formiga nos pés; **to put one's ~ down** bater pé; **to put one's ~ in it** meter os pés pelas mãos; **to put one's feet up** descansar; **to be rushed off one's feet** ser massacrado(da); **to set ~ in** pôr os pés em; **to stand on one's own two feet** ser dono de seu próprio nariz - **3.** [bottom] pé *m* - **4.** [of hill] sopé *m* - **5.** [unit of measurement] pé *m* (*30,48 cm*). ◇ *vt inf*: **to ~ the bill (for sthg)** pagar a conta (por algo).

footage ['fʊtɪdʒ] *n (U)* metragem *f*.

foot-and-mouth disease *n (U)* febre *f* aftosa.

football ['fʊtbɔ:l] *n* - **1.** *UK* [game] futebol *m* - **2.** *US* [American football] futebol *m* americano - **3.** [ball] bola *f* de futebol.

football club *n UK* time *m* de futebol.

footballer ['fʊtbɔ:lə'] *n UK* jogador *m*, -ra *f* de futebol, futebolista *mf*.

football field *n US* campo *m* de futebol americano.

football game *n US* partida *f* de futebol americano.

football ground *n UK* campo *m* de futebol.

football match *n UK* partida *f* de futebol.

football player *n* jogador *m*, -ra *f* de futebol.

football pools *npl UK* ≃ loteria *f* esportiva.

football supporter *n* torcedor *m*, -ra *f*.

footbrake ['fʊtbreɪk] *n* freio *m* de pé.

footbridge ['fʊtbrɪdʒ] *n* passarela *f*.

footer ['fʊtə'] *n* COMPUT rodapé *m*.

foot fault *n* TENNIS falta *f* de saque *(pé dentro da linha)*.

foothills ['fʊthɪlz] *npl* contraforte *m*.

foothold ['fʊthəʊld] *n* apoio *m* para os pés; **to get a ~** [on mountain, rockface] ter um ponto de apoio; [in organization, company] base *f* de operações.

footing ['fʊtɪŋ] *n* - **1.** [foothold] lugar *m* onde pôr o pé; **to lose one's ~** escorregar, perder a base - **2.** [basis] base *f*; **on an equal ~ (with sb/sthg)** em pé de igualdade (com alguém/algo).

footlights ['fʊtlaɪts] *npl* ribalta *f*.

footling *adj* dated & pej néscio(cia).

footman ['fʊtmən] (*pl* -men [-mən]) *n* lacaio *m*.

footmark ['fʊtmɑ:k] *n* pegada *f*.

footmen ['fʊtmən] *pl* ⊳ **footman**.

footnote ['fʊtnəʊt] *n* nota *f* de rodapé.

footpath ['fʊtpɑ:θ, *pl* -pɑ:ðz] *n* trilha *f*.

footprint ['fʊtprɪnt] *n* pegada *f*.

footsie *n*: **to play ~** tocar o pé de alguém com o próprio pé demonstrando interesse afetivo ou sexual.

Footsie *n UK* FIN inf = FTSE

footsore ['fʊtsɔ:'] *adj* com os pés doloridos.

footstep ['fʊtstep] *n* - **1.** [sound] passo *m* - **2.** [footprint] pegada *f*; **to follow in sb's ~s** seguir os passos de alguém.

footwear ['fʊtweə'] *n (U)* calçado *m*.

footwork ['fʊtwɜ:k] *n* SPORT jogo *m* de pernas.

for [fɔːr] *prep* **-1.** [expressing intention, purpose, reason] para; **this book is ~ you** este livro é para você; **what did you do that ~?** para que você fez isso?; **what's it ~?** para que é?; **to go ~ a walk** ir dar um passeio; **'~ sale'** 'vende-se'; **a town famous ~ its wine** uma cidade famosa pelo vinho; **~ this reason** por esta razão **-2.** [during] durante; **I'm going away ~ a while** vou estar fora durante OR por algum tempo; **I've lived here ~ ten years** vivo aqui há dez anos; **we talked ~ hours** falamos horas e horas **-3.** [by, before] para; **it'll be ready ~ tomorrow** estará pronto (para) amanhã; **be there ~ 8 p.m.** esteja lá antes das oito da noite **-4.** [on the occasion of] por; **I got socks ~ Christmas** ganhei meias de Natal; **~ the first time** pela primeira vez; **what's ~ dinner?** o que há para jantar?; **~ the moment** no momento **-5.** [on behalf of] por; **to do sthg ~ sb** fazer algo para alguém; **to work ~ sb** trabalhar para alguém **-6.** [with time and space] para; **there's no room ~ it** não há espaço para isso; **to have time ~ sthg** ter tempo para algo **-7.** [expressing distance]: **roadwork ~ 20 miles** obras na estrada ao longo de 32 quilômetros; **we drove ~ miles** dirigimos quilômetros e mais quilômetros **-8.** [expressing destination] para; **a ticket ~ Boston** um bilhete para Boston; **this train is ~ Newark only** este trem só vai até Newark **-9.** [expressing price] por; **I bought it ~ five dollars** comprei-o por cinco dólares **-10.** [expressing meaning]: **what's the Portuguese ~ boy?** como é que se diz boy em português? **-11.** [with regard to] para; **it's warm ~ November** para novembro está quente; **it's easy ~ you** para você é fácil; **respect ~ human rights** respeito pelos direitos humanos; **I feel sorry ~ them** sinto pena deles; **it's too far ~ us to walk** é longe demais para irmos a pé; **it's time ~ dinner** está na hora do jantar.

FOR (*abbr of* **free on rail**) FOR.

forage ['fɒrɪdʒ] *vi* [search] procurar; **to ~ for sthg** sair à procura de algo.

foray ['fɒreɪ] *n* **-1.** [raid] incursão *f* **-2.** *fig* [excursion] incursão *f*; **~ into sthg** incursão em algo.

forbad [fə'bæd], **forbade** [fə'beɪd] *pt* ⊳ **forbid**.

forbearing [fɔː'beərɪŋ] *adj* indulgente.

forbid [fə'bɪd] (*pt* **-bade** OR **-bad**, *pp* **forbid** OR **-bidden**, *cont* **-bidding**) *vt* [not allow] proibir; **to ~ sb to do sthg** proibir alguém de fazer algo; **God** OR **Heaven ~!** Deus me livre!

forbidden [fə'bɪdn] ⊳ *pp* ⊳ **forbid**. ⊳ *adj* proibido(da).

forbidding [fə'bɪdɪŋ] *adj* **-1.** [severe] repulsivo(va) **-2.** [threatening] ameaçador(ra).

force [fɔːs] ⊳ *n* **-1.** [gen] força *f*; **~ of habit** força do hábito; **by ~** à força **-2.** [power, influence] poder *m*; **a ~ to be reckoned with** um poder a ser reconhecido **-3.** [group] equipe *f*; **sales ~** a equipe de vendas; **security ~s** as equipes de segurança; **task ~** orça-tarefa *f*; **in ~** em grande número **-4.** [effect]: **to be in/come into ~** estar/entrar em vigor. ⊳ *vt* **-1.** [compel] forçar; **to ~ sb to do sthg** obrigar alguém a fazer algo; **to ~ sthg on sb** impor algo a alguém; **to ~ o.s.** forçar-se **-2.** [break open] forçar **-3.** [push] empurrar; **to ~ sthg open** forçar algo; **to ~ one's way through/into** abrir caminho (por entre) **-4.** [hurry] apressar **-5.** [smile, answer] arrancar.

  ➤ **forces** *npl*: **the ~s** as Forças Armadas; **to join ~s (with sb)** unir forças (com alguém).

  ➤ **by force of** *prep* mediante, por meio de.

  ➤ **force back** *vt sep* **-1.** [push back] fazer recuar **-2.** [suppress] reprimir.

  ➤ **force down** *vt sep* **-1.** [swallow] forçar-se a comer **-2.** [force to land] forçar a aterrissar.

forced [fɔːst] *adj* forçado(da).

forced landing *n* aterrissagem *f* forçada.

force-feed *vt* alimentar à força.

forceful ['fɔːsfʊl] *adj* **-1.** [strong, powerful] forte **-2.** [words, ideas] contundente **-3.** [support, recommendation] enérgico(ca).

forcefully ['fɔːsfʊlɪ] *adv* vigorosamente, energicamente.

forcemeat ['fɔːsmiːt] *n esp UK* recheio *m* de carne.

forceps ['fɔːseps] *npl* fórceps *m*.

forcible ['fɔːsəbl] *adj* **-1.** [using physical force] feito(ta) à força **-2.** [powerful] eficaz **-3.** [recommendation, argument] enérgico(ca).

forcibly ['fɔːsəblɪ] *adv* **-1.** [using physical force] à força **-2.** [powerfully] eficazmente **-3.** [eagerly] energicamente.

ford [fɔːd] ⊳ *n* vau *m*. ⊳ *vt* vadear.

fore [fɔːr] ⊳ *adj* NAUT dianteiro(ra). ⊳ *n*: **to come to the ~** *fig* tornar-se influente.

forearm ['fɔːrɑːm] *n* antebraço *m*.

forebears ['fɔːbeəz] *npl fml* antepassados *mpl*.

foreboding [fɔː'bəʊdɪŋ] *n* mau pressentimento *m*.

forecast ['fɔːkɑːst] (*pt & pp* **forecast** OR **-ed**) ⊳ *n* [prediction] previsão *f*. ⊳ *vt* [predict] prever.

forecaster ['fɔːkɑːstər] *n* **-1.** ECON analista *mf* **-2.** METEOR meteorologista *mf*.

foreclose [fɔː'kləʊz] ⊳ *vt* executar. ⊳ *vi*: **to ~ on sb** privar alguém do direito de resgatar uma hipoteca.

foreclosure [fɔː'kləʊʒər] *n* execução *f* de uma hipoteca.

forecourt ['fɔːkɔːt] *n* área *f* para estacionamento.

forefathers ['fɔːˌfɑːðəz] *npl* antepassados *mpl*.

forefinger ['fɔːˌfɪŋgər] *n* indicador *m*.

forefront ['fɔːfrʌnt] *n*: **in** OR **at the ~ of sthg** primeiro plano de algo.

forego [fɔː'gəʊ] *vt* = **forgo**.

foregoing [fɔː'gəʊɪŋ] ⊳ *adj* anterior, precedente. ⊳ *n fml*: **the ~** o supracitado.

foregone conclusion ['fɔːgɒn-] *n*: **it's a ~** é um resultado inevitável.

foreground ['fɔːgraʊnd] *n* primeiro plano *m*; **in the ~** em primeiro plano.

forehand ['fɔːhænd] *n* [tennis stroke] golpe *m* com a frente da mão.

forehead ['fɔːhed] *n* testa *f*.

foreign ['fɒrən] *adj* **-1.** [from abroad] estrangeiro(ra) **-2.** [external] exterior **-3.** [alien] estranho(nha).

foreign affairs *npl* relações *fpl* exteriores.

foreign aid *n* (U) ajuda *f* internacional.

foreign body *n* corpo *m* estranho.

foreign competition *n* (U) competição *f* internacional.

foreign currency n moeda m estrangeira.
foreigner ['fɒrənəʳ] n [from abroad] estrangeiro m, -ra f.
foreign exchange n (U) câmbio m; ~ **markets** mercados de câmbio; ~ **rates** taxas de câmbio.
foreign investment n (U) investimento m estrangeiro.
Foreign Legion n: the ~ a Legião Estrangeira.
foreign minister n ministro m de relações exteriores.
Foreign Office n UK: the ~ ≃ o Ministério das Relações Exteriores.
Foreign Secretary n UK ≃ Ministro m das Relações Exteriores.
foreleg ['fɔːleg] n perna f dianteira.
foreman ['fɔːmən] (pl -men **- 1.** [of workers] capataz m **- 2.** [of jury] primeiro jurado m.
foremost ['fɔːməʊst] <> adj principal. <> adv: **first and** ~ antes de mais nada.
forename ['fɔːneɪm] n prenome m.
forensic [fə'rensɪk] adj forense.
forensic medicine n (U) medicina f legal.
forensic science n (U) ciência f forense.
forerunner ['fɔːˌrʌnəʳ] n [precursor] precursor m, -ra f.
foresee [fɔː'siː] (pt -saw [-'sɔː], pp -seen) vt prever.
foreseeable [fɔː'siːəbl] adj previsível; **for/in the** ~ **future** num futuro próximo.
foreseen [fɔː'siːn] pp ▷ foresee.
foreshadow [fɔː'ʃædəʊ] vt prenunciar.
foreshortened [fɔː'ʃɔːtnd] adj condensado(da).
foresight ['fɔːsaɪt] n (U) previdência f.
foreskin ['fɔːskɪn] n prepúcio m.
forest ['fɒrɪst] n floresta f.
forestall [fɔː'stɔːl] vt prevenir.
forestry ['fɒrɪstrɪ] n (U) silvicultura f.
Forestry Commission n UK: the ~ departamento do governo britânico responsável pela proteção e pelo desenvolvimento das florestas e matas do país.
foretaste ['fɔːteɪst] n [sample] amostra f.
foretell [fɔː'tell] (pt & pp -told) vt predizer, prenunciar.
forethought ['fɔːθɔːt] n (U) premeditação f.
foretold [fɔː'təʊld] pt & pp ▷ foretell.
forever [fə'revəʳ] adv **- 1.** [eternally] para sempre **- 2.** inf [incessantly] sem parar, sempre **- 3.** inf [a long time] para sempre.
forewarn [fɔː'wɔːn] vt prevenir.
foreword ['fɔːwɜːd] n apresentação f.
forfeit ['fɔːfɪt] <> n **- 1.** [penalty] prenda f **- 2.** [fine] multa f. <> vt [lose] perder.
forgave [fə'geɪv] pt ▷ forgive.
forge [fɔːdʒ] <> n [place] forja f. <> vt **- 1.** [industry] forjar f **- 2.** fig [create] forjar **- 3.** [make illegal copy of] falsificar.
◆ **forge ahead** vi avançar continuamente.
forger ['fɔːdʒəʳ] n falsificador m, -ra f.
forgery ['fɔːdʒərɪ] (pl -ies) n falsificação f.
forget [fə'get] (pt - got, pp -gotten, cont -getting) <> vt **- 1.** [gen] esquecer; **to** ~ **to do sthg** esquecer-se de fazer algo; **to** ~ **o.s.** esquecer-se de si mesmo **- 2.** [leave behind] esquecer-se de. <>

vi esquecer-se; **to** ~ **about sthg** esquecer-se de algo.
forgetful [fə'getfʊl] adj esquecido(da).
forgetfulness [fə'getfʊlnɪs] n (U) esquecimento m.
forget-me-not n não-te-esqueças-de-mim f, miosótis f.
forgive [fə'gɪv] (pt -gave, pp -given) vt perdoar; **to** ~ **sb for sthg/for doing sthg** perdoar alguém por algo/por fazer algo.
forgiveness [fə'gɪvnɪs] n (U) perdão m.
forgiving [fə'gɪvɪŋ] adj que perdoa, clemente.
forgo [fɔː'gəʊ] (pt -went, pp -gone [-'gɒn]) vt renunciar a, abrir mão de.
forgot [fə'gɒt] pt ▷ forget.
forgotten [fə'gɒtn] pp ▷ forget.
fork [fɔːk] <> n **- 1.** [for food] garfo m **- 2.** [for gardening] forquilha f **- 3.** [in road, river] bifurcação f. <> vi bifurcar-se.
◆ **fork out** inf <> vt fus desembolsar; **to** ~ **out money on** OR **for sthg** desembolsar dinheiro em ou para algo. <> vi: **to** ~ **out (for sthg)** desembolsar uma grana (para algo).
forklift truck ['fɔːklɪft-] n empilhadeira f.
forlorn [fə'lɔːn] adj **- 1.** [face, expression, cry] desesperado(da) **- 2.** [desolate - person] desolado(da); [- place] abandonado(da) **- 3.** [hope, attempt] desesperança-do(da).
form [fɔːm] <> n **- 1.** [shape] forma f; **in the** ~ **of** na forma de; **to take the** ~ **of** tomar a forma de **- 2.** [type] tipo m **- 3.** (U) [fitness] aparência f; **on** ~ UK, **in** ~ US em forma; **off** ~ fora de forma **- 4.** [question-naire] formulário m **- 5.** [figure] imagem f **- 6.** UK SCH [class] série f **- 7.** (U) [usual behaviour]: **true to** ~ como era de se esperar. <> vt **- 1.** [gen] formar **- 2.** [constitute] constituir. <> vi formar-se.
formal ['fɔːml] adj **- 1.** [gen] formal **- 2.** [official] oficial.
formality [fɔː'mælətɪ] (pl -ies) n formalidade f.
formalize, -ise ['fɔːməlaɪz] vt formalizar.
formally ['fɔːməlɪ] adv **- 1.** formalmente **- 2.** [officially] oficialmente.
format ['fɔːmæt] (pt & pp -ted, cont -ting) <> n **- 1.** [of book, magazine] formato m **- 2.** [of meeting] estilo m **- 3.** COMPUT formato. <> vt COMPUT formatar.
formation [fɔː'meɪʃn] n **- 1.** [gen] formação f **- 2.** (U) [establishment] estrutura f.
formative ['fɔːmətɪv] adj formativo(va).
former ['fɔːməʳ] <> adj **- 1.** [earlier, previous] ex-; ~ **husband** ex-marido m **- 2.** [time] passado(da) **- 3.** [first] anterior. <> n: the ~ o primeiro.
formerly ['fɔːməlɪ] adv antigamente.
form feed n alimentação f de formulário.
Formica® [fɔː'maɪkə] n (U) fórmica® f.
formidable ['fɔːmɪdəbl] adj **- 1.** [frightening] pavoro-so(sa) **- 2.** [impressive] impressionante.
formless ['fɔːmlɪs] adj [shapeless] disforme, sem forma.
Formosa [fɔː'məʊsə] n Formosa f; **in** ~ em Formo-sa.
formula ['fɔːmjʊlə] (pl -as OR -ae [-iː]) n fórmula f.
formulate ['fɔːmjʊleɪt] vt formular.
formulation [ˌfɔːmjʊ'leɪʃn] n formulação f.

fornicate ['fɔ:nɪkeɪt] *vi fml* fornicar.

forsake [fə'seɪk] (*pt* **-sook**, *pp* **-saken**) *vt literary* abandonar.

forsaken [fə'seɪkn] *adj* abandonado(da).

forsook [fə'sʊk] *pt* ⊳ **forsake**.

forsythia [fɔ:'saɪθjə] *n (U)* forsítia *f.*

fort [fɔ:t] *n* forte *m*; **to hold the ~ (for sb)** tomar conta de algo (para alguém).

forte ['fɔ:tɪ] *n* forte *m.*

forth [fɔ:θ] *adv literary* -**1.** [outwards, onwards] adiante -**2.** [into future]: **from that day ~** daquele dia em diante.

forthcoming [fɔ:θ'kʌmɪŋ] *adj* -**1.** [imminent] próximo(ma) -**2.** [available] disponível -**3.** [helpful] prestimoso(sa).

forthright ['fɔ:θraɪt] *adj* franco(ca).

forthwith [ˌfɔ:θ'wɪθ] *adv fml* incontinenti.

fortieth ['fɔ:tɪɪθ] *num* quadragésimo(ma); *see also* sixth.

fortification [ˌfɔ:tɪfɪ'keɪʃn] *n MIL* -**1.** [act of fortifying] fortificação *f* -**2.** [structure] forte *m.*

fortified wine ['fɔ:tɪfaɪd-] *n* vinho *m* licoroso.

fortify ['fɔ:tɪfaɪ] (*pt & pp* **-ied**) *vt* -**1.** [place] fortificar -**2.** *fig* [person, resolve] fortalecer.

fortitude ['fɔ:tɪtju:d] *n (U)* fortaleza *f.*

fortnight ['fɔ:tnaɪt] *n* quinzena *f.*

fortnightly ['fɔ:tˌnaɪtlɪ] <> *adj* quinzenal. <> *adv* quinzenalmente.

fortress ['fɔ:trɪs] *n* fortaleza *f.*

fortuitous [fɔ:'tju:ɪtəs] *adj fml* [accidental] fortuito(-ta).

fortunate ['fɔ:tʃnət] *adj* feliz; **it's ~ that ...** por sorte ...

fortunately ['fɔ:tʃnətlɪ] *adv* felizmente.

fortune ['fɔ:tʃu:n] *n* -**1.** [large amount of money] fortuna *f* -**2.** [luck] sorte *f* -**3.** [future]: **to tell sb's ~** ler a sorte de alguém.
    ➡ **fortunes** *npl* vicissitudes *fpl.*

fortune-teller [-ˌtelə^r] *n* -**1.** adivinho *m*, -nha *f* -**2.** [using cards] cartomante *mf.*

forty ['fɔ:tɪ] *num* quarenta; *see also* sixty.

forum ['fɔ:rəm] (*pl* **-s**) *n* -**1.** *HISTORY* praça *f* pública -**2.** [meeting place] fórum *m.*

forward ['fɔ:wəd] <> *adj* -**1.** [position] dianteiro(ra) -**2.** [movement] para frente -**3.** [advanced] avançado(da) -**4.** [impudent] impudente. <> *adv* -**1.** [in space] para a frente -**2.** [to earlier time]: **to bring sthg ~** trazer algo à baila -**3.** [to later time]: **to put a clock ~** adiantar um relógio. <> *n SPORT* atacante *mf.* <> *vt* -**1.** [send on - letter] remeter; [- parcels, goods] expedir; [- information] enviar; **please ~ favor** enviar para novo endereço -**2.** [further] desenvolver.

forwarding address ['fɔ:wədɪŋ-] *n* endereço *m* para envio.

forward-looking [-'lʊkɪŋ] *adj* de visão.

forwardness ['fɔ:wədnɪs] *n (U)* [boldness] audácia *f.*

forwards ['fɔ:wədz] *adv* = **forward**.

forward slash *n TYPO* barra *f* inclinada (*para frente*).

forwent [fɔ:'went] *pt* ⊳ **forgo**.

fossil ['fɒsl] *n GEOL* fóssil *m.*

fossil fuel *n* combustível *m* fóssil.

fossilized, -ised ['fɒsɪlaɪzd] *adj GEOL* fossilizado(-da).

foster ['fɒstə^r] <> *adj* de criação; **~ brother** irmão de criação. <> *vt* -**1.** [child] criar, cuidar de -**2.** [idea, hope] fomentar.

foster child *n* filho *m*, -lha *f* de criação.

foster parent *n* pais *mpl* de criação.

fought [fɔ:t] *pt & pp* ⊳ **fight**.

foul [faʊl] <> *adj* -**1.** [dirty - linen] enlameado(da); [- water] imundo(da); [- air] poluído(da) -**2.** [food] estragado(da), podre; [taste] nojento(ta) ; [smell, breath] fétido(da) -**3.** [very unpleasant] péssimo(ma), horrível -**4.** [obscene] obsceno(na) -**5.** *phr*: **to fall ~ of sb** entrar em choque com alguém. <> *n SPORT* falta *f.* <> *vt* -**1.** [make dirty] sujar -**2.** *SPORT* cometer falta em -**3.** [entangle] enredar.
    ➡ **foul up** *vt sep inf* estragar.

foul-mouthed [-'maʊðd] *adj* desbocado(da).

foul play *n* -**1.** *SPORT* jogo *m* sujo -**2.** [criminal act] crime *m.*

found [faʊnd] <> *pt & pp* ⊳ **find**. <> *vt* -**1.** [provide funds for] fundar -**2.** [start building] assentar os alicerces de -**3.** [base]: **to ~ sthg on** basear algo em.

foundation [faʊn'deɪʃn] *n* -**1.** *(U)* [gen] fundação *f* -**2.** [basis] base *f* -**3.** *(U)* [cosmetic]: **~ (cream)** base *f.*
    ➡ **foundations** *npl CONSTR* alicerces *mpl.*

founder ['faʊndə^r] <> *n* [person] fundador *m*, -ra *f* <> *vi* -**1.** [sink] afundar -**2.** *fig* [fail] fracassar.

founder member *n* sócio-fundador *m*, sócia-fundadora *f.*

founding father *n* [founder] fundador *m.*

foundry ['faʊndrɪ] (*pl* **-ies**) *n* fundição *f.*

fount [faʊnt] *n* [origin] fonte *f.*

fountain ['faʊntɪn] *n* -**1.** [man-made] chafariz *m* -**2.** *fig* [source] fonte *f.*

fountain pen *n* caneta-tinteiro *f.*

four [fɔ:^r] *num* quatro; *see also* six; **on all ~s** de quatro.

four-leaved clover [-li:vd-] *n* trevo *m* de quatro folhas.

four-letter word *n* palavrão *m.*

four-poster (bed) *n* cama *f* com dossel.

foursome ['fɔ:səm] *n* quarteto *m.*

four-star *adj* (de) quatro estrelas.

fourteen [ˌfɔ:'ti:n] *num* quatorze; *see also* six.

fourteenth [ˌfɔ:'ti:nθ] *num* décimo quarto, décima quarta; *see also* sixth.

fourth [fɔ:θ] *num* quarto(ta); *see also* sixth.

Fourth of July *n*: **the ~** o 4 de julho (*dia da Independência norte-americana*).

FOURTH OF JULY

O 4 de julho, o dia da independência, é uma das mais importantes festas nacionais nos Estados Unidos. Como parte das comemorações, muitas cidades organizam paradas nas ruas e, à noite, queimas de fogos de artifício, em que predominam as cores azul, vermelho e branco. Os edifícios são decorados com enfeites nessas mesmas cores e com bandeiras americanas. Muita gente sai da cidade para fazer piquenique com a família e, conforme a tradição, comer cachorros-quentes e melancia.

four-way stop n US cruzamento m (de quatro vias).

four-wheel drive n -1. [vehicle] veículo m com tração nas quatro rodas -2. [system] tração f nas quatro rodas.

fowl [faʊl] (pl inv OR -s) n -1. CULIN ave f -2. [bird] ave f (doméstica).

fox [fɒks] <> n [animal] raposa f. <> vt -1. [outwit] lograr -2. [baffle] deixar atordoado(da).

foxcub n filhote m de raposa.

foxglove ['fɒksglʌv] n dedaleira f.

foxhole ['fɒkshəʊl] n -1. [for soldier] trincheira f -2. [for animal] toca f de raposa.

foxhound ['fɒkshaʊnd] n cão m de caça à raposa.

foxhunt ['fɒkshʌnt] n caça f à raposa.

foxhunting ['fɒks,hʌntɪŋ] n (U) caça f à raposa.

fox terrier n fox terrier m.

foxy ['fɒksɪ] adj [sexy] sexy.

foyer ['fɔɪeɪ] n -1. [of hotel, theatre] saguão m -2. US [of house] vestíbulo m.

FP n -1. (abbr of former pupil) ex-aluno m, -na f. -2. US (abbr of fireplug) hidrante m.

FPA (abbr of Family Planning Association) n associação britânica que oferece serviço de planejamento familiar.

fr. (abbr of franc) franco m.

Fr. (abbr of father) Pe.

fracas ['fræka:, US 'freɪkəs] (UK pl inv, US pl fracases) n rixa f.

fraction ['frækʃn] n -1. [gen] fração f -2. [a little bit]: it's a ~ too big é um pouquinho maior.

fractionally ['frækʃnəlɪ] adv levemente.

fractious ['frækʃəs] adj irritadiço(ça).

fracture ['fræktʃəʳ] MED <> n fratura f., <> vt fraturar.

fragile ['frædʒaɪl] adj frágil.

fragility [frə'dʒɪlətɪ] n fragilidade f.

fragment [n 'frægmənt, vb 'frægment] <> n fragmento m. <> vi fragmentar-se.

fragmentary ['frægməntrɪ] adj fragmentário(ria).

fragmented [fræg'mentɪd] adj fragmentado(da).

fragrance ['freɪgrəns] n fragrância f.

fragrant ['freɪgrənt] adj perfumado(da).

frail [freɪl] adj frágil.

frailty ['freɪltɪ] (pl -ies) n -1. (U) [gen] fragilidade f -2. [imperfection] fraqueza f.

frame [freɪm] <> n -1. [of picture] moldura f -2. [of glasses] armação f -3. [structure - of door] marco m; [- of boat] estrutura f; [- of window, bicycle] quadro m; [- of bed, chair] armação f -4. [physique] constituição f. <> vt -1. [put in a frame] emoldurar -2. fig [surround] cercar -3. [formulate, express] expressar -4. inf [falsely incriminate] incriminar falsamente.

frame of mind n estado m de espírito.

framework ['freɪmwɜ:k] n -1. [physical structure] estrutura f -2. [basis] base f.

France [frɑ:ns] n França f; in ~ na França.

franchise ['fræntʃaɪz] n -1. POL [right to vote] direito m de voto -2. COMM [right to sell goods] franquia f.

franchisee [,fræntʃaɪ'zi:] n franqueado m, -da f.

franchisor n franqueador m, -ra f.

frank [fræŋk] <> adj franco(ca). <> vt franquear.

Frankfurt ['fræŋkfət] n: ~ (am Main) Frankfurt (am Main); in ~ em Frankfurt.

frankfurter ['fræŋkfɜ:təʳ] n salsicha f defumada.

frankincense ['fræŋkɪnsens] n (U) olíbano m.

franking machine ['fræŋkɪŋ-] n máquina f de selagem.

frankly ['fræŋklɪ] adv francamente.

frankness ['fræŋknəs] n (U) franqueza f.

frantic ['fræntɪk] adj frenético(ca); **she was** ~ **ela estava fora de si.**

frantically ['fræntɪklɪ] adv -1. [in an upset manner] furiosamente -2. [busily] ativamente.

fraternal [frə'tɜ:nl] adj -1. [brotherly] fraterno(na) -2. [friendly] fraternal.

fraternity [frə'tɜ:nətɪ] (pl -ies) n -1. [community] comunidade f -2. US [of students] fraternidade f -3. (U) [friendship] fraternidade f.

FRATERNITY

Os clubes de estudantes, masculinos (fraternities) e femininos (sororities), são elementos de destaque na vida universitária norte-americana. Muitos estudantes associam-se a eles desde o primeiro ano de faculdade, permanecendo membros desses clubes mesmo após o término dos estudos. Cada clube possui seu próprio nome, composto de letras do alfabeto grego, e tem sua sede no edifício em que reside a maioria de seus membros. Os clubes realizam trabalhos para instituições de assistência social, mas são famosos também por suas bebedeiras e cerimônias secretas. Algumas universidades proibiram essas cerimônias de iniciação, porque elas promoviam trotes cruéis e perigosos.

fraternize, -ise ['frætənaɪz] vi [be on friendly terms] confraternizar; **to** ~ **with sb** confraternizar-se com alguém.

fraud [frɔ:d] n -1. (U) [crime] fraude f -2. [deceitful act] trapaça f -3. pej [impostor] impostor m, -ra f.

fraudulent ['frɔ:djʊlənt] adj fraudulento(ta).

fraught [frɔ:t] adj -1. [full]: ~ **with sthg** repleto(ta) de algo -2. UK [frantic] preocupado(da); **a** ~ **weekend** um fim de semana enlouquecido.

fray [freɪ] <> vi -1. [clothing, fabric, rope] esfiapar-se -2. fig [nerves, temper] desgastar-se. <> n literary rixa f.

frayed [freɪd] adj -1. [clothing, fabric, rope] esfiapado(da) -2. fig [nerves, temper] desgastado(da).

frazzled ['fræzld] adj inf [harassed] estafado(da).

FRB (abbr of Federal Reserve Board) n fundo de reserva federal norte-americano.

FRCP (abbr of Fellow of the Royal College of Physicians) membro do Royal College of Physicians, associação britânica de médicos.

FRCS (abbr of Fellow of the Royal College of Surgeons) membro do Royal College of Surgeons, associação britânica de cirurgiões.

freak [fri:k] <> adj imprevisto(ta). <> n -1. [strange creature - in appearance] aberração f; [- in behaviour] excêntrico m, -ca f -2. [unusual event] anomalia f -3. inf [fanatic] fanático m, -ca f.
➡ **freak out** inf <> vi -1. [get angry] baratinar-se -2. [panic] apavorar-se. <> vt sep baratinar.

freakish ['fri:kɪʃ] adj [strange] esquisito(ta).

freckle ['frekl] n sarda f.

free [fri:] (*compar* **freer**, *superl* **freest**, *pt* & *pp* **freed**) ⇔ *adj* **-1.** [gen] livre; **to be** ~ **to do sthg** ser livre para fazer algo; **feel** ~! sinta-se à vontade!; **to set sb/sthg** ~ libertar alguém/algo; **to give sb a** ~ **hand** dar a alguém carta branca **- 2.** [not paid for] grátis; ~ **of charge** sem despesas **- 3.** [unattached] solto(ta) **- 4.** [not affected by]; ~ **of additives** sem aditivos; ~ **from worry** sem preocupação **- 5.** [generous]: **to be** ~ **with sthg** [money] ser generoso(sa) com algo; [advice, affection] ser generoso(sa) em algo. ⇔ *adv* **-1.** [without payment] gratuitamente; **for** ~ de graça **- 2.** [without restraint] livremente. ⇔ *vt* **-1.** [release] pôr em liberdade, libertar **- 2.** [make available] liberar **- 3.** [remove] livrar; **to** ~ **sb of** OR **from sthg** livrar alguém de algo.

-free [fri:] *suffix*: **a salt-**~ **diet** uma dieta sem sal.

freebie ['fri:bɪ] *n inf* brinde *m*.

freedom ['fri:dəm] *n* liberdade *f*; ~ **from sthg** ausência *f* de algo; **the right to** ~ **from hunger** o direito de não se passar fome.

freedom fighter *n* lutador *m*, -ra *f* pela liberdade.

free enterprise *n (U)* livre iniciativa *f*.

free-fall *n (U)* queda *f* livre.

Freefone® ['fri:faun] *n UK (U)* discagem *f* gratuita.

free-for-all *n* **- 1.** [brawl] tumulto *m* generalizado **- 2.** [argument] discussão *f* generalizada.

free gift *n* oferta *f*.

freehand ['fri:hænd] ⇔ *adj* à mão livre. ⇔ *adv* à mão livre.

freehold ['fri:həʊld] ⇔ *adv*: **to buy** ~ comprar como propriedade alodial. ⇔ *n* propriedade *f* alodial.

freeholder ['fri:həʊldə'] *n* possuidor *m*, -ra *f* de propriedade alodial.

free house *n bar não-controlado por uma única cervejaria.*

free kick *n* tiro *m* livre; **to take a** ~ bater OR cobrar um tiro livre.

freelance ['fri:lɑ:ns] ⇔ *adj* frila, autônomo(ma). ⇔ *adv* como frila. ⇔ *n* frila *mf*, autônomo *m*, -ma *f*. ⇔ *vi* trabalhar como frila OR autônomo(-ma).

freeloader ['fri:ləʊdə'] *n inf* bicão *m*.

freely ['fri:lɪ] *adv* **-1.** [without constraint] livremente; ~ **available** fácil de obter **- 2.** [generously] generosamente.

freeman ['fri:mən] (*pl* **-men** [-mən]) *n* [citizen] cidadão *m* honorário.

free-market economy *n* economia *f* de livre mercado.

Freemason ['fri:ˌmeɪsn] *n* maçom *m*.

Freemasonry ['fri:ˌmeɪsnrɪ] *n* maçonaria *f*.

freemen ['fri:mən] *pl* ▷ **freeman**.

freephone ['fri:fəʊn] *n* = **freefone**.

freepost *n (U)* porte *m* pago.

free-range *adj UK* caipira; ~ **eggs** ovos caipira.

free sample *n* amostra *f* grátis.

freesia ['fri:zjə] *n* frésia *f*.

free speech *n (U)* liberdade *f* de expressão.

freestanding [ˌfri:'stændɪŋ] *adj* independente.

freestyle ['fri:staɪl] *n* [in swimming] estilo *m* livre.

freethinker [ˌfri:'θɪŋkə'] *n* livre-pensador *m*, -ra *f*.

free time *n* tempo *m* livre.

free trade *n (U)* livre comércio *m*.

freeway ['fri:weɪ] *n US* auto-estrada *f*.

freewheel [ˌfri:'wi:l] *vi* **-1.** [cyclist] andar sem pedalar **- 2.** [motorist] ir em ponto morto.

freewheeling [ˌfri:'wi:lɪŋ] *adj inf* [style, attitude] liberal.

free will *n (U)* vontade *f* própria; **to do sthg of one's own** ~ fazer algo por vontade própria.

free world *n*: **the** ~ o mundo livre.

freeze [fri:z] (*pt* **froze**, *pp* **frozen**) ⇔ *vt* **-1.** [gen] congelar **- 2.** [engine, lock] emperrar **- 3.** [pipes] entupir. ⇔ *vi* **-1.** [turn to ice] congelar-se **- 2.** METEOR esfriar muito **- 3.** [stop moving] parar **- 4.** *inf* [be cold] congelar. ⇔ *n* **-1.** [cold weather] frio *m* intenso **- 2.** [of wages, prices] congelamento *m*.
➥ **freeze over** *vi* congelar (*na superfície*).
➥ **freeze up** *vi* **-1.** [river, lake] congelar **- 2.** [lock, engine] emperrar.

freeze-dried [-'draɪd] *adj* congelado(da) a vácuo.

freeze frame *n* **- 1.** [photograph] pose *f* **- 2.** [on video] imagem *f* congelada.

freezer ['fri:zə'] *n* **- 1.** [machine] freezer *m*, frízer *m* **- 2.** [part of fridge] congelador *m*.

freezing ['fri:zɪŋ] ⇔ *adj* gelado(da); **it's** ~ **in here** está um gelo aqui; **I'm** ~ estou congelando. ⇔ *n* congelamento *m*; **5 degrees below** ~ *inf* 5 graus abaixo de zero.

freezing point *n* ponto *m* de congelamento.

freight [freɪt] *n (U)* [goods] carga *f*.

freight train *n* trem *m* de carga.

French [frentʃ] ⇔ *adj* francês(esa). ⇔ *n* francês *m*, -esa *f*. ⇔ *npl*: **the** ~ os franceses.

French bean *n* vagem *f*.

French bread *n (U)* pão *m* francês, bisnaga *f*.

French Canadian ⇔ *adj* franco-canadense. ⇔ *n* [person] franco-canadense *mf*.

French chalk *n (U)* giz *m* de alfaiate.

French doors *npl* = **French windows**.

French dressing *n* **- 1.** [in UK] molho *m* vinagrete **- 2.** [in US] molho *m* rosé.

French fries *npl esp US* batatas *fpl* fritas.

Frenchman ['frentʃmən] (*pl* **-men** [-mən]) *n* francês *m*.

French polish *n (U)* verniz *m* (*para móveis*).

French Riviera *n*: **the** ~ a Riviera Francesa.

French stick *n UK* baguete *f*.

French toast *n (U)* rabanada *f*.

French windows *npl* janela *f* de batente.

Frenchwoman ['frentʃˌwʊmən] (*pl* **-women** [ˌwɪmɪn]) *n* francesa *f*.

frenetic [frə'netɪk] *adj* frenético(ca).

frenzied ['frenzɪd] *adj* agitado(da), incontrolável.

frenzy ['frenzɪ] (*pl* **-ies**) *n* frenesi *m*.

frequency ['fri:kwənsɪ] (*pl* **-ies**) *n* frequência *f*.

frequency modulation *n (U)* freqüência *f* modulada.

frequent [*adj* 'fri:kwənt, *vb* frɪ'kwent] ⇔ *adj* freqüente. ⇔ *vt* freqüentar.

frequently ['fri:kwəntlɪ] *adv* freqüentemente.

fresco ['freskəʊ] (*pl* **-es** OR **-s**) *n* afresco *m*.

fresh [freʃ] ⇔ *adj* **-1.** [gen] fresco(ca); ~ **from**

recém-saído(da) de **-2.** [water] doce **-3.** [another] novo(va); **to make a ~ start** começar tudo de novo **-4.** [not tired] bem-disposto(ta) **-5.** [complexion] revigorado(da) **-6.** [refreshing] refrescante **-7.** [original] original **-8.** *inf dated* [cheeky] atrevido(da); **to get ~ with sb** ser atrevido(da) com alguém **-9.** [bright] vivo(va). ◇ *adv* [recently] recém-; **~ cut flowers** flores recém-cortadas; **to be ~ out of sthg** *inf* acabar de ficar sem algo.

freshen ['freʃn] ◇ *vt* [refresh] renovar. ◇ *vi* [wind] tornar-se mais frio (fria).
◆ **freshen up** ◇ *vt sep* **-1.** [person] refrescar **-2.** [room, house] tornar mais atrativo(va). ◇ *vi* [person] refrescar-se *(com água)*.

fresher ['freʃəʳ] *n UK inf* calouro *m*, -ra *f*.

freshly ['freʃlɪ] *adv* [recently] recentemente, recém-.

freshman ['freʃmən] (*pl* **-men** [-mən]) *n* calouro *m*.

freshness ['freʃnɪs] *n* **-1.** [gen] frescor *m* **-2.** [originality] originalidade *f*.

freshwater ['freʃˌwɔːtəʳ] *adj* de água doce.

fret [fret] (*pt* & *pp* **-ted**, *cont* **-ting**) *vi* [worry] preocupar-se.

fretful ['fretfʊl] *adj* irritadiço(ça); **a ~ night** uma noite agitada.

fretsaw ['fretsɔː] *n* serra *f* tico-tico.

Freudian *adj* freudiano(na); **~ slip** ato *m* falho.

FRG (*abbr of* **Federal Republic of Germany**) *n* RFA *f*.

Fri. (*abbr of* **Friday**) sex.

friar ['fraɪəʳ] *n* frei *m*.

friction ['frɪkʃn] *n (U)* **-1.** [rubbing] fricção *f* **-2.** [conflict] atrito *m*.

Friday ['fraɪdɪ] *n* sexta-feira *f*; *see also* **Saturday**.

fridge [frɪdʒ] *n esp UK* refrigerador *m*.

fridge-freezer *n UK* refrigerador *m* com freezer.

fried [fraɪd] ◇ *pt* & *pp* ▷ **fry**. ◇ *adj* frito(ta); **~ egg** ovo frito.

friend [frend] *n* amigo *m*, -ga *f*; **to be ~s (with sb)** ser amigo(ga) (de alguém); **to make ~s (with sb)** fazer amizade (com alguém).

friendless ['frendlɪs] *adj* sem amigos.

friendly ['frendlɪ] (*compar* **-ier**, *superl* **-iest**, *pl* **-ies**) ◇ *adj* **-1.** [kind, pleasant] amável; **to be ~ with sb** ser amigável com alguém **-2.** [not enemy] amigo(-ga) **-3.** [not serious] amistoso(sa). ◇ *n esp UK SPORT* amistoso *m*.

friendly society *n UK organização com a qual as pessoas contribuem regularmente e que lhes dá dinheiro quando se aposentam ou ficam doentes.*

friendship ['frendʃɪp] *n* **-1.** [between people] amizade *f* **-2.** [between countries] boas relações *fpl*.

fries [fraɪz] *npl* = **French fries**.

Friesian (cow) ['friːzjən-] *n* vaca *f* holandesa.

frieze [friːz] *n* friso *m*.

frigate ['frɪgət] *n* fragata *f*.

fright [fraɪt] *n* **-1.** (*U*) [fear] medo *m*; **to take ~** ter medo **-2.** [shock] susto *m*; **to give sb a ~** dar um susto em alguém.

frighten ['fraɪtn] *vt* assustar; **to ~ sb into doing sthg** forçar alguém a fazer algo por medo.
◆ **frighten away** *vt sep* espantar.
◆ **frighten off** *vt sep* espantar.

frightened ['fraɪtnd] *adj* amedrontado(da); **to be ~ of sthg/of doing sthg** ter medo de algo/de fazer algo.

frightening ['fraɪtnɪŋ] *adj* assustador(ra).

frightful ['fraɪtfʊl] *adj dated* horrendo(da).

frigid ['frɪdʒɪd] *adj* [sexually cold] frígido(da).

frill [frɪl] *n* **-1.** [decoration] babado *m* **-2.** *inf* [extra] frescura *f*.

frilly ['frɪlɪ] (*compar* **-ier**, *superl* **-iest**) *adj* com babados.

fringe [frɪndʒ] ◇ *n* **-1.** [gen] franja *f* **-2.** *fig* [edge] orla *f*, margem *f* **-3.** *fig* [extreme] facção *f*. ◇ *vt* [border] cercar.

fringe benefit *n* benefício *m* adicional.

fringe group *n* facção *f*.

fringe theatre *n UK* teatro *m* de vanguarda.

Frisbee® ['frɪzbɪ] *n* jogo *m* de Frisbee®.

Frisian Islands ['frɪʒən-] *npl*: **the ~** as Ilhas Frísias.

frisk [frɪsk] ◇ *vt* [search] revistar. ◇ *vi* [play] brincar.

frisky ['frɪskɪ] (*compar* **-ier**, *superl* **-iest**) *adj inf* brincalhão(lhona).

fritter ['frɪtəʳ] *n CULIN* bolinho *m* frito.
◆ **fritter away** *vt sep* desperdiçar; **to ~ money/time away on sthg** desperdiçar dinheiro/tempo com algo.

frivolity [frɪ'vɒlətɪ] (*pl* **-ies**) *n* frivolidade *f*.

frivolous ['frɪvələs] *adj* frívolo(la).

frizzy ['frɪzɪ] (*compar* **-ier**, *superl* **-iest**) *adj* crespo(pa).

fro [frəʊ] *adv* ▷ **to**.

frock [frɒk] *n dated* vestido *m*.

frog [frɒg] *n* [animal] rã *f*; **to have a ~ in one's throat** estar com a garganta irritada.

frogman ['frɒgmən] (*pl* **-men** [-mən]) *n* homem-rã *m*.

frogmarch ['frɒgmɑːtʃ] *vt* levar à força.

frogspawn ['frɒgspɔːn] *n (U)* ova *f* de rã.

frolic ['frɒlɪk] (*pt* & *pp* **-ked**, *cont* **-king**) ◇ *n* brincadeira *f*. ◇ *vi* brincar.

from [frɒm] *prep* **-1.** [expressing origin, source] de; **I'm ~ California** sou da Califórnia; **the train ~ Chicago** o trem de Chicago; **I bought it ~ a supermarket** comprei-o num supermercado **-2.** [expressing removal, deduction] de; **away ~ home** longe de casa; **to take sthg (away) ~ sb** tirar algo de alguém; **10% will be deducted ~ the total** será deduzido 10% do total **-3.** [expressing distance] de; **five miles ~ here** a oito quilômetros daqui; **it's not far ~ here** não é longe daqui **-4.** [expressing position] de; **~ here you can see the valley** daqui se vê o vale **-5.** [expressing what sthg is made with] de; **it's made ~ stone** é feito de pedra **-6.** [expressing starting time] desde; **~ the moment you arrived** desde que chegou; **~ now on** de agora em diante; **~ next year** a partir do próximo ano; **open ~ nine to five** aberto das nove às cinco **-7.** [expressing change] de; **the price has gone up ~ $1 to $2** o preço subiu de um dólar para dois; **to translate ~ German into English** traduzir do alemão para o inglês **-8.** [expressing range] de; **it could take ~ two to six months** pode levar de dois a seis meses **-9.** [as a result of] de; **I'm tired ~ walking**

estou cansado de andar **-10.** [expressing protection] de; **sheltered** ~ **the wind** protegido do vento **-11.** [in comparisons]: **different** ~ diferente de.

frond [frɒnd] *n* fronde *m*.

front [frʌnt] <> *n* **-1.** [gen] frente *f*; **at the** ~ **of** à frente de **-2.** MIL front *m*, frente *f* **-3.** [promenade]: **(sea)** ~ orla *f* marítima **-4.** [outward appearance] fachada *f* **-5.** [of book] capa *f*. <> *adj* [at front] da frente; ~ **page** primeira página; ~ **cover** capa. <> *vt* **-1.** [stand before] ser de frente para **-2.** [TV programme] estar à frente de. <> *vi*: **to** ~ **onto** sthg dar de frente para algo.
in front *adv* **-1.** [further forward] na frente **-2.** [winning]: **to be in** ~ estar na frente.
in front of *prep* **-1.** [close to front of] em frente de **-2.** [in the presence of] na frente de.

frontage [ˈfrʌntɪdʒ] *n* fachada *f* principal.

frontal [ˈfrʌntl] *adj* frontal.

frontbench [ˈfrʌntˈbentʃ] *n cadeiras dianteiras no parlamento britânico nas quais se sentam os líderes do governo e da oposição*.

front desk *n* recepção *f*.

front door *n* porta *f* da frente.

frontier [ˈfrʌnˌtɪəʳ, US frʌnˈtɪərl *n* **-1.** [border] fronteira *f* **-2.** *fig* [furthest limit] fronteira *f*.

frontispiece [ˈfrʌntɪspiːs] *n* frontispício *m*.

front line *n*: **the** ~ **a** linha de frente.

front man *n* **-1.** [of group] representante *mf* **-2.** [of programme] apresentador *m*, -ra *f*.

front-page *adj* de primeira página.

front room *n* sala *f* de estar.

front-runner *n* favorito *m*, -ta *f*.

front-wheel drive *n* **-1.** [vehicle] veículo com tração dianteira **-2.** [system] tração *f* dianteira.

frost [frɒst] <> *n* **-1.** (U) [layer of ice] geada *f* **-2.** [weather] frio *m* intenso. <> *vi*: **to** ~ **over** OR **up** cobrir-se de geada.

frostbite [ˈfrɒstbaɪt] *n* (U) enregelamento *m*.

frostbitten [ˈfrɒstˌbɪtn] *adj* enregelado(da).

frosted [ˈfrɒstɪd] *adj* **-1.** [opaque] fosco(ca) **-2.** US CULIN coberto(ta) com glacê.

frosting [ˈfrɒstɪŋ] *n* (U) US CULIN cobertura *f (de glacê)*.

frosty [ˈfrɒstɪ] (*compar* -ier, *superl* -iest) *adj* **-1.** [very cold] gelado(da) **-2.** [covered with frost] coberto(ta) de geada **-3.** *fig* [unfriendly] glacial.

froth [frɒθ] <> *n* (U) espuma *f*. <> *vi* espumar.

frothy [ˈfrɒθɪ] (*compar* -ier, *superl* -iest) *adj* [covered in froth] espumante.

frown [fraʊn] <> *n* cenho *m*. <> *vi* franzir as sobrancelhas.
frown (up)on *vt fus* não ver com bons olhos.

froze [frəʊz] *pt* ⊳ **freeze**.

frozen [ˈfrəʊzn] <> *pp* ⊳ **freeze**. <> *adj* **-1.** [gen] congelado(da) **-2.** [feeling very cold] gelado(da) **-3.** *fig* [rigid]: ~ **with fear** gelado(da) de medo **-4.** [prices, salaries, assets] congelado(da).

FRS *n* **-1.** (*abbr of* **Fellow of the Royal Society**) *membro da Royal Society, organização britânica para pesquisa científica.* **-2.** (*abbr of* **Federal Reserve System**) ≃ BACEN *m*.

frugal [ˈfruːgl] *adj* **-1.** [small] frugal **-2.** [careful] regrado(da).

fruit [fruːt] (*pl inv* OR **fruits**) <> *n* **-1.** [food] fruta *f* **-2.** *fig* [result] fruto *m*; **to bear** ~ dar resultados. <> *comp* de frutas; **a** ~ **tree** uma árvore frutífera. <> *vi* frutificar.

fruitcake [ˈfruːtkeɪk] *n* **-1.** bolo *m* com passas **-2.** *inf* [mad person] maluco *m*, -ca *f*.

fruiterer [ˈfruːtərəʳ] *n* UK fruteiro *m*, -ra *f*; ~ **'s (shop)** fruteira *f*.

fruitful [ˈfruːtfʊl] *adj* [successful] produtivo(va), proveitoso(sa).

fruition [fruːˈɪʃn] *n* (U): **to come to** ~ realizar-se.

fruit juice *n* suco *m* de fruta.

fruitless [ˈfruːtlɪs] *adj* [wasted] infrutífero(ra), vão (vã).

fruit machine *n* UK caça-níqueis *m inv*.

fruit salad *n* salada *f* de frutas.

frumpy [ˈfrʌmpɪ] (*compar* -ier, *superl* -iest) *adj inf* antiquado(da).

frustrate [frʌˈstreɪt] *vt* frustrar.

frustrated [frʌˈstreɪtɪd] *adj* frustrado(da).

frustrating [frʌˈstreɪtɪŋ] *adj* frustrante.

frustration [frʌˈstreɪʃn] *n* frustração *f*.

fry [fraɪ] (*pt* & *pp* **fried**) <> *vt* [food] fritar. <> *vi* [food] fritar.

frying pan [ˈfraɪŋ-] *n* frigideira *f*; **to jump out of the** ~ **into the fire** saltar da frigideira e cair no fogo, ir de mal a pior.

ft. *abbr of* **foot, feet**.

FT (*abbr of* **Financial Times**) *n jornal diário britânico de economia.*

FTC (*abbr of* **Federal Trade Commission**) *n órgão norte-americano responsável por se fazer cumprir a legislação sobre monopólios.*

FTSE (*abbr of* **Financial Times Stock Exchange**) *n* FTSE *m*; **the** ~ **index** o índice FTSE; **the** ~ **100** *as ações das 100 maiores empresas britânicas ponderadas com base em seu valor de mercado.*

fuchsia [ˈfjuːʃə] *n* fúcsia *f*.

fuck [fʌk] *vulg* <> *vt* [have sex with] trepar OR foder com. <> *vi* trepar, foder. <> *excl* merda!
fuck off *vulg* <> *vi* foder-se. <> *excl* vá se foder!

fucking [ˈfʌkɪŋ] *adj vulg* [for emphasis] de merda; **a** ~ **idiot** um idiota de merda.

fuddled [ˈfʌdld] *adj* [confused] confuso(sa).

fuddy-duddy [ˈfʌdɪˌdʌdɪ] (*pl* **fuddy-duddies**) *n inf* careta *mf*.

fudge [fʌdʒ] <> *n* (U) [sweet] fondant *m, doce de açúcar, leite e manteiga.* <> *vt* **-1.** *inf* [falsify, tamper with] falsificar **-2.** [avoid, confuse] escapar-se de.

fuel [fjʊəl] (*UK pt* & *pp* -**led**, *cont*-**ling**, *US pt* & *pp*-**ed**, *cont* -**ing**) <> *n* combustível *m*; **to add** ~ **to the fire** *fig* botar lenha na fogueira. <> *vt* **-1.** [supply with fuel] abastecer **-2.** [increase] aumentar.

fuel cell *n* célula *f* a combustível.

fuel pump *n* bomba *f* de combustível.

fuel tank *n* tanque *m* de combustível.

fugitive [ˈfjuːdʒətɪv] *n* fugitivo *m*, -va *f*.

fugue [fjuːg] *n* MUS fuga *f*.

fulcrum [ˈfʊlkrəm] (*pl* -**crums** OR -**cra** [-krə]) *n* fulcro *m*.

fulfil (*pt* & *pp* -**led**, *cont* -**ling**), **fulfill** *US* [fʊl'fɪl] *vt* -**1.** [carry out] cumprir; **to ~ one's role** desempenhar seu papel -**2.** [satisfy] satisfazer; **to ~ o.s.** realizar-se.

fulfilling [fʊl'fɪlɪŋ] *adj* gratificante.

fulfilment, fulfillment [fʊl'fɪlmənt] *n (U)* -**1.** [satisfaction] satisfação *f* -**2.** [carrying through - of ambition, dream] realização *f*; [- of role] desempenho *m*; [- of need, promise] cumprimento *m*.

full [fʊl] <> *adj* -**1.** [gen] cheio (cheia); **~ of** cheio (cheia) **de** -**2.** [with food] satisfeito(ta) -**3.** [complete - employment, use] integral; [- explanation, name, day, recovery] completo(ta), efetivo(va); [- member, professor] titular -**4.** [maximum] máximo(ma) -**5.** [sound] forte -**6.** [flavour] rico(ca) -**7.** [plump - mouth] cheio (cheia); [- figure] voluptuoso(sa) -**8.** [ample, wide] largo(ga). <> *adv* -**1.** [directly] em cheio -**2.** [very]: **to know ~ well that ...** saber muito bem que ... -**3.** [at maximum] no máximo. <> *n*: **in ~** [payment] na totalidade; [write] por extenso; **to the ~** ao máximo.

fullback ['fʊlbæk] *n* zagueiro *m*, -ra *f*.

full-blooded [-'blʌdɪd] *adj* -**1.** [pure-blooded] de raça pura -**2.** [wholehearted] vigoroso(sa).

full-blown [-'bləʊn] *adj* bem-caracterizado(da); **a ~ disease** uma doença bem-desenvolvida.

full board *n (U)* diária *f* completa.

full-bodied [-'bɒdɪd] *adj* [wine] encorpado(da).

full dress *n (U)* traje *m* a rigor.

full-face *adj* [portrait, photo] de frente.

full-fashioned *adj US* = **fully-fashioned**.

full-fledged *adj US* = **fully-fledged**.

full-frontal *adj* [photo, appearance] em nu frontal.

full-grown [-'grəʊn] *adj* adulto(ta).

full house *n* [at show, event] casa *f* cheia.

full-length <> *adj* -**1.** [portrait, mirror] de corpo inteiro -**2.** [dress, curtains] comprido(da) -**3.** [novel, film] extenso(sa); **a ~ film** um longa-metragem. <> *adv* ao comprido, completamente.

full moon *n* lua *f* cheia.

fullness ['fʊlnɪs] *n* -**1.** [of details, information] riqueza *f* -**2.** [of face, figure, lips] largura *f* -**3.** [of skirt, sleeves] comprimento *m* -**4.** *phr*: **in the ~ of time** no momento oportuno.

full-page *adj* de página inteira.

full-scale *adj* -**1.** [model, drawing, copy] em tamanho natural -**2.** [inquiry] completo(ta) -**3.** [war] total -**4.** [attack] maciço(ça).

full-size(d) *adj* -**1.** [life-size] de tamanho natural -**2.** [adult] adulto(ta) -**3.** *US AUT*: **~ car** carro *m* de passeio.

full stop <> *n* ponto *m* final. <> *adv UK* ponto final.

full time *n UK SPORT* final *m* de jogo.
➡ full-time <> *adj* de tempo integral. <> *adv* em tempo integral.

full up *adj* -**1.** [after meal] cheio(cheia) -**2.** [bus, train] lotado(da).

fully ['fʊlɪ] *adv* -**1.** [completely] completamente, totalmente; **to be ~ booked** estar com as reservas esgotadas -**2.** [in detail] em detalhes.

fully-fashioned *UK*, **full-fashioned** *US* [-'fæʃnd] *adj* justo(ta); **~ tights** meia-calça *f* justa.

fully-fledged *UK*, **full-fledged** *US* [-'fledʒd] *adj* *fig* [doctor, lawyer] experiente.

fulness ['fʊlnɪs] *n* = **fullness**.

fulsome ['fʊlsəm] *adj* exagerado(da).

fumble ['fʌmbl] *vi* tatear; **to ~ for sthg** procurar desajeitadamente por algo; **he ~d in his pockets for his keys** ele vasculhou os bolsos desajeitadamente à procura das chaves.

fume [fjuːm] *vi* [with anger] fumegar.
➡ fumes *npl* [gas - from car, fire] fumaça *f*; [- of paint] vapor *m*.

fumigate ['fjuːmɪgeɪt] *vt* desinfetar.

fun [fʌn] <> *n (U)* -**1.** [pleasure, amusement] diversão *f*; **we really had ~ at the party** nós realmente nos divertimos na festa; **what ~!** que divertido!; **for ~, for the ~ of it** por prazer, por brincadeira -**2.** [playfulness] alegria *f* -**3.** [ridicule]: **to make ~ of sb** caçoar de alguém; **to poke ~ at sb** zombar de alguém. <> *adj* divertido(da).

function ['fʌŋkʃn] <> *n* -**1.** [gen] função *f* -**2.** [formal social event] cerimônia *f*. <> *vi* funcionar; **to ~ as sthg** funcionar como algo.

functional ['fʌŋkʃnəl] *adj* -**1.** [furniture, design] funcional -**2.** [machine, system] operacional.

functionary ['fʌŋkʃnərɪ] (*pl* -**ies**) *n* funcionário *m* público, funcionária *f* pública.

function key *n COMPUT* tecla *f* de função.

fund [fʌnd] <> *n* -**1.** [amount of money] fundo *m* -**2.** *fig* [reserve] reserva *f*. <> *vt* financiar.
➡ funds *npl* recursos *mpl*.

fundamental [ˌfʌndə'mentl] *adj* -**1.** [basic] básico(-ca), fundamental -**2.** [vital] fundamental; **~ to sthg** fundamental para algo.
➡ fundamentals *npl* fundamentos *mpl*.

fundamentalism [ˌfʌndə'mentəlɪzm] *n (U)* fundamentalismo *m*.

fundamentally [ˌfʌndə'mentəlɪ] *adv* -**1.** [basically] basicamente, fundamentalmente -**2.** [radically] radicalmente.

funding ['fʌndɪŋ] *n (U)* recursos *mpl*.

fund-raising [-ˌreɪzɪŋ] <> *n (U)* angariação *f* de fundos. <> *comp* de angariação de fundos.

funeral ['fjuːnərəl] *n* funeral *m*.

funeral director *n* agente *mf* funerário, -ria.

funeral parlour *n* casa *f* funerária.

funeral service *n* cerimônia *f* de enterro.

funereal [fjuː'nɪərɪəl] *adj* fúnebre.

funfair ['fʌnfeəˠ] *n* parque *m* de diversões.

fungus ['fʌŋgəs] (*pl* -**gi** [-gaɪ], -**es**) *n BOT* fungo *m*.

funk [fʌŋk] *n (U)* -**1.** *MUS* funk *m* -**2.** *dated* [fear] pavor *m*.

funky ['fʌŋkɪ] (*compar* -**ier**, *superl* -**iest**) *adj MUS* ritmado(da), vibrante.

funnel ['fʌnl] (*UK pt* & *pp* -**led**, *cont* -**ling**, *US pt* & *pp* -**ed**, *cont* -**ing**) <> *n* -**1.** [tube] funil *m* -**2.** [on ship] chaminé *f*. <> *vt* -**1.** [liquid] passar por funil -**2.** [crowd, money] encaminhar. <> *vi* [crowd, people] encaminhar-se.

funnily ['fʌnɪlɪ] *adv* [strangely] estranhamente; **~ enough** curiosamente.

funny ['fʌnɪ] (*compar* -**ier**, *superl* -**iest**) *adj* -**1.** [amusing] engraçado(da) -**2.** [odd] esquisito(ta) -**3.** [ill]: **to feel ~** não se sentir bem.

➤ **funnies** *npl US* quadrinhos *mpl.*

funny bone *n* osso *m* do cotovelo.

funny farm *n esp US inf hum* pinel *f,* manicômio *m.*

fun run *n maratona que tem por objetivo angariar recursos para instituições de caridade.*

fur [fɜ:ʳ] *n* **-1.** [on animal] pêlo *m* **-2.** [garment] pele *f.*

fur coat *n* casaco *m* de pele.

furious [ˈfjʊərɪəs] *adj* **-1.** [very angry] furioso(sa) **-2.** [violent] violento(ta).

furiously [ˈfjʊərɪəslɪ] *adv* **-1.** [angrily] furiosamente **-2.** [fight, work, drive] violentamente.

furled [fɜ:ld] *adj* dobrado(da).

furlong [ˈfɜ:lɒŋ] *n medida correspondente a um oitavo de milha.*

furnace [ˈfɜ:nɪs] *n* [fire] fornalha *f.*

furnish [ˈfɜ:nɪʃ] *vt* **-1.** [fit out] mobiliar **-2.** *fml* [provide] fornecer; **to ~ sb with sthg** fornecer algo a alguém.

furnished [ˈfɜ:nɪʃt] *adj* [fitted out] mobiliado(da).

furnishings [ˈfɜ:nɪʃɪŋz] *npl* mobiliário *m.*

furniture [ˈfɜ:nɪtʃəʳ] *n (U)* móvel *m.*

furniture polish *n* lustrador *m* de móveis.

furore *UK* [fjʊˈrɔ:rɪ], **furor** *US* [ˈfjʊrɔ:r] *n* furor *m.*

furrier [ˈfʌrɪəʳ] *n* peleiro *m,* -ra *f.*

furrow [ˈfʌrəʊ] *n* **-1.** [in field] sulco *m* **-2.** [on forehead] ruga *f.*

furrowed [ˈfʌrəʊd] *adj* **-1.** [field, land] lavrado(da) **-2.** [brow] enrugado(da).

furry [ˈfɜ:rɪ] *(compar* -ier, *superl* -iest) *adj* **-1.** [animal] peludo(da) **-2.** [material, toy] de pelúcia.

further [ˈfɜ:ðəʳ] ◇ *compar* ▷ **far.** ◇ *adv* **-1.** [gen] mais adiante; **how much ~ is it?** a que distância fica?; **~ on/back** mais adiante/atrás **-2.** [complicate, develop, enquire] mais; **to take sth ~** levar algo adiante; **to go ~** ir adiante; **this mustn't go any ~** isso tem que ficar entre nós **-3.** [in addition] além disso. ◇ *adj* adicional, novo(va); **until ~ notice** até novas ordens. ◇ *vt* [career, cause, aims] impulsionar.

➤ **further to** *prep fml* com referência a.

further education *n UK educação para adultos após deixar a escola excluindo-se a universidade.*

furthermore [ˌfɜ:ðəˈmɔ:ʳ] *adv* além do mais, além disso.

furthermost [ˈfɜ:ðəməʊst] *adj* mais longe.

furthest [ˈfɜ:ðɪst] ◇ *superl* ▷ **far.** ◇ *adj* **-1.** [in distance] mais afastado(da) **-2.** [greatest] maior. ◇ *adv* **-1.** [in distance] mais longe **-2.** [to greatest degree, extent] maior.

furtive [ˈfɜ:tɪv] *adj* furtivo(va).

furtively [ˈfɜ:tɪvlɪ] *adv* furtivamente.

fury [ˈfjʊərɪ] *n* fúria *f;* **in a ~** num acesso de fúria.

fuse *esp UK,* **fuze** *US* [fju:z] ◇ *n* **-1.** *ELEC* fusível *m* **-2.** [of bomb, firework] detonador *m.* ◇ *vt* **-1.** [gen] fundir **-2.** *ELEC* queimar. ◇ *vi* **-1.** [gen] fundir-se **-2.** *ELEC* queimar.

fusebox *n* caixa *f* de fusíveis.

fused [fju:zd] *adj ELEC* [fitted with a fuse] com fusível.

fuselage [ˈfju:zəlɑ:ʒ] *n* fuselagem *f.*

fuse wire *n* fio *m* de chumbo *(para fusível).*

fusillade [ˌfju:zəˈleɪd] *n* fuzilaria *f.*

fusion [ˈfju:ʒn] *n* fusão *f.*

fuss [fʌs] ◇ *n* [bother, agitation] alvoroço *m;* **to make a ~** fazer um estardalhaço; **to kick up** *OR* **to make a ~ about sthg** causar *OR* fazer confusão por algo; **to make a ~ of sb** *UK* tratar alguém com atenção. ◇ *vi* [become agitated] alvoroçar-se.

➤ **fuss over** *vt fus* alvoroçar-se com.

fusspot [ˈfʌspɒt] *n inf* exagerado *m,* -da *f.*

fussy [ˈfʌsɪ] *(compar* -ier, *superl* -iest) *adj* **-1.** [fastidious] exigente **-2.** [over-ornate] exagerado(da).

fusty [ˈfʌstɪ] *(compar* -ier, *superl* -iest) *adj* **-1.** [room, clothes] com cheiro de mofo **-2.** [person, idea, attitude] antiquado(da).

futile [ˈfju:taɪl] *adj* fútil.

futility [fju:ˈtɪlətɪ] *n (U)* futilidade *f.*

futon [ˈfu:tɒn] *n* colchão japonês.

future [ˈfju:tʃəʳ] ◇ *n* **-1.** [time ahead] futuro *m;* **in (the) ~** no futuro **-2.** *GRAMM:* **~ (tense)** futuro *m.* ◇ *adj* futuro(ra).

➤ **futures** *npl COMM* mercado *m* de futuros.

futuristic [ˌfju:tʃəˈrɪstɪk] *adj* [design] futurístico(ca).

fuze *n, vt & vi US* = **fuse.**

fuzz [fʌz] *n* **-1.** [hair] penugem *f* **-2.** *inf* [police]**: the ~** os tiras.

fuzzy [ˈfʌzɪ] *(compar* -ier, *superl* -iest) *adj* **-1.** [hair] encrespado(da) **-2.** [image, ideas] difuso(sa).

fwd. *(abbr of* **forward**) encaminhar.

fwy *(abbr of* **freeway**) *US* auto-estrada *f.*

FY *(abbr of* **fiscal year**) *n* **-1.** *US* ano *m* fiscal. **-2.** *(abbr of* **financial year**) *UK* ano *m* fiscal.

FYI *(abbr of* **for your information**) para sua informação.

G

g¹ *(pl* **g's** *OR* **gs**), **G** *(pl* **G's** *OR* **Gs**) [dʒi:] *n* [letter] g, G *m.*

➤ **G** ◇ *n MUS* sol *m.* ◇ **-1.** *(abbr of* **good**) B *m* **-2.** [film certificate] *US (abbr of* **general (audience)**) censura *f* livre.

g² **-1.** *(abbr of* **gram**) g **-2.** *(abbr of* **gravity**) G.

GA *abbr of* **Georgia.**

gab [gæb] *n* ▷ **gift.**

gabardine [ˌgæbəˈdi:n] *n* **-1.** *(U)* [material] gabardine *f* **-2.** [raincoat] gabardina *f.*

gabble [ˈgæbl] ◇ *vt* tagarelar. ◇ *vi* tagarelar. ◇ *n* tagarelice *f.*

gable [ˈgeɪbl] *n* oitão *m.*

Gabon [gæˈbɒn] *n* Gabão *f;* **in ~** no Gabão.

Gabonese [ˌgæbəˈni:z] ◇ *adj* gabonense. ◇ *npl:* **the ~** os gabonenses.

gad ◆ **gad about** (*pt* & *pp* **-ded**, *cont* **-ding**) *vi inf* badalar.

gadget [ˈgædʒɪt] *n* aparelho *m*.

gadgetry [ˈgædʒɪtrɪ] *n (U)* aparelhagem *f*.

Gaelic [ˈgeɪlɪk] ◇ *adj* gaélico(ca). ◇ *n* gaélico *m*, -ca *f*.

gaffe [gæf] *n* gafe *f*.

gaffer [ˈgæfəʳ] *n UK inf* [boss] chefe *mf*.

gag [gæg] (*pt* & *pp* **-ged**, *cont* **-ging**) ◇ *n* **-1.** [for mouth] mordaça *f* **-2.** *inf* [joke] piada *f*. ◇ *vt* [put gag on] amordaçar. ◇ *vi* amordaçar.

gage *n* & *vt US* = **gauge**.

gaiety [ˈgeɪətɪ] *n (U)* alegria *f*.

gaily [ˈgeɪlɪ] *adv* **-1.** [cheerfully] alegremente **-2.** [without thinking] despreocupadamente.

gain [geɪn] ◇ *n* **-1.** [profit] ganho *m* **-2.** *(U)* [making a profit] lucro *m* **-3.** [increase] aumento *m*. ◇ *vt* **-1.** [gen] ganhar **-2.** [subj: watch, clock] adiantar-se; **my watch has ~ed ten minutes** meu relógio adiantou-se em dez minutos. ◇ *vi* **-1.** [increase]: **to ~ in sthg** crescer em algo **-2.** [profit] lucrar; **to ~ from/by sthg** lucrar com algo **-3.** [watch, clock] adiantar-se.
◆ **gain on** *vt fus* aproximar-se de.

gainful [ˈgeɪnfʊl] *adj fml* [activity, employment] lucrativo(va), vantajoso(sa).

gainfully [ˈgeɪnfʊlɪ] *adv fml* vantajosamente.

gainsay [ˌgeɪnˈseɪ] (*pt* & *pp* **-said**) *vt fml* contradizer.

gait [geɪt] *n* maneira *f* de andar.

gaiters [ˈgeɪtəz] *npl* polainas *fpl*.

gal. *abbr of* **gallon**.

gala [ˈgɑːlə] ◇ *n* **-1.** [celebration] festival *m* **-2.** *UK SPORT* festival *m*. ◇ *comp* [performance, occasion] de gala.

Galapagos Islands [gəˈlæpəgəs-] *npl*: **the ~** as Ilhas Galápagos; **in the ~** nas Ilhas Galápagos.

galaxy [ˈgæləksɪ] (*pl* **-ies**) *n* [group of planets and stars] galáxia *f*.

gale [geɪl] *n* [wind] ventania *f*.

Galicia [gəˈlɪʃɪə] *n* **-1.** [in Central Europe] Galícia; **in ~** na Galícia **-2.** [in Spain] Galiza; **in ~** na Galiza.

gall [gɔːl] ◇ *n (U)* [nerve]: **to have the ~ to do sthg** ter a audácia de fazer algo. ◇ *vt* incomodar.

gall. *abbr of* **gallon**.

gallant [*sense 1* ˈgælənt, *sense 2* gəˈlænt] *adj* **-1.** [courageous] valente **-2.** [polite to women] galante.

gallantry [ˈgæləntrɪ] *n (U)* **-1.** [courage] valentia *f* **-2.** [politeness to women] galanteio *m*.

gall bladder *n* vesícula *f* biliar.

galleon [ˈgælɪən] *n* galeão *m*.

gallery [ˈgælərɪ] (*pl* **-ies**) *n* galeria *f*.

galley [ˈgælɪ] (*pl* **galleys**) *n* **-1.** [ship] galé *f* **-2.** [kitchen] cozinha *f* (*de navio ou avião*) **-3.** *TYPO*: **~ (proof)** prova *f* de granel.

Gallic [ˈgælɪk] *adj* gaulês(lesa).

galling [ˈgɔːlɪŋ] *adj* **-1.** [annoying] irritante **-2.** [humiliating] vergonhoso(sa).

gallivant [ˌgælɪˈvænt] *vi inf* perambular.

gallon [ˈgælən] *n* galão *m*.

gallop [ˈgæləp] ◇ *n* **-1.** [pace of horse] galope *m* **-2.** [horse ride] galopada *f*. ◇ *vi* galopar.

galloping [ˈgæləpɪŋ] *adj fig* [soaring] galopante.

gallows [ˈgæləʊz] (*pl inv*) *n* forca *f*.

gallstone [ˈgɔːlstəʊn] *n* cálculo *m* biliar.

Gallup poll® [ˈgæləp-] *n UK* ≃ pesquisa *f* do ibope.

galore [gəˈlɔːʳ] *adv* em abundância.

galoshes [gəˈlɒʃɪz] *npl* galocha *f*.

galvanize, -ise [ˈgælvənaɪz] *vt* **-1.** *TECH* galvanizar **-2.** [impel]: **to ~ sb into action** estimular alguém a uma ação.

Gambia [ˈgæmbɪə] *n*: **(the) ~** a Gâmbia; **in (the) ~** na Gâmbia.

Gambian [ˈgæmbɪən] ◇ *adj* gambiano(na). ◇ *n* gambiano *m*, -na *f*.

gambit [ˈgæmbɪt] *n* **-1.** [remark, ploy] lábia *f* **-2.** [in chess] tática *f*, estratégia *f*.

gamble [ˈgæmbl] ◇ *n* [calculated risk] aposta *f*; **to take a ~** assumir o risco. ◇ *vi* **-1.** [bet] apostar; **to ~ on sthg** apostar em algo **-2.** [take risk]: **to ~ on sthg** arriscar em algo.

gambler [ˈgæmbləʳ] *n* jogador *m*, -ra *f*.

gambling [ˈgæmblɪŋ] *n (U)* jogo *m* (*de azar*).

gambol [ˈgæmbl] (*UK pt* & *pp* **-led**, *cont* **-ling**, *US pt* & *pp* **-ed**, *cont* **-ing**) *vi* cabriolar, saltar.

game [geɪm] ◇ *n* **-1.** [sport, amusement] jogo *m*; **a children's ~** uma brincadeira de criança **-2.** [contest, match] jogo *m*, partida *f* **-3.** [division of match - in tennis] game *m*; [- in bridge] jogada *f* **-4.** [playing equipment] brinquedo *m* **-5.** [scheme, trick] truque *m*; **stop playing ~s with me!** pare de brincar comigo! **-6.** *(U)* [hunted animals] caça *f* **-7.** *phr*: **to beat sb at their own ~** derrotar alguém usando suas próprias armas; **the ~'s up** acabou a brincadeira; **to give the ~ away** entregar o jogo. ◇ *adj* **-1.** [brave] corajoso(sa) **-2.** [willing] disposto(-ta); **~ for sthg/to do sthg** pronto(ta) para algo/para fazer algo.
◆ **games** ◇ *n SCH* [physical education] jogos *mpl*. ◇ *npl* [sporting contest] jogos *mpl*.

gamekeeper [ˈgeɪmˌkiːpəʳ] *n* guarda-caça *mf*.

gamely [ˈgeɪmlɪ] *adv* [bravely] corajosamente.

game reserve *n* reserva *f* de caça.

gamesmanship [ˈgeɪmzmənʃɪp] *n (U)* artimanha *f* (*no jogo*).

gamma rays [ˈgæmə-] *npl* raios *mpl* gama.

gammon [ˈgæmən] *n (U)* presunto *m*.

gammy [ˈgæmɪ] (*compar* **-ier**, *superl* **-iest**) *adj UK inf* manco(ca).

gamut [ˈgæmət] *n* gama *f*; **to run the ~ of sthg** recorrer a toda a gama de algo.

gander [ˈgændəʳ] *n* [male goose] ganso *m*.

gang [gæŋ] *n* **-1.** [of criminals] quadrilha *f*, gangue *f* **-2.** [of young people] turma *f*.
◆ **gang up** *vi inf* mancomunar-se; **to ~ up on sb** mancomunar-se contra alguém.

Ganges [ˈgændʒiːz] *n*: **the (River) ~** o Rio Ganges.

gangland [ˈgæŋlænd] *n (U)* submundo *m* (*do crime*).

gangling [ˈgæŋglɪŋ], **gangly** [ˈgæŋglɪ] (*compar* **-ier**, *superl* **-iest**) *adj* desajeitado(da).

gangplank [ˈgæŋplæŋk] *n* prancha *f* (*de desembarque*), passadiço *m*.

gangrene [ˈgæŋgriːn] *n (U)* gangrena *f*.

gangrenous [ˈgæŋgrɪnəs] *adj* gangrenado(da).

gangster [ˈgæŋstəʳ] *n* gângster *mf*.

gangway ['gæŋweɪ] *n* -**1.** *UK* [aisle] corredor *m* -**2.** [gangplank] passadiço *m*.

gannet ['gænɪt] (*pl inv OR* -**s**) *n* [bird] ganso-patola *m*.

gantry ['gæntrɪ] (*pl* -**ies**) *n* [for crane] cavalete *m*.

GAO (*abbr of* **General Accounting Office**) *n* departamento *m* de finanças públicas (*norte-americano*).

gaol [dʒeɪl] *n* & *vt UK* = **jail**.

gap [gæp] *n* -**1.** [empty space] espaço *m*, brecha *f*; **her death left a ~ in our lives** sua morte deixou um vazio em nossas vidas; **fill in the ~s** preencher as lacunas -**2.** [in time] intervalo *m* -**3.** *fig* [in knowledge, report] falha *f* -**4.** *fig* [between theory and practice etc.] disparidade *f*.

gape [geɪp] *vi* -**1.** [person]: **to ~ (at sb/ sthg)** ficar boquiaberto(ta) (diante de alguém/algo) -**2.** [hole, shirt] abrir.

gaping ['geɪpɪŋ] *adj* -**1.** [person] boquiaberto(ta) -**2.** [hole, shirt, wound] todo aberto, toda aberta.

garage [*UK* 'gæra:ʒ, *US* gəˈrɑːʒ] *n* -**1.** [for keeping car] garagem *f* -**2.** *UK* [for fuel] posto *m* de gasolina -**3.** [for car repair] oficina *f* (*mecânica*) -**4.** [for selling cars] revendedora *f*.

garage sale *n US* venda *f* de garagem.

garb [gɑːb] *n* (*U*) *fml* traje *m*.

garbage ['gɑːbɪdʒ] *n esp US* (*U*) -**1.** [refuse] lixo *m* -**2.** *inf* [nonsense] besteira *f*.

garbage can *n US* lata *f* de lixo.

garbage collector *n US* lixeiro *m*, -ra *f*.

garbage truck *n US* caminhão *m* de lixo.

garbled ['gɑːbld] *adj* [message, account] adulterado(-da).

Garda (Síochána) *n Irish*: **the ~** *a polícia irlandesa*.

garden ['gɑːdn] *◇ n* jardim *m*. *◇ comp* de jardim. *◇ vi* jardinar.
  ➡ **gardens** *npl* jardim *m*.

garden centre *n* loja *f* de jardinagem.

garden city *n UK* cidade-jardim *f*.

gardener ['gɑːdnəʳ] *n* jardineiro *m*, -ra *f*.

gardenia [gɑːˈdiːnjə] *n* gardênia *f*.

gardening ['gɑːdnɪŋ] *◇ n* (*U*) jardinagem *f*. *◇ comp* de jardinagem; **~ expert** perito *m*, -ta *f* em jardinagem.

garden party *n* festa *f* ao ar livre.

gargantuan [gɑːˈgæntjʊən] *adj* gigantesco(ca).

gargle ['gɑːgl] *vi* gargarejar.

gargoyle ['gɑːgɔɪl] *n* gárgula *f*.

garish ['geərɪʃ] *adj* espalhafatoso(sa).

garland ['gɑːlənd] *n* guirlanda *f* (*de flores*).

garlic ['gɑːlɪk] *n* alho *m*.

garlic bread *n* pão *m* de alho.

garlicky ['gɑːlɪkɪ] *adj inf* -**1.** [in smell] com cheiro de alho -**2.** [in taste] com gosto de alho.

garment ['gɑːmənt] *n* peça *f* de roupa.

garner ['gɑːnəʳ] *vt fml* colher.

garnet ['gɑːnɪt] *n* [red stone] granada *f*.

garnish ['gɑːnɪʃ] *CULIN ◇ n* decoração *f*. *◇ vt* decorar.

garret ['gærət] *n* sótão *m*.

garrison ['gærɪsn] *◇ n* [soldiers] guarnição *f*. *◇ vt* guarnecer.

garrulous ['gærələs] *adj* tagarela.

garter ['gɑːtəʳ] *n* -**1.** [band round leg] liga *f* -**2.** *US* [suspender] suspensório *m*.

gas [gæs] (*pl* **gases** *OR* **gasses**, *pt* & *pp* -**sed**, *cont* -**sing**) *◇ n* -**1.** *CHEM* gás *m* -**2.** [domestic fuel] gás *m* (*de cozinha*) -**3.** *US* [fuel for vehicle] gasolina *f*; **to step on the ~** *inf* pisar no acelerador. *◇ vt* [poison] envenenar (com gás).

gas chamber *n* câmara *f* de gás.

gas cooker *n UK* fogão *m* a gás.

gas cylinder *n* botijão *m* de gás.

gaseous *adj TECH* gasoso(sa).

gas fire *n UK* aquecedor *m* a gás.

gas fitter *n* encanador *m*, -ra *f* de gás.

gas gauge *n US* medidor *m* de gás.

gash [gæʃ] *◇ n* corte *m* (*na pele*), ferida *f*. *◇ vt* cortar (*a pele*), ferir.

gasket ['gæskɪt] *n* gaxeta *f*.

gasman ['gæsmæn] (*pl* -**men** [-men]) *n* vendedor *m*, -ra *f* de gás.

gas mask *n* máscara *f* antigás.

gasmen *pl* ⊳ **gasman**.

gas meter *n* medidor *m* de gás.

gasoline ['gæsəliːn] *n US* (*U*) gasolina *f*.

gasometer [gæˈsɒmɪtəʳ] *n* gasômetro *m*.

gas oven *n* -**1.** [for cooking] forno *m* a gás -**2.** [gas chamber] câmara *f* de gás.

gasp [gɑːsp] *◇ n* arfada *f*. *◇ vi* ofegar.

gas pedal *n US* acelerador *m*.

gasping ['gɑːspɪŋ] *adj UK inf* [in great need]: **to be ~ for sthg** estar louco(ca) por algo.

gas pump attendant *n US* frentista *mf*.

gas station *n US* posto *m* de gasolina.

gas stove *n* = **gas cooker**.

gassy ['gæsɪ] (*compar* -**ier**, *superl* -**iest**) *adj pej* [water, beer] com muito gás.

gas tank *n US* tanque *m* de gasolina.

gas tap *n* torneira *f* de gás.

gastric ['gæstrɪk] *adj* gástrico(ca).

gastric ulcer *n* úlcera *f* gástrica.

gastritis [gæsˈtraɪtɪs] *n* (*U*) gastrite *f*.

gastroenteritis ['gæstrəʊˌentəˈraɪtɪs] *n* (*U*) gastroenterite *f*.

gastronomic [ˌgæstrəˈnɒmɪk] *adj* gastronômico(-ca).

gastronomy [gæsˈtrɒnəmɪ] *n* (*U*) gastronomia *f*.

gasworks ['gæswɜːks] (*pl inv*) *n* fábrica *f* de gás.

gate [geɪt] *n* portão *m*.

-GATE

Desde o escândalo de Watergate, em 1972, que resultou na primeira renúncia de um presidente dos Estados Unidos - Richard Nixon -, o sufixo *-gate* vem sendo acrescentado a outras palavras, para designar escândalos políticos nos Estados Unidos e na Grã-Bretanha. Assim, a palavra *Irangate* foi cunhada para referir-se á venda ilegal de armas dos Estados Unidos para o Irã, na década de 1980; e, ao final da década de 1990, a palavra *Monicagate* foi inventada para designar o escândalo sexual envolvendo o presidente Bill Clinton e a ex-estagiária da Casa Branca, Monica Lewinski.

gâteau ['gætəʊ] (*pl* -**x** [-z]) *n UK* bolo *m* recheado.

gatecrash ['geɪtkræʃ] *inf* <> *vt* entrar como penetra em. <> *vi* entrar como penetra.

gatecrasher ['geɪt,kræʃə'] *n inf* penetra *mf.*

gatehouse ['geɪthaʊs, *pl* -haʊzɪz] *n* portaria *f.*

gatekeeper ['geɪt,ki:pə'] *n* porteiro *m*, -ra *f.*

gatepost ['geɪtpəʊst] *n* mourão *m.*

gateway ['geɪtweɪ] *n* - **1.** [entrance] portão *m* - **2.** *fig* [means of access]: ~ **to** entrada *f* para; ~ **airport** aeroporto *m* de entrada.

gather ['gæðə'] <> *vt* - **1.** [collect - gen] colher; [- courage, strength] reunir: **to** ~ **together** reunir - **2.** [speed, momentum] ganhar - **3.** [understand]: **to** ~ **(that)** compreender que - **4.** [into folds] franzir. <> *vi* [come together] reunir.

➡ **gather up** *vt sep* [objects] juntar.

gathering ['gæðərɪŋ] *n* [meeting] assembléia *f.*

GATT [gæt] (*abbr of* **General Agreement on Tariffs and Trade**) *n acordo geral de tarifas e comércio,* GATT *m.*

gauche [gəʊʃ] *adj* desajeitado(da).

gaudy ['gɔ:dɪ] (*compar* -**ier**, *superl* -**iest**) *adj* chamativo(va).

gauge, gage *US* [geɪdʒ] <> *n* - **1.** [measuring instrument - for rain] pluviômetro *m*; [- for tyre pressure] calibrador *m*; [- for fuel] medidor *m* de combustível - **2.** [calibre] calibre *m* - **3.** [of rail] bitola *f.* <> *vt* - **1.** [estimate, measure] estimar, calcular - **2.** [predict] prever.

Gaul [gɔ:l] *n* - **1.** [country] Gália - **2.** [person] gaulês *m*, -lesa *f.*

gaunt [gɔ:nt] *adj* - **1.** [person, face] esquelético(ca) - **2.** [landscape, building] desolado(da).

gauntlet ['gɔ:ntlɪt] *n* [medieval glove] manopla *f*; [for motorcyclist] luva *f (de material resistente e punho largo)*; **to run the** ~ **of sthg** expor-se a algo; **to throw down the** ~ **(to sb)** lançar um desafio (a alguém).

gauze [gɔ:z] *n (U)* [fabric] gaze *f.*

gave [geɪv] *pt* ▷ **give.**

gawky ['gɔ:kɪ] (*compar* -**ier**, *superl* -**iest**) *adj* desengonçado(da).

gawp [gɔ:p] *vi* embasbacar-se; **to** ~ **at sb/sthg** embasbacar-se diante de alguém/algo.

gay [geɪ] <> *adj* - **1.** [homosexual] gay - **2.** [cheerful, brightly coloured] alegre. <> *n* [homosexual] gay *mf.*

Gaza Strip ['gɑːzə-] *n*: **the** ~ a Faixa de Gaza.

gaze [geɪz] <> *n* olhar *m* fixo. <> *vi*: **to** ~ **(at sb/sthg)** olhar fixamente (para alguém/algo).

gazebo [gə'zi:bəʊ] (*pl* -**s**) *n* mirante *m.*

gazelle [gə'zel] (*pl inv OR* -**s**) *n* gazela *f.*

gazette [gə'zet] *n* [newspaper] gazeta *f.*

gazetteer [,gæzɪ'tɪə'] *n* dicionário *m* geográfico.

gazump [gə'zʌmp] *vt UK inf* concordar em vender uma casa a alguém e depois vendê-la a outro por um preço mais alto; **to be** ~**ed** ser passado(da) pra trás na compra de um imóvel.

GB (*abbr of* **Great Britain**) *n* GB.

GBH (*abbr of* **grievous bodily harm**) *n UK* lesão *f* corporal grave.

GC (*abbr of* **George Cross**) *n (titular da) maior condecoração de bravura concedida a civis na Grã-Bretanha.*

GCE (*abbr of* **General Certificate of Education**) *n antigo exame final do ensino médio na Grã-Bretanha.*

GCH (*abbr of* **gas central heating**) *n UK* aquecimento *m* central a gás.

GCHQ (*abbr of* **Government Communications Headquarters**) *n centro de informações dos serviços secretos britânicos.*

GCSE (*abbr of* **General Certificate of Secondary Education**) *n exame final do ensino médio na Grã-Bretanha, em substituição ao nível O do GCE.*

Gdns (*abbr of* **Gardens**) Jd.

GDP (*abbr of* **gross domestic product**) *n* PIB *m.*

GDR (*abbr of* **German Democratic Republic**) *n* RDA *f.*

gear [gɪə'] <> *n* - **1.** *TECH* [mechanism] engrenagem *f* - **2.** [on car, bicycle] marcha *f*; **in** ~ engatado(da), engrenado(da); **out of** ~ desengatado(da), fora de funcionamento - **3.** *(U).* [equipment, clothes] apetrechos *mpl.* <> *vt*: **to** ~ **sthg to sb/sthg** encaminhar algo a alguém/algo.

➡ **gear up** *vi*: **to** ~ **up for sthg/to do sthg** preparar-se para algo/para fazer algo.

gearbox ['gɪəbɒks] *n* caixa *f* de câmbio.

gearing *n* [assembly of gears] engrenagem *f.*

gear lever, gear stick *UK*, **gear shift** *US n* alavanca *f* de mudança.

gear wheel *n* roda *f* de engrenagem.

gee [dʒi:] *excl* - **1.** [to horse]: ~ **up!** eia! - **2.** *US inf* [expressing surprise, excitement]: ~ **(whizz)!** puxa!, nossa!

geese [gi:s] *pl* ▷ **goose.**

Geiger counter ['gaɪgə'-] *n* contador *m* Geiger.

geisha (girl) ['geɪʃə-] *n* gueixa *f.*

gel [dʒel] (*pt & pp* -**led**, *cont* -**ling**) <> *n* [for hair] gel *m.* <> *vi* - **1.** *fig* [idea, plan] tomar forma - **2.** [liquid] engrossar.

gelatin ['dʒelətɪn], **gelatine** [,dʒelə'ti:n] *n* gelatina *f.*

gelding ['geldɪŋ] *n* cavalo *m* castrado.

gelignite ['dʒelɪgnaɪt] *n (U)* gelignite *f.*

gem [dʒem] *n* - **1.** [jewel] gema *f*, pedra *f* preciosa - **2.** *fig* [person, thing] jóia *f.*

Gemini ['dʒemɪnaɪ] *n* - **1.** [sign] Gêmeos - **2.** [person] geminiano *m*, -na *f*; **I'm** ~ sou de Gêmeos.

gemstone ['dʒemstəʊn] *n* pedra *f* preciosa.

gen [dʒen] (*pt & pp* -**ned**, *cont* -**ning**) *n UK inf* informações *fpl.*

➡ **gen up** *vi UK inf*: **to** ~ **up (on sthg)** informar-se (sobre algo).

gen. - **1.** (*abbr of* **general**) ger. - **2.** (*abbr of* **generally**) em geral.

Gen. (*abbr of* **General**) Gen.

gender ['dʒendə'] *n* - **1.** [sex] sexo *m* - **2.** *GRAMM* gênero *m.*

gene [dʒi:n] *n* gene *m.*

genealogist [,dʒi:nɪ'ælədʒɪst] *n* genealogista *mf.*

genealogy [,dʒi:nɪ'ælədʒɪ] (*pl* -**ies**) *n* genealogia *f.*

genera ['dʒenərə] *pl* ▷ **genus.**

general ['dʒenərəl] <> *adj* geral. <> *n MIL* general *mf.*

➡ **in general** *adv* - **1.** [as a whole] em geral - **2.** [usually] geralmente.

general anaesthetic *n* anestesia *f* geral.

general delivery n (U) US posta-restante f.

general election n eleições fpl gerais.

generality [,dʒenə'rælətɪ] (pl -ies) n -1. [generalization] generalidade f- 2. [majority] maioria f.

generalization [,dʒenərələr'zeɪʃn] n generalização f.

generalize, -ise ['dʒenərəlaɪz] vi generalizar; **to ~ about** sthg generalizar sobre algo.

general knowledge n (U) cultura m geral.

generally ['dʒenərəlɪ] adv -1. [usually] geralmente - 2. [by most people] comumente - 3. [in a general way] em geral.

general manager n gerente mf geral.

general practice n clínica f geral.

general practitioner n clínico m, -ca f geral.

general public n: the ~ o público em geral.

general-purpose adj de uso geral.

general strike n greve f geral.

generate ['dʒenəreɪt] vt - 1. [energy, power, heat] gerar - 2. [interest, excitement] provocar ; [jobs, employment] gerar.

generation [,dʒenə'reɪʃn] n geração f; **first/second ~** primeira/segunda geração.

generation gap n conflito m de gerações.

generator ['dʒenəreɪtə'] n gerador m.

generic [dʒɪ'nerɪk] adj [of whole group] genérico(ca).

generosity [,dʒenə'rɒsətɪ] n (U) generosidade f.

generous ['dʒenərəs] adj generoso(sa).

generously ['dʒenərəslɪ] adv generosamente.

genesis ['dʒenəsɪs] (pl -eses [-əsi:z]) n [origin] gênese f.

genetic [dʒɪ'netɪk] adj genético(ca).

➡ **genetics** n (U) genética f.

genetically modified [dʒɪ'netɪkəlɪ'mɒdɪfaɪd] adj geneticamente modificado(da).

genetic engineering n (U) engenharia f genética.

genetic fingerprinting [-'fɪŋgəprɪntɪŋ] n impressão f genética.

Geneva [dʒɪ'ni:və] n Genebra; **in ~** em Genebra.

Geneva convention n: the ~ a convenção de Genebra.

genial ['dʒi:njəl] adj cordial, simpático(ca).

genie ['dʒi:nɪ] (pl genies OR genii ['dʒi:nɪaɪl]) n gênio m.

genitals ['dʒenɪtlz] npl genitais mpl.

genius ['dʒi:njəs] (pl -es) n - 1. [person] gênio m - 2. [special ability]: **a stroke of ~** um golpe de mestre; **~ for** sthg/for doing sthg dom para algo/para fazer algo.

Genoa ['dʒə'nəʊə] n Gênova; **in ~** em Gênova.

genocide ['dʒenəsaɪd] n (U) genocídio m.

genre ['ʒrə] n [in art, literature, film] gênero m.

gent [dʒentl] n UK dated inf cavalheiro m.

➡ **gents** n UK [toilets] banheiro m masculino.

genteel [dʒen'ti:l] adj - 1. [refined] fino(na), refinado(da) - 2. [affected] afetado(da).

gentile ['dʒentaɪl] <> adj gói, não-judeu(dia). <> n gói mf.

gentle ['dʒentl] adj - 1. [gen] suave - 2. [kind] gentil - 3. [discreet] leve.

gentleman ['dʒentlmən] (pl -men [-mən]) n - 1. [well-bred man] cavalheiro m, gentleman m; **~'s**

agreement acordo m de cavalheiros - 2. [man] senhor m.

gentlemanly ['dʒentlmənlɪ] adj cavalheiresco(ca).

gentleness ['dʒentlnɪs] n - 1. [gen] suavidade f - 2. [kindness] delicadeza f.

gently ['dʒentlɪ] adv - 1. [gen] suavemente - 2. [kindly] delicadamente, gentilmente - 3. [slowly] lentamente.

gentry ['dʒentrɪ] n alta burguesia f.

genuflect ['dʒenju:flekt] vi fml genuflectir.

genuine ['dʒenjʊɪn] adj - 1. [antique, work of art] genuíno(na) - 2. [person, feeling, mistake] autêntico(ca).

genuinely ['dʒenjʊɪnlɪ] adv - 1. [surprised, disappointed] genuinamente - 2. [spoken, believed] sinceramente.

genus ['dʒi:nəs] (pl genera ['dʒenərəl]) n gênero m.

geographer [dʒɪ'ɒgrəfə'] n geógrafo m, -fa f.

geographical [,dʒɪə'græfɪkl] adj geográfico(ca).

geography [dʒɪ'ɒgrəfɪ] n geografia f.

geological [,dʒɪə'lɒdʒɪkl] adj geológico(ca).

geologist [dʒɪ'ɒlədʒɪst] n geólogo m, -ga f.

geology [dʒɪ'ɒlədʒɪl] n geologia f.

geometric(al) [,dʒɪə'metrɪk(l)] adj geométrico(ca).

geometry [dʒɪ'ɒmətrɪ] n (U) geometria f.

geophysics [,dʒi:əʊ'fɪzɪks] n (U) geofísica f.

Geordie ['dʒɔ:dɪ] <> adj de ou relativo a Tyneside. <> n [person] natural ou habitante de Tyneside.

George Cross ['dʒɔ:dʒ-] n UK medalha de honra ao mérito.

Georgia ['dʒɔ:dʒə] n [in US, CIS] Geórgia f.

Georgian ['dʒɔ:dʒən] <> adj - 1. UK [of Georgian period] georgiano(na) - 2. GEOGR: [US, CIS] georgiano(na). <> n [in US, CIS] georgiano m, -na f.

geranium [dʒɪ'reɪnjəm] (pl -s) n gerânio m.

gerbil ['dʒɜ:bɪl] n gerbo m.

geriatric [,dʒerɪ'ætrɪk] adj - 1. [of old people] geriátrico(ca) - 2. pej [very old, inefficient] ultrapassado(da).

germ [dʒɜ:m] n - 1. BIO germe m - 2. MED bactéria f - 3. fig [of idea, plan] embrião m.

German ['dʒɜ:mən] <> adj alemão(mã). <> n - 1. [person] alemão m, -mã f - 2. [language] alemão m.

Germanic [dʒɜ:'mænɪk] adj germânico(ca).

German measles n (U) rubéola f.

German shepherd (dog) n pastor m alemão.

Germany ['dʒɜ:mənɪ] (pl -ies) n Alemanha; **in ~** na Alemanha.

germicide ['dʒɜ:mɪsaɪd] n germicida f, bactericida f.

germinate ['dʒɜ:mɪneɪt] <> vt germinar. <> vi germinar.

germination [,dʒɜ:mɪ'neɪʃn] n (U) germinação f.

germ warfare n (U) guerra f bacteriológica.

gerrymandering ['dʒerɪmændərɪŋ] n (U) divisão de uma zona eleitoral de forma a beneficiar um partido em prejuízo de outro.

gerund ['dʒerənd] n GRAM gerúndio m.

gestation [dʒe'steɪʃn] n gestação f.

gestation period n período m de gestação.

gesticulate [dʒes'tɪkjʊleɪt] vi gesticular.

gesticulation [dʒe‚stɪkjʊ'leɪʃn] n gesticulação f.

gesture ['dʒestʃəʳ] <> n gesto m. <> vi: **to ~ to** OR **towards sb** fazer gestos a alguém

get [get] (pt & pp **got**, US pp **gotten**) vt **-1.** [obtain] obter; [buy] comprar; **she got a job** ela arranjou emprego **-2.** [receive] receber; **I got a book for Christmas** ganhei um livro no Natal **-3.** [means of transportation] apanhar; **let's ~ a taxi** vamos apanhar um táxi **-4.** [find] ir buscar; **could you ~ me the manager?** [in store] podia chamar o gerente?; [on phone] pode me passar o gerente? **-5.** [illness] apanhar; **I got the flu over Christmas** peguei uma gripe no Natal **-6.** [cause to become]: **to ~ sthg done** mandar fazer algo; **to ~ sthg ready** preparar algo; **can I ~ my car repaired here?** posso mandar consertar o meu carro aqui? **-7.** [ask, tell]: **to ~ sb to do sthg** arranjar alguém para fazer algo **-8.** [move]: **to ~ sthg out of sthg** tirar algo de algo; **I can't ~ it through the door** não consigo passar com isso na porta **-9.** [understand] compreender; **to ~ a joke** contar uma piada **-10.** [time, chance] ter; **we didn't ~ the chance to see everything** não tivemos oportunidade de ver tudo **-11.** [idea, feeling] ter; **I ~ a lot of enjoyment from it** me divirto à beça com isso **-12.** [phone] atender **-13.** [in phrases]: **you ~ a lot of rain here in winter** chove muito aqui no inverno ⊳ **have**. <> vi **-1.** [become] ficar; **it's getting late** está ficando tarde; **to ~ ready** preparar-se; **to ~ lost** perder-se; **~ lost!** não enche o saco!, desapareça! **-2.** [into particular state, position] meter-se; **how do you ~ to El Paso from here?** como se vai daqui para El Paso?; **to ~ into the car** entrar no carro **-3.** [arrive] chegar; **when does the train ~ here?** quando é que o trem chega aqui? **-4.** [in phrases]: **to ~ to do sthg** ter a oportunidade de fazer algo. <> aux vb ser; **to ~ delayed** atrasar-se; **to ~ killed** ser morto.

➤ **get along (with sb)** vi dar-se bem (com alguém).

➤ **get back** vi [return] voltar.

➤ **get in** vi [arrive] chegar; (enter) entrar.

➤ **get off** vi [leave] sair.

➤ **get on** vi [enter train, bus] entrar.

➤ **get out** vi [of car, bus, train] sair.

➤ **get through** vi [on phone] completar a ligação.

➤ **get up** vi levantar-se.

getaway ['getəweɪ] n fuga f; **to make one's ~** escapar.

getaway car n carro m de fuga.

get-together n inf encontro m informal (entre amigos).

getup ['getʌp] n inf traje m.

get-up-and-go n (U) inf iniciativa f.

get-well card n cartão m de melhoras.

geyser ['gi:zəʳ] n [hot spring] gêiser m.

Ghana ['gɑːnə] n Gana; **in ~** em Gana.

Ghan(a)ian [gɑː'neɪən] <> adj ganense. <> n ganense mf.

ghastly ['gɑːstlɪ] (compar -ier, superl -iest) adj **-1.** inf [very bad, unpleasant] horrível **-2.** [horrifying, macabre] macabro(bra), horroroso(sa) **-3.** [ill] abatido(da).

gherkin ['gɜːkɪn] n pepino m em conserva.

ghetto ['getəʊ] (pl -s OR -es) n gueto m.

ghetto blaster [-'blɑː.stəʳ] n inf minisystem portátil de grande potência.

ghost [gəʊst] <> n [spirit] fantasma m; **he doesn't have a ~ of a chance** ele não tem a menor chance. <> vt = ghostwrite.

ghostly ['gəʊstlɪ] (compar -ier, superl -iest) adj fantasmagórico(ca).

ghost town n cidade-fantasma f.

ghostwrite ['gəʊstraɪt] (pt -wrote, pp -written) vt escrever anonimamente para outra pessoa.

ghostwriter ['gəʊst‚raɪtəʳ] n ghost-writer mf.

ghostwritten ['gəʊst‚rɪtn] pp ⊳ ghostwrite.

ghostwrote ['gəʊstrəʊt] pt ⊳ ghostwrite.

ghoul [gu:l] n **-1.** [spirit] espírito m do mal **-2.** pej [ghoulish person] demônio m.

ghoulish ['gu:lɪʃ] adj [morbid] macabro(bra).

GHQ (abbr of general headquarters) n QG m.

GI (abbr of government issue) n soldado raso norte-americano.

giant ['dʒaɪənt] <> adj gigantesco(ca). <> n **-1.** [gen] gigante m **-2.** [business, organization] gigante mf.

giant-size(d) adj de tamanho família.

gibber ['dʒɪbəʳ] vi tagarelar.

gibberish ['dʒɪbərɪʃ] n (U) asneira f.

gibbon ['gɪbən] n gibão m.

gibe [dʒaɪb] <> n zombaria f. <> vi: **to ~ at sb/sthg** zombar de alguém/algo.

giblets ['dʒɪblɪts] npl miúdos mpl (de ave).

Gibraltar [dʒɪ'brɔːltəʳ] n Gibraltar; **in ~** em Gibraltar; **the Rock of ~** o Rochedo de Gibraltar.

giddy ['gɪdɪ] (compar -ier, superl -iest) adj [dizzy] tonto(ta).

gift [gɪft] n **-1.** [present] presente m **-2.** [talent] dom m; **to have a ~ for sthg/for doing sthg** ter o dom para algo/para fazer algo; **to have the ~ of the gab** ter o dom da fala; pej ter lábia.

GIFT (abbr of gamete in fallopian transfer) n técnica de inseminação artificial.

gift certificate n US = gift token.

gifted ['gɪftɪd] adj **-1.** [gen] talentoso(sa), de talento **-2.** [child] superdotado(da).

gift token, gift voucher UK, **gift certificate** US n vale-presente m.

gift wrap n papel m de presente.

gift-wrapped [-ræpt] adj enrolado(da) para presente.

gig [gɪg] n inf [concert] show m.

gigabyte ['gaɪgəbaɪt] n COMPUT gigabyte m.

gigantic [dʒaɪ'gæntɪk] adj gigantesco(ca).

giggle ['gɪgl] <> n **-1.** [laugh] risadinha f, risada f **-2.** UK inf [fun] diversão f; **to do sthg for a ~** divertir-se fazendo algo tolo; **to have the ~s** ter um ataque de riso. <> vi [laugh] dar risadinhas bobas.

giggly ['gɪglɪ] (compar -ier, superl -iest) adj com riso bobo.

GIGO ['gaɪgəʊ] (abbr of garbage in, garbage out) COMPUT GIGO m, entra lixo, sai lixo.

gigolo ['ʒɪgələʊ] (pl -s) n pej gigolô m.

gigot ['ʒɪgəʊ] n perna f de carneiro.

gilded ['gɪldɪd] adj = gilt.

gill [dʒɪl] *n* [unit of measurement] *0,142 litros.*

gills [gɪlz] *npl* [of fish] guelras *fpl.*

gilt [gɪlt] <> *adj* [covered in gold] dourado(da). <> *n (U)* [gold layer] dourado *m.*

➡ **gilts** *npl* FIN títulos *mpl* de máxima garantia.

gilt-edged *adj* FIN de máxima garantia.

gimme ['gɪmɪ] *inf* = give me.

gimmick ['gɪmɪk] *n pej* artimanha *f.*

gin [dʒɪn] *n* [drink] gim *m*; ~ **and tonic** gim-tônica *m.*

ginger ['dʒɪndʒəʳ] <> *adj UK* [colour - of hair] ruivo(va); [- of cat] avermelhado(da). <> *n (U)* **-1.** [root] gengibre *m* **-2.** [powder] gengibre *m* em pó.

ginger ale *n* [mixer] jinjibirra *f.*

ginger beer *n* [slightly alcoholic] cerveja *f* de gengibre.

gingerbread ['dʒɪndʒəbredl] *n (U)* **-1.** [cake] pão *m* de gengibre **-2.** [biscuit] biscoito *m* de gengibre.

ginger group *n UK* grupo *m* de pressão.

ginger-haired [-'heəd] *adj* ruivo(va).

gingerly ['dʒɪndʒəlɪ] *adv* cuidadosamente.

gingham ['gɪŋəm] *n (U)* [cloth] guingão *m.*

gingivitis [‚dʒɪndʒɪ'vaɪtɪs] *n (U)* MED gengivite *f.*

ginseng ['dʒɪnseŋ] *n (U)* ginseng *m.*

gipsy ['dʒɪpsɪ] (*pl* -ies) <> *adj* cigano(na). <> *n* [nomad] cigano *m*, -na *f.*

giraffe [dʒɪ'rɑːf] (*pl inv OR* -s) *n* girafa *f.*

gird [gɜːd] (*pt* & *pp* -ed *OR* **girt**) *vt* ▷ **loin.**

girder ['gɜːdəʳ] *n* viga *f.*

girdle ['gɜːdl] *n* [corset] espartilho *m.*

girl [gɜːl] *n* **-1.** [young female child] menina *f*, garota *f* **-2.** [young woman] moça *f* **-3.** [daughter] menina *f* **-4.** [female friend]: **the** ~**s** as amigas, as meninas.

girl Friday *n* auxiliar *f* de escritório.

girlfriend ['gɜːlfrend] *n* **-1.** [female lover] namorada *f* **-2.** [female friend] amiga *f.*

girl guide *UK*, **girl scout** *US n* [individual] escoteira *f*, bandeirante *f.*

girlie magazine ['gɜːlɪ-] *n inf* revista *f* erótica.

girlish ['gɜːlɪʃ] *adj* de menininha.

girl scout *n US* = girl guide.

giro ['dʒaɪrəʊ] (*pl* -s) *n UK* **-1.** *(U)* [system] transferência *f* de crédito **-2.**: *inf* ~ **(cheque)** seguro-desemprego *m.*

girt *pt* & *pp* ▷ **gird.**

girth [gɜːθ] *n* **-1.** [circumference] circunferência *f* **-2.** [of horse] cincha *f.*

gist [dʒɪst] *n* essência *f*; **to get the** ~ **(of sthg)** pegar a essência (de algo).

give [gɪv] (*pt* **gave**, *pp* **given**) <> *vt* **-1.** [gen] dar; **to** ~ **sb sthg** dar algo para *or* a alguém **-2.** [hand over, pass] entregar; **to** ~ **sb sthg**, **to** ~ **sthg to sb** entregar algo para *or* a alguém **-3.** [pay]: **to** ~ **sthg (for sthg)** dar *or* pagar algo (por algo) **-4.** *phr*: **to be given to believe** *or* **understand that** *fml* ser levado(da) a acreditar *or* entender que; **I'd** ~ **anything** *or* **my right arm to do that** eu daria tudo *or* qualquer coisa para fazer isso. <> *vi* [collapse, break] ceder. <> *n (U)* [elasticity] elasticidade *f.*

➡ **give or take** *prep* mais ou menos.

➡ **give away** *vt sep* **-1.** [get rid of] desfazer-se de **-2.** [reveal] revelar.

➡ **give back** *vt sep* [return] devolver.

➡ **give in** *vi* **-1.** [admit defeat] render-se, dar-se por vencido(da) **-2.** [agree unwillingly]: **to** ~ **in to sthg** ceder frente a algo.

➡ **give off** *vt fus* [produce] exalar.

➡ **give out** <> *vt sep* [distribute] distribuir. <> *vi* **-1.** [be exhausted] esgotar-se **-2.** [fail] falhar, não funcionar.

➡ **give over** <> *vt sep* [dedicate]: **to be given over to sthg** ser destinado(da) a algo. <> *vi UK inf* [stop]: ~ **over!** já] chega!

➡ **give up** <> *vt sep* **-1.** [stop, abandon] abandonar; **to** ~ **up smoking** parar de fumar; **to** ~ **up chocolate** deixar de comer chocolate **-2.** [surrender]: **to** ~ **o.s. up (to sb)** render-se (a alguém). <> *vi* [admit defeat] render-se.

➡ **give up on** *vt fus* [abandon] abandonar *(por muito difícil).*

give-and-take *n (U)* [compromise] toma-lá-dá-cá *m.*

giveaway ['gɪvə‚weɪ] <> *adj* **-1.** [telltale] revelador(ra) **-2.** [very cheap] dado(da). <> *n* [telltale sign] sinal *m* óbvio.

given ['gɪvn] <> *pp* ▷ **give.** <> *adj* **-1.** [set, fixed] dado(da); **at any** ~ **time** num determinado momento **-2.** [prone]: **to be** ~ **to sthg/to doing sthg** ser dado(da) a algo/a fazer algo. <> *prep* [taking into account] dado(da); ~ **the circumstances** dadas as circunstâncias; ~ **that** dado que.

given name *n US* prenome *m.*

giver ['gɪvəʳ] *n* doador *m*, -ra *f.*

glacé cherry ['glæseɪ-] *n* cereja *f* glaçada.

glacial ['gleɪsjəl] *adj* glacial.

glacier ['glæsjəʳ] *n* geleira *f.*

glad [glæd] (*compar* -**der**, *superl* -**dest**) *adj* **-1.** [happy, pleased] feliz; **to be** ~ **about sthg** estar feliz por algo; **to be** ~ **that** estar feliz que **-2.** [willing]: **to be** ~ **to do sthg** ter vontade de fazer algo, desejar fazer algo **-3.** [grateful]: **to be** ~ **of sthg** ficar agradecido(da) por algo.

gladden ['glædn] *vt literary* contentar.

glade [gleɪd] *n literary* clareira *f.*

gladiator ['glædɪeɪtəʳ] *n* gladiador *m.*

gladioli [‚glædɪ'əʊlaɪ] *npl* gladíolos *mpl.*

gladly ['glædlɪ] *adv* **-1.** [happily, eagerly] com prazer, alegremente **-2.** [willingly] com satisfação.

glamor *n US* = glamour.

glamorize, -ise ['glæməraɪz] *vt* fantasiar.

glamorous ['glæmərəs] *adj* [gen] glamouroso(sa); [job] atraente.

glamour *UK*, **glamor** *US* ['glæməʳ] *n (U)* [gen] glamour *m*; [of job] encanto *m.*

glance [glɑːns] <> *n* [quick look] olhadela *f*; **to cast** *OR* **take a** ~ **at sthg** dar uma olhada rápida em algo; **at a** ~ de relance; **at first** ~ à primeira vista. <> *vi* [look quickly]: **to** ~ **at sb/sthg** olhar alguém/algo de relance; **to** ~ **at** *OR* **through sthg** passar os olhos em algo.

➡ **glance off** *vt fus* **-1.** [light] desviar **-2.** [ball] rebater **-3.** [bullet] ricochetear.

glancing ['glɑːnsɪŋ] *adj* [oblique] oblíquo(qua).

gland [glænd] *n* glândula *f.*

glandular fever ['glændjʊləʳ-] *n (U)* mononucleose *f* infecciosa.

glare [gleəʳ] <> *n* **-1.** [scowl] olhar *m* penetrante, encarada *f* **-2.** *(U)* [blaze, dazzle] brilho *m* **-3.** [of publicity] foco *m*. ⋄ *vi* **-1.** [scowl]: **to ~ at sb/sthg** fulminar alguém/algo com o olhar, lançar um olhar fulminante sobre alguém/algo **-2.** [blaze, dazzle] ofuscar.

glaring ['gleərɪŋ] *adj* **-1.** [very obvious] evidente **-2.** [blazing, dazzling] ofuscante.

glasnost ['glæznɒst] *n (U)* glasnost *f*.

glass [glɑ:s] ⋄ *n* **-1.** *(U)* [material] vidro *m* **-2.** [for drinking] copo *m* **-3.** *(U)* [glassware] objetos *mpl* de cristal. ⋄ *comp* de vidro.

➡ **glasses** *npl* [spectacles] óculos *m inv*; [binoculars] binóculos *mpl*.

glassblowing ['glɑ:s,bləʊɪŋ] *n (U)* modelagem *f* de vidro a quente.

glass fibre *n (U) UK* fibra *f* de vidro.

glasshouse ['glɑ:shaʊs, *pl* -haʊzɪz] *n UK* **-1.** [greenhouse] estufa *f* **-2.** *fig inf* [military prison] prisão *f* militar.

glassware ['glɑ:sweə^r] *n (U)* objetos *mpl* de cristal.

glassy ['glɑ:sɪ] (*compar* **-ier**, *superl* **-iest**) *adj* **-1.** [smooth, shiny] cristalino(na) **-2.** [blank, lifeless] vidrado(da).

Glaswegian [glæz'wi:dʒən] ⋄ *adj* de ou relativo a Glasgow. ⋄ *n* **-1.** [person] natural ou habitante de Glasgow **-2.** [dialect] dialeto falado em Glasgow.

glaucoma [glɔ:'kəʊmə] *n (U)* glaucoma *m*.

glaze [gleɪz] ⋄ *n* **-1.** [on pottery] verniz *m*, esmalte *m* **-2.** *CULIN* glacê *m*. ⋄ *vt* **-1.** [pottery] envernizar **-2.** *CULIN* cristalizar.

➡ **glaze over** *vi* apagar-se.

glazed [gleɪzd] *adj* **-1.** [dull, bored] vidrado(da) **-2.** [pottery] vitrificado(da) **-3.** *CULIN* cristalizado(da) **-4.** [with glass] envidraçado(da).

glazier ['gleɪzjə^r] *n* vidraceiro *m*, -ra *f*.

gleam [gli:m] ⋄ *n* **-1.** [glow] lampejo *m* **-2.** [fleeting expression] olhar *m*. ⋄ *vi* **-1.** [surface, object] reluzir **-2.** [light] brilhar **-3.** [face, eyes] olhar.

gleaming ['gli:mɪŋ] *adj* **-1.** [surface, object] reluzente **-2.** [light] brilhante **-3.** [face, eyes] reluzente.

glean [gli:n] *vt* [gather] coletar.

glee [gli:] *n (U)* [joy, delight] alegria *f*; [gloating] regozijo *m*.

gleeful ['gli:fʊl] *adj* [joyful] alegre; [gloating] de regozijo.

glen [glen] *n Scot & Irish* vale *m*.

glib [glɪb] (*compar* **-ber**, *superl* **-best**) *adj pej* **-1.** [answer, excuse] de momento **-2.** [person] de muita lábia.

glibly ['glɪblɪ] *adv pej* [talk, reply] com muita lábia.

glide [glaɪd] *vi* **-1.** [move smoothly] deslizar **-2.** [fly] planar.

glider ['glaɪdə^r] *n* [plane] planador *m*.

gliding ['glaɪdɪŋ] *n (U)* [sport] vôo *m* sem motor; **to go ~** voar de planador.

glimmer ['glɪmə^r] ⋄ *n* **-1.** [faint light] luz *f* fraca **-2.** *fig* [trace, sign] sinal *m* mínimo; **a ~ of hope** um fio de esperança. ⋄ *vi* tremeluzir.

glimpse [glɪmps] ⋄ *n* **-1.** [sight, look] vislumbre *m*; **to catch a ~ of sb/sthg** ver alguém/algo de relance **-2.** [perception, idea, insight] noção *f*. ⋄ *vt*

-1. [catch sight of] ver de relance **-2.** [perceive] vislumbrar.

glint [glɪnt] ⋄ *n* brilho *m*. ⋄ *vi* **-1.** [metal, sunlight] brilhar **-2.** [eyes - greed, anger] faiscar; [- amusement] brilhar.

glisten ['glɪsn] *vi* brilhar.

glitch [glɪtʃ] *n inf* [in plan] falha *f* técnica, pane *f*.

glitter ['glɪtə^r] ⋄ *n* [gen] brilho *m*. ⋄ *vi* **-1.** [object, light] brilhar **-2.** [eyes - with excitement] cintilar; [- with fury] faiscar.

glittering ['glɪtərɪŋ] *adj* **-1.** [object, light] reluzente, brilhante **-2.** [eyes] brilhante **-3.** [glamorous] deslumbrante.

glitzy ['glɪtsɪ] (*compar* **-ier**, *superl* **-iest**) *adj inf* [glamorous] deslumbrante.

gloat [gləʊt] *vi*: **to ~ (over sthg)** tripudiar (de algo).

global ['gləʊbl] *adj* [worldwide] mundial.

globalization [,gləʊbəlaɪ'zeɪʃn] *n* globalização *f*.

globally ['gləʊbəlɪ] *adv* **-1.** [worldwide] mundialmente **-2.** [generally] em geral.

global warming [-'wɔ:mɪŋ] *n (U)* aquecimento *m* global.

globe [gləʊb] *n* **-1.** [Earth]: **the ~** o globo **-2.** [spherical shape] globo *m*.

globetrotter ['gləʊb,trɒtə^r] *n inf* globe-trotter *mf*.

globule ['glɒbju:l] *n* gota *f*.

gloom [glu:m] *n* **-1.** [darkness] escuro *m*, escuridão *f* **-2.** [unhappiness] desânimo *m*.

gloomy ['glu:mɪ] (*compar* **-ier**, *superl* **-iest**) *adj* **-1.** [place, landscape] sombrio(bria) **-2.** [weather] sombrio(bria), escuro(ra) **-3.** [atmosphere] deprimente; [mood] pessimista **-4.** [outlook, news] desanimador(ra).

glorification [,glɔ:rɪfɪ'keɪʃn] *n (U)* [act of glorifying] glorificação *f*.

glorified ['glɔ:rɪfaɪd] *adj pej* [jumped-up] incrementado(da).

glorify ['glɔ:rɪfaɪ] (*pt & pp* **-ied**) *vt* [overpraise, overesteem] glorificar.

glorious ['glɔ:rɪəs] *adj* **-1.** [illustrious] glorioso(sa) **-2.** [wonderful] magnífico(ca).

glory ['glɔ:rɪ] (*pl* **-ies**) *n* **-1.** [gen] glória *f* **-2.** *(U)* [splendour] esplendor *m*.

➡ **glories** *npl* glórias *fpl*.

➡ **glory in** *vt fus* [relish] desfrutar de.

gloss [glɒs] *n* **-1.** *(U)* [shine - of wood, furniture] lustre *m*; [- of hair] brilho *m* **-2.**: **~ (paint)** esmalte *m*.

➡ **gloss over** *vt fus* falar por alto sobre.

glossary ['glɒsərɪ] (*pl* **-ies**) *n* glossário *m*.

glossy ['glɒsɪ] (*compar* **-ier**, *superl* **-iest**) *adj* **-1.** [gen] lustroso(sa) **-2.** *fig* [spectacle, display] de luxo.

glossy magazine *n* revista *f* impressa em papel de luxo.

glove [glʌv] *n* luva *f*.

glove compartment *n* porta-luvas *m inv*.

glove puppet *n UK* fantoche *m*.

glow [gləʊ] ⋄ *n* **-1.** [light] fulgor *m*, brilho *m* **-2.** [flush] rubor *m* **-3.** *fig* [feeling] arrebatamento *m*. ⋄ *vi* **-1.** [fire] arder **-2.** [sky, light, brass] brilhar **-3.** [with colour] resplandecer **-4.** [person]: **to ~ (with sthg)** resplanceder (de algo).

glower ['glaʊə^r] *vi*: **to ~ (at sb/sthg)** olhar ameaçadoramente (para alguém/algo).

glowing ['gləʊɪŋ] adj [very favourable] inflamado(da).

glow-worm n vaga-lume m.

glucose ['glu:kəʊs] n (U) glicose f.

glue [glu:] (cont glueing OR gluing) ⟨⟩ n (U) cola f. ⟨⟩ vt [stick with glue] colar; **to ~ sthg to sthg** colar algo em algo; **to be ~d to sthg** fig [absorbed by] ficar grudado(da) em algo.

glue-sniffing [-ˌsnɪfɪŋ] n (U) inalação f de cola.

glum [glʌm] (compar **-mer**, superl **-mest**) adj [unhappy] melancólico(ca).

glut [glʌt] n excesso m.

gluten ['glu:tən] n (U) glúten m.

glutinous ['glu:tɪnəs] adj **-1.** [mud] pegajoso(sa) **-2.** [milk pudding, stew] glutinoso(sa) **-3.** [rice] empapado(da).

glutton ['glʌtn] n [greedy person] glutão m, -tona f; **to be a ~ for punishment** gostar de sofrer.

gluttony ['glʌtənɪ] n (U) gula f.

glycerin ['glɪsərɪn], **glycerine** ['glɪsəri:n] n (U) glicerina f.

gm (abbr of **gram**) g.

GMAT (abbr of **Graduate Management Admissions Test**) n exame de admissão no segundo ciclo do ensino superior nos Estados Unidos.

GM foods npl alimentos mpl geneticamente modificados.

GMO (abbr of **genetically modified organism**) ⟨⟩ adj OGM. ⟨⟩ n OGM m.

GMT (abbr of **Greenwich Mean Time**) n horário oficial de Greenwich, GMT m.

gnarled [nɑːld] adj **-1.** [tree] nodoso(sa) **-2.** [hands] áspero(ra).

gnash [næʃ] vt : **to ~ one's teeth** ranger os dentes.

gnat [næt] n mosquito m.

gnaw [nɔː] ⟨⟩ vt [chew] roer. ⟨⟩ vi [worry] atormentar-se; **to ~ (away) at sb** atormentar alguém.

gnome [nəʊm] n gnomo m.

GNP (abbr of **gross national product**) n PNB m.

gnu [nu:] (pl inv OR **-s**) n gnu m.

GNVQ (abbr of **General National Vocational Qualification**) n EDUC curso de formação profissional com duração de dois anos para maiores de 16 anos na Inglaterra e no País de Gales.

go [gəʊ] (pt **went**, pp **gone**, pl **goes**) vi **-1.** [move, travel] ir; **to ~ home** ir para casa; **to ~ to Brazil** ir ao Brasil; **to ~ by bus** ir de ônibus; **to ~ for a walk** fazer um passeio; **to ~ and do sthg** ir fazer algo; **to ~ in** entrar; **to ~ out** sair **-2.** [leave] ir-se; **it's time for us to ~** é hora de irmos embora; **when does the bus ~?** quando é que ônibus sai?; **~ away!** vá embora! **-3.** [attend] ir; **to ~ to school** ir para a escola; **which school do you ~ to?** para que escola você vai? **- 4.** [become] ficar; **she went pale** empalideceu; **the milk has gone sour** o leite azedou **-5.** [expressing future tense]: **to be going to do sthg** ir fazer algo **-6.** [function] funcionar; **the car won't ~** o carro não pega **-7.** [stop working] ir-se; **the fuse has gone** o fusível queimou **-8.** [time] passar **-9.** [progress] correr; **to ~ well** correr bem **-10.** [bell, alarm] tocar **-11.** [match] condizer; **to ~ with** condizer com; **red wine doesn't ~ with fish** vinho tinto não combina com peixe **-12.** [be sold] ser vendido; **'everything must ~'** 'liquidação total' **-13.** [fit] caber **-14.** [lead] ir; **where does this path ~?** aonde vai dar este caminho? **-15.** [belong] ir; ser **-16.** [in phrases]: **to let ~** [drop] largar algo; **there are two days to ~** faltam dois dias; **to ~** US [to take away] para levar. ⟨⟩ n **-1.** [turn] vez f; **it's your ~** é a sua vez **-2.** [attempt] tentativa f; **to have a ~ at sthg** experimentar algo; **'50 cents a ~'** [for game] '50 centavos cada vez'.

➤ **go ahead** vi [take place] realizar-se; **~ ahead!** vá em frente!

➤ **go around** vi [revolve] rodar; **there isn't enough cake to ~ around** não tem bolo (suficiente) para todo mundo.

➤ **go back** vi voltar.

➤ **go down** vi [decrease] diminuir; [sun] pôr-se; [tire] esvaziar-se.

➤ **go in** vi entrar.

➤ **go off** vi [alarm, bell] tocar, soar; [go bad] azedar; [light, heating] apagar-se.

➤ **go on** vi [happen] passar-se; [light, heating] acender-se; **to ~ on doing sthg** continuar a fazer algo.

➤ **go out** vi [leave house] sair; [light, fire, cigarette] apagar-se; [have relationship]: **to ~ out with sb** sair com alguém; **to ~ out to eat** ir comer fora.

➤ **go over** vt fus [check] rever.

➤ **go through** vt fus [experience] passar por; [spend] gastar; [search] revistar.

➤ **go up** vi [increase] subir.

➤ **go without** vt fus passar sem.

goad [gəʊd] vt [provoke] provocar; **to ~ sb into doing sthg** incitar alguém a fazer algo.

go-ahead ⟨⟩ adj [dynamic] dinâmico(ca), empreendedor(ra). ⟨⟩ n [permission] permissão f; **to give sb the ~ (for sthg)** dar a luz verde a alguém (para algo).

goal [gəʊl] n **-1.** SPORT gol m; **to score a ~** fazer um gol, marcar um gol **-2.** [aim] meta f, objetivo m.

goalie ['gəʊlɪ] n inf goleiro m, -ra f.

goalkeeper ['gəʊlˌkiːpəʳ] n goleiro m, -ra f.

goalless ['gəʊllɪs] adj : **~ draw** empate sem gols.

goalmouth ['gəʊlmaʊθ, pl -maʊðz] n boca f do gol.

goalpost ['gəʊlpəʊst] n trave f.

goat [gəʊt] n [animal] cabra f, bode m; **to act the ~** UK comportar-se de forma tola; **to get (on) sb's ~** encher o saco de alguém.

goatee (beard) n cavanhaque m.

goat's cheese n queijo m de cabra.

gob [gɒb] (pt & pp **-bed**, cont **-bing**) v inf ⟨⟩ n **-1.** UK [mouth] matraca f, bico m **-2.** UK [spit] escarro m. ⟨⟩ vi [spit] escarrar.

gobble ['gɒbl] vt devorar.

➤ **gobble down, gobble up** vt sep engolir rapidamente.

gobbledygook ['gɒbldɪguːk] n **-1.** [incomprehensible language] linguagem f incompreensível, palavreado m sem sentido **-2.** inf [nonsense] asneiras fpl.

go-between n intermediário m, -ria f.

Gobi ['gəʊbɪ] n : **the ~ Desert** o Deserto de Gobi.

goblet ['gɒblɪt] n cálice m.

goblin ['gɒblɪn] *n* duende *m*.
gobsmacked ['gɒbsmækt] *adj UK v inf* embasbacado(da).
go-cart *n* = go-kart.
god [gɒd] *n* deus *m*.
◆ **God** ⬦ *n* Deus *m*; **God knows** só Deus sabe; **for God's sake!** pelo amor de Deus!; **thank God** graças a Deus; **God willing** se Deus quiser. ⬦ *excl*: **(my) God!** (meu) Deus!
◆ **gods** *npl UK inf*: **the ~ s** THEATRE as galerias.
godchild ['gɒdtʃaɪld] (*pl* **-children** [-ˌtʃɪldrən]) *n* afilhado *m*, -da *f*.
goddam(n) ['gɒdæm] *esp US v inf* ⬦ *adj* maldito(ta); **where's the ~ key?** cadê a porcaria da chave?; **what a ~ waste of time!** que perda de tempo imbecil! ⬦ *excl* maldito!, maldita!
goddaughter ['gɒdˌdɔːtəʳ] *n* afilhada *f*.
goddess ['gɒdɪs] *n* deusa *f*.
godfather ['gɒdˌfɑːðəʳ] *n* padrinho *m*.
godforsaken ['gɒdfəˌseɪkn] *adj* abandonado(da) por Deus, que Deus esqueceu.
godmother ['gɒdˌmʌðəʳ] *n* madrinha *f*.
godparents ['gɒdˌpeərənts] *npl* padrinhos *mpl*.
godsend ['gɒdsend] *n* dádiva *f* de Deus.
godson ['gɒdsʌn] *n* afilhado *m*.
goes [gəʊz] *vb* ➡ go.
gofer ['gəʊfəʳ] *n US inf* serviçal *m*.
go-getter [-ˈgetəʳ] *n* pessoa *f* dinâmica.
goggle ['gɒgl] *vi*: **to ~ (at sb/sthg)** arregalar os olhos (para alguém ou algo).
goggles ['gɒglz] *npl* óculos *m* de proteção.
go-go dancer *n* dançarina *sexy (de bar, boîte)*.
going ['gəʊɪŋ] ⬦ *adj* **-1.** [rate, salary] em vigor, atual **-2.** *UK* [available, in existence] disponível; **she's the biggest fool ~** ela é a maior trouxa do momento. ⬦ *n* **-1.** [progress] avanço *m*, marcha *f*; **that's good ~** isso é que é andar rápido; **it was slow ~** estava indo devagar; **to be heavy ~** ser pesado(da); **to be easy ~** ser fácil (de lidar) **-2.** [in riding, horse-racing] condições *fpl* (do chão de corrida).
going concern *n* empresa *f* lucrativa e próspera.
goings-on *npl inf* coisas *fpl* estranhas.
go-kart [-kɑːt] *n UK* kart *m*.
Golan Heights ['gəʊˌlæn-] *npl*: **the ~** os Altos de Golan.
gold [gəʊld] ⬦ *adj* [gold-coloured] dourado(da). ⬦ *n* **-1.** (U) [metal] ouro *m*; **to be as good as ~** ser bem comportado(da), ser de ouro **-2.** (U) [gold jewellery, ornaments, coins] riquezas *fpl* **-3.** [medal] dobrão *m*. ⬦ *comp* [made of gold] de ouro.
golden ['gəʊldən] *adj* **-1.** [made of gold] de ouro **-2.** [gold-coloured] dourado(da).
golden age *n* idade *f* de ouro.
golden eagle *n* águia-real *f*.
golden handshake *n* bolada *f*.
golden opportunity *n* oportunidade *f* de ouro.
golden retriever *n* golden retriever *m*.
golden rule *n* regra *f* de ouro.
golden wedding *n* bodas *fpl* de ouro.
goldfish ['gəʊldfɪʃ] (*pl inv*) *n* peixe-dourado *m*.

goldfish bowl *n* aquário *m* para peixes-dourados.
gold leaf *n* (U) ouro *m* em folha.
gold medal *n* medalha *f* de ouro.
goldmine ['gəʊldmaɪn] *n lit, fig* mina *f* de ouro.
gold-plated [-ˈpleɪtɪd] *adj* banhado(da) a ouro.
gold standard *adj* padrão-ouro *m*.
goldsmith ['gəʊldsmɪθ] *n* ourives *mf*.
golf [gɒlf] *n* (U) golfe *m*.
golf ball *n* **-1.** [for golf] bola *f* de golfe **-2.** [for typewriter] esfera *f*.
golf club *n* **-1.** [association, place] clube *m* de golfe **-2.** [stick] taco *m* de golfe.
golf course *n* campo *m* de golfe.
golfer ['gɒlfəʳ] *n* jogador *m*, -ra *f* de golfe.
golly ['gɒlɪ] *excl inf dated* Deus do céu!
gondola ['gɒndələ] *n* [boat] gôndola *f*.
gondolier [ˌgɒndəˈlɪəʳ] *n* gondoleiro *m*, -ra *f*.
gone [gɒn] ⬦ *pp* ➡ go. ⬦ *adj* [no longer here] que já se foi. ⬦ *prep* [past]: **it's just ~ mid-day** já passa do meio-dia; **she's ~ fifty** ela já passou dos cinqüenta.
gong [gɒŋ] *n* gongo *f*.
gonna ['gɒnə] *cont inf* = going to.
gonorrh(o)ea [ˌgɒnəˈrɪə] *n* (U) gonorréia *f*.
goo [guː] *n* (U) *inf* meleca *f*.
good [gʊd] (*compar* better, *superl* best) ⬦ *adj* **-1.** [gen] bom, boa; **it feels ~ to be in the fresh air** faz bem estar ao ar livre; **it's ~ that** ... é bom que ...; **to be ~ at sthg** ser bom em algo, ser boa em algo; **to be ~ with** [children, animals] ter jeito com; [one's hands] ter habilidade com **-2.** [kind] gentil; **to be ~ to sb** ser bom para alguém, ser boa para alguém; **to be ~ enough to do sthg** fazer o favor de fazer algo; **a ~ number of people** um bom número de pessoas **-3.** [morally correct] correto(ta) **-4.** [well-behaved] bem-comportado(da); **be ~!** comporte-se bem! **-5.** [beneficial]: **it's ~ for you** faz bem para você **-6.** [attractive] bonito(ta) **-7.** *phr*: **it's a ~ job** *OR* **thing (that)** ... ainda bem que ...; **~ for you!** que bom para você!; **to give as ~ as one gets** pagar na mesma moeda; **to make sthg ~** reparar algo. ⬦ *n* **-1.** (U) [benefit, welfare] bem *m*; **for the ~ of** para o bem de; **for your own ~** para o seu próprio bem; **it will do him ~** fará bem a ele **-2.** [use]: **it's no ~** não adianta; **what's the ~ of ...?** qual é a vantagem de ...?; **will this be any ~?** isto serve? **-3.** [morality, virtue] bem *m*; **to be up to no ~** estar com más intenções. ⬦ *excl* que bom!
◆ **goods** *npl* [merchandise] mercadorias *fpl*; **to come up with** *OR* **deliver the ~s** *UK inf* fazer o esperado.
◆ **as good as** *adv* quase; **it's as ~ as new** está praticamente novo.
◆ **for good** *adv* [forever] para sempre.
◆ **good afternoon** *excl* boa tarde!
◆ **good day** *excl dated* *OR* *Austr* tenha um bom dia!
◆ **good evening** *excl* boa noite!
◆ **good morning** *excl* bom dia!
◆ **good night** *excl* boa noite!
good behaviour *n* bom comportamento *m*.
goodbye [ˌgʊdˈbaɪ] ⬦ *excl* até logo! ⬦ *n* adeus *m*.

good deed n boa ação f.
good-for-nothing <> adj imprestável. <> n imprestável mf.
good fortune n boa sorte f.
Good Friday n Sexta-Feira f Santa.
good-humoured [-'hju:məd] adj bem-humorado(da).
good-looking [-'lʊkɪŋ] adj [person] bonito(ta).
good manners npl boas maneiras fpl.
good-natured [-'neɪtʃəd] adj -1. [person] de bom coração -2. [rivalry, argument] amigável.
goodness ['gʊdnɪs] <> n -1. [kindness] bondade f -2. [nutritive quality] valor m nutritivo. <> excl: (my) ~! minha nossa!; for ~ sake! pelo amor de Deus!; thank ~ graças a Deus!; ~ gracious! Santo Deus!
goods train [gʊdz-] n UK trem m de carga.
good-tempered [-'tempəd] adj calmo(ma).
good turn n: to do sb a ~ fazer um favor a alguém.
goodwill [,gʊd'wɪl] n -1. [kind feelings] boa vontade f -2. COMM fundo m de comércio.
goody ['gʊdɪ] (pl -ies) <> n inf [good person] mocinho m, -nha f. <> excl que ótimo!
→ **goodies** npl inf -1. [delicious food] guloseimas fpl -2. [desirable objects] coisas fpl atraentes.
gooey ['gu:ɪ] (compar gooier, superl gooiest) adj inf [sticky] grudento(ta).
goof [gu:f] US inf <> n -1. [mistake] mancada f -2. [person] palerma mf. <> vi dar uma mancada.
→ **goof off** vi US inf vadear.
goofy ['gu:fɪ] (compar -ier, superl -iest) adj -1. inf [person] pateta -2. inf [behaviour, clothes] simplório(ria).
goose [gu:s] (pl geese [gi:s]) n [bird] ganso m, -sa f.
gooseberry ['gʊzbərɪ] (pl -ies) n -1. [fruit] groselha f -2. UK inf [unwanted person]: to play ~ segurar a vela.
gooseflesh ['gu:sfleʃ], **goose pimples** UK n, **goosebumps** US ['gu:sbʌmps] npl arrepio m.
goosestep ['gu:s,step] (pt & pp -ped, cont -ping) <> n passo m de ganso. <> vi andar a passo de ganso.
GOP (abbr of Grand Old Party) n US partido republicano norte-americano.
gopher ['gəʊfə'] n pequeno roedor semelhante a uma ratazana encontrado nos Estados Unidos.
gore [gɔ:'] <> n (U) literary [blood] sangue m (derramado). <> vt [subj: bull] ferir com os chifres.
gorge [gɔ:dʒ] <> n garganta f, desfiladeiro m. <> vt: to ~ o.s. on OR with sthg empanturrar-se com algo.
gorgeous ['gɔ:dʒəs] adj -1. [place, present, weather] magnífico(ca), maravilhoso(sa) -2. inf [person] deslumbrante.
gorilla [gə'rɪlə] n gorila m.
gormless ['gɔ:mlɪs] adj UK inf burro(ra).
gorse [gɔ:s] n (U) tojo m.
gory ['gɔ:rɪ] (compar -ier, superl -iest) adj sangrento(ta).
gosh [gɒʃ] excl inf por Deus!

go-slow n UK operação f tartaruga.
gospel ['gɒspl] <> n -1. [doctrine] evangelho m -2.: ~ (truth) verdade absoluta. <> comp gospel inv; ~ music/singer música/cantor(ra) gospel.
→ **Gospel** n [in Bible] Evangelho m.
gossamer ['gɒsəmə'] n -1. [spider's thread] teia f de aranha -2. [material] tecido muito fino.
gossip ['gɒsɪp] <> n -1. [conversation] conversa f, bate-papo m; to have a ~ bater papo -2. [person] fofoca f. <> vi fofocar.
gossip column n coluna f social.
got [gɒt] pt & pp ▷ get.
Gothic ['gɒθɪk] adj gótico(ca).
gotta ['gɒtə] cont inf = got to.
gotten ['gɒtn] pp US ▷ get.
gouge [gaʊdʒ] → **gouge out** vt sep -1. [hole] abrir -2. [eyes] arrancar.
goulash ['gu:læʃ] n (U) gulash m (prato típico húngaro).
gourd [gʊəd] n cabaço m.
gourmet ['gʊəmeɪ] <> n gourmet m. <> comp gastrônomo m, -ma f.
gout [gaʊt] n (U) gota f.
govern ['gʌvən] <> vt -1. POL governar -2. [determine] controlar. <> vi POL governar.
governable adj POL governável.
governess ['gʌvənɪs] n governanta f.
governing ['gʌvənɪŋ] adj POL governante.
governing body n conselho m administrativo.
government ['gʌvnmənt] <> n -1. [group of people] governo m -2. (U) [process] governo m; the art of ~ a arte de governar. <> comp do governo.
governmental [,gʌvn'mentl] adj governamental.
government stock n títulos mpl do governo.
governor ['gʌvənə'] n -1. POL governador m, -ra f -2. [of school] diretor m, -ra f -3. [of prison] diretor m, -ra f.
governor-general (pl **governor-generals** OR **governors-general**) n governador geral m.
govt (abbr of government) gov.
gown [gaʊn] n -1. [dress] vestido m -2. UNIV & JUR beca f -3. MED avental m.
GP (abbr of general practitioner) n clínico m geral.
GPO n -1. (abbr of General Post Office) antigo serviço britânico de correios. -2. (abbr of Government Printing Office) departamento de imprensa do governo (norte-americano).
gr. -1. abbr of gross. -2. (abbr of gram) g.
grab [græb] (pt & pp -bed, cont -bing) <> vt -1. [with hands - person, arm] agarrar; [- money] pegar -2. fig [opportunity, sandwich] pegar; to ~ the chance to do sthg aproveitar a oportunidade de fazer algo -3. inf [appeal to] arrebatar; how does this ~ you? o que você me diz disso? <> vi: to ~ at sthg [with hands] tentar agarrar. <> n: to make a ~ at OR for sthg tentar apoderar-se de algo.
grace [greɪs] <> n -1. (U) [elegance] graça f, elegância f -2. [graciousness]: to have the ~ to do sthg ter finura para fazer algo; to do sthg with good ~ fazer algo de bom grado -3. (U) [extra time] prazo m -4. [prayer] graças fpl. <> vt -1. fml [honour] agraciar -2. [adorn] enfeitar.

Grace n [title] Eminência f.

graceful ['greɪsfʊl] adj -**1.** [beautiful] elegante -**2.** [gracious] amável.

graceless ['greɪslɪs] adj -**1.** [lacking charm] sem graça -**2.** [ill-mannered] deselegante.

gracious ['greɪʃəs] <> adj -**1.** [polite] afável -**2.** [elegant] elegante. <> excl: **(good)** ~! Santo Deus!, Nossa (Senhora)!

graciously ['greɪʃəslɪ] adv [politely] afavelmente.

gradation [grə'deɪʃn] n [of colour, light] gradação f.

grade [greɪd] <> n -**1.** [level] nível m -**2.** [quality] qualidade f; **high-**~ de alta qualidade; **low-**~ de baixa qualidade; **to make the** ~ obter sucesso -**3.** US [in school] série f -**4.** [mark] classificação f -**5.** US [gradient] declive m. <> vt -**1.** [classify] classificar -**2.** [mark, assess] avaliar.

grade crossing n US passagem f de nível.

grade school n US escola f primária.

grade school teacher n US professor m, -ra f de nível primário.

gradient ['greɪdjənt] n -**1.** [of road] declive m -**2.** MATH gradiente m.

gradual ['grædʒʊəl] adj gradual.

gradually ['grædʒʊəlɪ] adv gradualmente.

graduate [n 'grædʒʊət, vb 'grædʒʊeɪt] <> n -**1.** [person with a degree] graduado m, -da f, licenciado m, -da f -**2.** US: **to be a high-school** ~ ter completado o segundo grau. <> comp US [postgraduate] pós-graduado(da). <> vi -**1.** [with a degree]: **to** ~ graduar-se -**2.** US [from high school]: **to** ~ formar-se -**3.** [progress]: **to** ~ **from sthg (to sthg)** passar OR evoluir de algo (para algo).

graduated ['grædʒʊeɪtɪd] adj [gen] graduado(da); [pension, tax] retroativo(va).

graduate school n US escola f de pós-graduação.

graduation [ˌgrædʒʊ'eɪʃn] n -**1.** [completion of course] formatura f -**2.** [ceremony - at university] colação f de grau; US [at high school] formatura f.

graffiti [grə'fiːtɪ] n (U) pichação f.

graft [grɑːft] <> n -**1.** [gen] enxerto m -**2.** UK inf [hard work] labuta f -**3.** US inf [corruption] suborno m. <> vt -**1.** enxertar; **to** ~ **sthg onto sthg** enxertar algo em algo -**2.** [idea, system] combinar; **to** ~ **sthg onto sthg** combinar algo com algo.

grain [greɪn] n -**1.** [of corn, rice, salt] grão m -**2.** (U) [crops] cereais mpl -**3.** fig [small amount] parcela f mínima; **there wasn't a** ~ **of truth in what he said** não havia uma palavra de verdade no que ele disse -**4.** (U) [of wood] veio m; **it goes against the** ~ **for me** fig vai contra a minha natureza.

gram [græm] n grama f.

grammar ['græməʳ] n gramática f.

grammar school n -**1.** [in UK] ginásio m -**2.** [in US] escola f primária.

grammatical [grə'mætɪkl] adj gramatical.

gramme [græm] n UK = **gram**.

gramophone ['græməfəʊn] dated <> n gramofone m. <> comp de gramofone.

gran [græn] n UK inf vovó f.

Granada [grə'nɑːdə] n Granada; **in** ~ em Granada.

granary ['grænərɪ] (pl -ies) n celeiro m.

granary bread n pão m de trigo.

grand [grænd] (pl inv) <> adj -**1.** [impressive, imposing] magnífico(ca) -**2.** [ambitious, large-scale] ambicioso(sa) -**3.** [socially important] ilustre -**4.** inf dated [excellent] excelente. <> n inf [thousand pounds] mil libras fpl; [thousand dollars] mil dólares mpl.

grandad n inf vovô m.

Grand Canyon n: **the** ~ o Grand Canyon.

grandchild ['græntʃaɪld] (pl -**children** [-ˌtʃɪldrən]) n neto m, -ta f.

granddad ['grændæd] n inf = **grandad**.

granddaughter ['grænˌdɔːtəʳ] n neta f.

grand duchess n [noblewoman] grã-duquesa f.

grand duke n [nobleman] grão-duque m.

grandeur ['grændʒəʳ] n grandeza f.

grandfather ['grændˌfɑːðəʳ] n avô m.

grandfather clock n relógio m de pêndulo.

grandiose ['grændɪəʊz] adj pej espalhafatoso(sa).

grand jury n US júri m principal.

grandma ['grænmɑː] n inf vovó f, vó f.

grand master n grão-mestre m.

grandmother ['grænˌmʌðəʳ] n avó f.

Grand National n: **the** ~ a Grand National, corrida de cavalos realizada anualmente em Liverpool, na Inglaterra.

grandpa ['grænpɑː] n inf vovô m, vô m.

grandparents ['grænˌpeərənts] npl avós mpl.

grand piano n piano m de cauda.

grand prix [ˌgrɒn'priː] (pl **grands prix**) n grande prêmio m.

grand slam n SPORT grand slam m.

grandson ['grænsʌn] n neto m.

grandstand ['grændstænd] n tribuna f de honra.

grand total n total m geral.

granite ['grænɪt] n (U) granito m.

granny ['grænɪ] (pl -ies) n inf vovó f, vó f.

granny flat n UK local dentro ou próximo à casa de uma pessoa, feito para que um parente de idade possa viver nele.

granola [grə'nəʊlə] n US granola f.

grant [grɑːnt] <> n [money - for renovations] subsídio m; [- for study] bolsa f. <> vt fml -**1.** [agree to] conceder -**2.** [accept as true] admitir; **I** ~ **(that)** ... eu admito que ... -**3.** phr: **to take sb/sthg for** ~ **ed** não dar o devido valor a alguém/algo; **to take it for** ~ **ed that** ... tomar como certo que ...

granulated sugar ['grænjʊleɪtɪd-] n (U) açúcar m -cristal.

granule ['grænjuːl] n grânulo m.

grape [greɪp] n uva f.

grapefruit ['greɪpfruːt] (pl inv OR -s) n pomelo m.

grape picking [-ˌpɪkɪŋ] n (U) colheita f de uvas.

grapevine ['greɪpvaɪn] n -**1.** [plant] parreira f -**2.** fig [information channel]: **I heard on the** ~ **that** ... um passarinho me contou que ...

graph [grɑːf] n gráfico m.

graphic ['græfɪk] adj -**1.** [vivid] vívido(da) -**2.** ART pitoresco(ca).

graphics npl [pictures] artes fpl gráficas; **computer** ~ **s** gráfico m de computador.

graphic artist n artista mf gráfico, -ca.

graphic design n (U) projeto m gráfico.

graphic designer n projetista mf gráfico, -ca.
graphic equalizer n equalizador m gráfico.
graphics card n COMPUT placa f gráfica.
graphite ['græfaɪt] n (U) grafita f.
graphology [græ'fɒlədʒɪ] n (U) grafologia f.
graph paper n (U) papel m quadriculado.
grapple ['græpl] ⟶ **grapple with** vt fus **-1.** [physically] atracar-se com **-2.** fig [mentally] estar às voltas com.
grappling iron ['græplɪŋ-] n arpéu m.
grasp [grɑːsp] ⟨⟩ n **-1.** [grip] agarramento m **-2.** [power to achieve]: **in** OR **within one's** ~ ao alcance de alguém **-3.** [understanding] compreensão f; **to have a good** ~ **of sthg** ter um bom domínio de algo. ⟨⟩ vt **-1.** [with hands] segurar **-2.** [understand] compreender **-3.** fig [seize] agarrar.
grasping ['grɑːspɪŋ] adj pej [greedy - person] ganancioso(sa); [- attitude] avaro(ra).
grass [grɑːs] ⟨⟩ n **-1.** [common green plant] grama f **-2.** (U) drugs sl [marijuana] maconha f. ⟨⟩ vi UK crime sl: **to** ~ **(on sb)** dedurar alguém.
grasshopper ['grɑːs.hɒpə] n gafanhoto m.
grassland ['grɑːslænd] n pastagem f.
grass roots ⟨⟩ npl [ordinary people] plebe f. ⟨⟩ comp popular.
grass snake n cobra f d'água.
grassy ['grɑːsɪ] (compar -ier, superl -iest) adj coberto(ta) de grama.
grate [greɪt] ⟨⟩ n [fireplace] grade f. ⟨⟩ vt CULIN ralar. ⟨⟩ vi [irritate] irritar; **to** ~ **on sb's nerves** deixar alguém com os nervos à flor da pele.
grateful ['greɪtfʊl] adj agradecido(da); **to be** ~ **to sb (for sthg)** ser grato(ta) a alguém (por algo).
gratefully ['greɪtfʊlɪ] adv agradecidamente.
grater ['greɪtə] n ralador m.
gratification [ˌgrætɪfɪ'keɪʃn] n **-1.** [pleasure] gratificação f **-2.** [satisfaction] satisfação f.
gratify ['grætɪfaɪ] (pt & pp -ied) vt **-1.** [please]: **to be gratified** sentir-se gratificado(da) **-2.** [satisfy] satisfazer.
gratifying ['grætɪfaɪɪŋ] adj [pleasing] gratificante.
grating ['greɪtɪŋ] ⟨⟩ adj áspero(ra). ⟨⟩ n [grille] grade f.
gratitude ['grætɪtjuːd] n (U) gratidão f; ~ **to sb (for sthg)** gratidão por alguém (por algo).
gratuitous [grə'tjuːɪtəs] adj fml [unjustified] gratuito(ta).
gratuity [grə'tjuːɪtɪ] (pl -ies) n fml [tip] gratificação f.
grave [greɪv] ⟨⟩ adj grave. ⟨⟩ n túmulo m; **to turn in one's** ~ revirar-se no túmulo; **to dig one's own** ~ cavar a própria sepultura.
grave accent [grɑːv-] n acento m grave.
gravedigger ['greɪvˌdɪgə] n coveiro m, -ra f.
gravel ['grævl] ⟨⟩ n (U) cascalho m. ⟨⟩ comp de cascalho.
gravelled UK, **graveled** US ['grævld] adj de cascalho.
gravestone ['greɪvstəʊn] n lápide f.
graveyard ['greɪvjɑːd] n cemitério m.
gravitate ['grævɪteɪt] vi: **to** ~ **towards sb/sthg** fig [be attracted to] ser atraído(da) por alguém/algo.
gravity ['grævətɪ] n **-1.** [force] gravidade f **-2.** fml [seriousness, worrying nature] seriedade f, gravidade

f **-3.** [solemnity] gravidade f.
gravy ['greɪvɪ] n **-1.** [meat juice] molho m de carne; [sauce] caldo m de carne **-2.** US v inf [easy money] grana f fácil.
gravy boat n molheira f.
gravy train n inf: **the** ~ a mina de ouro.
gray adj & n US = grey.
grayscale n US = greyscale.
graze [greɪz] ⟨⟩ n [wound] machucado m, ferimento m. ⟨⟩ vt **-1.** [feed on] pastar **-2.** [cause to feed] pastorear **-3.** [break surface of] esfolar **-4.** [touch lightly] tocar de leve. ⟨⟩ vi [animals] pastar.
grease [griːs] ⟨⟩ n **-1.** [animal fat] gordura f **-2.** [lubricant] graxa f **-3.** [dirt] sebo m. ⟨⟩ vt **-1.** [gen] engraxar **-2.** [baking tray] untar.
grease gun n bomba f engraxadeira.
greasepaint ['griːspeɪnt] n (U) maquilagem f para o teatro.
greaseproof paper [ˌgriːspruːf-] n (U) UK papel m parafinado.
greasy ['griːzɪ] (compar -ier, superl -iest) adj **-1.** [food] gorduroso(sa); [tools] engordurado(da); [hair, hands, skin] seboso(sa) **-2.** [clothes] sujo(ja) **-3.** [road] escorregadio(dia).
greasy spoon n hum [cafe] boteco m.
great [greɪt] ⟨⟩ adj **-1.** [gen] grande **-2.** inf [really good, really nice] ótimo(ma). ⟨⟩ n grande mf. ⟨⟩ excl ótimo!
Great Barrier Reef n: **the** ~ a Grande Barreira.
Great Bear n: **the** ~ (a) Ursa Maior.
Great Britain n Grã-Bretanha; **in** ~ na Grã-Bretanha.
greatcoat ['greɪtkəʊt] n sobretudo m pesado.
Great Dane n pastor m dinamarquês.
Great Depression n: **the** ~ a Grande Depressão.
great-grandchild n bisneto m, -ta f.
great-grandfather n bisavô m.
great-grandmother n bisavó f.
Great Lakes npl: **the** ~ os Grandes Lagos.
greatly ['greɪtlɪ] adv imensamente; ~ **exaggerated** muito exagerado(da); ~ **different** extremamente diferente.
greatness ['greɪtnɪs] n grandeza f.
Great Wall of China n: **the** ~ a Grande Muralha da China.
Great War n: **the** ~ a Grande Guerra.
Greece [griːs] n Grécia; **in** ~ na Grécia.
greed [griːd] n **-1.** [for food] gula f **-2.** fig [for money, power]: ~ **(for sthg)** ganância (por algo).
greedily ['griːdɪlɪ] adv gulosamente.
greedy ['griːdɪ] (compar -ier, superl -iest) adj **-1.** [for food] guloso(sa) **-2.** fig [for money, power]: ~ **for sthg** ganancioso(sa) por algo.
Greek [griːk] ⟨⟩ adj grego(ga); **the** ~ **Islands** as Ilhas Gregas. ⟨⟩ n **-1.** [person] grego m, -ga f **-2.** [language] grego m.
green [griːn] ⟨⟩ adj **-1.** [gen] verde **-2.** inf [with nausea, fear] pálido(da) **-3.** inf [inexperienced] novato(-ta) **-4.** inf [jealous]: ~ **(with envy)** morto(ta) de ciúme. ⟨⟩ n **-1.** [colour] verde; **in** ~ de verde **-2.** [in village] praça f **-3.** GOLF green m.

Green n POL Verde; **the Greens** os Verdes.
greens npl [vegetables] verduras fpl.
greenback ['gri:nbæk] n US inf [banknote] nota f de dólar.
green bean n vagem f.
green belt n UK área f verde.
Green Beret n US inf: **the ~s** os Green Berets, *membros das Forças Especiais norte-americanas.*
green card n **-1.** UK [for insuring vehicle] *seguro que protege veículos e motoristas no exterior* **-2.** US [resident's permit] green card m, visto m permanente *(nos Estados Unidos).*

GREEN CARD

Assim se denomina o documento que permite a um estrangeiro viver e trabalhar nos Estados Unidos. A despeito do nome, hoje o *green card* já não é verde. O processo para sua obtenção é longo e complexo. O interessado deve possuir um parente próximo que seja cidadão estadunidense ou estar empregado numa companhia do país. Do contrário, precisará comprovar que tem condições de fazer investimentos financeiros nos Estados Unidos.

greenery ['gri:nəri] n (U) folhagem f.
green fingers npl UK: **to have ~** ter dom/mão boa para jardinagem.
greenfly ['gri:nflai] (pl inv OR -ies) n pulgão m.
greengage ['gri:ngeidʒ] n rainha-cláudia f.
greengrocer ['gri:n,grəʊsə'] n verdureiro(ra); **~'s (shop)** quitanda f.
greenhorn ['gri:nhɔ:n] n US **-1.** [immigrant, new arrival] recém-chegado m, -da f **-2.** [novice] novato m, -ta f.
greenhouse ['gri:nhaʊs, pl -haʊzɪz] n estufa f.
greenhouse effect n: **the ~** o efeito estufa.
greenhouse gas n gás m de efeito estufa.
greenish ['gri:nɪʃ] adj esverdeado(da).
Greenland ['gri:nlənd] n Groenlândia; **in ~** na Groenlândia.
Greenlander ['gri:nləndə'] n groenlandês m, -esa f.
green light n: **the ~** o sinal verde.
green paper n POL projeto de lei.
Green Party n: **the ~** o Partido Verde.
green salad n salada f verde.
green thumb n US: **to have a ~** ter dom/mão boa para jardinagem.
greet [gri:t] vt **-1.** [say hello to] cumprimentar **-2.** [speech, announcement, remark] saudar **-3.** [subj: sight, smell] receber.
greeting ['gri:tɪŋ] n [salutation] cumprimento m, saudação f.
greetings npl [on card] votos mpl.
greetings card UK ['gri:tɪŋz-], **greeting card** US n cartão m de comemoração.
gregarious [grɪ'geərɪəs] adj gregário(ria).
gremlin ['gremlɪn] n inf *duende que supostamente provoca o mau funcionamento de motores ou outros equipamentos,* gremlin m.
Grenada [grə'neidə] n Granada; **in ~** em Granada.

grenade [grə'neid] n: **(hand) ~** granada f (de mão).
Grenadian [grə'neidjən] <> adj granadino(na). <> n granadino m, -na f.
grenadier [,grenə'dɪə'] n granadeiro m.
grew [gru:] pt <> grow.
grey UK, **gray** US [grei] <> adj **-1.** [colour, weather] cinzento(ta) **-2.** [hair, beard] grisalho(lha); **to go ~** ficar grisalho(lha) **-3.** [complexion - with fatigue, nausea] desolado(da); [- skin] envelhecido(da) **-4.** fig [life, situation] preto(ta). <> n cinza m; **in ~** de cinza.
grey area n área f cinzenta.
grey-haired [-'heəd] adj grisalho(lha).
greyhound ['greihaʊnd] n galgo m.
greying UK, **graying** US ['greiɪŋ] adj acinzentado(da).
grey matter n **-1.** MED massa f cinzenta **-2.** inf [brain power] inteligência f.
greyscale UK, **grayscale** US ['greiskeil] n COMPUT escala f de tons.
grey squirrel n esquilo m cinzento.
grid [grid] n **-1.** [grating] gradeamento m **-2.** [system of squares] grade f **-3.** ELEC rede f.
griddle ['gridl] n chapa f de ferro *(para assar).*
gridiron ['grid,aɪən] n **-1.** [in cooking] grelha f **-2.** US [game] futebol m americano; [field] campo m de futebol americano.
gridlock ['gridlɒk] n empasse m.
grid reference n coordenadas fpl.
grief [gri:f] n **-1.** [sorrow] pesar m, tristeza f **-2.** inf [trouble] chateação f **-3.** phr: **to come to ~** fracassar; **good ~!** credo!
grief-stricken adj agoniado(da).
grievance ['gri:vns] n [complaint] queixa m, agravo m.
grieve [gri:v] <> vt fml: **it ~s me to say that** me dói dizer que. <> vi: **to ~ (for sb/sthg)** estar de luto por alguém/algo.
grieving ['gri:vɪŋ] n (U) luto m.
grievous ['gri:vəs] adj fml [serious, harmful] doloroso(sa).
grievous bodily harm n (U) lesão f corporal.
grievously ['gri:vəslɪ] adv fml gravemente.
grill [gril] <> n **-1.** [for cooking] grelha f **-2.** [food] grelhado m. <> vt **-1.** [cook on grill] grelhar **-2.** [interrogate] interrogar.
grille [gril] n grade f.
grim [grim] (compar -mer, superl -mest) adj **-1.** [stern] severo(ra), rígido(da) **-2.** [gloomy] deprimente.
grimace [grɪ'meis] <> n careta f. <> vi fazer caretas.
grime [graim] n (U) sujeira f.
grimly ['grimli] adv **-1.** [unhappily] severamente **-2.** [with determination] rigidamente.
grimy ['graimi] (compar -ier, superl -iest) adj imundo(da).
grin [grin] (pt & pp -ned, cont -ning) <> n sorriso m aberto. <> vi: **to ~ (at sb/sthg)** abrir um sorriso (para alguém/algo); **to ~ and bear it** aceitar (algo) e aguentar firme.
grind [graind] (pt & pp ground) <> vt **-1.** [coffee, pepper, grain] moer; **freshly ground coffee** café

moído na hora - **2.** [ash, dirt]: **to ~ sthg into sthg** esmagar algo em algo - **3.** [rub together] ranger. ◇ *vi* [scrape] arranhar. ◇ *n* - **1.** [hard, boring work] rotina *f* - **2.** *US inf*: **to go ~** ficar grisalho(lha).
- **grind down** *vt sep* [oppress] oprimir.
- **grind up** *vt sep* - **1.** [bottles] triturar - **2.** [knife] afiar - **3.** *US* [meat] picar - **4.** [gemstone] lapidar.

grinder ['graɪndəʳ] *n* [machine] moedor *m*.

grinding ['graɪndɪŋ] *adj* [oppressive] opressivo(va).

grinning *adj* sorridente.

grip [grɪp] (*pt* & *pp* **-ped**, *cont* **-ping**) ◇ *n* - **1.** [physical hold]: **to have a ~ on sb/sthg** ter o controle sobre alguém/algo; **to keep a ~ on the handrail** segurar-se no corrimão; **to get a good ~** dar um bom aperto; **to release one's ~ on sb/sthg** deixar de controlar alguém/algo - **2.** [control, domination] domínio *m*; **~ on sb/sthg** controle sobre alguém/algo; **in the ~ of sthg** nas garras de algo; **to get to ~s with sthg** encarar algo; **to get a ~ on o.s.** controlar-se; **to lose one's ~** *fig* perder a eficiência - **3.** *(U)* [adhesion] aderência *f* - **4.** [handle] punho *m* - **5.** *dated* [bag] valise *f*. ◇ *vt* - **1.** [grasp] agarrar - **2.** [subj: tyres] ter aderência a - **3.** [imagination, attention] controlar.

gripe [graɪp] *inf* ◇ *n* [complaint] queixa *f*; **the ~s** cólicas *fpl*. ◇ *vi*: **to ~ (about sthg)** resmungar (por causa de algo).

gripping ['grɪpɪŋ] *adj* [story, film] emocionante.

grisly ['grɪzlɪ] (*compar* **-ier**, *superl* **-iest**) *adj* [horrible, macabre] horrendo(da), medonho(nha).

grist [grɪst] *n (U)*: **it's all ~ to sb's** *OR* **the mill** tudo vale *OR* serve.

gristle ['grɪsl] *n (U)* cartilagem *f*.

gristly ['grɪslɪ] (*compar* **-ier**, *superl* **-iest**) *adj* cartilaginoso(sa).

grit [grɪt] (*pt* & *pp* **-ted**, *cont* **-ting**) ◇ *n* - **1.** [stones] areia *f* - **2.** *inf* [courage] coragem *f*. ◇ *vt* [road, steps] pôr areia em.
- **grits** *npl US* canjica *f*.

gritter ['grɪtəʳ] *n* veículo que espalha areia nas estradas congeladas.

gritty ['grɪtɪ] (*compar* **-ier**, *superl* **-iest**) *adj* - **1.** [stony] arenoso(sa) - **2.** *inf* [brave] corajoso(sa).

grizzled ['grɪzld] *adj* acinzentado(da).

grizzly ['grɪzlɪ] (*pl* **-ies**) *n*: **~ (bear)** urso-cinzento *m*.

groan [grəʊn] ◇ *n* gemido *m*. ◇ *vi* - **1.** [moan] gemer - **2.** [creak] ranger - **3.** [complain] resmungar.

grocer ['grəʊsəʳ] *n* dono *m*, -na *f* de mercearia; **~'s (shop)** mercearia *f*.

groceries ['grəʊsərɪz] *npl* [foods] comestíveis *mpl*.

grocery ['grəʊsərɪ] (*pl* **-ies**) *n* [shop] mercearia *f*.

groggy ['grɒgɪ] (*compar* **-ier**, *superl* **-iest**) *adj* grogue.

groin [grɔɪn] *n ANAT* virilha *f*.

groom [gruːm] ◇ *n* - **1.** [of horses] cavalariço *m* - **2.** [bridegroom] noivo *m*. ◇ *vt* - **1.** [horse, dog] tratar - **2.** [candidate]: **to ~ sb (for sthg)** preparar alguém (para algo).

groomed *adj*: **well/badly ~** bem/mal tratado(-da).

groove [gruːv] *n* - **1.** [in metal, wood] entalhe *m* - **2.** [in record] ranhura *f*.

grope [grəʊp] ◇ *vt* - **1.** [sexually] acariciar - **2.** [try to

find]: **to ~ one's way** tatear o caminho. ◇ *vi*: **to ~ (about) for sthg** [object] tatear por algo; *fig* [solution, remedy] tentar algo às cegas.

gross [grəʊs] (*pl inv OR* **-es**) ◇ *adj* - **1.** [total] bruto(ta) - **2.** *fml* [serious, inexcusable] grave - **3.** *inf* [coarse, vulgar] indecente - **4.** *inf* [obese] balofo(fa) - **5.** *inf* [disgusting] nojento(ta). ◇ *n* grosa *f*. ◇ *vt* [subj: person] receber em bruto; [subj: store, film] arrecadar em bruto.

gross domestic product *n* produto *m* interno bruto.

grossly ['grəʊslɪ] *adv* [for emphasis] extremamente.

gross national product *n* produto *m* nacional bruto.

gross profit *n* lucro *m* bruto.

grotesque [grəʊ'tesk] *adj* [strange, unnatural] grotesco(ca).

grotto ['grɒtəʊ] (*pl* **-es** *OR* **-s**) *n* gruta *f*.

grotty ['grɒtɪ] (*compar* **-ier**, *superl* **-iest**) *adj UK inf* asqueroso(sa).

grouchy ['graʊtʃɪ] (*compar* **-ier**, *superl* **-iest**) *adj inf* mal-humorado(da).

ground [graʊnd] ◇ *pt* & *pp* ▷ **grind**. ◇ *n* - **1.** [surface of earth] terra *f*, chão *m*; **above/below ~** em cima/embaixo da terra; **on the ~** no chão; **to be thin on the ~** ser pouco numeroso(sa); **to get sthg off the ~** *fig* iniciar algo com sucesso - **2.** *(U)* [area of land] terreno *m* - **3.** [area used for a particular purpose] campo *m* - **4.** [subject area] área *f*; **to break fresh** *OR* **new ~** dar o primeiro passo - **5.** [advantage]: **to gain/lose ~** ganhar/perder terreno - **6.** *phr*: **to cut the ~ from under sb's feet** puxar o tapete de alguém; **to go to ~** esconder-se; **to run sb/sthg to ~** encontrar alguém/algo; **to run o.s. into the ~** trabalhar até a exaustão; **to stand one's ~** defender seu ponto de vista. ◇ *vt* - **1.** [base]: **to be ~ed on** *OR* **in sthg** ter algo como base; **to be well-~ed in sthg** estar bem baseado em algo - **2.** [aircraft, pilot] ficar retido(da) - **3.** *esp US inf* [child] ficar de castigo - **4.** *US ELEC*: **to be ~ed** ter um fio-terra.
- **grounds** *npl* - **1.** [reason] razão *f*, motivo *m*; **~s for sthg/for doing sthg** motivo para algo/para fazer algo; **on the ~s of** com o pretexto de; **on the ~s that** com o motivo de que - **2.** [land round building] jardins *mpl* - **3.** [area for specific purpose] área *f* - **4.** [of coffee] borra *f*.

ground control *n* controle *m* de terra.

ground cover *n (U)* vegetação *f* rasteira.

ground crew *n* equipe *f* de terra.

ground floor *n* [andar *m* of] térreo *m*.

ground-in *adj* impregnado(da).

grounding ['graʊndɪŋ] *n*: **~ (in sthg)** conhecimentos *mpl* básicos (sobre algo).

groundless ['graʊndlɪs] *adj* infundado(da).

ground level *n*: **at ~** ao nível do solo.

groundnut ['graʊndnʌt] *n* amendoim *m*.

ground plan *n* [of building] planta *f* baixa.

ground rent *n* aluguel *m* residencial.

ground rules *npl* regras *fpl* básicas.

groundsheet ['graʊndʃiːt] *n* lona *f*.

groundsman ['graʊndzmən] (*pl* **-men** [-mən]) *n UK* zelador *m* de campo esportivo.

ground staff n -1. [at sports ground] equipe f de campo -2. UK [at airport] pessoal m de terra.

groundswell ['graʊndswel] n [of feeling] acirramento m.

groundwork ['graʊndwɜ:k] n (U) base f, fundamento m.

group [gru:p] <> n -1. [gen] grupo m -2. MUS banda f. <> vt agrupar; [classify] classificar. <> vi: to ~ (together) agrupar-se.

group captain n UK ≃ coronel m (de aviação).

groupie ['gru:pɪ] n inf tiete mf.

group practice n prática médica empreendida por um grupo de médicos associados que trabalham juntos como colegas ou como especialistas de áreas diferentes.

group therapy n (U) terapia f de grupo.

grouse [graʊs] (pl sense 1 inv OR -s, pl sense 2 -s) <> n -1. [bird] galo-silvestre m -2. inf [complaint] queixa f. <> vi inf queixar-se.

grove [graʊv] n -1. [of trees] arvoredo m -2. [of fruit trees] pomar m.

grovel ['grɒvl] (UK pt & pp -led, cont -ling, US pt & pp -ed, cont -ing) vi -1. pej [humble o.s.] humilhar-se; to ~ to sb humilhar-se diante de alguém -2. [crawl on floor] rastejar.

grow [graʊ] (pt grew, pp grown) <> vt -1. [plants] cultivar -2. [hair, beard] deixar crescer. <> vi -1. [plant, hair, person] crescer; [company, city, economy, plan] desenvolver-se -2. [seeds] germinar -3. [increase] aumentar -4. [become] tornar-se; to ~ tired of sthg cansar-se de algo -5. [do eventually]: to ~ to do sthg passar a fazer algo.

☞ **grow apart** vi [become less friendly] distanciar-se.

☞ **grow into** vt fus [clothes, shoes] crescer o suficiente para poder vestir.

☞ **grow on** vt fus inf [please more and more]: this book is growing on me gosto cada vez mais deste livro.

☞ **grow out** vi [perm, dye] desbotar.

☞ **grow out of** vt fus -1. [clothes, shoes]: he's grown out of all his clothes as roupas dele ficaram pequenas -2. [habit] perder.

☞ **grow up** vi crescer.

grower ['graʊər] n [person] produtor m, -ra f, agricultor m, -ra f.

growl [graʊl] <> n -1. [of dog] rosnar m -2. [of lion] rugido m -3. [of engine] rangido m -4. [of person] resmungo m. <> vi -1. [dog] rosnar -2. [lion] rugir -3. [engine] ranger -4. [person] resmungar.

grown [graʊn] <> pp > **grow**. <> adj crescido(da).

grown-up <> adj -1. [fully grown, full-sized] crescido(da) -2. [mature, sensible] maduro(ra). <> n adulto m, -ta f.

growth [graʊθ] n -1. (U) [development, increase] crescimento m -2. MED [lump] tumor m, abscesso m.

growth rate n taxa f de crescimento.

grub [grʌb] n -1. [insect] larva f -2. (U) inf [food] rango m.

grubby ['grʌbɪ] (compar -ier, superl -iest) adj encardido(da).

grudge [grʌdʒ] <> n ressentimento m; to bear sb a ~, to bear a ~ against sb guardar rancor contra alguém. <> vt ressentir, lamentar; to ~ sb sthg invejar alguém por algo; to ~ doing sthg fazer algo com má vontade.

grudging ['grʌdʒɪŋ] adj relutante.

grudgingly ['grʌdʒɪŋlɪ] adv com relutância.

gruelling UK, **grueling** US ['gruəlɪŋ] adj árduo(-dua).

gruesome ['gru:səm] adj horrível.

gruff [grʌf] adj -1. [hoarse] rouco(ca) -2. [rough, unfriendly] brusco(ca).

grumble ['grʌmbl] <> n -1. [complaint] resmungo m -2. [rumble - thunder, stomach] ronco m; [- train] rebôo m. <> vi -1. [complain] resmungar; to ~ about sthg resmungar por algo -2. [rumble - thunder, stomach] roncar; [- train] reboar.

grumbling ['grʌmblɪŋ] n -1. [complaining] resmungo m -2. [rumbling] ronco m.

grumpy ['grʌmpɪ] (compar -ier, superl -iest) adj -1. inf [person] resmungão(ona) -2. inf [face] rabugento(ta).

grunt [grʌnt] <> n -1. [of pig] grunhido m -2. [of person] resmungo m. <> vi -1. [pig] grunhir -2. [person] resmungar.

G-string n -1. MUS corda f G -2. [clothing] tanga f tapa-sexo.

Guadeloupe [,gwa:də'lu:p] n Guadalupe; in ~ em Guadalupe.

Guam n Guam; in ~ em Guam.

guarantee [,gærən'ti:] <> n garantia f; under ~ sob garantia. <> vt -1. COMM dar garantia para -2. [promise] garantir.

guarantor [,gærən'tɔ:ʳ] n fiador m, -ra f.

guard [ga:d] <> n -1. [person] guarda mf -2. [group of guards] guarda f -3. [supervision] vigilância f; to be on ~ estar em guarda; to stand ~ estar de guarda; to be on (one's) ~ (against sthg) estar alerta (em relação a algo); to catch sb off ~ pegar alguém desprevenido(da) -4. UK RAIL chefe mf de trem -5. [protective device] dispositivo m de segurança -6. [in boxing] proteção f. <> vt -1. [protect] proteger -2. [prevent from escaping] vigiar.

☞ **guard against** vt fus prevenir-se contra.

guard dog n cão m de guarda.

guarded ['ga:dɪd] adj [careful] cauteloso(sa).

guardian ['ga:djən] n -1. JUR [of child] guardião m, -diã f -2. [protector] curador m, -ra f.

guardian angel n anjo m da guarda.

guardianship ['ga:djənʃɪp] n (U) tutela f.

guard rail n US [on road] proteção f lateral.

guardsman ['ga:dzmən] (pl -men [-mən]) n sentinela mf.

guard's van n UK vagão m de freio.

Guatemala [,gwa:tə'ma:lə] n Guatemala; in ~ na Guatemala.

Guatemalan [,gwa:tə'ma:lən] <> adj guatemalteco(ca). <> n guatemalteco m, -ca f.

guava ['gwa:və] n -1. [fruit] goiaba f -2. [tree] goiabeira f.

guerilla [gə'rɪlə] n = **guerrilla**.

Guernsey ['gɜ:nzɪ] n -1. [place] Guernsey; in ~ em Guernsey -2. [sweater] pulôver m de lã (originalmente usado por pescadores) -3. [cow] Guernsey.

guerrilla [gəˈrɪlə] n guerrilheiro m, -ra f; **urban ~** guerrilheiro urbano, guerrilheira urbana.

guerrilla warfare n (U) guerrilha f.

guess [ges] ◇ n - **1.** [at facts, figures] suposição f; **to take a ~** adivinhar - **2.** [hypothesis] hipótese f; **it's anybody's ~** não há como saber. ◇ vt [assess correctly] adivinhar; **~ what!** adivinha! ◇ vi - **1.** [attempt to answer] chutar; **to ~ at sthg** tentar adivinhar algo; **to keep sb ~ing** não contar a alguém - **2.** [think, suppose]: **I ~ (so)** eu acho (que sim).

guesstimate [ˈgestɪmət] n inf estimativa f aproximada.

guesswork [ˈgeswɜːk] n (U) adivinhação f.

guest [gest] n - **1.** [visitor - at home] visita mf; [- at club, restaurant, concert] convidado m, -da f - **2.** [at hotel] hóspede mf - **3.** [in show] convidado m, -da f especial - **4.** phr: **be my ~**! seja meu convidado!

guesthouse [ˈgesthaʊs, pl -haʊzɪz] n pensão f.

guest of honour n convidado m, -da f de honra.

guestroom [ˈgestrʊm] n quarto m de hóspedes.

guest star n ator m convidado, atriz f convidada.

guffaw [gʌˈfɔː] ◇ n gargalhada f. ◇ vi gargalhar, dar gargalhadas.

Guiana [gaɪˈænə] n Guiana; **in ~** na Guiana.

guidance [ˈgaɪdəns] n - **1.** [help] orientação f - **2.** [leadership] liderança f; **under the ~ of** sob a orientação de.

guide [gaɪd] ◇ n - **1.** [person, book for tourist] guia mf - **2.** [manual] manual m - **3.** [indication] estimativa f (aproximada) - **4.** = **girl guide.** ◇ vt - **1.** [show by leading] guiar; **the waiter ~d them to a table** o garçom os conduziu até a mesa - **2.** [plane, missile] orientar - **3.** [influence]: **to be ~d by sb/sthg** ser orientado(da) por alguém/algo.

Guide Association n: **the ~** as Escoteiras.

guide book n guia m.

guided missile [ˈgaɪdɪd-] n míssil m guiado.

guide dog n cão-guia m.

guided tour n - **1.** [of city] excursão f guiada - **2.** [of cathedral, museum etc] visita f guiada.

guidelines [ˈgaɪdlaɪnz] npl princípios mpl, diretrizes fpl.

guiding [ˈgaɪdɪŋ] adj norteador(ra).

guild [gɪld] n - **1.** HIST guilda f - **2.** [association] associação f.

guildhall [ˈgɪldhɔːl] n guilda f.

guile [gaɪl] n (U) literary astúcia f.

guileless [ˈgaɪlɪs] adj literary cândido(da).

guillotine [ˈgɪləˌtiːn] ◇ n - **1.** [gen] guilhotina f - **2.** UK POL estipulação de um tempo determinado para discutir um projeto de lei. ◇ vt guilhotinar.

guilt [gɪlt] n culpa f.

guiltily [ˈgɪltɪlɪ] adv com a consciência pesada.

guilty [ˈgɪltɪ] (compar -ier, superl -iest) adj - **1.** [remorseful] culpado(da); **to have a ~ conscience** ter a consciência pesada - **2.** [causing remorse] condenável, que causa remorso - **3.** JUR culpado(da); **to be found ~/not ~** ser declarado culpado(da)/ inocente - **4.** fig [culpable] culpável; **to be ~ of sthg** ser culpado(da) de algo.

guinea [ˈgɪnɪ] n guinéu m.

Guinea [ˈgɪnɪ] n Guiné; **in ~** em Guiné.

Guinea-Bissau [-bɪˈsaʊ] n Guiné-Bissau; **in ~** em Guiné-Bissau.

guinea fowl n galinha f d'angola.

guinea pig [ˈgɪnɪ-] n - **1.** [animal] porquinho-da-Índia m - **2.** [subject of experiment] cobaia mf.

guise [gaɪz] n fml aparência f, aspecto m.

guitar [gɪˈtɑːr] n violão m, guitarra f.

guitarist [gɪˈtɑːrɪst] n violonista mf, guitarrista mf.

gulch [gʌltʃ] n US ravina f.

gulf [gʌlf] n - **1.** [sea] golfo m - **2.** [deep hole]: **~ (between)** abismo (entre) - **3.** fig [separation] abismo m.

  ➤ **Gulf** n: **the Gulf** o Golfo Pérsico; **the Gulf of Aden** o Golfo de Áden; **the Gulf of Mexico** o Golfo do México.

Gulf States npl: **the ~** [around Persian Gulf] os países do Golfo Pérsico; [in US] os estados norte-americanos que têm costa para o Golfo do México (Flórida, Alabama, Mississippi, Louisiana e Texas).

Gulf Stream n: **the ~** a corrente do Golfo.

gull [gʌl] n [bird] gaivota f.

gullet [ˈgʌlɪt] n esôfago m.

gullible [ˈgʌləbl] adj ingênuo(nua).

gully [ˈgʌlɪ] (pl -ies) n - **1.** [valley] barranco m - **2.** [ditch] vala f.

gulp [gʌlp] ◇ n gole m. ◇ vt engolir. ◇ vi engolir em seco.

  ➤ **gulp down** vt sep engolir.

gum [gʌm] (pt & pp -med, cont -ming) ◇ n - **1.** (U) [chewing gum] chiclete m - **2.** [adhesive] goma f - **3.** ANAT gengiva f. ◇ vt - **1.** [cover with adhesive] passar goma em - **2.** [stick] colar.

gumboil [ˈgʌmbɔɪl] n abscesso m nas gengivas.

gumboots [ˈgʌmbuːts] npl UK galocha f.

gummed adj adesivo(va).

gumption [ˈgʌmpʃn] n (U) inf [resourcefulness] senso m prático.

gumshoe [ˈgʌmʃuː] n US crime sl detetive mf.

gun [gʌn] (pt & pp -ned, cont -ning) n - **1.** [gen] arma f - **2.** [specific type - revolver] revólver m; [- pistol] pistola f; [- shotgun] espingarda m; [- rifle] rifle m; [- cannon] canhão m; **to stick to one's ~s** não dar o braço a torcer - **3.** SPORT [starting pistol] revólver m; **to jump the ~** fig precipitar-se - **4.** [tool] pistola f.

  ➤ **gun down** vt sep balear.

gunboat [ˈgʌnbəʊt] n canhoeira f.

gundog [ˈgʌndɒg] n cão m de caça.

gunfire [ˈgʌnfaɪər] n (U) tiroteio m.

gunge [gʌndʒ] n (U) UK inf substância f nojenta e pegajosa.

gung-ho [ˌgʌŋˈhəʊ] adj UK inf impulsivo(va).

gunk [gʌŋk] n inf meleca f.

gunman [ˈgʌnmən] (pl -men [-mən]) n pistoleiro m.

gunner [ˈgʌnər] n MIL artilheiro m, -ra f.

gunpoint [ˈgʌnpɔɪnt] n: **at ~** na mira.

gunpowder [ˈgʌnˌpaʊdər] n (U) pólvora f.

gunrunning [ˈgʌnˌrʌnɪŋ] n (U) contrabando m de armas.

gunshot [ˈgʌnʃɒt] n [firing of gun] tiro m.

gunsmith [ˈgʌnsmɪθ] n armeiro m, -ra f.

gurgle [ˈgɜːgl] ◇ n - **1.** [of water] gorgolejo m - **2.** [of baby] gugu *m*. ◇ *vi* **-1.** [water] gorgolejar **-2.** [baby] fazer gugu.

guru [ˈgʊruː] *n* **-1.** [spiritual leader] guru *m* **-2.** [adviser] conselheiro *m*, -ra *f*.

gush [gʌʃ] ◇ *n* jorro *m*. ◇ *vt* jorrar. ◇ *vi* **-1.** [flow out] verter **-2.** *pej* [enthuse] entusiasmar-se.

gushing [ˈgʌʃɪŋ] *adj pej* [over-enthusiastic] efusivo(va).

gusset [ˈgʌsɪt] *n* **-1.** *SEWING* nesga *f* **-2.** [in tights] entreperna *m*.

gust [gʌst] ◇ *n* rajada *f*. ◇ *vi* dar uma rajada.

gusto [ˈgʌstəʊ] *n (U)*: **with ~** com garra.

gusty [ˈgʌstɪ] (*compar* **-ier**, *superl* **-iest**) *adj* tempestuoso(sa).

gut [gʌt] (*pt & pp* **-ted**, *cont* **-ting**) ◇ *n* **-1.** *MED* intestino *m* **-2.** *inf* [stomach] bucho *m*. ◇ *vt* **-1.** [remove organs from] destripar **-2.** [destroy] destruir.

➤ **guts** *npl inf* **-1.** [intestines] tripas *fpl*; **to hate sb's ~ s** ter alguém atravessado(da) na garganta **-2.** [courage] coragem *f*; **to have ~ s** ter estômago.

gut feeling *n* pressentimento *m*.

gut reaction *n* reação *f* instintiva.

gutter [ˈgʌtər] *n* **-1.** [ditch] sarjeta *f* **-2.** [on roof] calha *f*.

guttering [ˈgʌtərɪŋ] *n (U)* calhas *fpl*.

gutter press *n pej* imprensa-marrom *f*.

guttural [ˈgʌtərəl] *adj* gutural.

guv [gʌv] *n UK inf* chefe *m*.

guy [gaɪ] *n* **-1.** *inf* [man] cara *mf* **-2.** *esp US* [person] galera *f inv* **-3.** *UK* [dummy] *boneco que se queima na Grã-Bretanha na Noite da Conspiração da Pólvora.*

Guyana [gaɪˈænə] *n* Guiana *f*; **in ~** na Guiana.

Guy Fawkes Night *n* Noite *f* da Conspiração da Pólvora.

guy rope *n* amarra *f*.

guzzle [ˈgʌzl] ◇ *vt pej* - [food] devorar com gula; [- drink] beber com gula. ◇ *vi* engolir com gula.

gym [dʒɪm] *n inf* **-1.** [gymnasium - in school] ginásio *m*; [- in hotel, health club] sala *f* de ginástica **-2.** *(U)* [exercises] ginástica *f*, ginásio *m*.

gymkhana [dʒɪmˈkɑːnə] *n* gincana *f*.

gymnasium [dʒɪmˈneɪzjəm] (*pl* **-siums** OR **-sia** [-zjə]) *n* ginásio *m*.

gymnast [ˈdʒɪmnæst] *n* ginasta *mf*.

gymnastics [dʒɪmˈnæstɪks] *n (U)* ginástica *f*.

gym shoes *npl* sapatilha *f* de ginástica.

gymslip [ˈdʒɪmˌslɪp] *n UK* bata *f* escolar.

gynaecological *UK*, **gynecological** *US* [ˌgaɪnəkəˈlɒdʒɪkl] *adj* ginecológico(ca).

gynaecologist *UK*, **gynecologist** *US* [ˌgaɪnəˈkɒlədʒɪst] *n* ginecologista *mf*.

gynaecology *UK*, **gynecology** *US* [ˌgaɪnəˈkɒlədʒɪl] *n (U)* ginecologia *f*.

gypsy [ˈdʒɪpsɪ] (*pl* **-ies**) *adj & n* = gipsy.

gyrate [dʒaɪˈreɪt] *vi* girar.

gyration [dʒaɪˈreɪʃn] *n* giro *m*, rotação *f*.

gyroscope [ˈdʒaɪrəskəʊp] *n* giroscópio *m*.

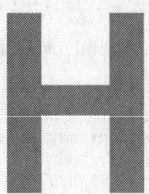

h (*pl* h's OR hs), **H** (*pl* H's OR Hs) [eɪtʃ] *n* [letter] h, H *m*.

ha [hɑː] *excl* ah!

habeas corpus [ˌheɪbjəsˈkɔːpəs] *n (U)* habeas corpus *m*.

haberdashery [ˈhæbədæʃərɪ] (*pl* **-ies**) *n* **-1.** *(U)* [goods] materiais *mpl* de costura, artigos *mpl* de armarinho **-2.** [shop] armarinho *m*.

habit [ˈhæbɪt] *n* **-1.** [customary practice] hábito *m*, costume *m*; **to be in the ~ of doing sthg** ter o hábito de fazer algo, ter o costume de fazer algo; **to make a ~ of sthg** tornar algo um hábito; **to make a ~ of doing sthg** ter por hábito fazer algo **-2.** [drug addiction] vício *m* **-3.** [garment] hábito *m*.

habitable [ˈhæbɪtəbl] *adj* habitável.

habitat [ˈhæbɪtæt] *n* habitat *m*.

habitation [ˌhæbɪˈteɪʃn] *n* **-1.** *(U)* [occupation] habitação *f* **-2.** *fml* [house] moradia *f*.

habit-forming [-ˌfɔːmɪŋ] *adj* que vicia; **marijuana is ~** a maconha vicia.

habitual [həˈbɪtʃʊəl] *adj* **-1.** [customary] habitual, costumeiro(ra) **-2.** [offender, smoker, drinker] inveterado(da).

habitually [həˈbɪtʃʊəlɪ] *adv* habitualmente.

hack [hæk] ◇ *n* **-1.** *pej* [writer] escritorzinho *m*, -razinha *f* **-2.** *US inf* [taxi] táxi *m*. ◇ *vt* **-1.** [cut] cortar **-2.** *inf* [cope with] enfrentar. ◇ *vi* [cut] talhar.

➤ **hack into** *vt fus COMPUT* invadir ilegalmente.

➤ **hack through** *vt fus* [cut] abrir caminho; **to ~ (one's way) through sthg** abrir caminho através de algo.

hacker [ˈhækər] *n COMPUT*: **(computer) ~** hacker *mf* (de computador).

hackie *n US inf* taxista *mf*.

hacking [ˈhækɪŋ] *n COMPUT* invasão *m* ilegal de sistemas de computação.

hacking cough *n* tosse *f* seca.

hackles [ˈhæklz] *npl* [on animal] pêlos *mpl* eriçados do dorso; **to make sb's ~ rise** enfurecer alguém.

hackney cab, hackney carriage [ˈhæknɪ-] *n fml* [taxi] carro *m* de praça.

hackneyed [ˈhæknɪd] *adj pej* batido(da), banal.

hacksaw [ˈhæksɔː] *n* serra *f* para metais.

had [weak form həd, strong form hæd] pt & pp ▷ have.

haddock ['hædək] (pl inv) n hadoque m.

hadn't ['hædnt] = had not.

haematology [ˌhiːmə'tɒlədʒɪ] n = hematology.

haemoglobin [ˌhiːmə'gləʊbɪn] n = hemoglobin.

haemophilia [ˌhiːmə'fɪlɪə] n = hemophilia.

haemophiliac [ˌhiːmə'fɪliæk] n = hemophiliac.

haemorrhage ['hemərɪdʒ] n & vi = hemorrhage.

haemorrhoids ['hemərɔɪdz] npl = hemorrhoids.

hag [hæg] n pej bruxa f, megera f.

haggard ['hægəd] adj abatido(da).

haggis ['hægɪs] n lingüiça escocesa, normalmente com o formato de uma bola, feita de carne de carneiro picada e embutida na pele do estômago do carneiro.

haggle ['hægl] vi pechinchar, regatear; **to ~ over** OR **about sthg** pechinchar acerca de algo; **to ~ with sb** pechinchar com alguém.

haggling ['hæglɪŋ] n (U) regateio m.

Hague [heɪg] n: **The ~** Haia.

hail [heɪl] ◇ n -1. (U) [frozen rain] granizo m -2. fig [torrent - of bullets] rajada f; [- of criticism] chuva f; [- of abuse] onda f. ◇ vt -1. [call] chamar -2. [acclaim]: **to ~ sb/sthg as sthg** aclamar alguém/algo como algo. ◇ v impers METEOR chover granizo.

hailstone ['heɪlstəʊn] n granizo m.

hailstorm n chuva f de granizo.

hair [heəʳ] ◇ n -1. (U) [on human head] cabelo m; **to do one's ~** pentear-se; **to let one's ~ down** relaxar e curtir; **to make sb's ~ stand on end** deixar alguém de cabelos em pé; **to split ~s** debater minúcias -2. [on animal, insect, plant] pêlo m -3. [on human skin] pêlo m. ◇ comp -1. [oil, lotion] capilar -2. [conditioner] de cabelos.

hairbrush ['heəbrʌʃ] n escova f de cabelo.

haircut ['heəkʌt] n corte m de cabelo.

hairdo ['heədu:] (pl -s) n inf penteado m.

hairdresser ['heəˌdresəʳ] n cabeleireiro m, -ra f; **~'s (salon)** (salão m de) cabeleireiro m.

hairdressing ['heəˌdresɪŋ] ◇ n (U) profissão f do cabeleireiro. ◇ comp de cabeleireiro.

hairdryer ['heəˌdraɪəʳ] n secador m de cabelos.

hair gel n (U) gel m fixador.

hairgrip ['heəgrɪp] n UK grampo m de cabelo.

hairline ['heəlaɪn] n [of the hair] contorno m do cabelo.

hairline fracture n fratura f muito fina.

hairnet ['heənet] n rede f de cabelo.

hairpiece ['heəpi:s] n cabelo m postiço.

hairpin ['heəpɪn] n grampo m de cabelo.

hairpin bend n curva f fechada.

hair-raising [-ˌreɪzɪŋ] adj assustador(ra); **a ~ story** uma história de deixar os cabelos em pé.

hair remover [-rɪˌmuːvəʳ] n (creme m) depilatório m.

hair-restorer n loção f capilar.

hair's breadth n: **by a ~** por um triz.

hair slide n UK passador m, presilha f.

hair-splitting n (U) pej sutilezas fpl.

hairspray ['heəspreɪ] n laquê m.

hairstyle ['heəstaɪl] n penteado m.

hairstylist ['heəˌstaɪlɪst] n cabeleireiro m, -ra f.

hairy ['heərɪ] (compar -ier, superl -iest) adj -1. [covered in hair - person] cabeludo(da); [- animal, legs] peludo(-da) -2. inf [dangerous] arriscado(da).

Haiti ['heɪtɪ] n Haiti; **in ~** no Haiti.

Haitian ['heɪʃn] ◇ adj haitiano(na). ◇ n haitiano m, -na f.

hake [heɪk] (pl inv OR -s) n merluza f.

halal [hə'lɑːl] ◇ adj que foi abatido conforme a lei islâmica. ◇ n (U) carne de animal abatido conforme a lei islâmica.

halcyon adj literary: **~ days** dias mpl venturosos.

hale [heɪl] adj: **~ and hearty** firme e forte.

half [UK hɑːf, US hæf] (pl senses 1, 2 and 3 halves, pl senses 4, 5 and 6 halves OR halfs) ◇ adj meio (meia); **~ my salary** metade f do meu salário. ◇ adv -1. [partly, almost] meio, quase; **I ~ expected him to say yes** eu meio que esperava que ele dissesse sim; **not ~!** UK inf e como! -2. [by half]: **to increase sthg by ~** acrescentar a metade ao valor de algo -3. [in equal measure] meio; **~-and-~** meio a meio -4. [in telling the time]: **~ past ten** UK, **~ after ten** US dez e meia; **it's ~ past ten/one** são dez e meia/é uma e meia. ◇ n -1. [one of two equal parts] metade f; **by ~** pela metade; **in ~** ao meio; **to be too clever by ~** pej ser muito astuto(ta); **he doesn't do things by halves** ele não faz as coisas pela metade; **to go halves (with sb)** rachar as despesas (com alguém) -2. [fraction] meio m -3. SPORT [of sports match] tempo m -4. SPORT [halfback] meio-campo mf -5. [of beer] meia cerveja f -6. [child's ticket] meia entrada f. ◇ pron [one of two equal parts] metade de; **~ of** metade de.

halfback ['hɑːfbæk] n meio-campo mf.

half-baked [-'beɪkt] adj inf mal-elaborado(da).

half board n (U) UK meia pensão f.

half-breed ◇ adj mestiço(ça). ◇ n mestiço m, -ça f.

half-brother n meio-irmão m.

half-caste [-kɑːst] ◇ adj mestiço(ça). ◇ n mestiço m, -ça f.

half cock n: **to go off (at) ~** ir com muita sede ao pote.

half-day n meio turno m.

half-fare n meia passagem f.

half-hearted [-'hɑːtɪd] adj desanimado(da).

half-heartedly [-'hɑːtɪdlɪ] adv sem entusiasmo.

half hour n meia hora f.
   ➡ **half-hour** adj = half-hourly.

half-hourly adj a cada meia hora.

half-length adj de meio corpo.

half-light n (U) meia-luz f.

half-mast n UK: **at ~** [flag] a meio pau.

half measures npl meios-termos mpl.

half moon n meia-lua f.

half note n US MUS mínima f.

halfpenny ['heɪpnɪ] (pl -pennies OR -pence) n meio pêni m.

half-price adj a metade do preço.
   ➡ **half price** adv pela metade do preço.

half-sister n meia-irmã f.

half step n US MUS semitom m.

half term n UK recesso m escolar.

half time n (U) meio-tempo m.

half tone n US MUS meio-tom m, semitom m.

half-truth n meia verdade f.

halfway [hɑːˈfweɪ] <> adj no meio do caminho. <> adv - **1.** [in space] a meio caminho - **2.** [in time] no meio - **3.** phr: **to meet sb** ~ fig [compromise] chegar a um acordo com alguém.

half-wit n idiota mf.

half-yearly adj semestral.

→ **half yearly** adv semestralmente.

halibut [ˈhælɪbət] (pl inv OR -s) n halibute m.

halitosis [ˌhælɪˈtəʊsɪs] n (U) halitose f.

hall [hɔːl] n - **1.** [in house] entrada f, hall m - **2.** [meeting room] salão m - **3.** [public building] sala f; **town** ~ prédio m da prefeitura - **4.** UK [UNIV & hall of residence] alojamento m, casa f do estudante; **to live in** ~ morar em casa do estudante - **5.** [country house] mansão m.

halleluja [ˌhælɪˈluːjə] excl aleluia!

hallmark [ˈhɔːlmɑːk] n - **1.** [typical feature] marca f distintiva - **2.** [on metal] selo m de autenticidade.

hallo [həˈləʊ] excl = hello.

hall of residence (pl halls of residence) n UK UNIV casa f do estudante.

hallowed [ˈhæləʊd] adj [respected] sagrado(da), santo(ta).

Hallowe'en, Halloween, [ˌhæləʊˈiːn] n Dia m das Bruxas.

HALLOWE'EN

O Halloween é celebrado nos Estados Unidos e na Grã-Bretanha na noite de 31 de outubro. As crianças, vestidas de bruxas, fantasmas etc., vão de porta em porta, pedindo doces às pessoas. Marca registrada dessa festa são as abóboras ocas, com o interior iluminado por uma vela.

---

hallucinate [həˈluːsɪneɪt] vi alucinar.

hallucination [ˌhəluːsɪˈneɪʃn] n alucinação f.

hallucinogenic [həˌluːsɪnəˈdʒenɪk] adj alucinógeno(na).

hallway [ˈhɔːlweɪ] n - **1.** [at entrance of house] saguão m, hall m - **2.** [corridor] corredor m.

halo [ˈheɪləʊ] (pl -es OR -s) n - **1.** [of saint, angel] auréola f - **2.** fig [circle of light] halo m.

halogen [ˈhælədʒen] <> n (U) halogênio m. <> comp halógeno m, -na f.

halt [hɔːlt] <> n [stop]: **to come to a** ~ [vehicle, horse] fazer uma parada; [development, activity] interromper-se; **to call a** ~ **to sthg** pôr fim a algo; **to grind to a** ~ [stop moving] parar lentamente; [stop working] estagnar-se. <> vt [stop - person] deter; [- development, activity] interromper. <> vi [stop - person, train] parar; [- development, activity] interromper-se.

halter [ˈhɔːltəʳ] n [for horse] cabresto m.

halterneck [ˈhɔːltənek] adj: ~ **dress** vestido m de frente-única.

halting [ˈhɔːltɪŋ] adj vacilante.

halve [UK hɑːv, US hæv] vt - **1.** [reduce by half] reduzir à metade - **2.** [divide] partir ao meio.

halves [UK hɑːvz, US hævz] pl ⊳ half.

ham [hæm] (pt & pp -med, cont -ming) <> n - **1.** [meat] presunto m - **2.** pej [actor] canastrão m - **3.**

[radio fanatic]: **(radio)** ~ radioamador m, -ra f. <> comp de presunto. <> vt: **to** ~ **it up** THEATRE exagerar na atuação.

Hamburg [ˈhæmbɜːg] n Hamburgo.

hamburger [ˈhæmbɜːgəʳ] n - **1.** [burger] hambúrguer m - **2.** US [mince] carne f moída.

ham-fisted [-ˈfɪstɪd] adj desajeitado(da).

hamlet [ˈhæmlɪt] n aldeia f.

hammer [ˈhæməʳ] <> n [tool] martelo m. <> vt - **1.** [with tool] martelar - **2.** [with fist] bater em - **3.** inf fig [fact, order]: **to** ~ **sthg into sb** meter algo na cabeça de alguém - **4.** inf fig [defeat] dar uma surra em. <> vi - **1.** [with tool] martelar - **2.** [with fist]: **to** ~ **(on sthg)** bater com insistência (em algo) - **3.** phr: **to** ~ **away at sthg** fig [task] trabalhar com afinco em algo.

→ **hammer into** vt sep: **to** ~ **sthg into sb** fig meter algo na cabeça de alguém.

→ **hammer out** <> vt fus [draw up] alcançar com muito esforço. <> vt sep [with tool] malhar.

hammock [ˈhæmək] n rede f de dormir.

hamper [ˈhæmpəʳ] <> n - **1.** [for picnic] cesta f - **2.** US [for laundry] cesto m de roupa. <> vt [impede] dificultar.

hamster [ˈhæmstəʳ] n hamster m.

hamstring [ˈhæmstrɪŋ] (pt & pp -strung [-strʌŋ]) <> n ANAT tendão m do jarrete. <> vt fig [thwart] impedir, dificultar.

hand [hænd] <> n - **1.** [part of body] mão f; **to hold** ~s dar as mãos; **by** ~ à mão; ~ **in** ~ [people] de mãos dadas; **with bare** ~s com suas próprias mãos; **at the** ~s **of** nas mãos de; ~s **up!** mãos ao alto!; **to change** ~s trocar de mãos; **to force sb's** ~ forçar alguém a agir; **to get** OR **lay one's** ~s **on sb** colocar OR pôr as mãos em alguém; **to get** OR **lay one's** ~s **on sthg** colocar OR pôr as mãos em algo; **to give sb a free** ~ dar carta branca a alguém; **to go** ~ **in** ~ [things] andar de mãos dadas; **to have one's** ~s **full** estar muito atarefado(da); **to try one's** ~ **at sthg** tentar fazer algo; **to wait on sb** ~ **and foot** dar tudo de bandeja para alguém; **to wash one's** ~s **of sthg** lavar as mãos sobre algo - **2.** [help] mão f; **to give** OR **lend sb a** ~ **(with sthg)** dar uma mão para alguém (em algo) - **3.** [control, management] mão f; **in the** ~s **of** nas mãos de; **to take sb in** ~ controlar alguém - **4.** [influence] dedo m; **to have a** ~ **in sthg/in doing sthg** interferir em algo/ao se fazer algo - **5.** [worker - on farm] peão m, -ona f; [- on ship] tripulante mf - **6.** [of clock, watch] ponteiro m - **7.** [handwriting] caligrafia f - **8.** [of cards] mão f; **I overplayed my** ~ fig superestimei minha situação - **9.** inf [applause] palmas fpl. <> vt: **to** ~ **sthg to sb, to** ~ **sb sthg** entregar algo a alguém.

→ **(close) at hand** adv próximo.

→ **in hand** adv - **1.** [time, money]: **to have sthg in** ~ ter algo sobrando - **2.** [problem, situation]: **to have sb/sthg in** ~ ter alguém/algo sob controle.

→ **on hand** adv em prontidão.

→ **on the one hand** adv por um lado.

→ **on the other hand** adv por outro lado.

→ **out of hand** <> adj [situation]: **to get out of** ~ sair de controle. <> adv [completely] completamente.

→ **to hand** adv à mão.

hand down *vt sep* [to next generation] legar.

hand in *vt sep* entregar.

hand on *vt sep* passar adiante.

hand out *vt sep* distribuir.

hand over ◇ *vt sep* **-1.** [baton, money] entregar **- 2.** [responsibility, power] transferir, ceder **- 3.** TELEC passar a ligação. ◇ *vi* [government minister, chairman] transferir; **to ~ over to sb** transferir para alguém.

handbag ['hændbæg] *n* bolsa *f*.

handball ['hændbɔːl] *n (U)* [game] handebol *m*.

handbill ['hændbɪl] *n* panfleto *m*.

handbook ['hændbʊk] *n* manual *m*.

handbrake ['hændbreɪk] *n* freio *m* de mão.

handclap ['hændklæp] *n*: **slow ~** aplauso lento e ritmado em forma de protesto.

handcrafted ['hænd,krɑːftɪd] *adj* artesanal.

handcuff ['hændkʌf] *vt* algemar.

handcuffs ['hændkʌfs] *npl* algemas *fpl*.

handful ['hændfʊl] *n* **-1.** *lit & fig* punhado *m* **- 2.** *inf* [difficult person, animal]**: to be a ~** ser um demônio.

handgun ['hændgʌn] *n* arma *f* de mão.

handheld PC ['hændheld-] *n* computador *m* de bolso, handheld *m*.

handicap ['hændɪkæp] *(pt & pp* **-ped,** *cont* **-ping)** ◇ *n* **- 1.** [physical or mental disability] deficiência *f* **- 2.** *fig* [disadvantage] obstáculo *m* **- 3.** SPORT handicap *m*. ◇ *vt* [hinder] estorvar, atrapalhar.

handicapped ['hændɪkæpt] ◇ *adj* [physically or mentally disabled] deficiente. ◇ *npl*: **the ~ os** deficientes.

handicraft ['hændɪkrɑːft] *n* [skill] artesanato *m*.

handiwork ['hændɪwɜːk] *n (U)* [work produced by o.s.] trabalho *m* manual.

handkerchief ['hæŋkətʃɪf] *(pl* **-chiefs** OR **-chieves** [-tʃiːvz]) *n* lenço *m*.

handle ['hændl] ◇ *n* **- 1.** [for opening and closing - of window] trinco *m*; [- of door] maçaneta *f* **- 2.** [for holding] cabo *m* **- 3.** [for carrying] alça *f*; **to fly off the ~** perder a cabeça. ◇ *vt* **- 1.** [with hands] manusear **- 2.** [control, operate - car] guiar; [- ship] comandar; [- gun] manejar; [- words] articular **- 3.** [manage, process] manejar **- 4.** [cope with] tratar de. ◇ *vi* **- 1.** governar **- 2.** [ship] comandar **- 3.** [car] guiar.

handlebars ['hændlbɑːz] *npl* guidom *m*.

handler ['hændlə^r] *n* **- 1.** [of animal] treinador *m*, -ra *f* **- 2.** [of luggage]**: (baggage) ~** carregador *m*, -ra *f* (de bagagem) **- 3.** [of stolen goods] receptor *m*, -ra *f*.

handling charges ['hændlɪŋ-] *npl* [at bank] taxas *fpl* de manutenção.

hand lotion *n* creme *m* para as mãos.

hand luggage *n* UK bagagem *f* de mão.

handmade [,hænd'meɪd] *adj* feito(ta) à mão.

hand-me-downs *npl* *inf* roupas *fpl* usadas.

handout ['hændaʊt] *n* **- 1.** [gift] donativo *m* **- 2.** [leaflet] folheto *m* informativo **- 3.** [for lecture, discussion] polígrafo *m*.

handover ['hændəʊvə^r] *n* transferência *f*.

handpicked [,hænd'pɪkt] *adj* [people] escolhido(da) a dedo.

handrail ['hændreɪl] *n* corrimão *m*.

handset ['hændset] *n* TELEC fone *m* (do telefone).

handshake ['hændʃeɪk] *n* aperto *m* de mão.

hands-off *adj* sem inteferência.

handsome ['hænsəm] *adj* **- 1.** [man] bonito(ta) **- 2.** *literary* [woman] bela, bonita **- 3.** [reward, profit] considerável.

handsomely ['hænsəmlɪ] *adv* [generously] generosamente.

hands-on *adj* [training, experience] prático(ca).

handstand ['hændstænd] *n*: **to do a ~** plantar bananeira.

hand-to-mouth *adj* precário(ria).

hand to mouth *adv* precariamente.

hand towel *n* toalha *f* de mão.

handwriting ['hænd,raɪtɪŋ] *n* letra *f*, caligrafia *f*.

handwritten ['hænd,rɪtn] *adj* escrito(ta) à mão.

handy ['hændɪ] *(compar* **-ier,** *superl* **-iest)** *adj* *inf* **- 1.** [useful] prático(ca); **to come in ~** vir a calhar **- 2.** [skilful] hábil **- 3.** [near] à mão; **to keep sthg ~** manter algo à mão.

handyman ['hændɪmæn] *(pl* **-men** [-menl)] *n* faz-tudo *mf*.

hang [hæŋ] *(pt & pp sense 1* **hung,** *pt & pp sense 2* **hung** OR **hanged)** ◇ *vt* **- 1.** [suspend] pendurar **- 2.** [execute] enforcar. ◇ *vi* **- 1.** [be suspended] estar suspenso(sa) **- 2.** [be executed] ser enforcado(da). ◇ *n*: **to get the ~ of sthg** *inf* pegar o jeito de algo.

hang about, hang around *vi* **- 1.** [loiter] demorar-se **- 2.** [wait] rondar.

hang down *vi* pender.

hang on ◇ *vt fus* [depend on] depender de. ◇ *vi* **- 1.** [keep hold]**: to ~ on (to sb/sthg)** segurar-se (em alguém/algo) **- 2.** *inf* [continue waiting] aguardar **- 3.** [persevere] resistir, agüentar.

hang onto *vt fus* **- 1.** [keep hold of] segurar-se a **- 2.** [keep] manter.

hang out ◇ *vt sep* [washing] estender. ◇ *vi inf* [spend time] passar um tempo, frequentar.

hang round *vi* = **hang about.**

hang together *vi* [alibi, argument] ser consistente.

hang up ◇ *vt sep* [suspend] pendurar. ◇ *vi* [on telephone] desligar.

hang up on *vt fus* TELEC desligar; **he hung up on me** ele desligou o telefone na minha cara.

hangar ['hæŋə^r] *n* hangar *m*.

hangdog ['hæŋdɒg] *adj* envergonhado(da).

hanger ['hæŋə^r] *n* [coat hanger] cabide *m*.

hanger-on *(pl* **hangers-on)** *n* bajulador *m*, -ra *f*, aproveitador *m*, -ra *f*.

hang glider *n* [apparatus] asa-delta *f*.

hang gliding *n (U)* vôo *m* livre (com asa delta).

hanging ['hæŋɪŋ] *n* **- 1.** *(U)* [form of punishment] forca *f* **- 2.** [execution] enforcamento *m* **- 3.** [drapery] tapeçaria *f* (para parede).

hangman ['hæŋmən] *(pl* **-men** [-mən]) *n* carrasco *m*, -ca *f*.

hangover ['hæŋ,əʊvə^r] *n* **- 1.** [from drinking] ressaca *f*; **to have a ~** estar de ressaca **- 2.** [from past]**: ~ (from sthg)** vestígio *m* (de algo).

hang-up *n inf* PSYCH complexo *m*.

hank *n* **- 1.** [of wool] novelo *m* **- 2.** [of rope, wire] meada *m*.

hanker ['hæŋkə^r] **hanker after, hanker for** *vt fus* ansiar por, desejar ardentemente.

hankering ['hæŋkərɪŋ] *n*: ~ **after** OR **for** anseio *m* por.

hankie, hanky ['hæŋkɪ] (*pl* -**ies**) (*abbr of* **handkerchief**) *n inf* lencinho *m*.

hanky-panky *n inf* [sexual behaviour] sem-vergonhice *f*.

Hanoi [hæ'nɔɪ] *n* Hanói.

Hansard ['hænsɑːd] *n atas oficiais dos debates realizados no parlamento britânico*, ≃ Diário Oficial.

haphazard [,hæp'hæzəd] *adj* caótico(ca), desordenado(da).

haphazardly [,hæp'hæzədlɪ] *adv* desordenadamente, de qualquer maneira.

hapless ['hæplɪs] *adj literary* desafortunado(da).

happen ['hæpən] *vi* -**1.** [occur] acontecer; **to** ~ **to sb** acontecer com alguém -**2.** [chance]: **I** ~**ed to see him yesterday** por acaso eu o vi ontem; **do you** ~ **to have a pen on you?** você não teria por acaso uma caneta?; **as it** ~**s** por acaso.

happening ['hæpənɪŋ] *n* [occurrence] acontecimento *m*.

happily ['hæpɪlɪ] *adv* -**1.** [contentedly]: **to be** ~ **doing sthg** fazer algo alegremente -**2.** [fortunately] felizmente -**3.** [willingly] com satisfação.

happiness ['hæpɪnɪs] *n* (U) felicidade *f*.

happy ['hæpɪ] (*compar* -**ier**, *superl* -**iest**) *adj* -**1.** [contented] feliz, contente -**2.** [causing contentment] feliz; **Happy Christmas/New Year/Birthday!** Feliz Natal/Ano Novo/Aniversário!; **to be** ~ **with** OR **about sthg** estar feliz com algo; **to be** ~ **to do sthg** estar muito disposto(ta) a fazer algo; **I'd be** ~ **to do it** eu faria isso com muito gosto.

happy event *n* nascimento *m*; **when's the** ~ **event** quando nasce a criança?

happy-go-lucky *adj* despreocupado(da).

happy hour *n inf* happy hour *f*.

happy medium *n* meio-termo *m*.

harangue [hə'ræŋ] <> *n* arenga *f*, ladainha *f*. <> *vt* arengar.

Harare [hə'rɑːrɪ] *n* Harare.

harass ['hærəs] *vt* [pester - with questions, problems] atormentar; [- sexually] molestar.

harassed ['hærəst] *adj* [stressed] tenso(sa).

harassment ['hærəsmənt] *n* -**1.** [persecution] perseguição *f* -**2.** [sexual] assédio *m*.

harbinger ['hɑːbɪndʒəʳ] *n literary* precursor *m*, -ra *f*.

harbour UK, **harbor** US ['hɑːbəʳ] <> *n* porto *m*. <> *vt* -**1.** [feeling] abrigar -**2.** [person] dar refúgio a.

harbour master *n* capitão *m*, -tã *f* do porto.

hard [hɑːd] <> *adj* -**1.** [very firm, not soft] duro(ra) -**2.** [difficult] difícil -**3.** [strenuous, stressful] duro(ra), pesado(da) -**4.** [forceful] forte -**5.** [harsh, unkind] ríspido(da); **to be** ~ **on sb/sthg** ser duro com alguém/algo -**6.** [winter, frost] rigoroso(sa) -**7.** [water] duro(ra) -**8.** [fact, news] concreto(ta) -**9.** UK POL [extreme]: ~ **left/right** extrema esquerda/direita. <> *adv* -**1.** [strenuously] muito, duro -**2.** [forcefully] com força -**3.** [rain, snow] intensamente -**4.** *phr*: **to be** ~ **pushed** OR **put** OR **pressed to do sthg** ver-se em apuros para fazer algo; **to feel** ~ **done by** sentir-se injustiçado(da) por.

hard-and-fast *adj* rígido(da).

hardback ['hɑːbæk] <> *adj* de capa dura. <> *n* [book] edição *f* de capa dura.

hard-bitten *adj* duro(ra), inflexível.

hardboard ['hɑːdbɔːd] *n* (U) madeira *f* compensada.

hard-boiled *adj* -**1.** [egg] cozido(da) -**2.** [person] impassível.

hard cash *n* (U) dinheiro *m* vivo.

hard cider *n* US sidra *f*.

hard copy *n* COMPUT cópia *f* impressa.

hard-core *adj* [pornography] explícito(ta).

➥ **hard core** *n* [of group] núcleo *m*.

hard court *n* quadra *f* rápida.

hard currency *n* moeda *f* forte.

hard disk *n* disco *m* rígido.

hard drugs *npl* drogas *fpl* pesadas.

harden ['hɑːdn] <> *vt* -**1.** [steel, arteries] endurecer -**2.** *fig* [person] endurecer -**3.** [attitude, ideas, opinion] fortalecer. <> *vi* -**1.** [glue, concrete, arteries] endurecer, endurecer-se -**2.** *fig* [person] endurecer-se -**3.** [attitude, ideas, opinion] fortalecer-se.

hardened ['hɑːdnd] *adj* -**1.** [steel, arteries] endurecido(da) -**2.** [criminal] habitual -**3.** [accustomed]: ~ **to sthg** acostumado(da) a algo.

hardening ['hɑːdnɪŋ] *n* -**1.** [of steel, arteries] endurecimento *m* -**2.** [of attitude, ideas, opinion] fortalecimento *m*.

hard hat *n* [for protection] capacete *m*.

hard-headed [-'hedɪd] *adj* realista.

hard-hearted [-'hɑːtɪd] *adj* insensível; **a** ~ **person** uma pessoa sem coração.

hard-hitting [-'hɪtɪŋ] *adj* chocante.

hard labour *n* (U) trabalhos *mpl* forçados.

hard line *n*: **to take a** ~ **on sthg** manter a linha dura em relação a algo.

➥ **hard-line** *adj* linha-dura.

➥ **hard lines** *npl* UK: **hard lines!** que azar!

hard-liner *n* linha-dura *mf*.

hardly ['hɑːdlɪ] *adv* -**1.** [scarcely, not really] dificilmente; ~ **ever/anything** quase nunca/nada; **I can** ~ **move/wait** mal posso me mover/esperar -**2.** [only just] apenas.

hardness ['hɑːdnɪs] *n* -**1.** [firmness, also of water] dureza *f* -**2.** [difficulty] dificuldade *f* -**3.** [of heart, person] insensibilidade *f*.

hard-nosed [-'nəʊzd] *adj* obstinado(da), contundente.

hard return *n* COMPUT retorno *m* de hardware.

hard sell *n* venda *f* agressiva.

hardship ['hɑːdʃɪp] *n* -**1.** (U) [difficult conditions] privações *fpl* -**2.** [difficult circumstance] dificuldade *f*.

hard shoulder *n* UK AUT acostamento *m*.

hard up *adj inf* desprovido(da); ~ **for sthg** desprovido(da) de algo.

hardware ['hɑːdweəʳ] *n* -**1.** [tools, equipment] ferragens *fpl* -**2.** COMPUT hardware *m*.

hardware shop *n* ferragem *f*.

hardwearing [,hɑːd'weərɪŋ] *adj* UK resistente.

hardwood ['hɑːdwʊd] *n* (U) madeira *f* de lei.

hardworking [,hɑːd'wɜːkɪŋ] *adj* trabalhador(ra).

hardy ['hɑːdɪ] (*compar* -**ier**, *superl* -**iest**) *adj* -**1.** [person, animal] forte, robusto(ta) -**2.** [plant] resistente.

hare [heə[r]] <> *n* lebre *f.* <> *vi UK inf:* to ~ off
correr a toda.
harebell *n* campainha *f.*
harebrained ['heə,breɪnd] *adj inf* tolo(la).
harelip [,heə'lɪp] *n* lábio *m* leporino.
harem [UK haːˈriːm, US ˈhærəm] *n* harém *m.*
haricot (bean) ['hærɪkəʊ-] *n* feijão *m.*
hark [haːk] ◆ **hark back** *vi:* to ~ back to sthg
voltar a algo.
harlequin ['haːləkwɪn] <> *n* arlequim *m.* <>
comp arlequinal, de arlequim.
Harley Street ['haːlɪ-] *n* rua no centro de
Londres famosa pelos seus médicos especialistas.
harm [haːm] <> *n* [physical] mal *m*; [psychological]
dano *m*; **to do** ~ **to sb/sthg**, **to do sb/sthg** ~
fazer mal a alguém/algo; **to mean no** ~ não ter
má intenção; **there's no** ~ **in it** não há mal
nenhum nisso; **to be out of** ~'s **way** estar a salvo;
to come to no ~ [person] chegar são e salvo,
chegar sã e salva; [thing] ficar a salvo. <> *vt* [phy-
sically] ferir; [psychologically] danificar, prejudicar.
harmful ['haːmfʊl] *adj* [physically] nocivo(va) ; [psy-
chologically] prejudicial.
harmless ['haːmlɪs] *adj* inofensivo(va).
harmlessly ['haːmlɪslɪ] *adv* [without causing damage]
sem causar dano.
harmonic [haːˈmɒnɪk] *adj* harmônico(ca).
harmonica [haːˈmɒnɪkə] *n* gaita-de-boca *f.*
harmonious [haːˈməʊnjəs] *adj* harmonioso(sa).
harmonium [haːˈməʊnjəm] (*pl* -s) *n* harmônio *m.*
harmonize, -ise ['haːmənaɪz] <> *vt* harmonizar.
<> *vi* harmonizar; **to** ~ **with sthg** harmonizar-se
com algo.
harmony ['haːmənɪ] (*pl* -ies) *n* harmonia *f*; **in** ~
with sthg em harmonia com algo.
harness ['haːnɪs] <> *n* -**1.** [for horse] arreio *m* -**2.**
[for person, child] andador *m.* <> *vt* -**1.** [horse] arrear,
pôr arreios em -**2.** [energy, solar power] aproveitar.
harp [haːp] *n* MUS harpa *f.*
◆ **harp on** *vi:* to ~ on (about sthg) bater
sempre na mesma tecla (sobre algo).
harpist ['haːpɪst] *n* harpista *mf.*
harpoon [haːˈpuːn] *n* arpão *m.* <> *vt* arpoar.
harpsichord ['haːpsɪkɔːd] *n* clavicórdio *m.*
harrowing ['hærəʊɪŋ] *adj* angustiante.
harry ['hærɪ] (*pt* & *pp* -**ied**) *vt* -**1.** [badger] importunar; **to** ~ **sb for sthg** importunar alguém para
obter algo -**2.** MIL [attack] saltear.
harsh [haːʃ] *adj* -**1.** [cruel, severe] severo(ra), duro(ra)
-**2.** [conditions, weather] duro(ra) -**3.** [cry, voice] áspe-
ro(ra) -**4.** [colour, contrast, light] forte -**5.** [landscape]
desolado(da) -**6.** [taste] azedo(da).
harshly ['haːʃlɪ] *adv* -**1.** [treat, punish, judge] severamente, duramente -**2.** [cry, shout] asperamente
-**3.** [shine] ofuscantemente.
harshness ['haːʃnɪs] *n* (U) -**1.** [of person, treatment]
severidade *f*, dureza *f* -**2.** [of climate] rigor *m* -**3.** [of
cry, voice] aspereza *f* -**4.** [of colour, contrast, light] forte
constraste *m* -**5.** [of landscape] desolação *f.*
harvest ['haːvɪst] <> *n* colheita *f.* <> *vt* [crops]
colher.
harvest festival *n* festividade religiosa que

celebra o início da colheita.
has [weak form həz, strong form hæz] *vb* ▷ **have**.
has-been *n inf pej:* that man is a ~ aquele
homem já era.
hash [hæʃ] *n* -**1.** (U) [meat] picadinho *m* -**2.** *inf* [mess]:
to make a ~ **of sthg** fazer uma confusão em algo
-**3.** *drugs sl* [hashish] haxixe *m.*
◆ **hash up** *vt sep UK inf* [make a mess of] fazer
uma confusão em.
hash browns *npl US* prato feito com batatas
esmagadas e fritas.
hashish ['hæʃiːʃ] *n* (U) haxixe *m.*
hasn't ['hæznt] = has not.
hassle ['hæsl] *inf* <> *n* [annoyance] amolação *f.* <>
vt amolar, aborrecer.
haste [heɪst] *n* (U) -**1.** [rush] pressa *f*; **to do sthg in** ~
fazer algo às pressas -**2.** [speed] rapidez *f*; **to**
make ~ *dated* apressar-se.
hasten ['heɪsn] <> *vt* acelerar. <> *vi* apressar-se;
I ~ **to add that ...** apresso-me a acrescentar que ...
hastily ['heɪstɪlɪ] *adv* -**1.** [rashly] apressadamente -**2.**
[quickly] rapidamente, às pressas.
hasty ['heɪstɪ] (*compar* -**ier**, *superl* -**iest**) *adj* -**1.** [rash]
precipitado(da) -**2.** [quick] breve.
hat [hæt] *n* chapéu *m*; **keep it under your** ~
mantenha isso entre nós; **to be talking through**
one's ~ só dizer besteira; **that's old** ~ isso é mais
velho que andar para frente.
hatbox ['hæt,bɒks] *n* chapeleira *f.*
hatch [hætʃ] <> *vt* -**1.** [chick] incubar -**2.** [egg]
chocar -**3.** *fig* [scheme, plot] conceber, idealizar.
<> *vi* -**1.** [chick] sair do ovo -**2.** [egg] chocar. <> *n*
[for serving food] portinhola *f*, janela *f* de comunicação.
hatchback ['hætʃ,bæk] *n* carro *m* com porta
traseira.
hatchet ['hætʃɪt] *n* machadinha *f*; **to bury the** ~
fazer as pazes.
hatchet job *n inf* crítica *f* destrutiva.
hatchway ['hætʃ,weɪ] *n* escotilha *f.*
hate [heɪt] <> *n* -**1.** [emotion] ódio *m* -**2.** [person, thing
hated] aversão *f.* <> *vt* [dislike] detestar, odiar; **to** ~
doing sthg odiar fazer algo.
hateful ['heɪtfʊl] *adj* detestável.
hatred ['heɪtrɪd] *n* (U) ódio *m.*
hat trick *n* SPORT série de três pontos marcados
pelo mesmo jogador na mesma partida.
haughty ['hɔːtɪ] (*compar* -**ier**, *superl* -**iest**) *adj* arrogante.
haul [hɔːl] <> *n* -**1.** [of drugs, stolen goods] carregamento *m* -**2.** [distance]: **long** ~ longo trajeto *m.* <>
vt -**1.** [pull] arrastar, puxar -**2.** [by lorry] transportar.
haulage ['hɔːlɪdʒ] *n* -**1.** [gen] transporte *m* -**2.** [cost]
gasto *m* com transporte.
haulage contractor *n* transportadora *f.*
haulier UK ['hɔːlɪə[r]], **hauler** US ['hɔːlər] *n* -**1.** [busi-
ness] transportadora *f* -**2.** [person] transportador
m, -ra *f.*
haunch [hɔːntʃ] *n* -**1.** [of person] quadril *m* -**2.** [of ani-
mal] lombo *m.*
haunt [hɔːnt] <> *n* [place] lugar *m* preferido. <> *vt*
-**1.** [subj: ghost] assombrar -**2.** [subj: memory, fear,
problem] perseguir.

haunted ['hɔːntɪd] adj -1. [house, castle] assombrado(da) - 2. [look] espantado(da).

haunting ['hɔːntɪŋ] adj inesquecível, obcecante.

Havana [hə'vænə] n Havana; **in** ~ em Havana.

have [hæv] (pt & pp **had**) aux vb -1. [to form perfect tenses]: **I** ~ **finished** acabei; ~ **you been there? - no, I** ~ **n't** você já esteve lá? - não; **they hadn't seen it** não o tinham visto; **we had already left** nós já tínhamos saído - 2. [must]: **to** ~ **(got) to do sthg** ter de fazer algo; **do you** ~ **to pay?** é preciso pagar? ◇ vt -1. [possess]: **to** ~ **(got) ter; do you** ~ OR ~ **you got a double room?** você tem um quarto de casal?; **she's got brown hair** ela tem o cabelo castanho - 2. [experience] ter; **to** ~ **a cold** estar resfriado; **to** ~ **a great time** divertir-se a valer - 3. [replacing other verbs] ter; **to** ~ **breakfast** tomar o café da manhã; **to** ~ **dinner** jantar; **to** ~ **lunch** almoçar; **to** ~ **a bath** tomar banho; **to** ~ **a drink** tomar qualquer coisa, tomar um drinque; **to** ~ **a shower** tomar um banho; **to** ~ **a swim** nadar - 4. [feel] ter; **I** ~ **no doubt about it** não tenho dúvida alguma OR nenhuma sobre isso - 5. [cause to be]: **to** ~ **sthg done** mandar fazer algo; **to** ~ **one's hair cut** cortar o cabelo - 6. [be treated in a certain way]: **I've had my wallet stolen** roubaram a minha carteira.

haven ['heɪvn] n [refuge] abrigo m.

haven't ['hævnt] = have not.

haversack ['hævəsæk] n dated mochila f.

havoc ['hævək] n (U) destruição f, estragos mpl; **to play** ~ **with sthg** causar estragos em algo.

Hawaii [hə'waɪiː] n Havaí; **in** ~ no Havaí.

Hawaiian [hə'waɪjən] ◇ adj havaiano(na). ◇ n havaiano m, -na f.

hawk [hɔːk] ◇ n -1. [bird] falcão m; **to watch sb like a** ~ observar alguém com olhos de lince - 2. POL não-pacifista m. ◇ vt [in the street] vender de forma ambulante ; [door to door] vender (de porta em porta).

hawker ['hɔːkəʳ] n -1. [street vendor] camelô mf - 2. [door-to-door] vendedor m, -ra f ambulante.

hawthorn ['hɔːθɔːn] n pilriteiro m.

hay [heɪ] n (U) feno m; **to make** ~ **while the sun shines** aproveitar uma oportunidade.

hay fever n (U) febre f do feno.

haymaking n (U) preparo m do feno.

haystack ['heɪstæk] n feixe m de feno.

haywire ['heɪwaɪəʳ] adj inf: **to go** ~ ficar louco (ca).

hazard ['hæzəd] ◇ n [danger] perigo m. ◇ vt -1. [life, reputation] arriscar, pôr em perigo - 2. [guess, suggestion] atrever-se a fazer.

hazardous ['hæzədəs] adj perigoso(sa), arriscado(-da).

hazard warning lights npl UK pisca-alerta m.

haze [heɪz] n -1. [mist] neblina f - 2. [state of confusion] confusão f mental.

hazel ['heɪzl] ◇ adj castanho-claro. ◇ n [tree] aveleira f.

hazelnut ['heɪzl,nʌt] n avelã f.

hazy ['heɪzɪ] (compar -ier, superl -iest) adj -1. [misty] nebuloso(sa) - 2. [vague, confused - ideas, memory] vago(ga); [- person, facts] confuso(sa).

H-bomb n bomba f H.

h & c (abbr of hot and cold (water)) (água) q e f.

HCA (abbr of health care assistant) n auxiliar mf de enfermagem.

he [hiː] ◇ pers pron ele; **he's tall** ele é alto.

HE -1. (abbr of high explosive) altamente explosivo(va). - 2. (abbr of His (or Her) Excellency) S.Exª.

head [hed] ◇ n -1. [gen] cabeça f; **a** OR **per** ~ por pessoa, por cabeça; **off the top of one's** ~ de improviso; **to bite** OR **snap sb's** ~ **off** xingar/insultar alguém sem motivos; **to laugh/sing/shout one's** ~ **off** rir/cantar/gritar a plenos pulmões; **to be banging one's** ~ **against a brick wall** dar murro em ponta de faca; **I can't make** ~ **nor tail of it** isto não tem pé nem cabeça; **on your own** ~ **be it** que seja por sua própria conta e risco, você que arque com as conseqüências; **to have a** ~ **for heights** não ter medo de altura; **to be off one's** ~ UK, **to be out of one's** ~ US estar fora de seu juízo; **we put our** ~**s together** tratamos de resolver juntos; **to go to one's** ~ subir à cabeça; **to keep one's** ~ manter a cabeça no lugar; **to lose one's** ~ perder a cabeça; **to be soft in the** ~ ter o miolo mole - 2. [of table, bed, river] cabeceira f - 3. [of page] cabeçalho m - 4. [of stairs] topo m - 5. [of queue, procession] frente f - 6. [of flower] corola f - 7. [head teacher] diretor m, -ra f - 8. ELEC cabeçote m - 9. phr: **to come to a** ~ chegar a um ponto crítico. ◇ vt -1. [be at front of, top of] encabeçar - 2. [be in charge of] comandar - 3. FTBL cabecear. ◇ vi dirigir-se, ir; **we gave up and** ~**ed home** nós desistimos e fomos para casa; **the ship was** ~**ing due north** o navio rumava para o norte.

➤ **heads** npl [on coin] cara f; ~**s or tails?** cara ou coroa?

➤ **head for** vt fus -1. [place] dirigir-se para - 2. fig [trouble, disaster] encaminhar-se para.

➤ **head off** ◇ vt sep -1. [intercept] deter - 2. [forestall] antecipar-se a. ◇ vi [leave] esquivar-se.

headache ['hedeɪk] n dor f de cabeça; **to have a** ~ ter uma dor de cabeça.

headband ['hedbænd] n faixa f (para a cabeça).

headboard ['hed,bɔːd] n cabeceira f.

head boy n UK [at school] representante m discente.

head cold n resfriado m.

head count n contagem f (das pessoas presentes).

headdress ['hed,dres] n touca f.

header ['hedəʳ] n -1. FTBL cabeçada f - 2. [at top of page] cabeçalho m.

headfirst [,hed'fɜːst] adv de cabeça.

headgear ['hed,gɪəʳ] n proteção f para a cabeça.

head girl n UK [in school] representante f discente.

headhunt ['hedhʌnt] vt [recruit] contratar (novos talentos).

headhunter ['hed,hʌntəʳ] n [recruiter] caça-talentos mf inv.

heading ['hedɪŋ] n título m, cabeçalho m.

headlamp ['hedlæmp] n UK farol m (de carro).

headland ['hedlənd] n promontório m.

headlight ['hedlaɪt] n farol m (de carro).

headline ['hedlaɪn] n -1. [in newspaper] manchete f - 2. [of news broadcast] notícia f principal.

headlong ['hedlɒŋ] ◇ *adv* **-1.** [at great speed] apressadamente **-2.** [impetuously] precipitadamente **-3.** [dive, fall] abruptamente. ◇ *adj* [impetuous] precipitado(da).

headmaster [ˌhed'mɑːstə^r] *n* diretor *m (de colégio)*.

headmistress [ˌhed'mɪstrɪs] *n* diretora *f (de colégio)*.

head office *n* sede *f*.

head-on ◇ *adj* frontal, de frente. ◇ *adv* de frente.

headphones ['hedfəʊnz] *npl* fones *mpl* de ouvido.

headquarters [ˌhed'kwɔːtəz] *npl* **-1.** FIN sede *f*, matriz *f* **-2.** MIL quartel-general *m*.

headrest ['hedrest] *n* apoio *m* para a cabeça.

headroom ['hedrʊm] *n* (U) **-1.** [in car] espaço *m* (entre a cabeça e o teto) **-2.** [below bridge] altura *f* livre.

headscarf ['hedskɑːf] (*pl* **-scarves** [-skɑːvz] OR **-scarfs**) *n* lenço *m* (para a cabeça).

headset ['hedset] *n* fones *mpl* de ouvido com microfone.

headship ['hedʃɪp] *n* direção *f (de colégio)*.

head start *n* vantagem *f* inicial; ~ **on** OR **over sb** vantagem sobre alguém.

headstone ['hedstəʊn] *n* lápide *f*.

headstrong ['hedstrɒŋ] *adj* cabeça-dura, obstinado(da).

head teacher *n* diretor *m*, -ra *f* de colégio.

head waiter *n* maître *m*.

headway ['hedweɪ] *n*: **to make** ~ fazer progressos.

headwind ['hedwɪnd] *n* vento *m* contrário.

headword *n* [in dictionary, reference book] entrada *f*, verbete *m*.

heady ['hedɪ] (*compar* **-ier**, *superl* **-iest**) *adj* **-1.** [exciting] emocionante **-2.** [causing giddiness] inebriante, estonteante.

heal [hiːl] ◇ *vt* **-1.** [mend, cure - person] curar; [- wound] cicatrizar **-2.** *fig* [breach, division] cicatrizar. ◇ *vi* [be mended, cured] cicatrizar.

➡ **heal up** *vi* [be mended, cured] cicatrizar.

healing ['hiːlɪŋ] ◇ *adj* curativo(va). ◇ *n* (U) cura *f*.

health [helθ] *n* (U) **-1.** [condition of body] saúde *f*; **to be in good/poor** ~ estar bem/mal de saúde; **to drink (to) sb's** ~ brindar à saúde de alguém **-2.** *fig* [of country, organization] bom estado *m*.

health centre *n* centro *m* de saúde.

health-conscious *adj* preocupado(da) com a saúde.

health farm *n* spa *m*.

health food *n* alimentos *mpl* naturais.

health food shop *n* loja *f* de alimentos naturais.

health hazard *n* risco *m* à saúde.

health service *n* serviço *m* de saúde.

health visitor *n* UK enfermeiro *m* comunitário, enfermeira *f* comunitária.

healthy ['helθɪ] (*compar* **-ier**, *superl* **-iest**) *adj* **-1.** [gen] saudável **-2.** *fig* [thriving] saneado(da) **-3.** [substantial] substancial.

heap [hiːp] ◇ *n* monte *m*, pilha *f*; **in a** ~

amontoado(da). ◇ *vt* **-1.** [pile up] amontoar; **to** ~ **sthg on (to) sthg** amontoar algo sobre algo **-2.** *fig* [lavish]: **to** ~ **sthg on sb** cobrir alguém de algo.

➡ **heaps** *npl inf*: ~ **s of** montes OR pilhas de.

hear [hɪə^r] (*pt* & *pp* **heard** [hɜːd]) ◇ *vt* **-1.** [perceive] ouvir **-2.** [learn of] escutar; **to** ~ **(that)** ouvir dizer que **-3.** JUR [listen to] ver. ◇ *vi* **-1.** [perceive sound] ouvir **-2.** [know]: **to** ~ **about sthg** ouvir falar sobre algo **-3.** [receive news] ter notícias de; **to** ~ **from sb** ter notícias de alguém **-4.** *phr*: **I've never heard of him/it!** nunca ouvi falar dele/disto!; **I won't** ~ **of it!** não quero saber nada sobre isto!

➡ **hear out** *vt sep* escutar *(sem interromper)*.

hearing ['hɪərɪŋ] *n* **-1.** [sense] audição *f*; **hard of** ~ com problemas de audição; **in/within sb's** ~ ao alcance dos ouvidos de alguém **-2.** JUR [trial] audiência *f*, julgamento *m*; **to give sb a fair** ~ *fig* dar a alguém a oportunidade de falar.

hearing aid *n* aparelho *m* auditivo.

hearsay ['hɪəseɪ] *n* (U) rumor *m*, boato *m*.

hearse [hɜːs] *n* carro *m* funerário.

heart [hɑːt] *n* **-1.** [gen] coração *m*; **to have a** ~ **of gold** ter um coração de ouro; **his** ~ **isn't in it** ele não colocou o coração nisto; **it's a subject close to my** ~ é um assunto que me encanta; **from the** ~ de coração; **from the bottom of my** ~ do fundo do meu coração; **in one's** ~ **of** ~ **s** no fundo do coração; **to do sthg to one's** ~ **'s content** fazer algo até que se tenha vontade; **my** ~ **leapt/sank** meu coração pulou/entristeceu-se; **to break sb's** ~ partir o coração de alguém; **to set one's** ~ **on sthg/on doing sthg** colocar o coração em algo/ao fazer algo; **to take sthg to** ~ levar algo a sério **-2.** (U) [courage]: **to have the** ~ **to do sthg** ter coragem de fazer algo; **to lose** ~ perder o ímpeto **-3.** [of problem] centro *m* **-4.** [of cabbage, celery, lettuce] miolo *m*.

➡ **hearts** *npl* [playing cards] copas *fpl*; **the six of** ~ **s** o seis de copas.

➡ **at heart** *adv* de coração.

➡ **by heart** *adv* de cor.

heartache ['hɑːteɪk] *n* sofrimento *m*, angústia *f*.

heart attack *n* ataque *m* cardíaco.

heartbeat ['hɑːtbiːt] *n* pulsação *f*.

heartbreaking ['hɑːtˌbreɪkɪŋ] *adj* de partir o coração.

heartbroken ['hɑːtˌbrəʊkn] *adj* de coração partido.

heartburn ['hɑːtbɜːn] *n* (U) azia *f*.

heart disease *n* (U) doença *f* cardíaca.

heartening ['hɑːtnɪŋ] *adj* animador(ra).

heart failure *n* (U) parada *f* cardíaca.

heartfelt ['hɑːtfelt] *adj* sincero(ra), de todo coração.

hearth [hɑːθ] *n* **-1.** [of fireplace] base *f* **-2.** [fireplace] lareira *f*.

heartland ['hɑːtlænd] *n* área *f* central.

heartless ['hɑːtlɪs] *adj* desumano(na); ~ **person** pessoa sem coração.

heartrending ['hɑːtˌrendɪŋ] *adj* consternador(ra).

heart-searching *n* (U) exame *m* de consciência.

heartthrob ['hɑːtθrɒb] *n* galã *m*.

heart-to-heart ◇ *adj* franco(ca). ◇ *n* conversa *f* franca.

heart transplant n transplante m de coração.
heartwarming ['hɑ:t,wɔ:mɪŋ] adj enternecedor(-ra), gratificante.
hearty ['hɑ:tɪ] (compar -ier, superl -iest) adj -1. [loud, energetic] caloroso(sa) -2. [substantial - meal] farto(ta); [- appetite] bom (boa) -3. [strongly felt] profundo(da).
heat [hi:t] ⋄ n -1. (U) [gen] calor m -2. (U) [specific temperature] temperatura f -3. (U) [fire, source of heat] fogo m -4. (U) fig: in the ~ of the moment no calor do momento -5. [eliminating round] rodada f -6. ZOOL: on ~ UK, in ~ no cio. ⋄ vt esquentar.
➡ **heat up** ⋄ vt sep [make warm] esquentar. ⋄ vi [become warm] ficar quente, esquentar.
heated ['hi:tɪd] adj -1. [room, swimming pool] aquecido(da) -2. [argument, discussion, person] esquentado(-da).
heater ['hi:tə'] n aquecedor m.
heath [hi:θ] n [open place] charneca f.
heathen ['hi:ðn] ⋄ adj pagão(gã). ⋄ n pagão m, -gã f.
heather ['heðə'] n (U) urze f.
heating ['hi:tɪŋ] n (U) calefação f.
heat rash n brotoeja f (pelo calor).
heat-resistant adj refratário(ria), resistente ao calor.
heat-seeking [-,si:kɪŋ] adj detector(ra) de calor.
heatstroke ['hi:tstrəʊk] n (U) insolação f.
heat wave n onda f de calor.
heave [hi:v] ⋄ vt -1. [pull] puxar, arrastar ; [push] empurrar -2. inf [throw] atirar, arremessar -3. [give out]: to ~ a sigh dar um suspiro. ⋄ vi -1. [pull] puxar -2. [rise and fall - boat, shoulders] sacudir-se; [- waves] ondular; [- chest] arfar -3. [retch] embrulhar. ⋄ n -1. [pull] puxão m -2. [push] empurrão m.
heaven ['hevn] n -1. [Paradise] paraíso m; ~ (alone) knows! sabe Deus! -2. (U) [something delightful] paraíso m.
➡ **heavens** ⋄ npl: the ~s literary os céus. ⋄ excl: (good) ~s! céus!
heavenly ['hevnlɪ] adj -1. inf dated [delightful] divino(na) -2. literary [of the skies] celestial.
heavily ['hevɪlɪ] adv -1. [for emphasis - to rain, smoke, drink, tax] excessivamente; [- laden, booked, dependent] totalmente; [- in debt] seriamente; [- populated] densamente -2. [solidly] solidamente -3. [noisily, ponderously] pesadamente -4. [deeply] profundamente.
heaviness ['hevɪnɪs] n -1. [of object] peso m -2. [of sleep] profundidade f -3. [of movement] dureza f, intensidade f -4. [of mixture] densidade f -5. [of feeling] abatimento m.
heavy ['hevɪ] (compar -ier, superl -iest) adj -1. [gen] pesado(da); how ~ is it? quanto pesa? -2. [intense, deep] intenso(sa); to be a ~ sleeper ter o sono muito profundo -3. [in quantity] em grande número -4. [person - fat] gordo(da); [- solidly built] sólido(da) -5. [laden]: ~ with fruit literary carregado(da) de fruta -6. [ponderous - movement] brusco(ca); [- fall] feio (feia) -7. [oppressive] carregado(da) -8. [sad]: with a ~ heart com o coração partido -9. [excessive]: to be a ~ smoker/drinker fumar/beber em excesso; this car's ~ on petrol este carro consome muita gasolina -10. [grave, serious]

grande -11. [busy] cheio (cheia).
heavy cream n US nata f para enfeitar.
heavy-duty adj para grandes cargas/esforços; [material] resistente.
heavy goods vehicle n UK veículo m de carga pesada.
heavy-handed [-'hændɪd] adj [clumsy - tactics, policy, person] desastrado(da); [- compliment, treatment] grosseiro(ra).
heavy industry n indústria f pesada.
heavy metal n (U) MUS heavy-metal m.
heavyweight ['hevɪweɪt] ⋄ adj SPORT peso pesado. ⋄ n peso m pesado.
Hebrew ['hi:bru:] ⋄ adj hebraico(ca). ⋄ n -1. [person] hebraico m, -ca f -2. [language] hebraico m.
Hebrides ['hebrɪdi:z] npl: the ~ as Hébridas; in the ~ nas Hébridas.
heck [hek] excl: what/where/why the ~ ...? o que/onde/por que diabos ...?; a ~ of a lot of uma montanha de; a ~ of a nice guy um cara e tanto.
heckle ['hekl] ⋄ vt ficar interrompendo. ⋄ vi ficar interrompendo.
heckler ['heklə'] n pessoa que fica interrompendo (um orador, um comediante, um político etc.)
hectare ['hekteə'] n hectare m.
hectic ['hektɪk] adj muito agitado(da).
hector ['hektə'] ⋄ vt intimidar com bravatas. ⋄ vi bravatear.
he'd [hi:d] = he had, he would.
hedge [hedʒ] ⋄ n [shrub] cerca f viva. ⋄ vi [prevaricate] dar evasivas.
hedgehog ['hedʒhɒg] n porco-espinho m.
hedgerow ['hedʒrəʊ] n linha f de cerca viva.
hedonism ['hi:dənɪzml] n (U) hedonismo m.
hedonist ['hi:dənɪst] n hedonista mf.
heed [hi:d] ⋄ n: to pay ~ to sb prestar atenção em alguém; to take ~ of sthg levar algo em consideração. ⋄ vt fml ter em conta.
heedless ['hi:dlɪs] adj: to be ~ of sthg não fazer caso de algo.
heel [hi:l] n -1. [of foot] calcanhar m; to dig one's ~s in fincar o pé; to follow hard on the ~s (of sb/sthg) ficar na cola (de alguém/algo); to take to one's ~s dar no pé; to turn on one's ~ dar meia volta -2. [of shoe] salto m.
hefty ['heftɪ] (compar -ier, superl -iest) adj inf -1. [person] robusto(ta) -2. [salary, fee, fine] vultoso(sa), alto(ta).
heifer ['hefə'] n vitela f, novilha f.
height [haɪt] n -1. [gen] altura f; in ~ de altura; what ~ is it/are you? que altura tem isto/você tem?; to gain/lose ~ ganhar/perder altura -2. [zenith] apogeu m; the ~ of [fight, fame, tourist season] o auge de; [stupidity, ignorance, bad manners] o cúmulo de.
➡ **heights** npl -1. [limits] limites mpl -2. [high places] alto m; are you afraid of ~? você tem medo de altura?; the Golan Heights o Planalto do Golã.
heighten ['haɪtn] ⋄ vt intensificar. ⋄ vi intensificar-se.
heinous ['heɪnəs] adj fml hediondo(da).

heir [eə^r] *n* herdeiro *m*.
heir apparent (*pl* **heirs apparent**) *n* sucessor *m* direto.
heiress ['eəris] *n* herdeira *f*.
heirloom ['eəlu:m] *n* herança *f* de família.
heist [haist] *n inf* roubo *m*.
held [held] *pt* & *pp* ▷ **hold**.
helices ['helisi:z] *pl* ▷ **helix**.
helicopter ['helikɒptə^r] *n* hepicóptero *m*.
heliport ['helipɔ:t] *n* heliporto *m*.
helium ['hi:liəm] *n* (U) hélio *m*.
helix ['hi:liks] (*pl* **-es** OR **helices**) *n* [spiral] hélice *f*.
hell [hel] ◇ *n* **-1.** inferno *m* **-2.** *inf* [for emphasis]: **what/where/why the ~ ...?** o que/onde/por que diabos ...?; **it was one ~ of a mess** estava uma bagunça total; **he's a ~ of a nice guy** ele é um cara simpático e tanto; **like ~** como o diabo; **like ~ you will!** com os diabos que você vai!; **let's get the ~ out (of here!)** vamos cair fora daqui! **-3.** *phr*: **to ~ with ...!** *v inf* pro inferno com ...!; **all ~ broke loose** *inf* o mundo veio abaixo; **to do sthg for the ~ of it** *inf* fazer algo por gosto; **to give sb ~** *inf* [verbally] fazer alguém passar poucas e boas; **go to ~!** *v inf* vá para o inferno!; **to play ~ with sthg** *inf* infernizar algo. ◇ *excl inf* diabos!, droga!
he'll [hi:l] = **he will**.
hell-bent *adj*: **to be ~ on doing sthg** estar totalmente decidido(da) a fazer algo.
hellish ['heliʃ] *adj inf* infernal.
hello [hə'ləu] *excl* [greeting] olá!, oi!; [answering telephone, attracting attention] alô!
helm [helm] *n* **-1.** [of ship] leme *m*, timão *m* **-2.** *fig* [of company, organization] direção *f*; **at the ~** na direção.
helmet ['helmit] *n* capacete *m*.
helmsman ['helmzmən] (*pl* **-men** [-mən]) *n* NAUT timoneiro *m*, -ra *f*.
help [help] ◇ *n* **-1.** (U) [assistance] ajuda *f*; **to be of ~** ajudar; **with the ~ of sb/sthg** com a ajuda de alguém/algo **-2.** (U) [in an emergency] socorro *m* **-3.** [useful person or object]: **to be a ~** ser útil. ◇ *vt* **-1.** [gen] ajudar; **to ~ sb (to) do sthg** ajudar alguém a fazer algo; **to ~ sb with sthg** ajudar alguém em algo; **can I ~ you?** [in shop, at reception] pois não? **-2.** [avoid] evitar; **I can't ~ feeling sad** não posso evitar ficar triste; **I couldn't ~ laughing** eu não conseguia parar de rir **-3.** *phr*: **to ~ o.s. (to sthg)** servir-se (de algo). ◇ *vi* [gen] ajudar; **to ~ with sthg** ajudar em algo. ◇ *excl* socorro!
▶ **help out** ◇ *vt sep* dar uma mão para. ◇ *vi* dar uma mão.
helper ['helpə^r] *n* ajudante *mf*.
helpful ['helpful] *adj* **-1.** [willing to help] prestativo(va) **-2.** [useful] proveitoso(sa).
helping ['helpiŋ] *n* porção *f* (*de comida*); **would you like a second ~?** quer repetir?
helping hand *n*: **if you need a ~, just call** se precisar de uma mãozinha, é só chamar.
helpless ['helplis] *adj* indefeso(sa).
helplessly ['helplisli] *adv* **-1.** [uncontrollably] sem parar **-2.** [in a helpless manner] sem se poder fazer nada.
helpline ['helplain] *n* (linha *f* de) suporte *m*.

Helsinki ['helsiŋki] *n* Helsinque; **in ~** em Helsinque.
helter-skelter [,heltə'skeltə^r] *UK* ◇ *n* tobogã *m* gigante. ◇ *adv* desordenadamente.
hem [hem] (*pt* & *pp* **-med**, *cont* **-ming**) ◇ *n* bainha *f*. ◇ *vt* abainhar, fazer a bainha de.
▶ **hem in** *vt sep* cercar.
he-man *n inf hum* macho *m*.
hematology [,hi:mə'tɒlədʒi] *n* (U) hematologia *f*.
hemisphere ['hemi,sfiə^r] *n* [of Earth] hemisfério *m*.
hemline ['hemlain] *n* (altura *f* da) bainha *f*.
hemoglobin [,hi:mə'gləubin] *n* (U) hemoglobina *f*.
hemophilia [,hi:mə'filiə] *n* (U) hemofilia *f*.
hemophiliac [,hi:mə'filiæk] *n* hemofílico *m*, -ca *f*.
hemorrhage ['heməridʒ] ◇ *n* hemorragia *f*. ◇ *vi* ter uma hemorragia.
hemorrhoids ['hemərɔidz] *npl* hemorróidas *fpl*.
hemp [hemp] *n* (U) [plant or fibre] cânhamo *m*.
hen [hen] *n* **-1.** [female chicken] galinha *f* **-2.** [female bird] fêmea *f*.
hence [hens] *adv fml* **-1.** [therefore] por isso, assim **-2.** [from now]: **ten years ~** daqui a dez anos.
henceforth [,hens'fɔ:θ] *adv fml* doravante.
henchman ['hentʃmən] (*pl* **-men** [-mən]) *n pej* capanga *m*, jagunço *m*.
henna ['henə] ◇ *n* (U) hena *f*. ◇ *vt* passar OR aplicar hena em.
hen party *n UK inf* despedida *f* de solteira.
henpecked ['henpekt] *adj pej* submisso(sa), dominado(da).
hepatitis [,hepə'taitis] *n* (U) hepatite *f*.
her [hɜ:^r] ◇ *pers pron* **-1.** (direct) a; **I know ~** eu a conheço **-2.** (indirect) lhe; **send it to ~** mande isso para ela; **tell ~** diga-lhe **-3.** (after prep) ela; **Lucy brought it with ~** a Lucy trouxe-o consigo OR com ela. ◇ *poss adj* o seu (a sua), dela; **~ books** o livros dela, os seus livros.
herald ['herəld] ◇ *n* [messenger] mensageiro *m*, -ra *f*. ◇ *vt fml* **-1.** [signify, usher in] anunciar **-2.** [proclaim] conclamar.
heraldry ['herəldri] *n* (U) heráldica *f*.
herb [*UK* hɜ:b, *US* ɜ:b] *n* erva *f*.
herbaceous [hɜ:'beiʃəs] *adj* herbáceo(cea).
herbal [*UK* 'hɜ:bl, *US* ɜ:bl] *adj* à base de ervas.
herbalist ['hɜ:blist] *n* herbanário *m*, -ria *f*.
herbicide *n* herbicida *f*.
herbivore ['hɜ:bivɔ:^r] *n* herbívoro *m*, -ra *f*.
herb tea *n* (U) infusão *f* de ervas.
herd [hɜ:d] ◇ *n* **-1.** [gen] rebanho *m*; [of elephants] manada *f* **-2.** [of people] multidão *f*. ◇ *vt* **-1.** [drive] pastorear **-2.** *fig* [push] conduzir (*em grupo*).
herdsman ['hɜ:dzmən] (*pl* **-men** [-mən]) *n* **-1.** [of sheep, goats] pastor *m* **-2.** [of cattle] boiadeiro *m*, vaqueiro *m*.
here [hiə^r] *adv* **-1.** [in, at this place] aqui; **~ he is/they are** aqui está ele/estão eles; **~ it is** aqui está; **~ you are!** toma!; **Christmas is nearly ~** o Natal está próximo; **~ and there** aqui e acolá **-2.** [from this place]: **from ~** daqui; **he left ~ a while ago** ele saiu daqui há pouco **-3.** [to this place]: **come ~!** vem aqui!; **~ they come** lá vêm eles **-4.** [in toasts]: **~'s to** um brinde a.

hereabouts UK [ˈhɪərəˌbaʊts], **hereabout** US [ˌhɪərəˈbaʊt] adv por aqui.

hereafter [ˌhɪərˈɑːftəʳ] ⬦ adv fml de agora em diante, a partir de agora. ⬦ n: the ~ o além.

hereby [ˌhɪəˈbaɪ] adv -1. fml [in documents] por meio deste (desta) -2. fml [when speaking]: I ~ declare this theatre open neste momento, declaro este teatro aberto.

hereditary [hɪˈredɪtrɪ] adj hereditário(ria).

heredity [hɪˈredətɪ] n (U) hereditariedade f.

heresy [ˈherəsɪ] (pl -ies) n heresia f.

heretic [ˈherətɪk] n -1. RELIG herege mf -2. fig [unorthodox thinker] rebelde mf.

herewith [ˌhɪəˈwɪð] adv fml [with letter]: please find ~ ... segue anexo ...

heritage [ˈherɪtɪdʒ] n (U) herança f.

heritage centre n museu m (em local histórico).

hermaphrodite [hɜːˈmæfrədaɪt] ZOOL ⬦ adj hermafrodita. ⬦ n hermafrodita mf.

hermetic [hɜːˈmetɪk] adj [airtight] hermético(ca).

hermetically [hɜːˈmetɪklɪ] adv: ~ sealed hermeticamente fechado(da).

hermit [ˈhɜːmɪt] n eremita mf.

hernia [ˈhɜːnjə] n hérnia f.

hero [ˈhɪərəʊ] (pl -es) n -1. [gen] herói m -2. [idol] ídolo m.

heroic [hɪˈrəʊɪk] adj heróico(ca).
➤ **heroics** npl pej patetices fpl.

heroin [ˈherəʊɪn] n [drug] (U) heroína f.

heroine [ˈherəʊɪn] n heroína f.

heroism [ˈherəʊɪzm] n (U) heroísmo m.

hero worship n (U) idolatria f, veneração f.

heron [ˈherən] (pl inv OR -s) n garça f real.

herpes [ˈhɜːpiːz] n (U) herpes m inv.

herring [ˈherɪŋ] (pl inv OR -s) n arenque m.

herringbone [ˈherɪŋbəʊn] adj [pattern] em espinha de peixe.

hers [hɜːz] poss pron o seu (a sua), (o/a) dela; a friend of ~ um amigo dela OR seu; those shoes are ~ estes sapatos são dela OR seus; these are mine - where are ~? estes são os meus - onde estão os dela?

herself [hɜːˈself] pron -1. (reflexive) se; she hurt ~ ela se machucou -2. (after prep) si própria OR mesma; she did it ~ foi ela mesma que o fez.

he's [hiːz] = he is, he has.

hesitant [ˈhezɪtənt] adj hesitante.

hesitate [ˈhezɪteɪt] vi [pause] hesitar; to ~ to do sthg hesitar em fazer algo.

hesitation [ˌhezɪˈteɪʃn] n hesitação f; without ~ sem hesitação; to have no ~ in doing sthg não ter dúvidas ao fazer algo.

hessian [ˈhesɪən] n UK aniagem f, juta f.

heterogeneous [ˌhetərəˈdʒiːnjəs] adj fml heterogêneo(nea).

heterosexual [ˌhetərəʊˈseksjʊəl] ⬦ adj heterossexual. ⬦ n heterossexual mf.

het up [het-] adj inf nervoso(sa), como uma pilha de nervos.

hew [hjuː] (pt -ed, pp -ed OR hewn) vt literary [stone, wood] talhar.

HEW (abbr of (Department of) Health, Education and Welfare) n ministério norte-americano de educação, saúde e bem-estar social.

hex [heks] n -1. [curse] praga f, urucubaca f -2. COMPUT: ~ (code) (código m) hexadecimal m.

hexagon [ˈheksəgən] n hexágono m.

hexagonal [hekˈsægənl] adj hexagonal.

hey [heɪ] excl ei!

heyday [ˈheɪdeɪ] n auge m, apogeu m.

hey presto [-ˈprestəʊ] excl tadá!

HF (abbr of high frequency) HF.

HGV (abbr of heavy goods vehicle) n veículos pesados, como ônibus e caminhão; an ~ licence ≃ uma carteira categoria C.

hi [haɪ] excl inf [hello] oi!, olá!

HI abbr of Hawaii.

hiatus [haɪˈeɪtəs] (pl -es) n fml [pause] pausa f.

hibernate [ˈhaɪbəneɪt] vi hibernar.

hibernation [ˌhaɪbəˈneɪʃn] n (U) hibernação f; to be in ~ estar hibernando.

hiccough, hiccup [ˈhɪkʌp] (pt & pp -ped, cont -ping) ⬦ n -1. [sound] soluço m; to have ~s estar com soluços -2. fig [difficulty] contratempo m. ⬦ vi soluçar.

hick [hɪk] n esp US inf pej caipira mf.

hid [hɪd] pt ⊳ hide.

hidden [ˈhɪdn] ⬦ pp ⊳ hide. ⬦ adj -1. [from view] escondido(da) -2. [not apparent - disadvantages, dangers] escondido(da); [- problems] não aparente; [- cost] embutido(do) -3. [deliberately concealed - weapons] secreto; [- feelings] oculto.

hidden agenda n pej segunda intenção f.

hide [haɪd] (pt hid, pp hidden) ⬦ n -1. [animal skin] pele f -2. [for watching birds, animals] esconderijo m. ⬦ vt -1. [conceal] esconder; to ~ sthg (from sb) esconder algo (de alguém) -2. [cover] cobrir. ⬦ vi [conceal o.s.] esconder-se.

hide-and-seek n (U) esconde-esconde m; to play ~ brincar de esconde-esconde.

hideaway [ˈhaɪdəweɪl] n inf refúgio m.

hidebound [ˈhaɪdbaʊnd] adj pej -1. [institution] antiquado(da) -2. [person] careta f.

hideous [ˈhɪdɪəs] adj horrível.

hideout [ˈhaɪdaʊt] n esconderijo m.

hiding [ˈhaɪdɪŋ] n -1. (U) [concealment]: to be in ~ estar escondido(da) -2. inf [beating]: to give sb a (good) ~ dar uma (boa) surra em alguém; to get a (good) ~ from sb levar uma (boa) surra de alguém.

hiding place n esconderijo m.

hierarchical [ˌhaɪəˈrɑːkɪkl] adj hierárquico(ca).

hierarchy [ˈhaɪərɑːkɪ] (pl -ies) n hierarquia f.

hieroglyphics [ˌhaɪərəˈglɪfɪks] npl hieróglifos mpl.

hi-fi [ˈhaɪfaɪ] n sistema f hi-fi.

higgledy-piggledy [ˌhɪɡldɪˈpɪɡldɪ] inf ⬦ adj desordenado(da). ⬦ adv desordenadamente, de qualquer maneira.

high [haɪ] ⬦ adj -1. [gen] alto(ta); to have a ~ opinion of sb/sthg ter alguém/algo em alta conta; how ~ is it? qual é a altura? -2. [greater than normal - speed] alto(ta); [- wind] forte; [- prices, unemployment] elevado(da); **temperatures in the ~ twenties** temperaturas bem acima dos 20 graus -3. [important, influential] importante -4. [honourable] nobre - **5.** [high-pitched] agudo(da) - **6.** *drugs sl* [on drugs] baratinado(da) - **7.** *inf* [drunk] alto(ta). <> *adv* - **1.** [above ground level] a grande altura - **2.** [in degrees] em alto grau; **to search ~ and low** procurar em tudo quanto é lugar. <> *n* [highest point] pico *m*; **to reach a new ~** atingir um novo pico; **to be on a ~** estar animadíssimo(ma).

highball ['haɪbɔːl] *n US* uísque *m* com soda e gelo.

highbrow ['haɪbraʊ] *adj* erudito(ta).

high chair *n* cadeira *f* de bebê.

high-class *adj* [superior - person] de alta classe; [- hotel, restaurant] de alta categoria; [- performance] de alto nível.

high command *n* alto comando *m*.

high commission *n* alta comissão *f*.

high commissioner *n* alto comissário *m*, alta comissária *f*.

High Court *n UK JUR* Corte *f* Suprema.

high-density *adj COMPUT* de alta densidade.

higher ['haɪə'] *adj* [exam, qualification] superior(ra).
➤ **Higher** *n*: **Higher (Grade)** *SCH* na *Escócia, exame realizado ao final da escola secundária.*

higher education *n (U)* ensino *m* superior.

high explosive *n* explosivo *m* de alta potência.

high-fidelity *adj* de alta-fidelidade.

high finance *n* altas finanças *fpl*.

high-flier *n* pessoa *f* ambiciosa.

high-flying *adj* [ambitious] ambicioso(sa).

high ground *n*: **to have** OR **hold the ~** ter OR levar vantagem; **to take the moral ~** acreditar possuir valores morais superiores.

high-handed [-'hændɪd] *adj* despótico(ca).

high-heeled [-'hiːld] *adj* de salto alto.

high horse *n inf*: **to get on one's ~** estar por cima.

high jump *n SPORT* salto *m* em altura; **to be for the ~** *UK inf* merecer uma punição.

Highland Games ['haɪlənd-] *npl* Jogos *mpl* das Terras Altas.

Highlands ['haɪləndz] *npl*: **the ~** [of Scotland] as Terras Altas.

high-level *adj* - **1.** [talks, discussions] de alto nível - **2.** [diplomats, officials] do alto escalão.

high life *n (U)*: **the ~** a vida da alta sociedade.

highlight ['haɪlaɪt] <> *n* [of event, occasion] ponto *m* alto, destaque *m*. <> *vt* - **1.** [with pen] realçar - **2.** [emphasize] enfatizar.
➤ **highlights** *npl* [in hair] realces *mpl*.

highlighter (pen) ['haɪlaɪtə'-] *n* caneta *f* marca-texto.

highly ['haɪlɪ] *adv* - **1.** [very, extremely] altamente - **2.** [very well, at high level] muito bem - **3.** [favourably] favoravelmente; **I ~ recommend it** realmente recomendo isso.

highly-strung *adj* irritadiço(ça).

high mass *n* missa *f* solene.

high-minded [-'maɪndɪd] *adj* nobre.

Highness ['haɪnɪs] *n*: **His/Her/Your (Royal) ~** Sua Alteza (Real); **Their (Royal) ~es** Suas Altezas (Reais).

high-octane *adj* de alto índice de octana.

high-pitched [-'pɪtʃt] *adj* [shrill] agudo(da).

high point *n* [of occasion] ponto *m* alto.

high-powered [-'paʊəd] *adj* - **1.** [powerful] de alta potência - **2.** [dynamic] dinâmico(ca).

high-pressure *adj* - **1.** [air, gas] de alta pressão - **2.** [persuasive] persuasivo(va).

high priest *n RELIG* sumo sacerdote *m*.

high-ranking [-'ræŋkɪŋ] *adj* de destaque.

high-resolution *adj COMPUT* de alta resolução.

high-rise *adj* de muitos andares; **a ~ building** um espigão.

high-risk *adj* de alto risco.

high school *n* - **1.** *UK* [for 11- to 18-year-olds] ≃ escola *f* secundária - **2.** *US* [for 15- to 18-year-olds] ≃ segundo grau *m*.

high seas *npl*: **the ~** o alto-mar.

high season *n (U)* alta estação *f*.

high-speed *adj* - **1.** [train] de alta velocidade - **2.** *PHOT* [film] para alta velocidade.

high-spirited *adj* [person] alegre, vivaz.

high spot *n* ponto *m* de relevo.

high street *n UK* avenida *f* principal.

hightail ['haɪteɪl] *vt esp US*: **they ~ed it back home** eles se mandaram rapidinho para casa.

high tea *n (U) UK* chá *f* ao fim da tarde (*servido no lugar do jantar*).

high-tech <> *adj* [method, industry] de alta tecnologia. <> *n* (*abbr of* **high technology**) alta tecnologia *f*.

high technology *n (U)* alta tecnologia *f*.

high-tension *adj* de alta tensão.

high tide *n (U)* [of sea] maré *f* alta.

high treason *n (U)* alta traição *f*.

high water *n (U)* preamar *f*.

highway ['haɪweɪ] *n* - **1.** *US* [main road between cities] auto-estrada *f* - **2.** *UK* [any main road] rodovia *f*.

Highway Code *n UK*: **the ~** ≃ o Código Nacional de Trânsito.

high wire *n* cabo *m* de aço.

hijack ['haɪdʒæk] <> *n* [of aircraft, car] seqüestro *m*. <> *vt* [aircraft, car] seqüestrar.

hijacker ['haɪdʒækə'] *n* seqüestrador *m*, -ra *f*.

hike [haɪk] <> *n* [long walk] caminhada *f*. <> *vi* [go for a long walk] caminhar.

hiker ['haɪkə'] *n* caminhante *mf*, andarilho *m*.

hiking ['haɪkɪŋ] *n (U)* excursões *fpl* a pé; **to go ~** fazer excursões.

hilarious [hɪ'leərɪəs] *adj* hilariante, engraçado(da).

hilarity [hɪ'lærətɪ] *n (U) fml* hilaridade *f*; **to cause much ~** causar muitos risos.

hill [hɪl] *n* - **1.** [mound] colina *f* - **2.** [slope] ladeira *f*.

hillbilly ['hɪl,bɪlɪ] (*pl* -ies) *n US inf pej* jeca *m*.

hillock ['hɪlək] *n* pequena colina *f*, outeiro *m*.

hillside ['hɪlsaɪd] *n* encosta *f*.

hill start *n* partida *f* do carro em uma lomba.

hilltop ['hɪltɒp] <> *adj* no topo do morro. <> *n* topo *m* do morro.

hilly ['hɪlɪ] (*compar* -ier, *superl* -iest) *adj* montanhoso(sa).

hilt [hɪlt] *n* punho *m*; **to the ~** ao extremo; **to support/defend sb to the ~** apoiar/defender alguém com unhas e dentes.

him [hɪm] *pers pron* - **1.** (*direct*) o; **I know ~** eu o conheço **-2.** *(indirect)* lhe; **tell ~** diga-lhe **-3.** *(after prep)* ele; **send it to ~** mande isso para ele; **Tony brought it with ~** Tony trouxe-o consigno OR com ele.

Himalayan [ˌhɪmə'leɪən] *adj* do Himalaia, himalaico(ca).

Himalayas [ˌhɪmə'leɪəz] *npl*: **the ~** as montanhas do Himalaia; **in the ~** nas montanhas do Himalaia.

himself [hɪm'self] *pron* **-1.** *(reflexive)* se; **he hurt ~** machucou-se **-2.** *(after prep)* si próprio OR mesmo; **he did it ~** foi ele mesmo que o fez.

hind [haɪnd] (*pl inv* OR **-s**) <> *adj* traseiro(ra). <> *n* [deer] corça *f.*

hinder ['hɪndə'] *vt* retardar, atrapalhar.

Hindi ['hɪndɪ] *n (U)* [language] hindi *m.*

hindmost ['haɪndməʊst] *adj* último(ma).

hindquarters ['haɪndkwɔ:təz] *npl* traseiro *m.*

hindrance ['hɪndrəns] *n* **-1.** [obstacle] obstáculo *m* **-2.** *(U)* [delay] atrasos *mpl.*

hindsight ['haɪndsaɪt] *n (U)*: **with the benefit of ~** olhando em retrospecto.

Hindu ['hɪndu:] (*pl* **-s**) <> *adj* hindu. <> *n* hindu *m.*

Hinduism ['hɪndu:ɪzm] *n (U)* hinduísmo *m.*

hinge [hɪndʒ] (*cont* **hingeing**) *n* [on door, window, lid] dobradiça *f.*
➡ **hinge (up)on** *vt fus* [depend on] depender de.

hint [hɪnt] <> *n* **-1.** [indirect suggestion] alusão *f*; **to drop a ~** dar uma indireta; **to take the ~** pegar uma indireta **-2.** [useful suggestion, tip] dica *f* **-3.** [small amount, trace] sinal *m.* <> *vi*: **to ~ at sthg** fazer alusão a algo. <> *vt*: **to ~ that** insinuar que.

hinterland ['hɪntəlænd] *n* [area around coast, river] hinterlândia *f*, interior *m.*

hip [hɪp] <> *adj inf* [fashionable] moderno(na). <> *n* [part of body] quadril *m.*

hip bath *n* banheira *f* de assento.

hip bone *n* osso *m* ilíaco.

hip flask *n* garrafa *f* de bolso.

hip-hop *n (U)* [music] hip-hop *m.*

hippie ['hɪpɪ] *n* hippie *m.*

hippo ['hɪpəʊ] (*pl* **-s**) *n* hipopótamo *m.*

hippopotamus [ˌhɪpə'pɒtəməs] (*pl* **-muses** OR **-mi** [-maɪ]) *n* hipopótamo *m.*

hippy ['hɪpɪ] (*pl* **-ies**) *n* = **hippie**.

hire ['haɪə'] <> *n (U)* [of car, equipment] aluguel *m*; **for ~** aluga-se; **bicycles for ~** alugam-se bicicletas; **taxi for ~** táxi livre. <> *vt* **-1.** [rent] alugar **-2.** [employ] contratar.
➡ **hire out** *vt sep* alugar.

hire car *n UK*: **to have a ~** alugar um carro.

hired help *n* [domestic staff] assessoria *f* doméstica.

hire purchase *n (U) UK* compra *f* a prazo; **to buy sthg on ~** comprar algo a prazo.

his [hɪz] <> *poss pron* o seu (a sua), (o/a) dele; **books** os livros dele, os seus livros <> *poss adj* o seu (a sua), dele; **a friend of ~** um amigo dele OR seu; **these shoes are ~** estes sapatos são dele OR seus; **these are mine - where are ~?** estes são os meus - onde estão os dele?

Hispanic [hɪ'spænɪk] <> *adj* hispânico(ca). <> *n esp US* hispânico *m*, -ca *f.*

hiss [hɪs] <> *n* **-1.** [of animal, person] silvo *m* **-2.** [of audience] vaia *f* **-3.** [of steam, gas] assobio *m.* <> *vt* [actor, speaker] vaiar. <> *vi* **-1.** [animal, person] silvar; **she ~ed angrily at him** ela o vaiou irritada **-2.** [steam, gas] assobiar.

histogram ['hɪstəgræm] *n* histograma *m.*

historian [hɪ'stɔ:rɪən] *n* historiador *m*, -ra *f.*

historic [hɪ'stɒrɪk] *adj* [significant] histórico(ca).

historical [hɪ'stɒrɪkəl] *adj* histórico(ca).

history ['hɪstərɪ] (*pl* **-ies**) *n* **-1.** [gen] história *f*; **to go down in ~** entrar para a história; **to make ~** fazer história **-2.** [past record] histórico *m.*

histrionics [hɪstrɪ'ɒnɪks] *npl pej* melodrama *m.*

hit [hɪt] (*pt & pp* **hit**, *cont* **-ting**) <> *n* **-1.** [blow] golpe *m*, pancada *f* **-2.** [successful strike] tiro *m* certeiro **-3.** [success] sucesso *m* **-4.** COMPUT [of website] visita *f.* <> *comp* de sucesso. <> *vt* **-1.** [strike a blow at] bater em **-2.** [crash into] bater contra **-3.** [score] ferir **-4.** [reach] alcançar; **the thought suddenly ~ me that ...** de repente me dei conta de que ... **-5.** [affect badly] atingir **-6.** *phr*: **to ~ it off (with sb)** dar-se bem (com alguém).
➡ **hit back** *vi*: **to ~ back (at sb/sthg)** *fig* revidar aos ataques (de alguém/algo).
➡ **hit on** *vt fus* **-1.** = **hit upon -2.** *US inf* [chat up] dar uma cantada em.
➡ **hit out** *vi*: **to ~ out at sb/sthg** [physically] tentar bater em alguém/algo; [in speech, writing] rebater veementemente.
➡ **hit upon** *vt fus* [think of] achar, descobrir.

hit-and-miss *adj* = **hit-or-miss**.

hit-and-run <> *adj* **-1.** [driver] que não presta socorro **-2.** [accident] em que se não presta socorro. <> *n* [accident] acidente no qual não se presta socorro.

hitch [hɪtʃ] <> *n* [problem, snag] dificuldade *f.* <> *vt* **-1.** [solicit]: **to ~ a lift** pegar carona **-2.** [fasten]: **to ~ sthg on(to) sthg** amarrar algo em algo. <> *vi* [hitchhike] viajar de carona.
➡ **hitch up** *vt sep* [pull up] levantar.

hitchhike ['hɪtʃhaɪk] *vi* viajar de carona.

hitchhiker ['hɪtʃhaɪkə'] *n* caroneiro *m*, -ra *f.*

hi-tech [ˌhaɪ'tek] *adj* = **high-tech**.

hither ['hɪðə'] *adv literary* aqui; **~ and thither** em muitas direções, aqui e acolá.

hitherto [ˌhɪðə'tu:] *adv fml* até agora.

hit list *n* lista *f* negra.

hit man *n* matador *m* de aluguel.

hit-or-miss *adj* aleatório(ria).

hit parade *n dated* parada *f* de sucessos.

HIV *(abbr of* human immunodeficiency virus*) n (U)* HIV *m*; **to be ~-positive** ser soropositivo(va).

hive [haɪv] *n* [for bees] colméia *f*; **a ~ of activity** *fig* um centro de atividades.
➡ **hive off** *vt sep* [separate] transferir.

HK *(abbr of* Hong Kong*)* HK.

hl *(abbr of* hectolitre*)* hl.

HM *(abbr of* His (or Her) Majesty*)* S.M.

HMG *(abbr of* His (or Her) Majesty's Government*)* *expressão utilizada nos documentos oficiais da Grã-Bretanha*, governo *m* de sua majestade.

HMI (*abbr of* **His (or Her) Majesty's Inspector**) *n* *inspetor de escolas na Grã-Bretanha.*

HMO (*abbr of* **health maintenance organization**) *n* órgão norte-americano de saúde pública.

HMS (*abbr of* **His (or Her) Majesty's Ship**) *prefixo utilizado nos navios da marinha real britânica*, navio *m* de sua majestade.

HMSO (*abbr of* **His (or Her) Majesty's Stationery Office**) *n serviço oficial de imprensa da Grã-Bretanha.*

HNC (*abbr of* **Higher National Certificate**) *n certificado de qualificação em disciplinas técnicas na Grã-Bretanha.*

HND (*abbr of* **Higher National Diploma**) *n diploma de qualificação em disciplinas técnicas na Grã-Bretanha.*

hoard [hɔːd] <> *n* [store] provisão *f.* <> *vt* [collect, save] estocar.

hoarding ['hɔːdɪŋ] *n UK* [for advertisements, posters] outdoor *m.*

hoarfrost ['hɔːfrɒst] *n (U)* geada *f.*

hoarse [hɔːs] *adj* rouco(ca).

hoax [həʊks] *n* trote *m.*

hoaxer ['həʊksər] *n* trotador *m*, -ra *f*; **bomb ~** *pessoa que passa um trote de bomba.*

hob [hɒb] *n UK* [on cooker] mesa *f.*

hobble ['hɒbl] *vi* [limp] coxear.

hobby ['hɒbɪ] (*pl* **-ies**) *n* [leisure activity] hobby *m.*

hobby horse *n* **-1.** [toy] cavalinho-de-pau *m* **-2.** [favourite topic] assunto *m* favorito.

hobnob ['hɒbnɒb] (*pt* & *pp* **-bed**, *cont* **-bing**) *vi* [socialize]: **to ~ with sb** enturmar-se com alguém.

hobo ['həʊbəʊ] (*pl* **-es** OR **-s**) *n US* [tramp] vagabundo *m*, -da *f.*

Ho Chi Minh City [,həʊ,tʃiː'mɪn-] *n* Ho Chi Minh.

hock [hɒk] *n (U)* [wine] vinho *m* branco do Reno.

hockey ['hɒkɪ] *n* **-1.** [on grass] hóquei *m* **-2.** *US* [ice hockey] hóquei *m* no gelo.

hockey stick *n* bastão *m* de hóquei.

hocus-pocus [,həʊkəs'pəʊkəs] *n (U)* [trickery] tapeação *f.*

hod [hɒd] *n* [for bricks] cocho *m* (*de pedreiro*).

hodgepodge *n US* = hotchpotch.

hoe [həʊ] <> *n* enxada *f.* <> *vt* capinar.

hog [hɒg] (*pt* & *pp* **-ged**, *cont* **-ging**) <> *n* **-1.** *US lit* & *fig* porco *m*, -ca *f* **-2.** *phr*: **to go the whole ~** ir até o fim. <> *vt inf* [monopolize] monopolizar.

Hogmanay ['hɒgmənɪ] *n denominação escocesa para a Noite de Ano Novo.*

hoi-polloi *npl pej*: **the ~** a gentalha, a ralé.

hoist [hɔɪst] <> *n* guindaste *f.* <> *vt* **-1.** [load, person] levantar **-2.** [sail, flag] içar.

hokum ['həʊkəm] *n US inf* palhaçada *f.*

hold [həʊld] (*pt* & *pp* **held**) <> *n* **-1.** [grasp, grip]: **to have a firm ~ on** sthg segurar algo firme; **to keep ~ of** sthg segurar algo; **to take** OR **lay ~ of** sthg começar a ter efeito de algo; **to get ~ of** sthg [obtain] arranjar algo; **to get ~ of sb** [find] encontrar **-2.** [of ship, aircraft] porão *m* **-3.** [control, influence] influência *f*; **to take ~** [fire] tomar conta. <> *vt* **-1.** [in hand, arms] segurar **-2.** [maintain in position] manter; **to ~ sb prisoner** manter alguém como

prisioneiro(ra); **to ~ sb hostage** tomar alguém como refém **-3.** [have, possess] ter, possuir **-4.** [conduct, stage] conduzir **-5.** *fml* [consider] julgar; **to ~ (that)** sustentar que; **to ~ sb responsible for** sthg responsabilizar alguém por algo; **to ~ sthg dear** ter afeição por algo **-6.** [on telephone]: **please ~ the line** aguarde na linha, por favor **-7.** [keep, sustain] manter **-8.** *MIL* ocupar **-9.** [support, have space for] suportar **-10.** [contain] guardar **-11.** *phr*: **~ it!**, **~ everything!** espera aí!; **to ~ one's own** virar-se. <> *vi* **-1.** [remain unchanged] manter-se; **to ~ still** OR **steady** segurar firme **-2.** [on phone] esperar.

<> **hold against** *vt sep*: **to ~** sthg **against sb** *fig* ter algo que pese contra alguém.

<> **hold back** <> *vi* [hesitate] hesitar; **to ~ back from doing sthg** hesitar em fazer algo. <> *vt sep* **-1.** [gen] reter **-2.** [prevent progress of]: **to ~ sb back (from doing sthg)** impedir alguém (de fazer algo).

<> **hold down** *vt sep* [job] manter.

<> **hold off** <> *vt sep* [fend off] manter à distância. <> *vi* [rain] parar.

<> **hold on** *vi* **-1.** [gen] esperar **-2.** [grip]: **to ~ on (to sthg)** segurar-se firme (em algo).

<> **hold onto** *vt fus* [retain] reter.

<> **hold out** <> *vt sep* [hand, arms] estender. <> *vi* **-1.** [last] durar **-2.** [resist]: **to ~ out (against sb/ sthg)** resistir (a alguém/algo).

<> **hold up** *vt sep* **-1.** [raise] levantar **-2.** [delay] atrasar **-3.** *inf* [rob] assaltar.

<> **hold with** *vt fus* [approve of] aprovar.

holdall ['həʊldɔːl] *n UK* mochila *f.*

holder ['həʊldər] *n* **-1.** [gen] suporte *m*, recipiente *m*; **cigarette ~** boquilha *f*; **candle ~** castiçal *m* **-2.** [owner - gen] titular *mf*; [- of ticket] portador *m*, -ra *f*; [- position, title] detentor *m*, -ra *f.*

holding ['həʊldɪŋ] <> *adj* [action, operation] controlador(ra). <> *n* **-1.** [investment] participação *f* acionária **-2.** [farm] propriedade *f.*

holding company *n* empresa *f* controladora, holding *f.*

hold-up *n* **-1.** [robbery] assalto *m* à mão armada **-2.** [delay] empecilho *m*, atraso *m.*

hole [həʊl] *n* **-1.** [gen] buraco *m*; **~ in one** um buraco numa só tacada; **to pick ~s in sthg** [criticize] achar defeito em algo; [in sock, shoe] furo *m* **-2.** *inf* [horrible place] buraco *m* **-3.** *inf* [predicament] apuro *m.*

<> **hole up** *vi* [hide, take shelter] hibernar.

holiday ['hɒlɪdeɪ] *n* **-1.** [vacation] férias *fpl*; **to be/go on ~** estar de/sair de férias **-2.** [public holiday] feriado *m.*

holiday camp *n UK* colônia *f* de férias.

holidaymaker ['hɒlɪdeɪ,meɪkər] *n UK* excursionista *mf.*

holiday pay *n UK* férias *fpl* remuneradas.

holiday resort *n UK* cidade *f* turística.

holiday season *n UK* têmporada *f* de férias.

holiness ['həʊlɪnɪs] *n (U)* [holy quality] santidade *f.*

<> **Holiness** *n* [in titles]: **His/Your Holiness** Sua Santidade.

holistic [həʊ'lɪstɪk] *adj* holístico(ca).

Holland ['hɒlənd] *n* Holanda *f*; **in ~** na Holanda.

hollandaise sauce [ˌhɒlənˈdeɪz-] *n (U)* molho *m* holandês.

holler [ˈhɒləʳ] *inf* <> *vt* gritar. <> *vi esp US* gritar.

hollow [ˈhɒləʊ] <> *adj* **-1.** [gen] oco (oca), vazio(-zia) **-2.** [gaunt - eyes] fundo(da); [- cheeks] magro(gra) **-3.** [empty of meaning or value - laugh, optimism] falso(sa); [- promise, victory] vão (vã). <> *n* **-1.** [gen] buraco *m* **-2.** [in ground, pillow] buraco *m*, cavidade *f*.

◆ **hollow out** *vt sep* **-1.** [make hollow] tornar oco (oca) **-2.** [make by hollowing] escavar.

holly [ˈhɒlɪ] *n (U)* azevinho *m*.

hollyhock *n* malva-rosa *f*.

Hollywood [ˈhɒlɪwʊd] <> *n* [film industry] Hollywood. <> *comp* de Hollywood.

holocaust [ˈhɒləkɔːst] *n* [destruction] holocausto *m*.
◆ **Holocaust** *n*: the Holocaust o Holocausto.

hologram [ˈhɒləɡræm] *n* holograma *m*.

hols [hɒlz] *npl UK inf* folgas *fpl*.

holster [ˈhəʊlstəʳ] *n* coldre *m*.

holy [ˈhəʊlɪ] (*compar* -ier, *superl* -iest) *adj* **-1.** [sacred] sagrado(da), santo(ta); ~ **water** água *f* benta **-2.** [pure and good] puro(ra).

Holy Communion *n (U)* Sagrada Comunhão *f*.

Holy Father *n*: the ~ o Papa.

Holy Ghost *n*: the ~ o Espírito Santo.

Holy Grail [-ˈɡreɪl] *n*: the ~ o Santo Graal.

Holy Land *n*: the ~ a Terra Santa.

holy orders *npl* votos *mpl* sagrados; **to take** ~ ordenar-se sacerdote.

Holy Spirit *n*: the ~ o Espírito Santo.

homage [ˈhɒmɪdʒ] *n fml* **-1.** [respect] homenagem *f*; **to pay** ~ **to sb/sthg** prestar homenagem a alguém/algo **-2.** [tribute] tributo *m*.

home [həʊm] <> *adj* **-1.** [not foreign] nacional **-2.** *SPORT* interno(na). <> *adv* **-1.** [to or at one's house] para casa **-2.** [from abroad] para casa (do exterior) **-3.** *phr*: **to bring sthg** ~ **(to sb)** fazer alguém enxergar algo; **to drive** *OR* **hammer sthg** ~ **(to sb)** deixar algo bem claro (para alguém). <> *n* **-1.** [one's house, place of residence] casa *f*; **to make one's** ~ fazer a casa; **it's a** ~ **from** ~ *UK*, **it's a** ~ **away from** ~ *US* é um lugar onde a gente se sente em casa **-2.** [place of origin] terra *f* natal **-3.** [family unit, Institution] lar *m*; **to leave** ~ sair de casa.

◆ **at home** *adv* **-1.** [gen] em casa; **at** ~ **with sthg** à vontade com algo; **to make o.s. at** ~ sentir-se à vontade *OR* em casa **-2.** [in one's own country] no meu país **-3.** *SPORT*: **to play at** ~ jogar em casa.

◆ **home in** *vi*: **to** ~ **in on sthg** dirigir-se diretamente a algo.

home address *n* endereço *m* residencial.

home banking *n (U)* home banking *m*.

home brew *n (U)* [beer] cerveja *f* caseira.

homecoming [ˈhəʊmˌkʌmɪŋ] *n* **-1.** [return] volta *f* ao lar **-2.** *US SCH & UNIV* regresso *m* dos ex-alunos às suas faculdades.

home computer *n* computador *m* pessoal.

home cooking *n* comida *f* caseira.

Home Counties *npl UK*: the ~ os condados ao redor de Londres.

home delivery *n* entrega *m* a domicílio.

home economics *n (U)* economia *f* doméstica.

home fries *npl US* batatas *fpl* fritas.

home ground *n* **-1.** [gen]: **to be on** ~ estar em seu território **-2.** *SPORT* campo *m* do time da casa.

home-grown *adj* plantado(da) em casa.

home help *n UK* empregada *que auxilia pessoas idosas ou doentes*.

home improvements *npl* reformas *fpl* na casa.

homeland [ˈhəʊmlænd] *n* **-1.** [country of birth] terra *f* natal **-2.** [in South Africa] gueto *m*.

homeless [ˈhəʊmlɪs] <> *adj* sem-teto. <> *npl*: **the** ~ os sem-teto, os desabrigados.

homelessness [ˈhəʊmlɪsnəs] *n (U)*: **the problem of** ~ o problema dos sem-teto.

home loan *n* financiamento *m* para habitação.

homely [ˈhəʊmlɪ] *adj* **-1.** [simple, unpretentious] simples **-2.** [ugly] feio (feia).

home-made *adj* caseiro(ra); ~ **bread** pão *m* feito em casa.

home movie *n* filmagem *f* caseira.

Home Office *n UK*: the ~ ≃ o Ministério do Interior.

homeopathic [ˌhəʊmɪəʊˈpæθɪk] *adj* homeopático(ca).

homeopathy [ˌhəʊmɪˈɒpəθɪ] *n (U)* homeopatia *f*.

homeowner [ˈhəʊmˌəʊnəʳ] *n* proprietário *m*, -ria *f* da casa.

home page *n COMPUT* homepage *f*, página *f* inicial.

home rule *n (U)* autonomia *f* interna.

home run *n US inf tacada que permite ao jogador de beisebol completar o circuito das bases.*

Home Secretary *n UK* ≃ Ministro *m*, -tra *f* do Interior.

homesick [ˈhəʊmsɪk] *adj* com saudade de casa; **to feel** ~ estar com saudades de casa.

homesickness [ˈhəʊmˌsɪknɪs] *n (U)* saudade *f* de casa.

homespun [ˈhəʊmspʌn] *adj fig* [unsophisticated] tosco(ca).

homestead [ˈhəʊmsted] *n US* fazenda *f*.

home straight *n*: the ~ [of race] a reta de chegada; [of task] última etapa *f*.

hometown [ˈhəʊmtaʊn] *n* cidade *f* natal.

home truth *n* verdades *fpl* desagradáveis; **to tell sb a few** ~**s** dizer algumas verdades para alguém.

homeward [ˈhəʊmwəd] <> *adj* de regresso. <> *adv* = **homewards**.

homewards [ˈhəʊmwədz] *adv* para casa.

homework [ˈhəʊmwɜːk] *n* **-1.** *SCH* dever *m* de casa, tema *m* **-2.** *inf fig* [preparation] dever *m* de casa.

homey, homy [ˈhəʊmɪ] *US adj US* familiar.

homicidal [ˈhɒmɪsaɪdl] *adj* homicida.

homicide [ˈhɒmɪsaɪd] *n fml* [act] homicídio *m*.

homily [ˈhɒmɪlɪ] (*pl* -ies) *n* [lecture] homilia *f*.

homing [ˈhəʊmɪŋ] *adj* **-1.** [instinct] que se refere ao instinto do lar; ~ **instinct** instinto *m* doméstico **-2.** [device] autodirecional.

homing pigeon *n* pombo-correio *m*.

homoeopathy *etc n* = **homeopathy** *etc*.

homogeneous [ˌhɒmə'dʒi:njəs] adj homogêneo(-nea).

homogenize, -ise [hə'mɒdʒənaɪz] vt UK homogeneizar.

homophobic ['hǝʊmǝʊ'fǝʊbɪk] adj homofóbico(-ca).

homosexual [ˌhɒmǝ'sekʃʊǝl] <> adj homossexual. <> n homossexual mf.

homosexuality [ˌhɒmǝˌsekʃʊ'ælǝtɪ] n (U) homossexualidade f.

homy adj US = homey.

Hon. -1. (abbr of **Honourable**) honorável -**2.** (abbr of **Honorary**) hon.

Honduran [hɒn'djʊǝrǝn] <> adj hondurenho(-nha). <> n hondurenho m, -nha f.

Honduras [hɒn'djʊǝrǝs] n Honduras; **in ~** em Honduras.

hone [hǝʊn] vt -**1.** [knife, sword] afiar -**2.** [intellect, wit] aprimorar.

honest ['ɒnɪst] <> adj -**1.** [trustworthy] honesto(ta) -**2.** [frank, truthful] sincero(ra); **to be ~, ...** para ser franco(ca), ... -**3.** [legal] legal. <> adv inf: **I didn't steal your pencil, ~!** eu não roubei o seu lápis, juro!

honestly ['ɒnɪstlɪ] <> adv -**1.** [in a trustworthy manner] honestamente -**2.** [frankly, truthfully] sinceramente. <> excl [expressing impatience, disapproval] ora, francamente!

honesty ['ɒnɪstɪ] n -**1.** (U) [trustworthiness] honestidade f -**2.** [frankness, truthfulness] sinceridade f.

honey ['hʌnɪ] n -**1.** (U) [food] mel m -**2.** esp US [dear] querido m, -da f.

honeybee ['hʌnɪbi:] n abelha f operária.

honeycomb ['hʌnɪkǝʊm] n -**1.** [in wax] favo m (de mel) -**2.:** **~ pattern** formato m de favo de mel.

honeymoon ['hʌnɪmu:n] <> n lit & fig lua-de-mel f. <> vi sair em lua-de-mel.

honeysuckle ['hʌnɪˌsʌkl] n madressilva f.

Hong Kong [ˌhɒŋ'kɒŋ] n Hong Kong; **in ~** em Hong Kong.

honk [hɒŋk] <> n -**1.** [of horn] buzinada f -**2.** [of goose] grasnada f. <> vi -**1.** [motorist] buzinar -**2.** [goose] grasnar. <> vt: **to ~ a horn** tocar a buzina.

honky ['hɒŋkɪ] (pl -**ies**) n US vinf offensive branquelo m, -la f.

Honolulu [ˌhɒnǝ'lu:lu:] n Honolulu; **in ~** em Honolulu.

honor etc n & vt US = honour etc.

honorary [UK 'ɒnǝrǝrɪ, US ɒnǝ'reǝrɪ] adj honorário(-ria).

honor roll n US [sch] [univ] relação f dos melhores alunos.

honour UK, **honor** US ['ɒnǝ^r] <> n honra f; **in ~ of sb/sthg** em honra de alguém/algo. <> vt honrar.
 ↪ **Honour** n [in titles]: **Your ~** Vossa Senhoria, Vossa Excelência.
 ↪ **honours** npl -**1.** [gen] honras fpl -**2.** UNIV tipo de grau universitário concedido por universidades britânicas -**3.** phr: **to do the ~s** fazer as honras da casa.

honourable UK, **honorable** US ['ɒnrǝbl] adj honrado(da).
 ↪ **Honourable** adj [in titles]: **the Honourable ...** o Honorável ...

honourably UK, **honorably** US ['ɒnǝrǝblɪ] adv honrosamente.

honour bound adj: **to be ~ to do sthg** ver-se moralmente obrigado(da) a fazer algo.

honours degree n UK [univ] = honours **2.**

honours list n UK na Inglaterra, relação de pessoas importantes que recebem condecorações como sinal de respeito.

Hons. (abbr of **honours degree**) n tipo de grau universitário concedido por universidades britânicas.

Hon. Sec. (abbr of **honorary secretary**) n secretário m honorário, secretária f honorária.

hooch [hu:tʃ] n inf bebida f alcoólica ilegal.

hood [hʊd] n -**1.** [on cloak, jacket] capuz f -**2.** US [of car] capota f -**3.** [of pram] toldo m -**4.** [of cooker] aba f -**5.** US [car bonnet] capô m.

hooded ['hʊdɪd] adj -**1.** [wearing a hood] encapuzado(da) -**2.** [eyes] mascarado(da).

hoodlum ['hu:dlǝm] n [youth] US inf arruaceiro m, -ra f; [gangster] gângster mf.

hoodwink ['hʊdwɪŋk] vt lograr.

hooey ['hu:ɪ] n US inf bobagem f.

hoof [hu:f, hʊf] (pl -s OR **hooves**) n pata f, casco m.

hook [hʊk] <> n -**1.** [for coat, picture, curtain] gancho m -**2.** [for catching fish] anzol m -**3.** [fastener] fecho m; **~ and eye** colchete m. <> vt -**1.** [fasten with hook] enganchar -**2.** [fish] fisgar -**3.** [arm, leg] dar um gancho em.
 ↪ **off the hook** adv -**1.** [phone] fora do gancho -**2.** [out of trouble] sem problemas; **to get sb off the ~** livrar alguém de um problema.
 ↪ **hook up** vt sep: **to ~ sthg up to sthg** COMPUT & TELEC conectar algo em algo.

hooked [hʊkt] adj -**1.** [shaped like a hook] curvado(da) -**2.** inf [addicted]: **to be ~ (on sthg)** ser viciado(da) (em algo).

hooker ['hʊkǝ^r] n US inf prostituta f.

hook(e)y ['hʊkɪ] n (U) US inf: **to play ~** matar aula.

hooligan ['hu:lɪgǝn] n arruaceiro m, -ra f, hooligan m.

hooliganism ['hu:lɪgǝnɪzm] n (U) arruaça f.

hoop [hu:p] n argola f.

hoop-la ['hu:plɑ:] n (U) [game] jogo m de argolas.

hooray [hʊ'reɪ] excl = hurray.

hoot [hu:t] <> n -**1.** [of owl] pio m -**2.** [of horn] buzinada f -**3.** [of laughter] grito m -**4.** UK inf [amusing thing, person]: **she's a real ~** ela é o máximo. <> vi -**1.** [owl] piar -**2.** [horn] buzinar -**3.** inf [person] gritar. <> vt [horn] buzinar.

hooter ['hu:tǝ^r] n -**1.** [horn - of car] buzina f; [- of factory] sirene f -**2.** UK inf [nose] narigão m.

Hoover® ['hu:vǝ^r] n UK aspirador m.
 ↪ **hoover** vt passar o aspirador em. <> vi passar o aspirador.

hooves [hu:vz] pl ▷ hoof.

hop [hɒp] (pt & pp -**ped**, cont -**ping**) <> n -**1.** [of person] pulo m num pé só -**2.** [of small animal, bird] pulinho m -**3.** inf [trip] viagem f rápida. <> vt inf

-1. US [bus, train] pegar **-2.** phr: ~ **it!** dê o fora. ◇ vi **-1.** [jump on one leg] pular com um pé só **-2.** [small animal, bird] dar pulinhos **-3.** inf [move nimbly] pular; **she ~ped on a plane to New York** ela foi dar um pulo em Nova York.

◆ **hops** npl [for making beer] lúpulos mpl.

hope [həʊp] ◇ n esperança f; **in the ~ of** na esperança de; **I don't hold out much ~** não tenho muita esperança; **to pin one's ~s on sb/sthg** depositar a esperança em alguém/algo; **to raise sb's ~s** dar esperança a alguém. ◇ vt: **to ~ (that)** esperar que; **to ~ to do sthg** esperar fazer algo. ◇ vi esperar; **to ~ for sthg** esperar (por) algo; **I ~ so/not** espero que sim/não; **to ~ for the best** esperar que tudo dê certo.

hope chest n US baú m do enxoval.

hopeful ['həʊpfʊl] ◇ adj **-1.** [full of hope] esperançoso(sa), otimista; **to be ~ of sthg/of doing sthg** ter esperanças de algo/de fazer algo **-2.** [encouraging] promissor(ra). ◇ n aspirante mf(a um cargo).

hopefully ['həʊpfəlɪ] adv **-1.** [in a hopeful way] esperançosamente **-2.** [with luck] com sorte.

hopeless ['həʊplɪs] adj **-1.** [despairing] desesperado(da) **-2.** [impossible] impossível **-3.** inf [useless] inútil.

hopelessly ['həʊplɪslɪ] adv **-1.** [despairingly] desesperançosamente **-2.** [completely] totalmente.

hopper ['hɒpə'] n [bin] tremonha f.

hopping ['hɒpɪŋ] adv: **to be ~ mad** estar soltando fogo pelas ventas.

hopscotch ['hɒpskɒtʃ] n (U) amarelinha f.

horde [hɔ:d] n horda f.

◆ **hordes** npl: ~ **s of** uma multidão de.

horizon [hə'raɪzn] n [of sky] horizonte m; **on the ~** no horizonte.

◆ **horizons** npl: **to broaden one's ~s** ampliar os horizontes.

horizontal [ˌhɒrɪ'zɒntl] ◇ adj horizontal. ◇ n: **the ~** a horizontal.

hormone ['hɔ:məʊn] n hormônio m.

hormone replacement therapy n terapia f de reposição hormonal.

horn [hɔ:n] n **-1.** [of animal] chifre m **-2.** MUS [instrument] trompa f **-3.** [of car] buzina f **-4.** [of ship] apito m.

hornet ['hɔ:nɪt] n vespão m.

horn-rimmed [-'rɪmd] adj feito(ta) com aros de chifre.

horny ['hɔ:nɪ] (compar -ier, superl -iest) adj **-1.** [scale, body, armour] feito(ta) de chifre **-2.** [hand] calejado(da) **-3.** vinf [sexually excited] com tesão.

horoscope ['hɒrəskəʊp] n horóscopo m.

horrendous [hɒ'rendəs] adj horrendo(da).

horrible ['hɒrəbl] adj horrível.

horribly ['hɒrəblɪ] adv **-1.** [horrifically] horrivelmente **-2.** inf [very] terrivelmente, muito.

horrid ['hɒrɪd] adj **-1.** esp UK [person] antipático(ca) **-2.** [idea, place] horroroso(sa).

horrific [hɒ'rɪfɪk] adj horroroso(sa), horrível.

horrify ['hɒrɪfaɪ] (pt & pp -ied) vt horrorizar.

horrifying ['hɒrɪfaɪɪŋ] adj horripilante.

horror ['hɒrə'] n **-1.** [gen] horror m; **to my/his ~** para o meu/seu espanto **-2.** [strong dislike]: **to**

have a ~ of sthg ter horror a algo.

horror film n filme m de terror.

horror-struck adj horrorizado(da).

hors d'oeuvre [ɔ:'dɜ:vr] (pl -s) n hors d'oeuvre m, entrada f.

horse [hɔ:s] n [animal] cavalo m.

horseback ['hɔ:sbæk] ◇ adj: ~ **riding** US equitação f. ◇ n: **on ~** a cavalo.

horsebox UK ['hɔ:sbɒks], **horsecar** US ['hɔ:ska:'] n reboque m para transportar cavalos.

horse chestnut n **-1.** [tree]: ~ **(tree)** castanheiro-da-índia m **-2.** [nut] castanha-da-índia f.

horse-drawn adj puxado(da) a cavalo.

horsefly ['hɔ:sflaɪ] (pl -flies) n mutuca f.

horsehair ['hɔ:sheə'] n (U) pêlo m de cavalo.

horseman ['hɔ:smən] (pl -men [-mən]) n **-1.** [non-professional] cavaleiro m **-2.** [professional] ginete m.

horse opera n US hum filme m de faroeste.

horseplay ['hɔ:spleɪ] n (U) grosseria f.

horsepower ['hɔ:sˌpaʊə'] n (U) cavalo-vapor m.

horse racing n (U) corrida f de cavalos.

horseradish ['hɔ:sˌrædɪʃ] n (U) [plant] raiz-forte f.

horse riding n (U) equitação f; **to go ~** andar a cavalo, montar.

horseshoe ['hɔ:sʃu:] n ferradura f.

horse show n concurso m hípico, rodeio m.

horse-trading n (U) fig & pej negociação f.

horse trials npl concurso m hípico, rodeio m.

horsewhip ['hɔ:swɪp] (pt & pp -ped, cont -ping) vt chicotear.

horsewoman ['hɔ:sˌwʊmən] (pl -women [-ˌwɪmɪn]) n amazona f.

horticultural [ˌhɔ:tɪ'kʌltʃərəl] adj hortícola.

horticulture ['hɔ:tɪkʌltʃə'] n (U) horticultura f.

hose [həʊz] ◇ n [hosepipe] mangueira f. ◇ vt regar com mangueira.

◆ **hose down** vt sep lavar com mangueira.

hosepipe ['həʊzpaɪp] n mangueira f.

hosiery ['həʊzɪərɪ] n (U) artigos mpl de malha, lingeries fpl.

hospice ['hɒspɪs] n [for the terminally ill] hospício m.

hospitable [hɒ'spɪtəbl] adj hospitaleiro(ra).

hospital ['hɒspɪtl] n hospital m.

hospitality [ˌhɒspɪ'tælətɪ] n (U) hospitalidade f.

hospitality suite n copa f livre (em conferência, hotel).

hospitalize, -ise ['hɒspɪtəlaɪz] vt hospitalizar.

host [həʊst] n **-1.** [at private party] anfitrião m, -ã f **-2.** [place, organization] sede f; ~ **city/country** cidade-/país-sede **-3.** [compere] apresentador m, -ra f **-4.** literary [large number]: **a ~ of sthg** um monte de algo. ◇ vt apresentar.

◆ **Host** n RELIG: **the ~** a hóstia.

hostage ['hɒstɪdʒ] n refém mf; **to be taken/held ~** ser levado(a)/mantido(a) como refém.

hostel ['hɒstl] n albergue m, alojamento m; **(youth) ~** albergue (da juventude).

hostelry ['hɒstəlrɪ] (pl -ries) n hum [pub] estalagem f.

hostess ['həʊstes] n **-1.** [at party] anfitriã f **-2.** [escort] acompanhante f.

hostile [UK 'hɒstaɪl, US 'hɒstl] adj **-1.** [gen] hostil; ~ **to sb/sthg** hostil com alguém/algo **-2.** [unfavourable] adverso(sa), desfavorável.

hostility [hɒ'stɪlətɪ] n (U) [antagonism, unfriendliness] hostilidade f.

➡ **hostilities** npl hostilidades fpl.

hot [hɒt] (compar -ter, superl -test, pt & pp -ted, cont -ting) adj **-1.** [gen] quente; **I'm** ~ estou com calor **-2.** [spicy] picante **-3.** inf [expert] bom (boa); **to be** ~ **on** OR **at sthg** ser bom (boa) em algo **-4.** [recent] recente, quente **-5.** [temper] veemente.

➡ **hot up** vi inf **-1.** [situation, campaign] esquentar **-2.** [party] animar-se **-3.** [pace]: **the pace is** ~**ting up** as coisas estão indo rápido demais.

hot-air balloon n balão m de ar quente.

hotbed ['hɒtbed] n fig [centre] foco m.

hotchpotch UK ['hɒtʃpɒtʃ], **hodgepodge** US ['hɒdʒpɒdʒ] n inf mixórdia f.

hot-cross bun n pão doce feito com passas e enfeitado com uma cruz que se come na Semana Santa.

hot dog n cachorro-quente m.

hotel [həʊ'tel] <> n hotel m. <> comp de hotel; ~ **industry** setor m hoteleiro.

hotelier [həʊ'telɪə'] n hoteleiro m, -ra f.

hot flush UK, **hot flash** US n calorão m (da menopausa).

hotfoot adv literary apressadamente.

hotheaded [,hɒt'hedɪd] adj temerário(ria).

hothouse ['hɒthaʊs, pl -haʊzɪz] <> n [greenhouse] estufa f. <> comp de estufa.

hot line n **-1.** [between government heads] linha f direta **-2.** [24-hour phone line] linha f de emergência.

hotly ['hɒtlɪ] adv **-1.** [argue, debate] calorosamente **-2.** [deny] veementemente **-3.** [pursue]: **to be** ~ **pursued** ser seguido(da) de perto.

hotplate ['hɒtpleɪt] n chapa f elétrica.

hotpot ['hɒtpɒt] n UK ensopado de cordeiro típico de Lancashire.

hot potato n inf fig [controversial topic] batata f quente.

hot rod n AUT carro m envenenado.

hot seat n inf: **to always be in the** ~ ser sempre quem tem de descascar o abacaxi.

hot spot n **-1.** [exciting place] lugar m da moda **-2.** [politically unsettled area] área f de tensão.

hot-tempered adj esquentado(da).

hot water n (U) inf fig: **to be in/get into** ~ estar/ficar em maus lençóis.

hot-water bottle n bolsa f de água quente.

hot-wire vt inf: **to** ~ **a car** dar partida num carro fazendo ligação direta.

hound [haʊnd] <> n [dog] cão m de caça. <> vt **-1.** [persecute] perseguir **-2.** [drive out]: **to** ~ **sb out (of somewhere)** conseguir tirar alguém (de algum lugar).

hour ['aʊə'] n **-1.** [gen] hora f; **half an** ~ meia hora; **per** OR **an** ~ por hora; **on the** ~ nas horas cheias, nas horas fechadas; **in the small** ~**s** em altas horas da madrugada **-2.** literary [specific moment] momento m.

➡ **hours** npl **-1.** [of business] expediente m; **bank** ~ expediente bancário **-2.** [routine] horário m; **to work long** ~ trabalhar por horas a fio.

hourly ['aʊəlɪ] <> adj **-1.** [happening every hour] de hora em hora, a cada hora **-2.** [per hour] por hora. <> adv **-1.** [every hour] a cada hora **-2.** [per hour] por hora **-3.** fig [constantly] continuamente.

house [n & adj haʊs, pl 'haʊzɪz, vb haʊz] <> adj **-1.** COMM caseiro(ra) **-2.** [wine] da casa. <> n **-1.** [gen] casa f; **it's on the** ~ é oferta da casa; **to put** OR **set one's** ~ **in order** pôr OR colocar as coisas em ordem; **to bring the** ~ **down** inf fazer a casa vir abaixo, ser muito aplaudido(da) **-2.** [people in house] família f **-3.** POL câmara f **-4.** [in debates]: **this** ~ **believes that ...** os participantes do debate acreditam que ... **-5.** [in school] dormitório m. <> vt [accommodate - people, family] alojar; [- department, library, office] abrigar.

house arrest n (U): **under** ~ sob prisão domiciliar.

houseboat ['haʊsbəʊt] n casa f flutuante.

housebound ['haʊsbaʊnd] adj confinado(da) em casa.

housebreaking ['haʊs,breɪkɪŋ] n (U) arrombamento m da casa.

housebroken ['haʊs,brəʊkn] adj US [pet] domesticado(da).

housecoat ['haʊskəʊt] n chambre m.

household ['haʊshəʊld] <> adj **-1.** [domestic] doméstico(ca) **-2.** [familiar] familiar. <> n família f, lar m.

householder ['haʊs,həʊldə'] n **-1.** [owner] dono m, -na f da casa **-2.** [head of family] chefe mf da casa.

househunting ['haʊs,hʌntɪŋ] n (U) procura f de casa; **to go** ~ procurar casa para morar/alugar.

househusband n dono m de casa.

housekeeper ['haʊs,ki:pə'] n governanta f.

housekeeping ['haʊs,ki:pɪŋ] n **-1.** [work] tarefas fpl domésticas **-2.** [budget]: ~ **(money)** dinheiro m para os gastos da casa.

houseman ['haʊsmən] (pl **-men** [-mən]) n UK interno m, -na f.

house martin n andorinha-de-casa f.

housemen pl ⊳ houseman.

house music n house music f.

House of Commons n UK: **the** ~ a Câmara dos Comuns.

HOUSE OF COMMONS

House of Commons e *House of Lords* são as duas casas que compõem o Parlamento britânico. A *House of Commons*, com seus *Members of Parliament* (MPs) são eleitos pelo povo para um mandato de cinco anos. O governo é formado pelos MPs pertencentes ao partido que obteve maioria nas eleições.

House of Lords n UK: **the** ~ a Câmara dos Lordes.

HOUSE OF LORDS

A *House of Lords* conta com mais de mil membros. Seus componentes não são eleitos: em sua maioria, eles ou herdaram seus títulos de nobreza ou desfrutam do título em caráter vitalício, mas não hereditário. A *House of Lords* tem menos poder do que a *House of Commons*, mas possui a prerrogativa de modificar leis aprovadas por essa última. É a mais alta corte de apelações do Reino Unido, excetuando-se a Escócia, que desfruta de sistema jurídico próprio.

House of Representatives *n US*: the ~ a Câmara dos Representantes.

HOUSE OF REPRESENTATIVES

Juntamente com o Senado, a *House of Representatives* constitui o corpo legislativo dos Estados Unidos. Seus deputados são eleitos em sistema de votação proporcional, de acordo com a população de cada estado.

house-owner *n* proprietário *m*, -ria *f* (*da casa*).

houseplant [ˈhaʊsplɑːnt] *n* planta *f* de interior.

house-proud *adj* fanático(ca) pela aparência da casa.

Houses of Parliament *npl UK*: the ~ o Parlamento britânico.

house-to-house *adj* de casa em casa.

house-train *vt UK* ensinar o local onde fazer as necessidades a (gato, cachorro).

housewarming (party) [ˈhaʊsˌwɔːmɪŋ-] *n* festa *f* de inauguração de uma casa.

housewife [ˈhaʊswaɪf] (*pl* -wives [-waɪvz]) *n* dona *f* de casa.

housework [ˈhaʊswɜːk] *n (U)* afazeres *mpl* domésticos.

housing [ˈhaʊzɪŋ] <> *n* -1. (*U*) [accommodation] alojamento *m* -2. (*U*) [topic, study] habitação *f* -3. TECH cárter *m*. <> *comp* habitacional.

housing association *n UK* organização que possui casas e ajuda seus membros a alugá-las ou comprá-las por um preço mais barato.

housing benefit *n UK* auxílio-moradia *m*.

housing development *n* conjunto *m* habitacional.

housing estate *UK*, **housing project** *US n* conjunto *m* habitacional.

hovel [ˈhɒvl] *n* [house] choupana *f*.

hover [ˈhɒvəʳ] *vi* -1. [fly] pairar, flutuar no ar -2. [linger] permanecer.

hovercraft [ˈhɒvəkrɑːft] (*pl inv OR* -s) *n* aerodeslizador *m*.

hoverport [ˈhɒvəpɔːt] *n* porto *m* para aerodeslizador.

how [haʊ] *adv* -1. [referring to way or manner] como; ~ **do you get there?** como se chega lá?; ~ **does it work?** como funciona?; **tell me** ~ **to do it** me diga como fazer isso. -2. [referring to health, quality] como; ~ **are you?** como vai?; ~ **are you doing?** como vai você?; ~ **are things?** como vão as coisas?; ~ **is your room?** como é o seu quarto? -3. [referring to degree, amount] quanto; ~ **far?** a que distância?; ~ **long?** quanto tempo?; ~ **many?**

quantos?; ~ **much?** quanto?; ~ **much is it?** quanto custa?; ~ **old are you?** quantos anos você tem? -4. [in phrases]: ~ **about a drink?** que tal uma bebida?; ~ **lovely!** que lindo!

howdy [ˈhaʊdɪ] *excl US inf* olá!

however [haʊˈevəʳ] <> *conj* [in whatever way] como quer que; ~ **you want** como quiser. <> *adv* -1. [nevertheless] contudo, no entanto -2. [no matter how]: ~ **difficult it is** por mais difícil que seja; ~ **many/much** não importa quantos/quanto -3. [how] de que modo, como.

howl [haʊl] <> *n* -1. [of pain, anger] grito *m* -2. [of laughter] gargalhada *f*. <> *vi* -1. [animal, wind] uivar -2. [person - in pain] gritar; [- with laughter] gargalhar.

howler [ˈhaʊləʳ] *n inf* asneira *f*.

howling [ˈhaʊlɪŋ] *adj inf* [success] imenso(sa).

hp (*abbr of* horsepower) *n* hp *m*.

HP *n* -1. *UK* (*abbr of* hire purchase) a prazo; **to buy sthg on** ~ comprar algo a prazo -2. = hp.

HQ (*abbr of* headquarters) *n* QG.

hr (*abbr of* hour) h.

HRH (*abbr of* His/Her Royal Highness) Sua A. Real.

hrs (*abbr of* hours) h.

HRT (*abbr of* hormone replacement therapy) *n* TRH *f*.

HS (*abbr of* high school) *US* escola de ensino médio.

HST (*abbr of* Hawaiian Standard Time) *horário oficial do Havái*.

ht (*abbr of* height) altura *f*.

HT (*abbr of* high tension) ELEC alta-tensão *f*.

hub [hʌb] *n* -1. [of wheel] cubo *m* -2. [of activity] centro *m*.

hub airport *n US* aeroporto *m* principal.

hubbub [ˈhʌbʌb] *n* algazarra *f*.

hubcap [ˈhʌbkæp] *n* calota *f*.

huddle [ˈhʌdl] <> *vi* -1. [crouch, curl up] amontoarse -2. [crowd together] apertar-se uns contra os outros. <> *n* [of people] amontoado *m*.

hue [hjuː] *n* [colour] matiz *f*.

huff [hʌf] <> *n*: in a ~ com raiva. <> *vi*: to ~ and puff estar ofegante, bufar.

huffy [ˈhʌfɪ] (*compar* -ier, *superl* -iest) *adj inf* -1. [offended] ressentido(da) -2. [touchy] sensível.

hug [hʌg] (*pt* & *pp* -ged, *cont* -ging) <> *n* abraço *m*; **to give sb a** ~ dar um abraço em alguém. <> *vt* -1. [embrace] abraçar -2. [stay close to] manter-se perto de.

huge [hjuːdʒ] *adj* enorme.

huh [hʌ] *excl* -1. [after questions] hein! -2. [expressing surprise] como!, hein! -3. [expressing scorn] hum!

hulk [hʌlk] *n* -1. [of ship] carcaça *f* -2. [person] brutamontes *mpl*.

hulking [ˈhʌlkɪŋ] *adj* gigantesco(ca).

hull [hʌl] *n* [of ship] casco *m*.

hullabaloo [ˌhʌləbəˈluː] *n inf* bagunça *f*.

hullo [həˈləʊ] *excl* = hello.

hum [hʌm] (*pt* & *pp* -med, *cont* -ming) <> *vi* -1. [buzz] zumbir -2. [sing] cantarolar -3. [be busy] estar em atividade -4. *phr*: to ~ and haw gaguejar, titubear. <> *vt* [tune] zunir. <> *n (U)* -1. [of bee, machine] zumbido *m* -2. [of car] barulho *m* -3. [of conversation] murmúrio *m*.

human [ˈhjuːmən] <> *adj* humano(na). <> *n*: ~ **(being)** (ser *m*) humano *m*.

humane [hju:'meɪn] *adj* [compassionate] humano(na), humanitário(ria).

humanely [hju:'meɪnlɪ] *adv* humanamente.

human error *n* (U) erro *m* humano.

humanist ['hju:mənɪst] *n* PHILOSOPHY humanista *mf*.

humanitarian [hju:ˌmænɪ'teərɪən] <> *adj* humanitário(ria). <> *n* pessoa *f* que luta pela justiça social.

humanity [hju:'mænətɪ] *n* humanidade *f*.
➥ **humanities** *npl*: **the humanities** as humanidades.

humanly ['hju:mənlɪ] *adv*: ~ **possible** humanamente possível.

human nature *n* (U) natureza *f* humana.

human race *n*: **the** ~ a raça humana.

human resources *npl* recursos *mpl* humanos.

human rights *npl* direitos *mpl* humanos.

humble ['hʌmbl] <> *adj* humilde. <> *vt* humilhar; **to** ~ **o.s.** humilhar-se.

humbly ['hʌmblɪ] *adv* humildemente.

humbug ['hʌmbʌg] *n* -**1.** (U) *dated* [hypocrisy] hipocrisia *f* -**2.** UK [sweet] caramelo *m* de menta.

humdrum ['hʌmdrʌm] *adj* monótono(na).

humid ['hju:mɪd] *adj* úmido(da).

humidity [hju:'mɪdətɪ] *n* (U) umidade *f*.

humiliate [hju:'mɪlɪeɪt] *vt* humilhar.

humiliating [hju:'mɪlɪeɪtɪŋ] *adj* humilhante.

humiliation [hju:ˌmɪlɪ'eɪʃn] *n* (U) humilhação *f*.

humility [hju:'mɪlətɪ] *n* (U) humildade *f*.

hummingbird ['hʌmɪŋbɜ:d] *n* beija-flor *m*.

humor *n* & *vt* US = **humour**.

humorist ['hju:mərɪst] *n* humorista *mf*.

humorous ['hju:mərəs] *adj* humorístico(ca).

humour UK, **humor** US ['hju:mər] <> *n* (U) [gen] humor *m*; **in bad/good** ~ *dated* de mau/bom humor. <> *vt* fazer a vontade de.

hump [hʌmp] <> *n* -**1.** [hill] elevação *f* -**2.** [on back of animal, person] corcova *f*. <> *vt inf* [carry] carregar.

humpbacked bridge ['hʌmpbækt-] *n* ponte *f* encurvada.

humus ['hju:məs] *n* (U) humo *m*. ·

hunch [hʌntʃ] <> *n inf* pressentimento *m*. <> *vt* curvar. <> *vi* curvar-se.

hunchback ['hʌntʃbæk] *n* corcunda *mf*.

hunched [hʌntʃt] *adj* encurvado(da).

hundred ['hʌndrəd] *num* cem; **a** OR **one hundred** cem; *see also* **six**.
➥ **hundreds** *npl* centenas *fpl*.

hundredth ['hʌndrətθ] *num* centésimo(ma); *see also* **sixth**.

hundredweight ['hʌndrədweɪt] *n* -**1.** [in UK] quintal *m* métrico (50,8 kg) -**2.** [in US] quintal *m* métrico (45,3 kg).

hung [hʌŋ] <> *pt* & *pp* ▷ **hang**. <> *adj* POL sem maioria.

Hungarian [hʌŋ'geərɪən] <> *adj* húngaro(ra). <> *n* -**1.** [person] húngaro *m*, -ra *f* -**2.** [language] húngaro *m*.

Hungary ['hʌŋgərɪ] *n* Hungria *f*; **in** ~ na Hungria.

hunger ['hʌŋgər] *n* -**1.** [desire for food, starvation] fome *f* -**2.** *literary* [strong desire] sede *f*.
➥ **hunger after, hunger for** *vt fus literary* ter fome de.

hunger strike *n* greve *f* de fome.

hung over *adj inf*: **to be** ~ estar com ressaca.

hungry ['hʌŋgrɪ] (*compar* -**ier**, *superl* -**iest**) *adj* -**1.** [for food] faminto(ta); **to go** ~ ficar com fome -**2.** *literary* [eager]: **to be** ~ **for sthg** ter sede de algo.

hung up *adj inf*: **to be** ~ **(on sb/sthg)**, **to be** ~ **(about sb/sthg)** ficar complexado(da) (por causa de alguém/algo).

hunk [hʌŋk] *n* -**1.** [large piece] naco *m* -**2.** *inf* [attractive man] pedaço *m* de mau caminho.

hunky-dory [ˌhʌŋkɪ'dɔːrɪ] *adj inf* satisfatório(ria) para todos.

hunt [hʌnt] <> *n* -**1.** [SPORT- activity] caça *f*; [- hunters] grupo *m* de caçadores -**2.** [search] busca *f*. <> *vi* -**1.** [for food, sport] caçar -**2.** [search]: **to** ~ **(for sthg)** procurar (algo). <> *vt* -**1.** [animals, birds] caçar -**2.** [person] procurar.
➥ **hunt down** *vt sep* encurralar.

hunter ['hʌntər] *n* caçador *m*, -ra *f*.

hunting ['hʌntɪŋ] <> *n* -**1.** SPORT caça *f* -**2.** UK [foxhunting] caça *f* à raposa -**3.** [pursuit] busca *f*. <> *comp* de caça.

huntsman ['hʌntsmən] (*pl* -**men** [-mən]) *n* caçador *m*.

hurdle ['hɜːdl] <> *n* -**1.** [in race] barreira *f* -**2.** [obstacle] obstáculo *m*. <> *vt* [jump over] saltar.
➥ **hurdles** *npl* SPORT corrida *f* de obstáculos.

hurl [hɜːl] *vt* -**1.** [throw] arremessar -**2.** [shout] proferir.

hurrah [hʊ'rɑː] *excl dated* viva!, hurra!

hurray [hʊ'reɪ] *excl* viva!

hurricane ['hʌrɪkən] *n* furacão *m*.

hurried ['hʌrɪd] *adj* [hasty] apressado(da), precipitado(da).

hurriedly ['hʌrɪdlɪ] *adv* apressadamente, precipitadamente.

hurry ['hʌrɪ] (*pt* & *pp* -**ied**) <> *vt* apressar. <> *vi* apressar-se; **to** ~ **to do sthg** apressar-se para fazer algo. <> *n* [rush] pressa *f*; **to be in a** ~ estar com pressa; **to do sthg in a** ~ fazer algo com pressa; **to be in no** ~ **to do sthg** [unwilling] não estar com pressa nenhuma de fazer algo.
➥ **hurry off** *vi* sair correndo.
➥ **hurry up** *vi* apressar-se; **hurry!** vamos de uma vez! <> *vt sep* apressar, acelerar.

hurt [hɜːt] (*pt* & *pp* **hurt**) <> *vt* -**1.** [cause physical pain to] machucar -**2.** [injure] ferir -**3.** [upset] magoar -**4.** [be detrimental to] prejudicar. <> *vi* -**1.** [gen] doer; **my feet** ~ os meus pés doem; **ouch, you're** ~ **ing!** ai, você está me machucando -**2.** [be detrimental] prejudicar. <> *adj* -**1.** [injured] machucado(da) -**2.** [upset] magoado(da). <> *n* (U) [emotional pain] dor *f*.

hurtful ['hɜːtfʊl] *adj* ofensivo(va).

hurtle ['hɜːtl] *vi* precipitar-se; **to** ~ **over** precipitar-se por; **to** ~ **past** passar como um raio.

husband ['hʌzbənd] *n* marido *m*.

husbandry ['hʌzbəndrɪ] *n* (U) *fml* criação *f*.

hush [hʌʃ] <> *n* [quietness] silêncio *m*. <> *vt* [silence] silenciar. <> *excl* silêncio!
➥ **hush up** *vt sep* -**1.** [affair] silenciar a respeito de -**2.** [noisy person] ficar quieto(ta).

hush money *n* (U) *inf* suborno *m* (*para comprar o silêncio de alguém*).

husk [hʌsk] *n* [of seed, grain] casca *f*.

husky ['hʌskɪ] (*compar* **-ier**, *superl* **-iest**) <> *adj* [hoarse] rouco(ca). <> *n* [dog] husky *m*.

hustings ['hʌstɪŋz] *npl UK* campanha *f* eleitoral.

hustle ['hʌsl] <> *vt* **-1.** [hurry] empurrar **-2.** *US* [persuade, trick]: **to ~ sb into doing sthg** pressionar alguém a fazer algo *OR* para que faça algo. <> *n (U)* [business]: **~ and bustle** grande atividade *f*.

hut [hʌt] *n* **-1.** [rough house] cabana *f* **-2.** [shed] barraca *f*.

hutch [hʌtʃ] *n* arapuca *f*.

hyacinth ['haɪəsɪnθ] *n* jacinto *m*.

hybrid ['haɪbrɪd] <> *adj* híbrido(da). <> *n* híbrido *m*.

hydrangea [haɪ'dreɪndʒə] *n* hortênsia *f*.

hydrant ['haɪdrənt] *n* hidrante *m*.

hydraulic [haɪ'drɔːlɪk] *adj* hidráulico(ca).
➡ **hydraulics** *n (U)* hidráulica *f*.

hydro *n UK* [spa] estância *f* hidromineral.

hydrocarbon [ˌhaɪdrə'kɑːbən] *n* hidrocarboneto *m*.

hydrochloric acid [ˌhaɪdrə'klɔːrɪk-] *n (U)* ácido *m* clorídrico.

hydroelectric [ˌhaɪdrəʊɪ'lektrɪk] *adj* hidrelétrico(-ca).

hydroelectricity [ˌhaɪdrəʊlek'trɪsətɪ] *n (U)* hidreletricidade *f*.

hydrofoil ['haɪdrəfɔɪl] *n* embarcação *f* com hidrofólio.

hydrogen ['haɪdrədʒən] *n (U)* hidrogênio *m*.

hydrogen bomb *n* bomba *f* de hidrogênio.

hydrophobia [ˌhaɪdrə'fəʊbjə] *n (U) fml* [rabies] hidrofobia *f*.

hydroplane ['haɪdrəpleɪn] *n* [speedboat] hidroplano *m*.

hyena [haɪ'iːnə] *n* hiena *f*.

hygiene ['haɪdʒiːn] *n (U)* higiene *f*.

hygienic [haɪ'dʒiːnɪk] *adj* higiênico(ca).

hygienist [haɪ'dʒiːnɪst] *n* [at dentist's] higienista *mf* bucal.

hymn [hɪm] *n* hino *m*.

hymn book *n* hinário *m*.

hype [haɪp] *inf* <> *n (U)* propaganda *f* exagerada. <> *vt* fazer propaganda exagerada de.

hyped up [haɪpd-] *adj inf* como uma pilha de nervos.

hyper ['haɪpə'] *adj inf* enérgico(ca), ativo(va).

hyperactive [ˌhaɪpər'æktɪv] *adj* hiperativo(va).

hyperbole [haɪ'pɜːbəlɪ] *n (U)* hipérbole *f*.

hyperinflation *n (U)* hiperinflação *f*.

hyperlink ['haɪpəˌlɪŋk] *n COMPUT* hyperlink *m*.

hypermarket ['haɪpəˌmɑːkɪt] *n* hipermercado *m*.

hypersensitive [ˌhaɪpə'sensɪtɪv] *adj* **-1.** [easily offended]: **~ (to/about sthg)** hipersensível (a algo) **-2.** *MED* hipersensível.

hypertension [ˌhaɪpə'tenʃn] *n MED (U)* hipertensão *f*.

hypertext ['haɪpətekst] *n COMPUT* hipertexto *m*.

hyperventilate [ˌhaɪpə'ventɪleɪt] *vi* hiperventilar.

hyphen ['haɪfn] *n* hífen *m*.

hyphenate ['haɪfəneɪt] *vt* hifenizar.

hypnosis [hɪp'nəʊsɪs] *n (U)* hipnose *f*; **under ~** hipnotizado(da).

hypnotic [hɪp'nɒtɪk] *adj* hipnótico(ca).

hypnotism ['hɪpnətɪzm] *n (U)* hipnotismo *m*.

hypnotist ['hɪpnətɪst] *n* hipnotizador *m*, -ra *f*.

hypnotize, -ise ['hɪpnətaɪz] *vt* hipnotizar.

hypoallergenic ['haɪpəʊˌælə'dʒenɪk] *adj* hipoalergênico(ca).

hypochondriac [ˌhaɪpə'kɒndriæk] *n* hipocondríaco *m*, -ca *f*.

hypocrisy [hɪ'pɒkrəsɪ] *n (U)* hipocrisia *f*.

hypocrite ['hɪpəkrɪt] *n* hipócrita *mf*.

hypocritical [ˌhɪpə'krɪtɪkl] *adj* hipócrita.

hypodermic needle [ˌhaɪpə'dɜːmɪk-] *n* agulha *f* hipodérmica.

hypodermic syringe [ˌhaɪpə'dɜːmɪk-] *n* seringa *f* hipodérmica.

hypothermia [ˌhaɪpəʊ'θɜːmɪə] *n (U)* hipotermia *f*.

hypothesis [haɪ'pɒθɪsɪs] (*pl* **-theses** [-θɪsiːzl]) *n* hipótese *f*.

hypothesize, -ise [haɪ'pɒθɪsaɪz] <> *vt* fazer hipóteses sobre. <> *vi* fazer hipóteses.

hypothetical [ˌhaɪpə'θetɪkl] *adj* hipotético(ca).

hysterectomy [ˌhɪstə'rektəmɪl] (*pl* **-ies**) *n* histerectomia *f*.

hysteria [hɪs'tɪərɪə] *n* histeria *f*.

hysterical [hɪs'terɪkl] *adj* **-1.** [gen] histérico(ca) **-2.** *inf* [very funny] hilariante.

hysterics [hɪs'terɪks] *npl* **-1.** [panic, excitement] crise *f* histérica, histeria *f* **-2.** *inf* [fits of laughter] ataque *m* de riso; **to be in ~** arrebentar-se de tanto rir.

Hz (*abbr of* **hertz**) Hz.

---

i (*pl* **i's** *OR* **is**), **I** (*pl* **I's** *OR* **Is**) [aɪ] *n* [letter] i, I *m*.

I¹ [aɪ] (*abbr of* **Island, Isle**) ilha *f*.

I² [aɪ] *pers pron* eu; **she and ~ were at college together** eu e ela fomos ao colégio juntos(tas); **it is ~** *fml* sou eu; **~ can't do it** eu não posso fazer isso.

IA *abbr of* **Iowa**.

IAEA (*abbr of* **International Atomic Energy Agency**) *n* AIEA *f*.

IATA (*abbr of* **International Air Transport Association**) *n associação internacional de transporte aéreo*, IATA *f*.

IBA (*abbr of* **Independent Broadcasting Authority**) *n órgão britânico de regulamentação das redes privadas de rádio e televisão*.

Iberian [aɪ'bɪːrɪən] <> *adj* ibérico(ca). <> *n* ibérico *m*, -ca *f*.

Iberian peninsula *n*: the ~ a Península Ibérica.

ibid (*abbr of* **ibidem**) ib.

i/c (*abbr of* **in charge**) resp.; **to be ~ sthg** ser responsável por.

ICA (*abbr of* **Institute of Contemporary Arts**) *n* *instituto de arte contemporânea de Londres*.

ICBM (*abbr of* **intercontinental ballistic missile**) *n* míssil *m* balístico intercontinental.

ICC *n* **-1.** (*abbr of* **International Chamber of Commerce**) ICC *f*, Câmara *f* de Comércio Internacional **-2.** (*abbr of* **Interstate Commerce Commission**) *órgão federal norte-americano que regula o comércio entre os estados*.

ice [aɪs] <> *n* **-1.** (*U*)[gen] gelo *m*; **to break the ~** *fig* quebrar o gelo; **to put sthg on ~** *fig* colocar algo de lado **-2.** *UK* [ice cream] sorvete *m*. <> *vt UK* [cover with icing] cobrir com glacê.
◆ **ice over, ice up** *vi* congelar.

ice age *n* era *f* glacial.

iceberg ['aɪsbɜːg] *n* iceberg *m*.

iceberg lettuce *n* alface *f* americana.

icebox ['aɪsbɒks] *n* **-1.** *UK* [in refrigerator] congelador *m* **-2.** *US* [refrigerator] geladeira *f*, refrigerador *m*.

icebreaker ['aɪs̩breɪkəʳ] *n* [ship] navio *m* quebra-gelo.

ice bucket *n* balde *m* de gelo.

ice cap *n* calota *f* glacial.

ice-cold *adj* gelado(da).

ice cream *n* sorvete *m*.

ice cream bar *n US* picolé *m* com casquinha de chocolate.

ice cube *n* cubo *m* de gelo.

iced [aɪst] *adj* **-1.** [cooled with ice] com gelo **-2.** [covered in icing] coberto(ta) com glacê.

ice floe *n* banquisa *f*.

ice hockey *n* (*U*) hóquei *m* sobre o gelo.

Iceland ['aɪslənd] *n* Islândia; **in ~** na Islândia.

Icelander ['aɪsləndəʳ] *n* islandês *m*, -esa *f*.

Icelandic [aɪs'lændɪk] <> *adj* islandês(esa). <> *n* [language] islandês *m*.

ice lolly *n UK* picolé *m*.

ice pick *n* picador *m* de gelo.

ice rink *n* rinque *m* (de patinação).

ice skate *n* patim *m* para o gelo.
◆ **ice-skate** *vi* patinar sobre o gelo.

ice-skater *n* patinador *m*, -ra *f* sobre o gelo.

ice-skating *n* (*U*) patinação *f* sobre o gelo; **to go ~** praticar patinação.

icicle ['aɪsɪkl] *n* pingente *m* de gelo.

icily ['aɪsɪlɪ] *adv* [in unfriendly way] friamente.

icing ['aɪsɪŋ] *n* (*U*) glacê *m*; **the third goal was the ~ on the cake** *fig* o terceiro gol foi para coroar a vitória.

icing sugar *n UK* açúcar *m* de confeiteiro.

ICJ (*abbr of* **International Court of Justice**) *n* TIJ *m*.

icon ['aɪkɒn] *n* ícone *m*.

iconoclast [aɪ'kɒnəklæst] *n* iconoclasta *mf*.

ICR (*abbr of* **Institute for Cancer Research**) *n* instituto norte-americano para pesquisa do câncer, ≃ INCA *m*.

ICU (*abbr of* **intensive-care unit**) *n* UTI *f*.

icy ['aɪsɪ] (*compar* **-ier**, *superl* **-iest**) *adj* **-1.** [very cold]

gelado(da) **-2.** [covered in ice] coberto(ta) de gelo **-3.** *fig* [unfriendly] frio (fria).

id [ɪd] *n* id *m*.

I'd [aɪd] = **I would, I had**.

ID <> *n* (*abbr of* **identification**) identificação *f*; **~ card** (carteira *f* de) *f* identidade, ≃ RG *m*. <> *abbr of* **Idaho**.

Idaho ['aɪdəˌhəʊ] *n* Idaho.

ID card *n* = **identity card**.

IDD (*abbr of* **international direct dialling**) *n* DDI *m*.

idea [aɪ'dɪə] *n* **-1.** [gen] idéia *f*; **to get the ~** *inf* pegar a idéia; **wherever did you get the ~ that I don't like him?** de onde você tirou a idéia de que eu não gosto dele?; **to have an ~ of sthg** ter idéia de algo; **to have an ~ that** ter a sensação de que; **to have no ~** não ter idéia; **the ~ is to...** a idéia é ... **-2.** [suspicion] impressão *f*.

ideal [aɪ'dɪəl] <> *adj* [perfect] ideal; **to be ~ for sthg** ser ideal para algo. <> *n* [principle] ideal *m*.

idealism [aɪ'dɪəlɪzm] *n* [high principles] idealismo *m*.

idealist [aɪ'dɪəlɪst] *n* idealista *mf*.

idealize, -ise [aɪ'dɪəlaɪz] *vt* idealizar.

ideally [aɪ'dɪəlɪ] *adv* **-1.** [perfectly] perfeitamente **-2.** [preferably] idealmente.

identical [aɪ'dentɪkl] *adj* idêntico(ca).

identical twins *npl* gêmeos *mpl* idênticos.

identifiable [aɪ'dentɪfaɪəbl] *adj* identificável.

identification [aɪˌdentɪfɪ'keɪʃn] *n* identificação *f*; **~ with sb/sthg** identificação com alguém/algo.

identify [aɪ'dentɪfaɪ] (*pt & pp* **-ied**) <> *vt* **-1.** [gen] identificar **-2.** [connect]: **to ~ sb with sthg** relacionar alguém a algo. <> *vi* [empathize]: **to ~ with sb/sthg** identificar-se com alguém/algo.

Identikit picture® [aɪ'dentɪkɪt-] *n* retrato *m* falado.

identity [aɪ'dentətɪ] (*pl* **-ies**) *n* identidade *f*.

identity card *n* (carteira *f* de) identidade *f*.

identity parade *n* identificação *f* (*de um criminoso*).

ideological [ˌaɪdɪə'lɒdʒɪkl] *adj* ideológico(ca).

ideology [ˌaɪdɪ'ɒlədʒɪ] (*pl* **-ies**) *n* ideologia *f*.

idiom ['ɪdɪəm] *n* **-1.** [phrase] expressão *f* idiomática **-2.** *fml* [style, language] linguagem *f*.

idiomatic [ˌɪdɪə'mætɪk] *adj* [natural-sounding] idiomático(ca).

idiosyncrasy [ˌɪdɪə'sɪŋkrəsɪ] (*pl* **-ies**) *n* idiossincrasia *f*.

idiot ['ɪdɪət] *n* [fool] idiota *mf*.

idiotic [ˌɪdɪ'ɒtɪk] *adj* idiota.

idle ['aɪdl] <> *adj* **-1.** [person - inactive] ocioso(sa); [- lazy] preguiçoso(sa) **-2.** [not in use] parado(da) **-3.** [empty] vão (vã) **-4.** [casual] casual **-5.** [futile] inútil. <> *vi* [engine] estar em ponto morto.
◆ **idle away** *vt sep* desperdiçar.

idleness ['aɪdlnɪs] *n* (*U*) [laziness] preguiça *f*.

idler ['aɪdləʳ] *n* preguiçoso(sa), desocupado(da).

idly ['aɪdlɪ] *adv* **-1.** [lazily] preguiçosamente **-2.** [casually] casualmente.

idol ['aɪdl] *n* ídolo *m*.

idolize, -ise ['aɪdəlaɪz] *vt* idolatrar.

idyll ['ɪdɪl] *n* idílio *m*.

idyllic [ɪ'dɪlɪk] *adj* idílico(ca).

i.e. (*abbr of* **id est**) i.e.

IEE (*abbr of* **Institution of Electrical Engineers**) *n* *instituto britânico de engenheiros eletricistas.*

if [ɪf] ◇ *conj* **-1.** [gen] se; ~ **I were you** se eu fosse você **-2.** [though] ainda que; **a good,** ~ **rather expensive, restaurant** um bom restaurante, ainda que caro **-3.** [that] que. ◇ *n:* ~ **s and buts** poréns *mpl.*
➡ **if not** *conj* se não.
➡ **if only** ◇ *conj* **-1.** [providing a reason] ao menos, nem que seja; **let's stop at the next services,** ~ **to stretch our legs** vamos parar no próximo posto, ao menos OR nem que seja para esticar as pernas **-2.** [expressing regret] se ao menos. ◇ *excl* quem dera!

iffy ['ɪfɪ] (*compar* -ier, *superl* -iest) *adj inf* inseguro(ra).

igloo ['ɪɡluː] (*pl* -s) *n* iglu *m.*

ignite [ɪɡ'naɪt] ◇ *vt* acender. ◇ *vi* acender, acender-se.

ignition [ɪɡ'nɪʃn] *n* ignição *f.*

ignition key *n* chave *f* de ignição.

ignoble [ɪɡ'nəʊbl] *adj fml* ignóbil.

ignominious [ˌɪɡnə'mɪnɪəs] *adj fml* ignominioso(-sa).

ignominy ['ɪɡnəmɪnɪ] *n (U) fml* ignomínia *f.*

ignoramus [ˌɪɡnə'reɪməs] (*pl* -es) *n* ignorante *mf.*

ignorance ['ɪɡnərəns] *n (U)* ignorância *f.*

ignorant ['ɪɡnərənt] *adj* **-1.** [uneducated] ignorante; [lacking information] desinformado(da) **-2.** *fml* [unaware]: **to be** ~ **of sthg** ignorar algo **-3.** *inf* [rude] ignorante.

ignore [ɪɡ'nɔːʳ] *vt* [take no notice of] ignorar.

iguana [ɪ'ɡwɑːnə] (*pl inv* OR -s) *n* iguana *f.*

ikon ['aɪkɒn] *n* = **icon.**

IL *abbr of* Illinois.

ILEA (*abbr of* **Inner London Education Authority**) *n antigo órgão responsável pela educacão em Londres.*

ileum ['ɪlɪəm] (*pl* ilea ['ɪlɪə]) *n* íleo *m.*

ilk [ɪlk] *n fml:* **of that** ~ [of that sort] do mesmo tipo.

ill [ɪl] ◇ *adj* **-1.** [sick, unwell] doente; **to feel** ~ sentir-se doente; **to be taken** ~, **to fall** ~ ficar doente **-2.** [bad, unfavourable] mau (má). ◇ *adv* mal; **to speak/think** ~ **of sb** falar/pensar mal de alguém; **we can** ~ **afford such luxuries** mal conseguimos pagar esses luxos.
➡ **ills** *npl* males *mpl.*

ill. (*abbr of* illustration) il.

I'll [aɪl] = **I will, I shall.**

ill-advised [-əd'vaɪzd] *adj* **-1.** [not sensible] imprudente, insensato(ta); **to be** ~ **to do sthg** ser imprudente fazer algo **-2.** [unwise] pouco aconselhável.

ill at ease *adj:* **he always felt shy and** ~ **at parties** ele sempre se sentia intimidado e pouco àvontade nas festas.

ill-bred *adj* malcriado(da).

ill-considered *adj* imponderado(da).

ill-disposed *adj:* **to be** ~ **towards sb** estar de má vontade com alguém.

illegal [ɪ'liːɡl] *adj* ilegal; ~ **immigrant/alien** imigrante/estrangeiro ilegal.

illegally [ɪ'liːɡəlɪ] *adv* ilegalmente.

illegible [ɪ'ledʒəbl] *adj* ilegível.

illegitimate [ˌɪlɪ'dʒɪtɪmət] *adj* ilegítimo(ma).

ill-equipped [-ɪ'kwɪpt] *adj* despreparado(da).

ill-fated [-'feɪtɪd] *adj* malfadado(da).

ill feeling *n (U)* ressentimento *f,* rancor *m.*

ill-founded [-'faʊndɪd] *adj* infundado(da).

ill-gotten gains [-'ɡɒtən-] *npl fml* ganhos *mpl* ilícitos.

ill health *n (U)* má saúde *f.*

illicit [ɪ'lɪsɪt] *adj* ilícito(ta).

illicitly [ɪ'lɪsɪtlɪ] *adv* ilicitamente.

ill-informed *adj* mal informado(da).

Illinois *n* Illinois; **in** ~ em Illinois.

illiteracy [ɪ'lɪtərəsɪ] *n (U)* analfabetismo *m.*

illiterate [ɪ'lɪtərət] ◇ *adj* analfabeto(ta). ◇ *n* analfabeto *m,* -ta *f.*

ill-mannered *adj* mal-educado(da).

illness ['ɪlnɪs] *n* doença *f.*

illogical [ɪ'lɒdʒɪkl] *adj* ilógico(ca).

ill-suited *adj* inadequado(da); **an** ~ **couple** um casal desajustado; **to be** ~ **to sthg** ser inadequado(da) para algo.

ill-tempered *adj* mal-humorado(da), genioso(-sa).

ill-timed [-'taɪmd] *adj* inoportuno(na).

ill-treat *vt* maltratar.

ill-treatment *n (U)* maus tratos *mpl.*

illuminate [ɪ'luːmɪneɪt] *vt* **-1.** [light up] iluminar **-2.** [explain] ilustrar, esclarecer.

illuminated [ɪ'luːmɪneɪtɪd] *adj* [sign, notice] iluminado(da).

illuminating [ɪ'luːmɪneɪtɪŋ] *adj* [enlightening] esclarecedor(ra).

illumination [ɪˌluːmɪ'neɪʃn] *n (U)* [lighting] iluminação *f.*
➡ **illuminations** *npl* UK luzes *fpl* decorativas.

illusion [ɪ'luːʒn] *n* **-1.** [gen] ilusão *f;* **to have no** ~ **s about sb/sthg** não ter ilusões com alguém/algo; **to be under the** ~ **that** estar com a ilusão de que **-2.** [magic trick] truque *m* de ilusionismo.

illusionist [ɪ'luːʒənɪst] *n fml* ilusionista *mf.*

illusory [ɪ'luːsərɪ] *adj fml* ilusório(ria).

illustrate ['ɪləstreɪt] *vt* ilustrar.

illustration [ˌɪlə'streɪʃn] *n* ilustração *f.*

illustrator ['ɪləstreɪtəʳ] *n* ilustrador *m,* -ra *f.*

illustrious [ɪ'lʌstrɪəs] *adj fml* ilustre.

ill will *n (U)* animosidade *f.*

ill wind [-wɪnd] *n:* **it's an** ~ **(that blows nobody any good)** *proverb* há males que vêm para o bem.

ILO (*abbr of* **International Labour Organization**) *n* OIT *f.*

I'm [aɪm] = **I am.**

image ['ɪmɪdʒ] *n* [gen] imagem *f;* **to be the** ~ **of sb** ser a cara de alguém.

imagery ['ɪmɪdʒrɪ] *n* imagens *fpl.*

imaginable [ɪ'mædʒɪnəbl] *adj* imaginável.

imaginary [ɪ'mædʒɪnrɪ] *adj* imaginário(ria).

imagination [ɪˌmædʒɪ'neɪʃn] *n* imaginação *f.*

imaginative [ɪ'mædʒɪnətɪv] *adj* imaginativo(va).

imagine [ɪ'mædʒɪn] *vt* imaginar; **to** ~ **doing sthg** imaginar fazer algo; ~ **(that)!** imagine!

imaginings [ɪ'mædʒɪnɪŋz] *npl literary* fantasias *fpl.*

imbalance [ˌɪm'bæləns] *n* desequilíbrio *m.*

imbecile [ˈɪmbɪsiːl] n imbecil mf.
imbue [ɪmˈbjuː] vt fml: **to be ~d with sthg** estar imbuído(da) de algo.
IMF (abbr of International Monetary Fund) n FMI m.
imitate [ˈɪmɪteɪt] vt imitar.
imitation [ˌɪmɪˈteɪʃn] ◇ n imitação f. ◇ adj de imitação.
imitator [ˈɪmɪteɪtər] n imitador m, -ra f.
immaculate [ɪˈnfækjʊlət] adj -1. [clean and tidy] imaculado(da) -2. [impeccable] impecável.
immaculately [ɪˈmækjʊlətlɪ] adv -1. [cleanly, tidily] de maneira imaculada -2. [impeccably] impecavelmente.
immaterial [ˌɪməˈtɪərɪəl] adj [irrelevant, unimportant] irrelevante.
immature [ˌɪməˈtjʊər] adj -1. [childish] imaturo(ra) -2. BOT & ZOOL jovem.
immaturity [ˌɪməˈtjʊərətɪ] n -1. [childishness] imaturidade f -2. BOT & ZOOL juventude f.
immeasurable [ɪˈmeʒrəbl] adj incomensurável.
immediacy [ɪˈmiːdjəsɪ] n (U) imediatidade f, urgência f.
immediate [ɪˈmiːdjət] adj -1. [gen] imediato(ta) -2. [closest in relationship] próximo(ma).
immediately [ɪˈmiːdjətlɪ] ◇ adv -1. [gen] imediatamente -2. [directly, closely] diretamente. ◇ conj [as soon as] assim que.
immemorial [ˌɪmɪˈmɔːrɪəl] adj: **from time ~** desde tempos imemoráveis.
immense [ɪˈmens] adj imenso(sa).
immensely [ɪˈmenslɪ] adv imensamente.
immensity [ɪˈmensətɪ] n (U) imensidão f.
immerse [ɪˈmɜːs] vt -1. [plunge into liquid]: **to ~ sthg in sthg** mergulhar algo em algo -2. fig [involve]: **to ~ o.s. in sthg** envolver-se em algo.
immersion heater [ɪˈmɜːʃn-] n ebulidor m.
immigrant [ˈɪmɪgrənt] ◇ n imigrante mf. ◇ comp de imigrantes.
immigration [ˌɪmɪˈgreɪʃn] ◇ n (U) imigração f. ◇ comp de imigração; **~ restrictions** restrições fpl para imigração.
imminence [ˈɪmɪnəns] n (U) iminência f.
imminent [ˈɪmɪnənt] adj iminente.
immobile [ɪˈməʊbaɪl] adj imóvel.
immobilization [ɪˌməʊbɪlaɪˈzeɪʃn] n (U) imobilização f.
immobilize, -ise [ɪˈməʊbɪlaɪz] vt imobilizar.
immobilizer n AUT corta-corrente m.
immodest [ɪˈmɒdɪst] adj -1. [vain] vaidoso(sa) -2. [indecent] indecente.
immoral [ɪˈmɒrəl] adj imoral.
immorality [ˌɪməˈrælətɪ] n (U) imoralidade f.
immortal [ɪˈmɔːtl] ◇ adj imortal. ◇ n -1. [god] deus m -2. [hero] imortal mf.
immortality [ˌɪmɔːˈtælətɪ] n imortalidade f.
immortalize, -ise [ɪˈmɔːtəlaɪz] vt imortalizar.
immovable [ɪˈmuːvəbl] adj -1. [fixed] fixo(xa) -2. [obstinate] inflexível.
immune [ɪˈmjuːn] adj -1. MED imune; **to be ~ to sthg** ser imune a algo -2. fig [impervious]: **to be ~ to sthg** não ser suscetível a algo -3. [exempt] isento(ta), livre; **to be ~ from sthg** estar protegido(da) de algo.

immune system n sistema m imunológico.
immunity [ɪˈmjuːnətɪ] n -1. (U) MED: **~ (to sthg)** imunidade f (a algo) -2. (U) fig [imperviousness]: **~ to sthg** falta f de suscetibilidade a algo -3. [exemption] isenção f; **~ from sthg** proteção f contra algo.
immunization [ˌɪmjuːnaɪˈzeɪʃn] n MED imunização f.
immunize, -ise [ˈɪmjuːnaɪz] vt: **to ~ sb (against sthg)** MED imunizar alguém (contra algo).
immunodeficiency [ˌɪmjuːnəʊdɪˈfɪʃənsɪ] n (U) imunodeficiência f.
immunology [ˌɪmjuːnˈɒlədʒɪ] n (U) imunologia f.
immutable [ɪˈmjuːtəbl] adj fml imutável.
imp [ɪmp] n -1. [creature] diabinho m -2. [naughty child] diabinho m, -nha f.
impact [n ˈɪmpækt, vb ɪmˈpækt] ◇ n impacto m; **on ~** ao impacto; **to make an ~ on sb/sthg** causar impacto em alguém/algo. ◇ vt -1. [collide with] colidir com -2. [influence] influenciar.
impair [ɪmˈpeər] vt prejudicar, debilitar.
impaired [ɪmˈpeəd] adj prejudicado(da), debilitado(da).
impale [ɪmˈpeɪl] vt perfurar; **to ~ sb/sthg on sthg** empalar alguém/algo em algo.
impart [ɪmˈpɑːt] vt fml -1. [information]: **to ~ sthg (to sb)** transmitir algo (a alguém) -2. [feeling, quality] conferir; **to ~ flavour to the dish** conferir sabor ao prato.
impartial [ɪmˈpɑːʃl] adj imparcial.
impartiality [ɪmˌpɑːʃɪˈælətɪ] n (U) imparcialidade f.
impassable [ɪmˈpɑːsəbl] adj intransitável.
impasse [æmˈpɑːs] n impasse m; **to reach an ~** chegar a um impasse.
impassioned [ɪmˈpæʃnd] adj veemente.
impassive [ɪmˈpæsɪv] adj impassível.
impatience [ɪmˈpeɪʃns] n impaciência f.
impatient [ɪmˈpeɪʃnt] adj impaciente; **to be ~ to do sthg** estar impaciente para fazer algo; **to be ~ for sthg** esperar algo com impaciência.
impatiently [ɪmˈpeɪʃntlɪ] adv impacientemente.
impeach [ɪmˈpiːtʃ] vt JUR impugnar.
impeachment [ɪmˈpiːtʃmənt] n (U) JUR impeachment m.
impeccable [ɪmˈpekəbl] adj impecável.
impeccably [ɪmˈpekəblɪ] adv impecavelmente.
impecunious [ˌɪmpɪˈkjuːnjəs] adj fml indigente.
impede [ɪmˈpiːd] vt impedir.
impediment [ɪmˈpedɪmənt] n impedimento m; **a speech ~** um defeito de fala.
impel [ɪmˈpel] (pt & pp -led, cont -ling) vt: **to ~ sb to do sthg** impelir alguém a fazer algo.
impending [ɪmˈpendɪŋ] adj iminente.
impenetrable [ɪmˈpenɪtrəbl] adj -1. [impossible to penetrate] impenetrável -2. [impossible to understand] incompreensível.
imperative [ɪmˈperətɪv] ◇ adj [essential] indispensável. ◇ n imperativo m.
imperceptible [ˌɪmpəˈseptəbl] adj imperceptível.
imperfect [ɪmˈpɜːfɪkt] ◇ adj [not perfect] imperfeito(ta). ◇ n GRAM: **~ (tense)** (pretérito m) imperfeito m.

imperfection [ˌɪmpə'fekʃn] *n* imperfeição *f.*

imperial [ɪm'pɪərɪəl] *adj* **-1.** [of an empire or emperor] imperial **-2.** [system of measurement]: ~ **system** *sistema britânico de medidas.*

imperialism [ɪm'pɪərɪəlɪzml] *n (U)* imperialismo *m.*

imperialist [ɪm'pɪərɪəlɪst] ⋄ *adj* imperialista. ⋄ *n* imperialista *mf.*

imperil [ɪm'perɪl] (*UK pt* & *pp* -**led**, *cont* -**ling**, *US pt* & *pp* -**ed**, *cont* -**ing**) *vt fml* pôr em perigo.

imperious [ɪm'pɪərɪəs] *adj* imperioso(sa).

impersonal [ɪm'pɜːsnl] *adj* impessoal.

impersonate [ɪm'pɜːsəneɪt] *vt* **-1.** [mimic, imitate] imitar **-2.** [pretend to be] fazer-se passar por.

impersonation [ɪmˌpɜːsə'neɪʃn] *n* [by mimic] imitação *f*; **to do ~s (of sb)** fazer imitações (de alguém).

impersonator [ɪm'pɜːsəneɪtə^r] *n* **-1.** [mimic] imitador *m*, -ra *f* **-2.** [impostor] impostor *m*, -ra *f.*

impertinence [ɪm'pɜːtɪnəns] *n (U)* impertinência *f.*

impertinent [ɪm'pɜːtɪnənt] *adj* [rude] impertinente.

imperturbable [ˌɪmpə'tɜːbəbl] *adj* imperturbável.

impervious [ɪm'pɜːvjəs] *adj* [not influenced]: ~ **to** sthg imune a algo.

impetuous [ɪm'petʃʊəs] *adj* impetuoso(sa).

impetus ['ɪmpɪtəs] *n* **-1.** [momentum] ímpeto *m* **-2.** [stimulus] estímulo *m.*

impinge [ɪm'pɪndʒ] *vi*: **to ~ on sb/sthg** afetar alguém/algo.

impish ['ɪmpɪʃ] *adj* travesso(sa).

implacable [ɪm'plækəbl] *adj* implacável.

implant [*n* 'ɪmplɑːnt, *vb* ɪm'plɑːnt] ⋄ *n* implante *m.* ⋄ *vt*: **to ~ sthg in(to) sb** implantar algo em alguém.

implausible [ɪm'plɔːzəbl] *adj* implausível.

implement [*n* 'ɪmplɪmənt, *vt* 'ɪmplɪment] ⋄ *n* [tool] ferramenta *f.* ⋄ *vt* implementar.

implementation [ˌɪmplɪmen'teɪʃn] *n (U)* implementação *f.*

implicate ['ɪmplɪkeɪt] *vt*: **to ~ sb in sthg** implicar alguém em algo.

implication [ˌɪmplɪ'keɪʃn] *n* **-1.** *(U)* [involvement] implicação *f*, envolvimento *m* **-2.** [inference] implicação *f*; **by ~** por conseqüência.

implicit [ɪm'plɪsɪt] *adj* **-1.** [inferred] implícito(ta) **-2.** [inherent]: ~ **in sthg** inerente a algo **-3.** [complete] absoluto(ta).

implicitly [ɪm'plɪsɪtlɪ] *adv* **-1.** [by inference] implicitamente **-2.** [completely] absolutamente.

implied [ɪm'plaɪd] *adj* subentendido(da).

implode [ɪm'pləʊd] *vi* implodir.

implore [ɪm'plɔː^r] *vt*: **to ~ sb (to do sthg)** implorar a alguém (para que faça algo).

imply [ɪm'plaɪ] (*pt* & *pp* -**ied**) *vt* **-1.** [suggest] pressupor **-2.** [involve] implicar.

impolite [ˌɪmpə'laɪt] *adj* descortês, indelicado(da).

imponderable [ɪm'pɒndrəbl] *adj* imponderável.
▶ **imponderables** *npl* imponderáveis *mpl.*

import [*n* 'ɪmpɔːt, *vt* ɪm'pɔːt] ⋄ *n* **-1.** COMM importação *f* **-2.** *fml* [meaning] significado *m*, sentido *m* **-3.** *(U) fml* [importance] importância *f.* ⋄

comp de importação. ⋄ *vt* importar.

importance [ɪm'pɔːtns] *n (U)* importância *f.*

important [ɪm'pɔːtnt] *adj* importante; **to be ~ to sb** ser importante para alguém.

importantly [ɪm'pɔːtntlɪ] *adv*: **more ~** o que é mais importante.

importation [ˌɪmpɔː'teɪʃn] *n (U)* importação *f.*

imported [ɪm'pɔːtɪd] *adj* importado(da).

importer [ɪm'pɔːtə^r] *n* importâdor *m*, -ra *f.*

impose [ɪm'pəʊz] ⋄ *vt* [force]: **to ~ sthg (on sb/sthg)** impor algo (a alguém/algo). ⋄ *vi* [cause trouble]: **to ~ (on sb)** causar problemas (para alguém).

imposing [ɪm'pəʊzɪŋ] *adj* imponente.

imposition [ˌɪmpə'zɪʃn] *n* imposição *f.*

impossibility [ɪmˌpɒsə'bɪlətɪ] (*pl* -**ies**) *n* impossibilidade *f.*

impossible [ɪm'pɒsəbl] ⋄ *adj* impossível. ⋄ *n*: **to do the ~** fazer o impossível.

impostor, imposter *US* [ɪm'pɒstə^r] *n* impostor *m*, -ra *f.*

impotence ['ɪmpətəns] *n* impotência *f.*

impotent ['ɪmpətənt] *adj* impotente.

impound [ɪm'paʊnd] *vt* JUR apreender.

impoverished [ɪm'pɒvərɪʃt] *adj lit* & *fig* empobrecido(da).

impracticable [ɪm'præktɪkəbl] *adj* impraticável.

impractical [ɪm'præktɪkl] *adj* pouco prático(ca).

imprecation [ˌɪmprɪ'keɪʃn] *n fml* imprecação *f.*

imprecise [ɪmprɪ'saɪs] *adj* impreciso(sa).

impregnable [ɪm'pregnəbl] *adj* **-1.** [impenetrable] invulnerável **-2.** *fig* [in very strong position] imbatível.

impregnate ['ɪmpregneɪt] *vt* **-1.** [introduce substance into]: **to ~ sthg with sthg** impregnar algo de algo **-2.** *fml* [fertilize] fecundar.

impresario [ˌɪmprɪ'sɑːrɪəʊ] (*pl* -**s**) *n* empresário *m*, -ria *f* teatral.

impress [ɪm'pres] ⋄ *vt* **-1.** [influence, affect] impressionar **-2.** [make clear]: **to ~ sthg on sb** convencer alguém da importância de algo. ⋄ *vi* impressionar.

impression [ɪm'preʃn] *n* **-1.** [gen] impressão *f*; **to make an ~** impressionar; **to be under the ~ (that)** ter a impressão de que **-2.** [impersonation] imitação *f.*

impressionable [ɪm'preʃnəbl] *adj* impressionável.

Impressionism *n (U)* ART Impressionismo *m.*

impressionist [ɪm'preʃənɪst] *n* [entertainer] imitador *m*, -ra *f.*
▶ **Impressionist** ART ⋄ *adj* impressionista. ⋄ *n* impressionista *mf.*

impressive [ɪm'presɪv] *adj* impressionante.

imprint ['ɪmprɪnt] ⋄ *n* **-1.** [mark] marca *f*, impressão *f* **-2.** [publisher's name] ≃ selo *m* da editora. ⋄ *vt* [mark] imprimir, marcar.

imprinted [ɪm'prɪntɪd] *adj* **-1.** [marked] marcado(da) **-2.** *fig* [on mind, memory]: ~ **on sthg** impresso(sa) em algo, marcado(da) em algo.

imprison [ɪm'prɪzn] *vt* [put in prison] aprisionar.

imprisonment [ɪm'prɪznmənt] *n (U)* aprisionamento *m.*

improbable [ɪmˈprɒbəbl] adj **-1.** [unlikely] improvável **- 2.** [strange] estranho(nha).

impromptu [ɪmˈprɒmptju:] adj de improviso, improvisado(da).

improper [ɪmˈprɒpəʳ] adj **-1.** [unsuitable] inadequado(da) **- 2.** [dishonest] desonesto(ta) **- 3.** [rude, shocking] impróprio(pria).

impropriety [ˌɪmprəˈpraɪətɪ] n indecoro m.

improve [ɪmˈpru:v] <> vi [get better] melhorar; to ~ **(up)on** sthg melhorar algo. <> vt **-1.** [gen] melhorar **- 2.** [cultivate] desenvolver.

improved [ɪmˈpru:vd] adj [better] melhorado(da).

improvement [ɪmˈpru:vmənt] n melhoria f; ~ in/on sthg melhoria em algo.

improvisation [ˌɪmprəvaɪˈzeɪʃn] n improvisação f.

improvise [ˈɪmprəvaɪz] vt & vi improvisar.

imprudent [ɪmˈpru:dənt] adj imprudente.

impudence n impudência f.

impudent [ˈɪmpjʊdənt] adj impudente.

impugn [ɪmˈpju:n] vt fml impugnar.

impulse [ˈɪmpʌls] n impulso m; on ~ sem pensar.

impulse buying [-ˈbaɪɪŋ] n (U) compra f impulsiva.

impulsive [ɪmˈpʌlsɪv] adj impulsivo(va).

impunity [ɪmˈpju:nətɪ] n impunidade f; with ~ impunemente.

impure [ɪmˈpjʊəʳ] adj impuro(ra).

impurity [ɪmˈpjʊərətɪ] (pl **-ies**) n impureza f.

IMRO [ˈɪmrəʊ] (abbr of **Investment Management Regulatory Organization**) n órgão britânico regulador de empresas que lidam com fundos de investimento e pensões.

in [ɪn] prep **-1.** [indicating place, position] em; **it comes ~ a box** vem numa caixa; ~ **the hospital** no hospital; ~ **Scotland** na Escócia; ~ **Boston** em Boston; ~ **the middle** no meio; ~ **the sun/rain** no sol/na chuva; ~ **here/there** aqui/ali (dentro); ~ **front** à frente. **- 2.** [appearing in] em; **who's ~ the play?** quem está na peça? **- 3.** [indicating arrangement] em; **they come ~ packs of three** vêm em embalagens de três; ~ **a row** em fila; **cut it ~ half** corte-o ao meio. **- 4.** [during] ~ **April** em abril; ~ **the afternoon** à OR de tarde; ~ **the morning** de manhã; **ten o'clock ~ the morning** dez (horas) da manhã; ~ **1994** em 1994; ~ **summer/winter** no verão/inverno. **- 5.** [within] em; [after] dentro de, daqui a; **it'll be ready ~ an hour** estará pronto daqui a OR dentro de uma hora; **she did everything ~ ten minutes** ela fez tudo em dez minutos; **they're arriving ~ two weeks** chegam dentro de OR daqui a duas semanas. **- 6.** [indicating means]: ~ **writing** por escrito; **they were talking ~ English** estavam falando (em) inglês; **write ~ ink** escreva a tinta. **- 7.** [wearing] de; **dressed ~ red** vestido de vermelho; **the man ~ the blue suit** o homem com o terno azul. **- 8.** [indicating state] em; **to be ~ a hurry** estar com pressa; **to be ~ pain** ter dores; **to cry out ~ pain** gritar de dor OR com dores; ~ **ruins** em ruínas; ~ **good health** com boa saúde. **- 9.** [with regard to] de; **a rise ~ prices** uma subida dos preços; **to be 50 meters ~ length** ter 50 metros de comprimento. **-10.** [with numbers]: **one ~ ten** um em cada dez. **-11.** [indicating age]: **she's ~ her twenties** ela está na casa dos

vinte. **-12.** [with colours]: **it comes ~ green or blue** vem em verde ou azul. **-13.** [with superlatives] de; **the best ~ the world** o melhor do mundo. <> adv **-1.** [inside] dentro; **you can go ~ now** pode entrar agora. **- 2.** [at home, work]: **she's not ~** (ela) não está; **to stay ~** ficar em casa. **- 3.** [train, bus, plane]: **the train's not ~ yet** o trem ainda não chegou. **- 4.** [tide]: **the tide is ~** a maré está cheia. <> adj inf [fashionable] na moda, in (inv).

in. abbr of **inch**.

IN abbr of **Indiana**.

inability [ˌɪnəˈbɪlətɪ] n incapacidade f; ~ **to do** sthg incapacidade para fazer algo.

inaccessible [ˌɪnəkˈsesəbl] adj inacessível.

inaccuracy [ɪnˈækjʊrəsɪ] (pl **-ies**) n imprecisão f.

inaccurate [ɪnˈækjʊrət] adj impreciso(sa).

inaction [ɪnˈækʃn] n inação f.

inactive [ɪnˈæktɪv] adj inativo(va).

inactivity [ˌɪnækˈtɪvətɪ] n (U) inatividade f.

inadequacy [ɪnˈædɪkwəsɪ] (pl **-ies**) n **-1.** (U) [state of being inadequate] insuficiência f **- 2.** [weakness - of system] imperfeição f; [- of person] incapacidade f.

inadequate [ɪnˈædɪkwət] adj **-1.** [insufficient] insuficiente **- 2.** [person] incapaz.

inadmissible [ˌɪnədˈmɪsəbl] adj inadmissível.

inadvertent [ˌɪnədˈvɜ:tnt] adj acidental.

inadvertently [ˌɪnədˈvɜ:təntlɪ] adv acidentalmente.

inadvisable [ˌɪnədˈvaɪzəbl] adj desaconselhável.

inalienable [ɪnˈeɪljənəbl] adj fml inalienável.

inane [ɪˈneɪn] adj vazio(zia), fútil.

inanely [ɪˈneɪnlɪ] adv futilmente.

inanimate [ɪnˈænɪmət] adj inanimado(da).

inanity [ɪˈnænətɪ] n (U) futilidade f.

inapplicable [ˌɪnəˈplɪkəbl] adj inaplicável.

inappropriate [ˌɪnəˈprəʊprɪət] adj inapropriado(da).

inarticulate [ˌɪnɑ:ˈtɪkjʊlət] adj **-1.** [person] incapaz de se expressar (bem) **- 2.** [words, sounds] inarticulado(da).

inasmuch [ˌɪnəzˈmʌtʃ] ⬥ **inasmuch as** conj fml [because] visto que; [to the extent that] na medida em que.

inattention [ˌɪnəˈtenʃn] n (U) desatenção f; ~ **to** sthg desatenção a algo.

inattentive [ˌɪnəˈtentɪv] adj desatento(ta); ~ **to** sthg desatento(ta) a algo.

inaudible [ɪˈnɔ:dɪbl] adj inaudível.

inaugural [ɪˈnɔ:gjʊrəl] adj [opening] inaugural.

inaugurate [ɪˈnɔ:gjʊreɪt] vt **-1.** [leader, president] empossar **- 2.** [building, system] inaugurar.

inauguration [ɪˌnɔ:gjʊˈreɪʃn] n **-1.** [of leader, president] posse f **- 2.** [of building, system] inauguração f.

inauspicious [ˌɪnɔ:ˈspɪʃəs] adj de mau agouro, pouco propício(cia).

in-between adj intermediário(ria).

inboard adj interno(na).

inborn [ˌɪnˈbɔ:n] adj inato(ta).

inbound [ˈɪnbaʊnd] adj US: **an ~ ship** um navio que se aproxima; **the ~ flight from Miami** o vôo que chega de Miami.

inbred [ˌɪn'bred] adj -1. [family, group] endogâmico(-ca), consangüíneo(nea) -2. [characteristic, quality] inato(ta).

inbreeding ['ɪnˌbriːdɪŋ] n (U) endogamia f.

inbuilt [ˌɪn'bɪlt] adj -1. [device] embutido(da), incorporado(da) -2. [quality, defect] inerente.

inc. (abbr of inclusive) inclusive.

Inc. [ɪŋk] (abbr of incorporated) ≃ S.A.

Inca ['ɪŋkə] <> adj inca. <> n inca mf.

incalculable [ɪn'kælkjʊləbl] adj [very great] incalculável.

incandescent [ˌɪnkæn'desnt] adj lit incandescente ; fig [with rage] vermelho(lha).

incantation [ˌɪnkæn'teɪʃn] n -1. [magic words] palavras fpl mágicas -2. [spell] feitiço m.

incapable [ɪn'keɪpəbl] adj -1. [unable]: **to be ~ of sthg/of doing sthg** ser incapaz de algo/de fazer algo -2. [incompetent] incompetente.

incapacitate [ˌɪnkə'pæsɪteɪt] vt incapacitar.

incapacitated [ˌɪnkə'pæsɪteɪtɪd] adj incapacitado(-da).

incapacity [ˌɪnkə'pæsətɪ] n (U) incapacidade f; **~ for sthg** incapacidade para algo.

incarcerate [ɪn'kɑːsəreɪt] vt fml encarcerar.

incarceration [ɪnˌkɑːsə'reɪʃn] n (U) fml encarceramento m.

incarnate [ɪn'kɑːneɪt] adj encarnado(da); **he is generosity ~** ele é a generosidade em pessoa.

incarnation [ˌɪnkɑː'neɪʃn] n encarnação f.

incendiary device [ɪn'sendjərɪ-] n artefato m incendiário.

incense [n 'ɪnsens, vt ɪn'sens] <> n (U) [perfume] incenso m. <> vt [anger] enfurecer, enraivecer.

incentive [ɪn'sentɪv] n incentivo m.

incentive scheme n plano m de incentivos.

inception [ɪn'sepʃn] n fml começo m, origem f.

incessant [ɪn'sesnt] adj incessante.

incessantly [ɪn'sesntlɪ] adv incessantemente.

incest ['ɪnsest] n incesto m.

incestuous [ɪn'sestjʊəs] adj -1. [sexual] incestuoso(-sa) -2. fig [too close] fechado em si mesmo, fechada em si mesma.

inch [ɪntʃ] <> n polegada f. <> vi avançar gradualmente.

incidence ['ɪnsɪdəns] n incidência f.

incident ['ɪnsɪdənt] n [occurrence, event] incidente m.

incidental [ˌɪnsɪ'dentl] adj [minor] acessório(ria), secundário(ria).

incidentally [ˌɪnsɪ'dentəlɪ] adv -1. [by chance] por acaso -2. [by the way] a propósito.

incidental music n música f de fundo.

incinerate [ɪn'sɪnəreɪt] vt incinerar.

incinerator [ɪn'sɪnəreɪtəʳ] n incinerador m.

incipient [ɪn'sɪpɪənt] adj fml incipiente.

incision [ɪn'sɪʒn] n fml incisão f.

incisive [ɪn'saɪsɪv] adj incisivo(va).

incisor [ɪn'saɪzəʳ] n incisivo m.

incite [ɪn'saɪt] vt incitar; **to ~ sb to do sthg** incitar alguém a fazer algo.

incitement [ɪn'saɪtmənt] n (U) incitamento m; **~ to sthg/to do sthg** incitamento a algo/a fazer algo.

incl. -1. (abbr of including) incluindo -2. (abbr of inclusive) inclusive.

inclement [ɪn'klemənt] adj fml [weather] inclemente.

inclination [ˌɪnklɪ'neɪʃn] n -1. (U) [liking, preference] vontade f -2. [tendency]: **~ to do sthg** tendência f OR inclinação f para fazer algo.

incline [n 'ɪnklaɪn, vb ɪn'klaɪn] <> n [slope] ladeira f. <> vt [lean, bend] inclinar. <> vi [tend]: **to ~ to sthg** tender para algo.

inclined [ɪn'klaɪnd] adj -1. [tending] inclinado(da), propenso(sa); **to be ~ to sthg** estar propenso(sa) a algo; **to be ~ to do sthg** estar inclinado(da) a fazer algo -2. [wanting, willing]: **to be ~ to do sthg** estar disposto(ta) a fazer algo -3. [sloping] inclinado(da).

include [ɪn'kluːd] vt -1. [contain] abranger -2. [add, count] incluir.

included [ɪn'kluːdɪd] adj incluído(da).

including [ɪn'kluːdɪŋ] prep inclusive; **six died, ~ a child** seis morreram, incluindo uma criança.

inclusion [ɪn'kluːʒn] n inclusão f.

inclusive [ɪn'kluːsɪv] adj inclusive; **1 to 9, ~** de um a nove, inclusive; **£150 ~ £150**, tudo incluído; **~ of** incluindo.

incognito [ˌɪnkɒg'niːtəʊ] adv incógnito(ta).

incoherent [ˌɪnkəʊ'hɪərənt] adj incoerente.

income ['ɪnkʌm] n -1. [earnings] renda f -2. [profit] lucro m.

incomes policy n UK política f de rendimentos.

income support n UK auxílio dado pelo governo a pessoas desempregadas ou de renda muito baixa.

income tax n imposto m de renda.

incoming ['ɪnˌkʌmɪŋ] adj -1. [tide] ascendente -2. [plane, passengers] de chegada -3. [mail, report, phone call] recebido(da) -4. [government, official] novo(va).

incommunicado [ˌɪnkəmjuːnɪ'kɑːdəʊ] adv incomunicável.

incomparable [ɪn'kɒmpərəbl] adj incomparável.

incompatible [ˌɪnkəm'pætɪbl] adj incompatível; **~ with sb/sthg** incompatível com alguém/algo.

incompetence [ɪn'kɒmpɪtəns] n (U) incompetência f.

incompetent [ɪn'kɒmpɪtənt] adj incompetente.

incomplete [ˌɪnkəm'pliːt] adj incompleto(ta).

incomprehensible [ɪnˌkɒmprɪ'hensəbl] adj incompreensível.

inconceivable [ˌɪnkən'siːvəbl] adj inconcebível.

inconclusive [ˌɪnkən'kluːsɪv] adj -1. [meeting, outcome, debate] sem conclusões claras -2. [evidence, argument] pouco convincente.

incongruous [ɪn'kɒŋgrʊəs] adj incongruente.

inconsequential [ˌɪnkɒnsɪ'kwenʃl] adj [insignificant] insignificante.

inconsiderable [ˌɪnkən'sɪdərəbl] adj: **not ~** nada desprezível.

inconsiderate [ˌɪnkən'sɪdərət] adj -1. [attitude, treatment] impensado(da), irrefletido(da) -2. [person] sem consideração.

inconsistency [ˌɪnkən'sɪstənsɪ] (pl -ies) n -1. (U)

[state of being inconsistent] **inconsistência** *f*-**2**. [contradictory point] contradição *f*.

inconsistent [,ınkən'sıstənt] *adj* -**1**. [not agreeing, contradictory] inconsistente; ~ **with sthg** contraditório(ria) com algo -**2**. [erratic] irregular.

inconsolable [,ınkən'səʊləbll] *adj* inconsolável.

inconspicuous [,ınkən'spıkjʊəs] *adj* discreto(ta).

incontinence [ın'kɒntınəns] *n (U)* incontinência *f*.

incontinent [ın'kɒntınənt] *adj* incontinente.

incontrovertible [,ınkɒntrə'vɜ:təbll] *adj* incontestável.

inconvenience [,ınkən'vi:njəns] <> *n* -**1**. *(U)* [difficulty, discomfort] incômodo *m* -**2**. [inconvenient thing] inconveniência *f*. <> *vt* incomodar.

inconvenient [,ınkən'vi:njənt] *adj* incoveniente.

incorporate [ın'kɔ:pəreıt] *vt* -**1**. [include] incorporar; **to** ~ **sb/sthg in (to) sthg** incluir alguém/algo em algo -**2**. [blend] combinar.

incorporated company *n* COMM sociedade *f* anônima.

incorporation [ın,kɔ:pə'reıʃn] *n* -**1**. [integration] integração *f*-**2**. COMM [of company] incorporação *f*.

incorrect [,ınkə'rekt] *adj* incorreto(ta).

incorrigible [ın'kɒrıdʒəbll] *adj* incorrigível.

incorruptible [,ınkə'rʌptəbll] *adj* [person] incorruptível.

increase [*n* 'ınkri:s, *vb* ın'kri:s] <> *n*: ~ **(in sthg)** aumento *m* (de algo); **to be on the** ~ estar aumentando, estar em crescimento. <> *vt & vi* aumentar.

increased [ın'kri:st] *adj* intensificado(da), em crescimento.

increasing [ın'kri:sıŋ] *adj* crescente.

increasingly [ın'kri:sıŋlı] *adv* cada vez mais.

incredible [ın'kredəbll] *adj inf* incrível.

incredulous [ın'kredjʊləs] *adj* incrédulo(la).

increment ['ınkrımənt] *n* incremento *m*.

incriminate [ın'krımıneıt] *vt* incriminar; **to** ~ **o.s.** incriminar-se.

incriminating [ın'krımıneıtıŋ] *adj* incriminatório(ria).

incrusted *adj* = **encrusted**.

incubate ['ınkjʊbeıt] *vt & vi* -**1**. [gen] incubar -**2**. [egg] chocar.

incubation [,ınkjʊ'beıʃn] *n* incubação *f*.

incubator ['ınkjʊbeıtəʳ] *n* [for baby] incubadora *f*.

inculcate ['ınkʌlkeıt] *vt fml*: **to** ~ **sthg in (to) sb** inculcar algo em alguém.

incumbent [ın'kʌmbənt] *fml* <> *adj*: **to be** ~ **(up)on sb to do sthg** incumbir alguém de fazer algo. <> *n* [postholder] titular *mf*.

incur [ın'kɜ:ʳ] *(pt & pp* -**red**, *cont* -**ring**) *vt* -**1**. [wrath, criticism] incorrer em -**2**. [expenses] contrair.

incurable [ın'kjʊərəbll] *adj lit & fig* incurável.

incursion [UK ın'kɜ:ʃn, US ın'kɜ:ʒn] *n* MIL incursão *f*; *fig* [unwelcome] invasão *f*.

indebted [ın'detıd] *adj* -**1**. [grateful]: **to be** ~ **to sb** estar em dívida com alguém -**2**. [owing money]: **to be** ~ **to sb** estar devendo a alguém.

indecency [ın'di:snsı] *n (U)* indecência *f*.

indecent [ın'di:snt] *adj* -**1**. [obscene] indecente -**2**. [unreasonable] inadequado(da).

indecent assault *n* atentado *m* contra o pudor.

indecent exposure *n (U)* ato *m* obsceno.

indecipherable [,ındı'saıfərəbll] *adj* indecifrável.

indecision [,ındı'sıʒn] *n (U)* indecisão *f*.

indecisive [,ındı'saısıv] *adj* indeciso(sa).

indeed [ın'di:d] *adv* -**1**. [certainly] realmente, certamente -**2**. [in fact] na verdade -**3**. [for emphasis] realmente; **very big** ~ estupidamente grande; **very few** ~ pouquíssimos(mas) -**4**. [to express surprise, disbelief] mesmo; ~? é mesmo?

indefatigable [,ındı'fætıgəbll] *adj* incansável.

indefensible [,ındı'fensəbll] *adj* [behaviour, argument] indefensável.

indefinable [,ındı'faınəbll] *adj* indefinível.

indefinite [ın'defınıt] *adj* -**1**. [indeterminate] indefinido(da) -**2**. [imprecise] impreciso(sa).

indefinitely [ın'defınıtlı] *adv* [for indeterminate period] indefinidamente.

indelible [ın'deləbll] *adj* -**1**. [gen] indelével -**2**. [memory] que não se pode apagar.

indelicate [ın'delıkət] *adj* indelicado(da).

indemnify [ın'demnıfaı] *(pt & pp* -**ied**) *vt* -**1**. [insure]: **to** ~ **sb for** OR **against sthg** segurar alguém contra algo -**2**. [compensate]: **to** ~ **sb for sthg** indenizar alguém por algo.

indemnity [ın'demnətı] *n* -**1**. *(U)* [insurance] garantia *f*-**2**. [compensation] indenização *f*.

indent [ın'dent] *vt* -**1**. [text] recuar -**2**. [edge, surface] recortar.

indentation [,ınden'teıʃn] *n* -**1**. [in text] recuo *m* de parágrafo novo -**2**. [in edge, coastline, surface] reentrância *f*.

indenture [ın'dentʃəʳ] *n* contrato *m* de aprendizagem.

independence [,ındı'pendəns] *n* independência *f*.

Independence Day *n festa nos Estados Unidos em comemoração à sua independência, no dia 4 de julho em 1776.*

independent [,ındı'pendənt] *adj* independente; ~ **of sb/sthg** independente de alguém/algo.

independently [,ındı'pendəntlı] *adv* -**1**. [govern, rule] independentemente; ~ **of sb/sthg** independentemente de alguém/algo -**2**. [live, think, act] de forma independente.

independent school *n* UK escola *f* privada.

in-depth *adj* em profundidade, exaustivo(va).

indescribable [,ındı'skraıbəbll] *adj* indescritível.

indestructible [,ındı'strʌktəbll] *adj* indestrutível.

indeterminate [,ındı'tɜ:mınət] *adj* [indefinite] indeterminado(da).

index ['ındeks] *(pl senses 1 and 2* -**es**, *pl sense 3* -**es** OR **indices**) <> *n* -**1**. [of book] índice *m* remissivo -**2**. [in library] catálogo *m* -**3**. ECON [value system] índice *m*. <> *vt* -**1**. [book] acrescentar índice remissivo a -**2**. [econ] indexar.

index card *n* ficha *f* de indexação.

index finger *n* (dedo *m*) indicador *m*.

index-linked [-lıŋkt] *adj* indexado(da).

India ['ındjə] *n* Índia *f*; **in** ~ na Índia.

India ink *n US* = **Indian ink**.

Indian ['ındjən] <> *adj* -**1**. [from India] indiano(na) -**2**. [from the Americas] índio(dia). <> *n* -**1**. [from India] indiano *m*, -na *f* **- 2.** [from the Americas] índio *m*, -dia *f*.

Indiana [ˌɪndɪˈænə] *n* Indiana; **in** ~ em Indiana.

Indian ink *UK*, **India ink** *US n* (tinta *f*) nanquim *m*.

Indian Ocean *n*: the ~ o Oceano Índico.

Indian summer *n* [warm weather] veranico *m*.

india rubber *n* borracha *f*.

indicate [ˈɪndɪkeɪt] <> *vt* **- 1.** [gen] indicar **- 2.** [suggest] sugerir. <> *vi* [when driving]: **to ~ left / right** sinalizar à esquerda/direita.

indication [ˌɪndɪˈkeɪʃn] *n* **- 1.** [suggestion] indicação *f* **- 2.** [sign] indício *m*.

indicative [ɪnˈdɪkətɪv] <> *adj*: ~ **of sthg** indicativo(va) de algo. <> *n GRAM* indicativo *m*.

indicator [ˈɪndɪkeɪtəʳ] *n* **- 1.** [sign] indicador *m* **- 2.** [on car] pisca-pisca *m*.

indices [ˈɪndɪsiːz] *pl* ⊳ **index**.

indict [ɪnˈdaɪt] *vt* indiciar; **to ~ sb for sthg** indiciar alguém por algo.

indictable [ɪnˈdaɪtəbl] *adj* passível de ser indiciado(da).

indictment [ɪnˈdaɪtmənt] *n* **- 1.** *JUR* indiciamento *m* **- 2.** [criticism] crítica *f* dura.

indie [ˈɪndɪ] *adj inf* independente.

indifference [ɪnˈdɪfrəns] *n* (U) indiferença *f*.

indifferent [ɪnˈdɪfrənt] *adj* **- 1.** [uninterested] indiferente; ~ **to sthg** indiferente a algo **- 2.** [mediocre] medíocre.

indigenous [ɪnˈdɪdʒɪnəs] *adj* nativo(va), indígena.

indigestible [ˌɪndɪˈdʒestəbl] *adj* **- 1.** [food] indigesto(ta) **- 2.** [facts] incompreensível.

indigestion [ˌɪndɪˈdʒestʃn] *n* (U) indigestão *f*.

indignant [ɪnˈdɪgnənt] *adj* indignado(da); **to be ~ at sthg** estar indignado(da) com algo.

indignantly [ɪnˈdɪgnəntlɪ] *adv* com indignação.

indignation [ˌɪndɪgˈneɪʃn] *n* (U) indignação *f*.

indignity [ɪnˈdɪgnətɪ] (*pl* -ies) *n* **- 1.** (U) [feeling of humiliation] afronta *f* **- 2.** [humiliating situation] indignidade *f*.

indigo [ˈɪndɪgəʊ] <> *adj* [in colour] da cor de anil. <> *n* [colour] anil *m*.

indirect [ˌɪndɪˈrekt] *adj* indireto(ta).

indirect costs *npl* gastos *mpl* indiretos.

indirect lighting *n* luz *f* *OR* iluminação *f* indireta.

indirectly [ˌɪndɪˈrektlɪ] *adv* indiretamente.

indirect speech *n GRAM* discurso *m* indireto.

indirect taxation *n* impostos *mpl* indiretos.

indiscreet [ˌɪndɪˈskriːt] *adj* indiscreto(ta); [tactless] indelicado(da).

indiscretion [ˌɪndɪˈskreʃn] *n* indiscrição *f*.

indiscriminate [ˌɪndɪˈskrɪmɪnət] *adj* indiscriminado(da).

indiscriminately [ˌɪndɪˈskrɪmɪnətlɪ] *adv* indiscriminadamente.

indispensable [ˌɪndɪˈspensəbl] *adj* indispensável.

indisposed [ˌɪndɪˈspəʊzd] *adj fml* [unwell] indisposto(ta).

indisputable [ˌɪndɪˈspjuːtəbl] *adj* inquestionável.

indistinct [ˌɪndɪˈstɪŋkt] *adj* **- 1.** [words] indistinto(ta) **- 2.** [memory] confuso(sa) **- 3.** [picture, marking] borrado(da).

indistinguishable [ˌɪndɪˈstɪŋgwɪʃəbl] *adj* indistinguível; ~ **from sb/sthg** indistinguível de alguém/algo.

individual [ˌɪndɪˈvɪdʒʊəl] <> *adj* **- 1.** [gen] individual **- 2.** [private] particular **- 3.** [distinctive] pessoal. <> *n* indivíduo *m*.

individualist [ˌɪndɪˈvɪdʒʊəlɪst] *n* individualista *mf*.

individualistic [ˈɪndɪˌvɪdʒʊəˈlɪstɪk] *adj* individualista.

individuality [ˈɪndɪˌvɪdʒʊˈælətɪ] *n* (U) individualidade *f*.

individually [ˌɪndɪˈvɪdʒʊəlɪ] *adv* [separately] individualmente.

indivisible [ˌɪndɪˈvɪzəbl] *adj* indivisível.

Indochina [ˌɪndəʊˈtʃaɪnə] *n* Indochina; **in** ~ na Indochina.

indoctrinate [ɪnˈdɒktrɪneɪt] *vt* doutrinar.

indoctrination [ɪnˌdɒktrɪˈneɪʃn] *n* (U) doutrinação *f*.

indolent [ˈɪndələnt] *adj fml* indolente.

indomitable [ɪnˈdɒmɪtəbl] *adj* indomável.

Indonesia [ˌɪndəˈniːzjə] *n* Indonésia; **in** ~ na Indonésia.

Indonesian [ˌɪndəˈniːzjən] <> *adj* indonésio(sia). <> *n* **- 1.** [person] indonésio *m*, -sia *f* **- 2.** [language] indonésio *m*.

indoor [ˈɪndɔːʳ] *adj* **- 1.** [plant] de interior **- 2.** [shoes] para dentro de casa **- 3.** [sports] em local coberto; ~ **swimming pool** piscina *f* coberta.

indoors [ˌɪnˈdɔːz] *adv* dentro de casa; **to go** ~ entrar, ir para dentro.

indubitably [ɪnˈdjuːbɪtəblɪ] *adv* indubitavelmente, sem dúvida.

induce [ɪnˈdjuːs] *vt*: **to ~ sb to do sthg** induzir alguém a fazer algo.

inducement [ɪnˈdjuːsmənt] *n* [incentive] estímulo *m*, incentivo *m*.

induction [ɪnˈdʌkʃn] *n* **- 1.** [into official position]: ~ **into sthg** posse *m* em algo **- 2.** (U) *MED*, *ELEC* indução *f* **- 3.** [introduction to job] apresentação *f*.

induction course *n* curso *m* de integração *OR* de iniciação.

indulge [ɪnˈdʌldʒ] <> *vt* **- 1.** [whim, passion] satisfazer **- 2.** [child, person] fazer a vontade de; **to ~ o.s.** permitir-se um luxo. <> *vi*: **to ~ in sthg** permitir-se algo.

indulgence [ɪnˈdʌldʒəns] *n* **- 1.** (U) [tolerance, kindness] indulgência *f* **- 2.** [special treat] vício *m*, prazer *m*.

indulgent [ɪnˈdʌldʒənt] *adj* [liberal, kind] indulgente.

Indus *n*: the (River) ~ o (Rio) Indus.

industrial [ɪnˈdʌstrɪəl] *adj* **- 1.** [of industry] industrial **- 2.** [industrialized] industrializado(da).

industrial action *n*: **to take** ~ declarar-se em greve.

industrial estate *UK*, **industrial park** *US n* parque *m* industrial.

industrial injury *n* acidente *m* de trabalho.

industrialist [ɪnˈdʌstrɪəlɪst] *n* industrialista *mf*.

industrialization [ɪnˌdʌstrɪəlaɪˈzeɪʃn] *n* industrialização *f*.

industrialize, -ise [ɪnˈdʌstrɪəlaɪz] <> *vt* industrializar. <> *vi* industrializar-se.

industrial park n US = industrial estate.

industrial relations npl relações fpl de trabalho.

industrial revolution n revolução f industrial.

industrial tribunal n justiça f do trabalho.

industrious [ɪn'dʌstrɪəs] adj trabalhador(ra), diligente.

industry ['ɪndəstrɪ] (pl -ies) n -1. [gen] indústria f; the coal ~ o setor carvoeiro -2. (U) [hard work] laboriosidade f.

inebriated [ɪ'ni:brɪeɪtɪd] adj fml inebriado(da).

inedible [ɪn'edɪbl] adj -1. [unpleasant to eat] não-comestível -2. [poisonous] venenoso(sa).

ineffective [ˌɪnɪ'fektɪv] adj ineficaz, inútil.

ineffectual [ˌɪnɪ'fektʃʊəl] adj ineficaz, inútil.

inefficiency [ˌɪnɪ'fɪʃnsɪ] n (U) ineficiência f.

inefficient [ˌɪnɪ'fɪʃnt] adj ineficiente.

inelegant [ɪn'elɪgənt] adj deselegante.

ineligible [ɪn'elɪdʒəbl] adj inelegível; to be ~ for sthg não estar qualificado(da) para algo.

inept [ɪ'nept] adj -1. [incompetent] inepto(ta); ~ at sthg incapaz de algo -2. [clumsy] malfeito(ta).

ineptitude [ɪ'neptɪtju:d] n (U) [incompetence] inépcia f, incompetência f.

inequality [ˌɪnɪ'kwɒlətɪ] (pl -ies) n desigualdade f.

inequitable [ɪn'ekwɪtəbl] adj fml injusto(ta).

ineradicable adj fml inextirpável.

inert [ɪ'nɜ:t] adj inerte.

inertia [ɪ'nɜ:ʃə] n inércia f.

inertia-reel seat belt n cinto m de segurança retrátil.

inescapable [ˌɪnɪ'skeɪpəbl] adj inevitável.

inessential [ˌɪnɪ'senʃl] adj: ~ (to sthg) dispensável (para algo).

inestimable [ɪn'estɪməbl] adj fml inestimável.

inevitable [ɪn'evɪtəbl] <> adj inevitável. <> n: the ~ o inevitável.

inevitably [ɪn'evɪtəblɪ] adv inevitavelmente.

inexact [ˌɪnɪg'zækt] adj inexato(ta).

inexcusable [ˌɪnɪk'skju:zəbl] adj imperdoável.

inexhaustible [ˌɪnɪg'zɔ:stəbl] adj inesgotável.

inexorable [ɪn'eksərəbl] adj fml [unpreventable] inexorável.

inexorably [ɪn'eksərəblɪ] adv inexoravelmente.

inexpensive [ˌɪnɪk'spensɪv] adj barato(ta), econômico(ca).

inexperience [ˌɪnɪk'spɪərɪəns] n (U) inexperiência f.

inexperienced [ˌɪnɪk'spɪərɪənst] adj inexperiente.

inexpert [ɪn'ekspɜ:t] adj inábil.

inexplicable [ˌɪnɪk'splɪkəbl] adj inexplicável.

inexplicably [ˌɪnɪk'splɪkəblɪ] adv inexplicavelmente.

inextricably [ˌɪnɪk'strɪkəblɪ] adv inextricavelmente.

infallible [ɪn'fæləbl] adj infalível.

infamous ['ɪnfəməs] adj infame.

infamy n (U) fml infâmia f.

infancy ['ɪnfənsɪ] n (U) primeira infância f; to be in its ~ fig estar engatinhando.

infant ['ɪnfənt] n -1. [baby] bebê m -2. [young child] criança f pequena.

infantile ['ɪnfəntaɪl] adj infantil.

infant mortality n mortalidade f infantil.

infantry ['ɪnfəntrɪ] n (U) infantaria f.

infantryman ['ɪnfəntrɪmən] (pl -men [-mən]) n soldado m de infantaria.

infant school n UK na Grã-Bretanha, escola para crianças entre 5 e 7 anos.

infatuated [ɪn'fætjʊeɪtɪd] adj: ~ (with sb/sthg) obcecado(da) (por alguém/algo).

infatuation [ɪnˌfætjʊ'eɪʃn] n: ~ (with sb/sthg) obsessão f (por alguém/algo).

infect [ɪn'fekt] vt -1. MED infectar; to become ~ed [wound] infeccionar; to ~ sb with sthg infectar alguém com algo -2. fig [spread to] contagiar.

infected [ɪn'fektɪd] adj -1. [food, patient] infectado(da); ~ with sthg infectado(da) por algo -2. [wound] infeccionado(da).

infection [ɪn'fekʃn] n -1. [disease] infecção f -2. (U) [spreading of germs] contágio m.

infectious [ɪn'fekʃəs] adj -1. [disease] infeccioso(sa) -2. fig [feeling, laugh] contagioso(sa).

infer [ɪn'fɜ:ʳ] (pt & pp -red, cont -ring) vt -1. [deduce]: to ~ (that) inferir que; to ~ sthg (from sthg) deduzir OR inferir algo (de algo) -2. inf [insinuate] insinuar.

inference ['ɪnfrəns] n -1. [conclusion] conclusão f -2. (U) [deduction]: by ~ por dedução.

inferior [ɪn'fɪərɪəʳ] <> adj [gen] inferior; ~ to sb/ sthg inferior a alguém/algo. <> n [in status] inferior mf.

inferiority [ɪnˌfɪərɪ'ɒrətɪ] n (U) inferioridade f.

inferiority complex n complexo m de inferioridade.

infernal adj inf dated infernal.

inferno [ɪn'fɜ:nəʊ] (pl -s) n inferno m, incêndio m incontrolável.

infertile [ɪn'fɜ:taɪl] adj -1. [woman, animal] estéril -2. [soil] infértil.

infertility [ˌɪnfə'tɪlətɪ] n (U) -1. [of woman, animal] esterilidade f -2. [of soil] infertilidade f.

infestation [ˌɪnfe'steɪʃn] n infestação f, praga f.

infested [ɪn'festɪd] adj: ~ with sthg infestado(da) por algo.

infidelity [ˌɪnfɪ'delətɪ] n [of partner] infidelidade f.

infighting ['ɪnˌfaɪtɪŋ] n (U) disputa f interna.

infiltrate ['ɪnfɪltreɪt] <> vt infiltrar. <> vi: to ~ into sthg infiltrar-se em algo.

infinite ['ɪnfɪnət] adj infinito(ta).

infinitely ['ɪnfɪnətlɪ] adv infinitamente.

infinitesimal [ˌɪnfɪnɪ'tesɪml] adj infinitesimal.

infinitive [ɪn'fɪnɪtɪv] n GRAM infinitivo m.

infinity [ɪn'fɪnətɪ] n -1. (U) [gen] infinito m -2. MATH [incalculable number] infinidade f.

infirm [ɪn'fɜ:m] <> adj [unhealthy] enfermo(ma). <> npl: the ~ os enfermos.

infirmary [ɪn'fɜ:mərɪ] (pl -ies) n -1. [hospital] hospital m -2. [room] enfermaria f.

infirmity [ɪn'fɜ:mətɪ] (pl -ies) n enfermidade f.

inflamed [ɪn'fleɪmd] adj MED inflamado(da).

inflammable [ɪn'flæməbl] adj [burning easily] inflamável.

inflammation [ˌɪnflə'meɪʃn] n MED inflamação f.

inflammatory [ɪnˈflæmətrɪ] *adj* [provocative] incendiante.

inflatable [ɪnˈfleɪtəbl] *adj* inflável.

inflate [ɪnˈfleɪt] *vt* -**1.** [fill with air] inflar -**2.** *ECON* [increase] inflacionar.

inflated [ɪnˈfleɪtɪd] *adj* -**1.** [filled with air] inflado(da) -**2.** *pej* [exaggerated] exagerado(da) -**3.** *ECON* [unreasonably high] inflacionado(da).

inflation [ɪnˈfleɪʃn] *n* (U) *ECON* inflação *f*.

inflationary [ɪnˈfleɪʃnrɪ] *adj* *ECON* inflacionário(ria).

inflationary spiral *n* espiral *f* inflacionária.

inflation-proof *adj* que não é afetado(da) pela inflação.

inflation rate *n* *ECON* taxa *f* de inflação.

inflection *n* *GRAM* flexão *f*.

inflexible [ɪnˈfleksəbl] *adj* -**1.** [gen] inflexível -**2.** [fixed] imutável.

inflict [ɪnˈflɪkt] *vt*: to ~ sthg on sb infligir algo a alguém.

in-flight *adj* de bordo.

inflow [ˈɪnfləʊ] *n* afluência *f*.

influence [ˈɪnfluəns] <> *n* -**1.** (U) [power]: ~ (on sb/sthg), ~ (over sb/sthg) influência *f* (sobre alguém/algo); **under the ~ of** [person, group] sob a influência de; [alcohol, drugs] sob o efeito de -**2.** [influential person, thing]: ~ (on sb/sthg) influência para alguém/algo. <> *vt* influenciar.

influential [ˌɪnfluˈenʃl] *adj* influente.

influenza [ˌɪnfluˈenzə] *n* (U) *fml* influenza *f*.

influx [ˈɪnflʌks] *n* afluxo *m*.

info [ˈɪnfəʊ] (*abbr of* information) *n* (U) *inf* info *f*.

inform [ɪnˈfɔːm] *vt* informar; to ~ sb of/about sthg informar alguém de/sobre algo.
◆ **inform on** *vt fus* denunciar, delatar.

informal [ɪnˈfɔːml] *adj* informal.

informally [ɪnˈfɔːməlɪ] *adv* informalmente.

informant [ɪnˈfɔːmənt] *n* informante *mf*.

information [ˌɪnfəˈmeɪʃn] *n* (U) informações *fpl*; **to give sb** ~ dar informações a alguém; **to get** ~ obter informações; **that's a useful piece of** ~ esta é uma informação útil; **to have some** ~ **on** *OR* **about sthg** ter alguma informação sobre algo; '**Information**' 'Informações'; **for your** ~ para seu conhecimento.

information desk *n* (balcão *m* de) informações *fpl*.

information office *n* (balcão *m* de) informações *fpl*.

information retrieval *n* recuperação *f* de informações.

information technology *n* tecnologia *f* da informação.

informative [ɪnˈfɔːmətɪv] *adj* instrutivo(va).

informed [ɪnˈfɔːmd] *adj* -**1.** [having information] informado(da) -**2.** [based on good information] bem-informado(da); ~ **guess** conjectura *f* bem-fundamentada.

informer [ɪnˈfɔːməʳ] *n* [denouncer] informante *mf*, delator *m*, -ra *f*.

infrared [ˌɪnfrəˈred] *adj* infravermelho(lha).

infrastructure [ˈɪnfrəˌstrʌktʃəʳ] *n* infra-estrutura *f*.

infrequent [ɪnˈfriːkwənt] *adj* infrequente.

infringe [ɪnˈfrɪndʒ] (*cont* infringeing) <> *vt* -**1.** [right] transgredir, violar -**2.** [law, agreement] infringir. <> *vi* -**1.** [on right]: to ~ on sthg transgredir *OR* violar algo -**2.** [on law, agreement]: to ~ on sthg infringir algo.

infringement [ɪnˈfrɪndʒmənt] *n* -**1.** [of right] transgressão *f*, violação *f* -**2.** [of law, agreement] infração *f*.

infuriate [ɪnˈfjʊərɪeɪt] *vt* enfurecer.

infuriating [ɪnˈfjʊərɪeɪtɪŋ] *adj* enfurecedor(ra).

infuse [ɪnˈfjuːz] <> *vt*: to ~ sb with sthg infundir algo em alguém. <> *vi* estar em infusão.

infusion [ɪnˈfjuːʒn] *n* infusão *f*.

ingenious [ɪnˈdʒiːnjəs] *adj* engenhoso(sa).

ingenuity [ˌɪndʒɪˈnjuːətɪ] *n* (U) engenhosidade *f*.

ingenuous [ɪnˈdʒenjʊəs] *adj* *fml* ingênuo(nua).

ingest [ɪnˈdʒest] *vt* *fml* ingerir.

ingot [ˈɪŋɡət] *n* lingote *m*.

ingrained [ˌɪnˈɡreɪnd] *adj* -**1.** [ground in] entranhado(da) -**2.** [deeply rooted] arraigado(da).

ingratiate [ɪnˈɡreɪʃɪeɪt] *vt*: to ~ o.s. with sb congraçar-se com alguém.

ingratiating [ɪnˈɡreɪʃɪeɪtɪŋ] *adj* insinuante, lisonjeiro(ra).

ingratitude [ɪnˈɡrætɪtjuːd] *n* (U) ingratidão *f*.

ingredient [ɪnˈɡriːdjənt] *n* ingrediente *m*.

ingrowing [ˈɪnˌɡrəʊɪŋ], **ingrown** [ˈɪnˌɡrəʊn] *adj* encravado(da).

inhabit [ɪnˈhæbɪt] *vt* habitar.

inhabitant [ɪnˈhæbɪtənt] *n* habitante *mf*.

inhalation [ˌɪnhəˈleɪʃn] *n* (U) inalação *f*.

inhale [ɪnˈheɪl] <> *vt* inalar. <> *vi* [breathe in - smoker] tragar; [- patient] inspirar.

inhaler [ɪnˈheɪləʳ] *n* *MED* inalador *m*.

inherent [ɪnˈhɪərənt, ɪnˈherənt] *adj* inerente; ~ in sthg inerente a algo.

inherently [ɪnˈhɪərəntlɪ, ɪnˈherəntlɪ] *adv* intrinsecamente.

inherit [ɪnˈherɪt] <> *vt*: to ~ sthg (from sb) herdar algo (de alguém). <> *vi* herdar.

inheritance [ɪnˈherɪtəns] *n* herança *f*.

inheritor [ɪnˈherɪtəʳ] *n* [of debt, problem, tradition] herdeiro *m*, -ra *f*.

inhibit [ɪnˈhɪbɪt] *vt* -**1.** [restrict] impedir -**2.** *PSYCH* [repress] inibir.

inhibited [ɪnˈhɪbɪtɪd] *adj* inibido(da).

inhibition [ˌɪnhɪˈbɪʃn] *n* inibição *f*.

inhospitable [ˌɪnhɒˈspɪtəbl] *adj* -**1.** [unwelcoming] inospitaleiro(ra) -**2.** [climate, area] inóspito(ta).

in-house <> *adj* -**1.** [journal, report, magazine] de circulação interna -**2.** [staff, group] interno(na), da casa; ~ **staff** quadro *m* interno. <> *adv* internamente.

inhuman [ɪnˈhjuːmən] *adj* -**1.** [cruel] desumano(na) -**2.** [not human] inumano(na).

inhumane [ˌɪnhjuːˈmeɪn] *adj* desumano(na).

inimitable [ɪˈnɪmɪtəbl] *adj* inimitável.

iniquitous [ɪˈnɪkwɪtəs] *adj* *fml* iníquo(qua).

iniquity [ɪˈnɪkwətɪ] (*pl* -ies) *n* -**1.** (U) *fml* [wickedness, injustice] iniqüidade *f* -**2.** [wicked or unjust act] injustiça *f*.

initial [ɪˈnɪʃl] (*UK* pt & pp -led, cont -ling, *US* pt & pp -ed, cont -ing) <> *adj* inicial. <> *vt* rubricar.
◆ **initials** *npl* iniciais *fpl*.

initialize, -ise [ɪˈnɪʃəlaɪz] vt COMPUT inicializar.

initially [ɪˈnɪʃəlɪ] adv inicialmente.

initiate [ɪˈnɪʃɪeɪt] <> vt -**1.** [start] iniciar - **2.** [teach]: **to ~ sb (into sthg)** iniciar alguém (em algo). <> n iniciado m, -da f.

initiation [ɪˌnɪʃɪˈeɪʃn] n (U) - **1.** [start] início m - **2.** [introduction, teaching] iniciação f.

initiative [ɪˈnɪʃətɪv] n -**1.** [gen] iniciativa f; **to use one's ~** fazer uso de sua própria iniciativa; **on one's own ~** por iniciativa própria - **2.** [first move]: **to take the ~** tomar a iniciativa - **3.** [advantage]: **to have the ~** ter a vantagem.

inject [ɪnˈdʒekt] vt -**1.** MED: **to ~ sb with sthg, to ~ sthg into sb** injetar algo em alguém - **2.** fig [add]: **to ~ sthg into sthg** injetar algo em algo.

injection [ɪnˈdʒekʃn] n injeção f.

injudicious [ˌɪndʒuːˈdɪʃəs] adj fml injudicioso(sa).

injunction [ɪnˈdʒʌŋkʃn] n JUR mandado m judicial, interdito m.

injure [ˈɪndʒəʳ] vt -**1.** [hurt physically] machucar; **to ~ o.s.** machucar-se, ferir-se - **2.** [reputation, chances] prejudicar - **3.** [offend] ferir.

injured [ˈɪndʒəd] <> adj -**1.** [physically hurt] machucado(da), ferido(da) - **2.** [reputation, chances] prejudicado(da) - **3.** [offended] ferido(da). <> npl: **the ~** os feridos.

injurious [ɪnˈdʒʊərɪəs] adj fml: **~ (to sb/sthg)** pernicioso(sa) (a alguém/algo).

injury [ˈɪndʒərɪ] (pl -ies) n -**1.** (U) [physical harm] lesão f - **2.** [wound] ferimento m; **to do o.s. an ~** machucar-se - **3.** (U) [to one's reputation] dano m - **4.** [to one's pride, feelings] golpe m.

injury time n (U) tempo m de descontos (num jogo).

injustice [ɪnˈdʒʌstɪs] n injustiça f; **to do sb an ~** fazer uma injustiça a alguém.

ink [ɪŋk] <> n (U) tinta f. <> comp de tinta; **~ pen** caneta-tinteiro f.
➤ **ink in** vt sep repassar a caneta.

ink-jet printer n impressora f jato de tinta.

inkling [ˈɪŋklɪŋ] n: **to have an ~ of sthg** ter uma vaga idéia de algo; **to have an ~ that** ter a vaga idéia de que.

inkpad [ˈɪŋkpæd] n almofada f para carimbos.

inkwell [ˈɪŋkwel] n tinteiro m.

INLA (abbr of **Irish National Liberation Army**) n grupo terrorista que luta pela reunificação da Irlanda, Exército m de Libertação Nacional Irlandês.

inlaid [ˌɪnˈleɪd] adj incrustado(da); **~ with sthg** incrustado(da) de algo.

inland [adj ˈɪnlənd, adv ɪnˈlænd] <> adj interior. <> adv -**1.** [drive, head, walk] para o interior - **2.** [be positioned] no interior.

Inland Revenue n UK: **the ~** o fisco, ≈ a Receita Federal.

in-laws npl inf sogros mpl.

inlet [ˈɪnlet] n -**1.** [stretch of water] enseada f - **2.** [way in] entrada f.

inmate [ˈɪnmeɪt] n -**1.** [mental hospital] interno m, -na f - **2.** [prison] preso m, -sa f.

inmost [ˈɪnməʊst] adj literary [deepest] mais íntimo(ma).

inn [ɪn] n pousada f.

innards [ˈɪnədz] npl entranhas fpl.

innate [ˌɪˈneɪt] adj inato(ta).

inner [ˈɪnəʳ] adj -**1.** [most central] interno(na); **Inner London** o centro de Londres - **2.** [unexpressed, secret - feelings, doubts] íntimo(ma); [- peace, meaning] interior.

inner city <> n: **the ~** o centro urbano decadente. <> comp do centro urbano decadente.

innermost [ˈɪnəməʊst] adj = **inmost**.

inner tube n câmara f de ar.

innings [ˈɪnɪŋz] (pl inv) n UK [in cricket] turno m; **to have had a good ~** fig ter aproveitado bem a vida.

innocence [ˈɪnəsəns] n (U) - **1.** JUR [gen] inocência f - **2.** [naivety] ingenuidade f.

innocent [ˈɪnəsənt] <> adj -**1.** [gen] inocente; **~ of sthg** inocente de algo - **2.** [harmless] ingênuo(nua). <> n [naive person] inocente mf.

innocuous [ɪˈnɒkjʊəs] adj [harmless] inócuo(cua).

innovation [ˌɪnəˈveɪʃn] n inovação f.

innovative [ˈɪnəvətɪv] adj inovador(ra).

innovator [ˈɪnəveɪtəʳ] n inovador m, -ra f.

innuendo [ˌɪnjuːˈendəʊ] (pl -es OR -s) n -**1.** [individual remark] insinuação f, indireta f - **2.** (U) [style of speaking] insinuações fpl.

innumerable [ɪˈnjuːmərəbl] adj inumerável.

inoculate [ɪˈnɒkjʊleɪt] vt inocular; **to ~ sb with sthg** inocular algo em alguém; **to ~ sb against sthg** vacinar alguém contra algo.

inoculation [ɪˌnɒkjʊˈleɪʃn] n -**1.** [injection] inoculação f - **2.** (U) [disease prevention] vacinação f.

inoffensive [ˌɪnəˈfensɪv] adj inofensivo(va).

inoperable [ɪnˈɒprəbl] adj -**1.** MED que não se pode operar - **2.** fml [unworkable] impraticável.

inoperative [ɪnˈɒprətɪv] adj -**1.** [unworkable] impraticável - **2.** [not working] que não funciona.

inopportune [ɪnˈɒpətjuːn] adj fml inoportuno(na).

inordinate [ɪˈnɔːdɪnət] adj fml -**1.** [gen] excessivo(va) - **2.** [pleasure] desmesurado(da).

inordinately [ɪˈnɔːdɪnətlɪ] adv fml [extremely] de forma desmesurada.

inorganic [ˌɪnɔːˈgænɪk] adj [substance] inorgânico(ca).

in-patient n paciente mf interno, -na.

input [ˈɪnpʊt] (pt & pp input OR -ted, cont -ting) <> n (U) - **1.** [contribution] contribuição f - **2.** COMPUT, ELEC entrada f. <> vt COMPUT entrar.

input/output n COMPUT entrada/saída f.

inquest [ˈɪnkwest] n JUR inquérito m.

inquire [ɪnˈkwaɪəʳ] <> vt: **to ~ when/whether/if/how ...** inquirir quando/se/como ... <> vi [ask for information] informar-se; **to ~ about sthg** pedir informações sobre algo.
➤ **inquire after** vt fus perguntar por.
➤ **inquire into** vt fus investigar.

inquiring [ɪnˈkwaɪərɪŋ] adj inquisitivo(va); **an ~ mind** uma mente curiosa.

inquiry [ɪnˈkwaɪərɪ] (pl -ies) n -**1.** [question] pergunta f; **'Inquiries'** 'Informações' - **2.** [investigation] investigação f, inquérito m - **3.** (U) [questioning]: **this spirit of ~** este espírito de questionar.

inquiry desk n (balcão m de) informações fpl.
inquisition [ˌɪnkwɪ'zɪʃn] n pej inquisição f.
➡ **Inquisition** n: **the Inquisition** a Inquisição.
inquisitive [ɪn'kwɪzətɪv] adj curioso(sa).
inroads ['ɪnrəʊdz] npl: **to make ~ into sthg** abrir caminho em algo.
insane [ɪn'seɪn] <> adj **-1.** MED [mad] insano(na) **-2.** fig [very stupid] louco(ca). <> npl: **the ~** os deficientes mentais.
insanitary [ɪn'sænɪtrɪ] adj insalubre, anti-higiênico(ca).
insanity [ɪn'sænətɪ] n (U) **-1.** MED [madness] insanidade f **-2.** fig [great stupidity] loucura f.
insatiable [ɪn'seɪʃəbl] adj insaciável.
inscribe [ɪn'skraɪb] vt **-1.** [on wall, headstone, plaque] escrever; **to ~ sthg with sthg** escrever algo com algo; **to ~ sthg on sthg** gravar algo em algo **-2.** [in book]: **to ~ sthg in sthg** escrever algo em algo.
inscription [ɪn'skrɪpʃn] n **-1.** [gen] inscrição f **-2.** [in book] dedicatória f.
inscrutable [ɪn'skruːtəbl] adj inescrutável, impenetrável.
insect ['ɪnsekt] n inseto m.
insect bite n picada f de inseto.
insecticide [ɪn'sektɪsaɪd] n inseticida m.
insect repellent n repelente m para insetos.
insecure [ˌɪnsɪ'kjʊəʳ] adj **-1.** [not confident] inseguro(ra) **-2.** [not safe] pouco seguro(ra).
insecurity [ˌɪnsɪ'kjʊərətɪ] n (U) **-1.** [lack of confidence] insegurança f **-2.** [uncertainty] instabilidade f.
insensible [ɪn'sensəbl] adj **-1.** [unconscious] inconsciente **-2.** [unaware]: **to be ~ of sthg** não ter consciência de algo **-3.** [unable to feel]: **to be ~ to sthg** ser insensível a algo.
insensitive [ɪn'sensətɪv] adj **-1.** [unkind, thoughtless] insensível **-2.** [unresponsive]: **~ to sthg** indiferente a algo **-3.** [unable to feel]: **~ to sthg** insensível a algo.
insensitivity [ɪnˌsensə'tɪvətɪ] n (U) **-1.** [unkindness, thoughtlessness] insensibilidade f **-2.** [lack of sensation]: **~ to sthg** insensibilidade a algo.
inseparable [ɪn'seprəbl] adj **-1.** [subjects, facts]: **~ (from sthg)** inseparável (de algo) **-2.** [people] inseparável.
insert [vb ɪn'sɜːt, n 'ɪnsɜːt] <> n encarte m. <> vt [put in]: **to ~ sthg (in OR into sthg)** inserir algo (em algo).
insertion [ɪn'sɜːʃn] n (U) inserção f.
in-service training n UK treinamento m no serviço.
inset ['ɪnset] n [detail] detalhe m.
inshore [adj 'ɪnʃɔːʳ, adv ɪn'ʃɔːʳ] <> adj costeiro(ra). <> adv **-1.** [towards shore] em direção à costa **-2.** [close to shore] perto da costa.
inside [ɪn'saɪd] <> adj [interior, near centre] interno(na). <> adv **-1.** [in, within - place, object, building] para dentro; **there was sthg ~** havia alguma coisa dentro; [- body, mind] por dentro **-2.** [prison] sl preso(sa). <> prep dentro de; **get some food ~ you!** coma alguma coisa!; **~ three weeks** em menos de três semanas. <> n **-1.** [interior, inner part]: **the ~** o lado de dentro; **~ out** [clothes] do avesso; **to know sthg ~ out** fig conhecer algo de

cabo a rabo; **to turn sthg ~ out** virar algo do avesso **-2.** AUT: **the ~** [in UK] a faixa da esquerda; [in mainland Europe, US, Brazil etc] a faixa da direita.
➡ **insides** npl inf [intestines] tripas fpl.
➡ **inside of** prep US [building, object] dentro de.
inside information n (U) informação f confidencial.
inside job n inf roubo cometido com a ajuda de um empregado da empresa ou do local roubado.
inside lane n AUT **-1.** [in UK] faixa f da esquerda **-2.** [in mainland Europe, US, Brazil etc] faixa f da direita.
insider [ˌɪn'saɪdəʳ] n pessoa f bem-informada (numa organização).
insider dealing, insider trading n (U) uso indevido de informações privilegiadas na bolsa de valores.
inside story n história f íntima.
insidious [ɪn'sɪdɪəs] adj insidioso(sa).
insight ['ɪnsaɪt] n **-1.** (U) [wisdom]: **~ (into sthg)** discernimento m (sobre algo) **-2.** [glimpse]: **~ (into sthg)** insight m (sobre algo); **the book gave me an ~ into the problem** o livro me fez ter algumas idéias sobre o problema.
insignia [ɪn'sɪgnɪə] (pl inv) n insígnia f.
insignificance [ˌɪnsɪg'nɪfɪkəns] n insignificância f.
insignificant [ˌɪnsɪg'nɪfɪkənt] adj insignificante.
insincere [ˌɪnsɪn'sɪəʳ] adj insincero(ra).
insincerity [ˌɪnsɪn'serətɪ] n (U) insinceridade f.
insinuate [ɪn'sɪnjʊeɪt] pej vt **-1.** [imply]: **to ~ (that)** insinuar que **-2.** [install]: **to ~ o.s. into sthg** infiltrar-se em algo.
insinuation [ɪnˌsɪnjʊ'eɪʃn] n pej **-1.** [suggestion] insinuação f **-2.** [act of insinuating] insinuação f.
insipid [ɪn'sɪpɪd] adj pej **-1.** [dull, boring] insosso(sa) **-2.** [flavourless - drink] insípido(da); [- food] insosso(sa).
insist [ɪn'sɪst] <> vt: **to ~ (that)** insistir que. <> vi: **to ~ on sthg** insistir em algo; **to ~ on doing sthg** insistir em fazer algo.
insistence [ɪn'sɪstəns] n (U) [act of demanding] insistência f; **~ on sthg/on doing sthg** insistência em algo/em fazer algo.
insistent [ɪn'sɪstənt] adj insistente; **~ on sthg** insistente em algo.
in situ [ˌɪn'sɪtjuː] adv no local.
insofar [ˌɪnsəʊ'fɑːʳ] ➡ **insofar as** conj na medida em que.
insole ['ɪnsəʊl] n [in shoe] palmilha f.
insolence ['ɪnsələns] n (U) insolência f.
insolent ['ɪnsələnt] adj insolente.
insoluble UK [ɪn'sɒljʊbl], **insolvable** US [ɪn'sɒlvəbl] adj insolúvel.
insolvable adj US insolúvel.
insolvency [ɪn'sɒlvənsɪ] n (U) insolvência f.
insolvent [ɪn'sɒlvənt] adj insolvente.
insomnia [ɪn'sɒmnɪə] n (U) insônia f.
insomniac [ɪn'sɒmnɪæk] n insone mf.
insomuch [ˌɪnsəʊ'mʌtʃ] ➡ **insomuch as** conj fml na medida em que.
inspect [ɪn'spekt] vt **-1.** [letter, person] examinar **-2.** [factory] inspecionar, vistoriar **-3.** [troops] passar revista em.

inspection [ɪnˈspekʃn] n - 1. [examination] exame m - 2. [official check] inspeção f, vistoria f.

inspector [ɪnˈspektəʳ] n - 1. [official] fiscal mf - 2. [of police] inspetor m, -ra f.

inspector of taxes n fiscal mf da Receita.

inspiration [ˌɪnspəˈreɪʃn] n - 1. (U) [source of ideas] inspiração f; ~ (for sthg) inspiração (para algo) - 2. [brilliant idea] idéia f.

inspire [ɪnˈspaɪəʳ] vt [stimulate, encourage]: to ~ sb (to do sthg) inspirar alguém (a fazer algo); to ~ sb with sthg, to ~ sthg in sb inspirar algo a alguém.

inspired [ɪnˈspaɪəd] adj inspirado(da).

inspiring [ɪnˈspaɪərɪŋ] adj [stimulating, exciting] inspirador(ra).

inst. [ɪnst] (abbr of instant) do corrente mês.

instability [ˌɪnstəˈbɪlətɪ] n (U) instabilidade f.

install UK, **instal** US [ɪnˈstɔːl] vt - 1. [machinery, equipment] instalar - 2. [appoint]: to ~ sb (as sthg) nomear alguém (como algo) - 3. [settle] instalar-se; to ~ o.s. in front of the fire acomodar-se em frente ao fogo.

installation [ˌɪnstəˈleɪʃn] n instalação f.

installment n US = instalment.

installment plan n US compra f a prazo.

instalment UK, **installment** US [ɪnˈstɔːlmənt] n - 1. [payment] prestação f; in ~s em prestações - 2. [episode] episódio m.

instance [ˈɪnstəns] n [example, case] caso m, exemplo m; for ~ por exemplo; in the first ~ fml em primeira instância.

instant [ˈɪnstənt] <> adj instantâneo(nea). <> n [moment] instante m; the ~ (that) ... no mesmo instante em que ...; at that OR the same ~ naquele OR no mesmo instante; this ~ agora mesmo.

instantaneous [ˌɪnstənˈteɪnjəs] adj instantâneo(nea).

instantly [ˈɪnstəntlɪ] adv instantaneamente.

instead [ɪnˈsted] adv em vez disso.

instead of prep em vez de, em lugar de.

instep [ˈɪnstep] n [of foot] peito m do pé.

instigate [ˈɪnstɪgeɪt] vt [initiate] instigar.

instigation [ˌɪnstɪˈgeɪʃn] n: at the ~ of por solicitação de.

instigator [ˈɪnstɪgeɪtəʳ] n instigador m, -ra f.

instil UK (pt & pp -led, cont -ling), **instill** US (pt & pp -ed, cont -ing) [ɪnˈstɪl] vt: to ~ sthg in(to) sb instilar algo em alguém.

instinct [ˈɪnstɪŋkt] n instinto m; first ~ primeiro impulso m.

instinctive [ɪnˈstɪŋktɪv] adj instintivo(va).

instinctively [ɪnˈstɪŋktɪvlɪ] adv instintivamente.

institute [ˈɪnstɪtjuːt] <> n [establishment] instituto m. <> vt instituir.

institution [ˌɪnstɪˈtjuːʃn] n instituição f.

institutional [ˌɪnstɪˈtjuːʃənl] adj - 1. [of organization] institucional - 2. [of psychiatric hospital, children's home] para uma instituição beneficente.

institutionalize vt institucionalizar.

institutionalized, -ised [ˌɪnstɪˈtjuːʃnəˌlaɪzd] adj institucionalizado(da).

instruct [ɪnˈstrʌkt] vt - 1. [tell, order]: to ~ sb to do sthg instruir alguém a fazer algo - 2. [teach]

instruir; to ~ sb in sthg instruir alguém em algo.

instruction [ɪnˈstrʌkʃn] n instrução f.

instructions npl [for use] instruções fpl.

instruction manual n manual m de instruções.

instructive [ɪnˈstrʌktɪv] adj instrutivo(va).

instructor [ɪnˈstrʌktəʳ] n - 1. [in driving, skiing] instrutor m - 2. [in swimming] professor m.

instructress [ɪnˈstrʌktrɪs] n - 1. [in driving, skiing] instrutora f - 2. [in swimming] professora f.

instrument [ˈɪnstrəmənt] n - 1. instrumento m - 2. literary [means] instrumento m.

instrumental [ˌɪnstrʊˈmentl] <> adj - 1. [important, helpful]: to be ~ in sthg desempenhar um papel fundamental em algo - 2. [music] instrumental. <> n MUS instrumental m.

instrumentalist [ˌɪnstrʊˈmentəlɪst] n MUS instrumentalista mf.

instrument panel n painel m de instrumentos.

insubordinate [ˌɪnsəˈbɔːdɪnət] adj fml insubordinado(da).

insubordination [ˈɪnsəˌbɔːdɪˈneɪʃn] n (U) fml insubordinação f.

insubstantial [ˌɪnsəbˈstænʃl] adj - 1. [fragile] frágil - 2. [unsatisfying] pouco substancioso(sa).

insufferable [ɪnˈsʌfərəbl] adj insuportável.

insufficient [ˌɪnsəˈfɪʃnt] adj fml insuficiente; ~ for sthg/to do sthg insuficiente para algo/para fazer algo.

insular [ˈɪnsjʊləʳ] adj - 1. [narrow-minded] limitado(da) - 2. [isolated] isolado(da).

insulate [ˈɪnsjʊleɪt] vt isolar; to ~ sb against OR from sthg isolar alguém de algo.

insulating tape [ˈɪnsjʊleɪtɪŋ-] n (U) UK fita f isolante.

insulation [ˌɪnsjʊˈleɪʃn] n (U) [material, substance] isolamento m.

insulin [ˈɪnsjʊlɪn] n (U) insulina f.

insult [vt ɪnˈsʌlt, n ˈɪnsʌlt] <> n insulto m; to add ~ to injury para piorar ainda mais as coisas. <> vt insultar, ofender.

insulting [ɪnˈsʌltɪŋ] adj ofensivo(va).

insuperable [ɪnˈsuːprəbl] adj fml insuperável.

insurance [ɪnˈʃʊərəns] <> n - 1. [against fire, accident, theft] seguro m; ~ against sthg seguro contra algo - 2. fig [safeguard, protection] proteção f; ~ against sthg proteção contra algo. <> comp de seguro.

insurance broker n corretor m, -ra f de seguros.

insurance policy n apólice f de seguros.

insurance premium n prêmio m do seguro.

insure [ɪnˈʃʊəʳ] <> vt - 1. [against fire, accident, theft]: to ~ sb/sthg against sthg segurar alguém/algo contra algo - 2. US [make certain] assegurar. <> vi [protect]: to ~ against sthg prevenir-se contra algo.

insured [ɪnˈʃɔːd] <> adj - 1. [against fire, accident, theft]: ~ (against OR for sthg) segurado(da) (contra algo) - 2. US [certain] assegurado(da). <> n: the ~ o segurado, a segurada.

insurer [ɪnˈʃʊərəʳ] n segurador m, -ra f.

insurgent [ɪn'sɜ:dʒənt] n insurgente mf.
insurmountable [ˌɪnsə'maʊntəbl] adj intransponível.
insurrection [ˌɪnsə'rekʃn] n insurreição f.
intact [ɪn'tækt] adj intacto(ta).
intake ['ɪnteɪk] n -1. [amount consumed] ingestão f - 2. [people recruited - SCH, UNIV] ingresso m; [- MIL] recrutamento m - 3. [inlet] entrada f.
intangible [ɪn'tændʒəbl] adj intangível.
integral ['ɪntɪgrəl] adj [essential] essencial; **to be ~ to sthg** ser parte integrante de algo.
integrate ['ɪntɪgreɪt] <> vi integrar; **to ~ with** OR **into sthg** integrar-se em algo. <> vt integrar; **to ~ sb with** OR **into sthg** integrar alguém em algo; **to ~ sthg with** OR **into sthg** integrar algo em algo.
integrated ['ɪntɪgreɪtɪd] adj [multiracial] integrado(-da).
integrated circuit n circuito m integrado.
integration [ˌɪntɪ'greɪʃn] n (U): **~ (with** OR **into sthg)** integração f (em algo).
integrity [ɪn'tegrətɪ] n (U) - 1. [honour] integridade f - 2. fml [wholeness] integridade f.
intellect ['ɪntəlekt] n - 1. [gen] inteligência f, intelecto m - 2. [mind] inteligência f.
intellectual [ˌɪntə'lektjʊəl] <> adj intelectual. <> n [person] intelectual mf.
intellectualize, -ise [ˌɪntə'lektjʊəlaɪz] vt intelectualizar.
intelligence [ɪn'telɪdʒəns] n (U) - 1. [ability to think and reason] inteligência f - 2. [information service] serviço m de inteligência - 3. [information] informações fpl secretas.
intelligence quotient n quociente m de inteligência.
intelligence test n teste m de inteligência.
intelligent [ɪn'telɪdʒənt] adj [clever] inteligente.
intelligent card n cartão m inteligente.
intelligently [ɪn'telɪdʒəntlɪ] adv inteligentemente.
intelligentsia [ɪnˌtelɪ'dʒentsɪə] n: **the ~** a intelligentsia.
intelligible [ɪn'telɪdʒəbl] adj inteligível.
intemperate [ɪn'tempərət] adj fml - 1. [excessive] excessivo(va) - 2. [uncontrolled] descomedido(da) - 3. [climate] intemperado(da).
intend [ɪn'tend] vt [mean] pretender, propor-se a; **to be ~ed for/as sthg** ser destinado(da) para algo; **to be ~ed for sb** ser destinado(da) a alguém; **it wasn't ~ed to be a criticism** não pretendia ser uma crítica; **it was ~ed to be a surprise** era para ser uma surpresa; **to ~ doing sthg/to do sthg** pretender fazer algo.
intended [ɪn'tendɪd] adj [planned] planejado(da); **the ~ victim** a vítima almejada.
intense [ɪn'tens] adj - 1. [gen] intenso(sa) - 2. [person - serious] muito sério(ria); [- emotional] forte.
intensely [ɪn'tenslɪ] adv - 1. [very] enormemente - 2. [very much] intensamente.
intensify [ɪn'tensɪfaɪ] (pt & pp -ied) <> vt intensificar. <> vi intensificar-se.
intensity [ɪn'tensətɪ] n - 1. [gen] intensidade f - 2. [of person - seriousness] seriedade f; [- of emotional nature] força f.
intensive [ɪn'tensɪv] adj [concentrated] intensivo(va).

intensive care n (U) tratamento m intensivo.
intensive care unit n unidade f de tratamento intensivo.
intent [ɪn'tent] <> adj - 1. [absorbed] atento(ta) - 2. [determined]: **to be ~ (up)on doing sthg** estar determinado(da) a fazer algo. <> n fml [intention] intenção f; **to all ~s and purposes** para todos os efeitos.
intention [ɪn'tenʃn] n intenção f.
intentional [ɪn'tenʃənl] adj intencional.
intentionally [ɪn'tenʃənəlɪ] adv intencionalmente.
intently [ɪn'tentlɪ] adv atentamente.
inter [ɪn'tɜ:ˈ] (pt & pp -red, cont -ring) vt fml sepultar.
interact [ˌɪntər'ækt] vi - 1. [people]: **to ~ (with sb)** interagir (com alguém) - 2. [forces, ideas]: **to ~ (with sthg)** interagir (com algo).
interaction [ˌɪntər'ækʃn] n interação f.
interactive [ˌɪntər'æktɪv] adj COMPUT interativo(va).
intercede [ˌɪntə'si:d] vi fml: **to ~ (with/for sb)** interceder (junto a/em favor de alguém).
intercept [ˌɪntə'sept] vt [message, missile] interceptar.
interception [ˌɪntə'sepʃn] n (U) interceptação f.
interchange [n 'ɪntətʃeɪndʒ, vb ˌɪntə'tʃeɪndʒ] <> n - 1. [exchange] intercâmbio m - 2. [road junction] trevo m rodoviário. <> vt trocar, intercambiar; **to ~ sthg with sb/sthg** trocar algo com alguém/algo.
interchangeable [ˌɪntə'tʃeɪndʒəbl] adj: **~ (with sb/sthg)** intercambiável (com alguém/algo).
intercity [ˌɪntə'sɪtɪ] adj UK intermunicipal.
intercom ['ɪntəkɒm] n interfone m.
interconnect [ˌɪntəkə'nekt] vi interligar-se; **to ~ with sthg** interligar-se com algo.
interconnecting adj [rooms] interligado(da).
intercontinental ['ɪntəˌkɒntɪ'nentl] adj intercontinental.
intercontinental ballistic missile n míssil m balístico intercontinental.
intercourse ['ɪntəkɔ:s] n (U) [sexual] relação f sexual.
interdenominational ['ɪntədɪˌnɒmɪ'neɪʃənl] adj de diferentes grupos religiosos.
interdepartmental ['ɪntəˌdi:pɑ:t'mentl] adj interdepartamental.
interdependent [ˌɪntədɪ'pendənt] adj interdependente.
interdict ['ɪntədɪkt] n - 1. JUR interdição m - 2. RELIG interdito m.
interest ['ɪntrəst] <> n - 1. [gen] interesse m; **~ in sb/sthg** interesse em alguém/algo - 2. [hobby] hobby m; **in the ~s of** [in order to benefit] em benefício de; [in order to achieve] com a finalidade de; **in the ~s of peace** em nome da paz - 3. (U) [financial charge] juro m - 4. [share in company] participação f. <> vt [appeal to] interessar; **to ~ sb in sthg/in doing sthg** chamar alguém para algo/para fazer algo; **can I ~ you in a drink?** posso te convidar para um drinque?
interested ['ɪntrəstɪd] adj interessado(da); **to be ~ in sb/sthg** estar interessado(da) em alguém/algo; **to be ~ in doing sthg** estar interessado(da) em fazer algo.
interest-free adj sem juros.

interesting ['ɪntrəstɪŋ] *adj* interessante.

interest rate *n* taxa *f* de juros.

interface [*n* 'ɪntəfeɪs, *vb* ɪntə'feɪs] ◇ *n* **-1.** *COMPUT* interface *f* **-2.** [junction, boundary] zona *f* de interação. ◇ *vt COMPUT* conectar por interface.

interfere [ˌɪntə'fɪə'] *vi* **-1.** [meddle] interferir, intrometer-se; **to ~ in sthg** interferir em algo, intrometer-se em algo **-2.** [cause disruption] interferir; **to ~ with sthg** interferir em algo.

interference [ˌɪntə'fɪərəns] *n (U)* **-1.** [meddling]: **~ (with OR in sthg)** intrometimento *m* (em algo) **-2.** *RADIO & TV* interferência *f*.

interfering [ˌɪntə'fɪərɪŋ] *adj pej* intrometido(da).

intergalactic *adj* intergaláctico(ca).

interim ['ɪntərɪm] ◇ *adj* provisório(ria). ◇ *n*: **in the ~** neste ínterim.

interior [ɪn'tɪərɪə'] ◇ *adj* **-1.** [inner] interno(na), interior **-2.** *POL* do interior. ◇ *n* **-1.** [inside] interior *m* **-2.** [of country]: **the ~** [inland part] o interior.

interior decorator *n* decorador *m*, -ra *f* de interiores.

interior designer *n* decorador *m*, -ra *f* de interiores.

interject [ˌɪntə'dʒekt] *fml* ◇ *vt* **-1.** [add] interpor **-2.** [interrupt] interromper. ◇ *vi* intervir.

interjection [ˌɪntə'dʒekʃn] *n* **-1.** [remark] interrupção *f* **-2.** *GRAM* interjeição *f*.

interleave [ˌɪntə'li:v] *vt*: **to ~ sthg with sthg** intercalar algo com algo.

interlock [ˌɪntə'lɒk] ◇ *vi* **-1.** *TECH* encaixar; **to ~ with sthg** encaixar com algo **-2.** [entwine] entrelaçar. ◇ *vt* **-1.** *TECH* engatar; **to ~ sthg with sthg** engatar algo em algo **-2.** [entwine] entrelaçar.

interloper ['ɪntələʊpə'] *n* intruso *m*, -sa *f*.

interlude ['ɪntəlu:d] *n* **-1.** [gen] intervalo *m* **-2.** *MUS* interlúdio *m*.

intermarry [ˌɪntə'mærɪ] (*pt & pp* **-ied**) *vi*: **to ~ (with sb)** unir-se (com alguém) pelo casamento *(parentes ou pessoas de raças, religiões, etc. distintas)*.

intermediary [ˌɪntə'mi:djərɪ] (*pl* **-ies**) *n* intermediário *m*, -ria *f*, mediador *m*, -ra *f*.

intermediate [ˌɪntə'mi:djət] *adj* intermediário *m*, -ria *f*.

interminable [ɪn'tɜ:mɪnəbl] *adj* interminável.

intermingle [ˌɪntə'mɪŋgl] *vi*: **to ~ (with people)** misturar-se (com as pessoas).

intermission [ˌɪntə'mɪʃn] *n* intervalo *m*.

intermittent [ˌɪntə'mɪtənt] *adj* intermitente.

intern [*vb* ɪn'tɜ:n, *n* 'ɪntɜ:n] ◇ *n US* [trainee - teacher] estagiário *m*, -ria *f*; [- doctor] interno *m*, -na *f*. ◇ *vt* internar.

internal [ɪn'tɜ:nl] *adj* interno(na); **~ affairs** relações *fpl* interiores.

internal-combustion engine *n* motor *m* de combustão interna.

internally [ɪn'tɜ:nəlɪ] *adv* internamente.

Internal Revenue *n US*: **the ~** a receita pública.

international [ˌɪntə'næʃənl] ◇ *adj* internacional. ◇ *n UK SPORT* **-1.** [match] partida *f* internacional **-2.** [player] atleta *mf* da seleção.

international date line *n*: **the ~** a linha internacional de data.

internationally [ˌɪntə'næʃnəlɪ] *adv* internacionalmente.

International Monetary Fund *n*: **the ~** o Fundo Monetário Internacional.

international relations *npl* relações *fpl* internacionais.

internecine [*UK* ˌɪntə'ni:saɪn, *US* ˌɪntər'ni:sn] *adj fml* interno(na); **the ~ quarrels in the party** as disputas internas no partido.

internee [ˌɪntɜ:'ni:] *n* recluso *m*, -sa *f (por motivos políticos)*.

Internet ['ɪntənet] *n*: **the ~** a Internet.

Internet access *n* acesso *m* à Internet.

Internet café *n* cibercafé *m*.

Internet connection *n* conexão *f* com a Internet.

Internet Service Provider *n* provedor *m* de serviços de Internet.

Internet start-up company *n* empresa *f* eletrônica que surgiu com a Internet.

Internet television, Internet TV *n* televisão *f* via Internet.

internment [ɪn'tɜ:nmənt] *n (U)* reclusão *f (por motivos políticos)*.

interpersonal [ˌɪntə'pɜ:sənl] *adj* interpessoal.

interplay ['ɪntəpleɪ] *n (U)*: **~ (of/between)** interação *f* (de/entre).

Interpol ['ɪntəpɒl] *n* Interpol *f*.

interpolate [ɪn'tɜ:pəleɪt] *vt fml* **-1.** [add]: **to ~ sthg (into sthg)** interpolar algo (em algo) **-2.** [interrupt] interpolar.

interpose [ˌɪntə'pəʊz] *vt fml* **-1.** [add] interpor **-2.** [interrupt] intervir.

interpret [ɪn'tɜ:prɪt] ◇ *vt* **-1.** [understand] interpretar; **to ~ sthg as** interpretar algo como **-2.** [translate] servir de intérprete em **-3.** *fml* [perform] interpretar. ◇ *vi* [translate] interpretar.

interpretation [ɪnˌtɜ:prɪ'teɪʃn] *n* interpretação *f*.

interpreted language *n COMPUT* linguagem *f* de programação interpretada.

interpreter [ɪn'tɜ:prɪtə'] *n* [person] intérprete *mf*.

interpreting [ɪn'tɜ:prɪtɪŋ] *n* [occupation] interpretação *f*.

interracial [ˌɪntə'reɪʃl] *adj* inter-racial.

interrelate [ˌɪntərɪ'leɪt] ◇ *vt* correlacionar. ◇ *vi*: **to ~ (with sthg)** correlacionar-se (com algo).

interrogate [ɪn'terəgeɪt] *vt* **-1.** [question] interrogar **-2.** *COMPUT* consultar.

interrogation [ɪnˌterə'geɪʃn] *n* **-1.** *(U)* [questioning] interrogação *f* **-2.** [interview] interrogatório *m*.

interrogation mark *n US* ponto *m* de interrogação.

interrogative [ˌɪntə'rɒgətɪv] *GRAM* ◇ *adj* interrogativo(va). ◇ *n* **-1.** [form]: **the ~** a forma interrogativa **-2.** [word] pronome *m* interrogativo.

interrogator [ɪn'terəgeɪtə'] *n* interrogador *m*, -ra *f*.

interrupt [ˌɪntə'rʌpt] ◇ *vt* interromper. ◇ *vi* interromper, incomodar.

interruption [ˌɪntə'rʌpʃn] *n* interrupção *f*.

interrupter *n ELEC* interruptor *m*.

intersect [ˌɪntəˈsekt] ◇ vi cruzar-se. ◇ vt cruzar.

intersection [ˌɪntəˈsekʃn] n [junction] interseção f.

intersperse [ˌɪntəˈspɜːs] vt: **to be ~ed with sthg** ser entremeado(da) por algo.

interstate (highway) n US rodovia f interestadual.

interval [ˈɪntəvl] n **-1.** [period of time]: **~ (between)** intervalo m (entrè); **at ~s** em intervalos; **at monthly/yearly ~s** em intervalos de um mês/um ano **-2.** UK [at play, concert] intervalo m **-3.** MUS pausa f.

intervene [ˌɪntəˈviːn] ◇ vt intervir. ◇ vi **-1.** [gen] intervir; **to ~ in sthg** intervir em algo **-2.** [time] transcorrer **-3.** [interrupt] interferir.

intervening [ˌɪntəˈviːnɪŋ] adj [period of time] transcorrido(da).

intervention [ˌɪntəˈvenʃn] n intervenção f.

interventionist [ˌɪntəˈvenʃənɪst] ◇ adj intervencionista. ◇ n intervencionista mf.

interview [ˈɪntəvjuː] ◇ n entrevista f. ◇ vt entrevistar.

interviewee [ˌɪntəvjuːˈiː] n entrevistado m, -da f.

interviewer [ˈɪntəvjuːəʳ] n entrevistador m, -ra f.

interweave [ˌɪntəˈwiːv] (pt **-wove**, pp **-woven**) fig ◇ vt entrelaçar. ◇ vi entrelaçar-se.

intestate [ɪnˈtesteɪt] adj: **to die ~** morrer intestado(da).

intestine [ɪnˈtestɪn] n intestino m.
◆ **intestines** npl intestinos mpl.

intimacy [ˈɪntɪməsɪ] (pl **-ies**) n (U) [closeness]: **~ (between/with)** intimidade f (entre/com).
◆ **intimacies** npl [personal thoughts] intimidades fpl.

intimate [adj & n ˈɪntɪmət, vb ˈɪntɪmeɪt] ◇ adj **-1.** íntimo(ma) **-2.** fml [sexually]: **to be ~ with sb** ter intimidades com alguém **-3.** [personal] pessoal **-4.** [thorough] profundo(da) **-5.** [direct] direto(ta). ◇ n fml [close friend] amigo m íntimo, amiga f íntima. ◇ vt fml [hint, imply] insinuar; **to ~ that** insinuar que, dar a entender que.

intimately [ˈɪntɪmətlɪ] adv intimamente.

intimation [ˌɪntɪˈmeɪʃn] n fml [suggestion] insinuação f.

intimidate [ɪnˈtɪmɪdeɪt] vt intimidar.

intimidation [ɪnˌtɪmɪˈdeɪʃn] n (U) intimidação f.

into [ˈɪntʊ] prep **-1.** [inside - referring to object] em; [- referring to place, vehicle] em direção a; **to get ~ a car** entrar num carro **-2.** [against] contra; **to bump ~ sb/sthg** tropeçar em alguém/algo; **to crash ~ sb/sthg** chocar-se com alguém/algo **-3.** [indicating transformation, change] em; **to translate ~ Spanish** traduzir para o espanhol **-4.** [concerning, about] sobre **-5.** MATH [indicating division] por; **6 ~ 2 is 3** 6 dividido por 2 é 3 **-6.** [indicating elapsed time]: **~ the night** noite adentro; **I was a week ~ my holiday when ...** eu estava há uma semana de férias quando ... **-7.** inf [interested in]: **to be ~ sthg** gostar de algo.

intolerable [ɪnˈtɒlrəbl] adj fml intolerável.

intolerance [ɪnˈtɒlərəns] n (U) [lack of respect] intolerância f.

intolerant [ɪnˈtɒlərənt] adj intolerante; **to be ~ of**

sb/sthg ser intolerante com alguém/algo.

intonation [ˌɪntəˈneɪʃn] n entonação f.

intone vt literary entoar.

intoxicated [ɪnˈtɒksɪkeɪtɪd] adj **-1.** [drunk]: **to be ~** estar embriagado(da) **-2.** fig [excited]: **to be ~ by** OR **with sthg** estar inebriado(da) com algo.

intoxicating [ɪnˈtɒksɪkeɪtɪŋ] adj **-1.** [alcoholic] embriagante **-2.** fig [exciting] inebriante.

intoxication [ɪnˌtɒksɪˈkeɪʃn] n (U) fml **-1.** [drunkenness] embriaguez f **-2.** [excitement] excitação f.

intractable [ɪnˈtræktəbl] adj fml **-1.** [stubborn] intratável **-2.** [insoluble] insolúvel.

intramural adj intramuros.

Intranet n COMPUT Intranet f.

intransigent [ɪnˈtrænzɪdʒəntl] adj fml intransigente.

intransitive [ɪnˈtrænzətɪv] adj intransitivo(va).

intrauterine device [ˌɪntrəˈjuːtəraɪn-] n dispositivo m intra-uterino.

intravenous [ˌɪntrəˈviːnəs] adj intravenoso(sa).

in-tray n bandeja f de entrada (para. documentos em escritório).

intrepid [ɪnˈtrepɪd] adj literary intrépido(da).

intricacy [ˈɪntrɪkəsɪ] (pl **-ies**) n **-1.** (U) [complexity] complexidade f **-2.** [detail] pormenor m.

intricate [ˈɪntrɪkət] adj intricado(da).

intrigue [ɪnˈtriːg] ◇ n intriga f. ◇ vt intrigar. ◇ vi: **to ~ against sb** fazer intriga contra alguém.

intriguing [ɪnˈtriːgɪŋ] adj intrigante.

intrinsic [ɪnˈtrɪnsɪk] adj intrínseco(ca).

intro [ˈɪntrəʊ] (pl **-s**) (abbr of **introduction**) n inf introdução f.

introduce [ˌɪntrəˈdjuːs] vt **-1.** [present, make aware of] apresentar; **to ~ sb to sb/sthg** apresentar alguém a alguém/algo **-2.** [bring in]: **to ~ sthg (to** OR **into)** introduzir algo (em).

introduction [ˌɪntrəˈdʌkʃn] n **-1.** [start, initiation] introdução f; **~ to sthg** introdução a algo **-2.** [presentation]: **~ (to sb)** apresentação f (a alguém).

introductory [ˌɪntrəˈdʌktrɪ] adj introdutório(ria).

introspective [ˌɪntrəˈspektɪv] adj introspectivo(va).

introvert [ˈɪntrəvɜːt] n introvertido m, -da f.

introverted [ˈɪntrəvɜːtɪd] adj introvertido(da).

intrude [ɪnˈtruːd] vi intrometer-se; **to ~ (up)on sb/sthg** intrometer-se em alguém/algo.

intruder [ɪnˈtruːdəʳ] n intruso m, -sa f.

intrusion [ɪnˈtruːʒn] n intrometimento m.

intrusive [ɪnˈtruːsɪv] adj **-1.** [person] intrometido(da) **-2.** [presence, interest] inoportuno(na).

intuition [ˌɪntjuːˈɪʃn] n intuição f.

intuitive [ɪnˈtjuːɪtɪv] adj intuitivo(va).

Inuit [ˈɪnʊɪt] ◇ adj inuit. ◇ n inuit mf.

inundate [ˈɪnʌndeɪt] vt inundar; **to be ~d with sthg** estar cheio (cheia) de algo.

inured [ɪˈnjʊəd] adj fml: **to be/become ~ to sthg** estar habituado(da)/habituar-se a algo.

invade [ɪnˈveɪd] vt invadir.

invader [ɪnˈveɪdəʳ] n MIL invasor m, -ra f.

invading adj invasor(ra).

invalid [adj ɪnˈvælɪd, n & vb ˈɪnvəlɪd] ◇ adj [not

acceptable] inválido(da). ◇ n [ill person] inválido m, -da f.

➡ **invalid out** vt sep: **to be ~ed out (of)** aposentar-se por invalidez (por).

invalidate [ɪn'vælɪdeɪt] vt **-1.** [claim, theory] invalidar; refutar **- 2.** [contract, agreement] anular.

invalid chair n cadeira f de rodas.

invaluable [ɪn'væljʊəbl] adj: **~ (to sb/sthg)** inestimável (para alguém/algo).

invariable [ɪn'veərɪəbl] adj invariável.

invariably [ɪn'veərɪəblɪ] adv [always] invariavelmente.

invasion [ɪn'veɪʒn] n invasão f.

invective [ɪn'vektɪv] n (U) fml invectiva f.

inveigle [ɪn'veɪgl] vt: **to ~ sb into sthg** aliciar alguém para algo; **to ~ sb into doing sthg** enganar alguém para que faça algo.

invent [ɪn'vent] vt inventar.

invention [ɪn'venʃn] n invenção f.

inventive [ɪn'ventɪv] adj inventivo(va).

inventor [ɪn'ventə^r] n inventor m, -ra f.

inventory ['ɪnventrɪ] (pl -ies) n **-1.** [list] inventário m **- 2.** US [goods] estoque m.

inventory control n controle m de estoque.

inverse [ɪn'vɜːs] ◇ adj [proportion, relation] inverso(sa). ◇ n fml inverso m.

invert [ɪn'vɜːt] vt fml inverter.

invertebrate [ɪn'vɜːtɪbreɪt] n invertebrado m.

inverted commas [ɪn'vɜːtɪd-] npl UK aspas fpl; **in ~** entre aspas.

inverted snob [ɪn'vɜːtɪd-] n pessoa que finge não gostar de coisas caras ou de boa qualidade.

invest [ɪn'vest] ◇ vt **-1.** [gen]: **to ~ sthg in sthg/in doing sthg** investir algo em algo/para fazer algo **- 2.** fml [endow]: **to ~ sb with sthg** outorgar algo a alguém, investir alguém de algo. ◇ vi **-1.** [financially] investir; **to ~ in sthg** investir em algo **- 2.** fig [in sthg useful]: **to ~ in sthg** investir em algo.

investigate [ɪn'vestɪgeɪt] vt & vi investigar.

investigation [ɪn,vestɪ'geɪʃn] n: **~ (into sthg)** investigação f (sobre algo).

investigative [ɪn'vestɪgətɪv] adj investigador(ra), de investigação.

investigator [ɪn'vestɪgeɪtə^r] n investigador m, -ra f.

investiture [ɪn'vestɪtʃə^r] n investidura f.

investment [ɪn'vestmənt] n investimento m.

investment analyst n analista mf financeiro, -ra.

investment trust n fundo m de investimento.

investor [ɪn'vestə^r] n investidor m, -ra f.

inveterate [ɪn'vetərət] adj inveterado(da).

invidious [ɪn'vɪdɪəs] adj **-1.** [unfair] injusto(ta) **- 2.** [unpleasant] desagradável.

invigilate [ɪn'vɪdʒɪleɪt] UK ◇ vt fiscalizar (um exame). ◇ vi fiscalizar um exame.

invigilator [ɪn'vɪdʒɪleɪtə^r] n UK fiscal mf.

invigorating [ɪn'vɪgəreɪtɪŋ] adj **-1.** [gen] revigorante **- 2.** [experience] estimulante.

invincible [ɪn'vɪnsɪbl] adj [unbeatable] invencível.

inviolate adj inviolado(da).

invisible [ɪn'vɪzɪbl] adj invisível.

invisible assets npl ativos mpl intangíveis.

invisible earnings npl ganhos mpl invisíveis.

invisible ink n (U) tinta f invisível.

invitation [,ɪnvɪ'teɪʃn] n convite m; **an ~ to sthg/ to do sthg** um convite para algo/para fazer algo.

invite [ɪn'vaɪt] vt **-1.** [request to attend] convidar; **to ~ sb to sthg** convidar alguém para algo **- 2.** [ask politely]: **to ~ sb to do sthg** convidar alguém para fazer algo **- 3.** [solicit] solicitar **- 4.** [encourage] estimular.

inviting [ɪn'vaɪtɪŋ] adj convidativo(va), tentador(-ra).

in vitro fertilization [,ɪn'viːtrəʊ-] n (U) fertilização f in vitro.

invoice ['ɪnvɔɪs] ◇ n fatura f. ◇ vt **-1.** [send an invoice to] enviar uma fatura para **- 2.** [prepare an invoice for] faturar.

invoke [ɪn'vəʊk] vt **-1.** fml [quote as justification] invocar **- 2.** [cause] evocar, suscitar.

involuntary [ɪn'vɒləntrɪ] adj [unintentional] involuntário(ria).

involve [ɪn'vɒlv] vt **-1.** [entail, require] envolver; **to ~ doing sthg** envolver fazer algo **- 2.** [concern, affect] atingir, afetar; **to be ~ed in sthg** estar envolvido(-da) em algo **- 3.** [make part of sthg]: **to ~ sb in sthg** envolver alguém em algo; **to ~ o.s. in sthg** meter-se em algo.

involved [ɪn'vɒlvd] adj **-1.** [complex] complicado(da) **- 2.** [participating]: **to be ~ in sthg** estar metido(da) em algo **- 3.** [in a relationship]: **to be/get ~ with sb** envolver-se com alguém **- 4.** [entailed]: **~ (in sthg)** envolvido(da) (em algo).

involvement [ɪn'vɒlvmənt] n (U) [gen] envolvimento m; **~ in sthg** envolvimento em algo.

invulnerable [ɪn'vʌlnərəbl] adj: **to be ~ (to sthg)** ser invulnerável (a algo).

inward ['ɪnwəd] ◇ adj **-1.** [feelings, satisfaction] interno(na), interior **- 2.** [flow, movement] para dentro. ◇ adv US = **inwards**.

inward investment n investimento m externo.

inwardly ['ɪnwədlɪ] adv [pleased, upset] por dentro.

inwards ['ɪnwədz], **inward** US adv para dentro.

I/O (abbr of input-output) n E/S f.

IOC (abbr of International Olympic Committee) n COI m.

iodine [UK 'aɪədiːn, US 'aɪədaɪn] n (U) iodo m.

ion ['aɪən] n íon m.

Ionian Sea [aɪ'əʊnjən-] n: **the ~** o Mar Jônio.

iota [aɪ'əʊtə] n pouquinho m; **not an ~** nem um pouquinho.

IOU (abbr of I owe you) n documento assinado no qual se reconhece uma dívida.

Iowa ['aɪəʊə] n Iowa; **in ~** em Iowa.

IPA (abbr of International Phonetic Alphabet) n AFI m.

IQ (abbr of intelligence quotient) n QI m.

IRA n **-1.** (abbr of Irish Republican Army) IRA m **- 2.** (abbr of individual retirement account) plano de previdência privada nos Estados Unidos.

Iran [ɪ'rɑːn] n Irã; **in ~** no Irã.

Iranian [ɪ'reɪnjən] ◇ adj iraniano(na). ◇ n [person] iraniano m, -na f.

Iraq [ɪ'rɑːk] n Iraque; **in ~** no Iraque.

Iraqi [ı'rɑːkı] <> *adj* iraquiano(na). <> *n* [person] iraquiano, -na *f.*

irascible [ı'ræsəbl] *adj* irascível.

irate [aı'reıt] *adj* irado(da).

Ireland ['aıələnd] *n* Irlanda; **in** ~ na Irlanda; **the Republic of** ~ a República da Irlanda.

iridescent [ˌırı'desənt] *adj literary* iridescente.

iris ['aıərıs] (*pl* -**es**) *n MED, BOT* íris *f inv.*

Irish ['aırıʃ] <> *adj* irlandês(esa). <> *n* [language] gaélico-irlandês *m.* <> *npl*: **the** ~ os irlandeses.

Irish coffee *n* café *m* irlandês.

Irishman ['aırıʃmən] (*pl* -**men** [-mən]) *n* irlandês *m.*

Irish Sea *n*: **the** ~ o Mar da Irlanda.

Irish setter *n* séter *m* irlandês.

Irish stew *n* ensopado de carne e verduras típico da Irlanda.

Irish wolfhound *n* wolfhound *m* irlandês.

Irishwoman ['aırıʃˌwumən] (*pl* -**women** [-ˌwımın]) *n* irlandesa *f.*

irk [ɜːk] *vt dated* aborrecer.

irksome ['ɜːksəm] *adj fml* aborrecido(da).

IRO *n* - **1.** (*abbr of* **International Refugee Organization**) organização humanitária para refugiados - **2.** (*abbr of* **Inland Revenue Office**) departamento britânico de arrecadação de impostos, ≃ Secretaria *f* da Fazenda.

iron ['aıən] <> *adj* - **1.** [made of iron] de ferro - **2.** *fig* [very strict] duro(ra). <> *n* - **1.** (*U*) [metal] ferro *m* - **2.** [for clothes] ferro *m* (de passar roupa) - **3.** [golf club] ferro *m.* <> *vt* passar (a ferro).

◆ **iron out** *vt sep fig* [overcome] resolver.

Iron Age <> *n*: **the** ~ a Idade do Ferro. <> *comp* da Idade do Ferro.

Iron Curtain *n*: **the** ~ a Cortina de Ferro.

ironic(al) [aı'rɒnık(l)] *adj* irônico(ca); **how** ~! que ironia!

ironically [aı'rɒnıklı] *adv* ironicamente.

ironing ['aıənıŋ] *n* (*U*) - **1.** [activity]: **to do the** ~ passar roupa - **2.** [clothes to be ironed] roupa *f* para passar.

ironing board *n* tábua *f* de passar roupa.

iron lung *n* pulmão *m* de aço.

ironmonger ['aıənˌmʌŋgəʳ] *n UK* ferrageiro *m*, -ra *f*; ~ **'s (shop)** ferragem *f.*

ironworks ['aıənwɜːks] (*pl inv*) *n* siderúrgica *f.*

irony ['aırənı] (*pl* -**ies**) *n* ironia *f*; **the** ~ **of it all is that ...** o curioso disso tudo é que ...

irradiate [ı'reıdıeıt] *vt* irradiar.

irrational [ı'ræʃənl] *adj* irracional.

irreconcilable [ıˌrekən'saıləbl] *adj* [completely different] irreconciliável.

irredeemable [ˌırı'diːməbl] *adj fml* - **1.** [irreplaceable] irrecuperável - **2.** [hopeless] irreparável.

irrefutable [ˌırı'fjuːtəbl] *adj fml* irrefutável.

irregular [ı'regjuləʳ] *adj* irregular.

irregularity [ıˌregjʊ'lærətı] (*pl* -**ies**) *n* irregularidade *f.*

irregularly [ı'regjʊləlı] *adv* [spasmodically] de forma irregular.

irrelevance [ı'reləvəns], **irrelevancy** [ı'reləvənsı] (*pl* -**ies**) *n* irrelevância *f.*

irrelevant [ı'reləvənt] *adj* irrelevante.

irreligious [ˌırı'lıdʒəs] *adj* descrente.

irremediable [ˌırı'miːdjəbl] *adj fml* irremediável.

irreparable [ı'repərəbl] *adj* irreparável.

irreplaceable [ˌırı'pleısəbl] *adj* insubstituível.

irrepressible [ˌırı'presəbl] *adj* irreprimível.

irreproachable [ˌırı'prəʊtʃəbl] *adj* irrepreensível.

irresistible [ˌırı'zıstəbl] *adj* irresistível.

irresolute [ı'rezəluːt] *adj fml* irresoluto(ta).

irrespective ◆ **irrespective of** *prep* independente de.

irresponsible [ˌırı'spɒnsəbl] *adj* irresponsável.

irretrievable [ˌırı'triːvəbl] *adj* - **1.** [data] irrecuperável - **2.** [loss, situation] irreparável.

irreverent [ı'revərənt] *adj* irreverente.

irreversible [ˌırı'vɜːsəbl] *adj* irreversível.

irrevocable [ı'revəkəbl] *adj* irrevogável.

irrigate ['ırıgeıt] *vt* [land] irrigar.

irrigation [ˌırı'geıʃn] <> *n* (*U*) [of land] irrigação *f.* <> *comp* de irrigação.

irritable ['ırıtəbl] *adj* [bad-tempered] irritável.

irritant ['ırıtənt] <> *adj* irritante. <> *n* - **1.** [irritating situation, person] motivo *m* de irritação - **2.** [substance] agente *m* irritante.

irritate ['ırıteıt] *vt* irritar.

irritated *adj* irritado(da).

irritating ['ırıteıtıŋ] *adj* irritante.

irritation [ˌırı'teıʃn] *n* - **1.** [gen] irritação *f* - **2.** [cause of anger] motivo *m* de irritação.

IRS (*abbr of* **Internal Revenue Service**) *n* departamento norte-americano de arrecadação de impostos, ≃ Secretaria *f* da Fazenda.

is [ız] *vb* ⊳ **be.**

ISA (*abbr of* **individual savings account**) *n* sistema britânico de aplicações financeiras isentas de impostos.

ISBN (*abbr of* **International Standard Book Number**) *n* ISBN *m.*

ISDN (*abbr of* **Integrated Services Delivery Network**) *n COMPUT* RDSI *f*, ISDN *f.*

Islam ['ızlɑːm] *n* (*U*) [religion] Islã *m.*

Islamabad [ız'læməbæd] *n* Islamabad; **in** ~ em Islamabad.

Islamic [ız'læmık] *adj* islâmico(ca).

island ['aılənd] *n* - **1.** [in water] ilha *f* - **2.** [in traffic] passagem *m* para pedestres.

islander ['aıləndəʳ] *n* ilhéu *m*, ilhoa *f.*

isle [aıl] *n* ilha *f*, ilhota *f.*

Isle of Man *n*: **the** ~ a Ilha de Man.

Isle of Wight [-waıt] *n*: **the** ~ a Ilha de Wight.

Isles of Scilly *npl* = **Scilly Isles.**

isn't ['ıznt] = **is not.**

ISO (*abbr of* **International Organization for Standardization**) *n* ISO *f.*

isobar ['aısəbɑːʳ] *n METEOR* isóbara *f.*

isolate ['aısəleıt] *vt*: **to** ~ **sthg/sb (from sthg)** isolar algo/alguém (de algo).

isolated ['aısəleıtıd] *adj* isolado(da).

isolation [ˌaısə'leıʃn] *n* (*U*) [solitariness] isolamento *m*; **in** ~ [live] em isolamento; [happen, consider] isoladamente.

isolationism [ˌaısə'leıʃənızm] *n* isolacionismo *m.*

isosceles triangle [aı'sɒsılıːz-] *n* triângulo *m* isósceles.

isotope ['aɪsətəʊp] *n* isótopo *m*.

ISP (*abbr of* **Internet Service Provider**) *n* ISP *m*.

Israel ['ɪzreɪəl] *n* Israel; **in** ~ em Israel.

Israeli [ɪz'reɪlɪ] ⟺ *adj* israelense. ⟺ *n* israelense *mf*.

Israelite ['ɪzrəlaɪt] ⟺ *adj* israelita. ⟺ *n* israelita *mf*.

issue ['ɪʃuː] ⟺ *n* **-1.** [important subject] assunto *m*, questão *f*; **at** ~ em questão; **to make an** ~ **of sthg** dar importância demasiada a algo **-2.** [edition] número *m*, edição *f* **-3.** [bringing out] emissão *f*. ⟺ *vt* **-1.** [statement, decree, warning] expedir **-2.** [stamps, bank notes, shares] emitir, pôr em circulação **-3.** [passport, documents, uniforms] expedir; **to** ~ **sthg to sb, to** ~ **sb with sthg** expedir algo a alguém. ⟺ *vi fml* [come out, go out]: **to** ~ **from** vir de.

Istanbul [ˌɪstæn'bʊl] *n* Istambul; **in** ~ em Istambul.

isthmus ['ɪsməs] *n* istmo *m*.

it [ɪt] *pron* **-1.** [referring to specific thing, subject after prep] ele *m*, ela *f* **-2.** [direct object] o *m*, a *f* **-3.** [indirect object] lhe; **a free book came with** ~ veio acompanhado de um livro grátis; **give** ~ **to me** me dê isso; **he gave** ~ **a kick** ele deu um chute nele; ~**'s big** é grande; ~**'s here** está aqui; **she hit** ~ ela deu uma pancada nele; **she lost** ~ ela o perdeu. **-4.** [referring to situation, fact]: ~**'s a difficult question** é uma questão difícil; **I can't remember** ~ não me lembro; **tell me about** ~ conte-me. **-5.** [used impersonally]: ~**'s hot** está calor; ~**'s six o'clock** são seis horas; ~**'s Sunday** é domingo. **-6.** [referring to person]: ~**'s me** sou eu; **who is** ~**?** quem é?

IT (*abbr of* **information technology**) *n* TI *f*.

Italian [ɪ'tæljən] ⟺ *adj* italiano(na). ⟺ *n* **-1.** [person] italiano *m*, -na *f* **-2.** [language] italiano *m*.

italic [ɪ'tælɪk] *adj* itálico *m*.

➡ **italics** *npl*: **in** ~ em itálico.

Italy ['ɪtəlɪ] *n* Itália; **in** ~ na Itália.

ITC (*abbr of* **Independent Television Commission**) *n* órgão britânico que monitora todos os canais de televisão independentes, a cabo e via satélite.

itch [ɪtʃ] ⟺ *n* coceira *f*. ⟺ *vi* **-1.** [be itchy] coçar **-2.** *fig* [be impatient]: **to be** ~**ing to do sthg** estar se coçando para fazer algo.

itchy ['ɪtʃɪ] (*compar* **-ier**, *superl* **-iest**) *adj* que coça.

it'd ['ɪtəd] = **it would, it had**.

item ['aɪtəm] *n* **-1.** [single thing] item *m* **-2.** [article in newspaper] artigo *m*.

itemize, -ise ['aɪtəmaɪz] *vt* detalhar, especificar.

itemized bill ['aɪtəmaɪzd-] *n* conta *f* discriminada.

itinerant [ɪ'tɪnərənt] *adj* itinerante.

itinerary [aɪ'tɪnərərɪ] (*pl* **-ies**) *n* itinerário *m*.

it'll [ɪtl] = **it will**.

ITN (*abbr of* **Independent Television News**) *n* agência britânica de notícias para os canais independentes de televisão.

its [ɪts] *poss adj* o seu (a sua), dele (dela).

it's [ɪts] = **it is, it has**.

itself [ɪt'self] *pron* **-1.** (*reflexive*) se **-2.** (*after prep*) si mesmo *m*, -ma *f* **-3.** (*stressed*): **the house** ~ **is fine** o casa em sí e boa.

ITV (*abbr of* **Independent Television**) *n* canal privado de televisão na Grã-Bretanha.

IUCD (*abbr of* **intrauterine contraceptive device**) *n* DIU *m*.

IUD (*abbr of* **intrauterine device**) *n* DIU *m*.

I've [aɪv] = **I have**.

IVF (*abbr of* **in vitro fertilization**) *n* FIV *f*.

ivory ['aɪvərɪ] ⟺ *adj* [ivory-coloured] marfim *inv*. ⟺ *n* (*U*) marfim *m*. ⟺ *comp* [made of ivory] de marfim.

Ivory Coast *n*: **the** ~ a Costa do Marfim; **in the** ~ na Costa do Marfim.

ivory tower *n fig* ≃ torre *f* de marfim.

ivy ['aɪvɪ] *n* (*U*) hera *f*.

Ivy League *n* US grupo formado pelas oito universidades mais prestigiadas do leste norte-americano.

J

j (*pl* **j's** OR **js**) **J** (*pl* **J's** OR **Js**) [dʒeɪ] *n* [letter] j, J *m*.

J/A (*abbr of* **joint account**) conta *f* conjunta.

jab [dʒæb] (*pt & pp* **-bed**, *cont* **-bing**) ⟺ *n* **-1.** [push] golpe *m* **-2.** UK *inf* [injection] injeção *f*. ⟺ *vt*: **to** ~ **sthg at sb/sthg** espetar algo em alguém/algo; **to** ~ **sthg into sb/sthg** cravar algo em alguém/algo. ⟺ *vi*: **to** ~ **at sb/sthg** apunhalar alguém/algo.

jabber ['dʒæbəʳ] ⟺ *vt* algaraviar. ⟺ *vi* tagarelar.

jack [dʒæk] *n* **-1.** [device] macaco *m* **-2.** [playing card] valete *m*.

➡ **jack in** *vt sep* UK *inf* largar.

➡ **jack up** *vt sep* **-1.** [lift with a jack] macaquear **-2.** [force up] aumentar.

jackal ['dʒækəl] *n* chacal *m*.

jackdaw ['dʒækdɔː] *n* gralha *f*.

jacket ['dʒækɪt] *n* **-1.** [garment] casaco *m*, jaqueta *f* **-2.** [potato skin] casca *f* **-3.** [book cover] sobrecapa *f* **-4.** US [of record] capa *f* **-5.** [of boiler] camisa *f*.

jacket potato *n* batata *f* assada com pele.

jackhammer ['dʒæk,hæməʳ] *n* US britadeira *f*.

jack-in-the-box *n* caixa *f* de surpresa.

jack knife *n* [tool] canivete *m* grande.

➡ **jack-knife** *vi* [truck, lorry] derrapar a parte dianteira.

jack-of-all-trades (*pl* **jacks-of-all-trades**) *n* pau-para-toda-obra *m*.

jack plug *n* pino *m*.

jackpot ['dʒækpɒt] *n* bolada *f*.

Jack Russell (terrier) *n* Jack Russell terrier *m*.

Jacobean [ˌdʒækə'bɪən] *adj* jacobino(na).

Jacobite ['dʒækəbaɪt] ⟺ *adj* jacobita. ⟺ *n* jacobita *mf*.

Jacuzzi® [dʒə'kuːzɪ] *n* banheira *f* de hidromassagem.

jade [dʒeɪd] ⬦ adj [jade-coloured] jade inv. ⬦ n -1. [stone] jade f -2. [colour] cor f jade. ⬦ comp [made of jade] de jade.

jaded ['dʒeɪdɪd] adj estafado(da).

jagged ['dʒægɪd] adj dentado(da).

jaguar ['dʒægjʊəʳ] n jaguar m.

jail [dʒeɪl] ⬦ n prisão f, cadeia f. ⬦ vt prender.

jailbird ['dʒeɪlbɜ:d] n inf preso m, -sa f reincidente.

jailbreak ['dʒeɪlbreɪk] n fuga f da prisão.

jailer ['dʒeɪləʳ] n carcereiro m, -ra f.

Jakarta [dʒə'kɑ:tə] n Jacarta; in ~ em Jacarta.

jam [dʒæm] (pt & pp -med, cont -ming) ⬦ n -1. (U) [preserve] geléia f -2. [of traffic] engarrafamento m -3. inf [difficult situation]: **to get into/be in a ~** meter-se/estar em apuros. ⬦ vt -1. [place roughly]: **to ~ sthg onto sthg** enfiar algo em algo -2. [fix, cause to stick - window]: **to ~ the window shut** trancar a janela; [- mechanism] emperrar -3. [fill, pack tightly] apinhar, abarrotar; **to ~ sthg into sthg** socar algo em algo -4. TELEC bloquear -5. RADIO interferir. ⬦ vi [stick] emperrar.
 ⬥ **jam on** vt [brakes] pisar.

Jamaica [dʒə'meɪkə] n Jamaica; in ~ na Jamaica.

Jamaican [dʒə'meɪkn] ⬦ adj jamaicano(na). ⬦ n jamaicano m, -na f.

jamb [dʒæm] n batente m.

jamboree [,dʒæmbə'ri:] n [celebration] farra f.

jamming ['dʒæmɪŋ] n RADIO interferência f.

jam-packed [-'pækt] adj inf apinhado(da).

jam session n sessão improvisada de jazz ou de rock.

Jan. [dʒæn] (abbr of January) jan.

jangle ['dʒæŋgl] ⬦ n [of keys, bells] som m estridente, estrépido m. ⬦ vt fazer soar de forma estridente. ⬦ vi retinir.

janitor ['dʒænɪtəʳ] n US & Scot [caretaker] zelador m, -ra f.

January ['dʒænjʊərɪ] n janeiro; see also September.

Japan [dʒə'pæn] n Japão; in ~ no Japão.

Japanese [,dʒæpə'ni:z] (pl inv) ⬦ adj japonês(esa). ⬦ n -1. [person] japonês m, -esa f -2. [language] jáponês m. ⬦ npl [people]: **the ~** os japoneses.

jape [dʒeɪp] n dated pilhéria f.

jar [dʒɑ:ʳ] (pt & pp -red, cont -ring) ⬦ n pote m. ⬦ vt [shake] sacudir. ⬦ vi -1. [noise, voice]: **to ~ (on sb)** dar nos nervos (de alguém) -2. [colours] destoar.

jargon ['dʒɑ:gən] n (U) jargão m.

jarring ['dʒɑ:rɪŋ] adj -1. [noise, voice] enervante -2. [colours] destoante.

jasmine ['dʒæzmɪn] n jasmim m.

jaundice ['dʒɔ:ndɪs] n (U) icterícia f.

jaundiced ['dʒɔ:ndɪst] adj fig [attitude, view] pessimista.

jaunt [dʒɔ:nt] n excursão f.

jaunty ['dʒɔ:ntɪ] (compar -ier, superl -iest) adj -1. [hat, wave] vistoso(sa) -2. [person] animado(da).

Java ['dʒɑ:və] n Java; in ~ em Java.

javelin ['dʒævlɪn] n dardo m.

jaw [dʒɔ:] ⬦ n -1. [of person] maxilar m -2. [of animal] mandíbula f. ⬦ vi inf tagarelar.

jawbone ['dʒɔ:bəʊn] n osso m maxilar.

jay [dʒeɪ] n gaio m.

jaywalk ['dʒeɪwɔ:k] vi atravessar a rua imprudentemente.

jaywalker ['dʒeɪwɔ:kəʳ] n pedestre mf imprudente.

jazz [dʒæz] n -1. MUS jazz m -2. US inf [insincere talk] balela f.
 ⬥ **jazz up** vt sep inf alegrar, animar.

jazz band n banda f de jazz.

jazz singer n cantor m, -ra f de jazz.

jazzy ['dʒæzɪ] (compar -ier, superl -iest) adj -1. [bright] chamativo(va) -2. [music] jazzístico(ca).

JCS (abbr of Joint Chiefs of Staff) n conselho militar do presidente dos Estados Unidos.

jealous ['dʒeləs] adj -1. [envious]: **to be ~ (of sb/sthg)** ter inveja (de alguém/algo) -2. [possessive]: **to be ~ (of sb/sthg)** estar com ciúmes (de alguém/algo).

jealously ['dʒeləslɪ] adv -1. [enviously] invejosamente -2. [possessively] zelosamente.

jealousy ['dʒeləsɪ] n (U) -1. [envy] inveja f -2. [resentment] ciúmes mpl.

jeans [dʒi:nz] npl jeans m inv.

Jeep® n jipe m.

jeer [dʒɪəʳ] ⬦ vt -1. [mock] zombar de -2. [boo] vaiar. ⬦ vi -1. [boo] vaiar; **to ~ at sb** vaiar alguém -2. [mock] zombar; **to ~ at sb** zombar de alguém.
 ⬥ **jeers** npl vaias fpl.

jeering ['dʒɪərɪŋ] ⬦ adj zombeteiro(ra). ⬦ n zombarias fpl.

Jehovah's Witness [dʒɪ'həʊvəz-] n Testemunha f de Jeová.

Jello® n (U) US ≃ gelatina f.

jelly ['dʒelɪ] (pl -ies) n -1. [dessert] gelatina f -2. [jam] geléia f.

jelly baby n UK caramelo em forma de boneco.

jelly bean n bala f de jujuba.

jellyfish ['dʒelɪfɪʃ] (pl inv OR -es) n água-viva f.

jelly roll n US rocambole m.

jemmy UK ['dʒemɪ], **jimmy** US ['dʒɪmɪl] (pl -ies) n pé-de-cabra m.

jeopardize, -ise ['dʒepədaɪz] vt pôr em perigo, arriscar.

jeopardy ['dʒepədɪ] n: in ~ em perigo.

jerk [dʒɜ:k] ⬦ n -1. [movement] guinada f, movimento m brusco -2. inf pej [fool] estúpido m, -da f. ⬦ vt mover abruptamente; **he ~ed the door open** ele abriu a porta bruscamente. ⬦ vi dar solavancos.

jerkily ['dʒɜ:kɪlɪ] adv abruptamente.

jerkin ['dʒɜ:kɪn] n colete m.

jerky ['dʒɜ:kɪ] (compar -ier, superl -iest) adj abrupto(ta).

jerry-built ['dʒerɪ-] adj mal construído(da).

jerry can n lata f.

jersey ['dʒɜ:zɪ] (pl jerseys) n -1. [sweater] suéter m -2. (U) [cloth] jérsei m.

Jersey ['dʒɜ:zɪ] n Jersey; in ~ em Jersey.

Jerusalem [dʒə'ru:sələm] n Jerusalém; in ~ em Jerusalém.

Jerusalem artichoke n tupinambor m.

jest [dʒest] n brincadeira f; in ~ de brincadeira.

jester ['dʒestəʳ] n bufão m.

Jesuit ['dʒezjʊɪt] ◇ adj jesuíta. ◇ n jesuíta m.
Jesus (Christ) ['dʒiːzəs-] ◇ n Jesus Cristo. ◇ interj inf Jesus Cristo!
jet [dʒetl (pt & pp -ted, cont -ting) ◇ n -1. [gen] jato m -2. [nozzle, outlet] cano m de descarga. ◇ vi [travel by jet] voar num avião a jato.
jet-black adj da cor de azeviche.
jet engine n motor m a jato.
jetfoil ['dʒetfɔɪl] n hidroavião m.
jet lag n (U) jet lag m.
jet-propelled [-prə'peldl adj de propulsão a jato.
jetsam ['dʒetsəm] n ▷ flotsam.
jet set n: the ~ o jet set.
jettison ['dʒetɪsən] vt -1. [cargo, bombs] alijar -2. fig [discard] descartar.
jetty ['dʒetɪ] (pl -ies) n quebra-mar m.
Jew [dʒuː] n judeu m.
jewel ['dʒuːəl] ◇ n -1. [gemstone] pedra f preciosa -2. [piece of jewellery] jóia f -3. [in watch] rubi m. ◇ comp de jóias.
jeweller UK, **jeweler** US ['dʒuːələʳ] n joalheiro m, -ra f; ~ 's (shop) joalheria f.
jewellery UK, **jewelry** US ['dʒuːəlrɪ] n (U) jóias fpl.
Jewish ['dʒuːɪʃl adj judeu(dia).
JFK (abbr of John Fitzgerald Kennedy International Airport) n (aeroporto m) JFK m.
jib [dʒɪbl (pt & pp -bed, cont -bing) ◇ n -1. [NAUT-beam] vau m; [- sail] bujarrona f -2. [of crane] braço m de guindaste. ◇ vi: to ~ at sthg hesitar em fazer algo.
jibe [dʒaɪbl n zombaria f.
jiffy ['dʒɪfɪl n inf: in a ~ num instante.
Jiffy bag® n envelope m acolchoado.
jig [dʒɪgl (pt & pp -ged, cont -ging) ◇ n [dance] jiga f. ◇ vi -1. [dance] dançar jiga -2. [jump] saracotear, gingar.
jiggle ['dʒɪgl] vt sacudir.
jigsaw (puzzle) ['dʒɪgsɔ-] n quebra-cabeça m.
jihad [dʒɪ'hɑːd] n jihad f.
jilt [dʒɪlt] vt deixar plantado(da).
jimmy n US = jemmy.
jingle ['dʒɪŋgl] ◇ n -1. [sound] tilintar m -2. [song] jingle m. ◇ vi tilintar.
jingoism ['dʒɪŋgəʊɪzm] n (U) jingoísmo m.
jinx [dʒɪŋks] n pé-frio m.
jinxed ['dʒɪŋkst] adj de má sorte.
jitters ['dʒɪtəz] npl inf: to have the ~ ficar com os nervos à flor da pele.
jittery ['dʒɪtərɪ] adj inf nervoso(sa).
jive [dʒaɪv] ◇ n -1. [dance] swing m -2. US inf [glib talk] burburinho m. ◇ vi dançar swing.
job [dʒɒbl n -1. [paid employment] emprego m -2. [task, piece of work] trabalho m; to do a good ~ fazer um bom trabalho; to make a good ~ of sthg fazer algo muito bem -3. [difficult time]: to have a ~ doing sthg ter trabalho para fazer algo -4. [function, role] tarefa f, função f -5. inf [plastic surgery]: to have a nose ~ fazer uma plástica no nariz -6. inf [crime] trabalho m -7. phr: that's just the ~ UK inf isso vem bem a calhar.
jobbing ['dʒɒbɪŋl adj UK que trabalha por empreitada.
job centre n UK agência f de empregos.

job creation scheme n projeto m de geração de empregos.
job description n descrição f do cargo.
jobless ['dʒɒblɪs] ◇ adj desempregado(da). ◇ npl: the ~ os desempregados.
job lot n lote m (de mercadorias variadas).
job satisfaction n (U) satisfação f profissional.
job security n (U) segurança f no trabalho.
Job Seekers Allowance n UK seguro-desemprego concedido a pessoas que comprovadamente estão buscando um novo trabalho.
jobsharing ['dʒɒbʃeərɪŋ] n (U) prática de dividir um trabalho de tempo integral entre duas pessoas de forma que cada uma cumpra apenas meio turno, especialmente para permitir que mulheres com filhos possam trabalhar.
Joburg, Jo'burg ['dʒəʊbɜːg] n inf Joanesburgo; in ~ em Joanesburgo.
jockey ['dʒɒkɪl (pl -s) ◇ n jóquei m. ◇ vi: to ~ for position competir por uma melhor posição.
jockstrap ['dʒɒkstræp] n sunga m.
jocular ['dʒɒkjʊləʳ] adj -1. [person] divertido(da) -2. [remark] engraçado(da).
jodhpurs ['dʒɒdpəz] npl culote m.
Joe Public [dʒəʊ-] n UK inf população f em geral.
jog [dʒɒg] (pt & pp -ged, cont -ging) ◇ n [run] corrida f, jogging m. ◇ vt [nudge] cutucar; to ~ the table sacudir a mesa; to ~ sb's memory refrescar a memória de alguém. ◇ vi [run] fazer cooper.
jogger ['dʒɒgəʳ] n [runner] corredor m, -ra f, praticante mf de cooper.
jogging ['dʒɒgɪŋ] n [running] cooper m.
joggle ['dʒɒgl] vt embalar.
Johannesburg [dʒəʊ'hænɪsbɜːg] n Joanesburgo; in ~ em Joanesburgo.
john [dʒɒn] n US inf [toilet] banheiro m.
John Hancock [-'hænkɒk] n US inf assinatura f, jamegão m.
join [dʒɔɪn] ◇ n junção f. ◇ vt -1. [connect] juntar -2. [get together with] juntar-se a; do ~ us for lunch venha almoçar com a gente -3. [become a member of - political party] filiar-se a; [- club] associar-se a; [- army] alistar-se em -4. [take part in] unir-se a; to ~ a queue UK, to ~ a line US entrar numa fila; to ~ forces juntar forças; ~ the club! juntem-se ao clube! ◇ vi -1. [connect - rivers] unir-se; [- pieces] encaixar-se -2. [become a member - of library] inscrever-se; [- of club] associar-se.
➤ **join in** vt fus & vi participar.
➤ **join up** vi MIL alistar-se.
joiner ['dʒɔɪnəʳ] n marceneiro m, -ra f.
joinery ['dʒɔɪnərɪ] n (U) marcenaria f.
joint [dʒɔɪntl ◇ adj conjunto(ta). ◇ n -1. ANAT articulação f -2. [where things are joined] encaixe m -3. UK [of meat] corte m -4. inf pej [place] espelunca f -5. drugs sl [cannabis cigarette] baseado m.
joint account n conta f conjunta.
Joint Chiefs of Staff npl: the ~ o Alto Comando das Forças Armadas (nos Estados Unidos).
jointed ['dʒɔɪntɪdl adj articulado(da).

jointly [ˈdʒɔɪntlɪ] adv conjuntamente.
joint ownership n (U) co-propriedade f.
joint-stock company n ≃ sociedade f anônima.
joint venture n joint-venture f.
joist [dʒɔɪst] n viga f de madeira.
jojoba [həˈhəʊbə] n (U) jojoba f.
joke [dʒəʊk] ◇ n -1. [funny story or action] piada f, anedota f; **to go beyond a** ~ perder a graça; **to play a** ~ **on sb** pregar uma peça em alguém; **it's no** ~ [not easy] não é fácil -2. [referring to situation, person]: **to be a** ~ ser uma piada. ◇ vi brincar; **to** ~ **about sthg** brincar em relação a algo; **to** ~ **with sb** brincar com alguém.
joker [ˈdʒəʊkəʳ] n -1. [person] brincalhão m, -lhona f -2. [playing card] curinga m.
jollity [ˈdʒɒlətɪ] n (U) alegria f.
jolly [ˈdʒɒlɪ] (compar -ier, superl -iest) ◇ adj alegre, divertido(da). ◇ adv UK inf muito; ~ **easy!** barbada!; ~ **good!** excelente!
jolt [dʒəʊlt] ◇ n -1. [jerk] empurrão m, solavanco m -2. [shock] sacudida f. ◇ vt -1. [jerk] sacudir -2. [shock] chocar; **to** ~ **sb into doing sthg** forçar alguém a fazer algo. ◇ vi sacolejar.
Joneses [ˈdʒəʊnzɪz] npl: **to keep up with the** ~ não ser menos que os outros.
Jordan [ˈdʒɔːdn] n Jordânia f; **in** ~ na Jordânia; **the (River)** ~ o (Rio) Jordão.
Jordanian [dʒɔːˈdeɪnjən] ◇ adj jordaniano(na). ◇ n jordaniano m, -na f.
joss stick [dʒɒs-] n incenso m aromático.
jostle [ˈdʒɒsl] ◇ vt acotovelar. ◇ vi acotovelar-se.
jot [dʒɒt] (pt & pp -ted, cont -ting) n tiquinho m; **there isn't a** ~ **of truth in** ... não há um pingo de verdade em ...; **I don't care a** ~ **what the rest of you think** não ligo a mínima para o que vocês pensam.
◆ **jot down** vt sep anotar.
jotter [ˈdʒɒtəʳ] n bloco m de anotações.
jottings [ˈdʒɒtɪŋz] npl recadinhos mpl.
journal [ˈdʒɜːnl] n -1. [magazine] revista f especializada -2. [diary] diário m.
journalese [ˌdʒɜːnəˈliːz] n (U) pej jargão m jornalístico, jornalês m.
journalism [ˈdʒɜːnəlɪzm] n (U) jornalismo m.
journalist [ˈdʒɜːnəlɪst] n jornalista mf.
journey [ˈdʒɜːnɪ] (pl -s) n jornada f.
joust [dʒaʊst] ◇ n justa f. ◇ vi justar.
jovial [ˈdʒəʊvjəl] adj jovial.
jowls [dʒaʊlz] npl bochechas fpl.
joy [dʒɔɪ] n -1. (U) [happiness] alegria f -2. [cause of happiness] prazer m, deleite m.
joyful [ˈdʒɔɪfʊl] adj alegre.
joyfully [ˈdʒɔɪfʊlɪ] adv alegremente.
joyous [ˈdʒɔɪəs] adj literary deleitante, jubiloso(sa).
joyously [ˈdʒɔɪəslɪ] adv literary com deleite.
joypad n COMPUT joystick m.
joyride [ˈdʒɔɪraɪd] ◇ n volta f num carro roubado. ◇ vi andar num carro roubado.
joyrider [ˈdʒɔɪraɪdəʳ] n ladrão m, -dra f de carro.
joystick [ˈdʒɔɪstɪk] n -1. [in aircraft] manche m -2. [for computers, video games] joystick m.

JP n abbr of Justice of the Peace.
Jr. (abbr of Junior) Jr.
jubilant [ˈdʒuːbɪlənt] adj jubilante.
jubilation [ˌdʒuːbɪˈleɪʃn] n (U) júbilo m.
jubilee [ˈdʒuːbɪliː] n jubileu m.
Judaism [dʒuːˈdeɪɪzm] n (U) judaísmo m.
judder [ˈdʒʌdəʳ] vi UK sacudir intensamente.
judge [dʒʌdʒ] ◇ n juíz m, -za f. ◇ vt -1. JUR julgar -2. [decide result of] sentenciar -3. [estimate] estimar. ◇ vi [decide] julgar; **to** ~ **from** OR **by** a julgar por, julgando-se por.
judg(e)ment [ˈdʒʌdʒmənt] n -1. JUR julgamento m; **to pass** ~ **(on sb)** condenar (alguém) -2. [opinion] parecer m; **to pass** ~ **(on sb/sthg)** julgar (alguém/algo); **to reserve** ~ adiar um julgamento -3. (U) [ability to form opinion] opinião f; **against my better** ~ contra a minha vontade -4. [punishment] sentença f.
judg(e)mental [dʒʌdʒˈmentl] adj pej crítico(ca).
judicial [dʒuːˈdɪʃl] adj judicial.
judiciary [dʒuːˈdɪʃərɪ] n: **the** ~ o judiciário.
judicious [dʒuːˈdɪʃəs] adj judicioso(sa).
judo [ˈdʒuːdəʊ] n (U) judô m.
jug [dʒʌg] n [container] jarro m.
juggernaut [ˈdʒʌgənɔːt] n [truck] jamanta f.
juggle [ˈdʒʌgl] ◇ vt -1. [throw] fazer malabarismos com -2. [rearrange] reorganizar -3. [commitments] equilibrar -4. [figures, ideas] maquiar. ◇ vi [as entertainment] fazer malabarismos.
juggler [ˈdʒʌgləʳ] n malabarista mf.
jugular (vein) [ˈdʒʌgjʊləʳ-] n (veia f) jugular f.
juice [dʒuːs] n -1. [from fruit, vegetables] suco m -2. [from meat] molho m.
◆ **juices** npl [in stomach] suco m gástrico.
juicy [ˈdʒuːsɪ] (compar -ier, superl -iest) adj -1. [full of juice] suculento(ta) -2. inf [scandalous] escandaloso(sa) -3. inf [enjoyable, desirable] desejável.
jujitsu [dʒuːˈdʒɪtsuː] n (U) jiu-jitsu m.
jukebox [ˈdʒuːkbɒks] n juke-box f.
Jul. (abbr of July) jul.
July [dʒuːˈlaɪ] n julho m; see also **September**.
jumble [ˈdʒʌmbl] ◇ n [mixture] mistura f. ◇ vt: **to** ~ **(up)** confundir.
jumble sale n UK venda f de objetos usados.
jumbo jet [ˈdʒʌmbəʊ-] n jumbo m.
jumbo-sized [ˈdʒʌmbəʊsaɪzd] adj gigantesco(ca).
jump [dʒʌmp] ◇ n -1. [leap] salto m -2. [fence in horse-jumping] obstáculo m -3. [rapid increase] alta m -4. phr: **to keep one** ~ **ahead of sb** manter um passo à frente de alguém. ◇ vt -1. [cross by leaping] pular; **the train** ~ **ed the rails** o trem descarrilhou -2. inf [attack] atacar -3. US [train, bus] viajar sem passagem em. ◇ vi -1. [leap] saltar -2. [make a sudden movement] sobressaltar; **the noise made me** ~ o barulho me fez dar um sobressalto -3. [increase rapidly] ter uma alta.
◆ **jump at** vt fus fig agarrar.
◆ **jump in** vi [get in quickly]: ~ **in!** entra rápido!
◆ **jump out** vi [get out quickly]: ~ **out!** salta fora!
◆ **jump up** vi [rise hurriedly] levantar-se rapidamente.
jumped-up [ˈdʒʌmpt-] adj UK inf pej pretencioso(sa).

jumper ['dʒʌmpəʳ] n -1. UK [pullover] suéter m - 2. US [dress] avental m.

jump jet n aeronave f de decolagem vertical.

jump leads npl cabos mpl para ligação da bateria.

jump-start vt fazer ligação direta.

jumpsuit ['dʒʌmpsuːtl] n macacão m.

jumpy ['dʒʌmpɪ] (compar -ier, superl -iest) adj nervoso(sa).

Jun. -1. (abbr of June) jun. - 2. = Junr.

junction ['dʒʌŋkʃn] n [meeting point] junção f, entroncamento m.

junction box n caixa f de ligação.

juncture ['dʒʌŋktʃəʳ] n fml: at this ~ nesta conjuntura.

June [dʒuːn] n junho; see also September.

jungle ['dʒʌŋgl] n selva f; the Amazon ~ a floresta amazônica.

jungle gym n US trepa-trepa f.

junior ['dʒuːnjəʳ] <> adj -1. [younger] jovem - 2. [lower in rank] júnior - 3. US [after name] júnior. <> n -1. [person of lower rank] júnior mf - 2. [younger person] jovem mf; he's five years her ~ ele é cinco anos mais jovem que ela - 3. US SCH & UNIV aluno m, -na f do penúltimo ano.

junior college n US escola f universitária para os dois primeiros anos de curso.

junior doctor n médico m, -ca f residente.

junior high school n US escola f de ensino intermediário (para alunos de 13 a 15 anos).

junior minister n UK subsecretário m, -ria f.

junior school n UK escola f primária.

juniper ['dʒuːnɪpəʳ] n junípero m.

junk [dʒʌŋk] <> n -1. inf [unwanted things] traste m - 2. [boat] junco m. <> vt jogar fora.

junket ['dʒʌŋkɪt] n -1. (U) [pudding] espécie de pudim feito com leite e coalho - 2. inf pej [trip] viagem f às custas do governo.

junk food n pej comida pronta e pouco saudável.

junkie ['dʒʌŋkɪ] n drugs sl drogado m, -da f.

junk mail n pej junk mail m.

junk shop n brechó m, brique m.

Junr (abbr of Junior) Jr.

junta [UK 'dʒʌntə, US 'hʊntəl] n junta f.

Jupiter ['dʒuːpɪtəʳ] n [planet] Júpiter.

jurisdiction [,dʒʊərɪs'dɪkʃn] n (U) jurisdição f.

jurisprudence [,dʒʊərɪs'pruːdəns] n (U) jurisprudência f.

juror ['dʒʊərəʳ] n jurado m, -da f.

jury ['dʒʊərɪ] (pl -ies) n júri m.

jury box n tribunal f do júri.

jury service n (U) trabalho m de jurado (num tribunal).

just [dʒʌstl] <> adj [fair] justo(ta). <> adv -1. [recently] agora mesmo; he's ~ left ele acabou de sair - 2. [at this or that moment]: I was ~ about to go out eu estava quase saindo; I'm ~ going to do it vou fazer isso agora mesmo; ~ then there was a knock at the door naquele momento houve uma batida na porta; she arrived ~ as I was leaving ela chegou no exato momento em que eu estava saindo; why do you always arrive ~ as I'm leaving? por que você sempre chega justamente quando estou saindo? - 3. [only, simply] apenas, simplesmente; in ~ a minute OR moment OR second num minuto OR instante OR segundo; ~ a minute! espera aí um pouquinho! - 4. [barely, almost not] mal; I can only ~ hear you mal consigo ouvir você; I only ~ caught the train quase perdi o trem; we have ~ enough time quase não temos tempo - 5. [for emphasis] simplesmente; I ~ can't believe it! simplesmente não consigo acreditar!; ~ look at this mess! dá só uma olhada na bagunça! - 6. [exactly, precisely] precisamente; ~ here exatamente aqui - 7. [in requests]: could I ~ borrow your pen? poderia me emprestar sua caneta, por favor?

➤ **just about** adv mais ou menos.

➤ **just as** adv [in comparisons]: ~ as well as you tão bem quanto você; ~ as bad as ever mal como sempre.

➤ **just now** adv -1. [a short time ago] agora mesmo - 2. [at this moment] neste momento.

justice ['dʒʌstɪs] n -1. [gen] justiça f - 2. [of a cause, claim] razão f - 3. [judge] juíz m - 4. phr: to do ~ to sthg [to a job] fazer justiça a algo; [to a meal] apreciar devidamente; to do ~ to sb fazer justiça a alguém; to do o.s. ~ desempenhar-se à altura.

Justice of the Peace (pl Justices of the Peace) n Juíz m, -za f de Paz.

justifiable ['dʒʌstɪfaɪəbl] adj justificável.

justifiable homicide n homicídio m em legítima defesa.

justifiably ['dʒʌstɪfaɪəblɪ] adv justificavelmente.

justification [,dʒʌstɪfɪ'keɪʃn] n -1. [good reason] justificativa f - 2. COMPUT: right-hand ~ alinhamento m justificado à direita.

justify ['dʒʌstɪfaɪ] (pt & pp -ied) vt -1. [give reasons for] justificar; to ~ doing sthg ter razões para fazer algo - 2. COMPUT & TYPO justificar.

justly ['dʒʌstlɪ] adv merecidamente, imparcialmente.

justness n (U) justiça f.

jut [dʒʌtl] (pt & pp -ted, cont -ting) vi: to ~ (out) projetar-se.

jute [dʒuːt] n (U) juta f.

juvenile ['dʒuːvənaɪl] <> adj -1. JUR juvenil - 2. pej [childish] infantil. <> n JUR [young person] menor mf.

juvenile court n juizado m de menores.

juvenile delinquent n delinquente mf juvenil.

juxtapose [,dʒʌkstə'pəʊz] vt: to ~ sthg with sthg justapor algo com algo.

juxtaposition [,dʒʌkstəpə'zɪʃn] n (U) justaposição f.

K

k (*pl* k's *OR* ks), **K** (*pl* K's *OR* Ks) [keɪ] *n* [letter] k, K *m*.
↠ **K** *n* **-1.** (*abbr of* **kilobyte**) K **-2.** (*abbr of* **Knight**) Cavaleiro *m* **-3.** (*abbr of* **thousand**) mil.

Kabul ['kɑːbʊl] *n* Cabul; **in ~** em Cabul.

kaftan ['kæftæn] *n* cafetã *f*.

Kalahari Desert [ˌkælə'hɑːrɪ-] *n*: **the ~** o Deserto de Kalahari.

kale [keɪl] *n* (U) couve *f* crespa.

kaleidoscope [kə'laɪdəskəʊp] *n* caleidoscópio *m*.

Kampala [kæm'pɑːlə] *n* Campala; **in ~** em Campala.

Kampuchea [ˌkæmpʊ'tʃɪə] *n* Camboja; **in ~** em Camboja.

Kampuchean ◇ *adj* cambojano(na). ◇ *n* cambojano *m*, -na *f*.

kangaroo [ˌkæŋgə'ruː] *n* canguru *m*.

Kansas ['kænzəs] *n* Kansas; **in ~** no Kansas.

kaolin ['keɪəlɪn] *n* (U) caulim *m*.

kaput [kə'pʊt] *adj inf* acabado(da).

karaoke [kɑːrə'əʊkɪ] *n* karaokê *m*.

karat ['kærət] *n US* quilate *m*.

karate [kə'rɑːtɪ] *n* (U) karatê *m*.

Kashmir [kæʃ'mɪə] *n* Cachemira; **in ~** na Cachemira.

Katmandu [ˌkætmæn'duː] *n* Katmandu; **in ~** em Katmandu.

kayak ['kaɪæk] *n* caiaque *m*.

Kazakhstan [ˌkæzæk'stɑːn] *n* Cazaquistão; **in ~** no Cazaquistão.

KB (*abbr of* **kilobyte(s)**) *n COMPUT* KB.

KBE (*abbr of* **Knight Commander of the Order of the British Empire**) *n (titular de) distinção britânica.*

KC (*abbr of* **King's Counsel**) *n título conferido a advogados de prestígio na Grã-Bretanha.*

kcal (*abbr of* **kilocalorie**) Kcal.

kebab [kɪ'bæb] *n churrasquinho picante servido com pão árabe e acompanhado de vegetais picados,* kebab *m*.

kedgeree ['kedʒərɪ] *n* (U) *UK prato indiano feito com arroz, peixe e ovos,* kedgeree *m*.

keel [kiːl] *n* quilha *f*; **on an even ~** em perfeito equilíbrio.
↠ **keel over** *vi* **-1.** [ship] emborcar **-2.** [person] desmaiar.

keen [kiːn] *adj* **-1.** [enthusiastic] entusiasta; **to be ~**

on sthg gostar muito de algo, ser aficionado(da) por algo; **to be ~ on sb** gostar muito de alguém; **to be ~ to do** *OR* **on doing sthg** estar muito a fim de fazer algo; **I'm not madly ~ on going** não estou com toda essa vontade de ir **-2.** [intense] intenso(sa) **-3.** [sharp, well-developed] apurado(da) **-4.** [wind] forte.

keenly ['kiːnlɪ] *adv* **-1.** [intensely] profundamente **-2.** [intently] atentamente.

keenness ['kiːnnɪs] *n* (U) **-1.** [enthusiasm] entusiasmo *m* **-2.** [intensity] intensidade *f* **-3.** [sharpness] perspicácia *f*.

keep [kiːp] (*pt & pp* kept) ◇ *vt* **-1.** [maintain in a particular place or state or position] manter; **to ~ sb waiting** fazer alguém esperar **-2.** [retain] ficar com; **please ~ the change** pode ficar com o troco; **they're ~ing the house in Scotland** eles estão mantendo a casa na Escócia **-3.** [continue]: **to ~ doing sthg** continuar fazendo algo; **to ~ talking** continuar falando; **to ~ going** continuar indo **-4.** [put aside, store] guardar **-5.** [prevent]: **to ~ sb/sthg from doing sthg** impedir alguém/algo de fazer algo **-6.** [detain] manter; **to ~ sb (from sthg)** privar alguém (de algo); **what kept you here?** o que te segurou aqui? **-7.** [fulfil, observe] cumprir; **to ~ a secret** guardar um segredo **-8.** [withhold news or fact of]: **to ~ sthg from sb** ocultar algo de alguém; **~ it to yourself for the moment** não conta isso para ninguém por enquanto **-9.** [diary, record, account] ter **-10.** [own - farm animals] criar; [- shop, car] ter **-11.** *phr*: **they ~ themselves to themselves** eles são muito reservados. ◇ *vi* **-1.** [remain, stay] manter-se **-2.** [continue moving] manter-se a **-3.** [last, stay fresh] conservar-se **-4.** *UK* [in health] manter-se. ◇ *n* (U) [food, board etc] sustento *m*.
↠ **for keeps** *adv* para valer.
↠ **keep at** *vt fus*: **to ~ at it** [work hard] empenhar-se.
↠ **keep back** *vt sep* conter.
↠ **keep down** *vt sep* **-1.** [stop from increasing] limitar **-2.** [food] controlar.
↠ **keep off** ◇ *vt sep* [fend off] manter afastado(da). ◇ *vt fus* [avoid] evitar; **'~ off the grass'** 'não pise na grama'.
↠ **keep on** ◇ *vi* **-1.** [continue] continuar **-2.** [talk incessantly]: **to ~ on (about sthg)** falar incessantemente (sobre algo). ◇ *vt* [continue]: **to ~ on doing sthg** [without stopping] continuar fazendo algo; [repeatedly] continuar fazendo algo sem parar.
↠ **keep on at** *vt fus UK* importunar.
↠ **keep out** ◇ *vt sep* manter-se fora. ◇ *vi*: **'~ out'** 'entrada proibida'.
↠ **keep to** ◇ *vt fus* **-1.** [observe, respect] respeitar **-2.** [not deviate from] manter-se em **-3.** [stay in] ficar em. ◇ *vt sep* [limit] limitar.
↠ **keep up** ◇ *vt sep* **-1.** [prevent from falling] segurar **-2.** [maintain, continue] manter **-3.** [prevent from going to bed] manter acordado(da). ◇ *vi* **-1.** [maintain pace, level] acompanhar; **to ~ up with sb/sthg** acompanhar alguém/algo **-2.** [remain in contact]: **to ~ up with sb** manter-se em contato com alguém.

keeper ['kiːpə] *n* **-1.** [in zoo] zelador *m*, -ra *f*, guarda *mf* **-2.** [curator] curador *m*, -ra *f*.

keep-fit *UK* ◇ *n (U)* ginástica *f.* ◇ *comp* de ginástica.

keeping ['ki:pɪŋ] *n* **-1.** [care] cuidado *m* **-2.** [conformity, harmony]: **in/out of ~ with sthg** [rules, regulations, decision] em acordo/desacordo com algo; [clothes, furniture, style] combinando/não combinando com algo.

keepsake ['ki:pseɪk] *n* lembrança *f.*

keg [keg] *n* barrilote *m.*

kelp [kelp] *n (U)* alga *f* marinha.

ken [ken] *n:* **beyond one's ~** além do alcance de alguém.

kennel ['kenl] *n* **-1.** [shelter for dog] canil *m* **-2.** *US* = **kennels.**

kennels *npl UK* [for boarding pets] canil *m.*

Kentucky [ken'tʌkɪ] *n* Kentucky; **in ~** em Kentucky.

Kenya ['kenjə] *n* Quênia; **in ~** no Quênia.

Kenyan ['kenjən] ◇ *adj* queniano(na). ◇ *n* queniano *m,* -na *f.*

kept [kept] *pt & pp* ▷ **keep.**

kerb [kɜ:b] *n UK* meio-fio *m.*

kerb crawler [-ˌkrɔ:lə^r] *n UK* pessoa que dirige o carro vagarosamente junto ao meio-fio em busca de prostitutas.

kerbstone ['kɜ:bstəʊn] *n UK* marco *m* de pedra.

kerfuffle [kə'fʌfl] *n UK inf* escarcéu *m.*

kernel ['kɜ:nl] *n* [of nut] amêndoa *f;* **the ~ of the issue** o cerne da questão.

kerosene ['kerəsi:n] *n (U)* querosene *f.*

kestrel ['kestrəl] *n* falcão *m* europeu.

ketch *n* brigue *m.*

ketchup ['ketʃəp] *n (U)* ketchup *m.*

kettle ['ketl] *n* chaleira *f.*

kettledrum ['ketldrʌm] *n* tímpano *m.*

key [ki:] ◇ *n* **-1.** [for lock] chave *f* **-2.** [of typewriter, computer] tecla *f* **-3.** [explanatory list] legenda *f* **-4.** [solution, answer]: **~ (to sthg)** chave (para algo) **-5.** [MUS - of piano, organ] tom *m;* [- scale of notes] clave *f.* ◇ *adj* [main] principal; **~ position** posição-chave; **~ issue** questão-chave.

key in *vt sep* digitar.

keyboard ['ki:bɔ:d] ◇ *n* teclado *m.* ◇ *vt* digitar.

keyboarder ['ki:bɔ:də^r] *n* digitador *m,* -ra *f.*

keyed up [ki:d-] *adj* excitado(da).

keyhole ['ki:həʊl] *n* buraco *m* da fechadura.

keynote ['ki:nəʊt] ◇ *n* [main point] tônica *f.* ◇ *comp:* **~ speech** conferência *f* de abertura.

keypad ['ki:pæd] *n COMPUT* teclado *m.*

keypunch ['ki:pʌntʃ] *n US* máquina *f* de perfurar cartões.

key ring *n* chaveiro *m.*

keystone ['ki:stəʊn] *n* pedra *f* angular.

keystroke ['ki:strəʊk] *n COMPUT* pressionamento *m* de tecla.

keyword *n* palavra-chave *f.*

kg (*abbr of* **kilogram**) Kg.

KGB *n* KGB *f.*

khaki ['kɑ:kɪ] ◇ *adj* cáqui *inv.* ◇ *n* **-1.** [colour] cáqui *m* **-2.** [cloth] tecido *m* cor de cáqui.

kHz (*abbr of* **kilohertz**) *n* kHz.

kibbutz [kɪ'bʊts] (*pl* **kibbutzim** [ˌkɪbʊt'si:m], **-es**) *n* kibutz *m.*

kick [kɪk] ◇ *n* **-1.** [with foot] chute *m* **-2.** *inf* [excitement]: **to do sthg for ~s** fazer algo para se divertir; **to get a ~ from sthg** desfrutar de algo **-3.** *inf* [of drink] efeito *m* estimulante. ◇ *vt* **-1.** [with foot] chutar; **to ~ o.s.** *fig* morder-se de raiva **-2.** *inf* [give up] largar. ◇ *vi* [person, baby, animal] dar pontapés.

kick about, kick around *vi UK inf* [lie around] rodear.

kick in *vi* fazer efeito.

kick off *vi* **-1.** *FTBL* dar o pontapé inicial **-2.** *inf fig* [start] começar.

kick out *vt sep inf* expulsar.

kick up *vt fus inf* protestar com violência.

kickoff ['kɪkɒf] *n* pontapé *m* inicial.

kick-start *vt* dar partida em; **to give sthg a ~** dar um grande impulso a algo.

kid [kɪd] (*pt & pp* **-ded**, *cont* **-ding**) ◇ *n* **-1.** *inf* [child, young person] criança *f;* **I've got four ~s** tenho quatro filhos **-2.** [young goat] cabrito *m* **-3.** [leather] pelica *f.* ◇ *comp inf* [brother, sister]: **my ~ brother** meu irmão mais novo; **my ~ sister** minha irmã mais nova. ◇ *vt inf* **-1.** [tease] caçoar **-2.** [delude]: **to ~ o.s.** iludir-se. ◇ *vi inf:* **to be kidding** estar brincando; **no kidding!** [in emphasis] não brinca!; [in disbelief] não acredito!

kiddie, kiddy ['kɪdɪ] (*pl* **-ies**) *n inf* guri *m,* -ria *f.*

kid gloves *npl:* **to treat** *OR* **handle sb with ~** tratar alguém com luvas de pelica.

kidnap ['kɪdnæp] (*UK pt & pp* **-ped**, *cont* **-ping**, *US pt & pp* **-ed**, *cont* **-ing**) *vt* seqüestrar.

kidnapper *UK,* **kidnaper** *US* ['kɪdnæpə^r] *n* seqüestrador *m,* -ra *f.*

kidnapping *UK,* **kidnaping** *US* ['kɪdnæpɪŋ] *n* seqüestro *m.*

kidney ['kɪdnɪ] (*pl* **-s**) *n* rim *m.*

kidney bean *n* feijão *m* roxo.

kidney machine *n* hemodialisador *m.*

Kilimanjaro [ˌkɪlɪmən'dʒɑ:rəʊ] *n* Kilimanjaro.

kill [kɪl] ◇ *n* **-1.** [of animal] abate *m;* **to move** *OR* **close in for the ~** dar o bote; *fig* dar o bote **-2.** [dead animal] presa *f.* ◇ *vt* **-1.** [gen] matar; **my feet are ~ing me** meus pés estão me matando; **to ~ o.s.** matar-se **-2.** [murder] assassinar **-3.** *fig* [cause to end, fail] acabar com **-4.** [pass]: **to ~ time** matar tempo. ◇ *vi* aniquilar.

kill off *vt sep* **-1.** [cause death of] aniquilar **-2.** *fig* [cause to end, fail] destruir.

killer ['kɪlə^r] *n* **-1.** [person] assassino *m,* -na *f* **-2.** [animal] matador *m,* -ra *f* **-3.** [disease] doença *f* fatal.

killer whale *n* orca *f,* baleia-assassina *f.*

killing ['kɪlɪŋ] ◇ *adj inf* [very funny] de matar. ◇ *n* **-1.** [of one person] assassinato *m* **-2.** [of several people] matança *f* **-3.** *inf* [profit]: **to make a ~** faturar uma grana.

killjoy ['kɪldʒɔɪ] *n* estraga-prazer *mf.*

kiln [kɪln] *n* fornalha *f.*

kilo ['ki:ləʊ] (*pl* **-s**) (*abbr of* **kilogram**) *n* quilo *m.*

kilo- [kɪlə] *prefix* quilo.

kilobyte ['kɪləbaɪt] *n* quilobyte *m.*

kilocalorie ['kɪləˌkælərɪ] *n* quilocaloria *f.*

kilogram(me) ['kɪləgræm] *n* quilograma *m.*

kilohertz ['kɪləhɜ:tz] (*pl inv*) *n* quilohertz *m.*

kilojoule [ˈkɪlədʒuːl] n quilojoule m.

kilometre UK [ˈkɪləˌmiːtəʳ], **kilometer** US [kɪˈlɒmɪtəʳ] n quilômetro m.

kilowatt [ˈkɪləwɒt] n quilowatt m.

kilt [kɪlt] n kilt m.

kimono [kɪˈməʊnəʊl] (pl -s) n quimono m.

kin [kɪn] n ⊳ **kith**.

kind [kaɪnd] ⊳ adj gentil, amável; **would you be so ~ as to ...?** será que você me faria a gentileza de ...? ⊳ n espécie f, tipo m; **a ~ of** uma espécie de; **~ of** inf de certo modo; **I ~ of thought that ...** eu meio que achei que ...; **of a ~** [sort of] do estilo; **an agreement of the ~** um acordo do estilo; [of same kind] do mesmo tipo; **in ~** [payment] em espécie; **nothing of the ~!** de jeito nenhum!; **it's one of a ~** é um em um milhão; **they're two of a ~** os dois são muito semelhantes.

kindergarten [ˈkɪndəˌgɑːtn] n jardim-de-infância m.

kind-hearted [-ˈhɑːtɪd] adj de bom coração.

kindle [ˈkɪndl] vt -1. [fire] pôr fogo em -2. fig [idea, feeling] inflamar.

kindling [ˈkɪndlɪŋ] n (U) [to light fire] gravetos mpl.

kindly [ˈkaɪndlɪ] (compar -ier, superl -iest) ⊳ adj bondoso(sa), gentil. ⊳ adv -1. [gen] bondosamente, gentilmente; **to look ~ on sb/sthg** olhar alguém/algo com bons olhos -2. [in sarcasm]: **~ leave the room!** faça o favor de sair da sala!; **will you ~ stop calling me that name!** pode fazer o favor de parar de me chamar por esse nome! -3. phr: **not to take ~ to sthg** não simpatizar com algo.

kindness [ˈkaɪndnɪs] n -1. (U) [gentleness] gentileza f, bondade f -2. [helpful act] generosidade f.

kindred [ˈkɪndrɪd] adj [similar] afim; **~ spirit** alma f gêmea.

kinetic [kɪˈnetɪk] adj cinético(ca).

kinfolk(s) [ˈkɪnfəʊk(s)] npl US = **kinsfolk**.

king [kɪŋ] n rei m.

kingdom [ˈkɪŋdəm] n reino m.

kingfisher [ˈkɪŋˌfɪʃəʳ] n martim-pescador m.

kingpin [ˈkɪŋpɪn] n -1. TECH pino-mestre m -2. fig [person] manda-chuva m.

king prawn n camarão m real.

king-size(d) [-saɪz(d)] adj de tamanho grande; **~ bed** cama f king-size.

kink [kɪŋk] n [in rope, hair] dobra f.

kinky [ˈkɪŋkɪ] (compar -ier, superl -iest) adj -1. inf [idea, behaviour] excêntrico(ca) -2. [sex] pervertido(da).

kinsfolk [ˈkɪnzfəʊk] npl parentes mpl.

kinship [ˈkɪnʃɪp] n -1. [relationship] parentesco m -2. [closeness] afinidade f.

kiosk [ˈkiːɒsk] n -1. [small shop] banca f -2. UK [telephone box] cabine f telefônica.

kip [kɪp] (pt & pp -ped, cont -ping) UK inf ⊳ n sesta f. ⊳ vi sestear.

kipper [ˈkɪpəʳ] n arenque m defumado.

Kirk [kɜːk] n Scot: **the ~** a igreja nacional escocesa.

kirsch [kɪəʃ] n quirche m.

kiss [kɪs] ⊳ n beijo m; **to give sb a ~** dar um beijo em alguém. ⊳ vt beijar; **to ~ sb goodbye** dar um beijo de despedida em alguém. ⊳ vi beijar-se.

kiss curl n UK pequeno anel de cabelo que se penteia para ficar reto na testa, na nuca ou na frente da orelha.

kiss of death n fig: **the ~** o beijo da morte.

kiss of life n [to resuscitate sb]: **to give sb the ~** fazer respiração boca-a-boca em alguém.

kissogram [ˈkɪsəgræm] n beijograma m, forma de homenagear uma pessoa contratando alguém para lhe dar um beijo, ao estilo das telemensagens.

kit [kɪt] (pt & pp -ted, cont -ting) n -1. [set] estojo m -2. (U) [clothes] equipamento m -3. [to be assembled] kit m, modelo m.
➝ **kit out** vt sep UK equipar.

kit bag n mochila f de viagem.

kitchen [ˈkɪtʃɪn] n cozinha f.

kitchenette [ˌkɪtʃɪˈnet] n kitchenette f, copa-cozinha f.

kitchen garden n horta f.

kitchen roll n papel-toalha m.

kitchen sink n pia f de cozinha.

kitchen unit n módulo m de cozinha.

kitchenware [ˈkɪtʃɪnweəʳ] n utensílios mpl para cozinha.

kite [kaɪt] n -1. [toy] pipa f -2. [bird] milhafre m.

Kite-mark n UK marca f de padrão de qualidade.

kith [kɪθ] n: **~ and kin** amigos mpl e parentes.

kitsch [kɪtʃ] n (U) kitsch mf.

kitten [ˈkɪtn] n gatinho m, -nha f.

kitty [ˈkɪtɪ] (pl -ies) n -1. [shared fund - for bills, drinks] vaquinha f; [- in card games] bolo m -2. [cat] gatinho m, -nha f.

kiwi [ˈkiːwiː] n -1. [bird] quivi m -2. inf [New Zealander] neozelandês m, -esa f.

kiwi fruit n quivi m.

KKK (abbr of Ku Klux Klan) n Ku Klux Klan f.

klaxon [ˈklæksn] n buzina f elétrica.

Kleenex® [ˈkliːneks] n lenço m de papel.

kleptomaniac [ˌkleptəˈmeɪnɪæk] n cleptomaníaco m, -ca f.

km (abbr of kilometre) km.

km/h (abbr of kilometres per hour) km/h.

knack [næk] n inclinação m, queda f; **to have the ~ (of doing sthg)** levar jeito (para fazer algo); **to have a ~ (for doing sthg)** ter uma queda (para fazer algo).

knacker [ˈnækəʳ] UK ⊳ n [horse slaughterer] matador m, -ra f de cavalos velhos. ⊳ vt inf [tire, break] acabar.

knackered [ˈnækəd] adj UK vinf [tired, broken] acabado(da).

knapsack [ˈnæpsæk] n mochila f.

knave [neɪv] n [playing card] valete m.

knead [niːd] vt [dough, clay] misturar.

knee [niː] n ANAT joelho m; **to be on one's ~s** [kneeling] ajoelhar-se; **to bring sb to their ~s** pôr alguém de joelhos.

kneecap [ˈniːkæp] n rótula f.

knee-deep adj -1. [snow, water] até o joelho -2. [person] enterrado(da) até o joelho.

knee-high adj à altura dos joelhos.

kneel [niːl] (UK pt & pp knelt, US pt & pp knelt OR -ed) vi ajoelhar-se.

kneel down *vi* ajoelhar, ajoelhar-se.

knee-length *adj* até o joelho.

knees-up *n UK inf* festa *f* barulhenta.

knell [nel] *n* -**1.** dobre *m* dos sinos -**2.** *fig*: **to sound the death ~ for sthg** decretar a sentença de morte para algo.

knelt [nelt] *pt & pp* ▷ **kneel**.

knew [nju:] *pt* ▷ **know**.

knickers ['nɪkəz] *npl* -**1.** *UK* [underwear] calcinha *f* -**2.** *US* [knickerbockers] calções *mpl* (presos à altura dos joelhos).

knick-knack ['nɪknæk] *n* penduricalho *m*.

knife [naɪf] (*pl* **knives**) ◇ *n* faca *f*. ◇ *vt* esfaquear.

knifing *n* facada *f*.

knight [naɪt] ◇ *n* -**1.** [gen] cavaleiro *m* -**2.** [in chess] cavalo *m*. ◇ *vt* nomear cavaleiro(ra).

knighthood ['naɪthʊd] *n* título *m* da classe dos cavaleiros.

knit [nɪt] (*pt & pp* **knit** *OR* **-ted**, *cont* **-ting**) ◇ *adj*: **closely** *OR* **tightly ~** *fig* fortemente unido(da). ◇ *vt* [make with wool] tricotar. ◇ *vi* -**1.** [with wool] fazer tricô, tricotar -**2.** [join] juntar-se.

knitted ['nɪtɪd] *adj* [scarf, hat] de malha.

knitting ['nɪtɪŋ] *n (U)* -**1.** [activity] trabalho *m* de tricô -**2.** [work produced] tricô *m*.

knitting machine *n* máquina *f* de tricô.

knitting needle *n* agulha *f* de tricô.

knitting pattern *n* molde *m* de tricô.

knitwear ['nɪtweə'] *n (U)* roupa *f* de tricô.

knives [naɪvz] *pl* ▷ **knife**.

knob [nɒb] *n* -**1.** [on door] maçaneta *f* -**2.** [on drawer] puxador *m* -**3.** [on walking stick, furniture] nó *m* -**4.** [on TV, radio] botão *m*.

knobbly *UK* ['nɒblɪ], **knobby** *US* ['nɒbɪ] (*compar* **-ier**, *superl* **-iest**) *adj* -**1.** [gen] nodoso(sa) -**2.** [knees] ossudo(da).

knock [nɒk] ◇ *n* -**1.** [blow] pancada *f*, batida *f* -**2.** *inf* [piece of bad luck] azar *m*. ◇ *vt* -**1.** [gen] bater contra; **to ~ one's head on sthg** bater com a cabeça em algo; **to ~ a hole in the wall** abrir um buraco na parede; **to ~ a nail into sthg** pregar um prego em algo -**2.** *inf fig* [criticize] criticar. ◇ *vi* -**1.** [on door]: **to ~ at** *OR* **on sthg** bater em algo -**2.** [car engine] bater.

knock about, knock around *inf* ◇ *vt sep* [beat up] tratar com violência. ◇ *vi* -**1.** *inf* [wander about] perambular -**2.** *inf* [spend time]: **to ~ about with sb** perder tempo com alguém.

knock back *vt sep inf* -**1.** [drink] enxugar -**2.** *inf* [cost] custar a.

knock down *vt sep* -**1.** [subj: car, driver] atropelar -**2.** [building] derrubar -**3.** [price] abater.

knock off ◇ *vt sep* -**1.** [lower price by] abaixar -**2.** *UK inf* [steal] abafar -**3.** *vinf* [sleep with] dormir com. ◇ *vi inf* [stop working] parar de trabalhar.

knock out *vt sep* -**1.** [make unconscious - subj: person, punch] pôr a nocaute; [- subj: drug] derrubar -**2.** [from competition] eliminar.

knock over *vt sep* -**1.** [push over] derrubar -**2.** [in car] atropelar.

knock up ◇ *vt sep* [produce hurriedly] preparar apressadamente. ◇ *vi TENNIS* bater bola.

knocker ['nɒkə'] *n* [on door] aldrava *f*.

knocking ['nɒkɪŋ] *n* -**1.** (U) [noise] pancadas *fpl* -**2.** *inf* [defeat] nocaute *m*; [criticism] crítica *f*.

knock-kneed [-'ni:d] *adj* de pernas tortas.

knock-on effect *n UK* efeito *m* dominó.

knockout ['nɒkaʊt] *n* -**1.** [in boxing] nocaute *m* -**2.** *inf* [sensation]: **she's a real ~** ela é de arrasar.

knockout competition *n UK* competição *f* com eliminatórias.

knock-up *n TENNIS* bate-bola *f*.

knot [nɒt] (*pt & pp* **-ted**, *cont* **-ting**) ◇ *n* -**1.** [gen] nó *m*; **to tie/untie a ~** fazer/desfazer um nó -**2.** [of people] grupo *m*. ◇ *vt* [rope, string] dar um nó em.

knotted *adj* -**1.** [tied in or with a knot] atado(da) com nós, emaranhado(da) -**2.** *phr UK*: **get ~!** *inf* te arranca!

knotty ['nɒtɪ] (*compar* **-ier**, *superl* **-iest**) *adj* [difficult] cabeludo(da).

know [nəʊ] (*pt* **knew**, *pp* **known**) ◇ *vt* -**1.** [become acquainted with] conhecer; **to get to ~ sb** conhecer alguém -**2.** [fact, information] saber; **to ~ (that)** saber que; **to get to ~ sthg** saber algo -**3.** [language, skill] ter conhecimento de; **to ~ how to do sthg** saber fazer algo -**4.** [recognize] reconhecer -**5.** [distinguish] diferenciar -**6.** [nickname, call]: **to be known as** ser conhecido(da) como. ◇ *vi* saber; **to ~ of sthg** saber de algo; **to ~ about sthg** [be aware of] saber sobre algo; [be expert in] saber de algo; **you ~** [for emphasis, to add information] você sabe; **there is no ~ing ...** é impossível saber ...; **to ~ sthg backwards** conhecer algo de cor e salteado; **not to ~ when one is well off** não saber a sorte que se tem; **to ~ better** não cair nessa. ◇ *n*: **to be in the ~** estar bem-informado(da) sobre.

know-all *n UK* sabichão *m*, -ona *f*.

know-how *n* experiência *f*, know-how *m*.

knowing ['nəʊɪŋ] *adj* [look, smile] de cumplicidade.

knowingly ['nəʊɪŋlɪ] *adv* -**1.** [look, smile] conscientemente -**2.** [act] de propósito.

know-it-all *n* = **know-all**.

knowledge ['nɒlɪdʒ] *n* conhecimento *m*; **it's common ~ that** é do senso comum que; **to my ~** que eu saiba; **to the best of my ~** até onde eu sei.

knowledgeable ['nɒlɪdʒəbl] *adj* entendido(da).

known [nəʊn] ◇ *pp* ▷ **know**. ◇ *adj* conhecido(da).

knuckle ['nʌkl] *n* -**1.** *ANAT* nó *m* (do dedo) -**2.** [of meat] mocotó *m*.

knuckle down *vi*: **to ~ down to sthg/to doing sthg** dedicar-se com afinco a algo/a fazer algo.

knuckle under *vi* dar-se por vencido(da).

knuckle-duster *n* soqueira *f* de metal.

KO (*abbr of* **knockout**) *n* K.O. *m*, nocaute *m*.

koala (bear) [kəʊ'ɑːlə-] *n* coala *m*.

kohl *n* cosmético usado no Oriente para escurecer as áreas acima e abaixo dos olhos.

kook [ku:k] *n US inf* biruta *mf*.

kooky ['ku:kɪ] (*compar* **-ier**, *superl* **-iest**) *adj US inf* biruta.

Koran [kɒ'rɑːn] *n*: **the ~** o Alcorão.

Korea [kə'rɪə] *n* Coréia *f*; **in ~** na Coréia.

Korean [kəˈrɪən] ◇ *adj* coreano(na). ◇ *n* -**1.** [person] coreano *m*, -na *f*- **2.** [language] coreano *m*.

kosher [ˈkəʊʃəʳ] *adj* -**1.** [meat] kosher - **2.** *fig inf* [reputable] limpo(pa), puro(ra).

Kosovan [ˈkɒsəvən], **Kosovar** [ˈkɒsəvɑː(r)] ◇ *adj* kosovar. ◇ *n* kosovar *mf*.

Kosovar Albanian ◇ *adj* albano-kosovar. ◇ *n* albano-kosovar *mf*.

Kosovo [ˈkɒsəvəʊ] *n* Kosovo; **in** ~ em Kosovo.

Koweit *n* = Kuwait; **in** ~ no Kuwait.

kowtow [ˌkaʊˈtaʊ] *vi*: **to** ~ **(to sb)** [behave humbly] humilhar-se (diante de alguém).

Krakow [ˈkrækaʊ] *n* = **Cracow**; **in** ~ em Cracow.

Kremlin [ˈkremlɪn] *n*: **the** ~ o Kremlin.

KS *abbr of* **Kansas**.

Kt (*abbr of* **Knight**) cav.

Kuala Lumpur [ˌkwɑːləˈlʊmpəʳ] *n* Cuala Lumpur; **in** ~ no Cuala Lumpur.

kudos [ˈkjuːdɒs] *n (U)* glória *f*.

Ku Klux Klan [kuːklʌksˈklæn] *n*: **the** ~ a Ku Klux Klan.

kumquat [ˈkʌmkwɒt] *n* árvore cítrica da China.

kung fu [ˌkʌŋˈfuː] *n (U)* kung fu *m*.

Kurd [kɜːd] *n* curdo *m*, -da *f*.

Kurdish [ˈkɜːdɪʃ] *adj* curdo(da).

Kurdistan [kɜːdɪˈstɑːn] *n* Curdistão; **in** ~ no Curdistão.

Kuwait [kjuːˈweɪt] *n* -**1.** [country] Kuwait; **in** ~ no Kuwait - **2.** [city] Kuwait.

Kuwaiti [kjuːˈweɪtɪ] ◇ *adj* kuwaitiano(na). ◇ *n* kuwaitiano *m*, -na *f*.

kW (*abbr of* **kilowatt**) Kw.

kWh (*abbr of* **kilowatt-hour**) kWh.

KY *abbr of* **Kentucky**.

l¹ (*pl* **l's** *OR* **ls**), **L** (*pl* **L's** *OR* **Ls**) [el] *n* [letter] l, L *m*.
◆ **L** -**1.** (*abbr of* **lake**) lago *m* - **2.** (*abbr of* **large**) G - **3.** (*abbr of* **left**) esq. - **4.** (*abbr of* **learner**) aprendiz *mf*.

l² (*abbr of* **litre**) l.

L

La *abbr of* **Louisiana**.

LA ◇ *n abbr of* **Los Angeles**. ◇ *abbr of* **Louisiana**.

lab [læb] *n inf* laboratório *m*.

label [ˈleɪbl] (*UK pt* & *pp* -**led**, *cont* -**ling**, *US pt* & *pp* -**ed**, *cont* -**ing**) ◇ *n* -**1.** [identification - on bottle] rótulo *m*; [- on luggage, clothing] etiqueta *f* - **2.** [of record] selo *m*. ◇ *vt* -**1.** [fix label to - bottle] rotular; [- luggage, clothing] etiquetar - **2.** [describe] descrever; **to** ~ **sb as sthg** rotular alguém de algo.

labor *etc n US* = **labour**.

laboratory [*UK* ləˈbɒrətrɪ, *US* ˈlæbrəˌtɔːrɪ] (*pl* -**ies**) ◇ *n* laboratório *m*. ◇ *comp* de laboratório.

Labor Day *n US* Dia *m* do Trabalho.

LABOR DAY

laborious [ləˈbɔːrɪəs] *adj* trabalhoso(sa).

labor union *n US* sindicato *m* (*de trabalhadores*).

labour *UK*, **labor** *US* [ˈleɪbəʳ] ◇ *n* -**1.** [work] trabalho *m*; **manual** ~ trabalho manual; **to withdraw one's** ~ abandonar o trabalho - **2.** [effort] esforço *m* - **3.** *(U)* [work force] mão-de-obra *f*; **parts and** ~ peças e mão-de-obra - **4.** *MED* [giving birth] trabalho *m* de parto; **to go into** ~ entrar em trabalho de parto. ◇ *vt* [insist on] insistir em. ◇ *vi* -**1.** [work] trabalhar - **2.** [struggle]: **to** ~ **at** *OR* **over sthg** trabalhar em algo; **to** ~ **under a delusion/misapprehension** estar redondamente enganado(da).
◆ **Labour** *UK POL* ◇ *adj* trabalhista. ◇ *n UK* o Partido Trabalhista.

labour camp *n* campo *m* de trabalhos forçados.

labour costs *npl* custos *mpl* com pessoal.

laboured *UK*, **labored** *US* [ˈleɪbəd] *adj* -**1.** [breathing] forçado(da) - **2.** [style] elaborado(da).

labourer *UK*, **laborer** *US* [ˈleɪbərəʳ] *n* peão *m*.

labour force *n* mão-de-obra *f*.

labour-intensive *adj* que exige muita mão-de-obra.

labour market *n* mercado *m* de trabalho.

labour of love *n* trabalho *m* por amor à arte.

labour pains *npl* dores *fpl* do parto.

Labour Party *n UK*: **the** ~ o Partido Trabalhista.

labour relations *npl* relações *fpl* trabalhistas.

laboursaving *UK*, **laborsaving** *US* [ˈleɪbəseɪvɪŋ] *adj*: ~ **device** mecanismo *m* que poupa trabalho.

Labrador [ˈlæbrədɔːʳ] *n* -**1.** [dog] labrador *m* - **2.** *GEOGR* Labrador.

laburnum *n* laburno *m*.

labyrinth [ˈlæbərɪnθ] *n* labirinto *m*.

lace [leɪs] ◇ *n* -**1.** *(U)* [fabric] renda *f* - **2.** [shoelace] cadarço *m*. ◇ *comp* de renda. ◇ *vt* -**1.** [shoe, boot] amarrar - **2.** [drink, food] misturar álcool em.
◆ **lace up** *vt sep* amarrar.

lacemaking [ˈleɪsˌmeɪkɪŋ] *n (U)* fabricação *f* de renda.

laceration [ˌlæsəˈreɪʃn] *n fml* & *MED* laceração *f*.

lace-up <> *adj* de cordões. <> *n UK* sapato *m* de amarrar.

lack [læk] <> *n* falta *f*; **for** *OR* **through** ~ **of** por falta de; **with no** ~ **of** sem falta de. <> *vt* sentir falta de, carecer de. <> *vi*: **you're** ~**ing in experience** te falta experiência; **to be** ~**ing** estar faltando.

lackadaisical [,lækə'deɪzɪkl] *adj pej* desinteressado(da), apático(ca).

lackey ['lækɪ] (*pl* -s) *n pej* pau-mandado *m*.

lacklustre *UK*, **lackluster** *US* ['læk,lʌstə'] *adj* sem brilho.

laconic [lə'kɒnɪk] *adj* lacônico(ca).

lacquer ['lækə'] <> *n* -**1.** [for wood, metal] verniz *m* -**2.** [for hair] fixador *m*. <> *vt* -**1.** [wood, metal] envernizar -**2.** [hair] aplicar fixador em.

lacrosse [lə'krɒs] *n* (U) *jogo canadense semelhante ao hóquei.*

lactic acid ['læktɪk-] *n* ácido *m* láctico.

lacy ['leɪsɪ] (*compar* -**ier**, *superl* -**iest**) *adj* rendado(da).

lad [læd] *n inf* -**1.** [young boy] rapaz *m* -**2.** [male friend] amigo *m*; **he went out for a drink with the** ~**s** ele saiu para beber com a rapazeada -**3.** *UK* [stable boy] empregado *m* de estábulo.

ladder ['lædə'] <> *n* -**1.** [for climbing] escada *f* de mão -**2.** *UK* [in tights] defeito *m*. <> *vt UK* [tights] puxar fio em. <> *vi UK* [tights] puxar fio.

laden ['leɪdn] *adj* carregado(da); ~ **with sthg** carregado com algo.

la-di-da [,lɑː'dɪ'dɑː] *adj inf pej* afetado(da).

ladies *UK* ['leɪdɪz], **ladies room** *US n* senhoras *fpl*, damas *fpl*.

lading ['leɪdɪŋ] *n* ▷ **bill**.

ladle ['leɪdl] <> *n* concha *f*. <> *vt* servir com concha.

lady ['leɪdɪ] (*pl* -**ies**) <> *n* -**1.** [woman] senhora *f* -**2.** [by birth or upbringing] dama *f* -**3.** *US inf* [to address woman] senhora *f*. <> *comp*: ~ **doctor** médica *f*.
➡ **Lady** *n* -**1.** [member of nobility] Lady *f* -**2.** *RELIG*: **Our Lady** Nossa Senhora.

ladybird *UK* ['leɪdɪbɜːd], **ladybug** *US* ['leɪdɪbʌg] *n* joaninha *f*.

lady-in-waiting [-'weɪtɪŋ] (*pl* ladies-in-waiting) *n* dama *f* de companhia.

lady-killer *n inf* mulherengo *m*, -ga *f*, conquistador *m*, -ra *f*.

ladylike ['leɪdɪlaɪk] *adj* elegante, refinado(da).

Ladyship ['leɪdɪʃɪp] *n*: **her/your** ~ Vossa Senhoria.

lag [læg] (*pt* & *pp* -**ged**, *cont* -**ging**) <> *n* [in time] atraso *m*, demora *f*. <> *vt* revestir com material isolante. <> *vi* [move more slowly]: **to** ~ **(behind)** ficar (para trás).

lager ['lɑːgə'] *n* cerveja *m* tipo Pilsen.

lager lout *n UK* beberrão *m*, -rona *f* jovem.

lagging ['lægɪŋ] *n* (U) revestimento *m*.

lagoon [lə'guːn] *n* lagoa *f*.

Lagos ['leɪgɒs] *n* Lagos; **in** ~ em Lagos.

lah-di-dah [,lɑː'dɪ'dɑː] *adj* = **la-di-da**.

laid [leɪd] *pt* & *pp* ▷ **lay**.

laid-back *adj inf* descontraído(da).

lain [leɪn] *pp* ▷ **lie**.

lair [leə'] *n* toca *f*.

laissez-faire [,leɪseɪ'feə'] <> *adj* do laissez-faire. <> *n* (U) laissez-faire *m*.

laity ['leɪtɪ] *n RELIG*: **the** ~ os laicos.

lake [leɪk] *n GEOGR* lago *m*.

Lake District *n*: **the** ~ a Região dos Lagos.

Lake Geneva *n* o Lago de Gênova.

lakeside ['leɪksaɪd] *adj* às margens do lago.

lama (*pl* -s) *n* lama *m*.

lamb [læm] *n* [animal, meat] cordeiro *m*.

lambast [læm'bæst], **lambaste** [læm'beɪst] *vt* criticar severamente.

lamb chop *n* costeleta *f* de cordeiro.

lambing ['læmɪŋ] *n* (U) parição *f* (*de ovelhas*).

lambskin ['læmskɪn] *n* pele *f* de cordeiro.

lambswool ['læmzwʊl] <> *n* (U) lã *f* de cordeiro. <> *comp* de lã de cordeiro.

lame [leɪm] *adj* -**1.** [person, horse] manco(ca) -**2.** [excuse, argument] pouco convincente.

lamé ['lɑːmeɪ] *n* (U) lamê *m*.

lame duck <> *adj US fig* [president] em final de mandato. <> *n* -**1.** *fig* [business] fracasso *m* -**2.** *fig* [person] inútil *mf*.

lamely ['leɪmlɪ] *adv* [unconvincingly] de forma não-convincente.

lament [lə'ment] <> *n* lamento *m*. <> *vt* lamentar.

lamentable ['læməntəbl] *adj* lamentável.

laminated ['læmɪneɪtɪd] *adj* laminado(da).

lamp [læmp] *n* lâmpada *f*.

lamplight ['læmplaɪt] *n* luz *f* de lâmpada.

lampoon [læm'puːn] <> *n* sátira *f*. <> *vt* satirizar.

lamppost ['læmppəʊst] *n* poste *m* de iluminação.

lampshade ['læmpʃeɪd] *n* quebra-luz *m*.

lance [lɑːns] <> *n* [spear] lança *f*. <> *vt MED* lancetar.

lance corporal *n UK* ≃ cabo *m*.

lancet ['lɑːnsɪt] *n MED* bisturí *m*, lanceta *f*.

land [lænd] <> *n* -**1.** [gen] terra *f* -**2.** [property, estate] terreno *m* -**3.** [nation] país *m*. <> *vt* -**1.** [plane] aterrissar -**2.** [cargo, passengers] desembarcar -**3.** [fish] recolher -**4.** *inf* [job, contract] fechar -**5.** *inf* [put, place]: **to** ~ **sb in trouble** pôr alguém em apuros; **to** ~ **sb in jail** fazer com que alguém acabe na cadeia -**6.** *inf* [encumber]: **to** ~ **sb with sb/sthg** incomodar alguém com alguém/algo. <> *vi* -**1.** [plane; passenger] aterrissar -**2.** [fall] cair -**3.** [from ship] desembarcar.
➡ **land up** *vi inf* acabar; **to** ~ **up in serious debt** acabar com um monte de dívidas; **to** ~ **up in** *OR* **at** [place] acabar em, ir parar em.

landed gentry ['lændɪd-] *npl* proprietários *mpl* de terra.

landing ['lændɪŋ] *n* -**1.** [of stairs] patamar *m* -**2.** [of aeroplane] aterrissagem *f* -**3.** [of goods from ship] desembarque *m*.

landing card *n* cartão *m* de desembarque.

landing craft *n* navio *m* de desembarque.

landing gear *n* (U) trem *m* de aterrissagem.

landing stage *n* cais *m inv* de desembarque.

landing strip *n* pista *f* de aterrissagem.

landlady ['lænd,leɪdɪ] (*pl* -**ies**) *n* [gen] senhoria *f*; [in guesthouse, pub] proprietária *f*.

landlocked [ˈlændlɒkt] *adj* cercado(da) de terra.
landlord [ˈlændlɔːd] *n* **-1.** [in lodgings] senhorio *m* **-2.** [of pub] proprietário *m*.
landmark [ˈlændmɑːk] *n* **-1.** [prominent feature] ponto *m* de referência **-2.** *fig* [in history] marco *m* divisório.
landmine [ˈlændmaɪn] *n* mina *f* terrestre.
landowner [ˈlændˌəʊnəʳ] *n* proprietário *m*, -ria *f* de terras.
landscape [ˈlændskeɪp] <> *n* paisagem *f.* <> *vt* ajardinar.
landscape gardener *n* paisagista *mf*.
landslide [ˈlændslaɪd] <> *n* **-1.** [of earth, rocks] desmoronamento *m* **-2.** *POL* vitória *f* esmagadora. <> *comp POL* esmagador(ra).
landslip [ˈlændslɪp] *n* deslizamento *m* de terra.
lane [leɪn] *n* **-1.** [road - in country] senda *f*; [- in town, village] ruela *f* **-2.** [division of road] pista *f*, faixa *f*; 'get/keep in ~' 'entrar/manter-se na pista' **-3.** [in swimming pool, on racetrack] raia *f* **-4.** [for shipping, aircraft] pista *f*.
langoustine *n* lagostim *m*.
language [ˈlæŋgwɪdʒ] *n* **-1.** [spoken, foreign] língua *f* **-2.** [style, mode of communication] linguagem *f*.
language laboratory *n* laboratório *m* de línguas.
languid [ˈlæŋgwɪd] *adj* lânguido(da).
languish [ˈlæŋgwɪʃ] *vi* **-1.** [suffer] sofrer **-2.** [become weak] debilitar-se.
languorous [ˈlæŋgərəs] *adj literary* langoroso(sa).
lank [læŋk] *adj* liso(sa).
lanky [ˈlæŋkɪ] (*compar* -ier, *superl* -iest) *adj* magricela.
lanolin(e) [ˈlænəlɪn] *n (U)* lanolina *f*.
lantern [ˈlæntən] *n* lanterna *f*.
Laos [laʊs] *n* Laos; in ~ em Laos.
Laotian [ˈlaʊʃən] <> *adj* laosiano(na). <> *n* **-1.** [person] laosiano *m*, -na *f* **-2.** [language] laosiano *m*.
lap [læp] (*pt & pp* -ped, *cont* -ping) <> *n* **-1.** [knees] colo *m* **-2.** *SPORT* volta *f.* <> *vt* **-1.** [subj: animal] lamber **-2.** *SPORT* [runner, car] estar uma volta à frente de. <> *vi* [water, waves] marulhar.
 lap up *vt sep* **-1.** [drink] beber com volúpia **-2.** *fig* [compliments, lies, information] receber com impaciência.
laparoscopy [ˌlæpəˈrɒskəpɪ] (*pl* -ies) *n* laparoscopia *f*.
La Paz [læˈpæz] *n* La Paz; in ~ em La Paz.
lapdog [ˈlæpdɒg] *n* [dog] cão *m* de estimação.
lapel [ləˈpel] *n* lapela *f*.
Lapland [ˈlæplænd] *n* Lapônia; in ~ na Lapônia.
Lapp [læp] <> *adj* lapão(ona). <> *n* **-1.** [person] lapão *m*, -ona *f* **-2.** [language] lapão *m*.
lapse [læps] <> *n* **-1.** [failing] lapso *m* **-2.** [in behaviour] deslize *m* **-3.** [of time] intervalo *m.* <> *vi* **-1.** [custom, licence] caducar **-2.** [passport] expirar **-3.** [law] prescrever **-4.** [deteriorate] decair **-5.** [subj: person]: to ~ into [coma] entrar em; [silence, dialect] mergulhar em; [bad habits] adquirir.
lapsed [læpst] *adj* descrente.
lap-top (computer) *n* (computador *m*) laptop *m*.

larceny [ˈlɑːsənɪ] *n (U)* furto *m*.
larch [lɑːtʃ] *n* larício *m*.
lard [lɑːd] *n (U)* toicinho *m*, banha *f (de porco)*.
larder [ˈlɑːdəʳ] *n* despensa *f*.
large [lɑːdʒ] *adj* grande.
 at large [escaped prisoner, animal] em liberdade. <> *adv* [as a whole] em geral.
largely [ˈlɑːdʒlɪ] *adv* em grande parte.
larger-than-life [ˈlɑːdʒəʳ-] *adj* exagerado(da).
large-scale *adj* **-1.** [wide-ranging] de grande escala **-2.** [map, diagram] em grande escala.
largesse, largess *US* [lɑːˈdʒes] *n (U)* grandeza *f*.
lark [lɑːk] *n* **-1.** [bird] cotovia *f* **-2.** *inf* [joke] brincadeira *f*; for a ~ de brincadeira.
 lark about *vi* fazer palhaçadas.
larva [ˈlɑːvə] (*pl* -vae [-viː]) *n* larva *f*.
laryngitis [ˌlærɪnˈdʒaɪtɪs] *n (U)* laringite *f*.
larynx [ˈlærɪŋks] (*pl* -es) *n* laringe *f*.
lasagna, lasagne [ləˈzænjə] *n (U)* lasanha *f*.
lascivious [ləˈsɪvɪəs] *adj* lascivo(va).
laser [ˈleɪzəʳ] *n* laser *m*.
laser beam *n* raio *m* laser.
laser printer *n* impressora *f* a laser.
laser show *n* show *m* com laser.
lash [læʃ] <> *n* **-1.** [eyelash] cílio *m* **-2.** [part of whip] chicote *m* **-3.** [blow with whip] chicotada *f.* <> *vt* **-1.** [whip] chicotear **-2.** [subj: wind, rain, waves] fustigar **-3.** [tie] atar; to ~ sthg to sthg atar algo em algo.
 lash out *vi* **-1.** [physically]: to ~ out (at *OR* against sb) atacar alguém com extrema violência **-2.** [verbally]: to ~ out (at *OR* against sb) atacar alguém verbalmente **-3.** *UK inf* [spend money]: to ~ out (on sthg) esbanjar dinheiro (em algo).
lass [læs] *n* [girl] moça *f*.
lasso [læˈsuː] (*pl* -s, *pt & pp* -ed, *cont* -ing) <> *n* laço *m.* <> *vt* laçar.
last [lɑːst] <> *adj* **-1.** [gen] último(ma); ~ but one penúltimo(ma); ~ but two antepenúltimo(ma) **-2.** [with dates, time of day] último(ma), passado(da); ~ week na semana passada, na última semana; ~ year no ano passado **-3.** [least likely]: you're the ~ person I expected to see você é a última pessoa que eu esperava ver. <> *adv* **-1.** [in final place] em último lugar **-2.** [most recently]: when did you ~ visit them? quando você os visitou pela última vez?; at ~ finalmente; at ~! até que enfim! <> *pron* o último, a última; to leave sthg till ~ deixar algo para o fim; the week before ~ na semana retrasada; the day before ~ anteontem. <> *n* [final thing]: the ~ I saw/heard of him a última coisa que eu soube dele. <> *vi* **-1.** [gen] durar; they only had food to ~ another week eles só tinham comida para mais uma semana **-2.** [survive] sobreviver.
 at (long) last *adv* por fim.
last-ditch *adj* derradeiro(ra).
lasting [ˈlɑːstɪŋ] *adj* duradouro(ra).
lastly [ˈlɑːstlɪ] *adv* **-1.** [to conclude] por fim **-2.** [at the end] finalmente.
last-minute *adj* de última hora.
last name *n* sobrenome *m*.
last post *n* **-1.** [postal collection] última coleta *f* **-2.** *MIL* toque *m* de recolher.

last rites *npl* últimos sacramentos *mpl.*
last straw *n*: it was the ~ foi a gota d'água.
Last Supper *n*: the ~ a Última Ceia.
last word *n*: to have the ~ ter a palavra final.
Las Vegas *n* Las Vegas; **in** ~ em Las Vegas.
lat. (*abbr of* latitude) lat.
latch [lætʃ] *n* trinco *m*; **on the** ~ fechado(da) com o trinco.
◆ **latch onto** *vt fus inf* agarrar-se a.
latchkey [ˈlætʃki:] (*pl* -s) ◇ *adj* [child] que fica sozinho(nha) em casa. ◇ *n* tranca *f (para porta exterior).*
late [leɪt] ◇ *adj* -**1.** [delayed] atrasado(da); **to be** ~ **for sthg** estar atrasado(da) para algo -**2.** [later than normal] tarde -**3.** [near end of]: **in** ~ **December** no final de dezembro -**4.** [dead] falecido(da). ◇ *adv* [not on time] tarde; **he arrived 20 minutes** ~ ele chegou 20 minutos atrasado; ~ **in December** no final de dezembro; **to work** ~ trabalhar até tarde.
◆ **of late** *adv* recentemente.
latecomer [ˈleɪtˌkʌmərˈ] *n* retardatário *m*, -ria *f.*
lately [ˈleɪtlɪ] *adv* ultimamente.
lateness [ˈleɪtnɪs] *n* -**1.** [of person, train] atraso *m* -**2.** [of meeting, event] hora *f* avançada.
late-night *adj* noturno(na), da noite; ~ **opening** aberto(ta) até tarde da noite.
latent [ˈleɪtənt] *adj* latente.
later [ˈleɪtərˈ] ◇ *adj* -**1.** [last, final] último(ma) -**2.** [subsequent, following] posterior -**3.** [train, bus, boat] que sai mais tarde. ◇ *adv* [at a later time]: ~ **(on)** mais tarde.
lateral [ˈlætərəl] *adj* lateral.
latest [ˈleɪtɪst] ◇ *adj* [most recent] último(ma). ◇ *n*: **at the** ~ no mais tardar.
latex [ˈleɪteks] ◇ *n* (U) látex *m inv.* ◇ *comp* de látex.
lath [lɑ:θ] *n* ripa *f*, sarrafo *m.*
lathe [leɪð] *n* torno *m* mecânico.
lather [ˈlɑ:ðərˈ] ◇ *n* espuma *f.* ◇ *vt* ensaboar. ◇ *vi* fazer espuma.
Latin [ˈlætɪn] ◇ *adj* latino(na). ◇ *n* [language] latim *m.*
Latin America *n* América Latina; **in** ~ na América Latina.
Latin American ◇ *adj* latino-americano(na). ◇ *n* [person] latino-americano *m*, -na *f.*
latitude [ˈlætɪtju:d] *n* -**1.** GEOGR latitude *f* -**2.** *fml* [freedom] liberdade *f (de expressão).*
latrine [ləˈtri:n] *n* latrina *f.*
latter [ˈlætərˈ] ◇ *adj* -**1.** [later] último(ma) -**2.** [second] segundo(da). ◇ *n*: **the** ~ o último, a última; **we prefer the** ~ **house to the former** preferimos esta casa àquela.
latter-day *adj* contemporâneo(nea).
latterly [ˈlætəlɪ] *adv* recentemente.
lattice [ˈlætɪs] *n* [fence, frame] treliça *f.*
lattice window *n* janela *f* de treliça.
Latvia [ˈlætvɪə] *n* Letônia; **in** ~ na Letônia.
Latvian [ˈlætvɪən] ◇ *adj* letão(ona). ◇ *n* -**1.** [person] letão *m*, -ona *f* -**2.** [language] letão *m.*
laudable [ˈlɔ:dəbl] *adj* louvável.
laugh [lɑ:f] ◇ *n* -**1.** [sound] riso *m*, risada *f*; to

have the last ~ rir por último -**2.** *inf* [fun, joke] piada *f*; **to do sthg for** ~**s** OR **a** ~ fazer algo por prazer. ◇ *vi* rir, gargalhar.
◆ **laugh at** *vt fus* [mock] rir-se de, gozar com.
◆ **laugh off** *vt sep* [dismiss] disfarçar. com um sorriso.
laughable [ˈlɑ:fəbl] *adj pej* [absurd] risível.
laughing gas [ˈlɑ:fɪŋ-] *n (U)* gás *m* hilariante.
laughingstock *n* motivo *m* de riso.
laughter [ˈlɑ:ftərˈ] *n (U)* risada *f*, risos *mpl.*
launch [lɔ:ntʃ] ◇ *n* -**1.** [gen] lançamento *m* -**2.** [start, initiation] início *m.* ◇ *vt* -**1.** [gen] lançar -**2.** [start, initiate] iniciar.
◆ **launch into** *vt fus* -**1.** [attack, fight] empreender -**2.** [lecture, explanation] proferir.
launching [ˈlɔ:ntʃɪŋ] *n* lançamento *m.*
launch(ing) pad [ˈlɔ:ntʃ(ɪŋ)-] *n* [for rocket, missile, satellite] plataforma *f* de lançamento.
launder [ˈlɔ:ndərˈ] *vt* -**1.** [clothes] lavar e passar -**2.** *inf* [money] lavar.
laund(e)rette [lɔ:nˈdret], **Laundromat®** US [ˈlɔ:ndrəmæt] *n* lavanderia *f* automatizada.
laundry [ˈlɔ:ndrɪ] (*pl* -ies) *n* -**1.** (U) [clothes - about to be washed] roupa *f* suja; [- newly washed] roupa *f* lavada -**2.** [room, business] lavanderia *f.*
laundry basket *n* cesto *m* de roupa suja.
laureate [ˈlɔ:rɪət] *n* ⊳ **poet laureate.**
laurel *n* louro *m.*
◆ **laurels** *npl*: **to rest on one's** ~**s** deitar na própria fama.
lava [ˈlɑ:və] *n (U)* lava *f.*
lavatory [ˈlævətrɪ] (*pl* -ies) *n* -**1.** [receptacle] privada *f* -**2.** [room] toalete *f.*
lavatory paper *n* UK papel *m* higiênico.
lavender [ˈlævəndərˈ] ◇ *adj* [colour] da cor da alfazema. ◇ *n* -**1.** [plant] alfazema *f*, lavanda *f* -**2.** [colour] lavanda *f.*
lavish [ˈlævɪʃ] ◇ *adj* -**1.** [generous] generoso(sa); **to be** ~ **with sthg** ser generoso(sa) com algo -**2.** [sumptuous] suntuoso(sa). ◇ *vt*: **to** ~ **sthg on sb/sthg** encher alguém/algo de algo.
lavishly [ˈlævɪʃlɪ] *adv* -**1.** [generously] generosamente -**2.** [sumptuously] suntuosamente.
law [lɔ:] ◇ *n* -**1.** [gen] lei *f*; **to break the** ~ transgredir a lei; **against the** ~ contra a lei; ~ **and order** lei e ordem; **the** ~ **of the jungle** a lei da selva -**2.** [system, subject] direito *m* -**3.** (U) *inf* [police]: **the** ~ a lei -**4.** *phr*: **to lay down the** ~ *pej* ditar as ordens. ◇ *comp* de direito.
law-abiding [-əˌbaɪdɪŋ] *adj* obediente à lei.
law-breaker *n* infrator *m*, -ra *f* da lei.
law court *n* tribunal *m* de justiça.
lawful [ˈlɔ:fʊl] *adj fml* lícito(ta).
lawfully [ˈlɔ:fʊlɪ] *adv fml* licitamente.
lawless [ˈlɔ:lɪs] *adj* -**1.** *fml* [illegal] ilegal -**2.** [without laws] sem lei -**3.** [person] indisciplinado(da).
Law Lords *npl* UK JUR: **the** ~ ≃ o Supremo Tribunal Federal.
lawmaker [ˈlɔ:ˌmeɪkərˈ] *n* legislador *m*, -ra *f.*
lawn [lɔ:n] *n* [grass] gramado *m.*
lawnmower [ˈlɔ:nˌməʊərˈ] *n* cortador *m* de grama.
lawn party *n* US recepção *f* ao ar livre.
lawn tennis *n* tênis *m inv* de gramado.

law school n escola f de direito.
lawsuit ['lɔ:su:t] n ação f judicial.
lawyer ['lɔ:jəᵣ] n advogado m, -da f.
lax [læks] adj negligente.
laxative ['læksətɪv] n laxante m.
laxity ['læksətɪ], **laxness** ['læksnɪs] n (U) negligência f.
lay [leɪ] (pt & pp laid) <> pt ⊳ lie. <> vt - 1. [in specified position] colocar - 2. [prepare - trap, snare] armar; [- plans] traçar; to ~ the table pôr a mesa - 3. [bricks] assentar; [carpet] colocar; [cable] afixar; [pipes, foundations] preparar - 4. [egg] pôr - 5. [blame, emphasis] aplicar. <> adj - 1. RELIG leigo(ga) - 2. [untrained, unqualified] desqualificado(da).
➡ **lay aside** vt sep - 1. [save] poupar - 2. [put down, abandon] abandonar.
➡ **lay before** vt sep [present] apresentar.
➡ **lay down** vt sep - 1. [formulate] formular - 2. [put down] depor.
➡ **lay into** vt fus inf [attack - physically] surrar; [- verbally] dar uma bronca em.
➡ **lay off** vt sep [make redundant] dispensar. <> vt fus inf - 1. [leave alone] deixar sozinho(nha) - 2. [stop, give up] parar de.
➡ **lay on** vt sep UK [provide, supply] providenciar.
➡ **lay out** vt sep - 1. [arrange, spread out] dispor - 2. [plan, design] projetar.
➡ **lay over** vi US pernoitar.
layabout ['leɪəbaʊt] n UK inf vadio m, -dia f.
lay-by (pl -s) n UK acostamento m.
lay days npl prazo estipulado para carga e descarga de um navio.
layer ['leɪəᵣ] n - 1. [of substance, material] camada f - 2. fig [level] nível m.
layette [leɪ'et] n enxoval m do bebê.
layman ['leɪmən] (pl -men [-mən]) n leigo m; in ~'s terms em termos gerais.
lay-off n [redundancy] demissão f.
layout ['leɪaʊt] n [design] leiaute m.
layover ['leɪəʊvəᵣ] n US parada f (durante uma viagem).
laze [leɪz] vi: to ~ (about OR around) vadiar.
lazily ['leɪzɪlɪ] adv [without effort] preguiçosamente.
laziness ['leɪzɪnɪs] n [idleness] preguiça f.
lazy ['leɪzɪ] (compar -ier, superl -iest) adj - 1. [person] preguiçoso(sa) - 2. [action] ocioso(sa).
lazybones ['leɪzɪbəʊnz] (pl inv) n inf preguiçoso m, -sa f.
lb abbr of pound.
lbw (abbr of leg before wicket) proteção ilegal do gol com a perna no jogo de cricket.
l.c. (abbr of lower case) caixa-baixa f.
L/C (abbr of letter of credit) carta f de crédito.
LCD (abbr of liquid crystal display) n tela f de cristal líquido, LCD m.
Ld (abbr of Lord) Lorde.
L-driver (abbr of learner driver) n UK ≃ auto-escola f (indicação no veículo).
LDS (abbr of Licentiate in Dental Surgery) n (titular de) graduação em odontologia na Grã-Bretanha.
LEA (abbr of local education authority) n órgão responsável pela educação numa área da Grã-Bretanha.

lead¹ [li:d] (pt & pp led) <> n - 1. (U) [winning position] dianteira f; to be in OR have the ~ estar na frente - 2. [amount ahead] vantagem f - 3. (U) [initiative, example] exemplo m; to take the ~ [do sthg first] tomar a iniciativa - 4. (U) [most important role]: the ~ o papel principal - 5. [clue] pista f - 6. [for dog] correia f - 7. [wire, cable] fio m. <> adj [most important] principal. <> vt - 1. [be in front of] dirigir - 2. [take, guide] conduzir - 3. [head, be in charge of] chefiar, comandar - 4. [organize] organizar; to ~ the way assumir a direção - 5. [life, existence] reger - 6. [cause, influence]: to ~ sb to do sthg induzir alguém a fazer algo. <> vi - 1. [go] levar - 2. [give access to]: that door ~s to the kitchen aquela porta dá para a cozinha - 3. [be winning] estar na frente - 4. [result in]: to ~ to sthg resultar em algo.
➡ **lead off** <> vt fus [subj: door, room] começar a partir de. <> vi - 1. [road, corridor]: to ~ off (from) começar (a partir de) - 2. [begin] começar.
➡ **lead up to** vt fus - 1. [precede] conduzir a - 2. [in conversation] levar a.
lead² [led] <> n - 1. (U) [metal] chumbo m - 2. [in pencil] grafite m. <> comp [made of or with lead] de chumbo.
leaded ['ledɪd] adj - 1. [petrol] com chumbo - 2. [window] com almofada de vidro.
leaden ['ledn] adj - 1. literary [dark grey] plúmbeo(bea) - 2. literary [heavy] soturno(na) - 3. [very dull] moroso(sa).
leader ['li:dəᵣ] n - 1. [gen] líder mf - 2. UK [in newspaper] editorial m.
leadership ['li:dəʃɪp] n - 1. [people in charge]: the ~ a liderança - 2. [position of leader] liderança f.
lead-free [led-] adj sem chumbo.
leading ['li:dɪŋ] adj - 1. [prominent] destacado(da) - 2. [main, principal]: to play the ~ part OR role in sthg lit & fig desempenhar o papel principal em algo - 3. SPORT [at front] primeiro(ra).
leading article n UK editorial m.
leading lady n atriz f principal, protagonista f.
leading light n figura f central.
leading man n ator m principal.
leading question n pergunta f com resposta induzida.
lead pencil [led-] n lápis m inv de grafita.
lead poisoning [led-] n saturnismo m.
lead time [li:d-] n COMM prazo m de entrega.
leaf [li:f] (pl leaves) n - 1. [gen] folha f - 2. [of table] aba f.
➡ **leaf through** vt fus folhear.
leaflet ['li:flɪt] <> n folder m, folheto m. <> vt distribuir folhetos em.
leafy ['li:fɪ] (compar -ier, superl -iest) adj - 1. [with many leaves] frondoso(sa) - 2. [with many trees] arborizado(da).
league [li:g] n liga f; to be in ~ with sb [work with] estar confabulado(da) com alguém.
league table n tabela f de classificação da liga.
leak [li:k] <> n - 1. [gen] vazamento m; a ~ in the roof uma goteira - 2. fig [disclosure] vazamento m (de informações). <> vt [make known] vazar. <> vi - 1. [gen] vazar; [boat, shoe]: to be ~ing estar com infiltração - 2. [roof] ter goteiras.

leak out *vi* [gen] vazar; **to ~ (out) from sthg** vazar de dentro de algo.

leakage ['liːkɪdʒ] *n* vazamento *m*.

leaky ['liːkɪ] (*compar* -**ier**, *superl* -**iest**) *adj* com furos; **a ~ roof** um teto com goteiras.

lean [liːn] (*pt* & *pp* **leant** OR -**ed**) <> *adj* -**1.** [gen] magro(gra) - **2.** *fig* [harvest, year] improdutivo(va). <> *vt* [support, prop]: **to ~ sthg against sthg** apoiar algo contra algo. <> *vi* -**1.** [bend, slope] inclinar-se - **2.** [rest]: **to ~ on/against sthg** apoiar-se em/contra algo.

lean back *vi* [person] recostar-se.

leaning ['liːnɪŋ] *n*: **~ (towards sthg)** inclinação *f* (para algo).

leant [lent] *pt* & *pp* ▷ **lean**.

lean-to (*pl* -**s**) *n* alpendre *m*.

leap [liːp] (*pt* & *pp* **leapt** OR -**ed**) <> *n* - **1.** [jump] salto *m*, pulo *m* - **2.** [increase] pulo *m*; **in ~s and bounds** com extrema rapidez. <> *vi* -**1.** [jump] saltar, pular - **2.** [increase] disparar; **to ~ to the eye** saltar aos olhos.

leap at *vt fus fig* não deixar escapar.

leapfrog ['liːpfrɒg] (*pt* & *pp* -**ged**, *cont* -**ging**) <> *n* (*U*) jogo *m* de pular carniça; **to play ~** brincar de pular carniça. <> *vi* -**1.** [jump]: **to ~ over sthg** saltar por cima de algo - **2.** *fig* aproveitar-se de.

leapt [lept] *pt* & *pp* ▷ **leap**.

leap year *n* ano *m* bissexto.

learn [lɜːn] (*pt* & *pp* -**ed** OR **learnt**) <> *vt* -**1.** [gen] aprender; **to ~ (how) to do sthg** aprender a fazer algo - **2.** [hear] ouvir; **to ~ that** ficar sabendo que. <> *vi* -**1.** [acquire knowledge, skill] aprender - **2.** [hear]: **to ~ of** OR **about sthg** ficar sabendo de algo.

learned ['lɜːnɪd] *adj* -**1.** [person] culto(ta), erudito(-ta) - **2.** [journal, paper, book] erudito(ta).

learner ['lɜːnəʳ] *n* aprendiz *mf*.

learner (driver) *n* aprendiz *mf* de direção.

learning ['lɜːnɪŋ] *n* - **1.** [knowledge] erudição *f* - **2.** [study] aprendizagem *f*.

learning curve *n* curva *f* de aprendizagem.

learnt [lɜːnt] *pt* & *pp* ▷ **learn**.

lease [liːs] <> *n* JUR arrendamento *m*, contrato *m* de locação; **to give sb a new ~ of life** UK, **to give a new ~ on life to sb** US dar uma nova vida a alguém. <> *vt* [premises] arrendar, alugar; **to ~ sthg from/to sb** arrendar algo de/para alguém; [car] fazer um leasing.

leaseback ['liːsbæk] *n contrato pelo qual o comprador aluga a propriedade comprada ao ex-proprietário.*

leasehold ['liːshəʊld] <> *adj* arrendado(da). <> *adv* em arrendamento.

leaseholder ['liːsˌhəʊldəʳ] *n* arrendatário *m*, -ria *f*.

leash [liːʃ] *n* [for dog] coleira *f*.

least [liːst] <> *adj* (*superl of little*) [smallest in amount, degree]: **the ~** o (a) menor; **he earns the ~ money of all** de todos ele é o que ganha menos. <> *pron* (*superl of little*) [smallest amount]: **the ~** o mínimo; **it's the ~ we'll have to spend** é o mínimo que teremos de gastar; **that's the ~ of my worries!** essa é a menor das minhas preocupações!; **it's the ~ (that) he can do** é o mínimo que ele podia fazer; **not in the ~** em absoluto, de modo algum;

to say the ~ para não dizer outra coisa. <> *adv* [to the smallest amount, degree] menos; **to aim for the ~ possible expenditure** desejar alcançar o menor gasto possível.

at least *adv* - **1.** [gen] pelo menos, no mínimo - **2.** [qualifying sthg one has said] pelo menos.

least of all *adv* muito menos.

not least *adv fml* em especial.

leather ['leðəʳ] <> *n* (*U*) couro *m*. <> *comp* de couro.

leathers *npl* [of motorbike rider] roupas *fpl* de couro.

leatherette [ˌleðə'ret] *n* (*U*) couro *m* sintético.

leave [liːv] (*pt* & *pp* **left**) <> *n* - **1.** [time off] licença *f*; **to be on ~** estar de licença - **2.** *fml* [permission] licença *f*, permissão *f* - **3.** *fml* [departure] partida *f*; **to take one's ~ (of sb)** *fml* despedir-se (de alguém). <> *vt* -**1.** [gen] deixar; **me alone!** me deixa em paz!; **it ~s me cold** isso me deixa indiferente; **it ~s a lot to be desired** isso deixa muito a desejar - **2.** [depart from] sair de - **3.** [entrust]: **to ~ it to sb to do sthg** deixar que alguém faça algo; **to ~ sthg/with sb** deixar algo com alguém; **~ it with me!** deixa (isso) comigo!; **to ~ sb sthg, to ~ sthg to sb** deixar algo para alguém - **4.** [husband, wife] deixar, largar. <> *vi* -**1.** [gen] partir, ir embora - **2.** [end relationship] ir embora.

leave behind *vt sep* - **1.** [abandon] abandonar - **2.** [forget] esquecer.

leave off *vt sep* - **1.** [omit] deixar fora, não incluir - **2.** [stop] parar de; **to ~ off doing sthg** parar de fazer algo; **~ off!** *inf* corta essa! <> *vi* [stop] deixar; **to carry on from where one left off** continuar de onde se havia parado.

leave out *vt sep* [omit] excluir, deixar de fora; **to feel left out** sentir-se ignorado(da).

leave of absence *n* licença *f*.

leaves [liːvz] *pl* ▷ **leaf**.

Lebanese [ˌlebə'niːz] (*pl inv*) <> *adj* libanês(esa). <> *n* [person] libanês *m*, -esa *f*.

Lebanon ['lebənən] *n* Líbano; **in (the) ~** no Líbano.

lecherous ['letʃərəs] *adj* lascivo(va).

lechery ['letʃərɪ] *n* (*U*) lascívia *f*.

lectern ['lektən] *n* atril *m*.

lecture ['lektʃəʳ] <> *n* - **1.** [talk - at university] aula *f*; [-at conference] palestra *f*, conferência *f*; **to give a ~ (on sthg)** dar uma palestra (sobre algo) - **2.** [criticism, reprimand] sermão *m*. <> *vt* [scold] dar um sermão em. <> *vi* [university]: **to ~ (on/in sthg)** dar uma aula (sobre algo); [at conference] dar uma palestra (sobre algo).

lecture hall *n* [in conference centre] - **1.** sala *f* de conferências - **2.** [in university] sala *f* de aula.

lecturer ['lektʃərəʳ] *n* - **1.** [teacher] professor *m*, -ra *f* - **2.** [speaker] palestrante *mf*, conferencista *mf*.

lecture theatre *n* anfiteatro *m*.

led [led] *pt* & *pp* ▷ **lead** [1].

LED (*abbr of* **light-emitting diode**) *n* LED *m*.

ledge [ledʒ] *n* - **1.** [of window] parapeito *m* - **2.** [of mountain] saliência *f*.

ledger ['ledʒəʳ] *n* livro *m* contábil.

lee [liː] *n* [shelter]: **in the ~ of sthg** ao abrigo de algo.

leech [liːtʃ] *n* - **1.** [creature] sanguessuga *f* - **2.**

fig & pej [person] sanguessuga *f.*

leek [li:k] *n* alho-poró *m.*

leer [lɪəʳ] ◇ *n* olhar *m* malicioso. ◇ *vi*: **to ~ at sb** olhar maliciosamente para alguém.

Leeward Islands ['li:wəd-] *npl*: **the ~** as Ilhas de Sotavento.

leeway ['li:weɪ] *n (U)* -**1.** [room to manoeuvre] liberdade *f* de ação -**2.** [time lost]: **to make up ~** recuperar o tempo perdido.

left [left] ◇ *pt & pp* ▷ **leave.** ◇ *adj* -**1.** [remaining] sobrando; **do you have any money ~?** tem algum dinheiro sobrando?; **to be ~** sobrar; **there's no milk ~** não sobrou leite -**2.** [side, hand, foot] esquerdo(da). ◇ *adv* para a esquerda. ◇ *n (U)* [direction]: **on/to the ~** à esquerda; **keep ~** mantenha-se à esquerda.
➡ **Left** *n POL*: **the Left** a esquerda.

left-hand *adj* esquerdo(da); **~ side** lado *m* esquerdo.

left-hand drive ◇ *adj* com direção do lado esquerdo. ◇ *n* veículo *m* com direção do lado esquerdo.

left-handed [-'hændɪd] ◇ *adj* -**1.** [person] canhoto(ta) -**2.** [implement] para canhotos -**3.** *US* [compliment] com duplo sentido. ◇ *adv* com a (mão) esquerda.

left-hander [-'hændəʳ] *n* canhoto *m*, -ta *f.*

Leftist *POL* ◇ *adj* esquerdista, de esquerda. ◇ *n* esquerdista *mf.*

left luggage (office) *n UK* guarda-bagagem *m.*

leftover ['leftəʊvəʳ] *adj* restante.
➡ **leftovers** *npl* sobras *fpl.*

left wing *n POL* esquerda *f.*
➡ **left-wing** *adj POL* esquerdista, de esquerda.

left-winger *n POL* esquerdista *mf.*

lefty ['leftɪ] (*pl* -ies) *n* -**1.** *UK inf pej & POL* esquerdista *mf* -**2.** *US* [left-handed person] canhoto *m*, -ta *f.*

leg [leg] *n* -**1.** [gen] perna *f*; **to be on one's last ~s** estar nas últimas; **you don't have a ~ to stand on** você não tem em que se basear; **to pull sb's ~** pegar no pé de alguém; [of animal, bird, insect] pata *f* -**2.** [*CULIN-* of chicken] coxa *f*; [- of frog, lamb] perna *f*; [- of pork] pernil *m* -**3.** [of journey, tournament] etapa *f.*

legacy ['legəsɪ] (*pl* -ies) *n* -**1.** [gift of money] legado *m* -**2.** *fig* [consequence] herança *f.*

legal ['li:gl] *adj* -**1.** [concerning the law] jurídico(ca) -**2.** [lawful] legal.

legal action *n* ação *f* legal; **to take ~ against sb** iniciar uma ação legal contra alguém.

legal aid *n (U)* auxílio *m* oficial de um advogado.

legality [li:'gælətɪ] *n (U)* legalidade *f.*

legalize, -ise ['li:gəlaɪz] *vt* legalizar.

legally ['li:gəlɪ] *adv* legalmente; **~ binding** com força da lei.

legal tender *n (U)* moeda *f* corrente.

legation [lɪ'geɪʃn] *n* legação *f.*

legend ['ledʒənd] *n* -**1.** [myth] lenda *f* -**2.** *fig* [person] lenda *f.*

legendary ['ledʒəndrɪ] *adj* lendário(ria).

leggings ['legɪŋz] *npl* calças *fpl* stretch.

leggy ['legɪ] (*compar* -ier, *superl* -iest) *adj* -**1.** [person] de pernas compridas e bonitas -**2.** [plant] de longo caule.

legible ['ledʒəbl] *adj* legível.

legibly ['ledʒəblɪ] *adv* de forma legível.

legion ['li:dʒən] ◇ *adj fml*: **to be ~** ser inumerável. ◇ *n* -**1.** *MIL* legião *f* -**2.** *fig* [large number] legião *f.*

legionnaire's disease [,li:dʒə'neəz-] *n (U)* doença *f* do legionário, *doença muito rara semelhante à pneumonia.*

legislate ['ledʒɪsleɪt] *vi* legislar, elaborar leis; **to ~ for/against sthg** elaborar leis a favor de/contra algo.

legislation [,ledʒɪs'leɪʃn] *n (U)* legislação *f.*

legislative ['ledʒɪslətɪv] *adj* legislativo(va).

legislator ['ledʒɪsleɪtəʳ] *n* legislador *m*, -ra *f.*

legislature ['ledʒɪsleɪtʃəʳ] *n* legislatura *f.*

legitimacy [lɪ'dʒɪtɪməsɪ] *n* legitimidade *f.*

legitimate [lɪ'dʒɪtɪmət] *adj* legítimo(ma).

legitimately [lɪ'dʒɪtɪmətlɪ] *adv* legitimamente.

legitimize, -ise [lɪ'dʒɪtəmaɪz] *vt* [make legal] legitimar.

legless ['legləs] *adj UK inf* [drunk] bêbado(da) como um gambá.

legroom ['legrʊm] *n (U)* espaço *m* para as pernas.

leg-warmers [-,wɔ:məz] *npl* polainas *fpl.*

legwork ['legwɜ:k] *n (U)*: **to do the ~** fazer o trabalho de campo.

leisure [*UK* 'leʒəʳ, *US* 'li:ʒər] *n (U)* lazer *m*; **do it at (your) ~** faça quando puder.

leisure centre *n* centro *m* de lazer.

leisurely [*UK* 'leʒəlɪ, *US* 'li:ʒərlɪ] ◇ *adj* calmo(ma). ◇ *adv* calmamente.

leisure time *n* (tempo *m* de) lazer *m.*

lemming ['lemɪŋ] *n* -**1.** [animal] lemingue *m* -**2.** *fig* [person] marionete *f.*

lemon ['lemən] *n* [fruit] limão *m.*

lemonade [,lemə'neɪd] *n* -**1.** *UK* [fizzy] soda *f* limonada -**2.** [made with fresh lemons] limonada *f.*

lemon curd *n (U) UK* espécie de geléia ou creme feito com suco de limão, açúcar, ovos e manteiga.

lemon juice *n* suco *m* de limão.

lemon sole *n* solha-limão *m.*

lemon squash *n UK* suco *m* de limão.

lemon squeezer [-,skwi:zəʳ] *n* espremedor *m* de limão.

lemon tea *n* chá *m* com limão.

lend [lend] (*pt & pp* **lent**) *vt* -**1.** [money, book] emprestar; **to ~ sb sthg, to ~ sthg to sb** emprestar algo para alguém -**2.** [support, assistance]: **to ~ sthg (to sb)** dar algo (a alguém) -**3.** [credibility, quality]: **to ~ sthg to sthg** conferir algo a algo -**4.** *phr*: **it doesn't ~ itself to that** não se presta para isso.

lender ['lendəʳ] *n* [of money] emprestador *m*, -ra *f.*

lending library ['lendɪŋ-] *n* biblioteca *f* pública.

lending rate ['lendɪŋ-] *n* taxa *f* de empréstimo.

length [leŋθ] *n* -**1.** [gen] comprimento *m*; **what ~ is it?** quanto tem de comprimento?; **it's five metres in ~** são cinco metros de comprimento; **she walked the ~ and breadth of England** ela caminhou por toda a Inglaterra -**2.** [of swimming pool] piscina *f* -**3.** [piece] pedaço *m* -**4.** *(U)* [duration] duração *f* -**5.** *phr*: **to go to great ~s to do sthg** não medir esforços para fazer algo.

at length adv -1. [eventually] no final das contas -2. [in detail] detalhadamente.

lengthen ['leŋθən] <> vt -1. [skirt] alongar -2. [life] prolongar. <> vi alongar-se, ficar mais longo(ga).

lengthways ['leŋθweɪz] adv ao comprido.

lengthy ['leŋθɪ] (compar -ier, superl -iest) adj longo(-ga).

leniency ['li:njənsɪ] n (U) leniência f, indulgência f.

lenient ['li:njənt] adj leniente, indulgente.

lens [lenz] n -1. [made of glass] lente f -2. [contact lens] lente f (de contato).

lent [lent] pt & pp ⊳ **lend**.

Lent [lent] n (U) quaresma f.

lentil ['lentɪl] n lentilha f.

Leo ['li:əʊ] n -1. [sign] leão m -2. [person] leonino(na); **I'm** ~ sou de Leão.

leopard ['lepəd] n leopardo m.

leopardess ['lepədɪs] n leoparda f.

leotard ['li:əta:d] n malha f (usada por dançarinos, acrobatas).

leper ['lepəʳ] n [person with leprosy] leproso m, -sa f.

leprechaun ['leprəkɔ:n] n leprechaun m, duende m.

leprosy ['leprəsɪ] n (U) lepra f.

lesbian ['lezbɪən] <> adj lésbico(ca). <> n lésbica f.

lesbianism ['lezbɪənɪzml] n (U) lesbianismo m.

lesion ['li:ʒn] n MED lesão f.

Lesotho [lə'səʊtəʊ] n Lesoto; **in** ~ no Lesoto.

less [les] (compar of little) <> adj [not as much] menos; ~ ... than menos ... (do) que; ~ and ~ cada vez menos. <> pron [not as much] menos; ~ than menos (do) que; **the** ~ **you work the** ~ **you earn** quanto menos você trabalha, menos você ganha; **no** ~ **than** nada menos que. <> adv [to a smaller extent] menos; ~ and ~ cada vez menos. <> prep [minus] menos.

lessee [le'si:] n fml arrendatário m, -ria f, locatário m, -ria f.

lessen ['lesn] vt & vi diminuir.

lesser ['lesəʳ] adj menor; **to a** ~ **extent** OR **degree** em menor grau.

lesson ['lesn] n -1. [class] aula f; **to give/take** ~ **s (in sthg)** dar/receber aulas (de algo) -2. [example] lição f; **to teach sb a** ~ ensinar uma lição a alguém.

lessor [le'sɔ:] n fml arrendador m, -ra f.

lest [lest] conj fml para que não; **I did what she asked,** ~ **she become even angrier** fiz o que ela pediu, temendo que ela ficasse ainda mais irritada.

let [let] (pt & pp let, cont -ting) vt -1. [allow]: **to** ~ **sb do sthg** deixar alguém fazer algo; **she** ~ **her hair grow** ela deixou o cabeço crescer; **to** ~ **go of sb/ sthg, to** ~ **sb/sthg go** soltar alguém/algo; [release] soltar alguém/algo; **to** ~ **sb know sthg** informar alguém de algo, informar algo a alguém -2. (in verb forms): ~'**s go!** vamos!; ~'**s see** agora vejamos; ~ **them wait!** eles que esperem! -3. [rent out] alugar; '**to** ~' 'aluga-se'.

let alone conj [much less]: **he couldn't walk,** ~ **alone jump** ele não conseguia caminhar, que dirá pular.

let down vt sep -1. [deflate] esvaziar -2. [disappoint] desapontar.

let in vt sep -1. [admit] deixar entrar -2. [air, water] deixar entrar.

let in for vt sep: **to** ~ **o.s. in for sthg** meter-se em algo.

let in on vt sep: **he** ~ **me in on his secret** ele me revelou o seu segredo.

let off vt sep -1. [excuse, allow not to do]: **to** ~ **sb off sthg** eximir alguém de algo -2. [criminal, pupil, child] deixar impune -3. [bomb, explosive] detonar -4. [firework] estourar.

let on vi contar (um segredo); **don't** ~ **on!** não conta nada!

let out vt sep -1. [gen] deixar sair -2. [sound, cry, laugh] emitir -3. [garment] alargar.

let up vi -1. [heat, rain] cessar -2. [person] relaxar.

letdown ['letdaʊn] n inf decepção f.

lethal ['li:θl] adj letal.

lethargic [lə'θɑ:dʒɪk] adj letárgico(ca).

lethargy ['leθədʒɪ] n (U) letargia f.

Letraset® n (U) letraset® f.

let's [lets] = **let us**.

letter ['letəʳ] n -1. [written message] carta f -2. [of alphabet] letra f.

letters npl fml [literature] letras fpl.

letter bomb n carta-bomba f.

letterbox ['letəbɒks] n UK -1. [in door] portinhola f para cartas -2. [in street] caixa f de correio.

letterhead ['letəhed] n cabeçalho m em papel timbrado.

lettering ['letərɪŋ] n (U) [characters] letras fpl.

letter of credit n carta f de crédito.

letter opener n abridor m de cartas.

letter-perfect adj US impecável.

letter quality n COMPUT qualidade f carta.

letters patent npl -1. JUR carta f patente -2. [of inventor] patente f.

lettuce ['letɪs] n alface f.

letup ['letʌp] n pausa f, intervalo m.

leuk(a)emia [lu:'ki:mɪə] n leucemia f.

levee ['levɪ] n US [embankment] barragem f.

level ['levl] (UK pt & pp -led, cont -ling, US pt & pp -ed, cont -ing) <> adj -1. [equal in height] nivelado(-da); **to be** ~ **(with sthg)** estar nivelado(da) (com algo) -2. [equal in standard] em pé de igualdade -3. [flat - floor, field] plano(na); [- spoon, cup] raso(sa). <> adv: **to draw** ~ **with sb** empatar com alguém, alcançar alguém. <> n -1. [gen] nível m; **to be on a** ~ **(with sthg)** estar no mesmo nível (de algo) -2. US [spirit level] nível m (de bolha) -3. [storey] andar m -4. phr: **to be on the** ~ inf ser sincero(ra). <> vt -1. [make flat] nivelar, aplainar -2. [demolish] derrubar -3. [aim]: **to** ~ **a gun at sb/sthg** apontar uma arma para alguém/algo; **to** ~ **an accusation at** OR **against sb** lançar uma acusação contra OR sobre alguém.

level off, level out vi estabilizar-se.

level with vt fus inf [be honest with] ser sincero(ra) com.

level crossing n UK passagem f de nível.

level-headed [-'hedɪd] adj equilibrado(da), sensato(ta).

level pegging [-'pegɪŋ] adj UK: **to be ~** estar igualado(da).

lever [UK 'liːvə', US 'levər] n alavanca f.

leverage [UK 'liːvərɪdʒ, US 'levərɪdʒ] n (U) **-1.** fig [influence] influência f **-2.** [force] alavancagem f, força f.

leviathan [lɪ'vaɪəθn] n [large body, organization] leviatã m, gigante m.

levitation [ˌlevɪ'teɪʃn] n (U) levitação f.

levity ['levətɪ] n (U) leviandade f.

levy ['levɪ] (pt & pp **-ied**) ⟷ n [financial contribution, tax]: **~ (on sthg)** taxa f (sobre algo). ⟷ vt [demand, collect] arrecadar.

lewd [ljuːd] adj [behaviour] lascivo(va), obsceno(na).

lexical ['leksɪkl] adj lexical.

liability [ˌlaɪə'bɪlətɪ] (pl **-ies**) n **-1.** [hindrance] estorvo m **-2.** JUR (U) [legal responsibility]: **~ (for sthg)** responsabilidade f (por algo).

➡ **liabilities** npl FIN [debts] passivos mpl, obrigações fpl.

liable ['laɪəbl] adj **-1.** [likely]: **she is ~ to do something stupid** é bem provável que ela faça algo estúpido **-2.** [prone]: **to be ~ to sthg** estar propenso(sa) a algo **-3.** JUR: **to be ~ (for sthg)** [legally responsible] ser legalmente responsável (-por algo); **to be ~ to sthg** [punishable] estar sujeito(ta) a algo.

liaise [lɪ'eɪz] vi: **to ~ (with)** fazer contato (com); **to ~ (between)** criar vínculos (entre).

liaison [lɪ'eɪzɒn] n **-1.** (U) [contact, cooperation]: **~ (with/between)** relação f (com/entre) **-2.** [affair, relationship]: **~ (with/between)** ligação f OR caso m (com/entre).

liar ['laɪə'] n mentiroso m, -sa f.

Lib -1. (abbr of **Liberal**) liberal **-2.** (abbr of **liberation**) liberação f.

libel ['laɪbl] (UK pt & pp **-led**, cont **-ling**, US pt & pp **-ed**, cont **-ing**) ⟷ n libelo m. ⟷ vt difamar.

libellous UK, **libelous** US ['laɪbələs] adj difamatório(ria).

liberal ['lɪbərəl] ⟷ adj **-1.** [tolerant] liberal **-2.** [generous] generoso(sa). ⟷ n liberal mf.

➡ **Liberal** POL ⟷ adj liberal. ⟷ n liberal mf.

liberal arts npl esp US ciências fpl humanas.

Liberal Democrat ⟷ adj liberal democrata. ⟷ n liberal democrata mf.

liberalize, -ise ['lɪbərəlaɪz] vt liberalizar.

liberal-minded [-'maɪndɪd] adj liberal.

Liberal Party n: **the ~** o Partido Liberal.

liberate ['lɪbəreɪt] vt libertar.

liberation [ˌlɪbə'reɪʃn] n (U) **-1.** [release] libertação f **-2.** fig [emancipation] libertação f.

liberator ['lɪbəreɪtə'] n libertador m, -ra f.

Liberia [laɪ'bɪərɪə] n Libéria; **in ~** na Libéria.

Liberian [laɪ'bɪərɪən] ⟷ adj liberiano(na). ⟷ n liberiano m, -na f.

libertine ['lɪbətiːn] n libertino m, -na f.

liberty ['lɪbətɪ] (pl **-ies**) n [gen] liberdade f; **at ~** em liberdade; **to be at ~ to do sthg** ter liberdade para fazer algo; **to take liberties (with sb)** tomar liberdades (com alguém).

libido [lɪ'biːdəʊ] (pl **-s**) n [sexual urge] libido f.

Libra ['liːbrə] n **-1.** [sign] libra f **-2.** [person] libriano m, -na f; **I'm ~** sou de Libra.

librarian [laɪ'breərɪən] n bibliotecário m, -ria f.

librarianship [laɪ'breərɪənʃɪp] n (U) biblioteconomia f.

library ['laɪbrərɪ] (pl **-ies**) n biblioteca f.

library book n livro m de biblioteca.

libretto [lɪ'bretəʊ] (pl **-s**) n libreto m.

Libya ['lɪbɪə] n Líbia; **in ~** na Líbia.

Libyan ['lɪbɪən] ⟷ adj líbio(bia). ⟷ n líbio m, -bia f.

lice [laɪs] pl ⟞ louse.

licence ['laɪsəns] ⟷ n **-1.** [permit - gen] licença f; [- for marriage] autorização f; [- for pilot] brevê m **-2.** COMM licença f; **under ~ from** com permissão de. ⟷ vt US = **license**.

license ['laɪsəns] ⟷ vt COMM autorizar. ⟷ n US = **licence**.

licensed ['laɪsənst] adj **-1.** [person]: **to be ~ to do sthg** estar autorizado(da) a fazer algo **-2.** [object - car, dog] com licença; [- gun] registrado(da) **-3.** UK [premises] autorizado(da) a vender álcool.

licensee [ˌlaɪsən'siː] n licenciado m, -da f.

license plate n US placa f (de automóvel).

licensing hours ['laɪsənsɪŋ-] npl UK horário de funcionamento dos bares.

LICENSING HOURS

Tradicionalmente, o horário de funcionamento dos pubs na Grã-Bretanha sempre esteve sujeito a regulamentação bastante estrita, vinculada à legislação sobre a venda de bebidas alcoólicas. Mas, a partir de 1988, as regras se tornaram mais flexíveis. Em vez de abrirem das 11:30 às 14:30h, e das 18 às 23:00h, os pubs passaram a abrir das 11 às 23h, menos aos domingos, quando funcionam das 11 às 15h e das 19 às 22:30h. Na Escócia, os horários são menos rigorosos.

---

licensing laws ['laɪsənsɪŋ-] npl UK leis que controlam a venda de bebidas alcoólicas.

licentious [laɪ'senʃəs] adj fml & pej licencioso(sa).

lichen ['laɪkən] n líquen m.

lick [lɪk] ⟷ n **-1.** [act of licking] lambida f **-2.** inf [small amount]: **a ~ of paint** uma demão de tinta. ⟷ vt **-1.** [with tongue] lamber; **to ~ one's lips** lamber os beiços **-2.** fig [subj: flames, waves] lamber **-3.** inf [defeat] derrotar.

licorice ['lɪkərɪs] n = **liquorice**.

lid [lɪd] n **-1.** [cover] tampa f **-2.** [eyelid] pálpebra f.

lido ['liːdəʊ] (pl **-s**) n **-1.** UK [swimming pool] piscina f pública **-2.** [beach] praia f.

lie [laɪ] (pt sense 1 lied, pt senses 2-7 lay, pp sense 1 lied, pp senses 2-7 lain, cont all senses lying) ⟷ n mentira f; **to tell ~s** contar mentiras. ⟷ vi **-1.** [tell untruth] mentir; **to ~ to sb** mentir para alguém **-2.** [to be lying down] estar deitado(da) **-3.** [lie down] deitar **-4.** [be situated] encontrar-se **-5.** [corpse] jazer **-6.** : **who knows what ~s ahead?** quem sabe o que nos espera? **-7.** phr: **to ~ low** ficar escondido(da).

➡ **lie about, lie around** vi **-1.** [people] andar sem fazer nada, vadiar **-2.** [things] estar jogado(-da).

➡ **lie down** vi deitar-se; **he won't take it lying down** ele não vai ficar agüentando isso.

➡ **lie in** vi UK ficar na cama até tarde.

Liechtenstein ['lɪktən‚staɪn] *n* Liechtenstein; **in** ~ em Liechtenstein.

lie detector *n* detector *m* de mentiras.

lie-down *n UK*: **to have a** ~ repousar.

lie-in *n UK*: **to have a** ~ ficar na cama até tarde.

lieu [lju:, lu:] ◆ **in lieu** *adv* em troca; **in** ~ **of** em vez de.

Lieut. (*abbr of* lieutenant) Ten.

lieutenant [*UK* lef'tenənt, *US* lu:'tenənt] *n* tenente *m*.

lieutenant colonel *n* tenente-coronel *m*.

life [laɪf] (*pl* lives) ◇ *n* -1. [gen] vida *f*; **to breathe** ~ **into sthg** dar vida a algo; **to come to** ~ criar vida; **that's** ~! é a vida!; **for** ~ para toda a vida; **for the** ~ **of me** *inf* por mais que eu tente; **to lay down one's** ~ entregar a vida; **to risk** ~ **and limb** arriscar a pele; **to scare the** ~ **out of sb** quase matar alguém do coração; **to take sb's/one's own** ~ tirar a vida de alguém/a própria vida - 2. (*U*) *inf* [life imprisonment] prisão *f* perpétua. ◇ *comp* vitalício(cia).

life-and-death *adj* de vida ou morte.

life annuity *n* renda *f* vitalícia.

life assurance *n* = life insurance.

life belt *n* cinto *m* salva-vidas.

lifeblood ['laɪfblʌd] *n* (*U*) *fig* [source of strength] força *f* vital.

lifeboat ['laɪfbəʊt] *n* -1. [on ship] bote *m* salva-vidas - 2. [on shore] lancha *f* de salvamento.

lifeboatman [-mən] (*pl* -men) *n* salva-vidas *m inv* (de barco).

life buoy *n* bóia *f* salva-vidas.

life cycle *n* ciclo *m* vital.

life expectancy *n* espectativa *f* de vida.

lifeguard ['laɪfgɑ:d] *n* salva-vidas *mf inv*.

life imprisonment [-ɪm'prɪznmənt] *n* prisão *f* perpétua.

life insurance *n* (*U*) seguro *m* de vida.

life jacket *n* colete *m* salva-vidas.

lifeless ['laɪflɪs] *adj* -1. [dead] sem vida, morto(ta) - 2. [listless] apagado(da).

lifelike ['laɪflaɪk] *adj* -1. [statue, doll] realista - 2. [portrait] fiel.

lifeline ['laɪflaɪn] *n* -1. [rope] corda *f* de segurança - 2. *fig* [with outside] cordão *m* umbilical.

lifelong ['laɪflɒŋ] *adj* de toda a vida.

life peer *n UK nobre britânico com título não-hereditário*.

life preserver [-prɪ‚zɜ:vər] *n US* -1. [belt] cinto *m* salva-vidas - 2. [jacket] colete *m* salva-vidas.

life raft *n* balsa *f* salva-vidas.

lifesaver ['laɪf‚seɪvər] *n* -1. [person] salva-vidas *mf inv* - 2. *fig* [relief, help] ajuda *f*.

life sentence *n* pena *f* de prisão perpétua.

life-size(d) [-saɪz(d)] *adj* em tamanho natural.

lifespan ['laɪfspæn] *n* -1. [of person, animal, plant] vida *f* - 2. [of product, machine] vida *f* útil.

lifestyle ['laɪfstaɪl] *n* estilo *m* de vida.

life-support system *n* sistema *m* de respiração artificial.

lifetime ['laɪftaɪm] *n* [length of time] vida *f*.

lift [lɪft] ◇ *n* -1. [ride] carona *f* - 2. *UK* [elevator] elevador *m*. ◇ *vt* -1. [gen] levantar; **he** ~**ed the**

books off the shelf ele tirou os livros da estante - 2. [ban, embargo] revogar - 3. [plagiarize] plagiar - 4. *inf* [steal] levantar. ◇ *vi* -1. [lid, top] levantar - 2. [mist, fog, clouds] dissipar-se - 3. [heart, spirits] melhorar.

◆ **lift up** ◇ *vt sep* [bag, baby, books] levantar. ◇ *vi* [lid, top] levantar.

lift-off *n* decolagem *f*.

ligament ['lɪgəmənt] *n ANAT* ligamento *m*.

light [laɪt] (*pt* & *pp* lit *OR* -ed) ◇ *adj* -1. [gen] leve - 2. [not dark] claro(ra). ◇ *adv*: **to travel** ~ viajar com pouca bagagem. ◇ *n* -1. [gen] luz *f* - 2. [for cigarette, pipe] fogo *m*; **to set** ~ **to sthg** atear fogo em algo - 3. [perspective]: **in the** ~ **of** *UK*, **in** ~ **of** *US* à luz de; **to see sb/sthg in a different** ~ ver alguém/algo de forma diferente - 4. *literary* [in sb's eyes] brilho *m* - 5. *phr*: **to come to** ~ vir à luz; **to see the** ~ [understand] ver claramente; **to throw** *OR* **cast** *OR* **shed** ~ **on sthg** lançar luz sobre algo; **there's a** ~ **at the end of the tunnel** há uma luz no fim do túnel; **to make** ~ **of sthg** não dar a devida importância a algo. ◇ *vt* -1. [ignite] acender - 2. [illuminate] iluminar.

◆ **light out** *vi US inf* dar no pé.

◆ **light up** ◇ *vt sep* -1. [illuminate] iluminar - 2. [start smoking] acender. ◇ *vi* -1. [look happy] iluminar-se - 2. *inf* [start smoking] pôr-se a fumar.

light aircraft (*pl inv*) *n* pequeno aeroplano *m*.

light ale *n* (*U*) *UK tipo de cerveja escura e suave*.

light bulb *n* lâmpada *f*.

light cream *n US* creme *m* light.

lighted ['laɪtɪd] *adj* -1. [illuminated] iluminado(da) - 2. [on fire] aceso(sa).

light-emitting diode [-ɪ'mɪtɪŋ-] *n* diodo *m* emissor de luz.

lighten ['laɪtn] ◇ *vt* -1. [make brighter] clarear - 2. [make less heavy] aliviar. ◇ *vi* -1. [brighten] iluminar-se - 2. [become happier, more relaxed] alegrar-se.

◆ **lighten up** *vi inf* levar na brincadeira.

lighter ['laɪtər] *n* [cigarette lighter] isqueiro *m*.

light-fingered [-'fɪŋgəd] *adj inf* gatuno(na); **to be** ~ ter mão leve.

light-headed [-'hedɪd] *adj* tonto(ta).

light-hearted [-'hɑ:tɪd] *adj* -1. [cheerful] despreocupado(da) - 2. [amusing] alegre.

lighthouse ['laɪthaʊs, *pl* -haʊzɪz] *n* farol *m*.

light industry *n* indústria *f* leve.

lighting ['laɪtɪŋ] *n* (*U*) iluminação *f*.

lighting-up time *n* (*U*) hora *f* de acendimento da iluminação pública.

lightly ['laɪtlɪ] *adv* -1. [tap, knock] suavemente - 2. [cook, grill] ligeiramente - 3. [remark, say] levianamente.

light meter *n PHOT* fotômetro *m*.

lightning ['laɪtnɪŋ] *n* (*U*) raio *m*, relâmpago *m*.

lightning conductor *UK*, **lightning rod** *US n* pára-raios *m inv*.

lightning strike *n UK* greve-relâmpago *f*.

light opera *n* opereta *f*.

light pen *n* caneta *f* óptica.

lightship *n* navio-farol *m*.

lights-out *n* (*U*) *hora em que se apagam as luzes*.

lightweight ['laɪtweɪt] <> adj -**1.** [object] leve -**2.** fig & pej [person] de pouca expressão. <> n -**1.** [boxer] peso m leve -**2.** fig & pej [person] joão-ninguém m.

light year n ano-luz m.

likable ['laɪkəbl] adj simpático(ca), agradável.

like [laɪk] <> prep -**1.** [similar to] como; **to look ~ sb/sthg** parecer-se com alguém/algo, parecer alguém/algo; **what did it taste ~?** tinha gosto de quê?; **what did it look ~?** como era?; **what did it sound ~?** como era o barulho?; **~ this/that** assim -**2.** [typical of]: **that's just ~ him** isso é típico dele -**3.** [such as] (tal) como. <> vt -**1.** [enjoy, find pleasant, approve of] gostar; **to ~ doing** OR **to do sthg** gostar de fazer algo -**2.** [want, wish] querer; **to ~ to do sthg** desejar fazer algo; **to ~ sb to do sthg** desejar que alguém faça algo; **I'd ~ you to come** gostaria que você viesse. <> adj [similar] igual. <> n: **the ~ of sb/sthg** alguém/algo do estilo; **and the ~** e similares, e coisas do estilo.
  ◆ **likes** npl [things one likes] gostos mpl.

likeable ['laɪkəbl] adj = **likable**.

likelihood ['laɪklɪhʊd] n (U) probabilidade f; **in all ~** com toda certeza.

likely ['laɪklɪ] adj -**1.** [probable] provável; **rain is ~ later on** é provável que chova mais tarde; **to be ~ to do sthg** ser provável que algo aconteça; **he's ~ to come** é provável que ele venha; **a ~ story!** iro pura invenção! -**2.** [suitable] indicado(da).

like-minded [-'maɪndɪd] adj de mesma opinião.

liken ['laɪkn] vt: **to ~ sb/sthg to** comparar alguém/algo a.

likeness ['laɪknɪs] n semelhança f; **~ to sb/sthg** semelhança com alguém/algo.

likewise ['laɪkwaɪz] adv [similarly] da mesma maneira; **to do ~** fazer o mesmo.

liking ['laɪkɪŋ] n: **~ for sb/sthg** afeição f por alguém/algo; **to have a ~ for sb/sthg** ter afeição por alguém/algo; **to be to sb's ~** estar ao gosto de alguém; **he's too confident for my ~** ele é muito atrevido para o meu gosto.

lilac ['laɪlək] <> adj [colour] lilás. <> n -**1.** [tree] lilás m -**2.** (U) [colour] lilás m.

Lilo® ['laɪləʊ] (pl -s) n UK colchão m inflável.

lilt [lɪlt] n [in voice] melodia f; [in melody] cadência f.

lilting ['lɪltɪŋ] adj [voice] melodioso(sa); [melody] cadenciado(da).

lily ['lɪlɪ] (pl -ies) n lírio m.

lily of the valley (pl **lilies of the valley**) n lírio-do-vale m.

Lima ['liːmə] n Lima.

limb [lɪm] n -**1.** [of body] membro m -**2.** [of tree] ramo m -**3.** phr: **to be out on a ~** estar em apuros.

limber ['lɪmbəʳ] ◆ **limber up** vi fazer aquecimento, aquecer.

limbo ['lɪmbəʊ] (pl -s) n -**1.** (U) [uncertain state]: **to be in ~** estar no limbo -**2.** [dance]: **the ~** dança caribenha na qual se passa por baixo de uma barra com o corpo inclinado para trás, dança f da cordinha.

lime [laɪm] n -**1.** [fruit] lima f; **~ (juice)** (suco m de) lima f -**2.** [linden tree] tília f -**3.** (U) [substance] cal f.

lime cordial n refresco m de lima.

lime-green adj de cor verde-limão.

limelight ['laɪmlaɪt] n: **to be in the ~** estar no/ser o centro das atenções.

limerick ['lɪmərɪk] n poema humorístico de cinco linhas.

limestone ['laɪmstəʊn] n (U) calcário m, pedra f calcária.

limey ['laɪmɪ] (pl -s) n US inf termo pejorativo que designa um inglês.

limit ['lɪmɪt] <> n limite m; **to be off ~s** ser/estar proibido(da); **within ~s** [to a certain extent] até certo ponto; **he's/she's the ~!** inf ele/ela é o cúmulo! <> vt limitar, restringir; **to ~ o.s. to sthg** limitar-se a algo.

limitation [ˌlɪmɪ'teɪʃn] n limitação f.

limited ['lɪmɪtɪd] adj [restricted] limitado(da); **to be ~ to sthg** estar limitado(da) a algo.

limited company n companhia f limitada.

limited edition n edição f limitada.

limited liability company n = **limited company.**

limitless ['lɪmɪtlɪs] adj ilimitado(da).

limo ['lɪməʊ] n inf limusine f.

limousine ['lɪməziːn] n limusine f.

limp [lɪmp] <> adj -**1.** [hand, handshake] sem firmeza -**2.** [body, lettuce] murcho(cha) -**3.** [excuse] mole. <> n manqueira f. <> vi mancar.

limpet ['lɪmpɪt] n lapa f.

limpid adj literary límpido(da).

limply ['lɪmplɪ] adv -**1.** [lie, hang] sem firmeza -**2.** [reply] de forma vacilante.

linchpin ['lɪntʃpɪn] n fig [important person, thing] peça-chave f.

linctus ['lɪŋktəs] n (U) UK expectorante m.

line [laɪn] <> n -**1.** [gen] linha f; **washing ~** corda f de varal; **power ~** cabo m de força; **to draw the ~ at doing sthg** fig estabelecer limites para fazer algo -**2.** [row] fileira f, linha f -**3.** [queue] fila f; **to stand** OR **wait in ~** ficar OR esperar em fila; **to be in ~ for promotion** estar a caminho da promoção -**4.** [alignment] alinhamento m; **in ~** alinhado(da); **in ~ with** em linha com; **to step out of ~** sair da linha -**5.** [RAIL - railway track] linha f (férrea); [- route] linha f -**6.** NAUT: **shipping ~** companhia f marítima -**7.** [in writing - of text] linha f; **to read between the ~s** ler nas entrelinhas; [- of poetry, song] verso m -**8.** [wrinkle] ruga f -**9.** TELEC [telephone connection] linha f (telefônica) -**10.** inf [short letter]: **to drop sb a ~** escrever umas linhas para alguém -**11.** [of ideas, reasoning] linha f de raciocínio; **along the same ~s** seguindo a mesma linha; **to be on the right ~s** estar num bom caminho -**12.** inf [field of activity] ramo m -**13.** [lineage, ancestry] linhagem f. <> vt -**1.** [form rows along] alinhar-se ao longo de; **crowds ~d the street** a multidão lotava a rua -**2.** [cover inside surface of] forrar.
  ◆ **lines** npl -**1.** SCH castigo que consiste em escrever a mesma frase inúmeras vezes -**2.** [actor's words] texto m.
  ◆ **on the line** adv: **to put sthg on the ~** pôr algo em jogo.
  ◆ **out of line** adj inaceitável.
  ◆ **line up** <> vt sep -**1.** [in rows] alinhar -**2.** inf [organize] arranjar, organizar. <> vi -**1.** [in a row]

alinhar-se **-2.** [in a queue] pôr-se na fila.
lineage ['lɪnɪdʒ] n *fml* linhagem f.
linear ['lɪnɪə'] adj linear.
lined [laɪnd] adj **-1.** [paper] pautado(da) **-2.** [face] enrugado(da).
line drawing n desenho m a traço.
line feed n COMPUT avanço m de linha.
linen ['lɪnɪn] (U) ⟨⟩ n **-1.** [cloth] linho m **-2.** [sheets] roupa f de cama **-3.** [tablecloths] toalha f *(de mesa)*. ⟨⟩ comp **-1.** [suit, napkins] de linho **-2.** [cupboard, drawer]: ~ cupboard *armário no qual se guardam as roupas de cama e de mesa*.
linen basket n cesto m de roupa suja.
line-out n RUGBY *formação para recomeço do jogo quando a bola saiu de campo*.
line printer n COMPUT impressora f de linha.
liner ['laɪnə'] n [ship] transatlântico m.
linesman ['laɪnzmən] (pl -men [-mən]) n SPORT juiz m de linha.
line-up n **-1.** [of players, competitors] seleção f **-2.** US [identification parade] fila f de identificação.
linger ['lɪŋgə'] vi **-1.** [dawdle] demorar-se **-2.** [persist] persistir.
lingerie ['lænʒərɪ] n (U) lingerie f.
lingering ['lɪŋgrɪŋ] adj **-1.** [persistent] persistente **-2.** [slow] lento(ta) **-3.** [long] prolongado(da).
lingo ['lɪŋgəʊ] (pl -es) n inf idioma f.
linguist ['lɪŋgwɪst] n **-1.** [someone good at languages] pessoa f com facilidade para os idiomas **-2.** [student or teacher of linguistics] lingüista mf.
linguistic [lɪŋ'gwɪstɪk] adj lingüístico(ca).
➤ **linguistics** n (U) lingüística f.
liniment ['lɪnɪmənt] n (U) linimento m.
lining ['laɪnɪŋ] n **-1.** [of coat, curtains, box] forro m **-2.** [of stomach, nose] paredes fpl internas **-3.** AUT [of brakes] revestimento m.
link [lɪŋk] ⟨⟩ n **-1.** [of chain] elo m **-2.** COMPUT linque m **-3.** [connection] conexão f; ~ between sb/sthg vínculo m OR ligação f entre alguém/algo; ~ with sb/sthg vínculo OR ligação com alguém/algo. ⟨⟩ vt **-1.** [relate] ligar, relacionar; to ~ sb/sthg with OR to sb/sthg ligar alguém/algo com OR a alguém/algo, relacionar alguém/algo com OR a alguém/algo **-2.** [connect physically] enlaçar.
➤ **link up** ⟨⟩ vt sep [connect] conectar; to ~ sthg up with sthg conectar algo a algo. ⟨⟩ vi [connect]: to ~ up (with sb/sthg) conectar-se (a alguém/algo).
linkage ['lɪŋkɪdʒ] n [connection] conexão f, vínculo m.
linked [lɪŋkt] adj **-1.** [related] relacionado(da) **-2.** [connected physically] enlaçado(da); arms ~ ed de braços dados.
links [lɪŋks] (pl inv) n SPORT campo m de golfe.
link-up n conexão f.
lino ['laɪnəʊ], **linoleum** [lɪ'nəʊljəm] n (U) linóleo m.
linseed oil ['lɪnsiːd-] n (U) óleo m de linhaça.
lint [lɪnt] n **-1.** [dressing] gaze f **-2.** US [fluff] fiapo m.
lintel ['lɪntl] n verga f *(de porta ou janela)*.
lion ['laɪən] n leão m.
lion cub n filhote m de leão.
lioness ['laɪənes] n leoa f.

lionize, -ise ['laɪənaɪz] vt tratar como celebridade, endeusar.
lip [lɪp] n **-1.** [of mouth] lábio m; to keep a stiff upper ~ manter-se firme; my ~s are sealed eu sou um túmulo **-2.** [of container] borda f.
liposuction ['lɪpəʊˌsʌkʃən] n lipoaspiração f.
lip-read vi ler nos lábios.
lip-reading n (U) leitura f dos lábios.
lip salve [-sælv] n UK pomada f para lábios.
lip service n: to pay ~ to sthg concordar com algo da boca para fora.
lipstick ['lɪpstɪk] n batom m.
liquefy ['lɪkwɪfaɪ] (pt & pp -ied) ⟨⟩ vt liquefazer. ⟨⟩ vi liquefazer-se.
liqueur [lɪ'kjʊə'] n licor m.
liquid ['lɪkwɪd] ⟨⟩ adj [fluid] líquido(da). ⟨⟩ n [fluid] líquido m.
liquid assets npl ativo m disponível.
liquidate ['lɪkwɪdeɪt] vt liquidar.
liquidation [ˌlɪkwɪ'deɪʃn] n (U) FIN falência f; to go into ~ abrir falência.
liquidator ['lɪkwɪdeɪtə'] n FIN liquidante mf.
liquid crystal display n tela f de cristal líquido.
liquidity [lɪ'kwɪdətɪ] n (U) **-1.** [having money] liquidez f **-2.** [being liquid] condição f de ser líquido.
liquidize, -ise ['lɪkwɪdaɪz] vt UK CULIN liquidificar.
liquidizer ['lɪkwɪdaɪzə'] n UK liquidificador m.
liquor ['lɪkə'] n US [alcohol] álcool m; [spirits] bebida f alcoólica.
liquorice ['lɪkərɪʃ, 'lɪkərɪs] n (U) alcaçuz m.
liquor store n US armazém m de bebidas alcoólicas.
lira ['lɪərə] n [Italian] lira f.
Lisbon ['lɪzbən] n Lisboa f; in ~ em Lisboa.
lisp [lɪsp] ⟨⟩ n ceceio m. ⟨⟩ vi cecear.
lissom(e) ['lɪsəm] adj *literary* grácil, esbelto(ta).
list [lɪst] ⟨⟩ n lista f. ⟨⟩ vt [in writing, speech] listar. ⟨⟩ vi NAUT adernar.
listed building [ˌlɪstɪd-] n UK prédio m tombado.
listed company [ˌlɪstɪd-] n UK sociedade f de capital aberto.
listen ['lɪsn] vi **-1.** [give attention] escutar, ouvir; to ~ to sb/sthg escutar alguém/algo; to ~ for sthg estar atento(ta) a algo **-2.** [heed advice] dar atenção a; to ~ to sb/sthg escutar alguém/algo.
➤ **listen in** vi **-1.** RADIO escutar um programa numa estação; to ~ in to sthg sintonizar em algo **-2.** [eavesdrop] escutar a conversa alheia; to ~ in on sthg [conversation] prestar atenção em algo; [phone call] interceptar algo.
➤ **listen up** vi US inf prestar atenção.
listener ['lɪsnə'] n ouvinte mf.
listing ['lɪstɪŋ] n listagem f.
➤ **listings** npl [of events] programação f cultural.
listless ['lɪstlɪs] adj apático(ca).
list price n preço m de catálogo.
lit [lɪt] pt & pp ⊳ light.
litany ['lɪtənɪ] (pl -ies) n **-1.** RELIG ladainha f, litania f **-2.** [series] ladainha f.
liter n US = litre.
literacy ['lɪtərəsɪ] n (U) alfabetização f.

literal ['lɪtərəl] *adj* literal.

literally ['lɪtərəlɪ] *adv* literalmente; **to take sthg ~** levar algo ao pé da letra.

literary ['lɪtərərɪ] *adj* literário(ria); **a ~ man** um literato.

literate ['lɪtərət] *adj* **-1.** [able to read and write] alfabetizado(da); **computer-~** que tem conhecimentos de informática **-2.** [well-read] letrado(da), culto(ta).

literature ['lɪtrətʃəʳ] *n* (U) **-1.** [novels, plays, poetry] literatura *f* **-2.** [books on a particular subject] literatura *f*, bibliografia *f* **-3.** [printed information] informações *fpl*.

lithe [laɪð] *adj* ágil.

lithium ['lɪθɪəm] *n* lítio *m*.

lithograph ['lɪθəgrɑːf] *n* litografia *f*.

lithography *n* (U) litografia *f*.

Lithuania [ˌlɪθjʊ'eɪnɪə] *n* Lituânia; **in ~** na Lituânia.

Lithuanian [ˌlɪθjʊ'eɪnjən] <> *adj* lituano(na). <> *n* **-1.** [person] lituano *m*, -na *f* **-2.** [language] lituano *m*.

litigant ['lɪtɪgənt] *n fml* litigante *mf*.

litigate ['lɪtɪgeɪt] *vi fml* litigar.

litigation [ˌlɪtɪ'geɪʃn] *n* (U) *fml* litígio *m*.

litmus paper ['lɪtməs-] *n* papel *m* tornassol.

litre UK, **liter** US ['liːtəʳ] *n* **-1.** [metric unit] litro *m* **-2.** [capacity of engine] cilindrada *f*.

litter ['lɪtəʳ] <> *n* **-1.** (U) [waste material] lixo *m* **-2.** [newborn animals] ninhada *f* **-3.** [for litter tray]: **(cat) ~** areia *f* química (*para fezes de gato*). <> *vt*: **to be ~ed with sthg** estar coberto(ta) de algo.

litter bin *n* UK cesto *m* de lixo.

litter lout UK, **litterbug** *n inf* pessoa que suja as vias públicas.

litter tray *n* recipiente com areia química para o gato fazer suas necessidades.

little ['lɪtl] <> *adj* **-1.** [gen] pequeno(na) **-2.** [younger] menor; **my ~ brother** meu irmão mais novo **-3.** [short in time or distance] curto(ta) **-4.** [not much] pouco(ca); **she has a ~ money left** ela tem pouco dinheiro sobrando. <> *pron* [small amount] pouco(ca); **a ~** um pouco; **a ~ (bit)** um pouquinho. <> *adv* **-1.** [to a limited extent] pouco; **he's ~ more than a waiter** ele é pouco mais do que um garçom; **~ by ~** pouco a pouco **-2.** [rarely] raramente; **we go there as ~ as possible** vamos lá o mínimo possível.

little finger *n* dedo *m* mínimo, minguinho *m*.

little-known *adj* pouco conhecido(da).

liturgy ['lɪtədʒɪ] (*pl* -ies) *n* [form of worship] liturgia *f*.

live [lɪv] <> *vi* **-1.** [gen] viver **-2.** [reside] morar, viver. <> *vt* viver; **to ~ it up** *inf* curtir a vida.

➤ **live down** *vt sep* redimir-se de.

➤ **live for** *vt fus* viver para.

➤ **live in** *vi* **-1.** [student] ser interno(na) **-2.** [servant, nanny] dormir na casa.

➤ **live off** *vt fus* **-1.** [savings] viver de **-2.** [parents, family] viver às custas de.

➤ **live on** <> *vt fus* **-1.** [money] viver **-2.** [food] viver de. <> *vi* [memory, feeling, works] perdurar.

➤ **live out** <> *vt fus* acabar; **she won't ~ out the month** ela não chega até o final do mês. <> *vi* dormir fora.

➤ **live together** *vi* [cohabit] viver juntos(tas).

➤ **live up to** *vt fus* estar à altura de.

➤ **live with** *vt fus* **-1.** [cohabit with] viver com **-2.** *inf* [accept] conviver com.

live [laɪv] <> *adj* **-1.** [living] vivo(va) **-2.** [burning] aceso(sa) **-3.** [unexploded] carregado(da) **-4.** ELEC com eletricidade **-5.** MUS, RADIO & TV ao vivo. <> *adv* ao vivo.

live-in [lɪv-] *adj* residente.

livelihood ['laɪvlɪhʊd] *n* meio *m* de vida, sustento *m*.

liveliness ['laɪvlɪnɪs] *n* **-1.** [of person] vivacidade *f* **-2.** [of debate] ânimo *m* **-3.** [of mind] sagacidade *f*.

lively ['laɪvlɪ] (*compar* -ier, *superl* -iest) *adj* **-1.** [gen] animado(da) **-2.** [mind, curiosity, imagination] sagaz, perspicaz **-3.** [colour] vivo(va).

liven ['laɪvn] ➤ **liven up** <> *vt sep* animar. <> *vi* [person] animar-se.

liver ['lɪvəʳ] *n* fígado *m*.

Liverpudlian [ˌlɪvə'pʌdlɪən] <> *adj* de ou relativo a Liverpool. <> *n* morador ou residente de Liverpool.

liver sausage UK, **liverwurst** US ['lɪvəwɜːst] *n* (U) salsicha *f* de fígado.

livery ['lɪvərɪ] (*pl* -ies) *n* **-1.** [uniform] libré *f* **-2.** [of a company] marca *f* distintiva.

lives [laɪvz] *pl* ⊳ **life**.

livestock ['laɪvstɒk] *n* (U) animais *mpl* de uma fazenda.

live wire [laɪv-] *n* **-1.** [wire] cabo *m* com corrente **-2.** *inf* [person] pessoa *f* dinâmica, empreendedor *m*, -ra *f*.

livid ['lɪvɪd] *adj* **-1.** *inf* [angry] furioso(sa) **-2.** [blue-grey] roxo(xa).

living ['lɪvɪŋ] <> *adj* vivo(va); **~ proof** prova *f* viva. <> *n* **-1.** [people]: **the ~** os vivos **-2.** [means of earning money]: **what do you do for a ~?** o que você faz para ganhar a vida; **to scrape a ~** mal ganhar a vida **-3.** (U) [lifestyle] (estilo *m* de) vida *f*; **healthy ~** vida *f* saudável.

living conditions *npl* condições *fpl* de vida.

living expenses *npl* despesas *fpl* básicas.

living room *n* sala *f* de estar.

living standards *npl* padrão *m* de vida.

living wage *n* salário *m* básico.

lizard ['lɪzəd] *n* **-1.** [large] lagarto *m* **-2.** [small] lagartixa *f*.

llama ['lɑːmə] (*pl inv* OR -s) *n* lhama *m*.

LLB (*abbr of* Bachelor of Laws) *n* (titular de) graduação em direito.

LLD (*abbr of* Doctor of Laws) *n* (titular de) doutorado em direito.

LMT (*abbr of* Local Mean Time) *n* horário *m* local.

lo [ləʊ] *excl*: **~ and behold** olha só!

load [ləʊd] <> *n* **-1.** [gen] carga *f*; **to take a ~ off one's mind** tirar um peso da consciência **-2.** [burden] fardo *m* **-3.** [large amount]: **~s of, a ~ of** *inf* um monte de; **a ~ of rubbish** *inf* um monte de bobagem. <> *vt* **-1.** [container, vehicle, person] carregar; **to ~ sb/sthg with sthg** carregar alguém/algo de algo **-2.** [gun]: **to ~ sthg (with sthg)** carregar algo (com algo) **-3.** [in camera, video recorder]: **to ~ a film** colocar filme (*na câmera*);

to ~ a tape colocar fita *(na filmadora)* **- 4.** COMPUT [program] carregar.

➤ **load up** ◇ *vt sep* carregar. ◇ *vi* [with furniture, boxes] carregar.

loaded ['ləʊdɪd] *adj* **-1.** [question, statement] com duplo sentido **- 2.** [gun, camera] carregado(da) **- 3.** *inf* [rich] forrado(da).

loading bay ['ləʊdɪŋ-] *n* zona *f* de carga e descarga.

loaf [ləʊf] *(pl* **loaves)** *n* [of bread] (pedaço *m* de) pão *m*.

➤ **loaf about** *vi* vagabundear.

loafer ['ləʊfəʳ] *n* **-1.** [shoe] mocassim *m* **- 2.** [lazy person] vadio *m*, -dia *f*.

loam [ləʊm] *n (U)* marga *f*.

loan [ləʊn] ◇ *n* empréstimo *m*; **on ~** por empréstimo. ◇ *vt* emprestar; **to ~ sthg to sb, to ~ sb sthg** emprestar algo a alguém.

loan account *n* conta *f* de empréstimo.

loan capital *n (U)* capital *f* de empréstimo.

loan shark *n inf pej* agiota *mf*.

loath [ləʊθ] *adj*: **to be ~ to do sthg** estar pouco inclinado(da) a fazer algo.

loathe [ləʊð] *vt* odiar, detestar; **to ~ doing sthg** odiar fazer algo.

loathing ['ləʊðɪŋ] *n (U)* ódio *m*.

loathsome ['ləʊðsəm] *adj* repugnante.

loaves [ləʊvz] *pl* ▷ **loaf**.

lob [lɒb] *(pt & pp* **-bed,** *cont* **-bing)** ◇ *n* TENNIS lob *m*. ◇ *vt* **-1.** [throw] lançar **- 2.** [TENNIS - ball] rebater com um lob; [- opponent] dar um lob em.

lobby ['lɒbɪ] *(pl* **-ies,** *pt & pp* **-ied)** ◇ *n* **-1.** [hall] saguão *m* **- 2.** [pressure group] lobby *m*, grupo *m* de pressão. ◇ *vt* pressionar.

lobbyist ['lɒbɪɪst] *n* lobista *mf*.

lobe [ləʊb] *n* ANAT lóbulo *m*.

lobelia [lə'bi:ljə] *n* lobélia *f*.

lobotomy [lə'bɒtəmɪ] *(pl* **-ies)** *n* lobotomia *f*.

lobster ['lɒbstəʳ] *n* lagosta *f*.

lobster pot *n* armadilha *f* para pegar lagostas.

local ['ləʊkl] ◇ *adj* local. ◇ *n inf* **-1.** [person]: **the ~s** os habitantes do lugar **- 2.** UK [pub] pub *m* local **- 3.** US [bus, train] municipal *m*.

local anaesthetic *n* anestesia *f* local.

local area network *n* COMPUT rede *f* local.

local authority *n* UK autoridade *f* local.

local call *n* chamada *f* local.

local colour *n (U)* cor *f* local.

local derby *n* UK clássico *m* local.

locale [ləʊ'kɑ:l] *n fml* local *m*.

local government *n (U)* governo *m* local.

locality [ləʊ'kælətɪ] *(pl* **-ies)** *n* localidade *f*.

localized, -ised ['ləʊkəlaɪzd] *adj* localizado(da).

locally ['ləʊkəlɪ] *adv* [in region] localmente ; [in neighbourhood] na região.

local time *n (U)* hora *f* local.

locate [UK ləʊ'keɪt, US 'ləʊkeɪt] ◇ *vt* localizar. ◇ *vi* US [settle] localizar-se.

location [ləʊ'keɪʃn] *n* **-1.** [place] localização *f* **- 2.** CINEMA: **on ~** em locação.

loc. cit. *(abbr of* **loco citato)** loc. cit.

loch [lɒk] *n* Scot lago *m*.

lock [lɒk] ◇ *n* **-1.** [of door, window, box] fechadura *f*; **under ~ and key** fechado(da) a sete chaves **- 2.** [on canal] eclusa *f* **- 3.** AUT [steering lock] ângulo *m* de giro **- 4.** [of hair] mecha *f* **- 5.** *phr*: **~, stock and barrel** com tudo. ◇ *vt* **-1.** [fasten securely] fechar com chave **- 2.** [keep safely] trancar **- 3.** [immobilize] bloquear **- 4.** [hold firmly]: **to be ~ed in an embrace** estar fortemente abraçado(da); **to be ~ed in combat** estar envolvido(da) em disputa. ◇ *vi* **-1.** [fasten securely] fechar com chave, chavear **- 2.** [become immobilized] trancar.

➤ **locks** *npl literary* [hair] cachos *mpl*.

➤ **lock away** *vt sep* trancar a sete chaves.

➤ **lock in** *vt sep* encerrar.

➤ **lock out** *vt sep* **-1.** [accidentally] trancar do lado de fora **- 2.** [deliberately] deixar na rua.

➤ **lock up** ◇ *vt sep* **-1.** [person] trancafiar **- 2.** [house] trancar **- 3.** [valuables] fechar com chave **- 4.** [with padlock] fechar com cadeado. ◇ *vi* trancar-se.

lockable ['lɒkəbl] *adj* com fechadura.

locker ['lɒkəʳ] *n* [for clothes, luggage, books] compartimento *m* com chave.

locker room *n* US vestiário *m*.

locket ['lɒkɪt] *n* medalhão *m*.

lockjaw *n (U)* tétano *m*.

lockout ['lɒkaʊt] *n* greve *f* patronal, lockout *m*.

locksmith ['lɒksmɪθ] *n* serralheiro *m*, -ra *f*.

lock-up *n* **-1.** [prison] prisão *f*, cárcere *m* **- 2.** UK [garage] garagem *f*.

loco ['ləʊkəʊ] *(pl* **-s)** *inf* ◇ *adj* US louco(ca). ◇ *n* UK [locomotive] locomotiva *f*.

locomotive ['ləʊkə,məʊtɪv] *n* locomotiva *f*.

locum ['ləʊkəm] *(pl* **-s)** *n* interino *m*, -na *f*.

locust ['ləʊkəst] *n* gafanhoto *m*.

lodge [lɒdʒ] ◇ *n* **-1.** [caretaker's room] portaria *f* **- 2.** [of manor house] guarita *f* **- 3.** [of Freemasons] loja *f* **- 4.** [for hunting] região *f* de caça. ◇ *vt* *fml* [register] apresentar. ◇ *vi* **-1.** [stay, live]: **to ~ with sb** hospedar-se na casa de alguém **- 2.** [become stuck] alojar-se **- 3.** *fig* [in mind] gravar-se na mente.

lodger ['lɒdʒəʳ] *n* pensionista *mf (em casa de família).*

lodging ['lɒdʒɪŋ] *n* ▷ **board**.

➤ **lodgings** *npl* alojamentos *mpl*.

loft [lɒft] *n* [attic] sótão *m*; **~ (apartment)** *apartamento transformado na cobertura de um armazém ou de uma fábrica, em geral amplo e sem divisórias internas.*

lofty ['lɒftɪ] *(compar* **-ier,** *superl* **-iest)** *adj* **-1.** [noble] elevado(da), nobre **- 2.** *pej* [haughty] arrogante **- 3.** *literary* [high] elevado(da).

log [lɒg] *(pt & pp* **-ged,** *cont* **-ging)** ◇ *n* **-1.** [of wood] tronco *m* **- 2.** [written record - of ship] diário *m* de bordo; [- of plane] diário *m* de vôo. ◇ *vt* **-1.** [information - on paper] registrar; [- in computer] registrar em log **- 2.** [speed, distance, time] anotar.

➤ **log in** *vi* COMPUT entrar (no sistema), efetuar login.

➤ **log out** *vi* COMPUT sair (do sistema), efetuar logout.

loganberry ['ləʊgənbərɪ] *(pl* **-ies)** *n* tipo de framboesa de maior tamanho.

logarithm ['lɒgərɪðm] *n* logaritmo *m*.

logbook ['lɒgbʊk] n -1. [of ship] diário m de bordo -2. [of plane] diário m de vôo -3. [of car] documentação f.

log cabin n cabana f.

log fire n fogueira f.

loggerheads ['lɒgəhedz] n: **at ~ with** em desavença com.

logic ['lɒdʒɪk] n lógica f.

logical ['lɒdʒɪkl] adj lógico(ca).

logically ['lɒdʒɪklɪ] adv logicamente.

logistical [lə'dʒɪstɪkl] adj logístico(ca).

logistics [lə'dʒɪstɪks] <> n MIL logística f. <> npl fig [organization] logística f.

logjam ['lɒgdʒæm] n fig problema m crônico.

logo ['ləʊgəʊ] (pl -s) n logotipo m.

logrolling ['lɒgrəʊlɪŋ] n (U) US troca f de favores.

logy adj US inf vagaroso(sa).

loin [lɔɪn] n lombo m.

➤ **loins** npl ANAT quadris mpl; **to gird one's ~s** fig preparar-se para a batalha.

loincloth ['lɔɪnklɒθ] n tanga f.

loiter ['lɔɪtə^r] vi -1. [hang about] demorar-se -2. [dawdle] vadiar.

loll [lɒl] vi -1. [sit, lie about] recostar-se, refestelar-se -2. [hang down] estar pendente.

lollipop ['lɒlɪpɒp] n pirulito m.

lollipop lady n UK guarda f escolar.

lollipop man n UK guarda m escolar.

lolly ['lɒlɪ] (pl -ies) n -1. [lollipop] pirulito m -2. UK [ice cream] picolé m -3. (U) UK inf [money] grana f.

London ['lʌndən] n Londres; **in ~** em Londres.

Londoner ['lʌndənə^r] n londrino m, -na f.

lone [ləʊn] adj solitário(ria).

loneliness ['ləʊnlɪnɪs] n (U) solidão f.

lonely ['ləʊnlɪ] (compar -ier, superl -iest) adj -1. [gen] solitário(ria), só -2. [place] isolado(da).

lone parent n UK pai m solteiro, mãe f solteira.

loner ['ləʊnə^r] n solitário m, -ria f.

lonesome ['ləʊnsəm] adj US inf -1. [person] solitário(ria), só -2. [place] isolado(da).

long [lɒŋ] <> adj -1. [in time] longo(ga); **two days ~** de dois dias de duração; **how ~ will it take?** quanto tempo vai demorar? -2. [in space] comprido(da), longo(ga); **10 metres ~** com 10 metros de comprimento; **it's five hundred pages ~** tem quinhentas páginas. <> adv [for a long time] por muito tempo; **how ~ have you been waiting?** há quanto tempo você está esperando?; **as** OR **so ~ as** desde que; **before ~** agora; **for ~** muito tempo; **no ~er** não mais; **I can't wait any ~er** não posso mais esperar; **so ~!** inf até logo! <> n: **the ~ and the short of it is that ...** em poucas palavras, o que aconteceu é que ... <> vt: **to ~ to do sthg** ansiar por fazer algo.

➤ **as long as, so long as** conj [if] desde que; **as ~ as you're happy about it** desde que você esteja feliz com isso.

➤ **long for** vt fus ansiar por.

long. (abbr of **longitude**) long.

long-awaited [-ə'weɪtɪd] adj tão esperado(da).

long-distance adj de longa distância.

long-distance call n chamada f de longa distância.

long division n (U) divisão f detalhada.

long-drawn-out adj interminável.

long drink n bebida resultante da mistura de álcool e refresco.

longevity [lɒn'dʒevətɪ] n [of person] longevidade f.

long-haired adj -1. [rabbit, sheep] de pêlo comprido -2. [person] de cabelo comprido.

longhand ['lɒŋhænd] n (U) escrita f à mão.

long-haul adj de grande distância.

longing ['lɒŋɪŋ] <> adj ansioso(sa). <> n desejo m; **~ (for sthg)** ânsia f (por algo).

longingly ['lɒŋɪŋlɪ] adv ansiosamente.

Long Island n Long Island.

longitude ['lɒndʒɪtju:d] n GEOGR (U) longitude f.

long johns npl ceroulas fpl.

long jump n salto m em distância.

long-lasting adj de longa duração, duradouro(-ra).

long-life adj longa-vida.

long-lost adj perdido(da) há muito tempo.

long-playing record [-'pleɪɪŋ-] n LP m.

long-range adj -1. [missile, bomber] de longo alcance -2. [plan, forecast] a longo prazo.

long-running adj -1. [play] de muita duração -2. [dispute] que já dura muito tempo -3. [programme] há muito tempo no ar.

longshoreman ['lɒŋʃɔːmən] (pl -men [-mən]) n US estivador m.

long shot n fig possibilidade f remota.

long-sighted adj -1. MED presbita -2. fig [having foresight] previdente.

long-standing adj de longa data.

long-suffering adj sofrido(da).

long term n: **in the ~** a longo prazo.

➤ **long-term** adj a longo prazo.

long vacation n UK UNIV férias fpl de verão.

long wave n (U) onda f longa.

longways ['lɒŋweɪz] adv ao comprido, longitudinalmente.

long-wearing adj US resistente, duradouro(ra).

long weekend n feriadão m.

long-winded adj cansativo(va).

loo [lu:] (pl -s) n UK inf toalete m.

loofa(h) ['lu:fə] n esponja f vegetal.

look [lʊk] <> n -1. [with eyes] olhada f; **to give sb a ~** dar uma olhada em alguém; **to have a ~ (for sthg)** dar uma olhada (procurando algo); **to take** OR **have a ~ (at sthg)** dar uma olhada (em algo) -2. [appearance] aparência f; **by the ~ (s) of things** pelo jeito. <> vi -1. [with eyes] olhar; **to ~ at sb/sthg** olhar alguém/algo -2. [search] procurar -3. [have stated appearance] parecer; **to ~ like** parecer como; **it ~s like rain** parece que vai chover; **to ~ as if** parecer como se; **you ~ as if you haven't slept** parece que você não dormiu. <> vt -1. [look at] olhar -2. [appear]: **to ~ one's age** aparentar a idade que se tem; **to ~ one's best** vestir-se elegantemente. <> excl: **~ (here)!** olha (só)!

➤ **looks** npl [attractiveness] aparência f, beleza f.

➤ **look after** vt fus [take care of] cuidar de; **to ~ after o.s.** cuidar-se.

look at *vt fus* **-1.** [examine] examinar **-2.** [analise] analisar **-3.** [regard, consider] olhar para.

look back *vi* [reminisce] recordar; **she's never ~ed back** ela nunca retrocedeu.

look down on *vt fus* [condescend to] desdenhar de, depreciar.

look for *vt fus* procurar (por).

look forward to *vt fus* aguardar (ansiosamente).

look into *vt fus* [examine] analisar, examinar.

look on <> *vt fus* = **look upon**. <> *vi* [watch] observar.

look onto *vi* [face] ter vista para, dar para.

look out *vi* [take care] tomar cuidado; **~ out!** cuidado!

look out for *vt fus* [try to spot] estar atento(ta) a.

look round <> *vt fus* [visit] visitar. <> *vi* **-1.** [look at surroundings] percorrer com o olhar ao redor **-2.** [turn] virar-se.

look through *vt fus* [report, document] examinar o conteúdo de.

look to *vt fus* **-1.** [depend on] contar com **-2.** [think about] pensar em.

look up <> *vt sep* **-1.** [in book] consultar **-2.** [visit] visitar. <> *vi* [improve] melhorar.

look upon *vt fus* [consider]: **I ~ upon him as my father** eu o considerava meu pai.

look up to *vt fus* [admire] prezar, respeitar.

look-alike *n* sósia *mf*.

look-in *n UK*: **to get a ~** [chance to participate] ter a possibilidade de participar *or* fazer parte.

lookout ['lʊkaʊt] *n* **-1.** [place] posto *m* de observação, guarita *f* **-2.** [person] vigia *mf* **-3.** [search]: **to be on the ~ for sthg** estar à espreita de algo.

look-up table *n COMPUT* tabela *f* de consulta.

loom [lu:m] <> *n* tear *m*. <> *vi* **-1.** [rise up] erguer-se **-2.** *fig* [be imminent] aproximar-se, ser iminente; **to ~ large** crescer em tamanho.

loom up *vi* despontar sombriamente.

looming ['lu:mɪŋ] *adj* iminente.

loony ['lu:nɪ] (*compar* -ier, *superl* -iest, *pl* -ies) *inf* <> *adj* lunático(ca). <> *n* lunático *m*, -ca *f*.

loop [lu:p] <> *n* **-1.** [shape] laço *m* **-2.** [contraceptive] DIU *m* **-3.** *COMPUT* loop *m*, laço *m*. <> *vt* [rope, string] enlaçar. <> *vi* [road, river] fazer uma curva acentuada.

loophole ['lu:phəʊl] *n* furo *m* (*na lei*).

loo roll *n UK inf* rolo *m* de papel higiênico.

loose [lu:s] <> *adj* **-1.** [not firmly fixed] frouxo(xa) **-2.** [unattached, unpackaged - sheets of paper] avulso(sa); [- sweets, nails] solto(ta) **-3.** [not tight-fitting] folgado(da) **-4.** [free, not restrained] solto(ta) **-5.** *pej* & *dated* [promiscuous] promíscuo(cua) **-6.** [inexact] impreciso(sa) **-7.** [informal] informal **-8.** *US inf* [relaxed]: **to stay ~** ficar relaxado(da). <> *n* (*U*): **to be on the ~** andar solto(ta).

loose change *n* (*U*) trocado *m*.

loose end *n* ponta *f* solta; **yet another ~ we can't explain** outra incógnita que a gente não consegue explicar; **to be at a ~ UK, to be at ~s US** estar entediado(da), não ter o que fazer.

loose-fitting *adj* folgado(da).

loose-leaf binder *n* pasta *f* de folhas soltas.

loosely ['lu:slɪ] *adv* **-1.** [not firmly] sem apertar **-2.** [inexactly] imprecisamente.

loosen ['lu:sn] <> *vt* [make less tight] afrouxar. <> *vi* [become less tight] afrouxar.

loosen up *vi* **-1.** [before game, race] aquecer-se **-2.** *inf* [relax] relaxar.

loot [lu:t] <> *n* (*U*) saque *m*. <> *vt* saquear.

looter ['lu:tə'] *n* saqueador *m*, -ra *f*.

looting ['lu:tɪŋ] *n* (*U*) saque *m*.

lop [lɒp] (*pt* & *pp* -ped, *cont* -ping) *vt* podar.

lop off *vt sep* cortar.

lope [ləʊp] *vi* **-1.** [animal] trotar **-2.** [person] andar a passos largos e ligeiros.

lop-sided [-'saɪdɪd] *adj* **-1.** [uneven] assimétrico(ca) **-2.** *fig* [biased] distorcido(da).

lord [lɔːd] <> *n UK* [man of noble rank] lorde *m*. <> *vt*: **to ~ it over** humilhar.

Lord *n* **-1.** *RELIG*: **the Lord** [God] o Senhor; **good Lord!** *UK* Deus meu! **-2.** [in titles] lorde *m* **-3.** [as form of address]: **my Lord** [bishop] Reverendíssimo *m*; [judge] Meritíssimo *m*, -ma *f*.

Lords *npl UK POL*: **the (House of) Lords** a Câmara dos Lordes.

Lord Chancellor *n UK POL* presidente da Câmara dos Lordes e responsável pela Justiça na Inglaterra e no País de Gales.

lordly ['lɔːdlɪ] (*compar* -ier, *superl* -iest) *adj* **-1.** [noble] nobre **-2.** *pej* [arrogant] arrogante.

Lord Mayor *n UK* prefeito da cidade de Londres e outras metrópoles.

Lordship ['lɔːdʃɪp] *n*: **your/his ~** Vossa/Sua Senhoria.

Lord's Prayer *n*: **the ~** o Pai Nosso.

lore [lɔː'] *n* (*U*) crença *f* popular.

lorry ['lɒrɪ] (*pl* -ies) *n UK* caminhão *m*.

lorry driver *n UK* motorista *mf* de caminhão.

lose [lu:z] (*pt* & *pp* lost) <> *vt* **-1.** [gen] perder; **to ~ sight of sb/sthg** perder alguém/algo de vista; **to ~ one's way** [get lost] perder-se; **to ~ weight** emagrecer, perder peso; **you have nothing to ~** *inf* você não tem nada a perder **-2.** [subj: clock, watch]: **my watch ~s 5 minutes a day** meu relógio atrasa 5 minutos por dia **-3.** [elude, shake off] escapar. <> *vi* **-1.** [fail to win] perder **-2.** [time] atrasar-se.

lose out *vi* sair perdendo; **to ~ out on sthg** sair perdendo em algo.

loser ['lu:zə'] *n* [gen] perdedor *m*, -ra *f*; **to be a good/bad ~** saber/não saber perder, ser um bom/mau perdedor.

losing ['lu:zɪŋ] *adj* vencido(da).

loss [lɒs] *n* **-1.** [gen] perda *f* **-2.** [failure to win] derrota *f* **-3.** *COMM* [of money] prejuízo *m*; **to make a ~** ter prejuízo; **to cut one's ~es** cortar a fonte de prejuízos **-4.** *phr*: **to be at a ~ to explain sthg** não saber como explicar algo.

loss adjuster [-ə'dʒʌstə'] *n* perito *m*, -ta *f* na determinação de avarias.

loss leader *n COMM* artigo *m* em liquidação, chamariz *m*.

lost [lɒst] <> *pt* & *pp* ▷ **lose**. <> *adj* **-1.** [gen] perdido(da); **to get ~** [lose way] perder-se; **get ~! *inf* te some! **-2.** [wasted]: **to be ~ on sb** não surtir efeito em alguém.

lost-and-found office *n US* setor *m* de achados e perdidos.

lost cause *n* causa *f* perdida.

lost property *n (U)* achados *mpl* e perdidos.

lost property office *n UK* setor *m* de achados e perdidos.

lot [lɒt] *n -* **1.** [large amount]: **a ~ of**, **~s of** muito(ta); **a ~ of people** muita gente, muitas pessoas; **~s of problems** muitos problemas; **he talks a ~** ele fala muito - **2.** *inf* [group of things]: **I bought two ~s of shares last week** comprei dois lotes de ações na semana passada; **put this ~ in my office** *inf* coloca tudo isso no meu escritório - **3.** *inf* [group of people]: **one ~ of refugees arrived yesterday** um grupo de refugiados chegou ontem; **what a mean ~ you are!** *inf* são todos uns mesquinhos! - **4.** [destiny] destino *m*, sorte *f* - **5.** [at auction] lote *m* - **6.** [entire amount]: **the ~** tudo - **7.** *US* [of land] lote *m*; [car park] estacionamento *m* - **8.** *phr*: **to draw ~s** tirar à sorte.

➤ **a lot** *adv* muito; **~ better** muito melhor.

loth [ləʊθ] *adj* = **loath**.

lotion ['ləʊʃn] *n* loção *f*.

lottery ['lɒtərɪ] (*pl* **-ies**) *n* loteria *f*.

LOTTO® ['lɒtəʊ] *n* loteria *f* nacional (britânica), ≃ loto *f*.

lotus position ['ləʊtəs-] *n* posição *f* de lótus.

loud [laʊd] <> *adj -* **1.** [person] barulhento(ta) - **2.** [voice, music, TV] alto(ta) - **3.** [bang] forte - **4.** [emphatic]: **to be ~ in sthg** ser enfático(ca) em algo - **5.** [garish] espalhafatoso(sa). <> *adv* alto; **~ and clear** alto e claro; **out ~** em voz alta.

loudhailer [ˌlaʊd'heɪləʳ] *n UK* megafone *m*.

loudly ['laʊdlɪ] *adv -* **1.** [shout] alto - **2.** [talk] em voz alta - **3.** [garishly] de forma espalhafatosa.

loudmouth ['laʊdmaʊθ, *pl* -maʊðz] *n inf* tagarela *mf*, gasguita *mf*.

loudness ['laʊdnɪs] *n (U)* intensidade *f* do som.

loudspeaker [ˌlaʊd'spiːkəʳ] *n* alto-falante *m*.

lough *n Irish* lago *m*.

Louisiana [luːˌiːzɪ'ænə] *n* Louisiana; **in ~** em Louisiana.

lounge [laʊndʒ] (*cont* **loungeing**) <> *n -* **1.** [in house] sala *f* de estar - **2.** [in airport] sala *f* de espera - **3.** *UK* [bar] = **lounge bar**. <> *vi* recostar-se.

➤ **lounge about, lounge around** *vi* vadiar.

lounge bar *n UK* sala *f* mais confortável *(num bar)*.

lounge lizard *n* parasita *mf* social.

lounge suit *n UK* traje *m* social, terno *m*.

louse [laʊs] (*pl sense 1* **lice**, *pl sense 2* **-s**) *n -* **1.** [insect] piolho *m* - **2.** *inf pej* [person] canalha *mf*.

➤ **louse up** *vt sep US vinf* melar.

lousy ['laʊzɪ] (*compar* **-ier**, *superl* **-iest**) *adj inf* **-1.** [poor quality] péssimo(ma); **his performance was ~** a apresentação dele foi uma porcaria - **2.** [ill]: **to feel ~** sentir-se mal.

lout [laʊt] *n* mal-educado *m*.

louvre *UK*, **louver** *US* ['luːvəʳ] *n*: **~ door** porta *f* de veneziana; **~ window** veneziana *f*.

lovable ['lʌvəbl] *adj* amável, encantador(ra).

love [lʌv] <> *n -* **1.** *(U)* [affection for person] amor *m*; **give her my ~** dá um abraço nela por mim; **a**

~-hate relationship uma relação de amor e ódio; **~ from** [at end of letter] um abraço, um beijo; **to be in ~** estar apaixonado(da); **to fall in ~** apaixonar-se; **to make ~** fazer amor - **2.** [liking for sthg, for activity] paixão *f*; **to have a ~ of** OR **for sthg** ter paixão por algo - **3.** [beloved person, thing] amor *m* - **4.** *inf* [term of address] amor *m* - **5.** *(U)* TENNIS: **30 ~ 30** a zero. <> *vt* **-1.** [gen] amar - **2.** [like] adorar; **to ~ to do sthg** OR **doing sthg** adorar fazer algo.

love affair *n* caso *m* (de amor).

lovebite ['lʌvbaɪt] *n* chupão *m*.

loveless ['lʌvlɪs] *adj* [marriage] sem amor.

love letter *n* carta *f* de amor.

love life *n* vida *f* amorosa.

lovely ['lʌvlɪ] (*compar* **-ier**, *superl* **-iest**) *adj -* **1.** [person, child - in looks] encantador(ra); [- in character] amável - **2.** [view, day, weather] adorável; [dress, surprise, holiday] maravilhoso(sa), adorável.

love-making *n (U)* relação *f* sexual.

lover ['lʌvəʳ] *n -* **1.** [sexual partner] amante *mf* - **2.** [enthusiast] amante *mf*, apaixonado *m*, -da *f*.

lovesick ['lʌvsɪk] *adj* doente de amor *(não-correspondido)*.

love song *n* canção *f* de amor.

love story *n* história *f* de amor.

loving ['lʌvɪŋ] *adj* carinhoso(sa), afetuoso(sa).

lovingly ['lʌvɪŋlɪ] *adv* carinhosamente, afetuosamente.

low [ləʊ] <> *adj -* **1.** [gen] baixo(xa); **we are ~ on milk** estamos com pouco leite - **2.** [poor - intelligence] pouco(ca); [- opinion] pobre; [- standard, quality, esteem] baixo(xa); [- health] debilitado(da) - **3.** [not loud or high] baixo(xa) - **4.** [light] fraco(ca) - **5.** [neckline] decotado(da) - **6.** [depressed] deprimido(da) - **7.** [vulgar] baixo(xa). <> *adv -* **1.** [gen] baixo - **2.** [situated, built] embaixo. <> *n -* **1.** [low point] baixa *f* - **2.** METEOR área *f* de baixa pressão.

low-alcohol *adj* de baixo teor alcoólico.

lowbrow ['ləʊbraʊ] *adj* de baixo nível intelectual.

low-calorie *adj* de baixa caloria.

Low Church *n* corrente *evangélica da Igreja Anglicana*.

Low Countries *npl*: **the ~** os Países Baixos.

low-cut *adj* decotado(da).

low-down *adj inf*: **~ trick** truque *m* baixo.

➤ **lowdown** *n inf*: **to give sb the lowdown (on sthg)** dar os detalhes concretos (sobre algo) a alguém.

lower[1] ['ləʊəʳ] <> *adj* inferior. <> *vt -* **1.** [gen] baixar - **2.** [reduce] reduzir.

lower[2] ['laʊəʳ] *vi -* **1.** [be dark] estar escuro(ra) - **2.** [frown]: **to ~ at sb** fechar a cara para alguém.

Lower Chamber [ˌləʊəʳ-] *n POL* ≃ Câmara *f* Baixa.

lower class [ˌləʊəʳ-] *n*: **the ~(es)** as classes baixas.

Lower House [ˌləʊəʳ-] *n POL* Câmara *f* Baixa.

lowest common denominator ['ləʊɪst-] *n*: **the ~** o menor denominador comum.

low-fat *adj* com baixo teor de gordura.

low-flying *adj* de vôo rasante.

low frequency *n* baixa freqüência *f*.

low gear *n US* primeira *f (marcha)*.

low-key adj discreto(ta).
Lowlands ['ləʊləndz] npl: **the ~** [of Scotland] as Terras Baixas (da Escócia).
low-level language n COMPUT linguagem f de baixo nível.
low-loader n veículo m com baixa plataforma de carga.
lowly ['ləʊlɪ] (compar -ier, superl -iest) adj humilde.
low-lying adj [land] baixo(xa).
Low Mass n missa f baixa.
low-necked [-'nekt] adj decotado(da).
low-paid adj mal pago(ga).
low-rise adj baixo(xa).
low season n baixa estação f.
low tide n maré f baixa.
loyal ['lɔɪəl] adj leal, fiel.
loyalist ['lɔɪəlɪst] n leal mf (ao governo).
➡ **Loyalist** n POL [in Northern Ireland] protestante que acredita que a Irlanda do Norte deva continuar fazendo parte do Reino Unido.
loyalty ['lɔɪəltɪ] (pl -ies) n lealdade f, fidelidade f.
loyalty card n cartão f de fidelização.
lozenge ['lɒzɪndʒ] n -1. [tablet] pastilha f -2. [shape] losango m.
LP (abbr of long-playing record) n LP m.
L-plate n UK ≃ auto-escola f (indicação no veículo), placa que contém a letra L em vermelho fixada no veículo conduzido por pessoa que está aprendendo a dirigir.
LPN (abbr of licensed practical nurse) n técnico em enfermagem nos Estados Unidos.
LPO (abbr of London Philharmonic Orchestra) n Orquestra f Filarmônica de Londres.
LRAM (abbr of Licentiate of the Royal Academy of Music) n membro da academia britânica de música.
LRB (abbr of London Review of Books) n jornal britânico de resenhas literárias e humanidades.
LSAT (abbr of Law School Admissions Test) n exame de acesso às escolas de direito nos Estados Unidos.
LSD n (abbr of lysergic acid diethylamide) LSD m.
LSE (abbr of London School of Economics) n escola londrina de ciências políticas e econômicas.
LSO (abbr of London Symphony Orchestra) n Orquestra f Sinfônica de Londres.
Lt. (abbr of lieutenant) Ten.
LT (abbr of low tension) n ELEC baixa tensão f.
Ltd, ltd (abbr of limited) Ltda.
lubricant ['lu:brɪkənt] n lubrificante m.
lubricate ['lu:brɪkeɪt] vt lubrificar.
lubrication [,lu:brɪ'keɪʃn] n (U) lubrificação f.
lucid ['lu:sɪd] adj -1. [easily understood] nítido(da) -2. [clear-headed] lúcido(da).
lucidly ['lu:sɪdlɪ] adv claramente, lucidamente.
luck [lʌk] n (U) sorte f; **good ~!** boa sorte!; **bad ~** [misfortune] azar m; **bad ~!** [said to commiserate] que azar!; **hard ~!** azar!; **to be in ~** estar com sorte; **to try one's ~ at sthg** tentar a sorte em algo; **with (any) ~** com (um pouco de) sorte.
➡ **luck out** vi US inf ter sorte.
luckily ['lʌkɪlɪ] adv afortunadamente.

luckless ['lʌklɪs] adj desafortunado(da).
lucky ['lʌkɪ] (compar -ier, superl -iest) adj -1. [fortunate - person] sortudo(da), com sorte; [- event] feliz -2. [bringing good luck] da sorte.
lucky charm n amuleto m.
lucky dip n UK saco m de surpresas.
lucrative ['lu:krətɪv] adj lucrativo(va).
ludicrous ['lu:dɪkrəs] adj -1. [appearance, situation] ridículo(la) -2. [decision, suggestion] absurdo(da).
ludo ['lu:dəʊ] n (U) UK ludo m.
lug [lʌg] (pt & pp -ged, cont -ging) vt inf arrastar, tirar com dificuldade.
luggage ['lʌgɪdʒ] n (U) UK bagagem f.
luggage rack n UK porta-bagagem m.
luggage van n UK RAIL vagão m de bagagem.
lugubrious [lu:'gu:brɪəs] adj fml lúgubre.
lukewarm ['lu:kwɔ:m] adj -1. [tepid] morno(na) -2. [unenthusiastic] desanimado(da), indiferente.
lull [lʌl] ⟨⟩ n -1. [in activity] pausa f; **the ~ before the storm** fig a bonança antes da tempestade -2. [in fighting] trégua f. ⟨⟩ vt -1. [make sleepy]: **to ~ sb to sleep** ninar alguém para dormir -2. [reassure]: **to ~ sb into a false sense of security** passar a alguém uma falsa sensação de segurança.
lullaby ['lʌləbaɪ] (pl -ies) n cantiga f de ninar.
lumbago [lʌm'beɪgəʊ] n (U) lumbago m.
lumber ['lʌmbə[r]] ⟨⟩ n -1. US [timber] madeira f serrada, tábua f -2. UK [bric-a-brac] trastes mpl. ⟨⟩ vi [large person, animal, vehicle] andar a custo.
➡ **lumber with** vt sep UK inf [encumber] encarregar.
lumbering ['lʌmbərɪŋ] adj desengoçado(da).
lumberjack ['lʌmbədʒæk] n lenhador m, -ra f.
lumbermill ['lʌmbə,mɪl] n US serraria f.
lumber-room n UK quarto f para guardar tralhas.
lumberyard ['lʌmbəja:d] n madeireira f.
luminous ['lu:mɪnəs] adj luminoso(sa).
lump [lʌmp] ⟨⟩ n -1. [piece - of coal] pedaço m; [- earth, sugar] torrão m; [- in sauce, soup] caroço m -2. MED [on body] tumor m. ⟨⟩ vt: **to ~ sthg together** agrupar algo; **you'll just have to ~ it** inf você vai ter de engolir isso!
lumpectomy [,lʌm'pektəmɪ] (pl -ies) n cirurgia para remoção de tumor do seio.
lump sum n soma f global.
lumpy ['lʌmpɪ] (compar -ier, superl -iest) adj encaroçado(da).
lunacy ['lu:nəsɪ] n (U) loucura f.
lunar ['lu:nə[r]] adj lunar.
lunatic ['lu:nətɪk] ⟨⟩ adj pej lunático(ca). ⟨⟩ n -1. pej [fool] idiota mf -2. [insane person] lunático m, -ca f.
lunatic asylum n hospício m, manicômio m.
lunatic fringe n minoria f extremista.
lunch [lʌntʃ] ⟨⟩ n almoço m; **to have ~** almoçar. ⟨⟩ vi almoçar.
luncheon ['lʌntʃən] n fml almoço m.
luncheonette n US lanchonete f.
luncheon meat n (U) fiambre m.
luncheon voucher n UK tíquete-refeição m.
lunch hour n hora f do almoço.
lunchtime ['lʌntʃtaɪm] n hora f do almoço.
lung [lʌŋ] n pulmão m.

lung cancer *n (U)* câncer *m* de pulmão.

lunge [lʌndʒ] *vi* arremessar-se; **to ~ at sb** investir contra alguém.

lupin *UK* [ˈluːpɪn], **lupine** *US* [ˈluːpaɪn] *n* tremoço *m.*

lurch [lɜːtʃ] <> *n* [movement] cambaleio *m*, solavanco *m*; **to leave sb in the ~** deixar alguém na mão. <> *vi* [in movement] cambalear, balançar.

lure [ljʊəʳ] <> *n* [attraction] fascínio *m.* <> *vt* [tempt] fascinar.

lurid [ˈljʊərɪd] *adj* **-1.** [brightly coloured] sensacional **-2.** [shockingly unpleasant] chocante.

lurk [lɜːk] *vi* espreitar.

lurking [ˈlɜːkɪŋ] *adj* que segue rondando.

Lusaka [luːˈsɑːkə] *n* Lusaka; **in ~** em Lusaka.

luscious [ˈlʌʃəs] *adj* **-1.** [fruit] suculento(ta) **-2.** [colour] vistoso(sa).

lush [lʌʃ] <> *adj* **-1.** [healthy, thick] viçoso(sa) **-2.** *inf* [sumptuous] luxuoso(sa). <> *n US inf* [drunkard] bêbado *m*, -da *f.*

lust [lʌst] *n* **-1.** *(U)* [sexual desire] luxúria *f* **-2.** [greed]: **~ for sthg** cobiça *f* por algo.
  ◆ lust after, lust for *vt fus* **-1.** [money, power] cobiçar **-2.** [person] desejar.

luster *n US* = lustre.

lustful [ˈlʌstfʊl] *adj* luxurioso(sa).

lustre *UK*, **luster** *US* [ˈlʌstəʳ] *n* [brightness] brilho *m.*

lusty [ˈlʌstɪ] *(compar* -ier, *superl* -iest) *adj* vigoroso(sa), forte.

lute [luːt] *n* alaúde *m.*

luv [lʌv] *n UK inf* amor *m.*

Luxembourg [ˈlʌksəmˌbɜːg] *n* Luxemburgo; **in ~** em Luxemburgo.

luxuriant [lʌgˈʒʊərɪənt] *adj* viçoso(sa), exuberante.

luxuriate [lʌgˈʒʊərɪeɪt] *vi* deleitar-se; **to ~ in sthg** deleitar-se com algo.

luxurious [lʌgˈʒʊərɪəs] *adj* **-1.** [expensive] luxuoso(sa) **-2.** [voluptuous] esplêndido(da).

luxury [ˈlʌkʃərɪ] *(pl* -ies) <> *n* luxo *m.* <> *comp* de luxo.

luxury goods *npl* artigos *mpl* de luxo.

LV *(abbr of* luncheon voucher) *n* vale-refeição *m.*

LW *(abbr of* long wave) *n* onda *f* longa.

lychee [ˌlaɪˈtʃiː] *n* lichia *f.*

Lycra® [ˈlaɪkrə] <> *n (U)* lycra® *f.* <> *comp* de lycra.

lying [ˈlaɪɪŋ] <> *adj* [dishonest] mentiroso(sa), falso(sa). <> *n* [dishonesty] mentiras *fpl.*

lymph gland [lɪmf-] *n* glândula *f* linfática.

lynch [lɪntʃ] *vt* linchar.

lynx [lɪnks] *(pl inv OR* -es) *n* lince *m.*

lyre [ˈlaɪəʳ] *n* lira *f.*

lyric [ˈlɪrɪk] *adj* lírico(ca).
  ◆ lyrics *npl* letra *f (de música).*

lyrical [ˈlɪrɪkl] *adj* **-1.** [poetic] lírico(ca) **-2.** [enthusiastic] entusiasmado(da).

m¹ *(pl* m's *OR* ms), **M** *(pl* M's *OR* Ms) [em] *n* [letter] m, M *m.*
  ◆ M -1. *UK (abbr of* motorway) rodovia *f* **-2.** *(abbr of* medium) M.

m² -1. *(abbr of* metre) m **-2.** *(abbr of* million) milhão *m.* **-3.** *abbr of* mile.

ma [mɑː] *n inf* mamã *f.*

MA <> *n (abbr of* Master of Arts) *(titular de) diploma de mestre em ciências humanas.* <> *abbr of* Massachusetts.

ma'am [mæm] *n* madame *f.*

mac [mæk] *(abbr of* mackintosh) *n UK inf* [coat] capa *f* de chuva.

macabre [məˈkɑːbrə] *adj* macabro(bra).

Macao [məˈkaʊ] *n* Macau; **in ~** em Macau.

macaroni [ˌmækəˈrəʊnɪ] *n (U)* macarrão *m.*

macaroni cheese *n (U)* macarrão *m* com molho de queijo.

macaroon [ˌmækəˈruːn] *n* biscoito doce preparado com amêndoas e coco.

mace [meɪs] *n* **-1.** [ornamental rod] maça *f* **-2.** *(U)* [spice] macis *m inv.*

Macedonia [ˌmæsɪˈdəʊnɪə] *n* Macedônia; **in ~** na Macedônia.

Macedonian [ˌmæsɪˈdəʊnɪən] <> *adj* macedônico(ca). <> *n* macedônico *m*, -ca *f.*

machete [məˈʃetɪ] *n* machete *m.*

Machiavellian [ˌmækɪəˈvelɪən] *adj* maquiavélico(ca).

machinations [ˌmækɪˈneɪʃnz] *npl* maquinações *fpl.*

machine [məˈʃiːn] <> *n* máquina *f.* <> *vt* **-1.** SEWING costurar à maquina **-2.** TECH usinar.

machine code *n* COMPUT código *m* de máquina.

machinegun [məˈʃiːngʌn] *(pt & pp* -ned, *cont* -ning) <> *n* metralhadora *f.* <> *vt* metralhar.

machine language *n* COMPUT linguagem *f* de máquina.

machine-readable *adj* COMPUT legível por máquina.

machinery [məˈʃiːnərɪ] *n (U)* **-1.** [machines] maquinário *m* **-2.** *fig* [system] mecanismo *m.*

machine shop *n* oficina *f* de máquinas.

machine tool *n* máquina *f* operatriz.

machine-washable *adj* lavável à máquina.

machinist [mə'ʃiːnɪst] *n* operador *m*, -ra *f* de máquina.

machismo [mə'tʃɪzməʊ] *n (U)* machismo *m*.

macho ['mætʃəʊ] *adj inf* machista.

mackerel ['mækrəl] (*pl inv OR* **-s**) *n* cavala *f*.

mackintosh ['mækɪntɒʃ] *n UK* capa *f* de chuva.

macramé [mə'krɑːmi] *n (U)* macramé *m*.

macro ['mækrəʊ] *n COMPUT* macro *f*.

macrobiotic [ˌmækrəʊbaɪ'ɒtɪk] *adj* macrobiótico(-ca).

macrocosm ['mækrəʊkɒzml] *n* macrocosmo *m*.

macroeconomics ['mækrəʊˌiːkə'nɒmɪks] *n (U)* macroeconomia *f*.

mad [mæd] (*compar* **-der**, *superl* **-dest**) *adj* **-1.** [insane] louco(ca); **to go ~** enlouquecer **-2.** *pej* [foolish] maluco(ca) **-3.** [furious] doido(da); **to go ~ at sb** ficar louco(ca) com alguém **-4.** [hectic] exaspera-do(da); **like ~** feito louco(ca) **-5.** [very enthusiastic]: **to be ~ about sb/sthg** ser louco(ca) por alguém/algo.

Madagascan [ˌmædə'gæskən] *adj* malgaxe. *n* **-1.** [person] malgaxe *mf* **-2.** [language] malgaxe *m*.

Madagascar [ˌmædə'gæskəʳ] *n* Madagascar; **in ~** em Madagascar.

madam ['mædəm] *n fml* [form of address] senhora *f*.

madcap ['mædkæp] *adj* doido(da).

madden ['mædn] *vt* enfurecer, exasperar.

maddening ['mædnɪŋ] *adj* enlouquecedor(ra).

made [meɪd] *pt & pp* ⇒ **make**.

-made [məɪd] *suffix:* French ~ feito(ta) na França.

Madeira [mə'dɪərə] *n* **-1.** *(U)* [wine] madeira *m* **-2.** *GEOGR* Ilha *f* da Madeira; **in ~** na Ilha da Madeira.

made-to-measure *adj* feito(ta) sob medida.

made-up *adj* **-1.** [with make-up] maquiado(da) **-2.** [prepared] já preparado(da) **-3.** [invented] falso(sa), esfarrapado(da).

madhouse ['mædhaʊs, *pl* -haʊzɪz] *n fig inf* hospício *m*.

madly ['mædlɪ] *adv* [frantically] alucinadamente; **~ in love** loucamente apaixonado(da).

madman ['mædmən] (*pl* **-men** [-mən]) *n* louco *m*.

madness ['mædnɪs] *n (U)* loucura *f*.

Madonna [mə'dɒnə] *n* **-1.** *RELIG:* **the ~** a Nossa Senhora **-2.** *ART* madona *f*.

Madrid [mə'drɪd] *n* Madrid; **in ~** em Madrid.

madrigal ['mædrɪgl] *n* madrigal *m*.

madwoman ['mædˌwʊmən] (*pl* **-women** [-ˌwɪmɪn]) *n* louca *f*.

maestro ['maɪstrəʊ] (*pl* **-tros** *OR* **-tri** [-trɪ]) *n* maestro *m*.

MAFF (*abbr of* **Ministry of Agriculture, Fisheries, and Food**) *n ministério britânico da agricultura, da pesca e dos alimentos,* ≃ Ministério *m* da Agricultura.

Mafia ['mæfɪə] *n:* **the ~** a Máfia.

mag [mæg] (*abbr of* **magazine**) *n inf* revista *f*.

magazine [ˌmægə'ziːn] *n* **-1.** [periodical] revista *f* **-2.** [news programme] programa *m* de variedades **-3.** [on a gun] câmara *f*.

magenta [mə'dʒentə] *adj* magenta. *n (U)* magenta *m*.

maggot ['mægət] *n* larva *f*.

Maghreb ['mʌɡreb] *n:* **the ~** o Magrebe.

magic ['mædʒɪk] *adj* **-1.** [gen] mágico(ca) **-2.** [referring to conjuring] de mágica. *n (U)* **-1.** [gen] magia *f* **-2.** [conjuring] mágica *f*.

magical ['mædʒɪkl] *adj* [using sorcery] mágico(ca).

magic carpet *n* tapete *m* mágico.

magic eye *n UK* olho *m* mágico.

magician [mə'dʒɪʃn] *n* **-1.** [conjurer] mágico *m*, -ca *f* **-2.** [wizard] mago *m*, -ga *f*.

magic wand *n* varinha *f* mágica.

magisterial [ˌmædʒɪ'stɪərɪəl] *adj* **-1.** *fml* [authoritative] dominador(ra) **-2.** *JUR* magistral.

magistrate ['mædʒɪstreɪt] *n* magistrado *m*, -da *f*.

magistrates' court *n UK* tribunal *m*.

Magna Carta [ˌmægnə'kɑːtə] *n:* **the ~** a Carta Magna.

magnanimous [mæg'nænɪməs] *adj* magnânimo(-ma).

magnate ['mægneɪt] *n* magnata *mf*.

magnesium [mæg'niːzɪəm] *n (U)* magnésio *m*.

magnet ['mægnɪt] *n* **-1.** *PHYSICS* ímã *m* **-2.** *fig* [attraction] atrativo *m*.

magnetic [mæg'netɪk] *adj* **-1.** *PHYSICS* magnético(ca) **-2.** *fig* [personality] atraente, carismático(ca).

magnetic disk *n* disco *m* magnético.

magnetic field *n* campo *m* magnético.

magnetic tape *n (U)* fita *f* magnética.

magnetism ['mægnɪtɪzm] *n (U)* magnetismo *m*.

magnification [ˌmægnɪfɪ'keɪʃn] *n (U)* **-1.** [process] ampliação *f* **-2.** [degree of enlargement] aumento *m*.

magnificence [mæg'nɪfɪsəns] *n (U)* magnificência *f*.

magnificent [mæg'nɪfɪsənt] *adj* **-1.** [clothes, splendour, building] grandioso(sa) **-2.** [idea, book, game] magnífico(ca), brilhante.

magnify ['mægnɪfaɪ] (*pt & pp* **-ied**) *vt* **-1.** [TECH - image] ampliar; [- sound] amplificar **-2.** *fig* [exaggerate] exagerar.

magnifying glass ['mægnɪfaɪɪŋ-] *n* lupa *f*, lente *f* de aumento.

magnitude ['mægnɪtjuːd] *n* magnitude *f*.

magnolia [mæg'nəʊljə] *n* **-1.** [tree, flower] magnólia *f* **-2.** [colour] creme *m*.

magnum ['mægnəm] (*pl* **-s**) *n* garrafa *f* de 1,5 *litro de capacidade.*

magpie ['mægpaɪ] *n* pega *f* (*ave*).

maharaja(h) [ˌmɑːhə'rɑːdʒə] *n* marajá *m*.

mahogany [mə'hɒgənɪ] *n* mogno *m*.

maid [meɪd] *n* [servant] empregada *f* doméstica.

maiden ['meɪdn] *adj* [voyage, speech] de estréia, inaugural. *n literary* [young girl] donzela *f*; [virgin] virgem *f*.

maiden aunt *n* tia *f* solteirona.

maiden name *n* nome *m* de solteira.

maiden speech *n POL* discurso *m* inaugural.

mail [meɪl] *n* **-1.** [letters, parcels] correio *m*; **by ~** pelo correio **-2.** [system] correios *mpl*. *vt* **-1.** [send] mandar pelo correio **-2.** [put in mail box] postar.

mailbag ['meɪlbæg] *n* sacola *f* do carteiro.

mailbox ['meɪlbɒks] *n* **-1.** *US* [for letters] caixa *f* de correio **-2.** *COMPUT* caixa *f* de entrada.

mailing list ['meɪlɪŋ-] *n* lista *f* de endereços.

mailman ['meɪlmən] (*pl* -men [-mən]) *n US* carteiro *m*.

mail order *n* (*U*) pedido *m* por reembolso postal.

mailshot ['meɪlʃɒt] *n* mala-direta *f*.

mail train *n* trem-correio *m*, trem *m* postal.

mail truck *n US* caminhão *m* dos correios.

mail van *n* [for delivering mail - by road] carro-correio *m*; [- by rail] vagão-correio *m*.

maim [meɪm] *vt* mutilar.

main [meɪn] ⬦ *adj* principal. ⬦ *n* [pipe] tubulação *f*.
➤ **mains** *npl*: the ~ s [gas, water] as tubulações; [electric] a rede elétrica.
➤ **in the main** *adv* em geral.

main course *n* prato *m* principal.

Maine [meɪn] *n* Maine; **in** ~ em Maine.

mainframe (computer) ['meɪnfreɪm-] *n* computador *m* mainframe.

mainland ['meɪnlənd] ⬦ *adj* continental. ⬦ *n*: **the** ~ o continente.

main line *n RAIL* linha-tronco *f*.
➤ **mainline** ⬦ *adj* [train, station] de linha-tronco. ⬦ *vt &vi* **drugs** *sl* injetar-se na veia.

mainly ['meɪnlɪ] *adv* principalmente.

main road *n* rodovia *f* principal.

mainsail ['meɪnseɪl] *n* vela-mestra *f*.

mainstay ['meɪnsteɪ] *n* meio *m* de subsistência.

mainstream ['meɪnstriːm] ⬦ *adj* predominante. ⬦ *n*: the ~ a tendência geral.

maintain [meɪn'teɪn] *vt* -**1.** [gen] manter -**2.** [support, provide for] sustentar, manter -**3.** [look after] manter em bom estado -**4.** [assert]: **to** ~ **(that)** sustentar que.

maintenance ['meɪntənəns] *n* (*U*) -**1.** [gen] manutenção *f* -**2.** [money] pensão *f*.

maintenance order *n UK JUR* obrigação *f* de pensão alimentícia.

maisonette [ˌmeɪzə'net] *n* duplex *m inv*.

maize [meɪz] *n* (*U*) milho *m*.

Maj. (*abbr of* **Major**) Maj.

majestic [mə'dʒestɪk] *adj* majestoso(sa).

majestically [mə'dʒestɪklɪ] *adv* majestosamente.

majesty ['mædʒəstɪ] (*pl* -ies) *n* [grandeur] majestade *f*.
➤ **Majesty** *n*: **His** OR **Her/Your Majesty** Sua/Vossa Majestade.

major ['meɪdʒəʳ] ⬦ *adj* -**1.** [gen] principal -**2.** MUS maior. ⬦ *n* [MIL - in army] major *m*; [- in air force] major-aviador *m*. ⬦ *vi US UNIV*: **to** ~ **in sthg** especializar-se em algo.

Majorca [mə'jɔːkə, mə'dʒɔːkə] *n* Maiorca; **in** ~ em Maiorca.

Majorcan [mə'jɔːkən, mə'dʒɔːkən] ⬦ *adj* maiorquino(na). ⬦ *n* maiorquino *m*, -na *f*.

majorette [ˌmeɪdʒə'ret] *n* baliza *f*.

major general *n* general-de-divisão *m*.

majority [mə'dʒɒrətɪ] (*pl* -ies) *n* maioria *f*; **in a** OR **the** ~ na maioria; **age of** ~ maioridade *f*.

majority shareholder *n* acionista *mf* majoritário, -ria.

major road *n* estrada *f* principal.

make [meɪk] (*pt & pp* made) *vt* -**1.** [produce, manufacture] fazer; **to be made of** ser feito de; **to** ~ **lunch/dinner** fazer o almoço/jantar; **made in Japan** fabricado no Japão. -**2.** [perform, do] fazer; **to** ~ **a mistake** cometer um erro, enganar-se; **to** ~ **a phone call** dar um telefonema. -**3.** [cause to be] tornar; **to** ~ **sthg better** melhorar algo; **to** ~ **sb happy** fazer alguém feliz; **to** ~ **sthg safer** tornar algo mais seguro. -**4.** [cause to do, force] fazer; **to** ~ **sb do sthg** obrigar alguém a fazer algo; **it made her laugh** isso a fez rir. -**5.** [amount to, total] ser; **that** ~ s **$5** são 5 dólares. -**6.** [calculate]: **I** ~ **it seven o'clock** calculo que sejam sete horas; **I** ~ **it $4** segundo os meus cálculos são 4 dólares. -**7.** [profit, loss] ter. -**8.** *inf* [arrive in time for]: **we didn't** ~ **the 10 o'clock train** não conseguimos apanhar o trem das 10. -**9.** [friend, enemy] fazer. -**10.** [have qualities for] dar; **this would** ~ **a lovely bedroom** isto dava um lindo quarto. -**11.** [bed] fazer. -**12.** [in phrases]: **to** ~ **do** contentar-se; [damage] reparar; **to** ~ **it** [arrive on time] conseguir chegar a tempo; [be able to go] poder ir; [survive a crisis] recuperar-se. ⬦ ~ **it** [of product] marca *f*.
➤ **make out** *vt sep* [check, receipt] passar; [form] preencher; [see] distinguir; [hear] perceber, entender.
➤ **make up** *vt sep* [invent] inventar; [comprise] constituir; [difference, extra] cobrir.
➤ **make up for** *vt fus* compensar.

make-believe *n* (*U*) faz-de-conta *m*.

makeover ['meɪkəʊvəʳ] *n* -**1.** [for person] tratamento *m* -**2.** [for company] aperfeiçoamento *m*.

maker ['meɪkəʳ] *n* -**1.** [of film] produtor *m*, -ra *f* -**2.** [of product] fabricante *mf*.

makeshift ['meɪkʃɪft] *adj* -**1.** [temporary] provisório(ria) -**2.** [improvised] improvisado(da).

make-up *n* (*U*) -**1.** [cosmetics] maquiagem *f*; ~ **bag** nécessaire *m*; ~ **remover** removedor *m* de maquiagem -**2.** [person's character] caráter *m* -**3.** [composition] composição *f*.

makeweight *n* contrapeso *m*.

making ['meɪkɪŋ] *n* [of cake] fabricação *f*; [of film] produção *f*; **in the** ~ em desenvolvimento; **this is history in the** ~ isto passará para a história; **your problems are of your own** ~ teus problemas são todos coisas da tua cabeça; **to be the** ~ **of sb/sthg** ser a causa do êxito de alguém/algo; **you have the** ~ s **of a diplomat** você tem tudo para ser um diplomata.

maladjusted [ˌmælə'dʒʌstɪd] *adj* desajustado(da).

malaise [mə'leɪz] *n* (*U*) *fml* [unease] mal-estar *m*.

malaria [mə'leərɪə] *n* (*U*) malária *f*.

Malawi [mə'lɑːwɪ] Maláui; **in** ~ no Maláui.

Malawian [mə'lɑːwɪən] ⬦ *adj* malauiano(na). ⬦ *n* malauiano *m*, -na *f*.

Malay [mə'leɪ] ⬦ *adj* malaio(ia). ⬦ *n* -**1.** [person] malaio *m*, -ia *f* -**2.** [language] malaio *m*.

Malaya [mə'leɪə] *n* Malásia; **in** ~ na Malásia.

Malayan [mə'leɪən] ⬦ *adj* malaio(ia). ⬦ *n* malaio *m*, -ia *f*.

Malaysia [mə'leɪzɪə] *n* Malásia; **in** ~ na Malásia.

Malaysian [mə'leɪzɪən] ⬦ *adj* malaio(ia). ⬦ *n* malaio *m*, -ia *f*.

malcontent *n fml* descontente *mf*.

Maldives ['mɔːldɪvz] *npl*: **the** ~ as Maldivas; **in the** ~ nas Maldivas.

male [meɪl] <> adj -**1.** [animal] macho; ~ **kangaroo** canguru m macho -**2.** [human] masculino(na) -**3.** [concerning men] do homem, masculino(na). <> n -**1.** [animal] macho m-**2.** [human] homem m.

male chauvinist (pig) n pej porco m chauvinista.

male nurse n enfermeiro m.

malevolent [mə'levələnt] adj malévolo(la).

malformed [mæl'fɔːmd] adj malformado(da).

malfunction [mæl'fʌŋkʃn] <> n mau funcionamento m. <> vi funcionar mal.

Mali ['mɑːlɪ] n Mali; **in** ~ em Mali.

malice ['mælɪs] n (U) malícia f.

malicious [mə'lɪʃəs] adj malicioso(sa).

malign [mə'laɪn] <> adj maligno(na). <> vt difamar, falar mal de.

malignant [mə'lɪgnənt] adj -**1.** [full of hate] malvado(da) -**2.** MED maligno(na).

malinger [mə'lɪŋgəʳ] vi pej fazer-se de doente.

malingerer [mə'lɪŋgərəʳ] n pej doente mf fingido, -da.

mall [mɔːl] n esp US: **(shopping)** ~ shopping m (center).

mallard n marreco m.

malleable ['mælɪəbl] adj -**1.** [easily influenced] influenciável -**2.** [that can be shaped] maleável.

mallet ['mælɪt] n [hammer] marreta f.

malnourished [mæl'nʌrɪʃt] adj subnutrido(da).

malnutrition [mælnjuː'trɪʃn] n (U) subnutrição f.

malpractice [mæl'præktɪs] n (U) JUR falta f profissional.

malt [mɔːlt] n -**1.** (U) [grain] malte m -**2.** [whisky] uísque m de malta.

Malta ['mɔːltə] n Malta; **in** ~ em Malta.

Maltese [mɔːl'tiːz] (pl inv) <> adj maltês(esa). <> n -**1.** [person] maltês m, -esa f-**2.** [language] maltês m.

maltreat [mæl'triːt] vt maltratar.

maltreatment [mæl'triːtmənt] n (U) maus-tratos mpl.

malt whisky n uísque m de malte.

mammal ['mæml] n mamífero m.

Mammon n fig riqueza f maléfica.

mammoth ['mæməθ] <> adj gigantesco(ca), descomunal. <> n mamute m.

man [mæn] (pl **men**, pt & pp -**ned**, cont -**ning**) <> n -**1.** [gen] homem m; **the** ~ **in the street** o homem comum; **to talk** ~ **to** ~ conversar de homem para homem; **to be** ~ **enough to do sthg** ser homem suficiente para fazer algo -**2.** [as form of address] cara m. <> vt -**1.** [ship, plane] tripular -**2.** [machine, switchboard, telephone] manejar.

manacles ['mænəklz] npl algemas fpl.

manage ['mænɪdʒ] <> vi -**1.** [cope] arranjar-se -**2.** [financially] virar-se. <> vt -**1.** [be responsible for, control - organization, business] dirigir, gerenciar; [- money] administrar; [- another person] representar; [- time] organizar -**2.** [succeed]: **to** ~ **to do sthg** conseguir fazer algo -**2.** [be available for]: **I can only** ~ **an hour tonight** eu só disponho de uma hora esta noite.

manageable ['mænɪdʒəbl] adj -**1.** [hair, inflation] controlável -**2.** [children] dominável -**3.** [task, operation] viável.

management ['mænɪdʒmənt] n -**1.** (U) [control, running] administração f, gestão f-**2.** [people in control] gerência f, direção f.

management consultant n assessor m, -ra f de administração.

manager ['mænɪdʒəʳ] n -**1.** [of organization] gerente mf, diretor m, -ra f-**2.** [of popstar] empresário m, -ria f-**3.** SPORT treinador m, -ra f.

manageress [mænɪdʒə'res] n UK gerente f.

managerial [mænɪ'dʒɪərɪəl] adj gerencial.

managing director ['mænɪdʒɪŋ-] n diretorgerente m, diretora-gerente f.

Managua [mə'nægwə] n Manágua; **in** ~ em Manágua.

Mancunian [mæŋ'kjuːnjən] <> adj manchesteriano(na). <> n [person] manchesteriano m, -na f.

mandarin ['mændərɪn] n -**1.** [fruit] tangerina f-**2.** [civil servant] mandarim m, -na f.

mandate ['mændeɪt] n -**1.** [elected right or authority] mandato m-**2.** [task] incumbência f, missão f.

mandatory ['mændətrɪ] adj obrigatório(ria).

mandolin ['mændəlɪn] n bandolim m.

mane [meɪn] n -**1.** [of horse] crina f-**2.** [of lion] juba f.

man-eating [-iːtɪŋ] adj antropófago(ga).

maneuver US = manoeuvre.

manfully ['mænfʊlɪ] adv valentemente.

manganese n (U) manganês m.

mange [meɪndʒ] n (U) sarna f.

manger ['meɪndʒəʳ] n manjedoura f.

mangetout (pea) [mɑːʒ'tuː-] n UK ervilha-torta f.

mangle ['mæŋgl] vt -**1.** [body, car] destroçar -**2.** fig [text] assassinar.

mango ['mæŋgəʊ] (pl -es OR -s) n manga f.

mangrove ['mæŋgrəʊv] n mangue m.

mangy ['meɪndʒɪ] (compar -**ier**, superl -**iest**) adj sarnento(ta).

manhandle ['mæn hændl] vt maltratar.

manhole ['mænhəʊl] n poço m de inspeção, boca-de-lobo m.

manhood ['mænhʊd] n (U) -**1.** [age] idade f adulta -**2.** [virility] virilidade f.

man-hour n hora-homem f.

manhunt ['mænhʌnt] n perseguição f (a um criminoso).

mania ['meɪnjə] n -**1.** (U) PSYCH mania f-**2.** [excessive liking]: ~ **(for sthg)** gosto m excessivo (por algo).

maniac ['meɪnɪæk] n -**1.** [madman] maníaco m, -ca f -**2.** [fanatic] fanático m, -ca f.

manic ['mænɪk] adj -**1.** [overexcited] doido(da) -**2.** PSYCH maníaco(ca).

manic-depressive <> adj maníaco-depressivo(va). <> n maníaco-depressivo m, -va f.

manicure ['mænɪkjʊəʳ] <> n [individual treatment]: **to give sb a** ~ fazer as unhas de alguém. <> vt: **to** ~ **one's nails** fazer as unhas.

manifest ['mænɪfest] fml <> adj manifesto(ta). <> vt manifestar.

manifestation [mænɪfes'teɪʃn] n fml manifestação f.

manifestly ['mænɪfestlɪ] adv fml evidentemente, claramente.

manifesto [ˌmænɪˈfestəʊ] (*pl* -s OR -es) *n* manifesto *m*.

manifold [ˈmænɪfəʊld] <> *adj literary* múltiplo(-pla). <> *n* AUT coletor *m*; **exhaust** ~ cano *m* de descarga.

manila *adj* de papel manilha.

Manila [məˈnɪlə] *n* Manila; **in** ~ em Manila.

manilla [məˈnɪlə] *adj* = manila.

manipulate [məˈnɪpjʊleɪt] *vt* - **1.** [control for personal benefit] manipular - **2.** [operate - machine, controls] operar; [- lever] acionar.

manipulation [məˌnɪpjʊˈleɪʃn] *n* (U) - **1.** [control for personal benefit] manipulação *f* - **2.** [operation - of machine, controls] operação *f*; [- of lever] acionamento *m*.

manipulative [məˈnɪpjʊlətɪv] *adj* manipulador(-ra).

Manitoba [ˌmænɪˈtəʊbə] *n* Manitoba; **in** ~ em Manitoba.

mankind [mænˈkaɪnd] *n* (U) humanidade *f*.

manly [ˈmænlɪ] (*compar* -ier, *superl* -iest) *adj* másculo(la), viril.

man-made *adj* - **1.** [problem, disaster] produzido(-da) pelo homem - **2.** [fibre, environment] artificial.

manna [ˈmænə] *n* (U) maná *m*.

manned [mænd] *adj* tripulado(da).

mannequin [ˈmænɪkɪn] *n* [dummy] manequim *m*.

manner [ˈmænəʳ] *n* - **1.** [method] maneira *f*, forma *f*; **in a** ~ **of speaking** por assim dizer - **2.** [bearing, attitude] jeito *m*, comportamento *m* - **3.** *literary* [type, sort]: **all** ~ **of** todos os tipos de.

➡ **manners** *npl* maneiras *fpl*; **to be good/bad** ~s **to do sthg** ser de boa/má educação fazer algo.

mannered [ˈmænəd] *adj fml* afetado(da).

mannerism [ˈmænərɪzm] *n* trejeito *m*.

mannish [ˈmænɪʃ] *adj* [woman] masculino(na).

manoeuvrable UK, **maneuverable** US [məˈnuːvrəbl] *adj* manobrável.

manoeuvre UK, **maneuver** US [məˈnuːvəʳ] <> *n* - **1.** [movement] manobra *f* - **2.** *fig* [clever move] manobra *f*. <> *vt* [control physically] manobrar, manejar. <> *vi* [move physically] manobrar.

➡ **manoeuvres** *npl* MIL manobras *fpl*.

manor [ˈmænəʳ] *n* [house] solar *m*.

manpower [ˈmænˌpaʊəʳ] *n* (U) mão-de-obra *f*.

manservant [ˈmænsɜːvənt] (*pl* **menservants**) *n* dated criado *m*.

mansion [ˈmænʃn] *n* mansão *f*.

man-size(d) *adj* de tamanho extragrande.

manslaughter [ˈmænˌslɔːtəʳ] *n* (U) homicídio *m* involuntário.

mantelpiece [ˈmæntlpiːs] *n* consolo *m* de lareira.

mantle [ˈmæntl] *n* - **1.** [layer, covering] camada *f* - **2.** [of leadership, high office] posição *f* (de comando).

man-to-man *adj* de homem para homem.

manual [ˈmænjʊəl] <> *adj* manual. <> *n* [handbook] manual *m*.

manually [ˈmænjʊəlɪ] *adv* manualmente.

manual worker *n* operário *m*, -ria *f*.

manufacture [ˌmænjʊˈfæktʃəʳ] <> *n* (U) manufatura *f*, fabricação *f*. <> *vt* - **1.** [make] manufaturar, fabricar - **2.** [invent] inventar.

manufacturer [ˌmænjʊˈfæktʃərəʳ] *n* fabricante *mf*.

manufacturing [ˌmænjʊˈfæktʃərɪŋ] *n* (U) manufatura *f*, fabricação *f*.

manufacturing industries *npl* indústrias *fpl* manufatureiras.

manure [məˈnjʊəʳ] *n* (U) esterco *m*.

manuscript [ˈmænjʊskrɪpt] *n* manuscrito *m*.

Manx [mæŋks] <> *adj* manx. <> *n* [language] manx *m*.

many [ˈmenɪ] (*compar* **more**, *superl* **most**) <> *adj* [a lot of, plenty of] muitos(tas); ~ **people** muitas pessoas, muita gente; **how** ~ ...? quantos(tas) ...?; **too** ~ ... demais; **there are too** ~ **books for me to read** há livros demais para eu ler; **as** ~ ... **as** tantos ... quantos, tantas ... quantas; **bring as** ~ **cups as you can** traga tantas xícaras quantas você puder; **so** ~ ... tantos(tas) ...; **a good** OR **great** ~ ... muitíssimos(mas) ..., um grande número de ... <> *pron* [a lot, plenty] muitos(tas); **how** ~? quantos(tas)?; **too** ~ muitos(tas); **as** ~ **as** tantos(-tas) quanto; **so** ~ tantos(tas); **a good** OR **great** ~ muitos(tas), um grande número.

Maori [ˈmaʊrɪ] <> *adj* maori. <> *n* maori *mf*.

map [mæp] (*pt* & *pp* -ped, *cont* -ping) <> *n* mapa *m*; **to put sb/sthg on the** ~ colocar alguém/algo no mapa. <> *vt* - **1.** [chart] fazer o mapa de - **2.** COMPUT associar.

➡ **map out** *vt sep* planejar, planificar.

maple [ˈmeɪpl] *n* bordo *m*.

maple leaf *n* folha *f* de bordo.

maple syrup *n* (U) xarope *m* de bordo.

Maputo [məˈpuːtəʊ] *n* Maputo; **in** ~ em Maputo.

mar [mɑːʳ] (*pt* & *pp* -red, *cont* -ring) *vt* prejudicar, frustrar.

Mar. (*abbr of* **March**) mar.

marathon [ˈmærəθn] <> *adj* exaustivo(va). <> *n* maratona *f*.

marathon runner *n* maratonista *mf*.

marauder [məˈrɔːdəʳ] *n* gatuno *m*, -na *f*, saqueador *m*, -ra *f*.

marauding [məˈrɔːdɪŋ] *adj* saqueador(ra).

marble [ˈmɑːbl] *n* - **1.** (U) [stone] mármore *m* - **2.** [for game] bolita *f* de gude.

➡ **marbles** *n* (U) [game] jogo *m* de gude.

march [mɑːtʃ] <> *n* - **1.** [gen] marcha *f* - **2.** [steady progress] avanço *m*. <> *vi* - **1.** [gen] marchar - **2.** [approach] avançar. <> *vt* conduzir, levar à força.

March [mɑːtʃ] *n* março *m*; *see also* **September**.

marcher [ˈmɑːtʃəʳ] *n* [protester] manifestante *mf*.

marching orders [ˈmɑːtʃɪŋ-] *npl*: **to give sb his** ~ mandar alguém passear, dar cartão vermelho para alguém.

marchioness [ˈmɑːʃənes] *n* [aristocrat] marquesa *f*.

march-past *n* parada *f*.

Mardi Gras [ˌmɑːdɪˈgrɑː] *n* Terça-Feira *f* de Carnaval.

mare [meəʳ] *n* égua *f*.

marg. (*abbr of* **margarine**) *n inf* margarina *f*.

margarine [ˌmɑːdʒəˈriːn, ˌmɑːgəˈriːn] *n* (U) margarina *f*.

marge [mɑːdʒ] *n* (U) *inf* margarina *f*.

margin [ˈmɑːdʒɪn] *n* - **1.** [gen] margem *f* - **2.** [of desert, forest] limite *m*.

marginal ['mɑːdʒɪnl] *adj* **-1.** [unimportant] secundá-rio(ria) **-2.** *UK POL*: ~ seat *OR* **constituency** *cadeira f ganha por uma pequena maioria de votos.*

marginally ['mɑːdʒɪnəlɪ] *adv* ligeiramente.

marigold ['mærɪgəʊld] *n* calêndula *f.*

marihuana, marijuana [ˌmærɪ'wɑːnə] *n (U)* maconha *f.*

marina [mə'riːnə] *n* marina *f.*

marinade [ˌmærɪ'neɪd] <> *n* marinada *f.* <> *vt & vi* = **marinate.**

marinate ['mærɪneɪt] <> *vt* marinar. <> *vi* ficar em marinada.

marine [mə'riːn] <> *adj* **-1.** [underwater] marinho(-nha) **-2.** [seafaring] marítimo(ma). <> *n MIL* fuzileiro *m* naval.

marionette [ˌmærɪə'net] *n* marionete *f.*

marital ['mærɪtl] *adj* conjugal.

marital status *n* estado *m* civil.

maritime ['mærɪtaɪm] *adj* marítimo(ma).

Maritime Provinces, Maritimes *npl*: **the** ~ as Províncias Marítimas.

marjoram ['mɑːdʒərəm] *n (U)* manjerona *f.*

mark [mɑːk] <> *n* **-1.** [stain] mancha *f*; [scratch] marca *f* **-2.** [in exam] nota *f* **-3.** [stage, level]: **the half-way** ~ o meio caminho; **beyond the billion** ~ acima de um bilhão **-4.** [sign, indication] sinal *f* **-5.** [currency] marco *m* **-6.** *CULIN* nível *m* de temperatura **-7.** *phr*: **to make one's** ~ deixar a marca; **to be quick/slow off the** ~ reagir rapidamente/lenta-mente; **wide of the** ~ longe da verdade. <> *vt* **-1.** [gen] marcar **-2.** [exam, essay] corrigir **-3.** [com-memorate] comemorar, celebrar **-4.** [stain] man-char.

  ◆ **mark down** *vt sep* **-1.** [*COMM* - prices] rebaixar; [- goods] baixar o preço de **-2.** [downgrade] baixar a nota de.

  ◆ **mark off** *vt sep* [cross off] assinalar.

  ◆ **mark up** *vt sep* [*COMM* - prices] aumentar; [- goods] remarcar.

marked [mɑːkt] *adj* [noticeable] notável.

markedly ['mɑːkɪdlɪ] *adv* [noticeably] notavelmente.

marker ['mɑːkəʳ] *n* **-1.** [sign] indicador *m* **-2.** *SPORT* marcador *m* **-3.** [of exam] avaliador *m*, -ra *f.*

marker pen *n* caneta *f* marcadora.

market ['mɑːkɪt] <> *n* [gen] mercado *m*; **on the** ~ à venda. <> *vt* comercializar, vender. <> *vi US* [shop]: **to go** ~**ing** ir às compras.

marketable ['mɑːkɪtəbl] *adj* vendável, comercia-lizável.

market analysis *n (U)* análise *f* de mercado.

market day *n* dia *f* da feira.

market forces *npl COMM* tendências *fpl* do mercado.

market garden *n esp UK* horta *f.*

marketing ['mɑːkɪtɪŋ] *n (U) COMM* marketing *m.*

marketplace ['mɑːkɪtpleɪs] *n* mercado *m.*

market price *n COMM* preço *m* de mercado.

market research *n (U)* pesquisa *f* de mercado.

market town *n* cidade *f* com feira livre.

market value *n COMM* valor *m* de mercado.

marking ['mɑːkɪŋ] *n (U) SCH & UNIV* correção *f.*

  ◆ **markings** *npl* **-1.** [of flower] manchas *fpl* **-2.** [of animal] pintas *fpl* **-3.** [of road] sinais *mpl.*

marksman ['mɑːksmən] (*pl* -men [-mən]) *n* atirador *m.*

marksmanship ['mɑːksmənʃɪp] *n (U)* pontaria *f.*

markup ['mɑːkʌp] *n* margem *m* de lucro.

marmalade ['mɑːməleɪd] *n (U)* geléia *f.*

maroon [mə'ruːn] *adj* de cor castanho-averme-lhado.

marooned [mə'ruːnd] *adj* abandonado(da).

marquee [mɑː'kiː] *n* toldo *m.*

marquess ['mɑːkwɪs] *n* = **marquis.**

marquetry *n (U)* marchetaria *f.*

marquis ['mɑːkwɪs] *n* marquês *m.*

marriage ['mærɪdʒ] *n* casamento *m.*

marriage bureau *n UK* agência *f* matrimonial.

marriage certificate *n* certidão *m* de casa-mento.

marriage guidance *n (U)* orientação *f* para casais.

marriage guidance counsellor *n* terapeuta *mf* para casais.

married ['mærɪd] *adj* **-1.** [having a spouse] casado(da) **-2.** [of marriage] de casado.

marrow ['mærəʊ] *n* **-1.** *UK* [vegetable] abóbora *f* **-2.** *(U)* [in bones] medula *f.*

marry ['mærɪ] (*pt & pp* -ied) <> *vt* casar; **will you** ~ **me?** quer se casar comigo? <> *vi* [get married] casar-se.

Mars [mɑːz] *n* [planet] Marte.

marsh [mɑːʃ] *n* pântano *m.*

marshal ['mɑːʃl] (*UK pt & pp* -led, *cont* -ling, *US pt & pp* -ed, *cont* -ing) <> *n* **-1.** *MIL* marechal *m* **-2.** [assis-tant] oficial *m* **-3.** *US* [law officer] oficial *mf* de justiça. <> *vt* **-1.** [people] dirigir, conduzir **-2.** [support, thoughts] ordenar, organizar.

marshalling yard ['mɑːʃlɪŋ-] *n* pátio *m* ferroviá-rio.

marshland ['mɑːʃlænd] *n (U)* pantanal *m.*

marshmallow [*UK* ˌmɑːʃ'mæləʊ, *US* 'mɑːrʃˌmeləʊ] *n* **-1.** [sweet] marshmallow *m* **-2.** *(U)* [substance] de marshmallow.

marshy ['mɑːʃɪ] (*compar* -ier, *superl* -iest) *adj* panta-noso(sa).

marsupial [mɑː'suːpjəl] *n* marsupial *m.*

martial ['mɑːʃl] *adj* marcial.

martial arts [ˌmɑːʃl-] *npl* artes *fpl* marciais.

martial law [ˌmɑːʃl-] *n (U)* lei *f* marcial.

Martian ['mɑːʃn] <> *adj* marciano(na). <> *n* marciano *m*, -na *f.*

martin ['mɑːtɪn] *n* martinete *m.*

martini [mɑː'tiːnɪ] *n* [cocktail] martini *m.*

Martinique [ˌmɑːtɪ'niːk] *n* Martinica; **in** ~ na Martinica.

martyr ['mɑːtəʳ] *n* mártir *mf.*

martyrdom ['mɑːtədəm] *n (U)* martírio *m.*

martyred ['mɑːtəd] *adj* martirizado(da).

marvel ['mɑːvl] (*UK pt & pp* -led, *cont* -ling, *US pt & pp* -ed, *cont* -ing) <> *n* **-1.** [sur-prise, miracle] milagre *m.* <> *vt*: **to** ~ **that** admirar--se que. <> *vi*: **to** ~ **(at sthg)** maravilhar-se (com algo).

marvellous *UK*, **marvelous** *US* ['mɑːvələs] *adj* maravilhoso(sa).

Marxism ['mɑːksɪzm] *n (U)* marxismo *m.*

Marxist [ˈmɑːksɪst] ◇ *adj* marxista. ◇ *n* marxista *mf*.

Maryland [ˈmeərɪlænd] *n* Maryland; **in** ~ em Maryland.

marzipan [ˈmɑːzɪpæn] *n (U)* maçapão *m*.

mascara [mæsˈkɑːrə] *n (U)* rímel *m*.

mascot [ˈmæskət] *n* mascote *f*.

masculine [ˈmæskjʊlɪn] *adj* masculino(na).

masculinity [ˌmæskjʊˈlɪnətɪ] *n (U)* masculinidade *f*.

mash [mæʃ] *vt* triturar, amassar.

MASH [mæʃ] (*abbr of* **mobile army surgical hospital**) *n hospital militar de campanha norte-americano*.

mashed potatoes [mæʃt-] *npl* purê *m* de batatas.

mask [mɑːsk] ◇ *n* -**1.** [covering face] máscara *f* -**2.** *fig* [dissimulation] máscara *f*. ◇ *vt* -**1.** [cover] mascarar -**2.** [conceal] disfarçar.

masked [mɑːskt] *adj* [face, man] mascarado(da).

masking tape [ˈmɑːskɪŋ-] *n (U)* fita *f* adesiva.

masochism [ˈmæsəkɪzm] *n (U)* masoquismo *m*.

masochist [ˈmæsəkɪst] *n* masoquista *mf*.

masochistic [ˌmæsəˈkɪstɪk] *adj* masoquista.

mason [ˈmeɪsn] *n* -**1.** [stonemason] pedreiro *m*, -ra *f* -**2.** [Freemason] maçom *m*.

masonic [məˈsɒnɪk] *adj* maçônico(ca).

masonry [ˈmeɪsnrɪ] *n (U)* [stones] alvenaria *f*.

masquerade [ˌmæskəˈreɪd] *vi*: **to** ~ **as** fazer-se passar por; **to** ~ **under the name of ...** esconder-se sob o nome de ...

mass [mæs] ◇ *n* -**1.** GEOGR, PHYSICS massa *f* -**2.** [large amount] grande quantidade *f* -**3.** [main part, majority]: **the** ~ **of** a maioria de. ◇ *adj* em massa. ◇ *vt* concentrar. ◇ *vi* concentrar-se.
➡ **Mass** *n* RELIG missa *f*.
➡ **masses** *npl* -**1.** *inf* [lots, plenty] montes *mpl*; ~ **es of sthg** montes de algo -**2.** [ordinary people]: **the** ~ **es** as massas.

Massachusetts [ˌmæsəˈtʃuːsɪts] *n* Massachusetts.

massacre [ˈmæsəkəʳ] ◇ *n* massacre *m*. ◇ *vt* massacrar.

massage [*UK* ˈmæsɑːʒ, *US* məˈsɑːʒ] ◇ *n* massagem *f*. ◇ *vt* massagear.

massage parlour *n* -**1.** [for massage] clínica *f* de massagem -**2.** *euphemism* [brothel] casa *f* de massagens.

masseur [mæˈsɜːʳ] *n* massagista *m*.

masseuse [mæˈsɜːz] *n* massagista *f*.

massive [ˈmæsɪv] *adj* [in size, amount] enorme; ~ **majority** maioria em massa.

massively [ˈmæsɪvlɪ] *adv* enormemente.

mass-market *adj* para mercados de massa.

mass media *n or npl*: **the** ~ os meios de comunicação de massas.

mass-produce *vt* produzir em série.

mass production *n (U)* produção *f* em série.

mast [mɑːst] *n* -**1.** [on boat] mastro *m* -**2.** RADIO & TV antena *f*.

mastectomy (*pl* -ies) *n* mastectomia *f*.

master [ˈmɑːstəʳ] ◇ *n* -**1.** [person in charge] senhor *m*; **a** ~ **and his servants** um amo e seus servos -**2.** *fig* [of subject, situation] dono *m* -**3.** *UK* [teacher] mestre *m* -**4.** [of ship] capitão *m* -**5.** [original copy] original *m*. ◇ *adj* -**1.** [in trade] mestre -**2.** [original] original. ◇ *vt* -**1.** [gain control of] dominar, controlar -**2.** [perfect] dominar.

master bedroom *n* quarto *m* principal.

master disk *n* COMPUT disco-mestre *m*.

masterful [ˈmɑːstəfʊl] *adj* dominante, autoritário(ria).

master key *n* chave-mestra *f*.

masterly [ˈmɑːstəlɪ] *adj* magistral.

mastermind [ˈmɑːstəmaɪnd] ◇ *n* cabeça *mf*; **he is the** ~ **behind the plan** ele é o cabeça do plano. ◇ *vt* ser o cabeça de.

Master of Arts (*pl* **Masters of Arts**) *n* -**1.** [degree] mestrado *m* em ciências humanas, *diploma de mestre em ciências humanas* -**2.** [person] mestre *mf* em ciências humanas, *titular de diploma de mestre em ciências humanas*.

master of ceremonies (*pl* **masters of ceremonies**) *n* mestre-de-cerimônias *mf*.

Master of Science (*pl* **Masters of Science**) *n* -**1.** [degree] mestrado *m* em ciências exatas, *diploma de mestre em ciências exatas* -**2.** [person] mestre *mf* em ciências exatas, *titular de diploma de mestre em ciências exatas*.

masterpiece [ˈmɑːstəpiːs] *n* obra-prima *f*.

master plan *n* plano-mestre *m*.

master's degree *n* mestrado *m*.

masterstroke [ˈmɑːstəstrəʊk] *n* golpe *m* de mestre.

master switch *n* chave *f* geral.

masterwork [ˈmɑːstəwɜːk] *n* obra-prima *f*.

mastery [ˈmɑːstərɪ] *n (U)* domínio *m*.

mastic [ˈmæstɪk] *n (U)* almécega *f*.

masticate [ˈmæstɪkeɪt] *fml vt* & *vi* mastigar.

mastiff [ˈmæstɪf] *n* mastim *m*.

masturbate [ˈmæstəbeɪt] *vi* masturbar-se.

masturbation [ˌmæstəˈbeɪʃn] *n (U)* masturbação *f*.

mat [mæt] *n* -**1.** [on floor] tapete *m*; **door** ~ capacho *m* -**2.** [on table]: **beer** ~ porta-copos *m inv*; **table** ~ jogo *m* americano.

match [mætʃ] ◇ *n* -**1.** [game] partida *f* -**2.** [for lighting] fósforo *m* -**3.** [equal]: **to be no** ~ **for sb** não ser páreo para alguém. ◇ *vt* -**1.** [be the same as] coincidir com -**2.** [coordinate with] combinar com -**3.** [equal] equiparar-se a. ◇ *vi* [be the same] combinar.

matchbox [ˈmætʃbɒks] *n* caixa *f* de fósforos.

matched [mætʃt] *adj*: **to be well** ~ [well suited] combinar bem; [equal in strength] estar igualado(da); **they are well** ~ **(as a couple)** eles formam um belo casal.

matching [ˈmætʃɪŋ] *adj* que combina bem.

matchless [ˈmætʃlɪs] *adj literary* incomparável, ímpar.

matchmaker [ˈmætʃˌmeɪkəʳ] *n* casamenteiro *m*, -ra *f*.

match play *n* GOLF partida de golfe entre duas equipes.

match point *n* TENNIS -**1.** *(U)* [situation] match point *m* -**2.** [score] match point *m*, ponto *m* do jogo.

matchstick [ˈmætʃstɪk] *n* palito *m*.

mate [meɪt] ◇ n -**1.** inf [friend] amigo m, -ga f, companheiro m, -ra f -**2.** UK inf [form of address] colega mf -**3.** [of animal] parceiro m, -ra f -**4.** NAUT: (first) ~ contramestre m. ◇ vi [animals] acasalar-se; to ~ with acasalar-se com.

material [mə'tɪərɪəl] ◇ adj -**1.** material -**2.** [important] substancial. ◇ n material m.
➡ **materials** npl materiais mpl.

materialism [mə'tɪərɪəlɪzm] n (U) [desire for possessions] materialismo m.

materialist [mə'tɪərɪəlɪst] n [person greedy for possessions] materialista mf.

materialistic [mə,tɪərɪə'lɪstɪk] adj materialista.

materialize, -ise [mə'tɪərɪəlaɪz] vi -**1.** [happen] concretizar-se -**2.** [appear] materializar-se.

materially [mə'tɪərɪəlɪ] adv -**1.** [physically] materialmente -**2.** [importantly, essentially] essencialmente.

maternal [mə'tɜːnl] adj maternal.

maternity [mə'tɜːnətɪ] n (U) maternidade f.

maternity benefit n (U) auxílio-maternidade m.

maternity dress n vestido m de gestante.

maternity hospital n maternidade f (no hospital).

maternity leave n licença-maternidade f.

maternity ward n maternidade f.

math n US = maths.

mathematical [,mæθə'mætɪkl] adj matemático(ca).

mathematician [,mæθəmə'tɪʃn] n matemático m, -ca f.

mathematics [,mæθə'mætɪks] n (U) [subject] matemática f.

maths UK [mæθs], **math** US [mæθ] (abbr of mathematics) inf ◇ n (U) [subject] matemática f. ◇ comp de matemática.

maths coprocessor [-,kəʊ'prəʊsesəʳ] n COMPUT coprocessador m matemático.

matinée ['mætɪneɪ] n matinê f.

matinée jacket n UK casaquinho m de bebê.

mating call ['meɪtɪŋ-] n chamado m do macho (para acasalamento).

mating season ['meɪtɪŋ-] n época f de acasalamento.

matriarch ['meɪtrɪɑːk] n -**1.** [of a society] matriarca f -**2.** literary [of a family] matriarca f.

matrices ['meɪtrɪsiːz] pl ▷ **matrix**.

matriculate [mə'trɪkjʊleɪt] vi UNIV matricular-se.

matriculation [mə,trɪkjʊ'leɪʃn] n (U) UNIV matrícula f.

matrimonial [,mætrɪ'məʊnjəl] adj matrimonial.

matrimony ['mætrɪmənɪ] n (U) matrimônio m.

matrix ['meɪtrɪks] (pl matrices OR -es) n -**1.** [gen] matriz f -**2.** TECH molde m para fundição.

matron ['meɪtrən] n -**1.** UK [in hospital] enfermeira-chefe f -**2.** [in school] enfermeira f -**3.** US [in prison] superintendente f -**4.** [middle-aged woman] matrona f.

matronly ['meɪtrənlɪ] adj euph matronal.

matt UK, **matte** US [mæt] adj fosco(ca).

matted ['mætɪd] adj embaraçado(da).

matter ['mætəʳ] ◇ n -**1.** [question, situation] questão f, assunto m; a ~ of life and death uma questão de vida ou morte; the fact OR truth of the ~ is ... o xis da questão é ...; that's another OR a different ~ isso é outra questão/coisa; a ~ of opinion uma questão de opinião; a ~ of time uma questão de tempo; to make ~ s worse piorar as coisas; and to make ~ s worse, ... e para piorar (ainda mais) as coisas, ...; as a ~ of course como algo natural; as a ~ of principle por uma questão de princípios; within a ~ of hours numa questão de horas -**2.** [trouble, cause of pain] problema m; what's the ~? qual é o problema?, o que (é que) houve?; what's the ~ with it/her? qual é o problema com isso /ela? -**3.** (U) PHYSICS matéria f -**4.** (U) [material] material/ m; **vegetable** ~ matéria vegetal. ◇ vi [be important] importar; it doesn't ~ não importa; it doesn't ~ what you decide não interessa o que você decidir.
➡ **as a matter of fact** adv aliás, na verdade.
➡ **for that matter** adv quanto a isso.
➡ **no matter** adv: no ~ how hard I try ... não importa quanto eu tente ...; no ~ what aconteça o que acontecer.

Matterhorn ['mætə,hɔːn] n: the ~ a Montanha Matterhorn.

matter-of-fact adj sem sentimento, prosaico(ca).

matting ['mætɪŋ] n (U) esteira f.

mattress ['mætrɪs] n colchão m.

mature [mə'tjʊəʳ] ◇ adj -**1.** [person] maduro(ra) -**2.** [food, drink] envelhecido(da), maturado(da) -**3.** [cheese] curado(da). ◇ vi -**1.** [gen] amadurecer -**2.** [animal, plant] crescer -**3.** [wine, spirit] envelhecer -**4.** [cheese] curar -**5.** [insurance policy] vencer.

mature student n UK UNIV estudante mf adulto, -ta.

maturity [mə'tjʊərətɪ] n maturidade f.

maudlin ['mɔːdlɪn] adj choroso(sa).

maul [mɔːl] vt [attack, savage] atacar gravemente.

Mauritania [,mɒrɪ'teɪnɪə] n Mauritânia; in ~ na Mauritânia.

Mauritanian [,mɒrɪ'teɪnɪən] ◇ adj mauritano(na). ◇ n mauritano m, -na f.

Mauritian [mə'rɪʃən] ◇ adj mauriciano(na). ◇ n mauriciano m, -na f.

Mauritius [mə'rɪʃəs] n Maurício; in ~ em Maurício.

mausoleum [,mɔːsə'lɪəm] (pl -s) n mausoléu m.

mauve [məʊv] ◇ adj da cor de malva. ◇ n (U) malva f.

maverick ['mævərɪk] ◇ adj inconformista. ◇ n inconformista mf.

mawkish ['mɔːkɪʃ] adj piegas.

max. [mæks] (abbr of maximum) máx.

maxim ['mæksɪm] (pl -s) n máxima f.

maxima ['mæksɪmə] pl ▷ **maximum**.

maximize, -ise ['mæksɪmaɪz] vt maximizar.

maximum ['mæksɪməm] (pl maxima OR -s) ◇ adj [highest, largest] máximo(ma). ◇ n [upper limit] máximo m.

may [meɪ] modal vb -**1.** poder; you ~ like it talvez você goste; he ~ well have said that ele pode muito bem ter dito aquilo; it ~ rain pode ser que chova; be that as it ~ seja como for; I would like to add, if I ~ ... eu gostaria de acrescentar, se possível ... **- 2.** *fml* [to express wish, hope]: **long ~ it last!** que dure por muito tempo!; **~ they be very happy!** que eles sejam muito felizes!; ➢ **might**.

May [meɪ] *n* maio; *see also* **September**.

Maya [ˈmaɪə] *n*: **the ~** os Maias.

maybe [ˈmeɪbiː] *adv* talvez.

Mayday *n* [SOS] mayday, sinal *m* de socorro.

May Day *n* Primeiro *m* de Maio.

mayfly [ˈmeɪflaɪ] (*pl* **-flies**) *n* efeméride *f*.

mayhem [ˈmeɪhem] *n* (*U*) caos *m inv*.

mayn't = may not.

mayonnaise [ˌmeɪəˈneɪz] *n* (*U*) maionese *f*.

mayor [meəʳ] *n* prefeito *m*.

mayoress [ˈmeərɪs] *n* [female mayor] prefeita *f*; [wife of mayor] esposa *f* do prefeito.

maypole [ˈmeɪpəʊl] *n mastro erigido para o dia 1° de maio ao redor do qual se dança.*

may've *cont* = may have.

maze [meɪz] *n* **- 1.** [system of paths] labirinto *m* **- 2.** *fig* [tangle] confusão *f*.

MB ⬦ *n* (*abbr of* **Bachelor of Medicine**) (*titular de*) *bacharelado em medicina.* ⬦ **- 1.** (*abbr of* **megabyte**) MB **- 2.** *abbr of* **Manitoba**.

MBA (*abbr of* **Master of Business Administration**) *n* MBA *m*.

MBBS (*abbr of* **Bachelor of Medicine and Surgery**) *n* (*titular de*) *bacharelado em medicina e cirurgia.*

MBE (*abbr of* **Member of the Order of the British Empire**) *n* (*beneficiário da*) *ordem do Império Britânico.*

MC (*abbr of* **master of ceremonies**) *n* mestre-de-cerimônias *m*.

MCAT (*abbr of* **Medical College Admissions `rest**) *n exame de admissão para a faculdade de medicina nos Estados Unidos.*

MCC (*abbr of* **Marylebone Cricket Club**) *n clube londrino de críquete, responsável pelas regras do jogo.*

McCarthyism [məˈkɑːrθiɪzəm] *n* macartismo *m*.

McCoy [məˈkɔɪ] *n* (*U*) *inf*: **the real ~** o produto genuíno.

MCP (*abbr of* **male chauvinist pig**) *n inf* machista *m*.

MD ⬦ *n* **- 1.** (*abbr of* **Doctor of Medicine**) (*titular de*) *doutorado em medicina* **- 2.** (*abbr of* **managing director**) diretor-gerente *m*. ⬦ *abbr of* **Maryland**.

MDT (*abbr of* **Mountain Daylight Time**) *n horário de verão na zona das Montanhas Rochosas nos Estados Unidos.*

me [miː] *pers pron* **- 1.** (*direct, indirect*) me; **she knows ~** ela me conhece; **it's ~** sou eu; **send it to ~** mande-o para mim; **tell ~** diga-me; **- 2.** (*after prep*) mim; **with ~** comigo; **it's for ~** é para mim.

ME ⬦ *n* (*abbr of* **myalgic encephalomyelitis**) EM *f*. ⬦ *abbr of* **Maine**.

meadow [ˈmedəʊ] *n* campina *f*.

meagre *UK*, **meager** *US* [ˈmiːgəʳ] *adj* magro(gra), insuficiente.

meal [miːl] *n* refeição *f*; **to go out for a ~** sair para jantar; **to make a ~ of sthg** *UK fig* & *pej* fazer algo parecer mais cansativo do que realmente é.

meals on wheels *npl UK* serviço de entrega

domiciliar de refeições para idosos e necessitados.

mealtime [ˈmiːltaɪm] *n* hora *f* da refeição; **at ~s** na hora das refeições.

mealy-mouthed [ˌmiːlɪˈmaʊðd] *adj pej* evasivo(-va), fingido(da).

mean [miːn] (*pt* & *pp* **meant**) ⬦ *adj* **- 1.** [miserly] mesquinho(nha); **to be ~ with sthg** ser avarento com algo **- 2.** [unkind] grosseiro(ra); **to be ~ to sb** ser malvado(da) com alguém **- 3.** [average] médio(dia) **- 4.** *iro* [inferior] inferior; **she's no ~ singer** [excellent] ela é uma cantora de primeira; **it's no ~ task** não é pouca coisa. ⬦ *n* [average] meio-termo *m*; ➢ **means**. ⬦ *vt* **- 1.** [signify, represent] significar **- 2.** [have in mind, intend] querer dizer; **to ~ to do sthg** ter a intenção de fazer algo, tencionar fazer algo; **to be meant for sb/sthg** ser feito(ta) para alguém/algo; **they're not meant to be there** eles não deveriam estar lá; **it was meant as a compliment** era para ser um elogio; **to be meant to do sthg** dever fazer algo; **to ~ well** ter boa vontade **- 3.** [be serious about] falar sério; **she meant every word she said** tudo o que ela disse era a sério **- 4.** [entail] acarretar **- 5.** *phr*: **I ~** quer dizer.

meander [mɪˈændəʳ] *vi* **- 1.** [river, road] serpentear **- 2.** [in walking] vagar **- 3.** [in speaking] divagar.

meaning [ˈmiːnɪŋ] *n* **- 1.** [sense] sentido *m*, significado *m* **- 2.** (*U*) [purpose, importance] sentido *m*.

meaningful [ˈmiːnɪŋfʊl] *adj* **- 1.** [expressive] significativo(va) **- 2.** [deep, profound] sério(ria).

meaningless [ˈmiːnɪŋlɪs] *adj* **- 1.** [devoid of sense] sem sentido **- 2.** [futile] fútil.

meanness [ˈmiːnnɪs] *n* (*U*) **- 1.** [stinginess] avareza *f* **- 2.** [unkindness] maldade *f*.

means [miːnz] (*pl inv*) ⬦ *n* [method, way] meio *m*; **a ~ to an end** um meio para um fim; **by ~ of** por meio de. ⬦ *npl* [money] recursos *mpl*.

➣ **by all means** *adv* claro que sim.

➣ **by no means** *adv* de modo algum.

means test *n esp UK* averiguação oficial quanto à carência de renda para fins de recebimento de pensão do governo.

meant [ment] *pt* & *pp* ➢ **mean**.

meantime [ˈmiːntaɪm] *n*: **in the ~** enquanto isso.

meanwhile [ˈmiːnwaɪl] *adv* **- 1.** [at the same time] enquanto isso **- 2.** [between two events] nesse ínterim.

measles [ˈmiːzlz] *n*: **to catch ~** pegar sarampo.

measly [ˈmiːzlɪ] (*compar* **-ier**, *superl* **-iest**) *adj inf* miserável.

measurable [ˈmeʒərəbl] *adj* [significant] considerável.

measurably [ˈmeʒərəblɪ] *adv* consideravelmente.

measure [ˈmeʒəʳ] ⬦ *n* **- 1.** [step, action] medida *f* **- 2.** (*U*) [degree, amount] grau *m*; **the film had a ~ of success** o filme até que teve sucesso; **for good ~** para se certificar **- 3.** [of alcohol] dose *f* **- 4.** [indication] indicação *f* **- 5.** [device] régua *f*. ⬦ *vt* [determine size of, gauge] medir. ⬦ *vi* [be of stated size] medir.

➣ **measure up** *vi* [be good enough] estar à altura; **to ~ up to sthg** estar à altura de algo.

measured [ˈmeʒəd] *adj literary* ponderado(da).

measurement [ˈmeʒəmənt] *n* **- 1.** [figure, amount]

medida *f* - **2.** *(U)* [act of measuring] medição *f.*
measurements *npl* [of sb's body] medidas *fpl.*
measuring jug ['meʒərɪŋ-] *n* jarro *m* de medidas.
measuring tape ['meʒərɪŋ-] *n* fita *f* métrica.
meat [miːt] *n (U)* carne *f.*
meatball ['miːtbɔːll] *n* almôndega *f.*
meat pie *n UK* torta *f* de carne.
meaty ['miːtɪ] (*compar* -**ier**, *superl* -**iest**) *adj fig* [full of ideas] rico(ca), sólido(da).
Mecca ['mekə] *n* - **1.** GEOGR Meca - **2.** *fig* [paradise]: **a** ~ **for** um paraíso para.
mechanic [mɪˈkænɪk] *n* mecânico *m*, -ca *f.*
mechanics ⬦ *n (U)* [study] mecânica *f.* ⬦ *npl* [way sthg works] mecânica *f.*
mechanical [mɪˈkænɪkl] *adj* mecânico(ca).
mechanical engineering *n (U)* engenharia *f* mecânica.
mechanism ['mekənɪzm] *n* mecanismo *m.*
mechanization *n* mecanização *f.*
mechanize, -ise ['mekənaɪz] ⬦ *vt* mecanizar. ⬦ *vi* mecanizar-se.
Med (*abbr of* **Mediterranean Sea**) *n UK inf* Mediterrâneo *m.*
MEd [ˌemˈed] (*abbr of* **Master of Education**) *n (titular de) mestrado em educação.*
medal ['medl] *n* medalha *f.*
medallion [mɪˈdæljən] *n* medalhão *m.*
medallist *UK*, **medalist** *US* ['medəlɪst] *n* medalhista *mf.*
meddle ['medl] *vi* meter-se; **to** ~ **in/with sthg** meter-se em/com algo.
meddlesome ['medlsəm] *adj* metido(da), intrometido(da).
media ['miːdjə] ⬦ *pl* ⊳ **medium.** ⬦ *n or npl*: **the** ~ a mídia.
mediaeval [ˌmedɪˈiːvl] *adj* = **medieval.**
media event *n* evento *m* da mídia.
median ['miːdjən] ⬦ *adj* MATH mediano(na). ⬦ *n US* [of road] canteiro *m* divisor.
mediate ['miːdɪeɪt] ⬦ *vt* [produce by arbitration] negociar. ⬦ *vi* [arbitrate]: **to** ~ **between** ser mediador(a) entre.
mediation [ˌmiːdɪˈeɪʃn] *n (U)* [arbitration] mediação *f.*
mediator ['miːdɪeɪtə'] *n* mediador *m*, -ra *f.*
medic ['medɪk] *n inf* - **1.** [medical student] estudante *mf* de medicina - **2.** [doctor] médico *m*, -ca *f.*
Medicaid ['medɪkeɪd] *n (U) US* auxílio-saúde *m.*

MEDICAID/MEDICARE

Em razão da falta de um sistema nacional de saúde nos Estados Unidos, foram criados, em 1965, os programas *Medicare* e *Medicaid*, visando a oferecer assistência médica a idosos e a pessoas sem recursos. O *Medicare* destina-se aos maiores de 65 anos e é financiado pelos impostos relativos à seguridade social. Além disso, cada participante paga uma contribuição mensal, e uma pequena taxa é cobrada cada vez que se utiliza o atendimento médico. O *Medicaid* volta-se para aqueles que não dispõem de recursos econômicos, sendo financiado pelos governos federal e estadual.

medical ['medɪkl] ⬦ *adj* médico(ca). ⬦ *n* [checkup] exame *m* médico, check-up *m.*
medical certificate *n* [result of medical exam] atestado *m* médico.
medical insurance *n (U)* seguro-saúde *m.*
medical student *n* estudante *mf* de medicina.
Medicare ['medɪkeə'] *n (U) US* seguro-saúde *m (para idosos).*
medicated ['medɪkeɪtɪd] *adj* medicinal.
medication [ˌmedɪˈkeɪʃn] *n* medicação *f.*
medicinal [meˈdɪsɪnl] *adj* [drink, herb, tea] medicinal.
medicine ['medsɪn] *n* - **1.** *(U)* [treatment of illness] medicina *f* - **2.** [substance] medicamento *m*, remédio *m.*
medicine man *n* curandeiro *m.*
medieval [ˌmedɪˈiːvl] *adj* medieval.
mediocre [ˌmiːdɪˈəʊkə'] *adj* medíocre.
mediocrity [ˌmiːdɪˈɒkrətɪ] *n (U)* [poor quality] mediocridade *f.*
meditate ['medɪteɪt] *vi* - **1.** [reflect, ponder] refletir; **to** ~ (**up**)**on sthg** refletir sobre algo - **2.** [practise meditation] meditar.
meditation [ˌmedɪˈteɪʃn] *n* meditação *f.*
Mediterranean [ˌmedɪtəˈreɪnjən] ⬦ *n* - **1.** [sea]: **the** ~ (**Sea**) o (Mar) Mediterrâneo - **2.** [area around sea]: **the** ~ o mediterrâneo. ⬦ *adj* mediterrâneo(nea).
medium ['miːdjəm] (*pl sense 1* -dia, *pl sense 2* -diums) ⬦ *adj* [middle, average] médio(dia). ⬦ *n* - **1.** [way of communicating] meio *m* de comunicação - **2.** [spiritualist] médium *mf.*
medium-dry *adj* semi-seco(ca).
medium-size(d) [-saɪzd] *adj* de tamanho médio.
medium wave *n (U)* onda *f* média.
medley ['medlɪ] (*pl* -**s**) *n* - **1.** [mixture] mistura *f* - **2.** [selection of music] coletânea *f.*
meek [miːk] *adj* dócil, meigo(ga).
meekly ['miːklɪ] *adv* docilmente.
meet [miːt] (*pt* & *pp* **met**) ⬦ *n US* [meeting] encontro *m*, competição *f.* ⬦ *vt* - **1.** [gen] encontrar; **she met his gaze defiantly** ela encarou o olhar dele de forma desafiadora - **2.** [by arrangement] encontrar-se com, reunir-se com - **3.** [make acquaintance of] conhecer; **I met a really interesting guy** conheci um cara muito interessante - **4.** [wait for - person] ir esperar; [- train, plane, bus, boat] esperar - **5.** [fulfil, satisfy] satisfazer, cumprir - **6.** [deal with] enfrentar - **7.** [pay] pagar em dia - **8.** [experience, come across] deparar-se com - **9.** [hit, touch] ir de encontro a. ⬦ *vi* - **1.** [gen] encontrar-se; **their eyes met across the room** os olhos deles se cruzaram na sala - **2.** [committee] reunir-se - **3.** [become acquainted] conhecer-se - **4.** [hit, touch] bater-se.
meet up *vi* [by arrangement] encontrar-se; **to** ~ **up with sb** encontrar-se com alguém.
meet with *vt fus* - **1.** [encounter] experimentar - **2.** *US* [by arrangement] encontrar.
meeting ['miːtɪŋ] *n* - **1.** [gen] reunião *f* - **2.** [coming together] encontro *m.*
meeting place *n* ponto *m* de encontro.
mega- [megə] *prefix* - **1.** [in measurements] mega - **2.** *inf* [very big] mega.

megabit n COMPUT megabit m.
megabyte ['megəbaɪt] n COMPUT megabyte m.
megahertz ['megəhɜːts] n RADIO megahertz m.
megalomania [ˌmegələ'meɪnjəl] n (U) megalomania f.
megalomaniac [ˌmegələ'meɪnɪæk] n megalomaníaco m, -ca f.
megaphone ['megəfəʊn] n megafone m.
megaton ['megətʌn] n megaton m.
megawatt ['megəwɒt] n megawatt m.
melamine ['meləmiːn] n (U) melanina f.
melancholy ['melənkəlɪ] <> adj [sad] melancólico(ca). <> n (U) melancolia f.
mellow ['meləʊ] <> adj -**1.** [gen] suave -**2.** [smooth, pleasant] melodioso(sa) -**3.** [gentle, relaxed] alegre, tranqüilo(la). <> vt: **to be ~ed by sthg** sentir-se amadurecido(da) por algo; **to be ~ed by wine** ficar alegre por causa do vinho. <> vi [become more gentle or relaxed] suavizar-se, tranqüilizar-se.
melodic [mɪ'lɒdɪk] adj MUS melódico(ca).
melodious [mɪ'ləʊdjəs] adj melodioso(sa).
melodrama ['melədrɑːmə] n melodrama m.
melodramatic [ˌmelədrə'mætɪk] adj melodramático(ca).
melody ['melədɪ] (pl -ies) n [tune] melodia f.
melon ['melən] n melão m.
melt [melt] <> vt -**1.** [make liquid] derreter -**2.** fig [soften] amolecer. <> vi -**1.** [become liquid] derreter -**2.** fig [soften] amolecer -**3.** fig [disappear]: **to ~ into sthg** desaparecer em algo, fundir-se em algo; **to ~ away** dissipar-se; **his savings ~ed away** suas economias se acabaram.
melt down vt sep fundir-se.
meltdown ['meltdaʊn] n -**1.** (U) [act of melting] fusão f -**2.** [incident] acidente m nuclear.
melting point ['meltɪŋ-] n ponto m de fusão.
melting pot ['meltɪŋ-] n fig [of cultures, races, ideas] cadinho m cultural.
member ['membər] <> adj -membro. <> n membro m.
Member of Congress (pl **Members of Congress**) n US Membro m do Congresso.
Member of Parliament (pl **Members of Parliament**) n [in UK] Membro m do Parlamento.
membership ['membəʃɪp] n -**1.** [gen - of party, union] associação f; [- of club] qualidade f de sócio; **I have to renew my ~** tenho que renovar o meu título -**2.** [number of members] número m de sócios -**3.** [people themselves]: **the ~** os sócios, os membros.
membership card n carteira f de sócio.
membrane ['membreɪn] n ANAT membrana f.
memento [mɪ'mentəʊ] (pl -s) n lembrança f.
memo ['meməʊ] (pl -s) n [at work] memorando m.
memoirs ['memwɑːz] npl memórias fpl.
memo pad n rascunho m de memorando.
memorabilia [ˌmemərə'bɪlɪə] npl memorabília f.
memorable ['memərəbll] adj memorável.
memorandum [ˌmemə'rændəm] (pl -**da**, -**dums**) n fml memorando m.
memorial [mɪ'mɔːrɪəl] <> adj comemorativo(va). <> n memorial m.

memorize, -ise ['meməraɪz] vt memorizar, decorar.
memory ['memərɪ] (pl -ies) n -**1.** [gen] memória f; **in ~ of** em memória de; **to lose one's ~** perder a memória; **from ~** de memória; **within living ~** de que se tem memória -**2.** [sthg remembered] lembrança f.
memory card n COMPUT placa f de memória.
men [men] pl ▷ **man.**
menace ['menəs] <> n -**1.** [gen] ameaça f -**2.** inf [nuisance, pest] praga f. <> vt ameaçar.
menacing ['menəsɪŋ] adj ameaçador(ra).
menacingly ['menəsɪŋlɪ] adv de forma ameaçadora.
menagerie [mɪ'nædʒərɪ] n reserva f particular de animais selvagens.
mend [mend] <> n (U) inf: **to be on the ~** estar convalescendo. <> vt [repair] consertar; **to ~ one's ways** corrigir-se.
mending ['mendɪŋ] n -**1.** [repairing]: **to do the ~** consertar -**2.** [clothes] roupas fpl a consertar.
menfolk ['menfəʊk] npl homens mpl em geral.
menial ['miːnjəl] adj simplório(ria), baixo(xa).
meningitis [ˌmenɪn'dʒaɪtɪs] n (U) MED meningite f.
menopause ['menəpɔːz] n (U): **the ~** a menopausa.
menservants ['mensɜːvənts] pl ▷ **manservant.**
men's room n US: **the ~** o banheiro dos homens.
menstrual ['menstrʊəl] adj menstrual.
menstruate ['menstrʊeɪt] vi menstruar.
menstruation [ˌmenstrʊ'eɪʃn] n (U) menstruação f.
menswear ['menzweər] n (U) roupa f masculina.
mental ['mentl] adj mental.
mental age n idade f mental.
mental block n: **to have a ~ about sthg** ter um bloqueio mental sobre algo.
mental hospital n hospital m psiquiátrico.
mentality [men'tælətɪ] n (U) [way of thinking] mentalidade f.
mentally ['mentəlɪ] adv mentalmente.
mentally handicapped ['mentəlɪ-] npl: **the ~** os deficientes mentais.
mentally-handicapped adj com deficiência mental.
mental note n: **to make a ~ to do sthg** gravar na memória para fazer algo.
menthol ['menθɒl] n (U) mentol m.
mentholated ['menθəleɪtɪd] adj mentolado(da).
mention ['menʃn] <> vt [say, talk about] mencionar; **to ~ sthg to sb** mencionar algo para alguém; **not to ~ sem** falar em; **don't ~ it!** não tem o quê! <> n [reference] menção f.
mentor ['mentɔː'] n fml mentor m, -ra f.
menu ['menjuː] n -**1.** [in restaurant] menu m, cardápio m -**2.** COMPUT menu m.
menu-driven adj COMPUT orientado(da) por menu.
meow n & vi US = **miaow.**
MEP (abbr of **Member of the European Parliament**) n membro do parlamento europeu.
mercantile ['mɜːkəntaɪl] adj mercantil.

mercenary ['mɜːsɪnrɪ] (pl -ies) <> adj mercená-rio(ria). <> n [soldier] mercenário m.

merchandise ['mɜːtʃəndaɪz] n (U) COMM mercado-ria f.

merchant ['mɜːtʃənt] <> adj mercantil. <> n comerciante mf.

merchant bank n UK banco m mercantil.

merchant navy UK, **merchant marine** US n marinha f mercante.

merciful ['mɜːsɪfʊl] adj -1. [person] piedoso(sa) -2. [death, release] misericordioso(sa).

mercifully ['mɜːsɪfʊlɪ] adv -1. [fortunately] graças a Deus -2. [with clemency] com clemência.

merciless ['mɜːsɪlɪs] adj impiedoso(sa).

mercilessly ['mɜːsɪlɪslɪ] adv impiedosamente.

mercurial [mɜːˈkjʊərɪəl] adj literary volúvel.

mercury ['mɜːkjʊrɪ] n (U) mercúrio m.

Mercury ['mɜːkjʊrɪ] n [planet] Mercúrio.

mercy ['mɜːsɪ] (pl -ies) n -1. (U) [kindness, pity] piedade f; **at the ~ of** fig à mercê de -2. [blessing] bênção f.

mercy killing n eutanásia f.

mere [mɪə^r] adj -1. [just, no more than] mero(ra); **she's a ~ child!** ela é só uma criança! -2. [for emphasis] simples, mero(ra) -3. [amount, quantity] apenas.

merely ['mɪəlɪ] adv -1. [simply, just, only] meramente, simplesmente -2. [of amount, quantity] apenas.

meretricious adj fml falacioso(sa).

merge [mɜːdʒ] <> n COMPUT intercalamento m. <> vt -1. COMM fundir -2. COMPUT intercalar. <> vi -1. COMM fundir-se; **to ~ with sthg** unir-se com algo -2. [roads, lines] unir-se -3. [blend, melt] misturar; **to ~ into sthg** incorporar-se em algo.

merger ['mɜːdʒə^r] n COMM fusão f.

meridian [məˈrɪdɪən] n GEOGR meridiano m.

meringue [məˈræŋ] n merengue m.

merino [məˈriːnəʊ] adj merino(na).

merit ['merɪt] <> n (U) [value] mérito m. <> vt merecer.
    ➤ **merits** npl [advantages, qualities] méritos mpl; **to judge sthg on its ~s** julgar algo por seus méritos.

meritocracy [ˌmerɪˈtɒkrəsɪ] (pl -ies) n [system] meritocracia f.

mermaid ['mɜːmeɪd] n sereia f.

merrily ['merɪlɪ] adv -1. [gen] divertidamente -2. iro [blithely] alegremente.

merriment ['merɪmənt] n (U) literary [laughter] risa-das fpl.

merry ['merɪ] (compar -ier, superl -iest) adj -1. literary [laugh, joke, person] alegre, divertido(da) -2. [fire, party] agradável; **Merry Christmas!** Feliz Natal! -3. inf [tipsy] alegre.

merry-go-round n carrossel m.

merrymaking ['merɪˌmeɪkɪŋ] n (U) literary pândega f, folia f.

mesh [meʃ] <> n (U) [netting] malha f. <> vi -1. [fit together] combinar -2. TECH encaixar.

mesmerize, -ise ['mezmərəraɪz] vt: **to be ~d by sb/sthg** ser hipnotizado(da) por alguém/algo.

mess [mes] n -1. [gen] bagunça f; **to be (in) a ~** estar uma bagunça, estar de pernas para o ar -2. [muddle, problem] confusão f -3. MIL rancho m.

➤ **mess about, mess around** inf <> vt sep embromar. <> vi -1. [gen] matar tempo -2. [tinker]: **to ~ about with sthg** mexer em algo.
➤ **mess up** vt sep inf -1. [make untidy, dirty - room, papers, objects] bagunçar; [- clothes] sujar -2. [spoil] estragar.
➤ **mess with** vt fus inf meter-se com.

message ['mesɪdʒ] n -1. [piece of information] mensa-gem f -2. [idea, moral] moral m -3. phr: **to get the ~** inf receber o recado.

message switching n COMPUT comutação f de mensagem.

messenger ['mesɪndʒə^r] n mensageiro m, -ra f; **by ~** por mensageiro.

Messiah [mɪˈsaɪə] n: **the ~** o Messias.

Messrs, Messrs. ['mesəz] (abbr of messieurs) Srs.

messy ['mesɪ] (compar -ier, superl -iest) adj -1. [dirty, untidy] desarrumado(da) -2. [person, activity] confu-so(sa) -3. [job] sujo(ja) -4. inf [complicated, confused] complicado(da).

met [met] pt & pp [arrow] meet.

Met [met] (abbr of Metropolitan Opera) n: **the ~** a Ópera Metropolitana de Nova Iorque.

metabolism [məˈtæbəlɪzm] n metabolismo m.

metal ['metl] <> n metal m. <> adj de metal.

metallic [mɪˈtælɪk] adj -1. [gen] metálico(ca) -2. TECH [of metal] metalífero(ra).

metallurgist n metalúrgico m, -ca f.

metallurgy [məˈtælədʒɪ] n (U) metalurgia f.

metalwork ['metlwɜːk] n (U) [craft] trabalho m em metal.

metalworker ['metlˌwɜːkə^r] n metalurgista mf.

metamorphose [ˌmetəˈmɔːfəʊz] vi: **to ~ (into sthg)** metamorfosear-se (em algo).

metamorphosis [ˌmetəˈmɔːfəsɪs, ˌmetəmɔːˈfəʊsɪs] (pl -phoses [-siːz]) n metamorfose f.

metaphor ['metəfə^r] n metáfora f.

metaphorical [ˌmetəˈfɒrɪkl] adj metafórico(ca).

metaphysical [ˌmetəˈfɪzɪkl] adj PHILOSOPHY metafísi-co(ca).

metaphysics [ˌmetəˈfɪzɪks] n (U) metafísica f.

mete [miːt] ➤ **mete out** vt sep: **to ~ sthg out to sb** impor algo a alguém.

meteor ['miːtɪə^r] n meteoro m.

meteoric [miːtɪˈɒrɪk] adj fig [rapid] meteórico(ca).

meteorite ['miːtjəraɪt] n meteorito m.

meteorological [ˌmiːtjərəˈlɒdʒɪkl] adj meteoroló-gico(ca).

meteorologist [ˌmiːtjəˈrɒlədʒɪst] n meteorologis-ta mf.

meteorology [ˌmiːtjəˈrɒlədʒɪ] n (U) meteorologia f.

meter ['miːtə^r] <> n -1. [device] medidor m; **taxi ~** taxímetro m; **electricity ~** relógio m de luz; **parking ~** parquímetro m -2. US = metre. <> vt [measure] medir.

methadone ['meθədəʊn] n (U) metadona f.

methane ['miːθeɪn] n (U) metano m.

method ['meθəd] n [way, system] método m.

methodical [mɪˈθɒdɪkl] adj metódico(ca).

methodically [mɪˈθɒdɪklɪ] adv metodicamente.

Methodist ['meθədɪst] <> adj metodista. <> n metodista mf.

methodology [ˌmeθəˈdɒlədʒɪl] (pl -ies) n fml metodologia f.

meths [meθs] n UK inf álcool m metilado.

methylated spirits [ˈmeθɪleɪtɪd-] n (U) álcool m metilado.

meticulous [mɪˈtɪkjʊləs] adj meticuloso(sa).

meticulously [mɪˈtɪkjʊləslɪ] adv meticulosamente.

Met Office (abbr of Meteorological Office) n instituto britânico de meteorologia.

metre UK, **meter** US [ˈmiːtəʳ] n -1. [unit of measurement] metro m - 2. [in poetry] métrica f.

metric [ˈmetrɪk] adj métrico(ca).

metrication [ˌmetrɪˈkeɪʃn] n UK conversão f ao sistema métrico.

metric system n: the ~ o sistema métrico.

metric ton n tonelada f métrica.

metro [ˈmetrəʊ] (pl -s) n metrô m.

metronome [ˈmetrənəʊm] n metrônomo m.

metropolis [mɪˈtrɒpəlɪs] (pl -es) n [large city] metrópole f.

metropolitan [ˌmetrəˈpɒlɪtn] adj [of a metropolis] metropolitano(na).

Metropolitan Police npl: the ~ a Polícia de Londres.

mettle [ˈmetl] n (U): to be on one's ~ estar preparado(da) para agir da melhor forma possível; to show OR prove one's ~ provar seu próprio valor.

mew [mjuː] n & vi = miaow.

mews [mjuːz] (pl inv) n UK estrebaria f.

Mexican [ˈmeksɪkn] <> adj mexicano(na). <> n mexicano m, -na f.

Mexico [ˈmeksɪkəʊ] n México; in ~ no México.

Mexico City n Cidade f do México.

mezzanine [ˈmetsəniːn] n mezanino m.

MFA (abbr of Master of Fine Arts) n (titular de) bacharelado em belas artes.

mfr (abbr of manufacturer) fabr. mf.

mg (abbr of milligram) mg.

Mgr -1. (abbr of Monseigneur, Monsignor) Mons. - 2. (abbr of manager) gerente mf.

MHR (abbr of Member of the House of Representatives) n membro do congresso norte-americano, ≃ deputado m, -da f federal.

MHz (abbr of megahertz) MHz.

MI abbr of Michigan.

MI5 (abbr of Military Intelligence 5) n órgão do serviço secreto britânico de contra-espionagem.

MI6 (abbr of Military Intelligence 6) n órgão do serviço secreto britânico de espionagem.

MIA (abbr of missing in action) US desaparecido em combate.

miaow UK [miːˈaʊ], **meow** US [mɪˈaʊ] <> n miado m, miau m. <> vi miar.

mice [maɪs] pl ⊳ mouse.

Mich. abbr of Michigan.

Michigan [ˈmɪʃɪgən] n Michigan; in ~ em Michigan.

mickey [ˈmɪkɪ] n: to take the ~ out of sb UK inf tirar sarro de alguém.

MICR (abbr of magnetic ink character recognition) n MICR f.

micro [ˈmaɪkrəʊ] (pl -s) n micro m.

micro- [ˈmaɪkrəʊ] prefix micro.

microbe [ˈmaɪkrəʊb] n micróbio m.

microbiologist [ˌmaɪkrəʊbaɪˈɒlədʒɪst] n microbiologista mf.

microbiology [ˌmaɪkrəʊbaɪˈɒlədʒɪl] n (U) microbiologia f.

microchip [ˈmaɪkrəʊtʃɪp] n microchip m.

microcircuit [ˈmaɪkrəʊˌsɜːkɪt] n microcircuito m.

microclimate n microclima m.

microcomputer [ˌmaɪkrəʊkəmˈpjuːtəʳ] n microcomputador m.

microcosm [ˈmaɪkrəkɒzml] n microcosmo m.

microfiche [ˈmaɪkrəʊfiːʃ] (pl inv OR -s) n microficha f.

microfilm [ˈmaɪkrəʊfɪlm] n microfilme m.

microlight [ˈmaɪkrəlaɪt] n ultraleve m.

micron [ˈmaɪkrɒn] n mícron m.

microorganism [ˌmaɪkrəʊˈɔːgənɪzml] n microorganismo m.

microphone [ˈmaɪkrəfəʊn] n microfone m.

microprocessor [ˈmaɪkrəʊˌprəʊsesəʳ] n microprocessador m.

micro scooter n patinete m.

microscope [ˈmaɪkrəskəʊp] n microscópio m.

microscopic [ˌmaɪkrəˈskɒpɪk] adj -1. [very small] microscópico(ca) - 2. [detailed] minucioso(sa).

microsecond n microssegundo m.

microsurgery [ˌmaɪkrəˈsɜːdʒərɪ] n (U) microcirurgia f.

microwave (oven) n forno m de microondas.

mid- [mɪd] prefix: ~height de meia altura; ~morning no meio da manhã; in ~August em meados de agosto; in ~winter em pleno inverno; she's in her ~twenties ela tem uns vinte e poucos anos.

midair [mɪdˈeəʳ] <> adj no ar. <> n (U): in ~ no ar.

midday [ˈmɪddeɪ] n (U) meio-dia m.

middle [ˈmɪdl] <> adj -1. [centre] do meio -2. [in time]: he was in his ~ forties ele estava nos seus quarenta e poucos anos. <> n -1. [centre] meio m, centro m; in the ~ (of sthg) no meio (de algo); in the ~ of nowhere no meio do nada -2. [in time] meio m; to be in the ~ of sthg estar no meio de algo; to be in the ~ of doing sthg estar fazendo algo; in the ~ of the night no meio da noite, em plena madrugada; in the ~ of September em meados de setembro -3. [waist] cintura f.

middle age n (U) meia-idade f.

middle-aged adj de meia-idade.

Middle Ages npl: the ~ a Idade Média.

middle-class adj da classe média.

middle classes npl: the ~ a classe média.

middle distance n: in the ~ em segundo plano.

Middle East n: the ~ o Oriente Médio.

Middle Eastern adj do Oriente Médio.

middle finger n dedo m médio.

middleman [ˈmɪdlmæn] (pl -men [-men]) n intermediário m.

middle management n (U) administração f intermediária.

middle name *n* segundo nome *m (num nome composto)*.

middle-of-the-road *adj* moderado(da).

middle school *n UK escola para crianças de 9 a 13 anos*.

middleweight ['mɪdlweɪt] *n* peso *m* médio.

middling ['mɪdlɪŋ] *adj* médio(dia), regular.

Mideast *n US*: **the ~** o Oriente Médio.

midfield [‚mɪd'fiːld] *n FTBL* meio-campo *m*.

midge [mɪdʒ] *n* mosquito-pólvora *m*.

midget ['mɪdʒɪt] *n* anão *m*, -nã *f*.

MIDI *(abbr of* **musical instrument digital interface***) n* MIDI *f*.

midi system ['mɪdɪ-] *n* sistema *m* MIDI.

Midlands ['mɪdləndz] *npl*: **the ~** *a região central da Inglaterra*.

midnight ['mɪdnaɪt] <> *n (U)* meia-noite *f*. <> *comp* da meia-noite.

midriff ['mɪdrɪf] *n* diafragma *m*.

midst [mɪdst] *n* [in space, time]: **in the ~ of** *literary* no meio de; **in our ~** entre nós.

midstream [‚mɪd'striːm] *n* **-1.** [of river]: **in ~** no meio da corrente **-2.** *fig* [when talking]: **in ~** no meio da conversa.

midsummer ['mɪd‚sʌmə^r] *n (U)* pleno verão *m*.

Midsummer Day *n* Dia *m* de São João *(24 de junho)*.

midway [‚mɪd'weɪ] *adv* **-1.** [in space]: **~ (between)** a meio caminho (entre) **-2.** [in time]: **~ (through)** na metade (de).

midweek [*adj* ‚mɪd'wiːk, *adv* 'mɪdwiːk] <> *adj* do meio da semana. <> *adv* no meio da semana.

Midwest [‚mɪd'west] *n*: **the ~** o Meio Oeste *(dos Estados Unidos)*.

Midwestern [‚mɪd'westən] *adj* do Meio-Oeste *(dos Estados Unidos)*.

midwife ['mɪdwaɪf] *(pl* **-wives** [-waɪvz]*) n* parteira *f*.

midwifery ['mɪd‚wɪfərɪ] *n (U)* trabalho *m* de parteira.

miffed [mɪft] *adj inf* amuado(da).

might [maɪt] <> *modal vb* **-1.** [expressing possibility]: **I think I ~ go to the pub tonight** acho que é possível eu ir ao bar hoje; **he ~ be armed** ele poderia estar armado **-2.** [expressing suggestion]: **you ~ have told me** você poderia ter me contado; **it ~ be better to wait** talvez fosse melhor esperar **-3.** *(past tense of may) fml* [asking permission]: **he asked if he ~ leave the room** ele me pediu permissão para sair da sala **-4.** [in polite questions, suggestions]: **~ I ...?** podia ...? **-5.** [contradicting a point of view]: **you ~ well be right, but ...** é bem possível que você tenha razão, mas ... **-6.** *phr*: **I ~ have known** *OR* **guessed** eu deveria ter suspeitado. <> *n* **-1.** [power] poder *m* **-2.** [physical strength] força *f*.

mightn't ['maɪtənt] = **might not**.

might've ['maɪtəv] = **might have**.

mighty ['maɪtɪ] *(compar* **-ier**, *superl* **-iest***)* <> *adj* **-1.** [powerful] poderoso(sa) **-2.** [very large] enorme. <> *adv US inf* muito.

migraine ['miːgreɪn, 'maɪgreɪn] *n* enxaqueca *f*.

migrant ['maɪgrənt] <> *adj* **-1.** [bird, animal] migratório(ria) **-2.** [worker] migrante. <> *n* **-1.** [bird,

animal] migratório *m*, -ria *f* **-2.** [person] emigrante *mf*.

migrate [*UK* maɪ'greɪt, *US* 'maɪgreɪt] *vi* **-1.** [bird, animal] migrar **-2.** [person] emigrar.

migration [maɪ'greɪʃn] *n* **-1.** [of birds, animals] migração *f* **-2.** [of people] emigração *f*.

migratory ['maɪgrətrɪ] *adj* [bird, animal] migratório(-ria).

mike [maɪk] *(abbr of* **microphone***) n inf* mike *m*.

mild [maɪld] <> *adj* **-1.** [food, shampoo, sedative] suave **-2.** [person, manner] sereno(na) **-3.** [weather] temperado(da) **-4.** [surprise, criticism, reproach] moderado(da) **-5.** [illness] leve. <> *n tipo de cerveja suave*.

mildew ['mɪldjuː] *n* **-1.** *(U)* [gen] mofo *m* **-2.** *(U) BOT* míldio *m*.

mildly ['maɪldlɪ] *adv* **-1.** [talk, complain, criticize] moderadamente; **to put it ~** para não dizer coisa pior **-2.** [slightly] bastante.

mild-mannered *adj* gentil, educado(da).

mildness ['maɪldnɪs] *n* **-1.** [of food, shampoo, sedative] suavidade *f* **-2.** [of person, manner] serenidade *f* **-3.** [of weather] calmaria *f* **-4.** [of criticism, reproach] moderação *f*.

mile [maɪl] *n* milha *f*; **we could see for ~s** conseguíamos ver quilômetros à frente; **to be ~s away** *fig* estar bem longe.
➡ **miles** *adv (in comparisons)* muito; **this is ~ better** sem dúvida alguma isto é realmente melhor.

mileage ['maɪlɪdʒ] *n* **-1.** [distance travelled] quilometragem *f* **-2.** *(U) inf* [advantage] vantagem *f*.

mileage allowance *n* pagamento *m* por quilômetros rodados.

mileometer [maɪ'lɒmɪtə^r] *n* odômetro *m*.

milestone ['maɪlstəʊn] *n* **-1.** [marker stone] marco *m* miliário **-2.** *fig* [event] marco *m*.

milieu [*UK* 'miːljɜː, *US* miː'ljuː] *(pl* **-s** *OR* **-x***) n* meio *m* (social).

militant ['mɪlɪtənt] <> *adj* militante. <> *n* militante *mf*.

militarism ['mɪlɪtərɪzml] *n (U)* militarismo *m*.

militarist ['mɪlɪtərɪst] *n* militarista *mf*.

militarized zone, militarised zone ['mɪlɪtəraɪzd-] *n* zona *f* militarizada.

military ['mɪlɪtrɪ] <> *adj* militar. <> *n*: **the ~** as forças armadas, os militares.

military police *npl* polícia *f* militar.

militate ['mɪlɪteɪt] *vi fml*: **to ~ against sthg** militar contra algo.

militia [mɪ'lɪʃə] *n* milícia *f*.

milk [mɪlk] <> *n* leite *m*. <> *vt* **-1.** [get milk from] ordenhar **-2.** *fig* [use for one's own ends] explorar.

milk chocolate <> *n (U)* chocolate *m* ao leite. <> *comp* de chocolate ao leite.

milk float *UK*, **milk truck** *US n* veículo usado na entrega domiciliar do leite.

milking ['mɪlkɪŋ] *n (U)* ordenha *f*.

milkman ['mɪlkmən] *(pl* **-men** [-mən]*) n* leiteiro *m*.

milk round *n UK* **-1.** [by milkman] entrega *f* de leite **-2.** *UNIV* [recruitment drive] recrutamento *m* de pessoal.

milk shake *n* milk-shake *m*.

milk tooth *n* dente-de-leite *m*.

milk truck n US = milk float.

milky ['mɪlkɪl (compar -ier, superl -iest) adj -1. UK [with milk] com leite -2. [like milk] leitoso(sa) -3. [pale white] pálido(da).

Milky Way n: the ~ a Via Láctea.

mill [mɪl] <> n -1. [flour mill] moinho m -2. [factory] fábrica f -3. [grinder] moedor m. <> vt [grain] moer.
➡ **mill about, mill around** vi aglomerar-se.

millennium [mɪ'lenɪəm] (pl -nnia [-nɪəl] n [thousand years] milênio m.

miller ['mɪləʳ] n moleiro m, -ra f.

millet ['mɪlɪt] n painço m.

milli- ['mɪlɪl prefix mili.

millibar ['mɪlɪbɑ:ʳ] n milibar m.

milligram(me) ['mɪlɪgræml n miligrama m.

millilitre UK, **milliliter** US ['mɪlɪ,li:təʳ] n mililitro m.

millimetre UK, **millimeter** US ['mɪlɪ,mi:təʳ] n milímetro m.

millinery ['mɪlɪnrɪl n (U) chapelaria f (para senhoras).

million ['mɪljən] n -1. [1,000,000] milhão m -2. [enormous number]: a ~, ~s of milhões de.

millionaire [,mɪljə'neəʳ] n milionário m, -ria f.

millionairess [,mɪljə'neərɪs] n milionária f.

millipede ['mɪlɪpi:d] n embuá m.

millisecond ['mɪlɪ,sekənd] n milissegundo m.

millstone ['mɪlstəʊn] n [for grinding] pedra f de moinho; a ~ round one's neck fig um grande peso sobre os ombros.

millwheel ['mɪlwi:l] n roda f de azenha.

milometer [maɪ'lɒmɪtəʳ] n = mileometer.

mime [maɪm] <> n (U) mímica f. <> vt imitar. <> vi fazer mímica.

mimic ['mɪmɪk] (pt & pp -ked, cont -king) <> n [person] imitador m, -ra f. <> vt [person, voice, gestures] imitar.

mimicry ['mɪmɪkrɪl n (U) imitação f.

mimosa [mɪ'məʊzəl n mimosa f.

min. [mɪn] -1. (abbr of minute) min. -2. (abbr of minimum) mín.

Min. (abbr of ministry) Min.

mince [mɪns] <> n (U) UK carne f picada. <> vt picar; not to ~ one's words não ter papas na língua. <> vi andar com passinhos.

mincemeat ['mɪnsmi:t] n (U) -1. [fruit] iguaria feita de sebo, frutas cristalizadas e passas -2. US [minced meat] picadinho m.

mince pie n torta com recheio de frutas secas preparada geralmente no Natal.

mincer ['mɪnsəʳ] n moedor m de carne.

mind [maɪnd] <> n -1. [gen] mente f; great ~s think alike duas cabeças pensam melhor que uma; to broaden one's ~ ampliar os horizontes de alguém; state of ~ estado de espírito -2. [thoughts] memória f; to come into/cross sb's ~ passar pela cabeça de alguém; to have sthg on one's ~ estar preocupado(da) com algo; to take sb's ~ off sthg fazer alguém esquecer algo; that was a load OR weight off my ~ isso tirou um peso da minha consciência; to put OR set sb's ~ at rest tranqüilizar alguém -3. [attention]: to concentrate the ~ concentrar a mente; to keep one's ~ on sthg concentrar-se em algo; to put one's ~ to sthg colocar empenho em algo -4. [opinion]: to my ~ na minha opinião; to change one's ~ mudar de idéia; to keep an open ~ manter a mente aberta; to make one's ~ up tomar uma decisão; to speak one's ~ dizer o que se pensa; to be in two ~s about sthg estar com dois corações sobre algo -5. [memory] memória f; to bear sthg in ~ ter algo em mente; to call sthg to ~ trazer algo à memória; to cast one's ~ back pensar no que já aconteceu (no passado); to slip one's ~ fugir da memória -6. [intention]: to have sthg in ~ ter algo em mente; to have a ~ to do sthg estar pensando em fazer algo. <> vi -1. [care, worry] importar-se; do you ~ if ...? você se importaria se ...?; I don't ~ eu não me importo; never ~ [don't worry] não faz mal; [it's not important] não tem importância -2. [be careful]: ~ out! UK cuidado! <> vt -1. [object to] importar-se em; I don't ~ waiting não me importo em esperar; I wouldn't ~ a ... eu aceitaria um ... -2. [bother about] preocupar-se com -3. [pay attention to] prestar atenção com -4. [take care of] tomar conta de.
➡ **mind you** adv: he didn't give me a Christmas present this year - ~, he never does ele não me deu um presente de Natal neste ano - bom, mas ele nunca dá mesmo.

mind-bending adj inf confuso(sa).

minder ['maɪndəʳ] n -1. [of child] pessoa f que cuida de crianças -2. UK [bodyguard] guarda-costas m inv.

mindful ['maɪndfʊl] adj: ~ of sthg ciente de algo.

mindless ['maɪndlɪs] adj -1. [stupid] absurdo(da), sem sentido -2. [not requiring thought] tedioso(sa).

mind reader n: I'm not a ~! eu não leio pensamentos!

mindset ['maɪndset] n mentalidade f.

mind's eye n: in one's ~ na imaginação de alguém.

mine¹ [maɪn] <> n -1. [gen] mina f -2. [source]: a ~ of information uma fonte de informação. <> vt -1. [excavate] extrair -2. [lay mines in] minar.

mine² [maɪn] poss pron o meu (a minha); a friend of mine um amigo meu; those shoes are mine esses sapatos são meus; mine are here - where are yours? os meus estão aqui - onde estão os seus?

mine detector n detector m de minas.

minefield ['maɪnfi:ld] n -1. [area containing mines] campo m minado -2. fig [dangerous topic] campo m minado.

minelayer ['maɪn,leɪəʳ] n lança-minas m inv.

miner ['maɪnəʳ] n mineiro m, -ra f.

mineral ['mɪnərəl] <> adj GEOL mineral. <> n GEOL mineral m.

mineralogy [,mɪnə'rælədʒɪ] n (U) mineralogia f.

mineral water n (U) água f mineral.

minestrone [,mɪnɪ'strəʊnɪ] n (U) sopa f minestrone.

minesweeper ['maɪn,swi:pəʳ] n caça-minas m inv.

mingle ['mɪŋgl] <> vt: to ~ sthg with sthg misturar algo com algo. <> vi -1. [combine] misturar-se; to ~ with sthg misturar-se com algo -2. [socially] misturar-se; to ~ with sb misturar-se com alguém.

mini ['mɪnɪ] *n* [skirt, dress] minissaia *f*.

miniature ['mɪnətʃə^r] ⋄ *adj* [reduced-scale] em miniatura. ⋄ *n* **-1.** [painting] miniatura *f* **-2.** [of alcohol] garrafa *f* em miniatura **-3.** [small scale]: **in** ~ em miniatura.

minibus ['mɪnɪbʌs] (*pl* **-es**) *n* microônibus *m inv*.

minicab ['mɪnɪkæb] *n UK* radiotáxi *m*.

minicomputer [,mɪnɪkəm'pju:tə^r] *n* minicomputador *m*.

MiniDisc® ['mɪdɪsk] *n* MiniDisc® *m*.

MiniDisc player® *n* reprodutor *m* de MiniDisc®.

minidish [m'mɪdɪʃ] *n* miniparabólica *f*.

minim ['mɪnɪm] *n MUS* mínima *f*.

minima ['mɪnɪmə] *pl* ⊳ **minimum**.

minimal ['mɪnɪml] *adj* mínimo(ma).

minimize, -ise ['mɪnɪmaɪz] *vt* [reduce] minimizar.

minimum ['mɪnɪməm] (*pl* **-mums** OR **-ma**) ⋄ *adj* mínimo(ma). ⋄ *n* mínimo *m*.

minimum lending rate [-'lendɪŋ-] *n* taxa *f* mínima de empréstimo.

minimum wage *n* salário *m* mínimo.

mining ['maɪnɪŋ] ⋄ *adj* mineiro(ra); ~ **engineer** engenheiro *m*, -ra *f* de minas. ⋄ *n* mineração *f*.

minion ['mɪnjən] *n hum or pej* lacaio *m*, -a *f*.

miniseries ['mɪnɪsɪərɪz] (*pl inv*) *n* minissérie *f*.

miniskirt ['mɪnɪskɜ:t] *n* minissaia *f*.

minister ['mɪnɪstə^r] *n* **-1.** POL: ~ **(for sthg)** ministro *m*, -tra *f* (de algo) **-2.** RELIG pastor *m*, -ra *f*.
 ➡ **minister to** *vt fus* **-1.** [person] atender **-2.** [needs] atender a.

ministerial [,mɪnɪ'stɪərɪəl] *adj* POL ministerial.

minister of state *n*: ~ **(for sthg)** secretário *m*, -ria *f* de estado (para algo).

ministry ['mɪnɪstrɪ] (*pl* **-ies**) *n* **-1.** POL ministério *m*; **Ministry of Defence** Ministério da Defesa **-2.** RELIG [clergy]: **the** ~ o sacerdócio.

mink [mɪŋk] (*pl inv*) *n* **-1.** (U) [fur] pele *f* de visom **-2.** [animal] visom *m*.

mink coat *n* casaco *m* de visom.

Minnesota [,mɪnɪ'səʊtə] *n* Minnesota; **in** ~ em Minnesota.

minnow ['mɪnəʊ] *n* [fish] peixinho *m* (*de água doce*).

minor ['maɪnə^r] ⋄ *adj* [gen] menor. ⋄ *n* [in age] menor *mf* de idade.

Minorca [mɪ'nɔ:kə] *n* Minorca; **in** ~ em Minorca.

minority [maɪ'nɒrətɪ] (*pl* **-ies**) ⋄ *adj* minoritário(ria). ⋄ *n* [gen] minoria *f*; **to be in a** OR **the** ~ estar em minoria, ser minoria.

minority government *n* governo *m* minoritário.

minor road *n* caminho *m* secundário.

minster ['mɪnstə^r] *n* catedral *f*.

minstrel ['mɪnstrəl] *n* menestrel *m*.

mint [mɪnt] ⋄ *n* **-1.** (U) [herb] hortelã *f* **-2.** [sweet] bala *f* de hortelã **-3.** [for coins]: **the Mint** a Casa da Moeda; **in** ~ **condition** novo(va) em folha. ⋄ *vt* [coins] cunhar.

mint sauce *n* (U) molho *m* de hortelã.

minuet [,mɪnjʊ'et] *n* minueto *m*.

minus ['maɪnəs] (*pl* **-es**) ⋄ *prep* **-1.** MATH [less]: **4** ~ **2 is 2** 4 menos 2 é 2 **-2.** [in temperatures]: **it's** ~ **5 degrees** está fazendo 5 graus abaixo de zero. ⋄

adj **-1.** MATH [less than zero] negativo(va) **-2.** SCH [in grades] menos. ⋄ *n* **-1.** MATH sinal *m* de menos **-2.** [disadvantage] desvantagem *f*.

minuscule ['mɪnəskju:l] *adj* minúsculo(la).

minus sign *n* sinal *m* de menos.

minute¹ ['mɪnɪt] *n* [gen] minuto *m*; **at any** ~ a qualquer momento; **at the last** ~ no último minuto; **this** ~ agora mesmo; **up to the** ~ [news, design] de última hora; [technology] de ponta; **wait a** ~! espere um pouco!
 ➡ **minutes** *npl* [of meeting] ata *f*.

minute² [maɪ'nju:t] *adj* [tiny] mínimo(ma).

minutiae [maɪ'nju:ʃɪaɪ] *npl* minúcias *fpl*.

miracle ['mɪrəkl] *n* milagre *m*.

miraculous [mɪ'rækjʊləs] *adj* milagroso(sa).

miraculously [mɪ'rækjʊləslɪ] *adv fig* [surprisingly] milagrosamente.

mirage [mɪ'rɑ:ʒ] *n* miragem *f*.

mire [maɪə^r] *n* (U) lamaçal *m*.

mirror ['mɪrə^r] ⋄ *n* espelho *m*. ⋄ *vt* **-1.** [copy] espelhar **-2.** *literary* [reflect] refletir.

mirror image *n* imagem *f* refletida.

mirth [mɜ:θ] *n* (U) *literary* alegria *f*.

misadventure [,mɪsəd'ventʃə^r] *n fml* [unfortunate accident] desventura *f*; **death by** ~ JUR morte *f* acidental.

misanthropist [mɪs'ænθrəpɪst] *n* misantropo *m*, -pa *f*.

misapplication *n* má aplicação *f*, abuso *m*.

misapprehension ['mɪs,æprɪ'henʃn] *n* mal-entendido *m*.

misappropriate [,mɪsə'prəʊprɪeɪt] *vt* desviar.

misappropriation ['mɪsə,prəʊprɪ'eɪʃn] *n* desvio *m*.

misbehave [,mɪsbɪ'heɪv] *vi* comportar-se mal.

misbehaviour *UK*, **misbehavior** *US* [,mɪsbɪ'heɪvjə^r] *n* (U) mau comportamento *m*, má conduta *f*.

misc (*abbr of* **miscellaneous**) variado(da).

miscalculate [,mɪs'kælkjʊleɪt] *vt* & *vi* calcular mal.

miscalculation [,mɪskælkjʊ'leɪʃn] *n* erro *m* de cálculo.

miscarriage [,mɪs'kærɪdʒ] *n* aborto *m* natural.

miscarriage of justice *n* erro *m* judicial.

miscarry [,mɪs'kærɪ] (*pt* & *pp* **-ied**) *vi* **-1.** [woman] abortar naturalmente **-2.** [plan] fracassar.

miscellaneous [,mɪsə'leɪnjəs] *adj* diverso(sa).

miscellany [*UK* mɪ'selənɪ, *US* 'mɪsəleɪnɪ] (*pl* **-ies**) *n* miscelânea *f*.

mischance [,mɪs'tʃɑ:ns] *n fml* azar *m*, infortúnio *m*; **by** ~ por azar.

mischief ['mɪstʃɪf] *n* (U) **-1.** [playfulness] malícia *f* **-2.** [naughty behaviour] travessuras *fpl* **-3.** [harm] dano *m*.

mischievous ['mɪstʃɪvəs] *adj* **-1.** [playful] cheio (cheia) de malícia **-2.** [naughty] travesso(sa).

misconceived [,mɪskən'si:vd] *adj* [plan, idea] mal concebido(da).

misconception [,mɪskən'sepʃn] *n* conceito *m* falho, idéia *f* equivocada.

misconduct [,mɪs'kɒndʌkt] *n* [bad behaviour] má conduta *f*.

misconstrue [ˌmɪskən'stru:l] *vt fml* interpretar erroneamente.

miscount [ˌmɪs'kaʊnt] *vt & vi* contar mal.

misdeed [ˌmɪs'di:d] *n literary* delito *m*.

misdemeanour *UK*, **misdemeanor** *US* [ˌmɪsdɪ'mi:nəʳ] *n JUR* contravenção *f*.

misdirected [ˌmɪsdɪ'rektɪd] *adj* -1. [letter] mal endereçado(da) -2. [misused] mal dirigido(da).

miser ['maɪzəʳ] *n* avarento *m*, -ta *f*.

miserable ['mɪzrəbl] *adj* -1. [unhappy] infeliz, triste -2. [depressing - conditions, life] miserável; [- weather, holiday, evening] horrível -3. [failure] lamentável.

miserably ['mɪzrəblɪ] *adv* -1. [unhappily] tristemente -2. [in depressing fashion] miseravelmente -3. [fail] de forma lamentável.

miserly ['maɪzəlɪ] *adj* mesquinho(nha), miserável.

misery ['mɪzərɪ] *(pl* -ies) *n* -1. [unhappiness] tristeza *f* -2. [poverty] miséria *f* -3. [gloomy person] desgraça *f*.

misfire [ˌmɪs'faɪəʳ] *vi* -1. [gun] não disparar -2. [car engine] não dar partida -3. [plan] fracassar.

misfit ['mɪsfɪt] *n* desajustado *m*, -da *f*.

misfortune [mɪs'fɔ:tʃu:n] *n* -1. *(U)* [bad luck] azar *m* -2. [piece of bad luck] infortúnio *m*, desgraça *f*.

misgivings [mɪs'gɪvɪŋz] *npl* receio *m*, desconfiança *f*.

misguided [ˌmɪs'gaɪdɪd] *adj* -1. [person] desencaminhado(da) -2. [attempt, opinion] equivocado(da).

mishandle [ˌmɪs'hændl] *vt* -1. [person, animal] maltratar -2. [negotiations, business] administrar mal.

mishap ['mɪshæp] *n* -1. *(U)* [accident]: **without ~** sem incidentes -2. [unfortunate event] incidente *m*, percalço *m*.

mishear [ˌmɪs'hɪəʳ] *(pt & pp* **-heard** [-'hɜ:d]) *vt & vi* ouvir mal.

mishmash ['mɪʃmæʃ] *n inf* mixórdia *f*.

misinform [ˌmɪsɪn'fɔ:m] *vt* informal mal.

misinformation [ˌmɪsɪnfə'meɪʃn] *n (U)* informação *f* errada.

misinterpret [ˌmɪsɪn'tɜ:prɪt] *vt* interpretar mal.

misjudge [ˌmɪs'dʒʌdʒ] *vt* -1. [calculate wrongly] calcular mal -2. [appraise wrongly] julgar mal.

misjudg(e)ment [ˌmɪs'dʒʌdʒmənt] *n* julgamento *m* errado.

mislay [ˌmɪs'leɪ] *(pt & pp* **-laid**) *vt* perder, extraviar.

mislead [ˌmɪs'li:d] *(pt & pp* **-led**) *vt* enganar.

misleading [ˌmɪs'li:dɪŋ] *adj* enganoso(sa).

misled [ˌmɪs'led] *pt & pp* ▷ **mislead**.

mismanage [ˌmɪs'mænɪdʒ] *vt* administrar mal.

mismanagement [ˌmɪs'mænɪdʒmənt] *n (U)* má administração *f*.

mismatch [ˌmɪs'mætʃ] *vt*: **to be ~ed** [colours] combinar mal; [in marriage] estar desencontrado(da).

misnomer [ˌmɪs'nəʊməʳ] *n* termo *m* impróprio.

misogynist [mɪ'sɒdʒɪnɪst] *n* misógino *m*, -na *f*.

misplace [ˌmɪs'pleɪs] *vt* extraviar, perder.

misplaced [ˌmɪs'pleɪst] *adj* [trust, confidence] inapropriado(da).

misprint ['mɪsprɪnt] *n* erro *m* de impressão.

mispronounce [ˌmɪsprə'naʊns] *vt* pronunciar mal.

misquote [ˌmɪs'kwəʊt] *vt* citar erroneamente.

misread [ˌmɪs'ri:d] *(pt & pp* **-read**) *vt* -1. [read wrongly] ler erroneamente -2. [misinterpret] interpretar mal.

misrepresent ['mɪsˌreprɪ'zent] *vt* -1. [person] dar uma imagem equivocada de -2. [facts] deturpar.

misrepresentation ['mɪsˌreprɪzen'teɪʃn] *n* -1. *(U)* [wrong interpretation] má interpretação *f* -2. [false account] deturpação *f*.

misrule [ˌmɪs'ru:l] *n* [misgovernment] mau governo *m*.

miss [mɪs] <> *vt* -1. [gen] perder -2. [fail to see] não ver, perder -3. [fail to hit] errar; **to ~ the target** não acertar o alvo -4. [feel absence of - person, home, family] sentir/estar com saudades de; [- things] sentir falta de -5. [fail to be present at] faltar a -6. [escape] evitar; **I just ~ed being run over** escapei de ser atropelado por pouco. <> *vi* [fail to hit] não acertar. <> *n*: **to give sthg a ~** *inf* deixar algo.
◆ **miss out** <> *vt sep* omitir. <> *vi*: **to ~ out (on sthg)** perder (algo).

Miss [mɪs] *n* senhorita *f*.

misshapen [ˌmɪs'ʃeɪpn] *adj* -1. [hands, fingers] deformado(da) -2. [object] disforme.

missile [*UK* 'mɪsaɪl, *US* 'mɪsəl] *n* -1. [weapon] míssil *m* -2. [thrown object] projétil *m*.

missile launcher [-ˌlɔ:ntʃəʳ] *n* lança-mísseis *m inv*.

missing ['mɪsɪŋ] *adj* -1. [object] perdido(da) -2. [person] desaparecido(da) -3. [not present] que falta; **who's ~?** quem está faltando?; **to go ~** desaparecer.

missing link *n*: **here was the ~ between ...** aqui está o elo que faltava entre ...

missing person *n* pessoa *f* desaparecida.

mission ['mɪʃn] *n* missão *f*.

missionary ['mɪʃənrɪ] *(pl* -ies) *n* missionário *m*, -ria *f*.

Mississippi [ˌmɪsɪ'sɪpɪ] *n* -1. [river]: **the ~ (River)** o (Rio) Mississippi -2. [state] Mississippi; **in ~** em Mississippi.

missive ['mɪsɪv] *n* missiva *f*.

Missouri [mɪ'zʊərɪ] *n* Missouri; **in ~** em Missouri.

misspell [ˌmɪs'spell] *(pt & pp* **-spelt** *OR* **-spelled**) *vt* soletrar erroneamente.

misspelling [ˌmɪs'spelɪŋ] *n* erro *m* de ortografia.

misspelt [ˌmɪs'spelt] *pt & pp* ▷ **misspell**.

misspend *(pt & pp* **-spent**) *vt* [money, talent, youth] desperdiçar.

mist [mɪst] *n* neblina *f*.
◆ **mist over, mist up** *vi* embaçar.

mistake [mɪ'steɪk] *(pt* **-took**, *pp* **-taken**) <> *n* erro *m*; **to make a ~** cometer um erro, equivocar-se; **by ~** por engano. <> *vt* -1. [misunderstand] entender mal -2. [fail to distinguish]: **to ~ sb/sthg for** confundir alguém/algo com; **there's no mistaking ...** não tem como confundir ...

mistaken [mɪ'steɪkn] <> *pp* ▷ **mistake**. <> *adj* -1. [person] equivocado(da), enganado(da); **to be ~ about sb/sthg** estar enganado(da) sobre alguém/algo -2. [belief, idea] equivocado(da).

mistaken identity *n*: **a case of ~** um caso de identificação equivocada.

mistakenly [mɪs'teɪknlɪ] *adv* equivocadamente.

mister ['mɪstə'] n inf amigo m.
➤ **Mister** n Senhor m.
mistime [ˌmɪs'taɪm] vt calcular mal o tempo de.
mistletoe ['mɪsltəʊ] n (U) visco m.
mistook [mɪ'stʊk] pt ▷ **mistake**.
mistranslation [ˌmɪstræns'leɪʃn] n tradução f incorreta.
mistreat [ˌmɪs'triːt] vt maltratar.
mistreatment [ˌmɪs'triːtmənt] n (U) maus tratos mpl.
mistress ['mɪstrɪs] n -1. [of house, situation] dona f -2. [female lover] amante f -3. [schoolteacher] professora f.
mistrial ['mɪstraɪəl] n processo m nulo.
mistrust [ˌmɪs'trʌst] ◇ n (U) desconfiança f, receio m. ◇ vt desconfiar de.
mistrustful [ˌmɪs'trʌstfʊl] adj desconfiado(da); ~ of sb/sthg desconfiado(da) de alguém/algo.
misty ['mɪstɪ] (compar -ier, superl -iest) adj nebuloso(sa).
misunderstand [ˌmɪsʌndə'stænd] (pt & pp -stood) vt & vi entender mal.
misunderstanding [ˌmɪsʌndə'stændɪŋ] n -1. (U) [lack of understanding] equívoco m -2. [wrong interpretation] mal-entendido m -3. [disagreement] desentendimento m.
misunderstood [ˌmɪsʌndə'stʊd] pt & pp ▷ **misunderstand**.
misuse [n ˌmɪs'juːs, vb ˌmɪs'juːz] ◇ n -1. (U) [wrong use] uso m indevido -2. [abuse] abuso m. ◇ vt -1. [use wrongly] usar indevidamente -2. [abuse] abusar de.
MIT (abbr of Massachusetts Institute of Technology) n MIT m.
mite [maɪt] n -1. ZOOL ácaro m -2. inf [small amount]: a ~ um pouquinho -3. inf [small child] criancinha f.
miter n US = mitre.
mitigate ['mɪtɪgeɪt] vt fml mitigar.
mitigating ['mɪtɪgeɪtɪŋ] adj fml: ~ circumstances circunstâncias fpl atenuantes.
mitigation [ˌmɪtɪ'geɪʃn] n (U) fml mitigação f, atenuante f.
mitre UK, **miter** US ['maɪtə'] n -1. [hat] mitra f -2. [joint] meia-esquadria f.
mitt [mɪt] n -1. = **mitten** -2. [in baseball] luva f.
mitten ['mɪtn] n [with fingers joined] luva f (com separação somente para o polegar); [with fingers cut off] mitene f.
mix [mɪks] ◇ vt misturar; to ~ sthg with sthg misturar algo com algo. ◇ vi misturar-se, combinar-se; to ~ with sb misturar-se com alguém. ◇ n -1. [gen] mistura f -2. COMM: marketing ~ mix m de marketing, composto m mercadológico.
➤ **mix up** vt sep -1. [confuse] confundir -2. [disorder] misturar.
mixed [mɪkst] adj -1. [of different kinds] misturado(da) -2. [of different sexes] misto(ta).
mixed-ability adj UK de vários níveis.
mixed blessing n: it was a ~ teve um lado bom e um lado ruim.
mixed doubles n (U) duplas fpl mistas.
mixed economy n economia f mista.

mixed grill n prato grelhado com carnes e vegetais.
mixed marriage n casamento m misto.
mixed up adj -1. [confused] confuso(sa) -2. [involved]: to be ~ in sthg estar envolvido(da) em algo.
mixer ['mɪksə'] n -1. [machine - for food] f batedeira; [- for drinks] misturador m; [- for cement] betoneira f -2. [soft drink] bebida não-alcoólica usada para se misturar com bebidas alcoólicas.
mixer tap n UK torneira f (para o fluxo de água fria e quente).
mixing bowl ['mɪksɪŋ-] n tigela f.
mixture ['mɪkstʃə'] n mistura f.
mix-up n inf engano m, confusão f.
mk, MK (abbr of mark) marco m.
mkt (abbr of market) mercado m.
ml (abbr of millilitre) n ml.
MLitt [ˌem'lɪt] (abbr of Master of Literature, Master of Letters) n (titular de) mestrado em literatura.
MLR (abbr of minimum lending rate) taxa mínima de juros praticada para empréstimos pelo Banco da Inglaterra, referência para os demais bancos.
mm (abbr of millimetre) mm.
MMR (abbr of measles, mumps, and rubella) n MMR f, SCR f.
MN ◇ n (abbr of Merchant Navy) marinha f mercante. ◇ abbr of **Minnesota**.
mnemonic [nɪ'mɒnɪk] n mnemônica f.
MO ◇ n (abbr of medical officer) médico encarregado dos serviços de saúde. ◇ abbr of **Missouri**.
moan [məʊn] ◇ n -1. [of pain, sadness] gemido m -2. inf [complaint] resmungo m, queixa f. ◇ vi -1. [in pain, sadness] gemer -2. inf [complain] resmungar, queixar-se; to ~ about sb/sthg resmungar OR queixar-se sobre alguém/algo.
moaning ['məʊnɪŋ] n -1. [pain, sadness] gemidos mpl -2. (U) [complaining] reclamação f, queixas fpl.
moat [məʊt] n fosso m.
mob [mɒb] (pt & pp -bed, cont -bing) ◇ n -1. multidão f -2. pej: the ~ a ralé, a plebe. ◇ vt cercar, amontoar-se ao redor de.
mobile ['məʊbaɪl] ◇ adj -1. [able to move] móvel -2. inf [having transport] motorizado(da). ◇ n -1. [phone] (telefone) celular m -2. [decoration] móbile m.
mobile home n trailer m.
mobile library n biblioteca f móvel OR ambulante.
mobile phone n (telefone) celular m.
mobile shop n unidade f móvel de vendas.
mobility [mə'bɪlətɪ] n mobilidade f.
mobility allowance n UK ajuda financeira que recebem os deficientes físicos para poderem se locomover.
mobilization [ˌməʊbɪlaɪ'zeɪʃn] n mobilização f.
mobilize, -ise ['məʊbɪlaɪz] ◇ vt mobilizar. ◇ vi mobilizar-se.
moccasin ['mɒkəsɪn] n mocassim m.
mock [mɒk] ◇ adj falso(sa); a ~ exam um simulado. ◇ vt [deride] zombar de. ◇ vi zombar.

mockery ['mɒkərı] n -1. (U) [scorn] zombaria f -2. [travesty] paródia f; **to make a ~ of sthg** pôr algo em ridículo.

mocking ['mɒkıŋ] adj zombeteiro(ra).

mockingbird ['mɒkıŋbɜ:dl n tordo m imitador.

mock-up n modelo m em tamanho natural.

mod [mɒd] n jovem britânico dos anos 60 que vestia roupas alinhadas e gostava da música soul americana.

MoD (abbr of Ministry of Defence) n ministério m da defesa (britânico).

mod cons [,mɒd-] (abbr of modern conveniences) npl UK inf: **all ~** todas as comodidades modernas.

mode [məʊd] n -1. [gen] modo m -2. [of transport] meio m.

model ['mɒdl] (UK pt & pp -led, cont -ling, US pt & pp -ed, cont -ing) <> adj -1. [miniature] em miniatura -2. [exemplary] modelo. <> n [gen] modelo m. <> vt -1. [shape] moldar -2. [in fashion show] desfilar com -3. [copy]: **to ~ o.s. on sb** ter alguém como modelo, espelhar-se em alguém. <> vi [in fashion show] desfilar.

modem ['məʊdem] COMPUT n modem m.

moderate [adj & n 'mɒdərət, vb 'mɒdəreıt] <> adj moderado(da). <> n POL moderado m, -da f. <> vt moderar. <> vi moderar-se.

moderately ['mɒdərətlı] adv moderadamente.

moderation [,mɒdə'reıʃn] n moderação f; **in ~** com moderação.

moderator ['mɒdəreıtər] n -1. [of debate] moderador m, -ra f -2. RELIG presidente duma assembleia protestante.

modern ['mɒdən] adj moderno(na).

modern-day adj dos dias de hoje.

modernism ['mɒdənızm] n (U) modernismo m.

modernization [,mɒdənaɪ'zeıʃn] n modernização f.

modernize, -ise ['mɒdənaız] <> vt modernizar. <> vi modernizar-se.

modern languages npl línguas fpl modernas.

modest ['mɒdıst] adj modesto(ta).

modestly ['mɒdıstlı] adv -1. [to small extent] ligeiramente -2. [not proudly] modestamente.

modesty ['mɒdıstı] n (U) modéstia f.

modicum ['mɒdıkəm] n fml quantia f módica; **a ~ of** um mínimo de.

modification [,mɒdıfı'keıʃn] n -1. [minor alteration] modificação f -2. (U) [alteration] alteração f, modificação f.

modify ['mɒdıfaı] (pt & pp -ied) vt -1. [alter] modificar -2. [tone down] moderar.

modular ['mɒdjʊlər] adj -1. [furniture] modular -2. [course] em módulos.

modulated ['mɒdjʊleıtıd] adj [voice] modulado(da).

modulation [,mɒdjʊ'leıʃn] n TECH modulação f.

module ['mɒdju:l] n módulo m.

Mogadishu [,mɒgə'dıʃu:] n Mogadíscio; **in ~** em Mogadíscio.

moggy ['mɒgı] (pl -ies) n UK inf gato m, -ta f.

mogul ['məʊgl] n [magnate] magnata m.

MOH (abbr of Medical Officer of Health) n secretário municipal de saúde na Grã-Bretanha.

mohair ['məʊheər] <> n mohair m. <> comp de mohair.

Mohammedan [mə'hæmıdn] <> adj maometano(na). <> n maometano m, -na f.

Mohican [məʊ'hi:kən] <> adj moicano(na). <> n -1. [indian] moicano m, -na f -2. [haircut] corte de cabelo punk em que a cabeça é raspada nas laterais.

moist [mɔıst] adj úmido(da); **~ cake** bolo m fofo.

moisten ['mɔısn] vt umedecer.

moisture ['mɔıstʃər] n (U) umidade f.

moisturize, -ise ['mɔıstʃəraız] vt umectar.

moisturizer ['mɔıstʃəraızər] n (creme) hidratante m.

molar ['məʊlər] n molar m.

molasses [mə'læsız] n (U) melaço m.

mold etc n & vt US = mould.

Moldavia [mɒl'deıvıə] n Moldávia; **in ~** na Moldávia.

mole [məʊl] n -1. [animal] toupeira f -2. [on skin] sinal m -3. [spy] espião m, -ã f.

molecular [mə'lekjʊlər] adj molecular.

molecule ['mɒlıkju:l] n molécula f.

molehill ['məʊlhıl] n montículo de terra deixado pelas toupeiras ao cavar seus túneis.

molest [mə'lest] vt -1. [attack sexually - child] molestar; [- person] assediar -2. [bother] incomodar.

molester [mə'lestər] n molestador m, -ra f; **child ~** perverso m, -ra f de menores.

mollify ['mɒlıfaı] (pt & pp -ied) vt fml tranqüilizar.

mollusc, mollusk US ['mɒləsk] n molusco m.

mollycoddle ['mɒlı,kɒdl] vt inf mimar.

Molotov cocktail ['mɒlətɒf-] n coquetel m Molotov.

molt vt & vi US = moult.

molten ['məʊltn] adj derretido(da), fundido(da).

mom [mɒm] n US inf mãe f.

moment ['məʊmənt] n -1. [gen] momento m; **~ of truth** hora f da verdade; **for one ~** por um momento; **at any ~** a qualquer momento; **at the ~** no momento; **at the last ~** no último momento; **for the ~** por enquanto -2. [importance] importância f.

momentarily ['məʊməntərılı] adv -1. [for a short time] momentaneamente -2. US [immediately] imediatamente.

momentary ['məʊməntrı] adj momentâneo(nea).

momentous [mə'mentəs] adj significativo(va).

momentum [mə'mentəm] n -1. PHYSICS momento m -2. fig [speed, force] força f.

momma ['mɒmə], **mommy** ['mɒmı] n US mamãe f, mãezinha f.

Mon. (abbr of Monday) seg.

Monaco ['mɒnəkəʊ] n Mônaco; **in ~** em Mônaco.

monarch ['mɒnək] n monarca mf.

monarchist ['mɒnəkıst] n monarquista mf.

monarchy ['mɒnəkı] (pl -ies) n monarquia f; **the ~** a monarquia.

monastery ['mɒnəstrı] (pl -ies) n monastério m.

monastic [mə'næstık] adj monástico(ca).

Monday ['mʌndı] n segunda-feira f; see also Saturday.

monetarism ['mʌnıtərızm] n (U) monetarismo m.

monetarist [ˈmʌnɪtərɪst] n monetarista mf.

monetary [ˈmʌnɪtrɪ] adj monetário(ria).

money [ˈmʌnɪ] n (U) dinheiro m; **to make** ~ ganhar dinheiro; **to get one's** ~ '**s worth** fazer o dinheiro OR investimento valer a pena.

moneybox [ˈmʌnɪbɒks] n cofrinho m.

moneyed adj fml abastado(da).

moneylender [ˈmʌnɪˌlendəʳ] n prestamista mf.

moneymaker [ˈmʌnɪˌmeɪkəʳ] n mina f (de ouro).

moneymaking [ˈmʌnɪˌmeɪkɪŋ] adj rentável, lucrativo(va).

money market n mercado m financeiro.

money order n ordem f de pagamento.

money-spinner [-ˌspɪnəʳ] n esp UK inf mina f (de ouro).

money supply n oferta f de moeda.

mongol [ˈmɒŋgəl] dated & offensive <> adj mongolóide. <> n mongolóide mf.

➠ **Mongol** adj & n = **Mongolian**.

Mongolia [mɒŋˈgəʊlɪə] n Mongólia; **in** ~ na Mongólia.

Mongolian [mɒŋˈgəʊlɪən] <> adj mongol. <> n **-1.** [person] mongol mf **-2.** [language] mongol m.

mongoose [ˈmɒŋguːs] (pl -s) n mangusto m.

mongrel [ˈmʌŋgrəl] n [dog] vira-lata m.

monitor [ˈmɒnɪtəʳ] <> n TECH monitor m. <> vt monitorar.

monk [mʌŋk] n monge m.

monkey [ˈmʌŋkɪ] (pl -s) n [animal] macaco m, -ca f.

monkey nut n amendoim m.

monkey wrench n chave f inglesa.

monkfish [ˈmʌŋkfɪʃ] (pl inv OR -es) n peixe-pescador m.

mono [ˈmɒnəʊ] <> adj monofônico(ca), mono inv. <> n inf **-1.** [sound] som m mono **-2.** US [glandular fever] mononucleose f infecciosa.

monochrome [ˈmɒnəkrəʊm] adj [TV, photograph] monocromo(ma).

monocle [ˈmɒnəkl] n monóculo m.

monogamous [mɒˈnɒgəməs] adj monógamo(ma).

monogamy [mɒˈnɒgəmɪ] n (U) monogamia f.

monogrammed [ˈmɒnəgræmd] adj bordado(da) com as iniciais.

monolingual [ˌmɒnəˈlɪŋgwəl] adj monolíngue.

monolithic [ˌmɒnəˈlɪθɪk] adj monolítico(ca).

monologue, monolog US [ˈmɒnəlɒg] n **-1.** THEATRE monólogo m **-2.** inf [long speech] palestra f longa.

mononucleosis [ˌmɒnəʊˌnjuːklɪˈəʊsɪs] n US mononucleose f.

monoplane [ˈmɒnəpleɪn] n monoplano m.

monopolize, -ise [məˈnɒpəlaɪz] vt monopolizar.

monopoly [məˈnɒpəlɪ] (pl -ies) n monopólio m; ~ **on** OR **of sthg** monopólio em OR de algo; **the Monopolies and Mergers Commission** UK organização que investiga a possível formação de monopólio pelas empresas.

monorail [ˈmɒnəreɪl] n monotrilho m.

monosodium glutamate [ˌmɒnəˈsəʊdjəmˈgluːtəmeɪt] n (U) glutamato m monossódico.

monosyllabic [ˌmɒnəsɪˈlæbɪk] adj monossilábico(ca).

monosyllable [ˈmɒnəˌsɪləbl] n monossílabo m.

monotone [ˈmɒnətəʊn] n: **he speaks in a** ~ ele fala com uma voz monótona.

monotonous [məˈnɒtənəs] adj [voice, job, life] monótono(na).

monotonously [məˈnɒtənəslɪ] adv de forma monótona.

monotony [məˈnɒtənɪ] n (U) monotonia f.

monoxide [mɒˈnɒksaɪd] n monóxido m.

Monrovia [mɒnˈrəʊvɪə] n Monróvia; **in** ~ em Monróvia.

Monsignor [ˌmɒnˈsiːɲəʳ] n Monsenhor m.

monsoon [mɒnˈsuːn] n [rainy season] monção f.

monster [ˈmɒnstəʳ] <> adj gigantesco(ca), enorme. <> n monstro m.

monstrosity [mɒnˈstrɒsətɪ] (pl -ies) n monstruosidade f.

monstrous [ˈmɒnstrəs] adj **-1.** [appalling] espantoso(sa) **-2.** [hideous] monstruoso(sa) **-3.** [very large] gigantesco(ca).

montage [ˈmɒntɑːʒ] n montagem f.

Montana [mɒnˈtænə] n Montana; **in** ~ em Montana.

Mont Blanc [mɒ̃tl] n Monte m Branco.

Montenegro [ˌmɒntɪˈniːgrəʊ] n Montenegro; **in** ~ em Montenegro.

Montevideo [ˌmɒntɪvɪˈdeɪəʊ] n Montevidéu; **in** ~ em Montevidéu.

month [mʌnθ] n mês m.

monthly [ˈmʌnθlɪ] (pl -ies) <> adj mensal. <> adv mensalmente. <> n [publication] revista f mensal.

Montreal [mɒntrɪˈɔːl] n Montreal; **in** ~ em Montreal.

monument [ˈmɒnjʊmənt] n monumento m.

monumental [ˌmɒnjʊˈmentl] adj **-1.** [gen] monumental **-2.** [extremely bad] descomunal.

moo [muː] (pl -s) <> n mugido m. <> vi mugir.

mooch [muːtʃ] ➠ **mooch about, mooch around** vi inf perambular, vaguear.

mood [muːd] n [state of feelings] humor m; **in a (bad)** ~ de mau humor; **in a good** ~ de bom humor.

moody [ˈmuːdɪ] (compar -ier, superl -iest) adj pej **-1.** [changeable] temperamental, de humor variável **-2.** [bad-tempered] mal-humorado(da).

moon [muːn] n lua f; **to be over the** ~ inf dar pulos de alegria.

moonbeam [ˈmuːnbiːm] n raio m de luar.

moonlight [ˈmuːnlaɪt] (pt & pp -ed) <> n (U) luar m, luz f da lua. <> vi inf [have second job] ter um trabalho extra.

moonlighting [ˈmuːnlaɪtɪŋ] n (U) [illegal work] trabalho m extra, bico m.

moonlit [ˈmuːnlɪt] adj enluarado(da).

moonscape [ˈmuːnskeɪp] n paisagem f lunar.

moon shot n viagem para a lua em espaçonave.

moonstone n pedra-da-lua f.

moonstruck [ˈmuːnstrʌk] adj inf lunático(ca).

moony (compar -ier, superl -iest) adj UK inf sonhador(ra).

moor [mɔːʳ] <> n esp UK brejo m vt & vi atracar, ancorar.

Moor [mɔːʳ] n mouro m, -ra f.

moorhen n frango-d'água m.

moorings ['mɔ:rɪŋz] *npl* [of boat, ship - ropes, chains] amarras *fpl*; [- place] ancoradouro *m*.
Moorish ['mɔ:rɪʃ] *adj* mouro(ra), mourisco(ca).
moorland ['mɔ:lənd] *n (U) esp UK* charneca *f*.
moose [mu:s] (*pl inv*) *n* [North American] alce *m*.
moot [mu:t] *vt* propor.
moot point *n* questão *f* controversa.
mop [mɒp] (*pt & pp* -ped, *cont* -ping) ⬦ *n* -1. [for cleaning] esfregão *m* -2. *inf* [of hair] mecha *f*. ⬦ *vt* -1. [floor] esfregar, passar o esfregão em -2. [brow, face] enxugar.
➡ **mop up** *vt sep* -1. [clean up] limpar *(com esfregão)* -2. *fig* [clear away] eliminar.
mope [məʊp] *vi pej* lastimar-se.
➡ **mope about, mope around** *vi pej* vaguear desanimado(da).
moped ['məʊpɛd] *n* bicicleta *f* motorizada.
moral ['mɒrəl] ⬦ *adj* moral; ~ **support** apoio *m* moral. ⬦ *n* [lesson] moral *f*.
➡ **morals** *npl* [principles] princípios *mpl*.
morale [mə'rɑ:l] *n (U)* moral *m*.
moralistic [ˌmɒrə'lɪstɪk] *adj pej* moralista.
morality [mə'rælətɪ] (*pl* -ies) *n* moralidade *f*.
moralize, -ise ['mɒrəlaɪz] *vi pej*: to ~ (**about** OR **on** sthg) moralizar (sobre algo).
morally ['mɒrəlɪ] *adv* moralmente.
Moral Majority *n* grupo de pressão ultraconservador apoiado pelas igrejas fundamentalistas nos EUA.
morass [mə'ræs] *n* [mass] emaranhado *m*, confusão *f*.
moratorium [ˌmɒrə'tɔ:rɪəm] (*pl* -ria [-rɪə]) *n fml* moratória *f*; ~ **on** sthg moratória em algo.
morbid ['mɔ:bɪd] *adj* [unhealthy] mórbido(da).
more [mɔ:r] ⬦ *adj* -1. [a larger amount of] mais; **there are** ~ **tourists than usual** há mais turistas que o normal. -2. [additional] mais; **is there any** ~ **cake?** tem mais bolo?; **I'd like two** ~ **bottles** queria mais duas garrafas; **there's no** ~ **wine** já não tem mais vinho. ⬦ *adv* -1. [in comparatives] mais; **it's** ~ **difficult than before** é mais difícil do que antes; **speak** ~ **clearly** fale de forma mais clara; **we go there** ~ **often now** agora vamos lá mais freqüentemente. -2. [to a greater degree] mais; **we ought to go to the movies** ~ deviámos ir mais vezes ao cinema. -3. [in phrases]: **once** ~ mais uma vez; **we'd be** ~ **than happy to help** teríamos muito prazer em ajudar.
➡ **more and more** *adv, adj & pron* cada vez mais.
➡ **more or less** *adv* mais o menos.
moreover [mɔ:'rəʊvər] *adv fml* além disso.
morgue [mɔ:g] *n* [mortuary] necrotério *m*.
MORI ['mɔ:rɪ] (*abbr of* **Market & Opinion Research Institute**) *n instituto britânico de pesquisa de mercado e opinião.*
moribund ['mɒrɪbʌnd] *adj fml* moribundo(da).
Mormon ['mɔ:mən] *n* mórmon *mf*.
morning ['mɔ:nɪŋ] *n* -1. [first part of day] manhã *f*; **in the** ~ [before lunch] de OR pela manhã; [tomorrow morning] pela manhã -2. [between midnight and noon] manhã *f*.
➡ **mornings** *adv US* de manhã.
morning-after pill *n* pílula *f* do dia seguinte.

morning dress *n esp UK* [formal clothes] *paletó preto com calça listrada.*
morning sickness *n (U)* náusea *f* matinal.
Moroccan [mə'rɒkən] ⬦ *adj* marroquino(na). ⬦ *n* marroquino *m*, -na *f*.
Morocco [mə'rɒkəʊ] *n* Marrocos; **in** ~ em Marrocos.
moron ['mɔ:rɒn] *n inf* [stupid person] idiota *mf*, imbecil *mf*.
moronic [mə'rɒnɪk] *adj* [stupid] idiota, imbecil.
morose [mə'rəʊs] *adj* melancólico(ca).
morphing *n* morphing *m*.
morphine ['mɔ:fi:n] *n (U)* morfina *f*.
morris dancing ['mɒrɪs-] *n (U) dança folclórica inglesa em que os homens representam personagens lendários.*
Morse (code) [mɔ:s-] *n (U)* código *m* Morse.
morsel ['mɔ:sl] *n* pedacinho *m*.
mortal ['mɔ:tl] ⬦ *adj* mortal. ⬦ *n* mortal *mf*.
mortality [mɔ:'tælətɪ] *n (U)* mortalidade *f*.
mortality rate *n* taxa *f* de mortalidade.
mortally ['mɔ:təlɪ] *adv* -1. [fatally] mortalmente -2. [deeply] profundamente.
mortar ['mɔ:tər] *n* -1. (U) [cement mixture] argamassa *f* -2. [gun] morteiro *m* -3. [bowl] almofariz *m*.
mortarboard ['mɔ:təbɔ:d] *n* -1. CONSTR padiola *f (para argamassa)* -2. UNIV barrete *m* de formatura.
mortgage ['mɔ:gɪdʒ] ⬦ *n* hipoteca *f*. ⬦ *comp* hipotecário(ria). ⬦ *vt* hipotecar.
mortgagee [ˌmɔ:gɪ'dʒi:] *n* credor *m* hipotecário, credora *f* hipotecária.
mortgagor [ˌmɔ:gɪ'dʒɔ:r] *n* devedor *m* hipotecário, devedora *f* hipotecária.
mortician [mɔ:'tɪʃn] *n US* agente *mf* funerário, -ria.
mortified ['mɔ:tɪfaɪd] *adj* mortificado(da).
mortify *vt* mortificar.
mortise lock ['mɔ:tɪs-] *n* fechadura *f* embutida.
mortuary ['mɔ:tʃʊərɪ] (*pl* -ies) *n* necrotério *m*.
mosaic [mə'zeɪk] *n* mosaico *m*.
Moscow ['mɒskəʊ] *n* Moscou; **in** ~ em Moscou.
Moslem ['mɒzləm] *adj & n* = **Muslim**.
mosque [mɒsk] *n* mesquita *f*.
mosquito [mə'ski:təʊ] (*pl* -es OR -s) *n* mosquito *m*.
mosquito net *n* mosquiteiro *m*.
moss [mɒs] *n (U)* musgo *m*.
mossy ['mɒsɪ] (*compar* -ier, *superl* -iest) *adj* coberto(ta) de musgo.
most [məʊst] ⬦ *adj* (*superl of many & much*) -1. [the majority of] a maioria de; ~ **people** a maioria das pessoas -2. [largest amount of]: **(the)** ~ mais; **who's got (the)** ~ **money?** quem é que tem mais dinheiro?; **what gave me (the)** ~ **satisfaction was ...** o que me deu a maior satisfação foi ... ⬦ *pron* -1. [the majority] a maioria; **(the)** ~ **of** a maioria de; ~ **of the time** a maior parte do tempo -2. [largest amount]: **(the)** ~ o máximo; **at** ~ no máximo -3. *phr*: **to make the** ~ **of** sthg tirar o máximo de algo. ⬦ *adv* -1. [to the greatest extent]: **what I like (the)** ~ o que eu mais gosto -2. *fml* [very] muito; ~ **certainly** com toda a certeza -3. *US* [almost] quase.

mostly ['məʊstlɪ] *adv* **-1.** [in the main] principalmente **-2.** [usually] normalmente.

MOT ◇ *n* (*abbr of* **Ministry of Transport (test)**) vistoria anual obrigatória realizada pelo Ministério dos Transportes britânico em carros com mais de 3 anos de fabricação. ◇ *vt*: **to have one's car ~ 'd** realizar a vistoria no carro.

motel [məʊ'tel] *n* hotel *m* de beira de estrada.

moth [mɒθ] *n* **-1.** ZOOL mariposa *f* **-2.** [in clothes] traça *f*.

mothball ['mɒθbɔːl] *n* (bola de) naftalina *f*.

moth-eaten *adj* roído(da) pelas traças.

mother ['mʌðəʳ] ◇ *n* mãe *f* ◇ *vt pej* [spoil] mimar.

motherboard ['mʌðəˌbɔːd] *n* COMPUT placa-mãe *f*.

motherhood ['mʌðəhʊd] *n* (U) maternidade *f*.

Mothering Sunday ['mʌðərɪŋ-] *n* Dia *m* das Mães.

mother-in-law (*pl* mothers-in-law OR mother-in-laws) *n* sogra *f*.

motherland ['mʌðəlænd] *n* pátria *f*.

motherless ['mʌðəlɪs] *adj* órfão(fã) de mãe.

motherly ['mʌðəlɪ] *adj* maternal, materno(na).

Mother Nature *n* Mãe *f* Natureza.

mother-of-pearl ◇ *n* (U) madrepérola *f*. ◇ *comp* de madrepérola.

Mother's Day *n* Dia *m* das Mães.

mother ship *n* nave-mãe *f*.

mother superior *n* madre *f* superiora.

mother-to-be (*pl* mothers-to-be) *n* futura mãe *f*.

mother tongue *n* língua *f* materna.

motif [məʊ'tiːf] *n* motivo *m*.

motion ['məʊʃn] ◇ *n* **-1.** (U) [process of moving] movimento *m*; **to set sthg in ~** colocar algo em marcha; **to go through the ~s** [act insincerely] fingir, mostrar um falso interesse **-2.** [proposal] proposta *f*. ◇ *vt*: **to ~ sb to do sthg** fazer sinal para alguém fazer algo. ◇ *vi*: **to ~ to sb** fazer sinal (*com a mão*) para alguém.

motionless ['məʊʃənlɪs] *adj* imóvel.

motion picture *n* US filme *m*.

motivate ['məʊtɪveɪt] *vt* **-1.** [give cause] motivar **-2.** [give incentive] incentivar; **to ~ sb to do sthg** incentivar alguém a fazer algo.

motivated ['məʊtɪveɪtɪd] *adj* motivado(da).

motivation [,məʊtɪ'veɪʃn] *n* **-1.** [cause] razão *f* **-2.** (U) [sense of purpose] motivação *f*.

motive ['məʊtɪv] *n* motivo *m*, razão *f*.

motley ['mɒtlɪ] *adj pej* heterogêneo(nea).

motocross ['məʊtəkrɒs] *n* (U) motocross *m*.

motor ['məʊtəʳ] ◇ *adj UK* [relating to cars - industry, accident] automobilístico(ca); [- mechanic] de automóveis. ◇ *n* [engine] motor *m*. ◇ *vi dated* viajar de automóvel.

Motorail® ['məʊtəreɪl] *n UK* serviço ferroviário de transporte de automóveis.

motorbike ['məʊtəbaɪk] *n* moto *f*.

motorboat ['məʊtəbəʊt] *n* barco *m* a motor.

motorcade ['məʊtəkeɪd] *n* caravana *f*.

motorcar ['məʊtəkaːʳ] *n UK fml* automóvel *m*.

motorcycle ['məʊtəˌsaɪkl] *n* motocicleta *f*.

motorcyclist ['məʊtəˌsaɪklɪst] *n* motociclista *mf*.

motoring ['məʊtərɪŋ] ◇ *adj UK* automobilístico

(ca); **~ offence** infração *f* de trânsito. ◇ *n* (U) dated automobilismo *m*.

motorist ['məʊtərɪst] *n* motorista *mf*.

motorize, -ise ['məʊtəraɪz] *vt* motorizar.

motor lodge *n US* hotel *m* em beira de estrada.

motor racing *n* (U) corrida *f* automobilística.

motor scooter *n* lambreta *f*.

motor vehicle *n* veículo *m* motorizado.

motorway ['məʊtəweɪ] ◇ *n UK* auto-estrada *f*. ◇ *comp* na auto-estrada.

mottled ['mɒtld] *adj* com manchas, pintado(da).

motto ['mɒtəʊ] (*pl* -s OR -es) *n* [maxim] lema *m*.

mould, mold *US* [məʊld] ◇ *n* **-1.** (U) BOT mofo *m* **-2.** [shape] fôrma *f*, molde *m*. ◇ *vt* **-1.** [influence] moldar **-2.** [shape physically] moldar, modelar.

moulding, molding *US* ['məʊldɪŋ] *n* [decoration] cornija *f*.

mouldy, moldy *US* (*compar* -ier, *superl* -iest) ['məʊldɪ] *adj* mofado(da).

moult, molt *US* [məʊlt] ◇ *vt* trocar. ◇ *vi* **-1.** [bird] trocar as penas **-2.** [dog] trocar o pêlo.

mound [maʊnd] *n* **-1.** [small hill] morro *m* **-2.** [untidy pile] montanha *f*.

mount [maʊnt] ◇ *n* **-1.** [support, frame] moldura *f* **-2.** [horse, pony] montaria *f* **-3.** [mountain] monte *m*. ◇ *vt* **-1.** [climb onto] montar **-2.** *fml* [climb up] subir **-3.** [organize] montar; **to ~ guard over sb/sthg** montar guarda para vigiar alguém/algo **-4.** [photograph] emoldurar **-5.** [trophy] pôr em posição de destaque **-6.** [jewel] engastar. ◇ *vi* **-1.** [increase] aumentar **-2.** [climb on horse] montar.
➡ **mount up** *vi* [increase] aumentar.

mountain ['maʊntɪn] *n* [gen] montanha *f*; **to make a ~ out of a molehill** fazer uma tempestade num copo d'água.

mountain bike *n* mountain bike *f*.

mountaineer [,maʊntɪ'nɪəʳ] *n* montanhista *mf*, alpinista *mf*.

mountaineering [,maʊntɪ'nɪərɪŋ] *n* (U) montanhismo *m*, alpinismo *m*.

mountainous ['maʊntɪnəs] *adj* [full of mountains] montanhoso(sa).

mountain range *n* cadeia *f* de montanhas, cordilheira *f*.

mountain rescue *n* (U) resgate *m* nas montanhas.

mounted ['maʊntɪd] *adj* [on horseback] montado(da).

Mountie ['maʊntɪ] *n inf* membro da polícia montada canadense.

mourn [mɔːn] ◇ *vt* **-1.** [the loss of] lamentar **-2.** [the death of] lamentar a morte de. ◇ *vi*: **to ~ for sb** fazer luto por alguém.

mourner ['mɔːnəʳ] *n* enlutado *m*, -da *f*.

mournful ['mɔːnfʊl] *adj* lamuriento(ta), desolado(da).

mourning ['mɔːnɪŋ] *n* **-1.** [period] luto *m* **-2.** [clothes] traje *m* de luto; **in ~** em luto.

mouse [maʊs] (*pl* mice) *n* **-1.** [animal] camundongo *m* **-2.** COMPUT mouse *m*.

mouse mat, mouse pad *n* COMPUT mouse pad *m*.

mousetrap ['maʊstræp] *n* ratoeira *f*.

moussaka [muːˈsɑːkə] *n prato grego à base de beringela e carne moída*.

mousse [muːs] *n* -**1.** [food] musse *f* -**2.** [for hair] mousse *m*.

moustache *UK* [məˈstɑːʃ], **mustache** *US* [ˈmʌstæʃ] *n* bigode *m*.

mouth [*n* maʊθ, *vt* maʊð] *n* -**1.** ANAT boca *f*; **to keep one's ~ shut** *inf* ficar de boca fechada -**2.** [entrance - of cave, hole] boca *f*; [- of river] foz *f*. *vt* -**1.** [silently]: **to ~ a reply** articular uma resposta -**2.** [pompously] dizer pomposamente.

mouthful [ˈmaʊθfʊl] *n* -**1.** [amount - of food] bocado *m*; [- of water] gole *m* -**2.** *inf* [difficult word] palavra *f* difícil de ser pronunciada, palavrão *m*.

mouthorgan [ˈmaʊθˌɔːgən] *n* harmônica *f*, gaita-de-boca *f*.

mouthpiece [ˈmaʊθpiːs] *n* -**1.** [of object] bocal *m* -**2.** [spokesperson] porta-voz *mf*.

mouth-to-mouth *adj*: **~ resuscitation** respiração *f* boca-a-boca.

mouth ulcer *n* úlcera *f* bucal.

mouthwash [ˈmaʊθwɒʃ] *n* antiséptico *m* bucal.

mouth-watering [-ˌwɔːtərɪŋ] *adj* de dar água na boca.

movable [ˈmuːvəbl] *adj* móvel.

move [muːv] *n* -**1.** [movement] movimento *m*; **to be always on the ~** [travelling around] estar sempre viajando; [beginning to move] estar a caminho; **to get a ~ on** *inf* apressar-se -**2.** [change] mudança *f* -**3.** [in board game - turn to play] vez *f*; [- action] jogada *f* -**4.** [course of action] medida *f*. *vt* -**1.** [shift] mudar, mexer; **to ~ the car** tirar o carro -**2.** [change - job, office] mudar de; [- house] mudar-se de -**3.** [affect emotionally] tocar, comover -**4.** [in debate]: **to ~ that ...** sugerir que ... -**5.** *fml* [cause]: **to ~ sb to do sthg** impelir alguém a fazer algo. *vi* -**1.** [shift] mover-se, mexer-se -**2.** [act] agir -**3.** [to new house, job] mudar-se.

move about *vi* -**1.** [fidget] remexer-se, ir de lá para cá -**2.** [travel] viajar.

move along *vt sep* circular. *vi* continuar andando.

move around *vi* = move about.

move away *vi* -**1.** [go in opposite direction] afastar-se -**2.** [live elsewhere] ir-se embora.

move in *vt sep* [troops] chegar. *vi* -**1.** [to new house] instalar-se -**2.** [take control, attack] preparar-se para o ataque.

move off *vi* [train, bus, car] sair.

move on *vt sep* fazer circular. *vi* -**1.** [after stopping] prosseguir -**2.** [in discussion] passar para outro tema.

move out *vt sep* [troops] retirar. *vi* [from house] mudar-se.

move over *vi* chegar mais para lá/cá.

move up *vi* [on seat] chegar mais para lá/cá.

moveable *adj* = movable.

movement [ˈmuːvmənt] *n* -**1.** [gen] movimento *m* -**2.** [transportation] movimentação *f*.

movie [ˈmuːvɪ] *n esp US* filme *m*.

movie camera *n* câmara *f* cinematográfica.

moviegoer [ˈmuːvɪˌgəʊəˀ] *n US* cinéfilo *m*, -la *f*.

movie star *n US* estrela *f* de cinema.

movie theater *n US* cinema *f*.

moving [ˈmuːvɪŋ] *adj* -**1.** [touching] tocante, comovente -**2.** [not fixed] móvel.

moving staircase *n* escada *f* rolante.

mow [məʊl] (*pt* -ed, *pp* -ed OR mown) *vt* [cut - grass, lawn] cortar; [- corn, wheat] ceifar.

mow down *vt sep* dizimar.

mower [ˈməʊəˀ] *n* [machine] ceifadeira *f*.

mown [məʊn] *pp* mow.

Mozambican [ˌməʊzəmˈbiːkən] *adj* moçambicano(na). *n* moçambicano *m*, -na *f*.

Mozambique [ˌməʊzəmˈbiːk] *n* Moçambique; **in ~** em Moçambique.

MP *n* -**1.** (*abbr of* Member of Parliament) *membro do Parlamento Britânico* -**2.** (*abbr of* Military Police) *polícia militar*, ≃ PE *f* -**3.** *Can* (*abbr of* Mounted Police) Polícia *f* Montada.

MP3 (*abbr of* MPEG-1 Audio Layer-3) *n* COMPUT MP3 *m*.

MPEG (*abbr of* Moving Pictures Expert Group) *n* COMPUT MPEG *m*.

mpg (*abbr of* miles per gallon) *n* milhas *fpl* por galão.

mph (*abbr of* miles per hour) *n* milhas *fpl* por hora.

MPhil [ˌemˈfɪl] (*abbr of* Master of Philosophy) *n* (*titular de*) *mestrado em filosofia*.

MPS (*abbr of* Member of the Pharmaceutical Society) *n* *membro da sociedade britânica de farmacêuticos*.

Mr [ˈmɪstəˀ] (*abbr of* Mister) *n* Sr.

MRC (*abbr of* Medical Research Council) *n* *organização do governo britânico de incentivo à pesquisa médica*.

MRCP (*abbr of* Member of the Royal College of Physicians) *n* *membro do colégio real de médicos britânicos*.

MRCS (*abbr of* Member of the Royal College of Surgeons) *n* *membro do colégio real de cirurgiões britânicos*.

MRCVS (*abbr of* Member of the Royal College of Veterinary Surgeons) *n* *membro do colégio real de veterinários britânicos*.

Mrs [ˈmɪsɪz] (*abbr of* Missus) *n* Sra.

ms. (*abbr of* manuscript) *n* manuscrito *m*.

Ms [mɪz] *n* *abreviatura usada diante do nome de mulher quando não se quer especificar seu estado civil, válida para senhora ou senhorita*.

MS *n* -**1.** (*abbr of* manuscript) manuscrito *m* -**2.** (*abbr of* Master of Science) (*titular de*) *mestrado em ciências* -**3.** (*abbr of* multiple sclerosis) esclerose *f* múltipla. *abbr of* Mississippi.

MSA (*abbr of* Master of Science in Agriculture) *n* (*titular de*) *mestrado em agronomia*.

MSB (*abbr of* most significant bit/byte) *n* MSB *m*.

MSc (*abbr of* Master of Science) *n* (*titular de*) *mestrado em ciências*.

MSC (*abbr of* Manpower Services Commission) *n* *antiga organização do governo britânico que tratava de mão-de-obra*.

MSG (*abbr of* monosodium glutamate) *n* glutamato *m* monossódico.

Msgr (*abbr of* Monsignor) Mons.

MST (*abbr of* Mountain Standard Time) *n* *horário oficial da região das Montanhas Rochosas nos Estados Unidos*.

MSW *(abbr of* **Master of Social Work***) n (titular de) mestrado em serviço social.*

Mt *(abbr of* **mount***)* Mte.

MT ◇ *n (abbr of* **machine translation***)* tradução *f* automática. ◇ *abbr of* **Montana**.

much [mʌtʃ] *(compar* **more**, *superl* **most***)* ◇ *adj* muito(ta); **as** ~ **(...) as** tanto (...) quanto; **how** ~ **...?** quanto ...?; **too** ~ ... demais. ◇ *pron* muito; **how** ~ **have you got?** quanto você tem?; **I don't think** ~ **of it** não me parece grande coisa; **as** ~ **as** tanto quanto; **how** ~ **?** quanto?; **too** ~ demais; **this isn't** ~ **of a party** essa festa não está grande coisa; **I'm not** ~ **of a cook** não sou um grande cozinheiro; **so** ~ **for my hard work!** tanto desgaste por meu trabalho!; **I thought as** ~ já imaginava; **it's not up to** ~ *inf* não é nenhuma maravilha, não é aquilo tudo. ◇ *adv* muito; **thank you very** ~ muito obrigado(da); **it's** ~ **too cold** está frio demais; **it's** ~ **the same** é praticamente a mesma coisa; **'what did you think of the film?' - 'not** ~ **'** 'o que você achou do filme?' - 'não gostei muito'; **he's not so** ~ **stupid as lazy** ele é muito mais preguiçoso que bobo; **too** ~ demais; **without so** ~ **as ...** sem nem sequer ...; ~ **as** (exatamente) como; **nothing** ~ nada de mais.

muchness [ˈmʌtʃnɪs] *n:* **to be much of a** ~ vir a ser a mesma coisa.

muck [mʌk] *n inf* **-1.** [dirt] sujeira *f* **-2.** [manure] esterco *m*.
◆ **muck about, muck around** *UK inf* ◇ *vt sep* fazer perder tempo. ◇ *vi* fazer cera.
◆ **muck in** *vi UK inf* trabalhar juntos(tas).
◆ **muck out** *vt sep* limpar.
◆ **muck up** *vt sep UK inf* estragar.

muckraking [ˈmʌkreɪkɪŋ] *n (U) fig* sensacionalismo *m*.

mucky [ˈmʌkɪ] *(compar* **-ier**, *superl* **-iest***) adj inf* sujo(ja).

mucus [ˈmjuːkəs] *n (U)* muco *m*.

mud [mʌd] *n (U)* lama *f*, barro *m*.

muddle [ˈmʌdl] ◇ *n* **-1.** [disorder] desordem *f*; **to be in a** ~ estar em desordem **-2.** [confusion] confusão *f*; **to be in a** ~ estar confuso(sa). ◇ *vt* **-1.** [put into disorder] desordenar **-2.** [confuse] confundir, misturar.
◆ **muddle along** *vi* prosseguir de forma confusa.
◆ **muddle through** *vi* conseguir de qualquer jeito.
◆ **muddle up** *vt sep* misturar.

muddle-headed [-ˌhedɪd] *adj* **-1.** [person] incapaz de pensar com clareza **-2.** [thinking] confuso(sa).

muddy [ˈmʌdɪ] *(compar* **-ier**, *superl* **-iest**, *pt & pp* **-ied***)* ◇ *adj* **-1.** [covered with mud - floor, boots] embarrado(da); [- river] lamacento(ta) **-2.** [in colour] turvo(va). ◇ *vt fig* [issue, situation] complicar.

mudflap [ˈmʌdflæp] *n* pára-lama *m*.

mudflat [ˈmʌdflæt] *n* estirâncio *m*.

mudguard [ˈmʌdɡɑːd] *n* pára-lama *m*.

mud pack *n* lama *f* medicinal.

mud-slinging *n (U) fig* difamação *f*.

muesli [ˈmjuːzlɪ] *n UK* granola *f*.

muff [mʌf] ◇ *n* [for hands] regalo *m*; [for ears]

protetor *m* de orelhas *(contra o frio)*. ◇ *vt inf* perder.

muffin [ˈmʌfɪn] *n* **-1.** *UK* [bread roll] pãozinho redondo e chato que se come quente com manteiga **-2.** *US* [cake] bolinho *m* doce com frutas/chocolate.

muffle [ˈmʌfl] *vt* [quieten] abafar.

muffled [ˈmʌfld] *adj* **-1.** [sound] abafado(da) **-2.** [wrapped up warmly]: ~ **(up)** agasalhado(da).

muffler [ˈmʌfləʳ] *n US* [for car] silenciador *m*.

mug [mʌɡ] *(pt & pp* **-ged**, *cont* **-ging***)* ◇ *n* **-1.** caneca *f* **-2.** *inf* [fool] tolo *m*, -la *f*. ◇ *vt* [attack and rob] assaltar.

mugger [ˈmʌɡəʳ] *n* assaltante *mf*.

mugging [ˈmʌɡɪŋ] *n* assalto *m*.

muggy [ˈmʌɡɪ] *(compar* **-ier**, *superl* **-iest***) adj* mormacento(ta), quente e úmido(da).

mugshot [ˈmʌɡʃɒt] *n inf* fotografia tirada pela polícia de frente e de perfil quando se é fichado.

mujaheddin [ˌmuːdʒəheˈdiːn] *npl* mujaheddin *mpl*.

mulatto [mjuːˈlætəʊ] *(pl* **-s** *OR* **-es***) n* mulato *m*, -ta *f*.

mule [mjuːl] *n* **-1.** [animal] mula *f* **-2.** [slipper] tamanco *m*.

mull [mʌl] ◆ **mull over** *vt sep* refletir sobre.

mullah [ˈmʌlə] *n* mulá *m*.

mulled [mʌld] *adj:* ~ **wine** quentão *m*.

mullet [ˈmʌlɪt] *(pl inv OR* **-s***) n* tainha *f*.

mulligatawny [ˌmʌlɪɡəˈtɔːnɪ] *n (U)* sopa indiana feita com caril.

mullioned *adj* de caixilhos.

multi- [ˈmʌltɪ] *prefix* mult(i)-.

multi-access *adj COMPUT* de multiacesso.

multicoloured *UK*, **multicolored** *US* [ˌmʌltɪˈkʌləd] *adj* multicor.

multicultural [ˌmʌltɪˈkʌltʃərəl] *adj* multicultural.

multifarious [ˌmʌltɪˈfeərɪəs] *adj* variado(da).

multilateral [ˌmʌltɪˈlætərəl] *adj* multilateral.

multilingual *adj* multilíngüe.

multimedia [ˌmʌltɪˈmiːdjə] *adj* multimídia.

multimillionaire [ˈmʌltɪˌmɪljəˈneəʳ] *n* multimilionário *m*, -ria *f*.

multinational [ˌmʌltɪˈnæʃənl] ◇ *adj* multinacional. ◇ *n* multinacional *f*.

multiple [ˈmʌltɪpl] ◇ *adj* múltiplo(pla). ◇ *n* MATH múltiplo *m*.

multiple-choice *adj* de múltipla escolha.

multiple injuries *npl* lesões *fpl* múltiplas.

multiple pileup *n* acidentes *mpl* múltiplos *(de veículos)*.

multiple sclerosis [-sklɪˈrəʊsɪs] *n (U)* esclerose *f* múltipla.

multiplex cinema [ˈmʌltɪpleks-] *n* cinema *m* multi-salas, cinema *m* multiplex.

multiplication [ˌmʌltɪplɪˈkeɪʃn] *n* multiplicação *f*.

multiplication sign *n* sinal *m* de multiplicação.

multiplication table *n* tabuada *f*.

multiplicity [ˌmʌltɪˈplɪsətɪ] *n* multiplicidade *f*.

multiply [ˈmʌltɪplaɪ] *(pt & pp* **-ied***)* ◇ *vt* multiplicar. ◇ *vi* **-1.** MATH multiplicar **-2.** [increase] multiplicar-se.

multi-purpose *adj* multiuso.
multiracial [ˌmʌltɪ'reɪʃl] *adj* multirracial.
multiscreen cinema *n* cinema *m* multi-salas.
multi-storey *UK*, **multistory** *US* <> *adj* com muitos andares. <> *n* edifício-garagem *m*.
multitude ['mʌltɪtjuːd] *n* -1. [large number] multi-plicidade *f* - 2. [crowd] multidão *f*.
mum [mʌm] *UK inf* <> *n* [mother] mamãe *f*. <> *adj*: to keep ~ não dar um pio.
mumble ['mʌmbl] *vt* & *vi* murmurar.
mumbo jumbo ['mʌmbəʊ'dʒʌmbəʊ] *n* (U) *pej* palavreado *m*, enrolação *f*.
mummify ['mʌmɪfaɪ] (*pt* & *pp* -ied) *vt* mumificar.
mummy ['mʌmɪ] (*pl* -ies) *n* -1. *UK inf* [mother] mamãe *f*, mãe *f* - 2. [preserved body] múmia *f*.
mumps [mʌmps] *n* (U) caxumba *f*.
munch [mʌntʃ] *vt* & *vi* mascar.
mundane [mʌn'deɪn] *adj* trivial.
mung bean [mʌŋ-] *n* feijão-fradinho *m*.
municipal [mju:'nɪsɪpl] *adj* municipal.
municipality [mju:ˌnɪsɪ'pælətɪ] (*pl* -ies) *n* [city, district] município *m*.
munificent [mju:'nɪfɪsənt] *adj fml* munificente.
munitions [mju:'nɪʃnz] *npl* munições *fpl*.
mural ['mjuːərəl] *n* (pintura *f*) mural *m*.
murder ['mɜːdəʳ] <> *n* assassinato *m*; **to get away with** ~ fazer o que bem entender sem ser punido(da). <> *vt* assassinar.
murderer ['mɜːdərəʳ] *n* assassino *m*.
murderess ['mɜːdərɪs] *n* assassina *f*.
murderous ['mɜːdərəs] *adj* assassino(na), homicida.
murky ['mɜːkɪ] (*compar* -ier, *superl* -iest) *adj* -1. [gen] sombrio(bria) - 2. [water] turvo(va).
murmur ['mɜːməʳ] <> *n* -1. [low sound] murmúrio *m* - 2. *MED* [of heart] sopro *m*. *vt* & *vi* murmurar.
MusB, MusBac (*abbr of* Bachelor of Music) *n* (*titular de*) bacharelado em *música*.
muscle ['mʌsl] *n* -1. músculo *m* - 2. (U) *fig* [power] poder *m*.
◆ **muscle in** *vi* intrometer-se.
muscleman ['mʌslmən] (*pl* -men [-mən]) *n* [strong man] homem *m* musculoso.
Muscovite ['mʌskəvaɪt] <> *adj* moscovita. <> *n* moscovita *mf*.
muscular ['mʌskjʊləʳ] *adj* -1. [of muscles] muscular - 2. [strong] musculoso(sa).
muscular dystrophy [-'dɪstrəfɪ] *n* (U) distrofia *f* muscular.
MusD, MusDoc (*abbr of* Doctor of Music) *n* (*titular de*) doutorado em *música*.
muse [mju:z] <> *n* [source of inspiration] musa *f*. <> *vi* meditar, refletir.
museum [mju:'ziːəm] *n* museu *m*.
mush [mʌʃ] *n* (U) *inf* -1. [gunge] mingau *m* - 2. [drivel] pieguice *f*.
mushroom ['mʌʃrʊm] <> *n* cogumelo *m*. <> *vi* [grow quickly] expandir-se rapidamente.
mushroom cloud *n* cogumelo *m* nuclear.
mushy ['mʌʃɪ] (*compar* -ier, *superl* -iest) *adj* -1. [very soft] mole - 2. [over-sentimental] água-com-açúcar, sentimentalóide.

music ['mju:zɪk] *n* -1. [gen] música *f* - 2. [written set of notes] partitura *f*.
musical ['mju:zɪkl] <> *adj* -1. [relating to music] [melodious] musical - 2. [talented in music] com talento para música. <> *n* musical *m*.
musical box *UK*, **music box** *US* *n* caixinha *f* de música.
musical chairs *n* (U) dança *f* da cadeira.
musical instrument *n* instrumento *m* musical.
music box *n US* = musical box.
music centre *n* [machine] aparelho *m* de som.
music hall *n UK* -1. [theatre] sala *f* de espetáculo - 2. (U) [variety entertainment] teatro *m* de variedades.
musician [mju:'zɪʃn] *n* músico *m*, -ca *f*.
music stand *n* atril *m* (*para partituras*).
musk [mʌsk] *n* (U) almíscar *m*.
musket ['mʌskɪt] *n* mosquete *m*.
muskrat ['mʌskræt] *n* rato-almiscarado *m*.
Muslim ['mʊzlɪm] <> *adj* muçulmano(na). <> *n* muçulmano *m*, -na *f*.
muslin ['mʌzlɪn] *n* (U) musselina *f*.
musquash ['mʌskwɒʃ] *n* -1. [animal] rato-almiscarado *m* - 2. (U) [fur] pele *f* de rato-almiscarado.
muss [mʌs] *vt US*: to ~ sthg (up) desarrumar algo.
mussel ['mʌsl] *n* mexilhão *m*.
must [mʌst] <> *modal vb* -1. [have to] dever, ter que; I ~ go eu preciso ir - 2. [intend to] ter que - 3. [as suggestion] precisar, ter que - 4. [to express likelihood] dever. <> *n* (U) *inf* [necessity]: **the film is a** ~ você tem que ver o filme.
mustache *n US* = moustache.
mustard ['mʌstəd] *n* (U) mostarda *f*; ~ **and cress** *UK* brotos *mpl* de mostarda e agrião.
mustard gas *n* (U) gás *m* de mostarda.
muster ['mʌstəʳ] <> *vt* -1. [assemble] reunir - 2. [summon - strength, energy] juntar; [- support] reunir. <> *vi* reunir-se.
◆ **muster up** *vt fus* -1. [courage] armar-se de - 2. [strength] juntar - 3. [support] reunir.
mustn't ['mʌsnt] = must not.
must've ['mʌstəv] = must have.
musty ['mʌstɪ] (*compar* -ier, *superl* -iest) *adj* -1. [gen] mofado(da) - 2. [smell] com cheiro de mofo.
mutant ['mju:tənt] <> *adj* mutante. <> *n* mutante *mf*.
mutate [mju:'teɪt] *vi* mutar; to ~ into sthg mutar-se para algo.
mutation [mju:'teɪʃn] *n* mutação *f*.
mute [mju:t] <> *adj* mudo(da). <> *n* [person who cannot speak] mudo *m*, -da *f*. <> *vt* [muffle] abafar, amortecer.
muted ['mju:tɪd] *adj* -1. [soft] suave - 2. [less strong - reaction] discreto(ta); [- feelings] contido(da).
mutilate ['mju:tɪleɪt] *vt* mutilar.
mutilation [ˌmju:tɪ'leɪʃn] *n* mutilação *f*.
mutineer [ˌmju:tɪ'nɪəʳ] *n* amotinado *m*, -da *f*.
mutinous ['mju:tɪnəs] *adj* [disobedient] rebelde.
mutiny ['mju:tɪnɪ] (*pl* -ies, *pt* & *pp* -ied) <> *n* motim *m*. <> *vi* amotinar-se.
mutt [mʌt] *n inf* -1. [fool] tolo *m*, -la *f*, bobo *m*, -ba *f* - 2. *US* [dog] vira-lata *m*.

mutter ['mʌtə^r] ⬦ *vt* murmurar. ⬦ *vi* resmungar; **to ~ to sb** sussurrar para alguém; **to ~ to o.s.** ficar resmungando.

muttering ['mʌtərɪŋ] *n* -**1.** [muttered remark] resmungo *m* -**2.** *(U)* [muttering sound] murmúrio *m*.

mutton ['mʌtn] *n (U)* (carne *f* de) carneiro *m*; **~ dressed as lamb** *UK* lobo *m* em pele de cordeiro.

mutual ['mju:tʃʊəl] *adj* -**1.** [reciprocal] mútuo(tua) -**2.** [common] comum.

mutual fund *n US* fundo *m* mútuo.

mutually ['mju:tʃʊəlɪ] *adv* [reciprocally] mutuamente; **~ exclusive** mutuamente excludente.

Muzak® ['mju:zæk] *n (U) gravação de música suave que toca continuamente em locais públicos.*

muzzle ['mʌzl] ⬦ *n* -**1.** [dog's nose and jaws] focinho *m* -**2.** [wire guard] focinheira *f* -**3.** [of gun] boca *f*. ⬦ *vt* -**1.** [put guard on] colocar focinheira em -**2.** *fig* [silence] amordaçar.

muzzy ['mʌzɪ] *(compar* -**ier**, *superl* -**iest)** *adj* [groggy] atordoado(da), confuso(sa).

MVP *(abbr of* **most valuable player**) *n nos Estados Unidos, título dado ao melhor jogador de um time.*

MW *(abbr of* **medium wave**) onda *f* média.

my [maɪ] *poss adj* meu (minha); **~ books** os meus livros; **~ name is Joe** o meu nome é Joe.

mynah bird *n* mainá *m*.

myopic [maɪ'ɒpɪk] *adj* míope.

myriad ['mɪrɪəd] *literary* ⬦ *adj* incontável. ⬦ *n* miríade *f*.

myrrh [mɜ:^r] *n (U)* mirra *f*.

myrtle ['mɜ:tl] *n* mirto *m*.

myself [maɪ'self] *pron* -**1.** *(reflexive)* me; **I hurt ~** machuquei-me -**2.** *(after prep)* mim -**3.** *(stressed)* eu mesmo (eu mesma); **I did it ~** eu mesmo o fiz.

mysterious [mɪ'stɪərɪəs] *adj* misterioso(sa); **to be ~ about sthg** andar cheio (cheia) de mistérios sobre algo.

mysteriously [mɪ'stɪərɪəslɪ] *adv* misteriosamente.

mystery ['mɪstərɪ] *(pl* -**ies)** ⬦ *adj* misterioso(sa). ⬦ *n* mistério *m*.

mystery story *n* história *f* de suspense.

mystery tour *n* viagem *f* surpresa, *passeio turístico de ônibus no qual as pessoas não conhecem o roteiro.*

mystic ['mɪstɪk] ⬦ *adj* místico(ca). ⬦ *n* místico *m*, -ca *f*.

mystical ['mɪstɪkl] *adj* [spiritual] místico(ca).

mysticism ['mɪstɪsɪzm] *n (U)* misticismo *m*.

mystified ['mɪstɪfaɪd] *adj* [puzzled] perplexo(xa), desconcertado(da).

mystifying ['mɪstɪfaɪɪŋ] *adj* [puzzling] desconcertante.

mystique [mɪ'sti:k] *n (U)* mística *f*.

myth [mɪθ] *n* mito *m*.

mythic ['mɪθɪk] *adj* [like a myth] mítico(ca).

mythical ['mɪθɪkl] *adj* -**1.** [imaginary] mítico(ca) -**2.** [untrue] falso(sa).

mythological [ˌmɪθə'lɒdʒɪkl] *adj* [legendary] mitológico(ca).

mythology [mɪ'θɒlədʒɪ] *(pl* -**ies)** *n* -**1.** *(U)* [collection of myths] mitologia *f* -**2.** [set of false beliefs] mito *m*.

myxomatosis [ˌmɪksəmə'təʊsɪs] *n (U)* mixomatose *f*.

n *(pl* **n's** *OR* **ns)**, **N** *(pl* **N's** *OR* **Ns)** [en] *n* [letter] n, N *m*.
➡ **N** *(abbr of* **north**) N.

n/a, N/A -**1.** *(abbr of* **not applicable**) não-aplicável -**2.** *(abbr of* **not available**) n/d.

NA *(abbr of* **Narcotics Anonymous**) *n organização norte-americana de ajuda a toxicômanos.*

NAACP *(abbr of* **National Association for the Advancement of Colored People**) *n organização norte-americana de defesa dos direitos de pessoas negras.*

NAAFI ['næfɪ] *(abbr of* **Navy, Army & Air Force Institute**) *n organização governamental encarregada das provisões das forças armadas britânicas.*

nab [næb] *(pt & pp* -**bed**, *cont* -**bing)** *vt inf* -**1.** [arrest] pegar -**2.** [claim quickly] pegar rapidamente.

NACU *(abbr of* **National Association of Colleges and Universities**) *n associação nacional de faculdades e universidades norte-americanas.*

nadir ['neɪˌdɪə^r] *n* -**1.** *ASTRON* nadir *m* -**2.** *fig* [low point] ponto *m* mais baixo.

naff [næf] *adj UK inf* -**1.** [untrendy] brega -**2.** [mediocre] medíocre -**3.** [stupid] idiota.

NAFTA *(abbr of* **North American Free Trade Agreement**) *n* NAFTA *f*.

nag [næg] *(pt & pp* -**ged**, *cont* -**ging)** ⬦ *n inf* -**1.** [person] estorvo *m* -**2.** *UK* [horse] rocim *m*. ⬦ *vt* [pester, find fault with] incomodar; **to ~ sb to do sthg/into doing sthg** incomodar alguém para fazer algo. ⬦ *vi*: **to ~ (at sb)** incomodar (alguém).

nagging ['nægɪŋ] *adj* -**1.** [thought, doubt, pain] perturbador(ra), persistente -**2.** [person] briguento(ta).

nail [neɪl] ⬦ *n* -**1.** [for fastening] prego *m*; **to hit the ~ on the head** acertar na mosca -**2.** [of finger, toe] unha *f*. ⬦ *vt* [fasten]: **to ~ sthg to sthg** pregar algo em algo.
➡ **nail down** *vt sep* -**1.** [fasten] pregar -**2.** *fig* [person]: **to ~ sb down to a date** pressionar alguém a fixar uma data.
➡ **nail up** *vt sep* -**1.** [fasten on wall] fixar -**2.** [close with nails] pregar.

nail-biting *adj* cheio (cheia) de suspense, muito emocionante.

nail brush *n* escova *f* de unhas.

nail clippers *npl* cortador *m* de unhas.

nail file *n* lixa *f* de unha.

nail polish *n (U)* esmalte *m* de unhas.

nail scissors *npl* tesoura *f* para unhas.

nail varnish *n (U)* esmalte *m* de unhas.

nail varnish remover [-rɪ'muːvəʳ] *n (U)* removedor *m* de esmalte.

Nairobi [naɪ'rəʊbɪ] *n* Nairóbi.

naive, naïve [naɪ'iːv] *adj* ingênuo(nua).

naivety, naïvety [naɪ'iːvtɪ] *n (U)* ingenuidade *f*.

naked ['neɪkɪd] *adj* **-1.** [nude] nu (nua), pelado(da) **-2.** [exposed] descoberto(ta); ~ **truth** verdade *f* nua e crua; ~ **flame** chama *f* sem proteção; **with the** ~ **eye** a olho nu **-3.** [obvious, blatant - emotions] óbvio(via); [- aggression] aberto(ta).

NALGO ['nælgəʊ] (*abbr of* **National and Local Government Officers' Association**) *n antigo sindicato de funcionários britânicos*.

Nam [næm] (*abbr of* **Vietnam**) *n US* Vietnam *m*.

name [neɪm] <> *n* nome *m*; **what's your** ~ **?** como você se chama?; **by** ~ pelo nome; **is there anyone here by the** ~ **of ...?** há alguém aqui que se chame ...?; **in the** ~ **of** em nome de; **in my/his** ~ em meu/seu nome; **in** ~ **only** só de nome; **to call sb** ~**s** chamar alguém de tudo; **to make a** ~ **for o.s.** conquistar uma boa reputação. <> *vt* **-1.** [christen] batizar; **to** ~ **sb after sb** *UK*, **to** ~ **sb for sb** *US* dar nome a alguém em homenagem a alguém; **to** ~ **sthg after sthg** *UK*, **to** ~ **sthg for sthg** *US* dar um nome a algo em homenagem a algo **-2.** [reveal identity of] dizer o nome de **-3.** [choose] escolher.

name-dropping *n (U) menção do nome de pessoas famosas que se conheceu, com o intuito de impressionar*.

nameless ['neɪmlɪs] *adj* **-1.** [unknown - person] anônimo(ma); [- disease] desconhecido(da) **-2.** [indescribable] indescritível.

namely ['neɪmlɪ] *adv* a saber.

nameplate ['neɪmpleɪt] *n* placa *f* de identificação (*em portas*).

namesake ['neɪmseɪk] *n* [with same name] xará *mf*.

Namibia [naː'mɪbɪə] *n* Namíbia; **in** ~ na Namíbia.

Namibian [naː'mɪbɪən] <> *adj* namibiano(na). <> *n* namibiano *m*, -na *f*.

nan(a) [næn(ə)] *n UK inf* vó *f*.

nan bread [næn-] *n (U) pão indiano sem fermento*.

nanny ['nænɪ] (*pl* -ies) *n* [childminder] babá *f*.

nanny goat *n* cabra *f*.

nanny state *n* estado *m* protetor.

nap [næp] (*pt & pp* -ped, *cont* -ping) <> *n* [sleep] soneca *f*, cochilo *m*; **to take** OR **have a** ~ tirar uma soneca OR um cochilo. <> *vi* [sleep] cochilar; **to be caught napping** *inf* ser pego de surpresa.

napalm ['neɪpɑːm] *n (U)* napalm *m*.

nape [neɪp] *n*: ~ **(of the neck)** nuca *f*.

napkin ['næpkɪn] *n* [serviette] guardanapo *m*.

nappy ['næpɪ] (*pl* -ies) *n UK* fralda *f*.

nappy liner *n espécie de papel descartável que mantém o bebê seco quando o restante da fralda está molhada*.

narcissi [naː'sɪsaɪ] *pl* ⊳ **narcissus**.

narcissism ['naːsɪsɪzm] *n (U)* narcisismo *m*.

narcissistic [ˌnaːsɪ'sɪstɪk] *adj* narcisista.

narcissus [naː'sɪsəs] (*pl* **-cissuses** OR **-cissi**) *n* narciso *m*.

narcotic [naː'kɒtɪk] *n* narcótico *m*.

nark [naːk] *UK inf* <> *n* [police informer] informante *mf*, dedo-duro *mf*. <> *vt* irritar.

narky ['naːkɪ] (*compar* -ier, *superl* -iest) *adj UK inf* enjoado(da), mal-humorado(da).

narrate [*UK* nə'reɪt, *US* 'næreɪt] *vt* narrar.

narration [*UK* nə'reɪʃn, *US* næ'reɪʃn] *n* narração *f*.

narrative ['nærətɪv] <> *adj* narrativo(va). <> *n* narrativa *f*.

narrator [*UK* nə'reɪtəʳ, *US* 'næreɪtər] *n* [speaker] narrador *m*, -ra *f*.

narrow ['nærəʊ] <> *adj* **-1.** [thin, not wide] estreito(ta) **-2.** [limited, restricted] limitado(da) **-3.** [marginal, close - victory, majority] apertado(da); [- escape]: **to have a** ~ **escape** escapar por um triz. <> *vt* **-1.** [eyes] apertar **-2.** [difference] diminuir, reduzir. <> *vi* **-1.** [road, river] estreitar-se **-2.** [eyes] estreitar-se **-3.** [difference] diminuir, reduzir.

➡ **narrow down** *vt sep* [restrict] diminuir, reduzir.

narrow-gauge *adj* RAIL de bitola estreita.

narrowly ['nærəʊlɪ] *adv* **-1.** [win, lose, miss] por muito pouco **-2.** [escape, miss] por um triz.

narrow-minded [-'maɪndɪd] *adj* de visão limitada.

NAS (*abbr of* **National Academy of Sciences**) *n organização norte-americana de incentivo à pesquisa científica*.

NASA ['næsə] (*abbr of* **National Aeronautics and Space Administration**) *n* NASA *f*.

nasal ['neɪzl] *adj* nasal.

nascent ['neɪsənt] *adj fml* nascente.

NASDAQ (*abbr of* **National Association of Securities Dealers Automated Quotations**) *n* NASDAQ *f*.

nastily ['naːstɪlɪ] *adv* [unkindly] com má intenção; **to fall** ~ ter uma queda feia.

nastiness ['naːstɪnɪs] *n (U)* [unkindness] má intenção *f*.

nasturtium [nəs'tɜːʃəm] (*pl* -s) *n* capuchinha *f*.

nasty ['naːstɪ] (*compar* -ier, *superl* -iest) *adj* **-1.** [unkind, unpleasant] mal-intencionado(da) **-2.** [disgusting, unattractive] horrível, desagradável; **cheap and** ~ barato(ta) e de mau gosto **-3.** [tricky] complicado(da) **-4.** [serious - injury, disease] sério(ria); [- fall, accident] feio (feia).

Natal [nə'tæl] *n* Natal; **in** ~ em Natal.

nation ['neɪʃn] *n* [country] nação *f*.

national ['næʃənl] <> *adj* nacional. <> *n* cidadão *m*, -dã *f*.

national anthem *n* hino *m* nacional.

national curriculum *n*: **the** ~ *o currículo nacional do ensino na Inglaterra e no País de Gales*.

national debt *n* dívida *f* pública.

national dress *n (U)* roupas *fpl* típicas (*de um país*).

National Front *n UK* Frente *f* Nacional, *partido político minoritário de extrema direita na Grã-Bretanha*.

national grid *n UK* rede *f* elétrica.

National Guard *n US:* the ~ a Guarda Nacional norte-americana.

National Health Service *n (U) UK:* the ~ o Serviço Nacional de Saúde, *órgão britânico gestor da saúde pública.*

National Heritage Minister *n ministro da cultura, do turismo e do desporto britânico.*

National Insurance *n (U) UK* **-1.** [system] ≃ Instituto Nacional de Seguro Social **-2.** [payments] contribuição *f* para a previdência social.

nationalism ['næʃnəlɪzm] *n (U)* nacionalismo *m*.

nationalist ['næʃnəlɪst] <> *adj* [pro-independence] nacionalista. <> *n* [supporter of independence movement] nacionalista *mf*.

nationality [ˌnæʃə'nælətɪ] *(pl* **-ies)** *n* nacionalidade *f*.

nationalization [ˌnæʃnəlaɪ'zeɪʃn] *n* [of company, industry] nacionalização *f*.

nationalize, -ise ['næʃnəlaɪz] *vt* [company, industry] nacionalizar.

nationalized ['næʃnəlaɪzd] *adj* [company, industry] nacionalizado(da).

National Lottery *n:* the ~ a loteria britânica.

national park *n* parque *m* nacional.

national service *n (U) UK* MIL serviço *m* militar.

National Trust *n (U) UK:* the ~ *organização britânica que promove a preservação e o acesso público a edifícios de interesse histórico ou arquitetônico e a locais de beleza natural,* ≃ o Patrimônio Nacional.

nation state *n* estado *m* nação.

nationwide ['neɪʃənwaɪd] <> *adj* em âmbito nacional. <> *adv* **-1.** [travel] por todo o país **-2.** [being shown] em todo o país **-3.** [being broadcast] para todo o país.

native ['neɪtɪv] <> *adj* **-1.** [country, area] natal **-2.** nativo(va); ~ **language** língua *f* materna; ~ **to** nativo(va) de. <> *n* **-1.** [person born in area, country] natural *mf* **-2.** *offensive* [original inhabitant] nativo *m*, -va *f*.

Native American <> *adj* indígena norte-americano(na). <> *n* indígena *mf* norte-americano, -na.

NATIVE AMERICAN

Entre os séculos XVII e XIX, as tribos aborígenes que povoavam o território norte-americano viram-se obrigadas a defender suas terras dos colonos europeus, muitas vezes tendo de lutar para mantê-las. Muitos índios morreram em combate ou por contrair doenças trazidas pelos europeus para a América. Outros foram obrigados a viver em reservas, territórios destinados especialmente a eles. Ao longo do século XX, o governo dos EUA procurou conceder mais direitos aos grupos étnicos nativos, demonstrando cada vez maior interesse por sua história e cultura tradicional.

Nativity [nə'tɪvətɪ] *n:* the ~ a Natividade.

nativity play *n* natividade *f*.

NATO ['neɪtəʊ] *(abbr of* **North Atlantic Treaty Organization)** *n* OTAN *f*.

natter ['nætəʳ] *UK inf* <> *n:* to have a ~ bater um papo, trovar fiado. <> *vi* papear, bater um papo.

natty ['nætɪ] *(compar* **-ier,** *superl* **-iest)** *adj* **-1.** *inf* [person] boa-pinta **-2.** [dresser, appearance] elegante, chique.

natural ['nætʃrəl] <> *adj* **-1.** [gen] natural; **to die of** ~ **causes** morrer de causas naturais **-2.** [inborn, instinctive] nato(ta) **-3.** [biological] biológico(ca) **-4.** : **C** ~ dó bequadro. <> *n* [talented person]: **to be a** ~ ter um talento natural.

natural childbirth *n (U)* parto *m* natural.

natural gas *n (U)* gás *m* natural.

natural history *n (U)* história *f* natural.

naturalist ['nætʃrəlɪst] *n* [biologist] naturalista *mf*.

naturalize, -ise ['nætʃrəlaɪz] *vt* [make citizen] naturalizar; **to be** ~ **d** naturalizar-se.

naturally ['nætʃrəlɪ] *adv* **-1.** [as expected, understandably] naturalmente **-2.** [unaffectedly] com naturalidade **-3.** [instinctively] por natureza; **to come** ~ **to sb** ser inato(ta) em alguém.

naturalness ['nætʃrəlnɪs] *n (U)* naturalidade *f*.

natural resources *npl* recursos *mpl* naturais.

natural science *n* ciências *fpl* naturais.

natural wastage *n* demissão *f* voluntária.

natural yoghurt *n* iogurte *m* natural.

nature ['neɪtʃəʳ] *n* natureza *f*; **by** ~ por natureza.

nature reserve *n* reserva *f* natural.

nature trail *n* trilha *f* ecológica.

naturist ['neɪtʃərɪst] *n* naturista *mf*.

naughty ['nɔːtɪ] *(compar* **-ier,** *superl* **-iest)** *adj* **-1.** [badly behaved] malcriado(da) **-2.** [rude, indecent] obsceno(na), atrevido(da).

nausea ['nɔːsjə] *n (U)* náusea *f*.

nauseam ['nɔːzɪæm] ⊳ **ad nauseam.**

nauseate ['nɔːsɪeɪt] *vt* **-1.** [cause nausea in] nausear, causar náuseas em **-2.** *fig* [disgust]: **it really** ~ **s me** isso (realmente) me dá nojo.

nauseating ['nɔːsɪeɪtɪŋ] *adj* **-1.** [sickening] enjoativo(va) **-2.** *fig* [disgusting] repugnante.

nauseous ['nɔːsjəs] *adj* **-1.** [sick] enjoado(da) **-2.** *fig* [revolting] repugnante.

nautical ['nɔːtɪkl] *adj* náutico(ca).

nautical mile *n* milha *f* náutica.

naval ['neɪvl] *adj* naval.

naval officer *n* oficial *mf* da marinha.

nave [neɪv] *n* nave *f (da igreja).*

navel ['neɪvl] *n* umbigo *m*.

navigable ['nævɪgəbl] *adj* [deep, wide] navegável.

navigate ['nævɪgeɪt] <> *vt* **-1.** [steer - plane] pilotar; [- ship] comandar **-2.** [travel safely across] navegar por. <> *vi* **-1.** [ship] comandar **-2.** [car] ser co-piloto(ta) **-3.** [plane] pilotar.

navigation [ˌnævɪ'geɪʃn] *n (U)* [piloting, steering - plane] pilotagem *f*; [- ship] navegação.

navigator ['nævɪgeɪtəʳ] *n* **-1.** [on a ship] navegador *m*, -ra *f* **-2.** [on a plane] comandante *mf*.

navvy ['nævɪ] *(pl* **-ies)** *n UK inf* operário *m (em escavações).*

navy ['neɪvɪ] *(pl* **-ies)** <> *adj* [in colour] azul-marinho. <> *n* **-1.** [armed force] marinha *f (de guerra)* **-2.** = navy blue.

navy blue <> *adj* azul-marinho. <> *n* azul-marinho *m*.

Nazareth *n* Nazaré; **in** ~ em Nazaré.

Nazi ['nɑːtsɪ] *(pl* **-s)** <> *adj* nazista. <> *n* nazista *mf*.

NB -1. (*abbr of* **nota bene**) NB **-2.** *abbr of* **New Brunswick.**

NBA *n* **-1.** (*abbr of* **National Basketball Association**) NBA *f* **-2.** (*abbr of* **National Boxing Association**) *federação de boxe norte-americana.*

NBC (*abbr of* **National Broadcasting Company**) *n rede de televisão norte-americana*, NBC *f*.

NBS (*abbr of* **National Bureau of Standards**) *n organização norte-americana de normatização de unidades de medida.*

NC -1. (*abbr of* **no charge**) grátis **-2.** *abbr of* **North Carolina.**

NCC (*abbr of* **National Curriculum Council**) *n na Grã-Bretanha, órgão responsável pelo currículo escolar,* ≃ Conselho *m* Nacional de Educação.

NCCL (*abbr of* **National Council for Civil Liberties**) *n organização britânica que defende os direitos do cidadão.*

NCO (*abbr of* **non-commissioned officer**) *n* oficial *m* subalterno.

ND *abbr of* **North Dakota.**

NE -1. *abbr of* **Nebraska -2.** *abbr of* **New England -3.** (*abbr of* **northeast**) NE.

Neanderthal [nɪ'ændəta:l] <> *adj* neandertal. <> *n* (homem *m* de) neandertal *m*.

neap tide [ni:p-] *n* maré *f* morta OR de quadratura.

near [nɪəʳ] <> *adj* **-1.** [in space] perto **-2.** [in time, relationship] próximo(ma); **in the ~ future** em breve; **the nearest thing to sthg** o mais próximo de algo **-3.** [almost happened] quase; **it was a ~ thing** faltou pouco. <> *adv* **-1.** [in space] perto; **come ~er!** chegue mais perto! **-2.** [in time] próximo(ma) **-3.** [almost] quase; **we're nowhere ~ finding a solution** nem estamos nem perto de encontrar uma solução. <> *prep* **-1.** : **~ (to)** perto de; **phone ~er the time** ligue quando chegar a hora **-2.** [on the point of]: **~ (to)** à beira de **-3.** [similar to]: **~ (to)** próximo(ma) de. <> *vt* aproximar-se de. <> *vi* aproximar-se.

nearby [nɪə'baɪ] <> *adj* próximo(ma). <> *adv* perto, nas redondezas.

Near East *n*: **the ~** o Oriente Próximo.

nearly ['nɪəlɪ] *adv* [almost] quase; **I ~ cried** quase chorei; **not ~** nem de longe; **not ~ enough** muito pouco; **you don't make ~ enough effort** você não se esforça o suficiente OR o bastante; **he doesn't study ~ enough** ele não estuda o suficiente.

near miss *n* [nearly a collision] quase-colisão *f*.

nearness ['nɪənɪs] *n* [in distance] proximidade *f*.

nearside ['nɪəsaɪd] <> *adj* do lado oposto ao do condutor. <> *n* lado *m* oposto ao do condutor.

nearsighted [,nɪə'saɪtɪd] *adj US* míope.

neat [ni:t] *adj* **-1.** [tidy] arrumado(da) **-2.** [skilful] hábil **-3.** [undiluted] puro(ra) **-4.** *US inf* [very good] ótimo(ma), maravilhoso(sa).

neatly ['ni:tlɪ] *adv* **-1.** [tidily] com capricho **-2.** [skilfully] habilmente.

neatness ['ni:tnɪs] *n* **-1.** [of room] arrumação *f* **-2.** [of appearance] asseio *m* **-3.** [of handwriting] clareza *f*.

Nebraska [nɪ'bræskə] *n* Nebrasca; **in ~** em Nebrasca.

nebulous ['nebjʊləs] *adj fml* nebuloso(sa).

NEC (*abbr of* **National Exhibition Centre**) *n centro de convenções em Birmingham, Inglaterra.*

necessarily [*UK* 'nesəsrəlɪ, ,nesə'serəlɪ] *adv* inevitavelmente, necessariamente; **not ~** não necessariamente.

necessary ['nesəsrɪ] *adj* **-1.** [required] necessário(ria) **-2.** [inevitable] inevitável.

necessitate [nɪ'sesɪteɪt] *vt fml* necessitar de.

necessity [nɪ'sesətɪ] (*pl* **-ies**) *n* necessidade *f*; **of ~** por necessidade.

neck [nek] <> *n* **-1.** ANAT pescoço *m*; **to be up to one's ~ (in sthg)** estar até o pescoço (de algo); **to breathe down sb's ~** ficar na cola de alguém; **to stick one's ~ out** arriscar-se **-2.** [of shirt, dress] gola *f* **-3.** [of bottle] gargalo *m*. <> *vi inf* agarrar-se. ⏵ **neck and neck** *adj* **-1.** [horses] cabeça a cabeça **-2.** [competitors] emparelhado(da).

neckerchief ['nekətʃɪf] (*pl* **-chiefs** OR **-chieves** [-tʃɪvz]) *n* echarpe *f*.

necklace ['neklɪs] *n* colar *m*.

neckline ['neklaɪn] *n* decote *m*.

necktie ['nektaɪ] *n US* gravata *f*.

nectar ['nektəʳ] *n* (U) [from flowers] néctar *m*.

nectarine ['nektərɪn] *n* [fruit] nectarina *f*.

née [neɪ] *adj* em solteira.

need [ni:d] <> *n* necessidade *f*; **~ for sthg** necessidade por algo; **~ to do sthg** necessidade de fazer algo; **to be in** OR **have ~ of sthg** necessitar de algo; **to have no ~ of sthg** não precisar de algo; **if ~ be** se necessário for; **in ~** em necessidade. <> *vt* precisar de, necessitar de; **to ~ to do sthg** precisar fazer algo. <> *modal vb*: **~ we go?** precisamos ir mesmo?; **it ~ not happen** não tem que ser assim. ⏵ **needs** *adv*: **if ~s must** se preciso for.

needle ['ni:dl] <> *n* agulha *f*; **it's like looking for a ~ in a haystack** é como procurar uma agulha em um palheiro. <> *vt inf* alfinetar, importunar.

needlecord ['ni:dlkɔ:d] *n* (U) veludo *m* cotelê.

needlepoint ['ni:dlpɔɪnt] *n* (U) bordado *m*.

needless ['ni:dlɪs] *adj* desnecessário(ria); **~ to say** ... desnecessário dizer que ...

needlessly ['ni:dlɪslɪ] *adv* desnecessariamente.

needlework ['ni:dlwɜ:k] *n* (U) **-1.** [work produced] bordado *m* **-2.** [activity] costura *f*.

needn't ['ni:dnt] = **need not.**

needy ['ni:dɪ] (*compar* **-ier**, *superl* **-iest**) <> *adj* necessitado(da), carente. <> *npl*: **the ~** os necessitados.

nefarious [nɪ'feərɪəs] *adj fml* execrável.

negate [nɪ'geɪt] *vt fml* [cancel out] anular, invalidar.

negation [nɪ'geɪʃn] *n fml* [cancelling out] anulação *f*, invalidação *f*.

negative ['negətɪv] <> *adj* negativo(va). <> *n* **-1.** PHOT negativo *m* **-2.** LING negação *f*; **to answer in the ~** dizer não.

neglect [nɪ'glekt] <> *n* **-1.** [of duty] não-cumprimento *m* **-2.** [of work, children] desleixo *m*, descuido *m*; **in a state of ~** num estado de total abandono. <> *vt* **-1.** [not take care of] abandonar **-2.** [not do - duty] não cumprir com; [- work] não fazer; **to ~ to do sthg** deixar de fazer algo.

neglected [nɪˈglektɪd] *adj* [child, garden] abandonado(da).

neglectful [nɪˈglektfʊl] *adj* negligente; ~ **of sb/ sthg** negligente com alguém/algo.

negligee [ˈneglɪʒeɪ] *n* chambre *m*.

negligence [ˈneglɪdʒəns] *n (U)* negligência *f*.

negligent [ˈneglɪdʒənt] *adj* negligente.

negligently [ˈneglɪdʒəntlɪ] *adv* negligentemente.

negligible [ˈneglɪdʒəbl] *adj* insignificante.

negotiable [nɪˈgəʊʃjəbl] *adj* [which can be discussed] negociável.

negotiate [nɪˈgəʊʃɪeɪt] <> *vt* **-1.** [obtain through negotiation] negociar **-2.** [get over] transpor **-3.** [get around - obstacle] contornar; [- bend] tomar. <> *vi* negociar; **to** ~ **with sb for sthg** negociar algo com alguém.

negotiation [nɪˌgəʊʃɪˈeɪʃn] *n (U)* [talking, discussion] negociação *f*.
➧ **negotiations** *npl* negociações *fpl*.

negotiator [nɪˈgəʊʃɪeɪtəʳ] *n* negociador *m*, -ra *f*.

neigh [neɪ] *vi* relinchar.

neighbor etc *n US* = neighbour etc.

neighbour UK, **neighbor** US [ˈneɪbəʳ] *n* vizinho *m*, -nha *f*.

neighbourhood UK, **neighborhood** US [ˈneɪbəhʊd] *n* **-1.** [of town] vizinhança *f*; **in the** ~ na vizinhança; **in the** ~ **of sthg** nas proximidades de algo **-2.** [approximate area]: **in the** ~ **of** [approximately] por volta de.

neighbourhood watch *n UK* vigilância *f* comunitária.

neighbouring UK, **neighboring** US [ˈneɪbərɪŋ] *adj* vizinho(nha).

neighbourly UK, **neighborly** US [ˈneɪbəlɪ] *adj* de boa vizinhança; **to be** ~ ser um bom vizinho.

neither [ˈnaɪðəʳ, ˈniːðəʳ] <> *adj* nenhum(ma). <> *adv* nem; ~ **... nor ...** nem ... nem ...; **that's** ~ **here nor there** isso não importa. <> *pron* nenhum(ma) dos dois; ~ **of us** nenhum de nós dois. <> *conj*: ~ **do I** nem eu.

neo- [ˈniːəʊ] *prefix* neo-.

neoclassical [ˌniːəʊˈklæsɪkl] *adj* neoclássico(ca).

neolithic [ˌniːəʊˈlɪθɪk] *adj* neolítico(ca).

neologism [niːˈɒlədʒɪzm] *n* neologismo *m*.

neon [ˈniːɒn] *n (U)* neônio *m*.

neon light *n* lâmpada *f* OR luz *f* de néon.

neon sign *n* letreiro *m* de néon.

Nepal [nɪˈpɔːl] *n* Nepal; **in** ~ no Nepal.

Nepalese [ˌnepəˈliːz] (*pl inv*) <> *adj* nepalês(esa). <> *n* [person] nepalês *m*, -esa *f*.

Nepali [nɪˈpɔːlɪ] *n* [language] nepali *m*, nepalês *m*.

nephew [ˈnefjuː] *n* sobrinho *m*.

nepotism [ˈnepətɪzm] *n (U)* nepotismo *m*.

Neptune [ˈneptjuːn] *n* [planet] Netuno *m*.

nerd *n* pessoa estúpida e ridícula.

nerve [nɜːv] *n* **-1.** ANAT nervo *m* **-2.** [courage] coragem *f*; **to lose one's** ~ perder a coragem **-3.** [cheek] petulância *f*; **to have the** ~ **to do sthg** ter a petulância de fazer algo.
➧ **nerves** *npl* nervos *mpl*; **to get on sb's** ~ **s** dar nos nervos de alguém.

nerve centre *n* **-1.** ANAT centro *m* nervoso **-2.** fig [headquarters] centro *m* nevrálgico.

nerve gas *n (U)* gás *m* asfixiante.

nerve-racking [-ˌrækɪŋ] *adj* angustiante.

nervous [ˈnɜːvəs] *adj* nervoso(sa); **to be** ~ **of sthg/ of doing sthg** ter medo de algo/de fazer algo; **to be** ~ **about sthg** ficar nervoso(sa) por algo.

nervous breakdown *n* crise *f* nervosa.

nervously [ˈnɜːvəslɪ] *adv* nervosamente.

nervousness [ˈnɜːvəsnɪs] *n* nervosismo *m*.

nervous system *n* sistema *m* nervoso.

nervous wreck *n* pilha *f* de nervos.

nervy [ˈnɜːvɪ] (*compar* -ier, *superl* -iest) *adj inf* **-1.** [nervous] nervoso(sa) **-2.** US [cheeky] petulante *mf*.

nest [nest] <> *n* **-1.** [gen] ninho *m* **-2.** [of ants] formigueiro *m* **-3.** [of wasps] vespeiro *m* **-4.** [of tables] conjunto *m*. <> *vi* [make a nest] fazer um ninho, aninhar-se.

nest egg *n* pé-de-meia *m*.

nestle [ˈnesl] *vi* **-1.** [make o.s. comfortable] aconchegar-se **-2.** [be sheltered] estar abrigado(da).

nestling [ˈneslɪŋ] *n* [baby bird] filhote *m*.

net [net] (*pt & pp* -ted, *cont* -ting) <> *adj* **-1.** [gen] líquido(da) **-2.** [final] final. <> *n* **-1.** [gen] rede *f* **-2.** [type of fabric] malha *f*. <> *vt* **-1.** [catch] enredar **-2.** *fig* [acquire because of skill] alcançar **-3.** [bring in as profit] render.
➧ **Net** *n*: **the Net** COMPUT a Rede.

netball [ˈnetbɔːl] *n (U)* esporte feminino semelhante ao basquete, bola-ao-cesto *m*.

net curtains *npl* cortinas *fpl* de voile.

Netherlands [ˈneðələndz] *npl*: **the** ~ os Países Baixos; **in the** ~ nos Países Baixos.

netiquette [ˈnetɪket] *n* COMPUT netiqueta *f*.

net profit *n* lucro *m* líquido.

net revenue *n* receita *f* líquida.

nett *adj* = net.

netting [ˈnetɪŋ] *n (U)* **-1.** [of metal, plastic] tela *f* **-2.** [fabric] voile *m*.

nettle [ˈnetl] <> *n* urtiga *f*. <> *vt* [irritate] irritar.

network [ˈnetwɜːk] <> *n* **-1.** [gen] rede *f* **-2.** [group of people] grupo *m*; **a** ~ **of contacts** uma rede de contatos. <> *vt* **-1.** RADIO & TV [broadcast] transmitir em rede **-2.** COMPUT ligar em rede. <> *vi* [give mutual aid] criar uma rede de contatos.

networking [ˈnetwɜːkɪŋ] *n* COMM estabelecimento *m* de uma rede de contatos.

neuralgia [njʊəˈrældʒə] *n (U)* neuralgia *f*.

neurological [ˌnjʊərəˈlɒdʒɪkl] *adj* neurológico (ca).

neurologist [njʊəˈrɒlədʒɪst] *n* neurologista *mf*.

neurology [njʊəˈrɒlədʒɪ] *n (U)* neurologia *f*.

neurosis [ˌnjʊəˈrəʊsɪs] (*pl* -ses [-siːz]) *n* neurose *f*.

neurosurgery [ˌnjʊərəʊˈsɜːdʒərɪ] *n (U)* neurocirurgia *f*.

neurotic [ˌnjʊəˈrɒtɪk] <> *adj* [person] neurótico(ca). <> *n* neurótico *m*, -ca *f*.

neuter [ˈnjuːtəʳ] <> *adj* **-1.** GRAM neutro(tra) **-2.** [sexless] castrado(da). <> *vt* castrar.

neutral [ˈnjuːtrəl] <> *adj* **-1.** [non-allied] [pale greybrown & ELEC] neutro(tra) **-2.** [inexpressive] indiferente **-3.** [colourless] incolor. <> *n* **-1.** (U) AUT ponto *m* morto **-2.** [POL - country] país *m* neutro; [- person] pessoa *f* neutra.

neutrality [njuːˈtrælɪt] *n (U)* POL neutralidade *f*.

neutralize, -ise [ˈnjuːtrəlaɪz] vt [effects] neutralizar.

neutron [ˈnjuːtrɒn] n nêutron m.

neutron bomb n bomba f de nêutrons.

Nevada [nɪˈvɑːdə] n Nevada; **in** ~ em Nevada.

never [ˈnevəʳ] adv **-1.** [at no time] nunca; ~ **ever** jamais **- 2.** inf [in surprise, disbelief] nunca; **you** ~ **did!** não (me diga)! **- 3.** phr: **well I** ~! não acredito!

never-ending adj interminável.

never-never n UK inf: **on the** ~ a perder de vista.

never-never land n país m das maravilhas.

nevertheless [ˌnevəðəˈles] adv contudo, todavia.

new [njuː] adj novo(va); **as good as** ~ como se fosse novo; **to be** ~ **to sthg** ser novo em algo.

◆ **news** n (U)**-1.** [information] notícia f; **the** ~ **s** as notícias; **a piece of** ~ **s** uma notícia; **that's** ~ **s to me** isto é novidade para mim; **to break the** ~ **s to sb** dar a má notícia a alguém **- 2.** RADIO & TV noticiário m.

New Age n New Age f, Nova Era f.

new blood n (U) fig sangue m novo.

newborn [ˈnjuːbɔːn] adj recém-nascido(da).

New Brunswick [-ˈbrʌnzwɪk] n New Brunswick.

New Caledonia [-ˌkælɪˈdəʊnjə] n Nova Caledônia; **in** ~ em Nova Caledônia.

New Caledonian [-ˌkælɪˈdəʊnjən] ⋄ adj neocaledônio(nia). ⋄ n neocaledônio m, -nia f.

newcomer [ˈnjuːˌkʌməʳ] n: ~ **(to sthg)** novato m, -ta f (em algo); ~ **(to somewhere)** recém-chegado m, -da f (em algum lugar).

New Delhi n Nova Déhli; **in** ~ em Nova Déhli.

New England n Nova Inglaterra; **in** ~ na Nova Inglaterra.

newfangled [ˌnjuːˈfæŋgld] adj inf pej modernoso(sa).

new-found adj recém-descoberto(ta); ~ **friend** amigo m recente.

Newfoundland [ˈnjuːfəndlənd] n Terra f Nova.

New Guinea n Nova Guiné; **in** ~ na Nova Guiné.

New Hampshire [-ˈhæmpʃəʳ] n New Hampshire; **in** ~ em New Hampshire.

New Hebrides npl: **the** ~ as Novas Hébridas; **in the** ~ nas Novas Hébridas.

New Jersey n Nova Jérsei; **in** ~ em Nova Jérsei.

newly [ˈnjuːlɪ] adv recém-.

newly-weds npl recém-casados mpl, -das fpl.

New Mexico n Novo México; **in** ~ no Novo México.

new moon n lua f nova.

New Orleans [-ˈɔːlɪənz] n Nova Orleans; **in** ~ em Nova Orleans.

New Quebec n Nova Quebec; **in** ~ em Nova Quebec.

news agency n agência f de notícias.

newsagent UK [ˈnjuːzeɪdʒənt], **newsdealer** US [ˈnjuːzdiːlər] n [person] jornaleiro m, -ra f; ~ **'s (shop)** banca f de jornais.

news bulletin n boletim m de notícias.

newscast [ˈnjuːzkɑːst] n noticiário m, jornal m.

newscaster [ˈnjuːzkɑːstəʳ] n **-1.** [television] apresentador m, -ra f de jornal **- 2.** [radio] locutor(ra).

news conference n entrevista f coletiva.

newsdealer n US = newsagent.

newsflash [ˈnjuːzflæʃ] n plantão m de notícias.

newsgroup [ˈnjuːzgruːp] n COMPUT grupo m de notícias.

newshound [ˈnjuːzhaʊnd] n repórter mf, caçador m, -ra f de notícias.

newsletter [ˈnjuːzˌletəʳ] n boletim m de notícias.

newsman [ˈnjuːzmæn] (pl -men [-men]) n repórter m.

New South Wales n Nova Gales do Sul.

newspaper [ˈnjuːzˌpeɪpəʳ] n jornal m.

newspaperman [ˈnjuːzˌpeɪpəmæn] (pl -men [-men]) n [journalist] **-1.** jornalista m **- 2.** [seller] jornaleiro m, -ra f.

newsprint [ˈnjuːzprɪnt] n (U) papel m jornal.

newsreader [ˈnjuːzˌriːdəʳ] n **-1.** [TV] apresentador m, -ra f de jornal **- 2.** [radio] locutor(ra).

newsreel [ˈnjuːzriːl] n cinejornal m.

newsroom [ˈnjuːzruːm] n sala f de redação.

news-sheet n folheto m informativo.

news-stand n banca f de revistas.

newsworthy [ˈnjuːzˌwɜːðɪ] adj que vale a pena ser noticiado(da), de interesse jornalístico.

newt [njuːt] n tritão m.

new technology n (U) nova tecnologia f.

New Testament n: **the** ~ o Novo Testamento.

new town n UK cidade f planejada.

new wave n **-1.** CINEMA nova onda f **- 2.** [in pop music] new wave f.

New World n: **the** ~ o Novo Mundo.

New Year n Ano m Novo; **Happy** ~! Feliz Ano Novo!

New Year's Day n dia m de Ano Novo, primeiro m do ano.

New Year's Eve n véspera f de Ano Novo.

New York [-ˈjɔːk] n **-1.** [city] Nova Iorque; ~ **(City)** (cidade f de) Nova Iorque **- 2.** [state]: ~ **(State)** (Estado m de) Nova Iorque.

New Yorker [-ˈjɔːkəʳ] n nova-iorquino m, -na f.

New Zealand [-ˈziːlənd] n Nova Zelândia; **in** ~ na Nova Zelândia.

New Zealander [-ˈziːləndəʳ] n neozelandês(esa).

next [nekst] ⋄ adj **-1.** [in time] próximo(ma); ~ **week** semana que vem; **the** ~ **week** na semana que vem; **the day after** ~ depois de amanhã; **the week after** ~ sem ser a próxima semana, na outra **- 2.** [in space - turning, page, street] próximo(ma); [- room] ao lado. ⋄ adv **-1.** [afterwards] depois; **when are you** ~ **going to Brazil?** quando você irá novamente ao Brasil? **- 2.** [next time] da próxima vez (que); **when we** ~ **meet** da próxima vez que nos encontrarmos **- 3.** (with superlatives): ~ **best / biggest** o segundo melhor/maior. ⋄ prep US ao lado de. ⋄ n próximo m, -ma f.

◆ **next to** prep **-1.** [physically near] ao lado de, junto a **- 2.** (in comparisons) próximo(ma) de **- 3.** [almost] quase; ~ **to nothing** quase nada.

next-door ⋄ adj: ~ **neighbour** vizinho m, -nha f do lado. ⋄ adv ao lado.

next of kin n parente m mais próximo.

NF ⋄ n (abbr of **National Front**) pequeno partido político britânico de extrema direita. ⋄ abbr of **Newfoundland**.

NFL (*abbr of* **National Football League**) *n* federação norte-americana de futebol americano.

NG (*abbr of* **National Guard**) *n* força militar existente em cada estado norte-americano, ≃ Guarda *f* Nacional.

NGO (*abbr of* **non-governmental organization**) *n* ONG *f*.

NH *abbr of* **New Hampshire**.

NHL (*abbr of* **National Hockey League**) *n* federação norte-americana de hóquei sobre o gelo.

NHS (*abbr of* **National Health Service**) *n* órgão estatal britânico de saúde pública.

NI ⬦ *n* (*abbr of* **National Insurance**) *sistema britânico de seguridade social*, ≃ INSS *m.* ⬦ *abbr of* **Northern Ireland**.

Niagara [naɪˈægrə] *n*: ~ **Falls** as cataratas do Niágara.

nib [nɪb] *n* pena *f (de caneta)*.

nibble [ˈnɪbl] ⬦ *vt* -**1.** [subj: person, caterpillar] beliscar; [subj: rodent, goat, sheep] roer - **2.** [playfully] mordiscar. ⬦ *vi*: **to** ~ **at sthg** mordiscar algo.

Nicaragua [ˌnɪkəˈrægjʊəl] *n* Nicarágua; **in** ~ na Nicarágua.

Nicaraguan [ˌnɪkəˈrægjʊən] ⬦ *adj* nicaraguano(-na). ⬦ *n* nicaraguano *m*, -na *f*.

nice [naɪs] *adj* -**1.** [expressing approval - dress, picture] belo(la); [- day, weather] agradável; [- car, food] bom (boa) - **2.** [kind, pleasant] gentil; **it was** ~ **of you to help** foi muita gentileza de sua parte ajudar.

nice-looking [-ˈlʊkɪŋ] *adj* [attractive] bonito(ta); ~ **person** pessoa *f* atraente.

nicely [ˈnaɪslɪ] *adv* -**1.** [well, attractively, satisfactorily] bem; **that will do** ~ será o suficiente - **2.** [politely] educadamente.

nicety [ˈnaɪsətɪ] (*pl* -**ies**) *n* [refinement] delicadeza *f*.

niche [niːʃ] *n* -**1.** [gen] nicho *m* - **2.** [in life] boa colocação *f*.

nick [nɪk] ⬦ *n* -**1.** [cut] talha *f*, corte *m* - **2.** *UK inf* [jail]: **he did four days in the** ~ **for burglary** ele ficou quatro dias enjaulado por roubo - **3.** *inf* [condition]: **in good/bad** ~ *UK* em bom/mau estado - **4.** *phr*: **in the** ~ **of time** em cima da hora. ⬦ *vt* -**1.** [cut] talhar, cortar - **2.** *UK inf* [steal] passar a mão em - **3.** *UK inf* [arrest] enjaular.

nickel [ˈnɪkl] *n* -**1.** (*U*) [metal] níquel *m* - **2.** *US* [coin] moeda *f* de 5 centavos.

nickname [ˈnɪkneɪm] ⬦ *n* apelido *m.* ⬦ *vt* apelidar.

Nicosia [ˌnɪkəˈsiːə] *n* Nicósia.

nicotine [ˈnɪkətiːn] *n* (*U*) nicotina *f*.

niece [niːs] *n* sobrinha *f*.

nifty [ˈnɪftɪ] (*compar* -**ier**, *superl* -**iest**) *adj inf* chique.

Niger [ˈnaɪdʒəʳ] *n* -**1.** [country] Níger; **in** ~ em Níger - **2.** [river]: **the (River)** ~ o (Rio) Níger.

Nigeria [naɪˈdʒɪərɪə] *n* Nigéria; **in** ~ na Nigéria.

Nigerian [naɪˈdʒɪərɪən] ⬦ *adj* nigeriano(na). ⬦ *n* nigeriano *m*, -na *f*.

Nigerien [naɪˈdʒɪərɪən] ⬦ *adj* nigerino(na). ⬦ *n* nigerino *m*, -na *f*.

niggardly [ˈnɪgədlɪ] *adj* -**1.** [person] mesquinho(-nha) - **2.** [amount] miserável.

niggle [ˈnɪgl] ⬦ *n* [worry] preocupação *f*. ⬦ *vt* -**1.** [worry] preocupar - **2.** [criticize] incomodar. ⬦ *vi*

-**1.** [worry]: **it** ~ **d at me all day** isso ficou me dando volta o dia inteiro - **2.** [criticize] reclamar.

nigh [naɪ] *adv* -**1.** *literary* [near] próximo(ma) -**2.** : **well** ~ [almost] praticamente.

night [naɪt] *n* -**1.** [not day] noite *f*; **at** ~ à *or* de noite; ~ **and day**, **day and** ~ noite e dia, dia e noite -**2.** *phr*: **to have an early/a late** ~ ir dormir cedo/tarde.
  ➡ **nights** *adv* -**1.** *US* [at night] à *or* de noite -**2.** *UK* [night shift]: **to work** ~**s** trabalhar durante a noite.

nightcap [ˈnaɪtkæp] *n* -**1.** [drink] bebida que se toma antes de se ir dormir -**2.** [hat] touca *f* de dormir.

nightclothes [ˈnaɪtkləʊðz] *npl* roupa *f* de dormir.

nightclub [ˈnaɪtklʌb] *n* casa *f* noturna, nightclub *m*.

nightdress [ˈnaɪtdres] *n* camisola *f*.

nightfall [ˈnaɪtfɔːl] *n* (*U*) anoitecer *m*.

nightgown [ˈnaɪtgaʊn] *n* camisola *f*.

nightie [ˈnaɪtɪ] *n inf* camisola *f*.

nightingale [ˈnaɪtɪŋgeɪl] *n* rouxinol *m*.

nightlife [ˈnaɪtlaɪf] *n* (*U*) vida *f* noturna.

nightlight [ˈnaɪtlaɪt] *n* luz *f* fraca *(que se deixa acesa à noite)*.

nightly [ˈnaɪtlɪ] ⬦ *adj* noturno(na). ⬦ *adv* à noite.

nightmare [ˈnaɪtmeəʳ] *n lit* & *fig* pesadelo *m*

nightmarish [ˈnaɪtmeərɪʃ] *adj* horripilante.

night owl *n fig* notívago *m*, -ga *f*, coruja *mf*.

night porter *n* porteiro *m*, -ra *f* do turno da noite.

night safe *n* caixa externo de banco para depósitos fora do horário de expediente.

night school *n* (*U*) escola *f* noturna.

night shift *n* [period] turno *m* da noite.

nightshirt [ˈnaɪtʃɜːt] *n* camisolão *m*.

nightspot [ˈnaɪtspɒt] *n* clube *m* noturno.

nightstick [ˈnaɪtstɪk] *n US* cassetete *m*.

night-time *n* (*U*) noite *f*.

night watchman *n* guarda-noturno *m*.

nightwear *n* (*U*) roupa *f* de dormir.

nihilism [ˈnaɪəlɪzml] *n* (*U*) [rejection of authority] niilismo *m*.

nil [nɪl] *n* (*U*) -**1.** [nothing] nada *m* -**2.** *UK sport* zero *m*.

Nile [naɪl] *n*: **the** ~ o Nilo.

nimble [ˈnɪmbl] *adj* ágil.

nimbly [ˈnɪmblı] *adv* agilmente.

nine [naɪn] *num* nove; *see also* **six**.

nineteen [ˌnaɪnˈtiːn] *num* dezenove; *see also* **six**.

nineteenth [naɪnˈtiːnθ] *num* décimo nono, décima nona; *see also* **sixth**.

ninetieth [ˈnaɪntɪəθ] *num* nonagésimo(ma); *see also* **sixth**.

ninety [ˈnaɪntɪ] *num* noventa; *see also* **sixty**.

ninny (*pl* -**ies**) *n inf* bobo(ba).

ninth [naɪnθ] *num* nono(na); *see also* **sixth**.

nip [nɪp] (*pt* & *pp* -**ped**, *cont* -**ping**) ⬦ *n* -**1.** [pinch] beliscão *m* -**2.** [bite] mordiscada *f* -**3.** [of drink] trago *m.* ⬦ *vt* -**1.** [pinch] beliscar -**2.** [bite] mordiscar. ⬦ *vi UK inf* [dash] dar uma saída.

nipper [ˈnɪpəʳ] *n UK inf* criancinha *f*.

nipple ['nɪpl] n -1. [of breast] mamilo m -2. [of baby's bottle] bico m.

nippy ['nɪpɪ] (compar -ier, superl -iest) adj -1. [cold] fresquinho(nha) -2. [quick] rápido(da).

NIREX (abbr of Nuclear Industry Radioactive Waste Executive) n órgão britânico que regula o lixo radiativo da indústria nuclear, ≃ CNEN m.

Nissen hut n refúgio m militar.

nit [nɪt] n -1. [in hair] lêndea f -2. UK inf [idiot] idiota mf.

nit-picking inf <> adj minucioso(sa). <> n (U) detalhismo m.

nitrate ['naɪtreɪt] n nitrato m.

nitric acid ['naɪtrɪk-] n (U) ácido m nítrico.

nitrogen ['naɪtrədʒən] n (U) nitrogênio m.

nitroglycerin(e) [ˌnaɪtrəʊ'glɪsərɪːn] n (U) nitroglicerina f.

nitty-gritty [ˌnɪtɪ'grɪtɪ] n inf: to get down to the ~ ir ao que interessa.

nitwit ['nɪtwɪt] n inf idiota mf.

NJ abbr of New Jersey.

NLF (abbr of National Liberation Front) n FLN f.

NLRB (abbr of National Labor Relations Board) n órgão norte-americano de justiça do trabalho.

NM abbr of New Mexico.

no [nəʊ] (pl -es) <> adv [gen] não; ~, thanks não obrigado(da). <> adj nenhum(ma), algum(ma); I have ~ money left não tehno mais um tostão. <> n não m.

No., no. (abbr of number) no.

Noah's ark ['nəʊəz-] n arca f de Noé.

nobble ['nɒbl] vt -1. [racehorse] drogar -2. [bribe] subornar -3. [grab, catch] apanhar.

Nobel prize [nəʊ'bel-] n prêmio m Nobel.

nobility [nə'bɪlətɪ] n -1. [aristocracy]: the ~ a nobreza -2. (U) [nobleness] nobreza f.

noble ['nəʊbl] <> adj -1. [aristocratic, distinguished] nobre -2. [brave] grandioso(osa). <> n nobre mf.

nobleman ['nəʊblmən] (pl -men [-mən]) n homem m nobre.

noblewoman ['nəʊblˌwʊmən] (pl -women [-ˌwɪmɪn]) n mulher f nobre.

nobly ['nəʊblɪ] adv [generously] generosamente.

nobody ['nəʊbədɪ] (pl -ies) <> pron ninguém. <> n pej [insignificant person] joão-ninguém m.

no-claim(s) bonus n bonificação f de seguro.

nocturnal [nɒk'tɜːnl] adj noturno(na).

nod [nɒd] (pt & pp -ded, cont -ding) <> n inclinação f de cabeça. <> vt [in agreement]: to ~ one's head assentir com a cabeça; [as greeting] cumprimentar com a cabeça. <> vi -1. [in agreement] assentir com a cabeça -2. [to indicate sthg] indicar com a cabeça -3. [as greeting]: to ~ to sb cumprimentar alguém com a cabeça.
◆ **nod off** vi cabecear.

node [nəʊd] n -1. [gen] nó m -2. COMPUT nó m, nodo m.

nodule ['nɒdjuːl] n nódulo m.

no-fly zone n zona f de exclusão aérea.

no-go area n UK zona f proibida.

noise [nɔɪz] n [sound] barulho m.

noiseless ['nɔɪzlɪs] adj silencioso(osa).

noiselessly ['nɔɪzlɪslɪ] adv silenciosamente.

noisily ['nɔɪzɪlɪ] adv ruidosamente, fazendo barulho.

noisy ['nɔɪzɪ] (compar -ier, superl -iest) adj barulhento(ta).

nomad ['nəʊmæd] n nômade mf.

nomadic [nə'mædɪk] adj nômade.

no-man's-land n (U) terra f de ninguém.

nom de plume n pseudônimo m.

nominal ['nɒmɪnl] adj -1. [in name only] apenas no nome; a ~ Catholic um católico só no nome; a ~ leader um líder de fachada -2. [very small] simbólico(ca).

nominally ['nɒmɪnəlɪ] adv [in theory] teoricamente.

nominate ['nɒmɪneɪt] vt -1. [propose]: to ~ sb (for/as sthg) designar alguém (para algo) -2. [appoint]: to ~ sb (sthg) nomear alguém (algo); to ~ sb (to sthg) nomear alguém (para algo).

nomination [ˌnɒmɪ'neɪʃn] n -1. [proposal] indicação f -2. (U) [appointment]: ~ (to sthg) nomeação f (para algo).

nominee [ˌnɒmɪ'niː] n nomeado m, -da f.

non- [nɒn] prefix [not] não-.

non-addictive adj que não provoca dependência.

non-aggression n (U) não-agressão f.

non-alcoholic adj não alcoólico(ca).

non-aligned adj não-alinhado(da).

non-believer n descrente mf.

nonchalant [UK 'nɒnʃələnt, US ˌnɒnʃə'lɑːnt] adj indiferente.

nonchalantly [UK 'nɒnʃələntlɪ, US ˌnɒnʃə'lɑːntlɪ] adv com indiferença.

non-combatant n não-combatente mf.

non-commissioned officer n oficial mf subalterno, -na, funcionário m, -ria f não-comissionado, -da f.

non-committal adj evasivo(va).

non-competitive adj não-competitivo(va).

non compos mentis [-ˌkɒmpəs'mentɪs] adj fora do juízo perfeito, que não está em posse de suas faculdades mentais.

nonconformist [ˌnɒnkən'fɔːmɪst] <> adj inconformista. <> n inconformista mf.

nonconformity n (U) inconformismo m.

noncontributory [ˌnɒnkən'trɪbjʊtərɪ] adj não-contributivo(va).

non-cooperation n (U) não-cooperação f.

nondescript [UK 'nɒndɪskrɪpt, US ˌnɒndɪ'skrɪpt] adj desinteressante.

non-drinker n abstêmio m, -mia f.

non-drip adj que não pinga.

non-driver n: he's a ~ ele não sabe dirigir.

none [nʌn] pron nehum m, -ma f; there's ~ left não resta nada; ~ of this is your fault nada disso foi culpa sua.

nonentity [nɒ'nentətɪ] (pl -ies) n nulidade f, zero mf à esquerda.

non-essential adj supérfluo(flua).

nonetheless [ˌnʌnðə'les] adv contudo, não obstante.

non-event n decepção f, fracasso m.

non-executive director n diretor ou diretora não-responsável pela tomada de decisões

em sua instituição ou empresa.
non-existent *adj* inexistente.
non-fattening *adj* que não engorda.
non-fiction *n (U)* não-ficção *f*.
non-flammable *adj* não-inflamável.
non-infectious *adj* não-infeccioso(sa).
non-inflammable *adj* não-inflamável.
non-interference, non-intervention *n (U)* não-intervenção *f*.
non-iron *adj* que não precisa passar.
non-malignant *adj* não-maligno(na).
non-member *n* não-sócio *m*, não-membro *m*.
non-negotiable *adj* não-negociável.
no-no *n inf*: it's a ~ isso é algo que não se faz.
no-nonsense *adj* prático(ca).
non-operational *adj* inoperante.
non-participation *n (U)* não-participação *f*.
non-payment *n (U)* inadimplência *f*, não-pagamento *m*.
nonplussed, nonplused *US* [ˌnɒnˈplʌst] *adj* perplexo(xa).
non-profit-making *UK*, **non-profit** *US adj* sem fins lucrativos.
non-proliferation *n (U)* não-proliferação *f*.
non-renewable *adj* **-1.** [contract, agreement] não-prorrogável **-2.** [natural resources, fossil fuels] não-renovável.
non-resident *n* **-1.** [of country] não-residente *mf* **-2.** [of hotel]: **open to** ~**s** aberto ao público.
non-returnable *adj* [bottle] não-retornável, sem retorno.
nonsense ['nɒnsəns] <> *n (U)* **-1.** [meaningless words] bobagem *f*, asneira *f* **-2.** [foolish idea] besteira *f*; it is ~ **to suggest that ...** é um absurdo sugerir que ... **-3.** [foolish behaviour] idiotice *f*; **stop this** ~ **at once** pára com essas criancices agora mesmo; **to make (a)** ~ **of sthg** ridicularizar algo. <> *excl* bobagem!, que nada!
nonsensical [nɒnˈsensɪkl] *adj* sem sentido, absurdo(da).
non sequitur [-ˈsekwɪtəʳ] *n* non sequitur *m*, incoerência *f*.
non-shrink *adj* que não encolhe.
non-skid *adj* antiderrapante.
non-slip *adj* antiderrapante.
non-smoker *n* não-fumante *mf*.
non-starter *n UK inf* [plan]: **to be a** ~ estar condenado(da) ao fracasso.
non-stick *adj* antiaderente.
non-stop <> *adj* **-1.** [gen] contínuo(nua), incessante **-2.** [flight] sem escalas. <> *adv* sem parar, continuamente.
non-taxable *adj* isento(ta) de impostos.
non-toxic *adj* atóxico(ca).
non-transferable *adj* não-transferível.
non-U *adj UK dated* popular, pouco refinado(da).
non-violence *n (U)* não-violência *f*.
non-voter *n* pessoa *f* que não vota.
non-voting *adj* **-1.** [person] que não vota **-2.** *FIN* [shares] sem direito a voto.
non-white <> *adj* que não é da raça branca. <> *n* pessoa *f* que não é da raça branca.

noodles ['nu:dlz] *npl* talharim *m*.
nook [nʊk] *n* [of room] canto *m*; **every** ~ **and cranny** todos os cantos.
noon [nu:n] <> *n (U)* meio-dia *m*. <> *comp* do meio-dia.
noonday ['nu:ndeɪ] <> *n* meio-dia *m*. <> *comp* do meio-dia.
no one *pron* = **nobody**.
noose [nu:s] *n* [lasso] nó *m* corrediço.
no-place *adv US* = **nowhere**.
nor [nɔːʳ] *conj* **-1.** ▷ **neither** **-2.** [and not] nem; **I don't smoke** -~ **do I** eu não fumo - nem eu; **I don't know,** ~ **do I care** não sei, nem quero saber.
Nordic ['nɔːdɪk] *adj* nórdico(ca).
norm [nɔːm] *n* norma *f*; **the** ~ o normal.
normal ['nɔːml] *adj* normal.
normality [nɔːˈmælɪtɪ], **normalcy** *US* ['nɔːmlsɪ] *n (U)* normalidade *f*.
normalize, -ise ['nɔːməlaɪz] <> *vt* normalizar. <> *vi* normalizar-se.
normally ['nɔːməlɪ] *adv* normalmente.
Norman <> *adj* normando(da). <> *n* normando(da).
Normandy ['nɔːməndɪ] *n* Normandia; **in** ~ na Normandia.
Norse [nɔːs] *adj* nórdico(ca).
north [nɔːθ] <> *adj* norte; **North London** o norte de Londres. <> *adv* para o norte; ~ **of** ao norte de. <> *n* [direction] norte *m*.
North Africa *n* África do Norte; **in** ~ na África do Norte.
North America *n* América do Norte; **in** ~ na América do Norte.
North American <> *adj* **-1.** da América do Norte **-2.** [of USA] norte-americano(na). <> *n* **-1.** pessoa *f* da América do Norte **-2.** [of USA] norte-americano *m*, -na *f*.
northbound ['nɔːθbaʊnd] *adj* com direção norte.
North Carolina [-ˌkærəˈlaɪnə] *n* Carolina *f* do Norte; **in** ~ na Carolina do Norte.
North Country *n*: **the** ~ *UK* a região norte da Inglaterra.
North Dakota [-dəˈkəʊtə] *n* Dakota do Norte; **in** ~ em Dakota do Norte.
northeast [ˌnɔːθˈiːst] <> *adj* nordeste. <> *n* [direction] nordeste *m*. <> *adv* para o nordeste; ~ **of** ao nordeste de.
northeasterly [ˌnɔːθˈiːstəlɪ] *adj* **-1.** [towards northeast, in northeast] a nordeste **-2.** [from northeast] do nordeste.
northerly ['nɔːðəlɪ] *adj* **-1.** [towards north, in north] ao norte **-2.** [from north] do norte.
northern ['nɔːðən] *adj* do norte.
Northerner ['nɔːðənəʳ] *n* pessoa que nasceu ou vive no norte.
Northern Ireland *n* Irlanda do Norte; **in** ~ na Irlanda do Norte.
Northern Lights *npl*: **the** ~ a aurora boreal.
northernmost ['nɔːðənməʊst] *adj* mais setentrional, mais ao norte.
Northern Territory *n* Território *m* do Norte.
North Korea *n* Coréia do Norte; **in** ~ na Coréia do Norte.

North Korean ◇ *adj* norte-coreano(na). ◇ *n* norte-coreano *m*, -na *f*.

North Pole *n*: the ~ o Pólo Norte.

North Sea ◇ *n*: the ~ o Mar do Norte. ◇ *comp* -**1.** [oil, oilrig] do Mar do Norte -**2.** [fishing] no Mar do Norte.

North Star *n*: the ~ a estrela Polar.

North Vietnam *n* Vietnã do Norte; **in** ~ no Vietnã do Norte.

North Vietnamese ◇ *adj* norte-vietnamita. ◇ *n* norte-vietnamita *mf*.

northward ['nɔːθwəd] ◇ *adj* para o norte. ◇ *adv* = **northwards**.

northwards ['nɔːθwədz] *adv* para o norte.

northwest [ˌnɔːθ'west] ◇ *adj* -**1.** [in the northwest, facing the northwest] noroeste -**2.** [from the northwest] do noroeste. ◇ *n* [direction] noroeste *m*. ◇ *adv* para noroeste; ~ **of** a noroeste de.

northwesterly [ˌnɔːθ'westəlɪ] *adj* -**1.** [towards northwest, in northwest] a noroeste -**2.** [from northwest] do noroeste.

Northwest Territories *npl Can*: the ~ os Territórios do Noroeste.

North Yemen *n* Iêmen do Norte; **in** ~ no Iêmen do Norte.

Norway ['nɔːweɪ] *n* Noruega; **in** ~ na Noruega.

Norwegian [nɔː'wiːdʒən] ◇ *adj* norueguês(esa). ◇ *n* -**1.** [person] norueguês *m*, -esa *f* -**2.** [language] norueguês *m*.

Nos., nos. (*abbr of* **numbers**) nos.

nose [nəʊz] *n* -**1.** ANAT nariz *m*; **under one's** ~ debaixo do nariz de alguém; **to cut one's** ~ **off to spite one's face** prejudicar-se ao tentar prejudicar outra pessoa; **to have a** ~ **for sthg** sentir o cheiro de algo; **he gets up my** ~ *inf* ele me deixa muito irritado(da); **to keep one's** ~ **out of sthg** não meter o nariz em algo; **to look down one's** ~ **at sb/sthg** *fig* olhar de cima para alguém/algo; **to pay through the** ~ pagar os olhos da cara; **to poke** *OR* **stick one's** ~ **into sthg** *inf* meter o nariz em algo; **to turn up one's** ~ **at sthg** torcer o nariz para algo -**2.** [of car] ponta *f*.

◆ **nose about, nose around** *vi* bisbilhotar.

nosebag ['nəʊzbæg] *n* embornal *m*.

nosebleed ['nəʊzbliːd] *n* hemorragia *f* nasal.

nosecone ['nəʊzkəʊn] *n* ogiva *f*.

nosedive ['nəʊzdaɪv] ◇ *n* [of plane] mergulho *m*. ◇ *vi* -**1.** [plane] mergulhar -**2.** *fig* [prices, popularity] despencar.

nose ring *n* argola *f* de nariz.

nose stud *n* piercing *m* de nariz.

nosey ['nəʊzɪ] *adj* = **nosy**.

nosh [nɒʃ] *n UK inf* [food] rango *m*.

nosh-up *n UK inf* comilança *f*.

nostalgia [nɒ'stældʒə] *n (U)*: ~ **(for sthg)** nostalgia *f* (de algo).

nostalgic [nɒ'stældʒɪk] *adj* nostálgico(ca).

nostril ['nɒstrəl] *n* narina *f*.

nosy ['nəʊzɪ] (*compar* -**ier**, *superl* -**iest**) *adj* curioso(sa), abelhudo(da).

not [nɒt] *adv* não; **I hope** ~ espero que não; ~ **a** nem um (uma); ~ **even a** nem mesmo um (uma); ~ **all/every** nem todos(das); ~ **always** nem

sempre; **it's** ~ **every day we get sunshine** não é todo dia que tem sol; **it's** ~ **that I'm jealous, but** ... não que eu seja ciumento, mas ...; ~ **at all** em absoluto, de maneira nenhuma; [to acknowledge thanks] de nada.

notable ['nəʊtəbl] ◇ *adj* notável; **to be** ~ **for sthg** destacar-se por algo. ◇ *n fml* celebridade *f*.

notably ['nəʊtəblɪ] *adv* -**1.** [in particular] especialmente -**2.** [noticeably] claramente, obviamente.

notary ['nəʊtərɪ] (*pl* -**ies**) *n*: ~ **(public)** notário *m*, -ria *f*.

notation [nəʊ'teɪʃn] *n* notação *f*.

notch [nɒtʃ] *n* -**1.** [cut] corte *m*, entalhe *m* -**2.** *fig* [on scale] ponto *m*.

◆ **notch up** *vt fus* conseguir.

note [nəʊt] ◇ *n* -**1.** [gen] nota *f* -**2.** [written reminder, record] anotação *f*, nota *f*; **to take** ~ **of sthg** prestar atenção em algo; **to compare** ~**s** trocar idéias -**3.** [short letter] bilhete *m* -**4.** [tone] tom *m* -**5.** [importance]: **of** ~ digno(na) de nota. ◇ *vt* -**1.** [observe] notar, observar -**2.** [mention] apontar, mencionar.

◆ **notes** *npl* [in book] anotações *fpl*.

◆ **note down** *vt sep* anotar.

notebook ['nəʊtbʊk] *n* -**1.** [for writing in] caderno *m* -**2.** COMPUT notebook *m*.

noted ['nəʊtɪd] *adj* conhecido(da), destacado(da); ~ **for sthg** conhecido(da) por algo.

notepad ['nəʊtpæd] *n* bloco *m* de notas.

notepaper ['nəʊtpeɪpəʳ] *n (U)* papel *m* de carta.

noteworthy ['nəʊtˌwɜːðɪ] (*compar* -**ier**, *superl* -**iest**) *adj* digno(na) de menção.

nothing ['nʌθɪŋ] ◇ *pron* nada; ~ **new/interesting** nada de novo/interessante; **she did** ~ ela não fez nada; **for** ~ [free] de graça; [in vain] para nada.

nothingness ['nʌθɪŋnɪs] *n (U)* nada *m*.

notice ['nəʊtɪs] ◇ *n* -**1.** *(U)* [attention] atenção *f*; **to come to one's** ~ chegar até alguém; **to escape one's** ~ passar desapercebido(da); **to take** ~ **(of sb/sthg)** dar bola (para alguém/algo); **to take no** ~ **(of sb/sthg)** não dar bola (para alguém/algo), fazer pouco caso (de alguém/algo); **he didn't take a blind bit of** ~ ele não fez nem mesmo o mais remoto caso -**2.** *(U)* [warning, announcement] aviso *m*; **at short** ~ em cima da hora; **until further** ~ até segunda ordem -**3.** *(U)* [at work]: **to be given one's** ~ receber aviso prévio; **to hand in one's** ~ apresentar pedido de demissão. ◇ *vt* perceber, notar; **to** ~ **sb doing sthg** ver que alguém está fazendo algo. ◇ *vi* perceber.

noticeable ['nəʊtɪsəbl] *adj* notável, digno(na) de nota.

noticeably ['nəʊtɪsəblɪ] *adv* notavelmente.

notice board *n* quadro *m* de avisos.

notification [ˌnəʊtɪfɪ'keɪʃn] *n (U)* notificação *f*.

notify ['nəʊtɪfaɪ] (*pt & pp* -**ied**) *vt*: **to** ~ **sb (of sthg)** notificar alguém (de algo).

notion ['nəʊʃn] *n* [concept, idea] noção *f*.

◆ **notions** *npl US* [haberdashery] aviamentos *mpl*.

notional ['nəʊʃənl] *adj* [hypothetical] hipotético(ca).

notoriety [ˌnəʊtə'raɪətɪ] *n (U)* notoriedade *f*.

notorious [nəʊ'tɔːrɪəs] *adj* notório(ria); ~ **for sthg** notório(ria) por algo.

notoriously [nəʊˈtɔːrɪəslɪ] *adv* notoriamente.

notwithstanding [ˌnɒtwɪθˈstændɪŋ] *fml* <> *prep* não obstante. <> *adv* no entanto, não obstante.

nougat [ˈnuːgɑː] *n* nugá *m*.

nought [nɔːt] *num* zero *m*; ~**s and crosses** jogo *m* da velha.

noun [naʊn] *n* substantivo *m*.

nourish [ˈnʌrɪʃ] *vt* -**1.** [feed] nutrir - **2.** [entertain, foster] alimentar.

nourishing [ˈnʌrɪʃɪŋ] *adj* nutritivo(va).

nourishment [ˈnʌrɪʃmənt] *n* (U) alimento *m*.

nouveau riche <> *adj* de novo-rico. <> *n* novo-rico *m*, nova-rica *f*.

Nov. (*abbr of* November) nov.

Nova Scotia [ˌnəʊvəˈskəʊʃə] *n* Nova Escócia; **in** ~ na Nova Escócia.

Nova Scotian [ˌnəʊvəˈskəʊʃn] <> *adj* neoescocês(esa). <> *n* neoescocês *m*, -esa *f*.

novel [ˈnɒvl] <> *adj* original. <> *n* romance *m*.

novelist [ˈnɒvəlɪst] *n* romancista *mf*.

novelty [ˈnɒvltɪ] (*pl* -**ies**) *n* -**1.** (U) [quality] originalidade *f* -**2.** [unusual object, event] novidade *f* -**3.** [cheap object] bugiganga *f*.

November [nəˈvembə^r] *n* novembro *m*; *see also* September.

novice [ˈnɒvɪs] *n* -**1.** [inexperienced person] novato *m*, -ta *f*, principiante *mf* -**2.** RELIG noviço *m*, -ça *f*.

Novocaine® [ˈnəʊvəkeɪn] *n* (U) novocaína® *f*.

now [naʊ] <> *adv* -**1.** [at this time] agora; **from** ~ **on I'm in charge** de agora em diante eu estou no comando; **any day** ~ qualquer dia destes; **any time** ~ a qualquer momento; ~ **and then** *or* **again** de vez em quando; **for** ~ por ora - **2.** [already, before this time] já; **they should be here by** ~ eles já deveriam ser estar aqui; **he's been away for two weeks** ~ já faz duas semanas que ele foi embora - **3.** [at a particular time in the past] então; **we were all singing** ~ estávamos todos cantando naquele momento - **4.** [to introduce statement] agora - **5.** [nowadays] atualmente; ~ **many people use computers to work** atualmente muitas pessoas usam computadores para trabalhar. <> *conj*: ~ **(that)** agora que.

NOW [naʊ] (*abbr of* National Organization for Women) *n* importante organização feminista norte-americana.

nowadays [ˈnaʊədeɪz] *adv* hoje em dia, atualmente.

nowhere UK [ˈnəʊweə^r], **no-place** US *adv* em nenhum lugar; **to appear out of** *or* **from** ~ aparecer do nada; ~ **near** nem de longe; **to be getting** ~ indo a lugar nenhum; **this is getting us** ~ isto não está nos levando a nada.

no-win situation *n* beco *m* sem saída.

noxious [ˈnɒkʃəs] *adj* nocivo(va).

nozzle [ˈnɒzl] *n* bocal *m*, bico *m*.

NP (*abbr of* notary public) tabelião *m*, -liã *f*.

NS *abbr of* Nova Scotia.

NSC (*abbr of* National Security Council) *n* conselho federal que coordena a defesa e a política externa norte-americanas.

NSF <> *n* (*abbr of* National Science Foundation)

fundação norte-americana de pesquisa científica. <> (*abbr of* not sufficient funds) sem fundos.

NSPCC (*abbr of* National Society for the Prevention of Cruelty to Children) *n* organização britânica de prevenção a maus tratos a crianças.

NSU (*abbr of* non-specific urethritis) *n* uretrite *f* não-específica.

NSW *abbr of* New South Wales.

NT *n* -**1.** (*abbr of* New Testament) NT *m* -**2.** (*abbr of* National Trust) organização britânica encarregada da preservação de edifícios históricos e locais de interesse público.

nth [enθ] *adj inf* [umpteenth] enésimo(ma).

nuance [ˈnjuːˈɑːns] *n* [of word, meaning] nuança *f*.

nub [nʌb] *n* [crux] essência *f*.

Nubian Desert *n*: **the** ~ o Deserto Núbio.

nubile [UK ˈnjuːbaɪl, US ˈnuːbəl] *adj fml or hum* núbil.

nubuck *n* nubuck *m*, tipo de camurça muito fina usada na fabricação de sapatos.

nuclear [ˈnjuːklɪə^r] *adj* nuclear.

nuclear bomb *n* bomba *f* nuclear.

nuclear disarmament *n* (U) desarmamento *m* nuclear.

nuclear energy *n* (U) energia *f* nuclear.

nuclear family *n* família *f* nuclear.

nuclear fission *n* (U) fissão *f* nuclear.

nuclear-free zone *n* zona *f* livre de energia nuclear.

nuclear fusion *n* (U) fusão *f* nuclear.

nuclear physics *n* (U) física *f* nuclear.

nuclear power *n* (U) energia *f* nuclear.

nuclear reactor *n* reator *m* nuclear.

nuclear war *n* guerra *f* nuclear.

nuclear winter *n* inverno *m* nuclear.

nucleus [ˈnjuːklɪəs] (*pl* -**lei** [-lɪaɪ]) *n* núcleo *m*.

nude [njuːd] <> *adj* nu (nua). <> *n* [figure, painting] nu *m*; **in the** ~ em pêlos.

nudge [nʌdʒ] <> *n* -**1.** [with elbow] cutucada *f* - **2.** *fig* [to encourage] empurrada *f*. <> *vt* -**1.** [with elbow] cutucar - **2.** *fig* [to encourage] empurrar; **to** ~ **sb's memory** puxar a memória de alguém.

nudist [ˈnjuːdɪst] <> *adj* nudista. <> *n* nudista *mf*.

nudity [ˈnjuːdətɪ] *n* (U) nudez *f*.

nugget [ˈnʌgɪt] *n* -**1.** [of gold] pepita *f* - **2.** *fig* [valuable piece] pérola *f*.

nuisance [ˈnjuːsns] *n* -**1.** [annoying thing, situation] chatice *f* - **2.** [annoying person] chato *m*, -ta *f* de galocha; **to make a** ~ **of o.s.** amolar.

nuke [njuːk] *inf* <> *n* arma *f* nuclear. <> *vt* bombardear com armas nucleares.

null [nʌl] *adj*: ~ **and void** nulo e sem valor.

nullify [ˈnʌlɪfaɪ] (*pt* & *pp* -**ied**) *vt* anular.

numb [nʌm] <> *adj* [shoulder, hand] adormecido(da); [person] paralisado(da); **to be** ~ **with cold** estar congelado(da) de frio. <> *vt* [subj: cold, anaesthetic] paralisar.

number [ˈnʌmbə^r] <> *n* -**1.** [gen] número *m*; **a** ~ **of** vários(as); **I've told you any** ~ **of times ...** já te disse um milhão de vezes ... - **2.** [of car] placa *f* -**3.** [song] música *f*. <> *vt* -**1.** [amount to] chegar a -**2.** [give a number to] numerar -**3.** [include]: **to be** ~**ed among** figurar entre.

number-crunching [-ˌkrʌntʃɪŋ] n (U) inf cálculo m em grande escala.

numberless ['nʌmbəlɪs] adj inumerável.

number one ◇ adj [main] número um, principal. ◇ n -1. [priority] o mais importante -2. inf [oneself]: **to look after** ~ cuidar de si mesmo(ma).

numberplate ['nʌmbəpleɪt] n placa f do carro.

Number Ten n: ~ (Downing Street) a casa número 10 de Downing Street, residência oficial do primeiro ministro britânico; fig o governo britânico.

numbness ['nʌmnɪs] n -1. dormência f-2. fig [with shock, fear] paralisia f.

numbskull ['nʌmskʌl] n = numskull.

numeracy ['njuːmərəsɪ] n UK facilidade f com números.

numeral ['njuːmərəl] n algarismo m.

numerate ['njuːmərət] adj UK que sabe fazer cálculos elementares.

numerical [njuːˈmerɪkl] adj numérico(ca).

numerous ['njuːmərəs] adj inúmero(ra).

numskull ['nʌmskʌl] n inf besta mf, imbecil mf.

nun [nʌn] n freira f.

nuptial ['nʌpʃl] adj fml nupcial.

nurse [nɜːs] ◇ n enfermeiro m, -ra f. ◇ vt -1. MED [care for] cuidar de, atender -2. [harbour, foster] nutrir -3. [breast-feed] amamentar.

nursemaid ['nɜːsmeɪd] n babá f.

nursery ['nɜːsərɪ] (pl -ies) ◇ adj pré-escolar. ◇ n -1. [for children] creche f-2. [for plants, trees] viveiro m -3. [at home] quarto m das crianças.

nursery nurse n UK ama-seca f.

nursery rhyme n cantiga f infantil.

nursery school n pré-escola f.

nursery slopes npl SKIING pista f para principiantes.

nursing ['nɜːsɪŋ] n -1. [profession] enfermagem f-2. [care] cuidados mpl.

nursing auxiliary n auxiliar mf de enfermagem.

nursing home n -1. [for old people] clínica f de repouso -2. [for childbirth] maternidade f (privada).

nurture ['nɜːtʃəʳ] vt -1. [children, plants] criar -2. [hope, desire, plan] alimentar.

nut [nʌt] n -1. [to eat] noz f-2. TECH porca f; **the ~ s and bolts** fig [basics] o básico -3. inf [mad person] maluco m, -ca f-4. inf [enthusiast] aficionado m, -da f-5. inf [head] cuca f.

➨ **nuts** inf ◇ adj: **to be ~ s** estar louco(ca). ◇ excl US maldito seja!

nutcase ['nʌtkeɪs] n inf pirado m, -da f.

nutcrackers ['nʌtˌkrækəz] npl quebra-nozes m.

nutmeg ['nʌtmeg] n (U) noz-moscada f.

nutrient ['njuːtrɪənt] n nutriente m.

nutrition [njuːˈtrɪʃn] n (U) nutrição f.

nutritional [njuːˈtrɪʃənl] adj nutritivo(va).

nutritionist [njuːˈtrɪʃənɪst] n nutricionista mf.

nutritious [njuːˈtrɪʃəs] adj nutritivo(va).

nutshell ['nʌtʃel] n casca f de noz; **in a ~** em poucas palavras.

nutter ['nʌtəʳ] n UK inf louco m, -ca f.

nuzzle ['nʌzl] ◇ vt [with nose] fuçar. ◇ vi [nestle]: to ~ (up) against sb/sthg aconchegar-se em alguém/algo.

NV abbr of Nevada.

NVQ (abbr of National Vocational Qualification) n na Inglaterra e no País de Gales, certificado de qualificação vocacional obtido pelos estudantes de 15 a 16 anos, ≃ diploma m de segundo grau.

NW (abbr of northwest) NO.

NY abbr of New York.

Nyasaland n Nyasaland; **in ~** em Nyasaland.

NYC abbr of New York City.

nylon ['naɪlɒn] ◇ n (U) [fabric] náilon m. ◇ comp de náilon.

➨ **nylons** npl dated [stockings] meias fpl de náilon.

nymph [nɪmf] n ninfa f.

nymphomaniac [ˌnɪmfəˈmeɪnɪæk] ◇ adj ninfomaníaco(ca). ◇ n ninfomaníaco m, -ca f.

NYRB (abbr of New York Review of Books) n conceituada revista norte-americana com artigos de crítica literária.

NYSE (abbr of New York Stock Exchange) n Bolsa f de Nova Iorque.

NZ abbr of New Zealand.

o (pl o's OR os), **O** (pl O's OR Os) [əʊ] n -1. [letter] o, O m -2. [zero] zero m.

oaf [əʊf] n imbecil mf.

oak [əʊk] ◇ n: ~ (tree) carvalho m. ◇ comp de carvalho.

OAP (abbr of old age pensioner) n UK idoso que recebe pensão do estado.

oar [ɔːʳ] n remo m; **to put** OR **stick one's ~ in** fig meter o bedelho em.

oarlock ['ɔːlɒk] n US [rowlock] tolete m.

oarsman ['ɔːzmən] (pl -men [-mən]) n remador m.

oarswoman ['ɔːzˌwʊmən] (pl -women [-ˌwɪmɪn]) n remadora f.

OAS (abbr of Organization of American States) n OEA f.

oasis [əʊˈeɪsɪs] (pl oases [əʊˈeɪsiːz]) n -1. [in desert] oásis m inv -2. fig [pleasant place] oásis m inv.

oatcake ['əʊtkeɪk] n biscoito m de aveia.

oath [əʊθ] n -1. [promise] juramento m; **on** OR **under ~** sob juramento -2. [swearword] blasfêmia f.

oatmeal ['əʊtmiːl] ◇ n [food] farinha f de aveia. ◇ comp de aveia.

oats [əʊts] npl [grain] aveia f.

OAU (*abbr of* **Organization of African Unity**) *n* OUA f.

obdurate [ˈɒbdjʊərət] *adj fml* contumaz.

OBE (*abbr of* **Order of the British Empire**) *n* (*beneficiário da*) *ordem honorífica do Império Britânico*.

obedience [əˈbiːdjəns] *n* (*U*): ~ **(to sb)** obediência f (a alguém).

obedient [əˈbiːdjənt] *adj* obediente.

obediently [əˈbiːdjəntlɪ] *adv* obedientemente.

obelisk [ˈɒbəlɪsk] *n* [column] obelisco m.

obese [əʊˈbiːs] *adj* obeso(sa).

obesity [əʊˈbiːsətɪ] *n* (*U*) obesidade f.

obey [əˈbeɪ] <> *vt* obedecer a. <> *vi* obedecer.

obituary [əˈbɪtʃʊərɪ] (*pl* **-ies**) *n* obituário m.

object [*n* ˈɒbdʒɪkt, *vb* ɒbˈdʒekt] <> *n* **- 1.** [gen] objeto m **- 2.** [aim] objetivo m **- 3.** *GRAM* objeto m, complemento m. <> *vt*: **to ~ (that)** objetar (que). <> *vi* objetar; **to ~ to sthg/to doing sthg** opor a algo/a fazer algo.

objection [əbˈdʒekʃn] *n* [argument against] objeção f; **to have no ~ to sthg/to doing sthg** não ter nenhuma objeção a algo/a fazer algo.

objectionable [əbˈdʒekʃənəbl] *adj* desagradável.

objective [əbˈdʒektɪv] <> *adj* objetivo(va). <> *n* objetivo m.

objectively [əbˈdʒektɪvlɪ] *adv* objetivamente.

objectivity [ˌɒbdʒekˈtɪvətɪ] *n* (*U*) objetividade f.

object lesson [ˈɒbdʒɪkt-] *n*: **an ~ in sthg** um exemplo perfeito de algo.

objector [əbˈdʒektəʳ] *n* opositor m, -ra f.

obligate [ˈɒblɪgeɪt] *vt fml* obrigar; **to ~ sb to do sthg** obrigar alguém a fazer algo.

obligation [ˌɒblɪˈgeɪʃn] *n* obrigação f.

obligatory [əˈblɪgətrɪ] *adj* obrigatório(ria).

oblige [əˈblaɪdʒ] <> *vt* **- 1.** [force]: **to ~ sb to do sthg** obrigar alguém a fazer algo **- 2.** *fml* [do a favour to] fazer um favor a. <> *vi* fazer um favor.

obliging [əˈblaɪdʒɪŋ] *adj* prestativo(va).

oblique [əˈbliːk] <> *adj* **- 1.** [indirect - look] enviesado(da); [- reference, hint, compliment] indireto(ta) **- 2.** [slanting] oblíquo(qua). <> *n TYPO* barra f.

obliquely [əˈbliːklɪ] *adv* [indirectly] indiretamente.

obliterate [əˈblɪtəreɪt] *vt* [destroy] obliterar.

obliteration [əˌblɪtəˈreɪʃn] *n* (*U*) [destruction] obliteração f.

oblivion [əˈblɪvɪən] *n* (*U*) **- 1.** [unconsciousness] inconsciência f **- 2.** [state of being forgotten] esquecimento m.

oblivious [əˈblɪvɪəs] *adj* inconsciente; **to be ~ to** OR **of sthg** não ter consciência de algo.

oblong [ˈɒblɒŋ] <> *adj* oblongo(ga). <> *n* retângulo m.

obnoxious [əbˈnɒkʃəs] *adj* repulsivo(va), repugnante.

o.b.o. (*abbr of* **or best offer**) ou a melhor oferta.

oboe [ˈəʊbəʊ] *n* oboé m.

oboist [ˈəʊbəʊɪst] *n* oboísta mf.

obscene [əbˈsiːn] *adj* obsceno(na).

obscenity [əbˈsenətɪ] (*pl* **-ies**) *n* obscenidade f.

obscure [əbˈskjʊəʳ] <> *adj* **- 1.** [not well-known] desconhecido(da) **- 2.** [difficult to see/understand] obscuro(ra). <> *vt* **- 1.** [make difficult to understand] obscurecer **- 2.** [hide] esconder.

obscurity [əbˈskjʊərətɪ] *n* (*U*) obscuridade f.

obsequious [əbˈsiːkwɪəs] *adj fml* & *pej* servil.

observable [əbˈzɜːvəbl] *adj* visível, observável.

observably [əbˈzɜːvəblɪ] *adv* visivelmente.

observance [əbˈzɜːvns] *n* (*U*) observância f, cumprimento m.

observant [əbˈzɜːvnt] *adj* observador(ra).

observation [ˌɒbzəˈveɪʃn] *n* observação f.

observation post *n* ponto m de observação.

observatory [əbˈzɜːvətrɪ] (*pl* **-ies**) *n* observatório m.

observe [əbˈzɜːv] *vt* observar.

observer [əbˈzɜːvəʳ] *n* **- 1.** [gen] observador m, -ra f **- 2.** [political commentator] analista mf.

obsess [əbˈses] *vt* obsedar, obcecar; **to be ~ed by** OR **with sb/sthg** estar obcecado(da) com OR por alguém/algo.

obsession [əbˈseʃn] *n* obsessão f.

obsessional [əbˈseʃənl] *adj* obsessivo(va).

obsessive [əbˈsesɪv] *adj* obsessivo(va).

obsolescence [ˌɒbsəˈlesns] *n* (*U*) obsolescência f.

obsolescent [ˌɒbsəˈlesnt] *adj* antiquado(da).

obsolete [ˈɒbsəliːtl] *adj* obsoleto(ta).

obstacle [ˈɒbstəkl] *n* obstáculo m.

obstacle race *n* corrida f de obstáculos.

obstetrician [ˌɒbstəˈtrɪʃn] *n* obstetra mf.

obstetrics [ɒbˈstetrɪks] *n* (*U*) obstetrícia f.

obstinacy [ˈɒbstɪnəsɪ] *n* [stubbornness] obstinação f, teimosia f.

obstinate [ˈɒbstənət] *adj* **- 1.** [stubborn] obstinado(da), teimoso(sa) **- 2.** [persistent] persistente.

obstinately [ˈɒbstənətlɪ] *adv* [stubbornly] obstinadamente, teimosamente.

obstreperous [əbˈstrepərəs] *adj fml or hum* escandaloso(sa).

obstruct [əbˈstrʌkt] *vt* **- 1.** [road, path, traffic] obstruir, bloquear **- 2.** [progress, justice] impedir.

obstruction [əbˈstrʌkʃn] *n* **- 1.** [blockage, obstacle] obstrução f, obstáculo m **- 2.** (*U*) [act of impeding] impedimento m **- 3.** *SPORT* obstrução f.

obstructive [əbˈstrʌktɪv] *adj* obstrutivo(va).

obtain [əbˈteɪn] *vt* [get] obter.

obtainable [əbˈteɪnəbl] *adj* disponível.

obtrusive [əbˈtruːsɪv] *adj* **- 1.** [person, behaviour] inconveniente **- 2.** [smell] penetrante **- 3.** [colour] gritante.

obtrusively [əbˈtruːsɪvlɪ] *adv* indiscretamente, inconvenientemente.

obtuse [əbˈtjuːs] *adj* obtuso(sa).

obverse [ˈɒbvɜːs] *n* **- 1.** [front side] reverso m **- 2.** [opposite] contrapartida f.

obviate [ˈɒbvɪeɪt] *vt fml* evitar, prevenir.

obvious [ˈɒbvɪəs] <> *adj* **- 1.** [evident] óbvio(via) **- 2.** [unsubtle] evidente. <> *n*: **to state the ~** afirmar o óbvio.

obviously [ˈɒbvɪəslɪ] *adv* **- 1.** [of course] evidentemente, obviamente; **~ not** claro que não **- 2.** [clearly] evidentemente; **he's ~ lying** é óbvio que ele está mentindo.

obviousness [ˈɒbvɪəsnɪs] *n* (*U*) obviedade f.

OCAS (*abbr of* **Organization of Central American**

States) n Organização f dos Estados da América Central.

occasion [ə'keɪʒn] <> n -1. [circumstance, time] ocasião f; **on several** ~s em várias ocasiões; **on** ~ **fml** de vez em quando; **special** ~ ocasião especial; **to rise to the** ~ mostrar-se à altura da ocasião -2. **fml** [reason, motive] razão f. <> vt fml [cause] ocasionar.

occasional [ə'keɪʒnl] adj ocasional.

occasionally [ə'keɪʒnəlɪ] adv de vez em quando, ocasionalmente.

occasional table n mesa f auxiliar.

occluded front n METEOR frente f oclusa.

occult [ɒ'kʌlt] <> adj oculto(ta). <> n: **the** ~ o oculto.

occupancy ['ɒkjʊpənsɪ] n (U) fml ocupação f.

occupant ['ɒkjʊpənt] n ocupante mf.

occupation [,ɒkjʊ'peɪʃn] n -1. [job] ocupação f, emprego m -2. [pastime] passatempo m -3. (U) MIL ocupação f.

occupational [,ɒkju:'peɪʃnl] adj ocupacional.

occupational disease n MED doença f ocupacional.

occupational hazard n risco m da profissão.

occupational therapist n terapeuta mf ocupacional.

occupational therapy n (U) terapia f ocupacional.

occupied ['ɒkjʊpaɪd] adj ocupado(da).

occupier ['ɒkjʊpaɪə'] n ocupante mf.

occupy ['ɒkjʊpaɪ] (pt & pp -ied) vt -1. [gen] ocupar -2. [keep busy]: **to** ~ **o.s.** ocupar-se.

occur [ə'kɜː'] (pt & pp -red, cont -ring) vi -1. [happen] ocorrer -2. [exist] existir -3. [be found] ser encontrado(da) -4. [come to mind]: **to** ~ **to sb** ocorrer a alguém.

occurrence [ə'kʌrəns] n -1. [event] acontecimento m -2. (U) [fact or instance of occurring] ocorrência f.

ocean ['əʊʃn] n oceano m.

oceangoing ['əʊʃn,gəʊɪŋ] adj de grande autonomia.

Oceania [,əʊʃɪ'ɑːnɪə] n Oceania; **in** ~ na Oceania.

Oceanian [,əʊʃɪ'ɑːnɪən] <> adj oceânico(ca). <> n oceânico m, -ca f.

ochre UK, **ocher** US ['əʊkə'] adj [colour] ocre.

o'clock [ə'klɒk] adv: **five** ~ cinco horas; **it's four** ~ são quatro horas; **it's one** ~ é uma hora.

OCR n -1. (abbr of optical character reader) OCR m -2. (abbr of optical character recognition) OCR f.

Oct. (abbr of October) out.

octagon ['ɒktəgən] n octógono m.

octagonal [ɒk'tægənl] adj octogonal.

octane ['ɒkteɪn] n octano m.

octane number, octane rating n índice m de octana.

octave ['ɒktɪv] n MUS oitava f.

octet [ɒk'tet] n MUS octeto m.

October [ɒk'təʊbə'] n outubro m; see also September.

octogenarian [,ɒktəʊdʒɪ'neərɪən] n octogenário m, -ria f.

octopus ['ɒktəpəs] (pl -puses OR -pi [-paɪ]) n polvo m.

OD <> n inf (abbr of overdose) overdose f. <> vi -1.

inf (abbr of **overdose**) tomar uma overdose -2. **fig, hum** exagerar. <> adj (abbr of **overdrawn**) no negativo, referente a conta bancária.

odd [ɒd] adj -1. [strange] estranho(nha) -2. [not part of pair] sem par -3. [number] ímpar -4. [leftover] avulso(sa) -5. [occasional] ocasional -6. inf [approximately]: **20** ~ **years** 20 e tantos anos.

<> **odds** npl -1. [probability] probabilidades fpl; **the** ~s **are that** ... as previsões são de que ...; **against the** ~s apesar de todas as dificuldades -2. [bits]: ~**s and ends** miudezas fpl -3. phr: **to be at** ~ **s with sb/sthg** discordar de algo/alguém.

oddball ['ɒdbɔːl] n inf esquisitão m, -tona f.

oddity ['ɒdɪtɪ] (pl -ies) n -1. [strange person, thing] esquisitice f -2. (U) [strangeness] estranheza f.

odd-job man UK, **odd-jobber** US n faz-tudo mf.

odd jobs npl biscates mpl.

oddly ['ɒdlɪ] adv [strangely] estranhamente; ~ **enough, I didn't care** surpreendentemente, não me importei.

oddments ['ɒdmənts] npl retalhos mpl.

odds-on ['ɒdz-] adj inf: **the** ~ **favourite** o grande favorito.

ode [əʊd] n ode f.

odious ['əʊdjəs] adj odioso(sa).

odometer [əʊ'dɒmɪtə'] n [in car] velocímetro m.

odor n US = odour.

odorless adj US = odourless.

odour UK, **odor** US ['əʊdə'] n odor m.

odourless UK, **odorless** US ['əʊdəlɪs] adj inodoro(ra).

odyssey ['ɒdɪsɪ] (pl -s) n literary odisséia f.

OECD (abbr of Organization for Economic Cooperation and Development) n organização que reúne um grupo de países desenvolvidos que trabalham pelo desenvolvimento do comércio e crescimento econômico, OECD f.

oesophagus UK, **esophagus** US [ɪ'sɒfəgəs] n esôfago m.

oestrogen UK, **estrogen** US [iː'strədʒən] n (U) estrogênio m.

of [ɒv] prep -1. [belonging to] de; **the colour** ~ **the car** a cor do carro. -2. [expressing amount] de; **a piece** ~ **cake** uma fatia de bolo; **a fall** ~ **20%** uma queda de 20%; **lots** ~ **people** muita gente. -3. [containing, made from] de; **a glass** ~ **beer** um copo de cerveja; **a house** ~ **stone** uma casa de pedra; **it's made** ~ **wood** é de madeira. -4. [regarding, relating to, indicating cause] de; **fear** ~ **spiders** medo de aranhas; **he died** ~ **cancer** ele morreu de câncer. -5. [referring to time] de; **the summer** ~ **1969** o verão de 1969; **the 26th** ~ **August** o 26 de agosto. -6. [with cities, countries] de; **the city** ~ **San Francisco** a cidade de San Francisco. -7. [on the part of] de; **that was very kind** ~ **you** foi muito amável da sua parte. -8. US [in telling the time] menos, para; **it's ten** ~ **four** são dez para as quatro.

off [ɒf] <> adv -1. [away]: **to drive/walk** ~ ir-se embora; **to get** ~ [from bus, train, etc] descer; **we're** ~ **to Austria next week** vamos para a Áustria na próxima semana. -2. [expressing removal]: **to take sthg** ~ tirar algo. -3. [so as to stop working]: **to turn sthg** ~ [TV, radio, engine] desligar algo; [tap]

fechar algo. **- 4.** [expressing distance or time away]: **it's a long way** ~ [in distance] é muito longe; [in time] ainda falta muito; **it's two months** ~ é daqui a dois meses. **- 5.** [not at work] de folga; **I'm taking a week** ~ vou tirar uma semana de férias. <> *prep* **-1.** [away from]: **to get** ~ **sthg** descer de algo; ~ **the coast** ao largo da costa; **just** ~ **the main road** perto da estrada principal. **- 2.** [indicating removal]: **take the lid** ~ **the jar** tire a tampa do frasco; **we'll take $20** ~ **the price** descontaremos 20 dólares do preço. **- 3.** [absent from]: **to be** ~ **work** não estar trabalhando. **- 4.** *inf* [from] a; **I bought it** ~ **her** eu comprei isso dela. <> *adj* **-1.** [TV, radio, light] apagado(da), desligado(da); [tap] fechado(da); [engine] desligado(da). **- 2.** [cancelled] cancelado(da).

offal ['ɒfl] *n (U)* vísceras *fpl (do animal abatido)*.

off-balance *adv* **-1.** [not standing firmly] sem equilíbrio **- 2.** [unprepared] desprevenido(da).

offbeat ['ɒfbiːt] *adj inf* original, excêntrico(ca).

off-centre <> *adj* descentralizado(da). <> *adv* fora do centro.

off-chance *n*: he called on the ~ of seeing her ele ligou com a remota esperança de vê-la.

off-colour *adj* **-1.** [ill] indisposto(ta) **- 2.** [rude, offensive] ofensivo(va).

offcut ['ɒfkʌt] *n* retalho *m*.

off-day *n inf* dia *m* de folga.

off duty *adv*: when do you get ~? quando você fica de folga?
➡ **off-duty** *adj* de folga.

offence *UK*, **offense** *US* [ə'fens] *n* **-1.** [crime] infração *f*, delito *m* **- 2.** [displeasure, hurt] insulto *m*, ofensa *f*; **to take** ~ ofender-se.

offend [ə'fend] <> *vt* [upset] ofender. <> *vi* **-1.** [contravene]: **to** ~ **against** transgredir; [decency] pecar contra **- 2.** [commit a crime] cometer (um) crime.

offended [ə'fendɪd] *adj* ofendido(da).

offender [ə'fendə^r] *n* **-1.** [criminal] transgressor *m*, -ra *f* **- 2.** [culprit] infrator *m*, -ra *f*.

offending [ə'fendɪŋ] *adj* ofensor(ra).

offense [sense 2 'ɒfens] *n US* **-1.** = offence **- 2.** *SPORT* ataque *m*.

offensive [ə'fensɪv] <> *adj* **-1.** [causing offence] ofensivo(va) **- 2.** [aggressive] agressivo(va). <> *n* **-1.** *MIL* ofensiva *f* **- 2.** *fig* [attack]: **to go on** *OR* **take the** ~ partir para a ofensiva.

offensiveness [ə'fensɪvnɪs] *n (U)* caráter *m* ofensivo.

offer ['ɒfə^r] <> *n* **-1.** [something offered] oferta *f*; **on** ~ [available] em oferta **- 2.** [bid, proposal] proposta *f*. <> *vt* **-1.** [present, give] oferecer; **to** ~ **sthg to sb, to** ~ **sb sthg** oferecer algo a alguém **- 2.** [propose]: **to** ~ **to do sthg** oferecer-se para fazer algo. <> *vi* oferecer-se.

offering ['ɒfərɪŋ] *n* **-1.** [something offered] oferta *f* **- 2.** *RELIG* [sacrifice] oferenda *f*.

off guard *adv* desprevenido(da).

off-hand <> *adj* [unfriendly] brusco(ca). <> *adv* [at this moment] de imediato.

office ['ɒfɪs] *n* **-1.** [room] escritório *m*, gabinete *m* **- 2.** [building] edifício *m* de escritórios **- 3.** [staff] pessoal *m* **- 4.** [government department] departamento

m **- 5.** [distribution point - for tickets] bilheteria *f*; [- for information] guichê *m*; [- for enquiries] serviço *m* de informações **- 6.** [position of authority] cargo *m*; **in** ~ no poder; **to take** ~ tomar posse.

office automation *n* automatização *f*.

office block *n* prédio *m* de escritórios.

office boy *n* contínuo *m*, bói *m*.

officeholder ['ɒfɪsˌhəʊldə^r] *n* detentor *m*, -ra *f* de cargo público.

office hours *npl* horário *m* de expediente.

office junior *n UK* assistente *mf* de escritório.

Office of Fair Trading *n* ≃ Delegacia *f* de Defesa do Consumidor.

officer ['ɒfɪsə^r] *n* **-1.** *MIL* oficial *mf* **- 2.** [in organization] diretor *m*, -ra *f* **- 3.** [in police force] (agente) policial *m*.

office work *n (U)* trabalho *m* de escritório.

office worker *n* funcionário *m*, -ria *f* de escritório.

official [ə'fɪʃl] <> *adj* oficial. <> *n* [public] funcionário *m*, -ria *f*; *SPORT* oficial *mf*.

officialdom [ə'fɪʃəldəm] *n (U)* burocracia *f*.

officially [ə'fɪʃəlɪ] *adv* oficialmente.

official receiver *n* síndico *m*, -ca *f* em falências.

officiate [ə'fɪʃɪeɪt] *vi* oficiar; **to** ~ **at sthg** celebrar algo.

officious [ə'fɪʃəs] *adj pej* intrometido(da).

offing ['ɒfɪŋ] *n*: in the ~ num futuro próximo.

off-key *MUS* <> *adj* desafinado(da). <> *adv* de maneira desafinada.

off-licence *n UK* loja *f* de bebidas alcoólicas.

off limits *adj esp US* proibido(da).

off-line *adj COMPUT* off-line, desconectado(da).

offload ['ɒfləʊd] *vt inf*: **to** ~ **sthg (onto sb)** livrar-se de algo (passando para alguém).

off-peak <> *adj* de tarifa reduzida. <> *adv* fora do horário de pico.

off-putting [-ˌpʊtɪŋ] *adj* desconcertante.

off sales *npl UK* venda *f* de bebidas alcoólicas.

off season *n*: the ~ a baixa temporada.
➡ **off-season** *adj* de baixa temporada.

offset ['ɒfset] (*pt* & *pp* offset, *cont* **-ting**) *vt* contrabalançar.

offshoot ['ɒfʃuːt] *n* [spin-off] ramificação *f*; **to be an** ~ **of sthg** ser uma ramificação de algo.

offshore ['ɒfʃɔː^r] <> *adj* **-1.** [in or on the sea] em alto mar **- 2.** [near coast] costeiro(ra). <> *adv* **-1.** [out at sea] ao largo **- 2.** [near coast] a pouca distância da costa.

offside [*adj* & *adv* ˌɒf'saɪd, *n* 'ɒfsaɪd] <> *adj* **-1.** [part of vehicle] do lado do motorista **- 2.** *SPORT* impedido(da). <> *n* [of vehicle] lado *m* do motorista.

offspring ['ɒfsprɪŋ] (*pl inv*) *n* **-1.** *fml or hum* [of people] descendência *f* **- 2.** [of animals] prole *f*.

offstage [ˌɒf'steɪdʒ] <> *adj* dos bastidores. <> *adv* nos bastidores.

off-the-cuff <> *adj* improvisado(da). <> *adv* de improviso.

off-the-peg *adj UK* pronto(ta), confeccionado(-da).

off-the-record <> *adj* extra-oficial. <> *adv* extra-oficialmente.

off-the-wall *adj* não usual, excêntrico(ca).

off-white *adj* de cor não totalmente branca.

OFSTED (*abbr of* **Office for Standards in Education**) *n órgão britânico que inspeciona a educação.*

OFT (*abbr of* **Office of Fair Trading**) *n órgão britânico que controla as transações comerciais.*

often ['ɒfn, 'ɒftn] *adv* **-1.** [many times] muitas vezes; **how ~?** quantas vezes?; **how ~ do you visit her?** com que freqüência você a visita? **-2.** [in many cases] freqüentemente.
➤ **as often as not** *adv* geralmente.
➤ **every so often** *adv* de vez em quando.
➤ **more often than not** *adv* freqüentemente.

ogle ['əʊgl] *vt pej* comer com os olhos.

ogre ['əʊgə'] *n* [in fairy tales] ogro *m.*

oh [əʊ] *excl* **-1.** [to introduce comment] ah!; **~ really?** é mesmo? **-2.** [expressing emotion] ah!; **~ no!** essa não!

OH *abbr of* Ohio.

Ohio [əʊ'haɪəʊ] *n* Ohio; **in ~** em Ohio.

ohm [əʊm] *n* ohm *m.*

OHMS (*abbr of* **On His (or Her) Majesty's Service**) *na Grã-Bretanha, expressão que indica o caráter oficial de um documento.*

oil [ɔɪl] <> *n* **-1.** [gen] óleo *m* **-2.** (U) [petroleum] petróleo *m* **-3.** (U) [olive oil] azeite *m.* <> *vt* [lubricate] lubrificar.
➤ **oils** *npl* ART tintas *fpl* a óleo.

oilcan ['ɔɪlkæn] *n* almotolia *f.*

oil change *n* troca *f* de óleo.

oilcloth ['ɔɪlklɒθ] *n* (U) oleado *m.*

oilfield ['ɔɪlfiːld] *n* campo *m* petrolífero.

oil filter *n* filtro *m* de óleo.

oil-fired [-,faɪəd] *adj* a óleo.

oil industry *n*: **the ~** a indústria petrolífera, o setor petroleiro.

oilman ['ɔɪlmən] (*pl* **-men** [-mən]) *n* **-1.** [worker] trabalhador *m* do setor petroleiro **-2.** [businessman] executivo *m* do setor petroleiro.

oil paint *n* tinta *f* a óleo.

oil painting *n* **-1.** [art] pintura *f* a óleo **-2.** [picture] quadro *m* a óleo.

oilrig ['ɔɪlrɪg] *n* plataforma *f* petrolífera.

oilskins ['ɔɪlskɪnz] *npl* capa *f* de oleado.

oil slick *n* mancha *f* de óleo.

oil tanker *n* **-1.** [ship] petroleiro *m* **-2.** [lorry] caminhão *m* -tanque.

oil well *n* poço *m* de petróleo.

oily ['ɔɪlɪ] (*compar* **-ier**, *superl* **-iest**) *adj* **-1.** [covered in oil] gorduroso(sa) **-2.** *pej* [smarmy] bajulador(ra).

ointment ['ɔɪntmənt] *n* pomada *f.*

oiro (*abbr of* **offers in the region of**) ofertas em torno de.

OK (*pl* OKs, *pt* & *pp* OKed, *cont* OKing), **okay** [,əʊ'keɪ] *inf* <> *adj*: **are you ~?** você está bem?; **to be ~ with** OR **by sb** estar tudo bem com alguém. <> *adv* [well] bem. <> *n*: **to give (sb) the ~** dar sinal verde (a alguém). <> *excl* **-1.** [asking for, expressing agreement] está bem!, tá (bem/bom)! **-2.** [fair enough] certo! **-3.** [to introduce new topic] bom! <> *vt* aprovar.

Oklahoma [,əʊklə'həʊmə] *n* Oklahoma; **in ~** em Oklahoma.

okra ['əʊkrə] *n* (U) quiabo *m.*

old [əʊld] <> *adj* **-1.** [aged, ancient, longstanding]

velho(lha) **-2.** [referring to age]: **how ~ are you?** quantos anos você tem? **-3.** [former, ancient, out-of-date] antigo(ga); **in the ~ days** antigamente **-4.** *inf* [for emphasis]: **any ~ clothes will do** qualquer roupa serve; **any ~ how** de qualquer jeito. <> *npl*: **the ~** os idosos.

old age *n* (U) velhice *f.*

old age pension *n* UK pensão *f* por idade.

old age pensioner *n* UK aposentado *m*, -da *f* por idade.

Old Bailey [-'beɪlɪ] *n*: **the ~** o prédio do Tribunal Criminal (de Londres).

olden ['əʊldn] *adj*: **in the ~ days** antigamente.

old-fashioned [-'fæʃnd] *adj* **-1.** [outmoded] antiquado(da) **-2.** [traditional] tradicional.

old flame *n* paixão *f* antiga.

old hat *adj inf pej*: **to be ~** estar fora de moda.

old maid *n pej* [spinster] solteirona *f.*

old master *n* **-1.** [painter] grande mestre *m* **-2.** [painting] obra-prima *f.*

old people's home *n* lar *m* de idosos.

Old Testament *n*: **the ~** o Antigo Testamento.

old-time *adj* de antigamente.

old-timer *n* **-1.** [veteran] veterano *m*, -na *f* **-2.** *esp* US [old man] velho(lha).

old wives' tale *n* conto *m* da carochinha.

Old World *n*: **the ~** o Velho Mundo.

O level (*abbr of* **ordinary level**) *n* UK até há pouco tempo, primeira etapa do GCE, exame prestado pelos estudantes britânicos aos 16 anos, agora substituído pelo GCSE.

oligarchy ['ɒlɪgɑːkɪ] (*pl* **-ies**) *n* oligarquia *f.*

olive ['ɒlɪv] <> *adj* da cor de oliva. <> *n* **-1.** [fruit] azeitona *f* **-2.** [tree]: **~ (tree)** oliveira *f.*

olive green *adj* verde-oliva.

olive oil *n* (U) azeite *m* de oliva.

Olympic [ə'lɪmpɪk] *adj* olímpico(ca).
➤ **Olympics** *npl*: **the ~s** as Olimpíadas.

Olympic Games *npl*: **the ~** os Jogos Olímpicos.

OM (*abbr of* **Order of Merit**) *n* (beneficiário da) ordem do mérito britânica.

O & M (*abbr of* **organization and method**) *n* O & M *f.*

Oman [əʊ'mɑːn] *n* Omã; **in ~** em Omã.

OMB (*abbr of* **Office of Management and Budget**) *n órgão norte-americano que assessora o presidente em questões orçamentárias.*

ombudsman ['ɒmbʊdzmən] (*pl* **-men** [-mən]) *n* ombudsman *mf.*

omelet(te) ['ɒmlɪt] *n* omelete *f.*

omen ['əʊmen] *n* presságio *m.*

ominous ['ɒmɪnəs] *adj* **-1.** ominoso(sa) **-2.** [threatening] ameaçador(ra).

ominously ['ɒmɪnəslɪ] *adv* ominosamente.

omission [ə'mɪʃn] *n* omissão *f.*

omit [ə'mɪt] (*pt* & *pp* **-ted**, *cont* **-ting**) *vt* omitir; **to ~ to do sthg** deixar de fazer algo.

omnibus ['ɒmnɪbəs] *n* **-1.** [book] antologia *f* **-2.** UK RADIO & TV programa *f* de variedades.

omnipotence [ɒm'nɪpətəns] *n* (U) *fml* onipotência *f.*

omnipotent [ɒm'nɪpətənt] *adj fml* onipotente.

omnipresent [,ɒmnɪ'prezntl] *adj fml* onipresente.

omniscience *n fml* onisciência *f.*

omniscient [ɒmˈnɪsɪənt] *adj fml* onisciente.

omnivorous [ɒmˈnɪvərəs] *adj ZOOL* onívoro(ra).

on [ɒn] ⋄ *prep* **-1.** [expressing position, location] em, sobre; **it's ~ the table** está na mesa, está sobre a mesa; **put it ~ the table** ponha-o na *or* sobre a mesa; **~ my right** à minha direita; **~ the right** à direita; **a picture ~ the wall** um quadro na parede; **the exhaust ~ the car** o cano de descarga do carro; **we stayed ~ a farm** ficamos numa fazenda. **-2.** [with forms of transportation]: **~ the plane** no avião; **to get ~ a bus** subir num ônibus. **-3.** [expressing means, method] em; **~ foot** a pé; **~ the radio** no rádio; **~ TV** na televisão; **paid ~ an hourly basis** pago por hora. **-4.** [using] a; **it runs ~ unleaded gas** funciona com gasolina sem chumbo; **to be ~ drugs** drogar-se; **to be ~ medication** estar tomando medicamentos. **-5.** [about] sobre; **a book ~ Germany** um livro sobre a Alemanha. **-6.** [expressing time]: **~ arrival** ao chegar; **~ Tuesday** na terça-feira; **~ August 25th** no dia 25 de agosto. **-7.** [with regard to] em, sobre; **a tax ~ imports** um imposto sobre as importações; **the effect ~ the country** o impacto no país. **-8.** [describing activity, state]: **~ vacation** de férias; **~ sale** à venda. **-9.** [in phrases]: **do you have any money ~ you?** *inf* você tem dinheiro?; **the drinks are ~ me** as bebidas são por minha conta. ⋄ *adv* **-1.** [in place, covering]: **to put one's clothes ~** vestir-se; **to put the lid ~** tapar. **-2.** [movie, play, programme]: **the news is ~** está passando o telejornal; **what's ~ at the movies?** o que é que está passando no cinema? **-3.** [with transportation]: **to get ~** subir. **-4.** [functioning]: **to turn sthg ~** [TV, radio, light] ligar *or* acender algo; [tap] abrir algo; [engine] pôr algo para trabalhar. **-5.** [taking place]: **how long is the festival ~?** quanto tempo dura o festival?; **the game is already ~** o jogo já começou. **-6.** [farther forward]: **to drive ~** continuar a dirigir. **-7.** [in phrases]: **I already have something ~ tonight** já tenho planos para esta noite. ⋄ *adj* [TV, radio, light] ligado(da), aceso(sa); [tap] aberto(ta); [engine] funcionando.

ON *abbr of* Ontario.

ONC (*abbr of* Ordinary National Certificate) *n* diploma técnico em nível secundário na Grã-Bretanha.

once [wʌns] ⋄ *adv* **-1.** [on one occasion] uma vez; **~ again** *or* **more** [one more time] outra vez; [yet again] novamente; **~ and for all** de uma vez por todas; **~ in a while** de vez em quando; **~ or twice** uma vez ou duas; **for ~** ao menos uma vez **-2.** [previously, formerly] outrora; **~ upon a time** era uma vez. ⋄ *conj* assim que, quando.
 ➤ **at once** *adv* **-1.** [immediately] imediatamente **-2.** [at the same time] ao mesmo tempo; **all at ~** de repente.

once-over *n inf*: **to give sb/sthg the ~** dar uma olhada rápida em alguém/algo.

oncoming [ˈɒnˌkʌmɪŋ] *adj* **-1.** [traffic, vehicle] em sentido contrário **-2.** [danger] iminente.

OND (*abbr of* Ordinary National Diploma) *n* diploma técnico em nível superior na Grã-Bretanha, obtido em curso de 3 anos.

one [wʌn] ⋄ *num* um (uma); **thirty-~** trinta e um;

~ fifth um quinto. ⋄ *adj* [only] único(ca); **~ day** um dia. ⋄ *pron* [referring to a particular thing or person] um *m*, uma *f*; **the green ~** o verde; **that ~** aquele *m*, aquela *f*.

one-armed bandit *n* caça-níqueis *m*.

one-liner *n* piada *f* curta.

one-man *adj* individual, solo.

one-man band *n* **-1.** [musician] homem *m* -orquestra **-2.** [business, operation] faz-tudo *m*.

one-night stand *n* **-1.** [performance] apresentação *f* única **-2.** *inf* [sexual relationship] ficada *f* de uma noite só, transa *f* passageira.

one-off *inf* ⋄ *adj* único(ca). ⋄ *n* **-1.** [unique event, person] único *m*, -ca *f* **-2.** [unique product] exemplar *m* único.

one-on-one *adj US* = one-to-one.

one-parent family *n* família *f* que possui apenas um dos pais.

one-piece *adj* de uma peça só; **a ~ swimsuit** um maiô inteiro.

onerous [ˈəʊnərəs] *adj* oneroso(sa), difícil.

one's *poss adj*: **to do ~ duty** fazer o seu dever; **to be on ~ own** estar sozinho(nha).

oneself [wʌnˈself] *pron fml* **-1.** (*reflexive*) se **-2.** (*after prep*) si próprio(pria), si mesmo(ma).

one-sided [-ˈsaɪdɪd] *adj* **-1.** [unequal] desigual, unilateral **-2.** [biased] parcial.

onetime [ˈwʌntaɪm] *adj* [former] antigo(ga).

one-to-one *UK*, **one-on-one** *US adj* **-1.** [discussion] entre dois **-2.** [tuition] individual.

one-touch dialling *UK*, **one-touch dialing** *US n* discagem *f* automática.

one-upmanship [ˌwʌnˈʌpmənʃɪp] *n* (*U*) capacidade de parecer ser melhor que os outros.

one-way *adj* **-1.** [moving in one direction] de mão única **-2.** [for outward travel only] só de ida.

ongoing [ˈɒnˌgəʊɪŋ] *adj* em andamento, atual.

onion [ˈʌnjən] *n* cebola *f*.

online [ˈɒnlaɪn] *COMPUT adj & adv* on-line.

online banking *n* serviço *m* de banco on-line.

online shopping *n* compras *fpl* on-line.

onlooker [ˈɒnˌlʊkər] *n* espectador *m*, -ra *f*.

only [ˈəʊnlɪ] ⋄ *adj* único(ca); **an ~ child** um filho único. ⋄ *adv* **-1.** [exclusively] só **-2.** [merely, just] apenas, só **-3.** [for emphasis] só; **I was ~ too willing to help** eu queria tanto ajudar; **it's ~ natural you should be upset** é bastante natural que você fique perturbado; **not ~ ... but also** não apenas ... mas também; **~ just** por pouco. ⋄ *conj* só que.

o.n.o., ono (*abbr of* or near (est) offer) ou a oferta mais próxima.

onrush [ˈɒnrʌʃ] *n* [of feeling] irrupção *f*.

on-screen *COMPUT adj & adv* na tela.

onset [ˈɒnset] *n* começo *m*.

onshore [ˈɒnʃɔːr] ⋄ *adj* **-1.** [on land] terrestre **-2.** [moving towards land] em direção à costa. ⋄ *adv* **-1.** [on land] em terra **-2.** [towards land] para a praia.

onside [ɒnˈsaɪd] *adj & adv SPORT* em posição legal.

onslaught [ˈɒnslɔːt] *n* investida *f*.

Ont. *abbr of* Ontario.

Ontario [ɒnˈteərɪəʊ] *n* [province] Ontário *m*; **in ~** em Ontário.

on-the-job *adj* no trabalho, prático(ca).

on-the-spot *adj* no ato, no local.

onto [*unstressed before consonant* 'ɒntə, *unstressed before vowel* 'ɒntʊ, *stressed* 'ɒntu:] *prep* ⊳ **on**.

onus ['əʊnəs] *n* ônus *m*.

onward ['ɒnwəd] ⟨⟩ *adj* [advancing - in time] para a frente; [- in space] adiante, para a frente. ⟨⟩ *adv* = **onwards**.

onwards ['ɒnwədz] *adv* [forwards - in space] para a frente; [- in time] em diante.

onyx ['ɒnɪks] *n (U)* ônix *m*.

oodles ['u:dlz] *npl inf*: ∼ **of sthg** um montão de algo.

oof *excl inf* uff!

ooh [u:] *excl inf* aah!

oops [ʊps, u:ps] *excl inf* ôpa!

ooze [u:z] ⟨⟩ *vt fig* exalar. ⟨⟩ *vi* exsudar; **to** ∼ **from** OR **out of sthg** transpirar por algo; **sweat** ∼ **d from every pore** o suor transpirava-lhe por todos os poros. ⟨⟩ *n (U)* lodo *m*.

opacity [ə'pæsətɪ] *n* **-1.** [non-transparency] opacidade *f* **-2.** *fig* [obscurity] obscuridade *f*.

opal ['əʊpl] *n* [gem] opala *m*.

opaque [əʊ'peɪk] *adj* **-1.** [not transparent] opaco(ca) **-2.** *fig* [obscure] obscuro(ra).

OPEC ['əʊpek] *(abbr of* Organization of the Petroleum Exporting Countries*) n* OPEP *f*.

open ['əʊpn] ⟨⟩ *adj* **-1.** [gen] aberto(ta); **to be** ∼ **to sthg** [ready to accept] ser aberto(ta) a algo; **to be** ∼ **to sb** [opportunity, choice] estar aberto(ta) a alguém; **to lay o.s.** ∼ **to criticism** manter-se aberto(ta) à crítica **-2.** [frank] franco(ca) **-3.** [unfastened] descobrado(da) **-4.** [not enclosed] amplo(pla) **-5.** [uncovered] descoberto(ta) **-6.** [meeting, competition, invitation] aberto(ta) a todos **-7.** [unconcealed] manifesto(ta). ⟨⟩ *n*: **in the** ∼ [in the fresh air] ao ar livre; **to bring sthg out into the** ∼ pôr algo para fora. ⟨⟩ *vt* **-1.** [gen] abrir **-2.** [inaugurate] inaugurar **-3.** [unblock] desbloquear. ⟨⟩ *vi* abrir.

➤ **open on to** *vt fus* [subj: room, door] dar para.

➤ **open out** *vi* **-1.** [bud, petals] abrir-se **-2.** [road, path, river] alargar-se **-3.** [view, valley] revelar-se.

➤ **open up** ⟨⟩ *vt* [unlock door] destrancar a porta. ⟨⟩ *vi* **-1.** [gen] abrir-se **-2.** [shop, house] abrir.

open-air *adj* ao ar livre; ∼ **swimming pool** piscina descoberta.

open-and-shut *adj* evidente.

opencast ['əʊpnkɑ:st] *adj*: ∼ **mining** lavra *f* a céu aberto.

open day *n* dia em que uma escola, universidade etc. podem ser visitados pelo público em geral.

open-ended [-'endɪd] *adj* sem prazo para acabar, aberto(ta).

opener ['əʊpnə'] *n* abridor *m*.

open-handed [-'hændɪd] *adj* generoso(sa).

openhearted [,əʊpn'hɑ:tɪd] *adj* de coração aberto.

open-heart surgery *n (U)* cirurgia *f* de coração aberto.

opening ['əʊpnɪŋ] ⟨⟩ *adj* [first] primeiro(ra). ⟨⟩ *n* **-1.** [beginning] lançamento *m* **-2.** [gap] abertura *f* **-3.** [opportunity] oportunidade *f*; ∼ **for sthg**

oportunidade para algo **-4.** [job vacancy] vaga *f*.

opening hours *npl* horário *m* de funcionamento.

opening night *n* (noite de) estréia *f*.

opening time *n* UK hora *f* de abrir.

open letter *n* carta *f* aberta.

openly ['əʊpənlɪ] *adv* abertamente.

open market *n* mercado *m* aberto.

open marriage *n* casamento *m* aberto.

open-minded [-'maɪndɪd] *adj* compreensivo(va), sem preconceitos.

open-mouthed [-'maʊðd] *adj* boquiaberto(ta); **in** ∼ **admiration** numa admiração de deixar de boca aberta.

open-necked [-'nekt] *adj* aberto(ta) no colo.

openness ['əʊpnnɪs] *n (U)* [frankness] franqueza *f*.

open-plan *adj* sem divisórias.

open prison *n* prisão *f* de regime aberto.

open sandwich *n* sanduíche *m* aberto.

open season *n* temporada *f*.

open shop *n* local de trabalho onde não é necessário pertencer a um sindicato.

Open University *n* UK: **the** ∼ universidade britânica para alunos adultos que estudam em casa, através de uma combinação de programas de rádio e televisão e ensino à distância.

open verdict *n* JUR júri *m* pendente.

opera ['ɒpərə] *n* ópera *f*.

opera glasses *npl* binóculos *mpl* de teatro.

opera house *n* teatro *m* lírico.

opera singer *n* cantor *m*, -ra *f* de ópera.

operate ['ɒpəreɪt] ⟨⟩ *vt* **-1.** [cause to work] operar **-2.** COMM [manage] dirigir. ⟨⟩ *vi* **-1.** [function] funcionar **-2.** COMM dirigir **-3.** MED operar; **to** ∼ **on sb/sthg** operar alguém/algo.

operatic [,ɒpə'rætɪk] *adj* de ópera, lírico(ca).

operating room ['ɒpəreɪtɪŋ-] *n* US = **operating theatre**.

operating system ['ɒpəreɪtɪŋ-] *n* COMPUT sistema *m* operacional.

operating theatre UK, **operating room** US ['ɒpəreɪtɪŋ-] *n* sala *f* de operações.

operation [,ɒpə'reɪʃn] *n* **-1.** [gen] operação *f* **-2.** MIL manobra *f* **-3.** COMM administração *f* **-4.** (U) [functioning] funcionamento *m*; **in** ∼ [machine, device] em funcionamento; [law, system] em vigor **-5.** MED operação *f*, cirurgia *f*; **to have an** ∼ **on one's knee** ser operado(da) no joelho; **to perform a kidney transplant** ∼ fazer uma cirurgia de transplante renal.

operational [,ɒpə'reɪʃənl] *adj* operacional.

operative ['ɒprətɪv] ⟨⟩ *adj* [law] em vigor; [system] vigente. ⟨⟩ *n* [in factory] operário *m*, -ria *f*.

operator ['ɒpəreɪtə'] *n* **-1.** TELEC telefonista *mf* **-2.** [technician] operador *m*, -ra *f* **-3.** COMM [person in charge] encarregado *m*, -da *f*.

operetta [,ɒpə'retə] *n* opereta *f*.

ophthalmic optician [ɒf'θælmɪk-] *n* oculista *mf*.

ophthalmologist [,ɒfθæl'mɒlədʒɪst] *n* oftalmologista *mf*.

opinion [ə'pmjən] *n* opinião *f*; **to be of the** ∼ **that** ser da opinião de que; **in my** ∼ na minha opinião.

opinionated [ə'pınjəneıtıd] *adj pej* teimoso(sa), cabeça-dura.

opinion poll *n* pesquisa *f* de opinião.

opium ['əupjəm] *n (U)* ópio *m*.

opponent [ə'pəunənt] *n* adversário *m*, -ria *f*.

opportune ['ɒpətju:n] *adj* oportuno(na).

opportunism [,ɒpə'tju:nızm] *n (U)* oportunismo *m*.

opportunist [,ɒpə'tju:nıst] *n* oportunista *mf*.

opportunity [,ɒpə'tju:nətı] *(pl* -ies) *n* oportunidade *f*; **to get the** ~ **(to do sthg)** ter a oportunidade (de fazer algo); **to take the** ~ **to do** OR **of doing sthg** aproveitar a oportunidade para fazer algo.

oppose [ə'pəuz] *vt* opor-se a.

opposed [ə'pəuzd] *adj* oposto(ta); **to be** ~ **to sthg** opor-se a algo; **as** ~ **to** em oposição a, em vez de; **I like beer** ~ **wine** prefiro vinho e não cerveja.

opposing [ə'pəuzıŋ] *adj* oposto(ta), contrário(ria).

opposite ['ɒpəzıt] <> *adj* -1. [facing] em frente; **the** ~ **side (of the street/house/door)** o outro lado (da rua/casa/porta) -2. [very different]: ~ **(to sthg)** oposto(ta) (a algo). <> *adv* [lá] em frente. <> *prep* [facing] em frente a. <> *n* [contrary] contrário *m*.

opposite number *n* número *m* equivalente.

opposite sex *n*: **the** ~ o sexo oposto.

opposition [,ɒpə'zıʃn] *n* -1. *(U)* [gen] oposição *f* -2. [opposing team] adversário *m*, -ria *f*.

◆ **Opposition** *n UK* POL: **the Opposition** a Oposição.

oppress [ə'pres] *vt* -1. [tyrannize] oprimir -2. [subj: anxiety, atmosphere] deprimir.

oppressed [ə'prest] <> *adj* [people, minorities] oprimido(da). <> *npl*: **the** ~ os oprimidos.

oppression [ə'preʃn] *n (U)* opressão *f*.

oppressive [ə'presıv] *adj* -1. [gen] opressivo(va) -2. [heat, weather] sufocante.

oppressor [ə'presə°] *n* opressor *m*, -ra *f*.

opprobrium [ə'prəubrıəm] *n (U) fml* opróbrio *m*.

opt [ɒpt] <> *vt*: **to** ~ **to do sthg** optar por OR preferir fazer algo. <> *vi*: **to** ~ **for sthg** optar por OR escolher algo.

◆ **opt in** *vi*: **to** ~ **in (to sthg)** optar por participar (de algo).

◆ **opt out** *vi*: **to** ~ **out (of sthg)** optar por não participar (de algo); [give up] abrir mão (de algo).

optic ['ɒptık] *adj* óptico(ca).

◆ **optics** *n (U)* óptica *f*.

optical ['ɒptıkl] *adj* -1. [relating to light] óptico(ca) -2. [visual] visual.

optical character reader *n* COMPUT leitora *f* óptica de caracteres.

optical character recognition *n* COMPUT reconhecimento *m* óptico de caracteres.

optical fibre *n* TELEC fibra *f* óptica.

optical illusion *n* ilusão *f* de óptica.

optician [ɒp'tıʃn] *n* oculista *mf*; ~ **'s** óptica *f*.

optimism ['ɒptımızm] *n (U)* otimismo *m*.

optimist ['ɒptımıst] *n* otimista *mf*.

optimistic [,ɒptı'mıstık] *adj* otimista; **to be** ~ **about sthg** ser/estar otimista sobre algo.

optimize, -ise ['ɒptımaız] *vt* otimizar.

optimum ['ɒptıməm] *adj* ótimo(ma).

option ['ɒpʃn] *n* [choice] opção *f*; **to have the** ~ **to do** OR **of doing sthg** ter a opção de fazer algo.

optional ['ɒpʃənl] *adj* opcional.

opulence ['ɒpjuləns] *n (U)* opulência *f*.

opulent ['ɒpjulənt] *adj* opulento(ta).

opus ['əupəs] *(pl* -es OR **opera**) *n* MUS opus *m*.

or [ɔ:°] *conj* -1. [gen] ou -2. [after negative] nem; **he can't read** ~ **write** ele não sabe ler nem escrever -3. [otherwise] senão; **I'd better go now** ~ **I'll miss my plane** acho melhor eu ir logo, senão vou perder o vôo.

OR *abbr of* Oregon.

oracle ['ɒrəkl] *n* [prophet] oráculo *m*.

oral ['ɔ:rəl] <> *adj* -1. [spoken] oral -2. [relating to the mouth] bucal. <> *n* exame *m* oral.

orally ['ɔ:rəlı] *adv* -1. [in spoken form] oralmente -2. [via the mouth] por via oral.

orange ['ɒrındʒ] <> *adj* [colour] laranja. <> *n* -1. [fruit] laranja *f* -2. *(U)* [colour] laranja *m inv*.

orangeade [,ɒrındʒ'eıd] *n* laranjada *f*.

orange blossom *n* [flowers] flor *f* de laranjeira.

orange juice *n* suco *m* de laranja.

Orangeman ['ɒrındʒmən] *(pl* -men [-mən]) *n UK* orangista *mf*.

orange tree *n* laranjeira *f*.

orangutang [ɔ:,ræŋu'tæŋ] *n* orangotango *m*.

oration [ɔ:'reıʃn] *n fml* discurso *m*.

orator ['ɒrətə°] *n* orador *m*, -ra *f*.

oratorio [,ɒrə'tɔ:rıəu] *(pl* -s) *n* oratório *m*.

oratory ['ɒrətrı] *n* -1. *(U)* [eloquence] oratória *f* -2. [prayer room] oratório *m*.

orb [ɔ:b] *n* -1. [sphere] orbe *m* -2. [ornamental ball] esfera *f*.

orbit ['ɔ:bıt] <> *n* órbita *f*; **to be in/go into** ~ **(around sthg)** estar/entrar em órbita (ao redor de algo); **to put sthg into** ~ **(around sthg)** pôr algo em órbita (ao redor de algo). <> *vt* orbitar.

orbital road *n UK* estrada *que circunda uma cidade*.

orchard ['ɔ:tʃəd] *n* pomar *m*.

orchestra ['ɔ:kıstrə] *n* orquestra *f*.

orchestral [ɔ:'kestrəl] *adj* orquestral.

orchestra pit *n* fosso *m* da orquestra.

orchestrate ['ɔ:kıstreıt] *vt* -1. MUS orquestrar -2. *fig* [organize] osquestrar.

orchestration [,ɔ:ke'streıʃn] *n* MUS & *fig* orquestração *f*.

orchid ['ɔ:kıd] *n* orquídea *f*.

ordain [ɔ:'deın] *vt* -1. *fml* [decree] ordenar, decretar -2. RELIG: **to be** ~**ed** ser ordenado(da).

ordeal [ɔ:'di:l] *n* experiência *f* traumática, provação *f*.

order ['ɔ:də°] <> *n* -1. [gen] ordem *f*; **to be under** ~**s to do sthg** receber ordens para fazer algo; **in** ~ em ordem; **in working** ~ em funcionamento; **to be out of** ~ [not working] estar fora de operação, não estar funcionando; [in meeting, debate] agir de forma inaceitável; [behaviour] ser improcedente; **to keep** ~ manter a ordem -2. COMM [request] pedido *m*; **to place an** ~ **with sb for sthg** encomendar algo com alguém; **on** ~ reservado(-da); **to** ~ sob encomenda -3. *US* [portion] porção *f*. <> *vt* -1. [command] ordenar; **to** ~ **sb to do sthg** ordenar alguém a fazer algo; **to** ~ **that** ordenar que **-2.** [request - drink, food, shopping item] pedir; [- taxi] chamar. <> *vi* pedir, fazer o pedido *(em restaurante)*.

➡ **orders** *npl* RELIG: **(holy)** ~**s** ordens *fpl* (sagradas).

➡ **in the order of** UK, **on the order of** US *prep* da ordem de.

➡ **in order that** *conj* a fim de que, para que.

➡ **in order to** *conj* para.

➡ **order about, order around** *vt sep*: **he's always** ~**ing people about** ele está sempre mandando nas pessoas.

order book *n* livro *m* de encomendas.

order form *n* formulário *m* de encomenda.

orderly ['ɔːdəlɪ] *(pl* -**ies)** <> *adj* -**1.** [person] obediente -**2.** [room, office] ordenado(da). <> *n* [in hospital] assistente *mf*.

order number *n* número *m* do pedido.

ordinal ['ɔːdɪnl] <> *adj* ordinal. <> *n* ordinal *m*.

ordinarily ['ɔːdənrəlɪ] *adv* [normally] geralmente.

ordinary ['ɔːdənrɪ] <> *adj* -**1.** [normal] comum, normal -**2.** *pej* [unexceptional] medíocre. <> *n*: **out of the** ~ fora do comum.

ordinary level *n* UK nível *m* fundamental *(na escola)*.

ordinary seaman *n* UK marinheiro *m*.

ordinary shares *npl* UK FIN ações *fpl* ordinárias.

ordination [ˌɔːdɪ'neɪʃn] *n (U)* ordenação *f*.

ordnance ['ɔːdnəns] *n* -**1.** [military supplies] arsenal *f* bélico -**2.** [artillery] artilharia *f*.

Ordnance Survey *n* UK & *Irish* serviço oficial de topografia e cartografia.

ore [ɔːʳ] *n* minério *m*.

oregano [ˌɒrɪ'gɑːnəʊ] *n (U)* orégano *m*.

Oregon ['ɒrɪgən] *n* Oregon; **in** ~ no Oregon.

organ ['ɔːgən] *n* -**1.** [gen] órgão *m* -**2.** *fig* [mouthpiece] órgão *m*.

organic [ɔː'gænɪk] *adj* orgânico(ca).

organically [ɔː'gænɪklɪ] *adv* AGR organicamente.

organic chemistry *n (U)* química *f* orgânica.

organism ['ɔːgənɪzm] *n* BIOL organismo *m*.

organist ['ɔːgənɪst] *n* organista *mf*.

organization [ˌɔːgənaɪ'zeɪʃn] *n* organização *f*.

organization chart *n* organograma *m*.

organizational [ˌɔːgənaɪ'zeɪʃnl] *adj* organizacional.

organize, -ise ['ɔːgənaɪz] <> *vt* organizar. <> *vi* organizar-se.

organized ['ɔːgənaɪzd] *adj* organizado(da).

organized crime *n (U)* crime *m* organizado.

organized labour *n (U)* mão-de-obra *f* sindicalizada.

organizer ['ɔːgənaɪzəʳ] *n* [person] organizador *m*, -ra *f*.

organza [ɔː'gænzə] *n (U)* organza *f*.

orgasm ['ɔːgæzm] *n* orgasmo *m*.

orgy ['ɔːdʒɪ] *(pl* -**ies)** *n* orgia *f*.

orient ['ɔːrɪənt] *vt esp* US = **orientate**.

Orient ['ɔːrɪənt] *n*: **the** ~ o Oriente.

oriental [ˌɔːrɪ'entl] <> *adj* oriental. <> *n* [non-PC term for East-Asian] oriental *mf*.

orientate ['ɔːrɪənteɪt] *vt*: **to be** ~**d towards sb/**

sthg ser orientado(da) para alguém/algo; **to** ~ **o.s.** orientar-se.

orientation [ˌɔːrɪen'teɪʃn] *n (U)* orientação *f*.

orienteering [ˌɔːrɪən'tɪərɪŋ] *n (U)* esporte no qual as pessoas utilizam um mapa e uma bússola para se orientar, corrida *f* de orientação.

orifice ['ɒrɪfɪs] *n* orifício *m*.

origami [ˌɒrɪ'gɑːmɪ] *n (U)* origami *m*.

origin ['ɒrɪdʒɪn] *n* origem *f*; **country of** ~ país *m* de origem.

➡ **origins** *npl* origens *fpl*.

original [ə'rɪdʒənl] <> *adj* original. <> *n* original *m*.

originality [əˌrɪdʒə'nælətɪ] *n (U)* originalidade *f*.

originally [ə'rɪdʒənlɪ] *adv* [initially] originalmente.

original sin *n (U)* pecado *m* original.

originate [ə'rɪdʒəneɪt] <> *vt* originar, produzir. <> *vi*: **to** ~ **(in)** originar-se (em), surgir (de); **to** ~ **from** originar-se de.

origination *n (U)* [invention, creation] origem *f*, criação *f*.

originator [ə'rɪdʒəneɪtəʳ] *n* autor *m*, -ra *f*, inventor *m*, -ra *f*.

Orinoco [ˌɒrɪ'nəʊkəʊ] *n*: **the (River)** ~ o (Rio) Orinoco.

Orkney Islands ['ɔːknɪ-], **Orkneys** ['ɔːknɪz] *npl*: **the** ~ as Ilhas Órcadas; **in the** ~ nas Ilhas Órcadas.

ornament ['ɔːnəmənt] *n* ornamento *m*.

ornamental [ˌɔːnə'mentl] *adj* ornamental.

ornamentation [ˌɔːnəmen'teɪʃn] *n (U)* ornamentação *f*.

ornate [ɔː'neɪt] *adj* ornado(da).

ornately [ɔː'neɪtlɪ] *adv* vistosamente, de forma requintada.

ornery ['ɔːnərɪ] *adj* US *inf* genioso(sa).

ornithologist [ˌɔːnɪ'θɒlədʒɪst] *n* ornitólogo *m*, -ga *f*.

ornithology [ˌɔːnɪ'θɒlədʒɪ] *n (U)* ornitologia *f*.

orphan ['ɔːfn] <> *n* órfão *m*, -fã *f*. <> *vt*: **to be** ~**ed** ficar órfão(fã).

orphanage ['ɔːfənɪdʒ] *n* orfanato *m*.

orthodontist [ˌɔːθə'dɒntɪst] *n* ortodontista *mf*.

orthodox ['ɔːθədɒks] *adj* ortodoxo(xa).

Orthodox Church *n*: **the** ~ a Igreja Ortodoxa.

orthodoxy ['ɔːθədɒksɪ] *n* ortodoxia *f*.

orthopaedic [ˌɔːθə'piːdɪk] *adj* ortopédico(ca).

orthopaedics [ˌɔːθə'piːdɪks] *n (U)* ortopedia *f*.

orthopaedist [ˌɔːθə'piːdɪst] *n* ortopedista *mf*.

orthopedic etc [ˌɔːθə'piːdɪk] *adj* = **orthopaedic etc**.

OS <> *n* *(abbr of* **Ordnance Survey)** *organização oficial britânica que elabora mapas detalhados da Grã-Bretanha e da Irlanda*. <> -**1.** *(abbr of* **outsize)** GGG -**2.** *(abbr of* **out of stock)** fora de estoque.

Oscar ['ɒskəʳ] *n* CINEMA Oscar *m*.

oscillate ['ɒsɪleɪt] *vi* -**1.** [from side to side] oscilar -**2.** *fig* [vacillate]: **to** ~ **between** oscilar entre.

oscilloscope [ɒ'sɪləskəʊp] *n* osciloscópio *m*.

OSD *(abbr of* optical scanning device) *n* OSD *m*.

OSHA *(abbr of* Occupational Safety and Health

Administration) n órgão norte-americano responsável pela saúde e pela segurança no trabalho.

Oslo ['ɒzləʊl] n Oslo; **in** ~ em Oslo.

osmosis [ɒz'məʊsɪs] n (U) osmose f.

osprey ['ɒspri] (pl -s) n gavião-pescador m.

Ostend [ɒs'tend] n Ostend; **in** ~ em Ostend.

ostensible [ɒ'stensəbl] adj ostensivo(va).

ostensibly [ɒ'stensəbli] adv ostensivamente.

ostentation [ˌɒstən'teɪʃn] n (U) ostentação f.

ostentatious [ˌɒstən'teɪʃəs] adj ostentoso(sa).

osteoarthritis [ˌɒstɪəʊɑː'θraɪtɪs] n (U) osteoartrite f.

osteopath ['ɒstɪəpæθ] n osteopático m, -ca f.

osteopathy [ˌɒstɪ'ɒpəθɪ] n osteopatia f.

ostracize, -ise ['ɒstrəsaɪz] vt condenar ao ostracismo;

ostrich ['ɒstrɪtʃ] n avestruz mf.

OT n **- 1.** (abbr of Old Testament) AT m **- 2.** (abbr of occupational therapy) TO f.

OTC (abbr of Officer Training Corps) n unidade de formação de oficiais da reserva do exército britânico.

OTE (abbr of on target earnings) prêmios obtidos mediante cumprimento de objetivos.

other ['ʌðəʳ] <> adj **-1.** [gen] outro(tra); **the** ~ **one** o outro, a outra **- 2.** phr: **the** ~ **day** no outro dia; **the** ~ **week** na outra semana. <> adv: ~ **than** a não ser; **to be none** ~ **than** ser nem mais nem menos que. <> pron: **the** ~ o outro, a outra; ~**s** outros(tras); **the** ~**s** os outros, as outras; **one after the** ~ um atrás do outro, uma atrás da outra; **one or** ~ **of you must help me** um de vocês dois deve me ajudar.

➤ **something or other** pron uma coisa ou outra.

➤ **somehow or other** adv de um jeito ou de outro.

otherwise ['ʌðəwaɪz] <> adv **-1.** [apart from that] de resto, tirando isso **- 2.** [differently, in a different way] de outra maneira; **deliberately or** ~ intencionalmente ou não. <> conj [or else] senão, do contrário.

other world n: **the** ~ o outro mundo.

otherworldly [ˌʌðə'wɜːldlɪ] adj místico(ca), espiritual.

OTT (abbr of over the top) adj UK inf além dos limites; **it's a bit** ~ está um pouco além dos limites.

Ottawa ['ɒtəwə] n Ottawa; **in** ~ em Ottawa.

otter ['ɒtəʳ] n lontra f.

OU (abbr of Open University) n universidade f aberta.

ouch [aʊtʃ] excl ai!

ought [ɔːt] aux vb dever; **I really** ~ **to go** eu realmente deveria ir; **you** ~ **not to have done that** você não deveria ter feito isso; **she** ~ **to pass her exam** ela tem chance de passar no exame.

oughtn't [ɔːtnt] cont = ought not.

Ouija board® ['wiːdʒə] n ≃ jogo m do copo.

ounce [aʊns] n **-1.** [unit of measurement] onça f **- 2.** fig [small amount]: **an** ~ **of**, um pouco de.

our ['aʊəʳ] poss adj nosso(a); ~ **books** os nossos livros.

ours ['aʊəz] poss pron o nosso (a nossa); **a friend of** ~ um amigo nosso; **those shoes are** ~ estes sapatos são (os) nossos; ~ **are here - where are yours?** os nossos estão aqui - onde estão os seus?

ourselves [aʊə'selvz] pron pl **-1.** (reflexive) nos **-2.** (after prep) nós mesmos(mas), nós próprios(prias); **we did it** ~ nós mesmos OR próprios o fizemos.

oust [aʊst] vt fml: **to** ~ **sb (from sthg)** expulsar alguém (de algo).

ouster ['aʊstəʳ] n US **-1.** [from country] expulsão f **-2.** [from office] destituição f.

out [aʊt] <> adj [light, cigarette] apagado(da); [not in fashion] fora de moda; **cargo pants are so** ~ as calças cargo estão tão fora de moda. <> adv **-1.** [outside] fora; **to get/go** ~ **(of)** sair (de); **it's cold** ~ **today** está frio lá fora hoje; **he looked** ~ ele olhou para fora. **-2.** [not at home, work] fora; **to be** ~ não estar em casa; **to go** ~ sair. **-3.** [so as to be extinguished]: **to turn sthg** ~ apagar algo; **put your cigarette** ~ apague o cigarro. **-4.** [expressing removal]: **to pour sthg** ~ despejar algo, jogar algo fora; **to take money** ~ [from cashpoint] retirar dinheiro; **to take sthg** ~ **(of)** tirar algo (de). **-5.** [outwards]: **to stick** ~ sobressair. **-6.** [expressing distribution]: **to hand sthg** ~ distribuir algo. **-7.** [in phrases]: **to get enjoyment** ~ **of sthg** divertir-se com algo; **stay** ~ **of the sun** não se exponha ao sol; **made** ~ **of wood** (feito) de madeira; **five** ~ **of ten women** cinco em cada dez mulheres; **I'm** ~ **of cigarettes** não tenho cigarros.

out-and-out adj completo(ta), absoluto(ta).

outback ['aʊtbæk] n: **the** ~ o interior da Austrália.

outbid [ˌaʊt'bɪd] (pt & pp outbid, cont -ding) vt: **to** ~ **sb (for sthg)** sobrepujar alguém (em algo).

outboard (motor) ['aʊtbɔːd-] n motor m de popa.

outbound ['aʊtbaʊnd] adj **-1.** [train, flight] de ida **-2.** [traffic] de saída.

outbreak ['aʊtbreɪk] n **-1.** [of crime, violence] explosão f **-2.** [of disease] surto m **-3.** [of war] deflagração f.

outbuildings ['aʊtbɪldɪŋz] npl dependências fpl.

outburst ['aʊtbɜːst] n **-1.** [of emotion] manifestação f **-2.** [sudden occurrence] explosão f.

outcast ['aʊtkɑːst] n rejeitado m, -da f.

outclass [ˌaʊt'klɑːs] vt exceder, ultrapassar.

outcome ['aʊtkʌm] n resultado m.

outcrop ['aʊtkrɒp] n afloramento m.

outcry ['aʊtkraɪ] (pl -ies) n protestos mpl.

outdated [ˌaʊt'deɪtɪd] adj ultrapassado(da), fora de moda.

outdid [ˌaʊt'dɪd] pt ▷ outdo.

outdistance [ˌaʊt'dɪstəns] vt **-1.** [in race] deixar para trás **-2.** fig [in business, development] ultrapassar.

outdo [ˌaʊt'duː] (pt -did, pp -done [-dʌn]) vt ultrapassar, superar.

outdoor ['aʊtdɔːʳ] adj ao ar livre.

outdoors [aʊt'dɔːz] adv ao ar livre; **let's eat** ~ vamos comer fora.

outer ['aʊtə'] *adj* externo(na); **Outer London** a Grande Londres.

outermost ['aʊtəməʊst] *adj* mais externo(na); ~ **planet of the solar system** o planeta mais afastado do sistema solar.

outer space *n (U)* espaço *m* exterior.

outerwear *n* roupa *f* de cima.

outfit ['aʊtfɪt] *n* -**1.** [clothes] vestimenta *f*; [fancy dress] traje *m* -**2.** *inf* [organization] agrupamento *m*, grupo *m*.

outfitters ['aʊt̩fɪtəz] *n UK dated* confecção *f*.

outflank [,aʊt'flæŋk] *vt* -**1.** *MIL* surpreender pela retaguarda -**2.** *fig* [in argument, business] superar.

outgoing ['aʊt̩gəʊɪŋ] *adj* -**1.** [leaving] de partida -**2.** [friendly, sociable] extrovertido(da), aberto(ta).

➡ **outgoings** *npl UK* despesas *fpl*.

outgrow [,aʊt'grəʊ] (*pt* -**grew**, *pp* -**grown**) *vt* -**1.** [grow too big for]: **he has ~n his shirts** as camisas ficaram pequenas para ele -**2.** [grow too old for] ser muito grande para.

outhouse ['aʊthaʊs, *pl* -haʊzɪz] *n* dependência *f*.

outing ['aʊtɪŋ] *n* -**1.** [trip] excursão *f* -**2.** *(U)* [of homosexuals] *revelação da homossexualidade de uma pessoa famosa*.

outlandish [aʊt'lændɪʃ] *adj* estranho(nha), extravagante.

outlast [,aʊt'lɑːst] *vt* sobreviver a, durar mais tempo que.

outlaw ['aʊtlɔː] ⬦ *n* fora-da-lei *mf*. ⬦ *vt* -**1.** [make illegal] declarar ilegal -**2.** [declare an outlaw] proscrever.

outlay ['aʊtleɪ] *n* despesa *f*, desembolso *m*.

outlet ['aʊtlet] *n* -**1.** [for feelings] escape *m* -**2.** [hole, pipe] saída *f* -**3.** [shop] ponto *m* de venda -**4.** *US ELEC* tomada *f*.

outline ['aʊtlaɪn] ⬦ *n* -**1.** [brief description] linhas *fpl* gerais, esboço *m*; **in ~** em linhas gerais -**2.** [silhouette] contorno *m*. ⬦ *vt* -**1.** [describe briefly] resumir, esboçar -**2.** [silhouette]: **to be ~d against** sthg delinear-se contra algo.

outlive [,aʊt'lɪv] *vt* -**1.** [subj: person] viver mais que -**2.** *fig* [subj: idea, object] sobreviver.

outlook ['aʊtlʊk] *n* -**1.** [attitude, disposition] postura *f*, atitude *f* -**2.** [prospect] perspectiva *f*.

outlying ['aʊt̩laɪɪŋ] *adj* distante, remoto(ta).

outmanoeuvre *UK*, **outmaneuver** *US* [,aʊtmə'nuːvə'] *vt* passar a perna em.

outmoded [,aʊt'məʊdɪd] *adj* antiquado(da), fora de moda.

outnumber [,aʊt'nʌmbə'] *vt* exceder em número.

out-of-date *adj* -**1.** [passport, season ticket] expirado(da) -**2.** [clothes, belief] antiquado(da).

out of doors *adv* ao ar livre.

out-of-the-way *adj* [isolated] remoto(ta).

outpace [,aʊt'peɪs] *vt* -**1.** [subj: person] deixar para trás -**2.** *fig* [subj: technology] deixar para trás.

outpatient ['aʊt̩peɪʃnt] *n* paciente *mf* ambulatorial.

outplacement *n COMM* recolocação *f* (*em outra empresa*).

outplay [,aʊt'pleɪ] *vt SPORT* superar, jogar melhor que.

outpost ['aʊtpəʊst] *n fig* [bastion] posto *m* avançado.

outpouring ['aʊt̩pɔːrɪŋ] *literary n* efusão *f*.

output ['aʊtpʊt] ⬦ *n* -**1.** [production] produção *f* -**2.** [*COMPUT* - printing out] saída *f*; [- printout] cópia *f* impressa. ⬦ *vt COMPUT* gerar como saída.

outrage ['aʊtreɪdʒ] ⬦ *n* -**1.** *(U)* [anger, shock] indignidade *f* -**2.** [atrocity] atrocidade *f*, ultraje *m*. ⬦ *vt* ultrajar.

outraged ['aʊtreɪdʒd] *adj* indignado(da).

outrageous [aʊt'reɪdʒəs] *adj* -**1.** [offensive, shocking] ultrajante -**2.** [extravagant, wild] extravagante.

outran [,aʊt'ræn] *pt* ▷ **outrun.**

outrank [,aʊt'ræŋk] *vt* exceder em hierarquia.

outrider ['aʊt̩raɪdə'] *n* escolta *f*.

outright [*adj* 'aʊtraɪt, *adv* ,aʊt'raɪt] ⬦ *adj* -**1.** [categoric, direct] claro(ra), categórico(ca) -**2.** [total, complete - disaster] completo(ta); [- victory, winner] indiscutível. ⬦ *adv* -**1.** [ask] abertamente, francamente -**2.** [win, fail] indiscutivelmente, completamente -**3.** [deny] categoricamente -**4.** [be killed]: **to be killed ~** morrer no ato.

outrun [,aʊt'rʌn] (*pt* -**ran**, *pp* -**run**, *cont* -**ning**) *vt* correr mais que.

outsell [,aʊt'sell] (*pt & pp* -**sold**) *vt* vender mais que.

outset ['aʊtset] *n*: **at the ~** no princípio; **from the ~** desde o princípio.

outshine [,aʊt'ʃaɪn] (*pt & pp* -**shone** [-ʃɒn]) *vt* [do better than] eclipsar.

outside [*adv* ,aʊt'saɪd, *adj, prep & n* 'aʊtsaɪd] ⬦ *adj* -**1.** [gen] externo(na) -**2.** [unlikely] remoto(ta). ⬦ *adv* (lá) fora; **to look ~** olhar para fora; **to run ~** correr lá fora; **to go ~** ir lá para fora. ⬦ *prep* -**1.** [not inside] fora de; **we live half an hour ~ London** moramos a meia hora de Londres -**2.** [beyond] além de. ⬦ *n* -**1.** [exterior] exterior *m* -**2.** [limit]: **at the ~** no máximo.

➡ **outside of** *prep US* [apart from] exceto.

outside broadcast *n UK RADIO & TV* (transmissão *f*) externa *f*.

outside lane *n AUT* -**1.** [in UK] faixa *f* da direita -**2.** [in mainland Europe, US, Brazil etc] faixa *f* da esquerda.

outside line *n* linha *f* externa.

outsider [,aʊt'saɪdə'] *n* -**1.** *SPORT* azarão *m* -**2.** [from outside social group] estranho *m*, -nha *f*, desconhecido *m*, -da *f*.

outsize ['aʊtsaɪz] *adj* -**1.** [book, portion] enorme -**2.** [clothes] extra-grande.

outsized ['aʊtsaɪzd] *adj* enorme.

outskirts ['aʊtskɜːts] *npl*: **the ~** os arredores.

outsmart [,aʊt'smɑːt] *vt* passar a perna em.

outsold [,aʊt'səʊld] *pt & pp* ▷ **outsell.**

outsource ['aʊtsɔːs] *vt COMM* terceirizar.

outsourcing ['aʊtsɔːsɪŋ] *n COMM* terceirização *f*.

outspoken [,aʊt'spəʊkn] *adj* franco(ca).

outspread [,aʊt'spred] *adj* estendido(da).

outstanding [,aʊt'stændɪŋ] *adj* -**1.** [excellent] destacado(da), notável -**2.** [very obvious, important] notável -**3.** [pending] pendente.

outstay [,aʊt'steɪ] *vt*: **to ~ one's welcome** abusar da hospitalidade de alguém.

outstretched [,aʊt'stretʃt] *adj* estendido(da).

outstrip [,aʊt'strɪp] (*pt* & *pp* **-ped**, *cont* **-ping**) *vt* **-1.** [do better than] superar **- 2.** [run faster than] ultrapassar, deixar para trás.

out-take *n* **-1.** CINEMA sobras *fpl* de filme **- 2.** TV sobras *fpl* de programa.

out-tray *n* bandeja *f* de saída.

outvote [,aʊt'vəʊt] *vt*: **to ~ sb** vencer alguém por receber mais votos; **the proposal was ~d by fifty to forty (votes)** a proposta foi derrotada por cinqüenta (votos) a quarenta.

outward ['aʊtwəd] ◇ *adj* **-1.** [going away] de ida **- 2.** [apparent] aparente **- 3.** [visible] visível. ◇ *adv* US = outwards.

outwardly ['aʊtwədlɪ] *adv* [apparently] aparentemente.

outwards UK ['aʊtwədz], **outward** US *adv* para fora.

outweigh [,aʊt'weɪ] *vt* pesar mais que.

outwit [,aʊt'wɪt] (*pt* & *pp* **-ted**, *cont* **-ting**) *vt* ser mais esperto(ta) que.

outworker ['aʊt,wɜ:kəʳ] *n* colaborador *m* externo, colaboradora *f* externa.

oval ['əʊvl] ◇ *adj* oval. ◇ *n* oval *m*.

Oval Office *n*: **the ~** o Salão Oval.

ovarian [əʊ'veərɪən] *adj* ovariano(na); **~ cancer** câncer de ovário.

ovary ['əʊvərɪ] (*pl* **-ies**) *n* ANAT ovário *m*.

ovation [əʊ'veɪʃn] *n* ovação *f*; **a standing ~** ovação com o público de pé.

oven ['ʌvn] *n* [for cooking] forno *m*.

oven glove *n* luva *f* para o forno.

ovenproof ['ʌvnpru:f] *adj* refratário(ria).

oven-ready *adj* pronto(ta) para ir ao forno.

ovenware ['ʌvnweəʳ] *n* (U) louça *f* refratária.

over ['əʊvəʳ] ◇ *prep* **-1.** [gen] sobre; **put your coat ~ that chair** ponha o seu casaco naquela cadeira; **to rule ~ a country** governar um país **- 2.** [directly above] sobre, em cima de **- 3.** [on the far side of] ao outro lado de **- 4.** [across the surface of] por; **she walked ~ the lawn** ela caminhou pelo gramado **- 5.** [across the top or edge of] por cima de **- 6.** [more than] mais de; **~ and above** bem acima de **- 7.** [by means of] por **- 8.** [concerning, due to] por; **it was a fight ~ a woman, I think** era uma disputa por uma mulher, acho eu **- 9.** [during] durante **-10.** [recovered from] recuperado(da) (de). ◇ *adv* **-1.** [distance away] lá; **~ here/there** por aqui, lá **- 2.** [across]: **to cross ~** cruzar; **they flew ~ to America** eles voaram para a América; **~ at mum's** na casa da minha mãe; **to ask sb ~** convidar alguém para ir lá em casa **- 3.** [to the ground] para baixo **- 4.** [to face a different way]: **to turn sth ~** virar algo **- 5.** [more] mais **- 6.** [remaining]: **that leaves £2 ~** isso nos sobra £2; **I ate the piece of cake left ~** comi o pedaço de bolo que sobrou **- 7.** RADIO câmbio; **~ and out!** câmbio e desligo! **- 8.** [involving repetitions]: **(all) ~ again** (tudo) novamente; **~ and ~ (again)** várias e várias vezes. ◇ *adj* [finished] acabado(da); **the meeting was ~ by seven** a reunião acabou às sete horas. ◇ *n* UK [cricket] *série de seis lançamentos de um único jogador.*

◆ all over ◇ *prep* por todo(da). ◇ *adv* [everywhere] por todas as partes. ◇ *adj* [finished] acabado(da).

over- ['əʊvəʳ] *prefix* muito, sobre-.

overabundance [,əʊvərə'bʌndəns] *n* (U) superabundância *f*.

overact [,əʊvər'ækt] *vi pej* [in play] exagerar na atuação.

overactive [,əʊvər'æktɪv] *adj* muito ativo(va).

overall [*adj* & *n* 'əʊvərɔːl, *adv* ,əʊvər'ɔːl] ◇ *adj* [total] global, total. ◇ *adv* **-1.** [in total] no geral **- 2.** [in general] normalmente, em geral. ◇ *n* **-1.** [coat] avental *m*, guarda-pó *m* **- 2.** US [with trousers] macacão *m*.

◆ overalls *npl* macacão *m*.

overambitious [,əʊvəræm'bɪʃəs] *adj* muito ambicioso(sa).

overanxious [,əʊvər'æŋkʃəs] *adj* muito nervoso(sa).

overarm ['əʊvərɑːm] ◇ *adj* por cima do ombro. ◇ *adv* por cima do ombro.

overate [,əʊvər'et] *pt* ⊳ **overeat**.

overawe [,əʊvər'ɔː] *vt* intimidar.

overbalance [,əʊvə'bæləns] *vi* perder o equilíbrio.

overbearing [,əʊvə'beərɪŋ] *adj pej* arrogante.

overblown [,əʊvə'bləʊn] *adj pej* exagerado(da).

overboard ['əʊvəbɔːd] *adv* **-1.** NAUT: **to fall ~** cair ao mar **- 2.** *fig*: **to go ~ (about sb/sthg)** [be overenthusiastic about] empolgar-se (com alguém/algo).

overbook [,əʊvə'bʊk] *vi* ter mais reservas que lugares; **the plane was ~** deu overbook no avião.

overburden [,əʊvə'bɜːdn] *vt*: **to be ~ed with sthg** estar sobrecarregado(da) de algo.

overcame [,əʊvə'keɪm] *pt* ⊳ **overcome**.

overcapitalize, -ise [,əʊvə'kæpɪtəlaɪz] *vi* FIN sobrecapitalizar.

overcast ['əʊvəkɑːst] *adj* carregado(da), nublado(da).

overcharge [,əʊvə'tʃɑːdʒ] ◇ *vt*: **to ~ sb (for sthg)** cobrar de alguém em excesso (por algo). ◇ *vi*: **to ~ (for sthg)** cobrar em excesso (por algo).

overcoat ['əʊvəkəʊt] *n* sobretudo *m*.

overcome [,əʊvə'kʌm] (*pt* **-came**, *pp* **-come**) *vt* **-1.** [control, deal with] superar, vencer **- 2.** [overwhelm]: **to be ~ (by OR with sthg)** [emotion] estar tomado(da) (por algo); [smoke, fumes] estar asfixiado(da) (por algo).

overcompensate [,əʊvə'kɒmpənseɪt] *vi*: **to ~ (for sthg)** compensar em excesso (por algo).

overconfident [,əʊvə'kɒnfɪdənt] *adj* confiante em excesso.

overcooked *adj* cozido(da) demais.

overcrowded [,əʊvə'kraʊdɪd] *adj* **-1.** [room, building] superlotado(da) **- 2.** [city, country] superpovoado(da).

overcrowding [,əʊvə'kraʊdɪŋ] *n* **-1.** (U) [of room, building] superlotação *f* **- 2.** (U) [of city, country] superpovoamento *m*.

overdeveloped [,əʊvədə'veləpt] *adj* **-1.** PHOT submetido a longo tempo de revelação **- 2.** [exaggerated] exagerado(da).

overdo [,əʊvə'duː] (*pt* **-did** [-dɪd], *pp* **-done**) *vt* **-1.** *pej* [exaggerate] exagerar **-2.** [do too much]: **to ~ the walking** caminhar demais; **the doctor told her not to ~ it** o médico disse para ela pegar leve OR não exagerar **-3.** [overcook] cozinhar demais.

overdone [,əʊvə'dʌn] <> pp |> **overdo**. <> adj: it's ~ cozinhou demais.

overdose [n 'əʊvədəʊs , vb əʊvə'dəʊs] <> n overdose f. <> vi: **to ~ on sthg** tomar uma overdose de algo.

overdraft ['əʊvədrɑ:ft] n saldo m negativo.

overdrawn [,əʊvə'drɔːn] adj **-1.** [person]: **to be ~** ter saldo negativo **-2.** [account] no negativo.

overdress [,əʊvə'dres] vi arrumar-se demais.

overdrive ['əʊvədraɪv] n (U) fig: **to go into ~** trabalhar a todo vapor.

overdue [,əʊvə'dju:] adj **-1.** [gen] atrasado(da); **I'm ~ for a dental checkup** já está na hora de eu fazer a revisão no dentista **-2.** [needed, awaited]: **(long) ~** (há muito) esperado(da).

overeager [,əʊvər'i:gə'] adj ansioso(sa) demais.

over easy adj US CULIN: **eggs ~** ovos mpl fritos (dos dois lados).

overeat [,əʊvər'i:t] (pt -ate, pp -eaten) vi comer demais, atracar-se.

overemphasize, -ise [,əʊvər'emfəsaɪz] vt enfatizar demais.

overenthusiastic ['əʊvərɪn,θju:zɪ'æstɪk] adj entusiasta demais.

overestimate [,əʊvər'estɪmeɪt] vt superestimar.

overexcited [,əʊvərɪk'saɪtɪd] adj sobreexaltado(-da).

overexpose [,əʊvərɪk'spəʊz] vt PHOT superexpor.

overfeed [,əʊvə'fi:d] (pt & pp -fed [-fedl) vt superalimentar.

overfill [,əʊvə'fɪl] vt encher demais.

overflow [vb ,əʊvə'fləʊ, n 'əʊvəfləʊl] <> vi transbordar; **to be ~ing (with sthg)** estar transbordando (de algo); **full to ~ing** entupido(da). <> vt transbordar. <> n ladrão m.

overgrown [,əʊvə'grəʊn] adj coberto(ta) de mato.

overhang [n 'əʊvəhæŋ, vb ,əʊvə'hæŋ] (pt & pp -hung) <> n saliência f. <> vt sobressair-se de, projetar-se de. <> vi sobressair, projetar.

overhaul [n 'əʊvəhɔ:l, vb ,əʊvə'hɔ:ll <> n revisão f. <> vt **-1.** [service] fazer a revisão de **-2.** [revise] revisar.

overhead [adv ,əʊvə'hed, adj & n 'əʊvəhedl <> adj aéreo(rea). <> adv por cima, pelo alto. <> n US despesas fpl gerais, gastos mpl gerais.

➠ **overheads** npl UK despesas fpl gerais, gastos mpl gerais.

overhead projector n retroprojetor m.

overhear [,əʊvə'hɪə'] (pt & pp -heard [-hɜ:dl) vt entreouvir.

overheat [,əʊvə'hi:t] <> vt superaquecer. <> vi superaquecer-se.

overhung [,əʊvə'hʌŋ] pt & pp |> **overhang**.

overindulge [,əʊvərɪn'dʌldʒ] <> vt ser indulgente demais com, mimar demais. <> vi: **to ~ (in sthg)** abusar (com algo).

overjoyed [,əʊvə'dʒɔɪd] adj: **to be ~ (at sthg)** estar contentíssimo(ma) (com algo).

overkill ['əʊvəkɪl] n (U) exagero m.

overladen [,əʊvə'leɪdn] <> pp |> **overload**. <> adj sobrecarregado(da).

overlaid [,əʊvə'leɪd] pt & pp |> **overlay**.

overland ['əʊvəlænd] <> adj terrestre. <> adv por terra.

overlap [n 'əʊvəlæp, vb ,əʊvə'læpl (pt & pp -ped, cont -ping) <> n **-1.** (U) [similarity] coincidência f **-2.** [overlapping part, amount] sobreposição f. <> vt sobrepor-se a. <> vi **-1.** [cover each other] sobrepor-se **-2.** [be similar] coincidir; **to ~ (with sthg)** coincidir em parte (com algo).

overlay [,əʊvə'leɪ] (pt & pp -laid) vt: **to be overlaid with sthg** estar revestido(da) de algo.

overleaf [,əʊvə'li:f] adv no verso.

overload [,əʊvə'ləʊd] (pp -loaded OR -laden) vt sobrecarregar; **to be ~ed (with sthg)** estar sobrecarregado(da) de algo.

overlong [,əʊvə'lɒŋ] <> adj muito comprido(da). <> adv tempo demais.

overlook [,əʊvə'lʊk] vt **-1.** [look over] dar para **-2.** [disregard, miss] fazer vista grossa para **-3.** [excuse] desculpar.

overlord ['əʊvəlɔ:d] n literary senhor m.

overly ['əʊvəlɪ] adv demais; **not ~** não muito.

overmanning [,əʊvə'mænɪŋ] n (U) excesso m de mão-de-obra.

overnight [adj 'əʊvənaɪt, adv ,əʊvə'naɪtl <> adj **-1.** [stay, guest, parking] por uma noite **-2.** [clothes] para uma noite **-3.** [journey] de uma noite; **~ bag** bolsa f de viagem **-4.** [very sudden] da noite para o dia. <> adv **-1.** [for all of night] durante a noite **-2.** [very suddenly] da noite para o dia.

overpaid [,əʊvə'peɪd] <> pt & pp |> **overpay**. <> adj pago(ga) em excesso.

overpass ['əʊvəpɑ:s] n US viaduto m.

overpay [,əʊvə'peɪ] (pt & pp -paid) vt pagar demais.

overplay [,əʊvə'pleɪ] vt exagerar; **to ~ one's hand** exagerar (tentando tirar mais vantagem).

overpopulated [,əʊvə'pɒpjʊleɪtɪd] adj superpopulado(da).

overpower [,əʊvə'paʊə'] vt **-1.** [in fight] subjugar **-2.** fig [overwhelm] vencer, sobrepujar.

overpowering [,əʊvə'paʊərɪŋ] adj **-1.** [desire, feeling] dominante **-2.** [smell] asfixiante **-3.** [heat, sensation] sufocante **-4.** [personality] opressor(ra).

overpriced [,əʊvə'praɪst] adj muito caro(ra).

overproduction [,əʊvəprə'dʌkʃn] n (U) superprodução f, excesso m de produção.

overprotective [,əʊvəprə'tektɪv] adj superprotetor(ra).

overran [,əʊvə'ræn] pt |> **overrun**.

overrated [,əʊvə'reɪtɪd] adj superestimado(da).

overreach [,əʊvə'ri:tʃ] vt: **to ~ o.s.** ir longe demais, dar o passo maior que a perna.

overreact [,əʊvərɪ'ækt] vi: **to ~ (to sthg)** reagir exageradamente (a algo).

override [,əʊvə'raɪd] (pt -rode, pp -ridden) vt **-1.** [be more important than] passar por cima de, não fazer caso de **-2.** [overrule] desautorizar.

overriding [,əʊvə'raɪdɪŋ] adj predominante.

overripe [ˌəʊvəˈraɪp] *adj* **-1.** [fruit] maduro(ra) demais **- 2.** [cheese] passado(da).

overrode [ˌəʊvəˈrəʊd] *pt* ▷ **override**.

overrule [ˌəʊvəˈruːl] *vt* **-1.** [person, decision] desautorizar **- 2.** [objection] negar.

overrun [ˌəʊvəˈrʌn] (*pt* **-ran**, *pp* **-run**, *cont* **-running**) ◇ *vt* **-1.** MIL [occupy] invadir **- 2.** fig [cover, fill]: **to be ~ with sthg** estar repleto(ta) de algo. ◇ *vi* passar do tempo previsto.

oversaw [ˌəʊvəˈsɔː] *pt* ▷ **oversee**.

overseas [*adj* ˈəʊvəsiːz, *adv* ˌəʊvəˈsiːz] ◇ *adj* **-1.** [market] exterior **- 2.** [network, branches] no exterior **- 3.** [sales, aid] para o exterior **- 4.** [from abroad] estrangeiro(ra). ◇ *adv* **-1.** [travel, sell] para o exterior **- 2.** [study, live] no exterior.

oversee [ˌəʊvəˈsiː] (*pt* **-saw**, *pp* **-seen** [-ˈsiːn]) *vt* supervisionar.

overseer [ˈəʊvəˌsiːəʳ] *n* supervisor *m*, -ra *f*.

overshadow [ˌəʊvəˈʃædəʊ] *vt* **-1.** [make darker] fazer sombra em **- 2.** fig [outweigh, eclipse]: **to be ~ ed by sb/sthg** ser eclipsado(da) por alguém/algo **- 3.** fig [mar, cloud]: **to be ~ ed by sthg** ser ofuscado(da) por algo.

overshoot [ˌəʊvəˈʃuːt] (*pt* & *pp* **-shot**) *vt* passar.

oversight [ˈəʊvəsaɪt] *n* deslize *m*, descuido *m*.

oversimplification [ˌəʊvəˌsɪmplɪfɪˈkeɪʃn] *n* simplificação *f* excessiva.

oversimplify [ˌəʊvəˈsɪmplɪfaɪ] (*pt* & *pp* **-ied**) ◇ *vt* simplificar demais ◇ *vi* simplificar demais.

oversleep [ˌəʊvəˈsliːp] (*pt* & *pp* **-slept** [-ˈslept]) *vi* dormir demais, ficar dormindo.

overspend [ˌəʊvəˈspend] (*pt* & *pp* **-spent** [-ˈspent]) *vi* gastar além da conta.

overspill [ˈəʊvəspɪl] *n* (U) excesso *m* de população.

overstaffed [ˌəʊvəˈstɑːft] *adj* com excesso de funcionários.

overstate [ˌəʊvəˈsteɪt] *vt* exagerar.

overstay [ˌəʊvəˈsteɪ] *vt*: **to ~ one's welcome** abusar da hospitalidade de alguém.

overstep [ˌəʊvəˈstep] (*pt* & *pp* **-ped**, *cont* **-ping**) *vt* passar por cima de; **to ~ the mark** passar dos limites.

overstock [ˌəʊvəˈstɒk] *vt* abarrotar, entupir.

overstrike [ˈəʊvəstraɪk] (*pt* & *pp* **-struck**) COMPUT ◇ *n* sobreposição *f* de caracteres. ◇ *vt* sobrepor caracteres.

oversubscribed [ˌəʊvəsʌbˈskraɪbd] *adj* subscrito (ta) em excesso.

overt [ˈəʊvɜːt] *adj* aberto(ta), manifesto(ta).

overtake [ˌəʊvəˈteɪk] (*pt* **-took**, *pp* **-taken** [-ˈteɪkn]) ◇ *vt* **-1.** AUT ultrapassar **- 2.** [subj: disaster, misfortune] surpreender, pegar de surpresa. ◇ *vi* AUT ultrapassar.

overtaking [ˌəʊvəˈteɪkɪŋ] *n* (U) ultrapassagem *f*; 'no ~' 'proibido ultrapassar'.

overthrow [*n* ˈəʊvəθrəʊ, *vb* ˌəʊvəˈθrəʊ] (*pt* **-threw**, *pp* **-thrown**) ◇ *n* deposição *f*, destituição *f*. ◇ *vt* **-1.** [government, president] depor, destituir **- 2.** [concept, idea, standard] derrubar.

overtime [ˈəʊvətaɪm] ◇ *n* **-1.** [extra time worked] hora *f* extra **- 2.** US SPORT prorrogação *f*.

◇ *adv*: **to work ~** fazer hora extra.

overtly [ˈəʊvɜːtlɪ] *adv* abertamente, publicamente.

overtones [ˈəʊvətəʊnz] *npl* insinuações *fpl*.

overtook [ˌəʊvəˈtʊk] *pt* ▷ **overtake**.

overture [ˈəʊvəˌtjʊəʳ] *n* MUS abertura *f*.

➤ **overtures** *npl*: **to make ~ s to sb** fazer uma proposta a alguém.

overturn [ˌəʊvəˈtɜːn] ◇ *vt* **-1.** [turn over] virar **- 2.** [overrule] invalidar **- 3.** [overthrow] depor. ◇ *vi* **-1.** [boat] virar **- 2.** [lorry, car] capotar.

overuse [ˌəʊvəˈjuːz] *vt* usar demais.

overview [ˈəʊvəvjuː] *n* visão *f* geral.

overweening [ˌəʊvəˈwiːnɪŋ] *adj* desmedido(da).

overweight [ˌəʊvəˈweɪt] *adj* obeso(sa), gordo(da).

overwhelm [ˌəʊvəˈwelm] *vt* **-1.** [make helpless] subjugar **- 2.** MIL [gain control of] dominar, passar a controlar.

overwhelming [ˌəʊvəˈwelmɪŋ] *adj* **-1.** [feeling, quality] impressionante **· - 2.** [victory, defeat, majority] esmagador(ra).

overwhelmingly [ˌəʊvəˈwelmɪŋlɪ] *adv* em peso, em massa.

overwork [ˌəʊvəˈwɜːk] ◇ *n* (U) trabalho *m* excessivo. ◇ *vt* **-1.** [give too much work to] fazer trabalhar demais **- 2.** fig [overuse] usar demais. ◇ *vi* trabalhar demais.

overwrought [ˌəʊvəˈrɔːt] *adj* muito nervoso(sa).

ovulate [ˈɒvjʊleɪt] *vi* ovular.

ovulation [ˌɒvjʊˈleɪʃn] *n* (U) ovulação *f*.

ow [aʊ] *excl* ai!

owe [əʊ] *vt*: **to ~ sthg to sb**, **to ~ sb sthg** dever algo a alguém.

owing [ˈəʊɪŋ] *adj* que se deve.

➤ **owing to** *prep* por causa de, devido a.

owl [aʊl] *n* coruja *f*.

own [əʊn] ◇ *adj* [indicating possession] próprio(pria); **my/your ~ car** meu/teu próprio carro; **he doesn't need a lift, he has his ~ car** ele não precisa de carona, tem seu próprio carro; **she has her ~ style** ela tem um estilo próprio. ◇ *pron* [indicating possession]: **my ~** o(a) meu(minha); **your ~** o(a) seu(sua); **a house of my ~** minha própria casa; **the city has a special atmosphere of its ~** a cidade tem uma atmosfera especial que lhe é própria; **on one's ~** [alone] sozinho(nha); **to get one's ~ back** dar o troco, vingar-se. ◇ *vt* possuir, ter.

➤ **own up** *vi*: **to ~ up (to sthg)** confessar (algo), admitir (algo).

own brand *n* COMM marca *f* própria.

owner [ˈəʊnəʳ] *n* proprietário *m*, -ria *f*, dono *m*, -na *f*.

owner-occupier *n* esp UK morador *m* proprietário, moradora *f* proprietária.

ownership [ˈəʊnəʃɪp] *n* (U) posse *f*, propriedade *f*.

own goal *n* esp UK **-1.** FTBL gol *m* contra; **to score an ~** marcar um gol contra **- 2.** UK fig [foolish mistake] gol *m* contra.

ox [ɒks] (*pl* **oxen**) *n* boi *m*.

Oxbridge [ˈɒksbrɪdʒ] *n* (U) as universidades de Oxford e Cambridge.

OXBRIDGE

Oxbridge é o termo utilizado para designar conjuntamente as universidades de Oxford e Cambridge. Essas duas universidades, fundadas no século XIII, são as mais antigas e as mais respeitadas da Grã-Bretanha. Ambas se subdividem em *colleges*, muitos dos quais abrigados em belíssimos edifícios, e mantêm suas antigas tradições. Há grande rivalidade entre as duas universidades, sobretudo no que se refere ás disputas esportivas.

oxen ['ɒksn] *pl* ⊳ **ox**.

OXFAM *n organização britânica de caridade para ajuda a países subdesenvolvidos.*

oxide ['ɒksaɪd] *n* óxido *m*.

oxidize, -ise ['ɒksɪdaɪz] *vi* oxidar.

oxtail soup ['ɒksteɪl-] *n (U)* rabada *f.*

ox tongue *n (U)* língua *f* de boi.

oxyacetylene [,ɒksɪə'setɪliːn] ◇ *n (U)* oxiacetileno *m.* ◇ *comp* oxiacetilênico(ca).

oxygen ['ɒksɪdʒən] *n (U)* oxigênio *m.*

oxygenate ['ɒksɪdʒəneɪt] *vt* oxigenar.

oxygen mask *n* máscara *f* de oxigênio.

oxygen tent *n* tenda *f* de oxigênio.

oyster ['ɔɪstə'] *n* ostra *f.*

oz. *abbr of* ounce.

ozone ['əʊzəʊn] *n* ozônio *m.*

ozone-friendly *adj* não-prejudicial à camada de ozônio.

ozone layer *n* camada *f* de ozônio.

P

p¹ (*pl* **p's** OR **ps**), **P** (*pl* **P's** OR **Ps**) [piː] *n* [letter] p *m.*
 ➡ **P** - **1.** (*abbr of* **president**) Pres. - **2.** (*abbr of* **prince**) Pr.

p² - **1.** (*abbr of* page) p. - **2.** *abbr of* penny, pence.

P45 *n documento oficial que o empregado recebe do empregador na Grã-Bretanha ao deixar o emprego e repassa ao próximo empregador, contendo informações salariais.*

P60 *n documento oficial fornecido pelo empregador ao empregado na Grã-Bretanha com informações sobre salário recebido e impostos pagos durante aquele ano,* ≃ *declaração f de rendimentos.*

pa [pɑː] *n inf esp US* pai *m.*

p.a. (*abbr of* per annum) p.a.

PA ◇ *n* - **1.** *UK* (*abbr of* **personal assistant**) assessor *m,* -ra *f* pessoal - **2.** (*abbr of* **public address system**) sistema *m* de alto-falantes - **3.** (*abbr of* **Press Association**) *agência de notícias britânica.*

◇ *abbr of* **Pennsylvania**.

PABX (*abbr of* **private automatic branch exchange**) *n* PABX *m.*

PAC *n* - **1.** (*abbr of* **political action committee**) *comitê de levantamento de fundos para causas políticas nos Estados Unidos* - **2.** (*abbr of* **Pan Africanist Congress**) Congresso *m* Pan-Africano.

pace [peɪs] ◇ *n* - **1.** *(U)* [speed, rate] ritmo *m,* andamento *m;* **at one's own** ~ no próprio ritmo de alguém; **to keep** ~ **(with sb/sthg)** acompanhar o ritmo (de alguém/algo) - **2.** [step] passo *m.* ◇ *vt* andar por. ◇ *vi* andar de um lado para o outro.

pacemaker ['peɪs,meɪkə'] *n* - **1.** *MED* marca-passo *m* - **2.** [in race] *competidor que estabelece o ritmo da corrida.*

pacesetter ['peɪs,setə'] *n US SPORT atleta que estabelece o ritmo da corrida.*

pachyderm ['pækɪdɜːm] *n* paquiderme *m.*

Pacific [pə'sɪfɪk] ◇ *adj* do Pacífico. ◇ *n:* **the** ~ **(Ocean)** o (Oceano) Pacífico.

pacification [,pæsɪfɪ'keɪʃn] *n (U) fml* - **1.** [of person] apaziguamento *m* - **2.** [of country, region] pacificação *f.*

Pacific Rim *n:* **the** ~ a Região do Pacífico.

pacifier ['pæsɪfaɪə'] *n US* bico *m.*

pacifism ['pæsɪfɪzm] *n (U)* pacifismo *m.*

pacifist ['pæsɪfɪst] *n* pacifista *mf.*

pacify ['pæsɪfaɪ] (*pt & pp* -ied) *vt* - **1.** [person] acalmar - **2.** [country, region] pacificar.

pack [pæk] ◇ *n* - **1.** [rucksack] mochila *f* - **2.** [bundle] pacote *m,* embrulho *m* - **3.** [of cigarettes] maço *m* - **4.** *esp US* [washing powder, tissues] caixa *f* - **5.** [of cards] baralho *m* - **6.** [of animals - dogs] matilha *f;* [- wolves] alcatéia *f;* [- of thieves] quadrilha *f* - **7.** *CYCLING, RUGBY* pelotão *m* - **8.** *phr:* **that's a** ~ **of lies!** é um monte de mentiras! ◇ *vt* - **1.** [bag, suitcase] fazer - **2.** [clothes, etc] colocar na mala - **3.** [put in container, parcel] embalar - **4.** [crowd into] lotar; **to be** ~**ed into sthg** estar socado(da) em algo. ◇ *vi* - **1.** [for journey, holiday] fazer as malas - **2.** [push tightly] apertar-se, amontoar-se.
 ➡ **pack in** ◇ *vt sep UK inf* [job, boyfriend, smoking] deixar; ~ **it in!** [stop annoying me] pare com isso!, chega!; [shut up] boca fechada! ◇ *vi inf* pifar.
 ➡ **pack off** *vt sep inf* enviar, mandar.
 ➡ **pack up** ◇ *vt sep* arrumar. ◇ *vi* - **1.** [pack one's suitcase] fazer as malas - **2.** *inf* [finish work] cair fora (do trabalho) - **3.** *UK inf* [break down] pifar.

package ['pækɪdʒ] ◇ *n* - **1.** [gen] pacote *m* - **2.** [box] caixa *f* - **3.** *US* [of cigarettes] maço *m,* carteira *f* OR *m* - **4.** [set, group] pacote *m.* ◇ *vt* embalar, empacotar.

package deal *n* pacote *m* de acordo.

package holiday *n* pacote *m* de férias.

packager ['pækɪdʒə'] *n* - **1.** [person packaging] embalador *m,* -deira *f* - **2.** *COMM* produtora *f* independente.

package tour *n* pacote *m* turístico.

packaging ['pækɪdʒɪŋ] *n (U)* embalagem *f.*

packed [pækt] *adj* - **1.** [place]: ~ **(with)** lotado(da) (de) - **2.** [magazine, information pack]: ~ **with** repleto(ta) de.

packed lunch n UK **-1.** [for school] f merenda f **-2.** [for work] marmita f.

packed out adj UK inf apinhado(da).

packet ['pækɪt] n **-1.** [gen] pacote m **-2.** [box] caixa f **-3.** [of cigarettes] maço m, carteira f **-4.** UK inf [lot of money] bolada f, dinheirama f.

packhorse n cavalo m de carga.

pack ice n (U) gelo m flutuante.

packing ['pækɪŋ] n (U) **-1.** [protective material] embalagem f **-2.** [for journey, holiday]: **to do the ~** fazer as malas.

packing case n caixote m de embalagem.

pact [pækt] n pacto m.

pad [pæd] (pt & pp **-ded**, cont **-ding**) <> n **-1.** [for clothes, body]: **shoulder ~** ombreira f; **knee ~** joelheira f; **shin ~** tornozeleira f **-2.** [notepad] bloco m de anotações **-3.** [for absorbing liquid - cotton wool] chumaço m; [- sanitary] absorvente m higiênico **-4.** SPACE: **(launch) ~** plataforma f (de lançamento) **-5.** [of cat or dog] almofadinha f **-6.** inf dated [home] casa f. <> vt **-1.** [clothing, furniture] revestir, forrar **-2.** [wound] cobrir **-3.** fig [speech, letter, essay] alongar de forma desnecessária. <> vi andar com suavidade.

~ pad out vt sep **-1.** [clothing, furniture] revestir, forrar **-2.** [speech, letter, essay] alongar de forma desnecessária.

padded ['pædɪd] adj **-1.** [jacket] revestido(da), forrado(da) **-2.** [shoulders] com ombreiras **-3.** [chair] acolchoado(da).

padded cell n cela f acolchoada.

padding ['pædɪŋ] n (U) **-1.** [in jacket] revestimento m **-2.** [in shoulders] ombreira f **-3.** [in chair] enchimento m **-4.** [in speech, essay, letter] enrolação f.

paddle ['pædl] <> n **-1.** [for canoe, dinghy] remo m **-2.** [wade]: **to have a ~** patinhar na água. <> vt remar. <> vi **-1.** [in canoe, dinghy] remar **-2.** [wade] patinhar.

paddle boat, paddle steamer n vapor m movido a rodas.

paddling pool ['pædlɪŋ-] n **-1.** [in park] piscina f infantil **-2.** [inflatable] piscina f inflável.

paddock ['pædək] n **-1.** [small field] manejo m **-2.** [at racecourse] paddock m.

paddy field ['pædɪ-] n arrozal m.

paddy wagon ['pædɪ-] n US inf camburão m.

padlock ['pædlɒk] <> n cadeado m. <> vt fechar com cadeado.

paederast ['pedəræst] n = **pederast**.

paediatric [ˌpiːdɪˈætrɪk] adj = **pediatric**.

paediatrician [ˌpiːdɪəˈtrɪʃn] n = **pediatrician**.

paediatrics [ˌpiːdɪˈætrɪks] n = **pediatrics**.

paedophile UK ['piːdəfaɪl], **pedophile** US n pedófilo m, -la f.

paella [paɪˈelə] n (U) paelha f.

paeony ['piːənɪ] (pl **-ies**) n = **peony**.

pagan ['peɪgən] <> adj pagão(gã). <> n pagão m, -gã f.

paganism ['peɪgənɪzm] n (U) paganismo m.

page [peɪdʒ] <> n página f. <> vt chamar (pelo alto-falante).

page [peɪdʒ] vt [using pager]: **to be ~d** receber chamadas pelo pager; **to ~ sb** chamar

alguém pelo pager.

pageant ['pædʒənt] n desfile m, cortejo m cívico.

pageantry ['pædʒəntrɪ] n (U) fausto m, pompa f.

page boy n **-1.** UK [at wedding] pajem m **-2.** [hairstyle] chanel m.

page break n COMPUT quebra f de página.

pager ['peɪdʒə'] n pager m.

pagination [ˌpædʒɪˈneɪʃn] n (U) paginação f.

pagoda [pəˈgəʊdə] n pagode m.

paid [peɪd] <> pt & pp ⊳ **pay**. <> adj pago(ga); **badly/well ~** bem/mal pago(ga).

paid-up adj UK remido(da).

pail [peɪl] n balde m.

pain [peɪn] <> n **-1.** dor f; **to be in ~** sentir dor; **a ~ in the neck** inf uma mala-sem-alça **-2.** (U) [mental suffering] sofrimento m, pena f **-3.** inf [annoyance]: **it's such a ~!** é tão chato!; **he is a real ~!** ele é um saco! <> vt fml fazer sofrer, atormentar; **to ~ sb to do sthg** ser muito difícil para alguém fazer algo.

~ pains npl esforços mpl; **to be at ~s to do sthg** empenhar-se para fazer algo; **to take ~s to do sthg** esforçar-se para fazer algo; **he got absolutely nothing for his ~s** tanto esforço e ele não conseguiu absolutamente nada.

pained [peɪnd] adj aflito(ta), consternado(da).

painful ['peɪnfʊl] adj **-1.** [sore] dolorido(da) **-2.** [causing pain] doloroso(sa) **-3.** [distressing] penoso(sa), doloroso(sa).

painfully ['peɪnfʊlɪ] adv **-1.** [distressingly] dolorosamente **-2.** [for emphasis] terrivelmente.

painkiller ['peɪnˌkɪlə'] n analgésico m, calmante m.

painless ['peɪnlɪs] adj indolor, fácil.

painlessly ['peɪnlɪslɪ] adv **-1.** [without hurting] sem dor **-2.** [unproblematically] de forma fácil, de forma indolor.

painstaking ['peɪnzˌteɪkɪŋ] adj meticuloso(sa), minucioso(sa).

painstakingly ['peɪnzˌteɪkɪŋlɪ] adv meticulosamente, minuciosamente.

paint [peɪnt] <> n tinta f. <> vt **-1.** pintar; **to ~ the wall white** pintar o teto de branco **-2.** [with make-up] maquiar. <> vi pintar.

paintbox ['peɪntbɒks] n ART estojo m de tintas.

paintbrush ['peɪntbrʌʃ] n **-1.** [of artist] pincel m **-2.** [of decorator] broxa f.

painted ['peɪntɪd] adj pintado(da).

painter ['peɪntə'] n pintor m, -ra f.

painting ['peɪntɪŋ] n **-1.** [picture] pintura f, quadro m **-2.** (U) ACTIVITY pintura f.

paint stripper n (U) removedor m (de tinta).

paintwork ['peɪntwɜːk] n (U) pintura f.

pair [peə'] n par m; **a ~ of idiots** uma dupla de idiotas; **a ~ of scissors** uma tesoura; **a ~ of trousers** uma calça; **a ~ of spectacles** um óculos.

~ pair off <> vt sep fazer par com. <> vi: **let's ~ and meet back here later** vamos nos separar aos pares e nos encontrar aqui mais tarde.

pajamas [pəˈdʒɑːməz] npl US = **pyjamas**.

Pakistan [UK ˌpɑːkɪˈstɑːn, US ˌpækɪˈstæn] n Paquistão; **in ~** no Paquistão.

Pakistani [UK ˌpɑːkɪˈstɑːnɪ, US ˌpækɪˈstænɪ] <> adj

paquistanês(esa). <> n paquistanês, -esa f.

pal [pæl] n inf **-1.** [friend] camarada mf, companheiro m, -ra f **-2.** [as term of address]: **now wait a minute, ~, I was first!** espera um pouco, meu chapa, eu cheguei primeiro!

PAL (abbr of **phase alternate line**) n PAL f.

palace ['pælɪs] n palácio m.

palaeontology UK, **paleontology** US [ˌpælɪɒn'tɒlədʒɪl] n (U) paleontologia f.

palatable ['pælətəbl] adj **-1.** [pleasant to taste] saboroso(sa) **-2.** [acceptable] aceitável, admissível.

palate ['pælət] n **-1.** ANAT palato m **-2.** [sense of taste] paladar m.

palatial [pə'leɪʃl] adj palaciano(na).

palaver [pə'lɑ:və'] n inf **-1.** [talk] palavrório m **-2.** [fuss] bagunça f, rebuliço m.

pale [peɪl] <> adj **-1.** [colour] fosco(ca) **-2.** [light] ênue **-3.** [clothes] claro(ra) **-4.** [face, complexion] pálido(da). <> vi **-1.** [become pale] empalidecer **-2.** [become insignificant]: **to ~ into insignificance (beside sb/ sthg)** perder toda importância (junto a alguém/algo).

pale ale n UK tipo de cerveja clara.

paleness ['peɪlnɪs] n (U) palidez f.

paleontology n US = paleontology.

Palestine ['pælɪˌstaɪn] n Palestina; **in ~** na Palestina.

Palestinian [ˌpælə'stɪnɪən] <> adj palestino(na). <> n palestino m, -na f.

palette ['pælət] n paleta f.

palette knife n espátula f.

palimony ['pælɪmənɪ] n (U) pensão alimentícia paga à ex-amante.

palindrome n palíndromo m.

palings ['peɪlɪŋz] npl cerca f.

pall [pɔ:l] <> n **-1.** [of smoke] nuvem f, cortina f **-2.** US [coffin] caixão m. <> vi perder a graça.

pallbearer ['pɔ:lˌbeərə'] n carregador m, -ra f de caixão.

pallet ['pælɪt] n palete m, plataforma f de carga.

palliative ['pælɪətɪv] n fml paliativo m.

pallid ['pælɪd] adj pálido(da).

pallor ['pælə'] n palor m.

palm [pɑ:m] n **-1.** [tree] palmeira f **-2.** [of hand] palma f.

➤ **palm off** vt sep inf: **to ~ sthg off on sb** empurrar algo para alguém; **to ~ sb off with sthg** enganar alguém com algo; **to ~ sthg off as sthg** fazer passar algo como algo.

palmistry ['pɑ:mɪstrɪ] n (U) quiromancia f.

palm oil n (U) azeite-de-dendê m.

Palm Sunday n Domingo m de Ramos.

palmtop ['pɑ:mtɒp] n COMPUT palmtop m.

palm tree n palmeira f.

palomino [ˌpælə'mi:nəʊ] (pl -s) n palomino m.

palpable ['pælpəbl] adj palpável.

palpably ['pælpəblɪ] adv obviamente.

palpitate ['pælpɪteɪt] vi palpitar.

palpitations [ˌpælpɪ'teɪʃənz] npl palpitações fpl.

palsy n (U) paralisia f.

paltry ['pɔ:ltrɪ] (compar -ier, superl -iest) adj irrisório(ria).

pampas ['pæmpəz] n: **the ~** o pampa.

pampas grass n (U) capim-dos-pampas m inv.

pamper ['pæmpə'] vt mimar.

pamphlet ['pæmflɪt] <> n panfleto m. <> vi panfletar.

pamphleteer [ˌpæmflə'tɪə'] n POL panfletário m, -ria f, panfletista mf.

pan [pæn] (pt & pp -ned, cont -ning) <> n **-1.** [for frying] frigideira **-2.** [for boiling] panela f **-3.** US [for baking] assadeira f **-4.** [of scales] prato m **-5.** [of toilet] vaso m sanitário. <> vt inf esculachar. <> vi **-1.** [for gold] batear **-2.** CINEMA capturar uma vista panorâmica.

panacea [ˌpænə'sɪə] n fig: **a ~ (for sthg)** uma panacéia (para algo).

panache [pə'næʃ] n (U) bravata f, elã m.

panama n: **~ (hat)** panamá m.

Panama ['pænəˌmɑː] n Panamá; **in ~** no Panamá.

Panama Canal n: **the ~** o Canal do Panamá.

Panama City n Cidade f do Panamá.

Panamanian [ˌpænə'meɪnɪən] <> adj panamenho(nha). <> n panamenho m, -nha f.

pan-American adj pan-americano(na).

pancake ['pænkeɪk] n panqueca f.

Pancake Day n UK ≃ Terça-feira f de Carnaval.

pancake roll n rolinho m primavera.

Pancake Tuesday n = Pancake Day.

pancreas ['pæŋkrɪəs] n pâncreas m inv.

panda ['pændə] (pl inv OR -s) n panda m.

Panda car n UK patrulha f policial.

pandemonium [ˌpændɪ'məʊnjəm] n (U) pandemônio m.

pander ['pændə'] vi: **to ~ to sb/sthg** fazer concessões a alguém/algo.

pane [peɪn] n vidraça f, vidro m de vidraça.

panel ['pænl] n **-1.** [group of people] equipe f **-2.** TECH painel m.

panel game n UK jogo televisivo em que um grupo de pessoas deve realizar determinada tarefa.

panelling UK, **paneling** US ['pænəlɪŋ] n (U) apainelamento m.

panellist UK, **panelist** US ['pænəlɪst] n painelista mf.

panel pin n UK prego m sem cabeça.

pang [pæŋ] n acesso m (de fome, de culpa etc).

panic ['pænɪk] (pt & pp -ked, cont -king) <> n (U) pânico m. <> vi entrar em pânico.

panicky ['pænɪkɪ] adj **-1.** [person] aterrorizado(da) **-2.** [feeling] aterrorizante.

panic stations n (U) inf: **it was ~** foi uma verdadeira loucura.

panic-stricken adj em pânico.

pannier ['pænɪə'] n **-1.** [on back, horse] alforje m **-2.** [bicycle] cesto m.

panoply ['pænəplɪ] n (U) fml panóplia f.

panorama [ˌpænə'rɑːmə] n panorama m.

panoramic [ˌpænə'ræmɪk] adj panorâmico(ca).

pansy (pl -ies) n **-1.** [flower] amor-perfeito m **-2.** inf pej [man] veado m.

pant [pænt] vi ofegar.

➤ **pants** npl **-1.** UK [underpants] calcinha f **-2.** US [trousers] calças fpl.

panther ['pænθə'] (pl inv OR -s) n pantera f.

panties ['pæntɪz] *npl inf* calcinha *f.*

pantihose ['pæntɪhəʊz] *npl* = **panty hose.**

panto ['pæntəʊ] (*pl* -**s**) *n UK inf* = **pantomime.**

pantomime ['pæntəmaɪm] *n UK* peça de teatro *pàra crianças realizada no Reino Unido no Natal.*

pantry ['pæntrɪ] (*pl* -**ies**) *n* despensa *f.*

panty hose ['pæntɪ-] *npl US* meia-calça *f.*

papa [*UK* pə'pɑː, *US* 'pæpə] *n* papá *m.*

papacy (*pl* -**ies**) *n* -**1.** [period] papado *m* -**2.** [office, institution]: **the ~** o papado, o pontificado.

papadum ['pæpədəm] *n* = **popadum.**

papal ['peɪpl] *adj* papal.

paparazzi [ˌpæpə'rætsɪ] *npl pej* paparazzi *mpl.*

papaya [pə'paɪə] *n* papaia *m.*

paper ['peɪpə'] ◇ *n* -**1.** (*U*) [material] papel *m*; **a piece of ~** uma folha de papel; **on ~** [written down] no papel; [in theory] teoricamente -**2.** [newspaper] jornal *m* -**3.** [in exam] trabalho *m* -**4.** [essay] ensaio *m* -**5.** [at conference] apostila *f,* polígrafo *m.* ◇ *adj* -**1.** [cup, napkin, hat] de papel -**2.** [theoretical] no papel. ◇ *vt* empapelar.

◆ **papers** *npl* -**1.** [identity papers] documentos *mpl* (de identidade) -**2.** [documents] documentação *f.*

◆ **paper over** *vt fus fig* encobrir, disfarçar.

paperback ['peɪpəbæk] *n*: **~ (book)** brochura *f*; **in ~** em brochura.

paper bag *n* saco *m* de papel.

paperboy ['peɪpəbɔɪ] *n* jornaleiro *m.*

paper clip *n* clipe *m.*

papergirl ['peɪpəgɜːl] *n* jornaleira *f.*

paper handkerchief *n* lenço *m* de papel.

paper knife *n* abridor *m* de cartas.

paper mill *n* fábrica *f* de papel.

paper money *n* (*U*) papel-moeda *m.*

paper shop *n UK* banca *f* de jornais.

paperweight ['peɪpəweɪt] *n* peso *m* para papel.

paperwork ['peɪpəwɜːk] *n* (*U*) papelada *f.*

papier-mâché [ˌpæpjeɪ'mæʃeɪ] ◇ *n* (*U*) papel *m* machê. ◇ *comp* de papel machê.

papist ['peɪpɪst] *n pej* papista *mf.*

paprika ['pæprɪkə] *n* (*U*) páprica *f.*

Papua *n* Papua.

Papuan ['pæpjʊən] ◇ *adj* papua. ◇ *n* papua *mf.*

Papua New Guinea *n* Papua Nova Guiné; **in ~** em Papua Nova Guiné.

par [pɑː'] *n* -**1.** [parity]: **on a ~ with sb/sthg** no mesmo nível que alguém/algo -**2.** (*U*) *GOLF* par *m*; **under/over ~** abaixo/acima do par -**3.** [good health]: **below** *OR* **under ~** indisposto(ta) -**4.** *FIN* valor *m* (ao par).

para ['pærə] *n UK inf* paraquedista *mf* (*do exército*).

parable ['pærəbl] *n* parábola *f.*

parabola [pə'ræbələ] *n TECH* parábola *f.*

paracetamol [ˌpærə'siːtəmɒl] *n* paracetamol *m.*

parachute ['pærəʃuːt] ◇ *n* pára-quedas *m inv.* ◇ *vi* saltar de pára-quedas.

parade [pə'reɪd] ◇ *n* -**1.** [procession] desfile *m* -**2.** *MIL* parada *f*; **on ~** em revista -**3.** *UK* [street of shops] via *f* comercial -**4.** [street, path] passeio *m* público. ◇ *vt* -**1.** [*MIL* - soldiers] fazer desfilar; [- prisoners] apresentar -**2.** [object] exibir -**3.** *fig*

[flaunt] fazer alarde de, mostrar-se com. ◇ *vi* desfilar.

parade ground *n* praça *f* de armas.

paradigm ['pærədaɪm] *n* paradigma *m.*

paradigmatic *adj* paradigmático(ca).

paradise ['pærədaɪs] *n* paraíso *m.*

◆ **Paradise** *n* Paraíso *m.*

paradox ['pærədɒks] *n* paradoxo *m.*

paradoxical [ˌpærə'dɒksɪkl] *adj* paradoxal.

paradoxically [ˌpærə'dɒksɪklɪ] *adv* paradoxalmente.

paraffin ['pærəfɪn] *n* (*U*) querosene *m.*

paraffin wax *n* (*U*) parafina *f.*

paragliding ['pærəˌglaɪdɪŋ] *n* vôo *m* de paraglider.

paragon *n* modelo *m.*

paragraph ['pærəgrɑːf] *n* parágrafo *m.*

Paraguay ['pærəgwaɪ] *n* Paraguai; **in ~** no Paraguai.

Paraguayan [ˌpærə'gwaɪən] ◇ *adj* paraguaio(ia). ◇ *n* paraguaio *m,* -ia *f.*

parakeet ['pærəkiːt] *n* periquito *m.*

paralegal [ˌpærə'liːgl] *n US secretária altamente especializada que auxilia os advogados em seu trabalho.*

parallel ['pærəlel] (*pt* & *pp* -**led,** *cont* -**ling**) ◇ *adj* [gen] paralelo(la); **~ to** *OR* **with sthg** paralelo(la) a algo. ◇ *n* paralelo *m*; **to have no ~** não ter precedente *OR* paralelo. ◇ *vt* igualar-se a.

parallel bars *npl* barras *fpl* paralelas.

paralyse *UK,* **paralyze** *US* ['pærəlaɪz] *vt* paralisar.

paralysed *UK,* **paralyzed** *US* ['pærəlaɪzd] *adj MED* paralisado(da).

paralysis [pə'rælɪsɪs] (*pl* -**lyses** [-lɪsiːz]) *n* -**1.** *MED* paralisia *f* -**2.** [of industry, traffic] imobilidade *f.*

paralytic [ˌpærə'lɪtɪk] ◇ *adj* -**1.** *MED* paralítico(ca) -**2.** *UK inf* [drunk] bêbado(da) feito um gambá. ◇ *n* paralítico *m,* -ca *f.*

paralyze *vt US* = **paralyse.**

paralyzed *adj US* = **paralysed.**

paramedic [ˌpærə'medɪk] *n* paramédico *m,* -ca *f.*

paramedical [ˌpærə'medɪkl] *adj* paramédico(ca).

parameter [pə'ræmɪtə'] *n* parâmetro *m.*

paramilitary [ˌpærə'mɪlɪtrɪ] *adj* paramilitar.

paramount ['pærəmaʊnt] *adj* vital, fundamental; **of ~ importance** de suma importância.

paranoia [ˌpærə'nɔɪə] *n* (*U*) paranóia *f.*

paranoiac [ˌpærə'nɔɪæk] *MED* ◇ *adj* paranóico(ca). ◇ *n* paranóico *m,* -ca *f.*

paranoid ['pærənɔɪd] *adj* -**1.** [person] paranóico(ca) -**2.** [disorder] paranóico(ca).

paranormal [ˌpærə'nɔːml] *adj* paranormal.

parapet ['pærəpɪt] *n* parapeito *m.*

paraphernalia [ˌpærəfə'neɪljə] *n* (*U*) parafernália *f.*

paraphrase ['pærəfreɪz] ◇ *n* paráfrase *f.* ◇ *vt* & *vi* parafrasear.

paraplegia *n* (*U*) paraplegia *f.*

paraplegic [ˌpærə'pliːdʒɪk] ◇ *adj* paraplégico (ca). ◇ *n* paraplégico *m,* -ca *f.*

parapsychology [ˌpærəsaɪ'kɒlədʒɪ] *n* (*U*) parapsicologia *f.*

paraquat® *n* (*U*) *CHEM* paraquat *m.*

parascending [,pærə'sendıŋ] n vôo m de para-pente.

parasite ['pærəsaɪt] n parasita m.

parasitic [,pærə'sɪtɪk] adj parasita.

parasol ['pærəsɒl] n sombrinha f.

paratrooper ['pærətru:pəʳ] n pára-quedista mf (do exército).

parboil ['pɑ:bɔɪl] vt aferventar.

parcel ['pɑ:sl] (UK pt & pp -led, cont-ling, US pt & pp-ed, cont-ing) n pacote m, encomenda f.

➤ **parcel up** vt sep empacotar.

parcel post n (U) serviço de encomenda f postal.

parched [pɑ:tʃt] adj -1. [grass, plain] seco(ca) -2. [throat, lips] ressecado(da) -3. inf [very thirsty] seco(-ca).

parchment ['pɑ:tʃmənt] n (U) pergaminho m.

pardon ['pɑ:dn] <> n -1. JUR indulto m -2. (U) [for-giveness] perdão m; **I beg your ~?** [showing surprise or offence] como é?, o que foi?; [what did you say?] como?, o que você disse?; **I beg your ~!** [to apolo-gize] perdão!, desculpe! <> vt -1. JUR indultar -2. [forgive] perdoar; **to ~ sb for sthg** perdoar alguém por algo; **~ me!** me desculpe!

pardonable ['pɑ:dnəbl] adj perdoável.

pare [peəʳ] vt -1. [apple] descascar -2. [fingernail] aparar, cortar.

➤ **pare down** vt sep -1. [remove layer] aparar -2. [reduce] reduzir.

parent ['peərənt] n -1. [mother] mãe f -2. [father] pai m.

➤ **parents** npl pais mpl.

parentage ['peərəntɪdʒ] n (U) ascendência f, origem f.

parental [pə'rentl] adj dos pais.

parent company n matriz f.

parenthesis [pə'renθɪsɪs] (pl -theses [-θɪsi:z]) n parêntese m.

parenthetical adj entre parênteses.

parenthood ['peərənthʊd] n (U) paternidade f, maternidade f.

parenting ['peərəntɪŋ] n (U) cuidados mpl dos pais.

parent-teacher association n associação f de pais e mestres.

par excellence adj por excelência.

pariah [pə'raɪə] n pej pária mf.

Paris ['pærɪs] n Paris; **in ~** em Paris.

parish ['pærɪʃ] n -1. [of church] paróquia f -2. UK [area of local government] distrito m.

parish council n UK conselho m distrital.

parishioner [pə'rɪʃənəʳ] n paroquiano m, -na f.

parish priest n pároco m.

Parisian [pə'rɪzjən] <> adj parisiense. <> n parisiense mf.

parity ['pærətɪ] n (U) igualdade f; **~ with** igualdade com; **~ between** paridade f de or entre.

park [pɑ:k] <> n -1. [public] parque m -2. US AUT posição da alavanca de carro hidramático usada para estacionar. <> vt & vi estacionar.

parka ['pɑ:kə] n parca f.

parking ['pɑ:kɪŋ] n (U) estacionamento m; **I find ~ very difficult** acho muito difícil estacionar; **'no ~'** 'proibido estacionar'.

parking garage n US edifício-garagem m.

parking light n US luz m de estacionamento.

parking lot n US área f de estacionamento.

parking meter n parquímetro m.

parking place n vaga f para estacionar.

parking ticket n multa f por estacionamento proibido.

Parkinson's (disease) ['pɑ:kɪnsnz-] n (U) mal m de Parkinson.

park keeper n UK guarda mf de parque.

parkland ['pɑ:klænd] n (U) parque m.

parkway ['pɑ:kweɪ] n US alameda f.

parky ['pɑ:kɪ] (compar -ier, superl -iest) adj UK inf frio (fria), fresco(ca).

parlance ['pɑ:ləns] n (U): **in common/legal ~** em linguagem coloquial/legal.

parliament ['pɑ:ləmənt] n -1. [gen] parlamento m -2. [session] legislatura f.

parliamentarian [,pɑ:ləmen'teərɪən] n parlamen-tar mf.

parliamentary [,pɑ:lə'mentərɪ] adj parlamentar.

parlour UK, **parlor** US ['pɑ:ləʳ] n -1. dated [in house] sala f de visitas -2. [cafe]: **ice cream ~** sorveteria f.

parlour game n jogo m de salão.

parlous ['pɑ:ləs] adj fml precário(ria).

Parmesan (cheese) [,pɑ:mɪ'zæn-] n (U) queijo m parmesão.

parochial [pə'rəʊkjəl] adj pej provinciano(na).

parochial school n US escola f particular católica.

parody ['pærədɪ] (pl -ies, pt & pp -ied) <> n paródia f. <> vt parodiar.

parole [pə'rəʊl] <> n (U) liberdade f condicional; **on ~** em liberdade condicional. <> vt pôr em liberdade condicional.

paroxysm ['pærəksɪzm] n -1. [feeling] paroxismo m -2. [movement] acesso m.

parquet ['pɑ:keɪ] n (U) parquê m.

parrot ['pærət] n papagaio m.

parrot fashion adv como um papagaio.

parry ['pærɪ] (pt & pp -ied) vt -1. [blow] desviar -2. [question] esquivar-se de.

parsimonious [,pɑ:sɪ'məʊnjəs] adj fml & pej ava-rento(ta).

parsley ['pɑ:slɪ] n (U) salsa f.

parsnip ['pɑ:snɪp] n chirivia f.

parson ['pɑ:sn] n pároco m.

parson's nose n UK inf sambiquira f.

part [pɑ:t] <> n -1. [gen] parte f; **in ~** em parte; **for the most ~** em sua maioria; **~ and parcel of** parte integrante de; **that's only ~ of the story** isso é só uma parte da história; **the best or better ~ of** a maior parte de -2. [component] peça f -3. [acting role] papel m -4. [involvement]: **~ in sthg** participa-ção f em algo; **to take ~ in sthg** participar de algo; **to play an important ~ in sthg** ter um papel importante em algo; **to want no ~ in sthg** não querer se envolver em algo; **for my/your** etc **~** por minha/sua parte; **on my/your** etc **~** de minha/sua parte -5. US [hair parting] linha f. <> adv em parte. <> vt -1. [separate] separar -2. [move apart, open] abrir -3. [hair] repartir. <> vi

-1. [leave one another] separar-se **-2.** [move apart, open] abrir-se.
➥ **parts** *npl* terras *fpl.*
➥ **part with** *vt fus* desfazer-se de.
partake [pɑː'teɪk] (*pt* **-took**, *pp* **-taken**) *vi fml*: **to** ~ **of** [wine] beber; [food] comer.
part exchange *n* **-1.** [deal] *negociação em que se paga parte do valor de um produto com um artigo usado* **-2.** (*U*) [system] *sistema através do qual se paga parte do valor do produto com um artigo usado*; **in** ~ *como parte do pagamento.*
partial ['pɑːʃl] *adj* **-1.** [gen] parcial **-2.** [fond]: ~ **to sthg** afeiçoado(da) a algo.
partiality [ˌpɑːʃɪ'ælətɪ] *n* **-1.** (*U*) [bias] parcialidade *f* **-2.** [fondness]: ~ **for sthg** afeição *f* a algo, predileção *f* a algo.
partially ['pɑːʃəlɪ] *adv* parcialmente, em parte.
partially sighted *adj* com visão parcial.
participant [pɑː'tɪsɪpənt] *n* participante *mf.*
participate [pɑː'tɪsɪpeɪt] *vi* participar; **to** ~ **in sthg** participar de algo.
participation [pɑːˌtɪsɪ'peɪʃn] *n* (*U*) participação *f.*
participle ['pɑːtɪsɪpl] *n* particípio *m.*
particle ['pɑːtɪkl] *n* partícula *f.*
parti-coloured *adj* multicor, matizado(da).
particular [pə'tɪkjʊlə^r] *adj* **-1.** [gen] especial **-2.** [fussy] exigente.
➥ **particulars** *npl* particularidades *fpl.*
➥ **in particular** *adv* em especial, em particular.
particularity (*pl* **-ies**) *n fml* particularidade *f.*
particularly [pə'tɪkjʊləlɪ] *adv* **-1.** [in particular] especialmente **-2.** [very] muito.
parting ['pɑːtɪŋ] *n* **-1.** (*U*) despedida *f* **-2.** *UK* [in hair] repartição *f.*
parting shot *n* tirada *f* final; **to deliver a** ~ fazer um último comentário antes de sair, dar uma tirada final.
partisan [ˌpɑːtɪ'zæn] ◇ *adj* partidário(ria). ◇ *n* guerrilheiro *m*, -ra *f.*
partition [pɑː'tɪʃn] ◇ *n* **-1.** [wall] divisória *f* **-2.** [screen] separação *f* **-3.** [of a country] divisão *f.* ◇ *vt* **-1.** [room] separar com divisórias **-2.** [country] dividir.
partly ['pɑːtlɪ] *adv* em parte.
partner ['pɑːtnə^r] ◇ *n* parceiro *m*, -ra *f.* ◇ *vt* ser parceiro de.
partnership ['pɑːtnəʃɪp] *n* parceria *f.*
partook [pɑː'tʊk] *pt* ⊳ **partake.**
partridge ['pɑːtrɪdʒ] (*pl inv OR* **-s**) *n* perdiz *f.*
part-time ◇ *adj* de meio período. ◇ *adv* em meio período.
part-timer *n* funcionário *m*, -ria *f* de meio período.
party ['pɑːtɪ] (*pl* **-ies**, *pt* & *pp* **-ied**) ◇ *n* **-1.** *POL* partido *m* **-2.** [social gathering] festa *f* **-3.** [group] grupo *m* **-4.** *JUR, COMM* [individual] parte *f* **-5.** [involved person]: **to be a** ~ **to sthg** ter parte em algo. ◇ *vi inf* festejar.
party line *n* **-1.** *POL* linha *f* (política) do partido **-2.** *TELEC* extensão *f* de linha telefônica.
party piece *n inf* espetáculo *m* particular.
party political broadcast *n UK* propaganda

f política em rádio e TV.
party politics *n* (*U*) política *f* partidária.
party wall *n* parede-meia *f.*
parvenu ['pɑːvənjuː] *n pej* novo-rico *m*, nova-rica *f.*
pass [pɑːs] ◇ *n* **-1.** [gen] passe *m* **-2.** *UK* [successful result] aprovação *f*; **to get a** ~ ser aprovado *m*, -da *f* em algo **-3.** [route between mountains] desfiladeiro *m* **-4.** *phr*: **to make a** ~ **at sb** *inf* passar-se com alguém. ◇ *vt* **-1.** [gen] passar; **to** ~ **sthg to sb, to** ~ **sb sthg** passar algo a alguém **-2.** [move past] passar por **-3.** *AUT* [overtake] ultrapassar **-4.** [exceed] passar de **-5.** [exam, test] passar em **-6.** [approve] aprovar **-7.** [express - opinion, judgment] formular; [- sentence] ditar. ◇ *vi* **-1.** [gen] passar **-2.** *AUT* [overtake] ultrapassar **-3.** *SPORT* fazer passes **-4.** [occur] ocorrer.
➥ **pass around** *vt sep* = **pass round.**
➥ **pass as** *vt fus* passar por.
➥ **pass away** *vi* falecer.
➥ **pass by** ◇ *vt sep fig* passar desapercebido (da) por. ◇ *vi* passar.
➥ **pass for** *vt fus* = **pass as.**
➥ **pass off** *vt sep*: **to pass sb/sthg off as sthg** fazer alguém/algo passar por algo.
➥ **pass on** ◇ *vt sep* **-1.** [object]: **to pass sthg on (to sb)** passar algo adiante (para alguém) **-2.** [characteristic, tradition, information] transmitir. ◇ *vi* **-1.** [move on]: **to** ~ **on to the next question** passar para a próxima questão **-2.** = **pass away.**
➥ **pass out** *vi* **-1.** [faint] desmaiar **-2.** *UK MIL* graduar-se.
➥ **pass over** *vt fus* passar por cima.
➥ **pass round** *vt sep* ir passando, passar.
➥ **pass to** *vt fus* passar para.
➥ **pass up** *vt sep* deixar passar.
passable ['pɑːsəbl] *adj* **-1.** [satisfactory] passável, aceitável **-2.** [not blocked] livre.
passably ['pɑːsəblɪ] *adv* aceitavelmente.
passage ['pæsɪdʒ] *n* **-1.** [gen] passagem *f* **-2.** *ANAT* trato *m* **-3.** [sea journey] travessia *f.*
passageway ['pæsɪdʒweɪ] *n* passagem *f*, corredor *m.*
passbook ['pɑːsbʊk] *n* caderneta *f* de conta bancária.
passé *adj pej* ultrapassado(da).
passenger ['pæsɪndʒə^r] *n* passageiro *m*, -ra *f.*
passerby [ˌpɑːsə'baɪ] (*pl* **passersby** [ˌpɑːsəz'baɪ]) *n* passante *mf*, transeunte *mf.*
passing ['pɑːsɪŋ] ◇ *adj* passageiro(ra). ◇ *n* (*U*) passagem *f.*
➥ **in passing** *adv* de passagem.
passion ['pæʃn] *n* (*U*) paixão *f*; ~ **for sthg** paixão por algo.
➥ **Passion** *n*: **the Passion** a Paixão de Cristo.
➥ **passions** *npl* paixões *fpl.*
passionate ['pæʃənət] *adj* apaixonado(da).
passionately ['pæʃənətlɪ] *adv* apaixonadamente.
passionfruit ['pæʃənfruːt] *n* (*U*) maracujá *m.*
passive ['pæsɪv] ◇ *adj* passivo(va). ◇ *n*: **the** ~ a passiva.
passively ['pæsɪvlɪ] *adv* passivamente.
passive resistance *n* (*U*) resistência *f* passiva.
passive smoker *n* (*U*) fumante *mf* passivo, -va.
passivity [pæ'sɪvətɪ] *n* (*U*) passividade *f.*

passkey ['pɑːskiː] n -1. [particular] chave f pessoal -2. [universal] chave-mestra f.

Passover ['pɑːsˌəʊvəʳ] n: (the) ~ a Páscoa Judia.

passport ['pɑːspɔːt] n -1. [document] passaporte m -2. [means]: ~ to sthg passaporte para algo.

passport control n controle m de passaportes.

password ['pɑːswɜːd] n senha f.

past [pɑːst] <> adj -1. [former] passado(da) -2. [last] último(ma); over the ~ week durante a última semana -3. [finished] terminado(da), passado(da); our problems are now ~ nossos problemas terminaram. <> adv -1. [telling the time]: it's ten ~ eleven são onze e dez -2. [by] por; to walk ~ passar por; to run ~ passar correndo por; he didn't see me as I drove ~ ele não me viu quando passei por ele de carro. <> n -1. [time]: the ~ o passado; in the ~ no passado -2. [personal history] passado m. <> prep -1. [telling the time]: at five ~ nine às nove e cinco; it's half ~ eight são oito e meia -2. [by] pela frente de -3. [beyond] além de; the post office is ~ the bank o correio é passando o banco; to be ~ it inf passar da idade disso; I wouldn't put it ~ him inf tratando-se dele eu não me surpreenderia.

pasta ['pæstə] n (U) massa f, macarrão m.

paste [peɪst] <> n -1. [smooth mixture] pasta f -2. (U) CULIN patê m -3. (U) [glue] cola f -4. (U) [jewellery] bijuteria f. <> vt [gen] colar.

pastel ['pæstl] <> adj pastel. <> n pastel m.

paste-up n TYPO colagem f.

pasteurize, -ise ['pɑːstʃəraɪz] vt pasteurizar.

pastiche [pæ'stiːʃ] n -1. [work of imitation] imitação f -2. [mixed work] pastiche m.

pastille ['pæstɪl] n pastilha f.

pastime ['pɑːstaɪm] n passatempo m.

pasting ['peɪstɪŋ] n inf surra f.

pastor ['pɑːstəʳ] n pastor m.

pastoral ['pɑːstərəl] adj -1. RELIG pastoral -2. [countryside] bucólico(ca).

past participle n particípio m passado.

pastrami [pə'strɑːmɪ] n (U) carne de vaca defumada e muito condimentada.

pastry ['peɪstrɪ] (pl -ies) n -1. (U) [mixture] massa f -2. [cake] torta f.

past tense n passado m.

pasture ['pɑːstʃəʳ] n pasto m.

pastureland ['pɑːstʃəlænd] n pastagem f.

pasty¹ ['peɪstɪ] (compar -ier, superl -iest) adj pálida (da).

pasty² ['pæstɪ] (pl -ies) n UK CULIN pastelão m de carne.

pasty-faced ['peɪstɪ-] adj com rosto pálido.

pat [pæt] (compar -ter, superl -test, pt & pp -ted, cont-ting) <> adj preparado(da), ensaiado(da). <> adv: to have sthg off ~ ter algo na ponta da língua. <> n -1. [light stroke] palmadinha f -2. [small portion] porção f pequena. <> vt -1. [surface] bater de leve em -2. [dog] acariciar -3. [back, shoulder, hand] dar uma palmadinha em.

Patagonia [ˌpætə'gəʊnɪə] n Patagônia; in ~ na Patagônia.

Patagonian <> adj patagônio(nia). <> n patagônio m, -nia f.

patch [pætʃ] <> n -1. [piece of material] remendo m -2. [to cover eye] venda f -3. [small area] área f -4. [of land] pedaço m -5. [period of time] período m -6. phr: not to be a ~ on sb/sthg inf não se comparar nem de longe com alguém/algo. <> vt remendar.

→ **patch together** vt sep [assemble hastily - government] formar a duras penas; [- agreement] alcançar a duras penas.

→ **patch up** vt sep -1. [mend] consertar, remendar -2. fig [resolve] resolver.

patchwork ['pætʃwɜːk] <> adj de retalhos; a ~ quilt uma colcha de retalhos. <> n -1. colcha f de retalhos -2. fig [mixed collection - of fields] mosaico m; [- cultures, religions] mistura m; inf [hotchpotch] salada m.

patchy ['pætʃɪ] (compar -ier, superl -iest) adj -1. [gen] irregular -2. [incomplete] incompleto(ta).

pâté ['pæteɪ] n patê m.

patent [UK 'peɪtənt, US 'pætənt] <> adj evidente. <> n patente f. <> vt patentear.

patented [UK 'peɪtəntɪd, US 'pætəntɪd] adj patenteado(da).

patentee [UK ˌpeɪtən'tiː, US ˌpætən'tiː] n detentor m, -ra f de uma patente.

patent leather n (U) couro m envernizado.

patently [UK 'peɪtəntlɪ, US 'pætəntlɪ] adv evidentemente.

Patent Office n: the ~ o Registro de Patentes.

paternal [pə'tɜːnl] adj -1. [love, attitude] paternal -2. [relation] paterno(na).

paternalistic [pəˌtɜːnə'lɪstɪk] adj pej paternalista.

paternity [pə'tɜːnətɪ] n (U) paternidade f.

paternity leave n licença-paternidade f.

paternity suit n ação f de paternidade.

path [pɑːθ, pl pɑːðz] n -1. [track] trilha f -2. [way ahead] caminho m; our ~s had crossed before nossos caminhos já se haviam cruzado antes -3. [trajectory] trajetória f -4. [course of action] curso m.

pathetic [pə'θetɪk] adj -1. [causing pity] patético(ca) -2. [useless] inútil, infeliz.

pathetically [pə'θetɪklɪ] adv -1. [causing pity] pateticamente -2. [uselessly] inutilmente.

pathological [ˌpæθə'lɒdʒɪkl] adj patológico(ca).

pathologist [pə'θɒlədʒɪst] n patologista mf.

pathology [pə'θɒlədʒɪ] n (U) patologia f.

pathos ['peɪθɒs] n (U) patos m.

pathway ['pɑːθweɪ] n caminho m.

patience ['peɪʃns] n (U) paciência f; to try sb's ~ testar a paciência de alguém.

patient ['peɪʃnt] <> adj paciente. <> n paciente mf.

patiently ['peɪʃntlɪ] adv pacientemente.

patina ['pætɪnə] n pátina f.

patio ['pætɪəʊ] (pl -s) n pátio m.

patio doors npl portas de vidros que dão para um pátio.

patisserie [pə'tiːsərɪ] n loja f de bolos e tortas.

Patna rice ['pætnə-] n (U) arroz m Patna.

patois ['pætwɑː] (pl inv) n patoá m.

patriarch ['peɪtrɪɑːk] n patriarca m.

patriarchy ['peɪtrɪɑːkɪ] (pl -ies) n patriarcado m.

patrimony [*UK* 'pætrɪmənɪ, *US* 'pætrɪməʊnɪ] *n* (*U*) *fml* patrimônio *m*.

patriot [*UK* 'pætrɪət, *US* 'peɪtrɪət] *n* patriota *mf*.

patriotic [*UK* ˌpætrɪ'ɒtɪk, *US* ˌpeɪtrɪ'ɒtɪk] *adj* patriótico(ca).

patriotism [*UK* 'pætrɪətɪzm, *US* 'peɪtrɪətɪzm] *n* (*U*) patriotismo *m*.

patrol [pə'trəʊl] (*pt* & *pp* -**led**, *cont* -**ling**) ⬦ *n* patrulha *f*; **on** ~ de guarda. ⬦ *vt* patrulhar.

patrol car *n* radiopatrulha *f*.

patrolman [pə'trəʊlmən] (*pl* -**men** [-mən]) *n US* patrulheiro *m*, policial *m*.

patrol wagon *n US* camburão *m*.

patrolwoman [pə'trəʊlˌwʊmən] (*pl* -**women** [-ˌwɪmɪn]) *n US* patrulheira *f*.

patron ['peɪtrən] *n* -**1.** [gen] patrono *m*, -nesse *f* -**2.** *fml* [customer] cliente *mf*.

patronage ['pætrənɪdʒ] *n* (*U*) patrocínio *m*.

patronize, -ise ['pætrənaɪz] *vt* -**1.** *pej* [talk down to] tratar com condescendência -**2.** *fml* [be a customer of] ser cliente de -**3.** *fml* [back financially] patrocinar.

patronizing ['pætrənaɪzɪŋ] *adj pej* condescendente.

patron saint *n* [santo *m*] padroeiro *m*, [santa *f*] padroeira *f*.

patter ['pætər] ⬦ *n* -**1.** [sound of feet] passinhos *mpl* -**2.** *fig*: **the** ~ **of raindrops on the roof** o barulhinho da chuva no telhado -**3.** [talk] arenga *f*. ⬦ *vi* -**1.** [dog] dar passinhos rápidos -**2.** [rain] tamborilar.

pattern ['pætən] ⬦ *n* -**1.** [gen] padrão *m* -**2.** [for sewing, knitting] molde *m* -**3.** [model] modelo *m*. ⬦ *vt*: **to be** ~**ed on sthg** ser baseado(ada) em algo.

patterned ['pætənd] *adj* estampado(da).

patty ['pætɪ] (*pl* -**ies**) *n* -**1.** [pasty] empanada *f* -**2.** [savoury cake] tortinha *f*.

paucity ['pɔːsətɪ] *n fml* escassez *f*.

paunch [pɔːntʃ] *n* pança *f*, barriga *f*.

paunchy ['pɔːntʃɪ] (*compar* -**ier**, *superl* -**iest**) *adj* barrigudo(da).

pauper ['pɔːpər] *n* indigente *mf*.

pause [pɔːz] ⬦ *n* -**1.** [short silence] pausa *f* -**2.** [break, rest] interrupção *f*. ⬦ *vi* fazer uma pausa.

pave [peɪv] *vt* pavimentar; **to** ~ **the way for sb/sthg** preparar o terreno para alguém/algo.

paved [peɪvd] *adj* calçado(da), pavimentado(da).

pavement ['peɪvmənt] *n* -**1.** *UK* [at side of road] calçada *f* -**2.** *US* [roadway] rua *f*.

pavement artist *n UK* artista *mf* de rua.

pavilion [pə'vɪljən] *n* pavilhão *m*.

paving ['peɪvɪŋ] *n* (*U*) -**1.** [material] material *m* para pavimentação -**2.** [paved surface] pavimento *m*, calçamento *m*.

paving stone *n* paralelepípedo *m*.

paw [pɔː] ⬦ *n* pata *f*. ⬦ *vt* -**1.** [subj: animal] dar patadas em -**2.** *pej* [subj: person] apalpar.

pawn [pɔːn] ⬦ *n* -**1.** [chesspiece] peão *m* -**2.** [unimportant person] joguete *m*, marionete *f*. ⬦ *vt* empenhar.

pawnbroker ['pɔːnˌbrəʊkər] *n* penhorista *mf*.

pawnshop ['pɔːnʃɒp] *n* casa *f* de penhores.

pay [peɪ] (*pt* & *pp* **paid**) ⬦ *vt* -**1.** [gen] pagar; **to** ~ **sb/sth for sthg** pagar alguém/algo por algo; **to** ~ **one's way** pagar as despesas -**2.** *UK* [into bank account]: **to** ~ **sthg into sthg** depositar algo em algo -**3.** [be profitable to] ser rentável para; **it won't** ~ **you to sell just now** não vale a pena vender agora -**4.** [be advantageous to] ser proveitoso(sa) para; **it will** ~ **you not to say anything** é melhor você não dizer nada -**5.** [compliment, respects, attention] prestar; [visit, call] fazer. ⬦ *vi* -**1.** [gen] pagar; **to** ~ **for sthg** pagar algo; **the work** ~**s well** o trabalho é bem remunerado; **crime doesn't** ~ o crime não compensa -**2.** *fig* [suffer] pagar; **to** ~ **dearly for sthg** pagar caro por algo. ⬦ *n* -**1.** [wage] paga *f* -**2.** [salary] salário *m*.

➡ **pay back** *vt sep* -**1.** [return loan of money to] devolver -**2.** [revenge o.s. on]: **to** ~ **sb back (for sthg)** pagar a alguém na mesma moeda (por algo).

➡ **pay off** ⬦ *vt sep* -**1.** [repay] saldar, liquidar -**2.** [dismiss] despedir com indenização -**3.** [bribe] subornar, comprar. ⬦ *vi* obter êxito.

➡ **pay out** ⬦ *vt sep* -**1.** [spend] desembolsar -**2.** [let out] soltar. ⬦ *vi* gastar.

➡ **pay up** *vi* saldar dívida.

payable ['peɪəbl] *adj* -**1.** [to be paid] a pagar -**2.** [on cheque]: ~ **to sb** para crédito de alguém.

pay as you earn *n* (*U*) *UK* imposto *m* de renda retido na fonte.

pay-as-you-go *n* [for mobile phone, Internet, etc] *sistema de pagamento por tempo de uso*.

paybed ['peɪbed] *n UK* leito *m* pago (*em hospital público*).

paycheck ['peɪtʃek] *n US* [cheque] contracheque *m*; [money] salário *m*.

pay cheque *n UK* contracheque *m*.

payday ['peɪdeɪ] *n* (*U*) dia *m* de pagamento.

PAYE (*abbr of* **pay as you earn**) *n* (*U*) imposto *m* de renda retido na fonte.

payee [peɪ'iː] *n* beneficiário *m*, -ria *f*.

pay envelope *n US* envelope *m* de pagamento.

payer ['peɪər] *n* pagador *m*, -ra *f*.

paying guest ['peɪɪŋ-] *n* pensionista *mf*.

paying-in book *n UK* formulário *m* para depósitos.

payload ['peɪləʊd] *n* -**1.** [load] carga *f* útil -**2.** MIL, AERON carga *f*.

paymaster ['peɪˌmɑːstər] *n aquele que detém o controle econômico sobre alguém*.

paymaster general *n UK* responsável do governo britânico encarregado de pagar os funcionários do governo.

payment ['peɪmənt] *n* pagamento *m*.

payoff ['peɪɒf] *n* -**1.** [result] resultado *m* -**2.** *UK* [redundancy payment] indenização *f* (*por demissão*).

payola [peɪ'əʊlə] *n* [bribing] (*U*) *inf US* suborno *m*.

pay packet *n UK* -**1.** [envelope] envelope *m* de pagamento -**2.** [wages] pagamento *m*.

pay-per-view ⬦ *adj* [channel] pay-per-view. ⬦ *n* pay-per-view *m*.

pay phone, pay station *US n* telefone *m* público.

payroll ['peɪrəʊl] *n* folha *f* de pagamento.

payslip UK ['peɪslɪp], **paystub** US n contracheque m.

pay station n US = pay phone.

paystub ['peɪstʌb] n US = payslip.

PBS (abbr of Public Broadcasting Service) n compa- nhia de televisão norte-americana que produz programas de qualidade.

PBX (abbr of private branch exchange) n PBX m.

pc <> n (abbr of postcard) cartão-postal m. <> (abbr of per cent) por cento.

p/c (abbr of petty cash).

PC <> n -1. (abbr of personal computer) PC m -2. (abbr of police constable) policial mf. <> adj (abbr of politically correct) politicamente correto.

PCB (abbr of printed circuit board) n placa f de circuito impresso.

pcm (abbr of per calendar month) por mês (do calendário).

PCV (abbr of passenger-carrying vehicle) n veículo m de passageiros.

pd (abbr of paid) pg.

PD (abbr of police department) ≃ DP f.

PDA (abbr of personal digital assistant) n COMPUT PDA m.

PDF (abbr of portable document format) n COMPUT PDF m.

pdq (abbr of pretty damn quick) adv inf muito rápido.

PDSA (abbr of People's Dispensary for Sick Animals) n organização britânica que oferece atendimento veterinário gratuito.

PDT (abbr of Pacific Daylight Time) n horário de verão na costa oeste dos Estados Unidos.

PE (abbr of physical education) n UK ≃ Ed.Fís.

pea [pi:] n CULIN ervilha f.

peace [pi:s] n (U) -1. [gen] paz f; to be at ~ with sb/ o.s./sthg estar em paz com alguém/consigo mesmo/com algo; to make (one's) ~ with sb/sthg fazer as pazes com alguém/algo -2. [law and order] paz f, ordem f.

peaceable ['pi:səbl] adj pacífico(ca).

peaceably ['pi:səblɪ] adv pacificamente.

Peace Corps n organização norte-americana que colabora com os projetos dos países em desenvolvimento.

peaceful ['pi:sfʊl] adj -1. [tranquil] tranqüilo(la) -2. [non-violent] pacífico(ca).

peacefully ['pi:sfʊlɪ] adv -1. [tranquilly] tranqüila- mente -2. [without violence] pacificamente.

peacefulness ['pi:sfʊlnɪs] n (U) tranqüilidade f.

peacekeeping force ['pi:sˌki:pɪŋ-] n força f de paz.

peacemaker ['pi:sˌmeɪkəʳ] n pacificador m, -ra f, conciliador m, -ra f.

peace offering n inf bandeira f branca.

peacetime ['pi:staɪm] n (U) tempo m de paz.

peach [pi:tʃ] <> adj da cor de pêssego. <> n -1. [fruit] pêssego m -2. [colour] cor f de pêssego. <> comp de pêssego.

Peach Melba [-'melbə] n pêche m melba, compo- ta de pêssego servida com sorvete de baunilha.

peacock ['pi:kɒk] n pavão m.

peahen ['pi:hen] n pavoa f.

peak [pi:k] <> adj -1. [time] de pico -2. [productiv- ity, condition] máximo(ma). <> n -1. [mountain top] pico m -2. [highest point] cume m, apogeu m -3. [of cap] viseira f. <> vi atingir o máximo.

peaked [pi:kt] adj com viseira; ~ cap boné m (com viseira).

peak hour n hora f de pico.

peak period n período m de pico.

peak rate n tarifa f máxima.

peaky ['pi:kɪ] (compar -ier, superl -iest) adj UK inf acabado(da).

peal [pi:l] <> n -1. [of bells] repique m -2. [of thunder] estrondo m; ~ (of laughter) gargalhada f. <> vi repicar.

peanut ['pi:nʌt] n amendoim m.

peanut butter n (U) manteiga f de amendoim.

pear [peəʳ] n pêra f.

pearl [pɜ:l] n pérola f.

pearly ['pɜ:lɪ] (compar -ier, superl -iest) adj perolado (da).

peasant ['peznt] n -1. [in countryside] camponês m, -esa f -2. pej [ignorant person] caipira mf.

peasantry ['pezntrɪ] n: the ~ os camponeses.

peashooter ['pi:ˌʃu:təʳ] n sarabatana f.

peat [pi:t] n (U) turfa f.

peaty ['pi:tɪ] (compar -ier, superl -iest) adj turfoso(sa).

pebble ['pebl] n cascalho m, seixo m.

pebble-dash n UK argamassa f com cascalho.

pecan (nut) ['pi:kæn-] n noz-pecã f.

pecan pie n torta f de noz-pecã.

peck [pek] <> n -1. [with beak] bicada f -2. [kiss] bicota f. <> vt -1. [with beak] bicar -2. [kiss] dar uma bicota. <> vi bicar.

pecking order ['pekɪŋ-] n hierarquia f.

peckish ['pekɪʃ] adj UK inf esfomeado(da).

pectin ['pektɪn] n (U) pectina f.

pectoral ['pektərəl] adj peitoral.

peculiar [pɪ'kju:ljəʳ] adj -1. [odd] esquisito(ta) -2. [slightly ill] estranho(nha) -3. [characteristic]: to be ~ to sb/sthg ser característico(ca) de alguém/algo.

peculiarity [pɪˌkju:lɪ'ærətɪ] (pl -ies) n -1. [strange ha- bit] peculiaridade f -2. [individual characteristic] singu- laridade f -3. [oddness] excentricidade f.

peculiarly [pɪ'kju:lɪjəlɪ] adv -1. [especially] particu- larmente -2. [oddly] estranhamente -3. [character- istically] tipicamente.

pecuniary [pɪ'kju:njərɪ] adj pecuniário(ria).

pedagogical [ˌpedə'gɒdʒɪkl] adj pedagógico(ca).

pedagogy [ˌpedə'gɒdʒɪ] n (U) pedagogia f.

pedal ['pedl] (UK pt & pp -led, cont -ling, US pt & pp -ed, cont -ing) <> n pedal m; brake ~ freio m. <> vi pedalar.

pedal bin n lixeira f com pedal.

pedalo ['pedələʊ] (pl -s OR -es) n UK pedalinho m.

pedant ['pedənt] n pej pedante mf, formalista mf.

pedantic [pɪ'dæntɪk] adj pej pedante.

pedantry ['pedəntrɪ] n (U) pej pedantismo m.

peddle ['pedl] vt -1. [sell] traficar -2. [spread] espalhar.

peddler ['pedləʳ] n -1. [drug dealer] traficante mf -2. US = pedlar.

pederast ['pedəræst] n pederasta m.

pedestal ['pedɪstl] n pedestal m; **to put sb on a ~** colocar alguém num pedestal.

pedestrian [pɪ'destrɪən] <> adj pej enfadonho (nha). <> n pedestre mf.

pedestrian crossing n UK faixa f para pedestres.

pedestrianize, -ise [pɪ'destrɪənaɪz] vt transformar em área só para pedestres.

pedestrian precinct UK, **pedestrian zone** US n área f só para pedestres.

pediatric [ˌpiːdɪ'ætrɪk] adj pediátrico(ca).

pediatrician [ˌpiːdɪə'trɪʃn] n pediatra mf.

pediatrics [ˌpiːdɪ'ætrɪks] n (U) pediatria f.

pedicure ['pedɪˌkjʊəᵈ] n pedicure mf.

pedigree ['pedɪgriː] <> adj com pedigree. <> n -1. [of animal] pedigree m -2. [of person] linhagem f.

pedlar UK, **peddler** US ['pedlᵃᵈ] n vendedor m, -ra f ambulante.

pedophile ['piːdəfaɪl] n = paedophile.

pee [piː] inf <> n xixi m; **to have a ~** fazer xixi. <> vi fazer xixi.

peek [piːk] inf <> n espiadela f. <> vi espiar.

peel [piːl] <> n (U) casca f. <> vt & vi descascar.
◆ **peel off** vt sep -1. [pull off] arrancar, desgrudar -2. [take off] tirar.

peeler ['piːlᵃᵈ] n descascador m.

peelings ['piːlɪŋz] npl cascas fpl.

peep [piːp] <> n -1. [look] espiada f -2. inf [sound] pio m. <> vi dar uma espiada em.
◆ **peep out** vi surgir.

peephole ['piːphəʊl] n vigia f (em porta).

peeping Tom [ˌpiːpɪŋ'tɒm] n voyeur m.

peep show n cineminha f, caixa que contém imagens em movimento que se pode ver através de um pequeno buraco.

peer [pɪəᵈ] <> n -1. [noble] nobre m -2. [equal] par m. <> vi: **to ~ at** observar; **to ~ through the clouds** observar por entre as nuvens.

peerage ['pɪərɪdʒ] n pariato m; **the ~** o pariato.

peeress ['pɪərɪs] n -1. [woman peer] nobre f -2. [wife or widow of peer] esposa f de nobre.

peer group n grupo de mesma faixa etária ou classe social.

peer pressure n (U) pressão exercida pelo grupo da mesma faixa etária ou classe social a que se pertence.

peeved [piːvd] adj inf aborrecido(da).

peevish ['piːvɪʃ] adj irritadiço(ça), mal-humorado (da).

peg [peg] (pt & pp -ged, cont -ging) <> n -1. [hook] cabide m -2. [for washing line] prendedor m (de roupa) -3. [for tent] pino m. <> vt [price, increase] fixar.
◆ **peg out** <> vt sep estender. <> vi UK inf esticar as canelas.

PEI n abbr of Prince Edward Island.

pejorative [pɪ'dʒɒrətɪv] adj pejorativo(va).

pekinese (pl inv OR -s) n [dog] pequinês m.
◆ **Pekinese, Pekingese** <> adj pequinês(e-sa). <> n pequinês m, -esa f.

Peking [piː'kɪŋ] n Pequim; **in ~** em Pequim.

pekingese (pl inv OR -s) n = pekinese.

pelican ['pelɪkən] (pl inv OR -s) n pelicano m.

pelican crossing n UK faixa f de segurança (com semáforo acionado pelo pedestre).

pellet ['pelɪt] n -1. [small ball - of paper] bolinha f; [- of food, mud] bolo m -2. [for gun] chumbinho m.

pell-mell [ˌpel'mel] adv atropeladamente.

pelmet ['pelmɪt] n UK bandô m.

Peloponnese [ˌpeləpə'niːz] n: **the ~** o Peloponeso.

pelt [pelt] <> n -1. [animal skin] pele f -2. [speed]: **(at) full ~** a toda velocidade. <> vt: **to ~ sb with sthg** arremessar algo em alguém. <> vi -1. [rain] chover a cântaros -2. [run very fast] correr a toda.

pelvic ['pelvɪk] adj pélvico(ca).

pelvis ['pelvɪs] (pl -vises OR -ves [-viːz]) n pélvis f inv.

pen [pen] (pt & pp -ned, cont -ning) <> n -1. [for writing] caneta f -2. [enclosure] curral m. <> vt -1. literary [write] redigir, escrever -2. [enclose - livestock] cercar; [- people] encurralar.

penal ['piːnl] adj JUR penal.

penalize, ise ['piːnəlaɪz] vt -1. [gen] penalizar -2. [put at a disadvantage] prejudicar.

penal settlement n colônia f penal.

penalty ['penltɪ] (pl -ies) n -1. [punishment] penalidade f; **to pay the ~ (for sthg)** fig pagar pena (por algo) -2. [fine] pena f -3. SPORT pênalti m; **~ (kick)** pênalti.

penalty area, penalty box n UK SPORT área f de pênalti, grande área f.

penalty clause n cláusula f penal.

penalty goal n gol m de pênalti.

penalty kick n ⊳ penalty.

penance ['penəns] n (U) penitência f.

pen-and-ink adj à tinta.

pence [pens] UK pl ⊳ penny.

penchant [UK pɑːʃɒ, US 'pentʃənt] n: **to have a ~ for sthg/for doing sthg** ter uma queda por algo/por fazer algo.

pencil ['pensl] (UK pt & pp -led, cont -ling, US pt & pp -ed, cont -ing) <> n lápis m inv; **in ~** a lápis. <> vt escrever a lápis.
◆ **pencil in** vt sep -1. [person] inscrever provisoriamente -2. [date] marcar provisoriamente.

pencil case n estojo m (de canetas).

pencil sharpener n apontador m de lápis.

pendant ['pendənt] n pendente m.

pending ['pendɪŋ] fml <> adj -1. [about to happen] iminente -2. [waiting to be dealt with] pendente. <> prep à espera de.

pending tray n UK bandeja f de assuntos pendentes.

pendulum ['pendjʊləm] (pl -s) n pêndulo m.

penetrate ['penɪtreɪt] <> vt -1. [get through - subj: person, object] penetrar em, adentrar-se em; [- rain] infiltrar-se em -2. [infiltrate - party] entrar sorrateiramente em; [- terrorist group, spy ring] infiltrar-se em. <> vi inf [be understood] cair a ficha.

penetrating ['penɪtreɪtɪŋ] adj -1. [gen] penetrante -2. [wind, cold] cortante.

penetration [ˌpenɪ'treɪʃn] n (U) -1. [gen] penetração f -2. fml [insight] perspicácia f.

penfriend ['penfrend] n amigo m, -ga f por correspondência.

penguin ['peŋgwɪn] n pingüim m.

penicillin [ˌpenɪˈsɪlɪn] *n (U)* penicilina *f.*
peninsula [pəˈnɪnsjʊlə] *(pl -s) n* península *f.*
penis [ˈpiːnɪs] *(pl penises* [ˈpiːnɪsɪz]) *n* pênis *m inv.*
penitent [ˈpenɪtənt] *adj fml* penitente.
penitentiary [ˌpenɪˈtenʃərɪ] *(pl -ies) n US* penitenciária *f.*
penknife [ˈpennaɪf] *(pl -knives* [-naɪvz]) *n* canivete *m,* navalha *f.*
pen-name *n* pseudônimo *m.*
pennant [ˈpenənt] *n* bandeirola *f.*
penniless [ˈpenɪlɪs] *adj* sem dinheiro.
Pennines [ˈpenaɪnz] *npl:* the ~ as Pennines.
Pennsylvania [ˌpensɪlˈveɪnɪə] *n* Pensilvânia.
penny [ˈpenɪ] *(pl senses 1 & 2 -ies, pl sense 3* **pence**) *n* **-1.** *UK* [coin] pêni *m* **-2.** *US* [coin] centavo *m* **-3.** *UK* [value] centavo *m* **-4.** *phr:* a ~ **for your thoughts** um centavo por seus pensamentos; **the** ~ **dropped** *UK inf* caiu a ficha; **to spend a** ~ *UK inf* fazer xixi; **two** OR **ten a** ~ *UK inf* a preço de banana.
penny-pinching [-ˌpɪntʃɪŋ] <> *adj* avarento(ta). <> *n (U)* avareza *f.*
pen pal *n inf* amigo *m,* -ga *f* por correspondência.
pension [ˈpenʃn] *n* **-1.** *UK* [on retirement - state scheme] pensão *f;* [- private scheme] previdência *f* privada **-2.** [for disability] pensão *f* por invalidez.
→ **pension off** *vt sep* aposentar-se.
pensionable [ˈpenʃənəbl] *adj* com direito à aposentadoria; ~ **age** idade *f* de se aposentar.
pension book *n UK carnê dado pelo governo britânico a todos os pensionistas e cujos cupons podem ser trocados semanalmente por dinheiro nas agências dos correios.*
pensioner [ˈpenʃənəʳ] *n UK:* (old-age) ~ pensionista *mf.*
pension fund *n* fundo *m* de pensão.
pension plan, pension scheme *n* plano *m* de aposentadoria.
pensive [ˈpensɪv] *adj* pensativo(va).
pentagon [ˈpentəgən] *n* pentágono *m.*
→ **Pentagon** *n US:* the **Pentagon** o Pentágono.

PENTAGON

O Pentágono, imenso edifício de cinco faces situado em Washington, abriga o ministério da Defesa dos EUA. De modo geral, o termo é empregado também para designar o poder militar estadunidense.

pentathlete [penˈtæθliːt] *n* pentatleta *mf.*
pentathlon [penˈtæθlən] *(pl -s) n* pentatlo *m.*
Pentecost [ˈpentɪkɒst] *n* Pentecostes *m inv.*
penthouse [ˈpenthaʊs, pl -haʊzɪz] *n* cobertura *f.*
pent up [pent-] *adj* contido(da), reprimido(da).
penultimate [peˈnʌltɪmət] *adj* penúltimo(ma).
penury [ˈpenjʊrɪ] *n (U) fml* penúria *f.*
peony [ˈpɪənɪ] *(pl -ies) n* peônia *f.*
people [ˈpiːpl] <> *n* [nation, race] povo *m.* <> *npl* **-1.** [gen] pessoas *fpl;* ~ **say that ...** dizem que ... **-2.** [inhabitants] habitantes *mpl* **-3.** POL: **the** ~ o povo. <> *vt:* **to be** ~**d by** OR **with** ser povoado(da) por.
people carrier *n* monovolume *m.*
pep [pep] *(pt & pp -ped, cont -ping) n inf* vigor *m,* vitalidade *f.*

→ **pep up** *vt sep* **-1.** [person] revigorar **-2.** [party, event] animar.
PEP *(abbr of* **personal equity plan)** *n plano de poupança popular na Grã-Bretanha.*
pepper [ˈpepəʳ] *n* **-1.** *(U)* [spice] pimenta *f;* **black / white** ~ pimenta preta/branca **-2.** [vegetable] pimentão *m;* **red/green** ~ pimentão vermelho/verde.
pepperbox *n US =* pepper pot.
peppercorn [ˈpepəkɔːn] *n* grão *m* de pimenta.
peppered [ˈpepəd] *adj* **-1.** [sprinkled]: ~ **(with sthg)** salpicado(da) (de algo) **-2.** [hit repeatedly]: ~ **(with sthg)** crivado(da) (de algo).
pepper mill *n* moedor *m* de pimenta.
peppermint [ˈpepəmɪnt] *n* **-1.** [sweet] menta *f* **-2.** *(U)* [herb] hortelã-pimenta *f.*
pepper pot *UK,* **pepperbox** *US* [ˈpepəbɒks] *n* pimenteira *f.*
peppery [ˈpepərɪ] *adj* apimentado(da).
pep talk *n inf* palavras *fpl* de ânimo OR incentivo.
peptic ulcer [ˈpeptɪk-] *n* úlcera *f* péptica.
per [pɜːʳ] *prep* por; ~ **hour/day/kilo/person** por hora/dia/quilo/pessoa; **as** ~ **instructions** conforme/segundo as instruções.
per annum *adv* por ano.
p/e ratio *(abbr of* **price-earnings ratio)** *n* índice *m* de benefício.
per capita [pəˈkæpɪtə] *adj, adv* per capita.
perceive [pəˈsiːv] *vt* **-1.** [see] distinguir **-2.** [notice, realize] perceber, ver **-3.** [conceive, consider]: **to** ~ **sb/sthg as** ver alguém/algo como.
per cent *adv* por cento.
percentage [pəˈsentɪdʒ] *n* porcentagem *f.*
perceptible [pəˈseptəbl] *adj* perceptível.
perception [pəˈsepʃn] *n* **-1.** *(U)* [gen] distinção *f* **-2.** *(U)* [insight, understanding] percepção *f,* perspicácia *f* **-3.** [opinion] idéia *f.*
perceptive [pəˈseptɪv] *adj* perspicaz.
perceptively [pəˈseptɪvlɪ] *adv* de modo perspicaz.
perch [pɜːtʃ] *(pl sense 3 only inv* OR **-es)** <> *n* **-1.** [for bird] poleiro *m* **-2.** [high position] posição *f* elevada **-3.** [fish] perca *f.* <> *vi:* **to** ~ **(on sthg)** [bird] pousar (em algo); [person] empoleirar-se (em algo).
percolate [ˈpɜːkəleɪt] *vi* **-1.** [brew] coar **-2.** [seep - water] infiltrar-se; [- news] vazar.
percolator [ˈpɜːkəleɪtəʳ] *n* cafeteira *f.*
percussion [pəˈkʌʃn] *n (U)* MUS percussão *f;* **the** ~ **(section)** a percussão.
percussionist [pəˈkʌʃənɪst] *n* percussionista *mf.*
peremptory [pəˈremptərɪ] *adj* peremptório(ria), categórico(ca).
perennial [pəˈrenjəl] <> *adj* perene. <> *n* BOT planta *f* perene.
perestroika [ˌperəˈstrɔɪkə] *n (U)* perestroika *f.*
perfect [*adj & n* ˈpɜːfɪkt, *vb* pəˈfekt] <> *adj* perfeito(ta); **it makes** ~ **sense** é perfeitamente lógico (ca). <> *n* GRAMM: ~ **(tense)** o perfeito. <> *vt* aperfeiçoar.
perfect competition *n (U)* ECON concorrência *f* perfeita.
perfection [pəˈfekʃn] *n* perfeição *f;* **to** ~ à perfeição.
perfectionist [pəˈfekʃənɪst] *n* perfeccionista *mf.*

perfectly ['pɜːfɪktlɪ] *adv* perfeitamente; ' ~ **hon-est/ridiculous** totalmente honesto/ridículo, totalmente honesta/ridícula.

perforate ['pɜːfəreɪt] *vt* perfurar.

perforations [,pɜːfə'reɪʃnz] *npl* perfurações *fpl*.

perform [pə'fɔːm] <> *vt* -**1.** [carry out] realizar, levar a cabo -**2.** [in front of audience - play] representar, interpretar; [- music, dance] apresentar. <> *vi* -**1.** [function - car, machine] funcionar; [- person, team] sair-se -**2.** [in front of audience] apresentar-se, atuar.

performance [pə'fɔːməns] *n* -**1.** (U) [carrying out, doing] execução *f*, realização *f* -**2.** [show] apresentação *f* -**3.** [rendition] performance *f*, desempenho *m* -**4.** (U) [of car, engine] desempenho *m*, rendimento *m*.

performance art *n* (U) *expressão artística em que se combina diversas atividades como teatro, música, dança, escultura, fotografia etc*.

performance car *n* carro *m* de alto desempenho.

performer [pə'fɔːmə'] *n* performer *mf*.

performing arts [pə'fɔːmɪŋ-] *npl*: **the** ~ as artes performáticas.

perfume ['pɜːfjuːm] *n* -**1.** [for woman] perfume *m* -**2.** [pleasant smell] aroma *f*.

perfumed [*UK* 'pɜːfjuːmd, *US* pər'fjuːmd] *adj* perfumado(da).

perfunctory [pə'fʌŋktərɪ] *adj* superficial, feito(ta) às pressas.

perhaps [pə'hæps] *adv* talvez; ~ **you're right** talvez você esteja certo; ~ **so/not** talvez sim/não; ~ **you should go and see her?** quem sabe você vai dar uma olhada nela?

peril ['perɪl] *n* (U) *literary* perigo *m*; **at one's** ~ por sua conta e risco.

perilous ['perələs] *adj literary* perigoso(sa).

perilously ['perələslɪ] *adv* perigosamente.

perimeter [pə'rɪmɪtə'] *n* perímetro *m*; ~ **fence/wall** alambrado *m*, cerca *f*.

period ['pɪərɪəd] <> *n* -**1.** [gen] período *m*; **free** ~ período livre -**2.** *HISTORY* era *f* -**3.** [menstruation] período *m* menstrual -**4.** *US* [full stop] ponto *m*. <> *comp* [dress, furniture] de época.

periodic [,pɪərɪ'ɒdɪk] *adj* periódico(ca).

periodical [,pɪərɪ'ɒdɪkl] <> *adj* = **periodic**. <> *n* periódico *m*.

periodic table *n* tabela *f* periódica.

period pains *npl* cólicas *fpl* menstruais.

period piece *n* obra *f* de época.

peripatetic [,perɪpə'tetɪk] *adj* itinerante.

peripheral [pə'rɪfərəl] <> *adj* -**1.** [of little importance] secundário(ria) -**2.** [at edge] periférico(ca). <> *n COMPUT* periférico *m*.

periphery [pə'rɪfərɪ] (*pl* -**ies**) *n* -**1.** [edge] periferia *f* -**2.** [unimportant area] margens *fpl*.

periscope ['perɪskəʊp] *n* periscópio *m*.

perish ['perɪʃ] *vi* -**1.** [die] perecer -**2.** [decay] deteriorar-se.

perishable ['perɪʃəbl] *adj* perecível.

➡ **perishables** *npl* produtos *mpl* perecíveis.

perishing ['perɪʃɪŋ] *adj UK inf* -**1.** [cold] frio (fria) de

rachar; **it's** ~ está fazendo um frio de rachar -**2.** [for emphasis] danado(da).

peritonitis [,perɪtə'naɪtɪs] *n* (U) peritonite *f*.

perjure ['pɜːdʒə'] *vt JUR*: **to** ~ **o.s.** perjurar-se.

perjury ['pɜːdʒərɪ] *n* (U) *JUR* perjúrio *m*.

perk [pɜːk] *n inf* mordomia *m*, regalia *f*.

➡ **perk up** *vi* animar-se.

perky ['pɜːkɪ] (*compar* -**ier**, *superl* -**iest**) *adj inf* animado(da), alegre.

perm [pɜːm] <> *n* permanente *m*. <> *vt* fazer permanente.

permanence ['pɜːmənəns] *n* (U) permanência *f*.

permanent ['pɜːmənənt] <> *adj* -**1.** [not temporary - job] fixo(xa); [- damage, feature] permanente -**2.** [continuous, constant] permanente, constante. <> *n US* permanente *m*.

permanently ['pɜːmənəntlɪ] *adv* -**1.** [forever] permanentemente -**2.** [continuously] permanentemente.

permeable ['pɜːmjəbl] *adj* permeável.

permeate ['pɜːmɪeɪt] *vt* permear.

permissible [pə'mɪsəbl] *adj* permissível.

permission [pə'mɪʃn] *n* (U) permissão *f*; ~ **to do sthg** permissão para fazer algo.

permissive [pə'mɪsɪv] *adj* permissivo(va), tolerante.

permissiveness [pə'mɪsɪvnɪs] *n* (U) tolerância *f*.

permit [*vb* pə'mɪt, *n* 'pɜːmɪt] (*pt & pp* -**ted**, *cont* -**ting**) <> *n* autorização *f*. <> *vt* permitir; **to** ~ **sb to do sthg** permitir que alguém faça algo; **my mother won't** ~ **me to go out** minha mãe não vai me deixar sair; **to** ~ **sb sthg** permitir algo a alguém. <> *vi* permitir; **weather permitting** se o tempo deixar.

permutation [,pɜːmju'teɪʃn] *n* permutação *f*.

pernicious [pə'nɪʃəs] *adj fml* pernicioso(sa).

pernickety *UK* [pə'nɪkətɪ], **persnickety** *US adj inf* meticuloso(sa).

peroxide [pə'rɒksaɪd] *n* (U) peróxido *m*.

peroxide blonde *n* loura *f* oxigenada *OR* de farmácia.

perpendicular [,pɜːpən'dɪkjʊlə'] <> *adj* -**1.** *MATH* perpendicular; ~ **to sthg** perpendicular a algo -**2.** [upright] vertical. <> *n MATH* perpendicular *f*.

perpetrate ['pɜːpɪtreɪt] *vt fml* perpetrar.

perpetration [,pɜːpɪ'treɪʃn] *n* (U) *fml* perpetração *f*.

perpetrator ['pɜːpɪtreɪtə'] *n fml* perpetrador *m*, -ra *f*.

perpetual [pə'petʃʊəl] *adj* -**1.** *pej* [continuous] constante -**2.** [everlasting - darkness] perpétuo(tua); [- hunger] eterno(na).

perpetually [pə'petʃʊəlɪ] *adv* -**1.** *pej* [continuously] constantemente, continuamente -**2.** [forever] perpetuamente, eternamente.

perpetual motion *n* (U) moto-contínuo *m*.

perpetuate [pə'petʃʊeɪt] *vt* perpetuar.

perpetuation [pə,petʃʊ'eɪʃn] *n* (U) perpetuação *f*.

perpetuity [,pɜːpɪ'tjuːətɪ] *n* (U): **in** ~ *fml* para sempre.

perplex [pə'pleks] *vt* desconcertar, deixar perplexo(xa).

perplexed [pə'plekst] *adj* perplexo(xa).

perplexing [pə'pleksɪŋ] *adj* desconcertante.
perplexity [pə'pleksətɪ] *n (U)* perplexidade *f.*
perquisite ['pɜːkwɪzɪt] *n fml* privilégios *mpl* adicionais.
per se [pɜː'seɪ] *adv* **-1.** [as such] como tal **-2.** [in itself] em si.
persecute ['pɜːsɪkjuːt] *vt* perseguir, oprimir.
persecution [ˌpɜːsɪ'kjuːʃn] *n* **-1.** [act of cruelty] perseguição *f* **-2.** [cruel treatment] opressão *f.*
persecutor ['pɜːsɪkjuːtəʳ] *n* opressor *m*, -ra *f,* perseguidor *m*, -ra *f.*
perseverance [ˌpɜːsɪ'vɪərəns] *n (U)* perseverança *f.*
persevere [ˌpɜːsɪ'vɪəʳ] *vi* **-1.** [with difficulty] perseverar; **to ~ with sthg** persistir em algo **-2.** [with determination]: **to ~ in doing sthg** insistir em fazer algo.
Persia ['pɜːʃə] *n* Pérsia; **in ~** na Pérsia.
Persian ['pɜːʃn] ⬦ *adj* persa. ⬦ *n* **-1.** [person] persa *mf* **-2.** [language] persa *m.*
Persian cat *n* gato *m*, -ta *f* persa.
Persian Gulf *n*: **the ~** o Golfo Pérsico.
persist [pə'sɪst] *vi* **-1.** [problem, situation, rain] persistir **-2.** [person]: **to ~ in doing sthg** insistir em fazer algo.
persistence [pə'sɪstəns] *n (U)* **-1.** [continuation] persistência *f* **-2.** [determination] obstinação *f,* determinação *f.*
persistent [pə'sɪstənt] *adj* **-1.** [constant] constante **-2.** [determined] obstinado(da) determinado(da).
persistently [pə'sɪstəntlɪ] *adv* **-1.** [constantly] constantemente **-2.** [determinedly] obstinadamente, de forma determinada.
persnickety [pə'snɪkɪtɪ] *adj US* = **pernickety.**
person ['pɜːsn] *(pl* **people** *OR* **persons** *fml) n* **-1.** [man or woman] pessoa *f*; **in ~** pessoalmente, em pessoa; **in the ~ of** na pessoa de **-2.** [body]: **about one's ~** em seu corpo **-3.** *GRAMM* pessoa *f.*
persona [pə'səʊnə] *(pl* **-s** *OR* **-ae** [-iː]*) n* imagem *f.*
personable ['pɜːsnəbl] *adj* bem-apessoado(da).
personage ['pɜːsənɪdʒ] *n fml* personalidade *f.*
personal ['pɜːsənl] ⬦ *adj* **-1.** [gen] pessoal **-2.** [letter, message] particular **-3.** *pej* [rude] ofensivo (va). ⬦ *n US* [advert] nota *f* pessoal *(em jornal).*
personal account *n* conta *f* pessoal.
personal allowance *n FIN* desconto *m* simplificado *(na declaração do imposto de renda).*
personal assistant *n* assistente *mf* particular.
personal call *n* telefonema *m* particular, chamada *f* pessoal.
personal column *n* seção *f* de recados *(em jornal).*
personal computer *n* computador *m* pessoal.
personal estate *n* bens *mpl* móveis.
personal hygiene *n (U)* higiene *f* pessoal.
personality [ˌpɜːsə'nælətɪ] *(pl* **-ies***) n* personalidade *f.*
personalize, -ise ['pɜːsənəlaɪz] *vt* **-1.** [mark with name, initials] personalizar **-2.** *pej* [issue, argument] levar para o lado pessoal.
personalized ['pɜːsənəlaɪzd] *adj* personalizado (da).
personally ['pɜːsnəlɪ] *adv* pessoalmente; **to take**

sthg ~ levar algo para o lado pessoal.
personal organizer *n* agenda *f* pessoal.
personal pension plan *n* plano *m* de previdência particular.
personal pronoun *n* pronome *m* pessoal.
personal property *n (U) JUR* bens *mpl* móveis.
personal stereo *n* walkman *m.*
persona non grata [-'grɑːtəl] *(pl* **personae non gratae** [-'grɑːtiːl]*) n* persona non grata *f.*
personify [pə'sɒnɪfaɪ] *(pt & pp* **-ied***) vt* personificar.
personnel [ˌpɜːsə'nel] ⬦ *n (U)* [in firm, organization] equipe *f.* ⬦ *npl* [staff] funcionários *mpl.*
personnel department *n* departamento *m* de pessoal.
personnel officer *n* funcionário *m*, -ria *f* do departamento pessoal.
person-to-person *adj TELEC* de pessoa a pessoa.
perspective [pə'spektɪv] *n* perspectiva *f*; **to get sthg in ~** *fig* pôr algo em perspectiva.
Perspex® ['pɜːspeks] *n UK* plexiglás® *m.*
perspicacious [ˌpɜːspɪ'keɪʃəs] *adj fml* perspicaz.
perspiration [ˌpɜːspə'reɪʃn] *n* transpiração *f.*
perspire [pə'spaɪəʳ] *vi* transpirar.
persuade [pə'sweɪd] *vt* persuadir; **to ~ sb to do sthg** persuadir alguém a fazer algo; **to ~ sb that** convencer alguém de que; **to ~ sb of sthg** convencer alguém de algo.
persuasion [pə'sweɪʒn] *n* **-1.** *(U)* [act of persuading] persuasão *f* **-2.** [belief] crença *f.*
persuasive [pə'sweɪsɪv] *adj* persuasivo(va).
persuasively [pə'sweɪsɪvlɪ] *adv* persuasivamente.
pert [pɜːt] *adj* **-1.** [person, reply] vivo(va), atrevido(va) **-2.** [nose, bottom] gracioso(sa).
pertain [pə'teɪn] *vi fml*: **~ing to sb/sthg** relacionado(da) a alguém/algo.
pertinence ['pɜːtɪnəns] *n (U)* pertinência *f,* relevância *f.*
pertinent ['pɜːtɪnənt] *adj* pertinente, relevante.
perturb [pə'tɜːb] *vt fml* perturbar.
perturbed [pə'tɜːbd] *adj fml* perturbado(da).
Peru [pə'ruː] *n* Peru; **in ~** no Peru.
perusal [pə'ruːzl] *n* **-1.** [thorough reading] leitura *f* **-2.** [quick reading] leitura *f* rápida.
peruse [pə'ruːz] *vt* **-1.** [read thoroughly] ler com atenção **-2.** [read quickly] ler por cima.
Peruvian [pə'ruːvjən] ⬦ *adj* peruano(na). ⬦ *n* peruano *m*, -na *f.*
pervade [pə'veɪd] *vt* impregnar.
pervasive [pə'veɪsɪv] *adj* penetrante.
perverse [pə'vɜːs] *adj* perverso(sa).
perversely [pə'vɜːslɪ] *adv* perversamente.
perversion [*UK* pə'vɜːʃn, *US* pə'vɜːrʒn] *n* perversão *f.*
perversity [pə'vɜːsətɪ] *n (U)* perversidade *f.*
pervert [*n* 'pɜːvɜːt, *vb* pə'vɜːt] ⬦ *n* pervertido *m*, -da *f.* ⬦ *vt* **-1.** [distort] distorcer **-2.** [corrupt morally] perverter.
perverted [pə'vɜːtɪd] *adj* **-1.** [sexually deviant] pervertido(da) **-2.** [distorted] distorcido(da).
peseta [pə'seɪtə] *n* peseta *f.*

peso ['peɪsəʊ] (*pl* -s) *n* peso *m*.

pessary ['pesərɪ] (*pl* -ies) *n* pessário *m*.

pessimism ['pesɪmɪzm] *n (U)* pessimismo *m*.

pessimist ['pesɪmɪst] *n* pessimista *mf*.

pessimistic [,pesɪ'mɪstɪk] *adj* pessimista.

pest [pest] *n* [gen] praga *f*, peste *f*.

pester ['pestə'] *vt* importunar, incomodar.

pesticide ['pestɪsaɪd] *n* pesticida *f*.

pestle ['pesl] *n* pilão *m*.

pet [pet] (*pt & pp* -ted, *cont* -ting) <> *adj* [favourite] predileto(ta), preferido(da). <> *n* -1. [domestic animal] animal *m* de estimação -2. [favourite person] preferido *m*, -da *f*. <> *vt* acariciar, afagar. <> *vi* acariciar-se.

petal ['petl] *n* pétala *f*.

peter ['pi:tə'] ◆ **peter out** *vi* -1. [food, interest] esgotar-se -2. [path] desaparecer.

pethidine ['peθɪdi:n] *n (U)* petidina *f*.

petit bourgeois [pə,ti:'bʊəʒwa:] (*pl* petits bourgeois [pə,ti:'bʊəʒwa:]) <> *adj* pequeno-burguês (guesa). <> *n* pequeno-burguês *m*, -guesa *f*.

petite [pə'ti:t] *adj* diminuto(ta).

petit four [,peti-] (*pl* petits fours [,peti-]) *n* bolo pequeno ou biscoito servido com café no final da refeição.

petition [pɪ'tɪʃn] <> *n* -1. [supporting campaign] abaixo-assinado *m* -2. JUR petição *f*. <> *vt* peticionar. <> *vi* -1. [campaign]: **to ~ for/against sthg** fazer um abaixo-assinado a favor de/contra algo -2. JUR: **to ~ for divorce** pedir o divórcio.

petitioner [pɪ'tɪʃənə'] *n* -1. JUR [in divorce] requerente *mf* -2. [on petition] peticionário *m*, -ria *f*.

pet name *n* apelido *m* carinhoso.

petrified ['petrɪfaɪd] *adj* petrificado(da).

petrify ['petrɪfaɪ] (*pt & pp* -ied) *vt* petrificar.

petrochemical [,petrəʊ'kemɪkl] *adj* petroquímico(ca).

petrodollar ['petrəʊ,dɒlə'] *n* FIN petrodólar *m*.

petrol ['petrəl] *n (U)* UK gasolina *f*.

petrolatum *n* US vaselina *f (líquida)*.

petrol bomb *n* UK coquetel *m* molotov.

petrol can *n* UK lata *f* de gasolina.

petrol cap *n* UK tampa *f* do tanque de combustível.

petroleum [pɪ'trəʊljəm] *n (U)* petróleo *m*.

petroleum jelly *n* UK vaselina *f*.

petrol pump *n* UK bomba *f* de gasolina.

petrol pump attendant *n* UK frentista *mf*.

petrol station *n* UK posto *m* de gasolina.

petrol tank *n* UK tanque *m* de gasolina.

pet shop *n* pet shop *f*, loja *f* de produtos para animais de estimação.

petticoat ['petɪkəʊt] *n* anágua *f*.

pettiness ['petɪnɪs] *n (U)* mesquinharia *f*.

petty ['petɪ] (*compar* -ier, *superl* -iest) *adj* -1. [small-minded] mesquinho(nha) -2. [trivial] insignificante.

petty cash *n (U)* dinheiro *m* para pequenas despesas, trocado *m*.

petty officer *n* suboficial *mf*.

petulant ['petjʊlənt] *adj* petulante.

petunia [pɪ'tju:njə] *n* petúnia *f*.

pew [pju:] *n* banco *m (de igreja)*.

pewter ['pju:tə'] *n (U)* peltre *m*.

PG (*abbr of* **parental guidance**) *para menores acompanhados*.

PGA (*abbr of* **Professional Golfers' Association**) *n associação de jogadores profissionais de golfe nos Estados Unidos*.

p & h (*abbr of* **postage and handling**) *n* US *valor m de postagem*.

pH (*abbr of* **potential of hydrogen**) *n* CHEM ph.

PH (*abbr of* **Purple Heart**) *n (beneficiário de) honraria concedida pelo governo norte-americano a soldados feridos em ação*.

PHA (*abbr of* **Public Housing Administration**) *n órgão norte-americano encarregado de fornecer alojamento a pessoas necessitadas*.

phallic ['fælɪk] *adj* fálico(ca); **~ symbol** símbolo *m* fálico.

phallus ['fæləs] (*pl* -es OR **phalli** ['fælaɪ]) *n* falo *m*.

phantom ['fæntəm] <> *adj* [imaginary] ilusório(ria). <> *n* [ghost] fantasma *m*.

phantom pregnancy *n* gravidez *f* psicológica.

pharaoh ['feərəʊ] *n* faraó *m*.

Pharisee ['færɪsi:] *n* fariseu *m*.

pharmaceutical [,fɑ:mə'sju:tɪkl] *adj* farmacêutico(ca).

◆ **pharmaceuticals** *npl* produtos *mpl* farmacêuticos.

pharmacist ['fɑ:məsɪst] *n* farmacêutico *m*, -ca *f*.

pharmacology [,fɑ:mə'kɒlədʒɪl] *n (U)* farmacologia *f*.

pharmacy ['fɑ:məsɪ] (*pl* -ies) *n* farmácia *f*.

phase [feɪz] <> *n* fase *f*. <> *vt* dividir em etapas, escalonar.

◆ **phase in** *vt sep* introduzir gradualmente.

◆ **phase out** *vt sep* retirar gradualmente.

PhD (*abbr of* **Doctor of Philosophy**) *n (titular de) doutorado em ciências humanas*.

pheasant ['feznt] (*pl inv* OR -s) *n* faisão *m*.

phenobarbitone UK [,fi:nəʊ'bɑ:bɪtəʊn], **phenobarbitol** US [,fi:nəʊ'bɑ:bɪtl] *n (U)* fenobarbital *m*.

phenomena [fɪ'nɒmɪnə] *pl* ⊳ **phenomenon**.

phenomenal [fɪ'nɒmɪnl] *adj* fenomenal.

phenomenon [fɪ'nɒmɪnən] (*pl* -mena) *n* fenômeno *m*.

phew [fju:] *excl* ufa!

phial ['faɪəl] *n* frasco *m*.

Philadelphia [,fɪlə'delfɪə] *n* Filadélfia *f*.

philanderer [fɪ'lændərə'] *n* galanteador *m*, sedutor *m*.

philanthropic [,fɪlən'θrɒpɪk] *adj* filantrópico(ca).

philanthropist [fɪ'lænθrəpɪst] *n* filantropo *m*.

philately [fɪ'lætəlɪ] *n (U)* filatelia *f*.

philharmonic [,fɪlɑ:'mɒnɪk] *adj* filarmônico(ca).

Philippine ['fɪlɪpi:n] *adj* filipino(na); **the ~ Islands** as (Ilhas) Filipinas.

◆ **Philippines** *npl*: **the ~ s** as Filipinas.

philistine [UK 'fɪlɪstaɪn, US 'fɪlɪsti:n] *n* filisteu *m*, -éia *f*.

Phillips® ['fɪlɪps] *comp*: **~ screw** parafuso *m* Phillips; **~ screwdriver** chave *f* Phillips.

philosopher [fɪ'lɒsəfə'] *n* filósofo *m*, -fa *f*.

philosophical [,fɪlə'sɒfɪkl] *adj* filosófico(ca).

philosophize, -ise [fɪ'lɒsəfaɪz] *vi* filosofar.
philosophy [fɪ'lɒsəfɪ] (*pl* -ies) *n* filosofia *f*.
phlegm [flem] *n (U)* fleuma *f*.
phlegmatic [fleg'mætɪk] *adj* fleumático(ca).
Phnom Penh [ˌnɒm'pen] *n* Phnom Penh.
phobia ['fəʊbjə] *n* fobia *f*; **to have a ~ about sthg** ter fobia a algo.
phoenix ['fiːnɪks] *n* fênix *f*.
phone [fəʊn] <> *n* telefone *m*; **to be on the ~** [speaking] estar no telefone; *UK* [connected to network] ter telefone. <> *comp* telefônico(ca). <> *vt* telefonar, ligar para. <> *vi* telefonar, ligar.
  ◆ **phone back** *vt sep* & *vi* ligar de volta.
  ◆ **phone up** *vt sep* & *vi* ligar.
phone book *n* lista *f* telefônica.
phone booth *n US* cabine *f* telefônica.
phone box *n UK* cabine *f* telefônica.
phone call *n* ligação *f*, chamada *f* telefônica; **to make a ~** fazer uma ligação.
phonecard ['fəʊnkaːd] *n* cartão *m* telefônico.
phone-in *n* RADIO, TV programa *para o qual as pessoas ligam e suas perguntas ou opiniões vão para o ar*.
phone line *n* -1. [wire] cabo *m* telefônico -2. [connection] linha *f* telefônica.
phone number *n* número *m* de telefone.
phone-tapping [-ˌtæpɪŋ] *n (U)* grampo *m (no telefone)*.
phonetics [fə'netɪks] *n (U)* fonética *f*.
phoney *UK*, **phony** *US* ['fəʊnɪ] (*compar* -ier, *superl* -iest, *pl* -ies) <> *adj* falso(sa). <> *n* farsante *mf*.
phoney war *n período entre o início da segunda guerra mundial e abril de 1940 em que houve pouca atividade militar entre a Alemanha e a Grã-Bretanha*.
phony *adj* & *n US* = **phoney**.
phosphate ['fɒsfeɪt] *n* fosfato *m*.
phosphorus ['fɒsfərəs] *n (U)* fósforo *m*.
photo ['fəʊtəʊ] *n* foto *f*; **to take a ~ (of sb/sthg)** tirar OR bater uma foto (de alguém/algo).
photo booth *n* cabine *f* de foto automática.
photocall ['fəʊtəʊkɔːl] *n* sessão *f* de fotos.
photocopier ['fəʊtəʊˌkɒpɪ] *n* fotocopiadora *f*.
photocopy ['fəʊtəʊˌkɒpɪ] (*pl* -ies, *pt* & *pp* -ied) <> *n* fotocópia *f*. <> *vt* fotocopiar.
photoelectric cell [ˌfəʊtəʊɪ'lektrɪk-] *n* célula *f* fotoelétrica.
photo finish *n* SPORT photo finish *f, decisão do vencedor de uma corrida através de fotografia*.
photofit® *n*: **~ (picture)** *retrato de alguém procurado pela polícia montado a partir de outras fotos ou feito com desenhos de diversas partes do rosto*.
photogenic [ˌfəʊtəʊ'dʒenɪk] *adj* fotogênico(ca).
photograph ['fəʊtəgraːf] <> *n* fotografia *f*; **to take a ~ (of sb/sthg)** tirar OR bater uma fotografia (de alguém/algo). <> *vt* fotografar.
photographer [fə'tɒgrəfəʳ] *n* fotógrafo *m*, -fa *f*.
photographic [ˌfəʊtə'græfɪk] *adj* fotográfico(ca).
photographic memory *n* memória *f* fotográfica.
photography [fə'tɒgrəfɪ] *n (U)* fotografia *f*.

photojournalism [ˌfəʊtəʊ'dʒɜːnəlɪzm] *n (U)* fotojornalismo *m*.
photon ['fəʊtɒn] *n* fóton *m*.
photo opportunity *n oportunidade, planejada ou acidental, que um político ou uma celebridade tem de ser fotografado em um contexto que o favorece*.
photosensitive [ˌfəʊtəʊ'sensɪtɪv] *adj* fotossensível.
Photostat® ['fəʊtəstæt] (*pt* & *pp* -ted, *cont* -ting) *n* cópia *f* fotostática.
  ◆ **photostat** *vt* tirar cópia fotostática.
photosynthesis [ˌfəʊtəʊ'sɪnθəsɪs] *n (U)* fotossíntese *f*.
photovoltaic cell [ˌfəʊtəʊvɒl'teɪk-] *n* célula *f* fotovoltaica.
phrasal verb ['freɪzl-] *n combinação de um verbo e de uma preposição ou um advérbio, que juntos possuem sentido único*.
phrase [freɪz] <> *n* -1. [part of sentence] frase *f* -2. [expression] expressão *f*. <> *vt* [express - letter] redigir; [- apology, refusal] expressar; **sorry, I've ~d that badly** desculpe, eu me expressei mal.
phrasebook ['freɪzbʊk] *n* manual *m* de conversação.
phraseology [ˌfreɪzɪ'ɒlədʒɪ] *n (U)* fraseologia *f*.
physical ['fɪzɪkl] <> *adj* físico(ca). <> *n* exame *m* médico.
physical chemistry *n (U)* físico-química *f*.
physical education *n (U)* SCH educação *f* física.
physical examination *n* exame *m* médico.
physical geography *n (U)* geografia *f* física.
physically ['fɪzɪklɪ] *adv* fisicamente.
physically handicapped <> *adj* portador(-ra) de deficiência física. <> *npl*: **the ~** os portadores de deficiência física.
physical science *n (U)* ciência *f* física.
physical training *n* treinamento *m* físico.
physician [fɪ'zɪʃn] *n* médico *m*, -ca *f*.
physicist ['fɪzɪsɪst] *n* físico *m*, -ca *f*.
physics ['fɪzɪks] *n (U)* física *f*.
physio ['fɪzɪəʊ] (*pl* -s) *n inf* -1. [physiotherapist] fisioterapeuta *mf* -2. [physiotherapy] fisioterapia *f*.
physiognomy [ˌfɪzɪ'ɒnəmɪ] (*pl* -ies) *n fml* fisionomia *f*.
physiology [ˌfɪzɪ'ɒlədʒɪ] *n* fisiologia *f*.
physiotherapist [ˌfɪzɪəʊ'θerəpɪst] *n* fisioterapeuta *mf*.
physiotherapy [ˌfɪzɪəʊ'θerəpɪ] *n (U)* fisioterapia *f*.
physique [fɪ'ziːk] *n* físico *m*.
pianist ['pɪənɪst] *n* pianista *mf*.
piano [pɪ'ænəʊ] (*pl* -s) *n* piano *m*; **to play the ~** tocar piano.
piano accordion *n* acordeão *m*.
Picardy ['pɪkədɪ] *n* Picardia *(região da França)*.
piccalilli [ˌpɪkə'lɪlɪ] *n (U)* molho quente feito com vegetais e servido com carne fria.
piccolo ['pɪkələʊ] (*pl* -s) *n* flautim *m*.
pick [pɪk] <> *n* -1. [tool] picareta *f* -2. [selection]: **to take one's ~** escolher o que quiser -3. [best]: **the ~ of** o melhor de. <> *vt* -1. [select, choose] escolher; **to ~ one's way across/through sthg** atravessar algo com cuidado -2. [gather] colher

- **3.** [remove] tirar - **4.** [nose]: **to ~ one's nose** pôr o dedo no nariz - **5.** [teeth]: **to ~ one's teeth** palitar os dentes - **6.** [provoke] provocar; **to ~ a fight (with sb)** arranjar briga (com alguém) - **7.** [lock] forçar *(com instrumento ou ferramenta).* <> *vi* escolher; **to ~ and choose** ser exigente *(na escolha).*

◆ **pick at** *vt fus* [food] beliscar.

◆ **pick on** *vt fus* meter-se com.

◆ **pick out** *vt sep* - **1.** [recognize] reconhecer - **2.** [select, choose] escolher.

◆ **pick up** <> *vt sep* - **1.** [lift up] pegar, apanhar; **to ~ up the pieces** *fig* juntar os pedaços, voltar à normalidade - **2.** [collect] pegar - **3.** [acquire] adquirir; **to ~ up speed** pegar velocidade - **4.** [subj: police]: **to ~ sb up for sthg** pegar alguém por algo - **5.** *inf* [start relationship with] dar em cima de - **6.** [detect, receive] captar - **7.** [resume] retomar. <> *vi* - **1.** [improve] melhorar - **2.** [resume] retomar.

pickaxe *UK*, **pickax** *US* ['pıkæks] *n* picareta *f.*

picker ['pıkə'] *n* colheiteiro *m*, -ra *f.*

picket ['pıkıt] <> *n* [at place of work - person] piqueteiro *m*, -ra *f*; [- instance of picketing] piquete *m.* <> *vt* fazer piquete em.

picketing ['pıkətıŋ] *n (U)* piquetes *mpl.*

picket line *n* piquete *m* de grevistas.

pickings ['pıkıŋz] *npl*: **easy/rich ~** dinheiro *m* fácil.

pickle ['pıkl] <> *n* - **1.** [food] picles *m inv* - **2.** *inf* [difficult situation]: **to be in a ~** estar numa enrascada. <> *vt* fazer conserva de.

pickled ['pıkld] *adj* em conserva.

pick-me-up *n inf* estimulante *m*, tônico *m.*

pickpocket ['pık,pɒkıt] *n* batedor *m*, -ra *f* de carteiras.

pick-up *n* - **1.** [of record player] pickup *f* - **2.** [truck] picape *f.*

pick-up truck *n* picape *f.*

picky ['pıkı] *(compar* -**ier**, *superl* -**iest***) adj* difícil de contentar, enjoado(da).

picnic ['pıknık] *(pt & pp* -**ked**, *cont* -**king***) <> *n* piquenique *m.* <> *vi* fazer piquenique.

picnicker ['pıknıkə'] *n* excursionista *mf.*

Pict [pıkt] *n*: **the ~s** os Pictos.

pictorial [pık'tɔ:rıəl] *adj* ilustrado(da).

picture ['pıktʃə'] <> *n* - **1.** [painting, drawing] quadro *m* - **2.** [photograph] fotografia *f* - **3.** [image] imagem *f* - **4.** [movie] filme *m* - **5.** [prospect] cenário *m* - **6.** [epitome]: **he's the ~ of misery** ele é a personificação da miséria - **7.** *phr*: **to get the ~** *inf* entender; **to put sb in the ~** colocar alguém a par; **to be in/out of the ~** estar por dentro/fora. <> *vt* - **1.** [in mind] imaginar - **2.** [in photo] fotografar - **3.** [in painting, drawing] retratar.

◆ **pictures** *npl UK*: **the ~s** o cinema.

picture book *n* livro *m* ilustrado.

picture rail *n* moldura *f* para pendurar quadros.

picturesque [,pıktʃə'resk] *adj* pitoresco(ca).

picture window *n* janela *f* panorâmica.

piddling ['pıdlıŋ] *adj inf pej* irrisório(ria).

pidgin ['pıdʒın] <> *n* pídgin *m.* <> *comp*: **~ English** inglês *m* macarrônico.

pie [paı] *n* - **1.** [sweet] torta *f* - **2.** [savoury] pastelão

m; **~ in the sky** castelos no ar.

piece [pi:s] *n* - **1.** [gen] pedaço *m*; **to be smashed to ~s** ser esmagado(da) em pedaços; **to fall to ~s** ficar em pedaços; **to pull** *OR* **tear sb/sthg to ~s** [criticize] arrasar com alguém/algo; **to take sthg to ~s** desmontar algo; **in ~s** em pedaços; **in one ~** [intact] sem um arranhão, intacto(ta); [unharmed] são e salvo, sã e salva; **to go to ~s** *fig* vir abaixo - **2.** [of food] pedaço *f* - **3.** *(with uncountable noun)* [gen] peça *f*; **~ of paper** folha *f* de papel; **~ of luck** golpe *m* de sorte; **~ of information** informação *f* - **4.** [of journalism] artigo *m* - **5.** [coin] moeda *f.*

◆ **piece together** *vt sep* reunir.

pièce de résistance [,pjesdərezıs'tãs] *(pl* **pièces de résistance** [,pjesdərezıs'tãs]*) n* [main attraction] atração *m* principal.

piecemeal ['pi:smi:l] <> *adj* pouco sistemático (ca). <> *adv* aos poucos, gradualmente.

piecework ['pi:swз:k] *n (U)* trabalho *m* por tarefas.

pie chart *n* gráfico *m* circular.

pied-à-terre *(pl* **pieds-à-terre***) n pequena casa ou apartamento para uso ocasional como segunda residência.*

pie-eyed *adj inf* bêbum.

pie plate *n US* prato *m* para torta.

pier [pıə'] *n* píer *m.*

pierce [pıəs] *vt* - **1.** [subj: bullet, needle] furar; **to have one's ears ~d** furar as orelhas - **2.** [subj: noise, light, pain] romper.

pierced [pıəst] *adj* furado(da).

piercing ['pıəsıŋ] <> *adj* - **1.** [sound, voice] agudo (da), estridente - **2.** [wind] cortante - **3.** [look, eyes] penetrante. <> *n* piercing *m.*

piety ['paıətı] *n* piedade *f.*

piffle ['pıfl] *n inf* asneira *f.*

piffling ['pıflıŋ] *adj inf* ridículo(la).

pig [pıg] *(pt & pp* -**ged**, *cont* -**ging***) n* - **1.** [animal] porco *m*, -ca *f* - **2.** *inf pej* [greedy eater] glutão *m*, -ona *f*; **to make a ~ of o.s.** empanturrar-se - **3.** *inf pej* [unkind person] grosseirão *m*, -rona *f.*

◆ **pig out** *vi inf* empanturrar-se.

pigeon ['pıdʒın] *(pl inv OR* -**s***) n* pomba *f.*

pigeon-chested [-'tʃestıd] *adj* de peito para frente.

pigeonhole ['pıdʒınhəʊl] <> *n* [compartment] escaninho *m.* <> *vt* [classify] classificar.

pigeon-toed [-'təʊd] *adj com pés voltados para dentro.*

piggish ['pıgıʃ] *adj inf* porcalhão(lhona).

piggy ['pıgı] *(compar* -**ier**, *superl* -**iest**, *pl* -**ies***) <> *adj* de porco. <> *n inf* [piglet] porquinho *m*, -nha *f.*

piggyback ['pıgıbæk] *n*: **to give sb a ~** levar alguém na garupa.

piggybank ['pıgıbæŋk] *n* porquinho *m (de moedas).*

pig-headed *adj* cabeçudo(da).

piglet ['pıglıt] *n* leitão *m*, -toa *f*, porquinho *m*, -nha *f.*

pigment ['pıgmənt] *n* pigmento *m.*

pigmentation [,pıgmən'teıʃn] *n* pigmentação *f.*

pigmy *(pl* -**ies***) n* = **pygmy.**

pigpen *n US* = **pigsty.**

pigskin ['pɪgskɪn] ⬥ n (U) couro m de porco. ⬥ comp de couro de porco.

pigsty ['pɪgstaɪ] (pl -ies), **pigpen** US ['pɪgpen] n chiqueiro m.

pigswill ['pɪgswɪl] n (U) lavagem f.

pigtail ['pɪgteɪl] n trança f.

pike [paɪk] (pl sense 1 only inv OR -s) n -1. [fish] lúcio m -2. [spear] pique m.

pikestaff ['paɪkstɑ:f] n: **plain as a** ~ claro como um dia de sol.

pilaster [pɪ'læstə'] n pilastra f.

pilchard ['pɪltʃəd] n sardinha f.

pile [paɪl] ⬥ n -1. [heap] monte m; **a** ~ OR ~**s of** sthg inf um monte de algo -2. [neat stack] pilha f -3. [of carpet, fabric] felpa f. ⬥ vt empilhar; **to be** ~**d with** sthg estar entulhado(da) de algo.
  ➤ **piles** npl MED hemorróidas fpl.
  ➤ **pile in** vi inf apinhar-se.
  ➤ **pile into** vt fus inf amontoar-se.
  ➤ **pile out** vi inf debandar; **to** ~ **out of** sthg debandar de algo.
  ➤ **pile up** ⬥ vt sep amontoar, empilhar. ⬥ vi acumular-se.

pile driver n bate-estaca m.

pile-up n engavetamento m.

pilfer ['pɪlfə'] ⬥ vt: **to** ~ sthg (from) furtar algo (de). ⬥ vi: **to** ~ (from) furtar (de), surrupiar (de).

pilgrim ['pɪlgrɪm] n peregrino m, -na f.

PILGRIM FATHERS

Assim é chamado o grupo de puritanos ingleses que, perseguido por suas crenças religiosas, embarcou para a América, em 1620, a bordo do navio Mayflower. Os Pilgrim Fathers fundaram a primeira colônia inglesa, onde hoje é o estado de Massachussetts. Durante o primeiro inverno que passaram no novo mundo, muitos morreram de fome. Mas, a partir do segundo ano na América, os nativos da região os ensinaram a plantar trigo e outras lavouras. Dessa forma, no outono, quando os colonos viram que tinham comida suficiente para sobreviver ao inverno, celebraram uma refeição de Ação de Graças com os nativos. Muitos anos depois, em 1863, o presidente Lincoln transformou o dia de Ação de Graças em feriado nacional, em comemoração ao sucesso daquela primeira colheita.

---

pilgrimage ['pɪlgrɪmɪdʒ] n peregrinação f.

pill [pɪl] n -1. MED pílula f -2. [contraceptive]: **the** ~ a pílula anticoncepcional; **to be on the** ~ tomar pílula (anticoncepcional).

pillage ['pɪlɪdʒ] ⬥ n (U) pilhagem f. ⬥ vt pilhar.

pillar ['pɪlə'] n -1. ARCHIT pilar m -2. fig [of community, church etc] bastião m; **to be a** ~ **of strength** ser uma fortaleza; **to be a** ~ **of the church** ser um bastião da igreja.

pillar box n UK caixa f coletora (do correio).

pillbox ['pɪlbɒks] n -1. [box for pills] caixa f de comprimidos -2. MIL casamata f.

pillion ['pɪljən] n assento m traseiro; **to ride** ~ ir na garupa.

pillock ['pɪlək] n UK inf imbecil.

pillory ['pɪlərɪ] (pl -ies, pt & pp -ied) ⬥ n [form of punishment] pelourinho m. ⬥ vt fig [ridicule]: **to be pilloried** ser ridicularizado(da).

pillow ['pɪləʊ] n -1. [for bed] travesseiro m -2. US [on sofa, chair] almofada f.

pillowcase ['pɪləʊkeɪs], **pillowslip** ['pɪləʊslɪp] n fronha f.

pilot ['paɪlət] ⬥ n piloto m. ⬥ comp [trial] piloto; ~ **project** projeto-piloto m. ⬥ vt -1. [gen] pilotar -2. [bill] pôr em prática -3. [scheme] aplicar.

pilot light, pilot burner n [on gas appliance] piloto m.

pilot scheme n projeto-piloto m.

pilot study n estudo m -piloto.

pimento [pɪ'mentəʊ] (pl inv OR -s) n pimentão m.

pimp [pɪmp] n inf cafetão m.

pimple ['pɪmpl] n espinha f.

pimply ['pɪmplɪ] (compar -ier, superl -iest) adj espinhento(ta), cheio (cheia) de espinhas.

pin [pɪn] (pt & pp -ned, cont -ning) ⬥ n -1. [for sewing] alfinete m; **to have** ~**s and needles** fig estar com formigamento; **to be on** ~**s and needles** US estar uma pilha -2. [drawing pin] percevejo m -3. [safety pin] alfinete m de segurança -4. [of plug, grenade] pino m -5. TECH pino m, cavilha f -6. US [brooch] broche m; [badge] bottom m -7. GOLF: **the** ~ a bandeira. ⬥ vt -1. [attach]: **to** ~ sthg **to** OR **on** sthg prender OR colocar algo em algo -2. [immobilize]: **to** ~ sb **against** OR **to** sthg prender alguém contra/em algo -3. [apportion]: **to** ~ sthg **on** sb botar a culpa de algo em alguém, culpar alguém de algo.
  ➤ **pin down** vt sep -1. [identify] determinar, identificar -2. [force to make a decision] obrigar a se decidir.
  ➤ **pin up** vt sep -1. [poster, list of results] afixar -2. [hem, hair] prender.

PIN [pɪn] (abbr of **personal identification number**) n senha f.

pinafore ['pɪnəfɔ:'] n -1. [apron] avental m -2. UK [dress] jardineira f.

pinball ['pɪnbɔ:l] n (U) fliperama f.

pinball machine n máquina f de fliperama.

pincers ['pɪnsəz] npl -1. [tool] torquês f -2. [front claws] pinças fpl.

pinch [pɪntʃ] ⬥ n -1. [nip] beliscão m; **to feel the** ~ apertar o cinto -2. [small quantity] pitada f. ⬥ vt -1. [nip] beliscar -2. inf [steal - money, clothes] passar a mão em; [- car] pegar.
  ➤ **at a pinch** UK, **in a pinch** US adv em último caso.

pinched [pɪntʃt] adj -1. [thin, pale] abatido(da); ~ **with cold/hunger** pálido(da) de frio/fome -2. [short of]: ~ **for** sthg escasso(sa) de algo.

pincushion ['pɪn,kʊʃn] n alfineteira f.

pine [paɪn] ⬥ n -1. [tree] pinheiro m -2. (U) [wood] pinho m. ⬥ comp [furniture] de pinho. ⬥ vi: **to** ~ **for** sb/sthg suspirar por alguém/algo.
  ➤ **pine away** vi consumir-se (de desgosto).

pineapple ['paɪnæpl] n abacaxi m.

pine cone n pinha f.

pine needle n agulha f de pinheiro.

pine tree n pinheiro m.

pinewood ['paɪnwʊd] n -1. [forest] pinheiral m -2. (U) [material] madeira f de pinho.

ping [pɪŋ] <> n tinido m. <> vi retinir.

Ping-Pong® [-pɒŋ] n (U) ping-pong m.

pinhole ['pɪnhəʊl] n buraquinho m.

pinion ['pɪnjən] <> n TECH pinhão m. <> vt imobilizar.

pink [pɪŋk] <> adj -1. [in colour] cor-de-rosa -2. [with embarrassment] vermelho(lha); **to turn ~** ficar vermelho(lha). <> n -1. [colour] rosa m -2. [flower] cravina f, cravo m.

pinkie ['pɪŋkɪ] n US & Scot minguinho m.

pinking scissors, pinking shears npl tesoura f de picotar.

pink pound UK, **pink dollar** n: **the ~** poder aquisitivo da comunidade gay.

pin money n (U) pequena quantia de dinheiro extra recebido (geralmente do marido) para despesas pessoais.

pinnacle ['pɪnəkl] n -1. fig [of career, success] auge m -2. [mountain peak] topo m -3. ARCHIT [spire] pináculo m.

pinny ['pɪnɪ] (pl -ies) n inf avental m.

pinpoint ['pɪnpɔɪnt] vt -1. [difficulty, cause] determinar, identificar -2. [position, target, leak] identificar.

pinprick ['pɪnprɪk] n -1. [mark, hole] pontinho m -2. fig [slight irritation] chateação f.

pin-striped [-ˌstraɪpt] adj riscado(da).

pint [paɪnt] n -1. UK [unit of measurement] quartilho m (0,568 litro) -2. US [unit of measurement] pint m (0,473 litro) -3. UK [beer] cerveja f.

pintable n UK máquina f de fliperama.

pint-size(d) adj inf minúsculo(la).

pin-up n pin-up f.

pioneer [ˌpaɪə'nɪəʳ] <> n -1. [first settler] pioneiro m, -ra f -2. [innovator] pioneiro m, -ra f <> vt lançar, ser pioneiro(na) de.

pioneering [ˌpaɪə'nɪərɪŋ] adj pioneiro(ra).

pious ['paɪəs] adj -1. [religious] piedoso(sa) -2. pej [sanctimonious] devoto(ta).

piously ['paɪəslɪ] adv -1. [religiously] piedosamente -2. pej [sanctimoniously] devotadamente.

pip [pɪp] n -1. [seed] semente f -2. UK [bleep] sinal m.

pipe [paɪp] <> n -1. [for gas, water] tubo m, cano m -2. [for smoking] cachimbo m -3. MUS flauta f. <> vt canalizar.

➡ **pipes** npl MUS [bagpipes] gaita f de foles.

➡ **pipe down** vi inf fechar a matraca.

➡ **pipe up** vi inf: **there was silence and then she ~d up with a suggestion** fez-se silêncio e então ela saiu com uma sugestão.

pipe cleaner n limpador m para cachimbo.

piped music [paɪpt-] n UK música f ambiente.

pipe dream n castelo m no ar, sonho m impossível.

pipeline ['paɪplaɪn] n -1. [for oil] oleoduto m -2. [for gas] gasoduto m; **to be in the ~** fig estar a caminho.

piper ['paɪpəʳ] n MUS tocador m, -ra f de gaita de foles.

piping hot ['paɪpɪŋ-] adj extremamente quente.

pipsqueak ['pɪpskwiːk] n pej coisa f insignificante.

piquant ['piːkənt] adj -1. [spicy] picante -2. [interesting] intrigante.

pique [piːk] n (U) ressentimento m; **a fit of ~** um ataque de despeito.

piracy ['paɪrəsɪ] n pirataria f.

piranha [pɪ'rɑːnə] n piranha f.

pirate ['paɪrət] <> adj [illegally copied] pirateado(da). <> n -1. [sailor] pirata m -2. [illegal copy] cópia f pirata. <> vt piratear.

pirate radio n UK rádio f pirata.

pirouette [ˌpɪru'et] <> n pirueta f. <> vi fazer pirueta.

Pisces ['paɪsiːz] n -1. [sign] peixes m -2. [person] pisciano(na); **I'm ~** sou de Peixes.

piss [pɪs] vulg <> n -1. [urine] mijo m; **to take the ~ out of sb/sthg** tirar um sarro de algo/alguém -2. [urination]: **to have a ~** dar uma mijada. <> vi -1. [urinate] mijar -2. [rain]: **it's ~ing with rain** está chovendo canivete.

➡ **piss down** vi UK vulg [rain]: **the rain was ~ing down** chovia a cântaros.

➡ **piss off** vulg <> vt sep encher o saco. <> vi UK ir à merda; **~ off!** vai à merda!

pissed [pɪst] adj vulg -1. UK [drunk] mamado(da) -2. US [annoyed] puto(ta) da cara.

pissed off adj vulg de saco cheio.

pistachio [pɪ'stɑːʃɪəʊ] (pl -s) n pistache m.

piste [piːst] n SKIING pista f.

pistol ['pɪstl] n pistola f.

piston ['pɪstən] n pistom m.

pit [pɪt] (pt & pp -ted, cont -ting) <> n -1. [large hole] cova f -2. [small, shallow hole] marca f -3. [for orchestra] fosso m da orquestra -4. [mine] mina f -5. [quarry] canteiro m -6. US [of fruit] caroço m -7. phr: **the ~ of one's stomach** a boca do estômago. <> vt: **to be ~ted against sb** ser incitado(da) contra alguém; **to ~ one's wits against sb/sthg** medir forças contra alguém/algo.

➡ **pits** npl -1. [in motor racing]: **the ~s** o box -2. inf [awful]: **the ~s** o fim da picada.

pit bull (terrier) n pit bull terrier m.

pitch [pɪtʃ] <> n -1. SPORT campo m -2. MUS tom m -3. (U) [level, degree] grau m -4. [street vendor's place] ponto m -5. inf [spiel]: **sales ~** papo m de vendedor -6. [of ship, aircraft] arfagem f -7. [of slope, roof] (grau m de) inclinação f -8. [throw] arremesso m -9. [tar] piche m. <> vt -1. [throw] arremessar; **to be ~ed into sthg** [person] ser posto(ta) em algo da noite para o dia -2. [set level of - price] estabelecer um preço para; [- speech] dar um tom a -3. [camp, tent] armar. <> vi -1. [fall over] despencar; **to ~ forward** precipitar-se para frente -2. [ship, plane] arfar.

➡ **pitch in** vi inf -1. [start work] botar a mão na massa -2. [lend a hand] colaborar.

pitch-black adj preto(ta) como carvão.

pitched [pɪtʃt] adj inclinado(da).

pitched battle [ˌpɪtʃt-] n batalha f campal.

pitcher ['pɪtʃəʳ] n US -1. [jug] jarro m -2. [in baseball] lançador m.

pitchfork ['pɪtʃfɔːk] n forcado m.

piteous ['pɪtɪəs] adj lastimável, comovente.

piteously ['pɪtɪəslɪ] adv de forma comovente.

pitfall ['pɪtfɔːl] n armadilha f, perigo m.

pith [pɪθ] n (U) parte branca da casca de uma fruta.

pithead ['pɪthed] *n* boca *f* da mina.

pith helmet *n* chapéu *m* de palha.

pithy ['pɪθɪ] (*compar* -ier, *superl* -iest) *adj* denso(sa), contundente.

pitiable ['pɪtɪəbll] *adj* -1. [arousing pity] lastimoso(sa) -2. [arousing contempt] lamentável.

pitiful ['pɪtɪfʊl] *adj* -1. [arousing pity] lastimável -2. [arousing contempt] lastimoso(sa).

pitifully ['pɪtɪfʊlɪ] *adv* -1. [arousing pity] comovedoramente -2. [arousing contempt]: **a ~ lame excuse** uma desculpa lamentável.

pitiless ['pɪtɪlɪs] *adj* impiedoso(sa).

pit stop *n* pit stop *m*.

pitta bread ['pɪtə-] *n (U)* pão *m* sírio; *tipo de pão oval sem levedura.*

pittance ['pɪtəns] *n* miséria *f.*

pitted ['pɪtɪd] *adj* -1. descaroçado(da) -2.: **~ with** sthg marcado(da) com algo.

pitter-patter ['pɪtə,pætə'] *n* ruído *m (de passos, de chuva).*

pituitary [pɪ'tjʊɪtrɪ] (*pl* -ies) *n*: **~ (gland)** glândula *f* pituitária.

pity ['pɪtɪ] (*pt & pp* -ied) <> *n* -1. [sympathy, sorrow] compaixão *f*; **to take** OR **have ~ on sb** ficar com pena de alguém -2. [shame] pena *f*; **what a ~!** que pena! <> *vt* sentir pena de.

pitying ['pɪtɪɪŋ] *adj* compassivo(va).

pivot ['pɪvət] <> *n* -1. TECH eixo *m* -2. *fig* [crux] centro *m*, eixo *m.* <> *vi*: **to ~ (on sthg)** girar (sobre algo).

pixel ['pɪksll] *n* COMPUT píxel *m.*

pixie, pixy ['pɪksɪ] (*pl* -ies) *n* duende *m.*

pizza ['pi:tsə] *n* pizza *f.*

pizzazz [pɪ'zæz] *n (U) inf* vitalidade *f*, energia *f.*

Pk (*abbr of* **park**) parque *m.*

pl. *abbr of* **please**.

P & L (*abbr of* **profit and loss**) *n* perdas *fpl* e lucros *mpl.*

PLA (*abbr of* **People's Liberation Army**) *n* forças armadas da República Popular da China.

placard ['plækɑ:dl] *n* cartaz *m.*

placate [plə'keɪtl] *vt* aplacar, acalmar.

placatory [plə'keɪtərɪ] *adj* apaziguante.

place [pleɪs] <> *n* -1. [gen] lugar *m*; **~ of birth** local de nascimento; **to put sb in their ~** colocar alguém em seu lugar; **to fall into ~** fazer sentido -2. [suitable occasion] momento *m* -3. [home] casa *f*; **decimal ~** MATH casa decimal -4. [post, vacancy] vaga *f* -5. [role, function] papel *m* -6. [rank] posição *f* -7. [instance]: **why didn't you say so in the first ~?** por que você não disse isso logo?; **in the first ~ ..., and in the second ~ ...** em primeiro lugar ..., e em segundo lugar ... -8. *phr*: **the market takes ~ every Sunday** a feira acontece todos os domingos; **the events that took ~ that day became infamous** os acontecimentos que tiveram lugar naquele dia tornaram-se notórios; **to take the ~ of sb/sthg** tomar o lugar de alguém/algo, substituir alguém/algo. <> *vt* -1. [position, put] colocar -2. [lay, apportion]: **to ~ blame on sb/sthg** colocar a culpa em alguém/algo; **to ~ emphasis on sb/sthg** dar ênfase a alguém/algo; **to ~ pressure on sb/sthg** exercer pressão sobre alguém/algo; **to**

~ responsibility on sb/sthg pôr a responsabilidade em alguém/algo -3. [identify] identificar -4. [make]: **to ~ an order** COMM fazer um pedido; **to ~ a bet** fazer uma aposta -5. [situate] situar; **how are we ~d for money?** como estamos de dinheiro? -6. [in race]: **to be ~d** classificar-se.

➡ **all over the place** *adv* por todo lado.

➡ **in place** *adv* -1. [in proper position] no lugar -2. [established, set up] estabelecido(da).

➡ **in place of** *prep*: **in ~ of me** em meu lugar.

➡ **out of place** *adv* -1. [in wrong position] fora do lugar -2. [unsuitable] fora de propósito.

placebo [plə'si:bəʊ] (*pl* -s OR -es) *n* placebo *m.*

place card *n* cartão *m* de reserva *(de mesa em jantar).*

place kick *n* tiro *m* livre *(com a bola colocada).*

place mat *n* toalha *f* de mesa individual.

placement ['pleɪsmənt] *n* -1. *(U)* [positioning] disposição *f* -2. [work experience] estágio *m.*

placement service *n* US serviço *m* de colocação profissional.

placenta [plə'sentə] (*pl* -s OR -tae [-ti:]) *n* placenta *f.*

place setting *n* jogo *m* de mesa para uma pessoa.

placid ['plæsɪd] *adj* -1. [even-tempered] plácido(da) -2. [peaceful] sereno(na).

placidly ['plæsɪdlɪ] *adv* calmamente.

plagiarism ['pleɪdʒərɪzm] *n (U)* plágio *m.*

plagiarist ['pleɪdʒərɪst] *n* plagiador *m*, -ra *f.*

plagiarize, -ise ['pleɪdʒəraɪz] *vt* plagiar.

plague [pleɪg] <> *n* praga *f*; **to avoid sb/sthg like the ~** fugir de alguém/algo como uma praga. <> *vt*: **to ~ sb with sthg** importunar alguém com algo; **to be ~d by sthg** ser/estar atormentado(da) por algo.

plaice [pleɪs] (*pl inv*) *n* linguado *m.*

plaid [plæd] *n (U)* tecido *m* em xadrez da Escócia.

Plaid Cymru [,plaɪd'kʌmrɪ] *n* UK POL Plaid Cymru *(partido nacionalista galês).*

plain [pleɪn] <> *adj* -1. [not patterned] liso(sa) -2. [simple, not fancy] simples; **~ yoghurt** iogurte *m* natural -3. [clear] claro(ra); **to make sthg ~ to sb** deixar algo claro para alguém -4. [blunt] direto (ta) -5. [absolute] absoluto(ta) -6. [not pretty] sem atrativos. <> *adv inf* [completely] claramente. <> *n* GEOGR planície *f.*

plain chocolate *n* UK chocolate *m* meio amargo.

plain-clothes *adj* à paisana.

plain flour *n* UK farinha *f* sem fermento.

plainly ['pleɪnlɪ] *adv* -1. [upset, angry] completamente -2. [remember, hear] claramente -3. [frankly] francamente, abertamente -4. [simply] de forma simples.

plain sailing *n (U)* caminho *m* livre.

plain-spoken *adj* franco(ca).

plaintiff ['pleɪntɪf] *n* querelante *mf.*

plaintive ['pleɪntɪv] *adj* triste, melancólico(ca).

plait [plæt] <> *n* trança *f.* <> *vt* trançar.

plan [plæn] (*pt & pp* -ned, *cont* -ning) <> *n* -1. [strategy] plano *m*; **to go according to ~** sair de acordo com o planejado -2. [outline] esboço *m* -3. [diagram, map - of garden, building] planta *f*; [- of inside of

a machine] esquema *m* de montagem. <> *vt* **-1.** [organize] planejar **-2.** [intend] pretender; **to ~ to do sthg** pensar em fazer algo **-3.** [design, devise] projetar. <> *vi* fazer planos; **to ~ for sthg** fazer planos para algo.
 ➡ **plans** *npl* planos *mpl*; **to have ~s for** ter planos para.
 ➡ **plan on** *vt fus*: **to ~ on doing sthg** pretender fazer algo.
 ➡ **plan out** *vt sep* traçar.
plane [pleɪn] <> *adj* plano(na). <> *n* **-1.** [aircraft] avião *m* **-2.** GEOM plano *m* **-3.** *fig* [level] patamar *m* **-4.** [tool] plaina *f* **-5.** [tree] plátano *m.* <> *vt* aplainar.
planet [ˈplænɪt] *n* planeta *f.*
planetarium [ˌplænɪˈteərɪəm] (*pl* **-riums** OR **-ria** [-rɪə]) *n* planetário *m.*
planetary [ˈplænɪtrɪ] *adj* planetário(ria).
plane tree *n* plátano *m.*
plank [plæŋk] *n* **-1.** [piece of wood] tábua *f* **-2.** POL [main policy] item *m.*
plankton [ˈplæŋktən] *n (U)* plâncton *m.*
planned [plænd] *adj* planejado(da).
planner [ˈplænəʳ] *n* planejador *m*, -ra *f*; **town ~** urbanista *mf.*
planning [ˈplænɪŋ] *n* planejamento *m.*
planning permission *n (U)* autorização *f* para construir.
plan of action *n* plano *m* de ação.
plant [plɑːnt] <> *n* **-1.** BOT planta *f* **-2.** [factory] fábrica *f*; **nuclear ~** usina *f* nuclear **-3.** *(U)* [heavy machinery] maquinários *mpl.* <> *vt* **-1.** [seed, tree] plantar; [field, garden] semear; **to ~ sthg with sthg** semear algo com algo **-2.** [blow, kiss] dar **-3.** [place oneself] plantar-se; [- object] fincar **-4.** [offload] despachar **-5.** [spy] infiltrar **-6.** [bomb, microphone] colocar secretamente; **to ~ sthg on sb** esconder algo em alguém **-7.** [thought, idea] incutir.
 ➡ **plant out** *vt sep* transplantar.
plantain [ˈplæntɪn] *n* banana-da-terra *f.*
plantation [plænˈteɪʃn] *n* plantação *f.*
planter [ˈplɑːntəʳ] *n* **-1.** [farmer] fazendeiro *m*, -ra *f* **-2.** [container] jardineira *f.*
plant pot *n* vaso *m* para plantas.
plaque [plɑːk] *n* placa *f.*
plasma [ˈplæzmə] *n (U)* plasma *m.*
plaster [ˈplɑːstəʳ] <> *n* **-1.** [gen] gesso *m*; **in ~** engessado(da) **-2.** UK [for cut]: **(sticking) ~** esparadrapo *m*, Band-Aid® *m.* <> *vt* **-1.** [put plaster on] revestir com gesso **-2.** [cover]: **to ~ sthg with sthg** cobrir algo com algo **-3.** [make stick] fixar.
plasterboard [ˈplɑːstəbɔːd] *n (U)* chapa *f* de gesso.
plaster cast *n* molde *m* de gesso.
plastered [ˈplɑːstəd] *adj inf* [drunk] de porre.
plasterer [ˈplɑːstərəʳ] *n* rebocador *m*, -ra *f.*
plastering [ˈplɑːstərɪŋ] *n (U)* ato *m* de rebocar.
plaster of paris *n* gesso *m* de Paris.
plastic [ˈplæstɪk] <> *adj* de plástico. <> *n* **-1.** [material] plástico *m* **-2.** *inf* [credit cards] cartão *m* (de crédito).
plastic bullet *n* bala *f* de borracha.
plastic explosive *n* explosivo *m* plástico.

Plasticine® UK [ˈplæstɪsiːn], **play dough** US *n (U)* plasticina *f.*
plastic money *n* cartões *mpl* de crédito.
plastic surgeon *n* cirurgião *m* plástico, cirurgiã *f* plástica.
plastic surgery *n (U)* cirurgia *f* plástica.
plastic wrap *n US* filme *m* de PVC transparente.
plate [pleɪt] <> *n* **-1.** [gen] prato *m*; **to have a lot on one's ~** ter muito com o que se preocupar; **to be handed sthg on a ~** receber algo de mão beijada **-2.** [on wall, door or surgical] placa *f* **-3.** *(U)* [gold, silver etc] baixela *f* **-4.** [photograph] chapa *f* **-5.** [in dentistry] dentadura *f* **-6.** [in baseball] base *f.* <> *vt*: **to be ~d (with sthg)** ser banhado (a algo).
Plate [pleɪt] *n*: **the River ~** o Rio da Prata.
plateau [ˈplætəʊ] (*pl*-s OR -x [-z]) *n* **-1.** GEOGR planalto *m* **-2.** *fig* [steady level] nível *m* estável.
plateful [ˈpleɪtfʊl] *n* pratada *f.*
plate-glass *adj* de vidro laminado.
platelet [ˈpleɪtlɪt] *n* plaqueta *f.*
plate rack *n* escorredor *m* de pratos.
platform [ˈplætfɔːm] *n* **-1.** [gen] plataforma *f* **-2.** [for speaker, performer] palanque *m* **-3.** *fig* [arena] veículo *m.*
platform game *n* COMPUT jogo *m* de obstáculos.
platform ticket *n* UK bilhete *m* de plataforma.
platinum [ˈplætɪnəm] <> *adj* platinado(da). <> *n* platina *f.* <> *comp* de platina.
platinum blonde *n* loira *f* platinada.
platitude [ˈplætɪtjuːd] *n* lugar-comum *m*, chavão *m.*
platonic [pləˈtɒnɪk] *adj* platônico(ca).
platoon [pləˈtuːn] *n* pelotão *m.*
platter [ˈplætəʳ] *n* travessa *f.*
platypus [ˈplætɪpəs] (*pl* -es) *n* ornitorrinco *m.*
plaudits [ˈplɔːdɪts] *npl* aclamações *fpl*, aplausos *mpl.*
plausible [ˈplɔːzəbl] *adj* [reason, excuse] plausível; [person] convincente.
plausibly [ˈplɔːzəblɪ] *adv* plausivelmente, convincentemente.
play [pleɪ] <> *n* **-1.** *(U)* [amusement] brincadeira *f*; **children at ~** crianças brincando **-2.** [piece of drama] peça *f* **-3.** SPORT: **in/out of ~** em/fora de jogo **-4.** [consideration]: **to come into ~** *fig* entrar em jogo **-5.** [pun]: **~ on words** trocadilho *m* **-6.** TECH folga *f.* <> *vt* **-1.** [gen] jogar; **to ~ hide-and-seek** brincar de esconde-esconde **-2.** [opposing player or team] jogar contra **-3.** [joke, trick] pregar **-4.** [perform] desempenhar, representar; **to ~ a part** OR **role in sthg** *fig* desempenhar um papel em algo **-5.** [MUS - instrument, CD] tocar; [- tune] executar **-6.** [pretend to be] fingir **-7.** *phr*: **to ~ it cool** agir com calma. <> *vi* **-1.** [amuse o.s.] brincar; **to ~ with sb/sthg** brincar com alguém/algo **-2.** SPORT jogar; **to ~ for sb** jogar para alguém; **to ~ against sb** jogar contra alguém **-3.** PERFORM: **to ~ in sthg** atuar em algo **-4.** [music] tocar **-5.** *literary* [breeze, sun, light] brincar com **-6.** *phr*: **to ~ safe** não se arriscar.
 ➡ **play along** *vi*: **to ~ along (with sb)** fazer o jogo (de alguém).
 ➡ **play at** *vt fus* fazer de conta que.
 ➡ **play back** *vt sep* colocar de novo.

play down vt sep menosprezar.

play off ⬦ vt sep: **to ~ sb/sthg off against sb/sthg** colocar alguém/algo contra alguém/algo. ⬦ vi SPORT enfrentar-se novamente (para obter um desempate).

play (up)on vt fus tirar proveito de.

play up ⬦ vt sep enfatizar. ⬦ vi **-1.** [cause problems] dar trabalho **-2.** [misbehave] descomportar-se.

playable ['pleɪəbll] adj em condições de jogo.

play-act vi fazer fita.

playbill ['pleɪbɪll] n cartaz m de lançamento.

playboy ['pleɪbɔɪl] n playboy m.

play dough n US = Plasticine®.

player ['pleɪə'] n **-1.** [of game, sport] jogador m, -ra f **-2.** MUS músico m, -ca f; **guitar ~** guitarrista mf; **saxophone ~** saxofonista mf **-3.** dated & THEATRE ator m, atriz f.

playfellow ['pleɪˌfeləʊl] n amigo m, -ga f de infância.

playful ['pleɪfʊll] adj **-1.** [good-natured] divertido(da) **-2.** [frisky] brincalhão(lhona).

playfully ['pleɪfʊlɪl] adv divertidamente.

playgoer ['pleɪˌɡəʊə'] n freqüentador m, -ra f de teatro.

playground ['pleɪɡraʊndl] n [at school] pátio m de recreio; [in park] parque m de diversões.

playgroup ['pleɪɡru:pl] n jardim-de-infância m.

playhouse ['pleɪhaʊs, pl -haʊzɪz] n **-1.** [toy house] casa f de brinquedo **-2.** dated [theatre] teatro m.

playing card ['pleɪɪŋ-] n carta f de baralho.

playing field ['pleɪɪŋ-] n quadra f de esportes.

playlist ['pleɪlɪstl] n UK lista f de músicas (para tocar num programa de rádio).

playmate ['pleɪmeɪtl] n amigo m, -ga f de infância.

play-off n partida f de desempate.

playpen ['pleɪpenl] n cercadinho m para crianças, chiqueirinho m.

playroom ['pleɪrʊml] n sala f de recreação.

playschool ['pleɪsku:ll] n jardim-de-infância m.

plaything ['pleɪθɪŋl] n **-1.** [toy] brinquedo m **-2.** fig [person] joguete m.

playtime ['pleɪtaɪml] n (U) (hora f do) recreio m.

playwright ['pleɪraɪtl] n dramaturgo m, -ga f.

plaza ['plɑːzəl] n **-1.** [public square] praça f **-2.** [building complex] complexo m.

plc (abbr of public limited company) UK companhia f pública limitada.

plea [pliː] n **-1.** [appeal] apelo m **-2.** JUR contestação f.

plea bargaining n (U) acordo segundo o qual o réu se declara culpado por uma acusação menor e o promotor público, em troca, o inocenta de uma acusação mais grave.

plead [pliːd] (pt & pp -ed OR pled) ⬦ vt **-1.** JUR defender; **to ~ insanity** alegar insanidade mental; **to ~ guilty** declarar culpado(da) **-2.** [give as excuse] alegar. ⬦ vi **-1.** [beg] implorar; **to ~ with sb to do sthg** implorar a alguém que faça algo; **to ~ for sthg** implorar algo **-2.** JUR responder a uma acusação.

pleading ['pliːdɪŋl] ⬦ adj de súplica. ⬦ n súplica f.

pleasant ['plezntl] adj agradável.

pleasantly ['plezntlɪl] adv agradavelmente.

pleasantry ['plezntrɪl] (pl -ies) n: **to exchange pleasantries** trocar amabilidades.

please [pliːzl] ⬦ adv por favor. ⬦ vt agradar; **to ~ o.s.** fazer o que se deseja; **~ yourself!** como queira! ⬦ vi **-1.** [give satisfaction] agradar **-2.** [choose]: **to do as one ~s** fazer como quiser; **if you ~** se quiser.

pleased [pliːzd] adj contente, feliz; **to be ~ about sthg** estar satisfeito(ta) com algo; **to be ~ with sb/ sthg** estar satisfeito(ta) com alguém/algo; **~ to meet you!** prazer em conhecê-lo(-la)!

pleasing ['pliːzɪŋl] adj agradável.

pleasingly ['pliːzɪŋlɪl] adv agradavelmente.

pleasurable ['pleʒərəbll] adj agradável.

pleasure ['pleʒə'] n **-1.** (U) [feeling of happiness] alegria f; **with ~** com (muito) prazer **-2.** [enjoyment] prazer m; **it's a ~** OR **my ~!** é um prazer!, não tem de quê!

pleat [pliːt] ⬦ n prega f. ⬦ vt fazer prega em.

pleated ['pliːtɪdl] adj pregueado(da).

plebeian [plə'biːanl] adj pej plebeu(béia).

plebiscite ['plebɪsaɪtl] n plebiscito m.

plectrum ['plektrəml] (pl -s) n palheta f.

pled [pledl] pt & pp ⬦ **plead**.

pledge [pledʒl] ⬦ n **-1.** [promise] promessa f **-2.** [token] símbolo m **-3.** [as a security] garantia f. ⬦ vt **-1.** [promise to provide] prometer **-2.** [commit]: **to be ~d to sthg** estar comprometido(da) com algo; **to ~ o.s. to sthg** comprometer-se com algo **-3.** [pawn] penhorar.

plenary session ['pliːnərɪ-] n sessão f plenária.

plentiful ['plentɪfʊll] adj abundante.

plenty ['plentɪl] ⬦ n (U) fartura f. ⬦ pron bastante; **~ of** bastante; **~ of time** bastante tempo; **~ of reasons** inúmeras razões. ⬦ adv US [very] muito.

plethora ['pleθərəl] n excesso m.

pleurisy ['plʊərəsɪl] n (U) pleurisia f.

Plexiglas® ['pleksɪɡlɑːsl] n (U) US Plexiglas® m.

pliable ['plaɪəbll], **pliant** ['plaɪəntl] adj **-1.** [supple] flexível **-2.** [adaptable] dócil.

pliers ['plaɪəzl] npl alicate m.

plight [plaɪtl] n péssima situação f; **in a ~** em apuros.

plimsoll ['plɪmsəll] n UK calçados mpl para prática de esportes.

Plimsoll line n linha f de flutuação.

plinth [plɪnθl] n plinto m.

PLO (abbr of Palestine Liberation Organization) n OLP f.

plod [plɒdl] (pt & pp -ded, cont -ding) vi **-1.** [walk slowly] arrastar-se **-2.** [work slowly] trabalhar vagarosamente.

plodder ['plɒdə'] n pej trabalhador m lerdo e pouco criativo.

plonk [plɒŋkl] n UK inf vinho m fajuto.

plonk down vt sep inf deixar cair.

plop [plɒpl] (pt & pp -ped, cont -ping) ⬦ n chape m. ⬦ vi estatelar-se.

plot [plɒtl] (pt & pp -ted, cont -ting) ⬦ n **-1.** [conspiracy] compô m; **the ~ thickens** a coisa está se complicando **-2.** [story] enredo m, trama f **-3.** [of land] lote *m* **-4.** *US* [house plan] planta *f.* ◇ *vt* **-1.** [conspire] tramar; **to ~ to do sthg** tramar para fazer algo **-2.** [chart] traçar **-3.** MATH traçar, plotar. ◇ *vi* conspirar; **to ~ against sb** conspirar contra alguém.

plotter ['plɒtə'] *n* [schemer] conspirador *m*, -ra *f.*

plough *UK*, **plow** *US* [plaʊ] ◇ *n* arado *m.* ◇ *vt* **-1.** AGR arar, lavrar **-2.** [invest]: **to ~ money into sthg** investir muito dinheiro em algo. ◇ *vi*: **to ~ into sthg** colidir contra algo.
➤ **plough on** *vi* prosseguir.
➤ **plough up** *vt sep* arar.

ploughman's ['plaʊmənz] (*pl inv*) *n UK*: **~ (lunch)** refeição que consiste em pão, queijo, cebola e picles.

ploughshare *UK*, **plowshare** *US* ['plaʊʃeə'] ·*n* relha *f* de arado.

plow etc *n* & *vt US* = **plough etc.**

ploy [plɔɪ] *n* estratagema *f.*

PLR (*abbr of* **Public Lending Right**) *n valor que o autor recebe na Grã-Bretanha quando um livro seu é retirado nas bibliotecas públicas.*

pls (*abbr of* **please**) por favor.

pluck [plʌk] ◇ *vt* **-1.** [flower, fruit] colher **-2.** [pull] apanhar; **the helicopter ~ed the survivors off the ship** o helicóptero resgatou os sobreviventes do navio **-3.** [chicken] depenar **-4.** [eyebrows] depilar **-5.** [musical instrument] dedilhar. ◇ *n* (*U*) *dated* [courage] garra *f.*
➤ **pluck up** *vt fus*: **to ~ up the courage to do sthg** criar coragem para fazer algo.

plucky ['plʌkɪ] (*compar* -**ier**, *superl* -**iest**) *adj dated* valente.

plug [plʌg] (*pt* & *pp* -**ged**, *cont* -**ging**) ◇ *n* **-1.** ELEC tomada *f*; [socket] plugue *m* **-2.** [for bath or sink] tampa *f*, válvula *f* **-3.** *inf* [in advertising] lance *m* de marketing. ◇ *vt* **-1.** [block] tampar **-2.** *inf* [advertise] fazer propaganda de.
➤ **plug in** *vt sep* ligar.

plughole ['plʌghəʊl] *n* ralo *m.*

plum [plʌm] ◇ *adj* **-1.** [colour] da cor de ameixa **-2.** [choice]: **a ~ job** uma jóia de emprego. ◇ *n* **-1.** [fruit] ameixa *m* **-2.** [colour] cor *m* de ameixa.

plumage ['plu:mɪdʒ] *n* (*U*) plumagem *f.*

plumb [plʌm] ◇ *adv* **-1.** *UK* [exactly] exatamente **-2.** *US* [completely] totalmente. ◇ *vt*: **to ~ the depths of sthg** atingir o auge de algo.
➤ **plumb in** *vt sep UK* instalar.

plumber ['plʌmə'] *n* encanador *m*, -ra *f.*

plumbing ['plʌmɪŋ] *n* (*U*) **-1.** [fittings] encanamento *m* **-2.** [work] trabalho *m* do encanador.

plumb line *n* prumo *m.*

plume [plu:m] *n* **-1.** [on bird] pluma *f* **-2.** [on hat, helmet] penacho *m* **-3.** [column]: **a ~ of smoke** um penacho de fumaça.

plummet ['plʌmɪt] *vi* **-1.** [dive] mergulhar (*em direção ao solo*) **-2.** [decrease rapidly] despencar.

plummy ['plʌmɪ] (*compar* -**ier**, *superl* -**iest**) *adj UK inf pej* afetado(da).

plump [plʌmp] ◇ *adj* roliço(ça). ◇ *vi*: **to ~ for sthg** optar por algo.
➤ **plump up** *vt sep* afofar.

plum pudding *n* pudim *m* de passas.

plum tree *n* ameixeira *f.*

plunder ['plʌndə'] ◇ *n* **-1.** [pillaging] pilhagem *f* **-2.** [booty] saque *m.* ◇ *vt* saquear.

plunge [plʌndʒ] ◇ *n* **-1.** [rapid decrease] caída *f* **-2.** [dive] mergulho; **to take the ~** mergulhar de cabeça, dar um passo decisivo. ◇ *vt* **-1.** [immerse]: **to ~ sthg into sthg** mergulhar algo em algo **-2.** *fig* [thrust]: **to ~ sthg into sthg** enfiar algo em algo; **the room was ~d into darkness** a sala mergulhou na escuridão. ◇ *vi* **-1.** [dive, throw o.s.] mergulhar **-2.** [decrease rapidly] despencar.

plunger ['plʌndʒə'] *n* desentupidor *m.*

plunging ['plʌndʒɪŋ] *adj* profundo(da).

pluperfect [,plu:'pɜ:fɪkt] *n*: **the ~ (tense)** o (tempo) mais-que-perfeito.

plural ['plʊərəl] ◇ *adj* plural. ◇ *n* plural *m.*

pluralistic [,plʊərə'lɪstɪk] *adj* pluralista.

plurality [plʊ'rælətɪ] *n* **-1.** [large number]: **a ~ of** uma pluralidade de **-2.** *US* [majority] maioria *f.*

plus [plʌs] (*pl* -**es** *OR* -**ses**) ◇ *adj* mais; **thirty-five ~** trinta e cinco ou mais. ◇ *n* **-1.** MATH sinal *m* de adição, sinal *m* de mais **-2.** *inf* [bonus] vantagem *f.* ◇ *prep* mais. ◇ *conj* [moreover] além disso.

plus fours *npl* calças *fpl* de golfe/de caça.

plush [plʌʃ] *adj* suntuoso(sa).

plus sign *n* sinal *m* de mais.

Pluto ['plu:təʊ] *n* Plutão.

plutonium [plu:'təʊnɪəm] *n* (*U*) plutônio *m.*

ply [plaɪ] (*pt* & *pp* **plied**) ◇ *n* espessura. ◇ *vt* **-1.** [work] trabalhar em **-2.** [supply, provide]: **to ~ sb with sthg** prover alguém com algo **-3.** [travel] navegar em. ◇ *vi* [travel] navegar em.

-ply *adj* de espessura.

plywood ['plaɪwʊd] *n* (*U*) compensado *m.*

p.m., pm (*abbr of* **post meridiem**): **at three ~** às três da tarde.

PM (*abbr of* **prime minister**) *n* primeiro-ministro *m*, primeira-ministra *f.*

PMS (*abbr of* **premenstrual syndrome**) *n* SPM *f.*

PMT (*abbr of* **premenstrual tension**) *n* TPM *f.*

pneumatic [nju:'mætɪk] *adj* **-1.** [air-powered] pneumático(ca) **-2.** [air-filled] de ar.

pneumatic drill *n* perfuratriz *f.*

pneumonia [nju:'məʊnjə] *n* (*U*) pneumonia *f.*

Po *n*: **the (River) ~** o (Rio) Pó.

PO *n* **-1.** (*abbr of* **Post Office**) correio *m* **-2.** (*abbr of* **postal order**) vale *m* postal.

poach [pəʊtʃ] ◇ *vt* **-1.** [hunt illegally] caçar ilegalmente **-2.** [copy] plagiar **-3.** [CULIN - salmon] escaldar; [- egg] escalfar. ◇ *vi* caçar ilegalmente.

poacher ['pəʊtʃə'] *n* **-1.** [person] caçador *m* furtivo, caçadora *f* furtiva **-2.** CULIN panela *f* para cozinhar ovos.

poaching ['pəʊtʃɪŋ] *n* (*U*) caça *f* ilegal.

PO Box (*abbr of* **Post Office Box**) *n* caixa *f* postal.

pocket ['pɒkɪt] ◇ *n* **-1.** [in clothes] bolso *m*; **to live in each other's ~s** estar sempre juntos(tas); **the deal left us £10 out of ~** o negócio nos deu um prejuízo de £10; **to pick sb's ~** roubar do bolso de alguém **-2.** [in car door etc] porta-mapas *m* **-3.** [small area] foco *m* **-4.** [of snooker, pool table] caçapa *f.* ◇ *adj* [pocket-sized] de bolso. ◇ *vt* **-1.** [place in pocket] pôr no bolso -**2**. [steal] embolsar -**3**. [in snooker, pool] encaçapar.

pocketbook [ˈpɒkɪtbʊk] n -**1**. [notebook] livro m de bolso -**2**. US [handbag] carteira f.

pocketbook computer n computador m de bolso.

pocket calculator n calculadora f de bolso.

pocketful [ˈpɒkɪtfʊl] n bolso m cheio.

pocket-handkerchief n lenço m de bolso.

pocketknife [ˈpɒkɪtnaɪf] (pl **-knives** [-naɪvz]) n canivete m.

pocket money n (U) mesada m.

pocket-size(d) adj de bolso.

pockmark [ˈpɒkmɑːk] n sinal m de varíola.

pod [pɒd] n -**1**. [of plants] vagem f -**2**. [of spacecraft] módulo m.

podgy [ˈpɒdʒɪ] (compar **-ier**, superl **-iest**) adj inf atarracado(da).

podiatrist [pəˈdaɪətrɪst] n US podiatra mf.

podium [ˈpəʊdɪəm] (pl **-diums** OR **-dia** [-dɪə]) n pódio m.

poem [ˈpəʊɪm] n poema f.

poet [ˈpəʊɪt] n poeta mf, poetisa f.

poetic [pəʊˈetɪk] adj poético(ca).

poetic justice n (U) justiça f poética.

poet laureate n poeta mf laureado, poetisa f laureada.

poetry [ˈpəʊɪtrɪ] n (U) -**1**. [poems] poesia f -**2**. fig [beauty] beleza f.

pogo stick n pula-pula m.

pogrom [ˈpɒgrəm] n massacre m organizado (de um grupo étnico em particular).

poignancy [ˈpɔɪnjənsɪ] n (U) comoção f.

poignant [ˈpɔɪnjənt] adj comovente.

poinsettia [pɔɪnˈsetɪə] n poinsétia f.

point [pɔɪnt] ⬦ n -**1**. [gen] ponto m; **at this ~ in time** neste momento; **~ of no return** ponto sem volta; **to have a ~** ter razão; **to make a ~** fazer uma observação; **to make one's ~** dar sua opinião; **a sore ~** questão dolorosa -**2**. [tip] ponta f -**3**. [essence, heart] parte f essencial; **to get** OR **come to the ~** ir ao ponto principal; **beside the ~** irrelevante; **to the ~** objetivo(va) -**4**. [feature, characteristic] característica f -**5**. [purpose] propósito m, razão f -**6**. [of compass] ponto m cardeal -**7**. UK ELEC ponto m -**8**. US [full stop] ponto m final -**9**. phr: **to make a ~ of doing sthg** fazer questão de fazer algo. ⬦ vt: **to ~ sthg (at sb/sthg)** apontar algo (para alguém/algo); **to ~ the way (to sthg)** mostrar a direção (para algo). ⬦ vi apontar; **to ~ at sb/sthg**, **to ~ to sb/sthg** apontar para alguém/algo.

➡ **points** npl UK RAIL pontos mpl.

➡ **up to a point** adv até certo ponto.

➡ **on the point of** prep prestes a.

➡ **point out** vt sep -**1**. [indicate] indicar -**2**. [call attention to] salientar.

point-blank ⬦ adj -**1**. [direct] categórico(ca) -**2**. [close-range] à queima-roupa. ⬦ adv -**1**. [directly] categoricamente -**2**. [at close range] à queima-roupa.

point duty n (U) UK serviço m de controle de trânsito.

pointed [ˈpɔɪntɪd] adj -**1**. [sharp] pontiagudo(da) -**2**. [meaningful] sugestivo(va).

pointedly [ˈpɔɪntɪdlɪ] adv sugestivamente.

pointer [ˈpɔɪntəʳ] n -**1**. [tip, hint] dica f -**2**. [needle on dial] agulha f -**3**. [stick] indicador m -**4**. [dog] pointer m -**5**. COMPUT ponteiro m.

pointing [ˈpɔɪntɪŋ] n (U) rejuntamento m.

pointless [ˈpɔɪntlɪs] adj inútil.

point of order (pl **points of order**) n questão f de ordem.

point of sale (pl **points of sale**) n COMM ponto m de venda.

point of view (pl **points of view**) n ponto m de vista.

point-to-point n UK corrida de cavalos que atravessa uma região, sinalizada com banderinhas.

poise [pɔɪz] n (U) compostura f.

poised [pɔɪzd] adj -**1**. [ready] pronto(ta), preparado(da); **to be ~ to do sthg** estar pronto(ta) para fazer algo; **to be ~ for sthg** estar pronto(ta) para algo -**2**. [calm and dignified] equilibrado(da).

poison [ˈpɔɪzn] ⬦ n veneno m. ⬦ vt -**1**. [gen] envenenar -**2**. [pollute] poluir -**3**. fig [spoil, corrupt] corromper.

poisoning [ˈpɔɪzniŋ] n (U) envenenamento m, intoxicação f.

poisonous [ˈpɔɪznəs] adj -**1**. [gas, chemical] tóxico(ca) -**2**. [snake, mushroom, plant] venenoso(sa) -**3**. fig [corrupting] pernicioso(sa).

poison-pen letter n carta f anônima.

poke [pəʊk] ⬦ n remexida f. ⬦ vt -**1**. [prod, jab] remexer, cutucar -**2**. [stick, thrust] enfiar em -**3**. [fire] atiçar, remexer. ⬦ vi projetar-se; **his head ~d round the corner** a cabeça dele apareceu na esquina.

➡ **poke about, poke around** vi inf escarafunchar.

➡ **poke at** vt fus: **he ~d at my eye with his finger** ele cutucou meu olho com seu dedo.

poker [ˈpəʊkəʳ] n -**1**. [game] pôquer m -**2**. [for fire] atiçador m.

poker-faced [-ˌfeɪst] adj de rosto inexpressivo.

poky [ˈpəʊkɪ] (compar **-ier**, superl **-iest**) adj pej apertado(da).

Poland [ˈpəʊlənd] n Polônia f; **in ~** na Polônia.

polar [ˈpəʊləʳ] adj GEOGR polar.

polar bear n urso m polar.

polarity [pəʊˈlærətɪ] n polaridade f.

polarization [ˌpəʊləraɪˈzeɪʃn] n (U) polarização f.

polarize, -ise [ˈpəʊləraɪz] vt polarizar.

Polaroid® [ˈpəʊlərɔɪd] n polaróide® f.

Polaroids® [ˈpəʊlərɔɪdz] npl [sunglasses] óculos mpl de sol (Polaroid).

pole [pəʊl] n -**1**. [gen] pólo m; **to be ~s apart** ser totalmente diferente(s) -**2**. [rod, post] poste m.

Pole [pəʊl] n polonês m, -esa f.

poleaxe [ˈpəʊlæks] vt nocautear.

poleaxed [ˈpəʊlækst] adj atordoado(da).

polecat [ˈpəʊlkæt] n [in Europe and Asia] furão-bravo m.

polemic [pəˈlemɪk] n fml polêmica f.

pole position n SPORT (U) pole position f.

Pole Star *n*: the ~ a Estrela Polar.
pole vault *n*: the ~ o salto com vara.
pole-vault *vi* saltar com vara.
pole-vaulter [-ˌvɔːltər] *n* saltador(ra) com vara.
police [pəˈliːs] <> *npl* -**1.** [police force]: the ~ a polícia -**2.** [policemen, policewomen] policial *mf.* <> *vt* policiar.
police car *n* rádio-patrulha *f.*
police constable *n UK* policial *mf.*
police department *n US* departamento *m* de polícia, polícia *f.*
police dog *n* cão *m* policial.
police force *n* força *f* policial.
policeman [pəˈliːsmən] (*pl* -**men** [-mən]) *n* policial *m.*
police officer *n* oficial *mf* de polícia.
police record *n* ficha *f* policial; **to have a** ~ ter ficha na polícia.
police state *n* estado *m* policial.
police station *n UK* delegacia *f.*
policewoman [pəˈliːsˌwʊmən] (*pl* -**women** [-ˌwɪmɪn]) *n* policial *f.*
policy [ˈpɒləsɪ] (*pl* -**ies**) *n* -**1.** [plan, practice] política *f* -**2.** [document, agreement] apólice *f.*
policy-holder *n* segurado *m*, -da *f.*
polio [ˈpəʊlɪəʊ] *n* (*U*) poliomelite *f*, paralisia *f* infantil.
polish [ˈpɒlɪʃ] <> *n* -**1.** [cleaning material] polidor *m* -**2.** [shine] polimento *m* -**3.** *fig* [refinement] requinte *m.* <> *vt* -**1.** polir -**2.** *fig* [perfect]: **to** ~ **sthg (up)** refinar algo.
➤ **polish off** *vt sep inf* -**1.** [meal] comer/beber rapidamente -**2.** [job, book] dar um fim rápido em.
Polish [ˈpəʊlɪʃ] <> *adj* polonês(esa) <> *n* [language] polonês *m.* <> *npl*: the ~ os poloneses.
polished [ˈpɒlɪʃt] *adj* -**1.** [gen] polido(da) -**2.** [performer, performance] elegante.
polite [pəˈlaɪt] *adj* -**1.** [person, remark] educado(da), cortês(tesa) -**2.** [society] polido(da).
politely [pəˈlaɪtlɪ] *adv* educadamente.
politeness [pəˈlaɪtnɪs] *n* (*U*) educação *f*, cortesia *f.*
politic [ˈpɒlətɪk] *adj fml* prudente.
political [pəˈlɪtɪkl] *adj* político(ca).
political asylum *n* (*U*) asilo *m* político.
political football *n* debate *m* político acirrado.
political geography *n* (*U*) geografia *f* política.
politically [pəˈlɪtɪklɪ] *adv* politicamente.
politically correct [pəˌlɪtɪklɪ-] *adj* politicamente correto(ta).
political prisoner *n* prisioneiro *m* político, prisioneira *f* política.
political science *n* (*U*) ciência *f* política.
politician [ˌpɒlɪˈtɪʃn] *n* político *m*, -ca *f.*
politicize, -ise [pəˈlɪtɪsaɪz] *vt* politizar.
politics [ˈpɒlətɪks] <> *n* política *f.* <> *npl* [of a person, group] política *f.*
polka [ˈpɒlkə] *n* polca *f*; **to do the** ~ dançar a polca.
polka dot *n* bolinhas *fpl* (*em um padrão de tecido*).
poll [pəʊl] <> *n* -**1.** [election] eleição *f* -**2.** [survey]

pesquisa *f.* <> *vt* -**1.** [people] entrevistar -**2.** [votes] receber, obter.
➤ **polls** *npl*: **to go to the** ~ **s** ir às urnas.
pollen [ˈpɒlən] *n* (*U*) pólen *m.*
pollen count *n* contagem *f* de pólen.
pollinate [ˈpɒləneɪt] *vt* polinizar.
pollination [ˌpɒlɪˈneɪʃn] *n* (*U*) polinização *f.*
polling [ˈpəʊlɪŋ] *n* (*U*) votação *f.*
polling booth [ˈpəʊlɪŋ-] *n* cabine *f* de votação.
polling day [ˈpəʊlɪŋ-] *n UK* dia *f* de eleição.
polling station [ˈpəʊlɪŋ-] *n* zona *f* eleitoral.
pollster [ˈpəʊlstər] *n* especialista *mf* em sondagem pública.
poll tax *n* imposto *m* per capita.
➤ **Poll Tax** *n UK* *imposto sobre votantes na Grã-Bretanha.*
pollutant [pəˈluːtnt] *n* poluente *m.*
pollute [pəˈluːt] *vt* poluir.
pollution [pəˈluːʃn] *n* poluição *f.*
polo [ˈpəʊləʊ] *n* (*U*) pólo *m.*
polo neck *n UK* -**1.** [collar] gola *f* alta -**2.** [jumper] blusão *m* de gola alta.
➤ **polo-neck** *adj UK* de gola alta.
polo shirt *n* camisa *f* pólo.
poltergeist [ˈpɒltəgaɪst] *n* *fantasma que move objetos e faz barulhos.*
polyanthus [ˌpɒlɪˈænθəs] (*pl* -**thuses** *OR* -**thi** [-θaɪ]) *n* primavera-dos-jardins *f.*
poly bag *n UK inf* saco *m* plástico.
polyester [ˌpɒlɪˈestər] *n* (*U*) poliéster *m.*
polyethylene *n US* = **polythene**.
polygamist [pəˈlɪgəmɪst] *n* polígamo *m*, -ma *f.*
polygamy [pəˈlɪgəmɪ] *n* (*U*) poligamia *f.*
polygon [ˈpɒlɪgən] *n* polígono *m.*
polymer [ˈpɒlɪmər] *n* polímero *m.*
Polynesia [ˌpɒlɪˈniːʒə] *n* Polinésia; **in** ~ na Polinésia; **French** ~ Polinésia Francesa.
Polynesian [ˌpɒlɪˈniːʒən] <> *adj* polinésio(sia). <> *n* -**1.** [person] polinésio *m*, -sia *f* -**2.** [language] polinésio *m.*
polyp [ˈpɒlɪp] *n* pólipo *m.*
polystyrene [ˌpɒlɪˈstaɪriːn] *n* (*U*) poliestireno *m*, isopor *m.*
polytechnic [ˌpɒlɪˈteknɪk] *n UK* politécnica *f.*
polythene *UK* [ˈpɒlɪθiːn], **polyethylene** *US* [ˈpɒlɪˈeθɪliːn] *n* (*U*) polietileno *m.*
polythene bag *n UK* saco *m* de polietileno.
polyunsaturated [ˌpɒlɪʌnˈsætʃəreɪtɪd] *adj* poliinsaturado(da).
polyurethane [ˌpɒlɪˈjʊərəθeɪn] *n* (*U*) poliuretano *m.*
pom [pɒm] *n Austr pej* inglês(esa).
pomander [pəˈmændər] *n* sachê *m* (aromático).
pomegranate [ˈpɒmɪˌgrænɪt] *n* romã *f.*
pommel [ˈpɒml] *n* -**1.** [on saddle] maçaneta *f* -**2.** [on sword] botão *m.*
pomp [pɒmp] *n* (*U*) pompa *f.*
pompom [ˈpɒmpɒm] *n* pompom *m.*
pompous [ˈpɒmpəs] *adj* [pretentious - speech, style] pomposo(sa); [- person] pretensioso(sa).
ponce [pɒns] *n UK v inf pej* -**1.** [effeminate man] marica *m* -**2.** [pimp] gigolô *m.*

poncho ['pɒntʃəʊ] (*pl* -s) *n* poncho *m*.
pond [pɒnd] *n* lago *m (natural ou artificial)*; the ~ *inf* o Atlântico.
ponder ['pɒndə'] <> *vt* ponderar. <> *vi* ponderar; to ~ on *or* over sthg meditar sobre algo.
ponderous ['pɒndərəs] *adj* -**1.** [dull, solemn] ponderoso(sa) -**2.** [large and heavy] pesado(da) -**3.** [slow, clumsy] enfadonho(nha).
pong [pɒŋ] *UK inf* <> *n* fedor *m*. <> *vi* feder.
pontiff ['pɒntɪf] *n* pontífice *m*.
pontificate [pɒn'tɪfɪkeɪt] *vi pej* pontificar; to ~ about *or* on sthg pontificar sobre algo.
pontoon [pɒn'tu:n] *n* -**1.** [bridge] barcaça *f* -**2.** *UK* [game] vinte-e-um *m*.
pony ['pəʊnɪ] (*pl* -ies) *n* pônei *m*.
ponytail ['pəʊnteɪl] *n* rabo-de-cavalo *m*.
pony-trekking [-,trekɪŋ] *n* (*U*) excursão *f* em pôneis.
poodle ['pu:dl] *n* poodle *m*.
poof [pʊf] *n UK v inf offensive* veado *m*.
pooh-pooh *vt inf* fazer pouco caso de, desdenhar.
pool [pu:l] <> *n* -**1.** [natural] lago *m* -**2.** [swimming pool] piscina *f* -**3.** [of liquid, light] poça *f* -**4.** [of workers, cars, talent] grupo *m* -**5.** (*U*) *SPORT* bilhar *m*. <> *vt* juntar.
 ◆ **pools** *npl UK*: the ~ s ≃ a loteria esportiva.
pooped [pu:pt] *adj inf* esgotado(da).
poor [pɔ:'] <> *adj* pobre. <> *npl*: the ~ os pobres.
poorhouse ['pɔ:haʊs, *pl* -haʊzɪz] *n* albergue *m (para pobres)*.
poorly ['pɔ:lɪ] <> *adj UK inf* [ill] mal. <> *adv* mal.
poor relation *n fig* primo *m* pobre.
pop [pɒp] (*pt* & *pp* -ped, *cont* -ping) <> *n* -**1.** (*U*) [music] pop *m* -**2.** (*U*) *inf* [fizzy drink] gasosa *f* -**3.** *esp US inf* [father] pai *m* -**4.** [noise] estouro *m*. <> *vt* -**1.** [burst] estourar -**2.** [put quickly] pôr rapidamente. <> *vi* -**1.** [burst] estourar -**2.** [spring, fly off] soltar-se -**3.** [eyes] arregalar -**4.** [go quickly] dar uma passada; he ~ ped from behind the sofa ele apareceu de atrás do sofá.
 ◆ **pop in** *vi* entrar por um momento.
 ◆ **pop up** *vi* aparecer de repente.
popadum ['pɒpədəm] *n* pão *indiano frito em óleo*.
pop art *n* (*U*) arte *f* pop.
pop concert *n* concerto *m* pop.
popcorn ['pɒpkɔ:n] *n* (*U*) pipoca *f*.
pope [pəʊp] *n* papa *m*.
pop group *n* grupo *m* pop.
poplar ['pɒplə'] *n* choupo *m*.
poplin ['pɒplɪn] *n* (*U*) popeline *m*.
popper ['pɒpə'] *n UK* presilha *f*.
poppy ['pɒpɪ] (*pl* -ies) *n* papoula *f*.
poppycock ['pɒpɪkɒk] *n* (*U*) *inf* papo *m* furado.
Poppy Day *n UK* Dia *m* do Armistício.

POPPY DAY

O *Poppy Day* ou *Remembrance Day* é celebrado no segundo domingo de novembro. Nesse dia, os britânicos carregam uma amapola de papel na lapela, em memória de seus soldados mortos nas guerras mundiais.

Popsicle® ['pɒpsɪkl] *n US* picolé *m*.
pop singer *n* cantor *m*, -ra *f* pop.
populace ['pɒpjʊləs] *n*: the ~ o populacho.
popular ['pɒpjʊlə'] *adj* popular.
popularity [,pɒpjʊ'lærətɪ] *n* (*U*) popularidade *f*.
popularize, -ise ['pɒpjʊləraɪz] *vt* popularizar.
popularly ['pɒpjʊləlɪ] *adv* popularmente.
populate ['pɒpjʊleɪt] *vt* -**1.** [inhabit] povoar -**2.** [colonize] urbanizar.
populated ['pɒpjʊleɪtɪd] *adj* povoado(da).
population [,pɒpjʊ'leɪʃn] *n* população *f*.
population explosion *n* explosão *f* demográfica.
populist ['pɒpjʊlɪst] *n* populista *mf*.
pop-up *adj* -**1.** [toaster] com sistema de ejeção -**2.** [book] com ilustrações tridimensionais.
porcelain ['pɔ:səlɪn] *n* (*U*) porcelana *f*.
porch [pɔ:tʃ] *n* -**1.** [entrance] átrio *m* -**2.** *US* [veranda] alpendre *m*.
porcupine ['pɔ:kjʊpaɪn] *n* porco-espinho *m*.
pore [pɔ:'] *n* poro *m*.
 ◆ **pore over** *vt fus* examinar minuciosamente.
pork [pɔ:k] *n* (*U*) carne *f* de porco.
pork chop *n* costeleta *f* de porco.
pork pie *n* pastelão *m* de porco.
porn [pɔ:n] *n* (*U*) *inf* pornô *m*; hard ~ pornografia pesada; soft ~ pornografia leve.
pornographic [,pɔ:nə'græfɪk] *adj* pornográfico(ca).
pornography [pɔ:'nɒgrəfɪ] *n* (*U*) pornografia *f*.
porous ['pɔ:rəs] *adj* poroso(sa).
porpoise ['pɔ:pəs] *n* porco-do-mar *m*.
porridge ['pɒrɪdʒ] *n* (*U*) mingau *m* com cereais.
port [pɔ:t] <> *n* -**1.** [gen] porto *m* -**2.** (*U*) *NAUT* bombordo *m*; to ~ a bombordo -**3.** (*U*) [drink] vinho *m* do Porto -**4.** *COMPUT* porta *f*. <> *comp* -**1.** [relating to a harbour] porteiro(ra) -**2.** *NAUT* a bombordo.
portable ['pɔ:təbl] *adj* portável.
Portacrib® ['pɔ:tə,krɪb] *n US* moisés *m*.
portal ['pɔ:tl] *n* -**1.** *literary* portada *f* -**2.** *COMPUT* portal *m*.
Port-au-Prince [,pɔ:təʊ'prɪns] *n* Porto-Príncipe.
portcullis [,pɔ:t'kʌlɪs] *n* portão *m* levadiço *(em um castelo)*.
portend [pɔ:'tend] *vt literary* prognosticar.
portent ['pɔ:tənt] *n literary* prognóstico *m*.
porter ['pɔ:tə'] *n* -**1.** *UK* [doorman] porteiro *m*, -ra *f* -**2.** [for luggage] carregador *m*, -ra *f* -**3.** *US* [on train] cabineiro *m*, -ra *f*.
portfolio [,pɔ:t'fəʊljəʊ] (*pl* -s) *n* -**1.** [case] pasta *f* -**2.** [sample of work] portfólio *m* -**3.** *FIN* carteira *f*.
porthole ['pɔ:thəʊl] *n* vigia *mf*.
portion ['pɔ:ʃn] *n* -**1.** [part, share] porção *f* -**2.** [set amount of food] parte *f*.
portly ['pɔ:tlɪ] (*compar* -ier, *superl* -iest) *adj* corpulento(ta).
port of call *n* -**1.** *NAUT* porto *m* de escala -**2.** *fig* [on journey] ponto *m* de parada.
Port of Spain *n* Porto *m* de Espanha.
portrait ['pɔ:trɪt] *n* retrato *m*.

portraitist [ˈpɔːtrɪtɪst] n retratista mf.

portray [pɔːˈtreɪ] vt **- 1.** [in a play, film] interpretar **- 2.** [describe, represent] descrever **- 3.** [subj: artist] retratar.

portrayal [pɔːˈtreɪəl] n **- 1.** [in a play, film] interpretação f **- 2.** [description, representation] descrição f **- 3.** [painting, photograph] retrato m.

Portugal [ˈpɔːtʃʊgl] n Portugal; **in** ~ em Portugal.

Portuguese [ˌpɔːtʃʊˈgiːz] (pl inv) <> adj português(guesa). <> n [language] português m. <> npl: **the** ~ os portugueses.

POS (abbr of point of sale) n UK ponto m de venda.

pose [pəʊz] <> n **- 1.** [position, stance] pose f **- 2.** pej [pretence, affectation] pose f. <> vt **- 1.** [problem, danger, threat] constituir **- 2.** [question] fazer. <> vi **- 1.** [model] posar **- 2.** pej [behave affectedly] fazer-se **- 3.** [pretend to be]: **to** ~ **as sb/sthg** fazer-se passar por alguém/algo.

poser [ˈpəʊzəʳ] n **- 1.** pej [person] fingido m, -da f **- 2.** inf [hard question] quebra-cabeça f.

poseur [pəʊˈzɜːʳ] n pej fingido m, -da f.

posh [pɒʃ] adj inf **- 1.** [hotel, clothes] chique **- 2.** [upperclass] chique.

posit [ˈpɒzɪt] vt fml postular.

position [pəˈzɪʃn] <> n **- 1.** [gen] posição f; **in** ~ em posição **- 2.** [job] cargo m **- 3.** [state, situation] posição f, situação f; **to be in a/no** ~ **to do sthg** estar/não estar em condições de fazer algo **- 4.** [stance, opinion]: ~ **on sthg** posição sobre algo. <> vt posicionar; **to** ~ **o.s.** posicionar-se.

positive [ˈpɒzətɪv] adj **- 1.** [gen] positivo(va); **to be** ~ **about sthg** ser positivo(va) sobre algo; **be** ~ **about the exam!** seja otimista em relação à prova! **- 2.** [irrefutable] irrefutável **- 3.** [for emphasis]: **a** ~ **joy** uma ótima brincadeira; **a** ~ **nightmare** um pesadelo terrível.

positive discrimination n (U) discriminação f positiva.

positively [ˈpɒzətɪvlɪ] adv **- 1.** [gen] positivamente **- 2.** [irrefutably] irrefutavelmente **- 3.** [for emphasis] definitivamente.

positive vetting n (U) UK investigação completa a que é submetido um candidato a cargo público relacionado com a segurança nacional.

posse [ˈpɒsɪ] n **- 1.** [of sheriff] US destacamento m **- 2.** inf [gang] bando m armado.

possess [pəˈzes] vt **- 1.** [gen] possuir **- 2.** [subj: emotion] levar a.

possessed [pəˈzest] adj possuído(da).

possession [pəˈzeʃn] n (U) posse f; **to have sthg in one's** ~, **to be in** ~ **of sthg** estar em posse de algo.
   possessions npl posses fpl, bens mpl.

possessive [pəˈzesɪv] <> adj **- 1.** pej [clinging] possessivo(va) **- 2.** GRAMM possessivo(va). <> n GRAMM possessivo m.

possessively [pəˈzesɪvlɪ] adv possessivamente.

possessor [pəˈzesəʳ] n fml proprietário m, -ria f.

possibility [ˌpɒsəˈbɪlətɪ] (pl -ies) n possibilidade f.

possible [ˈpɒsəbl] <> adj possível; **as soon as** ~ o mais cedo possível; **as much as** ~ o máximo possível. <> n possível m.

possibly [ˈpɒsəblɪ] adv **- 1.** [perhaps, maybe] possivelmente **- 2.** [conceivably]: **I'll do all I** ~ **can** vou fazer tudo que estiver ao meu alcance; **how could he** ~ **do that?** como ele foi capaz de fazer isso?; **I can't** ~ **take the money!** simplesmente não posso aceitar o dinheiro!

possum [ˈpɒsəm] (pl inv OR -s) n US gambá m.

post [pəʊst] <> n **- 1.** [mail service]: **the** ~ o correio; **by** ~ pelo correio; **in the** ~ no correio **- 2.** (U) [letters etc] correio m **- 3.** [delivery] mala f postal **- 4.** UK [collection] coleta f **- 5.** [pole] poste m **- 6.** [position, job] posto m **- 7.** MIL guarnição f **- 8.** phr: **to pip sb at the** ~ vencer alguém na última hora. <> vt **- 1.** [by mail] postar, pôr no correio **- 2.** [transfer] transferir **- 3.** phr: **to keep sb** ~ **ed** manter alguém informado(da).

post [pəʊst] vt COMPUT [message, query] enviar.

post- [pəʊst] prefix pós-.

postage [ˈpəʊstɪdʒ] n (U) franquia f; ~ **and packing** despesas fpl de envio.

postage stamp n fml selo m (postal).

postal [ˈpəʊstl] adj postal.

postal order n vale m postal.

postbag [ˈpəʊstbæg] n **- 1.** UK [bag] sacola f de correio **- 2.** inf [letters received] mala f de cartas.

postbox [ˈpəʊstbɒks] n UK caixa f de correio.

postcard [ˈpəʊstkɑːd] n cartão m postal.

postcode [ˈpəʊstkəʊd] n UK código m (de endereçamento) postal.

post-date vt pós-datar.

poster [ˈpəʊstəʳ] n cartaz m, pôster m.

poste restante [ˌpəʊstˈrestɑːnt] n (U) esp UK posterestante f.

posterior [pɒˈstɪərɪəʳ] <> adj posterior. <> n hum traseiro m.

posterity [pɒˈsterətɪ] n (U) posteridade f.

poster paint n têmpera f.

post-free adj esp UK com porte pago.

postgraduate [ˌpəʊstˈgrædʒʊət] <> adj pós-graduado(da). <> n pós-graduado m, -da f.

post-haste adv dated de pronto.

posthumous [ˈpɒstjʊməs] adj póstumo(ma).

posthumously [ˈpɒstjʊməslɪ] adv postumamente.

post-industrial adj pós-industrial.

posting [ˈpəʊstɪŋ] n [assignment] nomeação f.

postman [ˈpəʊstmən] (pl -men [-mən]) n carteiro m.

postmark [ˈpəʊstmɑːk] <> n carimbo m (postal). <> vt carimbar.

postmaster [ˈpəʊstˌmɑːstəʳ] n agente m de correio.

Postmaster General (pl Postmasters General) n diretor m geral dos correios.

postmistress [ˈpəʊstˌmɪstrɪs] n agente f de correio.

postmortem [ˌpəʊstˈmɔːtəm] <> adj post-mortem. <> n **- 1.** [autopsy] autópsia f **- 2.** fig [analysis] análise f detalhada.

postnatal [ˌpəʊstˈneɪtl] adj pós-natal.

post office n **- 1.** [organization]: **the Post Office** a Agência dos Correios **- 2.** [building] correio m.

post office box n caixa f postal.

post-operative adj pós-operatório(ria).

post-paid *adj* com porte pago.

postpone [pəs'pəʊn] *vt* adiar.

postponement [,pəʊst'pəʊnmənt] *n* adiamento *m*.

postscript ['pəʊstskrɪpt] *n* **-1.** [to letter] pós-escrito *m* **-2.** *fig* [additional information] adendo *m*.

postulate [*n* 'pɒstjʊlət, *vb* 'pɒstjʊleɪt] *vt fml* postular.

posture ['pɒstʃə^r] ◇ *n* postura *f*; ~ **on sthg** postura em relação a algo. ◇ *vi*: **he's always posturing** ele está sempre bancando pose.

posturing *n* (U) pose *f*, atitude *f*.

postviral syndrome [,pəʊst'vaɪrəl-] *n* síndrome *f* pós-virótica.

postwar [,pəʊst'wɔ:^r] *adj* pós-guerra.

posy ['pəʊzɪ] (*pl* -ies) *n* ramalhete *m*.

pot [pɒt] (*pt* & *pp* -ted, *cont* -ting) ◇ *n* **-1.** [for cooking] panela *f*; **to go to** ~ ir para o brejo; **the** ~ **calling the kettle black** rir-se o roto do esfarrapado **-2.** [for tea, coffee] bule *m* **-3.** [for paint, jam] frasco *m* **-4.** [flowerpot] vaso *m* **-5.** (U) *drugs sl* [cannabis] maconha *f*. ◇ *vt* **-1.** [plant] plantar (*em vaso*) **-2.** [billiards ball] encaçapar.

potash ['pɒtæʃ] *n* (U) potassa *f*.

potassium [pə'tæsɪəm] *n* (U) potássio *m*.

potato [pə'teɪtəʊ] (*pl* -es) *n* batata *f*.

potato crisps UK, **potato chips** US *npl* batatinhas *fpl* fritas.

potato peeler [-,pi:lə^r] *n* descascador *m* de batatas.

pot-bellied [-,belɪd] *adj* barrigudo(da).

potboiler ['pɒt,bɔɪlə^r] *n pej* livro, quadro ou outro artigo de pouco valor artístico, produzido rapidamente com fins apenas comerciais.

pot-bound *adj* sufocado(da) com muitas raízes.

potency ['pəʊtənsɪ] *n* (U) **-1.** [of argument] força *f* **-2.** [of drink, drug] teor *m* **-3.** [virility] potência *f*, virilidade *f*.

potent ['pəʊtənt] *adj* **-1.** [argument] forte **-2.** [drink, drug] de alto teor, poderoso(sa) **-3.** [virile] potente, viril.

potentate ['pəʊtənteɪt] *n* potentado *m*.

potential [pə'tenʃl] ◇ *adj* potencial, em potencial. ◇ *n* [of person] potencial *m*; **to have** ~ ter potencial.

potentially [pə'tenʃəlɪ] *adv* potencialmente.

pothole ['pɒthəʊl] *n* buraco *m*.

potholer ['pɒt,həʊlə^r] *n UK* espeleologista *mf*.

potholing ['pɒt,həʊlɪŋ] *n UK* espeleologia; **to go** ~ explorar cavernas.

potion ['pəʊʃn] *n* poção *f*.

potluck [,pɒt'lʌk] *n*: **to take** ~ [at meal] contentar-se com o que houver para comer; [in choice] arriscar *or* tentar a sorte.

pot plant *n* planta *f* de vaso.

potpourri [,pəʊ'pʊərɪ] *n* pot-pourri *m*.

pot roast *n* carne *f* assada.

potshot ['pɒt,ʃɒt] *n*: **to take a** ~ (**at sthg**) atirar a esmo (em algo).

potted ['pɒtɪd] *adj* **-1.** [grown in pot] de vaso **-2.** [preserved] em conserva **-3.** UK *fig* [condensed] condensado(da).

potter ['pɒtə^r] *n* oleiro *m*, -ra *f*.

➡ **potter about, potter around** *vi UK*

ocupar-se em trabalhos pequenos.

Potteries ['pɒtərɪz] *npl*: **the** ~ os Potteries (*distrito na Inglaterra típico por sua cerâmica*).

potter's wheel *n* roda *f* de oleiro.

pottery ['pɒtərɪ] (*pl* -ies) *n* **-1.** [gen] cerâmica *f* **-2.** [factory] olaria *f*.

potting compost ['pɒtɪŋ-] *n* (U) adubo *m* para plantas de interiores.

potty ['pɒtɪ] (*compar* -ier, *superl* -iest, *pl* -ies) UK *inf* ◇ *adj* doido(da); **to be** ~ **about sb/sthg** ser doido(da) por alguém/algo. ◇ *n* [for children] penico *m*.

potty-trained [-,treɪnd] *adj*: **a** ~ **child** uma criança que já sabe pedir para ir ao banheiro.

pouch [paʊtʃ] *n* bolsa *f*.

pouffe [pu:f] *n UK* [seat] pufe *m*.

poultice ['pəʊltɪs] *n* cataplasma *m*.

poultry ['pəʊltrɪ] ◇ *n* (U) [meat] carne *f* de aves (*domésticas*). ◇ *npl* [birds] aves *fpl* domésticas.

pounce [paʊns] *vi* **-1.** [subj: animal, bird]: **to** ~ (**on** *OR* **upon sthg**) agarrar (algo) **-2.** [subj: person, police]: **to** ~ (**on** *OR* **upon sb**) lançar-se (sobre alguém) **-3.** *fig* [on mistake, suggestion]: **to** ~ (**up**)**on sthg** precipitar-se sobre algo.

pound [paʊnd] ◇ *n* **-1.** UK [unit of money] libra *f* **-2.** UK [currency system]: **the** ~ a libra **-3.** [unit of weight] libra *f* **-4.** [for dogs] canil **-5.** [for cars] depósito *m* (*para automóveis apreendidos*). ◇ *vt* **-1.** [strike loudly] esmurrar **-2.** [pulverize] pulverizar. ◇ *vi* **-1.** [strike loudly]: **to** ~ **on sthg** esmurrar algo **-2.** [beat, throb - heart] palpitar; [- head] latejar.

pound coin *n* moeda *f* de libra.

pounding ['paʊndɪŋ] *n* **-1.** [of drums, fists] surra *f* **-2.** [of heart] palpitação *f* **-3.** [of head] latejamento *m* **-4.** *phr*: **to get** *OR* **take a** ~ [be severely damaged] ser seriamente atingido(da); [be heavily defeated] levar uma surra.

pound sterling *n* libra *f* esterlina.

pour [pɔ:^r] ◇ *vt* **-1.** [cause to flow] despejar; **to** ~ **sthg into sthg** despejar algo em algo; **to** ~ **sb a drink, to** ~ **a drink for sb** servir um drinque a alguém **-2.** *fig* [invest]: **to** ~ **money into sthg** investir muito dinheiro em algo. ◇ *vi* **-1.** [flow quickly] fluir, correr **-2.** *fig* [rush] correr. ◇ *v impers* [rain hard] chover a cântaros.

➡ **pour in** *vi* vir em enxurrada.

➡ **pour out** *vt sep* **-1.** [empty] esvaziar **-2.** [serve] servir **-3.** *fig* [emotions] abrir.

pouring ['pɔ:rɪŋ] *adj* [rain] torrencial.

pout [paʊt] ◇ *n* beiço *m*. ◇ *vi* fazer beiço.

poverty ['pɒvətɪ] *n* (U) **-1.** [hardship] miséria *f* **-2.** [lack]: ~ **of sthg** pobreza de algo.

poverty line *n* linha *f* da pobreza.

poverty-stricken *adj* carente, necessitado(da).

poverty trap *n UK* situação na qual uma pessoa pobre não tem vantagem em arrumar emprego por perder os benefícios do governo.

pow [paʊ] *excl inf* paf!

POW (*abbr of* prisoner of war) *n* prisioneiro *m*, -ra *f* de guerra.

powder ['paʊdə^r] ◇ *n* [tiny particles] pó *m*; **face** ~

pó-de-arroz m; **gun**~ pólvora f; **washing** ~ detergente m. <> vt [make-up] maquiar; **to** ~ **o.s.** maquiar-se.

powder compact n estojo m (de pó-de-arroz).
powdered ['paʊdəd] adj [in powder form] em pó.
powder puff n esponja f de pó-de-arroz.
powder room n toalete m.
powdery ['paʊdərɪ] adj -1. [like powder] poeirento (ta) -2. [covered in powder] cheio (cheia) de pó.
power ['paʊəʳ] <> n -1. (U) [control, influence] poder m; **to be in** ~ estar no poder; **to come to** ~ chegar ao poder; **to have** ~ **over sb** ter poder sobre alguém; **to take** ~ assumir o poder -2. [ability, capacity] força f; **mental** ~**s** poderes mpl mentais; **to be (with)in one's** ~ **to do sthg** competir a alguém fazer algo -3. [legal authority] autoridade f; **to have the** ~ **to do sthg** ter autoridade para fazer algo -4. [strength] força f; **the** ~**s that be** os poderes constituídos -5. (U) TECH energia f -6. (U) [electricity] luz f. <> vt alimentar.
power base n reduto m (de força).
powerboat ['paʊəbəʊt] n powerboat m, pequeno barco de corrida muito veloz.
power broker n pessoa que exerce grande influência através do controle de votos ou de indivíduos.
power cut n corte m de energia.
power failure n falha f no sistema elétrico.
powerful ['paʊəfʊl] adj -1. [influential] poderoso(sa) -2. [strong] poderoso(sa), forte -3. [very convincing, very moving] vigoroso(sa).
powerhouse ['paʊəhaʊs, pl -haʊzɪz] n fig fonte f de influência.
powerless ['paʊəlɪs] adj fraco(ca); **to be** ~ **to do sthg** ser impotente para fazer algo.
power line n linha f de força.
power of attorney n procuração f.
power plant n central f elétrica.
power point n UK ponto m de força, tomada f.
power-sharing n POL divisão f de poder (entre partidos políticos).
power station n estação f de força.
power steering n (U) direção f hidráulica.
power worker n eletricitário m, -ria f.
Powys ['paʊɪs] n Powys.
pp (abbr of per procurationem) p/.
p & p (abbr of postage and packing) n postagem f e empacotamento.
PPE (abbr of philosophy, politics and economics) n filosofia, política e economia, famoso curso oferecido pela Universidade de Oxford.
ppm (abbr of parts per million) ppm.
PPS <> n (abbr of parliamentary private secretary) deputado britânico que assessora um ministro. <> (abbr of post postscriptum) P.P.S.
PQ abbr of Province of Quebec.
PR <> n -1. (abbr of public relations) RP mf -2. (abbr of proportional representation) representação f proporcional. <> abbr of Puerto Rico.
practicable ['præktɪkəbl] adj praticável.
practical ['præktɪkl] <> adj -1. [gen] prático(ca) -2. [practicable] praticável. <> n prática f.

practicality [ˌpræktɪ'kælətɪ] n (U) praticabilidade f.
➡ **practicalities** npl aspectos mpl práticos.
practical joke n peça f, trote m.
practically ['præktɪklɪ] adv praticamente.
practice ['præktɪs], **practise** US n -1. (U) [gen] prática f; **to be out of** ~ estar destreinado(da); **the athlete is out of** ~ estar fora de forma -2. (U) [implementation]: **to put sthg into** ~ pôr algo em prática; **in** ~ [in fact] na prática -3. [training session] sessão f de treino.
practiced adj US = practised.
practicing adj US = practising.
practise, practice US ['præktɪs] <> vt praticar. <> vi -1. [train] treinar -2. [professional] exercer.
practised, practiced US ['præktɪst] adj experiente, treinado(da); **to be** ~ **at doing sthg** ser competente ao fazer algo.
practising, practicing US ['præktɪsɪŋ] adj -1. [doctor, lawyer] que exerce -2. [Christian, Catholic] praticante -3. [homosexual] assumido(da).
practitioner [præk'tɪʃnəʳ] n MED: **a medical** ~ um profissional da área médica.
pragmatic [præg'mætɪk] adj pragmático(ca).
pragmatism ['prægmətɪzml] n (U) pragmatismo m.
pragmatist ['prægmətɪst] n pragmatista m.
Prague [prɑːg] n Praga; **in** ~ em Praga.
prairie ['preərɪ] n pradaria f.
praise [preɪz] <> n -1. (U) [commendation] elogio m -2. RELIG louvor m; ~ **be to God!** louvado seja Deus! -3. phr: **to sing sb's** ~**s** tecer elogios a alguém. <> vt -1. [commend] elogiar -2. RELIG louvar.
praiseworthy ['preɪzˌwɜːðɪ] adj louvável.
praline ['prɑːliːn] n pralina f.
pram [præm] n UK carrinho m de bebê.
PRAM (abbr of programmable random access memory) n RAM f programável.
prance [prɑːns] vi empinar-se.
prang [præŋ] UK inf dated <> n desastre m. <> vt espatifar-se.
prank [præŋk] n peça f.
prat [præt] n UK v inf palerma mf.
prattle ['prætl] pej <> n tagarelice m. <> vi tagarelar; **to** ~ **on about sthg** tagarelar sobre algo.
prawn [prɔːn] n pitu m.
prawn cocktail n coquetel m de pitus.
prawn cracker n petisco de origem chinesa parecido com batatas fritas.
pray [preɪ] vi RELIG rezar; **to** ~ **to sb** rezar para alguém; **to** ~ **for sthg** rezar por algo.
prayer [preəʳ] n -1. (U) [act of praying] prece f -2. [set of words] oração f; **to say one's** ~**s** fazer suas orações -3. fig [strong hope] pedido m.
➡ **prayers** npl [service] preces fpl.
prayer book n missal m.
prayer meeting n serviço m de oração.
pre- [priː] prefix pré-.
preach [priːtʃ] <> vt pregar. <> vi -1. RELIG pregar; **to** ~ **to sb** fazer sermões a alguém -2. pej [pontificate] dar sermões em; **to** ~ **at sb** dar sermões em alguém.

preacher ['pri:tʃə'] n pregador m, -ra f.
preamble [pri:'æmbl] n preâmbulo m.
prearranged [ˌpri:ə'reɪndʒd] adj já combinado(-da).
precarious [prɪ'keərɪəs] adj precário(ria).
precariously [prɪ'keərɪəslɪ] adv precariamente.
precast [ˌpri:'kɑ:st] adj pré-moldado(da).
precaution [prɪ'kɔ:ʃn] n precaução f; **as a ~ against** sthg como precaução contra algo.
precautionary [prɪ'kɔ:ʃənərɪ] adj de precaução.
precede [prɪ'si:d] vt -1. [gen] preceder -2. [walk in front of] adiantar-se.
precedence ['presɪdəns] n: **to take ~ over** sthg ter prioridade sobre algo; **to take ~ over sb** ter precedência sobre alguém.
precedent ['presɪdənt] n precedente m.
preceding [prɪ'si:dɪŋ] adj -1. [previous] anterior -2. [written before] anterior, precedente.
precept ['pri:sept] n preceito m.
precinct ['pri:sɪŋkt] n -1. UK [shopping area] zona f comercial -2. US [district] distrito m.
➡ **precincts** npl [around building] arredores mpl.
precious ['preʃəs] adj -1. [friendship, moment, time] precioso(sa), querido(da) -2. [jewel, object, material] precioso(sa) -3. inf iro [damned] maldito(ta); **~ little** muito pouco -4. [affected] afetado(da).
precious metal n metal m precioso.
precious stone n pedra f preciosa.
precipice ['presɪpɪs] n precipício m.
precipitate [adj prɪ'sɪpɪtət , vb prɪ'sɪpɪteɪt] fml ⟨⟩ adj precipitado(da). ⟨⟩ vt precipitar.
precipitation [prɪˌsɪpɪ'teɪʃn] n precipitação f.
precipitous [prɪ'sɪpɪtəs] adj -1. [very steep] íngreme -2. [hasty] precipitado(da).
précis [UK 'preɪsi:, US 'preɪsi:] (pl inv) n resumo m.
precise [prɪ'saɪs] adj preciso(sa), exato(ta); **to be ~** [speaking exactly] para ser preciso.
precisely [prɪ'saɪslɪ] adv exatamente; **to describe/explain** sthg **~** descrever/explicar algo com precisão.
precision [prɪ'sɪʒn] ⟨⟩ n (U) precisão f; **to do** sthg **with ~** fazer algo com precisão. ⟨⟩ comp de precisão.
preclude [prɪ'klu:d] vt fml impedir, evitar; **to ~ sb/sthg from doing** sthg impedir alguém/algo de fazer algo.
precocious [prɪ'kəʊʃəs] adj precoce.
precocity [prɪ'kɒsətɪ] n (U) precocidade f.
preconceived [ˌpri:kən'si:vd] adj preconcebido(-da).
preconception [ˌpri:kən'sepʃn] n idéia f preconcebida.
precondition [ˌpri:kən'dɪʃn] n fml precondição f, condição f prévia; **to be a ~ for** OR **of** sthg ser um pré-requisito para algo.
precooked [pri:'kʊkt] adj pré-cozido(da).
precursor [ˌpri:'kɜ:sə'] n fml precursor m, -ra f; **to be a ~ of** OR **to** sthg ser um precursor de algo.
predate [pri:'deɪt] vt preceder, ser anterior a.
predator ['predətə'] n -1. [animal, bird] predador m, -ra f -2. fig [exploitative person] explorador m, -ra f.
predatory ['predətrɪ] adj predatório(ria).
predecease [ˌpri:dɪ'si:s] vt fml morrer antes de.

predecessor ['pri:dɪsesə'] n -1. [person] predecessor m, -ra f, antecessor m, -ra f -2. [thing] antecessor m, -ra f.
predestination [pri:ˌdestɪ'neɪʃn] n (U) RELIG predestinação f.
predestine [ˌpri:'destɪn] vt: **to be ~d to sthg to do** sthg estar predestinado(da) a algo/a fazer algo.
predetermine [ˌpri:dɪ'tɜ:mɪn] vt predeterminar.
predetermined [ˌpri:dɪ'tɜ:mɪnd] adj predetermi-nado(da).
predicament [prɪ'dɪkəmənt] n aperto m; **to be in a ~** estar num aperto.
predicate ['predɪkət] n GRAMM predicado m.
predict [prɪ'dɪkt] vt prever.
predictable [prɪ'dɪktəbl] adj previsível.
predictably [prɪ'dɪktəblɪ] adv -1. [in an expected way] de forma previsível -2. [as was expected] como era de se imaginar.
prediction [prɪ'dɪkʃn] n -1. [something foretold] previsão f, prognóstico m -2. (U) [foretelling] previsão f.
predictor [prɪ'dɪktə'] n indicador m.
predigest [ˌpri:daɪ'dʒest] vt fig simplificar; **~ed** mastigado (mastigada).
predilection [ˌpri:dɪ'lekʃn] n: **~ for** sthg predile-ção f por algo.
predispose [ˌpri:dɪs'pəʊz] vt: **to be ~d to sthg to do** sthg estar predisposto(ta) a algo/a fazer algo.
predisposition ['pri:ˌdɪspə'zɪʃn] n: **~ to(wards)** sthg predisposição f a algo; **~ to do** sthg predisposição para fazer algo.
predominance [prɪ'dɒmɪnəns] n -1. [preponder-ance] predominância f, predomínio m -2. [control] predomínio m.
predominant [prɪ'dɒmɪnənt] adj predominante.
predominantly [prɪ'dɒmɪnəntlɪ] adv predomi-nantemente.
predominate [prɪ'dɒmɪneɪt] vi -1. [be greater in number] predominar -2. [prevail] predominar, pre-valecer.
pre-eminent adj preeminente.
pre-empt [-'empt] vt antecipar-se a.
pre-emptive [-'emptɪv] adj preventivo(va).
pre-emptive strike n ataque m preventivo.
preen [pri:n] vt -1. [subj: bird] alisar com o bico -2. fig [subj: person]: **to ~ o.s.** arrumar-se, ajeitar-se.
pre-exist vi preexistir.
prefab ['pri:fæb] n inf casa f pré-fabricada.
prefabricate [ˌpri:'fæbrɪkeɪt] vt pré-fabricar.
preface ['prefɪs] ⟨⟩ n [in book] prefácio m; **~ to** sthg [to text] prefácio a algo; [to speech] preâmbulo m. ⟨⟩ vt: **to ~** sthg **with** sthg/**by doing** sthg introduzir algo com algo/fazendo algo.
prefect ['pri:fekt] n UK monitor m, -ra f, prefeito m, -ta f (em escola).
prefer [prɪ'fɜ:'] (pt & pp **-red**, cont **-ring**) vt preferir; **to ~** sthg **to** sthg preferir algo a algo; **to ~ to do** sthg preferir fazer algo.
preferable ['prefrəbl] adj: **to be ~ (to** sthg**)** ser preferível(a algo).
preferably ['prefrəblɪ] adv preferivelmente.

preference ['prefərənsl] *n*: ~ **(for sthg)** preferência *f*(por algo); **to give sb/sthg** ~ , **to give** ~ **to sb/ sthg** dar preferência a alguém/algo.

preference shares *UK npl*, **preferred stock** *US n* ações *fpl* preferenciais.

preferential [ˌprefə'renʃl] *adj* preferencial.

preferred [prɪ'fɜːd] *adj* preferido(da).

preferred stock *n US* = **preference shares**.

prefigure [priː'fɪɡəʳ] *vt fml* prefigurar, anunciar.

prefix ['priːfiks] *n GRAMM* prefixo *m*.

pregnancy ['pregnənsɪ] (*pl* -ies) *n* gravidez *f*.

pregnancy test *n* teste *m* de gravidez.

pregnant ['pregnənt] *adj* -**1.** [carrying unborn baby - human] grávido(da); [- animal] prenho(ha) -**2.** *fig* [significant] significativo(va).

preheated [ˌpriː'hiːtɪd] *adj* preaquecido(da).

prehistoric [ˌpriːhɪ'stɒrɪk] *adj* pré-histórico(ca).

prehistory [ˌpriː'hɪstərɪ] *n (U)* pré-história *f*.

pre-industrial *adj* pré-industrial.

prejudge [ˌpriː'dʒʌdʒ] *vt* prejulgar.

prejudice ['predʒʊdɪs] <> *n* -**1.** [bias] preconceito *m*; ~ **in favour of sb/sthg** tendência *f* de favorecer alguém/algo; ~ **against sb/sthg** preconceito contra alguém/algo -**2.** [harm] prejuízo *m*. <> *vt* -**1.** [bias] ter preconceito em relação a; **to** ~ **sb in favour of/against sthg** predispor alguém a favor de/contra algo -**2.** [jeopardize] prejudicar.

prejudiced ['predʒʊdɪst] *adj* preconceituoso(sa), parcial; **to be** ~ **in favour of sb/sthg** favorecer alguém/algo; **to be** ~ **against sb/sthg** ser preconceituoso(sa) em relação a alguém/algo.

prejudicial [ˌpredʒʊ'dɪʃl] *adj* prejudicial; **to be** ~ **to sb/sthg** ser prejudicial para alguém/algo.

prelate ['prelɪt] *n RELIG* prelado *m*.

preliminary [prɪ'lɪmɪnərɪ] (*pl* -ies) *adj* preliminar.
◆ **preliminaries** *npl* -**1.** [preliminary events or stages] preliminares *fpl* -**2.** [eliminating contests] eliminatórias *fpl* -**3.** *US POL* prévias *fpl*.

prelims ['priːlɪmz] *npl UK* [exams] exames *mpl* preliminares.

prelude ['preljuːd] *n*: ~ **to sthg** prelúdio *m* de algo.

premarital [ˌpriː'mærɪtl] *adj* pré-marital, antes do casamento.

premature ['premə,tjʊəʳ] *adj* prematuro(ra).

prematurely [ˌpremə'tjʊəlɪ] *adv* prematuramente.

premeditated [ˌpriː'medɪteɪtɪd] *adj* premeditado (da).

premenstrual syndrome, premenstrual tension [priː'menstrʊəl-] *n* síndrome *f* pré-menstrual.

premier ['premjəʳ] <> *adj* principal, primeiro(ra). <> *n* [prime minister] primeiro-ministro *m*, primeira-ministra *f*.

premiere ['premɪeəʳ] *n* estréia *f*.

premiership ['premɪəʃɪp] *n* [office] cargo *m* de primeiro-ministro; [term of office] mandato *m* (*do primeiro-ministro*).
◆ **Premiership** *n UK FTBL*: **the** ~ ≃ o Clube dos 13.

premise ['premɪs] *n* premissa *f*; **on the** ~ **that** com a premissa de que.

◆ **premises** *npl* [site] local *m*; **on the** ~**s** no local.

premium ['priːmjəm] *n* -**1.** [gen] prêmio *m*; **at a** ~ [above usual value] *a um valor superior ao nominal*; [in great demand] muito disputado(da) -**2.** *phr*: **to put** *OR* **place a high** ~ **on sthg** dar grande importância a algo.

premium bond *n UK* obrigação emitida pelo governo que dá direito a prêmios mensais em dinheiro mediante sorteio.

premonition [ˌpremə'nɪʃn] *n* premonição *f*.

prenatal [ˌpriː'neɪtl] *adj US* pré-natal.

preoccupation [priː,ɒkjʊ'peɪʃn] *n* preocupação *f*; ~ **with sthg** preocupação com algo.

preoccupied [priː'ɒkjʊpaɪd] *adj* preocupado(da); **to be** ~ **with sthg** estar preocupado(da) com algo.

preoccupy [priː'ɒkjʊpaɪ] (*pt* & *pp* -ied) *vt* preocupar.

preordain [ˌpriːɔː'deɪn] *vt* predeterminar; **to be** ~**ed to do sthg** estar predestinado(da) a fazer algo.

prep [prep] *n UK inf* [homework]: **to do one's** ~ fazer o dever de casa.

pre-packed *adj* pré-embalado(da).

prepaid ['priːpeɪd] *adj* com porte pago.

preparation [ˌprepə'reɪʃn] *n* -**1.** (*U*) [act of preparing] preparação *f*; **in** ~ **for sthg** em preparação para algo -**2.** [prepared mixture] preparado *m*.
◆ **preparations** *npl* [plans] preparativos *mpl*; **to make** ~**s for sthg** fazer preparativos para algo.

preparatory [prɪ'pærətrɪ] *adj* preparatório(ria).

preparatory school *n* -**1.** [in UK] colégio pago para crianças de 7 a 13 anos -**2.** [in US] *escola particular que prepara alunos para entrar na universidade*.

prepare [prɪ'peəʳ] <> *vt* preparar; **to** ~ **to do sthg** preparar-se para fazer algo. <> *vi*: **to** ~ **for sthg** preparar-se para algo.

prepared [prɪ'peəd] *adj* [organized, done beforehand] preparado(da); **to be** ~ **for sthg** *OR* **to do sthg** estar preparado(da) para algo/para fazer algo.

preponderance [prɪ'pɒndərəns] *n* predomínio *m*.

preponderantly [prɪ'pɒndərəntlɪ] *adv* predominantemente, majoritariamente.

preposition [ˌprepə'zɪʃn] *n* preposição *f*.

prepossessing [ˌpriːpə'zesɪŋ] *adj fml* atraente, agradável.

preposterous [prɪ'pɒstərəs] *adj* absurdo(da).

preppy ['prepɪ] (*pl* -ies) *US inf* <> *adj* -**1.** [male] de mauricinho -**2.** [female] de patricinha. <> *n* -**1.** [male] mauricinho *m* -**2.** [female] patricinha *f*.

prep school (*abbr of* **preparatory school**) *n escola particular que prepara crianças de 7 a 12 anos na Grã-Bretanha*.

Pre-Raphaelite [ˌpriː'ræfəlaɪt] <> *adj* pré-rafaelita. <> *n* pré-rafaelita *mf*.

pre-recorded *adj* pré-gravado(da).

prerequisite [ˌpriː'rekwɪzɪt] *n* pré-requisito *m*; ~ **of** *OR* **for sthg** pré-requisito para algo.

prerogative [prɪ'rɒɡətɪv] *n* prerrogativa *f*.

presage ['presɪdʒ] *vt fml* pressagiar.

Presbyterian [ˌprezbɪ'tɪərɪən] ◇ *adj* presbiteriano(na). ◇ *n* presbiteriano *m*, -na *f*.

presbytery ['prezbɪtrɪ] *n* presbitério *m*.

pre-school ◇ *adj* pré-escolar. ◇ *n US* pré-escola *f*.

prescient ['presɪənt] *adj fml* presciente.

prescribe [prɪ'skraɪb] *vt* **-1.** *MED* prescrever **-2.** [order] ordenar, mandar.

prescription [prɪ'skrɪpʃn] *n* [*MED* - written form] receita *f* (médica); [- medicine] prescrição *f*; **on ~** com receita (médica).

prescription charge *n UK* no *Reino Unido, quantia fixa que se paga por quaisquer remédios receitados por um médico.*

prescriptive [prɪ'skrɪptɪv] *adj GRAMM* prescritivo (va).

presence ['prezns] *n* presença *f*; **in the ~ of sb** na presença de alguém; **to have ~** ter presença.

presence of mind *n* presença *f* de espírito.

present [*adj* & *n* 'preznt, *vb* prɪ'zent] ◇ *adj* **-1.** [gen] presente, atual **-2.** [in attendance] presente; **to be ~ at sthg** estar presente em algo. ◇ *n* **-1.:** **the ~** o presente; **at ~** atualmente; **for the ~** no momento **-2.** *GRAMM:* **~ (tense)** presente *m*. ◇ *vt* **-1.** [gen] apresentar; **to ~ sb to sb** apresentar alguém para alguém **-2.** [give] presentear; **to ~ sb with sthg, to ~ sthg to sb** presentar alguém com algo **-3.** [provide, pose] deparar-se com; **to ~ sb with sthg, to ~ sthg to sb** representar algo para alguém **-4.** [arrive, go]: **to ~ o.s.** apresentar-se.

presentable [prɪ'zentəbl] *adj* apresentável.

presentation [ˌprezn'teɪʃn] *n* **-1.** [gen] apresentação *f* **-2.** [ceremony] cerimônia *f* **-3.** [performance] representação *f*.

presentation copy *n* cópia *f* de apresentação, exemplar *m* gratuito.

present day *n*: **the ~** o momento atual.

➤ **present-day** *adj* atual, de hoje em dia.

presenter [prɪ'zentə'] *n UK* apresentador *m*, -ra *f*.

presentiment [prɪ'zentɪmənt] *n fml* pressentimento *m*.

presently ['prezntlɪ] *adv* **-1.** [soon] em breve, daqui a pouco **-2.** [now] atualmente.

preservation [ˌprezə'veɪʃn] *n (U)* **-1.** [gen] preservação *f* **-2.** [of food] conservação *f*.

preservation order *n esp UK* ordem *f* de tombamento.

preservative [prɪ'zɜ:vətɪv] *n* **-1.** [for food] conservante *m* **-2.** [for wood] revestimento *m*.

preserve [prɪ'zɜ:v] ◇ *n* [jam] compota *f*, conserva *f*. ◇ *vt* **-1.** [gen] preservar **-2.** [food] conservar.

preserved [prɪ'zɜ:vd] *adj* **-1.** [food] em conserva **-2.** [building] preservado(da) **-3.** [furniture, wood] conservado(da).

preset [ˌpri:'set] (*pt* & *pp* **preset**, *cont* **-ting**) *vt* programar.

pre-shrunk *adj* pré-encolhido(da).

preside [prɪ'zaɪd] *vi* presidir; **to ~ over OR at sthg** presidir algo.

presidency ['prezɪdənsɪ] (*pl* **-ies**) *n* presidência *f*.

president ['prezɪdənt] *n* presidente *mf*.

President-elect *n* presidente *mf* eleito, -ta.

presidential [ˌprezɪ'denʃl] *adj* presidencial.

press [pres] ◇ *n* **-1.** [push] pressionamento *m* **-2.** [journalism]: **the ~** a imprensa; **to get a good ~** ser elogiado(da) na/pela imprensa; **to get a bad ~** ser criticado(da) na/pela imprensa, **-3.** [printing machine] imprensa *f* **-4.** [pressing machine] prensa *f*. ◇ *vt* **-1.** [push firmly - switch] ligar; [- accelerator] pisar em; **to ~ sthg against sthg** prensar algo contra algo **-2.** [squeeze] espremer **-3.** [iron] passar **-4.** [press person, button] pressionar; **he didn't need much ~ and readily agreed** ele não precisava de muita pressão e concordou prontamente; **to ~ sb for sthg** pressionar alguém buscando algo; **to ~ sb to do sthg** OR **into doing sthg** pressionar alguém a fazer algo; **to ~ sthg (up)on sb** empurrar algo a alguém, obrigar alguém a aceitar algo **-5.** [pursue] insistir em **-6.** *JUR*: **to ~ charges (against sb)** fazer acusações (contra alguém). ◇ *vi* **-1.** [push] apertar; **to ~ (on sthg)** apertar (algo) com força **-2.** [surge] comprimir-se; **to ~ forwards** empurrar para frente.

➤ **press on** *vi* [continue] continuar; **to ~ on with sthg** continuar com algo.

press agency *n* assessoria *f* de imprensa.

press agent *n* acessor *m*, -ra *f* de imprensa.

press baron *n UK* magnata *m* da imprensa.

press box *n* cabine *f* de imprensa.

press conference *n* entrevista *f* coletiva.

press corps *n US* equipe *f* de jornalistas.

press cutting *n UK* recorte *m* de jornal.

pressed [prest] *adj*: **to be ~ (for time/money)** estar meio apertado(da) (de tempo/dinheiro).

press fastener *n UK* botão *m* de pressão.

press gallery *n* tribuna *f* de imprensa.

pressgang ['presgæŋ] ◇ *n* grupo de homens que recrutavam marinheiros à força. ◇ *vt UK*: **to ~ sb into doing sthg** forçar alguém a fazer algo.

pressing ['presɪŋ] *adj* urgente, premente.

pressman ['presmæn] (*pl* **-men** [-men]) *n UK* jornalista *m*.

press officer *n* acessor *m*, -ra *f* de imprensa.

press release *n* press-release *m*, comunicado *m* de imprensa.

press-stud *n UK* botão *m* de pressão.

press-up *n UK* flexão *f*, apoio *m* (*como exercício*).

pressure ['preʃə'] ◇ *n* pressão *f*; **to put ~ on sb (to do sthg)** pressionar alguém (a fazer algo OR para que faça algo), exercer pressão sobre alguém (para fazer algo). ◇ *vt*: **to ~ sb to do** OR **into doing sthg** pressionar alguém a fazer algo.

pressure cooker *n* panela *f* de pressão.

pressure gauge *n* manômetro *m*.

pressure group *n* grupo *m* de pressão.

pressurize, -ise ['preʃəraɪz] *vt* **-1.** *TECH* pressurizar **-2.** *UK* [force]: **to ~ sb to do** OR **into doing sthg** pressionar alguém a fazer algo.

Prestel® ['prestel] *n UK* serviço público de videotexto oferecido pela British Telecom.

prestige [pre'sti:ʒ] ◇ *n (U)* prestígio *m*. ◇ *comp* de prestígio.

prestigious [pre'stɪdʒəs] *adj* prestigioso(sa).

prestressed concrete [,pri:'strest-] *n (U)* concreto *m* protendido.

presumably [prɪ'zju:məblɪ] *adv* presumivelmente; ~ **you've read the book** suponho que você já tenha lido o livro.

presume [prɪ'zju:m] *vt* presumir, supor; **to be ~d dead/innocent** ser julgado(da) morto(ta)/inocente; **to ~ (that)** supor *or* imaginar que.

presumption [prɪ'zʌmpʃn] *n* -1. [assumption] pressuposição *f*, suposição *f* -2. *(U)* [audacity] presunção *f*.

presumptuous [prɪ'zʌmptʃʊəs] *adj* presunçoso (sa).

presuppose [,pri:sə'pəʊz] *vt* pressupor.

pre-tax *adj* bruto(ta).

pretence, pretense US [prɪ'tens] *n* fingimento *m*; **under false ~s** com falsos pretextos.

pretend [prɪ'tend] <> *vt* -1. [make believe]: **to ~ to be/to do sthg** fingir ser/fazer algo; **to ~ (that)** fingir (que), fazer de conta (que) -2. [claim]: **to ~ to do sthg** fingir fazer algo. <> *vi* fingir.

pretense *n* US = **pretence**.

pretension [prɪ'tenʃn] *n* pretensão *f*; **to have ~s to sthg/to be sthg** ter pretensões de algo/de ser algo.

pretentious [prɪ'tenʃəs] *adj* pretencioso(sa).

pretentiously [prɪ'tenʃəslɪ] *adv* pretenciosamente.

pretentiousness [prɪ'tenʃəsnɪs] *n (U)* pretensão *f*, caráter *m* pretencioso.

preterite ['pretərət] *n* pretérito *m*.

pretext ['pri:tekst] *n* pretexto *m*; **on** *or* **under the ~ that** com o pretexto de que; **on** *or* **under the ~ of doing sthg** com o pretexto de estar fazendo algo.

Pretoria [prɪ'tɔ:rɪə] *n* Pretória.

prettify ['prɪtɪfaɪ] *(pt & pp -ied)* *vt* embelezar.

prettily ['prɪtɪlɪ] *adv* de uma forma encantadora.

pretty ['prɪtɪ] *(compar -ier, superl -iest)* <> *adj* bonito(ta). <> *adv* [quite, rather] bastante; ~ **much** *or* **well** mais ou menos.

pretzel ['pretsl] *n* rosca salgada em forma de nó, pretzel *m*.

prevail [prɪ'veɪl] *vi* -1. [be widespread] prevalecer, predominar -2. [triumph] prevalecer; **to ~ over sb/sthg** prevalecer sobre alguém/algo -3. [persuade]: **to ~ (up)on sb to do sthg** persuadir alguém a fazer algo *or* para que faça algo.

prevailing [prɪ'veɪlɪŋ] *adj* predominante.

prevalence ['prevələns] *n* predomínio *m*.

prevalent ['prevələnt] *adj* predominante, prevalecente.

prevaricate [prɪ'værɪkeɪt] *vi* prevaricar.

prevent [prɪ'vent] *vt* evitar, impedir; **to ~ sb (from) doing sthg** impedir alguém de fazer algo; **to ~ sthg (from) doing sthg** evitar que algo faça algo; **they tried to ~ any pain to the animal** eles tentaram não causar nenhuma dor ao animal.

preventable [prɪ'ventəbl] *adj* evitável.

preventative [prɪ'ventətɪv] *adj* = **preventive**.

prevention [prɪ'venʃn] *n (U)* prevenção *f*; ~ **is better than cure** é melhor prevenir do que remediar.

preventive [prɪ'ventɪv] *adj* preventivo(va).

preview ['pri:vju:] *n* -1. [early showing] pré-estréia *f* -2. [trailer] trailer *m*.

previous ['pri:vjəs] *adj* -1. [earlier, prior] anterior, prévio(via); ~ **convictions** antecedentes *mpl* criminais; **it was the ~ President who did it** foi o ex-presidente que fez isso -2. [days and dates] anterior.

previously ['pri:vjəslɪ] *adv* -1. [formerly] anteriormente, antes -2. [with days and dates] antes.

prewar [,pri:'wɔ:ʳ] *adj* anterior à guerra.

pre-wash *n* pré-lavagem *f*.

prey [preɪ] *n (U)* presa *f*, vítima *f*; **to fall ~ to sb/ sthg** ser vítima de alguém/algo.
 ⏍ **prey on** *vt fus* -1. [live off] caçar, alimentar-se de -2. [trouble]: **to ~ on sb's mind** atormentar alguém.

price [praɪs] <> *n* -1. preço *m*; **at a ~** a que preço; **at any ~** a qualquer preço, a todo custo -2. *fig* [penalty]: **to pay the ~ for sthg** pagar o preço por algo. <> *vt* pôr preço em; **it was ~d highly** seu preço era muito elevado.

price-cutting *n (U)* redução *f* de preços.

price-fixing [-,fɪksɪŋ] *n (U)* cartel *m*.

priceless ['praɪslɪs] *adj* -1. [very valuable] inestimável, que não tem preço -2. *inf* [funny] impagável.

price list *n* lista *f* de preços.

price tag *n* -1. [label] etiqueta *f* de preço -2. [sacrifice] *fig* preço *m*.

price war *n* guerra *f* de preços.

pricey ['praɪsɪ] *(compar -ier, superl -iest)* *adj* inf caro(ra).

prick [prɪk] <> *n* -1. [scratch, wound] picada *f* -2. *vulg* [penis] cacete *m*, caralho *m* -3. *vulg* [stupid person] pau-no-cu *m*. <> *vt* -1. [jab, pierce] espetar -2. [sting] arder.
 ⏍ **prick up** *vt fus*: **to ~ up one's ears** [subj: animal] levantar as orelhas; [subj: person] aguçar os ouvidos.

prickle ['prɪkl] <> *n* -1. [thorn] espinho *m* -2. [sensation] formigamento *m*, comichão *f*. <> *vi* formigar, comichar.

prickly ['prɪklɪ] *(compar -ier, superl -iest)* *adj* -1. [thorny] espinhoso(sa), espinhento(ta) -2. *fig* [touchy] suscetível.

prickly heat *n (U)* brotoeja *f*.

pride [praɪd] <> *n* orgulho *m*; **to swallow one's ~** engolir o orgulho; **to take ~ in sthg/in doing sthg** sentir-se orgulhoso(a) em algo/ao fazer algo; **his new car was his ~ and joy** seu novo carro era a menina dos olhos dele; **to have ~ of place** ter lugar de honra. <> *vt*: **to ~ o.s. on sthg** orgulhar-se de algo.

priest [pri:st] *n* -1. [Christian] padre *m*, sacerdote *m* -2. [non-Christian] homem *m* religioso.

priestess ['pri:stɪs] *n* sacerdotisa *f*.

priesthood ['pri:sthʊd] *n (U)* -1. [position, office]: **the ~** o sacerdócio -2. [priests collectively]: **the ~** o clero.

prig [prɪg] *n* moralista *mf*, puritano *m*, -na *f*.

prim [prɪm] *(compar -mer, superl -mest)* *adj* afetado

(da), empertigado(da).
primacy ['praɪməsɪ] *n (U)* primazia *f*.
prima donna [ˌpriːməˈdɒnə] (*pl* -s) *n* -**1.** [female singer] prima-dona *f* -**2.** *pej* [self-important person] prima-dona *f*.
primaeval [praɪˈmiːvəl] *adj* = **primeval**.
prima facie [ˌpraɪməˈfeɪʃɪ] *adj* à primeira vista.
primal ['praɪml] *adj* -**1.** [original] primário(ria) -**2.** [most important] principal.
primarily ['praɪmərɪlɪ] *adv* primeiramente, principalmente.
primary ['praɪmərɪ] (*pl* -ies) ⟨⟩ *adj* primário(ria). ⟨⟩ *n US POL* prévias *fpl*.

primary colour *n* cor *f* primária.
primary election *n US* prévias *fpl*.
primary school *n* escola *f* primária.
primary teacher *n* [in UK] professor *m* primário, professora *f* primária.
primate ['praɪmeɪt] *n* -**1.** *ZOOL* primata *m* -**2.** *RELIG* primaz *m*.
prime [praɪm] ⟨⟩ *adj* -**1.** [main] primeiro(ra) principal -**2.** [excellent] excelente, de primeira. ⟨⟩ *n* [peak] auge *m*, plenitude *f*; **in one's** ~ na flor da idade. ⟨⟩ *vt* -**1.** [inform]: **to** ~ **sb about sthg** instruir alguém sobre algo -**2.** [paint] imprimar, preparar para pintura -**3.** [make ready - gun] carregar; [- machine] aprontar; [- pump] escorvar.
prime minister *n* primeiro-ministro *m*, primeira-ministra *f*.
prime mover [-ˈmuːvəʳ] *n fig* força *f* motora.
prime number *n* número *m* primo.
primer ['praɪməʳ] *n* -**1.** [paint] imprimadura *f* -**2.** [textbook] manual *m*.
prime time *n (U)* horário *m* nobre.
⟶ **prime-time** *adj* -**1.** [TV] de maior audiência -**2.** [viewing, advertising] no horário nobre.
primeval [praɪˈmiːvl] *adj* primitivo(va).
primitive ['prɪmɪtɪv] *adj* -**1.** [not civilized, of an early type] primitivo(va) -**2.** [simple, basic] rudimentar.
primordial [praɪˈmɔːdjəl] *adj fml* primordial.
primrose ['prɪmrəʊz] *n* prímula *f*.
Primus stove® ['praɪməs-] *n* fogareiro *m*.
prince [prɪns] *n* príncipe *m*; **Prince of Wales** Príncipe de Gales.
Prince Charming *n hum* príncipe *m* encantado.
princely ['prɪnslɪ] (*compar* -ier, *superl* -iest) *adj* -**1.** [of a prince] principesco(ca) -**2.** [generous, lavish] generoso(sa).
princess [prɪnˈses] *n* princesa *f*; **Princess Royal** Princesa Real.
principal ['prɪnsəpl] ⟨⟩ *adj* principal. ⟨⟩ *n* -**1.** [of school] diretor *m*, -ra *f* -**2.** [of college] reitor *m*, -ra *f*.
principality [ˌprɪnsɪˈpælɪtɪ] (*pl* -ies) *n* principado *m*.

principally ['prɪnsəplɪ] *adv* especialmente, principalmente.
principle ['prɪnsəpl] *n* -**1.** princípio *m* -**2.** *(U)* [integrity] princípios *mpl*; **he lacks** ~ ele não tem princípios; **(to do sthg) on** ~ *OR* **as a matter of** ~ fazer algo por (uma questão de) princípios.
⟶ **in principle** *adv* em princípio.
principled ['prɪnsəpld] *adj* de princípio.
print [prɪnt] ⟨⟩ *n* -**1.** *(U)* [type] caracteres *mpl (de imprensa)*; **the book is still in** ~ o livro ainda está disponível *(não esgotado)*; **he saw his name in** ~ ele viu seu nome impresso; **to be out of** ~ estar esgotado(da) -**2.** *ART* gravura *f* -**3.** [photograph] cópia -**4.** [fabric] estampado *m* -**5.** [footprint] pegada *f*; [fingerprint] impressão *f* digital. ⟨⟩ *vt* -**1.** [produce by printing] imprimir -**2.** [publish] publicar -**3.** [on fabric] estampar -**4.** [write clearly] escrever em letra de forma. ⟨⟩ *vi* -**1.** [in handwriting] escrever em letra de forma -**2.** [printer] imprimir.
⟶ **print out** *vt sep COMPUT* imprimir.
printed circuit ['prɪntɪd-] *n* circuito *m* impresso.
printed matter ['prɪntɪd-] *n (U)* impresso *m*.
printer ['prɪntəʳ] *n* -**1.** [person, firm] impressor *m*, -ra *f* -**2.** *COMPUT* impressora *f*.
printing ['prɪntɪŋ] *n* impressão *f*.
printing press *n* prensa *f*, máquina *f* impressora.
printout ['prɪntaʊt] *n* saída *f* de impressora, impressão *f*.
prior ['praɪəʳ] ⟨⟩ *adj* -**1.** [previous] prévio(via), anterior -**2.** [more important] mais importante. ⟨⟩ *n* [monk] prior *m*.
⟶ **prior to** *prep* antes de; ~ **to doing sthg** antes de fazer algo.
prioress ['praɪəres] *n* prioresa *f*.
prioritize, -ise [praɪˈɒrɪtaɪz] *vt* priorizar, dar prioridade a.
priority [praɪˈɒrətɪ] (*pl* -ies) ⟨⟩ *adj* prioritário (ria). ⟨⟩ *n* prioridade *f*; **to have** *OR* **take** ~ **(over sthg)** ter prioridade (sobre algo).
⟶ **priorities** *npl* prioridades *fpl*.
priory ['praɪərɪ] (*pl* -ies) *n* convento *m (dirigido por um prior)*.
prise [praɪz] *vt*: **to** ~ **sthg open** abrir algo com força; **to** ~ **sthg away** separar algo usando força.
prism ['prɪzm] *n* prisma *m*.
prison ['prɪzn] *n* prisão *f*.
prison camp *n* campo *m* de prisioneiros.
prisoner ['prɪznəʳ] *n* prisioneiro *m*, -ra *f*; **to be taken** ~ ser levado prisioneiro, ser levada prisioneira.
prisoner of war (*pl* prisoners of war) *n* prisioneiro *m*, -ra *f* de guerra.
prissy ['prɪsɪ] (*compar* -ier, *superl* -iest) *adj* fresco(ca).
pristine ['prɪstiːn] *adj* imaculado(da).
privacy [*UK* 'prɪvəsɪ, *US* 'praɪvəsɪ] *n* privacidade *f*.
private ['praɪvɪt] ⟨⟩ *adj* -**1.** [confidential, not for the public] privado(da) -**2.** [not state-controlled] privado (da), particular -**3.** [personal] privado(da), pessoal -**4.** [secluded] afastado(da), retirado(da) -**5.** [reserved] reservado(da). ⟨⟩ *n* -**1.** [soldier] soldado *m* raso -**2.** [secrecy]: **(to do sthg) in** ~ fazer algo em particular.

➡ **privates** *npl inf* ANAT partes *fpl (pudendas)*.

private company *n* empresa *f* privada.

private detective *n* detetive *mf* particular.

private enterprise *n (U)* empresa *f* privada.

private eye *n* detetive *mf* particular.

private income *n UK* renda *f* pessoal.

private investigator *n* detetive *mf* particular.

private limited company *n* COMM companhia *f* privada limitada.

privately ['praɪvɪtlɪ] *adv* -1. [not by the state] de forma privada; ~ **owned** de propriedade privada; ~ **educated** educado(da) em escola particular -2. [confidentially] privadamente, em particular -3. [personally] no fundo.

private member's bill *n UK* projeto *de lei apresentado ao parlamento britânico por um deputado sem cargo no governo*.

private parts *npl inf* partes *fpl* pudendas.

private practice *n (U) UK* prática *f* privada *(de uma profissão)*.

private property *n* propriedade *f* privada.

private school *n* escola *f* particular.

private sector *n (U)*: **the** ~ o setor privado.

privation [praɪ'veɪʃn] *n* privação *f*.

privatization [ˌpraɪvɪtaɪ'zeɪʃn] *n (U)* privatização *f*.

privatize, -ise ['praɪvɪtaɪz] *vt* privatizar.

privet ['prɪvɪt] *n (U)* alfena *f*.

privilege ['prɪvɪlɪdʒ] *n* -1. [special advantage] privilégio *m* -2. [honour] privilégio *m*, honra *f*.

privileged ['prɪvɪlɪdʒd] *adj* privilegiado(da).

privy ['prɪvɪ] *adj*: **to be** ~ **to sthg** *fml* inteirar-se de algo.

Privy Council *n UK*: **the** ~ *conselho privado que aconselha o monarca em questões políticas*.

Privy Purse *n*: **the** ~ *quantia aprovada pelo parlamento britânico e destinada a cobrir os gastos do monarca*.

prize [praɪz] <> *adj* -1. [prizewinning] premiado(da) -2. [perfect] perfeito(ta) -3. [valued] de estimação. <> *n* prêmio *m*. <> *vt* apreciar, valorizar.

prize day *n UK* (dia *m* de) entrega *f* de prêmios.

prizefight ['praɪzfaɪt] *n* luta *f* de boxe profissional.

prize-giving [-ˌgɪvɪŋ] *n UK* entrega *f* de prêmios.

prize money *n* dinheiro *m* ganho em prêmio.

prizewinner ['praɪzˌwɪnər] *n* premiado *m*, -da *f*.

pro [prəʊ] *(pl -s) n* -1. *inf* [professional] profissional *mf* -2. [advantage]: **the** ~**s and cons** os prós e os contras.

pro- [prəʊ] *prefix* pró-.

PRO *n* -1. *(abbr of* **public relations officer)** chefe *mf* de relações públicas -2. *(abbr of* **public Record Office)** *arquivo público na Grã-Bretanha*.

pro-am <> *adj* de profissionais e amadores. <> *n competição mista entre profissionais e amadores*.

probability [ˌprɒbə'bɪlətɪ] *(pl -ies) n* probabilidade *f*; **in all** ~ **they will win** é muito provável que eles vençam.

probable ['prɒbəbl] *adj* provável.

probably ['prɒbəblɪ] *adv* provavelmente.

probate ['prəʊbeɪt] JUR <> *n* legitimação *f* de testamento. <> *vt US* legitimar *(um testamento)*.

probation [prə'beɪʃn] *n (U)* -1. [of prisoner] liberdade *f* condicional; **to put sb on** ~ colocar alguém em liberdade condicional -2. [trial period] período *m* de experiência; **to be on** ~ estar em período de experiência.

probationary [prə'beɪʃnrɪ] *adj* -1. [teacher, nurse] em período de experiência -2. [year] de experiência; ~ **period** período *m* de experiência.

probationer [prə'beɪʃnə'] *n* -1. [employee] funcionário *m*, -ria *f* em período de experiência -2. [offender] pessoa *f* em liberdade condicional.

probation officer *n pessoa encarregada de vigiar detentos em liberdade condicional*.

probe [prəʊb] <> *n* -1. [investigation] sindicância *f*, investigação *f*; ~ **into sthg** sindicância sobre algo -2. MED, TECH sonda *f*. <> *vt* -1. [investigate] investigar -2. [prod] explorar. <> *vi*: **to** ~ **for/ into sthg** investigar para encontrar algo.

probing ['prəʊbɪŋ] *adj* inquiridor(ra).

probity ['prəʊbətɪ] *n (U) fml* probidade *f*.

problem ['prɒbləm] <> *n* problema *f*; **no** ~! *inf* sem problema! <> *comp* problemático(ca).

problematic(al) [ˌprɒblə'mætɪk(l)] *adj* problemático(ca), difícil.

problem page *n* página *f* com perguntas dos leitores *(em revistas, jornais)*.

procedural [prə'si:dʒərəl] *adj* processual.

procedure [prə'si:dʒə'] *n* procedimento *m*.

proceed [*vb* prə'si:d, *npl* 'prəʊsi:dz] <> *vt* [do subsequently]: **to** ~ **to do sthg** passar a fazer algo. <> *vi* -1. [continue] prosseguir, continuar; **to** ~ **with sthg** prosseguir com algo -2. *fml* [go, advance] dirigir-se para.

➡ **proceeds** *npl* proventos *mpl*.

proceedings [prə'si:dɪŋz] *npl* -1. [series of events] ação *f* -2. [legal action] processo *m*.

process ['prəʊses] <> *n* processo *m*; **in the** ~ no decorrer; **to be in the** ~ **of doing sthg** estar em vias de fazer algo. <> *vt* processar.

processed cheese ['prəʊsest-] *n* queijo *m* processado.

processing ['prəʊsesɪŋ] *n* processamento *m*.

procession [prə'seʃn] *n* -1. [ceremony] cortejo *m* -2. [demonstration] passeata *f* -3. [continuous line] procissão *f*.

processor ['prəʊsesə'] *n* -1. COMPUT processador *m* -2. CULIN processador *m* de alimentos.

pro-choice *adj* favorável ao direito da mulher de optar ou não pelo aborto.

proclaim [prə'kleɪm] *vt* -1. [declare] proclamar, declarar -2. [law] promulgar.

proclamation [ˌprɒklə'meɪʃn] *n* -1. proclamação *f* -2. [of law] promulgação *f*.

proclivity [prə'klɪvɪtɪ] *(pl -ies) n fml*: ~ **(to** OR **towards sthg)** propensão *f* OR tendência *f* (a algo).

procrastinate [prə'kræstɪneɪt] *vi* procrastinar, protelar.

procrastination [prəˌkræstɪ'neɪʃn] *n (U)* procrastinação *f*, protelação *f*.

procreate ['prəʊkrɪeɪt] *vi* procriar.

procreation [ˌprəʊkrɪ'eɪʃn] *n (U)* procriação *f*.

procurator fiscal [ˈprɒkjʊreɪtəˈ-] *n Scot* oficial público responsável por levar as pessoas a julgamento.

procure [prəˈkjʊəˈ] *vt* conseguir, obter.

procurement [prəˈkjʊəmənt] *n (U)* aquisição *f*.

prod [prɒd] (*pt* & *pp* **-ded**, *cont* **-ding**) <> *n* **-1.** [push, poke] cutucão *m*, empurrão *m* **-2.** *fig* [reminder] toque *m*. <> *vt* **-1.** [push, poke] cutucar, empurrar **-2.** [remind, prompt]: **to ~ sb (into doing sthg)** dar um toque em alguém (para fazer algo *OR* para que faça algo).

prodigal [ˈprɒdɪgl] *adj* pródigo(ga).

prodigious [prəˈdɪdʒəs] *adj* prodigioso(sa).

prodigy [ˈprɒdɪdʒɪ] (*pl* **-ies**) *n* prodígio *m*.

produce [*n* ˈprɒdjuːs, *vb* prəˈdjuːs] <> *n* **-1.** [goods] produtos *mpl* **-2.** [fruit and vegetables] produtos *mpl* agrícolas. <> *vt* **-1.** [gen] produzir **-2.** *BIOL* gerar **-3.** [yield - raw materials, crop] produzir; [- interest, profit] gerar **-4.** [present, show] apresentar.

producer [prəˈdjuːsəˈ] *n* **-1.** [gen] produtor *m*, -ra *f* **-2.** [theatre] diretor *m*, -ra *f*.

product [ˈprɒdʌkt] *n* **-1.** [thing manufactured or grown] produto *m* **-2.** [result]: **to be a ~ of sthg** ser resultado *OR* produto de algo.

production [prəˈdʌkʃn] *n* produção *f*; **to put sthg/go into ~** começar a produzir *OR* fabricar algo.

production line *n* linha *f* de produção.

production manager *n* gerente *mf* de produção.

productive [prəˈdʌktɪv] *adj* produtivo(va).

productively [prəˈdʌktɪvlɪ] *adv* de forma produtiva.

productivity [ˌprɒdʌkˈtɪvətɪ] *n (U)* produtividade *f*.

productivity deal *n* acordo *m* de produtividade.

Prof. [prɒf] (*abbr of* **Professor**) *n* Prof.

profane [prəˈfeɪm] *adj* obsceno(na).

profanity [prəˈfænətɪ] (*pl* **-ies**) *n* **-1.** [of language, behaviour] obscenidade *f*, indecência *f* **-2.** [word] blasfêmia *f*.

profess [prəˈfes] *vt* **-1.** [claim] alegar; **to ~ to do/to be sthg** alegar fazer/ser algo **-2.** [declare] declarar.

professed [prəˈfest] *adj* **-1.** [avowed] declarado(da) **-2.** [alleged] pretenso(sa).

profession [prəˈfeʃn] *n* **-1.** [career] profissão *f*; **by ~** por profissão **-2.** [body of people] categoria *f* (profissional).

professional [prəˈfeʃənl] <> *adj* profissional. <> *n* profissional *mf*.

professional foul *n* falta *f* intencional.

professionalism [prəˈfeʃnəlɪzm] *n* [high quality] profissionalismo *m*.

professionally [prəˈfeʃnəlɪ] *adv* profissionalmente; **to be ~ trained** receber orientação profissional.

professor [prəˈfesəˈ] *n* **-1.** *UK* [head of department] chefe *mf* de departamento **-2.** *US* & *Can* [teacher, lecturer] professor *m* (universitário), professora *f* (universitária).

professorship [prəˈfesəʃɪp] *n UK* cátedra *f*; *US* cargo de professor universitário.

proffer [ˈprɒfəˈ] *vt*: **to ~ sthg (to sb)** oferecer algo (a alguém).

proficiency [prəˈfɪʃənsɪ] *n (U)* proficiência *f*; **~ in sthg** proficiência em algo.

proficient [prəˈfɪʃnt] *adj* proficiente, competente; **to be ~ in** *OR* **at sthg** ter competência em algo; **to be ~ in a foreign language** ter proficiência em uma língua estrangeira.

profile [ˈprəʊfaɪl] *n* perfil *m*; **in ~** de perfil; **to keep a low profile** *fig* não chamar a atenção.

profit [ˈprɒfɪt] <> *n* **-1.** [financial gain] lucro *m*; **to make a ~** ter lucro; **to sell sthg at a ~** vender algo com lucro **-2.** *(U)* [advantage] proveito *m*, benefício *m*. <> *vi*: **to ~ (from** *OR* **by sthg)** tirar proveito (de algo).

profitability [ˌprɒfɪtəˈbɪlətɪ] *n (U)* lucratividade *f*, rentabilidade *f*.

profitable [ˈprɒfɪtəbl] *adj* **-1.** [making a profit] lucrativo(va), rentável **-2.** [beneficial] proveitoso (sa).

profitably [ˈprɒfɪtəblɪ] *adv* **-1.** [at a profit] com lucro **-2.** [usefully] de forma proveitosa.

profiteering [ˌprɒfɪˈtɪərɪŋ] *n (U)* especulação *f*.

profit-making <> *adj* com fins lucrativos. <> *n (U)* obtenção *f* de lucros.

profit margin *n* margem *f* de lucro.

profit sharing [-ˌʃeərɪŋ] *n (U)* participação *f* nos lucros.

profligate [ˈprɒflɪgɪt] *adj* **-1.** [extravagant] extravagante **-2.** [immoral] libertino(na).

pro forma [-ˈfɔːmə] *adj* pro forma.

profound [prəˈfaʊnd] *adj* profundo(da).

profoundly [prəˈfaʊndlɪ] *adv* **-1.** [intensely] profundamente **-2.** [wisely] com profundidade.

profuse [prəˈfjuːs] *adj* **-1.** [abundant] abundante **-2.** [generous, extravagant] profuso(sa).

profusely [prəˈfjuːslɪ] *adv* **-1.** [abundantly] abundantemente **-2.** [generously, extravagantly] profusamente.

profusion [prəˈfjuːʒn] *n* profusão *f*.

progeny [ˈprɒdʒənɪ] (*pl* **-ies**) *n fml* progênie *f*.

progesterone [prəˈdʒestərəʊn] *n (U)* progesterona *f*.

prognosis [prɒgˈnəʊsɪs] (*pl* **-noses** [-ˈnəʊsiːz]) *n* prognóstico *m*.

prognostication [prɒgˌnɒstɪˈkeɪʃn] *n* prognóstico *m*.

program [ˈprəʊgræm] (*pt* & *pp* **-med** *OR* **-ed**, *cont* **-ming** *OR* **-ing**) <> *n* **-1.** *COMPUT* programa *m* **-2.** *US* = **programme**. <> *vt* **-1.** *COMPUT* programar **-2.** *US* = **programme**.

programer *n US* = **programmer**.

programmable [prəʊˈgræməbl] *adj* programável.

programme *UK*, **program** *US* [ˈprəʊgræm] <> *n* programa *m*. <> *vt* programar; **to ~ sthg to do sthg** programar algo para fazer algo *OR* para que faça algo.

programmer *UK*, **programer** *US* [ˈprəʊgræməˈ] *n COMPUT* programador *m*, -ra *f*.

programming [ˈprəʊgræmɪŋ] *n COMPUT* programação *f*.

programming language *n* linguagem *f* de programação.

progress [n 'prəʊgres, vb prə'gres] ⟷ n -1. [gen] progresso m;to make ~ [improve] fazer progresso; to make ~ in sthg [get on] progredir em algo; in ~ em andamento -2. [physical movement] avanço m. ⟷ vi -1. [gen] progredir -2. [move forward]: to ~ to sthg prosseguir para algo.

progression [prə'greʃn] n -1. [advance] progressão f -2. [series] sucessão f.

progressive [prə'gresɪv] adj -1. [forward-looking] progressista -2. [gradual] progressivo(va).

progressively [prə'gresɪvlɪ] adv progressivamente.

progress report n -1. [on student] relatório m de desempenho -2. [on patient] boletim m médico -3. [on work, on project] relatório m de acompanhamento.

prohibit [prə'hɪbɪt] vt proibir; to ~ sb from doing sthg proibir alguém de fazer algo.

prohibition [ˌprəʊɪ'bɪʃn] n proibição f.

prohibitive [prə'hɪbətɪv] adj exorbitante.

project [n 'prɒdʒekt, vb prə'dʒekt] ⟷ n -1. [plan, idea] projeto m -2. SCH projeto m, estudo m; ~ on sthg projeto estudo sobre algo. ⟷ vt -1. [gen] projetar; to ~ sthg on to sthg projetar algo em algo -2. [estimate] projetar, estimar -3. [present] apresentar, dar uma imagem de. ⟷ vi projetar.

projectile [prə'dʒektaɪl] n projétil m.

projection [prə'dʒekʃn] n -1. [gen] projeção f -2. [protrusion] saliência f.

projectionist [prə'dʒekʃənɪst] n operador m, -ra f de projeção (no cinema).

projection room n sala f de projeção.

projector [prə'dʒektər] n projetor m.

proletarian [ˌprəʊlɪ'teərɪən] adj proletário(ria).

proletariat [ˌprəʊlɪ'teərɪət] n proletariado m.

pro-life adj pró-vida.

proliferate [prə'lɪfəreɪt] vi proliferar.

prolific [prə'lɪfɪk] adj prolífico(ca).

prologue, prolog US['prəʊlɒg] n -1. [introduction] prólogo m -2. fig [preceding event]: ~ to sthg preâmbulo m para algo.

prolong [prə'lɒŋ] vt prolongar.

prom [prɒm] n -1. UK inf (abbr of promenade) [at seaside] caminho junto ao mar -2. US [ball] baile de gala estudantil -3. UK inf (abbr of promenade concert): the Proms concertos que acontecem no Albert Hall, em Londres, no verão.

promenade [ˌprɒmə'nɑːd] n UK [at seaside] calçadão. m.

promenade concert n UK concerto sinfônico ao qual boa parte das pessoas assiste de pé.

prominence ['prɒmɪnəns] n (U) -1. [importance] importância f -2. [conspicuousness] notoriedade f, proeminência f.

prominent ['prɒmɪnənt] adj -1. [important - person, politician] destacado(da); [- ideas, issues] proeminente -2. [noticeable - building, landmark] em evidência; [- cheekbones] saliente.

prominently ['prɒmɪnəntlɪ] adv em evidência.

promiscuity [ˌprɒmɪs'kjuːətɪ] n (U) promiscuidade f.

promiscuous [prɒ'mɪskjʊəs] adj promíscuo(cua).

promise ['prɒmɪs] ⟷ n promessa f; to make (sb) a ~ fazer uma promessa (a alguém); to show ~ ser promissor(ra). ⟷ vt -1. [pledge]: to ~ (sb) sthg prometer algo (a alguém); to ~ (sb) to do sthg prometer (a alguém) fazer algo -2. [indicate]: to ~ sthg prometer algo; it ~ s to be a wonderful day promete ser um dia maravilhoso. ⟷ vi prometer.

promising ['prɒmɪsɪŋ] adj promissor(ra).

promissory note ['prɒmɪsərɪ-] n nota f promissória.

promo ['prəʊməʊ] (pl -s) n inf filme m promocional.

promontory ['prɒməntrɪ] (pl -ies) n promontório m.

promote [prə'məʊt] vt -1. [foster] promover, fomentar -2. [push, advertise] promover -3. [in job]: to ~ sb (to sthg) promover alguém (a algo) -4. SPORT: to be ~ d to the First Division subir para a Primeira Divisão.

promoter [prə'məʊtər] n -1. [organizer] patrocinador m, -ra f -2. [supporter] defensor m, -ra f.

promotion [prə'məʊʃn] n promoção f; to get OR be given ~ ser promovido(da).

prompt [prɒmpt] ⟷ adj -1. [quick] pronto(ta), rápido(da) -2. [punctual] pontual. ⟷ adv pontualmente. ⟷ n [THEATRE - line] deixa f; [- person] ponto m. ⟷ vt -1. [provoke, persuade]: to ~ sb (to do sthg) levar alguém (a fazer algo) -2. THEATRE dar a deixa.

prompter ['prɒmptər] n ponto m (no teatro).

promptly ['prɒmptlɪ] adv -1. [quickly] prontamente, rapidamente -2. [punctually] pontualmente.

promptness ['prɒmptnɪs] n (U) -1. [quickness] rapidez f -2. [punctuality] pontualidade f.

promulgate ['prɒmlgeɪt] vt -1. [law, decree] promulgar -2. [belief, idea] propagar.

prone [prəʊn] adj -1. [susceptible]: to be ~ to sthg/ to do sthg ser propenso(sa) a algo/a fazer algo -2. [lying flat] (deitado(da)) de bruços.

prong [prɒŋ] n dente m (de garfo).

pronoun ['prəʊnaʊn] n pronome m.

pronounce [prə'naʊns] ⟷ vt -1. [say aloud] pronunciar -2. [declare, state] declarar. ⟷ vi: to ~ on sthg pronunciar-se sobre algo.

pronounced [prə'naʊnst] adj pronunciado(da), marcado(da).

pronouncement [prə'naʊnsmənt] n pronunciamento m.

pronto ['prɒntəʊ] adv inf imediatamente.

pronunciation [prəˌnʌnsɪ'eɪʃn] n pronúncia f.

proof [pruːf] n -1. [gen] prova f -2. [of alcohol] teor m alcoólico.

proofread ['pruːfriːd] (pt & pp -read [-red]) vt revisar.

proofreader ['pruːfˌriːdər] n revisor m, -ra f.

prop [prɒp] (pt & pp -ped, cont -ping) ⟷ n -1. [physical support] escora f, estaca f -2. fig [supporting thing, person] apoio m -3. RUGBY pilar m. ⟷ vt: to ~ sthg against sthg apoiar algo em OR contra algo.
➭ **props** npl [in film, play] acessórios mpl.
➭ **prop up** vt sep -1. [support physically] escorar, sustentar -2. fig [sustain] apoiar.

Prop. (abbr of proprietor) proprietário m, -ria f.

propaganda [ˌprɒpə'gændə] n (U) propaganda f.

propagate ['prɒpəgeɪt] <> *vt* propagar. <> *vi* propagar-se.

propagation [,prɒpə'geɪʃn] *n* -1. *BOT* propagação *f* -2. [dissemination] propagação *f*, disseminação *f*.

propane ['prəʊpeɪn] *n (U)* propano *m*.

propel [prə'pel] (*pt* & *pp* -led, *cont* -ling) *vt* -1. [drive forward] impulsionar -2. *fig* [urge] impelir.

propeller [prə'pelə'] *n* hélice *f*.

propelling pencil [prə'pelɪŋ-] *n UK* lapiseira *f*.

propensity [prə'pensətɪ] (*pl* -ies) *n fml*: ~ **for** *OR* **to** sthg propensão *f* a algo; ~ **to do sthg** propensão para fazer algo.

proper ['prɒpə'] *adj* -1. [real] verdadeiro(ra) -2. [correct] correto(ta), exato(ta) -3. [decent] decente, apropriado(da) -4. [specifically] próprio(pria) -5. *UK inf* [for emphasis]: **a** ~ **idiot** um perfeito idiota.

properly ['prɒpəlɪ] *adv* -1. [satisfactorily] adequadamente, bem -2. [correctly] direito -3. [decently] adequadamente.

proper noun *n* nome *m* próprio.

property ['prɒpətɪ] (*pl* -ies) *n* -1. [gen] propriedade *f* -2. *(U)* [buildings] imóveis *mpl* -3. *(U)* [land] terrenos *mpl.*

property developer *n* (empresa *f*) construtora *f.*

property owner *n* proprietário *m*, -ria *f* de um imóvel.

property tax *n* imposto *m* predial e territorial.

prophecy ['prɒfɪsɪ] (*pl* -ies) *n* profecia *f.*

prophesy ['prɒfɪsaɪ] (*pt* & *pp* -ied) *vt* profetizar.

prophet ['prɒfɪt] *n* profeta *mf.*

prophetic [prə'fetɪk] *adj* profético(ca).

propitious [prə'pɪʃəs] *adj fml* propício(cia).

proponent [prə'pəʊnənt] *n* defensor *m*, -ra *f*, partidário *m*, -ria *f.*

proportion [prə'pɔ:ʃn] *n* -1. [part] parte *f* -2. [ratio, comparison] proporção *f*; **in** ~ **to** em proporção a; **out of all** ~ **to** totalmente fora de proporção em relação a -3. *(U) ART*: **in** ~ proporcional; **out of** ~ fora de proporção; **a sense of** ~ *fig* senso *m* de proporção; **to get sthg out of** ~ *fig* fazer uma tempestade em um copo d'água sobre algo.

proportional [prə'pɔ:ʃənl] *adj* proporcional, em proporção a; **to be** ~ **to sthg** ser proporcional a algo.

proportional representation *n (U)* representação *f* proporcional.

proportionate [prə'pɔ:ʃnət] *adj* proporcional; ~ **to sthg** proporcional a algo.

proposal [prə'pəʊzl] *n* proposta *f*; **marriage** ~ proposta *f (de casamento).*

propose [prə'pəʊz] <> *vt* -1. [suggest] propor -2. [introduce] apresentar -3. [toast] brindar a -4. [intend]: **to** ~ **doing** *OR* **to do sthg** ter a intenção de fazer algo. <> *vi* [make offer of marriage] pedir em casamento; **to** ~ **to sb** pedir a mão de alguém em casamento.

proposed [prə'pəʊzd] *adj* proposto(ta).

proposition [,prɒpə'zɪʃn] <> *n* -1. [statement of theory] proposição *f* -2. [suggestion] proposta *f*; **to make sb a** ~ fazer uma proposta a alguém. <> *vt fml* fazer uma proposta indecorosa a.

propound [prə'paʊnd] *vt fml* expor.

proprietary [prə'praɪətrɪ] *adj fml COMM* registrado (da).

proprietor [prə'praɪətə'] *n* proprietário *m*, -ria *f.*

proprietorial [prə,praɪə'tɔ:rɪəl] *adj* possessivo(va).

propriety [prə'praɪətɪ] *n (U) fml* retidão *f.*

propulsion [prə'pʌlʃn] *n (U)* propulsão *f.*

pro rata [-'rɑ:tə] *adj* & *adv* pro rata.

prosaic [prəʊ'zeɪk] *adj* prosaico(ca).

proscenium (arch) [prə'si:njəm-] *n* proscênio *m.*

proscribe [prəʊ'skraɪb] *vt fml* proscrever.

prose [prəʊz] <> *n (U)* prosa *f.* <> *comp* em prosa.

prosecute ['prɒsɪkju:t] <> *vt JUR* processar; **to be** ~ **d for sthg** ser processado(da) por algo. <> *vi* -1. [bring a charge] promover ação penal -2. [represent in court] sustentar acusação em juizo.

prosecution [,prɒsɪ'kju:ʃn] *n* -1. [criminal charge] acusação *f* -2. [lawyers]: **the** ~ a acusação.

prosecutor ['prɒsɪkju:tə'] *n* promotor *m*, -ra *f.*

prospect [*n* 'prɒspekt, *vb* prə'spekt] <> *n* -1. [hope] possibilidade *f* -2. [probability] perspectiva *f.* <> *vi* prospectar; **to** ~ **for sthg** prospectar algo.
➥ **prospects** *npl* [chances of success]: ~ **s (for sthg)** perspectivas *fpl* (de algo).

prospecting [prə'spektɪŋ] *n (U)* prospecção *f.*

prospective [prə'spektɪv] *adj* provável, possível.

prospector [prə'spektə'] *n* prospector *m*, -ra *f.*

prospectus [prə'spektəs] (*pl* -es) *n* prospecto *m*, folheto *m* informativo.

prosper ['prɒspə'] *vi* prosperar.

prosperity [prɒ'sperətɪ] *n (U)* prosperidade *f.*

prosperous ['prɒspərəs] *adj* próspero(ra).

prostate (gland) ['prɒsteɪt-] *n* próstata *f.*

prosthesis [prɒs'θi:sɪs] (*pl* -theses ['θi:si:z]) *n* prótese *f.*

prostitute ['prɒstɪtju:t] *n* prostituta *f*; **male** ~ prostituto *m.*

prostitution [,prɒstɪ'tju:ʃn] *n (U)* prostituição *f.*

prostrate [*adj* 'prɒstreɪt, *vb* prɒ'streɪt] <> *adj* prostrado(da). <> *vt*: **to** ~ **o.s. (before sb)** prostrar-se (diante de alguém).

protagonist [prə'tægənɪst] *n* protagonista *mf.*

protect [prə'tekt] *vt* proteger; **to** ~ **sb/sthg from**, **to** ~ **sb/sthg against** proteger alguém/algo de/contra.

protection [prə'tekʃn] *n (U)* proteção *f*; ~ **from sb/sthg,** ~ **against sb/sthg** proteção de *OR* contra alguém/algo.

protectionism [prə'tekʃənɪzm] *n (U)* protecionismo *m.*

protectionist [prə'tekʃənɪst] *adj* protecionista.

protection money *n (U)* dinheiro *m* pago em troca de proteção.

protective [prə'tektɪv] *adj* protetor(ra); **to be/feel** ~ **towards sb** ser/sentir-se protetor(ra) em relação a alguém.

protective custody *n (U)* custódia *f* preventiva.

protectiveness [prə'tektɪvnɪs] *n (U)* sentimento *m* de proteção.

protector [prə'tektə'] *n* -1. [person] protetor *m*, -ra *f* -2. [on machine] dispositivo *m* de proteção.

protectorate [prə'tektərət] *n* protetorado *m.*

protégé ['prɒteʒeɪ] *n* protegido *m.*

protégée ['prɒteʒeɪ] *n* protegida *f.*

protein ['prəʊtiːn] *n (U)* proteina *f.*

protest [*n* 'prəʊtest, *vb* prə'test] <> *n* protesto *m.* <> *vt* -**1.** [state] protestar, declarar -**2.** *US* [protest against] protestar contra. <> *vi* [complain] protestar; **to ~ about/against sthg** protestar por/contra algo.

Protestant ['prɒtɪstənt] <> *adj* protestante. <> *n* protestante *mf.*

Protestantism ['prɒtɪstəntɪzm] *n (U)* protestantismo *m.*

protestation [ˌprɒte'steɪʃn] *n fml* -**1.** [declaration] declaração *f* -**2.** [protest] protesto *m.*

protester [prə'testə'] *n* manifestante *mf.*

protest march *n* marcha *f* de protesto, manifestação *f.*

protocol ['prəʊtəkɒl] *n (U)* protocolo *m.*

proton ['prəʊtɒn] *n* próton *m.*

prototype ['prəʊtətaɪp] *n* protótipo *m.*

protracted [prə'træktɪd] *adj* prolongado(da).

protractor [prə'træktə'] *n* transferidor *m.*

protrude [prə'truːd] *vi* salientar-se, sobressair-se; **to ~ from sthg** sobressair-se em algo.

protrusion [prə'truːʒn] *n* saliência *f.*

protuberance [prə'tjuːbərəns] *n* protuberância *f.*

proud [praʊd] *adj* -**1.** [gen] orgulhoso(sa); **to be ~ of sb/sthg** estar orgulhoso(sa) de alguém/algo; **to be ~ to do sthg** ter a honra de fazer algo -**2.** *pej* [arrogant] orgulhoso(sa), arrogante.

proudly ['praʊdlɪ] *adv* -**1.** [with satisfaction] orgulhosamente -**2.** *pej* [arrogantly] arrogantemente.

provable ['pruːvəbl] *adj* demonstrável.

prove [pruːv] (*pp*-**d** OR **proven**) *vt* -**1.** [show to be true] provar, demonstrar -**2.** [show o.s. to be]: **to ~ (to be) sthg** demonstrar ser algo; **to ~ o.s. to be sthg** mostrar-se algo.

proven ['pruːvn, 'prəʊvn] <> *pp* ▷ **prove.** <> *adj* comprovado(da).

Provençal [ˌprɒvɒn'sɑːl] <> *adj* provençal. <> *n* [language] provençal *m.*

Provence [prɒ'vɒns] *n* Provença *f*; **in ~** na Provença.

proverb ['prɒvɜːb] *n* provérbio *m.*

proverbial [prə'vɜːbjəl] *adj* proverbial.

provide [prə'vaɪd] *vt* fornecer, prover; **to ~ sb with sthg** proporcionar algo a alguém; **to ~ sthg for sb** oferecer algo a alguém.

➡ **provide for** *vt fus* -**1.** [support] sustentar, manter -**2.** *fml* [make arrangements for] prever, tomar medidas para.

provided [prə'vaɪdɪd] ➡ **provided (that)** *conj* desde que, contanto que.

providence ['prɒvɪdəns] *n (U)* providência *f.*

providential [ˌprɒvɪ'denʃl] *adj fml* providencial.

provider [prə'vaɪdə'] *n* provedor *m*, -ra *f.*

providing [prə'vaɪdɪŋ] ➡ **providing (that)** *conj* desde que.

province ['prɒvɪns] *n* -**1.** [part of country] província *f* -**2.** [specialist subject] campo *m*, ramo *m* do conhecimento; [area of responsibility] alçada *f.*

➡ **provinces** *npl*: **the ~ s** o interior.

provincial [prə'vɪnʃl] *adj* -**1.** [of a province] da província -**2.** *pej* [narrow-minded] provinciano(na).

provision [prə'vɪʒn] *n* -**1.** *(U)* [act of supplying] provisão *f* -**2.** *(U)* [arrangement] providência *f*; **to make ~ for/sthg** tomar providências para algo; **to make ~ for/sb** garantir o sustento de alguém -**3.** [in agreement, law] cláusula *f.*

➡ **provisions** *npl* [supplies] provisões *fpl.*

provisional [prə'vɪʒənl] *adj* provisório(ria).

Provisional IRA *n*: **the ~** braço armado do *Sinn Féin, Irlanda do Norte.*

provisional licence *n UK* carteira *f* provisória.

provisionally [prə'vɪʒnəlɪ] *adv* temporariamente.

proviso [prə'vaɪzəʊ] (*pl*-**s**) *n* condição *f*; **with the ~ that** com a condição de que.

provocation [ˌprɒvə'keɪʃn] *n* provocação *f.*

provocative [prə'vɒkətɪv] *adj* -**1.** [controversial] provocativo(va) -**2.** [sexy] provocante.

provocatively [prə'vɒkətɪvlɪ] *adv* -**1.** [controversially] provocativamente -**2.** [sexily] provocantemente.

provoke [prə'vəʊk] *vt* provocar.

provoking [prə'vəʊkɪŋ] *adj* provocador(ra).

provost *n* -**1.** *UK* [head of college] reitor *m*, -ra *f* -**2.** *Scot* [head of town council] prefeito *m*, -ta *f.*

prow [praʊ] *n* proa *f.*

prowess ['praʊɪs] *n (U) fml* façanha *f.*

prowl [praʊl] <> *n*: **on the ~** de ronda, rondando. <> *vt* rondar por. <> *vi* fazer a ronda.

prowl car *n US* carro *m* patrulha.

prowler ['praʊlə'] *n* gatuno *m*, -na *f.*

proximity [prɒk'sɪmətɪ] *n (U) fml* proximidade *f*; **~ to sthg** proximidade a algo; **in the ~ of sthg** nas proximidades de algo.

proxy ['prɒksɪ] (*pl*-**ies**) *n*: **by ~** por procuração.

prude [pruːd] *n* pessoa *f* pudica, puritano *m*, -na *f.*

prudence ['pruːdns] *n (U) fml* prudência *f.*

prudent ['pruːdnt] *adj* prudente.

prudently ['pruːdntlɪ] *adv* prudentemente.

prudish ['pruːdɪʃ] *adj* pudico(ca).

prune [pruːn] <> *n* ameixa *f* seca. <> *vt* podar.

prurient ['prʊərɪənt] *adj fml* lascivo(va).

Prussian ['prʌʃn] <> *adj* prussiano(na). <> *n* prussiano *m*, -na *f.*

pry [praɪ] (*pt* & *pp* **pried**) *vi* bisbilhotar; **to ~ into sthg** intrometer-se em algo.

PS (*abbr of* **postscript**) *n* PS.

psalm [sɑːm] *n* salmo *m.*

pseud [sjuːd] *n UK inf* intelectualóide *mf.*

pseudo- [ˌsjuːdəʊ] *prefix* pseudo(-).

pseudonym ['sjuːdənɪm] *n* pseudônimo *m.*

psi (*abbr of* **pounds per square inch**) psi *f.*

psoriasis [sɒ'raɪəsɪs] *n (U)* psoríase *f.*

psst [pst] *excl* psiu!

PST (*abbr of* **Pacific Standard Time**) *n horário oficial da costa oeste dos Estados Unidos.*

psych [saɪk] ➡ **psych up** *vt sep inf* preparar psicologicamente; **to ~ o.s. up** preparar-se psicologicamente.

psyche ['saɪkɪ] *n* psique *f.*

psychedelic [ˌsaɪkɪ'delɪk] *adj* psicodélico(ca).

psychiatric [ˌsaɪkɪ'ætrɪk] *adj* psiquiátrico(ca).

psychiatric nurse *n* enfermeiro *m* psiquiátrico, enfermeira *f* psiquiátrica.

psychiatrist [saɪ'kaɪətrɪst] *n* psiquiatra *mf.*

psychiatry [saɪˈkaɪətrɪ] *n (U)* psiquiatria *f.*
psychic [ˈsaɪkɪk] <> *adj* - **1.** [clairvoyant] paranormal - **2.** [mental] psíquico(ca). <> *n* paranormal *mf*, médium *mf.*
psychoanalyse, -yze *US* [ˌsaɪkəʊˈænəlaɪz] *vt* psicanalisar.
psychoanalysis [ˌsaɪkəʊəˈnæləsɪs] *n (U)* psicanálise *f.*
psychoanalyst [ˌsaɪkəʊˈænəlɪst] *n* psicanalista *mf.*
psychological [ˌsaɪkəˈlɒdʒɪkl] *adj* psicológico(ca).
psychological warfare *n (U)* guerra *f* psicológica.
psychologist [saɪˈkɒlədʒɪst] *n* psicólogo *m*, -ga *f.*
psychology [saɪˈkɒlədʒɪ] *n* psicologia *f.*
psychopath [ˈsaɪkəpæθ] *n* psicopata *mf.*
psychosis [saɪˈkəʊsɪs] (*pl* -**choses** [ˈkəʊsiːz]) *n* psicose *f.*
psychosomatic [ˌsaɪkəʊsəˈmætɪk] *adj* psicossomático(ca).
psychotherapy [ˌsaɪkəʊˈθerəpɪ] *n (U)* psicoterapia *f.*
psychotic [saɪˈkɒtɪk] <> *adj* psicótico(ca). <> *n* psicótico *m*, -ca *f.*
pt - **1.** *abbr of* **pint** - **2.** (*abbr of* **point**) pt.
Pt. (*abbr of* **Point**) [on map] Pta.
PT (*abbr of* **physical training**) *n* treinamento *m* físico.
PTA (*abbr of* **parent-teacher association**) *n* ≃ APM *f.*
Pte. (*abbr of* **Private**) soldado do exército britânico.
PTO (*abbr of* **please turn over**) vide verso.
PTV *n* (*abbr of* **pay television**) televisão *f* por assinatura.
pub [pʌb] *n* pub *m*, bar *m.*

PUB

Em toda a Grã-Bretanha, o *pub* é um dos grandes centros da vida social, mas sua importância varia de acordo com a região (Inglaterra, Escócia, Irlanda ou País de Gales) e com a cidade ou povoado em que se encontra. Esses estabelecimentos, de acesso proibido a menores de 16 anos desacompanhados, eram conhecidos por seus horários rígidos de funcionamento, embora tenham se tornado mais flexíveis, de alguns anos para cá (ver *licensing hours*). Em geral, os *pubs* oferecem grande variedade de cervejas e bebidas alcoólicas. Batatinhas fritas em saquinhos eram aperitivos tradicionais nos *pubs*, mas muitos hoje servem pratos rápidos também.

---

pub. (*abbr of* **published**) publicado.
pub-crawl *n UK*: **to go on a** ~ andar de bar em bar.
puberty [ˈpjuːbətɪ] *n (U)* puberdade *f.*
pubescent [pjuːˈbesnt] *adj* púbere.
pubic [ˈpjuːbɪk] *adj* pubiano(na).
public [ˈpʌblɪk] <> *adj* - **1.** [gen] público(ca); **to go** ~ **on sthg** *inf* levar a público; **to make sthg** ~ tornar algo público - **2.** *COMM*: **to go** ~ abrir o capital. <> *n*: **the** ~ o público; **in** ~ em público.
public-address system *n* sistema *m* de autofalantes.
publican [ˈpʌblɪkən] *n UK* dono *m*, -na *f* de um pub.
publication [ˌpʌblɪˈkeɪʃn] *n* publicação *f.*

public company *n* sociedade *f* anônima (*com ações na Bolsa*).
public convenience *n UK* sanitário *m* público.
public domain *n*: **in the** ~ em domínio público.
public holiday *n* feriado *m* nacional.
public house *n UK fml* bar *m*, pub *m.*
publicist [ˈpʌblɪsɪst] *n* publicitário *m*, -ria *f.*
publicity [pʌbˈlɪsɪtɪ] <> *n* publicidade *f.* <> *comp* publicitário(ria).
publicity stunt *n* golpe *f* publicitário, jogada *f* de marketing.
publicize, -ise [ˈpʌblɪsaɪz] *vt* divulgar.
public limited company *n* sociedade *f* anônima (*com ações na Bolsa*).
publicly [ˈpʌblɪklɪ] *adv* publicamente.
public office *n* cargo *m* público.
public opinion *n (U)* opinião *f* pública.
public ownership *n (U)* bem *m* público.
public prosecutor *n* promotor *m* público, promotora *f* pública.
public relations <> *n (U)* relações *fpl* públicas. <> *npl* relações *f* públicas.
public relations officer *n* agente *mf* de relações públicas.
public school *n* - **1.** *UK* [private school] escola *f* particular - **2.** *US* & *Scot* [state school] escola *f* pública.

PUBLIC SCHOOL

Na Inglaterra e no País de Gales, a *public school* é uma escola privada tradicional. Algumas delas, como Eton e Harrow, gozam de grande fama e são muito procuradas. Considera-se que as *public schools* formam a elite da nação. Nos Estados Unidos e, por vezes, também na Escócia, o termo designa uma escola pública.

---

public sector *n* setor *m* público.
public servant *n* servidor *m* público, servidora *f* pública.
public service vehicle *n UK* veículo *m* do serviço público.
public-spirited *adj* com espírito cívico.
public transport *n (U)* transporte *m* público.
public utility *n* utilidade *f* pública.
public works *npl* obras *fpl* públicas.
publish [ˈpʌblɪʃ] <> *vt* - **1.** [gen] publicar - **2.** [make known] divulgar, tornar público(ca). <> *vi* publicar.
publisher [ˈpʌblɪʃəʳ] *n* - **1.** [company] editora *f* - **2.** [person] editor *m*, -ra *f.*
publishing [ˈpʌblɪʃɪŋ] *n (U)* setor *m* editorial.
publishing company, publishing house *n* editora *f.*
pub lunch *n* almoço servido em um pub.
puce [pjuːs] *adj* marrom-avermelhado(da).
puck [pʌk] *n* [ice hockey] disco *m.*
pucker [ˈpʌkəʳ] <> *vt* franzir. <> *vi* enrugar.
pudding [ˈpʊdɪŋ] *n* - **1.** [food - sweet] pudim *m*; [- savoury] pastelão *m* - **2.** (U) *UK* [part of meal] sobremesa *f.*
puddle [ˈpʌdl] *n* poça *f.*
pudgy [ˈpʌdʒɪ] *adj* = **podgy**.

puerile ['pjʊəraɪl] *adj fml* pueril.
Puerto Rican [ˌpwɜ:təʊ'ri:kən] ◇ *adj* porto-riquenho(nha). ◇ *n* porto-riquenho *m*, -nha *f*.
Puerto Rico [ˌpwɜ:təʊ'ri:kəʊ] *n* Porto Rico.
puff [pʌf] ◇ *n* **- 1.** [of cigarette, pipe] baforada *f* **- 2.** [of air, smoke] golfada *f*. ◇ *vt* baforar. ◇ *vi* **-1.** [smoke]: **to ~ at** *or* **on sthg** dar tragadas em algo **- 2.** [pant] ofegar.
➡ **puff out** *vt sep* **-1.** [chest, cheeks] inflar **- 2.** [feathers] eriçar.
➡ **puff up** *vi* **-1.** [eyes, skin] inchar **- 2.** [feathers] eriçar.
puffed [pʌft] *adj* **-1.** [swollen]: **~ up** inchado(da) **- 2.** *UK inf* [out of breath]: **~ (out)** ofegante.
puffed sleeve *n* manga *f* bufante.
puffin ['pʌfɪn] *n* papagaio-do-mar *m*.
puffiness ['pʌfɪnɪs] *n* inchação *f*.
puff pastry, puff paste *US n (U)* massa *f* folhada.
puffy ['pʌfɪ] (*compar* -ier, *superl* -iest) *adj* inchado(-da).
pug [pʌg] *n* dogue *m*.
pugnacious [pʌg'neɪʃəs] *adj fml* belicoso(sa).
puke [pju:k] *vi v inf* vomitar.
pull [pʊl] ◇ *n* **- 1.** [tug with hand] puxão *m* **- 2.** [influence] prestígio *m*. ◇ *vt* **- 1.** [gen] puxar; **to ~ sthg to pieces** despedaçar algo **- 2.** [curtains - open] abrir; [- close] puxar **- 3.** [take out - cork, tooth] arrancar; [- gun] sacar; **she ~ ed herself out of the water** ela se afastou da água **- 4.** [muscle, hamstring] distender **- 5.** [attract] atrair. ◇ *vi* [tug with hand] puxar.
➡ **pull ahead** *vi* ultrapassar; **to ~ ahead of sb/sthg** passar a frente de alguém/algo.
➡ **pull apart** *vt sep* desmontar.
➡ **pull at** *vt fus* puxar, dar puxões em.
➡ **pull away** *vi* **-1.** [from roadside]: **to ~ away (from)** afastar-se (da margem da estrada) **- 2.** [in race]: **to ~ away (from)** disparar na frente (de).
➡ **pull back** *vi* recuar.
➡ **pull down** *vt sep* demolir.
➡ **pull in** *vi* [vehicle] encostar.
➡ **pull off** *vt sep* **-1.** [take off] tirar rapidamente **- 2.** [succeed in] conseguir levar a cabo.
➡ **pull on** *vt sep* **-1.** [clothes] vestir rapidamente **- 2.** [shoes] calçar rapidamente.
➡ **pull out** ◇ *vt sep* retirar. ◇ *vi* **-1.** [train] partir **- 2.** [vehicle] entrar na estrada **- 3.** [withdraw] retirar.
➡ **pull over** *vi* [vehicle, driver] encostar.
➡ **pull through** ◇ *vi* [patient] restabelecer-se, recuperar-se. ◇ *vt sep* [subj: doctor] ajudar na recuperação de.
➡ **pull together** ◇ *vt sep*: **to ~ o.s. together** acalmar-se. ◇ *vi* cooperar, unir forças.
➡ **pull up** ◇ *vt sep* **-1.** [raise] levantar **- 2.** [move closer] aproximar **- 3.** [stop]: **to ~ sb up short** deter alguém. ◇ *vi* parar, deter.
pull-down menu *n COMPUT* menu *m* suspenso.
pulley ['pʊlɪ] (*pl* pulleys) *n* roldana *f*.
pullout ['pʊlaʊt] *n* **-1.** [of troops] retirada *f* **- 2.** [in magazine] encarte *m*.
pullover ['pʊlˌəʊvəʳ] *n* pulôver *m*.
pulp [pʌlp] ◇ *adj* barato(ta), de má qualidade. ◇ *n* **-1.** [soft mass] pasta *f* **- 2.** [of fruit] polpa *f* **- 3.** [of wood] cerne *m*. ◇ *vt* reduzir à pasta de papel.
pulpit ['pʊlpɪt] *n* púlpito *m*.
pulsar ['pʌlsɑ:ʳ] *n* pulsar *m*.
pulsate [pʌl'seɪt] *vi* **-1.** [heart] pulsar, palpitar **- 2.** [air, sound] vibrar; **pulsating rhythm** ritmo *m* vibrante.
pulse [pʌls] ◇ *n* **-1.** [in body] pulso *m*; **to take sb's ~** tomar o pulso de alguém **- 2.** *TECH* impulso *m*. ◇ *vi* [throb - blood] pulsar; [- music, room] vibrar.
➡ **pulses** *npl* [food] grãos *mpl*.
pulverize, -ise ['pʌlvəraɪz] *vt* pulverizar.
puma ['pju:mə] (*pl inv* or -s) *n* puma *m*.
pumice (stone) ['pʌmɪs-] *n (U)* pedra-pomes *f*.
pummel ['pʌml] (*UK pt* & *pp* -led, *cont* -ling, *US pt* & *pp* -ed, *cont* -ing) *vt* esmurrar.
pump [pʌmp] ◇ *n* bomba *f*. ◇ *vt* **-1.** [convey by pumping] bombear **- 2.** *inf* [invest]: **to ~ money into sthg** injetar dinheiro em algo **- 3.** *inf* [interrogate] sondar. ◇ *vi* **-1.** [machine] bater **- 2.** [person] arfar **- 3.** [heart] palpitar.
➡ **pumps** *npl* [shoes] sapatilhas *fpl*.
pumpernickel ['pʌmpənɪkl] *n (U)* pão *m* de centeio.
pumpkin ['pʌmpkɪn] *n* abóbora *f*.
pumpkin pie *n* torta *f* de abóbora.
pun [pʌn] *n* jogo *m* de palavras.
punch [pʌntʃ] ◇ *n* **-1.** [blow] soco *m* **- 2.** [tool] punção *m* **-3.** (U) [drink] ponche *m*. ◇ *vt* **-1.** [hit] esmurrar, soquear **- 2.** [perforate - paper, ticket] picar; [- hole] perfurar.
➡ **punch in** *vi US* bater o ponto *(na entrada)*.
➡ **punch out** *vi US* bater o ponto *(na saída)*.
Punch-and-Judy show [-'dʒu:dɪ-] *n* teatro *de fantoches para crianças apresentado normalmente na praia*.
punch-bag, punching bag *US n* saco *m* de pancadas.
punch ball *n* saco *m* de pancadas.
punch bowl *n* poncheira *f*.
punch-drunk *adj* zonzo(za), grogue.
punch(ed) card [pʌntʃ(t)-] *n* cartão *m* perfurado.
punching bag *n US* = punch-bag.
punch line *n* frase *f* final, arremate *m (de uma história)*.
punch-up *n UK inf* briga *f*.
punchy ['pʌntʃɪ] (*compar* -ier, *superl* -iest) *adj inf* incisivo(va).
punctilious [pʌŋk'tɪlɪəs] *adj fml* escrupuloso(sa), meticuloso(sa).
punctual ['pʌŋktʃʊəl] *adj* pontual.
punctually ['pʌŋktʃʊəlɪ] *adv* pontualmente.
punctuate ['pʌŋktʃʊeɪt] *vt* **-1.** [add punctuation to] pontuar **- 2.** [interrupt]: **to be ~ d by** *or* **with sthg** ser interrompido(da) por algo.
punctuation [ˌpʌŋktʃʊ'eɪʃn] *n (U)* pontuação *f*.
punctuation mark *n* sinal *m* de pontuação.
puncture ['pʌŋktʃəʳ] ◇ *n* furo *m*. ◇ *vt* **-1.** [tyre, ball] furar **- 2.** [lung, skin] perfurar.
pundit ['pʌndɪt] *n* especialista *mf*, autoridade *f (em algum assunto)*.
pungent ['pʌndʒənt] *adj* **-1.** [strong-smelling] forte, penetrante **- 2.** *fig* [powerful] pujente.
punish ['pʌnɪʃ] *vt* punir; **to ~ sb for sthg/for doing**

sthg punir alguém por algo/por fazer algo.
punishable [ˈpʌnɪʃəbl] adj punível, castigável.
punishing [ˈpʌnɪʃɪŋ] adj penoso(sa).
punishment [ˈpʌnɪʃmənt] n -**1.** [gen] punição f, castigo m -**2.** [heavy use]: **to take a lot of** ~ sofrer estragos.
punitive [ˈpjuːnətɪv] adj punitivo(va).
Punjab [ˌpʌnˈʒɑːb] n: **the** ~ o Punjab; **in the** ~ no Punjab.
Punjabi [ˌpʌnˈʒɑːbɪ] ◇ adj punjabi. ◇ n -**1.** [person] punjabi mf -**2.** [language] punjabi m.
punk [pʌŋk] ◇ adj punk. ◇ n -**1.** (U) [music]: ~ (**rock**) rock m punk -**2.** [person]: ~ (**rocker**) roqueiro m, -ra f punk -**3.** US inf [lout] rebelde mf.
punnet [ˈpʌnɪt] n UK cesto m.
punt [pʌnt] ◇ n -**1.** [boat] barco m a remo -**2.** [Irish currency] libra f irlandesa. ◇ vi [in boat] navegar em barco a remo.
punter [ˈpʌntəʳ] n -**1.** [someone who bets] apostador m, -ra f -**2.** UK inf [customer] cliente mf.
puny [ˈpjuːnɪ] (compar-ier, superl-iest) adj -**1.** [person] raquítico(ca) -**2.** [limbs] fraco(ca) -**3.** [effort] débil.
pup [pʌp] n -**1.** [young dog] cachorrinho m, -nha f -**2.** [young seal, otter] filhote m.
pupil [ˈpjuːpl] n -**1.** [student] aluno m, -na f -**2.** [follower] pupilo m, -la f -**3.** [of eye] pupila f.
puppet [ˈpʌpɪt] n -**1.** [string puppet] marionete f -**2.** [glove puppet] fantoche m -**3.** pej [person, country] fantoche mf.
puppet government n governo m de marionetes.
puppet show n teatro m de marionetes.
puppy [ˈpʌpɪ] (pl-ies) n cachorrinho m, -nha f.
puppy fat n (U) inf dobrinhas fpl (do bebê).
purchase [ˈpɜːtʃəs] fml ◇ n -**1.** (U) [act of buying] compra f, aquisição f -**2.** [thing bought] aquisição f -**3.** [grip] apoio m. ◇ vt comprar, adquirir.
purchase order n ordem f de compra.
purchase price n preço m de compra.
purchaser [ˈpɜːtʃəsəʳ] n comprador m, -ra f.
purchase tax n UK imposto m de compras.
purchasing power [ˈpɜːtʃəsɪŋ-] n (U) poder m de compra.
purdah [ˈpɜːdə] n (U) RELIG prática muçulmana de manter as mulheres longe do contato com os homens.
pure [pjʊəʳ] adj -**1.** [gen] puro(ra) -**2.** [clear] cristalino(na) -**3.** literary [chaste] puro(ra) -**4.** [for emphasis] mero(ra), puro(ra).
purebred [ˈpjʊəbred] adj puro-sangue.
puree [ˈpjʊəreɪ] ◇ n purê m. ◇ vt amassar.
purely [ˈpjʊəlɪ] adv puramente.
pureness [ˈpjʊənɪs] n (U) pureza f.
purgative [ˈpɜːgətɪv] n purgante m.
purgatory [ˈpɜːgətrɪ] n (U) hum [suffering] purgatório m.
➡ **Purgatory** n [place] Purgatório m.
purge [pɜːdʒ] ◇ n POL expurgo m. ◇ vt -**1.** POL purgar -**2.** [rid]: **to** ~ **sthg (of sthg)** livrar algo (de algo); **to** ~ **o.s. (of sthg)** livrar-se (de algo).
purification [ˌpjʊərɪfɪˈkeɪʃn] n (U) purificação f.
purifier [ˈpjʊərɪfaɪəʳ] n purificador m.

purify [ˈpjʊərɪfaɪ] (pt & pp -ied) vt purificar.
purist [ˈpjʊərɪst] n purista mf.
puritan [ˈpjʊərɪtən] ◇ adj puritano(na). ◇ n puritano m, -na f.
puritanical [ˌpjʊərɪˈtænɪkl] adj pej puritano(na).
purity [ˈpjʊərətɪ] n (U) -**1.** pureza f -**2.** literary [chastity] pureza f.
purl [pɜːl] ◇ n laçada f. ◇ vt dar uma laçada.
purloin [pɜːˈlɔɪn] vt fml surrupiar.
purple [ˈpɜːpl] ◇ adj purpúreo(rea). ◇ n púrpura f.
purport [pəˈpɔːt] vi fml: **to** ~ **to do/be sthg** pretender fazer/ser algo.
purpose [ˈpɜːpəs] n -**1.** [objective, reason] objetivo m, propósito m -**2.** [use] propósito m; **to no** ~ em vão -**3.** [determination] determinação f.
➡ **on purpose** adv de propósito.
purpose-built adj especialmente construído (da), feito(ta) sob medida.
purposeful [ˈpɜːpəsfʊl] adj determinado(da), resoluto(ta).
purposely [ˈpɜːpəslɪ] adv deliberadamente, intencionalmente.
purr [pɜːʳ] ◇ n -**1.** [of cat] ronrom m -**2.** [of engine] ronco m. ◇ vi -**1.** [gen] roncar -**2.** [cat] ronronar.
purse [pɜːs] ◇ n -**1.** [for money] carteira f -**2.** US [handbag] bolsa f. ◇ vt franzir (em desagrado).
purser [ˈpɜːsəʳ] n comissário m, -ria f de bordo.
purse snatcher [-ˌsnætʃəʳ] n US trombadinha mf.
purse strings npl: **to hold the** ~ controlar os gastos, administrar o dinheiro.
pursue [pəˈsjuː] vt -**1.** [follow] perseguir -**2.** [hobby] dedicar-se a -**3.** [interest, aim] buscar, ir atrás de -**4.** [take further] aprofundar-se em.
pursuer [pəˈsjuːəʳ] n perseguidor m, -ra f.
pursuit [pəˈsjuːt] n -**1.** [gen] perseguição f; **in** ~ **of sb/sthg** de busca de alguém/algo; **to be in hot** ~ perseguir de perto -**2.** [of happiness, security etc] fml busca f -**3.** [occupation, activity] atividade f.
purveyor [pəˈveɪəʳ] n fml fornecedor m, -ra f.
pus [pʌs] n (U) pus m.
push [pʊʃ] ◇ n -**1.** [shove] empurrão m -**2.** [on button, bell] pressionamento m -**3.** [campaign] pressão f -**4.** phr: **to give sb the** ~ UK inf [end relationship] dar o fora em alguém; [dismiss] mandar alguém embora. ◇ vt -**1.** [press, move - door, person] empurrar; [- button] apertar -**2.** [encourage] incitar; **to** ~ **sb to do sthg** incitar alguém a fazer algo -**3.** [force] impelir; **to** ~ **sb into doing sthg** impelir alguém a fazer algo -**4.** inf [promote] promover -**5.** drugs sl [sell illegally] traficar -**6.** inf [approach]: **we were** ~ **ing 90 miles an hour** estávamos beirando as 90 milhas por hora. ◇ vi -**1.** [shove] empurrar; **to** ~ **through** abrir caminho aos empurrões em -**2.** [on button, bell] apertar -**3.** [campaign]: **to** ~ **for sthg** fazer pressão por algo.
➡ **push ahead** vi prosseguir; **to** ~ **ahead with sthg** seguir em frente com algo.
➡ **push around** vt sep inf fig [bully] mandar.
➡ **push in** vi [in queue] furar.
➡ **push off** vi inf [go away] largar-se.
➡ **push on** vi [continue] seguir em frente sem parar.
➡ **push over** vt sep derrubar.

push through *vt sep* [force to be accepted] conseguir que se aprove.

pushbike ['puʃbaɪk] *n UK* bici *f*.

push-button *adj* de botão.

pushcart ['puʃkɑːt] *n* carrinho *m* de mão.

pushchair ['puʃtʃeəʳ] *n UK* carrinho *m* de bebê.

pushed [puʃt] *adj inf*: to be ~ for sthg andar meio curto(ta) de algo; to be hard ~ to do sthg estar com dificuldades para fazer algo.

pusher ['puʃəʳ] *n drugs sl* traficante *mf*, vendedor *m*, -ra *f* de drogas.

pushover ['puʃ,əuvəʳ] *n inf* otário *m*, -ria *f*.

push-start *vt* arrancar empurrando.

push-up *n US* flexão *f*.

pushy ['puʃɪ] (*compar* -ier, *superl* -iest) *adj pej* agressivo(va).

puss [pus], **pussy (cat)** ['pusɪ-] *n inf* gatinho *m*, bichano *m*.

pussy willow ['pusɪ-] *n* salgueiro *m*.

put [put] (*pt* & *pp* put, *cont* -ting) *vt* - **1**. [gen] colocar, pôr - **2**. [express] colocar, expressar; to ~ it to sb that expor a alguém que, colocar para alguém que - **3**. [ask] colocar, perguntar - **4**. [cause to be] colocar; to ~ sb out of work deixar alguém sem trabalho - **5**. [estimate]: to ~ sthg at avaliar algo em - **6**. [invest]: to ~ sthg into sthg investir algo em algo, colocar algo em algo - **7**. [apply - responsibility]: to ~ responsiblity on sb/sthg colocar responsabilidade em alguém/algo; to ~ pressure on sb/sthg pressionar alguém/algo; to ~ tax on sthg colocar impostos sobre algo - **8**. [write] escrever.

➡ **put across** *vt sep* expor.

➡ **put aside** *vt sep* - **1**. [place on one side] colocar de lado - **2**. [save] poupar - **3**. [disregard] deixar de lado.

➡ **put away** *vt sep* - **1**. [tidy away] colocar no lugar, organizar - **2**. *inf* [lock up] encerrar (*na prisão*).

➡ **put back** *vt sep* - **1**. [replace] repor no lugar - **2**. [postpone] adiar - **3**. [clock, watch] atrasar.

➡ **put by** *vt sep* [money] poupar.

➡ **put down** *vt sep* - **1**. [lay down] largar, pôr no chão - **2**. [quell] sufocar - **3**. *inf* [criticize] humilhar, rebaixar - **4**. [write down] apontar - **5**. *UK* [kill] sacrificar.

➡ **put down to** *vt sep* atribuir a.

➡ **put forward** *vt sep* - **1**. [propose] apresentar, propor - **2**. [advance] adiar - **3**. [clock, watch] adiantar.

➡ **put in** *vt sep* - **1**. [spend] dedicar - **2**. [submit] apresentar.

➡ **put off** *vt sep* - **1**. [postpone] adiar - **2**. [switch off - radio, light] desligar; [- light] desligar - **3**. [cause to wait] fazer esperar - **4**. [discourage] desanimar; dissuadir - **5**. [disturb] distrair - **6**. [cause to dislike] desanimar, desestimular; to ~ sb off sthg desestimular alguém de algo.

➡ **put on** *vt sep* - **1**. [wear - trousers, hat] vestir; [- shoes] calçar - **2**. [arrange] montar - **3**. [gain in weight]: to ~ on weight engordar - **4**. [switch on - radio, light] ligar; [- brake] acionar - **5**. [play] tocar, pôr - **6**. [start cooking] colocar no fogo - **7**. [pretend] fingir - **8**. [bet] apostar - **9**. [add] acrescentar - **10**. *US inf* [tease] zombar de.

➡ **put onto** *vt sep* [tell about]: to ~ sb onto sthg indicar algo a alguém.

➡ **put out** *vt sep* - **1**. [place outside] colocar *OR* pôr para fora - **2**. [issue] tornar público(ca) - **3**. [extinguish] apagar - **4**. [switch off] desligar - **5**. [extend] espichar - **6**. *inf* [injure] deslocar - **7**. [annoy, upset]: to be ~ out ficar chateado(da) - **8**. [inconvenience] importunar, incomodar; to ~ o.s. out incomodar-se.

➡ **put over** *vt sep* = put across.

➡ **put through** *vt sep TELEC* transferir.

➡ **put together** *vt sep* - **1**. [assemble] montar - **2**. [combine] juntar, misturar - **3**. [organize] organizar.

➡ **put up** ⟨⟩ *vt sep* - **1**. [build] erguer - **2**. [raise and open - umbrella] abrir; [- flag] hastear - **3**. [fix to wall] afixar - **4**. [provide] pôr - **5**. [propose] indicar - **6**. [increase] aumentar - **7**. [provide accommodation for] hospedar. ⟨⟩ *vt fus* [offer, present] manifestar.

➡ **put upon** *vt fus UK*: to be ~ upon ser explorado(da).

➡ **put up to** *vt sep*: to ~ sb up to sthg induzir alguém a algo.

➡ **put up with** *vt fus* suportar, agüentar.

putative ['pjuːtətɪv] *adj fml* suposto(ta).

put-down *n inf* comentário *m* maldoso.

putrefaction [,pjuːtrɪ'fækʃn] *n* (U) putrefação *f*.

putrefy ['pjuːtrɪfaɪ] (*pt* & *pp* -ied) *vi fml* putrefazer.

putrid ['pjuːtrɪd] *adj fml* putrefato(ta).

putsch [putʃ] *n* golpe *m* de estado.

putt [pʌt] ⟨⟩ *n* tacada *f* leve (*no golfe*). ⟨⟩ *vt* dar uma tacada leve em. ⟨⟩ *vi* dar uma tacada leve.

putter ['pʌtəʳ] *n* taco *m* de golfe (*para tacadas leves*).

➡ **putter about, putter around** *US vi* = potter about.

putting green ['pʌtɪŋ-] *n* minicampo *m* sem obstáculos (*para jogar golfe*).

putty ['pʌtɪ] *n* (U) massa *f* de vidraceiro.

put-up job *n inf* embuste *m*.

put-upon *adj inf* explorado(da); to feel ~ sentir-se usado (usa) da.

puzzle ['pʌzl] ⟨⟩ *n* - **1**. [toy, game] quebra-cabeça *m* - **2**. [mystery] enigma *m*. ⟨⟩ *vt* deixar perplexo(xa). ⟨⟩ *vi*: to ~ over sthg quebrar a cabeça com algo.

➡ **puzzle out** *vt sep* decifrar.

puzzled ['pʌzld] *adj* confuso(sa), perplexo(xa).

puzzling ['pʌzlɪŋ] *adj* desconcertante.

PVC (*abbr of* polyvinyl chloride) *n* PVC *m*.

Pvt. (*abbr of* Private) soldado *m* raso.

p.w. (*abbr of* per week) por semana.

PWR (*abbr of* pressurized-water reactor) *n* reator de água pressurizada.

PX (*abbr of* post exchange) *n* loja em base militar norte-americana.

Pygmy (*pl* -ies) *n* pigmeu *m*, -méia *f*.

pyjama *comp* de pijama.

pyjamas [pə'dʒɑːməz] *npl* pijama *m*.

pylon ['paɪlən] *n ELEC* torre *f* (*de eletricidade*).

PYO (*abbr of* pick your own) *n* colha você mesmo, cartaz em fazendas convidando a pessoa a colher vegetais ou frutas a preços inferiores aos cobrados em supermercados.

pyramid ['pɪrəmɪd] n pirâmide f.
pyramid selling n (U) vendas fpl em pirâmide.
pyre ['paɪə^r] n pira f.
Pyrenean [,pɪrə'niːən] adj pirenaico(ca).
Pyrenees [,pɪrə'niːz] npl: the ~ os Pireneus.
Pyrex® ['paɪreks] <> n (U) pírex® m inv. <> comp de pírex.
pyromaniac [,paɪrəʊ'meɪnɪæk] n piromaníaco m, -ca f.
pyrotechnics [,paɪrəʊ'tekniks] <> n (U) [science] pirotécnica f. <> npl fig [show of brilliance] espetáculo m pirotécnico.
python ['paɪθn] (pl inv OR -s) n píton m.

q (pl q's OR qs), **Q** (pl Q's OR Qs) [kjuː] n [letter] q, Q m.
Qatar [kæ'taː^r] n Qatar; **in** ~ no Qatar.
QC (abbr of **Queen's Counsel**) n advogado que representa clientes nas cortes superiores britânicas.
QED (abbr of **quod erat demonstrandum**) q.e.d., c.q.d.
QM (abbr of **quartermaster**) n quartelmestre m.
q.t., QT (abbr of **quiet**) inf: **on the** ~ em segredo.
Q-tip® n US cotonete m.
qty (abbr of **quantity**) qtd f.
quack [kwæk] <> n -1. [noise] grasnido m -2. inf pej [doctor] curandeiro m charlatão, curandeira f charlatona. <> vi grasnir.
quad [kwɒd] n -1. (abbr of **quadruplet**) quádruplos mpl, -plas fpl -2. (abbr of **quadrangle**) pátio cercado por edifícios, em geral em escola ou universidade.
quadrangle ['kwɒdræŋgl] n -1. [figure] quadrângulo m -2. [courtyard] pátio m.
quadrant ['kwɒdrənt] n quadrante m.
quadraphonic [,kwɒdrə'fɒnɪk] adj quadrafônico(ca).
quadrilateral [,kwɒdrɪ'lætərəl] <> adj quadrilateral. <> n quadrilátero m.
quadruped ['kwɒdrʊped] n quadrúpede m.
quadruple [kwɒ'druːpl] <> adj quadruplicado(da). <> vt & vi quadruplicar.
quadruplets ['kwɒdrʊplɪts] npl quadrigêmeos mpl, -meas fpl.
quads [kwɒdz] npl inf quadrigêmeos mpl, -meas fpl.
quaff [kwɒf] vt dated emborcar (bebida alcoólica).
quagmire ['kwægmaɪə^r] n pântano m.
quail [kweɪl] (pl inv OR -s) <> n codorna f. <> vi literary amedrontar-se.

quaint [kweɪnt] adj pitoresco(ca), singular.
quaintness n (U) singularidade f.
quake [kweɪk] <> n (abbr of **earthquake**) inf terremoto m. <> vi tremer.
Quaker ['kweɪkə^r] n quacre m.
qualification [,kwɒlɪfɪ'keɪʃn] n -1. [examination, certificate] qualificação f, título m -2. [quality, skill] qualificação f -3. [qualifying statement] restrição f, ressalva f.
qualified ['kwɒlɪfaɪd] adj -1. [trained] qualificado(da) -2. [able]: **to be** ~ **to do sthg** estar qualificado(da) para fazer algo -3. [limited] com ressalvas.
qualify ['kwɒlɪfaɪ] (pt & pp -ied) <> vt -1. [modify] restringir -2. [entitle]: **to** ~ **sb to do sthg** qualificar alguém para fazer algo. <> vi -1. [pass exams] habilitar-se -2. [be entitled]: **to** ~ **(for sthg)** qualificar-se(para algo) -3. SPORT classificar-se.
qualifying ['kwɒlɪfaɪɪŋ] adj -1. [modifying] qualificativo(va) -2. [entitling] qualificador(ra) -3. SPORT classificatório(ria); ~ **round** fase f classificatória, eliminatórias fpl.
qualitative ['kwɒlɪtətɪv] adj qualitativo(va).
quality ['kwɒlətɪ] (pl -ies) <> n qualidade f. <> comp de qualidade.
quality control n (U) controle m de qualidade.
quality press n UK: **the** ~ a imprensa não-sensacionalista or de qualidade.
qualms [kwaːmz] npl receio m, escrúpulos mpl.
quandary ['kwɒndərɪ] (pl -ies) n dilema m; **to be in a** ~ **about** OR **over sthg** estar num dilema sobre algo.
quango ['kwæŋgəʊ] (abbr of **quasi-autonomous non-governmental organization**) (pl -s) n UK usu pej na Grã-Bretanha, conselho administrativo não-eleito, indicado pelo governo para administrar um serviço público.
quantifiable [kwɒntɪ'faɪəbl] adj quantificável.
quantify ['kwɒntɪfaɪ] (pt & pp -ied) vt quantificar.
quantitative ['kwɒntɪtətɪv] adj quantitativo(va).
quantity ['kwɒntətɪ] (pl -ies) n -1. quantidade f; **in** ~ em quantidade -2. phr: **an unknown** ~ uma incógnita.
quantity surveyor n calculista mf de obra.
quantum leap ['kwɒntəm-] n avanço m impressionante.
quantum theory ['kwɒntəm-] n teoria f quântica.
quarantine ['kwɒrəntiːn] <> n quarentena f; **to be in** ~ estar em OR de quarentena. <> vt pôr em quarentena.
quark [kwaːk] n -1. PHYSICS quark m -2. CULIN queijo m tipo quark.
quarrel ['kwɒrəl] (UK pt & pp -led, cont -ling, US pt & pp -ed, cont -ing) <> n discussão f; **to have no** ~ **with sb/sthg** não ter nada contra alguém/algo. <> vi discutir; **to** ~ **with sb** discutir com alguém; **to** ~ **with sthg** não estar de acordo sobre algo.
quarrelsome ['kwɒrəlsəm] adj briguento(ta).
quarry ['kwɒrɪ] (pl -ies, pt & pp -ied) <> n -1. [place] pedreira f -2. [prey] presa f. <> vt extrair.
quarry tile n ladrilho m.
quart [kwɔːt] n -1. UK [unit of measurement] quarto m de galão (1,14 litro) -2. US [unit of measurement]

quarto m de galão *(0,95 litro)*.

quarter ['kwɔ:təʳ] n **-1.** [fraction] quarto m **-2.** [in telling time]: **it's a ~ past two** UK, **it's a ~ after two** US são duas e quinze; **it's a ~ to two** UK, **it's a ~ of two** US faltam quinze para as duas **-3.** [of year] trimestre m **-4.** US [coin] moeda f de 25 centavos **-5.** [four ounces] quarto m de libra *(113,396 gr)* **-6.** [area in town] quarteirão m **-7.** [direction] lugar m, parte f; **they came from all ~s of the globe** eles vieram de todos os cantos da terra.
  quarters npl [rooms] alojamentos mpl.
  at close quarters adv de perto.

quarterback ['kwɔ:təbæk] n US jogador de futebol americano que lança a bola nas jogadas ofensivas.

quarterdeck ['kwɔ:tədek] n tombadilho m superior.

quarter-final n quarta-de-final f.

quarter-hour adj de quinze minutos.

quarter-light n UK janelinha f para ventilação *(no automóvel)*.

quarterly ['kwɔ:təlɪ] *(pl -ies)* ⟨⟩ adj trimestral. ⟨⟩ adv trimestralmente. ⟨⟩ n revista f trimestral.

quartermaster ['kwɔ:tə,mɑ:stəʳ] n MIL quartelmestre m.

quarter note n US MUS semínima f.

quartet [kwɔ:'tet] n quarteto m. ·

quarto ['kwɔ:təʊ] *(pl -s)* n in quarto m inv.

quartz [kwɔ:ts] n (U) quartzo m.

quartz watch n relógio m de quartzo.

quasar ['kweɪzɑ:ʳ] n quasar m.

quash [kwɒʃ] vt **-1.** [reject] revogar, anular **-2.** [quell] sufocar, reprimir.

quasi- ['kweɪzaɪ] prefix quase-.

quaver ['kweɪvəʳ] ⟨⟩ n **-1.** MUS colcheia f **-2.** [in voice] tremor m. ⟨⟩ vi tremer.

quavering ['kweɪvərɪŋ] adj trêmulo(la).

quay [ki:] n cais m.

quayside ['ki:saɪd] n cais m.

queasy ['kwi:zɪ] *(compar -ier, superl -iest)* adj enjoado(da).

Quebec [kwɪ'bek] n [province, city] Québec; **in ~** em Québec.

Quebecer, Quebecker [kwɪ'bekəʳ] n quebequense mf.

queen [kwi:n] n **-1.** [gen] rainha f **-2.** [playing card] dama f.

queen bee n (abelha f) rainha f.

queen mother n: **the ~** a rainha-mãe.

Queen's Counsel n UK advogado inglês de alta ordem.

Queen's English n UK: **the ~** o inglês falado com perfeição na Grã-Bretanha.

queen's evidence n UK: **to turn ~** testemunhar *(um criminoso)* frente a um tribunal contra outros criminosos em troca de diminuição da pena.

queer [kwɪəʳ] ⟨⟩ adj [odd] esquisito(ta), estranho(nha). ⟨⟩ n inf pej [homosexual] veado m, bicha f.

quell [kwel] vt **-1.** [rebellion] sufocar, reprimir **-2.** [unease, anger] dominar, conter.

quench [kwentʃ] vt: **to ~ one's thirst** matar a sede.

querulous ['kwerʊləs] adj fml lamuriante.

query ['kwɪərɪ] *(pl -ies, pt & pp -ied)* ⟨⟩ n pergunta f, dúvida f. ⟨⟩ vt pôr em dúvida.

quest [kwest] n literary busca f; **~ for sthg** busca por algo.

question ['kwestʃn] ⟨⟩ n **-1.** [gen] questão f **-2.** [query] pergunta f; **to ask (sb) a ~** fazer uma pergunta a alguém **-3.** [doubt] dúvida f; **to** OR **call sthg into ~** por OR colocar algo em dúvida; **to** OR **bring sthg into ~** colocar algo em questão; **beyond ~** sem nenhuma dúvida; **open to ~** debatível; **without ~** sem dúvida **-4.** phr: **there's no ~ of ...** não há dúvida de (que) ... ⟨⟩ vt **-1.** [interrogate] interrogar **-2.** [express doubt about] questionar.
  in question adv: **the matter in ~** o assunto em questão.
  out of the question adj fora de questão.

questionable ['kwestʃənəbl] adj questionável.

questioner ['kwestʃənəʳ] n interrogador m, -ra f.

questioning ['kwestʃənɪŋ] ⟨⟩ adj de interrogação. ⟨⟩ n (U) interrogatório m.

question mark n ponto m de interrogação.

question master esp UK, **quizmaster** ['kwɪz,mɑ:stəʳ] esp US n apresentador m, -ra f *(de um show de perguntas)*.

questionnaire [,kwestʃə'neəʳ] n questionário m.

question time n UK POL audiência no parlamento britânico na qual os ministros respondem a perguntas dos parlamentares.

queue [kju:] UK ⟨⟩ n fila f; **to jump the ~** furar a fila. ⟨⟩ vi fazer fila; **to ~ (up) for sthg** fazer fila para algo.

queue-jump vi UK furar a fila.

quibble ['kwɪbl] pej ⟨⟩ n chorumela f. ⟨⟩ vi queixar-se por bobagem, lamuriar-se; **to ~ over** OR **about sthg** queixar-se por bobagem sobre algo.

quiche [ki:ʃ] n quiche f.

quick [kwɪk] ⟨⟩ adj rápido(da). ⟨⟩ adv depressa, rápido.

quicken ['kwɪkn] ⟨⟩ vt [make faster] apressar, acelerar. ⟨⟩ vi [get faster] acelerar(-se).

quickly ['kwɪklɪ] adv **-1.** [rapidly] rapidamente **-2.** [without delay] depressa, rápido.

quickness ['kwɪknɪs] n rapidez f.

quicksand ['kwɪksænd] n areia f movediça.

quicksilver ['kwɪk,sɪlvəʳ] n (U) dated mercúrio m.

quickstep ['kwɪkstep] n: **the ~** dança de salão de passos rápidos.

quick-tempered adj irritadiço(ça).

quick-witted [-'wɪtɪd] adj arguto(ta).

quid [kwɪd] *(pl inv)* n UK inf libra f *(esterlina)*.

quid pro quo [-'kwəʊ] *(pl quid pro quos)* n compensação f, troca f.

quiescent [kwar'esnt] adj fml quiescente.

quiet ['kwaɪət] ⟨⟩ adj **-1.** [gen] quieto(ta); **in a ~ voice** numa voz baixa; **to keep ~ about sthg** guardar silêncio sobre algo; **be ~!** fique quieto(ta)! **-2.** [tranquil] tranqüilo(la) **-3.** [not busy] parado(da) **-4.** [discreet] suave, discreto(ta); **to have a ~**

word with sb falar discretamente com alguém
- **5.** [intimate] íntimo(ma). <> *n (U)* tranqüilidade
f, silêncio *m*; **on the** ~ *inf* na surdina, às
escondidas. <> *vt US* acalmar, tranqüilizar.
➡ **quiet down** <> *vt sep US* acalmar, tranqüilizar. <> *vi* acalmar-se, tranqüilizar-se.

quieten [ˈkwaɪətn] *vt* acalmar, tranqüilizar.
➡ **quieten down** <> *vt sep* acalmar, tranqüilizar. <> *vi* acalmar-se, tranqüilizar-se.

quietly [ˈkwaɪətlɪ] *adv* - **1.** [without noise] sem fazer
barulho - **2.** [without excitement] tranqüilamente
- **3.** [without fuss] discretamente.

quietness [ˈkwaɪətnɪs] *n (U)* quietude *f*, tranqüilidade *f*.

quiff [kwɪf] *n UK* topete *m*.

quill (pen) [kwɪl-] *n* pena *f (de escrever)*.

quilt [kwɪlt] *n* acolchoado *m*, edredom *m*.

quilted [ˈkwɪltɪd] *adj* acolchoado(da).

quince [kwɪns] *n* marmelo *m*.

quinine [kwɪˈniːn] *n (U)* quinina *f*.

quins *UK* [kwɪnz], **quints** *US* [kwɪnts] *npl inf*
quíntuplos *mpl*, -plas *fpl*.

quintessential [ˌkwɪntəˈsenʃl] *adj* puro(ra); **this**
passage is ~ **Dickens** esta passagem é Dickens
puro.

quintet [kwɪnˈtet] *n* quinteto *m*.

quints *npl US* = quins.

quintuplets [kwɪnˈtjuːplɪts] *npl* quíntuplos *mpl*,
-plas *fpl*.

quip [kwɪp] *(pt & pp* -ped, *cont* -ping) <> *n* gracejo
m. <> *vi* gracejar.

quire [kwaɪəʳ] *n* mão *f* de papel.

quirk [kwɜːk] *n* - **1.** [habit] mania *f*, esquisitice *f* - **2.**
[strange event] estranha coincidência *f*; **by a** ~ **of**
fate por um capricho do destino.

quirky [ˈkwɜːkɪ] *(compar* -ier, *superl* -iest) *adj* peculiar.

quit [kwɪt] *(UK pt & pp* quit *OR* -ted, *cont* -ting, *US pt*
& *pp* quit, *cont* -ting) <> *vt* - **1.** [resign from]
abandonar, deixar - **2.** [stop]: **to** ~ **smoking** deixar
de fumar. <> *vi* - **1.** [resign] demitir-se - **2.** [give up]
desistir.

quite [kwaɪt] *adv* - **1.** [completely] completamente,
totalmente - **2.** [fairly] bem; ~ **a lot of people**
bastante gente; ~ **a few times** várias vezes - **3.**
[after negative]: **I don't** ~ **understand** não entendo
muito bem; **this room is not** ~ **big enough** essa
sala não é tão grande quanto deveria ser - **4.** [for
emphasis]: **she's** ~ **a singer** ela é uma cantora e
tanto - **5.** [to express agreement]: ~ **(so)!** exatamente!

Quito [ˈkiːtəʊ] *n* Quito.

quits [kwɪts] *adj inf*: **to be** ~ **(with sb)** estar
quite (com alguém); **to call it** ~ ficar quite.

quitter [ˈkwɪtəʳ] *n inf pej*: **she's not a** ~ ela não é
das que desistem fácil.

quiver [ˈkwɪvəʳ] <> *n* - **1.** [shiver] estremecimento
m - **2.** [for arrows] aljava *f*. <> *vi* estremecer.

quivering [ˈkwɪvərɪŋ] *adj* trêmulo(la).

quixotic [kwɪkˈsɒtɪk] *adj literary* quixotesco(ca).

quiz [kwɪz] *(pl* -zes, *pt & pp* -zed, *cont* -zing) <> *n* - **1.**
[competitions, game] jogo *m* de perguntas e respos-
tas - **2.** *US SCH* exame *m*. <> *vt*: **to** ~ **sb (about**

sthg) interrogar alguém (sobre algo).

quizmaster [ˈkwɪzmɑːstəʳ] *n esp US* = **question mas-**
ter.

quizzical [ˈkwɪzɪkl] *adj* interrogativo(va).

quoits [kwɔɪts] *n (U)* jogo *m* das argolas.

Quonset hut® [ˈkwɒnsɪt-] *n US* barracão *m* do
exército.

quorate [ˈkwɔːreɪt] *adj UK* que tem quorum.

quorum [ˈkwɔːrəm] *n* quórum *m*.

quota [ˈkwəʊtə] *n* cota *f*.

quotation [kwəʊˈteɪʃn] *n* - **1.** [citation] citação *f* - **2.**
COMM cotação *f*.

quotation marks *npl* aspas *fpl*; **in** ~ entre
aspas.

quote [kwəʊt] <> *n* - **1.** [citation] citação *f* - **2.** *COMM*
cotação *f*. <> *vt* - **1.** [cite] citar - **2.** *COMM* cotar; **she**
~ **d £100** ela fixou um preço de £100. <> *vi*
- **1.** [cite] citar; **to** ~ **from sthg** citar de algo - **2.**
COMM: **to** ~ **for sthg** estabelecer um preço para
algo.
➡ **quotes** *npl inf* aspas *fpl*; **single/double** ~ **s**
aspas simples/duplas; **in** ~ **s** entre aspas.

quoted company [ˈkwəʊtɪd-] *n UK* empresa *f*
registrada em bolsa.

quotient [ˈkwəʊʃnt] *n* quociente *m*.

q.v. *(abbr of* quod vide) veja.

qwerty keyboard [ˈkwɜːtɪ-] *n UK* teclado *m*
qwerty.

R

r *(pl* r's *OR* rs), **R** *(pl* R's *OR* Rs) [ɑːʳ] *n* [letter] r, R *m*.
➡ **R** - **1.** *(abbr of* right) dir. - **2.** *(abbr of* River) R. - **3.**
(abbr of restricted) não recomendado(da) para
menores - **4.** *US (abbr of* Republican) republicano
m, -na *f*.

RA *(abbr of* Royal Academy) *n (membro da)* Academia Real de Artes na Grã-Bretanha.

RAAF *(abbr of* Royal Australian Air Force) *n* força
aérea real australiana.

Rabat [rəˈbɑːt] *n* Rabat.

rabbi [ˈræbaɪ] *n* rabino *m*.

rabbit [ˈræbɪt] *n* - **1.** [animal] coelho *m*, -lha *f* - **2.** *(U)*
[food] coelho *m*.

rabbit hole *n* toca *f* de coelho.

rabbit hutch *n* coelheira *f*.

rabbit warren *n* - **1.** [for rabbits] coelheira *f* - **2.**
[building] labirinto *m*.

rabble [ˈræbl] *n* - **1.** [disorderly crowd] povaréu *m* - **2.**
[riffraff] gentalha *f*.

rabble-rousing *adj* que agita a multidão.

rabid [ˈræbɪd, ˈreɪbɪd] *adj* - **1.** [infected with rabies]

raivoso(sa) **-2.** *pej* [fanatical] ferrenho(nha), fanáti-
co(ca).
rabies ['reɪbiːz] *n (U)* raiva *f.*
RAC (*abbr of* **Royal Automobile Club**) *n automóvel
clube britânico.*
raccoon [rə'kuːn] *n* racum *m.*
race [reɪs] ⬦ *n* **-1.** [ethnicity] raça *f* **-2.** [competition]
corrida *f*; **a ~ against time** uma corrida contra o
tempo. ⬦ *vt* competir com *(em corrida).* ⬦ *vi*
-1. [compete]: **to ~ against sb** bater uma corrida
com alguém **-2.** [rush] ir correndo **-3.** acelerar.
race car *n US* = racing car.
racecourse ['reɪskɔːs] *n* hipódromo *m.*
race driver *n US* = racing driver.
racehorse ['reɪshɔːs] *n* cavalo *m* de corrida.
race meeting *n* concurso *m* hípico.
race relations *npl* relações *fpl* inter-raciais.
race riot *n* conflito *m* racial.
racetrack ['reɪstræk] *n* autódromo *m.*
racial ['reɪʃl] *adj* racial.
racial discrimination *n (U)* discriminação *m*
racial.
racialism ['reɪʃəlɪzm] *n* = racism.
racing ['reɪsɪŋ] *n (U) SPORT* corrida *f.*
racing car *UK,* **race car** *US n* carro *m* de corrida.
racing driver *UK,* **race driver** *US n* piloto *m* de
corrida.
racism ['reɪsɪzm] *n (U)* racismo *m.*
racist ['reɪsɪst] ⬦ *adj* racista. ⬦ *n* racista *mf.*
rack [ræk] ⬦ *n* **-1.** [frame - for plates] escorredor *m*
de louça; [- for toast] prateleira *f*; [- for bottles]
porta-garrafas *m inv* **-2.** [for luggage] porta-baga-
gens *m inv.* ⬦ *vt literary:* **to be ~ ed by** *OR* **with
sthg** estar atormentado(da) por algo.
racket ['rækɪt] *n* **-1.** [noise] algazarra *f*, zoeira *f* **-2.**
[illegal activity] golpe *m*, fraude *f* **-3.** *SPORT* raquete *f.*
racketeering [ˌrækə'tɪərɪŋ] *n (U) pej:* **to be indicted
on ~ charges** ser acusado(da) de extorquir
dinheiro.
raconteur [ˌrækɒn'tɜː] *n pessoa que sabe contar
piadas.*
racoon *n* = raccoon.
racquet ['rækɪt] *n* raquete *f.*
racy ['reɪsɪ] (*compar* -ier, *superl* -iest) *adj* vivaz.
RADA ['rɑːdə] (*abbr of* **Royal Academy of Dramatic
Art**) *n academia britânica de arte dramática.*
radar ['reɪdɑː] *n (U)* radar *m.*
radar trap *n* radar *m (usado pela polícia).*
radial (tyre) ['reɪdjəl-] *n* pneu *m* radial.
radian ['reɪdjən] *n (U)* radiano *m.*
radiance ['reɪdjəns] *n* **-1.** [of face, smile] brilho *m* **-2.**
literary [brilliance] brilho *m.*
radiant ['reɪdjənt] *adj* **-1.** [happy] radiante **-2.** *literary* [brilliant] brilhante **-3.** *TECH* por radiação.
radiate ['reɪdɪeɪt] ⬦ *vt* irradiar. ⬦ *vi* **-1.** [be
emitted] irradiar **-2.** [spread from centre] sair, partir
do centro.
radiation [ˌreɪdɪ'eɪʃn] *n* radiação *f.*
radiation sickness *n (U)* doença *f* causada
pela radiação.
radiator ['reɪdɪeɪtə] *n* **-1.** [in house] aquecedor *m* **-2.**
AUT radiador *m.*
radiator grille *n* grade *f* do radiador.

radical ['rædɪkl] ⬦ *adj* radical. ⬦ *n POL* radical
mf.
radically ['rædɪklɪ] *adv* radicalmente.
radii ['reɪdɪaɪ] *pl* ⬦ **radius.**
radio ['reɪdɪəʊ] (*pl* -s) ⬦ *n* **-1.** [gen] rádio *m* **-2.**
[station] rádio *f.* ⬦ *comp* de rádio. ⬦ *vt* transmitir por rádio.
radioactive [ˌreɪdɪəʊ'æktɪv] *adj* radioativo(va).
radioactive waste *n (U)* lixo *m* radioativo.
radioactivity [ˌreɪdɪəʊæk'tɪvətɪ] *n (U)* radioatividade *f.*
radio alarm *n* rádio-relógio *m.*
radio-controlled [-kən'trəʊld] *adj* de controle
remoto.
radio frequency *n* radiofreqüência *f.*
radiogram ['reɪdɪəʊˌgræm] *n* radiograma *m.*
radiographer [ˌreɪdɪ'ɒgrəfə] *n* radiologista *mf.*
radiography [ˌreɪdɪ'ɒgrəfɪ] *n (U)* radiografia *f.*
radiology [ˌreɪdɪ'ɒlədʒɪ] *n (U)* radiologia *f.*
radiotherapist [ˌreɪdɪəʊ'θerəpɪst] *n* radioterapeu-
ta *mf.*
radiotherapy [ˌreɪdɪəʊ'θerəpɪ] *n (U)* radioterapia
f.
radish ['rædɪʃ] *n* rabanete *m.*
radium ['reɪdɪəm] *n (U)* rádio *m.*
radius ['reɪdɪəs] (*pl* radii) *n* **-1.** *MATH* raio *m* **-2.** *ANAT*
rádio *m.*
radon ['reɪdɒn] *n (U)* radônio *m.*
RAF [ɑː'reɪ'ef, ræf] (*abbr of* **Royal Air Force**) *n força
aérea real britânica.*
raffia ['ræfɪə] *n (U)* ráfia *f.*
raffish ['ræfɪʃ] *adj* que é atraente e tem estilo,
*apesar de não ser muito respeitável ou conven-
cional.*
raffle ['ræfl] ⬦ *n* rifa *f.* ⬦ *vt* rifar.
raffle ticket *n* bilhete *m* de rifa.
raft [rɑːft] *n* **-1.** [of wood] jangada *f* **-2.** [of rubber, plas-
tic] bote *m* **-3.** [large number] monte *m*; **a ~ of policies**
POL um monte de políticas.
rafter ['rɑːftə] *n* viga *f.*
rag [ræg] *n* **-1.** [piece of cloth] trapo *m*; **it was like a red
~ to a bull** estava pedindo pra levar **-2.** *pej*
[newspaper] jornaleco *m.*
➡ **rags** *npl* [clothes] trapos *mpl*; **from ~s to
riches** da pobreza à riqueza.
ragamuffin ['rægəˌmʌfɪn] *n* maltrapilho *m*, -lha *f.*
rag-and-bone man *n pessoa que compra e
vende roupas e móveis velhos na rua.*
ragbag ['rægbæg] *n fig* salada *f*, mixórdia *f.*
rag doll *n* boneca *f* de pano.
rage [reɪdʒ] ⬦ *n* **-1.** [fury] fúria *f*; **to fly into a ~**
ficar enraivecido(da) **-2.** *inf* [fashion]: **all the ~** a
última moda. ⬦ *vi* **-1.** [person] enfurecer-se **-2.**
[storm, argument] recrudescer.
ragged ['rægɪd] *adj* **-1.** [wearing torn clothes] mal-
trapilho(lha) **-2.** [torn] esfarrapado(da) **-3.** [wavy]
irregular **-4.** [poor-quality] pobre.
raging ['reɪdʒɪŋ] *adj* terrível.
ragout ['ræguː] *n* ragu *m.*
rag trade *n inf*: **the ~** a indústria do vestuário.
rag week *n UK semana em que as universidades britânicas organizam atividades diver-
tidas para fins beneficentes.*

raid [reɪd] <> n -1. MIL [attack] incursão f -2. [forced entry - by robbers] assalto m; [- by police] batida f. <> vt -1. MIL [attack] atacar de surpresa -2. [enter by force - robbers] assaltar; [- police] fazer uma batida em.

raider ['reɪdə'] n -1. [attacker] invasor m, -ra f -2. [thief] ladrão m, -dra f, assaltante mf.

rail [reɪl] <> n -1. [on staircase] corrimão m -2. [on walkway] ferro m de proteção -3. [on bridge] parapeito m -4. [on ship] amurada f -5. [bar] barra f -6. [of railway line] trilho m -7. (U) [form of transport] trem m. <> comp ferroviário(a).

railcard ['reɪlkɑ:d] n UK cartão m de desconto (no trem).

railing ['reɪlɪŋ] n -1. [round basement] grade f -2. [on walkway] ferro m de proteção -3. [on ship] amurada f -4. [on bridge] parapeito m.

railway UK ['reɪlweɪ], **railroad** US ['reɪlrəʊd] n -1. [track] estrada f de ferro -2. [company] companhia f ferroviária -3. [system] sistema m ferroviário.

railway engine n locomotiva f.

railway line n -1. [route] linha f de trem -2. [track] via f férrea, trilhos mpl.

railwayman ['reɪlweɪmən] (pl -men [-mən]) n UK ferroviário m.

railway station n estação f de trem.

railway track n via f férrea, trilhos mpl.

rain [reɪn] <> n (U) chuva f. <> v impers METEOR chover. <> vi [fall like rain] cair como chuva.
➡ **rain down** vi chover.
➡ **rain off** UK, **rain out** US vt sep: the match was ~ed off o jogo foi cancelado devido ao mau tempo.

rainbow ['reɪnbəʊ] n arco-íris m.

rainbow trout n truta-arco-íris f.

rain check n US: to take a ~ (on sthg) deixar (algo) para outra hora or para a próxima.

raincoat ['reɪnkəʊt] n capa f de chuva.

raindrop ['reɪndrɒp] n pingo m de chuva.

rainfall ['reɪnfɔ:l] n (U) precipitação f.

rain forest n floresta f tropical.

rain gauge n pluviômetro m.

rainproof ['reɪnpru:f] adj impermeável.

rainstorm ['reɪnstɔ:m] n pancada f or temporal m de chuva.

rainwater ['reɪn,wɔ:tə'] n (U) água f da chuva.

rainy ['reɪnɪ] (compar -ier, superl -iest) adj chuvoso(-sa).

raise [reɪz] <> n US aumento m. <> vt -1. [gen] levantar -2. [lift up] levantar, erguer; to ~ o.s. levantar-se -3. [increase] aumentar; to ~ one's voice levantar a voz -4. [improve] elevar -5. [evoke] evocar -6. [child, animals] criar -7. [crop] cultivar -8. [build] erguer.

raisin ['reɪzn] n passa f (de uva).

Raj [rɑ:dʒ] n: the ~ o Império Britânico na Índia.

rajah ['rɑ:dʒə] n rajá m.

rake [reɪk] <> n -1. [implement] rastelo m -2. dated & literary [immoral man] devasso m, libertino m. <> vt -1. [smooth] rastelar -2. [gather] juntar com o rastelo.
➡ **rake in** vt sep inf faturar.
➡ **rake up** vt sep [past] remexer em.

rake-off n inf propina f, lucro m ilícito.

rakish ['reɪkɪʃ] adj -1. [dissolute] libertino(na) -2. [jaunty] charmoso(sa).

rally ['rælɪ] (pl -ies, pt & pp -ied) <> n -1. [gen] rali m -2. [meeting] comício m. <> vt reunir. <> vi -1. [come together] reunir-se -2. [recover] recuperar-se.
➡ **rally round** <> vt fus mobilizar. <> vi mobilizar-se.

rallying ['rælɪŋ] n (U) rali m.

rallying cry n grito m de guerra.

rallying point n ponto m de encontro.

ram [ræm] (pt & pp -med, cont -ming) <> n carneiro m. <> vt -1. [crash into] bater contra or em -2. [force] enfiar -3. phr: to ~ sthg home deixar algo bem claro.

RAM [ræm] (abbr of random-access memory) n RAM f.

Ramadan [,ræmə'dæn] n (U) ramadã m.

ramble ['ræmbl] <> n passeio m no campo. <> vi -1. [walk] passear -2. [talk] divagar.

rambler ['ræmblə'] n excursionista mf.

rambling ['ræmblɪŋ] adj -1. [building] cheio (cheia) de voltas e curvas -2. [conversation, book] desconexo(xa).

RAMC (abbr of Royal Army Medical Corps) n corpo médico das forças armadas reais britânicas.

ramekin ['ræmɪkɪn] n recipiente f individual (para ir ao forno).

ramification [,ræmɪfɪ'keɪʃn] n ramificação f.

ramp [ræmp] n -1. [slope] rampa f -2. AUT [in road] viaduto m.

rampage [ræm'peɪdʒ] <> n: to go on the ~ sair em debandada, debandar-se. <> vi sair em debandada, debandar-se.

rampant ['ræmpənt] adj desenfreado(da).

ramparts ['ræmpɑ:ts] npl muralha f.

ramshackle ['ræm,ʃækl] adj desmantelado(da).

ran [ræn] pt ▷ run.

RAN (abbr of Royal Australian Navy) n marinha real australiana.

ranch [rɑ:ntʃ] n fazenda m, rancho m.

rancher ['rɑ:ntʃə'] n fazendeiro m, -ra f.

ranch house n US -1. [house on ranch] casa f na fazenda -2. [ranch-style house] casa f de campo.

rancid ['rænsɪd] adj rançoso(sa).

rancour UK, **rancor** US ['ræŋkə'] n (U) rancor m.

random ['rændəm] <> adj aleatório(ria). <> n: at ~ aleatoriamente.

random access memory n (U) COMPUT memória f de acesso aleatório, memória f RAM.

randomly ['rændəmlɪ] adv ao acaso.

R and R (abbr of rest and recreation) n US termo militar norte-americano para licença.

randy ['rændɪ] (compar -ier, superl -iest) adj inf tarado(da).

rang [ræŋ] pt ▷ ring.

range [reɪndʒ] <> n -1. [distance covered - of telescope, gun] alcance m; [- of ship, plane] autonomia f; to be out of ~ estar fora de alcance; to be within ~ of sthg estar ao alcance de algo; at close ~ à queima-roupa -2. [variety] variedade f -3. [bracket] faixa f -4. [of mountains, hills] cadeia f -5. [shooting area] linha *f* - **6.** *MUS* alcance *m.* <> *vt* [place in row] enfileirar. <> *vi* - **1.** [vary]: **to ~ from ... to ...** variar de ... a ...; **to ~ between ... and ...** oscilar entre ... e ... - **2.** [deal with, include]: **to ~ over sthg** passar por algo.

ranger ['reɪndʒər'] *n* guarda-florestal *mf.*

Rangoon [ræŋ'guːn] *n* Rangum.

rank [ræŋk] <> *adj* - **1.** [utter, absolute - disgrace, stupidity] completo(ta); [- injustice, bad luck] total - **2.** [offensive] rançoso(sa). <> *n* - **1.** [in army, police] posto *m*; **the ~ and file** *MIL* soldados rasos; [of political party, organization] bases *fpl*; **to pull ~** abusar da autoridade; **to close ~s** *fig* estreitar os laços - **2.** [social class] nível *m* - **3.** [row, line] fila *f.* <> *vt* - **1.** [classify] classificar - **2.** *US* [outrank] ocupar posição mais alta que. <> *vi* classificar-se; **to ~ as/ among** classificar-se como/entre.

   ranks *npl* - **1.** *MIL*: **the ~s** os soldados rasos - **2.** *fig* [members] filas *fpl.*

ranking ['ræŋkɪŋ] <> *n* classificação *f.* <> *adj US* [highest-ranking] do alto escalão.

rankle ['ræŋkl] *vi* causar dor; **it still ~s with me!** isso ainda me dói!

ransack ['rænsæk] *vt* - **1.** [plunder] saquear - **2.** [search] revistar.

ransom ['rænsəm] *n* resgate *m*; **to hold sb to ~** [keep prisoner] pedir resgate por alguém; *fig* [put in impossible position] chantagear alguém.

rant [rænt] *vi* falar asneira.

ranting ['ræntɪŋ] *n* falatório *m.*

rap [ræp] (*pt & pp* -**ped**, *cont* -**ping**) <> *n* - **1.** [knock] batidinha *f* - **2.** *MUS* rap *m* - **3.** *phr*: **to take the ~** pagar o pato. <> *vt* [knock] dar batidinhas em. <> *vi* - **1.** [knock]: **to ~ on sthg** dar batidinhas em algo - **2.** *MUS* cantar rap.

rapacious [rə'peɪʃəs] *adj fml* voraz.

rapacity [rə'pæsɪtɪ] *n* (U) *fml* voracidade *f.*

rape [reɪp] <> *n* - **1.** [gen] estupro *m* - **2.** *fig* [destruction] destruição *f* - **3.** (U) [plant] colza *f.* <> *vt* estuprar.

rapeseed *n* semente *f* de colza.

rapid ['ræpɪd] *adj* rápido(da).

   rapids *npl* corredeira *f.*

rapid-fire *adj* - **1.** *MIL* de fogo cerrado - **2.** *fig* [spoken quickly] feito um atrás do outro, feita uma atrás da outra.

rapidity [rə'pɪdətɪ] *n* (U) rapidez *f.*

rapidly ['ræpɪdlɪ] *adv* rapidamente.

rapidness *n* = rapidity.

rapist ['reɪpɪst] *n* estuprador *m*, -ra *f.*

rapper ['ræpər'] *n MUS* rapper *mf.*

rapport [ræ'pɔːr'] *n* afinidade *f*; **a ~ with/between** uma afinidade com/entre.

rapprochement *n* reaproximação *f.*

rapt [ræpt] *adj* absorto(ta).

rapture ['ræptʃər'] *n* arrebatamento *m*; **to go into ~s over sb/sthg**, **to go into ~s about sb/sthg** desfazer-se em elogios por alguém/algo.

rapturous ['ræptʃərəs] *adj* arrebatador(ra).

rare [reər'] *adj* - **1.** [gen] raro(ra) - **2.** *CULIN* [underdone] malpassado(da).

rarefied ['reərɪfaɪd] *adj* - **1.** [air, atmosphere] rarefeito(ta) - **2.** [refined] exclusivo(va).

rarely ['reəlɪ] *adv* raramente.

rareness ['reənɪs] (U) *n* - **1.** [scarcity, uncommonness] raridade *f* - **2.** [infrequency] infreqüência *f* - **3.** *CULIN* qualidade *f* de malpassado.

raring ['reərɪŋ] *adj*: **to be ~ to go** estar ansioso(sa) para começar.

rarity ['reərətɪ] (*pl* -**ies**) *n* raridade *f.*

rascal ['rɑːskl] *n* patife *m*, malandro *m*, -dra *f.*

rash [ræʃ] <> *adj* precipitado(da). <> *n* - **1.** *MED* erupção *f* - **2.** [spate] onda *f.*

rasher ['ræʃər'] *n* fatia *f* fina *(de bacon).*

rashly ['ræʃlɪ] *adv* precipitadamente.

rashness ['ræʃnɪs] *n* (U) precipitação *f.*

rasp [rɑːsp] <> *n* rangido *m.* <> *vi* esganiçar-se.

raspberry ['rɑːzbərɪ] (*pl* -**ies**) *n* - **1.** [fruit] framboesa *f* - **2.** [rude noise]: **to blow a ~** debochar fazendo barulho com a boca.

rasping ['rɑːspɪŋ] *adj* áspero(ra) e estridente.

rasta ['ræstə] *n inf* rasta *mf.*

rastafarian [ˌræstə'feərɪən] *n* rastafári *mf.*

rat [ræt] *n* - **1.** [animal] rato *m*, ratazana *f*; **to smell a ~** suspeitar que há algo errado - **2.** *pej* [person] tratante *mf.*

ratbag ['rætbæg] *n UK inf pej* canalha *mf.*

ratchet ['rætʃɪt] *n* catraca *f.*

rate [reɪt] <> *n* - **1.** [speed] velocidade *f*; **at this ~** nesse ritmo - **2.** [ratio, proportion - birth, death, inflation] taxa *f*; [- unemployment] índice *m* - **3.** [price] tarifa *f.* <> *vt* - **1.** [consider]: **to ~ sb/sthg (as)** considerar alguém/algo; **to ~ sb/sthg (among)** classificar alguém/algo (entre) - **2.** [deserve] merecer.

   at any rate *adv* pelo menos.

rateable value ['reɪtəbl-] *n UK* valor *m* tributável.

rate of exchange *n* (taxa *f* de) câmbio *m.*

ratepayer ['reɪtˌpeɪər'] *n UK* contribuinte *mf.*

rather ['rɑːðər'] *adv* - **1.** [slightly, a bit] um pouco - **2.** [for emphasis] bem, bastante - **3.** [expressing a preference]: **I would ~ wait** eu preferiria esperar - **4.** [more exactly]: **or ~ ...** ou melhor ... - **5.** [on the contrary]: **(but) ~ ...** (senão) pelo contrário ...

   rather than *conj* em vez de.

ratification [ˌrætɪfɪ'keɪʃn] *n* (U) ratificação *f.*

ratify ['rætɪfaɪ] (*pt & pp* -**ied**) *vt* ratificar.

rating ['reɪtɪŋ] *n* - **1.** [standing - high, low, popularity] índice *m*; [- opinion poll] posição *f* - **2.** *UK* [sailor] marinheiro *m*, -ra *f.*

   ratings *npl TV* índices *mpl* de audiência.

ratio ['reɪʃɪəʊ] (*pl* -**s**) *n* razão *f*, proporção *f.*

ration ['ræʃn] <> *n* ração *f.* <> *vt* [goods] racionar.

   rations *npl* ração *f.*

rational ['ræʃnl] *adj* racional.

rationale [ˌræʃə'nɑːl] *n* lógica *f*, fundamento *m* lógico.

rationalization [ˌræʃənəlaɪ'zeɪʃn] *n* racionalização *f.*

rationalize, -ise ['ræʃənəlaɪz] *vt* racionalizar.

rationing ['ræʃənɪŋ] *n* (U) racionamento *m.*

rat race *n* competição *f* acirrada *(no mundo dos negócios).*

rattle ['rætl] <> *n* - **1.** [noise] barulho *m*, ruído *m* - **2.** [toy] chocalho *m.* <> *vt* - **1.** [make rattling noise with]

chacoalhar **-2.** [unsettle] desconcertar. ◇ *vi*
[make rattling noise] chacoalhar.
 ▶ **rattle off** *vt sep* repetir de memória.
 ▶ **rattle on** *vi*: **to ~ on (about sthg)** tagarelar
(sobre algo).
 ▶ **rattle through** *vt fus* tratar de encerrar.
rattlesnake [ˈrætlsneɪk], **rattler** *US* [ˈrætləʳ] *n*
cascavel *f*.
ratty [ˈrætɪ] (*compar* -ier, *superl* -iest) *adj inf* -1. *UK* [in
bad mood] rabugento(ta) **-2.** *US* [in bad condition]
surrado(da), roto(ta).
raucous [ˈrɔːkəs] *adj* -1. [laughter, voice] rouco(ca) e
estridente **-2.** [behaviour] escandaloso(sa).
raunchy [ˈrɔːntʃɪ] (*compar* -ier, *superl* -iest) *adj*
insinuante.
ravage [ˈrævɪdʒ] *vt* devastar.
 ▶ **ravages** *npl* estragos *mpl*.
rave [reɪv] ◇ *adj* entusiasmado(da). ◇ *n UK inf*
[party] rave *f*. ◇ *vi* -1. [talk angrily]: **to ~ at sb**
xingar alguém; **to ~ against sthg** vociferar contra
algo **-2.** [talk enthusiastically]: **to ~ about sthg** falar
com entusiasmo sobre algo.
raven [ˈreɪvn] ◇ *adj* totalmente negro(gra). ◇ *n*
corvo *m*.
ravenous [ˈrævənəs] *adj* -1. [person, animal] faminto
(ta) **-2.** [appetite] voraz.
raver [ˈreɪvəʳ] *n UK inf* festeiro *m*, -ra *f*.
rave-up *n UK inf* rave *f*.
ravine [rəˈviːn] *n* ravina *f*.
raving [ˈreɪvɪŋ] *adj* [for emphasis] delirante; **~ lunatic**
doido *m* varrido, doida *f* varrida.
 ▶ **ravings** *npl* delírios *mpl*.
ravioli [ˌrævɪˈəʊlɪ] *n (U)* ravióli *m*.
ravish [ˈrævɪʃ] *vt* -1. *literary* [rape] violentar **-2.** [de-
light] extasiar.
ravishing [ˈrævɪʃɪŋ] *adj* -1. [sight, beauty] extasiante
-2. [person] belíssimo(ma).
raw [rɔː] *adj* -1. [uncooked] cru (crua) **-2.** [untreated]
bruto(ta) **-3.** [painful] em carne viva **-4.** [inexper-
ienced] inexperiente **-5.** [cold] frio (fria).
raw deal *n*: **to get a ~** receber um tratamento
injusto.
Rawlplug® [ˈrɔːlplʌg] *n* bucha *f*.
raw material *n* -1. [natural substance] matéria-
prima *f* **-2.** *(U) fig* [basis] base *f*.
ray [reɪ] *n* -1. [beam] raio *m* **-2.** *fig* [glimmer] resquício
m.
rayon [ˈreɪɒn] *n (U)* raiom *m*.
raze [reɪz] *vt* destruir completamente, arrasar.
razor [ˈreɪzəʳ] *n* -1. [electric] barbeador *m* elétrico **-2.**
[disposable] barbeador *m*, aparelho *m* de barbear.
razor blade *n* lâmina *f* de barbear.
razor-sharp *adj* -1. [very sharp] muito afiado(da)
-2. *fig* [very quick - person] ágil; [- mind] afiado(da),
perspicaz.
razzle [ˈræzl] *n UK inf*: **to go on the ~** cair na
gandaia.
razzmatazz [ˈræzəmətæz] *n (U) inf* auê *m*.
R & B (*abbr of* rhythm and blues) *n* mistura de
ritmos de blues e jazz precursora do rock and
roll.
RC (*abbr of* Roman Catholic) *adj* católico romano,
católica romana.

RCA (*abbr of* Royal College of Art) *n* escola londrina
de belas artes.
RCAF (*abbr of* Royal Canadian Air Force) *n* força
aérea real canadense.
RCMP (*abbr of* Royal Canadian Mounted Police) *n*
polícia montada canadense.
RCN *n* (*abbr of* Royal Canadian Navy) marinha real
canadense.
Rd (*abbr of* Road) estrada *f*.
R & D (*abbr of* research and development) *n* P & D.
RDC (*abbr of* Rural District Council) *n* câmara de
vereadores de uma comunidade rural britânica.
re [riː] *prep* referente a.
RE *n* -1. (*abbr of* religious education) educação *f*
religiosa **-2.** (*abbr of* Royal Engineers) unidade de
engenharia do exército britânico responsável
pela construção de fortes, pontes e outras obras.
reach [riːtʃ] ◇ *n* [of arm, boxer] alcance *m*; **within
(sb's) ~** [easily touched] ao alcance (de alguém);
[easily travelled to] a pouca distância (de alguém);
out of *OR* **beyond sb's ~** [not easily touched] fora/
além do alcance de alguém; [not easily travelled to]
fora/além do alcance de alguém. ◇ *vt* -1. [arrive
at] chegar a, alcançar **-2.** [be able to touch] alcançar
-3. [contact] contatar, entrar em contato com **-4.**
[extend as far as] atingir **-5.** [attain, achieve] chegar a.
◇ *vi* -1. [person]: **to ~ out/across** alcançar; **to ~
down** abaixar-se **-2.** [land] alcançar, ir até.
 ▶ **reaches** *npl*: **the upper/lower ~es** a parte
alta/baixa.
reachable [ˈriːtʃəbl] *adj* -1. [accessible] acessível **-2.**
[contactable] localizável; **he's ~ by phone** ele pode
ser contatado por telefone.
react [rɪˈækt] *vi* -1. [respond]: **to ~ (to sthg)** reagir
(a algo) **-2.** [rebel]: **to ~ against sthg** reagir contra
algo **-3.** *CHEM*: **to ~ with sthg** reagir com algo.
reaction [rɪˈækʃn] *n* -1. reação *f* **-2.** [response]: **~
(to sthg)** reação *f* (a algo) **-3.** [rebellion]: **~ (against
sthg)** reação *f* (contra algo).
reactionary [rɪˈækʃənrɪ] ◇ *adj* reacionário(ria).
◇ *n* reacionário *m*, -ria *f*.
reactivate [rɪˈæktɪveɪt] *vt* reativar.
reactor [rɪˈæktəʳ] *n* [nuclear reactor] reator *m*.
read [riːd] (*pt & pp* read [red]) ◇ *n*: **to be a good
~** ser uma boa leitura. ◇ *vt* -1. [gen] ler; **to ~
sb's mind** ler os pensamentos de alguém; **to ~
events** ver os acontecimentos; **the man came to
~ the electricity meter** o funcionário veio tirar a
leitura da luz; **to be well ~ in a subject** conhecer
bem um assunto **-2.** [subj: sign, notice] dizer; [subj:
gauge, meter, barometer] marcar **-3.** *UK UNIV* estudar.
◇ *vi* -1. [person] ler; **to ~ (to sb)** ler (para
alguém); **to ~ between the lines** ler nas entrelinhas; **to ~ sb like a book** compreender alguém
perfeitamente **-2.** [text]: **it ~s well/badly** isto
está bem/mal escrito.
 ▶ **read into** *vt sep*: **I wouldn't ~ much into
what he said** eu não levaria muito a sério o que
ele disse; **what do you ~ into the minister's decision?** como você vê a decisão do ministro?
 ▶ **read out** *vt sep* ler em voz alta.
 ▶ **read up on** *vt fus* estudar.
readable [ˈriːdəbl] *adj* -1. [book] interessante de se
ler **-2.** *COMPUT* [disk] legível.

readdress [ˌriːəˈdres] *vt* reendereçar.
reader [ˈriːdəʳ] *n* leitor *m*, -ra *f*.
readership [ˈriːdəʃɪp] *n* público *m* leitor.
readily [ˈredɪlɪ] *adv* -1. [willingly] de boa vontade -2. [easily] facilmente.
readiness [ˈredɪnɪs] *n* (U) -1. [preparedness] prontidão *f*-2. [willingness]: ~ (to do sthg) presteza (para fazer algo).
reading [ˈriːdɪŋ] *n* -1. [gen] leitura *f* -2. [recital] recital *m* -3. [from gauge, meter, thermometer] marcação *f*-4. POL [of bill] revisão *f*.
reading lamp *n* lâmpada *f* de leitura.
reading room *n* sala *f* de leitura.
readjust [ˌriːəˈdʒʌst] <> *vt* reajustar. <> *vi*: to ~ (to sthg) reorganizar-se (para algo).
readmit [ˌriːədˈmɪt] *vt* readmitir.
readout [ˈriːdaʊt] *n* COMPUT exibição *f* de dados.
read-through [riːd-] *n* olhada *f* geral.
ready [ˈredɪ] (*pt* & *pp* -ied) <> *adj* -1. [prepared] pronto(ta); **to be** ~ **to do sthg** estar pronto(ta) para fazer algo; **to be** ~ **for sthg** estar pronto(ta) para algo; **to get** ~ preparar-se; **to get sthg** ~ preparar algo -2. [willing]: **to be** ~ **to do sthg** estar disposto(ta) a fazer algo -3. [in need of]: **to be** ~ **for sthg** precisar de algo -4. [likely]: **to be** ~ **to do sthg** estar prestes a fazer algo -5. [easily accessible] à mão. <> *vt* preparar.
ready cash *n* (U) dinheiro *m* em mão.
ready-made *adj* pronto(ta).
ready money *n* (U) dinheiro *m* à vista.
ready-to-wear *adj* prêt-à-porter.
reaffirm [ˌriːəˈfɜːm] *vt* reafirmar.
reafforest [ˌriːəˈfɒrɪst] *vt* reflorestar.
reafforestation [ˈriːəˌfɒrɪˈsteɪʃn] *n* (U) reflorestamento *m*.
real [ˈrɪəl] <> *adj* -1. [gen] real; **in** ~ **terms** em termos reais -2. [authentic - problem, situation] real; [- gold, jewels] legítimo(ma); **the** ~ **thing** a verdade; **a** ~ **job** um emprego de verdade; **it's for** ~ é real -3. [for emphasis] verdadeiro(ra). <> *adv US* bem.
real ale *n* (U) UK cerveja *f* artesanal.
real estate *n* (U) bens *mpl* imobiliários.
realign [ˌriːəˈlaɪn] *vt* -1. POL reorganizar -2. [brakes] realinhar.
realignment [ˌriːəˈlaɪnmənt] *n* -1. POL reestruturação *f*-2. [of wheels] realinhamento *m*.
realism [ˈrɪəlɪzm] *n* (U)-1. [common sense] bom senso *m*-2. [artistic style] realismo *m*.
realist [ˈrɪəlɪst] *n* realista *mf*.
realistic [ˌrɪəˈlɪstɪk] *adj* realista; ~ **chance** chance real; **to be** ~ **about sthg** ser realista em relação a algo.
realistically [ˌrɪəˈlɪstɪklɪ] *adv* -1. [reasonably] realisticamente -2. [accurately] de forma realista.
reality [rɪˈælətɪ] (*pl* -ies) *n* [gen] realidade *f*, **in** ~ [in fact] na realidade; [in real life] na vida real.
reality TV *n* (U) reality shows *mpl*.
realization [ˌrɪəlaɪˈzeɪʃn] *n* (U) -1. [awareness, recognition] percepção *f*-2. [achievement] realização *f*.
realize, -ise [ˈrɪəlaɪz] *vt* -1. [become aware of, understand] perceber, dar-se conta de -2. [achieve] concretizar -3. COMM atingir.

reallocate [ˌriːˈæləkeɪt] *vt* realocar.
really [ˈrɪəlɪ] <> *adv* -1. [gen] realmente -2. [to reduce force of negative statements] na real. <> *excl* -1. [expressing doubt]: **really?** é mesmo?, não é mesmo? -2. [expressing surprise, disbelief]: **really?** mesmo? -3. [expressing disapproval]: **really!** francamente!
realm [relm] *n* -1. [field] domínio *m* -2. [kingdom] reino *m*.
real-time *adj* COMPUT de tempo real.
realtor [ˈrɪəltəʳ] *n* US corretor *m*, -ra *f* de imóveis.
ream [riːm] *n* resma *f*.
➤ **reams** *npl fig* [a lot] páginas *fpl* e páginas.
reap [riːp] *vt* colher; **you** ~ **what you sow** você colhe o que planta.
reappear [ˌriːəˈpɪəʳ] *vi* reaparecer.
reappearance [ˌriːəˈpɪərəns] *n* reaparecimento *m*.
reapply [ˌriːəˈplaɪ] (*pt* & *pp* -ied) *vi* reaplicar; **to** ~ **for sthg** recandidatar-se a algo.
reappraisal [ˌriːəˈpreɪzl] *n* reavaliação *f*.
reappraise [ˌriːəˈpreɪz] *vt* reavaliar.
rear [rɪəʳ] <> *adj* -1. [door, window] dos fundos -2. [wheel] traseiro(ra). <> *n* -1. [back - of building] fundos *mpl*; [- of vehicle] traseira *f*; **to be at the** ~ estar no final; **to bring up the** ~ fechar a raia -2. *inf* [buttocks] bunda *f*. <> *vt* -1. [children, animals, plants] criar -2. *fig* [lift up]: **it has** ~**ed its head again** ele deu as caras novamente. <> *vi*: **to** ~ **(up)** empinar, empinar-se.
rear admiral *n* contra-almirante *m*.
rearguard action [ˈrɪəgɑːd-] *n* ação *f* pela retaguarda.
rear light *n* lanterna *f* traseira.
rearm [riːˈɑːm] *vt* & *vi* rearmar.
rearmament [rɪˈɑːməmənt] *n* (U) rearmamento *m*.
rearmost [ˈrɪəməʊst] *adj* último(ma).
rearrange [ˌriːəˈreɪndʒ] *vt* -1. [arrange differently] reorganizar -2. [reschedule] reajustar.
rearrangement [ˌriːəˈreɪndʒmənt] *n* -1. [different arrangement] reorganização *f* -2. [rescheduling] reajuste *m*.
rearview mirror [ˈrɪəvjuː-] *n* espelho *m* retrovisor.
reason [ˈriːzn] <> *n* -1. [cause] razão *f*, motivo *m*; ~ **for sthg** razão para algo; **by** ~ **of** *fml* em razão de; **for some** ~ por alguma razão -2. (U) [justification]: **to have** ~ **to do sthg** ter razões para fazer algo -3. (U) [rationality, common sense] razão *f*; **to listen to** ~ ouvir à razão; **it stands to** ~ é lógico. <> *vt* concluir. <> *vi* raciocinar.
➤ **reason with** *vt fus* argumentar com.
reasonable [ˈriːznəbl] *adj* -1. [sensible] sensato(ta) -2. [acceptable] razoável -3. [fairly large] aceitável.
reasonably [ˈriːznəblɪ] *adv* -1. [quite] razoavelmente -2. [sensibly] sensatamente.
reasoned [ˈriːznd] *adj* racional.
reasoning [ˈriːznɪŋ] *n* (U) raciocínio *m*.
reassemble [ˌriːəˈsembl] <> *vt* -1. [machinery] remontar -2. [people] reagrupar. <> *vi* reunir-se novamente.
reassess [ˌriːəˈses] *vt* reavaliar.
reassessment [ˌriːəˈsesmənt] *n* reavaliação *f*.

reassurance [ˌriːəˈʃɔːrəns] n -1. (U) [comfort] reconforto m -2. [promise] nova garantia f.
reassure [ˌriːəˈʃɔːr] vt tranqüilizar.
reassuring [ˌriːəˈʃɔːrɪŋ] adj tranqüilizador(ra).
reawaken [ˌriːəˈweɪkn] vt redespertar.
rebate [ˈriːbeɪt] n restituição f.
rebel [n ˈrebl, vb rɪˈbel] (pt & pp -led, cont -ling) <> n rebelde mf. <> vi -1. [revolt]: to ~ (against sb/sthg) rebelar-se (contra alguém/algo) -2. [not conform]: to ~ (against sb/sthg) revoltar-se (contra alguém/algo).
rebellion [rɪˈbeljən] n -1. [armed revolt] rebelião f -2. [opposition] oposição f -3. (U) [nonconformity] revolta f.
rebellious [rɪˈbeljəs] adj rebelde.
rebirth [ˌriːˈbɜːθ] n (U) renascimento m.
rebound [n ˈriːbaʊnd, vb rɪˈbaʊnd] <> n: on the ~ [ball] no ricochete; [person] no impulso. <> vi -1. [ball] ricochetear -2. [harm]: to ~ (up)on sb recair sobre alguém.
rebuff [rɪˈbʌf] <> n recusa f. <> vt recusar.
rebuild [ˌriːˈbɪld] (pt & pp -built) vt reconstruir.
rebuke [rɪˈbjuːk] <> n reprimenda f. <> vt: to ~ sb (for sthg) repreender alguém (por algo).
rebut [riːˈbʌt] (pt & pp -ted, cont -ting) vt refutar.
rebuttal [riːˈbʌtl] n refutação f.
rec n inf -1. (abbr of recreation ground) UK playground m -2. (abbr of recreation) US recreação f.
rec. (abbr of received) recebido.
recalcitrant [rɪˈkælsɪtrənt] adj obstinado(da).
recall [rɪˈkɔːl] <> n -1. (U) [memory] recordação f -2. [on faulty goods] recall m -3. [change]: beyond ~ impossível de ser alterado(da). <> vt -1. [remember] relembrar-se de -2. [summon back - parliament] reconvocar; [- ambassador] chamar de volta.
recant [rɪˈkænt] <> vt -1. [faith, religion] renegar -2. [statement] retirar -3. [opinion] reconsiderar. <> vi retratar-se.
recap [ˈriːkæp] (pt & pp -ped, cont -ping) inf <> n recapitulação f. <> vt -1. [summarize] recapitular -2. US [tyre] recauchutar. <> vi [summarize] recapitular.
recapitulate [ˌriːkəˈpɪtjʊleɪt] vt & vi recapitular.
recapture [ˌriːˈkæptʃər] <> n recaptura f. <> vt -1. [prisoner, town] recapturar -2. [mood, feeling] resgatar.
recd, rec'd (abbr of received) recebido.
recede [riːˈsiːd] vi -1. [move away] afastar-se -2. fig [disappear, fade] desaparecer -3. [subj: hair] formar entradas.
receding [rɪˈsiːdɪŋ] adj -1. [hair]: ~ hairline entrada f (no cabelo) -2. [chin]: ~ chin queixo m retraído.
receipt [rɪˈsiːt] n -1. [piece of paper] recibo m -2. (U) [act of receiving] recebimento m.
➡ **receipts** npl receita f.
receivable [rɪˈsiːvəbl] adj a receber.
receive [rɪˈsiːv] <> vt -1. [gen] receber -2. [welcome] recepcionar -3. [greet]: to be well/badly ~d ser bem/mal recebido(da). <> vi [in tennis etc] receber.
receiver [rɪˈsiːvər] n -1. [of telephone] fone m -2. [radio, TV set] receptor m -3. [criminal] receptador m, -ra f -4. FIN [official] curador m, -ra f.

receivership [rɪˈsiːvəʃɪp] n (U): to go into ~ ir para curadoria.
receiving end [rɪˈsiːvɪŋ-] n: to be on the ~ (of sthg) estar na linha de tiro (de algo).
recent [ˈriːsnt] adj recente.
recently [ˈriːsntlɪ] adv recentemente; until ~, no one knew of his existence até pouco tempo atrás, ninguém sabia da existência dele.
receptacle [rɪˈseptəkl] n recipiente m.
reception [rɪˈsepʃn] n recepção f.
reception centre n UK (centro m de) alojamento m.
reception class n aula f de boas-vindas.
reception desk n recepção f.
receptionist [rɪˈsepʃənɪst] n recepcionista mf.
reception room n recepção f.
receptive [rɪˈseptɪv] adj receptivo(va); to be ~ to sthg ser receptivo a algo.
receptiveness n (U) receptividade f.
recess [ˈriːses, UK rɪˈses] n -1. [vacation] recesso m; to be in/go into ~ estar/entrar em recesso -2. [alcove] reentrância f, vão m -3. [of mind, memory] refluxo m -4. US SCH recreio m, intervalo m.
recessed [ˈriːsest, UK rɪˈsest] adj embutido(da).
recession [rɪˈseʃn] n recessão f.
recessionary [rɪˈseʃənrɪ] adj recessivo(va).
recessive [rɪˈsesɪv] adj recessivo(va).
recharge [ˌriːˈtʃɑːdʒ] vt recarregar.
rechargeable [ˌriːˈtʃɑːdʒəbl] adj recarregável.
recipe [ˈresɪpɪ] n receita f.
recipient [rɪˈsɪpɪənt] <> adj recebedor(ra), receptor(ra). <> n -1. [of letter] destinatário(ria) -2. [of cheque] beneficiário(ria) -3. [of award] ganhador(ra).
reciprocal [rɪˈsɪprəkl] adj recíproco(ca).
reciprocate [rɪˈsɪprəkeɪt] <> vt retribuir a. <> vi retribuir.
recital [rɪˈsaɪtl] n recital m.
recitation [ˌresɪˈteɪʃn] n recitação f.
recite [rɪˈsaɪt] vt -1. [perform aloud] recitar -2. [list] enumerar.
reckless [ˈrekləs] adj imprudente.
recklessness [ˈrekləsnɪs] n (U) imprudência f.
reckon [ˈrekn] vt -1. inf [think] achar -2. [consider, judge]: he was ~ed to be too old for the job ele foi considerado velho demais para o trabalho -3. [expect]: to ~ to do sthg esperar fazer algo -4. [calculate] calcular.
➡ **reckon on** vt fus contar com.
➡ **reckon with** vt fus -1. [expect] esperar -2. [face, deal with]: a force to be ~ed with uma força a ser considerada.
➡ **reckon without** vt fus não levar em conta.
reckoning [ˈrekənɪŋ] n cálculo m; day of ~ dia do ajuste de contas.
reclaim [rɪˈkleɪm] vt -1. [claim back] recuperar -2. [make fit for use] desbravar.
reclamation [ˌrekləˈmeɪʃn] n (U) aproveitamento m.
recline [rɪˈklaɪn] vi reclinar-se.
reclining [rɪˈklaɪnɪŋ] adj reclinável.
recluse [rɪˈkluːs] n recluso m, -sa f.
reclusive [rɪˈkluːsɪv] adj recluso(sa).
recognition [ˌrekəɡˈnɪʃn] n -1. [identification]

reconhecimento *m*; **beyond** *OR* **out of all** ~ irreconhecível- **2.** [acknowledgment] identificação *f*; **in** ~ **of** em reconhecimento a.

recognizable [ˈrekəgnaɪzəbl] *adj* reconhecível; **he was barely** ~ mal dava para reconhecê-lo.

recognize, -ise [ˈrekəgnaɪz] *vt* reconhecer.

recoil [*vb* rɪˈkɔɪl, *n* ˈriːkɔɪl] <> *n* coice *m*. <> *vi* recuar; **to** ~ **from/at sthg** recuar diante de algo; **she** ~ **ed at his suggestion** ela recuou diante da sugestão dele.

recollect [ˌrekəˈlekt] *vt* recordar-se de, lembrar-se de.

recollection [ˌrekəˈlekʃn] *n* recordação *f*, lembrança *f*.

recommence [ˌriːkəˈmens] *vt* & *vi* recomeçar.

recommend [ˌrekəˈmend] *vt* - **1.** [commend, speak in favour of]: **to** ~ **sb/sthg (to sb)** recomendar alguém/algo (para alguém) - **2.** [advise] recomendar.

recommendation [ˌrekəmenˈdeɪʃn] *n* recomendação *f*.

recommended retail price [ˌrekəˈmendɪd-] *n* preço *m* sugerido ao varejo.

recompense [ˈrekəmpens] <> *n*: ~ **(for sthg)** recompensa (por algo). <> *vt*: **to** ~ **sb (for sthg)** recompensar alguém (por algo).

reconcile [ˈrekənsaɪl] *vt* - **1.** [beliefs, ideas] conciliar; **to** ~ **sthg with sthg** conciliar algo com algo - **2.** [people] reconciliar; **to be** ~**d with sb** reconciliar-se com alguém- **3.** [resign]: **to** ~ **o.s. to sthg** resignar-se a algo.

reconciliation [ˌrekənsɪlɪˈeɪʃn] *n* - **1.** [of beliefs, ideas] conciliação *f*- **2.** [of people] reconciliação *f*.

recondite [ˈrekəndaɪt] *adj fml* recôndito(ta).

reconditioned [ˌriːkənˈdɪʃnd] *adj* recondicionado(da).

reconnaissance [rɪˈkɒnɪsəns] *n* (U) reconhecimento *m*.

reconnect [ˌriːkəˈnekt] *vt* religar.

reconnoitre *UK*, **reconnoiter** *US* [ˌrekəˈnɔɪtəʳ] <> *vt* reconhecer. <> *vi* fazer um reconhecimento.

reconsider [ˌriːkənˈsɪdəʳ] *vt* & *vi* reconsiderar.

reconstitute [ˌriːˈkɒnstɪtjuːt] *vt*- **1.** [re-form] reconstituir - **2.** [dried food] hidratar.

reconstruct [ˌriːkənˈstrʌkt] *vt* reconstruir.

reconstruction [ˌriːkənˈstrʌkʃn] *n* - **1.** [gen] reconstrução *f*- **2.** [of event, crime] reconstituição *f*.

reconvene [ˌriːkənˈviːn] *vt* reunir-se novamente.

record [*n* & *adj* ˈrekɔːd, *vb* rɪˈkɔːd] <> *adj* recorde. <> *n* - **1.** [gen] registro *m*; **off the** ~ em off; **on** ~ [on file] em registro; [ever recorded] já registrado(da); **to go on** ~ [say publicly] ir a público - **2.** [vinyl disc] disco *m* - **3.** [best achievement] recorde *m* - **4.** *phr*: **to set** *OR* **put the** ~ **straight** corrigir um mal-entendido. <> *vt* - **1.** [write down] registrar - **2.** [put on tape etc] gravar.

record-breaker *n* recordista *mf*.

record-breaking *adj* que quebra recordes.

recorded delivery [rɪˈkɔːdɪd-] *n (U)*: **to send sthg by** ~ enviar algo como carta registrada.

recorder [rɪˈkɔːdəʳ] *n* - **1.** [machine] gravador *m*- **2.** [musical instrument] flauta *f* doce.

record holder *n* detentor *m*, -ra *f* do recorde.

recording [rɪˈkɔːdɪŋ] *n* gravação *f*.

recording studio *n* estúdio *m* de gravação.

record library *n* discoteca *f*.

record player *n* toca-discos *m*.

recount [*n* ˈriːkaʊnt, *vt sense 1* rɪˈkaʊnt, *sense 2* ˌriːˈkaʊnt] <> *n* recontagem *f*. <> *vt* - **1.** [narrate] relatar - **2.** [count again] recontar.

recoup [rɪˈkuːp] *vt* recuperar.

recourse [rɪˈkɔːs] *n (U) fml*: **to have** ~ **to sthg** recorrer a algo.

recover [rɪˈkʌvəʳ] <> *vt* - **1.** [stolen goods, money] recuperar; **to** ~ **sthg (from sb/somewhere)** recuperar algo (de alguém/algum lugar) - **2.** [consciousness, one's breath] recobrar; **to** ~ **o.s.** recuperar-se. <> *vi* - **1.** [from illness, accident] [finances]: **to** ~ **(from sthg)** recuperar-se (de algo)- **2.** [from shock, setback, sb's death]: **to** ~ **(from sthg)** refazer-se (de algo).

recoverable [rɪˈkʌvrəbl] *adj FIN* recuperável.

recovery [rɪˈkʌvərɪ] (*pl* -ies) *n* - **1.**: ~ **(from sthg)** recuperação (de algo) - **2.** recuperação *f*.

recovery vehicle *n UK* guincho *m*.

recreate [ˈriːkrɪˌeɪt] *vt* recriar.

recreation [ˌrekrɪˈeɪʃn] *n (U)* recreação *f*, divertimento *m*.

recreational [ˌrekrɪˈeɪʃənl] *adj* recreativo(ta); ~ **facilities** local para recreação.

recreation room *n* - **1.** [in public building] sala *f* de recreação - **2.** *US* [in house] sala *f* de jogos.

recrimination [rɪˌkrɪmɪˈneɪʃn] *n (U)* recriminação *f*.

    ◆ **recriminations** *npl* recriminações *fpl*.

recrudescence [ˌriːkruːˈdesns] *n fml* recrudescimento *m*.

recruit [rɪˈkruːt] <> *n* recruta *mf*. <> *vt* recrutar; **to** ~ **sb (for sthg/to do sthg)** recrutar alguém (para algo/para fazer algo). <> *vi* [take on new staff] recrutar gente.

recruitment [rɪˈkruːtmənt] *n (U)* recrutamento *m*.

rectangle [ˈrekˌtæŋgl] *n* retângulo *m*.

rectangular [rekˈtæŋgjʊləʳ] *adj* retangular.

rectification [ˌrektɪfɪˈkeɪʃn] *n (U) fml* retificação *f*.

rectify [ˈrektɪfaɪ] (*pt* & *pp* -ied) *vt fml* retificar.

rectitude [ˈrektɪtjuːd] *n (U) fml* retidão *f*.

rector [ˈrektəʳ] *n* - **1.** [priest] pároco *m*- **2.** *Scot* [head - of school] diretor *m*, -ra *f*; [- of college, university] reitor *m*, -ra *f*.

rectory [ˈrektərɪ] (*pl* -ies) *n* residência *f* paroquial.

rectum [ˈrektəm] (*pl* -s) *n* reto *m*.

recuperate [rɪˈkuːpəreɪt] *vi fml*: **to** ~ **(from sthg)** restabelecer-se (de algo).

recuperation [rɪˌkuːpəˈreɪʃn] *n (U)* recuperação *f*, restabelecimento *m*.

recur [rɪˈkɜːʳ] (*pt* & *pp* -red, *cont* -ring) *vi* repetir-se.

recurrence [rɪˈkʌrəns] *n fml* recorrência *f*.

recurrent [rɪˈkʌrənt] *adj* recorrente.

recurring [rɪˈkɜːrɪŋ] *adj* - **1.** [often repeated] recorrente - **2.** *MATH* periódico(ca).

recyclable [ˌriːˈsaɪkləbl] *adj* reciclável.

recycle [ˌriːˈsaɪkl] *vt* reciclar.

recycling *n* reciclagem *f*.

red [red] (*compar* -der, *superl* -dest) <> *adj* - **1.** [gen]

vermelho(lha) **-2.** [hair] ruivo(va). ⋄ *n (U)* [colour] vermelho *m*; **to be in the ~** *inf* estar no vermelho; **to see ~** enfurecer-se.

➤ **Red** *pej* ⋄ *adj* [left-wing, communist] vermelho(lha). ⋄ *n* [left-winger, communist] vermelho *m*, lha *f.*

red alert *n* **-1.** *(U)* [state of readiness]: **on ~** em alerta vermelho **-2.** [order to be ready] alerta *f* vermelho.

red blood cell *n* glóbulo *m* vermelho.

red-blooded [-'blʌdɪd] *adj hum* com aquilo roxo.

red-brick *adj UK* [building] de tijolo à vista.

➤ **redbrick** *adj UNIV*: **redbrick university** *universidade construída em grandes centros fora de Londres nos séculos XIX e XX.*

red card *n FTBL*: **to be shown the ~**, **to get a ~** receber cartão vermelho.

red carpet *n*: **to roll out the ~ for sb** estender o tapete vermelho para alguém.

➤ **red-carpet** *adj*: **to give sb the red-carpet treatment** dar tratamento VIP para alguém.

Red Crescent *n*: **the ~** o Crescente Vermelho.

Red Cross *n*: **the ~** a Cruz Vermelha.

redcurrant ['redkʌrənt] *n* **-1.** [fruit] groselha *f* **-2.** [bush] groselheira *f.*

red deer *n* veado *m.*

redden ['rednl] ⋄ *vt* [make red] avermelhar. ⋄ *vi* [flush] ruborizar-se, ficar ruborizado(da).

redecorate [ˌriː'dekəreɪt] ⋄ *vt* redecorar. ⋄ *vi* redecorar a casa.

redeem [rɪ'diːm] *vt* **-1.** [save, rescue] redimir; **to ~ o.s.** redimir-se **-2.** [from pawnbroker] resgatar.

redeemer *n RELIG*: **the Redeemer** o Redentor.

redeeming [rɪ'diːmɪŋ] *adj* redentor, que redime.

redefine [ˌriːdɪ'faɪn] *vt* redefinir.

redemption [rɪ'dempʃn] *n (U) RELIG* redenção *f*, salvação *f*; **beyond** *OR* **past ~** *fig* irrecuperável.

redeploy [ˌriːdɪ'plɔɪ] *vt* remanejar.

redeployment [ˌriːdɪ'plɔɪmənt] *n (U)* remanejamento *m.*

redesign [ˌriːdɪ'zaɪn] *vt* **-1.** [replan, redraw] remodelar **-2.** [reorganize, rethink] repensar.

redevelop [ˌriːdɪ'veləp] *vt* renovar.

redevelopment [ˌriːdɪ'veləpmənt] *n (U)* renovação *f.*

red-faced [-'feɪst] *adj* **-1.** [after exercise, with heat] vermelho(lha) **-2.** [with embarrassment] corado(da).

red-haired [-'heəd] *adj* ruivo(va).

red-handed [-'hændɪd] *adj*: **to catch sb ~** pegar alguém com a mão na massa.

redhead ['redhed] *n* ruiva *f.*

red herring *n fig* pista *f* falsa.

red-hot *adj* **-1.** [extremely hot] em brasa **-2.** [very enthusiastic] apaixonado(da) **-3.** *inf* [very good] supimpa.

redid [ˌriː'dɪd] *pt* ⊳ **redo**.

Red Indian ⋄ *adj* dos peles-vermelhas. ⋄ *n* pele-vermelha *mf.*

redirect [ˌriːdɪ'rekt] *vt* **-1.** [mail] redirecionar **-2.** [traffic, aircraft] desviar **-3.** [one's energies, money, aid] direcionar.

rediscover [ˌriːdɪs'kʌvəʳ] *vt* **-1.** [re-experience] redescobrir **-2.** [make popular, famous again]: **to be ~ed** ser redescoberto(ta).

redistribute [ˌriːdɪs'trɪbjuːt] *vt* redistribuir.

red-letter day *n* dia *m* memorável.

red light *n* [traffic signal] luz *f* vermelha.

red-light district *n* zona *f* do baixo meretrício.

red meat *n (U)* carne *f* vermelha.

red mullet *n* salmonete *m.*

redness ['rednɪs] *n (U)* vermelhidão *f.*

redo [ˌriː'duː] *(pt* **-did**, *pp* **-done)** *vt* **-1.** [do again] refazer **-2.** *inf* [redecorate] redecorar.

redolent ['redələnt] *adj literary* **-1.** [reminiscent]: **~ of sthg** rememorativo(va) de algo **-2.** [smelling]: **~ of sthg** com aroma de algo.

redone *pp* ⊳ **redo**.

redouble [ˌriː'dʌbl] *vt*: **to ~ one's efforts (to do sthg)** redobrar os esforços (para fazer algo).

redoubtable [rɪ'daʊtəbl] *adj fml* formidável.

redraft [ˌriː'drɑːft] *vt* reescrever.

redraw [ˌriː'drɔː] *(pt* **-drew**, *pp* **-drawn** [-'drɔːn]) *vt* redesenhar.

redress [rɪ'dres] *fml* ⋄ *n (U)* retificação *f.* ⋄ *vt*: **to ~ the balance** compensar.

redrew [ˌriː'druː] *pt* ⊳ **redraw**.

Red Sea *n*: **the ~** o Mar Vermelho.

red setter *n* cão *m* perdigueiro.

Red Square *n* Praça *f* Vermelha.

red squirrel *n* esquilo *m* vermelho.

red tape *n (U) fig* burocracia *f.*

reduce [rɪ'djuːs] ⋄ *vt* **-1.** [make smaller, less] reduzir; **to ~ sthg to a pulp** reduzir algo à essência **-2.** *CULIN* engrossar no fogo **-3.** [force, bring]: **to be ~d to doing sthg** ser forçado(da) a fazer algo; **to be ~d to sthg** estar reduzido(da) a algo. ⋄ *vi US* [lose weight] emagrecer.

reduced [rɪ'djuːst] *adj* reduzido(da); **in ~ circumstances** em circunstâncias limitadas.

reduction [rɪ'dʌkʃn] *n* **-1.** [decrease]: **~ (in sthg)** redução (em algo) **-2.** [amount of decrease]: **~ (of)** redução de.

redundancy [rɪ'dʌndənsɪ] *(pl* **-ies)** *n UK* **-1.** [job loss] demissão *f* **-2.** *(U)* [jobless state] desemprego *m.*

redundancy payment *n UK* indenização *f (por demissão sem justa causa).*

redundant [rɪ'dʌndənt] *adj* **-1.** *UK* [jobless]: **to be made ~** ficar desempregado(da) **-2.** [superfluous] supérfluo(a).

redwood ['redwʊd] *n*: **a ~ (tree)** uma sequóia.

re-echo ⋄ *vt* [repeat] repetir. ⋄ *vi* [echo] repercutir, ecoar.

reed [riːd] ⋄ *n* **-1.** [plant] junco *m* **-2.** [of musical instrument] palheta *f.* ⋄ *comp* [made of reeds] de junco.

re-educate *vt* reabilitar.

reedy ['riːdɪ] *(compar* **-ier**, *superl* **-iest)** *adj* [voice] estridente.

reef [riːf] *n* recife *m.*

reek [riːk] ⋄ *n* fedor *m.* ⋄ *vi*: **to ~ (of sthg)** feder (a algo).

reel [riːl] ⋄ *n* **-1.** [roll] rolo *m* **-2.** [on fishing rod] molinete *m.* ⋄ *vi* **-1.** [stagger] cambalear **-2.** [head, mind] girar; **to ~ from sthg** estar confuso(sa) por (causa de) algo.

➤ **reel in** *vt sep* enrolar.

reel off *vt sep* [list] enumerar.

re-elect *vt*: **to ~ sb (as) sthg** reeleger alguém (como algo).

re-election *n (U)* reeleição *f*.

re-emphasize *vt* reenfatizar.

re-enact *vt* reviver.

re-enter *vt* **-1.** [room, country] reentrar em **-2.** COMPUT [data] reinserir em.

re-entry *n* **-1.** [into room, country] reentrada *f* **-2.** COMPUT [of data] reinserção *f*.

re-examine *vt* **-1.** [question, case] reexaminar **-2.** [witness] reinquirir **-3.** [candidate] rever.

re-export COMM ◇ *n* **-1.** *(U)* [act of exporting] reexportação *f* **-2.** [goods exported] reexportações *fpl.* ◇ *vt* reexportar.

ref [ref] *n* **-1.** *inf* (*abbr of* referee) SPORT árbitro *m* **-2.** (*abbr of* reference) ADMIN ref.

refectory [rɪˈfektərɪ] (*pl* -ies) *n* **-1.** [in school, college] cantina *f* **-2.** [in monastery] refeitório *m*.

refer [rɪˈfɜːʳ] (*pt & pp* -red, *cont* -ring) *vt* **-1.** [person]: **to ~ sb to sthg** encaminhar alguém para algo **-2.** [report, case, decision]: **to ~ sthg to sb/sthg** encaminhar algo para alguém/algo.

   ◆ **refer to** *vt fus* **-1.** [mention, speak about] referir-se a **-2.** [apply to, concern] aplicar-se a **-3.** [consult] consultar.

referee [ˌrefəˈriː] ◇ *n* **-1.** SPORT árbitro *m*, -tra *f* **-2.** UK [for job application] referência *f*. ◇ *vt & vi* SPORT apitar.

reference [ˈrefrəns] *n* **-1.** [gen] referência *f* **-2.** *(U)* [act of mentioning]: **to make ~ to sb/sthg** referência a alguém/algo; **with ~ to** *fml* com referência a **-3.** [mention]: **~ (to sb/sthg)** menção a alguém /algo **-4.** *(U)* [for advice, information]: **~ (to sb/sthg)** referência a alguém/algo; **for future ~** para consulta futura **-5.** COMM [in letter] referências *fpl*.

reference book *n* livro *m* de consulta.

reference library *n* biblioteca *f* de consulta.

reference number *n* número *m* de referência.

referendum [ˌrefəˈrendəm] (*pl* -s OR -da [-də]) *n* POL plebiscito *m*.

referral [rɪˈfɜːrəl] *n fml* referência *f*.

refill [*n* ˈriːfɪl, *vb* ˌriːˈfɪl] ◇ *n* **-1.** [for pen, lighter] carga *f* nova **-2.** *inf* [drink] dose *f* extra. ◇ *vt* [fill again - bottle, glass] encher novamente; [- petrol tank] reabastecer.

refillable [ˌriːˈfɪləbl] *adj* recarregável.

refine [rɪˈfaɪn] *vt* **-1.** [purify] refinar **-2.** [details, speech] aprimorar.

refined [rɪˈfaɪnd] *adj* refinado(da).

refinement [rɪˈfaɪnmənt] *n* **-1.** [improvement]: **~ (on sthg)** refinamento (de algo) **-2.** *(U)* [gentility] requinte *m*.

refinery [rɪˈfaɪnərɪ] (*pl* -ies) *n* refinaria *f*.

refit [*n* ˈriːfɪt, *vb* ˌriːˈfɪt] (*pt & pp* -ted, *cont* -ting) ◇ *n* [of ship] reaparelhamento *m*. ◇ *vt* [ship] reaparelhar.

reflate [ˌriːˈfleɪt] *vt* ECON reinflacionar.

reflation [ˌriːˈfleɪʃn] *n (U)* ECON reflação *f*.

reflationary [riːˈfleɪʃənrɪ] *adj* ECON reflacionário(ria).

reflect [rɪˈflekt] ◇ *vt* refletir; **to be ~ed in sthg** estar refletido(da) em algo, refletir-se em algo; **to**

~ that ... refletir que ... ◇ *vi* [think, consider]: **to ~ (on OR upon sthg)** refletir (sobre algo).

reflection [rɪˈflekʃn] *n* **-1.** [gen] reflexo *m* **-2.** [comment, thought] reflexão *f*; **~ on sthg** reflexão sobre algo; **on ~** pensando bem.

reflective [rɪˈflektɪv] *adj* **-1.** [thoughtful] reflexivo(va) **-2.** [shiny] brilhante.

reflector [rɪˈflektəʳ] *n* refletor *m*.

reflex [ˈriːfleks] *n*: **~ (action)** (ato) reflexo *m*.

   ◆ **reflexes** *npl* reflexos *mpl*.

reflex camera *n* câmera *f* reflex.

reflexive [rɪˈfleksɪv] *adj* GRAMM reflexivo(va).

reflexology [ˌriːflekˈsɒlədʒɪ] *n* reflexoterapia *f*.

reforest [ˌriːˈfɒrɪst] *vt esp US* = **reafforest**.

reforestation [riːˌfɒrɪˈsteɪʃn] *n esp US* = **reafforestation**.

reform [rɪˈfɔːm] ◇ *n* reforma *f*. ◇ *vt* **-1.** [change] reformar **-2.** [improve behaviour of] corrigir. ◇ *vi* corrigir-se.

reformat [ˌriːˈfɔːmæt] (*pt & pp* -ted, *cont* -ting) *vt* COMPUT reformatar.

Reformation [ˌrefəˈmeɪʃn] *n*: **the ~** a Reforma.

reformatory [rɪˈfɔːmətrɪ] (*pl* -ies) *n US* reformatório *m*.

reformed [rɪˈfɔːmd] *adj* regenerado(da).

reformer [rɪˈfɔːməʳ] *n* reformador *m*, -ra *f*.

reformist [rɪˈfɔːmɪst] ◇ *adj* reformista. ◇ *n* reformista *mf*.

refract [rɪˈfrækt] ◇ *vt* refratar. ◇ *vi* refratar-se.

refrain [rɪˈfreɪn] ◇ *n* refrão *m*. ◇ *vi fml*: **to ~ from doing sthg** abster-se de fazer algo.

refresh [rɪˈfreʃ] *vt* refrescar; **to ~ sb's memory** refrescar a memória de alguém.

refreshed [rɪˈfreʃt] *adj* revigorado(da).

refresher course [rɪˈfreʃəʳ-] *n* curso *m* de aperfeiçoamento OR atualização.

refreshing [rɪˈfreʃɪŋ] *adj* **-1.** [pleasantly different] reconfortante **-2.** [cooling, energy-giving] refrescante.

refreshments [rɪˈfreʃmənts] *npl* comes *mpl* e bebes, lanche *m*.

refrigerate [rɪˈfrɪdʒəreɪt] *vt* refrigerar.

refrigeration [rɪˌfrɪdʒəˈreɪʃn] *n (U)* refrigeração *f*.

refrigerator [rɪˈfrɪdʒəreɪtəʳ] *n* geladeira *f*, refrigerador *m*.

refuel [ˌriːˈfjʊəl] (*UK pt & pp* -led, *cont* -ling, *US pt & pp* -ed, *cont* -ing) ◇ *vt* reabastecer. ◇ *vi* reabastecer-se (*de combustível*).

refuge [ˈrefjuːdʒ] *n* **-1.** [place of safety] refúgio *m* **-2.** *(U)* [safety]: **to seek OR take ~** [hide] procurar refúgio, refugiar-se; **to seek OR take ~ in sthg** *fig* procurar refúgio em algo, refugiar-se em algo.

refugee [ˌrefjʊˈdʒiː] *n* refugiado *m*, -da *f*.

refugee camp *n* campo *m* de refugiados.

refund [*n* ˈriːfʌnd, *vb* rɪˈfʌnd] ◇ *n* reembolso *m*. ◇ *vt*: **to ~ sthg to sb, to ~ sb sthg** reembolsar algo a alguém.

refurbish [ˌriːˈfɜːbɪʃ] *vt* **-1.** [shop, office] reformar **-2.** [building] restaurar.

refurbishment [ˌriːˈfɜːbɪʃmənt] *n* **-1.** [of shop, office] reforma *f* **-2.** [building] restauração *f*.

refurnish [ˌriːˈfɜːnɪʃ] *vt* mobiliar novamente.

refusal [rɪ'fjuːzl] *n* recusa *f*; **her ~ to accept the conditions** o fato de ela não ter aceitado as condições; **to meet with ~** ser rechaçado(da).

refuse[1] [rɪ'fjuːz] ◇ *vt* -1. [withhold, deny]: **to ~ sb sthg, to ~ sthg to sb** negar algo a alguém -2. [decline] recusar; **to ~ to do sthg** recusar-se a fazer algo, negar-se a fazer algo. ◇ *vi* negar-se, dizer que não.

refuse[2] ['refjuːs] *n (U)* lixo *m*, refugo *m*.

refuse collection ['refjuːs-] *n* coleta *f* de lixo.

refuse collector ['refjuːs-] *n* lixeiro *m*, -ra *f*.

refuse dump ['refjuːs-] *n* depósito *m* de lixo, lixeira *f*.

refute [rɪ'fjuːt] *vt fml* refutar.

reg. (*abbr of* **registered**): **~ trademark** marca *f* registrada.

regain [rɪ'geɪn] *vt* recuperar.

regal ['riːgl] *adj* régio(gia).

regale [rɪ'geɪl] *vt*: **to ~ sb with sthg** entreter alguém com algo.

regalia [rɪ'geɪljə] *n (U) fml* insígnias *fpl* reais.

regard [rɪ'gɑːd] ◇ *n* -1. *(U) fml* [respect, esteem] respeito *m*, estima *f*; **~ (for sb/sthg)** respeito *or* estima (por alguém/algo) -2. [aspect]: **in this/ that ~** a este respeito. ◇ *vt* considerar; **to ~ o.s. intelligent** considerar-se inteligente; **to ~ sb/ sthg as** considerar alguém/algo; **to ~ sb/sthg with** ver alguém/algo com; **to be highly ~ed** ser muito bem considerado(da).
➣ **regards** *npl* [in greetings] lembranças *fpl*; **with my best ~s** cordialmente.
➣ **as regards** *prep* em relação a, no que se refere a.
➣ **in regard to, with regard to** *prep* a respeito de, em relação a.

regarding [rɪ'gɑːdɪŋ] *prep* a respeito de, em relação a.

regardless [rɪ'gɑːdlɪs] *adv* apesar de tudo.
➣ **regardless of** *prep* independentemente de; **~ the cost** custe o que custar.

regatta [rɪ'gætə] *n* regata *f*.

regd. = **reg**.

Regency ['riːdʒənsɪ] *adj* (com período) regencial.

regenerate [rɪ'dʒenəreɪt] ◇ *vt* regenerar. ◇ *vi* -1. [organs, tissue] regenerar-se -2. [economy] recuperar-se -3. [project] ser reformado(da).

regeneration [rɪ,dʒenə'reɪʃn] *n* -1. *(U)* [of organs, tissue] regeneração *f* -2. *(U)* [of economy] recuperação *f* -3. *(U)* [of project] reforma *f*.

regent ['riːdʒənt] ◇ *adj* regente. ◇ *n* regente *mf*.

reggae ['regeɪ] *n (U)* reggae *m*.

regime [reɪ'ʒiːm] *n pej* regime *m*.

regiment ['redʒɪmənt] *n* MIL regimento *m*.

regimental [,redʒɪ'mentl] *adj* MIL do regimento, regimental.

regimented ['redʒɪmentɪd] *adj* -1. *pej* [workforce] estritamente controlado(da) -2. [in rows] ordenado(da) em fileiras.

region ['riːdʒən] *n* -1. [gen] região *f* -2. [range]: **in the ~ of** por volta de.

regional ['riːdʒənl] *adj* regional.

register ['redʒɪstə[r]] ◇ *n* registro *f*. ◇ *vt* -1.

registrar -2. [express] expressar, mostrar. ◇ *vi* -1. [enroll]: **to ~ as/for sthg** inscrever-se como/ para algo -2. [book in] registrar-se -3. *inf* [be properly understood] assimilar.

registered ['redʒɪstəd] *adj* -1. [officially listed] oficialmente inscrito(ta) -2. [letter, parcel] registrado (da).

registered nurse *n* enfermeira *f* formada.

registered post *UK*, **registered mail** *US n (U)*: **to send sthg by ~** enviar algo registrado (pelo correio).

registered trademark *n* marca *f* registrada.

registrar ['redʒɪstrɑː[r]] *n* -1. [keeper of records] escrivão *m*, -vã *f*, oficial *mf* de registro -2. *UNIV* [administrator] secretário *m*, -ria *f* geral -3. *UK* [doctor] médico *m*, -ca *f* em estágio de especialização.

registration [,redʒɪ'streɪʃn] *n* -1. [course enrolment] matrícula *f* -2. [of births, marriages and deaths] registro *m* -3. *AUT* = **registration number**.

registration document *n* certificado *m* de registro de veículo.

registration number *n* AUT número *m* de licença.

registry ['redʒɪstrɪ] (*pl* -ies) *n* registro *m*.

registry office *n* registro *m* civil.

regress [rɪ'gres] *vi fml*: **to ~ (to sthg)** regredir (a algo).

regression [rɪ'greʃn] *n (U) fml* regressão *f*.

regressive [rɪ'gresɪv] *adj fml* regressivo(va).

regret [rɪ'gret] (*pt & pp* -ted, *cont* -ting) ◇ *n* -1. *(U) fml* [sorrow] pesar *m* -2. [sad feeling]: **to have no ~a about sthg** não lamentar algo em absoluto. ◇ *vt*: **to ~ sthg/doing sthg** lamentar algo/ter feito algo; **we ~ to announce ...** lamentamos comunicar ...

regretful [rɪ'gretfʊl] *adj* -1. [smile look] de arrependimento -2. [person] arrependido(da).

regretfully [rɪ'gretfʊlɪ] *adv* pesarosamente; **~ we have to announce ...** lamentamos ter que anunciar ...

regrettable [rɪ'gretəbl] *adj fml* lamentável.

regrettably [rɪ'gretəblɪ] *adv* lamentavelmente.

regroup [,riː'gruːp] *vi* reagrupar-se.

regt (*abbr of* **regiment**) regto.

regular ['regjʊlə[r]] ◇ *adj* -1. [gen] regular -2. [frequent - occurrence] freqüente; [- customer] habitual; [- visitor] assíduo(dua) -3. [usual] habitual, normal -4. *US* [in size] médio(dia) -5. *US* [pleasant] amigável -6. *US* [normal] normal. ◇ *n* [customer, client] cliente *mf* habitual.

regular army *n* exército *m* ativo.

regularity [,regjʊ'lærətɪ] *n (U)* regularidade *f*.

regularly ['regjʊləlɪ] *adv* -1. [equally spaced] de maneira uniforme -2. [repeated at expected time] regularmente.

regulate ['regjʊleɪt] *vt* regular.

regulation [,regjʊ'leɪʃn] ◇ *adj* regulamentar. ◇ *n* -1. [rule] regra *f*, lei *f* -2. *(U)* [control] regulamento *m*, regulamentação *f*.

regurgitate [rɪ'gɜːdʒɪteɪt] *vt* -1. [bring up] regurgitar -2. *fig & pej* [repeat] repetir maquinalmente.

rehabilitate [,riːə'bɪlɪteɪt] *vt* -1. [convict, addict] reabilitar -2. [patient, invalid] recuperar.

rehabilitation [ˌriːəˌbɪlɪ'teɪʃn] n -1. [of convict, addict] reabilitação f -2. [of patient, invalid] recuperação f.

rehash [ˌriː'hæʃ] inf <> vt pej retocar. <> n retoque m.

rehearsal [rɪ'hɜːsl] n ensaio m.

rehearse [rɪ'hɜːs] <> vt ensaiar. <> vi: to ~ (for sthg) ensaiar (para algo).

reheat [ˌriː'hiːt] vt reaquecer, esquentar de novo.

rehouse [ˌriː'haʊz] vt: to be ~d ser realojado (da).

reign [reɪn] <> n reinado m. <> vi: to ~ (over sb/sthg) reinar (sobre alguém/algo).

reigning ['reɪnɪŋ] adj atual.

reimburse [ˌriːɪm'bɜːs] vt: to ~ sb (for sthg) reembolsar alguém (por algo).

reimbursement [ˌriːɪm'bɜːsmənt] n (U) fml: ~ (for sthg) reembolso m (por algo).

rein [reɪn] n fig: to give (a) free ~ to sb, to give sb free ~ dar carta branca a alguém; to keep a tight ~ on sb/sthg controlar alguém/algo com firmeza.
➤ **reins** npl -1. [for horse] rédeas fpl -2. [for child] andadeira f.
➤ **rein in** vt sep [horse] puxar as rédeas de.

reincarnation [ˌriːɪnkɑː'neɪʃn] n (U) reencarnação f.

reindeer ['reɪnˌdɪəʳ] (pl inv) n rena f.

reinforce [ˌriːɪn'fɔːs] vt: to ~ sthg (with sthg) reforçar algo (com algo).

reinforced concrete [ˌriːɪn'fɔːst-] n (U) concreto m armado.

reinforcement [ˌriːɪn'fɔːsmənt] n reforço m.
➤ **reinforcements** npl reforços mpl.

reinstate [ˌriːɪn'steɪt] vt -1. [person - in job] readmitir; [- in position, office] reempossar, reintegrar -2. [payment, idea, policy] restabelecer.

reinstatement [ˌriːɪn'steɪtmənt] n -1. [of person - in job] readmissão f; [- in position, office] reintegração f -2. [of payment, idea, policy] restabelecimento m.

reinterpret [ˌriːɪn'tɜːprɪt] vt reinterpretar.

reintroduce ['riːˌɪntrə'djuːs] vt reintroduzir.

reintroduction [riːˌɪntrə'dʌkʃn] n (U) reintrodução f.

reissue [riː'ɪʃuː] <> n reedição f, reimpressão f. <> vt reeditar, reimprimir.

reiterate [riː'ɪtəreɪt] vt fml reiterar.

reiteration [riːˌɪtə'reɪʃn] n fml reiteração f.

reject [n 'riːdʒekt, vb rɪ'dʒekt] <> n [in factory, shop] refugo m, rejeito m. <> vt -1. [not agree to] rejeitar, não concordar com -2. [dismiss, not accept] rejeitar -3. [for job] recusar.

rejection [rɪ'dʒekʃn] n -1. (U) [act of refusal] rejeição f -2. [for job] recusa f.

rejig [ˌriː'dʒɪg] (pt & pp -ged, cont -ging) vt UK inf modificar ou alterar um pouco.

rejoice [rɪ'dʒɔɪs] vi: to ~ (at or in sthg) regozijar-se or alegrar-se (por algo).

rejoicing [rɪ'dʒɔɪsɪŋ] n (U) regozijo m, alegria f; ~ at or over sthg regozijo m por algo.

rejoin [rɪ'dʒɔɪn] vt -1. [group, friends] reunir-se novamente com -2. [regiment] reingressar em -3. [motorway] pegar novamente -4. [club, society] voltar a ser sócio(cia) de -5. [reply] replicar, retorquir.

rejoinder [rɪ'dʒɔɪndəʳ] n réplica f.

rejuvenate [rɪ'dʒuːvəneɪt] vt rejuvenescer.

rejuvenation [rɪˌdʒuːvə'neɪʃn] n (U) rejuvenescimento m.

rekindle [ˌriː'kɪndl] vt fig reacender, reavivar.

relapse [rɪ'læps] <> n recaída f; to have a ~ ter uma recaída. <> vi: to ~ into [coma] entrar novamente em; [drunken stupor, old ways] voltar a cair em; [crime] reincidir em.

relate [rɪ'leɪt] <> vt -1. [connect]: to ~ sthg to sthg relacionar algo a algo -2. [tell] contar. <> vi -1. [connect]: to ~ to sthg relacionar-se a algo -2. [concern]: to ~ to sthg referir-se a algo -3. [empathize]: to ~ (to sb/sthg) ter muito em comum (com alguém/algo).
➤ **relating to** prep sobre, acerca de.

related [rɪ'leɪtɪd] adj -1. [in same family] aparentado (da); to be ~ to sb ser aparentado(da) de alguém -2. [connected] relacionado(da).

relation [rɪ'leɪʃn] n -1. (U) [connection]: ~ (to/between) relação f (com/entre); to bear no ~ to não ter nada a ver com; in ~ to [state, size] em relação a -2. [family member] parente mf, familiar mf.
➤ **relations** npl [relationship] relações fpl; ~ between/with relações entre/com.

relational [rɪ'leɪʃənl] adj COMPUT relacional.

relationship [rɪ'leɪʃnʃɪp] n -1. [gen] relação f -2. [relations] relação f, relacionamento m -3. [connection] ligação f.

relative ['relətɪv] <> adj relativo(va). <> n parente mf, familiar mf.
➤ **relative to** prep fml -1. [compared to] em comparação com -2. [connected with] relativo(va) a, com relação a.

relatively ['relətɪvlɪ] adv relativamente.

relativity [ˌrelə'tɪvətɪ] n (U) relatividade f.

relax [rɪ'læks] <> vt -1. [gen] relaxar -2. [loosen, free up] afrouxar. <> vi -1. [person] relaxar, descontrair-se; ~! It's OK! relaxe! Está tudo bem! -2. [grip] afrouxar-se.

relaxation [ˌriːlæk'seɪʃn] n (U) -1. [rest] relaxamento m -2. [of rule, discipline, regulation] afrouxamento m.

relaxed [rɪ'lækst] adj -1. [person] relaxado(da), descontraído(da) -2. [meeting, evening, mood] descontraído(da).

relaxing [rɪ'læksɪŋ] adj relaxante.

relay ['riːleɪ] (pt & pp senses 1 & 2 -ed, pt & pp sense 3 relaid) <> n -1. SPORT: ~ (race) corrida f de revezamento; in ~s fig em turnos -2. [broadcast] retransmissão f. <> vt -1. [broadcast] retransmitir -2. [message, news]: to ~ sthg (to sb) transmitir algo (a alguém) -3. [cable, carpet, tiles] repor.

release [rɪ'liːs] <> n -1. (U) [from captivity] soltura f, libertação f -2. (U) [from pain, suffering] liberação f -3. [statement] comunicado m -4. (U) [of gas, fumes] escapamento m, emissão f -5. (U) [of film, video, CD] lançamento m; on ~ CINEMA em exibição -6. [film, video, CD]: new ~ novo lançamento. <> vt -1. [set free] soltar, libertar; to ~ sb from prison/captivity libertar or soltar alguém da prisão/do cativeiro; to ~ sb from sthg [promise, contract] liberar alguém de algo **- 2.** [make available] liberar **- 3.** [control, grasp, mechanism] soltar **- 4.** [let out, emit]: **heat is ∼ d from the liquid into the air** o calor é liberado do líquido para o ar **- 5.** [film, video, CD] lançar; [statement, news story] divulgar.

relegate ['relɪgeɪt] *vt* **-1.** [demote]: **to ∼ sb/sthg (to)** relegar alguém/algo (a) **- 2.** *SPORT*: **to be ∼ d** *UK* ser rebaixado(da).

relegation [ˌrelɪ'geɪʃn] *n (U)* **-1.** [demotion]: **∼ (to)** relegação *f* (a) **- 2.** *SPORT*: **∼ (to)** rebaixamento *m* (a).

relent [rɪ'lent] *vi* **-1.** [person] condescender **- 2.** [wind, storm] abrandar-se, acalmar-se.

relentless [rɪ'lentlɪs] *adj* implacável.

relentlessly [rɪ'lentlɪslɪ] *adv* implacavelmente.

relevance ['reləvəns] *n (U)* **-1.** [connection]: **∼ (to sb/ sthg)** relevância *f* (a alguém/algo) **- 2.** [significance]: **∼ (to sb/sthg)**, **∼ (for sb/sthg)** importância *f* (para alguém/algo).

relevant ['reləvənt] *adj* **-1.** [gen] relevante; **∼ (to sb/sthg)** relevante (a alguém/algo) **- 2.** [important]: **∼ (to sb/sthg)** importante (a alguém/algo).

reliability [rɪˌlaɪə'bɪlətɪ] *n (U)* confiabilidade *f*.

reliable [rɪ'laɪəbl] *adj* **-1.** [dependable] confiável **- 2.** [correct, true] seguro(ra).

reliably [rɪ'laɪəblɪ] *adv* **-1.** [dependably] de forma confiável **- 2.** [correctly, truly]: **to be ∼ informed that ...** saber de fonte segura que ...

reliance [rɪ'laɪəns] *n (U)*: **∼ (on sb/sthg)** dependência *f* (de alguém/algo).

reliant [rɪ'laɪənt] *adj*: **∼ on sb/sthg** dependente de alguém/algo.

relic ['relɪk] *n* relíquia *f*.

relief [rɪ'li:f] *n* **-1.** [comfort] alívio *m*; **she sighed with ∼** ela suspirou aliviada **- 2.** *(U)* [for poor, refugees] auxílio *m* **- 3.** *US* [social security] subsídio *m*.

relief map *n* mapa *m* em relevo.

relief road *n UK* desvio *m*.

relieve [rɪ'li:v] *vt* **-1.** [ease, lessen] aliviar; **to ∼ sb of sthg** aliviar alguém de algo **- 2.** [take over from] substituir **- 3.** [give help to] auxiliar.

relieved [rɪ'li:vd] *adj* aliviado(da).

religion [rɪ'lɪdʒn] *n* religião *f*.

religious [rɪ'lɪdʒəs] *adj* religioso(sa).

reline [ˌri:'laɪn] *vt* **-1.** [gen] revestir novamente **- 2.** [brakes] trocar o forro de.

relinquish [rɪ'lɪŋkwɪʃ] *vt* **-1.** [power, post, claim] renunciar a **- 2.** [hold] soltar.

relish ['relɪʃ] <> *n* **-1.** *(U)* [enjoyment]: **with (great) ∼** com(grande)satisfação **- 2.** [pickle] picles *mpl*. <> *vt* desfrutar de; **to ∼ the thought** *OR* **idea** *OR* **prospect of doing sthg** desfrutar de antemão da idéia *OR* da perspectiva de fazer algo.

relive [ˌri:'lɪv] *vt* reviver.

relocate [ˌri:ləʊ'keɪt] <> *vt* realocar, transferir. <> *vi* transferir-se.

relocation [ˌri:ləʊ'keɪʃn] *n (U)* realocação *f*.

relocation expenses *npl* gastos *mpl* com transferência.

reluctance [rɪ'lʌktəns] *n (U)* relutância *f*; **with ∼** com relutância.

reluctant [rɪ'lʌktənt] *adj* relutante; **to be ∼ to do sthg** estar pouco disposto(ta) a fazer algo.

reluctantly [rɪ'lʌktəntlɪ] *adv* relutantemente.

rely [rɪ'laɪ] *(pt & pp* -ied*)* ◆ **rely on** *vt fus* **-1.** [count on] contar com; **to ∼ on sb/sthg to do sthg** estar certo(ta) de que alguém/algo fará algo **- 2.** [be dependent on]: **to ∼ on sb/sthg for sthg** depender de alguém/algo para algo.

REM *(abbr of* rapid eye movement*)* *n* REM *m*.

remain [rɪ'meɪn] *vi* **-1.** [stay] permanecer, ficar; **to ∼ the same** continuar sendo igual **- 2.** [be left] ficar; **the problem ∼** o problema continua; **to ∼ to be done** ficar para ser feito(ta); **it ∼ s to be seen ...** isso ainda tem que ver ... ◆ **remains** *npl* **-1.** [of meal, fortune, body] restos *mpl* **- 2.** [corpses] corpos *mpl* **- 3.** [of ancient civilization, buildings] ruínas *fpl*.

remainder [rɪ'meɪndə'] *n* **-1.** [rest]: **the ∼** o resto **- 2.** *MATH* resto *m*; **three into ten goes three ∼ one** dez (dividido) por três é igual a três e sobra um.

remaining [rɪ'meɪnɪŋ] *adj* restante; **it's my last ∼ pound!** é a última libra que eu tenho!

remake [*n* ˌri:'meɪk, *vb* ˌri:'meɪk] *CINEMA* <> *n* nova versão *f*, remake *m*. <> *vt* fazer uma nova versão de.

remand [rɪ'mɑ:nd] *JUR* <> *n*: **on ∼** sob prisão preventiva. <> *vt* recolocar em prisão preventiva; **to be ∼ ed in custody** estar sob custódia.

remand centre *n UK* instituição para a qual são enviadas as pessoas que aguardam julgamento.

remark [rɪ'mɑ:k] <> *n* comentário *m*. <> *vt*: **to ∼ (that)** comentar que. <> *vi*: **to ∼ on sthg** fazer comentários sobre algo.

remarkable [rɪ'mɑ:kəbl] *adj* excepcional, extraordinário(ria).

remarkably [rɪ'mɑ:kəblɪ] *adv* excepcionalmente, extraordinariamente.

remarry [ˌri:'mærɪ] *(pt & pp* -ied*)* *vi* casar-se de novo.

remedial [rɪ'mi:djəl] *adj* **-1.** [pupil] atrasado(da) **- 2.** [teacher, class] de reforço **- 3.** [corrective] corretivo (va).

remedy ['remədɪ] *(pl* -ies, *pt & pp* -ied*)* <> *n* **-1.** [for ill health]: **∼ (for sthg)** remédio *m* (para algo) **- 2.** *fig* [solution]: **∼ (for sthg)** *OR* solução *f* (para algo). <> *vt* remediar.

remember [rɪ'membə'] <> *vt* **-1.** lembrar-se de, lembrar; **to ∼ doing sthg** lembrar-se de ter feito algo; **to ∼ to do sthg** lembrar-se de fazer algo **- 2.** [as greeting]: **∼ me to your wife** dê lembranças minhas à sua esposa. <> *vi* lembrar(-se).

remembrance [rɪ'membrəns] *n (U)* *fml*: **in ∼ of** em memória de.

Remembrance Day *n* na Grã-Bretanha, dia em memória das pessoas mortas nas duas guerras mundiais.

remind [rɪ'maɪnd] *vt* **-1.** [tell]: **to ∼ sb (about sthg/ to do sthg)** lembrar alguém (de algo/de fazer algo) **- 2.** [be reminiscent of]: **to ∼ sb of sb/sthg** fazer alguém se lembrar de alguém/algo; **she ∼ s me of my sister** ela me faz lembrar a minha irmã.

reminder [rɪ'maɪndə'] *n* **-1.** [to jog memory]: **∼ of sthg/to do sthg** lembrança *f* de algo/de fazer algo **- 2.** [for bill, membership, licence] lembrete *m*.

reminisce [ˌremɪ'nɪs] *vi*: **to ~ (about sthg)** rememorar(algo).

reminiscences [ˌremɪ'nɪsənsɪz] *npl* reminiscências *fpl*.

reminiscent [ˌremɪ'nɪsnt] *adj*: **~ of sb/sthg** que faz lembrar alguém/algo.

remiss [rɪ'mɪs] *adj* descuidado(da), negligente.

remission [rɪ'mɪʃn] *n* -**1.** JUR redução *f* de pena - **2.** MED remissão *f*.

remit ['ri:mɪt] (*pt* & *pp* -**ted**, *cont* -**ting**) ◇ *n UK* alçada *f*; **that's outside my ~** isto está fora da minha alçada. ◇ *vt* remeter.

remittance [rɪ'mɪtns] *n* -**1.** [payment] remessa *f* -**2.** COMM [settlement of invoice] remessa *f* de valores.

remnant ['remnənt] *n* [of cloth] sobra *f*; [of beauty, culture] resto *m*.

remodel [ˌri:'mɒdl] (*UK pt* & *pp* -**led**, *cont* -**ling**, *US pt* & *pp* -**ed**, *cont* -**ing**) *vt* -**1.** [change shape of] remodelar - **2.** *US* [renovate] reformar.

remold *n US* = **remould**.

remonstrate ['remənstreɪt] *vi fml*: **to ~ (with sb about sthg)** protestar (com alguém sobre algo).

remorse [rɪ'mɔ:s] *n* (U) remorso *m*.

remorseful [rɪ'mɔ:sfʊl] *adj* cheio (cheia) de remorso.

remorseless [rɪ'mɔ:slɪs] *adj* -**1.** [pitiless] desapiedado(da) - **2.** [unstoppable] impiedoso(sa), implacável.

remorselessly [rɪ'mɔ:slɪslɪ] *adv* -**1.** [pitilessly] de forma desapiedada - **2.** [unstoppably] impiedosamente, implacavelmente.

remote [rɪ'məʊt] *adj* -**1.** [gen] remoto(ta) - **2.** [unconnected, detached]: **~ from** distante de.

remote control *n* controle *m* remoto.

remote-controlled [-kən'trəʊld] *adj* operado(-da) por controle remoto.

remotely [rɪ'məʊtlɪ] *adv* remotamente.

remoteness [rɪ'məʊtnɪs] *n* (U) -**1.** [distance - in space] isolamento *f*; [- in time] distanciamento *m* - **2.** [aloofness] indiferença *m*.

remould *UK*, **remold** *US* ['ri:məʊld] *n* pneu *m* recauchutado.

removable [rɪ'mu:vəbl] *adj* desmontável.

removal [rɪ'mu:vl] *n* -**1.** *UK* [change of house] mudança *f* - **2.** (U) [act of removing] remoção *f*.

removal man *n UK* encarregado *m* da mudança.

removal van *n UK* caminhão *m* de mudança.

remove [rɪ'mu:v] *vt* -**1.** [gen]: **to ~ sthg (from)** remover algo (de) - **2.** [take off garment] tirar - **3.** [from a job, post]: **to ~ sb (from)** demitir alguém (de) - **4.** [injustice, difficulty] eliminar - **5.** [problem] resolver - **6.** [suspicion] dissipar.

removed [rɪ'mu:vd] *adj*: **to be far ~ from** estar muito distante de.

remover [rɪ'mu:vəʳ] *n* removedor *m*.

remuneration [rɪˌmju:nə'reɪʃn] *n fml* (U) remuneração *f*.

Renaissance [rə'neɪsəns] ◇ *n*: **the ~** o Renascimento. ◇ *comp* do Renascimento.

rename [ˌri:'neɪm] *vt* renomear.

rend ['rend] (*pt* & *pp* **rent**) *vt fml* rasgar, despedaçar.

render ['rendəʳ] *vt* -**1.** [make, change] tornar; **to ~ sthg useless** tornar algo inútil; **to ~ sb speechless**

deixar alguém boquiaberto(ta) - **2.** [give] dar, prestar; **to ~ good services** prestar bons serviços - **3.** COMPUT exibir.

rendering ['rendərɪŋ] *n* -**1.** [performance - of play] interpretação *f*; [- of song, piece of music] execução *f* - **2.** [translation] tradução *f* - **3.** COMPUT exibição *f*.

rendezvous ['rɒndɪvu:] (*pl inv*) *n* -**1.** [meeting] encontro *m* - **2.** [place] ponto *m* de encontro.

rendition [ren'dɪʃn] *n* -**1.** [of piece of music] execução *f* - **2.** [of poem] declamação *f*.

renegade ['renɪgeɪd] ◇ *adj* renegado(da). ◇ *n* renegado *m*, -da *f*.

renege [rɪ'ni:g] *vi fml*: **to ~ on sthg** deixar de cumprir algo.

renegotiate [ˌri:nɪ'gəʊʃɪeɪt] *vt* & *vi* renegociar.

renew [rɪ'nju:] *vt* -**1.** [gen] renovar - **2.** [start again] reiniciar.

renewable [rɪ'nju:əbl] *adj* renovável.

renewal [rɪ'nju:əl] *n* renovação *f*.

rennet ['renɪt] *n* (U) coalheira *f*.

renounce [rɪ'naʊns] *vt* renunciar a.

renovate ['renəveɪt] *vt* renovar, reformar.

renovation [ˌrenə'veɪʃn] *n* (U) reforma *f*, renovação *f*.

➡ **renovations** *npl* reformas *fpl*.

renown [rɪ'naʊn] *n* (U) renome *m*.

renowned [rɪ'naʊnd] *adj*: **~ (for sthg)** renomado(da) (por algo).

rent [rent] ◇ *pt* & *pp* ➡ **rend**. ◇ *n* aluguel *m*. ◇ *vt* alugar.

➡ **rent out** *vt sep* alugar.

rental ['rentl] ◇ *adj* de aluguel. ◇ *n* [money] aluguel *m*.

rent book *n* livro *m* de registro do aluguel.

rent boy *n UK inf* garoto *m* de programa.

rented ['rentɪd] *adj* alugado(da).

rent-free ◇ *adj* isento(ta) de aluguel. ◇ *adv* sem pagar aluguel.

renumber [ˌri:'nʌmbəʳ] *vt* renumerar.

renunciation [rɪˌnʌnsɪ'eɪʃn] *n* (U) renúncia *f*.

reoccurrence [ˌri:ə'kʌrəns] *n* nova ocorrência *f*, repetição *f*.

reopen [ˌri:'əʊpn] ◇ *vt* -**1.** [open again] reabrir - **2.** [start again] recomeçar. ◇ *vi* -**1.** [open again] reabrir - **2.** [start again] recomeçar.

reorganization ['ri:ˌɔ:gənər'zeɪʃn] *n* (U) reorganização *f*.

reorganize, -ise [ˌri:'ɔ:gənaɪz] ◇ *vt* reorganizar. ◇ *vi* reorganizar-se.

rep [rep] *n* -**1.** (*abbr of* **representative**) *inf* representante *mf* - **2.** (*abbr of* **repertory**) *apresentação de uma série de peças teatrais em seqüência por uma mesma companhia teatral em um mesmo teatro*.

Rep. -**1.** (*abbr of* **Representative**) *US* deputado *m*, -da *f* - **2.** (*abbr of* **Republican**) republicano *m*, -na *f*.

repaid [ri:'peɪd] *pt* & *pp* ➡ **repay**.

repaint [ˌri:'peɪnt] *vt* repintar.

repair [rɪ'peəʳ] ◇ *n* -**1.** (U) [act of mending] reparo *m*, conserto *m*; **it's beyond ~** não tem conserto; **ingood/bad ~** em bom/mau estado - **2.** [instance of mending] reparo *m*. ◇ *vt* reparar.

repair kit *n* caixa *f* de ferramentas (*de bicicleta*).

repaper [ˌriːˈpeɪpə^r] *vt*: to ~ **the wall** trocar o papel de parede.

reparations [ˌrepəˈreɪʃnz] *npl* indenizações *fpl*.

repartee [ˌrepɑːˈtiː] *n* (*U*) troca *f* de réplicas engenhosas.

repatriate [ˌriːˈpætrɪeɪt] *vt* repatriar.

repay [riːˈpeɪ] (*pt* & *pp* **repaid**) *vt* -**1.** [money] reembolsar, devolver; to ~ **sb sthg, to ~ sthg to sb** reembolsar *or* devolver algo a alguém - **2.** [favour] retribuir; to ~ **sb for sthg** retribuir alguém por algo.

repayment [riːˈpeɪmənt] *n* -**1.** (*U*) [act of paying back] reembolso *m*, devolução *f* -**2.** [sum] pagamento *m*.

repeal [rɪˈpiːl] <> *n* revogação *f*. <> *vt* revogar.

repeat [rɪˈpiːt] <> *vt* -**1.** [gen] repetir; to ~ **o.s.** repetir-se - **2.** [broadcast] reprisar. <> *n* [broadcast] reprise *f*.

repeated [rɪˈpiːtɪd] *adj* repetido(da).

repeatedly [rɪˈpiːtɪdlɪ] *adv* repetidamente.

repel [rɪˈpel] (*pt* & *pp* -**led**, *cont* -**ling**) *vt* -**1.** [disgust] repugnar - **2.** [drive away] repelir.

repellent [rɪˈpelənt] <> *adj* repugnante. <> *n* repelente *m*.

repent [rɪˈpent] <> *vt* arrepender-se de. <> *vi*: to ~ **of sthg** arrepender-se de algo.

repentance [rɪˈpentəns] *n* (*U*) arrependimento *m*.

repentant [rɪˈpentənt] *adj* -**1.** [person] arrependido(da) - **2.** [smile] de arrependimento.

repercussions [ˌriːpəˈkʌʃnz] *npl* repercussões *fpl*.

repertoire [ˈrepətwɑː^r] *n* repertório *m*.

repertory [ˈrepətrɪ] *n* (*U*) repertório *m*.

repertory company *n* companhia *f* teatral de repertório.

repetition [ˌrepɪˈtɪʃn] *n* repetição *f*.

repetitious [ˌrepɪˈtɪʃəs], **repetitive** [rɪˈpetɪtɪv] *adj* repetitivo(va).

rephrase [ˌriːˈfreɪz] *vt* -**1.** [question] reformular - **2.** [statement] dizer com outras palavras.

replace [rɪˈpleɪs] *vt* -**1.** [take the place of] substituir; to ~ **sthg (with sthg)** substituir *or* trocar algo (por algo); to ~ **sb (with sb)** substituir alguém (por alguém); **if I lose your book, I'll ~ it** se eu perder o teu livro, eu te dou outro - **2.** [put back] recolocar no lugar.

replacement [rɪˈpleɪsmənt] *n* -**1.** (*U*) [act of replacing] reposição *f*, substituição *f* - **2.** [new person, object]: ~ **(for sthg)** substituto *m*, -ta *f* (para algo); ~ **(for sb)** suplente *mf* (para alguém).

replacement part *n* peça *f* de reposição.

replay [*n* ˈriːpleɪ, *vb* ˌriːˈpleɪ] <> *n* -**1.** [recording] replay *m* - **2.** [game] partida *f* de desempate. <> *vt* -**1.** [match, game] jogar de novo - **2.** [film, tape] reprisar.

replenish [rɪˈplenɪʃ] *vt* fml: to ~ **sthg (with sthg)** reabastecer *or* prover novamente algo (com algo).

replete [rɪˈpliːt] *adj* -**1.** fml [object] cheio(a) - **2.** fml [person] satisfeito(ta), saciado(da).

replica [ˈreplɪkə] *n* réplica *f*, cópia *f*.

replicate [ˈreplɪkeɪt] *vt* fml duplicar, reproduzir com exatidão.

replication [ˌreplɪˈkeɪʃn] *n* fml -**1.** (*U*) [process of copying] reprodução *f* exata - **2.** [copy] réplica *f*, cópia *f*.

reply [rɪˈplaɪ] (*pl* -ies, *pt* & *pp* -ied) <> *n* resposta *f*; **in ~ to sthg** em resposta a algo. <> *vt* responder; to ~ **that** responder que. <> *vi* responder; to ~ **to sb/sthg** responder a alguém/algo.

reply coupon *n* cupom *m* de resposta.

reply-paid *adj* pré-pago(ga), com porte pago.

report [rɪˈpɔːt] <> *n* -**1.** [description, account] relatório *m* - **2.** PRESS reportagem *f* - **3.** UK SCH boletim *m* de avaliação. <> *vt* -**1.** [news, crime] informar, comunicar - **2.** [make known]: to ~ **that** informar que; to ~ **sthg (to sb)** relatar algo (a alguém) - **3.** [complain about]: to ~ **sb (to sb)** denunciar alguém (a alguém); to ~ **sb for sthg** denunciar alguém por algo. <> *vi* -**1.** [give account] relatar; to ~ **on sthg** fazer um relatório sobre algo - **2.** PRESS: to ~ **on sthg** fazer uma reportagem sobre algo - **3.** [present o.s.]: to ~ **to** apresentar-se a; to ~ **for sthg** apresentar-se para algo.
◆ **report back** *vi*: to ~ **back (to sb)** dar retorno (para alguém).

reportage [ˌrepɔːˈtɑːʒ] *n* reportagem *f*.

report card *n* US SCH boletim *m*, caderneta *f* escolar.

reportedly [rɪˈpɔːtɪdlɪ] *adv* segundo se diz; **he is ~ not intending to return to this country** sabe-se que ele não pretende voltar a este país.

reported speech [rɪˈpɔːtɪd-] *n* (*U*) discurso *m* indireto.

reporter [rɪˈpɔːtə^r] *n* repórter *mf*.

repose [rɪˈpəʊz] *n* (*U*) *literary* repouso *m*.

repository [rɪˈpɒzɪtrɪ] (*pl* -ies) *n* depósito *m*, armazém *m*.

repossess [ˌriːpəˈzes] *vt* retomar a posse de.

repossession [ˌriːpəˈzeʃn] *n* (*U*) reintegração *f* de posse.

repossession order *n* ordem *f* de despejo.

reprehensible [ˌreprɪˈhensəbl] *adj* fml repreensível.

represent [ˌreprɪˈzent] *vt* -**1.** [gen] representar - **2.** [describe]: to ~ **sb/sth gas** descrever *or* representar alguém/algo como - **3.** phr: **to be well** *or* **strongly** ~ **ed** estar bem representado(da).

representation [ˌreprɪzenˈteɪʃn] *n* (*U*) representação *f*.
◆ **representations** *npl* fml: **to make ~s to sb** apresentar reclamações a alguém.

representative [ˌreprɪˈzentətɪv] <> *adj* representativo(va); ~ **(of sb/sthg)** representativo(va) (de alguém/algo). <> *n* -**1.** [of company, organization, group] representante *mf* - **2.** COMM: **(sales)** ~ representante *mf* (de vendas) - **3.** US POL deputado *m*, -da *f*.

repress [rɪˈpres] *vt* reprimir.

repressed [rɪˈprest] *adj* reprimido(da).

repression [rɪˈpreʃn] *n* (*U*) repressão *f*.

repressive [rɪˈpresɪv] *adj* repressivo(va).

reprieve [rɪˈpriːv] <> *n* -**1.** [of death sentence] indulto *m* - **2.** [respite] trégua *f*. <> *vt* indultar.

reprimand [ˈreprɪmɑːnd] <> *n* reprimenda *f*, repreensão *f*. <> *vt* repreender.

reprint [n'ri:prɪnt, vb ˌri:'prɪntl] <> n reimpressão f. <> vt reimprimir.

reprisal [rɪ'praɪzl] n retaliação f, represália f.

reproach [rɪ'prəʊtʃ] <> n **-1.** (U) [disapproval] censura f, repreensão f **-2.** [words of blame] acusação f. <> vt: **to ~ sb (for OR with sthg)** censurar OR repreender alguém (por algo).

reproachful [rɪ'prəʊtʃfʊl] adj de reprovação.

reprobate ['reprəbeɪt] n hum réprobo m, -ba f.

reproduce [ˌri:prə'dju:sl] <> vt reproduzir. <> vi reproduzir-se.

reproduction [ˌri:prə'dʌkʃn] n reprodução f.

reproductive [ˌri:prə'dʌktɪv] adj BIOL reprodutor (ra).

reprogram [ˌri:'prəʊɡræm] (pt & pp **-ed** OR **-med**, cont**-ing** OR **-ming**) vt reprogramar.

reproof [rɪ'pru:f] n **-1.** [words of blame] censura f **-2.** (U) [disapproval] reprovação f.

reprove [rɪ'pru:f] vt: **to ~ sb (for sthg)** reprovar alguém (por algo).

reproving [rɪ'pru:vɪŋ] adj reprovador(ra), de reprovação.

reptile ['reptaɪl] n réptil m.

Repub. (abbr of **Republican**) n republicano m, -na f.

republic [rɪ'pʌblɪk] n república f.

republican [rɪ'pʌblɪkən] <> adj republicano(na). <> n republicano m, -na f.
 ➤ Republican <> adj **-1.** [in USA] republicano (na); **the Republican Party** o Partido Republicano **-2.** [in Northern Ireland] independentista. <> n **-1.** [in USA] republicano m, -na f **-2.** [in Northern Ireland] independentista mf.

repudiate [rɪ'pju:dɪeɪt] vt fml repudiar.

repudiation [rɪˌpju:dɪ'eɪʃn] n (U) fml repúdio m.

repugnant [rɪ'pʌɡnənt] adj fml repugnante.

repulse [rɪ'pʌls] vt repelir.

repulsion [rɪ'pʌlʃn] n (U) **-1.** [disgust] repulsa f **-2.** PHYSICS repulsão f.

repulsive [rɪ'pʌlsɪv] adj repulsivo(va).

reputable ['repjʊtəbl] adj de boa reputação.

reputation [ˌrepjʊ'teɪʃn] n reputação f; **to have a ~ for sthg/for being sthg** ter fama de algo/de ser algo.

repute [rɪ'pju:t] n (U) fml **-1.** [reputation]: **of good/ ill ~** de boa/má reputação **-2.** [distinction]: **of ~** de renome.

reputed [rɪ'pju:tɪd] adj de renome; **to be ~ to be/ do sthg** ter fama de ser/fazer algo.

reputedly [rɪ'pju:tɪdlɪ] adv supostamente, segundo dizem.

reqd (abbr of **required**) requerido.

request [rɪ'kwest] <> n: **~ (for sthg)** solicitação f (de algo); **on ~** através de solicitação; **at sb's ~** por solicitação de alguém. <> vt solicitar, pedir; **to ~ sb to do sthg** solicitar a alguém que faça algo.

request stop n UK parada f de ônibus não-obrigatória.

requiem (mass) ['rekwɪəm-] n réquiem m.

require [rɪ'kwaɪəʳ] vt **-1.** [need] requerer, necessitar de **-2.** [demand] exigir; **to ~ sb to do sthg** exigir que alguém faça algo; **employees are ~d to wear**

a **uniform** exige-se que os funcionários usem uniformes.

required [rɪ'kwaɪəd] adj necessário(ria); **formal dress is ~d** exigem-se trajes formais.

requirement [rɪ'kwaɪəmənt] n **-1.** [need] necessidade f **-2.** [condition] requisito m, condição f.

requisite ['rekwɪzɪt] adj fml necessário(ria), requerido(da).

requisition [ˌrekwɪ'zɪʃn] vt requisitar.

reran [ˌri:'ræn] pt ⊳ rerun.

reread [ˌri:'ri:d] (pt & pp reread [ˌri:'redl] vt reler.

rerecord [ˌri:rɪ'kɔ:d] vt regravar.

reroute [ˌri:'ru:t] vt redirecionar.

rerun [n 'ri:ˌrʌn, vb ri:'rʌn] (pt reran, pp rerun, cont-ning) <> n **-1.** [film, programme] reprise f **-2.** [similar situation] repetição f. <> vt **-1.** [race, competition] voltar a participar de **-2.** [film, programme] reprisar **-3.** [tape] pôr novamente.

resale price maintenance ['ri:seɪl-] n (U) UK FIN manutenção f do preço de revenda.

resat [ˌri:'sæt] pt & pp ⊳ resit.

reschedule [UK ˌri:'ʃedjʊl, US ˌri:'skedʒʊl] vt FIN renegociar.

rescind [rɪ'sɪnd] vt [JUR - contract] rescindir; [- law] revogar.

rescue ['reskju:] <> n **-1.** [help] auxílio f; **to go/ come to sb's ~** ir/vir em auxílio de alguém **-2.** [successful attempt] resgate m, salvamento m. <> vt resgatar, salvar; **to ~ sb from sb/sthg** resgatar OR salvar alguém de alguém/algo; **to ~ sthg from sb/sthg** salvar algo de alguém/algo.

rescue operation n operação f de resgate.

rescuer ['reskjʊəʳ] n resgatador m, -ra f.

reseal [ˌri:'si:l] vt fechar novamente.

resealable [ˌri:'si:ləbl] adj que se pode fechar novamente.

research [rɪ'sɜ:tʃ] <> n (U): **~ (on OR into sthg)** pesquisa f (sobre algo); **~ and development** pesquisa e desenvolvimento. <> vt pesquisar, fazer uma pesquisa sobre. <> vi: **to ~ (into sthg)** fazer uma pesquisa (sobre algo).

researcher [rɪ'sɜ:tʃəʳ] n pesquisador m, -ra f.

research work n (U) trabalho m de pesquisa.

resell [ˌri:'sell (pt & pp resold) vt revender.

resemblance [rɪ'zembləns] n semelhança f; **~ to sb/sthg** semelhança com alguém/algo; **~ between** semelhança entre.

resemble [rɪ'zembl] vt assemelhar-se a, parecer-se com.

resent [rɪ'zent] vt ofender-se com, ressentir-se de.

resentful [rɪ'zentfʊl] adj ressentido(da).

resentfully [rɪ'zentfʊlɪ] adv com ressentimento.

resentment [rɪ'zentmənt] n (U) ressentimento m.

reservation [ˌrezə'veɪʃn] n **-1.** [gen] reserva f; **without ~** sem reserva **-2.** US [for Native Americans] reserva f (indígena).
 ➤ reservations npl [doubts] reservas fpl, dúvidas fpl.

reserve [rɪ'zɜ:v] <> n reserva f; **in ~** de reserva. <> vt **-1.** [keep for particular purpose]: **to ~ sthg for sb/sthg** reservar algo para alguém/algo **-2.** [retain]: **to ~ the right to do sthg** reservar-se o direito de fazer algo.

reserve bank n US banco m de reserva federal.
reserve currency n moeda f de reserva.
reserved [rɪ'zɜ:vd] adj reservado(da).
reserve price n UK preço m mínimo (de venda).
reserve team n UK time m reserva.
reservist [rɪ'zɜ:vɪst] n reservista mf.
reservoir ['rezəvwɑ:ʳ] n -1. [lake] reservatório m natural -2. [large supply] reservatório m.
reset [ˌri:'set] (pt & pp reset, cont -ting) <> vt -1. [clock, meter, controls] reajustar -2. [bone] recolocar no lugar -3. COMPUT reinicializar. <> vi COMPUT reinicializar.
resettle [ˌri:'setl] <> vt -1. [land] ocupar -2. [people] reassentar. <> vi [people] reassentar-se.
resettlement [ˌri:'setlmənt] n (U) -1. [of land] ocupação f -2. [of people] reassentamento m.
reshape [ˌri:'ʃeɪp] vt reformar, remodelar.
reshuffle [ˌri:'ʃʌfl] <> n POL reorganização f, reforma f; **cabinet** ~ reforma f do gabinete. <> vt ADMIN & POL reformar.
reside [rɪ'zaɪd] vi fml residir; **happiness does not** ~ **in wealth** a felicidade não reside na riqueza.
residence ['rezɪdəns] n -1. [house] residência f -2. (U) [fact of residing]: **to apply for** ~ solicitar visto de residência; **to take up** ~ fml estabelecer residência (em), instalar-se -3. (U) [residing at a particular time]: **to be in** ~ fml estar presente -4. (U) UNIV: **writer in** ~ escritor(ra) residente (que atua temporariamente numa universidade).
residence permit n visto m de residência.
resident ['rezɪdənt] <> adj residente; **she's been** ~ **in france for two years** faz dois anos que ela está morando na França. <> n residente mf.
residential [ˌrezɪ'denʃl] adj em regime de internato.
residential area n zona f residencial.
residents' association n associação f de moradores.
residual [rɪ'zɪdjʊəl] adj residual.
residue ['rezɪdju:] n CHEM resíduo m.
resign [rɪ'zaɪn] <> vt -1. [give up - job] demitir-se de; [- post] renunciar a -2. [accept calmly]: **to** ~ **o.s. to sthg** resignar-se a algo. <> vi pedir demissão, demitir-se; **to** ~ **(from sthg)** pedir demissão OR demitir-se (de algo).
resignation [ˌrezɪg'neɪʃn] n -1. [from job] demissão f -2. [from post] renúncia f -3. (U) [calm acceptance] resignação f.
resigned [rɪ'zaɪnd] adj: ~ **(to sthg)** resignado(da) (a algo).
resilience [rɪ'zɪlɪəns] n (U) capacidade f de recuperação.
resilient [rɪ'zɪlɪənt] adj -1. [rubber, metal] elástico(ca) -2. [person] que se recupera rapidamente, resistente.
resin ['rezɪn] n (U) resina f.
resist [rɪ'zɪst] vt -1. [gen] resistir a -2. [oppose] opor-se a.
resistance [rɪ'zɪstəns] n (U) -1. [to enemy, attack, infection] resistência f; ~ **to sthg** resistência a algo -2. [to change, proposal, attempt] oposição f.
resistant [rɪ'zɪstənt] adj -1. MED [immune]: ~ **(to**

sthg) resistente (a algo) -2. [opposed]: ~ **to sthg** que se opõe a algo.
resistor [rɪ'zɪstəʳ] n ELEC resistor m.
resit [n 'ri:sɪt, vb ˌri:'sɪt] (pt & pp resat, cont -ting) UK <> n exame m de recuperação. <> vt fazer de novo (um exame).
resold [ˌri:'səʊld] pt & pp ▷ resell.
resolute ['rezəlu:t] adj resoluto(ta), determinado (da).
resolutely ['rezəlu:tlɪ] adv resolutamente, com determinação.
resolution [ˌrezə'lu:ʃn] n -1. [gen] resolução f -2. [vow, promise] promessa f.
resolve [rɪ'zɒlv] <> n (U) resolução f. <> vt [solve] resolver; [vow, promise]: **to** ~ **that** prometer que; **to** ~ **to do sthg** resolver fazer algo.
resonance ['rezənəns] n (U) ressonância f.
resonant ['rezənənt] adj ressonante.
resonate ['rezəneɪt] vi ressoar.
resort [rɪ'zɔ:t] n -1. [for holidays] estância f de férias -2. [solution]: **as a last** ~ como último recurso; **in the last** ~ em última instância.
◆ **resort to** vt fus apelar para.
resound [rɪ'zaʊnd] vi -1. [noise] ressoar, retumbar -2. [place]: **the room** ~ed **with laughter** as risadas ressoavam em toda a sala.
resounding [rɪ'zaʊndɪŋ] adj -1. [gen] retumbante -2. [extremely loud] estrondoso(sa) -3. [unequivocal] clamoroso(sa).
resource [rɪ'sɔ:s] n recurso m.
resourceful [rɪ'sɔ:sfʊl] adj versátil, habilidoso(sa).
resourcefulness [rɪ'sɔ:sfʊlnɪs] n (U) versatilidade f.
respect [rɪ'spekt] <> n (U) respeito m; ~ **(for sb/ sthg)** respeito m OR admiração f (por alguém/algo); **with** ~, ... com todo o respeito, ...; **in this** ~ a este respeito; **in that** ~ quanto a isso. <> vt respeitar; **to** ~ **sb for sthg** respeitar alguém por algo.
◆ **respects** npl saudações fpl, cumprimentos mpl; **to pay one's last** ~ **s to sb** prestar uma última homenagem a alguém.
◆ **with respect to** prep com respeito a.
respectability [rɪˌspektə'bɪlətɪ] n (U) respeitabilidade f.
respectable [rɪ'spektəbl] adj respeitável.
respectably [rɪ'spektəblɪ] adv de forma respeitável.
respected adj respeitado(da).
respectful [rɪ'spektfʊl] adj respeitoso(sa).
respectfully [rɪ'spektfʊlɪ] adv respeitosamente.
respective [rɪ'spektɪv] adj respectivo(va).
respectively [rɪ'spektɪvlɪ] adv respectivamente.
respiration [ˌrespə'reɪʃn] n (U) respiração f.
respirator ['respəreɪtəʳ] n -1. [gas mask] máscara f antigás -2. [machine] respirador m.
respiratory [UK rɪ'spɪrətrɪ, US 'respərətɔ:rɪ] adj respiratório(ria).
respire [rɪ'spaɪəʳ] vi respirar.
respite ['respaɪt] n -1. [pause] descanso m -2. [delay] adiamento m, novo prazo m.
resplendent [rɪ'splendənt] adj literary resplandescente.

respond [rɪ'spɒnd] ◇ vt responder. ◇ vi: to ~ **(to sthg)** responder (a algo); **to ~ by doing sthg** responder fazendo algo.

response [rɪ'spɒns] n resposta f; **in ~** em resposta.

responsibility [rɪ,spɒnsə'bɪlətɪ] (pl -**ies**) n: ~ **(for sthg)** responsabilidade f (por algo); ~ **(to sb)** responsabilidade f (diante de alguém).

responsible [rɪ'spɒnsəbl] adj -**1.** [gen]: ~ **(for sthg)** responsável (por algo) -**2.** [answerable]: ~ **to sb** que presta contas a alguém -**3.** [requiring sense] de responsabilidade.

responsibly [rɪ'spɒnsəblɪ] adv de forma responsável.

responsive [rɪ'spɒnsɪv] adj que responde muito bem; ~ **(to sthg)** sensível OR atencioso(sa) (a algo).

respray [n 'riː:spreɪ, vb ,riː:'spreɪ] ◇ n nova pintura f. ◇ vt repintar.

rest [rest] ◇ n -**1.** [remainder]: **the ~** o resto; **the ~ of** o resto de -**2.** (U) [relaxation] descanso m -**3.** [break] pausa f, descanso m -**4.** [support] apoio m -**5.** phr: **to lay** OR **put sthg to ~** sepultar algo; **to come to ~** deter-se. ◇ vt -**1.** [relax] descansar -**2.** [support, lean]: **to ~ sthg on/against sthg** apoiar OR descansar algo em algo -**3.** phr: ~ **assured (that)** fique descansado(da) que. ◇ vi -**1.** [relax, be still] descansar -**2.** [depend]: **to ~ (up)on sb/sthg** depender de alguém/algo -**3.** [duty, responsibility]: **to ~ with sb** pesar sobre alguém -**4.** [be supported]: **to ~ on/against sthg** apoiar-se em/contra algo.

rest area n US & Austr área f de descanso (numa estrada).

restart [n ,riː:'stɑːt, vb ,riː:'stɑːt] ◇ n COMPUT reinício m. ◇ vt -**1.** [vehicle, engine] ligar novamente -**2.** [work] recomeçar -**3.** COMPUT reiniciar. ◇ vi -**1.** [play, film] recomeçar -**2.** [vehicle] dar partida, pegar -**3.** [engine] ligar novamente.

restate [,riː:'steɪt] vt reformular, expor novamente.

restaurant ['restərɒnt] n restaurante m.

restaurant car n UK vagão-restaurante m.

rest cure n cura f pelo descanso forçado.

rested ['restɪd] adj descansado(da).

restful ['restfʊl] adj tranqüilo(la), sossegado(da).

rest home n -**1.** [for the elderly] lar m de idosos -**2.** [for the sick] casa f de repouso.

resting place ['restɪŋ-] n última morada f.

restitution [,restɪ'tjuːʃn] n (U) fml restituição f.

restive ['restɪv] adj inquieto(ta).

restless ['restlɪs] adj -**1.** [bored, dissatisfied] impaciente -**2.** [fidgety] inquieto(ta), agitado(da) -**3.** [sleepless]: **a ~ night** uma noite em claro.

restlessly ['restlɪslɪ] adv -**1.** [impatiently] impacientemente -**2.** [sleeplessly] sem conseguir dormir.

restock [,riː:'stɒk] ◇ vt reabastecer. ◇ vi reabastecer-se.

restoration [,restə'reɪʃn] n (U) restauração f.

restorative [rɪ'stɒrətɪv] adj fml revigorante.

restore [rɪ'stɔː] vt -**1.** [reestablish, bring back] restabelecer; **the king was ~ed to power** o rei foi reconduzido ao poder; **I feel completely ~ed to health** sinto-me totalmente recuperado(da); **to ~ sthg to sb/sthg** devolver algo a alguém/algo

-**2.** [renovate] restaurar -**3.** [give back] restituir.

restorer [rɪ'stɔːrə] n -**1.** [person] restaurador m, -ra f -**2.** (U) [substance] tônico m.

restrain [rɪ'streɪn] vt -**1.** [gen] reprimir; **to ~ o.s. from doing sthg** conter-se para não fazer algo -**2.** [overpower, bring under control] controlar.

restrained [rɪ'streɪnd] adj comedido(da).

restraint [rɪ'streɪnt] n -**1.** [rule, check] restrição f, limitação f -**2.** (U) [control] controle m.

restrict [rɪ'strɪkt] vt restringir, limitar; **to ~ sb to sthg** restringir alguém a algo; **to ~ sthg to sb/ sthg** restringir algo a alguém/algo; **to ~ o.s. to sthg** limitar-se a algo.

restricted [rɪ'strɪktɪd] adj -**1.** [not public] restrito(ta) -**2.** [limited] limitado(da).

restriction [rɪ'strɪkʃn] n -**1.** [limitation, regulation] restrição f; **to place ~s on sthg** impor restrições a algo -**2.** (U) [impediment, hindrance] limitação f.

restrictive [rɪ'strɪktɪv] adj restritivo(va).

restrictive practices npl práticas fpl restritivas.

rest room n US banheiro m.

restructure [,riː:'strʌktʃə] vt reestruturar.

result [rɪ'zʌlt] ◇ n resultado m; **as a ~** como resultado, por conseguinte; **as a ~ of sthg** como resultado de algo. ◇ vi: **to ~ in sthg** ter algo como resultado; **to ~ from sthg** ser resultado de algo.

resultant [rɪ'zʌltənt] adj fml resultante.

resume [rɪ'zjuːm] ◇ vt -**1.** [activity] recomeçar -**2.** fml [place, position] retomar. ◇ vi recomeçar, continuar.

résumé ['rezjuːmeɪ] n -**1.** [summary] resumo m -**2.** US [of career, qualifications] currículo m.

resumption [rɪ'zʌmpʃn] n (U) retomada f.

resurface [,riː:'sɜːfɪs] ◇ vt repavimentar. ◇ vi vir à tona.

resurgence [rɪ'sɜːdʒəns] n (U) ressurgimento m.

resurrect [,rezə'rekt] vt ressuscitar.

resurrection [,rezə'rekʃn] n (U) ressurreição f.

  ➤ **Resurrection** n RELIG: **the Resurrection** a Ressurreição.

resuscitate [rɪ'sʌsɪteɪt] vt -**1.** [bring back to life] ressuscitar -**2.** [prevent from dying] reanimar.

resuscitation [rɪ,sʌsɪ'teɪʃn] n (U) ressuscitação f, reanimação f.

retail ['riː:teɪl] ◇ n (U) varejo m. ◇ adv no varejo. ◇ vi: **to ~ at** ser vendido(da) no varejo.

retailer ['riː:teɪlə] n varejista mf.

retail outlet n ponto m de venda.

retail price n preço m no varejo.

retail price index n UK índice m de preço ao consumidor.

retain [rɪ'teɪn] vt reter.

retainer [rɪ'teɪnə] n -**1.** [fee] adiantamento m -**2.** [servant] criado m, -da f (com muitos anos de serviço numa casa).

retaining wall [rɪ'teɪnɪŋ-] n muro m de arrimo.

retaliate [rɪ'tælɪeɪt] vi retaliar.

retaliation [rɪ,tælɪ'eɪʃn] n retaliação f.

retarded [rɪ'tɑːdɪd] adj mentalmente retardado(da).

retch [retʃ] vi fazer força para vomitar.

retd (*abbr of* **retired**) aposentado(da).
retention [rɪ'tenʃn] *n* **-1.** [of pride, power, independence] manutenção *f* **- 2.** [of heat, water] retenção *f*.
retentive [rɪ'tentɪv] *adj* retentivo(va).
rethink [*n* 'ri:θɪŋk, *vb* ˌri:'θɪŋk] (*pt & pp* **-thought** [-'θɔ:tl] <> *n*: **to have a ~ about sthg** ter que repensar algo; **to have a ~** dar uma repensada. <> *vt* repensar, reconsiderar. <> *vi* repensar, reconsiderar.
reticence ['retɪsəns] *n* (*U*) reticência *f*.
reticent ['retɪsənt] *adj* reticente.
retina ['retɪnə] (*pl* **-nas** OR **-nae** [-ni:]) *n* retina *f*.
retinue ['retɪnju:] *n* séquito *m*.
retire [rɪ'taɪəᵊ] *vi* **-1.** [from work] aposentar-se **- 2.** *fml* [to another place] retirar-se **- 3.** *fml* [to bed] recolher-se.
retired [rɪ'taɪəd] *adj* aposentado(da).
retirement [rɪ'taɪəmənt] *n* aposentadoria *f*.
retirement age *n* idade *f* de aposentadoria OR de se aposentar.
retirement pension *n* aposentadoria *f*.
retiring [rɪ'taɪərɪŋ] *adj* **-1.** [shy] retraído(da), tímido(da) **- 2.** [from work] *que está a ponto de se aposentar.*
retort [rɪ'tɔ:tl] <> *n* réplica *f*. <> *vt*: **to ~ (that)** retrucar (que).
retouch [ˌri:'tʌtʃl] *vt* retocar.
retrace [rɪ'treɪs] *vt*: **to ~ one's steps** refazer o mesmo caminho.
retract [rɪ'trækt] <> *vt* **-1.** [take back] retratar **- 2.** [draw in] recolher. <> *vi* **-1.** [recant] retratar-se **- 2.** [be drawn in] recolher-se.
retractable [rɪ'træktəbl] *adj* retrátil.
retraction [rɪ'trækʃn] *n* (*U*) retratação *f*.
retrain [ˌri:'treɪn] <> *vt* reabilitar. <> *vi* reabilitar-se, reciclar-se.
retraining [ˌri:'treɪnɪŋ] *n* (*U*) reciclagem *f*.
retread ['ri:tred] *n* pneu *m* recauchutado.
retreat [rɪ'tri:t] <> *n* **-1.** MIL [withdrawal]: **~ (from)** retirada *f* (de) **- 2.** *fig* [from principle, policy, lifestyle]: **to beat a (hasty) ~** bater em retirada **- 3.** [refuge] refúgio *m*. <> *vi*: **to ~ (to/from)** retirar-se (para/de).
retrenchment [ri:'trentʃmənt] *n fml* redução *f* OR corte *m* de gastos.
retrial [ˌri:'traɪəl] *n* novo julgamento *m*.
retribution [ˌretrɪ'bju:ʃn] *n* (*U*) castigo *m* merecido.
retrieval [rɪ'tri:vl] *n* (*U*) COMPUT recuperação *f*.
retrieve [rɪ'tri:v] *vt* **-1.** [get back] reaver **- 2.** COMPUT recuperar **- 3.** [rescue, rectify] reparar, remediar.
retriever [rɪ'tri:vəᵊ] *n* [dog] perdigueiro *m*; [of specific breed] labrador *m*.
retroactive [ˌretrəʊ'æktɪv] *adj fml* retroativo(va).
retrograde ['retrəgreɪd] *adj fml* retrógrado(da); **a ~ step** um passo para trás.
retrogressive [ˌretrə'gresɪv] *adj fml & pej* retrógrado(da).
retrospect ['retrəspekt] *n* (*U*): **in ~** em retrospecto.
retrospective [ˌretrə'spektɪv] <> *adj* **-1.** [mood, look] retrospectivo(va) **- 2.** [law, pay rise] retroativo (va). <> *n* retrospectiva *f*.

retrospectively [ˌretrə'spektɪvlɪ] *adv* **-1.** [describe, feel] retrospectivamente **- 2.** [come into force, pay] de forma retroativa.
return [rɪ'tɜ:n] <> *n* **-1.** (*U*) [arrival back] volta *f*, regresso *m*; **~ (to)** regresso *m* (para); **~ to sthg** *fig* volta a algo **- 2.** [giving back] devolução *f* **- 3.** TENNIS rebatida *f* **- 4.** UK [ticket] passagem *f* de ida e volta **- 5.** [profit] retorno *m* **- 6.** COMPUT [on keyboard] tecla *f* Return. <> *comp* [journey] de volta. <> *vt* **-1.** [gen] devolver **- 2.** [reciprocate, give in exchange] retribuir **- 3.** JUR dar **- 4.** POL eleger. <> *vi*: **to ~ (from/to)** voltar (de/a).
➡ **returns** *npl* **-1.** COMM retorno *m*, rendimentos *mpl* **- 2.** [on birthday]: **many happy ~s (of the day)!** que a data se repita por muitos e muitos anos!
➡ **in return** *adv* em troca.
➡ **in return for** *prep* em troca de.
returnable [rɪ'tɜ:nəbl] *adj* retornável.
returning officer [rɪ'tɜ:nɪŋ-] *n* UK *oficial existente em cada distrito eleitoral da Grã-Bretanha que organiza a eleição para o Parlamento e anuncia o resultado oficial.*
return key *n* COMPUT tecla *f* Return.
return match *n* partida *f* de volta.
return ticket *n* UK passagem *f* de ida e volta.
reunification [ˌri:ju:nɪfɪ'keɪʃn] *n* (*U*) reunificação *f*.
reunion [ˌri:'ju:njən] *n* reunião *f*.
Reunion [ˌri:'ju:njən] *n*: **~ (Island)** Ilha Réunion; **in ~** na Ilha Réunion.
reunite [ˌri:ju:'naɪt] *vt* reunir; **to be ~d with sb/sthg** estar reunido com alguém/algo.
reupholster [ˌri:ʌp'həʊlstəᵊ] *vt* estofar novamente.
reusable [ri:'ju:zəbl] *adj* reutilizável, reciclável.
reuse [*n* ˌri:'ju:s, *vb* ˌri:'ju:z] <> *n* (*U*) reutilização *f*. <> *vt* reutilizar.
rev [rev] (*pt & pp* **-ved**, *cont* **-ving**) *inf* <> *n* (*abbr of* **revolution**) rotação *f*. <> *vt*: **to ~ sthg (up)** acelerar algo. <> *vi*: **to ~ (up)** acelerar o motor.
Rev. (*abbr of* **Reverend**) Revdo.
revalue [ˌri:'vælju:] *vt* **-1.** [reassess] reavaliar **- 2.** FIN [increase value of] valorizar.
revamp [ˌri:'væmp] *vt inf* **-1.** [reorganize] reformar **- 2.** [redecorate] redecorar.
rev counter *n* tacómetro *m*.
reveal [rɪ'vi:l] *vt* revelar.
revealing [rɪ'vi:lɪŋ] *adj* **-1.** [clothes]: **a ~ dress** um vestido que mostra tudo **- 2.** [comment] revelador(ra), esclarecedor(ra).
reveille [UK rɪ'vælɪ, US 'revəlɪ] *n* toque *m* de alvorada.
revel ['revl] (*UK pt & pp* **-led**, *cont* **-ling**, *US pt & pp* **-ed**, *cont* **-ing**) *vi*: **to ~ in sthg** desfrutar de algo, deleitar-se com algo.
revelation [ˌrevə'leɪʃn] *n* **-1.** [surprising fact] revelação *f* **- 2.** [surprising experience] surpresa *f*.
reveller UK, **reveler** US ['revələᵊ] *n* farrista *mf*.
revelry ['revəlrɪ] *n* (*U*) farra *f*.
revenge [rɪ'vendʒ] <> *n* (*U*) vingança *f*; **to take ~ (on sb)** vingar-se (de alguém). <> *comp* por vingança. <> *vt* vingar; **to ~ o.s. on sb/sthg** vingar-se de alguém/algo.

revenue ['revənju:] n **-1.** [income] receita f **-2.** [from investment] rendimento f **-3.** *UK FIN*: **the Inland Revenue** a Receita Federal.

reverberate [rɪ'vɜːbəreɪt] vi **-1.** [re-echo] ressoar, retumbar **-2.** [have repercussions] repercutir.

reverberations [rɪˌvɜːbə'reɪʃnz] npl **-1.** [echoes] reverberação f **-2.** [repercussions] repercussões fpl.

revere [rɪ'vɪər] vt *fml* reverenciar, venerar.

reverence ['revərəns] n (U) *fml* reverência f.

Reverend ['revərənd] n reverendo m.

Reverend Mother n madre f superiora.

reverent ['revərənt] adj reverente.

reverential [ˌrevə'renʃl] adj *fml* reverencial.

reverie ['revərɪ] n *fml* devaneio m.

reversal [rɪ'vɜːsl] n **-1.** [of trend, policy, decision] reviravolta f **-2.** [of roles, order, position] inversão f **-3.** [piece of ill luck] contratempo m.

reverse [rɪ'vɜːs] ◇ adj reverso(sa), inverso(sa). ◇ n **-1.** *AUT*: ~ **(gear)** marcha f a ré; **to be in** ~ estar com a marcha a ré engatada; **to go into** ~ dar ré **-2.** [opposite]: **the** ~ o contrário **-3.** [back, other side - of paper] verso m; [- of coin] outro lado m. ◇ vt **-1.** *AUT* dar marcha a ré em **-2.** [trend, policy, decision] reverter **-3.** [roles, order, position] inverter **-4.** [turn over] virar **-5.** *UK TELEC*: **to** ~ **the charges** fazer uma ligação a cobrar. ◇ vi *AUT* dar marcha a ré.

reverse-charge call n *UK* chamada f a cobrar.

reversible [rɪ'vɜːsəbl] adj reversível.

reversing light [rɪ'vɜːsɪŋ-] n *UK* luz f de ré.

reversion [rɪ'vɜːʃn] n (U) reversão f, volta f; ~ **to sthg** reversão *OR* volta a algo.

revert [rɪ'vɜːt] vi: **to** ~ **to sthg** voltar a algo.

review [rɪ'vju:] ◇ n **-1.** [examination] revisão f, reavaliação f; **to come up for** ~ ser revisado(da), ser reavaliado(da); **the situation is under** ~ a situação está sendo avaliada **-2.** [critique] crítica f, resenha f. ◇ vt **-1.** [reassess] reavaliar **-2.** [write an article on] fazer resenha *OR* crítica de **-3.** [troops] passar em revista **-4.** *US* [study] revisar.

reviewer [rɪ'vju:ər] n crítico m, -ca f.

revile [rɪ'vaɪl] vt *literary* insultar, injuriar.

revise [rɪ'vaɪz] ◇ vt **-1.** [reconsider] revisar **-2.** [rewrite] corrigir, alterar **-3.** *UK* [study] revisar. ◇ vi *UK*: **to** ~ **(for sthg)** fazer revisão (para algo).

revised [rɪ'vaɪzd] adj revisado(da).

revision [rɪ'vɪʒn] n **-1.** [alteration] alteração f, correção f **-2.** (U) [study] revisão f.

revisionist [rɪ'vɪʒnɪst] ◇ adj revisionista. ◇ n revisionista mf.

revisit [ˌri:'vɪzɪt] vt revisitar.

revitalize, -ise [ˌri:'vaɪtəlaɪz] vt revitalizar.

revival [rɪ'vaɪvl] n **-1.** *COMM* reativação f **-2.** [of interest, cultural activity] renovação f **-3.** [of play] revival m.

revive [rɪ'vaɪv] ◇ vt **-1.** [resuscitate] ressuscitar **-2.** [revitalize - plant, economy] revitalizar; [- interest, hopes] despertar **-3.** [bring back into use, being - tradition] restabelecer; [- musical, play] reviver; [- memories] trazer à baila. ◇ vi **-1.** [regain consciousness] voltar a si, recobrar os sentidos **-2.** [be revitalized - plant, economy] revitalizar-se; [- interest, hopes] renovar-se.

revoke [rɪ'vəʊk] vt *fml* revogar.

revolt [rɪ'vəʊlt] ◇ n revolta f, rebelião f. ◇ vt revoltar. ◇ vi: **to** ~ **(against sb/sthg)** revoltar-se *OR* rebeliar-se (contra alguém/algo).

revolting [rɪ'vəʊltɪŋ] adj revoltante, repugnante.

revolution [ˌrevə'lu:ʃn] n revolução f; ~ **in sthg** revolução em algo.

revolutionary [ˌrevə'lu:ʃnərɪ] (pl **-ies**) ◇ adj revolucionário(ria). ◇ n *POL* revolucionário m, -ria f.

revolutionize, -ise [ˌrevə'lu:ʃənaɪz] vt revolucionar.

revolve [rɪ'vɒlv] vi girar, dar voltas; **to** ~ **(a)round sthg** girar em torno de algo; **to** ~ **(a)round sb** girar em torno de alguém.

revolver [rɪ'vɒlvər] n revólver m.

revolving [rɪ'vɒlvɪŋ] adj giratório(ria).

revolving door n porta f giratória.

revue [rɪ'vju:] n teatro m de revista.

revulsion [rɪ'vʌlʃn] n (U) repugnância f, asco m.

reward [rɪ'wɔːd] ◇ n **-1.** [recompense] recompensa f **-2.** [sum of money] recompensa f, gratificação f. ◇ vt recompensar; **to** ~ **sb for/with sthg** recompensar alguém por/com algo.

rewarding [rɪ'wɔːdɪŋ] adj gratificante.

rewind [ˌri:'waɪnd] (pt & pp rewound) vt rebobinar.

rewire [ˌri:'waɪər] vt trocar a fiação elétrica de.

reword [ˌri:'wɜːd] vt expressar com outras palavras.

rework [ˌri:'wɜːk] vt reelaborar.

rewound [ˌri:'waʊnd] pt & pp ▷ rewind.

rewrite [ˌri:'raɪt] (pt rewrote [ˌri:'rəʊt], pp rewritten [ˌri:'rɪtnl]) vt reescrever.

REX (abbr of **real-time executive routine**) n [comput] programa em tempo real.

Reykjavik ['rekjəvɪk] n Reykjavik.

RFC (abbr of **Rugby Football Club**) n clube de rugby britânico.

RGN (abbr of **registered general nurse**) n titular de diploma em enfermagem na Grã-Bretanha.

r.h. (abbr of **right hand**) mão f direita.

Rh (abbr of **rhesus**) Rh.

rhapsody ['ræpsədɪ] (pl **-ies**) n **-1.** *MUS* rapsódia f **-2.** [strong approval] entusiasmo m.

Rheims n Rheims.

Rhesus ['ri:səs] n: ~ **positive/negative** Rh positivo/negativo.

rhetoric ['retərɪk] n (U) retórica f.

rhetorical question [rɪ'tɒrɪkl-] n pergunta f retórica.

rheumatic [ru:'mætɪk] adj reumático(ca).

rheumatism ['ru:mətɪzml] n (U) reumatismo m.

rheumatoid arthritis ['ru:mətɔɪd-] n (U) artrite f reumatóide.

Rhine [raɪn] n: **the** ~ o Reno.

Rhineland ['raɪnlænd] n Renânia f.

rhinestone ['raɪnstəʊn] n diamante m falso.

rhino ['raɪnəʊ] (pl inv *OR* **-s**) n inf rino m.

rhinoceros [raɪ'nɒsərəs] (pl inv *OR* **-es**) n rinoceronte m.

Rhode Island [rəʊd-] n Rhode Island.

Rhodes [rəʊdz] n Rodes.

Rhodesia [rəʊ'di:ʃə] n Rodésia f.

Rhodesian [rəʊ'di:ʃn] <> *adj* rodesiano(na). <> *n* rodesiano *m*, -na *f*.

rhododendron [ˌrəʊdə'dendrən] *n* rododendro *m*.

Rhone *n*: the (River) ~ o Rio Ródano.

rhubarb ['ru:bɑ:b] *n (U)* ruibarbo *m*.

rhyme [raɪm] <> *n* -**1.** [word] rima *f*; in ~ em verso -**2.** [poem] poesia *f*, versos *mpl.* <> *vi* rimar; to ~ with sthg rimar com algo.

rhyming slang ['raɪmɪŋ-] *n (U)* UK tipo de gíria do leste londrino que consiste em contrapor duas palavras que dão significado a uma terceira, rimando a segunda com essa terceira.

rhythm ['rɪðm] *n* ritmo *m*.

rhythm and blues *n (U)* rhythm *m* and blues.

rhythmic(al) ['rɪðmɪk(l)] *adj* ritmado(da).

RI <> *n* (*abbr of* **religious instruction**) educação *f* religiosa. <> *abbr of* **Rhode Island**.

rib [rɪb] *n* -**1.** ANATcostela *f* -**2.** [of metal or wood] vareta *f*.

RIBA (*abbr of* **Royal Institute of British Architects**) *n* instituto real dos arquitetos britânicos.

ribald ['rɪbəld] *adj* grosseiro(ra).

ribbed [rɪbd] *adj* canelado(da).

ribbon ['rɪbən] *n* fita *f*.

rib cage *n* caixa *f* torácica.

rice [raɪs] *n (U)* arroz *m*.

rice field *n* arrozal *m*.

rice paper *n (U)* papel *m* de palha de arroz.

rice pudding *n* arroz-doce *m*, arroz-de-leite *m*.

rich [rɪtʃ] <> *adj* -**1.** [gen] rico(ca); to be ~ in sthg ser rico(ca) em algo -**2.** [indigestible] pesado(da) -**3.** [vibrant] vibrante -**4.** [sumptuous, expensive] suntuoso(sa). <> *npl*: the ~ os ricos.
> riches *npl* -**1.** [natural resources] riquezas *fpl* -**2.** [wealth] riqueza *f*.

richly ['rɪtʃlɪ] *adv* [gen] ricamente; ~ deserved bem merecido(da).

richness ['rɪtʃnɪs] *n (U)* -**1.** [gen] riqueza *f* -**2.** [of food] peso *m*.

Richter scale ['rɪktə'-] *n*: the ~ a escala Richter.

rickets ['rɪkɪts] *n (U)* raquitismo *m*.

rickety ['rɪkətɪ] *adj* instável, sem solidez.

rickshaw ['rɪkʃɔ:] *n* jinriquixá *m*.

ricochet ['rɪkəʃeɪ] (*pt & pp* -ed OR -ted, *cont* -ing OR -ting) <> *n* ricochete *m*. <> *vi* ricochetear; to ~ off sthg ricochetear em algo.

rid [rɪd] (*pt* rid OR -ded, *pp* rid, *cont* -ding) <> *adj*: to be ~ of sb/sthg estar livre de alguém/algo. <> *vt*: to ~ sb/sthg of sthg livrar alguém/algo de algo; to ~ o.s. of sthg livrar-se de algo; to get ~ of sb/sthg livrar-se de alguém/algo.

riddance ['rɪdəns] *n inf*: good ~! já vai tarde!, que bons ventos o levem!

ridden ['rɪdn] *pp* **>** ride.

riddle ['rɪdl] *n* -**1.** [verbal puzzle] adivinhação *f* -**2.** [mystery] enigma *m*.

riddled ['rɪdld] *adj* -**1.** [holes, errors] cheio (cheia) -**2.** [bullet holes] crivado(da) -**3.** [woodworm] infestado(da).

ride [raɪd] (*pt* rode, *pp* ridden) <> *n* -**1.** [gen] passeio *m*; to go for a OR horse/bike ~ dar um passeio a cavalo/de bicicleta; to go for a car ~ dar uma volta OR um passeio de carro -**2.** *phr*: to take sb for a ~ *inf* [trick] levar alguém no bico. <> *vt* -**1.** [horse] montar em -**2.** [bicycle, motorbike] andar de -**3.** [distance] percorrer -**4.** US [travel in] ir de. <> *vi* -**1.** [on horseback] montar -**2.** [on bicycle] andar de bicicleta -**3.** [on motorbike] andar de moto -**4.** [in car, bus]: to ~ in sthg andar de algo.
> ride up *vi* subir.

rider ['raɪdə'] *n* -**1.** [on horseback - male] jinete *m*; [- female] amazona *f* -**2.** [on bicycle] ciclista *mf* -**3.** [on motorbike] motoqueiro *m*, -ra *f*.

ridge [rɪdʒ] *n* -**1.** [on mountain] crista *f* -**2.** [on flat surface - in sand, of muscles] saliência *f*; [- in fabric] ruga *f*.

ridicule ['rɪdɪkju:l] <> *n (U)* zombaria *f.* <> *vt* ridicularizar.

ridiculous [rɪ'dɪkjʊləs] *adj* ridículo(la).

ridiculously [rɪ'dɪkjʊləslɪ] *adv* ridiculamente.

riding ['raɪdɪŋ] <> *n (U)* equitação *f.* <> *comp* de equitação.

riding crop *n* chicote *m*, rebenque *m*.

riding habit *n* traje *m* de montar.

riding school *n* escola *f* de equitação.

rife [raɪf] *adj* muito comum; to be ~ with sthg estar cheio(cheia) de algo.

riffraff ['rɪfræf] *n (U)* gentalha *f*, ralé *f*.

rifle ['raɪfl] <> *n* rifle *m.* <> *vt* roubar.
> rifle through *vt fus* vasculhar.

rifle range *n* estande *m* de tiro ao alvo.

rift [rɪft] *n* -**1.** GEOL fenda *f* -**2.** [quarrel] desavença *f*; ~ between/in desavença entre/em.

Rift Valley *n*: the ~ o Rift Valley.

rig [rɪg] (*pt & pp* -ged, *cont* -ging) <> *n* [structure - onshore] torre *f* de perfuração; [- offshore] plataforma *f* petrolífera. <> *vt* manipular.
> rig up *vt sep* armar, construir.

rigging ['rɪgɪŋ] *n* -**1.** [of ship] *(U)* cordame *m* -**2.** [of votes] fraude *f* em uma votação.

right [raɪt] <> *adj* -**1.** [gen] certo(ta), correto(ta); to be ~ about sthg estar certo(ta) sobre algo, ter razão sobre algo; to get sthg ~ acertar algo; to be ~ to do sthg estar certo(ta) ao fazer algo -**2.** [going well] bem -**3.** [socially desirable, appropriate] apropriado(da) -**4.** [not left] direito(ta) -**5.** UK inf [complete] perfeito(ta). <> *adv* -**1.** [correctly] corretamente, bem -**2.** [not left] para a direita -**3.** [emphatic use]: ~ here aqui mesmo; ~ down bem para baixo; ~ in the middle bem no meio -**4.** [immediately]: I'll be ~ back eu já volto; ~ after Christmas logo depois do Natal; ~ now [immediately] agora; [at this very moment] já; ~ away em seguida. <> *n* -**1.** *(U)* [moral correctness] certo *m*; to be in the ~ ter razão -**2.** [entitlement, claim] direito *m*; by ~s por direito; in one's own ~ por seus próprios méritos -**3.** [right-hand side] direita *f*; on the ~ à direita. <> *vt* -**1.** [correct] corrigir -**2.** [make upright] endireitar. <> *excl* certo!
> Right *n* POL: the Right a direita.

right angle *n* ângulo *m* reto; at ~s to sthg em ângulo reto com algo.

righteous ['raɪtʃəs] *adj* -**1.** [anger, indignation] justo(ta) -**2.** [person] honrado(da).

righteousness ['raɪtʃəsnɪs] *n (U)* honradez *f*, retidão *f*.

rightful ['raɪtfʊl] *adj* legítimo(ma).

rightfully [ˈraɪtfʊlɪ] *adv* legitimamente.

right-hand *adj* direito(ta); ~ **side** o lado direito.

right-hand drive *adj* com direção do lado direito.

right-handed [-ˈhændɪd] *adj* destro(tra).

right-hand man *n* braço *m* direito.

rightly [ˈraɪtlɪ] *adv* -**1.** [gen] corretamente -**2.** [justifiably] com razão.

right-minded [-ˈmaɪndɪd] *adj* honrado(da).

rightness *n (U)* -**1.** [soundness] correção *f* -**2.** [appropriateness] conveniência *f*.

righto [ˈraɪtəʊ] *excl inf* certo!

right of way *n* -**1.** *AUT* preferência *f* -**2.** [access] direito *m* de passagem.

rights issue *n* emissão *f* de bônus de subscrição.

right-thinking *adj* correto(ta), sensato(ta).

right wing *n*: **the** ~ a direita.
  ➠ **right-wing** *adj* de direita.

right-winger *n* direitista *mf*.

rigid [ˈrɪdʒɪd] *adj* -**1.** [gen] rígido(da) -**2.** [inflexible] inflexível.

rigidity [rɪˈdʒɪdətɪ] *n (U)* rigidez *f*.

rigidly [ˈrɪdʒɪdlɪ] *adv* -**1.** [fixedly] firmemente -**2.** [harshly, strictly] rigidamente.

rigmarole [ˈrɪgmərəʊl] *n inf pej* -**1.** [process] ritual *m* -**2.** [story] ladainha *f*.

rigor *n US* = **rigour**.

rigor mortis [-ˈmɔːtɪs] *n (U)* rigidez *f* cadavérica.

rigorous [ˈrɪgərəs] *adj* rigoroso(sa).

rigorously [ˈrɪgərəslɪ] *adv* rigorosamente.

rigour *UK*, **rigor** *US* [ˈrɪgəˈ] *n (U)* rigor *m*.
  ➠ **rigours** *npl* rigores *mpl*.

rig-out *n UK inf* traje *m*, beca *f*.

rile [raɪl] *vt* irritar.

rim [rɪm] *n* -**1.** [top edge of container] borda *f* -**2.** [outer edge of round object - of spectacles, glass] moldura *f*; [- of wheel] aro *m*.

rind [raɪnd] *n* casca *f*.

ring [rɪŋ] (*pt* **rang**, *pp vt senses 1 & 2 & vi* **rung**, *pt & pp vt senses 3 & 4 only* **ringed**) ⬦ *n* -**1.** [telephone call]: **to give sb a** ~ dar uma ligada para alguém -**2.** [sound of bell] toque *m* -**3.** [quality, tone] tom *m*; **it has a familiar** ~ soa familiar -**4.** [circular object - for curtains, napkin] argola *f*; **napkin** ~ argola *f* para guardanapo; [- hoop] aro *m* -**5.** [piece of jewellery] anel *m* -**6.** [of people, trees] círculo *m* -**7.** [for boxing] ringue *m* -**8.** [people working together] cartel *m* -**9.** *phr*: **to run** ~**s round sb** *fig* superar alguém facilmente. ⬦ *vt* -**1.** *UK* [phone] telefonar para, ligar para -**2.** [bell, doorbell] tocar -**3.** [draw a circle round] fazer um círculo ao redor de -**4.** [surround] cercar, rodear; **to be** ~**ed with sthg** estar cercado(da) de algo. ⬦ *vi* -**1.** *UK* [phone] telefonar, ligar -**2.** [bell, doorbell] tocar -**3.** [to attract attention]: **to** ~ **(for sb/sthg)** chamar (por alguém/algo) -**4.** [resound]: **to** ~ **with sthg** ressoar com algo -**5.** *phr*: **to** ~ **true** soar verdadeiro(ra).
  ➠ **ring back** *UK* ⬦ *vt sep* voltar a ligar para. ⬦ *vi* voltar a ligar.
  ➠ **ring off** *vi UK* desligar.
  ➠ **ring out** *vi* -**1.** [sound] soar claramente -**2.** *UK TELEC* ligar.

  ➠ **ring up** *vt sep UK* ligar.

ring binder *n* fichário *m* com aros de metal.

ringer [ˈrɪŋəˈ] *n*: **to be a dead** ~ **for sb** ser o retrato vivo de alguém.

ring finger *n* (dedo *m*) anular *m*.

ringing [ˈrɪŋɪŋ] ⬦ *adj* [clear, loud] alto e claro, alta e clara. ⬦ *n* -**1.** *(U)* [of bell] toque *m* -**2.** *(U)* [in ears] zumbido *m*.

ringing tone *n UK TELEC* tom *m* de discagem.

ringleader [ˈrɪŋliːdəˈ] *n* cabeça *m*.

ringlet [ˈrɪŋlɪt] *n* anel *m* de cabelo.

ringmaster [ˈrɪŋmɑːstəˈ] *n* diretor *m*, -ra *f* de circo.

ring road *n UK* anel *m* rodoviário.

ringside [ˈrɪŋsaɪd] ⬦ *n*: **the** ~ o ringue. ⬦ *comp* de primeira fila.

ring tone *n* [for mobile phone] toque *m* musical.

ringway [ˈrɪŋweɪ] *n UK* anel *m* rodoviário.

ringworm [ˈrɪŋwɜːm] *n (U)* tinha *f*.

rink [rɪŋk] *n* rinque *m*.

rinse [rɪns] ⬦ *n* enxágue *m*. ⬦ *vt* enxaguar; **to** ~ **one's mouth out** enxaguar a boca.

Rio (de Janeiro) [ˌriːəʊ(dədʒəˈnɪərəʊ)] *n* Rio de Janeiro.

Rio Grande [ˌriːəʊˈgrændɪ] *n*: **the** ~ o Rio Grande.

Rio Negro *n*: **the** ~ o Rio Negro.

riot [ˈraɪət] ⬦ *n* desordem *f*; **to run** ~ descontrolar-se. ⬦ *vi* amotinar-se.

rioter [ˈraɪətəˈ] *n* desordeiro *m*, -ra *f*.

rioting [ˈraɪətɪŋ] *n (U)* desordem *f*.

riotous [ˈraɪətəs] *adj* -**1.** [party] barulhento(ta) -**2.** [behaviour, mob] desordeiro(ra).

riot police *npl* tropa *f* de choque.

riot shield *n* escudo *m* antimotim.

rip [rɪp] (*pt & pp* -**ped**, *cont* -**ping**) ⬦ *n* rasgão *m*. ⬦ *vt* -**1.** [tear, shred] rasgar -**2.** [remove] arrancar. ⬦ *vi* rasgar.
  ➠ **rip off** *vt sep inf* -**1.** [cheat] trapacear, passar a perna em -**2.** [steal] roubar.
  ➠ **rip up** *vt sep* rasgar, fazer em pedaços.

RIP (*abbr of* **rest in peace**) descanse em paz.

ripcord [ˈrɪpkɔːd] *n* corda *f* de abertura.

ripe [raɪp] *adj* maduro(ra); **to be** ~ **(for sthg)** *fig* estar pronto(ta) (para algo).

ripen [ˈraɪpn] *vt & vi* amadurecer.

ripeness [ˈraɪpnɪs] *n (U)* maturação *f*.

rip-off *n inf* -**1.** [swindle] assalto *m* -**2.** [imitation] imitação *f* barata.

ripple [ˈrɪpl] ⬦ *n* -**1.** [in water] ondulação *f* -**2.** [of laughter, applause] onda *f*. ⬦ *vt* ondular.

rip-roaring *adj inf* estrondoso(sa).

rise [raɪz] (*pt* **rose**, *pp* **risen** [ˈrɪzn]) ⬦ *n* -**1.** *UK* [increase in amount] aumento *m*, subida *f* -**2.** *UK* [increase in salary] aumento *m* -**3.** [to power, fame] ascensão *f* -**4.** [slope] ladeira *f* -**5.** *phr*: **to give** ~ **to sthg** originar algo. ⬦ *vi* -**1.** [gen] elevar-se -**2.** [sun, moon] nascer, sair -**3.** *UK* [increase] aumentar, subir -**4.** [stand up] levantar-se -**5.** *literary* [get out of bed] levantar-se -**6.** [to a challenge]: **to** ~ **to sthg** mostrar-se à altura de algo; **to** ~ **to the occasion** elevar-se à altura (de algo) -**7.** [rebel] sublevar-se -**8.** [in status] ascender; **to** ~ **to sthg** ascender a algo -**9.** [bread, soufflé] crescer.

➤ **rise above** vt fus superar, mostrar-se superior a.

riser ['raɪzəʳ] n: **an early** ~ um madrugador; **a late** ~ pessoa f que se levanta tarde.

risible ['rɪzəbl] adj fml risível.

rising ['raɪzɪŋ] ⬦ adj **-1.** [gen] em ascensão **-2.** [sloping upwards] em aclive **-3.** [tide] que sobe. ⬦ n [rebellion] levante m, rebelião f.

rising damp n (U) umidade f proveniente do solo.

risk [rɪsk] ⬦ n risco m; **to run the** ~ **of sthg/of doing sthg** correr o risco de algo/de fazer algo; **to take a** ~ arriscar-se; **it's at your own** ~ é por sua conta e risco; **at** ~ em perigo; **at the** ~ **of** sob risco de. ⬦ vt **-1.** [put in danger] arriscar **-2.** [take the chance of]: **to** ~ **doing sthg** arriscar-se a fazer algo; **go on,** ~ **it!** vamos, arrisque-se!

risk capital n (U) capital m de risco.

risk-taking n (U) aceitação f de riscos.

risky ['rɪskɪ] (compar **-ier**, superl **-iest**) adj arriscado (da).

risotto [rɪ'zɒtəʊ] (pl **-s**) n risoto m.

risqué ['ri:skeɪ] adj picante.

rissole ['rɪsəʊl] n UK bolinho m de carne, rissole m.

rite [raɪt] n rito m.

ritual ['rɪtʃʊəl] ⬦ adj ritual. ⬦ n ritual m.

rival ['raɪvl] (UK pt & pp **-led**, cont **-ling**, US pt & pp **-ed**, cont **-ing**) ⬦ adj **-1.** [gen] rival **-2.** [company] concorrente. ⬦ n **-1.** [gen] rival mf **-2.** [company] concorrente mf. ⬦ vt rivalizar OR competir com.

rivalry ['raɪvlrɪ] n rivalidade f.

river ['rɪvəʳ] n rio m.

river bank n margem f do rio.

riverbed ['rɪvəbed] n leito m do rio.

riverside ['rɪvəsaɪd] n: **the** ~ a margem do rio.

rivet ['rɪvɪt] ⬦ n rebite m. ⬦ vt **-1.** [fasten with rivets] rebitar **-2.** fig [fascinate]: **to be** ~ **ed by sthg** estar fascinado(da) por algo.

riveting ['rɪvɪtɪŋ] adj fascinante.

Riviera [ˌrɪvɪ'eərə] n: **the French** ~ a Riviera Francesa; **the Italian** ~ a Riviera Italiana.

Riyadh ['ri:æd] n Riyadh.

RM (abbr of **Royal Marines**) n fuzileiros navais britânicos.

RN n **-1.** (abbr of **Royal Navy**) marinha f real britânica **-2.** (abbr of **registered nurse**) titular de diploma de enfermagem na Grã-Bretanha.

RNA (abbr of **ribonucleic acid**) n RNA m.

RNLI (abbr of **Royal National Lifeboat Institution**) n organização de voluntários na Grã-Bretanha e na Irlanda que oferece resgate marítimo.

RNZAF (abbr of **Royal New Zealand Air Force**) n força aérea real neozelandesa.

RNZN (abbr of **Royal New Zealand Navy**) n marinha real neozelandesa.

roach [rəʊtʃ] (pl sense 1 inv OR **-es**, pl senses 2 & 3 **-es**) n **-1.** [fish] peixe semelhante à carpa **-2.** drugs sl bagana f de baseado **-3.** US [cockroach] barata f.

road [rəʊd] n **-1.** [major] estrada f; **by** ~ por estrada; **on the** ~ [travelling] na estrada; **on the** ~ **to** fig a caminho de **-2.** [minor] caminho m **-3.** [street] rua f.

road atlas n guia f rodoviário.

roadblock ['rəʊdblɒk] n barreira f policial.

road-fund licence n UK ≃ imposto m sobre veículos automotores, ≃ IPVA m.

road haulage n transportes mpl rodoviários.

road hog n inf pej dono m, -na f da estrada.

roadholding ['rəʊdˌhəʊldɪŋ] n (U) estabilidade f (na estrada).

roadie ['rəʊdɪ] n inf roadie mf.

road map n mapa m rodoviário.

road rage n raiva f no trânsito.

road roller n rolo m compressor.

road safety n (U) segurança f no trânsito.

road sense n (U) senso m de direção.

roadshow ['rəʊdʃəʊ] n programa de rádio transmitido diretamente por um disc-jóquei itinerante.

roadside ['rəʊdsaɪd] ⬦ n: **the** ~ a beira da estrada. ⬦ comp de beira da estrada.

road sign n placa f de trânsito.

roadsweeper ['rəʊdˌswi:pəʳ] n [vehicle] caminhão m de limpeza das ruas.

road tax n ≃ imposto m sobre veículos automotores, ≃ IPVA m.

road test n teste m de direção.

➤ **road-test** vt fazer um teste de direção com.

road transport n (U) transporte m rodoviário.

roadway ['rəʊdweɪ] n pista f (da estrada).

road works npl obras fpl na pista.

roadworthy ['rəʊdˌwɜːðɪ] adj em condições de tráfego.

roam [rəʊm] ⬦ vt vagar por. ⬦ vi vagar.

roar [rɔːʳ] ⬦ vi **-1.** [lion] rugir **-2.** [traffic, plane, engine] roncar **-3.** [person] urrar; **to** ~ **with laughter** rir às gargalhadas **-4.** [wind] bramir. ⬦ vt bradar. ⬦ n **-1.** [of lion] rugido m **-2.** [of engine] ronco m **-3.** [of traffic] barulho m **-4.** [of wind] sopro m **-5.** [of person] urro m.

roaring ['rɔːrɪŋ] ⬦ adj **-1.** [traffic, wind] barulhento(ta) **-2.** [fire] crepitante **-3.** [for emphasis] estrondoso(sa); **a** ~ **success** um sucesso estrondoso; **to do a** ~ **trade** vender bem. ⬦ adv [for emphasis] completamente.

roast [rəʊst] ⬦ adj assado(da). ⬦ n assado m. ⬦ vt **-1.** [meat, potatoes] assar **-2.** [coffee beans, nuts] torrar.

roast beef n (U) rosbife m.

roasting ['rəʊstɪŋ] inf ⬦ adj muito quente; **I'm** ~! estou derretendo de calor! ⬦ adv: **it's a** ~ **hot day!** hoje está um inferno de quente!

roasting tin n assadeira f.

rob [rɒb] (pt & pp **-bed**, cont **-bing**) vt roubar; **to** ~ **sb of sthg** [money, goods] roubar algo de alguém; fig [of opportunity, glory] privar alguém de algo.

robber ['rɒbəʳ] n ladrão m, -dra f.

robbery ['rɒbərɪ] (pl **-ies**) n roubo m.

robe [rəʊb] n **-1.** [of priest] túnica f **-2.** [judge] toga f **-3.** [monarch] manto m **-4.** US [dressing gown] robe m.

robin ['rɒbɪn] n pintarroxo m.

robot ['rəʊbɒt] n robô m.

robotics [rəʊ'bɒtɪks] n (U) robótica f.

robust [rəʊ'bʌst] adj [person] **-1.** robusto(ta) **-2.** [economy] forte **-3.** [health] de ferro **-4.** [criticism, defence] vigoroso(sa).

robustly [rəʊ'bʌstlɪ] *adv* vigorosamente.
rock [rɒk] <> *n* -**1.** *(U)* [substance] rocha *f* -**2.** [boulder] rochedo *m*, penhasco *m* -**3.** *US* [pebble] pedregulho *m* -**4.** *(U)* [music] rock *m* -**5.** *(U) UK* [sweet] barra *f* de caramelo. <> *comp* [music] de rock. <> *vt* -**1.** [cause to move] balançar -**2.** [shock] abalar. <> *vi* balançar-se.
 on the rocks *adv* -**1.** [drink] com gelo, on the rocks -**2.** [marriage, relationship] que vai mal.
rock and roll *n (U)* rock and roll *m*.
rock bottom *n (U)* nível *m* baixíssimo; **to hit ~** atingir o fundo do poço.
 rock-bottom *adj* baixíssimo(ma).
rock cake *n UK* bolo com frutas secas.
rock climber *n* alpinista *mf*.
rock-climbing *n (U)* alpinismo *m*.
rocker ['rɒkə'] *n* [chair] embaladeira *f*; **to be off one's ~** *inf* ter um parafuso a menos.
rockery ['rɒkərɪ] *(pl* -ies*) n* jardim *m* de pedras.
rocket ['rɒkɪt] <> *n* foguete *m*. <> *vi* disparar.
rocket launcher [-ˌlɔ:ntʃə'] *n* lança-foguetes *m inv*.
rock face *n* parede *f* de pedra.
rockfall ['rɒkfɔ:l] *n* deslizamento *m* de pedras.
rock-hard *adj* duro(ra) como pedra.
Rockies ['rɒkɪz] *npl*: **the ~** as Montanhas Rochosas.
rocking chair ['rɒkɪŋ-] *n* cadeira *f* de balanço.
rocking horse ['rɒkɪŋ-] *n* cavalinho *m* de balanço.
rock music *n (U)* rock *m*.
rock 'n' roll *n* = **rock and roll**.
rock pool *n piscina formada por pedras na praia.*
rock salt *n (U)* sal-gema *m*.
rock singer *n* cantor *m*, -ra *f* de rock, roqueiro *m*, -ra *f*.
rocky ['rɒkɪ] *(compar* -ier, *superl* -iest*) adj* -**1.** [full of rocks] rochoso(sa) -**2.** [unsteady] instável.
Rocky Mountains *npl*: **the ~** as Montanhas Rochosas.
rococo [rə'kəʊkəʊ] *adj* rococó.
rod [rɒd] *n* -**1.** [wooden] vara *f* -**2.** [metal] barra *f*.
rode [rəʊd] *pt* ⊳ **ride**.
rodent ['rəʊdənt] *n* roedor *m*.
rodeo ['rəʊdɪəʊ] *(pl* -s*) n* rodeio *m*.
roe [rəʊ] *n* ova *f (de peixe).*
roe deer *n* corço *m*, -ça *f*.
rogue [rəʊg] <> *adj* -**1.** [animal] solitário e perigoso, solitária e perigosa -**2.** *fig* [person] rebelde. <> *n* -**1.** [likable rascal] malandro *m*, -dra *f* -**2.** *dated* [dishonest person] vigarista *mf*.
roguish ['rəʊgɪʃ] *adj* malandro(dra).
role [rəʊl] *n* -**1.** [position, function] função *f*, papel *m* -**2.** *CINEMA, THEATRE* papel *m*.
roll [rəʊl] <> *n* -**1.** [of material, paper, film] rolo *m* -**2.** [of banknotes] maço *m* -**3.** [of cloth] peça *f* -**4.** [of bread] pãozinho *m* -**5.** [list] lista *f* -**6.** [sound - of drum] rufar *m*; [- of thunder] estrondo *m*. <> *vt* -**1.** [turn over] rolar; **to ~ one's eyes** [in fear, despair] revirar os olhos -**2.** [make into cylinder] enrolar; **~ed into one** *fig* tudo num só. <> *vi* -**1.** [of a round object] rolar -**2.** [move] andar -**3.** [sway from side to side] balançar

- **4.** [sound - drum] rufar; [- thunder] retumbar.
 roll about, roll around *vi* rolar.
 roll back *vt sep US* [prices] reduzir.
 roll in *vi inf* -**1.** [money] chegar de balde -**2.** [person] pintar.
 roll over *vi* virar-se.
 roll up <> *vt sep* -**1.** [make into cylinder] enrolar -**2.** [sleeves] arregaçar. <> *vi* -**1.** [vehicle] chegar -**2.** *inf* [person] pintar.
roll bar *n* santantônio *m*.
roll call *n* toque *m* de chamada.
rolled gold [rəʊld-] *n (U)* plaquê *m*.
roller ['rəʊlə'] *n* -**1.** [cylinder] cilindro *m* -**2.** [curler] rolo *m*.
Rollerblades® ['rəʊləˌbleɪdz] *npl* patins *mpl* em linha.
rollerblading ['rəʊləˌbleɪdɪŋ] *n* patinação *f (com patins em linha)*; **to go ~** praticar patinação *(com patins em linha)*.
roller blind *n* persiana *f* de enrolar.
roller coaster *n* montanha-russa *f*.
roller skate *n* patim *m* de rodas.
 roller-skate *vi* patinar.
roller towel *n* toalha *f* de rolo.
rollicking ['rɒlɪkɪŋ] *adj* divertido(da).
rolling ['rəʊlɪŋ] *adj* -**1.** [undulating] ondulado(da) -**2.** [swaying from side to side] bamboleante -**3.** *phr*: **to be ~ in it** *inf* estar nadando em dinheiro.
rolling mill *n* laminador *m*.
rolling pin *n* rolo *m* de massa.
rolling stock *n (U)* material *m* rodante.
roll-neck *adj* com gola rulê.
roll of honour *n* lista *f* de honra.
roll-on <> *adj* de rolo, roll-on. <> *n* desodorante *m* de rolo *OR* roll-on.
roll-on roll-off *adj UK*: **a ~ ferry** uma balsa para veículos.
roly-poly *(pl* -ies*) n UK*: **~ (pudding)** rocambole *m*.
ROM [rɒm] *(abbr of* read-only memory*) n* ROM *f*.
romaine lettuce [rəʊ'meɪn-] *n US* alface *f (de folha larga).*
Roman ['rəʊmən] <> *adj* romano(na). <> *n* romano *m*, -na *f*.
Roman candle *n* pistolão *m*.
Roman Catholic <> *adj* católico (romano), católica (romana). <> *n* católico *m* (romano), católica *f* (romana).
romance [rəʊ'mæns] *n* -**1.** [gen] romance *m* -**2.** *(U)* [romantic quality] romantismo *m*.
Romanesque [ˌrəʊmə'nesk] *adj* românico(ca).
Romani *adj* & *n* = **Romany**.
Romania [rə'meɪnjə] *n* Romênia; **in ~** na Romênia.
Romanian [rə'meɪnjən] <> *adj* romeno(na). <> *n* -**1.** [person] romeno *m*, -na *f* -**2.** [language] romeno *m*.
Roman numerals *npl* algarismos *mpl* romanos.
romantic [rəʊ'mæntɪk] *adj* romântico(ca).
romanticism [rəʊ'mæntɪsɪzm] *n* romantismo *m*.
romanticize, **-ise** [rəʊ'mæntɪsaɪz] <> *vt* romantizar. <> *vi* romantizar, fantasiar.
Romany ['rəʊmənɪ] *(pl* -ies*)* <> *adj* cigano(na).

◇ *n* **-1.** [person] cigano *m*, -na *f* **-2.** [language] romani *m*.

Rome [rəʊm] *n* Roma.

romp [rɒmp] ◇ *n* travessura *f.* ◇ *vi* brincar ruidosamente.

rompers ['rɒmpəz] *npl*, **romper suit** ['rɒmpəʳ-] *n* macacão *m* de criança.

roof [ru:f] *n* **-1.** [covering - of vehicle] capota *f*; [- of building] telhado *m*; **not under my ~ !** não na minha casa!; **under the same ~** sob o mesmo teto; **to have a ~ over one's head** ter onde morar; **to go through** OR **hit the ~** subir pelas paredes **-2.** [upper part - of cave] teto *m*; [- of mouth] céu *m* da boca.

roof garden *n* jardim *m* de cobertura.

roofing ['ru:fɪŋ] *n (U)* material *m* para cobertura.

roof rack *n* bagageiro *m (na capota do carro)*.

rooftop ['ru:ftɒp] *n* telhado *m*.

rook [rʊk] *n* **-1.** [bird] gralha *f* **-2.** [chess piece] torre *f*.

rookie ['rʊkɪ] *n US* novato *m*, -ta *f*.

room [ru:m, rʊm] *n* **-1.** [in building] sala *f* **-2.** [bedroom] quarto *m* **-3.** *(U)* [space] espaço *m*; **to make ~ for sb/sthg** abrir espaço para alguém/algo **-4.** *(U)* [opportunity, possibility] possibilidade *f*; **~ to** OR **for manoeuvre** espaço para manobrar.

rooming house ['ru:mɪŋ-] *n US* pensão *f*.

roommate ['ru:mmeɪt] *n* companheiro *m*, -ra *f* de quarto.

room service *n* serviço *m* de quarto.

room temperature *n* temperatura *f* ambiente.

roomy ['ru:mɪ] *(compar* -ier, *superl* -iest) *adj* espaçoso(sa), amplo(pla).

roost [ru:st] ◇ *n* poleiro *m*; **to rule the ~** cantar de galo. ◇ *vi* empoleirar-se.

rooster ['ru:stəʳ] *n* galo *m*.

root [ru:t] ◇ *adj* básico(ca), fundamental. ◇ *n* [gen] raiz *f*; **to put down ~s** [person] criar raízes; **to take ~** [plant] pegar; [idea] consolidar-se. ◇ *vi* remexer.

➤ **roots** *npl* raízes *fpl*.

➤ **root for** *vt fus esp US inf* torcer por.

➤ **root out** *vt sep* arrancar até a raiz, extirpar.

root beer *n US* cerveja sem álcool feita de raízes.

root crop *n* tubérculos *mpl*.

rooted ['ru:tɪd] *adj*: **to be ~ to the spot** ficar paralisado(da) (de medo).

rootless ['ru:tlɪs] *adj* sem raízes, desarraigado(da).

root vegetable *n* tubérculo *m*.

rope [rəʊp] ◇ *n* corda *f*; **to know the ~s** estar por dentro do assunto. ◇ *vt* amarrar com corda.

➤ **rope in** *vt sep inf* arrastar para.

➤ **rope off** *vt sep* isolar com cordas.

rop(e)y ['rəʊpɪ] *(compar* -ier, *superl* -iest) *adj UK inf* **-1.** [poor-quality] ruim **-2.** [unwell] indisposto(ta), mal.

rosary ['rəʊzərɪ] *(pl* -ies) *n* rosário *m*.

rose [rəʊz] ◇ *pt* ▷ **rise**. ◇ *adj* [pink] rosa, cor-de-rosa. ◇ *n* [flower] rosa *f*; **it's not a bed of ~s** não é feito de rosas.

rosé ['rəʊzeɪ] *n (U)* vinho *m* rosé.

rosebed ['rəʊzbed] *n* canteiro *m* de rosas.

rosebud ['rəʊzbʌd] *n* botão *m* de rosa.

rose bush *n* roseira *f*.

rose-coloured *adj* cor-de-rosa.

rose hip *n* rosa-mosqueta *f*.

rosemary ['rəʊzmərɪ] *n (U)* alecrim *m*.

rose-tinted *adj*: **to look through ~ glasses** ver tudo cor-de-rosa.

rosette [rəʊ'zet] *n* roseta *f*.

rosewater ['rəʊz,wɔ:təʳ] *n (U)* água-de-rosas *f*.

rosewood ['rəʊzwʊd] *n (U)* pau-rosa *m*.

RoSPA *(abbr of* Royal Society for the Prevention of Accidents) *n organização britânica para prevenção de acidentes.*

roster ['rɒstəʳ] *n* lista *f*.

rostrum ['rɒstrəm] *(pl* -trums OR -tra [-trə]) *n* tribuna *f*, rostro *m*.

rosy ['rəʊzɪ] *(compar* -ier, *superl* -iest) *adj* **-1.** [pink] rosado(da) **-2.** [hopeful] promissor(ra).

rot [rɒt] *(pt* & *pp* -ted, *cont* -ting) ◇ *n* **-1.** [decay - of wood, food] putrefação *f*; [- in society, organization] decadência *f* **-2.** *UK dated* [nonsense] besteira *f*, bobagem *f*. ◇ *vt* [cause to decay] corroer, decompor. ◇ *vi* apodrecer.

rota ['rəʊtə] *n* lista *f* de turnos.

rotary ['rəʊtərɪ] ◇ *adj* rotatório(ria). ◇ *n US* [roundabout] rotatória *f*.

Rotary Club *n*: **the ~** o Rotary Club.

rotate [rəʊ'teɪt] ◇ *vt* **-1.** [gen] alternar **-2.** [turn] girar. ◇ *vi* **-1.** [turn] girar, dar voltas **-2.** [in sequence - jobs] alternar-se; [- crops] alternar.

rotation [rəʊ'teɪʃn] *n* **-1.** [turning movement] rotação *f* **-2.** *(U)* [sequence - of jobs] revezamento *m*, alternância *f*; [- of crops] rodízio *m*; **in ~** por turnos.

rote [rəʊt] *n (U)*: **by ~** de cor OR memória.

rote learning *n* decoreba *f*.

rotor ['rəʊtəʳ] *n* rotor *m*.

rotten ['rɒtn] *adj* **-1.** [decayed] podre **-2.** *inf* [poor-quality, unskilled] péssimo(ma) **-3.** *inf* [unpleasant, nasty] perverso(sa), ruim **-4.** *inf* [unenjoyable] detestável **-5.** *inf* [unwell]: **to feel ~** sentir-se péssimo(ma) **-6.** [unhappy, bad]: **to feel ~ (about sthg)** sentir-se péssimo(ma) (por algo).

rotund [rəʊ'tʌnd] *adj fml* rotundo(da).

rouble ['ru:bl] *n* rublo *m*.

rouge [ru:ʒ] *n (U)* ruge *m*.

rough [rʌf] ◇ *adj* **-1.** [not smooth - surface] áspero(ra); [- road] acidentado(da) **-2.** [violent] rude, grosseiro(ra) **-3.** [crude, basic - people, manners] rústico(ca); [- shelter, conditions, situation] precário(ria) **-4.** [approximate - not detailed] rudimentar; [- not exact] aproximado(da) **-5.** [unpleasant, tough - life, time] duro(ra), difícil; [- area, town etc] tumultuoso(sa) **-6.** [stormy - weather] tormentoso(sa); [- sea] agitado(da); [- wind] violento(ta); [- day] tempestuoso(sa) **-7.** [sounding harsh] áspero(ra) **-8.** [tasting harsh] azedo(da) **-9.** [tired, ill] abatido(da). ◇ *adv*: **to sleep ~** dormir na rua. ◇ *n* **-1.** GOLF: **the ~** o rough **-2.** [undetailed form]: **in ~** em rascunho. ◇ *vt phr*: **to ~ it** viver sem comodidades.

➤ **rough out** *vt sep* esboçar.
➤ **rough up** *vt sep* bater em, atacar.
roughage ['rʌfɪdʒ] *n* fibras *fpl*.
rough and ready *adj* rústico(ca), feito(ta) às pressas.
rough-and-tumble *n (U)* tumulto *m*.
roughcast *n (U)* reboco *m* grosso.
rough diamond *n UK fig* diamante *m* bruto.
roughen ['rʌfn] *vt* tornar áspero(ra).
rough justice *n (U)* injustiça *f*.
roughly ['rʌflɪ] *adv* **-1.** [not gently] bruscamente **-2.** [crudely] rusticamente **-3.** [approximately] aproximadamente, mais ou menos.
roughneck ['rʌfnek] *n* **-1.** [oilrig worker] *petroleiro que trabalha em campo de perfuração* **-2.** *US inf* [ruffian] casca-grossa *mf*.
roughness ['rʌfnɪs] *n (U)* **-1.** [lack of smoothness] aspereza *f* **-2.** [lack of gentleness] rudeza *f*, grosseria *f*.
roughshod ['rʌfʃɒd] *adv*: **to ride ~ over sb/sthg** tratar alguém/algo a pontapés.
roulette [ru:'let] *n (U)* roleta *f*.
round [raʊnd] ◇ *adj* **-1.** [gen] redondo(da) **-2.** [fat, curved - cheeks, hips] roliço(ça), redondo(da); [- bulge] redondo(da). ◇ *prep* **-1.** [surrounding] ao redor de **-2.** [near] em volta de; **~ here** por aqui **-3.** [all over] por todo(da) **-4.** [in circular movement, in circumference] ao redor de; **she measures 70 cm ~ the waist** ela mede *OR* tem 70 cm de cintura **-5.** [to/on the other side of]: **to drive ~ the corner** dobrar a esquina; **I live just ~ the corner** eu moro logo ali **-6.** [so as to avoid - hole, obstacle]: **to go ~ an obstacle** contornar um obstáculo; [- problem]: **to find a way ~ sthg** achar um jeito de contornar algo. ◇ *adv* **-1.** [surrounding]: **all ~** por toda a volta, por todos os lados **-2.** [near]: **~ about** [in distance] por perto; [in number, amount] aproximadamente **-3.** [all over]: **to travel ~** viajar por aí **-4.** [in circular movement]: **~ (and ~)** em círculos; **to go ~** circular; **to spin ~** girar **-5.** [in circumference]: **it's at least 3 km ~** tem no mínimo 3 km de circunferência **-6.** [to the other side or direction] ao redor; **to turn ~** virar; **to go ~** dar a volta **-7.** [on a visit]: **come ~ sometime!** apareçam uma hora dessas! ◇ *n* **-1.** [gen] rodada *f*; **a ~ of applause** uma salva de palmas **-2.** [professional visit] percurso *m* **-3.** [of ammunition] cartucho *m* **-4.** *BOXING* assalto *m* **-5.** *GOLF* partida *f*. ◇ *vt* [turn] dobrar, virar.
➤ **rounds** *npl* [professional visits] percurso *m*; **to do** *OR* **go the ~s** *fig* espalhar-se, propagar-se.
➤ **round off** *vt sep* encerrar, terminar.
➤ **round up** *vt sep* **-1.** [gather together] reunir **-2.** *MATH* arredondar.
roundabout ['raʊndəbaʊt] ◇ *adj* indireto(ta). ◇ *n UK* **-1.** [on road] rotatória *f* **-2.** [at fairground] carrossel *m* **-3.** [at playground] gira-gira *m*.
rounded ['raʊndɪd] *adj* redondo(da).
rounders ['raʊndəz] *n (U) UK* bete *m*.
Roundhead ['raʊndhed] *n HIST* seguidor de *Oliver Cromwell na guerra civil inglesa*, Cabeça *m* Redonda.
roundly ['raʊndlɪ] *adv* totalmente, terminantemente.
round-neck *adj* de gola redonda.

round-shouldered [-'ʃəʊldəd] *adj* de ombros caídos.
round-table *adj* em igualdade de condições.
round the clock *adv* durante as 24 horas do dia.
➤ **round-the-clock** *adj* contínuo(nua), 24 horas do dia.
round trip ◇ *adj US* de ida e volta. ◇ *n* viagem *f* de ida e volta.
round-up *n* resumo *m*.
rouse [raʊz] *vt* **-1.** [wake up] despertar **-2.** [impel]: **to ~ sb to do sthg** animar alguém a fazer algo; **to ~ o.s. to do sthg** animar-se a fazer algo **-3.** [excite] estimular **-4.** [give rise to] suscitar.
rousing ['raʊzɪŋ] *adj* estimulante.
rout [raʊt] ◇ *n* derrota *f* esmagadora. ◇ *vt* derrotar de forma esmagadora.
route [ru:t] ◇ *n* **-1.** [line of travel - of journey] rota *f*; [- of or person, procession] trajeto *m*, percurso *m* **-2.** [of bus, train] linha *f* **-3.** [of plane, ship] rota *f* **-4.** *fig* [to achievement] caminho *m*. ◇ *vt* **-1.** [flight, traffic] direcionar **-2.** [goods] enviar.
route map *n* mapa *m (de localização)*.
route march *n* marcha *f*.
routine [ru:'ti:n] ◇ *adj* **-1.** [normal] de rotina **-2.** *pej* [humdrum, uninteresting] rotineiro(ra). ◇ *n* **-1.** *(U)* [normal pattern of activity] rotina *f* **-2.** *pej* [boring repetition] rotina *f*.
routinely [ru:'ti:nlɪ] *adv* freqüentemente.
rove [raʊv] *literary* ◇ *vt* errar, vagar por. ◇ *vi*: **to ~ around** vagar.
roving ['raʊvɪŋ] *adj* itinerante; **~ eyes** olhar *m* errante.
row¹ [raʊ] ◇ *n* **-1.** [gen] fileira *f* **-2.** [succession] seqüência *f*, série *f*; **four in a ~** quatro seguidos. ◇ *vt* **-1.** [boat] remar **-2.** [person] conduzir de barco a remo. ◇ *vi* [in boat] remar.
row² [raʊ] ◇ *n* **-1.** [quarrel] briga *f* **-2.** *inf* [noise] alvoroço *m*, barulho *m*. ◇ *vi* [quarrel] discutir, brigar.
rowboat ['raʊbəʊt] *n US* barco *m* a remo.
rowdiness ['raʊdɪnɪs] *n (U)* alvoroço *m*, tumulto *m*.
rowdy ['raʊdɪ] *(compar -ier, superl -iest) adj* **-1.** [person] brigão(gona) **-2.** [party, atmosphere] barulhento(ta).
rower ['raʊə'] *n* remador *m*, -ra *f*.
row house [raʊ-] *n US* casa *f* geminada.
rowing ['raʊɪŋ] *n (U)* remo *m*.
rowing boat *n UK* barco *m* a remo.
rowing machine *n* remo *m* seco.
royal ['rɔɪəl] ◇ *adj* real. ◇ *n inf* membro *m* da família real.
Royal Air Force *n (U)*: **the ~** a Força Aérea Britânica.
royal blue *adj* azul-imperial.
royal family *n* família *f* real.
royalist ['rɔɪəlɪst] *n* monarquista *mf*.
royal jelly *n (U)* geléia *f* real.
Royal Mail *n UK*: **the ~** os Correios da Grã-Bretanha.
Royal Marines *n UK*: **the ~** os Fuzileiros Navais Britânicos.

Royal Navy *n*: the ~ a Marinha Real Britânica.
royalty ['rɔɪəltɪ] *n (U)* realeza *f.*
➤ **royalties** *npl* direitos *mpl* autorais.
RP (*abbr of* **received pronunciation**) *n* pronúncia padrão do inglês.
RPI (*abbr of* **retail price index**) *n* ≃ IPC *m.*
rpm (*abbr of* **revolutions per minute**) *npl* rpm.
RR (*abbr of* **railroad**) *US* ferrovia *f.*
RRP (*abbr of* **recommended retail price**) *n UK* preço *m* sugerido.
RSA *n* **-1.** (*abbr of* **Republic of South Africa**) República *f* da África do Sul **-2.** (*abbr of* **Royal Society of Arts**) sociedade britânica para o fomento às artes, à indústria e ao comércio.
RSC (*abbr of* **Royal Shakespeare Company**) *n* importante companhia teatral britânica especializada em Shakespeare.
RSI (*abbr of* **repetitive strain injury**) *n* LER *f.*
RSJ (*abbr of* **rolled steel joist**) *n* vigamento *m* folheado a aço.
RSPB (*abbr of* **Royal Society for the Protection of Birds**) *n* organização britânica para a proteção de pássaros em seu habitat.
RSPCA (*abbr of* **Royal Society for the Prevention of Cruelty to Animals**) *n* sociedade britânica protetora de animais.
RSVP (*abbr of* **répondez s'il vous plaît**) RSVP.
rub [rʌb] (*pt* & *pp* -**bed**, *cont* -**bing**) ⬦ *vt* esfregar; **to ~ shoulders with** acotovelar-se com; **to ~ sthg against sthg** esfregar algo em *OR* contra algo; **to ~ sthg on sthg** [polish] esfregar algo em algo; **to ~ sthg in (to) sthg** esfregar algo em algo; **to ~ it in** *inf fig* trazer à tona; **to ~ sb up the wrong way** *UK*, **to ~ sb the wrong way** *US* ofender alguém sem intenção. ⬦ *vi*: **to ~ (against** *OR* **on sthg)** roçar (em algo); **to ~ (together)** esfregar-se; **to ~ along** dar-se bem com.
➤ **rub off on** *vt fus* influir em.
➤ **rub out** *vt sep* apagar.
rubber ['rʌbə'] ⬦ *adj* de borracha. ⬦ *n* **-1.** *(U)* [substance] borracha *f* **-2.** *UK* [eraser] borracha *f* **-3.** [in bridge] rubber *m* **-4.** *US inf* [condom] camisinha *f* **-5.** *US* [overshoe] galocha *f.*
rubber band *n* atilho *m*, borrachinha *f (para papel).*
rubber boot *n US* bota *f* de borracha.
rubber dinghy *n* bote *m* de borracha.
rubberize, -ise ['rʌbəraɪz] *vt* revestir de borracha.
rubberneck ['rʌbənek] *vi US inf* [stare] olhar com curiosidade.
rubber plant *n* goma-elástica *f.*
rubber stamp *n* carimbo *m.*
➤ **rubber-stamp** *vt* aprovar sem questionar.
rubber tree *n* seringueira *f.*
rubbery ['rʌbərɪ] *adj* borrachento(ta).
rubbing ['rʌbɪŋ] *n* [of brass] calcografia *f.*
rubbish ['rʌbɪʃ] ⬦ *n* **-1.** [refuse] lixo *m* **-2.** *inf fig* [worthless matter] porcaria *f* **-3.** *inf* [nonsense] besteira *f*, bobagem *f.* ⬦ *vt inf* rebaixar. ⬦ *excl* bobagem!
rubbish bag *n UK* saco *m* de lixo.
rubbish bin *n UK* lata *f* de lixo.

rubbish dump, rubbish tip *n UK* depósito *m* de lixo.
rubbishy ['rʌbɪʃɪ] *adj inf* porcaria.
rubble ['rʌbl] *n (U)* entulho *m.*
rubella [ruː'belə] *n (U)* rubéola *f.*
ruby ['ruːbɪ] *(pl* -**ies**) *n* rubi *m.*
RUC (*abbr of* **Royal Ulster Constabulary**) *n* força policial na Irlanda do Norte.
ruck *n* **-1.** *inf* [fight] arruaça *f* **-2.** *RUGBY* luta *f* pela posse da bola.
rucksack ['rʌksæk] *n* mochila *f.*
ructions ['rʌkʃnz] *npl inf* alvoroço *m*, tumulto *m.*
rudder ['rʌdə'] *n* leme *m.*
ruddy ['rʌdɪ] (*compar* -**ier**, *superl* -**iest**) *adj* **-1.** [reddish] corado(da) **-2.** *UK dated* [for emphasis] maldito(ta).
rude [ruːd] *adj* **-1.** [impolite] rude, grosseiro(ra) **-2.** [dirty, naughty - joke] sujo(ja); [- word] grosseiro(ra); [- noise] violento(ta) **-3.** [unexpected] brusco(ca); **~ awakening** um despertar brusco **-4.** *literary* [primitive] rústico(ca).
rudely ['ruːdlɪ] *adv* **-1.** [gen] de forma grosseira **-2.** [unexpectedly] bruscamente, violentamente.
rudeness ['ruːdnɪs] *n (U)* grosseria *f.*
rudimentary [ˌruːdɪ'mentərɪ] *adj* rudimentar.
rudiments ['ruːdɪmənts] *npl* rudimentos *mpl*, noções *fpl* básicas.
rue [ruː] *vt* lamentar, arrepender-se de.
rueful ['ruːfʊl] *adj* arrependido(da).
ruff [rʌf] *n* gola *f* franzida.
ruffian ['rʌfjən] *n* rufião *m*, -ona *f.*
ruffle ['rʌfl] ⬦ *n* rufo *m.* ⬦ *vt* **-1.** [mess up - hair, fur] revolver; [- water] agitar **-2.** [upset] enervar.
rug [rʌg] *n* **-1.** [carpet] tapete *m (pequeno)* **-2.** [blanket] manta *f.*
rugby ['rʌgbɪ] *n (U)* rúgbi *m.*
Rugby League *n* rúgbi profissional disputado com equipes de 13 jogadores.
Rugby Union *n* rúgbi amador disputado com equipes de 15 jogadores.
rugged ['rʌgɪd] *adj* **-1.** [rocky, uneven] acidentado(da) **-2.** [sturdy] potente **-3.** [roughly handsome] rústico(ca) e atraente.
ruggedness ['rʌgɪdnɪs] *n (U)* aspereza *f.*
rugger ['rʌgə'] *n (U) UK inf* rúgbi *m.*
ruin ['ruːɪn] ⬦ *n* ruína *f.* ⬦ *vt* **-1.** [spoil] arruinar, estragar **-2.** [bankrupt] arruinar.
➤ **in ruin(s)** *adv* em ruínas.
ruination [ruːɪ'neɪʃn] *n (U)* arruinação *f*, ruína *f.*
ruinous ['ruːɪnəs] *adj* dispendioso(sa).
rule [ruːl] ⬦ *n* **-1.** [regulation - *SPORT*] regra *f*; **to bend the ~s** abrir uma exceção nas regras; [- *SCH*] norma *f* **-2.** [convention, guideline] regra *f*; **as a ~ of thumb** por experiência (própria) **-3.** [norm]: **the ~** a regra, a norma; **as a ~** via de regra **-4.** *(U)* [control] domínio *m* **-5.** [ruler] régua *f.* ⬦ *vt* **-1.** [control, guide] comandar **-2.** [govern] governar **-3.** [decide]: **to ~ that** ordenar *OR* decretar que. ⬦ *vi* **-1.** [give decision] deliberar **-2.** *fml* [be paramount] dominar **-3.** [govern] governar.
➤ **rule out** *vt sep* **-1.** [reject as unsuitable] descartar **-2.** [prevent, make impossible - possibility, circumstances] descartar; [- event, decision] impedir.
rulebook ['ruːlbʊk] *n*: the ~ o regulamento.

ruled [ruːld] *adj* pautado(da).

ruler ['ruːlə'] *n* -**1.** [for measurement] régua *f* -**2.** [leader] soberano *m*, -na *f*.

ruling ['ruːlɪŋ] ◇ *adj* no poder, dominante. ◇ *n* sentença *f*, parecer *m*.

rum [rʌm] (*compar* -**mer**, *superl* -**mest**) ◇ *adj UK inf dated* esquisito(ta). ◇ *n* (U) rum *m*.

Rumania [ruːˈmeɪnjə] *n* = **Romania**.

Rumanian [ruːˈmeɪnjən] *adj* & *n* = **Romanian**.

rumba ['rʌmbə] *n* rumba *f*.

rumble ['rʌmbl] ◇ *n* -**1.** [noise - of thunder] estrondo *m*; [- of stomach, train] ronco *m*; [- of traffic] barulho *m* -**2.** *US inf* [fight] arruaça *f*. ◇ *vt UK inf dated* revelar, descobrir. ◇ *vi* -**1.** [thunder] trovejar -**2.** [stomach, train] roncar -**3.** [traffic] fazer barulho.

rumbustious [rʌmˈbʌstʃəs] *adj UK* esfuziante, enérgico(ca).

ruminate ['ruːmɪneɪt] *vi fml*: to ~ (about OR on sthg) ruminar (algo).

rummage ['rʌmɪdʒ] *vi* escarafunchar.

rummage sale *n US* bazar *m* beneficente (de artigos usados).

rummy ['rʌmɪ] *n* (U) jogo de cartas semelhante à canastra e ao buraco.

rumour *UK*, **rumor** *US* ['ruːmə'] *n* rumor *m*, boato *m*.

rumoured *UK*, **rumored** *US* ['ruːməd] *adj*: to be ~ed that comenta-se que.

rump [rʌmp] *n* -**1.** [of animal] anca *f*, garupa *f* -**2.** *inf* [of person] nádegas *fpl*.

rumple ['rʌmpl] *vt* -**1.** [clothes] amarrotar -**2.** [hair] despentear.

rump steak *n* filé *m* de alcatra.

rumpus ['rʌmpəs] *n inf* bafafá *m*, rolo *m*.

rumpus room *n US* sala *f* de jogos.

run [rʌn] (*pt* ran, *pp* run, *cont* -ing) ◇ *n* -**1.** [on foot] corrida *f*; **to go for a** ~ ir dar uma corrida; **to break into a** ~ sair em disparada; **to take the dog for a** ~ levar o cão para um passeio; **on the** ~ em fuga -**2.** [in car] passeio *f*; **it's a long** ~ **down to Cornwall** é um longo caminho até Cornwall -**3.** [series - of luck] alternância *f*; [- of disasters, wins] série *f* -**4.** *THEATRE* temporada *f* -**5.** [great demand]: ~ **on sthg** procura *f* OR demanda *f* por algo -**6.** [in tights] fio *m* puxado -**7.** [in cricket, baseball] ponto *m* -**8.** [sports track] pista *f* -**9.** [term, period]: **in the short/ long** ~ a curto/longo prazo. ◇ *vt* -**1.** [on foot] correr -**2.** [manage, control] dirigir, administrar -**3.** [machine] operar -**4.** [car] dirigir, fazer andar -**5.** [water, bath, tap] abrir -**6.** [publish] publicar -**7.** *inf* [drive] levar -**8.** [move, pass]: **to** ~ **sthg along/over sthg** passar algo em/sobre algo. ◇ *vi* -**1.** [gen] passar; **to be running late** estar atrasado(da) -**2.** [on foot] correr; **to** ~ **for it** fugir -**3.** *US* [in election]: **to** ~ (**for sthg**) concorrer (a algo) -**4.** [progress, develop]: **to** ~ **smoothly** ir bem -**5.** [machine, factory, engine] funcionar; **to** ~ **on** OR **off sthg** funcionar com algo -**6.** [liquid, river] escorrer; **to** ~ **dry** secar -**7.** [nose] escorrer -**8.** [tap] pingar -**9.** [colour] borrar -**10.** [continue] continuar; **to have two months to** ~ o contrato ainda é válido por dois meses; **feelings are** ~**ning high** os ânimos estão exaltados.

◆ **run about** *vi* -**1.** [from place to place] correr (de um lugar para outro) -**2.** [associate] andar.

◆ **run across** *vt fus* encontrar-se com.

◆ **run along** *vi dated*: ~ **along now!** andando!

◆ **run around** *vi* = **run about**.

◆ **run away** *vi* -**1.** [flee]: **to** ~ **away (from sb/ sthg)** fugir (de alguém/algo) -**2.** *fig* [avoid]: **to** ~ **away from sthg** fugir de algo.

◆ **run away with** *vt fus*: **he lets his enthusiasm** ~ **away with him** ele se deixa levar pelo entusiasmo.

◆ **run down** ◇ *vt sep* -**1.** [in vehicle] atropelar -**2.** [criticize] falar mal de -**3.** [allow to decline] enfraquecer. ◇ *vi* perder força.

◆ **run in** *vt sep* [car] amaciar.

◆ **run into** *vt fus* -**1.** [encounter - problem] deparar-se com; [- person] topar com -**2.** [in vehicle] chocar-se com OR contra -**3.** [amount to] chegar a, atingir.

◆ **run off** ◇ *vt sep* [a copy] imprimir. ◇ *vi* [abscond, elope]: **to** ~ **off (with sb/sthg)** fugir (com alguém/algo).

◆ **run on** *vi* continuar.

◆ **run out** *vi* -**1.** [become used up] esgotar -**2.** [expire] vencer, caducar.

◆ **run out of** *vt fus* ficar sem; **we've** ~ **out of food** acabou a nossa comida.

◆ **run over** *vt sep* atropelar.

◆ **run through** *vt fus* -**1.** [spread through] permear -**2.** [practise] ensaiar, praticar -**3.** [read through] passar os olhos em.

◆ **run to** *vt fus* -**1.** [amount to] chegar a -**2.** [afford]: **my budget doesn't** ~ **to a new car** meu orçamento não me permite comprar um carro novo.

◆ **run up** *vt fus* contrair.

◆ **run up against** *vt fus* deparar-se com.

run-around *n inf*: **to give sb the** ~ enrolar alguém.

runaway ['rʌnəweɪ] ◇ *adj* [out of control - train, inflation] descontrolado(da); [- victory] fácil. ◇ *n* fugitivo *m*, -va *f*.

rundown ['rʌndaʊn] *n* -**1.** [report] relatório *m* detalhado -**2.** [decline] desmantelamento *m* gradual.

◆ **run-down** *adj* -**1.** [dilapidated] arruinado(da), em ruínas -**2.** [tired] esgotado(da).

rung [rʌŋ] ◇ *pp* ▷ **ring**. ◇ *n* degrau *m*.

run-in *n inf* rixa *f*.

runner ['rʌnə'] *n* -**1.** [athlete] corredor *m*, -ra *f* -**2.** [smuggler - guns] contrabandista *mf*; [- drugs] traficante *mf* -**3.** [wood or metal strip - of sledge, skate] lâmina *f*; [- of drawer] corrediça *f*.

runner bean *n UK* feijão-trepador *m*.

runner-up (*pl* runners-up) *n* segundo colocado *m*, segunda colocada *f*.

running ['rʌnɪŋ] ◇ *adj* -**1.** [continuous] constante -**2.** [consecutive] consecutivo(va) -**3.** [water - not stagnant] corrente; [- in pipes] encanado(da). ◇ *n* -**1.** (U) *SPORT* corrida *f*; **she loves** ~ **in the park** ela gosta de correr no parque -**2.** [management, control] gestão *f*, direção *f* -**3.** [of machine] funcionamento *m* -**4.** *phr*: **to make the** ~ tomar as rédeas; **to be in/out of the** ~ (**for sthg**) ter/não ter possibilidades (de algo). <> *comp SPORT* de corrida.

running commentary *n* comentário *m* ao vivo.

running costs *npl* despesas *fpl* de manutenção.

running mate *n US* candidato *m*, -ta *f* a vice-presidente.

running repairs *npl* pequenos reparos *mpl*.

runny ['rʌnɪ] (*compar* -ier, *superl* -iest) *adj* -1. [food - eggs] mal-passado(da); [- jam, honey] mole; [- butter, chocolate] derretido(da) -2. [nose] escorrendo -3. [eyes] lacrimejante.

run-of-the-mill *adj* corriqueiro(ra).

runt [rʌnt] *n* -1. [animal] filhote *m* mais fraco -2. *pej* [person] tampinha *mf*.

run-through *n* ensaio *m*.

run-up *n* -1. [preceding time] período *m* anterior -2. *SPORT* impulso *m*.

runway ['rʌnweɪ] *n* pista *f* (de pouso/decolagem).

rupture ['rʌptʃəʳ] *n* -1. *MED* hérnia *f* -2. [of relationship] rompimento *m*.

rural ['rʊərəl] *adj* rural.

ruse [ru:z] *n* ardil *m*.

rush [rʌʃ] <> *n* -1. [hurry] pressa *f*; there's no ~ não há pressa; to make a ~ for sthg disparar até algo -2. [demand]: ~ (for OR on sthg) procura *f* excessiva (por algo); ~ to do sthg corrida para fazer algo -3. [busiest period] corre-corre *m* -4. [surge - physical] fluxo *m*; ~ of air corrente *m* de ar; [- mental, emotional] torrente *f*. <> *vt* -1. [hurry] apressar; to ~ sb into sthg apressar alguém em algo; to ~ sb into doing sthg apressar alguém para que faça algo -2. [send quickly] levar com urgência -3. [attack suddenly] investir repentinamente contra. <> *vi* -1. [hurry] apressar-se; to ~ into sthg entrar de cabeça em algo -2. [crowd] correr.

➤ **rushes** *npl* -1. *BOT* juncos *mpl* -2. *CINEMA* primeiras cópias *fpl*.

rushed [rʌʃt] *adj* -1. [person] apressado(da) -2. [work] feito(ta) às pressas.

rush hour *n* hora *f* do rush.

rush job *n* -1. [urgent job] trabalho *m* urgente -2. [bad work] trabalho *m* feito às pressas.

rusk [rʌsk] *n* biscoito *m* seco.

russet ['rʌsɪt] *adj* ferrugíneo(nea).

Russia ['rʌʃə] *n* Rússia; in ~ na Rússia.

Russian ['rʌʃn] <> *adj* russo(sa). <> *n* -1. [person] russo *m*, -sa *f* -2. [language] russo *m*.

Russian roulette *n* (U) roleta *f* russa.

rust [rʌst] <> *n* (U) ferrugem *f*. <> *vi* enferrujar.

rustic ['rʌstɪk] *adj* rústico(ca).

rustle ['rʌsl] <> *n* ruído *m*. <> *vt* -1. [paper, leaves] farfalhar -2. *US* [cattle] roubar. <> *vi* farfalhar.

rustproof ['rʌstpru:f] *adj* inoxidável.

rusty ['rʌstɪ] (*compar* -ier, *superl* -iest) *adj* enferrujado(da).

rut [rʌt] *n* -1. [furrow] sulco *m*; to get into/be in a ~ tornar-se/ser escravo(va) da rotina -2. [animal] cio *m*.

rutabaga [ˌru:tə'beɪgə] *n US* nabo *m* sueco.

ruthless ['ru:θlɪs] *adj* impiedoso(sa).

ruthlessly ['ru:θlɪslɪ] *adv* impiedosamente.

ruthlessness ['ru:θlɪsnɪs] *n* (U) crueldade *f*.

RV *n* -1. (*abbr of* revised version) tradução da Bíblia para o inglês no final do século XIX -2. (*abbr of* recreational vehicle) *US* motor-home *m*.

Rwanda [rʊ'ændə] *n* Ruanda; in ~ em Ruanda.

Rwandan [rʊ'ændən] <> *adj* ruandês(esa). <> *n* ruandês *m*, -esa *f*.

rye [raɪ] *n* (U) centeio *m*.

rye bread *n* (U) pão *m* de centeio.

rye grass *n* (U) azevém *m*.

rye whiskey *n* (U) uísque *m* de centeio.

S

s (*pl* ss OR s's), **S** (*pl* Ss OR S's) [es] *n* [letter] s, S *m*.

➤ **S** (*abbr of* south) S.

SA -1. (*abbr of* South Africa) África *f* do Sul -2. (*abbr of* South America) América *f* do Sul -3. (*abbr of* South Australia) região sul da Austrália.

Saar *n*: the ~ o Sarre.

Sabbath ['sæbəθ] *n*: the ~ o sabá.

sabbatical [sə'bætɪkl] *n* período *m* sabático; on ~ em período sabático.

saber ['seɪbəʳ] *n US* = sabre.

sable *n* zibelina *f*.

sabotage ['sæbətɑ:ʒ] <> *n* (U) sabotagem *f*. <> *vt* sabotar.

saboteur [ˌsæbə'tɜːʳ] *n* sabotador *m*, -ra *f*.

sabre UK, **saber** US ['seɪbəʳ] *n* sabre *m*.

saccharin(e) ['sækərɪn] *n* (U) sacarina *f*.

sachet ['sæʃeɪ] *n* sachê *m*.

sack [sæk] <> *n* -1. [bag] saco *m* -2. *UK inf* [dismissal]: to get OR be given the ~ ser despedido(da). <> *vt* *UK inf* [dismiss] despedir, mandar embora.

sackful ['sækfʊl] *n* saca *f*.

sacking ['sækɪŋ] *n* (U) linhagem *f*.

sacrament ['sækrəmənt] *n* sacramento *m*.

sacred ['seɪkrɪd] *adj* sagrado(da).

sacrifice ['sækrɪfaɪs] <> *n* sacrifício *m*. <> *vt* sacrificar.

sacrilege ['sækrɪlɪdʒ] *n* (U) sacrilégio *m*.

sacrilegious [ˌsækrɪ'lɪdʒəs] *adj* sacrílego(ga).

sacrosanct ['sækrəʊsæŋkt] *adj* sacrossanto(ta).

sad [sæd] (*compar* -der, *superl* -dest) *adj* triste.

sadden ['sædn] *vt* entristecer.

saddle ['sædl] <> *n* -1. [for horse] sela *f* -2. [of bicycle, motorcycle] selim *m*. <> *vt* -1. [put saddle on] selar -2. *fig* [burden]: to ~ sb with sthg encarregar alguém de algo.

➤ **saddle up** <> *vt fus* selar. <> *vi* selar.

saddlebag ['sædlbæg] *n* -1. [for horse] alforje *m* -2.

[for bicycle, motorcycle] bolsa *f*.
saddler ['sædlə'] *n* seleiro *m*, -ra *f*.
sadism ['seɪdɪzm] *n (U)* sadismo *m*.
sadist ['seɪdɪst] *n* sádico *m*, -ca *f*.
sadistic [sə'dɪstɪk] *adj* sádico(ca).
sadly ['sædlɪ] *adv* **-1.** [sorrowfully] tristemente **-2.** [regrettably] lamentavelmente.
sadness ['sædnɪs] *n* tristeza *f*.
sadomasochistic *adj* sadomasoquista.
s.a.e., sae (*abbr of* **stamped addressed envelope**) *n* envelope-resposta com porte pago.
safari [sə'fɑːrɪ] *n* safári *m*; **to go on ~** fazer um safári.
safari park *n* parque-safári *m*.
safe [seɪf] *adj* **-1.** [not causing harm or danger] seguro(ra); **in ~ hands** em boas mãos **-2.** [not in danger] protegido(da); **to be ~ from attack** estar a salvo de ataques; **~ and sound** são e salvo, sã e salva **-3.** [not causing disagreement] pacífico(ca); **it's ~ to say that ...** pode-se dizer com segurança que ... **-4.** [not involving any risk] seguro(ra); **to be on the ~ side** por precaução **-5.** [secret] bem guardado(da). *n* cofre *m*.
safe-breaker *n* arrombador *m*, -ra *f* de cofre.
safe-conduct *n* **-1.** [document giving protection] salvo-conduto *m* **-2.** *(U)* [protection] salvaguarda *f*.
safe-deposit box *n* caixa-forte *f*.
safeguard ['seɪfgɑːd] *n* salvaguarda *f*, proteção *f*; **~ against sthg** proteção contra algo. *vt*: **to ~ sb/sthg (against sthg)** proteger *or* salvaguardar alguém/algo (de algo).
safe haven *n* refúgio *m*.
safe house *n* esconderijo *m*.
safe keeping *n (U)* proteção *f*, custódia *f*; **in sb's ~** aos cuidados de alguém.
safely ['seɪflɪ] *adv* **-1.** [gen] com segurança **-2.** [unharmed] ileso(sa), a salvo **-3.** [for certain]: **I can ~ say (that) ...** posso dizer seguramente que ...
safe sex *n (U)* sexo *m* seguro.
safety ['seɪftɪ] *n* segurança *f*. *comp* de segurança.
safety belt *n* cinto *m* de segurança.
safety catch *n* trava *f* de segurança.
safety curtain *n* cortina *f* corta-fogo, cortina *f* de amianto.
safety-deposit box *n* = **safe-deposit box**.
safety island *n US* ilha *f (na rua)*.
safety match *n* fósforo *m* de segurança.
safety net *n* **-1.** [in circus] rede *f* de segurança **-2.** *fig* [means of protection] proteção *f*.
safety pin *n* alfinete *m* de segurança.
safety valve *n* **-1.** *TECH* válvula *f* de segurança **-2.** *fig* [for emotions] válvula *f* de escape.
saffron ['sæfrən] *n (U)* **-1.** [spice] açafrão *m* **-2.** [colour] amarelo-laranja *m*.
sag [sæg] (*pt & pp* **-ged**, *cont* **-ging**) *vi* **-1.** [sink downwards] afundar, ceder **-2.** *fig* [lessen] diminuir.
saga ['sɑːgə] *n* **-1.** *LITERATURE* saga *f* **-2.** *pej* [drawn-out account] novela *f*.
sage [seɪdʒ] *adj* [wise] sábio(bia). *n* **-1.** *(U)* [herb] sálvia *f* **-2.** [wise man] sábio *m*.
saggy ['sægɪ] (*compar* **-ier**, *superl* **-iest**) *adj* [bed] afundado(da); [breasts] caído(da).

Sagittarius [ˌsædʒɪ'teərɪəs] *n* **-1.** [sign] Sagitário *m* **-2.** [person] sagitariano *m*, -na *f*; **I'm ~** sou de Sagitário.
Sahara [sə'hɑːrə] *n*: **the ~ (Desert)** o (Deserto do) Saara.
Saharan [sə'hɑːrən] *adj* saariano(na).
said [sed] *pt & pp* say.
sail [seɪl] *n* **-1.** [of boat] vela *f*; **to set ~** zarpar **-2.** [journey by boat]: **let's go for a ~** vamos velejar. *vt* **-1.** [boat] governar **-2.** [sea] cruzar. *vi* **-1.** [to depart] zarpar **-2.** [sport] velejar **-3.** [to travel, move - person] navegar; [- boat] singrar **-4.** *fig* [through air] voar.
sail through *vt fus* passar fácil por.
sailboard ['seɪlbɔːd] *n* prancha *f* de windsurfe.
sailboat *n US* = **sailing boat**.
sailcloth ['seɪlklɒθ] *n (U)* lona *f*.
sailing ['seɪlɪŋ] *n* **-1.** *(U)* *SPORT* navegação *f* a vela, vela *f*; **I like to go ~** eu gosto de (ir) velejar; **plain ~** sem maiores dificuldades **-2.** [trip by ship] travessia *f*.
sailing boat *UK*, **sailboat** *US* ['seɪlbəʊt] *n* barco *m* a vela.
sailing dinghy *n* dinga *f*.
sailing ship *n* veleiro *m*.
sailor ['seɪlə'] *n* marinheiro *m*, -ra *f*; **to be a good ~** não ficar mareado(da).
saint [seɪnt] *n* **-1.** *RELIG* santo *m*, -ta *f* **-2.** *inf* [very good person] santo *m*, -ta *f*.

SAINT PATRICK'S DAY

Em 17 de março, comemora-se o dia de são Patrício, o patrono da Irlanda. Lá, esse dia é feriado nacional, mas a data é celebrada também em várias partes do mundo pelos irlandeses ou seus descendentes, sobretudo nos Estados Unidos. Nesse dia, a tradição manda usar um *shamrock*, uma espécie de trevo, que é o emblema nacional da Irlanda; ou vestir verde, que é a cor que representa o país.

Saint Helena *n* Santa Helena.
Saint Lawrence *n*: **the ~ (River)** o (Rio) São Lourenço.
Saint Lucia *n* Santa Lúcia.
saintly ['seɪntlɪ] (*compar* **-ier**, *superl* **-iest**) *adj* santo(ta), santificado(da).
Saint Petersburg *n* São Petersburgo.
sake [seɪk] *n* **-1.** [benefit, advantage]: **for the ~ of** para o bem de; **for my ~** por mim **-2.** [purpose]: **for the ~ of** pelo bem de; **let us say, for the ~ of argument, that ...** digamos, só para argumentar, que ... **-3.** *phr*: **to do sthg for its own ~** fazer algo só por fazer; **for God's** *or* **Heaven's ~!** pelo amor de Deus!
salad ['sæləd] *n* salada *f*.
salad bowl *n* saladeira *f*.
salad cream *n (U)* *UK* molho *m* para salada *(à base de maionese)*.
salad dressing *n (U)* molho *m* para salada *(à base de vinagre, óleo e ervas)*.
salad oil *n (U)* azeite *m* para salada.
salamander ['sæləˌmændə'] *n* salamandra *f*.
salami [sə'lɑːmɪ] *n (U)* salame *m*.

salaried ['sælərɪd] *adj* **-1.** [employee] assalariado(da) **-2.** [job] remunerado(da).

salary ['sælərɪ] (*pl* **-ies**) *n* salário *m*.

salary scale *n* escala *f* salarial.

sale [seɪl] *n* **-1.** [gen] venda *f*; **on** ~ à venda; **(up)for** ~ à venda; **'for** ~**'** 'vende-se' **-2.** [at reduced prices] liquidação *f*, saldo *m* **-3.** [auction] leilão *m*.
◆ **sales** *npl* **-1.** [quantity sold] vendas *fpl* **-2.** [at reduced prices]: **the** ~**s** os saldos. *comp* de vendas.

saleroom *UK* ['seɪlruml, **salesroom** *US* ['seɪlzrum] *n* sala *f* de leilão.

sales assistant ['seɪlz-], **salesclerk** *US* ['seɪlzklɜːrk] *n* balconista *mf*, vendedor *m*, -ra *f (em loja)*.

sales conference *n* conferência *f* de vendas.

sales drive *n* campanha *f* de vendas.

sales force *n* força *f* de vendas.

salesman ['seɪlzmən] (*pl* **-men** [-mən]) *n* [gen] vendedor *m*; [representative] representante *m* de vendas.

sales pitch *n* lábia *f* de vendedor.

sales rep *n inf* representante *mf* de vendas.

sales representative *n* representante *mf* de vendas.

salesroom *n US* = saleroom.

sales slip *n* recibo *m*.

sales tax *n* (*U*) imposto pago ao governo sobre mercadorias ou bens comprados.

sales team *n* equipe *f* de vendas.

saleswoman ['seɪlz,wumən] (*pl* **-women** [-,wɪmɪn]) *n* [gen] vendedora *f*; [representative] representante *f* de vendas.

salient ['seɪljənt] *adj fml* evidente, notável.

saline ['seɪlam] *adj* salino(na).

saliva [sə'laɪvə] *n* (*U*) saliva *f*.

salivate ['sælɪveɪt] *vi* salivar.

sallow ['sæləʊ] *adj* amarelado(da).

sally ['sælɪ] (*pl* **-ies**, *pt & pp* **-ied**) *n* gracejo *m*, chiste *m*.
◆ **sally forth** *vi hum or literary* sair com garra e ímpeto.

salmon ['sæmən] (*pl inv OR* **-s**) *n* salmão *m*.

salmonella [,sælmə'nelə] *n* (*U*) salmonela *f*.

salmon pink *adj* rosa-salmão. *n* rosa-salmão *f*.

salon ['sælɒn] *n* **-1.** [hairdresser's] salão *m* **-2.** [clothes shop] butique *f*.

saloon [sə'luːn] *n* **-1.** *UK* [car] sedã *m* **-2.** *US* [bar] bar *m* **-3.** *UK* [in pub]: ~ **(bar)** em alguns pubs e hotéis, bar finamente decorado e de preços mais altos do que os do public bar **-4.** [on ship] salão *m*.

salopettes [,sælə'pets] *npl* calças *fpl* de ski.

salt [sɔːlt, sɒlt] *n* **-1.** sal *m* **-2.** *phr*: **the** ~ **of the earth** o sal da terra; **to rub** ~ **into sb's wounds** pôr o dedo na ferida (de alguém); **to take sthg with a pinch of** ~ ficar com o pé atrás em relação a algo, considerar algo com uma certa reserva. *comp* salgado(da). *vt* **-1.** [food] salgar **-2.** [roads] jogar sal em (para derreter o gelo).
◆ **salt away** *vt sep inf* guardar.

SALT [sɔːlt] (*abbr of* Strategic Arms Limitation Talks/Treaty) *n* SALT *m*.

salt cellar *UK*, **salt shaker** *US* [-,ʃeɪkə'] *n* saleiro *m*.

salted ['sɔːltɪd] *adj* salgado(da), com sal.

saltpetre *UK*, **saltpeter** *US* [,sɔːlt'piːtə'] *n* (*U*) salitre *m*.

salt shaker *n US* = salt cellar.

saltwater ['sɔːlt,wɔːtə'] *adj* de água salgada. *n* (*U*) água *f* salgada, água *f* do mar.

salty ['sɔːltɪ] (*compar* **-ier**, *superl* **-iest**) *adj* salgado(da).

salubrious [sə'luːbrɪəs] *adj* salubre.

salutary ['sæljʊtrɪ] *adj* salutar.

salute [sə'luːt] *n* **-1.** MIL [with hand] continência *f* **-2.** MIL [firing of guns] salva *f* **-3.** (*U*) [act of saluting] cumprimento *m* **-4.** [formal acknowledgment] saudação *f*. *vt* **-1.** MIL [with hand] fazer continência a **-2.** [acknowledge formally, honour] cumprimentar. *vi* MIL [with hand] fazer continência.

Salvadorean, Salvadorian [,sælvə'dɔːrɪən] *adj* salvadorenho(nha). *n* salvadorenho *m*, -nha *f*.

salvage ['sælvɪdʒ] *n* **-1.** [rescue of ship] salvamento *m* **-2.** [property rescued] objetos *mpl* recuperados. *vt* **-1.** [rescue]: **to** ~ **sthg (from)** salvar algo (de) **-2.** *fig* [gain from failure]: **to** ~ **sthg (from)** preservar algo (de).

salvage vessel *n* barco *m* de salvamento.

salvation [sæl'veɪʃn] *n* salvação *f*.

Salvation Army *n*: **the** ~ o Exército da Salvação.

salve [sælv] *vt*: **to do sthg to** ~ **one's conscience** fazer algo para aliviar a consciência.

salver ['sælvə'] *n* salva *f*, bandeja *f*.

salvo ['sælvəʊ] (*pl* **-s** *OR* **-es**) *n* salva *f*.

Samaritan [sə'mærɪtn] *n*: **good** ~ bom samaritano *m*.

samba ['sæmbə] *n* samba *m*.

same [seɪm] *adj* [gen] mesmo(ma); **at the** ~ **time** [simultaneously] ao mesmo tempo; [yet] mesmo assim; **one and the** ~ o mesmo, a mesma. *adv*: **the** ~ o mesmo, a mesma. *pron* [unchanged, identical]: **the** ~ o mesmo, a mesma; **the hats they were wearing were the** ~ os chapéus que eles estavam usando eram iguais; **all** *OR* **just the** ~ [nevertheless, anyway] mesmo assim; **it's all the** ~ **to me** para mim dá no mesmo, para mim tanto faz; **it's not the** ~ não é a mesma coisa.

sameness ['seɪmnɪs] *n* **-1.** (*U*) [lack of variety] mesmice *f* **-2.** [similarity] uniformidade *f*.

Samoa [sə'məʊə] *n* Samoa *f*; **in** ~ em Samoa; **American** ~ Samoa Americana *OR* Oriental.

Samoan [sə'məʊən] *adj* samoano(na). *n* samoano *m*, -na *f*.

samosa [sə'məʊsə] *n* espécie de pastel indiano feito de vegetais, temperos e carne.

sample ['saːmpl] *n* amostra *f*. *vt* **-1.** [taste] provar *n* **-2.** [try out, test] experimentar **-3.** MUS amostrar.

sampler ['saːmplə'] *n* SEWING bordado com palavras e figuras bordadas, normalmente feito como prova da habilidade de quem o confeccionou.

sanatorium (*pl* **-riums** *OR* **-ria** [-rɪə]), **sanitorium** *US* (*pl* **-riums** *OR* **-ria** [-rɪə]) [,sænə'tɔːrɪəm] *n* sanatório *m*.

sanctify ['sæŋktɪfaɪ] (*pt* & *pp* **-ied**) *vt* **-1.** RELIG santificar - **2.** [approve] abençoar.

sanctimonious [,sæŋktɪ'məʊnjəs] *adj pej* santarrão(rrona).

sanction ['sæŋkʃn] <> *n* sanção *f.* <> *vt* sancionar.

<> **sanctions** *npl* POL sanções *fpl.*

sanctity ['sæŋktətɪ] *n* (U) santidade *f.*

sanctuary ['sæŋktʃʊərɪ] (*pl* **-ies**) *n* **-1.** [gen] santuário *m* - **2.** [place of safety] abrigo *m* - **3.** (U) [safety, refuge] refúgio *m.*

sanctum ['sæŋktəm] (*pl* **-s**) *n inf* lugar *m* sagrado, santuário *m.*

sand [sænd] <> *n* (U) areia *f.* <> *vt* lixar.

<> **sands** *npl* [beach] areias *fpl.*

<> **sand down** *vt sep* lixar.

sandal ['sændl] *n* sandália *f.*

sandalwood ['sændlwʊd] *n* (U) sândalo *m.*

sandbag ['sændbæg] *n* saco *m* de areia.

sandbank ['sændbæŋk] *n* banco *m* de areia.

sandblast ['sændblɑːst] *vt limpar com jato de areia.*

sandbox *n US* = **sandpit.**

sandcastle ['sænd,kɑːsl] *n* castelo *m* de areia.

sand dune *n* duna *f.*

sander ['sændəʳ] *n* lixadeira *f.*

sandpaper ['sænd,peɪpəʳ] <> *n* (U) lixa *f.* <> *vt* lixar.

sandpit UK ['sændpɪt], **sandbox** US ['sændbɒks] *n* caixa *f* de areia.

sandstone ['sændstəʊn] *n* (U) arenito *m.*

sandstorm ['sændstɔːm] *n* tempestade *f* de areia.

sand trap *n US* GOLF armadilha *f* de areia.

sandwich ['sænwɪdʒ] <> *n* sanduíche *m.* <> *vt* *fig*: to be ~ ed between ser prensado(da) entre.

sandwich course *n UK curso universitário que inclui um certo tempo de experiência profissional.*

sandy ['sændɪ] (*compar* **-ier**, *superl* **-iest**) *adj* **-1.** [made of sand] arenoso(sa) - **2.** [sand-coloured] cor-de-areia.

sane [seɪn] *adj* **-1.** [not mad] são(sã) - **2.** [sensible] sensato(ta).

sang [sæŋ] *pt* <> **sing.**

sanguine ['sæŋgwɪn] *adj* esperançoso(sa), otimista.

sanitary ['sænɪtrɪ] *adj* **-1.** [connected with health] sanitário(ria) - **2.** [clean, hygienic] higiênico(ca).

sanitary towel, sanitary napkin US *n* absorvente *m* higiênico.

sanitation [,sænɪ'teɪʃn] *n* **-1.** [in streets] saneamento *m* - **2.** [in houses] instalações *fpl* sanitárias.

sanitation worker *n US* lixeiro *m*, -ra *f.*

sanitize, -ise ['sænɪtaɪz] *vt* suavizar.

sanitorium *n US* = **sanatorium.**

sanity ['sænətɪ] *n* **-1.** [saneness] sanidade *f* - **2.** [good sense] sensatez *f.*

sank [sæŋk] *pt* <> **sink.**

San Marino [,sænmə'riːnəʊ] *n* San Marino; **in** ~ em San Marino.

San Salvador [,sæn'sælvədɔːʳ] *n* São Salvador.

Sanskrit ['sænskrɪt] *n* sânscrito *m.*

Santa (Claus) ['sæntə(,klɔːz)] *n* Papai *m* Noel.

São Paulo [,saʊ'paʊləʊ] *n* São Paulo.

sap [sæp] (*pt* & *pp* **-ped**, *cont* **-ping**) <> *n* **-1.** (U) [of plant] seiva *m* - **2.** US inf [gullible person] bobo(ba). <> *vt* enfraquecer, consumir.

sapling ['sæplɪŋ] *n* árvore *m* nova, arvorezinha *f.*

sapphire ['sæfaɪəʳ] *n* safira *f.*

Sarajevo [,særə'jeɪvəʊ] *n* Sarajevo.

sarcasm ['sɑːkæzm] *n* (U) sarcasmo *m.*

sarcastic [sɑː'kæstɪk] *adj* sarcástico(ca).

sarcophagus [sɑː'kɒfəgəs] (*pl* **-gi** [-gaɪ], **-es**) *n* sarcófago *m.*

sardine [sɑː'diːn] *n* sardinha *f.*

Sardinia [sɑː'dɪnjə] *n* Sardenha; **in** ~ na Sardenha.

sardonic [sɑː'dɒnɪk] *adj* mordaz.

Sargasso Sea [sɑː'gæsəʊ-] *n*: **the** ~ o Mar de Sargaço.

sari ['sɑːrɪ] *n* sári *m.*

sarong [sə'rɒŋ] *n* sarongue *m.*

sarsaparilla [,sɑːspə'rɪlə] *n* salsaparrilha *f.*

sartorial [sɑː'tɔːrɪəl] *adj fml* no vestir.

SAS (*abbr of* **Special Air Service**) *n unidade especial do exército britânico encarregada de operações de antiterrorismo e sabotagem.*

SASE (*abbr of* **self-addressed stamped envelope**) *n US envelope auto-endereçado e já selado.*

sash [sæʃ] *n* faixa *f.*

sash window *n* janela *f* de guilhotina.

Saskatchewan [,sæs'kætʃɪwən] *n* Saskatchewan.

sassy ['sæsɪ] *adj US inf* descarado(da), atrevido(da).

sat [sæt] *pt* & *pp* <> **sit.**

Sat. (*abbr of* **Saturday**) sáb.

SAT [sæt] *n* **-1.** (*abbr of* **Standard Assessment Test**) *exames de aptidão que os estudantes da Inglaterra e do País de Gales prestam aos 7, 11 e 14 anos de idade* - **2.** (*abbr of* **Scholastic Aptitude Test**) *exame prestado por estudantes no último ano da escola secundária nos Estados Unidos, importante ao se ingressar na universidade.*

SAT

O *Scholastic Aptitude Test* (SAT) é uma prova de conhecimentos gerais aplicada nos EUA àqueles que desejam ingressar na universidade. A prova é realizada em certas datas fixas, ao longo do ano letivo, e pode ser prestada mais de uma vez. Embora seja pré-requisito importante para o ingresso na universidade, o SAT não é o único critério de admissão. Qualificações e atividades do estudante também são levadas em consideração.

Satan ['seɪtn] *n* Satã *m*, Satanás *m.*

satanic [sə'tænɪk] *adj* satânico(ca).

satchel ['sætʃəl] *n* pasta *f*, mochila *f* escolar.

sated ['seɪtɪd] *adj fml* saciado(da); ~ **with sthg** saciado(da) com algo.

satellite ['sætəlaɪt] <> *n* satélite *m.* <> *comp* **-1.** TELEC por satélite - **2.** [dependent]: ~ **city** cidade-satélite *f.*

satellite dish *n* [for TV] antena *f* parabólica.

satellite TV *n* tevê *f* via satélite.

satiate ['seɪʃɪeɪt] *vt fml* saciar.

satin ['sætɪn] <> *n* (U) cetim *m.* <> *comp* **-1.** [made

of satin] de cetim **-2.** [smooth] acetinado(da).
satire ['sætaɪə'] n sátira f.
satirical [sə'tɪrɪkl] adj satírico(ca).
satirist ['sætərɪst] n satirista mf.
satirize, -ise ['sætəraɪz] vt satirizar.
satisfaction [,sætɪs'fækʃn] n **-1.** [gen] satisfação f;
to do sthg to sb's ~ fazer algo ao gosto de
alguém **-2.** *(U)* [fulfilment of need] atendimento m,
cumprimento m; ~ **guaranteed** satisfação garan-
tida.
satisfactory [,sætɪs'fæktərɪ] adj satisfatório(ria).
satisfied ['sætɪsfaɪd] adj **-1.** [happy] satisfeito(ta); **to
be ~ with** sthg estar satisfeito(ta) com algo **-2.**
[convinced] convencido(da); **to be ~ (that)** estar
convencido(da) de que.
satisfy ['sætɪsfaɪ] (pt & pp **-ied**) vt **-1.** [make happy]
satisfazer **-2.** [convince] convencer; **to ~ sb that**
convencer alguém de que; **to ~ o.s.** that
convencer-se de que **-3.** [fulfil] satisfazer, atender
a.
satisfying ['sætɪsfaɪɪŋ] adj satisfatório(ria), agradável.
satsuma [,sæt'su:mə] n tipo de tangerina proveniente do Japão.
saturate ['sætʃəreɪt] vt **-1.** [drench] ensopar, empapar; **to ~** sthg **with** sthg ensopar OR empapar algo
com algo **-2.** [fill completely, swamp] inundar; **to ~**
sthg **with** sthg saturar algo com algo.
saturated adj **-1.** [drenched] ensopado(da), empa-
pado(da) **-2.** [fat] saturado(da).
saturation [,sætʃə'reɪʃn] <> n **-1.** [drenching] enso-
pamento m **-2.** [complete filling] saturamento m. <>
comp [bombing] por saturação; [TV] ~ **coverage**
cobertura f exaustiva.
saturation point n: **to reach ~** alcançar o
ponto de saturação.
Saturday ['sætədɪ] <> n sábado m; **what day is it?
- it's ~** que dia é hoje? - é sábado; **are you going
~?** inf você vai sábado?; **see you ~!** inf até
sábado!; **on ~** no sábado; **on ~s** aos sábados; **to
work ~s** trabalhar aos sábados; **last ~** sábado
passado; **this ~** este sábado; **next ~** sábado da
semana que vem; **every ~** todos os sábados;
every other ~ um sábado sim, outro não; **the ~
before** no sábado anterior; **the ~ before last** há
dois sábados; **the ~ after next, ~ week, a week on
~** não no próximo sábado, no outro. <> comp
aos sábados; **~ morning/afternoon/night** sábado
de manhã/tarde/noite; **~ evening** no fim da
tarde de sábado; **a ~ job** um trabalho aos
sábados.
Saturn ['sætɜ:n] n Saturno.
sauce [sɔ:s] n **-1.** CULIN molho m **-2.** UK inf [cheek]
atrevimento m.
sauce boat n molheira f.
saucepan ['sɔ:spən] n panela f com um cabo.
saucer ['sɔ:sə'] n pires m inv.
saucy ['sɔ:sɪ] (compar **-ier**, superl **-iest**) adj inf atrevi-
do(da).
Saudi Arabia [,saʊdɪə'reɪbjə] n Arábia Saudita; **in
~** na Arábia Saudita.
Saudi (Arabian) ['saʊdɪ-] <> adj árabe-saudita.
<> n árabe-saudita mf.

sauna ['sɔ:nə] n sauna f.
saunter ['sɔ:ntə'] vi passear (tranqüilamente).
sausage ['sɒsɪdʒ] n **-1.** *(U)* [meat] lingüiça f **-2.**
[shaped piece of meat] salsicha f.
sausage roll n UK enroladinho m de salsicha.
sauté [UK 'saʊteɪ, US saʊ'teɪ] (pt & pp **sautéed** OR **sa-
utéd**) <> adj sauté. <> vt fritar levemente.
savage ['sævɪdʒ] <> adj selvagem. <> n selvagem
mf. <> vt **-1.** [attack physically] atacar ferozmente
-2. [criticize] atacar.
savageness ['sævɪdʒnɪs], **savagery** ['sævɪdʒrɪ] n
(U) selvageria f.
savanna(h) [sə'vænə] n savana f.
save [seɪv] <> n SPORT defesa f. <> prep fml: ~ **(for)**
exceto. <> vt **-1.** [gen] salvar; **to ~ sb from** sthg/
from doing sthg salvar alguém de algo/de fazer
algo; **to ~ sb's life** salvar a vida de alguém **-2.**
[prevent waste of] economizar **-3.** [set aside] guardar
-4. [make unnecessary] poupar; **to ~ sb/sthg from
doing** sthg poupar alguém/algo de fazer algo
-5. SPORT defender. <> vi economizar.
 save up vi economizar.
save as you earn n UK forma de poupança em
que a contribuição mensal gera renda livre de
impostos.
saveloy ['sævələɪ] n UK salsichão m de porco.
saver ['seɪvə'] n **-1.** [object]: **a time/money ~** algo
que economiza tempo/dinheiro **-2.** FIN [at bank,
building society] poupador m, -ra f.
saving grace ['seɪvɪŋ-] n mérito m.
savings ['seɪvɪŋz] npl economias fpl.
savings account n US (caderneta f de) poupança f.
savings and loan association n US sociedade
f de empréstimos imobiliários.
savings bank n caixa f econômica, banco m só
de cadernetas de poupança.
saviour UK, **savior** US ['seɪvjə'] n salvador m, -ra f.
 Saviour n: **the Saviour** o Salvador.
savoir-faire [,sævwa:'feə'] n *(U)* savoir-faire m.
savour UK, **savor** US ['seɪvə'] vt **-1.** [enjoy taste of]
saborear **-2.** fig [enjoy greatly] saborear, aproveitar.
savoury UK (pl **-ies**), **savory** (pl **-ies**) US ['seɪvərɪ]
<> adj **-1.** [not sweet] condimentado(da) **-2.** [re-
spectable, pleasant] agradável. <> n tira-gosto m.
Savoy n Savoy.
savoy (cabbage) n repolho m crespo.
saw [sɔ:] (UK pt **-ed**, pp **sawn**, US pt & pp **-ed**) <> pt
▷ **see**. <> n serra f. <> vt serrar.
 saw up vt sep serrar.
sawdust ['sɔ:dʌst] n *(U)* serragem f.
sawed-off shotgun n US = **sawn-off shotgun**.
sawmill ['sɔ:mɪl] n serraria f.
sawn [sɔ:n] pp UK ▷ **saw**.
sawn-off shotgun UK, **sawed-off shotgun**
US [sɔ:d-] n arma f de cano serrado.
sax [sæks] n inf sax m.
Saxon ['sæksn] <> adj saxão(xã). <> n saxão m,
-xã f.
saxophone ['sæksəfəʊn] n saxofone m.
saxophonist [UK ,sæks'ɒfənɪst, US 'sæksəfəʊnɪst] n
saxofonista mf.
say [seɪ] (pt & pp **said**) <> vt **-1.** [gen] dizer; **to ~**

sthg again repetir algo; **to ~ yes** dizer que sim; **to ~ to o.s.** dizer para si mesmo(ma); **to ~ nothing of** sem mencionar; **to ~ (that)** dizer que; **he's said to be the best footballer in the world** dizem que ele é o melhor jogador do mundo - **2.** [giving information] mostrar; **the clock ~s two thirty** o relógio está marcando duas e meia - **3.** [assume, suppose] supor; **let's ~ you win** digamos que você vença - **4.** *phr:* **that goes without ~ing** nem precisa dizer isso; **I'll ~ this for him/her ...** há que se admitir OR dizer que ele/ela ...; **it has a lot to be said for it** tem muitos pontos em seu favor; **she didn't have much to ~ for herself** *inf* ela era uma pessoa muito reservada; **what have you got to ~ for yourself?** o que você tem a dizer para se defender?; **you don't ~!** não diga!, não é verdade! <> *n* [power of decision]: **to have a/no ~ (in sthg)** ter/não ter voz nem vez (em algo); **let me have my ~** deixe-me dizer o que eu penso.
◆ **that is to say** *adv* quer dizer.

SAYE (*abbr of* **save as you earn**) *n* tipo de poupança na Grã-Bretanha com vantagens em relação a impostos.

saying ['seɪŋ] *n* ditado *m* popular, dito *m*.

say-so *n inf* [permission] permissão *f*.

SBA (*abbr of* **Small Business Administration**) *n* órgão do governo norte-americano de ajuda à pequena empresa.

s/c (*abbr of* **self-contained**) *UK* acomodação, normalmente um apartamento, que contém cozinha, banheiro e geralmente porta externa próprios.

SC <> *n* (*abbr of* **supreme court**) ≃ STF *m*. <> *abbr of* **South Carolina**.

scab [skæb] *n* - **1.** [of wound] casca *f*, crosta *f* - **2.** *pej* [non-striker] fura-greve *mf*.

scabby ['skæbɪ] (*compar* -ier, *superl* -iest) *adj* coberto(ta) de feridas.

scabies ['skeɪbi:z] *n* (U) sarna *f*.

scaffold ['skæfəʊld] *n* - **1.** [frame] andaime *m* - **2.** [for executions] cadafalso *m*, patíbulo *m*.

scaffolding ['skæfəldɪŋ] *n* (U) andaime *m*.

scalawag *n US* = **scallywag**.

scald [skɔːld] <> *n* escaldadura *f*. <> *vt* escaldar.

scalding ['skɔːldɪŋ] *adj* escaldante.

scale [skeɪl] <> *n* - **1.** [gen] escala *f*; **to ~ em** escala - **2.** [size, extent] tamanho *m*; **on a large ~** de grande escala - **3.** [of fish, snake] escama *f* - **4.** *US* = **scales**. <> *vt* - **1.** [climb] escalar - **2.** [remove scales from] escamar.
◆ **scales** *npl* balança *f*.
◆ **scale down** *vt fus* reduzir.

scale diagram *n* diagrama *m* em escala.

scale model *n* maquete *f*.

scallion ['skæljən] *n US & Irish* [spring onion] cebolinha *f* verde.

scallop ['skɒləp] <> *n* [shellfish] vieira *f*. <> *vt* [decorate edge of] guarnecer.

scallywag *UK* ['skælɪwæg], **scalawag** *US* ['skæləwæg] *n* - **1.** *inf* [child] pestinha *mf* - **2.** [adult] safado(-da).

scalp [skælp] <> *n* - **1.** ANAT couro *m* cabeludo - **2.** [removed from head] escalpo *m*. <> *vt* escalpelar.

scalpel ['skælpəl] *n* bisturi *m*.

scalper ['skælpəʳ] *n US* [tout] cambista *mf*.

scam [skæm] *n inf* esquema *f*, estratagema *m*.

scamp [skæmp] *n inf* pestinha *mf*, moleque *mf*.

scamper ['skæmpəʳ] *vi* fugir rapidamente.

scampi ['skæmpɪ] *n* (U) camarão-castanho *m*.

scan [skæn] (*pt & pp* -ned, *cont* -ning) <> *n* MED & TECH exame *m*, escaneamento *m*. <> *vt* - **1.** [gen]
• **escanear - 2.** [examine carefully] examinar cuidadosamente - **3.** [glance at] correr os olhos por. <> *vi* - **1.** LITERATURE estar bem escandido(da) - **2.** COMPUT escanear.

scandal ['skændl] *n* escândalo *m*.

scandalize, ise ['skændəlaɪz] *vt* escandalizar.

scandalous ['skændələs] *adj* - **1.** [shocking] escandaloso(sa) - **2.** [infuriating] exasperador(ra).

Scandinavia [ˌskændɪ'neɪvjə] *n* Escandinávia; **in ~** na Escandinávia.

Scandinavian [ˌskændɪ'neɪvjən] <> *adj* escandinavo(va). <> *n* escandinavo *m*, -va *f*.

scanner ['skænəʳ] *n* escaneador *m*, scanner *m*.

scant [skænt] *adj* insuficiente, escasso(sa).

scanty ['skæntɪ] (*compar* -ier, *superl* -iest) *adj* - **1.** [dress] mínimo(ma) - **2.** [amount, resources] escasso(sa) - **3.** [meal] insuficiente.

scapegoat ['skeɪpgəʊt] *n* bode *m* expiatório.

scar [skɑːʳ] (*pt & pp* -red, *cont* -ring) <> *n* - **1.** [physical] cicatriz *f* - **2.** *fig* [mental] seqüela *f*. <> *vt* - **1.** [physically] deixar cicatriz em - **2.** *fig* [mentally] deixar seqüelas em.

scarce ['skeəs] *adj* escasso(sa); **to make o.s. ~** manter-se afastado(da).

scarcely ['skeəslɪ] *adv* apenas; **~ anyone/ever** quase ninguém/nunca.

scarcity ['skeəsətɪ] *n* (U) escassez *f*.

scare [skeəʳ] <> *n* - **1.** [sudden fright] susto *m* - **2.** [public panic] ameaça *f*; **bomb ~** ameaça de bomba. <> *vt* assustar.
◆ **scare away, scare off** *vt sep* afugentar.

scarecrow ['skeəkrəʊ] *n* espantalho *m*.

scared ['skeəd] *adj* - **1.** [very frightened] apavorado(da); **to be ~ stiff** OR **to death** estar morrendo de medo - **2.** [nervous, worried]: **to be ~ that ...** estar com medo de que ...

scaremonger *n* alarmista *mf*.

scarey ['skeərɪ] *adj* = **scary**.

scarf [skɑːf] (*pl* -s OR **scarves**) *n* - **1.** [long - to keep warm] cachecol *m*; [- as accessory] echarpe *f* - **2.** [square] lenço *m*.

scarlet ['skɑːlət] <> *adj* escarlate. <> *n* escarlate *m*.

scarlet fever *n* (U) escarlatina *f*.

scarper *vi UK inf* fugir.

scarves [skɑːvz] *pl* > **scarf**.

scary ['skeərɪ] (*compar* -ier, *superl* -iest) *adj inf* apavorante.

scathing ['skeɪðɪŋ] *adj* mordaz; **to be ~ about sb/sthg** fazer uma crítica mordaz a alguém/algo.

scatter ['skætəʳ] <> *vt* espalhar. <> *vi* dispersar-se.
◆ **scatter about, scatter around** *vt sep* espalhar.

scatterbrained ['skætəbreɪnd] *adj inf* desmiolado(da), avoado(da).

scattered ['skætəd] *adj* disperso(sa).

scattering ['skætərɪŋ] *n*: **a ~ of snow** uma fina camada de neve.

scatty ['skætɪ] (*compar* **-ier**, *superl* **-iest**) *adj UK inf* desmiolado(da), avoado(da).

scavenge ['skævɪndʒ] <> *vt* [subj: animal, bird]: **to ~ sthg** cavucar algo; *fig* [subj: person] cavucar algo. <> *vi* [animal, bird]: **to ~ for sthg** cavucar por algo; *fig* [person] cavucar por algo.

scavenger ['skævɪndʒə^r] *n* **-1.** [animal] *animal que se alimenta de carniça* **-2.** *fig* [person] catador *m*, -ra *f* de lixo.

SCE (*abbr of* **Scottish Certificate of Education**) *n* *exame de conhecimentos em três níveis prestado pelos estudantes na Escócia.*

scenario [sɪ'nɑːrɪəʊ] (*pl* **-s**) *n* cenário *m*.

scene [siːn] *n* **-1.** [gen] cena *f*; **on the ~** no local; **a change of ~** uma mudança de ares *or* ambiente; **behind the ~s** nos bastidores **-2.** [picture of place] paisagem *f*, cenário *m* **-3.** [sight, impression] vista *f* **-4.** [area of activity] área *f* **-5.** [embarrassing fuss] cena *f*, escândalo *m* **-6.** *phr*: **to set the ~** [for person] descrever a cena; [for event] preparar o cenário.

scenery ['siːnərɪ] *n (U)* **-1.** [of countryside] paisagem *f* **-2.** THEATRE cenário *m*.

scenic ['siːnɪk] *adj* **-1.** [view] pitoresco(ca) **-2.** [tour] turístico(ca).

scenic route *n* rota *f* turística.

scent [sent] <> *n* **-1.** [smell - of flowers] perfume *m*, fragrância *f*; [- of animal] cheiro *m*, odor *m* **-2.** *fig* [track] rastro *m*, pista *f* **-3.** *(U)* [perfume] perfume *m*. <> *vt* **-1.** [subj: animal] farejar **-2.** *fig* [subj: person] sentir cheiro de.

scented ['sentɪd] *adj* perfumado(da).

scepter *n US* = **sceptre**.

sceptic *UK*, **skeptic** *US* ['skeptɪk] *n* céptico(ca).

sceptical *UK*, **skeptical** *US* ['skeptɪkl] *adj* céptico(ca); **to be ~ about sthg** ser céptico(ca) em relação a algo.

scepticism *UK*, **skepticism** *US* ['skeptɪsɪzm] *n (U)* ceticismo *m*.

sceptre *UK*, **scepter** *US* ['septə^r] *n* cetro *m*.

SCF (*abbr of* **Save the Children Fund**) *n organização internacional de caridade pelo bem-estar das crianças.*

schedule [*UK* 'ʃedjuːl, *US* 'skedʒʊl] <> *n* **-1.** [plan] plano *m*; **(according) to ~** de acordo com o planejado; **to be ahead of ~** estar adiantado(da); **to be behind ~** estar atrasado(da); **on ~** sem atraso **-2.** [written list - of prices, contents] lista *f*; [- of times] horários *mpl*. <> *vt*: **to ~ sthg (for)** marcar algo(para).

scheduled flight [*UK* 'ʃedjuːld-, *US* 'skedʒʊld-] *n* vôo *m* regular.

schematic [skɪ'mætɪk] *adj* esquemático(ca).

scheme [skiːm] <> *n* **-1.** [plan] projeto *m* **-2.** *pej* [dishonest plan] esquema *f* **-3.** [arrangement, decoration] disposição *f*; **colour ~** combinação *f* de cores **-4.** *phr*: **in the ~ of things** na ordem das coisas. <> *vt pej*: **to ~ to do sthg** conspirar para fazer algo. <> *vi pej* tramar.

scheming ['skiːmɪŋ] *adj* que faz intriga.

schism ['sɪzm, 'skɪzm] *n* cisma *m*.

schizophrenia [ˌskɪtsə'friːnjə] *n (U)* esquizofrenia *f*.

schizophrenic [ˌskɪtsə'frenɪk] <> *adj* esquizofrênico(ca). <> *n* esquizofrênico *m*, -ca *f*.

schlepp *US inf* <> *vt* arrastar. <> *vi*: **to ~ (around)** ficar de papo pro ar.

schmal(t)z [ʃmɔːlts] *n (U) inf* sentimentalismo *m*.

schmuck [ʃmʌk] *n US inf* idiota *mf*.

scholar ['skɒlə^r] *n* **-1.** [expert]: **he's a Greek ~** ele é perito em grego **-2.** *dated* [student] aluno *m*, -na *f* **-3.** [holder of scholarship] bolsista *mf*.

scholarship ['skɒləʃɪp] *n* **-1.** [grant] bolsa *f* **-2.** *(U)* [learning] erudição *f*.

scholastic [skə'læstɪk] *adj fml* educacional.

school [skuːl] *n* **-1.** [place of education] escola *f*, colégio *m* **-2.** [hours spent in school] escola *f* **-3.** UNIV [department] faculdade *f* **-4.** *US* [university] universidade *f* **-5.** [group of fish] cardume *m* **-6.** [of whales, dolphins] grupo *m*.

school age *n (U)* idade *f* escolar.

schoolbook ['skuːlbʊk] *n* livro *m* escolar.

schoolboy ['skuːlbɔɪ] *n* aluno *m*.

schoolchild ['skuːltʃaɪld] (*pl* **-children** [-tʃɪldrən]) *n* aluno *m*, -na *f*.

schooldays ['skuːldeɪz] *npl* tempos *mpl* de colégio *or* escola.

school dinner *n* refeição *f* escolar.

school district *n US autoridade local nos Estados Unidos com competência em termos de educação primária e secundária.*

school friend *n* colega *mf* (de escola).

schoolgirl ['skuːlgɜːl] *n* aluna *f*.

schooling ['skuːlɪŋ] *n (U)* educação *f*, ensino *m*.

schoolkid ['skuːlkɪd] *n inf* aluno *m*, -na *f*.

school-leaver [-ˌliːvə^r] *n UK jovem que concluiu o ensino obrigatório.*

school-leaving age [-'liːvɪŋ-] *n (U) UK idade de conclusão do ensino obrigatório.*

schoolmarm *n US* professora *f* antiquada.

schoolmaster ['skuːlˌmɑːstə^r] *n dated* mestre *m*.

schoolmistress ['skuːlˌmɪstrɪs] *n dated* mestra *f*.

school of thought *n* escola *f* de pensamento.

school report *n* boletim *m* escolar.

schoolroom ['skuːlrʊm] *n dated* classe *f*.

schoolteacher ['skuːlˌtiːtʃə^r] *n* professor *m*, -ra *f*.

school uniform *n* uniforme *m* escolar.

schoolwork ['skuːlwɜːk] *n (U)* trabalho *m* escolar.

school year *n* ano *m* letivo.

schooner ['skuːnə^r] *n* **-1.** [ship] escuna *f* **-2.** *UK* [sherry glass] caneca *f* (*para xerez*).

sciatica [saɪ'ætɪkə] *en (U)* ciática *f*.

science ['saɪəns] <> *n* ciência *f*. <> *comp* **-1.** [student] de ciências **-2.** [degree] em ciências.

science fiction *n (U)* ficção *f* científica.

science park *n* complexo *m* científico (*em empresas*).

scientific [ˌsaɪən'tɪfɪk] *adj* científico(ca).

scientist ['saɪəntɪst] *n* cientista *mf*.

sci-fi ['saɪfaɪ] (*abbr of* **science fiction**) *n inf* ficção *f* científica.

Scilly Isles ['sɪlɪ-], **Scillies** ['sɪlɪz] *npl*: **the ~** as Ilhas Scilly; **in the ~** nas Ilhas Scilly.

scintillating ['sɪntɪleɪtɪŋ] *adj* brilhante.
scissors ['sɪzəz] *npl* tesoura *f*; **a pair of ~** uma tesoura.
sclerosis *n* ▷ **multiple sclerosis.**
scoff [skɒf] ◇ *vt UK inf* devorar, engolir. ◇ *vi* zombar; **to ~ at sb/sthg** zombar de alguém/algo.
scold [skəʊld] *vt* repreender, xingar.
scone [skɒn] *n bolinho geralmente tomado à hora do chá com manteiga ou geléia.*
scoop [sku:p] ◇ *n* **-1.** [kitchen implement - for sugar] colher *f*; [- for ice cream] pá *f* **-2.** [scoopful] concha *f*, colher *f* grande; **two ~s of ice cream** duas bolas de sorvete **-3.** [news report] furo *m*. ◇ *vt* **-1.** [with hands] tirar com as mãos **-2.** [with implement] tirar com colher.
◆ **scoop out** *vt sep* tirar com colher.
scoot [sku:t] *vi inf* correr com muita pressa.
scooter ['sku:tə^r] *n* **-1.** [toy] patinete *f* **-2.** [motorcycle] lambreta *f*.
scope [skəʊp] *n (U)* **-1.** [opportunity] possibilidades *fpl* **-2.** [range] escopo *m*.
scorch [skɔ:tʃ] ◇ *vt* **-1.** [clothes, food, skin] chamuscar **-2.** [grass, fields] queimar. ◇ *vi* **-1.** [clothes, food] chamuscar **-2.** [face, skin] queimar.
scorched earth policy [skɔ:tʃt-] *n* política *f* de terra queimada.
scorcher ['skɔ:tʃə^r] *n inf* dia *m* escaldante.
scorching ['skɔ:tʃɪŋ] *adj inf* escaldante.
score [skɔ:^r] ◇ *n* **-1.** *SPORT* placar *m* **-2.** [in test, competition] nota *f* **-3.** *dated* [twenty] vintena *f* **-4.** *MUS* partitura *f* **-5.** [subject]: **on that ~** a esse respeito. ◇ *vt* **-1.** *SPORT* marcar **-2.** [achieve] conseguir, obter **-3.** [win in an argument] ganhar **-4.** [cut] gravar, entalhar. ◇ *vi* **-1.** *SPORT* marcar **-2.** [in an argument]: **to ~ over sb** levar vantagem sobre alguém.
◆ **scores** *npl* [lots]: **~s (of sthg)** um monte (de algo).
◆ **score out** *vt sep UK* riscar.
scoreboard ['skɔ:bɔ:d] *n* placar *m*.
scorecard ['skɔ:kɑ:d] *n* cartão *m* para marcação de pontos.
score-draw *n FTBL* empate *m* com gols.
scorer ['skɔ:rə^r] *n* **-1.** [official] anotador *m*, -ra *f* de pontos **-2.** [player - football] goleador *m*, -ra *f*; [- basketball] cestinha *mf*; [- sports in general] jogador(ra) que marca mais pontos.
scorn [skɔ:n] ◇ *n (U)* desdém *m*, menosprezo *m*; **to pour ~ on sb/sthg** menosprezar alguém/algo, desdenhar de alguém/algo. ◇ *vt* **-1.** [despise] desprezar **-2.** *fml* [refuse to accept] desdenhar.
scornful ['skɔ:nfʊl] *adj* desdenhoso(osa); **to be ~ of sthg** desdenhar de algo.
Scorpio ['skɔ:pɪəʊ] (*pl* **-s**) *n* **-1.** [sign] Escorpião *m* **-2.** [person] escorpiano *m*, -na *f*; **I'm ~** sou de Escorpião.
scorpion ['skɔ:pjən] *n* escorpião *m*.
Scot [skɒt] *n* escocês *m*, -esa *f*.
scotch [skɒtʃ] *vt* **-1.** [idea] acabar com **-2.** [rumour] desmentir.
Scotch [skɒtʃ] ◇ *adj* escocês(esa). ◇ *n* [whisky] uísque *m* escocês.
Scotch egg *n UK ovo cozido coberto com lingüiça e farinha de rosca e depois frito em óleo quente.*
Scotch (tape)® *n US* fita *f* adesiva, durex® *m*.
scot-free *adj inf*: **to get off ~** sair impune.
Scotland ['skɒtlənd] *n* Escócia; **in ~** na Escócia.
Scotland Yard *n* Scotland Yard *f*.
Scots [skɒts] ◇ *adj* escocês(esa). ◇ *n (U)* [dialect] escocês *m*.
Scotsman ['skɒtsmən] (*pl* **-men** [-mən]) *n* escocês *m*.
Scotswoman ['skɒtswʊmən] (*pl* **-women** [-ˌwɪmɪn]) *n* escocesa *f*.
Scottish ['skɒtɪʃ] *adj* escocês(esa).
Scottish National Party *n*: **the ~** o Partido Nacionalista Escocês.
scoundrel ['skaʊndrəl] *n dated* canalha *mf*.
scour [skaʊə^r] *vt* **-1.** [clean] esfregar **-2.** [search] esquadrinhar.
scourer ['skaʊrə^r] *n* esponja *f* de aço, bombril® *m*.
scourge [skɜ:dʒ] *n* **-1.** [cause of suffering] flagelo *m* **-2.** [critic] tormento *m*.
Scouse *n inf* **-1.** [person] *pessoa proveniente de Liverpool* **-2.** [accent] *dialeto falado pelas pessoas provenientes de Liverpool.*
scout [skaʊt] *n MIL* batedor *m*, explorador *m*.
◆ **Scout** *n* escoteiro *m*.
◆ **scout around** *vi*: **to ~ around (for sthg)** explorar a área (em busca de algo).
scoutmaster *n* chefe *m* dos escoteiros.
scowl [skaʊl] ◇ *n* carranca *f*, cara *f* feia. ◇ *vi* franzir o cenho; **to ~ at sb** fazer cara feia para alguém.
scrabble ['skræbl] *vi* **-1.** [scramble] escalar com dificuldade; **to ~ up/down** subir/descer escalando **-2.** [scrape]: **to ~ at sthg** arranhar algo **-3.** [feel around] escarafunchar; **to ~ around for sthg** escarafunchar à procura de algo.
Scrabble® ['skræbl] *n (U)* Palavras *fpl* Cruzadas *(jogo)*.
scraggy ['skrægɪ] (*compar* **-ier**, *superl* **-iest**) *adj inf* magricela.
scram [skræm] (*pt* & *pp* **-med**, *cont* **-ming**) *vi inf* chispar.
scramble ['skræmbl] ◇ *n* briga *f*. ◇ *vi* **-1.** [climb] trepar em **-2.** [move clumsily] caminhar cambaleando; **she ~d for her handbag in the crush** ela teve que brigar pela bolsa no meio do tumulto.
scrambled eggs ['skræmbld-] *npl* ovos *mpl* mexidos.
scrambler ['skræmblə^r] *n COMPUT* misturador *m*.
scrap [skræp] (*pt* & *pp* **-ped**, *cont* **-ping**) ◇ *n* **-1.** [small piece] pedaço *m*; **~ of conversation** trecho *m*; **~ of information** uma informação; **there isn't a ~ of evidence** não há prova alguma; **it won't make a ~ of difference** não fará a mínima diferença **-2.** [metal] sucata *f* **-3.** *inf* [fight, quarrel] briga *f*. ◇ *vt* abandonar.
◆ **scraps** *npl* sobras *fpl*.
scrapbook ['skræpbʊk] *n* album *m* de recortes.
scrap dealer *n* ferro-velho *m*, sucateiro *m*, -ra *f*.
scrape [skreɪp] ◇ *n* **-1.** [scraping noise] rangido *m*, arranhão *m* **-2.** *dated* [difficult situation] enrascada *f*. ◇ *vt* **-1.** [remove]: **to ~ sthg off sthg** raspar algo de algo **-2.** [peel] raspar **-3.** [rub against - car, bumper, glass] riscar; [- knee, elbow, skin] arranhar. ◇ *vi* **-1.**

[rub]: **to ~ against/on sthg** raspar contra/em algo - **2.** [save money] economizar.

 scrape through *vt fus* passar com as calças na mão.

 scrape together, scrape up *vt sep* juntar a duras penas.

scraper ['skreɪpəʳ] *n* raspador *m*.

scrap heap *n* - **1.** [of waste metal] monte *m* de sucata - **2.** *fig*: **to end up on the** [of people] ~ acabar rejeitado(da); [of ideas] acabar na lata de lixo.

scrapings ['skreɪpɪŋz] *npl* raspas *fpl*.

scrap merchant *n UK* sucateiro *m*, -ra *f*.

scrap metal *n (U)* sucata *f*, ferro-velho *m*.

scrap paper *UK*, **scratch paper** *US n (U)* papel *m* rascunho.

scrappy ['skræpɪ] (*compar* -ier, *superl* -iest) *adj pej* desconexo(xa).

scrapyard ['skræpjɑːd] *n* ferro-velho *m*.

scratch [skrætʃ] <> *n* - **1.** [gen] arranhão *m* - **2.** *phr*: **to do sthg from** ~ fazer algo começando do nada; **to be up to** ~ estar à altura. <> *vt* - **1.** [wound] arranhar - **2.** [surface] riscar - **3.** [rub] coçar; **to ~ o.s.** coçar-se. <> *vi* - **1.** [branch, knife, thorn]: **to ~ at/against sthg** roçar em algo - **2.** [person, animal] coçar-se.

scratchpad ['skrætʃpæd] *n US* bloco *m* de anotações.

scratch paper *n US* = scrap paper.

scratchy ['skrætʃɪ] (*compar* -ier, *superl* -iest) *adj* - **1.** [sound] arranhado(da) - **2.** [material] que pinica.

scrawl [skrɔːl] <> *n* rabisco *m*. <> *vt* rabiscar.

scrawny ['skrɔːnɪ] (*compar* -ier, *superl* -iest) *adj* esquelético(ca).

scream [skriːm] <> *n* - **1.** [of person] grito *m*; ~ **s of laughter** gargalhadas *fpl* - **2.** [of tyres, machine] guincho *m* - **3.** *inf* [funny person] pessoa *f* divertida. <> *vt* gritar. <> *vi* - **1.** [person] gritar, vociferar - **2.** [tyres, machine] guinchar.

scree [skriː] *n (U)* acúmulo *de pedras soltas na encosta de uma montanha*.

screech [skriːtʃ] <> *n* - **1.** [gen] guincho *m* - **2.** [of person] grito *m*; **a ~ of laughter** gargalhadas *fpl*. <> *vt* berrar, gritar. <> *vi* - **1.** [gen] guinchar - **2.** [person] gritar, berrar.

screen [skriːn] <> *n* - **1.** [viewing surface] tela *f* - **2.** *CINEMA*: **the (big)** ~ a tela de cinema - **3.** [protective or dividing panel] biombo *m*. <> *vt* - **1.** [gen] exibir - **2.** [hide, shield] proteger; **to ~ sb/sthg (from sb/sthg)** proteger alguém/algo (de alguém/algo) - **3.** [question, examine] examinar; **to ~ sb for sthg** fazer exames em alguém em busca de algo.

 screen off *vt sep* separar com biombo.

screen door *n* porta *f* com tela.

screen dump *n COMPUT* despejo *m* de tela.

screening ['skriːnɪŋ] *n* - **1.** [in cinema] exibição *f*, projeção *f* - **2.** [on TV] exibição *f* - **3.** *(U)* [for security] triagem *f* - **4.** *(U) MED* [examination] exame *m* médico.

screenplay ['skriːnpleɪ] *n* roteiro *m*.

screen print *n* serigrafia *f*.

screen saver *n COMPUT* protetor *m* de tela.

screen test *n* teste *m* de filmagem.

screenwriter ['skriːnˌraɪtəʳ] *n* roteirista *mf*.

screw [skruː] <> *n* parafuso *m*. <> *vt* - **1.** [fix with screws]: **to ~ sthg to sthg** aparafusar algo em algo - **2.** [twist] enroscar - **3.** *vulg* [have sex with] trepar com, foder. <> *vi* - **1.** [fix together] enroscar - **2.** *vulg* [have sex] trepar, foder.

 screw up *vt sep* - **1.** [crumple up] amassar - **2.** [contort, twist] contrair - **3.** *inf* [ruin] ferrar.

screwball ['skruːbɔːl] *n US inf* cabeça *mf* oca.

screwdriver ['skruːˌdraɪvəʳ] *n* chave *f* de fenda.

screwtop jar ['skruːtɒp-] *n* pote *m* com tampa de rosca.

screwy ['skruːɪ] *adj US inf* maluco(ca).

scribble ['skrɪbl] <> *n* rabisco *m*, garrancho *m*. <> *vt & vi* rabiscar.

scribe [skraɪb] *n fml* escriba *m*.

scrimp [skrɪmp] *vi*: **to ~ and save (to do sthg)** apertar o cinto (para fazer algo).

script [skrɪpt] *n* - **1.** [of play, film] script *m*, roteiro *m* - **2.** [system of writing] escrita *f* - **3.** [handwriting] letra *f*.

scripted ['skrɪptɪd] *adj* com roteiro.

Scriptures ['skrɪptʃəz] *npl*: **the** ~ as Escrituras.

scriptwriter ['skrɪptˌraɪtəʳ] *n* roteirista *mf*.

scroll [skrəʊl] <> *n* rolo *m* de papel *OR* pergaminho. <> *vt COMPUT* rolar.

 scroll down *vi COMPUT* mover para baixo, baixar.

 scroll up *vi COMPUT* mover para cima, subir.

scroll bar *n COMPUT* barra *f* de rolagem.

scrooge [skruːdʒ] *n inf pej* avarento *m*, -ta *f*, miserável.

scrotum ['skrəʊtəm] (*pl* -ta [-tə], -tums) *n* escroto *m*.

scrounge [skraʊndʒ] *inf* <> *vt*: **to ~ sthg (off sb)** filar algo (de alguém). <> *vi* filar; **to ~ off sb** *UK* viver às custas de alguém.

scrounger ['skraʊndʒəʳ] *n inf* parasita *mf*.

scrub [skrʌb] (*pt & pp* -bed, *cont* -bing) <> *n* - **1.** [rub] esfregação *f*; **give it a good** ~ dá uma boa esfregada (nisso) - **2.** *(U)* [undergrowth] moita *f*. <> *vt* esfregar.

scrubbing brush *UK* ['skrʌbɪŋ-], **scrub brush** *US n* escovão *m*.

scruff [skrʌf] *n ANAT*: **by the ~ of the neck** pelo cangote.

scruffy ['skrʌfɪ] (*compar* -ier, *superl* -iest) *adj* - **1.** [gen] sujo(ja) - **2.** [room, part of town] bagunçado(da).

scrum(mage) ['skrʌm(ɪdʒ)] *n RUGBY* disputa *f* de bola.

scrumptious ['skrʌmpʃəs] *adj inf* delicioso(sa).

scrumpy ['skrʌmpɪ] *n UK* cidra *f (de alto teor alcoólico)*.

scrunch [skrʌntʃ] *inf* <> *vt* amassar. <> *vi* ranger, estalar.

scrunchy ['skrʌntʃɪ] (*pl* -ies) *n* rabicó *m*.

scruples ['skruːplz] *npl* escrúpulos *mpl*.

scrupulous ['skruːpjʊləs] *adj* - **1.** [fair] escrupuloso (sa) - **2.** [thorough] completo(ta).

scrupulously ['skruːpjʊləslɪ] *adv* - **1.** [fairly] com escrúpulos - **2.** [thoroughly] totalmente.

scrutinize, -ise ['skruːtɪnaɪz] *vt* escrutinar.

scrutiny ['skruːtɪnɪ] *n (U)* escrutínio *m*.

scuba diving ['skuːbə-] *n (U)*: **to go** ~ mergulhar com tubo de oxigênio.

scud [skʌd] (*pt* & *pp* -**ded**, *cont* -**ding**) *vi literary* deslizar rapidamente.

scuff [skʌf] *vt* -**1**. [drag] arrastar -**2**. [damage - shoes] gastar; [- surface] riscar.

scuffle ['skʌfl] <> *n* briga *f*. <> *vi* brigar; **to ~ with sb** brigar com alguém.

scull [skʌl] <> *n* ginga *f*. <> *vi* remar.

scullery ['skʌlərɪ] (*pl* -**ies**) *n* copa *f (para lavar e guardar louça)*.

sculpt [skʌlpt] *vt* esculpir.

sculptor ['skʌlptə^r] *n* escultor *m*, -ra *f*.

sculpture ['skʌlptʃə^r] <> *n* escultura *f*. <> *vt* esculpir.

scum [skʌm] *n* -**1**. [froth] espuma *f* -**2**. *v inf pej* [worthless people] escória *f*.

scupper ['skʌpə^r] *vt* -**1**. *NAUT* [sink] afundar -**2**. *UK fig* [ruin] arruinar.

scurf [skɜːf] *n (U)* caspa *f*.

scurrilous ['skʌrələs] *adj fml* difamatório(ria).

scurry ['skʌrɪ] (*pt* & *pp* -**ied**) *vi*: **to ~ off** escapulir-se.

scurvy ['skɜːvɪ] *n (U)* escorbuto *m*.

scuttle ['skʌtl] <> *n* balde *m* para carvão. <> *vi* correr.

scuzzy (*compar* -**ier**, *superl* -**iest**) *adj inf* chulo(la).

scythe [saɪð] <> *n* foice *f*. <> *vt* ceifar.

SD *abbr of* South Dakota.

SDI (*abbr of* Strategic Defense Initiative) *n plano estratégico norte-americano de defesa anti-míssil, conhecido também como Star Wars*.

SDLP (*abbr of* Social Democratic and Labour Party) *n partido político da Irlanda do Norte que defende a integração pacífica com a República da Irlanda*.

SE (*abbr of* southeast) SE.

sea [siː] <> *n* mar *m*; **to be at ~** [ship, sailor] estar no mar; **to be all at ~** *fig* [person] estar totalmente perdido(da); **by ~** pelo mar; **by the ~** junto ao mar; **out to ~** [away from land] para alto mar. <> *comp* -**1**. [travel, voyage] marítimo(ma) -**2**. [animal] marinho(nha).

  seas *npl*: **the ~s** os mares.

sea air *n (U)* ar *m* do mar.

sea anemone *n* anêmona *f* do mar.

seabed ['siːbed] *n*: **the ~** o fundo do mar.

seabird ['siːbɜːd] *n* ave *f* marinha.

seaboard ['siːbɔːd] *n fml* litoral *m*.

sea breeze *n* brisa *f* do mar.

seafaring ['siːˌfeərɪŋ] *adj* -**1**. [man] do mar -**2**. [nation] de navegantes.

seafood ['siːfuːd] *n (U)* frutos *mpl* do mar.

seafront ['siːfrʌnt] *n* orla *f* marítima.

seagoing ['siːˌɡəʊɪŋ] *adj* de alto-mar.

seagull ['siːɡʌl] *n* gaivota *f*.

seahorse ['siːhɔːs] *n* cavalo *m* marinho.

seal [siːl] (*pl sense 1 only inv OR* -**s**) <> *n* -**1**. [gen] selo *m*; **~ of approval** carimbo *m* de aprovação; **to put** *OR* **set the ~ on sthg** selar algo -**2**. [animal] foca *f* -**3**. *TECH* vedação *f*. <> *vt* -**1**. [stick down] selar -**2**. [block up] vedar.

  seal off *vt sep* interditar.

sealable ['siːləbl] *adj* vedável.

sea lane *n* rota *f* marítima.

sealant ['siːlənt] *n* selador *m*.

sea level *n (U)* nível *m* do mar.

sealing wax ['siːlɪŋ-] *n (U)* lacre *m*.

sea lion (*pl inv OR* -**s**) *n* leão-marinho *m*.

sealskin ['siːlskɪn] *n (U)* pele *f* de foca.

seam [siːm] *n* -**1**. *SEWING* costura *f*; **the room was bursting at the ~s** a sala estava entupida de gente -**2**. [of coal] veio *m*.

seaman ['siːmən] (*pl* -**men** [-mən]) *n* marinheiro *m*.

seamanship ['siːmənʃɪp] *n (U)* náutica *f*.

sea mist *n (U)* nevoeiro *m* do mar.

seamless ['siːmlɪs] *adj* -**1**. [gen] sem costuras -**2**. *fig* [faultless] perfeito(ta).

seamstress ['semstrɪs] *n* costureira *f*.

seamy ['siːmɪ] (*compar* -**ier**, *superl* -**iest**) *adj* sórdido(-da).

séance ['seɪɒns] *n* sessão *f* espírita.

seaplane ['siːpleɪn] *n* hidroavião *m*.

seaport ['siːpɔːt] *n* porto *m* de mar.

search [sɜːtʃ] <> *n* -**1**. [for lost person, object] procura *f*, busca *f*; **~ for sthg** busca *OR* procura por algo; **in ~ of** a procura de, em busca de -**2**. [of person, luggage, house] procura *f*. <> *vt* -**1**. [gen] procurar; **to ~ sthg for sthg** procurar algo em algo -**2**. [mind, memory] vascular -**3**. [frisk] revistar. <> *vi* -**1**. [look for] procurar; **to ~ for sb/sthg** procurar (por) alguém/algo -**2**. [try to recall]: **to ~ for sthg** tentar lembrar algo.

  search out *vt sep* descobrir, encontrar.

search engine *n COMPUT* mecanismo *m* de busca.

searcher ['sɜːtʃə^r] *n* investigador *m*, -ra *f*.

searching ['sɜːtʃɪŋ] *adj* -**1**. [question] perspicaz -**2**. [examination, review] minucioso(sa) -**3**. [look] penetrante.

searchlight ['sɜːtʃlaɪt] *n* holofote *m*.

search party *n* equipe *f* de busca.

search warrant *n* mandado *m* de busca.

searing ['sɪərɪŋ] *adj* -**1**. [intense] intenso(sa) -**2**. [highly critical] contundente.

sea salt *n (U)* sal *m* marinho.

seashell ['siːʃel] *n* concha *f* (marinha).

seashore ['siːʃɔː^r] *n*: **the ~** o litoral.

seasick ['siːsɪk] *adj* mareado(da).

seaside ['siːsaɪd] *n*: **the ~** a praia.

seaside resort *n* local *m* de veraneio *(na praia)*.

season ['siːzn] <> *n* -**1**. [time of year] estação *f* -**2**. [for particular activity] período *m*, época *f* -**3**. [of holiday] temporada *f*; **out of ~** fora de temporada -**4**. [of food]: **in ~** da estação; **out of ~** fora da estação -**5**. [series - of films] festival *m*; [- of lectures] série *f*. <> *vt* temperar.

seasonal ['siːzənl] *adj* sazonal.

seasoned ['siːznd] *adj* experiente.

seasoning ['siːznɪŋ] *n* tempero *m*.

season ticket *n* bilhete *m* para a temporada.

season-ticket holder *n* pessoa *que comprou um bilhete que lhe dá direito de assistir a todos os jogos da temporada*.

seat [siːt] <> *n* -**1**. [gen] assento *m* -**2**. [place to sit] banco *m* -**3**. [of clothing] fundilho *m* -**4**. *POL* [in parliament] cadeira *f*. <> *vt* -**1**. [sit down] sentar; **to ~ o.s.** sentar-se -**2**. [subj: building, vehicle] acomodar.

seat belt n cinto m de segurança.

seated ['si:tɪd] adj sentado(da).

-seater ['si:tə'] suffix: **a two ~ car** um carro com dois lugares.

seating ['si:tɪŋ] ◇ n (U) acomodação f. ◇ comp de acomodação; **~ plan** distribuição f dos lugares (na mesa).

SEATO ['si:təʊl (abbr of South-East Asia Treaty Organization) n OTSEA f.

sea urchin n ouriço-do-mar m.

seawall ['si:'wɔ:ll n quebra-mar m, dique m.

seawater ['si:ˌwɔ:tə'] n (U) água f do mar.

seaweed ['si:wi:dl n (U) alga f marinha.

seaworthy ['si:ˌwɜ:ðɪl adj em condições de navegar.

sebaceous [sɪ'beɪʃəsl adj sebáceo(cea).

sec. (abbr of second) n seg.

Sec. (abbr of secretary) secretário m, -ria f.

SEC (abbr of Securities and Exchange Commission) n organismo do governo norte-americano que supervisiona as transações da bolsa.

secateurs [ˌsekə'tɜ:z] npl UK tesoura f para podar.

secede [sɪ'si:dl vi fml separar-se; **to ~ from sthg** separar-se de algo.

secession [sɪ'seʃn] n (U) fml secessão f.

secluded [sɪ'klu:dɪd] adj isolado(da), afastado(da).

seclusion [sɪ'klu:ʒn] n (U) isolamento m.

second¹ ['sekənd] ◇ n **- 1.** [gen] segundo m **- 2.** UK UNIV diploma m com louvor **- 3.** AUT: **~ (gear)** segunda f. ◇ num segundo(da); **what are you doing on the ~?** o que você vai fazer no dia dois (deste mês)?; **the ~ of March** dia 2 de Março; **... ~ only to Boris** ... perdendo apenas para Boris; **he is ~ to none** ele não perde para ninguém; see also **sixth**. ◇ vt secundar.

◆ **seconds** npl **- 1.** COMM artigos mpl de segunda-linha **- 2.** [of food] repetição f.

second² [sɪ'kɒndl vt UK transferir provisoriamente.

secondary ['sekəndrɪl adj secundário(ria); **to be ~ to sthg** ser secundário para algo.

secondary picketing n (U) piquete feito por pessoas não envolvidas na categoria reivindicante.

secondary school n escola f secundária.

second best ['sekənd-] adj segundo(da) melhor; **to settle for ~** contentar-se com a segunda opção.

second-class ['sekənd-] adj **- 1.** [gen] de segunda classe **- 2.** pej [less important] de segunda classe **- 3.** UK UNIV tipo de grau universitário com louvor concedido por universidades britânicas.

second cousin ['sekənd-] n primo m, -ma f em segundo grau.

second-degree burn ['sekənd-] n queimadura f de segundo grau.

seconder ['sekəndə'] n pessoa f que secunda.

second floor ['sekənd-] n **- 1.** UK [third storey] terceiro andar m **- 2.** US [second storey] segundo andar m.

second-guess ['sekənd-] vt **- 1.** US [with hindsight] julgar a posteriori **- 2.** [predict] prever.

second-hand ['sekənd-] ◇ adj **- 1.** [gen] de segunda mão **- 2.** [shop] de objetos usados. ◇ adv **- 1.** [not new] de segunda mão **- 2.** fig [indirectly]: **to hear sthg ~** ouvir algo de terceiros.

second hand ['sekənd-] n ponteiro m dos segundos.

second-in-command ['sekənd-] n suplente mf.

secondly ['sekəndlɪl adv em segundo lugar.

secondment [sɪ'kɒndmənt] n UK transferência f temporária.

second nature ['sekənd-] n (U) segunda natureza f.

second-rate ['sekənd-] adj pej de segunda categoria.

second thought ['sekənd-] n: **to have ~s about sthg** estar em dúvida sobre algo; **on ~s** UK, **on ~ US** pensando bem.

secrecy ['si:krəsɪ] n (U) sigilo m.

secret ['si:krɪtl ◇ adj secreto(ta); **to keep sthg ~** manter algo em segredo. ◇ n segredo m; **in ~** em segredo.

secret agent n agente mf secreto.

secretarial [ˌsekrə'teərɪəl] adj **- 1.** [course] de secretário **- 2.** [staff] de secretários **- 3.** [training] para secretariado.

secretariat [ˌsekrə'teərɪət] n secretariado m.

secretary [UK 'sekrətrɪ, US 'sekrəˌterɪl (pl -ies) n **- 1.** [gen] secretário m, -ria f **- 2.** POL [minister] ministro m, -tra f.

secretary-general (pl secretaries-general) n secretário m, -ria f geral.

Secretary of State n **- 1.** UK [minister]: **~ (for sthg)** ministro m (de algo) **- 2.** US [in charge of foreign affairs] secretário m, -ria f das relações exteriores.

secrete [sɪ'kri:t] vt **- 1.** [produce] secretar **- 2.** fml [hide] ocultar.

secretion [sɪ'kri:ʃn] n secreção f.

secretive ['si:krətɪv] adj **- 1.** [person] reservado(da) **- 2.** [organization] secreto(ta).

secretly ['si:krɪtlɪl adv secretamente, em segredo.

secret police n (U) polícia f secreta.

secret service n serviço m secreto.

sect [sektl n seita f.

sectarian [sek'teərɪən] adj sectário(ria).

section ['sekʃn] ◇ n seção f. ◇ vt **- 1.** GEOM seccionar **- 2.** fml [cut] seccionar.

sector ['sektə'] n setor m.

secular ['sekjʊlə'] adj secular.

secure [sɪ'kjʊə'] ◇ adj **- 1.** [tightly locked up] seguro(ra), protegido(da) **- 2.** [fixed in place] seguro(ra), firme **- 3.** [safe, not likely to change] garantido(da) **- 4.** [strong, solid] firme **- 5.** [free of anxiety, confident] confiante. ◇ vt **- 1.** [obtain] conseguir, obter **- 2.** [make safe] proteger **- 3.** [fasten] fechar bem.

securely [sɪ'kjʊəlɪl adv firmemente.

security [sɪ'kjʊərətɪ] (pl -ies) ◇ n **- 1.** [gen] segurança f **- 2.** (U) [legal protection] segurança f, garantia f; **~ of tenure** cargo m vitalício. ◇ comp de segurança.

◆ **securities** npl FIN papéis mpl negociáveis.

security blanket n cobertor ou outro obejeto de estimação com o qual a pessoa se sente protegida.

Security Council *n*: the ~ o Conselho de Segurança.

security forces *npl* forças *fpl* de segurança.

security guard *n* (guarda *mf* de) segurança *mf*.

security risk *n* ameaça *f* à segurança.

sedan [sɪˈdæn] *n US* sedã *m*.

sedan chair *n* liteira *f*.

sedate [sɪˈdeɪt] <> *adj* calmo(ma), sossegado(da). <> *vt* sedar.

sedation [sɪˈdeɪʃn] *n* (U) sedação *f*.

sedative [ˈsedətɪv] <> *adj* sedativo(va). <> *n* sedativo *m*.

sedentary [ˈsedntrɪ] *adj* sedentário(ria).

sediment [ˈsedɪmənt] *n* sedimento *m*.

sedition [sɪˈdɪʃn] *n* (U) sedição *f*.

seditious [sɪˈdɪʃəs] *adj* sedicioso(sa).

seduce [sɪˈdjuːs] *vt* seduzir; **to** ~ **sb into doing sthg** persuadir alguém a fazer algo.

seduction [sɪˈdʌkʃn] *n* sedução *f*.

seductive [sɪˈdʌktɪv] *adj* sedutor(ra).

see [siː] (*pt* saw, *pp* seen) <> *vt* -**1.** [gen] ver; **we're going to** ~ **each other tonight** vamos nos ver hoje à noite; ~ **you!** até mais!; ~ **you soon/later/to-morrow!** até breve/mais tarde/amanhã! -**2.** [friend, doctor] visitar -**3.** [realize]: **to** ~ **(that)** perceber que -**4.** [understand] entender -**5.** [accompany] levar, acompanhar -**6.** [find out, ascertain] descobrir; **I'll** ~ **what I can do** verei o que posso fazer -**7.** [make sure]: **I'll** ~ **(that the work gets done)** vou providenciar (para que o trabalho fique pronto) -**8.** [judge, consider] ver, considerar -**9.** [subj: day, date]: **today saw ...** hoje aconteceu ... <> *vi* -**1.** [perceive with eyes] enxergar -**2.** [understand] entender; **I** ~ entendo; **you** ~, **...** veja bem, ... -**3.** [find out] ver; **to** ~ **if one can do sthg** ver se se pode fazer algo; **let's** ~, **let me** ~ vamos ver, vejamos.

◆ **seeing as, seeing that** *conj inf* já que, como.

◆ **see about** *vt fus* -**1.** [organize]: **I'll** ~ **about getting you some work** vou dar um jeito de te arrumar algum trabalho -**2.** [think about] ver.

◆ **see off** *vt sep* -**1.** [say goodbye to] despedir-se de -**2.** *UK* [chase away] afugentar.

◆ **see through** <> *vt fus* [not be deceived by] não se deixar enganar por. <> *vt sep* [to conclusion] levar a termo.

◆ **see to** *vt fus* cuidar de.

seed [siːd] <> *n* -**1.** [of plant] semente *f* -**2.** *SPORT* pré-selecionado *m*, -da *f*. <> *vt*: **she's** ~ **ed first in the world** ela é a número um do mundo.

◆ **seeds** *npl* fig [beginnings] semente *f*.

seedless [ˈsiːdlɪs] *adj* sem semente/caroço.

seedling [ˈsiːdlɪŋ] *n* muda *f*.

seedy [ˈsiːdɪ] (*compar*-ier, *superl*-iest) *adj* -**1.** [person] maltrapilho(lha) -**2.** [room, area] usado(da).

seek [siːk] (*pt* & *pp* sought) *fml* <> *vt* procurar; **to** ~ **to do sthg** procurar fazer algo. <> *vi* -**1.** [search]: **to** ~ **for sthg** procurar (por) algo -**2.** [request]: **to** ~ **for sthg** pedir algo.

◆ **seek out** *vt sep* perseguir.

seem [siːm] <> *vi* parecer; **it** ~**s too good to be true** parece bom demais para ser verdade; **I** ~ **to remember that ...** parece que eu me lembro de

que ...; **I can't** ~ **to do that** por mais que eu tente, não consigo fazer isso. <> *v impers*: **it** ~**s (that)** parece que.

seeming [ˈsiːmɪŋ] *adj fml* aparente.

seemingly [ˈsiːmɪŋlɪ] *adv* aparentemente.

seemly (*compar*-ier, *superl*-iest) *adj literary* decoroso(sa).

seen [siːn] *pp* ▷ **see**.

seep [siːp] *vi* infiltrar-se, penetrar.

seersucker [ˈsɪəˌsʌkəʳ] *n* (U) *tecido leve de algodão listado*.

seesaw [ˈsiːsɔː] *n* gangorra *f*.

seethe [siːð] *vi* fervilhar; **to be seething with sthg** estar fervilhando com algo.

seething [ˈsiːðɪŋ] *adj* -**1.** [furious] furioso(sa) -**2.** [teeming] fervilhante.

see-through *adj* transparente.

segment [ˈsegmənt] *n* -**1.** [of market, report, audience] segmento *m* -**2.** [of fruit] gomo *m*.

segregate [ˈsegrɪgeɪt] *vt* segregar.

segregation [ˌsegrɪˈgeɪʃn] *n* (U) segregação *f*.

Seine [seɪn] *n*: **the (River)** ~ o (Rio) Sena.

seismic [ˈsaɪzmɪk] *adj* sísmico(ca).

seize [siːz] *vt* -**1.** [grab] agarrar, pegar -**2.** [win, capture] tomar -**3.** [arrest] prender, deter -**4.** [take advantage of] aproveitar.

◆ **seize (up)on** *vt fus* valer-se de.

◆ **seize up** *vi* -**1.** [body] enrijecer -**2.** [engine] emperrar.

seizure [ˈsiːʒəʳ] *n* -**1.** *MED* ataque *m* -**2.** (U) [taking, capturing] tomada *f*.

seldom [ˈseldəm] *adv* raramente.

select [sɪˈlekt] <> *adj* -**1.** [carefully chosen] selecionado(da) -**2.** [exclusive] seleto(ta). <> *vt* selecionar.

select committee *n* comissão *f* parlamentar de inquérito.

selected [sɪˈlektɪd] *adj* escolhido(da).

selection [sɪˈlekʃn] *n* -**1.** [gen] seleção *f* -**2.** [range of goods] coleção *f*.

selective [sɪˈlektɪv] *adj* seletivo(va).

selector [sɪˈlektəʳ] *n SPORT* selecionador *m*, -ra *f*.

self [self] (*pl* selves) *n*: **she's her old** ~ ela volta a ser ela mesma; **the** ~ o eu.

self- [self] *prefix* auto-; ~ **defence** *UK*, ~ **defense** *US* autodefesa *f*; ~ **accusation** auto-acusação *f*.

self-addressed envelope [-əˈdrest-] *n* envelope *m* de resposta.

self-addressed stamped envelope [-əˌdrestˈstæmpt-] *n US* envelope *m* de resposta pré-pago.

self-adhesive *adj* auto-adesivo(va).

self-appointed [-əˈpɔɪntɪd] *adj pej* autodesignado(da).

self-assembly *adj UK* desmontável.

self-assertive *adj* seguro(ra) de si.

self-assurance *n* (U) autoconfiança *f*.

self-assured *adj* confiante em si mesmo(ma), seguro(ra) de si.

self-catering *adj* sem refeições incluídas.

self-centred [-ˈsentəd] *adj* egocêntrico(ca).

self-cleaning *adj* autolimpante.

self-coloured *adj UK* unicolor.

self-confessed [-kənˈfest] *adj* assumido(da).

self-confidence n autoconfiança f.
self-confident adj -**1.** [person] seguro(ra) de si -**2.** [remark, attitude] que passa segurança.
self-conscious adj inibido(da).
self-contained [-kən'teɪnd] adj -**1.** [person] reservado(da) -**2.** [flat] independente.
self-control n (U) autocontrole m.
self-controlled adj controlado(da), sereno(na).
self-defence n (U) legítima defesa f; **in** ~ em legítima defesa.
self-denial n (U) abnegação f.
self-destruct [-dɪs'trʌkt] <> adj autodestrutivo (va). <> vi autodestruir-se.
self-determination n (U) autodeterminação f.
self-discipline n (U) autodisciplina f.
self-doubt n (U) insegurança f.
self-drive adj UK alugado(da) sem motorista.
self-educated adj autodidata.
self-effacing [-ɪ'feɪsɪŋ] adj modesto(ta), humilde.
self-employed [-ɪm'plɔɪd] adj autônomo(ma), que trabalha por conta própria.
self-esteem n (U) amor-próprio m.
self-evident adj óbvio(via).
self-explanatory adj claro(ra), manifesto(ta).
self-expression n (U) expressão f própria.
self-focusing [-'fəʊkəsɪŋ] adj com foco automático.
self-government n (U) governo m autônomo.
self-help n (U) auto-ajuda f.
self-important adj pej presunçoso(sa), convencido(da).
self-imposed [-ɪm'pəʊzd] adj imposto a si mesmo, imposta a si mesma.
self-indulgent adj pej comodista, que se permite excessos.
self-inflicted [-ɪn'flɪktɪd] adj auto-infligido(da).
self-interest n (U) pej interesse m pessoal OR próprio.
selfish ['selfɪʃ] adj egoísta.
selfishness ['selfɪʃnɪs] n (U) egoísmo m.
selfless ['selflɪs] adj desinteressado(da).
self-locking [-'lɒkɪŋ] adj de fechamento automático.
self-made adj que se fez por si mesmo(ma).
self-opinionated adj pej presunçoso(sa).
self-perpetuating [-pə'petʃʊeɪtɪŋ] adj que se perpetua a si mesmo(ma).
self-pity n (U) pej autocomiseração f.
self-portrait n auto-retrato m.
self-possessed [-pə'zest] adj dono de si mesmo, dona de si mesma.
self-preservation n autopreservação f.
self-proclaimed [-prə'kleɪmd] adj pej autodenominado(da).
self-raising flour UK [-,reɪzɪŋ-], **self-rising flour** US n (U) farinha f com fermento.
self-regard n (U) -**1.** [self-esteem] amor-próprio m -**2.** pej [conceit] narcisismo m.
self-regulating [-'regjʊleɪtɪŋ] adj auto-regulador (ra).
self-reliant adj independente.
self-respect n (U) amor m próprio.

self-respecting [-rɪs'pektɪŋ] adj que se presta, digno(na).
self-restraint n (U) autocontrole m.
self-righteous adj pej hipócrita.
self-rising flour n US = self-raising flour.
self-rule n (U) autonomia f (de um governo).
self-sacrifice n (U) abnegação f.
selfsame ['selfseɪm] adj mesmíssimo(míssima).
self-satisfied adj pej convencido(da).
self-sealing [-'si:lɪŋ] adj auto-adesivo(va).
self-seeking [-'si:kɪŋ] pej adj interesseiro(ra).
self-service <> n (U) auto-serviço m, self-service m. <> comp de auto-serviço, self-service; **a** ~ **shop** uma loja self-service.
self-starter n -**1.** AUT arranque m automático -**2.** [person] empreendedor m, -ra f.
self-styled [-'staɪld] adj pej pretenso(sa).
self-sufficient adj: ~ (**in** sthg) auto-suficiente (em algo).
self-supporting [-sə'pɔ:tɪŋ] adj economicamente independente.
self-tanning adj autobronzeador(ra).
self-taught adj autodidata.
self-test vi COMPUT autotestar.
self-willed adj pej obstinado(da).
sell [sell (pt & pp **sold**) <> vt -**1.** vender; **to** ~ sthg **to sb, to** ~ **sb** sthg vender algo para alguém; **to** ~ sthg **for** vender algo por; **to** ~ **o.s.** vender-se; **to** ~ **o.s. short** desmerecer-se -**2.** fig [make enthusiastic about]: **to** ~ sthg **to sb, to** ~ **sb** sthg vender algo a alguém; **to** ~ **sb an idea** vender uma idéia a alguém; **I'm not really sold on the idea** não consigo comprar essa idéia. <> vi vender; **to** ~ **for** OR **at** ser vendido(da) por OR a.
⇒ **sell off** vt sep liquidar.
⇒ **sell out** <> vt sep: **to be sold out** estar esgotado(da). <> vi -**1.** [shop, ticket office]: **to** ~ **out** (**of** sthg) vender todo o estoque (de algo) -**2.** [betray one's principles] vender-se.
⇒ **sell up** vi vender tudo.
sell-by date n UK prazo m de validade.
seller ['selə^r] n vendedor m, -ra f.
seller's market n mercado m de demanda OR favorável ao vendedor.
selling ['selɪŋ] n (U) venda f.
selling price ['selɪŋ-] n preço m de venda.
Sellotape® ['seləteɪp] n UK fita f adesiva, durex® m.
⇒ **sellotape** vt segurar com fita adesiva.
sell-out n -**1.** [performance, match] sucesso m de bilheteria -**2.** [of principles] traição f.
sell-through n US COMM venda f direta (ao consumidor).
seltzer n US água f de soda.
selves [selvz] pl ⊳ **self.**
semantic [sɪ'mæntɪk] adj semântico(ca).
⇒ **semantics** n (U) semântica f.
semaphore ['seməfɔ:^r] n (U) semáforo m.
semblance ['sembləns] n fml aparência f.
semen ['si:mən] n (U) sêmen m.
semester [sɪ'mestə^r] n semestre m.
semi ['semɪ] n -**1.** UK inf [house] casa f geminada -**2.** US [lorry] caminhão m articulado.

semi- ['semɪ] *prefix* semi-.
semi-automatic *adj* semi-automático(ca).
semicircle ['semɪˌsɜːkl] *n* semicírculo *m*.
semicircular [ˌsemɪ'sɜːkjʊləʳ] *adj* semicircular.
semicolon [ˌsemɪ'kəʊlən] *n* ponto-e-vírgula *m*.
semi-conscious *adj* semiconsciente.
semi-detached ⋄ *adj UK* geminado(do). ⋄ *n UK* casa *f* geminada.
semi-final *n* semifinal *f*.
semi-finalist *n* semifinalista *mf*.
seminal *adj* -1. [important] muito influente -2. [of semen] seminal.
seminar ['semɪnɑːʳ] *n* seminário *m*.
seminary ['semɪnərɪ] (*pl* -ies) *n RELIG* seminário *m*.
semiotics *n (U)* semiótica *f*.
semi-precious *adj* semiprecioso(sa).
semi-skilled *adj* semi-especializado(da).
semi-skimmed [-'skɪmd] *adj* semidesnatado(-da).
semi-trailer *n* -1. [trailer] reboque *m* -2. *US* [lorry] caminhão *m* articulado.
semolina [ˌseməˈliːnə] *n (U)* semolina *f*.
Sen. -1. (*abbr of* **senator**) Sen. -2. (*abbr of* **Senior**) sênior.
Senate ['senɪt] *n POL*: **the** ~ o Senado; **the United States** ~ o Senado dos Estados Unidos.

senator ['senətəʳ] *n* senador *m*, -ra *f*.
send [send] (*pt* & *pp* **sent**) *vt* -1. [letter, message, money] enviar, mandar; **to** ~ **sb sthg**, **to** ~ **sthg to sb** enviar *OR* mandar algo para alguém -2. [tell to go]: **to** ~ **sb (to)** mandar alguém (para); **to** ~ **sb for sthg** mandar alguém buscar algo -3. [propel] lançar -4. [into a specific state] deixar; **to** ~ **sb mad** deixar alguém louco(ca); **to** ~ **to sleep** dar sono em alguém; **to** ~ **sb flying** arremessar alguém longe.
 send back *vt sep* devolver; **to** ~ **sb back** fazer alguém voltar.
 send down *vt sep inf* encarcerar.
 send for *vt fus* -1. [person] mandar chamar -2. [by post] encomendar.
 send in *vt sep* -1. [visitor] fazer entrar -2. [troops, police] enviar; mandar -3. [submit] enviar.
 send off *vt sep* -1. [by post] enviar , (*pelo correio*) -2. *SPORT* expulsar.
 send off for *vt fus* encomendar (*pelo correio*).
 send up *vt sep inf* -1. *UK* [imitate] arremedar, imitar -2. *US* [send to prison] mandar para a prisão.
sender ['sendəʳ] *n* remetente *mf*.
send-off *n* despedida *f*.
send-up *n UK inf* paródia *f*, sátira *f*.
Senegal [ˌsenɪ'gɔːl] *n* Senegal; **in** ~ no Senegal.
Senegalese [ˌsenɪgə'liːz] ⋄ *adj* senegalês(esa). ⋄ *npl*: **the** ~ os senegaleses.

senile ['siːnaɪl] *adj* senil.
senile dementia *n (U)* demência *f* senil.
senility [sɪ'nɪlətɪ] *n (U)* senilidade *f*.
senior ['siːnjəʳ] ⋄ *adj* -1. [highest-ranking] superior(ra) -2. [higher-ranking]: ~ **to sb** superior a alguém -3. *SCH* [pupils, classes] veterano(na); ~ **year** *US* último ano do ensino secundário e das universidades nos Estados Unidos. ⋄ *n* -1. [older person] mais velho(lha); **I'm five years his** ~ sou cinco anos mais velho do que ele -2. *SCH* & *UNIV* veterano *m*, -na *f*.
senior citizen *n* idoso *m*, -sa *f*.
senior high school *n US* escola *f* de ensino médio (*dos 16 aos 18 anos*).
seniority [ˌsiːnɪ'ɒrətɪ] *n (U)* grau *m* de poder ou competência.
sensation [sen'seɪʃn] *n* sensação *f*.
sensational [sen'seɪʃənl] *adj* -1. [causing a stir] sensacional -2. *inf* [wonderful] sensacional -3. [sensationalist] sensacionalista.
sensationalist [sen'seɪʃnəlɪst] *adj pej* sensacionalista.
sense [sens] ⋄ *n* -1. [gen] sentido *m*; **to make** ~ [have clear meaning] fazer sentido; [be logical] ser lógico(ca); **to make** ~ **of sthg** entender algo -2. [feeling, sensation - of guilt, terror, honour] sentimento *m*; [- of justice, duty, urgency] senso *m* -3. [natural ability]: ~ **of direction** senso *m* de direção; ~ **of style** idéia *f* de estilo -4. *(U)* [wisdom, reason] bom senso *m*, sabedoria *f*; **to talk** ~ falar seriamente; **there's no** ~ **in arguing/fighting** não faz sentido brigar/lutar -5. *phr*: **to come to one's** ~**s** [be sensible again] recobrar o juízo; [regain consciousness] recobrar os sentidos; **to be out of one's** ~**s** perder o juízo. ⋄ *vt* sentir; **to** ~ **that** sentir que.
 in a sense *adv* de certo modo, em certo sentido.
senseless ['senslɪs] *adj* -1. [stupid] sem sentido, estúpido(da) -2. [unconscious] inconsciente; **to knock sb** ~ bater em alguém até ficar inconsciente.
sensibilities [ˌsensɪ'bɪlətɪz] *npl* sensibilidade *f*.
sensible ['sensəbl] *adj* -1. [reasonable, practical] prático(ca) -2. [person] sensato(ta).
sensibly ['sensəblɪ] *adv* sensatamente.
sensitive ['sensɪtɪv] *adj* -1. [eyes, skin]: ~ **(to sthg)** sensível (a algo) -2. [understanding, aware]: ~ **(to sthg)** compreensivo(va) (com algo) -3. [easily hurt, touchy]: ~ **(to/about sthg)** sensível *OR* suscetível (a algo) -4. [controversial] delicado(da) -5. [instrument] sensível.
sensitivity [ˌsensɪ'tɪvətɪ] *n* sensibilidade *f*.
sensor ['sensəʳ] *n* sensor *m*.
sensual ['sensjʊəl] *adj* sensual.
sensuous ['sensjʊəs] *adj* sensual.
sent [sent] *pt* & *pp* ⋏ **send**.
sentence ['sentəns] ⋄ *n* -1. [group of words] frase *f*, oração *f* -2. *JUR* sentença *f*. ⋄ *vt*: **to** ~ **sb (to sthg)** condenar alguém (a algo).
sententious [sen'tenʃəs] *adj pej* sentencioso(sa).
sentiment ['sentɪmənt] *n* -1. [feeling] sentimento *m* -2. [opinion] opinião *f* -3. *(U) pej* [sentimentality] sentimentalismo *m*.

sentimental [ˌsentɪ'mentl] *adj* **-1.** *pej* [over-emotional] sentimental **-2.** [emotional] sentimental.
sentimentality [ˌsentɪmen'tælətɪ] *n* (U) *pej* sentimentalismo *m*.
sentinel ['sentɪnl] *n* sentinela *mf*.
sentry ['sentrɪ] (*pl* **-ies**) *n* sentinela *mf*.
Seoul [səʊl] *n* Seul.
separable ['seprəbl] *adj*: ~ **(from sthg)** separável (de algo).
separate [*adj* & *n* 'seprət, *vb* 'sepəreɪt] <> *adj* **-1.** [not joined, apart] separado(da); ~ **from sthg** separado(da) de algo **-2.** [individual] separado(da), diferente **-3.** [distinct] distinto(ta). <> *vt* separar; **to** ~ **sb/sthg from** separar alguém/algo de; **to** ~ **sb/sthg into** separar alguém/algo em; **to** ~ **sb/ sthg from** separar alguém/algo de. <> *vi* **-1.** [gen] separar-se; **to** ~ **into sthg** separar-se em algo **-2.** [go different ways]: **to** ~ **(from sb/sthg)** separar-se (de alguém/algo).
➤ **separates** *npl* UK peças *fpl* avulsas (de roupa).
separated ['sepəreɪtɪd] *adj* separado(da).
separately ['seprətlɪ] *adv* separadamente.
separation [ˌsepə'reɪʃn] *n* separação *f*; ~ **(from sb/sthg)** separação (de alguém/algo).
separatism *n* separatismo *m*.
separatist ['seprətɪst] *n* separatista *mf*.
sepia ['si:pjə] *adj* sépia.
Sept. (*abbr of* September) set.
September [sep'tembəʳ] <> *n* setembro; **when are you going? -** ~ quando você vai? - em setembro; **one of the hottest** ~**s on record** um dos setembros mais quentes que já se registrou; **in** ~ em setembro; **last/this/next** ~ em setembro do ano passado/deste ano/do ano que vem; **by** ~ até setembro; **every** ~ todos os anos em setembro; **during** ~ em setembro, durante o mês de setembro; **at the beginning/end of** ~ no início/ fim de setembro; **in the middle of** ~ em meados de setembro, no meio do mês de setembro. <> *comp* de setembro; ~ **birthday** aniversário *m* em setembro.
septet *n* septeto *m*.
septic ['septɪk] *adj* séptico(ca); **to go** ~ infeccionar.
septicaemia UK, **septicemia** US [ˌseptɪ'si:mɪə] *n* (U) septicemia *f*.
septic tank *n* fossa *f* séptica.
sepulchre UK, **sepulcher** US ['sepʌlkəʳ] *n literary* sepulcro *m*.
sequel ['si:kwəl] *n* **-1.** [book, film]: ~ **to sthg** continuação *f* de algo **-2.** [consequence]: ~ **to sthg** seqüela *f* de algo.
sequence ['si:kwəns] *n* **-1.** [gen] seqüência *f*; **in** ~ em seqüência **-2.** [series] seqüência *f*, sucessão *f*.
sequester, sequestrate *vt* JUR confiscar, colocar sob custódia.
sequin ['si:kwɪn] *n* lantejoula *f*.
sera ['sɪərə] *pl* ▷ **serum**.
Serb *adj* & *n* = **Serbian**.
Serbia ['sɜ:bjə] *n* Sérvia; **in** ~ na Sérvia.
Serbian ['sɜ:bjən], **Serb** [sɜ:b] <> *adj* sérvio(via). <> *n* **-1.** [person] sérvio *m*, -via *f* **-2.** [language] sérvio *m*.

Serbo-Croat [ˌsɜ:bəʊ'krəʊæt], **Serbo-Croatian** [ˌsɜ:bəʊkrəʊ'eɪʃn] <> *adj* servo-croata. <> *n* [language] servo-croata *m*.
serenade [ˌserə'neɪd] <> *n* serenata *f*. <> *vt* fazer uma serenata para.
serene [sɪ'ri:n] *adj* sereno(na).
serenely [sɪ'ri:nlɪ] *adv* serenamente.
serenity [sɪ'renətɪ] *n* (U) serenidade *f*.
serf [sɜ:f] *n* HIST servo *m*, -va *f*.
serge [sɜ:dʒ] *n* (U) sarja *f*.
sergeant ['sɑ:dʒənt] *n* **-1.** MIL sargento *m* **-2.** POLICE tenente *m*.
sergeant major *n* primeiro-sargento *m*.
serial ['sɪərɪəl] *n* série *f*, seriado *m*.
serialize, -ise ['sɪərɪəlaɪz] *vt* publicar em folhetim.
serial killer *n* assassino *m*, -na *f* em série, serial killer *m*.
serial number *n* número *m* de série.
series ['sɪəri:z] (*pl inv*) *n* **-1.** [sequence] série *f* **-2.** RADIO & TV série *f*, seriado *m*.
serious ['sɪərɪəs] *adj* **-1.** [gen] sério(ria); **are you** ~? fala sério? **-2.** [problem, illness] grave.
serious crime *n* crime *m* grave.
seriously ['sɪərɪəslɪ] *adv* **-1.** [earnestly] seriamente; **to take sb/sthg** ~ levar alguém/algo a sério **-2.** [very badly] gravemente.
seriousness ['sɪərɪəsnɪs] *n* (U) **-1.** [of person, expression, voice] seriedade *f*; **in all** ~ seriamente **-2.** [of illness, situation, loss] gravidade *f*.
sermon ['sɜ:mən] *n* **-1.** RELIG sermão *m* **-2.** *fig* & *pej* [lecture] sermão *m*.
serpent ['sɜ:pənt] *n literary* serpente *f*.
serrated [sɪ'reɪtɪd] *adj* serrilhado(da), dentado(da).
serum ['sɪərəm] (*pl* serums OR sera) *n* soro *m*.
servant ['sɜ:vənt] *n* criado *m*, -da *f*, empregado *m*, -da *f*.
serve [sɜ:v] <> *n* SPORT serviço *m*, saque *m*. <> *vt* **-1.** [gen] servir; **to** ~ **sthg to sb**, **to** ~ **sb sthg** servir algo a alguém **-2.** [have effect]: **to** ~ **to do sthg** servir para fazer algo; **to** ~ **a purpose** cumprir o propósito **-3.** [provide] abastecer; **which motorway** ~**s Birmingham** que rodovia atende à região de Birmingham? **-4.** JUR: **to** ~ **sb with sthg**, **to** ~ **sthg on sb** entregar algo a alguém **-5.** [complete, carry out] cumprir; **he's serving time** ele está cumprindo pena **-6.** SPORT servir, sacar **-7.** *phr*: **it** ~**s you right** bem feito! <> *vi* **-1.** [be employed - as soldier] servir o exército; [- in profession, on committee] prestar serviços **-2.** [function]: **to** ~ **as sthg** servir como algo **-3.** [in shop, bar etc] servir **-4.** SPORT sacar.
➤ **serve out, serve up** *vt sep* servir.
server ['sɜ:vəʳ] *n* COMPUT servidor *m*.
service ['sɜ:vɪs] <> *n* **-1.** [gen] serviço *m*; **in** ~ em funcionamento; **out of** ~ fora de serviço **-2.** (U) [in shop, bar etc] atendimento *m* **-3.** [mechanical check] revisão *f* **-4.** RELIG serviço *m*, culto *m* **-5.** [set of tableware] jogo *m* **-6.** [dinner] ~ aparelho *m* de jantar **-6.** SPORT serviço *m*, saque *m* **-7.** [use, help]: **to be of** ~ **(to sb)** servir a (alguém). <> *vt* **-1.** [car, machine] fazer a revisão de **-2.** FIN [debt, loan] pagar os juros de.
➤ **services** *npl* **-1.** [on motorway] estação *f* de serviços **-2.** [armed forces]: **the** ~**s** as forças

armadas **-3.** [help] serviços *mpl*.

serviceable ['sɜ:vɪsəbl] *adj* resistente, prático(ca).

service area *n* estação *f* de serviços.

service charge *n* taxa *f* de serviço.

service industries *npl* setor *m* de prestação de serviços.

serviceman ['sɜ:vɪsmən] (*pl* **-men** [-mən]) *n* MIL militar *m*.

service provider *n* COMPUT provedor *m*.

service station *n* posto *m* de gasolina, posto *m* de serviços.

servicewoman ['sɜ:vɪsˌwʊmən] (*pl* **-women**) *n* MIL militar *f*.

serviette [ˌsɜ:vɪ'et] *n* guardanapo *m*.

servile ['sɜ:vaɪl] *adj* servil.

servility [sɜ:'vɪlətɪ] *n (U)* servilismo *m*.

serving ['sɜ:vɪŋ] <> *adj* **-1.** [spoon, dish, fork] de servir **-2.** [member, chairman] que presta serviços. <> *n* [portion] porção *f*.

sesame ['sesəmɪ] *n (U)* gergelim *m*, sésamo *m*; **open ~!** abre-te, sésamo!

session ['seʃn] *n* **-1.** [gen] sessão *f*; **in ~** em sessão **-2.** *US* [school term] período *m* letivo.

set [set] (*pt* & *pp* set, *cont* -ting) <> *adj* **-1.** [specified, prescribed] estabelecido(da) **-2.** [fixed, rigid] fixo(xa); **~ phrase** frase *f* feita; **to be ~ in one's ways** ter costumes arraigados **-3.** [ready] pronto(ta); **~ for sthg/to do sthg** pronto(ta) para algo/para fazer algo **-4.** [determined]: **to be ~ on sthg/on doing sthg** estar empenhado(da) em algo/em fazer algo; **to be dead ~ against sthg** ser completamente contra algo. <> *n* **-1.** [collection, group - stamps] série *f*; [- chess, tea] jogo *m* (de); [- keys, tyres, saucepans] conjunto *m*; [- books] coleção *f* (de) **-2.** [apparatus] aparelhagem *f* **-3.** [of film, play] cenário *m* **-4.** TENNIS set *m*. <> *vt* **-1.** [put in specified position, place] pôr, colocar **-2.** [fix, insert]: **to ~ sthg in(to) sthg** fixar algo em algo **-3.** [indicating change of state or activity] pôr; **to ~ sb free** pôr alguém em liberdade; **to ~ sb's mind at rest** tranqüilizar alguém; **to ~ sthg in motion** pôr algo em movimento; **to ~ sthg right** emendar algo; **to ~ sb thinking** fazer alguém pensar; **to ~ sthg on fire** pôr fogo em algo **-4.** [lay, prepare in advance] pôr, colocar **-5.** [adjust] ajustar, botar; **she ~ the meter at zero** ela ajustou o medidor para zero **-6.** [decide on] estabelecer, fixar **-7.** [establish, create - example] dar; [- precedent] abrir; [- trend] impor; [- record] estabelecer **-8.** [assign - target, problem] determinar; [- school work] passar; [- exam, test work] aplicar **-9.** MED [mend] recompor **-10.** MUS [arrange]: **to ~ sthg to music** musicar algo **-11.** [story] passar-se; **the film is ~ in Scotland** o filme se passa na Escócia **-12.** [hair] fazer mise-en-plis. <> *vi* **-1.** [sun] pôr-se **-2.** [solidify - jelly] endurecer; [- glue, cement] secar.

◆ **set about** *vt fus*: **to ~ about sthg** começar algo; **to ~ about doing sthg** pôr-se a fazer algo.

◆ **set against** *vt sep* **-1.** [compare] comparar **-2.** [put in opposition] pôr contra; **the war ~ brother against brother** a guerra colocou irmão contra irmão **-3.** FIN compensar com; **we can ~ our expenses against tax** podemos deduzir nossos gastos do imposto de renda.

◆ **set ahead** *vt sep US* [clock] adiantar.

◆ **set apart** *vt sep* distinguir; **to ~ sb/sthg apart from** distinguir alguém/algo de.

◆ **set aside** *vt sep* **-1.** [keep, save] guardar **-2.** [not consider] deixar de lado.

◆ **set back** *vt sep* **-1.** [delay] atrasar **-2.** *inf* [cost]: **this book ~ me back £20** este livro me custou £20.

◆ **set down** *vt sep* **-1.** [write down] pôr por escrito **-2.** [put down] deixar.

◆ **set in** *vi* manifestar-se.

◆ **set off** <> *vt sep* **-1.** [initiate, cause] provocar **-2.** [ignite] fazer explodir. <> *vi* pôr-se a caminho.

◆ **set on** *vt sep* atiçar em; **he ~ the dogs on her** ele atiçou os cachorros nela.

◆ **set out** <> *vt sep* **-1.** [arrange, spread out] dispor **-2.** [clarify, explain] expor. <> *vt fus*: **to ~ out to do sthg** propor-se a fazer algo. <> *vi* pôr-se a caminho.

◆ **set up** <> *vt sep* **-1.** [gen] montar **-2.** [establish, arrange - company] montar, fundar; [- committee, organization] criar; [- interview, meeting] organizar; **to ~ o.s. up** estabelecer-se; **to ~ up house** OR **home** instalar-se **-3.** *inf* [make appear guilty] convencer; **to ~ sb up** armar contra alguém; **I was ~ up!** me armaram uma! <> *vi* estabelecer-se.

setback ['setbæk] *n* contratempo *m*.

set menu *n* cardápio *m* a preço fixo.

set piece *n* ART & LITERATURE parte de um filme, romance ou música de grande efeito dramático e que normalmente não é parte essencial da história principal.

set square *n UK* esquadro *m*.

settee [se'ti:] *n* sofá *m*.

setter ['setə'] *n* cão *m* de caça.

setting ['setɪŋ] *n* **-1.** [surroundings] cenário *m* **-2.** [of dial, control] posição *f*.

settle ['setl] <> *vt* **-1.** [conclude, decide] resolver **-2.** [pay] saldar **-3.** [make comfortable] acomodar; **to ~ o.s. somewhere** acomodar-se em algum lugar **-4.** [calm] acalmar, tranqüilizar. <> *vi* **-1.** [go to live] instalar-se **-2.** [make o.s. comfortable] acomodar-se **-3.** [come to rest] depositar-se; **to ~ on sthg** pousar em algo.

◆ **settle down** *vi* **-1.** [give one's attention]: **to ~ down (to sthg/to doing sthg)** dedicar-se (a algo/a fazer algo) **-2.** [become stable] estabelecer-se **-3.** [make o.s. comfortable] acomodar-se; **to ~ down (for sthg)** preparar-se (para algo) **-4.** [become calm] acalmar-se.

◆ **settle for** *vt fus* conformar-se com.

◆ **settle in** *vi* **-1.** [new house] instalar-se **-2.** [in new job] adaptar-se.

◆ **settle on** *vt fus* decidir-se por.

◆ **settle up** *vi*: **to ~ up (with sb)** ajustar as contas (com alguém).

settled ['setld] *adj* estável.

settlement ['setlmənt] *n* **-1.** [agreement] acordo *m* **-2.** [village] povoado *m* **-3.** [payment] pagamento *m*.

settler ['setlə'] *n* colonizador *m*, -ra *f*.

set-to *n inf* briga *f*.

set-up *n inf* **-1.** [system, organization] estrutura *f* **-2.** [deception to incriminate] armação *f*.

seven ['sevn] *num* sete; *see also* **six**.

seventeen [ˌsevn'tiːn] num dezessete; see also **six**.

seventeenth [ˌsevn'tiːnθ] num décimo sétimo, décima sétima; see also **sixth**.

seventh ['sevnθ]. num sétimo(ma); see also **sixth**.

seventh heaven n (U): **to be in** ~ estar no sétimo céu.

seventieth ['sevntjəθ] num septuagésimo(ma); see also **sixth**.

seventy ['sevntɪ] num setenta; see also **sixty**.

sever ['sevəʳ] vt -**1.** [rope, limb] cortar -**2.** [relationship] romper.

several ['sevrəl] <> adj vários(rias). <> pron vários mpl, -rias fpl.

severance ['sevrəns] n (U) fml rompimento m.

severance pay n (U) indenização m por demissão.

severe [sɪ'vɪəʳ] adj -**1.** [extreme, bad - shock] forte; [- weather] ruim; [- pain] agudo(da); [- injury, illness] grave -**2.** [stern] severo(ra).

severely [sɪ'vɪəlɪ] adv -**1.** [extremely, badly] gravemente -**2.** [sternly] severamente.

severity [sɪ'verətɪ] n (U) -**1.** [seriousness] gravidade f -**2.** [strength] força f -**3.** [sternness] severidade f.

sew [səʊ] (UK pp sewn, US pp sewed OR sewn) vt & vi costurar.

➤ **sew up** vt sep -**1.** [join] costurar -**2.** inf [arrange, fix] costurar; **it's all sewn up!** está tudo muito bem costurado!

sewage ['suːɪdʒ] n (U) águas fpl residuais.

sewage farm n estação f de tratamento de esgoto.

sewage works n estação f de tratamento de esgoto.

sewer ['suəʳ] n esgoto m; **the city's** ~ **system** o sistema de esgotos da cidade.

sewerage ['suərɪdʒ] n (U) rede f de esgotos.

sewing ['səʊɪŋ] n (U) -**1.** [activity] trabalho m de costura -**2.** [items] costura f.

sewing machine n máquina f de costura.

sewn [səʊn] pp ⊳ **sew**.

sex [seks] n sexo m; **to have** ~ **(with sb)** fazer sexo (com alguém).

sex appeal n (U) sex appeal m, atração f sexual.

sex education n (U) educação f sexual.

sexism ['seksɪzm] n (U) sexismo m.

sexist ['seksɪst] <> adj sexista. <> n sexista mf.

sex life n vida f sexual.

sex object n objeto m sexual.

sex shop n sex shop m.

sextet [seks'tet] n sexteto m.

sextuplet [seks'tjuːplɪt] n sêxtuplo m.

sexual ['seksʊəl] adj sexual.

sexual assault n ataque m sexual.

sexual discrimination n discriminação f sexual.

sexual harassment n (U) assédio m sexual.

sexual intercourse n (U) relações fpl sexuais.

sexuality [ˌseksʊ'ælətɪ] n (U) sexualidade f.

sexually transmitted disease n doença f sexualmente transmissível.

sexy ['seksɪ] (compar -ier, superl -iest) adj inf sexy, sexualmente atraente.

Seychelles [seɪ'ʃelz] npl: **the** ~ as Ilhas Seychelles; **in the** ~ nas Ilhas Seychelles.

sf, SF (abbr of **science fiction**) n ficção f científica.

SFO (abbr of **Serious Fraud Office**) n departamento de polícia britânico que investiga questões econômicas.

SG (abbr of **Surgeon General**) n autoridade responsável pela saúde pública nos Estados Unidos.

Sgt. (abbr of **sergeant**) Sgt.

sh [ʃ] excl psiu!

shabby ['ʃæbɪ] (compar -ier, superl -iest) adj -**1.** [in bad condition - clothes, briefcase] em mau estado; [- street] abandonado(da) -**2.** [wearing old clothes] esfarrapado(da) -**3.** [mean] mesquinho(nha).

shack [ʃæk] n cabana f.

shackle ['ʃækl] vt -**1.** [chain] algemar -**2.** literary [restrict] impedir.

➤ **shackles** npl -**1.** [metal restraints] algemas pl -**2.** literary [restrictions] impedimentos mpl.

shade [ʃeɪd] <> n -**1.** (U) [shadow] sombra f -**2.** [lampshade] abajur m, quebra-luz m -**3.** [colour] tonalidade f -**4.** [nuance] tom m. <> vt -**1.** [from light] fazer sombra em, proteger do sol; **to** ~ **one's eyes** proteger os olhos do sol (usando a mão) -**2.** [by drawing lines] sombrear. <> vi: **to** ~ **into sthg** fundir-se em algo.

➤ **shades** npl inf óculos mpl escuros.

shading ['ʃeɪdɪŋ] n sombreado m.

shadow ['ʃædəʊ] <> n -**1.** [dark area] sombra f -**2.** [under eyes] olheiras fpl -**3.** phr: **to be a** ~ **of one's former self** ser uma sombra do que se era; **there's nota** OR **the** ~ **of a doubt** não há sombra de dúvida. <> adj UK POL na sombra.

shadow cabinet n gabinete-sombra m, gabinete do principal partido de oposição na Grã-Bretanha.

shadowy ['ʃædəʊɪ] adj -**1.** [dark] escuro(ra) -**2.** [hard to see] vago(ga) -**3.** [unknown, sinister] obscuro(ra).

shady ['ʃeɪdɪ] (compar -ier, superl -iest) adj -**1.** [sheltered from sun] sombreado(da) -**2.** [providing shade] que dá sombra -**3.** inf [dishonest, sinister] suspeito(ta).

shaft [ʃɑːft] <> n -**1.** [vertical passage] poço m -**2.** [rod] haste f -**3.** [of light] feixe m. <> vt v inf [dupe, treat unfairly] ludibriar.

shaggy ['ʃægɪ] (compar -ier, superl -iest) adj -**1.** [hair, beard] desgrenhado(da) -**2.** [dog] peludo(da) -**3.** [carpet, rug] felpudo(da).

shaggy-dog story n piada f longa e boba.

shake [ʃeɪk] (pt shook, pp shaken ['ʃeɪkən]) <> vt -**1.** [gen] abalar -**2.** [move vigorously] sacudir; **to** ~ **sb's hand** apertar a mão de alguém; **to** ~ **hands** apertar as mãos; **to** ~ **one's head** [to say no] negar com a cabeça. <> vi tremer. <> n sacudida f.

➤ **shake down** vt sep US inf -**1.** [rob] chantagear -**2.** [search] revistar.

➤ **shake off** vt sep livrar-se de.

➤ **shake up** vt sep abalar.

shakedown n US inf -**1.** [extortion] extorsão f -**2.** [search] revista f.

shaken ['ʃeɪkn] pp ⊳ **shake**.

shake-out n -**1.** FIN [slight recession] ligeira recessão f -**2.** [shake-up] reestruturação f.

Shakespearean [ʃeɪk'spɪərɪən] *adj* shakespearia-no(na).

shake-up *n inf* reestruturação *f*.

shaky ['ʃeɪkɪ] (*compar* **-ier**, *superl* **-iest**) *adj* **- 1.** [unsteady - chair, table] frágil, instável; [- hand, writing, voice] trêmulo(la); [- person] abalado(da) **- 2.** [weak, uncertain] débil.

shale [ʃeɪl] *n (U)* xisto *m*.

shall [*weak form* ʃəl, *strong form* ʃæl] *aux vb* **- 1.** [to express future tense]: **we ~ be in Scotland in June** estaremos na Escócia em junho; **I ~ ring next week** vou ligar semana que vem **- 2.** [in questions]: **~ we have our tea now?** vamos tomar nosso chá agora?; **where ~ I put this?** onde eu coloco isto?; **~ I give her a ring, then?** ligo para ela, então?; **I'll do that, ~ I?** eu faço isso, pode ser? **- 3.** [will definitely]: **we ~ overcome!** venceremos!; **you ~ go to the ball, Cinderella!** você irá ao baile, Cinderela! **- 4.** [in orders]: **you ~ tell me what happened!** você deve me contar o que aconteceu!

shallot [ʃə'lɒt] *n* cebolinha *f*.

shallow ['ʃæləʊ] *adj* **- 1.** [in size] raso(sa) **- 2.** *pej* [superficial] superficial **- 3.** [breathing] não-profundo(da).
  shallows *npl* baixio *m*.

sham [ʃæm] (*pt & pp* **-med**, *cont* **-ming**) ⇔ *adj* falso(sa), fingido(da). ⇔ *n* farsa *f*. ⇔ *vi* fingir.

shambles ['ʃæmblz] *n* **- 1.** [disorder] confusão *f* **- 2.** [fiasco] fiasco *m*.

shame [ʃeɪm] ⇔ *n* **- 1.** *(U)* [remorse] vergonha *f* **- 2.** *(U)* [dishonour]: **to bring ~ (up)on sb** trazer desonra *or* vergonha a alguém **- 3.** [pity]: **it's a ~ (that)** é uma pena *or* lástima que; **what a ~!** que pena! ⇔ *vt* **- 1.** [fill with shame] envergonhar **- 2.** [force by making ashamed]: **I ~d him into telling the truth** eu o forcei a dizer a verdade ao fazê-lo sentir-se envergonhado por não dizer.

shamefaced [ʃeɪm'feɪst] *adj* envergonhado(da).

shameful ['ʃeɪmfʊl] *adj* vergonhoso(sa).

shameless ['ʃeɪmlɪs] *adj* desavergonhado(da).

shammy ['ʃæmɪ] (*pl* **-ies**) *n inf*: **~ (leather)** camurça *f*.

shampoo [ʃæm'puː] (*pl* **-s**, *pt & pp* **-ed**, *cont* **-ing**) ⇔ *n* **- 1.** [liquid - for hair] xampu *m*; [- for carpet] detergente *m* **- 2.** [act of shampooing] lavada *f* com xampu. ⇔ *vt* lavar.

shamrock ['ʃæmrɒk] *n (U)* trevo *m*.

shandy ['ʃændɪ] (*pl* **-ies**) *n* shandy *m*, *bebida preparada com limonada e cerveja*.

shan't [ʃɑːnt] *cont* = **shall not**.

shanty town *n* ≃ favela *f*.

shape [ʃeɪp] ⇔ *n* **- 1.** [form] forma *f*; **to take ~** tomar forma **- 2.** [figure, silhouette] silhueta *f* **- 3.** [guise]: **in the ~ of** na forma de; **not in any ~ or form** de maneira nenhuma **- 4.** [form, health]: **to be in good/bad ~** estar em boa/má forma; **to lick** *or* **knock sb/sthg into ~** deixar alguém no ponto. ⇔ *vt* **- 1.** [mould physically]: **to ~ sthg (into)** dar a algo forma (de); **a birthmark ~d like a strawberry** uma marca de nascença com a forma de morango **- 2.** [influence] influenciar.
  shape up *vi* desenvolver-se.

SHAPE [ʃeɪp] (*abbr of* **Supreme Headquarters Allied Powers Europe**) *n* quartel-general das potências aliadas na Europa.

-shaped ['ʃeɪpt] *suffix com forma de*; **star~** em forma de estrela.

shapeless ['ʃeɪplɪs] *adj* sem forma.

shapely ['ʃeɪplɪ] (*compar* **-ier**, *superl* **-iest**) *adj* bem formado(da); **~ legs** pernas *fpl* bem torneadas.

shard [ʃɑːd] *n* caco *m*.

share [ʃeəʳ] ⇔ *n*: **~ (of/in sthg)** parte *f* (em/de algo); **to have/do one's ~ of sthg** ter/fazer a parte que toca a alguém de algo; **everyone must do his ~ of the work** todo mundo deve fazer a parte que lhe toca do trabalho; **to have a ~ in the profits** ter participação nos lucros. ⇔ *vt* **- 1.** [gen] compartilhar; **to ~ sthg (with sb)** compartilhar algo (com alguém) **- 2.** [reveal] revelar; **to ~ sthg (with sb)** revelar algo (a alguém). ⇔ *vi* dividir, compartilhar; **to ~ in sthg** compartilhar algo.
  shares *npl* FIN ações *fpl*.
  share out *vt sep* dividir, compartilhar.

share capital *n (U)* capital *m* acionário.

share certificate *n* cautela *f* de ações.

shareholder ['ʃeəˌhəʊldəʳ] *n* acionista *mf*.

share index *n* índice *m* de cotações.

share-out *n* compartilhamento *m*, divisão *f*.

shareware ['ʃeəˌweəʳ] *n* shareware *m*.

shark [ʃɑːk] (*pl inv or* **-s**) *n* **- 1.** [fish] tubarão *m* **- 2.** *fig* [dishonest person] trapaceiro *m*, -ra *f*.

sharp [ʃɑːp] ⇔ *adj* **- 1.** [not blunt - teeth, pencil] apontado(da); [- needle] pontudo(da); [- knife, razor] afiado(da) **- 2.** [well-defined] claro(ra), bem-definido(da) **- 3.** [intelligent, keen - person, mind] inteligente, esperto(ta); [- eyesight] penetrante; [- hearing] atento(ta) **- 4.** [abrupt, sudden] abrupto(ta), brusco(ca) **- 5.** [angry, severe] seco(ca) **- 6.** [sound, pain] agudo(da) **- 7.** [cold, wind] cortante **- 8.** [bitter] acre **- 9.** MUS sustenido(da); **C ~** dó sustenido. ⇔ *adv* **- 1.** [punctually] pontualmente; **at eight o'clock ~** pontualmente às oito horas **- 2.** [quickly, suddenly] de repente. ⇔ *n* MUS sustenido *m*.

sharpen ['ʃɑːpn] ⇔ *vt* **- 1.** [make sharp - knife, tool] afiar; [- pencil] apontar **- 2.** [heighten - sense, abilities] apurar; [- disagreements, differences] aumentar. ⇔ *vi* **- 1.** [become keener, quicker - senses, abilities] apurar; [- appetite, disagreements] aumentar **- 2.** [become more piercing, louder] esganiçar-se.

sharp end *n UK fig*: **to be at the ~ of sthg** levar todo o peso de algo nas costas.

sharpener ['ʃɑːpnəʳ] *n* **- 1.** [for pencil] apontador *m* **- 2.** [for knife] amolador *m*.

sharp-eyed [-'aɪd] *adj* perspicaz.

sharply ['ʃɑːplɪ] *adv* **- 1.** [distinctly] claramente **- 2.** [suddenly] de repente, repentinamente **- 3.** [harshly] duramente.

sharpness ['ʃɑːpnɪs] *n (U)* **- 1.** [of point, edge - of pencil] ponta *f*; [- of knife, razor] fio *m* **- 2.** [of outline, image] nitidez *f* **- 3.** [of mind, senses, sound] agudeza *f* **- 4.** [of pain] intensidade *f* **- 5.** [of remarks, criticism, tone] dureza *f*, aspereza *f* **- 6.** [of taste, smell] acridez *f*.

sharpshooter *n* atirador *m*, -ra *f* de primeira.

sharp-tongued *adj* de língua afiada, mordaz.

sharp-witted [-'wɪtɪd] *adj* perspicaz, sagaz.

shat [ʃæt] *pt & pp* ⊳ **shit**.

shatter ['ʃætəʳ] ⇔ *vt* **- 1.** [glass, window] estilhaçar **- 2.** *fig* [beliefs, hopes, dreams] destruir, arrasar; **to**

be **~ed (by sthg)** ficar arrasado(da) (com algo). ◇ *vi* estilhaçar-se.

shattered ['ʃætəd] *adj* **-1.** [shocked, upset] arrasado(da) **-2.** *UK inf* [very tired] podre.

shattering ['ʃætərɪŋ] *adj* **-1.** [gen] arrasador(ra) **-2.** *UK* [very tiring] extenuante.

shatterproof ['ʃætəpru:f] *adj* que não estilhaça.

shave [ʃeɪv] ◇ *n*: **to have a ~** fazer a barba; **to be a close ~** *fig* ser por pouco *OR* por um triz. ◇ *vt* **-1.** [with razor - face] barbear, fazer a barba de; [- body] depilar, raspar **-2.** [cut pieces off] cortar. ◇ *vi* barbear-se, fazer a barba.
➡ shave off *vt sep* raspar.

shaven ['ʃeɪvn] *adj* raspado(da).

shaver ['ʃeɪvə'] *n* barbeador *m*, aparelho *m* de barbear.

shaving brush ['ʃeɪvɪŋ-] *n* pincel *m* de barba.

shaving cream ['ʃeɪvɪŋ-] *n (U)* creme *m* de barbear.

shaving foam ['ʃeɪvɪŋ-] *n (U)* espuma *f* de barbear.

shavings ['ʃeɪvɪŋz] *npl* **-1.** [of wood] cavacos *mpl*, lascas *fpl* **-2.** [of metal] cisalha *f*.

shaving soap ['ʃeɪvɪŋ-] *n (U)* sabão *m* de barbear.

shawl [ʃɔ:l] *n* xale *m*.

she [ʃi:] ◇ *pers pron* ela; **~'s tall** ela é alta.

sheaf [ʃi:f] *(pl sheaves) n* **-1.** [of papers, letters] maço *m* **-2.** [of corn, grain] feixe *m*.

shear [ʃɪə'] *(pt -ed, pp -ed OR shorn) vt* tosquiar.
➡ shears *npl* **-1.** [for garden] tesoura *f* de podar **-2.** [for dressmaking] tesoura *f*.
➡ shear off ◇ *vt sep* romper. ◇ *vi* romper-se.

sheath [ʃi:θ] *(pl -s) n* **-1.** [for sword, dagger] bainha *f* **-2.** *UK* [condom] camisinha *f*.

sheathe [ʃi:ð] *vt* **-1.** [sword, dagger] embainhar **-2.** [cable, pipe]: **~d in sthg** revestido(da) de algo.

sheath knife *n* faca *f* com bainha.

sheaves [ʃi:vz] *pl* ⊳ sheaf.

shed [ʃed] *(pt & pp shed, cont -ding) n* galpão *m*. ◇ *vt* **-1.** [lose naturally] perder **-2.** [discard, get rid of] desfazer-se de; **the company decided to ~ 100 employees** a empresa decidiu despedir 100 funcionários; **after a drink she ~s any inhibition** depois de um drinque, ela deixa de lado qualquer inibição **-3.** [accidentally lose] perder **-4.** [tears, blood] derramar.

she'd [weak form ʃɪd, strong form ʃi:d] = **she had**, **she would**.

sheen [ʃi:n] *n* brilho *m*.

sheep [ʃi:p] *(pl inv) n* **-1.** [animal] ovelha *f*, **-2.** *fig* [person] cordeiro *m*.

sheepdog ['ʃi:pdɒg] *n* cão *m* pastor.

sheepfold *n* aprisco *m*, redil *m*.

sheepish ['ʃi:pɪʃ] *adj* encabulado(da).

sheepishly ['ʃi:pɪʃlɪ] *adv* encabuladamente.

sheepskin ['ʃi:pskɪn] *n (U)* pele *f* de carneiro.

sheepskin jacket *n* jaqueta *f* de couro *(de carneiro)*.

sheepskin rug *n* tapete *m* de pele de carneiro.

sheer [ʃɪə'] *adj* **-1.** [absolute] puro(ra) **-2.** [very steep - cliff] escarpado(da); [- drop] vertical **-3.** [delicate] diáfano(na).

sheet [ʃi:t] *n* **-1.** [for bed] lençol *m*; **as white as a ~** branco(ca) como uma folha de papel **-2.** [of paper] folha *f* **-3.** [of glass, metal, wood] lâmina *f*.

sheet feed *n* alimentador *m* de papel.

sheet ice *n (U)* capa *f* de gelo.

sheeting ['ʃi:tɪŋ] *n (U)* chapa *f*.

sheet lightning *n (U)* relâmpago *m* irradiado entre nuvens.

sheet metal *n (U)* metal *m* em chapas.

sheet music *n (U)* partituras *fpl* soltas.

sheik(h) [ʃeɪk] *n* xeque *m*.

shelf [ʃelf] *(pl shelves) n* prateleira *f*.

shelf life *n* validade *f (de um produto)*.

shell [ʃel] ◇ *n* **-1.** [gen] casca *f* **-2.** [of tortoise] carapaça *f* **-3.** [on beach] concha *f* **-4.** [of building] estrutura *f* **-5.** [of boat] casco *m* **-6.** [of car] chassi *m* **-7.** *MIL* granada *f*. ◇ *vt* **-1.** [remove covering] descascar **-2.** *MIL* [fire shells at] bombardear.
➡ shell out *inf* ◇ *vt sep* desembolsar. ◇ *vi*: **to ~ out for sthg** desembolsar para algo.

she'll [ʃi:l] *cont* = **she will**, **she shall**.

shellfish ['ʃelfɪʃ] *(pl inv) n* **-1.** [creature] molusco *m*, crustáceo *m* **-2.** *(U)* [food] marisco *m*.

shelling ['ʃelɪŋ] *n (U)* bombardeio *m*.

shell shock *n (U)* trauma *f* de guerra.

shell suit *n UK* conjunto de calça e jaqueta de náilon à prova d'água.

shelter ['ʃeltə'] ◇ *n* **-1.** [building, structure] abrigo *m*, refúgio *m* **-2.** *(U)* [cover, protection] abrigo *m*, proteção *f* **-3.** *(U)* [accommodation] abrigo *m*. ◇ *vt* **-1.** [from rain, sun, bombs]: **to be ~ed by/from sthg** estar protegido(da) por/de algo **-2.** [give asylum to] abrigar. ◇ *vi*: **to ~ from/in sthg** abrigar-se de/em algo.

sheltered ['ʃeltəd] *adj* **-1.** [protected] protegido(da) **-2.** [supervised] assistencial.

shelve [ʃelv] ◇ *vt* engavetar. ◇ *vi* inclinar-se.

shelves [ʃelvz] *pl* ⊳ shelf.

shelving ['ʃelvɪŋ] *n (U)* prateleiras *fpl*.

shenanigans *npl inf* **-1.** [trickery] trapaça *f* **-2.** [mischief] travessura *f*.

shepherd ['ʃepəd] ◇ *n* pastor *m*. ◇ *vt fig* acompanhar.

shepherd's pie ['ʃepədz-] *n (U)* gratinado de carne moída temperada com ervas e coberto com purê de batatas.

sherbet ['ʃɜ:bət] *n* **-1.** *(U) UK* [sweet powder] pó efervescente ingerido como doce **-2.** *US* [sorbet] sorvete *m* de frutas.

sheriff ['ʃerɪf] *n* **-1.** *US* [law officer] xerife *m* **-2.** *Scot* [judge] juiz *m*, -íza *f*.

sherry ['ʃerɪ] *(pl -ies) n* xerez *m*.

she's [ʃi:z] = **she is**, **she has**.

Shetland ['ʃetlənd] *n*: **~, the ~ Islands** as Ilhas Shetland; **in ~, in the ~ Islands** nas Ilhas Shetland.

shh [ʃ] *excl* = sh.

shield [ʃi:ld] ◇ *n* **-1.** [armour] escudo *m* **-2.** *UK* [sports trophy] troféu *m* *(na forma de escudo)* **-3.** [protection]: **~ against sthg** proteção *f* contra algo. ◇ *vt*: **to ~ sb (from sthg)** proteger alguém (de algo); **to ~ o.s. (from sthg)** proteger-se (de algo).

shift [ʃɪft] ◇ *n* **-1.** [gen] turno *m* **-2.** [slight change] mudança f. ⬦ vt **-1.** [move, put elsewhere] mover, mudar de lugar **-2.** [change slightly] mudar de **-3.** *fig* [blame, responsibility]: **to ~ sthg (onto sb)** transferir algo (a alguém) **-4.** *US AUT* [gear] trocar **-5.** [stain] remover, limpar. ⬦ vi **-1.** [move] mover-se **-2.** [change slightly] mudar **-3.** *US AUT* trocar de marcha **-4.** [stain] sair.

shift key n tecla f shift.

shiftless ['ʃɪftlɪs] *adj* folgado(da).

shift stick n *US* alavanca f de mudanças, alavanca f de marcha.

shifty ['ʃɪftɪ] (*compar* -ier, *superl* -iest) *adj inf* matreiro(ra).

Shiite ['ʃiːaɪt] ⬦ *adj* xiita. ⬦ n xiita *mf*.

shilling ['ʃɪlɪŋ] n *UK* xelim m.

shilly-shally ['ʃɪlɪˌʃælɪ] (*pt* & *pp* -ied) *vi* vacilar, titubear.

shimmer ['ʃɪməʳ] ⬦ n reflexo m trêmulo, cintilação f. ⬦ vi cintilar, tremeluzir.

shin [ʃɪn] (*pt* & *pp* -ned, *cont* -ning) n canela f (*na perna*).

➠ **shin up** *UK*, **shinny up** *US* vt fus trepar em.

shin bone n tíbia f.

shine [ʃaɪn] (*pt* & *pp* shone) ⬦ n brilho m. ⬦ vt **-1.** [focus] direcionar **-2.** [polish] lustrar. ⬦ vi **-1.** [give out light] brilhar **-2.** [excel]: **to ~ at sthg** sobressair-se em algo.

shingle ['ʃɪŋgl] n (U) cascalhos m, pedrinhas *fpl*.

➠ **shingles** n *MED* herpes-zoster m.

shining ['ʃaɪnɪŋ] *adj* brilhante.

shinny ➠ **shinny up** vt fus *US* = shin up.

shin pads *npl* caneleira f.

shiny ['ʃaɪnɪ] (*compar* -ier, *superl* -iest) *adj* brilhante.

ship [ʃɪp] (*pt* & *pp* -ped, *cont* -ping) ⬦ n navio m, barco m. ⬦ vt enviar por via marítima.

shipbuilder ['ʃɪpˌbɪldəʳ] n empresa f de construção naval.

shipbuilding ['ʃɪpˌbɪldɪŋ] n (U) construção f naval.

ship canal n canal m de navegação.

shipment ['ʃɪpmənt] n carregamento m.

shipper ['ʃɪpəʳ] n **-1.** [person] exportador(ra) **-2.** [company] empresa f exportadora.

shipping ['ʃɪpɪŋ] n (U) **-1.** [transport] envio m, transporte m **-2.** [ships] navegação f.

shipping agent n **-1.** [person] agente m marítimo **-2.** [company] agência f marítima.

shipping company n companhia f de navegação.

shipping forecast n previsão f das condições marítimas.

shipping lane n rota f marítima.

shipshape ['ʃɪpʃeɪp] *adj* em ordem.

shipwreck ['ʃɪprek] ⬦ n **-1.** [destruction of ship] naufrágio m **-2.** [wrecked ship] navio m naufragado. ⬦ vt: **to be ~ ed** naufragar.

shipwrecked ['ʃɪprekt] *adj* naufragado(da).

shipyard ['ʃɪpjɑːd] n estaleiro m.

shire [ʃaɪəʳ] n condado m.

➠ **Shire** n: **the Shires** the Shires, *os condados centrais da Inglaterra*.

shire horse n cavalo m de tiro.

shirk [ʃɜːk] vt escapar a.

shirker ['ʃɜːkəʳ] n vadio m, -dia f.

shirt [ʃɜːt] n camisa f.

shirtsleeves ['ʃɜːtsliːvz] *npl*: **to be in (one's) ~** estar em mangas de camisa.

shirt tail n fralda f (*da camisa*).

shirty ['ʃɜːtɪ] (*compar* -ier, *superl* -iest) *adj UK inf* estúpido(da).

shit [ʃɪt] (*pt* & *pp* shit *OR* -ted *OR* shat, *cont* -ting) *vulg* ⬦ n merda f. ⬦ vi cagar. ⬦ *excl* merda!

shiver ['ʃɪvəʳ] ⬦ n tremer; **to give sb the ~ s** dar arrepios a alguém. ⬦ vi: **to ~ (with sthg)** tremer (de algo).

shoal [ʃəʊl] n cardume m.

shock [ʃɒk] ⬦ n **-1.** [gen] choque m **-2.** (U) *MED*: **to be suffering from ~, to be in (a state of) ~** estar em estado de choque **-3.** [thick mass] mecha f. ⬦ vt **-1.** [upset] chocar **-2.** [offend] ofender. ⬦ vi chocar.

shock absorber [-əbˌzɔːbəʳ] n amortecedor m.

shocked [ʃɒkt] *adj* **-1.** [upset] chocado(da) **-2.** [offended] chocado(da), ofendido(da).

shocking ['ʃɒkɪŋ] *adj* **-1.** [very bad] péssimo(ma) **-2.** [scandalous] escandaloso(sa) **-3.** [horrifying] chocante.

shockproof ['ʃɒkpruːf] *adj* à prova de choque.

shock tactics *npl* **-1.** *MIL* tática f de choque **-2.** *fig* [surprising manoeuvre] tratamento m de choque.

shock therapy, shock treatment n (U) *MED* terapia f à base de eletrochoques.

shock troops *npl* tropas *fpl* de choque.

shock wave n onda f de choque.

shod [ʃɒd] ⬦ *pt* & *pp* ⊳ shoe. ⬦ *adj* calçado(da).

shoddy ['ʃɒdɪ] (*compar* -ier, *superl* -iest) *adj* **-1.** [badly done or made] de segunda qualidade **-2.** *fig* [poor, unworthy] inferior.

shoe [ʃuː] (*pt* & *pp* -ed *OR* shod, *cont* -ing) ⬦ n **-1.** [for person] sapato m **-2.** [for horse] ferradura f **-3.** [brake] sapata f. ⬦ vt ferrar.

shoebrush ['ʃuːbrʌʃ] n escova f para sapato.

shoe cleaner n [liquid] líquido m para limpar sapatos.

shoehorn ['ʃuːhɔːn] n calçadeira f.

shoelace ['ʃuːleɪs] n cadarço m.

shoemaker ['ʃuːˌmeɪkəʳ] n sapateiro m, -ra f.

shoe polish n (U) graxa f de sapato.

shoe repairer n sapateiro m, -ra f.

shoe shop n sapataria f.

shoestring ['ʃuːstrɪŋ] ⬦ *adj* restrito(ta). ⬦ n *fig*: **on a ~** com orçamento mínimo.

shoetree ['ʃuːtriː] n fôrma f para sapato.

shone [ʃɒn] *pt* & *pp* ⊳ shine.

shoo [ʃuː] ⬦ vt enxotar. ⬦ *excl* xô!

shook [ʃʊk] *pt* ⊳ shake.

shoot [ʃuːt] (*pt* & *pp* shot) ⬦ vt **-1.** [fire gun at - killing] matar a tiros, balear; [- wounding] ferir a tiros, balear; **to ~ o.s.** [kill o.s.] dar-se um tiro, atirar em si mesmo(ma) **-2.** *UK* [hunt] caçar **-3.** [arrow, question] disparar **-4.** [glance, look] relancear **-5.** *CINEMA* filmar, rodar **-6.** *US* [pool] jogar. ⬦ vi **-1.** [fire gun]: **to ~ (at sb/sthg)** atirar (em alguém/algo) **-2.** *UK* [hunt] caçar **-3.** [move quickly]: **to ~ in/**

out/past entrar/sair/passar rapidamente; **to ~ ahead** sair na frente; **to ~ off** partir rapidamente - **4.** CINEMA filmar, rodar - **5.** [SPORT- football] chutar; [- basketball, netball etc] arremessar. <> *n* -**1.** UK [hunting expedition] caçada *f* - **2.** [new growth] brote *m*. <> *excl US inf* - **1.** [go ahead] manda! - **2.** [damn] droga!

shoot down *vt sep* - **1.** [person] matar a tiros - **2.** [plane] derrubar - **3.** *fig* [reject] derrubar por terra.

shoot up *vi* - **1.** [grow quickly] dar um pulo - **2.** [increase quickly] disparar - **3.** *drugs sl* [take drugs] drogar-se.

shooting ['ʃuːtɪŋ] *n* - **1.** [firing of gun] tiroteio *m* - **2.** (U) [hunting] caça *f*.

shooting range *n* área *f* de tiro.

shooting star *n* estrela *f* cadente.

shooting stick *n* bastão que serve como assento.

shoot-out *n* tiroteio *m*.

shop [ʃɒp] (*pt & pp* -ped, *cont* -ping) <> *n* - **1.** [store] loja *f*; **to talk ~** falar sobre trabalho - **2.** [workshop] oficina *f*, seminário *m*. <> *vi* comprar; **to go shopping** fazer compras.

shop around *vi* comparar preços.

shop assistant *n* UK vendedor *m*, -ra *f* (de loja).

shop floor *n*: the ~ o chão de fábrica, os operários.

shopkeeper ['ʃɒpˌkiːpəʳ] *n* lojista *mf*.

shoplifter ['ʃɒpˌlɪftəʳ] *n* ladrão *m*, -dra *f* de lojas.

shoplifting ['ʃɒpˌlɪftɪŋ] *n* (U) roubo *m* numa loja.

shopper ['ʃɒpəʳ] *n* comprador *m*, -ra *f*.

shopping ['ʃɒpɪŋ] *n* compras *fpl*; **to go ~** fazer compras.

shopping bag *n* sacola *f* de compras.

shopping basket *n* UK - **1.** [in supermarket] cesta *f* - **2.** [for online shopping] cesta *f* de compras.

shopping cart *n* US - **1.** [in supermarket] carrinho *m* - **2.** [for online shopping] carrinho *m* de compras.

shopping centre UK, **shopping mall** US, **shopping plaza** US [-ˌplɑːzə] *n* shopping (center) *m*, centro *m* comercial.

shopping list *n* lista *f* de compras.

shopping mall, shopping plaza *n* US = shopping centre.

shopsoiled UK ['ʃɒpsɔɪld], **shopworn** US ['ʃɒpwɔːn] *adj* deteriorado(da) por ficar exposto numa loja.

shop steward *n* representante *mf* sindical.

shopwalker *n* UK supervisor *m*, -ra *f* (de loja).

shopwindow [ˌʃɒpˈwɪndəʊ] *n* vitrina *f*.

shopworn *adj* US = shopsoiled.

shore [ʃɔːʳ] *n* - **1.** [land by water] beira *f*, margem *f*; **sea ~** litoral *m* - **2.** (U) [not at sea]: **on ~** em terra.

shore up *vt sep* - **1.** [prop up] reforçar, sustentar - **2.** *fig* [sustain] sustentar.

shore leave *n* (U) licença *f* para desembarcar.

shoreline ['ʃɔːlaɪn] *n* linha *f* costeira.

shorn [ʃɔːn] <> *pp* ⊳ shear. <> *adj* - **1.** [grass] cortado(da) - **2.** [hair] raspado(da); **~ of** *fig* desprovido(da) de, despojado(da) de; **she was shorn of her responsibility** retiraram todo o poder dela.

short [ʃɔːt] <> *adj* - **1.** [in length, distance] curto(ta) - **2.** [in height] baixo(xa) - **3.** [in time] curto(ta), breve; **in two ~ days we'll be in Spain!** em apenas dois dias, estaremos na Espanha! - **4.** [curt]: **to be ~ (with sb)** ser seco(ca) (com alguém) - **5.** [lacking]: **money is always ~ around Christmas** o dinheiro anda sempre curto no Natal; **we're a pound ~** falta (-nos) uma libra; **she's a bit ~ on brain power** falta a ela um pouco de agilidade mental; **to be ~ of sthg** andar mal de algo; **to be ~ of breath** estar com falta de ar - **6.** [abbreviated]: **to be ~ for sthg** ser o diminutivo de algo. <> *adv* - **1.** [lacking]: **we're running ~ of food** está acabando a comida - **2.** [suddenly, abruptly]: **to cut sthg ~** interromper algo antes do fim; **to stop ~** parar de repente; **to bring** OR **pull sb up ~** fazer alguém parar de repente. <> *n* - **1.** UK [alcoholic drink] drinque *m* (bebida forte) - **2.** CINEMA [film] curta *f*.

shorts *npl* - **1.** [short trousers] shorts *mpl* - **2.** US [underwear] cuecas *fpl*.

for short *adv* para abreviar, para simplificar.

in short *adv* enfim.

nothing short of *prep*: **it was nothing ~ of madness** foi uma verdadeira loucura.

short of *prep*: **~ of doing sthg** a não ser fazendo algo.

shortage ['ʃɔːtɪdʒ] *n* falta *f*, escassez *f*.

short back and sides *n* UK corte *m* de cabelo do exército.

shortbread ['ʃɔːtbred] *n* (U) biscoito *m* amanteigado.

short-change *vt* - **1.** [in shop, restaurant] dar mal o troco a - **2.** *fig* [reward unfairly] passar para trás.

short circuit *n* curto-circuito *m*, curto *m*.

short-circuit <> *vt* provocar curto-circuito em. <> *vi* dar curto-circuito.

shortcomings ['ʃɔːtˌkʌmɪŋz] *npl* defeitos *mpl*.

shortcrust pastry ['ʃɔːtkrʌst-] *n* (U) massa *f* podre.

short cut *n* - **1.** [quick route] atalho *m* - **2.** [quick method] método *m* rápido.

shorten ['ʃɔːtn] <> *vt* encurtar; **'Robert' can be ~ed to 'Bob'** Bob é a forma reduzida de Robert. <> *vi* encurtar.

shortening ['ʃɔːtnɪŋ] *n* (U) CULIN gordura *f* vegetal.

shortfall ['ʃɔːtfɔːl] *n* déficit *m*; **~ in** OR **of sthg** déficit em OR de algo.

shorthand ['ʃɔːthænd] *n* (U) - **1.** [writing system] taquigrafia *f*, estenografia *f* - **2.** [short form]: **~ (for sthg)** maneira *f* suave (de dizer algo).

shorthanded [ˌʃɔːtˈhændɪd] *adj*: **to be ~** estar com falta de pessoal.

shorthand typist *n* UK taquígrafo *m*, -fa *f*, estenógrafo *m*, -fa *f*.

short-haul *adj* de curta distância.

short list *n* UK - **1.** [for job] lista *f* de candidatos selecionados - **2.** [for prize] relação *f* dos finalistas.

short-list *vt* UK: **to be short-listed (for sthg)** [for job] estar entre os candidatos selecionados (para algo); [for prize] estar entre os finalistas (de algo).

short-lived [-'lɪvd] *adj* fugaz, efêmero(ra).

shortly ['ʃɔːtlɪ] *adv* - **1.** [soon] em breve, logo; ~

before/after pouco antes/depois de **-2.** [curtly, abruptly] bruscamente, secamente.

shortness [ˈʃɔːtnɪs] n (U)**-1.** [in time] brevidade f**-2.** [in length] curteza f**-3.** [in height] baixa estatura f**-4.** [in distance] proximidade f.

short-range adj **-1.** [missile, weapon] de curto alcance **-2.** [forecast] a curto prazo.

short shrift [-ˈʃrɪft] n: **to give sb** ~ prestar pouca atenção a alguém.

shortsighted [ˌʃɔːtˈsaɪtɪd] adj **-1.** [myopic] míope **-2.** fig [lacking foresight] de visão curta.

short-staffed [-ˈstɑːft] adj: **to be** ~ estar com falta de pessoal.

short-stay adj: **a** ~ **car park** estacionamento para curtos períodos de tempo, geralmente 2-3 horas; ~ **accommodation** acomodação para poucos dias; **a** ~ **patient** paciente hospitalizado por três dias ou menos.

short story n conto m.

short-tempered [-ˈtempəd] adj irritadiço(ça).

short-term adj **-1.** [happening soon] a curto prazo **-2.** [of short duration] de curto prazo.

short time n UK: **to be on** ~ trabalhar com jornada reduzida.

short wave n onda f curta.

shot [ʃɒt] <> pt & pp ⊳ **shoot**. <> n **-1.** [gunshot] tiro m; **like a** ~ [quickly] como um raio **-2.** [marksman] atirador m, -ra f **-3.** SPORT chute m **-4.** [photograph] foto f **-5.** CINEMA tomada f **-6.** inf [try, go] tentativa f **-7.** [injection] injeção f**-8.** [of alcohol] dose f.

shotgun [ˈʃɒtɡʌn] n espingarda f.

shot put n: **the** ~ o lançamento de peso.

should [ʃʊd] aux vb **-1.** [indicating duty, necessity]: **we** ~ **leave now** deveríamos ir agora **-2.** [seeking advice, permission]: ~ **I go too?** eu vou também? **-3.** [as suggestion]: **I** ~ **deny everything** eu negaria tudo **-4.** [indicating probability]: **she** ~ **be home soon** ela deve chegar em casa logo **-5.** [was or were expected to]: **they** ~ **have won the match** eles deveriam ter ganhado o jogo **-6.** (as conditional): **I** ~ **like to come with you** eu gostaria de ir com você; **how** ~ **I know?** como é que eu poderia saber?; ~ **you be interested, ...** caso você esteja interessado, ... **-7.** (in subordinate clauses): **we decided that you** ~ **meet him** decidimos que você deveria encontrá-lo **-8.** [expressing uncertain opinion]: **I** ~ **think he's about 50 years old** eu diria que ele tem uns 50 anos **-9.** (after who or what) [expressing surprise]: **and who** ~ **I see but Ann!** e então quem é que eu vejo? A Ann!

shoulder [ˈʃəʊldəʳ] <> n **-1.** [part of body] ombro m; **to look over one's** ~ olhar para trás; **a** ~ **to cry on** um ombro no qual chorar; **to rub** ~**s with sb** conviver com alguém (rico e famoso) **-2.** [part of clothing] ombreira f **-3.** CULIN [joint] quarto m dianteiro. <> vt **-1.** [load] carregar nos ombros **-2.** [responsibility] arcar com.

shoulder bag n mochila f.

shoulder blade n omoplata f.

shoulder-length adj na altura dos ombros.

shoulder pad n ombreira f.

shoulder strap n alça f.

shouldn't [ˈʃʊdnt] = **should not**.

should've [ˈʃʊdəv] = **should have**.

shout [ʃaʊt] <> n grito m. <> vt gritar. <> vi gritar; **to** ~ **at sb** [tell off] gritar com alguém.
◆ **shout down** vt sep calar com gritos.
◆ **shout out** vt sep gritar.

shouting [ˈʃaʊtɪŋ] n (U) gritos mpl; **a lot of** ~ uma gritaria.

shove [ʃʌv] inf <> n: **to give sb/sthg a** ~ dar um empurrão em alguém/algo. <> vt empurrar; **to** ~ **sb in** colocar alguém para dentro aos empurrões; **to** ~ **sb out** tirar alguém aos empurrões.
◆ **shove off** vi **-1.** [in boat] afastar-se da costa **-2.** inf [go away] cair fora.

shovel [ˈʃʌvl] (UK pt & pp-**led**, cont-**ling**, US pt & pp-**ed**, cont -**ing**) <> n pá f. <> vt **-1.** [with a shovel] tirar com pá **-2.** fig [food, meal] devorar; **they** ~**led down their food and left** eles engoliram a janta e saíram.

show [ʃəʊ] (pt-**ed**, pp **shown** OR -**ed**) <> n **-1.** [piece of entertainment - theatre] espetáculo m; [- TV, radio] show m, programa m **-2.** CINEMA sessão f **-3.** [exhibition] exposição f; **on** ~ à mostra **-4.** [display] demonstração f; **for** ~ para bonito **-5.** [pretence] demonstração f falsa. <> vt **-1.** [gen] mostrar; **to** ~ **sb sthg, to** ~ **sthg to sb** mostrar algo para alguém; **to** ~ **sb how to do sthg** mostrar a alguém como fazer algo; **to have something to** ~ **for sthg** ganhar uma coisa por algo; **to have nothing to** ~ **for sthg** não ter ganhado nada por algo; **to** ~ **o.s.** apresentar-se; **it just goes to** ~ **(that) ...** isso só prova que ... **-2.** [reveal] mostrar, revelar; **to** ~ **sb sthg** demostrar algo por alguém **-3.** [escort]: **to** ~ **sb to sthg** levar OR acompanhar alguém até algo **-4.** [broadcast] apresentar, passar **-5.** [profit, loss] registrar **-6.** [work of art, produce] mostrar, exibir. <> vi **-1.** [indicate, make clear] mostrar, indicar **-2.** [be visible] aparecer; **inside he was very angry but it didn't** ~ por dentro ele estava muito bravo mas não aparentava **-3.** CINEMA passar.
◆ **show around** vt sep = **show round**.
◆ **show in** vt sep mandar entrar.
◆ **show off** <> vt sep exibir. <> vi exibir-se.
◆ **show out** vt sep levar até à porta.
◆ **show round** vt sep mostrar (uma cidade, um apartamento); **to** ~ **sb round town** mostrar a cidade a alguém.
◆ **show up** <> vt sep: **to** ~ **sb up in public** fazer alguém passar vergonha em público. <> vi **-1.** [stand out] destacar-se **-2.** [arrive] aparecer. ·

showbiz [ˈʃəʊbɪz] n (U) inf showbiz m.

show business n (U) showbusiness m, mundo m dos espetáculos.

showcase [ˈʃəʊkeɪs] n **-1.** [glass case] vitrina f **-2.** fig [advantageous setting] prato m cheio.

showdown [ˈʃəʊdaʊn] n: **to have a** ~ **with sb** ter um acerto final de contas com alguém.

shower [ˈʃaʊəʳ] <> n **-1.** [gen] chuva f **-2.** [device] chuveiro m **-3.** [wash]: **to have** OR **take a** ~ tomar uma ducha **-4.** US [for wedding] chá m de panela **-5.** [for a baby] chá m de fralda. <> vt **-1.** [sprinkle] jogar; **the newlyweds were** ~**ed with confetti** os recém-casados ganharam uma chuva de confetes **-2.** [bestow]: **to** ~ **sb with sthg, to** ~ **sthg**

(up)on sb encher alguém de algo. <> *vi* tomar banho.

shower cap *n* touca *f* de banho.

showerproof [ˈʃaʊəpruːf] *adj* resistente à chuva, impermeável.

showery [ˈʃaʊərɪ] *adj* chuvoso(sa).

showing [ˈʃəʊɪŋ] *n* sessão *f*.

show jumping [-ˌdʒʌmpɪŋ] *n (U)* concurso *m* hípico de saltos.

showman [ˈʃəʊmən] *(pl* -men [-mən]) *n* -1. [at fair, circus] apresentador *m* -2. *fig* [publicity-seeker] astro *m*, showman *m*.

showmanship [ˈʃəʊmənʃɪp] *n (U)* encenação *f*; **to be pure** ~ ser um verdadeiro show OR espetáculo.

shown [ʃəʊn] *pp* ▷ **show.**

show-off *n inf* exibido(da).

show of hands *n*: **they voted by a** ~ eles votaram levantando as mãos.

showpiece [ˈʃəʊpiːs] *n* atração *f* principal.

showroom [ˈʃəʊrʊm] *n* salão *m* de exposição.

showy [ˈʃəʊɪ] *(compar* -ier, *superl* -iest) *adj* chamativo(va).

shrank [ʃræŋk] *pt* ▷ **shrink.**

shrapnel [ˈʃræpnl] *n (U)* metralha *f*.

shred [ʃred] *(pt & pp* -ded, *cont* -ding) <> *n* -1. [small piece] pedaço *m* -2. *fig* [scrap]: **there was not a** ~ **of evidence that ...** não havia a mais remota evidência de que ...; **a** ~ **of truth** um pingo de verdade. <> *vt* -1. CULIN picar -2. [paper] picar, rasgar.

shredder [ˈʃredəʳ] *n* -1. CULIN [in food processor] triturador *m* -2. [for documents] picadora *f* de papel.

shrew [ʃruː] *n* musaranho *m*.

shrewd [ʃruːd] *adj* perspicaz, astuto(ta).

shrewdness [ˈʃruːdnɪs] *n (U)* perspicácia *f*, astúcia *f*.

shriek [ʃriːk] <> *n* grito *m*; **a** ~ **of laughter** uma gargalhada. <> *vt* gritar. <> *vi*: **to** ~ **(with/in)** gritar (de); **to** ~ **with laughter** gargalhar.

shrill [ʃrɪl] *adj* agudo(da).

shrimp [ʃrɪmp] *n* camarão *m*.

shrine [ʃraɪn] *n* santuário *m*.

shrink [ʃrɪŋk] *(pt* shrank, *pp* shrunk) <> *vt* encolher. <> *vi* -1. [become smaller] encolher -2. *fig* [contract, diminish] diminuir -3. [recoil]: **to** ~ **away from sthg** recuar frente a algo -4. [be reluctant]: **to** ~ **from sthg/from doing sthg** fugir de algo/de fazer algo. <> *n inf* [psychoanalyst] psicanalista *mf*.

shrinkage [ˈʃrɪŋkɪdʒ] *n (U)* -1. [loss in size] encolhimento *m* -2. *fig* [contraction] redução *f*.

shrink-wrap *vt* embalar com plástico termorretrátil.

shrivel [ˈʃrɪvl] *(UK pt & pp* -led, *cont* -ling, *US pt & pp* -ed, *cont* -ing) <> *vt*: **to** ~ **(up)** secar, murchar. <> *vi*: **to** ~ **(up)** secar, murchar.

shroud [ʃraʊd] <> *n* mortalha *f*. <> *vt*: **to be** ~ **ed in sthg** [darkness, fog] estar encoberto(ta) em algo; [mystery] estar envolto(ta) em algo.

Shrove Tuesday [ˈʃrəʊv-] *n* terça-feira *f* de Carnaval.

shrub [ʃrʌb] *n* arbusto *m*.

shrubbery [ˈʃrʌbərɪ] *(pl* -ies) *n* arbustos *mpl*.

shrug [ʃrʌg] *(pt & pp* -ged, *cont* -ging) <> *n* encolhimento *m* dos ombros; **to give a** ~ dar de ombros. <> *vt* encolher. <> *vi* dar de ombros, encolher os ombros.

➤ **shrug off** *vt sep* não dar bola para.

shrunk [ʃrʌŋk] *pp* ▷ **shrink.**

shrunken [ˈʃrʌŋkn] *adj* -1. [person] enrugado(da) -2. [business] reduzido(da) -3. [fruit] seco(ca).

shucks [ʃʌks] *excl US inf* -1. [it was nothing] ora bolas! -2. [damn] droga!

shudder [ˈʃʌdəʳ] <> *n* calafrio *m*. <> *vi* -1. [person]: **to** ~ **(with sthg)** estremecer-se (de algo); **I** ~ **to think** me dá calafrios só de pensar -2. [machine, vehicle] tremer, balançar.

shuffle [ˈʃʌfl] <> *n* -1. [of feet] arrasto *m* -2. [of cards] baralhamento *m*; **to give the cards a** ~ embaralhar as cartas. <> *vt* -1. [feet] arrastar -2. [cards] embaralhar -3. [papers] mudar de lugar. <> *vi* -1. [walk]: **to** ~ **(in/out/along)** entrar/sair/andar arrastando os pés -2. [fidget] remexer-se nervosamente.

shun [ʃʌn] *(pt & pp* -ned, *cont* -ning) *vt* evitar.

shunt [ʃʌnt] *vt* -1. RAIL manobrar, trocar de via férrea -2. *fig* [move]: **we were** ~ **ed from one room to another** ficamos nos mandando de uma sala para outra.

shunter *n* -1. [engine] locomotiva *f* de manobras -2. [person] guarda-chaves *mf inv*.

shush [ʃʊʃ] *excl* psit!

shut [ʃʌt] *(pt & pp* shut, *cont* -ting) <> *adj* fechado(da). <> *vt & vi* fechar; ~ **your mouth** OR **face!** *v inf* fecha o bico OR a matraca.

➤ **shut away** *vt sep* -1. [criminal] trancafiar; **to** ~ **o.s. away** encerrar-se -2. [valuables] guardar.

➤ **shut down** <> *vt sep & vi* fechar.

➤ **shut in** *vt sep* trancar; **to** ~ **o.s. in** trancar-se em.

➤ **shut out** *vt sep* -1. [of building, room] não deixar entrar -2. [block out of mind] bloquear.

➤ **shut up** <> *vt sep* -1. [shop, factory] fechar -2. [silence] calar, fazer calar. <> *vi* -1. *inf* [be quiet] calar a boca -2. [close] fechar.

shutter [ˈʃʌtəʳ] *n* -1. [on window] veneziana *f* -2. [in camera] obturador *m*.

shuttle [ˈʃʌtl] <> *adj*: ~ **service** [of planes] ponte *f* aérea; [of buses, train] linha *f* regular. <> *n* -1. [train, bus] linha *f* regular -2. [plane] avião *m* da ponte aérea. <> *vi* ir e vir. <> *vt* transportar.

shuttlecock [ˈʃʌtlkɒk] *n* peteca *f*.

shy [ʃaɪ] *(pt & pp* shied) <> *adj* tímido(da); **to be** ~ **of doing sthg** não se atrever a fazer algo. <> *vi* espantar-se.

➤ **shy away from** *vt fus*: **to** ~ **away from sthg** fugir de algo; **to** ~ **away from doing sthg** negar-se a fazer algo.

shyly [ˈʃaɪlɪ] *adv* timidamente.

shyness [ˈʃaɪnɪs] *n (U)* timidez *f*.

Siam *n* Sião; **in** ~ no Sião.

Siamese [ˌsaɪəˈmiːz] *(pl inv)* <> *adj* siamês(esa). <> *n* -1. [person] siamês *m*, -esa *f* -2. [cat] gato *m* siamês.

Siamese twins *npl* irmãos *mpl* siameses, irmãs *fpl* siamesas.

SIB (*abbr of* **Securities and Investment Board**) *n* organismo britânico regulador de investimentos na bolsa.

Siberia [saɪ'bɪərɪə] *n* Sibéria; **in** ~ na Sibéria.

Siberian [saɪ'bɪərɪən] <> *adj* siberiano(na). <> *n* siberiano *m*, -na *f*.

sibling ['sɪblɪŋ] *n* irmão *m*, -mã *f*.

Sicilian [sɪ'sɪljən] <> *adj* siciliano(na). <> *n* siciliano *m*, -na *f*.

Sicily ['sɪsɪlɪ] *n* Sicília; **in** ~ na Sicília.

sick [sɪk] *adj* - **1.** [unwell] doente - **2.** [nauseous]: **to feel** ~ sentir-se mal - **3.** [vomiting]: **to be** ~ *UK* vomitar - **4.** [fed up]: **to be** ~ **of sthg/of doing sthg** estar farto(ta) de algo/de fazer algo - **5.** [angry, disgusted]: **to make sb** ~ *fig* deixar alguém doente - **6.** [offensive] de mau gosto.

sickbay ['sɪkbeɪ] *n* enfermaria *f*.

sickbed ['sɪkbed] *n* leito *m* de doente.

sicken ['sɪkn] <> *vt* deixar doente. <> *vi UK*: **to be** ~ **ing for sthg** estar ficando doente de algo.

sickening ['sɪknɪŋ] *adj* - **1.** [disgusting] repugnante - **2.** *hum* [infuriating] irritante, exasperante.

sickle ['sɪkl] *n* foice *f*.

sick leave *n* (*U*) licença *f* de saúde.

sickly ['sɪklɪ] (*compar* -**ier**, *superl* -**iest**) *adj* - **1.** [unhealthy] doentio(tia) - **2.** [nauseating] nauseante.

sickness ['sɪknɪs] *n* - **1.** (*U*) [general illness] doença *f*, enfermidade *f* - **2.** *UK* (*U*) [nausea, vomiting] náusea *f*, enjôo *m* - **3.** [specific illness] doença *f*.

sickness benefit *n* (*U*) ≃ auxílio-doença *m*.

sick pay *n* (*U*) espécie de auxílio-doença pago pelo empregador.

sickroom ['sɪkrʊm] *n* enfermaria *f*.

side [saɪd] <> *n* - **1.** [gen] lado *m*; **on every** ~, **on all** ~ **s** por todos os lados; **from** ~ **to** ~ de um lado a outro; **to put sthg to** *or* **on one** ~ pôr *or* colocar algo de lado; **at** *or* **by sb's** ~ ao lado de alguém; ~ **by** ~ lado a lado; **on my mother's** ~ por parte da minha mãe - **2.** [surface] lateral *f* - **3.** [of table, river] borda *f*, beira *f* - **4.** [slope] ladeira *f*, encosta *f* - **5.** [in sport] equipe *f* - **6.** [viewpoint] ponto *m* de vista; **to take sb's** ~ ficar do lado de alguém; **to be on sb's** ~ estar do lado de alguém - **7.** [aspect] aspecto *m*; **to be on the safe** ~ por via das dúvidas - **8.** *phr*: **on the large/small** ~ um pouco grande/ pequeno demais; **to do sthg on the** ~ [in addition] fazer algo para ganhar um dinheiro extra; [dishonestly] fazer algo por fora (*sem que a Receita saiba*); **to keep** *or* **stay on the right** ~ **of sb** ficar quieto(ta) ao lado de alguém. <> *adj* lateral.
   side with *vt fus* pôr-se ao lado de.

sideboard ['saɪdbɔːd] *n* armário *m*, guarda-louça *m*.

sideboards *UK* ['saɪdbɔːdz], **sideburns** *US* ['saɪdbɜːnz] *npl* suíças *fpl*, costeletas *fpl*.

sidecar ['saɪdkɑːʳ] *n* side-car *m*.

side dish *n* acompanhamento *m*, guarnição *f*.

side effect *n* efeito *m* colateral.

sidekick ['saɪdkɪk] *n inf* cupincha *mf*, comparsa *mf*.

sidelight ['saɪdlaɪt] *n* luz *f* lateral.

sideline ['saɪdlaɪn] *n* - **1.** [extra business] ocupação *f* secundária - **2.** *SPORT* [painted line] linha *f* lateral - **3.** [periphery]: **on the** ~ **s** nas margens.

sidelong ['saɪdlɒŋ] <> *adj* de lado. <> *adv*: **to look** ~ **at sb/sthg** olhar de lado para alguém/ algo.

side-on <> *adj* lateral. <> *adv* de lado.

side plate *n* prato *m* para pão.

side road *n* estrada *f* secundária.

sidesaddle ['saɪd,sædl] *adv*: **to ride** ~ montar de silhão.

sideshow ['saɪdʃəʊ] *n* área de jogos ou de espetáculos paralelos numa feira ou num circo.

sidestep ['saɪdstep] (*pt* & *pp* -**ped**, *cont* -**ping**) *vt* - **1.** [step to one side to avoid] desviar, evitar - **2.** *fig* [problem, question] esquivar-se de.

side street *n* rua *f* secundária.

sidetrack ['saɪdtræk] *vt*: **to be** ~ **ed** desviar (dos objetivos).

sidewalk ['saɪdwɔːk] *n US* calçada *f*.

sideways ['saɪdweɪz] <> *adj* - **1.** [movement] lateral - **2.** [look] de soslaio. <> *adv* - **1.** [move] de lado - **2.** [look] de soslaio.

siding ['saɪdɪŋ] *n* - **1.** *UK* [for shunting] via *f* morta - **2.** *US* [loop line] tapume *m*.

sidle ['saɪdl]   **sidle up** *vi*: **to** ~ **up to sb** aprochegar-se furtivamente de alguém.

SIDS (*abbr of* **sudden infant death syndrome**) *n* morte súbita de recém-nascido.

siege [siːdʒ] *n* cerco *m*.

Sierra Leone [si:,eərəli'əʊn] *n* Serra Leoa; **in** ~ em Serra Leoa.

Sierra Leonean [si:,eərəli'əʊnɪən] <> *adj* serra-leonês(esa). <> *n* serra-leonês *m*, -esa *f*.

siesta [si:'estə] *n* sesta *f*.

sieve [sɪv] <> *n* peneira *f*; **to have a head** *or* **memory like a** ~ ter uma memória terrível. <> *vt* peneirar.

sift [sɪft] <> *vt* - **1.** [sieve] peneirar - **2.** *fig* [examine carefully] examinar cuidadosamente. <> *vi*: **to** ~ **through sthg** analisar algo minuciosamente.

sigh [saɪ] <> *n* suspiro *m*; **to heave a** ~ **of relief** suspirar aliviado(da). <> *vi* suspirar.

sight [saɪt] <> *n* - **1.** [gen] visão *f*; **his first** ~ **of the sea** a primeira vez que ele viu o mar; **in** ~ à vista; **out of** ~ longe de vista; **to catch** ~ **of sb/sthg** avistar alguém/algo; **to know sb by** ~ conhecer alguém de vista; **to lose** ~ **of sb/sthg** perder algo/alguém de vista; **to shoot on** ~ atirar sem aviso; **at first** ~ à primeira vista - **2.** [spectacle] espetáculo *m* - **3.** [on gun] mira *f*; **to set one's** ~ **s on doing sthg** propor-se a fazer algo; **to set one's** ~ **on sthg** botar algo na cabeça - **4.** [a lot]: **a** ~ **better/worse** muito melhor/pior. <> *vt* avistar, divisar.
   sights *npl* pontos *mpl* turísticos.

sighting ['saɪtɪŋ] *n*: **there have been two** ~ **s of the prisoner** o prisioneiro foi visto duas vezes.

sightseeing ['saɪt,siːɪŋ] *n* (*U*) turismo *m*; **to do some** ~ fazer turismo.

sightseer ['saɪt,siːəʳ] *n* turista *mf*.

sign [saɪn] <> *n* - **1.** [gen] sinal *m* - **2.** [in music] símbolo *m* - **3.** [notice] placa *f*. <> *vt* - **1.** [document] assinar - **2.** *SPORT* [player] contratar.
   sign away *vt sep* ceder (*assinando um documento*).

➧ **sign for** *vt fus* -**1.** [sign receipt for] assinar o recibo de -**2.** [sign contract for] assinar um contrato com.

➧ **sign in** *vi* dar entrada.

➧ **sign on** *vi* -**1.** [enrol]: **to ~ on (for sthg)** [for course] inscrever-se (em algo); MIL alistar-se (em algo) -**2.** [register as unemployed] cadastrar-se para receber o seguro desemprego.

➧ **sign out** *vi* dar saída.

➧ **sign up** ◇ *vt sep* -**1.** [employee] contratar -**2.** [soldier] recrutar. ◇ *vi* [enrol]: **to ~ up (for sthg)** [for course] inscrever-se (em algo); MIL alistar-se (em algo).

signal ['sɪɡnl] (*UK pt* & *pp* -led, *cont* -ling, *US pt* & *pp* -ed, *cont* -ing) ◇ *n* sinal *m*. ◇ *vt* -**1.** [send signals to] enviar sinais a -**2.** [indicate - a turn] sinalizar; [- a warning] indicar; **to ~ sb (to do sthg)** fazer sinal para alguém (fazer algo) -**3.** *fig* marcar, anunciar. ◇ *adj fml* marcante. ◇ *vi* -**1.** AUT sinalizar -**2.** [indicate]: **to ~ to sb (to do sthg)** fazer sinal para alguém (fazer algo); **he ~ led to the waiter for the bill** ele fez um sinal para o garçom pedindo a conta.

signal box *UK*, **signal tower** *US n* cabina *f* de sinaleiro.

signalman ['sɪɡnlmən] (*pl* -men [-mən]) *n* sinaleiro *m*.

signal tower *n US* = **signal box.**

signatory ['sɪɡnətrɪ] (*pl* -ies) *n* signatário *m*, -ria *f*.

signature ['sɪɡnətʃəʳ] *n* assinatura *f*.

signature tune *n* tema *m*.

signet ring ['sɪɡnɪt-] *n* anel *m* com sinete.

significance [sɪɡ'nɪfɪkəns] *n* (U) -**1.** [importance] importância *f* -**2.** [meaning] significado *m*.

significant [sɪɡ'nɪfɪkənt] *adj* significativo(va).

significantly [sɪɡ'nɪfɪkəntlɪ] *adv* -**1.** [improve, increase, change] significativamente -**2.** [smile, nod, wink] sugestivamente.

signify ['sɪɡnɪfaɪ] (*pt* & *pp* -ied) *vt* significar.

signing ['saɪnɪŋ] *n UK* contratação *f*.

sign language *n* (U) linguagem *f* de sinais.

signpost ['saɪnpəʊst] *n* placa *f* de sinalização.

Sikh [si:k] ◇ *adj* sique. ◇ *n* sique *mf*.

Sikhism ['si:kɪzm] *n* (U) siquismo *m*.

silage ['saɪlɪdʒ] *n* (U) silagem *f*.

silence ['saɪləns] ◇ *n* silêncio *m*; **in ~** em silêncio. ◇ *vt* silenciar, calar.

silencer ['saɪlənsəʳ] *n* -**1.** [on gun] silenciador *m* -**2.** AUT silenciador *m*, silencioso *m*.

silent ['saɪlənt] *adj* -**1.** [gen] silencioso(sa) -**2.** [taciturn] silencioso(sa), taciturno(na) -**3.** [not revealing anything]: **to be ~ about sthg** ser discreto(ta) sobre algo -**4.** CINEMA & LING mudo(da).

silently ['saɪləntlɪ] *adv* -**1.** [without speaking] em silêncio -**2.** [noiselessly] silenciosamente.

silent partner *n US* sócio *m* comanditário, sócia *f* comanditária.

silhouette [ˌsɪlu:'et] ◇ *n* silhueta *f*. ◇ *vt*: **to be ~ d against sthg** destacar-se (contra algo).

silicon ['sɪlɪkən] *n* (U) silício *m*.

silicon chip [ˌsɪlɪkən-] *n* chip *m* de silício.

silicone ['sɪlɪkəʊn] *n* (U) silicone *m*.

Silicon Valley *n* Vale do Silício.

silk [sɪlk] ◇ *n* (U) seda *f*. ◇ *comp* de seda.

silk screen printing *n* (U) serigrafia *f*.

silkworm ['sɪlkwɜ:m] *n* bicho-da-seda *m*.

silky ['sɪlkɪ] (*compar* -ier, *superl* -iest) *adj* sedoso(sa).

sill [sɪl] *n* peitoril *m*.

silliness ['sɪlɪnɪs] *n* (U) imbecilidade *f*, estupidez *f*.

silly ['sɪlɪ] (*compar* -ier, *superl* -iest) *adj* -**1.** [foolish] bobo(ba) -**2.** [comical] bobo(ba), ridículo(la).

silo ['saɪləʊ] (*pl* -s) *n* silo *m*.

silt [sɪlt] *n* (U) sedimento *m*, lodo *m*.

➧ **silt up** *vi* assorear.

silver ['sɪlvəʳ] ◇ *adj* prateado(da). ◇ *n* (U) -**1.** [metal] prata *f* -**2.** [coins] moedas *fpl* -**3.** [silverware] prataria *f*. ◇ *comp* [made of silver] de prata.

silver-plated [-'pleɪtɪd] *adj* prateado(da).

silver screen *n inf*: **the ~** o cinema.

silversmith ['sɪlvəsmɪθ] *n* prateiro *m*, -ra *f*.

silverware ['sɪlvəweəʳ] *n* -**1.** [objects made of silver] prataria *f* -**2.** *US* [cutlery] prataria *f*.

silver wedding *n* bodas *fpl* de prata.

silvery ['sɪlvərɪ] *adj* prateado(da).

similar ['sɪmɪləʳ] *adj* parecido(da), semelhante; **~ to sthg** parecido(da) *or* similar a algo.

similarity [ˌsɪmɪ'lærətɪ] (*pl* -ies) *n*: **~ (between)** semelhança *f* (entre), similaridade *f* (entre); **~ to sthg** semelhança *f* com algo.

similarly ['sɪmɪləlɪ] *adv* igualmente, da mesma forma.

simile ['sɪmɪlɪ] *n* símile *m*.

simmer ['sɪməʳ] *vt* & *vi* cozinhar em fogo baixo.

➧ **simmer down** *vi inf* sossegar o facho.

simper ['sɪmpəʳ] ◇ *n* sorriso *m* bobo. ◇ *vi* sorrir de forma boba.

simpering ['sɪmpərɪŋ] *adj* -**1.** [person] que sorri com cara de bobo(ba) -**2.** [smile] bobo(ba).

simple ['sɪmpl] *adj* -**1.** [gen] simples -**2.** *inf* [mentally retarded] simplório(ria).

simple-minded [-'maɪndɪd] *adj* simplório(ria).

simpleton ['sɪmpltən] *n dated* basbaque *mf*.

simplicity [sɪm'plɪsətɪ] *n* simplicidade *f*.

simplification [ˌsɪmplɪfɪ'keɪʃn] *n* simplificação *f*.

simplify ['sɪmplɪfaɪ] (*pt* & *pp* -ied) *vt* simplificar.

simplistic [sɪm'plɪstɪk] *adj* simplista.

simply ['sɪmplɪ] *adv* -**1.** [gen] simplesmente; **you must go and see the film** você só tem que ir ver o filme -**2.** [in an uncomplicated way] de forma simples.

simulate ['sɪmjʊleɪt] *vt* -**1.** [feign] simular, fingir -**2.** [produce effect, appearance of] simular.

simulation [ˌsɪmjʊ'leɪʃn] *n* -**1.** [feigning] simulação *f*, fingimento *m* -**2.** [simulated appearance, effect] simulacro *m* -**3.** COMPUT simulação *f*.

simulator ['sɪmjʊleɪtəʳ] *n* simulador *m*.

simultaneous [*UK* ˌsɪmʊl'teɪnjəs, *US* ˌsaɪməl'teɪnjəs] *adj* simultâneo(nea).

simultaneously [*UK* ˌsɪmʊl'teɪnjəslɪ, *US* ˌsaɪməl'teɪnjəslɪ] *adv* simultaneamente.

sin [sɪn] (*pt* & *pp* -ned, *cont* -ning) ◇ *n* pecado *m*; **to live in ~** viver em pecado. ◇ *vi*: **to ~ (against sb/sthg)** pecar (contra alguém/algo).

sin bin *n inf* ICE HOCKEY banco *m* para os suspensos do jogo.

since [sɪns] ◇ *adv*: **~ (then)** desde então; **long ~**

há muito tempo. ◇ *prep* desde. ◇ *conj* **-1.** [in time]: **it's ages ~ I saw him** faz séculos que eu não o vejo **-2.** [because] já que, como.

sincere [sɪnˈsɪəʳ] *adj* sincero(ra).

sincerely [sɪnˈsɪəlɪ] *adv* sinceramente; **Yours ~** [at end of letter] atenciosamente.

sincerity [sɪnˈserətɪ] *n (U)* sinceridade *f.*

sine [saɪn] *n* MATH seno *m.*

sinecure [ˈsaɪnɪˌkjʊəʳ] *n* sinecura *f.*

sinew [ˈsɪnjuː] *n* tendão *m.*

sinewy [ˈsɪnjuːɪ] *adj* musculoso(sa).

sinful [ˈsɪnfʊl] *adj* **-1.** [guilty of sin] pecador(ra) **-2.** [wicked, immoral] pecaminoso(sa).

sing [sɪŋ] (*pt* sang, *pp* sung) ◇ *vt* cantar; **to ~ sb a song, to ~ a song to sb** cantar uma música para alguém. ◇ *vi* cantar.

Singapore [ˌsɪŋəˈpɔːʳ] *n* Cingapura.

Singaporean [ˌsɪŋəpəˈrɪən] ◇ *adj* cingapuriano(-na). ◇ *n* cingapuriano *m*, -na *f.*

singe [sɪndʒ] (*cont* singeing) *vt* chamuscar.

singer [ˈsɪŋəʳ] *n* cantor *m*, -ra *f.*

Singhalese [ˌsɪŋəˈliːz] ◇ *adj* cingalês(esa). ◇ *n* **-1.** [person] cingalês *m*, -esa *f* **-2.** [language] cingalês *m.*

singing [ˈsɪŋɪŋ] ◇ *adj* de canto. ◇ *n* canto *m.*

singing telegram *n* telegrama *m* cantado.

single [ˈsɪŋgl] ◇ *adj* **-1.** [sole] único(ca); **to sweep up every ~ leaf** varrer todas as folhas, sem deixar nenhuma; **every ~ day** todo santo dia **-2.** [unmarried] solteiro(ra) **-3.** *UK* [one-way] de ida. ◇ *n* **-1.** *UK* [one-way ticket] passagem *f* de ida **-2.** MUS single *m.*

◆ **singles** *npl* TENNIS simples *f inv.*

◆ **single out** *vt sep*: **to ~ sb out (for sthg)** escolher alguém (para algo).

single bed *n* cama *f* de solteiro.

single-breasted [-ˈbrestɪd] *adj* não-trespassado(da).

single cream *n (U) UK* creme *m* leve.

single-decker (bus) *n UK* ônibus *m inv* de um andar.

Single European Market *n*: **the ~** o Mercado Comum Europeu.

single file *n*: **in ~** em fila indiana.

single-handed [-ˈhændɪd] *adv* sem ajuda.

single-minded [-ˈmaɪndɪd] *adj* determinado(da), resoluto(ta); **to be ~ about sthg** ter um objetivo muito claro em relação a algo.

single parent *n* pai *m* solteiro, mãe *f* solteira.

single-parent family *n* família *f* em que falta um dos pais.

single room *n* quarto *m* simples.

singles bar *n* bar *m* para solteiros.

singlet [ˈsɪŋglɪt] *n* camiseta *f* (sem mangas).

single ticket *n UK* passagem *f* de ida.

singsong [ˈsɪŋsɒŋ] *inf* ◇ *adj* monótono(na). ◇ *n UK* reunião *f* para cantar.

singular [ˈsɪŋgjʊləʳ] ◇ *adj* **-1.** GRAMM no singular **-2.** [unusual, remarkable] singular. ◇ *n* singular *m.*

singularly [ˈsɪŋgjʊləlɪ] *adv* notavelmente.

Sinhalese [ˈsɪnhəliːz] *adj & n* = **Singhalese**.

sinister [ˈsɪnɪstəʳ] *adj* sinistro(tra).

sink [sɪŋk] (*pt* sank, *pp* sunk) ◇ *n* pia *f.* ◇ *vt* **-1.**

[cause to go underwater] afundar **-2.** [cause to penetrate]: **to ~ sthg into sthg** cravar algo em algo. ◇ *vi* **-1.** [gen] afundar; **to ~ without trace** sumir sem deixar vestígio **-2.** [below ground - person] afundar-se; [- sun] pôr-se **-3.** [slump]: **he sank back into his chair** ele se afundou na cadeira; **she sank to her knees** ela caiu sobre os joelhos **-4.** *fig* [heart, spirits] congelar **-5.** [fall] baixar; **her voice sank to a whisper** sua voz foi baixando até ficar um sussurro **-6.** *fig* [slip]: **to ~ into sthg** [despair, poverty] cair em algo; [depression, coma] entrar em algo.

◆ **sink in** *vi*: **it hasn't sunk in yet** ainda não caiu a ficha.

sinking [ˈsɪŋkɪŋ] *n* afundamento *m.*

sinking fund *n* fundo *m* de amortização.

sink unit *n* pia *f.*

sinner [ˈsɪnəʳ] *n* pecador *m*, -ra *f.*

Sinn Fein [ˌʃɪnˈfeɪn] *n* Sinn Fein *m*, *braço político do IRA.*

sinuous [ˈsɪnjʊəs] *adj* sinuoso(sa).

sinus [ˈsaɪnəs] (*pl* -es) *n* seio *m (paranasal).*

sinusitis [ˌsaɪnəˈsaɪtɪs] *n* sinusite *f.*

sip [sɪp] (*pt & pp* -ped, *cont* -ping) ◇ *n* gole *m.* ◇ *vt* bebericar.

siphon [ˈsaɪfn] ◇ *n* sifão *m.* ◇ *vt* **-1.** [draw off] tirar com sifão **-2.** *fig* [transfer] desviar.

◆ **siphon off** *vt sep* **-1.** [draw off] tirar com sifão **-2.** *fig* [transfer] desviar.

sir [sɜːʳ] *n* **-1.** [form of address] senhor *m* **-2.** [in titles] sir *m.*

siren [ˈsaɪərən] *n* sirene *f.*

sirloin (steak) [ˈsɜːlɔɪn] *n* bife *m* de lombo de vaca.

sissy [ˈsɪsɪ] (*pl* -ies) *n inf* fresco *m.*

sister [ˈsɪstəʳ] ◇ *adj* **-1.** [organization] congênere **-2.** [ship] gêmeo(mea). ◇ *n* **-1.** [gen] irmã *f* **-2.** [nun] irmã *f*, freira *f* **-3.** *UK* [senior nurse] (enfermeira *f*) supervisora *f.*

sisterhood [ˈsɪstəhʊd] *n (U)* irmandade *f.*

sister-in-law (*pl* sisters-in-law OR sister-in-laws) *n* cunhada *f.*

sisterly [ˈsɪstəlɪ] *adj* de irmã.

sit [sɪt] (*pt & pp* sat, *cont* -ting) ◇ *vt* **-1.** [place] sentar **-2.** *UK* [examination] fazer. ◇ *vi* **-1.** [gen] sentar-se **-2.** [be member]: **to ~ on sthg** integrar algo, fazer parte de algo **-3.** [be in session] reunir-se **-4.** [be situated] ficar **-5.** *phr*: **to ~ tight** ficar onde se está.

◆ **sit about, sit around** *vi* ver o tempo passar.

◆ **sit back** *vi* **-1.** [relax] recostar-se, relaxar **-2.** [not act] ficar sentado(da).

◆ **sit down** ◇ *vt sep* sentar. ◇ *vi* sentar-se.

◆ **sit in on** *vt fus* estar presente (sem tomar parte).

◆ **sit out** *vt sep* **-1.** [tolerate] agüentar *(até o final)* **-2.** [not participate in] *não participar de.*

◆ **sit through** *vt fus* agüentar até o final.

◆ **sit up** *vi* **-1.** [be sitting upright] sentar-se reto(ta); [move into upright position] endireitar-se **-2.** [stay up] ficar acordado(da).

sitcom [ˈsɪtkɒm] *n inf* comédia *f* de situação, sitcom *f.*

sit-down ⟨⟩ *adj* [gen] com os participantes sentados à mesa; **a ~ strike** uma greve de braços cruzados. ⟨⟩ *n UK*: **to have a ~** sentar-se um pouco.

site [saɪt] ⟨⟩ *n* -**1.** [piece of land - archaelogy] sítio *m*; [- building] lote *m*; [- missile] campo *m*; [- camp] área *f* -**2.** [location, place] local *m* -**3.** *COMPUT* site *m*. ⟨⟩ *vt* localizar-se, situar-se.

sit-in *n* greve *f* branca.

sitter ['sɪtə'] *n* -**1.** *ART* modelo *mf* vivo, -va -**2.** [baby-sitter] babá *f*.

sitting ['sɪtɪŋ] *n* -**1.** [serving of meal] turno *m* para as refeições -**2.** [session] sessão *f*.

sitting duck *n inf* alvo *m* fácil, presa *f* fácil.

sitting room *n* sala *f* de estar.

sitting tenant *n UK* inquilino que tem o direito de permanecer numa casa mesmo após sua venda.

situate ['sɪtjʊeɪt] *vt* -**1.** [locate] situar -**2.** [put in context] contextualizar.

situated ['sɪtjʊeɪtɪd] *adj*: **to be ~** estar localizado (da), localizar-se.

situation [,sɪtjʊ'eɪʃn] *n* -**1.** [gen] situação *f* -**2.** [location] localização *f* -**3.** [job] emprego *m*, colocação *f*; **'Situations Vacant'** *UK* 'Empregos'.

situation comedy *n* comédia *f* de situação.

sit-up *n* abdominal *m*.

SI unit (*abbr of* Système international d'unités unit) *n* unidade do sistema internacional de medidas, como o metro, o litro etc.

six [sɪks] ⟨⟩ *num adj* -**1.** [numbering six] seis -**2.** [referring to age]: **she's ~ (years old)** ela tem seis anos (de idade). ⟨⟩ *num pron* seis; **I want ~** quero seis; **~ of us went** seis do nosso grupo foram; **there were ~ of us** éramos seis; **groups of ~** grupos *mpl* de seis. ⟨⟩ *num* -**1.** [gen] seis; **two hundred and ~** duzentos e seis -**2.** [six o'clock] seis (horas); **we arrived at ~** chegamos às seis -**3.** [six degrees]: **it's ~ below** faz seis graus abaixo de zero -**4.** [in addresses]: **~ Peyton Place** Praça Peyton, casa *OR* número 6; **we sell them in ~es** são vendidos(das) de seis em seis; **to form into ~es** formar grupos de seis; **~-nil** seis a zero.

six-shooter [-'ʃuːtə'] *n US* revólver *m* (de seis tiros).

sixteen [sɪks'tiːn] *num* dezesseis; *see also* **six**.

sixteenth [sɪks'tiːnθ] *num* décimo sexto, décima sexta; *see also* **sixth**.

sixth [sɪksθ] ⟨⟩ *num adj* sexto(ta). ⟨⟩ *num adv* sexto. ⟨⟩ *num pron* sexto(ta). ⟨⟩ *n* -**1.** [fraction] sexto *m* -**2.** [in dates]: **the ~** o dia seis; **the ~ of September** o dia seis de setembro.

sixth form *n UK SCH* curso opcional de dois anos no ensino secundário britânico oferecido aos alunos de 16 anos a fim de ingressarem na universidade.

sixth form college *n UK* escola pública na Inglaterra para adolescentes de 16 a 18 anos na qual se preparam para ingressar na universidade ou para fazer testes de formação profissional.

sixth sense *n* sexto sentido *m*.

sixtieth ['sɪkstɪəθ] *num* sexagésimo(ma); *see also* **sixth**.

sixty ['sɪkstɪ] (*pl* -ies) *num* sessenta; *see also* **six**.

sixties *npl* -**1.** [decade]: **the sixties** os anos sessenta -**2.** [in ages]: **to be in one's sixties** estar na casa dos sessenta.

size [saɪz] *n* -**1.** tamanho *m*; **an organization of that ~** uma organização daquele porte -**2.** *phr*: **to cut sb down to ~** colocar alguém em seu devido lugar.

size up *vt sep* -**1.** [situation] avaliar -**2.** [person] julgar.

sizeable ['saɪzəbl] *adj* considerável.

-sized [saɪzd] *suffix*: **life ~ models** modelos *mpl* em tamanho natural; **medium ~ companies** empresas *fpl* de médio porte.

sizzle ['sɪzl] *vi* chiar.

SK *abbr of* Saskatchewan.

skate [skeɪt] (*pl sense 3 only inv OR* -**s**) ⟨⟩ *n* -**1.** [gen] patim *m* -**2.** [fish] raia *f*. ⟨⟩ *vi* -**1.** [on ice skates] patinar no gelo -**2.** [on roller skates] patinar, andar de patins.

skate over, skate round *vt fus* evitar, fugir de.

skateboard ['skeɪtbɔːd] *n* skate *m*.

skateboarder ['skeɪtbɔːdə'] *n* skatista *mf*.

skater ['skeɪtə'] *n* patinador *m*, -ra *f*.

skating ['skeɪtɪŋ] *n (U)* -**1.** [on ice] patinação *f* no gelo; **to go ~** patinar no gelo -**2.** [on roller skates] patinação *f*; **to go ~** andar de patins.

skating rink *n* [for ice skating] pista *f* de patinação no gelo; [for roller skating] rinque *m*, pista *f* de patinação.

skein [skeɪn] *n* madeixa *f*.

skeletal ['skelɪtl] *adj* esquelético(ca).

skeleton ['skelɪtn] ⟨⟩ *adj* básico(ca), mínimo (ma). ⟨⟩ *n* esqueleto *m*; **to have a ~ in the cupboard** *fig* ter o rabo preso.

skeleton key *n* chave-mestra *f*.

skeleton staff *n* contingente *m* mínimo de pessoal.

skeptic etc *n US* = **sceptic etc**.

sketch [sketʃ] ⟨⟩ *n* -**1.** [drawing] esboço *m*, croqui *m* -**2.** [brief description] resumo *m* -**3.** [on TV, radio, stage] esquete *m*. ⟨⟩ *vt* -**1.** [draw] fazer um esboço de -**2.** [describe] resumir. ⟨⟩ *vi* fazer croquis.

sketch in, sketch out *vt sep* dar uma rápida idéia de.

sketchbook ['sketʃbʊk] *n* caderno *m* de desenhos.

sketchpad ['sketʃpæd] *n* bloco *m* de desenhos.

sketchy ['sketʃɪ] (*compar* -**ier**, *superl* -**iest**) *adj* incompleto(ta), pouco detalhado(da).

skew [skjuː] ⟨⟩ *n UK*: **on the ~** torcido(da). ⟨⟩ *vt* distorcer. ⟨⟩ *vi* atravessar-se.

skewer ['skjʊə'] ⟨⟩ *n* espeto *m*. ⟨⟩ *vt* espetar.

skew-whiff [,skjuː'wɪf] *adj UK inf* torto(ta).

ski [skiː] (*pt & pp* skied, *cont* skiing) ⟨⟩ *n* esqui *m*. ⟨⟩ *comp* de esqui. ⟨⟩ *vi* esquiar.

ski boots *npl* botas *fpl* de esqui.

skid [skɪd] (*pt & pp* -**ded**, *cont* -**ding**) ⟨⟩ *n AUT* derrapagem *f*; **to go into a ~** derrapar. ⟨⟩ *vi* derrapar.

skid mark *n* marca *f* de derrapagem.

skid row [-rəʊ] *n (U) US inf*: **to be on ~** estar na rua da amargura.

skier ['skiːəᶜ] *n* esquiador *m*, -ra *f*.
skiing ['skiːɪŋ] ⬦ *n (U)* esqui *m*; **to go** ~ ir esquiar. ⬦ *comp* -1. [holiday, accident] de esqui -2. [enthusiast] do esqui.
ski instructor *n* instrutor *m*, -ra *f* de esqui.
ski jump *n* -1. [slope] rampa *f* para saltos de esqui -2. [sporting event] salto *m* de esqui.
skilful, skillful *US* ['skɪlfʊl] *adj* hábil.
skilfully, skillfully *US* ['skɪlfʊlɪ] *adv* habilmente.
ski lift *n* teleférico *m*.
skill [skɪl] *n* -1. *(U)* [expertise] experiência *f*, destreza *f* -2. [craft, technique] habilidade *f*.
skilled [skɪld] *adj* -1. [skilful] habilidoso(sa); **to be** ~ **in** *OR* **at doing sthg** ter muito jeito para fazer algo -2. [trained] especializado(da), qualificado(da).
skillet ['skɪlɪt] *n US* frigideira *f*.
skillful *etc adj US* = skilful *etc*.
skim [skɪm] *(pt & pp* -med, *cont* -ming) ⬦ *vt* -1. [remove - cream] tirar a nata de; [- fat] tirar a gordura de; [- sap] extrair -2. [glide over] roçar -3. [glance through] passar os olhos em. ⬦ *vi* -1. **: to** ~ **over sthg** [bird] dar uma rasante em algo; [stone] ricochetear em algo -2. [read]**: to** ~ **through sthg** ler algo por cima.
skim(med) milk [skɪm(d)mɪlk] *n (U)* leite *m* desnatado.
skimp [skɪmp] *vi***: to** ~ **on sthg** [food, material, time] restringir algo; [money] economizar em algo; [work] fazer algo correndo.
skimpy ['skɪmpɪ] *(compar* -ier, *superl* -iest) *adj* -1. [meal] parco(ca) -2. [clothes] justo(ta) -3. [facts] insuficiente.
skin [skɪn] *(pt & pp* -ned, *cont* -ning) ⬦ *n* -1. *(U)* [gen] pele *f*; **to do sthg by the** ~ **of one's teeth** fazer algo por um triz; **to jump out of one's** ~ *UK* perder o chão; **it makes my** ~ **crawl** me dá calafrios; **to save one's own** ~ salvar a própria pele -2. [of fruit, vegetable, on paint, pudding] casca *f* -3. [on milk] nata *f*. ⬦ *vt* -1. [remove skin from - fruit] descascar; [- dead animal] pelar -2. [graze] esfolar.
skin-deep *adj* superficial.
skin diver *n* mergulhador *m*, -ra que pratica mergulho livre *f*.
skin diving *n (U)***: to go** ~ praticar mergulho *m* livre.
skinflint ['skɪnflɪnt] *n* pão-duro *m*.
skin graft *n* enxerto *m* de pele.
skinhead ['skɪnhed] *n UK* skinhead *m*.
skinny ['skɪnɪ] *(compar* -ier, *superl* -iest) *adj inf* magricela.
skint [skɪnt] *adj UK v inf* pelado(da), sem um tostão.
skin test *n* teste *m* de pele.
skin-tight *adj* muito justo(ta).
skip [skɪp] *(pt & pp* -ped, *cont* -ping) ⬦ *n* -1. [little jump] pulinho *m* -2. *UK* [large container] caçamba *f (para entulho)*. ⬦ *vt* -1. [page] pular -2. [class] perder -3. [meal] faltar a. ⬦ *vi* -1. [move in little jumps] ir pulando -2. *UK* [using rope] pular.
ski pants *npl* calças *fpl* de esqui.
ski pole *n* bastão *m* de esqui.
skipper ['skɪpəᶜ] *n* capitão *m*, -tã *f*.
skipping ['skɪpɪŋ] *n UK***: to do some** ~ pular corda.
skipping rope ['skɪpɪŋ-] *n UK* corda *f* de pular.

ski resort *n* estação *f* de esqui.
skirmish ['skɜːmɪʃ] ⬦ *n* -1. *MIL* escaramuça *f* -2. *fig* [disagreement] desavença *f*. ⬦ *vi MIL* & *fig* ter uma escaramuça.
skirt [skɜːt] ⬦ *n* [garment] saia *f*. ⬦ *vt* -1. [go round] contornar -2. [avoid dealing with] evitar.
◆ **skirt round** *vt fus* -1. [go round]**: to** ~ **round sb/sthg** desviar de alguém/algo -2. [avoid dealing with]**: to** ~ **round sthg** evitar algo.
skirting board ['skɜːtɪŋ-] *n UK* rodapé *m*.
ski stick *n* bastão *m* de esqui.
skit [skɪt] *n***:** ~ **on sthg** sátira *f OR* paródia *f* sobre algo.
ski tow *n* ski lift *m*.
skittish ['skɪtɪʃ] *adj* -1. [person] esquivo(va) -2. [animal] arisco(ca).
skittle ['skɪtl] *n UK* pino *m* de boliche.
◆ **skittles** *n (U) UK* boliche *m*.
skive [skaɪv] *vi UK inf***: to** ~ **(off)** [at school] matar aula; [at work] matar o serviço.
skivvy ['skɪvɪ] *(pl* -ies, *pt & pp* -ied) *UK inf* ⬦ *n* serviçal *mf*. ⬦ *vi***: to** ~ **(for sb)** servir de empregada(da) *(para alguém)*.
skulduggery [skʌl'dʌgərɪ] *n (U)* trapaça *f*.
skulk [skʌlk] *vi* esconder-se.
skull [skʌl] *n* -1. *ANAT* crânio *m* -2. [on skeleton] caveira *f*.
skullcap ['skʌlkæp] *n* solidéu *m*.
skunk [skʌnk] *n* gambá *m*.
sky [skaɪ] *(pl* skies) *n* céu *m*.
skycap *n US* carregador *m*, -ra *f* de bagagem *(no aeroporto)*.
skydiver ['skaɪˌdaɪvəᶜ] *n* pára-quedista *mf*.
skydiving ['skaɪˌdaɪvɪŋ] *n (U)* pára-quedismo *m*.
sky-high *inf* ⬦ *adj* nas alturas. ⬦ *adv***: to blow sthg** ~ [bridge, building] mandar algo para os ares; *fig* [argument, theory] mandar algo para o espaço; **to go** ~ ir para as alturas.
skylark ['skaɪlɑːk] *n* calandra *f*.
skylight ['skaɪlaɪt] *n* clarabóia *f*.
skyline ['skaɪlaɪn] *n* linha *f* do horizonte.
skyscraper ['skaɪˌskreɪpəᶜ] *n* arranha-céu *m*.
slab [slæb] *n* -1. [of concrete, stone] laje *f* -2. [of meat, cake] fatia *f* -3. [of chocolate] barra *f*.
slack [slæk] ⬦ *adj* -1. [not tight] frouxo(xa) -2. [not busy] parado(da) -3. [not efficient] desleixado(da), negligente. ⬦ *n (U)* ponta *f* solta.
◆ **slacks** *npl dated* slack *m*.
slacken ['slækn] ⬦ *vt* -1. [make slower] reduzir -2. [make looser] afrouxar. ⬦ *vi* -1. [become slower] reduzir -2. [become looser] afrouxar.
◆ **slacken off** *vi* -1. [rain, storm] abrandar -2. [work, trade] desacelerar.
slag [slæg] *n* -1. *(U)* [waste material] escombros *mpl* -2. *inf pej* [promiscuous woman] vagabunda *f*.
slagheap ['slæghiːp] *n* monte *m* de entulho.
slain [sleɪn] *pp* ⮑ slay.
slalom ['slɑːləm] *n* corrida *f* com obstáculos *(de esqui e canoagem)*.
slam [slæm] *(pt & pp* -med, *cont* -ming) ⬦ *vt* -1. [shut] bater -2. [place roughly]**: to** ~ **sthg on (to) sthg** jogar algo com violência sobre algo -3. *fig* [criticize] criticar. ⬦ *vi* [shut] bater.

slander ['slɑ:ndə^r] ⬦ n (U) calúnia f. ⬦ vt caluniar.

slanderous ['slɑ:ndrəs] adj calunioso(sa).

slang [slæŋ] ⬦ adj popular. ⬦ n (U) gíria f.

slant [slɑ:nt] ⬦ n -1. [diagonal angle - of table, shelf] inclinação f; [- of land] declive m; **on** OR **ata** ~ inclinado(da) -2. [point of view] perspectiva f; enfoque m. ⬦ vt [bias] distorcer. ⬦ vi [slope] inclinar-se.

slanting ['slɑ:ntɪŋ] adj inclinado(da).

slap [slæp] (pt & pp -ped, cont -ping) ⬦ n -1. [on face] bofetada f; **a** ~ **in the face** [fig] uma bofetada -2. [on back] tapa m. ⬦ vt -1. [smack - on face] esbofetear; [- on back] dar um tapa em -2. [put]: **to** ~ **sthg on** dar uma retocada em. ⬦ adv inf [exactly] em cheio; ~ **in the middle of the city** bem no meio da cidade.

slapdash ['slæpdæʃ], **slaphappy** ['slæp,hæpɪ] adj relaxado(da).

slapstick ['slæpstɪk] n (U) pastelão m; **the film is pure** ~ este filme é um pastelão só.

slap-up adj UK inf farto(ta); **a** ~ **dinner** um jantar formidável.

slash [slæʃ] ⬦ n -1. [long cut] rasgão m, corte m -2. [oblique stroke] barra f oblíqua; **forward** ~ barra f (inclinada) -3. UK inf [pee]: **to have a** ~ fazer xixi. ⬦ vt -1. [cut - material, tyres] rasgar; [- wrists] cortar -2. inf [reduce drastically] cortar.

slat [slæt] n ripa f, sarrafo m.

slate [sleɪt] ⬦ n -1. (U) [material] ardósia f -2. [on roof] telha f de ardósia; **to wipe the** ~ **clean** sacudir a poeira; **put it on the** ~ põe na conta. ⬦ vt [criticize] malhar.

slatted adj com ripas.

slaughter ['slɔ:tə^r] ⬦ n -1. [of animals] matança f -2. [of people] chacina f. ⬦ vt -1. [animals] matar, carnear -2. [people] chacinar.

slaughterhouse ['slɔ:təhaʊs, pl -haʊzɪz] n matadouro m.

Slav [slɑ:v] ⬦ adj eslavo(va). ⬦ n eslavo m, -va f.

slave [sleɪv] ⬦ n escravo m, -va f; **to be a** ~ **to sthg** ser escravo(va) de algo. ⬦ vi [work hard]: **to** ~ **(over sthg)** trabalhar como um escravo em algo, trabalhar como uma escrava em algo.

slaver ['sleɪvə^r] vi babar.

slavery ['sleɪvərɪ] n (U) escravidão f.

slave trade n: **the** ~ o tráfico OR comércio de escravos.

Slavic ⬦ adj eslavo(va). ⬦ n -1. [language] eslavo m -2. HIST eslavo m, -va f.

slavish ['sleɪvɪʃ] adj pej [unoriginal, servile] servil.

Slavonic [slə'vɒnɪk] adj & n = **Slavic**.

slay [sleɪ] (pt slew, pp slain) vt literary assassinar.

sleaze n sujeira f.

sleazy ['sli:zɪ] (compar -ier, superl -iest) adj sujo(ja).

sledge [sledʒ], **sled** US [sled] n trenó m.

sledgehammer ['sledʒ,hæmə^r] n marreta f.

sleek [sli:k] adj -1. [hair] sedoso(sa) -2. [fur] brilhoso(sa) -3. [animal, bird] lustroso(sa) -4. [car, plane] vistoso(sa) -5. [person] polido(da).

sleep [sli:p] (pt & pp slept) ⬦ n -1. (U) [rest] sono m; **to go to** ~ [doze off] adormecer; [go numb] ficar dormente; **to put to** ~ [patient] anestesiar; [animal]

sacrificar -2. [period of sleeping] sono m. ⬦ vi dormir.

➤ **sleep around** vi inf pej dormir com qualquer um(ma).

➤ **sleep in** vi dormir até mais tarde.

➤ **sleep off** vt sep: **to** ~ **sthg off** curar algo dormindo.

➤ **sleep through** vt fus: **to** ~ **through sthg** não despertar com algo.

➤ **sleep together** vi euphemism dormir juntos(tas).

➤ **sleep with** vt fus euphemism dormir com.

sleeper ['sli:pə^r] n -1. [person]: **to be a heavy/light** ~ ter sono pesado/leve -2. [sleeping compartment] leito m -3. [train] trem-leito m -4. UK [on railway track] dormente m.

sleepily ['sli:pɪlɪ] adv sonolentamente, quase dormindo.

sleeping bag ['sli:pɪŋ-] n saco m de dormir.

sleeping car ['sli:pɪŋ-] n vagão-leito m.

sleeping partner ['sli:pɪŋ-] n UK sócio m comanditário, sócia f comanditária.

sleeping pill ['sli:pɪŋ-] n pílula f para dormir.

sleeping policeman ['sli:pɪŋ-] n UK inf quebra-molas m inv.

sleeping tablet ['sli:pɪŋ-] n comprimido m para dormir.

sleepless ['sli:plɪs] adj em claro, sem dormir.

sleeplessness ['sli:plɪsnɪs] n (U) falta f de sono, insônia f.

sleepwalk ['sli:pwɔ:k] vi sonambular.

sleepy ['sli:pɪ] (compar -ier, superl -iest) adj -1. [person] sonolento(ta) -2. [place] pacato(ta).

sleet [sli:t] ⬦ n (U) granizo m. ⬦ v impers chover granizo.

sleeve [sli:v] n -1. [of garment] manga f; **to have sthg up one's** ~ ter uma carta escondida na manga -2. [for record] capa f.

sleeveless ['sli:vlɪs] adj sem mangas.

sleigh [sleɪ] n trenó m.

sleight of hand [,slaɪt-] n (U) -1. [skill with hands] prestidigitação f -2. fig [deception] artimanha f.

slender ['slendə^r] adj -1. [thin - person, figure] esbelto(ta); [- legs] delgado(da) -2. [scarce] escasso(sa).

slept [slept] pt & pp ⬐ **sleep**.

sleuth [slu:θ] n inf hum detetive mf.

slew [slu:] ⬦ pt ⬐ **slay**. ⬦ vi: **the car** ~ed off **the road** o carro rodopiou para fora da estrada.

slice [slaɪs] ⬦ n -1. [gen] fatia f -2. [of lemon] rodela f -3. [proportion] parte f -4. SPORT cortada f. ⬦ vt -1. [cut into slices] fatiar -2. SPORT cortar. ⬦ vi: **to** ~ **through/into sthg** cortar algo com facilidade.

➤ **slice off** vt sep [sever] arrancar fora.

➤ **slice up** vt sep [food] fatiar, cortar em fatias.

sliced bread [slaɪst-] n (U) pão m fatiado.

slick [slɪk] ⬦ adj -1. [smoothly efficient - performance, teamwork] talentoso(sa); [- technique, crime] engenhoso(sa) -2. pej [glib] ardiloso(sa). ⬦ n local m escorregadio.

slicker n US capa f de chuva.

slide [slaɪd] (pt & pp slid [slɪd]) ⬦ n -1. PHOT eslaide m -2. [in playground] escorregador m -3. [for microscope] lâmina f -4. UK [for hair] passador m -5.

[decline] declínio *m.* <> *vt* [move smoothly] deslizar. <> *vi* **-1.** [on ice, slippery surface] escorregar **-2.** [move quietly] deslizar **-3.** [decline gradually] sucumbir a; **to let things** ~ deixar que as coisas piorem.

slide projector *n* projetor *m* de eslaides.

slide rule *n* régua *f* de cálculo.

sliding door [,slaɪdɪŋ-] *n* porta *f* de correr.

sliding scale [,slaɪdɪŋ-] *n* escala *f* móvel.

slight [slaɪt] <> *adj* **-1.** [minor] ligeiro(ra); **not in the** ~**est** nem de leve; **I haven't got the** ~**est interest in his car** eu não tenho o menor interesse no carro dele **-2.** [slender] de aspecto frágil. <> *n* menosprezo *m.* <> *vt* [offend] menosprezar.

slightly [ˈslaɪtlɪ] *adv* **-1.** [to small extent] ligeiramente, levemente **-2.** [slenderly]: ~ **built** magrinho(nha).

slim [slɪm] (*compar* **-mer**, *superl* **-mest**, *pt* & *pp* **-med**, *cont* **-ming**) <> *adj* **-1.** [person] esbelto(ta) **-2.** [object] fino(na) **-3.** [chance, possibility] remoto(ta). <> *vi* [lose weight] emagrecer; **I'm** ~ **ming** estou de dieta; [diet] emagrecer.

slime [slaɪm] *n (U)* muco *m.*

slimline *adj* mais fino(na) *(que o normal).*

slimmer [ˈslɪməʳ] *n* pessoa *f* de dieta.

slimming [ˈslɪmɪŋ] <> *n (U)* emagrecimento *m.* <> *adj* **-1.** [magazine] de dieta **-2.** [product] para emagrecer.

slimness [ˈslɪmnɪs] *n (U)* esbelteza *f*, elegância *f.*

slimy [ˈslaɪmɪ] (*compar* **-ier**, *superl* **-iest**) *adj* **-1.** [covered in slime] coberto(ta) com lodo OR muco **-2.** *pej* [servile] fingido(da).

sling [slɪŋ] (*pt* & *pp* **slung**) <> *n* **-1.** [for injured arm] tipóia *f.* **-2.** [for carrying things] linga *f.* <> *vt* **-1.** [hang roughly] pendurar **-2.** *inf* [throw] atirar, jogar **-3.** [hang by both ends] pendurar.

slingback [ˈslɪŋbæk] *n* sandália *f.*

slingshot [ˈslɪŋʃɒt] *n US* catapulta *f.*

slink [slɪŋk] (*pt* & *pp* **slunk**) *vi*: **to** ~ **(away** OR **off)** escapulir-se.

slip [slɪp] (*pt* & *pp* **-ped**, *cont* **-ping**) <> *n* **-1.** [mistake] deslize *m*, descuido *m*; **a** ~ **of the pen** um erro de ortografia; **a** ~ **of the tongue** um lapso verbal **-2.** [form] formulário *m* **-3.** [of paper] folha *f* **-4.** [underwear] combinação *f*, anágua *f* **-5.** *phr*: **to give sb the** ~ *inf* safar-se de alguém. <> *vt* **-1.** [slide] enfiar, meter **-2.** [clothes]: **to** ~ **sthg on** vestir algo rapidamente; ~ **your clothes off** tira fora essas tuas roupas **-3.** [escape] fugir; **it** ~ **ped my mind** me esqueci. <> *vi* **-1.** [lose balance] escorregar **-2.** [move unexpectedly] escapulir **-3.** [move gradually] entrar em **-4.** [decline] baixar; **to let things** ~ deixar escapar algo *(falando)* **-5.** [move discreetly] escapulir-se; **to** ~ **into/out of sthg** [clothes] vestir/tirar algo **-6.** AUT [clutch] patinar **-7.** *phr*: **to let sthg** ~ dizer algo sem querer.

  slip away *vi* [leave] ir embora.

  slip on *vt sep* [clothes, shoes] enfiar.

  slip up *vi* [make a mistake] cometer um deslize.

slip-on *adj* [shoes] sem cadarço.

  slip-ons *npl* [shoes] mocassim *m.*

slippage *n (U)* deslizamento *m.*

slipped disc [,slɪpt-] *n* hérnia *f* de disco.

slipper [ˈslɪpəʳ] *n* pantufa *f.*

slippery [ˈslɪpərɪ] *adj* **-1.** [surface, soap] escorregadio(dia) **-2.** *pej* [person] evasivo(va).

slip road *n UK* acesso *m (na estrada).*

slipshod [ˈslɪpʃɒd] *adj* desleixado(da).

slipstream [ˈslɪpstriːm] *n* rastro *m.*

slip-up *n inf* mancada *f.*

slipway [ˈslɪpweɪ] *n* carreira *f (para navios).*

slit [slɪt] (*pt* & *pp* **slit**, *cont* **-ting**) <> *n* **-1.** [opening] fenda *f* **-2.** [cut] corte *m.* <> *vt* **-1.** [cut open] cortar **-2.** [cut through] fender.

slither [ˈslɪðəʳ] *vi* **-1.** [car, person] arrastar-se **-2.** [snake] rastejar.

sliver [ˈslɪvəʳ] *n* **-1.** [gen] caco *f* **-2.** [of ice, wood] lasca *f.*

slob [slɒb] *n inf* [disgusting person - in habits] porcalhão *m*, -lhona *f*; [- in appearance] porco *m*, -ca *f.*

slobber [ˈslɒbəʳ] *vi* babar.

slog [slɒg] (*pt* & *pp* **-ged**, *cont* **-ging**) *inf* <> *n* **-1.** [tiring work] chatice *f* **-2.** [tiring journey] maçada *f.* <> *vi* **-1.** [work]: **to** ~ **(away) at sthg** trabalhar sem descanso em algo **-2.** [walk, move] andar a custo.

slogan [ˈsləʊgən] *n* slogan *m.*

slop [slɒp] (*pt* & *pp* **-ped**, *cont* **-ping**) <> *vt* derramar. <> *vi* transbordar.

slope [sləʊp] <> *n* **-1.** [of roof, ground] inclinação *f* **-2.** [hill] encosta *f* **-3.** *phr*: **he's on the slippery** ~ **to alcoholism** ele está indo direto para o alcoolismo. <> *vi* inclinar-se.

sloping [ˈsləʊpɪŋ] *adj* inclinado(da).

sloppy [ˈslɒpɪ] (*compar* **-ier**, *superl* **-iest**) *adj* **-1.** [careless] desleixado(da), relaxado(da) **-2.** *inf* [sentimental] meloso(sa), piegas.

slosh [slɒʃ] <> *vt* **-1.** [spill] chapinhar **-2.** [pour] despejar **-3.** [apply] espalhar. <> *vi* **-1.** [liquid] chapinhar **-2.** [through liquid, mud] patinhar.

sloshed [slɒʃt] *adj UK inf* com a cara cheia.

slot [slɒt] (*pt* & *pp* **-ted**, *cont* **-ting**) *n* **-1.** [opening] abertura *f* **-2.** [groove] ranhura *f* **-3.** [place in schedule] espaço *m* **-4.** COMPUT slot *m.*

  slot in <> *vt sep* [insert] encaixar. <> *vi* [fit neatly] encaixar.

sloth [sləʊθ] *n* **-1.** [animal] bicho-preguiça *m* **-2.** *(U) literary* [laziness] preguiça *f.*

slot machine *n* **-1.** [vending machine] máquina *f* automática *(de bebidas, cigarros etc)* **-2.** [arcade machine] caça-níqueis *m inv.*

slot meter *n UK* medidor *m (de luz ou gás)* que funciona com moedas.

slouch [slaʊtʃ] <> *n* [person] incompetente *mf.* <> *vi* [in posture] ter má postura.

slough *vt sep* **-1.** [shed] trocar OR mudar *(de pele)* **-2.** *fig* [get rid of] livrar-se de.

Slovak [ˈsləʊvæk] <> *adj* eslavo(va). <> *n* **-1.** [person] eslavo *m*, -va *f* **-2.** [language] eslavo *m.*

Slovakia [sləˈvækɪə] *n* Eslováquia; **in** ~ na Eslováquia.

Slovakian [sləˈvækɪən] <> *adj* eslovaco(ca). <> *n* eslovaco *m*, -ca *f.*

Slovenia [sləˈviːnjə] *n* Eslovênia; **in** ~ na Eslovênia.

Slovenian [sləˈviːnjən] <> *adj* esloveno(na). <> *n* esloveno *m*, -na *f.*

slovenly [ˈslʌvnlɪ] *adj* **-1.** [person, work] desmazelado(da) **-2.** [appearance] desleixado(da) **-3.** [dress] desalinhado(da).

slow [sləʊ] ◇ *adj* -**1.** [not fast] lento(ta) -**2.** [clock, watch] atrasado(da) -**3.** [not busy] parado(da) -**4.** [not intelligent] lerdo(da). ◇ *adv*: **to go** ~ [driver] ir devagar; [workers] fazer operação-tartaruga. ◇ *vt* retardar. ◇ *vi* ir mais devagar, desacelerar.
◆ **slow down, slow up** ◇ *vt sep* -**1.** [growth] retardar -**2.** [car] reduzir a velocidade de. ◇ *vi* -**1.** [car] reduzir a velocidade de -**2.** [walker] diminuir a marcha.

slow-acting *adj* de ação lenta.

slowcoach ['sləʊkəʊtʃ], **slowpoke** *US n inf* molenga *mf*.

slowdown ['sləʊdaʊn] *n* desaceleração *f*.

slow handclap *n* aplauso lento e ritmado em sinal de protesto.

slowly ['sləʊlɪ] *adv* devagar; ~ **but surely** devagar e sempre.

slow motion *n* (U) câmera *f* lenta.
◆ **slow-motion** *adj* em câmera lenta.

slowpoke *n US* = slowcoach.

SLR (*abbr of* single-lens reflex) *n* tipo de câmera fotográfica que usa uma lente única.

sludge [slʌdʒ] *n* -**1.** [mud] lama *f* -**2.** [sediment] lodo *m*.

slug [slʌg] (*pt & pp* -**ged**, *cont* -**ging**) ◇ *n* -**1.** ZOOL lesma *f* -**2.** *inf* [of alcohol] trago *m* -**3.** *US inf* [bullet] bala *f* (*de revólver*). ◇ *vt inf* [hit] esmurrar.

sluggish ['slʌgɪʃ] *adj* -**1.** [lethargic] vagaroso(sa) -**2.** [reaction, business] moroso(sa).

sluice [sluːs] ◇ *n* [lock] comporta *f*. ◇ *vt* [rinse]: **to** ~ **sthg down/out** lavar algo com muita água.

slum [slʌm] (*pt & pp* -**med**, *cont* -**ming**) ◇ *n* [area of poor housing] favela *f*, cortiço *m*. ◇ *vt*: **to** ~ **it** *inf* baixar o padrão de vida.

slumber ['slʌmbə^r] *literary* ◇ *n* (U) sono *m*. ◇ *vi* adormecer.

slump [slʌmp] ◇ *n* -**1.** [decline]: ~ **(in sthg)** queda *f* (em algo) -**2.** ECON crise *f* econômica. ◇ *vi* -**1.** [business, prices, market] cair -**2.** [person] afundar-se.

slung [slʌŋ] *pt & pp* ⊳ **sling**.

slunk [slʌŋk] *pt & pp* ⊳ **slink**.

slur [slɜː^r] (*pt & pp* -**red**, *cont* -**ring**) ◇ *n* -**1.** [in voice] balbuceio *m* -**2.** [insult]: ~ **(on sb/sthg)** ultraje *m* OR afronta *f* (a alguém/algo). ◇ *vt* [speech] balbuciar; **to** ~ **one's words** engolir as palavras.

slurp [slɜːp] *vt* sorver fazendo barulho.

slurred [slɜːd] *adj* ininteligível.

slurry *n* (U) purina *f*.

slush [slʌʃ] *n* (U) neve *f* meio derretida.

slush fund, slush money *US n* caixa *m* dois.

slut [slʌt] *n* -**1.** *inf* [dirty or untidy woman] mulher *f* relaxada -**2.** *v inf* [sexually immoral woman] rameira *f*.

sly [slaɪ] (*compar* slyer OR slier, *superl* slyest OR sliest) ◇ *adj* -**1.** [look, smile, grin] dissimulado(da) -**2.** [cunning] astuto(ta) -**3.** [secretive] fingido(da). ◇ *n*: **on the** ~ às escondidas.

slyness ['slaɪnɪs] *n* (U) dissimulação *f*.

S & M (*abbr of* sadism and masochism) *n* SM *m*.

smack [smæk] ◇ *n* -**1.** [slap] palmada *f* -**2.** [impact] batida *f*. ◇ *vt* -**1.** [slap] dar uma palmada em -**2.** [put] colocar bruscamente -**3.** [make sound]: **to** ~

one's lips estalar os lábios. ◇ *vi*: **to** ~ **of sthg** cheirar a algo. ◇ *adv inf* [exactly]: ~ **in the middle** bem no meio.

small [smɔːl] ◇ *adj* -**1.** [gen] pequeno(na); **in a** ~ **way** em pequena escala -**2.** [person] baixo(xa) -**3.** [importance] pouco(ca) -**4.** [matter, alteration] de pouca importância. ◇ *n*: **the** ~ **of the back** a região lombar.
◆ **smalls** *npl UK inf dated* roupa *f* de baixo.

small ads [-ædz] *npl UK* classificados *mpl*.

small arms *npl* armas *fpl* portáteis OR de mão.

small change *n* (U) trocado *m*.

small fry *n* (U) peixe *m* pequeno, fichinha *f*.

smallholder ['smɔːlˌhəʊldə^r] *n UK* minifundiário *m*, -ria *f*.

smallholding ['smɔːlˌhəʊldɪŋ] *n UK* minifúndio *m*.

small hours *npl* primeiras horas *fpl* da manhã.

small letters *npl*: **in** ~ em minúscula.

smallness ['smɔːlnɪs] *n* -**1.** (U) [of building, person] pequenez *f* -**2.** [rise, amount] escassez *f*.

smallpox ['smɔːlpɒks] *n* (U) varíola *f*.

small print *n*: **the** ~ as letras miúdas (*de um contrato*).

small-scale *adj* em pequena escala.

small talk *n* (U): **to make** ~ conversar amenidades.

small-time *adj* de segunda; **a** ~ **criminal** um ladrão de galinha.

smarmy ['smɑːmɪ] (*compar* -**ier**, *superl* -**iest**) *adj inf* adulador(ra).

smart [smɑːt] ◇ *adj* -**1.** [elegant] elegante -**2.** [clever] inteligente -**3.** [fashionable, exclusive] chique, elegante -**4.** [rapid] rápido(da) -**5.** [impertinent] insolente. ◇ *vi* -**1.** [sting] pungir, arder -**2.** [feel anger, humiliation] ofender-se.

smart card *n* cartão *m* inteligente.

smarten ['smɑːtn] ◆ **smarten up** *vt sep* arrumar; **to** ~ **o.s. up** arrumar-se.

smash [smæʃ] ◇ *n* -**1.** [sound] estilhaço *m* -**2.** *inf* [car crash] acidente *m* -**3.** *inf* [success] estouro *m* -**4.** TENNIS cortada *f*. ◇ *vt* -**1.** [break into pieces] quebrar -**2.** [hit, crash] bater em; **to** ~ **one's fist into sthg** dar um soco em algo -**3.** *fig* [defeat] derrotar. ◇ *vi* -**1.** [break into pieces] quebrar-se -**2.** [crash, collide]: **to** ~ **through/into sthg** espatifar-se contra/em algo.
◆ **smash up** *vt sep* destruir completamente.

smash-and-grab (raid) *n UK* saque *m* após arrombamento (*numa loja*).

smashed [smæʃt] *adj inf* mamado(da) (*de bêbado*).

smash hit *n* sucesso *m* absoluto.

smashing ['smæʃɪŋ] *adj inf* fabuloso(sa), fenomenal.

smash-up *n* choque *m* violento, desastre *m*.

smattering ['smætərɪŋ] *n* noções *fpl*; **to have a** ~ **of Welsh** falar meia dúzia de palavras de galês.

SME (*abbr of* small and medium-sized enterprise) *n* pequena e média empresa *f*.

smear [smɪə^r] ◇ *n* -**1.** [dirty mark] mancha *f* (*de gordura*) -**2.** MED esfregaço *m* -**3.** [slander] calúnia *f*. ◇ *vt* -**1.** [smudge - page] manchar; [- painting] borrar -**2.** [spread]: **to** ~ **sthg onto sthg** espalhar algo sobre algo; **to** ~ **sthg with sthg** untar algo com algo **-3.** [slander] caluniar.

smear campaign n campanha f de difamação.

smear test n esfregaço m.

smell [smel] (pt & pp -ed OR **smelt**) <> n **-1.** [odour] cheiro m, odor m **-2.** (U) [sense of smell] olfato m. <> vt **-1.** [notice an odour of] sentir cheiro de **-2.** [sniff at] cheirar **-3.** fig [sense] pressentir. <> vi **-1.** [have sense of smell] sentir cheiro **-2.** [have particular smell]: **to ~ of sthg** cheirar a algo; **to ~ like sthg** cheirar como algo; **to ~ good/bad** cheirar bem/mal **-3.** [smell unpleasantly] feder.

smelling salts npl sais mpl aromáticos.

smelly [ˈsmelɪ] (compar **-ier**, superl **-iest**) adj fedorento(ta).

smelt [smelt] <> pt & pp ▷ **smell**. <> vt TECH fundir.

smile [smaɪl] <> n sorriso m. <> vi sorrir. <> vt sorrir; **to ~ one's thanks** sorrir em agradecimento.

smiley [ˈsmaɪlɪ] n COMPUT smiley m.

smiling [ˈsmaɪlɪŋ] adj sorridente, risonho(nha).

smirk [smɜːk] <> n sorriso m afetado. <> vi sorrir de forma afetada.

smith [smɪθ] n ferreiro m, -ra f.

smithereens [ˌsmɪðəˈriːnz] npl inf: **to be smashed to ~** ser quebrado(da) em pedacinhos OR em mil pedaços.

smithy [ˈsmɪðɪ] (pl **-ies**) n ferraria f.

smitten [ˈsmɪtn] adj inf hum: **to be ~ (with sb/ sthg)** estar apaixonado(da) (por alguém/algo).

smock [smɒk] n avental m, guarda-pó m.

smog [smɒg] n (U) bruma f.

smoke [sməʊk] <> n **-1.** (U) [from burning] fumaça f **-2.** [act of smoking]: **to have a ~** fumar. <> vt **-1.** [cigarette, cigar] fumar **-2.** [fish, meat, cheese] defumar. <> vi **-1.** [chimney, engine, lamp] fumegar **-2.** [person] fumar.

smoked [sməʊkt] adj [food] defumado(da).

smokeless fuel [ˈsməʊklɪs-] n (U) combustível m limpo.

smokeless zone [ˈsməʊklɪs-] n área na qual se proíbe o uso de combustíveis que produzam fumaça.

smoker [ˈsməʊkəʳ] n **-1.** [person who smokes] fumante mf **-2.** inf RAIL [compartment] vagão m para fumantes.

smokescreen [ˈsməʊkskriːn] n fig cortina f de fumaça.

smoke shop n US tabacaria f.

smokestack n chaminé f.

smokestack industry n US indústria f pesada OR de base.

smoking [ˈsməʊkɪŋ] n (U): **~ is bad for you** fumar não te faz bem; **'no ~'** 'é proibido fumar'.

smoking compartment UK, **smoking car** US n vagão m para fumantes.

smoky [ˈsməʊkɪ] (compar **-ier**, superl **-iest**) adj **-1.** [full of smoke] enfumaçado(da) **-2.** [resembling smoke - taste] com gosto de fumaça; [- colour] cinzento(ta).

smolder vi US = **smoulder**.

smooch [smuːtʃ] vi inf dar amassos.

smooth [smuːð] <> adj **-1.** [surface - skin, fabric] macio(cia); [- stone] liso(sa); [- water, sea] calmo(ma) **-2.** CULIN [texture] uniforme **-3.** [flow, supply] fluido(da)

-4. [pace] tranqüilo(la) **-5.** [taste, ride] suave **-6.** [engine] macio(cia) **-7.** pej [person, manner] lisonjeiro(ra) **-8.** [trouble-free] tranqüilo(la), sem problemas. <> vt **-1.** [gen] alisar; **to ~ the way** preparar o terreno **-2.** [rub] passar.

➡ **smooth out** vt sep **-1.** [gen] alisar **-2.** fig [difficulties] resolver-se.

➡ **smooth over** vt fus resolver.

smoothly [ˈsmuːðlɪ] adv **-1.** [gen] suavemente **-2.** [talk] calmamente, sem se alterar **-3.** [without problems] tranqüilamente, sem problemas.

smoothness [ˈsmuːðnɪs] n (U) **-1.** [gen - skin, fabric, engine] maciez f; [- road, stone] lisura f; [- sea, water, flight] tranqüilidade f; [- finish] perfeição f **-2.** CULIN [texture] uniformidade f **-3.** [of flow, supply] fluidez f **-4.** [of pace] tranqüilidade f, calma f.

smooth-talking adj de lábia fácil.

smother [ˈsmʌðəʳ] vt **-1.** [cover thickly]: **to ~ sthg in** OR **with sthg** cobrir algo de algo **-2.** [suffocate] sufocar **-3.** [extinguish] abafar **-4.** fig [repress] reprimir **-5.** [suffocate with love] mimar demais.

smoulder UK, **smolder** US [ˈsməʊldəʳ] vi **-1.** [fire] fumegar **-2.** fig [feelings] arder.

SMS (abbr of **short message service**) n COMPUT SMS m, mensagens fpl curtas de texto.

smudge [smʌdʒ] <> n [dirty mark] borrão m. <> vt [spoil - by blurring] borrar; [- by dirtying] manchar.

smug [smʌg] (compar **-ger**, superl **-gest**) adj pej presunçoso(sa).

smuggle [ˈsmʌgl] vt **-1.** [across frontiers] contrabandear **-2.** [against rules]: **to ~ sthg in/out** trazer algo escondido.

smuggler [ˈsmʌgləʳ] n contrabandista mf.

smuggling [ˈsmʌglɪŋ] n (U) contrabando m.

smugness [ˈsmʌgnɪs] n (U) pej presunção f.

smut [smʌt] n **-1.** [of soot, dirt] sujeira f, fuligem f **-2.** (U) inf pej [lewd matter] obscenidade f.

smutty [ˈsmʌtɪ] (compar **-ier**, superl **-iest**) adj inf pej obsceno(na), indecente.

snack [snæk] <> n lanche m. <> vi US lanchar.

snack bar n lancheria f.

snag [snæg] (pt & pp **-ged**, cont **-ging**) <> n **-1.** [small problem] dificuldade f **-2.** [in nail, tights, fabric] ponta f saliente. <> vt enganchar. <> vi: **to ~ (on sthg)** enganchar-se (em algo).

snail [sneɪl] n caracol m.

snail mail n correio m tradicional.

snake [sneɪk] <> n cobra f, serpente f. <> vi serpentear.

snap [snæp] (pt & pp **-ped**, cont **-ping**) <> adj atropelado(da), repentino(na). <> n **-1.** [act or sound of snapping] estalo m **-2.** inf [photograph] foto f **-3.** [card game] jogo de cartas semelhante ao burro mecânico. <> vt **-1.** [break] partir (em dois) **-2.** [make cracking sound with]: **to ~ sthg open/shut** abrir/fechar algo com um golpe; **to ~ one's fingers** estalar os dedos **-3.** [speak sharply] falar bruscamente **-4.** inf [photograph] bater foto. <> vi **-1.** [break] partir (em dois) **-2.** [make cracking sound] estalar; **to ~ into place** ir para o lugar com uma pancada **-3.** [attempt to bite]: **to ~ (at sb/sthg)** tentar morder (alguém/algo) **-4.** [speak sharply]: **to ~ (at sb)** ficar brabo(ba) (com alguém) **-5.** phr: **to ~ out of it** animar-se de repente.

snap up *vt sep* não deixar escapar.

snap fastener *n esp US* botão *m* de pressão.

snappy ['snæpɪ] (*compar* -ier, *superl* -iest) *adj inf* - **1.** [stylish] chique - **2.** [quick] rápido(da); **make it ~!** anda logo!

snapshot ['snæpʃɒt] *n* instantânea *f.*

snare [sneə^r] ⇔ *n* armadilha *f.* ⇔ *vt* pegar numa armadilha.

snarl [snɑːll] ⇔ *n* rosnado *m.* ⇔ *vi* - **1.** [animal] rosnar - **2.** [person] resmungar.

snarl-up *n* rolo *m*, confusão *f.*

snatch [snætʃ] ⇔ *n* [fragment] trecho *m.* ⇔ *vt* - **1.** [grab] agarrar - **2.** *fig* [sleep, opportunity, look] aproveitar; **to ~ some sleep** tirar um tempo para dormir. ⇔ *vi* [grab]: **to ~ (at sthg)** tentar agarrar (algo).

snazzy ['snæzɪ] (*compar* -ier, *superl* -iest) *adj inf* chamativo(va).

sneak [sniːk] (*US pt* snuck) ⇔ *n UK inf* mexeriqueiro *m*, -ra *f.* ⇔ *vt* levar escondido(da); **to ~ a look at sb/sthg** espiar alguém/algo. ⇔ *vi* [move quietly] esgueirar-se.

sneakers ['sniːkəz] *npl US* tênis *m inv.*

sneaking ['sniːkɪŋ] *adj* [feeling, suspicion] secreto(ta).

sneak preview *n* pré-estréia *f.*

sneaky ['sniːkɪ] (*compar* -ier, *superl* -iest) *adj inf* sorrateiro(ra).

sneer [snɪə^r] ⇔ *n* escárnio *m.* ⇔ *vi* - **1.** [smile unpleasantly] sorrir com escárnio - **2.** [ridicule]: **to ~ (at sthg)** zombar (de algo).

sneeze [sniːz] ⇔ *n* espirro *m.* ⇔ *vi* espirrar; **it's not to be ~d at** *inf* não é de se jogar fora.

snicker ['snɪkə^r] *vi* rir por dentro.

snide [snaɪd] *adj* sarcástico(ca).

sniff [snɪf] ⇔ *n* fungada *f.* ⇔ *vt* - **1.** [smell] fungar - **2.** [drug] cheirar. ⇔ *vi* - **1.** [to clear nose] assoar - **2.** [to show disapproval] torcer o nariz.

sniff out *vt sep* - **1.** [detect by sniffing] farejar - **2.** *inf* [seek out] descobrir.

sniffer dog ['snɪfə^r-] *n* cão *m* farejador.

sniffle ['snɪfl] *vi* fungar.

snigger ['snɪgə^r] ⇔ *n* escárnio *m.* ⇔ *vi* rir por dentro.

snip [snɪp] (*pt & pp* -ped, *cont* -ping) ⇔ *n inf* [bargain] pechincha *f.* ⇔ *vt* [cut] cortar (em pedaços).

snipe [snaɪp] *vi* - **1.** [shoot]: **to ~ (at sb/sthg)** disparar (em alguém/algo) - **2.** [criticize]: **to ~ at sb** criticar alguém.

sniper ['snaɪpə^r] *n* franco-atirador *m*, -ra *f.*

snippet ['snɪpɪt] *n* fragmento *m.*

snivel ['snɪvl] (*UK pt & pp* -led, *cont* -ling, *US pt & pp* - ed, *cont* -ing) *vi* choramingar.

snob [snɒb] *n* esnobe *mf.*

snobbery ['snɒbərɪ] *n (U)* esnobismo *m.*

snobbish ['snɒbɪʃ], **snobby** ['snɒbɪ] (*compar* -ier, *superl* -iest) *adj* esnobe.

snog (*pt & pp* -ged, *cont* -ging) *vi UK inf* agarrar-se.

snooker ['snuːkə^r] ⇔ *n (U)* snooker *m.* ⇔ *vt UK inf* [thwart]: **to be ~ ed** estar com as mãos atadas.

snoop [snuːp] *vi inf* bisbilhotar.

snooper ['snuːpə^r] *n inf* bisbilhoteiro *m*, -ra *f.*

snooty ['snuːtɪ] (*compar* -ier, *superl* -iest) *adj* presunçoso(sa).

snooze [snuːz] ⇔ *n* cochilo *m*, soneca *f*; **to have a ~** tirar uma soneca *OR* um cochilo. ⇔ *vi* cochilar.

snore [snɔː^r] ⇔ *n* ronco *m.* ⇔ *vi* roncar.

snoring ['snɔːrɪŋ] *n (U)* roncos *mpl.*

snorkel ['snɔːkl] *n* (tubo *m*) snorkel *m.*

snorkelling *UK*, **snorkeling** *US* ['snɔːklɪŋ] *n (U)* mergulho *m* com (tubo) snorkel.

snort [snɔːt] ⇔ *n* bufo *m.* ⇔ *vi* bufar. ⇔ *vt drugs sl* cheirar.

snotty ['snɒtɪ] (*compar* -ier, *superl* -iest) *adj inf* [snooty] presunçoso(sa).

snout [snaʊt] *n* focinho *m.*

snow [snəʊ] ⇔ *n (U)* neve *f.* ⇔ *v impers* nevar.

snow in *vt sep*: **to be ~ ed in** estar preso(sa) por causa da neve.

snow under *vt sep*: **to be ~ ed under (with sthg)** estar atolado(da) (de algo).

snowball ['snəʊbɔːl] ⇔ *n* bola *f* de neve. ⇔ *vi fig* [increase rapidly] crescer como bola de neve.

snow blindness *n* ofuscação *f (da neve).*

snowboard ['snəʊbɔːd] *n* snowboard *m.*

snowboarding ['snəʊbɔːdɪŋ] *n* snowboard *m*; **to go ~** praticar snowboard.

snowbound ['snəʊbaʊnd] *adj* bloqueado(da) pela neve.

snow-capped [-ˌkæpt] *adj* com o pico coberto de neve.

snowdrift ['snəʊdrɪft] *n* monte *m* de neve.

snowdrop ['snəʊdrɒp] *n* campainha *f* branca.

snowfall ['snəʊfɔːl] *n* - **1.** [fall of snow] nevada *f* - **2.** [amount of snow over time] quantidade *f* de neve.

snowflake ['snəʊfleɪk] *n* floco *m* de neve.

snowman ['snəʊmæn] (*pl* -men [-menl]) *n* boneco *m* de neve.

snow pea *n US* ervilha *f* torta.

snowplough *UK*, **snowplow** *US* ['snəʊplaʊ] *n* [vehicle] limpa-neve *m.*

snowshoe ['snəʊʃuː] *n* raquete *f* de neve.

snowstorm ['snəʊstɔːm] *n* nevasca *f.*

snowy ['snəʊɪ] (*compar* -ier, *superl* -iest) *adj* - **1.** [weather, day] de muita neve - **2.** [road, landscape] com muita neve.

SNP (*abbr of* **Scottish National Party**) *n partido nacional escocês que prega a independência da Grã-Bretanha.*

Snr, snr (*abbr of* **senior**) sênior.

snub [snʌb] (*pt & pp* -bed, *cont* -bing) ⇔ *n* repulsa *f.* ⇔ *vt* desprezar.

snuck [snʌk] *pt US* ⊳ **sneak.**

snuff [snʌf] ⇔ *n (U)* [tobacco] rapé *m.* ⇔ *vt*: **to ~ it** *inf* morrer.

snuffle ['snʌfl] *vi* fungar.

snuff movie *n* filme pornográfico com um assassinato como desenlace.

snug [snʌg] (*compar* -ger, *superl* -gest) *adj* - **1.** [person, feeling] agradável - **2.** [place] confortável - **3.** [close-fitting] cômodo(da).

snuggle ['snʌgl] *vi* aconchegar-se; **to ~ down** cobrir-se (com coberta).

so [səʊ] ⇔ *adv* - **1.** [emphasizing degree] tão; **don't be ~ stupid!** não seja tão idiota!; **it's ~ difficult (that ...,)** é tão difícil (que ...); **~ much** tanto(ta); **~ many**

tantos(tas). **- 2.** [referring back]: **I don't think** ~ acho que não; **I'm afraid** ~ receio que sim; ~ **you knew already** então você já sabia; **if** ~ nesse caso. **- 3.** [also] também; ~ **do I** eu também. **- 4.** [in this way] deste modo, assim. **- 5.** [expressing agreement]: ~ **there is** pois é, é verdade. **- 6.** [in phrases]: **or** ~ mais ou menos; ~ **as** para; ~ **that** para. <> conj **- 1.** [therefore] por isso; **I'm away next week** ~ **I won't be there** viajo na semana que vem, portanto não estarei lá. **- 2.** [summarizing] então; ~ **what have you been up to?** então, o que é que você tem feito? **- 3.** [in phrases]: ~ **what?** inf e daí?; ~ **there!** inf pronto!, nada a fazer!

SO (abbr of **standing order**) débito m em conta.

soak [səʊk] <> vt **- 1.** [leave immersed] pôr de molho **- 2.** [wet thoroughly] ensopar; **to be** ~**ed with sthg** estar ensopado(da) de algo. <> vi **- 1.** [become thoroughly wet]: **to leave sthg to** ~, **to let sthg** ~ deixar algo de molho **- 2.** [spread]: **to** ~ **into sthg** espalhar-se por algo; **to** ~ **through (sthg)** infiltrar-se em algo.

  soak up vt sep [liquid] absorver.

soaked [səʊkt] adj ensopado(da); **to be** ~ **through** ficar ensopado(da) dos pés à cabeça.

soaking [ˈsəʊkɪŋ] adj ensopado(da).

so-and-so n inf **- 1.** [to replace a name] fulano m, -na f **- 2.** [annoying person] filho m, -lha f da mãe.

soap [səʊp] <> n **- 1.** (U) [for washing] sabão m **- 2.** TV novela f. <> vt ensaboar.

soap bubble n bolha f de sabão.

soap dish n saboneteira f.

soap flakes npl sabão m em flocos.

soap opera n novela f.

soap powder n (U) sabão m em pó.

soapsuds [ˈsəʊpsʌdz] npl espuma f de sabão.

soapy [ˈsəʊpɪ] (compar -ier, superl -iest) adj **- 1.** [full of soap] ensaboado(da) **- 2.** [resembling soap] de sabão.

soar [sɔːʳ] vi **- 1.** [bird] levantar vôo **- 2.** [rise into the sky] subir **- 3.** [increase rapidly] aumentar rapidamente **- 4.** literary [be impressively high] elevar-se **- 5.** [rise in volume or pitch] aumentar de intensidade.

soaring [ˈsɔːrɪŋ] adj **- 1.** [rapidly increasing] cada vez mais alto(ta) **- 2.** [spire, tower] altíssimo(ma) **- 3.** [rising in volume or pitch] cada vez mais intenso(sa).

sob [sɒb] (pt & pp -bed, cont -bing) <> n soluço m. <> vt soluçar. <> vi [cry] soluçar.

sobbing [ˈsɒbɪŋ] n (U) soluços mpl.

sober [ˈsəʊbəʳ] adj **- 1.** [not drunk] sóbrio(bria) **- 2.** [serious] sério(ria) **- 3.** [plain] simples.

  sober up vi ficar sóbrio(bria).

sobering [ˈsəʊbərɪŋ] adj que faz refletir.

sobriety [səʊˈbraɪətɪ] n (U) fml sobriedade f.

Soc. (abbr of **Society**) Soc.

so-called [-kɔːld] adj **- 1.** [misleadingly named] suposto(ta) **- 2.** [widely known as] chamado(da).

soccer [ˈsɒkəʳ] n (U) futebol m.

sociable [ˈsəʊʃəbl] adj sociável.

social [ˈsəʊʃl] adj social.

social climber n pej arrivista mf.

social club n clube m social.

social conscience n consciência f social.

social democracy n (U) social-democracia f.

social event n evento m social.

social fund n na Grã-Bretanha, fundo de auxílio em casos de extrema necessidade.

socialism [ˈsəʊʃəlɪzml] n (U) socialismo m.

socialist [ˈsəʊʃəlɪst] <> adj socialista. <> n socialista mf.

socialite [ˈsəʊʃəlaɪt] n socialite m.

socialize, -ise [ˈsəʊʃəlaɪz] vi: **to** ~ **(with sb)** socializar-se (com alguém).

socialized medicine n US saúde f pública.

social life n **- 1.** [of individual] vida f social **- 2.** (U) [in general] vida f em sociedade.

socially [ˈsəʊʃəlɪ] adv **- 1.** [towards society] socialmente **- 2.** [outside business] fora do trabalho.

social order n ordem f social.

social science n ciência f social; **the** ~**s** as ciências sociais.

social security n (U) previdência f social.

social services npl assistência f social.

social studies n estudos mpl sociais.

social work n (U) trabalho m social.

social worker n assistente mf social.

society [səˈsaɪətɪ] (pl -ies) n sociedade f.

socioeconomic [ˈsəʊsɪəʊˌiːkəˈnɒmɪk] adj POL socioeconômico(ca).

sociological [ˌsəʊsɪəˈlɒdʒɪkl] adj sociológico(ca).

sociologist [ˌsəʊsɪˈɒlədʒɪst] n sociólogo m, -ga f.

sociology [ˌsəʊsɪˈɒlədʒɪ] n (U) sociologia f.

sock [sɒk] n meia f; **to pull one's** ~**s up** inf fig empenhar-se.

socket [ˈsɒkɪt] n **- 1.** ELEC tomada f **- 2.** [de lâmpada] soquete m **- 3.** [ANAT - of arm, hipbone] concavidade f, [- of eye] órbita f.

sod [sɒd] n **- 1.** [of turf] torrão m **- 2.** v inf [person] sujeito m.

soda [ˈsəʊdə] n **- 1.** [gen] soda f **- 2.** US [fizzy drink] refrigerante m.

soda syphon n garrafa d'água com sifão para servir soda.

soda water n (U) soda f, água f com gás.

sodden [ˈsɒdn] adj encharcado(da).

sodium [ˈsəʊdɪəm] n (U) sódio m.

sofa [ˈsəʊfə] n sofá m.

sofabed n sofá-cama m.

Sofia [ˈsəʊfjə] n Sofia.

soft [sɒft] adj **- 1.** [gen] mole **- 2.** [to touch] macio(cia) **- 3.** [gentle] suave **- 4.** [kind, caring] meigo(ga), bondoso(sa) **- 5.** [not strict] flexível.

softball n SPORT espécie de beisebol que se joga com uma bola mais macia e maior.

soft-boiled adj: ~ **eggs** ovos mpl quentes:

soft drink n **- 1.** [fruit juice] refresco m **- 2.** [fizzy drink] refrigerante m.

soft drugs npl drogas fpl leves.

soften [ˈsɒfn] <> vt **- 1.** [substance] suavizar **- 2.** [blow, impact, effect] amortecer **- 3.** [attitude] enternecer. <> vi **- 1.** [substance] amaciar **- 2.** [attitude] amolecer **- 3.** [eyes, voice, expression] suavizar.

  soften up vt sep inf [make amenable] amaciar.

softener [ˈsɒfnəʳ] n [for washing] amaciante m.

soft focus n (U) foco m enevoado; **in** ~ em foco enevoado.

soft furnishings *npl* UK complementos *mpl* para decoração.

softhearted [‚sɒft'hɑːtɪd] *adj* de bom coração.

softly ['sɒftlɪ] *adv* -**1.** [gently, without violence] com delicadeza -**2.** [quietly] suavemente -**3.** [dimly] tenuamente -**4.** [fondly] carinhosamente.

softness ['sɒftnɪs] *n (U)* -**1.** [malleability] maleabilidade *f* -**2.** [to touch] maciez *f* -**3.** [gentleness] suavidade *f* -**4.** [kindness] bondade *f*.

soft-pedal *vi inf*: to ~ on sthg maneirar em algo.

soft return *n* COMPUT quebra *f* de linha condicional.

soft sell *n inf sistema de venda em que não se pressiona o comprador*.

soft-spoken *adj* de voz suave.

soft toy *n* bichinho *m* de pelúcia.

software ['sɒftweəʳ] *n (U)* COMPUT software *m*.

software package *n* COMPUT pacote *m* de software.

softwood *n* [timber] madeira *f* branca.

softy ['sɒftɪ] *(pl* -**ies)** *n inf* -**1.** *pej* [weak person] fracote *mf* -**2.** [sensitive person] manteiga-derretida *mf*.

soggy ['sɒgɪ] *(compar* -**ier,** *superl* -**iest)** *adj* empapado(da), encharcado(da).

soil [sɔɪl] <> *n* -**1.** [earth] terra *f*, solo *m* -**2.** *fig* [territory] solo *m*. <> *vt* [dirty] sujar.

soiled [sɔɪld] *adj* sujo(ja).

solace ['sɒləs] *n literary* consolo *m*.

solar ['səʊləʳ] *adj* solar.

solar energy *n* energia *f* solar.

solarium [sə'leərɪəm] *(pl* -**riums** OR -**ria** [-rɪəl) *n* solário *m*.

solar panel *n* painel *m* solar.

solar plexus [-'pleksəs] *n* plexo *m* solar.

solar power *n* energia *f* solar.

solar system *n* sistema *f* solar.

sold [səʊld] *pt & pp* ▷ **sell**.

solder ['səʊldəʳ] <> *n (U)* solda *f*. <> *vt* soldar.

soldering iron ['səʊldərɪŋ-] *n* ferro *m* de soldar.

soldier ['səʊldʒəʳ] *n* soldado(da).

➤ **soldier on** *vi* UK agüentar firme.

sold out *adj* esgotado(da).

sole [səʊl] *(pl sense 2 only inv* OR -**s)** <> *adj* -**1.** [only] único(ca) -**2.** [exclusive] exclusivo(va). <> *n* -**1.** [of foot] sola *f* -**2.** [fish] linguado *m*.

solely ['səʊllɪ] *adv* [entirely] unicamente.

solemn ['sɒləm] *adj* solene.

solemnly ['sɒləmlɪ] *adv* solenemente.

sole trader *n* UK COMM comerciante *mf* individual.

solicit [sə'lɪsɪt] <> *vt fml* [request] solicitar. <> *vi* [prostitute] oferecer seus serviços.

solicitor [sə'lɪsɪtəʳ] *n* UK solicitador *m*, -ra *f*.

solicitous [sə'lɪsɪtəs] *adj* -**1.** [caring] solícito(ta) -**2.** [anxious]: ~ of OR for sthg desejoso(sa) de algo.

solid ['sɒlɪd] <> *adj* -**1.** [gen] sólido(da) -**2.** [of a single substance] maciço(ça) -**3.** [reliable, respectable] coerente -**4.** [unbroken, continuous] ininterrupto(ta). <> *adv*: to be packed ~ estar superlotado(da). <> *n* [not liquid or gas] sólido *m*.

➤ **solids** *npl* [food] sólidos *mpl*; she can't eat ~s ela não pode comer nada sólido.

solidarity [‚sɒlɪ'dærətɪ] *n (U)* solidariedade *f*.

solid fuel *n* combustível *m* sólido.

solidify [sə'lɪdɪfaɪ] *(pt & pp* -**ied)** *vi* solidificar-se.

solidly ['sɒlɪdlɪ] *adv* -**1.** [sturdily] solidamente -**2.** [completely, definitely] inteiramente -**3.** [without interruption] ininterruptamente.

soliloquy [sə'lɪləkwɪ] *(pl* -**ies)** *n* LITER solilóquio *m*.

solitaire [‚sɒlɪ'teəʳ] *n* -**1.** [jewel] solitário *m* -**2.** [card game] paciência *f*.

solitary ['sɒlɪtrɪ] *adj* -**1.** [gen] solitário(ria) -**2.** [single] isolado(da).

solitary confinement *n (U)* solitária *f*.

solitude ['sɒlɪtjuːd] *n (U)* solidão *f*.

solo ['səʊləʊ] *(pl* -**s)** <> *adj* -**1.** MUS solo *inv* -**2.** [attempt, flight] único(ca). <> *n* MUS solo *m*. <> *adv* -**1.** MUS em solo -**2.** [fly, climb] sozinho(nha).

soloist ['səʊləʊɪst] *n* solista *mf*.

Solomon Islands ['sɒləmən-] *npl*: **the** ~ as Ilhas Salomão; **in the** ~ nas Ilhas Salomão.

solstice ['sɒlstɪs] *n* solstício *m*.

soluble ['sɒljʊbl] *adj* -**1.** [substance] solúvel -**2.** [problem] solucionável.

solution [sə'luːʃn] *n* -**1.** [to problem, puzzle]: ~ **(to sthg)** solução *f* (para algo) -**2.** [liquid] solução *f*.

solve [sɒlv] *vt* resolver.

solvency ['sɒlvənsɪ] *n (U)* FIN solvência *f*.

solvent ['sɒlvənt] <> *adj* FIN solvente. <> *n* [substance] solvente *m*.

solvent abuse [-ə'bjuːs] *n (U)* inalação *f* de cola e solventes.

Somali [sə'mɑːlɪ] <> *adj* somali. <> *n* -**1.** [person] somali *mf* -**2.** [language] somali *m*.

Somalia [sə'mɑːlɪə] *n* Somália *f*; **in** ~ na Somália.

sombre UK, **somber** US ['sɒmbəʳ] *adj* -**1.** [person, mood] lúgubre -**2.** [colour, place] sombrio(bria).

some [sʌm] <> *adj* -**1.** [certain, large amount of] algum (alguma); ~ **meat** um pouco de carne; ~ **money** um pouco de dinheiro; **I had** ~ **difficulty getting here** tive algumas dificuldades para chegar aqui. -**2.** [certain, large number of] alguns (algumas); ~ **sweets** alguns doces; ~ **people** algumas pessoas; **I've known him for** ~ **years** já o conheço há alguns anos. -**3.** [not all] alguns (algumas); ~ **jobs are better paid than others** alguns empregos são mais bem pagos que outros. -**4.** [in imprecise statements] um (uma) ... qualquer; ~ **woman phoned** telefonou uma mulher. <> *pron* -**1.** [certain amount] algum *m*, alguma *f*, parte *f*; **can I have** ~**?** posso ficar com uma parte?; ~ **of the money** algum dinheiro, parte do dinheiro. -**2.** [certain number] alguns *mpl*, algumas *fpl*; **can I have** ~**?** posso ficar com alguns?; ~ **(of them) left early** alguns (deles) foram embora cedo. <> *adv* [approximately] aproximadamente; **there were** ~ **7,000 people there** havia umas 7.000 pessoas.

somebody ['sʌmbədɪ] *pron* alguém.

someday ['sʌmdeɪ] *adv* algum dia.

somehow ['sʌmhaʊ], **someway** US ['sʌmweɪ] *adv* -**1.** [by some action] de alguma maneira -**2.** [for some reason] por alguma razão; ~ **I don't think he'll come** tenho a impressão de que ele não virá.

someone ['sʌmwʌn] *pron* = **somebody**.

someplace adv US = somewhere.

somersault ['sʌməsɔːlt] <> n salto m mortal. <> vi dar um salto mortal.

Somerset n Somerset.

something ['sʌmθɪŋ] <> pron -**1.** algo, alguma coisa; **or** ~ **inf** ou (qualquer) coisa parecida -**2.** phr: it's really ~! é demais! <> adv [in approximations]: ~ **like** uns(umas), qualquer coisa como.

sometime ['sʌmtaɪm] adv: ~ **in** June em junho.

sometimes ['sʌmtaɪmz] adv às OR por vezes.

someway adv US = somehow.

somewhat ['sʌmwɒt] adv um tanto.

somewhere UK ['sʌmweəʳ], **someplace** US ['sʌmpleɪs] adv -**1.** [unknown place] em algum lugar, em alguma parte -**2.** [specific place] a alguma parte -**3.** [in approximations]: ~ **around** OR **between** aproximadamente.

son [sʌn] n filho m.

sonar ['səʊnɑːʳ] n (U) sonar m.

sonata [sə'nɑːtə] n sonata f.

song [sɒŋ] n -**1.** [piece of music] música f; **for a** ~ [cheaply] por uma bagatela; **to make a** ~ **and dance about sth** inf fazer uma tempestade num copo d'água em relação a algo -**2.** (U) [act of singing]: **they burst into** ~ desataram a cantar -**3.** [of bird] canto m.

songbook ['sɒŋbʊk] n cancioneiro m.

sonic ['sɒnɪk] adj sônico(ca).

sonic boom n ruído m sônico.

son-in-law (pl sons-in-law OR son-in-laws) n genro m.

sonnet ['sɒnɪt] n soneto m.

sonny ['sʌnɪ] n inf filhinho m.

soon [suːn] adv -**1.** [in a short time] logo -**2.** [early] cedo; **how** ~ **can you finish it?** para quando você consegue terminar?; **as** ~ **as** assim que; **as** ~ **as possible** o quanto antes -**3.** phr: **I'd just as** ~ ... eu preferiria (que) ...

sooner ['suːnəʳ] adv -**1.** [earlier] mais cedo; **no** ~ **did he arrive than** ... ele tinha acabado de chegar quando ...; ~ **or later** mais cedo ou mais tarde; **the** ~ **the better** quanto mais cedo, melhor -**2.** [expressing preference]: **I'd** ~ ... preferiria ...

soot [sʊt] n (U) fuligem f.

soothe [suːð] vt -**1.** [relieve] aliviar -**2.** [calm] acalmar.

soothing ['suːðɪŋ] adj -**1.** [pain-relieving] analgésico(ca), calmante -**2.** [calming] tranqüilizante.

sooty ['sʊtɪ] (compar -ier, superl -iest) adj fuliginoso(-sa).

sop n pej compensação f de pouco valor; ~ **to sb/ sth** compensação de pouco valor para alguém/ algo.

SOP (abbr of standard operating procedure) n procedimento m habitual.

sophisticated [sə'fɪstɪkeɪtɪd] adj -**1.** [stylish] sofisticado(da) -**2.** [intelligent] inteligente -**3.** [complicated] complicado(da).

sophistication [sə,fɪstɪ'keɪʃn] n (U) -**1.** [stylishness] sofisticação f -**2.** [intelligence] inteligência f -**3.** [complexity] complexidade f.

sophomore ['sɒfəmɔːʳ] n US estudante do segundo ano de faculdade.

soporific [,sɒpə'rɪfɪk] adj soporífero(ra).

sopping ['sɒpɪŋ] adj: ~ **(wet)** encharcado(da).

soppy ['sɒpɪ] (compar -ier, superl -iest) adj inf pej sentimentalóide.

soprano [sə'prɑːnəʊ] (pl -s) n -**1.** [person] soprano mf -**2.** [voice] soprano f.

sorbet ['sɔːbeɪ] n sorbet m.

sorcerer ['sɔːsərəʳ] n feiticeiro m.

sorceress n feiticeira f.

sordid ['sɔːdɪd] adj sórdido(da).

sore [sɔːʳ] <> adj -**1.** [painful] dolorido(da); **a** ~ **throat** uma dor de garganta -**2.** US inf [angry] zangado(da) -**3.** literary [dire, great] imenso(sa). <> n MED inflamação f.

sorely ['sɔːlɪ] adv literary imensamente.

sorority [sə'rɒrətɪ] (pl -ies) n US irmandade feminina numa universidade.

sorrel ['sɒrəl] n (U) azeda-miúda f.

sorrow ['sɒrəʊ] n -**1.** [feeling of sadness] mágoa f -**2.** [cause of sadness] desgosto m.

sorrowful ['sɒrəfʊl] adj magoado(da), triste.

sorry ['sɒrɪ] (compar -ier, superl -iest) <> adj -**1.** [expressing apology]: **I'm** ~ desculpe; **to be** ~ **about sth** lamentar algo; **to be** ~ **for sth** estar arrependido(da) por algo; **to be** ~ **to do sth** desculpar-se por fazer algo -**2.** [expressing disappointment]: **to be** ~ **(that)** lamentar que; **to be** ~ **about sth** ficar sentido(da) por algo -**3.** [expressing regret]: **I'm** ~ **to have to say that** ... lamento ter que dizer que ...; **to be** ~ **to do sth** estar triste por fazer algo -**4.** [expressing sympathy]: **to be** OR **feel** ~ **for sb** estar com/sentir pena de alguém; **to be** OR **feel** ~ **for o.s.** estar com/sentir pena de si mesmo -**5.** [expressing polite disagreement]: **I'm** ~, **but I think that** ... me desculpa, mas eu acho que ... -**6.** [poor, pitiable] lamentável. <> excl -**1.** [expressing apology] desculpe! -**2.** [asking for repetition] como! -**3.** [to correct o.s.]: **a boy,** ~, **a man** um garoto, quer dizer, um homem.

sort [sɔːt] <> n -**1.** [gen] tipo m; **a** ~ **of** um tipo de, uma espécie de -**2.** [act of sorting out] escolha f. <> vt [classify, separate] classificar.

  sorts npl: **a lawyer of** ~s um advogado medíocre, um advogadozinho; **to be out of** ~s não se sentir bem.

  sort of adv [rather] mais ou menos.

  sort out vt sep -**1.** [into groups] classificar -**2.** [tidy up] pôr em ordem -**3.** [solve] resolver -**4.** [work out] concluir.

sortie ['sɔːtiː] n [MIL - by troops] surtida f; [- by aircraft] ação f de reconhecimento.

sorting office ['sɔːtɪŋ-] n centro f de triagem.

sort-out n UK inf: **to have a** ~ dar uma geral.

SOS (abbr of save our souls) n SOS f.

so-so inf adj, adv mais ou menos.

soufflé ['suːfleɪ] n suflê m.

sought [sɔːt] pt & pp ▷ seek.

sought-after adj solicitado(da).

soul [səʊl] n -**1.** [gen] alma f -**2.** [emotional depth] sentimento m -**3.** [perfect example] exemplo m perfeito -**4.** (U) [music] (música f) soul m.

soul-destroying [-dɪ,strɔɪŋ] adj [boring] massante; [discouraging] desmoralizador(ra).

soul food n US comida tradicional dos negros do sul dos Estados Unidos.

soulful [ˈsəʊlfʊl] adj cheio (cheia) de sentimentos.

soulless [ˈsəʊlɪs] adj desalmado(da).

soul mate n alma f gêmea.

soul music n (U) música f soul.

soul-searching n (U) exame m de consciência.

sound [saʊnd] ◇ adj -1. [healthy] sadio(dia) -2. [sturdy] sólido(da) -3. [reliable] confiável, seguro(ra) -4. [thorough] completo(ta). ◇ adv: **to be ~ asleep** estar num sono profundo. ◇ n -1. [particular noise] barulho m -2. (U) [in general] som m -3. (U) [volume] volume m -4. [impression, idea] tom m. ◇ vt [alarm, bell, horn] tocar. ◇ vi -1. [make a noise] fazer barulho; **to ~ like sthg** soar como algo -2. [seem] parecer; **to ~ like sthg** parecer algo.

  sound out vt sep: **to ~ sb out (on** OR **aboutsthg)** sondar alguém(sobre algo).

sound barrier n barreira f do som.

sound bite n declaração f mordaz (feita por políticos no rádio ou na tevê).

sound card n COMPUT placa f de som.

sound effects npl efeitos mpl sonoros.

sounding board n -1. caixa f de ressonância -2. fig [person]: **he needs a ~, rather than thinking alone** ele precisa de alguém com quem possa trocar idéias, em vez de pensar sozinho.

sounding [ˈsaʊndɪŋ] n -1. NAUT [measurement] prumada f -2. fig [investigation] sondagem f.

soundly [ˈsaʊndlɪ] adv -1. [thoroughly] completamente -2. [deeply] profundamente.

soundness [ˈsaʊndnɪs] n (U) [reliability] solidez f.

soundproof [ˈsaʊndpruːf] adj à prova de som.

soundtrack [ˈsaʊndtræk] n trilha f sonora.

sound wave n onda f sonora.

soup [suːp] n sopa f, caldo m.

  soup up vt sep inf [car] envenenar.

soup kitchen n bandejão m público.

soup plate n prato m fundo.

soup spoon n colher f de sopa.

sour [saʊəʳ] ◇ adj -1. [acidic] ácido(da) -2. [milk] azedo(da); **to go** OR **turn sour** [milk] azedar; fig [be spoiled] degringolar -3. [ill-tempered] mal-humorado(da). ◇ vt & vi [person, relationship] azedar.

source [sɔːs] n -1. [gen] fonte f -2. [cause] origem f -3. [of river] nascente f.

soured cream n (U) nata f azeda.

sour grapes n (U) inf inveja f pura.

sourness [ˈsaʊənɪs] n (U) -1. [gen] azedume m -2. [acidity] acidez f.

south [saʊθ] ◇ adj sul. ◇ adv para o sul; **~ of** ao sul de. ◇ n -1. [direction] sul m -2. [region]: **the ~** o sul.

South Africa n África f do Sul; **in ~** na África do Sul; **the Republic of ~** a República da África do Sul.

South African ◇ adj sul-africano(na). ◇ n [person] sul-africano m, -na f.

South America n América f do Sul; **in ~** na América do Sul.

South American ◇ adj sul-americano(na). ◇ n [person] sul-americano m, -na f.

southbound [ˈsaʊθbaʊnd] adj para o sul.

South Carolina n Carolina f do Sul.

South Dakota n Dakota f do Sul.

south-east ◇ adj sudeste. ◇ adv para o sudeste; **~ of** a sudeste de. ◇ n -1. [direction] sudeste m -2. [region]: **the ~** o sudeste.

South-East Asia n Sudeste m Asiático; **in ~** no Sudeste Asiático.

south-easterly adj -1. [in the south-east] sudeste -2. [towards the south-east] para o sudeste -3. [from the south-east] do sudeste.

south-eastern adj do sudeste.

southerly [ˈsʌðəlɪ] adj -1. [in the south] ao sul -2. [towards the south] para o sul -3. [from the south] do sul.

southern [ˈsʌðən] adj sulista.

Southern Africa n África Meridional; **in ~** na África Meridional.

Southerner [ˈsʌðənəʳ] n sulista mf.

South Korea n Coréia f do Sul; **in ~** na Coréia do Sul.

South Korean ◇ adj sul-coreano(na). ◇ n sul-coreano m, -na f.

South Pole n: **the ~** o Pólo Sul.

South Vietnam n Vietnã m do Sul; **in ~** no Vietnã do Sul.

South Vietnamese ◇ adj sul-vietnamita. ◇ n sul-vietnamita mf.

southward [ˈsaʊθwəd] ◇ adj sul. ◇ adv = southwards.

southwards [ˈsaʊθwədz] adv para o sul.

south-west ◇ adj sudoeste. ◇ adv para o sudoeste; **~ of** a sudoeste de. ◇ n -1. [direction] sudoeste m -2. [region]: **the ~** o sudoeste.

south-westerly adj -1. [in the south-west] ao sudoeste -2. [towards the south-west] para o sudoeste -3. [from the south-west] do sudoeste.

south-western adj do sudoeste.

South Yemen n Iêmen m do Sul; **in ~** no Iêmen do Sul.

South Yorkshire n South Yorkshire.

souvenir [ˌsuːvəˈnɪəʳ] n suvenir m, lembrança f.

sou'wester [saʊˈwestəʳ] n [hat] sueste m.

sovereign [ˈsɒvrɪn] ◇ adj -1. [state, territory] soberano(na) -2. [excellent] magnífico(ca). ◇ n -1. [ruler] soberano m, -na f -2. [coin] soberano m.

sovereignty [ˈsɒvrɪntɪ] n [supreme power] soberania f.

soviet n soviético(ca).

  Soviet ◇ adj soviético m, -ca f. ◇ n [person] soviético m, -ca f.

Soviet Union n: **the (former) ~** a (antiga) União Soviética; **in the ~** na União Soviética.

sow[1] [səʊ] (pt -ed, pp sown OR -ed) vt semear.

sow[2] [saʊ] n [pig] porca f.

sown [səʊn] pp ▷ sow.

sox npl US ▷ bobby sox.

soya [ˈsɔɪə] n (U) soja f.

soy(a) bean [ˈsɔɪ(ə)-] n grão m de soja.

soy sauce [sɔɪ-] n (U) molho m de soja.

sozzled [ˈsɒzld] adj UK inf pinguço(ça).

spa [spɑː] n -1. [mineral spring] termas fpl -2. [for health care] spa m.

space [speɪs] ◇ n -1. [gen] espaço m; **to stare into**

~ olhar para o nada - **2.** [gap] lugar *m*, espaço *m* - **3.** [period of time] intervalo *m* - **4.** [seat, place] lugar *m*. <> *comp* espacial. <> *vt* espaçar.

space out *vt sep* [arrange] espaçar.

space age *n*: the ~ a era espacial.

space-age *adj inf* da era espacial.

space bar *n* barra *f* de espaço.

space capsule *n* cápsula *f* espacial.

spacecraft ['speɪskrɑːft] (*pl inv*) *n* espaçonave *f*.

spaceman ['speɪsmæn] (*pl* -men [-men]) *n inf* [astronaut] astronauta *m*.

space probe *n* sonda *f* espacial.

spaceship ['speɪʃɪp] *n* nave *f* espacial, astronave *f*.

space shuttle *n* ônibus *m inv* espacial.

space station *n* estação *f* espacial.

spacesuit ['speɪssuːt] *n* roupa *f* espacial.

spacewoman ['speɪs,wʊmən] (*pl* -women [-,wɪmɪn]) *n inf* [astronaut] astronauta *f*.

spacing ['speɪsɪŋ] *n* (U) TYPO espaçamento *m*.

spacious ['speɪʃəs] *adj* espaçoso(sa).

spade [speɪd] *n* - **1.** [tool] pá *f* - **2.** [playing card] espada *f*.

spades *npl* espadas *fpl*; **the six of** ~**s** o seis de espadas.

spadework ['speɪdwɜːk] *n* (U) *inf* trabalho *m* preliminar.

spaghetti [spə'getɪ] *n* (U) espaguete *m*.

Spain [speɪn] *n* Espanha *f*; **in** ~ na Espanha.

spam [spæm] (*pt* & *pp* -med, *cont* -ming) COMPUT <> *n* spam *m*. <> *vt* enviar spam para.

span [spæn] (*pt* & *pp* -ned, *cont* -ning) <> *pt* > **spin**. <> *n* - **1.** [in time] período *m*; **concentration** ~ tempo *m* de concentração - **2.** [range] gama *f* - **3.** [of hand] palmo *m* - **4.** [of arms] braçada *f* - **5.** [of wings] envergadura *f* - **6.** [of bridge, arch] extensão *f*. <> *vt* - **1.** [encompass] cobrir um período de - **2.** [cross] atravessar, cruzar.

spandex *n* spandex *m*.

spangled ['spæŋgld] *adj literary*: ~ **(with sthg)** adornado(da) (de algo).

Spaniard ['spænjəd] *n* espanhol *m*, -la *f*.

spaniel ['spænjəl] *n* cocker *m* spaniel.

Spanish ['spænɪʃ] <> *adj* espanhol(la). <> *n* [language] espanhol *m*. <> *npl*: **the** ~ os espanhóis.

Spanish America *n* América Espanhola.

Spanish American <> *adj* - **1.** [in US] hispano(na) - **2.** [in Latin America] hispano-americano(na). <> *n* - **1.** [in US] hispano *m*, -na *f* - **2.** [in Latin America] hispano-americano *m*, -na *f*.

spank [spæŋk] <> *n* palmada *f*. <> *vt* dar palmadas em.

spanner ['spænə'] *n* chave *f* inglesa.

spar [spɑː'] (*pt* & *pp* -red, *cont* -ring) *vi* - **1.** BOXING treinar boxe - **2.** [verbally]: **to** ~ **(with sb)** discutir amigavelmente (com alguém).

spare [speə'] <> *adj* - **1.** [surplus] sobressalente, de sobra; **have you got a** ~ **pencil?** você tem um lápis sobrando? - **2.** [free] livre. <> *n* [surplus object] sobressalente *mf*. <> *vt* - **1.** [put aside, make available] dispor de; **to have sthg to** ~ [extra] ter algo de sobra - **2.** [not harm] preservar - **3.** [economize]

poupar; **to** ~ **no expense** não poupar despesas - **4.** [save, protect from]: **to** ~ **sb sthg** poupar alguém de algo.

spare part *n* peça *f* sobressalente.

spare tyre *n* estepe *m*.

spare wheel *n* roda *f* sobressalente.

spare room *n* quarto *m* de hóspedes.

spare time *n* (U) tempo *m* livre.

sparing ['speərɪŋ] *adj*: **to be** ~ **with** OR **of sthg** ser econômico(ca) em algo.

sparingly ['speərɪŋlɪ] *adv* com moderação.

spark [spɑːk] <> *n* - **1.** [from fire] fagulha *f* - **2.** [from electricity] faísca *f* - **3.** *fig* [of interest, humour etc] lampejo *m*. <> *vt* [trigger] provocar.

sparking plug ['spɑːkɪŋ-] *n UK* = spark plug.

sparkle ['spɑːkl] <> *n* - **1.** [gen] brilho *m* - **2.** [of person, conversation, wit] estilo *m*, brilho *m*. <> *vi* - **1.** [gen] brilhar - **2.** [person, conversation, wit] ser brilhante, brilhar.

sparkler ['spɑːklə'] *n* [firework] estrelinha *f*.

sparkling *adj* - **1.** [mineral water] com gás, gaseificado(da) - **2.** [wit] brilhante.

sparkling wine ['spɑːklɪŋ-] *n* vinho *m* espumante.

spark plug *n* vela *f* (*de ignição*).

sparrow ['spærəʊ] *n* pardal *m*.

sparse [spɑːs] *adj* esparso(sa).

spartan ['spɑːtn] *adj* espartano(na).

spasm ['spæzm] *n* - **1.** MED [muscular contraction] espasmo *m* - **2.** [fit] acesso *m*.

spasmodic [spæz'mɒdɪk] *adj* [intermittent] espasmódico(ca).

spastic ['spæstɪk] MED <> *adj* espástico(ca). <> *n* espasmofílico *m*, -ca *f*.

spat [spæt] *pt* & *pp* > spit.

spate [speɪt] *n* série *f*, sucessão *f*.

spatial ['speɪʃl] *adj* espacial; ~ **awareness** noção *f* de espaço.

spatter ['spætə'] *vt* & *vi* respingar.

spatula ['spætjʊlə] *n* CULIN, MED espátula *f*.

spawn [spɔːn] <> *n* (U) [of frogs, fish] ovas *fpl*. <> *vt* *fig* [produce] gerar. <> *vi* ZOOL desovar.

spay [speɪ] *vt* castrar (*fêmea*).

speak [spiːk] (*pt* spoke, *pp* spoken) <> *vt* - **1.** [say] dizer - **2.** [express opinion]: **to** ~ **ill of sb** falar mal de alguém - **3.** [language] falar. <> *vi* - **1.** [say words] falar; **to** ~ **to** OR **with sb** falar com alguém; **to** ~ **to sb about sthg** falar com alguém sobre algo; **to** ~ **about sb/sthg** falar sobre alguém/algo; **to** ~ **well** OR **highly of sb** falar bem de alguém; **nobody/ nothing to** ~ **of** ninguém/nada em especial - **2.** [make a speech]: **to** ~ **to sb** discursar para alguém; **to** ~ **on sthg** falar OR discursar sobre algo - **3.** [in giving an opinion]: **generally** ~**ing** falando em termos gerais; **personally** ~**ing** pessoalmente falando; ~**ing as** [in the position of] falando como; ~**ing of** [on the subject of] falando sobre.

so to speak *adv* por assim dizer.

speak for *vt fus* [represent] falar em nome de; **it** ~**s for itself** isso fala por si mesmo; ~ **for yourself!** fala isso por ti!

speak out *vi* falar publicamente; **to** ~ **out**

against sb/sthg fazer declarações contra alguém/algo.
➡ **speak up** vi -**1.** [say something] falar claro; **to ~ up for sb/sthg** sair em defesa de alguém/algo -**2.** [speak louder] falar mais alto.

speaker ['spi:kə'] n -**1.** [person talking, of a language] falante mf -**2.** [in lecture] orador m, -ra f, conferencista mf -**3.** [loudspeaker] alto-falante m -**4.** [in stereo system] caixa f de som.
➡ **Speaker** n UK [in House of Commons] Presidente mf da Câmara dos Comuns.

speaking ['spi:kıŋ] n discurso m.

speaking clock n UK serviço m de hora certa.

spear [spıə'] ◇ n [weapon] lança f. ◇ vt lancear.

spearhead ['spıəhed] ◇ n ponta-de-lança f. ◇ vt encabeçar.

spec [spek] n UK inf: **to buy sthg on ~** comprar algo sem garantia; **to go on ~** ir sem ter feito reserva.

special ['speʃl] ◇ adj especial. ◇ n -**1.** [on menu]: **today's ~** prato m do dia -**2.** [on TV] especial m -**3.** [train] trem m especial.

special agent n agente mf especial.

special constable n UK policial mf voluntário, -ria.

special correspondent n correspondente mf especial.

special delivery n (U) [service] entrega f especial.

special effects npl efeitos mpl especiais.

specialist ['speʃəlıst] ◇ adj especializado(da). ◇ n [expert] especialista mf.

speciality [ˌspeʃɪ'ælətı] (pl -ies), **specialty** US ['speʃltı] (pl -ies) n especialidade f.

specialize, -ise ['speʃəlaız] vi especializar-se; **to ~ in sthg** especializar-se em algo.

specially ['speʃəlı] adv -**1.** [on purpose, specifically] especialmente -**2.** [really] realmente; **do you want to go? - not ~** quer ir? - na verdade não.

special offer n oferta f especial, promoção f.

special school n escola f especial.

specialty n US = speciality.

species ['spi:ʃi:z] (pl inv) n espécie f.

specific [spə'sıfık] adj [particular, precise] específico(ca); **~ to sb/sthg** específico(ca) de alguém/algo.
➡ **specifics** npl [details] detalhes mpl específicos.

specifically [spə'sıfıklı] adv especificamente.

specification [ˌspesıfı'keıʃn] n [plan] especificação f.
➡ **specifications** npl TECH especificações fpl técnicas.

specify ['spesıfaı] (pt & pp -ied) vt especificar.

specimen ['spesımən] n -**1.** [example] espécime m, exemplar m -**2.** [sample] amostra f.

specimen copy n cópia f de amostra.

specimen signature n assinatura f reconhecida em cartório.

speck [spek] n -**1.** [small stain] mancha f pequena -**2.** [small particle] partícula f.

speckled ['spekld] adj manchado(da); **~ with sthg** pintado(da) de algo.

specs [speks] npl inf [glasses] óculos m inv.

spectacle ['spektəkl] n -**1.** [sight] visão f -**2.** [event] espetáculo m.
➡ **spectacles** npl UK [glasses] óculos m inv.

spectacular [spek'tækjulə'] ◇ adj espetacular. ◇ n espetáculo m.

spectate [spek'teıt] vi assistir como espectador(-ra).

spectator [spek'teıtə'] n espectador m, -ra f.

spectator sport n esporte m de multidões.

spectre UK, **specter** US ['spektə'] n -**1.** fml [ghost] espectro m -**2.** fig [frightening prospect]: **the ~ of famine** o fantasma da fome.

spectrum ['spektrəm] (pl -tra [-trə]) n -**1.** PHYS espectro m -**2.** fig [range] gama f.

speculate ['spekjuleıt] ◇ vt: **to ~ that** especular que. ◇ vi especular.

speculation [ˌspekju'leıʃn] n especulação f.

speculative ['spekjulətıv] adj especulativo(va).

speculator ['spekjuleıtə'] n FIN especulador m, -ra f.

sped [sped] pt & pp ⊳ speed.

speech [spi:tʃ] n -**1.** [gen] fala f -**2.** [formal talk]: **to give OR make a ~ (on sthg)** dar OR fazer um discurso (sobre algo); **to give OR make a ~ (to sb)** dar OR fazer um discurso (para alguém) -**3.** [manner of speaking] maneira f de falar -**4.** (U) [dialect] dialeto m, maneira f de falar -**5.** GRAMM discurso m.

speech day n UK dia de encerramento do ano letivo quando são proferidos discursos e os estudantes recebem prêmios.

speech impediment n defeito m na fala.

speechless ['spi:tʃlıs] adj: **to be ~ (with sthg)** ficar emudecido(da) (de algo).

speech processing n COMPUT processamento m da fala.

speech therapist n fonoaudiólogo m.

speech therapy n (U) fonoaudiologia f.

speed [spi:d] (pt & pp -ed OR sped) ◇ n -**1.** [rate, pace] velocidade f; **at ~** a grande velocidade -**2.** (U) [rapid rate] rapidez f -**3.** [gear] marcha f. ◇ vi -**1.** [move fast]: **to ~ (along/away/by)** ir/acelerar/passar a toda velocidade -**2.** AUT [go too fast] exceder a velocidade.
➡ **speed up** ◇ vt sep acelerar. ◇ vi acelerar.

speedboat ['spi:dbəut] n lancha f.

speed-dial button n [on phone, fax] tecla m de discagem rápida.

speeding ['spi:dıŋ] n (U) excesso m de velocidade.

speed limit n limite m de velocidade.

speedo (pl -s) n UK inf velocímetro m.

speedometer [spı'domıtə'] n velocímetro m.

speed trap n -**1.** [radar] radar m -**2.** [camera] pardal m.

speedway ['spi:dweı] n -**1.** SPORT corrida f de motos -**2.** US [road] pista f de corrida.

speedy ['spi:dı] (compar -ier, superl -iest) adj rápido(da).

speleology [ˌspi:lı'ɒlədʒı] n (U) fml espeleologia f.

spell [spel] (UK pt & pp spelt OR -ed, US pt & pp -ed) ◇ n -**1.** [period of time] período m -**2.** [enchantment] feitiço m, encanto m -**3.** [magic words] palavras fpl mágicas. ◇ vt -**1.** [write] soletrar -**2.** fig [signify] significar. ◇ vi escrever corretamente.

spell out *vt sep* -1. [read aloud] soletrar -2. [explain]: **to ~ sthg out (for** *or* **to sb)** explicar algo em detalhes (para alguém).

spellbound ['spelbaʊnd] *adj* encantado(da).

spellcheck ['speltʃek] *vt* COMPUT passar o corretor ortográfico em.

spellchecker ['speltʃekə'] *n* COMPUT corretor *m* ortográfico.

spelling ['spelɪŋ] *n* ortografia *f.*

spelt [spelt] *pt & pp UK* ⊳ **spell.**

spend [spend] (*pt & pp* **spent**) *vt* -1. [pay out] gastar; **to ~ sthg on sb/sthg** gastar algo em alguém/algo -2. [time, life] passar -3. [energy] gastar.

spender ['spendə'] *n* [person] esbanjador *m*, -ra *f*, gastador *m*, -ra *f.*

spending ['spendɪŋ] *n (U)* gastos *mpl.*

spending money *n (U)* dinheiro *m* para pequenos gastos pessoais.

spending power *n (U)* poder *m* aquisitivo.

spendthrift ['spendθrɪft] *n* perdulário *m*, -ria *f.*

spent [spent] ⟨⟩ *pt & pp* ⊳ **spend.** ⟨⟩ *adj* [consumed, burned out - matches, ammunition] usado(da); [- force, patience, energy] esgotado(da).

sperm [spɜːm] (*pl inv* OR **-s**) *n* esperma *m.*

spermicidal cream [,spɜːmi'saɪdl-] *n* creme *m* espermicida.

sperm whale *n* baleia *f* cachalote.

spew [spjuː] ⟨⟩ *vt* [cause to flow, spread] expelir, cuspir. ⟨⟩ *vi* [flow, spread]: **to ~ (out) from sthg** lançar-se(para fora)de algo; **flames ~ed out of the volcano** o vulcão cuspia chamas.

sphere [sfɪə'] *n* esfera *f.*

spherical ['sferɪkl] *adj* esférico(ca).

sphincter ['sfɪŋktə'] *n* esfíncter *m.*

sphinx [sfɪŋks] (*pl* **-es**) *n* esfinge *f.*

spice [spaɪs] ⟨⟩ *n* tempero *m.* ⟨⟩ *vt* -1. CULIN: **to ~ sthg (with sthg)** temperar algo (com algo) -2. *fig* [add excitement to]: **to ~ sthg (up)** dar sabor a algo.

spick-and-span [,spɪkən'spæn] *adj* asseado(da).

spicy ['spaɪsɪ] (*compar* **-ier**, *superl* **-iest**) *adj* picante.

spider ['spaɪdə'] *n* aranha *f.*

spider's web, spiderweb US ['spaɪdəweb] *n* teia *f* de aranha.

spidery ['spaɪdərɪ] *adj* aranhoso(sa).

spiel [ʃpiːl] *n* lábia *f.*

spike [spaɪk] ⟨⟩ *n* -1. [on railings] prego *m* -2. [on shoe] cravo *m* -3. [on plant] espigão *m* -4. [of hair] corte *m* escovinha. ⟨⟩ *vt* reforçar com mais álcool.

➡ **spikes** *npl UK* tênis *m inv* com travas.

spiky ['spaɪkɪ] (*compar* **-ier**, *superl* **-iest**) *adj* -1. [branch] pontudo(da) -2. [plant] espinhento(ta) -3. [hair] eriçado(da).

spill [spɪl] (*UK pt & pp* **spilt** OR **-ed**, *US pt & pp* **-ed**) ⟨⟩ *vt* derramar. ⟨⟩ *vi* -1. [liquid] derramar; **the wine ~ed all over the carpet** o vinho esparramou por todo o carpete -2. [salt, sugar, etc] esparramar -3. [crowd]: **the fans ~ed out of stadium** os torcedores saíram em massa do estádio; **the crowd ~ed into the main square** a multidão espalhou-se pela praça principal.

spillage ['spɪlɪdʒ] *n* derramamento *m.*

spilt [spɪlt] *pt & pp UK* ⊳ **spill.**

spin [spɪn] (*pt* **span** OR **spun**, *pp* **spun**, *cont* **-ning**) ⟨⟩ *n* -1. [turn] giro *m*, volta *f* -2. AERON parafuso *m* -3. *inf* [in car] volta *f* -4. SPORT [on ball] efeito *m.* ⟨⟩ *vt* -1. [cause to rotate] rodar, girar -2. [in spin-dryer] centrifugar -3. [thread, cloth, wool] fiar -4. SPORT [ball] fazer girar. ⟨⟩ *vi* -1. [rotate] girar, dar voltas -2. [feel dizzy]: **to be spinning** estar rodando -3. [spinner] fiar -4. [in spin-dryer] centrifugar.

➡ **spin out** *vt sep* -1. [story, explanation] prorrogar -2. [food, money] esticar.

spina bifida [,spaɪnə'bɪfɪdə] *n (U)* espinha *f* bífida.

spinach ['spɪnɪdʒ] *n (U)* espinafre *m.*

spinal column ['spaɪnl-] *n* coluna *f* vertebral.

spinal cord *n* medula *f* espinhal.

spindle ['spɪndl] *n* -1. [machine rod] eixo *m* -2. [for spinning] fuso *m.*

spindly ['spɪndlɪ] (*compar* **-ier**, *superl* **-iest**) *adj* longo e fino, longa e fina.

spin doctor *n pej* pessoa encarregada das relações com a imprensa, geralmente para um político ou partido, e que manipula as informações a serem dadas.

spin-dry *vt UK* centrifugar.

spin-dryer *n UK* centrifugadora *f (de roupas).*

spine [spaɪn] *n* -1. ANAT espinha *f* dorsal -2. [of book] lombada *f* -3. [spike, prickle] espinho *m.*

spine-chilling *adj* de arrepiar, horripilante.

spineless ['spaɪnlɪs] *adj* [feeble] pobre de espírito.

spinner ['spɪnə'] *n* [of thread] fiandeiro *m*, -ra *f.*

spinning ['spɪnɪŋ] *n (U)* fiação *f.*

spinning top *n* pião *m.*

spin-off *n* [by-product] subproduto *m.*

spinster ['spɪnstə'] *n* solteirona *f.*

spiral ['spaɪərəl] (*UK pt & pp* **-led**, *cont* **-ling**, *US pt & pp* **-ed**, *cont* **-ing**) ⟨⟩ *adj* espiral. ⟨⟩ *n* -1. [curve] espiral *f* -2. [increase] escalada *f* -3. [decrease] queda *f.* ⟨⟩ *vi* -1. [move in spiral curve] mover-se em espiral -2. [increase rapidly] subir vertiginosamente -3. [decrease rapidly]: **to ~ downwards** despencar.

spiral staircase *n* escada *f* caracol.

spire [spaɪə'] *n* pináculo *m.*

spirit ['spɪrɪt] ⟨⟩ *n* espírito *m*; **to enter into the ~ of sthg** entrar no espírito de algo. ⟨⟩ *vt*: **to ~ sb into/out ofsthg** colocar/tirar alguém às escondidas de algo.

➡ **spirits** *npl* -1. [mood] astral *m*; **to be in high/low ~ s** estar de alto/baixo astral -2. [alcohol] bebidas *fpl* destiladas.

spirited ['spɪrɪtɪd] *adj* animado(da).

spirit level *n* nível *m* de pedreiro OR bolha.

spiritual ['spɪrɪtʃʊəl] *adj* espiritual.

spiritualism ['spɪrɪtʃʊəlɪzm] *n (U)* espiritualismo *m.*

spiritualist ['spɪrɪtʃʊəlɪst] *n* espiritualista *mf.*

spit [spɪt] (*UK pt & pp* **spat**, *cont* **-ting**, *US pt & pp* **spit**, *cont* **-ting**) ⟨⟩ *n* -1. *(U)* [saliva] cuspe *m* -2. [skewer] espeto *m.* ⟨⟩ *vi* [from mouth] cuspir. ⟨⟩ *v impers UK* [rain lightly] chuviscar.

➡ **spit out** *vt sep* cuspir; **come on, ~ it out!** vamos, desembucha!

spite [spaɪt] ⟨⟩ *n (U)* rancor *m*; **to do sthg out of** OR **from ~** fazer algo por maldade. ⟨⟩ *vt* magoar.

➡ **in spite of** *prep* apesar de; **to do sthg in ~ of**

o.s. [unintentionally] fazer algo a contragosto.

spiteful ['spaɪtfʊl] *adj* maldoso(sa), mal-intencionado(da).

spitting image ['spɪtɪŋ-] *n*: **to be the ~ of sb** ser o retrato cuspido e escarrado de alguém.

spittle ['spɪtl] *n (U)* cuspe *m*.

splash [splæʃ] ⇔ *n* **-1.** [sound] chape *m*, pancada *f* na água **-2.** [small quantity] respingo *m*; **a ~ of lemonade** uma esguichada de limonada **-3.** [patch] mancha *f.* ⇔ *vt* **-1.** [subj: person] respingar **-2.** [subj: water] molhar **-3.** [apply haphazardly] espalhar. ⇔ *vi* **-1.** [person]: **to ~ about** OR **around** patinhar **-2.** [water, liquid]: **to ~ on/against sthg** espirrar em/contra algo.

➦ **splash down** *vi* amerissar.

➦ **splash out** *inf* ⇔ *vt sep*: **to ~ sthg out on sthg** gastar algo em algo. ⇔ *vi*: **to ~ out (on sthg)** gastar um dinheirão (em algo).

splashdown ['splæʃdaʊn] *n* amerissagem *f.*

splash guard *n US* pára-lama *m.*

splay [spleɪ] ⇔ *vt* esticar. ⇔ *vi*: **to ~ (out)** esticar.

spleen [spliːn] *n* **-1.** ANAT baço *m* **-2.** *(U)* *fig* [anger] cólera *f.*

splendid ['splendɪd] *adj* **-1.** [very good] esplêndido(da) **-2.** [magnificent, beautiful] esplendoroso(sa).

splendidly ['splendɪdlɪ] *adv* **-1.** [perform, write, behave] maravilhosamente **-2.** [design, dress, entertain] magnificamente, esplendidamente.

splendour *UK*, **splendor** *US* ['splendə'] *n* **-1.** *(U)* [beauty, magnificence] esplendor *m* **-2.** [magnificent feature] maravilha *f.*

splice [splaɪs] *vt* [join - rope] juntar, unir; [- film, tape] montar.

splint [splɪnt] *n* tala *f.*

splinter ['splɪntə'] ⇔ *n* lasca *f.* ⇔ *vt*: **to be ~ ed** estar lascado(da). ⇔ *vi* [glass, bone, wood] lascar.

splinter group *n* grupo *m* dissidente.

split [splɪt] (*pt* & *pp* **split**, *cont* **-ting**) ⇔ *n* **-1.** [crack] racha *f*, fenda *f*; **~ (in sthg)** fenda (em algo) **-2.** [tear] rasgão *m*; **~ in sthg** rasgão em algo **-3.** [division, schism] separação *f*; **~ in sthg** racha *m* em algo; **~ between** divisão *f* entre. ⇔ *vt* **-1.** [crack] rachar, partir **-2.** [tear] rasgar **-3.** [divide - group, organization] rachar; [- road] dividir-se **-4.** [share] dividir; **to ~ the difference** rachar a diferença. ⇔ *vi* **-1.** [crack] rachar-se **-2.** [tear] rasgar-se **-3.** *inf* [leave] sair.

➦ **splits** *npl*: **to do the ~s** fazer espacato OR grande écart.

➦ **split off** (*pt* & *pp* **split**) ⇔ *vt sep* [snap off]: **to ~ sthg off (from sthg)** separar algo (de algo). ⇔ *vi* **-1.** [snap off]: **to ~ off (from sthg)** desprender-se (de algo) **-2.** [separate]: **to ~ off (from sb)** separar-se (de alguém).

➦ **split up** ⇔ *vt sep*: **to ~ sthg up (into sthg)** dividir algo (em algo). ⇔ *vi* separar-se; **to ~ up with sb** romper com alguém.

split end *n* ponta *f* dupla *(no cabelo).*

split-level *adj* **-1.** [building, house, room] dúplex *inv* **-2.** [grill] duplo.

split peas *npl* ervilhas *fpl* secas.

split personality *n* dupla personalidade *f.*

split screen *n* **-1.** CINEMA & TV tela *f* múltipla **-2.** COMPUT divisão *f* de tela.

split second *n* fração *f* de segundo.

splitting ['splɪtɪŋ] *adj*: **~ headache** enxaqueca *f.*

splutter ['splʌtə'] ⇔ *n* [of person] balbucio *m.* ⇔ *vi* **-1.** [person] balbuciar **-2.** [car, engine] estalar **-3.** [spit] crepitar.

spoil [spɔɪl] (*pt* & *pp* **-ed** OR **spoilt**) *vt* **-1.** [ruin] estragar **-2.** [pamper] mimar; **to ~ sb** fazer um agrado a alguém; **to ~ o.s.** dar-se um capricho.

➦ **spoils** *npl* butim *m*; **~ of war** despojos *mpl* de guerra.

spoiled [spɔɪld] *adj* = **spoilt.**

spoiler ['spɔɪlə'] *n* spoiler *m.*

spoilsport ['spɔɪlspɔːt] *n* desmancha-prazeres *mf inv.*

spoilt [spɔɪlt] ⇔ *pt* & *pp* ⊳ **spoil.** ⇔ *adj* **-1.** [child] mimado(da) **-2.** [food, dinner] estragado(da).

spoke [spəʊk] ⇔ *pt* ⊳ **speak.** ⇔ *n* raio *m (da roda).*

spoken ['spəʊkn] *pp* ⊳ **speak.**

spokesman ['spəʊksmən] (*pl* **-men** [-mən]) *n* porta-voz *m.*

spokesperson ['spəʊks,pɜːsn] (*pl* **spokespeople**) *n* porta-voz *mf.*

spokeswoman ['spəʊks,wʊmən] (*pl* **-women** [-,wɪmɪn]) *n* porta-voz *f.*

sponge [spʌndʒ] (*UK cont* **spongeing**, *US cont* **sponging**) ⇔ *n* **-1.** [for cleaning, washing] esponja *f* **-2.** [cake] pão-de-ló *m.* ⇔ *vt* limpar com esponja. ⇔ *vi inf*: **to ~ off sb** viver às custas de alguém.

sponge bag *n UK* nécessaire *m.*

sponge cake *n* pão-de-ló *m.*

sponge pudding *n UK* pudim *de bolacha feito ao banho-maria.*

sponger ['spʌndʒə'] *n inf pej* parasita *mf.*

spongy ['spʌndʒɪ] (*compar* **-ier**, *superl* **-iest**) *adj* esponjoso(sa).

sponsor ['spɒnsə'] ⇔ *n* patrocinador *m*, -ra *f.* ⇔ *vt* **-1.** patrocinar **-2.** [bill, appeal, proposal] dar o respaldo a.

sponsored walk [,spɒnsəd-] *n* marcha *f* beneficente.

sponsorship ['spɒnsəʃɪp] *n (U)* patrocínio *m.*

spontaneity [,spɒntə'neɪətɪ] *n (U)* espontaneidade *f.*

spontaneous [spɒn'teɪnjəs] *adj* espontâneo(nea).

spontaneously [spɒn'teɪnjəslɪ] *adv* espontaneamente.

spoof [spuːf] *n*: **~ (of** OR **on sthg)** sátira *f* (de OR sobre algo).

spook [spuːk] *vt US* assustar.

spooky ['spuːkɪ] (*compar* **-ier**, *superl* **-iest**) *adj* **-1.** *inf* [place, house] assombrado(da) **-2.** *inf* [film] aterrorizante.

spool [spuːl] ⇔ *n* **-1.** [of thread, tape, film] carretel *m* **-2.** COMPUT spool *m.* ⇔ *vi* COMPUT direcionar trabalho de impressão para o spool.

spoon [spuːn] ⇔ *n* **-1.** [piece of cutlery] colher *f* **-2.** [spoonful] colherada *f.* ⇔ *vt*: **to ~ sthg onto/into sthg** pôr OR colocar uma colherada de algo em algo.

spoon-feed *vt* **-1.** [feed with spoon] dar de comer

com colher a **-2.** *fig* [give too much help to] dar mastigado *OR* de mão beijada a.

spoonful ['spu:nfʊl] (*pl*-s *OR* **spoonsful** ['spu:nzfʊl]) *n* colherada *f*.

sporadic [spə'rædɪk] *adj* esporádico(ca).

sport [spɔ:t] ◇ *n* **-1.** [gen] esporte *m* **-2.** *dated* [cheerful person] pessoa *f* amável. ◇ *vt* [wear] exibir, ostentar.
➧ **sports** ◇ *npl UK* ▷ **sports day**. ◇ *comp* esportivo(va).

sporting ['spɔ:tɪŋ] *adj* **-1.** [relating to sport] esportivo(va) **-2.** [generous, fair] nobre; **that's very ~ of you** é muita bondade sua.

sports car ['spɔ:ts-] *n* carro *m* esporte.

sports day *n UK dia dedicado a competições esportivas na escola.*

sports jacket ['spɔ:ts-] *n* jaqueta *f* esportiva.

sportsman ['spɔ:tsmən] (*pl* **-men** [-mən]) *n* esportista *m*.

sportsmanship ['spɔ:tsmənʃɪp] *n (U)* espírito *m* esportivo.

sports pages *npl* página *f OR* seção *f* de esportes.

sportswear ['spɔ:tsweə'] *n (U)* roupas *fpl* esportivas.

sportswoman ['spɔ:ts,wʊmən] (*pl* **-women** [-,wɪmɪn]) *n* esportista *f*.

sporty ['spɔ:tɪ] (*compar*-ier, *superl* -iest) *adj inf* **-1.** [person] aficcionado(da) por esportes **-2.** [car, clothes] esportivo(va).

spot [spɒt] (*pt* & *pp* **-ted**, *cont* -ting) ◇ *n* **-1.** [mark, dot] mancha *f* **-2.** [pimple] sinal *m* **-3.** *inf:* **a ~ of sleep** uma dormida; **a ~ of work** um pouco de trabalho; [- of milk, liquid] gole *m*; [- of rain] pingo *m*, gota *f* **-4.** [place] local *m*; **on the ~** no local; **to do sthg on the ~** fazer algo no ato **-5.** *RADIO & TV* espaço *m* **-6.** *phr:* **to have a soft ~ for sb** ter uma leve caída por alguém; **to put sb on the ~** colocar alguém em maus lençóis. ◇ *vt* [notice] enxergar.

spot check *n* controle *m* aleatório.

spotless ['spɒtlɪs] *adj* [clean] impecável.

spotlight ['spɒtlaɪt] *n* [bright light] refletor *m*; **to be in the ~** *fig* ser o centro das atenções.

spot-on *adj UK inf* certeiro(ra).

spot price *n* preço *m* para entrega imediata.

spotted ['spɒtɪd] *adj* de bolinhas.

spotty ['spɒtɪ] (*compar*-ier, *superl* -iest) *adj* **-1.** *UK* [skin] sardento(ta) **-2.** *US* [patchy] de remendos, irregular.

spouse [spaʊs] *n* esposo *m*, -sa *f*.

spout [spaʊt] ◇ *n* **-1.** [of container] bico *m* **-2.** [of water - from fountain, geyser] jorro *m*; [- from whale] esguicho *m*. ◇ *vt pej* [churn out] jorrar. ◇ *vi:* **to ~ from** *OR* **out of sthg** jorrar de algo.

sprain [spreɪn] ◇ *n* torção *f*, distensão *f*. ◇ *vt* torcer, distender.

sprang [spræŋ] *pt* ▷ **spring.**

sprat [spræt] *n* espadilha *f*.

sprawl [sprɔ:l] ◇ *n (U)* expansão *f*; **urban ~** expansão *f* urbana descontrolada. ◇ *vi* **-1.** [person] estirar-se **-2.** [city, suburbs] expandir-se.

sprawling ['sprɔ:lɪŋ] *adj* [city, suburbs] de expansão descontrolada.

spray [spreɪ] ◇ *n* **-1.** *(U)* [droplets] borrifo *m* **-2.** [pressurized liquid] spray *m* **-3.** [insect] pulverizador *m* **-4.** [can, container] vaporizador *m* **-5.** [of flowers] ramo *m*. ◇ *vt* & *vi* **-1.** [treat] pulverizar **-2.** [apply] borrifar.

spray can *n* spray *m*, aerosol *m*.

spray paint *n* tinta *f* spray.

spread [spred] (*pt* & *pp* **spread**) ◇ *n* **-1.** *(U)* *CULIN* [paste] pasta *f* **-2.** [diffusion, growth] propagação *f* **-3.** [range] extensão *f* **-4.** *PRESS* chapado *m* **-5.** [buffet] banquete *m* **-6.** *US* [bedspread] colcha *f*. ◇ *vt* **-1.** [open out, unfold - map, tablecloth, rug] estender; [- arms, legs, fingers] abrir **-2.** [apply - butter, jam] untar; **to ~ sthg over sthg** untar algo com algo; [- glue] passar; **to ~ sthg over sthg** passar algo em algo **-3.** [diffuse, disseminate] espalhar **-4.** [over a period of time]: **to be ~ over ...** ter uma duração de ... **-5.** [over an area] espalhar; **the floor was ~ with straw** o chão estava coberto de palha **-6.** [distribute evenly] expandir. ◇ *vi* [gen] espalhar-se; [disease, infection] alastrar-se.
➧ **spread out** ◇ *vt sep* **-1.** [distribute]: **to be ~ out** [far apart] estar espalhado(da); [sprawling] estender-se **-2.** [open out, unfold - fingers, arms] abrir; [- map, tablecloth, rug] estender. ◇ *vi* [disperse] dispersar-se.

spread-eagled [-,i:gld] *adj* de braços e pernas abertos.

spreadsheet ['spredʃi:t] *n COMPUT* panilha *f* eletrônica.

spree [spri:] *n* farra *f*.

sprig [sprɪg] *n* broto *m*, ramo *m*.

sprightly ['spraɪtlɪ] (*compar*-ier, *superl* -iest) *adj* ativo(va).

spring [sprɪŋ] (*pt* **sprang**, *pp* **sprung**) ◇ *n* **-1.** [season] primavera *f*; **in ~** na primavera **-2.** [coil] mola *f* **-3.** [leap] pulo *m* **-4.** [water source] fonte *f*. ◇ *comp* **-1.** [rain, weather, colours] de primavera **-2.** [mattress] de mola **-3.** [water] de nascente. ◇ *vt* **-1.** [make known suddenly]: **to ~ sthg on sb** revelar subitamente algo a alguém **-2.** [develop]: **to ~ a leak** começar a fazer água. ◇ *vi* **-1.** [leap] saltar; **to ~ into action/to life** pôr-se em marcha/funcionamento **-2.** [be released] soltar-se; **to ~ shut/open** fechar/abrir rapidamente **-3.** [originate]: **to ~ from sthg** originar-se de algo.
➧ **spring up** *vi* **-1.** [get up] levantar-se **-2.** [grow in size, height] elevar-se **-3.** [appear] surgir de repente.

springboard ['sprɪŋbɔ:d] *n fig* [launch pad]: **~ for/ to sthg** trampolim *m* para algo.

spring-clean ◇ *vt* fazer uma faxina geral em. ◇ *vi* fazer uma faxina geral.

spring-loaded *adj* de mola.

spring onion *n UK* cebolinha *f* verde.

spring roll *n UK* rolinho *m* primavera.

spring tide *n* maré *f* viva.

springtime ['sprɪŋtaɪm] *n (U):* **in (the) ~** na primavera.

springy ['sprɪŋɪ] (*compar*-ier, *superl* -iest) *adj* **-1.** [carpet, mattress, ground] flexível **-2.** [rubber] elástico(ca).

sprinkle ['sprɪŋkl] *vt* **-1.** salpicar; **to ~ sthg over** *OR* **on sthg** salpicar algo sobre *OR* em algo; **to ~ sthg with sthg** regar algo com algo **-2.** [powder]

polvilhar **-3.** [liquid] borrifar.

sprinkler [ˈsprɪŋkləʳ] n **-1.** [for gardens] regador m **-2.** [for extinguishing fires] extintor m.

sprinkling [ˈsprɪŋklɪŋ] n **-1.** [of water] borrifo m **-2.** [of sand] punhado m **-3.** [of people] grupo m pequeno **-4.** [of salt] pitada f.

sprint [sprɪnt] <> n *SPORT* [race] corrida f de velocidade. <> vi correr a toda (velocidade).

sprinter [ˈsprɪntəʳ] n [runner] corredor m, -ra f de velocidade.

sprite n fada f.

spritzer [ˈsprɪtsəʳ] n vinho com água mineral.

sprocket [ˈsprɒkɪt] n [wheel] roda f dentada.

sprout [spraʊt] <> n **-1.** *CULIN:* **(brussels) ~s** couve-de-bruxelas f **-2.** [shoot] broto m. <> vt **-1.** [germinate] germinar **-2.** [bud] brotar **-3.** [grow] crescer. <> vi **-1.** [germinate] germinar **-2.** [bud] brotar **-3.** [grow] crescer **-4.** [appear]: **to ~ (up)** surgir rapidamente.

spruce [spru:s] <> adj alinhado(da). <> n [tree] abeto m.

➡ **spruce up** vt sep arrumar; **to ~ o.s. up** arrumar-se.

sprung [sprʌŋ] pp ⊳ **spring**.

spry [spraɪ] (compar -ier, superl -iest) adj ativo(va).

SPUC (abbr of Society for the Protection of the Unborn Child) n organização antiaborto.

spud [spʌd] n inf batata f.

spun [spʌn] pt & pp ⊳ **spin**.

spunk [spʌŋk] n (U) inf [courage] coragem f.

spur [spɜ:ʳ] (pt & pp -red, cont -ring) <> n **-1.** [incentive]: **~ (to sthg)** estímulo m (a algo) **-2.** [on rider's boot] espora f. <> vt **-1.** [encourage]: **to ~ sb to do sthg** incentivar alguém a fazer algo **-2.** [horse] esporear.

➡ **on the spur of the moment** adv sem pensar duas vezes.

➡ **spur on** vt sep [encourage] estimular.

spurious [ˈspʊərɪəs] adj **-1.** [not genuine] espúrio(ria) **-2.** [based on false reasoning] falso(sa).

spurn [spɜ:n] vt rejeitar, desprezar.

spurt [spɜ:t] <> n **-1.** [of steam] jato m **-2.** [of water] jorro m **-3.** [of flame] labareda f **-4.** [of activity, energy] acesso m **-5.** [burst of speed] acelerada f; **to put on a ~** [while running, cycling] dar uma acelerada; [while working] dar um esforço. <> vi **-1.** [water]: **to ~ (out of OR from sthg)** jorrar (de algo); [steam] sair um jato de vapor (de algo); [flame] sair uma labareda (de algo) **-2.** [run] acelerar.

sputter [ˈspʌtəʳ] vi **-1.** [engine] estalar **-2.** [stutter] gaguejar **-3.** [fire] crepitar **-4.** [oil in pan] espirrar.

spy [spaɪ] (pl spies, pt & pp spied) <> n espião m, -ã f. <> vt inf espionar. <> vi **-1.** [work as spy] espionar **-2.** [watch secretly]: **to ~ on sb** espionar alguém.

spying [ˈspaɪɪŋ] n (U) espionagem f.

spy satellite n satélite m espião.

Sq., sq. (abbr of square) pça.

squabble [ˈskwɒbl] <> n rinha f, discussão f. <> vi: **to ~ (about OR over sthg)** discutir (sobre algo).

squad [skwɒd] n **-1.** [of police] esquadrão m **-2.** *MIL* pelotão m **-3.** [*SPORT*, group of players - of club] time m; [- of national team] seleção f.

squad car n radiopatrulha f.

squadron [ˈskwɒdrən] n esquadrão m.

squadron leader n UK comandante m de aviação.

squalid [ˈskwɒlɪd] adj **-1.** [filthy] esquálido(da), sórdido(da) **-2.** [base, dishonest] depreciável.

squall [skwɔ:l] n [storm] tempestade f.

squalor [ˈskwɒləʳ] n (U) sordidez f, miséria f.

squander [ˈskwɒndəʳ] vt desperdiçar.

square [skweəʳ] <> adj **-1.** quadrado(da) **-2.** [not owing money]: **we're ~ now** estamos quites agora. <> n **-1.** [shape] quadrado m **-2.** [in town, city] praça f **-3.** inf [unfashionable person] quadrado m, -da f **-4.** phr: **to be back to ~ one** voltar ao ponto de partida. <> vt **-1.** *MATH* [multiply by itself] elevar ao quadrado **-2.** [balance, reconcile]: **to ~ sthg with sthg** conciliar algo com algo.

➡ **square up** vi **-1.** [settle up]: **to ~ up with sb** acertar-se com alguém, acertar as contas com alguém **-2.** [confront]: **to ~ up to sb/sthg** fazer frente a alguém/algo.

squared [skweəd] adj quadriculado(da).

square dance n quadrilha f (de dança).

square deal n negócio m limpo.

squarely [ˈskweəlɪ] adv **-1.** [directly] exatamente **-2.** [honestly] honestamente, abertamente.

square meal n boa refeição f.

square root n raiz f quadrada.

squash [skwɒʃ] <> n **-1.** (U) *SPORT* squash m **-2.** UK [drink]: **lemon/orange ~** refresco m de limão/laranja **-3.** US [vegetable] abóbora f. <> vt [squeeze, flatten] esmagar.

squat [skwɒt] (compar -ter, superl -test, pt & pp -ted, cont -ting) <> adj atarracado(da). <> n UK [building] moradia f ilegal. <> vi **-1.** [crouch]: **to ~ (down)** agachar-se **-2.** UK [be a squatter] viver num lugar ilegalmente.

squatter [ˈskwɒtəʳ] n UK [in empty building] posseiro m, -ra f.

squawk [skwɔ:k] <> n [of bird] grasnado m. <> vi [bird] grasnar.

squeak [skwi:k] <> n **-1.** [of animal] guincho m **-2.** [of door, hinge] rangido m. <> vi **-1.** [animal] guinchar **-2.** [floorboard, bed, hinge] ranger.

squeaky [ˈskwi:kɪ] (compar -ier, superl -iest) adj **-1.** [floorboard, bed, hinge] que range **-2.** [voice] estridente.

squeal [skwi:l] <> n **-1.** [of person, animal] grito m agudo **-2.** [of brakes, tyres] guincho m. <> vi **-1.** [person, animal] gritar **-2.** [brakes, tyres] guinchar.

squeamish [ˈskwi:mɪʃ] adj apreensivo(va).

squeeze [skwi:z] <> n **-1.** [pressure] aperto m **-2.** inf [crush of people] aperto m. <> vt **-1.** [press firmly] apertar **-2.** [extract, press out] espremer **-3.** [cram]: **to ~ sthg into sthg** [into place] espremer algo dentro de algo; [into time] virar-se para fazer algo em algo **-4.** fig [information]: **to ~ sthg out of sb** arrancar algo de alguém. <> vi: **to ~ into/through sthg** conseguir se enfiar em algo.

squeezebox n UK acordeão m.

squeezer [ˈskwi:zəʳ] n espremedor m.

squelch [skweltʃ] vi chapinhar.

squib [skwɪb] n: **damp ~** decepção f.

squid [skwɪd] (*pl inv OR* **-s**) *n* lula *f*.

squiffy (*compar* **-ier**, *superl* **-iest**) *adj UK inf dated* embriagado(da).

squiggle ['skwɪgl] *n* rabisco *m*.

squint [skwɪnt] <> *n* MED estrabismo *m*. <> *vi* **-1.** MED ser estrábico(ca) - **2.** [half-close one's eyes]: **to** ~ **at sthg** olhar com os olhos semicerrados para algo.

squire ['skwaɪə^r] *n* [landowner] proprietário *m*, -ria *f* rural.

squirm [skwɜːml] *vi* **-1.** [wriggle] contorcer-se - **2.** [wince]: **to** ~ **(with sthg)** demostrar mal-estar (com algo).

squirrel [*UK* 'skwɪrəl, *US* 'skwɜːrəl] *n* esquilo *m*.

squirt [skwɜːt] <> *vt* **-1.** [force out] esguichar - **2.** [cover with liquid]: **to** ~ **sb/sthg with sthg** esguichar algo em alguém/algo. <> *vi*: **to** ~ **(out of sthg)** esguichar (para fora de algo).

Sr - **1.** (*abbr of* **senior**) *forma utilizada após o nome de um homem para indicar que ele é pai de alguém com o mesmo nome* - **2.** (*abbr of* **sister**) *irmã f (de caridade)*.

SRC *n* - **1.** (*abbr of* **Science Research Council**) *conselho britânico de pesquisa científica* - **2.** (*abbr of* **Students' Representative Council**) *diretório acadêmico britânico*.

Sri Lanka [ˌsriːˈlæŋkə] *n* Sri Lanka; **in** ~ em Sri Lanka.

Sri Lankan <> *adj* de Sri Lanka. <> *n* [person] *habitante de Sri Lanka*.

SS (*abbr of* **steamship**) SS.

SSA (*abbr of* **Social Security Administration**) *n organismo norte-americano de previdência social*.

SSSI (*abbr of* **Site of Special Scientific Interest**) *n área de especial interesse científico na Grã-Bretanha*.

St (*abbr of* **saint**) Sto.

ST (*abbr of* **Standard Time**) *n* hora *f* oficial.

stab [stæb] (*pt & pp* **-bed**, *cont* **-bing**) <> *n* **-1.** [with knife] punhalada *f* - **2.** *inf* [attempt]: **to have a** ~ **(at sthg)** ter uma experiência (em algo) - **3.** [twinge] pontada *f*. <> *vt* **-1.** apunhalar, esfaquear - **2.** [jab] fincar. <> *vi* [jab]: **to** ~ **at sthg** fincar em algo.

stabbing ['stæbɪŋ] <> *adj* lancinante. <> *n* punhalada *f*.

stability [stəˈbɪlətɪ] *n (U)* estabilidade *f*.

stabilize, -ise ['steɪbəlaɪz] <> *vt* estabilizar. <> *vi* estabilizar-se.

stabilizer ['steɪbəlaɪzə^r] *n* [on ship, aircraft, bicycle] estabilizador *m*.

stable ['steɪbl] <> *adj* **-1.** [gen] estável - **2.** [solid, anchored] firme. <> *n* [building] estábulo *m*; [horses] cavalariça *f*.

stable lad *n* cavalariço *m*.

staccato [stəˈkɑːtəʊ] <> *adj* staccato. <> *adv* em staccato.

stack [stæk] <> *n* **-1.** [pile] pilha *f* - **2.** *inf* [a lot, lots]: ~**s** *OR* **a** ~ **of sthg** um monte de algo. <> *vt* **-1.** [pile up] empilhar - **2.** [fill]: **to be** ~ **ed with sthg** estar empilhado(da) de algo.

  ◆ **stack up** *vi* **-1.** *inf* [add up, work out] encaixar-se - **2.** *inf* [compare]: **to** ~ **up against** *OR* **to sb/sthg** comparar-se com relação a alguém/algo.

stadium ['steɪdjəm] (*pl* **-diums** *OR* **-dia** [-djə]) *n* estádio *m*.

staff [stɑːf] <> *n* [employees] pessoal *m*, quadro *m*. <> *vt*: **the shop was** ~ **ed by women** a equipe da loja era composta de mulheres.

staffing ['stɑːfɪŋ] *n (U)* contratação *f* de pessoal.

staff nurse *n UK* enfermeiro *m*, -ra *f* assistente.

staff room *n* sala *f* dos professores.

stag [stæg] (*pl inv OR* **-s**) *n* ZOOL veado *m*.

stage [steɪdʒ] <> *n* **-1.** [period, phase] etapa *f*, estágio *m* - **2.** [platform] palco *m*; **on** ~ em cena; **to set the** ~ **for sthg** preparar o terreno para algo - **3.** [acting profession]: **the** ~ o teatro. <> *vt* **-1.** THEATRE representar - **2.** [organize] organizar.

stagecoach ['steɪdʒkəʊtʃ] *n* diligência *f*.

stage door *n* entrada *f* de artistas.

stage fright *n (U)* medo *m* do palco.

stagehand ['steɪdʒhænd] *n* assistente *mf* de palco.

stage-manage *vt* **-1.** THEATRE dirigir - **2.** *fig* [orchestrate] orquestrar.

stage manager *n* contra-regra *mf*, diretor *m*, -ra *f* de cena.

stage name *n* nome *m* artístico.

stagflation *n* POL estagflação *f*.

stagger ['stægə^r] <> *vt* **-1.** [astound] abalar, chocar - **2.** [arrange at different times] escalonar. <> *vi* [totter] cambalear.

staggering ['stægərɪŋ] *adj* assombroso(sa).

staging ['steɪdʒɪŋ] *n* **-1.** THEATRE encenação *f* - **2.** [performing, organizing] organização *f*.

stagnant ['stægnənt] *adj* **-1.** [water, air] estancado(da) - **2.** [business, career, economy] estagnado(da).

stagnate [stægˈneɪt] *vi* **-1.** [water, air] estancar - **2.** [business, career, economy] estagnar-se.

stagnation [stægˈneɪʃn] *n* **-1.** [of water, air] estancamento *m* - **2.** [of business, career, economy] estagnação *f*.

stag night *OR* **party** *n* despedida *f* de solteiro.

staid [steɪd] *adj* sério(ria), recatado(da).

stain [steɪn] <> *n* [mark] mancha *f*. <> *vt* [discolour] manchar.

stained [steɪnd] *adj* **-1.** [soiled, marked] manchado(da) - **2.** [wood] tingido(da).

stained glass [ˌsteɪnd-] *n (U)* vitral *m*.

stained-glass window *n* janela *f* de vitral.

stainless steel [ˌsteɪnlɪs-] *n (U)* aço *m* inoxidável.

stain remover [-rɪˌmuːvə^r] *n* removedor *m* de manchas.

stair [steə^r] *n* [step] degrau *m*.

  ◆ **stairs** *npl* [flight] escada *f*.

staircase ['steəkeɪs] *n* escadas *fpl*.

stairway ['steəweɪ] *n* escadas *fpl*, escadaria *f*.

stairwell ['steəwell] *n* vão *m OR* poço *m* das escadas.

stake [steɪk] <> *n* **-1.** [share]: **to have a** ~ **in sthg** ter interesses em algo - **2.** [wooden post] estaca *f* - **3.** [in gambling] aposta *f*. <> *vt* **-1.** [risk]: **to** ~ **sthg (on** *OR* **upon sthg)** arriscar algo (com algo) - **2.** [in gambling] apostar - **3.** [state]: **to** ~ **a claim to sthg** reivindicar algo.

  ◆ **stakes** *npl* **-1.** [prize] prêmio *m* - **2.** [contest] disputa *f*.

  ◆ **at stake** *adv*: **to be at** ~ estar em jogo.

stakeout ['steɪkaʊt] *n esp US* [police surveillance] vigilância *f.*

stalactite ['stæləktaɪt] *n* estalactite *f.*

stalagmite ['stæləgmaɪt] *n* estalagmite *f.*

stale [steɪl] *adj* **-1.** [food] passado(da) **-2.** [air] viciado(da) **-3.** [bread] amanhecido(da) **-4.** [breath] velho(lha) **-5.** [athlete] esgotado(da) **-6.** [artist] sem inspiração **-7.** [idea] batido(da).

stalemate ['steɪlmeɪt] *n* **-1.** [deadlock] impasse *m* **-2.** *CHESS* empate *m.*

staleness ['steɪlnɪs] *n* **-1.** [person, news, idea, air] envelhecimento *m* **-2.** [of bread] dureza *f* **-3.** [of food] rancidez *f.*

stalk [stɔ:k] ⬦ *n* **-1.** [of flower, plant] caule *m* **-2.** [of leaf] talo *m* **-3.** [of fruit] cabo *m.* ⬦ *vt* [hunt] tocaiar. ⬦ *vi* [walk] andar de forma irritada.

stall [stɔ:l] ⬦ *n* **-1.** [table] estande *m*, banca *f* **-2.** [in stable] baia *f.* ⬦ *vt* **-1.** *AUT* fazer morrer **-2.** [delay] ganhar tempo. ⬦ *vi* **-1.** *AUT* morrer **-2.** [delay] ganhar tempo.

⬤ **stalls** *npl UK* platéia *f.*

stallholder ['stɔ:lˌhəʊldə^r] *n UK* dono *m*, -na *f* de banca *(no mercado).*

stallion ['stæljən] *n* garanhão *m.*

stalwart ['stɔ:lwət] ⬦ *adj* [loyal] leal, fiel. ⬦ *n* leal partidário *m*, -ia *f.*

stamen ['steɪmən] *n* estame *m.*

stamina ['stæmɪnə] *n (U)* resistência *f.*

stammer ['stæmə^r] ⬦ *n* gagueira *f.* ⬦ *vi* gaguejar.

stamp [stæmp] ⬦ *n* **-1.** [postage stamp] selo *m* **-2.** [rubber stamp] carimbo *m* **-3.** *fig* [hallmark] selo *m.* ⬦ *vt* **-1.** [mark, word, sign] carimbar **-2.** [pattern] timbrar **-3.** [stomp]: **to ~ one's foot** bater com o pé no chão **-4.** [stick stamp on] selar **-5.** *fig* [with characteristic quality] estampar. ⬦ *vi* **-1.** [walk] andar com passos pesados **-2.** [with one foot]: **to ~ on sthg** pisar em algo.

⬤ **stamp out** *vt sep* **-1.** [fire] abafar **-2.** [opposition] sufocar **-3.** [crime, disease] erradicar.

stamp album *n* álbum *m* de selos.

stamp-collecting *n (U)* filatelia *f.*

stamp collector *n* filatelista *mf.*

stamp duty *n (U) UK* imposto *m* de selo.

stamped addressed envelope ['stæmptə.dr-est-] *n UK* envelope selado e endereçado ao remetente, que o usa para enviar algo a si próprio através de outra pessoa.

stampede [stæm'pi:d] ⬦ *n* **-1.** [of animals] debandada *f* **-2.** [of people] fuga *f* em pânico. ⬦ *vi* [animals] debandar.

stamp machine *n* máquina *f* de selos.

stance [stæns] *n* **-1.** [posture] atitude *f*, postura *f* **-2.** [attitude]: **~ (on sthg)** postura (sobre algo) **-3.** *Scot* [for bus] ponto *m.*

stand [stænd] (*pt* & *pp* **stood**) ⬦ *n* **-1.** [stall] banca *f*, barraca *f* **-2.** [for umbrella, hat] cabide *m* **-3.** [for bicycle, lamp] suporte *m* **-4.** *SPORT* arquibancada *f* **-5.** *MIL* posição *f*; **to make a ~** resistir ao inimigo **-6.** [position] posição *f*; **to take a ~ on sthg** tomar uma posição em algo **-7.** *US JUR* depoimento *m*; **to take the ~** tomar o depoimento. ⬦ *vt* **-1.** [place] colocar **-2.** [withstand] agüentar **-3.** [put up with] suportar **-4.** [treat]: **to ~ sb sthg** convidar algo

para alguém **-5.** *JUR*: **to ~ trial** ser processado(da). ⬦ *vi* **-1.** [be on one's feet] ficar em pé **-2.** [rise to one's feet] levantar-se **-3.** [be located] estar **-4.** [be left undisturbed] repousar **-5.** [be valid] seguir de pé **-6.** [indicating current situation]: **as things ~ ...** do jeito que as coisas andam; **unemployment ~s at three million** o desemprego já atinge três milhões de pessoas **-7.** [on issue]: **where do you ~ on ...?** qual é a sua opinião sobre ...? **-8.** *UK POL* [be a candidate], candidatar-se (a) **-9.** [be likely]: **I ~ to win** é provável que eu ganhe **-10.** *US* [stop]: 'no **~ing'** proibido parar e estacionar.

⬤ **stand aside** *vi* [move aside] ficar de lado.

⬤ **stand back** *vi* [get out of way] afastar-se.

⬤ **stand by** ⬦ *vt fus* **-1.** [person] estar ao lado de **-2.** [promise, decision, offer] manter. ⬦ *vi* **-1.** [in readiness]: **to ~ by (for sthg/to do sthg)** estar preparado (da) (a algo/a fazer algo) **-2.** [not intervene] ficar de lado.

⬤ **stand down** *vi* [resign] retirar-se.

⬤ **stand for** *vt fus* **-1.** [signify] significar, representar **-2.** [tolerate] agüentar.

⬤ **stand in** *vi*: **to ~ in (for sb)** substituir (alguém).

⬤ **stand out** *vi* **-1.** [be clearly visible] sobressair **-2.** [be distinctive] destacar-se.

⬤ **stand up** ⬦ *vt sep inf* [miss appointment with] deixar plantado(da). ⬦ *vi* **-1.** [be on one's feet, upright] ficar de pé **-2.** [rise to one's feet] levantar-se **-3.** [be accepted as true] ser convincente.

⬤ **stand up for** *vt fus* sair em defesa de.

⬤ **stand up to** *vt fus* **-1.** [weather, heat, bad treatment] resistir a **-2.** [person, boss] peitar.

standard ['stændəd] ⬦ *adj* **-1.** [gen] normal **-2.** [type, feature] comum **-3.** [size] padronizado **-4.** [text, work] -padrão; **~ practice** prática-padrão *f.* ⬦ *n* **-1.** [level] nível *m* **-2.** [point of reference] padrão *m*, critério *m* **-3.** [flag] estandarte *m.*

⬤ **standards** *npl* [principles] valores *mpl* morais.

standard-bearer *n fig* porta-estandarte *mf.*

standardize, -ise ['stændədaɪz] *vt* padronizar.

standard lamp *n UK* abajur *m* de pé.

standard of living (*pl* **standards of living**) *n* padrão *m* de vida.

standard time *n (U)* hora *f* oficial.

standby ['stændbaɪ] (*pl* **standbys**) ⬦ *n* [substitute] reserva *f*; **to be on ~** estar a postos. ⬦ *comp* stand-by.

stand-in *n* **-1.** [replacement] suplente *mf*, **-2.** [stunt person] dublê *mf.*

standing ['stændɪŋ] ⬦ *adj* [permanent] permanente; **a ~ joke** uma piada manjada; **a ~ invitation** um convite em aberto. ⬦ *n* **-1.** [reputation] reputação *f* **-2.** [duration] duração *f*; **friends of 20 years' ~** amigos há mais de 20 anos.

standing charge *n* taxa *f* fixa.

standing committee *n* comissão *f* permanente.

standing order *n* débito *m* automático em conta.

standing ovation *n* ovação *f* em pé.

standing room *n (U)* lugar *m* em pé.

standoffish [ˌstænd'ɒfɪʃ] *adj* reservado(da).

standpipe *n* tubo *m* ascendente.

standpoint ['stændpɔɪntl *n* ponto *m* de vista.

standstill ['stændstɪl] *n*: **at a ~** [not moving] parado(da); *fig* [not active] paralisado(da); **to come to a ~** [stop moving] parar; *fig* [cease] estancar.

stand-up *adj*: **~ comedian** comediante *mf* de platéia; **~ fight** briga *f* violenta.

stank [stæŋk] *pt* ⊳ **stink**.

Stanley knife® *n* estilete *m*.

stanza ['stænzə] *n* estrofe *f*.

staple ['steɪpll] ⟨⟩ *adj* [principal] básico(ca), de primeira necessidade. ⟨⟩ *n* -**1.** [for paper] grampo *m* -**2.** [principal commodity] produto *m* de primeira necessidade. ⟨⟩ *vt* grampear.

staple diet *n* dieta *f* básica.

staple gun *n* grampeador *m* industrial.

stapler ['steɪplə'] *n* grampeador *m*.

star [stɑːʰ] (*pt* & *pp* **-red**, *cont* **-ring**) ⟨⟩ *n* -**1.** [gen] estrela *f* -**2.** [asterisk] asterisco *m*. ⟨⟩ *comp* de estrela. ⟨⟩ *vt* [include as celebrity]: **the film ~ s** Mel Gibson o filme é estrelado por Mel Gibson. ⟨⟩ *vi* [actor]: **to ~ (in sthg)** ser protagonista(de algo).
➤ **stars** *npl* [horoscope] horóscopo *m*.

star attraction *n* atração *f* principal.

starboard ['stɑːbəd] ⟨⟩ *adj* de estibordo. ⟨⟩ *n* (U) estibordo *m*; **~ a** estibordo.

starch [stɑːtʃ] *n* -**1.** [stiffening substance] goma *f* -**2.** [in food] amido *m*.

starched [stɑːtʃt] *adj* engomado(da).

starchy ['stɑːtʃɪ] (*compar* **-ier**, *superl* **-iest**) *adj* [foods] amiláceo(cea).

stardom ['stɑːdəm] *n* (U) estrelato *m*.

stare [steəʰ] ⟨⟩ *n* olhar *m* fixo. ⟨⟩ *vi*: **to ~ (at sb/ sthg)** olhar fixamente (para alguém/algo).

starfish ['stɑːfɪʃ] (*pl inv* OR **-es**) *n* estrela-do-mar *f*.

stark [stɑːk] ⟨⟩ *adj* -**1.** [bare, bleak] desolado(da) -**2.** [rock] áspero(ra) -**3.** [decoration] desguarnecido(da) -**4.** [room] sem mobília -**5.** [contrast] duro(ra) -**6.** [reality] nu(a) e cru(a) -**7.** [fact] às claras. ⟨⟩ *adv*: **~ naked** em pêlo.

starlet *n pej* estrelinha *f*.

starlight ['stɑːlaɪt] *n* (U) luz *f* das estrelas.

starling ['stɑːlɪŋ] *n* estorninho *m*.

starlit ['stɑːlɪt] *adj* iluminado(da) pelas estrelas.

starry ['stɑːrɪ] (*compar* **-ier**, *superl* **-iest**) *adj* estrelado(da).

starry-eyed [-'aɪd] *adj* [naive] iludido(da).

Stars and Stripes *n*: **the ~** a bandeira dos Estados Unidos.

star sign *n* signo *m* (do horóscopo).

star-studded *adj*: **a ~ cast** um elenco de estrelas.

start [stɑːt] ⟨⟩ *n* -**1.** [beginning] início *m*, começo *m*; **for a ~** para começar -**2.** [jump] sobressalto *m*, susto *m* -**3.** SPORTS saída *f* -**4.** [lead] vantagem *f*. ⟨⟩ *vt* -**1.** [begin] começar; **to ~ doing** OR **to do sthg** começar a fazer algo -**2.** [turn on] ligar -**3.** [set up - ger] criar, formar; [- business] montar -**4.** [initiate, instigate] iniciar. ⟨⟩ *vi* -**1.** [begin] começar; **to ~ with sb/sthg** começar com alguém/algo; **to ~ with**, ... [at first] para começar, ... -**2.** [car] pegar -**3.** [engine] pôr-se em funcionamento -**4.** [tape] ligar -**5.** [set out] sair -**6.** [jump] sobressair-se, assustar-se -**7.** *inf* [be annoying]: **don't you ~!** não começa!

➤ **start off** ⟨⟩ *vt sep* [cause to start - person] pôr -se a caminho; **this should be enough work to ~ you off** com isso já tem trabalho suficiente para começar; [- meeting] começar; [- rumour, discussion] desencadear. ⟨⟩ *vi* -**1.** [begin] começar -**2.** [set out] sair.

➤ **start on** *vt fus* [begin] começar; **she finished off the biscuits and ~ ed on the cake** ela terminou com os biscoitos e partiu para o bolo.

➤ **start out** *vi* -**1.** [in life, career] começar -**2.** [set out] partir.

➤ **start up** ⟨⟩ *vt sep* -**1.** [set up - business] montar; [- shop] botar; [- women's group] criar, formar -**2.** [car, engine, machine] ligar. ⟨⟩ *vi* -**1.** [guns, music, noise] começar -**2.** [car, engine, machine] ligar -**3.** [set up business] estabelecer-se.

starter ['stɑːtə'] *n* -**1.** UK [hors d'oeuvre] entrada *f*, primeiro prato *m* -**2.** AUT (motor *m* de) arranque *m* -**3.** [SPORT- official] juiz *m*, -íza *f*; [- competitor] corredor *m*, -ra *f*.

starter motor *n* (motor *m* de) arranque *m*.

starter pack *n* pacote *m* inicial.

starting block ['stɑːtɪŋ-] *n* bloco *m* de partida (numa corrida).

starting point ['stɑːtɪŋ-] *n* ponto *m* de partida.

starting price *n* preço *m* de inauguração.

startle ['stɑːtl] *vt* assustar.

startling ['stɑːtlɪŋ] *adj* assustador(ra), surpreendente.

starvation [stɑːˈveɪʃn] *n* (U) fome *f*, inanição *f*.

starve [stɑːv] ⟨⟩ *vt* -**1.** [deprive of food] não dar comida para -**2.** [deprive]: **to ~ sb of sthg** privar alguém de algo. ⟨⟩ *vi* -**1.** [have no food] passar fome -**2.** *inf* [be hungry]: **I'm starving to death!** estou morrendo de fome!

starving *adj* -**1.** [without food] esfomeado(da) -**2.** *inf* [hungry] faminto(ta).

star wars *n* guerra *f* nas estrelas, *programa espacial militar norte-americano.*

state [steɪt] ⟨⟩ *n* -**1.** [condition] estado *m*; **not to be in a fit ~ to do sthg** não estar em condições de fazer algo; **to be in a ~** estar com os nervos à flor da pele -**2.** [authorities]: **the ~** o Estado. ⟨⟩ *comp* de estado. ⟨⟩ *vt* [declare] afirmar, declarar; **to ~ that** afirmar que; [specify] estabelecer.
➤ **State** *n* [government]: **the State** o Estado.
➤ **States** *npl* [USA]: **the States** os Estados Unidos.

state-controlled *adj* controlado(da) pelo estado.

State Department *n* US ≃ Ministério *m* das Relações Exteriores.

state education *n* UK ensino *m* público.

stateless *adj* sem pátria.

stately ['steɪtlɪ] (*compar* **-ier**, *superl* **-iest**) *adj* [dignified] majestoso(sa).

stately home *n* UK *casa grande de campo aberta à visitação.*

statement ['steɪtmənt] *n* -**1.** [declaration] afirmação *f*, declaração *f* -**2.** JUR declaração *f* -**3.** [from bank] extrato *m*.

state of affairs *n* situação *f* em geral.

state of emergency *n* estado *m* de emergência.

state of mind (pl **states of mind**) n estado m de espírito.

state-of-the-art adj de vanguarda, moderno(-na).

state-owned [-'ɔʊnd] adj estatal.

state school n escola f pública.

state secret n segredo m de estado.

state's evidence n US: **to turn** ~ testemunhar a favor de um delinqüente num tribunal contra outros em troca de uma redução na pena.

stateside ['steɪtsaɪd] <> adj dos Estados Unidos. <> adv -**1**. [travel] para os Estados Unidos -**2**. [live] nos Estados Unidos.

statesman ['steɪtsmən] (pl **-men** [-mən]) n estadista m, homem m de estado.

statesmanship ['steɪtsmənʃɪp] n (U) competência f para governar.

static ['stætɪk] <> adj [unchanging] estável. <> n (U) ELEC estática f.

static electricity n (U) eletricidade f estática.

station ['steɪʃn] <> n -**1**. [gen] estação f; **police** ~ delegacia f; **fire** ~ corpo m de bombeiros -**2**. [position] posto m -**3**. fml [rank] posição f. <> vt -**1**. [position] situar, colocar -**2**. MIL estacionar.

stationary ['steɪʃnərɪ] adj estacionário(ria).

stationer n dono m, -na f de papelaria; ~'s **(shop)** papelaria f.

stationery ['steɪʃnərɪ] n (U) artigos mpl de escritório.

station house n US distrito m policial.

stationmaster ['steɪʃn,mɑːstəʳ] n chefe mf da estação.

station wagon n US perua f (camioneta).

statistic [stə'tɪstɪk] n [number] estatística f.

➡ **statistics** n (U) [science] estatística f.

statistical [stə'tɪstɪkl] adj estatístico(ca).

statistician [ˌstætɪ'stɪʃn] n estatístico m, -ca f.

statue ['stætʃuː] n estátua f.

statuesque [ˌstætjʊ'esk] adj escultural.

statuette [ˌstætjʊ'et] n estatueta f.

stature ['stætʃəʳ] n (U) -**1**. [height, size] estatura f -**2**. [importance] categoria f.

status ['steɪtəs] n (U) -**1**. [legal or social position] condição f, estado m -**2**. [prestige] status m inv.

status bar n COMPUT barra f de status.

status quo [-'kwəʊ] n: **the** ~ o status quo.

status symbol n símbolo m de status.

statute ['stætjuːt] n estatuto m.

statute book n: **the** ~ o código de leis.

statutory ['stætjʊtrɪ] adj estatutário(ria).

staunch [stɔːntʃ] <> adj leal, fiel. <> vt estancar.

stave [steɪv] (pt & pp **-d** OR **stove**) n MUS pauta f.

➡ **stave off** vt sep afastar temporariamente.

stay [steɪ] <> n [visit] estada f, estadia f. <> vi -**1**. [remain] ficar; **to** ~ **put** ficar no lugar -**2**. [reside temporarily] ficar, permanecer -**3**. [continue to be] permanecer; **I don't want to** ~ **a teacher all my life** não quero ser professor toda a minha vida; **she** ~ **ed awake till midnight** ficou acordada até a meia-noite -**4**. Scot [reside permanently] hospedar-se.

➡ **stay away** vi: **to** ~ **away from sb/some- where** ficar longe de alguém/algum lugar.

➡ **stay in** vi [stay at home] ficar em casa.

➡ **stay on** vi ficar, permanecer.

➡ **stay out** vi -**1**. [not come home] ficar fora -**2**. [strikers] permanecer em greve -**3**. [not get involved]: **to** ~ **out of sthg** ficar fora de algo.

➡ **stay up** vi -**1**. [not go to bed] ficar acordado(da) -**2**. [not fall] ficar de pé.

stayer n UK -**1**. [horse] cavalo m resistente -**2**. [person] pessoa f resistente.

staying power ['steɪɪŋ-] n (U) resistência f.

St Bernard [UK -'bɜːnəd, US -bərˈnɑːrd] n [dog] são-bernardo m.

STD n -**1**. (abbr of **subscriber trunk dialling**) sistema de chamadas telefônicas diretas de longa distância na Grã-Bretanha -**2**. (abbr of **sexually transmitted disease**) DST f.

stead [sted] n: **to stand sb in good** ~ servir muito a alguém.

steadfast ['stedfɑːst] adj -**1**. [supporter] fiel -**2**. [resolve] resoluto(ta) -**3**. [gaze] fixo(xa).

steadily ['stedɪlɪ] adv -**1**. [gradually] gradualmente -**2**. [regularly] normalmente -**3**. [calmly - look, stare] fixamente; [- say] calmamente.

steady ['stedɪ] (compar **-ier**, superl **-iest**, pt & pp **-ied**) <> adj -**1**. [gradual] gradual -**2**. [regular, constant] constante -**3**. [not shaking] firme -**4**. [calm - voice] calmo(ma); [- stare] fixo(xa) -**5**. [stable - boyfriend, girlfriend] firme; [- relationship] sério(ria); [- job] estável -**6**. [sensible] sensato(ta). <> vt -**1**. [stabilize] estabilizar; **to** ~ **o.s.** equilibrar-se -**2**. [calm] controlar; **to** ~ **o.s.** acalmar-se, controlar os nervos.

steak [steɪk] n -**1**. (U) [meat] bife m -**2**. [piece of meat or fish] filé m.

steakhouse ['steɪkhaʊs, pl -haʊzɪz] n churrascaria f.

steal [stiːl] (pt **stole**, pp **stolen**) <> vt roubar; **to** ~ **a glance at sb** lançar um olhar furtivo em alguém. <> vi -**1**. [take illegally] roubar -**2**. [move stealthily] mover-se furtivamente.

stealing ['stiːlɪŋ] n (U) roubo m.

stealth [stelθ] n (U): **by** ~ furtivamente, às escondidas.

stealthy ['stelθɪ] (compar **-ier**, superl **-iest**) adj furtivo(va).

steam [stiːm] <> n (U) vapor m; **to let off** ~ desabafar; **to run out of** ~ ficar sem forças. <> comp a vapor. <> vt CULIN cozinhar no vapor. <> vi -**1**. [gen] largar vapor -**2**. [train, ship] partir largando fumaça.

➡ **steam up** <> vt sep -**1**. [mist up] embaçar -**2**. fig [get angry]: **to get** ~ **ed up about sthg** soltar fumaça pelas ventas por causa de algo. <> vi [window, glasses] embaçar.

steamboat ['stiːmbəʊt] n barco m a vapor.

steam engine n máquina f a vapor.

steamer ['stiːməʳ] n -**1**. [ship] navio m a vapor -**2**. CULIN panela f que cozinha no vapor.

steam iron n ferro m a vapor.

steamroller ['stiːm,rəʊləʳ] n rolo m compressor.

steam shovel n US escavadeira f a vapor.

steamy ['stiːmɪ] (compar **-ier**, superl **-iest**) adj -**1**. [full of steam] cheio (cheia) de vapor -**2**. inf [erotic] quente.

steel [sti:l] ⇔ *n (U)* aço *m*. ⇔ *comp* de aço. ⇔ *vt*: **to ~ o.s. (for sthg)** encher-se de forças (para algo).

steel industry *n* indústria *f* do aço.

steel wool *n (U)* palha *f* de aço.

steelworker ['sti:l,wɜːkəʳ] *n* operário *m* siderúrgico, operária *f* siderúrgica.

steelworks ['sti:lwɜːks] *(pl inv) n* (usina *f*) siderúrgica *f*.

steely ['sti:lɪ] (*compar* **-ier**, *superl* **-iest**) *adj* **-1.** [steel-coloured] azerado(da) **-2.** [strong, determined] inflexível, inabalável.

steep [sti:p] ⇔ *adj* **-1.** [hill, road] íngreme **-2.** [increase, fall] acentuado(da) **-3.** *inf* [expensive] abusivo(va) **-4.** *inf* [unreasonable] exagerado(da). ⇔ *vt* **-1.** [soak] embeber, molhar **-2.** [fruit] macerar.

steeped [sti:pt] *adj fig*: **~ in sthg** imerso(sa) em algo.

steeple ['sti:pl] *n* agulha *f (do campanário)*.

steeplechase ['sti:pltʃeɪs] *n* corrida *f* de obstáculos.

steeplejack *n* consertador *m*, -ra *f* de chaminés e campanários.

steeply ['sti:plɪ] *adv* **-1.** [at steep angle] vertiginosamente **-2.** [considerably] consideravelmente.

steer ['stɪəʳ] ⇔ *n* [bullock] boi *m*. ⇔ *vt* conduzir, guiar. ⇔ *vi* conduzir; **the car ~s well** é um carro bom de dirigir; **the bus ~ed into the hedge** o ônibus foi direto para a cerca viva; **to ~ clear (of sb/sthg)** *fig* ficar longe (de alguém/algo).

steering ['stɪərɪŋ] *n (U) AUT* direção *f*.

steering column *n* coluna *f* de direção.

steering committee *n* comitê *m* de direção.

steering lock *n* capacidade *f* de giro.

steering wheel *n* volante *m*, direção *f*.

stellar ['steləʳ] *adj* estelar.

stem [stem] (*pt* & *pp* **-med**, *cont* **-ming**) ⇔ *n* **-1.** [of plant] caule *m* **-2.** [of glass] pé *m*, base *f* **-3.** [of pipe] tubo *m* **-4.** *GRAMM* raiz *f*. ⇔ *vt* [stop - flow] conter; [- blood] estancar.

➡ **stem from** *vt fus* derivar-se de, ser o resultado de.

stench [stentʃ] *n* fedor *m*.

stencil ['stensl] (*UK pt* & *pp* **-led**, *cont* **-ling**, *US pt* & *pp* **-ed**, *cont* **-ing**) ⇔ *n* [template] matriz *f*. ⇔ *vt* reproduzir com matriz.

stenographer [stə'nɒɡrəfəʳ] *n* estenógrafo *m*, -fa *f*.

stenography [stə'nɒɡrəfɪ] *n (U)* estenografia *f*.

step [step] (*pt* & *pp* **-ped**, *cont* **-ping**) ⇔ *n* **-1.** [pace] passo *m*; **in ~ with** *fig* [in touch with] em acordo com; **out of ~ with** *fig* [out of touch with] em desacordo com; **to watch one's ~** [when walking] olhar onde se pisa; *fig* [be cautious] tomar cuidado **-2.** [action] medida *f* **-3.** [stage, degree] grau *m*; **~ by ~** passo a passo **-4.** [stair, ladder] degrau *m* **-5.** *US MUS* tom *m*. ⇔ *vi* **-1.** [take a single step] dar um passo; **to ~ forward** dar um passo à frente; **watch where you ~** olhe onde você pisa; **to ~ off sthg** descer de algo; **to ~ over sthg** pisar em algo **-2.** [put one's foot down]: **to ~ on sthg** pisar em algo; **~ on it!** [drive fast, hurry up] acelera!; **to ~ in sthg** meter o pé em algo.

➡ **steps** *npl* **-1.** [stairs] escadas *fpl* **-2.** *UK* [stepladder] escada *f* de mão.

➡ **step aside** *vi* **-1.** [move to one side] afastar-se, ficar de lado **-2.** [resign] renunciar.

➡ **step back** *vi* [pause to reflect] parar para pensar.

➡ **step down** *vi* [resign] renunciar.

➡ **step in** *vi* [intervene] intervir.

➡ **step up** *vt sep* [increase] aumentar.

step aerobics *n* step *m*.

stepbrother ['step,brʌðəʳ] *n* meio-irmão *m*.

stepchild ['steptʃaɪld] (*pl* **-children** [-,tʃɪldrən]) *n* enteado *m*, -da *f*.

stepdaughter ['step,dɔːtəʳ] *n* enteada *f*.

stepfather ['step,fɑːðəʳ] *n* padrasto *m*.

stepladder ['step,lædəʳ] *n* escada *f* de mão.

stepmother ['step,mʌðəʳ] *n* madrasta *f*.

stepping-stone ['stepɪŋ-] *n* **-1.** [in river] passadeira *f* **-2.** *fig* [way to success] trampolim *m*.

stepsister ['step,sɪstəʳ] *n* meia-irmã *f*.

stepson ['stepsʌn] *n* enteado *m*.

stereo ['sterɪəʊ] (*pl* **-s**) ⇔ *adj* estéreo(rea). ⇔ *n* **-1.** [stereo system] (aparelho *m* de) som *m* **-2.** *(U)* [stereo sound] estéreo *m*.

stereophonic *adj* estereofônico(ca).

stereotype ['sterɪətaɪp] ⇔ *n* estereótipo *m*. ⇔ *vt* estereotipar.

sterile ['steraɪl] *adj* **-1.** [germ-free] esterilizado(da) **-2.** [unable to produce offspring] estéril **-3.** *pej* [unimaginative] improdutivo(va).

sterility [ste'rɪlətɪ] *n (U)* **-1.** [gen] esterilidade *f* **-2.** *pej* [lack of imagination] improdutividade *f*.

sterilization [,sterəlaɪ'zeɪʃn] *n (U)* [gen] esterilização *f*.

sterilize, -ise ['sterəlaɪz] *vt* esterilizar.

sterilized milk ['sterəlaɪzd-] *n (U)* leite *m* esterilizado.

sterling ['stɜːlɪŋ] ⇔ *adj* **-1.** [of British money] esterlino(na) **-2.** [excellent] excelente. ⇔ *n (U)* libra *f* esterlina. ⇔ *comp* em libras esterlinas.

sterling silver *n (U)* prata *f* de lei.

stern [stɜːn] ⇔ *adj* severo(ra). ⇔ *n* popa *f*.

sternly ['stɜːnlɪ] *adv* [disapprovingly] em desaprovação.

steroid ['stɪərɔɪd] *n* esteróide *m*.

stethoscope ['steθəskəʊp] *n* estetoscópio *m*.

stetson ['stetsn] *n* chapéu *m* de vaqueiro.

stevedore ['sti:vədɔːʳ] *n US* estivador *m*, -ra *f*.

stew [stju:] ⇔ *n* ensopado *m*, refogado *m*. ⇔ *vt* ensopar, refogar. ⇔ *vi*: **to let sb ~** *fig* deixar alguém cozinhando.

steward ['stjʊəd] *n* **-1.** *UK* [on plane] comissário *m* de bordo **-2.** *UK* [ship, train] camareiro *m* **-3.** *UK* [marshal] coordenador *m*, -ra *f (de uma corrida, um desfile etc)*.

stewardess ['stjʊədɪs] *n* comissária *f* de bordo.

stewing steak *UK* ['stju:ɪŋ-], **stewbeef** *US* ['stju:bi:f] *n (U)* carne *f* para refogar.

St. Ex. *(abbr of* **stock exchange**) bolsa *f* de valores.

stg *(abbr of* **sterling**) libra *f* esterlina.

stick [stɪk] (*pt* & *pp* **stuck**) ⇔ *n* **-1.** [piece of wood] graveto *m* **-2.** [of chalk] (pedaço *m* de) giz *m* **-3.** [of dynamite] (banana *f*) de dinamite **-4.** [of celery] talho *m* de aipo **-5.** [walking stick] bastão *m* **-6.** *SPORT* taco *m* **-7.** *phr:* **to get the wrong end of the** ~ entender justamente o contrário. <> *vt* **-1.** [jab]: **to** ~ **sthg in(to) sthg** fincar *OR* espetar algo em algo; **to** ~ **sthg through sthg** atravessar algo com algo **-2.** [with adhesive] colar; **to** ~ **sthg on** *OR* **to sthg** colar algo em algo **-3.** *inf* [put] socar **-4.** *UK inf* [tolerate] agüentar; **to** ~ **it** conseguir agüentar. <> *vi* **-1.** [arrow, dart, spear]: **I've got a splinter stuck in my finger** há uma felpa enfiada no meu dedo **-2.** [adhere]: **to** ~ **(to sthg)** colar (em algo) **-3.** [become jammed] emperrar **-4.** [remain]: **to** ~ **in one's mind** ficar na cabeça de alguém.

➤ **sticks** *npl pej* [country]: **(out) in the** ~**s** lá nos cafundós, no fim do mundo.

➤ **stick around** *vi inf* ficar.

➤ **stick at** *vt fus* continuar firme em; **to** ~ **at it** continuar firme.

➤ **stick by** *vt fus* **-1.** [person] ficar ao lado de **-2.** [decision] manter.

➤ **stick out** <> *vt sep* **-1.** [extend] colocar para fora; **to** ~ **one's tongue out at sb** botar a língua (para alguém) **-2.** *inf* [endure]: **to** ~ **it out** agüentar. <> *vi* **-1.** [protrude] sobressair **-2.** *inf* [be noticeable] destacar-se, chamar a atenção.

➤ **stick out for** *vt fus UK* insistir até conseguir.

➤ **stick to** *vt fus* **-1.** [person, path] não abandonar **-2.** [principles, decision] ser fiel a; **if I were you, I'd ~ to French** se eu fosse tu, ficaria apenas com o francês **-3.** [promise] cumprir.

➤ **stick together** *vi* [people] manter-se unidos(-das).

➤ **stick up** <> *vt sep* **-1.** [sign, notice, postcard] fixar na parede **-2.** [with gun]: ~ **'em up!** mãos ao alto! <> *vi* sobressair; **to be** ~**ing up** estar espetado(da).

➤ **stick up for** *vt fus* defender.

➤ **stick with** *vt fus* **-1.** [activity, decision] manter **-2.** [person] ficar perto de.

sticker ['stɪkə'] *n* [piece of paper] adesivo *m*.

sticking plaster ['stɪkɪŋ-] *n* **-1.** *(U)* [bandaging material] esparadrapo *m* **-2.** [bandage] curativo *m*.

stick insect *n* bicho-pau *m*.

stick-in-the-mud *n inf* retrógrado *m*, -da *f*.

stickleback ['stɪklbæk] *n* esgana-gata *m*.

stickler ['stɪklə'] *n*: ~ **for sthg** obsessivo(va) por algo.

stick-on *adj* adesivo(va).

stickpin *n US* alfinete *m* de gravata.

stick shift *n US* [gear lever] alavanca *f* da marcha *OR* mudança; [car] carro *m* com câmbio manual.

stick-up *n inf* assalto *m* à mão armada.

sticky ['stɪkɪ] (*compar* **-ier**, *superl* **-iest**) *adj* **-1.** [tacky] grudento(ta) **-2.** [adhesive] adesivo(va) **-3.** *inf* [awkward] chato(ta) **-4.** [humid] abafado(da).

stiff [stɪf] <> *adj* **-1.** [inflexible] duro(ra) **-2.** [difficult to move] emperrado(da) **-3.** [difficult to stir] consistente **-4.** [aching] dolorido(da); ~ **neck** torcicolo *m* **-5.** [formal] formal **-6.** [severe] severo(ra) **-7.** [difficult] duro(ra) **-8.** *inf* [drink] forte **-9.** [breeze] forte. <> *adv inf* [for emphasis] muito; **to be bored** ~ estar completamente entediado(da); **to be scared/frozen** ~ estar morrendo de medo/de frio.

stiffen ['stɪfn] <> *vt* **-1.** [paper, fabric] endurecer **-2.**

[resistance, resolve] reforçar. <> *vi* **-1.** [tense up - people] ficar tenso(sa); [- joints, muscles, back] enrijecer **-2.** [become difficult to move] emperrar **-3.** [become more severe, intense - competition] ficar mais acirrado(da); [- resistance, resolve] fortalecer-se **-4.** [breeze] ficar mais forte.

stiffener ['stɪfnə'] *n* [in collar] *tira fina de plástico ou cartão inserida num colar para manter os pontos compactados*.

stiffness ['stɪfnɪs] *n (U)* **-1.** [of paper, fabric] rigidez *f* **-2.** [of hinge, handle, door] emperramento *m* **-3.** [of joints, limbs, back] enrijecimento *m*, tensão *f* **-4.** [of manner, smile, welcome] formalidade *f*, frieza *f* **-5.** [of sentence, punishment] rigorosidade *f* **-6.** [of resistance, resolve] firmeza *f* **-7.** [of exam] dificuldade *f*.

stifle ['staɪfl] <> *vt* **-1.** [suffocate] sufocar **-2.** [suppress] sufocar, reprimir. <> *vi* [suffocate] sufocar.

stifling ['staɪflɪŋ] *adj* sufocante.

stigma ['stɪgmə] *n* estigma *m*.

stigmatize, -ise ['stɪgmətaɪz] *vt* estigmatizar.

stile [staɪl] *n escada para passar sobre uma cerca.*

stiletto (heel) [stɪ'letəʊ-] *n UK* salto *m* alto.

still [stɪl] <> *adv* **-1.** [in time] ainda; **do you** ~ **live in ...?** você ainda mora em ...? **-2.** [all the same] ainda assim **-3.** *(with comparatives)* ainda; **more interesting** ~, ... ainda mais interessante que isso, ... **-4.** [motionless] sem se mover; **sit** ~! te senta e fica quieto! <> *adj* **-1.** [not moving] parado(da) **-2.** [calm, quiet] calmo(ma), tranqüilo(la) **-3.** [not windy] sem vento **-4.** [not fizzy] sem gás. <> *n* **-1.** *PHOT* foto *f* fixa **-2.** [for making alcohol] alambique *m*.

stillborn ['stɪlbɔ:n] *adj* nado-morto(ta).

still life (*pl* **-s**) *n* natureza-morta *f*.

stillness ['stɪlnɪs] *n (U)* quietude *f*.

stilted ['stɪltɪd] *adj* forçado(da).

stilts [stɪlts] *npl* **-1.** [for person] pernas *fpl* de pau **-2.** [for building] estacas *fpl*.

stimulant ['stɪmjʊlənt] *n* estimulante *m*.

stimulate ['stɪmjʊleɪt] *vt* **-1.** [gen] estimular **-2.** [physically] excitar.

stimulating ['stɪmjʊleɪtɪŋ] *adj* estimulante.

stimulation [‚stɪmjʊ'leɪʃn] *n (U)* estímulo *m*.

stimulus ['stɪmjʊləs] (*pl* **-li** [-laɪ]) *n* estímulo *m*.

sting [stɪŋ] (*pt & pp* **stung**) <> *n* **-1.** [from bee] ferroada *f*; **to take the** ~ **out of sthg** *fig* atenuar algo **-2.** [from insect] picada *f* **-3.** [from nettle] urticária *f* **-4.** [part of bee, wasp, scorpion] ferrão *m*. <> *vt* **-1.** [subj: bee, wasp, scorpion] picar; [subj: nettle] queimar; [subj: smoke, acid] irritar **-2.** *fig* [subj: remark, criticism] ferir. <> *vi* **-1.** [bee, wasp, scorpion] picar; [nettle] queimar; [smoke, acid] irritar **-2.** [eyes, skin] arder.

stinging nettle ['stɪŋɪŋ-] *n UK* urtiga *f*.

stingy ['stɪndʒɪ] (*compar* **-ier**, *superl* **-iest**) *adj* **-1.** [person] sovina **-2.** *inf* [amount] escasso(sa).

stink [stɪŋk] (*pt* **stank** *OR* **stunk**, *pp* **stunk**) <> *n* fedor *m*. <> *vi* **-1.** [smell] feder **-2.** *inf fig* [be worthless] ser uma porcaria, não valer nada.

stink-bomb *n* bomba *f* de cheiro.

stinking ['stɪŋkɪŋ] *inf* <> *adj* **-1.** [smelly] fedorento(ta) **-2.** *fig* [for emphasis] maldito(ta). <> *adv* extremamente; **he's** ~ **rich** está podre de rico.

stint [stɪnt] <> n[period of time] período m. <> vi: **to ~ on sthg** pechinchar algo.

stipend ['staɪpend] n estipêndio m.

stipulate ['stɪpjʊleɪt] vt estipular.

stipulation [ˌstɪpjʊ'leɪʃn] n -1. (U) [stating of conditions] estipulação f -2. [condition] condição f.

stir [stɜː^r] (pt & pp -red, cont -ring) <> n -1. [act of mixing] mexida f -2. [public excitement] agitação f, alvoroço m. <> vt -1. [mix] mexer, misturar -2. [move physically] mexer; **to ~ o.s.** mexer-se (para fazer algo) -3. [rouse, excite] instigar. <> vi -1. [move gently] mover-se, mexer-se -2. [awaken] despertar.

➤ **stir up** vt sep -1. [dust, mud] levantar -2. [trouble, dissent, feelings, memories] provocar.

stir-fry vt refogar.

stirring ['stɜːrɪŋ] <> adj instigante. <> n [feeling] indício m.

stirrup ['stɪrəp] n estribo m.

stitch [stɪtʃ] <> n -1. GEN ponto m -2. [pain]: **to have a ~** sentir pontadas de dor -3. phr: **to be in ~es** chorar de tanto rir. <> vt costurar.

stitching ['stɪtʃɪŋ] n (U) costura f.

stoat [stəʊt] n arminho m.

stock [stɒk] <> n -1. [gen] estoque m; **in ~** em estoque; **out of ~** esgotado(da) -2. [FIN - of company] capital m; [- of government] títulos mpl do governo; **~s and shares** títulos mpl mobiliários, ações fpl -3. (U) [ancestry] estirpe f, linhagem f -4. CULIN caldo m -5. (U) [livestock] rebanho m -6. [of gun] coronha f -7. phr: **to take ~ (of sthg)** refletir (sobre algo). <> adj [typical] típico(ca). <> vt -1. COMM ter em estoque -2. [fill] encher (de); **to be ~ed with** estar cheio (cheia) de.

➤ **stock up** vi: **to ~ up (on OR with sthg)** fazer estoque (de algo).

stockade [stɒ'keɪd] n paliçada f.

stockbroker ['stɒkˌbrəʊkə^r] n corretor m, -ra f da bolsa.

stockbroking ['stɒkˌbrəʊkɪŋ] n (U) corretagem f na bolsa.

stockcar n stockcar m.

stock company n US sociedade f anônima de capital acionário.

stock control n controle m de estoque.

stock cube n UK caldo m em cubo.

stock exchange n bolsa f de valores.

stockholder ['stɒkˌhəʊldə^r] n US acionista mf.

Stockholm ['stɒkhəʊm] n Estocolmo; **in ~** em Estocolmo.

stocking ['stɒkɪŋ] n meia f.

stock-in-trade n -1. (U) [usual behaviour] mote m -2. (U) [work] ferramenta f de trabalho.

stockist ['stɒkɪst] n UK varejista mf.

stock market n mercado m de ações.

stock phrase n frase f feita.

stockpile ['stɒkpaɪl] <> n estoque m. <> vt estocar, armazenar.

stockroom ['stɒkrʊm] n depósito m.

stock-still adv imóvel.

stocktaking ['stɒkˌteɪkɪŋ] n (U) inventário m.

stocky ['stɒkɪ] (compar -ier, superl -iest) adj reforça-do(da), corpulento(ta).

stodgy ['stɒdʒɪ] (compar -ier, superl -iest) adj -1. [indigestible] pesado(da) -2. pej [uninteresting] enfadonho(-nha).

stoic ['stəʊɪk] <> adj estóico(ca). <> n estóico m, -ca f.

stoical ['stəʊɪkl] adj estóico(ca).

stoicism ['stəʊɪsɪzm] n estoicismo m.

stoke [stəʊk] vt [keep burning] alimentar.

stole [stəʊl] <> pt ▷ steal. <> n [shawl] estola f.

stolen ['stəʊln] pp ▷ steal.

stolid ['stɒlɪd] adj impassível.

stomach ['stʌmək] <> n -1. [organ] estômago m; **on a full/an empty stomach** com o estômago cheio/vazio -2. [abdomen] ventre m. <> vt [tolerate] tolerar.

stomach ache n dor f de estômago.

stomach pump n bomba f para lavagem estomacal.

stomach ulcer n úlcera f de estômago.

stomach upset [-'ʌpset] n indigestão f.

stomp [stɒmp] vi pisar forte.

stone [stəʊn] (pl sense 5 only inv OR -s) <> n -1. [gen] pedra f; **a ~'s throw from** bem perto de -2. [jewel] pedra f preciosa -3. [in fruit] caroço m -4. [unit of measurement] equivalent to 6,35kg. <> comp de pedra. <> vt apedrejar.

Stone Age n: **the ~** a Idade da Pedra.

stone-cold adj gelado(da) como pedra.

stoned [stəʊnd] adj vinf -1. [drunk] mamado(da) -2. [drugged] chapado(da).

stonemason ['stəʊnˌmeɪsn] n canteiro m, -ra f.

stonewall [ˌstəʊn'wɔːl] vi [avoid questions] andar com evasivas.

stoneware n (U) faiança f.

stonewashed ['stəʊnwɒʃt] adj estonado(da).

stonework ['stəʊnwɜːk] n (U) cantaria f.

stony ['stəʊnɪ] (compar -ier, superl -iest) adj -1. [covered with stones] pedregoso(sa) -2. [unfriendly] impassível, frio (fria).

stood [stʊd] pt & pp ▷ stand.

stooge [stuːdʒ] n -1. inf [manipulated person] fantoche m -2. [in comedy act] comparsa mf.

stool [stuːl] n [seat] mocho m, banquinho m.

stoop [stuːp] <> n -1. [bent back]: **to walk with a ~** caminhar encurvado(da) -2. US [of house] varanda f. <> vi -1. [bend forwards and down] abaixar-se -2. [hunch shoulders] encurvar-se -3. fig [debase o.s.]: **to ~ to sthg** rebaixar-se a algo.

stop [stɒp] (pt & pp -ped, cont -ping) <> n -1. [gen] parada f -2. [standstill]: **to come to a ~** dar uma parada -3. [end]: **to put a ~ to sthg** dar um basta em algo -4. [in punctuation] ponto m -5. phr: **to pull out all the ~s** fig remover todos os empecilhos -6. TECH trava f, ferrolho m. <> vt -1. [gen] parar; **to ~ doing sthg** parar de fazer algo -2. [prevent] impedir; **to ~ sb/sthg from doing sthg** impedir alguém/algo de fazer algo -3. [interrupt - wages] suspender; [- cheque] sustar; [- match] interromper; [- newspaper] parar -4. [hole, gap] tapar. <> vi -1. [gen] parar; **to ~ at nothing (to do sthg)** não parar por nada (para conseguir algo) -2. [stay] ficar.

➤ **stop off** vi dar uma parada.

◆ **stop over** *vi* passar a noite.

◆ **stop up** ⬦ *vt sep* [block] entupir. ⬦ *vi UK* ficar acordado(da).

stopcock ['stɒpkɒk] *n* torneira *f* de passagem.

stopgap ['stɒpgæp] *n* quebra-galho *m*.

stopover ['stɒp,əʊvə'] *n* parada *f*.

stoppage ['stɒpɪdʒ] *n* - **1.** [strike] paralização *f* - **2.** *UK* [deduction] dedução *f*.

stopper ['stɒpə'] *n* rolha *f*.

stopping *adj UK*: ~ **train** trem com parada em todas as estações.

stop press *n* notícias *fpl* de última hora.

stop sign *n* AUT sinal *m* de parada.

stopwatch ['stɒpwɒtʃ] *n* cronômetro *m*.

storage ['stɔːrɪdʒ] *n (U)* armazenamento *m*.

storage heater *n UK* aquecedor que acumula calor à noite, quando a eletricidade é mais barata, e libera calor durante o dia.

store [stɔː'] ⬦ *n* - **1.** *esp US* [shop] loja *f* - **2.** [supply] reserva *f*, provisão *f* - **3.** [storage place] depósito *m* - **4.** *phr*: **to set great** ~ **by** OR **on sthg** dar muita importância a algo. ⬦ *vt* - **1.** [gen] armazenar - **2.** [details, address, ideas] guardar.

◆ **in store** *adv* [imminent]: **who knows what the future has in** ~ **for us?** quem sabe o que o futuro nos reserva?

◆ **store up** *vt sep* - **1.** [objects] armazenar - **2.** [facts, information] guardar.

store card *n* cartão *m* de crédito *(de lojas)*.

store detective *n* segurança *mf* de loja.

storehouse ['stɔːhaʊs, *pl* -haʊzɪz] *n* - **1.** *esp US* [warehouse] depósito *m* - **2.** *fig* [treasury] mina *f*.

storekeeper ['stɔː,kiːpə'] *n US* lojista *mf*.

storeroom ['stɔːruːm] *n* - **1.** [gen] almoxarifado *m* - **2.** [for food] despensa *f*.

storey *UK (pl* **storeys**), **story** *US (pl* **-ies**) ['stɔːrɪ] *n* andar *m*.

stork [stɔːk] *n* cegonha *f*.

storm [stɔːm] ⬦ *n* - **1.** [bad weather] temporal *m*, tempestade *f*; **a** ~ **in a teacup** uma tempestade num copo d'água - **2.** [violent reaction] torrente *f*. ⬦ *vt* - **1.** MIL tomar de assalto - **2.** [say angrily] esbravejar. ⬦ *vi* [go angrily]: **to** ~ **into/out of** entrar/sair intempestivamente.

storm cloud *n* [bringing rain] nuvem *f* de chuva.

storming *n* - **1.** [assault] assalto *m*, investida *f* - **2.** [capture] tomada *f*.

stormy ['stɔːmɪ] *(compar* **-ier**, *superl* **-iest**) *adj* - **1.** [weather, sea] tempestuoso(sa) - **2.** *fig* [relationship, meeting] turbulento(ta).

story ['stɔːrɪ] *(pl* **-ies**) *n* - **1.** [tale] história *f*, conto *m*; **it's the (same) old** ~ é a velha história de sempre; **to cut a long** ~ **short,** ... para encurtar a história ... - **2.** HIST & *euphemism* história *f* - **3.** [article - newspaper] artigo *m*; [- TV, radio] reportagem *f* - **4.** *US* = **storey**.

storybook ['stɔːrɪbʊk] *adj* de novela.

storyteller ['stɔːrɪ,telə'] *n* - **1.** [teller of story] contador *m*, -ra *f* de histórias - **2.** *euphemism* [liar] mentiroso *m*, -sa *f*.

stout [staʊt] ⬦ *adj* - **1.** [corpulent] corpulento(ta) - **2.** [strong] forte, resistente - **3.** [brave] firme, forte. ⬦ *n (U)* cerveja *f* escura, stout *f*.

stoutness ['staʊtnɪs] *n (U)* [corpulence] corpulência *f*.

stove [stəʊv] ⬦ *pt* & *pp* ⊳ **stave.** ⬦ *n* - **1.** [for cooking] forno *m* - **2.** [for heating] estufa *f*.

◆ **stow away** *vi* [on ship, plane] embarcar como clandestino(na).

stowaway ['stəʊəweɪl] *n* clandestino *m*, -na *f*.

straddle ['strædl] *vt* - **1.** [subj: person] escarranchar-se em - **2.** [subj: bridge, town] atravessar, cruzar.

strafe *vt* MIL metralhar.

straggle ['strægl] *vi* - **1.** [buildings, hair, plant] espalhar-se - **2.** [person, group] ficar para trás.

straggler ['stræglə'] *n* retardatário *m*, -ria *f*.

straggly ['stræglɪ] *(compar* **-ier**, *superl* **-iest**) *adj* emaranhado(da).

straight [streɪt] ⬦ *adj* - **1.** [gen] reto(ta) - **2.** [not curly] liso(sa) - **3.** [honest, frank] direto(ta), franco(ca) - **4.** [tidy] arrumado(da) - **5.** [simple] fácil, simples - **6.** [undiluted] puro(ra) - **7.** *inf* [conventional] convencional - **8.** *gay sl* [heterosexual] heterossexual - **9.** [quits] quite - **10.** *phr*: **to get something** ~ deixar uma coisa clara. ⬦ *adv* - **1.** [in a straight line]: ~ **ahead** bem na frente; **I couldn't see** ~ não podia ver direito - **2.** [upright] reto(ta); **why won't that painting hang** ~ por que aquele quadro não fica reto? - **3.** [directly, immediately] imediatamente; **I'll go** ~ **to bed** vou direto para a cama - **4.** [honestly, frankly] com toda a franqueza - **5.** [undiluted]: **I drink my whisky** ~ tomo meu uísque puro - **6.** *phr*: **to go** ~ corrigir-se. ⬦ *n* SPORT: **the** ~ a reta final.

◆ **straight off** *adv* no ato.

◆ **straight out** *adv* sem rodeios.

straightaway *adv* em seguida.

straighten ['streɪtn] ⬦ *vt* - **1.** [tidy] arrumar, organizar - **2.** [make straight] endireitar - **3.** [make level] pôr reto(ta), endireitar. ⬦ *vi* [stand or sit up]: **to** ~ **(up)** endireitar-se.

◆ **straighten out** *vt sep* [sort out - mess] arrumar; [- problem] resolver.

straight face *n*: **to keep a** ~ ficar sério(ria).

straightforward [,streɪt'fɔːwəd] *adj* - **1.** [easy] simples - **2.** [honest, frank - answer] direto(ta); [- person] aberto(ta), franco(ca).

strain [streɪn] ⬦ *n* - **1.** [mental] tensão *f* - **2.** MED [of muscle, back] distenção *f* - **3.** [TECH - weight] peso *m*; [- pressure] pressão *f*; [- force] força *f* - **4.** [type, variety] variedade *f*. ⬦ *vt* - **1.** [work hard] forçar - **2.** MED [injure] distender - **3.** [overtax - resources, budget] esticar; [- enthusiasm] acabar; [- patience] esgotar - **4.** [drain - vegetables] escorrer; [- tea] coar - **5.** TECH [rope, girder, ceiling] estirar. ⬦ *vi* [try very hard]: **to** ~ **to do sthg** esforçar-se para fazer algo.

◆ **strains** *npl literary* [of music] acordes *mpl*.

strained [streɪnd] *adj* - **1.** [forced] forçado(da) - **2.** [tense] tenso(sa) - **3.** MED [sprained] distendido(da) - **4.** [culin - liquid] coado(da); [- vegetables] escorrido (da).

strainer ['streɪnə'] *n* coador *m*.

strait [streɪt] *n* GEOGR estreito *m*.

◆ **straits** *npl*: **in dire** OR **desperate** ~ **s** em sérios apuros.

straitened ['streɪtnd] *adj fml*: ~ **circumstances** dificuldades financeiras.

straitjacket ['streɪtˌdʒækɪt] n [garment] camisa f de força.

straitlaced [ˌstreɪt'leɪst] adj pej puritano(na).

Strait of Gibraltar n: the ~ o Estreito de Gibraltar.

Strait of Hormuz n: the ~ o Estreito de Hormuz.

strand [strænd] n -1. [of hair, cotton, wool] mecha f; a ~ of hair um fio de cabelo -2. [of story, argument, plot] linha f.

stranded ['strændɪd] adj -1. [person] preso(sa) -2. [car] atolado(da) -3. [boat] encalhado(da).

strange [streɪndʒ] adj -1. [unusual, unexpected] estranho(nha) -2. [unfamiliar] desconhecido(da), estranho(nha).

strangely ['streɪndʒlɪ] adv -1. [in an odd manner] de forma estranha -2. [unexpectedly, mysteriously] inesperadamente -3. [surprisingly]: ~ (enough) por mais estranho que pareça.

stranger ['streɪndʒə'] n -1. [unknown person] estranho m, -nha f; to be a/no ~ to sthg estar/não estar familiarizado com algo -2. [person from elsewhere] forasteiro m, -ra f.

strangle ['stræŋgl] vt -1. [kill - person] estrangular; [- chicken] torcer o pescoço de -2. fig [stifle] sufocar.

stranglehold ['stræŋglhəʊld] n -1. [round neck] gravata f -2. fig [strong influence]: ~ (on sb/sthg) controle m total (sobre alguém/algo).

strangulation [ˌstræŋgjʊ'leɪʃn] n (U) [act of killing] estrangulamento m.

strap [stræp] (pt & pp -ped, cont -ping) <> n -1. [for carrying] correia f, tira f -2. [for fastening] alça f -3. [of watch] pulseira f. <> vt [fasten] prender (com correia).

strapless ['stræplɪs] adj [garment] sem alça.

strapping ['stræpɪŋ] adj robusto(ta).

Strasbourg ['stræzbɜːg] n Estrasburgo; in ~ em Estrasburgo.

strata ['strɑːtə] pl ⊳ stratum.

stratagem ['strætədʒəm] n estratagema m.

strategic [strə'tiːdʒɪk] adj estratégico(ca).

strategist ['strætɪdʒɪst] n MIL estrategista mf.

strategy ['strætɪdʒɪ] (pl -ies) n estratégia f.

stratified ['strætɪfaɪd] adj estratificado(da).

stratosphere ['strætəˌsfɪə'] n: the ~ a estratosfera.

stratum ['strɑːtəm] (pl -ta) n -1. GEOL estrato m -2. fig [of society] estrato m social.

straw [strɔː] <> n -1. (U) [dried corn] palha f -2. [for drinking] canudinho m -3. phr: to clutch at ~s agarrar-se a qualquer coisa em desespero; the last ~ a gota d'água. <> comp de palha.

strawberry ['strɔːbərɪ] (pl -ies) <> n [fruit] morango m. <> comp de morango.

straw poll n sondagem f de opinião.

stray [streɪ] <> adj perdido(da). <> n [animal] animal m perdido. <> vi -1. [from group] perder-se -2. [from path] desviar-se -3. [thoughts, mind]: to ~ from the point desviar-se do tema.

streak [striːk] <> n -1. [of grease] faixa f -2. [of lightning] raio m -3. [in hair] luz f -4. [in character] traço m -5. [period]: a winning/losing ~ período m em que só se ganha/perde. <> vi [move

quickly] passar como um raio.

streaked [striːkt] adj [marked]: ~ with sthg manchado(da) de algo.

streaky ['striːkɪ] (compar -ier, superl -iest) adj [colour, surface] riscado(da), listrado(da).

streaky bacon n UK bacon m.

stream [striːm] <> n -1. [brook] riacho m -2. [of liquid] curso m -3. [of air] corrente f -4. [of light] raio m, faixa f -5. [of liquid, air, light] rio m -6. [of people, traffic] torrente f -7. [of abuse, queries, complaints, books] série f -8. UK SCH grupo m. <> vt UK SCH agrupar de acordo com o rendimento escolar. <> vi -1. [gen] jorrar -2. [air] fluir -3. [people]: to ~ in/out entrar/sair em massa -4. [traffic] mover-se rapidamente.

streamer ['striːmə'] n [for party] serpentina f, flâmula f.

streamline ['striːmlaɪn] vt -1. [make aerodynamic] dar forma aerodinâmica a -2. [make efficient] racionalizar.

streamlined ['striːmlaɪnd] adj -1. [aerodynamic] aerodinâmico(ca) -2. [efficient] racional.

street [striːt] n rua f; to be right up sb's ~ UK inf ser exatamente o que se precisa; to be ~s ahead of sb/sthg UK estar muito além de alguém/algo.

streetcar ['striːtkɑː'] n US bonde m.

street-cred(ibility) n (U) inf imagem f, aceitação f (entre as pessoas jovens).

street lamp, street light n lâmpada f de rua.

street lighting n (U) iluminação f pública.

street map n mapa m (da cidade).

street market n feira f ao ar livre.

street plan n mapa m viário.

street value n preço m de venda (de uma droga).

streetwise ['striːtwaɪz] adj esperto(ta); she's very ~ ela se vira muito bem na rua.

strength [streŋθ] n -1. (U) [gen] força f -2. (U) [power, influence] poder m; on the ~ of com base em; to go from ~ to ~ ir de vento em popa -3. [quality, ability] ponto m forte -4. (U) [solidity] solidez f -5. [intensity - gen] intensidade f; [- of alcohol] teor m alcoólico; [- of drug] potência f -6. FIN [of currency] solidez f -7. (U) [number] número m; to be at full ~ estar com força total; to be below ~ não estar com força total; in ~ em grande número.

strengthen ['streŋθn] <> vt -1. [gen] fortalecer -2. [reinforce] reforçar -3. [intensify] intensificar -4. [make braver, more confident] encorajar. <> vi -1. [physically - body, muscle] fortalecer-se; [- voice] tornar-se mais forte -2. [intensify] intensificar-se -3. FIN [currency] fortalecer-se.

strenuous ['strenjʊəs] adj extenuante.

stress [stres] <> n -1. [emphasis]: ~ (on sthg) ênfase f (em algo) -2. [tension, anxiety] estresse m; to be under ~ estar estressado(da) -3. TECH [physical pressure]: ~ (on sthg) pressão f (sobre algo) -4. LING [on word, syllable] acento m tônico. <> vt -1. [emphasize] enfatizar, realçar -2. LING [word, syllable] acentuar (na pronúncia).

stressed [strest] adj estressado(da).

stressful ['stresfʊl] adj estressante.

stretch [stretʃ] <> n -1. [area] extensão f -2. [period

of time] período *m* - **3.** [effort]: **by no ~ of the imagination** por mais que se queira. ◇ *vt* - **1.** [gen] esticar - **2.** [pull taut] estirar - **3.** [rules, meaning, truth] distorcer - **4.** [challenge] fazer render ao máximo. ◇ *vi* - **1.** [gen] esticar-se - **2.** [area]: **to ~ over** estender-se por; **to ~ from ... to** estender-se de ... até - **3.** [person] espreguiçar-se. ◇ *adj* elástico(ca).

➟ **at a stretch** *adv* sem parar.

➟ **stretch out** ◇ *vt sep* estender, esticar. ◇ *vi* esticar-se *(deitando)*.

stretcher ['stretʃə'] *n* maca *f*.

stretcher party *n* (equipe *f* de) padioleiros *mpl*.

stretchmarks ['stretʃmɑːks] *npl* estrias *fpl*.

stretchy ['stretʃɪ] (*compar* **-ier**, *superl* **-iest**) *adj* elástico(ca).

strew [struː] (*pt* **-ed**, *pp* **strewn** [struːn], **-ed**) *vt*: **to be strewn on** *or* **over sthg** estar esparramado(da) em/sobre algo; **to be strewn with sthg** estar coberto(ta) de algo.

stricken ['strɪkn] *adj*: **to be ~ by** *or* **with sthg** [grief] estar abalado(da) por algo; [doubt, horror, panic] ser tomado(da) por algo; [illness, complaint] estar atacado(da) por algo.

strict [strɪkt] *adj* - **1.** [severe] rígido(da) - **2.** [inflexible] rigoroso(sa) - **3.** [exact, precise] exato(ta), preciso(sa).

strictly ['strɪktlɪ] *adv* - **1.** [severely] rigidamente - **2.** [rigidly, absolutely] estritamente - **3.** [precisely, exactly] exatamente, precisamente; **~ speaking** a rigor - **4.** [exclusively] exclusivamente.

strictness ['strɪktnɪs] *n* (*U*) - **1.** [severity] rigidez *f* - **2.** [rigidity] rigor *m*.

stride [straɪd] (*pt* **strode**, *pp* **stridden** ['strɪdn]) ◇ *n* passada *f*; **to take sthg in one's ~** *fig* encarar algo com tranqüilidade. ◇ *vi* caminhar a passos largos.

➟ **strides** *npl*: **to make (great) ~s** fazer (grandes) progressos.

strident ['straɪdnt] *adj* - **1.** [voice, sound] estridente - **2.** [demand] rigoroso(sa).

strife [straɪf] *n* (*U*) *fml* conflitos *mpl*.

strike [straɪk] (*pt* & *pp* **struck**) ◇ *n* - **1.** [gen] greve *f*; **to be (out) on ~** estar em greve; **to go on ~** entrar em greve - **2.** *MIL* [attack] ataque *m* - **3.** [find] descoberta *f*. ◇ *comp* de greve. ◇ *vt* - **1.** [hit - deliberately] bater, golpear; [- accidentally] atingir, pegar em - **2.** [subj: hurricane, disaster, lightning] atingir - **3.** [subj: thought] ocorrer; **to ~ sb as sthg** parecer algo a alguém - **4.** [impress]: **to be struck by** *or* **with sthg** ficar impressionado(da) com algo - **5.** [reach, arrive at] fechar - **6.** [ignite] acender - **7.** [find] descobrir; **to ~ a balance (between)** encontrar um ponto de equilíbrio (entre); **to ~ a serious/happy note** passar uma idéia séria/alegre - **8.** [chime] bater - **9.** *phr*: **to be struck blind/dumb** ficar cego/mudo, ficar cega/muda; **to ~ fear** *or* **terror into sb** infundir medo/terror em alguém; **to ~ (it) lucky** ter sorte; **to ~ it rich** ficar rico(ca). ◇ *vi* - **1.** [stop working] entrar em greve - **2.** [hit accidentally]: **to ~ against sthg** bater em algo - **3.** [happen suddenly - hurricane, disaster] ocorrer; [- lightning] cair - **4.** [attack] atacar - **5.** [chime]: **the clock struck seven** o relógio bateu sete horas.

➟ **strike back** *vi* revidar.

➟ **strike down** *vt sep* derrubar.

➟ **strike off** *vt sep*: **to be struck off** perder a licença profissional.

➟ **strike out** ◇ *vt sep* rasurar. ◇ *vi* - **1.** [head out] partir, pôr-se a caminho - **2.** [do sthg different] partir para outra.

➟ **strike up** ◇ *vt fus* - **1.** [friendship, conversation] travar - **2.** [music] começar a tocar. ◇ *vi* começar a tocar.

strikebound ['straɪkbaʊnd] *adj* paralisado(da) pela greve.

strikebreaker ['straɪk‚breɪkə'] *n* fura-greve *mf*.

strike pay *n* (*U*) fundo *m* de greve.

striker ['straɪkə'] *n* - **1.** [person on strike] grevista *mf* - **2.** *FTBL* atacante *mf*.

striking ['straɪkɪŋ] *adj* - **1.** [noticeable, unusual] impressionante, chocante - **2.** [attractive] que chama a atenção.

striking distance *n* (*U*): **within ~ (of sthg)** muito perto (de algo).

string [strɪŋ] (*pt* & *pp* **strung**) ◇ *n* - **1.** (*U*) [thin rope] cordão *m*, barbante *m* - **2.** [piece of thin rope] cordel *m*; **(with) no ~s attached** sem restrições; **to pull ~s** mexer os pauzinhos - **3.** [row, chain - of beads, pearls] colar *m*; [- of onions] réstia *f* - **4.** [series] série *f*, sucessão *f* - **5.** [for bow, tennis racket] corda *f*; **to be highly strung** *fig* ter o pavio curto - **6.** *COMPUT* string *m*. ◇ *comp* [vest, bag] de cordão.

➟ **strings** *npl* *MUS*: **the ~s** as cordas.

➟ **string along** *vt sep inf* dar falsas esperanças a.

➟ **string out** *vt sep*: **to be strung out** estar disperso(sa).

➟ **string together** *vt sep fig* juntar.

➟ **string up** *vt sep inf* enforcar.

string bean *n* vagem *f*.

stringed instrument ['strɪŋd-] *n* instrumento *m* de corda.

stringent ['strɪndʒənt] *adj* rigoroso(sa).

string quartet *n* quarteto *m* de cordas.

stringy (*compar* **-ier**, *superl* **-iest**) *adj* fibroso(sa).

strip [strɪp] (*pt* & *pp* **-ped**, *cont* **-ping**) ◇ *n* - **1.** [of fabric, paper, carpet] tira *f*; **to tear a ~ off sb**, **to tear sb off a ~** *UK* dar uma bronca em alguém - **2.** [of land, water, forest] faixa *f* - **3.** *UK SPORT* camiseta *f* *(de time)*. ◇ *vt* - **1.** [undress] despir; **~ped to the waist** nu (nua) até o peito - **2.** [remove layer of] descascar - **3.** [take away from]: **to ~ sb of sthg** despojar alguém de algo. ◇ *vi* - **1.** [undress] despir-se - **2.** [do a striptease] fazer um striptease.

➟ **strip off** ◇ *vt sep* tirar. ◇ *vi* despir-se.

strip cartoon *n* *UK* tira *f* em quadrinhos.

stripe [straɪp] *n* - **1.** [band of colour] lista *f*, faixa *f* - **2.** [sign of rank] galão *m*.

striped [straɪpt] *adj* listado(da).

strip lighting *n* (*U*) iluminação *f* fluorescente.

stripper ['strɪpə'] *n* - **1.** [performer of striptease] stripper *mf* - **2.** [tool, liquid] removedor *m*.

strip-search ◇ *n* revista *f* policial *(fazendo tirar a roupa)*. ◇ *vt* revistar *(fazendo tirar a roupa)*.

strip show *n* show *m* de striptease.

striptease ['striptiːz] *n* striptease *m*.

stripy ['straɪpɪ] (*compar* -ier, *superl* -iest) *adj* listado(-da).

strive [straɪv] (*pt* strove, *pp* striven ['strɪvnl]) *vi fml*: to ~ for sthg/to do sthg lutar por algo/para fazer algo.

strobe (light) ['strəʊb-] *n* luz *f* estroboscópica.

strode [strəʊd] *pt* ⊳ stride.

stroke [strəʊk] ⋄ *n* -**1.** MED derrame *m* cerebral -**2.** [of brush] pincelada *f* -**3.** [of pen] traço *m* -**4.** [in swimming - movement] braçada *f*; [- style] nado *m* -**5.** [movement in rowing] remada *f* -**6.** [in tennis] raquetada *f* -**7.** [in golf] tacada *f* -**8.** [of clock] batida *f* -**9.** [of bell] dobre *m* -**10.** UK TYPO [slash] barra *f* -**11.** [piece]: **a ~ of genius** um lance de gênio; **a ~ of luck** um golpe de sorte; **not to do a ~ of work** não levantar um dedo; **at a ~** de um golpe só. ⋄ *vt* acariciar.

stroll [strəʊl] ⋄ *n* passeio *m*. ⋄ *vi* passear.

stroller ['strəʊlə^r] *n US* [for baby] carrinho *m* de bebê.

strong [strɒŋ] ⋄ *adj* -**1.** [gen] forte; **I've never been ~ in mathematics** matemática nunca foi o meu forte; **~ point** ponto forte; **~ nerves** nervos *mpl* de aço -**2.** [solid, sturdy] reforçado(da) -**3.** [in number] de ... pessoas; **the crowd was 2000 ~** a multidão tinha 2000 pessoas. ⋄ *adv*: **to be still going ~** [person, group] ser forte ainda; [machine] funcionar bem ainda.

strongarm ['strɒŋɑːm] *adj*: **to use ~ tactics** ter pulso firme.

strongbox ['strɒŋbɒks] *n* caixa-forte *f*.

stronghold ['strɒŋhəʊld] *n fig* baluarte *m*.

strong language *n* (U) *euphemism* linguagem *f* pesada.

strongly ['strɒŋlɪ] *adv* -**1.** [sturdily, solidly - built] solidamente; [- protected] fortemente -**2.** [in degree or intensity] intensamente; **the kitchen smells ~ of onions** tem um cheiro forte de cebola na cozinha -**3.** [very definitely] totalmente; **to feel ~ about sthg** ter uma opinião firme sobre algo.

strong man *n* homem *m* forte.

strong-minded [-'maɪndɪd] *adj* de caráter.

strong room *n* casa-forte *f*.

strong-willed [-'wɪld] *adj* obstinado(da).

stroppy ['strɒpɪ] (*compar* -ier, *superl* -iest) *adj* UK *inf* emburrado(da).

strove [strəʊv] *pt* ⊳ strive.

struck [strʌk] *pt* & *pp* ⊳ strike.

structural ['strʌktʃərəl] *adj* estrutural.

structurally ['strʌktʃərəlɪ] *adv* estruturalmente.

structure ['strʌktʃə^r] ⋄ *n* -**1.** [organization, arrangement] estrutura *f* -**2.** [building, construction] construção *f*. ⋄ *vt* estruturar.

struggle ['strʌgl] ⋄ *n* -**1.** [gen]: **~ (for sthg/to do sthg)** luta *f* (por algo/por fazer algo) -**2.** [fight] briga *f*. ⋄ *vi* -**1.** [try hard, strive] esforçar-se; **to ~ free** lutar para ser solto(ta); **to ~ (for sthg/to do sthg)** lutar (por algo/por fazer algo) -**2.** [fight]: **to ~ (with sb)** brigar (com alguém) -**3.** [move with difficulty] mover-se com dificuldade; **he ~d to his feet** ele conseguiu se levantar a duras penas.
➡ **struggle on** *vi*: **to ~ on (with sthg)** continuar (algo) a duras penas.

struggling ['strʌglɪŋ] *adj* esforçado(da).

strum [strʌm] (*pt* & *pp* -med, *cont* -ming) ⋄ *vt*

dedilhar. ⋄ *vi*: **to ~ (on sthg)** dedilhar (algo).

strung [strʌŋ] *pt* & *pp* ⊳ string.

strut [strʌt] (*pt* & *pp* -ted, *cont* -ting) ⋄ *n* -**1.** CONSTR escora *f* -**2.** AERON montante *m*. ⋄ *vi* andar empertigado(da).

strychnine ['strɪkniːn] *n* (U) estricnina *f*.

stub [stʌb] (*pt* & *pp* -bed, *cont* -bing) ⋄ *n* -**1.** [of cigarette, pencil] toco *m* -**2.** [of ticket, cheque] canhoto *m*. ⋄ *vt*: **to ~ one's toe (on)** dar uma topada com o dedo do pé (em).
➡ **stub out** *vt sep* apagar.

stubble ['stʌbl] *n* (U) -**1.** [in field] restolho *m* -**2.** [on chin] barba *f* curta.

stubborn ['stʌbən] *adj* -**1.** [person] teimoso(sa), cabeçudo(da) -**2.** [stain] persistente, difícil.

stubbornly ['stʌbənlɪ] *adv* -**1.** [wait] teimosamente -**2.** [refuse] resistentemente -**3.** [declare] resolutamente.

stubby ['stʌbɪ] (*compar* -ier, *superl* -iest) *adj* atarracado(da).

stucco ['stʌkəʊ] *n* (U) estuque *m*.

stuck [stʌk] ⋄ *pt* & *pp* ⊳ stick. ⋄ *adj* -**1.** [gen] preso(sa) -**2.** [window] emperrado(da) -**3.** [stumped]: **can you help with this problem? I'm ~** pode me ajudar com esse problema? (eu) empaquei.

stuck-up *adj inf pej* convencido(da), metido(da).

stud [stʌd] *n* -**1.** [metal decoration] tachão *m* -**2.** [earring] pingente *m* -**3.** UK [on boot, shoe] taco *m* -**4.** (U) [of horses] plantel *m*; **to be put out to ~** ser usado(da) para reprodução.

studded ['stʌdɪd] *adj*: **~ (with sthg)** adornado(da) (com algo); **a ~ jacket** uma jaqueta adornada; **~ with precious stones** cravejado(da) de pedras preciosas.

student ['stjuːdnt] ⋄ *n* -**1.** [at college, university] estudante *mf* -**2.** [scholar] estudioso *m*, -sa *f*. ⋄ *comp* -**1.** [nurse, teacher] em estágio -**2.** [politics] estudantil -**3.** [lifestyle] de estudante -**4.** [disco] para estudantes.

student loan *n* UK crédito *m* educativo.

students' union *n* grêmio *m* estudantil.

stud farm *n* haras *m inv*.

studied ['stʌdɪd] *adj* -**1.** [answer] pensado(da) -**2.** [smile] estudado(da).

studio ['stjuːdɪəʊ] (*pl* -s) *n* estúdio *m*.

studio apartment *n US* = studio flat.

studio audience *n* público *m* no auditório.

studio flat UK, **studio apartment** US *n* (apartamento *m*) JK *m*.

studious ['stjuːdjəs] *adj* estudioso(sa).

studiously ['stjuːdjəslɪ] *adv* cuidadosamente.

study ['stʌdɪ] (*pl* -ies, *pt* & *pp* -ied) ⋄ *n* -**1.** (U) [gen] estudo *m* -**2.** [room] sala *f* de estudos. ⋄ *vt* -**1.** [learn] estudar -**2.** [examine] examinar, estudar. ⋄ *vi* estudar.
➡ **studies** *npl* estudos *mpl*.

stuff [stʌf] ⋄ *n* (U) *inf* -**1.** [matter, things] coisa *f*; **to know one's ~** entender do riscado; **and all that ~** e tudo isso -**2.** [substance]: **what's that ~ in your pocket?** o que é isso aí no seu bolso? -**3.** [belongings] coisas *fpl*. ⋄ *vt* -**1.** [push, put] enfiar -**2.** [fill, cram]: **to ~ sthg (with sthg)** encher algo (com algo) -**3.** [with food]: **to ~ o.s. (with OR on sthg)** *inf* empanturrar-se (de algo) **- 4.** CULIN rechear.

stuffed [stʌftl] *adj* **-1.** [filled, crammed]: ~ **with sthg** atulhado(da) de algo **- 2.** *inf* [with food] empanturrado(da) **- 3.** CULIN recheado(da) **- 4.** [animal] empalhado(da) **- 5.** *phr*: **get** ~ **!** *UK v inf* vai te catar!

stuffing ['stʌfɪŋ] *n* (U) **-1.** [filling - for furniture] estofamento *m*; [- for toys] enchimento *m* **- 2.** CULIN recheio *m*.

stuffy ['stʌfɪ] (*compar* **-ier**, *superl* **-iest**) *adj* **-1.** [room] abafado(da) **- 2.** [formal, old-fashioned] retrógrado(da).

stumble ['stʌmbl] *vi* **-1.** [trip] tropeçar **- 2.** [hesitate, make mistake] equivocar-se.
➤ **stumble across, stumble on** *vt fus* **-1.** [person] topar com **- 2.** [objects] encontrar por acaso.

stumbling block ['stʌmblɪŋ-] *n* pedra *f* no caminho, obstáculo *m*.

stump [stʌmp] ◇ *n* **-1.** [of tree] toco *m* **- 2.** [of limb] coto *m*. ◇ *vt* deixar perplexo(xa). ◇ *vi* caminhar com passo firme; **he** ~**ed up the steps** ele subiu a escada com passo firme.
➤ **stumps** *npl* CRICKET varetas *fpl* verticais.
➤ **stump up** *vt fus inf UK* desembolsar.

stun [stʌn] (*pt* & *pp* **-ned**, *cont* **-ning**) *vt* **-1.** [knock unconscious] deixar sem sentidos **- 2.** [shock, surprise] atordoar.

stung [stʌŋ] *pt* & *pp* ▷ **sting**.

stun grenade *n* granada *f* de efeito moral.

stunk [stʌŋk] *pt* & *pp* ▷ **stink**.

stunned *adj* **-1.** [unconscious] inconsciente **- 2.** [shocked, surprised] atordoado(da).

stunning ['stʌnɪŋ] *adj* **-1.** [very beautiful] imponente **- 2.** [very shocking, surprising] espantoso(sa).

stunt [stʌnt] ◇ *n* **-1.** [for publicity] golpe *m* publicitário **- 2.** CINEMA cena *f* arriscada, cena *f* perigosa. ◇ *vt* inibir.

stunted ['stʌntɪd] *adj* mirrado(da).

stunt man *n* dublê *m*.

stunt woman *n* dublê *f*.

stupefy ['stju:pɪfaɪ] (*pt* & *pp* **-ied**) *vt* **-1.** [tire, bore] entorpecer **- 2.** [surprise] deixar estupefato(ta).

stupendous [stju:'pendəs] *adj inf* **-1.** [wonderful] estupendo(da) **- 2.** [very large] enorme.

stupid ['stju:pɪd] *adj* **-1.** [foolish] estúpido(da) **- 2.** *inf* [wretched, damned] idiota.

stupidity [stju:'pɪdətɪ] *n* (U) estupidez *f*.

stupidly ['stju:pɪdlɪ] *adv* estupidamente.

stupor ['stju:pəˡ] *n* estupor *m*.

sturdy ['stɜ:dɪ] (*compar* **-ier**, *superl* **-iest**) *adj* **-1.** [person] forte, robusto(ta) **- 2.** [furniture, platform] sólido(da), firme.

sturgeon ['stɜ:dʒən] (*pl inv*) *n* esturjão *m*.

stutter ['stʌtəˡ] ◇ *n* gagueira *f*. ◇ *vi* gaguejar.

sty [staɪ] (*pl* **sties**) *n* chiqueiro *m*.

stye [staɪ] *n* terçol *m*.

style [staɪl] ◇ *n* **-1.** [manner] estilo *m*; **in the** ~ **of** ao estilo de **- 2.** (U) [smartness, elegance] classe *f* **- 3.** [fashion, design] modelo *m*. ◇ *vt* pentear de acordo com a moda.

styling mousse *n* (U) mousse *f* modeladora.

stylish ['staɪlɪʃ] *adj* de estilo.

stylist ['staɪlɪst] *n* estilista *mf*.

stylized, -ised ['staɪlaɪzd] *adj* estilizado(da).

stylus ['staɪləs] (*pl* **-es**) *n* **-1.** [on record player] agulha *f* **- 2.** COMPUT caneta *f* gráfica.

stymie ['staɪmɪ] *vt inf*: **to be** ~**d** estar entravado(da).

suave [swɑ:v] *adj* afável.

sub [sʌb] *n inf* **-1.** SPORT (*abbr of* **substitute**) reserva *mf* **- 2.** (*abbr of* **submarine**) submarino *m* **- 3.** *UK* (*abbr of* **subscription**) assinatura *f* **- 4.** *UK* (*abbr of* **advance payment**) adiantamento *m* **- 5.** *US* [sandwich] *tipo de sanduíche*.

sub- [sʌb] *prefix* sub(-).

subcommittee ['sʌbkəˌmɪtɪ] *n* subcomissão *f*.

subconscious [ˌsʌb'kɒnʃəs] ◇ *adj* subconsciente. ◇ *n*: **the** ~ o subconsciente.

subconsciously [ˌsʌb'kɒnʃəslɪ] *adj* de forma subconsciente.

subcontinent [ˌsʌb'kɒntɪnənt] *n* subcontinente *m*.

subcontract [ˌsʌbkən'trækt] *vt* subcontratar.

subculture ['sʌbˌkʌltʃəˡ] *n* subcultura *f*.

subdivide [ˌsʌbdɪ'vaɪd] *vt* subdividir.

subdue [səb'dju:] *vt* **-1.** [enemy, rioters, crowds] subjugar **- 2.** [feelings, passions] conter, dominar.

subdued [səb'dju:d] *adj* **-1.** [person] desanimado(da) **- 2.** [feelings] reprimido(da) **- 3.** [light, sound, colour] fraco(ca).

subeditor [ˌsʌb'edɪtəˡ] *n* copidesque *mf*.

subgroup ['sʌbgru:p] *n* subgrupo *m*.

subheading ['sʌbˌhedɪŋ] *n* subtítulo *m*.

subhuman [ˌsʌb'hju:mən] *adj pej* subumano(na).

subject [*adj, n* & *prep* 'sʌbdʒekt, *vt* səb'dʒekt] ◇ *adj*: ~ **(to sthg)** sujeito(ta) (a algo). ◇ *n* **-1.** [topic, person under consideration] assunto *m*, tema *m* **- 2.** GRAMM sujeito *m* **- 3.** SCH & UNIV cadeira *f* **- 4.** [citizen] súdito *m*, -ta *f*. ◇ *vt* **-1.** [bring under strict control] sujeitar, dominar **- 2.** [force to experience]: **to** ~ **sb to sthg** sujeitar alguém a algo.
➤ **subject to** *prep* sujeito(ta) a; ~ **to the budget** dependendo do orçamento.

subjection [səb'dʒekʃn] *n* sujeição *f*, subordinação *f*.

subjective [səb'dʒektɪv] *adj* subjetivo(va).

subjectively [səb'dʒektɪvlɪ] *adv* subjetivamente.

subject matter ['sʌbdʒekt-] *n* (U) temática *f*, tema *m*.

sub judice *adj* JUR sub judice.

subjugate ['sʌbdʒʊgeɪt] *vt fml* **-1.** [gen] subjugar **- 2.** [feelings, desires] dominar.

subjunctive [səb'dʒʌŋktɪv] *n* GRAMM: ~ **(mood)** (modo *m*) subjuntivo *m*.

sublet [ˌsʌb'let] (*pt* & *pp* **sublet**, *cont* **-ting**) *vt* sublocar.

sublime [sə'blaɪm] *adj* sublime; **from the** ~ **to the ridiculous** do sublime ao ridículo.

sublimely [sə'blaɪmlɪ] *adv* totalmente, completamente.

subliminal [ˌsʌb'lɪmɪnl] *adj* subliminar.

submachine gun [ˌsʌbmə'ʃi:n-] *n* metralhadora *f*.

submarine [ˌsʌbmə'ri:n] *n* submarino *m*.

submerge [səb'mɜ:dʒ] ◇ *vt* **-1.** [flood] inundar **- 2.** [plunge into liquid] submergir **- 3.** *fig* [in activity]: **to** ~ **o.s. in sthg** mergulhar em algo. ◇ *vi* mergulhar.

submission [səb'mɪʃn] *n (U)* **-1.** [obedience, capitulation] submissão *f* **-2.** [presentation] apresentação *f.*

submissive [səb'mɪsɪv] *adj* submisso(sa).

submit [səb'mɪt] (*pt* & *pp* **-ted**, *cont* **-ting**) <> *vt* submeter. <> *vi*: **to ~ (to sb)** render-se (a alguém); **to ~ (to sthg)** submeter-se (a algo).

subnormal [ˌsʌb'nɔːml] *adj* subnormal.

subordinate [*adj* & *n* sə'bɔːdɪnət, *vt* sə'bɔːdɪneɪt] <> *adj fml*: **~ (to sthg)** subordinado(da) (a algo). <> *n* subordinado *m*, -da *f.* <> *vt fml* subordinar.

subordinate clause [sə'bɔːdɪnət-] *n* oração *f* subordinada.

subordination [səˌbɔːdɪ'neɪʃn] *n (U)*: **~ (of/to sthg)** subordinação *f*(de/a algo).

subpoena [sə'piːnə] (*pt* & *pp* **-ed**) *JUR* <> *n* intimação *f (para comparecimento em juízo).* <> *vt* intimar *(para comparecimento em juízo).*

sub-post office *n UK pequena agência de correios local que oferece menos serviços que uma agência central.*

subroutine [ˈsʌbruːˌtiːn] *n COMPUT* sub-rotina *f.*

subscribe [səb'skraɪb] <> *vi* **-1.** [to magazine, newspaper]: **to ~ (to sthg)** fazer assinatura (de algo) **-2.** [to view, belief]: **to ~ to sthg** concordar com algo. <> *vt* contribuir com, doar.

subscriber [səb'skraɪbə'] *n* **-1.** [to magazine, newspaper] assinante *mf* **-2.** [to service] usuário *m*, -ria *f* **-3.** [to charity, campaign] doador *m*, -ra *f.*

subscription [səb'skrɪpʃn] *n* **-1.** [to newspaper, magazine] assinatura *f* **-2.** [to club, organization - monthly] mensalidade *f*; [- yearly] anuidade *f.*

subsection [ˈsʌbˌsekʃn] *n* subseção *f.*

subsequent [ˈsʌbsɪkwənt] *adj* subseqüente.

subsequently [ˈsʌbsɪkwəntlɪ] *adv* subseqüentemente, por conseguinte.

subservient [səb'sɜːvjənt] *adj* **-1.** [servile]: **~ (to sb)** subserviente (a alguém) **-2.** [less important]: **~ (to sthg)** subordinado(da) (a algo).

subset *n MATH* subconjunto *m.*

subside [səb'saɪd] *vi* **-1.** [storm, anger] acalmar; [pain, grief] passar **-2.** [floods] baixar; [swelling] diminuir **-3.** *CONSTR* ceder.

subsidence [səb'saɪdns, 'sʌbsɪdns] *n (U) CONSTR*: **the problems were caused by ~** os problemas foram causados pelo fato de o terreno tȇr cedido.

subsidiarity [səbsɪdɪ'ærɪtɪ] *n política de permitir que as próprias pessoas numa organização tomem decisões sobre questões que as afetam, em vez de deixá-las para o grupo todo.*

subsidiary [səb'sɪdjərɪ] (*pl* **-ies**) <> *adj* subsidiário(ria). <> *n*: **~ (company)** (empresa *f)* subsidiária *f.*

subsidize, -ise [ˈsʌbsɪdaɪz] *vt* subsidiar.

subsidy [ˈsʌbsɪdɪ] (*pl* **-ies**) *n* subsídio *m.*

subsist [səb'sɪst] *vi*: **to ~ (on sthg)** sobreviver (à base de algo).

subsistence [səb'sɪstəns] *n (U)* subsistência *f.*

subsistence allowance *n UK* diária *f.*

subsistence farming *n (U)* agricultura *f* de subsistência.

subsistence level *n* nível *m* mínimo de subsistência.

substance [ˈsʌbstəns] *n* **-1.** [gen] substância *f* **-2.** [essence, gist] essência *f* **-3.** *(U)* [importance] importância *f.*

substandard [ˌsʌb'stændəd] *adj* inferior.

substantial [səb'stænʃl] *adj* **-1.** [large, considerable] substancial **-2.** [solid, well-built] sólido(da).

substantially [səb'stænʃəlɪ] *adv* **-1.** [quite a lot] substancialmente, consideravelmente **-2.** [mainly] basicamente.

substantiate [səb'stænʃɪeɪt] *vt fml* fundamentar.

substantive *adj fml* pertinente, substancioso(-sa).

substitute [ˈsʌbstɪtjuːt] <> *n* **-1.** [replacement]: **~ (for sb/sthg)** substituto *m*, -ta *f*(de alguém/algo); **to be no ~ (for sthg)** não estar à altura (de algo) **-2.** *SPORT* reserva *mf*, suplente *mf.* <> *vt*: **to ~ sb for sb** substituir alguém por alguém; **to ~ sthg for sthg** substituir algo por algo. <> *vi*: **to ~ for sb/sthg** substituir alguém/algo.

substitute teacher *n US* professor *m*, -ra *f* suplente.

substitution [ˌsʌbstɪ'tjuːʃn] *n* substituição *f.*

subterfuge [ˈsʌbtəfjuːdʒ] *n* subterfúgio *m.*

subterranean [ˌsʌbtə'reɪnjən] *adj* subterrâneo(-nea).

subtitle [ˈsʌbˌtaɪtl] *n* subtítulo *m.*
 ◆ **subtitles** *npl CINEMA* legenda *f.*

subtle [ˈsʌtl] *adj* sutil.

subtlety [ˈsʌtltɪ] *n* **-1.** [gen] sutileza *f* **-2.** [delicacy, understatement] delicadeza *f.*

subtly [ˈsʌtlɪ] *adv* sutilmente.

subtotal [ˈsʌbtəʊtl] *n* subtotal *m.*

subtract [səb'trækt] *vt*: **to ~ sthg (from sthg)** subtrair algo (de algo).

subtraction [səb'trækʃn] *n* subtração *f.*

subtropical [ˌsʌb'trɒpɪkl] *adj* subtropical.

suburb [ˈsʌbɜːb] *n* periferia *f.*
 ◆ **suburbs** *npl*: **the ~ s** a periferia.

suburban [sə'bɜːbn] *adj* **-1.** [of suburbs] da periferia **-2.** *pej* [boring] suburbano(na).

suburbia [sə'bɜːbɪə] *n (U)* bairros *mpl* residenciais.

subversion [səb'vɜːʃn] *n (U)* subversão *f.*

subversive [səb'vɜːsɪv] <> *adj* subversivo(va). <> *n* subversivo *m*, -va *f.*

subvert [səb'vɜːt] *vt* subverter.

subway [ˈsʌbweɪ] *n* **-1.** *UK* [underground walkway] passagem *f* subterrânea **-2.** *US* [underground railway] metrô *m.*

sub-zero *adj* abaixo de zero.

succeed [sək'siːd] <> *vt* **-1.** [person] suceder a **-2.** [event, emotion]: **to be ~ ed by sthg** ser sucedido(-da) por algo. <> *vi* **-1.** [achieve desired result]: **to ~ in sthg/in doing sthg** conseguir algo/fazer algo **-2.** [work well, come off] dar bons resultados, sair-se bem **-3.** [go far in life] triunfar.

succeeding [sək'siːdɪŋ] *adj* seguinte.

success [sək'ses] *n* sucesso *m.*

successful [sək'sesfʊl] *adj* **-1.** [attempt] bem-sucedido(da) **-2.** [film, book etc] de sucesso **-3.** [person] bem-sucedido(da), de sucesso.

successfully [sək'sesfʊlɪ] *adv* com sucesso.

succession [sək'seʃn] *n* **-1.** [series] sucessão *f*; **to**

follow in (quick OR **close)** ~ ocorrer numa (rápida) seqüência - **2.** (U) fml [to high position] sucessão f.

successive [sək'sesɪv] adj sucessivo(va).

successor [sək'sesə'] n sucessor m, -ra f.

success story n história f de sucesso.

succinct [sək'sɪŋkt] adj sucinto(ta).

succinctly [sək'sɪŋktlɪ] adv sucintamente.

succulent ['sʌkjʊlənt] adj suculento(ta).

succumb [sə'kʌm] vi: **to** ~ **(to sthg)** sucumbir (a algo).

such [sʌtʃ] ◇ adj - **1.** [referring back] tal, semelhante; **I never heard** ~ **nonsense!** nunca ouvi tal absurdo! - **2.** [referring forward] assim; **have you got** ~ **a thing as a tin opener?** você teria algo como um abridor de latas?; ~ **words as 'duty' and 'honour'** palavras como dever e honra - **3.** [whatever]: **I've spent** ~ **as I had** gastei o pouco dinheiro que eu tinha - **4.** [so great, so extreme]: ~ ... **that** tal ... que; **the state of the economy is** ~ **that** ... tal é o estado da economia que ... ◇ adv tão; ~ **nice people** essas pessoas tão gentis; ~ **a lot of books** tantos livros; ~ **a long time** tanto tempo. ◇ pron [referring back]: **and** ~ **(like)** e coisas do gênero; **this is my car,** ~ **as it is** este é o meu carro, embora não seja grande coisa; **help yourself to wine,** ~ **as there is** sirva-se de vinho, ainda que não tenha muito.

➡ **as such** adv propriamente dito(ta).

➡ **such and such** adj: **at** ~ **and** ~ **a time** de tal em tal hora.

suchlike ['sʌtʃlaɪk] ◇ adj deste tipo, do estilo. ◇ pron - **1.** [things] coisas do estilo - **2.** [people] gente desse tipo.

suck [sʌk] vt - **1.** [by mouth] chupar - **2.** [draw in] aspirar, sugar - **3.** fig [involve]: **to be** ~ **ed into sthg** estar absorvido(da) em algo.

➡ **suck up** vi inf: **to** ~ **up (to sb)** puxar o saco (de alguém).

sucker ['sʌkə'] n - **1.** [suction pad] ventosa f - **2.** inf [gullible person] trouxa mf.

suckle ['sʌkl] ◇ vt amamentar. ◇ vi amamentar.

sucrose ['su:krəʊz] n (U) sacarose f.

suction ['sʌkʃn] n (U) - **1.** [drawing in] sucção f - **2.** [adhesion] adesão f.

suction pump n bomba f de sucção.

Sudan [su:'dɑ:n] n Sudão m; **in (the)** ~ no Sudão.

Sudanese [ˌsu:də'ni:z] ◇ adj sudanês(esa). ◇ n sudanês m, -esa f. ◇ npl: **the** ~ os sudaneses.

sudden ['sʌdn] adj - **1.** [quick] repentino(na); **all of a** ~ de repente - **2.** [unforeseen] inesperado(da).

sudden death n FTBL morte f súbita.

suddenly ['sʌdnlɪ] adv de repente.

suddenness ['sʌdnnɪs] n (U) rapidez f repentina OR inesperada.

suds [sʌdz] npl espuma f de sabão.

sue [su:] vt: **to** ~ **sb (for sthg)** processar alguém (por algo).

suede [sweɪd] ◇ n (U) camurça f. ◇ comp de camurça.

suet ['sʊɪt] n (U) sebo m.

Suez ['su:ɪz] n Suez.

Suez Canal n: **the** ~ o Canal de Suez.

suffer ['sʌfə'] ◇ vt sofrer. ◇ vi - **1.** [feel physical pain] sofrer de; **to** ~ **from sthg** MED sofrer de algo - **2.** [experience difficulties or loss] sair prejudicado(-da).

sufferance ['sʌfrəns] n (U): **on** ~ por condescendência OR tolerância.

sufferer ['sʌfrə'] n paciente mf.

suffering ['sʌfrɪŋ] n sofrimento m.

suffice [sə'faɪs] vi fml ser suficiente, bastar.

sufficient [sə'fɪʃnt] adj suficiente.

sufficiently [sə'fɪʃntlɪ] adv suficientemente.

suffix ['sʌfɪks] n sufixo m.

suffocate ['sʌfəkeɪt] ◇ vt sufocar, asfixiar. ◇ vi sufocar-se, asfixiar-se.

suffocation [ˌsʌfə'keɪʃn] n (U) asfixia f.

suffrage ['sʌfrɪdʒ] n (U) sufrágio m.

suffuse [sə'fju:z] vt: ~ **d with sthg** banhado(da) de algo.

sugar ['ʃʊgə'] ◇ n (U) açúcar m. ◇ vt adoçar.

sugar beet n (U) beterraba f (açucareira).

sugar bowl n açucareiro m.

sugarcane ['ʃʊgəkeɪn] n (U) cana-de-açúcar f.

sugar-coated [-'kəʊtɪd] adj cristalizado(da).

sugared ['ʃʊgəd] adj adoçado(da).

sugar lump n torrão m de açúcar.

sugar refinery n refinaria f de açúcar.

sugary ['ʃʊgərɪ] adj - **1.** [high in sugar] açucarado(da), muito doce - **2.** fig & pej [sentimental] meloso(sa).

suggest [sə'dʒest] vt - **1.** [propose] sugerir, propor; **to** ~ **that sb do sthg** sugerir que alguém faça algo - **2.** [imply] insinuar.

suggestion [sə'dʒestʃn] n - **1.** [gen] sugestão f - **2.** (U) [implication] insinuação f.

suggestive [sə'dʒestɪv] adj - **1.** [implying sexual connotation] insinuante, provocante - **2.** [implying a certain conclusion]: ~ **(of sthg)** indicativo(va) (de algo) - **3.** [reminiscent]: ~ **of sthg** evocativo(va) de algo.

suicidal [suːˈsaɪdl] adj suicida.

suicide ['su:ɪsaɪd] n (U) suicídio m; **to commit** ~ cometer suicídio, suicidar-se.

suicide attempt n tentativa f de suicídio.

suit [su:t] n - **1.** [of matching clothes - for man] terno m; [- for woman] conjunto m - **2.** SPORT [outfit] traje m - **3.** [in cards] naipe m; **to follow** ~ seguir no mesmo naipe; fig seguir o exemplo - **4.** JUR processo m. ◇ vt - **1.** [look attractive on] cair bem - **2.** [be convenient or agreeable to] convir; ~ **yourself!** como quiser! - **3.** [be appropriate to]: **that job** ~ **s you perfectly!** este trabalho é a sua cara! ◇ vi [be convenient or agreeable]: **does that** ~? está bom para ti?

suitability [ˌsu:tə'bɪlətɪ] n (U) adequação f, conveniência f.

suitable ['su:təbl] adj adequado(da), apropriado (da); **the most** ~ **person** a pessoa mais indicada.

suitably ['su:təblɪ] adv adequadamente, apropriadamente.

suitcase ['su:tkeɪs] n mala f.

suite [swi:t] n - **1.** [of rooms] suíte f - **2.** [of furniture] conjunto m.

suited ['su:tɪd] adj - **1.** [suitable]: ~ **to/for sthg** adequado(da) para algo - **2.** [compatible]: **they are well** ~ eles combinam muito bem.

suitor ['su:tə'] n dated pretendente m.

sulfate *n US* = sulphate.
sulfur *n US* = sulphur.
sulfuric acid *n US* = sulphuric acid.
sulk [sʌlk] *n*: **to go into a** ~ ficar emburrado(da).
◇ *vi* emburrar-se.
sulky ['sʌlkɪ] (*compar* -ier, *superl* -iest) *adj* emburrado(da).
sullen ['sʌlən] *adj* mal-humorado(da), atacado(da).
sulphate *UK*, **sulfate** *US* ['sʌlfeɪt] *n (U)* sulfato *m*.
sulphur *UK*, **sulfur** *US* ['sʌlfəʳ] *n (U)* enxofre *m*.
sulphuric acid *UK*, **sulfuric acid** *US* [sʌl'fjʊərɪk-] *n (U)* ácido *m* sulfúrico.
sultan ['sʌltən] *n* sultão *m*.
sultana [səl'tɑːnə] *n UK* [dried grape] passa *f* branca.
sultry ['sʌltrɪ] (*compar* -ier, *superl* -iest) *adj* -1. [hot] abafado(da), mormacento(ta) -2. [sexy] quente.
sum [sʌm] (*pt* & *pp* -med, *cont* -ming) *n* soma *f*.
◆ **sum up** *vt sep* [summarize] resumir. ◇ *vi* recapitular.
Sumatra *n* Sumatra; **in** ~ em Sumatra.
Sumatran *adj de ou relativo a Sumatra.* ◇ *n habitante ou natural de Sumatra.*
summarily ['sʌmərəlɪ] *adv* sumariamente.
summarize, -ise ['sʌməraɪz] *vt* resumir. ◇ *vi* resumir.
summary ['sʌmərɪ] (*pl* -ies) *adj fml* sumário(ria). ◇ *n* resumo *m*.
summation [sʌ'meɪʃn] *n* -1. [summing-up] recapitulação *f* -2. [total] soma *f*.
summer ['sʌməʳ] *n* verão *m*; **in** ~ no verão. ◇ *comp* de verão.
summer camp *n US* colônia *f* de férias.
summer house *n* -1. [in garden] quiosque *m (em jardim)* -2. [for holidays] casa *f* de veraneio.
summer school *n* escola *f* de verão.
summertime ['sʌmətaɪm] *adj* de verão. ◇ *n*: (**the**) ~ o verão.
Summer Time *n UK* horário *m* de verão.
summery ['sʌmərɪ] *adj* de verão.
summing-up [ˌsʌmɪŋ-] (*pl* **summings-up**) *n JUR* recapitulação *f*.
summit ['sʌmɪt] *n* -1. [mountaintop] topo *m*, cume *m* -2. [meeting] reunião *f* de cúpula.
summon ['sʌmən] *vt* convocar.
◆ **summon up** *vt sep* armar-se de.
summons ['sʌmənz] (*pl* **summonses**) *JUR n* intimação *f*. ◇ *vt* intimar.
sumo (wrestling) ['suːməʊ-] *n* sumô *m*.
sump [sʌmp] *n AUT* cárter *m*.
sumptuous ['sʌmptʃʊəs] *adj* suntuoso(sa).
sum total *n* soma *f* total.
sun [sʌn] (*pt* & *pp* -ned, *cont* -ning) *n*: **the** ~ o sol. ◇ *vt*: **to** ~ **o.s.** tomar sol.
Sun. (*abbr of* Sunday) dom.
sunbathe ['sʌnbeɪð] *vi* tomar (banho de) sol.
sunbather ['sʌnbeɪðəʳ] *n* banhista *mf*.
sunbeam ['sʌnbiːm] *n* raio *m* de sol.
sunbed ['sʌnbed] *n* câmara *f* de bronzeamento artificial.
sunburn ['sʌnbɜːn] *n (U)* queimadura *f* de sol.
sunburned ['sʌnbɜːnd], **sunburnt** ['sʌnbɜːnt] *adj* queimado(da) de sol.

sun cream *n (U)* protetor *m* solar.
sundae ['sʌndeɪ] *n* sundae *m*.
Sunday ['sʌndɪ] *n* domingo *m*; *see also* **Saturday**.
Sunday paper *n UK* edição *f* dominical *(de um jornal)*.
Sunday school *n* catequese *f*.
sundial ['sʌndaɪəl] *n* relógio *m* de sol.
sundown ['sʌndaʊn] *n (U)* crepúsculo *m*.
sun-dried *adj* seco(ca), desidratado(da).
sundry ['sʌndrɪ] *adj fml* diversos(sas); **all and** ~ todos(das) sem exceção.
◆ **sundries** *npl fml* artigos *mpl* diversos.
sunflower ['sʌnˌflaʊəʳ] *n* girassol *m*.
sung [sʌŋ] *pp* ▷ **sing**.
sunglasses ['sʌnˌglɑːsɪz] *npl* óculos *mpl* escuros OR de sol.
sunhat ['sʌnhæt] *n* chapéu *m* de praia.
sunk [sʌŋk] *pp* ▷ **sink**.
sunken ['sʌŋkən] *adj* -1. [in water] submerso(sa) -2. [low-level - garden] rebaixado(f da); [- bath] embutido(da) -3. [cheeks] encovado(da) -4. [eyes] fundo(-da).
sunlamp ['sʌnlæmp] *n* lâmpada *f* ultravioleta.
sunlight ['sʌnlaɪt] *n (U)* luz *f* do sol OR solar.
sunlit ['sʌnlɪt] *adj* ensolarado(da).
Sunni ['sʊnɪ] (*pl* -s) *adj* sunita. ◇ *n* sunita *mf*.
sunny ['sʌnɪ] (*compar* -ier, *superl* -iest) *adj* -1. [full of sun] ensolarado(da) -2. *fig* [cheerful] luminoso(sa) -3. *phr*: ~ **side up** *US* [fried egg] com a gema para cima.
sunray lamp *n* lâmpada *f* ultravioleta.
sunrise ['sʌnraɪz] *n* -1. [time of day] amanhecer *m* -2. [event] nascer *m* do sol.
sunroof ['sʌnruːf] *n* teto *m* solar.
sunset ['sʌnset] *n* -1. *(U)* [time of day] anoitecer *m* -2. [event] pôr-do-sol *m*, crepúsculo *m*.
sunshade ['sʌnʃeɪd] *n* guarda-sol *m*.
sunshine ['sʌnʃaɪn] *n (U)* (luz *f* do) sol *m*.
sunspot ['sʌnspɒt] *n* -1. *ASTRON* mancha *f* solar -2. [holiday resort] *local ensolarado para se passar as férias.*
sunstroke ['sʌnstrəʊk] *n (U)* insolação *f*.
suntan ['sʌntæn] *n* bronzeado *m*. ◇ *comp* bronzeador(ra).
suntanned ['sʌntænd] *adj* bronzeado(da).
suntrap ['sʌntræp] *n* local *m* muito ensolarado.
sun-up *n US inf* nascer *m* do sol.
super ['suːpəʳ] *adj inf* excelente. ◇ *n* [petrol] gasolina *f* premium.
superabundance [ˌsuːpərə'bʌndəns] *n* superabundância *f*.
superannuation ['suːpəˌrænjʊ'eɪʃn] *n* -1. *(U)* [pension] aposentadoria *f*, pensão *f* -2. [contribution] contribuição *f* para a previdência.
superb [suː'pɜːb] *adj* soberbo(ba).
superbly [suː'pɜːblɪ] *adv* soberbamente.
Super Bowl *n US*: **the** ~ *a final do campeonato de futebol americano.*
supercilious [ˌsuːpə'sɪlɪəs] *adj* convencido(da), arrogante.
superficial [ˌsuːpə'fɪʃl] *adj* superficial.
superfluous [suː'pɜːflʊəs] *adj* supérfluo(flua).

superglue ['su:pəglu:] *n (U)* superbonder® *f.*

superhuman [ˌsu:pə'hju:mən] *adj* sobre-humano (na).

superimpose [ˌsu:pərɪm'pəʊz] *vt*: **to ~ sthg on sthg** sobrepor algo a algo.

superintend [ˌsu:pərɪn'tend] *vt* superintender.

superintendent [ˌsu:pərɪn'tendənt] *n* **-1.** *UK* [of police] chefe *mf* de polícia **-2.** *fml* [of department] superintendente *mf.*

superior [su:'pɪərɪəʳ] *adj* **-1.** [gen] superior; **~ to sthg/sb** superior a algo/alguém **-2.** *pej* [arrogant] arrogante. ⋄ *n* superior *m*, -ra *f.*

superiority [su:ˌpɪərɪ'ɒrətɪ] *n (U)* **-1.** [gen] superioridade *f.* **-2.** *pej* [arrogance] arrogância *f.*

superlative [su:'pɜ:lətɪv] *adj* [of the highest quality] excelente. ⋄ *n* GRAMM superlativo *m.*

superloo *n* toalete público com dispositivos especiais e muitas vezes automatizado.

superman *n* super-homem *m.*

supermarket ['su:pəˌmɑ:kɪt] *n* supermercado *m.*

supernatural [ˌsu:pə'nætʃrəl] *adj* sobrenatural. ⋄ *n*: **the ~** o sobrenatural.

superpower ['su:pəˌpaʊəʳ] *n* superpotência *f.*

superscript *adj* sobrescrito(ta).

supersede [ˌsu:pə'si:d] *vt* suplantar.

supersonic [ˌsu:pə'sɒnɪk] *adj* supersônico(ca).

superstar ['su:pəstɑ:ʳ] *n* superstar *mf.*

superstition [ˌsu:pə'stɪʃn] *n* **-1.** *(U)* [superstitious beliefs] superstição *f.* **-2.** [particular belief] crendice *f.*

superstitious [ˌsu:pə'stɪʃəs] *adj* supersticioso(sa).

superstore ['su:pəstɔ:ʳ] *n* hipermercado *m.*

superstructure ['su:pəˌstrʌktʃəʳ] *n* superestrutura *f.*

supertanker ['su:pəˌtæŋkəʳ] *n* superpetroleiro *m.*

supertax ['su:pətæks] *n* sobretaxa *f.*

supervise ['su:pəvaɪz] *vt* supervisionar.

supervision [ˌsu:pə'vɪʒn] *n (U)* supervisão *f.*

supervisor ['su:pəvaɪzəʳ] *n* supervisor *m*, -ra *f.*

supper ['sʌpəʳ] *n* **-1.** [main evening meal] jantar *m* **-2.** [snack before bedtime] lanche *m* antes de dormir.

supplant [sə'plɑ:nt] *vt fml* suplantar.

supple ['sʌpl] *adj* flexível.

supplement [*n* 'sʌplɪmənt, *vb* 'sʌplɪment] *n* **-1.** [addition] acréscimo *m* **-2.** [in book] suplemento *m*; [of newspaper] suplemento *m*, encarte *m.* ⋄ *vt* complementar.

supplementary [ˌsʌplɪ'mentərɪ] *adj* suplementar.

supplier [sə'plaɪəʳ] *n* fornecedor *m*, -ra *f.*

supply [sə'plaɪ] *(pl* -ies, *pt & pp* -ied) *n* **-1.** [store, reserve] estoque *m*; **to be in short ~** estar escasso(sa) **-2.** *(U)* [network] abastecimento *m* **-3.** *(U)* ECON oferta *f.* ⋄ *vt*: **to ~ sthg (to sb)** fornecer algo (a alguém); **if you ~ the food, I'll bring the drink** se você entrar com a comida, eu trago a bebida; **to ~ sb (with sthg)** prover alguém (com algo); **to ~ sthg with sthg** abastecer algo com algo.

➥ **supplies** *npl* **-1.** [food] provisões *fpl* **-2.** [office equipment] material *m* **-3.** MIL apetrechos *mpl.*

supply teacher *n UK* professor *m* substituto, professora *f* substituta.

support [sə'pɔ:t] *n* **-1.** [gen] apoio *m* **-2.** *(U)* [financial] ajuda *f.* **-3.** *(U)* [substantiation] embasamento *m* **-4.**

[object, person] suporte *m.* ⋄ *vt* **-1.** [physically] sustentar, apoiar **-2.** [back, back up] apoiar **-3.** [financially] ajudar **-4.** [theory] fundamentar **-5.** SPORT torcer para.

supporter [sə'pɔ:təʳ] *n* **-1.** [of person, plan] partidário *m*, -ria *f.* **-2.** SPORT torcedor *m*, -ra *f.*

supportive [sə'pɔ:tɪv] *adj* incentivador(ra).

suppose [sə'pəʊz] *vt* **-1.** [assume] supor; **I don't ~ ...?** [in polite requests] eu não sei se você poderia ...?; **you don't ~ ...?** [asking opinion] você não acha que ...? **-2.** [concede reluctantly] supor, achar. ⋄ *vi* **-1.** [assume] crer; **I ~ (so)** suponho que sim; **I ~ not** suponho que não **-2.** [admit] admitir; **I ~ so/not** admito que sim/que não. ⋄ *conj* [what if]: **~ we went out?** que tal OR e se a gente saísse?

supposed [sə'pəʊzd] *adj* **-1.** [doubtful] suposto(posta) **-2.** [intended]: **you weren't ~ to be outside** não era para você estar na rua **-3.** [reputed]: **he was ~ to be here at eight** era para ele estar aqui às oito horas; **it's ~ to be very good** dizem que é muito bom.

supposedly [sə'pəʊzɪdlɪ] *adv* supostamente.

supposing [sə'pəʊzɪŋ] *conj*: **~ we went out?** que tal OR e se a gente saísse?

supposition [ˌsʌpə'zɪʃn] *n* suposição *f.*

suppository [sə'pɒzɪtrɪ] *(pl* -ies) *n* supositório *m.*

suppress [sə'pres] *vt* **-1.** [uprising, revolt] reprimir **-2.** [information, report] ocultar **-3.** [emotions] conter.

suppression [sə'preʃn] *n (U)* **-1.** [of uprising, revolt] repressão *f.* **-2.** [of information, report] ocultação *f.* **-3.** [of emotions] dissimulação *f.*

suppressor *n* ELEC supressor *m.*

supranational *adj* supranacional.

supremacy [sʊ'preməsɪ] *n (U)* supremacia *f.*

supreme [sʊ'pri:m] *adj* **-1.** [highest in rank] supremo(ma) **-2.** [great] extraordinário(ria).

Supreme Court *n* [in US]: **the ~** a Suprema Corte.

supremely [sʊ'pri:mlɪ] *adv*: **~ important** de suma importância.

supremo [sʊ'pri:məʊ] *(pl* -s) *n UK inf* manda-chuva *mf.*

Supt *(abbr of* **superintendent)** superintendente *mf.*

surcharge ['sɜ:tʃɑ:dʒ] *n*: **~ (on sthg)** sobretaxa *f* (a algo). ⋄ *vt*: **to ~ sb (on sthg)** sobretaxar alguém (em algo).

sure [ʃʊəʳ] *adj* **-1.** [reliable] confiável, seguro(ra) **-1.** [certain] certo(ta); **to be ~ about sthg** ter certeza sobre algo; **to be ~ of sthg** estar certo de algo; **be ~ of doing sthg** ter certeza de que vai fazer algo; **the dollar is ~ to fall soon** [be certain] com (toda) certeza o dólar vai cair em breve; [remember] certificar-se de; **to make ~ (that) ...** certificar-se de que ...; **I'm ~ (that) ...** tenho certeza de que

... **- 3.** [confident]: **to be ~ of o.s.** estar seguro(ra) de si mesmo(ma). **<>** adv **- 1.** inf [yes] com certeza, claro **- 2.** US [really] realmente.
➡ for sure adv com (toda) certeza.
➡ sure enough adv de fato.

surefire ['ʃʊəfaɪəʳ] adj inf certeiro(ra).

surefooted [ˌʃʊə'fʊtɪd] adj com os pés firmes.

surely ['ʃʊəlɪ] adv com certeza; **~ you can't be serious!** você não pode estar falando a verdade!

sure thing excl US inf [expressing assent] claro!

surety ['ʃʊərətɪ] n garantia f, fiança f.

surf [sɜːf] n (U) espuma f (das ondas do mar). **<>** vi surfar. **<>** vi: **to ~ the Internet** navegar na Internet.

surface ['sɜːfɪs] n **- 1.** superfície f; **on the ~** à primeira vista; **below** OR **beneath the ~** abaixo OR acima da superfície **- 2.** phr: **to scratch the ~** encher lingüiça. **<>** vi **- 1.** [from water] emergir, vir à tona **- 2.** [become generally known] vir à tona **- 3.** inf hum [appear, reappear - after sleep] acordar; [- after prolonged absence] dar o ar da graça.

surface mail n correio m terrestre OR marítimo.

surface-to-air adj terra-ar.

surfboard ['sɜːfbɔːd] n prancha f de surfe.

surfeit ['sɜːfɪt] n fml excesso m.

surfer ['sɜːfəʳ] n surfista mf.

surfing ['sɜːfɪŋ] n (U) surfe m; **to go ~** ir surfar.

surge [sɜːdʒ] n **- 1.** [gen] onda f; [of electricity] sobretensão f **- 2.** [of water] torrente f **- 3.** [of sales, applications] onda f, aumento m. **<>** vi **- 1.** [gen] aumentar **- 2.** [people, vehicles] avançar em massa **- 3.** [water] subir **- 4.** [emotion] intensificar-se **- 5.** [interest, support] crescer.

surgeon ['sɜːdʒən] n cirurgião m, -giã f.

surgery ['sɜːdʒərɪ] (pl -ies) n **- 1.** (U) MED [activity, operation] cirurgia f **- 2.** UK MED [place] consultório m **- 3.** UK MED [consulting period] consulta f **- 4.** UK POL audiência f.

surgical ['sɜːdʒɪkl] adj **- 1.** [connected with surgery] cirúrgico(ca) **- 2.** [worn as treatment] ortopédico(ca).

surgical spirit n (U) UK anti-séptico m.

Surinam n Suriname; **in ~** no Suriname.

surly ['sɜːlɪ] (compar -ier, superl -iest) adj ríspido(da).

surmise [sɜː'maɪz] vt fml presumir.

surmount [sɜː'maʊnt] vt superar, vencer.

surname ['sɜːneɪm] n sobrenome m.

surpass [sə'pɑːs] vt fml ultrapassar, superar.

surplus ['sɜːpləs] adj excedente; **he was ~ to requirements** ele estava além do que se precisava. **<>** n **- 1.** [gen] excedente m **- 2.** [in budget] superávit m.

surprise [sə'praɪz] n surpresa f; **to take sb by ~** pegar alguém de surpresa. **<>** vt surpreender.

surprised [sə'praɪzd] adj surpreso(fsa); **I wouldn't be ~ (if ...)** não me surpreenderia (se ...).

surprising [sə'praɪzɪŋ] adj surpreendente.

surprisingly [sə'praɪzɪŋlɪ] adv surpreendentemente.

surreal [sə'rɪəl] adj surreal.

surrealism [sə'rɪəlɪzm] n (U) surrealismo m.

surrealist [sə'rɪəlɪst] adj surrealista. **<>** n surrealista mf.

surrender [sə'rendəʳ] n rendição f. **<>** vt **- 1.**

[weapons, passport] entregar **- 2.** [liberty, right, claims] renunciar a. **<>** vi **- 1.** [stop fighting]: **to ~ (to sb)** render-se (a alguém) **- 2.** fig [give in]: **to ~ (to sthg)** sucumbir OR ceder (a algo).

surreptitious [ˌsʌrəp'tɪʃəs] adj clandestino(na), furtivo(va).

surrogate ['sʌrəgeɪt] adj suplente. **<>** n substituto m, -ta f.

surrogate mother n mãe f de aluguel.

surround [sə'raʊnd] n borda f. **<>** vt **- 1.** [encircle] circundar, rodear **- 2.** [trap] cercar **- 3.** fig [be associated with] rondar.

surrounding [sə'raʊndɪŋ] adj **- 1.** [all around] circundante **- 2.** [associated] relacionado(da).
➡ surroundings npl **- 1.** [physical] arredores mpl **- 2.** [social] ambiente m.

surtax ['sɜːtæks] n (U) sobretaxa f.

surveillance [sɜː'veɪləns] n (U) vigilância f.

survey [n 'sɜːveɪ, vb sə'veɪ] n **- 1.** [statistical investigation] pesquisa f, levantamento m **- 2.** [physical examination - of land] medição f; [- of building] vistoria f, inspeção f. **<>** vt **- 1.** [contemplate] contemplar **- 2.** [investigate statistically] fazer um levantamento de **- 3.** [examine, assess - land] medir; [- building] vistoriar, inspecionar.

surveyor [sə'veɪəʳ] n [of land] agrimensor m, -ra f; [of building] vistoriador m, -ra f.

survival [sə'vaɪvl] n **- 1.** (U) [continuing to live] sobrevivência f **- 2.** [relic] relíquia f.

survive [sə'vaɪv] vt **- 1.** [live through] sobreviver a **- 2.** [live longer than] sobreviver. **<>** vi **- 1.** [gen] sobreviver **- 2.** inf [cope successfully] sobreviver.
➡ survive on vt fus sustentar-se OR manter-se com.

survivor [sə'vaɪvəʳ] n **- 1.** [gen] sobrevivente mf **- 2.** fig [fighter] lutador m, -ra f.

susceptible [sə'septəbl] adj **- 1.** [likely to be influenced]: **~ (to sthg)** suscetível (a algo) **- 2.** MED: **~ (to sthg)** propenso(sa) (a algo).

suspect [adj & n 'sʌspekt, vb sə'spekt] adj suspeito(ta). **<>** n suspeito m, -ta f. **<>** vt **- 1.** suspeitar; **I ~ corruption in the system** imagino que haja corrupção no sistema **- 2.** [consider guilty]: **to ~ sb (of sthg)** suspeitar de alguém (em algo).

suspend [sə'spend] vt **- 1.** [gen] suspender **- 2.** [temporarily discontinue] suspender, interromper.

suspended animation [sə'spendɪd-] n (U) morte f aparente.

suspended sentence [sə'spendɪd-] n condenação f condicional.

suspender belt [sə'spendəʳ-] n UK cinta-liga f.

suspenders [sə'spendəz] npl **- 1.** UK [for stockings] cintas-ligas fpl **- 2.** US [for trousers] suspensórios mpl.

suspense [sə'spens] n (U) suspense m; **to keep sb in ~** deixar alguém em suspense.

suspension [sə'spenʃn] n suspensão f.

suspension bridge n ponte f suspensa.

suspicion [sə'spɪʃn] n suspeita f; **under ~** sob suspeita.

suspicious [sə'spɪʃəs] adj **- 1.** [having suspicions] desconfiado(da) **- 2.** [causing suspicion] suspeito(ta).

suspiciously [sə'spɪʃəslɪ] adv **- 1.** [showing a suspicious attitude] desconfiadamente; **he asked me ~ if ...** ele me perguntou desconfiado se ... **-2.** [causing suspicion] de forma suspeita.

suss ➼ **suss out** *UK inf vt sep* sacar; **I can't suss him out at all** ainda não saquei qual é a dele.

sustain [sə'steɪn] *vt* **-1.** [gen] manter **-2.** [nourish spiritually] sustentar **-3.** [suffer] sofrer **-4.** [withstand] suportar.

sustenance ['sʌstɪnəns] *n (U) fml* subsistência *f*.

suture ['su:tʃə^r] *n* sutura *f*.

svelte [svelt] *adj* esbelto(ta).

SW -1. (*abbr of* **short wave**) OC *f* **-2.** (*abbr of* **southwest**) SO.

swab [swɒb] *n* (bucha *f* de) algodão *m*.

swagger ['swægə^r] *n* andar *m* garboso. ◇ *vi* andar com ar garboso.

Swahili [swɑ:'hi:lɪ] *adj* suaíli. ◇ *n* [language] suaíli *m*.

swallow ['swɒləʊ] *n* **-1.** [bird] andorinha *f* **-2.** [of food] bocado *m* **-3.** [of drink] gole *m*. ◇ *vt* **-1.** [gen] engolir **-2.** *fig* [hold back] engolir em seco. ◇ *vi* engolir.

swam [swæm] *pt* ▷ **swim**.

swamp [swɒmp] *n* pântano *m*, brejo *m*. ◇ *vt* **-1.** [flood] inundar **-2.** [overwhelm]**: to ~ sb/sthg (with sthg)** sobrecarregar alguém/algo (de algo).

swan [swɒn] *n* cisne *m*.

swap [swɒp] (*pt & pp* **-ped**, *cont* **-ping**) *n* troca *f*. ◇ *vt* **: to ~ sthg (with sb)** trocar algo com alguém; **to ~ sthg (over** OR **round)** trocar algo; **to ~ sthg for sthg** trocar algo por algo. ◇ *vi* trocar.

swap meet *n US* mercado *m* de trocas.

swarm [swɔːm] *n* **-1.** [of bees] enxame *m* **-2.** *fig* [of people] mundaréu *m*. ◇ *vi* **-1.** [bees] enxamear **-2.** *fig* [people] apinhar-se **-3.** *fig* [place]**: to be ~ing (with)** estar fervilhando de.

swarthy ['swɔːðɪ] (*compar* **-ier**, *superl* **-iest**) *adj* moreno(f na).

swashbuckling ['swɒʃˌbʌklɪŋ] *adj* de aventura.

swastika ['swɒstɪkə] *n* suástica *f*.

swat [swɒt] (*pt & pp* **-ted**, *cont* **-ting**) *vt* golpear.

swatch [swɒtʃ] *n* amostra *f*.

swathe [sweɪð] *n* vastidão *f*.

swathed [sweɪðd] *adj literary*: **~ in sthg** enrolado(da) em algo.

swatter ['swɒtə^r] *n* mata-moscas *m inv*.

sway [sweɪ] *vt* **-1.** [cause to swing] balançar **-2.** [influence] persuadir, convencer. ◇ *vi* oscilar. ◇ *n (U) fml*: **to come under the ~ of sb/sthg** ficar sob influência de alguém/algo; **to hold ~ (over sb/sthg)** exercer influência (sobre alguém/algo).

Swazi *n* suazi *mf*.

Swaziland ['swɑːzɪlænd] *n* Suazilândia; **in ~ na** Suazilândia.

swear [sweə^r] (*pt* **swore**, *pp* **sworn**) *vt* **-1.** [gen] jurar; **to ~ to do sthg** jurar fazer algo **-2.** [pronounce]**: to ~ an oath** prestar juramento **-3.** *inf* [state emphatically] jurar. ◇ *vi* **-1.** [state emphatically] jurar **-2.** [use swearwords] praguejar.

➼ **swear by** *vt fus inf* confiar totalmente em.

➼ **swear in** *vt sep* JUR prestar juramento a.

swearword ['sweəwɜːd] *n* blasfêmia *f*, palavrão *m*.

sweat [swet] *n* **-1.** (*U*) [perspiration] suor *m* **-2.** (*U*) *inf*

[hard work] trabalheira *f* **-3.** *inf* [state of anxiety] suador *m*; **to be in a cold ~** suar frio. ◇ *vi* **-1.** [perspire] suar **-2.** *inf* [worry] preocupar-se com.

sweatband ['swetbænd] *n* **-1.** [for wrist] munhequeira *f* **-2.** [for head] faixa *f* para cabeça.

sweater ['swetə^r] *n* suéter *m*.

sweatshirt ['swetʃɜːt] *n* moletom *m*.

sweatshop ['swetʃɒp] *n estabelecimento que oferece más condições de trabalho e baixos salários aos empregados*.

sweaty ['swetɪ] (*compar* **-ier**, *superl* **-iest**) *adj* **-1.** [skin, clothes] suado(f da) **-2.** [place] abafado(f da) **-3.** [activity] exaustivo(f va).

swede [swi:d] *n UK* rutabaga *f*.

Swede [swi:d] *n* sueco *m*, -ca *f*.

Sweden ['swi:dn] *n* Suécia; **in ~ na** Suécia.

Swedish ['swi:dɪʃ] *adj* sueco(ca). ◇ *n* [language] sueco *m*. ◇ *npl*: **the ~** os suecos.

sweep [swi:p] (*pt & pp* **swept**) *n* **-1.** [sweeping movement] movimento *m* (circular) **-2.** [with brush] varrida *f* **-3.** [electronic examination] varredura *f* **-4.** [chimneysweep] limpador *m*, -ra *f* de chaminé. ◇ *vt* **-1.** [gen] varrer **-2.** [with eyes] examinar **-3.** [spread through] disseminar **-4.** [for bugs or bombs] vasculhar, examinar **-5.** [force] arrastar; **to ~ sb off his/her feet** abarrotar o coração dele/dela **-6.** [push with hand] afastar; **she swept the papers off her desk** ela tirou os papéis do escritório. ◇ *vi* **-1.** [wind, rain] precipitar-se **-2.** [vehicle] ir a toda velocidade **-3.** [emotion, laughter, rumour] espalhar-se; **fear swept through the crowd** o medo se espalhou pela multidão **-4.** [walk quickly] passar como um raio.

➼ **sweep aside** *vt sep* afastar.

➼ **sweep away** *vt sep* varrer do mapa.

➼ **sweep up** ◇ *vt sep & vi* escovar.

sweeper ['swi:pə^r] *n* FTBL líbero *m*.

sweeping ['swi:pɪŋ] *adj* **-1.** [effect] radical **-2.** [statement] muito genérico(ca) **-3.** [curve] amplo(pla).

sweepstake ['swi:psteɪk] *n loteria que se baseia nas corridas de cavalo*.

sweet [swi:t] *adj* **-1.** [gen] doce **-2.** [smell] doce, perfumado(da) **-3.** [sound] doce, melodioso(sa) **-4.** [gentle, kind] amável; **that's very ~ of you** é muita gentileza de sua parte **-5.** [attractive] meigo(ga). ◇ *n UK* **-1.** [candy] doce *m* **-2.** [dessert] sobremesa *f*.

sweet-and-sour *adj* agridoce.

sweet corn *n (U)* milho *m* verde.

sweeten ['swi:tn] *vt* adoçar.

sweetener ['swi:tnə^r] *n* **-1.** [substance] adoçante *m* **-2.** *inf fig* [bribe] suborno *m*.

sweetheart ['swi:thɑːt] *n* **-1.** [term of endearment] querido *m*, -da *f* **-2.** [boyfriend or girlfriend] namorado *m*, -da *f*.

sweetness ['swi:tnɪs] *n (U)* **-1.** [gen] doçura *f* **-2.** [of feelings] prazer *f* **-3.** [of smell] aroma *f* **-4.** [of sound] melodia *f*.

sweet pea *n* ervilha-de-cheiro *f*.

sweet potato *n* batata-doce *f*.

sweet shop *n UK* confeitaria *f*.

sweet-talk *vt*: **to ~ sb (into doing sthg)** levar alguém na conversa (para fazer algo).

sweet tooth *n inf:* to have a ~ ser louco(ca) por doce.

swell [swel] (*pt* -ed, *pp* swollen *OR* -ed) *vi* -1. [become larger]: to ~ (up) inchar -2. [fill with air] inflar -3. [increase in number] aumentar -4. [become louder] intensificar-se -5. [with pride] encher-se. <> *vt* aumentar. <> *n* elevação *f;* sea ~ vaivém *m* do mar. <> *adj US inf* genial, excelente.

swelling ['swelɪŋ] *n* -1. (*U*) [swollenness] inchamento *m* -2. [swollen area] inchaço *m.*

sweltering ['sweltərɪŋ] *adj* -1. [weather] abafado(da) -2. [person] sufocado(da).

swept [swept] *pt & pp* ⊳ sweep.

swerve [swɜːv] *vi* -1. [car, lorry] dar uma guinada -2. [person] desviar repentinamente.

swift [swɪft] *adj* -1. [fast] veloz -2. [prompt, ready] rápido(da). <> *n* [bird] andorinhão *m* preto.

swiftly ['swɪftlɪ] *adj* -1. [rapidly] velozmente -2. [without delay] rapidamente.

swiftness ['swɪftnɪs] *n* (*U*) rapidez *f.*

swig [swɪg] (*pt & pp* -ged, *cont* -ging) *inf vt* beber a grandes goles. <> *n* trago *m.*

swill [swɪl] *n* (*U*) lavagem *f.* <> *vt UK* enxaguar.

swim [swɪm] (*pt* swam, *pp* swum, *cont* -ming) *n* banho *m (de mar, de piscina)*; to have a ~ nadar; to go for a ~ ir nadar *OR* tomar banho *(de mar, de piscina)*. <> *vi* -1. [move through water] nadar; can you ~? você sabe nadar? -2. [feel dizzy] dar voltas; my head was ~ming minha cabeça estava girando.

swimmer ['swɪmə^r] *n* nadador *m,* -ra *f.*

swimming ['swɪmɪŋ] *n* [bathing] natação *f;* to go ~ ir nadar.

swimming baths *npl UK* piscina *f* pública coberta.

swimming cap *n* touca *f* de natação.

swimming costume *n UK* traje *m* de banho.

swimming pool *n* piscina *f.*

swimming trunks *npl* sunga *m.*

swimsuit ['swɪmsuːt] *n* traje *m* de banho.

swindle ['swɪndl] *n* logro *m,* fraude *f.* <> *vt* lograr; to ~ sb out of sthg lograr alguém em algo.

swine [swaɪn] *n inf pej* [person] porco *m,* -ca *f.*

swing [swɪŋ] (*pt & pp* swung) *n* -1. [child's toy] balanço *m* -2. [change] virada *f,* mudança *f* -3. [swaying movement] rebolado *m* -4. *inf* [blow]: to take a ~ at sb dar um golpe em alguém -5. *phr:* to be in full ~ estar a todo vapor; to get into the ~ of sthg entrar no ritmo de algo. <> *vt* -1. [move back and forth] balançar -2. [turn] virar bruscamente. <> *vi* -1. [move back and forth] balançar -2. [turn] girar; to ~ open abrir-se -3. [hit out]: to ~ at sb dar um golpe em alguém -4. [change] virar, mudar.

swing bridge *n* ponte *f* giratória.

swing door *n* porta *f* corrediça.

swingeing ['swɪndʒɪŋ] *adj* severo(ra).

swinging ['swɪŋɪŋ] *adj inf* -1. [party] divertido(da), alegre -2. [era, lifestyle] descontraído(da).

swipe [swaɪp] <> *n:* to take a ~ at sb/sthg tentar bater em algo/alguém. <> *vt* -1. *inf* [steal] roubar -2. [plastic card] passar. <> *vi:* to ~ at sthg tentar golpear algo.

swirl [swɜːl] <> *n* -1. [swirling movement] rodopio *m* -2. [eddy] redemoinho *m.* <> *vt* girar como um redemoinho. <> *vi* girar.

swish [swɪʃ] <> *adj inf* [posh] bacana. <> *n* [movement - of dress] ruge-ruge *m*; [- of tail] meneio *m.* <> *vt* [tail] balançar, agitar. <> *vi* [move] menear.

Swiss [swɪs] <> *adj* suíço(ça). <> *n* [person] suíço *m,* -ça *f.* <> *npl:* the ~ os suíços.

Swiss chard *n* acelga *f.*

swiss roll *n UK* rocambole *m.*

switch [swɪtʃ] <> *n* -1. [control device] chave *f,* interruptor *m* -2. [change] mudança *f,* virada *f* -3. *US RAIL* desvio *m.* <> *vt* -1. [transfer] trocar; to ~ one's attention to sthg dirigir a atenção a algo -2. [swap, exchange] trocar de; to ~ sthg round trocar algo de lugar. <> *vi* [transfer] trocar; to ~ to/from sthg transferir para/de algo.

⟐ **switch off** <> *vt sep* desligar. <> *vi inf* [person] desconcentrar-se.

⟐ **switch on** *vt sep* ligar.

Switch® [swɪtʃ] *n UK* cartão de débito automático *Switch.*

switchblade ['swɪtʃbleɪd] *n US* canivete *m.*

switchboard ['swɪtʃbɔːd] *n* mesa *f* telefônica.

switchboard operator *n* telefonista *mf.*

switched-on *adj inf* [person] antenado(da).

Switzerland ['swɪtsələnd] *n* Suíça; in ~ na Suíça.

swivel ['swɪvl] (*UK pt & pp* -led, *cont* -ling, *US pt & pp* -ed, *cont* -ing) *vt & vi* girar.

swivel chair *n* cadeira *f* giratória.

swollen ['swəʊln] <> *pp* ⊳ swell. <> *adj* -1. [ankle, arm] inchado(da) -2. [river] cheio (cheia).

swoon [swuːn] *vi literary or hum* desmaiar.

swoop [swuːp] <> *n* -1. [downward flight] arremetida *f;* in one fell ~ de uma só vez -2. [raid] ataque -surpresa *m.* <> *vi* -1. [fly downwards] precipitar-se, mergulhar -2. [pounce] atacar de surpresa.

swop [swɒp] *n, vt & vi* = swap.

sword [sɔːd] *n* espada *f;* to cross ~s (with sb) discutir (com alguém).

swordfish ['sɔːdfɪʃ] (*pl inv OR* -es) *n* peixe-espada *m.*

swordsman ['sɔːdzmən] (*pl* -men [-mən]) *n* esgrimista *m,* espadachim *m.*

swore [swɔː^r] *pt* ⊳ swear.

sworn [swɔːn] <> *pp* ⊳ swear. <> *adj* -1. [committed]: to be ~ enemies ser inimigos declarados -2. *JUR* sob juramento.

swot [swɒt] (*pt & pp* -ted, *cont* -ting) *UK inf* <> *n pej* cê-dê-efe *mf.* <> *vi:* to ~ (for sthg) matar-se de estudar (para algo).

⟐ **swot up** *inf* <> *vt sep* matar-se de estudar. <> *vi:* to ~ up (on sthg) matar-se de estudar (algo).

swum [swʌm] *pp* ⊳ swim.

swung [swʌŋ] *pt & pp* ⊳ swing.

sycamore ['sɪkəmɔː^r] *n* falso-plátano *m.*

sycophant ['sɪkəfænt] *n* bajulador *m,* -ra *f.*

Sydney ['sɪdnɪ] *n* Sydney.

syllable ['sɪləbl] *n* sílaba *f.*

syllabub ['sɪləbʌb] *n* doce feito de creme, claras de ovos e vinho ou suco de frutas.

syllabus ['sɪləbəs] (pl **-buses** OR **-bi** [-baɪ]) n programa m da disciplina.

symbol ['sɪmbl] n símbolo m.

symbolic [sɪm'bɒlɪk] adj simbólico(ca); **to be ~ of** sthg ser símbolo de algo.

symbolism ['sɪmbəlɪzm] n (U) simbolismo m.

symbolize, -ise ['sɪmbəlaɪz] vt simbolizar.

symmetrical [sɪ'metrɪkl] adj simétrico(ca).

symmetry ['sɪmətrɪ] n (U) simetria f.

sympathetic [ˌsɪmpə'θetɪk] adj **-1.** [understanding] compreensivo(va) **-2.** [willing to support] favorável; **~ to** sthg favorável a algo **-3.** [likable] simpático(ca), agradável.

sympathize, -ise ['sɪmpəθaɪz] vi **-1.** [feel sorry] compadecer-se; **to ~ with** sb solidarizar-se com alguém, compadecer-se de alguém **-2.** [understand] compreender; **to ~ with** sthg compreender algo **-3.** [support]: **to ~ with** sthg apoiar algo.

sympathizer, -iser ['sɪmpəθaɪzə'] n simpatizante mf.

sympathy ['sɪmpəθɪ] n **-1.** [understanding] empatia f; **~ for** sb empatia por alguém **-2.** [agreement] simpatia f; **in ~ (with** sthg) de acordo (com algo) **-3.** [support]: **in ~** em solidariedade; **in ~ with** sb em solidariedade a alguém.

➡ **sympathies** npl **-1.** [approval] simpatias fpl **-2.** [condolences] pêsames mpl.

symphonic [sɪm'fɒnɪk] adj sinfônico(ca).

symphony ['sɪmfənɪ] (pl **-ies**) n sinfonia f.

symphony orchestra n orquestra f sinfônica.

symposium [sɪm'pəʊzjəm] (pl **-siums** OR **-sia** [-zjəl] n fml simpósio m.

symptom ['sɪmptəm] n sintoma m.

symptomatic [ˌsɪmptə'mætɪk] adj sintomático(ca); **to be ~ of** sthg ser um sintoma de algo.

synagogue ['sɪnəgɒg] n sinagoga f.

sync [sɪŋk] n (U) inf: **out of ~** fora de sincronia; **in ~** sincronizado(da).

synchronize, -ise ['sɪŋkrənaɪz] vt, vi sincronizar.

synchronized swimming ['sɪŋkrənaɪzd-] n (U) nado m sincronizado.

syncopated ['sɪŋkəpeɪtɪd] adj sincopado(da).

syncopation [ˌsɪŋkə'peɪʃn] n (U) síncope f.

syndicate [n 'sɪndɪkət, vb 'sɪndɪkeɪt] <> n sindicato m. <> vt PRESS distribuir em cadeia.

syndrome ['sɪndrəʊm] n síndrome f.

synergy (pl **-ies**) n sinergia f.

synod n sínodo m.

synonym ['sɪnənɪm] n sinônimo m; **~ for** OR **of** sthg sinônimo para OR de algo.

synonymous [sɪ'nɒnɪməs] adj **-1.** [having the same meaning] sinônimo(ma) **-2.** [associated]: **~ with** sthg sinônimo de algo.

synopsis [sɪ'nɒpsɪs] (pl **-ses** [-si:z]) n sinopse f.

syntax ['sɪntæks] n LING sintaxe f.

synthesis ['sɪnθəsɪs] (pl **-ses** [-si:z]) n síntese f.

synthesize, -ise ['sɪnθəsaɪz] vt sintetizar.

synthesizer ['sɪnθəsaɪzə'] n MUS sintetizador m.

synthetic [sɪn'θetɪk] adj **-1.** [man-made] sintético(ca) **-2.** pej [insincere] artificial.

syphilis ['sɪfɪlɪs] n (U) sífilis f inv.

syphon ['saɪfn] n & vt = siphon.

Syria ['sɪrɪə] n Síria f; **in ~** na Síria.

Syrian ['sɪrɪən] <> adj sírio(ria). <> n sírio m, -ria f.

syringe [sɪ'rɪndʒ] (cont **syringeing** OR **syringing**) <> n seringa f. <> vt lavar, limpar.

syrup ['sɪrəp] n (U) **-1.** [sugar and water] calda f **-2.** UK [golden syrup] melado m **-3.** [medicine] xarope m.

system ['sɪstəm] n **-1.** [gen] sistema m **-2.** [network, structure - road] rede f; [- railway] malha f **-3.** inf [government]: **the ~** o sistema **-4.** (U) [methodical approach] sistemática f **-5.** phr: **to get** sthg **out of one's ~** inf parar de se preocupar com algo.

systematic [ˌsɪstə'mætɪk] adj sistemático(ca).

systematize, -ise ['sɪstəmətaɪz] vt UK sistematizar.

system disk n COMPUT disco m de sistema.

systems analyst ['sɪstəmz-] n COMPUT analista mf de sistemas.

systems engineer ['sɪstəmz-] n COMPUT engenheiro m, -ra f de sistemas.

system software n COMPUT software m de sistema.

t (pl **t's** OR **ts**), **T** (pl **T's** OR **Ts**) [ti:] n t, T m.

ta [tɑ:] excl UK inf brigado(da!); **~ very much** brigado(da)!

TA (abbr of **Territorial Army**) n organização militar britânica de pessoas que não são membros regulares do exército.

tab [tæb] n **-1.** [of cloth] etiqueta f **-2.** [of metal] lingüeta f **-3.** US [bill] conta f; **to pick up the ~** pagar a conta **-4.** (abbr of **tabulator**) [on keyboard] (tecla f) tab m **-5.** phr: **to keep ~s on** sb ficar de olho em alguém.

tabby ['tæbɪ] (pl **-ies**) n: **~ (cat)** gato m tigrado.

tabernacle ['tæbənækl] n tabernáculo m.

tab key n tecla f tab.

table ['teɪbl] <> n **-1.** [piece of furniture] mesa f **-2.** [diagram] tabela f **-3.** phr: **to turn the ~s on** sb inverter as posições com alguém. <> vt **-1.** UK [propose] apresentar **-2.** US [postpone] adiar.

tableau ['tæbləʊ] (pl **-x** ['tæbləʊz], **-s**) n quadro m vivo.

tablecloth ['teɪblklɒθ] n toalha f de mesa.

table d'hôte ['tɑ:bl,dəʊt] n: **the ~** o cardápio do dia.

table football n pebolim m.

table lamp n luminária f.

table licence n licença para venda de bebidas alcoólicas apenas com a refeição.

table linen n (U) roupa f de mesa.
table manners npl modos mpl à mesa.
table mat n descanço m para panelas.
table of contents n sumário m.
table salt n (U) sal m de mesa.
tablespoon ['teiblspu:n] n -1. [spoon] colher f (de sopa) -2. [spoonful] colherada f de sopa.
tablet ['tæblɪt] n -1. [pill] comprimido m, pastilha f -2. [piece of stone] pedra f lascada -3. [piece of soap] barra f.
table tennis n (U) tênis m inv de mesa.
tableware n (U) utensílios mpl de mesa.
table wine n (U) vinho m de mesa.
tabloid ['tæblɔɪd] n: ~ (newspaper) tablóide m; the ~ press a imprensa sensacionalista.

TABLOID

Nos países anglo-saxões, o formato pequeno, ou tablóide, é característico dos jornais sensacionalistas. No Reino Unido, são publicações diárias desse tipo o *Daily Express*, o *Daily Mail*, *Daily Mirror*, *The Star* e *The Sun*. Nos Estados Unidos, esse tipo de jornal também existe, embora sua publicação seja, em geral, semanal. Os mais conhecidos são *The National Enquirer*, *The Star* e *The Globe*.

---

taboo [tə'bu:] (pl -s) <> adj tabu. <> n tabu m.
tabulate ['tæbjʊleɪt] vt dispor em formato de tabela.
tachograph ['tækəgrɑːf] n tacógrafo m.
tachometer [tæ'kɒmɪtə'] n tacômetro m.
tacit ['tæsɪt] adj fml tácito(ta).
taciturn ['tæsɪtɜːn] adj fml taciturno(na).
tack [tæk] <> n -1. [nail] tacha f -2. NAUT rumo m -3. fig [course of action] tática f; **to change** ~ mudar de tática. <> vt -1. [fasten with nail] afixar (com tachas) -2. [in sewing] alinhavar. <> vi NAUT virar.
⬥ **tack on** vt sep inf [add as afterthought] anexar.
tackle ['tækl] <> n -1. FTBL entrada f -2. RUGBY obstrução f -3. [equipment, gear] apetrechos mpl -4. [for lifting] guincho m. <> vt -1. [job] lidar com -2. [problem] atacar -3. FTBL roubar a bola de -4. RUGBY derrubar -5. [attack] enfrentar -6. [talk to]: **to** ~ **sb about** OR **on sthg** pegar alguém para falar sobre algo.
tacky ['tækɪ] (compar -ier, superl -iest) adj -1. inf [cheap and nasty] barato(ta) -2. [sticky] grudento(ta), pegajoso(sa).
taco ['tækəʊl] (pl -s) n taco m.
tact [tækt] n (U) tato m.
tactful ['tæktfʊl] adj discreto(ta); **that wasn't very** ~ **of you** você não agiu com muito tato.
tactfully ['tæktfʊlɪ] adv discretamente.
tactic ['tæktɪk] n tática f.
⬥ **tactics** n MIL tática f.
tactical ['tæktɪkl] adj -1. [gen] estratégico(ca) -2. MIL tático(ca).
tactical voting n (U) UK votação f tática.
tactile adj tátil.
tactless ['tæktlɪs] adj indiscreto(ta); **he's so** ~ falta tato nele.
tactlessly ['tæktlɪslɪ] adv indiscretamente.
tadpole ['tædpəʊl] n girino m.

Tadzhikistan [tɑːˌdʒɪkɪ'stɑːn] n Tadjiquistão; **in** ~ no Tadjiquistão.
taffeta ['tæfɪtə] n (U) tafetá m.
taffy ['tæfɪ] (pl -ies) n US puxa-puxa m.
tag [tæg] (pt & pp -ged, cont -ging) <> n -1. [gen] etiqueta f -2. (U) [game] pega-pega f -3. COMPUT tag f, marca f. <> vt etiquetar.
⬥ **tag along** vi inf: **she always has to** ~ **along** ela sempre tem de vir junto.
Tagus n: **the** ~ o Tejo.
Tahiti [tɑː'hiːtɪ] n Taiti; **in** ~ no Taiti.
Tahitian <> adj taitiano(na). <> n taitiano m, -na f.
tail [teɪl] <> n -1. [gen] rabo m; **with one's** ~ **between one's legs** [person] com o rabo entre as pernas -2. [of coat, shirt] fralda f -3. [of comet, plane] cauda f -4. [of car] parte f traseira. <> comp [rear] traseiro(ra). <> vt inf ir atrás de.
⬥ **tails** <> adv [when tossing a coin] coroa f. <> npl [coat] fraque m.
⬥ **tail off** vi diminuir.
tailback ['teɪlbæk] n UK fila f (de carros).
tailcoat ['teɪlˌkəʊt] n fraque m.
tail end n final m, parte f final.
tailgate ['teɪlgeɪt] n tampa f traseira.
taillight ['teɪlaɪt] n luz f traseira.
tailor ['teɪlə'] <> n alfaiate m. <> vt adaptar.
tailored ['teɪləd] adj [well-fitting] feito(ta) sob medida.
tailor-made adj fig [role, job] sob medida.
tail pipe n US cano m de descarga.
tailplane ['teɪlpleɪn] n leme m (do avião).
tailwind ['teɪlwɪnd] n vento m de cauda.
taint [teɪnt] <> n mancha f. <> vt manchar.
tainted ['teɪntɪd] adj -1. [reputation] manchado(da) -2. US [food] estragado(da).
Taiwan [ˌtaɪ'wɑːn] n Taiwan; **in** ~ em Taiwan.
Taiwanese [ˌtaɪwə'niːz] <> adj taiwanês(esa). <> n taiwanês m, -esa f.
take [teɪk] (pt took, pp taken) <> vt -1. [gen] levar -2. [accompany] levar, acompanhar -3. [capture, undergo, swallow, measure] tomar -4. [receive] receber; **to** ~ **a seat** sentar-se; **to** ~ **control/command** tomar o controle/comando -5. [rent] alugar -6. [object, hand, road, means of transport] pegar -7. [accept, take on] aceitar; ~ **my word for it** acredita em mim; **what batteries does it** ~? que pilha vai aí? -8. [contain] suportar -9. [bear] agüentar -10. [require] precisar; **it could** ~ **years** pode levar anos -11. [holiday] tirar; **to** ~ **a walk** dar uma caminhada; **to** ~ **a bath** tomar um banho; **to** ~ **a photo** tirar OR bater uma foto -12. [pity, interest] ter; **to** ~ **offence** ofender-se; **I** ~ **the view that** ... sou da opinião de que ...; **to** ~ **sthg seriously/badly** levar algo a sério/a mal -13. [wear as a particular size - shoe] calçar; [- dress] vestir -14. [consider] pensar em, considerar -15. [assume]: **I** ~ **it (that)** ... presumo que ... <> vi [have intended effect - dye] tingir; [- fire] prender. <> n TOMADA f.
⬥ **take aback** vt sep surpreender; **to be taken aback** ficar espantado(da).
⬥ **take after** vt fus parecer-se com.
⬥ **take apart** vt sep desmontar.
⬥ **take away** vt sep -1. [remove] levar embora

- 2. [deduct] subtrair, tirar.

● **take back** *vt sep* **-1.** [return] devolver **- 2.** [accept] aceitar de volta **- 3.** [statement, accusation] retirar.

● **take down** *vt sep* **-1.** [dismantle] desmontar **- 2.** [write down] escrever, tomar nota de **- 3.** [lower] baixar.

● **take in** *vt sep* **-1.** [deceive] enganar **- 2.** [understand] compreender **- 3.** [include] incluir **- 4.** [provide accommodation for] acolher.

● **take off** ◇ *vt sep* **-1.** [remove] tirar **- 2.** [have as holiday] tirar de folga; **she took the afternoon off** ela tirou a tarde de folga; **to ~ time off** tirar uma folga **- 3.** *UK inf* [imitate] imitar **- 4.** *inf* [go away suddenly]: **to ~ o.s. off** mandar-se (embora). ◇ *vi* **-1.** [gen] decolar **- 2.** [go away suddenly] mandar-se (embora), ir-se embora.

● **take on** ◇ *vt sep* **-1.** [accept - work, job] aceitar; [- responsibility] assumir **- 2.** [employ] admitir **- 3.** [confront] desafiar. ◇ *vt fus* [assume, develop] adquirir.

● **take out** *vt sep* **-1.** [from container] tirar **- 2.** [delete] suprimir, tirar **- 3.** [go out with] convidar para sair **- 4.** *phr*: **to ~ it** *OR* **a lot out of one** *inf* esgotar alguém.

● **take out on** *vt sep* descarregar em, descontar em.

● **take over** ◇ *vt sep* **-1.** [take control of] tomar o controle de, assumir **- 2.** [job, role] assumir. ◇ *vi* **-1.** [take control] tomar o poder **- 2.** [in job] assumir.

● **take to** *vt fus* **-1.** [feel a liking for - person] ter afeição especial por; [- activity] gostar de **- 2.** [begin]: **to ~ to doing sthg** começar a fazer algo.

● **take up** *vt fus* **-1.** [begin - acting, singing] começar a se dedicar a; [- post, job] assumir **- 2.** [continue] prosseguir **- 3.** [discuss further] voltar a discutir **- 4.** [use up - time] tomar; [- space] ocupar; [- effort] exigir.

● **take up on** *vt sep* **-1.** [an offer] aceitar **- 2.** [ask to explain]: **I'd like to ~ you up on that point** gostaria que você explicasse melhor esse ponto.

● **take upon** *vt sep*: **to ~ it upon o.s. to do sthg** permitir-se fazer algo.

takeaway *UK* ['teɪkə,weɪ], **takeout** *US* ['teɪkaʊt] ◇ *n* **-1.** [shop] *estabelecimento que vende comida para levar* **- 2.** [food] comida *f* para levar. ◇ *comp* [food] para levar.

take-home pay *n (U)* salário *m* líquido.

taken ['teɪkn] ◇ *pp* ▷ **take**. ◇ *adj* [pleased]: **~ with sb/sthg** contente com alguém/algo.

takeoff ['teɪkɒf] *n* decolagem *f*.

takeout *n US* = **takeaway**.

takeover ['teɪk,əʊvəʳ] *n* **-1.** [of company] aquisição *f* **- 2.** [of government] tomada *f* do poder.

takeover bid *n* oferta *f* pública de compra de ações.

taker ['teɪkəʳ] *n* interessado *m*, -da *f*.

takeup ['teɪkʌp] *n* [of shares] resposta *f*.

taking *adj dated* gracioso(sa).

takings *npl* féria *f*, arrecadação *f*.

talc [tælk], **talcum (powder)** ['tælkəm-] *n (U)* talco *m*.

tale [teɪl] *n* **-1.** [fictional story] conto *m* **- 2.** [anecdote] história *f*.

talent ['tælənt] *n*: **~ (for sthg)** talento *m* (para algo).

talented ['tæləntɪd] *adj* talentoso(sa).

talent scout *n* caçador *m*, -ra *f* de talentos.

talisman ['tælɪzmən] (*pl* **-s**) *n* talismã *m*.

talk [tɔːk] ◇ *n* **-1.** [conversation] conversa *f* **- 2.** *(U)* [gossip] boatos *mpl*, falatório *m* **- 3.** [lecture] palestra *f*. ◇ *vi* **-1.** [gen] falar; **to ~ to sb** falar *OR* conversar com alguém; **to ~ about sb/sthg** falar sobre alguém/algo; **~ing of sb/sthg, ...** falando de alguém/algo, ..., por falar em alguém/algo, ...; **to ~ big** contar vantagem **- 2.** [gossip] fofocar **- 3.** [make a speech] dar palestra; **to ~ on** *OR* **about sthg** falar sobre algo. ◇ *vt* **-1.** [discuss] tratar de **- 2.** [spout] falar.

● **talks** *npl* negociações *fpl*.

● **talk down to** *vt fus* desmerecer.

● **talk into** *vt sep*: **to ~ sb into sthg/into doing sthg** convencer alguém de algo/a fazer algo.

● **talk out of** *vt sep*: **to ~ sb out of sthg/out of doing sthg** dissuadir alguém de algo/de fazer algo.

● **talk over** *vt sep* discutir.

talkative ['tɔːkətɪv] *adj* loquaz.

talker ['tɔːkəʳ] *n* orador *m*, -ra *f*.

talking point ['tɔːkɪŋ-] *n* tema *m* da conversa.

talking-to ['tɔːkɪŋ-] *n inf* bronca *f*.

talk show *US* ◇ *n* programa *m* de entrevistas, talk-show *m*. ◇ *comp* de programa de entrevistas.

talk time *n (U)* [on mobile phone] tempo *m* de conversação.

tall [tɔːl] *adj* [in height] alto(ta); **she's two metres ~** ela mede dois metros (de altura); **how ~ are you?** qual é a sua altura?

tallboy ['tɔːlbɔɪ] *n* cômoda *f*.

tall order *n* tarefa *f* impossível.

tall story *n* história *f* fantasiosa.

tally ['tælɪ] (*pl* **-ies**, *pt* & *pp* **-ied**) ◇ *n* [record] conta *f*; **to keep a ~ of sthg** manter registro de algo. ◇ *vi* [correspond] fechar.

talon ['tælən] *n* garra *f*.

tambourine [,tæmbə'riːn] *n* pandeiro *m*.

tame [teɪm] ◇ *adj* **-1.** [animal, bird] domesticado(da) **- 2.** *pej* [person] parado(da) **- 3.** *pej* [unexciting] monótono(na). ◇ *vt* **-1.** [animal, bird] domesticar **- 2.** [person] dominar.

tamely ['teɪmlɪ] *adv* docilmente.

tamer ['teɪməʳ] *n* domador *m*, -ra *f*.

Tamil ['tæmɪl] ◇ *adj* tâmil. ◇ *n* **-1.** [person] tâmil *mf* **- 2.** [language] tâmil *m*.

tamper ['tæmpəʳ] ● **tamper with** *vt fus* **-1.** [gen] mexer em **- 2.** [lock] forçar.

tampon ['tæmpɒn] *n* absorvente *m* interno.

tan [tæn] (*pt* & *pp* **-ned**, *cont* **-ning**) ◇ *adj* castanho(nha). ◇ *n* bronzeado *m*; **to get a ~** bronzear-se. ◇ *vi* bronzear-se.

tandem ['tændəm] *n* [bicycle] bicicleta *f* de dois lugares; **in ~** em colaboração com.

tandoori [tæn'dʊərɪ] ◇ *n (U)* *método indiano de assar a carne em forno de barro*. ◇ *comp* cozido(da) em forno de barro.

tang [tæŋ] n [smell] cheiro m forte; [taste] gosto m forte.

tangent ['tændʒənt] n GEOM tangente f; **to go off at a ~** fig sair pela tangente.

tangerine [ˌtændʒə'riːn] n tangerina f.

tangible ['tændʒəbl] adj tangível.

Tangier [tæn'dʒɪə^r] n Tânger.

tangle ['tæŋgl] <> n -1. [mass] emaranhado m -2. fig [mess] rolo m; **they got into a ~** eles se meteram num rolo. <> vt: **to get ~d (up)** emaranhar-se. <> vi emaranhar-se.
➣ **tangle with** vt fus inf meter-se com.

tangled ['tæŋgld] adj -1. [gen] emaranhado(da) -2. fig [life, relationship] enrolado(da).

tango ['tæŋgəʊ] (pl -s, pt & pp -ed, cont -ing) <> n tango m. <> vi dançar tango.

tangy ['tæŋɪ] (compar -ier, superl -iest) adj forte.

tank [tæŋk] n tanque m.

tankard ['tæŋkəd] n canecão m (para cerveja).

tanker ['tæŋkə^r] n -1. [ship] navio-tanque m; oil ~ petroleiro m -2. [truck] caminhão-tanque m -3. [train] vagão-tanque m.

tankful ['tæŋkfʊl] n tanque m.

tanned [tænd] adj bronzeado(da).

tannin ['tænɪn] n (U) tanino m.

Tannoy® ['tænɔɪ] n alto-falante m.

tantalize, -ise ['tæntəlaɪz] vt tentar, provocar.

tantalizing ['tæntəlaɪzɪŋ] adj tentador(ra).

tantamount ['tæntəmaʊnt] adj: ~ **to sthg** equivalente a algo.

tantrum ['tæntrəm] (pl -s) n acesso m de fúria.

Tanzania [ˌtænzə'nɪə] n Tanzânia; **in ~** na Tanzânia.

Tanzanian [ˌtænzə'nɪən] <> adj tanzaniano(na). <> n tanzaniano m, -na f.

Taoiseach n primeiro ministro da República da Irlanda.

tap [tæp] (pt & pp -ped, cont -ping) <> n -1. [device] torneira f -2. [light blow] batida f leve, palmadinha f. <> vt -1. [knock] bater de leve; **to ~ one's fingers on sthg** tamborilar em algo -2. [make use of] utilizar -3. [listen secretly to] grampear. <> vi bater.

tap dance n sapateado m.

tap dancer n sapateador m, -ra f.

tape [teɪp] <> n -1. [gen] fita f -2. SPORT [at finishing line] fita f de chegada -3. [adhesive material] fita f adesiva. <> vt -1. [record] gravar -2. [fasten with adhesive tape] juntar com fita adesiva -3. US [bandage] enfaixar.

tape deck n deck m.

tape measure n fita f métrica.

taper ['teɪpə^r] <> n vela f fina. <> vi estreitar-se, afilar-se.
➣ **taper off** vi ir diminuindo.

tape-record [-rɪˌkɔːd] vt gravar.

tape recorder n gravador m.

tape recording n gravação f.

tapered ['teɪpəd] adj afilado(da).

tapestry ['tæpɪstrɪ] (pl -ies) n -1. [gen] tapeçaria f -2. fig [of life] trama f.

tapeworm ['teɪpwɜːm] n solitária f.

tapioca [ˌtæpɪ'əʊkə] n (U) tapioca f.

tapir ['teɪpə^r] (pl inv OR -s) n anta f, tapir m.

tappet n tucho m.

tar [tɑː^r] n (U) alcatrão m.

tarantula [tə'ræntjʊlə] n tarântula f.

target ['tɑːgɪt] <> n -1. [gen] alvo m -2. fig [goal] meta f; **to be on ~ to do sthg** fazer algo de acordo com o previsto. <> vt -1. [as object of attack] mirar -2. [as customer] visar.

tariff ['tærɪf] n -1. [tax] tarifa f -2. UK [price list] tabela f de preços.

Tarmac® ['tɑːmæk] n alcatrão m.
➣ **tarmac** n AERON: **the tarmac** a pista.

tarnish ['tɑːnɪʃ] <> vt -1. [make dull] embaciar -2. fig [damage] manchar. <> vi [become dull] embaciar.

tarnished ['tɑːnɪʃt] adj -1. [dull] embaciado(da) -2. fig [damaged] manchado(da).

tarot ['tærəʊ] n: **the ~** o tarô.

tarot card n carta f de tarô.

tarpaulin [tɑː'pɔːlɪn] n -1. (U) [material] encerado m -2. [sheet] lona f alcatroada.

tarragon ['tærəgən] n (U) estragão m.

tart [tɑːt] <> adj -1. [bitter-tasting] azedo(da) -2. [sarcastic] mordaz. <> n -1. [sweet pastry] torta f -2. UK vinf [prostitute] piranha f.
➣ **tart up** vt sep UK inf pej [smarten up]: **to ~ o.s. up** emperiquitar-se.

tartan ['tɑːtn] <> n -1. [pattern] xadrez m -2. (U) [cloth] tartan m. <> comp de tartan.

tartar n tártaro m.

tartar(e) sauce ['tɑːtə^r-] n (U) molho m tártaro.

tartness ['tɑːtnɪs] n (U) -1. [of taste] acidez f -2. [of comment] mordacidade f.

task [tɑːsk] n tarefa f.

task force n força-tarefa f.

taskmaster ['tɑːskˌmɑːstə^r] n capataz m; **a hard ~** um tirano.

Tasmania [tæz'meɪnjə] n Tasmânia.

Tasmanian [tæz'meɪnjən] <> adj tasmaniano(na). <> n tasmaniano m, -na f.

tassel ['tæsl] n borla f.

taste [teɪst] <> n -1. [gen] gosto m; **in bad/good ~** de mau/bom gosto -2. fig [liking, preference]: ~ **(for sthg)** gosto (por algo) -3. fig [experience]: **I've had a ~ of success** eu senti o gostinho do sucesso -4. (U) [sense of taste] paladar m -5. [try]: **have a ~** dá uma provada. <> vt -1. [gen] sentir o gosto de -2. [test, try] provar. <> vi: **it ~s horrible** tem um gosto horrível; **to ~ of/like sthg** ter gosto de algo.

taste bud n papila f gustativa.

tasteful ['teɪstfʊl] adj de bom gosto.

tastefully ['teɪstfʊlɪ] adv com bom gosto.

tasteless ['teɪstlɪs] adj -1. [cheap and unattractive] sem graça -2. [offensive] de mau gosto -3. [without flavour] sem gosto.

taster ['teɪstə^r] n degustador m, -ra f.

tasty ['teɪstɪ] (compar -ier, superl -iest) adj saboroso(sa).

tat [tæt] n (U) UK inf pej bugigangas fpl.

tattered ['tætəd] adj -1. [clothes] esfarrapado(da) -2. [paper] gasto(ta).

tatters ['tætəz] npl: **in ~** [clothes] em farrapos; fig [confidence, reputation] em frangalhos.

tattle-tale *n US* = telltale.
tattoo [tə'tu:] (*pl* -s) ◇ *n* -1. [design] tatuagem *f* -2. [rhythmic beating] rufar *m* de tambores -3. *UK* [military display] parada *f* OR desfile *m* militar. ◇ *vt* tatuar.
tattooist [tə'tu:ɪst] *n* tatuador *m*, -ra *f*.
tatty ['tætɪ] (*compar* -ier, *superl* -iest) *adj UK inf pej* -1. [clothes] surrado(da) -2. [area] enxovalhado(da).
taught [tɔ:t] *pt* & *pp* ▷ teach.
taunt [tɔ:nt] ◇ *n* insulto *m*. ◇ *vt* insultar.
Taurus ['tɔ:rəs] *n* -1. [sign] Touro *m* -2. [person] taurino(na); **I'm** ~ sou de Touro.
taut [tɔ:t] *adj* retesado(da).
tauten ['tɔ:tn] ◇ *vt* retesar. ◇ *vi* retesar.
tautology [tɔ:'tɒlədʒɪ] *n* tautologia *f*.
tavern ['tævn] *n dated* taberna *f*.
tawdry ['tɔ:drɪ] (*compar* -ier, *superl* -iest) *adj pej* de mau gosto.
tawny ['tɔ:nɪ] *adj* fulvo(va).
tax [tæks] ◇ *n* imposto *m*. ◇ *vt* -1. [gen] tributar -2. [strain, test] esgotar.
taxable ['tæksəbl] *adj* tributável.
tax allowance *n* limite *m* de isenção fiscal.
taxation [tæk'seɪʃn] *n* (U) -1. [system] sistema *m* tributário -2. [amount] tributação *f*.
tax avoidance [-ə'vɔɪdəns] *n* (U) dedução *f* fiscal.
tax collector *n* cobrador *m*, -ra *f* de impostos.
tax cut *n* redução *f* tributária.
tax-deductible [-dɪ'dʌktəbl] *adj* dedutível.
tax disc *n UK* disco fixado no pára-brisa do veículo para mostrar que o imposto já foi pago.
tax evasion *n* (U) sonegação *f* de impostos.
tax-exempt *adj US* = tax-free.
tax exemption *n* (U) isenção *f* de impostos.
tax exile *n UK* pessoa que vive no exterior para evitar o pagamento de impostos.
tax-free *UK*, **tax-exempt** *US adj* isento(ta) de imposto.
tax haven *n* paraíso *m* fiscal.
taxi ['tæksɪ] ◇ *n* táxi *m*. ◇ *vi* taxiar.
taxicab ['tæksɪkæb] *n* táxi *m*.
taxidermist ['tæksɪdɜ:mɪst] *n* empalhador *m*, -ra *f*.
taxi driver *n* motorista *mf* de táxi, taxista *mf*.
taximeter *n* taxímetro *m*.
taxing ['tæksɪŋ] *adj* árduo(a).
tax inspector *n* inspetor *m*, -ra *f* da Receita.
taxi rank *UK*, **taxi stand** *n* ponto *m* de táxi.
taxman ['tæksmæn] (*pl* -men [-men]) *n* -1. [tax collector] coletor *m* de impostos -2. *inf* [tax office]: **the** ~ ≃ o Leão, ≃ o Fisco.
taxpayer ['tæks,peɪə'] *n* contribuinte *mf*.
tax relief *n* (U) dedução *f* tributária.
tax return *n* declaração *f* de renda.
tax year *n* ano *m* fiscal.
TB (*abbr of* **tuberculosis**) *n* tuberculose *f*.
T-bone steak *n* bisteca *f* de boi.
tbs., tbsp. (*abbr of* **tablespoon(ful)**) colher *f* de sopa.
TD *n* -1. (*abbr of* **Treasury Department**) *departamento do tesouro norte-americano* -2. (*abbr of* **touchdown**) *jogada do futebol norte-americano e do rugby*.

tea [ti:] *n* -1. [gen] chá *m* -2. *UK* [afternoon meal] lanche *m* -3. *UK* [evening meal] chá *m*.
teabag ['ti:bæg] *n* saquinho *m* de chá.
tea ball *n US esfera metálica perfurada na qual são colocadas as folhas de chá para infusão.*
tea break *n UK* pausa *f* para o chá.
tea caddy [-,kædɪ] *n* caixa *f* para chá.
teacake ['ti:keɪk] *n UK* bolinho *m* (*que acompanha o chá*).
teach [ti:tʃ] (*pt* & *pp* taught) ◇ *vt* -1. [instruct] ensinar; **to** ~ **sb sthg**, **to** ~ **sthg to sb** ensinar algo a alguém; **to** ~ **sb to do sthg** ensinar alguém a fazer algo; **to** ~ **(sb) that** ensinar (a alguém) que -2. [give lessons in] dar aulas de -3. [advocate] preconizar. ◇ *vi* lecionar.
teacher ['ti:tʃə'] *n* professor *m*, -ra *f*.
teachers college *n US* = teacher training college.
teacher's pet *n pej* queridinho *m*, -nha *f* da classe.
teacher training college *UK*, **teachers college** *US n* curso *f* de licenciatura.
teaching ['ti:tʃɪŋ] *n* -1. (U) [profession, work] magistério *m* -2. [thing taught] ensinamento *m*.
teaching aid *n* material *m* pedagógico.
teaching hospital *n UK* hospital-escola *m*.
teaching practice *n* (U) prática *f* de ensino.
teaching staff *n* corpo *m* docente.
tea cloth *n* -1. [tablecloth] toalha *f* de mesa -2. [tea towel] pano *m* de prato.
tea cosy *UK*, **tea cozy** *US n* abafador *m* (*de chá*).
teacup ['ti:kʌp] *n* xícara *f* de chá.
teak [ti:k] ◇ *n* (U) teca *f*. ◇ *comp* de teca.
tealeaves *npl* borra *f* de chá.
team [ti:m] *n* -1. *SPORT* time *m* -2. [group] equipe *f*.
◆ **team up** *vi* montar uma equipe; **to** ~ **up with sb** associar-se a alguém.
team game *n* esporte *m* de equipe.
teammate ['ti:meɪt] *n* companheiro *m*, -ra *f* de equipe.
team spirit *n* (U) espírito *m* de equipe.
teamster ['ti:mstə'] *n US* caminhoneiro *m*, -ra *f*.
teamwork ['ti:mwɜ:k] *n* (U) trabalho *m* em equipe.
tea party *n* chá *m* da tarde.
teapot ['ti:pɒt] *n* bule *m* de chá.
tear¹ [tɪə'] *n* lágrima *f*; **in** ~ **s** aos prantos; **to burst into** ~ **s** debulhar-se em lágrimas.
tear² [teə'] (*pt* tore, *pp* torn) ◇ *vt* -1. [rip] rasgar; **to** ~ **sthg open** abrir algo rasgando; **to** ~ **sb/sthg to pieces** *fig* [criticize] demolir alguém/algo; **to be torn between** *fig* estar dividido(da) entre -2. [remove roughly] arrancar. ◇ *vi* -1. [rip] rasgar -2. *inf* [move quickly] ir a toda -3. *phr*: **to** ~ **loose** [get free] soltar-se. ◇ *n* [rip] rasgão *m*.
◆ **tear apart** *vt sep* -1. [rip up] destroçar -2. *fig* [disrupt greatly] desmantelar -3. [upset greatly] magoar.
◆ **tear at** *vt fus* avançar contra.
◆ **tear away** *vt sep*: **to** ~ **o.s. away (from sthg)** desvencilhar-se (de algo).
◆ **tear down** *vt sep* -1. [demolish] demolir -2. [remove] remover.
◆ **tear off** *vt sep* [clothes] arrancar.
◆ **tear out** *vt sep* [coupon, page] arrancar.

tear up *vt sep* despedaçar, fazer em pedaços.

tearaway ['teərə,weɪl] *n UK inf* arruaceiro *m*, -ra *f*.

teardrop ['tɪədrɒpl] *n* lágrima *f*.

tearful ['tɪəfʊl] *adj* **-1.** [person] choroso(rosa) **-2.** [event] triste.

tear gas [tɪəʳ-] *n (U)* gás *m* lacrimogêneo.

tearing ['teərɪŋ] *adj inf* apressado(da).

tear jerker *n hum* dramalhão *m*.

tearoom ['ti:rʊm] *n* salão *f* de chá.

tease [ti:z] <> *n inf* **-1.** [joker] gozador *m*, -ra *f* **-2.** [sexually] provocador *m*, -ra *f.* <> *vt*: **to ~ sb (about sthg)** gozar de alguém (sobre algo).

tea shop *n* casa *f* de chá.

teasing ['ti:zɪŋ] *adj* importuno(na).

teaspoon ['ti:spu:n] *n* colher *f* de chá.

tea strainer *n* coador *m* de chá.

teat [ti:t] *n* **-1.** [of animal] teta *f* **-2.** [of bottle] bico *m*.

teatime ['ti:taɪm] *n (U) UK* hora *f* do chá.

tea towel *n* pano *m* de prato.

tea urn *n cilindro dotado de torneira usado para preparar grandes quantidades de chá.*

technical ['teknɪkl] *adj* técnico(ca).

technical college *n UK* escola *f* técnica.

technical drawing *n (U)* desenho *m* técnico.

technicality [,teknɪ'kælətɪ] *(pl* -ies*) n* detalhe *m* técnico.

technically ['teknɪklɪ] *adv* tecnicamente.

technician [tek'nɪʃn] *n* **-1.** [worker] técnico *m*, -ca *f* **-2.** [artist] especialista *mf*.

Technicolor® ['teknɪ,kʌləʳ] *n (U)* tecnicolor® *m*.

technique [tek'ni:k] *n* técnica *f*.

techno ['teknəʊ] *n MUS* tecno *m*.

technocrat ['teknəʊkræt] *n* tecnocrata *mf*.

technological [,teknə'lɒdʒɪkl] *adj* tecnológico(ca).

technologist [tek'nɒlədʒɪst] *n* tecnologista *mf*, tecnólogo *m*, -ga *f*.

technology [tek'nɒlədʒɪ] *(pl* -ies*) n* tecnologia *f*.

teddy ['tedɪ] *(pl* -ies*) n*: **~ (bear)** ursinho *m* de pelúcia.

tedious ['ti:djəs] *adj* tedioso(sa).

tedium ['ti:djəm] *n fml* tédio *m*.

tee [ti:] *n GOLF* **-1.** [area] tee *m*, ponto *m* de partida **-2.** [for ball] tee *m*.

tee off *vi GOLF* dar a tacada inicial.

teem [ti:m] *vi* **-1.** [rain] chover torrencialmente; **the rain ~ed down** caiu uma chuva torrencial **-2.** [be busy]: **to be ~ing with** estar inundado(da) de.

teen [ti:n] *adj inf* adolescente.

teenage ['ti:neɪdʒ] *adj* adolescente.

teenager ['ti:n,eɪdʒəʳ] *n* adolescente *mf*.

teens [ti:nz] *npl* adolescência *f*.

teeny (weeny) [,ti:nɪ('wi:nɪ)], **teensy (weensy)** [,ti:nzɪ('wi:nzɪ)] *adj inf* pequenininho(-nha).

tee shirt *n* camiseta *f*.

teeter ['ti:təʳ] *vi* **-1.** [wobble] balançar, oscilar **-2.** *fig* [be in danger]: **to ~ on the brink of bankruptcy** estar à beira da falência.

teeter-totter *n US* gangorra *f*.

teeth [ti:θ] *pl* ⊳ **tooth**.

teethe [ti:ð] *vi* começar a ter dentes.

teething ring ['ti:ðɪŋ-] *n* mordedor *m*.

teething troubles ['ti:ðɪŋ-] *npl fig* dificuldades *fpl* iniciais.

teetotal [ti:'təʊtl] *adj* abstêmio(mia).

teetotaller *UK*, **teetotaler** *US* [ti:'təʊtləʳ] *n* abstêmio *m*, -mia *f*.

TEFL ['tefl] *(abbr of* **teaching of English as a foreign language***) n* ensino *de inglês para estrangeiros.*

Teflon® ['teflɒn] <> *n (U)* teflon® *m.* <> *comp* de teflon®.

Teh(e)ran *n* Teerã.

tel. *(abbr of* **telephone***)* tel. *m*.

Tel-Aviv [,telə'vi:vl] *n*: **~ (-Jaffa)** Tel-Aviv(-Jafa).

tele- ['telɪ] *prefix* [over a distance] tele-.

telecast ['telɪkɑ:st] *n* programa *m* de televisão.

telecom ['telɪkɒm] *n UK*, **telecoms** ['telɪkɒmz] *npl inf* telecom.

telecommunications ['telɪkə,mju:nɪ'keɪʃnz] *npl* telecomunicações *fpl*.

telecon *(abbr of* **telephone conversation***) n*.

telegram ['telɪgræm] *n* telegrama *m*.

telegraph ['telɪgrɑ:f] <> *n* telégrafo *m.* <> *vt* telegrafar.

telegraph pole, telegraph post *UK n* poste *m* de telégrafo.

telepathic [,telɪ'pæθɪk] *adj* telepático(ca).

telepathy [tɪ'lepəθɪ] *n (U)* telepatia *f*.

telephone ['telɪfəʊn] <> *n (U)* telefone *m*; **to be on the ~** *UK* [have a telephone line] ter telefone; [be talking on the telephone] estar no telefone. <> *vt* telefonar. <> *vi* telefonar.

telephone banking *n* serviço *m* de banco por telefone.

telephone book *n* lista *f* telefônica.

telephone booth *n UK* telefone *m* público.

telephone box *n UK* cabine *f* telefônica.

telephone call *n* telefonema *m*.

telephone directory *n* lista *f* telefônica.

telephone exchange *n* central *f* telefônica.

telephone kiosk *n UK* cabine *f* telefônica.

telephone line *n* linha *f* de telefone.

telephone number *n* número *m* de telefone.

telephone operator *n* telefonista *mf*.

telephone tapping *n (U)* escuta *f* telefônica.

telephonist [tɪ'lefənɪst] *n UK* telefonista *mf*.

telephoto lens [,telɪ'fəʊtəʊ-] *n* (lente *f*) tele-objetiva *f*.

teleprinter ['telɪ,prɪntəʳ], **teletypewriter** *US* [,telɪ'taɪp,raɪtəʳ] *n* teleimpressor *m*, teletipo *m*.

Teleprompter® [,telɪ'prɒmptəʳ] *n* teleprompter *m*.

telesales ['telɪseɪlz] *npl* televendas *fpl*.

telescope ['telɪskəʊp] *n* telescópio *m*.

telescopic [,telɪ'skɒpɪk] *adj* telescópico(ca).

teleshopping *n* telecompras *fpl*.

teletext ['telɪtekst] *n (U)* teletexto *m*.

telethon ['telɪθɒn] *n* teleton *m*.

teletypewriter *n US* = **teleprinter**.

televideo [telɪ'vɪdɪəʊ] *n* televisor *m* com videocassete.

televise ['telɪvaɪz] *vt* televisionar.

television ['telɪ,vɪʒn] *n* televisão *f*; **on ~** na televisão.

television licence *n UK taxa paga ao governo para ter acesso à televisão.*

television programme *n* programa *f* de televisão.

television set *n* (aparelho *m* de) televisão *f.*

teleworker ['teliwɜːkəʳ] *n* teletrabalhador *m*, -ra *f.*

teleworking *n* teletrabalho *m.*

telex ['teleks] <> *n* telex *m.* <> *vt* transmitir por telex.

tell [tel] (*pt* & *pp* **told**) <> *vt* **-1.** [gen] contar; **to ~ sb (that)** contar a alguém que; **to ~ sb sthg, to ~ sthg to sb** contar algo a alguém; **I told you so!** eu te falei! **-2.** [instruct, judge, reveal] dizer; **do as you're told!** faça como lhe disseram!; **to ~ sb to do sthg** dizer para alguém fazer algo; **to ~ sb (that)** dizer a alguém que; **to ~ what sb is thinking** saber o que alguém está pensando; **there's no ~ing ...** nunca se sabe ... <> *vi* **-1.** [speak] falar **-2.** [judge] dizer **-3.** [have effect] surtir efeito.

◆ **tell apart** *vt sep* distinguir, diferenciar.

◆ **tell off** *vt sep* repreender.

teller ['teləʳ] *n* **-1.** [of votes] escrutinador *m*, -ra *f* **-2.** [in bank] caixa *mf.*

telling ['telıŋ] *adj* **-1.** [relevant] contundente **-2.** [revealing] revelador(ra).

telling-off (*pl* **tellings-off**) *n* bronca *f.*

telltale ['telteıl] <> *adj* revelador(ra). <> *n* mexeriqueiro *m*, -ra *f.*

telly ['telı] (*pl* **-ies**) *n UK inf* televisão *f*; **on ~** na televisão.

temerity [tı'merətı] *n (U) fml* temeridade *f.*

temp *UK* [temp] *inf* <> *n* (*abbr of* **temporary (employee)**) funcionário *m* temporário, funcionária *f* temporária. <> *vi* trabalhar em emprego temporário.

temp. (*abbr of* **temperature**) temp. *f.*

temper ['tempəʳ] <> *n* **-1.** [state of mind, mood] humor *m*; **to be in a good/bad ~** estar de bom/mau humor; **to lose one's ~** perder a cabeça; **to have a short ~** ter pavio curto **-2.** [temperament] temperamento *m.* <> *vt fml* controlar, conter.

temperament ['tempromənt] *n* temperamento *m.*

temperamental [ˌtempro'mentl] *adj* temperamental.

temperance ['temprəns] *n (U)* **-1.** *fml* [moderation] temperança *f* **-2.** [not drinking alcohol] abstinência *f.*

temperate ['temprət] *adj* temperado(da).

temperature ['temprətʃəʳ] *n* temperatura *f*; **to have a ~** ter febre; **to take sb's ~** tirar a temperatura de alguém.

tempered ['tempəd] *adj* contido(da), comedido(da).

tempest ['tempıst] *n literary* tempestade *f.*

tempestuous [tem'pestjʊəs] *adj* **-1.** *literary* [stormy] turbulento(ta) **-2.** *fig* [emotional] tempestuoso(sa).

tempi ['tempiː] *pl* ➞ **tempo.**

template ['templıt] *n* **-1.** [of shape, pattern] molde *m*, modelo *m* **-2.** *COMPUT* gabarito *m.*

temple ['templ] *n* **-1.** *RELIG* templo *m* **-2.** *ANAT* têmpora *f.*

templet *n* = **template.**

tempo ['tempəʊ] (*pl* **-pos** *OR* **-pi**) *n* **-1.** *MUS* ritmo *m,*

velocidade *f* **-2.** [of an event] tempo *m.*

temporarily [ˌtempə'rerəlı] *adv* temporariamente.

temporary ['tempərərı] *adj* temporário(ria).

tempt [tempt] *vt* tentar; **to ~ sb to do sthg** tentar alguém a fazer algo; **to be** *OR* **feel ~ed to do sthg** estar/sentir-se tentado(da) a fazer algo.

temptation [temp'teıʃn] *n* tentação *f.*

tempting ['temptıŋ] *adj* tentador(ra).

ten [ten] *num* dez; *see also* **six.**

tenable ['tenəbl] *adj* **-1.** [reasonable, credible] sustentável **-2.** [job, post] seguro(ra), estável; **the post is ~ for one year** o cargo terá duração de um ano.

tenacious [tı'neıʃəs] *adj* tenaz.

tenacity [tı'næsətı] *n (U)* tenacidade *f.*

tenancy ['tenənsı] (*pl* **-ies**) *n* **-1.** [period] aluguel *m* **-2.** *(U)* [possession] locação *f.*

tenant ['tenənt] *n* **-1.** [of a house] inquilino *m*, -na *f* **-2.** [of a pub] locatário *m*, -ria *f.*

Ten Commandments *npl*: **the ~** os Dez Mandamentos.

tend [tend] *vt* **-1.** [have tendency]: **to ~ to do sthg** ter a tendência a fazer algo; **I ~ to think (that) ...** sou levado(da) a crer que ... **-2.** [look after] cuidar.

tendency ['tendənsı] (*pl* **-ies**) *n* **-1.** [gen]: **~ towards sthg/to do sthg** tendência *f* a algo/a fazer algo; **~ towards sthg** tendência *f* a algo **-2.** [leaning, habit] tendência *f.*

tender ['tendəʳ] <> *adj* **-1.** [caring, gentle] terno(na), meigo(ga) **-2.** [meat] macio(cia) **-3.** [sore] dolorido(da) **-4.** [young, innocent]: **at a ~ age** em tenra idade. <> *n COMM* proposta *f*, oferta *f.* <> *vt fml* oferecer.

tenderize, -ise ['tendəraız] *vt* amaciar.

tenderly ['tendəlı] *adv* carinhosamente.

tenderness ['tendənıs] *n (U)* **-1.** [care, compassion] ternura *f*, meiguice *f* **-2.** [soreness] sensibilidade *f.*

tendon ['tendən] *n* tendão *m.*

tendril ['tendrıl] *n* gavinha *f.*

tenement ['tenəmənt] *n* cortiço *m.*

Tenerife *n* Tenerife; **in ~** em Tenerife.

tenet ['tenıt] *n fml* dogma *m.*

tenner ['tenəʳ] *n UK inf* **-1.** [amount]: **it cost a ~** custou dez libras **-2.** [note] nota *f* de dez libras.

Tennessee *n* Tennessee.

tennis ['tenıs] <> *n (U)* tênis *m.* <> *comp* de tênis.

tennis ball *n* bola *f* de tênis.

tennis court *n* quadra *f* de tênis.

tennis player *n* jogador *m*, -ra *f* de tênis.

tennis racket *n* raquete *f* de tênis.

tenor ['tenəʳ] <> *adj* de tenor. <> *n* **-1.** [singer] tenor *m* **-2.** *fml* [meaning, mood] teor *m.*

tenpin bowling *UK* ['tenpın-], **tenpins** *US* ['tenpınz] *n (U)* boliche *m* (com dez pinos).

tense [tens] <> *adj* tenso(sa). <> *n GRAMM* tempo *m* (verbal). <> *vt* tencionar; retesar. <> *vi* endurecer-se.

tensed up [tenst-] *adj* tenso(sa).

tension ['tenʃn] *n* tensão *f.*

◆ **tensions** *npl* conflitos *mpl.*

ten-spot *n US* nota *f* de dez dólares.

tent [tent] *n* tenda *f*, barraca *f.*

tentacle ['tentəkl] *n* tentáculo *m.*

tentative ['tentətɪv] *adj* **-1.** [unconfident, hesitant - person] indeciso(sa); [- handshake] vacilante **-2.** [temporary, not final] provisório(ria).

tentatively ['tentətɪvlɪ] *adv* **-1.** [hesitantly] hesitantemente **-2.** [not finally] provisoriamente.

tenterhooks ['tentəhʊks] *npl*: **to be on** ~ estar com os nervos à flor da pele.

tenth [tenθ] *num* décimo(ma); *see also* **sixth.**

tent peg *n* estaca *f* de barraca.

tent pole *n* mastro *m* de barraca.

tenuous ['tenjʊəs] *adj* **-1.** [argument] pouco convincente **-2.** [connection] de pouca importância **-3.** [hold] tênue.

tenuously ['tenjʊəslɪ] *adv* sutilmente.

tenure ['tenjəʳ] *n (U) fml* **-1.** [of property] posse *f*-**2.** [of job] estabilidade *f*.

tepee ['ti:pi:] *n* tenda *f* indígena.

tepid ['tepɪd] *adj* **-1.** [liquid] tépido(da), morno(na) **-2.** *pej* [lacking gusto] morno(na).

tequila [tɪ'ki:lə] *n* tequila *f*.

Ter. *abbr of* **terrace.**

term [tɜ:m] ◇ *n* **-1.** [word, expression] termo *m* **-2.** *SCH* & *UNIV* [third of school year] semestre *m* - **3.** *POL* [period in political office]: ~ **(of office)** mandato *m* - **4.** [stretch of time] período *m*; **in the long/short** ~ a longo/curto prazo. ◇ *vt* designar.

　　terms *npl* **-1.** [of contract, agreement] termos *mpl* **-2.** [conditions]: **in international/real** ~ **s** em termos internacionais/reais **-3.** [of relationship]: **on equal** *OR* **the same** ~ **s** de igual para igual, em condições de igualdade; **to be on good** ~ **s (with sb)** dar-se bem (com alguém); **are you on speaking** ~ **s?** vocês estão se falando? **- 4.** *phr*: **to come to** ~ **s with sthg** aceitar algo.

　　in terms of *prep* no que diz respeito a; **to think in** ~ **s of doing sthg** pensar em fazer algo.

terminal ['tɜ:mɪnl] ◇ *adj* terminal. ◇ *n* terminal *m*.

terminally ['tɜ:mɪnəlɪ] *adv*: **to be** ~ **ill** ser um doente (em fase) terminal.

terminate ['tɜ:mɪneɪt] ◇ *vt* **-1.** [agreement, discussion] *fml* pôr fim a, encerrar **-2.** [pregnancy] interromper **-3.** [contract] rescindir. ◇ *vi* **-1.** [bus, train]: **this bus** ~ **s in the city centre** este ônibus pára no centro na cidade **-2.** [contract] terminar.

termination [ˌtɜ:mɪ'neɪʃn] *n* **-1.** *(U) fml* [ending] término *m* - **2.** [abortion] interrupção *f* da gravidez.

termini ['tɜ:mɪnaɪ] *pl* ▷ **terminus.**

terminology [ˌtɜ:mɪ'nɒlədʒɪ] *n* terminologia *f*.

terminus ['tɜ:mɪnəs] *(pl -ni OR -nuses) n* terminal *m*.

termite ['tɜ:maɪt] *n* cupim *m*.

terrace ['terəs] *n* **-1.** *UK* [of houses] fileira *f* de casas geminadas **-2.** [patio] terraço *m* - **3.** [on hillside] terraço *m*, socalco *m*.

　　terraces *npl FTBL*: **the** ~ **s** as arquibancadas.

terraced ['terəst] *adj* escalonado(da).

terraced house *n UK* casa *f* geminada.

terracotta [ˌterə'kɒtə] *n (U)* terracota *f*.

terrain [te'reɪn] *n (U)* terreno *m*.

terrapin ['terəpɪn] *(pl inv OR -s) n* tartaruga *f* aquática.

terrestrial [tə'restrɪəl] *adj fml* terrestre.

terrible ['terəbl] *adj* terrível.

terribly ['terəblɪ] *adv* **-1.** [very badly] terrivelmente **-2.** [extremely] imensamente.

terrier ['terɪəʳ] *n* terrier *m*.

terrific [tə'rɪfɪk] *adj* **-1.** [wonderful] fabuloso(sa), maravilhoso(so) **-2.** [enormous] enorme.

terrified ['terɪfaɪd] *adj*: ~ **(of sb/sthg)** aterrorizado(da) (com alguém/algo); **to be** ~ **of sthg** ter horror a algo.

terrify ['terɪfaɪ] *(pt & pp -ied) vt* aterrorizar.

terrifying ['terɪfaɪɪŋ] *adj* aterrorizante.

terrine [te'ri:n] *n* terrina *f*.

territorial [ˌterɪ'tɔ:rɪəl] *adj* territorial.

Territorial Army *n UK*: **the** ~ o *exército voluntário da Grã-Bretanha.*

territorial waters *npl* águas *fpl* territoriais.

territory ['terətrɪ] *(pl -ies) n* **-1.** [political area] território *m* - **2.** [terrain] terreno *m* - **3.** [area of knowledge] campo *m*, área *f*.

terror ['terəʳ] *n* **-1.** *(U)* [fear] terror *m* - **2.** [something feared] horror *m* - **3.** *inf* [rascal] pestinha *mf*.

terrorism ['terərɪzm] *n (U)* terrorismo *m*.

terrorist ['terərɪst] *n* terrorista *mf*.

terrorize, -ise ['terəraɪz] *vt* aterrorizar.

terror-stricken *adj* em pânico, aterrorizado(da).

terry (cloth) *n (U)* tecido *m* atoalhado.

terse [tɜ:s] *adj* seco(ca).

tersely ['tɜ:slɪ] *adv* secamente.

tertiary ['tɜ:ʃərɪ] *adj fml* terciário(ria).

tertiary education *n (U)* educação *f* de terceiro grau.

Terylene® ['terəli:n] *n (U)* tergal® *m*.

TES *(abbr of* **Times Education Supplement**) *n suplemento semanal do Times britânico direcionado à educação.*

TESL ['tesl] *(abbr of* **teaching of English as a second language**) *n ensino de inglês como segunda língua.*

TESOL *(abbr of* **teaching of English to speakers of other languages**) *n ensino de inglês para falantes de outras línguas.*

TESSA ['tesə] *(abbr of* **tax-exempt special savings account**) *n sistema de poupança britânica que tem isenção de impostos sobre o juro do capital depositado a prazo fixo.*

test [test] ◇ *n* **-1.** [trial] teste *m*; **to put sb/sthg to the** ~ colocar alguém/algo à prova **-2.** [*MED*, examination of knowledge, skill] exame *m*; *SCH* prova *f*, teste *m*. ◇ *vt* **-1.** [try out] testar **-2.** [examine, check] examinar; **to** ~ **sb on sthg** examinar algo de alguém.

testament ['testəmənt] *n* **-1.** [gen] testamento *m* **-2.** [proof]: ~ **to sthg** testemunho *m* de algo.

test ban *n* suspensão *f* de testes nucleares.

test card *n UK* mira *f*.

test case *n JUR* caso *m* precedente.

test-drive *vt* test-drive *m*.

tester ['testəʳ] *n* **-1.** [person testing] provador *m*, -ra *f* **-2.** [sample] amostra *f*.

test flight *n* vôo *m* de prova.

testicles ['testɪklz] *npl* testículos *mpl*.

testify ['testɪfaɪ] *(pt & pp -ied)* ◇ *vt* declarar; **to** ~

that testemunhar que. ◇ *vi* **-1.** JUR declarar sob juramento **-2.** [be proof]: **to ~ to sthg** evidenciar algo.

testimonial [ˌtestɪˈməʊnjəl] *n* ` **-1.** [reference] carta *f* de recomendação **-2.** [tribute] homenagem *f*.

testimony [*UK* 'testɪmənɪ, *US* 'testəməʊnɪ] *n (U)* **-1.** JUR depoimento *m*, testemunho *m*; **to bear ~** testemunhar **-2.** [proof, demonstration]: **~ to sthg** testemunho de algo.

testing ['testɪŋ] *adj* [trying, difficult] duro(ra).

testing ground *n* área *f* de testes.

test match *n UK* partida *f* internacional.

testosterone *n* testosterona *f*.

test paper *n* **-1.** SCH teste *m* escrito **-2.** CHEM papel *m* reativo.

test pattern *n US* padrão *m* de teste.

test pilot *n* piloto *m* de prova.

test tube *n* tubo *m* de ensaio, proveta *f*.

test-tube baby *n* bebê *m* de proveta.

testy ['testɪ] (*compar* **-ier**, *superl* **-iest**) *adj* **-1.** [person] irritadiço(ça) **-2.** [remark, comment] agressivo(va).

tetanus ['tetənəs] *n (U)* tétano *m*.

tetchy ['tetʃɪ] (*compar* **-ier**, *superl* **-iest**) *adj* irritável, rabugento(ta).

tête-à-tête [ˌteɪtɑːˈteɪt] *n* tête-à-tête *m*.

tether ['teðəʳ] ◇ *vt* **-1.** [horse] apear **-2.** [dog] amarrar. ◇ *n*: **to be at the end of one's ~** estar no limite.

Texan ['teksn] *n* texano *m*, -na *f*.

Texas ['teksəs] *n* Texas.

Tex-Mex *adj* mexicano(na) do Texas.

text [tekst] *n* texto *m*.

textbook ['tekstbʊk] *n* livro-texto *m*.

textile ['tekstaɪl] ◇ *n* tecido *m*. ◇ *comp* **-1.** [industry] têxtil **-2.** [worker] da indústria têxtil.

texting ['tekstɪŋ] *n inf* mensagens *fpl* de texto.

text message *n* [on mobile phone] mensagem *m* de texto.

text messaging [-'mesɪdʒɪŋ] *n* [on mobile phone] mensagem *f* de texto.

texture ['tekstʃəʳ] *n* textura *f*.

Thai [taɪ] ◇ *adj* tailandês(esa). ◇ *n* **-1.** [person] tailandês *m*, -esa *f* **-2.** [language] tailandês *m*.

Thailand ['taɪlænd] *n* Tailândia; **in ~** na Tailândia.

thalidomide [θəˈlɪdəmaɪd] *n (U)* talidomida *f*.

Thames [temz] *n*: **the ~** o Tâmisa.

than [weak form ðən, strong form ðæn] ◇ *conj* que; **more ~ ten** mais de dez; **I'd rather stay in ~ go out** prefiro ficar em casa a sair.

thank [θæŋk] *vt*: **to ~ sb (for sthg)** agradecer alguém (por algo); **~ God** OR **goodness** OR **heavens!** graças a Deus/aos céus!

➡ **thanks** ◇ *npl* agradecimento *m*. ◇ *excl* obrigado(da)!

➡ **thanks to** *prep* graças a.

thankful ['θæŋkfʊl] *adj* agradecido(da); **~ for sthg** agradecido(da) por algo.

thankfully ['θæŋkfʊlɪ] *adv* **-1.** [with gratitude] agradecidamente **-2.** [thank goodness] graças a Deus.

thankless ['θæŋklɪs] *adj* ingrato(ta).

thanksgiving *n* ação *f* de graças.

➡ **Thanksgiving (Day)** *n* Dia *m* de Ação de Graças.

THANKSGIVING

Nos Estados Unidos, o dia de Ação de Graças, a quarta quinta-feira de novembro, comemora o estabelecimento dos primeiros colonos no país. O almoço em família, que geralmente marca essa data, consiste em peru com mirtilos, acompanhado de batatas, e, para terminar, torta de abóbora. No Canadá, comemoração similar acontece em 1° de outubro.

thank you *excl* obrigado(da); **~ for** obrigado(da) por.

➡ **thankyou** *n* agradecimento *m*.

that [ðæt, weak form of pron & conj ðət] (*pl* **those**) ◇ *adj* **-1.** [referring to thing, person mentioned] esse (essa); **I prefer ~ book** prefiro esse livro. **-2.** [referring to thing, person farther away] aquele (aquela); **~ book at the back** aquele livro lá atrás; **I'll have ~ one** quero aquele (ali) OR esse. ◇ *pron* **-1.** [referring to thing, person mentioned] esse *m*, essa *f*; [indefinite] isso; **what's ~?** o que é isso?; **who's ~?** [on the phone] quem fala?; [pointing] e esse, quem é?; **~'s interesting** que interessante. **-2.** [referring to thing, person farther away] aquele *m*, aquela *f*; [indefinite] aquilo; **is ~ Lucy?** [pointing] aquela é a Lucy?; **I want those at the back** quero aqueles lá atrás; **what's ~ on the roof?** o que é aquilo no telhado? **-3.** [introducing relative clause] que; **a shop ~ sells antiques** uma loja que vende antiguidades; **the movie ~ I saw** o filme que eu vi; **the room ~ I slept in** o quarto onde OR em que dormi. ◇ *adv* assim tão; **it wasn't ~ bad/good** não foi assim tão mau/bom; **it didn't cost ~ much** não custou tanto assim. ◇ *conj* que; **tell him ~ I'm going to be late** diga-lhe que vou chegar atrasado.

thatched [θætʃt] *adj* com telhado de palha.

Thatcherism ['θætʃərɪzm] *n (U)* thatcherismo *m*.

that's [ðæts] = **that is**.

thaw [θɔː] ◇ *vt* **-1.** [ice] derreter **-2.** [frozen food] descongelar. ◇ *vi* **-1.** [ice] derreter **-2.** [food] descongelar **-3.** *fig* [people, relations] tornar-se um pouco mais amistoso. ◇ *n* [warm spell] degelo *m*.

the [weak form ðə, before vowel ðɪ, strong form ðiː] *definite article* **-1.** [gen] o (a), os (as) (*pl*); **~ book** o livro; **~ apple** a maçã; **~ girls** as meninas; **~ Wilsons** os Wilson; **to play ~ piano** tocar piano. **-2.** [with an adjective to form a noun] o (a), os (as) (*pl*); **~ British** os britânicos; **~ young** os jovens; **~ impossible** o impossível. **-3.** [in dates]: **~ twelfth** o dia doze; **~ forties** os anos quarenta. **-4.** [in titles]: **Elizabeth ~ Second** Elizabeth Segunda.

theatre, theater *US* ['θɪətəʳ] *n* **-1.** [building] teatro *m* **-2.** [art, industry]: **the ~** o teatro **-3.** [in hospital] sala *f* de cirurgia **-4.** *US* [cinema] cinema *m*.

theatregoer, theatergoer *US* ['θɪətəˌɡəʊəʳ] *n* aficionado *m*, -da *f* por teatro.

theatrical [θɪˈætrɪkl] *adj* teatral.

theft [θeft] *n* roubo *m*.

their [ðeəʳ] *adj* seu (sua), deles (delas); **~ house** a sua casa, a casa deles.

theirs [ðeəz] *pron* o/a deles (o/a delas); **a friend of** ~ um amigo deles; **these books are** ~ estes livros são (os) deles; **these are ours - where are** ~? estes são os nossos - onde estão os deles?

them [*weak form* ðəm, *strong form* ðem] *pron* **-1.** *(direct)* os *mpl*, as *fpl*; **I know** ~ eu os conheço **-2.** *(indirect)* lhes; **send this to** ~ mande-lhes isso; **tell** ~ diga-lhes **-3.** *(after prep)* eles *mpl*, elas *fpl*; **Anna and Sam brought it with** ~ a Anna e o Sam trouxeram-no com eles.

thematic [θɪˈmætɪk] *adj* temático(ca).

theme [θiːm] *n* **-1.** [gen] tema *m* **-2.** [signature tune] sintonia *f*.

theme park *n* parque *m* temático.

theme song *n* música-tema *f*, tema *m* musical.

theme tune *n* música-tema *f*, tema *f* musical.

themselves [ðemˈselvz] *pron* **-1.** *(reflexive)* se; **they hurt** ~ eles machucaram-se **-2.** *(after prep)* eles *mpl* próprios, elas *fpl* próprias, si *mpl* próprios, si *fpl* próprias; **they blame** ~ eles culpam-se a si próprios; **they did it** ~ fizeram-no eles mesmos OR próprios.

then [ðen] <> *adv* **-1.** [later, as a result] então; **if you help me out now,** ~ **I'll return the favour** se você me ajudar agora, eu te devolvo o favor; **it starts at eight - I'll see you** ~ começa às oito - te vejo a essa hora **-2.** [next, afterwards] depois **-3.** [in that case] então, neste caso; **all right** ~ então, tudo certo **-4.** [therefore] então, portanto **-5.** [furthermore, also] além disso. <> *adj* então.

thence [ðens] *adv fml & literary* de lá.

theologian [θɪəˈləʊdʒən] *n* teólogo *m*, -ga *f*.

theology [θɪˈɒlədʒɪ] *n* teologia *f*.

theorem [ˈθɪərəm] *n* teorema *f*.

theoretical [θɪəˈretɪkl] *adj* teórico(ca).

theoretically [θɪəˈretɪklɪ] *adv* teoricamente, em teoria.

theorist [ˈθɪərɪst] *n* teórico *m*, -ca *f*.

theorize, -ise [ˈθɪəraɪz] *vi*: **to** ~ **(about sthg)** teorizar (sobre algo).

theory [ˈθɪərɪ] *(pl* -ies) *n* teoria *f*; **in** ~ em teoria.

therapeutic [θerəˈpjuːtɪk] *adj* terapêutico(ca).

therapist [ˈθerəpɪst] *n* terapeuta *mf*.

therapy [ˈθerəpɪ] *n* (U) terapia *f*.

there [ðeəʳ] <> *pron* [indicating existence of sthg]: ~ **is/are** há; ~'**s someone at the door** tem alguém na porta <> *adv* **-1.** [in existence, available] lá, ali; **is Sam** ~, **please?** [when telephoning] o Sam está? **-2.** [referring to place] lá; **I'm going** ~ **next week** vou lá para a semana; **over** ~ ali; **it's right** ~ **by the phone** está aí bem ao lado do telefone.

  ➤ **there you are** *adv* handing sthg to sb] aqui está.

thereabouts [ˌðeərəˈbaʊts], **thereabout** US [ˌðeərəˈbaʊt] *adv*: **or** ~ ou por ali; **by 1998 or** ~ mais ou menos em 1998.

thereafter [ˌðeərˈɑːftəʳ] *adv fml* conseqüentemente, depois disso.

thereby [ˌðeəʳˈbaɪ] *adv fml* desse modo.

therefore [ˈðeəfɔːʳ] *adv* portanto, por isso.

therein [ˌðeərˈɪn] *adv fml* **-1.** [inside] lá dentro **-2.** [in that matter]: ~ **lies the problem** aí é que está o problema.

there's [ðeəz] *cont* = there is.

thereupon [ˌðeərəˈpɒn] *adv fml* **-1.** [as a result] em razão disso **-2.** [then] por isso.

thermal [ˈθɜːml] *adj* térmico(ca); ~ **waters** águas *fpl* termais.

thermal reactor *n* reator *m* térmico.

thermal underwear *n* (U) roupa *f* térmica.

thermodynamics [ˌθɜːməʊdaɪˈnæmɪks] *n* (U) termodinâmica *f*.

thermoelectric *adj* termoelétrico(ca).

thermometer [θəˈmɒmɪtəʳ] *n* termômetro *m*.

thermonuclear [ˌθɜːməʊˈnjuːklɪəʳ] *adj* termonuclear.

thermoplastic [ˌθɜːməʊˈplæstɪk] <> *adj* termoplástico(ca). <> *n* (polímero *m*) termoplástico *m*.

Thermos (flask)® [ˈθɜːməs-] *n* garrafa *f* térmica.

thermostat [ˈθɜːməstæt] *n* termostato *m*.

thesaurus [θɪˈsɔːrəs] *(pl* -es) *n* tesauro *m*.

these [ðiːz] *pl* ➤ **this**.

thesis [ˈθiːsɪs] *(pl* **theses** [ˈθiːsiːzl]) *n* tese *f*.

they [ðeɪ] *pers pron pl* eles *mpl*, elas *fpl*.

they'd [ðeɪd] = they had, they would.

they'll [ðeɪl] = they shall, they will.

they're [ðeəʳ] = they are.

they've [ðeɪv] = they have.

thick [θɪk] <> *adj* **-1.** [bulky] grosso(sa); **it's 6 cm** ~ tem 6 cm de grossura; **how** ~ **is that wall?** qual é a espessura da parede? **-2.** [dense] denso(sa) **-3.** *inf* [stupid] estúpido(da) **-4.** [viscous] espesso(sa) **-5.** [voice - with anger] enraivecido(da); [- with emotion] embargado(da); [- with drink] enrolado(da) **-6.** [full, covered]: **to be** ~ **with sthg** estar cheio (cheia) de algo. <> *n*: **to be in the** ~ **of sthg** estar no centro de algo.

  ➤ **thick and fast** *adv*: questions came ~ and fast choviam perguntas de todos os lados.

  ➤ **through thick and thin** *adv*: **I'll do it through** ~ **and thin!** vou fazer isso de qualquer maneira!

thicken [ˈθɪkn] <> *vt* engrossar. <> *vi* **-1.** [become denser] ficar mais denso(sa) **-2.** [become more solid] engrossar.

thicket [ˈθɪkɪt] *n* moita *f*.

thickly [ˈθɪklɪ] *adv* **-1.** [not thinly - spread] em camadas grossas; [- cut] em fatias grossas **-2.** [voice - with anger] com voz enraivecida; [- with emotion] com voz embargada; [- with drink] com voz enrolada **-3.** [densely] densamente.

thickness [ˈθɪknɪs] *n* **-1.** [width, depth] espessura *f* **-2.** [density - of forest, hedge] densidade *f*; [- of hair] grossura *f* **-3.** [of soup, sauce] consistência *f*.

thickset [ˌθɪkˈset] *adj* robusto(ta).

thick-skinned [-ˈskɪnd] *adj* insensível.

thief [θiːf] *(pl* **thieves**) *n* ladrão *m*, -dra *f*.

thieve [θiːv] <> *vt* roubar. <> *vi* roubar.

thieves [θiːvz] *pl* ➤ **thief**.

thieving ['θi:vɪŋ] ⋄ adj ladrão(dra). ⋄ n (U) roubo m, furto m.

thigh [θaɪl n coxa f.

thighbone ['θaɪbəʊn] n fêmur m.

thimble ['θɪmbl] n dedal m.

thin [θɪn] (compar -ner, superl -nest, pt & pp -ned, cónt -ning) ⋄ adj -1. [in width, depth] fino(na) -2. [skinny] magro(gra) -3. [watery] ralo(la), aguado(da) -4. [sparse - crowd, vegetation] disperso(sa); [- hair] ralo(la); to be ~ on top estar ficando calvo(va) -5. [excuse] fraco(ca). ⋄ adv: to be wearing ~ [becoming boring] estar perdendo o interesse; [beginning to fail] my patience is wearing ~ está acabando a minha paciência. ⋄ vi: my hair is ~ning meu cabelo está começando a cair.
➡ **thin down** vt sep diluir.

thin air n (U): to appear out of ~ aparecer do nada; to disappear into ~ desaparecer sem deixar vestígio.

thing [θɪŋ] n -1. [gen] coisa f; you poor ~! coitadinho(nha); the next ~ on the list o próximo item da lista; the (best) ~ to do would be ... o melhor a fazer seria ...; for one ~ em primeiro lugar; (what) with one ~ and another entre uma coisa e outra; the ~ is ... a questão é ..., acontece que ...; it's just one of those ~s inf é apenas uma dessas coisas que acontecem; to have a ~ about sb/sthg inf [like] gostar muito de alguém/algo; [dislike] não suportar alguém/algo; to make a ~ (out) of sthg inf fazer um alarde de algo -2. [anything]: not a ~ nada; I don't know a ~ (about) não sei nada (sobre or de) -3. inf [fashion]: the ~ a última moda.
➡ **things** npl -1. [clothes, possessions] coisas fpl -2. inf [life] coisas fpl.

thingamabob ['θɪŋəmə,bɒb], **thingamajig** ['θɪŋəmədʒɪg], **thingummy(jig)** UK ['θɪŋəmɪ-], **thingy** UK ['θɪŋɪ] n -1. [thing] coisa f -2. [person] fulano(na).

think [θɪŋk] (pt & pp thought) ⋄ vt -1. [believe]: to ~ (that) achar or acreditar que; I ~ so acho que sim; I don't ~ so acho que não -2. [have in mind] pensar -3. [imagine] entender, imaginar -4. [remember] pensar, lembrar -5. [in polite requests]: do you ~ you could help me? você acha que pode me ajudar? ⋄ vi -1. [use mind] pensar -2. [have stated opinion]: what do you ~ of or about his new film? o que você acha do novo filme dele?; I don't ~ much of them/it não tenho uma opinião muito boa sobre eles/ele; to ~ a lot of sb/sthg ter alguém/algo em grande estima -3. phr: to ~ better of sthg/of doing sthg pensar melhor sobre algo/sobre fazer algo; he ~s nothing of doing it ele tira isso de letra; to ~ twice pensar duas vezes. ⋄ n inf: to have a ~ (about sthg) pensar (sobre algo).
➡ **think about** vt fus [consider] pensar em; I'll have to ~ about it vou ter que pensar sobre isso.
➡ **think back** vi: to ~ back (to sthg) recordar-se (de algo).
➡ **think of** vt fus -1. [gen] pensar em; to ~ of doing sthg pensar em fazer algo -2. [remember] lembrar-se de -3. [show consideration for]: it was

kind of you to ~ of me foi muito gentil de tua parte se lembrar de mim.
➡ **think out, think through** vt sep -1. [plan] elaborar -2. [problem] examinar.
➡ **think over** vt sep refletir sobre.
➡ **think up** vt sep imaginar, bolar.

thinker ['θɪŋkə'] n pensador m, -ra f.

thinking ['θɪŋkɪŋ] ⋄ adj: the ~ man o homem que pensa. ⋄ n (U) -1. [opinion] opinião f; to my way of ~ na minha opinião -2. [reflection] reflexão f; I'll have to do a lot of hard ~ about your proposal vou ter que pensar bastante sobre a tua proposta -3. [theory] teoria f.

think tank n assessoria f técnica.

thinly ['θɪnlɪ] adv -1. [in width, depth - slice] em fatias finas; [- spread] numa camada fina -2. [forested] escassamente -3. [barely] pouco.

thinner ['θɪnə'] n (U) tíner m, solvente m.

thinness ['θɪnnɪs] n -1. [in width, depth] finura f -2. [slim build] magreza f.

thin-skinned [-'skɪnd] adj suscetível.

third [θɜ:d] ⋄ num terceiro(ra). ⋄ n -1. [fraction] terço m -2. UK UNIV ≃ nota f C (num título universitário); see also sixth.

third-class adj UK UNIV ≃ nota f C (num título universitário).

third-degree burns npl queimaduras fpl de terceiro grau.

thirdly ['θɜ:dlɪ] adv em terceiro lugar.

third party n terceiros mpl.

third party insurance n seguro m contra terceiros.

third-rate adj pej de terceira categoria.

Third World n: the ~ o Terceiro Mundo.

thirst [θɜ:st] n sede f; ~ for sthg fig sede de algo.

thirsty ['θɜ:stɪ] (compar -ier, superl -iest) adj -1. [parched]: to be or feel ~ estar com or sentir sede -2. [causing thirst] que dá sede.

thirteen [,θɜ:'ti:n] num treze; see also six.

thirteenth [,θɜ:'ti:nθ] num décimo terceiro, décima terceira; see also sixth.

thirtieth ['θɜ:tɪəθ] num trigésimo(ma); see also sixth.

thirty ['θɜ:tɪ] (pl -ies) num trinta; see also sixty.

thirty-something adj típico das pessoas que já passaram dos trinta anos e vivem confortavelmente.

this [ðɪs] (pl these) ⋄ adj -1. [referring to thing, person] este (esta); these chocolates are delicious estes chocolates são deliciosos; ~ morning/week esta manhã/semana; I prefer ~ book prefiro este livro; I'll take ~ one quero este -2. inf [used when telling a story]: there was ~ man ... havia um homem ... ⋄ pron [referring to thing, person] este m, esta f; [indefinite] isto; ~ is for you isto é para você; what are these? o que é isto?, o que é que são estas coisas?; ~ is David Gregory [introducing someone] este é o David Gregory; [on telephone] aqui fala David Gregory. ⋄ adv: it was ~ big era deste tamanho; I don't remember it being ~ tiring não me lembro de ser tão cansativo assim.

thistle ['θɪsl] n cardo m.

thither ['ðiðə^r] *adv* ⊳ **hither**.

tho' [ðəʊ] *conj* & *adv* = **though**.

thong [θɒŋ] *n* -**1.** [piece of leather] correia *f*, tira *f* de couro -**2.** [bikini] tanga *f* -**3.** *US* [sandal] sandália *f*.

thorn [θɔːn] *n* -**1.** [prickle] espinho *m*; **to be a ~ in sb's flesh** *OR* **side** ser um tormento na vida de alguém -**2.** [bush, tree] espinheiro *m*.

thorny ['θɔːnɪ] (*compar* **-ier**, *superl* **-iest**) *adj* -**1.** [prickly] espinhoso(sa), cheio (cheia) de espinhos -**2.** *fig* [tricky, complicated] espinhoso(sa).

thorough ['θʌrə] *adj* -**1.** [gen] completo(ta) -**2.** [meticulous] minucioso(sa).

thoroughbred ['θʌrəbred] *n* puro-sangue *m*.

thoroughfare ['θʌrəfeə^r] *n fml* via *f* pública.

thoroughly ['θʌrəlɪ] *adv* -**1.** [fully, in detail] a fundo, exaustivamente -**2.** [completely, utterly] completamente, totalmente.

thoroughness ['θʌrənɪs] *n* (*U*) -**1.** [exhaustiveness] profundidade *f*, meticulosidade *f* -**2.** [meticulousness] minúcia *f*.

those [ðəʊz] *pl* ⊳ **that**.

though [ðəʊ] ⬦ *conj* -**1.** [in spite of the fact that] embora -**2.** [even if] ainda que; **even ~** embora. ⬦ *adv* no entanto.

thought [θɔːt] ⬦ *pt* & *pp* ⊳ **think**. ⬦ *n* -**1.** [notion] idéia *f* -**2.** (*U*) [act of thinking] reflexão *f* -**3.** (*U*) [philosophy] pensamento *m* -**4.** [gesture] intenção *f*.

➡ **thoughts** *npl* -**1.** [reflections] opiniões *fpl*; **she keeps her ~ to herself** ela não expressa o que pensa; **to collect one's ~s** concentrar-se -**2.** [views] opiniões *fpl*, idéias *fpl*.

thoughtful ['θɔːtfʊl] *adj* -**1.** [pensive] pensativo(va) -**2.** [considerate] atencioso(sa).

thoughtfulness ['θɔːtfʊlnɪs] *n* (*U*) -**1.** [pensiveness] ar *m* pensativo -**2.** [considerateness] atenção *f*, consideração *f*.

thoughtless ['θɔːtlɪs] *adj* indelicado(da).

thoughtlessness ['θɔːtlɪsnɪs] *n* (*U*) indelicadeza *f*.

thousand ['θaʊznd] *num*: **a ~** mil; **two ~** dois mil; **~s of** milhares de.

thousandth ['θaʊzntθ] *num* -**1.** milésimo(ma) -**2.** [fraction] milésimo(ma); *see also* **sixth**.

thrash [θræʃ] *vt* -**1.** [beat, hit] surrar, dar uma surra em -**2.** *inf* [trounce] dar uma surra em.

➡ **thrash about, thrash around** *vi* debater-se; **to be ~ing about in one's sleep** ter um sono agitado.

➡ **thrash out** *vt sep* esgotar *(um assunto)*.

thrashing ['θræʃɪŋ] *n* -**1.** [beating, hitting] surra *f* -**2.** *inf* [trouncing] surra *f*.

thread [θred] ⬦ *n* -**1.** [of cotton, wool] fio *m* -**2.** [of screw] rosca *f* -**3.** *fig* [theme] fio *m* da meada. ⬦ *vt* -**1.** [pass thread through] enfiar -**2.** [move]: **to ~ one's way through** abrir caminho.

threadbare ['θredbeə^r] *adj* -**1.** [clothes, carpet] surrado(da) -**2.** [argument, joke] manjado(da).

threat [θret] *n* -**1.** [warning] ameaça *f* -**2.** [menace]: **~ (to sb/sthg)** ameaça (a alguém/algo) -**3.** [risk]: **~ (of sthg)** ameaça (de algo).

threaten ['θretn] ⬦ *vt* -**1.** [issue threat]: **to ~ sb (with sthg)** ameaçar alguém (com algo); **to ~ to do sthg** ameaçar fazer algo -**2.** [endanger]

ameaçar. ⬦ *vi* ameaçar.

threatening ['θretnɪŋ] *adj* ameaçador(ra).

three [θriː] *num* três; *see also* **six**.

three-D *adj* tridimensional.

three-day event *n* concurso hípico de três dias.

three-dimensional [-dɪ'menʃənl] *adj* tridimensional.

threefold ['θriːfəʊld] ⬦ *adj* triplo(pla). ⬦ *adv* três vezes; **to increase ~** triplicar.

three-legged race [-'legɪd-] *n* corrida *f* de três pernas.

three-piece *adj* de três peças.

three-ply *adj* -**1.** [wood] com três espessuras -**2.** [wool] com três fios.

three-point turn *n UK* volta *f* de três pontos.

three-quarters *npl* três quartos *mpl*.

threesome ['θriːsəm] *n* trio *m*.

three-star *adj* de três estrelas.

three-wheeler [-'wiːlə^r] *n* triciclo *m*.

thresh [θreʃ] *vt* debulhar.

threshing machine ['θreʃɪŋ-] *n* debulhadora *f*.

threshold ['θreʃhəʊld] *n* -**1.** [doorway] soleira *f* -**2.** [level] limiar *m* -**3.** *fig* [verge]: **to be on the ~ of sthg** estar no limiar de algo.

threshold agreement *n* acordo *m* para indexação salarial.

threw [θruː] *pt* ⊳ **throw**.

thrift [θrɪft] *n* -**1.** [prudent expenditure] economia *f*, poupança *f* -**2.** *US* [savings bank] = **thrift institution**.

thrift institution *n US* ≃ banco *m* de poupança.

thrift shop *n US* loja *f* beneficente.

thrifty ['θrɪftɪ] (*compar* **-ier**, *superl* **-iest**) *adj* econômico(ca).

thrill [θrɪl] ⬦ *n* -**1.** [sudden feeling - of joy] vibração *f*; [- of horror] estremecimento *m* -**2.** [exciting experience] emoção *f*. ⬦ *vt* emocionar, entusiasmar. ⬦ *vi*: **to ~ to sthg** emocionar-se *OR* entusiasmar-se com algo.

thrilled [θrɪld] *adj*: **~ (with sthg/to do sthg)** encantado(da) (com algo/por fazer algo).

thriller ['θrɪlə^r] *n* suspense *m* *(enquanto obra)*.

thrilling ['θrɪlɪŋ] *adj* emocionante.

thrive [θraɪv] (*pt* **-d** *OR* **throve**, *pp* **-d**) *vi* -**1.** [person, plant] desenvolver-se -**2.** [business] prosperar.

thriving ['θraɪvɪŋ] *adj* -**1.** [person, plant] próspero(ra) -**2.** [plant] que se desenvolve.

throat [θrəʊt] *n* -**1.** [inside mouth] garganta *f*; **to ram** *OR* **force sthg down sb's ~** *fig* empurrar algo goela abaixo (em alguém); **to stick in sb's ~** *fig* ficar preso(sa) na garganta de alguém -**2.** [front of neck] pescoço *m*; **to be at each other's ~s** estar batendo boca; **to cut sb's ~** [kill] cortar a garganta de alguém.

throaty ['θrəʊtɪ] (*compar* **-ier**, *superl* **-iest**) *adj* rouco(ca).

throb [θrɒb] (*pt* & *pp* **-bed**, *cont* **-bing**) ⬦ *n* -**1.** [of pulse] pulsação *f* -**2.** [of head] latejamento *m* -**3.** [of heart] palpitação *f*; [of engine, machine, drums] vibração *f*. ⬦ *vi* -**1.** [beat - pulse, blood] pulsar; [- heart] palpitar; [- engine, machine] vibrar; [- music, drums] vibrar, ressoar -**2.** [be painful] latejar.

throes [θrəʊz] *npl*: **death ~** agonia *f* da morte; **to**

be in the ~ of sthg estar no meio de algo.

thrombosis [θrɒm'bəʊsɪs] (*pl* -boses [-si:z]) *n* trombose *f*.

throne [θrəʊn] *n* -1. [chair] trono *m* -2. [position, authority]: **the** ~ o trono.

throng [θrɒŋ] <> *n* aglomeração *f*. <> *vt* aglomerar. <> *vi* aglomerar-se.

throttle ['θrɒtl] <> *n* -1. [valve] válvula *f* de estrangulamento -2. [lever] alavanca *f (da válvula de estrangulamento)*; [pedal] afogador *m*. <> *vt* estrangular.

through [θru:] <> *adj* [finished] terminado(da); **to be** ~ **with sthg** ter terminado algo; **to be** ~ **with sb** terminar com alguém. <> *adv* -1. [from one end to another] até o fim; **they let us** ~ nos deixaram passar -2. [until] até; **I slept** ~ **till ten** dormi até as dez. <> *prep* -1. [from one side to another] através de; **to cut** ~ cortar algo; **to get** ~ **sthg** passar por algo -2. [during, throughout] durante; **to go** ~ **an experience** passar por uma experiência -3. [because of] por; **to happen** ~ **sthg** acontecer devido a algo -4. [by means of] graças a -5. *US* [up till and including]: **Monday** ~ **Friday** de segunda a sexta.
➤ **through and through** *adv* -1. [completely] dos pés à cabeça -2. [thoroughly]: **to know sthg** ~ **and** ~ conhecer algo de cima a baixo.

throughout [θru:'aʊt] <> *prep* -1. [during] durante todo(da) -2. [everywhere in] por todo(da). <> *adv* -1. [all the time] o tempo todo -2. [everywhere] por todo o lado.

throughput [θru:ˌpʊt] *n UK* -1. rendimento *m* -2. *COMPUT* throughput *m*.

throve [θrəʊv] *pt* ▷ **thrive**.

throw [θrəʊ] (*pt* threw, *pp* thrown) <> *vt* -1. [gen] atirar; **to** ~ **one's arms around sb/sthg** abraçar alguém/algo -2. [move suddenly]: **to** ~ **o.s.** jogar -se, atirar-se; **to** ~ **o.s. into sthg** *fig* atirar-se em algo -3. [rider] derrubar, desmontar -4. *fig* [force into]: **we were all thrown into confusion** ficamos todos muito confusos; **he was thrown into the job at short notice** largaram o trabalho nas costas dele sem avisar -5. [shadow, light]: **to** ~ **sthg on sthg** projetar algo em algo -6. [tantrum, fit]: **to** ~ **a tantrum/fit** ter um acesso de fúria/um ataque -7. *fig* [confuse] deixar confuso(sa). <> *n* [toss, pitch] arremesso *m*, lançamento *m*.
➤ **throw away** *vt sep* jogar fora.
➤ **throw in** *vt sep* incluir *(como brinde)*.
➤ **throw out** *vt sep* -1. [discard] jogar fora -2. *fig* [reject] rejeitar -3. [force to leave] expulsar.
➤ **throw up** <> *vt sep* [cause to rise] jogar. <> *vi inf* [vomit] vomitar, botar para fora.

throwaway ['θrəʊəˌweɪ] *adj* -1. [disposable] descartável -2. [casual] fortuito(ta), casual.

throwback ['θrəʊbæk] *n*: ~ **(to sthg)** retrocesso *m* (a algo).

throw-in *n UK FTBL* arremesso *m* lateral.

thrown [θrəʊn] *pp* ▷ **throw**.

thru [θru:] *adj, adv & prep US inf* = **through**.

thrush [θrʌʃ] *n* -1. [bird] tordo *m* -2. *MED* cândida *f*.

thrust [θrʌst] (*pt & pp* thrust) <> *n* -1. [forward movement of knife, sword] golpe *m*; [- of army] investida *f*; [- of body] impulso *m* -2. (*U*) [forward force] (força *f* de) propulsão *f* -3. [main aspect]

essência *f*. <> *vt* -1. [shove, jab] empurrar -2. [jostle]: **to** ~ **one's way** abrir caminho à força.
➤ **thrust upon** *vt sep*: **to** ~ **sthg upon sb** impor algo a alguém.

thrusting ['θrʌstɪŋ] *adj* agressivo(va).

thruway ['θru:weɪ] *n US* rodovia *f*.

thud [θʌd] (*pt & pp* -ded, *cont* -ding) <> *n* baque *m*. <> *vi* dar um baque seco.

thug [θʌg] *n* marginal *mf*.

thumb [θʌm] <> *n* [of hand] polegar *m*; **to twiddle one's** ~ **s** ficar à toa. <> *vt inf* [hitch]: **to** ~ **a lift** pedir carona *(com o dedo)*.
➤ **thumb through** *vt fus* folhear.

thumb index *n* índice *m* alfabético.

thumbnail ['θʌmneɪl] <> *adj* breve. <> *n* unha *f* do polegar.

thumbnail sketch *n* descrição *f* breve.

thumbs down [ˌθʌmz-] *n*: **to get** OR **be given the** ~ ser recebido(da) com desaprovação, não ser bem recebido(da).

thumbs up [ˌθʌmz-] *n* [go-ahead]: **to give sb/sthg the** ~ dar luz verde a alguém/algo.

thumbtack ['θʌmtæk] *n US* percevejo *m (para fixar)*.

thump [θʌmp] <> *n* -1. [blow] soco *m* -2. [thud] baque *m*. <> *vt* -1. [punch] dar um soco em -2. [place heavily]: **he** ~ **ed the books down on the table** ele bateu os livros na mesa com força. <> *vi* -1. [move heavily] caminhar pesadamente; **to** ~ **in/ out** entrar/sair com passos pesados -2. [pound - heart] palpitar; [- head] latejar.

thunder ['θʌndə^r] <> *n* (*U*) -1. *METEOR* trovão *m* -2. *fig* [loud sound] estrondo *m*. <> *vt* [say angrily] vociferar, esbravejar. <> *vi* [make loud sound] fazer um estrondo. <> *v impers METEOR* trovejar.

thunderbolt ['θʌndəbəʊlt] *n* -1. *METEOR* raio *m* -2. *fig* [shock] choque *m*.

thunderclap ['θʌndəklæp] *n* trovão *m*.

thundercloud ['θʌndəklaʊd] *n* nuvem *f* de temporal.

thundering *adj* enorme, descomunal.

thunderous ['θʌndərəs] *adj* ensurdecedor(ra).

thunderstorm ['θʌndəstɔ:m] *n* temporal *m*.

thunderstruck ['θʌndəstrʌk] *adj fig* atônito(ta).

thundery ['θʌndəri] *adj* carregado(da).

Thur, Thurs (*abbr of* Thursday) qui.

Thursday ['θɜ:zdɪ] *n* quinta-feira *f*; *see also* **Saturday**.

thus [ðʌs] *adv fml* -1. [as a consequence] assim, por isso -2. [in this way] desse modo -3. [as follows] assim.

thwart [θwɔ:t] *vt* frustrar, impedir.

thyme [taɪm] *n* (*U*) tomilho *m*.

thyroid ['θaɪrɔɪd] *n* tireóide *f*.

tiara [tɪ'ɑ:rə] *n* tiara *f*.

Tiber ['taɪbə^r] *n*: **the (River)** ~ o (Rio) Tibre.

Tibet [tɪ'bet] *n* Tibete *m*; **in** ~ no Tíbete.

Tibetan [tɪ'betn] <> *adj* tibetano(na). <> *n* -1. [person] tibetano *m*, -na *f* -2. [language] tibetano *m*.

tibia ['tɪbɪə] (*pl* -biae [-bɪi:], -s) *n* tíbia *f*.

tic [tɪk] *n* tique *m*.

tick [tɪk] <> *n* -1. [written mark] (sinal *m* de) visto *m* -2. [sound] tiquetaque *m*; **I shan't be a** ~ não vou demorar **-3.** [insect] carrapato *m.* <> *vt* marcar *(com sinal de visto).* <> *vi* **-1.** [make ticking sound] fazer tiquetaque **-2.** *fig* [behave in a certain way]: **what makes him ~?** o que o motiva? ◆ **tick away, tick by** *vi* passar.

◆ **tick off** *vt sep* **-1.** [mark off] marcar *(com sinal de visto)* **-2.** [tell off]: **to ~ sb off (for sthg)** dar uma bronca em alguém (por algo).

◆ **tick over** *vi* funcionar em marcha lenta.

ticked [tıkd] *adj US inf* [annoyed] incomodado(da).

ticker tape *n* (*U*) fita *f* de teleimpressor; **~ parade** desfile *m* com confete e serpentinas.

ticket ['tıkıt] *n* **-1.** [for entry, access - plane] bilhete *m*; [- bus, train] passagem *f*; [- for footbal match, concert] entrada *f*, ingresso *m* **-2.** [label on product] etiqueta *f* **-3.** [notice of traffic offence] multa *f* **-4.** *POL* chapa *f*.

ticket agency *n* agência que vende entradas de teatro ou passagens de trem, avião etc.

ticket collector *n UK* revisor *m*, -ra *f* (no trem).

ticket holder *n* portador *m*, -ra *f* do ingresso.

ticket inspector *n UK* revisor *m*, -ra *f* (no trem).

ticket machine *n* máquina *f* automática que vende ingressos.

ticket office *n* **-1.** [in theatre] bilheteria *f* **-2.** [in station] guichê *m* de venda.

ticking off ['tıkıŋ-] (*pl* tickings off) *n*: **to get a ~** levar uma bronca; **to give sb a ~** dar uma bronca em alguém.

tickle ['tıkl] <> *vt* **-1.** [touch lightly] fazer cócegas em **-2.** *fig* [amuse] divertir. <> *vi*: **my feet are tickling** sinto cócegas nos pés.

ticklish ['tıklıʃ] *adj* **-1.** [sensitive to touch]: **to be ~** sentir cócegas **-2.** *fig* [delicate] delicado(da).

tick-tack-toe *n US* [game] jogo-da-velha *m*.

tidal ['taıdl] *adj* da maré.

tidal wave *n* maremoto *m*.

tidbit *n US* = titbit.

tiddler ['tıdlə'] *n UK* [fish] peixinho *m*.

tiddly ['tıdlı] (*compar*-ier, *superl*-iest) *adj inf* **-1.** [tipsy] grogue **-2.** [tiny] pequenininho(nha).

tiddlywinks ['tıdlıwıŋks], **tiddledywinks** *US* ['tıdldıwıŋks] *n* (*U*) [game] jogo *m* da pulga.

tide [taıd] *n* **-1.** [of sea] maré *f* **-2.** *fig* [trend] tendência *f*; **the ~ of history** o curso da história **-3.** *fig* [large quantity] corrente *f*.

◆ **tide over** *vt sep* dar uma força *(por um certo tempo).*

tidemark *n* **-1.** [of sea] linha *f* da maré alta **-2.** *UK* [round bath] marca *f* do nível da água escoada.

tidily ['taıdılı] *adv* [nearly] ordenadamente.

tidiness ['taıdınıs] *n* **-1.** [or room, desk] (*U*) ordem *f* **-2.** [of appearance] asseio *m*.

tidings ['taıdıŋz] *npl literary* novas *fpl.*

tidy ['taıdı] (*compar*-ier, *superl*-iest, *pt* & *pp*-ied) <> *adj* **-1.** [gen] arrumado(da) **-2.** [in habits] asseado(da) **-3.** *inf* [sizeable] razoável. <> *vt* arrumar.

◆ **tidy away** *vt sep* pôr em ordem.

◆ **tidy up** <> *vt sep* arrumar. <> *vi*: **I'll have to ~ up before going out** [objects] vou ter que arrumar tudo antes de sair.; [hair, appearance] vou ter que me arrumar antes de sair.

tie [taı] (*pt* & *pp* tied, *cont* tying) <> *n* **-1.** [necktie] gravata *f* **-2.** [string, cord] nó *m*, laçada *f* **-3.** [bond, link]

laço *m*, vínculo *m* **-4.** [in game, competition] empate *m* **-5.** *US RAIL* dormente *m.* <> *vt* **-1.** [attach]: **to ~ sthg (on) to sthg** amarrar algo (em algo); **to ~ sthg round sthg** amarrar algo em volta de algo; **to ~ sthg with sthg** amarrar algo com algo **-2.** [do up, fasten - shoelaces] atar, amarrar; [- knot] dar **-3.** *fig* [link]: **to be ~d to sthg/sb** estar ligado(da) a alguém/algo **-4.** *fig* [restricted]: **to be ~d to sthg** estar limitado(da) a algo. <> *vi* [draw]: **to ~ (with sb)** empatar (com alguém).

◆ **tie down** *vt sep fig* [restrict] prender; **to feel tied down by sthg** sentir-se preso(sa) a algo.

◆ **tie in with** *vt fus* concordar com, ajustar-se com.

◆ **tie up** *vt sep* **-1.** [secure with string, rope] amarrar **-2.** *fig* [restrict use of] limitar o uso de **-3.** *fig* [link]: **to be ~d up with sthg** estar ligado(da) a algo.

tiebreak(er) ['taıbreık(ə')] *n* **-1.** *TENNIS* tie-break *m* **-2.** [extra question] desempate *m.*

tied [taıd] *adj SPORT* empatado(da).

tied cottage *n UK* casa que o agricultor aluga a um de seus trabalhadores enquanto durar o serviço.

tied up *adj* [busy] ocupado(da).

tie-dye *vt* tie-dye.

tie-in *n* **-1.** [link]: **~ between/with sthg** ligação *f* entre/com algo **-2.** [promotional product] produto *m* promocional *(de um filme, programa de televisão).*

tiepin ['taıpın] *n* alfinete *m* de gravata.

tier [tıə'] *n* **-1.** [of seats, shelves] fileira *f* **-2.** [cake] camada *f.*

Tierra del Fuego *n* Terra do Fogo; **in ~** na Terra do Fogo.

tie-up *n* **-1.** [link]: **~ between/with sthg** relação *f* próxima entre/com algo **-2.** *US* [interruption - in work] suspensão *f*; [- in traffic] engarrafamento *m* rápido.

tiff [tıf] *n* desavença *f*, briguinha *f.*

tiger ['taıgə'] *n* tigre *m.*

tiger cub *n* filhote *m* de tigre.

tight [taıt] <> *adj* **-1.** [gen] apertado(da); **a ~ fit** justo(ta) **-2.** [taut] esticado(da), teso(sa) **-3.** [close together] comprimido(da) **-4.** [painful]: **my chest feels ~** sinto uma dor forte no peito **-5.** [strict] rigoroso(sa) **-6.** [at sharp angle] cerrado(da) **-7.** *inf* [drunk] bêbado(da) **-8.** *inf* [miserly] sovina. <> *adv* **-1.** [firmly, securely] com força; **to hold ~** segurar bem; **to shut** *OR* **close sthg ~** fechar bem algo **-2.** [tautly] bem esticado(da).

◆ **tights** *npl* meia-calça *f.*

tighten ['taıtn] <> *vt* **-1.** [knot, belt, rules] apertar **-2.** [make tauter] esticar **-3.** [strengthen]: **to ~ one's hold** *OR* **grip on sthg** agarrar *OR* segurar algo com força **-4.** [security] intensificar. <> *vi* [make tighter] apertar.

◆ **tighten up** *vt sep* **-1.** [belt, screw, rule] apertar **-2.** [control, security] intensificar.

tightfisted [,taıt'fıstıd] *adj inf pej* pão-duro.

tightknit [,taıt'nıt] *adj* muito unido(da).

tight-lipped [-'lıpt] *adj* **-1.** [with lips pressed together] de lábios cerrados **-2.** [silent] calado(da).

tightly ['taıtlı] *adv* **-1.** [closely]: **the dress fitted her**

~ o vestido entrava bem apertado nela **- 2.** [firmly, securely] com força; [fasten, tie] bem **- 3.** [tautly] bem esticado(da).

tightness ['taɪtnɪs] *n (U)* **- 1.** [gen] aperto *m* **- 2.** [strictness] rigor *m* **- 3.** [of schedule] pressão *f* de tempo.

tightrope ['taɪtrəʊp] *n* corda *f* bamba; **to be on** OR **walking a** ~ estar OR andar na corda bamba.

tightrope walker *n* funâmbulo *m*, -la *f*.

Tigré *n* Tigre; **in** ~ em Tigre.

tigress ['taɪgrɪs] *n* tigresa *f*.

Tigris *n*: **the (River)** ~ o (Rio) Tigre.

tilde ['tɪldə] *n* til *m*.

tile [taɪl] *n* **- 1.** [on roof] telha *f* **- 2.** [on floor] piso *m* **- 3.** [on wall] azulejo *m*.

tiled [taɪld] *adj* **- 1.** [roof] telhado(da) **- 2.** [floor] ladrilhado(da) **- 3.** [wall] azulejado(da).

tiling ['taɪlɪŋ] *n (U)* **- 1.** [act of tiling - roof, floor, wall] colocação *f* **- 2.** [tiled surface - roof] telhas *fpl*; [- floor] piso *m*; [- wall] azulejos *mpl*.

till [tɪl] <> *prep* até; ~ **now** até agora. <> *conj* até; **wait ~ I come back** espere até eu voltar OR que eu volte. <> *n* caixa *f* (registradora).

tiller ['tɪlə'] *n* cana *f* do leme.

tilt [tɪlt] <> *n* inclinação *f*. <> *vt* inclinar. <> *vi* inclinar-se.

timber ['tɪmbə'] *n* **- 1.** *(U)* [wood] madeira *f (para a construção)* **- 2.** [beam - of ship] viga *f* mestra; [- of house] madeiramento *m*.

timbered ['tɪmbəd] *adj* revestido(da) com madeira.

time [taɪm] <> *n* **- 1.** *(U)* [general measurement, spell] tempo *m*; **to get the** ~ **to do sthg** ter tempo para fazer algo; **to take** ~ levar tempo; **to take** ~ **out to do sthg** tirar tempo para fazer algo; **it's high** ~ ... já é hora de ...; **to get** ~ **and a half** receber o pagamento combinado mais a metade; **to have no** ~ **for sb/sthg** não ter tempo a perder com alguém/algo; **to make good** ~ fazer uma boa média (de tempo); **to pass the** ~ passar o tempo; **to play for** ~ tentar ganhar tempo; **to take one's** ~ **(doing sthg)** dar-se seu tempo (para fazer algo); **it was a long** ~ **before he came** passou muito tempo antes que ele viesse; **for a** ~ por um tempo **- 2.** [as measured by clock, moment] hora *f*; **the** ~ **is three o'clock** são três horas; **what** ~ **is it?**, **what's the** ~? que horas são?, tem horas?; **in a week's/year's** ~ daqui a uma semana/um mês; **to keep** ~ manter a hora certa; **to lose** ~ atrasar; **to tell the** ~ dizer as horas; **now would be a good** ~ **to ask** seria uma boa hora para perguntar **- 3.** [point in time in past] época *f*; **at that** ~ naquela época **- 4.** [era] era *f*; **in ancient** ~**s** na antiguidade; **to be ahead of one's** ~ estar à frente de seu tempo; **before my** ~ [before I was born] antes de eu nascer; [before I worked here] antes de eu trabalhar ali; **to be behind the** ~**s** estar parado(da) no tempo **- 5.** [occasion] vez *f*; **at the best of** ~**s** até nos melhores momentos; **from** ~ **to** ~ de vez em quando; ~ **after** ~, ~ **and again** uma e outra vez **- 6.** [experience]: **we had a good** ~ nos divertimos muito; **we had a terrible** ~ foi uma situação horrível; **to have a hard** ~ **trying to do sthg** ter dificuldade tentando fazer algo **- 7.** [degree of lateness]: **in good** ~ na hora certa;

ahead of ~ cedo; **on** ~ na hora **- 8.** MUS compasso *m*. <> *vt* **- 1.** [schedule] marcar **- 2.** [measure duration, speed of] cronometrar **- 3.** [choose appropriate moment for] escolher o momento certo para.

➡ **times** <> *npl*: **four** ~ **s as much as me** quatro vezes mais do que eu. <> *prep* MATH: **four** ~ **s five is twenty** quatro vezes cinco é vinte.

➡ **about time** *adv*: **it's about** ~ já era hora.

➡ **at a time** *adv*: **for months at a** ~ por meses seguidos; **one at a** ~ um (uma) por vez; **I always read several maganizes at a** ~ sempre leio várias revistas ao mesmo tempo.

➡ **at (any) one time** *adv* em qualquer momento.

➡ **at times** *adv* às vezes.

➡ **at the same time** *adv* ao mesmo tempo.

➡ **for the time being** *adv* por enquanto.

➡ **in time** *adv* **- 1.** [not late]: **in** ~ **(for sthg)** a tempo (para algo) **- 2.** [eventually] com o tempo.

time-and-motion study *n* estudo de métodos e técnicas para o rendimento no trabalho.

time bomb *n* bomba-relógio *f*.

time-consuming [-kən‚sju:mɪŋ] *adj* que exige muito tempo.

timed [taɪmd] *adj* **- 1.** [race, test] cronometrado(da) **- 2.** [opportune]: **well** ~ oportuno(na); **badly** ~ pouco oportuno(na).

time difference *n* diferença *f* de fuso horário.

time-honoured *adj* consagrado(da).

timekeeping ['taɪm‚ki:pɪŋ] *n (U)* pontualidade *f*; **he was sacked for bad** ~ foi demitido por chegar atrasado.

time lag *n* intervalo *m*.

time-lapse *adj* PHOT time-lapse.

timeless ['taɪmlɪs] *adj* eterno(na).

time limit *n* prazo *m*, limite *m* de tempo.

timely ['taɪmlɪ] (*compar* **-ier**, *superl* **-iest**) *adj* oportuno(na).

time machine *n* máquina *f* do tempo.

time off *n (U)* (tempo *m* de) folga *f*; ~ **(from) sthg** folga (de algo); **I'm owed** ~ me devem alguns dias de folga.

time-out (*pl* **time-outs** OR **times-out**) *n* US SPORT intervalo *m*.

timepiece ['taɪmpi:s] *n dated* relógio *m*.

timer ['taɪmə'] *n* temporizador *m*.

timesaving ['taɪm‚seɪvɪŋ] *adj* que economiza tempo.

time scale *n* escala *f* de tempo.

time-share *n* UK propriedade *f* comprada em sociedade.

time sheet *n* folha *f* de ponto.

time signal *n* sinal *m* horário (*emitido nas rádios*).

time switch *n* temporizador *m* (*numa máquina*).

timetable ['taɪm‚teɪbl] *n* **- 1.** [gen] horário *m* **- 2.** [schedule] programação *f*, programa *m*.

time zone *n* fuso *m* horário.

timid ['tɪmɪd] *adj* tímido(da).

timidly ['tɪmɪdlɪ] *adv* timidamente.

timing ['taɪmɪŋ] *n (U)* **- 1.** [of actor, musician, tennis player] timing *m* **-2.** [chosen moment]: **she made her comment with perfect** ~ ela fez seu comentário no momento certo **-3.** *SPORT* [measuring] cronometragem *f.*

timing device *n* dispositivo *m* de retardamento *(numa bomba).*

timpani ['tɪmpənɪ] *npl* timbales *mpl*, tímpanos *mpl.*

tin [tɪn] <> *n* **-1.** *(U)* [metal] estanho *m*; ~ **plate** folha-de-fandres *f* **-2.** *UK* [for food, storage] lata *f* **-3.** [for cooking] assadeira *f.* <> *comp* **-1.** [tin] de estanho **-2.** [tinplate] de folha-de-flandres.

tin can *n* lata *f.*

tinder *n (U)* isca *f (para acender o fogo).*

tinfoil ['tɪnfɔɪl] *n (U)* papel *m* OR folha *f* de estanho.

tinge [tɪndʒ] *n* **-1.** [of colour] tom *m*, matiz *m* **-2.** [of feeling] rápida sensação *f*; **a** ~ **of guilt** uma ponta de culpa.

tinged [tɪndʒd] *adj* **-1.** [colour]: ~ **with sthg** com um toque de algo **-2.** [feeling]: ~ **with sthg** com uma pontinha de algo.

tingle ['tɪŋgl] *vi* formigar; **to** ~ **with sthg** agitar-se com algo.

tingling ['tɪŋglɪŋ] *n* formigamento *m.*

tinker ['tɪŋkəʳ] <> *n* **-1.** *pej* [gipsy] cigano *m*, -na *f* **-2.** [rascal] diabinho *m*, -nha *f.* <> *vi* atamancar; **to** ~ **with sthg** fuçar em algo.

tinkle ['tɪŋkl] <> *n* **-1.** [of bell] tilintar *m* **-2.** *UK inf* [phone call]: **to give sb a** ~ bater um fio para alguém. <> *vi* **-1.** [bell] tilintar **-2.** [phone] tocar.

tin mine *n* mina *f* de estanho.

tinned [tɪnd] *adj UK* enlatado(da), em conserva.

tinny ['tɪnɪ] *(compar* **-ier**, *superl* **-iest)** *adj* **-1.** [sound] metálico(ca) **-2.** *inf pej* [badly made] malfeito(ta).

tin opener *n UK* abridor *m* de lata.

tinpot *adj UK pej* de araque.

tinsel ['tɪnsl] *n (U)* lantejoula *f*, ouropel *m.*

tint [tɪnt] <> *n* matiz *m* <> *vt* **-1.** [gen] matizar **-2.** [window, glass] colorir **-3.** [hair] tingir.

tinted ['tɪntɪd] *adj* **-1.** [window, glass] colorido(da) **-2.** [hair] tingido(da).

tiny ['taɪnɪ] *(compar* **-ier**, *superl* **-iest)** *adj* minúsculo(-la), diminuto(ta).

tip [tɪp] *(pt & pp* **-ped**, *cont* **-ping)** <> *n* **-1.** [end] ponta *f*; **it's on the** ~ **of my tongue** está na ponta da língua **-2.** *UK* [dump]: **rubbish** ~ lixão *m*, depósito *m* de lixo **-3.** [gratuity] gorjeta *f* **-4.** [piece of advice] dica *f.* <> *vt* **-1.** [tilt] inclinar **-2.** [spill] derramar **-3.** [give a gratuity to] dar gorjeta a. <> *vi* **-1.** [tilt] inclinar-se **-2.** [spill] derramar **-3.** [give a gratuity] dar gorjeta.

◆ **tip off** *vt sep* avisar, alertar.

◆ **tip over** *vt sep & vi* virar.

◆ **tip up** *vi* virar.

tip-off *n* informação *f (secreta).*

tipped [tɪpt] *adj* **-1.** [spear] com ponta de aço **-2.** [cigarette] com filtro **-3.** [pen]: **felt-**~ **pen** caneta *f* hidrográfica.

Tipp-Ex® ['tɪpeks] *n UK* ≃ errorex® corretivo *m.*

◆ **tipp-ex** *vt UK* corrigir com corretivo.

tipple ['tɪpl] *n inf* bebida *f.*

tipsy ['tɪpsɪ] *(compar* **-ier**, *superl* **-iest)** *adj inf* alto(ta) *(por ingerir bebida alcóolica),* tocado(da).

tiptoe ['tɪptəʊ] <> *n*: **on** ~ nas pontas dos pés.

<> *vi* andar nas pontas dos pés.

tip-top *adj inf dated* ótimo(ma).

tirade [taɪ'reɪd] *n* descascadela *f.*

Tirana, Tiranë *n* Tirana.

tire ['taɪəʳ] <> *n US* = **tyre**. <> *vt* cansar. <> *vi* **-1.** [get tired] cansar-se, ficar cansado(da) **-2.** [get fed up]: **to** ~ **ofsb/sthg** cansar-se de alguém/algo.

◆ **tire out** *vt sep* esgotar.

tired ['taɪəd] *adj* **-1.** [sleepy] cansado(da) **-2.** [fed up]: ~ **of sthg/of doing sthg** cansado(da) de algo/de fazer algo.

tiredness ['taɪədnɪs] *n (U)* cansaço *m.*

tireless ['taɪəlɪs] *adj* incansável.

tiresome ['taɪəsəm] *adj* cansativo(va), enfadonho(-nha).

tiring ['taɪərɪŋ] *adj* cansativo(va).

Tirol *n* = Tyrol.

tissue ['tɪʃuː] *n* **-1.** [paper handkerchief] lenço *m* de papel **-2.** *(U)* BIOL tecido *m* **-3.** *phr*: **a** ~ **of lies** um emaranhado de mentiras.

tissue paper *n (U)* papel *m* de seda.

tit [tɪt] *n* **-1.** [bird] chapim *m* **-2.** *vulg* [breast] teta *f.*

titbit *UK* ['tɪtbɪt], **tidbit** *US* ['tɪdbɪt] *n* **-1.** [of food] petisco *m* **-2.** *fig* [of news]: **a** ~ **of gossip** uma pequena fofoca.

tit for tat [-'tæt] *n*: **it's** ~ é olho por olho.

titillate ['tɪtɪleɪt] <> *vt* excitar. <> *vi* excitar-se.

titivate ['tɪtɪveɪt] *vt* arrumar, enfeitar.

title ['taɪtl] *n* título *m.*

titled ['taɪtld] *adj* com título de nobreza.

title deed *n* título *m* de propriedade.

titleholder ['taɪtl,həʊldəʳ] *n SPORT* campeão *m*, -peã *f.*

title page *n* página *f* de rosto.

title role *n* papel *m* principal.

titter ['tɪtəʳ] *vi* rir baixinho.

tittle-tattle ['tɪtl,tætl] *n (U) inf pej* mexerico *m.*

titular ['tɪtjʊləʳ] *adj* honorário(ria), nominal.

T-junction *n* junção-tê *f.*

TLS *(abbr of* **Times Literary Supplement)** *n* suplemento semanal do *Times* britânico direcionado à literatura.

TM <> *n* **-1.** *(abbr of* **transcendental meditation)** meditação *f* transcendental **-2.** *(abbr of* **translation memory)** MT *f.* <> *abbr of* **trademark**.

TN *abbr of* **Tennessee**.

TNT *(abbr of* **trinitrotoluene)** *n* TNT *m.*

to [unstressed before consonant tə, unstressed before vowel tʊ, stressed tuː] <> *prep* **-1.** [indicating direction] para; **to go** ~ **Brazil** ir ao Brasil; **to go** ~ **school** ir para a escola. **-2.** [indicating position]: ~ **the left/right** à esquerda/direita. **-3.** [expressing indirect object] a; **to give sthg** ~ **sb** dar algo a alguém; **give it** ~ **me** dê-me isso; **to listen** ~ **the radio** ouvir rádio. **-4.** [indicating reaction, effect]: ~ **my surprise** para surpresa minha; **it's** ~ **your advantage** é em seu benefício. **-5.** [until] até; **to count** ~ **ten** contar até dez; **we work from nine** ~ **five** trabalhamos das nove (até) às cinco. **-6.** [in stating opinion] para; ~ **me, he's lying** para mim, ele está mentindo. **-7.** [indicating change of state]: **to turn** ~ **sthg** transformar-se em algo; **it could lead** ~ **trouble** pode vir a dar problemas. **-8.** *UK* [in expressions of time] para; **it's ten ~ three** são dez para as três; **at quarter ~ seven** às quinze para as sete. **- 9.** [in ratios, rates]: **40 miles ~ the gallon** 40 milhas por galão. **-10.** [of, for]: **the answer ~ the question** a resposta à pergunta; **the key ~ the car** a chave do carro; **a letter ~ my daughter** uma carta para a minha filha. **-11.** [indicating attitude] (para) com; **to be rude ~ sb** ser grosseiro com alguém. ◇ **with** infinitive **-1.** [forming simple infinitive]: **~ walk** andar; **~ laugh** rir. **-2.** [following another verb]: **to begin ~ do sthg** começar a fazer algo; **to try ~ do sthg** tentar fazer algo. **-3.** [following an adjective]: **difficult ~ do** difícil de fazer; **pleased ~ meet you** prazer em conhecê-lo; **ready ~ go** pronto para partir. **-4.** [indicating purpose] para; **we came here ~ look at the castle** viemos para ver o castelo.

toad [tǝʊd] n sapo m.

toadstool ['tǝʊdstu:l] n cogumelo m venenoso.

toady ['tǝʊdɪ] (pl **-ies**, pt & pp **-ied**) pej ◇ n bajulador m, -ra f. ◇ vi: **to ~ (to sb)** puxar o saco (de alguém).

toast [tǝʊst] ◇ n **-1.** (U) [bread] torrada f, pão m torrado **-2.** [drink] brinde m; **to drink a ~ to sb/sthg** fazer um brinde a alguém/algo **-3.** [person]: **the ~ of the town** o herói da cidade. ◇ vt **-1.** [bread] tostar, torrar **-2.** [person] brindar a.

toasted sandwich [,tǝʊstɪd-] n misto-quente m.

toaster ['tǝʊstǝʳ] n torradeira f.

toast rack n porta-torradas m inv.

tobacco [tǝ'bækǝʊ] n tabaco m.

tobacconist n charuteiro m, -ra f, vendedor m, -ra f de fumo OR tabaco; **~'s (shop)** tabacaria f.

Tobago [tǝ'beɪgǝʊ] n ▷Trinidad and Tobago.

toboggan [tǝ'bɒgǝn] ◇ n tobogã m. ◇ vi deslizar-se em tobogã.

today [tǝ'deɪ] ◇ adv (U) **-1.** [this day] hoje **-2.** [nowadays] de hoje, atual; **~'s technology** a tecnologia hoje em dia. ◇ adv **-1.** [this day] hoje **-2.** [nowadays] hoje (em dia).

toddle ['tɒdl] vi **-1.** [walk unsteadily] dar os primeiros passos **-2.** inf [go]: **to ~ off** OR **along** cair fora.

toddler ['tɒdlǝʳ] n criança f pequena (que começa a andar).

toddy ['tɒdɪ] (pl **-ies**) n ponche m.

to-do (pl **-s**) n inf dated tumulto m, alvoroço m.

toe [tǝʊ] ◇ n **-1.** [of foot] dedo m (do pé) **-2.** [of sock] ponta f **-3.** [of shoe] biqueira f. ◇ vt: **to ~ the line** cumprir as normas.

toehold ['tǝʊhǝʊld] n **-1.** [in rock] ponto m de apoio **-2.** fig [in market]: **to gain a ~ in** conseguir uma brecha em.

toenail ['tǝʊneɪl] n unha f do pé.

toffee ['tɒfɪ] n **-1.** [sweet] tofe m, caramelo m **-2.** (U) [substance] tofe m.

toffee apple n UK maçã f do amor.

tofu ['tǝʊfu:] n (U) tofu m.

toga ['tǝʊgǝ] n toga f.

together [tǝ'geðǝʳ] ◇ adj inf sensato(ta). ◇ adv juntos(tas); **to go ~** combinar.
➡ **together with** prep junto com.

togetherness [tǝ'geðǝnɪs] n (U) união f, camaradagem f.

toggle switch ['tɒgl-] n **-1.** ELECTRON chave f articulada **-2.** COMPUT comutador m (alternado).

Togo ['tǝʊgǝʊ] n Togo; **in ~** no Togo.

Togolese ◇ adj togolês(esa). ◇ n togolês m, -esa f.

togs [tɒgz] npl inf traje m, roupa f.

toil [tɔɪl] fml ◇ n trabalho m duro. ◇ vi trabalhar duro.
➡ **toil away** vi: **to ~ away (at sthg)** trabalhar duro (em algo).

toilet ['tɔɪlɪt] n vaso m sanitário; **to go to the ~** ir ao banheiro.

toilet bag n nécessaire m.

toilet paper n (U) papel m higiênico.

toiletries ['tɔɪlɪtrɪz] npl artigos mpl de toalete.

toilet roll n **-1.** (U) [paper] papel m higiênico **-2.** [roll] rolo m de papel higiênico.

toilet soap n (U) sabonete f.

toilet tissue n (U) papel m higiênico.

toilet-trained [-,treɪnd] adj que já sabe ir ao banheiro.

toilet water n (U) água-de-colônia f, colônia f.

to-ing and fro-ing [,tu:ɪŋǝn'frǝʊɪŋ] n (U) idas fpl e vindas.

token ['tǝʊkn] ◇ adj simbólico(ca). ◇ n **-1.** [voucher, disc - for machines] ficha f; [- for books, records] vale m; **-2.** [symbol] símbolo m, mostra f.
➡ **by the same token** adv da mesma forma.

Tokyo ['tǝʊkjǝʊ] n Tóquio; **in ~** em Tóquio.

told [tǝʊld] pt & pp ▷ tell.

tolerable ['tɒlǝrǝbl] adj tolerável, passável.

tolerably ['tɒlǝrǝblɪ] adv razoavelmente.

tolerance ['tɒlǝrǝns] n tolerância f.

tolerant ['tɒlǝrǝnt] adj **-1.** [not bigoted]: **~ of sb/sthg** tolerante com alguém/algo **-2.** [resistant]: **~ to sthg** resistente a algo.

tolerate ['tɒlǝreɪt] vt **-1.** [put up with] suportar, tolerar **-2.** [permit] tolerar.

toleration [,tɒlǝ'reɪʃn] n (U) tolerância f.

toll [tǝʊl] ◇ n **-1.** [number]: **death ~** número m de vítimas fatais **-2.** [fee] pedágio m **-3.** phr: **to take its ~** ter suas implicações. ◇ vt [bell] tocar, badalar. ◇ vi [bell] tocar, dobrar.

tollbooth ['tǝʊlbu:θ] n cabine f de pedágio.

toll bridge n ponte f com pedágio.

toll-free US ◇ adj gratuito(ta). ◇ adv: **to call ~** telefonar OR ligar gratuitamente.

tomato [UK tǝ'mɑ:tǝʊ, US tǝ'meɪtǝʊ] (pl **-es**) n tomate m.

tomb [tu:m] n túmulo m, tumba f.

tombola [tɒm'bǝʊlǝ] n esp UK tômbola f.

tomboy ['tɒmbɔɪ] n menina que gosta de jogos e brincadeiras de meninos.

tombstone ['tu:mstǝʊn] n lápide f.

tomcat ['tɒmkæt] n gato m (macho).

tomfoolery [tɒm'fu:lǝrɪ] n (U) tolice f.

tomorrow [tǝ'mɒrǝʊ] ◇ n **-1.** [day after today] amanhã m **-2.** fig [future] futuro m. ◇ adv **-1.** [the day after today] amanhã; **~ week** uma semana a contar de amanhã **-2.** [in future] no futuro.

ton [tʌn] *(pl inv OR* -s) *n* -1. *UK* [imperial unit of measurement] tonelada *f* inglesa *OR* longa *(1016,05 kg)* -2. *US* [unit of measurement] tonelada *f (907,19 kg)* -3. [metric unit of measurement] tonelada *f* métrica - 4. *phr*: **to weigh a** ~ *inf* pesar uma tonelada; **to come down on sb like a** ~ **of bricks** soltar os cachorros em cima de alguém.
➤ **tons** *npl UK inf*: ~**s (of)** um monte de.

tonal ['təʊnl] *adj* tonal.

tone [təʊn] *n* -1. [gen] tom *m* -2. *TELEC* sinal *m*; **dialling** ~ linha *f* de discagem -3. *phr*: **to lower the** ~ **of** sthg baixar o nível de algo.
➤ **tone down** *vt sep* suavizar, moderar.
➤ **tone in** *vi* combinar; **to** ~ **in with sthg** combinar com algo.
➤ **tone up** *vt sep* pôr em forma.

tone-deaf *adj* que não tem ouvido musical.

toner ['təʊnə'] *n* -1. [for photocopier, printer] toner *m* -2. [cosmetic] tônico *m*, tonificante *m*.

tongs [tɒŋz] *npl* -1. [for sugar] pinça *f* para açúcar -2. [for hair] pinças *fpl*.

tongue [tʌŋ] *n* -1. [gen] língua *f*; **to have one's** ~ **in one's cheek** *inf* falar brincando; **to hold one's** ~ *fig* fechar o bico; ~**s will wag** as pessoas vão falar a respeito -2. *fml* [language] língua *f* -3. [of shoe] lingüeta *f*.

tongue-in-cheek *adj* em tom de brincadeira.

tongue-tied [-ˌtaɪd] *adj* mudo(da) *(por timidez ou nervosismo)*.

tongue twister [-ˌtwɪstə'] *n* trava-língua *m*.

tonic ['tɒnɪk] *n* -1. [gen] tônico *m* -2. (U) [tonic water] (água *f*) tônica *f* -3. *fig* [beneficial thing] bálsamo *m*.

tonic water *n* (U) (água *f*) tônica *f*.

tonight [tə'naɪt] ◇ *n* (U) esta noite *f*. ◇ *adv* hoje à noite, esta noite.

tonnage ['tʌnɪdʒ] *n* (U) *NAUT* -1. [weight] tonelagem *f* -2. [amount of cargo] tonelagem *f* (de arqueação).

tonne [tʌn] *(pl inv OR* -s) *n* tonelada *f* métrica.

tonsil ['tɒnsl] *n* amígdala *f*.

tonsil(l)itis [ˌtɒnsɪ'laɪtɪs] *n* (U) amigdalite *f*.

too [tuː] *adv* -1. [also] também -2. [excessively]: ~ **much** demais; ~ **old** velho demais; ~ **many things** muitas e muitas coisas; ~ **long a book** um livro longo demais; **all** ~ **soon** cedo demais; **only** ~ ... muito ...; **I'd be only** ~ **happy to help** eu adoraria ajudar -3. *(with negatives)*: **not** ~ **bad** nada mal; **I wasn't** ~ **impressed** não fiquei muito impressionado.

took [tʊk] *pt* ⊳ take.

tool [tuːl] *n* -1. [implement] ferramenta *f*; **to down** ~**s** *UK* parar de trabalhar em protesto -2. *fig* [means] ferramenta *f*, instrumento *m*; **the** ~**s of one's trade** as ferramentas de trabalho de alguém.
➤ **tool around** *vi US inf* passear.

tool box *n* caixa *f* de ferramentas.

tool kit *n* jogo *m* de ferramentas.

toot [tuːt] ◇ *n* buzinada *f*. ◇ *vt* buzinar. ◇ *vi* buzinar.

tooth [tuːθ] *(pl* teeth) *n* dente *m*; **to be long in the** ~ *UK pej* estar um pouco passado(da); **to be fed up to the back teeth with sthg** *UK inf* estar até aqui com algo; **to grit one's teeth** cerrar os dentes; **to have no teeth** *fig* [be powerless] não ter poder

algum; **to lie through one's teeth** mentir até não poder mais.

toothache ['tuːθeɪk] *n* (U) dor *f* de dente.

toothbrush ['tuːθbrʌʃ] *n* escova *f* de dentes.

toothless ['tuːθlɪs] *adj* desdentado(da).

toothpaste ['tuːθpeɪst] *n* (U) pasta *f* de dentes.

toothpick ['tuːθpɪk] *n* palito *m*.

tooth powder *n* (U) pó *m* dentifrício.

tootle ['tuːtl] *vi inf* [move unhurriedly] passear.

top [tɒp] *(pt & pp* -ped, *cont* -ping) ◇ *adj* -1. [highest] de cima, superior -2. [most important, successful] importante; **she got the** ~ **mark** ela tirou a melhor nota -3. [maximum] máximo(ma). ◇ *n* -1. [gen] topo *m*, parte *f* de cima; **from** ~ **to bottom** de cima a baixo; **on** ~ em cima; **to go over the** ~ *UK* passar um pouco dos limites; **at the** ~ **of one's voice** a toda voz -2. [highest point - of list, class] primeiro(ra); [- of tree] copa *f*; [- of hill] cume *m*; [- of page] topo *m* -3. [lid, cap] tampa *f* -4. [upper side] superfície *f* -5. [clothing - bikini, pyjama] parte *f* de cima; [- blouse] blusa *f* -6. [toy] pião *m* -7. [highest rank - of an organization] topo *m*; [- of a league, class] primeiro(ra). ◇ *vt* -1. [to be first in - league, poll] liderar, estar em primeiro lugar em; [- table, chart] liderar, encabeçar -2. [better] superar -3. [exceed] passar de -4. [put on top of] cobrir.
➤ **on top of** *prep* -1. [in space] em cima de -2. [in addition to] além de; **on** ~ **of that** como se não bastasse -3. [in control of]: **to be** ~ **of sthg** ter algo sob controle -4. *phr*: **to get on** ~ **of sb** deixar alguém preocupado(da).
➤ **top up** *UK*, **top off** *US vt sep* encher novamente.

topaz ['təʊpæz] *n* topázio *m*.

top brass *n* (U) *inf*: **the** ~ os altos cargos, os figurões.

topcoat ['tɒpkəʊt] *n* -1. [item of clothing] sobretudo *m* -2. [paint] última demão *f*.

top dog *n inf* manda-chuva *mf*.

top-flight *adj* de primeira qualidade.

top floor *n* último andar *m*.

top gear *n* marcha *f* mais rápida *(de um veículo)*.

top hat *n* cartola *f*.

top-heavy *adj* muito pesado(da) na parte de cima.

topic ['tɒpɪk] *n* tópico *m*.

topical ['tɒpɪkl] *adj* atual, da atualidade.

topknot ['tɒpnɒt] *n* coque *m*.

topless ['tɒplɪs] *adj* [barebreasted] topless; **to go** ~ fazer topless.

top-level *adj* do mais alto nível.

topmost ['tɒpməʊst] *adj* mais alto(ta).

top-notch *adj inf* de primeira.

topographer *n* topógrafo *m*, -fa *f*.

topography [tə'pɒgrəfi] *n* (U) topografia *f*.

topped [tɒpt] *adj*: ~ **by** *OR* **with sthg** com algo em cima.

topping ['tɒpɪŋ] *n* cobertura *f*.

topple ['tɒpl] ◇ *vt* derrubar. ◇ *vi* vir abaixo.
➤ **topple over** *vi* vir abaixo.

top-ranking [-'ræŋkɪŋ] *adj* do mais alto nível.

TOPS [tɒps] *(abbr of* Training Opportunities Scheme)

n programa de formação vocacional do governo britânico.

top-secret *adj* ultra-secreto(ta).

top-security *adj* de segurança máxima.

topsoil ['tɒpsɔɪl] *n (U)* solo *m* arável, camada *f* superficial do solo.

topspin *n (U)* topspin *m*.

topsy-turvy [ˌtɒpsɪ'tɜːvɪ] ◇ *adj* -1. [messy] de pernas para o ar -2. [haywire] louco(ca). ◇ *adv* [upside down] de ponta-cabeça.

top-up card *n* [for mobile phone] cartão *m* de recarga.

tor *n esp UK* [hill] colina *f* rochosa *(típica da Inglaterra)*.

torch [tɔːtʃ] *n* -1. *UK* [electric] lanterna *f* -2. [flaming stick] tocha *f*.

tore [tɔːʳ] *pt* ▷ **tear** ².

torment [*n* 'tɔːment, *vb* tɔː'ment] ◇ *n* tormento *m*. ◇ *vt* atormentar.

tormentor [tɔː'mentəʳ] *n* atormentador *m*, -ra *f*.

torn [tɔːn] *pp* ▷ **tear** ².

tornado [tɔː'neɪdəʊ] *(pl* -es *OR* -s*) n* tornado *m*.

Toronto *n* Toronto; **in ~** em Toronto.

torpedo [tɔː'piːdəʊ] *(pl* -es*)* ◇ *n* torpedo *m*. ◇ *vt* torpedear.

torpedo boat *n* torpedeiro *m*.

torpor ['tɔːpəʳ] *n (U)* torpor *m*.

torque [tɔːk] *n TECH* torque *m*.

torrent ['tɒrənt] *n* torrente *f*.

torrential [tə'renʃl] *adj* torrencial.

torrid ['tɒrɪd] *adj* tórrido(da).

torso ['tɔːsəʊ] *(pl* -s*) n* torso *m*.

tortoise ['tɔːtəs] *n* tartaruga *f* terrestre.

tortoiseshell ['tɔːtəʃell] ◇ *adj* [cat] escama-de-tartaruga. ◇ *n (U)* [material] tartaruga *f*. ◇ *comp* de tartaruga.

tortuous ['tɔːtʃʊəs] *adj* -1. [twisty] sinuoso(sa) -2. [over-complicated] tortuoso(sa).

torture ['tɔːtʃəʳ] ◇ *n* tortura *f*. ◇ *vt* torturar.

torturer ['tɔːtʃərəʳ] *n* torturador *m*, -ra *f*.

Tory ['tɔːrɪ] *(pl* -ies*)* ◇ *adj* tóri, do partido conservador britânico. ◇ *n* tóri *mf*, membro *m* do partido conservador britânico.

toss [tɒs] ◇ *vt* -1. [throw carelessly] atirar, jogar -2. [head] sacudir -3. [food] misturar -4. [coin] jogar *(ao ar)*; **to ~ a coin** tirar no cara ou coroa -5. [throw about] jogar, arremessar. ◇ *vi* -1. [with coin] tirar no cara ou coroa -2. [move about]: **to ~ and turn** rolar na cama. ◇ *n* -1. [of coin] arremesso *m (de moeda)* -2. [of head] sacudida *f*, meneio *m*.

▸ **toss up** *vi* disputar no cara ou coroa.

toss-up *n inf*: **it's a ~ whether they win or lose** impossível dizer *OR* saber se eles ganham ou perdem.

tot [tɒt] *(pt & pp* -ted, *cont* -ting*) n* -1. *inf* [small child] nenezinho *f*, -nha -2. [of drink] golinho *m*.

▸ **tot up** *vt sep inf* somar.

total ['təʊtl] *(UK pt & pp* -led, *cont* -ling, *US pt & pp* -ed, *cont* -ing*)* ◇ *adj* total. ◇ *n* total *m*; **in ~** no total. ◇ *vt* -1. [add up] somar -2. [amount to] totalizar -3. *US inf* [wreck] arruinar.

totalitarian [ˌtəʊtælɪ'teərɪən] *adj* totalitário(ria).

totality [təʊ'tælətɪ] *n* totalidade *f*.

totally ['təʊtəlɪ] *adv* totalmente.

tote bag [təʊt-] *n US* sacola *f* de compras.

totem pole ['təʊtəm-] *n* totem *m*.

totter ['tɒtəʳ] *vi* cambalear.

toucan ['tuːkən] *n* tucano *m*.

touch [tʌtʃ] ◇ *n* -1. [gen] toque *m*; **to put the finishing ~s to sthg** dar os últimos retoques a algo -2. [contact]: **to get in ~ (with sb)** entrar em contato (com alguém); **to keep in ~ (with sb)** manter contato (com alguém); **to lose ~ (with sb)** perder o contato (com alguém); **to be out of ~ with sthg** estar por fora de algo -3. [small amount]: **a ~ (of sthg)** um pouco (de algo) -4. *SPORT*: **in ~** na lateral -5. *phr*: **it was ~ and go whether we left or stayed** a gente não sabia se saía ou ficava; **to be a soft ~** [for money] não saber dizer que não *(empresta dinheiro)* -6. *(U)* [sense] tato *m*; **soft to the ~** suave ao toque; **the ~ of her lips** o toque de seus lábios. ◇ *vt* -1. [make contact with] tocar -2. [move emotionally] tocar, comover -3. [eat] comer -4. [drink] beber. ◇ *vi* -1. [make contact] tocar -2. [be in contact] tocar-se.

▸ **a touch** *adv* um pouco.

▸ **touch down** *vi* [plane] aterrissar.

▸ **touch on** *vt fus* tocar por cima.

▸ **touch up** *vt sep* [paintwork] retocar.

touch-and-go *adj* incerto(ta), duvidoso(sa).

touchdown ['tʌtʃdaʊn] *n* -1. [on land, sea] aterrissagem *f* -2. [in American football] touchdown *m*.

touched [tʌtʃt] *adj* -1. [grateful] comovido(da), emocionado(da) -2. *inf* [slightly mad] tantã.

touching ['tʌtʃɪŋ] *adj* tocante, comovente.

touch judge *n RUGBY* bandeirinha *m*, juiz *m*, -íza *f* de linha.

touchline ['tʌtʃlaɪn] *n SPORT* linha *f* lateral.

touchpaper ['tʌtʃˌpeɪpəʳ] *n* estopim *m*.

touch screen *n* tela *f* tátil.

touch-type *vi* -1. [typewriter] datilografar sem olhar para o teclado -2. [computer] digitar sem olhar para o teclado.

touchy ['tʌtʃɪ] *(compar* -ier, *superl* -iest*) adj* -1. [person] suscetível; **to be ~ about sthg** ser sensível em relação a algo -2. [subject, question] delicado(da).

tough [tʌf] *adj* -1. [gen] duro(ra) -2. [person, character] forte -3. [material] resistente -4. [decision, life] difícil -5. [criminal, neighbourhood] da pesada -6. *inf* [unfortunate] difícil; **~ luck** má sorte; [as exclamation] que azar!

toughen ['tʌfn] *vt* endurecer.

toughened ['tʌfnd] *adj* temperado(da).

toughness ['tʌfnɪs] *n (U)* -1. [of character - strength] força *f*; [- hardness] firmeza *f* -2. [of material] resistência *f* -3. [of meat] dureza *f*.

toupee ['tuːpeɪ] *n* peruca *f*.

tour [tʊəʳ] ◇ *n* -1. [trip] excursão *f*, viagem *f* -2. [of building, town, museum] visita *f*; **guided ~** visita *f* guiada -3. [official journey] turnê *f*. ◇ *vt* -1. [visit] visitar -2. *SPORT & THEATRE* fazer uma turnê por. ◇ *vi* [go on trip] fazer uma excursão, viajar; **to ~ round somewhere** fazer uma excursão em algum lugar, viajar por algum lugar.

tourer ['tʊərəʳ] *n* [car] carro *m* de turismo.

touring ['tʊərɪŋ] <> *adj* -1. [exhibition] itinerante - 2. [show, theatre group] em turnê. <> *n (U)* viagens *fpl* turísticas; **to go** ~ fazer turismo.
tourism ['tʊərɪzm] *n (U)* turismo *m*.
tourist ['tʊərɪst] *n* turista *mf*.
tourist class *n (U)* classe *f* econômica OR turística.
tourist (information) office *n* (serviço *m* de) informações *fpl* turísticas.
touristy ['tʊərɪstɪ] *adj pej* muito turístico(ca).
tournament ['tɔːnəmənt] *n* CHESS & SPORT torneio *m*.
tourniquet ['tʊənɪkeɪ] *n* torniquete *m*.
tour operator *n* agência *f* de viagens.
tousle *vt* -1. [hair] despentear - 2. [fur, feathers] desarrumar.
tout [taʊt] <> *n* cambista *mf*. <> *vt* [tickets, goods] revender *(como cambista)*. <> *vi*: **to** ~ **for sthg** angariar algo; **to** ~ **for trade** tentar obter algo; **to** ~ **for clients** aliciar algo; **to** ~ **for investment** buscar algo.
tow [taʊ] <> *n* reboque *m*; **on** ~ UK a reboque; **with sb in** ~ com alguém a reboque. <> *vt* rebocar.
towards UK [tə'wɔːdz], **toward** US [tə'wɔːd] *prep* - 1. [in the direction of] para, em direção a - 2. [indicating attitude] em relação a - 3. [near in time, space] perto de - 4. [as contribution to] para.
towaway zone ['taʊəweɪ-] *n* US zona *f* de estacionamento proibido.
towbar ['taʊbɑː] *n* engate *m* para reboque.
towel ['taʊəl] *n* toalha *f*.
towelling UK, **toweling** US ['taʊəlɪŋ] <> *n (U)* tecido *m* atoalhado. <> *comp* atoalhado(da).
towel rail *n* toalheiro *m*.
tower ['taʊəʳ] <> *n* torre *f*; **a** ~ **of strength** UK um forte apoio. <> *vi* destacar-se; **to** ~ **over sb** ser muito mais alto(ta) do que alguém; **to** ~ **over/sthg** destacar-se por cima de algo.
tower block *n* UK prédio *m* alto de escritórios.
towering ['taʊərɪŋ] *adj* [very tall] altíssimo(ma).
town [taʊn] *n* -1. [population centre] cidade *f* - 2. (U) [centre of town, city] centro *m* (da cidade); **to go out on the** ~ ir divertir-se; **to go to** ~ *fig* botar para quebrar.
town centre *n* centro *m* (da cidade).
town clerk *n* secretário *m*, -ria *f* da câmara municipal.
town council *n* câmara *f* municipal.
town hall *n* -1. [building] prefeitura *f* -2. (U) fig [council] prefeitura *f*.
town house *n* [fashionable house] mansão *f*.
town plan *n* -1. [map] mapa *m* da cidade -2. [project, plan] projeto *m* de urbanização.
town planner *n* urbanista *mf*.
town planning *n (U)* -1. [study] urbanismo *m* -2. [practice] urbanização *f*.
townsfolk ['taʊnzfəʊk], **townspeople** ['taʊnz,piːpl] *npl*: **the** ~ os habitantes *(de uma cidade)*, os cidadãos.
township ['taʊnʃɪp] *n* -1. [in South Africa] *zona urbana atribuída antigamente pelo governo à população negra* -2. [in US] ≃ município *m*.
towpath ['taʊpɑːθ, *pl* -pɑːðz] *n* caminho *m* de sirga.

towrope ['taʊrəʊp] *n* cabo *m* para reboque.
tow truck *n* US guincho *m*, reboque *m*.
toxic ['tɒksɪk] *adj* tóxico(ca).
toxin ['tɒksɪn] *n* toxina *f*.
toy [tɔɪ] *n* brinquedo *m*.
    ➡ **toy with** *vt fus* -1. [idea]: **to** ~ **with sthg** pensar em algo - 2. [play]: **to** ~ **with sthg** brincar com algo.
toyboy *n inf* amante *m* de uma coroa.
toy shop *n* loja *f* de brinquedos.
trace [treɪs] <> *n* -1. [evidence, remains] vestígio *m*; **without** ~ sem deixar vestígio -2. [small amount] vestígio *m*. <> *vt* -1. [find] localizar - 2. [follow progress of] traçar - 3. [mark outline of] traçar ; [with tracing paper] decalcar.
trace element *n* CHEM elemento-traço *m*.
tracer bullet ['treɪsəʳ-] *n* projétil *m* luminoso.
tracing ['treɪsɪŋ] *n* [on paper] decalque *m*.
tracing paper ['treɪsɪŋ-] *n (U)* papel *m* de decalque.
track [træk] <> *n* -1. [path] trilha *f*; **off the beaten** ~ isolado(da) - 2. SPORT pista *f* - 3. RAIL trilho *m* - 4. [mark, trace] pegada *f*; **to hide** OR **cover one's** ~s não deixar rasto; **to stop dead in one's** ~s parar atônito(ta) - 5. [on record, tape, CD] faixa *f* - 6. *phr*: **to keep** ~ **of sb/sthg** não perder alguém/algo de vista; **to lose** ~ **of sb/sthg** perder alguém/algo de vista; **to be on the right/wrong** ~ estar no caminho certo/errado. <> *vt* [follow] seguir a pista de. <> *vi* [camera] seguir.
    ➡ **track down** *vt sep* localizar.
tracker dog ['trækəʳ-] *n* cão *m* de caça OR policial.
track event *n* prova *f* de atletismo *(na pista)*.
tracking station ['trækɪŋ-] *n* estação *f* de rastreamento.
track record *n* histórico *m (de reputação)*.
track shoes *npl* calçados *mpl* de corrida.
tracksuit ['træksuːt] *n* abrigo *m* esportivo.
tract [trækt] *n* -1. [pamphlet] panfleto *m* -2. [of land, forest] extensão *f* -3. MED trato *m*; **digestive** ~ aparelho *m* digestivo.
traction ['trækʃn] *n (U)* -1. PHYSICS tração *f* -2. MED tração *f*; **to have one's leg in** ~ fazer tração na perna.
traction engine *n* veículo *m* de carga pesada.
tractor ['træktəʳ] *n* trator *m*.
tractor-trailer *n* US veículo *m* articulado.
trade [treɪd] <> *n* -1. (U) [commerce] comércio *m* -2. [job] profissão *f*, ofício *m*; **by** ~ por formação. <> *vt* [exchange] negociar; **to** ~ **sthg for sthg** trocar algo por algo. <> *vi* -1. COMM [do business] negociar; **to** ~ **with sb** negociar com alguém -2. US [shop]: **to** ~ **at** OR **with** comprar em.
    ➡ **trade in** *vt sep* [exchange] dar como entrada.
trade barrier *n* barreira *f* comercial.
trade deficit *n* déficit *m* comercial.
trade discount *n (U)* desconto *m* para revendedor.
trade fair *n* feira *f* industrial.
trade gap *n* déficit *m* na balança comercial.
trade-in *n* objeto ou artigo que se entrega como entrada ao se comprar um novo, base *f* de troca.

trademark ['treɪdmɑ:k] n -1. COMM marca f regis-trada -2. fig [characteristic] marca f registrada.
trade name n COMM razão f social.
trade-off n equilíbrio m.
trade price n preço m de atacado.
trader ['treɪdəʳ] n comerciante mf.
trade route n rota f de comércio.
trade secret n segredo m comercial.
tradesman ['treɪdzmən] (pl -men [-mən]) n [shop-keeper, trader] comerciante m.
tradespeople ['treɪdz,pi:pl] npl comerciantes mfpl.
trades union n UK = trade union.
Trades Union Congress n UK: the ~ a associação britânica dos sindicatos.
trades unionist n UK = trade unionist.
trade union n sindicato m.
trade unionist n sindicalista mf.
trading ['treɪdɪŋ] n (U) comércio m.
trading estate n UK distrito m industrial.
trading stamp n cupom m promocional.
tradition [trə'dɪʃn] n -1. (U) [system of customs] tradição f -2. [established practice] costume m.
traditional [trə'dɪʃənl] adj tradicional.
traditionally [trə'dɪʃnəlɪ] adv tradicionalmente.
traffic ['træfɪk] (pt & pp -ked, cont -king) <> n (U) -1. [vehicles] tráfego m -2. [illegal trade] tráfico m; ~ in sthg tráfico de algo. <> vi: to ~ in sthg traficar algo.
traffic circle n US rotatória f.
traffic island n canteiro m central.
traffic jam n congestionamento m.
trafficker ['træfɪkəʳ] n traficante mf; ~ in sthg traficante de algo.
traffic lights npl semáforo m.
traffic offence UK, **traffic violation** US n infração f de trânsito.
traffic sign n sinal m de trânsito.
traffic violation n US = traffic offence.
traffic warden n UK guarda mf de trânsito.
tragedy ['trædʒədɪ] (pl -ies) n -1. (U) [ill fate, dramatic form] tragédia f -2. [terrible event, play] tragédia f.
tragic ['trædʒɪk] adj trágico(ca).
tragically ['trædʒɪklɪ] adv tragicamente.
trail [treɪl] <> n -1. [path] trilha f; to blaze a ~ fig abrir caminho -2. [traces] rastro m; on the ~ of sb/sthg na pista de alguém/algo. <> vt -1. [drag behind, tow] arrastar -2. [lag behind] estar atrás de. <> vi -1. [drag behind] arrastar -2. [move slowly] andar lentamente -3. SPORT [lose] perder.
trail away, trail off vi apagar-se.
trailblazing ['treɪl,bleɪzɪŋ] adj pioneiro(ra).
trailer ['treɪləʳ] n -1. [vehicle for luggage] reboque m -2. esp US [for living in] trailer m -3. CINEMA trailer m.
trailer court, trailer park n US camping m (para trailers).
train [treɪn] <> n -1. RAIL trem m -2. [of dress] cauda f -3. [connected sequence]: ~ of thought linha f de raciocínio. <> vt -1. [teach] treinar; to ~ sb to do sthg treinar alguém para fazer algo; to ~ sb in sthg treinar alguém em algo -2. [for job]: to ~ sb as sthg preparar OR formar alguém para ser algo -3. SPORT treinar; to ~ sb for sthg treinar alguém para algo -4. [plant] dirigir -5. [gun, camera] apontar. <> vi -1. [for job] preparar-se; to ~ as sthg estudar para algo -2. SPORT treinar; to ~ for sthg treinar para algo.
train driver n maquinista mf.
trained [treɪnd] adj -1. [psychologist] formado(da) -2. [singer] profissional -3. [cartographer] qualificado(-da) -4. [doctor] especializado(da).
trainee [treɪ'ni:] <> adj estagiário(ria). <> n estagiário m, -ria f, trainee mf.
trainer ['treɪnəʳ] n -1. [of animals] amestrador m, -ra f -2. SPORT treinador m, -ra f.
trainers npl UK [shoes] tênis m inv para a prática desportiva.
training ['treɪnɪŋ] n (U) -1. [for job]: ~ in sthg formação f em algo, treinamento m para algo -2. SPORT treinamento m.
training college n UK escola f profissionalizan-te.
training course n curso m de formação profis-sional.
training shoes npl UK tênis m inv para a prática desportiva.
train set n trenzinho m.
train spotter [-,spɒtəʳ] n aficcionado por trens que vai até as estações para contar o número que trens que passam.
train station n US & Scot estação f ferroviária.
traipse [treɪps] vi vaguear.
trait [treɪt] n traço m.
traitor ['treɪtəʳ] n traidor m, -ra f; ~ to sthg traidor(ra) de algo.
trajectory [trə'dʒektərɪ] (pl -ies) n TECH trajetória f.
tram [træm], **tramcar** ['træmkɑ:ʳ] n UK bonde m.
tramcar n UK fml bonde m.
tramlines ['træmlaɪnz] npl -1. [for trams] trilhos mpl do bonde -2. TENNIS linha f lateral de duplas.
tramp [træmp] <> n vagabundo m, -da f. <> vt caminhar a pé por. <> vi andar com passos pesados.
trample ['træmpl] <> vt esmagar com os pés, pisar em. <> vi -1. [tread]: to ~ on sthg pisar em algo -2. fig [act cruelly]: to ~ on sb espezinhar alguém.
trampoline ['træmpəli:n] n trampolim m.
trance [trɑ:ns] n [hypnotic state] transe m; in a ~ em transe.
tranquil ['træŋkwɪl] adj literary plácido(da).
tranquility n US = tranquillity.
tranquilize vt US = tranquillize.
tranquilizer n US = tranquillizer.
tranquillity UK, **tranquility** US [træŋ'kwɪlətɪ] n (U) tranqüilidade f.
tranquillize, -ise UK, **tranquilize** US ['træŋkwɪ-laɪz] vt tranqüilizar.
tranquillizer UK, **tranquilizer** US ['træŋkwɪd laɪzəʳ] n tranqüilizante m.
transact [træn'zækt] vt fml fazer, levar a cabo.
transaction [træn'zækʃn] n transação f.
transatlantic [,trænzət'læntɪk] adj -1. [crossing the Atlantic] transatlântico(ca) -2. [on the other side of the Atlantic] de além-mar.

transceiver [træn'si:vəˈ] *n* rádio *m* transmissor-receptor.

transcend [træn'send] *vt fml* [go beyond] transcender.

transcendental meditation [ˌtrænsen'dentl-] *n (U)* meditação *f* transcedental.

transcribe [træn'skraɪb] *vt* transcrever.

transcript ['trænskrɪpt] *n* [of speech, conversation] transcrição *f*.

transept ['trænsept] *n* transepto *m*.

transfer [*n* 'trænsfɜːˈ, *vb* træns'fɜːr] (*pt* & *pp* -red, *cont* -ring) <> *n* -1. [gen] transferência *f* -2. [design] decalcomania *f* -3. *US* [ticket] passagem *f* válida para conexão. <> *vt* transferir. <> *vi* transferir-se.

transferable [træns'fɜːrəbl] *adj* transferível.

transference ['trænsfərəns] *n (U) fml* [act of transferring] transferência *f*.

transfer fee *n UK SPORT* (valor *m* do) passe *m*.

transfigure [træns'fɪgəˈ] *vt literary* transfigurar.

transfix [træns'fɪks] *vt* [immobilize] paralisar.

transform [træns'fɔːm] *vt* transformar; **to ~ sb/sthg into sthg** transformar alguém/algo em algo.

transformation [ˌtrænsfə'meɪʃn] *n* transformação *f*.

transformer [træns'fɔːməˈ] *n ELEC* transformador *m*.

transfusion [træns'fju:ʒn] *n* transfusão *f*.

transgress [træns'gres] *fml* <> *vt* transgredir. <> *vi* cometer uma transgressão.

transgression [træns'greʃn] *n fml* transgressão *f*.

transient ['trænzɪənt] <> *adj fml* [fleeting] transitório(ria). <> *n US* [person] pessoa *f* em trânsito.

transistor [træn'zɪstəˈ] *n ELECTRON* transistor *m*.

transistor radio *n dated* (rádio *m*) transistor *m*.

transit ['trænsɪt] *n*: **in ~** de passagem.

transit camp *n* acampamento *m* provisório.

transition [træn'zɪʃn] *n* -1. [change] transição *f* -2. *(U)* [act of changing] transição *f*; **~ from sthg to sthg** transição de algo para algo; **in ~** em transição.

transitional [træn'zɪʃənl] *adj* de transição.

transitive ['trænzɪtɪv] *adj GRAMM* transitivo(va).

transit lounge *n* sala *f* de trânsito.

transitory ['trænzɪtrɪ] *adj* transitório(ria).

translate [træns'leɪt] <> *vt* -1. [languages] traduzir -2. *fig* [transform]: **to ~ sthg into sthg** transformar algo em algo. <> *vi* -1. [words] traduzir-se; **to ~ from sthg into sthg** traduzir de algo para algo -2. [person] traduzir.

translation [træns'leɪʃn] *n* tradução *f*.

translator [træns'leɪtəˈ] *n* tradutor *m*, -ra *f*.

translucent [trænz'lu:snt] *adj* translúcido(da).

transmission [trænz'mɪʃn] *n* transmissão *f*.

transmit [trænz'mɪt] (*pt* & *pp* -ted, *cont* -ting) *vt* transmitir.

transmitter [trænz'mɪtəˈ] *n ELECTRON* transmissor *m*.

transparency [trans'pærənsɪ] (*pl* -ies) *n* transparência *f*.

transparent [trans'pærənt] *adj* -1. [gen] transparente -2. [obvious] óbvio(via).

transpire [træn'spaɪəˈ] *fml* <> *vt*: **it ~s that ...** descobre-se que ... <> *vi* [happen] acontecer, ocorrer.

transplant [*n* 'trænsplɑːnt, *vb* træns'plɑːnt] <> *n* transplante *m*. <> *vt* -1. [gen] transplantar -2. [population] transferir.

transport [*n* 'trænspɔːt, *vb* træn'spɔːt] <> *n* transporte *m*. <> *vt* [goods, people] transportar.

transportable [træn'spɔːtəbl] *adj* transportável.

transportation [ˌtrænspɔː'teɪʃn] *n (U) esp US* = transport.

transport cafe ['trænspɔːt-] *n UK* lanchonete *m* deestrada.

transporter [træn'spɔːtəˈ] *n* caminhão *m* para transporte de automóveis.

transpose [træns'pəʊz] *vt* [change round] inverter.

transsexual [træns'sekʃʊəl] *n* transexual *mf*.

transvestite [trænz'vestaɪt] *n* travesti *mf*.

trap [træp] (*pt* & *pp* -ped, *cont* -ping) <> *n* -1. [for animal, bird] armadilha *f* -2. *fig* [trick] cilada *f*. <> *vt* -1. [animal, bird] apanhar em armadilha -2. *fig* [trick] armar uma cilada -3. [immobilize, catch]: **to be ~ped in sthg** ficar preso(sa) em algo -4. [retain] guardar.

trapdoor [ˌtræp'dɔːˈ] *n* alçapão *m*.

trapeze [trə'pi:z] *n* trapézio *m*.

trapper ['træpəˈ] *n* caçador *m*, -ra *f* que pôe armadilhas.

trappings ['træpɪŋz] *npl* pompas *fpl*.

trash [træʃ] <> *n (U)* -1. *US* [refuse] lixo *m* -2. *inf pej* [sthg of poor quality] lixo *m*, porcaria *f*. <> *vt US* -1. [criticize] acabar com, demolir -2. [damage] arrasar.

trashcan ['træʃkæn] *n US* lata *f* de lixo.

trashy ['træʃɪ] (*compar* -ier, *superl* -iest) *adj inf* imprestável.

trauma ['trɔːmə] *n* -1. [distressing experience] trauma *m* -2. *(U)* [distress] trauma *m*.

traumatic [trɔː'mætɪk] *adj* traumático(ca).

traumatize, -ise ['trɔːmətaɪz] *vt* [shock] traumatizar.

travel ['trævl] (*UK pt* & *pp* -led, *cont* -ling, *US pt* & *pp* -ed, *cont* -ing) <> *n (U)* viagem *f*; **I'm keen on ~** eu adoro viajar. <> *vt* -1. [place] viajar por -2. [distance] viajar. <> *vi* -1. [gen] viajar -2. [news] voar.
    ◆ **travels** *npl* viagens *fpl*.

travel agency *n* agência *f* de viagens.

travel agent *n* agente *mf* de viagens; **~ 's** agência *f* de viagens.

travel brochure *n* catálogo *m* de viagens.

travel card *n* passe *m*.

traveler *etc n US* = **traveller** *etc*.

travelled *UK*, **traveled** *US* ['trævld] *adj* -1. [person] viajado(da) -2. [road, route] movimentado(da).

traveller *UK*, **traveler** *US* ['trævləˈ] *n* -1. [gen] viajante *mf* -2. [sales representative] representante *mf* comercial.

traveller's cheque *n* cheque *m* de viagem, traveler's cheque *m*.

travelling *UK*, **traveling** *US* ['trævlɪŋ] *adj* -1. [itinerant] itinerante, ambulante -2. [portable, of travel] de viagem.

travelling expenses *npl* despesas *fpl* de viagem.

travelling salesman *n* caixeiro-viajante *m*.

travelogue, travelog *US* ['trævəlɒg] *n* -1. [talk]

conferência f sobre uma viagem **-2.** [film] documentário m sobre viagem.

travelsick ['trævəlsɪk] adj enjoado(da) *(pela viagem)*.

traverse ['trævəs, ˌtrə'vɜːs] vt fml atravessar.

travesty ['trævəstɪ] (pl -ies) n paródia f.

trawl [trɔːl] ◇ n **-1.** [fishing net] rede f de arrasto **-2.** [search] busca f. ◇ vt **-1.** [fish]: **to ~ sthg (for sthg)** vasculhar algo (à procura de algo) **-2.** [search]: **to ~ sthg for sthg** conferir algo à procura de algo. ◇ vi **-1.** [fish]: **to ~ for sthg** pescar com rede de arrasto à procura de algo **-2.** [search]: **to ~ for sthg** procurar (por) algo.

trawler ['trɔːlər] n traineira f.

tray [treɪ] n bandeja f.

treacherous ['tretʃərəs] adj **-1.** [person] traidor(ra) **-2.** [plan, behaviour] traiçoeiro(ra) **-3.** [dangerous] perigoso(sa).

treachery ['tretʃərɪ] n (U) traição f.

treacle ['triːkl] n (U) UK melado m.

tread [tred] (pt trod, pp trodden) ◇ n **-1.** [on tyre] banda f de rodagem **-2.** [shoe] sola f **-3.** [sound or way of walking] passos mpl. ◇ vt [crush] esmagar com os pés; **to ~ sthg into sthg** esmagar algo em algo. ◇ vi **-1.** [place foot]: **to ~ on sthg** pisar em algo **-2.** [walk, progress] andar; **to ~ carefully** fig andar com cuidado.

treadle ['tredl] n pedal m.

treadmill ['tredmɪl] n **-1.** [wheel] roda f de moinho **-2.** fig [dull routine] rotina f.

treas. (abbr of treasurer) tesoureiro m, -ra f.

treason ['triːzn] n (U) traição f.

treasure ['treʒər] ◇ n lit & fig tesouro m. ◇ vt dar valor a.

treasure hunt n caça f ao tesouro.

treasurer ['treʒərər] n tesoureiro m, -ra f.

treasure trove n (U) JUR tesouro m escondido.

treasury ['treʒərɪ] (pl -ies) n [room] sala f do tesouro.

➤ **Treasury** n: **the Treasury** ≃ o Ministério da Fazenda.

treasury bill n letra f do Tesouro.

treat [triːt] ◇ vt **-1.** [handle, deal with] tratar; **to ~ sb/sthg as sthg, to ~ sb/sthg like sthg** tratar alguém/algo como algo **-2.** [give sthg special]: **to ~ sb (to sthg)** invitar alguém (para algo); **to ~ o.s. to sthg** presentear-se com algo **-3.** [MED, process] tratar. ◇ n **-1.** [food] delícia f **-2.** [gift] prazer m.

treatise ['triːtɪs] n fml: **~ (on sthg)** tratado m (sobre algo).

treatment ['triːtmənt] n tratamento m.

treaty ['triːtɪ] (pl -ies) n [written agreement] tratado m.

treble ['trebl] ◇ adj **-1.** MUS de soprano **-2.** [with numbers]: **my phone extension is ~ 4** meu ramal é 444. ◇ n MUS soprano m. ◇ vt & vi triplicar.

treble clef n clave f de sol.

tree [triː] n árvore f; **to be barking up the wrong ~** acusar erroneamente.

tree-lined adj arborizado(da).

tree surgeon n especialista no cuidado de árvores.

treetop ['triːtɒp] n copa f (de árvore).

tree-trunk n tronco m (de árvore).

trek [trek] (pt & pp -ked, cont -king) ◇ n expedição f. ◇ vi **-1.** [go on long journey] fazer uma expedição **-2.** inf [walk laboriously] caminhar com dificuldade.

trellis ['trelɪs] n treliça f.

tremble ['trembl] vi tremer.

tremendous [trɪ'mendəs] adj **-1.** [impressive, large] tremendo(da), enorme **-2.** inf [really good] fabuloso(sa).

tremendously [trɪ'mendəslɪ] adv [impressively, hugely] enormemente.

tremor ['tremər] n tremor m.

tremulous ['tremjʊləs] adj literary trêmulo(la).

trench [trentʃ] n **-1.** [narrow channel] vala f **-2.** MIL trincheira f.

trenchant ['trentʃənt] adj fml mordaz.

trench coat n capa f de chuva.

trench warfare n (U) guerra f de trincheiras.

trend [trend] n [tendency] tendência f.

trendsetter ['trendˌsetər] n iniciador m, -ra f de modas.

trendy ['trendɪ] (compar -ier, superl -iest, pl -ies) inf ◇ adj **-1.** [person] moderno(na) **-2.** [clothes, music] da moda. ◇ n pessoa f moderna.

trepidation [ˌtrepɪ'deɪʃn] n (U) fml: **in** OR **with ~** com ansiedade.

trespass ['trespəs] vi [on sb's land] invadir; **'no ~ing'** 'entrada proibida'.

trespasser ['trespəsər] n invasor m, -ra f; **'~s will be prosecuted'** 'os invasores serão punidos por lei'.

trestle ['tresl] n cavalete m.

trestle table n mesa f de cavalete.

trial ['traɪəl] n **-1.** JUR julgamento m; **to be on ~ (for sthg)** ser processado(da) (por algo) **-2.** [test, experiment] teste m; **on ~** em testes; **by ~ and error** por tentativa e erro **-3.** [unpleasant experience] suplício m; **~s and tribulations** dificuldades fpl e problemas.

trial basis n: **on a ~** como experiência.

trial period n período m de experiência.

trial run n ensaio m.

trial-size(d) adj em tamanho de amostra.

triangle ['traɪæŋgl] n **-1.** [gen] triângulo m **-2.** US [set square] esquadro m.

triangular [traɪ'æŋgjʊlər] adj [in triangle shape] triangular.

triathlon [traɪ'æθlɒn] (pl -s) n triatlo m.

tribal ['traɪbl] adj tribal.

tribe [traɪb] n [social group] tribo f.

tribulation [ˌtrɪbjʊ'leɪʃn] n ▷ trial.

tribunal [traɪ'bjuːnl] n tribunal m.

tribune ['trɪbjuːn] n HIST tribuno m.

tributary ['trɪbjʊtrɪ] (pl -ies) n GEOGR afluente m.

tribute ['trɪbjuːt] n **-1.** [act of respect, admiration] tributo m; **to be a ~ to sb/sthg** ser um tributo para alguém/algo; **to pay ~ (to sb/sthg)** prestar homenagem a (alguém/algo) **-2.** [evidence] prova f **-3.** (U) [respect, admiration] homenagem f; **to pay ~ (to sb/sthg)** prestar homenagem (a alguém/algo).

trice [traɪs] n: **in a ~** num abrir e fechar de olhos.

triceps ['traɪseps] (pl inv OR -cepses) n tríceps m inv.

trick [trɪk] ◇ *n* **-1.** [to deceive] trapaça *f*; **to play a** ~ **on sb** pregar uma peça em alguém **-2.** [to entertain] truque *m* **-3.** [ability, knack] hábito *m*; **to do the** ~ dar resultado. ◇ *adj* **-1.** [knife] de brincadeira **-2.** [moustache] postiço(ça). ◇ *vt* enganar; **to** ~ **sb into sthg** enrolar alguém sobre algo; **to** ~ **sb into doing sthg** enrolar alguém para que faça algo.

trickery [ˈtrɪkərɪ] *n (U)* trapaça *f*.

trickle [ˈtrɪkl] ◇ *n* **-1.** [of liquid] fio *m* **-2.** [of people or things] pingo *m*. ◇ *vi* **-1.** [liquid] gotejar, pingar **-2.** [people, things]: **to trickle in/out** entrar/sair aos poucos.

trick or treat *n (U)* gostosuras *fpl* ou travessuras.

trick question *n* pega-ratão *m*.

tricky [ˈtrɪkɪ] (*compar* **-ier**, *superl* **-iest**) *adj* [difficult] enrolado(da), complicado(da).

tricycle [ˈtraɪsɪkl] *n* triciclo *m*.

trident [ˈtraɪdnt] *n* tridente *m*.

tried [traɪd] ◇ *pt & pp* ▷ **try**. ◇ *adj*: ~ **and tested** testado e aprovado, testada e aprovada.

trier [ˈtraɪə[r]] *n* batalhador *m*, -ra *f*.

trifle [ˈtraɪfl] *n* **-1.** CULIN sobremesa de biscoito feito com gelatina, creme, frutas e nata **-2.** [unimportant thing] ninharia *f*.
➠ **a trifle** *adv fml* ligeiramente, um pouco.
➠ **trifle with** *vt fus*: **he's not a person to be** ~**d with** não é uma pessoa com a qual se possa brincar.

trifling [ˈtraɪflɪŋ] *adj pej* insignificante.

trigger [ˈtrɪgə[r]] ◇ *n* [on gun] gatilho *m*. ◇ *vt* **-1.** [mechanism] acionar **-2.** [explosion, reaction] desencadear **-3.** [revolution, protest] provocar.
➠ **trigger off** *vt sep* = **trigger**.

trigger-happy *adj* provocador(ra).

trigonometry [ˌtrɪgəˈnɒmətrɪ] *n (U)* trigonometria *f*.

trilby [ˈtrɪlbɪ] (*pl* **-ies**) *n UK* chapéu *m* de feltro.

trill [trɪl] ◇ *n* **-1.** MUS tremolo *m* **-2.** [of birds] trinado *m*. ◇ *vi* trinar.

trillions [ˈtrɪljənz] *npl inf* milhares *mpl*; ~ **of** um monte de.

trilogy [ˈtrɪlədʒɪ] (*pl* **-ies**) *n* trilogia *f*.

trim [trɪm] (*compar* **-mer**, *superl* **-mest**, *pt & pp* **-med**, *cont* **-ming**) ◇ *adj* **-1.** [neat and tidy] bem cuidado(da) **-2.** [slim] esbelto(ta). ◇ *n* **-1.** [cut - hair] corte *m*; [- hedge] poda *f* **-2.** [decoration] enfeite *m*. ◇ *vt* **-1.** [cut - hair, nails, lawn] cortar; [- hedge] podar; [- moustache] aparar **-2.** [decorate] enfeitar; **to** ~ **sthg with sthg** enfeitar algo com algo.
➠ **trim away, trim off** *vt sep* cortar.

trimmed [trɪmd] *adj*: ~ **with sthg** enfeitado(da) com algo.

trimming *n* [on clothing] enfeite *m*.
➠ **trimmings** *npl* **-1.** CULIN guarnição *f* **-2.** [scraps] aparas *fpl*.

Trinidad and Tobago [ˈtrɪnɪdæd-] *n* Trinidad e Tobago; **in** ~ em Trinidad e Tobago.

Trinidadian ◇ *adj* trinitário(ria). ◇ *n* trinitário *m*, -ria *f*.

Trinity [ˈtrɪnətɪ] *n* RELIG: **the** ~ a Trindade.

trinket [ˈtrɪŋkɪt] *n* adorno *m*.

trio [ˈtriːəʊ] (*pl* **-s**) *n* trio *m*.

trip [trɪp] (*pt & pp* **-ped**, *cont* **-ping**) ◇ *n* **-1.** [journey] viagem *f* **-2.** *drugs sl* [experience] viagem *f*. ◇ *vt* [make stumble] fazer tropeçar, passar uma rasteira em. ◇ *vi* [stumble]: **to** ~ **(over)** tropeçar (em); **to** ~ **over sthg** tropeçar em algo.
➠ **trip up** *vt sep* **-1.** [make stumble] fazer tropeçar **-2.** [catch out] passar uma rasteira em.

tripartite [ˌtraɪˈpɑːtaɪt] *adj fml* [agreement, talks] tripartite.

tripe [traɪp] *n (U)* **-1.** CULIN dobradinha *f* **-2.** *inf* [nonsense] bobajada *f*.

triple [ˈtrɪpl] ◇ *adj* triplo(pla). ◇ *vt & vi* triplicar.

triple jump *n*: **the** ~ o salto triplo.

triplets [ˈtrɪplɪts] *npl* trigêmeos *mpl*, -meas *fpl*.

triplicate [ˈtrɪplɪkət] ◇ *adj fml* em triplicata. ◇ *n*: **in** ~ em três vias.

tripod [ˈtraɪpɒd] *n* tripé *m*.

Tripoli [ˈtrɪpəlɪ] *n* Tripoli.

tripper [ˈtrɪpə[r]] *n esp UK* excursionista *mf*, turista *mf*.

tripwire [ˈtrɪpwaɪə[r]] *n* fio *m* de armadilha.

trite [traɪt] *adj pej* banal.

triumph [ˈtraɪəmf] ◇ *n* **-1.** [success] triunfo *m* **-2.** *(U)* [satisfaction] triunfo *m*. ◇ *vi* triunfar; **to** ~ **over sb/sthg** triunfar sobre alguém/algo.

triumphal [traɪˈʌmfl] *adj fml* triunfal.

triumphant [traɪˈʌmfənt] *adj* [exultant] triunfante.

triumphantly [trɪˈʌmfəntlɪ] *adv* triunfalmente.

triumvirate *n* HIST triunvirato *m*.

trivet *n* **-1.** [over fire] trempe *f* **-2.** [to protect table] suporte *m* para pratos.

trivia [ˈtrɪvɪə] *n (U)* trivialidades *fpl*.

trivial [ˈtrɪvɪəl] *adj pej* trivial.

triviality [ˌtrɪvɪˈælɪtɪ] (*pl* **-ies**) *n* **-1.** [sthg unimportant] trivialidade *f* **-2.** *(U)* [lack of importance] trivialidade *f*.

trivialize, -ise [ˈtrɪvɪəlaɪz] *vt* banalizar.

trod [trɒd] *pt* ▷ **tread**.

trodden [ˈtrɒdn] ◇ *pp* ▷ **tread**. ◇ *adj* pisoteado(da).

Trojan [ˈtrəʊdʒən] ◇ *adj* HIST troiano(na). ◇ *n* **-1.** HIST troiano *m*, -na *f* **-2.** *fig* [hard worker]: **to work like a** ~ trabalhar como um escravo.

troll [trəʊl] *n* [goblin] troll *m*, trasgo *m*.

trolley [ˈtrɒlɪ] (*pl* **trolleys**) *n* **-1.** *UK* [gen] carrinho *m* **-2.** *US* [vehicle] bonde *m*.

trolleybus [ˈtrɒlɪbʌs] *n* ônibus *m inv* elétrico.

trolley case *n* mala *f* com rodinhas.

trombone [trɒmˈbəʊn] *n* trombone *m*.

troop [truːp] ◇ *n* [band] bando *m*, grupo *m*. ◇ *vi* [march] andar em bando; **to** ~ **in/out** entrar/sair em bando.
➠ **troops** *npl* MIL tropas *fpl*.

trooper [ˈtruːpə[r]] *n* **-1.** MIL soldado *m* de cavalaria **-2.** *US* [policeman] policial *mf* militar.

troopship [ˈtruːpʃɪp] *n* navio-transporte *m*.

trophy [ˈtrəʊfɪ] (*pl* **-ies**) *n* SPORT troféu *m*.

tropical [ˈtrɒpɪkl] *adj* tropical.

Tropic of Cancer [ˈtrɒpɪk-] *n*: **the** ~ o Trópico de Cancer.

Tropic of Capricorn [ˈtrɒpɪk-] *n*: **the** ~ o Trópico de Capricórnio.

tropics [ˈtrɒpɪks] *npl*: **the** ~ os trópicos.

trot [trɒt] (*pt* & *pp* -ted, *cont* -ting) ⬥ *n* -1. [of horse] trote *m* -2. [of person] passo *m* apressado. ⬥ *vi* -1. [horse] trotar -2. [person] andar apressadamente.
➤ **on the trot** *adv inf*: four times on the ~ quatro vezes seguidas.
➤ **trot out** *vt sep pej*: to ~ out the same old excuses ficar repetindo as mesmas desculpas manjadas.

Trotskyism ['trɒtskɪzm] *n* (*U*) trotskismo *m*.

trotter ['trɒtə'] *n* [pig's foot] pé *m* de porco.

trouble ['trʌbl] ⬥ *n* -1. (*U*) [difficulty] problema *m*; **to be in** ~ [having problems] estar com problemas; **to get into** ~ [with sb in authority] ter conflitos; **the** ~ **with sb/sthg is ...** o problema com alguém/algo é ... -2. [bother] incômodo *m*; **to take the** ~ **to do sthg** dar-se ao trabalho de fazer algo; **to be asking for** ~ procurar problema -3. (*U*) [pain, illness] problema *m* -4. (*U*) [fighting] confusão *f* -5. POL [unrest] agitação *f*. ⬥ *vt* -1. [worry, upset] preocupar -2. [interrupt, disturb] importunar -3. [cause pain to] incomodar.
➤ **troubles** *npl* -1. [worries] problemas *mpl*, preocupações *fpl* -2. POL [unrest] conflitos *mpl*.

troubled ['trʌbld] *adj* -1. [worried, upset] preocupado(da) -2. [disturbed - sleep] agitado(da); [- life, place, time] tumultuado(da).

trouble-free *adj* sem problemas.

troublemaker ['trʌbl,meɪkə'] *n* agitador *m*, -ra *f*.

troubleshooter ['trʌbl,ʃuːtə'] *n* solucionador *m*, -ra *f* de problemas; **he's the** ~ **here** é ele quem resolve os problemas aqui.

troublesome ['trʌblsəm] *adj* problemático(ca).

trouble spot *n* área *f* de conflito.

trough [trɒf] *n* -1. [for animals] cocho *m* -2. [low point] baixa *f*.

trounce [traʊns] *vt inf* [team, rivals] dar uma surra em, derrubar.

troupe [truːp] *n* trupe *f*.

trouser press ['traʊzə'-] *n* máquina *f* de passar calças.

trousers ['traʊzəz] *npl* calças *fpl*.

trouser suit ['traʊzə'-] *n UK* terninho *m*.

trousseau ['truːsəʊ] (*pl* -x [-z], -s) *n* enxoval *m*.

trout [traʊt] (*pl inv OR* -s) *n* truta *f*.

trove [trəʊv] ⊳ **treasure trove**.

trowel ['traʊəl] *n* -1. [for the garden] pá *f* de jardim -2. [for cement, plaster] colher *f* de pedreiro.

truancy ['truːənsɪ] *n* (*U*) gazeio *m*, falta *f* às aulas.

truant ['truːənt] *n* [child] criança *f* que mata às aulas; **to play** ~ gazear OR matar aula.

truce [truːs] *n* trégua *f*; ~ **between** trégua entre.

truck [trʌk] ⬥ *n* -1. *esp US* [lorry] caminhão *m* -2. RAIL vagão *m*. ⬥ *vt US* transportar de caminhão.

truck driver *n esp US* motorista *mf* de caminhão.

trucker ['trʌkə'] *n US* caminhoneiro *m*, -ra *f*.

truck farm *n US* chácara *f*.

trucking ['trʌkɪŋ] *n* (*U*) *US* transporte *m* por caminhão.

truck stop *n US* restaurante *m* para caminhoneiros.

truculent ['trʌkjʊlənt] *adj* truculento(ta).

trudge [trʌdʒ] ⬥ *n* caminhada *f* difícil. ⬥ *vi* arrastar-se.

true [truː] *adj* -1. [factual] verdadeiro(ra); **I can't believe it's** ~ não acredito que seja verdade; **to come** ~ tornar-se realidade -2. [faithful, genuine] verdadeiro(ra); [- friend] de verdade -3. [precise, exact] exato(ta).

true-life *adj* baseado(da) na vida real.

truffle ['trʌfl] *n* trufa *f*.

truism ['truːɪzm] *n* truísmo *m*.

truly ['truːlɪ] *adv* -1. [in fact] verdadeiramente -2. [sincerely] realmente; ~, **I didn't do it** com toda sinceridade eu não fiz isso -3. [for emphasis] realmente -4. *phr*: **yours** ~ [at end of letter] cordialmente; **and who do you think did that? - yours** ~, **of course!** e quem você acha que fez isso? - euzinho em pessoa, obviamente!

trump [trʌmp] ⬥ *n* [card] trunfo *m*. ⬥ *vt* trunfar.

trump card *n fig* trunfo *m*.

trumped-up ['trʌmpt-] *adj pej* forjado(da).

trumpet ['trʌmpɪt] ⬥ *n* MUS trompete *m*. ⬥ *vi* [elephant] barrir.

trumpeter ['trʌmpɪtə'] *n* trompetista *mf*.

truncate *vt fml* truncado(da).

truncheon ['trʌntʃən] *n* cassetete *m*.

trundle ['trʌndl] ⬥ *vt* empurrar lentamente. ⬥ *vi* rodar lentamente.

trunk [trʌŋk] *n* -1. [gen] tronco *m* -2. [of elephant] tromba *f* -3. [box] baú *m* (de viagem) -4. *US* [of car] porta-malas *m inv*.
➤ **trunks** *npl* [for swimming] calção *m* de banho, sunga *f*.

trunk road *n UK* ≃ rodovia *f* nacional.

truss [trʌs] *n* -1. MED funda *f* OR cinta *f* para hérnia -2. CONSTR viga *f*.

trust [trʌst] ⬥ *vt* -1. [have confidence in] confiar em; **to** ~ **sb to do sthg** confiar em alguém para fazer algo; ~ **you!** *iro* conto com você! -2. [entrust]: **to** ~ **sb with sthg** confiar algo a alguém -3. *fml* [hope]: **to** ~ **(that)** esperar que. ⬥ *n* -1. (*U*) [faith] confiança *f*; ~ **in sb/sthg** confiança em alguém/algo; **to put** OR **place one's** ~ **in sb/sthg** pôr OR depositar sua confiança em alguém/algo; **to take sthg on** ~ tomar algo como verdade -2. (*U*) [responsibility] confiança *f* -3. FIN fideicomisso *m*; **in** ~ em fideicomisso -4. COMM truste *m*.

trust company *n* sociedade *f* fiduciária.

trusted ['trʌstɪd] *adj* de confiança.

trustee [trʌs'tiː] *n* -1. FIN & JUR fideicomissário *m*, -ria *f* -2. [of institution] curador *m*, -ra *f*.

trusteeship [,trʌs'tiːʃɪp] *n* (*U*) fideicomisso *m*.

trust fund *n* fundo *m* fiduciário.

trusting ['trʌstɪŋ] *adj* crédulo(la).

trustworthy ['trʌst,wɜːðɪ] *adj* (digno(na)) de confiança.

trusty ['trʌstɪ] (*compar* -ier, *superl* -iest) *adj hum* fiel.

truth [truːθ] *n* -1. [gen]: **the** ~ a verdade; **to tell the** ~ dizer a verdade; **to tell the** ~, **...** para dizer a verdade, ... -2. (*U*) [veracity] veracidade *f*; **in (all)** ~ em verdade, na realidade.

truth drug *n* droga *f* da verdade.

truthful ['truːθfʊl] *n* -1. [person] sincero(ra), verdadeiro(ra) -2. [story] verídico(ca).

try [traɪ] (*pt* & *pp* -ied, *pl* -ies) ⬥ *vt* -1. [attempt]

tentar; **to ~ to do sthg** tentar fazer algo **- 2.** [sample, test] experimentar **- 3.** *JUR* levar a juízo **- 4.** [tax, strain] cansar; **to ~ sb's patience** esgotar a paciência de alguém. <> *vi* tentar; **to ~ for sthg** tratar de conseguir algo. <> *n* **-1.** [attempt] tentativa *f*; **to give sthg a ~** provar algo; **to have a ~ at sthg** tentar fazer algo **- 2.** *RUGBY* ato de levar a bola até a linha de fundo do adversário e posicioná-la no solo para se marcar pontos.

try on *vt sep* [clothes] experimentar.

try out *vt sep* **-1.** [car, machine] testar **- 2.** [plan] pôr à prova.

trying ['traɪɪŋ] *adj* difícil, árduo(dua).

try-out *n inf*: **can I have a ~ of the car?** posso experimentar o carro?

tsar [zɑːʳ] *n* czar *m*.

T-shirt *n* camiseta *f*.

tsp. (*abbr of* **teaspoon**) colher *f* de chá.

T-square *n* régua-tê *f*.

TT (*abbr of* **teetotal**) *adj* abstêmio(mia).

Tuareg *npl* [people] tuaregue *mf*.

tub [tʌb] *n* **-1.** [container - for ice cream, margarine] pote *m*; [- for water] tina *f* **- 2.** *inf* [bath] banheira *f*.

tuba ['tjuːbə] *n* tuba *f*.

tubby ['tʌbɪ] (*compar* **-ier**, *superl* **-iest**) *adj inf* rolha-de-poço, gorducho(cha).

tube [tjuːb] *n* **-1.** [gen] tubo *m* **- 2.** *UK* [underground train] metrô *m*; [underground system]: **the ~** o metrô; **by ~** de metrô.

tubeless ['tjuːblɪs] *adj* [tyre] sem câmara (de ar).

tuber ['tjuːbəʳ] *n* tubérculo *m*.

tuberculosis [tjuːˌbɜːkjʊˈləʊsɪs] *n (U)* tuberculose *f*.

tube station *n UK* estação *f* de metrô.

tubing ['tjuːbɪŋ] *n (U)* tubulação *f*.

tubular ['tjuːbjʊləʳ] *adj* tubular.

TUC (*abbr of* **Trades Union Congress**) *n federação dos sindicatos na Grã-Bretanha*, ≃ CUT *f*.

tuck [tʌk] <> *n SEWING* prega *f*. <> *vt* [place neatly] enfiar, meter.

tuck away *vt sep* [store] guardar; **to be ~ed away** [hidden] estar escondido(da).

tuck in <> *vt sep* **-1.** [child, patient in bed] ajeitar na cama **- 2.** [clothes] meter para dentro. <> *vi inf* comer com apetite.

tuck up *vt sep* enfiar, meter.

tuck shop *n UK* confeitaria *f* (*perto de um colégio*).

Tudor ['tjuːdəʳ] <> *adj* **-1.** *HIST* da dinastia Tudor **- 2.** *ARCHIT* da era Tudor. <> *n*: **the ~s** os Tudors.

Tue., Tues. (*abbr of* **Tuesday**) ter.

Tuesday ['tjuːzdɪ] *n* terça-feira *f*; *see also* **Saturday**.

tuft [tʌft] *n* tufo *m*.

tug [tʌg] (*pt* & *pp* **-ged**, *cont* **-ging**) <> *n* **-1.** [pull] puxão *m* **- 2.** [boat] rebocador *m*. <> *vt* dar um puxão em. <> *vi* dar um puxão; **to ~ at sthg** dar um puxão em algo.

tugboat ['tʌgbəʊt] *n* (barco *m*) rebocador *m*.

tug-of-love *n UK inf conflito pela custódia de uma criança*.

tug-of-war *n* cabo-de-guerra *m*.

tuition [tjuːˈɪʃn] *n (U)* ensino *m*; **private ~** aulas *fpl* particulares.

tulip ['tjuːlɪp] *n* tulipa *f*.

tulle *n (U)* tule *m*.

tumble ['tʌmbl] <> *vi* **-1.** [person] tombar **- 2.** [water] jorrar **- 3.** *fig* [prices] despencar. <> *n* tombo *m*.

tumble down *vi* [building] vir abaixo.

tumble to *vt fus UK inf* sacar, tocar-se de.

tumbledown ['tʌmbldaʊn] *adj* em ruínas.

tumble-dry *vt* secar em secadora.

tumble-dryer [-ˌdraɪəʳ] *n* secadora *f* (de roupa).

tumbler ['tʌmbləʳ] *n* [glass] copo *m*.

tummy ['tʌmɪ] (*pl* **-ies**) *n inf* **-1.** [outside of stomach] barriga *f* **- 2.** [inside of stomach] barriga *f*.

tumour *UK*, **tumor** *US* ['tjuːməʳ] *n* tumor *m*.

tumult ['tjuːmʌlt] *n fml* tumulto *m*.

tumultuous ['tjuːmʌltjʊəs] *adj fml* [applause] efusivo(va).

tuna [*UK* 'tjuːnə, *US* 'tuːnə] (*pl inv OR* **-s**), **tuna fish** (*pl* **tuna fish**) *n* **-1.** [fish] atum *m* **- 2.** *(U)* [food] atum *m*.

tundra ['tʌndrə] *n* tundra *f*.

tune [tjuːn] <> *n* [song, melody] melodia *f*; **to the ~ of** *fig* no montante de; **to change one's ~** *inf* virar a casaca. <> *vt* **-1.** *MUS* afinar **- 2.** *RADIO* & *TV* sintonizar; **to ~ sthg to sthg** sintonizar algo em algo **- 3.** [engine] ajustar, regular. <> *vi RADIO* & *TV*: **to ~ to sthg** sintonizar em algo.

tune in *vi RADIO* & *TV* sintonizar-se; **to ~ in to sthg** sintonizar-se em algo.

tune up *vi MUS* afinar *OR* consertar os instrumentos.

in tune <> *adj MUS* afinado(da). <> *adv* **-1.** *MUS* harmonicamente **- 2.** [in agreement]: **in ~ with sb/sthg** em sintonia com alguém/algo.

out of tune <> *adj MUS* desafinado(da). <> *adv* **-1.** *MUS* desarmonicamente **- 2.** [not in agreement]: **out of ~ with sb/sthg** fora de sintonia com alguém /algo.

tuneful ['tjuːnfʊl] *adj* melodioso(sa).

tuneless ['tjuːnlɪs] *adj* desarmônico(ca).

tuner ['tjuːnəʳ] *n* **-1.** *RADIO* & *TV* sintonizador *m* **- 2.** *MUS* afinador *m*.

tuner amplifier *n* amplificador *m* sintonizador.

tungsten ['tʌŋstən] <> *n (U)* tungstênio *m*. <> *comp* de tungstênio.

tunic ['tjuːnɪk] *n* [clothing] túnica *f*.

tuning fork ['tjuːnɪŋ-] *n* diapasão *m*.

Tunis ['tjuːnɪs] *n* Túnis.

Tunisia [tjuːˈnɪzɪə] *n* Tunísia *f*; **in ~** na Tunísia.

Tunisian [tjuːˈnɪzɪən] <> *adj* tunisiano(na). <> *n* [person] tunisiano *m*, -na *f*.

tunnel ['tʌnl] (*UK pt* & *pp* **-led**, *cont* **-ling**, *US pt* & *pp* **-ed**, *cont* **-ing**) <> *n* túnel *m*. <> *vi*: **to ~ through sthg** atravessar um túnel por algo.

tunnel vision *n (U)* **-1.** *MED* visão *f* em túnel **- 2.** *fig* & *pej* [narrow-mindedness] visão *f* estreita.

tunny ['tʌnɪ] (*pl inv OR* **-ies**) *n* [fish] tuna *f*.

tuppence *n UK dated* (moeda *f* de) dois pennies *mpl*.

turban ['tɜːbən] *n* [man's headdress] turbante *m*.

turbid ['tɜːbɪd] *adj* túrbido(da).

turbine ['tɜːbaɪn] *n* turbina *f*.

turbo ['tɜːbəʊ] (*pl* **-s**) *n* turbo *m*.

turbocharged ['tɜːbəʊtʃɑːdʒd] *adj* com turbo; ~ car carro-turbo *m*.

turbojet [ˌtɜːbəʊ'dʒet] *n* -1. [engine] turborreator *m* -2. [plane] turbojacto *m*.

turboprop *n* -1. [engine] turbopropulsor *m* -2. [plane] avião *m* com turbopropulsor.

turbot ['tɜːbət] (*pl inv OR* -s) *n* linguado *m*.

turbulence ['tɜːbjʊləns] *n (U)* turbulência *f*.

turbulent ['tɜːbjʊlənt] *adj* turbulento(ta).

tureen [tə'riːn] *n* sopeira *f*.

turf [tɜːf] (*pl* -s *OR* **turves**) ◇ *n* -1. (U) [grass surface] gramado *m* -2. [clod] turfa *f*. ◇ *vt* [with grass] gramar.
➤ **turf out** *vt sep UK inf* -1. [evict] chutar, dar patadas em -2. [throw away] jogar fora.

turf accountant *n UK fml* agenciador *m*, -ra *f* de apostas.

turgid ['tɜːdʒɪd] *adj fml* [style, prose] empolado(da).

Turk [tɜːk] *n* turco *m*, -ca *f*.

Turkestan, Turkistan [ˌtɜːkɪ'stɑːn] *n* Turquistão; **in** ~ no Turquistão.

turkey ['tɜːkɪ] (*pl* **turkeys**) *n* -1. [bird] peru *m* -2. (U) [meat] peru *m*.

Turkey ['tɜːkɪ] *n* Turquia; **in** ~ na Turquia.

Turkish ['tɜːkɪʃ] ◇ *adj* turco(ca). ◇ *n* [language] turco *m*. ◇ *npl*: **the** ~ os turcos.

Turkish bath *n* banho *m* turco.

Turkish delight *n (U)* doce feito de substância gelatinosa em cubos com cobertura de açúcar ou chocolate.

Turkistan *n* = Turkestan.

Turkmenian *adj* turcomano(na).

Turkmenistan [ˌtɜːkmenɪ'stɑːn] *n* Turcomênia.

turmeric ['tɜːmərɪk] *n (U)* [spice] açafrão-da-terra *m*.

turmoil ['tɜːmɔɪl] *n (U)* desordem *f*.

turn [tɜːn] ◇ *n* -1. [in road, river] curva *f* -2. [revolution, twist] volta *f* -3. [change] reviravolta *f*; **to take a** ~ **for the better/worse** mudar para melhor/pior -4. [in game]: **it's my** ~ é a minha vez -5. [in order] vez *f*; **in** ~ por vez; **to take (it in)** ~ s **to do sthg** revezar-se para fazer algo -6. [end] virada *f*; **the** ~ **of the century** a virada do século -7. [performance] número *m*, apresentação *f* -8. *MED* ataque *m*, crise *f* -9. *phr*: **to do sb a good** ~ fazer uma boa ação a alguém. ◇ *vt* -1. [cause to rotate] girar -2. [move round, turn over] virar -3. [go round] dobrar -4. [direct]: **to** ~ **sthg to sb/sthg** voltar algo para alguém/algo -5. [change]: **to** ~ **sthg into sthg** transformar algo em algo -6. [make, cause to become] deixar; **to** ~ **sthg inside out** virar algo pelo avesso. ◇ *vi* -1. [change direction] virar, dobrar; **to** ~ **to sb/sthg** voltar-se para alguém/algo -2. [rotate] girar -3. [move round] voltar-se -4. [in book]: ~ **to page 102** vão até a página 102 -5. [for consolation]: **to** ~ **to sb/sthg** buscar consolo em alguém/algo -6. [become] tornar-se; **my hair's** ~ing **grey** meu cabelo está ficando branco; **to** ~ **into sthg** transformar-se em algo.
➤ **turn against** *vt fus* voltar-se contra.
➤ **turn around** *vt sep* & *vi* = **turn round**.
➤ **turn away** ◇ *vt sep* [refuse entry to] não deixar entrar. ◇ *vi* distanciar-se.
➤ **turn back** ◇ *vt sep* -1. [force to return] fazer voltar -2. [fold back] dobrar. ◇ *vi* [return] voltar atrás.
➤ **turn down** *vt sep* -1. [reject] recusar -2. [heating, lighting] diminuir -3. [sound] abaixar.
➤ **turn in** *vi inf* [go to bed] ir dormir.
➤ **turn off** ◇ *vt fus* [road, path] sair de. ◇ *vt sep* [switch off - appliance, engine] desligar; [- gas, tap] fechar. ◇ *vi* [leave road, path] dobrar.
➤ **turn on** ◇ *vt sep* -1. [make work - appliance, engine] ligar; [- gas, tap] abrir; [- light] acender -2. *inf* [excite sexually] acender. ◇ *vt fus* [attack] avançar em.
➤ **turn out** ◇ *vt sep* -1. [switch off] apagar -2. *inf* [produce] fazer; **the factory** ~ s **out cars** a fábrica produz carros -3. [eject] expulsar -4. [empty] esvaziar. ◇ *vt fus*: **to** ~ **out to be** acabar sendo, vir a ser; **it** ~ s **out that ...** acontece que ... ◇ *vi* -1. [end up] acabar, terminar -2. [attend]: **to** ~ **out (for sthg)** comparecer (em algo).
➤ **turn over** ◇ *vt sep* -1. [playing card, stone, page] virar -2. [consider]: **I** ~ ed **his ideas over in my mind** fiquei com as idéias dele dando voltas na minha cabeça -3. [hand over] entregar; **to** ~ **sb/sthg over to sb** entregar alguém/algo para alguém. ◇ *vi* -1. [roll over] revirar-se -2. *UK TV* mudar de canal.
➤ **turn round** ◇ *vt sep* -1. [chair, picture] virar -2. [wheel] girar -3. [words, sentence] expressar de outra maneira -4. [quantity of work] aliviar -5. [company] reerguer. ◇ *vi* [person] virar-se.
➤ **turn up** ◇ *vt sep* [heat, lighting, radio, TV] aumentar. ◇ *vi inf* -1. [gen] aparecer -2. [opportunity, solution] surgir.

turnabout ['tɜːnəbaʊt] *n* mudança *f* radical.

turnaround *n US* = **turnround**.

turncoat ['tɜːnkəʊt] *n pej* vira-casaca *mf*.

turning ['tɜːnɪŋ] *n* [side road]: **the first** ~ **to the left** a primeira (rua) à esquerda.

turning circle *n* raio *m* de viragem.

turning point *n* momento *m* decisivo.

turnip ['tɜːnɪp] *n* nabo *m*.

turnout ['tɜːnaʊt] *n* [attendance] comparecimento *m*, número *m* de participantes.

turnover ['tɜːnˌəʊvə] *n (U)* -1. [of personnel] rotatividade *f* -2. *FIN* volume *m* de vendas.

turnpike ['tɜːnpaɪk] *n US* rodovia *f* com pedágio.

turnround *UK* ['tɜːnraʊnd], **turnaround** *US* ['tɜːnərəʊnd] *n* -1. *COMM* tempo *m* de carga e descarga (*de um barco, avião*) -2. [change] reviravolta *f*.

turn signal lever *n US* pisca-pisca *m*.

turnstile ['tɜːnstaɪl] *n* borboleta *f* (*em ônibus*).

turntable ['tɜːnˌteɪbl] *n* [on record player] prato *m* (giratório).

turn-up *n UK* -1. [on trousers] bainha *f* -2. *inf* [surprise]: **a** ~ **for the books** *inf* uma surpresa total.

turpentine ['tɜːpəntaɪn] *n (U)* terebintina *f*.

turps [tɜːps] *n UK inf* aguarrás *f inv*.

turquoise ['tɜːkwɔɪz] ◇ *adj* turquesa. ◇ *n* -1. (U) [mineral, gem] turquesa *f* -2. [colour] turquesa *m*.

turret ['tʌrɪt] *n* [on castle] torre *f* pequena.

turtle ['tɜːtl] (*pl inv OR* -s) *n* tartaruga *f*.

turtledove ['tɜːtldʌv] *n* pomba-rola *f*.

turtleneck [ˈtɜːtlnek] n **- 1.** [garment] blusa f de gola olímpica **- 2.** [neck] gola f olímpica.

turves [tɜːvz] UK pl ➤ **turf**.

tusk [tʌsk] n [of animal] presa f.

tussle [ˈtʌsl] ⇔ n briga f. ⇔ vi brigar; **to ~ over** sthg brigar por algo.

tut [tʌt] excl tsc!

tutor [ˈtjuːtəʳ] ⇔ n **- 1.** [private] professor m, -ra f particular **- 2.** UNIV professor m universitário, professora f universitária. ⇔ vt: **to ~ sb in sthg** dar aulas particulares de algo para alguém. ⇔ vi dar aulas particulares.

tutorial [tjuːˈtɔːrɪəl] ⇔ adj: **~ group** grupo reduzido de estudantes que assiste a uma aula. ⇔ n aula f para grupos pequenos.

tutu [ˈtuːtuː] n tutu f.

tux [tʌks] n inf smoking m.

tuxedo [tʌkˈsiːdəʊ] (pl -s) n US smoking m.

TV (abbr of **television**) ⇔ n **- 1.** [medium, industry, apparatus] TV f; **on ~** na TV. ⇔ comp de TV.

TV dinner n refeição f completa em porção individual pronta para esquentar.

TVP (abbr of **textured vegetable protein**) n proteína f vegetal.

twaddle [ˈtwɒdl] n inf pej lorota f.

twang [twæŋ] ⇔ n **- 1.** [sound - of guitar] som m metálico; [- of string, elastic] som m vibrante **- 2.** [accent] som m nasalado. ⇔ vt **- 1.** [guitar] vibrar **- 2.** [wire, string] fazer vibrar. ⇔ vi produzir um som vibrante.

tweak [twiːk] vt inf [pull] beliscar.

twee [twiː] adj UK pej piegas inv.

tweed [twiːd] ⇔ n (U) tweed m. ⇔ comp de tweed.

tweet [twiːt] vi inf piar.

tweezers [ˈtwiːzəz] npl pinças fpl.

twelfth [twelfθ] num décimo segundo, décima segunda; see also **sixth**.

Twelfth Night n Noite f de Reis.

twelve [twelv] num doze; see also **six**.

twentieth [ˈtwentɪəθ] num vigésimo(ma); see also sixth.

twenty [ˈtwentɪ] (pl -ies) num vinte; see also **sixty**.

twenty-twenty vision n (U) visão f perfeita.

twerp [twɜːp] n UK inf imbecil mf.

twice [twaɪs] adv duas vezes; **~ a week** duas vezes por semana; **he earns ~ as much as me** ele ganha o dobro que eu.

twiddle [ˈtwɪdl] ⇔ vt girar (entre os dedos). ⇔ vi: **to ~ with** sthg brincar com algo entre os dedos.

twig [twɪg] n graveto m.

twilight [ˈtwaɪlaɪt] n **- 1.** [in evening] crepúsculo m vespertino **- 2.** fig [last stages, end] ocaso m.

twill [twɪl] n (U) sarja f.

twin [twɪn] ⇔ adj **- 1.** [child, sibling] gêmeo(mea) **- 2.** [beds] duplo(pla) **- 3.** [towns, towers] gêmeos(meas). ⇔ n [sibling] gêmeos mpl, -meas fpl.

twin-bedded [-ˈbedɪd] adj com duas camas.

twin carburettor n carburador m duplo.

twine [twaɪn] ⇔ n (U) barbante m. ⇔ vt: **to ~** sthg round sthg enrolar algo em algo.

twin-engined [-ˈendʒɪndl] adj bimotor.

twinge [twɪndʒ] n **- 1.** [of pain] pontada f **- 2.** [of guilt] remorso m.

twinkle [ˈtwɪŋkl] ⇔ n brilho m. ⇔ vi **- 1.** [star, light] cintilar **- 2.** [eyes] brilhar.

twin room n quarto m com duas camas.

twinset n UK conjunto de blusa e casaquinho.

twin town n cidade-irmã f.

twin tub n máquina f de lavar e secar.

twirl [twɜːl] ⇔ vt **- 1.** [spin] girar **- 2.** [twist] torcer. ⇔ vi rodopiar.

twist [twɪst] ⇔ n **- 1.** [gen] volta f **- 2.** [turn, twirl] giro m; **to give sthg a ~** girar algo **- 3.** fig [in plot] reviravolta f. ⇔ vt **- 1.** [gen] retorcer **- 2.** [face, frame] torcer **- 3.** [head] voltar **- 4.** [lid, knob, dial] girar **- 5.** [words, meaning] distorcer. ⇔ vi **- 1.** [road, river] dar voltas **- 2.** [body, part of body] torcer.

twisted [ˈtwɪstɪd] adj pej [bizarre] deturpado(da).

twister [ˈtwɪstəʳ] n US tornado m.

twisty [ˈtwɪstɪ] (compar -ier, superl -iest) adj inf cheio (cheia) de curvas.

twit [twɪt] n UK inf idiota mf, imbecil mf.

twitch [twɪtʃ] ⇔ n espasmo m; **nervous ~** tique m nervoso. ⇔ vt [ears, nose] tremer. ⇔ vi contrair-se.

twitter [ˈtwɪtəʳ] vi **- 1.** [bird] cantar, pipilar **- 2.** pej [person] cantar vantagem.

two [tuː] num dois (duas); **in ~** em dois; see also **six**.

two-bit adj US pej barato(ta); **a ~ little dictator** um ditadorzinho de meia-tigela or de araque.

two-dimensional adj **- 1.** [picture] em duas dimensões, bidimensional **- 2.** pej [report, description] simples, sem profundidade.

two-door adj [car] de duas portas.

twofaced [ˌtuːˈfeɪst] adj pej de duas caras.

twofold [ˈtuːfəʊld] ⇔ adj duplo(pla). ⇔ adv: **to increase ~** duplicar-se.

two-handed [-ˈhændɪd] adj **- 1.** [sword] que se usa com as duas mãos **- 2.** [backhand] que se dá com as duas mãos.

two-piece adj [suit, swimsuit] de duas peças.

two-ply adj de duas camadas.

two-seater [-ˈsiːtəʳ] n carro m esporte (com apenas dois lugares).

twosome [ˈtuːsəm] n inf dupla f.

two-stroke ⇔ adj **- 1.** [engine] de dois tempos **- 2.** [oil] para motor de dois tempos. ⇔ n motor m de dois tempos.

two-time vt inf botar chifre em.

two-tone adj bicolor.

two-way adj **- 1.** [traffic] de mão dupla **- 2.** [discussion, debate] de duas vias **- 3.** [cooperation] mútuo(-tua) **- 4.** TELEC: **~ radio** aparelho m emissor e receptor.

TX abbr of **Texas**.

tycoon [taɪˈkuːn] n magnata mf.

type [taɪp] ⇔ n **- 1.** [gen] tipo m **- 2.** (U) TYPO: **in bold / italic ~** em negrito/itálico. ⇔ vt & vi **- 1.** [on typewriter] datilografar **- 2.** [on computer] digitar; **to ~ sthg into sthg** inserir algo em algo.

  ➡ **type up** vt sep **- 1.** [on typewriter] datilografar **- 2.** [on computer] digitar.

typecast [ˈtaɪpkɑːst] (pt & pp typecast) vt escalar sempre para o mesmo tipo de papel; **to be ~ as**

sthg ser sempre escalado(da) (para atuar) como algo.

typeface ['taɪpfeɪs] n TYPO tipo m, letra f.

typescript ['taɪpskrɪpt] n cópia f datilografada.

typeset ['taɪpset] (pt & pp typeset, cont -ting) vt TYPO compor.

typesetter n [company] tipografia f.

typesetting n composição f (para impressão).

typewriter ['taɪp,raɪtə'] n máquina f de escrever.

typhoid (fever) ['taɪfɔɪd-] n (U) febre f tifóide.

typhoon [taɪ'fu:n] n tufão m.

typhus ['taɪfəs] n (U) tifo m.

typical ['tɪpɪkl] adj típico(ca); ~ of sb/sthg típico(-ca) de alguém/algo.

typically ['tɪpɪklɪ] adv -1. [usually] geralmente, normalmente -2. [characteristically] tipicamente.

typify ['tɪpɪfaɪ] (pt & pp -ied) vt -1. [be characteristic of] tipificar -2. [embody, symbolize] simbolizar.

typing ['taɪpɪŋ] n -1. (U) [on typewriter] datilografia f -2. (U) [on computer] digitação f.

typing error n -1. [on typewriter] erro m de datilografia -2. [on computer] erro m de digitação.

typing pool n -1. [typewriter] serviço m de datilografia -2. [computer] serviço m de digitação.

typist ['taɪpɪst] n -1. [on typewriter] datilógrafo m, -fa f -2. [on computer] digitador m, -ra f.

typo ['taɪpəʊ] n inf erro m tipográfico.

typographic(al) error [,taɪpə'græfɪk(l)-] n erro m tipográfico.

typography [taɪ'pɒgrəfɪ] n -1. (U) [process, job] tipografia f -2. [format] composição f tipográfica.

tyrannical [tɪ'rænɪkl] adj tirânico(ca).

tyranny ['tɪrənɪ] n (U) [of person, government] tirania f.

tyrant ['taɪrənt] n tirano m, -na f.

tyre UK, **tire** US ['taɪə'] n pneu m.

tyre pressure n (U) pressão f do pneu.

Tyrol, Tirol [tɪ'rəʊl] n: the ~ o Tirol.

Tyrolean [tɪrə'li:ən], **Tyrolese** [,tɪrə'li:z] <> adj tirolês(esa). <> n tirolês m, -esa f.

Tyrrhenian Sea [tɪ'ri:nɪən-] n: the ~ o Mar Tirreno.

tzar [zɑ:'] n = tsar.

u (pl u's OR us), **U** (pl U's OR Us) [ju:] n [letter] u, U m.
➥ **U** (abbr of universal) livre.

U (abbr of universal) filme de censura livre.

UAE (abbr of United Arab Emirates) n EAU mpl.

UB40 (abbr of unemployment benefit form 40) n

certificado de recebimento do seguro-desemprego na Grã-Bretanha.

U-bend n sifão m.

ubiquitous [ju:'bɪkwɪtəs] adj fml ubíquo(qua).

u.c. (abbr of upper case) n caixa-alta f.

UCAS (abbr of Universities and Colleges Admissions Service) n organização britânica que trata da admissão às faculdades e universidades.

UCL (abbr of University College, London) n uma das faculdades da Universidade de Londres.

UDA (abbr of Ulster Defence Association) n organização paramilitar protestante da Irlanda do Norte, favorável à permanência da Irlanda do Norte no Reino Unido.

UDC (abbr of Urban District Council) n câmara de vereadores britânica de comunidade urbana.

udder ['ʌdə'] n úbere m.

UDI (abbr of unilateral declaration of independence) n -1. HIST declaração unilateral de independência (na Rodésia) -2. hum: to declare ~ on sb passar alguém para trás.

UDR (abbr of Ulster Defence Regiment) n antigo regimento de reservistas na Irlanda do Norte, agora parte do Regimento Real Irlandês.

UEFA [ju:'eɪfə] (abbr of Union of European Football Associations) n UEFA f.

UFC (abbr of Universities Funding Council) n órgão britânico responsável por gerir as doações universitárias.

UFO (abbr of unidentified flying object) n OVNI m.

Uganda [ju:'gændə] n Uganda; **in** ~ em Uganda.

Ugandan [ju:'gændən] <> adj ugandense. <> n [person] ugandense mf.

ugh [ʌg] excl puf!

ugliness ['ʌglɪnɪs] n (U) -1. [unattractiveness] feiúra f -2. fig [unpleasantness] repulsa f.

ugly ['ʌglɪ] (compar -ier, superl -iest) adj -1. [unattractive] feio (feia) -2. fig [unpleasant] desagradável.

UHF (abbr of ultra-high frequency) n UHF m.

UHT (abbr of ultra-heat treated) adj UHT; ~ **milk** leite m longa-vida.

UK (abbr of United Kingdom) n RU m.

UKAEA (abbr of United Kingdom Atomic Energy Authority) n órgão responsável pelo controle da energia atômica no Reino Unido.

Ukraine [ju:'kreɪn] n: the ~ a Ucrânia; **in the** ~ na Ucrânia.

Ukrainian [ju:'kreɪnjən] <> adj ucraniano(na). <> n -1. [person] ucraniano m, -na f -2. [language] ucraniano m.

ulcer ['ʌlsə'] n -1. [in stomach] úlcera f -2. [in mouth] afta f.

ulcerated ['ʌlsəreɪtɪd] adj ulcerado(da).

Ulster ['ʌlstə'] n Irlanda f do Norte; **in** ~ na Irlanda do Norte.

Ulster Unionist Party n partido político norte-irlandês que defende a permanência da Irlanda do Norte como parte do Grã-Bretanha.

ulterior [ʌl'tɪərɪə'] adj: ~ **motive** motivo m ulterior.

ultimata [,ʌltɪ'meɪtə] pl ➪ ultimatum.

ultimate ['ʌltɪmət] <> adj -1. [success, objetive] final,

definitivo(va) **-2.** [failure] último(ma) **-3.** [most powerful] máximo(ma). <> *n:* **the ~ in sthg** a última palavra em algo.
ultimately [ˈʌltɪmətlɪ] *adv* **-1.** [finally, in the long term] finalmente, por fim **-2.** [fundamentally] no fundo.
ultimatum [ˌʌltɪˈmeɪtəm] (*pl* **-tums** OR **-ta**) *n* ultimato *m.*
ultra- [ˈʌltrə] *prefix* ultra-.
ultramarine [ˌʌltrəməˈriːn] *adj* ultramarino(na).
ultrasonic [ˌʌltrəˈsɒnɪk] *adj* ultra-sônico(ca).
ultrasound [ˈʌltrəsaʊnd] *n (U)* ultra-som *m.*
ultraviolet [ˌʌltrəˈvaɪələt] *adj* ultravioleta.
um [ʌm] *excl* hum!
umbilical cord [ʌmˈbɪlɪkl-] *n* cordão *m* umbilical.
umbrage [ˈʌmbrɪdʒ] *n:* **to take ~ (at sthg)** ofender-se (com algo).
umbrella [ʌmˈbrelə] <> *n* **-1.** [gen] guarda-chuva *m;* **-2.** [fixed] guarda-sol *m.* <> *adj* guarda-chuva; **~ word** palavra guarda-chuva.
UMIST (*abbr of* **University of Manchester Institute of Science and Technology**) *n* instituto de ciência e tecnologia da Universidade de Manchester, UMIST *m.*
umpire [ˈʌmpaɪəʳ] <> *n* árbitro *m.* <> *vt & vi* arbitrar, apitar.
umpteen [ˌʌmpˈtiːn] *num adj inf:* **~ times** um milhão de vezes.
umpteenth [ˌʌmpˈtiːnθ] *num adj inf* enésimo(ma).
UN (*abbr of* **United Nations**) *n:* **the ~** a ONU.
unabashed [ˌʌnəˈbæʃt] *adj* imperturbável.
unabated [ˌʌnəˈbeɪtɪd] *adj* incessante.
unable [ʌnˈeɪbl] *adj* incapaz; **to be ~ to do sthg** não poder fazer algo.
unabridged [ˌʌnəˈbrɪdʒd] *adj* integral.
unacceptable [ˌʌnəkˈseptəbl] *adj* inaceitável.
unaccompanied [ˌʌnəˈkʌmpənɪd] *adj* **-1.** [child] sozinho(nha) **-2.** [luggage] desacompanhado(da) **-3.** [song] sem acompanhamento.
unaccountable [ˌʌnəˈkaʊntəbl] *adj* **-1.** [inexplicable] incompreensível **-2.** [not responsible] que não é responsável; **to be ~ for sthg** não ser responsável por algo; **to be ~ to sb** não ter de dar satisfações para alguém.
unaccountably [ˌʌnəˈkaʊntəblɪ] *adv* [inexplicably] inexplicavelmente.
unaccounted [ˌʌnəˈkaʊntɪd] *adj:* **~ for** desaparecido(da).
unaccustomed [ˌʌnəˈkʌstəmd] *adj* **-1.** [unused]: **to be ~ to sthg/to doing sthg** estar desacostumado(da) a algo/a fazer algo **-2.** *fml* [not usual] inusual.
unacquainted [ˌʌnəˈkweɪntɪd] *adj:* **to be ~ with sb/sthg** não conhecer alguém/algo.
unadulterated [ˌʌnəˈdʌltəreɪtɪd] *adj* **-1.** [unspoiled] não-adulterado(da) **-2.** [absolute] puro(ra).
unadventurous [ˌʌnədˈventʃərəs] *adj* pouco aventureiro(ra).
unaffected [ˌʌnəˈfektɪd] *adj* **-1.** [unchanged] intacto(ta); **to be ~ by sthg** não ser atingido(da) por algo **-2.** [natural] natural.
unafraid [ˌʌnəˈfreɪd] *adj* destemido(da).
unaided [ˌʌnˈeɪdɪd] <> *adj* feito(ta) sem ajuda. <> *adv* sem ajuda.

unambiguous [ˌʌnæmˈbɪgjʊəs] *adj* inequívoco(-ca).
un-American [ˈʌn-] *adj* antiamericano(na).
unanimity [ˌjuːnəˈnɪmətɪ] *n (U) fml* unanimidade *f.*
unanimous [juːˈnænɪməs] *adj* unânime.
unanimously [juːˈnænɪməslɪ] *adv* unanimemente.
unannounced [ˌʌnəˈnaʊnst] <> *adj* não-anunciado(da). <> *adv* sem anunciar.
unanswered [ˌʌnˈɑːnsəd] *adj* não-respondido(da).
unappealing [ˌʌnəˈpiːlɪŋ] *adj* desagradável.
unappetizing, -ising [ˌʌnˈæpɪtaɪzɪŋ] *adj* **-1.** [food] pouco apetitoso(sa) **-2.** [sight, thought] pouco apetecível.
unappreciated [ˌʌnəˈpriːʃɪeɪtɪd] *adj* não-reconhecido(da).
unappreciative [ˌʌnəˈpriːʃɪətɪv] *adj* ingrato(ta); **to be ~ of sthg** ser incapaz de apreciar algo.
unapproachable [ˌʌnəˈprəʊtʃəbl] *adj* [person] inacessível.
unarmed [ˌʌnˈɑːmd] *adj* desarmado(da).
unarmed combat *n (U)* combate *m* sem armas.
unashamed [ˌʌnəˈʃeɪmd] *adj* descarado(da).
unassisted [ˌʌnəˈsɪstɪd] *adj* sem ajuda.
unassuming [ˌʌnəˈsjuːmɪŋ] *adj* despretensioso(-sa).
unattached [ˌʌnəˈtætʃt] *adj* **-1.** [not fastened, linked] independente; **~ to sthg** separado(da) de algo **-2.** [without partner] sem compromisso.
unattainable [ˌʌnəˈteɪnəbl] *adj* inatingível.
unattended [ˌʌnəˈtendɪd] *adj* **-1.** [luggage, children] desacompanhado(da) **-2.** [fire, shop] sem vigilância.
unattractive [ˌʌnəˈtræktɪv] *adj* **-1.** [person, building, place] sem atrativos **-2.** [idea, prospect] sem brilho.
unauthorized, -ised [ˌʌnˈɔːθəraɪzd] *adj* não-autorizado(da).
unavailable [ˌʌnəˈveɪləbl] *adj* que não está disponível.
unavoidable [ˌʌnəˈvɔɪdəbl] *adj* inevitável.
unavoidably [ˌʌnəˈvɔɪdəblɪ] *adv* inevitavelmente.
unaware [ˌʌnəˈweəʳ] *adj* desconhecedor(ra); **to be ~ of sb/sthg** não estar consciente de alguém/algo.
unawares [ˌʌnəˈweəz] *adv:* **to catch** OR **take sb ~** pegar alguém desprevenido(da).
unbalanced [ˌʌnˈbælənst] *adj* **-1.** [biased] parcial **-2.** [deranged] desequilibrado(da).
unbearable [ʌnˈbeərəbl] *adj* insuportável, insustentável.
unbearably [ʌnˈbeərəblɪ] *adv* insuportavelmente, insustentavelmente.
unbeatable [ˌʌnˈbiːtəbl] *adj* imbatível.
unbecoming [ˌʌnbɪˈkʌmɪŋ] *adj fml* [dress, colour] pouco favorecedor(ra).
unbeknown(st) [ˌʌnbɪˈnəʊn(st)] *adv:* **~ to** sem o conhecimento de.
unbelievable [ˌʌnbɪˈliːvəbl] *adj* **-1.** [amazing] incrível **-2.** [not believable] inacreditável.
unbelievably [ˌʌnbɪˈliːvəblɪ] *adv* [extremely] extremamente.
unbend [ˌʌnˈbend] (*pt & pp* **unbent**) *vi* [relax] relaxar.
unbending [ˌʌnˈbendɪŋ] *adj* [intransigent] resoluto(-ta).

unbent [ˌʌn'bentl] *pt* & *pp* ▷ **unbend**.
unbia(s)sed [ˌʌn'baɪəst] *adj* imparcial.
unblemished [ˌʌn'blemɪʃt] *adj* *fig* irretocável.
unblock [ˌʌn'blɒk] *vt* **-1.** [drain, tunnel] desbloquear **-2.** [pipe] desentupir.
unbolt [ˌʌn'bəʊlt] *vt* [door] destrancar.
unborn [ˌʌn'bɔːn] *adj* [child] nascituro(ra).
unbreakable [ˌʌn'breɪkəbl] *adj* inquebrável.
unbridled [ˌʌn'braɪdld] *adj* desenfreado(da).
unbuckle [ˌʌn'bʌkl] *vt* desafivelar.
unbutton [ˌʌn'bʌtn] *vt* desabotoar.
uncalled-for [ˌʌn'kɔːld-] *adj* injusto(ta), desnecessário(ria).
uncanny [ʌn'kænɪ] (*compar* **-ier**, *superl* **-iest**) *adj* sinistro(tra).
uncared-for [ˌʌn'keəd-] *adj* abandonado(da).
uncaring [ˌʌn'keərɪŋ] *adj* insensível.
unceasing [ˌʌn'siːsɪŋ] *adj* *fml* incessante.
unceremonious ['ʌnˌserɪ'məʊnjəs] *adj* [abrupt] abrupto(ta).
unceremoniously ['ʌnˌserɪ'məʊnjəslɪ] *adj* [abruptly] abruptamente.
uncertain [ʌn'sɜːtn] *adj* **-1.** [gen] incerto(ta) **-2.** [person] indeciso(sa); **in no ~ terms** sem meias palavras.
unchain [ˌʌn'tʃeɪn] *vt* desacorrentar.
unchallenged [ˌʌn'tʃælɪndʒd] *adj* [authority, leadership, version] inquestionável.
unchanged [ˌʌn'tʃeɪndʒd] *adj* sem alterar.
unchanging [ˌʌn'tʃeɪndʒɪŋ] *adj* imutável.
uncharacteristic ['ʌnˌkærəktə'rɪstɪk] *adj* não-característico(ca).
uncharitable [ˌʌn'tʃærɪtəbl] *adj* mesquinho(nha).
uncharted [ˌʌn'tʃɑːtɪd] *adj* **-1.** [not recorded on maps] não-cartografado(da) **-2.** *fig* [unfamiliar] desconhecido(da).
unchecked [ˌʌn'tʃektl] ◇ *adj* [unrestrained] desenfreado(da). ◇ *adv* [unrestrained] sem restrições.
uncivilized, -ised [ˌʌn'sɪvɪlaɪzd] *adj* [barbaric] não-civilizado(da).
unclassified [ˌʌn'klæsɪfaɪd] *adj* **-1.** [not confidential] não-confidencial **-2.** [not categorised] não-classificado.
uncle ['ʌŋkl] *n* tio *m*.
unclean [ˌʌn'kliːn] *adj* **-1.** [dirty] sujo(ja) **-2.** *RELIG* impuro(ra).
unclear [ˌʌn'klɪər] *adj* **-1.** [meaning, instructions] confuso(sa), pouco claro(ra) **-2.** [future] obscuro(ra) **-3.** [motives, details] confuso(sa) **-4.** [person]: **to be ~ about sthg** não ter algo claro.
unclothed [ˌʌn'kləʊðd] *adj* *fml* despido(da).
uncomfortable [ˌʌn'kʌmftəbl] *adj* **-1.** [giving discomfort] desconfortável **-2.** *fig* [awkward] desagradável **-3.** [person - in physical discomfort] desconfortável; [- ill at ease] incomodado(da).
uncomfortably [ˌʌn'kʌmftəblɪ] *adv* **-1.** [in physical discomfort] desconfortavelmente **-2.** *fig* [uneasily] de forma incômoda **-3.** [unpleasantly] desagradavelmente.
uncommitted [ˌʌnkə'mɪtɪd] *adj* não-comprometido(da).
uncommon [ʌn'kɒmən] *adj* **-1.** [rare] raro(ra) **-2.** *fml* [extreme] fora do comum.

uncommonly [ʌn'kɒmənlɪ] *adv* *fml* extraordinariamente.
uncommunicative [ˌʌnkə'mjuːnɪkətɪv] *adj* reservado(da).
uncomplicated [ˌʌn'kɒmplɪkeɪtɪd] *adj* descomplicado(da).
uncomprehending ['ʌnˌkɒmprɪ'hendɪŋ] *adj* atônito(ta).
uncompromising [ˌʌn'kɒmprəmaɪzɪŋ] *adj* resoluto(ta), inflexível.
unconcerned [ˌʌnkən'sɜːnd] *adj* [not anxious] indiferente.
unconditional [ˌʌnkən'dɪʃənl] *adj* incondicional.
uncongenial [ˌʌnkən'dʒiːnjəl] *adj* *fml* desagradável.
unconnected [ˌʌnkə'nektɪd] *adj* desconexo(xa).
unconquered [ˌʌn'kɒŋkəd] *adj* não-conquistado(da).
unconscious [ʌn'kɒnʃəs] ◇ *adj* **-1.** [gen] inconsciente **-2.** *fig* [unaware]: **to be ~ of sthg** não estar ciente de algo. ◇ *n* *PSYCH*: **the ~** o inconsciente.
unconsciously [ʌn'kɒnʃəslɪ] *adv* inconscientemente.
unconstitutional ['ʌnˌkɒnstɪ'tjuːʃənl] *adj* inconstitucional.
uncontested [ˌʌnkən'testɪd] *adj* **-1.** [gen] incontestado(da) **-2.** [election] sem oponente.
uncontrollable [ˌʌnkən'trəʊləbl] *adj* incontrolável.
uncontrolled [ˌʌnkən'trəʊld] *adj* descontrolado(da).
unconventional [ˌʌnkən'venʃənl] *adj* não-convencional.
unconvinced [ˌʌnkən'vɪnst] *adj* não-convencido(da).
unconvincing [ˌʌnkən'vɪnsɪŋ] *adj* não-convincente.
uncooked [ˌʌn'kʊktl] *adj* cru (crua).
uncooperative [ˌʌnkəʊ'ɒpərətɪv] *adj* não-disposto(ta) a ajudar.
uncork [ˌʌn'kɔːk] *vt* desarrolhar.
uncorroborated [ˌʌnkə'rɒbəreɪtɪd] *adj* não-confirmado(da).
uncouth [ʌn'kuːθ] *adj* grosseiro(ra).
uncover [ʌn'kʌvər] *vt* **-1.** [saucepan] destampar **-2.** [corruption, truth] revelar, expor.
uncurl [ˌʌn'kɜːl] *vi* **-1.** [hair] alisar **-2.** [wire] esticar **-3.** [animal] desenroscar-se.
uncut [ˌʌn'kʌt] *adj* **-1.** [film] sem cortes **-2.** [jewel] bruto(ta).
undamaged [ˌʌn'dæmɪdʒd] *adj* intacto(ta).
undaunted [ˌʌn'dɔːntɪd] *adj* inabalável, destemido(da).
undecided [ˌʌndɪ'saɪdɪd] *adj* **-1.** [person] indeciso(sa) **-2.** [issue] pendente.
undemanding [ˌʌndɪ'mɑːndɪŋ] *adj* **-1.** [task] que exige pouco esforço **-2.** [person] pouco exigente.
undemonstrative [ˌʌndɪ'mɒnstrətɪv] *adj* [person] reservado(da).
undeniable [ˌʌndɪ'naɪəbl] *adj* inegável.
under ['ʌndər] ◇ *prep* **-1.** [beneath, below] embaixo de; **they walked ~ the bridge** passaram por baixo da ponte **-2.** [less than] menos de **-3.** [indicating

conditions or circumstances]: ~ **the circumstances** dadas as circunstâncias; **I'm ~ the impression that ...** tenho a impressão de que ... - **4.** [undergoing]: ~ **discussion** em discussão - **5.** [directed, governed by]: **he has ten people ~ him** tem dez pessoas trabalhando sob seu comando - **6.** [according to] de acordo com - **7.** [in classification, name, title]: **he filed it ~ 'D'** arquivou na letra D; ~ **an alias** sob outro nome. <> *adv* -**1.** [beneath] embaixo; **to go ~** fracassar - **2.** [less]: **children of five years and ~** crianças de cinco anos ou menos.

under- ['ʌndə'] *prefix* sub-.

underachiever [ˌʌndərə'tʃiːvə'] *n* pessoa que não rende tudo o que pode.

underage [ʌndər'eɪdʒ] *adj* -**1.** [person] menor de idade - **2.** [drinking, sex] para menor de idade.

underarm ['ʌndərɑːm] <> *adj* -**1.** [deodorant, hair] para as axilas - **2.** SPORT [bowling] com a mão por baixo do ombro. <> *adv* [throw, bowl] por baixo do ombro.

underbrush ['ʌndəbrʌʃ] *n* US vegetação *f* rasteira *(numa floresta)*.

undercarriage ['ʌndə,kærɪdʒ] *n* trem *m* de aterrissagem.

undercharge [ˌʌndə'tʃɑːdʒ] *vt* cobrar menos que o estipulado.

underclothes ['ʌndəkləʊðz] *npl* roupas *fpl* íntimas OR de baixo.

undercoat ['ʌndəkəʊt] *n* [of paint] primeira demão *f*.

undercook [ˌʌndə'kʊk] *vt* não cozinhar suficientemente.

undercover ['ʌndə,kʌvə'] <> *adj* secreto(ta). <> *adv* na clandestinidade.

undercurrent ['ʌndə,kʌrənt] *n* fig [tendency] sentimento *m* oculto.

undercut [ˌʌndə'kʌt] (*pt & pp* **undercut**, *cont* -**ting**) *vt* [in price] vender mais barato que.

underdeveloped [ˌʌndədɪ'veləpt] *adj* subdesenvolvido(da), em desenvolvimento.

underdog ['ʌndədɒg] *n*: **the ~** os menos favorecidos.

underdone [ˌʌndə'dʌn] *adj* [food] meio cru (crua).

underemployment [ˌʌndərɪm'plɔɪmənt] *n (U)* subemprego *m*.

underestimate [*n* ˌʌndər'estɪmət, *vb* ˌʌndər'estɪmeɪt] <> *n* subestimação *f*. <> *vt* subestimar.

underexposed [ˌʌndərɪk'spəʊzd] *adj* PHOT subexposto(ta).

underfinanced [ˌʌndə'faɪnænst] *adj* insuficientemente financiado(da).

underfoot [ˌʌndə'fʊt] *adv* debaixo dos pés; **the ground is wet ~** o chão está molhado.

undergo [ˌʌndə'gəʊ] (*pt* -**went**, *pp* -**gone**) *vt* -**1.** [change, difficulties] passar por - **2.** [operation, examination] submeter-se a.

undergraduate [ˌʌndə'grædʒʊət] <> *adj* de graduação. <> *n* universitário *m*, -ria *f* *(que ainda não colou grau)*.

underground [*adj & n* 'ʌndəgraʊnd, *adv* ˌʌndə'graʊnd] <> *adj* -**1.** [below the ground] subterrâneo(nea) - **2.** fig [secret, illegal] clandestino(na). <> *adv*: **to go ~** passar à clandestinidade; **to be**

forced ~ ter de passar à clandestinidade. <> *n* -**1.** UK [transport system] metrô *m* - **2.** [activist movement] resistência *f*.

undergrowth ['ʌndəgrəʊθ] *n (U)* vegetação *f* rasteira *(numa floresta)*.

underhand [ˌʌndə'hænd] *adj* clandestino(na).

underinsured [ˌʌndərɪn'ʃʊəd] *adj* segurado(da) abaixo do valor corrente.

underlay ['ʌndəleɪ] *n* [for carpet] forração *f*.

underline [ˌʌndə'laɪn] *vt* -**1.** [draw line under] sublinhar - **2.** fig [stress] salientar.

underling *n* subalterno *m*, -na *f*.

underlying [ˌʌndə'laɪɪŋ] *adj* subjacente.

undermanned [ˌʌndə'mænd] *adj* com falta de mão-de-obra.

undermentioned [ˌʌndə'menʃnd] *adj* fml abaixo mencionado(da).

undermine [ˌʌndə'maɪn] *vt* fig [weaken] minar.

underneath [ˌʌndə'niːθ] <> *prep* debaixo de. <> *adv* -**1.** [beneath] por baixo - **2.** fig [within oneself] por dentro, no fundo. <> *adj* inf de baixo. <> *n* [underside]: **the ~** a parte de baixo; **on the ~** no fundo; **on the ~ of the box** na parte de baixo da caixa.

undernourished [ˌʌndə'nʌrɪʃt] *adj* subnutrido(-da).

underpaid [*pt & pp* ˌʌndə'peɪd, *adj* 'ʌndəpeɪd] <> *pt & pp* ⊳ **underpay**. <> *adj* mal pago(ga).

underpants ['ʌndəpænts] *npl* cueca *f*.

underpass ['ʌndəpɑːs] *n* passagem *f* subterrânea.

underpay [ˌʌndə'peɪ] (*pt & pp* -**paid**) *vt* pagar mal.

underpin [ˌʌndə'pɪn] (*pt & pp* -**ned**, *cont* -**ning**) *vt* fig [back up] embasar.

underplay [ˌʌndə'pleɪ] *vt* [minimize the importance of] minimizar.

underprice [ˌʌndə'praɪs] *vt* cotar algo abaixo de seu valor real.

underprivileged [ˌʌndə'prɪvɪlɪdʒd] *adj* [children] desamparado(da).

underproduction [ˌʌndəprə'dʌkʃn] *n (U)* produção *f* insuficiente.

underrated [ˌʌndə'reɪtɪd] *adj* subestimado(da).

underscore [ˌʌndə'skɔː'] *vt* -**1.** [underline] sublinhar - **2.** fig [emphasize] salientar.

undersea ['ʌndəsiː] *adj* submarino(na).

undersecretary [ˌʌndə'sekrətərɪ] (*pl* -**ies**) *n* subsecretário *m*, -ria *f*.

undersell [ˌʌndə'sel] (*pt & pp* -**sold**) *vt* -**1.** COMM [sell at lower prices than] vender mais barato que - **2.** fig [undervalue]: **to ~ o.s.** vender-se barato.

undershirt ['ʌndəʃɜːt] *n* US camiseta *f*.

underside ['ʌndəsaɪd] *n*: **the ~** a parte de baixo.

undersigned ['ʌndəsaɪnd] *n* fml: **the ~** o abaixo-assinado.

undersize(d) [ˌʌndə'saɪz(d)] *adj* menor que o normal.

underskirt ['ʌndəskɜːt] *n* anágua *f*.

undersold [ˌʌndə'səʊld] *pt & pp* ⊳ **undersell**.

understaffed [ˌʌndə'stɑːft] *adj* com falta de pessoal.

understand [ˌʌndə'stænd] (*pt & pp* -**stood**) <> *vt* -**1.** entender, compreender; **to make o.s. understood** fazer-se entender - **2.** fml [believe]: **to ~ that**

acreditar que. <> *vi* entender, compreender.

understandable [ˌʌndəˈstændəbl] *adj* compreensível.

understandably [ˌʌndəˈstændəblɪ] *adv* naturalmente; **he was ~ upset** é compreensível que ele estivesse chateado.

understanding [ˌʌndəˈstændɪŋ] <> *n* **-1.** [knowledge, insight] compreensão *f*, entendimento *m* **-2.** *(U)* [sympathy] compreensão *f* mútua **-3.** [interpretation, conception]: **it is my ~ that ...** tenho a impressão de que ... **-4.** [informal agreement] entendimento *m*; **on the ~ that ...** à condição de que ... <> *adj* [sympathetic] compreensivo(va).

understate [ˌʌndəˈsteɪt] *vt* [minimize] atenuar.

understated *adj* [elegance, clothes] sóbrio(bria).

understatement [ˌʌndəˈsteɪtmənt] *n* **-1.** [inadequate statement] atenuação *f* **-2.** *(U)* [quality of understating] atenuação *f*; **he is a master of ~** ele é o rei dos eufemismos.

understood [ˌʌndəˈstʊd] *pt* & *pp* ▷ **understand**.

understudy [ˈʌndəˌstʌdɪ] (*pl* **-ies**, *pt* & *pp* **-ied**) <> *n* ator *m* substituto, atriz *f* substituta. <> *vt* : **to ~ the role of Macbeth** substituit alguém no papel de Macbeth.

undertake [ˌʌndəˈteɪk] (*pt* **-took**, *pp* **-taken**) *vt* **-1.** [take on - responsibility, control] assumir; [- task] incumbir-se de **-2.** [promise]: **to ~ to do sthg** comprometer-se a fazer algo.

undertaker [ˈʌndəˌteɪkəʳ] *n* agente *mf* funerário, -ria; **~'s** [place] funerária *f*.

undertaking [ˌʌndəˈteɪkɪŋ] *n* **-1.** [task] incumbência *f* **-2.** [promise] promessa *f*.

undertone [ˈʌndətəʊn] *n* **-1.** [quiet voice] voz *f* baixa **-2.** [vague feeling] traço *m*; **an ~ of sadness** um traço de tristeza.

undertook [ˌʌndəˈtʊk] *pt* ▷ **undertake**.

undertow [ˈʌndətəʊ] *n* ressaca *f* (*no mar*).

undervalue [ˌʌndəˈvæljuː] *vt* **-1.** [person] subestimar **-2.** [house, object] avaliar algo abaixo de seu real valor.

underwater [ˌʌndəˈwɔːtəʳ] <> *adj* submarino(na). <> *adv* debaixo d'água.

underwear [ˈʌndəweəʳ] *n* *(U)* roupa *f* íntima *or* de baixo.

underweight [ˌʌndəˈweɪt] *adj* abaixo do peso.

underwent [ˌʌndəˈwent] *pt* ▷ **undergo**.

underwired *adj* [bra] com suporte.

underworld [ˈʌndəˌwɜːld] *n* [criminal society]: **the ~** o submundo.

underwrite [ˈʌndəraɪt] (*pt* **-wrote**, *pp* **-written**) *vt* **-1.** *fml* [guarantee] comprometer-se com **-2.** [in insurance business] subscrever.

underwriter [ˈʌndəˌraɪtəʳ] *n* segurador *m*, -ra *f*.

underwritten [ˈʌndəˌrɪtn] *pp* ▷ **underwrite**.

underwrote [ˈʌndərəʊt] *pt* ▷ **underwrite**.

undeserved [ˌʌndɪˈzɜːvd] *adj* não-merecido(da).

undesirable [ˌʌndɪˈzaɪərəbl] *adj* indesejável.

undeveloped [ˌʌndɪˈveləpt] *adj* **-1.** [country] subdesenvolvido(da), em desenvolvimento **-2.** [land, resource] não explorado(da).

undid [ʌnˈdɪd] *pt* ▷ **undo**.

undies [ˈʌndɪz] *npl* *inf* roupas *fpl* íntimas *or* de baixo.

undignified [ʌnˈdɪɡnɪfaɪd] *adj* indecoroso(sa), impróprio(pria).

undiluted [ˌʌndaɪˈljuːtɪd] *adj* **-1.** [quality, emotion] puro(ra) **-2.** [liquid] não-diluído(da).

undiplomatic [ˌʌndɪpləˈmætɪk] *adj* pouco diplomático(ca), indelicado(da).

undischarged [ˌʌndɪsˈtʃɑːdʒd] *adj* **-1.** [debt] pendente **-2.** [person]: **~ bankrupt** pessoa *f* falida não-reabilitada.

undisciplined [ʌnˈdɪsɪplɪnd] *adj* indisciplinado(da).

undiscovered [ˌʌndɪsˈkʌvəd] *adj* [unknown] não-descoberto(ta).

undisputed [ˌʌndɪˈspjuːtɪd] *adj* indiscutível.

undistinguished [ˌʌndɪsˈtɪŋɡwɪʃt] *adj* sem graça.

undivided [ˌʌndɪˈvaɪdɪd] *adj* [whole] inteiro(ra); **my ~ attention** toda a minha atenção.

undo [ʌnˈduː] (*pt* **-did**, *pp* **-done**) *vt* **-1.** [knot] desfazer, desatar **-2.** [buttons] desabotoar **-3.** [garment] desamarrar **-4.** [good work, efforts] anular.

undoing [ʌnˈduːɪŋ] *n* *(U)* *fml* ruína *f*, perdição *f*.

undone [ʌnˈdʌn] <> *pp* ▷ **undo**. <> *adj* **-1.** [coat] desabotoado(da) **-2.** [shoe] desamarrado(da) **-3.** *fml* [not done] por fazer.

undoubted [ʌnˈdaʊtɪd] *adj* indubitável.

undoubtedly [ʌnˈdaʊtɪdlɪ] *adv* indubitavelmente.

undreamed-of [ʌnˈdriːmdɒv], **undreamt-of** [ʌnˈdremtɒv] *adj* [unimaginable] jamais imaginado(da).

undress [ʌnˈdres] <> *vt* despir. <> *vi* despir-se.

undressed [ʌnˈdrest] *adj* [person] despido(da); **to get ~** tirar a roupa, despir-se.

undrinkable [ʌnˈdrɪŋkəbl] *adj* **-1.** [dangerous to drink] não-potável **-2.** [bad-tasting] intragável.

undue [ʌnˈdjuː] *adj* *fml* desmedido(da).

undulate [ˈʌndjʊleɪt] *vi* *fml* ondular.

unduly [ʌnˈdjuːlɪ] *adv* *fml* demasiadamente.

undying [ʌnˈdaɪɪŋ] *adj* *literary* imperecível.

unearned income [ʌnˈɜːnd-] *n* *(U)* renda *f* diferida.

unearth [ʌnˈɜːθ] *vt* **-1.** [dig up] desenterrar **-2.** *fig* [discover] descubrir.

unearthly [ʌnˈɜːθlɪ] *adj* **-1.** [ghostly] sobrenatural **-2.** *inf* [time of day]: **at an ~ hour in the morning** num horário absurdo da manhã.

unease [ʌnˈiːz] *n* *(U)* inquietação *f*, apreensão *f*.

uneasy [ʌnˈiːzɪ] (*compar* **-ier**, *superl* **-iest**) *adj* **-1.** [troubled] apreensivo(va) **-2.** [embarrassed] constrangido(da); **an ~ silence** um silêncio constrangedor **-3.** [peace, truce] duvidoso(sa).

uneatable [ʌnˈiːtəbl] *adj* **-1.** [dangerous to eat] *que não se pode comer* **-2.** [bad-tasting] indigesto(ta).

uneaten [ʌnˈiːtn] *adj*: **lots of ~ food** muita comida que sobrou.

uneconomic [ˈʌnˌiːkəˈnɒmɪk] *adj* pouco rentável.

uneducated [ʌnˈedjʊkeɪtɪd] *adj* **-1.** [person] inculto(ta), sem instrução **-2.** [behaviour, manners, speech] em que se percebe falta de instrução.

unemotional [ˌʌnɪˈməʊʃənl] *adj* **-1.** [person] impassível **-2.** [voice, tone] frio (fria) **-3.** [statement] objetivo(va).

unemployable [ˌʌnɪm'plɔɪəbl] *adj* que dificilmente encontrará trabalho.

unemployed [ˌʌnɪm'plɔɪd] ⟨⟩ *adj* [out-of-work]
desempregado(da). ⟨⟩ *npl*: **the ~** os desempregados.

unemployment [ˌʌnɪm'plɔɪmənt] *n* desemprego
m.

unemployment benefit *UK*, **unemployment compensation** *US* *n (U)* ≃ seguro-
desemprego *m*.

unenviable [ˌʌn'envɪəbl] *adj* nada de invejável.

unequal [ˌʌn'i:kwəl] *adj* desigual.

unequalled *UK*, **unequaled** *US* [ˌʌn'i:kwəld] *adj*
igualável.

unequivocal [ˌʌnɪ'kwɪvəkl] *adj fml* inequívoco(ca).

unerring [ˌʌn'ɜ:rɪŋ] *adj* infalível.

UNESCO [ju:'neskəʊ] (*abbr of* United Nations Educational, Scientific and Cultural Organization) *n*
UNESCO *f*.

unethical [ʌn'eθɪkl] *adj* antiético(ca).

uneven [ˌʌn'i:vn] *adj* **-1.** [surface] irregular **-2.** [road]
acidentado(da) **-3.** [performance, coverage *etc*] desigual, desparelho(lha) **-4.** [competition] injusto(ta).

uneventful [ˌʌnɪ'ventfʊl] *adj* sem maiores incidentes.

unexceptional [ˌʌnɪk'sepʃənl] *adj* sem nada de
mais, normal.

unexpected [ˌʌnɪk'spektɪd] *adj* inesperado(da).

unexpectedly [ˌʌnɪk'spektɪdlɪ] *adv* inesperadamente.

unexplained [ˌʌnɪk'spleɪnd] *adj* inexplicado(da).

unexploded [ˌʌnɪk'spləʊdɪd] *adj* [bomb] que não
detonou.

unexpurgated [ˌʌn'ekspəgeɪtɪd] *adj* sem cortes,
na íntegra.

unfailing [ʌn'feɪlɪŋ] *adj* [loyalty, support, good humour]
infalível.

unfair [ˌʌn'feəʳ] *adj* injusto(ta).

unfair dismissal *n (U)* demissão *f* sem justa
causa.

unfairly *adv* injustamente.

unfairness [ˌʌn'feənɪs] *n* injustiça *f*.

unfaithful [ˌʌn'feɪθfʊl] *adj* [sexually] infiel.

unfamiliar [ˌʌnfə'mɪljəʳ] *adj* **-1.** [not well-known]
desconhecido(da) **-2.** [not acquainted]: **to be ~ with
sb/sthg** desconhecer alguém/algo.

unfashionable [ʌn'fæʃnəbl] *adj* ultrapassado(-
da).

unfasten [ˌʌn'fɑ:snl] *vt* **-1.** [garment, buttons] desabotoar **-2.** [rope] desamarrar.

unfavourable *UK*, **unfavorable** *US* [ˌʌn'feɪvrəbl]
adj desfavorável.

unfeeling [ʌn'fi:lɪŋ] *adj* insensível.

unfinished [ˌʌn'fɪnɪʃt] *adj* inacabado(da).

unfit [ˌʌn'fɪt] *adj* **-1.** [not in good shape] fora de forma
-2. [not suitable]: **~ (for sthg)** inadequado(da)
(para algo).

unflagging [ˌʌn'flægɪŋ] *adj* **-1.** [support, enthusiasm]
inesgotável **-2.** [supporter] incansável.

unflappable [ˌʌn'flæpəbl] *adj esp UK* inabalável.

unflattering [ˌʌn'flætərɪŋ] *adj* pouco favorece-
dor(ra).

unflinching [ʌn'flɪntʃɪŋ] *adj* impávido(da).

unfold [ʌn'fəʊld] ⟨⟩ *vt* **-1.** [open out] desdobrar **-2.**
[explain] expor. ⟨⟩ *vi* [become clear] esclarecer-se.

unforeseeable [ˌʌnfɔ:'si:əbl] *adj* imprevisível.

unforeseen [ˌʌnfɔ:'si:n] *adj* imprevisto(ta).

unforgettable [ˌʌnfə'getəbl] *adj* inesquecível.

unforgivable [ˌʌnfə'gɪvəbl] *adj* imperdoável.

unformatted [ˌʌn'fɔ:mætɪd] *adj COMPUT* não-forma-
tado(da).

unfortunate [ʌn'fɔ:tʃnət] *adj* **-1.** [unlucky] azaren-
to(ta) **-2.** [regrettable] lamentável.

unfortunately [ʌn'fɔ:tʃnətlɪ] *adv* infelizmente.

unfounded [ˌʌn'faʊndɪd] *adj* infundado(da).

unfriendly [ˌʌn'frendlɪ] (*compar* -**ier**, *superl* -**iest**) *adj*
hostil.

unfulfilled [ˌʌnfʊl'fɪld] *adj* **-1.** [ambition, promise,
prophecy] que não se realizou **-2.** [person] insatis-
feito(ta).

unfurl [ˌʌn'fɜ:l] *vt* **-1.** [flag, sail] desfraldar **-2.** [um-
brella] abrir.

unfurnished [ˌʌn'fɜ:nɪʃt] *adj* desmobiliado(da),
sem móveis.

ungainly [ʌn'geɪnlɪ] *adj* desajeitado(da).

ungenerous [ˌʌn'dʒenərəs] *adj* **-1.** [mean] miserável; **a not ~ gift** um presente bastante generoso
-2. [uncharitable] pouco generoso(sa).

ungodly [ˌʌn'gɒdlɪ] *adj* **-1.** [irreligious] ímpio(pia) **-2.**
inf [unreasonable]: **why are you phoning me at this
~ hour?** por que você está me ligando nesta
hora da madrugada?

ungrateful [ʌn'greɪtfʊl] *adj* mal-agradecido(da).

ungratefulness [ʌn'greɪtfʊlnɪs] *n (U)* ingratidão *f*.

unguarded [ˌʌn'gɑ:dɪd] *adj* **-1.** [not guarded] des-
protegido(da) **-2.** [careless]: **in an ~ moment** num
momento de descuido.

unhappily [ʌn'hæpɪlɪ] *adv* **-1.** [sadly] tristemente
-2. *fml* [unfortunately] lamentavelmente.

unhappiness [ʌn'hæpɪnɪs] *n (U)* infelicidade *f*.

unhappy [ʌn'hæpɪ] (*compar* -**ier**, *superl* -**iest**) *adj* **-1.**
[sad] triste **-2.** [uneasy]: **to be ~ (with OR about
sthg)** estar descontente(com algo) **-3.** *fml* [unfortu-
nate] lamentável, infeliz.

unharmed [ˌʌn'hɑ:md] *adj* ileso(sa).

UNHCR (*abbr of* United Nations High Commission
for Refugees) *n organização internacional que
faz parte da ONU responsável pela ajuda a
refugiados.*

unhealthy [ʌn'helθɪ] (*compar* -**ier**, *superl* -**iest**) *adj*
-1. [in bad health] doentio(tia) **-2.** [causing bad health]
insalubre **-3.** *fig* [undesirable] prejudicial.

unheard [ˌʌn'hɜ:d] *adj*: **to be OR go ~** passar sem
ser ouvido(da).

unheard-of [ˌʌn'hɜ:d-] *adj* **-1.** [unknown, completely
absent] inaudito(ta) **-2.** [unprecedented] sem precedente.

unheeded [ˌʌn'hi:dɪd] *adj*: **to go ~** passar desa-
percebido(da).

unhelpful [ˌʌn'helpfʊl] *adj* **-1.** [unwilling to help - per-
son] pouco prestativo(va); [- attitude] com má
vontade **-2.** [not useful] inútil.

unhindered [ʌn'hɪndəd] *adj* sem impedimentos.

unhook [ˌʌn'hʊk] *vt* **-1.** [unfasten hooks of] desengan-
char **-2.** [remove from hook] desprender.

unhurt [ˌʌn'hɜ:t] *adj* ileso(sa).

unhygienic [ˌʌnhaɪˈdʒiːnɪk] adj anti-higiênico(ca).

uni (abbr of **university**) n UK inf universidade f.

UNICEF [ˈjuːnɪˌsef] (abbr of **United Nations Children's Fund**) n UNICEF f.

unicorn [ˈjuːnɪkɔːn] n unicórnio m.

unicycle [ˈjuːnɪsaɪkl] n monociclo m.

unidentified [ˌʌnaɪˈdentɪfaɪd] adj não-identificado(da).

unidentified flying object n objeto m voador não-identificado.

unification [ˌjuːnɪfɪˈkeɪʃn] n (U) unificação f.

uniform [ˈjuːnɪfɔːm] <> adj uniforme. <> n uniforme m.

uniformity [ˌjuːnɪˈfɔːmətɪ] n (U) uniformidade f.

uniformly [ˈjuːnɪfɔːmlɪ] adv uniformemente.

unify [ˈjuːnɪfaɪ] (pt & pp -ied) vt unificar.

unifying [ˈjuːnɪfaɪɪŋ] adj unificador(ra).

unilateral [ˌjuːnɪˈlætərəl] adj unilateral.

unimaginable [ˌʌnɪˈmædʒɪnəbl] adj inimaginável.

unimaginative [ˌʌnɪˈmædʒɪnətɪv] adj sem imaginação.

unimpaired [ˌʌnɪmˈpeəd] adj -1. [gen] intacto(ta) -2. [health] inalterado(da).

unimpeded [ˌʌnɪmˈpiːdɪd] adj desimpedido(da), sem obstáculos.

unimportant [ˌʌnɪmˈpɔːtənt] adj insignificante, sem importância.

unimpressed [ˌʌnɪmˈprest] adj pouco impressionado(da).

uninhabited [ˌʌnɪnˈhæbɪtɪd] adj desabitado(da).

uninhibited [ˌʌnɪnˈhɪbɪtɪd] adj desinibido(da).

uninitiated [ˌʌnɪˈnɪʃɪeɪtɪd] npl: the ~ os inexperientes.

uninjured [ˌʌnˈɪndʒəd] adj ileso(sa).

uninspiring [ˌʌnɪnˈspaɪrɪŋ] adj nada inspirador(ra).

unintelligent [ˌʌnɪnˈtelɪdʒənt] adj pouco inteligente.

unintentional [ˌʌnɪnˈtenʃənl] adj involuntário(ria).

uninterested [ˌʌnˈɪntrəstɪd] adj desinteressado(da).

uninterrupted [ˌʌnˌɪntəˈrʌptɪd] adj ininterrupto(ta).

uninvited [ˌʌnɪnˈvaɪtɪd] adj não-convidado(da).

union [ˈjuːnjən] <> n -1. [trade union] sindicato m -2. [alliance] união f. <> comp sindical.

Unionist [ˈjuːnjənɪst] n UK POL membro de partido político que deseja que a Irlanda do Norte continue fazendo parte do Reino Unido, unionista mf.

unionize, -ise [ˈjuːnjənaɪz] vt sindicalizar.

unionized, -ised adj sindicalizado(da).

Union Jack n: the ~ a bandeira do Reino Unido.

union shop n US empresa na qual todos os empregados devem pertencer a um sindicato.

unique [juːˈniːk] adj -1. [unparalleled] incomparável, único(ca) -2. fml [peculiar, exclusive]: ~ to sb/sthg peculiar a alguém/algo.

uniquely [juːˈniːklɪ] adv -1. fml [exclusively] unicamente -2. [exceptionally] excepcionalmente.

unisex [ˈjuːnɪseks] adj unissex inv.

unison [ˈjuːnɪzn] n (U) [agreement] harmonia f; in ~ [simultaneously] em uníssono.

UNISON [ˈjuːnɪzn] n sindicato gigante que reúne a maioria dos funcionários britânicos, ≃ CUT f.

unit [ˈjuːnɪt] n -1. [gen] unidade f -2. [piece of furniture] módulo m.

unit cost n custo m unitário.

unite [juːˈnaɪt] <> vt unificar. <> vi unir-se, juntar-se.

united [juːˈnaɪtɪd] adj -1. [in harmony] unido(da); they are ~ on this point eles estão todos de acordo neste ponto -2. [unified] unificado(da).

United Arab Emirates npl: the ~ os Emirados Árabes Unidos.

united front n: to present a ~ fazer frente única.

United Kingdom n: the ~ o Reino Unido.

United Nations n: the ~ as Nações Unidas.

United States n: the ~ (of America) os Estados Unidos (da América); in the ~ nos Estados Unidos.

unit price n preço m unitário.

unit trust n UK fundo m de investimento.

unity [ˈjuːnətɪ] n -1. [union] união f, unidade f -2. [harmony] união f.

Univ. (abbr of **University**) univ.

universal [ˌjuːnɪˈvɜːsl] adj [belief, truth] universal.

universal joint n junta f universal.

universe [ˈjuːnɪvɜːs] n ASTRON universo m.

university [ˌjuːnɪˈvɜːsətɪ] (pl -ies) <> n universidade f. <> comp universitário(ria); ~ student estudante m universitário, -ria f.

unjust [ˌʌnˈdʒʌst] adj injusto(ta).

unjustifiable [ʌnˈdʒʌstɪˌfaɪəbl] adj injustificável.

unjustified [ʌnˈdʒʌstɪfaɪd] adj injustificado(da).

unkempt [ˌʌnˈkempt] adj [hair, beard, appearance] desajeitado(da).

unkind [ʌnˈkaɪnd] adj -1. [gen] indelicado(da) -2. fig [climate] rigoroso(sa).

unkindly [ʌnˈkaɪndlɪ] adv de forma indelicada.

unknown [ˌʌnˈnəʊn] <> adj desconhecido(da). <> n -1. [unknown thing]: the ~ o desconhecido -2. [unknown person] desconhecido m, -da f, estranho m, -nha f.

unlace [ˌʌnˈleɪs] vt desamarrar.

unladen [ˌʌnˈleɪdn] adj sem carga.

unlawful [ˌʌnˈlɔːfʊl] adj ilegal.

unleaded [ˌʌnˈledɪd] adj sem chumbo.

unleash [ˌʌnˈliːʃ] vt literary desencadear.

unleavened [ˌʌnˈlevnd] adj [bread] sem fermento.

unless [ənˈles] conj a menos que; ~ I'm mistaken, ... a não ser que eu esteja enganado, ...

unlicensed, unlicenced US [ˌʌnˈlaɪsənst] adj -1. [fishing, hunting] proibido(da) -2. [car] não-licenciado(da) -3. [premises, restaurant] sem licença.

unlike [ˌʌnˈlaɪk] prep -1. [different from] diferente de -2. [in contrast to] ao contrário de -3. [not typical of] atípico(ca); it's very ~ you to complain você não é de reclamar.

unlikely [ʌnˈlaɪklɪ] adj -1. [not probable] improvável -2. [bizarre] estranho(nha).

unlimited [ʌnˈlɪmɪtɪd] adj ilimitado(da).

unlisted [ʌn'lɪstɪd] *adj US* [phone number] fora da lista.

unlit [ˌʌn'lɪt] *adj* **-1.** [not burning] apagado(da) **-2.** [dark] sem luz.

unload [ˌʌn'ləʊd] *vt* **-1.** [gen] descarregar **-2.** *fig* [unburden]: **to ~ sthg on(to) sb** descarregar algo em alguém.

unlock [ˌʌn'lɒk] *vt* destrancar, abrir *(com chave)*.

unloved [ˌʌn'lʌvd] *adj*: **to be/feel ~** não ser/se sentir amado(da).

unluckily [ʌn'lʌkɪlɪ] *adv* infelizmente; **~ for us, ...** para nosso azar, ...

unlucky [ʌn'lʌkɪ] *(compar* **-ier,** *superl* **-iest)** *adj* **-1.** [unfortunate] infeliz **-2.** [bringing bad luck] de mau agouro.

unmanageable [ʌn'mænɪdʒəbl] *adj* **-1.** [vehicle, situation] fora de controle **-2.** [size, parcel] de difícil manuseio.

unmanly [ʌn'mænlɪ] *(compar* **-ier,** *superl* **-iest)** *adj* [behaviour, attitude] indigno(na) de um homem.

unmanned [ˌʌn'mænd] *adj* não-tripulado(da).

unmarked [ˌʌn'mɑːkt] *adj* **-1.** [uninjured] sem marca **-2.** [unidentified] não-identificado(da).

unmarried [ˌʌn'mærɪd] *adj* solteiro(ra).

unmask [ˌʌn'mɑːsk] *vt* desmascarar.

unmatched [ˌʌn'mætʃt] *adj* inigualável.

unmentionable [ʌn'menʃnəbl] *adj* indizível.

unmistakable [ˌʌnmɪ'steɪkəbl] *adj* inconfundível.

unmitigated [ʌn'mɪtɪgeɪtɪd] *adj* completo(ta), absoluto(ta); **he's talking ~ nonsense!** ele não está dizendo coisa com coisa!

unmoved [ˌʌn'muːvd] *adj*: **to be ~ by sthg** ser indiferente a algo.

unnamed [ˌʌn'neɪmd] *adj* [anonymous] anônimo(ma).

unnatural [ʌn'nætʃrəl] *adj* **-1.** [unusual, strange] estranho(nha) **-2.** [affected] pouco natural.

unnecessary [ʌn'nesəsərɪ] *adj* desnecessário(ria).

unnerving [ˌʌn'nɜːvɪŋ] *adj* enervante.

unnoticed [ˌʌn'nəʊtɪst] *adj* despercebido(da).

UNO (*abbr of* **United Nations Organization**) *n* ONU *f*.

unobserved [ˌʌnəb'zɜːvd] *adj* despercebido(da).

unobtainable [ˌʌnəb'teɪnəbl] *adj* inacessível.

unobtrusive [ˌʌnəb'truːsɪv] *adj* discreto(ta).

unoccupied [ˌʌn'ɒkjʊpaɪd] *adj* desocupado(da).

unofficial [ˌʌnə'fɪʃl] *adj* não-oficial.

unopened [ˌʌn'əʊpənd] *adj* fechado(da).

unorthodox [ˌʌn'ɔːθədɒks] *adj* não-ortodoxo(xa).

unpack [ˌʌn'pæk] *<>* *vt* **-1.** [bag, suitcase] desfazer **-2.** [clothes, books, shopping] desembrulhar. *<>* *vi* desfazer as malas.

unpaid [ˌʌn'peɪd] *adj* não-remunerado(da).

unpalatable [ʌn'pælətəbl] *adj* **-1.** [unpleasant to taste] intragável **-2.** *fig* [difficult to accept] desagradável.

unparalleled [ʌn'pærəleld] *adj* sem paralelo.

unpatriotic ['ʌnˌpætrɪ'ɒtɪk] *adj* antipatriótico(ca).

unpick [ˌʌn'pɪk] *vt* descosturar.

unpin [ˌʌn'pɪn] *(pt & pp* **-ned,** *cont* **-ning)** *vt* [remove pin from] desprender.

unplanned [ˌʌn'plænd] *adj* não-planejado(da).

unpleasant [ʌn'pleznt] *adj* desagradável.

unpleasantness [ʌn'plezntnɪs] *n (U)* **-1.** [of person, experience, weather] dissabor *m* **-2.** [discord] desentendimento *m*.

unplug [ʌn'plʌg] *(pt & pp* **-ged,** *cont* **-ging)** *vt ELEC* desligar.

unpolished [ˌʌn'pɒlɪʃt] *adj* **-1.** [furniture, brass, shoes] não-polido(da) **-2.** [person, manner] grosseiro(ra).

unpolluted [ˌʌnpə'luːtɪd] *adj* despoluído(da).

unpopular [ˌʌn'pɒpjʊlə'] *adj* impopular.

unprecedented [ʌn'presɪdəntɪd] *adj* sem precedente.

unpredictable [ˌʌnprɪ'dɪktəbl] *adj* imprevisível.

unprejudiced [ˌʌn'predʒʊdɪst] *adj* imparcial.

unprepared [ˌʌnprɪ'peəd] *adj*: **to be ~ (for sthg)** não estar preparado(da) (para algo).

unprepossessing ['ʌnˌpriːpə'zesɪŋ] *adj* pouco atraente.

unpretentious [ˌʌnprɪ'tenʃəs] *adj* despretencioso(sa).

unprincipled [ʌn'prɪnsəpld] *adj* inescrupuloso(sa).

unprintable [ˌʌn'prɪntəbl] *adj* impublicável.

unproductive [ˌʌnprə'dʌktɪv] *adj* improdutivo(va).

unprofessional [ˌʌnprə'feʃnl] *adj* não-profissional.

unprofitable [ˌʌn'prɒfɪtəbl] *adj* [not making a profit] não-lucrativo(va).

unprompted [ˌʌn'prɒmptɪd] *adj* espontâneo(nea).

unpronounceable [ˌʌnprə'naʊnsəbl] *adj* impronunciável.

unprotected [ˌʌnprə'tektɪd] *adj* [person, skin] desprotegido(da); **~ sex** relação *f* sexual desprotegida.

unprovoked [ˌʌnprə'vəʊkt] *adj* não-provocado(da), espontâneo(nea).

unpublished [ˌʌn'pʌblɪʃt] *adj* inédito(ta).

unpunished [ˌʌn'pʌnɪʃt] *adj*: **to go ~** ficar impune.

unqualified [ˌʌn'kwɒlɪfaɪd] *adj* **-1.** [not qualified] desqualificado(da) **-2.** [total, complete] absoluto(ta).

unquestionable [ʌn'kwestʃənəbl] *adj* inquestionável.

unquestioning [ʌn'kwestʃənɪŋ] *adj* incondicional.

unravel [ʌn'rævl] *(UK pt & pp* **-led,** *cont* **-ling,** *US pt & pp* **-ed,** *cont* **-ing)** *<>* *vt* **-1.** [undo] desembaraçar **-2.** *fig* [solve] elucidar. *<>* *vi* [become undone] desembaraçar-se.

unreadable [ˌʌn'riːdəbl] *adj* **-1.** [gen] ilegível **-2.** [difficult, tedious to read] difícil de ler.

unreal [ˌʌn'rɪəl] *adj* [strange] irreal.

unrealistic [ˌʌnrɪə'lɪstɪk] *adj* pouco realista.

unreasonable [ʌn'riːznəbl] *adj* **-1.** [unfair, not sensible] injusto(ta) **-2.** [not justifiable] absurdo(da), irracional.

unrecognizable [ˌʌn'rekəgnaɪzəbl] *adj* irreconhecível.

unrecognized [ˌʌn'rekəgnaɪzd] *adj* **-1.** [not known, noticed] não-reconhecido(da); **to be ~** não ser reconhecido(da) **-2.** [unacknowledged] inconfesso(sa).

unrecorded [ˌʌnrɪˈkɔːdɪd] *adj* **-1.** [remark, fact, event] não-registrado(da) **-2.** [music, voice] desconhecido(-da).

unrefined [ˌʌnrɪˈfaɪnd] *adj* **-1.** [petrol, sugar, flour] não-refinado(da) **-2.** [person, manners] impolido(da).

unrehearsed [ˌʌnrɪˈhɜːst] *adj* improvisado(da).

unrelated [ˌʌnrɪˈleɪtɪd] *adj*: **to be ~ (to sthg)** não estar relacionado(da) (a algo).

unrelenting [ˌʌnrɪˈlentɪŋ] *adj* **-1.** [pressure] contínuo(nua) **-2.** [questions] implacável.

unreliable [ˌʌnrɪˈlaɪəbl] *adj* inconfiável.

unrelieved [ˌʌnrɪˈliːvd] *adj* **-1.** [pain] que não alivia **-2.** [gloom, boredom]: **a period of ~ boredom** um período de tédio sem fim.

unremarkable [ˌʌnrɪˈmɑːkəbl] *adj* comum.

unremitting [ˌʌnrɪˈmɪtɪŋ] *adj* incessante.

unrepeatable [ˌʌnrɪˈpiːtəbl] *adj* **-1.** [not fit to be repeated] irrepetível **-2.** [exceptional] excepcional.

unrepentant [ˌʌnrɪˈpentənt] *adj* não-arrependido(da).

unrepresentative [ˌʌnreprɪˈzentətɪv] *adj* pouco representativo(va); **~ of sthg** pouco representativo de algo.

unrequited [ˌʌnrɪˈkwaɪtɪd] *adj* não-correspondido(da).

unreserved [ˌʌnrɪˈzɜːvd] *adj* **-1.** [admiration, support, approval] integral **-2.** [seat, place] não-reservado(-da).

unresolved [ˌʌnrɪˈzɒlvd] *adj* sem solução.

unresponsive [ˌʌnrɪˈspɒnsɪv] *adj*: **to be ~ to sthg** ser indiferente a algo.

unrest [ˌʌnˈrest] *n* (U) agitação *f*.

unrestrained [ˌʌnrɪˈstreɪnd] *adj* desenfreado(da).

unrestricted [ˌʌnrɪˈstrɪktɪd] *adj* irrestrito(ta).

unrewarding [ˌʌnrɪˈwɔːdɪŋ] *adj* pouco compensador(ra).

unripe [ˌʌnˈraɪp] *adj* verde.

unrivalled *UK*, **unrivaled** *US* [ʌnˈraɪvld] *adj* incomparável.

unroll [ˌʌnˈrəʊl] *vt* [unfold] desenrolar.

unruffled [ˌʌnˈrʌfld] *adj* [calm] sereno(na).

unruly [ʌnˈruːlɪ] (*compar* -ier, *superl* -iest) *adj* **-1.** [wayward] indisciplinado(da) **-2.** [untidy] desarrumado(da).

unsafe [ˌʌnˈseɪf] *adj* **-1.** [dangerous] perigoso(sa) **-2.** [in danger] inseguro(ra).

unsaid [ˌʌnˈsed] *adj*: **to leave sthg ~** não falar algo.

unsaleable, unsalable *US* [ˌʌnˈseɪləbl] *adj* invendável.

unsatisfactory [ˈʌnˌsætɪsˈfæktərɪ] *adj* insatisfatório(ria).

unsavoury, unsavory *US* [ʌnˈseɪvərɪ] *adj* **-1.** [behaviour, person, habits] *(moralmente)* ofensivo(va) **-2.** [smell] repugnante.

unscathed [ˌʌnˈskeɪðd] *adj* ileso(sa), são e salvo, sã e salva.

unscheduled [*UK* ˌʌnˈʃedjʊld, *US* ˌʌnˈskedʒʊld] *adj* imprevisto(ta).

unscientific [ˈʌnˌsaɪənˈtɪfɪk] *adj* não-científico(ca).

unscrew [ˌʌnˈskruː] *vt* **-1.** [lid, bottle top] desenroscar **-2.** [sign, mirror] desparafusar.

unscripted [ˌʌnˈskrɪptɪd] *adj* de improviso.

unscrupulous [ʌnˈskruːpjʊləs] *adj* inescrupuloso(sa).

unseat [ˌʌnˈsiːt] *vt* **-1.** [rider] derrubar *(da sela)* **-2.** *fig* [politician] depor.

unseeded [ˌʌnˈsiːdɪd] *adj* [player, team] que não é cabeça de chave.

unseemly [ʌnˈsiːmlɪ] (*compar* -ier, *superl* -iest) *adj* inconveniente.

unseen [ˌʌnˈsiːn] <> *adj* [not observed] despercebido(da); [not visible] escondido(da). <> *adv* despercebido(da).

unselfish [ˌʌnˈselfɪʃ] *adj* desinteressado(da).

unselfishly [ˌʌnˈselfɪʃlɪ] *adv* desinteressadamente.

unsettle [ˌʌnˈsetl] *vt* inquietar.

unsettled [ˌʌnˈsetld] *adj* **-1.** [unstable - person] inquieto(ta); [- weather] instável **-2.** [unfinished, unresolved - argument] incerto(ta); [- issue] vago(ga) **-3.** [account, bill] duvidoso(sa) **-4.** [area, region] despovoado(da).

unsettling [ˌʌnˈsetlɪŋ] *adj* inquietante.

unshak(e)able [ʌnˈʃeɪkəbl] *adj* inabalável.

unshaven [ˌʌnˈʃeɪvn] *adj* [face, chin] com a barba por fazer.

unsheathe [ˌʌnˈʃiːð] *vt* desembainhar.

unsightly [ʌnˈsaɪtlɪ] *adj* de péssima aparência.

unskilled [ˌʌnˈskɪld] *adj* [worker] não-especializado(da), incapaz; [work] não-especializado(da).

unsociable [ʌnˈsəʊʃəbl] *adj* [person, place] anti-social.

unsocial [ʌnˈsəʊʃl] *adj*: **to work ~ hours** trabalhar fora de hora.

unsold [ˌʌnˈsəʊld] *adj* não-vendido(da).

unsolicited [ˌʌnsəˈlɪsɪtɪd] *adj* que não foi pedido(da).

unsolved [ˌʌnˈsɒlvd] *adj* não-solucionado(da).

unsophisticated [ˌʌnsəˈfɪstɪkeɪtɪd] *adj* **-1.** [gen] simples **-2.** [person - in dress, style] pouco sofisticado(da); [- in attitudes] simples, natural.

unsound [ˌʌnˈsaʊnd] *adj* **-1.** [based on false ideas] equivocado(da) **-2.** [in poor condition] inseguro(ra); **to be of ~ mind** estar fora de si.

unspeakable [ʌnˈspiːkəbl] *adj* terrível.

unspeakably [ʌnˈspiːkəblɪ] *adv* terrivelmente.

unspecified [ˌʌnˈspesɪfaɪd] *adj* indefinido(da).

unspoiled [ˌʌnˈspɔɪld], **unspoilt** [ˌʌnˈspɔɪlt] *adj* **-1.** [person] incólume **-2.** [place] intocado(da).

unspoken [ˌʌnˈspəʊkən] *adj* **-1.** [not expressed openly] subentendido(da) **-2.** [tacit] tácito(ta).

unsporting [ˌʌnˈspɔːtɪŋ] *adj* pouco esportivo(va).

unstable [ˌʌnˈsteɪbl] *adj* instável.

unstated [ˌʌnˈsteɪtɪd] *adj* não-afirmado(da).

unsteady [ˌʌnˈstedɪ] (*compar* -ier, *superl* -iest) *adj* **-1.** [person, step, voice] inseguro(ra) **-2.** [chair, ladder] pouco seguro(ra).

unstinting [ˌʌnˈstɪntɪŋ] *adj* irrestrito(ta).

unstoppable [ˌʌnˈstɒpəbl] *adj* inevitável.

unstrap [ˌʌnˈstræp] (*pt & pp* -ped, *cont* -ping) *vt* desapertar.

unstructured [ˌʌnˈstrʌktʃəd] *adj* desorganizado(-da).

unstuck [ˌʌnˈstʌk] *adj*: **to come ~** [notice, stamp,

label] descolar-se; *fig* [plan, system] degringolar; *fig* [person] dar-se mal.

unsubstantiated [ˌʌnsəb'stænʃieitid] *adj* **-1.** [statement, story, report] que não foi confirmado(da) **-2.** [accusation] sem provas.

unsuccessful [ˌʌnsək'sesfʊl] *adj* malsucedido(da).

unsuccessfully [ˌʌnsək'sesfʊlɪ] *adv* em vão.

unsuitable [ʌn'suːtəbl] *adj* inconveniente; **to be ~ for sthg** ser inapropriado(da) para algo.

unsuited [ʌn'suːtɪd] *adj* **-1.** [not appropriate]: **to be ~ to** *OR* **for sthg** ser inadequado(da) para algo **-2.** [not compatible]: **to be ~ (to each other)** ser totalmente incompatível (um em relação ao outro).

unsung [ˌʌn'sʌŋ] *adj* [deed, hero] não-aclamado(da).

unsure [ˌʌn'ʃɔː'] *adj* **-1.** [not confident]: **to be ~ (of o.s.)** não ser seguro(ra) (de si) **-2.** [not certain]: **to be ~ (about/of sthg)** não ter certeza (sobre/de algo).

unsurpassed [ˌʌnsə'pɑːst] *adj* incomparável.

unsuspecting [ˌʌnsə'spektɪŋ] *adj* insuspeitável.

unsweetened [ˌʌn'swiːtnd] *adj* sem açúcar.

unswerving [ʌn'swɜːvɪŋ] *adj* resoluto(ta).

unsympathetic ['ʌnˌsɪmpə'θetɪk] *adj* [unfeeling] insensível.

untamed [ˌʌn'teimd] *adj* **-1.** [not domesticated] não-domesticado(da) **-2.** [not cultivated] não-cultivado(da) **-3.** [not subjugated] indômito(ta).

untangle [ˌʌn'tæŋgl] *vt* [disentangle] desemaranhar.

untapped [ˌʌn'tæpt] *adj* [unexploited] inexplorado(da).

untaxed [ˌʌn'tækst] *adj* isento(ta) de imposto.

untenable [ˌʌn'tenəbl] *adj* insustentável.

unthinkable [ʌn'θɪŋkəbl] *adj* [inconceivable] inconcebível.

unthinkingly [ʌn'θɪŋkɪŋlɪ] *adv* sem pensar.

untidy [ʌn'taɪdɪ] (*compar* **-ier**, *superl* **-iest**) *adj* **-1.** [gen] desarrumado(da) **-2.** [person, work] desleixado(da).

untie [ˌʌn'taɪ] (*cont* **untying**) *vt* [string, knot, bonds] desatar; [prisoner] soltar.

until [ən'tɪl] ⬦ *prep* **-1.** [up to, till] até **-2.** *(after negative)* antes de; **I can't come ~ tomorrow** eu não posso vir antes de amanhã. ⬦ *conj* **-1.** [up to, till] até; **we were told to wait ~ he arrived** pediram-nos para esperar até que ele chegasse *OR* até ele chegar **-2.** *(after negative)* antes de, até; **they never help ~ I tell them to** eles só ajudam quando eu peço; **don't sign ~ you've checked everything** não assine nada antes de ter verificado tudo.

untimely [ʌn'taɪmlɪ] *adj* **-1.** [premature] prematuro(ra) **-2.** [inopportune] inoportuno(na).

untiring [ʌn'taɪərɪŋ] *adj* incansável.

untold [ˌʌn'təʊld] *adj* [incalculable, vast] inimaginável.

untouched [ˌʌn'tʌtʃt] *adj* intocado(da).

untoward [ˌʌntə'wɔːd] *adj* [unfortunate] inconveniente.

untrained [ˌʌn'treɪnd] *adj* destreinado(da).

untrammelled *UK*, **untrammeled** *US* [ʌn'træməld] *adj fml* irrestrito(ta); **~ by** não restrito(ta) a, livre de.

untranslatable [ˌʌntræns'leɪtəbl] *adj* intraduzível.

untreated [ˌʌn'triːtd] *adj* **-1.** *MED* não-tratado(da) **-2.** [unprocessed] sem tratamento.

untried [ˌʌn'traɪd] *adj* [not tested] não-testado(da).

untroubled [ˌʌn'trʌbld] *adj* [undisturbed]: **to be ~ by sthg** ficar calmo(ma) diante de algo.

untrue [ˌʌn'truː] *adj* **-1.** [inaccurate] falso(sa) **-2.** [unfaithful, disloyal]: **to be ~ to sb** ser infiel a alguém.

untrustworthy [ˌʌn'trʌstˌwɜːðɪ] *adj* indigno(na) de confiança.

untruth [ˌʌn'truːθ] *n* inverdade *f*.

untruthful [ˌʌn'truːθfʊl] *adj* mentiroso(sa).

untutored [ˌʌn'tjuːtəd] *adj* [untrained] destreinado(da).

unusable [ˌʌn'juːzəbl] *adj* inutilizável, imprestável.

unused [*sense 1* ˌʌn'juːzd, *sense 2* ʌn'juːst] *adj* **-1.** [new] novo(va) **-2.** [unaccustomed]: **to be ~ to sthg/to doing sthg** não estar acostumado(da) a algo/a fazer algo.

unusual [ʌn'juːʒl] *adj* [rare] raro(ra).

unusually [ʌn'juːʒəlɪ] *adv* [exceptionally] excepcionalmente.

unvarnished [ʌn'vɑːnɪʃt] *adj fig* [plain, straightforward] cru.

unveil [ˌʌn'veɪl] *vt* **-1.** [remove covering from] desvelar **-2.** *fig* [reveal, divulge] expor.

unwaged [ˌʌn'weɪdʒd] *adj UK* desassalariado(da).

unwanted [ˌʌn'wɒntɪd] *adj* indesejado(da).

unwarranted [ˌʌn'wɒrəntɪd] *adj* injustificado(da).

unwavering [ʌn'weɪvərɪŋ] *adj* firme.

unwelcome [ʌn'welkəm] *adj* **-1.** [news, experience] desagradável **-2.** [visitor] desconfortável.

unwell [ˌʌn'wel] *adj*: **to be/feel ~** estar/sentir-se indisposto(ta).

unwholesome [ˌʌn'həʊlsəm] *adj* **-1.** [food, drink] insalubre **-2.** [behaviour, thought] doentio(tia) **-3.** [appearance] doente.

unwieldy [ʌn'wiːldɪ] (*compar* **-ier**, *superl* **-iest**) *adj* **-1.** [cumbersome] pesado(da) **-2.** *fig* [inefficient] ineficiente.

unwilling [ˌʌn'wɪlɪŋ] *adj* [reluctant] relutante; **to be ~ to do sthg** estar relutante para/em fazer algo.

unwind [ˌʌn'waɪnd] (*pt* & *pp* **-wound**) ⬦ *vt* desenrolar. ⬦ *vi fig* [person] relaxar.

unwise [ˌʌn'waɪz] *adj* imprudente.

unwitting [ʌn'wɪtɪŋ] *adj fml* inadvertido(da), impremeditado(da).

unwittingly [ʌn'wɪtɪŋlɪ] *adv fml* inadvertidamente.

unworkable [ˌʌn'wɜːkəbl] *adj* impraticável.

unworldly [ˌʌn'wɜːldlɪ] *adj* [spiritual, ascetic] espiritual.

unworthy [ʌn'wɜːðɪ] (*compar* **-ier**, *superl* **-iest**) *adj* [undeserving]: **to be ~ of sb/sthg** ser indigno(na) de alguém/algo.

unwound [ˌʌn'waʊnd] *pt* & *pp* ⊳ **unwind**.

unwrap [ˌʌn'ræp] (*pt* & *pp* **-ped**, *cont* **-ping**) *vt* desembrulhar.

unwritten law [ˌʌn'rɪtn-] *n* lei *f* não-escrita.

unyielding [ʌn'jiːldɪŋ] *adj* inflexível.

unzip [ˌʌn'zɪp] (*pt* & *pp* **-ped**, *cont* **-ping**) *vt* abrir o zíper de.

unzip [ˌʌn'zɪp] *vt* descompactar.

up [ʌp] ⬦ *adv* **-1.** [toward higher position, level] para cima; **to go ~** subir; **prices are going ~** os preços estão subindo; **we walked ~ to the top** subimos até o topo; **to pick sthg ~** apanhar algo. **- 2.** [in higher position]: **she's ~ in her bedroom** está lá em cima no seu quarto; **~ there** ali *OR* lá em cima. **- 3.** [into upright position]: **to stand ~** pôr-se em *OR* de pé; **to sit ~** [from lying position] sentar-se; [sit straight] sentar-se direito. **- 4.** [northward]: **~ in Canada** no Canadá. **- 5.** [in phrases]: **to walk ~ and down** andar de um lado para o outro; **to jump ~ and down** dar pulos; **~ to six weeks** até seis semanas; **~ to ten people** até dez pessoas; **are you ~ to travelling?** você está em condições de viajar?; **what are you ~ to?** o que você está tramando?; **it's ~ to you** depende de você; **~ until ten o'clock** até às dez horas. <> *prep* **-1.** [toward higher position]: **to walk ~ a hill** subir um monte; **I went ~ the stairs** subi as escadas. **- 2.** [in higher position] no topo de; **~ a hill** no topo de um monte; **~ a ladder** no topo de uma escada. **- 3.** [at end of]: **they live ~ the block from us** eles vivem no final da nossa rua. <> *adj* **-1.** [out of bed] levantado(da); **I got ~ at six today** levantei-me às seis hoje. **- 2.** [at an end]: **time's ~** acabou-se o tempo. **- 3.** [rising]: **the ~ escalator** a escada rolante ascendente. <> *n:* **~s and downs** altos e baixos *mpl*.

up-and-coming *adj* promissor(ra).

up-and-up *n:* **to be on the ~** *UK* [improving] estar para cima; *US* [honest] ser confiável.

upbeat [ˈʌpbiːt] *adj* otimista.

upbraid [ʌpˈbreɪd] *vt fml:* **to ~ sb (for sthg/for doing sthg)** repreender alguém por algo/por fazer algo.

upbringing [ˈʌpˌbrɪŋɪŋ] *n* (U) educação *f*.

update [ˌʌpˈdeɪt] *vt* [bring up-to-date] atualizar.

upend [ʌpˈend] *vt* [stand on end] pôr de pé; [turn upside down] virar de ponta-cabeça.

upfront [ˌʌpˈfrʌnt] <> *adj:* **to be ~ (about sthg)** ser franco(ca) sobre algo. <> *adv* adiantado(da).

upgrade [ˌʌpˈgreɪd] *vt* **-1.** [improve - facilities] melhorar; [- computer system] fazer um upgrade em **- 2.** [promote] promover.

upheaval [ʌpˈhiːvl] *n* convulsão *f*.

upheld [ʌpˈheld] *pt & pp* ⊳ **uphold**.

uphill [ˌʌpˈhɪl] <> *adj* **-1.** [rising] íngreme **- 2.** *fig* [difficult] árduo(dua). <> *adv* para cima.

uphold [ʌpˈhəʊld] (*pt & pp* **-held**) *vt* [support] apoiar.

upholster [ʌpˈhəʊlstəʳ] *vt* estofar.

upholstery [ʌpˈhəʊlstərɪ] *n* (U) estofamento *m*.

upkeep [ˈʌpkiːp] *n* (U) manutenção *f*.

upland [ˈʌplənd] *adj* no planalto.
⟜ **uplands** *npl* planaltos *mpl*.

uplift [ʌpˈlɪft] *vt* [cheer] extasiar.

uplifting [ʌpˈlɪftɪŋ] *adj* [cheering] extasiante, edificante.

uplighter *n* *ELEC* luminária *que projeta a luz para cima.*

up-market *adj* de alta categoria.

upon [əˈpɒn] *prep fml* **-1.** [gen] sobre; **the weekend is ~ us** o final de semana já está em cima da gente; **summer is ~ us** o verão está chegando **- 2.** [when] após.

upper [ˈʌpəʳ] <> *adj* **-1.** [gen] superior **- 2.** *GEOGR* [inland] alto(ta). <> *n* [of shoe] gáspea *f*.

upper class *n:* **the ~** a alta classe.
⟜ **upper-class** *adj* de alta classe.

upper-crust *adj* da alta roda.

uppercut [ˈʌpəkʌt] *n* direto *m* no queixo.

upper hand *n:* **to have the ~** ter a palavra final; **to gain** *OR* **get the ~** obter o controle.

Upper House *n UK POL* Câmara *f* dos Lordes.

uppermost [ˈʌpəməʊst] *adj* **-1.** [highest] mais alto(ta) **- 2.** [most important]: **to be ~ in one's mind** ser o mais importante na cabeça de alguém.

Upper Volta [-ˈvɒltə] *n* Alto Volta; **in ~** em Alto Volta.

uppity [ˈʌpətɪ] *adj inf* arrogante.

upright [*adj senses 1 & 2 & adv* ˈʌpraɪt, *n* ˈʌpraɪt] <> *adj* **-1.** [erect] vertical **- 2.** *fig* [honest] honesto(ta). <> *adv* verticalmente. <> *n* **-1.** [of door] marco *m* **- 2.** [of bookshelf] pilar *m* **- 3.** [of goal] poste *m*.

upright piano *n* piano *m* de armário.

uprising [ˈʌpˌraɪzɪŋ] *n* revolta *f* rebelião *f*.

uproar [ˈʌprɔːʳ] *n* **-1.** [commotion] algazarra *f* **- 2.** [protest] protesto *m*.

uproarious [ʌpˈrɔːrɪəs] *adj* [noisy] barulhento(ta).

uproot [ʌpˈruːt] *vt* **-1.** [force to leave] arrancar; **to ~ o.s.** desarraigar-se **- 2.** *BOT* [tear out of ground] arrancar.

upset [ʌpˈset] (*pt & pp* **upset**, *cont* **-ting**) <> *adj* **-1.** [distressed] descontrolado(da); [offended] chateado(da) **- 2.** *MED:* **to have an ~ stomach** ter um estômago fraco. <> *n* **-1.** *MED:* **to have a stomach ~** ficar com dor de estômago **- 2.** [surprise result] surpresa *f*. <> *vt* **-1.** [distress] deixar nervoso(sa), irritar **- 2.** [mess up] atrapalhar **- 3.** [overturn, knock over] virar.

upsetting [ʌpˈsetɪŋ] *adj* [distressing] desconcertante.

upshot [ˈʌpʃɒt] *n* desfecho *m*.

upside down [ˌʌpsaɪd-] <> *adj* [inverted] invertido(da), ao contrário. <> *adv* de cabeça para baixo; **to turn sthg ~** *fig* [disorder] virar algo de pernas para o ar.

upstage [ˌʌpˈsteɪdʒ] *vt fig* roubar a cena de.

upstairs [ˌʌpˈsteəz] <> *adj* de cima. <> *adv* **-1.** [not downstairs] em cima **- 2.** [on one of the floors above] de cima. <> *n* andar *m* de cima.

upstanding [ˌʌpˈstændɪŋ] *adj* [honest] honrado(da).

upstart [ˈʌpstɑːt] *n* novo-rico *m*, nova-rica *f*.

upstate [ˌʌpˈsteɪt] *US* <> *adj:* **~ New York** do interior de Nova Iorque. <> *adv* no interior.

upstream [ˌʌpˈstriːm] <> *adj:* **the bridge is a few miles ~ (from here)** a ponte fica poucas milhas rio acima (a partir daqui). <> *adv* correnteza acima.

upsurge [ˈʌpsɜːdʒ] *n:* **~ of/in sthg** aumento *m* de/em algo.

upswing [ˈʌpswɪŋ] *n:* **~ (in sthg)** impulso *m* (em algo).

uptake [ˈʌpteɪk] *n:* **to be quick/slow on the ~** ter um raciocínio rápido/lento.

uptight [ʌpˈtaɪt] *adj inf* nervoso(sa).

up-to-date *adj* **-1.** [machinery, methods] moderno(na) **- 2.** [news, information] atualizado(da); **to keep ~ with sthg** manter-se a par de algo.

up-to-the-minute *adj* mais recente.

uptown [ˌʌp'taʊn] *US* ◇ *adj* da parte alta da cidade. ◇ *adv* na parte alta da cidade.

upturn ['ʌptɜ:n] *n:* ~ **(in sthg)** melhoria *f* (em algo).

upturned [ʌp'tɜ:nd] *adj* **-1.** [pointing upwards] virado(da) para cima; ~ **nose** nariz *m* arrebitado **-2.** [upside down] virado(da) de cabeça para baixo.

upward ['ʌpwəd] ◇ *adj* [movement, trend] para cima. ◇ *adv US* = **upwards**.

upwardly-mobile *adj* de franca ascensão.

upwards ['ʌpwədz] *adv* para cima.
◆ **upwards of** *prep* mais de.

upwind [ˌʌp'wɪnd] *adj:* **to be** ~ **of sb/sthg** estar fora do raio de ação de alguém/algo.

URA (*abbr of* **Urban Renewal Administration**) *n* órgão norte-americano responsável pelo desenvolvimento das áreas urbanas menos favorecidas.

Urals ['jʊərəlz] *npl:* **the** ~ os Urais; **in the** ~ nos Urais.

uranium [jʊ'reɪnjəm] *n (U)* urânio *m*.

Uranus ['jʊərənəs] *n* [planet] Urano *m*.

urban ['ɜ:bən] *adj* urbano(na).

urbane [ɜ:'beɪn] *adj* gentil.

urbanize, -ise ['ɜ:bənaɪz] *vt* urbanizar.

urban renewal *n* reurbanização *f*.

Urdu ['ʊədu:] *n (U)* urdu *m*.

urge [ɜ:dʒ] ◇ *n* impulso *m*; **to have an** ~ **to do sthg** ter um impulso de fazer algo. ◇ *vt* **-1.** [try to persuade]: **to** ~ **sb to do sthg** incitar alguém a fazer algo **-2.** [advocate] defender.

urgency ['ɜ:dʒənsɪ] *n (U)* urgência *f*.

urgent ['ɜ:dʒənt] *adj* **-1.** [pressing] urgente **-2.** [desperate] insistente.

urgently ['ɜ:dʒəntlɪ] *adv* [as soon as possible] urgentemente.

urinal [jʊə'raɪnl] *n* [receptacle] urinol *m*; [room] mictório *m*.

urinary ['jʊərɪnərɪ] *adj* urinário(ria).

urinate ['jʊərɪneɪt] *vi* urinar.

urine ['jʊərɪn] *n (U)* urina *f*.

URL (*abbr of* **uniform resource locator**) *n COMPUT* URL *f*.

urn [ɜ:n] *n* **-1.** [for ashes] urna *f* funerária **-2.** [for tea, coffee] chaleira *f*.

Uruguay ['jʊərəgwaɪ] *n* Uruguai *m*; **in** ~ no Uruguai.

Uruguayan [ˌjʊərə'gwaɪən] ◇ *adj* uruguaio(-guaia). ◇ *n* uruguaio *m*, -guaia *f*.

us [ʌs] *pers pron* (*direct*) nos; (*indirect, after prep*) nós; **they know** ~ conhecem-nos; **it's** ~ somos nós; **send it to** ~ envie-nos isso; **tell** ~ diga-nos; **we brought it with** ~ trouxemo-lo conosco.

US (*abbr of* **United States**) *n:* **the** ~ os EUA; **in the** ~ nos EUA.

USA *n* **-1.** (*abbr of* **United States of America**): **the** ~ os EUA; **in the** ~ nos EUA **-2.** (*abbr of* **United States Army**) forças armadas norte-americanas.

usable ['ju:zəbl] *adj* utilizável, usável.

USAF (*abbr of* **United States Air Force**) *n* força aérea norte-americana.

usage ['ju:zɪdʒ] *n* **-1.** (*U*) [use of language] uso *m* **-2.**

[meaning] sentido *m* **-3.** (*U*) [handling, treatment] uso *m*.

USB (*abbr of* **Universal Serial Bus**) *n COMPUT* USB *m*.

USB port *n COMPUT* porta *f* USB.

USCG (*abbr of* **United States Coast Guard**) *n* guarda-costeira norte-americana.

USDA (*abbr of* **United States Department of Agriculture**) *n* ministério da agricultura norte-americano.

USDI (*abbr of* **United States Department of the Interior**) *n* ministério do interior norte-americano.

use [*n* & *aux vb* ju:s, *vt* ju:z] ◇ *n* **-1.** [gen] uso *m*; **to be in** ~ estar em uso; **to be out of** ~ estar fora de uso; **to make** ~ **of sthg** fazer uso de algo; **to let sb have the** ~ **of sthg** deixar que alguém utilize algo **-2.** [purpose, usefulness] utilidade *f*; **to be of** ~ ser útil; **to be no** ~ ser inútil; **what's the** ~ **(of doing sthg)?** qual é a utilidade(de se fazer algo)? ◇ *aux vb* costumar; **I** ~ **d to live in London** eu morava em Londres; **there** ~ **d to be a tree here** havia uma árvore aqui. ◇ *vt* **-1.** [utilize] usar, utilizar **-2.** *pej* [exploit] usar.
◆ **use up** *vt sep* esgotar.

used [*sense 1* ju:zd, *sense 2* ju:st] *adj* **-1.** [object, car *etc*] usado(da) **-2.** [accustomed]: **to be** ~ **to sthg/to doing sthg** estar acostumado(da) a algo/a fazer algo; **to get** ~ **to sthg** acostumar-se a algo.

useful ['ju:sfʊl] *adj* útil; **to come in** ~ mostrar-se útil.

usefulness ['ju:sfʊlnɪs] *n (U)* utilidade *f*.

useless ['ju:slɪs] *adj* **-1.** [gen] inútil **-2.** *inf* [hopeless] incorrigível.

uselessness ['ju:slɪsnɪs] *n (U)* inutilidade *f*.

user ['ju:zər] *n* usuário *m*, -ria *f*.

user-friendly *adj* de fácil utilização.

USES (*abbr of* **United States Employment Service**) *n* ministério do trabalho norte-americano.

usher ['ʌʃər] ◇ *n* **-1.** [at wedding] recepcionista *m* **-2.** [at theatre, concert] lanterninha *m*. ◇ *vt* conduzir.

usherette [ˌʌʃə'ret] *n* **-1.** [at wedding] recepcionista *f* **-2.** [at theatre, concert] lanterninha *f*.

USIA (*abbr of* **United States Information Agency**) *n* agência de informações norte-americana.

USM *n* **-1.** (*abbr of* **United States Mail**) serviço de correio norte-americano **-2.** (*abbr of* **United States Mint**) casa da moeda norte-americana **-3.** (*abbr of* **unlisted securities market**) parte da bolsa de valores de Londres que negocia os papéis das empresas menores.

USN (*abbr of* **United States Navy**) *n* marinha norte-americana.

USPHS (*abbr of* **United States Public Health Service**) *n* ministério norte-americano de saúde e previdência social.

USS (*abbr of* **United States Ship**) navio de guerra norte-americano.

USSR (*abbr of* **Union of Soviet Socialist Republics**) *n:* **the (former)** ~ a (ex-)URSS.

usu. (*abbr of* **usually**) usualmente.

usual ['ju:ʒəl] *adj* usual, habitual; **as** ~ [as normal] como de costume; [as often happens] como sempre.

usually ['ju:ʒəlɪ] *adv* geralmente, normalmente; **more than** ~ mais do que normalmente.

usurp [juːˈzɜːp] *vt fml* usurpar.
usury [ˈjuːʒʊrɪ] *n (U) fml* usura *f.*
UT *abbr of* Utah.
Utah [ˈjuːtɑː] *n* Utah.
utensil [juːˈtensl] *n* utensílio *m.*
uterus [ˈjuːtərəs] (*pl* -**ri** [-raɪ], -**ruses**) *n* útero *m.*
utilitarian [ˌjuːtɪlɪˈteərɪən] *adj* [functional] utilitário (ria), funcional.
utility [juːˈtɪlətɪ] (*pl* -**ies**) *n* -**1.** (*U*)[usefulness]utilidade *f* -**2.** [public service] serviço *m* público -**3.** COMPUT utilitário *m.*
utility room *n* área *f* de serviços.
utilize, -ise [ˈjuːtəlaɪz] *vt* utilizar.
utmost [ˈʌtməʊst] <> *adj* máximo(ma), supremo(ma). <> *n* -**1.** [best effort]**: to do one's ~** fazer o impossível -**2.** [maximum] máximo *m*; **to the ~** ao máximo, até não poder mais.
utopia [juːˈtəʊpjə] *n* utopia *f.*
utter [ˈʌtəʳ] <> *adj* total, completo(ta). <> *vt* -**1.** [sound, cry] emitir -**2.** [word] proferir.
utterly [ˈʌtəlɪ] *adv* totalmente, completamente.
U-turn *n* -**1.** [turning movement] retorno *m* -**2.** *fig* [complete change] guinada *f* de 180 graus.
UV (*abbr of* ultraviolet) U.V.
Uzbek <> *adj* usbeque. <> *n* -**1.** [person] usbeque *mf* -**2.** [language] usbeque *m.*
Uzbekistan [ʊzˌbekɪˈstɑːn] *n* Usbequistão; **in ~** no Usbequistão.

v¹ (*pl* v's *OR* vs), **V** (*pl* V's *OR* Vs) [viː] *n* [letter] v, V *m.*
v² -**1.** (*abbr of* verse) v -**2.** (*abbr of* vide) [cross-reference] vide -**3.** (*abbr of* versus) versus -**4.** (*abbr of* volt) v.
VA *abbr of* Virginia.
vacancy [ˈveɪkənsɪ] (*pl* -**ies**) *n* -**1.** [job, position] vaga *f* -**2.** [room available] quarto *m* livre; **'vacancies'** 'há vagas'; **'no vacancies'** 'lotação esgotada'.
vacant [ˈveɪkənt] *adj* -**1.** [gen] vago(ga) -**2.** [look, expression] distraído(da).
vacant lot *n* lote *m* disponível.
vacantly [ˈveɪkəntlɪ] *adv* distraidamente.
vacate [vəˈkeɪt] *vt* -**1.** [give up, resign] deixar vago(ga) -**2.** [leave empty, stop using] desocupar.
vacation [vəˈkeɪʃn] *n* -**1.** UNIV [period when closed] férias *fpl* -**2.** US [holiday] férias *fpl.*
vacationer [vəˈkeɪʃənəʳ] *n US* veranista *mf.*
vacation resort *n US* colônia *f* de férias.
vaccinate [ˈvæksɪneɪt] *vt*: **to ~ sb (against sthg)** vacinar alguém (contra algo).

vaccination [ˌvæksɪˈneɪʃn] *n* vacinação *f*; **have you had your ~?** já tomou sua vacina?
vaccine [UK ˈvæksiːn, US vækˈsiːn] *n* vacina *f.*
vacillate [ˈvæsəleɪt] *vi*: **to ~ (between)** oscilar (entre); **she ~d for a long time before making up her mind** ela hesitou por muito tempo antes de se decidir.
vacuum [ˈvækjʊəm] <> *n* -**1.** [gen] vácuo *m* -**2.** [machine]: **~ (cleaner)** aspirador *m* (de pó). <> *vt* aspirar, passar o aspirador em.
vacuum cleaner *n* aspirador *m* de pó.
vacuum-packed *adj* embalado(da) a vácuo.
vacuum pump *n* bomba *f* de vácuo.
vagabond [ˈvægəbɒnd] *n literary* vagabundo *m*, -da *f.*
vagaries [ˈveɪgərɪz] *npl fml* caprichos *mpl.*
vagina [vəˈdʒaɪnə] *n* vagina *f.*
vaginal *adj* vaginal.
vagrancy [ˈveɪgrənsɪ] *n (U)* vagabundagem *f.*
vagrant [ˈveɪgrənt] *n* vagabundo *m*, -da *f.*
vague [veɪg] *adj* -**1.** [imprecise] vago(ga), impreciso(sa) -**2.** [feeling] leve -**3.** [evasive] evasivo(va) -**4.** [absent-minded] distraído(da) -**5.** [indistinct] vago(ga).
vaguely [ˈveɪglɪ] *adv* -**1.** [imprecisely] vagamente -**2.** [slightly, not very] levemente -**3.** [absent-mindedly] distraidamente -**4.** [indistinctly]: **I could ~ make out a ship on the horizon** mal dava para distinguir um navio no horizonte.
vain [veɪn] *adj* -**1.** *pej* [conceited] vaidoso(sa) -**2.** [futile, worthless] vão (vã).
➤ **in vain** *adv* em vão.
vainly [ˈveɪnlɪ] *adv* -**1.** [in vain] em vão -**2.** [conceitedly] vaidosamente.
valance [ˈvæləns] *n* -**1.** [on bed] dossel *m* -**2.** US [on curtains] sanefa *f.*
vale [veɪl] *n literary* vale *m.*
valedictory [ˌvælɪˈdɪktərɪ] *adj fml* de adeus.
valentine card [ˈvæləntaɪn-] *n* cartão *m* de dia dos namorados.
Valentine's Day [ˈvæləntaɪnz-] *n*: **(St) ~ Dia** *m* dos Namorados.
valet [ˈvæleɪ, ˈvaelɪt] *n* [manservant] camareiro *m.*
valet parking *n*: **'~'** serviço *m* de manobrista.
valet service *n* serviço *m* de lavanderia.
valiant [ˈvæljənt] *adj* valente.
valid [ˈvælɪd] *adj* válido(da).
validate [ˈvælɪdeɪt] *vt* -**1.** [argument, claim] validar, corroborar -**2.** [document] validar, legitimar.
validity [vəˈlɪdətɪ] *n* validade *f.*
Valium® [ˈvælɪəm] *n (U)* valium® *m.*
valley [ˈvælɪ] (*pl* valleys) *n* vale *m.*
valour UK, **valor** US [ˈvæləʳ] *n (U) fml* & *literary* valor *m.*
valuable [ˈvæljʊəbl] *adj* valioso(sa).
➤ **valuables** *npl* objetos *mpl* de valor.
valuation [ˌvæljʊˈeɪʃn] *n* avaliação *f.*
value [ˈvæljuː] <> *n* -**1.** (*U*)[gen] valor *m*; **to place a high ~ on sthg** dar muita importância a algo -**2.** [financial] valor *m*; **to be good ~** estar com o preço muito bom; **to be ~ for money** estar bem em conta; **to take sb/sthg at face ~** levar alguém/algo ao pé da letra. <> *vt* -**1.** [estimate price of] avaliar -**2.** [cherish] valorizar.

➤ **values** npl [morals] valores mpl morais, princípios mpl.

value added tax n ≃ imposto m sobre circulação de mercadorias e serviços.

valued ['vælju:d] adj estimado(da).

value judg(e)ment n juízo m de valor.

valuer ['væljʊəʳ] n avaliador mf, -ra de preços.

valve [vælv] n válvula f.

vamoose [vəˈmu:s] vi inf dar o fora.

vamp n vampe f.

vampire ['væmpaɪəʳ] n vampiro m.

van [væn] n -1. AUT caminhonete f, van f -2. UK RAIL vagão m de carga.

vandal ['vændl] n vândalo m, -la f.

vandalism ['vændəlɪzml] n (U) vandalismo m.

vandalize, -ise ['vændəlaɪz] vt destruir.

vanguard ['vænɡɑ:d] n vanguarda f; in the ~ of sthg na vanguarda de algo.

vanilla [vəˈnɪlə] ⬦ n (U) baunilha f. ⬦ comp de baunilha.

vanish ['vænɪʃ] vi desaparecer.

vanishing point ['vænɪʃɪŋ-] n ponto m de fuga.

vanity ['vænətɪ] n (U) pej vaidade f.

vanity unit n armário m de banheiro.

vanquish ['væŋkwɪʃ] vt literary vencer.

vantage point ['vɑ:ntɪdʒˌpɔɪnt] n -1. [for view] ponto m de observação -2. fig [advantageous position] posição f vantajosa.

vapour UK, **vapor** US ['veɪpəʳ] n (U) vapor m.

vapour trail n risco m de fumaça (de avião no céu).

variable ['veəriəbll] ⬦ adj variável. ⬦ n -1. [indefinite thing] variáveis fpl -2. MATH variável f.

variance ['veəriəns] n fml: at ~ with sthg em desacordo com algo.

variant ['veəriənt] ⬦ adj [different] variante. ⬦ n [different form, spelling] variante f.

variation [ˌveəriˈeɪʃn] n -1. (U) [fact of difference] variação f; ~ in sthg variação em algo -2. [degree of difference] variação f; ~ in sthg variação em algo -3. [different version & MUS] variação f; ~ on sthg variação em algo.

varicose veins ['værɪkəʊs-] npl varizes fpl.

varied ['veərɪd] adj variado(da).

variety [vəˈraɪətɪ] n (pl -ies) n -1. (U) [difference in type] variedade f -2. [selection] variedade f -3. [type] tipo m -4. (U) THEATRE (teatro m de) variedades fpl.

variety show n programa m de variedades.

various ['veərɪəs] adj -1. [several] vários(rias) -2. [different] variados(das).

varnish ['vɑ:nɪʃ] ⬦ n -1. [for wood] verniz m -2. [for nails] esmalte m. ⬦ vt -1. [wood] envernizar -2. [nails] pintar.

varnished ['vɑ:nɪʃt] adj -1. [wood, pottery] envernizado(da) -2. [nails] pintado(da).

vary ['veərɪ] (pt & pp -ied) ⬦ vt variar. ⬦ vi; to ~ in sthg variar em algo; to ~ with sthg variar de acordo com algo.

varying ['veərɪɪŋ] adj [different] variado(da); [fluctuating] diverso(sa).

vascular ['væskjʊləʳ] adj vascular.

vase [UK vɑ:z, US veɪz] n vaso m.

vasectomy [vəˈsektəmɪ] (pl -ies) n -1. (U) [process] vasectomia f -2. [operation] vasectomia f.

Vaseline® ['væsəli:n] n (U) vaselina® f.

vast [vɑ:st] adj enorme, imenso(sa).

vastly ['vɑ:stlɪ] adv enormemente, muito.

vastness ['vɑ:stnɪs] n (U) [hugeness] imensidão f.

vat [væt] n tina f.

Vatican ['vætɪkən] n: the ~ o Vaticano.

Vatican City n Cidade f do Vaticano; in ~ na Cidade do Vaticano.

vault [vɔ:lt] ⬦ n -1. [in bank] caixa-forte f -2. [in church] cripta f -3. [roof] abóbada f -4. [jump] salto m. ⬦ vt saltar. ⬦ vi: to ~ over sthg pular por cima de algo.

vaulted ['vɔ:ltɪd] adj ARCHIT abobadado(da).

vaulting horse ['vɔ:ltɪŋ-] n SPORT cavalo-de-pau m (na ginástica).

vaunted ['vɔ:ntɪd] adj fml alardeado(da).

veal [vi:l] n (U) vitela f.

veer [vɪəʳ] vi -1. [vehicle, road, wind] virar -2. fig [conversation, mood] alternar-se.

veg [vedʒ] n UK inf -1. (abbr of vegetable) verduras fpl -2. (U) (abbr of vegetables) verduras fpl.

vegan ['vi:ɡən] ⬦ adj vegan. ⬦ n vegan mf.

vegetable ['vedʒtəbl] ⬦ n -1. BOT vegetal m -2. [food] hortaliças fpl, legume m. ⬦ adj -1. [protein] vegetal -2. [soup] de legumes.

vegetable garden n horta f.

vegetable oil n (U) óleo m vegetal.

vegetarian [ˌvedʒɪˈteərɪən] ⬦ adj vegetariano(-na). ⬦ n vegetariano m, -na f.

vegetarianism [ˌvedʒɪˈteərɪənɪzml] n (U) vegetarianismo m.

vegetate ['vedʒɪteɪt] vi pej vegetar.

vegetation [ˌvedʒɪˈteɪʃn] n (U) vegetação f.

veggie ['vedʒɪ] UK inf ⬦ adj vegetariano(na). ⬦ n vegetariano m, -na f.

vehement ['vi:əmənt] adj -1. [gesture, attack] violento(ta) -2. [person, denial] veemente.

vehemently ['vi:əməntlɪ] adv -1. [attack] violentamente -2. [deny, refuse] veementemente.

vehicle ['vi:əkl] n -1. [for transport] veículo m -2. fig [medium]: a ~ for sthg um meio para algo.

vehicular [vɪˈhɪkjʊləʳ] adj fml de veículos automotores.

veil [veɪl] n -1. [for face] véu m -2. fig [obscuring thing] manto m.

veiled [veɪld] adj [hidden] velado(da).

vein [veɪn] n -1. ANAT veia f -2. [of leaf] nervura f -3. [of mineral] veio m -4. [style, mood] estilo m; in the same ~ no mesmo estilo.

Velcro® ['velkrəʊ] n (U) velcro® m.

vellum ['veləm] n (U) papel m velino.

velocity [vɪˈlɒsətɪ] (pl -ies) n PHYSICS velocidade f.

velour [vəˈlʊəʳ] n (U) tecido m aveludado.

velvet ['velvɪt] ⬦ n (U) veludo m. ⬦ comp de veludo.

vend vt -1. fml [sell] vender -2. JUR vender.

vendetta [venˈdetə] n vendeta f.

vending machine ['vendɪŋ-] n máquina f de venda automática.

vendor ['vendɔ:ʳ] n vendedor m, -ra f.

veneer [vəˈnɪəʳ] n -**1.** (U) [of wood] compensado m - **2.** fig [appearance] aparência f.
venerable [ˈvenərəbl] adj fml venerável.
venerate [ˈvenəreɪt] vt fml & RELIG venerar.
venereal disease [vɪˈnɪərɪəl-] n (U) doença f venérea.
Venetian [vɪˈniːʃn] <> adj veneziano(na). <> n veneziano m, -na f.
venetian blind n persiana f.
Venezuela [ˌvenɪzˈweɪlə] n Venezuela; **in** ~ **na** Venezuela.
Venezuelan [ˌvenɪzˈweɪlən] <> adj venezuelano(-na). <> n venezuelano m, -na f.
vengeance [ˈvendʒəns] n (U) vingança f; **it started raining with a** ~ começou a chover para valer.
vengeful [ˈvendʒfʊl] adj literary vingativo(va).
Venice [ˈvenɪs] n Veneza; **in** ~ em Veneza.
venison [ˈvenɪzn] n (U) carne f de veado.
venom [ˈvenəm] n (U) - **1.** [poison] veneno m - **2.** fig [spite, bitterness] veneno m.
venomous [ˈvenəməs] adj venenoso(sa).
vent [vent] <> n saída f de ar, abertura f de ar; **to give** ~ **to sthg** dar vazão a algo. <> vt [express] descarregar; **to** ~ **sthg on sb/sthg** descarregar algo em alguém/algo.
ventilate [ˈventɪleɪt] vt ventilar.
ventilation [ˌventɪˈleɪʃn] n (U) ventilação f.
ventilator [ˈventɪleɪtəʳ] n ventilador m.
ventriloquist [venˈtrɪləkwɪst] n ventríloquo m, -qua f.
venture [ˈventʃəʳ] <> n empreendimento m. <> vt [proffer] arriscar; **to** ~ **to do sthg** arriscar-se a fazer algo. <> vi -**1.** [go somewhere dangerous] aventurar-se -**2.** [embark]: **to** ~ **into sthg** lançar-se em algo.
venture capital n (U) capital m de risco.
venturesome adj -**1.** [person] aventureiro(ra) -**2.** [action] arriscado(da).
venue [ˈvenjuː] n local m (em que se realiza algo).
Venus [ˈviːnəs] n [planet] Vênus.
veracity [vəˈræsətɪ] n (U) fml veracidade f.
veranda(h) [vəˈrændə] n varanda f.
verb [vɜːb] n verbo m.
verbal [ˈvɜːbl] adj verbal.
verbally [ˈvɜːbəlɪ] adv [in spoken words] verbalmente.
verbatim [vɜːˈbeɪtɪm] <> adj literal. <> adv literalmente, palavra por palavra.
verbose [vɜːˈbəʊs] adj fml prolixo(xa).
verdict [ˈvɜːdɪkt] n -**1.** JUR veredito m -**2.** [opinion] parecer m; ~ **on sthg** parecer sobre algo.
verge [vɜːdʒ] n -**1.** [edge, side] acostamento m -**2.** [brink]: **on the** ~ **of sthg** à beira de algo; **on the** ~ **of doing sthg** a ponto de fazer algo.
 verge (up)on vt fus beirar.
verger [ˈvɜːdʒəʳ] n sacristão m.
verification [ˌverɪfɪˈkeɪʃn] n -**1.** [check] (U) verificação f -**2.** [confirmation] confirmação f.
verify [ˈverɪfaɪ] (pt & pp -ied) vt -**1.** [check] verificar -**2.** [confirm] confirmar.
veritable [ˈverɪtəbl] adj fml or hum legítimo(ma).
vermilion [vəˈmɪljən] <> adj vermelho-alaranjado(da). <> n vermelhão m.

vermin [ˈvɜːmɪn] npl -**1.** [ZOOL - rodents] bichos mpl; [- insects] insetos mpl nocivos -**2.** pej [people] parasita mf.
Vermont n Vermonte.
vermouth [ˈvɜːməθ] n (U) vermute m.
vernacular [vəˈnækjʊləʳ] <> adj LING vernacular. <> n: **the** ~ o vernáculo.
verruca [vəˈruːkə] (pl -cas OR -cae [-kaɪ]) n verruga f.
versa > vice versa.
versatile [ˈvɜːsətaɪl] adj -**1.** [multitalented] versátil -**2.** [multipurpose] multifuncional.
versatility [ˌvɜːsəˈtɪlətɪ] n (U) -**1.** [multitalented nature] versatilidade f -**2.** [multipurpose nature] multifuncionalidade f.
verse [vɜːs] n -**1.** (U) [poetry] versos mpl, poesia f -**2.** [stanza] estrofe m -**3.** [in Bible] versículo m.
versed [vɜːst] adj: **to be well** ~ **in sthg** ser bem versado(da) em algo.
version [ˈvɜːʃn] n -**1.** [gen] versão f -**2.** [translation] tradução f.
versus [ˈvɜːsəs] prep -**1.** SPORT contra -**2.** [as opposed to] em oposição a.
vertebra [ˈvɜːtɪbrə] (pl -brae [-briː]) n vértebra f.
vertebrate [ˈvɜːtɪbreɪt] n vertebrado m.
vertical [ˈvɜːtɪkl] adj vertical.
vertical integration n (U) FIN integração f vertical.
vertically [ˈvɜːtɪklɪ] adv verticalmente.
vertigo [ˈvɜːtɪɡəʊ] n (U) vertigem f.
verve [vɜːv] n (U) vivacidade f, entusiasmo m.
very [ˈverɪ] <> adv -**1.** [for emphasis] muito; **to like sthg** ~ **much** gostar muito de algo -**2.** [as euphemism]: **he's not** ~ **intelligent** ele não é muito inteligente. <> adj mesmíssimo(ma); **the** ~ **book I've been looking for** justo o livro que eu estava procurando; **the** ~ **thought make me bad** só de pensar eu já fico mal; **fighting for his** ~ **life** lutando por sua própria vida; **the** ~ **best** o melhor de todos; **a house of my** ~ **own** minha própria casa.
 very well adv muito bem; **you can't** ~ **well stop him now** é um pouco tarde para impedi-lo.
vespers [ˈvespəz] n (U) vésperas fpl.
vessel [ˈvesl] n fml -**1.** [boat] embarcação f -**2.** [container] recipiente m, vasilha f.
vest [vest] n -**1.** UK [undershirt] camiseta f -**2.** US [waistcoat] colete m.
vested interest [ˈvestɪd-] n capital m investido; ~ **in sthg** capital investido em algo.
vestibule [ˈvestɪbjuːl] n -**1.** fml [entrance hall] vestíbulo m -**2.** US [on train] vestíbulo m.
vestige [ˈvestɪdʒ] n fml vestígio m.
vestry [ˈvestrɪ] (pl -ies) n sacristia f.
Vesuvius [vɪˈsuːvjəs] n Vesúvio m.
vet [vet] (pt & pp -ted, cont -ting) <> n -**1.** UK (abbr of **veterinary surgeon**) veterinário m, -ria f -**2.** US (abbr of **veteran**) veterano m, -na f de guerra. <> vt UK [check] submeter a uma investigação.
veteran [ˈvetrən] <> adj [experienced] veterano(na). <> n veterano m, -na f.
veteran car n UK carro m de época (feito antes de 1905).
Veterans Day n US Dia m dos Veteranos, 11 de

*novembro, dia em que os Estados Unidos come-
moram o fim das duas guerras mundiais e
homenageiam seus veteranos.*

veterinarian [ˌvetərɪ'neərɪən] *n US* veterinário *m*,
-ria *f*.

veterinary science ['vetərɪnrɪ-] *n (U)* veterinária
f.

veterinary surgeon ['vetərɪnrɪ-] *n UK fml* veterinário *m*, -ria *f*.

veto ['vi:təʊ] (*pl* -es, *pt* & *pp* -ed, *cont* -ing) ⟨⟩ *n* -1.
(U) [power to forbid] veto *m* -2. [act of forbidding] veto *m*.
⟨⟩ *vt* vetar.

vetting ['vetɪŋ] *n (U)* investigação *f (sobre o
passado de uma pessoa).*

vex [veks] *vt fml* [annoy] importunar.

vexed question [ˌvekst-] *n* pomo *m* de discórdia.

VI *abbr of* Virgin Islands.

via ['vaɪə] *prep* -1. [travelling through] via; **they flew to
China ~ Karachi** eles viajaram para a China
(passando) por Karachi -2. [by means of] através
de; **~ satellite** via satélite.

viability [ˌvaɪə'bɪlətɪ] *n* viabilidade *f.*

viable ['vaɪəbl] *adj* viável.

viaduct ['vaɪədʌkt] *n* viaduto *m*.

vibrant ['vaɪbrənt] *adj* -1. [colour, light] forte -2. [per-
son] dinâmico(ca) -3. [city, atmosphere] animado(da)
-4. [sound] vibrante.

vibrate [vaɪ'breɪt] *vi* vibrar.

vibration [vaɪ'breɪʃn] *n* vibração *f.*

vicar ['vɪkər] *n* vigário *m*, pároco *m*.

vicarage ['vɪkərɪdʒ] *n* casa *f* paroquial.

vicarious [vɪ'keərɪəs] *adj* indireto(ta).

vice [vaɪs] *n* -1. *(U)* [immorality] vício *m* -2. [moral fault]
vício *m* -3. [tool] torno *m* de mesa.

vice- [vaɪs] *prefix* vice-.

vice-admiral *n* vice-almirante *m*.

vice-chairman *n* vice-presidente *m*.

vice-chancellor *n UK UNIV* reitor *m*, -ra *f*.

vice-president *n* vice-presidente *mf*.

vice squad *n* delegacia *f* de costumes.

vice versa [ˌvaɪsɪ'vɜ:sə] *adv* vice-versa.

vicinity [vɪ'sɪnətɪ] *n* -1. [neighbourhood] proximidades *fpl*, redondezas *fpl*; **in the ~ (of)** nas
proximidades *or* redondezas(de) -2. [approximate
figures]: **in the ~ of** cerca de.

vicious ['vɪʃəs] *adj* -1. [attack, blow] violento(ta) -2.
[person, gossip] cruel -3. [dog] feroz, brabo(ba).

vicious circle *n* círculo *m* vicioso.

viciousness ['vɪʃəsnɪs] *n* -1. [of attack] violência *f*
-2. [of person, gossip] crueldade *f* -3. [of dog] ferocidade *f.*

vicissitudes [vɪ'sɪsɪtju:dz] *npl fml* vicissitudes *fpl.*

victim ['vɪktɪm] *n* vítima *f.*

victimize, -ise ['vɪktɪmaɪz] *vt* vitimar.

victor ['vɪktər] *n* vencedor *m*, -ra *f.*

Victoria Cross [vɪk'tɔ:rɪə-] *n condecoração militar britânica.*

Victoria Falls [vɪk'tɔ:rɪə-] *npl*: **the ~** as Cataratas
de Vitória.

Victorian [vɪk'tɔ:rɪən] *adj* -1. [from Victorian era]
vitoriano(na) -2. *usu pej* [overstrict] vitoriano(na).

Victoriana [ˌvɪktɔ:rɪ'ɑ:nə] *n (U)* antiguidades *fpl* da
era vitoriana.

victorious [vɪk'tɔ:rɪəs] *adj* [winning] vitorioso(sa).

victory ['vɪktərɪ] (*pl* -ies) *n* -1. *(U)* [act of winning]
vitória *f* -2. [win] vitória *f*; **~ over sb/sthg** vitória
sobre alguém/algo.

video ['vɪdɪəʊ] (*pl* -s, *pt* & *pp* -ed, *cont* -ing) ⟨⟩ *n* -1.
(U) [medium] vídeo *m* -2. [recording, machine] vídeo *m*
-3. [cassette] videocassete *m*. ⟨⟩ *comp* de vídeo.
⟨⟩ *vt* -1. [using videorecorder] gravar em vídeo -2.
[using camera] gravar um vídeo de.

video camera *n* câmera *f* de vídeo.

video cassette *n* vídeocassete *m*, vídeo *m*.

videodisc *UK*, **videodisk** *US* ['vɪdɪəʊdɪsk] *n* vi-
deodisco *m*.

video game *n* video game *m*.

video machine *n* vídeo *m*.

videophone ['vɪdɪəʊfəʊn] *n* videofone *m*.

videorecorder ['vɪdɪəʊrɪˌkɔ:dər] *n* videocassete
m, vídeo *m*.

video recording *n* -1. [copy on video] cópia *f* em
vídeo -2. *(U) TV* gravação *f* em vídeo.

video shop *n* videolocadora *f.*

videotape ['vɪdɪəʊteɪp] *n* -1. [cassette] videoteipe *m*
-2. *(U)* [ribbon] fita *f.*

vie [vaɪ] (*pt* & *pp* vied, *cont* vying) *vi*: **to ~ for sthg**
competir por algo; **to ~ with sb (for sthg/to do
sthg)** competir com alguém (por algo/para fazer
algo).

Vienna [vɪ'enə] *n* Viena.

Viennese [ˌvɪə'ni:z] ⟨⟩ *adj* vienense. ⟨⟩ *n*
vienense *mf.*

Vietnam [*UK* ˌvjet'næm, *US* ˌvjet'nɑ:m] *n* Vietnã; **in
~** no Vietnã.

Vietnamese [ˌvjetnə'mi:z] ⟨⟩ *adj* vietnamita. ⟨⟩
n -1. [person] vietnamita *mf* -2. [language] vietnamita
m. ⟨⟩ *npl*: **the ~** os vietnamitas.

view [vju:] ⟨⟩ *n* -1. [opinion] visão *f*, opinião *f*; **~ of
sthg** visão de algo; **~ on sb/sthg** opinião sobre
alguém/algo; **in my ~** na minha opinião; **to take
the ~ that** ser da opinião de que -2. [vista] vista *f*
-3. [ability to see] visão *f*; **to come into ~** aparecer.
⟨⟩ *vt* -1. [consider] ver -2. *fml* [house] visitar -3. [so-
lar system] observar.
➥ **in view of** *prep* em vista de.
➥ **with a view to** *conj* com o intuito de.

viewer ['vju:ər] *n* -1. [person] telespectador *m*, -ra *f*
-2. [apparatus] visor *m.*

viewfinder ['vju:ˌfaɪndər] *n* visor *m*.

viewpoint ['vju:pɔɪnt] *n* -1. [opinion] ponto *m* de
vista -2. [place] mirante *m*.

vigil ['vɪdʒɪl] *n* vigília *f.*

vigilance ['vɪdʒɪləns] *n (U)* vigilância *f.*

vigilant ['vɪdʒɪlənt] *adj* vigilante.

vigilante [ˌvɪdʒɪ'læntɪ] *n* vigilante *mf.*

vigor *n US* = vigour.

vigorous ['vɪgərəs] *adj* -1. [gen] vigoroso(sa) -2. [at-
tempt] enérgico(ca) -3. [person, animal] vivaz -4.
[plant] viçoso(sa).

vigour *UK*, **vigor** *US* ['vɪgər] *n (U)* vigor *m.*

Viking ['vaɪkɪŋ] ⟨⟩ *adj* viking, viquingue. ⟨⟩ *n*
viking *mf*, viquingue *mf.*

vile [vaɪl] *adj* -1. [person] vil -2. [mood] muito ruim
-3. [act] desprezível -4. [food] repugnante.

vilify ['vɪlɪfaɪ] (*pt* & *pp* -ied) *vt fml* difamar.

villa ['vɪlə] n casa f de campo, chalé m.
village ['vɪlɪdʒ] n vilarejo m povoado m.
villager ['vɪlɪdʒəʳ] n população f de um vilarejo.
villain ['vɪlən] n -1. [of film, book, play] vilão m, -lã f -2. dated [criminal] criminoso m, -sa f.
vinaigrette [,vɪnɪ'gret] n (U) molho m vinagrete.
vindicate ['vɪndɪkeɪt] vt [confirm] vindicar; [justify] justificar.
vindication [,vɪndɪ'keɪʃn] n [confirmation] vindicação f; [justification] justificação f.
vindictive [vɪn'dɪktɪv] adj vingativo(va).
vine [vaɪn] n [grapevine] videira f, parreira f.
vinegar ['vɪnɪgəʳ] n (U) vinagre m.
vine leaf n folha f de parreira.
vineyard ['vɪnjəd] n vinhedo m.
vintage ['vɪntɪdʒ] <> adj -1. [wine] de boa safra -2. fig [classic] clássico(ca). <> n [wine] safra f.
vintage car n UK carro m de época (feito entre 1919 e 1930).
vintage wine n vinho m de uma boa safra.
vintner n comerciante mf de vinhos.
vinyl ['vaɪnɪl] <> n (U) vinil m. <> comp de vinil.
viola [vɪ'əʊlə] n -1. MUS viola f -2. BOT violeta f.
violate ['vaɪəleɪt] vt -1. [disregard] violar -2. [disrupt] invadir -3. [break into] profanar.
violation [,vaɪə'leɪʃn] n -1. (U) [disregarding] violação f -2. [disruption] invasão f -3. [breaking into] profanação f.
violence ['vaɪələns] n (U) -1. [physical force] violência f -2. [of words, reaction] violência f.
violent ['vaɪələnt] adj -1. [gen] violento(ta) -2. [emotion, colour] intenso(sa).
violently ['vaɪələntlɪ] adv violentamente.
violet ['vaɪələt] <> adj violeta. <> n -1. [flower] violeta f -2. (U) [colour] violeta f.
violin [,vaɪə'lɪn] n violino m.
violinist [,vaɪə'lɪnɪst] n violinista mf.
viper ['vaɪpəʳ] n víbora f.
viral ['vaɪrəl] adj viral, virótico(ca).
virgin ['vɜːdʒɪn] <> adj literary -1. [sexually] virgem -2. [forest, snow, soil] virgem. <> n virgem mf.
Virginia [və'dʒɪnjə] n Virgínia f.
Virginia creeper n videira f virgem.
Virgin Islands n: the ~ as Ilhas Virgens; in the ~ nas Ilhas Virgens.
virginity [və'dʒɪnətɪ] n (U) virgindade f.
Virgo ['vɜːgəʊ] (pl -s) n -1. [sign] Virgem m -2. [person] virginiano m, -na f; I'm ~ sou de Virgem.
virile ['vɪraɪl] adj viril.
virility [vɪ'rɪlətɪ] n (U) virilidade f.
virtual ['vɜːtʃʊəl] adj [certainty, necessity] virtual.
virtually ['vɜːtʃʊəlɪ] adv [almost] praticamente.
virtual memory n COMPUT memória f virtual.
virtual reality n realidade f virtual.
virtue ['vɜːtjuː] n -1. (U) [goodness] virtude f -2. [merit, quality] virtude f -3. [benefit] vantagem f; ~ in sthg vantagem em algo.
➡ **by virtue of** prep fml em virtude de.
virtuoso [,vɜːtjʊ'əʊzəʊ] (pl -sos OR -si [-siː]) n virtuoso m, -sa f.
virtuous ['vɜːtʃʊəs] adj virtuoso(sa).
virulent ['vɪrʊlənt] adj -1. fml [bitter and hostile]

virulento(ta) -2. MED [very powerful] virulento(ta).
virus ['vaɪrəs] n vírus m inv.
visa ['viːzə] n visto m.
vis-à-vis [,viːzɑː'viː] prep fml em relação a.
viscose ['vɪskəʊs] n (U) -1. [solution] viscose f -2. [material] viscose f.
viscosity [vɪ'skɒsətɪ] n CHEM viscosidade f.
viscount ['vaɪkaʊnt] n visconde m.
viscous ['vɪskəs] adj CHEM viscoso(sa).
vise [vaɪs] n US torno m de mesa.
visibility [,vɪzɪ'bɪlətɪ] n visibilidade f.
visible ['vɪzəbl] adj visível.
visibly ['vɪzəblɪ] adv [clearly] visivelmente.
vision ['vɪʒn] n -1. (U) [ability to see] visão f, vista f -2. (U) fig [foresight] visão f -3. [impression, dream] visão f -4. (U) TV imagem f.
visionary ['vɪʒənrɪ] (pl -ies) <> adj [full of foresight] visionário(ria). <> n [person] visionário m, -ria f.
visit ['vɪzɪt] <> n visita f; on a ~ to numa visita a. <> vt visitar.
➡ **visit with** vt fus US -1. [talk with] conversar com -2. [go and see] visitar, ir ver.
visiting card ['vɪzɪtɪŋ-] n cartão m de visita.
visiting hours ['vɪzɪtɪŋ-] npl hora f de visita.
visitor ['vɪzɪtəʳ] n -1. [to person] visita mf -2. [to place] visitante mf.
visitors' book n livro m de visitantes.
visitor's passport n UK passaporte m temporário.
visor ['vaɪzəʳ] n [on helmet] viseira f.
vista ['vɪstə] n -1. [view] vista f, perspectiva f -2. fig [perspective] perspectiva f.
visual ['vɪʒʊəl] adj -1. [gen] visual -2. [examination] de vista.
visual aids npl recursos mpl visuais.
visual display unit n monitor m.
visualize, -ise ['vɪʒʊəlaɪz] vt visualizar; to ~ (sb) doing sthg imaginar (alguém) fazendo algo.
visually ['vɪʒʊəlɪ] adv visualmente; ~ handicapped person pessoa f com problemas visuais.
vital ['vaɪtl] adj -1. [essential] vital, essencial -2. [full of life] cheio (cheia) de vida.
vitality [vaɪ'tælətɪ] n (U) vitalidade f.
vitally ['vaɪtəlɪ] adv extremamente.
vital statistics npl inf [of figure] medidas fpl (do corpo de uma mulher).
vitamin [UK 'vɪtəmɪn, US 'vaɪtəmɪn] n vitamina f.
vitreous adj vítreo(trea).
vitriolic [,vɪtrɪ'ɒlɪk] adj fml acrimonioso(osa), virulento(ta).
viva ['vaɪvə] n UNIV = viva voce.
vivacious [vɪ'veɪʃəs] adj vivaz, animado(da).
vivacity [vɪ'væsətɪ] n (U) vivacidade f.
viva voce [,vaɪvə'vəʊsɪ] n UNIV exame m oral.
vivid ['vɪvɪd] adj -1. [bright] vivo(va) -2. [clear] vívido(da).
vividly ['vɪvɪdlɪ] adv -1. [brightly] com cores muito vivas -2. [clearly] vividamente.
vivisection [,vɪvɪ'sekʃn] n (U) vivissecção f.
vixen ['vɪksn] n raposa f (fêmea).
viz [vɪz] (abbr of videlicet) a saber.
VLF (abbr of very low frequency) n VLF f.

V-neck *n* **-1.** [sweater, dress] decote *m* em V **-2.** [neck] gola *f* em V.

VOA (*abbr of* Voice of America) *n emissora oficial de rádio norte-americana com transmissões para todo o mundo em inglês e outras línguas.*

vocabulary [vəˈkæbjʊlərɪ] (*pl* -ies) *n* vocabulário *m*.

vocal [ˈvəʊkl] *adj* **-1.** [outspoken] sincero(ra) **-2.** [of the voice] vocal.

➤ **vocals** *npl* vocais *mpl*; **on** ~ **s** no vocal.

vocal cords *npl* cordas *fpl* vocais.

vocalist [ˈvəʊkəlɪst] *n* vocalista *mf*.

vocation [vəʊˈkeɪʃn] *n* [calling] vocação *f*.

vocational [vəʊˈkeɪʃənl] *adj* vocacional.

vociferous [vəˈsɪfərəs] *adj fml* vociferante.

vodka [ˈvɒdkə] *n* vodca *f*.

vogue [vəʊg] <> *adj* em voga. <> *n* moda *f*; ~ **for** sthg moda de algo; **in** ~ na moda, em voga.

voice [vɔɪs] <> *n* **-1.** [gen] voz *f*; **to raise/lower one's** ~ levantar/baixar a voz; **to keep one's** ~ **down** manter a voz baixa **-2.** [influence] influência *f*. <> *vt* [opinion, emotion] manifestar.

voice box *n* laringe *f*.

Voice of America *n* Voz *f* da América (*emissora de rádio dos Estados Unidos*).

voice-over *n* narração *f* (*num comercial para tevê*).

void [vɔɪd] <> *adj* **-1.** [invalid] inválido(da) ▷ **null -2.** *fml* [empty]: ~ **of** sthg desprovido(da) de algo. <> *n literary* vazio *m*.

voile [vɔɪl] *n* (*U*) voile *m*.

vol. (*abbr of* volume) vol.

volatile [*UK* ˈvɒlətaɪl, *US* ˈvɒlətl] *adj* [unpredictable - situation] imprevisível; [- person] volúvel; [- market] volátil.

vol-au-vent [ˈvɒləʊvɒ̃] *n petisco de massa folhada com recheio.*

volcanic [vɒlˈkænɪk] *adj* [of volcanoes] vulcânico(ca).

volcano [vɒlˈkeɪnəʊ] (*pl* -es *OR* -s) *n* vulcão *m*.

vole [vəʊl] *n* rato-calunga *m*.

Volga [ˈvɒlɡə] *n*: **the (River)** ~ o (Rio) Volga.

volition [vəˈlɪʃn] *n fml*: **of one's own** ~ por vontade própria.

volley [ˈvɒlɪ] (*pl* volleys) <> *n* **-1.** [of gunfire] rajada *f*, saraivada *f* **-2.** *fig* [rapid succession] torrente *f* **-3.** *SPORT* voleio *m*. <> *vt* dar de voleio em.

volleyball [ˈvɒlɪbɔːl] *n* (*U*) voleibol *m*, vôlei *m*.

volt [vəʊlt] *n* volt *m*.

Volta [ˈvɒltə] *n* **-1.** [river]: **the (River)** ~ o (Rio) Volta **-2.** [lake]: **Lake** ~ Lago *m* Volta.

voltage [ˈvəʊltɪdʒ] *n* voltagem *f*.

voluble [ˈvɒljʊbl] *adj fml* loquaz.

volume [ˈvɒljuːm] *n* (*U*) volume *m*.

volume control *n* controle *m* de volume.

voluminous [vəˈluːmɪnəs] *adj fml* **-1.** [garment] volumoso(sa) **-2.** [container] espaçoso(sa).

voluntarily [*UK* ˈvɒləntrɪlɪ, *US* ˌvɒlənˈterəlɪ] *adv* voluntariamente.

voluntary [ˈvɒləntrɪ] *adj* voluntário(ria); ~ **organization** organização *f* beneficente.

voluntary liquidation *n* (*U*) liquidação *f* voluntária.

voluntary redundancy *n UK* demissão *f* voluntária.

voluntary work *n* trabalho *m* voluntário.

volunteer [ˌvɒlənˈtɪəʳ] <> *n* voluntário *m*, -ria *f*. <> *vt* **-1.** [offer of one's free will]: **to** ~ **to do** sthg oferecer-se (de livre e espontânea vontade) para fazer algo **-2.** [information, advice] oferecer. <> *vi* **-1.** [freely offer one's services]: **to** ~ **(for** sthg**)** oferecer-se (para algo) **-2.** *MIL* alistar-se como voluntário(ria).

voluptuous [vəˈlʌptjʊəs] *adj* voluptuoso(sa).

vomit [ˈvɒmɪt] <> *n* (*U*) vômito *m*. <> *vi* vomitar.

voodoo *n* vodu *m*.

voracious [vəˈreɪʃəs] *adj* voraz.

vortex [ˈvɔːteks] (*pl* -texes *OR* -tices [-tɪsiːz]) *n* **-1.** *TECH* vórtice *m* **-2.** *fig* [of events] turbilhão *m*.

vote [vəʊt] <> *n* **-1.** [individual decision] voto *m*; ~ **for** sb/sthg voto em alguém/algo; ~ **against** sb/sthg voto contra alguém/algo **-2.** [session, ballot] votação *f*; **to put** sthg **to the** ~ levar algo à votação **-3.** [result of ballot]: **the** ~ a votação **-4.** [section of voters] eleitorado *m* **-5.** [suffrage] voto *m*. <> *vt* **-1.** [declare, elect] eleger **-2.** [choose in ballot] votar em; **they** ~ **ed to return to work** eles votaram pela volta ao trabalho **-3.** [suggest] votar. <> *vi* [express one's choice] votar; **to** ~ **for/against** sb votar em/contra alguém; **to** ~ **for/against** sthg votar a favor de/contra algo.

➤ **vote in** *vt sep* eleger.

➤ **vote out** *vt sep* derrotar (nas urnas).

vote of confidence (*pl* votes of confidence) *n* voto *m* de confiança.

vote of no confidence (*pl* votes of no confidence) *n* voto *m* de censura.

vote of thanks (*pl* votes of thanks) *n*: **to give a** ~ fazer um discurso de agradecimento.

voter [ˈvəʊtəʳ] *n* votante *mf*.

voting [ˈvəʊtɪŋ] *n* votação *f*.

vouch [vaʊtʃ] ➤ **vouch for** *vt fus* **-1.** [take responsibility for] responsabilizar-se por **-2.** [declare belief in] dar testemunho de.

voucher [ˈvaʊtʃəʳ] *n* [for restaurant, purchase, petrol] vale *m*.

vow [vaʊ] <> *n* **-1.** juramento *m*, promessa *f* solene **-2.** *RELIG* voto *m*. <> *vt*: **to** ~ **to do** sthg jurar fazer algo; **to** ~ **(that)** jurar que.

vowel [ˈvaʊəl] *n* vogal *f*.

voyage [ˈvɔɪdʒ] *n* viagem *f*.

voyeur [vwɑːˈjɜːʳ] *n* voyeur *m*, -euse *f*.

voyeurism [vwɑːˈjɜːrɪzm] *n* (*U*) voyeurismo *m*.

VP *n* (*abbr of* vice-president) vice-presidente *mf*.

vs (*abbr of* versus) vs.

VSO (*abbr of* Voluntary Service Overseas) *n organização britânica de voluntários para ajuda a países em desenvolvimento.*

VSOP (*abbr of* very special old pale) *expressão que indica que uma bebida tem de 20 a 25 anos.*

VT *abbr of* Vermont.

VTOL (*abbr of* vertical takeoff and landing) *n decolagem e aterrissagem na vertical.*

VTR (*abbr of* videotape recorder) *n* vídeo *m*.

vulgar [ˈvʌlɡəʳ] *adj* **-1.** [common] comum **-2.** [rude] vulgar, baixo(xa).

vulgarity [vʌlˈɡærətɪ] *n* (*U*) **-1.** [commonness] vulgaridade *f* **-2.** [rudeness] grosseria *f*, vulgaridade *f*.

vulnerability [ˌvʌlnərə'bɪlətɪ] *n* vulnerabilidade *f.*

vulnerable ['vʌlnərəbl] *adj* **-1.** [easily hurt] vulnerável; **~ to sthg** [to being hurt] vulnerável a algo **-2.** [easily influenced]: **~ (to sthg)** facilmente influenciável (por algo).

vulture ['vʌltʃəʳ] *n* **-1.** [bird] abutre *m*, urubu *m* **-2.** *fig* [exploitative person] abutre *m.*

w (*pl* **w's** OR **ws**), **W** (*pl* **W's** OR **Ws**) ['dʌblju:] *n* w, W *m.*
W -1. (*abbr of* **west**) O. **- 2.** (*abbr of* **watt**) W *m.*

WA *abbr of* **Washington**.

wacky ['wækɪ] (*compar* **-ier**, *superl* **-iest**) *adj inf* excêntrico(ca), extravagante.

wad [wɒd] *n* **-1.** [of cotton wool] chumaço *m*; [of paper, bank notes, documents] pilha *f*; [of tobacco] masca *f* **-2.** [of chewing gum] pedaço *f.*

wadding ['wɒdɪŋ] *n* [stuffing] enchimento *m.*

waddle ['wɒdl] *vi* caminhar se balançando.

wade [weɪd] *vi* patinhar.
➤ wade through *vt fus fig*: **he was wading through the documents** ele penava muito para ler os documentos.

wadge [wɒdʒ] *n* **-1.** *UK inf* [gen] pilha *f*, porção *f* **-2.** [of cotton wool] chumaço *m*; [of papers] feixe *m*; [of pie] fatia *f.*

wading pool ['weɪdɪŋ-] *n US* piscina *f* para crianças.

wafer ['weɪfəʳ] *n* [thin biscuit] wafer *m.*

wafer-thin *adj* finíssimo(ma).

waffle ['wɒfl] ⟨⟩ *n* **-1.** CULIN waffle *m* **-2.** (*U) UK inf* [vague talk] lengalenga *f*, ladainha *f.* ⟨⟩ *vi inf* enrolar.

waft [wɑːft, wɒft] *vi* flutuar.

wag [wæg] (*pt* & *pp* **-ged**, *cont* **-ging**) ⟨⟩ *vt* sacudir. ⟨⟩ *vi* [tail] abanar.

wage [weɪdʒ] ⟨⟩ *n* salário *m.* ⟨⟩ *vt*: **to ~ war against sb/sthg** guerrear com alguém/algo.
➤ wages *npl* [of worker] pagamento *m*, salário *m*; **I always get my ~ s at the end of the week** eu recebo sempre nos finais de semana.

wage claim *n* reivindicação *f* salarial.

wage differential *n* diferença *f* salarial.

wage earner [-ˌɜːnəʳ] *n* assalariado *m*, -da *f.*

wage freeze *n* congelamento *m* de salário.

wage packet *n* **-1.** [envelope] envelope *m* de pagamento **-2.** [pay] pagamento *m.*

wager ['weɪdʒəʳ] *n* aposta *f.*

wage rise *n UK* aumento *m* de salário.

waggish *adj* **-1.** *inf* [remark, mood, behaviour] jocoso(sa) **-2.** *inf* [person] divertido(da).

waggle ['wægl] *inf vt* & *vi* balançar.

wagon ['wægən], **waggon** *UK n* **-1.** [horse-drawn vehicle] carroça *f* **-2.** *UK RAIL* vagão *m.*

wagtail *n* lavandisca *f.*

waif [weɪf] *n literary* criança *f* abandonada.

wail [weɪl] ⟨⟩ *n* lamento *m*, gemido *m.* ⟨⟩ *vi* **-1.** [baby] choramingar **-2.** [person] gemer **-3.** [wind, siren] soar.

wailing ['weɪlɪŋ] *n* **-1.** [of baby] choramingo *m* **-2.** [of person] gemido *m* **-3.** [of wind, siren] som *m.*

waist [weɪst] *n* cintura *f.*

waistband ['weɪstbænd] *n* cintura *f*, cós *m.*

waistcoat ['weɪskəʊt] *n* colete *m.*

waistline ['weɪstlaɪn] *n* cintura *f.*

wait [weɪt] ⟨⟩ *n* espera *f*; **to lie in ~ for sb** esperar alguém numa emboscada. ⟨⟩ *vi* esperar; **to ~ and see** esperar para ver; **~ a minute** OR **second** OR **moment** [interrupting sb] espere um minuto/segundo/momento; [interrupting o.s.] espera (aí) um pouquinho; **(just) you ~!** espere que você vai ver! ⟨⟩ *vt* **-1.**: **I/he** *etc* **couldn't ~ to do sthg** eu/ele mal podia esperar para fazer algo **-2.** *US* [delay]: **don't ~ dinner for me** não precisa me esperar para jantar.
➤ wait about, wait around *vi* esperar, aguardar.
➤ wait for *vt fus* esperar; **to ~ for sb to do sthg** esperar que alguém faça algo.
➤ wait on *vt fus* [serve food to] servir; **she ~ s on her family hand and foot** ela responde a todas as necessidades da família.
➤ wait up *vi* ficar acordado(da) esperando.

waiter ['weɪtəʳ] *n* garçom *m.*

waiting game ['weɪtɪŋ-] *n*: **to play a ~** esperar o momento certo.

waiting list ['weɪtɪŋ-] *n* lista *f* de espera.

waiting room ['weɪtɪŋ-] *n* sala *f* de espera.

waitress ['weɪtrɪs] *n* garçonete *f.*

waive [weɪv] *vt* **-1.** *fml* [rule] não aplicar **-2.** *fml* [entrance fee] abrir mão de.

waiver ['weɪvəʳ] *n JUR* renúncia *f.*

wake [weɪk] (*pt* **woke** OR **-d**, *pp* **woken** OR **-d**) ⟨⟩ *n* **-1.** [of ship, boat] esteira *f*; **in one's ~** *fig* pelo caminho; **in the ~ of** *fig* nas águas de **-2.** [for dead person] velório *m.* ⟨⟩ *vt* acordar. ⟨⟩ *vi* acordar-se.
➤ wake up ⟨⟩ *vt sep* acordar. ⟨⟩ *vi* **-1.** [wake] acordar-se **-2.** *fig* [become aware]: **to ~ up (to sthg)** conscientizar-se (de algo).

waken ['weɪkən] *fml* ⟨⟩ *vt* despertar. ⟨⟩ *vi* despertar-se.

waking hours ['weɪkɪŋ-] *npl* horas *fpl* de vigília.

Wales [weɪlz] *n* País de Gales; **in ~** no País de Gales.

walk [wɔːk] ⟨⟩ *n* **-1.** [stroll] passeio *m*, caminhada *f*; **to go for a ~** dar um passeio **-2.** [path] caminho *m* **-3.** [gait] jeito *m* de andar. ⟨⟩ *vt* **-1.** [escort] acompanhar **-2.** [take out for exercise] levar para passear **-3.** [cover on foot] caminhar; **to ~ the streets** [be homeless] vagar pela rua; [in search of sthg] percorrer as ruas; [prostitute] prostituir-se. ⟨⟩ *vi* caminhar, andar.
➤ walk away with *vt fus inf fig* [carry off] levar.
➤ walk in on *vt fus* [interrupt] interromper.

walk off *vt sep* [headache, cramp, meal] dar uma volta para aliviar.

walk off with *vt fus inf* -**1.** [steal] levar -**2.** [win easily] levar de barbada.

walk out *vi* -**1.** [leave suddenly] sair -**2.** [go on strike] entrar em greve branca.

walk out on *vt fus* deixar, abandonar.

walkabout ['wɔ:kə,baʊt] *n UK* [by politician] caminhada *f* pelas ruas; **to go on a ~** caminhar entre as pessoas *(nas ruas)*.

walker ['wɔ:kəʳ] *n* [for pleasure, sport] caminhante *mf*.

walkie-talkie [,wɔ:kɪ'tɔ:kɪ] *n* walkie-talkie *m*.

walk-in *adj* -**1.** [cupboard] espaçoso(sa) -**2.** *US* [easy] fácil.

walking ['wɔ:kɪŋ] *n* [for pleasure, sport] caminhada *f*; **to go ~** dar uma caminhada.

walking shoes *npl* sapatos *mpl* de caminhada.

walking stick *n* bengala *f*.

Walkman® ['wɔ:kmən] *n* walkman® *m*.

walk of life (*pl* walks of life) *n* -**1.** [job] profissão *f* -**2.** [social position] posição *f* social.

walk-on *adj* de figurante.

walkout ['wɔ:kaʊt] *n* [of members, spectators, workers] greve *f* branca.

walkover ['wɔ:k,əʊvəʳ] *n UK inf* [victory] barbada *f*, vitória *f* fácil.

walkway ['wɔ:kweɪ] *n* passadiço *m*, passagem *f*.

wall [wɔ:l] *n* -**1.** [interior] parede *f* -**2.** [exterior] muro *m*; **to come up against a brick ~** chegar a um beco sem saída; **to drive sb up the ~** deixar alguém louco -**3.** ANAT parede *f*.

wallaby ['wɒləbɪ] (*pl* -ies) *n* marsupial australiano parecido com um pequeno canguru.

wallchart ['wɔ:ltʃɑ:t] *n* mural *m*.

wall cupboard *n* armário *m* embutido.

walled [wɔ:ld] *adj* cercado(da) *(com muros)*.

wallet ['wɒlɪt] *n* carteira *f*.

wallflower ['wɔ:l,flaʊəʳ] *n* -**1.** [plant] aleli *m* -**2.** *inf fig* [person] azeite *m*.

Walloon <> *adj* valão(ona). <> *n* -**1.** [person] valão *m*, -ona *f* -**2.** [language] valão *m*.

wallop ['wɒləp] *inf* <> *n* surra *f*. <> *vt* [hit] surrar.

wallow ['wɒləʊ] *vi* -**1.** [in water] mergulhar -**2.** [in mud] chafurdar -**3.** [in emotion]: **to ~ in sthg** afundar-se em algo.

wall painting *n* afresco *m*, mural *m*.

wallpaper ['wɔ:l,peɪpəʳ] <> *n (U)* papel *m* de parede. <> *vt* forrar com papel de parede.

Wall Street *n* Wall Street; **on ~** em Wall Street.

wall-to-wall *adj*: **~ carpet** carpete *m*.

wally ['wɒlɪ] (*pl* -ies) *n UK inf* pateta *mf*.

walnut ['wɔ:lnʌt] *n* -**1.** [nut] noz *m* -**2.** [tree, material] nogueira *f*.

walrus ['wɔ:lrəs] (*pl inv OR* -es) *n* morsa *f*.

waltz [wɔ:ls] <> *n* valsa *f*. <> *vi* -**1.** [dance] dançar uma valsa -**2.** *inf* [walk confidently]: **to ~ in/out** entrar/sair de fininho.

wan [wɒn] (*compar* -ner, *superl* -nest) *adj* abatido(da).

wand [wɒnd] *n* varinha *f* mágica.

wander ['wɒndəʳ] *vi* -**1.** [person] perambular -**2.** [mind, thoughts] divagar.

wanderer ['wɒndərəʳ] *n* andarilho *m*, -lha *f*.

wandering ['wɒndərɪŋ] *adj* [itinerant] ambulante.

wanderlust ['wɒndəlʌst] *n (U)* paixão *f* por viajar.

wane [weɪn] <> *n*: **on the ~** em declínio. <> *vi* -**1.** [influence, interest] declinar -**2.** [moon] minguar.

wangle ['wæŋgl] *vt inf* arranjar, conseguir.

wanna ['wɒnə] *cont esp US* = want a, want to.

wannabe *adj inf* que gostaria de ser igual a outra pessoa ou grupo de pessoas.

want [wɒnt] <> *n* -**1.** [need] necessidade *f* -**2.** [lack] falta *f*; **for ~ of** por falta de -**3.** *(U)* [deprivation] penúria *f*; **to be in ~** passar necessidades. <> *vt* -**1.** [desire] querer; **to ~ to do sthg** querer fazer algo; **to ~ sb to do sthg** querer que alguém faça algo -**2.** *inf* [need] precisar.

want ad *n US inf* anúncio *m* (classificado).

wanted ['wɒntɪd] *adj*: **to be ~ (by the police)** ser procurado(da) (pela polícia).

wanting ['wɒntɪŋ] *adj fml* [inadequate]: **to be ~ (in sthg)** carecer (de algo); **the play is ~ in humour** está faltando humor na peça; **to be found ~** deixar a desejar.

wanton ['wɒntən] *adj* -**1.** *fml* [malicious] gratuito(ta), sem motivo -**2.** [immoral] libertino(na).

WAP [wæp] (*abbr of* wireless application protocol) *n* WAP *m*.

WAP phone *n* telefone *m* WAP.

war [wɔ:ʳ] (*pt & pp* -red, *cont* -ring) *n* guerra *f*; **at ~** em guerra; **to go to ~** entrar em guerra; **to have been in the ~s** *UK* estar num estado deplorável.

warble ['wɔ:bl] *vi literary* [bird] trinar, chilrear.

war crime *n* crime *m* de guerra.

war criminal *n* criminoso *m*, -sa *f* de guerra.

war cry *n* [in battle] grito *m* de guerra.

ward [wɔ:d] *n* -**1.** [in hospital] ala *f* -**2.** *UK POL* distrito *m* eleitoral -**3.** *JUR* tutelado *m*, -da *f*.

ward off *vt fus* proteger-se de.

war dance *n* dança *f* de guerra.

warden ['wɔ:dn] *n* -**1.** [of park] guarda *mf* -**2.** *UK* [of youth hostel, hall of residence] diretor *m*, -ra *f* -**3.** *US* [prison governor] diretor *m*, -ra *f*.

warder ['wɔ:dəʳ] *n* [in prison] carcereiro *m*, -ra *f*.

ward of court *n* menor *mf* sob tutela judicial.

wardrobe ['wɔ:drəʊb] *n* -**1.** [piece of furniture] guarda-roupa *m*, armário *m* -**2.** [collection of clothes] guarda-roupa *m*.

wardrobe mistress *n UK* figurinista *f*.

warehouse ['weəhaʊs, *pl* -haʊzɪz] *n* armazém *m*, depósito *m*.

wares [weəz] *npl literary* mercadorias *fpl*.

warfare ['wɔ:feəʳ] *n* combate *m*; **gang ~** disputa *f* entre gangues.

war game *n* -**1.** [military exercise] manobra *f OR* exercício *m* militar -**2.** [game of strategy] jogo *m* de estratégia militar.

warhead ['wɔ:hed] *n MIL* ogiva *f*.

warily ['weərəlɪ] *adv* com desconfiança.

warlike ['wɔ:laɪk] *adj* guerreiro(ra), belicoso(sa).

warm [wɔ:m] ◇ *adj* -1. [gen] quente; **I'm ~ estou com calor; are you ~ enough?** não está com frio, certo? - 2. [clothing, blanket] que protege do frio - 3. [sound] cálido(da) - 4. [person] afetuoso(sa), caloroso(sa) - 5. [friendly - congratulations] efusivo(va); [- attitude, smile, handshake] caloroso(sa). ◇ *vt* [heat gently] aquecer.

➡ **warm over** *vt sep US* -1. [food] requentar - 2. [ideas] insistir em.

➡ **warm to** *vt fus* tomar simpatia por.

➡ **warm up** ◇ *vt sep* -1. [heat] esquentar - 2. [audience] esquentar. ◇ *vi* -1. [get warmer - gen] esquentar; [- person] esquentar-se - 2. [prepare - for exercise] aquecer, aquecer-se; [- for performance] preparar-se.

warm-blooded [-'blʌdɪd] *adj* de sangue quente.

war memorial *n* memorial *m* de guerra.

warm front *n* frente *f* quente.

warm-hearted [-'hɑ:tɪd] *adj* afetuoso(sa).

warmly ['wɔ:mlɪ] *adv* -1. [in warm clothes]: **to dress ~** agasalhar-se bem - 2. [in a friendly way] calorosamente, efusivamente.

warmness ['wɔ:mnɪs] *n (U)* [friendliness] cordialidade *f*.

warmonger ['wɔ:ˌmʌŋgəʳ] *n* belicista *mf*.

warmth [wɔ:mθ] *n (U)* -1. [of temperature] calor *m* - 2. [of welcome, smile, support] cordialidade *f*.

warm-up *n* [preparation] aquecimento *m*.

warn [wɔ:n] ◇ *vt* -1. [advise] advertir, prevenir; **to ~ sb of** *OR* **about sthg** advertir alguém de/sobre algo; **to ~ sb against doing sthg** advertir alguém sobre (os riscos de) fazer algo; **to ~ sb not to do sthg** avisar a alguém para que não faça algo - 2. [inform] avisar. ◇ *vi* [forecast]: **to ~ of sthg** alertar para a possbilidade de algo.

warning ['wɔ:nɪŋ] ◇ *adj* de advertência. ◇ *n* -1. [official caution] advertência *f* - 2. [prior notice] aviso *m*.

warning light *n* luz *f* de advertência.

warning triangle *n UK* triângulo *m* luminoso (do carro).

warp [wɔ:p] ◇ *n* [of cloth] urdidura *f*. ◇ *vt* -1. [wood] empenar - 2. [personality, mind] desvirtuar; [judgement] distorcer. ◇ *vi* [wood] empenar.

warpath ['wɔ:pɑ:θ] *n*: **to be/go on the ~** *fig* estar procurando briga.

warped [wɔ:pt] *adj* -1. [wood] empenado(da) - 2. [person] corrompido(da).

warrant ['wɒrənt] ◇ *n JUR* [written order] mandado *m* (judicial). ◇ *vt fml* [justify] merecer.

warrant officer *n* -1. *MIL* suboficial *mf* - 2. *NAUT* subtenente *mf*.

warranty ['wɒrəntɪ] (*pl* -ies) *n* garantia *f*.

warren ['wɒrən] *n* [of rabbit] toca *f*.

warring ['wɔ:rɪŋ] *adj* rival.

warrior ['wɒrɪəʳ] *n literary* guerreiro *m*, -ra *f*.

Warsaw ['wɔ:sɔ:] *n* Varsóvia; **in ~** em Varsóvia; **the ~ Pact** o Pacto de Varsóvia.

warship ['wɔ:ʃɪp] *n* navio *m* de guerra.

wart [wɔ:t] *n* verruga *f*.

wartime ['wɔ:taɪm] ◇ *adj* de guerra. ◇ *n (U)* tempos *mpl* de guerra; **in ~** em tempos de guerra.

war widow *n* viúva *f* de guerra.

wary ['weərɪ] (*compar* -ier, *superl* -iest) *adj* receoso(sa); **~ of sthg/of doing sthg** receoso(sa) de algo/de fazer algo.

was [*weak form* wəz, *strong form* wɒz] *pt* ▷ **be**.

wash [wɒʃ] ◇ *n* -1. [act of washing] lavada *f*; **to have a ~** lavar-se; **to give sthg a ~** dar uma lavada em algo - 2. [clothes to be washed] roupa *f* para lavar *OR* suja - 3. [from boat] esteira *f*. ◇ *vt* -1. [clean] lavar - 2. [subj: current, sea, rain] levar, arrastar. ◇ *vi* [clean o.s.] lavar-se.

➡ **wash away** *vt sep* levar, arrastar.

➡ **wash down** *vt sep* -1. [food] regar - 2. [clean] lavar.

➡ **wash out** *vt sep* -1. [stain, dye] tirar lavando - 2. [container] enxaguar.

➡ **wash up** ◇ *vt sep* -1. *UK* [dishes] lavar - 2. [subj: sea, river] trazer, arrastar. ◇ *vi* -1. *UK* [wash the dishes] lavar os pratos - 2. *US* [wash o.s.] lavar-se.

washable ['wɒʃəbl] *adj* lavável.

wash-and-wear *adj* que não precisa ser passado.

washbasin *UK* ['wɒʃˌbeɪsn], **washbowl** *US* ['wɒʃbəʊl] *n* lavatório *m*.

washcloth ['wɒʃˌklɒθ] *n US* toalha *f* de rosto.

washed-out [wɒʃt-] *adj* -1. [pale] desbotado(da) - 2. [exhausted] exausto(ta).

washed-up [wɒʃt-] *adj inf* acabado(da).

washer ['wɒʃəʳ] *n* -1. *TECH* arruela *f* - 2. [washing machine] lavadora *f* (de roupa).

washer-dryer *n* lavadora *f* e secadora.

washing ['wɒʃɪŋ] *n (U)* -1. [act] lavagem *f* - 2. [clothes] roupa *f* para lavar *OR* suja.

washing line *n* varal *m*.

washing machine *n* lavadora *f* (de roupa).

washing powder *n (U) UK* sabão *m* em pó.

Washington ['wɒʃɪŋtən] *n* -1. [state]: **~ State** Estado de Washington - 2. [city]: **~ D.C.** Washington D.C.

washing-up *n* -1. *UK* [crockery, pans *etc*] louça *f* para lavar *OR* suja - 2. [act]: **to do the ~** lavar a louça.

washing-up liquid *n UK* detergente *m*.

washout ['wɒʃaʊt] *n inf* fracasso *m*, desastre *m*.

washroom ['wɒʃrʊm] *n US* lavabo *m*.

wasn't [wɒznt] = **was not**.

wasp [wɒsp] *n* [insect] vespa *f*.

Wasp, WASP [wɒsp] (*abbr of* White Anglo-Saxon Protestant) *n inf* nos *Estados Unidos e no Canadá, pessoa branca de origem anglo-saxônica e protestante*.

waspish ['wɒspɪʃ] *adj* mordaz.

wastage ['weɪstɪdʒ] *n* desperdício *m*.

waste [weɪst] ◇ *adj* -1. [material, fuel] de sobra - 2. [area of land] improdutivo(va). ◇ *n* -1. [misuse] desperdício *m*; **to go to ~** perder-se; **a ~ of time** uma perda de tempo - 2. [refuse] resíduos *mpl*. ◇ *vt* [misuse] desperdiçar; **it would be ~d on me** eu não saberia aproveitar isso.

➡ **wastes** *npl literary* [wastelands] desertos *mpl*.

➡ **waste away** *vi* definhar.

wastebasket n US cesto m de lixo.
wasted adj [misused] perdido(da).
waste disposal unit n triturador m de lixo.
wasteful ['weɪstfʊl] adj: **to be very ~ to do sthg** ser muito desperdício fazer algo.
waste ground n (U) terra f improdutiva, descampados mpl.
wasteland ['weɪstˌlænd] n terreno m deserto.
waste paper n (U) papel m usado.
wastepaper basket [ˌweɪstˈpeɪpəʳ-], **wastepaper bin** [ˌweɪstˈpeɪpəʳ-], **wastebasket** US ['weɪstˌbɑːskɪt] n cesto m para papel.
watch [wɒtʃ] <> n -**1.** [timepiece] relógio m -**2.** [act of guarding]: **to keep ~** ficar de guarda; **to keep ~ on sb/sthg** vigiar alguém/algo -**3.** [guard] guarda mf. <> vt -**1.** [look at - television, programme, match] ver; [- scene, activity] contemplar -**2.** [spy on] vigiar -**3.** [be careful about] cuidar; **~ what you're doing** presta atenção no que você está fazendo; **~ it!** inf cuidado! <> vi [observe] observar.
◆ watch for vt fus esperar.
◆ watch out vi -**1.** [be careful]: **to ~ out (for sthg)** ter cuidado (com algo); **~ out!** cuidado! -**2.** [keep a lookout]: **to ~ out for sthg** prestar atenção em algo.
◆ watch over vt fus [look after] cuidar de.
watchdog ['wɒtʃdɒg] n -**1.** [dog] cão m de guarda -**2.** fig [organization] comissão que fiscaliza as empresas e impede que realizem ações ilegais ou irresponsáveis.
watchful ['wɒtʃfʊl] adj [vigilant] atento(ta); **to keep a ~ eye on sb/sthg** estar atento(ta) a alguém/algo.
watchmaker ['wɒtʃˌmeɪkəʳ] n relojoeiro m, -ra f.
watchman ['wɒtʃmən] (pl -men [-mən]) n segurança m, vigia m.
watchword ['wɒtʃwɜːd] n palavra f de ordem, lema m.
water ['wɔːtəʳ] <> n -**1.** [gen] água f; **to pour** OR **throw cold ~ on sthg** fig dar um banho de água fria em algo; **to tread ~** [in sea, pool] boiar mexendo as pernas; fig [do same thing] marcar passo; **that's ~ under the bridge** são águas passadas -**2.** [urine]: **to pass ~** tirar água do joelho. <> vt [plants, soil] regar. <> vi -**1.** [eyes] lacrimejar -**2.** [mouth]: **it makes my mouth ~** fico com água na boca.
◆ waters npl águas fpl.
◆ water down vt sep -**1.** [dilute] diluir -**2.** usu pej [moderate] suavizar, moderar.
water bed n colchão m d'água.
water bird n ave f aquática.
water biscuit n bolacha f de água e sal.
waterborne ['wɔːtəbɔːn] adj transmitido(da) pela água.
water bottle n garrafa f d'água, cantil m.
water buffalo n búfalo-da-índia m.
water cannon n canhão m de água.
water chestnut n castanha-d'água f.
water closet n dated w.c. m.
watercolour ['wɔːtəˌkʌləʳ] n aquarela f.
water-cooled [-ˌkuːld] adj refrigerado(da) a água.
watercourse ['wɔːtəkɔːs] n [river, stream] córrego m.
watercress ['wɔːtəkres] n (U) agrião m.

watered-down [ˌwɔːtəd-] adj usu pej suavizado(-da).
waterfall ['wɔːtəfɔːl] n queda-d'água f, cachoeira f.
waterfront ['wɔːtəfrʌnt] n orla f marítima.
water heater n aquecedor m de água.
waterhole ['wɔːtəhəʊl] n cacimba f.
watering can ['wɔːtərɪŋ-] n regador m.
water jump n valado m de água (nas corridas de cavalo).
water level n nível m de água.
water lily n nenúfar m.
waterline ['wɔːtəlaɪn] n NAUT linha-d'água f.
waterlogged ['wɔːtəlɒgd] adj -**1.** [land] alagado(-da) -**2.** [vessel] inundado(da).
water main n adutora f.
watermark ['wɔːtəmɑːk] n -**1.** [in paper] marca f d'água -**2.** [showing water level] linha-d'água f.
watermelon ['wɔːtəˌmelən] n melancia f.
water pipe n [in building] cano m de água.
water pistol n pistola f d'água.
water polo n (U) pólo m aquático.
waterproof ['wɔːtəpruːf] <> adj à prova d'água. <> n capa f impermeável; **~s** roupa f à prova d'água. <> vt impermeabilizar.
water rates npl UK tarifa f de água.
water-resistant adj resistente à água.
watershed ['wɔːtəʃed] n -**1.** GEOGR linha f divisória das águas -**2.** fig [turning point] divisor m de águas.
waterside ['wɔːtəsaɪd] <> adj ribeirinho(nha). <> n: **the ~** a orla.
water skiing n (U) esqui m aquático.
water softener n abrandador m de água.
water-soluble adj solúvel em água.
watersports npl esportes mpl aquáticos.
waterspout n tromba f d'água.
water supply n fornecimento m de água.
water table n (nível m do) lençol m freático.
water tank n caixa f d'água.
watertight ['wɔːtətaɪt] adj -**1.** [waterproof] hermético(ca) -**2.** fig [faultless] infalível.
water tower n torre f d'água.
waterway ['wɔːtəweɪ] n via f navegável, canal m.
waterworks ['wɔːtəwɜːks] (pl inv) n [building] instalações fpl para a distribuição de água.
watery ['wɔːtərɪ] adj -**1.** [food, drink] aguado(da) -**2.** [light, sun, moon] pálido(da).
watt [wɒt] n watt m.
wattage ['wɒtɪdʒ] n potência f em watts.
wave [weɪv] <> n -**1.** GEN onda f -**2.** [of people] leva f -**3.** [in hair] ondulação f -**4.** [gesture] aceno m. <> vt -**1.** [brandish - hand, flag] agitar; [- stick, pistol, gun] empunhar -**2.** [gesture to] fazer sinal para -**3.** [hair] ondular. <> vi -**1.** [with hand] abanar; **to ~ at** OR **to sb** abanar para alguém -**2.** [flag] tremular -**3.** [tree] balançar -**4.** [hair] ondular.
◆ wave aside vt sep fig [dismiss] rejeitar.
◆ wave down vt sep fazer sinal para parar.
wave band n faixa f de onda.
wavelength ['weɪvleŋθ] n comprimento m de onda; **to be on the same ~** fig estar em sintonia.

waver ['weɪvə'] *vi* **-1.** [gen] vacilar; **to ~ in sthg** hesitar em algo **-2.** [light, temperature] oscilar **-3.** [flame] tremer.

wavy ['weɪvɪ] (*compar* **-ier**, *superl* **-iest**) *adj* **-1.** [hair] ondulado(da) **-2.** [line] sinuoso(sa).

wax [wæks] ◇ *n* [gen] cera *f.* ◇ *vt* **-1.** [floor, table] encerar ; [skis] passar cera em **-2.** [legs] depilar com cera. ◇ *vi* **-1.** *dated or hum* [become] tornar -se; **to ~ and wane** aumentar e diminuir **-2.** [moon] crescer.

waxen ['wæksən] *adj* [face, complexion] pálido(da).

wax paper *n US* papel *m* encerado.

waxworks ['wækswɜ:ks] (*pl inv*) *n* [museum] museu *m* de cera.

way [weɪ] ◇ *n* **-1.** [means, method] maneira *f*, modo *m*; **~s and means** meios *mpl*; **to get** *or* **have one's ~** conseguir o que se quer; **to have everything one's own ~** ter o que se quer **-2.** [manner, style] jeito *m*, maneira *f*; **in the same ~** da mesma forma; **this/that ~** dessa/daquela forma; **in a ~** de certa forma *OR* maneira; **in a big/small ~** em grande/pequena escala; **to fall for sb in a big ~** apaixonar-se loucamente por alguém; **to be in a bad ~** ficar mal; **in no ~** de maneira alguma **-3.** [skill]: **to have a ~ with sb/sthg** ter jeito para lidar com alguém/algo; **to have a ~ of doing sthg** ter o costume de fazer algo **-4.** [thoroughfare, path] caminho *m*; **across** *OR* **over the ~** do outro lado da rua; '**give ~**' *UK AUT* dê passagem **-5.** [route leading to a specified place] caminho *m*; **do you know the ~ to the cathedral?** sabe como se faz para chegar na catedral?; **to lose one's ~** perder-se; **out of one's ~** [place] fora do caminho de alguém; **can you post this letter on the** *OR* **one's ~ (to the shops)** quando você for (fazer compras), pode colocar esta carta no correio?; **to be under ~** [ship] estar navegando; [project, meeting] estar em andamento; **to get under ~** [ship] zarpar; [project, meeting] estar em andamento; **to be in the ~** estar na passagem *OR* frente; **to be out of the ~** [finished] estar pronto(ta); [not blocking] **if you put your suitcase over there, it will be out of the ~** se colocar sua mala lá, ela não vai ficar atrapalhando; **to go out of one's ~ to do sthg** não poupar esforços para fazer algo; **to keep out of sb's ~** não cruzar o caminho de alguém; **keep out of the ~!** saia do caminho!; **to make one's ~** dirigir-se; **to make ~ for sb/sthg** abrir espaço para alguém/algo; **to stand in sb's ~** *fig* ficar no caminho de alguém; **to work one's ~** abrir caminho para chegar a **-6.** [route leading in a specified direction]: **come this ~** vem por aqui; **~ in** entrada; **~ out** saída **-7.** [side] lado *m*; **the right/wrong ~ round** do jeito certo/errado; **the right/wrong ~ up** com o lado certo/errado para cima **-8.** [distance]: **all the ~** todo o caminho; **most of the ~** quase todo o caminho; **a long ~** um longo caminho; **to go a long ~ towards doing sthg** *fig* contribuir muito no sentido de se fazer algo **-9.** *phr*: **to give ~** [under weight, pressure] ceder; **no ~!** de maneira alguma! ◇ *adv inf* [by far] muito; **it's ~ too big!** é enorme de grande!

➧ **ways** *npl* [customs, habits] costumes *mpl*, hábitos *mpl*.

➧ **by the way** *adv* a propósito, aliás.

➧ **by way of** *prep* **-1.** [via] passando por **-2.** [as a sort of] como forma de.

➧ **in the way of** *prep* [in the form of]: **what do you have in the of ~ red wine?** o que tem de vinho branco?

waylay [ˌweɪˈleɪ] (*pt & pp* **-laid**) *vt* abordar.

way of life *n* estilo *m* *OR* modo *m* de vida.

way-out *adj inf* arrojado(da).

wayside ['weɪsaɪd] *n* [roadside] beira *f* da estrada; **to fall by the ~** *fig* ir por água abaixo.

wayward ['weɪwəd] *adj* incorrigível.

WC (*abbr of* water closet) *n* WC *m*.

WCC (*abbr of* **World Council of Churches**) *n* conselho mundial de igrejas.

we [wi:] *pers pron pl* nós **~'re young** (nós) somos jovens.

weak [wi:k] *adj* **-1.** [gen] fraco(ca) **-2.** [lacking knowledge, skill]: **to be ~ on sthg** ser fraco(ca) em algo).

weaken ['wi:kn] ◇ *vt* **-1.** [gen] enfraquecer; *FIN* [devalue] desvalorizar **-2.** [debilitate] debilitar. ◇ *vi* **-1.** [person - physically] debilitar-se; [- morally] desgastar-se; **no signs of ~ing** nenhum sinal de desgaste **-2.** [influence, power] diminuir **-3.** [structure] enfraquecer-se **-4.** *FIN* [dollar, mark] desvalorizar-se.

weak-kneed [-'ni:d] *adj inf pej* sem iniciativa.

weakling ['wi:klɪŋ] *n pej* fraco *m*, -ca *f (de corpo e mente)*.

weakly ['wi:klɪ] *adv* fracamente.

weak-minded [-'maɪndɪd] *adj* fraco(ca) de caráter.

weakness ['wi:knɪs] *n* **-1.** (*U*) [of person - physical] fraqueza *f*; [- moral] ponto *m* fraco; **to have a ~ for sthg** ter um fraco por algo **-2.** [of government, structure, plan] debilidade *f* **-3.** *FIN* [of currency] fragilidade *f*.

weal [wi:l] *n* vergão *m*.

wealth [welθ] *n* **-1.** (*U*) [riches] riqueza *f* **-2.** [abundance]: **a ~ of sthg** uma profusão de algo.

wealth tax *n UK* imposto *m* sobre bens.

wealthy ['welθɪ] (*compar* **-ier**, *superl* **-iest**) *adj* rico(ca).

wean [wi:n] *vt* **-1.** [from mother's milk] desmamar **-2.** [from habit]: **to ~ sb from** *OR* **off sthg** afastar alguém gradualmente de algo.

weapon ['wepən] *n* arma *f*.

weaponry ['wepənrɪ] *n* (*U*) armamento *m*.

wear [weə'] (*pt* **wore**, *pp* **worn**) ◇ *n* **-1.** [type of clothes] roupa *f* **-2.** [damage] desgaste *m*; **~ and tear** desgaste **-3.** [use] uso *m*; **to be the worse for ~** [tired] estar um trapo; [drunk] estar num estado deplorável. ◇ *vt* **-1.** [gen] usar **-2.** [clothes] vestir **-3.** [shoes] calçar **-4.** [damage - gen] danificar; [- holes] abrir. ◇ *vi* **-1.** [deteriorate] gastar **-2.** [last]: **to ~ well/badly** durar bastante/pouco **-3.** *phr*: **to ~ thin** ficar gasto(ta).

➧ **wear away** ◇ *vt sep* desgastar. ◇ *vi* desgastar-se.

➧ **wear down** ◇ *vt sep* **-1.** [reduce size of] gastar **-2.** [weaken] esgotar. ◇ *vi* gastar, desgastar.

➧ **wear off** *vi* passar.

➧ **wear on** *vi* transcorrer.

➧ **wear out** ◇ *vt sep* **-1.** [clothing, machinery]

usar até estragar **-2.** [patience, strength, reserves] esgotar **-3.** [person] ficar esgotado(da). <> *vi* [clothing, shoes] gastar.

wearable ['weərəbl] *adj* que se pode usar.

wearily ['wɪərɪlɪ] *adv* com cansaço.

weariness ['wɪərɪnɪs] *n (U)* exaustão *f*, cansaço *m*.

wearing ['weərɪŋ] *adj* [exhausting] fatigante.

weary ['wɪərɪ] (*compar* -ier, *superl* -iest) *adj* **-1.** [exhausted] exausto(ta) **-2.** [fed up]: **to be ~ of sthg/of doing sthg** estar farto(ta) de algo/de fazer algo.

weasel ['wi:zl] *n* doninha *f*.

weather ['weðə'] <> *n* tempo *m*; **to make heavy ~ of sthg** complicar algo desnecessariamente; **to be under the ~** estar se sentindo um pouco indisposto(ta). <> *vt* [survive] superar. <> *vi* ser resistente.

weather-beaten [-ˌbi:tn] *adj* **-1.** [stone, rocks] desgastado(da) **-2.** [face, skin] desgastado(da) pelo tempo.

weathercock ['weðəkɒk] *n* cata-vento *m (em forma de galo)*.

weathered ['weðəd] *adj* **-1.** [face] marcado(da) **-2.** [wood, building, stone] deteriorado(da).

weather forecast *n* previsão *f* do tempo.

weatherman ['weðəmæn] (*pl* -men [-men]) *n* meteorologista *m*.

weather map *n* mapa *m* do tempo.

weatherproof ['weðəpru:f] *adj* **-1.** [clothing] impermeável **-2.** [building] resistente às intempéries.

weather report *n* previsão *f* do tempo.

weather ship *n* navio *m* meteorológico.

weather vane [-veɪn] *n* cata-vento *m*.

weave [wi:v] (*pt* wove, *pp* woven) <> *n* trama *f (do tecido).* <> *vt* **-1.** [using loom] tecer **-2.** [move along]: **to ~ one's way** costurar *(no trânsito).* <> *vi* [move]: **to ~ in and out** ziguezaguear.

weaver ['wi:və'] *n* tecelão *m*, -lã *f*.

web [web] *n* **-1.** [cobweb] teia *f* **-2.** *fig* [of lies, intrigue] rede *f* **-3.** COMPUT Web *f*, Rede *f*.

webbed [webd] *adj* palmado(da).

webbing ['webɪŋ] *n (U)* [material] tira *f* de tecido resistente.

web browser *n* COMPUT navegador *m*.

webcam ['webkæm] *n* câmera *f* web, webcam *f*.

webcast ['webkɑ:st] *n* transmissão *f* ao vivo pela Internet.

web designer *n* web designer *mf*.

web-footed [-'fʊtɪd] *adj* palmípede.

web page *n* página *f* da Web.

webphone ['webfəʊn] *n* webphone *m*.

website ['websaɪt] *n* site *m* da Web.

wed [wed] (*pt* & *pp* wed OR -ded) *literary* <> *vt* [marry] desposar. <> *vi* casar.

we'd [wi:d] = we had, we would.

Wed. (*abbr of* Wednesday) qua.

wedded ['wedɪd] *adj* [committed]: **~ to sthg** dedicado(da) a algo.

wedding ['wedɪŋ] *n* casamento *m (cerimônia).*

wedding anniversary *n* aniversário *m* de casamento.

wedding cake *n* bolo *m* de casamento.

wedding dress *n* vestido *m* de noiva.

wedding night *n* noite *f* de núpcias.

wedding reception *n* recepção *f* de casamento.

wedding ring *n* aliança *f*.

wedge [wedʒ] <> *n* **-1.** [gen] cunha *f*; **to drive a ~ between** piorar o relacionamento entre; **the thin end of the ~** a ponta do iceberg **-2.** [of cheese, cake, pie] fatia *f*, porção *f*. <> *vt* **-1.** [make fixed or steady] calçar com cunha **-2.** [squeeze, push] enfiar; **she sat ~d between us** ela se sentou enfiada entre nós.

wedlock ['wedlɒk] *n (U) literary* matrimônio *m*.

Wednesday ['wenzdɪ] *n* quarta-feira *f*; *see also* **Saturday**.

wee [wi:] <> *adj* Scot pequenino(na). <> *n inf* xixi *m*. <> *vi inf* fazer xixi.

weed [wi:d] <> *n* **-1.** [wild plant] erva *f* daninha **-2.** *UK inf* [feeble person] fracote *m*, -ta *f*. <> *vt* capinar.

⬥ **weed out** *vt sep* eliminar.

weeding ['wi:dɪŋ] *n (U)* capina *f*.

weedkiller ['wi:dˌkɪlə'] *n* herbicida *m*.

weedy ['wi:dɪ] (*compar* -ier, *superl* -iest) *adj* **-1.** [overgrown with weeds] com muito inço **-2.** *UK inf* [feeble] fracote(ta).

week [wi:k] *n* [gen] semana *f*; **during the ~** durante a semana; **in three ~s' time** dentro de três semanas; **a ~ on Saturday** OR **Saturday ~** sem ser este sábado, no outro; **a ~ last Saturday** uma semana antes de sábado.

weekday ['wi:kdeɪ] *n* dia *m* da semana.

weekend [ˌwi:k'end] *n* fim *m* de semana; **at the ~** no fim de semana.

weekend bag *n* bolsa *f* pequena *(para sair no fim de semana).*

weekly ['wi:klɪ] (*pl* -ies) <> *adj* semanal. <> *adv* semanalmente. <> *n* semanário *m*.

weeny *adj UK inf* pouquinho(nha); **a ~ bit** um pouquinho.

weep [wi:p] (*pt* & *pp* wept) <> *n*: **to have a ~** chorar. <> *vt* derramar. <> *vi* chorar.

weeping willow [ˌwi:pɪŋ-] *n* salgueiro-chorão *m*.

weepy ['wi:pɪ] (*compar* -ier, *superl* -iest) <> *adj* choroso(sa), triste. <> *n* [sentimental film] dramalhão *m*.

weft *n* trama *f*.

weigh [weɪ] <> *vt* **-1.** [gen] pesar **-2.** [raise]: **to ~ anchor** levantar âncora. <> *vi* [have specific weight] pesar.

⬥ **weigh down** *vt sep* **-1.** [physically] sobrecarregar **-2.** [mentally]: **to be ~ed down by** OR **with sthg** estar prostrado(da) por algo.

⬥ **weigh (up)on** *vt fus* oprimir.

⬥ **weigh out** *vt sep* pesar.

⬥ **weigh up** *vt sep* [situation, pros and cons] pesar; [person, opposition] fazer uma idéia de.

weighbridge ['weɪbrɪdʒ] *n UK* balança *f* para veículos.

weighing machine ['weɪɪŋ-] *n* balança *f*.

weight [weɪt] <> *n* **-1.** [gen] peso *m*; **to put on** OR **gain ~** engordar; **to lose ~** perder peso; **to take the ~ off one's feet** descansar **-2.** *fig* [power, influence]: **the ~ of public opinion** a opinião pública em peso; **to carry** ~ ter peso; **to pull one's** ~ fazer sua parte; **to throw one's** ~ **about** ficar dando ordens. <> *vt*: **to** ~ **sthg (down)** colocar lastro em algo.

weighted ['weɪtɪd] *adj*: **to be** ~ **in favour of/ against sb** pesar a favor de/contra alguém; **to be** ~ **in favour of/against sthg** pesar a favor de/ contra algo.

weighting ['weɪtɪŋ] *n (U)* pagamento adicional por se viver numa cidade com alto custo de vida.

weightlessness ['weɪtlɪsnɪs] *n (U)* imponderabilidade *f*, ausência *f* de peso.

weight lifter *n* levantador *m*, -ra *f* de peso, halterofilista *mf*.

weight lifting *n (U)* levantamento *m* de peso.

weight training *n (U)* levantamento *m* de peso.

weighty ['weɪtɪ] (*compar* **-ier**, *superl* **-iest**) *adj* [serious, important] de peso.

weir [wɪəʳ] *n* represa *f*.

weird [wɪəd] *adj* estranho(nha), esquisito(ta).

weirdo ['wɪədəʊ] (*pl* **-s**) *n inf* excêntrico *m*, -ca *f*.

welcome ['welkəm] <> *adj* **-1.** [gen] bem-vindo(-da); **to make sb** ~ receber alguém muito bem **-2.** [free]: **to be** ~ **to do sthg** ter toda a liberdade para fazer algo **-3.** [in reply to thanks]: **you're** ~ de nada. <> *n* acolhida *f*. <> *vt* [gen] acolher. <> *excl* bem-vindo(da)!

welcoming ['welkəmɪŋ] *adj* cordial.

weld [weld] <> *n* solda *f*. <> *vt* soldar.

welder ['weldəʳ] *n* soldador *m*, -ra *f*.

welfare ['welfeəʳ] <> *adj* de assistência social. <> *n* **-1.** [state of wellbeing] bem-estar *m* **-2.** *US* [income support] assistência *f* social (do governo).

welfare state *n* estado *m* de bem-estar social.

well [wel] (*compar* **better**, *superl* **best**) <> *adj* bem; **to get** ~ ficar bem; **all is** ~ está tudo bem; **(all)** ~ **and good** tudo bem; **just as** ~ ainda bem que. <> *adv* **-1.** [gen] bem; **to go** ~ ir bem; ~ **done!** muito bem!; ~ **and truly** completamente; **to be** ~ **in with sb** *inf* ser muito amiguinho(nha) de alguém; **you're** ~ **out of it** *inf* ainda bem que você caiu fora **-2.** [definitely, certainly] certamente, definitivamente; **it was** ~ **worth it** claro que valeu a pena; **she's** ~ **over 40** ela tem muito mais de 40 **-3.** [easily, possibly] (muito) bem. <> *n* [water, oil] poço *m*. <> *excl* **-1.** [in hesitation] bem!, bom! **-2.** [to correct o.s.] bem **-3.** [to express resignation]: **oh** ~! enfim! **-4.** [in surprise] quem diria!, olha só!
➤ **as well** *adv* [in addition] também; **you may/ might as** ~ **tell the truth** e por que você não conta a verdade?
➤ **as well as** *conj* além de.
➤ **well up** *vi* brotar.

we'll [wi:l] = **we shall**, **we will**.

well-adjusted *adj* [psychologically] sensato(ta).

well-advised [-əd'vaɪzd] *adj* prudente; **he/you would be** ~ **to do sthg** seria prudente que ele/ você fizesse algo.

well-appointed [-ə'pɔɪntɪd] *adj* bem equipado(-da).

well-balanced *adj* **-1.** [mentally healthy] equilibrado(da) **-2.** [nutritious] balanceado(da).

well-behaved [-bɪ'heɪvd] *adj* bem-comportado(-da).

wellbeing [,wel'bi:ɪŋ] *n (U)* bem-estar *m*.

well-bred [-'bred] *adj* bem-educado(da).

well-built *adj* [person] robusto(ta), fornido(da).

well-chosen *adj* bem escolhido(da).

well-disposed *adj*: **to be** ~ **to(wards) sb/sthg** ser favorável a alguém/algo.

well-done *adj* [thoroughly cooked] bem passado(-da).

well-dressed [-'drest] *adj* bem vestido(da).

well-earned [-'ɜːnd] *adj* merecido(da).

well-established *adj* **-1.** [custom, tradition] antigo(ga) **-2.** [company] de sólida reputação.

well-fed *adj* bem alimentado(da).

well-groomed [-'gruːmd] *adj* bem-apresentado(da).

wellhead *n* nascente *f*.

well-heeled [-hiːld] *adj inf* rico(ca).

wellies ['welɪz] *npl UK inf* botas *fpl* impermeáveis.

well-informed *adj*: **to be** ~ **(about/on sthg)** estar bem informado(da) (sobre algo).

wellington (boot) *n* bota *f* impermeável.

well-intentioned [-ɪn'tenʃnd] *adj* bem-intencionado(da).

well-kept *adj* **-1.** [garden, village] bem cuidado(da) **-2.** [secret] bem guardado(da).

well-known *adj* conhecido(da).

well-mannered [-'mænəd] *adj*: **to be** ~ ter boas maneiras.

well-meaning *adj* bem-intencionado(da).

well-nigh [-naɪ] *adv* quase.

well-off *adj* **-1.** [financially] rico(ca), próspero(ra) **-2.** [in a good position]: **to be** ~ **for sthg** estar bem de algo; **not to know when one is** ~ *inf* não se dar conta da própria sorte.

well-paid *adj* bem pago(ga).

well-preserved *adj fig* [person] bem conservado(da).

well-proportioned [-prə'pɔːʃnd] *adj* bem-proporcionado(da).

well-read [-'red] *adj* instruído(da), culto(ta).

well-rounded [-'raʊndɪd] *adj* [varied] variado(da).

well-spoken *adj*: **to be** ~ falar bem.

well-thought-of *adj* de boa reputação.

well-thought-out *adj* bem elaborado(da).

well-timed *adj* oportuno(na).

well-to-do *adj* abastado(da), de dinheiro.

well-wisher *n* simpatizante *mf*.

well-woman clinic *n UK* clínica para o bem-estar da mulher.

welly (*pl* **-ies**) (*abbr of* **wellington**) *n UK inf* botas *fpl* de borracha.

we'll [wi:l] = **we shall**, **we will**.

Welsh [welʃ] <> *adj* galês(esa). <> *n (U)* [language] galês *m*. <> *npl*: **the** ~ os galeses.

Welshman ['welʃmən] (*pl* **-men** [-mən]) *n* galês *m*.

Welsh rarebit [-'reəbɪt] *n* torrada coberta com queijo derretido.

Welshwoman ['welʃ,wʊmən] (*pl* **-women** [-,wɪmɪn]) *n* galesa *f*.

welter ['weltəʳ] *n* confusão *f*, rebuliço *m*.

welterweight ['weltəweɪt] *n* peso *m* meio-médio.

wend [wend] *vt literary*: **to ~ one's way** dirigir-se vagarosamente.

wendy house ['wendɪ-] *n UK* casa *f* de bonecas.

went [went] *pt* ⊳ **go**.

wept [wept] *pt & pp* ⊳ **weep**.

were [wɜːʳ] *vb* ⊳ **be**.

we're [wɪəʳ] = **we are**.

weren't [wɜːnt] = **were not**.

werewolf ['wɪəwʊlf] (*pl* **-wolves** [-wʊlvz]) *n* lobisomem *m*.

west [west] ⟨⟩ *n* **-1.** [direction] oeste *m*; **the ~** o oeste **-2.** [region]: **the ~** o Oeste. ⟨⟩ *adj* oeste. ⟨⟩ *adv* para o oeste; **~ of** ao oeste de.
➡ **West** *n POL*: **the West** o Ocidente.

West Bank *n*: **the ~** a Cisjordânia; **on the ~** na Cisjordânia.

westbound ['westbaʊnd] *adj* em direção ao oeste.

West Country *n*: **the ~** o sudoeste da Inglaterra.

westerly ['westəlɪ] *adj* **-1.** [towards the west]: **in a ~ direction** para o oeste **-2.** [in the west] ocidental **-3.** [from the west] oeste.

western ['westən] ⟨⟩ *adj* **-1.** [part of country, continent] ocidental **-2.** *POL* [relating to the West] do Ocidente. ⟨⟩ *n* [book, film] western *m*.

Westerner ['westənəʳ] *n* **-1.** *POL* [inhabitant of the West] ocidental *mf* **-2.** [inhabitant of west of country] habitante *mf* do oeste.

westernize, -ise ['westənaɪz] *vt* ocidentalizar.

Western Isles *npl* Western Isles.

Western Samoa *n* Samoa Ocidental; **in ~** em Samoa Ocidental.

West German ⟨⟩ *adj* da Alemanha Ocidental. ⟨⟩ *n* [person] alemão *m*, -mã *f* ocidental.

West Germany *n*: (former) **~** a (antiga) Alemanha Ocidental; **in ~** na Alemanha Ocidental.

West Indian ⟨⟩ *adj* antilhano(na). ⟨⟩ *n* [person] antilhano *m*, -na *f*.

West Indies [-'ɪndɪːz] *npl*: **the ~** as Antilhas; **in the ~** nas Antilhas.

Westminster ['westmɪnstəʳ] *n* **-1.** [area] Westminster **-2.** *fig* [British parliament] parlamento *m* britânico.

West Virginia *n* Virgínia Ocidental.

westward ['westwəd] ⟨⟩ *adj* para o oeste. ⟨⟩ *adv* = **westwards**.

westwards ['westwədz] *adv* para o oeste.

wet [wet] (*compar* **-ter**, *superl* **-test**, *pt & pp* **wet** *OR* **-ted**, *cont* **-ting**) ⟨⟩ *adj* **-1.** [damp] úmido(da) **-2.** [soaked] molhado(da) **-3.** [rainy] chuvoso(sa) **-4.** [ink, concrete] fresco(ca); **' ~ paint'** tinta fresca **-5.** *UK inf pej* [weak, feeble] fraco(ca). ⟨⟩ *n inf UK POL* político conservador moderado. ⟨⟩ *vt* **-1.** [soak] molhar

-2. [dampen] umedecer **-3.** [bed]: **to ~ the bed** fazer xixi na cama; **to ~ o.s.** mijar-se.

wet blanket *n inf pej* desmancha-prazeres *mf inv*.

wet-look *adj* brilhante.

wetness ['wetnɪs] *n* **-1.** [dampness] umidade *f* **-2.** *UK inf pej* [feebleness] fraqueza *f*.

wet nurse *n* ama-de-leite *f*.

wet rot *n* [decay] apodrecimento *f* (*devido à umidade*).

wet suit *n* roupa *f* de mergulho.

WEU (*abbr of* **Western European Union**) *n* união de países da Europa Ocidental formada em 1955 para elaboração de políticas de defesa.

we've [wiːv] = **we have**.

whack [wæk] *inf* ⟨⟩ *n* **-1.** [hit] pancada *f* **-2.** *inf* [share]: **one's ~ of the profits** a sua parte nos lucros. ⟨⟩ *vt* dar pancadas em.

whacked [wækt] *adj UK inf* [exhausted] demolido(da).

whacky *adj* = **wacky**.

whale [weɪl] *n* [animal] baleia *f*; **to have a ~ of a time** *inf* divertir-se para valer.

whaling ['weɪlɪŋ] *n (U)* caça *f* às baleias.

wham [wæm] *excl inf* bum!

wharf [wɔːf] (*pl* **-s** *OR* **wharves** [wɔːvz]) *n* cais *m inv*.

what [wɒt] ⟨⟩ *adj* **-1.** [in questions] que; **~ colour is it?** de que cor é?; **he asked me ~ colour it was** ele perguntou-me de que cor era. **-2.** [in exclamations] que; **~ a surprise!** mas que surpresa!; **~ a beautiful day!** mas que dia lindo! ⟨⟩ *pron* **-1.** [in questions] o que; **~ is going on?** o que é que está acontecendo?; **~ is that?** o que é isso?; **~ is that thing called?** como é que se chama aquilo?; **~ is the problem?** qual é o problema?; **she asked me ~ had happened** ela perguntou-me o que é que tinha acontecido; **she asked me ~ I was thinking about** ela me perguntou em que eu estava pensando. **-3.** [introducing relative clause] o que; **I didn't see ~ happened** não vi o que aconteceu; **you can't have ~ you want** você não pode ter o que quer. **-4.** [in phrases]: **~ for?** para quê?; **~ about going out for a meal?** que tal irmos comer fora? ⟨⟩ *excl* quê!

whatever [wɒt'evəʳ] ⟨⟩ *adj* qualquer; **eat ~ food you find** coma o que encontrar; **no chance ~** nem a mais remota chance; **nothing ~** absolutamente nada. ⟨⟩ *pron* **-1.** [no matter what] o que quer que; **~ they may offer** ofereçam o que oferecerem **-2.** [indicating surprise]: **~ did you say?** o que foi que você disse? **-3.** [indicating lack of precision]: **~ that is** seja lá o que for; **or ~** ou o que seja.

whatnot ['wɒtnɒt] *n inf* [something, anything]: **and ~** e coisas assim.

what's-her-name *n inf* a tal fulana.

what's-his-name *n inf* o tal fulano.

whatsit *n inf* treco *m*.

whatsoever [ˌwɒtsəʊ'evəʳ] *adj* absolutamente.

wheat [wiːt] *n* trigo *m*.

wheat germ *n (U)* germe *m* de trigo.

wheatmeal ['wi:tmi:l] *n (U)* farinha *f* de trigo integral.

wheedle ['wi:dl] *vt*: **to** ~ **sb into doing sthg** bajular alguém para que faça algo; **to** ~ **sthg out of sb** conseguir algo de alguém por bajulação.

wheel [wi:l] <> *n* **-1.** [of bicycle, car, train] roda *f* **-2.** AUT [steering wheel] direção *f* (do carro). <> *vt* empurrar *(algo com rodas)*. <> *vi* **-1.** [move in circle] dar voltas **-2.** [turn round]: **to** ~ **round** dar a volta.

wheelbarrow ['wi:l,bærəʊ] *n* carrinho *m* de mão.

wheelbase *n* distância *f* entre eixos.

wheelchair ['wi:l,tʃeəᶦ] *n* cadeira *f* de rodas.

wheel clamp *n* grampo posto nas rodas de veículo estacionado em lugar proibido.

➤ **wheel-clamp** *vt* grampear a roda *(de veículo mal estacionado)*.

wheeler-dealer ['wi:lə'-] *n pej* negociante *mf* astuto, -ta.

wheelie bin *n UK* lixeira *f* com rodas.

wheeling and dealing ['wi:lɪŋ-] *n (U) pej* negócios *m* escusos.

wheeze [wi:z] <> *n* [sound of wheezing] respiração *f* ofegante. <> *vi* resfolegar.

wheezy ['wi:zɪ] (*compar* -ier, *superl* -iest) *adj* resfolegante.

whelk [welk] *n* caramujo *m*.

when *adv* & *conj* quando.

whenever [wen'evəᶦ] <> *conj* sempre que. <> *adv* **-1.** [indicating surprise] quando é que **-2.** [indicating lack of precision]: **or** ~ ou quando quiser.

where [weəᶦ] *adv* & *conj* onde.

whereabouts [*adv* ,weərə'baʊts, *n* 'weərəbaʊts] <> *adv* por onde. <> *npl* paradeiro *m*.

whereas [weər'æz] *conj* enquanto que, ao passo que.

whereby [weə'baɪ] *conj fml* através do (da) qual, pelo(la) qual.

wheresoever *conj* & *adv* = **wherever**.

whereupon [,weərə'pɒn] *conj fml* depois do que.

wherever [weər'evəᶦ] <> *conj* **-1.** [no matter where, everywhere] em todo o lugar que **-2.** [anywhere, in whatever place] onde quer que; **sit** ~ **you like** senta onde quiser **-3.** [in any situation] sempre que **-4.** [indicating ignorance]: ~ **that is** seja lá onde for. <> *adv* **-1.** [indicating surprise] onde é que **-2.** [indicating lack of precision] em qualquer lugar.

wherewithal ['weəwɪðɔ:l] *n fml*: **to have the** ~ **to do sthg** dispor dos meios necessários para fazer algo.

whet [wet] (*pt* & *pp* **-ted**, *cont* **-ting**) *vt*: **to** ~ **sb's appetite (for sthg)** despertar o interesse de alguém (por algo).

whether ['weðəᶦ] *conj* **-1.** [indicating choice, doubt] se **-2.** [no matter if]: ~ **I want to or not** queira ou não queira.

whew [hwju:] *excl* uau!

whey *n (U)* soro *m* do leite.

which [wɪtʃ] <> *adj* [in questions] qual, que; ~ **room do you want?** qual é o quarto que você quer?, que quatro você quer?; ~ **one?** qual (deles)?; **she**

asked me ~ **room I wanted** ela perguntou-me qual *or* que quarto eu queria <> *pron* **-1.** [in questions] qual; ~ **one is the cheapest?** qual é o mais barato?; ~ **one do you prefer?** qual (é o que) você prefere?; **he asked me** ~ **one I preferred** ele perguntou-me qual é que eu preferia **-2.** [introducing relative clause: subject]: **I can't remember** ~ **was better** não me lembro qual era o melhor **-3.** [introducing relative clause: object, after prep] que; **the sofa on** ~ **I'm sitting** o sofá em que estou sentado **-4.** [to refer back to a clause] o.que; **he's late,** ~ **annoys me** ele está atrasado, o que me aborrece; **he's always late,** ~ **I don't like** ele está sempre atrasado, coisa que eu detesto

whichever [wɪtʃ'evəᶦ] <> *adj* **-1.** [no matter which]: ~ **route you take** por qualquer dos caminhos que você for **-2.** [the one which]: ~ **colour you prefer** a cor que preferir. <> *pron* **-1.** [the one which] o (a) que, os (as) que **-2.** [no matter which one] qualquer um(ma).

whiff [wɪf] *n* **-1.** [smell] cheirinho *m* **-2.** *fig* [sign] cheiro *m*.

while [waɪl] <> *n* algum tempo *m*; **it's a long** ~ **since I did that** faz muito tempo que não faço isso; **for a** ~ por algum tempo; **after a** ~ depois de algum tempo; **to be worth one's** ~ valer a pena para alguém. <> *conj* **-1.** [as long as, during the time that] enquanto **-2.** [whereas] enquanto (que), ao passo que.

➤ **while away** *vt sep* passar o tempo *(de forma agradável)*.

whilst [waɪlst] *conj* = **while**.

whim [wɪm] *n* capricho *m*.

whimper ['wɪmpəᶦ] <> *n* choradeira *f*. <> *vt* lamuriar-se. <> *vi* choramingar.

whimsical ['wɪmzɪkl] *adj* **-1.** [idea, story] fantasioso(sa) **-2.** [look] estranho(nha) **-3.** [remark] esquisito(ta).

whine [waɪn] <> *n* **-1.** [child] gemido *m* **-2.** [dog] ganido *m* **-3.** [siren] grito *m* **-4.** [engine] zunido *m*. <> *vi* **-1.** [child] gemer **-2.** [dog] ganir **-3.** [siren] gritar **-4.** [engine] zunir **-5.** [complain]: **to** ~ **(about sb/sthg)** queixar-se (de alguém/algo).

whinge [wɪndʒ] (*cont* **whingeing**) *vi UK*: **to** ~ **(about sb/sthg)** queixar-se (de alguém/algo).

whip [wɪp] (*pt* & *pp* **-ped**, *cont* **-ping**) <> *n* **-1.** [for hitting] chicote *m* **-2.** *UK* POL membro do partido político responsável por fazer com que seus correligionários compareçam a votações importantes no parlamento. <> *vt* **-1.** [beat with whip] chicotear **-2.** *fig* [subj: rain, wind] açoitar **-3.** [take quickly]: **to** ~ **sthg out/off** arrancar algo de **-4.** CULIN bater.

➤ **whip up** *vt sep* [provoke] incitar.

whiplash injury ['wɪplæʃ-] *n* lesão *f* por efeito chicote.

whipped cream [wɪpt-] *n* creme *m* batido.

whippet ['wɪpɪt] *n* galgo *m*.

whip-round *n UK inf*: **to have a** ~ fazer uma vaquinha.

whirl [wɜ:l] <> *n* **-1.** [rotating movement] redemoinho *m*; **to be in a** ~ estar totalmente confuso(sa) **-2.** *fig* [flurry, round] turbilhão *m*, agitação *f* **-3.** *phr*: **let's give it a** ~ *inf* vamos tentar. <> *vt*: **to** ~

sb/sthg round rodopiar alguém/algo. ◇ *vi* **-1.** [move around] rodopiar **- 2.** *fig* [be confused, excited] dar voltas.

whirlpool ['wɜ:lpu:l] *n* redemoinho *m*.

whirlwind ['wɜ:lwɪnd] ◇ *adj fig* vertiginoso(sa). ◇ *n* furacão *m*.

whirr [wɜ:ʳ] ◇ *n* zumbido *m*. ◇ *vi* zumbir.

whisk [wɪsk] ◇ *n CULIN* batedeira *f.* ◇ *vt* **-1.** [put or take quickly - away]: **to ~ sb/sthg away** levar alguém/algo rapidamente; [- out]: **to ~ sthg out** tirar algo rapidamente **- 2.** *CULIN* bater.

whisker ['wɪskəʳ] *n* [of animal] bigode *m*.

  ◆ **whiskers** *npl* [of man] suíças *fpl*.

whiskey (*pl* **whiskeys**) *n* uísque *m* (de cevada).

whisky *UK* (*pl* **-ies**), **whiskey** *US* & *Irish* (*pl* **-s**) ['wɪskɪ] *n* uísque *m*.

whisper ['wɪspəʳ] ◇ *n* sussurro *m*, cochicho *m*. ◇ *vt* sussurrar, cochichar. ◇ *vi* sussurrar, cochichar.

whispering ['wɪspərɪŋ] *n (U)* cochichos *mpl*, sussurros *mpl*.

whist [wɪst] *n (U)* uíste *m*.

whistle ['wɪsl] ◇ *n* **-1.** [gen] apito *m* **- 2.** [through lips] assobio *m* **- 3.** [of bird] piado *m*, pio *m* **- 4.** [of kettle] chiar *m*. ◇ *vt* assobiar. ◇ *vi* **-1.** [gen] assobiar; **to ~ at sb** assobiar para alguém **- 2.** [using whistle] apitar **- 3.** [bird] piar **- 4.** [kettle] chiar.

whistle-stop tour *n* percurso rápido com várias paradas no caminho.

whit *n*: **not a ~** nem um pouco.

Whit [wɪt] *n UK* Pentecostes *m*.

white [waɪt] ◇ *adj* **-1.** [gen] branco(ca); **to go** *OR* **turn ~** [hair] ficar branco(ca); [face] empalidecer **- 2.** [milky] com leite. ◇ *n* **-1.** [gen] branco *m* **- 2.** [person] branco *m*, -ca *f* **- 3.** [of egg] clara *f.*

  ◆ **whites** *npl* roupas *fpl* brancas.

white blood cell *n* glóbulo *m* branco.

whiteboard ['waɪtbɔ:d] *n* quadro *m* branco.

white Christmas *n* Natal *m* com neve.

white-collar *adj* de colarinho branco.

white elephant *n fig* elefante *m* branco.

white goods *npl* [household machines] eletrodomésticos *mpl*.

white-haired [-'heəd] *adj* de cabelos brancos.

Whitehall ['waɪthɔ:l] *n* Whitehall.

white horses *npl UK* [on sea] crista *f* da onda.

white-hot *adj* incandescente.

White House *n*: **the ~** a Casa Branca.

white knight *n* pessoa ou organização que auxilia uma empresa em dificuldades.

white lie *n* mentira *f* branca.

white light *n* luz *f* branca.

white magic *n (U)* magia *f* branca.

white meat *n (U)* carne *f* branca.

whiten ['waɪtn] ◇ *vt* **-1.** [clothes] branquear **- 2.** [shoes] clarear **- 3.** [wall] caiar. ◇ *vi* branquear.

whitener ['waɪtnəʳ] *n* **-1.** [for clothes] alvejante *m* **- 2.** [for shoes] branqueador *m*.

whiteness ['waɪtnɪs] *n (U)* brancura *f.*

white noise *n* ruído *m* branco.

whiteout ['waɪtaʊt] *n* perda total de visibilidade devido à neve, whiteout *m*.

white paper *n POL* relatório *m* oficial do governo.

white sauce *n (U)* molho *m* branco.

White Sea *n*: **the ~** o Mar Branco.

white spirit *n (U) UK* aguarrás *f inv*.

white-tie *adj* de gala.

white trash *n US pej* [people] branquelo *m*, -la *f.*

whitewash ['waɪtwɒʃ] ◇ *n* **-1.** *(U)* [paint] (água *f* de) cal *f* **- 2.** *pej* [cover-up] disfarce *m*. ◇ *vt* **-1.** [paint] caiar, pintar com cal **- 2.** *pej* [cover up] disfarçar.

whitewater rafting ['waɪt,wɔ:təʳ-] *n* rafting *m*.

white wedding *n* casamento *m* tradicional.

whiting ['waɪtɪŋ] (*pl inv OR* **-s**) *n* merlúcio *m*.

Whit Monday *n* segunda-feira *f* de Pentecostes.

Whitsun ['wɪtsn] *n* [day] Pentecostes *m inv*.

whittle ['wɪtl] *vt*: **to ~ sthg away** *OR* **down** reduzir algo gradualmente.

whiz (*pt* & *pp* **-zed**, *cont* **-zing**), **whizz** [wɪz] ◇ *n inf*: **to be a ~ at sthg** ser uma fera em algo. ◇ *vi* passar zunindo.

whiz(z) kid *n inf* (menino *m*) prodígio *m*, (menina *f*) prodígia *f.*

who [hu:] *pron* **-1.** *(in direct, indirect questions)* quem **- 2.** *(in relative clauses)* que.

WHO (*abbr of* **World Health Organization**) *n* OMS *f.*

who'd [hu:d] = **who had**, **who would**.

whodu(n)nit [ˌhu:'dʌnɪt] *n inf* romance *m* policial.

whoever [hu:'evəʳ] *pron* **-1.** [gen] quem quer que; **I don't like him, ~ he is** não gosto dele, quem quer que ele seja **- 2.** [indicating surprise] quem será que; **~ can that be?** quem poderá ser?

whole [həʊl] ◇ *adj* **-1.** [entire, complete] inteiro(ra) **- 2.** [for emphasis]: **a ~ lot of** muitos e muitos, muitas e muitas, ; **a ~ lot bigger** muitíssimo maior. ◇ *adv* [for emphasis] totalmente. ◇ *n* **-1.** [all, entirety]: **the ~ of the summer** o verão todo **- 2.** [unit, complete thing] todo *m*.

  ◆ **as a whole** *adv* como um todo.

  ◆ **on the whole** *adv* em geral.

wholefood ['həʊlfu:d] *n UK* comida *f* integral.

whole-hearted [-'hɑ:tɪd] *adj* sincero(ra).

wholemeal *UK* ['həʊlmi:l], **whole wheat** *US adj* integral.

wholemeal bread *n UK* pão *m* integral.

whole note *n US* semibreve *f.*

wholesale ['həʊlseɪl] ◇ *adj* **-1.** [bulk] por atacado **- 2.** *pej* [excessive - slaughter] exagerado(da); [- destruction] em massa, em grande escala; [- theft] indiscriminado(da). <> *adv* **-1.** [in bulk] por atacado **- 2.** *pej* [excessively] indiscriminadamente.

wholesaler [ˈhəʊlˌseɪləʳ] *n* atacadista *mf*.

wholesome [ˈhəʊlsəm] *adj* saudável.

whole wheat *adj US* = wholemeal.

who'll [huːl] = who will.

wholly [ˈhəʊlɪ] *adv* totalmente, completamente.

whom [huːm] *pron fml* **-1.** *(in direct, indirect questions)* quem **- 2.** *(in relative clauses)* que; **to** ~ a quem.

whoop [wuːp] <> *n* grito *m*; **a** ~ **of glee** um grito de alegria. <> *vi* gritar.

whoopee [wʊˈpiː] *excl* hip hurra!

whooping cough [ˈhuːpɪŋ-] *n (U)* coqueluche *f*.

whoops [wʊps] *excl* opa!

whoosh [wʊʃ] *inf* <> *n* [sudden rush - of air] rajada *f*; [- of water] esguicho *m*. <> *vi* **-1.** [air] soprar forte **- 2.** [water] esguichar.

whop (*pt* & *pp* **-ped**, *cont* **-ping**) *vt inf* [defeat] derrubar, derrotar.

whopper [ˈwɒpəʳ] *n inf* **-1.** [something big] exagero *m* **- 2.** [lie] mentira *f* deslavada.

whopping [ˈwɒpɪŋ] *inf* <> *adj* tremendo(da), enorme. <> *adv*: **a** ~ **great lie** uma mentira enorme.

whore [hɔːʳ] *n pej* puta *f*, vagabunda *f*.

who're [ˈhuːəʳ] = who are.

whose [huːz] <> *pron* de quem <> *adj* **-1.** *(in direct, indirect questions)* de quem; ~ **book is this?** de quem é este livro? **- 2.** *(in relative clauses)* cujo(ja).

whosoever [ˌhuːsəʊˈevəʳ] *pron literary*: ~ **it is** quem quer que seja, seja quem for.

who's who [huːz-] *n* [book] quem é quem *m*, *livro contendo informações sobre as pessoas mais ricas e famosas do mundo*.

who've [huːv] = who have.

why [waɪ] <> *adv* & *conj* porque; ~ **not?** porque não?; **I know** ~ **Tom isn't here** eu sei porque é que o Tom não está; **tell me** ~ (diga-me) porquê.

WI <> *n* (*abbr of* **Women's Institute**) *associação britânica de mulheres que se reúnem para atividades sociais e culturais, principalmente em áreas rurais*. <> **-1.** *abbr of* **West Indies - 2.** *abbr of* **Wisconsin**.

wick [wɪk] *n* **-1.** pavio *m* **- 2.** *phr*: **to get on sb's** ~ *UK inf* dar nos nervos de alguém.

wicked [ˈwɪkɪd] *adj* **-1.** [evil] malvado(da) **- 2.** [mischievous, devilish] perverso(sa) **- 3.** *inf* [very good] bárbaro(ra).

wickedness *n* **-1.** [evil] maldade *f* **- 2.** [mischievousness] perversidade *f*.

wicker [ˈwɪkəʳ] *adj* de vime.

wickerwork [ˈwɪkəwɜːk] <> *n (U)* trabalho *m* em vime. <> *comp* de vime.

wicket [ˈwɪkɪt] *n CRICKET* **-1.** [stumps] meta *f* **- 2.** [pitch] wicket *m* **- 3.** [dismissal] demissão *f* do batedor.

wicket keeper *n* guarda-meta *mf*.

wide [waɪd] <> *adj* **-1.** [gen] largo(ga); **it's 6 metres** ~ tem 6 metros de largura; **how** ~ **is the room?** qual é a largura da sala? **- 2.** [eyes] arregalado(da) **- 3.** [coverage, selection] amplo(pla) **- 4.** [implications, issues] maior **- 5.** [shot, punch, ball] desviado(da). <> *adv* **-1.** [as far as possible] amplamente; **open** ~! abra bem! **- 2.** [off-target]: **to go** ~ desviar-se.

wide-angle lens *n PHOT* (objetiva *f*) grande-angular *f*.

wide-awake *adj* desperto(ta), bem acordado(da).

wide boy *n UK inf pej* pilantra *m*.

wide-eyed [-ˈaɪd] *adj* **-1.** [surprised, frightened] de olhos arregalados **- 2.** [innocent, gullible] ingênuo(nua).

widely [ˈwaɪdlɪ] *adv* **-1.** [gen] muito; ~ **known** amplamente conhecido(da) **- 2.** [considerably] bastante.

widen [ˈwaɪdn] <> *vt* **-1.** [make broader] alargar **- 2.** [increase scope or variety of] ampliar **- 3.** [gap, difference] aumentar. <> *vi* **-1.** [become broader] alargar **- 2.** [increase in scope or variety] estender **- 3.** [eyes] arregalar **- 4.** [gap, difference] aumentar.

wide open *adj* **-1.** [window, door] escancarado(da) **- 2.** [eyes] arregalado(da) **- 3.** [spaces] extenso(sa).

wide-ranging [-ˈreɪndʒɪŋ] *adj* de amplo alcance.

widescreen TV [ˈwaɪdskriːn-] *n* tv *f* widescreen.

widespread [ˈwaɪdspred] *adj* disseminado(da), geral.

widow [ˈwɪdəʊ] *n* viúva *f*.

widowed [ˈwɪdəʊd] *adj* viúvo(va).

widower [ˈwɪdəʊəʳ] *n* viúvo *m*.

width [wɪdθ] *n* **-1.** [breadth] largura *f*; **in** ~ de largura **- 2.** [in swimming pool] largura *f*; **she swam 20** ~ **s** ela nadou 20 piscinas.

widthways [ˈwɪdθweɪz] *adv* na transversal, transversalmente.

wield [wiːld] *vt* **-1.** [weapon] manejar **- 2.** [power] controlar, exercer.

wife [waɪf] (*pl* **wives**) *n* esposa *f*.

wig [wɪg] *n* peruca *f*.

wiggle [ˈwɪgl] *inf* <> *n* **-1.** [movement] balanço *m* **- 2.** [wavy line] linha *f* ondulada. <> *vt* balançar, agitar. <> *vi* balançar.

wiggly [ˈwɪglɪ] (*compar* **-ier**, *superl* **-iest**) *adj inf* **-1.** [wavy] ondulado(da) **- 2.** [movable] solto(ta).

wigwam [ˈwɪgwæm] *n* tenda *f* indígena (*em forma de cone*).

wild [waɪld] <> *adj* **-1.** [animal, land] selvagem **- 2.** [person, dog, attack] violento(ta) **- 3.** [plant] silvestre **- 4.** [scenery, landscape] agreste **- 5.** [sea] revolto(ta) **- 6.** [weather] turbulento(ta) **- 7.** [laughter, crowd, applause] frenético(ca); **the crowd went** ~ a multidão foi à loucura; **to run** ~ descontrolar-se **- 8.** [hair] desarrumado(da) **- 9.** [eyes, features] inquieto(ta) agitado(ta) **- 10.** [dream, scheme] maluco(ca) **- 11.** [estimate]: **a** ~ **guess** uma vaga idéia **- 12.** *inf* [very enthusiastic]: **to be** ~ **about sthg** ser louco(ca) por algo. <> *n*: **in the** ~ na natureza, em seu habitat natural.

➡ **wilds** *npl*: **the** ~ **s** as regiões selvagens.

wild card *n COMPUT* **-1.** curinga *m* **- 2.** [person]: **to be a** ~ ser completamente imprevisível.

wildcat [ˈwaɪldkæt] *n* gato-mourisco *m*.

wildcat strike *n* greve-relâmpago *f*.

wildebeest [ˈwɪldɪbiːst] (*pl inv OR* **-s**) *n* gnu *m*.

wilderness [ˈwɪldənɪs] *n* **-1.** [barren land] sertão *m* **- 2.** [overgrown land] matagal *m* **- 3.** *fig* [unimportant place]: **in the political** ~ no ostracismo político.

wildfire [ˈwaɪldˌfaɪəʳ] *n*: **to spread like** ~

espalhar-se como fogo na mata.

wild flower *n* flor *f* silvestre.

wildfowl *n* aves *fpl* silvestres.

wild-goose chase *n inf* busca *m* infrutífera.

wildlife ['waɪldlaɪf] *n (U)* fauna *f*.

wildly ['waɪldlɪ] *adv* **-1.** [enthusiastically, fanatically] freneticamente **-2.** [without reason or control] inadvertidamente **-3.** [very] extremamente **-4.** [menacingly] ameaçadoramente.

wild rice *n (U)* arroz *m* silvestre.

wild west *n inf*: the ~ o oeste selvagem.

wiles [waɪlz] *npl* artimanhas *fpl*.

wilful *UK*, **willful** *US* ['wɪlfʊl] *adj* **-1.** [determined] que sempre apronta das suas **-2.** [deliberate] proposital, intencional.

will¹ [wɪl] ⋄ *n* **-1.** [wish, desire] vontade *f*; **against my** ~ contra a minha vontade **-2.** [document] testamento *m*.

will² [wɪl] *aux vb* **-1.** [expressing future tense]: **it** ~ **be difficult to repair** vai ser difícil de consertar; ~ **you be here next Friday?** você vai estar aqui na próxima sexta?; **I** ~ **see you next week** vejo-lhe para a semana; **yes I** ~ sim; **no I won't** não. **-2.** [expressing willingness]: **I won't do it** recuso-me a fazê-lo. **-3.** [expressing polite question]: ~ **you have some more tea?** você quer mais um chá? **-4.** [in commands, requests]: ~ **you please be quiet!** pode ficar calado, por favor!; **close that window,** ~ **you?** feche a janela, por favor.

willful *adj US* = wilful.

willing ['wɪlɪŋ] *adj* **-1.** [prepared] disposto(ta); **to be** ~ **to do sthg** estar disposto(ta) a fazer algo **-2.** [eager] prestativo(va).

willingly ['wɪlɪŋlɪ] *adv* de bom grado.

willingness ['wɪlɪŋnɪs] *n* **-1.** [preparedness] disposição *f*, boa vontade *f*; ~ **to do sthg** disposição para fazer algo **-2.** [keenness] determinação *f*, ânsia *f*.

willow (tree) ['wɪləʊ-] *n* salgueiro *m*.

willowy ['wɪləʊɪ] *adj* longilíneo(nea).

willpower ['wɪl.paʊəʳ] *n (U)* força *f* de vontade.

willy ['wɪlɪ] (*pl* -ies) *n UK inf* piu-piu *m*.

willy-nilly [.wɪlɪ'nɪlɪ] *adv* **-1.** [at random] ao acaso **-2.** [wanting to or not] quer queria quer não.

wilt [wɪlt] *vi* **-1.** [plant] murchar **-2.** *fig* [person] definhar.

wily ['waɪlɪ] (*compar* -ier, *superl* -iest) *adj* ardiloso (sa).

wimp [wɪmp] *n inf pej* bunda-mole *mf*.

win [wɪn] (*pt* & *pp* won, *cont* -ning) ⋄ *n* vitória *f*. ⋄ *vt* **-1.** [gen] ganhar **-2.** [game, fight, competition] vencer. ⋄ *vi* ganhar; **you/I** *etc* **can't** ~ não tem jeito.

➡ **win over, win round** *vt sep* convencer.

wince [wɪns] ⋄ *vi* contrair-se; **to** ~ **at sthg** perturbar-se com algo; **to** ~ **with sthg** retrair-se de algo. ⋄ *n* contração *f* de dor.

winch [wɪntʃ] ⋄ *n* guindaste *m*. ⋄ *vt* levantar *OR* suspender com guindaste.

Winchester disk *n COMPUT* winchester *m*, disco *m* rígido.

wind¹ [wɪnd] ⋄ *n* **-1.** *METEOR* vento *m* **-2.** *(U)* [breath] fôlego *m*; **to get one's second** ~ *fig* recobrar o

folêgo **-3.** *(U)* [in stomach] gases *mpl*; **to break** ~ *euphemism* soltar gases **-4.** [in orchestra] instrumento *m* de sopro **-5.** *phr*: **to get** ~ **of sthg** *inf* tomar conhecimento de algo; **to sail close to the** ~ andar na corda bamba; **to put the** ~ **up sb** *inf* fazer alguém tremer nas bases; **it really put the** ~ **up me** *inf* realmente tremi nas bases. ⋄ *vt* **-1.** [knock breath out of] ficar sem fôlego **-2.** *UK* [baby] arrotar.

wind² [waɪnd] (*pt* & *pp* wound) ⋄ *vt* **-1.** [string, thread] enrolar **-2.** [clock] dar corda em **-3.** *phr*: **to** ~ **one's way** serpentear. ⋄ *vi* [river, road] serpentear.

➡ **wind back** *vt sep* [tape] rebobinar.

➡ **wind down** ⋄ *vt sep* **-1.** [car window] baixar **-2.** [business] fechar aos poucos. ⋄ *vi* **-1.** [clock] parar **-2.** [relax] espairecer.

➡ **wind forward** *vt sep* [tape] avançar.

➡ **wind on** *vt sep* rebobinar.

➡ **wind up** ⋄ *vt sep* **-1.** [finish - meeting] encerrar; [- business] fechar, liquidar **-2.** [clock] dar corda em **-3.** [car window] levantar **-4.** *UK inf* [deliberately annoy] azucrinar **-5.** *inf* [end up]: **to** ~ **up doing sthg** acabar fazendo algo. ⋄ *vi inf* [end up] acabar em.

windbreak ['wɪndbreɪk] *n* quebra-vento *m*.

windcheater *UK* ['wɪnd.tʃiːtəʳ], **windbreaker** *US* ['wɪnd.breɪkəʳ] *n dated* japona *f*.

windchill ['wɪndtʃɪl] *n (U)* sensação *m* térmica.

winded ['wɪndɪd] *adj* sem fôlego.

windfall ['wɪndfɔːl] *n* **-1.** [fruit] fruto *m* caído *(da árvore)* **-2.** [unexpected gift] dinheiro *m* que caiu do céu.

wind farm [wɪnd-] *n* parque *m* eólico.

winding ['waɪndɪŋ] *adj* sinuoso(sa).

wind instrument [wɪnd-] *n* instrumento *m* de sopro.

windmill ['wɪndmɪl] *n* moinho *m* de vento.

window ['wɪndəʊ] *n* **-1.** [gen] janela *f* **-2.** [of shop] vitrina *f* **-3.** [free time] tempo *m* livre.

window box *n* floreira *f* de janela.

window cleaner *n* limpador *m* de vidros.

window display *n* vitrina *f*.

window dressing *n* **-1.** [in shop] decoração *m* de vitrina **-2.** *fig* [non-essentials] fachada *f*.

window envelope *n* envelope *m* de janela.

window frame *n* caixilho *m* de janela.

window ledge *n* parapeito *m*.

windowpane *n* vidraça *f*.

window shade *n US* persiana *f*.

window-shopping *n (U)*: **to go** ~ ir olhar vitrinas.

window sill *n* parapeito *m*.

windpipe ['wɪndpaɪp] *n* traquéia *f*.

windscreen *UK* ['wɪndskriːn], **windshield** *US* ['wɪndʃiːld] *n* pára-brisa *m*.

windscreen washer *n* lavador *m* de pára-brisa.

windscreen wiper *n* limpador *m* de pára-brisa.

windshield *n US* = windscreen.

windsock ['wɪndsɒk] *n* biruta *f*.

windsurfer ['wɪnd.sɜːfəʳ] *n* **-1.** [person] windsurfista mf - **2.** [board] prancha f de windsurfe.

windsurfing ['wɪnd,sɜːfɪŋ] n (U) windsurfe m; **to go** ~ praticar windsurfe.

windswept ['wɪndsweptl] adj - **1.** [scenery] varrido(-da) ao vento - **2.** [person, hair] em desalinho.

wind tunnel [wɪnd-] n tunel m aerodinâmico.

wind turbine [wɪnd-] n turbina f eólica.

windy ['wɪndɪ] (compar -ier, superl -iest) adj - **1.** [weather, day] de muito vento; **it's** ~ está ventando - **2.** [place] exposto(ta) ao vento.

wine [waɪn] n vinho m; **red/rosé/white** ~ vinho tinto/rosé/branco.

wine bar n UK cantina f.

wine bottle n garrafa f de vinho.

wine box n garrafão m de vinho.

wine cellar n adega f.

wineglass ['waɪnglɑːs] n copo m de vinho.

wine list n carta f de vinhos.

wine merchant n UK mercador m, -ra f de vinhos.

winepress ['waɪnpres] n lagar m.

wine rack n suporte m para vinhos.

wine tasting [-,teɪstɪŋ] n (U) degustação f de vinhos.

wine waiter n sommelier m.

wing [wɪŋ] n - **1.** [gen] asa f - **2.** [of car] flanco m - **3.** [of building, organization] ala f.
- **wings** npl THEATRE: **the** ~ **s** os bastidores.

wing commander n UK tenente-coronel m (de aviação).

winger ['wɪŋəʳ] n SPORT ala f; **left-** ~ ponta-esquerda mf; **right-** ~ ponta-direita mf.

wing nut n porca f borboleta.

wingspan ['wɪŋspæn] n envergadura f.

wink [wɪŋk] <> n - **1.** [of eye] piscada f; **to have forty** ~ **s** inf tirar uma soneca; **not to sleep a** ~, **not to get a** ~ **of sleep** inf não pregar o olho. <> vi - **1.** [eye] piscar, pestanejar; **to** ~ **at sb** piscar para alguém - **2.** literary [lights] cintilar.

winkle ['wɪŋkl] n caramujo m.
- **winkle out** vt sep - **1.** [remove] arrancar - **2.** fig [extract]: **to** ~ **sthg out of sb** arrancar algo de alguém.

winner ['wɪnəʳ] n - **1.** [person] vencedor m, -ra f, ganhador m, -ra f - **2.** inf [success] vencedor m, -ra f; **to be onto a** ~ ser bem-sucedido(da).

winning ['wɪnɪŋ] adj - **1.** [victorious, successful] vencedor(ra), vitorioso(sa) - **2.** [pleasing] encantador(ra).
- **winnings** npl ganhos mpl (de aposta).

winning post n meta f.

Winnipeg n Winnipeg.

winsome ['wɪnsəm] adj literary encantador(ra).

winter ['wɪntəʳ] <> n inverno m; **in** ~ no inverno. <> comp de inverno.

winter sports npl esportes mpl de inverno.

wintertime ['wɪntətaɪm] n (U) inverno m; **in** ~ no inverno.

wint(e)ry ['wɪntrɪ] adj invernal, de inverno.

wipe [waɪp] <> n [clean]: **to give sthg a** ~ dar uma limpada em algo. <> vt - **1.** [rub to clean] limpar, passar um pano em - **2.** [rub to dry] secar.
- **wipe away** vt sep [tears] enxugar.

- **wipe out** vt sep - **1.** [erase] limpar - **2.** [kill] aniquilar - **3.** [eradicate] erradicar.
- **wipe up** <> vt sep - **1.** [dirt, mess] limpar - **2.** [water] secar. <> vi limpar.

wiper ['waɪpəʳ] n [windscreen wiper] limpador m de pára-brisa.

wire ['waɪəʳ] <> n - **1.** (U) [metal] cabo m, fio m - **2.** [length of wire] fio m - **3.** US [telegram] telegrama m. <> comp de arame. <> vt - **1.** [fasten, connect]: **to** ~ **sthg to sthg** ligar algo em algo - **2.** ELEC ligar à rede elétrica; **he** ~ **d the whole house himself** ele mesmo fez a instalação elétrica da casa - **3.** US [send telegram to] passar um telegrama para.
- **wire up** vt sep [house] fazer a instalação elétrica.

wire brush n escova f de aço.

wire cutters npl alicate m de arame.

wireless ['waɪəlɪs] n dated radiofone m.

wire netting n (U) tela f de arame.

wire-tapping [-,tæpɪŋ] n (U) escuta f telefônica.

wire wool n UK esponja f de aço.

wiring ['waɪərɪŋ] n (U) instalação f elétrica.

wiry ['waɪərɪ] (compar -ier, superl -iest) adj - **1.** [hair] eriçado(da) - **2.** [body, man] esguio(guia).

Wisconsin n Wisconsin.

wisdom ['wɪzdəm] n (U) sabedoria f.

wisdom tooth n dente m do juízo.

wise [waɪz] adj sábio(bia); **to get** ~ **to sthg** inf manjar algo; **to be no** ~ **r** OR **none the** ~ **r** continuar sem entender.
- **wise up** vi US compreender.

wisecrack ['waɪzkræk] n pej gafe f, mancada f.

wisely adv sabiamente.

wish [wɪʃ] <> n - **1.** [desire] desejo m; ~ **to do sthg** desejo de fazer algo; ~ **for sthg** desejo por algo - **2.** [magic request] pedido m. <> vt - **1.** [want]: **to** ~ **to do sthg** fml desejar fazer algo; **to** ~ **(that)** esperar que - **2.** [desire, request by magic]: **to** ~ **(that)** desejar que; **I** ~ **I were rich** ah, se eu fosse rico - **3.** [in greeting]: **to** ~ **sb sthg** desejar algo a alguém. <> vi [by magic]: **to** ~ **for sthg** pedir algo.
- **wishes** npl: **best** ~ **es** cumprimentos mpl, parabéns mpl; **(with) best** ~ **es** [at end of letter] com os cumprimentos.
- **wish on** vt sep: **to** ~ **sthg on sb** desejar algo para alguém.

wishbone ['wɪʃbəʊn] n osso m da sorte.

wishful thinking [,wɪʃfʊl-] n (U) fantasia f, ilusão f.

wishy-washy ['wɪʃɪ,wɒʃɪ] adj inf pej [vague] sem graça.

wisp [wɪsp] n - **1.** [tuft - of hair] mecha f, tufo m; [- of grass] bola f - **2.** [small cloud] nuvem f.

wispy ['wɪspɪ] (compar -ier, superl -iest) adj ralo(la).

wisteria n glicínia f.

wistful ['wɪstfʊl] adj melancólico(ca), triste.

wit [wɪt] n - **1.** (U) [humour] presença f de espírito, gracejo m - **2.** [funny person] brincalhão m, -na f - **3.** [intelligence]: **to have the** ~ **to do sthg** ter astúcia para fazer algo.
- **wits** npl [intelligence, mind]: **to have** OR **keep one's** ~ **s about one** manter-se alerta; **to be scared out of one's** ~ **s** inf estar morto(ta) de medo;

to be at one's ~s end estar à beira da loucura.
witch [wɪtʃ] *n* bruxa *f.*
witchcraft ['wɪtʃkrɑ:ft] *n (U)* bruxaria *f.*
witchdoctor ['wɪtʃˌdɒktə^r] *n* curandeiro *m,* -ra *f.*
witch-hazel *n* -**1.** *(U)* [liquid] água *f* de hamamélis - **2.** [tree] hamamélis *f inv.*
witch-hunt *n pej* caça *f* às bruxas.
with [wɪð] *prep* -**1.** [in company of] com; **come ~ me/ us** venha comigo/conosco; **can I go ~ you?** posso ir com você?; **we stayed ~ friends** ficamos em casa de amigos. -**2.** [in descriptions] com; **a man ~ a beard** um homem de barba; **a room ~ a bath- room** um quarto com banheiro. -**3.** [indicating means, manner] com; **I washed it ~ detergent** lavei-o com detergente; **they won ~ ease** ga- nharam com facilidade. -**4.** [indicating emotion] de; **to tremble ~ fear** tremer de medo. -**5.** [regarding] com; **be careful ~ that!** tenha cuidado com isso! -**6.** [indicating opposition] com; **to argue ~ sb** discutir com alguém. -**7.** [indicating covering, con- tents]: **to fill sthg ~ sthg** encher algo com *OR* de algo; **packed ~ people** cheio de gente; **topped ~ cream** coberto com creme.
withdraw [wɪð'drɔ:] (*pt* -**drew,** *pp* -**drawn**) ◇ *vt* -**1.** [remove] afastar; **to ~ sthg from sthg** remover algo de algo -**2.** *FIN* sacar -**3.** [troops, statement, of- fer] retirar. ◇ *vi* -**1.** [gen] retirar-se; **to ~ from** retirar-se de; **to ~ to** retirar-se para -**2.** [quit, give up] afastar-se; **to ~ from sthg** afastar-se de algo.
withdrawal [wɪð'drɔ:əl] *n* -**1.** *(U)* [gen] retirada *f,* **~ from sthg** afastamento *m* de algo -**2.** *(U)* [re- moval] remoção *f* -**3.** *(U)* [retraction] retratação *f* -**4.** *(U) MED* (síndrome *f* da) abstinência *f* -**5.** *FIN* saque *m.*
withdrawal symptoms *npl* síndrome *f* de abstinência.
withdrawn [wɪð'drɔ:n] ◇ *pp* ⊳ **withdraw.** ◇ *adj* [shy, quiet] retraído(da).
withdrew [wɪð'dru:] *pt* ⊳ **withdraw.**
wither ['wɪðə^r] ◇ *vt* secar. ◇ *vi* -**1.** [dry up] murchar -**2.** [become weak] debilitar-se.
withered ['wɪðəd] *adj* -**1.** [plant] murcho(cha) -**2.** [skin] seco(ca).
withering ['wɪðərɪŋ] *adj* -**1.** [look] fulminante -**2.** [remark] mordaz.
withhold [wɪð'həʊld] (*pt* & *pp* -**held** [-'held]) *vt* reter.
within [wɪ'ðɪn] ◇ *prep* -**1.** [gen] dentro de -**2.** [less than - distance]: **~ 5 quilometers of London** a menos de 5 quilômetros de Londres; [- time] em menos de. ◇ *adv* dentro.
without [wɪð'aʊt] ◇ *prep* sem; **~ doing sthg** sem fazer algo. ◇ *adv*: **to go** *OR* **do ~ (sthg)** ficar sem (algo).
withstand [wɪð'stænd] (*pt* & *pp* -**stood** [-'stʊd]) *vt* resistir a, agüentar.
witness ['wɪtnɪs] ◇ *n* -**1.** testemunha *f;* **to be ~ to sthg** ser testemunha de algo -**2.** *(U)* [testimony]: **to bear ~ to sthg** [give testimony of] dar testemu- nho de algo; [be proof of] testemunhar algo. ◇ *vt* -**1.** [see] testemunhar -**2.** [countersign] assinar como testemunha.
witness box *UK,* **witness stand** *US n* banco *m* das testemunhas.

witter ['wɪtə^r] *vi UK inf pej* dizer abobrinhas.
witticism ['wɪtɪsɪzm] *n* sagacidade *f.*
witty ['wɪtɪ] (*compar* -**ier,** *superl* -**iest**) *adj* espirituo- so(sa).
wives [waɪvz] *pl* ⊳ **wife.**
wizard ['wɪzəd] *n* -**1.** [man with magic powers] feiticeiro *m,* mago *m* -**2.** *fig* [skilled person] gênio *m.*
wizened ['wɪznd] *adj* envelhecido(da).
wk (*abbr of* **week**) semana *f.*
WO (*abbr of* **warrant officer**) *n* posto *militar.*
wobble ['wɒbl] *vi* -**1.** [chair] cambalear -**2.** [hands] tremer -**3.** [aeroplane] balançar.
wobbly ['wɒblɪ] (*compar* -**ier,** *superl* -**iest**) *adj* -**1.** [table, chair] *inf* bambo(ba) -**2.** [jelly] molenga.
woe [wəʊ] *n literary* lamúria *f,* infortúnio *m.*
wok [wɒk] *n* panela *f* wok.
woke [wəʊk] *pt* ⊳ **wake.**
woken ['wəʊkn] *pp* ⊳ **wake.**
wolf [wʊlf] (*pl* **wolves**) ◇ *n* -**1.** [animal] lobo *m* -**2.** [man] gavião *m,* paquerador *m.* ◇ *vt inf:* **to ~ sthg (down)** devorar algo.
wolf whistle *n* fiu-fiu *m (para as mulheres),* assobio *m (para as mulheres).*
wolves ['wʊlvz] *pl* ⊳ **wolf.**
woman ['wʊmən] (*pl* **women**) ◇ *n* mulher *f.* ◇ *comp:* **a ~ doctor** uma doutora; **a ~ governor** uma governadora; **a ~ teacher** uma professora; **a ~ footballer** uma jogadora de futebol; **a ~ prime minister** uma primeira-ministra.
womanhood ['wʊmənhʊd] *n* -**1.** [adult life] maioridade *f* feminina -**2.** [all women] mulheres *fpl.*
womanizer, -iser *n pej* paquerador *m.*
womanly ['wʊmənlɪ] *adj* feminino(na).
womb [wu:m] *n* ventre *m.*
wombat ['wɒmbæt] *n* vombatídeo *m.*
women ['wɪmɪn] *pl* ⊳ **woman.**
women's group *n* grupo *m* feminista.
Women's Institute *n UK:* **the ~** organização de mulheres, especialmente da área rural, que se encontram regularmente e participam de atividades culturais e trabalho social.
women's lib [-'lɪb] *n inf* libertação *f* da mulher.
women's liberation *n* -**1.** [aim] libertação *f* da mulher -**2.** [movement] movimento *m* pela liberta- ção da mulher.
won [wʌn] *pt* & *pp* ⊳ **win.**
wonder ['wʌndə^r] ◇ *n* -**1.** *(U)* [amazement] espanto *m* -**2.** [cause for surprise]: **it's a ~ (that) ...** é de se admirar que ...; **no** *OR* **little** *OR* **small ~** não é de se admirar -**3.** [amazing thing, person] maravilha *f;* **to work** *OR* **do ~s** realizar milagres. ◇ *vt* -**1.** [spec- ulate] perguntar-se; **to ~ if** *OR* **whether** perguntar- -se a si próprio(pria) se -**2.** [in polite requests]: **I ~ whether you would mind shutting the window?** será que você se importaria de fechar a janela? ◇ *vi* -**1.** [speculate] perguntar; **why did you ask?** - **oh, I just ~ ed** por que você perguntou isso? - ah, foi só por perguntar; **to ~ about sthg** pensar sobre algo -**2.** *literary* [be amazed]: **to ~ at sthg** admirar-se com algo.
wonderful ['wʌndəfʊl] *adj* maravilhoso(sa).

wonderfully ['wʌndəfʊlɪ] *adv* maravilhosa-mente.

wonderland ['wʌndələændl] *n* [fairyland] paraíso *m*.

wonky ['wɒŋkɪ] (*compar* -ier, *superl* -iest) *adj UK inf* [wobbly] cambaleante; [crooked] torto(ta).

wont [wəʊnt] ⟷ *adj*: to be ~ to do sthg estar acostumado(da) a fazer algo. ⟷ *n dated or literary*: as is one's ~ como é do feitio de alguém.

won't [wəʊnt] = will not.

woo [wuː] *vt* -1. *literary* [court] cortejar - 2. *fig* [try to win over] persuadir.

wood [wʊd] ⟷ *n* -1. (U) [timber] madeira *f* - 2. [group of trees] bosque *m*, floresta *f* - 3. *GOLF* bastão *m (de madeira)* - 4. *phr.* not to see the ~ for the trees *UK* prender-se às partes e não ver o todo; touch ~! bata na madeira! ⟷ *comp* de madeira.
➡ **woods** *npl* floresta *f*.

wooded ['wʊdɪd] *adj* arborizado(da).

wooden ['wʊdn] *adj* -1. [of wood] de madeira - 2. *pej* [actor] sem expressão.

wooden spoon *n* colher *f* de pau; to win *OR* get the ~ *UK fig* vir na rabeira.

woodland ['wʊdlənd] *n* floresta *f*.

woodlouse (*pl* -lice) *n* bicho-de-conta *m*.

woodpecker ['wʊd,pekə⟨r⟩] *n* pica-pau *m*.

wood pigeon *n* pombo *m* torcaz.

woodshed ['wʊdʃed] *n* depósito *m* para madeira.

woodwind ['wʊdwɪnd] ⟷ *adj* instrumento *m* doce *(de madeira)*. ⟷ *n*: the ~ os instrumentos doces.

woodwork ['wʊdwɜːk] *n* -1. [wooden objects] obra *f* de madeira - 2. [craft] carpintaria *f*.

woodworm ['wʊdwɜːm] *n* caruncho *m*.

woof [wuːf] ⟷ *n* uivo *m*. ⟷ *excl* auu!

wool [wʊl] *n* -1. [gen] lã *f* - 2. *phr.* he is pulling the ~ over your eyes *inf* ele está te vendendo gato por lebre.

woollen *UK*, **woolen** *US* ['wʊlən] *adj* [garment] de lã.
➡ **woollens** *npl* produtos *mpl* de lã.

woolly ['wʊlɪ] (*compar* -ier, *superl* -iest, *pl* -ies) ⟷ *adj* -1. [woollen] de lã, lanoso(sa) - 2. *inf* [fuzzy, unclear] desatinado(da). ⟷ *n inf* roupas *fpl* de lã.

woolly-headed [-'hedɪd] *adj inf pej* desatinado (desatina) da.

woozy ['wuːzɪ] (*compar* -ier, *superl* -iest) *adj inf* atordoado(da).

Worcester sauce ['wʊstə⟨r⟩-] *n* (U) molho *m* inglês.

word [wɜːd] ⟷ *n* -1. [gen] palavra *f*; ~ for ~ ao pé da letra; in other ~s em outras palavras; in your own ~s em suas próprias palavras; not in so many ~s não com todas as palavras; in a ~ em uma palavra; too ... for ~s ser extremamente ...; by ~ of mouth oralmente; to put in a (good) ~ for sb recomendar alguém; just say the ~ é só avisar; to have a ~ (with sb) ter uma palavra (com alguém), falar (com alguém); to have ~s with sb *inf* bater boca com alguém; to have the last ~ ter a última palavra; she doesn't mince her ~s ela não tem papas na língua; to weigh one's ~s medir as palavras; I couldn't get a ~ in edgeways eu não pude entrar na conversa; to give sb one's ~ dar a palavra a alguém; to be as good as one's ~, to be true to one's ~ cumprir bem a palavra - 2. (U) [news] notícias *fpl*. ⟷ *vt* redigir.

word game *n* qualquer jogo que envolva a construção ou a seleção de palavras.

wording ['wɜːdɪŋ] *n* (U) palavreado *m*.

word-perfect *adj* de cor e salteado.

wordplay ['wɜːdpleɪ] *n* (U) jogo *m* de palavras.

word processing *n* (U) processamento *m* de texto.

word processor [-'prəʊsesə⟨r⟩] *n* processador *m* de texto.

wordwrap ['wɜːdræp] *n* *COMPUT* marginação *f* automática.

wordy ['wɜːdɪ] (*compar* -ier, *superl* -iest) *adj pej* floreado(da).

wore [wɔː⟨r⟩] *pt* ⊳ wear.

work [wɜːk] ⟷ *n* -1. (U) [employment] emprego *m*; temporary/casual ~ trabalho temporário; in/out of ~ empregado/desempregado; at ~ no trabalho - 2. (U) [activity, tasks] trabalho *m*; at ~ em atividade; to have one's ~ cut out doing sthg *OR* to do sthg ser extremamente difícil para alguém fazer algo - 3. [something made, created, composed] obra *f* - 4. *phr.* he's a nasty piece of ~ *inf* ele é uma pessoa detestável. ⟷ *vt* -1. [person, staff] fazer trabalhar - 2. [machine] operar - 3. [shape, manipulate] trabalhar em - 4. [cultivate] cultivar - 5. [cause to become]: to ~ o.s. into sthg contrair-se em algo - 6. [make]: to ~ one's way [progress physically] avançar; [in career] progredir. ⟷ *vi* -1. [do a job] trabalhar - 2. [function, succeed] funcionar - 3. [have effect]: to ~ against sb/sthg ir contra alguém/algo - 4. [gradually become] tornar-se; to ~ loose soltar-se; to ~ into a tangle entrelaçar-se.
➡ **works** ⟷ *n* [factory] usina *f*. ⟷ *npl* -1. [mechanism] mecanismo *m* - 2. [digging, building] obras *fpl* - 3. *inf* [everything]: the ~s os aparatos.
➡ **work at** *vt fus* tentar melhorar.
➡ **work off** *vt sep* libertar-se de.
➡ **work on** *vt fus* -1. [concentrate on] dedicar-se a - 2. [take as basis] basear-se em - 3. [try to persuade] tentar persuadir.
➡ **work out** ⟷ *vt sep* -1. [formulate] elaborar - 2. [calculate] calcular. ⟷ *vi* -1. [figure, total]: to ~ out at totalizar; the bill ~s out at £5 a head a conta dá 5 libras para cada um - 2. [turn out] surtir efeito - 3. [be successful] dar certo - 4. [train, exercise] treinar.
➡ **work up** *vt sep* -1. [excite]: to ~ o.s. up into a frenzy excitar-se de tal forma - 2. [generate] gerar.

workable ['wɜːkəbl] *adj* viável.

workaday ['wɜːkədeɪ] *adj pej* prosaico(ca).

workaholic [,wɜːkə'hɒlɪk] *n* burro *m* de carga, workaholic *mf*.

workbasket *n* cesta *f* de costura.

workbench ['wɜːkbentʃ] *n* bancada *f*.

workbook ['wɜːkbʊk] *n* livro-texto *m*.

workday ['wɜːkdeɪ] *n* -1. [day's work] dia *m* de trabalho - 2. [not weekend] dia *m* útil.

worked up [,wɜːkt-] *adj* exaltado(da).

worker ['wɜ:kə'] *n* trabalhador *m*, -ra *f*, operário *m*, -ria *f*; **an office** ~ um empregado de escritório; **a hard/good** ~ um ótimo/bom trabalhador.

workforce ['wɜ:kfɔ:s] *n* força *f* de trabalho.

workhouse ['wɜ:khaʊs] *n* **-1.** *UK* [poorhouse] albergue *m* **-2.** *US* [prison] casa *f* de correção.

working ['wɜ:kɪŋ] *adj* **-1.** [in operation] em operação; **to be** ~ estar funcionando **-2.** [having employment - mothers, children] que trabalha; [- population] ativo(va) **-3.** [relating to work] de trabalho.
◆ **workings** *npl* **-1.** [of system, machine] operação *f* **-2.** *fig* [of mind] funcionamento *m*.

working capital *n* **-1.** [assets minus' liabilities] capital *m* de giro **-2.** [assets] ativo *m* circulante **-3.** [available money] dinheiro *m* em caixa.

working class *n*: **the** ~ a classe operária.
◆ **working-class** *adj* da classe operária.

working day *n* = **workday**.

working group *n* grupo *m* de trabalho.

working knowledge *n* conhecimento *m* de causa.

working man *n* trabalhador *m*.

working model *n* maquete *m*.

working order *n* *(U)*: **in** ~ em funcionamento.

working party *n* grupo *m* de trabalho.

working week *n* semana *f* de trabalho.

work-in-progress *n* trabalho *m* em andamento.

workload ['wɜ:kləʊd] *n* carga *f* de trabalho.

workman ['wɜ:kmən] (*pl* **-men** [-mən]) *n* trabalhador *m*, operário *m*.

workmanship ['wɜ:kmənʃɪp] *n* *(U)* acabamento *m*.

workmate ['wɜ:kmeɪt] *n* colega *mf* de trabalho.

work of art *n* obra *f* de arte.

workout ['wɜ:kaʊt] *n* treinamento *m*.

work permit [-,pɜ:mɪt] *n* visto *m* de trabalho.

workplace ['wɜ:kpleɪs] *n* local *m* de trabalho.

work placement *n* colocação *f* no mercado de trabalho.

workroom ['wɜ:krʊm] *n* sala *f* de trabalho.

works council *n* comissão *f* de trabalhadores.

workshop ['wɜ:kʃɒp] *n* **-1.** [room] oficina *f* **-2.** [building] fábrica *f* **-3.** [discussion] oficina *f*, workshop *f*.

workshy ['wɜ:kʃaɪ] *adj* *UK* avesso(sa) ao trabalho.

workstation ['wɜ:k,steɪʃn] *n* *COMPUT* estação *f* de trabalho.

work surface *n* superfície *f* de trabalho.

worktable ['wɜ:k,teɪbl] *n* mesa *f* de trabalho.

worktop ['wɜ:ktɒp] *n* *UK* superfície *f* de trabalho.

work-to-rule *n* *UK* paralisação *f* de trabalho extra.

world [wɜ:ld] ⬦ *n* **-1.** [gen] mundo *m*; **to be dead to the** ~ estar ferrado(da) no sono; **the best of both** ~**s** o melhor de dois mundos; **the** ~ o mundo; **how/what/in the** ~ **...?** como/o que é que ..., pelo amor de Deus?; **where/why in the** ~ **...?** onde/por que diabos ...?; **the** ~ **over** no mundo inteiro **-2.** [great deal]: **to think the** ~ **of sb** ter grande afeição por alguém; **to do one the** ~ **of good** fazer alguém se sentir extremamente feliz;

a ~ **of difference** toda uma diferença. ⬦ *comp* mundial.

World Bank *n*: **the** ~ o Banco Mundial.

world-class *adj* muito superior(ra).

World Cup *FTBL* ⬦ *n*: **the** ~ a Copa do Mundo. ⬦ *comp* da Copa do Mundo.

world-famous *adj* famoso(sa) no mundo todo.

worldly ['wɜ:ldlɪ] *adj* mundano(na); ~ **goods** coisas mundanas.

world music *n* *(U)* música *f* mundial.

world power *n* força *f* OR potência *f* mundial.

World Series *n* *US*: **the** ~ o Campeonato Nacional de Beisebol.

WORLD SERIES

A *World Series* é a grande final do campeonato norte-americano de beisebol. Ela é disputada em até sete partidas, nas quais, ao final da temporada, se enfrentam os campeões das duas mais importantes ligas do país: a *National League* e a *American League*. O campeão será o time que primeiro obtiver quatro vitórias. Trata-se de um dos mais importantes acontecimentos esportivos anuais do país. Conforme a tradição, a primeira bola do jogo é lançada pelo presidente da República.

World Service *n* serviço da BBC que transmite programas de rádio e TV em inglês e em vários idiomas para o mundo todo.

world-weary *adj* entediado(da).

worldwide ['wɜ:ldwaɪd] ⬦ *adj* mundial. ⬦ *adv* no mundo inteiro.

worm [wɜ:m] ⬦ *n* [animal - in stomach] lombriga *f*, verme *m*; [- earthwork] minhoca *f*. ⬦ *vt*: **to** ~ **one's way** mover-se; **to** ~ **one's way into sb's confidence** engambelar alguém.
◆ **worms** *npl* vermes *mpl*.
◆ **worm out** *vt sep*: **to** ~ **sthg out of sb** arrancar algo de alguém.

worn [wɔ:n] ⬦ *pp* ⊳ **wear**. ⬦ *adj* **-1.** [threadbare] surrado(da) **-2.** [tired] exausto(ta).

worn-out *adj* **-1.** [old, threadbare] usado(da), gasto(ta) **-2.** [tired] exausto(ta).

worried ['wʌrɪd] *adj* preocupado(da); **to be** ~ **about sb/sthg** estar preocupado(da) com alguém/algo; **to be** ~ **sick** estar profundamente preocupado(da).

worrier ['wʌrɪə'] *n*: **he's a terrible** ~ ele se preocupa com tudo.

worry ['wʌrɪ] (*pl* **-ies**, *pt* & *pp* **-ied**) ⬦ *n* **-1.** *(U)* [feeling] preocupação *f* **-2.** [problem] problema *m*. ⬦ *vt* [cause to be troubled] preocupar. ⬦ *vi* preocupar-se; **to** ~ **about sb/sthg** preocupar-se com alguém/algo; **not to** ~**!** nada com o que se preocupar!

worrying ['wʌrɪɪŋ] *adj* preocupante.

worse [wɜ:s] ⬦ *adj* pior; **to get** ~ piorar. ⬦ *adv* pior; ~ **off** em pior situação. ⬦ *n* pior *m*; **for the** ~ para o pior.

worsen ['wɜ:sn] *vt* & *vi* agravar, piorar.

worsening ['wɜ:snɪŋ] *adj* agravante, que piora.

worship ['wɜ:ʃɪp] (*UK pt* & *pp* **-ped**, *cont* **-ping**, *US pt*

& *pp* -ed, *cont* -ing) ⬦ *vt* -1. RELIG adorar - 2. [admire, adore] admirar, adorar. ⬦ *n (U)* adoração *f.*
➤ **Worship** *n*: Your/Her/His Worship Vossa Excelência.

worshipper *UK,* **worshiper** *US* ['wɜːʃɪpəʳ] *n* -1. RELIG devoto *m,* -ta *f* - 2. [admirer] admirador *m,* -ra *f.*

worst [wɜːst] ⬦ *adj* & *adv* pior. ⬦ *n*: **the** ~ o pior; **if the** ~ **comes to the** ~ se o pior acontecer; **to get the** ~ **of it** ficar com o pior.
➤ **at (the) worst** *adv* na pior das hipóteses.

worsted ['wʊstɪd] *n (U)* lã *f* penteada.

worth [wɜːθ] ⬦ *prep* - 1. [having the value of] valor *m*; **it's** ~ **£50** vale £50 - 2. [deserving of]: **it's** ~ **going to Brazil** vale a pena ir para a Brasil; **it's** ~ **a visit** vale a visita; **to be** ~ **doing sthg** valer a pena fazer algo. ⬦ *n* - 1. [value] valor *m* - 2. [supply] provisão *f.*

worthless ['wɜːθlɪs] *adj* - 1. [object] sem valor - 2. [person] inútil.

worthwhile [ˌwɜːθ'waɪl] *adj* que vale a pena.

worthy ['wɜːðɪ] (*compar* -ier, *superl* -iest) *adj* - 1. [deserving of respect] respeitável - 2. [deserving]: **to be** ~ **of sthg** ser merecedor(ra) de algo - 3. *pej* [good but unexciting] adequado(da).

would [wʊd] *modal vb* - 1. [in reported speech]: **she said she** ~ **come** ela disse que viria; **he promised he** ~ **help me** ele prometeu que me ajudaria - 2. [indicating likely result]: **what** ~ **you do if he phoned?** o que você faria se ele ligasse?; **I doubt she** ~ **have noticed** duvido que ela percebesse; **if he had lost, he** ~ **have resigned** se tivesse perdido, ele teria renunciado - 3. [indicating willingness]: **she** ~**n't go** ela não queria ir embora; **he** ~ **do anything for her** ele faria qualquer coisa por ela; **she** ~**n't give an answer even if ...** ela não teria respondido mesmo que ... - 4. [in polite questions]: ~ **you like a drink?** você gostaria de tomar um drinque?; ~ **you mind closing the window?** você poderia fechar a janela, por favor?; **help me shut the door,** ~ **you?** me ajuda a fechar a porta, por favor? - 5. [indicating inevitability]: **he** ~ **say that** não me surpreende que ele tenha dito isso; **I said yes - well, you** ~ eu disse sim - bem, era o esperado - 6. [expressing opinions]: **I** ~ **have thought that she'd be pleased** eu pensava que ela tivesse gostado; **I** ~ **prefer a blue one** eu preferia um azul - 7. [in giving advice]: **I'd report it if I were you** no teu lugar, eu denunciaria - 8. [describing habitual past actions]: **I** ~ **go for a walk every evening** eu costumava dar uma caminhada todas as tardes; **we** ~ **meet and he** ~ **say...** a gente se encontrava e ele dizia ...

would-be *adj* aspirante.

wouldn't ['wʊdnt] = would not.

would've ['wʊdəv] = would have.

wound¹ [wauːnd] ⬦ *n* ferida *f,* ferimento *m*; **to lick one's** ~**s** recuperar-se. ⬦ *vt* ferir.

wound² [waʊnd] *pt* & *pp* ▷ wind ².

wounded ['wuːndɪd] ⬦ *adj* ferido(da). ⬦ *npl*: **the** ~ os feridos.

wounding ['wuːndɪŋ] *adj* prejudicial.

wove [wəʊv] *pt* ▷ weave.

woven ['wəʊvn] *pp* ▷ weave.

wow [waʊ] *inf* ⬦ *n* estouro *m.* ⬦ *vt* empolgar. ⬦ *excl* uau!

WP ⬦ *n* - 1. (*abbr of* word processing) processamento *m* de textos - 2. (*abbr of* word processor) processador *m* de textos. ⬦ (*abbr of* weather permitting) se o tempo permitir.

WPC (*abbr of* woman police constable) *n policial feminina britânica de posto inferior.*

wpm (*abbr of* words per minute) ppm.

WRAC [ræk] (*abbr of* Women's Royal Army Corps) *n corporação feminina do exército britânico.*

WRAF [ræf] (*abbr of* Women's Royal Air Force) *n corporação feminina da força aérea real britânica.*

wrangle ['ræŋgl] ⬦ *n* disputa *f,* briga *f.* ⬦ *vi* brigar; **to** ~ **with sb (over sthg)** discutir com alguém (sobre algo).

wrap [ræp] (*pt* & *pp* -ped, *cont* -ping) ⬦ *vt* - 1. [cover in paper or cloth] embrulhar; **to** ~ **sthg in sthg** enrolar algo em algo; **to** ~ **sthg (a)round sthg** enrolar algo ao redor de algo - 2. [encircle]: **to** ~ **sthg (a)round sthg** enrolar algo em algo. ⬦ *n* [garment] xale *m.*
➤ **wrap up** ⬦ *vt sep* - 1. [cover in paper or cloth] embrulhar - 2. *inf* [complete] terminar. ⬦ *vi* [put warm clothes on]: ~ **up well** OR **warmly!** agasalhe-se bem!

wrapped up [ræpt-] *adj inf*: **to be** ~ **in sb/sthg** estar afundado(da) em alguém/algo.

wrapper ['ræpəʳ] *n* embalagem *f.*

wrapping ['ræpɪŋ] *n* embrulho *m,* invólucro *m.*

wrapping paper *n (U)* papel *m* de embrulho.

wrath [rɒθ] *n (U) literary* ira *f.*

wreak [riːk] *vt* causar.

wreath [riːθ] *n* coroa *f (de flores).*

wreathe [riːð] *vt literary* envolver.

wreck [rek] ⬦ *n* - 1. [car, plane] destroços *mpl* - 2. [ship] restos *mpl* - 3. *inf* [person] caco *m.* ⬦ *vt* - 1. [break, destroy] destruir - 2. NAUT [cause to run aground] naufragar - 3. [spoil, ruin] arruinar.

wreckage ['rekɪdʒ] *n* - 1. [of plane, car] restos *mpl* - 2. [of building] escombros *mpl.*

wrecker ['rekəʳ] *n US* reboque *m.*

wren [ren] *n* garriça *f.*

wrench [rentʃ] ⬦ *n* - 1. [tool] chave *f* inglesa - 2. [injury, twist] torcedura *f,* distensão *f* - 3. [cause of sadness] tristeza *f.* ⬦ *vt* - 1. [pull violently] arrancar - 2. [twist and injure] torcer, distender - 3. [force away] arrebatar; **to** ~ **sthg away from sthg** varrer algo para longe de algo.

wrest [rest] *vt literary*: **to** ~ **sthg from sb** extorquir algo de alguém.

wrestle ['resl] ⬦ *vt* derrubar. ⬦ *vi* - 1. [fight] lutar; **to** ~ **with sb** lutar com alguém - 2. *fig* [struggle]: **to** ~ **with sthg** lutar contra algo.

wrestler ['resləʳ] *n* lutador *m,* -ra *f* de luta livre.

wrestling ['reslɪŋ] *n (U)* luta *f* livre.

wretch [retʃ] *n* [unhappy person] desgraçado *m,* -da *f.*

wretched ['retʃɪd] *adj* - 1. [miserable] infeliz - 2. *inf* [damned] maldito(ta).

wriggle ['rɪgl] ⬦ *vt* mexer. ⬦ *vi* - 1. [move about] mexer-se - 2. [twist] retorcer-se.

wriggle out of *vt fus:* **to ~ out of sthg/of doing sthg** safar-se de algo/de fazer algo.

wring [rɪŋ] *(pt & pp* **wrung)** *vt* **-1.** [squeeze out water from] torcer **-2.** *literary* [hands] esfregar **-3.** [neck] virar.

wring out *vt sep* arrancar.

wringing ['rɪŋɪŋ] *adj:* **~ (wet)** encharcado(da), ensopado(da).

wrinkle ['rɪŋkl] *n* **-1.** [on skin] ruga *f* **-2.** [in cloth] prega *f.* *vt* [screw up] enrugar. *vi* [crease] dobrar-se.

wrinkled ['rɪŋkld], **wrinkly** ['rɪŋklɪ] *adj* **-1.** [skin] enrugado(da) **-2.** [cloth] com prega.

wrist [rɪst] *n* pulso *m.*

wristband ['rɪstbænd] *n* [of watch] pulseira *f.*

wristwatch ['rɪstwɒtʃ] *n* relógio *m* de pulso.

writ [rɪt] *n* mandado *m* judicial.

write [raɪt] *(pt* **wrote,** *pp* **written)** *vt* **-1.** [gen] escrever; **to ~ sb a letter** escrever uma carta para alguém **-2.** *US* [person] escrever para **-3.** [cheque, prescription] preencher **-4.** *COMPUT* gravar. *vi* **-1.** [gen] escrever; **to ~ to sb** escrever para alguém **-2.** *COMPUT* gravar.

write back *vt sep* escrever de volta. *vi* responder.

write down *vt sep* anotar.

write in *vi* [to radio or TV station, shop] responder.

write into *vt sep* [contract] acrescentar.

write off *vt sep* **-1.** [project] cancelar **-2.** [debt, investment] cancelar, reduzir **-3.** [person] descartar **-4.** *UK inf* [vehicle] destroçar. *vi* [for information] solicitar *(informações)*; **to ~ off to sb/sthg** solicitar informações a alguém; **to ~ off for sthg** solicitar algo.

write out *vt sep* [list, names] escrever por extenso.

write up *vt sep* [notes] redigir.

write-off *n* [car] perda *f* total.

write-protect *vt COMPUT* proteger contra gravação.

writer ['raɪtə'] *n* escritor *m*, -ra *f.*

write-up *n inf* crítica *f.*

writhe [raɪð] *vi* contorcer-se.

writing ['raɪtɪŋ] *n* **-1.** [gen] escrita *f*; **I couldn't see the ~** não conseguia ler o que estava escrito; **in ~** por escrito **-2.** [handwriting] caligrafia *f*; **I can't read your ~** não consigo ler o que você escreveu.

writings *npl* escritos *mpl.*

writing case *n UK* estojo *m* para escrever.

writing desk *n* escrivaninha *f.*

writing paper *n (U)* papel *m* de carta.

written ['rɪtn] *pp* write. *adj* **-1.** [not oral] escrito(ta) **-2.** [official] por escrito.

WRNS *(abbr of* **Women's Royal Naval Service)** *n* corporação feminina da marinha real britânica.

wrong [rɒŋ] *adj* **-1.** [gen] errado(da); **to be ~ to do sthg** enganar-se ao fazer algo **-2.** [morally bad] feio (feia). *adv* [incorrectly] errado; **to get sthg ~** enganar-se sobre algo; **to go ~** [make a mistake] errar; [stop functioning] funcionar mal; **don't get me ~** *inf* não me interprete mal. *n* erro *m*; **to be in the ~** estar equivocado(da). *vt literary* ofender.

wrong-foot *vt UK* **-1.** *SPORT* fintar **-2.** *fig* [surprise] surpreender.

wrongful ['rɒŋfʊl] *adj* injusto(ta).

wrongly ['rɒŋlɪ] *adv* **-1.** [unsuitably] inadequadamente **-2.** [mistakenly] erroneamente.

wrong number *n* número *m* errado.

wrote [rəʊt] *pt* write.

wrought iron [rɔ:t-] *n (U)* ferro *m* forjado.

wrung [rʌŋ] *pt & pp* wring.

WRVS *(abbr of* **Women's Royal Voluntary Service)** *n* associação de voluntárias britânicas para ajuda a necessitados em emergências.

wry [raɪ] *adj* **-1.** [amused] entretido(da) **-2.** [displeased] desgostoso(sa).

wt. *(abbr of* **weight)** peso *m.*

WV *abbr of* **West Virginia.**

WW *(abbr of* **world war)** GM *f.*

WWF *(abbr of* **World Wildlife Fund)** *n* organização internacional de proteção a plantas, animais selvagens e áreas naturais, WWF *m.*

WY *abbr of* **Wyoming.**

Wyoming *n* Wyoming.

WYSIWYG ['wɪzɪwɪg] *(abbr of* **what you see is what you get)** *adj* WYSIWYG.

x *(pl* **x's** *OR* **xs),** **X** *(pl* **X's** *OR* **Xs)** [eks] *n* **-1.** [letter] x, X *m* **-2.** [unknown name] X *m* **-3.** [unknown quantity] x *m* **-4.** [in algebra] x *m* **-5.** [at end of letter] beijos *mpl.*

xenophobia [ˌzenə'fəʊbjə] *n (U)* xenofobia *f.*

Xerox® *n* Xerox® *f.*

xerox *vt* xerocar.

Xmas ['eksməs] *n (U)* Natal *m.* *comp* de Natal.

X-ray *n* **-1.** [ray] raio *m* X **-2.** [picture] raio-X *m.* *vt* tirar um raio-X de, tirar uma radiografia de.

xylophone ['zaɪləfəʊn] *n* xilofone *m.*

y (*pl* y's *OR* ys), **Y** (*pl* Y's *OR* Ys) [waɪ] *n* [letter] y, Y *m*.
yacht [jɒt] *n* iate *m*.
yachting [ˈjɒtɪŋ] *n* (U) iatismo *m*.
yachtsman [ˈjɒtsmən] (*pl* -men [-mən]) *n* iatista *m*.
yachtswoman [ˈjɒts،wʊmən] (*pl* -women [-،wɪmɪn]) *n* iatista *f*.
yahoo [،jæˈhuː] *n* brutamontes *mf inv.*
yak [jæk] *n* iaque *m*.
Yale lock® [jeɪl-] *n* fechadura *f* cilíndrica.
yam [jæm] *n* inhame *m*.
Yangon *n* = Rangoon.
yank [jæŋk] *vt* arrancar.
Yank [jæŋk] *n UK inf pej* ianque *mf*.
Yankee [ˈjæŋkɪ] *n* -**1.** *UK inf pej* [American] ianque *mf* -**2.** *US* [northerner] *pessoa oriunda dos Estados do norte.*

> **YANKEE**
>
> Em sua origem, o termo *yankee* referia-se aos imigrantes holandeses que se estabeleceram sobretudo no noroeste dos Estados Unidos. Mais tarde, passou a designar qualquer pessoa proveniente dessa região. Assim, 'ianques' eram chamados os soldados nortistas, durante a Guerra de Secessão nos Estados Unidos. Nos dias atuais, sulistas ainda empregam a palavra em tom pejorativo, para referir-se aos americanos do norte do país.

yap [jæp] (*pt & pp* -ped, *cont* -ping) *vi* -**1.** [dog] ganir, latir - **2.** *pej* [person] tagarelar.
yard [jɑːd] *n* -**1.** [unit of measurement] jarda *f* - **2.** [walled area] pátio *m* - **3.** [place of work] oficina *f* - **4.** *US* [attached to house] jardim *m*.
yardstick [ˈjɑːdstɪk] *n* padrão *m* de medida.
yarn [jɑːn] *n* -**1.** (U) [thread] fio *m* - **2.** *inf* [story] lorota *f*; **to spin sb a** ~ contar lorotas para alguém.
yashmak [ˈjæʃmæk] *n* burca *f*.
yawn [jɔːn] <> *n* -**1.** [when tired] bocejo *m* - **2.** *UK inf* [boring event] chateação *f*. <> *vi* -**1.** [when tired] bocejar - **2.** [gape] abrir-se.
yd *abbr of* yard.
yeah [jeə] *adv inf* sim; **bring us something to drink** - ~, ~! traz algo para a gente beber - tá, já trago!
year [jɪə^r] *n* ano *m*; **all (the)** ~ **round** durante todo o ano; ~ **in** ~ **out** entra ano, sai ano.

◆ **years** *npl* [ages] séculos *mpl*.
yearbook [ˈjɪəbʊk] *n* anuário *m*.
yearling [ˈjɪəlɪŋ] *n* -**1.** [horse] potro *m* -**2.** [sheep, calves] filhote *m*.
yearly [ˈjɪəlɪ] <> *adj* anual. <> *adv* anualmente.
yearn [jɜːn] *vi:* **to** ~ **for sthg/to do sthg** ansiar por algo/para fazer algo.
yearning [ˈjɜːnɪŋ] *n* ânsia *f*; ~ **for sb/sthg** ânsia por alguém/algo.
yeast [jiːst] *n* (U) levedura *f*.
yell [jel] <> *n* grito *m*. <> *vi* gritar. <> *vt* gritar.
yellow [ˈjeləʊ] <> *adj* -**1.** [in colour] amarelo(la) -**2.** *inf* [cowardly] covarde. <> *n* amarelo *m*. <> *vi* amarelar.
yellow card *n FTBL* cartão *m* amarelo.
yellow fever *n* (U) febre *f* amarela.
yellow lines *n* faixa *f* amarela.
yellowness *n* (U) amarelidão *m*.
Yellow Pages® *n UK*: **the** ~ as Páginas Amarelas.
Yellow River *n*: **the** ~ o Rio Amarelo.
Yellow Sea *n*: **the** ~ o Mar Amarelo.
yelp [jelp] <> *n* latido *m*. <> *vi* latir.
Yemen [ˈjemən] *n*: **(the)** ~ o Iêmen; **in (the)** ~ no Iêmen.
Yemeni [ˈjemənɪ] <> *adj* iemenita. <> *n* iemenita *mf*.
yen [jen] (*pl sense 1 inv*) *n* -**1.** [Japanese currency] iene *m* -**2.** [longing]: **to have a** ~ **for sthg/to do sthg** desejar muito algo/fazer algo.
yeoman of the guard (*pl* -men of the guard) *n* membro *m* da guarda real.
yep *adv inf* sim.
yes [jes] <> *adv* sim; ~, **please** sim, por favor; **to say** ~ **to sthg** dizer sim para algo. <> *n* [vote in favour] sim *m*.
yes-man *n pej* capacho *m*.
yesterday [ˈjestədɪ] <> *n* ontem *m*; **the day before yesterday** anteontem. <> *adv* -**1.** [day before today] ontem -**2.** [the past] passado.
yet [jet] <> *adv* -**1.** [gen] ainda; **not** ~ ainda não -**2.** [up until now] já; **as** ~ até agora -**3.** [in the future] até -**4.** [to emphasize number, frequency] mais; ~ **again** mais uma vez. <> *conj* porém.
yeti *n* ieti *m*.
yew [juː] *n* teixo *m*.
Y-fronts *npl UK* cueca *f* com abertura na frente.
YHA (*abbr of* Youth Hostels Association) *n* associação britânica de albergues da juventude.
Yiddish [ˈjɪdɪʃ] <> *adj* relativo(va) ao iídiche. <> *n* (U) iídiche *m*.
yield [jiːld] <> *n* lucro *m*, rendimento *m*. <> *vt* -**1.** [produce - fruit, answer, clue] produzir; [- profits, result] gerar -**2.** [give up] ceder. <> *vi* -**1.** [open, give way, break] ceder -**2.** *fml* [give up, surrender] render-se; **to** ~ **to sb/sthg** ceder a alguém/algo.
yippee [*UK* jɪˈpɪ, *US* ˈjɪpɪ] *excl* iupi!
Y2K (*abbr of* year two thousand) *n* ano *m* 2000.
YMCA (*abbr of* Young Men's Christian Association) *n* ≃ ACM *f*.
yo *excl inf* oi!
yob(bo) [ˈjɒb(əʊ)] *n UK inf* bagunceiro *m*, -ra *f*.

yodel [ˈjəʊdl] (*UK pt* & *pp* **-led**, *cont* **-ling**, *US pt* & *pp* **-ed**, *cont* **-ing**) *vi* cantar à moda dos tiroleses.

yoga [ˈjəʊgə] *n (U)* ioga *f.*

yoghourt, yoghurt, yogurt [*UK* ˈjɒgət, *US* ˈjəʊgərt] *n* iogurte *m.*

yoke [jəʊk] *n* **-1.** [for oxen] junta *f* **-2.** *literary* [burden, suffering] jugo *m.*

yokel [ˈjəʊkl] *n pej* caipira *mf.*

yolk [jəʊk] *n* gema *f.*

yonder [ˈjɒndər] *adv literary* acolá.

Yorkshire pudding [ˈjɔːkʃər-] *n comida preparada com farinha, ovos e leite, e servida com carne.*

you [juː] *pron* **-1.** [subject: singular] você, tu; [subject: singular polite form] o senhor (a senhora); [subject: plural] vocês; [subject: plural polite form] os senhores (as senhoras); **do ~ speak Portuguese?** [singular] você fala português?; [polite form] (o senhor) fala português?; **~ Brazilians** os brasileiros. **-2.** [direct object: singular] o (a), te; [direct object: singular polite form] o senhor (a senhora); [direct object: plural] os (as), vos; [direct object: plural polite form] os (as), os senhores (as senhoras); **I saw ~** [singular] eu o vi; **can I help ~?** [polite form: singular] em que posso ajudá-lo?; [polite form: plural] em que posso ajudá-los?; **I'll see ~ later** [plural] vejo-os mais tarde. **-3.** [indirect object: singular] lhe, te; [indirect object: singular polite form] lhe; [indirect object: plural] lhes, vos; **I would like to ask ~ something** [polite form: singular] gostaria de perguntar algo a você; **didn't I tell ~ what happened?** [polite form: plural] não lhes contei o que aconteceu? **-4.** [after prep: singular] você, ti; [after prep: singular polite form] o senhor (a senhora), si; [after prep: plural] vocês; [after prep: plural polite form] os senhores (as senhoras), vós; **this is for ~** isto é para você/o senhor, etc; **with ~** [singular] com você, contigo; [singular: polite form] com o senhor (a senhora); [plural] com vocês; [plural: polite form] com os senhores (as senhoras). **-5.** [indefinite use: subject]: **the coffee ~ get in Brazil is very strong** o café que se bebe no Brasil é muito forte; **~ never know** nunca se sabe. **-6.** [indefinite use: object]: **exercise is good for ~** exercício faz bem (para a saúde).

you'd [juːd] = **you had**, **you would**.

you'll [juːl] = **you will**.

young [jʌŋ] <> *adj* **-1.** [person] jovem **-2.** [plant, wine, animal] novo(va). <> *npl* **-1.** [young people]: **the ~** a juventude **-2.** [baby animals] filhotes *mpl.*

younger *adj* mais novo(va); **Pitt the Younger** Pitt Júnior.

youngish [ˈjʌŋɪʃ] *adj* bem novo(va).

young man *n* moço *m*, rapaz *m.*

youngster [ˈjʌŋstər] *n* **-1.** [child] filho *m*, -lha *f* **-2.** [young person] jovem *mf.*

young woman *n* moça *f*, rapariga *f.*

your [jɔːr] *adj* **-1.** [singular subject] o seu (a sua), o teu (a tua); [singular subject: polite form] o/a do senhor (da senhora); [plural subject] o vosso (a vossa); [plural subject: polite form] o/a dos senhores (das senhoras); **~ dog** o seu/teu/vosso cão, o cão do senhor

(da senhora), o cão dos senhores (das senhoras); **~ house** a sua/tua/vossa casa, etc; **~ children** os seus/teus/vossos filhos, etc. **-2.** [indefinite subject]: **it's good for ~ health** é bom para a saúde.

you're [jɔːr] = **you are**.

yours [jɔːz] *pron* [singular subject] o seu (a sua), o teu (a tua); [plural subject] o vosso (a vossa); [formal - singular subject] o/a do senhor (da senhora); [- plural subject] o/a dos senhores (das senhoras); **a friend of ~** um amigo seu/teu/vosso/do senhor/da senhora/dos senhores/das senhoras; **these shoes are ~** estes sapatos são (os) teus/seus/vossos, etc; **these are mine – where are ~?** estes são os meus – onde estão os seus/teus/vossos, etc?

yourself [jɔːrˈself] *pron* **-1.** [reflexive: singular] se, te; [reflexive: plural] se; **did you hurt ~?** [singular] você se machucou? **-2.** [after prep: singular] você mesmo(-ma), tu mesmo(ma); [after prep: plural] você mesmos(mas); [after prep: plural polite form] os senhores mesmos (as senhoras mesmas), vós mesmos(mas); **did you do it ~?** [singular] você fez isso sozinho?; [polite form] foi o senhor mesmo que o fez?; **did you do it yourselves?** vocês fizeram isso sozinhos?; [polite form] foram os senhores mesmos que o fizeram?

youth [juːθ] *n* **-1.** [gen] juventude *f* **-2.** [boy, young man] mocidade *f* **-3.** *(U)* [young people] mocidade *f*, juventude *f.*

youth club *n* clube *m* da juventude.

youthful [ˈjuːθfʊl] *adj* juvenil.

youthfulness [ˈjuːθfʊlnɪs] *n (U)* juventude *f.*

youth hostel *n* albergue *m* da juventude.

youth hostelling [-ˈhɒstəlɪŋ] *n UK*: **to go youth hostelling** ir para albergues da juventude.

you've [juːv] *cont* = **you have**.

yowl [jaʊl] <> *n* **-1.** [dog] uivo *m* **-2.** [cat] miado *m.* <> *vi* **-1.** [dog] uivar **-2.** [cat] miar.

yo-yo [ˈjəʊjəʊ] *n* ioiô *m.*

yr (*abbr of* **year**) ano *m.*

YT *n abbr of* **Yukon Territory**.

Yucatan [jʌkəˈtɑːn] *n* Yucatan.

yucca *n* iúca *f.*

yuck [jʌk] *excl inf* argh!

Yugoslav *adj* & *n* = **Yugoslavian**.

Yugoslavia [juːgəˈslɑːvɪə] *n* Iugoslávia *f*; **in ~** na Iugoslávia.

Yugoslavian [juːgəˈslɑːvɪən], **Yugoslav** [juːgəˈslɑːv] <> *adj* iugoslavo(va). <> *n* iugoslavo *m*, -va *f.*

Yukon Territory *n* território *m* Yukon.

yule log *n* **-1.** [piece of wood] acha *f* de Natal **-2.** [cake] torta *f* de Natal.

yuletide [ˈjuːltaɪd] *n (U) literary* época *f* de Natal.

yummy [ˈjʌmɪ] (*compar* **-ier**, *superl* **-iest**) *adj inf* delicioso(sa).

yuppie, yuppy [ˈjʌpɪ] (*pl* **-ies**) (*abbr of* **young urban professional**) *n* yuppie *mf.*

YWCA (*abbr of* **Young Women's Christian Association**) *n ≃* ACM *f.*

z

[eagerness] vivacidade f - **3.** (U) [of orange, lemon] sabor m.

zigzag ['zɪgzæg] (pt & pp -ged, cont -ging) <> n ziguezague m. <> vi ziguezaguear.

zilch [zɪltʃ] n US inf: **I know she'll do ~ while I'm away** nada de nada, sei que ela não vai fazer nada de nada enquanto eu estiver fora.

Zimbabwe [zɪm'bɑːbwɪ] n Zimbábue; **in ~** no Zimbábue.

Zimbabwean [zɪm'bɑːbwɪən] <> adj zimbabuano(na). <> n zimbabuano m, -na f.

Zimmer frame® ['zɪməʳ-] n andador m.

zinc [zɪŋk] n (U) zinco m.

Zionism ['zaɪənɪzm] n sionismo m.

Zionist ['zaɪənɪst] <> adj sionista. <> n sionista mf.

zip [zɪp] (pt & pp -ped, cont -ping) <> n UK [fastener] fecho m ecler, zíper m. <> vt - **1.** [clothing] fechar com zíper - **2.** COMPUT zipar, compactar.

➤ **zip up** vt sep fechar o zíper de.

zip [zɪp]

zip code n US ≃ CEP m.

Zip disk® n COMPUT disco m Zip®.

Zip drive® n COMPUT unidade f Zip®.

zip fastener n UK = zip.

zipper ['zɪpəʳ] n US = zip.

zippy (compar -ier, superl -iest) adj inf [car] possante.

zit [zɪt] n esp US inf mancha f (na pele).

zither ['zɪðəʳ] n citara f.

zodiac ['zəʊdɪæk] n: **the ~** o zodíaco; **sign of the ~** signo m do zodíaco.

zombie ['zɒmbɪ] n [automaton] zumbi m.

zone [zəʊn] n [district] zona f.

zoo [zuː] n zoológico m.

zoological [ˌzəʊə'lɒdʒɪkl] adj zoológico(ca).

zoologist [zəʊ'ɒlədʒɪst] n zoólogo m, -ga f, zoologista mf.

zoology [zəʊ'ɒlədʒɪ] n (U) zoologia f.

zoom [zuːm] vi inf - **1.** [move quickly] arrancar-se - **2.** [rise rapidly] disparar.

➤ **zoom in** vi: **to ~ in (on sb/sthg)** dar um close em alguém/algo.

➤ **zoom off** vi inf arrancar-se.

zoom lens n (lentes fpl de) zum m.

zucchini [zuː'kiːnɪ] (pl inv OR -s) n US abobrinha f italiana.

Zulu ['zuːluː] <> adj zulu. <> n zulu mf.

Zürich ['zjʊərɪk] n Zurique; **in ~** em Zurique.

---

z (pl z's OR zs), **Z** (pl Z's OR Zs) [UK zed, US ziː] n [letter] z, Z m.

Zagreb n Zagreb.

Zaïre [zɑː'ɪəʳ] n Zaire; **in ~** no Zaire.

Zaïrese <> adj zairense. <> n zairense mf.

Zambesi, Zambezi n: **the ~** o Zambesi.

Zambia ['zæmbɪə] n Zâmbia; **in ~** no Zâmbia.

Zambian ['zæmbɪən] <> adj zambiano(na). <> n zambiano m, -na f.

zany ['zeɪnɪ] (compar -ier, superl -iest) adj inf bobo(ba).

Zanzibar n Zanzibar.

zap [zæp] (pt & pp -ped, cont -ping) inf <> vt - **1.** [kill] despachar - **2.** [in video games] destruir. <> vi - **1.** [rush] correr; **to ~ off to** correr para; **to ~ through sthg** passar os olhos por algo - **2.** TV zapear; **to ~ from channel to channel** ficar trocando de um canal para o outro.

zeal [ziːl] n (U) fml zelo m.

zealot ['zelət] n fml fanático m, -ca f.

zealous ['zeləs] adj fml zeloso(sa).

zebra [UK 'zebrə, US 'ziːbrə] (pl inv OR -s) n zebra f.

zebra crossing n UK faixa f de segurança.

zenith [UK 'zenɪθ, US 'ziːnəθ] n - **1.** ASTRON zênite m - **2.** fig [highest point] apogeu m.

zeppelin ['zepəlɪn] n zepelim m.

zero [UK 'zɪərəʊ, US 'ziːrəʊ] (pl -s OR -es, pt & pp -ed, cont -ing) <> adj zero. <> n zero m.

➤ **zero in on** vt fus - **1.** [subj: weapon] fazer mira em - **2.** [subj: person] concentrar-se em.

zero-rated [-ˌreɪtɪd] adj UK ≃ isento(ta) de IVA.

zest [zest] n - **1.** [excitement] entusiasmo m - **2.** (U)

PORTUGUESE VERBS
ENGLISH IRREGULAR VERBS

CONJUGAÇÃO DOS VERBOS PORTUGUESES
VERBOS IRREGULARES INGLESES

	1 ter	2 haver	3 ser
ind. presente	eu tenho, tu tens, ele tem, nós temos, vós tendes, eles têm	eu hei, tu hás, ele há, nós havemos/hemos, vós haveis/heis, eles hão	eu sou, tu és, ele é, nós somos, vós sois, eles são
ind. imperfeito	eu tinha	eu havia	eu era
ind. perfeito	eu tive	eu houve	eu fui
ind. m.-q.-p. simpl.	eu tivera	eu houvera	eu fora
ind. m.-q.-p. comp.	eu tinha tido	eu tinha havido	eu tinha sido
ind fut. do pres.	eu terei	eu haverei	eu serei
ind fut. do pret.	eu teria	eu haveria	eu seria
subj. presente	que eu tenha	que eu haja	que eu seja
subj. imperfeito	que eu tivesse	que eu houvesse	que eu fosse
subj. perfeito	que eu tenha tido	que eu tenha havido	que eu tenha sido
subj. m.-q.-perf.	que eu tivesse tido	que eu tivesse havido	que eu tivesse sido
subj. futuro	quando eu tiver	quando eu houver	quando eu for
inf. pessoal	eu ter, tu teres, ele ter, nós termos, vós terdes, eles terem	eu haver, tu haveres, ele haver, nós havermos, vós haverdes, eles haverem	eu ser, tu seres, ele ser, nós sermos, vós serdes, eles serem
imper. afirm.	tem (tu)	há (tu)	sê (tu)
imper. neg.	não tenhas	não hajas	não sejas
gerúndio	tendo	havendo	sendo
particípio	tido	havido	sido

	4 falar	5 comer	6 partir
ind. presente	eu falo, tu falas, ele fala, nós falamos, vós falais, eles falam	eu como, tu comes, ele come, nós comemos, vós comeis, eles comem	eu parto, tu partes, ele parte, nós partimos, vós partis, eles partem
ind. imperfeito	eu falava	eu comia	eu partia
ind. perfeito	eu falei	eu comi	eu parti
ind. m.-q.-p. simpl.	eu falara	eu comera	eu partira
ind. m.-q.-p. comp.	eu tinha falado	eu tinha comido	eu tinha partido
ind fut. do pres.	eu falarei	eu comerei	eu partirei
ind fut. do pret.	eu falaria	eu comeria	eu partiria
subj. presente	que eu fale	que eu coma	que eu parta
subj. imperfeito	que eu falasse	que eu comesse	que eu partisse
subj. perfeito	que eu tenha falado	que eu tenha comido	que eu tenha partido
subj. m.-q.-perf.	que eu tivesse falado	que eu tivesse comido	que eu tivesse partido
subj. futuro	quando eu falar	quando eu comer	quando eu partir
inf. pessoal	eu falar, tu falares, ele falar, nós falarmos, vós falardes, eles falarem	eu comer, tu comeres, ele comer, nós comermos, vós comerdes, eles comerem	eu partir, tu partires, ele partir, nós partirmos, vós partirdes, eles partirem
imper. afirm.	fala (tu)	come (tu)	parte (tu)
imper. neg.	não fales	não comas	não partas
gerúndio	falando	comendo	partindo
particípio	falado	comido	partido

	7 cortar-se	8 chamá-lo	9 ser amado
ind. presente	eu me corto, tu te cortas, ele se corta, nós nos cortamos, vós vos cortais, eles se cortam	eu o chamo, tu o chamas, ele o chama, nós o chamamos, vós o chamais, eles o chamam	eu sou amado, tu és amado, ele é amado, nós somos amados, vós sois amados, eles são amados
ind. imperfeito	eu me cortava	eu o chamava	eu era amado
ind. perfeito	eu me cortei	eu o chamei	eu fui amado
ind. m.-q.-p. simpl.	eu me cortara	eu o chamara	eu fora amado
ind. m.-q.-p. comp.	eu me tinha cortado	eu o tinha chamado	eu tinha sido amado
ind fut. do pres.	eu me cortarei	eu o chamarei	eu serei amado
ind fut. do pret.	eu me cortaria	eu o chamaria	eu seria amado
subj. presente	que eu me corte	que eu o chame	que eu seja amado
subj. imperfeito	que eu me cortasse	que eu o chamasse	que eu fosse amado
subj. perfeito	que eu me tenha cortado	que eu o tenha chamado	que eu tenha sido amado
subj. m.-q.-perf.	que eu me tivesse cortado	que eu o tivesse chamado	que eu tivesse sido amado
subj. futuro	quando eu me cortar	quando eu o chamar	quando eu for amado
inf. pessoal	eu me cortar, tu te cortares, ele se cortar, nós nos cortarmos, vós vos cortardes, eles se cortarem	eu o chamar, tu o chamares, ele o chamar, nós o chamarmos, vós o chamardes, eles o chamarem	eu ser amado, tu seres amado, ele ser amado, nós sermos amados, vós serdes amados, eles serem amados
imper. afirm.	corta-te (tu)	chama-o (tu)	sê amado (tu)
imper. neg.	não te cortes	não o chames	não sejas amado
gerúndio	cortando	chamando	amando
particípio	cortado	chamado	amado

	10 estar	11 dar	12 ficar
ind. presente	eu estou, tu estás, ele está, nós estamos, vós estais, eles estão	eu dou, tu dás, ele dá, nós damos, vós dais, eles dão	eu fico, tu ficas, ele fica, nós ficamos, vós ficais, eles ficam
ind. imperfeito	eu estava	eu dava	eu ficava
ind. perfeito	eu estive	eu dei	eu fiquei
ind. m.-q.-p. simpl.	eu estivera	eu dera	eu ficara
ind. m.-q.-p. comp.	eu tinha estado	eu tinha dado	eu tinha ficado
ind fut. do pres.	eu estarei	eu darei	eu ficarei
ind fut. do pret.	eu estaria	eu daria	eu ficaria
subj. presente	que eu esteja	que eu dê	que eu fique
subj. imperfeito	que eu estivesse	que eu desse	que eu ficasse
subj. perfeito	que eu tenha estado	que eu tenha dado	que eu tenha ficado
subj. m.-q.-perf.	que eu tivesse estado	que eu tivesse dado	que eu tivesse ficado
subj. futuro	quando eu estiver	quando eu der	quando eu ficar
inf. pessoal	eu estar, tu estares, ele estar, nós estarmos, vós estardes, eles estarem	eu dar, tu dares, ele dar, nós darmos, vós dardes, eles darem	eu ficar, tu ficares, ele ficar, nós ficarmos, vós ficardes, eles ficarem
imper. afirm.	está (tu)	dá (tu)	fica (tu)
imper. neg.	não estejas	não dês	não fiques
gerúndio	estando	dando	ficando
particípio	estado	dado	ficado

	13 dançar	14 pagar	15 passear
ind. presente	eu danço, tu danças, ele dança, nós dançamos, vós dançais, eles dançam	eu pago, tu pagas, ele paga, nós pagamos, vós pagais, eles pagam	eu passeio, tu passeias, ele passeia, nós passeamos, vós passeais, eles passeiam
ind. imperfeito	eu dançava	eu pagava	eu passeava
ind. perfeito	eu dancei	eu paguei	eu passeei
ind. m.-q.-p. simpl.	eu dançara	eu pagara	eu passeara
ind. m.-q.-p. comp.	eu tinha dançado	eu tinha pagado	eu tinha passeado
ind fut. do pres.	eu dançarei	eu pagarei	eu passearei
ind fut. do pret.	eu dançaria	eu pagaria	eu passearia
subj. presente	que eu dance	que eu pague	que eu passeie
subj. imperfeito	que eu dançasse	que eu pagasse	que eu passeasse
subj. perfeito	que eu tenha dançado	que eu tenha pagado	que eu tenha passeado
subj. m.-q.-perf.	que eu tivesse dançado	que eu tivesse pagado	que eu tivesse passeado
subj. futuro	quando eu dançar	quando eu pagar	quando eu passear
inf. pessoal	eu dançar, tu dançares, ele dançar, nós dançarmos, vós dançardes, eles dançarem	eu pagar, tu pagares, ele pagar, nós pagarmos, vós pagardes, eles pagarem	eu passear, tu passeares, ele passear, nós passearmos, vós passeardes, eles passearem
imper. afirm.	dança (tu)	paga (tu)	passeia (tu)
imper. neg.	não dances	não pagues	não passeies
gerúndio	dançando	pagando	passeando
particípio	dançado	pagado/pago	passeado

	16 enviar	17 odiar	18 comerciar
ind. presente	eu envio, tu envias, ele envia, nós enviamos, vós enviais, eles enviam	eu odeio, tu odeias, ele odeia, nós odiamos, vós odiais, eles odeiam	eu comerc(e)io, tu comerc(e)ias, ele comerc(e)ia, nós comerciamos, vós comerciais, eles comerc(e)iam
ind. imperfeito	eu enviava	eu odiava	eu comerciava
ind. perfeito	eu enviei	eu odiei	eu comerciei
ind. m.-q.-p. simpl.	eu enviara	eu odiara	eu comerciara
ind. m.-q.-p. comp.	eu tinha enviado	eu tinha odiado	eu tinha comerciado
ind fut. do pres.	eu enviarei	eu odiarei	eu comerciarei
ind fut. do pret.	eu enviaria	eu odiaria	eu comerciaria
subj. presente	que eu envie	que eu odeie	que eu comerc(e)ie
subj. imperfeito	que eu enviasse	que eu odiasse	que eu comerciasse
subj. perfeito	que eu tenha enviado	que eu tenha odiado	que eu tenha comerciado
subj. m.-q.-perf.	que eu tivesse enviado	que eu tivesse odiado	que eu tivesse comerciado
subj. futuro	quando eu enviar	quando eu odiar	quando eu comerciar
inf. pessoal	eu enviar, tu enviares, ele enviar, nós enviarmos, vós enviardes, eles enviarem	eu odiar, tu odiares, ele odiar, nós odiarmos, vós odiardes, eles odiarem	eu comerciar, tu comerciares, ele comerciar, nós comerciarmos, vós comerciardes, eles comerciarem
imper. afirm.	envia (tu)	odeia (tu)	comerc(e)ia (tu)
imper. neg.	não envies	não odeies	não comerc(e)ies
gerúndio	enviando	odiando	comerciando
particípio	enviado	odiado	comerciado

	19 saudar	20 doar	21 averiguar
ind. presente	eu saúdo, tu saúdas, ele saúda, nós saudamos, vós saudais, eles saúdam	eu dôo, tu doas, ele doa, nós doamos, vós doais, eles doam	eu averiguo, tu averiguas, ele averigua, nós averiguamos, vós averiguais, eles averiguam
ind. imperfeito	eu saudava	eu doava	eu averiguava
ind. perfeito	eu saudei	eu doei	eu averigüei
ind. m.-q.-p. simpl.	eu saudara	eu doara	eu averiguara
ind. m.-q.-p. comp.	eu tinha saudado	eu tinha doado	eu tinha averiguado
ind fut. do pres.	eu saudarei	eu doarei	eu averiguarei
ind fut. do pret.	eu saudaria	eu doaria	eu averiguaria
subj. presente	que eu saúde	que eu doe	que eu averigúe
subj. imperfeito	que eu saudasse	que eu doasse	que eu averiguasse
subj. perfeito	que eu tenha saudado	que eu tenha doado	que eu tenha averiguado
subj. m.-q.-perf.	que eu tivesse saudado	que eu tivesse doado	que eu tivesse averiguado
subj. futuro	quando eu saudar	quando eu doar	quando eu averiguar
inf. pessoal	eu saudar, tu saudares, ele saudar, nós saudarmos, vós saudardes, eles saudarem	eu doar, tu doares, ele doar, nós doarmos, vós doardes, eles doarem	eu averiguar, tu averiguares, ele averiguar, nós averiguarmos, vós averiguardes, eles averiguarem
imper. afirm.	saúda (tu)	doa (tu)	averigua (tu)
imper. neg.	não saúdes	não does	não averigúes
gerúndio	saudando	doando	averiguando
particípio	saudado	doado	averiguado

	22 enxaguar	23 adequar	24 relampaguear
ind. presente	eu enxáguo, tu enxáguas, ele enxágua, nós enxaguamos, vós enxaguais, eles enxáguam	nós adequamos, vós adequais	relampagueia, relampagueiam
ind. imperfeito	eu enxaguava	eu adequava	
ind. perfeito	eu enxagüei	eu adeqüei	
ind. m.-q.-p. simpl.	eu enxaguara	eu adequara	
ind. m.-q.-p. comp.	eu tinha enxaguado	eu tinha adequado	
ind fut. do pres.	eu enxaguarei	eu adequarei	
ind fut. do pret.	eu enxaguaria	eu adequaria	
subj. presente	que eu enxágüe		
subj. imperfeito	que eu enxaguasse	que eu adequasse	
subj. perfeito	que eu tenha enxaguado	que eu tenha adequado	
subj. m.-q.-perf.	que eu tivesse enxaguado	que eu tivesse adequado	
subj. futuro	quando eu enxaguar	quando eu adequar	
inf. pessoal	eu enxaguar, tu enxaguares, ele enxaguar, nós enxaguarmos, vós enxaguardes, eles enxaguarem	eu adequar, tu adequares, ele adequar, nós adequarmos, vós adequardes, eles adequarem	relampaguear
imper. afirm.	enxágua (tu)	adequai (vós)	
imper. neg.	não enxágües		
gerúndio	enxaguando	adequando	relampagueando
particípio	enxaguado	adequado	relampagueado

	25 agradecer	26 eleger	27 erguer
ind. presente	eu agradeço, tu agradeces, ele agradece, nós agradecemos, vós agradeceis, eles agradecem	eu elejo, tu eleges, ele elege, nós elegemos, vós elegeis, eles elegem	eu ergo, tu ergues, ele ergue, nós erguemos, vós ergueis, eles erguem
ind. imperfeito	eu agradecia	eu elegia	eu erguia
ind. perfeito	eu agradeci	eu elegi	eu ergui
ind. m.-q.-p. simpl.	eu agradecera	eu elegera	eu erguera
ind. m.-q.-p. comp.	en tinha agradecido	en tinha elegido	eu tinha erguido
ind fut. do pres.	eu agradecerei	eu elegerei	eu erguerei
ind fut. do pret.	eu agradeceria	eu elegeria	eu ergueria
subj. presente	que eu agradeça	que eu eleja	que eu erga
subj. imperfeito	que eu agradecesse	que eu elegesse	que eu erguesse
subj. perfeito	que eu tenha agradecido	que eu tenha elegido	que eu tenha erguido
subj. m.-q.-perf.	que eu tivesse agradecido	que eu tivesse elegido	que eu tivesse erguido
subj. futuro	quando eu agradecer	quando eu eleger	quando eu erguer
inf. pessoal	eu agradecer, tu agradeceres, ele agradecer, nós agradecermos, vós agradecerdes, eles agradecerem	eu eleger, tu elegeres, ele eleger, nós elegermos, vós elegerdes, eles elegerem	eu erguer, tu ergueres, ele erguer, nós erguermos, vós erguerdes, eles erguerem
imper. afirm.	agradece (tu)	elege (tu)	ergue (tu)
imper. neg.	não agradeças	não elejas	não ergas
gerúndio	agradecendo	elegendo	erguendo
particípio	agradecido	elegido, eleito	erguido

	28 roer	29 dizer	30 trazer
ind. presente	eu rôo, tu róis, ele rói, nós roemos, vós roeis, eles roem	eu digo, tu dizes, ele diz, nós dizemos, vós dizeis, eles dizem	eu trago, tu trazes, ele traz, nós trazemos, vós trazeis, eles trazem
ind. imperfeito	eu roía	eu dizia	eu trazia
ind. perfeito	eu roí	eu disse	eu trouxe
ind. m.-q.-p. simpl.	eu roera	eu dissera	eu trouxera
ind. m.-q.-p. comp.	eu tinha roído	eu tinha dito	eu tinha trazido
ind fut. do pres.	eu roerei	eu direi	eu trarei
ind fut. do pret.	eu roeria	eu diria	eu traria
subj. presente	que eu roa	que eu diga	que eu traga
subj. imperfeito	que eu roesse	que eu dissesse	que eu trouxesse
subj. perfeito	que eu tenha roído	que eu tenha dito	que eu tenha trazido
subj. m.-q.-perf.	que eu tivesse roído	que eu tivesse dito	que eu tivesse trazido
subj. futuro	quando eu roer	quando eu disser	quando eu trouxer
inf. pessoal	eu roer, tu roeres, ele roer, nós roermos, vós roerdes, eles roerem	eu dizer, tu dizeres, ele dizer, nós dizermos, vós dizerdes, eles dizerem	eu trazer, tu trazeres, ele trazer, nós trazermos, vós trazerdes, eles trazerem
imper. afirm.	rói (tu)	diz, dize (tu)	traz, traze (tu)
imper. neg.	não roas	não digas	não tragas
gerúndio	roendo	dizendo	trazendo
particípio	roído	dito	trazido

	31 fazer	32 aprazer	33 jazer
ind. presente	eu faço, tu fazes, ele faz, nós fazemos, vós fazeis, eles fazem	eu aprazo, tu aprazes, ele apraz, nós aprazemos, vós aprazeis, eles aprazem	eu jazo, tu jazes, ele jaz, nós jazemos, vós jazeis, eles jazem
ind. imperfeito	eu fazia	eu aprazia	eu jazia
ind. perfeito	eu fiz	eu aprouve	eu jazi
ind. m.-q.-p. simpl.	eu fizera	eu aprouvera	eu jazera
ind. m.-q.-p. comp.	eu tinha feito	eu tinha aprazido	eu tinha jazido
ind fut. do pres.	eu farei	eu aprazerei	eu jazerei
ind fut. do pret.	eu faria	eu aprazeria	eu jazeria
subj. presente	que eu faça	que eu apraza	que eu jaza
subj. imperfeito	que eu fizesse	que eu aprouvesse	que eu jazesse
subj. perfeito	que eu tenha feito	que eu tenha aprazido	que eu tenha jazido
subj. m.-q.-perf.	que eu tivesse feito	que eu tivesse aprazido	que eu tivesse jazido
subj. futuro	quando eu fizer	quando eu aprouver	quando eu jazer
inf. pessoal	eu fazer, tu fazeres, ele fazer, nós fazermos, vós fazerdes, eles fazerem	eu aprazer, tu aprazeres, ele aprazer, nós aprazermos, vós aprazerdes, eles aprazerem	eu jazer, tu jazeres, ele jazer, nós jazermos, vós jazerdes, eles jazerem
imper. afirm.	faz, faze (tu)	apraz, apraze (tu)	jaz, jaze (tu)
imper. neg.	não faças	não aprazas	não jazas
gerúndio	fazendo	aprazendo	jazendo
particípio	feito	aprazido	jazido

	34 caber	35 saber	36 poder
ind. presente	eu caibo, tu cabes, ele cabe, nós cabemos, vós cabeis, eles cabem	eu sei, tu sabes, ele sabe, nós sabemos, vós sabeis, eles sabem	eu posso, tu podes, ele pode, nós podemos, vós podeis, eles podem
ind. imperfeito	eu cabia	eu sabia	eu podia
ind. perfeito	eu coube	eu soube	eu pude
ind. m.-q.-p. simpl.	eu coubera	eu soubera	eu pudera
ind. m.-q.-p. comp.	eu tinha cabido	eu tinha sabido	eu tinha podido
ind fut. do pres.	eu caberei	eu saberei	eu poderei
ind fut. do pret.	eu caberia	eu saberia	eu poderia
subj. presente	que eu caiba	que eu saiba	que eu possa
subj. imperfeito	que eu coubesse	que eu soubesse	que eu pudesse
subj. perfeito	que eu tenha cabido	que eu tenha sabido	que eu tenha podido
subj. m.-q.-perf.	que eu tivesse cabido	que eu tivesse sabido	que eu tivesse podido
subj. futuro	quando eu couber	quando eu souber	quando eu puder
inf. pessoal	eu caber, tu caberes, ele caber, nós cabermos, vós caberdes, eles caberem	eu saber, tu saberes, ele saber, nós sabermos, vós saberdes, eles saberem	eu poder, tu poderes, ele poder, nós podermos, vós poderdes, eles poderem
imper. afirm.		sabe (tu)	
imper. neg.		não saibas	
gerúndio	cabendo	sabendo	podendo
particípio	cabido	sabido	podido

	37 crer	38 querer	39 requerer
ind. presente	eu creio, tu crês, ele crê, nós cremos, vós credes, eles crêem	eu quero, tu queres, ele quer, nós queremos, vós quereis, eles querem	eu requeiro, tu requeres, ele requer, nós requeremos, vós requereis, eles requerem
ind. imperfeito	eu cria	eu queria	eu requeria
ind. perfeito	eu cri	eu quis	eu requeri
ind. m.-q.-p. simpl.	eu crera	eu quisera	eu requerera
ind. m.-q.-p. comp.	eu tinha crido	eu tinha querido	eu tinha requerido
ind fut. do pres.	eu crerei	eu quererei	eu requererei
ind fut. do pret.	eu creria	eu quereria	eu requereria
subj. presente	que eu creia	que eu queira	que eu requeira
subj. imperfeito	que eu cresse	que eu quisesse	que eu requeresse
subj. perfeito	que eu tenha crido	que eu tenha querido	que eu tenha requerido
subj. m.-q.-perf.	que eu tivesse crido	que eu tivesse querido	que eu tivesse requerido
subj. futuro	quando eu crer	quando eu quiser	quando eu requerer
inf. pessoal	eu crer, tu creres, ele crer, nós crermos, vós crerdes, eles crerem	eu querer, tu quereres, ele querer, nós querermos, vós quererdes, eles quererem	eu requerer, tu requereres, ele requerer, nós requerermos, vós requererdes, eles requererem
imper. afirm.	crê (tu)	quer (tu)	requer (tu)
imper. neg.	não creias	não queiras	não requeiras
gerúndio	crendo	querendo	requerendo
particípio	crido	querido	requerido

	40 ver	**41 prover**	**42 ler**
ind. presente	eu vejo, tu vês, ele vê, nós vemos, vós vedes, eles vêem	eu provejo, tu provês, ele provê, nós provemos, vós provedes, eles provêem	eu leio, tu lês, ele lê, nós lemos, vós ledes, eles lêem
ind. imperfeito	eu via	eu provia	eu lia
ind. perfeito	eu vi	eu provi	eu li
ind. m.-q.-p. simpl.	eu vira	eu provera	eu lera
ind. m.-q.-p. comp.	eu tinha visto	eu tinha provido	eu tinha lido
ind fut. do pres.	eu verei	eu proverei	eu lerei
ind fut. do pret.	eu veria	eu proveria	eu leria
subj. presente	que eu veja	que eu proveja	que eu leia
subj. imperfeito	que eu visse	que eu provesse	que eu lesse
subj. perfeito	que eu tenha visto	que eu tenha provido	que eu tenha lido
subj. m.-q.-perf.	que eu tivesse visto	que eu tivesse provido	que eu tivesse lido
subj. futuro	quando eu vir	quando eu prover	quando eu ler
inf. pessoal	eu ver, tu veres, ele ver, nós vermos, vós verdes, eles verem	eu prover, tu proveres, ele prover, nós provermos, vós proverdes, eles proverem	eu ler, tu leres, ele ler, nós lermos, vós lerdes, eles lerem
imper. afirm.	vê (tu)	provê (tu)	lê (tu)
imper. neg.	não vejas	não provejas	não leias
gerúndio	vendo	provendo	lendo
particípio	visto	provido	lido

	43 valer	44 perder	45 pôr
ind. presente	eu valho, tu vales, ele vale, nós valemos, vós valeis, eles valem	eu perco, tu perdes, ele perde, nós perdemos, vós perdeis, eles perdem	eu ponho, tu pões, ele põe, nós pomos, vós pondes, eles põem
ind. imperfeito	eu valia	eu perdia	eu punha
ind. perfeito	eu vali	eu perdi	eu pus
ind. m.-q.-p. simpl.	eu valera	eu perdera	eu pusera
ind. m.-q.-p. comp.	eu tinha valido	eu tinha perdido	eu tinha posto
ind fut. do pres.	eu valerei	eu perderei	eu porei
ind fut. do pret.	eu valeria	eu perderia	eu poria
subj. presente	que eu valha	que eu perca	que eu ponha
subj. imperfeito	que eu valesse	que eu perdesse	que eu pusesse
subj. perfeito	que eu tenha valido	que eu tenha perdido	que eu tenha posto
subj. m.-q.-perf.	que eu tivesse valido	que eu tivesse perdido	que eu tivesse posto
subj. futuro	quando eu valer	quando eu perder	quando eu puser
inf. pessoal	eu valer, tu valeres, ele valer, nós valermos, vós valerdes, eles valerem	eu perder, tu perderes, ele perder, nós perdermos, vós perderdes, eles perderem	eu pôr, tu pores, ele pôr, nós pormos, vós pordes, eles porem
imper. afirm.	vale (tu)	perde (tu)	põe (tu)
imper. neg.	não valhas	não percas	não ponhas
gerúndio	valendo	perdendo	pondo
particípio	valido	perdido	posto

	46 acontecer	47 chover	48 doer
ind. presente	acontece, acontecem	chove	dói, doem
ind. imperfeito	acontecia, aconteciam	chovia	doía, doíam
ind. perfeito	aconteceu, aconteceram	choveu	doeu, doeram
ind. m.-q.-p. simpl.	acontecera, aconteceram	chovera	doera, doeram
ind. m.-q.-p. comp.	tinha acontecido	tinha chovido	tinha doído
ind. fut. do pres.	acontecerá, acontecerão	choverá	doerá, doerão
ind. fut. do pret.	aconteceria, aconteceriam	choveria	doeria, doeriam
subj. presente	que ele aconteça	chova	doa, doam
subj. imperfeito	que ele acontecesse	chovesse	doesse, doessem
subj. perfeito	que ele tenha acontecido	tenha chovido	tenha doído
subj. m.-q.-perf.	que ele tivesse acontecido	tivesse chovido	tivesse doído
subj. futuro	quando ele acontecer	quando chover	quando doer
inf. pessoal	ele acontecer, eles acontecerem	chover	doer, doerem
imper. afirm.			
imper. neg.			
gerúndio	acontecendo	chovendo	doendo
particípio	acontecido	chovido	doído

	49 prazer	50 precaver	51 reaver
ind. presente	praz, prazem	nós precavemos, vós precaveis	nós reavemos, vós reaveis
ind. imperfeito	prazia, praziam	eu precavia	eu reavia
ind. perfeito	prouve, prouveram	eu precavi	eu reouve
ind. m.-q.-p. simpl.	prouvera, prouveram	eu precavera	eu reouvera
ind. m.-q.-p. comp.	tinha prazido	eu tinha precavido	eu tinha reavido
ind fut. do pres.	prazerá, prazerão	eu precaverei	eu reaverei
ind fut. do pret.	prazeria, prazeriam	eu precaveria	eu reaveria
subj. presente	praza, prazam		
subj. imperfeito	prouvesse, prouvessem	que eu precavesse	que eu reouvesse
subj. perfeito	que ele tenha prazido	que eu tenha precavido	que eu tenha reavido
subj. m.-q.-perf.	que ele tivesse prazido	que eu tivesse precavido	que eu tivesse reavido
subj. futuro	quando ele prouver	quando eu precaver	quando eu reouver
inf. pessoal	prazer, prazerem	eu precaver, tu precaveres, ele precaver, nós precavermos, vós precaverdes, eles precaverem	eu reaver, tu reaveres, ele reaver, nós reavermos, vós reaverdes, eles reaverem
imper. afirm.	praza (você)	precavei (vós)	reavei (vós)
imper. neg.	não praza (você)		
gerúndio	prazendo	precavendo	reavendo
particípio	prazido	precavido	reavido

	52 fingir	53 distinguir	54 servir
ind. presente	eu finjo, tu finges, ele finge, nós fingimos, vós fingis, eles fingem	eu distingo, tu distingues, ele distingue, nós distinguimos, vós distinguis, eles distinguem	eu sirvo, tu serves, ele serve, nós servimos, vós servis, eles servem
ind. imperfeito	eu fingia	eu distinguia	eu servia
ind. perfeito	eu fingi	eu distingui	eu servi
ind. m.-q.-p. simpl.	eu fingira	eu distinguira	eu servira
ind. m.-q.-p. comp.	eu tinha fingido	eu tinha distinguido	eu tinha servido
ind fut. do pres.	eu fingirei	eu distinguirei	eu servirei
ind fut. do pret.	eu fingiria	eu distinguiria	eu serviria
subj. presente	que eu finja	que eu distinga	que eu sirva
subj. imperfeito	que eu fingisse	que eu distinguisse	que eu servisse
subj. perfeito	que eu tenha fingido	que eu tenha distinguido	que eu tenha servido
subj. m.-q.-perf.	que eu tivesse fingido	que eu tivesse distinguido	que eu tivesse servido
subj. futuro	quando eu fingir	quando eu distinguir	quando eu servir
inf. pessoal	eu fingir, tu fingires, ele fingir, nós fingirmos, vós fingirdes, eles fingirem	eu distinguir, tu distinguires, ele distinguir, nós distinguirmos, vós distinguirdes, eles distinguirem	eu servir, tu servires, ele servir, nós servirmos, vós servirdes, eles servirem
imper. afirm.	finge (tu)	distingue (tu)	serve (tu)
imper. neg.	não finjas	não distingas	não sirvas
gerúndio	fingindo	distinguindo	servindo
particípio	fingido	distinguido	servido

	55 seguir	56 sentir	57 ferir
ind. presente	eu sigo, tu segues, ele segue, nós seguimos, vós seguis, eles seguem	eu sinto, tu sentes, ele sente, nós sentimos, vós sentis, eles sentem	eu firo, tu feres, ele fere, nós ferimos, vós feris, eles ferem
ind. imperfeito	eu seguia	eu sentia	eu feria
ind. perfeito	eu segui	eu senti	eu feri
ind. m.-q.-p. simpl.	eu seguira	eu sentira	eu ferira
ind. m.-q.-p. comp.	eu tinha seguido	eu tinha sentido	eu tinha ferido
ind fut. do pres.	eu seguirei	eu sentirei	eu ferirei
ind fut. do pret.	eu seguiria	eu sentiria	eu feriria
subj. presente	que eu siga	que eu sinta	que eu fira
subj. imperfeito	que eu seguisse	que eu sentisse	que eu ferisse
subj. perfeito	que eu tenha seguido	que eu tenha sentido	que eu tenha ferido
subj. m.-q.-perf.	que eu tivesse seguido	que eu tivesse sentido	que eu tivesse ferido
subj. futuro	quando eu seguir	quando eu sentir	quando eu ferir
inf. pessoal	eu seguir, tu seguires, ele seguir, nós seguirmos, vós seguirdes, eles seguirem	eu sentir, tu sentires, ele sentir, nós sentirmos, vós sentirdes, eles sentirem	eu ferir, tu ferires, ele ferir, nós ferirmos, vós ferirdes, eles ferirem
imper. afirm.	segue (tu)	sente (tu)	fere (tu)
imper. neg.	não sigas	não sintas	não firas
gerúndio	seguindo	sentindo	ferindo
particípio	seguido	sentido	ferido

	58 prevenir	59 dormir	60 polir
ind. presente	eu previno, tu prevines, ele previne, nós prevenimos, vós prevenis, eles previnem	eu durmo, tu dormes, ele dorme, nós dormimos, vós dormis, eles dormem	eu pulo, tu pules, ele pule, nós polimos, vós polis, eles pulem
ind. imperfeito	eu prevenia	eu dormia	eu polia
ind. perfeito	eu preveni	eu dormi	eu poli
ind. m.-q.-p. simpl.	eu prevenira	eu dormira	eu polira
ind. m.-q.-p. comp.	eu tinha prevenido	eu tinha dormido	eu tinha polido
ind fut. do pres.	eu prevenirei	eu dormirei	eu polirei
ind fut. do pret.	eu preveniria	eu dormiria	eu poliria
subj. presente	que eu previna	que eu durma	que eu pula
subj. imperfeito	que eu prevenisse	que eu dormisse	que eu polisse
subj. perfeito	que eu tenha prevenido	que eu tenha dormido	que eu tenha polido
subj. m.-q.-perf.	que eu tivesse prevenido	que eu tivesse dormido	que eu tivesse polido
subj. futuro	quando eu prevenir	quando eu dormir	quando eu polir
inf. pessoal	eu prevenir, tu prevenires, ele prevenir, nós prevenirmos, vós prevenirdes, eles prevenirem	eu dormir, tu dormires, ele dormir, nós dormirmos, vós dormirdes, eles dormirem	eu polir, tu polires, ele polir, nós polirmos, vós polirdes, eles polirem
imper. afirm.	previne (tu)	dorme (tu)	pule (tu)
imper. neg.	não previnas	não durmas	não pulas
gerúndio	prevenindo	dormindo	polindo
particípio	prevenido	dormido	polido

	61 subir	62 fugir	63 frigir
ind. presente	eu subo, tu sobes, ele sobe, nós subimos, vós subis, eles sobem	eu fujo, tu foges, ele foge, nós fugimos, vós fugis, eles fogem	eu frijo, tu friges, ele frige, nós frigimos, vós frigis, eles frigem
ind. imperfeito	eu subia	eu fugia	eu frigia
ind. perfeito	eu subi	eu fugi	eu frigi
ind. m.-q.-p. simpl.	eu subira	eu fugira	eu frigi
ind. m.-q.-p. comp.	eu tinha subido	eu tinha fugido	eu tinha frigido
ind fut. do pres.	eu subirei	eu fugirei	eu frigirei
ind fut. do pret.	eu subiria	eu fugiria	eu frigiria
subj. presente	que eu suba	que eu fuja	que eu frija
subj. imperfeito	que eu subisse	que eu fugisse	que eu frigisse
subj. perfeito	que eu tenha subido	que eu tenha fugido	que eu tenha frigido
subj. m.-q.-perf.	que eu tivesse subido	que eu tivesse fugido	que eu tivesse frigido
subj. futuro	quando eu subir	quando eu fugir	quando eu frigir
inf. pessoal	eu subir, tu subires, ele subir, nós subirmos, vós subirdes, eles subirem	eu fugir, tu fugires, ele fugir, nós fugirmos, vós fugirdes, eles fugirem	eu frigir, tu frigires, ele frigir, nós frigirmos, vós frigirdes, eles frigirem
imper. afirm.	sobe (tu)	foge (tu)	frige (tu)
imper. neg.	não subas	não fujas	não frijas
gerúndio	subindo	fugindo	frigindo
particípio	subido	fugido	frigido, frito

	64 convergir	65 refletir	66 ir
ind. presente	eu convirjo, tu converges, ele converge, nós convergimos, vós convergis, eles convergem	eu reflito, tu refletes, ele reflete, nós refletimos, vós refletis, eles refletem	eu vou, tu vais, ele vai, nós vamos, vós ides, eles vão
ind. imperfeito	eu convergia	eu refletia	eu ia
ind. perfeito	eu convergi	eu refleti	eu fui
ind. m.-q.-p. simpl.	eu convergira	eu refletira	eu fora
ind. m.-q.-p. comp.	eu tinha convergido	eu tinha refletido	eu tinha ido
ind fut. do pres.	eu convergirei	eu refletirei	eu irei
ind fut. do pret.	eu convergiria	eu refletiria	eu iria
subj. presente	que eu convirja	que eu reflita	que eu vá
subj. imperfeito	que eu convergisse	que eu refletisse	que eu fosse
subj. perfeito	que eu tenha convergido	que eu tenha refletido	que eu tenha ido
subj. m.-q.-perf.	que eu tivesse convergido	que eu tivesse refletido	que eu tivesse ido
subj. futuro	quando eu convergir	quando eu refletir	quando eu for
inf. pessoal	eu convergir, tu convergires, ele convergir, nós convergirmos, vós convergirdes, eles convergirem	eu refletir, tu refletires, ele refletir, nós refletirmos, vós refletirdes, eles refletirem	eu ir, tu ires, ele ir, nós irmos, vós irdes, eles irem
imper. afirm.	converge (tu)	reflete (tu)	vai (tu)
imper. neg.	não convirjas	não reflitas	não vás
gerúndio	convergindo	refletindo	indo
particípio	convergido	refletido	ido

	67 vir	68 sair	69 rir
ind. presente	eu venho, tu vens, ele vem, nós vimos, vós vindes, eles vêm	eu saio, tu sais, ele sai, nós saímos, vós saís, eles saem	eu rio, tu ris, ele ri, nós rimos, vós rides, eles riem
ind. imperfeito	eu vinha	eu saía	eu ria
ind. perfeito	eu vim	eu saí	eu ri
ind. m.-q.-p. simpl.	eu viera	eu saíra	eu rira
ind. m.-q.-p. comp.	eu tinha vindo	eu tinha saído	eu tinha rido
ind fut. do pres.	eu virei	eu sairei	eu rirei
ind fut. do pret.	eu viria	eu sairia	eu riria
subj. presente	que eu venha	que eu saia	que eu ria
subj. imperfeito	que eu viesse	que eu saísse	que eu risse
subj. perfeito	que eu tenha vindo	que eu tenha saído	que eu tenha rido
subj. m.-q.-perf.	que eu tivesse vindo	que eu tivesse saído	que eu tivesse rido
subj. futuro	quando eu vier	quando eu sair	quando eu rir
inf. pessoal	eu vir, tu vires, ele vir, nós virmos, vós virdes, eles virem	eu sair, tu saires, ele sair, nós sairmos, vós sairdes, eles saírem	eu rir, tu rires, ele rir, nós rirmos, vós rirdes, eles rirem
imper. afirm.	vem (tu)	sai (tu)	ri (tu)
imper. neg.	não venhas	não saias	não rias
gerúndio	vindo	saindo	rindo
particípio	vindo	saído	rido

	70 pedir	71 ouvir	72 produzir
ind. presente	eu peço, tu pedes, ele pede, nós pedimos, vós pedis, eles pedem	eu ouço/oiço, tu ouves, ele ouve, nós ouvimos, vós ouvis, eles ouvem	eu produzo, tu produzes, ele produz, nós produzimos, vós produzis, eles produzem
ind. imperfeito	eu pedia	eu ouvia	eu produzia
ind. perfeito	eu pedi	eu ouvi	eu produzi
ind. m.-q.-p. simpl.	eu pedira	eu ouvira	eu produzira
ind. m.-q.-p. comp.	eu tinha pedido	eu tinha ouvido	eu tinha produzido
ind fut. do pres.	eu pedirei	eu ouvirei	eu produzirei
ind fut. do pret.	eu pediria	eu ouviria	eu produziria
subj. presente	que eu peça	que eu ouça	que eu produza
subj. imperfeito	que eu pedisse	que eu ouvisse	que eu produzisse
subj. perfeito	que eu tenha pedido	que eu tenha ouvido	que eu tenha produzido
subj. m.-q.-perf.	que eu tivesse pedido	que eu tivesse ouvido	que eu tivesse produzido
subj. futuro	quando eu pedir	quando eu ouvir	quando eu produzir
inf. pessoal	eu pedir, tu pedires, ele pedir, nós pedirmos, vós pedirdes, eles pedirem	eu ouvir, tu ouvires, ele ouvir, nós ouvirmos, vós ouvirdes, eles ouvirem	eu produzir, tu produzires, ele produzir, nós produzirmos, vós produzirdes, eles produzirem
imper. afirm.	pede (tu)	ouve (tu)	produz, produze (tu)
imper. neg.	não peças	não ouças	não produzas
gerúndio	pedindo	ouvindo	produzindo
particípio	pedido	ouvido	produzido

	73 construir	74 atribuir	75 argüir
ind. presente	eu construo, tu constróis, ele constrói, nós construímos, vós construís, eles constroem	eu atribuo, tu atribuis, ele atribui, nós atribuímos, vós atribuís, eles atribuem	eu arguo, tu argúis, ele argúi, nós argüimos, vós argüis, eles argúem
ind. imperfeito	eu construía	eu atribuía	eu argüia
ind. perfeito	eu construí	eu atribuí	eu argüi
ind. m.-q.-p. simpl.	eu construíra	eu atribuíra	eu argüira
ind. m.-q.-p. comp.	eu tinha construído	eu tinha atribuído	eu tinha argüido
ind fut. do pres.	eu construirei	eu atribuirei	eu argüirei
ind fut. do pret.	eu construiria	eu atribuiria	eu argüiria
subj. presente	que eu construa	que eu atribua	que eu argua
subj. imperfeito	que eu construísse	que eu atribuísse	que eu argüisse
subj. perfeito	que eu tenha construído	que eu tenha atribuído	que eu tenha argüido
subj. m.-q.-perf.	que eu tivesse construído	que eu tivesse atribuído	que eu tivesse argüido
subj. futuro	quando eu construir	quando eu atribuir	quando eu argüir
inf. pessoal	eu construir, tu construíres, ele construir, nós construirmos, vós construirdes, eles construírem	eu atribuir, tu atribuíres, ele atribuir, nós atribuirmos, vós atribuirdes, eles atribuírem	eu argüir, tu argüires, ele argüir, nós argüirmos, vós argüirdes, eles argüirem
imper. afirm.	constrói (tu)	atribui (tu)	argúi (tu)
imper. neg.	não construas	não atribuas	não arguas (tu)
gerúndio	construindo	atribuindo	argüindo
particípio	construído	atribuído	argüido

	76 reunir	77 proibir	78 emergir
ind. presente	eu reúno, tu reúnes, ele reúne, nós reunimos, vós reunis, eles reúnem	eu proíbo, tu proíbes, ele proíbe, nós proibimos, vós proibis, eles proíbem	eu emerjo, tu emerges, ele emerge, nós emergimos, vós emergis, eles emergem
ind. imperfeito	eu reunia	eu proibia	eu emergia
ind. perfeito	eu reuni	eu proibi	eu emergi
ind. m.-q.-p. simpl.	eu reunira	eu proibira	eu emergira
ind. m.-q.-p. comp.	eu tinha reunido	eu tinha proibido	eu tinha emergido
ind fut. do pres.	eu reunirei	eu proibirei	eu emergirei
ind fut. do pret.	eu reuniria	eu proibiria	eu emergiria
subj. presente	que eu reúna	que eu proíba	que eu emerja
subj. imperfeito	que eu reunisse	que eu proibisse	que eu emergisse
subj. perfeito	que eu tenha reunido	que eu tenha proibido	que eu tenha emergido
subj. m.-q.-perf.	que eu tivesse reunido	que eu tivesse proibido	que eu tivesse emergido
subj. futuro	quando eu reunir	quando eu proibir	quando eu emergir
inf. pessoal	eu reunir, tu reunires, ele reunir, nós reunirmos, vós reunirdes, eles reunirem	eu proibir, tu proibires, ele proibir, nós proibirmos, vós proibirdes, eles proibirem	eu emergir, tu emergires, ele emergir, nós emergirmos, vós emergirdes, eles emergirem
imper. afirm.	reúne (tu)	proíbe (tu)	emerge (tu)
imper. neg.	não reúnas	não proíbas	não emerjas
gerúndio	reunindo	proibindo	emergindo
particípio	reunido	proibido	emergido, emerso

	79 falir	80 remir
ind. presente	nós falimos, vós falis	nós remimos, vós remis
ind. imperfeito	eu falia	eu remia
ind. perfeito	eu fali	eu remi
ind. m.-q.-p. simpl.	eu falira	eu remira
ind. m.-q.-p. comp.	eu tinha falido	eu tinha remido
ind fut. do pres.	eu falirei	eu remirei
ind fut. do pret.	eu faliria	eu remiria
subj. presente		
subj. imperfeito	que eu falisse	que eu remisse
subj. perfeito	que eu tenha falido	que eu tenha remido
subj. m.-q.-perf.	que eu tivesse falido	que eu tivesse remido
subj. futuro	quando eu falir	quando eu remir
inf. pessoal	eu falir, tu falires, ele falir, nós falirmos, vós falirdes, eles falirem	eu remir, tu remires, ele remir, nós remirmos, vós remirdes, eles remirem
imper. afirm.	fali (vós)	remi (vos)
imper. neg.		
gerúndio	falindo	remindo
particípio	falido	remido

Infinitive	Past Tense	Past Participle
arise	arose	arisen
awake	awoke	awoken
be	was, were	been
bear	bore	born(e)
beat	beat	beaten
become	became	become
begin	began	begun
bend	bent	bent
beseech	besought	besought
bet	bet (*also* betted)	bet (*also* betted)
bid	bid (*also* bade)	bid (*also* bidden)
bind	bound	bound
bite	bit	bitten
bleed	bled	bled
blow	blew	blown
break	broke	broken
breed	bred	bred
bring	brought	brought
build	built	built
burn	burnt (*also* burned)	burnt (*also* burned)
burst	burst	burst
buy	bought	bought
can	could	-
cast	cast	cast
catch	caught	caught
choose	chose	chosen
cling	clung	clung
come	came	come
cost	cost	cost
creep	crept	crept
cut	cut	cut
deal	dealt	dealt
dig	dug	dug
do	did	done
draw	drew	drawn
dream	dreamed (*also* dreamt)	dreamed (*also* dreamt)
drink	drank	drunk
drive	drove	driven
dwell	dwelt	dwelt
eat	ate	eaten
fall	fell	fallen
feed	fed	fed
feel	felt	felt
fight	fought	fought
find	found	found
flee	fled	fled
fling	flung	flung
fly	flew	flown
forbid	forbade	forbidden
forget	forgot	forgotten
forsake	forsook	forsaken
freeze	froze	frozen
get	got	got (*US* gotten)

Infinitive	Past Tense	Past Participle
give	gave	given
go	went	gone
grind	ground	ground
grow	grew	grown
hang	hung (*also* hanged)	hung (*also* hanged)
have	had	had
hear	heard	heard
hide	hid	hidden
hit	hit	hit
hold	held	held
hurt	hurt	hurt
keep	kept	kept
kneel	knelt (*also* kneeled)	knelt (*also* kneeled)
know	knew	known
lay	laid	laid
lead	led	led
lean	leant (*also* leaned)	leant (*also* leaned)
leap	leapt (*also* leaped)	leapt (*also* leaped)
learn	learnt (*also* learned)	learnt (*also* learned)
leave	left	left
lend	lent	lent
let	let	let
lie	lay	lain
light	lit (*also* lighted)	lit (*also* lighted)
lose	lost	lost
make	made	made
may	might	-
mean	meant	meant
meet	met	met
mistake	mistook	mistaken
mow	mowed	mown (*also* mowed)
pay	paid	paid
put	put	put
quit	quit (*also* quitted)	quit (*also* quitted)
read	read	read
rend	rent	rent
rid	rid	rid
ride	rode	ridden
ring	rang	rung
rise	rose	risen
run	ran	run
saw	sawed	sawn
say	said	said
see	saw	seen
seek	sought	sought
sell	sold	sold
send	sent	sent
set	set	set
shake	shook	shaken
shall	should	-
shear	sheared	shorn (*also* sheared)
shed	shed	shed
shine	shone	shone

Infinitive	Past Tense	Past Participle
shoot	shot	shot
show	showed	shown
shrink	shrank	shrunk
shut	shut	shut
sing	sang	sung
sink	sank	sunk
sit	sat	sat
slay	slew	slain
sleep	slept	slept
slide	slid	slid
sling	slung	slung
slit	slit	slit
smell	smelt (*also* smelled)	smelt (*also* smelled)
sow	sowed	sown (*also* sowed)
speak	spoke	spoken
speed	sped (*also* speeded)	sped (*also* speeded)
spell	spelt (*also* spelled)	spelt (*also* spelled)
spend	spent	spent
spill	spilt (*also* spilled)	spilt (*also* spilled)
spin	spun	spun
spit	spat	spat
split	split	split
spoil	spoiled (*also* spoilt)	spoiled (*also* spoilt)
spread	spread	spread
spring	sprang	sprung
stand	stood	stood
steal	stole	stolen
stick	stuck	stuck
sting	stung	stung
stink	stank	stunk
stride	strode	stridden
strike	struck	struck (*also* stricken)
strive	strove	striven
swear	swore	sworn
sweep	swept	swept
swell	swelled	swollen (*also* swelled)
swim	swam	swum
swing	swung	swung
take	took	taken
teach	taught	taught
tear	tore	torn
tell	told	told
think	thought	thought
throw	threw	thrown
thrust	thrust	thrust
tread	trod	trodden
wake	woke (*also* waked)	woken (*also* waked)
wear	wore	worn
weave	wove (*also* weaved)	woven (*also* weaved)
wed	wedded	wedded
weep	wept	wept
win	won	won
wind	wound	wound
wring	wrung	wrung
write	wrote	written

Achevé d'imprimer par l'imprimerie
Maury-Imprimeur - 45330 Malesherbes en avril 2014
N° de projet : 11028701/03-541039
Dépôt légal : janvier 2008 - N° d'imprimeur : 189003

Imprimé en France